Index to
THE
LONDON STAGE
1660–1800

EDITED WITH CRITICAL INTRODUCTIONS BY

WILLIAM VAN LENNEP, EMMETT L. AVERY, ARTHUR H. SCOUTEN,

GEORGE WINCHESTER STONE, JR.,

and

CHARLES BEECHER HOGAN

Compiled, with an Introduction by

Ben Ross Schneider, Jr.

Foreword by George Winchester Stone, Jr.

———

SOUTHERN ILLINOIS UNIVERSITY PRESS
Carbondale and Edwardsville

Feffer and Simons, Inc.
London and Amsterdam

PN
2592
L63
S3

Printed by offset lithography in the United States of America

ISBN 0-8093-0907-6

CONTENTS

FOREWORD

By George Winchester Stone, Jr

The London Stage, 1660–1800 calendar of performances in eleven volumes was thirty-five years in the making, and has run to 8,026 pages. Divided into five chronological parts, each volume was provided by its editors with an index of sorts, but from the beginning the five editors envisioned the appearance ultimately of a combined index to make accessible all the information about plays, persons, and places as they appeared in each performance entry from volume to volume and part to part. Such is the *Index* that appears here, in 506,014 references to the calendar under twenty-five thousand entries, and this has been seven years in the making.

Although the *Index* is not analytical in the fullest sense, the editors alive at the time of compiling it have provided identifiers for plays, operas, oratorios, songs, specialty acts, pantomimes, burlettas, and masques. They have also identified the persons listed in the playbills and the extant theatre account books according to their primary functions in the theatres (actor, dancer, singer, musician, composer, box-keeper, treasurer, renter, and wardrobe-keeper), and for others, prominent members of the audience and business men of London, according to their occupations (from ambassador and statesman to carpenter, chandler, rope-maker, printer, lawyer, coffee-house manager, and tavern-keeper). Thus at a glance the *Index* points to the variety and richness of a broad range of London life for 140 years as it impinged on, supported, or drew sustenance from the theatres. Some ninety-six trades, for example, were described in R. Campbell's *The London Tradesman in 1747*, and the masters who operated eighty-nine of them prove to have maintained some profitable connection with the theatres. The *Index* enables the curious reader to follow through with ease the span of time during which any company or person was attached to a theatre.

It also provides direction for following the careers of the hundreds of actors, actresses, dancers, and musicians whose entertainment cheered the London populace nightly. All in all, the *Index* demonstrates what a wide-ranging document for social, economic, legal, artistic, and dramatic history *The London Stage, 1660–1800* is. The sheer bulk of the information therein recommended to its editors the usefulness of applying modern computer technology to organizing the *Index*. This technology has ultimately proved to be invaluable, but the whole project, with its starts and stops, and periods of experimentation could neither have been undertaken nor brought to successful conclusion without the financial support accorded to the compiler and his expert staff of young editors by numerous foundations and individuals.

It is a pleasure, therefore, to acknowledge such aid from The National Endowment for the Humanities (both for the pilot and the completion phases), The American Council of Learned Societies, The American Philosophical Society, The Andrew Mellon Foundation, The United States Steel Foundation, The Billy Rose Foundation, Lawrence University, and generous gifts from Mrs John A. Logan, Charles Beecher Hogan, Miss Faith Bradford,

Dr and Mrs J. Merrill Knapp, Jr, and a Friend of Lawrence University. Lawrence University has given strong support by its allocation of space and computer resources and by administering the grants in aid. Special thanks are due to Thomas Smith, President; Marvin Wrolstad, Vice President for Business Affairs; and Thomas Headrick and Rik Warch, Vice Presidents for Academic Affairs. Mr John Church and Mr John Bachuber, Directors of Computing at The Institute of Paper Chemistry in Appleton, Wisconsin, and Mr Michael Hall, Director of Lawrence's Computer Center, have helped at every step of the long process.

Before the text could be typed into the computer, extensive marking of the eleven volumes to assure the capture of index items was necessary. The project is much indebted to four eighteenth-century scholars who generously gave their time and labour for this task: Muriel Friedman, Mark Auburn, Leonard Leff, and Marcia Heineman Saunders. Devon and Ben Schneider III, and Dorothy Church also helped substantially at this stage. Many thanks are due also to Philip Hui of China Data Systems, Hong Kong, and to Tom Grainger, Barry Layfield, and Nicholas Blacklock of Computer Services Center, London, for expediting the conversion of text to machine-readable form. For solving a tape-conversion problem thanks are due to Wheaton College Computer Services, Lloyd Michalsen, Director, and Jacques LaFrance, consultant.

Gratitude must be expressed to two talented programmer-analysts who each devoted more than a year's work to the design and implementation of programs for compiling and editing the *Index*: Will Daland and Reid M. Watts. Walter Brown and Nicholas Schneider added improvements to the system. Christopher Gibbons, Andrew Reibs, Paul Konig, and Bruce Grodnik of the Lawrence Computer Center helped processing with advice and technical information. Thanks are also due to Sally and Walter Sedelow, Department of Computer Science, University of Kansas, for useful advice and help in identifying well-qualified programmer-analysts.

The basic text of *The London Stage, 1660–1800*, compiled as it was by five different scholars, adheres in general to a consistent format for entries and commentary, but no machine could automatically compile an index from such a diversified record. Only human intelligence could standardize, identify, and edit some fifty thousand raw index items for compiling. Hence abundant thanks must go to the scrupulous, efficient and tireless Lawrence students who performed these editing tasks— Catherine Boggs, Catherine Steiner, Marc Weinberger, Joseph Jacobs, and Ruth Steiner —each of whom gave more than two years to the project. Marc Weinberger also coordinated the editing staff and mapped out strategies. Suzanne Fusso contributed materially during the early stages and Melinda Young during the final phase. The following student editors also made substantial contributions—Connie Hansen, Sarah Larsen, Laurie Johnson, Sue Koch, Peter Pretkel, Lynn Seifert, Louise Freiberg, Elizabeth O'Brien, Jan Surkamp, Mark Burrows, and Kathy Rosner. Debbie Watts, Ben Ross Schneider III, Mackay Taylor Schneider, and Scott Farnsworth have served the project as computer operators.

The workers and editors deeply appreciate the pragmatic advice given throughout the life of the project by the exceptional director of the Southern Illinois University Press, Vernon Sternberg, whose initiative brought forth the original volumes of *The London Stage, 1660–1800*. Future generations of scholars in many fields will be indebted to Professor Ben Ross Schneider, Jr, for planning and administering the work of his dedicated staff and for bringing the *Index* to completion.

INTRODUCTION

By Ben Ross Schneider, Jr

THE INDEX

This *Index* contains all references to each name and title appearing in the calendar of *The London Stage, 1660–1800*, listed alphabetically in one merged index. References are to the date and theatre of the calendar entry containing the item, rather than to the page, because it was felt that index entries would thus convey more information and that citations would be easier to locate in the volumes themselves, since they are arranged chronologically. The names are those of persons, places, business establishments, clubs, and institutions mentioned in casts lists or commentary. The titles are those of plays, books, dances, songs, music, and entertainment, whether performed or commented on. Approximate date references are represented by the number "o": "June o" means "sometime in June." "Sept o" usually refers to the list of plays probably performed in a given season that is contained in the preface to some seasons. In other words, we have made these lists part of the calendar even though the month of the performance is not known and even though the year may be doubtful. Otherwise, references are to the calendar sections of *The London Stage, 1660–1800*. Prefaces to seasons and general introductions to the separate parts have not been indexed. Exhaustive tables of contents provided for these introductions refer to the great number of topics covered in them. Variants of names and titles are given in parentheses after the standard form when a variation is considered so great as to cause difficulty in finding the item in the text. Cross references from wide variants in common usage to the standard forms are made.

To avoid excessive cross references we have observed one overriding general principle: whenever a title is generic rather than specific we have indexed it under the most specific word describing the piece. For example "Dance of Furies" is listed as "Furies Dance," "Concerto on the violin" as "Violin concerto." We have observed the same principle for names with modifiers, listing, for instance, "Order of Albions" as "Albions, Order of" and "Theatre Royal, Bath" as "Bath Theatre." The user of the *Index* should look for generic terms and modified names under the most specific word in the item. Main entries for plays, operas, and oratorios will be found under their authors' names, but cross references from each title and variant title will direct the user to the author. No attempt has been made to assign titles of songs, dances, musical pieces, and entertainments to authors; such items will be found under their titles.

Nearly all persons have been identified by first name or initials; performing specialties, trades, professions, or titles are given when known. Those acquainted with the calendar are aware of the fact that a majority of performers go by their last names alone. When the last name is common to a number of persons, identification must be deduced from the available evidence, which is sometimes scarce. The user is warned, therefore, that references to persons may be misassigned, especially when a considerable number of people bear the same last name. Details of our methods for identifying persons will be found in the section on editing process, below. It was decided not to complicate the process of identification by merging the entries for an actress's maiden name and her married name. The user must therefore refer to both names for an actress's full career—for example, Raftor, Catherine, and Clive, Mrs Catherine.

When proof indexes showed that the great bulk of references to items of marginal interest threatened to overwhelm the user in his search for important information, the decision was made to eliminate certain kinds of entries altogether. General descriptions of pieces or persons have been systematically excluded: for example "Concerto," "Dance," "Song," "A Young Gentleman," "The Gentleman who played Hamlet." No roles or scene titles are indexed. Place references to London, to England, and to the London theatres have been excluded, but not references to other countries or cities or to theatres outside London. Titles of sources for calendar information, such as the *Public Advertiser*, have been dropped since they are listed in the frontmatter of *London Stage* volumes. References to items in "blind" cast lists have been dropped. About 80 percent of the cast lists in *The London Stage* are referred to in the following manner: "Romeo and Juliet. As 22 Sept., but Romeo-Wilks; Nurse omitted." In such an entry, the reference to "Wilks" would appear in the *Index* for this performance, but the actors from the cast of 22 September would not. If an actor is referred to more than once on the same day at the same theatre, only one reference has been retained. Therefore the user is warned that a given item may occur more than once in a performance entry.

Users whose needs go beyond the limits of the *Index* may consult the London Stage Information Bank at Lawrence University, Appleton, Wisconsin 54911, B. R. Schneider, Jr, Director. A computer-readable version of *The London Stage* calendar will be maintained at Lawrence with programs for extracting, rearranging, and displaying any kind of information contained in the calendar, including the "Comment" sections.

THE COMPUTER PROCESS

Soon after the last volumes came into print, it was decided to create a computer version of *The London Stage, 1660–1800*, that would facili-

tate a comprehensive index to the eleven volumes and serve as an easily-accessible information base for scholars. For the purpose, an advisory board was constituted, consisting of the surviving editors, the publisher, and scholars especially interested in eighteenth-century theatre history: George Winchester Stone, Jr, Chairman, Dean Emeritus of Libraries, New York University; the late Emmett L. Avery, Professor of English, Washington State University; Arthur H. Scouten, Professor of English, University of Pennsylvania; Charles Beecher Hogan, Research Associate, Yale University; Vernon Sternberg, Director, the Southern Illinois University Press; the late Professor Allardyce Nicoll, Colwall, Malvern, England; Sybil Rosenfeld, Editor, British Society for Theatre Research; Cecil Price, Professor of English, University College, Swansea, Wales; J. F. Arnott, Professor of Drama, University of Glasgow; John Robinson, Professor of English, University of Nebraska; William A. Armstrong, Professor of English, Birkbeck College, University of London; and Simon Trussler, Editor, *Theatre Quarterly*, London. Ben Ross Schneider, Jr, Professor of English, Lawrence University, was commissioned project director. In the spring of 1970 a proposal was drafted for a pilot study to ascertain the ultimate scope of the task and the best method of carrying it out. In due course, funds materialized, a programmer was appointed, and in September 1970 the work began.

The project developed in three phases: 1) entering the text of *The London Stage* into the computer and writing programs to retrieve information from it, 2) editing the computer version of the text, and 3) editing the index. The first phase was completed in the period 1970–72. The second lasted from 1973 to 1976. The final phase continued from 1976 into 1978. For editing the text and *Index* the project employed a staff of three to six student assistants working full time in summers and part time during the academic years 1974–78. Phases one and two each employed a fulltime programmer-analyst for one year.

Entering the Text

In the first phase the goal was to develop a computer system capable of searching a computer version of the text of *The London Stage* and to discover the best way of feeding this text into the computer. This phase was sufficiently funded to have the text professionally typed in Hong Kong and converted to computer tape by optical scanning of the typed pages. Several general principles were established at the start. 1. The full text was to be entered: this measure would assure the capture of each kind of information available, in case a decision was eventually made to include it in the index; and it would provide an information bank that could be searched for any information not eventually indexed, such as roles and topics in commentary. Lawrence University would conduct such searches for scholars at cost. 2. The comprehensive index was to contain names (of persons and places) and titles (defined as the designation of any performed piece). 3. The computer version would be as exact an image of the full text as mechanical methods would allow, which meant using upper and lower case, entering all punctuation, all headings, theatres, and dates. 4. As far as possible, the computer was to identify categories (actors, roles, titles, theatres, dates, songs, dances, and so forth) by interpreting the syntactical conventions (of order, punctuation, and key word) in which *The London Stage* habitually listed parts and performers in the various kinds of theatrical pieces. 5. Since commentary and parenthetical interruptions in cast lists had no regular syntax, they would be marked off so that routines for structural analysis could skip them. 6. Names and titles in these parenthetical interruptions and commentary were to be identified and marked editorially, to enable the computer to extract them. 7. Final adjustments of any deviations from the standard syntactical structure were to be made during the proofreading and editing of the text image.

The task of entering the text was tantamount to producing a new edition of *The London Stage*, revised according to the most rigorous syntactical principles. Programs were to depend on absolute precision in the use of punctuation and codes for identification by the computer. Failure to close a parenthesis, for example, could cause a whole performance entry to be unintelligible, and the omission of a dash could turn an actor into a role. It was determined that a great deal of redundant work would be avoided if typists did some normalizing of text as they typed (for example, changing the ambiguous "by" that linked performer to performance in singing and dancing sections to a dash, to conform to the linking of actor to role in play sections). To reduce errors, it was decided to mark the whole text for certain basic changes before it was typed. Index entries in parentheses and comments were identified and marked in the process. We were fortunate that four eighteenth-century scholars—Muriel Friedman (Loyola), Mark Auburn (Ohio State), Leonard Leff (Chicago), and Marcia Heinemann (Chicago)—answered a call in the project's *Newsletter* and volunteered to pre-edit most of the text for typing.

Will Daland (B.A., North Carolina) wrote the *London Stage* retrieval system in the programming language PL/1 for an IBM 360/44 that Lawrence shares with the Institute of Paper Chemistry. Limits of storage required that he break his retrieval system into five successive steps in which each step accomplished part of the work and passed it on computer tape to the next. The five programs work as follows. The first strips out commentary and parenthetical material, except for marked index entries, leaving a file that follows rigid syntactical rules. The second interprets this file on the basis of its syntactical structure, labeling each element as a section type, date, theatre, title, part, or performer. The third fills in casts not listed but referred to in various ways, such as, "Romeo and Juliet. As 22 Sept., but Romeo-Wilks, Nurse omitted." A fourth program extracts a "record" consisting of a section type, date, theatre, title (if any), part (if any), performer (if any) whenever an item in any of these categories satisfies a search request. Search requests may call for records having any combination of these elements, and several search requests can be executed in one pass through a file. The final step in the retrieval process sorts the retrieved records in any category, or set of categories, in any order. For example, the records may be sorted alphabetically by title and under each title sorted by theatre and under each theatre sorted by date. This form would be suited for studying the history of a set of plays, say Shakespeare's, in the London theatres. An index-compiling program, working from the same retrieved records was added in the next phase of the project.

A full account of entering text and designing retrieval programs is given in *Travels in Computerland* (Addison-Wesley, 1974), by B. R. Schneider.

Editing the Text

Supported by a second set of grants-in-aid, the project's goal was to perfect the information base entered in the first phase and produce an index to all names and titles. Some typographical errors occurred, of course, in the machine-readable *London Stage* calendar, the typing service in Hong Kong having promised no more than ninety-nine perfect lines out of one hundred. But typists had had to adapt the printed form to the capabilities of a typewriter, using an eleven-page set of guidelines that caused strange results in unforeseen circumstances. Furthermore, no attempt had been made to deal with exceptional ways of presenting performance data in the original text. The plan had been to make the typing process as simple as possible, to avoid delay and misinterpretation, and later to edit nonstandard passages to program specifications.

The first priority was to design an efficient editing system. It could not require editors to have prior computer experience, since that would make good editors harder to find. For this reason it had to be a "conversational" system, in which the computer helps the editor by asking for the information needed to perform the job, by denying erroneous responses, and by prompting correct ones. Most important, the editor should be able to inspect an actual segment of the computer version and alter that very segment upon identifying a deviation from the guidelines. Primitive systems in which the editor, by reference to a printout, must declare the line and position on the line where a change is to be made and then command the computer to insert, delete, or change something at that invisible spot in its memory would be too slow and error-prone for a task of this size. Finally, there should be a simple method of calling up segments of text for inspection and editing. This method should also be capable of retrieving any items not accessible by Will Daland's system, which had been limited to titles, parts, performers, and marked items in commentary.

For this purpose, Lawrence's conversational computer (a PDP/11 by Digital Equipment Company) was selected. A cathode-ray-tube terminal (a typewriter with a TV screen for a page, by Beehive Medical Electronics) provided a display on which text could be altered at will. And Reid Watts (B.A., Kansas, in math,

physics, and computer science) was appointed to write programs for servicing the editorial process. The System for Interactive Text-editing, Analysis, and Retrieval, "SITAR" as it came to be known, that Mr Watts brought into being is fully described and evaluated in *Communications of the Association for Computing Machinery* for June 1977.

Briefly, SITAR works as follows. To edit a passage on the screen of the terminal, one writes "EDIT" on the terminal keyboard. The computer asks, "What file?" unless it has already begun work on one. If not, the editor writes the name of the file, a word assigned to it when it was created on the computer. Then the computer asks, "Pattern?" In answer, the editor literally quotes the distinguishing features of the passage to be searched for, using ellipses to stand for unspecified text, and characters, words, word segments, or phrases to identify the passage desired and declare its desired limits. A typical "pattern" might contain a key word in the passage desired and characters matching its beginning and end. In the computer version of *The London Stage*, play entries are marked off by asterisks. To retrieve a performance of Macbeth, for example, the editor would simply quote in skeleton form that piece of text: "*. . . Macbeth . . .*" In the source, a dash is used for assigning a role to an actor. Thus the pattern for a performance in which Garrick plays Macbeth would be "* . . . Macbeth—Garrick . . .*"

Upon finding "Macbeth—Garrick" the computer would display the whole performance entry for the play, filling in the ellipses up to the boundary codes. By keyboard controls, the editor can move a visible pointer to any mistake he sees in the text on the terminal screen and correct it by inserting or deleting any amount of text or by writing over it. The text on the screen instantly adjusts to insertions or deletions. When the editor has made all changes to the entry that it requires, he presses a button and the revised entry replaces the original one in the computer. The process is as simple as pulling a book from a shelf, leafing through it to find a particular passage, and marking editorial changes in it with a pencil, with the inestimable advantage that the computer does the leafing with lightning speed, executes the pencilled corrections as fast as they are written, and in the same instant resets the whole book in type to accommodate the changes, no matter how much is added or subtracted.

The pattern search can also be used for collecting all examples of a pattern and storing them in a separate file from which they may be displayed or printed. Thus, one might make a file of all performances of Macbeth by Garrick. It will be seen that by virtue of these capabilities SITAR is a virtual concordance to the 8,026 pages of *The London Stage*, or to any other text on the computer, with the advantage that one can locate not simply all instances of a word but also of a word segment or phrase and define the context in which he wants them to appear in any way he chooses. In other words, SITAR can find information on any topic treated in *The London Stage* by searching for passages containing words associated with that topic.

After developing SITAR, we still lacked a system for compiling, formatting, and printing an index from the sorted records produced by Will Daland's retrieval system. The present *Index* was compiled and printed with programs created by Reid Watts for the IBM 360/44 during the editing phase of the project. The first step in editing the computer version of *The London Stage* was to print out the whole corpus and scan it for errors in the typists' rendering. Faulty passages were brought to the SITAR screen and corrected.

The uncompromising rigidity of the computer, coupled with the speed with which it "reads," actually contributes to the editorial process. Whenever a program encounters an arrangement of text that doesn't agree with specifications, it will quit, unless the programmer has included instructions for this emergency. When he writes instructions to cover the faulty circumstance, the programmer also arranges for the computer to report the erroneous condition. For this reason Will Daland's five programs could be used to "proofread" *The London Stage* for certain errors. Trial indexes were also useful in error detection. Any name or title that occurred only once in the *Index* was suspected of being a mistake, and checked against the original text. This source text was corrected five times on the basis of successive passes through the entire set of programs. The process was tantamount to producing five complete revisions by pre-computer methods, except that no new errors could be introduced, as would be the case if the revised

versions had to be typed out in the old way. Only erroneous text was affected. Since the programs could locate some eighty error conditions, and trial indexes detected spurious entries, the process was thorough.

Limitations of computer storage severely hampered the editing process. In the early stages of SITAR editing, Lawrence's PDP/11 computer had no means of keeping revised versions except on "DECtape," which meant dividing the text of *The London Stage* into sixty-three parts, each filling one tape. Furthermore, the IBM 360 which processed the edited tapes could not "read" DECtape. This defect necessitated two trips to a PDP/11 computer that could read DECtape and write IBM tape. Unfortunately the nearest such machine was two hundred miles away, at Wheaton College, Illinois. This problem was solved when Lawrence installed an IBM tape drive on its PDP/11. *The London Stage* could then fit on one IBM tape. But now storage on Lawrence's PDP/11 was the limiting feature: the disk allotted to SITAR (an RP05) would hold only one twenty-ninth of *The London Stage*, which meant loading and unloading tapes from the disk and passing them through the five IBM 360 programs twenty-nine times to produce one revised version of the full text. Keeping track of the resulting 145 tape files was a major task, and disaster prone.

In summary, the text-correction process consisted of passing each twenty-nine-part revision through five programs on the IBM 360, locating and marking new errors on printouts of the source, loading the parts, one at a time, onto the PDP/11 computer, and making the necessary changes to the computer version with SITAR. The source underwent this process five times.

The project employed from three to six student editors at a time during the three-year text-editing period; but they could not always be the same students. Actually, nineteen students participated in the work. Maintaining consistency was therefore a major task. What does one do if the theatre is not known? What if the text presents two cast lists for a single performance? Should "Their Majesties" be treated as a name or title? To provide definitive answers to such questions the director assembled a guide that eventually contained over 150 rules. This guide, a testimony to the great variety and complexity of *The London Stage*, went through a dozen editions, as rules were added and refined. The project's student editors merit highest praise for tireless attention to detail, total acceptance of responsibility, dedication to accuracy, and determination to comprehend, in the application of so many rules to so much material of such great diversity. It is impossible to convey how much they have accomplished, but the printouts they have inspected and marked, if piled on top of each other, would reach the fifteen-foot ceiling of the project's office twice.

Editing the Index

In the summer of 1976, the final phase, editing the *Index*, began. The greatest problems in this process were homonyms and synonyms: items with the same spelling but signifying two or more objects ("Bullock" in the calendar might signify Christopher, Hildebrand, Charles, William Jr, William Sr, or Billy); and items with different spellings but signifying the same object (Sir Fopling Flutter and The Man of Mode). In establishing a correct text of *The London Stage*, no attempt had been made to separate homonyms or normalize variants in the text itself: to have done so would have been to destroy some of the very evidence on which judgments of identity could be made. Without having all of the evidence on each case it would be difficult to decide which form to use as standard or make a reasoned attempt to sort out homonyms.

The strategy devised was to merge synonyms to standard forms on the basis of raw indexes showing the whole spread of variants. The problem of separating homonyms was complicated by the fact that the entries for several variants belonging to the homonym also appeared: not just an entry for a Bullock, who could be any of the six, but entries for each of the six as well. Here, the only solution was to merge the references to all six together and then divide them by editing based on careful study of the whole array. It was an easy enough job to change a name, but merging references to dates and theatres under the new name required altering each individual reference, sometimes several thousand per name, and sorting these again so that they might fall into their proper place in the new entry.

The merging process required a new program operating on sort records, written by Nick Schneider (Dartmouth 1979), which changed one item to another every time it found the first. The references could then be sorted so that the new index merged the synonyms. Some notion of the size of the task may be appreciated by the fact that eventually some twenty-three thousand merge instructions were written: about half of the raw entries were variants. The sheer number was not so much of a problem as the fact that careful study of text itself and of other reference works (such as the published volumes of Highfill, Burnim, Langhans *Dictionary of Actors, Actresses . . . in London, 1660–1800*) must take place to establish clear identities before merging. The attributions of references in the present *Index* required a great deal of research.

The project developed a research tool of its own to help with the one hundred-odd most difficult cases: a repertoire analysis by computer in which the roles of actors mingled under one name could be used to distinguish them from each other. Christopher Bullock's repertoire could be established from roles assigned to him under his full name. It was thereby possible to identify fairly well which references in the plain Bullock entry belonged to him and which to the other five.

The repertoire analysis revealed a general principle that could be used in assigning ambiguous references to particular actors: theatres hardly ever distinguish one actor from another unless two or more actors with the same name are concurrently performing at a theatre. In this case the senior actor goes by the last name alone, and the junior actor is distinguished by "Jr" or an initial. Two actors by the same name acting at different theatres are not distinguished. In sum, if an actor is senior or alone at a given theatre, he is "The" Bullock, Wilks, Cibber, and so on. Consequently, when Colley Cibber retired, he passed the title "Cibber" to Theophilus. The process of merging variants was considerably helped by SITAR's capacity to create and revise the file of merge instructions, and it can be said with some confidence that users can be quite sure that a Bullock in the calendar is the one we say it is in the *Index*.

Before struggling with the most difficult cases, the editors at Lawrence made the more obvious merges and sent proof indexes to original compilers, G. W. Stone, Jr, and C. B. Hogan (one name and one title index for each of the five parts). They checked these for errors and annotated each entry thoroughly, adding, where possible, first names, professions, and occupations from their vast store of knowledge. On receipt of their annotated proofs in the summer of 1977, merge instructions were completed, and final name and title indexes were produced in October. The task of correlating the annotations of the five parts (the sources did not always agree) on a printout of the complete index then began. Annotations were then added to the final index by SITAR. Counting some proof editions not mentioned above, the present *Index* is actually the fifth "edition."

EVALUATION OF THE COMPUTER PROCESS

It took seven years to produce this *Index* by computer and about two hundred thousand dollars. If Lawrence University had charged for computer time, the figure might have been double. There can be little doubt that making the vast resources of *The London Stage, 1660–1800,* accessible to students of the eighteenth century is worth this amount. It is a foundation on which scholars will build for years to come. The real question is whether it could have been done faster and for less without the services of the computer.

The answer is that without the computer the *Index* would probably never have been done at all; certainly not in seven years. Although combing the calendar for names and titles does not seem at first glance to be an insurmountable task, the sheer number of references (over five hundred thousand) does give pause. The number of names and titles before consolidation (fifty-two thousand) is also formidable. If a card were written for each reference, a box containing those cards would be one hundred yards long. A box containing one card for each name and title (but some actors performed as many as three thousand times) would be thirty feet long. Whether the compiler writes one card per reference and then sorts five hundred thousand cards, or searches a file averaging fifteen feet in length five hundred thousand times to add references to entries, his task is immense. But the way he spends his time is the real deterrent. Only the prospect of an OED could motivate such drudgery.

It must also be noted that, besides the *Index,* the project has produced programs and a computer version of *The London Stage* that may be as useful as the *Index* itself in coming to terms with such a mass of information. The computer system at Lawrence can rearrange the material of the calendar and produce displays that will enable scholars to investigate efficiently such things as trends in theatre offerings, stage careers of actors, histories of roles, songs, or dances. Since SITAR constitutes a virtual concordance to the whole corpus, the possibilities seem limitless; information on staging, costumes, the benefit system, the residences of actors, and finances are now accessible. Moreover, the whole computer system (except the machine-readable text available only through arrangement with Southern Illinois Press) is available for generating future reference works and indexing them.

It must be noted further that computer methods have saved substantial printing costs. The computer has formatted and printed the whole *Index* as it stands, without the help (or errors) of human typists or typesetters. The printer merely photographed the computer copy and printed it by photo-offset. Since this index is over one thousand pages long, the project has avoided approximately thirty thousand dollars in composition costs, it is estimated.

Elimination of errors provides further justification of computer methods. The ease with which proof copies of both index and text can be produced and the computer's indefatigable detection of errors result in an accuracy that would be very difficult to obtain without it. As this step-by-step account has shown, five editions of the text and five editions of the *Index* have been produced, each adding no errors and each more accurate than the last. If the text is correct, the computer cannot possibly mislocate an item; it must be there. Items may have been lost through failure to mark an item in commentary or through bad punctuation of a cast list, but after such rigorous mechanical and human scrutiny, such omissions must be very few.

Mechanical methods greatly assisted the process of sorting out homonyms and synonyms. In this process and in many other ways, mechanical memory comes to the aid of human memory. At the decision-making point the computer supplies all the information that bears on the decision. Before standardizing synonyms editors could consult the entire list of variants; before splitting up homonyms they could study the calendar history of all candidates. Proof indexes made the relevant facts easy to find. The computer printout of merge instructions was also a complete record of variants, enabling the editors to be sure of making all necessary cross references and annotations. Without proof indexes at several stages of the way, and other computer-produced documents, the person who compiles by hand must depend almost entirely on what he remembers. When the document he is dealing with contains five hundred thousand references to fifty-two thousand items, the mind boggles. To compete with a computer, a human being would have to be able to recall, without hesitation, things like the last time that D'Aigueville Senior performed, whether Smith danced or acted at Bartholomew Fair and when, and on what days, Jones played Romeo at Lincoln's Inn Fields.

And so, if the *Index* could have been compiled and annotated without a computer, it would probably have been less thorough and less accurate than the present one.

Because computer memory can substitute for human memory, editors using a computer need not be scholars in the field. Following a set of editorial guidelines, undergraduate student assistants with no other qualifications than dependability and intelligence, using early editions of the Index and ancillary printouts could index *The London Stage*. Of course, specialist knowledge, as provided by G. W. Stone and C. B. Hogan, in proofreading and annotating the *Index* has been indispensable. But the remaining work could not have been done without mechanical memory.

In retrospect, some economies might have been possible if the nature of the task could have been fully comprehended at the beginning. Entering the text by optical scanning of Hong Kong typing was probably the best available method under the circumstances, but it was difficult to get delivery on schedule and at the same time hold the service bureaus to the error rate they had promised. It would have been better to develop SITAR first and enter the full text at Lawrence with student typists. The typist's power to fix mistakes with ease would have allowed the project to employ people on the basis of intelligence and motivation instead of mechanical skill. And the director would have had better day-to-day control of the typing process.

Professionals have challenged the decision to put the source into upper and lower case. Keeping track of capitalization did indeed cost time and money. For this and other reasons the computer industry appears to have dispensed with lower case. However, capitalization does have meaning, and to lose the distinction is to lose information. Furthermore, it is difficult to read words written entirely in capitals, and if the project had used an all-capital text, it would have been a source of errors. Certainly many scholars for years to come will find it easier to scan an *Index* in upper and lower case.

KEY TO ABBREVIATIONS

NOTE: when two theatre abbreviations are linked, the same company performed at both theatres during the season indicated by the Index. At Bartholomew Fair, Mayfair, Southwark Fair, and Tottenham Court, the Index identifies the booth at which the performance took place by initials following the standard abbreviations, BF—, MF—, SF—, and TC—. These initials do not appear in the text of *The London Stage*, but may help the user locate the item in question.

AC	Angel Court	BPT	Blue Posts Tavern
ACA	Academy of Vocal and Instrumental Music	BR	Beveridge's Room
		BRA	Broughton's Amphitheatre
ACAD	Cibber's Histrionic Academy, Bowling Green, Richmond Hill	BRI/COUR	Bridge's Street Theatre and at Court
ACADEMY	Academy in Little Lincoln's Inn Fields	BRIDGES'	The First Drury Lane Theatre
		BRUSSELS	Brussels, Belgium
ACDL	Academy in Drury Lane	BT	Buffler Tavern
APH	Ashley's Dancing House	BUH	Buckingham House
ARME	Assembly Room, Mile End Road	CA	Caverley's Academy
ATCOURT	At Court	CAC	Crown and Cushion
AVT	Anchor and Vine Tavern	CAT	Not identified in London Stage
B&S	Barbers' and Surgeons' Hall	CC	Chelsea College
B-L	Bullock-Leigh Booth	CDR	Couch's Drawing Room
BANNSTER	John Bannister's House	CDS	Coignand's Dancing School
BB	Blue Boar, Holborn	CG	Covent Garden Theatre
BBT	Black Bull Tavern	CG/LIF	Covent Garden and Lincoln's Inn Fields Theatres
BCA	Bird Cage Alley		
BELH	Bellsize House	CGKING'S	Covent Garden and King's Theatres
BF	Bartholomew Fair		
BF—	Booth at BF identified by initials of proprietors	CGR	Coignand's Great Room
		CH	Charterhouse
BFT	Buffalo Tavern	CHA	Charterhouse
BG	Bedford Gate, Charles Street	CHAPEL	The Chapel at the Foundling's Hospital or at the Lock Hospital, Hyde Park Corner
BH	Boman's House		
BHB	Tiled Booth, Blackheath		
BHT	Bull's Head Tavern	CHE	Chelsea
BLA	Blackheath	CHELSEA	Priest's Boarding School, Chelsea
BLO	Bloomsbury	CHR	China Hall, Lower Road, Rotherhithe
BOS	Bow Street		

xvii

CII	Crown Inn, Lower Street, Islington	DLKING'S	Drury Lane and King's Theatres
CITY	The City, London	DLLIF	Drury Lane and Lincoln's Inn Fields Theatres
CL	Chancery Lane	DLORDG	Drury Lane or Dorset Garden Theatre
CLA	Clafton		
CLAR	Clare's Academy	DLORLIF	Drury Lane or Lincoln's Inn Fields Theatre
CLARK'S	Clark's School, Paul's Alley		
CLH	Clothworkers' Hall	DOVER	Dover, England
CLK	Clerkenwell	DR	Dancing Room
CLKCS	Clerkenwell Charity School	DS	Dancing School
COCKPIT	The Cockpit in Drury Lane	DT	Dog Tavern
COH	Coachmakers' Hall	EB	Essex Buildings
CORH	Corner House	EBH	Earl of Burlington's House
COURT	Whitehall or St James's	EC	Exeter Change, The Strand
CR	Crown and Anchor	EEH	Exchequer Eating House
CRT	Crown Tavern	EVELYN	John Evelyn's House
CS	Cannon Street	FALKLAND	Lord Falkland's Residence
CT	Castle Tavern	FE	Mr Fearnley's
CT/HAY	Castle Tavern and Haymarket Theatre	FH	Fishmongers' Hall
		FLR	Front Long Room
DC	Dorset Court	FS	Fleet Street
DEPT	Deptford	FT	Fleece Tavern
DG	Dorset Garden Theatre	FUL	Fulham
DG/IT	Dorset Garden Theatre and Inner Temple	GB	Golden Balls, Bow Street
		GF	Goodman's Fields Theatre
DGORDL	Dorset Garden or Drury Lane Theatre	GF/HAY	Goodman's Fields and Haymarket Theatres
DH	Drapers' Hall	GH	Girdlers' Hall
DL	Drury Lane Theatre	GLOBE	Globe and Marlborough's Head
DL/DG	Drury Lane and Dorset Garden Theatres	GO	Godwin's
		GR	Greenwich
DL/QUEEN	Drury Lane and Queen's Theatres	GROTTO	Grotto Gardens, St George's Fields
DL/DL	Drury Lane Theatre		
DL/DL/HA	Drury Lane and Haymarket Theatres	GRP	Great Room, Panton Street
		GRT	Great Room
DL/HAY	Drury Lane and Haymarket Theatres	GT	Greyhound Tavern
		GV	George and Vulture Tavern
DL/IT	Drury Lane Theatre and Inner Temple	H&P	Hand and Pen
		HA	Hampstead
DL/LIF	Drury Lane and Lincoln's Inn Fields Theatres	HAB	Haberdashers' Hall, Maiden Lane
		HAM	Long Room, Hampstead
DL/ORDG	Drury Lane and/or Dorset Garden Theatre	HAMM	Windsor Castle Inn, King Street, Hammersmith
DLANDLIF	Drury Lane and Lincoln's Inn Fields Theatres	HAW	Hampstead Wells
		HAY	Haymarket Theatre
DLDG	Drury Lane and Dorset Garden Theatres	HAY/GF	Haymarket and Goodman's Fields Theatres
DLDGLIF	Drury Lane, Dorset Garden, and Lincoln's Inn Fields Theatres	HAYGR	Great Room, Haymarket
		HC	Hampton Court

HDR	Hill's Dancing Room		MOORFL	Moorfields
HDS	Home's Dancing School		MR	Mercers' Hall
HC	Hampton Court		MS	Musical Society
HH	Haberdashers' Hall or Handel's Home		MT	Middle Temple
			MTH	Merchant Taylors' Hall
HIC	Hickford's		MTS	Merchant Taylors' School
HOUN	Hounslow		NH	North Hall
HT HUGHS'	Horseshoe Tavern in Freeman's Court		NONE	Calendar gives no theatre for performance
IT	Inner Temple		NTW	New Theatre, Mr Bradley's, Distiller, Old Gravel Lane, Wapping
JS	James Street			
KAT	King's Arms Tavern		NURSERY	In Moorfields, Bunhill, or Hatton Garden
KG	Kew Gardens			
KHS	King's Head Inn, Borough High Street, Southwark		NWC	New Wells, London Spa, Clerkenwell
KING/HAY	King's and Haymarket Theatres		NWGF	New Wells, Goodman's Fields
KING'S	King's Theatre		NWLS	New Wells, Lemon Street
KS	Kingston, The Playhouse by the Hand		NWMF	New Wells, Mayfair
			NWSM	New Wells, Shepherds' Market
LEI	Leicester House		OCH	Old Crown Inn, Highgate
LG	Leg Tavern		OLDFIELD	Mr Oldfield's Residence
LH	Loriner's Hall		OO	Outroper's Office
LI	Lincoln's Inn		ORMOND	Duke of Ormond's Residence
LIF	Lincoln's Inn Fields Theatre		OS	Orlibeer's School
LIF/QUEN	Lincoln's Inn Fields and Queen's Theatres		OSG	Old Spring Garden
			OXFORD	Oxford University
LIF/CG	Lincoln's Inn Fields and Covent Garden Theatres		PAN	Pantheon, Oxford Street
			PANT	The Pantheon
LIF/MT	Lincoln's Inn Fields Theatre and Middle Temple		PCGR	Great Room, Peter's Court
			PCR	Great Piazza Coffee Room, Covent Garden
LR	Long Room			
LRRH	Lecture Room, Robin Hood Tavern, near Temple Bar		PEPYS'S	Pepys's Residence
			PH	Pewterers' Hall
LRRH/PCR	Lecture Room, Robin Hood Tavern, and Great Piazza Coffee Room, Covent Garden		PM	Pall Mall
			PR	Powlet's Room
			PT	Pye Tavern
LS	Loe's School		PU	Punch's
LW	Lambeth Wells		PY	Palace Yard
MA	Mr Mayor's		QUEEN/DL	Queen's and Drury Lane Theatres
MARLY	Mary-le-Bone Gardens			
MBS	Mrs Bellamy's School		QUEEN'S	Queen's Theatre
MDS	Mrs Defenne's School		RANELAGH	Ranelagh Gardens
MEF	Mile End Fair		RDS	Roussau's Dancing School
MEG	Mile End Green		REDBULL	Red Bull Theatre
MF	Mayfair		RI	Richmond
MF—	Booth at MF identified by proprietors' initials		RICHMOND	New Wells, Richmond
			RIW	Richmond Wells
MH	Marlborough House		RIW/HAY	Richmond Wells and Haymarket Theatres
MO	Moorfields			

RL	Red Lion Street	TCJS	Tennis Court, James Street
RLSN	Red Lion Inn, Lordship Road, Stoke Newington	TC—	Booth at TC identified by proprietors' initials
ROBERT	Mrs Roberts's Home	TEC	Tennis Court
ROY	Royalty Theatre, Wells Street	TGB	Two Golden Balls
SALSBURY	Salisbury Court	THAMES	On the River Thames
SF	Southwark Fair	TT	Tower Tavern
SF—	Booth at SF identified by proprietors' initials	TTT	Three Tuns Tavern
		UM	Upper Moorfields
SG	Spring Garden	VAUX	Vauxhall Gardens
SH	Stationers' Hall	VENDU	Charles Street, Covent Garden
SHG	Somerset Hall Garden	VERE	Theatre in Vere Street
SJP	St James's Palace	VERE/RED	Vere Street and Red Bull Theatres
SLINGSBY	Mr Slingsby's residence		
SMITH'S	Mr Smith's residence	VH	Vintners' Hall
SML	St Martin's Lane	WCH	Wax Chandlers' Hall
SMMF	Shepherds' Market, Mayfair	WEYS'	Weys' Home
SOHO	Great Room, Dean Street, Soho	WF	Welch Fair
SOU	Southwark	WH	Whitehead
SOUGT	Southwark, Great Tiled Booth	WHF	White Horse Inn, Parsons Green, Fulham
SPS	St Paul's School		
SS	Soho Square	WINDSOR	Windsor Castle
ST	Swan Tavern	WINH	Windmill Hill
STA	St Alban's School	WLWS	White Lion Inn, Wych Street
STJAME	St James's Palace	WRSG	Wheatley's Riding School, Greenwich
STRAND	Society of Artists' Exhibition Room, Strand		
		WS	Westminster School
SUN	Sun Tavern	YB	York Buildings
SW	Sadlers' Wells	YB/HAY	York Buildings and Haymarket Theatre
TB	Temple Bar		
TC	Tottenham Court	YEB	Yates' Booth
TCD/BF	Tottenham Court booth and Bartholomew Fair	YH	York House
		YS	York Street, Covent Garden

A la Parisot (dance), 1797: CG, Jun 9
A la Plus Sage (dance), 1785: KING'S, Mar 3, Apr 5, 28
A Londre I was a Taylor nice (song), 1785: HAY, Aug 9
A me ritornate Speranze tu Care (song), 1748: KING'S, Apr 5
A Teneri Affetti (song), 1729: DL, Mar 26; 1734: DL, May 13, HAY, Jun 28, LIF,
  Aug 20
Abbot (musician), 1799: CG, Feb 8
Abbott (numberer), 1719: LIF, May 19
Abbott, Henry (stage doorkeeper), 1760: CG, Sep 22; 1763: CG, May 26; 1768: CG,
  Jun 3, 4; 1769: CG, May 6, 15; 1770: CG, May 18, 21; 1771: CG, May 22; 1772:
  CG, May 23; 1773: CG, May 22; 1774: CG, May 14; 1778: CG, May 21; 1779: CG,
  May 15; 1780: CG, May 24; 1781: CG, May 25; 1782: CG, May 08; 1783: CG, May
  31; 1784: CG, May 22
Abbott, James (house servant), 1767: CG, Dec 19; 1768: CG, Mar 18, Dec 12
Abbott, T (actor), 1788: HAY, Jun 10, Aug 2, 5, 9, 16, 18, 29, Sep 30; 1789:
  HAY, May 18, 20, 25, 27, Jun 1, 8, 10, 12, 22, 25, 30, Jul 1, 11, Aug 11, 25;
  1790: HAY, Jun 15, 25, 26, 28, 29, Jul 7, 16, Aug 12, 13, Sep 4; 1791: HAY,
  Jun 6, 8, 1, 9, 13, 15, 17, 22, 28, 30, Sep 1, 10, 13; 1793: HAY, Jun 13, 14,
  21, 25, 29, Jul 5, 9, 13, 17, 19, 20, Aug 3, 5, 6, 12, 13, 27, CG, Sep 23,
  30, Oct 7, 17, Nov 1, 13, 16, Dec 5; 1794: CG, Feb 22, Mar 25, May 9, 28, Jun
  10, HAY, Jul 8, 9, 10, 11, 12, 16, 17, 18, 21, 22, 25, Aug 11, 13, 27, CG,
  Sep 22, 26, Oct 20, 23; 1795: CG, Jan 31, Mar 19, Apr 8, May 1, 29, Jun 6,
  HAY, 9, 13, 15, 18, 20, Jul 1, 16, 18, 25, 30, 31, Aug 14, 27, 29, Sep 2, CG,
  14, 16, 21, 25, Oct 2, 7, 8, 9, 15, 16, 19, 23, 26, 30, Nov 4, 6, 7, 9, Dec
  4, 7, 9, 23; 1796: CG, Jan 13, 23, 26, Mar 15, 30, Apr 9, 26, May 16, Jun 4,
  HAY, 11, 13, 14, 18, 20, 22, 25, 29, 30, Jul 2, 4, 5, 6, 8, 9, 11, 12, 15,
  21, 23, 26, Aug 8, 9, 10, 11, 12, 13, 16, 18, 25, 29, Sep 5, 7, CG, 16, 19,
  21, 26, Oct 6, 7, 13, 14, 25, 29, Nov 19, 24, Dec 7, 19, 26; 1797: CG, Jan
  10, Feb 18, Mar 4, 7, 21, Apr 8, 19, 25, May 9, 16, 18, 31, Jun 1, 2, 9, HAY,
  12, 13, CG, 13, HAY, 15, 16, 17, 19, 20, 21, 22, 23, 24, 26, 28, Jul 3, 6,
  10, 15, 21, Aug 4, 9, 15, 30, 31, Sep 4, CG, 18, 22, 29, Oct 2, 16, Nov 2, 4,
  8, 10, 13, 15, 21, 23, 24, Dec 5, 8, 12, 18, 19, 23, 26; 1798: CG, Jan 4, 11,
  Feb 12, 13, Mar 19, 27, 31, Apr 9, 13, 14, 19, 20, 21, May 7, 12, 29, Jun 5,
  11, HAY, 12, 13, 14, 15, 16, 18, 19, 20, 21, 23, 30, Jul 6, 14, 21, Aug 3, 4,
  11, 21, 23, 25, 28, 29, Sep 3, CG, 19, 21, 26, 28, Oct 3, 8, 11, 15, Nov 7,
  9, 10, 12, 20, Dec 8, 11, 26; 1799: CG, Jan 3, 12, 14, 16, 17, 26, 29, Mar 2,
  16, 25, Apr 2, 8, 9, 12, 13, 19, 23, May 4, 6, 7, 13, 15, 22, 24, 25, 28, Jun
  12, HAY, 15, 17, 18, 19, 20, 21, 22, 24, 25, 28, 29, Jul 2, 9, 10, 12, 13,
  17, 20, 23, 27, Aug 5, 10, 13, 17, 21, CG, Sep 16, 18, 20, 23, 25, 27, Oct 2,
  7, 16, 18, 21, 24, 25, 31, Nov 4, 11, 13, 14, 15, 30, Dec 4, 16, 19, 23;
  1800: CG, Jan 16, Feb 4, 8, 10, Mar 1, 4, 17, 25, 27, Apr 5, 22, 23, 24, May
  1, 12, 13, 23, Jun 2, 5, 7, HAY, 13, 14, 16, 19, 20, 21, 28, Jul 2, 5, 15,
  Aug 7, 8, 14, 20, 23, 27, 29, Sep 1, 3, 11
Abbott's Academy, 1788: HAY, Sep 30
Abchurch Lane, 1749: CG, Apr 28
Abdelazar. See Behn, Aphra.
Abdicated Prince, The; or, The Adventures of Four Hours (play, anon), 1689:
  NONE, Sep 0
Abegg, Mrs (actor), 1758: SOHO, Mar 31, CG, Nov 23; 1759: CG, Jan 3, 29, Mar
  24, 26, Apr 3, Nov 30; 1760: CG, Jan 16, Apr 17, Sep 22, 29, Oct 20; 1761:
  CG, Jan 9, 28, Mar 5, Apr 2, 6, 11, Sep 16, 18, 21, 25; 1762: CG, Jan 12, Apr
  21, May 11, Sep 22
Abel Drugger's Return (entertainment), 1774: HAY, Aug 29, Sep 5, 6, 16, 19;
  1781: CII, Apr 5
Abel. See Arne, Dr Thomas A, The Sacrifice.
Abel, Karl Friedrich (musician, composer), 1761: SOHO, Jan 28; 1762: CG, Dec 8;
  1763: CG, Oct 22; 1767: KING'S, Mar 5, CG, May 23; 1771: GROTTO, Aug 30, Sep
  3, 9; 1772: HAY, Mar 30, Apr 27; 1773: HAY, Apr 19; 1775: DL, Mar 10, KING'S,
  Apr 5, 7; 1782: CG, Nov 25; 1783: CG, Jan 18
Abell, John (musician, singer), 1683: ATCOURT, Nov 0; 1688: ATCOURT, Jun 18;
  1700: DLORLIF, Jan 20; 1701: DG, May 21, RIW, Aug 11, HA, 25, RIW, Sep 8;
  1702: CC, Apr 25, SH, May 1, DL, 2, CC, 25, DL, Dec 29; 1715: SH, Jun 30
Abercomy, 1687: NONE, Feb 16
Aberdein (actor), 1782: HAY, Apr 9; 1783: DL, May 31; 1784: HAY, Feb 9, DL, May
  22; 1785: HAY, Jan 24, DL, May 20; 1786: DL, May 29; 1787: DL, Jun 1; 1792:
  HAY, Oct 22; 1793: HAY, Dec 26; 1794: DL, Oct 31; 1795: HAY, Sep 21; 1796:
  DL, Jan 11; 1800: DL, Jun 14

1

Abergavenny is fine (song), 1790: CG, Nov 23; 1791: CG, Sep 19; 1793: CG, May
    21; 1794: CG, Apr 12, Oct 29; 1795: CG, Oct 7; 1797: CG, Oct 2; 1799: CG, Mar
    16, Dec 9; see also Taffy and Griddy
Abergavenny, Lord. See Nevil, George.
Abgali (Abogly, Bogly), Sid Mahomet Ali (Moroccan ambassador), 1726: DL, Mar 8,
    LIF, 31, HAY, Apr 25, LIF, Aug 9, 19, 23, Sep 30, Oct 29
Abimelech. See Arnold, Dr Samuel.
Abingdon, Earl of. See Bertie, Willoughby.
Abington, Frances (actor, author), 1759: DL, Sep 25, 27, Oct 2, 4, 5, 6, 11,
    16, 17, 19, 30, 31, Nov 5, 19, 23; 1765: DL, Nov 27, Dec 5, 7; 1766: DL, Jan
    8, Feb 20, Apr 8, 14, 23, May 2, 10, Sep 25, Oct 4, 10, 17, 27, Nov 7, 17;
    1767: DL, Jan 2, 22, 24, Feb 21, 23, Mar 28, Apr 22, May 27, Sep 16, 18, 22,
    23, 25, Oct 8, 9, Nov 16, Dec 5, 12; 1768: DL, Jan 1, 19, 23, Feb 27, Apr 6,
    12, 14, May 10, Sep 27, Oct 1, 4, 8, 19, 31, Nov 5, 17, Dec 14, 17; 1769: DL,
    Feb 23, Mar 28, 31, Apr 25, 28, May 15, 16, 19, Sep 21, Oct 3, 4, 5, 6, 10,
    14, 16, 18, Nov 1, 15, Dec 4, 8, 16, 22, 23; 1770: DL, Jan 16, 17, 25, Mar 1,
    24, Apr 3, May 26, Sep 27, Oct 6, 15, 22, 23, 24, 26, Nov 15, 20, 24, Dec 5,
    12; 1771: DL, Jan 4, 19, Mar 14, 16, 18, 21, Apr 5, May 7, 22, 27, Sep 24,
    Oct 3, 26, 31, Nov 2, 9, 13, 14, 16, 22, 23, 26, 27, 30, Dec 7, 10, 14, 21,
    23, 28, 30; 1772: DL, Jan 1, 4, 11, 15, 17, 18, 25, Feb 1, 8, 22, 29, Mar 7,
    14, 21, 23, 28, 30, Apr 2, 4, 11, 22, 25, 27, May 2, 9, 12, 13, 16, 23, 30,
    Jun 6, 10, Sep 26, Oct 3, 8, 14, 15, 20, 30, Nov 30, Dec 14; 1773: DL, Jan 4,
    26, Feb 4, 18, 20, Mar 23, 27, Apr 3, 16, 21, May 13, Sep 23, 25, Oct 19, 22,
    30, Nov 15, Dec 4, 10, 11; 1774: DL, Jan 18, 22, Feb 15, Mar 15, May 5, 10,
    14, Sep 24, Oct 6, 12, 14, 26, Nov 3, 5, 7, 16, 24, CG, Dec 2, DL, 7, 19;
    1775: DL, Feb 8, Mar 6, 18, 27, Apr 4, 8, Oct 7, 11, 18, 20, 21, 31, Nov 6,
    27, 28, Dec 12, 19; 1776: DL, Jan 3, 20, Feb 5, 6, 8, 10, 12, Mar 12, 21, 28,
    Apr 8, 10, 17, 30, May 7, 23, Oct 10, 18, 30, Nov 6, 7, 19, 29, Dec 31; 1777:
    DL, Jan 16, Feb 24, Mar 22, 31, May 8, Oct 22, Dec 4; 1778: DL, Jan 23, Feb
    3, 4, Mar 5, Apr 9, Oct 6, 13, 19, Nov 18, Dec 21; 1779: DL, Jan 2, Feb 3,
    Mar 15, Apr 19, HAY, Aug 31, DL, Sep 21, 28, Oct 2, 12, 19, Nov 9, 11, 18,
    Dec 2; 1780: DL, Feb 28, Mar 6, Apr 1, 24, May 24, Oct 14, 25, 28, Dec 7, 20;
    1781: DL, Jan 22, 26, Feb 2, Mar 10, Apr 24, Sep 27, Oct 4, 18, 25, 30, Nov
    6, 15, 21; 1782: DL, Jan 9, 21, Feb 25, Mar 4, CG, 11, DL, Apr 1, CG, Nov 29,
    Dec 6, 20; 1783: CG, Jan 3, 17, Feb 19, Apr 25, May 22; 1784: CG, Jan 23, Feb
    13, 20, Mar 2, 6, Jun 2, Oct 6, 27, Nov 11; 1785: CG, Jan 14, 21, Feb 8, Mar
    5, May 26, Oct 5, 10, 19, 27, 29, Nov 2, 7, 19, 23, 26, Dec 7; 1786: CG, Feb
    10, Mar 11; 1787: CG, Jan 26, 31, Feb 9, Mar 15, 31, Apr 30, Oct 17, Nov 2,
    7, 14, 20, 26, Dec 5, 10; 1788: CG, Jan 2, 9, 11, 15, 17, 21, 23, Feb 4, 25,
    Mar 6, Apr 14, 25; 1789: CG, Jan 8, 15, 20, 23, 28, Feb 13, 20, 24, Mar 5,
    19, Apr 2, 29, May 8, 18, Nov 5, 12, 19, Dec 11; 1790: CG, Jan 13, Feb 4, Apr
    29; 1791: CG, May 10; 1797: CG, Jun 14, Oct 6, 11, 28, Nov 11, 18, Dec 8, 28,
    30; 1798: CG, Feb 6, Mar 31, Apr 27, May 16, HAY, Dec 17; 1799: CG, Apr 12
--Matrimony, 1798: CG, Apr 27
Abington, James (trumpeter, singer), 1756: DL, Feb 11
Abington, Joseph (violinist), 1711: GT, Apr 10; 1720: HIC, Mar 4; 1722: SH, Mar
    9; 1758: CHAPEL, Apr 27
Abogly, Sid Mahomet Ali. See Abgali, Sid Mahomet Ali.
Abos, Girolamo (composer), 1756: KING'S, Apr 10; 1758: KING'S, Apr 6; 1762: CG,
    Dec 8; 1763: CG, Oct 22
--Tito Manlio (opera), 1756: KING'S, Apr 10, 24
Abra Mule. See Trapp, Joseph.
Abraham believed in God (song), 1794: DL, Apr 10
Abraham enough (song), 1789: DL, Mar 18; 1790: DL, Feb 26; 1791: DL, Mar 23;
    1792: KING'S, Feb 24; 1793: KING/HAY, Feb 22; 1794: DL, Apr 10
Abrahams. See Abrams.
Abrahams, John (father of Harriet Abrams), 1775: DL, Nov 9; 1776: DL, Jan 3, 8,
    Feb 10, Mar 30
Abrams, Harriet (actor, singer, composer), 1775: DL, Oct 28, Dec 7; 1776: DL,
    Mar 30, Apr 20, May 1, Jun 10, Sep 24, Oct 18, Nov 4, 7, 25, Dec 10; 1777:
    DL, Jan 1, 4, 8, Feb 15, Apr 17, 22, Jun 6, Sep 20, Oct 23, 31, Nov 4, 10,
    12, Dec 3, 29; 1778: DL, Jan 1, 5, Feb 19, May 9, 21, 23, Sep 24, 26, Oct 8,
    13, 27, Nov 2, 9; 1779: DL, Jan 8, May 8, 11, Sep 30, Oct 5, 30, Nov 3, 20,
    Dec 14, 21, 27, 28; 1780: DL, Jan 28, Feb 28, Apr 18, 26, May 6; 1799: HAY,
    Sep 2, 16
Abrams, Miss G (singer, actor), 1779: DL, Jan 8, Mar 16, 25, Sep 30; 1780: DL,
    May 5, 9
Abroad and at Home. See Holman, Joseph George.
Absent Man, The. See Bickerstaff, Isaac.
Academy Lane, 1739: CL, Feb 12
Academy of Music, 1719: DL, May 9; 1720: KING'S, Feb 28
Academy, Chancery Lane, 1715: CL, Jun 13; 1732: CL, May 10

2

Academy, Drury Lane, 1733: ACDL, Mar 14
Academy, Little Lincoln's Inn Fields, 1676: ACADEMY, Dec 14
Academy, Soho Square, 1731: SS, Nov 8; 1732: SS, Nov 1; 1740: SS, Dec 10
Academy, The (dance), 1776: CG, May 3
Accomplished Maid, The. See Piccini, Niccolo.
Achilles in Petticoats. See Colman the elder, George.
Achilles. See Gay, John.
Achilles; or, Iphigenia in Aulis. See Boyer, Abel.
Achmet, Catherine Ann (actor), 1789: CG, Sep 14, 30, Nov 16, Dec 5; 1790: CG,
    Apr 29, May 11, 13, Jun 14
Achmet, Miss (actor), 1794: HAY, Jun 2
Achurch, Mrs (actor), 1734: JS, May 31
Achurch, Thomas (actor), 1730: HAY, Jan 21, Mar 30, SFP, Sep 9, SF, 14; 1749:
    CG, Apr 3
Aci e Galatea. See Bianchi Jr, Francesco.
Acis and Galatea (dance), 1750: DL, Feb 13, 19, 23
Acis and Galatea. See Handel, George Frederic.
Acis and Galatea; or, The Country Wedding. See Motteux, Peter Anthony.
Acis et Galatie (dance), 1797: KING'S, Jun 15, 17, 20, 27, Jul 4, 15, 22, 25
Ackery. See Akery.
Ackman, Ellis (actor), 1750: DL, Feb 24, Apr 23, Sep 28, Oct 30; 1751: DL, May
    4, 6, Sep 12, Oct 29; 1752: DL, Feb 6, Apr 1, 6, 25, Nov 25; 1753: DL, Jan 1,
    Feb 7, 22, Apr 12, 30, May 9, 18, Sep 13, 25, Oct 9, 17, 20; 1754: DL, Jan
    23, Apr 30, May 6, 13, Sep 14, Oct 10, 31, Nov 11; 1755: DL, Feb 18, May 2,
    Oct 7, Nov 8, 26; 1756: DL, Jan 21, May 6, Sep 25, 28, Nov 4, Dec 27; 1757:
    DL, Mar 24, May 9, Oct 7, 29, Nov 4, 25, Dec 22, 27; 1758: DL, Jan 13, May 8,
    Oct 17, Nov 16, 27, Dec 18, 28; 1759: DL, Jan 3, 4, Feb 1, May 4, 11, 14, 16,
    21, Sep 29, Oct 9, 27, 30, 31, Nov 19, 30, Dec 1, 7, 31; 1760: DL, Jan 24,
    Feb 21, Mar 4, 6, Apr 11, 22, 28, 30, May 8, Oct 2, 3, 7, 18, Nov 20, 27, Dec
    17; 1761: DL, Jan 3, 10, 31, Feb 12, Mar 26, Apr 6, 25, May 5, Sep 14, 15,
    17, 24, Oct 23, Nov 21, 28, Dec 11, 17, 30; 1762: DL, Mar 27, Apr 1, 3, 30,
    May 6, 12, 15, 17, Sep 21, 23, 25, Oct 5, 6, 7, 12, 15, 21, Nov 3, 4, 10, 23,
    25, Dec 6, 11, 22; 1763: DL, Jan 5, 15, 18, 19, 27, 29, Feb 24, Mar 15, 19,
    21, Apr 11, 20, 22, May 3, 23, Sep 17, 20, 22, 27, 29, Oct 4, 8, 17, 24, 28,
    31, Nov 4, 7, 8, 9, 14, 19, 23, 26, Dec 26; 1764: DL, Jan 4, 18, Feb 8, Mar
    20, 26, 29, 31, Apr 2, 12, 14, 24, May 8, 10, Sep 20, 22, 25, 27, Oct 15, 16,
    17, 19, 20, 22, 24, 26, 31, Nov 13, 17, 24, 27, Dec 26, 31; 1765: DL, Jan 18,
    22, 24, 26, Feb 4, Mar 19, Apr 13, 15, 20, May 9, 11, 17, 22, Sep 17, 24, 28,
    Oct 2, 5, 9, 11, 14, 15, 25, 28, Nov 11, 16, Dec 3, 5, 6, 14; 1766: DL, Jan
    6, 9, 13, 23, 24, Feb 11, Mar 15, 22, Apr 7, 12, 16, 25, May 6, 14, 19, HAY,
    Jun 26, DL, Sep 20, 23, 27, Oct 7, 8, 10, 16, 18, 23, 24, 29, Nov 4, 8, 24,
    Dec 2, 4; 1767: DL, Jan 24, Feb 7, Mar 7, 21, 30, Apr 22, 27, 28, May 1, 6,
    8, 15, Jun 1, Sep 15, 17, 19, 23, 25, 26, Oct 14, 20, 22, 23, 26, 28, Nov 4,
    7, 18, 19, 23, 24, 25, Dec 15, 26; 1768: DL, Jan 6, 9, 14, Mar 15, 21, Apr 6,
    14, May 2, Sep 8, 17, 20, 23, 26, 28, Oct 10, 11, 13, 19, 20, 21, 28, 31, Nov
    4, 5, 10, 24, Dec 7, 14, 17, 23, 28, 30; 1769: DL, Feb 13, Mar 18, 29, Apr
    12, 24, May 1, Sep 19, 21, 26, Oct 5, 7, 9, 10, 13, 23, 30, 31, Nov 4, 9, 11,
    14, 15, 17, 21, 24, 27, Dec 1, 6, 8, 12, 13, 16; 1770: DL, Jan 4, 8, 19, 27,
    Feb 21, Mar 1, 13, Apr 3, 7, 17, May 5, 9, 15, Sep 22, 29, Oct 3, 8, 9, 13,
    20, 26, 31, Nov 3, 5, 6, 9, 13, 14, HAY, 16, DL, 17, 19, 20, 21, 23, 24, 28,
    Dec 20, 22; 1771: DL, Jan 4, Mar 7, 9, 11, 12, 21, Apr 1, 5, 6, 9, 13, 30,
    May 1, 4, 28, Sep 21, 26, 28, Oct 1, 15, 17, 21, 30, 31, Nov 1, 4, 8, 9, 11,
    12, 13, 21, 22, 23, 25, 28, Dec 2, 4, 21, 26; 1772: DL, Jan 11, 15, Feb 27,
    29, Mar 19, 21, 26, 30, Apr 21, 25, May 12, 13, 18, 25, Jun 10, Sep 19, 22,
    24, 29, Oct 3, 6, 13, 14, 15, 16, 21, 24, 30, Nov 3, 4, 9, 17, 18, 20, 27,
    30, Dec 2, 7, 17, 18, 21, 26; 1773: DL, Jan 19, 21, Feb 2, 8, Mar 30, Apr 15,
    17, 23, 24, 27, May 4, 6, 10, 12, 13, Sep 18, 21, 25, 30, Oct 8, 14, 20, 22,
    23, 25, 26, 28, 30, Nov 2, 4, 6, 9, 13, 25, Dec 27; 1774: DL, Jan 10, 18, 19,
    22, Feb 2, 8, 15, Mar 12, 14, 22, Apr 4, 28, May 4, 10, 18, Sep 17, 22, 27,
    29, Oct 1, 4
Ackman, Mrs (house servant), 1779: CG, May 21
Ackroyde (Akeroyd, Aykerod), Samuel (composer), 1685: DL, May 9, Aug 0; 1686:
    DL, Jan 0, ATCOURT, Dec 1; 1693: DL, Feb 0, DG, May 0; 1695: DG, Nov 0; 1696:
    LIF, Jun 0; 1699: LIF, Mar 0, DL, May 0
Act of Grace, An; or, The Unhappy's Release (song), 1755: HAY, Aug 21
Acton (fishmonger), 1738: DL, Aay 12
Actors' Fund, 1776: DL, Mar 14
Adagio (dance), 1774: KING'S, Feb 22, Mar 12, Apr 14; 1776: KING'S, May 30
Adam St, 1779: CG, Mar 22; 1786: DL, Apr 24
Adam, Robert and James (architects), 1775: DL, Sep 23, 30; 1791: DL, Jun 4
Adamberger, Valentino (singer), 1777: KING'S, Nov 8; 1778: KING'S, Feb 7, Apr
    4, May 30, Nov 28; 1779: KING'S, Jan 23, Mar 25, May 29

3

Adams (actor), 1670: LIF, Nov 0; 1673: LIF, Dec 0
Adams (actor), 1728: HAY, Jul 1, Sep 6, Oct 15, 26, Nov 14, 19, Dec 7
Adams (actor), 1772: HAY, Sep 17
Adams (actor), 1788: HAY, Jul 24
Adams (coffee house proprietor), 1795: HAY, Apr 22
Adams, Charles (actor, dancer), 1736: HAY, Feb 16, Apr 26; 1740: BFLP, Aug 23;
   1741: DL, May 23, BFTY, Aug 22; 1743: JS, Mar 23, BFHC, Aug 23, BFGA, 23;
   1744: MFHNT, May 1, MF, 3, Jun 7; 1745: SMMF, Jul 11; 1746: HAY, Apr 30,
   BFYB, Aug 25; 1747: SF, Sep 14; 1748: HAY, Apr 30, BFLYY, Aug 24, SFLYYW, Sep
   7, BHB, Oct 1, 4, DL, Dec 23, 26, NWSM, 29; 1749: DL, Jan 2, NWMF, 5, HAY, 7,
   NWMF, 10, HAY, 16, DL, 17, SOU, Feb 13, DL, 21, NWSM, May 10, 15
Adams, James Sturgis (beneficiary), 1750: DL, Jan 11
Adams, Misses E, H and S (dancer), 1800: CG, May 27, Jun 13
Adams, Mrs (actor), 1731: LIF, Apr 1
Adams, Mrs (actor), 1748: SOU, Jul 4; 1749: HAY, Apr 29
Adams, Mrs (singer), 1750: HAY, Feb 16
Adams, Mrs, 1775: DL, Mar 23
Adams's Masquerade Warehouse, 1792: HAY, Aug 2
Adcock (actor, singer, manager), 1795: HAY, Sep 21; 1796: HAY, Feb 22, Apr 27
Adcock, Abraham (musician), 1740: DL, May 21; 1758: CHAPEL, Apr 27
Adcock, Mary (actor), 1758: HAY, Jan 18; 1765: DL, May 16
Adcock, Miss (singer), 1782: CG, Nov 18, Dec 6
Adcock, William (actor), 1758: HAY, Jan 16, 18; 1764: DL, Nov 12; 1765: DL, Jan
   2, 15, 23, Feb 4, Mar 16, Apr 22, 30, May 6, 7, 16, 21
Addinal (painter), 1779: HAY, Aug 24
Addington, Capt (author), 1773: DL, Dec 11
Addington, Sir William, 1774: CG, Apr 7
--Prince of Agra, The, 1774: CG, Apr 7
Addison, Elizabeth, Mrs John (singer, actor), 1792: CG, Feb 24, Mar 2, 14, 21;
   1796: CG, Sep 17, Oct 21, Nov 5, Dec 27
Addison, Joseph, 1705: DL, Apr 23; 1707: DL, Feb 1; 1713: DL, Apr 14, May 7;
   1715: YB, May 28; 1719: RI, Jul 6; 1721: DL, Dec 28; 1722: LIF, Feb 2, 5, Mar
   12, 13, DL, 31, LIF, Apr 4, 17, Oct 6, DL, 11, LIF, Nov 21, DL, Dec 12, LIF,
   22; 1723: LIF, Feb 12, Oct 14; 1724: HAY, Mar 23; 1730: GF, Jan 19, 20, Feb
   19, LIF, Apr 20, May 21; 1731: GF, Apr 19, Dec 1; 1732: GF, Feb 4, Nov 2;
   1733: LIF, Feb 22, Mar 7, Apr 5, HAY, Aug 20, DL/HAY, Nov 28; 1734: CG, Jan
   19, Mar 12, DL, Sep 14, 21, Oct 10, CG/LIF, Nov 28, DL, Dec 26; 1735: DL, Mar
   1, TC, May 28, DL, Jun 11, Sep 20, Dec 13, 17; 1736: DL, May 1, 12, Oct 27,
   Dec 3; 1737: DL, Feb 19, Mar 2, Sep 8; 1738: DL, Jan 2, Sep 12, Oct 3, 5, Nov
   23, CG, Dec 7; 1739: DL, Jan 19, Mar 24, May 7; 1740: DL, Mar 8, CG, Oct 17,
   Nov 20; 1741: DL, Feb 25, Mar 24; 1743: DL, Sep 27, CG, Oct 28; 1744: DL, Oct
   4; 1745: DL, Jan 31, Nov 9, GF, 22, Dec 9; 1747: DL, Jan 10; 1752: CG, Dec 8;
   1754: CG, Apr 26, DL, Oct 25; 1755: DL, Oct 3; 1767: CG, Apr 21; 1772: CG,
   Mar 27; 1773: CG, Sep 20; 1776: DL, Nov 28; 1786: CG, Apr 24; 1794: DL, Dec
   13
--Cato, 1713: DL, Apr 6, 14, 15, 16, 17, 18, 21, 22, 23, 24, 25, 28, 29, 30,
   May 1, 2, 5, 6, 7, 8, 9, Oct 19, 20, 29, Nov 12, Dec 3, 17, 29; 1714: DL, Jan
   16, Mar 15, Apr 6, 22, May 8, Sep 28, Oct 2, 23, Nov 10; 1715: DL, Jan 7, 19,
   SH, Mar 1, DL, May 3, Oct 21, Dec 29; 1716: DL, Feb 6, 14, Mar 19, Apr 13,
   May 21; 1717: DL, Jan 24, Mar 5, Oct 19; 1718: DL, Feb 22, Mar 8, 29, Apr 25,
   LIF, Oct 16, 17, DL, 25, Dec 26; 1719: DL, Feb 5, Apr 21, Oct 13; 1720: DL,
   Feb 9, May 13, Nov 29; 1721: DL, Feb 1, Mar 14, Dec 28; 1722: DL, Mar 31, Oct
   11, Dec 12; 1723: DL, May 1, CH, Aug 15, DL, Oct 31, GR, Nov 23, Dec 5; 1724:
   DL, Jan 2, Feb 25, Apr 9, Nov 12; 1725: DL, Feb 9, Mar 6, Apr 14, Oct 13;
   1726: DL, Feb 7, Apr 11; 1727: DL, Jan 19, 25, Mar 4, Apr 13, May 12, Oct 18,
   Dec 30; 1728: DL, Dec 14; 1729: DL, Feb 22, Oct 7, 27, Dec 27; 1730: LIF, Apr
   20, DL, May 6, LIF, 21, DL, Oct 1, GF, Nov 12, 13, 14, 16, Dec 3, DL, 29;
   1731: GF, Mar 15, Oct 26, Dec 2; 1732: DL, Jan 1, GF, Feb 18, DL, Mar 14, Oct
   5, KING'S, 31, Nov 4, 7, 11, 14, 18; 1733: DL, Apr 14, GF, 19, May 24, HAY,
   Aug 20, GF, Nov 2, DL/HAY, 28; 1734: CG, Jan 18, 19, Mar 12, 26, GF, Apr 25,
   DL, May 21, JS, 23, DL, Sep 14, 17, 21, GF, Oct 2, DL, 10, CG/LIF, Nov 28,
   29, Dec 2, 3, DL, 26; 1735: GF, Feb 5, DL, Mar 1, May 10, Jun 11, Sep 20, Dec
   13, 17; 1736: DL, Mar 6, LIF, 29, DL, May 1, GF, 5, DL, 12, CG, 17, DL, Oct
   27, LIF, 28, 30, Nov 2, 5, DL, Dec 3; 1737: HAY, Feb 14, DL, 19, Mar 2, May
   12, 17, CG, 31, DL, Sep 1, 8, Oct 4; 1738: DL, Jan 2, Sep 12, Nov 23, CG, Dec
   7; 1739: DL, Jan 19, 20, Mar 24, May 7, Sep 13, Oct 12, Nov 15; 1740: DL, Jan
   8, Mar 6, Oct 16, Nov 12, CG, 20; 1741: DL, Apr 27, JS, May 11, DL, Dec 8;
   1742: DL, Mar 4, CG, 25, DL, May 4, CG, Oct 18, Nov 18; 1743: DL, Feb 4, CG,
   12, Apr 22, DL, May 5, Sep 27, Oct 18, CG, 28, Dec 2; 1744: DL, Feb 3, CG,
   16, Mar 10, DL, Oct 4, CG, 18; 1745: CG, Jan 31, Mar 30, DL, Nov 9, GF, 22,
   Dec 9; 1746: HIC, Mar 14, CG, Oct 24, Dec 20; 1747: GF, Jan 22, Mar 14;
   1748: CG, Apr 16, Oct 25, Nov 12, Dec 21; 1749: DL, Jan 2, LEI, 7, DL, 20,

4

CG, Feb 4, Apr 6, Nov 11; 1750: CG, Jan 27, Mar 24, Dec 1, 29; 1751: CG, Feb
12; 1754: CG, Nov 27, Dec 6; 1755: CG, Feb 7; 1756: DL, Dec 11, 14; 1757: DL,
Jan 7, Feb 5; 1760: DL, Oct 18, 21; 1765: CG, Apr 16; 1766: CG, Apr 14; 1767:
CG, Mar 28, May 7; 1770: CG, Apr 30; 1771: DL, Apr 3; 1772: CG, May 11, 25;
1775: CG, Oct 21, Nov 17; 1776: CG, Feb 26, CHR, Oct 16; 1777: HAY, Aug 14,
18; 1779: CG, Jan 15, 18; 1784: DL, Apr 28, Nov 15; 1797: CG, May 31, HAY,
Dec 4
--Drummer, The; or, The Haunted House, 1716: DL, Mar 10, 13, 17; 1722: LIF, Feb
2, 3, 5, 6, 8, 10, 12, Mar 12, 13, Apr 4, 17, May 21, Oct 6, Nov 21, Dec 22;
1723: LIF, Feb 12, Mar 26, Oct 14, 16, Dec 20; 1724: LIF, Jan 18, Feb 7, 18,
Mar 21, HAY, 23, LIF, May 7, RI, Jun 27, LIF, Nov 27; 1725: LIF, Jan 23, Apr
2, May 19, Oct 27; 1726: LIF, Jan 18; 1727: LIF, Mar 4, Oct 13, Dec 20; 1728:
HAY, Jun 20; 1729: LIF, Jan 18, TT, Dec 29; 1730: LIF, Jan 9, GF, 19, 20, Feb
19, LIF, Oct 30; 1731: LIF, Feb 19, GF, 27, Apr 19, LIF, Nov 22, GF, Dec 1;
1732: LIF, Jan 14, GF, Feb 4, Nov 2, LIF/CG, 27; 1734: BLO, Jan 16, CG, 28,
RI, Sep 26, GF, Oct 30; 1735: CG/LIF, Feb 3, TC, May 28, CG, Oct 15; 1738:
DL, Oct 3, 5, 7; 1740: CG, Mar 22, 29, Apr 12, May 6, Oct 17, GF, 30; 1741:
CG, Oct 26, Dec 29; 1745: CG, Jan 23, GF, Nov 22, DL, 25; 1747: CG, Jan 17;
1749: CG, Dec 27; 1750: CG, Feb 8, 27, May 7, Nov 28; 1751: CG, Nov 11; 1752:
CG, Feb 11, 24, Dec 8; 1754: DL, Oct 25, 28, Nov 5, 9, Dec 2, 6, 26; 1755:
DL, Jan 4, 13, May 12, Oct 3; 1756: DL, Apr 24; 1758: DL, Feb 4; 1762: CG,
Jan 28, DL, 29, CG, Feb 1, DL, 1, 5, CG, 6, Apr 15; 1763: DL, May 14; 1764:
DL, Jan 23; 1765: CG, Dec 26; 1771: DL, Nov 6, 20; 1772: DL, Dec 29; 1774:
DL, Sep 17, Oct 25; 1776: DL, Nov 28; 1786: CG, Apr 24, 29, May 19, 23; 1790:
CG, May 11, 21; 1794: DL, Oct 18, Nov 7, Dec 12, 13
--Rosamond (musical), 1707: DL, Feb 1, Mar 4, 15, 22; 1733: LIF, Feb 22, Mar 7,
9, 14, 16, Apr 5, 9, 30, DL/HAY, Dec 3; 1734: HAY, Aug 16; 1735: GF, Apr 22;
1740: DL, Mar 8, 10, 11, 15, 18, 24, Apr 7, 11; 1741: DL, Feb 25, Mar 24;
1745: DL, Jan 31, Feb 1, 2, 4, 5, 6, 7, 8, 9, 13, 14, Mar 12, Apr 4, 25, May
6, 23; 1747: DL, Jan 10, 13, Mar 21; 1750: CG, Apr 30, MARLY, Aug 16; 1754:
DL, Mar 28, CG, Apr 26; 1765: DL, Apr 22, 29; 1767: CG, Apr 21
Addison, Mrs (dancer), 1747: DL, Nov 2, 13, 16, 17, Dec 15; 1748: DL, Jan 14,
18, Feb 9, Mar 14, Apr 14, 23, May 6, Sep 20, Oct 27, Nov 9, Dec 16, 21, 26,
27; 1749: DL, Jan 7, 9, Feb 2, 4, 21, Mar 13, Apr 12, 14, May 16, Sep 28, Oct
11, 18, 23, 24, 28, 30, Nov 1, 7, 9, 27, 29, 30, Dec 7, 13, 26, 27, 28; 1750:
DL, Jan 18, 19, 26, Feb 3, Apr 5, 16, NWC, 16, DL, Nov 27; 1751: DL, Apr 27,
Sep 21, Dec 26; 1752: DL, Apr 20, 27, Sep 19, Oct 10; 1753: DL, May 1; 1754:
DL, May 6, 7; 1755: DL, Apr 24, 29, May 5, Nov 8, 15; 1758: DL, May 2
Addison's Head (publishing house), 1750: DL, Oct 1
Addison's Hymn (song), 1772: CG, Apr 10
Address of Thanks (entertainment), 1777: KING'S, Jul 5; 1787: RLSN, Mar 26, 29;
1794: HAMM, Mar 24; 1795: WLWS, Jun 19
Address to the Audience (entertainment), 1763: CG, May 18; 1785: HAMM, Jun 17,
Jul 6; 1798: CG, Feb 9, May 11
Address to the Audience, Grand (entertainment), 1799: CG, May 15, 23
Address to the Humane Society (entertainment), 1789: HAY, Aug 5
Address to the Ladies (entertainment), 1778: HAY, Jan 26; 1794: HAMM, Mar 24;
1795: WLWS, Jun 19
Address to the Ladies on the Indecency of appearing at Immodest Plays, An
(pamphlet), 1756: DL, Jan 1
Address to the Town (entertainment), 1771: DL, Mar 16; 1773: DL, Apr 19; 1776:
HAY, Sep 18; 1778: CHR, Jun 3; 1779: HAY, Dec 20
Adela of Ponthieu (dance), 1782: KING'S, Apr 11, 16, 20, 27, 30, May 9, 17, Jun
15, 22, 29; 1788: KING'S, Apr 17, 19, Jun 3
Adelaide (dance), 1794: KING'S, Jan 11, 18, Feb 1, 11; see also Bergere des
Alpes, La
Adelaide de Brabant (dance), 1784: CG, May 8, 10, 12
Adelaide. See Pye, Henry James.
Adelaide, Mlle (dancer), 1789: KING'S, Jan 10, 31, Mar 3, 17, 31, May 26, Jun
13
Adelphi (play). See Terence.
Adelphi Tavern, 1776: DL, Jun 10
Adelphi Terrace, 1772: DL, Mar 3, 23
Adelphi, 1779: CG, Mar 22; 1786: DL, Apr 24; 1792: CG, Apr 12; 1793: CG, Apr
11; 1794: CG, Apr 30, May 6; 1795: CG, Apr 24, DL, Jun 3; 1796: CG, Apr 1,
DL, Jun 7; 1797: CG, Apr 29, DL, Jun 6
Adieu (song), 1798: HAY, Jul 11
Adieu thou partner (song), 1793: CG, Mar 20, 22
Adieux D'Arlequin, Pierrot et Colombine, Les (pantomime, anon), 1720: KING'S,
Jun 21
Adijah Effendi, Yussuf (Turkish ambassador), 1794: CG, May 7; 1795: CG, May 6
Admete (dance), 1789: KING'S, Mar 31, Apr 2, 4, 28, May 2, 5, 7, 12, 14

5

Admete and Alceste (dance), 1772: KING'S, Mar 3, 10, 12, 14, 17, 21, 28, Apr 9,
   May 5, 9, 16
Admeto. See Handel, George Frederic.
Admetus. See Handel, George Frederic.
Admiral Benbow (song), 1781: HAY, Aug 17, 31; 1783: HAY, Aug 27; 1788: HAY, Aug
   13; 1795: CG, Apr 28, May 1, 8; 1796: CG, Apr 15, 29, May 3, 24, Jun 2; 1797:
   CG, May 17, 20, 24, 30; 1798: CG, May 5, 9, 12; 1799: CG, Apr 9, May 24, 25,
   28, 31; 1800: CG, Apr 15, 26
Admiralty, Lords of the (spectators), 1722: GR, Apr 14
Adolphus, Rubin (renter), 1758: CG, Feb 23
Adonis Chace (music), 1734: HIC, Apr 5
Adopted Child, The. See Birch, Samuel.
Adriani (dancer), 1766: KING'S, Jan 25, Nov 25; 1767: KING'S, Feb 24
Adriano in Syria. See Ciampi, Lorenzo.
Adriano. See Veracini, Francis.
Advantage of Toping (song), 1798: DL, May 7; 1800: CG, May 7, 15
Adventure in St James's Park, An (play, anon), 1782: HAY, Jan 21
Adventurers, The. See Morris, Edward.
Adventures in Madrid. See Pix, Mary.
Adventures of a Buck (entertainment), 1784: CG, Jun 14
Adventures of a Night, The. See Hodson, William.
Adventures of Five Hours, The. See Tuke, Sir Samuel.
Adventures of Fribble, The. See Smart, Christopher.
Adventures of Half an Hour, The. See Bullock, Christopher.
Adventures of Harlequin in Spain, The (pantomime), 1741: TC, Aug 4
Adventures of Harlequin, The (pantomime), 1745: MF, May 6, 10
Adventures of Robin Hood, Earl of Huntington, and His Mate Little John, The
   (droll), 1724: SF, Sep 7
Adventures of Sir Lubberly Lackbrains, The (farce), 1749: BFC, Aug 23, 24, 25,
   26, 28
Adventures of the Haram of Ispahan (dance), 1774: KING'S, Feb 12
Adventures of Timur Koran, The. See Yates, Richard.
Advertisement, The; or, A Bold Stroke for a Husband. See Gardner, Sarah.
Advertisement, The; or, A New Way to Get a Husband. See Fennell, James.
Advice (song), 1799: DL, Apr 8
Advice to all Britons (song), 1744: CG, Apr 17
Advice to the Sons of Bacchus (song), 1741: GF, Apr 29
Advice to the Tatlers (song), 1739: DL, Mar 26
Aeneas and Dido. See Purcell, Henry.
Aeneas. See Porpora, Nicola.
Aerial Spirits' Dance (dance), 1747: DL, Dec 26; 1750: DL, Jan 1
Aerostation. See Pilon, Frederick.
Aeschylus, 1748: DL, Apr 23; 1781: DL, Feb 17
--Suppliants, The, 1781: DL, Feb 17
Aesop. See Vanbrugh, John.
Aesop's Concert of Animals (music), 1732: DL, Apr 25
Aethiopian Concert. See Smart, Christopher.
Aetius. See Handel, George Frederic.
Affani del Pensier (song), 1773: DL, Mar 10; 1789: DL, Mar 20
Affetti mici, Gli (song), 1788: KING'S, Feb 21
Affrighted Dwarf, The; or, Whimsical Transformation into Mad Moll (dance),
   1784: HAY, Nov 16; 1789: WHF, Nov 11
Africa, 1721: DL, May 2, LIF, 3, DL, 26; 1731: DL, Apr 24; 1749: HAY, Jan 16
African Prince, 1702: DL, Sep 18; 1759: DL, May 10
African singer, 1746: HIC, Mar 10
Aga, Cassem (Tripoline ambassador), 1728: DL, Nov 1, LIF, 23
Aga, Hadgie Saleh (Tripoline ambassador), 1715: LIF, Feb 22
Aga, Kister (entertainer), 1710: DL, Feb 2; 1723: DL, Jun 6; 1729: DL, May 28
Again the Philistines (song), 1794: DL, Apr 10
Agamemnon. See Thomson, James.
Agis. See Home, John.
Agitata (song), 1796: CG, Mar 2; 1798: CG, Apr 25
Aglaura. See Suckling, Sir John.
Aglionby, Dr William (spectator), 1698: LIF, Nov 0
Agmunda. See Brand, Hannah, Huniades.
Agnes de Castro. See Trotter, Catherine.
Agnes de Challiot. See Biancolelli, Pierre Francoise Dominique.
Agnetta, Miss (singer), 1748: BFSY, Aug 24; 1749: NWLS, Feb 27; 1750: NWSM, Aug
   20, SFP, Sep 7
Agreeable Disappointment, The. See Burnaby, William, Love Betrayed.
Agreeable Surprise, The. See O'Keeffe, John.
Agreement of the Gods (song), 1735: HAY, Aug 4

Agreement, The (song), 1737: CG, Apr 18, 21
Agrippina. See Handel, George Frederic.
Agus Jr, Joseph (musician, composer), 1773: HAY, Feb 26, Mar 3, 5, 17; 1774:
  HAY, Mar 23
Agus, Joseph? (musician, composer), 1762: CG, Dec 8; 1763: CG, Oct 22
Aguste, Mlle. See Auguste, Mlle.
Ah, Belinda I am pressed (song), 1700: LIF, Feb 0
Ah che nel petto io sento (song), 1793: DL, May 23; 1796: DL, Jun 9
Ah chi sa (song), 1792: KING'S, Mar 14, 23, 30
Ah, Corydon in vain you boast (song), 1672: DG, Aug 3
Ah! could Mandane yield her breath for thee! (song), 1791: DLKING'S, Nov 19
Ah! d'ascolta gia parmi (song), 1791: DL, Apr 13
Ah, false Amyntas (song), 1673: DG, Feb 6
Ah, how happy we are (song), 1695: DG, Apr 0
Ah, how sweet it is to love (song), 1694: NONE, Sep 0
Ah me! To many deaths decreed (song), 1692: DL, Jun 0, DLORDG, Aug 24
Ah! non lasciarmi no (song), 1749: KING'S, Mar 21
Ah Pardre Quel Golsomino (song), 1729: DL, Mar 26
Ah poor Oliver never boast (song), 1684: DLORDG, Aug 0
Ah queen, ah wretched queen, give o'er (song), 1698: LIF, Nov 0
Ah Se Amanti Fasti Mai (song), 1748: CG, Feb 13, Apr 27
Ah se un Cor Barbaro (song), 1760: CG, Mar 27; 1761: KING'S, Apr 28; 1762:
  KING'S, Mar 1; 1763: CG, Apr 23
Ah well-a-day, my poor heart (song), 1785: HAMM, Jul 25
Ah! Whither art thou fled? (song), 1796: DL, Jun 9
Aickin, Francis (actor), 1765: DL, May 17, Oct 28, Nov 20, Dec 3; 1766: DL, Jan
  9, 13, 14, 17, 22, 23, Feb 10, 13, 17, 20, Mar 15, 17, 20, Apr 9, 12, 16, 18,
  25, May 20, HAY, Jun 18, Jul 1, 3, 15, KING'S, Aug 8, 18, 20, 25, Sep 5, 13,
  19, DL, 23, 30, Oct 17, 21, 22, 23, Nov 4, 8, 17, 26, Dec 6; 1767: DL, Jan
  24, Feb 7, Mar 7, 21, 28, 30, May 4, 6, 8, Jun 3, Sep 12, 15, 21, 26, Oct 9,
  10, 14, 23, 26, 28, 29, Nov 4, 12, 13, 24, Dec 1, 5, 23; 1768: DL, Jan 6, 14,
  Feb 13, 27, Mar 15, 21, Apr 12, 27, May 24, HAY, Jul 18, 27, DL, Aug 18, HAY,
  19, DL, Sep 8, 17, 22, 24, 26, 28, 29, Oct 3, 6, 10, 15, 18, 20, 21, 31, Nov
  4, 9, Dec 3, 14, 17, HAY, 19; 1769: DL, Jan 27, Feb 23, Mar 11, 18, Apr 4, 7,
  28, HAY, May 24, 29, Jun 2, 5, Jul 12, 21, 24, Aug 7, 11, 14, 16, 18, 25, 30,
  Sep 11, DL, 16, 19, 23, Oct 10, 14, 31, Nov 4, 8, 11, 13, 14, 24, 27, 28, 29,
  Dec 6, 16; 1770: DL, Jan 4, 10, 27, Feb 8, Mar 3, 20, 26, 31, Apr 7, HAY, May
  16, 18, DL, 21, HAY, 2 , 25, 28, 30, Jun 15, 18, Jul 25, Aug 3, 24, 31, Sep
  3, DL, Oct 2, 12, 18, 19, 20, 25, Nov 5, 13, 14, 16, 17, 20, 23, Dec 13;
  1771: DL, Jan 12, 19, Mar 12, 16, Apr 1, 2, 3, 9, May 1, HAY, 15, 20, Jun 7,
  10, 12, 19, Jul 8, Aug 14, 26, Sep 2, DL, 24, Oct 5, 12, 17, 19, 28, 29, Nov
  4, 12, 15, 22, 25, Dec 23; 1772: DL, Jan 4, 15, Feb 26, Mar 18, 21, 23, 28,
  30, Apr 9, 25, May 4, 5, HAY, 18, 20, 22, 27, DL, 30, HAY, Jun 5, 8, 15, 22,
  Aug 10, Sep 8, DL, 26, Oct 6, 10, 13, 14, 16, 23, 29, Nov 3, 4, 12, 26, 27,
  Dec 16, 17, 30; 1773: DL, Jan 9, 21, Feb 11, 20, 27, Mar 20, Apr 12, 19, 23,
  30, May 10, 13, HAY, 17, DL, 19, HAY, 28, Jun 7, 11, 14, 18, Jul 2, 12, Aug
  4, 11, 27, Sep 20, DL, 23, 30, Oct 5, 20, 23, 26, 28, 30, Nov 4, Dec 3, 21;
  1774: DL, Feb 2, 19, Mar 3, 17, Apr 4, 26, May 3, 4, 5, HAY, 16, Jun 3, 6, 8,
  17, 27, Jul 15, Aug 26, Sep 5, 6, 12, DL, 17, HAY, 19, 30, DL, Nov 4, 5, 7,
  Dec 19, 26; 1775: DL, Jan 6, Mar 23, 25, CG, 30, HAY, May 15, 17, 19, 22, 26,
  29, Jun 5, 7, 12, Jul 21, 31, Aug 2, Sep 7, 18; 1782: HAY, Jun 10; see also
  Aickin, Francis and James
Aickin, Francis [at CG] and Aickin, James [at DL and HAY] (actors), 1775: CG,
  Sep 22, DL, 23, 28, 30, Oct 3, 5, 10, 11, CG, 12, 17, DL, 17, CG, 19, 21, DL,
  21, 23, 25, 28, CG, 30, DL, Nov 6, 14, 18, 21, 25, 28, 30, Dec 7, 19, CG, 29;
  1776: CG, Jan 15, DL, 26, CG, Feb 9, DL, 10, 12, 15, CG, 22, DL, 24, CG, 26,
  DL, Mar 16, CG, 18, Apr 9, DL, 16, 25, CG, 29, May 1, DL, 4, 11, CG, 17, DL,
  18, HAY, 22, 27, 28, 31, Jun 14, 19, Jul 5, 8, 10, 29, Aug 2, Sep 2, 17, DL,
  26, Oct 1, CG, 2, DL, 3, 8, CG, 8, DL, 10, 15, CG, 17, DL, 19, 23, 25, 26,
  30, CG, 31, Nov 1, DL, 7, CG, 21, DL, 25, 28, CG, Dec 2, 6, DL, 10, CG, 17,
  26; 1777: DL, Jan 4, 22, CG, Feb 5, DL, 20, CG, 22, DL, Mar 20, CG, 31, DL,
  Apr 11, CG, 11, DL, 17, May 8, CG, 13, HAY, 15, Jun 26, Jul 7, 11, 24, 30,
  Aug 7, 14, 19, 25, Sep 10, 17, 19, DL, 20, 23, 25, 30, Oct 2, CG, 6, DL, 7,
  CG, 10, DL, 17, CG, 21, DL, 22, 28, CG, 30, DL, 31, Nov 13, CG, 13, DL, 18,
  24, CG, 27, DL, 29, CG, Dec 3, DL, 4, CG, 10, DL, 13, 15, 18, CG, 19; 1778:
  DL, Jan 2, 5, 8, 10, CG, 21, DL, 24, Feb 10, CG, 16, 24, Mar 2, DL, 16, 30,
  CG, Apr 7, 11, 20, DL, 20, 21, CG, May 6, DL, 8, CG, 9, 15, HAY, 18, DL, 23,
  HAY, 27, 29, Jun 8, 19, Jul 9, 11, 30, Aug 21, Sep 2, 7, DL, 17, 19, 22, 24,
  CG, 25, 28, DL, 29, Oct 1, 3, 6, 8, CG, 12, 14, DL, 15, 20, CG, 22, DL, 23,
  26, 27, 28, 31, Nov 2, 4, CG, 4, DL, 14, 16, 18, CG, 19, Dec 3, 8, 17, DL,
  19, 22; 1779: CG, Jan 14, 18, DL, 23, CG, Feb 2, 23, Mar 9, DL, 13, 16, 22,
  27, CG, Apr 6, DL, 10, CG, 14, 16, DL, 28, CG, May 3, 6, 15, DL, 25, HAY, 31,

7

Jun 7, 10, 18, Jul 16, 31, Aug 18, 24, 27, 31, DL, Sep 18, 21, 25, 28, 30,
Oct 2, CG, 4, 11, 13, DL, 16, 25, 30, Nov 1, 3, CG, 10, DL, 15, 17, CG, 19,
DL, 19, 20, CG, 22, DL, 24, 27, CG, Dec 1, DL, 2, 9, CG, 9, DL, 13, CG, 16,
DL, 20, 27, 29; 1780: CG, Jan 17, DL, 24, 25, 26, 29, Feb 15, CG, 22, DL, 28,
CG, Mar 14, Apr 7, 10, DL, 17, 18, 21, CG, 21, DL, 26, CG, May 1, DL, 8, HAY,
30, Jun 2, 3, 5, 9, 13, 14, 26, Jul 1, 6, 10, 24, Aug 5, 14, 17, 29, 31, DL,
Sep 16, 23, 26, Oct 2, 5, 7, 10, 11, 12, 14, 17, CG, 18, DL, 19, 23, 25, CG,
26, DL, Nov 1, 3, CG, 4, DL, 8, CG, 8, DL, 18, CG, 27, DL, 29, Dec 6, 8, 15,
27, CG, 27; 1781: CG, Jan 4, DL, 6, 9, CG, 31, Feb 14, DL, 17, Mar 10, 19,
CG, Apr 2, DL, 21, CG, 27, DL, May 1, 5, CG, 7, DL, 8, CG, 10, DL, 17, HAY,
Jun 1, 5, 7, 8, 16, 26, Jul 18, 23, Aug 7, 22, DL, Sep 15, 18, CG, 19, DL,
22, 25, 27, 29, Oct 2, CG, 5, DL, 6, 19, 27, 29, 30, CG, 31, Nov 5, DL, 5,
13, 15, 20, 21, Dec 14, CG, 31; 1782: CG, Jan 1, 3, 10, DL, 21, CG, Feb 5,
Mar 14, DL, 16, 21, Apr 11, CG, 12, 20, DL, 23, CG, 23, DL, 25, 30, May 1, 8,
CG, 11, DL, 11, 14, HAY, Jun 4, 6, 15, 27, Jul 9, Aug 6, 9, 15, 24, 26, 27,
DL, Sep 17, 19, 20, CG, 23, DL, 24, 26, CG, 27, DL, 28, Oct 1, 3, CG, 4, DL,
12, 16, CG, 18, 19, 21, DL, 26, CG, 28, DL, Nov 2, 8, 16, 22, 26, CG, 29, DL,
29, Dec 5, CG, 9, DL, 14, CG, 19, 31; 1783: CG, Jan 1, DL, 11, 15, CG, 28,
DL, Feb 12, 18, Mar 3, 10, 17, 18, 20, CG, 29, 31, Apr 5, 7, DL, 7, CG, 26,
DL, 28, 29, CG, May 9, DL, 12, CG, 19, HAY, 31, Jun 4, 6, 7, 13, 16, 24, Jul
4, Aug 22, 26, 27, Sep 12, DL, 18, 20, 23, 25, CG, Oct 3, DL, 7, CG, 9, DL,
11, 16, 17, CG, 20, DL, 20, 21, 24, 30, Nov 3, CG, 8, DL, 12, CG, 13, 14, DL,
18, CG, 18, DL, 22, CG, 24, DL, 27, CG, 27, DL, Dec 10, CG, 11, DL, 11, 19,
CG, 31; 1784: DL, Jan 1, 3, CG, 3, DL, 14, CG, 14, 16, DL, 16, 20, CG, 22,
DL, 24, CG, 29, Feb 18, 19, DL, Mar 6, 23, CG, Apr 16, DL, 19, 21, CG, 26,
DL, 28, May 5, 17, 21, HAY, 29, 31, Jun 1, 2, 12, 16, Jul 7, 20, 28, Aug 2,
5, 10, 17, 18, 24, Sep 2, 13, DL, 16, CG, 20, DL, 23, CG, 24, DL, 28, Oct 5,
CG, 6, DL, 9, 14, 18, 23, 26, 28, CG, 28, 30, DL, Nov 3, CG, 4, DL, 4, 5, 9,
12, 15, 16, 17, 19, 20, 22, 23, 25, CG, 29, DL, Dec 2, CG, 13; 1785: CG, Jan
8, DL, 13, 14, 20, 27, Feb 2, 21, CG, Mar 3, DL, 8, CG, 15, DL, 17, CG, Apr
1, DL, 8, 9, 14, 18, 20, May 7, CG, 7, HAY, Jun 2, 4, 6, 7, 9, 17, 18, 21,
24, 28, 29, Jul 26, Aug 4, 23, Sep 2, 9, DL, 17, 20, 22, CG, 23, DL, 24, 27,
29, Oct 1, CG, 5, DL, 8, 11, CG, 13, DL, 17, CG, 17, DL, 20, 22, 26, 27, CG,
28, 29, DL, Nov 2, 3, 7, 8, CG, 9, DL, 12, 18, 21, 22, CG, Dec 1, 5, 10, 14,
DL, 26, CG, 29, DL, 30; 1786: CG, Jan 4, DL, 4, 14, CG, 18, Feb 7, 11, DL,
15, CG, 16, DL, 18, CG, 23, DL, 23, CG, 25, Mar 4, 6, 11, DL, 25, 28, Apr 4,
CG, 4, 26, May 3, 5, 9, 15, 20, DL, 24, HAY, Jun 9, 13, 15, 16, 19, 20, 21,
22, 23, 28, 29, Jul 3, 12, 13, 14, Aug 17, DL, Sep 16, CG, 18, 20, 25, DL,
28, 30, CG, Oct 2, DL, 3, CG, 6, DL, 7, 9, 16, 19, CG, 21, DL, 24, CG, 25,
DL, 27, 28, Nov 15, 18, CG, 18, DL, 22, CG, 27, DL, 29, Dec 2, CG, 4, DL, 5,
CG, 13, 15, DL, 19, CG, 27; 1787: CG, Jan 8, 15, DL, 18, 26, 29, Mar 12, CG,
26, 27, DL, Apr 10, 13, 14, CG, 16, 17, DL, 20, CG, 20, 27, DL, May 7, 11,
19, CG, 21, 28, DL, 31, HAY, Jun 11, 13, 14, 18, 20, 23, 27, 28, Jul 4, 7,
19, 23, 27, Aug 3, Sep 5, DL, 20, CG, 26, DL, 27, 29, CG, Oct 1, DL, 6, 13,
CG, 17, DL, 20, CG, 22, DL, 27, CG, 29, DL, 30, CG, 31, DL, Nov 3, CG, 5, DL,
5, 6, CG, 9, 14, DL, 16, CG, 19, DL, 20, CG, 22, 28, 30, Dec 3, DL, 7, 8, 10,
11, CG, 15, DL, 19, 26, CG, 27, 28; 1788: DL, Jan 2, 8, CG, 14, 18, DL, 21,
26, CG, Feb 4, DL, 25, CG, Mar 15, 24, DL, 29, CG, Apr 4, 8, 11, DL, 21, CG,
23, DL, 25, 30, May 1, 6, 23, HAY, Jun 10, 12, 17, 26, Jul 2, 7, 10, 14, 24,
Aug 2, 25, 27, 28, Sep 9, DL, 13, 16, CG, 17, DL, 25, Oct 2, CG, 8, DL, 9,
14, CG, 15, DL, 16, CG, 17, DL, 25, CG, 27, Nov 1, DL, 1, 6, CG, 6, DL, 17,
25, CG, 26, 28, DL, 28, Dec 9, CG, 27, 29, DL, 30; 1789: DL, Jan 6, 7, CG, 8,
21, DL, 26, CG, Feb 3, DL, 7, CG, 11, DL, 16, 18, 28, Mar 17, 21, CG, 28, Apr
4, DL, 14, CG, 15, DL, 21, CG, 28, DL, May 1, CG, 14, 22, DL, 27, 28, Jun 4,
13, HAY, 15, 17, 19, 22, 24, 29, Jul 15, 31, Aug 11, Sep 12, DL, 12, CG, 18,
DL, 19, 22, CG, 25, DL, 26, 29, Oct 1, CG, 6, DL, 10, CG, 12, DL, 13, 22, 28,
CG, Nov 2, DL, 4, 5, CG, 5, 6, 10, 16, DL, 21, CG, 23, DL, 27, CG, 30, DL,
30, Dec 14, CG, 14, 26; 1790: DL, Jan 15, CG, 23, Feb 11, DL, 23, CG, Mar 18,
Apr 20, 30, DL, May 8, 14, CG, 31, DL, Jun 1, HAY, 14, 15, 16, 18, 19, 22,
26, 30, Jul 5, 28, Aug 7, 16, DL, Sep 14, CG, 15, DL, 16, CG, 29, Oct 4, 6,
DL, 7, CG, 11, HAY, 13, CG, 18, 20, DL, 21, CG, 23, 27, DL, 27, CG, Nov 4,
DL, 4, 5, 10, CG, 11, DL, 12, CG, 27, 30, DL, Dec 3, CG, 6, 14; 1791: CG, Jan
3, 7, Feb 4, DL, Mar 21, 22, 28, Apr 4, 28, CG, 30, DL, May 14, CG, 18, 19,
24, DL, 31, Jun 4, HAY, 6, 8, 13, 16, 18, 20, 25, Jul 9, 15, 22, 30, Aug 15,
18, 24, 27, 30, 31, Sep 2, 5, CG, 21, DLKING'S, 27, Oct 3, 4, CG, 6, 7,
DLKING'S, 8, CG, 10, 17, 20, 24, 28, DLKING'S, 31, Nov 2, CG, 4, DLKING'S, 5,
7, 11, 14, CG, 24, DLKING'S, 30, Dec 2, CG, 26; 1792: DLKING'S, Jan 18, 24,
28, 31, Feb 4, CG, 6, DLKING'S, 8, 14, 18, 23, Mar 1, 6, 13, 17, 26, 29, 31,
CG, 31, Apr 12, DL, May 11, 19, 30, DLKING'S, Jun 15, HAY, 18, 20, 22, 23,
Jul 4, 16, Aug 6, 9, Sep 6, DL, 15, 20, 25, 27, 29, CG, Oct 10, 12, 15, DL,
16, CG, 17, DL, 18, 20, CG, 29, DL, Nov 2, CG, 3, DL, 5, CG, 5, 9; see also
Aickin, Francis; Aickin, James

Aickin, Graves (actor), 1797: HAY, Sep 18
Aickin, James (actor), 1767: DL, Mar 21, Nov 6, Dec 5, 12; 1768: DL, Apr 14,
    26, 27, 28, HAY, Jul 8, DL, Sep 26, 28, Oct 14, Nov 7; 1769: DL, Jan 24, 26,
    Feb 1, 7, 23, Mar 28, Apr 3, 18, 28, May 1, 18, 19, Sep 19, 28, Oct 2, 5, 6,
    10, 21, 30, Nov 4, 6, 14, 18, 23, Dec 13; 1770: DL, Jan 4, 27, Feb 21, 24,
    Mar 1, Apr 19, 23, 26, May 3, 9, 15, Oct 3, 4, 8, 22, 25, 29, Nov 3, 5, 10,
    13, 14, 16, 19, 24, 28, Dec 1, 5, 20, 31; 1771: DL, Jan 1, 4, 12, 19, Mar 14,
    16, 23, Apr 6, 15, 26, May 6, 17, 23, HAY, Jun 26, DL, Sep 28, Oct 3, 5, 10,
    15, 17, 19, 26, Nov 1, 4, 6, 8, 9, 13, 15, 18, 23, 28, Dec 4, 21, 26; 1772:
    DL, Jan 3, 7, 11, Feb 5, 17, 26, Mar 26, 28, Apr 6, 21, 25, May 4, 7, 8, 26,
    Sep 19, 22, Oct 1, 13, 16, 21, 23, 24, 31, Nov 3, 4, 7, 12, 16, 20, 30, Dec
    9, 18, 21, 29, 30; 1773: DL, Jan 1, 4, 13, 21, Feb 2, 13, 25, 27, Mar 9, Apr
    17, 21, May 1, 6, 10, 11, 12, 28, Jun 2, HAY, Jul 21, Sep 20, DL, 21, Oct 2,
    5, 6, 8, 9, 14, 22, 23, 28, Nov 4, 13, 15, 20, 24, 25, Dec 30; 1774: DL, Jan
    18, Feb 2, 8, 19, Mar 3, 12, 14, 17, 19, 21, 22, 26, Apr 4, 12, 19, 26, 27,
    29, May 4, 9, 20, Jun 2, HAY, 10, DL, Sep 17, 22, 27, Oct 4, 8, 13, 15, 20,
    21, 24, 28, Nov 17, 24, 25, Dec 7, 9; 1775: DL, Jan 2, Feb 17, 23, 28, Mar
    18, 20, Apr 17, 19, 22, 24, 28, May 1, 10, Sep 23, Nov 1; 1776: DL, May 13,
    HAY, 20; 1782: HAY, Jun 10; 1792: DL, Dec 15, 21, 26, 28; 1793: DL, Jan 4, 7,
    9, 29, Feb 5, 9, 12, 14, 16, 23, 26, Mar 4, 9, 12, Jun 5, HAY, 11, 12, 13,
    14, 15, 17, 21, 29, Aug 3, 6, 12, Sep 5, 19, 21, 24, 30, Oct 1, 4, 5, 8, 21,
    29, Nov 16, Dec 2, 30; 1794: HAY, Jan 14, 21, Feb 8, 22, Mar 1, 31, DL, Apr
    21, 25, 29, May 1, 8, 19, 22, Jun 4, 5, 9, 12, 16, 19, 26, 28, HAY, Jul 8, 9,
    10, 11, 12, 14, 17, 18, 21, 25, Aug 9, 20, 27, Sep 1, 3, DL, 16, HAY, 17, DL,
    20, 23, 27, 30, Oct 4, 7, 14, 18, 21, 28, 29, 31, Nov 12, 15, 18, 29, Dec 12,
    30; 1795: DL, Jan 20, 24, 26, Mar 14, 21, Apr 16, 17, HAY, Jun 9, 11, 12, 13,
    15, 16, 20, Jul 1, 22, 25, 31, Aug 7, 29, DL, Sep 24, 26, 29, Oct 1, 3, 5,
    12, 20, 21, 27, Nov 6, 12, 16, 17, 20, Dec 2, 9, 10, 11, 18, 30; 1796: DL,
    Jan 23, Feb 15, 29, Apr 13, 18, 20, 25, 26, 30, May 2, 11, 23, Jun 2, 8, HAY,
    13, DL, 14, HAY, 16, 17, 20, 22, 25, 30, Jul 5, 7, 9, 15, 18, 21, 23, 26, 30,
    Aug 3, 11, 13, 18, 29, 30, Sep 1, 7, 16, 17, DL, 20, 22, 24, 27, Oct 3, 6,
    10, 11, 27, Nov 1, 2, 5, 23, 24, 26, 28, Dec 9, 15, 17, 20, 27, 29, 30; 1797:
    DL, Jan 2, 10, 12, 14, 20, Feb 16, Mar 6, 20, Apr 6, 28, May 12, Jun 10, HAY,
    15, 17, 19, 21, 23, 24, 26, Jul 3, 6, 8, 10, 15, Aug 9, 14, 15, 28, Sep 4, 8,
    9, 12, 13, DL, 19, 23, Oct 3, 7, 14, Nov 2, 7, 9, 11, 15, 17, 23, 25, Dec 14;
    1798: DL, Jan 23, Feb 3, Mar 17, 24, May 7, 11, 19, 24, 29, 30, Jun 7, 8, CG,
    11, DL, 12, HAY, 12, 14, 15, 16, 20, 21, 23, 29, 30, Jul 5, 14, 16, Aug 3,
    21, 29, DL, Sep 15, 18, 20, 25, 27, 29, Oct 6, 11, 13, 20, 27, 30, Nov 6, 26,
    Dec 4, 5, 27; 1799: DL, Jan 8, 31, Feb 14, 26, Apr 22, 23, 27, May 20, 24,
    Jun 12, HAY, 20, 21, 22, 24, 25, Jul 2, 6, 9, 10, 12, 20, 23, 27, Aug 13, 21,
    DL, Oct 1, 7, 8, 12, 17, Nov 2, 6, 25, 27, 29, Dec 7, 9, 11; 1800: DL, Jan
    25, Feb 12, 14; see also Aickin, Francis and James
Aickin, Mrs Graves (actor), 1797: HAY, Sep 18
Ailesbury, Earl of. See Bruce, Thomas.
Aimable Vainqueur, L' (dance), 1743: CG, Apr 6, 19
Aime, Mlle (dancer), 1791: KING'S, Jun 2, 6
Aingel. See Angel.
Ainsworth (house servant), 1789: DL, Jun 10
Air Balloon, 1783: DL, Nov 8; 1784: CG, Feb 3, DL, 7
Air on the Recovery of the King (song), 1789: DL, Mar 6
Air St, 1779: CG, Apr 24, DL, May 5, HAY, Aug 27; 1780: DL, Apr 21, HAY, Aug
    31; 1781: DL, Apr 26
Airs. See Ayres.
Aitkin, John (singer), 1772: GROTTO, Aug 17; 1774: HAY, Sep 17
Akeroyd. See Ackroyde.
Akery (Ackery) (actor), 1783: CG, May 31; 1784: CG, May 22; 1786: CG, May 30;
    1787: CG, Jun 2; 1788: CG, May 27; 1800: CG, Jun 10
Al caro nume appresso (song), 1757: KING'S, Mar 24
Al Trionfo Duetto (song), 1729: DL, Mar 26
Aladin. See O'Keeffe, John.
Alard, Sieurs (dancers), 1716: DL, Mar 8, Oct 22
Alarm to Britons (entertainment), 1747: CG, Apr 20
Alas! Poor Sue (song), 1785: CG, Apr 18, May 18
Alas! when charming Sylvia's gone (song), 1696: DG, Aug 0
Alba Regalis, Court of, 1689: NONE, Sep 0
Albemarle St, 1782: KING'S, May 27
Albemarle, Earl and Countess of, 1723: GR, Dec 5
Albemarle, William, Earl of, 1729: GF, Dec 10
Albergatrice Vivace, L'. See Caruso, Lodovico.
Albergotti, Vittoria (singer), 1713: QUEEN'S, Feb 26
Albermarle, Duchess of. See Monck, Elizabeth Cavendish.
Albermarle, Duke of. See Monck, George.

9

Albero di Diana, L'. See Martin y Soler.
Albert and Adelaide. See Birch, Samuel.
Albertarelli, Francesco (singer), 1791: KING'S, Apr 16, 26, May 12, 19, 24, Jun
   2, 10
Alberti, Johann Friedrich (composer), 1729: HIC, Apr 16; 1752: KING'S, Mar 24
Albina, Countess Raimond. See Cowley, Hannah.
Albinoni, Tommaso (composer), 1711: GR, Aug 27; 1712: QUEEN'S, Nov 12; 1713:
   QUEEN'S, Mar 21; 1722: DL, Mar 14; 1723: DL, May 15
Albion and Albanius. See Dryden, John.
Albion Lodge, 1770: DL, May 5
Albion Queens, The. See Banks, John.
Albion Song (song), 1767: DL, May 13; 1768: DL, May 4; 1769: DL, May 5; 1770:
   DL, May 5
Albions, Honourable Order of Select, 1768: DL, May 4; 1769: DL, May 5; 1770:
   DL, May 5
Albrici, Bartholomeo (musician), 1679: SLINGSBY, Nov 20
Albumazar. See Tomkis, Thomas.
Albuzio (singer), 1754: KING'S, Jan 29, Feb 28
Alcanor. See Cumberland, Richard, The Arab.
Alceste (ballet). See Triomphe de L'Amour Conjugal.
Alceste (opera). See Lampugnani, Giovanni Battista; Smollett, Dr Tobias;
   Gresnick, Antoine Frederic.
Alceste; ossia, Il Trionfo dell' Amor Conjugale. See Gluck, Christoph
   Willibald von.
Alchemist, The. See Jonson, Ben.
Alcibiade. See Campistron, Jean Galbert de.
Alcibiades. See Otway, Thomas.
Alcides Name (song), 1753: CG, May 10
Alcina. See Handel, George Frederic; Gazzaniga, Giuseppe.
Alday, Paul (musician), 1793: KING/HAY, Mar 8, 15, 20, 22; 1800: CG, May 2
Alden (householder), 1789: CG, Feb 11
Aldermanbury, 1751: DL, Apr 26
Aldermen, Court of, 1700: BF, Jun 25; 1730: GF, Apr 28
Aldersgate Coffee House, 1750: DL, Nov 28
Aldersgate St, 1749: BF/SFP, Aug 23; 1750: DL, Nov 28; 1756: HAB, Dec 9; 1757:
   CG, Dec 15; 1759: CG, Jan 9; 1761: DL, Dec 15; 1762: CG, Dec 22; 1764: DL,
   Dec 19; 1765: CG, Dec 21; 1768: DL, Dec 20; 1769: CG, Dec 20
Aldgate, 1667: BF, Sep 6; 1724: PT, Nov 30; 1744: HAY, Apr 23
Aldridge, Mary Lee (actor), 1670: LIF, Jan 0
Aldridge, Robert (dancer), 1762: DL, Oct 23, Nov 23, 25; 1763: DL, Jan 3, 8,
   14, Feb 17, 24, Apr 9, 25, Sep 22, Oct 25, 28, Dec 1, 17, 26; 1764: DL, Jan
   23, Feb 24, May 2, 4, 11, Oct 6, 9, 11, 16, 29, Nov 2, 28; 1765: DL, Feb 13,
   15, Mar 2, 30, Apr 13, 20, May 1, 10, 11, Sep 24, Oct 1, 4, 8, Nov 16, 20;
   1766: DL, Jan 6, 23, Feb 7, Apr 12, 19, 28; 1767: CG, Sep 21, Oct 5, 9, 21,
   Nov 19; 1768: CG, Mar 7, Apr 22, Sep 20, 30, Nov 1, Dec 12; 1769: CG, Mar 14,
   Apr 27, May 6, Oct 5, 9, 18, Nov 23; 1770: CG, Mar 29, Apr 2, 17, May 1, Oct
   9, 15, 24, Nov 3, 12, 16, 23; 1771: CG, Mar 16, Apr 5, 18, 23, Oct 9, 16, 26,
   30, Nov 9, 12, Dec 21; 1772: CG, Mar 12, 23, 26, 28, Apr 6, 9, May 1, 5, Sep
   28, Oct 12, 28, Nov 6, 17; 1773: CG, Feb 6, Apr 16, 20, 26, May 3, 12, 18,
   19, Oct 5, 7, 14, 21, Nov 3, 12, 25, Dec 7, 8; 1774: CG, Feb 17, Mar 12, 26,
   Apr 12, 16, 27, May 3, 4, 17, 20, Oct 26, 27, 28, Nov 9, 19, Dec 2, 7, 9, 14,
   27; 1775: CG, Feb 1, Mar 30, Apr 22, 29, May 15, Dec 12, 20; 1776: CG, Jan 2,
   Feb 17, Mar 14, Apr 9, May 20, Oct 15, 31, Nov 6, 9, 20, Dec 23, 27; 1777:
   CG, Jan 22, Apr 19, 25, 29, Oct 8, 21, Nov 4, 25, Dec 22, 29; 1778: CG, Jan
   21, 28, Mar 9, 30, Apr 22, 24, May 2, Sep 25, Oct 14, Nov 27; 1779: CG, Feb
   16, 25, Apr 5, 21, 28, May 7, 13; 1780: CG, Sep 20, 27, Oct 11, 25, Nov 6,
   Dec 5; 1781: CG, Feb 8, 23, Apr 2, 20, 25, May 1, 2, Sep 21, 24, 28, Oct 24,
   Nov 8, Dec 13; 1782: CG, Feb 21, Apr 2, 27, May 17; 1796: CG, Jun 3
Aldus (Aldys) (actor), 1773: CG, Nov 18; 1775: CG, Feb 24
Alefounder, John (painter), 1783: HAY, Jul 26
Alessandri, Felice (composer), 1767: KING'S, Oct 27; 1768: KING'S, Feb 27;
   1769: KING'S, Mar 2; 1783: KING'S, Nov 29
--Moglie Fedele, La (opera), 1768: KING'S, Feb 27, Mar 1, 5, 12, 19, Apr 9, 23;
   1769: KING'S, Mar 16
--Re Alla Caccia, Il (opera), 1769: KING'S, Mar 2, 4, 7, 11, 18, Apr 1
Alessandro e Timoteo. See Sarti, Giuseppe.
Alessandro Nell Indie. See Metastasio, Pietro Bonaventura; Anfossi, Pasquale.
Alessandro Severo. See Zeno, Apostolo.
Aleworth, Joseph (musician), 1675: ATCOURT, Feb 15
Alexander (actor), 1666: NONE, Sep 0; 1668: BRIDGES, Sep 14; 1688: DL, May 3,
   NONE, Sep 0; 1689: NONE, Sep 0, DL, Nov 7, 20; 1690: DL, Jan 0, Mar 0, NONE,
   Sep 0, DL, Dec 0; 1691: DG, May 0, NONE, Sep 0; 1692: DL, Mar 0, Apr 0, Nov

Allison, Maria (actor), 1697: DL, Feb 0; 1698: DL, Dec 0; 1703: LIF, Mar 0, Nov
  0; 1704: DL, Jul 1; 1705: LIF, Aug 1
Allison's scholars (dancers), 1791: HAY, Sep 26; 1792: HAY, Oct 22
Allmack's Coffee House, 1756: DL, Nov 12
Allworthy (author), 1749: DL, Dec 4
Ally Croaker (song), 1753: DL, Oct 20; 1754: DL, May 13, 17, 18, 22; 1757: HAY,
  Sep 14; 1788: CG, Apr 14; 1796: DL, May 13, 30, Jun 9; 1797: DL, May 20, 31;
  1798: DL, May 24
Almack's Great Room, 1765: KING'S, Apr 24
Almahide. See Bononcini, Giovanni.
Almaine, D (house servant), 1774: CG, May 14
Almamia (song), 1729: LIF, Mar 5
Almena. See Rolt, Richard.
Almeyda, Queen of Granada. See Lee, Sophia.
Almida. See Celisia, Dorothea.
Almon, John (printer), 1780: CG, Apr 19; 1784: CG, Apr 17, Oct 12, DL, Nov 4,
  CG, Dec 27; 1785: CG, Mar 29; 1786: KING'S, Mar 11
Almyna. See Manley, Mary.
Alone by the Light of the Moon (song), 1790: CG, Jun 1
Alonso e Cora (dance), 1796: KING'S, Apr 2, 5, 12, May 3
Alonzo. See Home, John.
Alphonso. See Lampugnani, Giovanni Battista.
Alphonso, King of Naples. See Powell, George.
Alresford, 1747: CG, Feb 12
Alsatia Bully, The. See Shadwell, Thomas, The Squire of Alsatia.
Alternative, Tyranny or Liberty, The (play), 1746: DL, Jan 7
Alzira. See Hill, Aaron.
Alzuma. See Murphy, Arthur.
Amadei, Phillipo (composer), 1721: KING'S, Feb 1
--Arsaces; or, Amore e Maesta (opera), 1721: KING'S, Feb 1, 4, 8, 11, 15, 18,
  23, 28, May 10, Nov 1, 4, 8
Amadis. See Handel, George, Frederic.
Amadriade, L'; ou, La Nimphe des Bois (dance), 1791: KING'S, May 5, 7, 10, 12,
  17, 21, 24, 26, 28, 31, Jun 4, 6, 14, 17, Jul 9
Amans Reunis, Les (dance), 1781: KING'S, Nov 17, 20, 24, 28; 1782: KING'S, Mar
  9
Amans Trompes, Les (farce), 1721: HAY, Apr 20
Amant Deguise, L' (dance), 1791: PAN, Dec 17, 20
Amant Retrouve, L' (dance), 1795: KING'S, Jan 20, 24, Mar 3, May 12, 14, 22,
  Jun 16
Amant Statue, L' (dance), 1796: KING'S, Apr 21, 23, May 12, 17
Amanti Gelosi, Gli. See Cocchi, Gioacchino.
Amanti Ridicoli, Gli. See Galuppi, Baldassare.
Amants (dance), 1732: GF, Mar 4, Apr 12
Amants Consentants (dance), 1734: CG, May 8, 10, 15, 16, CG/LIF, Sep 25
Amants Constants (dance), 1733: DL/HAY, Oct 25, 27, 29, 31, HAY, Nov 19; 1734:
  DL/HAY, Jan 7, 23, 26
Amants Heureux (dance), 1742: CG, Mar 4; 1776: KING'S, Nov 2, 9, 16, 30, Dec 7,
  10, 14, 17, 21; 1777: KING'S, Jan 4, 11, 17, 21, Feb 1, Mar 4, 8, Apr 22, 29,
  May 1, 6, 8, 15, Jun 7
Amants Reunis, Les. See Beauchamp, Godart de.
Amants Surpris (dance), 1780: KING'S, Dec 16, 19; 1781: KING'S, Jan 13, 16, 29,
  Mar 8, Apr 5, May 1, 5, Jun 30; 1786: KING'S, Jun 1, 6, 20, 22, 24
Amants unis par l'Hymen (dance), 1778: KING'S, Apr 4, 11, May 30, Jun 20
Amants Volages (dance), 1743: DL, May 14
Amarath the Fourth (musical tale), 1798: HAY, Sep 17
Amasis, King of Egypt. See Marsh, Charles.
Amazon (song), 1742: JS, Apr 7
Amazon Queen, The. See Weston, John.
Ambarvalia (Roman festival pastiche), 1773: MARLY, Sep 3, 6, 9
Amber, Norton (banker, pit doorkeeper), 1747: DL, Apr 9; 1749: DL, May 16;
  1751: DL, Dec 17, 18; 1753: CG, Dec 21
Ambitious Slave, The. See Settle, Elkanah.
Ambitious Statesman, The. See Crowne, John.
Ambitious Stepmother, The. See Rowe, Nicholas.
Amboyna. See Dryden, John.
Ambroise (Ambroisiano, Ambrosia), Antonio (puppeteer), 1751: CT, Dec 3; 1752:
  CT/HAY, Feb 29; 1753: HAY, Mar 13
Ambrose, Miss (actor), 1761: DL, Jun 15, Jul 27
Ambrose, Miss (dancer), 1731: DL, Nov 25; 1732: DL, Feb 22, Mar 21, May 6;
  1736: CG, Jan 23, 24
Ambrose, Miss E (actor), 1761: DL, Jun 15, Jul 2, 27, Aug 8; 1771: HAY, Jun 5,

24, Jul 8, 24, Aug 7, 19, 26, Sep 16, DL, Oct 3, 19, Nov 13, 22, 27, Dec 17,
26, 31; 1772: DL, Jan 15, Feb 4, 27, Mar 18, 26, 28, Apr 2, 6, HAY, May 20,
22, Jun 1, 29, Aug 4, Sep 8, DL, Oct 6, 14, 16, 20, 21, 29, Nov 7, 17, 20,
30, Dec 7, 15; 1773: DL, Jan 1, 4, 26, Feb 4, Mar 23, Apr 23, May 1, 10, HAY,
17, 26, Jun 7, Jul 21, Aug 11, 27; 1774: HAY, May 16, 30, Jun 1, 3, 15, 27,
Aug 19, Sep 6, 19, 21; 1775: HAY, May 15, 22, 24, 26, Jun 5, Jul 7, 21, 31,
Sep 7, 18, CG, Oct 24, 25, 27, Nov 9, 10, 21, 28, 30, Dec 9; 1776: CG, Jan
12, 31, Feb 22, Mar 16, Apr 16, 19, 27, May 1, HAY, 20, 22, 27, 28, Jul 3,
Aug 2, Sep 2, CG, 23, 27, Oct 7, 31, Nov 4, 13, 15, 20, 25, 28, 30, Dec 18,
19, 21; 1777: CG, Jan 2, 17, Feb 22, 25, Apr 14, 22, 28, May 7, 8, 15, 20,
Sep 22, 24, Oct 6, 8, 10, 16, 20, 30, Nov 13; 1778: CG, Jan 3, 21, Feb 6, 25,
Mar 7, 9, Apr 24, May 7, 9, 19, Sep 28, Oct 2, 14, 15, 28, Nov 21, Dec 3, 11,
15; 1779: CG, Jan 2, Feb 12, Mar 22, Apr 21, 22, 26, 27, May 3, Sep 27,
Nov 4, 11, 19, 23, 25, Dec 16, 23; 1780: CG, Mar 18, Apr 7, 24, May 6, 18,
19, 24, Oct 3, 10, 13, Nov 2, Dec 4, 27; 1781: CG, Jan 10, Feb 14, 24, Mar 8,
May 11, 14, Sep 28, Oct 16, 23, 31, Nov 8, Dec 20; 1782: CG, Jan 7, 10, Apr
10, May 11, 28, 29, HAY, Sep 21; 1787: CG, May 5; 1788: CG, Feb 5; 1789: DL,
Feb 27, Mar 6, 18, 20, 25
Ambrosini, Antonia (singer), 1754: CG, Feb 11
Amelia wishes when she dies (song), 1734: DL, May 13
Amelia. See Carey, Henry; Cumberland, Richard.
Amelia, Princess, 1715: KING'S, Feb 19; 1728: KING'S, Feb 17, Mar 30, Apr 2,
DL, Nov 20, Dec 11, 12, 19, 26; 1729: DL, Jan 2, 15, 16, Feb 5, LIF, 12, DL,
Mar 6, 13, Apr 15, LIF, Oct 8, Nov 4, 18, Dec 18; 1730: DL, Oct 28, Nov 26,
KING'S, 28, DL, Dec 10; 1731: DL, Jan 21; 1732: KING'S, Dec 9; 1733: KING'S,
Apr 10, HAY, Jun 4, KING'S, 9; 1734: LIF, Jan 1, KING'S, Nov 2, 5, GF/HAY, 6,
Dec 5; 1735: GF/HAY, Jan 2, 9, LIF, Feb 27, CG/LIF, Apr 14, CG, May 14, Jul
2, DL, Nov 8; 1736: KING'S, Jan 27, CG, Feb 19, DL, May 8, CG, 19, LIF, Jul
7; 1746: CG, Oct 31, Nov 7, 10, 12, 25, Dec 9, 17; 1747: CG, Jan 13, 14, 27,
Feb 17; 1748: KING'S, Dec 17; 1750: DL, Jan 10, CG, Feb 14, DL, Mar 10, 17,
CG, 21; 1754: CG, Jan 28; 1786: NONE, Nov 1; see also Princesses
America, 1710: QUEEN'S, Apr 27, 28; 1775: CG, Jan 3; 1776: CG, Jan 3; 1779:
HAY, Jul 15, DL, Oct 16; 1798: CG, Sep 28
American Heroine, The; or, Ingratitude Punished (pantomime, anon), 1792:
DLKING'S, Mar 19
American Indians, 1790: DL, Jun 1
American Princes, 1719: LIF, Dec 21; 1720: LIF, Jan 5, YB, Apr 1; see also
Cherokee Chiefs; Indian Kings, American
Amherst by land, Boscawen by Sea (song), 1759: CG, Dec 13
Aminta. See Dancer, John; Tasso, Torquato.
Amintas that true-hearted swain (song), 1670: LIF, Sep 20
Amintas. See Oldmixon, John; Rolt, Richard.
Amitie a l'Epreuve, L'. See Favart, Charles Simon; Voisenon, Claude Henri de
Fusee de.
Amitie conduite a l'Amour (dance), 1784: KING'S, Feb 14
Amor che per te sento (song), 1728: LIF, May 8, 13, 18, 30; 1729: DL, Mar 26
Amor Costante, L'. See Leo, Leonardo.
Amor fra le Vendemmie, L'. See Guglielmi, Pietro.
Amor pui non Voglieo (song), 1714: QUEEN'S, May 29
Amor Vuol Sofferenza. See Leo, Leonardo.
Amore Artigiano, L'. See Gassmann, Florian Leopold.
Amore Contrastato, L'. See Paisiello, Giovanni.
Amore Inflame (music), 1714: QUEEN'S, May 29, Jun 23
Amore Soldato, L'. See Sacchini, Antonio Maria Gasparo.
Amoretti, Giustina (singer), 1748: KING'S, Nov 8
Amorevoli, Angelo (singer), 1741: KING'S, Oct 31, Nov 10, Dec 12, 19; 1742:
KING'S, Jan 19, Mar 2, Apr 13, 20, DL, May 6, KING'S, Nov 2, Dec 4; 1743:
KING'S, Jan 1, Feb 22, Mar 30, Apr 5
Amorous Adventure, The; or, The Plague of a Wanton Wife (play, anon), 1730:
HAY, Jul 17, 18, 21, 22, 23, 24, 28, Nov 16, Dec 28; 1731: HAY, Jan 1
Amorous Bigot, The. See Shadwell, Thomas.
Amorous Clowns, The; or, The Courtezan (dance), 1733: LIF/CG, May 3, 8, CG, Jun
26, 29; 1736: DL, May 14, 21
Amorous Contention, The; or, The Politic Maid (dance), 1740: BFH, Aug 23; 1742:
LIF, Nov 29
Amorous Couple (dance), 1733: GF, Oct 22, 23, 29, 30, Nov 1, 8
Amorous Follies, The (play, anon), 1720: KING'S, Mar 22; 1725: HAY, Apr 19; see
also Regnard, Jean Francois.
Amorous Gallant, The. See Bulteel, John.
Amorous Goddess, The; or, Harlequin Married (pantomime, anon), 1744: DL, Feb 1,
2, 3, 4, 6, 7, 9, 11, 13, 14, 16, 18, 20, 28, Mar 1, 3, 8, 15, 17, 26, 27,
30, 31, Apr 7, 12, 13, 14, 16, 19, 20, 27, May 2, 7, 24, 28, 31, Oct 17, 19,

20, 22, 23; <u>1746</u>: DL, Apr 25
Amorous Knife Grinders, The (dance), <u>1763</u>: CG, Oct 12
Amorous Lady, The; or, The Biter Bit (play, anon), <u>1733</u>: HAY, Jul 26
Amorous Old Widow, The (play, anon), <u>1736</u>: NONE, Sep 7
Amorous Old Woman, The. See Duffett, Thomas.
Amorous Prince, The. See Behn, Aphra.
Amorous Sportsman, The (dance), <u>1733</u>: GF, Dec 10, 17; <u>1734</u>: GF, Jan 5
Amorous Sportsman, The; or, Harlequin Triumphant (pantomime), <u>1744</u>: GF, Dec 26,
    27
Amorous Sportsman, The; or, The Death of the Stag (masque), <u>1732</u>: GF, Dec 20,
    21, 22, 26, 27, 28, 29, 30; <u>1733</u>: GF, Jan 1, 2, 3, 4, 5, 6, 11, 12, 19, Feb
    12, Apr 5, 11, 12, 16, 18, 19, 24, 25
Amorous Sportsman, The; or, The Jealous Farmer (pantomime), <u>1745</u>: GF, Feb 28,
    Mar 2
Amorous Swain, The; or, Rival Nymphs (dance), <u>1735</u>: DL, Mar 10, 13, 20, 22, 24,
    27, 29, Apr 11, 14, 15, 16, 17, 18, 21, 23, 24, 28, 29, May 1, 2, 5, 6, 8, 9,
    10, 13, 14, 20, 22, 29, Jun 3, 11; <u>1744</u>: CG, Apr 16, 23; <u>1748</u>: CG, Apr 20
Amorous Widow, The. See Betterton, Thomas.
Amour au Rendezvous, L' (dance), <u>1790</u>: DL, Jun 1
Amour dans la Vendange, L' (dance), <u>1778</u>: KING'S, May 19, 26, 28, Jun 2, 9
Amour et Psiche, L' (dance), <u>1788</u>: KING'S, Jan 29, Feb 5, 9, 12, 16, 19, 21,
    28, Mar 8, 11, 29, Apr 1, 26, May 6, 8, 15, Jun 26; <u>1796</u>: KING'S, Dec 13, 17,
    20, 23, 27, 31; <u>1797</u>: KING'S, Jan 3, 7, 17, 21, 24, Apr 8
Amour Jardinier, L' (dance), <u>1786</u>: KING'S, Apr 1, 6, 20, 27, 29, Jun 15, Jul 1,
    11
Amour Medicin, L'. See Moliere.
Amour Soldat, L' (dance), <u>1785</u>: KING'S, Apr 7
Amour Use, L'. See Destouches.
Amour Vange, L' (dance), <u>1796</u>: KING'S, Jun 2, 4, 7, Jul 2, 7
Amoureuses Follies. See Regnard, Jean Francois.
Amourous Fantasme, The. See Lower, William.
Amours d'Ete (dance), <u>1785</u>: KING'S, Apr 14
Amours de Colombine & de Scaramouche, Pedant, Scrupuleux, & Pierot Escallier,
    Les (pantomime, anon), <u>1725</u>: HAY, Mar 29
Amours de Nanterre, Les (farce, anon), <u>1734</u>: HAY, Nov 14, 21
Amours de Polichinelle and Dame Ragonde (dance), <u>1738</u>: CG, Mar 20
Amours of Alexander and Roxana (dance), <u>1783</u>: KING'S, Apr 10
Amours of Billingsgate, The. See Ryan, Lacy, The Cobler's Opera.
Amours of Harlequin, The; or, The Bottle-Conjuror Outdone (pantomime, anon),
    <u>1749</u>: BFYT, Aug 23, 24, 25, 26, 28, BHB, Oct 3, 5, 14
Amphion et Thalie; ou, L'Eleve des Muses (dance), <u>1791</u>: PAN, Feb 17, 19, 22,
    26, Mar 1, 3, 5, 8, 10, 12, 15, Apr 9, 12, 14, 28, 30, May 28
Amphitrion. See Moliere.
Amphitryo. See Plautus.
Amphitryon; or, The Two Sosias. See Dryden, John.
Amson, James (china merchant), <u>1767</u>: CG, Feb 25
Amsterdam Coffee House, <u>1752</u>: DL, Dec 19
Amsterdam Theatre, <u>1717</u>: DL, Apr 24
Amsterdam, <u>1669</u>: NONE, Jan 5; <u>1754</u>: CG, Feb 11, Dec 9
Amurath the Great, Emperor of the Turks (play, anon), <u>1730</u>: SFP, Sep 9; <u>1731</u>:
    TC, Aug 4, 5, 6, 7, 9, 10, 11, 12, 13, 14, 16, 17, 18, 19
Amusements Champetres (dance), <u>1776</u>: KING'S, Nov 2, 9, 12, Dec 17; <u>1777</u>:
    KING'S, Mar 1
Amusements of Strasburg (dance), <u>1771</u>: DL, Apr 22, 23, 25, Nov 18, 20; <u>1772</u>:
    DL, Jan 11, 29, Mar 21, Apr 6, 9
Amyntas led me to a grove (song), <u>1673</u>: DG, Feb 6
Amyntas. See Randolph, Thomas.
Anacreontic Society Revived, The (interlude, anon), <u>1798</u>: DL, May 23
Anacreontic Song (song), <u>1734</u>: CG, Apr 16; <u>1736</u>: CG, Apr 12, 17; <u>1748</u>: CG, Mar
    31; <u>1751</u>: CG, Apr 24; <u>1771</u>: GROTTO, Aug 30, Sep 9; <u>1785</u>: DL, Apr 18, May 5,
    HAY, Aug 19; <u>1786</u>: DL, Apr 4; <u>1787</u>: DL, Apr 9; <u>1788</u>: HAY, Aug 22; <u>1789</u>: CG,
    Apr 21, May 5, 29, HAY, Aug 25; <u>1790</u>: DL, May 20; <u>1791</u>: CG, May 5, DL, 18;
    <u>1792</u>: DLKING'S, Apr 10; <u>1795</u>: DL, May 27; <u>1800</u>: CG, May 6
Anatomist, The. See Ravenscroft, Edward.
Ancaster, Duchess of (spectator), <u>1767</u>: DL, Oct 14
Anchor and Vine Tavern, <u>1723</u>: AVT, Dec 31
Anchor Smiths (song), <u>1800</u>: CG, May 7, 15, 27, 30, Jun 5
Ancient Britons, Society of, <u>1773</u>: DL, Dec 18
Ancient History of Caradoc the Great, The; or, The Valiant Welshman (play,
    anon), <u>1727</u>: LIF, May 19
Ancient Music Academy, <u>1739</u>: CRT, Jan 18
Ancient Phillis has young Graces (song), <u>1693</u>: DL, Oct 0

15

And ever against eating cares (song), 1791: CG, Mar 18; 1792: CG, Feb 24
And he shall purify (song), 1793: KING/HAY, Feb 20; 1794: DL, Mar 19
And if I give thee Honor (song), 1794: CG, Mar 21
And in Each Tract of Glory (song), 1726: LIF, Jul 5
And in that air Behold! God is my salvation (song), 1792: KING'S, Mar 23, 28,
   30
And in that Day (song), 1792: KING'S, Mar 23, 28, 30
And Jesus went about (song), 1794: DL, Apr 10
And Miriam the Prophetess (song), 1793: CG, Feb 15, Mar 13; 1794: CG, Mar 14,
   Apr 9; 1798: CG, Mar 14, 30
And the Angel said unto them (song), 1790: DL, Mar 24
And the glory of the Lord (song), 1790: CG, Mar 26; 1793: KING/HAY, Feb 20;
   1794: DL, Mar 19; 1795: CG, Mar 27; 1798: CG, Mar 30
And the King shall Rejoice (anthem), 1775: DL, Mar 22
And the men of Judah (song), 1794: DL, Apr 10
And their aw nodding at our house at hame (song), 1791: CG, May 18
And we are Gayly yet (song), 1745: CG, May 1
And young and old (song), 1789: CG, Mar 20; 1790: DL, Mar 10; 1791: CG, Mar 18,
   DL, Apr 13; 1792: KING'S, Mar 14, 30; 1793: CG, Mar 20; 1794: CG, Mar 21, DL,
   Apr 9
Anderson (actor), 1732: HAY, May 8; 1738: CG, Mar 13, Apr 25, Aug 29, Dec 5,
   20; 1739: CG, May 11, 25, Sep 5, 21, 27, Oct 1, 2, 3, Nov 6, 20, Dec 10, 19;
   1740: CG, Feb 6, Mar 11, Apr 14, 18, 28, May 3, 9, 21, Sep 22, Oct 3, 6, 24,
   31, Nov 1, 4, 10, Dec 4, 29; 1741: CG, Jan 15, 27, Feb 5, 19, 26, Mar 2, 30,
   Apr 1, 24, 25, May 4, 5, 8, 12, Sep 23, 25; 1742: CG, Oct 9, 15, 18, 25, Nov
   4, Dec 7, 11; 1743: CG, May 4, 5, DL, Sep 15, 17, CG, 21, DL, 22, 24, CG, 28,
   DL, 29, CG, 30, DL, Oct 1, CG, 3, DL, 4, 11, 13, 15, CG, 17, 21, DL, 27, CG,
   28, DL, Nov 3, CG, 4, 7, 16, 19, 30, Dec 3, 8, 9, 12, 17, 31; 1744: CG, Jan
   11, 24, Feb 28, Mar 12, Apr 7, 28, 30, May 1, Sep 19, 24, 28, Oct 1, 3, 8,
   10, 15, 18, 20, 24, 31, Nov 5, 8, 9, 24, Dec 6, 12, 21, 28; 1745: CG, Feb 11,
   15, Apr 4, 20, 23, 26, May 1, 7, Sep 23, 25, 30, Oct 7, 14, 16, 31, Nov 4,
   15, 27, 28, Dec 20; 1746: CG, Jan 7, 9, 11, 13, Feb 5, 6, 8, 24, Mar 10, 13,
   15, 18, Apr 1, 3, 7, 21, 22, 23, 26, Sep 29, Oct 1, 3, 4, 6, 13, 20, 24, 29,
   Nov 3, 4, 11, Dec 6, 11, 26, 29; 1747: CG, Feb 6, 12, DL, 23, CG, Mar 9, 17,
   Apr 7, May 15, 20, 22, Oct 31, Nov 16, 18, Dec 9, 19, 28; 1748: CG, Jan 2, 7,
   8, 9, 14, 16, 27, Feb 10, Mar 8, 21, 24, 28, Apr 11, 13, 15, 16, 18, 21, 22,
   26, 27, 29, May 2, Sep 21, 26, 28, Oct 3, 7, 10, 14, 17, 24, 25, 28, 29, Nov
   3, 4, 9, 11, 12, 15, 16, 24, 28, Dec 9, 10, 20, 21, 26; 1749: CG, Jan 2, 3,
   11, 13, 25, 28, Feb 23, Mar 2, 13, 14, 29, 31, Apr 11, 17, 19, 20, May 4, Sep
   25, 27, 29, Oct 2, 4, 6, 9, 11, 12, 16, 19, 20, 23, 26, 30, Nov 3, 4, 8, 9,
   11, 16, 17, 18, 24, Dec 16, 26, 27, 28; 1750: CG, Jan 18, Feb 2, 5, 20, 22,
   Mar 1, 17, 20, 27, Apr 7, 23, May 1, Sep 24, 28, Oct 12, 13, 15, 17, 18, 19,
   24, 25, 26, 29, Nov 1, 5, 6, 8, 12, 17, 22, 24, 28, 29, 30, Dec 1, 18; 1751:
   CG, Jan 1, Mar 18, Apr 16, 22, May 6, 8, 16, Sep 23, 25, 27, Oct 7, 9, 11,
   17, 18, 25, 29, Nov 4, 6, 7, 11, 18, 22, 26, Dec 5, 14; 1752: CG, Jan 29, Mar
   16, 17, 30, Apr 28, 30, May 4, Sep 20, 22, 25, 29, Oct 2, 4, 6, 12, 16, 18,
   21, 23, 24, 27, 30, 31, Nov 1, 4, 7, 9, 10, 28, Dec 8, 9, 11, 13, 27; 1753:
   CG, Jan 20, 25, Feb 7, 12, Mar 19, 24, 26, 31, May 3, 7, 8, 18, Sep 12, 14,
   17, 21, 24, 26, Oct 3, 5, 10, 22, 24, 27, 30, 31, Nov 1, 5, 9, 12, 20, 22,
   26, 28, Dec 5; 1754: CG, Jan 10, 22, Mar 9, 18, 23, 26, Apr 6, 24, May 4, 6,
   13, 14, Sep 16, 20, 23, 25, 27, 30, Oct 2, 4, 7, 9, 15, 17, 18, 23, 24, Nov
   4, 12, 13, 16, 20, 23, 27, 28, Dec 10, 13; 1755: CG, Jan 4, 8, 10, 14, 22,
   28, Feb 4, 24, Mar 6, 22, Apr 2, 8, 9, 15, 18, May 7, 13, Sep 29, Oct 6, 8,
   11, 17, 18, 20, 24, 27, 30, 31, Nov 3, 4, 7, 8, 10, 11, 12, 13, 14, 17, 19,
   26, Dec 3, 5, 11, 12; 1756: CG, Jan 6, 15, Feb 19, 26, Mar 18, 22, 25, 27,
   30, Apr 1, 3, 6, 20, 29, May 17, Sep 20, 22, 27, 29, Oct 4, 6, 11, 13, 15,
   16, 18, 19, 20, 23, 25, 26, 27, 30, Nov 4, 8, 9, 11, 17, 22, 24, Dec 1, 7,
   10; 1757: CG, Jan 5, 14, 27, 28, Feb 9, 16, 19, 21, May 16, 20, Sep 16, 21,
   26, 28, 30, Oct 3, 5, 8, 10, 13, 14, 15, 17, 19, 21, 28, Nov 2, 4, 5, 7, 9,
   11, 14, 16, 18, 26, Dec 1, 5, 6, 7, 8, 9, 10, 14, 20; 1758: CG, Feb 1, Mar
   29, Apr 12, 14, 17, May 2, Sep 20, 22, 25, 27, 29, Oct 2, 4, 6, 9, 14, 20,
   23, 25, 26, 27, 30, Nov 1, 4, 7, 9, 13, 14, 16, 21, 23, Dec 2, 18; 1759: CG,
   Jan 11, 12, Feb 1, Mar 3, 5, 17, 20, Apr 5, 7, 28, May 3, 7, 8, 11, 17, Sep
   26, Oct 5, 8, 10, 22, 30, Nov 5, 28, 30, Dec 5, 6, 7, 8, 12, 21, 31; 1760:
   CG, Jan 4, 9, 14, 16, 24, 31, Feb 7, 28, Mar 18, 25, Apr 8, 9, May 2, 5, 6,
   7, 12, Sep 22, 24, Oct 1, 6, 10, 15, 18, 23, 25, Nov 18, 29, Dec 6, 9, 31;
   1761: CG, Jan 10, 23, Feb 16, 17, Mar 3, 5, 9, 25, 26, Apr 2, 13, 17, 20, 21,
   27, 29, May 5, 8, 11, Sep 9, 14, 21, 24, 28, Oct 1, 3, 5, 6, 7, 13, 17, 19,
   20, 21, 22, 23, 27, 31, Nov 2, 4, 9, 13, Dec 11, 28, 30; 1762: CG, Jan 18,
   Feb 3, 15, 22, Mar 13, 23, Apr 16, 24, 26, May 5, 6, 7, 14, Sep 22, 24, 30,
   Oct 1, 2, 6, 9, 12, 14, 16, 19, 21, 29, Nov 1, 30, Dec 4; 1763: CG, Jan 11,
   14, Feb 14, May 9, Sep 21, 23, 26, 30, Oct 14, Nov 4, 10, 16, 18, 22, Dec 9,

26, 27; <u>1764</u>: CG, Jan 17, Feb 11, 13, 15, Mar 27, Apr 10, 28, May 7, 9, 14,
18, 21, Sep 19, 21, 26, 28, Oct 5, 8, 15, 16, 17, 18, 19, 20, 22, 25, Nov 3,
5, 27, 30, Dec 7, 21; <u>1765</u>: CG, Jan 8, 9, 12, 14, 21, Feb 18, Mar 26, Apr 9,
11, 16, May 7, 15, Sep 16, 18, 20, 23, 27, 30, Oct 7, 9, 10, 15, 28, 30, Nov
13, 27, Dec 10; <u>1766</u>: CG, Jan 31, Feb 5, Mar 17, 31, Apr 14, 23, 25, May 6,
Sep 22, 26, Oct 6, 18, 21, 31, Nov 4, 8, 11, 18, 19, 25, Dec 4, 8, 9, 10, 13,
16, 20, 30, 31; <u>1767</u>: CG, Jan 23, Mar 21, 28, 31, Apr 6, May 8; <u>1768</u>: CG, Jan
21
Anderson (tailor), <u>1774</u>: CG, Jan 29
Anderson (watchmaker), <u>1747</u>: DL, Feb 18
Anderson, Miss (actor), <u>1782</u>: HAY, Mar 21
Anderson, Miss (dancer), <u>1733</u>: DL, Oct 24, Dec 1, 5, 11; <u>1734</u>: DL, Jan 1, Feb
4, Mar 7, DL/LIF, Apr 1, DL, 15, DL/HAY, 26, DL, May 15, DL/HAY, 17, DL, Oct
5, 10, 17, Nov 1, Dec 11, 21; <u>1735</u>: DL, Jan 18, 21, Feb 15, 18, Apr 11, May
14, Jul 1, GF/HAY, 15, 18, DL, Sep 25, 30, Oct 1, 7, 22, Nov 5, 17, 19, 20,
25, Dec 17, 18; <u>1736</u>: DL, Jan 3, 12, Apr 10, 15, 17, 26, May 7, 11, 14, 20,
25, 27, 28, Sep 7, Oct 5, 12, 23, 25, Nov 2, Dec 4, 31; <u>1737</u>: DL, Feb 14, Apr
29, 30, May 3, 4, 5, 9, 30
Anderson, Mrs (actor), <u>1724</u>: DL, Sep 26, Oct 16, Nov 2, 14, 23, Dec 7; <u>1725</u>:
DL, Jan 25, Feb 4, 20, Apr 7, 21, LIF, Nov 3, 13, 22, 29, 30, Dec 8; <u>1726</u>:
LIF, Jan 3, 14, Mar 21, Apr 12, 18, 21, May 9, Jun 17, 21, 24, Jul 1, 5, 15,
19, 22, 26, 29, Aug 2, 5, 9, 16, 19, 23, Sep 23, 30, Oct 3, 12, Nov 14, 21,
KING'S, Dec 10, 17, 21, 28; <u>1727</u>: KING'S, Mar 16, LIF, Oct 6, 12, 25, Nov 9;
<u>1728</u>: LIF, Apr 22, May 6, 11, 15, 22, 23, Jun 25, Jul 2, 12, Aug 2, HAY, Oct
15, Nov 19; <u>1729</u>: HAY, Jan 27; <u>1730</u>: LIF, Apr 10
Anderson, Mrs (actor, singer), <u>1749</u>: HAY, Apr 29; <u>1750</u>: HAY, Feb 16
Anderton Coffee House, <u>1751</u>: DL, May 14; <u>1752</u>: DL, Dec 19
Andre, Miss (dancer), <u>1785</u>: CG, Oct 10, Nov 7
Andreas, Miss (dancer), <u>1779</u>: KING'S, Dec 14; <u>1780</u>: KING'S, Apr 22, May 2, 12
Andrei, Antonio (librettist), <u>1778</u>: KING'S, May 5; <u>1782</u>: KING'S, Nov 2; <u>1784</u>:
KING'S, Mar 18
Andreoni (castrato singer), <u>1740</u>: HAY, Jan 22, Mar 15, May 10, LIF, Nov 22;
<u>1741</u>: LIF, Jan 10, HIC, 16, Feb 27, Mar 6, HAY, 9, HIC, 13, Apr 24, KING'S,
Oct 31; <u>1742</u>: KING'S, Jan 19, Mar 2, Apr 13
Andreozzi, Gaetano (composer), <u>1791</u>: PAN, Feb 17, CG, Jun 3; <u>1792</u>: DLKING'S,
May 23; <u>1793</u>: KING'S, Mar 19; <u>1794</u>: DL, Jun 9, Sep 27; <u>1795</u>: DL, Oct 1; <u>1796</u>:
CG, Mar 2; <u>1797</u>: DL, Feb 16; <u>1800</u>: DL, Jan 1
--Teodolinda (opera), <u>1793</u>: KING'S, Mar 12, 19, 23, Apr 2, 6, 13, 16, 20, 27,
May 11, Jun 4
Andrew and his Cutty Gun (song), <u>1798</u>: CG, Apr 28
Andrews (actor), <u>1760</u>: CG, May 14
Andrews (dresser) <u>1792</u>: DLKING'S, Jun 15; <u>1793</u>: DL, Jun 6
Andrews (haberdasher), <u>1771</u>: CG, Nov 28
Andrews (spectator), <u>1668</u>: LIF, Dec 30
Andrews, Hugh (music publisher), <u>1780</u>: DL, May 6; see also Birchall, Robert
Andrews, Miles Peter, <u>1774</u>: DL, Apr 29, Oct 19; <u>1778</u>: DL, Mar 16; <u>1779</u>: HAY,
Jul 1; <u>1780</u>: HAY, Jul 8, DL, Dec 4; <u>1781</u>: DL, Mar 10, HAY, Jul 9, DL, Nov 15;
<u>1782</u>: DL, Dec 11; <u>1784</u>: DL, Feb 14, CG, Dec 21; <u>1785</u>: CG, Dec 14; <u>1786</u>: CG,
Dec 20, 26; <u>1787</u>: CG, Feb 10, DL, Mar 12; <u>1788</u>: CG, Apr 25, Nov 28; <u>1789</u>: CG,
May 15, 26, Oct 7; <u>1790</u>: CG, Jan 28, May 18, Nov 3, DL, 17; <u>1791</u>: CG, Jan 7,
Apr 5, May 3, Nov 5; <u>1792</u>: CG, Apr 18, Oct 26, Nov 6, Dec 1; <u>1793</u>: CG, Jan
29, Mar 23, Apr 18, 24, Nov 19, Dec 18; <u>1794</u>: CG, Oct 30; <u>1795</u>: CG, Jan 31,
Nov 7; <u>1796</u>: CG, Jun 1, Oct 29; <u>1797</u>: CG, Jan 10, DL, Apr 19, CG, Sep 20;
<u>1798</u>: CG, Jan 11; <u>1799</u>: DL, May 17, HAY, Oct 21; <u>1800</u>: DL, Feb 1, CG, 8, Apr
23
--Baron Kinkvervankotsdorsprakengatchdern!, The (opera), <u>1781</u>: HAY, Jul 7, 9,
10, 11
--Belphegor; or, The Wishes (opera), <u>1778</u>: DL, Mar 16, 17, 19, 21, 23, 24, 28,
Apr 2, 4, 21, 24, Dec 16; <u>1779</u>: DL, Oct 9, 14, Dec 4; <u>1783</u>: DL, Apr 26, May
17, 31; <u>1789</u>: DL, Oct 27
--Best Bidder, The (farce), <u>1782</u>: DL, Nov 29, Dec 11, 12, 13, 17; <u>1783</u>: DL, Jan
18, 23, Feb 1, Apr 7
--Better Late than Never, <u>1790</u>: DL, Nov 17, 19, 23, 26, 30, Dec 3, 8, 29; <u>1791</u>:
DL, Jan 6, 17, 20, Feb 3, 11
--Conjuror, The, <u>1774</u>: DL, Apr 29
--Dissipation, <u>1781</u>: DL, Mar 10, 12, 13, 15, 22, 24, Apr 5, 19, 27, May 3, 14,
29, Nov 15, 23; <u>1782</u>: DL, Jan 2, Apr 15; <u>1783</u>: DL, Mar 20
--Election, The (interlude), <u>1774</u>: DL, Oct 19, 21, 22, 25, 26, 27, 29, 31, Nov
1, 11, 19, 21, 28, Dec 27; <u>1775</u>: DL, Mar 28; <u>1776</u>: DL, May 11, CHR, Oct 16;
<u>1777</u>: DL, Apr 1; <u>1780</u>: DL, Sep 16, 19, Oct 2, 3; <u>1782</u>: DL, Apr 3, 4; <u>1788</u>:
HAY, Aug 15, 26
--Enchanted Castle, The (Castle of Wonders, The) (pantomime), <u>1786</u>: CG, Dec 26,

27, 28, 29, 30; <u>1787</u>: CG, Jan 1, 2, 3, 4, 5, 6, 8, 9, 10, 11, 12, 13, 15, 16,
17, 18, 19, 20, 22, 23, 24, 25, 29, Feb 5, 10, 12, 16, 26, Mar 5, 8, 13, Apr
9, May 7, Nov 5, 9, 12, 19, Dec 3; <u>1796</u>: CG, Mar 15, Oct 24
--Fire and Water (opera), <u>1780</u>: HAY, Jul 8, 10, 12, 15, 19, 21, 22, 25, 28, Aug
11, 15, 16, Sep 1
--Mysteries of the Castle, The, <u>1795</u>: CG, Jan 31, Feb 2, 3, 4, 5, 6, 7, 9, 10,
11, 12, 13, 14, 16, Mar 3, 7, 10, Apr 17, Nov 4; <u>1796</u>: CG, Jan 1, Apr 8, May
31, Dec 22; <u>1797</u>: CG, Jan 5, Dec 18; <u>1799</u>: CG, Nov 11; <u>1800</u>: CG, Feb 3
--Reparation, The, <u>1784</u>: DL, Feb 14, 16, 17, 19, 20, 23, 26, Mar 1, 4, 11, 13,
15, Apr 23
--Summer Amusement; or, An Adventure at Margate (with William Augustus Miles)
(opera), <u>1779</u>: HAY, Jul 1, 2, 5, 6, 7, 8, 10, 12, 14, 20, 23, 28, 30, Aug 5,
12, 21, 25, Sep 7; <u>1780</u>: HAY, Jun 15, 20, 29, Jul 3, 20, 29, Aug 10, Sep 1;
<u>1781</u>: HAY, Jun 12, 14, 29, Jul 6, 14, 30, Aug 4, 28; <u>1782</u>: HAY, Jul 30, Aug
6, 7, 14, 24, 28, Sep 6, 13; <u>1783</u>: HAY, Jun 10, 24, Aug 8, 22; <u>1784</u>: HAY, Jun
4, 16, Jul 30, Aug 6, 20; <u>1785</u>: HAY, May 31, Jun 15, Jul 22; <u>1786</u>: HAY, Jun
26, Jul 5, Aug 22, 26; <u>1787</u>: HAY, Jun 16, 29, Aug 2; <u>1788</u>: HAY, Jun 16, 25,
30, Jul 14, Aug 20; <u>1789</u>: HAY, Jun 26, Jul 11, 13, 16, Aug 4; <u>1790</u>: HAY, Aug
20, 24; <u>1791</u>: HAY, Jun 14, 17, 22; <u>1792</u>: HAY, Jun 19, 27; <u>1793</u>: HAY, Jul 15,
26; <u>1794</u>: HAY, Aug 4, 8; <u>1795</u>: HAY, Jul 20, Aug 22
Andrews, Miss (actor, singer) <u>1796</u>: DL, May 13; <u>1797</u>: HAY, Jun 13, 16, 17, 19,
23, 26, 28, Jul 15, Aug 4, 9, 15, 23, 31, Sep 4; <u>1798</u>: HAY, Jan 15
Andrews, Mrs (actor), <u>1696</u>: DG, Jun 0; <u>1697</u>: DG, Jun 0, DL, Sep 0
Andria. See Terence.
Andromaca. See Jomelli, Niccolo; Nasolini, Sebastiano.
Andromache. See Crowne, John.
Andromana. See Shirley, James.
Andromaque. See Racine, Jean.
Andromeda (play, anon), <u>1662</u>: COCKPIT, Jan 20
Andronicus Comenius. See Wilson, John.
Andronicus. See Wilson, John.
Anfossi, Pasquale (composer), <u>1775</u>: KING'S, Jan 14, Mar 7; <u>1777</u>: KING'S, Feb 4;
<u>1778</u>: KING'S, Jan 20; <u>1779</u>: KING'S, Nov 27; <u>1781</u>: KING'S, Dec 11; <u>1782</u>:
KING'S, Nov 14, Dec 19; <u>1783</u>: KING'S, Mar 27, Jun 14, Nov 29, Dec 16; <u>1784</u>:
KING'S, Jan 17, Feb 24, May 8, Jun 12, Dec 18; <u>1785</u>: KING'S, Feb 26, May 12,
28; <u>1786</u>: KING'S, Feb 14, Mar 11, 16, May 4, 20, CG, Oct 16; <u>1788</u>: CG, Dec
13; <u>1789</u>: CG, Jan 26, Nov 24; <u>1792</u>: DL, Nov 21; <u>1793</u>: CG, May 11; <u>1794</u>: DL,
May 16, Oct 27, Dec 20, KING'S, 20; <u>1795</u>: DL, Oct 30
--Alessandro Nell Indie (opera), <u>1779</u>: KING'S, Nov 23, 27, 30, Dec 4, 7, 11,
18; <u>1780</u>: KING'S, Jan 8, 15
--Curioso Indiscreto, Il (opera), <u>1784</u>: KING'S, Dec 18, 21, 23, 28; <u>1785</u>:
KING'S, Jan 1, Mar 17, 29, Apr 7
--Didone Abbandonata (opera), <u>1786</u>: KING'S, Feb 11, 14, 18, 21, 25, 28, Mar 4,
7, Apr 6, 22; <u>1787</u>: KING'S, Mar 29; <u>1792</u>: DLKING'S, May 23
--Geloso in Cimento, Il (opera), <u>1777</u>: KING'S, Feb 4, 11, 18, Mar 4, 11, Apr
15, May 8
--Gemelle, Le (opera), <u>1784</u>: KING'S, Jun 12, 15, 22, 26
--Inglese in Italia, L' (opera), <u>1786</u>: KING'S, May 18, 20, 27
--Issipile (opera), <u>1784</u>: KING'S, May 8, 11, 22, 29, Jun 5, 19
--Marchesa Giardiniera, La (opera), <u>1775</u>: KING'S, Mar 7, 14, 18, 28, Apr 4, 18,
27, May 9, 25, Jun 2, 21
--Nitteti (opera), <u>1785</u>: KING'S, Feb 26, Mar 1, 5, 12, 19
--Silla (opera), <u>1783</u>: KING'S, Nov 29, Dec 2, 6, 9, 13, 20, 27, 30; <u>1784</u>:
KING'S, Jan 3
--Trionfo della Costanza, Il (opera), <u>1782</u>: KING'S, Dec 19, 21, 23, 28, 31;
<u>1783</u>: KING'S, Jan 4, 14, 18, 25, Feb 1, 8, 13, 25, Mar 8, 13, 20, 25, May 10
--Trionfo D'Arianna, Il (opera), <u>1784</u>: KING'S, Jan 17, 24, 31
--Vecchi Burlati, I (opera), <u>1783</u>: KING'S, Mar 27, Apr 1, 3, 8, 12, 24, May 6,
13
--Vera Costanza, La (opera), <u>1778</u>: KING'S, Jan 20, 27, Feb 3, 10, 17, 24, Apr
9, 28
--Viaggiatori Felici, I (opera), <u>1781</u>: KING'S, Dec 8, 11, 13, 20, 27, 29; <u>1782</u>:
KING'S, Jan 1, 8, 22, Feb 2, 5, 9, 16, 19, 21, 23, 28, Mar 2, 12, 14, 21, Apr
11, 18, 25, May 2, 16, 17, 27, Jun 3, 22, 25, 29; <u>1785</u>: KING'S, May 24, 28,
31, Jun 9, 14, 18, 28, Jul 2; <u>1786</u>: KING'S, Mar 16, 23, Apr 25, May 30, Jun
13, 27
--Zenobia in Palmira (opera), <u>1794</u>: KING'S, Dec 20, 23, 27, 30; <u>1795</u>: KING'S,
Jan 3, 6, 24
Angel (beneficiary), <u>1732</u>: LIF, Feb 25; <u>1736</u>: CAT, Feb 4
Angel (harpist), <u>1720</u>: LIF, Feb 27
Angel and Crown Tavern, <u>1743</u>: LIF, Mar 22
Angel and Trumpet, <u>1745</u>: CG, Mar 6

Angel Court, <u>1717</u>: SFBL, Sep 9; <u>1718</u>: SF, Sep 5; <u>1750</u>: HAY, Nov 10; <u>1788</u>:
   KING'S, May 15
Angel Inn, <u>1708</u>: DL, Sep 7; <u>1740</u>: CG, Mar 20; <u>1741</u>: CG, Mar 12; <u>1746</u>: DL, Apr
   3; <u>1747</u>: DL, Mar 31; <u>1752</u>: DL, Feb 22; <u>1785</u>: HAMM, Jul 2; <u>1786</u>: HAMM, Aug 5;
   <u>1787</u>: HAY, Mar 12
Angel Tavern, <u>1722</u>: SFM, Sep 5
Angel, Edward (actor), <u>1662</u>: ATCOURT, Nov 1; <u>1664</u>: LIF, Mar 7, Aug 13; <u>1665</u>:
   LIF, Apr 3; <u>1667</u>: LIF, Nov 7; <u>1668</u>: LIF, Feb 22, May 2, Dec 8, ATCOURT, 28;
   <u>1669</u>: LIF, Dec 14; <u>1670</u>: LIF, Sep 20, Nov 0; <u>1671</u>: LIF, Mar 6, 15, Jun 0;
   <u>1672</u>: DG, Feb 6, Jul 4, ATCOU/DG, Dec 2; <u>1673</u>: DG, Feb 6, Mar 12
Angelelli, Augusta (singer), <u>1798</u>: KING'S, Jan 23, 31, Mar 10, 22, Apr 10, 21,
   Jun 5
Angelic Fair (song), <u>1768</u>: CG, May 11
Angelica and Medoro. See Pescetti, Giovanni Battista.
Angelo, Henry Charles William (actor), <u>1792</u>: DLKING'S, Mar 29
Angelo, Sg (scene painter), <u>1723</u>: DL, Dec 5
Angelo, Sg. See Zanoni, Angelo.
Angels ever bright and fair (song), <u>1786</u>: DL, Mar 10; <u>1787</u>: DL, Feb 23; <u>1788</u>:
   DL, Feb 8; <u>1789</u>: CG, Mar 6, DL, 18, CG, May 20; <u>1790</u>: CG, Feb 24, DL, 26;
   <u>1791</u>: CG, Mar 11, DL, 23; <u>1792</u>: KING'S, Feb 24, CG, Mar 2, KING'S, 7; <u>1793</u>:
   KING/HAY, Feb 15, 22, CG, Mar 6; <u>1794</u>: DL, Mar 12, CG, 12, DL, 14, Apr 2, CG,
   4, DL, 10, CG, 11; <u>1795</u>: KING'S, Feb 20, 27, CG, 27, Mar 25; <u>1796</u>: CG, Feb
   26; <u>1797</u>: CG, Mar 10; <u>1798</u>: CG, Mar 14, 30; <u>1799</u>: CG, Feb 8
Angerstein, John Julius (merchant, banker), <u>1790</u>: DL, Nov 17; <u>1794</u>: DL, Jul 2;
   <u>1797</u>: KING'S, May 18, CG, Jun 14, DL, Oct 27
Angier (singer), <u>1784</u>: HAY, Mar 3, 17; <u>1785</u>: HAY, Feb 23
Angiolini, Pitrot (dancer), <u>1784</u>: KING'S, Dec 18; <u>1785</u>: KING'S, Mar 17
Angiolini, Sg and Sga Pitrot (dancer), <u>1784</u>: KING'S, Dec 18; <u>1785</u>: KING'S, Jan
   15, Mar 3, 12, May 12, Jun 18
Angiolini, Sga Pitrot (dancer), <u>1784</u>: KING'S, Dec 18; <u>1785</u>: KING'S, Feb 12, Mar
   3, 17, Apr 21; <u>1786</u>: KING'S, Mar 23
Anglais, L'. See Patrat, Joseph.
Anglesey, Lady. See Annesley, Elizabeth.
Angry Doctor and the Doubting Philosopher, The. See Centlivre, Susannah.
Animadversions on Mr Colman's True State (essay), <u>1768</u>: CG, Mar 9
Animadversions on Mr Congreve's late Answer to Mr Collier, <u>1697</u>: DL, Sep 0
Animal Magnetism. See Inchbald, Elizabeth.
Animal Pantomime, The (entertainment), <u>1752</u>: HAY, Dec 11, 12, 13, 14, 15, 16,
   18, 19, 20, 21, 22, 23, 26, 28, 29, 30; <u>1753</u>: HAY, Jan 2, 4, 6, 9, 11, 13,
   16, 18, 20, 23, 25, 27, 31, Feb 1, 3, 6, 8, 10, 13, 15, 17, 20, 21, 22, 23,
   24, 26, 27, 28, Mar 1, 3, 6, 10
Animated Statue (dance), <u>1800</u>: CG, Jun 13; see also Statues Animees
Animaux Raisonables, Les. See Fuzelier, Louis.
Animaux Raisonables, Les; ou, Ulysses & Circe. See Legrand, Marc-Antoine.
Anna Bullen. See Banks, John.
Anna. See Cuthbertson, Catherine.
Anna, Sga (singer), <u>1703</u>: YB, Mar 5
Anna's Love (song), <u>1792</u>: CG, May 15
Anna's Lullaby (song), <u>1795</u>: HAY, Mar 4
Annable, Benjamin (bellringer), <u>1756</u>: DL, Feb 9
Anne, Lady (spectator), <u>1737</u>: KING'S, Jan 8
Anne, Princess, <u>1675</u>: ATCOURT, Feb 15; <u>1678</u>: DL, Feb 0; <u>1679</u>: BRUSSELS, Oct 3;
   <u>1692</u>: DG, Jun 13, DLORDG, Jul 14; <u>1720</u>: KING'S, May 26; <u>1730</u>: KING'S, Jun 6;
   see also Princesses
Anne, Queen, <u>1733</u>: HAY, Nov 20; <u>1758</u>: CG, Mar 22; <u>1773</u>: DL, Jan 1; see also
   Highness; Majesties; Queen
Annereau, John (singer), <u>1794</u>: DL, May 16, 22, 23, Jun 25, Oct 27, 31, Nov 15,
   Dec 20; <u>1795</u>: DL, Feb 24, Oct 1, 30, Nov 11, Dec 10; <u>1796</u>: DL, Mar 12, Apr
   30, May 4, Sep 29, Oct 19, Dec 3; <u>1797</u>: DL, Jan 7, Feb 9, 10, 16, Apr 18
Annesley (Ansley), Mrs (dancer), <u>1744</u>: DL, Oct 2; <u>1745</u>: DL, Jan 14; <u>1747</u>: DL,
   Jan 24; <u>1748</u>: DL, Oct 27; <u>1749</u>: DL, Feb 21, BFCB, Aug 23
Annesley, Elizabeth Altharn, Lady Anglesey (commentator), <u>1663</u>: LIF, Jan 8
Annette and Lubin (dance), <u>1778</u>: KING'S, Nov 24, 28, Dec 1, 5, 8, 12, 15, 19,
   26; <u>1779</u>: KING'S, Jan 2, 9, 16, Feb 6, Apr 29, May 4, 11; <u>1789</u>: KING'S, Apr
   28, Jun 9
Annette and Lubin. See Dibdin, Charles.
Annibale in Capua (opera), <u>1746</u>: KING'S, Oct 30, Nov 4, 8, 18, 22, 25, 29
Annibali, Domenico (singer), <u>1736</u>: CG, Nov 27, Dec 8; <u>1737</u>: CG, Jan 12, Feb 16,
   May 18
Anniversary Ode for the Queen's Birthday (song), <u>1692</u>: ATCOURT, Apr 30
Anniversary, The (play, anon), <u>1758</u>: CG, Mar 29
Ansani, Giovanni (singer, composer), <u>1780</u>: KING'S, Dec 2, 23; <u>1781</u>: KING'S, Nov

17; <u>1782</u>: KING'S, Jan 12, Mar 7, 16, May 25, Jun 15, 18

Anseaume, Louis, <u>1793</u>: HAY, Dec 16

--Tableau Parlant, Le, <u>1793</u>: HAY, Dec 16

Ansell Jr (dancer), <u>1785</u>: CG, May 28

Ansell, John (box keeper), <u>1786</u>: CG, May 27; <u>1788</u>: CG, Jun 4; see also Ansell, John, Thomas, and William

Ansell, John, Thomas and William (house servants), <u>1760</u>: CG, Sep 22; <u>1762</u>: CG, May 19; <u>1763</u>: CG, May 25; <u>1764</u>: CG, May 25; <u>1765</u>: CG, May 23; <u>1766</u>: CG, May 16; <u>1767</u>: CG, May 22; <u>1768</u>: CG, Jun 2, 3; <u>1769</u>: CG, May 18; <u>1770</u>: CG, May 18, 21, 26, 28; <u>1771</u>: CG, May 24; <u>1772</u>: CG, May 27; <u>1773</u>: CG, May 27; <u>1774</u>: CG, May 19; <u>1775</u>: CG, May 24; <u>1776</u>: CG, May 18; <u>1777</u>: CG, May 22; <u>1778</u>: CG, May 20; <u>1779</u>: CG, May 18; <u>1780</u>: CG, May 19; <u>1781</u>: CG, May 22; <u>1782</u>: CG, May 22; <u>1783</u>: CG, May 30; <u>1784</u>: CG, May 27; <u>1786</u>: CG, May 31; <u>1787</u>: CG, Jun 5; <u>1794</u>: CG, Jun 17; <u>1795</u>: CG, Jun 17; <u>1799</u>: CG, Jun 8; <u>1800</u>: CG, Jun 11; see also Ansell, John; Ansell, Thomas; Ansell, William

Ansell, Miss (house servant), <u>1788</u>: CG, May 27

Ansell, Mrs (house servant), <u>1788</u>: CG, May 31; <u>1789</u>: CG, Jun 5

Ansell, Thomas (box-office keeper), <u>1771</u>: CG, May 22; <u>1772</u>: CG, May 23; <u>1773</u>: CG, May 22; <u>1774</u>: CG, May 7; <u>1775</u>: CG, May 30; <u>1776</u>: CG, May 21; <u>1777</u>: CG, May 23; <u>1778</u>: CG, May 21; <u>1779</u>: CG, May 15; <u>1780</u>: CG, May 24; <u>1781</u>: CG, May 25; <u>1782</u>: CG, May 28; <u>1783</u>: CG, May 31; <u>1784</u>: CG, May 22; see also Ansell, John, Thomas and William

Ansell, Widow (beneficiary), <u>1791</u>: CG, Jun 2; <u>1796</u>: CG, Jun 4

Ansell, William (billsticker), <u>1775</u>: CG, May 30; <u>1776</u>: CG, May 22; <u>1777</u>: CG, May 24; <u>1778</u>: CG, May 22; <u>1779</u>: CG, May 19; <u>1780</u>: CG, May 26; <u>1781</u>: CG, May 26; <u>1782</u>: CG, May 29; <u>1783</u>: CG, Jun 4; <u>1784</u>: CG, May 29; <u>1786</u>: CG, May 30; <u>1787</u>: CG, May 28; <u>1788</u>: CG, May 31; <u>1790</u>: CG, May 29; <u>1797</u>: CG, Jun 8; see also Ansell, John, Thomas and William

Anselmo (house servant), <u>1787</u>: CG, Jun 2; <u>1788</u>: CG, May 30; <u>1789</u>: CG, Jun 13; <u>1790</u>: CG, Jun 8; <u>1791</u>: CG, Jun 9; <u>1792</u>: CG, May 29; <u>1794</u>: CG, Jun 16; <u>1795</u>: CG, Jun 13; <u>1796</u>: CG, Jun 3; <u>1797</u>: CG, May 27; <u>1798</u>: CG, May 29; <u>1799</u>: CG, Jun 4; <u>1800</u>: CG, Jun 10

Anselmo, Widow (dresser), <u>1798</u>: CG, Jun 5

Anson, Commodore George (naval explorer), <u>1744</u>: JS, Dec 10

Anspach, Elizabeth Margravine of, <u>1780</u>: DL, May 24; <u>1781</u>: HAY, Jul 18; <u>1782</u>: DL, Mar 1; <u>1794</u>: HAMM, Mar 24; <u>1799</u>: CG, Apr 19; see also Craven, Elizabeth

Anspach, Margrave of, <u>1716</u>: HIC, Jun 9

Answer to that Important Question Whether it is lawful for the Professors of the Christian Religion to go to Plays (pamphlet), <u>1757</u>: DL, May 2

Answer to the Fly (song), <u>1746</u>: SOU, Oct 27

Antelope Inn, <u>1789</u>: KHS, Sep 16

Anthem (song), <u>1702</u>: SH, Jan 31, May 7; <u>1772</u>: CG, Apr 10; <u>1773</u>: HAY, Mar 3, 17; <u>1779</u>: DL, Mar 12; <u>1784</u>: CG, Mar 22; <u>1791</u>: CG, Mar 23; <u>1794</u>: DL, Apr 4; <u>1800</u>: CG, Mar 5

Anthony (French horn player), <u>1733</u>: HIC, Apr 20

Anti-Thespis, The (criticism), <u>1767</u>: DL, Jan 16

Anticipation (dance), <u>1782</u>: CG, May 17

Anticks' Dance (dance), <u>1703</u>: BFP, Aug 23; <u>1781</u>: DL, Apr 25, 26, May 7, 10

Antigallican Coffee House, <u>1762</u>: CG, May 6; <u>1787</u>: CG, Jun 15

Antigallican Procession, Grand (entertainment), <u>1781</u>: CG, May 1

Antigallicans, Ode in Honor of (ode), <u>1759</u>: DL, May 16

Antigona. See DeGiardini, Felice; Bianchi, Francesco Jr.

Antigone (pastiche), <u>1746</u>: KING'S, May 13, 20, 24, 27, 31, Jun 3, 7, 10, 14, 17, 21, 24

Antigono. See Conforto, Nicolo; Giordani, Tommaso.

Antinori, Luigi (singer), <u>1726</u>: KING'S, Jan 15, Mar 12, May 5

Antiochus the Great. See Wiseman, Jane.

Antipodes. See Brome, Sir Richard.

Antonia, Marie. See Marchesini, Maria Antonia.

Antonie (acrobat), <u>1719</u>: LIF, Jan 13, KING'S, Mar 2, 19

Antony and Cleopatra. See Shakespeare, William.

Anunciati, Sga (singer), <u>1766</u>: KING'S, Oct 21

ApArthur, Jeffrey (dancer), <u>1759</u>: HAY, Sep 21, 25

Apelles and Campaspe (dance), <u>1782</u>: KING'S, Jun 5, 6, 8, 11, 15, 18, 29, Nov 2, 9, 14, 19, 30, Dec 10, 17, 19, 28

Apertus (commentator), <u>1744</u>: DL, Nov 26

Apollo and Daphne (entertainment). See Cibber, Theophilus.

Apollo and Daphne (masque). See Hughes, John.

Apollo and Daphne; or, Harlequin's Metamorphoses. See Thurmond, John.

Apollo and Daphne; or, The Burgomaster Tricked. See Theobald, Lewis.

Apollo and Daphnis (music), <u>1734</u>: KING'S, Mar 23

Apollo and Venus (dance), <u>1773</u>: KING'S, Mar 30, Apr 3, 13, 17, May 3

20

Apollo Ed Issea. See Pugnani, Gaetano.
Apollo Society, 1736: DT, Apr 16
Apollon Berger (dance), 1796: KING'S, Dec 27; 1797: KING'S, Jan 3, 10, 14, 31,
    Mar 4, 28, Apr 25, Jun 20
Apollon e Daphne (dance), 1775: KING'S, Oct 31, Nov 4, 16, Dec 5; 1776: KING'S,
    Apr 30
Apollon et les Muses (dance), 1782: KING'S, May 2, 4, 7, 9, 11, 14, 21, Jun 1,
    25
Apology for Apologies (entertainment), 1773: DL, Apr 13
Apology to the Town for Himself and the Bottle, An (pamphlet), 1749: HAY, Feb
    10
Apothecaries Hall, 1661: LIF, Jun 28
Apparition, The. See Cross, John Cartwright.
Apparition, The; or, The Sham Wedding (play, anon), 1713: DL, Nov 25, 26
Appeal to the Publick in behalf of the Manager, An (pamphlet), 1763: DL, Feb 1
Appeal to the Publick, An (pamphlet), 1774: DL, Mar 1
Appear, all appear your kind mistress to show (song), 1693: NONE, Sep 0
Appearance is against Them. See Inchbald, Elizabeth.
Appius and Virginia. See Webster, John; Dennis, John.
Appius. See Moncrieff, John.
Apple Tree (public house), 1743: CG, Nov 17
Appleby (acrobat), 1696: SF, Sep 5
Appleby, Master (actor), 1798: DL, Jun 5
Appleby, William (messenger, porter), 1787: DL, Sep 25; 1788: DL, Jun 6, HAY,
    Aug 5; 1789: DL, Jun 10; 1790: DL, Jun 2; 1791: DL, May 31; 1792: DLKING'S,
    Jun 13; 1793: DL, May 31; 1795: DL, Jun 5; 1796: DL, Jun 15; 1797: DL, Jun
    15; 1798: DL, Jun 9; 1799: HAY, Apr 17, DL, Jul 3; 1800: DL, Jun 13
Apprentice, The. See Murphy, Arthur.
Apprentices Wardens and Masters Songs (song), 1735: TC, May 28
Aprice (Apreece) (sued Foote for libel), 1758: DL, Jan 30, Dec 18
April Fool, The. See Macnally, Leonard.
April-Day. See O'Hara, Kane.
ApShenkin children (dancer), 1742: GF, Mar 25, Apr 6, 24, May 27
ApShenkin, David (dancer), 1742: GF, Jan 13, Apr 22, 29
ApShenkin, David and Winifred (dancer), 1741: GF, Dec 23; 1742: GF, Jan 14, Feb
    8, 10, 24, Mar 22, Apr 19
ApShenkin, Winifred (dancer), 1742: GF, Jan 13, 14
Apsley, Sir Allen (producer of private plays), 1678: DL, Feb 0
Apsley, Frances (actor), 1678: DL, Feb 0; 1679: BRUSSELS, Oct 3
Aqua Triumphalis. See Tatham, John.
Aquilanti, Chiaretta (dancer), 1742: DL, Nov 8, 13, 17, 19, 22, 26, 30, Dec 1,
    11, 21, 31; 1743: DL, Jan 14, Feb 3, 26, Mar 10, 19, 24, Apr 8, May 16
Aquilius. See Ariosti, Attilio.
Arab, The. See Cumberland, Richard.
Arabin, Col (songwriter), 1789: DL, May 28
Arbaces. See Handel, George Frederic.
Arbour Dance (dance), 1704: DL, Jun 9
Arbuthnot, Dr John (author), 1746: DL, Mar 13
Arcacambis (play, anon), 1734: GF/HAY, Dec 18
Arcadia in Brenta, L'. See Galuppi, Baldassare.
Arcadia. See Sydney, Sir Philip.
Arcadia; or, The Shepherd's Wedding. See Lloyd, Robert.
Arcadian Festival (dance), 1781: CG, Nov 8, 10, 19
Arcadian Nuptials (dance), 1764: CG, Jan 19, Apr 25
Arch and French Lute (music), 1711: FE, Nov 7
Arch Lute (music), 1703: HA, May 18; 1707: YB, Apr 18
Arch Lute and Flute a la main Sonata (music), 1707: YB, Apr 18
Arch Lute and Violin (music), 1707: YB, Apr 18; 1708: SH, Feb 4, Mar 26
Arch Lute Cantata (music), 1707: YB, Apr 18
Arch Lute Solo (music), 1722: DL, Mar 14
Archambault, Louis Francois. See Dorvigny.
Archer (actor), 1735: YB, Jul 17; 1742: BFPY, Aug 25
Archer, Alexander (actor), 1798: DL, Nov 13, Dec 29; 1799: DL, Feb 26, Mar 2,
    25, Apr 17, May 16, 24, 25, Jul 2, Sep 19, Nov 8, 16, Dec 11; 1800: DL, Jan
    1, 14, Apr 29, May 16, Jun 11, 12
Archer, Elisha (violinist), 1792: KING'S, Feb 24, Mar 14; 1795: CG, Feb 20, 27;
    1796: CG, Feb 12; 1797: CG, Mar 3, DL, Dec 13; 1798: CG, Feb 23; 1799: CG,
    Feb 8
Archer, John (publisher), 1796: DL, Nov 15
Archers' Dance, Grand (dance), 1795: CG, Dec 21; 1796: CG, Jan 4
Archeveque (box-office keeper), 1772: DL, Sep 24; 1773: DL, Sep 21; 1774: DL,
    May 28, 30

Arcifanfano, L'. See Scolari, Giuseppi.
Arden of Feversham. See Haywood, Eliza; Lillo, George.
Argalus and Parthenia (droll, anon), 1745: MF, May 7
Argalus and Parthenia. See Glapthorne, Henry.
Argentina a Magician (entertainment), 1726: KING'S, Nov 12; 1727: KING'S, Jan
    12
Argentina Ortolana Contessa per Forza (entertainment), 1727: KING'S, Mar 23
Argentina Strega per Amore (entertainment), 1726: KING'S, Nov 23
Argentina, Sga (Vittora, Sga) (dancer), 1726: KING'S, Nov 26, Dec 17; 1727:
    KING'S, Feb 16, Apr 25
Argulus and Parthenia (play, anon), 1717: BF, Aug 24; 1745: MF, May 7
Argument Britannia (ode), 1761: SOHO, Apr 15
Argyle, Duke of (spectator), 1732: GF, Jan 29
Ariadne et Bacchus (dance), 1797: KING'S, Nov 28, Dec 2, 5, 9, 12, 16, 30;
    1798: KING'S, Jan 2, Mar 13, 31, Jul 10, Dec 8, 11; 1799: KING'S, Jan 1, Feb
    19
Ariadne in Crete. See Handel, George Frederic.
Ariadne in Naxus. See Porpora, Nicola.
Ariadne; or, The Marriage of Bacchus. See Perrin, Pierre.
Ariaja (composer), 1750: KING'S, Apr 10
Arianna E Teseo (pasticcio), 1760: KING'S, Nov 22, Dec 16, 20, 27; 1761:
    KING'S, Jan 3, 10, 17, 24, 31, Mar 7, Jun 3, 6; 1762: KING'S, Mar 1, 6, 8,
    13, Jun 5; 1768: KING'S, Oct 11, 22
Ariodante. See Handel, George Frederic.
Ariosti, Attilio (composer, violinist), 1716: KING'S, Jul 12; 1719: KING'S, Feb
    28, Mar 21, DL, Oct 1; 1721: KING'S, Apr 15; 1723: KING'S, Feb 19; 1724:
    KING'S, Jan 14, May 21, Dec 1; 1725: KING'S, Apr 10; 1727: KING'S, Jan 7, Oct
    21
--Aquilius (opera), 1724: KING'S, May 21, 26, 30, Jun 13
--Artaxerxes (opera), 1724: KING'S, Dec 1, 5, 8, 12, 15, 19, 22, 26, 29; 1725:
    KING'S, Jan 28
--Coriolanus (opera), 1723: KING'S, Feb 19, 23, 26, Mar 2, 5, 9, 12, 16, 19,
    23, Apr 23, May 7, 11; 1724: KING'S, Mar 17, Apr 16; 1732: KING'S, Mar 25,
    28, Apr 1, 11, 15
--Darius (opera), 1725: KING'S, Apr 10, 13, 17, 20, 24, 27
--Diana on Mount Latmos (cantata), 1719: DL, Oct 1, 13, Nov 4, 5, 17, Dec 10;
    1720: DL, Mar 5
--Lucius Verus (opera), 1727: KING'S, Jan 7, 10, 14, 21, 24, 28
--Teuzzone (opera), 1727: KING'S, Oct 21, 24, 28
--Vespasian (opera), 1724: KING'S, Jan 14, 18, 21, 25, 28, Feb 1, 8, 11, 15
Ariosto, Ludovico (poet), 1794: CG, May 30
Arise, O God with glory crowned (song), 1790: DL, Mar 17
Aristodemo (pastiche), 1744: KING'S, Apr 3, 7, 10, 14, 17, 21
Aristophanes, 1773: DL, Mar 22
Arlechino Pittor Alla Moda (pantomime, anon), 1727: KING'S, Mar 9
Arlechino Prencipe in Sogno (pantomime, anon), 1726: KING'S, Dec 14
Arlechino (Harlequin). See also Harlequin.
Arlequin a la Guinguette; ou, Les Amour de Village (farce, anon), 1721: HAY,
    Dec 28
Arlequin Balourd. See Procope, D M.
Arlequin Cabratier; ou, Les Auberges d'Arlequin (farce, anon), 1721: HAY, Feb 6
Arlequin Cartouche; ou, Les Voleurs. See Riccoloni, Lelio.
Arlequin Cartouche, Grand Provost et Juge (farce), 1735: GF/HAY, Jan 16, Mar 6
Arlequin Chasseur et Docteur Chinois (farce), 1720: KING'S, Jun 9; 1721: HAY,
    Jan 19, Feb 17, 20; 1725: HAY, Mar 1, Apr 1; 1726: HAY, May 3
Arlequin Conjurer, Statue, Enfant, Moor and Skeleton. See Lisle de la
    Drevetiere, L F.
Arlequin Courier de Batavia (farce), 1726: HAY, Apr 14
Arlequin Cru Colombine et Colombine Cru Arlequin (pantomime), 1721: HAY, Feb
    25, Mar 2
Arlequin Cru Prince par Magie (farce), 1725: HAY, Mar 18
Arlequin Cuisinier de la Guniquette (farce), 1725: HAY, Jan 27
Arlequin de Capite (farce, anon), 1726: HAY, Apr 27
Arlequin deux Visages (dance), 1740: DL, Apr 10; 1741: DL, Jan 21, 23, Mar 10,
    14, 21, Apr 13, 17
Arlequin Directeur (farce), 1721: HAY, Mar 27, 30
Arlequin Embassadeur D'Amour (farce), 1725: HAY, Apr 7
Arlequin Empereur de la Lune. See Fatouville, Nolant de.
Arlequin Esprit Folet (farce), 1719: LIF, Jan 8, KING'S, Feb 12; 1720: KING'S,
    May 17; 1721: HAY, Jan 16, Mar 13; 1725: HAY, Jan 1, Feb 1; 1734: HAY, Nov 8;
    1735: HAY, Feb 17, Mar 27, May 21
Arlequin et Octave, Persecutez par les Dames Inconues (farce, anon), 1725: HAY,

Jan 25

Arlequin et Sa Troupe Comediens Esclaves (pantomime, anon), 1734: GF/HAY, Dec
18

Arlequin et Scaramouch Soldats Deserteurs (pantomime, anon), 1721: HAY, Feb 20;
1724: HAY, Dec 30; 1725: HAY, Feb 5; 1726: HAY, May 2

Arlequin Feint Astrologue, Ramoneur, Statue, Enfant, Negre, Skellette
(pantomime, anon), 1724: HAY, Dec 28; 1725: HAY, Feb 8, 18, Apr 16; 1726:
HAY, Mar 31; 1734: HAY, Nov 7, 14, GF/HAY, Dec 6, HAY, 16; 1735: HAY, Jan 6,
LIF, Feb 27, HAY, Mar 24, Apr 28, May 26

Arlequin Femme Grosse (pantomime, anon), 1725: HAY, May 3

Arlequin Fourbe Anglois; ou, le Traiteur Mal-Traitte (pantomime), 1750: HAY,
Mar 13

Arlequin Galerien; ou, Le Port de Mer (farce), 1720: KING'S, Apr 26

Arlequin Gardien du Fleuve D'Oubly (farce), 1734: HAY, Nov 4, Dec 13; 1735:
HAY, Jan 3, Apr 11

Arlequin Gazettier Comique (farce), 1725: HAY, Jan 13, Apr 30

Arlequin Gentilhomme (farce), 1725: HAY, Jan 7, Feb 18, Apr 22

Arlequin Homme a Bonne Fortune. See Regnard, Jean Francois.

Arlequin Hulla (Nulla). See LeSage, Alain Rene.

Arlequin Invisible, a la Cour du Roy de la Chine. See LeSage, Alain Rene.

Arlequin Jouet de la Fortune (farce), 1719: LIF, Jan 20; 1721: HAY, Feb 16

Arlequin Laron, Juge et Prevost (farce), 1718: LIF, Nov 28; 1719: KING'S, Mar
5; 1720: KING'S, May 3; 1721: HAY, Jan 13; 1724: HAY, Dec 21

Arlequin Lawyer. See Fatouville, Nolant de.

Arlequin Limondier (farce), 1721: HAY, Apr 18

Arlequin Misantrope. See Biancolelli, Louis.

Arlequin Nouvelliste des Tuileries (farce), 1725: HAY, May 10

Arlequin Nouvelliste; ou, Le Retour de la Bezons (farce), 1721: HAY, Feb 9

Arlequin Perroquet (farce), 1721: HAY, Mar 23

Arlequin Petit Maitre (dance), 1742: DL, Feb 1, 3

Arlequin Petit Maitre a Bonne Fortune (farce), 1725: HAY, Jan 1

Arlequin Poli par l'Amour. See Marivaux, Pierre Carlet de Chamblain de.

Arlequin Prince by Enchantment; With His Comical Cavalcade (farce), 1726:
KING'S, Oct 5

Arlequin Prince par Magie (farce), 1719: KING'S, Mar 17; 1721: HAY, Jan 3

Arlequin Prodigal Merchant (farce), 1726: KING'S, Nov 9

Arlequin Protee. See Fatouville, Nolant de.

Arlequin Sauvage. See Lisle de la Drevetiere, L F.

Arlequin Tiresias; or, The Lovers Metamorphosed (farce), 1735: HAY, Jan 24, Apr
18

Arlequin Valet de deux Maitres. See Mandajors de Ours, Jean Pierre.

Arlequin Valet Etourdy (farce), 1725: HAY, Jan 6, Feb 22

Arlequin viconte de Bergamotte, Prince des Curieux (farce), 1725: HAY, Feb 3

Arlequino Triomphante (farce), 1745: HAY, Mar 5, 6, 12, 14

Arlequins (dance), 1742: DL, Feb 12, 18

Arlington St, 1761: DL, Jul 27

Arlington, Lord. See Bennet, Henry.

Arm, Arm, ye Brave (song), 1755: CG, May 8; 1789: CG, Apr 3; 1790: DL, Mar 10,
CG, 19; 1791: CG, Apr 15; 1792: CG, Mar 9; 1793: KING/HAY, Feb 15, CG, 15,
KING/HAY, 27, CG, Mar 13, 22; 1794: CG, Mar 7, DL, 26, Apr 4; 1795: CG, Feb
20; 1796: CG, Feb 26; 1797: CG, Mar 10; 1798: CG, Mar 28; 1799: CG, Feb 20;
1800: CG, Mar 19

Armenian Queen, The (play, anon), 1674: NONE, Sep 0

Armida. See Sacchini, Antonio Maria Gasparo; Mortellari, Michele.

Arminio. See Perez, Davide.

Arminius. See Steffani, Agostino; Patterson, William.

Armourer, The. See Cumberland, Richard.

Armoy, Miss. See Hamoir, Miss.

Armstead, Elizabeth Bridget (actor), 1774: CG, Oct 1, 7, Nov 19; 1775: CG, Jan
10; 1777: HAY, May 15, Jun 27

Armstrong (actor, singer), 1717: LIF, Jan 2, 25; 1718: LIF, Oct 25; 1719: LIF,
Apr 3; 1722: SOU, Sep 25; 1726: HAY, Feb 24

Armstrong, Elizabeth (dancer), 1771: DL, Apr 5, 16, 22, May 16, 27; 1772: DL,
Nov 21; 1773: DL, Mar 25, Apr 1; 1774: KING'S, Apr 28, May 12, CG, Sep 28,
Nov 19, Dec 26; 1775: CG, May 12, 26; 1776: CG, May 3, 15, DL, Nov 7; 1777:
DL, Apr 3, 22, May 2, Sep 20, Oct 2, Nov 7, 25; 1778: DL, Jan 17, 28, Mar 24,
May 15, Nov 2, Dec 11; 1779: CG, Apr 19, DL, May 8, 14, 17, CG, 21, DL, 25,
Nov 3; 1780: DL, Feb 24, 28, Apr 18, 24, May 2, CG, 18, DL, Sep 23, 30, Oct
2, 18, 19, Nov 11; 1781: DL, Jan 18, Apr 25, May 1, 5, 11, 14, KING'S, Jun 5,
DL, Sep 20, Oct 4, 19, Nov 13, 17, Dec 1, 11; 1782: DL, Jan 5, 11, 21, Feb
12, 19, May 14

Armstrong, Sir Thomas (murderer), 1675: DG, Aug 28

23

Armstrong, Widow (beneficiary), 1717: SH, Mar 27
Armuth und Edelsinn. See Kotzebue, August Friedrich Ferdinand von.
Arnauld (Arnaud) (dancer), 1764: CG, Oct 3, 4, Dec 12; 1765: CG, Mar 26, Sep
    25, Oct 12, 19, 28, Nov 15; 1766: HAY, Jun 20, Jul 15, KING'S, Aug 27, HAY,
    Sep 2, CG, Oct 8, 10, 25, Nov 18, 20; 1767: CG, Feb 21, Apr 2, 11, 20, May
    16, Sep 19, Oct 5, 8, 17, Nov 26, Dec 2, 31; 1768: CG, Jan 6, Apr 13, 16, May
    13, 24, 27, Sep 19, 20, Oct 7, 24, Nov 7, Dec 23, 26; 1769: CG, Jan 19, Feb
    4, Apr 8, 19, Sep 29, Oct 2, Nov 2, 4, 20, Dec 7, 19
Arne, Ann, Mrs Michael (singer), 1778: DL, Apr 7; 1780: CG, May 4, 11; 1784:
    HAY, Mar 3, 17; 1785: HAY, Feb 23; 1786: CG, May 27; 1787: CG, Jun 5; 1789:
    CG, Jun 13
Arne, Cecilia, Mrs Thomas Augustine (singer, actor), 1736: CG, Feb 19; 1737:
    HIC, Apr 1; 1738: HAY, Mar 3, DL, 4, Apr 12, May 15; 1739: KING'S, Jan 16,
    CG, Mar 10, DL, Nov 28; 1740: HIC, Jan 4, Feb 1, DL, 13, 14, HIC, 22, DL, Mar
    8, LIF, 26, HIC, 27, 28, Apr 2, DL, 16, HIC, 18, 25, DL, 25, May 7, Nov 28,
    Dec 10; 1741: HIC, Jan 16, DL, Feb 25, HAY, 26, HIC, 27, Mar 6, 13, DL, 17,
    24, Apr 13, 16, HIC, 24, DL, May 22, Oct 12, 15, 16, 24, Nov 24, Dec 3; 1742:
    DL, Feb 3, 4, 10, 22, Mar 8, 12, 13, 15, 20, 25, 30, Apr 17, 28; 1745: DL,
    Jan 14, 17, 31, Mar 16, 20, Apr 3, 4, 6, 15, 16, 17, 18, HAY, 20, DL, 25, 27,
    29, May 6, 10, 13, Sep 19, 21, 24, 26, 28, Oct 1, 3, 5, 31, Nov 1, 11, Dec
    17; 1746: DL, Jan 31, Mar 3, 17, 22, Apr 12; 1748: DL, Apr 20; 1751: HAY, Feb
    5, CG, Mar 1, May 3; 1752: CG, Feb 11, Mar 17, Apr 17; 1754: CG, Apr 26, HAY,
    May 29; 1779: CG, Apr 22; 1780: CG, May 23; 1781: CG, May 19; 1782: CG, May
    8; 1783: CG, May 28; 1784: CG, May 15
Arne, Elizabeth, Mrs Michael (singer), 1766: DL, Nov 14, 21, Dec 10, 11; 1767:
    DL, Jan 2, Feb 3, 11, CG, Mar 6, DL, Apr 4, May 4, 9, RANELAGH, Jun 1, DL, 3,
    Sep 12, 16, 22, Oct 23; 1768: DL, Jan 7, Feb 10, Mar 10, 22, Apr 11, 29,
    CHAPEL, May 25, DL, Aug 18, Sep 20, 27, 28, Oct 3, 19, 26, Nov 1, 3; 1769:
    DL, Mar 16
Arne, Michael (musician), 1750: CG, Apr 19, DL, 28; 1751: HAY, Feb 5, CG, May
    3; 1752: CG, Apr 17; 1755: DL, Mar 14, CG, Apr 2; 1756: DL, May 6, CG, Dec
    10; 1757: DL, Jan 21; 1758: DL, Mar 18; 1759: DL, Mar 23, 30, May 21; 1764:
    DL, Nov 2; 1766: DL, Nov 5, 14; 1767: DL, Jan 2, 15; 1772: DL, Nov 12; 1773:
    CG, Mar 20; 1777: HAY, Jul 18; 1778: DL, Jan 17, Apr 7, CG, May 11, DL, Nov
    30, Dec 23; 1779: CG, Sep 27, DL, Oct 21; 1780: CG, Feb 22, DL, Apr 14, Sep
    28; 1781: CG, Dec 26; 1782: CG, Feb 21, Mar 16, DL, Apr 18, CG, Sep 25, Oct
    10; 1783: CG, Jan 17, Apr 26, Sep 22; 1784: HAY, Mar 3; 1785: HAY, Feb 23;
    1789: CG, Dec 21; 1790: CG, Nov 15; 1796: CG, Mar 15, Oct 24; 1797: DL, May
    24; 1799: CG, May 13
Arne, Miss (singer) 1750: DL, Mar 28
Arne, Richard (singer), 1733: LIF, Mar 7, Apr 5, 30, HAY, Jun 4, DL/HAY, Oct
    10, 20, 25, 27, 29, Nov 9, 10, HAY, 19, DL/HAY, 24, 26, Dec 3, 20; 1734:
    DL/HAY, Jan 4, 5, 12, 28, Feb 22, Mar 4, 21, Apr 2, DL, 15, DL/HAY, 17, 26,
    DL, 29, May 15, HAY, Jun 3, 5, 28, Jul 5, LIF, Aug 20, HAY, 21, BFHBH, 24,
    DL, Sep 19, 24, Oct 5, 22, 25, Nov 8, 22, Dec 6; 1735: DL, Mar 6, May 6, 10,
    29, Sep 9
Arne, Sarah (actor, singer), 1794: DL, Apr 21, May 16, 23, Jun 9, Oct 27, Nov
    17; 1795: DL, Feb 6, Jun 1, Oct 22, 30, Nov 11, 23, Dec 10; 1796: DL, Jan 11,
    18, Mar 3, 12, Apr 30, May 28, Jun 1, Oct 19, Nov 9; 1797: DL, Jan 7, Feb 16,
    May 24, Dec 9; 1798: DL, Jan 16, Feb 20, May 11, 30, Jun 1, 18, Sep 18, Oct
    6, Nov 14, 26, Dec 4, 26, 29; 1799: DL, Jan 19, Mar 2, Apr 2, May 21, 24, Oct
    14, 31, Nov 14, Dec 11; 1800: DL, Jan 1, Mar 11, Apr 29, Jun 10
Arne, Susannah Maria (singer, actor), 1732: HAY, Mar 13, 24, Apr 21, May 17,
    LIF, Nov 20; 1733: LIF, Mar 7, KING'S, 17, LIF, Apr 9, DL/HAY, Oct 6, 13, 20,
    25, 27, 29, HAY, Nov 19, DL/HAY, 22, 24, 26, Dec 31; 1734: DL/HAY, Jan 4, 5,
    12, 26, 28, Feb 4, Mar 4, 21, 25, 28, 30, Apr 1, 2, DL, 4, HIC, 5, DL/HAY, 6,
    DL, 15; 1766: DL, Jan 30
Arne, Thomas (box numberer), 1732: LIF, Nov 20, 23, 30; 1733: LIF, Feb 22, HAY,
    May 31, DL/HAY, Oct 31, Nov 1, 3, 5, 6, 8, 12, 13, 15, 17, Dec 28; 1734:
    DL/HAY, Jan 12, 17, 19, 28, Feb 16, Mar 21, DL, Apr 29, LIF, Aug 20; 1735:
    DL, Jun 3, GF/HAY, Aug 21, HAY, 26, DL, Oct 18, 21, Nov 10, 13, 17; 1736: DL,
    Feb 28, Apr 22, May 25
Arne, Dr Thomas Augustine (composer, musician), 1736: DL, Dec 20; 1737: DL, Mar
    14, HIC, Apr 1, DL, 13; 1738: HAY, Mar 3, DL, 6, May 15; 1739: DL, Nov 15,
    28; 1740: DL, Feb 13, Mar 8, Apr 25, Nov 19, 28, Dec 10, 22; 1741: DL, Jan
    15, Feb 25, Mar 17, 24, HIC, Apr 24, DL, Oct 12, 15, Nov 21; 1742: DL, Feb
    15, 16, Mar 12, 19, Oct 19; 1743: DL, Feb 11; 1745: DL, Jan 14, 17, 31, Mar
    20, Apr 3, 15, 16, Sep 21, 28, Nov 5; 1746: DL, Jan 31, GF, Feb 18, DL, Mar
    3, 13, Apr 12, May 19, Dec 15; 1747: DL, Jan 10, 24, Mar 7, Nov 13; 1748: DL,
    Mar 21, Apr 20, Nov 15; 1749: DL, Feb 21, CG, Mar 9, 31, DL, Oct 11, Nov 17;
    1750: DL, Jan 5, Feb 3, 14, 15, 16, 17, CG, Apr 19, Sep 28; 1751: HAY, Feb 5,
    DL, 26, CG, Apr 23, May 3, Oct 7, Dec 14; 1752: DL, Jan 24, CG, Mar 7, DL,

21, Apr 25, CG, Dec 8; <u>1753</u>: DL, Mar 27, KING'S, May 12; <u>1754</u>: CG, Mar 25,
DL, 27, 28, CG, Apr 22, 26, HAY, May 29, Jun 4; <u>1755</u>: SOHO, Mar 11, DL, 12,
14, KING'S, 17, DL, 19, May 9; <u>1756</u>: DL, Feb 10, CG, Apr 19, CRT, Oct 28, DL,
Dec 20; <u>1757</u>: DL, Jan 21, CG, Apr 22, HAY, Oct 21, DL, Dec 2; <u>1758</u>: CG, Feb
1, 28, DL, Mar 3, CG, 13, DL, 31, CG, Apr 21, DL, May 2, Nov 15, CG, 23;
<u>1759</u>: DL, Feb 1, CG, 2, DL, Mar 23, CG, Apr 23, May 4, DL, Oct 17, CG, Nov 3,
30; <u>1760</u>: RANELAGH, Jun 18, CG, Sep 24, Nov 28, Dec 22; <u>1761</u>: DL, Feb 27,
KING'S, Mar 12, RANELAGH, Jun 12; <u>1762</u>: CG, Feb 2, DL, 26, Mar 5, HAY, 16,
DL, 17, CG, 20, DL, Apr 2, HAY, 22, DL, May 13, CG, Oct 1, Dec 8; <u>1763</u>: DL,
Apr 9, CG, 29, Oct 22; <u>1764</u>: CHAPEL, Feb 29, DL, Apr 12, RANELAGH, Jun 13,
CG, Dec 12; <u>1765</u>: KING'S, Feb 15, DL, Apr 22, KING'S, 27; <u>1766</u>: DL, Apr 15,
Nov 5; <u>1767</u>: DL, Jan 24, Apr 4, May 22; <u>1768</u>: MARLY, Jul 28, Aug 4, DL, Nov
1; <u>1769</u>: DL, Mar 16, Sep 30; <u>1770</u>: DL, Jan 8, HAY, Mar 12, DL, May 4, HAY,
21, DL, Jun 7, HAY, Aug 24, MARLY, 28, HAY, Dec 10, CG, 12, DL, 13; <u>1771</u>: CG,
Jun 6, HAY, Sep 2, CG, Nov 12, 16; <u>1772</u>: CG, Jan 27, HAY, Mar 16, CG, 31, May
26, HAY, Jun 10, DL, Sep 22, Oct 16, CG, Nov 21, DL, Dec 2, CG, 2, DL, 26;
<u>1773</u>: CG, Feb 23, 26, Mar 3, 19, 20, 26, Apr 12, DL, May 10, HAY, Jul 2, CG,
Sep 29, DL, Oct 9, 11, CG, Nov 5, Dec 16; <u>1774</u>: CG, Jan 10, HAY, Mar 15, CG,
Apr 13, HAY, Jun 7, CG, Oct 3; <u>1775</u>: HAY, Feb 16, DL, Apr 20, HAY, May 1, CG,
Oct 26, DL, 28, HAY, 30, DL, Dec 21; <u>1776</u>: HAY, Feb 22, Mar 5, CG, 16, HAY,
Apr 18, Sep 18, CG, Oct 23, Nov 25, Dec 6, 27; <u>1777</u>: CG, Jan 25, Mar 14, 19,
May 5, 13, 14, Oct 17, Nov 18; <u>1778</u>: CG, Feb 4, May 1; <u>1779</u>: HAY, Mar 17, CG,
Apr 7, May 13, HAY, Jul 1; <u>1780</u>: CG, Mar 14, Apr 10, 11, May 12; <u>1781</u>: CG,
Mar 23, Apr 3; <u>1782</u>: CG, May 6, Nov 2; <u>1783</u>: CG, Apr 5, 23, May 19; <u>1784</u>:
HAY, Mar 3, 17, CG, 27, DL, Nov 9; <u>1785</u>: HAY, Feb 23, DL, Apr 14, CG, Oct 17,
DL, 17; <u>1786</u>: CG, Apr 21, DL, Dec 5; <u>1788</u>: CG, Apr 1, DL, May 1, CG, 27;
<u>1789</u>: DL, Feb 27, Mar 20, CG, 31, DL, May 19, CG, Sep 23, DL, Oct 13, CG, Dec
21; <u>1790</u>: DL, Mar 5, CG, May 6, DL, Oct 11, CG, 19, Nov 15; <u>1791</u>: CG, Mar 18,
25, Apr 13, 30, May 2, Oct 3, DLKING'S, Nov 9; <u>1792</u>: CG, Mar 14, KING'S, 14,
CG, 21, Nov 24, DL, Dec 13, CG, 20; <u>1793</u>: KING/HAY, Feb 15, Mar 13, 15, CG,
23, Oct 2, HAY, Nov 19, CG, Dec 19; <u>1794</u>: HAY, Feb 24, CG, Mar 21, Apr 10,
DL, 21, CG, May 2, 23, HAY, Aug 1, 18, CG, Sep 17, 22, DL, Oct 7, CG, 20, Dec
26; <u>1795</u>: CG, Mar 13, Sep 21, DL, 29; <u>1796</u>: CG, Mar 16, Sep 19, DL, Oct 10;
<u>1797</u>: DL, Feb 22, Nov 7, Dec 9; <u>1798</u>: CG, Mar 2, 28, DL, Sep 18; <u>1799</u>: CG,
Feb 20, Mar 1, 15, DL, May 4, CG, 13, DL, Nov 14; <u>1800</u>: CG, Mar 21
--Artaxerxes (opera), <u>1762</u>: CG, Feb 2, 5, 9, 12, 16, 19, 23, HAY, Mar 16, CG,
Apr 1, 3, 14, HAY, 22, CG, 24, DL, May 13, HAY, 20, RANELAGH, Jun 11; <u>1763</u>:
CG, Feb 24, 25, Mar 8, 10, 22, Apr 7, 9, 14, 21, 28, May 3, 10, 19, Dec 12,
15, 19, 23, 30; <u>1764</u>: CG, Jan 2, 13, Mar 31, May 2, 10, Nov 23, Dec 5, 20;
<u>1765</u>: CG, Jan 4, 11, Apr 15, 22, May 1; <u>1768</u>: CG, Oct 22, 25, 28, DL, Nov 1,
CG, 3, 7, 11, 15, DL, 16, 23, CG, 23, DL, Dec 7; <u>1769</u>: CG, Mar 18, KING'S,
Jun 1, CG, Nov 24; <u>1770</u>: CG, Apr 7, May 4, HAY, Dec 14; <u>1771</u>: CG, Apr 6, 18,
GROTTO, Sep 9; <u>1772</u>: CG, Apr 23, Dec 19; <u>1773</u>: KING'S, Feb 25, Mar 18, 27,
CG, 27, Apr 14, 30; <u>1774</u>: CG, Mar 19, Apr 9, HAY, Jun 7, CG, Nov 29, Dec 2,
16; <u>1775</u>: CG, Mar 21, Apr 25, Oct 14, 18, 26, Nov 2, 8, 16, 18; <u>1776</u>: CG, Feb
17, Mar 25, Apr 20; <u>1777</u>: CG, Jan 18, 25, 31, Feb 11, DL, 13, CG, Mar 10, Apr
18; <u>1778</u>: CG, Jan 8; <u>1779</u>: CG, Apr 10, Dec 18; <u>1780</u>: CG, Jan 22, Apr 1, May
6, DL, Nov 11, 14, 16, 18, 21, Dec 1, 16; <u>1781</u>: DL, Jan 24, Apr 21, CG, May
2, DL, Oct 12, CG, 24, Nov 3; <u>1782</u>: CG, Feb 26, Apr 9; <u>1783</u>: CG, Jan 23, Feb
5, 18, HAY, Jul 16, 19, 23, 30, CG, Oct 16, Dec 3; <u>1784</u>: CG, Feb 4, 21; <u>1787</u>:
CG, Jan 6, 13, 19, 20, 29, Feb 17, 20, 26, Mar 6, Apr 12, May 3, 22, DL, Oct
25, 29, Nov 30, Dec 5; <u>1788</u>: DL, Mar 5, Apr 7, 12, 15, 19, 22, CG, 30, May 9,
DL, 9, 28, CG, Oct 16, 24, Dec 6, 20; <u>1789</u>: CG, Jan 17, DL, Mar 20; <u>1790</u>: DL,
Mar 5; <u>1791</u>: DLKING'S, Nov 17, 19, CG, 19, DLKING'S, 21, 22, CG, 26, Dec 17;
<u>1792</u>: CG, Jan 7, 21, Feb 17, May 1, DL, Nov 10, 14, 19, Dec 12, 15, 20; <u>1793</u>:
DL, Jan 21, KING/HAY, Mar 15, DL, May 23; <u>1794</u>: CG, Mar 21; <u>1796</u>: CG, Apr 30,
May 4, 11, 25; <u>1799</u>: CG, Feb 20, Mar 1, 15; <u>1800</u>: CG, May 22
--Beauty and Virtue (oratorio), <u>1762</u>: DL, Feb 26, Mar 3, 17, RANELAGH, Jun 11;
<u>1773</u>: CG, Mar 19
--Capochio and Dorinna (musical), <u>1768</u>: MARLY, Jul 28, Aug 4; <u>1770</u>: HAY, Mar 12
--Cooper, The (farce), <u>1772</u>: HAY, Jun 10, 12, 15, 17, 19, Jul 22, 24, Aug 19,
31; <u>1773</u>: HAY, Jul 2, 7
--Country Mad-Cap in London, The (musical), <u>1770</u>: DL, Jun 7, CG, Dec 12, 20,
22; <u>1771</u>: CG, Feb 25, Mar 4; <u>1772</u>: CG, Mar 31, May 5, 15, Oct 14, Nov 11;
<u>1773</u>: CG, Apr 20, May 24; <u>1774</u>: CG, Mar 26, Apr 5, 29, Dec 1; <u>1775</u>: CG, May
13, 23; <u>1776</u>: CG, May 13
--Dido and Aeneas (opera), <u>1734</u>: DL/HAY, Jan 12, 14, 15, 17, 19, 22, 24, 25,
29, DL/DL/HA, 31, HAY, Feb 1, DL/HAY, 7, 8, 11, 16, 18, 19
--Don Saverio (musical), <u>1750</u>: DL, Feb 3, 14, 15, 16, 17
--Eliza (opera), <u>1754</u>: HAY, May 29, Jun 4; <u>1756</u>: CRT, Oct 28, DL, Dec 20; <u>1757</u>:
DL, Jan 17, 21, 28, HAY, Aug 31, Sep 2; <u>1758</u>: DL, Mar 3; <u>1761</u>: KING'S, Mar
12; <u>1784</u>: HAY, Mar 17, 24, Apr 2, 27

25

--Henry and Emma; or, The Nut Brown Maid (farce), 1749: CG, Mar 31; 1750: MARLY, Aug 16
--Judith (oratorio), 1761: DL, Feb 27, Mar 4, 6, KING'S, 12; 1762: DL, Apr 2; 1764: CHAPEL, Feb 29; 1765: KING'S, Feb 15; 1767: CG, May 16; 1773: CG, Feb 26; 1784: HAY, Mar 3, 31; 1785: HAY, Mar 16; 1789: DL, Mar 20; 1800: CG, Mar 5
--Love and Resolution (musical dialogue), 1770: HAY, Dec 10, 13, 17
--Olimpiade, L' (opera), 1765: KING'S, Apr 27, 30
--Phoebe at Court (operetta), 1776: HAY, Feb 22, Mar 5
--Rose, The (musical), 1772: DL, Dec 1, 2; 1773: DL, Jan 1
--Sacrifice, The; or, The Death of Abel (oratorio), 1755: DL, Mar 12, 14, 19, 21; 1762: DL, Mar 5, 10; 1764: KING'S, Feb 8
--Sot, The (musical), 1775: HAY, Feb 16, Mar 9, May 1; 1776: HAY, Feb 22
--Squire Badger (musical), 1772: HAY, Mar 16
--Sultan, The (masque), 1758: CG, Nov 23, 24; 1759: CG, Jan 3, 18, Apr 18, Nov 30, Dec 1; 1760: CG, Apr 15
--Temple of Dulness, The (musical), 1745: DL, Jan 17, 18, 19, 21, 22, 23, 29
--Whittington's Feast (burlesque ode), 1776: HAY, Apr 18
Arne, Dr Thomas Augustine and Cecilia, 1738: DL, May 15
Arnick (tailor), 1773: DL, Oct 15
Arnold, (actor), 1696: LIF, Mar 0, Dec 0; 1697: LIF, Feb 20, Jun 0, Nov 0; 1698: LIF, Apr 0, May 0, Jun 0; 1699: LIF, Apr 0, Nov 7; 1700: LIF, Jan 9, Feb 0; 1701: LIF, Mar 0, Dec 0; 1702: LIF, Dec 31
Arnold, C (author), 1755: DL, Nov 13
Arnold, Elizabeth (actor), 1791: CG, May 26, Sep 19, 26, Oct 3, 20, Dec 21, 22; 1792: CG, Feb 28, Apr 12, 17, May 10, 11, 19, Oct 8, 19, Nov 26; 1794: CG, Sep 22, Oct 3, 20; 1795: CG, Jan 2, 14, 31, Mar 21, May 29, Jun 6, 10, 13
Arnold, Miss (actor), 1794: CG, Jun 3
Arnold, Dr Samuel (musician, composer), 1765: CG, Jan 31; 1766: CG, Apr 18, Dec 27; 1767: KING'S, Jan 23, CG, Apr 21; 1768: HAY, Feb 19, Mar 16, CG, Oct 10; 1769: HAY, Feb 24, CG, Jun 6; 1770: CG, Mar 2, 9, Apr 16, May 29, MARLY, Jun 16, Aug 7, 28, CG, Nov 22, Dec 26; 1771: CG, Feb 27, Mar 13, MARLY, Jul 6; 1772: CG, Mar 6, 20, 25, Apr 20, MARLY, Jul 2, Aug 25, Sep 1, 7; 1773: HAY, Mar 5, 24, CR, Apr 14; 1774: CHAPEL, Mar 26, PANT, Apr 4, MARLY, Jun 30; 1775: CG, Oct 17; 1776: STRAND, Jan 23, CG, Mar 6, 27, Nov 14; 1777: CG, Mar 19, Apr 29, HAY, May 15, Jun 19, Jul 18, 24, Aug 22, 30; 1778: CG, Feb 4, HAY, Jul 22, Aug 3; 1779: HAY, Jul 1, Aug 14; 1780: HAY, Jun 15, Jul 8, Aug 12, Sep 2; 1781: CG, Mar 23, HAY, Jun 12, 16, Jul 9, 18, Sep 4, CG, Nov 24, 28; 1782: HAY, Jun 4, Jul 2, 5, Aug 17, CG, Nov 2; 1783: CG, Feb 14, HAY, Jun 30, Aug 1, 12, 28; 1784: CG, Mar 25, 30, HAY, May 31, Jun 9, 19, Jul 30, Aug 21, Sep 6; 1785: HAY, May 28, 30, Jun 16, Jul 9, Aug 31; 1786: DL, Mar 3, HAY, Jul 3, Aug 12; 1787: KING'S, Mar 1, HAY, Jul 9, Aug 4; 1788: CG, Apr 1, HAY, Aug 5; 1789: CG, Jan 26, DL, Feb 27, Mar 20, 25, CG, 31, HAY, May 18, DL, 28, HAY, Aug 11, CG, Sep 23, DL, Nov 4, CG, Dec 21; 1790: DL, Feb 19, CG, May 13, HAY, Jul 16, Sep 4, CG, Nov 15; 1791: DL, Mar 11, 16, Apr 13, CG, May 2, 18, HAY, Jul 30; 1792: KING'S, Feb 24, 29, Mar 7, 14, 30, HAY, Jul 25, CG, Dec 20; 1793: KING/HAY, Feb 15, 27, Mar 6, 20, HAY, Aug 3, Sep 19, Oct 1, CG, 2, HAY, Nov 23, Dec 26; 1794: HAY, Feb 24, DL, Mar 26, Apr 25, HAY, Jul 21, Aug 9, 18, 20, DL, Oct 31; 1795: KING'S, Feb 7, 20, 27, DL, May 2, CG, 6, Jun 10, HAY, 20, Jul 31, Aug 21, 29, Sep 21; 1796: DL, Jan 11, May 13, HAY, Jun 11, 25, Sep 1, DL, Nov 26; 1797: DL, May 18, 23, HAY, Jul 8, Aug 15; 1798: HAY, Jan 15, DL, May 24, HAY, Jun 29, 30, Jul 6, 21, Aug 11; 1799: HAY, Jan 24, DL, May 9, CG, 13, HAY, Jul 9, 16, 20, Aug 13, 21; 1800: DL, Jun 3, HAY, 17, Jul 2, Sep 1
--Abimelech (oratorio), 1768: HAY, Mar 16, 18; 1772: CG, Mar 25
--Bohemienne, La (opera), 1778: HAY, Aug 3
--Cure of Saul, The (oratorio), 1763: CG, Mar 4, DL, Apr 27; 1767: KING'S, Jan 23; 1768: KING'S, Feb 5, HAY, 19, Mar 4; 1769: HAY, Feb 24, Mar 15; 1771: CG, Feb 27
--Don Quixote (entertainment), 1774: MARLY, Jun 30, Jul 2, 7, 11, 14, 25, 30, Aug 2, 11, 13, 18, 25, Sep 3, 8
--Prodigal Son, The (oratorio), 1773: HAY, Mar 5, 10, 12, 19, KING'S, 31, HAY, Apr 2; 1776: CG, Mar 27, 29; 1777: CG, Feb 28, Mar 5, 12; 1778: CG, Apr 1, 10; 1786: DL, Mar 8; 1788: DL, Mar 7
--Resurrection, The (oratorio), 1770: CG, Mar 9, 23, 30, Apr 6; 1771: CG, Mar 15, 22; 1772: CG, Mar 20; 1773: HAY, Mar 24, Apr 2; 1774: PANT, Mar 30, Apr 4; 1776: STRAND, Jan 23; 1787: DL, Mar 21; 1793: KING/HAY, Mar 15, 20; 1794: DL, Mar 26
Arnold, Samuel James, 1794: HAY, Jul 26; 1795: HAY, Jul 16; 1796: DL, Dec 10; 1797: HAY, Jun 26
--Auld Robin Grey (opera), 1794: HAY, Jul 26, 28, 30, 31, Aug 5, 6, 15, 26, Sep 5; 1795: HAY, Aug 21

26

--Irish Legacy, The (farce), 1797: HAY, Jun 24, 26, 27
--Shipwreck, The (opera), 1796: DL, Dec 10, 12, 13, 14, 15, 17, 19, 20, 21, 22,
  23; 1797: DL, Jan 10, 11, 12, 14, 21, 24, 26, Feb 7, 27, May 17, Oct 31, Nov
  2, 25, Dec 1; 1798: DL, Jan 8, 15, 29, Apr 21, May 2, 21, Jun 8, HAY, Aug 23,
  27, DL, Nov 3, 7, 30, Dec 6, 18; 1799: DL, Jan 5, 14, Mar 29, Apr 11, May 1,
  21, Jun 3, 12, HAY, Jul 19, Aug 6, 22, 29, DL, Nov 7, Dec 3, 12; 1800: DL,
  Jan 10, 24, May 30, Jun 10, 16
--Who Pays the Reckoning? (musical), 1795: HAY, Jul 16
Arnoldinus, Sixtus Petri (spectator), 1661: VERE, Aug 16, BF, 22, REDBULL, 22
Arnould, 1789: CG, Mar 16
--Mort du Capitaine Cook, La, 1789: CG, Mar 16
Around Her See Cupids Flying (song), 1717: LIF, Dec 12
Around let acclamations ring (song), 1793: CG, Feb 22, Mar 20; 1795: CG, Mar 4,
  18
Around the ever-honoured urn (song), 1800: CG, Jun 16
Around the Fair attending (song), 1789: DL, Mar 20
Around the Old Oak right Jolly and Gay (song), 1799: HAY, Sep 2
Arrah, my Judy (song), 1740: CG, May 5; 1741: CG, May 12; 1742: CG, May 4, 14,
  Oct 9; 1746: GF, Jan 31; 1747: DL, Apr 20; 1757: CG, Apr 18
Arran, Earl of. See Butler, Richard.
Arrigoni, Carlo (musician), 1733: HIC, Apr 20, LIF, May 7; 1735: HIC, Mar 27,
  Apr 11; 1736: HIC, Jan 21, Mar 5, LIF, 8
Arrived at Portsmouth. See Pearce, William.
Arrowsmith, Daniel (singer), 1784: HAY, Mar 3, 17; 1785: HAY, Feb 23; 1786: DL,
  Mar 3, 29; 1788: HAY, Apr 29
Arrowsmith, Joseph
--Reformation, The, 1673: DG, May 0
Arrowsmith, T (publisher), 1793: HAY, Dec 2; 1794: HAY, Jan 14
Arsaces. See Rolli, Paolo Antonio.
Arsaces; or, Amore e Maesta. See Amadei, Phillipo.
Arsinoe. See Clayton, Thomas.
Art and Nature. See Miller, James.
Art of Management, The. See Charke, Charlotte.
Artamene. See Gluck, Christoph Willibald von.
Artaserse. See Bertoni, Fernando Giuseppe; Vinci, Leonardo.
Artaserse; or, Le Pazzie D'Orlando. See Hasse, Johann Adolph.
Artaxerxes. See Ariosti, Attilio; Hasse, Johann Adolph; Arne, Dr Thomas A.
Artful Husband, The. See Taverner, William.
Artful Wife, The. See Taverner, William.
Arthur and Emmeline (entertainment), 1784: DL, Nov 22, 23, 25, 30, Dec 3, 8,
  10, 13, 16, 17, 28; 1785: DL, Jan 3, 8, 11, Feb 1, Apr 13, Oct 26, 28, Nov 3;
  1786: DL, Jan 5, 7, Mar 4, Apr 19, May 27, Sep 26, Oct 5, 7; 1788: DL, Oct 9,
  20, Nov 27, Dec 4; 1789: DL, Jan 27, Feb 17, May 8, Oct 24, 28, Nov 5; 1790:
  DL, Apr 30, May 18, 26; 1791: DL, Apr 28
Arthur O'Bradley (song), 1797: CG, May 17
Arthur, Henry (quarrels in theatre), 1699: DL, Nov 11
Arthur, John (actor, author), 1730: SFP, Sep 9; 1735: YB, Sep 18; 1737: CG, Nov
  2, 17; 1738: CG, Jan 18, 25, Feb 6, 23, Mar 13, Apr 24, May 10, Aug 29, Oct
  6, 16, Nov 13, 29, Dec 5, 18; 1739: CG, Jan 23, Feb 10, 14, Apr 12, 26, May
  2, 4, 7, 9, 17, 25, Aug 2, 21, BFHCL, 23, CG, 31, Sep 5, 7, 10, 12, 14, 22,
  27, Oct 1, 2, 3, 10, 22, 25, Nov 9, 20, Dec 7, 10, 19; 1740: CG, Jan 15, Feb
  2, Mar 11, 18, 25, 27, Apr 23, May 3, 5, 7, 14, 21, Jun 5, BFHC, Aug 23, CG,
  Sep 19, 22, 24, 26, 29, Oct 1, 6, 10, 24, Nov 6, 15, Dec 4, 5, 10, 13; 1741:
  CG, Jan 2, 5, 27, 28, 29, Feb 14, 19, Mar 2, 7, Apr 17, 22, 25, 27, May 1, 4,
  11, 12, BFTY, Aug 22, DL, Sep 5, Oct 9, 20, 21, Nov 11, 16, 21; 1742: DL, Mar
  29, May 3, 20, 22, Sep 11, 14, 18, 25, Oct 7, 9, 15, 16; 1743: DL, Jan 28,
  Feb 10, SOU, 18, 25, DL, Apr 8, May 5, 7, Dec 9, 17; 1744: DL, Jan 7, 12, 27,
  Mar 12, Apr 2, 3, May 5, 22, CG, Oct 1, 8, 20, 24, Nov 9, Dec 6; 1745: CG,
  Jan 4, 5, Apr 2, 4, 20, 23, May 13, Oct 7, 11, 31, Nov 15, 22, 23, 25, 28,
  Dec 5, 13, 20; 1746: CG, Jan 2, 9, 11, 13, 23, Feb 5, 17, Mar 10, 13, Apr 1,
  5, 28, Oct 1, 3, 6, 15, 20, 29, Nov 6, Dec 6, 9, 27, 29, 31; 1747: CG, Jan
  17, 29, Feb 3, 6, Mar 30, Apr 7, 21, May 12, 20, DL, Sep 19, Oct 3, 17, 21,
  24, Nov 17, Dec 16, 26; 1748: DL, Jan 9, Feb 3, Mar 19, Apr 12, Sep 13, 15,
  20, 22, CG, 26, 28, 30, Oct 7, 14, 17, 29, Nov 3, 11, 16, 24, 26, 28, Dec 20,
  21, 22, 26; 1749: CG, Jan 2, 10, 11, 25, Feb 23, Mar 2, 4, 9, 14, 29, 31, Apr
  7, 10, 11, 21, May 4, Sep 25, 27, 29, Oct 6, 9, 11, 12, 16, 18, 19, 20, 25,
  26, 27, 30, Nov 4, 8, 9, 18, HAY, 20, CG, 21, 23, Dec 8, 27; 1750: CG, Jan
  16, Feb 22, Mar 1, Apr 5, 23, DL, May 22, CG, Sep 24, 28, Oct 12, 13, 15, 18,
  22, 23, 29, Nov 5, 8, 12, 19, 22, 24, Dec 4, 10, 14; 1751: CG, Jan 17, Apr
  16, 24, May 8, 9, 14, Sep 23, 27, 30, Oct 18, 22, 29, Nov 4, 7, 11, 13, 14,
  16, Dec 4, 14; 1752: CG, Jan 3, 6, 18, 28, 29, Mar 3, 12, 16, 17, Apr 30, May
  4, Sep 20, Oct 2, 4, 6, 10, 18, 19, 26, 30, 31, Nov 1, 4, 9, 16, 23, 27, Dec

27

7, 11, 14, 19; 1753: CG, Jan 22, Feb 6, 12, Mar 19, Apr 2, May 7, Sep 10, 12,
17, 26, Oct 1, 3, 8, 17, 24, 30, Nov 1, 2, 5, 9, 12, Dec 5, 26; 1754: CG, Feb
12, Mar 9, 26, Apr 6, May 2, 7, 8, 13, Sep 16, 18, 23, 25, 30, Oct 2, 7, 9,
16, 17, 24, 29, Nov 1, 4, 6, 16, Dec 30; 1755: CG, Jan 4, 28, Feb 8, 18, Mar
22, Apr 4, 8, 10, 18, May 2, 3, 15, Oct 1, 6, 8, 10, 14, 16, 17, 18, 21, 22,
23, 27, Nov 4, 10, 12, 15, 17, 21, Dec 3, 5, 26; 1756: CG, Jan 6, Feb 19, Mar
25, Apr 5, Sep 20, 22, 27, 29, Oct 1, 6, 8, 14, 19, 20, 21, 22, 23, 26, 27,
28, Nov 4, 9, 13, 16, 17, Dec 10; 1757: CG, Jan 8, 28, Feb 9, 16, Apr 27, May
6, 16, Sep 14, 16, 21, 23, 26, 28, 30, Oct 5, 8, 12, 13, 14, 17, 22, 31, Nov
3, 4, 5, 7, 9, 14, Dec 1, 10; 1758: CG, Mar 11, 30, Apr 3, 5, 8, 14, 21, DL,
Sep 16; 1769: HAY, May 15, 22, 26, Jun 5, Aug 7, Sep 4
--Lucky Discovery, The; or, The Tanner of York, 1738: CG, Apr 24, 25, 27, Sep
25, Oct 23, Dec 6; 1739: CG, Mar 19, May 28; 1740: CG, Apr 9, May 14, Oct 1,
6, Nov 7, 11; 1741: CG, May 6, Sep 21, 23; 1756: CG, Apr 5
Arthur, Mrs (actor), 1769: HAY, May 15, 19, 22, 26, Jun 5, 12, 21
Arthur's Chocolate House, 1756: CG, Dec 8, DL, 18; 1758: DL, Mar 10
Artichoke Yard, 1733: MEG, Sep 28
Artifice, The. See Centlivre, Susannah; Miles, William Augustus.
Artificial Flower Warehouse, 1785: HAY, Feb 10
Artificial View of the World (entertainment), 1732: BF, Aug 25, SF, Sep 11
Arts and Sciences (dance), 1778: CG, May 9, 22
Arundel St, 1703: YB, Mar 12; 1752: DL, Jan 16
Arundel, John Lord (actor), 1697: LIF, Feb 27
Arundel, Lady. See Slingsby, Barbara.
Arviragus and Philicia. See Carlell, Lodowick.
As Amoret with Phyllis sat (song), 1676: DG, Mar 11
As burns the charger (song), 1799: DL, May 4
As Down in a Meadow (song), 1730: LIF, May 25
As from the power (song), 1789: CG, Mar 20; 1790: CG, Mar 3, 24; 1791: CG, Mar
25; 1792: CG, Mar 9, KING'S, 23, 30; 1793: CG, Feb 20; 1794: DL, Mar 21, CG,
26, DL, Apr 4; 1798: CG, Mar 28
As Hodge got drubbed (song), 1799: CG, Dec 9
As I grazed unaware (song), 1685: DL, May 9
As I saw fair Chlora (song), 1790: CG, Apr 21, May 24
As I saw fair Clara (song), 1737: CG, Mar 15, 17, 28, 31
As It Should Be. See Oulton, Walley Chamberlain.
As it was in the Beginning (song), 1789: DL, Mar 25
As on the pleasant banks of Tweed (song), 1793: DL, May 22
As pants the heart (song), 1761: KING'S, Mar 12; 1789: DL, Mar 25
As soon as the Chaos (song), 1692: DL, Jan 0
As steals the morn upon the night (song), 1791: CG, Mar 18; 1792: CG, Feb 24;
1794: CG, Mar 21
As when the Dove (song), 1784: CG, Apr 27; 1787: DL, Mar 7; 1790: CG, Mar 3,
DL, 10; 1791: DL, Apr 1; 1792: KING'S, Feb 29; 1793: CG, Mar 20, 22; 1794:
CG, Mar 12, DL, 26
As You Find It. See Boyle, Charles.
As You Like It. See Shakespeare, William.
As You Like It; or, Harlequin's Whim (pantomime, anon), 1745: JS, Sep 3; 1746:
NWC, Sep 15
Asbury (house servant), 1768: CG, Jun 4
Ascelin. See Asselin.
Ascension of the Bleeding Nun (dance), 1798: CG, Jun 4
Ascension, The. See Hook, James.
Ascot, 1759: DL, Jun 19
Ashbridge, John (kettle drummer), 1771: DL, Nov 11; 1786: DL, Jan 20; 1793:
KING/HAY, Feb 15; 1794: DL, Mar 12
Ashburnham, Lord (spectator), 1729: DL, Nov 6
Ashe, Andrew (musician), 1793: CG, Apr 25; 1794: DL, Mar 12, 19, 26, Apr 9;
1796: CG, Apr 15
Ashe, Dr Hoadly, 1797: CG, Apr 29
Ashley, Charles Jane (violoncellist), 1790: CG, Feb 19; 1791: CG, Mar 23; 1792:
CG, Mar 9; 1793: CG, Feb 15, Mar 6, 13, 20; 1794: CG, Mar 7, 12, 14, 21, Apr
11; 1795: CG, Feb 20, Mar 13, 25; 1796: CG, Feb 12, 17, 24, Mar 16; 1797: CG,
Mar 3, 10, 31; 1798: CG, Feb 23, 28, Mar 9, 14, 28, 30; 1799: CG, Feb 8, 15,
20, Mar 1, 15; 1800: CG, Feb 28, Mar 5, 14, 19, Apr 2
Ashley, General Christopher (violinist), 1790: CG, Feb 19, Mar 12; 1791: CG,
Mar 11, 18, Apr 15; 1792: CG, Feb 24; 1793: CG, Feb 15, Mar 1, 20, 22; 1794:
CG, Mar 7, 14, 21, Apr 2, 11; 1795: CG, Feb 20, Mar 4, 6, 25; 1796: CG, Feb
12, 17, 19, 26, Mar 4, 18; 1797: CG, Mar 3, 10; 1798: CG, Feb 23, 28, Mar 2,
16, 28, 30; 1799: CG, Feb 8, Mar 1; 1800: CG, Feb 28, Mar 14, 19, Apr 4
Ashley, General Christopher and Charles Jane (musicians), 1798: CG, Mar 23
Ashley, General Christopher, John James, and Richard Godfrey (musicians), 1789:

CG, Feb 27
Ashley, General Christopher, Richard Godfrey, and Charles Jane (musicians),
   1793: CG, Mar 20; 1799: CG, Feb 15
Ashley, John (oratorio director), 1789: CG, Feb 27; 1790: CG, Mar 26; 1791: CG,
   Mar 11; 1792: CG, Feb 24; 1794: CG, Apr 11; 1795: CG, Feb 27, Mar 27; 1796:
   CG, Mar 18; 1797: CG, Apr 7; 1798: CG, Mar 9, 30; 1799: CG, Feb 8, Mar 15;
   1800: CG, Feb 28, Mar 28, Apr 2, 4
Ashley, John James (organist), 1790: CG, Feb 19; 1791: CG, Mar 11; 1792: CG,
   Feb 24; 1793: CG, Feb 15, Mar 8; 1794: CG, Mar 7, 26; 1795: CG, Feb 20; 1796:
   CG, Feb 12; 1797: CG, Mar 3, 24; 1798: CG, Feb 23; 1799: CG, Feb 8; 1800: CG,
   Feb 28
Ashley, John, General Christopher, and John James (musicians), 1792: CG, Feb 24
Ashley, Richard Godfrey (viola player), 1794: CG, Mar 7; 1795: CG, Feb 20;
   1796: CG, Feb 12; 1797: CG, Mar 3; 1798: CG, Feb 23; 1799: CG, Feb 8; 1800:
   CG, Feb 28, Mar 14
Ashley's Punch House, 1740: APH, Mar 28
Ashmole, Elias (diarist), 1660: MT, Nov 2
Ashton (actor) 1698: DL, Dec 0
Ashton, Robert (violinist), 1675: ATCOURT, Feb 15
Ashurst, Sir William (Lord Mayor), 1693: CITY, Oct 30
Ashwell (spectator), 1663: BRIDGES, May 8
Ashwin (actor), 1795: CG, May 30; 1796: CG, May 31; 1797: CG, Jun 8; 1798: CG,
   May 18; 1799: CG, May 29; 1800: CG, Feb 17, Jun 10
Asilo D'Amore, L' (interlude), 1739: CG, Apr 11
Ask if yon damask rose be sweet (song), 1790: DL, Mar 10; 1792: KING'S, Mar 7;
   1794: DL, Apr 2
Aspey (Ashpey) (singer), 1742: GF, Feb 2; 1744: HAY, Jan 19
Assaf, Kausan Abon (Syrian prince), 1722: LIF, May 18
Assanni del pensier (song), 1734: HIC, Jul 10
Assault (dance), 1778: CG, May 22
Assayd, El Hadgee Mohammad (Algerian ambassador), 1731: DL, Jan 13
Asselin (Ansellin, Ascelin, Asolin) (dancer), 1772: CG, Nov 5, 17, KING'S, Dec
   1, 8; 1773: KING'S, Jan 2, 5, Feb 20, Mar 23, Apr 27, May 1, 11, Jun 1, 12,
   19; 1774: KING'S, Mar 24, Nov 19; 1775: KING'S, Apr 22, 25, May 6
Asselin, Mlle (dancer), 1759: KING'S, Nov 13; 1760: KING'S, Jan 15, Mar 1, 10,
   HAY, 27, KING'S, Apr 12, 17, 19, May 31, HAY, Jun 5, KING'S, Aug 25, Nov 22,
   Dec 16; 1761: KING'S, Jan 6, Feb 7, 26, Mar 9, Apr 28, Oct 13, Nov 10; 1762:
   KING'S, Mar 9, Apr 20; 1763: KING'S, Feb 19, May 7; 1765: KING'S, Dec 3
Assembla, L'. See Guglielmi, Pietro.
Assignation, The. See Dryden, John.
Astarita, G (composer), 1792: HAY, Mar 31
Astarto Re Di Tiro (pastiche), 1762: KING'S, Dec 4, 11, 18; 1763: KING'S, Jan
   22, 29; 1770: KING'S, Dec 15; 1771: KING'S, Jan 12, Feb 8; 1776: KING'S, Nov
   2, 9, 16, 23, Dec 14
Astartus. See Bononcini, Giovanni.
Astolphe dans L'isle de Alcina (dance), 1776: KING'S, Mar 12, 16, 23, 30, Apr
   9, 13, 16, 27, May 7, 14, 16, 28, Jun 11, 15, 18, 22, 29
Aston-Paget Booth, 1733: BFAP, Aug 23
Aston, Anthony (actor, manager, author), 1685: BF, Aug 0; 1697: LIF, Feb 20;
   1716: GLOBE, Dec 28; 1717: GLOBE, Mar 2; 1718: GLOBE, Dec 3; 1722: LIF, Jan
   13, 17, Feb 2, 10, 24, Mar 5, 8, 15, 29, 30, 31, Apr 4, May 17; 1723: DT, Nov
   1, 12, 26, KAT, Dec 4, CT, 10, BHT, 23, AVT, 31; 1724: BT, Jan 29, BPT, Feb
   21, RDS, Mar 4, BPT, 11, HT, 13, BPT, 18, HT, 20, WINH, Apr 13, BPT, 16, PY,
   20, TTT, 23, EEH, 27, HA, May 4, BFL, Aug 22, CT, Nov 24, PT, 30, DT, Dec 2;
   1729: FLR, Nov 29, Dec 1; 1731: LG, Mar 8, CRT, 10, LIF, Apr 1, 3, May 28,
   Dec 9; 1732: LIF, Jan 10, 28, HAY, Mar 8, BFMMO, Aug 23; 1733: SF/BFLH, Aug
   23; 1734: BLO, Jan 16, BFRLCH, Aug 24, Sep 2, SFL, 7, RI, 26; 1736: BFFH, Aug
   23, SF, Sep 7; 1738: GT, May 1,CG, 3; 1740: CAC, Mar 12, APH, 28, LG, Apr 7;
   1743: IT, Dec 26; 1744: IT, Feb 23, TB, 29, Mar 22
--Cleora; or, The Amorous Old Shepherdess, 1736: LIF, Apr 16
--Declamation (entertainment), 1738: GT, May 1
Aston, Anthony, Mrs and Walter (actor), 1717: GLOBE, Mar 2
Aston, Herbert (composer, commentator), 1669: BRIDGES, Jun 24
Aston, Jean, Mrs Walter (beneficiary) 1740: CAC, Mar 12
Aston, Mrs Anthony (actor), 1724: RDS, Mar 4; 1732: HAY, Mar 8
Aston, Walter (actor), 1724: RDS, Mar 4; 1729: FLR, Nov 29, Dec 1; 1731: BFLH,
   Aug 24; 1732: LIF, Jan 28; 1732: LIF, Jan 28, Mar 20, Apr 11, May 2, 22,
   LIF/CG, Nov 4; 1733: LIF/CG, Feb 5, 10, Mar 30, Apr 3, CG, 4, LIF/CG, 12, 17,
   21, 27, CG, May 1, LIF/CG, 10, CG, 16, LIF/CG, 19, Jun 1, CG, 26, Jul 6, 27,
   Aug 2, 14, DL, Sep 24, CG, 29, Oct 2, 6, 1 , 18, 19, 27, 31, Nov 8, 9, 10,
   14, DL, 14, CG, 16, DL, 23, CG, 24, 28, 30, Dec 3, 4, 15, 20, 31; 1734: CG,
   Jan 1, 5, 18, Mar 5, 28, May 3, 7, 16, 17, HAY, Jul 31, LIF, Oct 1, CG/LIF,

9, Nov 4, 11, 14, 25, Dec 26, 27; 1735: CG/LIF, Jan 4, 25, Feb 4, 11, Mar 11,
20, 29, Apr 10, May 5, 16, 26, LIF, Jul 16, 23, 30, Aug 1, 6, 22, 25, 29 Sep
2, 5, CG, 19, 24, 26, Oct 3, 13, 20, 22, 24, Nov 10, 15, 22, Dec 31; 1736:
CG, Jan 8, Feb 21, Mar 15, 18, 27, LIF, Apr 2, CG, 15, LIF, 16, CG, 30, May
17, 20, Jun 14, LIF, Jul 1, CG, Sep 20, 27, 29, Oct 15, 20, 22, 25, 30, Nov
1, 8, 15; 1737: CG, Jan 17, 25, Feb 3, 15, 26, Mar 14, 31, Apr 14, May 3, 6,
9, 31, Sep 16, 21, 23, 30, Oct 7, 10, 12, 24, 28, 31, Nov 2; 1738: CG, Jan 3,
13, 26, Feb 6, 13, 16, 23, Mar 13, 20, 25, Apr 10, 17, 25
Astre and Thieste. See Crebillon, Prosper.
Astrologer, The. See Ralph, James.
Astyanax. See Bononcini, Giovanni.
Asylum for Female Orphans, 1758: CG, Dec 19; 1760: RANELAGH, Jun 18; 1762:
KING'S, Apr 14; 1763: CG, Dec 06
At dawn of Life our Vows were plighted (song), 1795: CG, May 25; 1796: CG, Apr
5; 1797: CG, May 9; 1799: CG, Apr 26
At last divine Cecilia came (song), 1791: CG, Mar 25; 1792: CG, Mar 7; 1794:
CG, Mar 14
At London che've been (song), 1693: NONE, Sep 0
At the close of the evening the witches were set (song), 1690: NONE, Sep 0
At the dawn of Aurora (song), 1796: CG, May 16
At the peaceful Midnight Hour (song), 1799: DL, May 4
At Totterdown Hill (song), 1767: CG, May 5
Atalanta. See Handel, George Frederic.
Atalante and Hyppomenus; or, The Foot Race (dance), 1800: DL, May 14
Atcheson (actor), 1722: HAY, Jun 28
Athalia. See Handel, George Frederic.
Atheist, The. See Oakman, J.
Atheist, The; or, The Second Part of the Souldiers Fortune. See Otway, Thomas.
Athelstan. See Brown, Dr John.
Athelwold. See Hill, Aaron.
Atherton, Miss (actor) 1791: HAY, Mar 7
Atherton, Miss (actor, singer, dancer), 1732: DL, May 1, Aug 1, 17, BF, 22, DL,
Nov 17, Dec 6, 18; 1733: DL, Feb 1, 12, Mar 28, 31, Apr 19, 21, May 24,
BFCGBH, Aug 23, Sep 4, DL, Oct 12, 24, Nov 7, Dec 5, 26; 1734: DL, Jan 1, 8,
15, 28, Feb 4, HAY, Apr 5, 17; 1735: LIF, Jun 19, HAY, Dec 13, 17; 1736: HAY,
Jan 19, LIF, Mar 24, BFHC, Aug 23; 1740: BFLP, Aug 23, SF, Sep 9; 1743: BFFP,
Aug 23; 1744: JS, Mar 2, MF, Jun 7
Ati e Cibele. See Cimadoro, Giambattista.
Atkins (coal merchant), 1780: CG, Apr 27
Atkins (house servant), 1784: CG, May 15; 1786: CG, May 18; 1787: CG, May 19;
1788: CG, May 24, Jun 4; 1789: CG, Jun 6; 1790: CG, May 29; 1791: CG, Jun 2;
1792: CG, Jun 1; 1794: CG, Jun 12; 1795: CG, Jun 10; 1796: CG, May 21; 1797:
CG, May 26; 1798: CG, May 19; 1799: CG, May 17; 1800: CG, Jun 4
Atkins (pit doorkeeper), 1724: LIF, May 22
Atkins, Charles (dancer, actor), 1748: CG, Oct 19, Dec 26; 1749: CG, May 11,
SOU, Sep 18, CG, Oct 20, Nov 23; 1750: CG, Feb 22, NWSM, May 10, CG, Oct 29,
Nov 22, Dec 26; 1751: CG, May 3, 6, 14, DL, Oct 17, 29, Dec 26; 1753: DL, Apr
25, Oct 9, 17; 1754: DL, Oct 31; 1766: DL, Oct 11, 25; 1769: DL, Dec 6; 1770:
DL, Jan 6, Apr 20, May 17, Sep 22, 25, Nov 29, Dec 13; 1771: DL, Apr 6, May
20, Jun 1, Sep 26, Oct 8, 12, Nov 22, Dec 2, 4, 26; 1772: DL, Sep 19, Oct 3,
6, 23, Nov 12, 21, Dec 2, 26; 1773: DL, Mar 27, Apr 24, May 4, 11, 12, 17,
Sep 18, 21, 23, 25, 28, Oct 9, 13, 16, Nov 9, 25, Dec 27; 1774: DL, Apr 28,
Sep 17, 20, 29, Oct 1, 5, 14, 27, Nov 1, 5, 28; 1775: DL, Jan 2, Mar 28
Atkins, Eliza, Mrs William (singer, actor), 1797: HAY, Aug 16, 23, Sep 1, 4,
16; 1799: CG, Jan 5, 17, 22, 26, Feb 8, 15, 20, Mar 1, 2, 6, 8, Apr 2, 9, 16,
19, 30, May 3, 4, 7, 10, 13, 14, 15, 28, Jun 6, 7, Sep 16, 18, 25, 27, 30,
Oct 2, 4, 7, Nov 13, Dec 4, 10, 16; 1800: CG, Jan 11, Mar 4, 25, Apr 15, 17,
26, 30, May 1, 2, 13, 22, Jun 2, 5, 13, HAY, 14
Atkins, James (singer), 1794: DL, May 16, Oct 27, 31, Nov 15, Dec 20; 1795: DL,
Feb 9, Oct 30, Nov 11, Dec 10; 1796: DL, Mar 12, Apr 30, Sep 29, Oct 19, Nov
9; 1797: DL, Jan 7, Feb 9, May 18, Nov 8; 1798: DL, Jan 16, Feb 20, Oct 6,
Nov 14, 26, Dec 4, 29, 31; 1799: DL, Jan 19, 28
Atkins, Master (actor), 1759: DL, Apr 5
Atkins, Michael Sr (singer, actor), 1755: DL, Feb 3, Oct 7, 17, Nov 8, 15, 26;
1756: DL, Jan 21, Feb 11, Apr 29, May 7, 15, Nov 18, Dec 27, 29; 1757: DL,
Mar 24, Sep 17, 29, Oct 7, 29, Dec 22, 27; 1758: DL, Jan 13, May 2, 15, Nov
16; 1759: DL, Jan 3, Feb 26, Oct 4, 23, 26, 30, Dec 1, 28; 1760: DL, Apr 28,
29, May 7, 16, Jun 19, Sep 20, Oct 2, 3, Nov 29, Dec 12
Atkins, Miss. See Atkinson, Miss.
Atkins, Mrs (boxkeeper), 1722: HAY, Jun 28; 1723: HAY, Mar 6; 1725: LIF, May 7;
1726: LIF, May 12; 1727: LIF, May 17; 1728: LIF, May 18; 1729: LIF, May 9;
1730: LIF, May 25; 1731: LIF, May 28; 1732: LIF, May 12; 1735: CG/LIF, May

26; 1736: CG, May 25; 1737: CG, May 20; 1738: CG, May 12; 1739: CG, May 23
Atkins, Mrs (house servant), 1787: CG, Jun 2
Atkins, William (actor), 1799: CG, Sep 18, 20, 23, 27, Oct 21, 31, Nov 7, 14,
    30, Dec 3, 5, 16, 23; 1800: CG, Jan 16, Feb 8, 10, Mar 27, Apr 23, 25, 30,
    May 1, 7, 12, 13, 17, 23, 27, Jun 2, 10, 11, 12, HAY, 14, 16, 19, 20, 21, 27,
    Jul 2, 3, 5, 15, Aug 7, 14, 20, 22, Sep 1
Atkinson (actor), 1750: SFP, Sep 7
Atkinson (actor), 1781: HAY, Oct 16
Atkinson (doorkeeper), 1746: DL, May 1; 1748: DL, May 9; 1749: DL, May 5; 1750:
    DL, May 8; 1751: DL, May 9; 1752: DL, Apr 30, May 2
Atkinson, Joseph
--Mutual Deception, The, 1786: HAY, Aug 29; 1788: CG, May 12
Atkinson, Miss (actor), 1770: CG, Mar 22; 1771: HAY, Apr 15; 1773: HAY, May 24,
    31, Jun 4, 16, 18, 28, Jul 28, Aug 11, 27, Sep 16, 18; 1774: HAY, Apr 4;
    1782: HAY, May 6
Attalo. See Galuppi, Baldassare.
Attendez Moy sous L'Orme. See Regnard, Jean Francois.
Atterbury, Luffman (musician, composer), 1773: HAY, Apr 23; 1793: KING/HAY, Mar
    6; 1794: CG, Dec 26; 1795: CG, Jan 12
--Goliath (oratorio), 1773: HAY, Apr 23, May 5
Atterino (dancer), 1754: HAY, Jul 16, Aug 15, Sep 10
Attic Evening's Entertainment, An (entertainment), 1769: HAY, Feb 2, 9, 23
Attilio Regolo. See Jomelli, Niccolo.
Attwood, Thomas (musician, composer), 1790: DL, Mar 26; 1791: DL, May 3; 1792:
    KING'S, Mar 14, 23, DL, Oct 18; 1793: DL, Mar 7, May 10, HAY, Aug 12, Nov 30;
    1794: CG, May 13; 1795: DL, May 1, CG, 29, Oct 2; 1796: DL, Apr 13, Sep 29;
    1797: DL, May 13, HAY, Aug 24, DL, Oct 28, Nov 28, Dec 11, CG, 19; 1798: CG,
    Mar 17, May 23, Oct 5, 11, 25, Dec 11; 1799: CG, Jan 29, Apr 2, May 15, Jun
    7, HAY, Jul 13, Aug 21; 1800: CG, Feb 19, Mar 25, Apr 5, 26, HAY, Jun 14
Atwood (house servant), 1735: DL, May 23
Atwood (house servant), 1768: CG, Jan 4
Atwood, John (musician), 1735: HIC, Dec 11
Auberge D'Arlequin, L' (farce), 1720: KING'S, Jun 20; 1725: HAY, Mar 15
Aubert (dancer), 1715: LIF, Oct 7, 14, Nov 10
Aubert (Obert), Isabella (singer, author), 1715: KING'S, Aug 27; 1716: HIC, Mar
    15; 1717: LIF, Jan 2, Feb 27, HIC, Apr 3, LIF, Jun 1, DL, Nov 6, 11; 1719:
    LR, Jan 20, KING'S, Feb 26, Mar 2, HIC, Mar 6, LIF, May 27; 1720: LIF, Feb 5,
    YB, Jun 1
--Harlequin Hydaspes; or, The Greshamite (pantomime), 1719: LIF, May 22, 27
Aubin, Mrs (orator), 1724: LIF, Jan 2; 1729: YB, Apr 15, 22, 29; 1730: HAY, Dec
    9, 11
--Merry Masqueraders, The; or, The Humourous Cuckold, 1730: HAY, Dec 9, 11
Aubin, Penelope (author), 1737: YB, Apr 28
Aubrey, John, 1671: NONE, Oct 26; 1676: DG, May 25
--Country Revel, The; or, The Revel of Aldford, 1670: NONE, Sep 0; 1671: NONE,
    Oct 26
Auction of Pictures. See Foote, Samuel.
Audinot (French manager), 1783: CG, Oct 9
Audley St, 1738: GF, Sep 16
Augusta, Princess, 1736: CG, May 12; 1741: CG, Feb 28, Mar 7, Apr 6, DL, 21,
    CG, 24, May 15; 1743: CG, Apr 26; 1744: CG, May 10; 1745: HAY, Mar 5, CG, 11,
    28, May 4; 1746: CG, Nov 28, Dec 12; 1747: CG, May 14; 1748: CG, Oct 25, Nov
    10, Dec 21; 1749: LEI, Jan 7, CG, Feb 9, 27, May 4, Dec 16; 1750: CG, Mar 10,
    12; 1752: CG, Dec 30; 1754: DL, Dec 12; 1755: CG, Dec 18, DL, 31; 1756: DL,
    Jan 9, Mar 4; 1757: DL, Nov 3, CG, 5; 1758: CG, Jan 28, Feb 4; 1760: CG, Feb
    5, Apr 26, Dec 19; 1761: CG, Sep 24, Oct 8; 1764: DL, Jan 16, 20, 26; 1772:
    CG, Feb 8, DL, 8; see also Princesses; Wales, Princess of
Auguste (Aguste), Mlle (dancer), 1741: DL, Dec 4, CG, 7, DL, 7, CG, 8, 10, 12,
    14, 15, 21, 22, 28, 30; 1742: CG, Jan 4, 5, 8, 14, 18, 21, 25, Feb 6, 9, 10,
    12, 25, 26, Mar 18, 22, 29, Apr 5, 20, 21, 23, 28, May 21, Sep 29, Oct 4, 6,
    11, 15, Nov 1, 2, 5, 25, Dec 14, 15, 21, 30; 1743: CG, Jan 19, Feb 4, Mar 5,
    8, Apr 7, 22, 25, May 20; 1744: DL, Jan 28, Feb 2, 3, Mar 5, 13, 28, 29, Apr
    4, 6, 9, 10, 17, 21, 23, 30, May 1, 8, 11, 14, 15, 16, 17, 21, 22, 23; 1752:
    DL, Nov 25, 28, Dec 1, 8, 19, 21; 1753: DL, Jan 1, 10, 15, 24, Feb 19, Mar
    22, 24, 26, Apr 2, 24, 25, Sep 20, 22, 29, Oct 3, 12, 13, Nov 8, 10, 14, Dec
    14, 26; 1754: DL, Jan 7, 26, 31, Feb 11, Mar 16, 18, 19, Apr 2, 4, 17
Augustus Caesar, 1773: HAY, Aug 13
Auld Robin Grey (ballet), 1783: KING'S, Nov 29
Auld Robin Grey (song), 1781: CG, Apr 3, HAY, Aug 22, Oct 16; 1782: CG, Apr 9,
    12, 19, May 20; 1784: DL, Apr 26, 28, May 5; 1785: CG, Apr 18; 1788: HAY, Jul
    30; 1789: CG, May 20; 1792: CG, May 22; 1794: CG, May 26; see also Young
    Jamie loved me well

31

Auld Robin Grey. See Arnold, Samuel James.
Auletta, Pietro (composer), 1748: KING'S, Nov 29
Aumer, Jean Pierre (dancer), 1791: PAN, Feb 17, 26; 1793: KING'S, Jun 11, 15,
    18; 1794: KING'S, Jan 11, Mar 1, 4, Apr 1, May 31, DL, Oct 31, KING'S, Dec 6,
    20; 1795: KING'S, Jan 20, DL, Feb 12, 17, Mar 12, 14, KING'S, 26, DL, Apr 8,
    May 6, 20, KING'S, 28, Jun 20
Aumont, Duke of, 1713: CA, Mar 20
Aurasecchio (composer), 1758: KING'S, Apr 6
Aurelio and Miranda. See Boaden, James.
Aurelli, A, 1671: NONE, Sep 0
Aurengzebe. See Dryden, John.
Auretti, Anne (dancer), 1742: CG, Oct 25, Nov 8, Dec 10; 1743: CG, Mar 24, Apr
    6, 14, 16, 22; 1747: DL, Oct 31, Nov 2, 3, 23, 28, Dec 23, 30; 1748: DL, Jan
    1, 7, 12, 13, 18, 19, 23, 28, Feb 11, 12, 27, Mar 3, 5, 7, 8, 10, 12, 14, 17,
    24, 26, 31, Apr 14, 15, 16, 21, 23, 26, 29, May 3, 5, 11, 17, 25, Oct 27, Nov
    3, 12, 30, Dec 3; 1749: DL, Jan 7, 9, 10, 18, Feb 21, Mar 14, 30, Apr 8, 11,
    12, 14, May 6, 13, 16, Oct 24, 28, 31, Nov 1, 9, 27, 29, Dec 29; 1750: DL,
    Jan 18, Mar 10, 13, 15, 17, 22, 24, 26, 27, 29, 31, Apr 2, 5, 9, 17, 21, 23,
    27, May 7, 11, Oct 31, Nov 1, 2, 27, Dec 11, 18, 20, 22; 1751: DL, Jan 11,
    12, 14, 17, 19, 22, 23, 24, 25, 29, Feb 14, 18, 19, 21, 23, Mar 11, 12, 14,
    18, 19, Apr 8, 9, 10, 11, 12, 15, 17, 18, 23, 24, 25, 26, 29, 30, May 2, 17,
    18, 22, Oct 15, 17, 19, 28, Nov 5, Dec 7, 12, 21; 1752: DL, Jan 18, 22, 31,
    Feb 4, Mar 7, 9, 14, 16, 17, Apr 22, 28, Oct 17, 25, 26, Nov 2, 6, 16, 25,
    28, Dec 1; 1753: DL, Jan 1, 5, 15, 17, 24, Feb 23, Mar 1, 20, 22, 29, 31, Apr
    12, 24, May 19, Nov 23, Dec 19, 26; 1754: DL, Jan 7, 28, 31, Feb 23, Mar 12,
    16, 18, 23, 26, 30, Apr 1, 6, 16, May 30, Oct 8, 19, 28, Dec 5; 1755: DL, Apr
    7; 1764: KING'S, Jan 10, Feb 7, 14, 21, 25, Mar 20, 29, 31, Apr 10, 14, May
    5; 1765: KING'S, Jan 5
Auretti, Anne and Janeton (dancers), 1742: CG, Oct 23, Dec 17; 1743: CG, Feb 9,
    10, 17, 21, Apr 2, 6, May 20; 1748: DL, Jan 8, 14, Apr 2, Nov 7, Dec 21;
    1749: DL, Mar 7, 9, 11; 1754: DL, Apr 17
Auretti, Janeton (dancer), 1742: CG, Oct 25, Nov 9, Dec 1, 31; 1743: CG, Jan
    19, Apr 19, 22; 1747: DL, Nov 2, 13, 23, Dec 26; 1748: DL, Feb 9, 12, Mar 10,
    24, 26, 29, Apr 15, 20, 25, Oct 27, Nov 29, Dec 26; 1749: DL, Jan 10, Feb 21,
    Mar 13; 1751: DL, Oct 9, 15, 17, 18, 19, 28, Nov 5, 18, 19, Dec 7, 13, 14,
    16, 26; 1752: DL, Mar 5, 16, Apr 9, 11, 13, 16, 27, 29, May 5, Nov 13, 28;
    1753: DL, Jan 4, Mar 24, Apr 24, 27, May 1, 8
Aurora Borealis, Epilogue upon the (entertainment), 1716: DL, Mar 24
Austen, Miss (actor), 1767: CG, Jan 31
Austin, Joseph (actor), 1744: MF, Jun 27; 1757: DL, Feb 22, 28, May 9, Sep 27,
    29, Oct 15, 20, Nov 10, 15, 25; 1758: DL, Feb 1, May 4, Sep 16, 19, 21, 26,
    28, Oct 3, 13, 25, 30, Nov 4, 14, 18, 23; 1759: DL, Jan 3, Feb 1, Mar 6, 26,
    Apr 7, 21, May 11, 16, 23, 29, Sep 22, 25, CG, 28, DL, 29, Oct 4, 11, 12, 19,
    22, Nov 5, 10, CG, 13, DL, Dec 31; 1760: DL, Jan 19, Feb 21, Mar 6, 20, Apr
    9, 11, 28, May 1, 7, 8, 16, CG, Sep 22, DL, Oct 9, 18, 22, Nov 27, Dec 17;
    1761: DL, Jan 28, Mar 26, Apr 24, 25, 29, May 1, 11, 25, 28; 1769: CG, Apr 22
Austrian and Highland Broadsword Exercise (entertainment), 1800: DL, May 21
Austrian Dance (dance), 1743: BFHC, Aug 23
Author on the Wheel, An; or, a Piece cut in the Green-Room (entertainment),
    1785: DL, Apr 18
Author, The. See Foote, Samuel.
Author's Farce, The. See Fielding, Henry.
Author's Triumph, The; or, The Manager Managed (farce, anon), 1737: LIF, Apr 14
Avantures de la Foire St. Germain de Paris, Les (play), 1726: HAY, Apr 22
Avare, L'. See Moliere.
Avaro Deluso, L'. See Sacchini, Antonio Maria Gasparo.
Avemary Lane, 1759: CG, May 8
Aveugle Pretendu, L'. See Dorvigny.
Avison, Charles (composer), 1734: HIC, Mar 20; 1799: CG, Mar 1
--4th Concerto, 1795: CG, Mar 31; 1797: CG, Mar 1; 1799: CG, Mar 1
Avocat Patelin, L'. See Brueys, David Augustin de.
Avoglio, Christina Maria (singer), 1743: CG, Feb 18, Mar 23; 1744: DL, Feb 1,
    CG, 10, 24, DL, Oct 17
Avory (beneficiary), 1738: CG, Dec 8
Awake, Aeolian lyre (song), 1785: DL, Apr 22, May 3; 1791: DL, Apr 13; 1792:
    KING'S, Feb 29, Mar 7
Awake, O Constantine, awake (song), 1683: DL, Nov 12
Awake, the trumpet's lofty sound (song), 1790: DL, Feb 24; 1792: KING'S, Mar
    14; 1794: DL, Mar 21, CG, 26, DL, Apr 11; 1795: CG, Mar 25
Awake, unhappy man, awake (song), 1698: NONE, Sep 0
Away with the causes of riches and cares (song), 1676: DG, Nov 4
Awful pleasing being (song), 1796: CG, Mar 16; 1800: CG, Feb 28

Awkward Recruit (song), <u>1800</u>: CG, May 6
Axe and Battle Yard, <u>1735</u>: SFLP, Sep 4; <u>1737</u>: SF, Sep 7
Axt (Axe), John Mitchell (musician), <u>1748</u>: HAY, Dec 9
Aylett, Mrs (gallery doorkeeper), <u>1716</u>: LIF, Jul 18; <u>1719</u>: LIF, Jun 11; <u>1721</u>:
   LIF, Jun 7; <u>1722</u>: LIF, May 29; <u>1723</u>: LIF, Jun 3; <u>1724</u>: LIF, Jun 1; <u>1725</u>: LIF,
   May 21
Ayleworth, Jeoffrey (musician), <u>1681</u>: ATCOURT, Nov 15
Ayliff (Ayloffe), Mrs (actor, singer), <u>1692</u>: DG, May 2, DL, Jun 0, DLORDG, Aug
   24; <u>1693</u>: DL, Feb 0, Apr 0, ATCOURT, 30, DG, May 0, NONE, Sep 0, DL, Oct 0;
   <u>1694</u>: DL, Jan 0, DG, 10, DL, Feb 0, Apr 0, DG, May 0, NONE, Sep 0; <u>1695</u>: LIF,
   Apr 30, DL, Sep 0, LIF, Dec 0; <u>1696</u>: LIF, Nov 14
Ayliff St, <u>1736</u>: GF, Mar 25; <u>1740</u>: GF, Oct 15; <u>1742</u>: GF, Apr 19; <u>1746</u>: GF, Jan
   20, Feb 10, Mar 4
Ayliffe (carpenter), <u>1750</u>: DL, Jan 3
Aylmer, George (singer, actor), <u>1788</u>: HAY, Aug 5, 8; <u>1789</u>: HAY, Aug 11; <u>1791</u>:
   HAY, Jul 30, Aug 31, DLKING'S, Oct 15; <u>1792</u>: DLKING'S, May 23, HAY, Jun 23,
   DL, Oct 11, 18; <u>1793</u>: HAY, Jun 17, Jul 20; <u>1794</u>: DL, May 16, HAY, Aug 27, DL,
   Oct 27, Nov 15, Dec 20; <u>1795</u>: DL, Feb 9, HAY, Jun 13, 20, Jul 31, DL, Oct 30,
   Nov 11, Dec 10; <u>1796</u>: DL, Mar 12, Apr 6, 30, HAY, Jul 15, Aug 29, DL, Sep 29,
   Oct 19; <u>1797</u>: DL, Jan 7, May 18, HAY, Jun 23, Aug 14, 15, DL, Nov 8; <u>1798</u>:
   DL, Jan 16, Feb 20, HAY, Jun 30, Jul 21, Aug 11, DL, Oct 6, Nov 14, Dec 4,
   17, 29, 31; <u>1799</u>: DL, Jan 19, Feb 4, Mar 2, May 24, HAY, Jul 9, 13, 16, Aug
   21, Sep 2, 9, DL, Oct 14, Nov 14, Dec 11; <u>1800</u>: DL, Jan 1, Mar 11, 13, Apr
   29, May 3, HAY, Jun 14, Jul 2, 21, Aug 14, 29, Sep 1, 11
Aylward, Theodore (composer), <u>1794</u>: CG, Dec 26
Aynscombe (singer), <u>1762</u>: DL, Feb 26, Mar 3, 5, HAY, May 20
Ayre, R (printer), <u>1779</u>: KING'S, May 15; <u>1782</u>: KING'S, Dec 19
Ayrenhoff, Cornelius Hermann von, <u>1789</u>: HAY, Jun 22
--Postzug, Der; oder, Die Nobeln Passionen, <u>1789</u>: HAY, Jun 22
Ayres (Airs), James (actor), <u>1730</u>: HAY, Mar 30, Apr 20, SOU, Sep 24, HAY, Oct
   21, 23, Nov 9, 20, 30, Dec 28; <u>1731</u>: HAY, Jan 15, 18, 20, Feb 3, 10, 17, 26,
   Mar 17, 24, SF, Sep 8; <u>1734</u>: GF, Jan 19, 21, Feb 2, 11, May 7, 16, 20, Sep
   20, 25, Oct 14, 17, Dec 13; <u>1735</u>: GF, Jan 4, 6, 13, Mar 6, May 5; <u>1744</u>: HAY,
   Jan 19, Apr 16
Ayscough, George Edward, <u>1776</u>: DL, Dec 14
--Semiramis, <u>1776</u>: DL, Dec 14, 16, 20, 23, 30; <u>1777</u>: DL, Jan 3, 7, 8, 11, 15,
   20, Feb 1, 5; <u>1798</u>: DL, Apr 23
Azure God (song), <u>1775</u>: DL, Mar 20; <u>1776</u>: DL, Oct 29; <u>1779</u>: DL, Mar 25

B (actor), <u>1661</u>: NONE, Sep 0
B, B (author), <u>1748</u>: DL, Apr 19
B, E (secretary), <u>1757</u>: CG, Jan 13; <u>1759</u>: CG, Mar 7; <u>1760</u>: CG, Feb 27
B, J (author), <u>1750</u>: DL, Mar 16
B, M (author), <u>1768</u>: CG, Mar 15
B, Mrs (householder), <u>1760</u>: DL, Jan 16
B, Mrs (spectator), <u>1759</u>: CG, Oct 22
B, Mrs S (house servant), <u>1760</u>: CG, Sep 22
B, T (epiloguist), <u>1660</u>: NONE, Sep 0
Babb, Mrs (actor), <u>1707</u>: DL, Oct 18, 21, Nov 1
Babbini, Matteo (singer), <u>1785</u>: KING'S, Apr 16, 21, May 28; <u>1786</u>: KING'S, Jan
   24, Feb 14, Mar 11, 16, 21, 28, 30, May 20, 25
Babel, Mrs (merchant), <u>1772</u>: DL, Jan 6
Babel, William (musician, composer), <u>1711</u>: HDS, Apr 24; <u>1713</u>: HIC, Mar 25;
   <u>1717</u>: SH, Mar 27, May 10; <u>1718</u>: TEC, Mar 12, LIF, Apr 5, 26, May 1; <u>1719</u>:
   LIF, Feb 28, Apr 3; <u>1723</u>: SH, Mar 6; <u>1729</u>: HIC, Apr 16; <u>1732</u>: CL, Mar 17
Babel's scholar (musician), <u>1718</u>: LIF, Apr 5, May 1
Babett (merchant), <u>1772</u>: CG, Feb 18
Baccelli, Giovanna (dancer), <u>1774</u>: KING'S, Nov 8, 19, Dec 3, 13, 17; <u>1775</u>:
   KING'S, Jan 17, Feb 7, 14, 21, 28, Mar 23, Apr 6, 8, 18, 22, 25, May 11, 16,
   25, 30, Jun 6, 24, Oct 31, Nov 7; <u>1776</u>: KING'S, Jan 9, 27, Feb 3, 6, 13, 17,
   27, Mar 12, Apr 18, 20, Jun 8; <u>1777</u>: KING'S, Feb 25, Mar 15, Apr 12, May 1,
   8, 15, 24, Jul 5, Nov 4, 15, Dec 9; <u>1778</u>: KING'S, Feb 7, 24, Mar 3, 10, Apr
   4, 30, May 28; <u>1779</u>: KING'S, Feb 23, 27, Mar 25, Apr 15, May 15, 29, Jun 15,
   26; <u>1780</u>: KING'S, Jan 22, Feb 8, Apr 1, 20, 22, May 9, 27, Dec 16; <u>1781</u>:
   KING'S, Jan 23, Feb 22, Mar 15, 29, May 15, Jun 5, Jul 3, Nov 17, Dec 11;
   <u>1782</u>: KING'S, Jan 10, Feb 2, 5, 7, 14, 21, 23, Mar 19, Apr 11, May 2, 9, Jun
   1, 3, 15; <u>1783</u>: KING'S, Apr 10, May 1; <u>1786</u>: KING'S, Mar 23, Apr 1, 4, 27,
   May 23, Jun 1
Bacchanalian Divertissement Ballet (dance), <u>1800</u>: KING'S, Apr 15, 19, 22, May

24, Jun 7, Jul 8
Bacchanalian Jubilee (dance), 1773: DL, Nov 25
Bacchanalian Music (music), 1704: LIF, Jul 14
Bacchanalian Song (song), 1732: LIF, Mar 30, GF, Apr 17, LIF, 19, GF, 19, 21,
   May 1, 2, 12, 17, 18, 23; 1733: GF, May 18; 1739: CG, Nov 10, 16; 1740: CG,
   Jan 22; 1744: CG, Apr 7; 1746: CG, Apr 8; 1754: CG, May 2, 3; 1759: DL, Mar
   29, Apr 2
Bacchus and Ariadne (dance), 1734: CG, Apr 17, May 7; 1781: CG, Feb 8; 1797:
   KING'S, Dec 9; 1798: KING'S, Mar 31, DL, May 9
Bacchus and Circe (play), 1745: JS, Sep 3
Bacchus and Cupid. See Purcell, Henry, Cupid and Bacchus.
Bacchus and Venus (song), 1734: CG, Apr 16
Bacchus ever fair and young (song), 1790: CG, Mar 26; 1791: CG, Mar 25, Apr 13;
   1792: CG, Mar 7; 1793: KING/HAY, Mar 6; 1794: CG, Mar 14, DL, Apr 11
Bacchus Festival. See Jordan, Thomas.
Bacchus one day gaily striding (song), 1733: GF, Mar 17, May 14, 22; 1734: SFG,
   Sep 7; 1736: HAY, May 26
Bacchus Triumphant (song), 1741: CG, Apr 10
Bacchus' blessings (song), 1790: CG, Mar 26; 1791: CG, Apr 13; 1792: CG, Mar 7;
   1794: CG, Mar 14
Baccia per me la Mana Sgomtra dell Anima (song), 1729: DL, Mar 26
Bach (composer), 1763: KING'S, Feb 19, May 7; 1770: KING'S, Mar 22, Apr 7;
   1771: KING'S, Jan 10, Feb 8, Apr 30; 1772: KING'S, Feb 21, HAY, Apr 6; 1773:
   KING'S, Feb 5, CG, Mar 19; 1774: KING'S, Feb 10; 1775: KING'S, Jan 14, Mar 8,
   10, DL, 10, KING'S, 22, 24, 29, 31, Apr 5; 1776: DL, Mar 20; 1785: KING'S,
   May 12; 1792: CG, Feb 28; 1798: CG, Mar 23; 1799: CG, Feb 15
Bach, Ag, 1763: KING'S, Apr 25
Bach, Cecilia (actor), 1782: KING'S, May 27
Bach, Johann Christian (composer), 1765: KING'S, Jan 26, 29; 1767: CG, Jan 31;
   1777: KING'S, May 24; 1778: KING'S, Apr 4; 1782: KING'S, May 27; 1785: CG,
   May 12; 1787: CG, Mar 12; 1788: CG, Nov 6; 1789: CG, Sep 28; 1796: CG, Mar
   15, Oct 24
--Clemenza di Scipione, La (opera), 1778: KING'S, Apr 4, 11, 25, May 2, 9, 16,
   23, Jun 20
--Endimione (musical), 1772: HAY, Apr 6
--Gioas Re Di Giuda (oratorio), 1770: KING'S, Mar 22, 29, Apr 5; 1771: KING'S,
   Jan 10, 17, 24
--Orione (opera), 1763: KING'S, Feb 19, 26, 28, Mar 5, 12, 19, 26, Apr 9, 16,
   23, 30, May 16, Jun 2; 1770: KING'S, Feb 2; 1777: KING'S, May 24, 31, Jun 7,
   21
--Zanaida (opera), 1763: KING'S, May 7, 14, 20, 28, 31, Jun 11
Bach, Johann Christoph (musician), 1729: HIC, Apr 16
Bach, Johann Sebastian (composer), 1763: KING'S, Feb 3; 1767: KING'S, Feb 14
--Carattaco (opera), 1767: KING'S, Feb 14, 21, 28, Mar 7, 14, 28
Bacio, Il. See Giordani, Tommaso.
Bacon (lawyer), 1775: DL, Nov 15
Bacon, Dr Phanuel, 1756: NONE, Dec 25
--Taxes, The, 1756: NONE, Dec 25
Badcock (house servant), 1797: CG, Jun 6; 1798: CG, Jun 5
Baddeley, Richard (sub-treasurer), 1661: LIF/MT, Nov 1; 1663: MT, Feb 2
Baddeley, Robert (actor, author), 1760: HAY, Jun 28, DL, Oct 25, Nov 22; 1761:
   DL, Apr 6, 25, May 11, 26, 29, Jun 15, Jul 2, 21, 27, Aug 8; 1763: DL, Sep
   20, Oct 8, 12, 14, 17, 19, Nov 1, 23, 26, 28, 30, Dec 17; 1764: DL, Jan 2, 4,
   9, 13, 14, 17, 23, 27, Feb 21, Mar 26, Apr 12, May 9, 10, 11, 16, 22, Sep 22,
   25, 27, Oct 13, 15, 18, 19, 20, 22, Nov 13, 28, Dec 13, 18, 26; 1765: DL, Jan
   2, 23, Mar 2, 18, Apr 11, 13, 15, May 7, 18, Sep 19, Oct 11, 14, 22, 31, Nov
   16, Dec 7, 14, 20; 1766: DL, Jan 13, 24, Feb 20, Mar 17, 20, Apr 1, 8, 12,
   25, 29, May 2, 3, 10, 19, Sep 23, Oct 7, 9, 13, 17, 18, 23, 28, 29, 31, Nov
   8, 17, Dec 10, 30; 1767: DL, Feb 21, Mar 7, 21, 31, Apr 11, 22, 25, May 4, 6,
   8, 9, 23, 28, Sep 12, 15, 17, 19, 23, 25, 26, Oct 9, 14, 20, 28, Nov 7, 11,
   12, 23, 26, 28, Dec 1; 1768: DL, Jan 9, 14, Feb 20, Mar 8, 17, 19, Apr 6, 9,
   12, 14, 15, 22, 27, May 27, Sep 17, 22, 23, 24, 26, 27, 29, Oct 5, 11, 19,
   20, 25, Nov 1, 15; 1769: DL, Jan 6, 16, 24, 25, 27, Feb 4, Mar 16, 29, Apr 3,
   5, 11, 18, 24, May 1, Sep 16, 19, 21, 26, Oct 9, 10, 17, Nov 14, 15, 16, 22,
   29, Dec 4, 16, 23; 1770: DL, Jan 4, 26, Feb 8, Mar 1, 17, 27, Sep 29, Oct 2,
   3, 5, 18, 26, Nov 6, 13, 14, 16, 19, 20, 21, 24, Dec 4, 5, 6, 17, 20; 1771:
   DL, Jan 2, 4, 19, Mar 18, 21, Apr 1, 2, 5, 6, 10, 15, 17, 30, May 27, Sep 21,
   24, CG, 25, DL, 26, 28, Oct 12, 15, 17, 19, 28, 31, Nov 8, 9, 13, 22, Dec 2,
   3, 4, 21, 26, 31; 1772: DL, Jan 4, 8, 11, 15, 20, Mar 18, 21, 23, 26, Apr 6,
   CG, 21, DL, 25, 29, May 13, 14, HAY, 22, 27, Jun 1, 8, DL, 10, HAY, 10, 24,
   29, Jul 6, 15, Aug 10, DL, Sep 24, 26, 29, Oct 3, 13, 14, 15, 16, 17, 21, 23,
   28, 29, Nov 3, 16, 20, 30, Dec 15, 18; 1773: DL, Jan 1, 29, Feb 27, Mar 30,

Apr 1, 3, 28, 30, May 1, 6, 10, 12, 15, 17, 18, 24, Sep 18, 23, Oct 2, 8, 11,
14, 19, 22, 25, 28, 30, Nov 1, 6, 26, Dec 11, 20, 21, 30, 31; 1774: DL, Jan
5, 13, 22, Feb 8, 15, Mar 14, 15, 22, 26, Apr 4, 19, 25, May 7, 18, Sep 17,
24, 27, Oct 4, 5, 14, 20, 24, 28, Nov 7, 16, 24, 30, Dec 3, 19, 26; 1775: DL,
Jan 18, Feb 1, Mar 7, 18, 23, Apr 8, NONE, 10, DL, 17, 19, May 5, 6, 12, 27,
MARLY, 30, DL, Oct 3, 5, 7, 11, 23, 31, Nov 6, 9, 20, 23, 25, Dec 7, 11, 20,
25; 1776: DL, Jan 13, 27, Feb 9, 12, Mar 7, 18, 21, 23, 26, Apr 8, 26, 27,
May 4, 11, 16, 18, HAY, 20, 22, 27, 28, 31, DL, Jun 3, HAY, 14, 19, Jul 8,
24, Aug 2, 19, DL, Sep 21, Oct 5, 10, 15, 23, 30, Nov 7, 19, 25, 28, 29, Dec
14, 18, 28, 31; 1777: DL, Jan 1, 4, 16, Feb 24, Mar 13, 31, Apr 7, 22, 29,
May 8, Sep 20, 25, 27, 30, Oct 9, 22, 29, Nov 8, 14, 24, 29, Dec 11, 13;
1778: DL, Jan 2, 5, 22, 23, Feb 10, 24, Mar 5, 12, 30, Apr 20, 21, 27, May 2,
HAY, 18, Jun 10, Jul 11, Aug 20, Sep 7, DL, 17, 19, 24, 29, Oct 1, 6, 8, 13,
15, 19, 21, 28, Nov 2, 4, 18, 20, 28, 30, Dec 11, 21; 1779: DL, Jan 7, 29,
Mar 15, 18, 27, Apr 28, May 15, 19, 21, 25, HAY, 31, DL, Jun 1, HAY, 10, Jul
1, 16, Aug 13, 14, DL, Sep 18, 21, 23, 25, 30, Oct 2, 5, 12, 19, 21, 30, Nov
3, 6, 18, 22, 24, Dec 2, 4, 29; 1780: DL, Jan 11, 24, 26, Feb 22, 28, Mar 4,
Apr 4, 5, 17, 21, 26, May 10, HAY, 30, Jun 6, 13, 15, 23, Sep 5, 8, 11, DL,
16, 19, 21, 23, Oct 5, 10, 11, 12, 14, 17, 25, 31, Nov 1, 2, 3, 8, 10, 17,
22, Dec 1, 6, 7, 19, 27; 1781: DL, Jan 8, 16, Feb 17, Mar 10, 31, Apr 24, 28,
HAY, Jun 1, 8, 9, 12, 21, Jul 9, 18, 23, Aug 1, 24, DL, Sep 18, 20, 25, 27,
29, Oct 2, 6, 12, 13, 15, 16, 18, 24, 25, 26, 30, Nov 5, 6, 7, 13, 15; 1782:
DL, Jan 19, 21, 22, Feb 25, Apr 18, May 3, 10, HAY, Jun 4, 6, 10, 15, Jul 5,
30, Aug 5, 8, 13, 15, 16, DL, Sep 17, 18, 24, 26, Oct 15, 18, 29, Nov 1, 5,
22, 30, Dec 7, 11; 1783: DL, Jan 10, 15, 24, 29, Feb 12, Mar 3, 6, 20, 24,
Apr 28, 29, May 5, 12, 16, HAY, 31, Jun 4, 9, 10, Jul 5, Aug 22, 27, 29, DL,
Sep 16, 20, 30, Oct 2, 11, 14, 20, 22, 24, Nov 12, 13, 18, 20, 21, 27, 28;
1784: DL, Jan 3, 10, 16, 28, Feb 14, Apr 1, 16, 19, May 5, 10, HAY, 29, Jun
1, 2, 4, 10, 19, 25, Aug 19, 20, DL, Sep 16, 18, 21, 25, 28, 30, Oct 11, 12,
14, 18, 23, Nov 4, 9, 13, 22, 23, 25, Dec 11, 22, 28; 1785: DL, Jan 22, Feb
2, 21, Mar 30, Apr 11, 15, 18, 20, 26, 27, May 9, 11, 19, 26, HAY, 28, 31,
Jun 2, 13, 16, 17, 21, 24, 29, 30, Jul 21, 23, 26, 29, Aug 6, 16, 26, Sep 2,
DL, 20, 22, 24, 27, 29, Oct 1, 4, 13, 17, 25, 31, Nov 1, 17, 18, 26, Dec 30;
1786: DL, Jan 4, 9, 14, Feb 18, Mar 27, 28, Apr 4, 6, 26, May 17, 25, HAY,
Jun 9, 10, 12, 21, 23, 26, 28, 29, Jul 3, 7, 12, 24, 25, Aug 10, 17, Sep 9,
DL, 16, 19, 23, 26, 28, 30, Oct 3, 7, 9, 10, 25, 26, 28, Nov 15, 18, Dec 5,
11, 26, 28; 1787: DL, Jan 13, 24, Apr 23, May 3, 16, 21, 23, 31, HAY, Jun 14,
16, 20, 22, 23, 25, 27, 28, Jul 25, Aug 1, 4, 17, DL, Sep 18, 20, 22, 25, Oct
2, 9, 13, 15, 20, 24, 26, 30, Nov 27, Dec 7, 8, 28; 1788: DL, Jan 2, 5, Feb
7, 25, Mar 13, Apr 10, 11, 14, 30, May 6, 7, 21, 23, HAY, Jun 14, 16, 19, 20,
23, Jul 7, 14, Aug 9, 15, 25, Sep 3, DL, 23, 25, 27, 30, Oct 4, 7, 9, 11, 22,
25, Nov 5, 12, 25, 28; 1789: DL, Jan 1, 10, 26, Feb 7, 16, 21, Apr 30, May 5,
27, 28, HAY, Jun 19, 25, 26, 27, 29, 30, Jul 4, 6, 9, 11, Aug 10, 11, 27, DL,
Sep 12, 15, HAY, 15, DL, 19, 26, 29, Oct 1, 3, 13, 20, Nov 4, 24, 27, Dec 1;
1790: DL, Feb 10, 11, 15, 18, Mar 22, Apr 12, 14, 20, 29, HAY, Jun 14, 15,
16, 17, 19, 28, Jul 5, 22, Aug 10, 12, 13, 20, DL, Sep 11, 16, Oct 7, 11, 12,
HAY, 13, DL, 14, 18, 23, 25, 27, Nov 10, 17, Dec 3; 1791: DL, Jan 5, 25, Feb
22, Apr 28, May 10, 19, HAY, Jun 6, 8, 10, 17, 23, 30, Jul 9, 22, 26,
DLKING'S, Sep 22, 27, Oct 3, 10, 13, 25, 31, Nov 1, 2, 5, 9, 10, 22, 29, 30,
Dec 2; 1792: DLKING'S, Feb 8, Mar 26, 29, 31, Apr 12, May 17, 29, HAY, Jun
15, 18, 19, 20, 27, Jul 3, 7, 16, 23, Aug 9, 17, Sep 6, DL, 15, 18, 25, 27,
Oct 4, 9, 16, 20, 27, 31, Dec 3, 10, 13, 27, 28; 1793: DL, Jan 5, 9, 21, Feb
21, 23, Mar 7, 9, 11, 19, May 22, Jun 5, HAY, 11, 12, 13, Jul 5, 15, Sep 21,
24, Oct 4, 24, 29, Nov 19, Dec 16, 19; 1794: HAY, Feb 22, DL, May 1, 6, 30,
Jun 10, 12, 17, 19, 25, 26, HAY, Jul 9, 10, 11, 17, 18, 22, 29, Aug 4, 13,
Sep 17, DL, 18, 20, 23, 30, Oct 18, Nov 7, 12, 19
--Jewish Education (interlude), 1780: DL, Apr 17; 1782: DL, Apr 18; 1784: DL,
Apr 19; 1786: DL, Apr 26; 1788: DL, Apr 14; 1789: DL, May 5
--Lesson for Lawyers, A (interlude), 1789: DL, May 5
--Mordecai's Beard (interlude), 1790: DL, Apr 20; 1791: DL, Apr 28
--St Giles's Scrutiny, The; or, The Cries of London in a New Style (interlude),
1785: DL, Apr 11
--Swindlers, The, 1774: DL, Apr 25; 1792: DLKING'S, Apr 12
Baddeley, Robert and Sophia (actors), 1765: DL, May 7; 1766: DL, Apr 29; 1767:
DL, Jan 24; 1768: DL, Apr 15; 1769: DL, Apr 5
Baddeley, Sophia, Mrs Robert (actor, singer), 1764: DL, Sep 27; 1765: DL, Apr
27, May 7; 1766: DL, Jan 13, Mar 17, Apr 29, Sep 23, Dec 26; 1767: DL, Jan 2,
Feb 20, Mar 7, Apr 23, 24, May 4, 9, 18, 28, Sep 15, 21, 22, Oct 9, 10, 22,
28, Dec 4, 9; 1768: DL, Jan 23, Mar 24, Apr 11, 12, Sep 17, 24, 27, 30, Oct
1, HAY, 7, DL, 8, 10, 13, 14, 20, Nov 16; 1769: DL, Jan 27, Feb 4, 25, Mar
13, 16, 29, 31, Apr 3, 4, 11, CG, 13, 22, 28, DL, May 1, 9, 15, 23, HAY, Aug
31, DL, Sep 16, 19, 26, 28, 30, Oct 2, 4, 5, 9, 11, 13, 14, 18, Nov 1, 14,

15, 29, Dec 4, 8, 18, 28, 30; 1770: DL, Jan 16, Feb 7, 8, Mar 3, 22, 26, 29,
   Apr 5, 18, May 8, RANELAGH, Jul 20, DL, Sep 25, 27, Oct 2, 3, 5, 9, 13, 19,
   22, 24, 26, Nov 3, 6, 12, 24, Dec 8, 11, 13; 1771: DL, Jan 19, Mar 4, 7, 11,
   12, 16, Apr 8, 10, 12, 26, May 11, 14, 24, MARLY, Jul 18; 1772: DL, Mar 18,
   23; 1774: DL, Mar 26, May 9, Sep 24, Oct 1, 8, 14, 15, 28, Nov 5, 7, Dec 7;
   1775: DL, Jan 6, 11, Feb 1, 23, Apr 20, 24, 25, 26, May 1, 13; 1776: DL, Sep
   21, 26, Oct 1, 5, 9, 10, 12, 18, 23, 30, Nov 19, Dec 5; 1777: DL, Jan 16, 31,
   Mar 13, 20, 31, Oct 18, 23, 29, Nov 8, 11, Dec 15; 1778: DL, Jan 2, 8, 17,
   Feb 19, Mar 12, 30, Apr 11, 25, May 1, Oct 3, 13, 21, 23, 28, 29, 31, Nov 10,
   20, 28, 30, Dec 15, 23; 1779: DL, Jan 29, Oct 21, 23, 25, 26, 30, Nov 6, 15,
   19, 27, Dec 4, 18; 1780: DL, Jan 24, Feb 22, Apr 3, 21, Sep 16, 28, Oct 3, 5,
   Nov 2, 3, 11, 22, Dec 2, 16; 1781: DL, Mar 1
Baden, Prince Lewis of (German visitor), 1694: DG, Jan 10, YB, 25
Badinage Champetre (dance), 1725: DL, Nov 19, 20, 22, 24, 25, Dec 1, 2, 6, 13,
   17, 21; 1726: DL, Jan 8, 20, Nov 15, Dec 7; 1727: DL, Mar 23, Apr 14, Oct 12,
   17; 1728: DL, Feb 27, May 6, Sep 26, Oct 10; 1730: DL, Apr 8; 1732: GF, Jan
   15; 1734: DL, Feb 13, DL/LIF, Apr 1, LIF, 15, DL/HAY, 27, BFHBH, Aug 24;
   1737: BF, Aug 23; 1744: MFMCB, May 1
Badinage de Provence (dance), 1735: DL, Oct 22, Nov 8, 15, 17, 19, 22, 29, Dec
   3, 8, 17, 22, 29; 1736: DL, Jan 2, 3, Feb 9, 12, May 12; 1738: CG, Mar 20,
   DL, Dec 16, 18; 1739: CG, Oct 15, 27, 31, Nov 6, 7, 8, 14, 15, 20, 21, Dec 1,
   3, 6, 14, 18
Badinage, La (dance), 1759: CG, Apr 27
Badine (dance), 1733: DL, Oct 12, 15, 17, 19, Nov 21, Dec 1; 1734: DL, Mar 7,
   DL/LIF, 11, Apr 1
Badini, Carlo Francesco (librettist), 1769: KING'S, Apr 8; 1770: KING'S, May
   19; 1771: KING'S, Feb 23, Nov 23; 1772: KING'S, Jan 14; 1773: KING'S, Oct 23;
   1776: KING'S, Feb 29; 1779: KING'S, May 15; 1780: KING'S, May 9; 1782:
   KING'S, Apr 9, Dec 19; 1786: KING'S, Feb 14, May 20, Dec 23; 1787: KING'S,
   May 1; 1789: KING'S, Jun 2; 1791: KING'S, Jun 17
Badouin. See Baudouin.
Baer (musician), 1774: KING'S, Feb 10
Bagatelle (dance), 1733: DL/HAY, Oct 27, Nov 12, HAY, 19, DL/HAY, 23, 28, Dec
   1, 3, HAY, 13, DL/HAY, 20, 31; 1734: DL/HAY, Jan 1, 2, 10, Feb 6, Mar 9, Apr
   27; 1773: KING'S, Nov 20, 23, 30, Dec 7; 1774: KING'S, Jan 11, Apr 9, May 5,
   17
Bagg (doorkeeper), 1768: CG, Jun 3; 1769: CG, May 19
Baggs, Zachary (treasurer), 1702: DL, Oct 31; 1703: DL, Oct 16; 1704: DL, Jun
   27; 1705: DL, Jun 19; 1707: DL, Apr 14; 1708: DL, Oct 7; 1709: DL, Feb 24,
   Mar 26, 31, Apr 7; 1710: DL, Mar 9
Bagley (house servant), 1794: CG, Jun 16; 1796: CG, May 21; 1797: CG, May 25;
   1798: CG, May 19; 1799: CG, Jun 8; 1800: CG, Jun 11
Bagnio Lane, 1736: CG, Apr 28
Bagnolesi, Anna (singer), 1731: KING'S, Dec 7; 1732: KING'S, Jan 15, Feb 15,
   Mar 25, May 23, Jun 10
Bagpipe Song (song), 1731: LIF, Apr 29
Baguette de Vulcain, La. See Regnard, Jean Francois.
Baguette Enchantee, La (play, anon), 1724: HAY, Dec 18
Baildon, Thomas (singer, composer), 1745: DL, Apr 3; 1751: CG, Apr 24; 1754:
   CHAPEL, May 15; 1757: SOHO, Feb 1; 1758: CG, Mar 3, CHAPEL, Apr 27; 1762: CG,
   Dec 8; 1763: CG, Oct 22
Baildon Jr, Thomas (singer, composer), 1754: CHAPEL, May 15
Bailey, Abraham
--Spightful Sister, The, 1666: NONE, Sep 0
Bailey, Mrs William (actor), 1775: HAY, Oct 30; 1778: HAY, Mar 23, Apr 9, 29,
   CHR, Jun 8, 9, 18, 19, 22, 24, 26
Bailey (Bailie, Bayle), Samuel (actor), 1695: LIF, Dec 0; 1696: LIF, Mar 0, Jun
   0, Dec 0; 1697: LIF, Feb 20, Jun 0; 1698: LIF, Jan 0, Mar 0, Jun 0; 1700:
   LIF, Jan 9, Feb 0, Apr 0, Dec 0; 1701: LIF, Jan 0, Apr 0, Dec 0; 1702: LIF,
   Dec 31; 1703: LIF, May 0
Bailey, William (actor), 1769: HAY, Sep 19; 1775: HAY, Oct 30; 1778: HAY, Jan
   26, Feb 9, Mar 23, 24, 31, Apr 9, 29, CHR, May 25, 27, 29, Jun 1, 3, 8, 9,
   10, 15, 18, 19, 22, 24, 26; 1782: HAY, Nov 25; 1783: HAY, Sep 17
Baillie, Joanna, 1800: DL, Apr 29
--De Montfort, 1800: DL, Apr 29, 30, May 2, 3, 5, 6, 7, 9
Baily, Mrs (actor), 1743: JS, Jan 5; 1744: HAY, Sep 25, 27, Oct 4; 1746: DL,
   Aug 6, 8
Baily, 1735: CG/LIF, Mar 25
Baini, Cecilia (singer), 1763: KING'S, Nov 26; 1764: KING'S, Feb 21
Bains de la Porte de St Bernard, Les. See Boisfranc.
Bairam Feast Dance (dance), 1710: DL, Apr 25
Baker (actor), 1776: DL, Sep 28, Oct 18, Nov 28; 1777: DL, Jan 1, Feb 25, Apr

17, May 8, CHR, Jun 20, 23, 25, 30, Jul 2, 21
Baker (actor, singer, dancer), 1730: LIF, May 14, 21, 25; 1732: TC, Aug 4, HAY,
    Nov 16; 1733: HAY, Feb 28, DL, Dec 31; 1740: BFH, Aug 23; 1741: DL, May 9
Baker (French horn player), 1747: GF, Mar 24
Baker (house servant), 1760: CG, Sep 22
Baker (musician), 1766: DL, Oct 7
Baker (pit doorkeeper), 1742: DL, May 17; 1743: DL, May 16; 1744: DL, May 22;
    1745: DL, May 6
Baker, Benjamin (kettle drummer), 1730: DL, May 13, LIF, 14; 1732: DL, May 3,
    LIF, 9, 18; 1733: LIF/CG, Mar 30, May 7, 24, CG, Aug 9; 1734: CG, May 14, MR,
    Dec 13; 1735: CG/LIF, Mar 15, May 12, 27; 1736: MR, Feb 11, CG, May 11, 17,
    Jun 4; 1737: DL, May 4, CG, 10, 31
Baker, Charles (gallery office-keeper), 1752: DL, May 2; 1753: DL, May 17;
    1754: DL, May 21; 1755: DL, May 15; 1756: DL, May 18; 1757: DL, May 17; 1758:
    DL, May 16
Baker, Eliza, Mrs David Lionel Erskine (actor), 1762: DL, Apr 21, CG, Oct 6,
    19; 1763: CG, Jan 8, 14, Apr 26, 29, May 13, 17, Sep 30; 1764: CG, Feb 9, May
    9, Sep 28, Oct 3, Nov 30, Dec 7, 20, 21
Baker, Elizabeth, Mrs Thomas Sr (actor), 1761: CG, Oct 8; 1765: CG, Jan 4, 5,
    8, 15, 21, Feb 15, 19, Mar 12, 14, 16, Apr 9, 10, 19, 24, 29, May 6, 16, Sep
    27, Oct 3, 5, 7, 8, 9, 12, 14, 15, 19, 22, Nov 20, Dec 12, 20, 23, 26; 1766:
    CG, Feb 5, Mar 15, Apr 15, 28, May 8, 13, Oct 10, 14, 15, 18, 21, 22, 23, 25,
    28, Nov 4, 18, 21, Dec 3, 9, 20, 31; 1767: CG, Jan 29, Feb 14, Mar 24, Apr 6,
    21, May 4, 19, 21, Sep 17, 18, 19, 25, Oct 5, 6, 8, 9, 13, 17, 27, Nov 13,
    18, 19, 21, 26; 1768: CG, Jan 6, 18, 20, Feb 1, 25, Mar 15, Apr 19, 26, May
    3, 5, 13, 24, 26, Sep 19, 20, 21, 24, 26, 27, 29, 30, Oct 4, 5, 7, 10, 17,
    22, 24, Nov 18, 26, Dec 12, 26; 1769: CG, Jan 14, 19, Feb 13, 20, Mar 16, 29,
    30, Apr 7, 10, 11, 15, 18, Sep 18, 20, 27, 29, Oct 2, 6, 7, 14, 23, 27, Nov
    4, 11, 24, Dec 15, 22, 30; 1770: CG, Jan 3, 24, 27, Feb 23, 24, Mar 27, 29,
    Apr 7, 25, 27, May 1, 9, 17, HAY, Sep 20, CG, 24, 26, 28, Oct 1, 2, 5, 8, 15,
    Nov 8, 12, Dec 13, 17, 21; 1771: CG, Jan 15, 25, 26, Mar 12, 14, Apr 3, 5, 6,
    12, 18, 19, 22, 30, May 1, 3, 30, Sep 25, 30, Oct 2, 4, 22, 25, 28, 30, Nov
    1, 7, 8, 11, 12, 16, 19, Dec 9; 1772: CG, Jan 1, 8, 15, 27, 31, Mar 23, 30,
    Apr 4, 7, 21, 23, May 2, 22, 26, 27, Sep 21, 25, 30, Oct 14, 17, 30, Nov 2,
    4, 6, 14, 19, 21, Dec 26; 1773: CG, Jan 14, 16, 21, 23, Feb 6, 19, Mar 22,
    27, Apr 3, 13, 17, 23, 30, May 3, 11, 12, 22, 27, Sep 20, 22, 24, 29, Oct 1,
    4, 5, 6, 7, 8, 15, 16, 21, 23, 27, 30, Nov 11, 18, 23, 25, 26, Dec 1, 3, 7,
    13; 1774: CG, Jan 7, Feb 7, 11, Mar 12, 19, 26, HAY, Apr 4, CG, 5, 22, May 4,
    10, 12, Sep 19, 23, 28, Oct 3, 5, 11, 13, 15, 19, 20, 21, Nov 15, 19, 29;
    1775: CG, Jan 10, Apr 1, 4, 18, May 9, 11, 12, 15, 18, 19, 20, 26
Baker, Frances (actor), 1677: DL, Jun 0, Oct 0
Baker, Francis (actor), 1685: DLORDG, Jan 20, DG, Jul 0; 1689: DL, Mar 0, Nov
    20; 1690: DL, Oct 0
Baker, Sir George (physician), 1799: KING'S, Apr 6
Baker, Job (kettle drummer), 1727: LIF, May 10; 1729: LIF, May 6; 1730: LIF,
    Apr 2, May 9; 1731: GF, Mar 23, LIF, May 24, GF, Jun 3; 1732: GF, May 11, DL,
    Jul 7, HAY, 26; 1733: HAY, Feb 28, LIF/CG, Apr 25; 1734: HAY, Nov 14; 1735:
    CG/LIF, Apr 9, LIF, May 21, HAY, Dec 13; 1736: HAY, Jul 29; 1737: CG, Apr 26,
    HAY, May 3, CG, 16; 1742: HAY, Jun 16; 1743: JS, Jan 5, Mar 23; 1744: HAY,
    Feb 15, JS, Mar 2
Baker, Katherine (actor), 1677: DL, Mar 0, 17, Jun 0, Oct 0; 1678: DL, Mar 0;
    1683: DG, May 31; 1700: DL, Mar 0, Jul 9, Oct 0; 1701: DL, May 12, 31; 1705:
    LIF, Aug 1, LIF/QUEN, Oct 30, QUEEN'S, Dec 27; 1706: QUEEN'S, Feb 11, 21, Apr
    30, Jun 0; 1707: QUEEN'S, Jul 26; 1708: DL, Dec 20; 1709: DL, Mar 4, 17, May
    31, QUEEN'S, Oct 17; 1710: QUEEN'S, May 1, GR, Jun 24, Jul 8, 10, 12, 15, 20,
    Aug 3, 5, 10, 12, 19, 24, 26, 28, 29, 31, Sep 9; 1713: DL, Jun 19, Nov 25;
    1714: DL, Jun 4; 1715: DL, Feb 23, May 17, Jul 1, Aug 9, Dec 6; 1716: DL, Feb
    3, May 14, Jul 12; 1717: DL, Feb 25, May 11, 14, 25, Jun 24; 1718: DL, Feb
    19, May 14, 22, Jul 29, Aug 12; 1719: DL, Jan 16, Feb 14, May 5, Jun 9, 26;
    1720: DL, Jan 13, Apr 21, May 5, Nov 16; 1721: DL, Jan 11, Mar 23, May 5, Jul
    28, Aug 1, 4, Oct 6, 9, 18, Nov 17, 25, 29, 30, Dec 4; 1722: DL, Jan 9, Mar
    27, Apr 4, May 8, 15, Sep 27, Oct 24; 1723: DL, May 6, 16, Jun 4, Oct 3, Nov
    6; 1724: DL, Jan 8, Apr 10, 18, 28, 29, May 1, 22, Sep 29, Oct 28, 29; 1725:
    DL, Jan 4, 27, Apr 22, 30, May 8, Sep 14, 16, Oct 2, 12, 14, 23, 27, Nov 2,
    8, 27; 1726: DL, Apr 23, 26, May 11, 23, Sep 20, 29, Oct 27, Dec 17; 1727:
    DL, Apr 6, May 2, 3, 19, 26, Nov 21; 1728: DL, May 20; 1729: DL, Jan 6
Baker, L (author), 1678: DG, Mar 0
Baker, Miss (actor), 1779: HAY, Mar 15
Baker, Miss (actor, dancer), 1746: GF, Oct 27, Nov 13, 24, Dec 15; 1747: GF,
    Feb 10, 13, 16, 20, Mar 26; 1749: CG, Mar 9, DL, Oct 11, 24, Nov 9, 27, 29,
    30, Dec 2, 23, 28; 1750: DL, Jan 1, 4, 26, Feb 21, Mar 10, 13, 17, 27, 31,
    Apr 5; 1754: CG, Feb 12; 1759: DL, Sep 22, Oct 6, 16, 17, Nov 17, 24, Dec 31;

1760: DL, Oct 2, 7, 11, 14, Nov 17, Dec 3, 11, 13; 1761: DL, Jan 24, Feb 12,
Mar 7, Apr 3, 18, Sep 10, 17, 19, 25, 26, Oct 7, 10, 15, 20, 22, 26, Nov 3,
9, Dec 28; 1762: DL, Jan 15, Feb 3, 19, Mar 1, 30, Apr 24, 26, 30, May 10,
14, 25, 26, Sep 25, Oct 1, 5, 15, 22, 23, Nov 5, 23; 1763: DL, Jan 3, Feb 24,
Mar 26, Apr 5, 25, May 17, Sep 22, Oct 4, 6, 28, 31, Nov 10, 12, 15, 19, Dec
1, 17, 26; 1764: DL, Jan 23, Feb 16, 24, Mar 8, Apr 3, 5, 12, May 4, Sep 15,
25, 29, Oct 4, 6, 11, 13, 20, Nov 2, 13, 20, 28, Dec 13, 26; 1765: DL, Jan
18, 22, Feb 13, 15, Mar 2, Apr 13, 20, 27, May 1, 15, Sep 14, 24, 26, Oct 4,
5, 8, CG, Nov 13, DL, 14, 16, Dec 12; 1766: DL, Jan 6, 23, Feb 3, 7, Mar 22,
Apr 12, 15, 19, Sep 25; 1767: DL, Apr 4
Baker, Mrs (actor), 1753: CG, Nov 2, 3, 8, 22, 26; 1754: CG, Jan 10, Mar 26,
Apr 19, 20, 24, May 1, 7, 13, 15, DL, Jul 2, CG, Sep 30, Oct 14, 15, 16, 28,
Nov 7, 9, 27, 28, Dec 30; 1755: CG, Jan 8, 14, Feb 4, Mar 22, Apr 25, May 15,
Oct 8, 10, 11, 21, 22, 23, 24, 27, 31, Nov 7, 14, 22, 26, Dec 5, 11, 12;
1756: CG, Jan 15, Feb 9, Mar 25, Apr 6, 29, May 1, 10, Sep 20, 22, Oct 13,
14, 16, 18, 25, Nov 2, 16, 19, 27, 29, Dec 1; 1757: CG, Jan 5, 8, Feb 19, 21,
May 2, 4, 16, 24, Sep 21, 23, Oct 13, 15, 19, 28, 31, Nov 14, Dec 6, 9, 14,
20; 1758: CG, Mar 9, Apr 7, 21, Sep 25, Oct 2, 6, 16, 26, 30, Nov 3, 14, 16;
1759: CG, Jan 3, 4, Mar 5, 19, 20, 26, Apr 21, 27, 30, May 3, 8, DL, 17, CG,
23, Sep 26, Oct 1, DL, 2, CG, 5, 10, 11, Nov 23, 30, Dec 7, 8; 1760: CG, Jan
14, Feb 14, 21, Mar 20, 24, 25, Apr 28, 29, Sep 22, Oct 10
Baker, Mrs (actor), 1779: HAY, Oct 18, Dec 27; 1780: HAY, Jan 3, Apr 5, DL, May
10, HAY, Nov 13
Baker, Mrs (beneficiary), 1761: DL, May 14
Baker, Richard (author)
--Madhouse, The, 1737: LIF, Apr 22, 25
Baker, Richard (singer, actor), 1778: HAY, Jun 8, Sep 7; 1779: HAY, Mar 8, Aug
13, 27
Baker, Thomas (dramatist), 1701: DL, Mar 1; 1703: DL, Jan 27; 1705: DL, Oct 30;
1708: DL, Dec 14; 1709: DL, May 12; 1747: DL, Apr 20; 1748: CG, Mar 8; 1780:
CII, Mar 17; 1782: HAY, Aug 13
--Fine Lady's Airs, The; or, An Equipage of Lovers, 1708: DL, Dec 14, 15, 16,
17; 1709: GR, Jun 6; 1747: DL, Apr 20, 22
--Hampstead Heath, 1705: DL, Oct 30, 31, Nov 1
--Humours of the Age, The, 1701: DL, Mar 1, 13; 1703: DL, Jun 30
--Tunbridge Walks; or, The Yeoman of Kent, 1703: DL, Jan 27, Feb 12, Jun 16,
30, Jul 6, Oct 7, 25, Nov 22, Dec 28; 1704: DL, Jan 28, Feb 26, May 19, Sep
14, Nov 20; 1705: DL, Feb 15, May 24, Sep 27; 1706: DL, Jan 3; 1707: DL, Apr
3, 26, Oct 23, Dec 12; 1710: QUEEN'S, May 29, 31, GR, Jul 3, DL, Dec 22;
1711: GR, Aug 25; 1715: LIF, Mar 7; 1718: LIF, Aug 6, RI, 16; 1719: LIF, Jun
25, Jul 1, Oct 26; 1720: LIF, Mar 8; 1721: LIF, Feb 15; 1723: HA, Jul 23, DT,
Nov 1, KAT, Dec 4, CT, 10, AVT, 31; 1724: HT, Mar 13, PY, Apr 20; 1726: LIF,
Jul 5, 8, 12, Aug 9; 1727: LIF, May 4, Jun 14; 1728: LIF, Jul 2; 1729: LIF,
Apr 19, GF, Nov 6, 22, FLR, 29, GF, 29; 1730: GF, Jan 7, HAY, Nov 16; 1731:
GF, May 17, Oct 27, Nov 25; 1732: HAY, Mar 8, LIF/CG, Nov 8, Dec 26; 1733:
LIF/CG, Mar 26, 27; 1734: CG, Feb 4, DL, 18, 19, GF, May 23, CG/LIF, Nov 7;
1735: GF, May 8; 1736: LIF, Dec 17; 1737: LIF, Feb 7; 1738: CG, Jul 11, DL,
Dec 9, 13, 29; 1740: GF, Dec 5; 1743: JS, Apr 15; 1746: GF, Jan 17; 1747: DL,
Apr 20; 1748: CG, Mar 8, 10, 12, 22; 1749: SOU, Oct 9, BHB, 14, NWC, Nov 27;
1764: DL, Mar 24, May 7; 1782: HAY, Aug 13
Baker Jr, Thomas (actor, singer), 1785: CG, May 7; 1787: HAY, Mar 12, May 18,
25; 1789: HAY, Feb 23, DL, Dec 10; 1791: HAY, Sep 26, Oct 24, Dec 12, 26;
1792: HAY, Feb 6, 20, Dec 26; 1794: HAMM, Mar 24, HAY, Jun 2; 1796: HAY, Feb
22; 1797: HAY, Jan 23, 26, May 10, CG, Jun 21
Baker Sr, Thomas (actor, singer, dancer), 1745: DL, Apr 3, GF, Dec 4; 1746: GF,
Jan 13, Oct 29, Nov 4, 14, 19, Dec 5, 17; 1747: GF, Jan 5, 9, 16; 1748: CG,
Oct 27, Dec 10; 1749: CG, Feb 2, Mar 28, Oct 12, Nov 3, 4, 8, 23; 1750: CG,
Feb 24, Mar 27, Apr 26, Oct 29, Nov 8, 22, 29, Dec 26; 1751: CG, May 3, Sep
30, Nov 11, Dec 4, 9; 1752: CG, Feb 11, Mar 17, 30, Oct 10, 21, 26, 30, Dec
7, 28; 1753: CG, Jan 12, May 2, Oct 10, Dec 15; 1754: CG, Feb 5, Apr 20, May
2, Nov 5, 16, 20, Dec 30; 1755: CG, Apr 2, 9, Oct 20, 22, Nov 17, Dec 3;
1756: CG, Apr 5, 6, May 6, Oct 4, 6, 21, Dec 3, 10; 1757: CG, Mar 21, Apr 22,
23, 27, 30, May 11, 18, 25, Oct 12, Nov 4, 5, Dec 7, 10; 1758: CG, Feb 1, Mar
13, 29, Apr 24, Oct 6, Nov 1, 23; 1759: CG, Feb 1, Mar 19, Apr 7, 25, Oct 1,
10, Nov 5, 30, Dec 10; 1760: CG, Jan 16, 18, 31, Feb 14, Apr 8, 17, Sep 24,
29, Oct 8, 15, 20, Nov 18, Dec 11; 1761: CG, Apr 2, 27, Sep 7, 16, 25, 26,
Oct 9, 13; 1762: CG, Jan 28, May 11, Sep 22, 29, Oct 4, 8, 16, 19, Nov 1, 15,
Dec 8, 10; 1763: CG, Jan 24, 26, Sep 21, 23, Oct 3, 11, 14, Nov 10, 15, 22,
26, 30, Dec 28; 1764: CG, Jan 14, Feb 22, May 21, Sep 21, Oct 1, 17, 18, 26,
Nov 3, 5, 7, 15, 16, Dec 26; 1765: CG, Jan 31, Feb 15, 18, May 11, Sep 20,
23, DL, Oct 1, CG, 3, 7, 8, 9, 12, 14, 15, 22, 28, Nov 12, 20, 22, Dec 6, 9;
1766: CG, May 1, 5, Sep 22, Oct 8, 10, 21, 25, Nov 18, 21, Dec 20, 29; 1767:

CG, Jan 28, 29, Feb 14, 28, Mar 21, May 23, Sep 14, 18, 19, Oct 5, 9, 13, 17, 20, 23, 27, 30, Nov 4, 16, 18, 27; 1768: CG, Jan 4, 6, 20, Mar 22, Sep 26, 30, Oct 5, 7, 17, Nov 18; 1769: CG, May 9, 15, Sep 20, 29, Oct 6, Nov 4, 17; 1770: CG, Jan 3, 5, Feb 24, Mar 29, Sep 26, Oct 5, 8, 15, Nov 12, HAY, Dec 10, CG, 26; 1771: CG, Jan 1, 8, 11, Feb 21, Mar 14, Apr 6, 30, May 30, Sep 25, Oct 15, 25, Nov 9, 11, 12, Dec 11; 1772: CG, Jan 27, Feb 1, 17, 25, Mar 24, May 20, Oct 16, Nov 2, 28, 30, Dec 26; 1773: CG, Feb 6, 12, 13, Mar 22, Apr 3, 20, Sep 24, 29, Oct 16, 23, Nov 27, Dec 13, 16; 1774: CG, Jan 3, Feb 11, Mar 26, Apr 11, 22, 30, Sep 23, Oct 5, 11, 13, 19, 22, Nov 1; 1775: CG, Jan 21, Apr 1, May 17, HAY, Sep 18, CG, 22, 25, Oct 16, 19, 20, 31, Nov 13, 21, Dec 9, 26; 1776: CG, Jan 3, Feb 12, Mar 16, 25, Apr 9, 16, May 22, HAY, Sep 18, CG, Oct 7, DL, 18, CG, 25, Nov 9, 13, 14, Dec 2, 23, 26; 1777: CG, Jan 6, Mar 3, 31, Apr 23, Sep 29, Oct 1, 17, 29, Nov 25; 1778: CG, Jan 20, 29, Feb 23, Mar 30, May 6, 11, 22, Sep 18, Oct 14, 17, 26; 1779: CG, Mar 27, Apr 5, May 6, 19, Sep 20, 24, Oct 6, 18, 20, Nov 8, 13, 30, Dec 17; 1780: CG, Feb 1, Mar 27, Apr 27, May 6, Sep 25, Oct 2, 13, 19, 23, Nov 1, 15, Dec 27; 1781: CG, Feb 13, May 7, 16, Sep 24, Oct 19, 20, 31, Nov 2, 12, Dec 8, 17; 1782: CG, Mar 19, Apr 30, May 6, 11, 17, 27; 1784: CG, Oct 12, 18, 25, Nov 8, 19
Baker's Coffee House, 1754: CG, Jan 29
Bakewell, Mrs (actor), 1787: HAY, Apr 30
Baks (house servant), 1773: CG, Apr 15, May 24
Baks, Mrs (supernumerary), 1773: CG, Feb 27, May 21
Bal Masquer (dance), 1774: KING'S, Dec 13, 17; 1775: KING'S, Jan 17, 31, Feb 21, 28, Apr 18
Balatri, Filippo (singer), 1714: KING'S, Nov 16
Balbi, Rossina (dancer), 1754: CG, Nov 4, 19; 1755: CG, Jan 4, Apr 16, 22
Baldassari, Benedetto (singer), 1712: QUEEN'S, Mar 27, Apr 5, 26; 1719: DL, Mar 11, KING'S, 21; 1720: KING'S, Apr 2, 27, May 30; 1721: YB, Jan 9, KING'S, Dec 9; 1722: KING'S, Jan 10, Feb 15, 22, Mar 6, HAY, 16
Baldi (singer), 1726: KING'S, Jan 15, Mar 12, May 5; 1727: KING'S, Jan 7, 31, May 6, Oct 21, Nov 11; 1728: KING'S, Feb 17, Apr 30
Baldwin (actor), 1775: HAY, Feb 2
Baldwin, Mary (singer), 1704: LIF, Jul 10; 1706: QUEEN'S, Mar 7
Baldwin, R (printer), 1751: CG, Nov 16; 1756: DL, Jan 5; 1757: DL, Jan 29; 1781: DL, Nov 27; 1782: DL, Jan 21; 1786: DL, Mar 4
Balelli, Antonio (singer), 1786: KING'S, Dec 23; 1787: KING'S, Mar 1, 8, 15, 29, Apr 17, May 1, Dec 8; 1788: KING'S, Apr 5, May 8; 1789: KING'S, Jan 24, Feb 28, Mar 21, Apr 4, May 28, Jun 2
Baletti (dancer), 1755: DL, Nov 3, 4, 8
Balicourt (Bellicourt), Simon (flutist), 1735: ST, Nov 26; 1736: MR, Feb 11, GF, Apr 27; 1737: CT, Feb 18; 1745: HAY, Feb 14; 1747: CG, Apr 22; 1748: HAY, Dec 9
Ball (actor), 1747: RL, Jan 27
Ball Country Dance (dance), 1745: DL, Oct 12
Ball Dance (dance), 1727: LIF, Apr 27; 1728: LIF, May 6, 15, 20; 1735: CG/LIF, May 9; 1736: CG, May 8; 1737: LIF, Apr 18, CG, 25; 1738: CG, Mar 23, Apr 25; 1739: CG, Mar 26, DL, Apr 24, 25; 1740: CG, Mar 24, Dec 9; 1743: CG, Apr 9, 28; 1746: DL, Apr 3; 1752: CG, Mar 19; 1757: CG, Apr 27; 1761: CG, Apr 22; 1762: CG, Apr 28; 1766: RANELAGH, Jun 20; 1769: MARLY, Aug 10; 1771: DL, Apr 22
Ball Dance and Minuet (dance), 1733: LIF/CG, May 3; 1735: CG/LIF, Apr 17
Ball Dance, Grand (dance), 1737: DL, Mar 14; 1742: DL, Apr 8
Ball Minuet (dance), 1741: DL, Apr 4; 1747: CG, Apr 23; 1748: CG, Apr 20; 1754: CG, May 1
Ball, A; or, The Humours of a Masquerade (entertainment), 1739: TC, Aug 6
Ball, Miss (actor), 1781: HAY, Oct 16
Ball, Mrs (actor, singer), 1789: KHS, Sep 16
Ball, The. See Shirley, James.
Ballad (song), 1710: QUEEN'S, Jul 13; 1728: LIF, Mar 21, 28, YB, Apr 12; 1730: DL, May 18; 1734: CG, May 14; 1741: DL, Dec 10, 14, 15, 16, 17, 18, 19; 1742: DL, Jan 1, 8, 14, 18, 19, 26, 27, Feb 2, 4, 10, 11, 26, Mar 11, 13, 15, 22, 23, 25, Apr 6, 20, 24, 28; 1743: BFHC, Aug 23; 1745: CG, Dec 3, 30; 1746: CG, Feb 7; 1754: DL, Mar 28, Apr 1, CG, 22, DL, May 2, 7, 17; 1756: CG, May 4, 10; 1758: CG, Mar 13; 1759: DL, Mar 29; 1770: HAY, Aug 24; 1793: CG, May 15; 1795: CG, May 1; 1797: CG, May 2; 1798: CG, Apr 24, Jun 6; 1800: DL, Jun 7, HAY, Sep 3
Ballad Dance (dance), 1730: LIF, Dec 3, 5; 1739: CG, Sep 19; 1770: HAY, Dec 10
Ballad Dialogue (song), 1731: LIF, Apr 1, 8, 28, 29, May 12, 14; 1795: CG, Dec 21
Ballad Duetto (song), 1728: LIF, Apr 29, May 2
Ballad of Advice to a Friend (song), 1742: CG, Apr 22

Ballad of Mary Scot (song), 1738: DL, Mar 20, 21, 25, Apr 17
Ballad of Sally (song), 1717: DL, May 20; 1719: LIF, Apr 20
Ballad on a Lady's Twitcher (song), 1721: LIF, Apr 17
Ballard (animal trainer), 1752: HAY, Dec 11
Ballard, Jonathan (treasurer), 1756: CG, May 19; 1757: CG, May 4; 1758: CG, May
    1; 1759: CG, May 7; 1760: CG, May 2, Sep 22; 1761: CG, May 4; 1762: CG, May
    3; 1763: CG, May 6
Ballet d'Amour (dance), 1732: DL, Feb 21; 1736: DL, Feb 9, 10, Mar 23
Ballet d'Amour, Grand (dance), 1731: DL, Dec 22, 27, 28, 30
Ballet Dance between a Soldier, Sailor, Tinker, Tailor and Buxom Joan (dance),
    1737: SF, Sep 7
Ballet de Fleur, Le (dance), 1774: KING'S, Nov 8, 19, Dec 10
Ballet de la Paix Dance en presence de Monseigneur le President de Bordeaux
    (dance), 1659: NONE, Sep 0
Ballet et Musique (dance), 1674: NONE, Jan 5, ATCOURT, Feb 0
Ballet, Grand (dance), 1727: LIF, Apr 21; 1729: LIF, Apr 19; 1734: DL, Oct 17,
    19; 1735: GF/HAY, Jun 2, DL, Nov 17, 19, 20, 22, 25, 26, 27, 28, Dec 3, 4,
    18, HAY, 29; 1736: GF, Mar 29, DL, Apr 6, 29, May 14, 19, 21, 25, Jun 2, Oct
    26, 28, Nov 5, 13; 1737: DL, Mar 5, Apr 30, May 3, Sep 20, 27; 1738: DL, Jan
    13, Feb 20, 21, 25, Mar 2, CG, 7, DL, 13, 16, CG, 18, DL, 21, CG, 21, 25, Apr
    4, 6, 11, DL, 29, May 6, 10, 18, 19, 29, BFH, Aug 23, DL, Oct 12, 19, CG, 23,
    26, Nov 2, DL, 27, Dec 5, CG, 6, DL, 8, 11, 16; 1739: DL, Jan 13, 16, Feb 28,
    Mar 3, 8, 13, CG, 13, DL, 17, CG, 19, DL, 20, 22, CG, 22, 27, DL, Apr 2, CG,
    3, DL, 5, 9, CG, 9, DL, 10, 12, 24, Sep 13, CG, 28, DL, 29, CG, Oct 1, DL,
    11, 13, CG, 15, DL, 19, 22, 23, 26, CG, 27, 31, DL, 31, Nov 1, CG, 1, DL, 3,
    CG, 7, DL, 7, 8, CG, 10, DL, 10, 14, 16, 19, CG, 21, DL, 22, 23, CG, 28, Dec
    1, 8, DL, 8, 10, CG, 12, DL, 12, CG, 13, 15, 18, 19, 21, 22, DL, 22; 1740:
    DL, Jan 8, 11, 12, CG, 25, Feb 2, 6, 7, Mar 10, 20, 27, Apr 9, 14, 16, 18,
    28, May 5, 9, 13, 14, 16, 21, 23, 27, 29, DL, Oct 31, Nov 1, 3, 4, 6, 10, CG,
    13, DL, 17, Dec 10; 1741: DL, Apr 4, 6, 24, 27, 28, May 7, 9; 1742: DL, Feb
    24, 26, Mar 4, CG, Oct 25, Nov 4, 5, 8, 12, 19, 22, 24, 25, 26, Dec 1, 2, 8,
    9, 15; 1743: LIF, Feb 17, CG, 24, 28, LIF, Mar 3, CG, 7, LIF, 8, CG, 14, 24,
    Apr 14, 15, 20, 25, 29; 1744: CG, Apr 4, 9, 17, 23, May 1; 1746: CG, Apr 2,
    DL, Dec 8; 1747: CG, Apr 23, DL, Nov 2, 3, 7, 11, Dec 2, 12; 1752: CG, Mar
    19; 1753: DL, Mar 24, Apr 24; 1764: CG, Mar 20, 22, 26, 27; 1771: KING'S, Dec
    17, 21; 1772: KING'S, Jan 4, 7, 11, 14, May 14, 28, Nov 14, 21; 1773: KING'S,
    Jan 12, 15, 26, Feb 2, 25, Mar 9, 16, 18, 23, Apr 1, 17, 20, 24, 27, 29, May
    1, 3, 22, 25, Jun 3, 5, 12, 19; 1774: KING'S, Mar 26; 1775: KING'S, Jan 17;
    1776: KING'S, Apr 20; 1778: DL, Jan 17, Dec 23; 1779: KING'S, Dec 14, 21;
    1782: HAY, Aug 26, 29, Sep 4, 6, 13, 18, KING'S, Dec 17; 1783: HAY, Jun 30;
    1784: CG, Mar 27, Apr 27; 1785: HAY, Jul 13; 1789: DL, Dec 26
Ballet, Grand, with Chaconne (dance), 1773: KING'S, Apr 19, 20
Ballet, Grand, with Chorus (dance), 1773: KING'S, Jan 26, Feb 13, 20, 27, Mar
    16, Apr 19
Ballet, Grand, with Gavotte (dance), 1773: KING'S, Jun 1
Ballet, Grand, with Pas de Cinq (dance), 1773: KING'S, Mar 9, 16, 30, Apr 3,
    13, 17, 19
Ballet, Grand, with Passacaille and Chaconne (dance), 1773: KING'S, Apr 3, 13,
    19
Ballet, Grand, with Polonaise (dance), 1773: KING'S, Apr 20
Balletino, Sg and Sga (actors), 1754: BFSIY, Sep 3
Ballintine (house servant), 1772: CG, Jan 6
Balmerino, Lord (rebel), 1746: DL, Aug 4
Balmy hope (song), 1794: DL, Apr 4
Balmy sweetness (song), 1791: CG, Mar 25
Balon, Jean (dancer), 1699: LIF, Apr 8, 10, DL, 15, LIF, May 0; 1701: DL, Mar
    25; 1716: LIF, Oct 18
Balthazar (dancer), 1760: HAY, Jun 2, CG, Sep 22, Dec 11; 1761: CG, Mar 9, May
    8; 1762: DL, Apr 24, May 1, 24
Baltimore, Lord. See Calvert, Charles.
Bambaseno. See Bombazino.
Bambridge (Bembridge) (actor), 1731: GF, Nov 8, 18; 1736: BFHC, Aug 23; 1741:
    BFH, Aug 22, SF, Sep 14; 1743: SF, Sep 8; 1745: DL, Apr 27
Bambridge, Mrs (actor), 1731: GF, Oct 11, 13, 18, Dec 17; 1736: BFHC, Aug 23;
    1741: GF, Sep 25, Nov 9, 30, Dec 16, 26; 1742: GF, Jan 5, 23, 27, Mar 15, 27,
    Apr 26, May 12, LIF, Dec 1, 3, 22, 27, 28; 1743: LIF, Jan 7, 10, 14, Feb 2,
    14, 17, Apr 4, 5, 8, 11, HAY, 14, TCD/BFTD, Aug 23, SF, Sep 8; 1744: GF, Dec
    3, 5, 31; 1745: GF, Mar 7, 30, Oct 28, Nov 4, 11, 13, 14, 18, 19, 22, 23, 26,
    27, 28, 29, Dec 2, 6, 9, 11, 13, 16; 1746: GF, Jan 6, 13, 15, 17, 20, Feb 3,
    7, Mar 22, SOU, Sep 16, GF, Nov 18, 19, 20, 21, 26, 28, Dec 1, 3, 5, 9, 10,
    12, 17, 18, 22, 27; 1747: GF, Jan 2, 5, 9, Feb 2, 5, 25, Mar 2; 1748: NWC,
    Apr 4, HAY, May 2, CG, Oct 7, 14, 17, 24, 28, 29, Nov 3, 9, 15, 19, 26, 28,

Dec 1; 1749: CG, Jan 2, 11, 25, Mar 2, 4, 14, 29, Apr 7, 25, Sep 27, 29, Oct
2, 4, 11, 18, 20, 25, 26, 27, 30, Nov 3, 8, 21, 24, Dec 27; 1750: CG, Jan 16,
18, 31, Feb 20, Apr 23, 27, Sep 24, Oct 15, 17, 23, 24, 25, 26, Nov 24, 29,
Dec 4, 21; 1751: CG, Feb 16, Mar 12, 21, Apr 16, 29, May 9, Sep 25, Oct 8,
11, Dec 26; 1752: CG, Jan 1, 10, 18, Mar 30, Apr 28, 30, Sep 20, 22, 29, Oct
11, 23, 31, Nov 7, 9, 28, Dec 13; 1753: CG, Jan 22, Feb 12, May 7, Sep 10,
17, 21, 26, Oct 3, 5, 30, Nov 1, 9; 1754: CG, Mar 26, May 15, Sep 20, Oct 9,
11, 16, 24, 25, Nov 1; 1755: CG, Jan 16; 1760: CG, Sep 22
Bamfield (actor), 1671: LIF, Jun 0
Bamfield (Bamford), Edward (giant), 1767: CG, May 19
Banberigines (dancer), 1754: HAY, Jul 4, Aug 15, Sep 10
Banberry (actor, singer, dancer), 1746: GF, Jan 14, 24, 31, Mar 4, BFYB, Aug 25
Bancraft. See Bencraft, James.
Bancroft, John, 1690: DL, Nov 0; 1692: DL, Nov 8
--Edward III. See Mountfort, William.
--Henry II, 1690: DL, Nov 0; 1692: DL, Nov 8, 9, 10, 11, 12, NONE, 14; 1693:
DL, Jan 16
--Tragedy of Sertorius, The, 1679: DL, Mar 0
Bandettino, Teresa (librettist), 1793: KING'S, Jun 11
Banditti, The; or, A Ladies Distress. See D'Urfey, Thomas.
Banditti, The; or, Love's Labyrinth. See O'Keeffe, John.
Banished Duke, The; or, The Tragedy of Infortunatus (play, anon), 1689: NONE,
Sep 0
Banished General, The; or, The Distrest Lovers (play, anon), 1731: SF/BFMMO,
Aug 26, Sep 8
Banister, James (actor), 1785: HAMM, Jun 17, 27, Jul 2, 6, 8, 25, 26
Banister, Jeffery (violinist, schoolmaster), 1675: NONE, Sep 0
Banister, John (musician), 1663: LIF, Feb 23; 1668: LIF, Mar 26, BRIDGES, May
7, 18; 1669: LIF, Feb 25; 1670: NONE, Sep 0, LIF, 20, BRI/COUR, Dec 0; 1671:
LIF, Jun 0; 1672: DG, Feb 6, ATCOU/DG, Dec 2, WF, 30; 1674: WF, Sep 29; 1675:
WF, Jan 26, ATCOURT, Feb 15, NONE, Sep 0, BANNSTER, Nov 25; 1676: ACADEMY,
Dec 14; 1677: DG, May 12; 1678: EB, Nov 22, 25; 1679: EB, Jan 9; 1684: NONE,
Sep 0
--Musick; or, A Parley of Instruments (entertainment), 1676: ACADEMY, Dec 14
Banister Jr, John (musician), 1698: YB, Jan 10, 17, ROBERTS, Mar 23; 1702: DL,
Jul 7, 11, Oct 23; 1703: DL, Feb 11, YB, Mar 19, DL, Apr 19, Jun 18, YB, Dec
11; 1704: DL, Jan 17, YB, Mar 29, Apr 20, 28, May 18, DL, Dec 15; 1705: DL,
Apr 10; 1707: YB, Apr 18, May 23; 1715: LIF, May 9
Bank (renter), 1774: DL, May 30
Bank Coffee House, 1752: DL, Apr 22; 1787: HAY, Mar 12
Bank Note, The. See Macready, William.
Bank of England, 1798: CG, Feb 9
Bankrupt, The. See Foote, Samuel.
Banks (actor), 1723: HAY, Apr 15
Banks (actor), 1747: GF, Jan 5; 1749: NWLS, Feb 27
Banks (actor), 1789: KHS, Sep 16, WHF, Nov 9, 11
Banks (doorkeeper, supernumerary), 1738: CG, May 16; 1739: CG, May 29; 1740:
CG, May 27; 1741: CG, May 7; 1742: CG, May 11; 1743: CG, May 6; 1744: CG, May
14; 1745: CG, May 15; 1746: CG, May 7; 1747: CG, May 22; 1748: CG, May 6;
1749: CG, May 3; 1750: CG, May 7; 1751: CG, May 14
Banks of Invermay (song), 1777: HAY, Apr 22
Banks of the Tweed (song), 1777: HAY, Apr 22
Banks, John, 1692: NONE, Apr 13; 1693: NONE, Sep 0; 1695: LIF, Dec 0; 1704: DL,
Mar 6; 1722: DL, Jan 6; 1723: DL, May 10; 1766: CG, Apr 1, May 13
--Albion Queens, The; or, The Death of Mary Queen of Scotland, 1704: DL, Mar 6,
7, 9, 11, 13, 16, 21, Nov 22; 1711: DL, Mar 10, 13, Oct 18; 1713: DL, Mar 14,
Dec 10; 1714: DL, Mar 29, Nov 18; 1723: DL, Mar 2, 5; 1726: DL, Nov 19, 21,
24, Dec 26; 1727: DL, Apr 7, Nov 30; 1728: DL, Mar 23, 26, Dec 26; 1730: DL,
Jan 21; 1733: DL, Mar 8, 31; 1734: DL/HAY, Jan 12, 14, 15, Feb 11, DL, Mar 7,
CG/LIF, Sep 30, Oct 2, 4, Nov 19; 1735: DL, Apr 21; 1736: CG, Jan 7, Feb 21,
Oct 30, Nov 30; 1737: CG, Oct 31; 1738: CG, Nov 22; 1739: CG, Jan 1, DL, Apr
30, CG, Nov 28; 1742: CG, Feb 4, 24; 1743: CG, Feb 14, Oct 17; 1750: CG, Apr
5, 17; 1766: CG, May 13, 15, Nov 28; 1767: CG, May 4; 1769: CG, Mar 28, Apr
19, May 17; 1773: CG, Apr 16, May 18; 1779: CG, May 20
--Anna Bullen; or, Virtue Betrayed, 1682: DG, Mar 0, Aug 4; 1691: NONE, Sep 0;
1703: DL, Apr 23, Jun 9, Jul 3, Oct 12; 1704: DL, Jan 13; 1706: DL, Mar 27;
1707: DL/QUEEN, Dec 6, DL, 11; 1711: DL, Dec 3, 4, 27; 1713: DL, Mar 9; 1714:
DL, Jan 26; 1715: DL, Mar 28, Apr 19, Jun 17, Aug 5; 1725: DL, Jan 9, 11, 12,
13, 14, 15, 26, Mar 16, Dec 28; 1726: DL, Mar 22; 1727: DL, Apr 24, Nov 22,
23, 25, Dec 30; 1728: DL, Jan 1, 8; 1729: DL, Feb 25, Nov 22; 1731: DL, Nov
27; 1733: GF, Jan 8, 9, 10, 15, Feb 1, Mar 3, Apr 11, May 11, Sep 24, Dec 17;
1746: JS, Dec 29; 1750: CG, Jan 5, Mar 17, 22; 1758: CG, Apr 10; 1766: CG,

Apr 1, May 3; 1767: CG, May 6
--Cyrus the Great; or, The Tragedy of Love, 1695: LIF, Dec 0, 28
--Destruction of Troy, The, 1678: DG, Nov 0
--Innocent Usurper, The; or, The Death of the Lady Jane Gray, 1692: NONE, Apr 13; 1693: NONE, Sep 0
--Island Queens, The; or, The Death of Mary, Queen of Scotland, 1683: NONE, Sep 0; 1704: DL, Mar 6
--Rival Kings, The; or, The Loves of Oroondates and Statira, 1677: DL, Jun 0
--Unhappy Favourite, The; or, The Earl of Essex, 1681: DL, May 0; 1684: NONE, Sep 0; 1692: DL, Dec 9; 1698: NONE, Sep 0; 1699: DL, Dec 16; 1703: DL, Jan 9, Nov 2, Dec 10; 1704: DL, Feb 12, May 18, Sep 23, Nov 1; 1705: DL, May 15, Oct 3, Dec 27; 1706: QUEEN'S, Jan 10, May 29, Oct 16, Nov 29; 1707: QUEEN'S, Jan 3, 10, Feb 20, DL/QUEEN, Oct 25, Nov 12, Dec 4, 26; 1708: DL/QUEEN, Jan 22, May 1, DL, Sep 23; 1709: DL, Jan 15, May 10, QUEEN'S, Oct 4, Nov 23, DL, 25, QUEEN'S, Dec 26; 1710: QUEEN'S, Feb 17, May 25, DL, Nov 20, Dec 28; 1711: DL, May 14, Oct 2; 1712: DL, Feb 7, SML, Apr 11, May 21, DL, 29, SML, Jun 4, DL, Nov 1; 1713: DL, Mar 23, Oct 13; 1714: DL, Oct 26; 1715: LIF, Jan 1, 11, Oct 22, Nov 10; 1716: DL, Jan 5, Oct 17, LIF, 18, Nov 27; 1717: LIF, Apr 23, LIF, Nov 16; 1718: LIF, Jan 22, DL, Mar 17, LIF, Dec 6, 27; 1719: LIF, Mar 31, DL, May 13; 1720: LIF, May 25, DL, 30, LIF, Jun 7, DL, Dec 1, LIF, 27; 1721: LIF, Mar 14, DL, May 25, LIF, Oct 20; 1722: LIF, Jan 2, DL, 6, HAY, Feb 26, DL, Mar 12, LIF, Dec 7; 1723: HAY, Jan 4, DL, May 10, LIF, Dec 27; 1724: DL, Mar 14, May 14, Oct 6, Dec 3; 1725: LIF, Feb 9, DL, Mar 9, LIF, Nov 17, DL, 18; 1726: DL, Feb 15, May 12, Dec 15; 1727: DL, Apr 27, LIF, Dec 28; 1728: DL, Mar 11, HAY, Oct 19, LIF, Dec 26; 1729: GF, Nov 12, 26, LIF, Dec 29; 1730: GF, Feb 23, May 20, Jul 3, Oct 14, LIF, 27, GF, Dec 11, DL, 26; 1731: DL, Apr 19, GF, May 22, Dec 20; 1732: GF, Feb 3, Apr 20, Oct 9; 1733: LIF/CG, Jan 1, DL, 25, 31, GF, Oct 3, 11, CG, 23, DL, Nov 13, Dec 29; 1734: DL, Feb 4, GF, Apr 16, Sep 30, CG/LIF, Oct 9, DL, 12; 1735: GF, Jan 1, DL, 8, GF, Feb 13, DL, 25, CG/LIF, May 27, DL, Oct 7, GF, Nov 19, DL, Dec 11; 1736: GF, Feb 7, DL, 28, CG, Jun 14, DL, Nov 13, LIF, Dec 7; 1737: DL, Feb 18, Nov 19; 1738: DL, Oct 30; 1740: DL, Feb 16, Oct 27, GF, Dec 2; 1741: JS, Dec 28; 1742: CG, Feb 15, Mar 2, SOU, Sep 21; 1743: DL, Oct 8, 29; 1744: DL, Feb 1, CG, Dec 26; 1745: GF, Jan 2, 29, Dec 13; 1746: SOU, Sep 16, 17, GF, Dec 1; 1747: SF, Sep 14; 1748: SOU, Jul 18, BHB, Oct 4, SOU, 12; 1749: NWSM, May 16, SFGT, Sep 16, SOUGT, 22, CG, Dec 28; 1750: CG, Feb 10, SFY, Sep 14; 1751: SF, Sep 16; 1752: DL, Apr 20, CG, Dec 27
Banks, Mrs (actor), 1789: KHS, Sep 16, WHF, Nov 9, 11
Banks, Thomas (dancer, actor, scene painter), 1788: DL, Nov 8, 10, 15, 17, Dec 6, 22; 1789: DL, Feb 16, May 22, Sep 26, Oct 1, 20, 31, Nov 13, Dec 17, 22, 26; 1790: DL, Feb 27, Mar 22, May 14, 15, 27, Jun 4, Oct 7, 11, 16, 26, Nov 3, Dec 27; 1791: DL, Jan 10, May 10, 20, DLKING'S, Sep 27, Oct 29, 31, Nov 1, 5, 7, 10, 16, 28, 30, Dec 12; 1792: DLKING'S, Jan 6, 18, 24, 28, Feb 14, 18, Mar 12, 26, 29, Apr 12, 20, 24, 26, May 17, Jun 8, DL, Sep 25, 27, Oct 4, 13, 27, Nov 10, 16, 21, 26, Dec 3, 10, 26, 28; 1793: DL, Mar 9, Apr 3, 8, 17, May 3, Jun 1; 1794: DL, Apr 21, 29, May 1, 6, 8, 16, 22, 30, Jun 9, 11, 27, Sep 23, 27, Oct 7, 21, 27, Nov 8, 12, 18, 19, Dec 3, 5, 9, 20, 23; 1795: DL, Jan 19, 22, 28, Feb 6, 12, 28, Mar 5, 21, May 4, 27, Sep 29, Oct 1, 30, Nov 6, 11, 20, Dec 10, 12, 19, 23; 1796: DL, Jan 18, 23, Feb 27, Mar 12, 19, Apr 2, 11, 15, 18, 25, 27, 30, May 24, Jun 4, 11, 13, Sep 27, Oct 6, 10, 19, 28, Nov 11, Dec 15, 26; 1797: DL, Jan 24, Feb 7, 9, Mar 16, Apr 24; 1799: DL, Jan 19, May 24, Jul 4, 5, Nov 5, Dec 11; 1800: DL, Mar 11, Apr 29
Banks, W (dancer, actor), 1796: DL, Jan 18, Apr 4, Oct 1, 29, Nov 9, Dec 26; 1797: DL, Jun 10; 1798: DL, Jan 16, Feb 20, May 16, Oct 6, Nov 14, Dec 5; 1800: CG, Feb 17
Banks, Widow (beneficiary), 1752: CG, May 7; 1753: CG, May 21
Banks, William (dancer, actor, designer), 1766: CG, May 12, Nov 8, Dec 11; 1767: CG, Jan 1, DL, Apr 2, CG, Oct 5, 9, 17, 19, 20, Nov 19; 1768: CG, Jan 6, Feb 25, Sep 20, 24, Oct 24, Nov 8, 21; 1769: CG, Feb 21, Mar 4, Apr 10, May 19, Oct 23, Nov 4; 1770: CG, Jan 4, Apr 16, May 14, Nov 12, Dec 26; 1771: CG, Jan 1, Feb 21, Apr 22, Oct 15; 1772: CG, Jan 23, 31, Feb 17, 25, Apr 24, May 14, Oct 16, Nov 30; 1773: CG, Feb 15, Apr 24, Oct 6, 28, Nov 25, Dec 16; 1774: CG, Jan 3, Apr 11, 15, Sep 23, Nov 19, Dec 27; 1775: CG, Mar 30, DL, May 27, CG, Oct 13
Banks, William (house servant), 1792: DLKING'S, Jun 13; 1793: DL, May 31; 1795: DL, Jun 4; 1796: DL, Jun 10; 1797: DL, Jun 10
Bannian Day. See Brewer, George.
Bannister, Charles (actor), 1762: HAY, May 1; 1767: HAY, May 29, Jun 5, 8, 17, 22, 26, Jul 2, 6, 8, 10, 22, 31, Aug 5, 14, 21, 25, Sep 9, 12, 18, DL, 22, Oct 23, Nov 6, Dec 12, 19; 1768: DL, Jan 6, HAY, Jun 17, 23, 27, Jul 8, 18, 25, 27, Aug 10, 15, 19, 24, DL, Sep 22, 27, 28, Oct 3, HAY, 7, DL, 18, 31, Nov 17, Dec 17, 21; 1769: DL, Mar 11, 31, Apr 4, 28, HAY, May 15, 19, 26, 29,

Jun 2, 5, 21, Jul 12, Aug 7, 11, 14, 16, 28, 30, 31, Sep 11, 19, DL, 23, Oct
4, 14, 23, Nov 23, 24, 27, 28, Dec 13; 1770: DL, Jan 4, Feb 7, 8, Mar 22, Apr
7, 26, May 7, 8, MARLY, Jun 16, Jul 17, RANELAGH, 20, MARLY, 24, 31, Aug 7,
14, 21, 28, 30, Sep 4, 15, DL, 25, 27, Oct 2, 3, 4, 13, 19, 23, 25, 29, Nov
1, 3, 14, 16, 17, Dec 7, 13; 1771: DL, Jan 18, Mar 7, 12, 16, CG, Apr 5, DL,
12, 13, 16, 26, May 1, 4, 8, 9, MARLY, 23, Jun 4, 27, Jul 18, 27, Aug 3, 8,
HAY, 12, MARLY, 20, 22, 27, 29, Sep 3, 5, 10, 17, DL, Oct 1, 21, 22, 26, Dec
4, 17; 1772: DL, Jan 3, 11, Feb 29, Mar 18, 31, Apr 2, 21, May 2, 12, 18,
HAY, Aug 10, 17, MARLY, 20, HAY, 24, MARLY, 25, 28, Sep 1, 7, HAY, 17, DL,
19, 26, 29, Oct 10, 16, 20, Nov 6, 7, 12, 24, Dec 2; 1773: DL, Jan 9, 19, Feb
1, 10, Apr 14, 20, 23, May 1, 11, 13, 28, HAY, Jun 30, Jul 5, 12, 21, Aug 11,
20, 23, 27, 31, Sep 3, 16, 17, DL, 28, 30, Oct 5, 6, 9, 16, 19, Nov 2, 9, Dec
21, 27; 1774: DL, Jan 19, Mar 19, 24, 26, Apr 8, 9, 12, 18, 19, 27, 29, May
3, 5, 9, 10, HAY, 16, DL, 19, 20, 25, HAY, 30, DL, Jun 2, HAY, 7, 10, Jul 11,
15, MARLY, 28, HAY, Aug 8, MARLY, 18, HAY, 26, 29, Sep 5, 6, 16, 19, DL, 20,
24, 29, HAY, 30, DL, Oct 1, 5, 11, 19, Nov 4, 5, 7, Dec 9; 1775: DL, Feb 1,
Apr 22, 26, May 1, 3, 11, 13, HAY, 26, DL, 27, HAY, 31, Jul 31, Aug 21, 28,
Sep 4, 7, 16, 18, 19, 21, DL, Oct 5, 7, 10, 28, Nov 9, 11, 24, 28, Dec 11,
12, 18; 1776: DL, Feb 15, Apr 9, 12, 22, May 4, HAY, 20, 27, 28, Jun 12, 14,
19, 24, 26, Jul 1, 12, Aug 2, 19, 26, 27, Sep 2, 16, DL, 21, HAY, 23, DL, 24,
28, Oct 5, 10, 18, Nov 7, 9, 25, Dec 5, 28; 1777: DL, Jan 4, 8, Feb 20, Mar
1, 20, Apr 1, 21, 22, 28, May 9, HAY, 28, Jun 9, 19, Jul 3, 7, 15, 18, 24,
Aug 12, 22, 28, 30, Sep 3, 16, 17, 18, DL, 20, 23, Oct 7, 23, 29, Nov 8, 12,
19, Dec 4, 15, 30; 1778: DL, Jan 5, 8, 17, Feb 19, Mar 16, 30, Apr 25, May 1,
14, HAY, 22, Jun 8, 11, 12, 25, Jul 2, 9, 11, Aug 6, 7, 17, 20, 21, 27, Sep
2, 7, DL, 17, 24, 29, Oct 3, 6, 10, 13, 15, 22, Nov 2, Dec 23; 1779: DL, Jan
8, 27, Mar 16, 27, CG, Apr 24, May 6, HAY, Jun 7, 10, 12, 17, Jul 1, 17, Aug
6, 13, 14, 17, 18, 27, Sep 15, 17, DL, Nov 6, 12, 17, 18, 19, 27, Dec 20, 22,
CG, 22, DL, 30, 31; 1780: DL, Jan 3, Feb 28, Apr 3, 4, 11, 14, 21, CG, 22,
DL, 26, 29, HAY, May 30, Jun 3, 5, 13, 15, 24, 28, 29, Jul 8, 15, 27, Aug 10,
12, 17, 24, 29, 31, Sep 2, 8, 11, DL, 16, 23, 28, Oct 3, 5, 7, 10, 12, 17,
Nov 10, 28, Dec 6, 27; 1781: DL, Apr 21, 25, 26, CG, 30, May 7, DL, 7, 8, 10,
15, HAY, 30, Jun 1, 7, 8, 9, 12, 21, 26, Jul 6, 18, Aug 1, 7, 8, 15, 17, 21,
22, 24, 28, 29, Sep 4, DL, 15, HAY, 15, DL, 22, 25, 27, Oct 6, 19, Nov 5, 13,
20, 29, CG, Dec 5, 6, DL, 6, 13; 1782: DL, Apr 3, 15, 17, 18, 20, CG, 30, DL,
May 7, 18, HAY, Jun 3, 4, 6, 10, 11, 18, Jul 2, 17, 25, 30, Aug 5, 13, 17,
23, 24, 27, CG, Nov 8, 12, 19, 25, Dec 14, 20, 27, 31; 1783: CG, Feb 3, 14,
Apr 22, 28, May 3, 9, 17, 19, 21, HAY, 31, Jun 2, 4, 5, 7, 10, 20, 27, Jul 5,
8, 16, 28, Aug 1, 26, 27, 28, 29, CG, Sep 22, 24, Oct 2, 6, 8, 9, 28, Nov 4,
8, Dec 23; 1784: CG, Jan 29, Mar 6, 27, 30, Apr 17, 24, 26, May 1, 10, 17,
19, HAY, 28, 29, Jun 1, CG, 2, HAY, 2, 4, 19, 25, Jul 7, 19, 24, 27, 28, 30,
Aug 2, 10, 17, 24, 26, Sep 6, 17, DL, 25, 30, Oct 7, 14, 19, Nov 9, 12, 16,
22, 26; 1785: DL, Jan 6, 14, 17, HAY, 24, DL, Feb 2, 8, Mar 28, Apr 8, 11,
18, 22, 25, May 3, 11, 12, HAY, 28, 30, 31, Jun 2, 3, 7, 9, 18, 21, 28, HAMM,
Jul 4, HAY, 9, 11, 19, 20, 21, 26, Aug 2, 8, 19, 23, 26, Sep 16, DL, 17, Oct
1, 11, 13, 15, 17, 20, 26, 27, Nov 18, Dec 8; 1786: DL, Jan 6, Apr 4, May 2,
8, 15, Sep 23, 26, Oct 7, 9, 24, Dec 5, 6, 28; 1787: DL, Jan 26, Apr 9, 20,
25, 27, May 11, 14, 22, Sep 18; 1788: HAY, Jun 11, 12, 14, 16, 19, 20, 23,
28, Jul 10, 31, Aug 4, 5, 13, 15, 19, 22, Sep 2, CG, 15, 22, Oct 1, 13, 21,
28, Nov 1, 6, Dec 13, 15; 1789: CG, Feb 14, Mar 31, Apr 15, 21, 29, 30, May
2, 5, 6, 18, 20, 22, 29, Jun 8, 12, HAY, 19, 26, 27, 29, Jul 3, 7, 9, 29, Aug
10, 11, 25, CG, Sep 14, 23, 28, Oct 9, 12, 20, 24, 28, 31, Nov 10, 21, 24,
DL, 24, CG, 28, Dec 12, 21; 1790: CG, Jan 23, Mar 8, 18, 22, Apr 13, 16, 20,
21, May 5, 6, 7, 13, 18, 24, Jun 4, HAY, 15, 19, 22, 29, Jul 5, 16, 30, Aug
20, CG, Sep 13, 15, HAY, 15, CG, 17, Oct 1, 5, 6, 12, 13, 19, 30, Nov 12, 23,
Dec 2, 11, 20; 1791: CG, Jan 12, Feb 10, Apr 28, 30, May 3, 5, 14, 17, 18,
27, 31, Jun 3, 6, 7, 10, HAY, 13, 16, 17, 23, 30, Jul 1, 8, 15, 20, Aug 5,
10, 13, 16, 19, 24, 26, DLKING'S, Dec 27, 31; 1792: DLKING'S, Feb 7, 11, 18,
23, 27, Mar 6, 8, 10, 20, Apr 10, 19, May 23, HAY, Jun 15, 18, 20, 26, 27,
Jul 9, 14, 25, Aug 15, 22, DL, Dec 26; 1793: DL, Jan 2, 23, Feb 7, Apr 8, 18,
May 7, Jun 10, HAY, 12, Jul 9, 15, 25, Aug 3, 12, 16, 20, 27, 30, Sep 2, 19,
Oct 21, Nov 5, 6, 19, Dec 2, 14; 1794: HAY, Jan 21, Feb 8, 11, DL, Apr 21,
25, May 8, 9, 19, 22, 30, Jun 9, 12, 18, Jul 2, HAY, 8, 9, 14, 18, 21, Aug 4,
9, 11, 12, 20, 23, 27, 28, DL, Sep 23, 27, Oct 7, 14, 31, Dec 20; 1795: DL,
Jan 24, 26, Feb 6, HAY, Mar 4, DL, Apr 16, May 4, 18, 19, 27, 28, 29, 30,
HAY, Jun 9, 10, Jul 20, 30, 31, Aug 14, 18, Sep 2, DL, 29, Oct 1, 8, 27, 30,
Nov 23, Dec 30; 1796: DL, Mar 12, Apr 25, May 11, 21, 27, Jun 1, 3, HAY, 13,
14, 18, 22, 25, Jul 2, 11, 12, 23, Aug 11, 29, DL, Sep 22, Oct 10, 19, Nov
26; 1797: DL, Feb 16, 22, Mar 6, May 27, HAY, Jun 12, 13, 19, Aug 3, 4, 9,
14, 23, DL, Nov 7, 8, 10, 24, Dec 9, 20, 28; 1798: DL, Jan 4, 16, Feb 20, Jun
5, 7, HAY, 12, 18, 20, 23, Jul 5, 16, Aug 6, 9; 1799: HAY, Jun 17, 25, Jul
12, 23, 27, Aug 10, Sep 2; 1800: HAY, Jun 16, 20, 28, Aug 2, 7, 23

22, Nov 3, 12, 20; 1725: LIF, Jan 21, Mar 15, Apr 5, 15, Nov 13; 1726: LIF,
    Jan 14, Mar 28, Apr 15, 29, May 11, Sep 23, 30, Oct 5, 24, Nov 19, 26; 1727:
    LIF, Feb 13, Mar 16, Nov 7, 9; 1728: LIF, Feb 28, Mar 5, 9, 18, 21, 27, Apr
    22, May 3, 15, Oct 9, Nov 8, 23; 1729: LIF, Jan 18, Feb 6, Mar 5, 12, 19, Apr
    11, 15, 16, Oct 15, 24, 28, Nov 1, 4; 1730: LIF, Jan 2, Mar 16, Apr 8, 22,
    23, May 14, Jun 12; 1732: LIF, Mar 22, Nov 20; 1733: LIF, Mar 7, Apr 5, 16;
    1734: DL/HAY, Mar 21, DL, Apr 15, 29, May 13; 1740: CG, Dec 16
Barbiere di Siviglia, Il. See Paisiello, Giovanni.
Barclay (actor), 1741: DL, Oct 31, Nov 12, Dec 4; 1744: DL, May 16
Barclay, Caroline (actor, singer), 1792: KING'S, Feb 24, 29, Mar 7, 14, 23, 28,
    30, DLKING'S, May 23, HAY, Jul 23, Aug 17, 28, Sep 1, 10, 11, DL, 20, 27, Oct
    9, 13
Barclay, Mrs (house servant), 1746: DL, May 19; 1747: DL, May 11
Barcock (actor), 1730: BFOF, Aug 20; 1731: SF/BFMMO, Sep 8; 1732: HAY, Mar 8,
    Apr 1, 27, Jun 1, TC, Aug 4, BFMMO, 23; 1733: HAY, Mar 19
Bard, The (monologue), 1799: HAY, Sep 16
Bardin, Peter (actor), 1730: GF, Jan 13, 19, 22, 23, 26, Feb 2, 9, 10, Mar 5,
    17, 30, Apr 2, 6, 7, 15, 16, 28, May 14, 26, 27, 28, 29, Jun 3, 5, 12, 16,
    19, 26, Jul 1, 6, 10, 13, 17, 21, 22, BFPG, Aug 20, BFPG/TC, 24, GF, Sep 16,
    21, 23, 28, Oct 5, 9, 12, 14, 19, 27, 30, Nov 2, 5, 10, 11, 12, 18, 24, 26,
    27, 30, Dec 5, 7, 9, 11, 16, 21, 28, 30; 1731: GF, Jan 8, 20, 23, Feb 1, 8,
    18, 20, 22, 27, Mar 2, 8, 13, 15, 18, 27, 30, Apr 6, 20, 21, 27, May 5, 7,
    11, 13, 14, 15, 26, Jun 1, 2, 4, SF/BFMMO, Aug 26, Sep 8, GF, 27, Oct 11, 13,
    25, 26, Nov 1, 4, 5, 8, 12, 13, 15, 16, 22, 24, 26, Dec 1, 4, 6, 7, 9, 13,
    20, 21, 28, 30; 1732: GF, Feb 2, 21, 26, Mar 7, 20, 28, Apr 12, 13, 14, May
    4, RI, Aug 17, BFMMO, 23, GF, Oct 2, 5, 9, 11, 13, 16, 17, 18, 25, Nov 2, 23,
    27, 28, Dec 1, 18, 29; 1733: GF, Jan 17, 20, 27, Feb 5, 19, 20, Mar 5, 15,
    17, 28, 30, Apr 11, 13, 19, May 5, BFMMO, Aug 23, GF, Sep 14, 19, 20, 21, 25,
    27, 28, Oct 1, 3, 5, 9, 10, 12, 15, 19, 22, 24, 26, Nov 7, 10, 13, 14, 29,
    Dec 13, 15, 18, 31; 1734: GF, Jan 14, 19, 31, Feb 11, Apr 18, 24, 26, 27, May
    15, 17, RI, Jun 27, BFFO, Aug 24, GF, Sep 9, RI, 12, GF, 16, 20, Oct 16, 23,
    28, Nov 7, 18, 22, 25, 27, 29, Dec 2, 6, 13, 16, 31; 1735: GF, Jan 4, 6, 8,
    Feb 5, 8, 11, 17, 22, 24, Mar 6, 13, 17, 24, 29, Apr 9, 22, 30, May 3, 6,
    LIF, Aug 29, GF, Sep 10, 12, 15, 17, 19, 22, 24, 26, Oct 3, 6, 8, Nov 3, 6,
    11, 12, 17, 19, DL, Dec 16; 1736: DL, Jan 3, LIF, Apr 14, Jun 16, Dec 10, 11;
    1737: LIF, Jan 21, 24, Feb 12, 14, 21, Mar 1, 15, Apr 2, 18, 25, 27, 30, May
    4, Jun 15; 1738: DL, Apr 26, May 25; 1766: KING'S, Aug 13, 27, Sep 19
Bardoleau (singer), 1794: DL, May 16, 22, Jun 2, 21, Oct 27, 31, Nov 15, Dec
    20; 1795: DL, Feb 9, 24, Oct 30, Nov 11, Dec 10; 1796: DL, Jan 8, 11, Mar 3,
    12, Apr 30, May 4, Sep 29, Oct 19, Dec 3; 1797: DL, Jan 7, Feb 9, 10, Nov 8;
    1798: DL, Jan 16, Feb 1; 1799: DL, Jan 19, 23, Feb 4, 9, Mar 2, May 24, Oct
    14, Nov 14, Dec 11, 28; 1800: DL, Jan 1, Mar 11, 13, Apr 29, May 3
Bardoni, Cuzzoni (singer), 1728: KING'S, Apr 30
Bardoni, Faustina (singer), 1726: KING'S, May 5; 1727: KING'S, Jan 31, May 6,
    Oct 21, Nov 11; 1728: KING'S, Apr 30; see also Faustina, Sga
Bards' Chorus (song), 1795: CG, Apr 6
Barfield (actor), 1784: HAY, Feb 23
Barford, Richard
--Virgin Queen, The; or, The Captive Princess, 1728: LIF, Dec 5, 7, 9, 10
Barinton, Sir Charles (spectator), 1697: DLLIF, Feb 15
Barkeley, Lord (spectator), 1667: BRIDGES, Oct 19
Barker (spectator), 1667: BRIDGES, Apr 9
Barker and Son (printers), 1795: HAY, Sep 2
Barker, J (printer), 1780: CG, Oct 3; 1783: HAY, Aug 22; 1785: DL, Nov 21;
    1786: HAY, Aug 10; 1794: CG, May 28, HAY, Aug 20, Sep 3; 1796: DL, Apr 2, Nov
    5; 1798: CG, Mar 31, Oct 25; 1799: CG, Jan 29, Apr 16, May 4, Oct 7, Dec 23;
    1800: DL, Feb 1, CG, 19, DL, May 10
Barkinyoung (blacksmith), 1769: CG, Dec 16; 1773: CG, Oct 12
Barlace, Mrs (seamstress), 1750: DL, Feb 20
Barlocci, G (composer), 1749: KING'S, Jan 21
--Don Calascione (opera), 1749: KING'S, Jan 21, 24, 28, 31, Feb 4, 11, 25, Mar
    4, Apr 15, 22, May 6, 20; 1750: KING'S, Feb 10, 17, HAY, Apr 28
Barlow (actor, singer), 1745: GF, Oct 28, Nov 11, 12, 13, 14, 18, 19, 20, 21,
    22, 23, 26; 1746: GF, Jan 3, Feb 3, 20
Barlow, Edward (treasurer), 1786: CG, Jun 5; 1792: CG, Sep 17
Barnaby Brittle; or, A Wife at Her Wit's End (farce, anon), 1781: CG, Apr 18,
    19, 26, May 8, 19, 22; 1782: CG, Apr 4, 16, 23, 29, May 2, 3, 13, 29, Sep 30,
    Oct 18, 31, Nov 20, 23, Dec 13; 1783: CG, Jan 16, 28, Feb 11, 18, Mar 15, 31,
    May 14, 31, Oct 16, Dec 3; 1784: CG, Jan 21, 24, Feb 21, Apr 23, May 5, 24,
    Nov 20, Dec 2; 1785: CG, Feb 17, May 13, 21, Oct 7, Nov 24; 1786: CG, Mar 7,
    27, Nov 24; 1787: CG, Mar 6, HAY, 26, CG, Nov 23; 1788: CG, Apr 25, HAY, Sep
    30, CG, Oct 24; 1789: CG, Dec 2; 1790: CG, May 10; 1791: CG, Jun 6; 1792: CG,

Sep 20; <u>1793</u>: CG, Nov 16; <u>1794</u>: CG, May 29; <u>1797</u>: HAY, Jan 26; <u>1800</u>: CG, Feb 4

Barnard (actor), <u>1744</u>: HAY, Sep 29; <u>1748</u>: CG, Mar 28

Barnard (house servant), <u>1750</u>: CG, May 7; <u>1751</u>: CG, May 14; <u>1752</u>: CG, May 7; <u>1753</u>: CG, May 21; <u>1754</u>: CG, May 18

Barnard, Sir John (MP), <u>1735</u>: DL, Mar 6

Barnard, Miss (actor), <u>1783</u>: HAY, Dec 15; <u>1785</u>: HAY, Feb 10

Barnard, Mrs (actor), <u>1744</u>: JS, Dec 10

Barnard, Mrs (actor), <u>1779</u>: HAY, Oct 18; <u>1781</u>: CII, Mar 15, 27; <u>1782</u>: HAY, Mar 21; <u>1783</u>: HAY, Dec 15; <u>1784</u>: HAY, Dec 13

Barnard, Richard (detective), <u>1776</u>: DL, Apr 18

Barnardi. See Bernardi.

Barnes (actor), <u>1721</u>: LIF, Jan 19

Barnes (actor), <u>1778</u>: HAY, Feb 9; <u>1782</u>: HAY, May 6

Barnes (constable), <u>1758</u>: CG, May 12; <u>1759</u>: CG, May 25; <u>1760</u>: CG, Sep 22, Oct 11

Barnes (dancer), <u>1795</u>: CG, May 12; <u>1798</u>: CG, Mar 19

Barnes (house servant), <u>1794</u>: CG, Jun 10; <u>1795</u>: CG, Jun 13; <u>1796</u>: CG, Jun 6; <u>1797</u>: CG, Jun 6

Barnes' Booth, <u>1696</u>: SF, Sep 5; <u>1697</u>: BF, Aug 24

Barnes-Appleby Booth, <u>1698</u>: BF, Aug 25, SF, Sep 17; <u>1699</u>: BF, Aug 23

Barnes-Finley Booth, <u>1700</u>: BF, Aug 0; <u>1701</u>: MF, May 1, BF, Aug 25; <u>1702</u>: BFBF, Aug 24; <u>1703</u>: MF, May 0

Barnes, Edward (rope dancer), <u>1696</u>: SF, Sep 5; <u>1702</u>: BFBF, Aug 24

Barnes, Miss (actor, singer), <u>1781</u>: DL, May 10, Oct 19, Nov 5, 13, 15; <u>1782</u>: DL, Jan 3, Apr 12, 15, 25, 27, May 4, 7, Dec 16, 26; <u>1783</u>: DL, Mar 3, 20, May 12, 23, Oct 7, 13, Nov 3, 18, 27, Dec 2, 13; <u>1784</u>: DL, Jan 7, 13, Feb 3, Mar 29, May 3, 7, 24, Sep 18, 23, Oct 7, 26, Nov 9, 22, 23, 25, 26; <u>1785</u>: DL, Jan 20, HAY, 31, DL, Feb 2, Mar 17, Apr 1, 14, 20, 25, May 9, 19, Sep 27, Oct 17, 22, 26, Nov 2, 21, Dec 7, 26; <u>1786</u>: DL, Jan 6, 14, 16, Feb 18, May 24, 29, Sep 30, Oct 7, Nov 25, 29, Dec 5, 14, 16, 28; <u>1787</u>: DL, Jan 10, Mar 29, Apr 13, May 28, 30, Jun 7, Nov 6, Dec 6, 8, 26; <u>1788</u>: DL, Jan 22, Apr 8, 14, 25, May 6, 14, 22, 23, 26, Sep 13, 16, Oct 2, 13, 20, Nov 5, 10, 17, 27, Dec 4; <u>1789</u>: DL, Jan 13, 20, 21, 29, Feb 12, Apr 21, May 11, Jun 4, 9, 12, 13, Sep 15, 17, 22, 24, 26, Oct 13, Nov 13, 17, 18, 20, Dec 26; <u>1790</u>: DL, Jan 22, Feb 3, 5, Mar 2, 8, 13, 22, Apr 9, May 7, 14, 15, 18, 20, 27, Sep 14, Oct 7, 11, 14, 20, 27, Nov 19; <u>1791</u>: DL, Mar 17, May 10, 20, HAY, Dec 26

Barnes, Mrs (actor), <u>1782</u>: CG, Jan 21, Mar 14, Apr 17, 26, May 3, 11, DL, Dec 18; <u>1785</u>: HAY, Apr 25

Barnes, Richard (actor), <u>1689</u>: DL, Nov 20; <u>1691</u>: DL, Mar 0

Barnes, Widow-Evans-Finley Booth, <u>1706</u>: MF, May 1

Barnes, Widow, Booth of, <u>1705</u>: BF, Aug 27

Barnet (actor) <u>1782</u>: HAY, Nov 25; <u>1797</u>: HAY, Dec 4

Barnet, Jarvis (actor), <u>1748</u>: DL, Dec 2, 23, 26; <u>1749</u>: DL, Oct 17, Dec 28; <u>1750</u>: DL, Apr 2, 18, 23

Barnet, Master (actor), <u>1749</u>: DL, Dec 26

Barnet, Mrs (singer), <u>1795</u>: DL, Oct 30

Barnet, <u>1699</u>: DLLIF, Sep 12; <u>1702</u>: DL, Aug 22; <u>1704</u>: DL, Jun 5, 7; <u>1710</u>: DL, May 26

Barnett, Catherine (actor, singer), <u>1790</u>: CG, Dec 20; <u>1791</u>: CG, Sep 23, 26, Oct 3, 10, 20, Dec 10, 21, 22, 26; <u>1792</u>: CG, Feb 28, Mar 22, Apr 12, 17, May 10, Oct 8, 19, Nov 24, Dec 26, 31; <u>1793</u>: CG, Jan 2, Feb 25, Apr 4, 10, 11, May 24, Jun 1, 3, Sep 23, 30, Oct 2, 7, 9, 29, Nov 18, 19, 22, Dec 7, 30; <u>1794</u>: CG, Jan 27, Feb 6, Apr 7, May 2, 6

Barnett, Mrs (actor), <u>1729</u>: BFR, Aug 25

Barnett, Mrs (actor), <u>1780</u>: HAY, Jan 3, Mar 28

Barns, Mrs (actor), <u>1725</u>: HAY, Dec 27

Barnshaw, John (actor, singer), <u>1768</u>: CG, Apr 27, Sep 19, 26, 30, Oct 5, 10, 17, 18, Nov 5, 18, Dec 26; <u>1769</u>: CG, Jan 14, Feb 7, 16, May 10, 23, 24, 25, Sep 20, 22, 29, 30, Oct 6, 10, 23, Nov 4, 14, 30; <u>1770</u>: CG, Jan 3, 5, 23, 27, Feb 6, 9, Mar 29, May 1, 15, Sep 26, 28, Oct 8, 25, Nov 12, 23, Dec 26; <u>1771</u>: CG, Jan 1, 11, 21, 22, Mar 14, Apr 12, 30, May 10, 25, 30, GROTTO, Jun 22, Aug 8, 30, Sep 3, 9; <u>1772</u>: CG, Nov 28; <u>1777</u>: CHR, Jun 27, Jul 2

Barnstaple, <u>1798</u>: HAY, Aug 28

Baron (singer), <u>1800</u>: CG, Jan 16

Baron de la Crasse, Le. See Doisson, Raymond.

Baron Kinkvervankotsdorsprakengatchdern!, The. See Andrews, Miles Peter.

Baron, Michel, <u>1749</u>: HAY, Nov 17

--Homme a Bonne Fortune, L', <u>1718</u>: LIF, Dec 19; <u>1721</u>: HAY, Dec 26; <u>1722</u>: HAY, Jan 5; <u>1749</u>: HAY, Nov 17

Barone di Torre Forte, Il. See Piccini, Niccolo.

Baronet Bit, The; or, The Noble Englishman Rewarded (play), <u>1741</u>: SF, Sep 7

Barowby, Miss (actor), 1766: CG, Nov 7, 18
Barr (actor), 1788: DL, Dec 1
Barr (stage doorkeeper), 1750: CG, May 7
Barr, J S (printer), 1794: CG, Apr 10
Barratt (actor), 1722: HAY, Jun 28
Barre (choreographer), 1796: KING'S, Dec 13; 1797: KING'S, May 25; 1798:
   KING'S, Dec 26; 1799: KING'S, Jan 29
Barre, Catherine (actor), 1797: HAY, Sep 18
Barre, Mlle (dancer), 1796: KING'S, Feb 16, Apr 21, May 12, DL, 25
Barre, Mrs (actor), 1775: DL, May 1
Barren Island, The; or, Petticoat Government (play, anon), 1734: BFRLCH, Aug
   24, Sep 2
Barresford. See Berrisford.
Barresford, Mary (actor), 1788: HAY, Jul 23, 29, 30, 31, Aug 4, 21, 22, 28, Sep
   2, 13; 1789: HAY, May 18, 25, Jun 1, 15, 17, 19, 24, Aug 21, 22, Sep 15
Barret (actor), 1730: GF, Oct 19, 20, 30, Nov 5, 12; 1732: HAY, Nov 16
Barret (chandler), 1767: CG, Jan 6, Apr 27; 1772: CG, Feb 19, Apr 22, DL, Jun
   10; 1773: DL, Jun 2; 1774: DL, Jun 2; 1775: DL, Nov 3; 1776: DL, Jun 10;
   1781: CG, May 28; 1783: DL, Feb 22; 1786: CG, Apr 25; 1792: DLKING'S, Jan 2;
   1794: DL, May 6, Nov 14; 1796: DL, Jan 29
Barrett (actor), 1799: CG, Jun 12
Barrett (house servant), 1778: DL, May 25; 1779: DL, May 28; 1780: DL, May 20;
   1781: DL, May 5
Barrett (violinist), 1798: HAY, Jan 15; 1800: CG, Feb 28
Barrett, Giles Linnett (actor, manager), 1777: DL, Jan 28, Feb 3, Apr 24, May
   1, 26, 28, Jun 2, Sep 20, 23, 27, Nov 10, 24
Barrett, John (actor), 1779: HAY, Oct 13, 18, Dec 27; 1780: HAY, Jan 3, 17, Mar
   28, Apr 5, Jun 6, 9, 12, 13, 29, Jul 8, 15, 24, 29, Aug 12, 17, 30, Sep 5, 7,
   8, 11, Nov 13; 1781: HAY, Jan 22, Jun 7, 9, 21, Jul 9, 23, Aug 1, 7, 8, 17,
   21, 22, 25, 29; 1782: HAY, Jan 14, 21, Mar 21, May 6, Jun 3, 4, 10, 12, Aug
   5, 13, 17, 30, Sep 21; 1783: HAY, Jun 5, 20, 30, Jul 4, 8, 26, Aug 13, 23;
   1784: HAY, May 29, Jun 1, 2, 9, 14, 19, Aug 2, 10, 24, 28, 31, Sep 11, 14,
   17; 1785: HAY, May 28, Jun 2, 11, 16, 21, 24, Jul 11, 13, 19, 20, 21, 22, Aug
   2, 3, 6, 16, 23, 25, 26, 31, Sep 3; 1786: HAY, Jun 9, 12, 14, 16, 28, 29, Jul
   11, 12, 18, 21, 28, Aug 3, 4, Sep 7, 9, 13; 1787: HAY, May 23, 25, Jun 13,
   20, 21, 25, 26, 27, 28, Jul 13, 23, 27, Aug 7, 17, 20, 21, Sep 1, 8; 1788:
   HAY, Jun 10, 11, 13, 16, 20, 30, Jul 4, 10, Aug 5, 13, 27, Sep 13; 1789: HAY,
   May 25, 27, Jun 1, 3, 8, 17, 19, 22, 26, 27, 29, Jul 6, 7, 15, Aug 11, 27,
   Sep 8; 1790: HAY, Jun 14, 15, 16, 17, 18, 19, 22, 25, 26, 29, 30, Jul 5, 28,
   Aug 12, 13, 04, Sep 4; 1791: HAY, Jun 6, 8, 17, 18, 28, 22, 23, 30, Jul 14,
   15, 22, 30, Aug 2, 5, 10, 31; 1792: HAY, Jun 15, 18, 20, 23, 27, Jul 11, 14,
   23, 26, 30, Aug 6, 9, 17, 22; 1793: HAY, Jun 11, 12, 14, 17, 18, 21, 24, 26,
   29, Jul 13, 15, 18, 25, Aug 3, 7, 12, 27, Sep 12, 19, 21, 24, Oct 7; 1794:
   HAY, Jul 8, 9, 10, 11, 14, 17, 18, 21, 22, 25, 26, 29, 30, Aug 4, 9, 11, 14,
   16, 23, Sep 1, 10
Barrett, John (musician, composer), 1701: YB, May 5; 1712: DL, Jul 8; 1713: DL,
   Jun 12; 1714: DL, Jan 1, Jul 16; 1715: DL, Jul 8, Nov 11; 1720: DL, Jul 14,
   Aug 18, Oct 25; 1723: DL, Jun 4; 1724: DL, May 13, Oct 29; 1727: DL, Apr 3,
   Oct 30; 1729: DL, Dec 2
Barrett, Miss (actor), 1784: HAY, Nov 16
Barrett, Miss (actor, singer), 1776: HAY, Apr 22, May 2
Barrett, Mrs (actor), 1776: HAY, May 2
Barrett, Mrs (dancer, singer), 1790: DL, Oct 26; 1791: DLKING'S, Nov 5; 1792:
   DLKING'S, Mar 19, DL, Nov 21, Dec 27; 1794: DL, May 16, 30, Dec 20, 23; 1796:
   DL, Jan 18, Mar 1, Oct 1, 29, Dec 26; 1797: DL, Jun 10
Barrington (actor), 1783: DL, Jan 25
Barrington, John (actor), 1739: CG, Apr 5, 12, 30, DL, May 18; 1745: DL, Sep
   19, Nov 22, 25, Dec 5, 16, 30; 1746: DL, Jan 1, 2, 3, 14, 17, 18, GF, 31, DL,
   31, Feb 17, Mar 3, 18, Apr 5, 9, 11, 21, 22, 23, May 9, Oct 28, 31, Nov 1, 5,
   Dec 26; 1747: DL, Jan 15, 26, Feb 10, 28, Mar 3, 19, 24, 28, Apr 20, 25, Sep
   19, 24, Oct 3, 15, 29, Nov 17, 25, Dec 5, 16; 1748: DL, Jan 6, 9, May 4;
   1749: CG, Oct 11, Nov 23, 24; 1750: CG, Feb 19, 22, Mar 17, Oct 15, Nov 6,
   24, 29, Dec 14; 1751: CG, Apr 19, Sep 25, Nov 7; 1752: CG, Mar 30, Apr 1, 30,
   May 4, Sep 20, Oct 23, Dec 11; 1753: CG, Feb 12, Apr 23, May 7, Sep 26, Oct
   3, Nov 1; 1754: CG, Mar 9, Apr 25, May 15, Oct 2, 9, Dec 10, 30; 1755: CG,
   Jan 4, 28, Feb 8, Apr 2, 24, Oct 6, 10, 18, 24, Dec 3; 1756: CG, Apr 23, May
   17, Sep 24, 27, 29, Oct 20, 21, Dec 13; 1757: CG, Feb 9, Apr 22, Sep 21, 23,
   28, Oct 7, 12, 14, Nov 5, 24; 1758: CG, Feb 1, Mar 14, Apr 13, 14, Sep 22,
   Oct 4, 13, 20, 25, Nov 2, 13, 23; 1759: CG, Jan 5, 9, Feb 1, Apr 23, DL, May
   16, CG, Oct 5, 15, Nov 30, Dec 6, 10, 18, 20; 1760: CG, Feb 14, Apr 18, May
   2, 5, 16, Sep 22, Oct 6, 8, 14, Nov 18, Dec 19; 1761: CG, Apr 1, 10, May 25,
   Sep 9, Oct 26, Nov 17; 1762: CG, Feb 15, 22, Mar 20, Sep 20, Oct 8, 16, Nov

8, Dec 8, 21, 29; 1763: CG, Feb 14, May 9, Oct 18, 22, Nov 3, Dec 9; 1764:
CG, Feb 1, 9, 15, Apr 25, May 11, Oct 23, 25, Nov 3; 1765: CG, Feb 18, Apr
24, Sep 16, Oct 4, 15, Dec 6, 9; 1766: CG, Jan 31, Sep 22, Oct 18, Nov 11;
1767: CG, Apr 25, Sep 14, 18, 22, Nov 7, 17, 28; 1768: CG, Jan 16, Feb 13,
Apr 16, 20, 27, Oct 5, 14, Nov 4, 22; 1769: CG, Feb 25, Apr 4, 17, 28, May
15, Sep 22, Oct 18; 1770: CG, Apr 26, May 11, Oct 25; 1771: CG, May 11, Sep
27; 1772: CG, May 22
Barrington, John and Mrs (actors), 1753: CG, Apr 23; 1762: CG, Apr 22
Barrington, Mrs John (actor), 1749: CG, Sep 25, 29, Oct 6, 11, 12, 16, 18, 23,
25, 27, 30, Nov 9, 11, 16, 17, 24, Dec 7, 8; 1750: CG, Jan 16, Feb 20, 22,
Mar 20, Apr 3, 23, 25, Sep 24, 28, Oct 22, 29, Nov 8, 17, 19, Dec 4, 10, 18;
1751: CG, Jan 19, 28, Feb 1, Apr 24, May 2, 9, 16, Sep 23, 25, Oct 7, 8, 22,
29, Nov 6, 7, 13, 14, 16, 22, 26; 1752: CG, Jan 3, 18, Mar 3, 17, Apr 14, 28,
Sep 20, 22, 25, Oct 9, 10, 11, 19, 21, 23, 30, 31, Nov 9, 16, 22, 27, Dec 13,
14, 27; 1753: CG, Jan 17, 22, Mar 26, Apr 23, May 8, Sep 14, 17, 21, 26, Oct
1, 3, 5, 8, 10, 17, 31, Nov 2, 7, 9, 30, Dec 26; 1754: CG, Jan 10, Feb 12,
23, May 7, 13, Sep 18, 20, 23, 25, 27, 30, Oct 2, 4, 7, 9, 11, 14, 29, Nov
16, 20, Dec 13; 1755: CG, Feb 4, 20, Apr 2, 18, May 15, Oct 1, 3, 6, 20, 22,
23, 24, Nov 7, 10, 13, 17, 21, 25, Dec 4; 1756: CG, Feb 9, 19, Mar 23, 25,
30, Apr 6, 20, Sep 20, 24, 27, 29, Oct 1, 4, 6, 14, 28, Nov 9, 11, 16, 17,
Dec 7; 1757: CG, Jan 5, 14, 28, May 9, Sep 14, 23, 28, Oct 17, 20, 21, 22,
Nov 2, 9, 18, Dec 7, 9, 10; 1758: CG, Apr 12, Sep 18, 20, 25, Oct 20, Nov 1,
9, Dec 19, 28; 1759: CG, Jan 4, 9, 12, Mar 3, 22, May 25, Sep 26, Oct 3;
1760: CG, Jan 4, 9, Apr 8, 17, 29, May 2, Sep 22, Oct 13, 17, 25, Dec 6;
1761: CG, Apr 2, 6, 10, May 8, Sep 23, 30, Oct 2, 17, 23, Nov 2; 1762: CG,
Mar 27, Apr 21, May 11, 13, Oct 20; 1763: CG, May 26, Oct 17, Nov 10; 1764:
CG, Jan 26, May 12, 21, Sep 21, Oct 15, 17, Nov 8; 1765: CG, May 11, Oct 7,
23, 30, 31; 1766: CG, Apr 28, Oct 21, Nov 8; 1767: CG, Mar 2, Apr 4, 20, Sep
21, 25, Oct 29; 1768: CG, Feb 27, Sep 19, 26; 1769: CG, Oct 6, Nov 15; 1770:
CG, May 7, Sep 26; 1771: CG, Jan 10, Apr 30, Oct 25, Nov 21; 1772: CG, Apr
29, May 22, Nov 2
Barrois (dancer), 1755: CG, Jan 4
Barron, Mrs (charwoman), 1760: CG, Sep 22
Barronton (actor), 1748: HAY, May 2
Barrow and Co (oil merchants), 1766: DL, Dec 22; 1767: DL, Feb 20, May 19;
1771: DL, Nov 15, Dec 12; 1772: DL, Jan 6, Mar 26, Jun 10, Nov 18, Dec 8;
1773: DL, Jan 21, Mar 1, Jun 2, Dec 2; 1774: DL, Jan 7, 21, Feb 22, Jun 2,
Nov 18; 1775: DL, Jan 10, Feb 23, May 27, Nov 13, 24, Dec 8; 1776: DL, Jan 5,
26, Mar 25, Apr 11, Jun 10
Barrow, Thomas (singer), 1732: CR, Feb 23; 1758: CHAPEL, Apr 27
Barrowby, Dr (physician to performers), 1751: DL, Dec 30
Barrowby, Miss (dancer), 1765: CG, May 22; 1767: CG, Apr 27
Barry (actor), 1699: DL, Nov 11
Barry Jr (actor), 1799: CG, Jun 12
Barry, Ann, Mrs Spranger (actor), 1766: DL, Sep 30, Oct 8; 1767: DL, Mar 31,
Apr 28, May 2, Sep 18, Nov 4, 24; 1768: DL, Jan 23, Apr 6, 13, May 6, 30, Sep
22, 30, Oct 8, 11, 13, 15, 18, 21, 25, 31, Nov 4, 10, 15, 21, 24, Dec 3, 15,
28; 1769: DL, Jan 20, Feb 23, Mar 9, 11, 18, Apr 10, May 1, Oct 7, 12, 13,
14, 16, 18, 21, 26, 28, 31, Nov 2, 4, 8, 11, 16, 18, 21, 24, 28, Dec 1, 8,
13; 1770: DL, Jan 2, 4, 9, 22, 27, Feb 1, 13, Mar 3, 20, 26, Apr 2, 7, 19,
May 7, 9, Oct 9, 12, 17, 20, 25, 31, Nov 2, 5, 10, 14, 17, 20, 28, Dec 1, 4,
6, 12; 1771: DL, Jan 5, 12, Feb 25, Mar 9, 12, Apr 3, 9, 13, 26, May 1, Oct
1, 5, 10, 15, 25, 30, Nov 2, 4, 12, 15, 18, 21, 23, 28, Dec 4, 7, 31; 1772:
DL, Jan 7, 20, Feb 26, Mar 21, 23, Apr 6, 7, 11, May 4, Oct 6, 13, 23, 24,
Nov 4, 7, 14, 17, 28, Dec 8, 15, 17, 22, 30; 1773: DL, Jan 1, 16, 19, 21, Feb
2, 27, Mar 1, CG, 6, DL, 20, Apr 16, 19, 23, 27, 29, May 13, 19, Sep 30, Oct
5, 8, 23, 26, Nov 2, 4, 13, 20, 24, 26, Dec 3, 13, 16; 1774: DL, Jan 13, Feb
2, 19, 21, 28, Mar 12, 24, Apr 4, 21, 27, CG, Oct 31, Nov 8, 12, 24, Dec 3,
15, 17, 20; 1775: CG, Jan 7, Feb 11, 21, 28, Mar 18, 20, Apr 8, 17, 22, May
6, 13, 15, Oct 12, 17, 20, 25, 28, Nov 4, 10, 14, 24, Dec 1, 8; 1776: CG, Jan
15, Feb 5, 22, Mar 16, 18, Apr 24, Oct 2, 8, 15, 31, Nov 2, 7, 12, 21, 28;
1777: CG, Mar 3, 17, Apr 7, 14, Oct 16, 21, Nov 4, 6, 13, 27, Dec 10, 18;
1778: CG, Jan 21, Feb 10, 16, 24, 28, Mar 2, 7, 12, 23, 30, Apr 7, 11, Oct 24
Barry (Barrer), Elizabeth (actor), 1674: NONE, Sep 0; 1675: DG, Sep 0; 1676:
DG, Mar 11, Jul 3, 25, Aug 0, Nov 4, Dec 0; 1677: DG, Mar 24, May 31, Jun 0,
Jul 0; 1678: DG, Apr 5, May 28, Jun 0, Nov 0; 1679: DG, Mar 0, Sep 0, Oct 0;
1680: DG, Jan 0, Feb 0, Jun 0, Sep 0, Nov 1, Dec 8; 1681: DG, Jan 0, Mar 0,
Sep 0, Nov 0, DG/IT, 22; 1682: DG, Feb 9, Mar 0, Apr 0, NONE, Sep 0, ATCOURT,
Nov 15, DL, 16, 28; 1683: DG, Jul 0, DL, Nov 12; 1684: ATCOURT, Feb 11, DL,
Mar 0; 1685: DL, May 9; 1686: DL, Jan 0, Feb 4, Apr 0; 1687: DLORDG, Dec 20;
1688: DL, Feb 0, Apr 0, NONE, Sep 0; 1689: DLORDG, May 28, NONE, Sep 0, DL,
Nov 7, Dec 4; 1690: DLORDG, Jan 16, NONE, Sep 0, DL, Oct 0, DL/IT, 21, DL,

Nov 0, ATCOURT, 7, DL, Dec 0; 1691: DL, Apr 0, NONE, Sep 0, DL, Dec 0; 1692:
DL, Jan 0, NONE, 19, DL, Mar 3, Apr 0, Jun 0, Nov 8; 1693: DL, Jan 16, Feb 0,
Mar 0, Apr 0, ATCOURT, Jun 10, NONE, Sep 0, DL, Oct 0; 1694: DL, Jan 0, 13,
Feb 0, Mar 21, NONE, 22, DL, Apr 0, ATCOURT, 16; 1695: LIF, Apr 30, Sep 0,
Dec 0; 1696: LIF, Apr 0, Jun 0, Oct 0, Dec 0; 1697: LIF, Feb 20, Apr 0, May
0, Jun 0, Nov 0; 1698: LIF, Jan 0, Apr 0, May 0, Jun 0, Nov 0; 1699: LIF, Jan
5, Feb 0, Apr 0, May 0, Nov 7, Dec 0; 1700: LIF, Mar 0, 5, Apr 0, Dec 0;
1701: LIF, Jan 0, Mar 0, Apr 0, Nov 0, Dec 0; 1702: LIF, Dec 31; 1703: LIF,
Jan 0, Feb 0, Mar 0, Apr 28, May 0; 1704: LIF, Jan 0, Feb 3, ATCOURT, 7, LIF, 24,
ATCOURT, Apr 24, LIF, May 20, Nov 13, 18, Dec 4; 1705: LIF/QUEN, Feb 22, LIF,
Mar 10, LIF/QUEN, Oct 30, QUEEN'S, Nov 23; 1706: QUEEN'S, Feb 11, 21, Mar 4,
Jun 0, 26, Nov 2, 7, 9, 13, 19, 20, 21, 29, Dec 2, 5, 6, 11, 16, 30; 1707:
QUEEN'S, Jan 14, 20, 25, Feb 3, 15, Mar 6, Apr 21, May 2, 9, Jun 2, 25, Oct
16, 21, DL/QUEEN, 25, QUEEN'S, Nov 6, QUEEN/DL, 8, DL/QUEEN, 15, 18, 25,
QUEEN/DL, Dec 6, QUEEN'S, 13, DL/QUEEN, 27; 1708: DL, Jan 17, 31, Feb 3, 7,
9, 19, 23, Mar 15, 25, 27, Apr 15, 22, 29, Jun 17; 1709: DL, Apr 7, QUEEN'S,
Oct 4, 8, 21, 29, Nov 5, 9, 12, 15, 28, Dec 3; 1710: QUEEN'S, Mar 11, 13, Apr
13, 14
Barry, Jane (actor), 1766: DL, Oct 24, Nov 8; 1767: DL, Feb 9, Mar 31, Apr 24,
Oct 21; 1768: DL, Jan 19, Feb 27, Mar 21, Apr 27, May 26, Sep 23, 26, 28, 29,
Oct 3, 4, 6, 19, 25, Nov 4, 17, 21, Dec 3, 16; 1769: DL, Jan 19, Apr 10, 14,
May 17, 19, 20, Sep 21, Oct 3, 4, 7, 14; 1770: DL, Jan 17, 24, Feb 21, Mar
26, Apr 16, 19, 20, 30, May 3, 5, 9, 17, 19, 21, 30, Jun 4, Oct 11, 15, 16,
20, 23, 25, 26, 31, Nov 5, 9, 12, 15, 17, 23, Dec 4; 1771: DL, Jan 12, Apr 2,
9, 26, May 1, 17, 23, Sep 28, Oct 5, 12; 1772: DL, Mar 23
Barry, Mrs Thomas (actor), 1774: DL, Apr 21
Barry, Sir Nathaniel (songwriter), 1785: CG, May 12
Barry, Richard, 7th Earl of Barrymore, 1791: CG, Dec 21; 1793: HAY, Aug 20
Barry, Spranger (actor), 1746: DL, Oct 4, CG, Nov 6, DL, 7, 15, Dec 5, 15;
1747: DL, Jan 3, 15, Feb 2, 16, Mar 12, 24, 26, 28, Sep 22, 24, 26, Oct 20,
Nov 4, 5, 7, 18, 24, Dec 14, 16; 1748: DL, Jan 2, 20, Feb 1, 8, 13, 16, Mar
1, 3, 10, 15, Apr 2, 21, 22, 28, Sep 17, 24, Oct 1, 4, 6, 11, 13, 21, 28, Nov
2, 4, 8, 24, 29, Dec 10; 1749: DL, Jan 16, 20, 26, Feb 1, 6, Mar 9, Apr 5, 7,
Oct 3, 10, 17, 21, Nov 2, 4, 17, 20, 28, Dec 8; 1750: DL, Jan 6, Feb 7, 16,
24, Mar 10, 26, Apr 2, 19, Sep 8, CG, 28, DL, Oct 1, 2, CG, 8, 19, 23, 25,
27, Nov 1, 5, 12, 24, 29, Dec 1, 3, 7, 18; 1751: CG, Jan 3, 19, Feb 2, 23,
Mar 11, 16, 18, Apr 10, 22, May 1, DL, 14, CG, Oct 7, DL, 7, CG, 9, 11, 17,
21, 25, 26, Nov 4, 11, DL, 12, CG, 12, 25, 28, Dec 2, 5, 16, 21, DL, 30;
1752: CG, Jan 18, Feb 8, Mar 7, 16, 17, 30, Apr 6, 8, 15, 24, Oct 21, 24, 27,
30, 31, Nov 4, 10, 22, 28, Dec 9, 12, 21; 1753: CG, Jan 8, Feb 21, Mar 10,
17, 19, 26, Apr 9, May 7, Oct 10, 27, 30, DL, 30, CG, Nov 5, 8, 14, 19, 20,
22, 28, 30, Dec 11; 1754: CG, Jan 10, 21, 22, Feb 23, Mar 9, 21, 23, 25, 26,
Apr 17, 20, 24, DL, May 13, CG, 16; 1755: CG, Mar 12, Nov 12, DL, 12, CG, 14,
17, 19, 22, 29, Dec 1, 3, 5, 12, 27; 1756: CG, Jan 3, 15, Feb 26, Mar 18, 22,
30, Apr 1, 3, 6, Oct 4, 6, 8, 11, 13, 15, 25, 27, 30, Nov 4, 13, 29, Dec 1,
10; 1757: CG, Jan 5, 14, 27, Feb 4, 16, 21, Mar 14, 21, Apr 23, 27, May 4,
DL, Oct 8, Nov 28, CG, Dec 1, 5, DL, 5, CG, 5, 7, 10, 12, 14, 16, 20, 22, 27;
1758: CG, Jan 6, 10, 20, 27, 28, 31, Feb 2, 7, 11, 14, 18, 21, 25, 28, Mar 4,
7, 9, 13, 16, 18, 29, Apr 5, 10, 11, 12, 13, 14, 17, 25, May 3, 10, DL, Sep
16, 19; 1763: DL, Sep 27; 1766: HAY, Jul 12, KING'S, Aug 8, 13, 18, 25, 27,
Sep 5, 9, 15, 17, 19, DL, Oct 4, 31; 1767: DL, Jan 24, HAY, Jun 22, 26, 30,
Jul 6, 8, 15, 22, 31, Aug 5, 10, 14, 21, 26, 31, DL, Sep 12, HAY, 16, 18, 21,
CG, Oct 16, DL, 21, 27, 29, 31, Dec 15, 22; 1768: DL, Jan 2, 4, 6, 14, 28,
Feb 27, Mar 15, 21, 24, Apr 27, May 5, 11, 12, Oct 13, 21, 31, Nov 4, 21, 23,
24, Dec 3, 28; 1769: DL, Jan 9, 20, 24, Feb 23, Mar 11, 18, Apr 10, 12, 15,
17, May 5, Sep 21, Oct 7, 10, 12, 21, 26, 28, Nov 2, 4, 8, 11, 18, 21, 24,
28; 1770: DL, Jan 4, 9, 11, 22, 27, 31, Feb 1, 3, Mar 20, 26, Apr 7, May 7,
Oct 25, 31, Nov 2, 5, 10, 14, 17; 1771: DL, Jan 1, 12, Mar 23, Apr 13, 26,
May 6, Sep 26, Nov 4, 12, 15, 21, 23, 30, Dec 4; 1772: DL, Jan 7, 20, Feb 26,
Mar 21, 23, 31, Apr 11, 23, Sep 24, Oct 6, 13, 24, 28, 31, Nov 4, 10, 28, Dec
8, 17, 22, 30; 1773: DL, Jan 21, Feb 2, CG, Mar 6, DL, 20, 22, Apr 27, 29,
May 19, 29, Jun 2, Sep 28, Oct 16, 23, CG, 23, DL, 26, 29, Nov 4, 13, 20, 26,
Dec 3, 16; 1774: DL, Jan 15, Feb 2, 19, 21, Mar 12, 26, Apr 21, May 21, 30,
CG, Oct 31, Nov 4, 12, 24, Dec 3, DL, 5, CG, 15, 17, 20; 1775: CG, Jan 7, Feb
11, 21, Mar 2, 4, 27, Apr 22, Oct 12, 17, 25, 28, Nov 4, 10, 14, Dec 19;
1776: CG, Jan 15, Feb 5, 22, 27, Mar 16, 18, Apr 15, May 3, 20, DL, Jun 1,
CG, Oct 2, 8, Nov 28, Dec 3, 6; 1778: HAY, Sep 17
Barry, Spranger and Ann (actors), 1770: DL, Oct 5; 1771: DL, Nov 12, Dec 4;
1772: DL, Jun 6; 1775: CG, Feb 21, Oct 12; 1776: CG, Jan 5, Feb 7
Barry, Thomas (actor), 1767: HAY, Jun 26, Jul 6, 8, 15, Aug 21, Sep 16
Barry, William (actor), 1772: DL, May 28; 1773: DL, May 19
Barrymore, Earl of. See Barry, Richard.

Barrymore, Miss (actor), 1785: HAY, Mar 15
Barrymore, William (actor, singer), 1782: DL, Oct 3, 7, 16, 26, Nov 30, Dec 10,
  11, 26; 1783: DL, Jan 24, Feb 6, 7, 18, Mar 6, 24, Apr 7, 8, 24, May 10, Sep
  16, 18, 20, 25, 27, 30, Oct 7, 13, 20, 30, Nov 4, 18, 20, Dec 5, 10, 13;
  1784: DL, Jan 10, 13, 20, 23, Mar 8, 16, 30, Apr 12, 14, 16, 26, 28, May 3,
  10, 17, 21, Sep 18, 21, Oct 7, 12, 18, 19, 27, Nov 1, 4, 9, 12, 15, 19, Dec
  3; 1785: DL, Jan 6, 14, 27, Feb 2, 4, 8, Mar 31, Apr 2, 4, 11, 14, 18, 22,
  25, May 11, 24, Sep 20, 24, Oct 1, 6, 15, 17, 20, 22, 26, Nov 9, 17, 18, 21,
  22, Dec 1, 8, 26, 30; 1786: DL, Jan 4, 9, 24, Feb 15, 18, 23, Mar 4, 9, 27,
  Apr 4, 18, 26, May 3, 15, 25, 31, Sep 16, 19, 21, 23, 26, 28, 30, Oct 5, 7,
  9, 10, 12, 14, 23, 24, 27, 30, Nov 15, 18, 22, Dec 5, 6, 26; 1787: DL, Jan
  15, 18, 29, Feb 7, 15, 17, 24, Mar 12, 24, 29, Apr 9, 12, 18, 25, 27, May 8,
  19, 31, Jun 1, Sep 18, 20, 22, 25, Oct 3, 4, 11, 13, 18, 26, 27, 30, Nov 1,
  3, 5, 6, 8, 20, 29, 30, Dec 5, 8, 28; 1788: DL, Jan 2, 3, 8, 21, 28, 31, Mar
  29, Apr 8, 10, 11, 14, 21, 24, 28, 30, May 1, 5, 23, 27, 29, Jun 6, Sep 13,
  16, 18, 20, 23, 30, Oct 7, 9, 14, 16, 21, 22, 25, 28, Nov 4, 5, 8, 11, 17,
  21, 25, 28, Dec 1, 17, 18; 1789: DL, Jan 6, 7, 13, 19, 26, Feb 7, 14, 20, 23,
  28, Mar 17, 21, 23, Apr 4, 13, 16, 21, May 8, Jun 4, 5, 6, Sep 12, 17, 19,
  22, 26, 29, Oct 1, 17, 24, 26, 28, 31, Nov 7, 13, 21, 27, 30, Dec 2, 7, 14,
  26; 1790: DL, Jan 15, Feb 8, 10, 15, 18, Mar 8, 22, Apr 9, May 7, 14, 18, 26,
  27, Jun 1, Sep 30, Oct 7, 11, 14, 18, 21, 23, 25, Nov 2, 3, 10, 12, Dec 3, 7,
  14, 29; 1791: DL, Jan 14, Feb 15, Mar 28, 29, 31, Apr 2, 28, 29, 30, May 4,
  10, 14, 20, 28, 31, DLKING'S, Sep 22, 27, 29, Oct 3, 10, 24, 31, Nov 1, 4, 7,
  14, 15, 16, Dec 2, 5, 12, 13; 1792: DLKING'S, Jan 18, 21, 31, Feb 2, 8, 11,
  14, 18, Mar 1, 6, 10, 13, 17, 26, 29, 31, Apr 10, 12, 19, 20, May 3, 17, Jun
  15, DL, Sep 15, 25, 27, Oct 4, 13, 15, 18, 29, Nov 2, 5, 27, Dec 10, 17, 21,
  26, 28, 31; 1793: DL, Jan 1, 3, 5, 7, 16, Feb 5, 9, 12, 14, 16, 23, Mar 2, 4,
  5, 7, 9, 12, Apr 3, 9, 17, 22, 23, 25, 26, 27, 29, May 7, 10, 24, 25, 29, Jun
  5, 7, 10, HAY, 11, 12, 14, 15, 17, 18, 21, 22, 29, Jul 5, 15, 19, Aug 3, 6,
  12, 30, Sep 2, 19, 24, 26, 30, Oct 1, 4, 5, 8, 10, 15, 21, 22, 24, Nov 4, 5,
  16, 19, 23, Dec 2, 7, 19, 30; 1794: HAY, Jan 14, Feb 8, 13, 22, Mar 31, DL,
  Apr 21, 25, 26, May 1, 7, 17, 19, 22, Jun 6, 9, 12, 14, 16, 19, 21, 24, 27,
  28, Jul 2, 7, HAY, 9, 10, 11, 14, 16, 17, 19, 21, Aug 4, 9, 13, 20, Sep 1, 3,
  17, DL, 23, 27, 30, Oct 7, 9, 11, 14, 18, 20, 25, 27, 28, 29, 31, Nov 1, 8,
  12, 14, 15, 18, 29, Dec 3, 5, 6, 12, 16, 19, 20; 1795: DL, Jan 20, 21, 22,
  26, 28, Feb 9, 10, 17, Mar 3, 10, 14, 21, 24, Apr 16, 17, 22, 27, May 4, 26,
  Jun 6, HAY, 9, 10, 12, 13, 20, Jul 8, 16, 20, 22, 25, 31, Aug 3, 7, 31, DL,
  Oct 13, 15, 19, 30, Nov 6, 7, 10, 12, 13, 19, 20, 23, Dec 10, 18, 21, 23;
  1796: DL, Jan 12, 18, 20, 23, 29, Feb 1, 13, 15, 27, Mar 8, 12, 17, Apr 2, 4,
  18, 25, May 3, 20, Jun 6, 14, Sep 24, 27, Oct 3, 6, 10, 13, 15, 17, 19, 20,
  24, 25, 27, 28, Nov 2, 9, 10, 15, 23, Dec 6, 9, 16, 21, 23, 30; 1797: DL, Jan
  2, 7, 12, 14, 17, 20, 27, Feb 1, 3, 7, 16, Mar 6, 14, 20, Apr 28, May 1, 12,
  17, 19, 24, Jun 12, 14, CG, 14, DL, Sep 19, 28, Oct 3, 5, 7, 12, 14, Nov 18,
  20, 21, 25, 28, 29, Dec 2, 8, 9, 11, 14; 1798: DL, Jan 17, 23, 25, Feb 13,
  Mar 13, 24, Apr 14, 30, May 23, 24, 28, 30, Jun 4, 7, HAY, 12, 14, 20, 21,
  23, 28, 29, 30, Jul 14, 16, 21, 30, Aug 3, 11, 14, 21, 27, 29, Sep 3, 10, 12,
  DL, 15, 18, 20, 22, 25, 29, Oct 2, 4, 6, 9, 11, 13, 20, 27, 30, Nov 6, 13,
  14, 16, 26, Dec 3, 4, 5, 19, 21, 29; 1799: DL, Jan 8, 11, 19, Feb 4, 14, 23,
  26, Mar 2, 25, 26, Apr 8, 18, 19, 20, 22, 23, 24, May 3, 8, 24, Jul 1, HAY,
  6, 8, 9, 10, 12, 13, 16, 20, 23, 27, 30, Aug 13, 20, 21, 24, Sep 10, DL, 17,
  19, 21, 24, Oct 1, 3, 7, 12, 14, 17, 21, 22, 29, 31, Nov 2, 8, 16, 22, 25,
  27, 29, Dec 7, 9, 11; 1800: DL, Jan 1, 6, 18, 25, 27, Feb 10, 12, Mar 10, Apr
  1, 28, 29, May 1, 10, 13, 21, Jun 6, CG, 13, HAY, 14, 18, 19, 20, Jul 5, 15,
  Aug 7, 12, 15, 21, 22, 23, 29, Sep 10
Barsanti, Francesco (musician), 1750: DL, Apr 20
Barsanti, Jane (actor, singer), 1772: CG, Sep 21, Oct 23, 27; 1773: CG, Jan 28,
  May 10, Sep 22, Oct 6, 15, Nov 20, Dec 23; 1774: CG, Jan 5, 12, Mar 24, Apr
  5, 12, 23, DL, May 18, CG, 26, Oct 11, 26, Nov 25, Dec 12; 1775: CG, Jan 17,
  DL, Mar 6, CG, Apr 27, May 3, 5, Sep 20, 22, Dec 23; 1776: CG, Jan 24, Feb
  26, Apr 26, 30, May 13; 1777: HAY, Jun 11, Jul 15, Aug 19, 28, Sep 3, 19
Barthelemon, Cecilia Maria (singer), 1779: HAY, Mar 3; 1784: HAY, Apr 27
Barthelemon, Francois Hippolyte (musician, composer), 1764: CG, Jun 5; 1765:
  HAY, Mar 11; 1766: CG, Feb 14, 21, Mar 5, KING'S, May 22; 1767: DL, Oct 26,
  27; 1768: HAY, Feb 19, 24, Mar 3, 4, 9, 16, 18, Jun 3, 8, 17, DL, 21, HAY,
  23, Aug 24, Oct 7; 1770: DL, Mar 2, 7, HAY, 12, DL, 14, 21, 28, HAY, May 3,
  MARLY, Jul 17, Aug 7, 14, 21, 28, Sep 4, 15, 20, 21; 1771: DL, Feb 15, Apr
  27, May 13; 1773: CG, Feb 26, Mar 5, 19, 26, DL, Apr 22, HAY, 23, HIC, May
  18, MARLY, Jun 15, Jul 15, Aug 25, 26; 1774: HAY, Feb 18, 23, 25, Mar 2, 9,
  11, 16, 18, 23, 25, KING'S, Apr 19, DL, Oct 19, Nov 5, 30; 1775: DL, Mar 3,
  10, 15, 22, 25, 28, Apr 7, Nov 28; 1776: STRAND, Jan 23, HAY, Feb 22, Apr 18;
  1778: DL, Mar 16, HAY, Apr 30; 1779: HAY, Mar 3, 17; 1781: KING'S, Dec 11;
  1782: DL, Feb 1; 1783: KING'S, Apr 10, DL, 26, KING'S, Jun 3, Dec 6; 1784:

KING'S, Jan 17, Feb 3, 7, HAY, Mar 3, KING'S, 6, 25, HAY, Apr 27; 1785:
   KING'S, Jan 1, 11, Feb 5, Mar 3, 17; 1798: HAY, Jan 15; 1799: HAY, Jan 24
--Magic Girdle, The (musical), 1770: MARLY, Jul 17, 19, 21, 26, Aug 2, 4, 9,
   11, 21, Sep 1, 13, 17, 19, 21; 1773: MARLY, Jun 15
--Pelopida (opera), 1766: KING'S, May 22, 27, 31, Jun 3, 7, 14
--Wedding Day, The (musical), 1773: MARLY, Jul 15, 17, Aug 26, Sep 13
--Zingara, La; or, The Gipsey (musical), 1773: MARLY, Aug 25
Barthelemon, Mary, Mrs Francois Hippolyte (actor), 1767: KING'S, Jan 23, 31,
   RANELAGH, Jun 1; 1768: HAY, Mar 3, 4, Aug 24; 1769: DL, Apr 28, KING'S, Jun
   1; 1770: HAY, Mar 12, MARLY, Jun 16, Jul 17, 19, 24, Aug 7, 16, 21, 28, Sep
   11, 20; 1771: KING'S, Jan 10, Feb 28, Mar 14, DL, May 13, CG, Jun 6; 1773:
   CG, Mar 19, HAY, Apr 23, May 5, HIC, 18, MARLY, 27, Jul 15, Aug 5, 25, 26,
   27, Sep 3; 1774: HAY, Feb 18, 23, 25, KING'S, Mar 17; 1775: DL, Mar 10, CG,
   Oct 2, 26; 1776: HAY, Feb 22, Apr 18; 1778: HAY, Apr 30; 1779: HAY, Mar 3,
   17; 1780: CG, May 6, KING'S, Nov 25, 28, Dec 19; 1782: KING'S, Jan 10; 1784:
   HAY, Mar 3, Apr 27
Barthelemon, Master (singer), 1783: CG, May 6, 26
Bartholomew Fair (dance), 1731: DL, Aug 6, 20; 1732: DL, Apr 25, May 1, 6;
   1733: DL, May 5
Bartholomew Fair (poem), 1680: BF/SF, Aug 0
Bartholomew Fair (song), 1800: CG, Jun 6
Bartholomew Fair. See Jonson, Ben.
Bartholomew Fair, Comic Song about (song), 1799: HAY, Sep 16
Bartholomew Fair, 1660: SF, Sep 10; 1661: BF, Aug 22, 31; 1663: BF, Aug 25, Sep
   4; 1664: BF, Sep 2, 7; 1665: BF, Aug 7; 1666: NONE, Aug 3; 1667: BF, Aug 28,
   30, Sep 6; 1668: BF, Aug 29, Sep 7; 1672: BF, Aug 26; 1674: DL, Nov 30; 1675:
   BF, Sep 3; 1677: BF, Aug 27, 30; 1679: BF, Sep 1; 1680: BF, Aug 31; 1681: BF,
   Aug 0, Sep 9, DL, Oct 0; 1685: BF, Aug 0; 1688: BF, Aug 0; 1689: BF, Aug 26;
   1690: BF, Sep 1; 1691: BF, Aug 3, 8; 1693: BF, Aug 31; 1694: NONE, Mar 22,
   BF, Sep 1; 1696: BF, Aug 0, DG, 0; 1697: BF, Aug 24; 1698: BF, Aug 23, 25;
   1699: BFPD, Aug 23, BF, 23, 30, DLLIF, Sep 12; 1700: BF, Jun 25, Jul 6, Aug
   0; 1701: MF, May 1, DL, Aug 23; 1702: DL, Aug 22, BFGB, 24; 1704: DL, Jul 26;
   1706: QUEEN'S, Aug 23; 1714: SF, Aug 31; 1715: SF, Sep 5; 1716: DL, Jun 19;
   1717: BF, Aug 24, LIF, Dec 30; 1718: RI, Aug 23; 1721: BF/SF, Sep 2; 1722:
   SF, Sep 5; 1723: SF, Sep 5; 1726: BFLHS, Aug 24; 1731: SF/BFMMO, Aug 26, Sep
   8, SF/BFFHH, 8; 1732: GF, Oct 11; 1733: SF/BFLH, Sep 10; 1734: BFT, Aug 17;
   1737: SF, Sep 7; 1738: SFH, Sep 5; 1740: BF/WF/SF, Aug 29, Sep 8; 1742: BFPY,
   Aug 25, SF, Sep 8; 1747: BHB, Sep 26; 1748: BFSY, Aug 24, SFBCBV, Sep 7,
   SFLYYW, 7; 1749: NWSM, May 1, BF/SFP, Sep 7, SF/SF, 7, BF/SF, 8; 1753: BFSY,
   Sep 3, BFGI, 3; 1754: BFSIY, Sep 3; 1757: BF, Sep 3; 1759: BFY, Sep 3, SFS,
   18, 19, 20, 21; 1760: CG, Mar 20, NONE, Sep 0; 1762: BFY, Sep 3; 1776: CG,
   Mar 19
Bartholomew Lane, 1751: DL, May 2; 1752: DL, Apr 8
Bartholomew-Fair Song (play), 1735: GF/HAY, Jul 18
Bartholomew-tide Entertainment, A; or, A Trip to Chatham (play), 1778: HAY, Aug
   24
Bartholomon, J (actor), 1786: HAY, Mar 6
Barthrope (house servant), 1777: DL, May 30; 1778: DL, May 22; 1779: DL, May
   29; 1780: DL, May 23; 1781: DL, May 12; 1782: DL, May 16; 1783: DL, May 31;
   1784: DL, May 22; 1785: DL, May 21; 1786: DL, May 29
Bartleman, James (singer), 1784: CG, Apr 24; 1792: CG, Feb 24, Mar 2, 7, 9, 14,
   16, 21; 1793: CG, Feb 15, 20, 22, Mar 6, 8, 13, 20, 22; 1794: CG, Mar 7, 14,
   21; 1795: CG, Feb 20, 27, Mar 11, 13, 25, 27; 1796: CG, Feb 12, 26, Mar 16;
   1797: CG, Mar 3, 10, 22, 31; 1798: HAY, Jan 15; 1799: CG, Feb 8, 13, 15, 20,
   Mar 1, 6, 13, 15; 1800: CG, Apr 2
Bartleme (musician), 1675: ATCOURT, Feb 15
Bartlett (musician?), 1735: GF/HAY, Mar 21; 1741: DL, May 14
Bartolini, Vincenzio (singer), 1782: KING'S, Nov 2, 14, Dec 19; 1783: KING'S,
   Jan 7, Feb 18, 27, Mar 6, 27, Apr 29, Jun 3, 14, Nov 29, Dec 16; 1784:
   KING'S, Jan 6, 17, Feb 17, 24, Mar 4, 18, May 8, Jun 12; 1785: KING'S, Jan 4,
   8, Feb 26, Mar 17, Apr 16; 1786: KING'S, Feb 14, Mar 11, 21, 30, May 4, 25,
   Jun 13
Bartolomici, Louis (dancer), 1799: DL, Jul 1
Bartolotti, Girolamo (musician), 1731: HIC, Mar 19
Bartolozzi, Francesco (engraver), 1791: PAN, Feb 17, KING'S, May 19; 1795:
   KING'S, Apr 30
Barton (actor), 1736: HAY, Feb 16
Barton, Frances (actor), 1755: HAY, Sep 1, 9, 11, 15; 1756: DL, Oct 29, Nov 1,
   10, Dec 27; 1757: DL, Feb 5, Mar 24, May 4, Sep 15, Oct 7, 13, 15, 18, Dec 3;
   1758: DL, Apr 29, May 1, 2, Sep 19, 26, Oct 7, 21, 27, Nov 13, 16, 17, 27,
   Dec 20; 1759: DL, Jan 4, 20, Mar 6, 19, 20, 24, Apr 7, 27, May 21, 30, 31,
   Jun 19, 28, Jul 12

Barton, William (tavern keeper), 1752: DL, Apr 8
Barwick, Ann (servant), 1704: DL, Feb 5
Barwis, John (versifier), 1784: CG, Oct 25
Barzago. See Buzarglo.
Basant. See Bayzand.
Basanti. See Barsanti.
Bashaw, Admiral Perez (Moroccan ambassador), 1737: LIF, Sep 7
Bashful Lover, The. See Massinger, Phillip.
Bashful Maid (dance), 1720: LIF, Jan 11; 1723: HAY, Jan 28
Basile (tailor), 1773: CG, Dec 15
Basinghall St, 1703: GH, Apr 16; 1743: LIF, Mar 14
Basire, James (engraver), 1777: CG, Apr 5
Basket Maker, The. See O'Keeffe, John.
Basrier (musician), 1675: ATCOURT, Feb 15
Bass (actor), 1784: HAY, Mar 8
Bass Viol (music), 1713: SH, May 15; 1720: SH, Mar 9; 1721: LIF, May 2; 1723:
    LIF, May 7
Bass Viol Concerto (music), 1722: DL, Mar 14
Bass Viol Solo (music), 1715: GRT, Apr 25, May 9; 1719: HIC, Feb 18; 1725: LIF,
    Apr 12; 1732: HIC, May 10
Bassan (house servant), 1766: CG, May 15; 1767: CG, May 18; 1768: CG, Jun 3;
    1769: CG, May 20; 1770: CG, May 19; 1771: CG, May 25; 1772: CG, May 23, 29
Bassan, Miss (dancer), 1773: CG, Apr 24, May 21; 1774: CG, May 14, 18, 20;
    1775: CG, May 8; 1776: CG, May 11; 1777: CG, May 9; 1778: CG, May 12; 1779:
    CG, Apr 29; 1780: CG, May 23
Basset (actor), 1799: CG, Jun 12
Basset Table, The. See Centlivre, Susannah.
Bassingwhite (actor), 1779: HAY, Jan 11
Bassoon (music), 1714: SH, Feb 22; 1724: LIF, Mar 19, Apr 25; 1729: HIC, Apr
    16; 1732: LIF, Feb 25; 1737: DL, May 4, 27; 1744: LIF, Dec 11; 1757: HAY, Sep
    2, Oct 3; 1771: HAY, Apr 12; 1793: KING/HAY, Mar 13, 15; 1796: CG, Feb 26;
    1797: CG, Mar 17; 1798: CG, Mar 9
Bassoon Concerto (song), 1741: HIC, Mar 5, 6, KING'S, 14, HIC, Apr 10; 1743:
    KING'S, Mar 30; 1744: KING'S, Mar 28, HAY, Apr 4; 1745: DT, Mar 14, DL, May
    13; 1748: HAY, Dec 9; 1752: DL, Oct 16; 1753: KING'S, Apr 30; 1754: KING'S,
    Feb 28; 1755: KING'S, Mar 17; 1757: KING'S, Mar 24; 1758: KING'S, Apr 6;
    1761: KING'S, Mar 12; 1762: KING'S, May 11; 1763: KING'S, Apr 25; 1764: HAY,
    Nov 13; 1766: KING'S, Apr 10; 1769: HAY, Feb 9; 1770: KING'S, Feb 2; 1771:
    KING'S, Feb 8, 28; 1772: KING'S, Feb 21; 1773: KING'S, Feb 5; 1774: KING'S,
    Feb 10; 1775: KING'S, Jan 26; 1776: KING'S, Feb 15; 1782: DL, Mar 1; 1786:
    DL, Apr 5; 1788: DL, Feb 20; 1789: DL, Mar 6, 25; 1790: DL, Feb 24, Mar 24;
    1791: DL, Mar 30; 1792: KING'S, Feb 24, Mar 14, 21, 23; 1795: KING'S, Feb 27
Bassoon Obligato (music), 1795: KING'S, Jun 16; 1799: CG, Feb 20; 1800: CG, Mar
    19
Bassoon Solo (music), 1726: DL, Apr 28; 1732: TTT, Mar 3; 1745: HAY, Feb 14
Bassoon Solo Concerto (music), 1773: MARLY, Jun 15
Baster, Eleanor, Mrs John (actor, singer), 1800: CG, Jun 13
Bastille, 1790: CG, Dec 20
Baston, John (Bastion Sr) (musician), 1715: LIF, Mar 22, Apr 4, Nov 18; 1716:
    LIF, Apr 25, May 7, 31, Jul 20, Oct 17; 1717: LIF, Mar 1, Nov 11; 1718: LIF,
    May 20, Nov 10; 1719: LIF, Jan 2; 1720: HIC, Mar 4, LIF, Dec 23; 1722: DL,
    Mar 14, May 11, RI, Jul 23; 1723: DL, May 2, 28, Jun 6, 25, RI, Sep 2; 1724:
    DL, May 12; 1725: DL, Mar 31, May 19; 1726: DL, May 23, 25; 1727: DL, May 15;
    1728: YB, Mar 13; 1730: DL, Apr 16, 29, May 2; 1732: CL, Mar 17, Apr 5; 1733:
    DL, May 9
Baston, John and Thomas (musicians), 1709: SH, Aug 25; 1711: COH, Dec 20; 1712:
    SH, Dec 8; 1715: LIF, May 9; 1716: LIF, May 7, 31, Oct 17; 1717: LIF, Mar 1,
    Nov 11; 1719: LIF, Jan 2
Baston, Miss (dancer, harpsichordist), 1732: LIF/CG, Nov 9, Dec 8, CG/LIF, 19,
    LIF/CG, 28; 1733: LIF/CG, Jan 23, Mar 12, CG, 27, LIF/CG, 28, Apr 12, 16, 18,
    30, May 7, CG, 11, LIF/CG, 14, CG, 16, LIF/CG, 18, 21, 24, Jun 1, CG, 26, Aug
    9, 14, 16, 17, 21, Sep 22, Oct 4, 13, 16, 18, 27, Nov 12, Dec 7, 18, 28;
    1734: CG, Jan 17, 25, Feb 26, Mar 11, 16, Apr 1, 23, May 6, 8, 14, 16,
    CG/LIF, Sep 20, 25, Oct 2, 31, Dec 5, 12, 14, 19, 30; 1735: CG/LIF, Jan 13,
    14, 17, Feb 3, 13, 22, Mar 11, 15, Apr 11, 14, 17, May 16, 20, Jun 2
Baston, Thomas (Bastion Jr) (musician), 1714: SH, Jan 25; 1716: LIF, Apr 25;
    1720: LIF, May 5, 12
Batchelor (tailor), 1773: DL, Jan 22
Batchelor, Miss (dancer), 1750: CG, Dec 26; 1751: CG, Oct 28, Nov 11, Dec 4,
    20, 23; 1753: DL, May 2; 1754: DL, May 2
Bate (actor) 1779: HAY, Mar 15
Bate, Henry, 1774: CG, Apr 13; 1775: DL, Feb 1, 10, Apr 20, Nov 28; 1776: DL,

Feb 1, May 1; 1778: HAY, Aug 17; 1781: DL, Apr 23; 1782: CG, Feb 9; 1783: CG, Nov 8; 1791: CG, Feb 26; 1794: CG, Feb 22; see also Dudley, Henry Bate
--Blackamoor Wash'd White, The, 1776: DL, Feb 1, 2, 3, 5, May 1
--Dramatic Puffers, The (prelude), 1782: CG, Feb 9, 11, 12, 14, 16, 18, 19, 21, 23, 25, 28
--Flitch of Bacon, The (opera), 1778: HAY, Aug 17, 18, 19, 25, 26, 29, 31, Sep 1, 3, 4, 5, 8, 9, 11, 12, 14, 15, 16; 1779: CG, Apr 27, HAY, Jun 12, 14, 16, 18, 21, 22, 23, 25, 28, 29, 30, Jul 9, 13, 24, 29, Aug 4, 11, 13, 20, 24, 25, Sep 4, 11; 1780: CG, Jan 7, 11, 13, 14, 15, 21, 25, 27, Mar 18, Apr 10, 18, 22, HAY, Jun 28, Jul 5, 11, 14, 17, Aug 18, 21; 1781: CG, Mar 3, 15, 20, Apr 25, May 1, DL, 15, CG, 18, DL, 22, CG, 23, HAY, Aug 17, CG, Oct 13, Nov 6, 20, Dec 21; 1782: DL, May 7, 30, HAY, Jul 17, 23, Aug 9, 30, CG, Oct 23; 1783: CG, Apr 28, HAY, Jul 5, 29, CG, Oct 1, 31; 1784: CG, Apr 24, May 15, 21, 27, HAY, Jul 27, Aug 12; 1785: DL, May 3, HAY, Jul 19, DL, Oct 20, 29; 1786: DL, Jun 7, HAY, 13, Jul 1; 1787: HAY, Jul 19; 1788: HAY, Jun 19; 1789: CG, May 20, HAY, Jul 3, 11, 18; 1790: CG, Mar 18, Apr 13, May 3, Jun 1; 1791: CG, May 14, HAY, Jul 20, 27, DLKING'S, Dec 7; 1792: HAY, Aug 22, CG, Sep 28; 1793: HAY, Jul 9, 16, 30, Aug 24, CG, Nov 30, Dec 3, HAY, 14; 1794: HAY, Jul 8, 15, 19, 26, Aug 14; 1795: HAY, Aug 14, CG, Dec 9; 1796: CG, Jan 29, HAY, Jun 22; 1797: HAY, Aug 4; 1798: DL, May 23, HAY, Jun 23; 1799: CG, Jan 26, Mar 29, Apr 27, HAY, Jun 25, CG, Nov 11, 12, 13; 1800: HAY, Jun 20, 30, Jul 15
--Henry and Emma (interlude), 1774: CG, Apr 13; 1775: DL, Apr 20; 1779: HAY, Oct 18; 1780: HAY, Sep 5; 1781: DL, Apr 23; 1782: DL, Mar 23, Apr 24, May 2
--Magic Picture, The, 1783: CG, Nov 8, 14, 18, 21, 26, Dec 2; 1784: CG, Jan 2
--Pharnaces (opera), 1765: DL, Feb 11, 15, 18, 21, 25, 28, Mar 4; 1771: GROTTO, Aug 30
--Rival Candidates, The (opera), 1775: CG, Jan 6, DL, Feb 1, 2, 6, 8, 9, 10, 13, 14, 15, 22, 25, 27, Mar 4, 7, 9, 14, 18, May 25, Oct 10, 12, 20, 25; 1776: DL, Feb 9, 12, 20, 29, Mar 19, 21, Apr 27, 29, May 2, 9, 14, Oct 10, 12, 15, Dec 17, 20; 1777: DL, Oct 29; 1778: DL, Feb 20, Mar 2, May 19; 1779: DL, May 19, 28, Dec 4, 13; 1780: DL, Jan 26, Nov 3; 1781: DL, May 7, 25; 1783: DL, May 5, 30; 1784: DL, Apr 1, 20, 22, May 21; 1785: DL, Nov 1
--Travellers in Switzerland, The (opera), 1794: CG, Feb 22, 25, 26, 27, Mar 1, 3, 4, 6, 8, 10, 13, 15, 18, 20, 22, 31, Apr 8, 24, 28, May 5, Jun 6, Sep 26; 1796: CG, Apr 12, Jun 3; 1797: CG, May 24, Jun 8
--Woodman, The (opera), 1791: CG, Feb 26, 28, Mar 1, 2, 3, 4, 5, 7, 8, 10, 12, 14, 15, 17, 19, 21, 22, 24, 26, 28, 29, 31, Apr 2, 4, 12, 26, May 23, Jun 13, HAY, 13, CG, Dec 10, 13; 1792: CG, Jan 11, 19, 28, Feb 10, May 22, Oct 12, 19; 1793: CG, Dec 7; 1795: CG, Apr 28, Jun 16; 1796: CG, Apr 29, Oct 17, 25; 1797: CG, May 20; 1800: CG, Apr 15, May 7
Batelier, Mary (spectator), 1667: LIF, Sep 5; 1669: VERE, Apr 22
Batelier, W (spectator), 1666: MOORFLDS, Aug 29; 1668: LIF, Aug 31, Oct 19
Bateman (actor), 1782: HAY, Mar 4
Bateman; or, The Unhappy Marriage (or, The Fair Vow Breaker) (play, anon), 1694: BF, Sep 5; 1703: BFPD, Aug 23; 1715: SF, Sep 5; 1728: BFHM, Aug 24; 1733: TC, Jul 30, SF, Sep 10
Bateman, Sir Anthony (Lord Mayor), 1663: CITY, Oct 29
Bateman, Mrs (actor), 1730: SF, Sep 14
Bateman, Mrs (actor, singer, fencer), 1793: DL, Feb 14, Apr 26, May 1, 30
Bateman, Thomas (actor), 1660: REDBULL, Nov 5, VERE, Dec 0; 1669: BRIDGES, Apr 17
Bateman's Buildings, 1777: CG, Apr 26
Bateman's Ghost (droll), 1699: BF, Aug 30
Bates (actor), 1749: SOU, Jan 9
Bates (actor), 1797: HAY, May 10
Bates (householder), 1765: DL, Apr 26
Bates (musician), 1675: ATCOURT, Feb 15
Bates (songwriter), 1760: CG, Mar 15, RANELAGH, Jun 11; 1761: DL, Mar 30; 1763: CG, Apr 26; 1765: DL, Feb 15
Bates, James (actor), 1768: CG, Mar 17; 1769: CG, May 3; 1771: CG, Nov 25; 1779: CG, May 21; 1780: CG, May 23; 1781: CG, Sep 21, 24, Oct 23, Nov 17, 21, Dec 17, 31; 1782: CG, Jan 7, 8, 22, 29, Feb 5, Mar 16, 19, Apr 24, May 6, 11, HAY, Aug 17, Sep 18; 1783: HAY, Jun 30, CG, Oct 6, 11, 13, 20, 23, Nov 4; 1784: CG, Jan 9
Bates, Mrs (actor), 1678: DL, Feb 0
Bates, Mrs (supernumerary), 1770: CG, Mar 19, 22
Bates, Patty Ann, Mrs James (actor), 1783: CG, Oct 1, 6, 9, 13, 31, Nov 4, 8, Dec 26, 27; 1784: CG, Jan 23, Feb 10, Apr 26, 27, May 4, 13, 17, 26, Jun 10, 14, HAY, 17, Aug 19, Sep 13, CG, 20, 24, 27, 28, Oct 1, 6, 11, Nov 4, 11, 13, 27, 30, Dec 14, 27, 30; 1785: CG, Jan 8, 14, Feb 8, 12, Mar 5, 8, 29, Apr 2, 5, 11, 22, May 3, 4, 6, 7, HAY, Jun 11, 24, 29, Jul 23, Aug 4, Sep 2, 9, CG,

21, 23, 28, Oct 5, 10, 17, 19, 22, 26, 29, Nov 1, 7, 9, 19, Dec 7, 14, 26,
28, 30; 1786: CG, Jan 3, 4, 7, 14, 18, 20, 28, Feb 1, 4, 7, 11, 23, Mar 4,
Apr 18, 24, May 9, 15, 20, 26, DL, Jun 2, HAY, 13, 20, 29, Jul 3, 14, Aug 17,
CG, Sep 20, 29, Oct 6, 25, Nov 15, 29, Dec 13, 21; 1787: CG, Jan 4, 6, 11,
27, Mar 31, Apr 16, Oct 1
Bates, Robert (actor), 1767: CG, Oct 16, Nov 10, 20; 1768: CG, Feb 12, 27, Apr
12, 18, May 27, 31, Sep 30, Dec 22; 1769: CG, Apr 12, May 17, Dec 2, 7; 1770:
CG, Mar 23, Apr 24, DL, May 7, CG, 7, 22, Sep 26, Nov 1, Dec 26; 1771: CG,
Jan 1, Feb 21, May 1, 21, GROTTO, Jun 22, Aug 30, CG, Oct 2, 11, 15; 1772:
CG, Feb 25, May 25; 1773: CG, Mar 15, Apr 28, May 24, Oct 1, 28, Dec 4; 1774:
CG, Mar 22, May 6, 16, Oct 11, 21, Dec 2; 1775: HAY, Feb 2, DL, Sep 28; 1776:
CG, Jan 15, Apr 30, May 4, Nov 14, Dec 27; 1777: CG, Jan 8, May 3, 9, HAY,
Sep 3; 1778: CG, Mar 30, May 5, 14; 1779: CG, Apr 12, 23, May 3, Sep 27, HAY,
Oct 18, CG, 20, Nov 4; 1780: CG, Feb 1, 2, Apr 25, Sep 18, Oct 11, 19; 1781:
CG, Apr 28, May 12, Sep 24, 26; 1782: CG, Jan 5, Mar 16, 19, Apr 1, 10, May
17, Oct 3, 16, 17, Dec 12, 16; 1783: CG, Jan 1, Apr 23, Oct 11, 14, Nov 17;
1784: CG, Jan 29, Feb 23, Mar 27, Apr 13, May 15, 26, Sep 20, 29, Nov 13, Dec
14; 1785: CG, Feb 5, 15, 21, Mar 29, Apr 6, May 7, 11, Sep 26, 28, 30, Nov 1,
10; 1786: CG, Apr 24, May 18
Bates, William (actor), 1779: CG, Oct 16, Nov 4, 13, 26, 29, 30, Dec 3, 8, 11,
17; 1780: CG, Jan 19, Feb 22, 24, 26, Mar 18, Apr 17, 25, May 1, 6, 12, 26,
Sep 18, 20, 21, 25, Oct 2, 10, 11, 19, 24, Nov 1, 8, Dec 15; 1781: CG, Jan
15, Apr 28, May 7, 12, 16, Sep 19, 21, 26, 28, Oct 10, 20, 22, 23, 31, Nov 2,
Dec 7, 11, 26, 31; 1782: CG, Jan 5, 9, 18, 22, Feb 2, 9, Mar 19, Apr 30, May
11, 17, 29, Oct 3, 8, 14, 16, 17, 18, Nov 27, 30, Dec 12; 1783: CG, Jan 4,
Feb 19, Mar 29, Apr 7, 12, 22, May 16, 19, 23, 31; 1784: CG, Jan 9; 1787: DL,
Mar 12, Apr 12, 13, May 22, 31, Jun 1, Oct 6, 13, 26, Nov 6, Dec 26; 1788:
DL, Jan 17, 18, 21, 31, Mar 1, 29, 31, Apr 14, May 19, 21, Jun 6
Bates, William (music master, composer), 1768: DL, Nov 23; 1775: DL, Nov 24;
1777: CG, May 5; 1778: DL, Mar 30
Bath comedians, 1754: SFG, Sep 21
Bath Morris Dancers, 1743: BFYWR, Aug 23, SF, Sep 8
Bath Teazer (song), 1725: LIF, Apr 30; 1730: SOU, Sep 24
Bath Theatre, 1765: CG, Dec 3; 1768: HAY, Sep 17; 1770: HAY, Sep 20; 1777: HAY,
Jun 9, 11; 1778: HAY, Jan 26, Mar 24, Jul 1, Sep 17; 1779: HAY, Jun 18; 1781:
DL, Oct 15; 1782: DL, Oct 10; 1783: CG, Sep 19; 1785: CG, Oct 17; 1786: CG,
Dec 13; 1787: CG, Oct 3, 19; 1788: CG, Apr 26, HAY, Jul 7, CG, Sep 22, DL,
Oct 2; 1789: DL, Dec 23; 1790: CG, Feb 18, Jun 1, Sep 17; 1791: CG, Sep 19;
1793: HAY, Aug 6, 16; 1794: HAY, Feb 25, CG, Oct 7; 1795: CG, Jan 2, Sep 25;
1796: HAY, Jun 25, CG, Sep 21, 30, Oct 3, 12, DL, 31; 1797: HAY, Aug 16, CG,
Oct 12, DL, 17, CG, 20; 1798: CG, May 12, Sep 26, DL, 27; 1799: CG, Jan 5
Bath Unmasked, The. See Odingsells, Gabriel.
Bath, Knights of the, 1744: HAY, Oct 20; 1772: KING'S, Jun 11
Bath, The; or, The Western Lass. See D'Urfey, Thomas.
Bath, 1701, LIF, Aug 0; 1703: RIW, Aug 12; 1738: GT, May 1; 1744: KING'S, Jun
9; 1749: CG, Oct 4, DL, 5; 1751: DL, Sep 26; 1753: DL, Feb 23, CG, Mar 19,
DL, Oct 9, CG, Dec 10; 1756: DL, Apr 28; 1766: DL, Nov 4; 1767: DL, May 9,
CG, Dec 19; 1768: CG, Oct 24; 1769: DL, Mar 9, HAY, May 15; 1770: DL, Feb 27,
MARLY, Aug 21, DL, Sep 24, Nov 1, 13; 1772: DL, Feb 22, HAY, Mar 30; 1773:
DL, Feb 26; 1774: HAY, Jun 27, MARLY, Jul 2; 1776: DL, Apr 11; 1777: DL, Jan
20, HAY, Jun 26, Jul 15, 24, Aug 7, 19, 25, DL, Oct 14; 1778: DL, Jan 2, Feb
10, Mar 5, 31; 1779: DL, Mar 22; 1780: CG, Jan 12, Mar 14; 1781: HAY, Sep 11;
1782: CG, Oct 21; 1783: DL, Nov 3, Dec 10; 1784: DL, Mar 6; 1785: CG, Jan 19,
DL, Oct 20, Nov 26; 1786: CG, Mar 14, Apr 4; 1787: DL, Jan 29; 1789: DL, Mar
27, Apr 4, CG, May 22; 1790: CG, Nov 19, 23; 1791: DL, Jan 31, CG, May 20;
1792: KING'S, Feb 24, HAY, Jul 25; 1793: HAY, Dec 23; 1795: CG, Nov 9; 1796:
CG, Apr 20, DL, May 2, CG, Oct, 26, Nov 21; 1797: HAY, Aug 19, Sep 4, CG, Nov
11, 20, DL, 24; 1798: CG, May 12
Bathurst (printer), 1780: DL, Oct 19; 1782: DL, Sep 24; 1783: DL, Feb 22, Nov 3
Bathurst, Allen, Baron of Battlesden (speaks epilogue), 1695: WS, Dec 0
Bathurst, Villiers (commentator), 1700: LIF, Jan 28
Batichel. See Battishill.
Batiere, Mrs (actor), 1784: DL, Aug 20
Batson (actor), 1774: HAY, Jan 24
Batson, Mrs (actor), 1774: HAY, Jan 24
Batson's Coffee House, 1743: DL, Apr 29; 1750: DL, Feb 22, Apr 4; 1751: DL, Dec
17; 1759: DL, Mar 30
Batt (actor), 1734: YB, Jul 8
Batten (draper), 1761: CG, Mar 26
Batten, Lady. See Woodcock, Elizabeth.
Batten, Sir William (spectator), 1661: VERE, Oct 2
Batterino (actor), 1754: HAY/SFB, Sep 13

Battishill (Batichel), Jonathan (singer, organist, composer), 1756: SOHO, Mar
   16; 1762: CHAPEL, May 18; 1763: DL, Dec 26; 1764: DL, Nov 2; 1767: HAB, Dec
   10; 1773: HAY, Apr 23; 1777: CG, Nov 25; 1778: CG, Feb 4, 23, HAY, Sep 7;
   1799: HAY, Mar 29
Battle Dance (dance), 1791: CG, Jun 6
Battle in the Mediterranean (entertainment), 1744: MF, May 4
Battle of Dettingen, The (entertainment), 1743: TCY, Aug 4, BFFP, 23, BFHC, 23,
   SF, Sep 8, MEF, Oct 3; 1744: HAY, Apr 26
Battle of Eddington, The. See Penn, John.
Battle of Hastings, The. See Cumberland, Richard.
Battle of Hexham, The. See Colman the younger, George.
Battle of La Hogue, The (song), 1800: CG, Apr 5; see also Thursday in the Morn
   the Nineteenth of May
Battle of Parnassus, The (rehearsal), 1737: HAY, Jan 6
Battle of Poictiers, The; or, The English Prince. See Hoper, Mrs.
Battle of Rosbach, The (pantomime), 1758: HAY, Jan 6, 25
Battle of the Bawd's in the Theatre Royal Dec. 3, 1680, The (poem), 1680: DL,
   Dec 3
Battle of the Books, The. See Cooke, Thomas.
Battle of the Glorious First of August (entertainment), 1798: CG, Oct 31; 1799:
   CG, Nov 9
Battle of the Poets, The. See Cooke, Thomas.
Battle Royal, The (farce, anon), 1785: HAY, Dec 26
Battle Song (song), 1795: CG, May 1, 8; 1797: CG, May 2; 1798: CG, Apr 21;
   1799: CG, Apr 6; 1800: CG, Jun 2
Battlesden, Baron of. See Bathurst, Allen.
Bauday, King of, 1702: DL, Sep 18
Baudouin (Badoin, Baudvin, Boudouin) (dancer), 1735: GF/HAY, Apr 25, May 2, Jun
   2, HAY, Dec 17; 1736: HAY, Feb 16, 20, CG, Nov 9, 26, Dec 28; 1737: CG, Jan
   28, Feb 14, Mar 7, 24, May 12, BF, Aug 23, SF, Sep 7, CG, Oct 7; 1738: CG,
   Feb 13, DL, Oct 3, 21, 30; 1739: DL, Mar 10, Apr 10, May 2, 15, 23, 26, Sep
   8, 13, Oct 19, 26, Nov 1, 22, 28, Dec 6; 1740: DL, Jan 5, 15, Feb 13, Apr 11;
   1741: DL, Oct 12, 21, 27, Nov 4, 11, Dec 4; 1742: DL, Jan 6, Feb 18, Mar 8,
   Sep 21; 1743: DL, Feb 4, 11; 1744: DL, Feb 1, 3, May 5, Oct 2, 17; 1745: DL,
   Jan 14, May 8, 9
Baulk (dance), 1732: LIF, Jan 22, 28, Mar 9, Apr 12, 17, 19, 21, 22, 24, 27
Baumgarten, Karl Friedrich (musician), 1758: CHAPEL, Apr 27; 1761: KING'S, Mar
   12; 1762: KING'S, May 11; 1764: HAY, Nov 13; 1766: KING'S, Apr 10; 1770:
   KING'S, Feb 2; 1771: KING'S, Feb 8, 28, HAY, Apr 12; 1772: KING'S, Feb 21;
   1775: KING'S, Jan 26; 1776: KING'S, Feb 15; 1778: CG, Mar 6; 1779: CG, Nov
   12; 1784: DL, Jan 7, CG, Apr 17, DL, Sep 23, CG, Oct 12; 1787: DL, Dec 26;
   1788: DL, Nov 10; 1791: CG, Dec 10, 21; 1792: CG, Oct 8; 1794: CG, Apr 10,
   Sep 17, Nov 17, Dec 26
Baumgartner (beneficiary), 1742: JS, Jan 25
Bauquetiera de Village, La (dance), 1774: KING'S, May 12
Bauvais (watchmaker), 1735: DL, May 30
Baux, Master Julien (violinist), 1794: HAY, May 22
Bavaria, Duke Clemens of, 1761: KING'S, Oct 13
Bavaria, Elector of, 1699: DL, Apr 15
Bavarian Shoemakers (dance), 1762: DL, Oct 9, 11, 12, Nov 1, 2, 4, 12
Bawhoon, Hodgha (Persian envoy), 1703: DL, Apr 19
Baxter, Alice (commentator), 1699: STJAMES, Sep 0
Baxter, Mrs (actor), 1706: BF, Aug 27; 1710: GR, Sep 20, 28, 30; 1711: GR, May
   21; 1717: SF, Sep 14
Baxter, Mrs (actor), 1741: JS, Oct 6
Baxter, Richard (actor), 1660: COCKPIT, Oct 8, REDBULL, Nov 5; 1661: NONE, Sep
   0
Baxter, Richard (dancer, actor), 1703: DL, Oct 7; 1705: LIF, Oct 8; 1716: DL,
   Apr 4, 11, 20, May 7, 10, 12; 1732: DL, Mar 21; 1736: HAY, Feb 20
Bayes in Petticoats. See Clive, Catherine, The Rehearsal.
Bayes's Opera. See Odingsells, Gabriel.
Bayley, Mrs (singer), 1780: HAY, Sep 25
Bayne (house servant), 1778: DL, May 25; 1779: DL, May 29; 1780: DL, May 23;
   1781: DL, May 25; 1782: DL, May 4; 1787: DL, Jun 4; 1788: DL, Jun 6; 1789:
   DL, Jun 10; 1790: DL, May 29
Baynes (actor), 1800: CG, Jun 13
Bayswater, 1797: CG, Jun 21; 1798: CG, Jun 11; 1799: CG, Jun 12; 1800: CG, Jun
   13
Bayzand (Basant, Bisan), Elizabeth, Mrs William (singer), 1792: CG, Oct 8, 19,
   29, Dec 26; 1793: CG, Mar 11, Sep 30, Oct 7, 24, Nov 28, Dec 7, 27; 1794: CG,
   Sep 22, Oct 20; 1795: CG, Jan 31, Apr 24, May 18, Nov 4, 9, 16; 1796: CG, Jan
   1

Bayzand, William (dancer), <u>1791</u>: CG, Jun 13, Dec 22, 30, 31; <u>1792</u>: CG, Oct 8,
   Dec 20, 22; <u>1793</u>: CG, May 31; <u>1794</u>: CG, Apr 21, Jun 4, Sep 22; <u>1795</u>: CG, Jun
   4, Nov 16; <u>1796</u>: CG, Mar 15, May 10, Jun 6; <u>1798</u>: DL, Dec 6; <u>1799</u>: DL, Jan
   19, Feb 5, Oct 21; <u>1800</u>: DL, Mar 10, 11
Bazely (house servant), <u>1795</u>: CG, Jun 13
Bazinghall St, <u>1749</u>: DL, May 16
Be Thou Ruler (song), <u>1789</u>: DL, Mar 25
Beale (musician), <u>1760</u>: CG, Sep 22
Beale, John (singer), <u>1797</u>: CG, Mar 3; <u>1799</u>: CG, Feb 8
Bear and Harrow Tavern, <u>1728</u>: LIF, May 11; <u>1732</u>: LIF, Apr 27
Bear Yard, <u>1743</u>: LIF, Mar 14
Bear, <u>1660</u>: SF, Sep 10; <u>1778</u>: HAY, Mar 31
Beard, (Lady) Henrietta, Mrs John, <u>1767</u>: CG, May 23
Beard, John (singer, actor, manager, patentee), <u>1732</u>: CR, Feb 23; <u>1734</u>: CG/LIF,
   Nov 9; <u>1735</u>: CG, Jan 8, Mar 5, 28, Apr 1, 16; <u>1736</u>: CG, Jan 23, Feb 19, Mar
   6, HIC, Apr 8, CG, 12, HIC, 20, May 10, CG, 12, 13, Nov 26, Dec 8; <u>1737</u>: CG,
   Jan 12, Feb 14, 16, Mar 10, 14, 15, 17, 19, 23, 26, 28, 31, Apr 2, 11, 12,
   14, 18, 19, 21, 22, 25, 28, 29, May 2, 3, 5, 6, 9, 12, 18, DL, Aug 30, Sep 1,
   3, 8, 20, Oct 11, 13, 18, 22, 24, 25, 27, Nov 12, 15; <u>1738</u>: DL, Jan 19, 25,
   26, 31, Feb 23, Mar 2, 3, 4, Apr 17, 26, 27, May 3, 5, 9, 10, 12, 13, 16, 17,
   18, 19, 29, 30, Sep 7, 9, 12, 21, 23, Oct 10, 16, 20, 24, 25, 30, Nov 30, Dec
   7; <u>1739</u>: DL, Jan 1, 3, 6, 16, KING'S, 16, DL, 18, 24, 27, 31, Feb 1, 5, 7,
   Mar 1, 27, Apr 3, KING'S, 4, DL, 7, 24, 25, 26, 28, 30, May 3, 11, 14, 15,
   16, 17, 18, 23, 25, 28, Sep 1, 6, 18, 22, 27, Oct 9, 23, 24, 26, Nov 8, 20,
   LIF, 22, DL, 28, LIF, Dec 13, DL, 15; <u>1740</u>: HIC, Jan 4, Feb 22, LIF, 27, HIC,
   29, Mar 3, DL, 8, HIC, 19, DL, 22, 25, LIF, 26, DL, 27, HIC, 27, DL, 29, HIC,
   Apr 2, DL, 9, 10, 12, 14, 15, 16, 17, HIC, 18, DL, 18, 19, 21, 22, 24, 25,
   HIC, 25, DL, 26, 28; <u>1741</u>: DL, Sep 24, Oct 1, 8, 9, 12, 15, 24, 29, 31, Nov
   6, 9, 11, 13, 14, 17, 20, 21, 24, 27, Dec 5, 7, 8, 9, 10, 11, 12, 23, 26, 28,
   31; <u>1742</u>: DL, Jan 1, 11, 14, 16, 18, 19, 20, 22, 23, 26, 28, 29, Feb 2, 4,
   10, 11, 12, 13, 15, 17, 18, 19, 20, 23, 25, 26, 27, Mar 1, 2, 4, 6, 9, 11,
   12, 15, 16, 18, 20, 25, 27, 29, 30, Apr 1, 5, 6, 8, 17, 20, 21, 22, 23, 24,
   26, 27, 28, 29, 30, May 1, 3, 4, 6, 8, 11, 13, 14, 17, 18, 20, 22, 27, Oct 7,
   8, 9, 13, 14, 15, 16, 18, 19, 21, 22, 23, 25, 26, 27, 29, 30, Nov 5, 8, 9,
   11, 12, 15, 16, 19, 20, 22, 23, 25, 26, 27, 29, Dec 4, 9, 13, 15, 17; <u>1743</u>:
   DL, Jan 1, 3, 4, 6, 7, 14, 15, 17, 18, 20, Feb 11, CG, 18, 23, DL, Mar 3, 14,
   15, 21, 22, CG, 23, DL, 24, Apr 4, 5, 6, 7, 8, 9, 11, 13, 15, 20, 21, 27, May
   4, 5, 6, 7, 11, 16, LIF, Jun 3, CG, Nov 25, Dec 20, 23, 26; <u>1744</u>: CG, Jan 3,
   5, 19, Feb 9, 10, 14, 24, Mar 2, 3, 8, 13, 15, CR, 21, CG, 28, 29, 30, Apr 2,
   6, 7, 12, 16, 17, 19, 23, 24, 30, May 1, KING'S, Jun 9, CG, Sep 26, Oct 1, 8,
   22, 26, 31, KING'S, Nov 3, CG, 5, 8, 14, 28, Dec 29; <u>1745</u>: CG, Jan 1, KING'S,
   5, CG, 7, 10, 14, 22, 25, Feb 1, Mar 6, 18, KING'S, 27, CG, 28, Apr 2, 3, 4,
   10, 15, 20, May 1, 4, 29, DL, Jun 5, CG, Sep 25, 27, DL, 28, CG, 30, Oct 2,
   14, 18, 21, 29, Nov 4, 15, 22, 23, Dec 2, 3, 12, 30; <u>1746</u>: CG, Jan 1, 8, 15,
   24, 25, Feb 4, 7, GF, 7, CG, 14, 24, Mar 10, 13, 17, 18, Apr 7, 14, 15, 18,
   22, 25, 26, 28, Dec 11, 19, 20, 29, 30, 31; <u>1747</u>: CG, Jan 19, 27, Mar 7, 26,
   Apr 1, 24, Oct 31, Nov 24, Dec 17, 19, 26; <u>1748</u>: CG, Jan 29, Feb 15, Mar 3,
   8, 14, 21, 28, 31, Apr 6, 12, 13, 18, 20, 21, 23, 27, 28, DL, Sep 10, 20, Oct
   6, 15, 18, 25, Nov 3, 14, 23, Dec 26; <u>1749</u>: DL, Jan 2, 18, Feb 21, 28, Mar
   29, Apr 5, 15, HIC, 21, DL, Sep 21, 22, 26, 28, Oct 11, 17, 23, 26, Nov 30,
   Dec 2, 26; <u>1750</u>: DL, Jan 1, 4, 16, 18, 23, Feb 9, 15, 24, Mar 15, 24, 27, 28,
   Apr 25, 26, Sep 8, 11, 13, 18, 20, Oct 1, 13, 15, 20, 30, Nov 7, 13, Dec 13,
   15, 17, 22, 26; <u>1751</u>: DL, Jan 31, Feb 23, Mar 12, 20, Apr 10, 11, KING'S, 16,
   DL, May 14, Sep 7, 10, 17, 19, 20, 24, Oct 1, 11, 17, Nov 4, 19, Dec 17, 26;
   <u>1752</u>: DL, Jan 28, CG, Feb 26, DL, Mar 21, KING'S, 24, DL, Apr 11, 25, 29, Sep
   16, 19, 23, Oct 7, 13, 14, 16, 19, Nov 15, 25, 28, Dec 2, 18, 28; <u>1753</u>: DL,
   Mar 19, 22, 27, 29, Apr 5, 10, 26, 27, KING'S, 30, DL, May 4, Sep 8, 13, 15,
   27, Oct 3, 4, 9, 12, 29, 31, Nov 5, 6, 7, Dec 11, 14, 20, 22, 26; <u>1754</u>: DL,
   Jan 14, KING'S, Feb 28, DL, Mar 19, 23, 28, Apr 1, 16, 17, 24, May 2, 7, 10,
   13, CHAPEL, 15, DL, 17, Sep 14, 17, 19, 24, Oct 3, 5, 8, 10, 11, 14, Nov 4,
   22, 26, 28, Dec 4, 10; <u>1755</u>: DL, Jan 17, Feb 3, 18, Mar 13, 15, 17, KING'S,
   17, DL, 18, Apr 2, 3, 4, 16, 19, 21, 24, 25, 28, 29, May 3, 9, Sep 18, 20,
   23, 27, 30, Oct 7, 8, 10, 24, 27, Nov 1, 4, 26; <u>1756</u>: DL, Jan 20, 21, Feb 11,
   Mar 23, 27, 30, Apr 1, 3, 23, May 3, 5, 8, 21, 24, Sep 23, 28, Oct 9, 12, 16,
   19, Nov 2, 6, 11, 13, 23, 24, Dec 15, 20, 27; <u>1757</u>: DL, Jan 22, SOHO, Feb 1,
   CG, Mar 11, DL, 24, 28, 31, Apr 11, 12, 15, 20, 27, 30, May 5, 7, Sep 10, 27,
   29, Oct 1, 4, 6, 12, 20, 31, Nov 8, 19, Dec 2, 3, 22, 27; <u>1758</u>: DL, Jan 24,
   Feb 7, 21, CG, 22, Mar 1, 3, DL, 11, 16, 29, 31, SOHO, Apr 1, DL, 10, CHAPEL,
   27, DL, May 2, 3, 5, 18, Jun 22, Sep 16, 23, 28, 30, Oct 14, 20, 24, 30, Nov
   3, 15, 24, Dec 18; <u>1759</u>: DL, Jan 3, 6, 20, Feb 1, CG, 2, SOHO, Mar 1, DL, 20,
   29, Apr 2, 5, 7, 24, CG, May 4, DL, 7, 16, 17, 21, RANELAGH, Jun 13, DL, 19,
   HAM, Aug 13, DL, Sep 22, CG, Oct 10, 18, Nov 30, Dec 10, 13; <u>1760</u>: CG, Jan

18, Feb 14, 29, Mar 24, May 10, RANELAGH, Jun 11, CG, Sep 22, 24, 29, Oct 3,
Nov 28, Dec 11, 30; 1761: KING'S, Mar 12, CG, 14, Apr 2, 23, May 25, Sep 7,
12, 14, 16, 18, 25, 26, Oct 13, Nov 26; 1762: CG, Jan 28, Feb 2, Mar 30, Apr
19, CHAPEL, May 18, CG, Sep 22, 29, Oct 1, 4, 8, 26, Nov 1, 15, 29, Dec 8;
1763: CG, Jan 24, 28, Feb 24, Mar 1, DL, Apr 27, 29, CG, Sep 21, Oct 3, 8,
11, 14, 20, 22, Nov 3, 15, 22, Dec 2, 12, 13, 17; 1764: CG, Jan 19, 20, Feb
22, CHAPEL, 29, CG, May 1, Sep 21, Oct 1, 18, 23, 26, 27, 30, Nov 7, 23, Dec
12; 1765: CG, Jan 23, 26, 31, May 16, 20, Oct 3, 4, 7, 12, 15, 22, Nov 20,
Dec 3, 6; 1766: CG, Feb 5, May 5, KING'S, Sep 13, CG, Oct 10, 14, 18, 21, Nov
15, Dec 1, 20; 1767: CG, Jan 1, 29, Feb 5, 14, Mar 4, 16, 17, Apr 20, May 11,
16, 20, 23, Jun 9, Nov 27; 1769: DL, Mar 31; 1796: CG, Jun 7
Beatniffe (printer), 1792: DLKING'S, Jan 18
Beau (song), 1739: TC, Aug 8
Beau Defeated, The. See Pix, Mary.
Beau Demolished, The (play, anon), 1715: LIF, Feb 9, 10, 11, 15, 21, 22, 25,
Mar 1, 31, Apr 2, May 3; 1716: LIF, Feb 10, 28; 1724: LIF, Apr 9, May 6
Beau's Duel, The. See Centlivre, Susannah.
Beauchamp, Godart de
--Amants Reunis, Les, 1735: HAY, Jan 20, 24; 1749: HAY, Nov 14
Beauchamp, Lord (correspondent), 1743: DL, Jan 17, CG, Feb 25, KING'S, Nov 15
Beauclerk, Charles, Duke of St Albans, 1693: DL, Apr 0
Beaufield, Mrs (actor), 1783: HAY, Dec 15; 1784: HAY, Jan 21, Mar 8
Beauford (actor), 1741: TC, Aug 4
Beaufort (ticket deliverer), 1795: DL, Jun 4
Beaufort Buildings, 1711: YB, May 24; 1741: DL, Apr 22; 1742: DL, Dec 15; 1752:
DL, Apr 16; 1753: DL, Apr 25; 1754: DL, Apr 26; 1755: DL, Apr 1, 16; 1757:
DL, Apr 29; 1767: CG, Mar 23; 1777: DL, Mar 10; 1778: DL, Mar 26; 1779: DL,
Mar 15; 1780: DL, Mar 9; 1782: DL, Mar 18; 1786: DL, Mar 21; 1788: CG, Apr
25; 1789: CG, May 15; 1792: CG, May 5
Beaufort, Duke of. See Somerset, Henry.
Beaufort, Miss (actor), 1794: DL, Dec 20, 23; 1795: DL, May 6, Jun 4
Beauharnais, Fanny de
--Fausse Inconstance, La; ou, Le Triomphe de l'Honnetete, 1789: CG, Dec 5
Beaumarchais, Pierre Augustin Caron de, 1777: HAY, Aug 30; 1784: CG, Dec 14;
1785: CG, Feb 12, HAMM, Jul 25, CG, Oct 26; 1790: HAY, Jul 12
--Barbier de Seville, Le; ou, La Precaution Inutile, 1777: HAY, Aug 30
--Mariage de Figaro, Le, 1784: CG, Dec 14
Beaumaunt, Mlle (actor), 1736: HAY, Apr 29
Beaumont (actor), 1731: GF, Feb 22; 1745: GF, Apr 26; 1746: GF, Mar 11; 1747:
GF, Feb 25
Beaumont, Francis, 1662: REDBULL, Jan 22; 1666: BRIDGES, Dec 7; 1668: LIF, Aug
20; 1699: DL, Dec 0; 1704: LIF, Apr 28; 1705: QUEEN'S, May 28, DL, Jun 12,
Jul 25, 27; 1706: DL, Jan 4, QUEEN'S, Apr 26; 1707: QUEEN'S, Jan 4, 16, Feb
14, May 26, Oct 30; 1709: DL, Jan 3, QUEEN'S, Nov 11; 1710: QUEEN'S, Feb 11,
15, Mar 18, GR, Sep 23; 1711: DL, Jan 25, DL/QUEEN, Feb 8, DL, May 17,
DL/QUEEN, Jun 12, DL, Oct 11, 31; 1712: DL, Jan 4, 5, 25, Feb 11, 12, 16, Mar
31, Apr 3, Oct 2, Dec 18, 31; 1713: DL, Feb 12, Mar 17, May 21, Nov 13, Dec
18; 1714: DL, Jan 12, Feb 22, Apr 8, May 3, 19, Sep 24, Oct 25, 28, Nov 1, 9,
Dec 10, 17; 1715: DL, Jan 28, Feb 10, Aug 5, 9, 12, Oct 26, Nov 1, 30, Dec 3;
1716: DL, Jan 14, 28, Nov 13, 17; 1717: DL, Feb 19, Mar 26, Apr 2, 13, May
14, Jul 23, 30, Aug 2, Oct 25, Nov 29, Dec 3; 1718: DL, Jan 23, Feb 15, Jul
18, Aug 5, Oct 24, Dec 31; 1720: DL, Jan 8, Mar 31, May 7, 25, Jun 21, 30,
Jul 21; 1721: DL, Jan 3, 16, Mar 18, May 4, Jun 20, Sep 19, Oct 11, 21, 28,
Nov 13, 16, 20, 27, 30, Dec 18; 1722: DL, Jan 4, 5, 17, 19, 24, Apr 7, May 1,
17, 24, Oct 5, LIF, Nov 17, 19, DL, 29, 30, Dec 5, LIF, 6; 1723: DL, Jan 4,
LIF, 23, DL, Feb 4, 8, Apr 16, Oct 18; 1724: DL, Feb 20, Mar 5, LIF, 26; 1725:
DL, Jan 8, Apr 9, Oct 25, Dec 18; 1726: DL, Mar 24, Oct 22, Dec 8; 1727: DL,
May 24, Dec 4; 1728: DL, Apr 29; 1729: DL, Jan 21, Jul 15, Nov 18; 1730: DL,
Jan 3, Feb 24, GF, Apr 7, DL, Oct 8; 1731: DL, Apr 29, Sep 30, Dec 16; 1733:
DL, Feb 22, Oct 1, DL/HAY, 8, Nov 14, Dec 10, DL, 14, DL/HAY, 17; 1734: DL,
Jan 3, Oct 23, Dec 17; 1735: DL, Jan 28, 29, Feb 18, Oct 9, CG, Nov 17, DL,
29, Dec 1, 31; 1736: DL, Mar 2, CG, May 13, 14, Jun 3, Nov 25; 1737: DL, Mar
17, Sep 3, CG, Oct 26; 1738: CG, Apr 11, DL, Oct 21, Nov 30, Dec 11; 1739:
CG, Jan 25, Feb 5, Apr 14, DL, May 5, CG, 9, DL, 23, CG, Sep 10, DL, Oct 16,
CG, Nov 20, 30, Dec 27; 1740: DL, Jan 3, Mar 8; 1741: CG, Oct 7, DL, 10;
1743: DL, Nov 8, Dec 12; 1744: HAY, Jul 10; 1746: DL, Mar 17, Apr 21; 1747:
DL, Mar 7; 1749: DL, Oct 5, 7, 9, 19; 1750: CG, Apr 5; 1756: DL, Apr 26, CG,
Dec 10; 1757: CG, Jan 28, DL, Apr 30, CG, Oct 17; 1758: CG, Feb 1; 1763: DL,
Oct 8; 1767: CG, Dec 14; 1778: HAY, Jul 30; 1779: HAY, May 31; 1782: HAY, Nov
25; 1783: CG, Jan 17, Apr 23, May 10, HAY, Aug 13; 1785: DL, Jan 27, CG, Apr
11; 1787: DL, Oct 26; 1788: CG, Jan 14, Feb 25; 1791: DL, Mar 22, CG, Jun 1;
1792: DLKING'S, Apr 20; 1796: KING'S, Jul 7, CG, Nov 24

--Coxcomb, The. See Fletcher, John.
--King and No King. See Fletcher, John.
--Knight of the Burning Pestle, The. See Fletcher, John.
--Love's Cure. See Fletcher, John.
--Love's Pilgrimage. See Fletcher, John.
--Maid's Tragedy, The. See Fletcher, John.
--Philaster. See Fletcher, John.
--Scornful Lady, The. See Fletcher, John.
--Triumph of Honour, The, 1783: HAY, Aug 13, 19
--Wit at Several Weapons. See Fletcher, John.
--Wit without Money. See Fletcher, John.
--Woman Hater, The; or, The Hungry Courtier, 1667: NONE, Sep 0; 1668: LIF, Aug
   20
Beaumont, Mrs (actor), 1800: CG, Mar 17
Beaumont, Mrs (singer), 1770: HAY, Dec 10
Beaupre (dancer), 1789: KING'S, Jan 10, 31, Mar 3, 17, 31, Apr 28, May 26
Beauties Triumph. See Duffett, Thomas.
Beauty and Virtue. See Arne, Dr Thomas A.
Beauty at her levee. See Group of Lovers, The.
Beauty in Distress. See Motteux, Peter Anthony.
Beauty no more shall suffer eclipse (song), 1673: DG, May 0
Beaux' Lamentation (song), 1738: DL, May 13
Beaux' Stratagem, The. See Farquhar, George.
Beaw (Beau) (boxkeeper), 1731: DL, May 13; 1732: DL, May 10; 1733: DL, May 23;
   1734: DL/HAY, May 22; 1735: DL, May 23
Becket, T (printer, publisher), 1763: DL, Nov 10; 1769: CG, Feb 25; 1772: DL,
   Feb 29; 1775: DL, Jan 21, May 27, Nov 16; 1776: DL, Sep 21, Oct 18, Nov 21;
   1777: CG, Feb 22; 1778: CG, Jan 21, DL, Mar 16; 1779: DL, Oct 30; 1780: DL,
   Jan 11, Oct 5; 1781: DL, Jan 29, Mar 10; 1782: DL, Feb 25; 1783: DL, Jan 29;
   1795: KING'S, Apr 30; 1796: DL, Dec 26
Beckford, Alderman, 1767: HAY, Jun 19
Beckham (actor), 1731: GF, Nov 1; 1732: GF, Mar 7, May 10; 1733: GF, Jan 24;
   1734: RI, Jun 27; 1735: DL, Jan 22, Nov 15; 1736: DL, Jan 12; 1737: LIF, Jun
   15; 1738: DL, May 18; 1739: DL, May 19; 1740: DL, May 8; 1741: DL, May 15,
   BFH, Aug 22; 1742: GF, Apr 22; 1743: LIF, Apr 7; 1746: CG, Jun 16, GF, Oct
   27, 29; 1749: BFC, Aug 23
Beckham, Mrs (actor), 1735: LIF, Jun 12; 1746: GF, Oct 28, 29, 31, Nov 6, 7,
   13, 18, Dec 5, 17, 18; 1747: GF, Jan 5, Feb 25, Mar 26; 1748: NWC, Apr 4;
   1749: BFC, Aug 23
Beckham's Toy Shop, 1742: GF, Apr 22
Beckingham, Charles
--King Henry the Fourth of France, 1719: LIF, Nov 7, 9, 10, 11
--Scipio Africanus, 1718: LIF, Feb 14, 15, 18, 20, 21, 25
Beckington, Miss (actor), 1734: DL/HAY, May 17, JS, 29, 31, HAY, Jun 21, Aug 14
Bedcott (Becott) (wax chandler), 1747: CG, Apr 28; 1760: CG, Mar 8
Bedford Arms Tavern, 1730: DL, Dec 3; 1732: LIF, Mar 7; 1736: DL, Mar 22, Apr
   10; 1737: DL, Mar 19; 1741: GF, Dec 2; 1742: CG, May 4; 1759: DL, Apr 19;
   1783: KING'S, May 20
Bedford Buildings, 1758: DL, Apr 24
Bedford Coffee House, 1734: CG, Jan 12; 1742: DL, Apr 26; 1743: DL, Apr 18;
   1744: DL, Feb 25, Mar 5, 13, 29, Dec 13; 1745: CG, Mar 6; 1747: CG, Apr 20,
   HAY, 22; 1749: DL, Jan 20; 1750: DL, Mar 29; 1751: DL, Apr 19, CT, Dec 3, DL,
   18; 1752: DL, Jan 21, Apr 11, Nov 15; 1753: DL, May 22, CG, Oct 24, Nov 1, 3;
   1754: CG, Jan 29; 1755: DL, Apr 3; 1756: DL, Apr 24, Dec 18; 1757: DL, Apr
   12, CG, May 27, DL, Dec 21; 1758: DL, Mar 10, CG, Jul 6; 1760: CG, Jan 19,
   Mar 12; 1761: DL, Mar 30
Bedford Court, 1736: CG, Mar 27; 1738: DL, May 10; 1746: CG, Feb 18; 1778: HAY,
   Apr 9; 1798: HAY, Aug 18
Bedford Gate, 1691: BG, Feb 26, Sep 17
Bedford Head Tavern, 1758: CG, Jul 6
Bedford Row, 1733: LIF/CG, May 8; 1736: CG, May 6; 1737: CG, Apr 25; 1739: CG,
   Nov 7; 1786: DL, Jun 6; 1790: DL, May 7; 1791: DL, May 4; 1792: DLKING'S, May
   3; 1793: DL, Apr 25
Bedford Square, 1777: CG, May 2; 1785: HAY, Feb 10, DL, Apr 30; 1786: DL, Mar
   4, May 15; 1787: DL, Jan 29, Apr 17; 1788: DL, Jan 21, Mar 13, Apr 14, CG,
   23, DL, 29, May 2, 5, Dec 17; 1789: CG, Feb 11, DL, 16, Apr 21, CG, 28, DL,
   May 5, 11; 1790: DL, Apr 9, 20, CG, 30; 1791: DL, Apr 28, CG, May 11, Jun 3;
   1792: DLKING'S, Apr 12, CG, May 2; 1794: CG, May 14; 1795: CG, Apr 22, May
   13; 1796: DL, Apr 13, 18, CG, 20, DL, 29, May 23, HAY, Sep 5; 1797: DL, May
   8, 24; 1798: DL, May 7, 18, HAY, Aug 21; 1799: DL, Apr 8, 24, HAY, Aug 13;
   1800: DL, Apr 28, CG, May 20
Bedford St, 1738: DL, Mar 16; 1739: DL, Mar 8; 1740: DL, Mar 13, CG, 20; 1741:

CG, Mar 12; 1742: DL, Apr 21; 1743: DL, Apr 14; 1745: CG, Mar 11; 1746: DL,
  Mar 22; 1750: CG, Apr 5; 1751: DL, Dec 17; 1752: CG, Mar 30; 1780: HAY, Aug
  10; 1781: HAY, Aug 15; 1782: CG, Apr 30, DL, Jun 1; 1786: CG, Apr 19, DL, Jun
  6; 1787: CG, Apr 14; 1788: CG, Apr 26; 1790: CG, Apr 7, DL, May 7; 1791: DL,
  May 4; 1792: DLKING'S, May 3; 1793: DL, Apr 25; 1798: HAY, Aug 18; 1799: CG,
  May 31; 1800: CG, Apr 29, May 24
Bedford, Duchess of, 1753: CG, Mar 24
Bedford, Duke of, 1747: CG, May 27; 1750: DL, Apr 19; 1766: CG, Nov 18; 1767:
  CG, May 26; 1768: CG, Jun 1; 1771: DL, Dec 23; 1772: DL, May 1, Nov 20; 1773:
  DL, Jun 2, Dec 17; 1774: DL, Jun 2, Dec 16; 1775: DL, May 12, Nov 10; 1776:
  DL, May 3, Oct 25; 1777: DL, Dec 19; 1780: DL, Feb 26; 1781: DL, Dec 20;
  1783: DL, Oct 22; 1785: DL, Dec 21; 1787: CG, Jan 23; 1789: DL, Jun 13, CG,
  Nov 16; 1790: DL, Mar 18; 1791: CG, Nov 15; 1794: DL, Jul 2; 1796: CG, May
  25; 1797: KING'S, May 18, CG, Jun 14, DL, Oct 27, CG, Dec 6
Bedford, John Duke of, 1733: DL, Jun 4; 1743: KING'S, May 7
Bedingfield, Edward (commentator), 1685: DLORDG, Jan 1
Bedini, Sga (dancer), 1787: KING'S, Dec 8; 1788: KING'S, Jan 3, 12, 29, Mar 13
Bedlamites (dance), 1780: CG, Apr 21
Bedloe, Captain William
--Excommunicated Prince, The; or, The False Relique, 1678: NONE, Sep 0
Bedlow, Young (spectator), 1679: DG, Jun 21
Bedwell and Freeke (braziers), 1761: CG, Jan 2
Bedwell, Francis (renter), 1746: CG, Dec 10; 1758: CG, Jan 6, Feb 23
Bedwell, Martha (renter), 1758: CG, Jan 6, Feb 23
Beer of Old England (song), 1757: HAY, Sep 23
Beesley (actor), 1780: HAY, Nov 13
Beesomato Duet (song), 1752: CT/HAY, Apr 27, May 5
Beeson (house servant), 1730: GF, Jun 19; 1731: GF, May 14
Beeston (Beeson, Beezon) (actor), 1661: COCKPIT, Nov 13, SALSBURY, 26; 1663:
  NONE, Sep 0; 1667: BRIDGES, Oct 5, 19; 1668: NONE, Sep 0, BRIDGES, 15, Nov 6,
  Dec 18; 1669: BRIDGES, Feb 2, 6, Jun 24; 1670: BRIDGES, Aug 0, BRI/COUR, Dec
  0; 1673: LIF, May 0; 1674: LIF, Mar 0; 1675: DL, Jan 25
Beeston (house servant), 1783: CG, Jun 4; 1784: CG, May 29
Beeston (musician), 1711: WCH, Oct 17; 1712: OS, Nov 28
Beeston's scholar (musician), 1712: OS, Nov 28
Beete (proprietor), 1759: HAM, Aug 13
Beggar on Horseback, A. See O'Keeffe, John.
Beggar's Ballad (song), 1704: DL, Mar 20; 1795: CG, Dec 21; 1796: CG, Jan 4,
  May 20; 1797: CG, May 30, Jun 13; 1798: CG, May 25, 28, Jun 1; 1799: CG, May
  7; 1800: CG, Jun 2
Beggar's Bush, The. See Fletcher, John.
Beggar's Delight, The (song), 1684: DL, Mar 27
Beggar's Opera, The. See Gay, John.
Beggar's Opera, Tragedized, The (play, anon), 1734: HAY, Jun 3, 4, 21
Beggar's Pantomime, The; or, The Contending Colombines (pantomime, anon), 1736:
  LIF, Dec 7, 8, 9, 10, 13, 14, 15, 16, 17, 18, 20, 21, 22, 27, 28, 29, 30, 31;
  1737: LIF, Jan 1, 3, 4, 5, 6, 7, 10, 11, 12, 13, 14
Beggar's Wedding, The. See Coffey, Charles.
Begone, curst Fiends of Hell (song), 1695: DG, Apr 0
Begueule, La; or, She Would and She Would not (dance), 1783: KING'S, Mar 13,
  20, 22, 29, Apr 29, May 10, 13, 31, Jun 6, 14, 19
Behn, Aphra, 1669: BRIDGES, Jun 24; 1670: LIF, Sep 20; 1673: DG, Feb 18; 1676:
  NONE, Sep 0; 1677: DG, Sep 0; 1678: DG, Jan 17; 1679: DG, Mar 0; 1680: DG,
  Jun 0; 1682: DG, Mar 0, Aug 10, 12; 1683: NONE, Sep 0; 1684: ATCOURT, Feb 11;
  1694: NONE, Mar 22; 1695: DL, Apr 1; 1701: DL, Aug 13; 1715: LIF, Aug 11;
  1716: LIF, Jul 27, Aug 3, 8, Oct 31; 1717: LIF, Jan 7; 1718: LIF, Jul 9, 24;
  1721: LIF, Nov 17, DL, 23; 1722: DL, Jan 29, May 9, Oct 17, Dec 20; 1730: GF,
  Apr 6; 1762: CG, Mar 29; 1785: HAY, Dec 26; 1786: DL, Nov 25; 1790: DL, Mar 8
--Abdelazar; or, The Moor's Revenge, 1676: DG, Jul 3; 1692: NONE, Sep 0; 1695:
  DL, Apr 1
--Amorous Prince, The; or, The Curious Husband, 1671: LIF, Feb 24; 1785: HAY,
  Dec 26
--City Heiress, The; or, Sir Timothy Treatall, 1682: DG, Apr 0, May 17; 1697:
  NONE, Sep 0; 1701: DL, Aug 13; 1707: QUEEN'S, Jul 10
--Debauchee, The; or, The Credulous Cuckold, 1677: DG, Feb 0
--Disappointed Marriage, The; or, The Generous Mistress, 1686: DL, Apr 0
--Dutch Lover, The, 1673: DG, Feb 6
--Emperor of the Moon, The, 1687: DG, Mar 0, NONE, Sep 0, DLORDG, Dec 20; 1691:
  DLORDG, Nov 24; 1699: NONE, Sep 0; 1702: DL, Sep 18; 1703: DL, Apr 19, Oct
  18, Nov 24, 25, Dec 27, 31; 1704: DL, Feb 7, Jul 26, Aug 11, Oct 13, Dec 20;
  1705: DL, Jan 1, Apr 13, Nov 12; 1706: DG, Nov 16, DL/DG, 21; 1707: DL/DG,
  Jan 15, 28, DL, Nov 4; 1708: DL, Sep 3; 1709: DL, Mar 8, Dec 27, 28, 30;

1710: DL, Jan 7, 19, Feb 3, 15, Apr 10, 26, GR, Jul 22; 1714: DL, Nov 19, 20, 22, Dec 1, 15, 30; 1715: DL, Feb 26, Mar 1, Apr 5, LIF, 19, 20, Jun 7, Oct 1, Nov 22, DL, Dec 26; 1716: LIF, Jan 13, 31, DL, Mar 1, Apr 3, LIF, 6, May 28, Jul 6, Aug 17, Oct 17, Nov 30, Dec 28; 1717: DL, Feb 5, LIF, Apr 22, Jun 28, Oct 28, Nov 29, Dec 31; 1718: LIF, Jan 31, Mar 29, Jul 18, Oct 28, Nov 29, Dec 31; 1719: LIF, Feb 17, KING'S, Mar 7, LIF, 17, Oct 29, Dec 22; 1720: LIF, Jan 5, 19, Feb 19, Apr 23; 1721: LIF, Jan 19, 20, Feb 6, 28, Mar 21, Apr 21, Oct 25, Nov 17, Dec 6, 27; 1722: LIF, Apr 2, Jul 27, Nov 14, Dec 27; 1723: LIF, Feb 13, May 8, Oct 9; 1724: LIF, May 4, Nov 10; 1726: LIF, Jan 3, Mar 1; 1728: LIF, Nov 23, 25, Dec 12; 1729: LIF, May 20, Nov 11, Dec 1; 1730: LIF, May 19, Oct 1, Dec 29; 1731: LIF, Jan 26, Oct 30; 1735: GF, Oct 15, 17, 20, 22, 23, 24, 27, 28, 29, 30, 31, Nov 4, 5; 1739: CG, Feb 14, Mar 6, 12, 29, Jun 1, Oct 30; 1741: CG, Oct 30; 1748: DL, Dec 20, CG, 23, DL, 26, CG, 26, DL, 27, CG, 27, DL, 28

--False Count, The; or, A New Way to Play an Old Game, 1681: DG, Nov 0; 1696: NONE, Sep 0; 1715: LIF, Aug 11, 17, Oct 5; 1716: LIF, Feb 16, Apr 19; 1718: LIF, May 20, Jul 9; 1730: HAY, Nov 20, 23, Dec 4; 1762: CG, Mar 29

--Feigned Courtezans, The; or, A Night's Intrigue (Midnight's Intrigues, The), 1676: NONE, Sep 0; 1679: DG, Mar 0; 1680: ATCOURT, Mar 6; 1695: NONE, Sep 0; 1716: LIF, Jul 27, 28, Aug 3, 8, Oct 31; 1717: LIF, Jan 7

--Forced Marriage, The; or, The Jealous Bridegroom, 1670: LIF, Sep 20; 1671: LIF, Jan 9, 10; 1673: DG, Feb 18; 1687: NONE, Sep 0; 1689: NONE, Sep 0

--Like Father, Like Son; or, The Mistaken Brothers, 1682: DG, Mar 0

--Lucky Chance, The; or, An Alderman's Bargain, 1686: DL, Apr 0; 1697: NONE, Sep 0; 1718: LIF, Jul 23, 24; 1786: DL, Nov 25

--Merry Counterfeit, The; or, Viscount a la Mode, 1762: CG, Mar 29, Apr 3, May 11; 1771: CG, Apr 29

--Revenge, The; or, A Match in Newgate, 1680: DG, Jun 0

--Roundheads, The; or, The Good Old Cause, 1681: DG, Dec 0

--Rover, The; or, The Banished Cavaliers, 1677: DG, Mar 24; 1680: ATCOURT, Feb 11; 1685: DLORDG, Jan 22, ATCOURT, Oct 29; 1687: ATCOURT, Jan 19; 1690: ATCOURT, Nov 4; 1696: NONE, Sep 0; 1703: DL, Feb 18, Oct 15, Nov 9; 1704: DL, Jan 12, LIF, Feb 9, DL, Oct 21, Dec 5; 1705: DL, Jan 17, Oct 4, QUEEN'S, Dec 14; 1706: QUEEN'S, Oct 21; 1707: QUEEN'S, Jan 20; 1708: DL, Apr 22, May 29, Oct 19; 1709: DL, Feb 14, Mar 28, May 19, QUEEN'S, Oct 29, Dec 31; 1710: QUEEN'S, Apr 19, May 24, GR, Aug 26, DL, Nov 21; 1711: DL, Mar 6, 22, May 18, Oct 17; 1712: DL, May 3, Nov 19; 1713: DL, Oct 1, Dec 4; 1714: DL, Apr 16, Dec 21; 1715: DL, Nov 23, Dec 30; 1716: DL, Mar 6, May 31, Oct 24; 1717: DL, Feb 14, May 30, Oct 1; 1718: DL, Feb 10, Mar 20; 1720: DL, Jan 1, 7, 18, Mar 24, May 4, Nov 21; 1721: DL, Feb 23, Apr 10, May 16, Sep 9, Nov 23; 1722: DL, Jan 29, May 9, Oct 17, Dec 20; 1723: DL, Jan 31, Mar 25, May 18, Oct 21; 1724: DL, Feb 14, Apr 17, Nov 13; 1725: DL, Feb 16, LIF, Apr 5, 21, DL, May 10, Oct 20, LIF, Nov 11, DL, 24; 1726: LIF, Feb 12, Mar 31, Apr 19, DL, May 2, LIF, 24, DL, Sep 6, LIF, Nov 10, DL, Dec 6; 1727: LIF, Apr 15, 28, DL, May 10, LIF, 30, Sep 25, DL, Oct 23; 1728: DL, Apr 24, LIF, May 2, Oct 26; 1729: DL, Jan 1, Mar 13, LIF, Apr 16, DL, May 1, LIF, 14, Sep 29; 1730: LIF, Feb 2, GF, Apr 6, DL, 14, LIF, 23, DL, May 27, Sep 15, LIF, Nov 14; 1731: LIF, Jan 21, DL, Feb 5, GF, Mar 2, 4, 6, LIF, May 14, Oct 18, DL, Nov 23, GF, Dec 6, 17; 1732: DL, Jan 17, Apr 29, GF, May 8, LIF, 10, LIF/CG, Dec 15; 1733: DL, Apr 11, LIF/CG, May 14, CG, Oct 26; 1734: CG, Jan 4, GF, May 3; 1735: DL, Apr 28, May 6, Nov 6; 1736: CG, Mar 29, DL, May 4; 1737: CG, Jan 3, LIF, Mar 24, CG, Apr 11, Sep 26; 1738: CG, Apr 18, Nov 27; 1739: CG, Apr 27; 1740: CG, May 12; 1741: CG, Mar 16, Apr 21, Dec 7; 1742: CG, Jan 9, HAY, Jun 16, 23, CG, Dec 22; 1743: CG, Apr 23, Nov 2; 1748: CG, Mar 14, Nov 9; 1757: CG, Feb 19, 22, 26, Mar 3, 5, 8, 10, Apr 11, May 10, 24, Oct 19, Nov 19; 1758: CG, Apr 1, Nov 16, 17; 1759: CG, Apr 24; 1760: CG, Jan 14, Feb 26, Mar 15, May 15; 1790: DL, Mar 8

--Rover, The, Part II, 1681: DG, Jan 0, Apr 4

--Sir Patient Fancy, 1678: DG, Jan 0, 17

--Town Fop, The; or, Sir Timothy Tawdry, 1676: DG, Sep 0, Nov 1; 1698: NONE, Sep 0

--Wavering Nymph, The; or, Mad Amyntas, 1683: NONE, Sep 0

--Widow Ranter, The; or, The History of Bacon in Virginia, 1689: DL, Nov 20

--Young King, The; or, The Mistake, 1679: DG, Mar 0, Sep 0; 1697: NONE, Sep 0

--Younger Brother, The; or, The Amorous Jilt, 1696: DL, Feb 0

Behold, a ghastly band (song), 1791: CG, Mar 25; 1792: CG, Mar 7; 1794: CG, Mar 14

Behold, a virgin shall conceive (song), 1790: CG, Mar 26; 1793: KING/HAY, Feb 20; 1794: DL, Mar 19

Behold and see (song), 1793: KING/HAY, Feb 20; 1794: DL, Mar 19

Behold Darius great and good (song), 1790: DL, Feb 24; 1792: CG, Mar 7; 1794: CG, Mar 14

Behold I tell (song), 1792: KING'S, Mar 30; 1793: KING/HAY, Feb 20; 1794: DL, Mar 19; 1795: CG, Mar 27
Behold, it is Christ (song), 1794: DL, Apr 10
Behold, natty Sammy (song), 1798: CG, Apr 9
Behold the Lamb (song), 1793: KING/HAY, Feb 20; 1794: DL, Mar 19
Behold the Lord's arm is not shortened (song), 1794: DL, Mar 26
Behold the man with that gigantick might (song), 1693: DL, Apr 0
Behold the monster Polypheme (song), 1790: CG, Mar 3; 1791: CG, Apr 13
Behold the Nations (song), 1790: CG, Mar 17; 1792: CG, Mar 2; 1793: CG, Feb 15; 1794: CG, Mar 7; 1795: CG, Feb 20; 1797: CG, Mar 31; 1799: CG, Mar 15; 1800: CG, Mar 21
Behold the sweet Flowers (song), 1746: GF, Feb 18
Behold, ye powers, this bleeding fair (song), 1694: NONE, Sep 0
Belasyse (Belasses), Sir Henry (killed), 1667: BRIDGES, Aug 12
Belasyse (Bellasses), Baron John (spectator), 1666: ATCOURT, Dec 28; 1669: BRIDGES, Mar 4
Belasyse, Thomas, Viscount Fauconberg (spectator), 1663: BRIDGES, Jun 12
Belchier (banker), 1748: DL, May 2
Belenger (scene designer), 1795: KING'S, Mar 26
Belfille, Anne (actor), 1786: CG, Nov 13; 1787: ROY, Jun 20
Belfort, Mrs (dancer), 1760: CG, Oct 20; 1761: CG, Jan 12
Belguard (actor), 1738: BFP, Aug 23
Belingham (actor), 1775: HAY, Nov 20
Belisarius. See Phillips, William.
Belissen, Mrs (beneficiary), 1760: CG, Dec 20
Bell (singer), 1751: DL, Apr 22
Bell and Dragon (public house), 1776: CHR, Sep 30
Bell Savage Inn, 1749: HAY, Feb 10
Bell Tavern, 1749: CG, Apr 28
Bell, John (printer, publisher), 1771: DL, Dec 11; 1774: DL, Feb 1; 1776: DL, Oct 15, 29, Dec 5; 1777: DL, Oct 7, CG, Nov 18, DL, Dec 13; 1778: CG, Apr 27; 1784: DL, Mar 8; 1785: CG, Feb 28, DL, Dec 1, CG, 26; 1786: CG, Mar 18, Sep 25, Nov 15; 1787: DL, Feb 7; 1788: CG, Apr 23, DL, Sep 13; 1789: DL, Sep 24, 29, CG, Oct 24, Dec 31; 1790: CG, Jan 22, Oct 8, Nov 1, 4, DL, Dec 1, CG, 10; 1791: CG, Feb 11, May 11, DL, 20, CG, Oct 20, DLKING'S, Nov 8; 1792: DLKING'S, Feb 4; 1793: DL, Mar 18, CG, Oct 8; 1797: DL, Dec 14; 1798: HAY, Aug 11, DL, Dec 29; 1799: DL, Apr 22, Dec 7
Bell, Richard (actor), 1668: NONE, Sep 0, BRIDGES, Nov 6, Dec 18; 1669: BRIDGES, Jun 24; 1670: BRIDGES, Aug 0, BRI/COUR, Dec 0; 1671: BRIDGES, Mar 0, Jun 0; 1672: BRIDGES, Jan 0, 25
Bell, Thomas (actor), 1778: HAY, Mar 24; 1785: HAY, Apr 26
Bella Arsene, La. See Monsigny, Pierre Alexandre.
Bella Asteria et horla Tromba (song), 1726: LIF, Mar 28
Bella consola (song), 1746: KING'S, Mar 25
Bella mia Tiranna (song), 1762: KING'S, May 11
Bella notte (song), 1726: DL, Apr 28
Bella Pescatrice, La. See Guglielmi, Pietro.
Bella Sorge L'Esperanza (song), 1734: DL/HAY, Mar 30, Apr 1
Bellam (dancer), 1730: LIF, Apr 24
Bellamira. See Sedley, Sir Charles.
Bellamira, Her Dream. See Killigrew, Thomas.
Bellamy (publisher), 1796: CG, Mar 30
Bellamy and Settree (silk mercers), 1761: CG, Mar 3; 1771: CG, Nov 26; 1772: CG, Feb 3, Dec 8; 1774: CG, Jan 25, Apr 22
Bellamy, B P (actor), 1797: HAY, Dec 4
Bellamy, Daniel
--Love Triumphant; or, The Rival Goddesses (opera), 1722: MBS, Mar 26
Bellamy, Elizabeth (actor), 1736: CG, Sep 24, 29, Oct 8, 13, 25, 29, Nov 11, 22, 25, 29, Dec 6, 9, 20; 1737: CG, Jan 10, 17, Feb 1, 3, May 10, Sep 21, 26, Oct 12, 17, 26, 28, 29, Nov 9, 14, 16, 18; 1738: CG, Jan 6, 9, 25, Apr 17, May 18, Sep 22, 27, Oct 4, 9, 13, 16, 20, 26, 30, Nov 2, 7, 17, 18, 20, 27, 28, Dec 6, 12; 1739: CG, Jan 15, 22, 23, Feb 14, Mar 27, Apr 5, 12, May 1, 2, 3, 7, 25, Aug 21, Sep 5, 17, 1(, 21, 22, 28, Oct 2, 6, 8, 26, 29, 30, Nov 10, 20, Dec 1; 1740: CG, Jan 17, 25, Mar 18, 27, Apr 14, May 2, 5, 9, 12, 16, 23, 27, Sep 24, Oct 1, 3, 8, 22, 23, 29, Nov 1, 15, Dec 4, 19, 29; 1741: CG, Jan 12, 17, 21, 29, Mar 7, 16, Apr 11, 17, 20, 21, 22, 25, 28, May 1, 4, Oct 2, 10, 26, 30, Nov 7, 9, 26, Dec 1, 7, 11; 1742: CG, Feb 25, Mar 27, Apr 6, 19, May 8, Oct 27, 29, Nov 30, Dec 8, 22
Bellamy, George Anne (actor), 1744: CG, Nov 22; 1745: CG, Jan 31, Feb 11, 15, 19, Mar 7, 11, Apr 16; 1748: CG, Oct 22, 24, 25, Nov 15, 28, Dec 1, 3, 9, DL, 10, CG, 20, 26; 1749: CG, Jan 11, 13, Feb 18, 23, Mar 14, 29, Apr 5, 13, May 4; 1750: CG, Jan 23, 27, 31, Feb 2, 5, 20, 21, Mar 1, 6, 12, 20, 22, Apr 3,

23, 30, DL, Sep 28, Oct 1, 2, 24, Nov 1, 19, Dec 3; 1751: DL, Jan 16, 18, 21,
Feb 23, Mar 14, 18, Sep 20, Oct 7, 10, 14, 22, Nov 2, 4, 8, 28, Dec 3, 10,
30; 1752: DL, Jan 9, 21, 25, Feb 6, 13, 17, Mar 7, 12, 14, Apr 20, Sep 21,
Oct 3, 5, 11, 13, 28, Nov 3, 20; 1753: DL, Feb 1, 22, Mar 3, 22, 24, 29, Apr
2, 9, 30, May 7, CG, Oct 24, DL, 30, CG, Nov 19, 20, 22, 28, 30, Dec 15;
1754: CG, Jan 8, 10, Feb 23, Mar 26, 28, Apr 25, Oct 14, 17, 18, 29, Nov 20,
23, 27, 28, Dec 10; 1755: CG, Jan 10, 13, 14, 15, Feb 4, 20, Mar 6, 12, 18,
22, Apr 10, May 16, Oct 11, 14, 20, 30, Nov 4, 7, 14, 19, 22, 26, Dec 5;
1756: CG, Jan 15, Feb 3, 9, Mar 30, DL, Apr 8, CG, 29; 1757: CG, Mar 31, Dec
5, 7, 10, 12, 14, 20; 1758: CG, Jan 11, 16, 23, 26, 27, Mar 9, 13, 16, 29,
Apr 10, 12, 17, 25, Sep 29, Oct 2, 6, 14, 23, 26, 27, Nov 1, 14, Dec 2, 18;
1759: CG, Jan 12, Mar 24, 26, Apr 2, 5, 21, May 8, Nov 23; 1761: CG, Sep 12,
25, 28, Oct 1, 3, 5, 6, 13, 19, 20, 21, 23, 27, Nov 13; 1762: CG, Jan 12, 22,
Feb 3; 1764: CG, Dec 7, 21, 31; 1765: CG, Jan 14, 19, 21, 25, 28, Feb 18, Mar
14, 25, Apr 11, 16, May 7, 15, Sep 20, 23, 25, Oct 7, 11, 22, 28, Nov 13;
1766: CG, Jan 31, Feb 5, Mar 15, 17, 31, Apr 1, 14, 18, 28, May 6, 13, Nov
28, Dec 4, 9, 10, 26; 1767: CG, Jan 19, Feb 14, 16, Mar 2, 21, 23, 28, 31,
Apr 25, 27, May 4, 11, 13, 28, Sep 16, 23, 25, Oct 5, 16, 19, 29, 30; 1768:
CG, Mar 24, Apr 20, DL, Aug 18, Sep 8, CG, 26, 28, Nov 24, Dec 30; 1769: CG,
Jan 28, Mar 28, Apr 7, 15, May 3, Oct 6, 26, Nov 4, 15; 1770: CG, Feb 12, Mar
20, 24, 31, Apr 2, 24, Sep 24; 1780: CG, Jun 1; 1781: DL, May 29; 1782: CG,
May 27; 1785: DL, May 24
Bellamy, Mrs, school of, 1722: MBS, Mar 26
Bellamy, Richard (singer), 1786: DL, Mar 3, 24, 29
Bellamy, Thomas (author)
--Comet, The; or, How to Come at Her, 1789: HAY, Aug 10, 24, Sep 2, 9, 14;
1790: HAY, Aug 5
--Friends, The; or, The Benevolent Planters (prelude), 1789: HAY, Aug 5, 10
Bellamy, Thomas Ludford (singer), 1791: DL, Mar 11, 16, Apr 1; 1793: KING/HAY,
Feb 20, 22
Bellario (commentator), 1745: DL, Mar 18
Belle Esclave, La. See L'Estoile, Claude de.
Belle of the Village (dance), 1781: CG, Nov 1, 8; 1782: CG, May 25, Sep 25, Oct
29; 1783: CG, Sep 17; 1784: CG, Sep 17, Nov 6, 16; 1785: CG, Feb 14
Belle's Stratagem, The. See Cowley, Hannah.
Bellear (composer), 1734: GF, Mar 18
Bellerephon. See Terredellas, Domenico.
Bellers, Pettiplace (author)
--Injured Innocence, 1732: DL, Feb 3, 4, 5, 7, 8, 9
Belles have at ye all; or, Sketch of the Fashions (entertainment), 1784: CG,
Jun 14; 1786: DL, Mar 21; 1789: HAY, Aug 5; 1795: CG, Apr 29; 1796: CG, Apr 8
Belleur (jeweller), 1735: CG/LIF, Apr 24
Bellguard (actor), 1738: TC, Aug 7, SFH, Sep 5
Bellicourt. See Balicourt.
Bellman's Chaunt (song), 1795: CG, Dec 21, 26
Belloli, Marianna (singer), 1793: KING'S, Feb 5, 26, Mar 19, Apr 23, May 14,
Jun 8, 11
Belloy, Pierre Laurent Buirette de
--Gabrielle de Vergy, 1777: CG, Dec 10
Bells (music), 1757: HAY, Nov 2; 1796: CG, Jun 2
Bells of Aberdovy (song), 1789: DL, May 15; 1791: CG, May 18; 1798: CG, May 25
Belmira (opera, anon), 1734: LIF, Mar 23, 26, 30, Apr 2
Belmont (actor), 1792: HAY, Oct 15
Belon, Peter, 1675: DL, May 0
--Mock Duellist, The; or, The French Valet, 1675: DL, May 0
Belphegor; or, Arlequin Aux Enfers. See Legrand, Marc-Antoine.
Belphegor; or, The Marriage of the Devil. See Wilson, John.
Belphegor; or, The Wishes. See Andrews, Miles Peter.
Belshazzar. See Handel, George Frederic.
Belvoir, 1676: NONE, Sep 0
Bembridge. See Bambridge.
Ben and Mary (song), 1799: HAY, Sep 2
Ben Backstay lov'd the gentle Anna (song), 1790: CG, Nov 23, 26
Ben Jonson's Head Tavern, 1742: DL, Apr 21, 30; 1766: DL, Oct 2, 7, 14, 20, 27,
Nov 3, 10, 17, Dec 1, 8, 17, 22, 29; 1767: DL, Jan 6, 12, 26, Feb 9, 23, Mar
3, 9, 23, 31, Apr 6, 21, 27, May 4, 11, 25
Ben, Miss (actor), 1720: CGR, Jun 22
Benauki (spectator), 1734: LIF, Aug 20
Bence's Booth, 1750: SFB, Sep 8, 10, SF, 11, SFB, 12; 1752: SFB, Sep 22; 1754:
HAY/SFB, Sep 19, 20, 21, 23, 24; 1756: SFB, Sep 20, SF, 22, 23
Bence's Room, 1755: BF, Sep 6; 1757: BFB, Sep 5, 6
Bench of Justices, 1772: DL, Apr 24; 1773: DL, Sep 18

Benche mi siu crudele (song), <u>1751</u>: KING'S, Apr 16
Bencraft (Bancraft), James (actor), <u>1729</u>: LIF, Jan 1; <u>1730</u>: SFOF, Sep 9; <u>1731</u>: SF/BFMMO, Aug 26; <u>1732</u>: BFMMO, Aug 23; <u>1733</u>: BFMMO, Aug 23; <u>1734</u>: CG, May 14, BFRLCH, Aug 24, Sep 2, LIF, Oct 1, CG/LIF, Dec 30; <u>1735</u>: CG/LIF, Feb 8, LIF, Apr 19, CG, Oct 13, 17, Nov 6, 15, Dec 27; <u>1736</u>: CG, Jan 1, 9, 23, Mar 27, LIF, Apr 2, CG, 6, LIF, 16, CG, Jun 4, LIF, Jul 1, BFHC, Aug 23, CG, Sep 29, Oct 8, Nov 3; <u>1737</u>: CG, Feb 14, May 20, LIF, Jun 15, Jul 26, CG, Sep 30; <u>1738</u>: CG, Jan 25, Feb 13, 16, Mar 13, Apr 25, May 3, TC, Aug 7, BFP, 23, CG, 29, SFH, Sep 5, CG, Oct 4, 30, Nov 18, Dec 2, 4; <u>1739</u>: CG, Jan 20, Apr 9, 25, May 8, 21, BFH, Aug 23, CG, 31, Sep 7, 10, 12, 14, 17, 22, 27, Oct 3, 10, 20, 26, 31, Nov 20, Dec 4; <u>1740</u>: CG, Feb 12, Mar 27, Apr 30, May 5, 9, 13, Jun 5, BFHC, Aug 23, CG, Sep 19, 26, Oct 1, 3, 10, 22, 24, Nov 15, Dec 4, 13, 29; <u>1741</u>: CG, Jan 5, 7, 19, 21, 27, Feb 7, 16, 17, 24, 28, Mar 30, Apr 2, 6, 10, 11, 17, 18, 24, 28, 30, May 4, DL, Jun 4, BFH, Aug 22, CG, Sep 25, 28, 30, Oct 10, 13, 17, 20, 21, 24, Nov 26, Dec 18; <u>1742</u>: CG, Jan 2, 5, 21, Feb 22, Mar 6, Apr 29, May 4, 5, BFHC, Aug 25, CG, Oct 6, 9, 13, 16, 27, Nov 4, 25, Dec 7, 15, 21; <u>1743</u>: CG, Jan 8, 18, Feb 4, SOU, 18, 25, CG, Mar 8, Apr 13, 21, May 20, BFHC, Aug 23, CG, Sep 21, 28, 30, Oct 17, Nov 4, 7, 21, Dec 3, 8, 19, 20, 26, 27; <u>1744</u>: CG, Jan 14, Feb 14, Mar 30, Apr 2, 6, 13, 16, 19, 24, May 1, Sep 24, Oct 1, 15, 22, 24, 31, Nov 1, 5, 8, Dec 8, 13, 21; <u>1745</u>: CG, Jan 1, Mar 18, Apr 4, 26, 29, May 3, Sep 23, 30, Oct 11, 16, 29, Nov 4, 14, 15, 23, 28, Dec 13; <u>1746</u>: CG, Jan 1, 2, 9, 23, Feb 5, 24, Apr 1, 7, 8, 14, 17, 22, Sep 29, Oct 3, 4, 20, 27, 29, Nov 1, 4, 6, 12, Dec 8, 11, 17, 19, 31; <u>1747</u>: CG, Jan 29, Feb 3, 6, 12, 24, Mar 17, May 1, 22, Oct 31, Nov 16, 23, Dec 9, 19, 26, 28; <u>1748</u>: CG, Jan 2, 7, 27, Feb 29, Mar 3, 8, 14, 28, Apr 11, 13, 20, 21, 22, 29, Sep 23, 26, 30, Oct 3, 7, 14, 17, 27, Nov 4, 15, 16, 24, 26, Dec 22; <u>1749</u>: CG, Jan 2, 11, Mar 2, 7, 13, 14, 29, HAY, Apr 6, CG, 7, 12, 21, Sep 27, Oct 2, 6, 12, 18, 19, 20, 24, 25, 26, Nov 1, 8, 9, 23, 24, Dec 8; <u>1750</u>: CG, Feb 7, 22, Apr 16, 21, 23, Oct 12, 29, Nov 8, 12, 22, 24, 29, Dec 4, 21, 26; <u>1751</u>: CG, Apr 20, 23, 25, 29, May 1, 3, 9, Sep 23, 25, 27, 30, Oct 11, 28, Nov 11, Dec 4, 14; <u>1752</u>: CG, Mar 30, Apr 28, May 4, Oct 9, 10, 16, 18, 23, 26, 30, Nov 1, 2, 23, 28, Dec 7, 11, 13, 14; <u>1753</u>: CG, Mar 19, Apr 25, 27, May 7, 8, 18, Sep 12, 21, 26, Oct 17, 22, 24, 30, 31, Dec 15; <u>1754</u>: CG, Feb 12, Mar 9, Apr 2, 19, May 1, 7, Sep 16, 20, Oct 2, 14, 24, Nov 5, 14, 16, Dec 13, 30; <u>1755</u>: CG, Jan 28, Apr 2, 23, 25, May 6, 15, Oct 6, 17, 22, 24, Nov 10, 12, 13, 17, Dec 3, 27; <u>1756</u>: CG, Jan 6, Apr 24, 28, May 6, Sep 22, 27, 29, Oct 6, 19, 21, 29, Nov 4, 9, 24, 26, Dec 7, 10; <u>1757</u>: CG, Jan 27, 28, Feb 16, Apr 27, 29, May 20, Sep 16, 28, Oct 5, 13, 17, Nov 2, 5, 9, 11, 14, Dec 10; <u>1758</u>: CG, Jan 20, Apr 3, 14, 17, 19, Oct 4, 6, 9, 20, 25, 30; <u>1759</u>: CG, Feb 1, Mar 3, 17, Apr 7, 17, 28, May 11, Oct 10, Nov 5, 28, Dec 10; <u>1760</u>: CG, Sep 22, Oct 1, 6, 10, 15, 25; <u>1761</u>: CG, Apr 2, 14, 20, 28, May 8, 25, Sep 9, Oct 13, Nov 2; <u>1762</u>: CG, Apr 19; <u>1765</u>: CG, Jan 10, 21
Benda (composer), <u>1755</u>: HAY, Apr 18
Bendler, Salomon (singer), <u>1712</u>: QUEEN'S, Jan 23, Feb 27
Beneath a shady willow (song), <u>1676</u>: DG, Nov 4
Beneath that Shade (song), <u>1753</u>: KING'S, Apr 30
Beneath the myrtle shade (song), <u>1670</u>: BRI/COUR, Dec 0; <u>1692</u>: NONE, Sep 0
Beneditte (singer), <u>1720</u>: RI, Aug 29
Benefice, The. See Wild, Robert.
Benefit Ticket, The; or, The Self Rival (play, anon), <u>1719</u>: CGR, Nov 26
Benelli, Antonio Peregrino (singer), <u>1798</u>: KING'S, Apr 21, 26, 28, Jun 5, 19, Dec 8, 29; <u>1799</u>: KING'S, Jan 22, 26, Apr 20, May 30; <u>1800</u>: KING'S, Mar 18, 29, Apr 15, May 22, Jun 21
Benety, Anna (dancer), <u>1761</u>: KING'S, Feb 7
Benety, Giorgi (dancer), <u>1761</u>: KING'S, Feb 7
Benevolent Planters, The. See Bellamy, Thomas.
Benigni, Giuseppe (singer), <u>1790</u>: HAY, Apr 6, 29, May 29, Jun 3; <u>1791</u>: PAN, Feb 17, Apr 14, Jun 2
Benincasa, Bartolomeo (librettist), <u>1789</u>: KING'S, Feb 28
Benini, Anna (singer), <u>1787</u>: KING'S, Jan 9, Feb 17, Apr 17, Jun 5
Benjamin Bolus; or, The Newcastle Apothecary (entertainment), <u>1797</u>: DL, Apr 28, HAY, Aug 8
Benn and Pugh (merchants), <u>1773</u>: CG, Feb 1
Bennald (actor), <u>1736</u>: YB, Apr 26
Bennet (boxkeeper), <u>1796</u>: DL, Jun 15; <u>1797</u>: DL, Jun 13; <u>1798</u>: DL, Jun 9; <u>1799</u>: DL, Jul 3; <u>1800</u>: DL, Jun 14
Bennet St, <u>1779</u>: DL, May 11; <u>1780</u>: DL, May 5; <u>1782</u>: DL, May 3; <u>1786</u>: DL, May 10
Bennet, Claude (wine merchant), <u>1759</u>: CG, May 10
Bennet, Elizabeth (actor, singer), <u>1733</u>: HAY, Jun 4, Jul 26, BFMMO, Aug 23; <u>1734</u>: BFRLCH, Aug 24; <u>1735</u>: SOU, Apr 7, LIF, Jul 16, YB, 17, LIF, 23, Aug 1, 6, 25, 29, Sep 2, 5, YB/HAY, 17, DL, Oct 7, Nov 20; <u>1736</u>: DL, Jan 1, 12, Feb 28, May 7, Sep 14, 18, Oct 20, 23, 30, Nov 1, 13, Dec 22, 31; <u>1737</u>: DL, Jan

29, May 5, 17, 21, Sep 6, 17, 20, 27, 29, Oct 25, 27, Nov 11, 15, 16; 1738:
DL, Jan 5, 19, Feb 1, 2, 13, Mar 20, 21, May 6, 8, 13, 22, Sep 23, 28, Oct
30, Nov 2, 8, 9, 25, Dec 9, 15, 26; 1739: DL, Jan 3, 8, 13, 16, 26, Feb 5, 6,
8, Mar 1, 10, 20, 27, Apr 3, 10, 25, May 18, 19, 25, 28, Sep 4, 6, 8, 11, 15,
20, 24, 26, 27, Oct 1, 3, 4, 5, 6, 8, 9, 11, 15, 18, 23, 24, 27, 29, Nov 3,
7, 10, 20, 23, Dec 6, 11, 19; 1740: DL, Jan 5, 8, 19, Feb 13, 16, 23, Mar 17,
20, 27, Apr 15, 17, 19, 22, 23, 24, May 2, 6, 14, 15, Sep 11, 13, 18, 20, Oct
7, 10, 11, 14, 17, 27, 29, Nov 1, 6, 7, 24, 29, Dec 6, 15, 20; 1741: DL, Feb
2, Mar 30, 31, May 9, 12, 14, 27, BFTY, Aug 22, DL, Sep 10, 12, 15, 17, 19,
22, Oct 10, 15, Nov 11, Dec 7, 14, 15, 16, 19; 1742: DL, Jan 25, Feb 12, 13,
Mar 8, Apr 5, 20, 23, 28, May 6, 14, 28, Sep 11, 14, 16, 18, 25, 28, Oct 2,
5, 12, 13, 26, 27, Nov 1, 3, 8, 16, Dec 14; 1743: DL, Jan 11, Feb 17, Mar 1,
21, 24, SOU, 30, DL, Apr 7, 15, 29, May 4, 5, 12, 23, Sep 15, 17, 20, 22, 27,
29, Oct 4, 6, 8, 13, 15, 20, 22, 25, 27, Nov 8, 18, 23, 29, Dec 1, 12, 15,
16, 17, 19, 20; 1744: DL, Jan 7, 27, Mar 10, 12, Apr 3, 17, May 1, 4, 9, 14,
Sep 18, 20, 27, Oct 4, 9, 11, 13, 17, 20, 22, 24, 27, 30, Nov 1, 2, 3, 6, Dec
19; 1745: DL, Jan 26, Feb 11, 13, 20, Mar 30, Apr 17, 19, May 9, Sep 24, 26,
Oct 5, 8, 12, 15, Nov 9, 18, 19, 23, 25, 28, Dec 5, 11, 20; 1746: DL, Jan 2,
8, Mar 10, 13, Apr 5, 11, 14, 21, 23, 26, 28, May 9, Sep 23, 27, SOU, Oct 7,
DL, 11, 23, 25, 31, Nov 1, 21, Dec 20, 26, 29, 30; 1747: DL, Mar 12, 16, 23,
24, 28, May 18, Sep 15, 22, 24, 26, 29, Oct 3, 29, 30, Nov 2, 6, 7, 16, 17,
Dec 16; 1748: DL, Jan 22, Feb 3, Mar 15, 22, Apr 28, May 6, 18, Sep 15, Oct
31, Nov 1, 3, 5, 7, 28, 29, Dec 22, 23, 26, 31; 1749: DL, Jan 9, 16, 25, Apr
5, May 8, Sep 19, 21, 22, 26, Oct 13, 21, Nov 16, 28, Dec 7, 18, 20, 26, 28,
30; 1750: DL, Jan 22, 29, Mar 15, 19, Apr 2, 9, May 3, Sep 8, 11, 13, 15, 27,
28, Oct 15, 17, 23, Nov 1, 3, 8, 24, Dec 3, 31; 1751: DL, Jan 5, 12, 26, Feb
2, 15, 21, 23, Mar 12, 14, May 13, Sep 10, 12, 13, 14, 19, 20, 26, Oct 3, 4,
7, 29, Nov 2, 7, 16, Dec 10, 14, 26, 30; 1752: DL, Jan 1, 28, Mar 7, 9, Apr
6, 20, 27, Sep 19, 21, 23, 30, Oct 3, 5, 12, 13, 14, 26, 30, Nov 3, 8, 25,
27, Dec 18, 19, 29; 1753: DL, Jan 22, Mar 22, Apr 3, 14, May 1, 4, 22, Sep 8,
11, 13, 15, 20, 25, Oct 2, 3, 4, 9, 12, 16, 20, 24, 31, Nov 6, 14, 15, 26;
1754: DL, Jan 16, 23, Feb 1, 25, Mar 18, 23, Apr 16, 30, Sep 14, 17, 19, 21,
26, Oct 1, 5, 11, 12, 16, 21, 29, Nov 11; 1755: DL, Jan 15, 22, 25, Feb 18,
22, 25, Mar 4, Apr 2, 15, 25, May 6, Sep 13, 16, 20, 27, Oct 4, 7, 8, 23, 27,
31, Nov 12, 17, Dec 1, 4, 5, 11; 1756: DL, Jan 21, Feb 27, Mar 29, 30, Apr
24, May 5, 14, 18, 24, Sep 21, 30, Oct 12, 14, 21, 23, 28, Nov 11, 17, 19,
Dec 27; 1757: DL, Jan 3, 18, Feb 22, Mar 5, 7, 24, Apr 20, 30, Sep 10, 13,
17, 20, 22, 24, Oct 4, 6, 7, 8, Nov 10, 15, Dec 2, 3; 1758: DL, Jan 19, 27,
Feb 1, 20, Mar 11, 16, Apr 18, May 4, 17, Jun 1, Sep 16, 19, 23, 26, 28, Oct
3, 10, 12, 19, 25, 27, Nov 7, 14, 15, 23, 24, Dec 18, 20, 28; 1759: DL, Jan
6, 17, 20, Feb 15, Mar 6, 20, 24, Apr 26, May 11, 14, 24, Sep 22, 25, 29, Oct
2, 4, 9, 12, 17, 19, 22, 25, 31, Nov 2, 9, 10, 20, 23, Dec 5, 7, 12, 19, 29,
31; 1760: DL, Jan 11, 19, Mar 6, 20, Apr 12, 18 29, 30, May 13, Sep 20, 30,
Oct 2, 3, 9, 10, 11, 15, 17, 22, Nov 17, 26, 27, Dec 17, 29, 30; 1761: DL,
Mar 26, Apr 1, 16, 18, 28, 29, May 1, 5, 7, 11, 25, 28, Sep 8, 10, 12, 14,
15, 17, 18, 25, 26, Oct 26, 31, Nov 6, 18, 28, Dec 23; 1762: DL, Jan 15, 20,
23, 27, Mar 2, 6, 15, 20, 25, Apr 1, 22, 24, May 3, 6, 10, 12, Sep 18, 21,
23, 25, 28, 30, Oct 4, 5, 6, 12, 14, 15, Nov 1, 8, 10, 12, 16, 17, 18, 19,
26, 29, Dec 11, 14; 1763: DL, Jan 15, 17, Feb 17, Apr 11, 13, May 7, 12, 17,
26, Sep 17, 20, 24, 27, Oct 1, 14, 15, 24, 31, Nov 7, 19, 29, Dec 1, 5, 14,
17, 26; 1764: DL, Jan 9, 13, 14, 25, Feb 14, 18, Mar 3, 20, 24, 26, Apr 14,
24, Sep 15, 18, 20, 22, 27, 29, Oct 2, 4, 6, 9, 18, 20, 23, 25, Nov 7, 27,
Dec 8, 12, 18; 1765: DL, Jan 1, 15, 18, Feb 4, Mar 26, Apr 27, May 4, 11, 18,
Sep 14, 17, 21, 26, Oct 14, 18, 22, 23, 24, 28, 31, Nov 15, 16, 20, 22, Dec
3, 6; 1766: DL, Jan 13, 24, 29, Mar 20, Apr 9, 12, 25, May 10, Sep 20, 23,
25, 27, 30, Oct 21, 23, 29, 31, Nov 8, 20, 28, Dec 29, 30; 1767: DL, Jan 24,
Feb 7, 9, Mar 21, 30, Apr 11, May 4, 16, 23, 26, Jun 1
Bennet, Henry, Lord Arlington (Lord Chamberlain), 1668: LIF, Aug 29; 1680: DG,
Dec 8; 1683: DL, Jan 19
Bennet, Warner (actor, dancer), 1741: GF, Sep 16, Oct 9, 16, CG, Dec 11; 1742:
CG, Mar 15, May 5; 1743: HAY, Mar 24; 1744: DL, Feb 1, Oct 17; 1746: GF, May
1, BF, Aug 23, SFHP, Sep 8, SOU, 25, NWMF, Oct 6, DL, Nov 7; 1748: CG, Sep
26; 1749: CG, Jan 12, Apr 22, Oct 12, 20, Nov 9, 17, 23, Dec 29; 1750: DL,
Jan 1, CG, Feb 22, Apr 3, May 7, Oct 12, 22, 29, Nov 8, 23; 1751: CG, May 7,
Sep 27, 30; 1752: CG, Mar 17, Apr 28, 30, May 2, 4, Oct 18, 26, 30, Nov 1,
Dec 11, 13; 1753: CG, Feb 7, Apr 5, May 8, 9, 14, 15, 21, Sep 10, 12, 26, Oct
5, 10, 22; 1754: CG, Apr 18, 22, 30, May 7, 9, 15, Sep 16, Oct 2, 4, 7, Nov
1, 6, 16, 20, Dec 10; 1755: CG, Jan 8, Mar 6, 18, May 12, 15, Sep 29, Oct 6,
11, 16, 17, 20, 21, 22, Nov 3, 12, 17, Dec 3, 4, 30; 1756: CG, Jan 15, Feb
26, Mar 22, 25, 30, Apr 29, May 1, 13, 17, Sep 20, 22, 27, Oct 1, 4, 6, 15,
16, 22, 25, Nov 11, 16, 19, 22, 24, Dec 7, 10, 20; 1757: CG, Jan 21, 27, 28,
Feb 9, 16, 19, Mar 14, 29, 31, May 2, 4, 13, Sep 21, 23, 26, 28, Oct 7, 8,

10, 13, 14, 17, 19, Nov 5, 7, 11, Dec 5, 7, 8, 10, 20; 1758: CG, Jan 27, 28,
Feb 21, Mar 14, 16, Apr 3, 5, 21, May 3, Sep 22, 25, 27, Oct 4, 9, 13, 20,
30, Nov 1, 2, 9, 13, 14, 16, 18, 21; 1759: CG, Feb 1, 13, 26, Mar 3, 5, 17,
20, 27, Apr 7, 25, 30, May 7, 11, 15, Sep 26, 28, Oct 5, 10, 15, Nov 28, Dec
6, 18, 31; 1760: CG, Jan 4, 9, 14, 31, Feb 7, 14, Mar 18, 25, Apr 8, 18, 28,
29, May 2, 5, 6, 7, 8, 12, 14, 19, Sep 22, 24, 29, Oct 1, 10, 11, 14, 17, Nov
18, 21, 24, Dec 18, 31; 1761: CG, Jan 6, 7, Feb 17, Mar 3, 26, Apr 2, 17, 20,
27, May 1, 5, Sep 7, 14, 23, 25, 26, Oct 7, 14, 17, 26, 31, Nov 9, 10, 24,
Dec 28; 1762: CG, Feb 15, 22, Mar 2, 13, 20, 22, 23, 29, Apr 16, 26, May 5,
6, 7, 13, Sep 20, 22, 24, Oct 1, 4, 9, 16, 20, Nov 8, 29, Dec 8, 10, 21, 29;
1763: CG, Jan 11, 18, Feb 14, Apr 15, 27, May 9, 11, 16, Sep 21, 26, 30, Oct
7, 14, 18, 22, Nov 3, 10, 22, Dec 9, 26; 1764: CG, Jan 5, Feb 1, 9, 11, 15,
Mar 27, Apr 27, 28, May 7, 11, 18, 21, Sep 21, 26, Oct 3, 5, 8, 11, 17, 18,
20, 23, 25, Nov 3, Dec 29; 1765: CG, Feb 18, Apr 29, May 8, 15, Sep 16, 20,
30, Oct 2, 3, 4, 7, 10, 12, 15, 30, Nov 19, 27; 1766: CG, Apr 21, 25, May 2,
12, Sep 22, 26, Oct 6, 18, 21, 25, 30, Nov 8, 11, Dec 6, 16, 20; 1767: CG,
Jan 14, 19, 23, 27, Mar 21, Apr 24, May 1, 12, 15, 21, Sep 14, 18, Oct 13,
Nov 6, 7, 17, 27, Dec 26; 1768: CG, Feb 1, May 12, 28, 31
Bennett, Sir Henry (correspondent), 1664: BRIDGES, Sep 14
Benneval, Mlle (dancer), 1741: CG, Dec 30
Benonvilli (machinist), 1774: DL, Apr 22
Benskin (stationer), 1742: DL, Apr 21
Bensley, Robert (actor), 1765: DL, Oct 2, 25, Nov 25; 1766: DL, Jan 6, 8, 29,
Feb 4, Mar 18, Apr 16, Sep 27, Oct 10, 29, Nov 4, 6, 8, 24, 26, Dec 2, 13;
1767: DL, Jan 2, 31, Feb 7, Mar 21, 24, 28, 30, Apr 11, 20, 28, May 12, CG,
Sep 16, 23, Oct 5, 6, 16, 19, 22, 24, 31, Nov 4, 7, 11, 17, Dec 8, 14, 28;
1768: CG, Jan 9, 20, 29, Feb 20, Mar 17, Apr 25, May 11, Sep 20, 23, 28, Oct
12, 14, 17, 24, 26, Nov 8, 17, 24, Dec 3, 16; 1769: CG, Jan 2, 28, Mar 13,
29, 31, Apr 4, 17, DL, 19, CG, 26, May 3, Oct 3, 17, 18, 26, Nov 1, 4, 15,
23, 27, Dec 2, 19, 22; 1770: CG, Jan 19, Feb 3, 12, 24, Mar 22, 27, 29, 30,
31, Apr 18, 20, DL, 21, CG, 26, 30, May 7, Oct 1, 5, 8, 10, 12, 16, 18, 23,
27, 29, Nov 1, 5, 15, 29, 30, Dec 3, 4; 1771: CG, Jan 4, 9, 12, 26, 28, Feb
9, 23, Mar 12, Apr 3, 9, 23, 24, 27, May 6, Sep 23, 25, 27, Oct 2, 9, 11, 14,
18, 19, 22, 31, Nov 2, 5, 11, 21, 26, Dec 4, 21, 30; 1772: CG, Jan 1, 21, 23,
27, Feb 1, 22, Mar 5, 21, DL, 23, CG, 23, 24, 30, Apr 11, 30, May 4, 11, Sep
23, Oct 5, 16, 26, Nov 4, 6, 21, Dec 11, 22; 1773: CG, Jan 7, 16, 25, 28, Feb
23, Mar 1, 6, 22, Apr 3, 17, 19, May 3, 4, 7, 22, Sep 22, 24, Oct 9, 11, 18,
21, 23, Nov 4, 18, 27, Dec 23; 1774: CG, Jan 15, 29, Feb 11, Mar 12, 14, 22,
Apr 7, 11, May 9, 11, Oct 3, 15, 17, 21, 24, 31, Nov 3, 19, 24, Dec 2, 9, 12,
15, 17; 1775: CG, Jan 3, 7, Feb 11, Mar 2, 18, Apr 3, 8, 18, May 18, 20, DL,
Sep 28, Oct 2, 10, 14, 17, 28, 31, Nov 20, 23, Dec 11, CG, 19, DL, 22, 29;
1776: DL, Jan 13, 20, Feb 15, Mar 11, 14, 28, Apr 10, 19, Jun 1, Oct 1, 3, 5,
8, 18, 29, Nov 16, 19, 29, Dec 2, 14; 1777: DL, Jan 4, Apr 1, Oct 9, 11, 14,
17, CG, 23, DL, Nov 14, 24, 29, Dec 8, 18; 1778: DL, Jan 10, 23, 24, Feb 10,
21, Mar 5, 16, 30, Apr 20, 27, Sep 22, 29, Oct 1, 13, 17, 19, 21, 26, Nov 4,
11, 14, 27, 28, 30; 1779: DL, Feb 3, 8, CG, Mar 4, DL, 25, Apr 12, CG, 24,
May 1, DL, 8, 10, 15, HAY, 31, Jun 18, Jul 16, DL, Sep 23, 25, Oct 9, 12, 16,
19, Nov 3, 8, 9, 11, 17, 20, Dec 2, 13, 20; 1780: DL, Jan 20, Feb 15, Mar 4,
Apr 1, May 10, HAY, Jun 2, 14, Jul 1, 6, 10, 24, Aug 5, 17, 24, Sep 5, DL,
23, Oct 2, 10, 11, 17, 19, 23, 26, 28, Nov 22, 27, 29, Dec 4, 7, 15, 19, 20;
1781: DL, Jan 22, 26, Feb 17, Mar 19, Apr 17, May 5, 8, HAY, Jun 7, 16, Jul
18, Aug 7, DL, Sep 18, 20, Oct 4, 13, 27, Nov 6, 13, 27; 1782: DL, Jan 22,
26, Apr 9, 23, May 7, 10, 11, HAY, Jun 15, 19, 29, Jul 11, 16, Aug 15, 26,
DL, Sep 17, 18, 21, 24, Oct 1, 14, 30, Nov 2, 8, 29, Dec 14; 1783: DL, Jan 3,
Feb 22, Mar 3, 10, Apr 8, May 5, HAY, Jun 6, 16, 30, Jul 4, Aug 20, 27, Sep
12, DL, 23, 30, Oct 11, 14, 17, 18, 21, Nov 28, Dec 10, 12, 22; 1784: DL, Jan
22, 28, Feb 3, 10, Mar 22, Apr 1, 21, 24, 26, May 3, 21, HAY, 31, Jun 2, CG,
10, HAY, 17, Jul 12, 20, Aug 18, 19, Sep 13, DL, 18, 21, 30, Oct 9, 19, 23,
27, 28, Nov 5, 9, 16, 17, 20, Dec 22; 1785: DL, Feb 2, 3, 7, 21, Mar 8, Apr
7, 18, 20, HAY, Jun 2, 6, 16, 17, 24, 29, Aug 4, Sep 9, DL, 17, 22, Oct 1, 4,
6, 8, 15, 17, 25, CG, Nov 4, DL, 7, 8, 11, 12, 17, 18, 22, Dec 7, 26; 1786:
DL, Feb 15, Mar 9, 27, Apr 6, 22, May 17, CG, 20, DL, 25, HAY, Jun 9, 12, 13,
14, 15, 20, 21, 22, 29, Jul 3, 14, 19, 21, Aug 17, DL, Sep 19, CG, 27, DL,
Oct 3, 5, 9, 10, 16, 21, 23, 24, Nov 18, 22, Dec 5, 11, 19; 1787: DL, Jan 23,
24, Mar 8, Apr 14, 17, May 7, 23, 24, 30, Jun 1, HAY, 11, 14, 22, 28, Jul 4,
7, 19, 25, 27, Aug 29, Sep 5, DL, 18, Oct 6, 15, 18, 27, 30, Nov 3, 16, 24,
Dec 6, 10, 11; 1788: DL, Jan 8, 31, Feb 18, Apr 8, 11, 29, 30, May 1, 14, Jun
6, HAY, 12, 17, Jul 2, 14, Aug 28, Sep 9, DL, 16, 25, 30, Oct 4, 9, 11, 14,
16, 20, 22, Nov 1, 4, 6, 11, 12, 21, 25, 28, Dec 1, 9, 18; 1789: DL, Jan 17,
Apr 28, Sep 12, 15, 17, 26, 29, Oct 3, 13, 31, Nov 27, 30, Dec 14; 1790: DL,
Feb 8, 10, 18, Apr 9, May 14, HAY, Jun 14, 16, 22, Aug 11, 16, DL, Sep 14,
16, Oct 11, 12, 21, 25, Nov 3, Dec 14; 1791: DL, Mar 21, 28, Apr 4, May 7,

20, HAY, Jun 13, 20, 25, Jul 26, 30, Aug 2, 24, 27, DLKING'S, Oct 25, Nov 1,
4, 5, 7, 9, 14, Dec 1, 21; 1792: DLKING'S, Jan 24, 28, 31, Feb 2, 4, 11, 14,
18, 23, Mar 1, 10, 26, 29, Apr 11, 20, HAY, Jun 23, Jul 4, 25, Aug 6, DL, Oct
16, 22, Nov 2, 5, Dec 7, 13, 21, 26, 28, 31; 1793: DL, Jan 4, 14, 29, Feb 12,
14, 26, Mar 2, 5, 7, 9, Apr 9, 23, 25, May 17, 24, HAY, Jun 15, 17, 21, Aug
3, 6, Sep 19, 30, Oct 1, 21, Nov 19, Dec 30; 1794: HAY, Mar 31, DL, Apr 21,
May 1, 19, 22, Jun 6, 26, HAY, Jul 10, 17, 21, Aug 13, 20, 27, DL, Sep 20,
27, Oct 4, 7, 9, 14, 18, 21, 31, Nov 7, 14, 15, 18, 29, Dec 12, 16, 19; 1795:
DL, Jan 26, Mar 3, 10, 14, 21, Apr 27, 29, HAY, Jun 13, 20, Jul 9, 31, Aug 3,
7, 18, 29, DL, Sep 29, Oct 5, 19, 21, Nov 5, 6, 16, 19, 23, Dec 2, 10, 18;
1796: DL, Jan 11, Feb 1, Apr 2, 26, 29, May 6
Benson (actor), 1735: LIF, Jun 19
Benson (actor, entertainer, dancer), 1776: HAY, Oct 7; 1778: HAY, Feb 9, Apr
29; 1779: DL, Apr 7, Jun 1, Dec 20; 1780: DL, Apr 26, Oct 2; 1781: HAY, Jan
22, Mar 26; 1782: HAY, Mar 4, Sep 21; 1783: HAY, Sep 17; 1785: HAY, Feb 12,
Mar 15, Apr 26, HAMM, Jun 17, 27, Jul 2, 4, 6, 8, 15, 22, 25, 26, 27; 1786:
HAMM, Jun 28, 30, Jul 5, 7, 10, 19, 24, 26, Aug 5
Benson (house servant), 1798: DL, Jun 2; 1800: DL, Jun 13
Benson, Miss (actor), 1797: HAY, Aug 21; 1798: HAY, Jun 28, DL, Sep 29, Nov 14;
1799: DL, May 31, HAY, Jun 18, 19, DL, Sep 26
Benson, Miss, 1766: CG, Dec 10
Benson, Mrs (actor), 1728: LIF, Nov 19, 23; 1729: LIF, Apr 28, Oct 17; 1730:
LIF, May 15, Sep 25
Benson, Mrs (actor), 1785: HAY, Feb 12, Mar 15, Apr 26, HAMM, Jun 17, 27, Jul
1, 2, 4, 6, 8, 15, 22, 25, 26, 27; 1786: HAMM, Jun 5, 7, Jul 24, 26
Benson, Robert (actor, dancer, dramatist), 1778: HAY, Mar 24, Apr 9; 1780: DL,
May 20; 1781: DL, May 18; 1786: DL, Nov 13, 25, Dec 7, 19; 1787: DL, Feb 22,
Mar 8, Apr 12, 13, 14, May 21, 28, 31, Sep 18, Oct 4, 6, 26, 27, Nov 3, 5, 6,
10, 16, 21, Dec 4, 8, 10, 11, 26; 1788: DL, Jan 21, 22, 31, Mar 1, 3, 13, 25,
29, Apr 10, 14, 19, 21, May 5, 14, 22, 30, Jun 2, 12, Sep 30, Oct 2, 16, 20,
22, 23, 25, Nov 4, 6, 8, 19, 25, 28, 29, Dec 1, 6, 11, 17, 18, 22, 31; 1789:
DL, Jan 6, 8, 10, Feb 3, 7, 14, 16, Mar 17, 21, May 22, 23, 28, Jun 5, 9, 13,
Sep 24, 26, Oct 1, 31, Nov 4, 7, 12, 24, Dec 14, 17, 26, 28; 1790: DL, Jan
15, 23, 28, Feb 10, 27, Mar 2, 8, 18, 22, Apr 19, May 4, 7, 11, 14, 15, 28,
Jun 1, 2, 5, CG, 16, Jul 16, DL, Oct 2, 7, 14, 20, 21, 23, 26, 27, Nov 3, 5,
13, Dec 3, 8, 14, 27; 1791: DL, Jan 10, 27, 31, Mar 21, Apr 28, May 10, 14,
20, 26, DLKING'S, Sep 22, 24, 29, Oct 3, 20, 29, 31, Nov 2, 4, 5, 7, 8, 9,
14, 28, 30, Dec 1, 16, 19; 1792: DLKING'S, Jan 5, 7, 9, 13, 18, 20, 24, 28,
Feb 3, 11, 18, Mar 1, 3, 5, 6, 12, 13, 17, 26, 29, 31, Apr 10, 11, 12, 13,
14, 17, 20, 26, 28, May 2, 8, 17, 19, 24, Jun 4, 6, 13, 15, DL, Sep 19, 25,
27, Oct 2, 4, 9, 13, 18, Nov 5, 7, 13, 15, 16, 20, 21, 23, 26, Dec 1, 4, 10,
14, 21, 26, 27, 28, 31; 1793: DL, Jan 7, 16, Feb 5, 9, 12, 16, 23, 26, Mar 2,
4, 5, 9, 14, Apr 8, 9, 11, 17, 18, 20, 22, 23, 25, 26, 27, May 8, 10, 13, 14,
22, 24, 25, 29, 30, 31, Jun 1, 3, 5, 6, HAY, 12, 14, 15, 17, 18, 21, 26, 29,
Jul 1, 5, 13, 15, 18, 20, 25, Aug 3, 6, 7, 8, 12, 14, 16, 26, 28, Sep 7, 19,
21, 24, 26, 28, 30, Oct 1, 8, 10, 15, 18, 21, 29, 30, Nov 4, 5, 6, 13, 16,
22, 29, Dec 2, 9, 10, 13, 16, 19, 26, 30, 31; 1794: HAY, Jan 4, 14, 16, 17,
31, Feb 6, 10, 11, 13, 15, 17, 20, 22, Mar 1, 13, 15, 18, 27, 29, 31, DL, Apr
21, 25, 29, May 1, 3, 5, 6, 12, 13, 16, 19, 23, 30, Jun 4, 5, 9, 10, 11, 12,
14, 16, 24, 25, 26, 28, 30, Jul 2, 7, HAY, 8, 9, 10, 12, 14, 17, 18, 19, 21,
22, 26, Aug 4, 9, 18, 19, 20, 22, 27, 29, Sep 1, 3, 6, 13, DL, 16, HAY, 17,
DL, 18, 23, 27, Oct 2, 7, 14, 23, 27, Nov 10, 12, 14, 18, 21, 24, 26, 29, Dec
3, 9, 10, 12, 16, 19, 23; 1795: DL, Jan 1, 3, 12, 20, 21, 22, 27, 28, Feb 3,
5, 6, 12, 21, Mar 2, 21, Apr 16, May 4, Jun 1, 3, 6, HAY, 9, 10, 11, 12, 13,
15, 16, 20, 24, Jul 1, 4, 6, 8, 9, 16, 20, 22, 25, 31, Aug 3, 7, 8, 10, 11,
17, 18, 21, 29, Sep 2, 4, DL, 19, 22, 24, 26, 29, Oct 5, 10, 12, 13, 15, 19,
21, 22, 27, Nov 2, 5, 6, 10, 11, 12, 14, 19, 20, 23, Dec 10, 11, 12, 21;
1796: DL, Jan 13, 15, 16, 18, 22, 25, Feb 1, 13, 15, Mar 19, 28, 30, Apr 2,
5, 6, 8, 12, 13, 15, 18, 19, 25, 26, 29, 30, May 3, 6, 13, 31, Jun 9
--Britain's Glory; or, A Trip to Portsmouth (farce), 1794: HAY, Aug 20, 28, 30;
1795: DL, Jun 3
--Love and Money; or, The Fair Caledonian (farce), 1795: HAY, Aug 29, Sep 1, 7,
11, 12, 14, 15; 1796: DL, May 13, 31, HAY, Jul 14
Benson, Susannah, Mrs Robert (actor, singer), 1796: DL, Oct 19, Nov 9; 1797:
DL, Jan 7, 20, Feb 9, Jun 12, HAY, 23, Aug 14, 15, 24, DL, Nov 8, Dec 9;
1798: DL, Feb 24, HAY, Jun 13, 30, Jul 21, Aug 11, DL, Nov 14, 29, Dec 4, 29;
1799: DL, May 16, 24, HAY, Jul 9, Aug 10, 21, DL, Oct 14, 19, Nov 14, Dec 11,
28; 1800: DL, Mar 11, 13
Bent (gallery doorkeeper), 1794: CG, Jun 10; 1796: CG, Jun 4; 1797: CG, Jun 7;
1798: CG, Jun 5; 1799: CG, May 21; 1800: CG, Jun 10
Bentham (rat catcher), 1800: CG, Mar 1
Bentinck, Jane, Lady Portland (spectator), 1700: DLORLIF, Jan 20

Bentley (house servant), <u>1799</u>: DL, Jul 2
Bentley, Dr Richard (playwright), <u>1755</u>: DL, Feb 3; <u>1761</u>: DL, Jun 18, Jul 27;
   <u>1782</u>: CG, Oct 3, Dec 14; <u>1788</u>: CG, Dec 13
--Philodamus, <u>1761</u>: DL, Jul 27; <u>1782</u>: CG, Dec 14
--Prophet, The (opera), <u>1788</u>: CG, Dec 13, 15, 16; <u>1789</u>: CG, Feb 4, 5, 10, 12,
   26, Mar 24, Apr 27, Nov 24
--Wishes, The; or, Harlequin's Mouth Opened, <u>1761</u>: DL, Jun 18, Jul 27, 28, 30,
   Aug 3, 6; <u>1782</u>: CG, Oct 3, 4
Bentley, Dr Richard and Mrs, <u>1761</u>: DL, Jul 27
Bentley Jr, Richard (versifier), <u>1782</u>: CG, Dec 14
Benucci, Francesco (singer), <u>1789</u>: KING'S, May 9, 28, Jun 11
Beralta, Sga (singer), <u>1757</u>: CG, Mar 11
Berardi (dancer), <u>1764</u>: KING'S, Feb 21, Mar 10, 20, 29, May 5, DL, Oct 13, Nov
   2, 6, 13, 28, Dec 13; <u>1765</u>: DL, Jan 22, Feb 15, Mar 26, May 11, 16
Berecloth (doorkeeper), <u>1790</u>: CG, Jun 8; <u>1791</u>: CG, Jun 2; <u>1792</u>: CG, May 29;
   <u>1794</u>: CG, Jun 12; <u>1795</u>: CG, Jun 10; <u>1796</u>: CG, May 21; <u>1797</u>: CG, Jun 2; <u>1798</u>:
   CG, May 19; <u>1799</u>: CG, Jun 4; <u>1800</u>: CG, Jun 7
Beregani, N (author), <u>1737</u>: CG, Feb 16
Berenclow (composer), <u>1693</u>: DL, Mar 0; <u>1704</u>: YB, Mar 24
Berenger, Richard (versifier), <u>1781</u>: HAY, Aug 7
Berenice (pastiche), <u>1765</u>: KING'S, Jan 1, 5, 8, 12, 19
Berenice. See Handel, George Frederic.
Berenstadt, Gaetano (singer), <u>1717</u>: KING'S, Jan 5, Feb 2, HIC, Mar 13, 27,
   KING'S, May 18, YB, Jun 14; <u>1723</u>: KING'S, Jan 12, Feb 19, Mar 30, May 14, Nov
   27; <u>1724</u>: KING'S, Jan 14, Feb 20, Apr 18, May 21
Berg, George (composer), <u>1766</u>: KING'S, Apr 10
Berger Inconstant (dance), <u>1787</u>: KING'S, Jan 6, 16
Bergere (dance), <u>1757</u>: HAY, Jun 17, Sep 14; <u>1776</u>: KING'S, Mar 12
Bergere Capricieuse (dance), <u>1787</u>: KING'S, Mar 8
Bergere Constante (dance), <u>1782</u>: KING'S, Nov 5
Bergere Coquette (dance), <u>1780</u>: KING'S, Jan 22, Mar 9, Apr 8, 25, 27, May 2
Bergere des Alpes, La (dance), <u>1790</u>: HAY, Jan 7, Feb 6, 13, 20, 27, May 25, Jun
   3, 12, CG, Jul 6, 10, 17; <u>1794</u>: KING'S, Jan 11; see also Adelaide
Bergeres Champetres (dance), <u>1735</u>: CG/LIF, May 20
Bergeres Fideles (dance), <u>1740</u>: CG, Nov 19, Dec 12, 22; <u>1741</u>: CG, Jan 7
Bergeres Heureux (dance), <u>1734</u>: HAY, Aug 14, LIF, 20, HAY, 21
Bergeries (dance), <u>1732</u>: DL, Sep 23, 30, Oct 3, 12, 19, Nov 2, 4, 6, 9, 13, 15,
   16, Dec 7; <u>1733</u>: DL, Mar 29, Apr 16, 24, May 2, 7, 9, 14, 21, DL/HAY, Oct 6,
   12, 13, Nov 8, 9, Dec 1, 20, 28; <u>1734</u>: DL/HAY, Jan 2, HAY, Aug 16, DL, Sep
   19, 26, Oct 3, 8, 25, 26, Nov 16, CG/LIF, 18, 21, DL, Dec 4, 11, 19; <u>1736</u>:
   DL, Aug 26, 31, Sep 7, 11, 16; <u>1741</u>: GF, Sep 28
Berges, Les (dance), <u>1740</u>: GF, Dec 2, 3, 5, 12; <u>1765</u>: HAY, Jul 8, 19, Aug 28
Berington, Joseph, <u>1794</u>: DL, Oct 28
--Emilia Galotti, <u>1794</u>: DL, Oct 9, 16, 22, 25, 27, 28, 30, Nov 1, 4
Berkeley (house servant); <u>1772</u>: CG, Jan 7
Berkeley Square Coffee House, <u>1757</u>: DL, Dec 21
Berkeley Square, <u>1758</u>: CG, Jan 12; <u>1777</u>: KING'S, May 8, CG, 22; <u>1778</u>: CG, May
   20; <u>1779</u>: CG, May 18; <u>1780</u>: CG, May 19; <u>1786</u>: KING'S, Mar 16; <u>1788</u>: KING'S,
   Feb 21; <u>1789</u>: KING'S, May 28; <u>1790</u>: DL, May 26, HAY, 27; <u>1791</u>: KING'S, May
   23; <u>1793</u>: KING'S, Feb 19
Berkeley, G (correspondent), <u>1713</u>: DL, Apr 14, May 7
Berkeley, George Monck (author), <u>1787</u>: CG, Apr 24, May 1
Berkeley, Lord George (commentator), <u>1675</u>: DL, Aug 0
Berkeley, Samuel (renter), <u>1758</u>: CG, Mar 4
Berkeley (Bartley), Sir William, <u>1662</u>: VERE, Jun 2
--Cornelia, <u>1662</u>: VERE, Jun 2
--Lost Lady, The, <u>1661</u>: VERE, Jan 19, 28; <u>1669</u>: BRIDGES, Jan 12
Berkely Jr (property man), <u>1767</u>: DL, Jan 24
Berkley (actor), <u>1743</u>: DL, May 24; <u>1745</u>: DL, Apr 30, May 8
Berkley, Miss (house servant), <u>1762</u>: DL, May 8; <u>1764</u>: DL, May 12; <u>1765</u>: DL, May
   8; <u>1766</u>: DL, May 2, Nov 7; <u>1767</u>: DL, May 8; <u>1768</u>: DL, May 13; <u>1769</u>: DL, Apr
   19; <u>1770</u>: DL, May 16; <u>1771</u>: DL, May 27; <u>1772</u>: DL, Feb 7, May 25, Jun 10;
   <u>1773</u>: DL, May 24, Jun 2, Sep 23; <u>1774</u>: DL, May 16, Jun 2; <u>1775</u>: DL, Feb 1,
   May 8, 27; <u>1776</u>: DL, May 11
Berkley, Mrs, <u>1749</u>: DL, Dec 15
Berkly (rioter), <u>1721</u>: LIF, Feb 1
Berkshire, Lord. See Howard, Charles.
Berlin, <u>1741</u>: BFTY, Aug 22
Bern, <u>1769</u>: DL, Feb 2
Bernacchi, Antonio (singer), <u>1716</u>: KING'S, Mar 10, Apr 18, May 31, Jun 2; <u>1717</u>:
   KING'S, Jan 5, Feb 2, 16, HIC, Mar 13, 27, KING'S, May 13, YB, Jun 14; <u>1729</u>:
   KING'S, Dec 2; <u>1730</u>: KING'S, Feb 24, Apr 4, May 19

Bernard (actor), 1744: HAY, Sep 27, 29, Oct 4, 11; 1750: CG, May 3
Bernard (machinist), 1791: PAN, May 9
Bernard, John (actor, playwright), 1787: CG, Oct 19, Nov 8, 22, 24, 26, 28, 30,
    Dec 15; 1788: CG, Jan 2, 4, 10, 11, 29, Feb 25, Mar 1, 11, 28, Apr 8, 26, May
    19, Sep 19, Oct 10, 15, 17, 18, Nov 10, 28, Dec 26, 29; 1789: CG, Jan 2, 15,
    Feb 3, 24, Mar 5, 28, 31, Apr 14, 15, 20, 30, May 14, 15, 19, 22, Jun 5, Oct
    2, 7, 12, 20, 30, Nov 2, 6, 7, 13, 16, 20, 23, 27, Dec 2, 5, 11, 31; 1790:
    CG, Jan 23, Feb 4, 6, 25, Mar 13, 27, Apr 7, 20, 22, 29, May 5, 6, 7, 11, 14,
    31, Jun 1, 4, Sep 15, 17, Oct 1, 5, 6, 8, 11, 13, 19, 29, Nov 3, 6, 11, 19,
    23, Dec 2, 6, 11, 14, 17, 20; 1791: CG, Jan 3, 14, 26, Feb 4, 16, Mar 4, Apr
    30, May 2, 3, 6, 11, 18, 19, 20, 24, 31, Jun 3; 1793: CG, Sep 20, 23, Oct 9,
    10, 11, 17, 22, 29, 30, Nov 1, 11, 12, 16, 18, Dec 5, 6, 9, 17, 18, 19, 27;
    1794: CG, Jan 6, 22, Feb 5, 22, 26, Mar 18, Apr 12, 29, May 2, 24, Jun 9, Sep
    15, 17, 19, 22, 24, 26, 29, Oct 3, 7, 14, 23, 29, 30, Dec 6, 18, 26, 31;
    1795: CG, Jan 19, 23, 24, Feb 14, Mar 16, 19, Apr 8, May 2, 8, 14, 29, Jun 6,
    15, Sep 14, 16, 25, 28, Oct 2, 7, 14, 15, 19, 24, 30, Nov 2, 4, 30, Dec 2;
    1799: CG, Apr 12
--British Sailor, The; or, The Fourth of June (interlude), 1789: CG, May 22
--Poor Sailor, The; or, Little Bob and Little Ben (farce), 1795: CG, May 29,
    Jun 9, 11, 15, 17, Oct 2, Nov 13, 26, Dec 2, 7; 1796: CG, Jan 28, Jun 4, Dec
    15; 1797: CG, Mar 7, 14; 1798: CG, Feb 9, May 24; 1799: CG, Dec 5, 7
Bernard, John and Mrs (actors), 1788: CG, Apr 26; 1789: CG, May 22; 1790: CG,
    May 11; 1791: CG, May 24
Bernard, Master (singer), 1796: CG, Dec 19; 1797: CG, Jun 5; 1798: CG, Nov 12;
    1799: CG, Apr 13; 1800: CG, Jan 16, Feb 10
Bernard, Mrs John (actor), 1787: CG, Oct 19, Nov 8, 16, 20, 26, Dec 5, 10;
    1788: CG, Jan 2, 4, 10, 14, Feb 14, Mar 24, 27, Apr 8, 23, 26, May 12, Sep
    19, Oct 10, 17, 18, 29, Nov 12, Dec 19, 27, 29, 30; 1789: CG, Jan 2, 28, Feb
    3, Mar 28, 31, Apr 30, May 19, 22, Oct 2, 9, 16, Nov 5, 12, 21, 23, Dec 5;
    1790: CG, Feb 11, 25, Mar 18, Apr 7, 20, 29, May 11, Oct 8, 11, 13, 15, 29,
    Nov 6, 8, 30, Dec 6, 10, 31; 1791: CG, May 5, 11, 24, 31
Bernardi (Barnardi), Francisco (singer), 1720: KING'S, Nov 19, Dec 28; 1721:
    KING'S, Feb 1, Apr 15, May 20, Dec 9; 1722: KING'S, Jan 10, Feb 22; 1723:
    KING'S, Jan 12, Feb 19, Nov 27; 1724: KING'S, Oct 31, Dec 1; 1726: KING'S,
    Mar 12; 1727: KING'S, Oct 21; 1731: KING'S, Feb 2, Apr 6; 1734: LIF, Feb 26,
    May 11, KING'S, Oct 29; 1735: KING'S, Apr 8, May 3, Nov 25; 1736: KING'S, Jan
    24; see also Senesino, Francisco Bernardi
Bernardi, Sga (singer), 1770: KING'S, May 19
Bernasconi (composer), 1749: KING'S, Mar 21
Bernasconi, Antonia (singer), 1778: KING'S, Nov 28; 1779: KING'S, Jan 23, Mar
    25, May 29, Dec 14; 1780: KING'S, Feb 8, Apr 13, May 9, 25, Jun 27
Berner St, 1785: DL, May 5; 1796: CG, May 3
Berriman (Berryman), Joseph (actor), 1727: LIF, Apr 17, May 2, 18, 19; 1728:
    LIF, Jun 25, Jul 5, 12, 19, Dec 28; 1729: LIF, Mar 4
Berriman, Mrs Joseph (actor), 1726: LIF, Sep 28, Oct 3, 12, 17, 24, Nov 4, 8,
    10, 14, 30; 1727: LIF, Jan 4, 9, 16, Feb 2, 4, Apr 3, 5, 7, 17, 19, 26, 28,
    May 2, 9, 10, 19, 22, Sep 11, 13, Oct 31, Nov 4, 17, Dec 8, 14, 16; 1728:
    LIF, Jan 17, Mar 9, 21, 28, Apr 1, 4, 23, 24, 30, May 2, 11, 15, 18, 23, 30,
    Jun 25, Jul 5, 12, 19, Aug 2, Sep 30, Oct 23, Nov 1, 4, 11; 1729: LIF, Feb
    10, Mar 3, 4, 10, Apr 10, 11, 16, 17, 23, 26, May 15, Sep 17, 19, 22, 24, 29,
    Oct 3, 6, 13, 20, 22, 30, Nov 4, 8, 14, 25, Dec 15; 1730: LIF, Apr 27, 29,
    May 7, 9, 23, Sep 18, 21, Oct 5, 7, 19, 23, 26, 27, Nov 2, 3, 4, 6, 13, 23;
    1731: LIF, Jan 9, 21, Feb 3, 27, Mar 15, Apr 3, 21, May 10, 17, 20, Jun 2,
    Sep 20; 1732: LIF, Apr 25
Berrisford (Barresford), Robert (boxkeeper), 1746: DL, May 14; 1747: DL, May 8;
    1748: DL, May 9; 1749: DL, May 5; 1750: DL, May 10; 1751: DL, May 9; 1752:
    DL, Apr 30, May 2; 1753: DL, May 15; 1754: DL, May 17; 1755: DL, May 6; 1756:
    DL, May 10; 1757: DL, May 18; 1758: DL, May 9; 1759: DL, May 11; 1760: DL,
    May 13; 1761: DL, May 21; 1762: DL, May 20; 1763: DL, May 18; 1764: DL, May
    18; 1765: DL, May 20; 1766: DL, May 16; 1768: DL, May 27; 1769: DL, May 20;
    1771: DL, May 29; 1772: DL, Jun 10; 1773: DL, Jun 2; 1774: DL, May 28; 1775:
    DL, May 26; 1776: DL, May 22; 1777: DL, Jun 6
Berry, C (actor), 1780: CG, Oct 13, 26, Dec 8, 27; 1781: CG, Apr 18
Berry, Catherine (dancer), 1791: PAN, Feb 17, Mar 22; 1796: KING'S, Mar 10
Berry, Edward (actor, singer, dancer), 1729: DL, Feb 6, May 14, Jun 13, 20, 27,
    Jul 18, 25, Dec 8, 10; 1730: DL, Mar 30, Apr 20, May 11, 18, 27, BFOF, Aug
    20, SFOF, Sep 9, DL, Oct 20, 28; 1731: DL, Jan 20, Feb 8, Mar 20, Apr 19, 26,
    May 12, 31, Jun 7, 11, Jul 6, 20, 23, Aug 6, 11, 16, SF/BFFHH, 24, DL, Sep
    25, 30, Oct 2, Nov 25; 1732: DL, Jan 1, Feb 14, Mar 21, Apr 17, May 1, 8, Oct
    17, Nov 6, 7, 13, 17, 20, Dec 6, 11; 1733: DL, Jan 29, Feb 17, Mar 28, 31,
    Apr 19, 30, May 2, 3, 5, 7, 15, 21, BFCGBH, Aug 23, Sep 4, DL/HAY, 26, Oct 3,
    5, 8, 10, 12, 15, 17, 22, Nov 10, 14, 23, 24, 26, 28, Dec 17, 19, HAY, 26;

<u>1734</u>: DL/HAY, Jan 12, 17, 21, Mar 25, 30, Apr 1, 17, 20, 27, May 1, LIF, 23, BFHBH, Aug 24, DL, Sep 24, 26, Oct 21, 23, 26, Nov 8, 16, 20, 25, Dec 6; <u>1735</u>: DL, Jan 6, 13, 22, Mar 10, 22, Apr 21, 28, May 7, 10, Sep 11, 27, 30, Oct 7, 9, 11, 21, 25, 27, 31, Nov 3, 6, 7, 15, 19, 21, 24, 29; <u>1736</u>: DL, Jan 3, 12, Mar 13, 23, May 18, Sep 7, 9, 11, 23, Oct 12, 13, 19, 20, 27, Nov 2, 6, 8, 15, 22, Dec 15, 17, 30, 31; <u>1737</u>: DL, Jan 6, 10, 14, 17, 19, 21, 24, 26, 29, Feb 10, 19, 28, Mar 1, 10, 15, 22, Apr 29, May 2, 5, 7, 21, 23, Aug 30; <u>1739</u>: DL, May 15, Sep 4, 13, 14, 18, 24, Oct 9, Nov 5, 12, 15, 20, 23, Dec 11, 14, 22, 26, 31; <u>1740</u>: DL, Jan 8, CG, Feb 12, DL, Mar 6, 13, 27, Apr 16, 22, 24, May 2, 29, Sep 9, 20, 23, Oct 2, 4, 14, 16, Nov 4, 6, 19, 27, 28, 29, Dec 8, 20; <u>1741</u>: DL, Feb 14, Mar 14, Apr 3, 27, May 21, Jun 4, Sep 8, 10, Oct 8, 9, 15, 20, 21, Nov 2, 4, 11, 16, Dec 7, 16, 19, 26; <u>1742</u>: DL, Jan 6, 22, Feb 12, Mar 4, 15, 29, Apr 5, 24, 30, May 11, 12, 28, Sep 11, 14, 16, Oct 2, 5, 7, 9, 13, 16, 26, Nov 4, 8, Dec 14; <u>1743</u>: DL, Jan 11, 28, Feb 1, 4, 10, Mar 14, 21, 24, SOU, 30, DL, Apr 9, 21, 30, May 13, BFHC, Aug 23, DL, Sep 13, Dec 16; <u>1744</u>: DL, Jan 7, 27, Feb 21, Mar 10, 29, Apr 2, 3, 17, 23, May 1, 2, 22, 28, Oct 23, 30, Nov 6, Dec 19; <u>1745</u>: DL, Feb 20, Mar 7, Apr 24, May 8, Sep 28, Oct 1, 22, Nov 4, 9, 22, 23, Dec 5, 27; <u>1746</u>: DL, Jan 2, 18, 31, Apr 4, 10, 11, 14, 23, Sep 23, 25, 27, 30, Oct 4, 31, Nov 4, 7, Dec 11, 15, 26; <u>1747</u>: DL, Jan 15, Feb 10, 16, Mar 12, 16, 28, Apr 22, Sep 15, 17, 26, Oct 3, 15, 20, 21, 29, 30, Nov 2, 4, 7, 16, 17, 18, Dec 16, 26; <u>1748</u>: DL, Jan 6, 9, 20, Feb 1, Mar 19, Apr 19, 26, 28, Sep 10, 20, 22, 24, 27, 29, Oct 4, 6, 8, 11, 13, 15, 18, 22, 28, Nov 1, 3, 4, 7, 8, 9, 11, 14, 24, 29, Dec 21; <u>1749</u>: DL, Jan 9, 13, Feb 6, Mar 7, Apr 1, 15, May 8, 16, Sep 16, 21, 22, 26, 28, Oct 3, 13, 14, 17, 18, 21, 26, 28, Nov 2, 4, 15, 16, 21, 27, 28, Dec 11; <u>1750</u>: DL, Jan 6, 19, 31, Feb 6, 17, Mar 13, 15, 31, May 3, Sep 8, 11, 13, 18, 21, 22, 25, 27, 28, Oct 15, 16, 22, 24, 30, Nov 1, 2, 5, 7, 8, 13, 14, 24, 28, Dec 3, 22, 26; <u>1751</u>: DL, Jan 5, 7, Feb 23, Mar 14, Apr 15, 22, 29, May 1, Sep 7, 10, 17, 18, 19, 20, 26, Oct 2, 3, 7, 9, 11, 17, Nov 2, 8, 16, 29, Dec 26; <u>1752</u>: DL, Jan 6, 16, 28, Feb 13, 17, Mar 7, 12, 16, 30, Apr 1, 4, 20, 21, Sep 16, 19, 26, 28, 30, Oct 3, 5, 11, 13, 14, 16, 19, 23, 26, Nov 3, 8, 22, 25, 30, Dec 7, 18, 29; <u>1753</u>: DL, Jan 2, 8, Feb 6, 7, Mar 3, 19, 20, 22, Apr 2, 10, May 18, 25, Sep 8, 13, 15, 22, 25, 29, Oct 2, 3, 4, 6, 9, 10, 12, 13, 16, 23, 24, 30, 31, Nov 6, 15, Dec 26; <u>1754</u>: DL, Jan 7, 16, 23, Feb 20, Mar 19, Apr 4, 16, 20, Sep 14, 19, 24, 26, Oct 1, 3, 5, 10, 11, 12, 14, 16, 21, 22, 30, Nov 6, 11, 22, Dec 7, 13; <u>1755</u>: DL, Jan 6, 15, 25, Feb 18, 25, Mar 4, CG, 12, DL, 18, Apr 3, 10, 15, May 7, Sep 13, 18, 20, 23, 25, 27, Oct 2, 4, 8, 10, 13, 23, 28, Nov 1, 17, Dec 1, 4, 6, 11, 18; <u>1756</u>: DL, Jan 1, 10, 12, 21, Feb 24, Mar 25, 27, Apr 8, May 4, 10, 24, Sep 18, 21, 23, 25, 30, Oct 2, 7, 9, 12, 13, 14, 16, 19, 28, Nov 11, 12, 17, 23, Dec 10, 11, 27; <u>1757</u>: DL, Jan 18, Feb 22, Mar 7, 24, Apr 11, 19, 20, 23, 30, May 17, 23, CG, 27, DL, Sep 10, 13, 15, 17, 20, 24, 27, Oct 4, 6, 8, 15, 19, 20, 26, 29, Nov 8, 10, 19, 22, Dec 2, 3; <u>1758</u>: DL, Jan 19, 27, Feb 1, Mar 11, Apr 7, 17, May 15, Sep 16, 19, 21, 23, 26, 28, Oct 3, 12, 21, 24, 25, 27, 30, Nov 7, 14, 15, 23, 24, Dec 13, 29, 30; <u>1759</u>: DL, Jan 3, 6, 20, Feb 15, 24, Mar 15, Apr 16; <u>1760</u>: DL, Jan 8

Berry, Harriet (actor), <u>1797</u>: HAY, May 10
Berry, John (actor), <u>1791</u>: HAY, Oct 24; <u>1798</u>: HAY, Apr 23
Berry, Miss (actor), <u>1749</u>: BF/SFP, Aug 23
Berry, Thomas (actor), <u>1700</u>: LIF, Jan 9, Feb 0, Apr 0; <u>1701</u>: LIF, Mar 0
Berselli, Matteo (singer), <u>1720</u>: KING'S, Nov 19, Dec 28; <u>1721</u>: KING'S, Feb 1, Apr 15, May 20
Bertati, Giovanni (librettist), <u>1791</u>: PAN, Jun 16
Bertie, Lady Mary, <u>1671</u>: BRIDGES, Jan 2, NONE, Feb 4, ATCOURT, 6, 20, NONE, Mar 4, 16
Bertie, Peregrine (commentator), <u>1685</u>: DL, Dec 26, DLORDG, 30, OLDFIELD, 30; <u>1686</u>: NONE, Jan 7, DLORDG, 23, ATCOURT, 27, DL, Feb 4, DLORDG, 6, 11, ATCOURT, 16, DG, Mar 6; <u>1688</u>: DL, May 3, 5, 12
Bertie, Robert, Lord Willoughby, <u>1698</u>: DLLIF, Dec 13
Bertie, Willoughby, 4th Earl of Abingdon (composer), <u>1798</u>: HAY, Aug 23
Berto (dancer), <u>1675</u>: ATCOURT, Feb 15
Bertoldo. See Ciampi, Lorenzo.
Bertolli (Bertoldi), Francesca (singer), <u>1729</u>: KING'S, Dec 2; <u>1730</u>: KING'S, Feb 24, Apr 4, May 19, Nov 3; <u>1731</u>: KING'S, Feb 2, Apr 6; <u>1732</u>: KING'S, Jan 15, Feb 15, Mar 25, May 2, 23, Jun 10, Nov 4; <u>1733</u>: KING'S, Jan 27, Mar 17, LIF, Dec 29; <u>1734</u>: LIF, Feb 26, May 11, KING'S, Oct 29; <u>1735</u>: KING'S, Feb 1, Apr 8, May 3, Nov 25; <u>1736</u>: KING'S, Jan 24, Apr 13; <u>1737</u>: CG, Jan 12, Feb 16, May 18
Bertoni, Fernando Giuseppe (composer), <u>1749</u>: KING'S, Mar 21; <u>1758</u>: KING'S, Jan 31, Apr 6; <u>1761</u>: KING'S, Apr 28; <u>1775</u>: KING'S, Jan 14; <u>1778</u>: KING'S, Nov 28; <u>1779</u>: KING'S, Jan 23, Mar 11, May 15, 29, Nov 27, Dec 14; <u>1780</u>: KING'S, Jan 22, Mar 9, May 9, 31; <u>1781</u>: KING'S, Nov 17; <u>1782</u>: KING'S, Jan 12, Mar 7, May

25, CG, Nov 2, KING'S, 2, 14; 1783: KING'S, Jan 7, Feb 18; 1784: CG, Apr 17;
   1785: KING'S, Feb 24; 1786: CG, Oct 16; 1788: CG, Apr 1; 1789: CG, Mar 31,
   Sep 23; 1791: PAN, Jun 2
--Artaserse (opera), 1779: KING'S, Jan 23, 29, Feb 6, 13, 20, Mar 6; 1785:
   KING'S, Apr 16, 19, 21, 23, 30, May 7
--Cimene (opera), 1783: KING'S, Jan 7, 16, Mar 1
--Convito, Il (opera), 1782: KING'S, Nov 2, 5, 9, 16, 26, Dec 3, 7, 10, 17;
   1783: KING'S, Jan 25, 28, Feb 4, 15, Apr 26
--Demofoonte (opera), 1778: KING'S, Nov 28, Dec 5, 12, 19, 26; 1779: KING'S,
   Jan 2, 9, 16, Feb 9, 16, 27, Mar 11, 13, Jun 22, 26; 1784: KING'S, Mar 4, 6,
   13, 30, Apr 24, May 20, Jun 17; 1790: HAY, Apr 6
--Duca d'Atene, Il (opera), 1780: KING'S, May 9, 16, 23, 30, Jun 6, 13, 20
--Ezio (opera), 1781: KING'S, Nov 17, 20, 24, 28, Dec 1, 4, 8, 15, 22; 1782:
   KING'S, Jan 5, 19, 26, Feb 12, 16, 28, Jun 15
--Governante, La (opera), 1779: KING'S, May 15, 17, 25, Jun 1, 8, 15, 22
--Ifigenia in Aulide (opera), 1782: KING'S, May 25; 1783: KING'S, Feb 18, 22
--Junius Brutus (opera), 1782: KING'S, Jan 12, 31, Feb 12, 26
--Olimpiade, L' (opera), 1779: KING'S, May 29, Jun 5, 12, 19, 29, Jul 3; 1780:
   KING'S, Mar 9, 14, Apr 27, May 2
--Orfeo (opera), 1780: KING'S, May 31
--Pescatrici, La (opera), 1761: KING'S, Apr 25, 28, May 5, 12, 19, 28, Jun 1
--Quinto Fabio (opera), 1780: KING'S, Jan 22, 29, Feb 5, 12, 19, 26, 29, Mar 4,
   11, 18, Apr 8, 15, Jul 1; 1782: KING'S, Mar 7, 14; 1791: PAN, Jun 2
--Soldano Generoso, Il (opera), 1779: KING'S, Dec 14, 21, 23, 28; 1780: KING'S,
   Jan 1, 11, 25, Feb 1
Berwick St, 1742: DL, Apr 28; 1763: HAY, Sep 15
Berwillibald (Beswilleball), Giorgio Giacomo (singer), 1716: KING'S, Apr 18,
   HIC, Jun 9; see also Giacomo, Giorgio
Besford (actor), 1766: CG, Oct 9; 1768: CG, Jun 3
Besford, Esther (dancer, actor), 1766: CG, Apr 1, Oct 20; 1767: CG, Jan 31, Apr
   27, Sep 26, Nov 7; 1768: CG, Mar 1, 26, Apr 16, May 25, 26, 28, Sep 22, Nov
   23; 1769: CG, Jan 14, Apr 8, 26, May 12, 15, Oct 4, Nov 11, Dec 14, 30; 1770:
   CG, Jan 24, Mar 22, Apr 20, May 25, Sep 24, 26, 28; 1771: CG, Apr 12, 30, May
   9, 15, Sep 23, 30; 1772: CG, Apr 24, May 21, 29, Sep 21, 25, 30, Nov 2, Dec
   7, 26; 1773: CG, Jan 21, Feb 18, 19, Mar 15, Apr 24, 26, May 14, 19, Sep 29,
   Oct 4, Nov 12, 20, Dec 30; 1774: CG, Jan 7, Apr 11, 12, 16, 22, May 13, Oct
   5, 11, 20, 22, 28, Nov 21, Dec 14, 27; 1775: CG, Jan 2, Apr 17, 29, May 3,
   Dec 12, 15, 20; 1776: CG, Jan 1, 2, Feb 17, Mar 19, May 4, Sep 27, Oct 15,
   Nov 11, 20; 1777: CG, Apr 25, HAY, May 15, CG, Oct 8, 17, 21, Nov 25, Dec 22;
   1778: CG, Jan 28, Feb 23, Mar 9, May 2, Nov 25, Dec 12; 1779: CG, Feb 25, Mar
   20, Apr 28, May 8, Oct 22; 1780: CG, Feb 8, May 6, Sep 20, 21, 25, 27, Oct
   25, Nov 6, Dec 5; 1781: CG, Feb 8, 23, Apr 20, May 1, 18, Sep 24, 28, Oct 16,
   20, 24, Nov 8, Dec 13, 19; 1782: CG, Feb 21, Apr 2, 27, May 17, 25, Dec 6,
   11, 20, 31; 1783: CG, Apr 22, 25, May 28, Oct 1, 14; 1784: CG, Feb 13, Mar 6,
   Apr 27, Jun 10, Oct 27, Dec 1; 1785: CG, Jan 14, HAY, Mar 15, CG, Apr 6, 9,
   18, May 18, Sep 30, Oct 10, 12, Nov 2, 23; 1786: CG, Mar 4, May 17
Besford, Joseph (property man, porter), 1759: CG, Sep 28; 1760: CG, May 19, Sep
   22; 1763: CG, May 26; 1766: CG, Oct 10; 1767: CG, Oct 8; 1773: CG, May 31,
   Dec 16; 1774: CG, Apr 8; 1775: CG, May 11; 1776: CG, May 4; 1780: CG, May 23;
   1783: CG, May 28; 1787: CG, May 25; 1788: CG, Jun 3, HAY, Aug 5
Besford, Samuel (actor, dancer), 1764: CG, Mar 27, May 12, 15, Oct 8; 1765: CG,
   May 16, Sep 30, Oct 17; 1766: CG, Jan 31, May 15, Sep 26, Dec 23, 26; 1767:
   CG, Jan 31, May 18; 1768: CG, May 27; 1772: CG, Sep 28; 1773: CG, Nov 9;
   1775: CG, Nov 21, 22; 1777: CG, Apr 25, HAY, Jul 15, 24, Aug 25, Sep 10;
   1778: CG, Mar 9, 28; 1781: CG, May 1; 1782: CG, Apr 27, May 6, 10; 1783: CG,
   Oct 21; 1784: CG, Mar 11, Apr 27, May 26, Sep 28, Oct 27; 1785: HAY, Mar 15,
   CG, 29, May 11, HAY, Aug 31; 1788: HAY, Jul 10, Aug 5
Besozzi, Antonio and Carlo (oboists), 1757: DL, Mar 25
Bess of Bedlam (song), 1703: DL, Oct 16
Besswick, Miss (house servant), 1726: HAY, Apr 12
Bessy Bell (song), 1781: DL, May 9
Best (entertainer), 1779: HAY, Mar 15
Best Bidder, The. See Andrews, Miles Peter.
Best, 1771: DL, Dec 11
Beswilleball. See Berwillibald.
Besworth, Joseph (house servant), 1760: CG, Apr 8; 1761: CG, Feb 7, May 15
Bethell's Hatter and Hosier, 1750: DL, Nov 28
Bethun (dancer), 1733: HAY, Mar 27, CG, Aug 14, 16, 21, DL, Oct 15, Nov 13;
   1734: DL, Feb 4, Apr 15, May 15; 1736: DL, Oct 12; 1738: DL, Jan 24
Beton, Miss (actor), 1798: DL, Mar 24, Jun 5
Betson, A (author), 1751: DL, Feb 1
Bettenson, 1760: CG, Jan 19, Feb 16

71

Better Late than Never. See Andrews, Miles Peter.
Betterton, John (dancer), 1799: CG, May 14
Betterton, Julia (actor), 1797: CG, Oct 12, 21, Nov 3, 4, 23, Dec 23; 1798: CG,
Jan 9, Feb 9, 12, 13, Apr 17, 30, May 15, 16, 19, 31, Jun 4, Oct 1; 1799: CG,
Jan 12, Mar 16, Apr 9, 23, 26, 27, May 14, 22, Jun 7, Sep 20, 25, 30, Oct 11,
14, 25, Nov 8, Dec 23, 26; 1800: CG, Jan 29, Mar 27, Apr 17, 22, 29, May 2,
10

Betterton, Mary, Mrs Thomas (actor), 1661: LIF, Dec 16; 1662: LIF, Sep 30, Oct
18, ATCOURT, 27; 1663: LIF, Jan 8, Feb 23, Oct 0, ATCOURT, Dec 10, LIF, 22;
1664: BRIDGES, Feb 1, LIF, Mar 0, NONE, Apr 27, LIF, Jul 28, Aug 13, Nov 5,
Dec 2; 1665: LIF, Apr 3; 1668: LIF, Jul 6, NONE, Sep 0; 1669: LIF, May 12,
Dec 14; 1670: LIF, Apr 0, Sep 20, Nov 0; 1671: LIF, Jan 10, Mar 6, Jun 0, DG,
Nov 0; 1672: DG, Jan 31, Jul 4, Aug 3, ATCOU/DG, Dec 2; 1673: DG, Feb 18, May
0, Jul 3; 1674: DG, Nov 9; 1675: DG, May 28, NONE, Sep 0, DG, 0; 1676: DG,
Jan 10, Mar 0, 11, May 25, Jul 3, Aug 0, Dec 0; 1677: DG, Feb 12, Mar 24, May
12, Jul 0, Sep 0; 1678: DG, Jan 0, 17, Sep 0, Nov 0; 1679: DG, Apr 0; 1680:
DG, Feb 0, Sep 0, Nov 1, Dec 8; 1681: DG, Apr 0; 1682: DG, Jan 23; 1689: DL,
Nov 7; 1691: NONE, Sep 0; 1692: DL, Feb 0, Apr 0; 1693: DL, Feb 0, NONE, Sep
0; 1694: DL, Jan 0, NONE, Jul 0; 1696: LIF, Apr 0

Betterton, Thomas (actor, author), 1659: NONE, Sep 0; 1660: COCKPIT, Aug 18,
Oct 8, REDBULL, Nov 5; 1661: SALSBURY, Jan 29, Feb 9, 23, Mar 1, 19, LIF, Jun
28, Aug 15, 24, Sep 11, LIF/MT, Oct 21, LIF, Nov 4, Dec 16; 1662: LIF, Mar 1,
NONE, Sep 0, LIF, 30, Oct 18, ATCOURT, 27, Dec 1; 1663: LIF, Jan 6, 8, Feb
23, May 28, Jul 22, Oct 0, ATCOURT, Dec 10, LIF, 22; 1664: LIF, Mar 0, NONE,
Apr 27, LIF, Jul 28, Aug 13, Sep 10, Nov 5, Dec 2; 1665: LIF, Apr 3; 1666:
NONE, Sep 0, ATCOURT, Oct 29; 1667: LIF, Mar 7, ATCOURT, May 9, LIF, Sep 4,
Oct 15, 16, 24, Nov 6; 1668: LIF, Feb 11, Jul 6, Aug 12, 31, NONE, Sep 0;
1669: LIF, Feb 18, May 12, Dec 14; 1670: LIF, Feb 19, Apr 0, NONE, Sep 0,
LIF, 20; 1671: LIF, Jan 10, Jun 0, DG, Nov 0, 9; 1672: DG, Jan 31, Nov 4,
ATCOU/DG, Dec 2; 1673: DG, Feb 18, Jul 3; 1675: DG, Feb 27, Jun 12, Sep 0,
NONE, 0; 1676: DG, Jan 10, Mar 0, 11, May 25, Jun 8, Jul 3, Aug 0, NONE, Sep
0, DG, Nov 4, Dec 0; 1677: DG, Feb 12, Mar 24, May 12, Sep 0; 1678: DG, Jan
0, 17, Apr 5, May 28, Jun 0, Sep 0, Nov 0; 1679: DG, Mar 0, Apr 0, May 0, Oct
0, Dec 0; 1680: DG, Jan 0, Feb 0, Jun 0, Sep 0, Nov 1, Dec 8; 1681: DG, Mar
0, Apr 0; 1682: DG, Feb 9, Mar 0, Apr 0, NONE, Sep 0, DLORDG, Oct 9, ATCOURT,
Nov 15, DL, 16, 28; 1683: DG, Jul 0, DLORDG, Aug 14, NONE, Sep 0, DLORDG, 12,
DL, Nov 12; 1684: ATCOURT, Feb 11, DL, Apr 0, NONE, Aug 0; 1686: DL, Apr 0,
Nov 29; 1688: DL, Feb 0, NONE, Sep 0; 1689: DL, Apr 0, NONE, Sep 0, DL, Nov
7, Dec 4; 1690: DG, Jun 0, NONE, Sep 0, DL, Oct 0, DL/IT, 21; 1691: DG, May
0, NONE, Sep 0, DL, Dec 0; 1692: DL, Feb 0, NONE, 12, DL, Apr 0, Jun 0, Nov
8, Dec 9; 1693: DL, Mar 0, NONE, Sep 0, DL, Oct 0; 1694: DL, Jan 0, DG, 10,
DL, Feb 0, Apr 0, DG, May 0, NONE, Jul 0; 1695: LIF, Mar 25, DL, Apr 1, LIF,
30, DLANDLIF, May 0, DL, 0, LIF, Dec 0; 1696: LIF, Feb 0, Apr 0, Jun 0, Jul
0, Nov 14; 1697: LIF, Feb 20, Apr 0, May 0, Jun 0, Nov 0; 1698: LIF, Jan 0,
Apr 0, May 0, Jun 0, Jul 11, Nov 0; 1699: LIF, Feb 0, DLORLIF, 20, LIF, Apr
0, Nov 7, 26, Dec 0, 18; 1700: LIF, Jan 9, 28, Feb 0, DLLIF, 0, LIF, Mar 5,
Apr 0, NONE, Apr 11, DL, Jul 9, LIF, Dec 0; 1701: LIF, Jan 0, Apr 0, Dec 0;
1703: LIF, Jan 0, Apr 28, May 0, 21, DL, Jul 16; 1704: LIF, Jan 13, ATCOURT,
Feb 7, LIF, 10, 19, 24, ATCOURT, 28, LIF, Mar 30, ATCOURT, Apr 24, LIF, May
18, Nov 9, LIF/QUEN, 25, LIF, Dec 4; 1705: LIF/QUEN, Feb 22, Mar 3, QUEEN'S,
Nov 23, Dec 27; 1706: QUEEN'S, Jan 3, Feb 11, 21, Mar 28, Oct 26, 30, Nov 2,
13, 19, 21, 25, Dec 6, 10, 16; 1707: QUEEN'S, Jan 1, 14, 25, 28, Feb 3, 15,
18, Mar 6, 18, Apr 21, May 2, Nov 6, QUEEN/DL, 8, DL/QUEEN, 19, 25, Dec 27;
1708: QUEEN'S, Jan 10, DL, 17, Feb 19, Mar 11, 15, 22, Apr 15, Oct 16, 21,
Dec 30; 1709: DL, Jan 1, 7, 26, Feb 5, Mar 24, Apr 7, 9, 11, Jun 2, QUEEN'S,
Sep 15, 20, Dec 3, 8, 17; 1710: QUEEN'S, Feb 4, Apr 13; 1711: DL, Jun 4;
1720: DL, Dec 17, 19; 1721: DL, Dec 15; 1722: DL, May 5, Oct 12, Dec 13;
1727: DL, Feb 21, 25, Sep 9; 1728: DL, Oct 18; 1729: DL, May 7, Sep 23, Dec
30; 1730: DL, Feb 12, Sep 29; 1731: DL, May 19; 1732: GF, Oct 2, DL, 19;
1733: DL, May 7, 14, DL/HAY, Oct 12, Nov 9, 22, Dec 8; 1734: DL/HAY, Jan 19;
1736: DL, Mar 11; 1738: CG, Feb 16, DL, Mar 20, May 30; 1743: DL, Oct 15;
1753: DL, Mar 10, Oct 30; 1755: BF, Sep 6; 1758: CG, Feb 1

--Amorous Widow, The; or, The Wanton Wife, 1668: NONE, Sep 0; 1670: LIF, Nov 0;
1673: DG, Jan 10, Feb 4; 1675: DL, Oct 27; 1680: ATCOURT, Feb 13; 1683:
DLORDG, Jan 11; 1686: DLORDG, Dec 22; 1699: LIF, Dec 18; 1700: IT, Feb 2;
1704: LIF, Feb 16, Apr 20, Jun 26; 1705: LIF, Feb 20, QUEEN'S, Nov 12, 20;
1706: QUEEN'S, Apr 3, 20; 1707: QUEEN'S, Feb 7; 1709: QUEEN'S, Nov 19, 22,
26, Dec 22; 1710: QUEEN'S, Feb 2, Apr 29; 1711: DL, Jan 9, Apr 23, Sep 22,
Dec 11; 1712: DL, Jan 18, Apr 28, Sep 25, Dec 6; 1713: DL, Jan 16, 26, Apr
20, Oct 15; 1714: DL, Jan 20, 25, May 5, Sep 27; 1715: DL, Feb 15, LIF, Apr
9, DL, May 6, LIF, Jun 3, DL, Nov 16; 1716: DL, Feb 18, Apr 14, Oct 27; 1717:
DL, Mar 18; 1718: LIF, Jan 2, 4, 14, Feb 7, Mar 31, DL, Apr 19, LIF, Oct 24,

DL, Dec 10; 1719: LIF, Apr 9, DL, 16; 1720: DL, Jan 12, Apr 25, LIF, May 12,
DL, 14, LIF, Dec 6, 14; 1721: LIF, Jan 16, DL, 25, Apr 17, LIF, May 22, DL,
Oct 4, Dec 15; 1722: DL, Mar 13, LIF, Apr 19, DL, 30, LIF, May 16, DL, Oct
12, Dec 13; 1723: LIF, Apr 2, Oct 16, DL, 25, LIF, Nov 23; 1724: LIF, Jan 10,
DL, 24, LIF, Feb 3, Mar 17, BPT, 18, DL, May 1, LIF, 22, Oct 23, DL, Nov 10;
1725: LIF, Jan 9, Feb 3, Apr 3, DL, 10, Oct 23, LIF, Nov 10; 1726: DL, Jan
24, LIF, Feb 8, DL, Apr 13, Oct 27, Dec 9; 1727: DL, Feb 14, Mar 9, LIF, Oct
2, DL, Nov 14, LIF, Dec 13; 1728: DL, Nov 15; 1729: DL, Apr 16, LIF, 30, Dec
20; 1730: LIF, Apr 13, May 25, Dec 12; 1731: LIF, Jan 12, Feb 15, Apr 23, Nov
18; 1732: LIF, Jan 7, DL, 21, LIF, Mar 11, DL, May 4, LIF, 26, DL, Oct 10,
LIF/CG, Nov 10, DL, 28; 1733: DL, May 14, DL/HAY, Nov 9; 1734: CG, Jan 23,
Feb 12, 19, Mar 30; 1735: CG/LIF, Jan 23, Mar 27, Apr 23, CG, Dec 30; 1736:
DL, Dec 7, 8, 9; 1737: DL, May 30, CG, Nov 17; 1738: CG, Mar 11, DL, 20, May
30; 1739: CG, Jan 22, DL, May 19, CG, 28, DL, Nov 7; 1740: CG, May 7; 1741:
CG, Mar 7; 1742: CG, Apr 1, 27; 1746: CG, Feb 17, 20, Apr 17; 1752: CG, Jan
6, Apr 21; 1755: BF, Sep 6; 1758: CG, Mar 11, Apr 28; 1781: CG, Apr 18
--Woman Made a Justice, The, 1670: LIF, Feb 19
Betterton, Thomas and Mary, 1745: DL, Mar 18
Betterton, Thomas William (actor), 1781: CG, Apr 18; 1782: CG, Apr 4; 1797: CG,
Oct 20, 21, Nov 11, 18, 29, Dec 8; 1798: CG, Jan 5, Feb 9, Apr 27, May 10,
16, Sep 17, Oct 15, Nov 22, Dec 11; 1799: CG, Jan 3, 14, Apr 6, 9, 23, 27,
May 4, 14, 31, Jun 1, Sep 23, Oct 4, 31, Nov 11, 14, Dec 23; 1800: CG, Jan
18, Feb 8, Mar 27, Apr 5, 22, 23, 29, May 10, 13, 20, 23
Betterton, Thomas William and Julia (actors), 1798: CG, May 16; 1799: CG, May
14
Betterton, William (actor), 1659: NONE, Sep 0; 1661: SALSBURY, Jan 29
Betterton's Booth, 1698: DL, Feb 0
Betti. See Bitti.
Bettini (Bettina), Sga (dancer), 1741: KING'S, Dec 22; 1744: DL, Dec 14, 15,
17, 19, 21, 26, 28; 1745: DL, Jan 1, 8, 10, 11, 14, 21, 22, 26, 29, Feb 13,
Mar 11, 12, 14, Apr 17, 18, 20, 22, 24, 25, 27, 29, 30, May 1, 6, 7, 9, 13
Betts (actor), 1748: SFP, Sep 7
Betts (singer), 1798: HAY, Mar 26; 1799: CG, May 18
Betts, John Edward (violinist), 1798: HAY, Jan 15, CG, Feb 23; 1799: CG, Feb 8;
1800: CG, Feb 28
Betty. See Carey, Henry.
Beveridge's Room, 1719: BR, Apr 2
Beviamo tutti tre (song), 1781: DL, Apr 25, May 7; 1791: CG, May 18, 28; 1794:
CG, May 2; 1800: CG, May 6
Bevias, Mrs (landlady), 1794: HAMM, Mar 24
Bevill (boxkeeper), 1731: GF, May 11
Bevon, Mrs. See Kennedy, Polly.
Bew, Charles (actor), 1795: DL, May 29
Bewley (housekeeper), 1715: LIF, Nov 25; 1730: LIF, May 25; 1732: LIF, May 18;
1736: CG, May 31
Bewley, Elizabeth (house servant), 1716: LIF, Jul 18; 1717: LIF, May 23; 1719:
LIF, Jun 3; 1721: LIF, May 29
Beyond the desart mountains (song), 1697: NONE, Sep 0
Bianchi (Biancei), Francesco (singer), 1748: KING'S, Nov 8; 1769: KING'S, Sep
5, Nov 7; 1770: KING'S, Mar 1, 22
Bianchi Jr, Francesco (musician, composer), 1790: HAY, Feb 27; 1792: DL, Nov
21; 1794: KING'S, Apr 26, DL, May 16, Oct 27, KING'S, Dec 6, DL, 20; 1795:
KING'S, Feb 7, Mar 21, 28, Jun 16, DL, Oct 30; 1796: KING'S, Feb 9, May 24,
Dec 20; 1797: KING'S, Mar 11, Jun 10, Dec 20; 1798: KING'S, Feb 20; 1799:
KING'S, Jan 22; 1800: KING'S, Feb 8, Mar 18
--Aci e Galatea (pastoral), 1795: KING'S, Mar 21, 24, 28, Apr 11, 21, 25
--Antigona (opera), 1796: KING'S, May 24, 28, 31, Jun 2, 4, 7, 11, 21, 25, Jul
7, 12, 16, 19; 1798: KING'S, Jun 19, 23
--Cinna (opera), 1798: KING'S, Feb 20, 24, 27, Mar 3, 17, 27, 31, Apr 17, 19,
Jun 2
--Ines de Castro (opera), 1799: KING'S, Jan 22, 26, 29, Feb 2, 9, 16, 23, Mar
2, 9, 16, Apr 2, 23, 30, May 18, 21, Jun 4, 11, Jul 2, 23, 30; 1800: KING'S,
Mar 18, 22, 25, 29, Apr 5
--Merope (opera), 1797: KING'S, Jun 10, 13, 15, 17, 24, 27, Jul 1, 11, 15, 18,
25, 29, Dec 20, 23
--Nozze del Tamigi e Bellona, Le (cantata), 1797: KING'S, Mar 11
--Piramo e Tisbe (opera), 1796: KING'S, Feb 6, 9, 13, Mar 5
--Semiramide; o, La Vendetta di Nino (opera), 1794: KING'S, Apr 26, 29, May 3,
6, 10, 13, 24, 29, Jun 3, 6, 14, Jul 8; 1795: KING'S, Feb 7, 14, 28, Mar 7,
10, 14, 26, May 22, Jun 16, 23, 30, Jul 7; 1796: KING'S, Jan 2, 5, 9, 12, 16;
1798: KING'S, Jan 2, 9, 13, 20, Feb 3, Mar 22, 24, Apr 19; 1800: KING'S, Feb
8, 11, 15, Mar 1, Apr 1

--Sposa in Equivoco, La (opera), 1798: KING'S, Mar 22, 24
--Villanella Rapita, La (opera), 1790: HAY, Feb 27, Mar 2, 6, 9, 13, 20, 23,
   25, 27, Jun 10
Bianchi, Giovanni Battista (conductor, composer), 1780: KING'S, Nov 25, Dec 2,
   19; 1781: KING'S, Feb 22, Jun 5; 1782: KING'S, Nov 14
--Consiglio Imprudente, Il (opera), 1796: KING'S, Dec 20, 23, 27, 31; 1797:
   KING'S, Jan 3, Feb 7, 11, Mar 11; 1798: KING'S, Apr 10, 14
--Omaggio, L' (pastoral), 1780: KING'S, Nov 25; 1781: KING'S, Jun 5, 8, 14, 16
--Ricimero (opera), 1780: KING'S, Dec 2, 5, 9, 12, 16
Bianchini (house servant), 1744: CG, May 14; 1745: CG, May 15; 1746: CG, May 6;
   1747: CG, May 22
Biancolelli, Louis
--Arlequin Misantrope; or, Harlequin a Man-Hater (farce), 1719: KING'S, Mar 3;
   1734: GF/HAY, Nov 22
--Fausse Coquette, La (farce), 1718: LIF, Nov 14, 19; 1720: KING'S, May 12,
   HAY, Dec 30; 1726: HAY, Apr 25; 1734: GF/HAY, Nov 18; 1735: GF/HAY, Feb 24,
   HAY, Mar 19
--Tombeau de Maitre Andre, Le (pantomime), 1718: LIF, Nov 21, 26; 1720: KING'S,
   Jun 20; 1721: HAY, Jan 24, 31; 1724: HAY, Dec 21; 1725: HAY, Apr 9; 1734:
   HAY, Nov 25
Biancolelli, Pierre Francoise Dominique
--Agnes de Challiot, 1735: GF/HAY, Jan 17, Apr 10
--Harlequin always Harlequin, 1734: GF/HAY, Dec 18, 26; 1735: GF/HAY, Jan 9,
   LIF, Feb 27, GF/HAY, Mar 10, 20, May 12
--Sylphide, La (farce), 1734: HAY, Oct 28, Nov 27; 1735: HAY, Jan 23, GF/HAY,
   Mar 18, May 1
Bibb (sword cutler), 1767: CG, Jan 6, DL, 16; 1772: DL, Jan 6, CG, Feb 21, DL,
   Mar 3, Jun 10, CG, Dec 14; 1773: DL, Jun 2; 1774: CG, Jan 24, DL, Feb 22, Jun
   2; 1775: DL, Apr 25, May 27; 1776: DL, Jan 26, Jun 10
Bibby (actor, singer), 1746: DL, Mar 3, Apr 8, 25, 28, 30, May 1
Bible and Key (bookstore), 1759: CG, Mar 23; 1764: CG, Mar 14
Bible and Sun, 1751: DL, Mar 7
Bibson, Miss (actor), 1781: CII, Mar 15
Biche (musician), 1760: CG, Sep 22
Bickerstaff, Isaac, 1752: DL, Dec 22; 1760: CG, Dec 5; 1762: CG, Dec 8; 1764:
   CG, Oct 16; 1765: DL, Oct 8, Dec 7, 16; 1767: CG, Feb 21, 24, 28, Mar 3, 19;
   1768: CG, Feb 25, Mar 1, 8, 10, 14, DL, Oct 3, CG, 10, DL, Nov 17, 21; 1769:
   HAY, Jun 21, Aug 31; 1770: RANELAGH, May 28, CG, Oct 23, DL, Nov 24, Dec 7;
   1771: DL, Mar 16, Apr 12, May 8; 1772: CG, Nov 4; 1773: DL, Feb 1, CG, Oct 9,
   Nov 20; 1775: DL, Dec 12, 21; 1776: DL, Feb 27, CG, May 6; 1785: HAY, Apr 25;
   1788: DL, Nov 28; 1790: DL, Mar 22
--Absent Man, The, 1764: CG, Apr 28; 1768: DL, Mar 21, 24, Apr 4, 13, 28, 29,
   May 30, 31, Dec 16, 17; 1772: DL, Mar 12, 16, May 26; 1784: DL, Mar 29; 1795:
   CG, Mar 28
--Captive, The (musical), 1769: HAY, Jun 21, 23, 26, 28, 30, Jul 3, 10, 24, 31,
   Aug 2, 25, 28; 1770: HAY, Aug 31; 1771: DL, Mar 16, HAY, Aug 19
--Daphne and Amintor, 1765: DL, Oct 5, 8, 9, 10, 12, 14, 16, 17, 18, 19, 21,
   22, 23, 24, 25, 26, 28, 29, 30, 31, Nov 1, 11, 12, 14, 15, 20, Dec 11, 21;
   1766: DL, Feb 13, 17, Mar 15, Apr 5, 14, 19, Sep 23, 30, Oct 15, 17, Nov 14;
   1767: DL, Mar 9, 17, 28, Apr 4, 7, May 2, 9, Jun 3, Sep 12, 18, Oct 15, Dec
   18, 23; 1768: DL, Jan 16, Apr 5, May 5, Aug 18; 1769: DL, Mar 13, Dec 30;
   1770: DL, Nov 29, Dec 4, 12, 18; 1771: DL, Jan 19, Feb 7; 1772: CG, Nov 4, 5,
   12, 13, 16, 20; 1773: CG, Jan 18, Mar 16, 25, Apr 29, May 22, 26; 1774: CG,
   Oct 20, 22, 31; 1775: CG, Mar 2; 1777: DL, Nov 22, 24, Dec 18; 1778: DL, Jan
   24; 1786: DL, Apr 24, 29, May 13, Jun 7; 1790: HAY, Aug 6
--Doctor Last in his Chariot, The, 1769: HAY, Jun 21, 23, 26, 28, 30, Jul 3,
   31, Aug 18, 31; 1771: HAY, Mar 4; 1779: CG, Apr 26
--Ephesian Matron, The (interlude), 1769: HAY, Aug 31; 1770: RANELAGH, Jun 29,
   Jul 11, 18, Aug 1; 1771: DL, May 8; 1772: GROTTO, Aug 17; 1778: CG, May 13;
   1788: HAY, Apr 9
--He Would if He Could; or, An Old Fool Worse than Any, 1771: DL, Apr 12
--Hypocrite, The, 1768: DL, Nov 17, 18, 19, 22, 25, 28, 30, Dec 2, 8; 1769: DL,
   Jan 2, 5, 10, 17, Feb 1, Mar 28, May 12, Sep 21, Oct 16, Dec 11; 1770: DL,
   Jan 5, Feb 19, Oct 15; 1771: DL, May 13, Nov 27; 1773: DL, Jan 26, May 21,
   CG, Oct 9, 12; 1774: DL, Oct 6; 1775: DL, Mar 27; 1776: DL, Jan 3, Oct 10,
   12, 15, 18, Nov 15; 1779: DL, Nov 4, 11; 1780: DL, Feb 3, Apr 24; 1781: DL,
   Jan 26, 31, Feb 16, Apr 25, Oct 4; 1784: CG, Oct 6, 13, 20, 21, Nov 6, 24;
   1785: CG, Jan 7, Apr 14, Oct 29, Dec 17; 1786: CG, Jan 27; 1787: HAY, Apr 30,
   CG, Oct 17, Dec 18; 1789: CG, Jan 8, Nov 5, DL, Dec 2; 1790: DL, Jun 4; 1794:
   DL, Jun 23; 1795: DL, Jan 29
--Lionel and Clarissa (opera), 1768: CG, Feb 16, 25, 27, Mar 1, 3, 5, 8, 10,
   12, 14, DL, 21, CG, Apr 4, 14, 21; 1769: CG, Mar 16, Apr 8, 22, May 12, Oct

27; 1770: DL, Feb 8, 19, CG, Nov 8; 1771: CG, Mar 18; 1777: CG, Apr 29, May
9, Oct 3; 1778: CG, Mar 19, Apr 28, May 21; 1780: HAY, Aug 29; 1781: HAY, Jun
26; 1782: CG, May 1; 1783: CG, Oct 2, 10, 22; 1784: HAY, Aug 10; 1785: HAY,
Jun 18, 25, Aug 9; 1787: HAY, Aug 3; 1788: CG, Apr 25; 1790: CG, May 13;
1792: CG, May 22; 1798: CG, May 10, HAY, Jul 5, 11, 20
--Love in a Village (opera), 1762: CG, Dec 8, 9, 10, 11, 13, 14, 15, 16, 17,
18, 20, 21, 23, 29, 30; 1763: CG, Jan 1, 3, 5, 7, 10, 15, 18, 21, 22, 25, 29,
Feb 2, 4, 8, 10, 12, 17, 21, Mar 1, 7, 14, 24, Apr 4, 19, May 12, 28, Oct 22,
27, Nov 1, 3, 12, 19, 25, Dec 5; 1764: CG, Jan 6, Mar 12, 17, 19, Apr 23, May
17, 28, Oct 23, 31, Nov 10, 17, 26, Dec 8, 22, 29; 1765: CG, Jan 2, 9, 16,
23, DL, Feb 20, CG, 25, Mar 9, 16, 23, Apr 8, 20, May 14, Oct 4, 19, Nov 1,
15, 26, Dec 2; 1766: CG, Feb 1, 13, Mar 3, Apr 3, 17, May 8, HAY, Aug 21, CG,
Oct 18, 29, Nov 1, 12, 14, 20, Dec 12; 1767: CG, Jan 21, Feb 11, Mar 16, Apr
9, May 23, Sep 18, Oct 23, Nov 13, 26, Dec 1, 30; 1768: CG, Jan 12, Feb 15,
Mar 22, Apr 19, May 5, 7, 26, Sep 24, Oct 3, Nov 18, DL, 21, CG, Dec 12;
1769: CG, Jan 7, Feb 20, DL, Apr 3, CG, 10, DL, 22, CG, 28, DL, May 9, CG,
Sep 18, Oct 16, Nov 30, Dec 30; 1770: CG, Jan 17, 18, 24, Feb 6, 23, Mar 26,
Apr 27, May 17, HAY, Sep 20, CG, Oct 2, 4, 6, 9, 15, 17, Nov 2, 14, 20, Dec
8; 1771: CG, Jan 15, 19, 25, 31, Feb 8, 16, Mar 16, 21, May 1, DL, 14, CG,
17, 23, MARLY, Aug 27, 29, HAY, Sep 16, DL, Oct 8, 16, CG, Nov 1; 1772: CG,
Feb 21, Apr 29, May 14, DL, 18, HAY, Sep 18, CG, 30, Oct 1, 9, 22, Nov 10,
Dec 4; 1773: CG, Jan 23, Feb 19, Mar 29, Apr 26, HAY, Sep 17, CG, 29, Oct 1,
7, 13, Nov 3, 19, 30; 1774: CG, Jan 7, 8, Feb 4, Apr 15, May 13, DL, Jun 2,
CG, Sep 28, Oct 18, Nov 15, Dec 22; 1775: CG, Jan 25, HAY, Feb 2, CG, 24, Mar
13, 21, 25, DL, Apr 22, 27, CG, 28, DL, May 2, 22, Sep 30, CG, Oct 16, HAY,
30, DL, Nov 24; 1776: DL, May 20, Sep 26, CG, Oct 9, 11, DL, 31; 1777: CG,
Jan 1, HAY, Aug 12, 20, CG, Sep 26, DL, Oct 2; 1778: CG, Mar 31, Apr 6, DL,
25, CG, May 2, DL, 2, CG, 4, 12, HAY, 22, 23, DL, 25, HAY, 27, 29, Jun 3, 10,
22, CHR, 26, HAY, Jul 3; 1779: CG, Feb 13, 16, Mar 1, 8, 13, Apr 7, 9, 17,
May 8, HAY, Jun 7, 9, DL, Oct 25, CG, Dec 29; 1780: CG, Jan 5, 26, Apr 14,
May 11, 25, HAY, Jun 3, Jul 27, DL, Sep 26, 30, Oct 30, CG, Nov 15, 22, DL,
Dec 16; 1781: HAY, Jun 1, 6, Jul 28, Aug 25, DL, Sep 15, CG, Nov 7, HAY, 12,
DL, 24, CG, Dec 22; 1782: DL, May 4, HAY, Aug 24, Sep 4, 16, 19, CG, 30, DL,
Oct 3, 7, Nov 28; 1783: DL, Jan 31, Mar 6, HAY, Jun 2, 4, 7, 11, 14, 18, 21,
25, Jul 3, 21, Sep 3, CG, 17, DL, 25, Oct 9; 1784: CG, Apr 28, May 22, DL,
22, HAY, Jul 7, CG, Sep 22, DL, Oct 14, 21, Dec 27; 1785: DL, Jan 15, HAY,
Apr 25, DL, May 23, HAY, Jun 9, 13, 20, HAMM, Jul 1, CG, Dec 8; 1786: CG, Feb
13, 15, Mar 16, HAY, Jun 19, Jul 17, HAMM, 21, CG, Nov 14, 17, Dec 6, 16;
1787: CG, Jan 3, HAY, 8, CG, 10, 17, 22, Mar 13, 24, Apr 28, May 1, DL, 11,
CG, 12, DL, 15, HAY, Jul 23, DL, Sep 27, CG, Oct 3, 8, DL, Dec 12; 1788: DL,
Jan 14, CG, Feb 5, 12, DL, 21, CG, Mar 8, Apr 22, DL, Jun 10, CG, Sep 15, Oct
7, Nov 19, Dec 10; 1789: CG, Jan 13, HAY, Jun 5, CG, Oct 20, Nov 7, Dec 17;
1790: CG, Jan 9, 16, Mar 20, 25, Apr 24, Jun 3, Dec 11; 1791: CG, Jan 27, 29,
May 20, HAY, Aug 10, CG, Nov 15, 29; 1792: CG, Jan 3, 24, Feb 14, Apr 21, May
4; 1793: CG, Jan 25, Jun 1, Oct 26, Nov 2, 9, 21, Dec 14; 1794: CG, Jan 8,
HAY, 21, CG, 27, HAY, 28; 1795: CG, Oct 5, 9, 16, Dec 11; 1796: CG, May 30,
Sep 17; 1797: CG, May 24, Nov 9, 15, 17; 1798: CG, May 4, 17
--Love in the City (opera), 1767: CG, Feb 19, 21, 23, 24, 25, Mar 2, 19, May 27
--Maid of the Mill, The, 1764: CG, Oct 16; 1765: CG, Jan 31, Feb 1, 2, 4, 5, 6,
7, 8, 9, 11, 12, 13, 14, 16, 19, DL, 20, CG, 21, 23, 26, 28, Mar 2, 4, 5, 7,
11, 16, 28, Apr 13, May 4, 21, Oct 12, 25, Nov 21, 29, Dec 20, 28; 1766: CG,
Jan 7, Feb 8, 18, 25, Mar 11, Apr 10, DL, 19, CG, 24, May 1, 8, Oct 10, 15,
Nov 6, Dec 1, 31; 1767: CG, Jan 24, Feb 17, Mar 7, 26, Apr 2, 30, May 15, Oct
8, 20, Nov 19, Dec 4; 1768: CG, Jan 5, 23, Apr 8, 27, May 13, 24, Sep 19, Oct
18, DL, Nov 21, CG, Dec 7; 1769: CG, Jan 26, Mar 7, DL, 31, Apr 5, 12, CG,
13, DL, 15, 27, CG, May 9, 18, Sep 29, Oct 30, Nov 7, 14, 28; 1770: CG, Jan
13, Feb 9, Apr 3, 16, May 2, DL, Sep 25, CG, 28, DL, 29, Oct 30, CG, Dec 27;
1771: CG, Jan 21, Feb 18, Apr 10, DL, 19, CG, May 10, DL, Oct 22, CG, Nov 8,
Dec 23; 1772: CG, Feb 28, May 23, DL, Nov 6, 13, Dec 1; 1773: DL, Feb 22, CG,
Apr 13, May 12, HAY, Sep 20, DL, 28, Nov 27; 1774: CG, Feb 7, Apr 26, May 14,
DL, Sep 20, CG, 23, Dec 7; 1775: CG, Jan 6, May 12, 27, Sep 27; 1776: DL, Apr
20, CG, Dec 4; 1777: CG, May 22; 1778: CG, Feb 26, May 12, HAY, Jul 7, 9, 10,
21, 28, Aug 6, CG, Oct 27; 1779: CG, Jan 29, Oct 16, DL, Nov 27, Dec 16;
1780: HAY, Aug 31, DL, Oct 7, 18, Dec 23; 1781: CG, Jan 13, Feb 17, DL, Mar
6, May 26, CG, Sep 21, Oct 20, DL, Nov 20; 1782: CG, Feb 6, DL, May 16, HAY,
Sep 17, CG, 25, Oct 2, 25, DL, 26, 31; 1783: DL, Jan 18, Feb 27, Mar 31, Apr
22, CG, May 28, DL, 31, Sep 18, CG, Oct 24; 1784: DL, Feb 5, HAY, Aug 17;
1785: DL, Apr 8, May 27, HAY, Jun 28, Jul 2, HAMM, 6, 22, DL, Oct 11, Nov 14;
1786: HAY, Jun 9, 10, HAMM, Jul 7; 1787: DL, Jan 26, Feb 10, May 17; 1788:
DL, Jan 26, Sep 20; 1789: DL, Feb 18, CG, Dec 4, 12, 19; 1790: CG, Jan 5, Mar
2, Apr 17; 1795: CG, Jan 2, 14, Jun 13; 1797: CG, Oct 20, 23, 26; 1798: CG,
May 4, 11, DL, Sep 27, CG, 28; 1799: CG, Oct 4, DL, Nov 6; 1800: CG, Jun 4

--Padlock, The, <u>1768</u>: DL, Oct 3, 4, 5, 6, 8, 12, 13, 14, 17, 19, 26, 27, 29,
Nov 3, 4, 5, 7, 21, 28, 30, Dec 2, 3, 6, 12, 14, 22; <u>1769</u>: DL, Jan 3, 5, 9,
11, 12, 14, 21, 23, 31, Feb 16, 18, 20, 28, Mar 2, 4, 6, 7, 9, 16, 27, 30,
Apr 11, 13, 17, 20, 28, May 2, 6, 23, HAY, Aug 28, 30, 31, Sep 4, 11, 13, 15,
DL, 23, 28, Oct 5, 9, 13, Nov 14, 16, 22, 29, Dec 9; <u>1770</u>: DL, Jan 2, 27, Feb
6, 19, Mar 6, 20, 29, 31, Apr 2, 3, 7, 17, 19, 21, 25, May 3, 8, 9, 11, 19,
24, HAY, Jun 5, 13, 15, 18, 20, 29, Jul 2, 4, 6, 18, RANELAGH, 20, HAY, 25,
Aug 17, 29, Sep 10, 15, DL, Oct 2, 17, 20, CG, 23, 24, 25, 26, 27, HAY, 29,
CG, 31, Nov 6, 7, 10, 16, DL, 26, 27, Dec 3, 10, HAY, 14, CG, 18; <u>1771</u>: DL,
Jan 8, 14, 29, Feb 4, 12, 16, 19, 25, CG, 28, Mar 2, 12, 14, 16, DL, 19, CG,
23, Apr 4, 8, 9, DL, 10, CG, 16, 17, 19, 24, 25, May 7, DL, 8, 16, CG, 24,
DL, 24, HAY, Jun 5, 24, Jul 17, Aug 5, 30, Sep 9, DL, Oct 1, 3, 12, 18, CG,
Nov 5, 7, DL, 13, CG, Dec 16, DL, 18, CG, 20; <u>1772</u>: DL, Jan 24, Feb 1, 28,
CG, Apr 4, 24, DL, May 1, CG, 6, DL, 8, 15, CG, 16, 21, DL, 27, Jun 1, Sep
26, CG, Oct 7, DL, 29, CG, Nov 7, 18, Dec 19; <u>1773</u>: DL, Feb 1, CG, Mar 22,
30, Apr 1, DL, 20, CG, 24, DL, 26, CG, 28, DL, May 18, CG, 18, 21, HAY, Jul
5, 9, DL, Oct 16, 22, 28, CG, Nov 6, 12, DL, 23, CG, 24, DL, Dec 18; <u>1774</u>:
CG, Jan 7, DL, Mar 19, CG, Apr 8, 30, May 7, 18, HAY, 18, CG, 20, HAY, 30,
Jun 27, Jul 8, 25, CG, Sep 21, DL, 24, CG, Nov 10, DL, 16, CG, 26, DL, Dec
22, 23; <u>1775</u>: CG, Feb 13, Mar 9, 18, DL, May 11, CG, 30, Sep 20, 29, DL, Oct
5, CG, 28, DL, 31, CG, Nov 11, DL, Dec 7, 23; <u>1776</u>: DL, Jan 24, Feb 17, Apr
30, May 17, CG, 22, HAY, Jul 8, Aug 2, 14, CG, Sep 25, Oct 2, Nov 2, 7, 12,
28; <u>1777</u>: DL, Jan 8, CG, Mar 20, May 23, DL, 31, Jun 7, HAY, Sep 3, CG, 22,
Oct 10, DL, Nov 12, Dec 12; <u>1778</u>: DL, Jan 9, CG, 21, DL, Sep 26, 29; <u>1779</u>:
DL, May 7, HAY, Sep 17, DL, Oct 12, Dec 2; <u>1780</u>: DL, Apr 18, CG, May 23, DL,
Nov 10, 22; <u>1781</u>: HAY, Mar 26, CG, May 5; <u>1783</u>: DL, Jan 25, CG, Sep 19, Oct
3; <u>1784</u>: DL, Feb 24, Mar 2, Apr 16, 20, Oct 19, 28, Dec 23; <u>1785</u>: DL, Jan 27,
HAY, Aug 8, 15; <u>1786</u>: DL, May 2, HAMM, Jul 24, CG, Oct 4, 11, 13, Nov 28;
<u>1787</u>: RLSN, Mar 31, DL, Apr 27, CG, Sep 28, Oct 10; <u>1788</u>: CG, Apr 30, May 1,
HAY, Jul 10, 30, Aug 14; <u>1789</u>: DL, May 23, Jun 6, Sep 15, Nov 12, 30; <u>1790</u>:
CG, Apr 16, 22, Sep 13; <u>1791</u>: CG, Feb 10, DL, May 26, HAY, Aug 13, CG, Dec 3;
<u>1792</u>: CG, May 5; <u>1793</u>: HAY, Aug 20, Nov 5, 9; <u>1794</u>: HAY, Feb 13; <u>1796</u>: DL,
Jun 1; <u>1797</u>: HAY, Aug 23, 29
--Recruiting Serjeant, The (musical), <u>1770</u>: RANELAGH, Jul 20, 27, Aug 3, 29,
Sep 12, Oct 3, DL, Dec 7; <u>1771</u>: DL, Jan 18, May 1, GROTTO, Sep 9; <u>1773</u>: DL,
May 13, 22; <u>1776</u>: CG, May 6, MARLY, 23, 25, 30, Jun 1, 8, Aug 3, 10; <u>1777</u>:
HAY, Jul 3, 4, 8, 10, 31, Aug 8, Sep 1, 15; <u>1782</u>: DL, Apr 15, 30, HAY, Aug
23; <u>1783</u>: HAY, Aug 15; <u>1787</u>: ROY, Jul 3; <u>1789</u>: DL, Jun 3; <u>1790</u>: CG, May 7;
<u>1793</u>: CG, Dec 23
--School for Fathers, A (musical), <u>1770</u>: DL, Feb 8, 9, 12, 14, 16, 20, 23, Mar
15, Apr 18, May 4, Oct 19; <u>1773</u>: DL, Jan 9, 11, 15, 23, May 3; <u>1774</u>: DL, May
3; <u>1778</u>: DL, Jan 8, 12, 14, 16, Feb 18, May 5, Oct 3, Nov 25; <u>1779</u>: DL, Jan
1, Nov 19; <u>1780</u>: DL, Feb 7; <u>1781</u>: DL, Apr 21, May 4, Sep 15, 22; <u>1783</u>: DL,
Oct 30, Dec 23; <u>1784</u>: DL, Nov 12; <u>1785</u>: DL, May 13; <u>1787</u>: DL, Apr 20, 24, 30,
Dec 19; <u>1789</u>: DL, Oct 22; <u>1791</u>: DLKING'S, Nov 30
--Spoiled Child, The (farce), <u>1790</u>: DL, Mar 22, 27, Apr 10, 17, 26, 29, May 8,
Sep 16, Oct 18, Nov 5, 16, 25; <u>1791</u>: DL, Jan 29, Feb 2, 14, 26, Mar 3, Apr 2,
14, May 2, 9, 21, 27, Jun 3, DLKING'S, Oct 1, 20; <u>1792</u>: DLKING'S, Apr 11, May
8, 24; <u>1793</u>: DL, Apr 5, 10, May 8, 13, 28; <u>1795</u>: DL, Apr 24, 29, May 19, 27,
Jun 2, Dec 1, 8, 15, 22, 29; <u>1796</u>: DL, Jan 11, Mar 3, 14, Apr 9, 12, May 7;
<u>1797</u>: HAY, Feb 9, DL, Apr 28, May 30, Jun 12; <u>1798</u>: CG, Oct 3, 10, 12, 17,
19, 24, 26, Nov 2, DL, 28, Dec 1, CG, 8; <u>1799</u>: CG, Jan 9, 18, Apr 24, May 30,
HAY, Aug 17, CG, Oct 16, Nov 1, 6, 30; <u>1800</u>: CG, Jan 17, Feb 6, 18, May 29
--Sultan, The; or, A Peep into the Seraglio (musical), <u>1775</u>: DL, Dec 12, 13,
14, 15, 19, 20, 21; <u>1776</u>: DL, Feb 14, 19, 27, Mar 4; <u>1782</u>: CG, Dec 20; <u>1783</u>:
CG, Jan 3, 8, 10, Feb 12, 21; <u>1784</u>: CG, Mar 6, 11, 15, Apr 22, May 6, Oct 27;
<u>1785</u>: CG, Feb 12, Nov 23, Dec 7; <u>1786</u>: CG, Feb 2, Mar 11; <u>1787</u>: CG, Feb 9,
DL, 15, 17, 19, 24, Mar 1, 22, 24, 27, 31, Apr 13, 19, 24, May 2, Nov 1, 3,
7, 12, 19; <u>1788</u>: DL, Apr 16, May 13, Sep 18, Nov 19, Dec 10; <u>1789</u>: DL, Feb
18, CG, 19, DL, Mar 2, 19, CG, Apr 2, May 2, Nov 19; <u>1790</u>: DL, Feb 18, Sep
30, CG, Oct 23; <u>1791</u>: DLKING'S, Nov 7, 14, Dec 10, 21, 22; <u>1792</u>: DLKING'S,
Feb 1, 17, 28, Mar 5, 22, May 3, HAY, Aug 28, CG, Oct 3; <u>1793</u>: DL, Apr 1, 17,
CG, 17, DL, May 20, CG, Jun 1, Oct 5; <u>1794</u>: HAY, Sep 17, DL, Oct 27, Dec 26;
<u>1795</u>: DL, May 11, 21; <u>1796</u>: DL, Apr 12, 25, May 3, 11, 25, Jun 9; <u>1797</u>: DL,
Jun 14, CG, Nov 18, DL, 21; <u>1798</u>: HAY, Sep 12, 17; <u>1800</u>: DL, Apr 1, May 23,
26, CG, Jun 13
--Thomas and Sally; or, The Sailor's Return, <u>1760</u>: CG, Nov 27, 28, 29, Dec 1,
2, 3, 4, 5, 6, 9, 10; <u>1761</u>: CG, Jan 3, 16, 17, 27, Feb 7, 14, 17, 24, Mar 3,
27, Apr 4, 7, 8, 10, 18, 23, 27, Sep 14, 30, Oct 6, Dec 10; <u>1762</u>: CG, Jan 12,
15, 25, Apr 20, 23, Oct 1, 11, 12, 30, Nov 10, 19, 27; <u>1763</u>: DL, Apr 9, CG,
15, 26, DL, May 3, 14, 18, 23, CG, Oct 8, 12, 15, 29, Nov 24, Dec 3, 7, 16;
<u>1764</u>: CG, Jan 7, DL, Mar 31, CG, Apr 7, 25, DL, 28, May 1, CG, 4, 8, Oct 27,

29, Nov 1, 14, 24; 1765: CG, Jan 7, 19, DL, Feb 20, CG, Mar 18, 30, Apr 11,
DL, 23, CG, 29, May 6, Oct 7, Nov 16, DL, Dec 16; 1766: CG, Feb 4, Mar 17,
Apr 12, 18, 19, 22, Nov 15; 1767: CG, Jan 15, Feb 7, Mar 28, Apr 11, 20, May
7, 20, Dec 2, 31; 1768: CG, Feb 10, DL, Mar 10, CG, 24, DL, Apr 8, CG, 16,
26, DL, May 3, CG, 11, HAY, 30, Jun 1, CG, 2, HAY, 3, 6, 27, Jul 15, Aug 3,
5, CG, Sep 21, 27, HAY, Oct 7, CG, 13, Nov 2, 10, Dec 8, 13, 22; 1769: CG,
Apr 5, 14, 27, May 10, HAY, 19, Jul 28, CG, Sep 27, Oct 10, 25, Nov 2, Dec 5,
22; 1770: CG, Jan 23, Mar 8, Apr 20, May 5, 19, HAY, 21, CG, 23, HAY, Jul 30,
CG, Oct 5, Dec 11; 1771: DL, Jan 22, CG, Feb 23, Apr 2, 13, May 8, 25, DL,
Dec 6, 17, 23; 1772: DL, Feb 26, CG, Sep 23; 1773: CG, Mar 15, Oct 23, Nov
20, Dec 23; 1774: CG, Feb 1, HAY, Jul 11, 29, CG, Sep 19, HAY, 30; 1775: CG,
Jan 28, HAY, Jul 31; 1777: HAY, Aug 30; 1780: CG, Dec 12; 1783: DL, Nov 4, 6,
22; 1784: DL, Feb 14; 1787: RLSN, Mar 28; 1789: CG, Nov 24, 28; 1790: CG, Feb
13, Apr 14, 27; 1791: CG, Jun 7; 1794: HAY, Feb 24, Mar 6, 17, 31, Apr 3, DL,
28, 30, Jun 12, HAY, Aug 1; 1797: DL, Nov 13
--Tis Well It's No Worse, 1770: DL, Nov 22, 23, 24, 26, 27, 29, 30, Dec 3, 5,
7, 10; 1771: DL, Jan 1; 1785: HAY, Apr 25; 1788: DL, Nov 28
Bickerstaff, John (actor), 1702: DL, Nov 0; 1703: DL, Jun 23; 1704: DL, Jan 7,
26, Mar 6, May 0, Jul 5; 1705: DL, Mar 29, Jun 12, 26, Jul 25, Nov 20; 1706:
BF, Aug 27; 1707: DL, Mar 11, Apr 3, Oct 18, 23, 25, Nov 26, Dec 2; 1708: DL,
Jan 31, Feb 14, 24, Apr 19, 23, May 21, Jun 10, 17, 19, DL/QUEEN, 22, DL, Jul
3, 10, DL/QUEEN, 15, DL, 29, Aug 4, 31, Sep 3, 4, 7, 16, 18, 21, 25, 28, 30,
Oct 2, 12, 13, 25, Dec 21; 1709: DL, Jan 6, Feb 2, 5, 11, 19, 26, Mar 8, 21,
Apr 16, 27, May 7, 17, 18, Jun 2, Sep 6, Nov 24, Dec 3, 7; 1710: DL, Jan 9,
14, Feb 6, 25, Mar 14, 27, Apr 15, 21, May 23, GR, Aug 17, DL/QUEEN, Nov 7,
18, DL, Dec 21; 1711: DL, Mar 10, 20, May 17, 21, 22, DL/QUEEN, Jun 5, DL,
Jul 10, Nov 9, 23, Dec 31; 1712: DL, Jun 19, Jul 4, Oct 8, 21, 29; 1713: DL,
Jan 29, Feb 9, Mar 14, Jun 5, Dec 2; 1714: DL, Mar 29, Apr 27, May 17, 26,
Jun 4, 25, Jul 13; 1715: DL, Feb 4, 21, Mar 8, Apr 2, 19, May 27, Jun 6, 24,
28, Jul 1, Dec 9, 22; 1716: DL, Jan 13, Apr 2, 21, May 9, Jun 15, Oct 6, 9,
15, 19, 22; 1717: DL, Jan 5, 16, 28, 31, Apr 27, May 10, Jun 10, 14, 24, Jul
2, 16, Aug 6, 22, Oct 3, 21, 28, Nov 19, 25, Dec 4; 1718: DL, Jan 27, Apr 15,
29, May 22, 28, Jun 11, 27, Jul 8, 25, Aug 1, 8, Oct 15, 17, 28, Nov 12, 19,
24, Dec 11; 1719: DL, Jan 28, Apr 20, Aug 4, Oct 9, Nov 6, 11, 27, 30; 1720:
DL, Jan 13, Mar 19, Apr 25, Sep 13, Nov 7, 12; 1721: DL, Apr 12; 1722: DL,
Apr 25; 1723: DL, May 3
Bickerstaff, Mrs John, 1710: DL, Apr 12; 1723: DL, May 3
Bickerstaff's Burying, A. See Centlivre, Susannah.
Bickerstaff's Unburied Dead; or, Drums Demolished (play, anon), 1743: LIF, Jan
14, 17, 19, 21, 24, 26, Feb 2, 4, Mar 24; 1748: CG, Apr 27; 1796: CG, Mar 30
Bickerstaffe, Isaac, 1710: DL, Feb 4; see also Steele, Sir Richard
Bickerstaffe, John (beneficiary), 1710: DL, Feb 4
Bickham (beneficiary), 1733: HAY, Aug 20
Bicknell, Alexander (versifier), 1785: DL, May 24
Bicknell (Bignal), Margaret (actor, dancer), 1702: DL, Aug 20, Oct 20; 1703:
DL, Feb 12, YB, 24, DL, May 28, Jun 19, Jul 1, Oct 15, 16, 23, 25, 26, Nov 1,
5, 17, Dec 22, 27; 1704: DL, Oct 27, Nov 13, 27, 29, Dec 1; 1705: DL, Jan 1,
8, 12, 15, 26, Mar 19, 31, LIF/QUEEN, Dec 26; 1706: QUEEN'S, Jan 2, 7, 14, 18,
22, 23, Mar 25, Apr 3, LIF/QUEEN, 11, QUEEN'S, 15, 20, 30, May 15, Jun 0, 29,
Nov 7, 14, 25, Dec 13; 1707: QUEEN'S, Jan 13, 18, Feb 12, 14, Mar 8, Apr 30,
Jun 10, Jul 10, DL/QUEEN, Oct 27, 31, Nov 10, 14, QUEEN/DL, Dec 6; 1708:
DL/QUEEN, Jan 1, DL, Feb 3, 6, 7, DL/QUEEN, 21, DL, 26, Mar 15, DL/QUEEN, Apr
6, 8, DL, 19, 29, DL/QUEEN, May 19, DL, 21, Jun 5, Oct 7, 14, 22; 1709: DL,
Feb 24, Mar 2, 3, 21, Apr 14, 28, May 3, Sep 6, QUEEN'S, 22, 24, 29, Oct 6,
17, 22, 25, 31, Nov 8, 9, 12, 19, Dec 12; 1710: QUEEN'S, Jan 12, 18, 19, Feb
6, 11, Mar 16, Apr 20, May 15, 16, Jun 5, DL/QUEEN, Oct 5, Nov 4, QUEEN'S,
10, DL/QUEEN, 13, 15, DL, 27, Dec 9, 11, 14, 15, DL/QUEEN, 29; 1711: DL, Jan
9, DL/QUEEN, 12, DL, 15, 19, 20, 25, Feb 3, DL/QUEEN, 8, DL, 15, 19, Mar 5,
Apr 7, 27, May 4, 15, 22, DL/QUEEN, 25, DL, Sep 22, 25, Oct 10, 11, 19, 23,
31, Nov 1, 2, 5, 8, 26, Dec 31; 1712: DL, Apr 29, May 6, 15, 26, 29, Jun 9,
10, 12, 19, Sep 20, 25, 30, Oct 2, 7, 31, Dec 27; 1713: DL, Jan 6, 19, 26,
Feb 9, 13, 28, Mar 3, Apr 27, May 11, 12, 25, Jun 5, 9, 12, 17, 18, 19, Sep
29, Nov 9, 23, 28, Dec 2, 18; 1714: DL, Jan 28, May 3, 31, Jun 9, 18, Oct 6,
22, Nov 9, 26, 27, Dec 8; 1715: DL, Jan 5, Feb 11, 15, 22, 23, 28, Mar 19,
Apr 2, 9, 19, May 10, 13, 18, 20, 24, Jun 2, 6, Oct 13, 14, 22, 28, Nov 2, 4,
5, 11, 17, 19, 22, 23, 30, Dec 5, 9, 12, 19, 30; 1716: DL, Jan 11, 14, Feb 1,
9, 18, 21, 23, Apr 2, 9, 19, 21, May 1, 14, 18, 25, 31, Jun 15, Sep 29, Oct
9, 15, 16, 18, 22, 31, Nov 2, 3, 12, 14, 26, 27, Dec 7, 10, 13, 15; 1717: DL,
Jan 2, 3, 9, 16, 26, Feb 6, 15, Mar 1, 2, 14, 28, Apr 1, 2, 4, 9, 11, May 6,
10, 20, 24, Jun 3, 6, 24, Oct 3, 9, 10, 12, 16, 28, 29, 30, Nov 8, 18, 20,
22, 23, 27, Dec 3; 1718: DL, Jan 7, 14, 23, 27, 28, Feb 6, 10, Mar 18, 27,
Apr 5, 15, 25, 28, 29, May 2, 6, 7, 13, 14, 15, 16, 22, 27, 30, Oct 2, 7, 10,

14, 15, 18, 20, 22, 28, 29, 30, Nov 4, 6, 12, 14, 17, 19, Dec 11, 13, 15, 16,
29; 1719: DL, Jan 24, 29, Feb 3, 12, Mar 16, 19, Apr 6, 9, 11, 14, 17, 18,
20, 21, 24, 30, May 2, 4, 5, 7, 9, 11, 14, 15, 18, 27, Sep 15, 22, 29, Oct 3,
7, 9, 12, 15, 16, 17, 20, 23, 29, 30, Nov 6, 14, 25, Dec 2, 4, 7; 1720: DL,
Feb 29, Mar 15, 29, Apr 4, 9, 25, 28, 29, May 6, 9, 10, 11, 12, 19, 20, 21,
23, 26, 30, Jun 2, 6, Sep 10, 13, 20, 22, 27, Oct 6, 7, 8, 13, 22, Nov 7, Dec
5; 1721: DL, Jan 10, 13, 16, 23, 25, 27, Feb 14, Mar 13, 23, 30, Apr 13, 14,
15, 17, May 5, 8, 9, 19, 24, 29, Oct 2, 4, 6, 12, 13, 16, 17, 18, 20, 21, 23,
24, Nov 7, 11, 13, 17, 25, 27, 28, Dec 18, 22, 29; 1722: DL, Jan 10, 19, Feb
5, Mar 10, Apr 9, 10, 12, 18, 19, 26, 27, May 1, 7, 8, 23, 28, 29, Sep 8, 11,
20, 27, Oct 5, 8, 9, 10, 12, 13, 15, 16, 20, 22, 25, 29, Dec 4, 5, 7; 1723:
DL, Jan 29, 31, Feb 5, 11, Apr 17, May 24
Bicknell, Mrs (singer), 1755: BF, Sep 3
Bicknell, Mrs, sister of (dancer), 1716: DL, Apr 19; see also Younger,
Elizabeth
Biddle (beneficiary), 1741: GF, May 7
Biddy, Miss (dancer), 1728: DL, Mar 30, Nov 15
Bidotti (actor, dancer), 1789: DL, Dec 26; 1790: DL, Oct 26, Dec 27; 1791:
DLKING'S, Nov 5; 1792: DLKING'S, Mar 19, DL, Nov 21, Dec 27; 1794: DL, May 16
Bidwell (actor), 1779: DL, Apr 28, May 1
Bienfait (dancer), 1756: CG, Apr 22
Bigari (Bigar), Francesco (machinist), 1766: KING'S, Nov 25; 1768: KING'S, Mar
10; 1769: MARLY, Aug 10; 1770: KING'S, May 19; 1772: KING'S, Jan 14
Bigg, G (printer), 1778: KING'S, Nov 24, 28; 1779: KING'S, Jan 23, Feb 23, Mar
25; 1782: DL, May 10; 1784: KING'S, Mar 4; 1785: KING'S, Apr 16
Bigge (renter), 1793: CG, Sep 23
Biggerstaff. See Bickerstaff.
Biggs (actor), 1671: NONE, Sep 0
Biggs (actor, singer), 1794: DL, Apr 21, 28; 1797: HAY, May 10
Biggs, Anne (actor), 1797: DL, Oct 17, 21, Nov 2; 1798: DL, Feb 3, May 8, 12,
30, Jun 8, HAY, Aug 28, DL, Sep 15, Oct 8, 13, 18, 20, 30, Nov 10, Dec 5, 7,
8; 1799: DL, Jan 8, 11, 31, Apr 8, 17, 27, May 3, Jun 18, Sep 17, 19, Oct 1,
5, 7, 12, 17, 22, 29, Nov 2, 16, 27, Dec 7, 11; 1800: DL, Feb 1, 12, 20, May
10, 12, 22, Jun 9
Biggs, James (actor), 1798: DL, Sep 27, Oct 13, 16, Dec 7
Biggs, John (musician), 1731: SH, Mar 12; 1736: HAY, Feb 19; 1737: LIF, May 7
Biggs, Mrs (actor), 1719: LIF, Oct 26, Nov 3, 7, 12, 13, 18, 21, 23, 24; 1720:
LIF, Oct 11
Bigi, Giacinta (singer), 1796: KING'S, Feb 16, Apr 7, 16, May 24, Jun 14
Bignal (actor), 1732: TC, Aug 4
Bignel, Mrs (actor), 1732: HAY, Mar 17
Bigner (Bingner, Binger) (wigmaker), 1758: CG, Mar 2; 1760: CG, Feb 15; 1767:
CG, Feb 17; 1771: CG, Nov 28
Bigonzi (singer), 1724: KING'S, Jan 14, Feb 20, Apr 18
Bilker Bilked, The (droll), 1742: BFHC, Aug 25
Billingsgate, 1723: DT, Nov 1; 1745: CG, May 8
Billington, Elizabeth, Mrs James (actor, singer), 1786: CG, Feb 13, 21, 28, Mar
7, 16, 18, Apr 20, 29, May 2, 29, Oct 9, 16, 21, Nov 14, 15, 24, Dec 1, 23;
1787: CG, Jan 6, 13, 29, Mar 13, 31, Apr 24, May 15, Oct 3, 11, 18, Dec 21,
22; 1788: CG, Jan 28, Feb 12, Mar 10, 15, Apr 1, 30, May 22, Sep 15, Oct 1,
13, 16, 21, Nov 1, 19, Dec 13; 1789: CG, Jan 26, 31, Feb 14, 21, Mar 3, May
5, 20, Oct 13, 20, 24, 28, 31, Nov 10, 14, 21, 24, Dec 4, 12; 1790: CG, Mar
8, May 6, Jun 2; 1791: CG, Mar 11, 18, 23, 25, 30, Apr 6, 13, 15, Nov 1, 2,
12, 15, 19, Dec 2, 10; 1792: CG, Feb 2, 24, 25, 28, Mar 2, 7, 9, 14, 21, 31,
May 9, 22, 28
Billington, James (double-bass player), 1791: CG, Mar 11; 1792: CG, Feb 24
Billington, Thomas (singer), 1776: HAY, Feb 22; 1783: CG, May 6
Billiony (dancer), 1749: CG, Jan 11
Billoe, Miss (actor), 1741: JS, Oct 6
Bimson, John Mark (witness), 1745: CG, Feb 20
Bincks, Miss (actor, singer), 1731: LIF, Nov 2; 1732: LIF, Apr 18, May 3,
CG/LIF, Sep 22, LIF/CG, Oct 16, Dec 26; 1733: LIF/CG, Feb 10, Mar 26, CG/LIF,
26, LIF/CG, 30, CG, Apr 4, LIF/CG, 13, 27, 30, CG, May 16, LIF/CG, 19, 23,
CG/LIF, 28, BF, Aug 23, CG, Sep 17, 20, 22, Oct 18, 26, Nov 28, Dec 3, 4;
1734: CG, Jan 23, 25, Mar 5, 18, Apr 23, May 3, 7, BFFO, Aug 24, CG/LIF, Sep
18, 23, RI, 26, CG/LIF, 27, Oct 7, 9, LIF, 12, CG/LIF, 16, 18, 25, Nov 4, 11,
Dec 5; 1735: CG/LIF, Jan 6, 17, 23, Feb 3, 4, 11, 13, LIF, Mar 3, CG/LIF, 11,
29, CG, Apr 25, LIF, 30, CG/LIF, May 2, 5, 9, 16, LIF, 21, CG/LIF, 26, LIF,
Jun 19, CG, Sep 12, 16, 17, Oct 1, 8, 13, 22, 24, 31, Nov 6, 8, Dec 15, 29;
1736: CG, Feb 26, Mar 6, 15, 18, 25, 29, LIF, Apr 2, CG, 8, May 1, LIF, 5,
CG, 13, 18, 20, 24, 31, Jun 4, Sep 15, 17, 20, Oct 1, 4, 6, 8, LIF, 18, CG,
20, 22, 23, 25, 27, 29, Nov 3, 4, 25, 29, Dec 2, 20, 31; 1737: CG, Jan 7, 10,

17, 21, 25, Feb 26, Mar 10, 14, 15, 17, 24, Apr 11, 12, 15, 26, May 9, 10,
16, 31, LIF, Jul 26, Aug 2, 5, CG, Sep 16, 19, 21, 26, 30, Oct 3, 5, 12, 21,
22, 24, 26, 28, 29, Nov 1, 2, 4, 9, 14, 17, 18; 1738: CG, Jan 2, Apr 18, 24
Binetti (Binati, Binety), Anna (dancer), 1761: KING'S, Mar 9, Apr 28, Oct 13,
Nov 10; 1763: KING'S, Feb 19
Binetti, Giorgio (dancer), 1761: KING'S, Mar 9, Apr 28, Oct 13, Nov 10; 1763:
KING'S, Feb 19
Binetti, Giorgio and Anna (dancers), 1762: KING'S, Mar 9, 20
Binges, Mrs (dancer), 1700: DLORLIF, Jan 20
Bingham (actor), 1778: DL, Mar 16
Bingley (chandler), 1761: CG, Mar 10
Bingley, William (printer), 1789: KING'S, Feb 28
Bingner. See Bigner.
Binks, Elizabeth (actor), 1729: LIF, Jan 1
Birch, Samuel (actor, playwright), 1792: HAY, Apr 16; 1793: DL, May 10; 1794:
CG, May 13; 1795: DL, May 1; 1796: DL, Apr 13; 1797: DL, Oct 28; 1798: CG,
Dec 11
--Adopted Child, The (farce), 1795: DL, May 1, 5, 6, 12, 16, 25, Jun 5, Sep 24,
Nov 7, 14, Dec 10, 11, 23; 1796: DL, Jan 5, 7, 15, Mar 30, Nov 28, Dec 3;
1797: DL, Nov 7; 1799: DL, Apr 5, CG, May 14, DL, 22, Jun 14, 20
--Albert and Adelaide; or, The Victim of Constancy, 1798: CG, Dec 10, 11, 12,
14, 15, 17, 18, 19, 21, 22, 27, 29; 1799: CG, Jan 1, 2, 3, 14, May 4, 8, 16
--Fast Asleep (farce), 1797: DL, Oct 28, Nov 27, 28, 29
--Mariners, The (farce), 1793: DL, May 10, 15, 17, 24, 25, 27, Jun 1, HAY, Nov
30, Dec 3, 7, 19; 1794: HAY, Jan 7, 18, Feb 4, Mar 10, 15; 1796: DL, May 27
--Packet-Boat, The; or, A Peep behind the Veil (farce), 1794: CG, May 13, 17,
27
--Smugglers, The, 1796: DL, Apr 13, 15, 16, 19, 20, 21, 22, 23, 27, May 11, Oct
6, 8, 26, Nov 21; 1797: DL, Mar 30, Apr 3, May 24, Dec 11, 15; 1798: DL, Mar
19, Jun 11, Oct 15, Dec 22; 1799: DL, Jan 16
Birch, Thomas, 1741: DL, Feb 24
Birchall, Robert (music publisher), 1789: KING'S, May 9; see also Andrews, Hugh
Birchin Lane, 1753: DL, Dec 21; 1763: DL, Apr 27
Bird (actor), 1732: WINH, May 27, UM, Jun 19; 1734: MEG, Sep 30
Bird (beneficiary), 1757: CG, Nov 22
Bird and Animal Imitations (entertainment), 1755: BFGT, Sep 5
Bird Cage Alley, 1719: BCA, Sep 24; 1720: BCA, Sep 23, SOU, Oct 10, Nov 28;
1721: SFHL, Sep 2; 1722: SOU, Sep 25, 26, Oct 3; 1723: SOU, Feb 18, SF, Sep
5, SOU, 25; 1724: SF, Sep 2, 5, SOU, 24; 1730: SFOF, Sep 9, SF, 14
Bird Catchers (dance), 1746: CG, Mar 22, Apr 7, 10; 1750: DL, Nov 27, 28, 30,
Dec 1; 1772: CG, Dec 7, 8, 12, 14, 16, 23; 1773: CG, Jan 15, Feb 2, Apr 3, 17
Bird in a Cage, The. See Shirley, James.
Bird in a Cage, The; or, Money Works Wonders! (play, anon), 1786: CG, Apr 24,
May 11
Bird, Miss (actor), 1784: HAY, Nov 16; 1785: HAY, Apr 25, HAMM, Jun 17, Jul 1,
6, 8, 15, 22, 25, 26, 27
Bird, Theophilus (actor), 1659: NONE, Sep 0; 1660: NONE, Sep 0, REDBULL, Nov 5;
1661: NONE, Sep 0; 1662: VERE, Sep 24; 1663: BRIDGES, Nov 3; 1667: BRIDGES,
Oct 5; 1673: LIF, Dec 0
Bird Jr, Theophilus, 1663: BRIDGES, Nov 3
Bird, William (composer), 1732: HIC, Mar 31
Birkett (entertainer), 1788: HAY, Sep 30
Birkhead (Birket, Burkhead, Burkett), Matthew (actor), 1707: DL, Oct 18, 25,
Dec 26; 1708: DL, May 21, 31, Sep 3; 1709: DL, May 3, 17, Jun 2, Dec 7; 1710:
DL, Jan 3, 14, Mar 14, Apr 12, Jun 10; 1711: DL, Feb 6, Mar 17, Apr 7, May
21, 31, DL/QUEEN, Jun 5, Jul 13, DL, Aug 3, 10, 17, 24, 31, Oct 12, 13, 16,
22; 1712: DL, May 30, Jun 5, Oct 15, Nov 26; 1713: DL, Jun 10; 1714: DL, May
17, Jun 11, Jul 13, 16; 1715: DL, Feb 4, May 13, 20, 24, Jun 28, Jul 6, 8,
15, 19, Aug 2, 5, Oct 14, Nov 2, 5, 11, 14, 30, Dec 5; 1716: DL, Jan 23, Feb
3, Apr 9, May 16, Jul 12, 17, 19, 24, 26, Aug 16, Oct 18, 29, 31, Nov 26, Dec
13; 1717: DL, Jan 3, Feb 6, 13, Mar 2, 28, May 10, 16, 20, 29, Jun 3, 6, Jul
4, 16, Aug 6, 9, Oct 30, Nov 19; 1718: DL, Jan 21, May 7, Jul 1, 11, Aug 8,
Nov 12, Dec 1; 1719: DL, Feb 12, May 5, 6, Jun 2, 9, Jul 21; 1720: DL, May
18, Jul 7, Aug 4, 16, Dec 6; 1721: DL, Apr 13, May 6, 29, Dec 1; 1722: DL,
Jan 10, May 15, Dec 31
Birks of Invermay (song), 1776: HAY, Oct 7
Birmingham Theatre, 1776: CG, Oct 7, Nov 14; 1790: CG, Sep 17; 1796: CG, Sep
23; 1798: CG, Jan 4
Birmingham, 1774: DL, Oct 8; 1785: DL, May 24; 1789: DL, May 11; 1793: CG, Nov
18; 1796: CG, Mar 2, 16
Biron's Conspiracy. See Chapman, George.
Birt, Miss S (dancer), 1791: PAN, Feb 17, Mar 22, CG, Dec 21, 22

Birth and Adventures of Harlequin, The. See Theobald, Lewis, The Rape of
    Proserpine.
Birth Day, The. See Dibdin, Thomas John.
Birth Day, The; or, The Prince of Arragon. See O'Keeffe, John.
Birth of Harlequin, The; or, The Old Woman's Whim (pantomime), 1754: HAY/SFB,
    Sep 19, 20, 21, 23, 24
Birth of Merlin, The. See Rowley, William.
Birth-Day, The; or, The Arcadian Contest (burletta, anon), 1787: ROY, Jul 3
Birthday Ode. See Pye, Henry James.
Bisan. See Bayzand.
Biscaien (dance), 1736: DL, May 8
Bishop (boxkeeper), 1798: CG, Jun 5; 1799: CG, May 29; 1800: CG, Jun 7
Bishop (dancer), 1776: CG, Nov 23, Dec 26; 1777: CG, Feb 18, Apr 4, 26
Bishop (gallery keeper), 1738: DL, May 30; 1739: DL, May 31; 1740: DL, May 19;
    1741: DL, May 25; 1742: DL, May 24; 1744: DL, May 21
Bishop (singer), 1735: LIF, Aug 22; 1741: GF, May 5
Bishop, Mrs (actor), 1741: GF, Apr 28, Sep 16, 18, 25, 30, Oct 9, 16, 28, Nov
    4, 9, 27, Dec 10, 21, 26, 29; 1742: GF, Jan 18, 27, Feb 3, Apr 8, 22, 24, May
    6
Bishop, Mrs (actor), 1776: HAY, Sep 18; 1777: HAY, Oct 9
Bishopsgate St, 1705: HDR, Jan 2; 1749: CG, Apr 28; 1752: CG, Dec 12; 1792:
    HAY, Nov 26
Bishopsgate, 1798: HAY, Jan 15
Biter Bit, The; or, The Humours of Harlequin and Scaramouch (farce), 1731: GF,
    Jun 2, 4
Biter Bit, The; or, Vintner in the Suds (farce, anon), 1745: GF, Apr 17
Biter, The. See Rowe, Nicholas.
Bithmere, Augustin (dancer), 1783: CG, Oct 9; 1784: CG, May 8
--Rival Knights, The (ballet-pantomime), 1783: CG, Oct 9, 10, 11, 13, 14, 15,
    17, 21, 24, 27, 31, Nov 1, 6, 11; 1784: CG, Jan 19, 20, 21, 23, 24, Feb 7,
    14, 16, 18, 20, 21, 24, Mar 1, 4, 15, 16, 20, 22, 23, 29, 30, Apr 3, 12, 13,
    14, 16, 22, 23, 29, May 6, 8, 24; 1791: CG, Jun 6
Bithmere, Augustin and Mme (dancers), 1784: CG, May 8
Bithmere, Augustine Louis (dancer), 1791: PAN, Feb 17, 26, Mar 22
Bithmere, Marie Francoise (dancer), 1784: CG, Jan 29; 1791: PAN, Feb 17, 26,
    Mar 22, 24, Jun 10
Bithmere, Mme (dancer), 1783: CG, Oct 9; 1784: CG, May 8, 21, KING'S, Dec 18;
    1785: KING'S, Jan 1, Feb 5, Mar 3, May 12, Jun 14, 18; 1786: KING'S, Dec 23;
    1787: KING'S, Jan 16, 20, Mar 13, Jun 14
Bitti (Betti, Bitte, Bitty), Alexander (musician), 1715: HIC, Apr 6; 1716: DL,
    May 18; 1717: HIC, Apr 12, DL, May 25; 1718: DL, May 8, SH, Dec 23; 1722:
    LIF, May 4
Bizzana Universal (music), 1734: YB, Mar 8
Black and White Joke (entertainment), 1731: SOU, Sep 28; 1734: DL/HAY, Feb 4,
    Mar 9, DL, Apr 4, CG, 16, 19, 24, 27, May 1, 3, 4, 6, LIF, 29, HAY, Jun 5, 7,
    Jul 19, Aug 7, DL, Sep 7; 1735: DL, Jun 11, Dec 27; 1736: DL, Apr 16, 30, May
    4
Black Bird (song), 1797: DL, May 20
Black Boy Tavern, 1697: DG, Jul 1; 1763: HAY, Sep 15
Black Bull Tavern, 1749: BBT, Mar 1
Black Eyed Susan (song), 1731: LIF, Apr 28; 1740: DL, Apr 25; 1778: HAY, Mar
    31; 1791: CG, May 18, 20, 24, 31, Jun 6, 8; 1792: CG, May 9, 24, 28; 1793:
    CG, May 10, 27, Jun 3, 10; 1794: CG, May 2, 6, 10, 20; 1795: CG, Apr 24, May
    6, 16, 19, 29; 1796: CG, Apr 26, May 17, 27; 1797: CG, May 2, 11, 22; 1798:
    CG, Apr 21, May 8, 9, 12, 22, 23, Jun 1; 1799: CG, Mar 16, Apr 6, 9, 12, 19,
    26, May 3, 13, 14, 15, 25, Jun 1, 3, Oct 7; 1800: CG, Apr 15, 19, 30, May 10,
    22, 27, 29
Black Horse Tavern, 1752: DL, Apr 13; 1784: HAY, Jan 21
Black Joke (dance), 1730: RI, Jun 24, BFOF, Aug 20, SFOF, Sep 9; 1733: CG, Mar
    27, BFCGBH, Sep 4; 1734: JS, May 31, HAY, Aug 14, 21, DL, Sep 12, 19, 24, Dec
    26, 28, 31; 1735: DL, Jan 1, 11, 17, Apr 28, May 7, GF, 15, DL, 29, Jun 3,
    LIF, 19, Jul 11, 16, Aug 1, 25; 1736: DL, May 11, Sep 25, 30, Dec 9, 10, 17;
    1737: DL, Mar 4, Apr 29; 1738: DL, May 12, Oct 21, 26, 27; 1748: SFLYYW, Sep
    7, DL, Dec 27, 28; 1749: DL, Oct 30; 1750: DL, Apr 20, 23, 30, May 2, 4, 8,
    10
Black Lyon Tavern, 1745: CG, Apr 18; 1752: DL, Apr 10, Dec 20; 1771: DL, Oct 1;
    1772: DL, May 7, 25, Sep 29; 1773: DL, Jun 2, Oct 5; 1774: DL, Jun 2; 1775:
    DL, Apr 6; 1776: DL, Jun 10; 1777: HAY, Feb 11
Black Prince, The. See Boyle, Roger.
Black Prince's Festival (dance), 1774: CG, Apr 15
Black Swan Tavern, 1751: DL, May 2; 1752: DL, Apr 8
Black, a (dancer), 1702: LIF, Dec 29

Blackamoor Wash'd White, The. See Bate, Henry.
Blackbirds (song), 1770: CG, Apr 26
Blackburn (actor), 1780: HAY, Jan 3
Blackfriars Company, 1661: LIF, Aug 24
Blackfriars, 1661: SALSBURY, Jan 29; 1668: LIF, Oct 19; 1669: BRIDGES, Jan 12;
    1790: DL, May 25
Blackheath Fair, 1729: BLA, Sep 30; 1747: BHB, Sep 26
Blackheath, 1732: BLA, Jun 24; 1748: BHB, Oct 1, 4; 1749: BHB, Oct 3, 5, 10,
    14; 1762: DL, Sep 21
Blackly (singer), 1715: DL, Mar 12
Blackman St, 1749: DL, Apr 5; 1750: DL, Mar 22; 1751: DL, Mar 14; 1752: DL, Apr
    10
Blackmoor St, 1782: DL, May 8; 1785: HAY, Mar 15
Blackmoor, Lady (singer), 1767: HAY, Sep 7
Blackmoor's Head Tavern, 1739: DL, May 11
Blackmore (scene painter), 1795: CG, Dec 21; 1796: CG, Mar 15, Apr 9, Oct 24,
    Nov 5, Dec 19; 1797: CG, Mar 16, Nov 24, Dec 26; 1798: CG, Feb 12, Apr 9, Oct
    15, Nov 12, Dec 11; 1799: CG, Jan 29, DL, May 24, Dec 11
Blackmore, Master (actor), 1797: CG, Nov 24, Dec 26; 1799: CG, Mar 25
Blackmore, Masters (actors), 1799: CG, Jan 29
Blackmore, William (tailor), 1758: CG, Feb 18, Mar 2; 1759: CG, Nov 7, 13;
    1760: CG, Mar 11, Apr 12; 1761: CG, Jan 7, Feb 2, Apr 3, Sep 29, Oct 14;
    1766: CG, Nov 22
Blacksmith of Antwerp, The. See O'Keeffe, John.
Blacksmiths (dance), 1761: DL, Nov 19, 25
Bladderbridge (musician), 1774: HAY, Mar 15
Blade Bone, The. See Colman the elder, George.
Bladon, S (printer, publisher), 1770: DL, May 31; 1772: DL, Mar 2, 23; 1781:
    CG, Apr 18; 1783: CG, Apr 26; 1785: CG, May 7; 1790: DL, May 11
Blagden (renter), 1766: DL, Nov 4; 1767: DL, Mar 24
Blagden, Master (dancer), 1755: DL, Nov 8; 1759: DL, May 15, Jul 12, Dec 12;
    1760: DL, Jun 19
Blagden, Miss (dancer), 1759: DL, Dec 12; 1760: DL, Jun 19; 1761: DL, May 5;
    1762: DL, Apr 21
Blagden, Nicholas (actor), 1660: REDBULL, Nov 5; 1661: LIF, Jun 28; 1663: NONE,
    Sep 0
Blagge, Margaret (actor), 1673: HG, Sep 23; 1674: NONE, Sep 22, ATCOURT, Dec
    15, 22; 1675: SLINGSBY, Jan 19, ATCOURT, Feb 15
Blair (actor), 1772: HAY, Sep 21; 1782: HAY, Mar 18; 1785: HAY, Jan 24; 1791:
    HAY, Sep 26
Blake (dancer), 1783: KING'S, Dec 6; 1784: KING'S, Jan 17, Feb 26, Mar 6, 18,
    HAY, Apr 30; 1790: HAY, Jan 7, Feb 13, May 13, 27, 28; 1797: KING'S, Nov 28;
    1798: DL, May 9
Blake (hosier), 1767: DL, Apr 22
Blake, Mrs (dancer), 1761: CG, Jun 23
Blakeney, General (spectator), 1756: DL, Dec 9
Blakes (actor), 1770: HAY, Mar 19
Blakes (hatter), 1772: DL, Jun 10; 1773: DL, Jun 2; 1774: DL, Feb 22, Jun 2;
    1775: DL, May 27; 1776: DL, Jun 10; 1777: DL, Oct 24
Blakes-Penkethman Booth, 1698: BF, Aug 23
Blakes, Charles (actor), 1736: HAY, May 27; 1737: HAY, Mar 21, Apr 13; 1740:
    GF, Oct 21, 23, 28, 30, Nov 4, 15, 18, 25, 26, 28, 29, Dec 1, 6, 10, 12;
    1741: GF, Jan 15, 20, 27, 28, 29, Feb 2, 9, 10, 14, 19, Mar 7, 16, 19, Apr
    15, 27, BFTY, Aug 22, GF, Sep 16, 18, 21, 23, 28, 30, Oct 2, 13, 19, 23, 28,
    Nov 4, 9, 27, 30, Dec 2, 7, 9, 26, 31; 1742: GF, Jan 5, 11, 18, 26, Feb 3,
    19, 24, Mar 1, 27, 29, Apr 1, 8, May 10, 19, DL, Sep 14, Oct 7, 9, 13, 15,
    16, 25, 26, 30, Nov 3, 4, Dec 22; 1743: DL, Jan 11, 27, 28, Feb 10, 14, SOU,
    18, DL, Mar 3, 24, SOU, 30, DL, Apr 7, 16, 22, 27, May 5, 12, 24, BFHC, Aug
    23, DL, Sep 13, Oct 22, 25, 27, Nov 3, 4, 8, 12, 17, 18, 23, 24, 26, 29, Dec
    1, 6, 15, 17, 20, 22, 26, 27; 1744: DL, Jan 5, 7, 12, 13, 17, 27, Feb 1, 3,
    13, 21, Apr 2, 3, 9, 10, 21, May 16, 22, Sep 15, 18, 20, 22, Oct 2, 4, 6, 9,
    11, 13, 17, 19, 20, 22, 23, 24, 30, Nov 3, 5, 16, 24, Dec 11, 19; 1745: DL,
    Jan 4, 17, Feb 11, 13, 15, 20, Mar 7, 30, Apr 15, 19, 22, 30, Sep 21, 24, 26,
    Oct 1, 8, 15, 17, Nov 4, 9, 14, 18, GF, 18, DL, 19, 20, 22, 23, 26, 28, 30,
    Dec 5, 7, 12, 13, 20, 31; 1746: DL, Jan 3, 8, 11, 14, 15, 18, 31, Mar 3, 13,
    17, 18, Apr 11, 12, 15, 21, 23, 25, May 9, Jun 9, 11, Sep 23, 25, 30, Oct 2,
    4, 11, 31, Nov 1, 4, 5, 7, 15, 21, Dec 6, 15, 20, 26, 30; 1747: DL, Jan 2, 3,
    15, 26, Feb 2, 10, 16, Mar 3, 7, 10, 16, 19, 23, 24, 28, 30, Apr 27, May 5,
    Sep 15, 17, 19, 22, 24, 26, 29, Oct 3, 15, 17, 20, 21, 24, 29, 30, Nov 2, 4,
    6, 7, 10, 16, 17, 18, 25, 26, Dec 3, 4, 5, 16, 26; 1748: DL, Jan 2, 6, 9, 19,
    20, 22, Feb 1, Mar 17, 19, 22, 28, Apr 12, 14, 28, May 2, 16, 18, Sep 10, 13,
    15, 22, 24, 27, 29, Oct 1, 4, 6, 8, 11, 13, 15, 18, 19, 22, 28, 29, Nov 1, 2,

3, 4, 7, 8, 9, 11, 14, 28, 29, Dec 22, 23, 28; 1749: DL, Jan 9, Feb 6, 21,
Apr 4, 7, 29, May 1, 8, 11, 16, Sep 19, 21, 22, 26, 28, Oct 3, 10, 13, 14,
17, 18, 21, 23, 26, 28, 30, Nov 2, 4, 16, 28, 30, Dec 7, 8, 12, 18, 20; 1750:
DL, Jan 1, 6, Feb 15, Mar 13, 29, Apr 2, 18, 19, 25, May 3, Sep 11, 15, 18,
21, 22, 25, 27, 28, Oct 15, 16, 19, 20, 23, 24, 25, 29, 30, Nov 1, 3, 5, 7,
8, 13, 14, 24, 28, Dec 3, 14, 26; 1751: DL, Jan 5, 7, 26, 28, Feb 23, Mar 12,
14, 16, Apr 20, 29, May 1, Sep 7, 10, 14, 17, 18, 20, 24, 26, Oct 2, 3, 4, 7,
9, 11, 14, 16, 17, 22, 28, 29, Nov 2, 4, 7, 8, 16, 29, Dec 5, 14, 26; 1752:
DL, Jan 1, 11, 22, 24, 28, Feb 13, Mar 12, Apr 1, 3, 4, 10, 11, 13, 17, 20,
21, 27, 28, May 4, Sep 16, 19, 21, 26, 28, 30, Oct 3, 5, 7, 10, 11, 12, 13,
14, 16, 19, 21, 23, 28, Nov 3, 4, 8, 22, 25, 27, 30, Dec 8, 18, 19, 29; 1753:
DL, Jan 1, 8, 13, 15, 17, 22, Feb 6, 7, 19, Mar 3, 19, Apr 2, 3, 12, 14, 25,
30, May 2, 3, 4, 8, 18, 21, 22, 25, Sep 8, 11, 13, 25, 27, 29, Oct 2, 3, 4,
6, 9, 10, 12, 13, 16, 17, 18, 20, 23, 24, 25, 29, 31, Nov 1, 3, 5, 6, 8, 14,
15, 24, Dec 20, 22, 26; 1754: DL, Jan 7, 16, 23, 26, Feb 1, 9, 20, 25, Mar
16, 18, 25, Apr 4, 15, 16, 30, May 13, 24, Sep 14, 17, 24, 26, Oct 1, 3, 5,
10, 11, 12, 14, 15, 16, 18, 21, 23, 25, 30, 31, Nov 4, 7, 11, 22, 30, Dec 5,
7, 13; 1755: DL, Jan 6, 15, 25, Feb 18, 22, Mar 4, 15, 18, Apr 8, 14, 15, 19,
May 6, 27, Sep 13, 16, 18, 20, 23, 25, 27, 30, Oct 2, 3, 4, 7, 8, 10, 11, 17,
23, 24, 25, 28, 31, Nov 1, 4, 6, 12, 17, 22, 26, 28, Dec 1, 4, 6, 11; 1756:
DL, Jan 1, 2, 10, 21, Feb 10, 24, Mar 23, 27, 29, 30, Apr 3, 21, 24, May 5,
8, 10, 11, 12, 14, 24, Sep 18, 21, 23, 25, 28, 30, Oct 2, 5, 7, 9, 13, 14,
15, 16, 18, 19, 21, 28, 29, Nov 4, 11, 13, 17, 18, 19, Dec 10, 27; 1757: DL,
Jan 3, 6, 18, 22, 26, 27, Mar 7, 21, 24, Apr 11, 26, 27, May 2, 23, Sep 10,
13, 15, 17, 20, 22, 24, 27, 29, Oct 4, 6, 7, 8, 11, 15, 18, 19, 20, 25, 26,
29, Nov 1, 2, 4, 8, 10, 19, 22, Dec 3, 23, 27; 1758: DL, Jan 13, 27, 31, Feb
4, 11, 20, Mar 13, 16, 28, 30, Apr 3, 7, 10, 18, 21, 25, May 2, 8, 15, Sep
16, 19, 21, 23, 26, 28, Oct 3, 10, 18, 25, 27, 30, Nov 1, 2, 4, 7, 8, 13, 15,
16, 17, 21, 23, 24, 27, Dec 13, 14, 20, 27; 1759: DL, Jan 3, 4, 6, 20, Feb
26, 27, Mar 20, 24, 26, 31, Apr 7, 17, 19, 27, May 4, 7, 11, 14, 16, Sep 22,
25, 27, 29, Oct 2, 4, 9, 11, 12, 16, 22, 23, 30, Nov 1, 3, 10, 13, 19, 24,
Dec 1, 7, 12, 20, 31; 1760: DL, Jan 19, Feb 8, Mar 17, 27, Apr 9, 11, 21, 22,
24, 28, 29, May 7, 8, 16, 20, Sep 20, 23, 30, Oct 2, 3, 7, 8, 10, 11, 15, 23,
24, 25, Nov 27, Dec 2, 11, 17, 29, 30; 1761: DL, Jan 8, Feb 12, Mar 26, Apr
1, 17, 20, 23, 24, 25, 28, 29, May 1, 14, 28, Sep 5, 8, 10, 12, 14, 15, 17,
18, 23, 25, 28, 29, 30, Oct 1, 13, 14, 20, 23, 24, 29, 31, Nov 9, 10, 18, Dec
14, 23, 28; 1762: DL, Jan 7, 23, 27, 29, Feb 8, 22, Mar 1, 15, 20, 22, 25,
27, 30, Apr 1, 21, 22, 30, May 6, 7, 17, 18, Sep 21, 25, 28, 29, Oct 4, 5, 6,
7, 8, 11, 14, 15, 16, 20, 25, 28, 29, 30, Nov 3, 5, 10, 11, 12, 18, 19, 23,
25, 26, 27, Dec 11, 14, 18, 27; 1763: DL, Jan 14, 15, 17, 22, Feb 28, Mar 1,
14, 26, Apr 9, 29, May 2, 6, 7, 23, 28
Blakey (actor), 1743: LIF, Jan 10, 17, Feb 2, 11, 14, Apr 7, DL, Sep 22; 1745:
GF, Oct 28, Nov 4, 11, 13, 18, 19, 26, 27, 28, Dec 2, 4, 6, 9, 11, 13, 27;
1746: GF, Jan 1, 13, 15, 22, Feb 7, Mar 20, DL, Apr 4, GF, Dec 12; 1748: HAY,
May 2; 1750: HAY, Jul 26, DL, Sep 22, Oct 30; 1754: DL, Jul 2; 1755: HAY, Sep
1, 9, 11, 15; 1758: HAY, Jan 12, 16, 18, CG, Nov 9; 1759: CG, Nov 30, Dec 29;
1760: CG, Apr 15, HAY, Jun 28, CG, Sep 22; 1761: CG, Mar 26, DL, Jul 21, 27,
Aug 5, 8; 1763: HAY, Aug 1
Blakney's Head Tavern, 1757: CG, Dec 22
Blanchard, Charlotte, Mrs Thomas Jr (actor), 1792: CG, May 5, Sep 19, 21, 26,
Oct 3, 8, 19, 25, 27, 29, Nov 24, Dec 31; 1793: CG, Jan 9, Apr 11, Jun 1, 5
Blanchard, Misses (dancer), 1791: DL, May 25
Blanchard Jr, Thomas (actor), 1773: DL, Oct 13, Nov 25, Dec 27; 1774: DL, Jan
19, Feb 2, Mar 26, Apr 19, 20, 21, May 5, 16, Sep 22, HAY, 30, DL, Oct 5, 14,
26, Nov 1, 15; 1775: DL, Jan 2, Mar 20, Apr 17, May 1, 3, 12, 13, Sep 30, Oct
3, 11, Nov 11, 28, Dec 11; 1776: DL, Mar 11, May 4; 1787: CG, Oct 3, 12, 31,
Dec 26; 1788: CG, Jan 29, Feb 9, Apr 1, 29, 30, May 5, 12, 22, Sep 15, 19,
24, Nov 1, 4, 6, 27, 28, Dec 13, 15, 26; 1789: CG, Jan 27, Feb 3, 14, 21, 24,
Mar 3, 5, 31, Apr 4, 14, 20, 21, 30, May 2, 5, 14, 15, 22, 27, Jun 2, Sep 14,
18, 23, 28, 30, Oct 2, 7, 12, 16, 17, 20, 24, 30, 31, Nov 2, 10, 21, 24, Dec
3, 12, 31; 1790: CG, Feb 10, 25, Mar 8, 18, 22, 27, Apr 6, 16, 21, May 6, 7,
10, 11, 13, 19, 24, 26, 28, Jun 1, 4, Sep 13, 17, Oct 1, 5, 6, 8, 15, 19, 23,
29, 30, Nov 3, 4, 8, 11, 23, 27, 30, Dec 2, 8, 10, 11, 14, 17, 20; 1791: CG,
Jan 3, 12, 14, 15, 26, Mar 14, 15, Apr 11, 16, 28, 30, May 5, 6, 10, 17, 18,
24, 31, Jun 1, 3, 6, Sep 12, 14, 16, 19, 20, 21, 23, 30, Oct 3, 10, 12, 20,
27, Nov 7, 15, 19, 24, Dec 3, 10, 13; 1792: CG, Feb 2, 23, 25, 28, Mar 10,
Apr 21, May 5, 10, 18, 22, 28, Sep 17, 19, 20, 21, 26, 28, Oct 1, 3, 5, 12,
19, 27, 29, 31, Nov 3, 6, 7, 14, 24, Dec 5, 13; 1793: CG, Jan 25, Feb 25, Apr
4, 18, 24, May 1, 21, Jun 5, Sep 16, 17, 20, 23, 25, 27, 30, Oct 2, 5, 10,
12, 18, 19, 22, 25, 30, Nov 2, 7, 9, 16, 18, Dec 9, 19, 27; 1794: CG, Feb 22,
Mar 18, Apr 10, 12, May 9, 14
Blanchard Sr, Thomas (actor), 1773: DL, Dec 27; 1774: DL, Jan 19, Oct 14, 27,

Dec 9; 1775: DL, Jan 2, 21, Feb 23, Mar 2, 21, 23, May 1, 3, Oct 11, Nov 25,
Dec 7, 11; 1776: DL, Jan 16, Mar 14, Oct 15; 1779: HAY, Oct 18
Blanchet, Miss (dancer), 1787: DL, Jun 1, HAY, 13, Jul 6, Aug 7, DL, Sep 20;
1788: DL, Feb 1, 21, Apr 14, 16, Jun 5, Sep 16, 18, Oct 13, Nov 19, Dec 22;
1789: DL, Jan 7, 17, May 19, 22, 27, Nov 21, Dec 4, 9, 26; 1790: DL, Jan 23,
Feb 18, Mar 8, 23, Apr 5, May 15, 18, Jun 1, Sep 30, Oct 26, Dec 27; 1791:
CG, Jan 12, DLKING'S, Dec 31; 1792: DLKING'S, Mar 19
Blanchi (singer), 1770: KING'S, Feb 2
Bland and Weller (music publishers), 1797: CG, May 23, Oct 4
Bland, Esther, Mrs George (actor), 1742: CG, Mar 6, 8, 27, May 12, Nov 25;
1743: CG, May 4, BFHC, Aug 23; 1744: CG, Apr 4, May 4, Oct 3, Nov 1, 30, Dec
5, 6; 1745: CG, Jan 11, Apr 17, 18, 20, 25, 30, May 3, 8, 10, Oct 29, Nov 8,
14, 18, 19, 22, 23, 29, Dec 2, 12, 13, 23; 1746: CG, Jan 2, 7, 23, Feb 6, 15,
17, 24, Mar 15, 18, Apr 1, 2, 7, 12, 22, 28, Jun 11, 16, 20, 23, Oct 1, 10,
13, 27, 29, Nov 6, 11, 17, 26, Dec 17, 27; 1747: CG, Jan 29, Feb 2, 6, 9, 11,
Mar 10, Apr 4, May 12, 20, Nov 11, 13, 18, 23, 25, Dec 9, 15, 17, 19; 1748:
CG, Jan 1, 2, 7, 14, 15, 16, 19, 27, Feb 1, 10, 13, Mar 8, 14, 24, Apr 13,
18, 21, 26, 27, 29; 1750: DL, Sep 25; 1752: CG, Sep 18, 25, 29, Oct 4, 6, 9,
12, 14, 19, 23, Nov 3, 7, 10, 16, 23, Dec 8, 14, 19; 1753: CG, Feb 7, 21, Mar
22, 26, May 3, 7, 8, 9, 10, Sep 10, 14, 24, 26, Oct 1, 5, 8, 17, 22, 27, 29,
Nov 5, 26, Dec 11; 1754: CG, Jan 22, Feb 12, Mar 7, 9, 21, 23, Apr 6, 20, 24,
May 2, 4, 7, 13, 15, Oct 2
Bland, George (actor), 1751: CG, Oct 16, 17, Nov 18
Bland, George (actor), 1790: DL, Feb 10, CG, Jul 16, DL, Oct 7, 26, Nov 3, Dec
8, 27; 1791: DL, Jan 7, 25, Mar 22, Apr 29, May 11, HAY, Jun 6, 8, 10, 13,
20, Jul 7, 30, Aug 2, 24, 31, Sep 2, 3, DLKING'S, 27, Oct 3, 4, 13, 29, 31,
Nov 4, 5, 7, 14, Dec 3; 1792: DLKING'S, Jan 5, 9, 18, 21, Feb 11, 18, Mar 29,
May 8, HAY, Jun 18, 23, Jul 9, 25, Aug 1, 6, 9, 17, 22, DL, Sep 18, 19, 20,
25, 27, Oct 27, Nov 5, 21, Dec 4, 10, 17, 26, 28, 31; 1793: DL, Jan 16, 17,
23, Feb 5, 21, Mar 4, 9, Apr 8, 9, 10, 15, May 7, 10, 22, 24, 29, HAY, Jun
11, 12, 13, 14, 17, 18, 21, 24, 25, 26, 29, Jul 5, Aug 3, 6, 12, 16, 26, 27,
Sep 2, 19, 21, 24, 28, 30, Oct 5, 8, 15, 21, 30, Nov 19, 29, 30, Dec 7, 10,
14, 16, 19, 26, 30, 31; 1794: HAY, Jan 3, 4, 14, 16, 17, Feb 6, 19, 20, 22,
Mar 29, 31, DL, Apr 25, May 1, 6, 12, 16, 30, Jun 9, 28, HAY, Jul 8, 9, 10,
12, 17, 18, 21, 22, 25, 26, 29, Aug 4, 12, 18, 20, 27, DL, Sep 16, HAY, 17,
DL, 23, 27, Oct 11, 14, 16, 20, 23, 27, 29, 31, Nov 14, 18, 29, Dec 9, 12,
30; 1795: DL, Jan 1, 21, 26, 31, Feb 2, 3, 12, 28, Mar 5, 14, May 1, 18, 27,
Jun 3, HAY, 9, 10, 11, 13, 16, 18, 20, 24, Jul 1, 4, 25, 31, Aug 3, 19, 20,
Sep 1
Bland, James (actor), 1784: HAY, Feb 9
Bland, Maria Theresa, Mrs George (actor, singer), 1789: DL, Nov 24; 1790: DL,
Oct 26, 27, 28, Nov 19, 20, 24, 30, Dec 7, 8, 9, 14; 1791: DL, Jan 1, Feb 8,
10, 16, Mar 8, 31, Apr 28, May 3, 5, 10, HAY, Jun 10, 16, Jul 15, 30, Aug 16,
Sep 13, DLKING'S, Oct 15, 18, 24, 25, 29, Nov 2, 5, 9, 11, 12, 14, 16, 17,
28, 30, Dec 31; 1792: DLKING'S, Jan 5, 11, 21, Feb 7, 11, 18, KING'S, 24, 29,
Mar 7, DLKING'S, 10, KING'S, 14, DLKING'S, 17, KING'S, 23, DLKING'S, 26, 27,
KING'S, 28, DLKING'S, 29, KING'S, 30, DLKING'S, Apr 10, May 3, 8, 21, 31,
HAY, Jun 15, 18, 23, Jul 3, 14, 23, 25, Aug 9, 14, DL, Sep 18, 20, 27, 29,
Oct 9, 13, 18, Nov 2, 10, 21, 29, Dec 4, 13, 14, 17, 22, 26; 1793: DL, Jan
23, Feb 25, Mar 4, 5, 7, 9, 11, 21, Apr 1, 2, 8, May 7, 9, 10, 15, 21, Jun 3,
10, HAY, 12, 13, 17, 18, Aug 3, 12, Sep 2, 9, Oct 1, 4, 7, 8, 18, 22, Nov 19,
30, Dec 10, 16; 1794: HAY, Jan 7, 10, 21, 27, Feb 8, 11, DL, Mar 14, 19, 26,
HAY, 29, DL, Apr 2, 4, 9, 10, 11, 21, 25, 26, May 1, 3, 8, 12, 16, 19, Jun 9,
17, 24, HAY, Jul 11, 14, 18, 19, 21, 24, 26, Aug 20, 22, 23, Sep 2, 5, DL,
23, Oct 7, 11, 14, 18, 20, 27, 29, 31, Nov 3, 15, Dec 12, 20; 1795: DL, Jan
7, 13, 26, Mar 10, May 1, 2, 4, 6, 19, 27, 29, 30, Jun 3, HAY, 9, 10, 13, 15,
20, 27, Jul 16, 30, 31, Aug 3, 18, 21, Sep 2, DL, 17, 29, Oct 6, 8, 13, 15,
27, 30, Nov 2, 6, 7, 11, 12, 23, Dec 10, 18, 30; 1796: DL, Jan 18, Mar 17,
Apr 4, 30, May 11, 12, 17, 25, 27, Jun 1, 10, HAY, 11, 13, 15, 16, 18, 25,
Jul 2, 5, 8, 12, 15, 21, Aug 8, 23, 29, 30, Sep 1, 5, 16, 17, DL, 27, 29, Oct
3, 10, 15, 19, Nov 5, 10, 19, 26, 28, Dec 5, 10, 16; 1797: DL, Jan 7, 12, Feb
9, 11, 16, 17, 24, 27, Mar 14, 23, May 4, 12, 13, 22, 23, 31, Jun 6, 7, HAY,
16, 19, 21, 23, 26, Jul 3, 6, 8, 15, Aug 9, 10, 14, 15, 19, 28, Sep 1, 4, DL,
19, 23, 26, Oct 7, 19, 23, 28, 30, 31, Nov 7, 9, 11, 20, 24, Dec 2, 20; 1798:
DL, Jan 16, Mar 6, 24, 26, Apr 16, May 5, 24, 30, 31, Jun 5, 6, 7, HAY, 12,
DL, 12, HAY, 15, 16, 20, 28, 29, 30, Jul 10, 13, 14, 19, 21, Aug 6, 9, 11,
20, 21, 23, 29, Sep 7, 14, DL, 15, 27, 29, Oct 2, Nov 3, 5, 12, 13, 14, 26,
Dec 3, 4, HAY, 17, KING'S, 26, DL, 29; 1799: DL, Jan 1, 19, Feb 14, Mar 2,
KING'S, 26, DL, 26, Apr 2, 6, 25, May 4, 7, 16, 31, Jun 4, HAY, 18, 19, 20,
DL, 20, HAY, 28, Jul 2, DL, 2, HAY, 9, 12, 16, 19, 20, 23, 27, 30, Aug 13,
21, 24, 27, 28, Sep 2, 9, 16, DL, 19, 24, Oct 1, 3, 12, 14, Nov 6, 7, 8, 14,
15, 16, 22, 27, Dec 10, 19; 1800: DL, Jan 4, 21, Mar 4, 11, May 30, Jun 3, 5,

7, 9, 10, 11, 16, HAY, 16, 17, DL, 17, HAY, 18, DL, 18, HAY, 19, Aug 23, 26, 29

Blandford (actor, dancer), 1789: WHF, Nov 9, 11; 1792: HAY, Nov 26

Blandford (tallow chandler), 1749: DL, Nov 7, 14, 21, 28, Dec 5, 13, 19; 1750: DL, Jan 2, 9, 16, 23, 31, Feb 7, 13, 20, 27, Mar 13, 27, Apr 3; 1766: DL, Oct 17, Nov 14, Dec 12; 1767: DL, Jan 9, Feb 6, Mar 7, Apr 6, May 1; 1776: DL, Jun 1

Blandford Fire, 1731: DL, Dec 3

Blandy (constable), 1781: DL, May 12; 1782: DL, May 4; 1783: DL, May 31; 1784: DL, May 24; 1785: DL, May 23; 1786: DL, May 29

Blaney, Miss (actor), 1781: HAY, Nov 12; 1782: HAY, Jan 21

Blanfort, Marquis of. See Duras, Louis de.

Blant (house servant), 1788: CG, May 27

Blastock (actor), 1735: HAY, Dec 17; 1736: HAY, Jan 19, BFFH, Aug 23, SF, Sep 7

Blaythwaite, William (spectator), 1679: BF, Sep 3

Blazing Comet, The. See Johnson, Samuel.

Blendel (actor), 1772: HAY, Sep 21

Blenheim Mews, 1791: PAN, Feb 17, Dec 17

Bless the true Church and save the King (song), 1790: CG, Mar 3, 5, DL, 17, CG, May 24; 1791: CG, Mar 25; 1795: CG, Mar 18

Blest be the Lord (song), 1794: DL, Apr 10

Blest be the Man (song), 1786: DL, Mar 10; 1789: DL, Mar 18; 1790: DL, Feb 24, 26; 1791: DL, Mar 23; 1792: KING'S, Feb 24; 1793: KING/HAY, Feb 22; 1794: DL, Apr 10

Blest were the hours (play), 1797: DL, May 8

Blewitt, Jonas (composer), 1780: HAY, Sep 25; 1790: CG, Apr 6

Bligh (tallow chandler), 1786: CG, Oct 23

Blind Beggar of Bethnal Green, The. See Dodsley, Robert.

Blind Beggar of Bethnal Green, The; or, The Woman Never Vexed (Injured General, The) (droll), 1721: BF/SF, Aug 24, Sep 2; 1723: BFPJ, Aug 22, RI, Sep 2, SOU, 25; 1724: BFP, Aug 22; 1743: SF, Sep 8, MEF, Oct 3; 1744: MF, May 4

Blind Lady, The. See, Howard, Sir Robert.

Blind Man's Bluff (pantomime), 1723: DL, Mar 16

Blind Man's Buff (dance), 1757: HAY, Jun 17, Aug 13, 17, 24, 27, 31, Sep 2, 5, 28, Oct 12; 1764: CG, Oct 3, 8, 11, 12, Nov 1, 3, 14, 16, 20, 21, 23, 27, Dec 1, 3, 11, 28, 31; 1765: CG, Jan 7, 10, 17, 25, Mar 2, 4, 23, Apr 19, 22, 27, May 1, 14, 20, 22; 1767: CG, May 16, 19, 20

Bliss (actor), 1757: BFG, Sep 5

Blissett, Francis (actor), 1777: HAY, Jun 9, 11, 26, Jul 18, 24, Aug 7, 9, 14, 19, 25, 30, Sep 3, 10; 1778: HAY, Jun 8, 11, 12, 19, Jul 2, 11, Aug 3, 17, 22, 27, Sep 2, 17, 18; 1779: HAY, Jun 2, 10, 12, 17, Jul 17, 20, Aug 6, 17, 18, 24, 27, Sep 8; 1780: HAY, May 30, Jun 5, 9, 10, 12, 24, 28, Jul 8, 15, 24, Aug 17, 24, 30; 1781: HAY, Jun 8, 11, 16, Aug 1, 8, 15, 17, 22, 24, 29, 31, Sep 10; 1783: HAY, Jun 2, 3, 10, 20, Jul 5, Aug 1, 13, 26, 27, 30

Blithest Bird (song), 1747: DL, Mar 28

Block Heads' Dance (dance), 1795: CG, Nov 16

Blogg (singer), 1742: NWC, Dec 27; 1743: BFFP, Aug 23, NWLS, Nov 1; 1744: JS, Mar 16, MFHNT, May 1, MF, 3; 1745: GF, Oct 28

Blondel (dancer), 1742: BFHC, Aug 25

Bloody Brother, The. See Fletcher, John.

Bloomfield (actor), 1791: CG, Sep 19, 26, Nov 4; 1792: CG, Mar 6, May 30

Blooming virgins (song), 1791: CG, Mar 23; 1792: KING'S, Mar 28

Bloomsbury Square, 1738: DL, Aug 19; 1790: DL, May 4; 1791: DL, May 6; 1792: DLKING'S, May 1; 1799: HAY, Aug 22; 1800: DL, May 20

Bloomsbury, 1699: DLLIF, Dec 25; 1732: GF, Oct 11; 1733: LIF/CG, May 8; 1734: BFT, Aug 17, LIF, Oct 12; 1735: CG/LIF, Apr 14, May 12; 1736: CG, Apr 5; 1737: CG, May 10; 1738: DL, May 9; 1739: CG, Mar 26, DL, May 5; 1740: CG, Mar 24; 1749: DL, May 16; 1777: DL, Apr 1, HAY, Aug 19; 1778: DL, Apr 20, 23, HAY, Sep 10; 1779: DL, Apr 12, HAY, Sep 7; 1780: DL, Mar 16, Apr 1, HAY, Sep 5; 1782: HAY, Jan 14, CG, Apr 29, DL, May 3; 1785: DL, Apr 20; 1786: DL, Apr 22, May 1; 1787: DL, May 4, 8; 1791: DL, Apr 26, May 7; 1792: DLKING'S, Apr 9, 11; 1793: DL, Apr 9, 25, CG, May 23; 1794: CG, May 2; 1795: DL, Apr 22, CG, 28, DL, 29, CG, May 27; 1796: CG, Apr 12, DL, May 3, 6, CG, 12; 1797: CG, May 2, DL, Jun 2, 12; 1798: CG, Apr 21; 1799: CG, Apr 6; 1800: HAY, Aug 12

Blousabella (dance), 1703: LIF, Jun 8, 11; 1704: LIF, Jul 4, Aug 9; 1705: LIF, Jan 25; 1712: DL, Jun 12

Blow, Blow, thou Winter Wind (song), 1741: DL, Apr 13, 18, HIC, 24, DL, 28, CG, 30, DL, May 1, 4, 5, 7, 12, 13, 14, 22, 25, 26, 27, 28, Jun 4; 1743: JS, Mar 23; 1766: KING'S, Sep 13

Blow, Boreas, Blow (song), 1681: DL, Oct 0; 1795: DL, May 27

Blow high, Blow low (song), 1779: HAY, Dec 27; 1781: DL, Apr 25, 26, May 7, 10; 1793: CG, Apr 11; 1794: CG, Apr 7, 23, 25; 1795: CG, Apr 28

Blow, ye Bleak Winds around (song), 1746: GF, Feb 18
Blow, Dr John (composer), 1679: DG, Dec 0; 1680: DG, Sep 0; 1681: NONE, Sep 0;
  1682: DG, Jan 23; 1684: MS, Nov 22; 1686: DL, Apr 0; 1691: ATCOURT, Jan 1,
  SH, Nov 23; 1693: ATCOURT, Jan 1; 1695: DL, Oct 0; 1697: YB, Mar 3; 1698: YB,
  Mar 16, May 10; 1700: YB, Dec 11; 1702: SH, Jan 31, May 7, CC, 21; 1706: DL,
  Jan 7; 1709: SH, Nov 30; 1729: CRT, Dec 5
--Venus and Adonis (masque), 1681: NONE, Sep 0
Blower, Elizabeth (actor, singer), 1782: DL, Apr 27, Jun 1; 1787: CG, Sep 24,
  Oct 22, Dec 15, 17; 1788: CG, Jan 7, 14, May 31
Bludrick (actor), 1780: CG, Feb 21
Blue Beard; or, Female Curiosity. See Colman the younger, George.
Blue Beard; or, The Flight of Harlequin. See Delpini, Carlo Antonio.
Blue Bell of Scotland (song), 1800: DL, May 12, 23, 30, CG, Jun 13
Blue Boar Inn, 1750: BB, Jan 8
Blue Devils. See Colman the younger, George.
Blue Door, 1738: DL, May 17; 1742: CG, Mar 6, DL, Apr 30; 1743: DL, Mar 15
Blue Flower-pot (public house), 1740: DL, May 15
Blue Maid Alley, 1721: BF/SF, Sep 2; 1722: SF, Sep 5; 1724: SF, Sep 7; 1726:
  SFLH, Sep 8; 1733: SF/BFLH, Aug 23
Blue Post Coffee-house, 1792: HAY, Oct 15
Blue Post Tavern, 1724: BPT, Feb 21
Blunt, Mrs (actor), 1730: HAY, Mar 30
Blurton, James (actor, dancer, singer), 1767: CG, Apr 27, May 12, Sep 26, Oct
  10, Nov 14; 1768: CG, Mar 1, Apr 16, Sep 24, 28, Nov 23; 1769: CG, Jan 14,
  Apr 8, 26, May 12, Nov 11; 1770: CG, Jan 24, Dec 1, 5; 1771: CG, Apr 12, May
  9, 15, Sep 23, 30, Oct 11; 1772: CG, Apr 24, May 29, Sep 21, 25, 30, Nov 2,
  4, Dec 7, 26; 1773: CG, Feb 6, 18, Apr 24, May 14, 26, 28, Sep 29, Nov 25,
  Dec 30; 1774: CG, Jan 5, 7, Apr 11, 12, 15, 30, May 4, 7, 14, 16, 20, Oct 20,
  Nov 19, Dec 14; 1775: CG, Apr 18, 19, May 11, DL, Oct 3, 21, Nov 18, 28, Dec
  11, 20; 1776: DL, Feb 10, 14, 20, Apr 22, May 11, Jun 8, Sep 26, Oct 24, 31,
  Nov 6, 9, Dec 10; 1777: DL, Jan 4, Feb 10, Apr 19, May 15, Nov 8; 1778: DL,
  Feb 19, Apr 25, May 8; 1779: DL, Jan 29, May 25; 1780: DL, Dec 30; 1781: DL,
  Apr 18, 25, Oct 29; 1782: DL, Mar 14, Oct 5, 16, Nov 30; 1785: CG, May 18,
  Nov 2, Dec 26; 1786: CG, May 10, Oct 9; 1787: CG, Jan 31, Feb 10, Mar 31, Apr
  30, Dec 26; 1788: CG, Jan 14, 21, Mar 24, Apr 1, 12, Jun 4; 1789: CG, Mar 16,
  Jun 16, Sep 21, Oct 12, 20, Nov 23; 1790: CG, Mar 27, May 27, Oct 4, 6, Nov
  6, 26, Dec 4, 11, 20; 1791: CG, Feb 4, Mar 14, May 3, 7, 16, 26, 31, Jun 9,
  13, Sep 12, Oct 10, 20, 24, Nov 15, Dec 13, 21; 1792: CG, Mar 31, Apr 18, May
  10, 12, Oct 25, 27, 29, Nov 6, 24, Dec 26; 1793: CG, Jan 25, Mar 11, Apr 11,
  18, 24, May 27, Sep 17, 30, Oct 7, Nov 2, 13, Dec 19; 1794: CG, Jan 24, Feb
  5, 6, 22, Mar 25, Apr 23, 29, May 7, Jun 10, 12, Sep 22, Oct 6, 14, 20; 1795:
  CG, Jan 31, Mar 14, 19, Apr 7, 8, Jun 6, 10, Sep 14, 21, 25, Oct 5, 12, 30,
  Nov 4, 6, 7, 16, Dec 9; 1796: CG, Jan 1, 13, 23, Mar 15, 17, 30, Apr 9, 26,
  May 11, 23, Jun 7, Sep 16, 17, 19, 26, Oct 6, 7, 13, 24, 29, Nov 8, 19, Dec
  19, 27; 1797: CG, Jan 10, 11, Feb 18, Mar 4, 7, 16, Apr 8, 25, 27, May 3, 15,
  18, 22, 25, Oct 2, 12, 16, 18, 25, Nov 2, 8, 15, 24, Dec 18, 26; 1798: CG,
  Feb 9, 12, 13, Mar 19, 27, Apr 9, 21, May 8, 18, 28, Jun 5, Oct 8, 10, 11,
  15, 25, Nov 12, Dec 11, 15, 26; 1799: CG, Jan 12, 29, Mar 2, 5, 16, 25, Apr
  2, 13, 18, 19, May 17, 28, Jun 5, Sep 25, 30, Oct 7, 21, 24, 31, Nov 11, Dec
  9, 23; 1800: CG, Feb 10, Mar 4, 25, Apr 5, 23, 29, May 1, 7, 27, Jun 2, 10
Blurton, Mary, Mrs James (actor, singer), 1793: CG, Sep 30, Oct 2, 7, 9, 24,
  Dec 19, 27; 1794: CG, Jan 9, Feb 22, Sep 22, 29, Oct 20; 1795: CG, May 18,
  Jun 10, Sep 21, Oct 8, 19, 24, Nov 9, 16, 30; 1796: CG, Apr 9, May 10, Sep
  12, 19, 26, Oct 6, 7, 14, Dec 19; 1797: CG, Feb 18, Apr 25, Jun 5, Sep 25,
  Oct 16, Nov 2; 1798: CG, Feb 13, Apr 19, Sep 17, Oct 3, 8, 11, Nov 12, Dec
  11, 15, 26; 1799: CG, Jan 29, Mar 25, Apr 13, 19, Sep 18, 30, Oct 2, 7, 24,
  Dec 23; 1800: CG, Jan 16, Feb 17, Mar 25, Apr 28, Jun 2
Blush not redder than the Morning (song), 1679: DG, May 0
Boaden, James, 1784: HAY, Aug 18; 1793: DL, Mar 7; 1794: CG, Mar 25, DL, Apr
  21, CG, Oct 23; 1795: DL, Apr 17, CG, Jun 3; 1796: CG, Jan 8; 1797: HAY, Aug
  15, CG, Oct 11; 1798: HAY, Jul 21, DL, Dec 29
--Aurelio and Miranda, 1798: DL, Dec 29, 31; 1799: DL, Jan 1, 2, 3, 4
--Cambro-Britons, 1798: HAY, Jul 21, 23, 24, 25, 26, 27, 28, 31, Aug 2, 4, 7,
  23; 1799: HAY, Jul 20; 1800: HAY, Aug 29
--Fontainville Forest, 1794: CG, Mar 25, 27, 29, Apr 1, 3, 5, 10, 22, 26, May
  1, 3, Jun 2, 6, 18, Oct 6, Nov 18; 1796: CG, Jan 8
--Italian Monk, The, 1797: HAY, Aug 15, 16, 18, 19, 23, 26, 30, Sep 2, 6, 9,
  12, 14; 1798: DL, May 30, HAY, Jun 30, Jul 9, 13; 1799: HAY, Jul 9, 17
--Ozmyn and Daraxa, 1793: DL, Mar 7, 9, 12, 14, 16
--Secret Tribunal, The, 1795: CG, Jun 3, 9, 11, Oct 23, 31, Nov 5
Boadens, Charles, 1732: DL, Jan 10; 1760: DL, Mar 24
--Modish Couple, The; or, Marriage a la Mode, 1732: DL, Jan 10, 11, 12, 13;

    1760: DL, Mar 24; 1771: HAY, Apr 15
Boadicea, Queen of Britain (dabce), 1775: CG, May 12, 16
Boadicea, Queen of Britain. See Hopkins, Charles.
Boadicia. See Glover, Richard.
Boar's Head Tavern, 1738: DL, May 19
Board (actor), 1738: BFP, Aug 23
Boarding School Romps, The. See Coffey, Charles.
Boas (spectator), 1673: WF, Sep 27
Boccherini, Luigi (composer), 1794: CG, Dec 26
Bocchini (dancer), 1773: KING'S, Oct 23, Nov 20, 30, Dec 7; 1774: KING'S, Jan
    29, Feb 5, 12, 17, Mar 17, Apr 9, 19, 28, May 5, 12
Bochi, Giuseppe (singer), 1724: KING'S, Dec 1
Bodine (dancer), 1736: CG, Oct 20, Nov 3
Bodini (librettist), 1776: KING'S, Jan 9
Bodle, W (beneficiary), 1735: HAY, Sep 29
Bodvile, Elizabeth (spectator), 1661: LIF, Jul 1
Boggly, Mohamet Ben Ali. See Abgali, Sid Mahomet Ali.
Boham (actor), 1741: JS, Nov 9
Boheme, Anna Maria, Mrs Anthony (the first) (actor), 1723: LIF, Apr 16, 18, 19,
    23, 30, May 3, 4, 6, 10, 13, 14, 15, 17, 18, 23, 24, 27, 28, 29, 31, Jun 6
Boheme, Anthony (actor), 1718: LIF, Oct 16; 1719: LIF, Jan 16, May 7, Oct 2,
    Nov 7, 16, 17, 19, Dec 10, 15, 18, 28; 1720: LIF, Jan 7, 11, 21, Feb 11, 23,
    29, Mar 19, Apr 26, May 14, Jun 7, SFLH, Sep 5, LIF, Oct 1, 15, 20, 22, Nov
    1, 3, 10, 29, Dec 8, 17, 21, 31; 1721: LIF, Jan 7, 17, 19, 28, Feb 1, 9, 25,
    Mar 4, 11, 14, 18, Apr 13, 21, 25, May 29, BFLGB, Aug 24, SF, Sep 8, LIF, 23,
    29, Oct 3, 5, 7, 10, 14, 17, 21, 24, 26, 28, Nov 2, 4, 9, 11, 13, 16, 25, Dec
    2, 12; 1722: LIF, Jan 20, 22, Feb 13, Mar 8, 29, 31, May 7, 17, Jun 1, 13,
    Aug 1, BFPMB, 25, SF, Sep 5, LIF, 29, Oct 4, 13, 16, 18, 19, 20, 22, 23, 24,
    26, 27, 30, Nov 1, 2, 3, 5, 8, 16, 17, 22, 29, Dec 1, 15, 31; 1723: LIF, Jan
    11, 18, Feb 1, 7, 16, 22, Apr 6, 13, 23, May 3, Jul 10, Sep 28, 30, Oct 2, 4,
    10, 24, 31, Nov 2, 4, 12, 14, 16, 18, 21, 26, Dec 2, 7; 1724: LIF, Feb 24,
    Mar 19, 26, 28, Apr 9, 14, 28, 29, May 5, 19, 20, Jun 2, 3, 5, Aug 11, Sep
    23, 28, Oct 7, 9, 14, 22, Nov 4, 6, 12, 17, 18, 20, 24, 26; 1725: LIF, Jan
    16, 19, Feb 27, Mar 11, 29, Apr 5, 14, 23, May 21, Sep 24, Oct 1, 11, 15, 16,
    25, 26, 28, Nov 2, 9, 18, 30, Dec 2, 6, 15; 1726: LIF, Feb 19, Mar 24, Apr 2,
    11, 22, May 3, 11, Sep 21, 26, 28, Oct 17, 24, Nov 2, 4, 8, 11, 14, 18, 21;
    1727: LIF, Jan 4, 16, Feb 2, Apr 3, May 22, Sep 18, 20, Oct 9, 17, 19, 21,
    26, 31, Nov 4, 16, 17, Dec 11, 16; 1728: LIF, Jan 17, Mar 14, 21, Apr 1, 4,
    24, 30, Sep 16, 30, Oct 1, 7, 21, Nov 1, 4, 11, 19, 20, Dec 7; 1729: LIF, Sep
    12, 17, 22, Oct 3, 10, 13, 20, 24, 31, Nov 4, 8, 13, 14, 22, 25, Dec 15;
    1730: LIF, Jan 19, 26, Mar 30, Apr 20, May 6, 13, 15, 20, 23, Jun 1, 4, Sep
    16, 21, Oct 5, 7, 14, 19, 26, Nov 2, 3, 4, 13, Dec 4; 1731: LIF, Jan 7, 11
Boheme, Mrs Anthony (the second) (actor), 1730: LIF, Jun 4, Dec 4
Bohemia, Elizabeth Queen of (visitor), 1661: LIF, Aug 17
Bohemia, King and Queen of (visitors), 1661: LIF, Jul 2
Bohemia, King of (visitor), 1723: RI, Sep 2
Bohemian Peasant Dance (dance), 1757: HAY, Jul 1, 5
Bohemienne, La. See Arnold, Dr Samuel.
Bohemiens (dance), 1777: KING'S, Dec 16, 20, 23; 1778: KING'S, Jan 17, 20, 24,
    27, 31, Feb 3, 7, Mar 21, 28, Apr 28, May 12, 19
Bohun (actor), 1670: BRI/COUR, Dec 0
Boimaison (actor, dancer), 1794: DL, May 22, Jun 9, Sep 27, Dec 20; 1795: DL,
    Feb 12, May 6, Oct 1, 21, 30; 1796: DL, Jan 18, Jun 10
Boimaison, Mrs (actor, singer), 1794: DL, May 16, Jun 9, 24, Sep 27, Oct 6, 27,
    31, Nov 6, 15, Dec 20; 1795: DL, Jan 1, Oct 1, 22, 30, Nov 11, 23, Dec 10;
    1796: DL, Jan 11, 18, Mar 3, 12, Apr 30
Boin. See Bowen.
Bois. See Boyce, John.
Boisfranc
--Bains de la Porte de St Bernard, Les, 1719: LIF, Jan 22; 1720: KING'S, May
    27, Jun 1, 21; 1721: HAY, Jan 27
Boisgirard (dancer), 1791: PAN, Feb 17, 26
Boisgirard, Mme (dancer), 1791: PAN, Feb 17
Boissy, Louis de, 1789: DL, Apr 20
--Dehors Trompeurs, Les; ou, L'Homme du Jour, 1789: DL, Apr 20
--Francois a Londres, Le, 1734: HAY, Nov 29, Dec 4, GF/HAY, 5, 9, 28; 1735:
    GF/HAY, Jan 8, Feb 13, 24
--Vie est un Songe, La; ou, Arlequin Boufon a la Cour de Naples (Life is a
    Dream), 1735: GF/HAY, Jan 16, Feb 13, Mar 6
Boitar, Beatrice (actor), 1729: LIF, Jan 1
Bold Stroke for a Husband, A. See Cowley, Hannah.
Bold Stroke for a Wife, A. See Centlivre, Susannah.

Boldoni, G (author), 1736: KING'S, Apr 13
Bolingbroke, Mrs (actor), 1777: CHR, Jun 20, 23, 25, 27, 30, Jul 2
Bolla, Maria (singer), 1800: KING'S, Jan 11, Feb 18, Apr 24, May 13, DL, Jun 6,
   KING'S, 17, Jul 8
Bolney (householder), 1740: CG, Mar 10, DL, 25, Apr 15
Bologna, Barbara (dancer), 1798: CG, Oct 15; 1799: CG, Jan 29, Mar 2, Apr 13,
   May 22, Jun 4, Oct 21; 1800: CG, Feb 17, Mar 4, 25, Apr 28, May 1, 27, Jun 2,
   11
Bologna, John Peter (dancer), 1797: CG, Nov 24, Dec 26; 1798: CG, Feb 12, Mar
   19, Apr 9, Jun 4, Oct 15, 25, Nov 12, Dec 11, 26; 1799: CG, Jan 29, Mar 2, 7,
   Apr 11, 13, 22, 23, May 13, 22, 28, Jun 6, Oct 7, 21, 24, Dec 23; 1800: CG,
   Feb 10, Mar 4, Apr 23, 29, May 7, 27
Bologna, Louis (dancer), 1798: CG, Feb 12, Dec 11; 1799: CG, Jan 29, Mar 2, 25,
   Apr 13, 19, May 28, Oct 21, Dec 23; 1800: CG, Feb 10, Mar 4, 25, Apr 29, May
   1, 7, 27, Jun 2
Bologna, Mrs Louis (dancer), 1800: CG, Apr 29
Bologna, Mrs Pietro (dancer), 1797: CG, Dec 26; 1798: CG, Feb 12, Mar 19, Apr
   9, Oct 15, 25, Nov 12, Dec 11, 26; 1799: CG, Jan 29, Mar 2, 25, Apr 13, Oct
   21, 24, Dec 23; 1800: CG, Jan 24, Feb 10, Mar 4, 25, Apr 29, May 1, 27, Jun 2
Bologna, Pietro (dancer), 1797: CG, Nov 24, Dec 26; 1798: CG, Feb 12, Mar 19,
   Apr 9, 23, 25, Jun 4, Oct 15, 25, Nov 14, Dec 26; 1799: CG, Jan 29, Mar 2,
   25, Apr 13, May 22, 25, Jun 6, Oct 21, 24, Dec 23; 1800: CG, Mar 4, Apr 5,
   23, May 27, Jun 2, 5
Bolter, Mrs (mercer), 1771: DL, Dec 17
Bolton (actor), 1773: HAY, Jul 2, 5, 28, Aug 11, 27, Sep 3, 16
Bolton (smith), 1730: GF, Jul 14; 1731: GF, May 12
Bolton St, 1777: CG, May 14
Bolton, Mrs (actor), 1784: HAY, Mar 22; 1785: HAY, Feb 10, 12, Apr 26; 1788:
   HAY, Apr 29, Sep 30
Boman. See Bowman.
Boman's Chocolate-House, 1717: DL, Jun 18; 1718: LR, Dec 3
Bombastini (musician), 1759: HAY, Sep 17, 21
Bombastini, Sg and Sga (entertainer), 1759: HAY, Sep 25
Bombastini's daughter (entertainer), 1759: HAY, Oct 5
Bombasto (entertainer), 1752: CT/HAY, Jan 31, Mar 17, 21, Apr 1, 11, 16; 1753:
   HAY, Mar 13, Apr 7, 10; 1754: HAY, Aug 27; 1760: HAY, Feb 14
Bombazino (Bambaseno) (actor, dancer), 1752: CT/HAY, Jan 31, Mar 17, Apr 1, 11,
   16, May 5; 1753: HAY, Mar 13; 1754: HAY, Aug 27
Bon Andre (music), 1786: KING'S, Apr 27
Bon Prince, Le; ou, Les Infortunes Vertueux (dance), 1794: KING'S, May 31
Bon Ton. See Garrick, David.
Bond St, 1748: DL, Apr 13; 1765: DL, Nov 14
Bond, William (actor, author, proprietor), 1733: CG, Aug 20; 1735: YB, May 29,
   Jun 2
--Tuscan Treaty, The; or, Tarquin's Overthrow, 1733: CG, Aug 20, 21
Bondman, The; or, Love and Liberty. See Massinger, Phillip.
Bonds without Judgement. See Topham, Edward.
Bonduca. See Fletcher, John.
Bonduca, Music from (music), 1780: DL, Feb 18, Mar 3; 1781: DL, Mar 14, 16;
   1782: DL, Mar 15; 1784: DL, Mar 24
Boneway, Mlle (actor), 1746: BF, Aug 23
Bonfanti, Luigi (singer), 1794: KING'S, Dec 6; 1795: KING'S, Jan 27, Mar 21;
   1796: KING'S, Feb 16, Jun 14, 18; 1797: KING'S, Jan 10, Mar 21, Apr 27, Jun
   8, 10, Jul 15, 22, Dec 9, 12, 20; 1798: KING'S, Jan 23, Mar 10, 20
Bonham (actor), 1747: RL, Jan 27
Bonne Mere, La. See Florian, Jean Pierre Claris de.
Bonner, Miss (actor), 1791: HAY, Sep 26, Dec 12
Bonneval (Bonneville), Mlle (dancer), 1741: CG, Nov 11, 21, Dec 9, 28; 1742:
   CG, Jan 5, 8, 11, 21, 25, Feb 6, 10, 13, Mar 23, Apr 19, 21, May 1, DL, Oct
   5, 9, 25, Nov 8, 12, 13, 17, 26, Dec 11, 31; 1743: DL, Jan 14, Feb 3, 11, 26,
   Mar 8, Apr 7, 25, May 16, CG, Dec 20; 1744: CG, Feb 14, 28, Mar 1, 3, Apr 4,
   6, 14, 16, 17, 23
Bonnor, Charles (actor, dramatist), 1783: CG, Sep 19, 24, Oct 3, 10, Nov 10,
   Dec 5, 6, 23; 1784: CG, Jan 14, May 26, Jun 2, 14, Sep 17, 20, 24, 27, Oct
   25, 29, 30, Nov 3, 10, 11, 16, Dec 1, 14, 15; 1785: CG, Jan 12, 14, Feb 21,
   Mar 5, 29, Apr 1, 8, May 6, 11, 13, 26, 28; 1790: CG, Dec 20
--Picture of Paris, The, 1790: CG, Dec 20, 21, 22, 23, 27, 28, 29, 30, 31;
   1791: CG, Jan 1, 3, 5, 6, 7, 8, 10, 11, 13, 15, 17, 20, 21, 22, 24, 25, 27,
   28, 29, 31, Feb 1, 3, 4, 11, 25, Apr 25
--Transformation; or, The Manager an Actor in Spite of Himself (interlude),
   1784: CG, Jun 14; 1785: CG, May 6; 1787: DL, Apr 25, HAY, Aug 7; 1788: DL,
   Apr 21

87

Bonny Broom (song), 1757: DL, Mar 31
Bonny Christ Church Bells (song), 1788: HAY, Aug 22
Bonny Highlander (dance), 1700: DL, Jul 6
Bonny lad prithee lay thy pipe down (song), 1692: DL, Jan 0
Bonny lass gin thou wert mine (song), 1680: DG, Jun 0
Bonny Milkmaid (song), 1728: LIF, May 2
Bonomi, Giacinta (dancer), 1758: KING'S, Jan 10, 31, Nov 11; 1759: KING'S, Jan 16

Bononcini, Giovanni (composer), 1704: DL, Feb 21; 1705: DL, Dec 15, QUEEN'S, 31; 1706: DL, Jan 12; 1709: QUEEN'S, Jun 4; 1710: QUEEN'S, Jan 10, Mar 16; 1712: QUEEN'S, Nov 12; 1720: KING'S, Nov 19; 1721: KING'S, Apr 15; 1722: KING'S, Jan 10, Feb 22, Mar 6; 1723: BUH, Jan 11, KING'S, Mar 30, Nov 27; 1724: KING'S, Apr 18; 1727: LIF, Apr 5, KING'S, May 6; 1732: KING'S, Jun 24; 1734: LIF, Mar 2, Apr 16; 1789: KING'S, Feb 7
--Almahide (opera), 1710: QUEEN'S, Jan 10, 13, 17, 20, 24, 27, 31, Feb 10, 14, 17, 21, Mar 14, 21, 28, Apr 25, May 9, Jul 6; 1711: QUEEN'S, Apr 14, 18, 21, May 2, Nov 10, 14, 17, 28, Dec 1, 29; 1712: QUEEN'S, Jan 14
--Astartus (opera), 1720: KING'S, Nov 19, 23, 26, 30, Dec 3, 7, 10, 14, 17, 21; 1721: KING'S, Jan 7, 11, 14, 18, 28, Mar 4, 7, 11, 14, 18, Apr 1, 11, Jun 24, 28, Nov 11, 15, 18, 22; 1722: KING'S, Jun 6, 9; 1734: LIF, Feb 26, Mar 2, 5, 9, Apr 6, 16
--Astyanax (opera), 1727: KING'S, Apr 22, May 6, 9, 13, 16, 23, 27, 30, Jun 3, 6
--Calphurnia (opera), 1724: KING'S, Apr 18, 21, 25, 28, May 2, 5, 9, 14, 16, Jun 6, 9; 1729: HIC, Apr 16
--Crispus (opera), 1722: KING'S, Jan 10, 13, 17, 20, 24, 27, 31, Feb 3, 6, 10, Apr 11, 14, 18, 21, May 16, 19, Jun 13, 16, Dec 29; 1723: KING'S, Jan 2, 5, 8
--Erminia (opera), 1723: KING'S, Mar 30, Apr 2, 6, 16, 20, 27, 30, May 4
--Floro and Blesa (musical interlude), 1710: QUEEN'S, Mar 16
--Griselda (opera), 1722: KING'S, Feb 22, 24, 27, Mar 3, 10, 13, 17, 28, 31, Apr 4, 7, May 2, 5, 9, 30, Jun 2; 1729: HIC, Apr 16; 1733: KING'S, May 22, 26, 29, Jun 2, 5, 9
--Pastoral Entertainment, An (musical), 1732: KING'S, Jun 24
--Pharnaces (opera), 1723: KING'S, Nov 27, 30, Dec 4, 7; 1724: KING'S, Jan 4, 7, 11
Bonsor (doorkeeper), 1794: CG, Jun 17; 1795: CG, Jun 10; 1796: CG, May 21; 1797: CG, Jun 2; 1798: CG, May 19; 1799: CG, Jun 8; 1800: CG, Jun 10
Bonte du Seigneur (dance), 1788: KING'S, May 22, 31
Bonville (actor, singer), 1787: CG, Sep 26, Oct 1, 3, Dec 3, 17; 1788: CG, Jan 7, 14, Feb 5, Mar 1, May 21, 31, Sep 22, Oct 7, 8, Dec 15, 26, 29, 31
Boomar (singer), 1719: DL, May 2
Boone, Colonel (spectator), 1661: SALSBURY, Mar 26
Boor left in the Lurch (dance), 1716: DL, Jul 19
Bootell. See Bowtell.
Booth (actor), 1780: HAY, Mar 28; 1782: HAY, Jan 14, Sep 21
Booth (house servant), 1762: HAY, May 1; 1769: DL, Apr 25, Oct 14; 1770: DL, Jan 6, Mar 31, May 7, 14, 16, 18, Jun 7, Sep 25, 29, Oct 5, 13, 25, Nov 3, 17, 19, 23, 24, Dec 5, HAY, 14; 1771: DL, Mar 7, Apr 5, 6, 9, May 21, 27, Oct 28
Booth (householder), 1777: DL, Apr 21
Booth, Barton (actor, author), 1700: LIF, Dec 0; 1701: LIF, Jan 0, Mar 0, Apr 0, Aug 0, Nov 0, Dec 0; 1702: LIF, Jun 0, Dec 31; 1703: LIF, Jan 0, Feb 0, Nov 0; 1704: LIF, Feb 2, ATCOURT, 7, LIF, 24, ATCOURT, 28, DL, Mar 6, LIF, 25, Oct 2, Nov 13, Dec 4; 1705: LIF, Aug 1, LIF/QUEN, Oct 30, QUEEN'S, Nov 23, Dec 27; 1706: QUEEN'S, Jan 3, Feb 11, 21, Mar 7, Jun 0, Oct 26, Nov 19, 21, 22, 25, Dec 3, 6, 10, 11, 14, 30; 1707: QUEEN'S, Jan 1, 14, 18, 25, 28, 29, Feb 3, 4, 12, 14, 15, 18, Mar 1, Apr 3, 21, May 2, 9, Jun 18, 25, 27, Jul 4, 22, 26, 30, Aug 1, 12, 19, DL/QUEEN, Oct 18, 22, 23, 28, Nov 1, QUEEN/DL, 8, DL/QUEEN, 14, 15, 19, 20, QUEEN'S, 22, DL/QUEEN, 25, Dec 27; 1708: DL/QUEEN, Jan 1, DL, 15, 31, Feb 6, 7, 9, 14, 19, 24, Mar 15, 25, 27, Apr 15, 27, 29, May 31, Jun 17, 24, Jul 1, 3, 10, 20, 27, Oct 7, 13, 14, 16, 23, Dec 21, 22, 28, 30; 1709: DL, Jan 1, 3, 4, 7, 11, 22, 26, 29, Feb 1, 4, 5, 11, 12, 26, Mar 17, 19, 21, 24, Apr 9, 11, May 3, 17, 18, Jun 2, Sep 6, Nov 23, 25, 26, 28, 30, Dec 3, 6, 9, 10, 17, 22; 1710: DL, Jan 3, 14, 18, 21, 23, 26, 28, 31, Feb 11, 18, 23, 25, Mar 14, Apr 15, 21, May 23, DL/QUEEN, Nov 7, 9, 11, 14, 17, DL, 23, Dec 2, 7, 9; 1711: DL, Jan 18, 19, 20, 25, 27, Feb 3, DL/QUEEN, 17, DL, 27, Mar 10, 17, 20, DL/QUEEN, Apr 5, DL, 21, 24, DL/QUEEN, May 3, DL, 18, Jun 26, 29, DL/QUEEN, Jul 13, DL, 17, 24, 27, Aug 3, 17, Sep 27, 29, Oct 8, 11, 12, 16, 18, 20, 22, 24, 27, 29, 30, Nov 1, 3, 6, 7, 12, 24, 27, Dec 13; 1712: DL, Jan 19, Mar 17, Apr 25, May 8, 12, 13, Jun 2, Jul 1, 11, 18, 29, Aug 1, 12, Oct 4, 7, 10, 14, 21, 28, Nov 7, 25, 26, 28, Dec 27; 1713: DL, Jan 5, 6, 10, 15, 23, 29, Feb 13, 19, 28, Mar 3, 14, 16, 23,

88

26, 28, Apr 14, May 13, 18, Jun 3, 5, 12, 17, 18, 19, Nov 9, 11, 25, 27, Dec
18; 1714: DL, Jan 5, Feb 2, Mar 15, 29, Apr 23, 26, May 7, 17, 21, 26, 28,
Jun 2, 11, 14, 18, Oct 13, 22, 26, Nov 3, 9, 15, Dec 4, 6, 9; 1715: DL, Jan
5, 15, 24, Feb 4, 19, 21, 25, Mar 8, 14, 21, Apr 4, 20, May 17, 18, 20, Jun
6, Oct 13, Nov 9, 12, 17, 29, Dec 16; 1716: DL, Jan 7, 10, 13, 21, 23, 24,
25, Feb 23, 25, Mar 3, 22, Apr 2, 16, 17, May 9, Sep 29, Oct 2, 6, 9, 11, 12,
13, 18, 22, 23, Nov 1, 3, 12, 26, Dec 4, 14, 17, 27, 29; 1717: DL, Jan 5, 9,
24, Feb 2, 25, Mar 28, May 2, 10, 11, Jun 18, Sep 28, Oct 10, 11, 14, 15, 22,
26, Nov 19, 25, 27, 28, 30, Dec 6, 31; 1718: DL, Jan 20, 23, 27, 29, Feb 14,
Mar 1, 8, 22, Apr 5, May 2, 13, 20, NONE, Jul 30, DL, Sep 20, 25, Oct 4, 7,
11, 15, 21, 22, 25, 28, 31, Nov 4, 8, 12, 13, 18, 25, 27, Dec 2, 3, 19; 1719:
DL, Jan 3, 9, Feb 14, Mar 7, May 7, 8, 13, Jul 31, Sep 12, 17, 19, 29, Oct 8,
10, 13, 21, 22, 23, 31, Nov 3, 6, 7, 10, 11, 14, 17, 19, 20, 21, 24, 26, Dec
2, 5, 8, 11; 1720: DL, Jan 5, 27, Feb 5, 17, Apr 2, May 30, Jun 2, Sep 10,
13, 15, 17, 24, 29, Oct 1, 3, 4, 6, 8, 18, Nov 1, 2, 4, 10, 19, 22, 26, 29,
Dec 5, 6, 8; 1721: DL, Jan 13, 16, 17, 19, 24, Feb 3, 14, Mar 2, Apr 14, 18,
26, May 13, Sep 12, 14, 16, 21, 23, 26, 30, Oct 3, 5, 7, 10, 12, 14, 16, 19,
20, 21, 28, 31, Nov 3, 4, 14, 15, 18, 28, Dec 1, 12, 28; 1722: DL, Jan 9, 26,
Feb 19, Mar 12, 13, Apr 10, 13, 17, 27, May 5, 18, 22, Sep 11, 13, 15, 18,
22, 25, 29, Oct 6, 9, 11, 16, 18, 19, 23, 24, 27, 30, Nov 1, 5, 7, Dec 5, 7,
22, 26; 1723: DL, Jan 8, 9, 28, Feb 5, 6, 15, Mar 2, 11, 21, Apr 1, 22, May
11, 20, Sep 14, 17, 21, 24, 26, 28, Oct 5, 8, 12, 15, 19, 22, 23, 26, 28, 29,
31, Nov 4, 6, 7, 12, 14, Dec 5, 20, 30; 1724: DL, Jan 15, 27, Feb 6, 12, 15,
17, 22, Apr 8, 25, May 14, Sep 12, 15, 19, 22, 24, 26, Oct 14, 17, 20, 22,
27, 28, 31, Nov 2, 4, 7, 14, 19, Dec 3, 9, 22; 1725: DL, Jan 4, 9, 25, 27,
Feb 1, 3, 9, Apr 20, 22, 24, May 11, Sep 4, 9, 11, 16, 18, 30, Oct 2, 5, 7,
13, 16, 21, 25, 26, 27, Nov 1, LIF, 4, DL, 4, 8, 10, 12, 20, 27, Dec 7, 18,
22; 1726: DL, Jan 3, 11, Feb 2, 18, Mar 17, May 7, 11, 12, 18, 23, Sep 3, 8,
13, 15, 30; 1727: DL, Jan 16, 19, 21, Feb 4, 9, 11, 16, 21, 23, Mar 20, 25,
Apr 8, 12, 13, 15, 17, 24, 27, 29, May 5, 8, Sep 7, 9, 12, 16, 21, 23, 26,
Oct 3, 6, 7, 9, 13, 18, 21, 26, Nov 4, 9, 22, 27, Dec 13, 19; 1728: DL, Jan
9; 1730: DL, Nov 3, 21; 1731: DL, Oct 30; 1732: DL, Jul 14, NONE, Dec 25, DL,
28; 1733: DL, May 10; 1734: DL/HAY, Jan 12, 17, 19, Feb 16; 1747: CG, Feb 28;
1753: DL, Mar 10, Oct 30; 1772: DL, Sep 24; 1777: HAY, Aug 14
--Burgomaster Tricked, The, 1734: DL/HAY, Jan 12, 14, 15, 17, 19, 22, 24, 25,
29, DL/DL/HA, 31, HAY, Feb 1, DL/HAY, 7, 8, 11, 16, 18, 19, May 1, 3, DL, Sep
19, 21, 24, 30, Oct 3, 28, 30, Nov 18; 1736: DL, Nov 2, 3, 4, 11, Dec 3, 10,
30; 1737: DL, Jan 20, 26, 28, Nov 19; 1738: DL, Jan 2, 3, 4, 5, 6, 7, 9, 10,
11, Feb 7, 8, 10, 20, Dec 4, 5; 1746: SFHP, Sep 8, NWMF, Oct 6
Booth, Barton and Hester (actors), 1745: DL, Mar 18
Booth, Barton, on the Death of (poem), 1733: DL, Jun 23
Booth, Cockran Joseph (actor), 1774: CG, Oct 4, 13, 14, 22, 24, 26, 31, Nov 1,
3, 4, 8, 19, Dec 6, 9, 12, 20; 1775: CG, Mar 4, Apr 19, 28, May 4, 17, 20,
27, Sep 25, 29, Oct 9, 20, 25, 28, 30, Nov 4, 8, 13, 21, Dec 1, 7, 9, 22, 26,
27, 29; 1776: CG, Jan 1, 24, Mar 5, 18, 23, 30, Apr 11, 19, 30, May 10, Sep
27, Oct 7, 8, 9, 16, 17, 25, Nov 13, 14, 19, 22, 25, 26, 28, 30, Dec 5, 17,
19, 26, 27, 30; 1777: CG, Jan 1, 8, 9, 15, Feb 22, Mar 17, Apr 7, 16, 28, May
5, 14, Sep 29, Oct 6, 10, 15, 16, 20, 21, 27, 30, Nov 1, 6, 7, 12, 13, Dec 4,
19; 1778: CG, Jan 15, 21, Feb 11, 23, 25, 28, Mar 14, Apr 7, 11, 22, 25, 27,
28, May 9, 11, 15, Sep 18, Oct 2, 5, 7, 9, 14, 16, 21, 24, 26, 29, Nov 4, 21,
Dec 3, 21, 26; 1779: CG, Jan 5, 8, 11, 13, 25, 26, 29, Feb 11, Mar 4, 22, 23,
Apr 9, 21, 24, 26, 27, 28, 29, May 3, 6, 10, 13, 15, 18, 20, Sep 20, 22, Oct
1, 20, 23, Nov 1, 6, 8, 10, 11, 13, 16, 22, 23, 25, 30, Dec 3, 11, 16, 17,
18, 20, 31; 1780: CG, Jan 7, 12, 25, Feb 1, 8, 22, Mar 18, 27, 29, DL, Apr 5,
CG, 7, DL, 11, CG, 12, 19, 21, 25, May 12, 19, 24, Sep 18, 20, 21, 22, Oct 2,
3, 6, 9, 10, 11, 13, 19, 24, 26, 30, Nov 1, 4, 6, 10, 20, 22, 25, Dec 16, 28;
1781: CG, Jan 1, 15, 25, Feb 14, 15, Mar 13, 19, Apr 28, May 7, 10, 12, Sep
17, 19, 24, 26, 28, Oct 5, 31, Nov 2, 5, 7, 8, Dec 5, 8, 11, 17, 31; 1782:
CG, Jan 4, 5, 7, 9, 11, 16, 22, Feb 2, 4, 5, Mar 16, 19, Apr 1, 4, 9, 10, 12,
24, May 3, 6, 11, 17, 20, 22, 25, 28, Sep 23, DL, 28, CG, 30, Oct 3, 7, 9,
14, 15, 16, 17, 19, 21, 22, 29, Nov 1, 2, 4, 18, 19, 25, 27, 30, Dec 2, 6,
12, 14, 30; 1783: CG, Jan 3, 27, Feb 19, Mar 29, May 9, 10, 13, 14, 15, 17,
19, 20, 21, Jun 3, HAY, 6, CG, Sep 22, 24, Oct 1, 3, 6, 10, 11, 13, 14, 16,
17, 20, 21, 23, Nov 4, 6, 10, 19, 25, 27, Dec 5, 11; 1784: CG, Jan 7, 9, 13,
16, 29, 31, Feb 5, 19, 20, Mar 6, 22, Apr 13, 17, 23, 24, 26, 27, May 1, 8,
19, 21, 24, 25, 26, 27, Sep 17, 20, 21, 22, 27, 29, Oct 4, 8, 12, 27, 28, Nov
10, 13, 20, 29, Dec 1, 4, 10, 11, 22, 27; 1785: CG, Jan 1, 14, 19, 21, Feb 7,
19, Mar 5, 12, 29, 30, Apr 6, 8, 11, 18, May 7, 26, HAY, Jun 2, 16, 24, 29,
30, Jul 13, 20, 29, Aug 2, 10, 16, 19, 31, Sep 2, CG, 19, 21, 23, 26, 30, Oct
3, 7, 10, 14, 19, 26, 27, 31, Nov 1, 2, 7, 17, 19, 22, 25, 29, Dec 2, 7, 14,
16, 19, 26; 1786: CG, Jan 7, 11, 14, 28, 31, Feb 1, 8, 11, 17, 18, 21, 25,
28, Mar 18, Apr 1, 4, 18, 19, 26, 28, 29, May 9, 10, 11, 13, 15, 29, HAY, Jun

12, 14, 15, 19, 26, 28, 29, Jul 3, 7, 11, 12, 19, 28, Aug 3, 4, 12, 25, 29,
Sep 4, 9, CG, 18, 20, 25, 29, Oct 9, 12, 25, 31, Nov 13, 14, 15, 22, 24, 25,
30, Dec 1, 12, 15, 21, 23, 30; 1787: CG, Jan 2, 4, 6, 11, 31, Feb 6, 13, 20,
Mar 15, 26, 27, Apr 11, 16, 25, May 11, 14, 21, Sep 17, 19, 21, Oct 1, 5, 10,
12, 17, 18, 19, 29, 31, Nov 2, 5, 7, 8, 20, 23, 30, Dec 20, 22; 1788: CG, Jan
3, 5, 10, 18, 28, Feb 14, 25, Mar 8, 11, 26, 29, Apr 1, 2, 8, 11, May 12, 14,
Sep 19, DL, 20, CG, 22, 24, 26, Oct 1, 8, 18, 21, 24, 28, 29, Nov 6, 12, 20,
21, 26, 28, Dec 5, 13, 30, 31; 1789: CG, Jan 2, 15, 20, Feb 3, 11, Mar 31,
Apr 4, 14, 27, Jun 3, 17
Booth, Great Theatrical, 1722: SOU, Sep 26; 1730: SF, Sep 14; 1731: SFGT, Sep
8; 1736: NONE, Sep 7; 1742: UM, Apr 26, SOU, Sep 27; 1743: SOU, Feb 18, 25,
Mar 30; 1745: GF, Feb 4; 1754: SFG, Sep 21, 23, 24; 1757: BFG, Sep 5, 6
Booth, Great, 1702: BFGB, Aug 24; 1703: BFG, Aug 23; 1720: SOU, Oct 3; 1723:
SOU, Feb 18; 1730: SFG, Sep 8; 1731: UM, Apr 19; 1732: WINH, May 27; 1734:
SFG, Sep 7; 1735: SOU, Apr 7; 1739: TC, Aug 6
Booth, Grey Tiled, 1743: MEF, Oct 3
Booth, Hester, Mrs Barton (actor, dancer), 1719: DL, Sep 12, 17, 24, 29, Oct 3,
15, 22, 23, 26, 27, 29, Nov 3, 6, 16, 18, 19, 25, Dec 1, 2, 4, 7; 1720: DL,
Jan 1, 12, 14, 19, Feb 1, 10, 12, 29, Mar 15, 19, 24, 28, 31, Apr 2, 5, 19,
25, 26, May 5, 6, 9, 10, 11, 12, 16, 17, 18, 20, 21, 23, 24, 25, Sep 13, 17,
20, 22, 27, Oct 1, 3, 5, 8, 12, 15, 17, 22, 28, Nov 1, 4, 8, 10, 11, 12, 21,
22; 1721: DL, Jan 13, 23, Feb 14, Mar 13, 16, 25, 30, Apr 11, 12, 13, 14, 15,
17, 25, May 5, 23, 24, 31, Jun 6, Sep 9, 12, 26, 28, 30, Oct 7, 13, 16, 18,
28, Nov 1, 4, 13, 25, 27, 28, Dec 18, 20, 22, 29; 1722: DL, Jan 8, 10, 19,
22, 26, Feb 19, Mar 10, 15, 27, Apr 5, 9, 10, 12, 14, 24, 27, 28, 30, May 4,
5, 7, 8, 16, 19, 23, 24, 29, 30, Sep 15, 27, 29, Oct 5, 10, 12, 13, 16, 17,
22, 25, 26, 30, Nov 5, 7, Dec 3, 11, 27; 1723: DL, Jan 9, 17, Feb 5, Mar 2,
18, 21, Apr 29, May 2, 4, 9, 10, 11, 13, 15, 16, 17, 21, 23, 24, 30, 31, Sep
14, 26, 28, Oct 3, 5, 8, 16, 21, 30, Nov 1, 4, 9, 14, 15, 16, 18, 20, 21, 22,
23, Dec 31; 1724: DL, Jan 3, 27, Feb 10, 11, 17, 20, 27, Mar 5, 9, 16, 23,
26, Apr 7, 13, 15, 17, May 2, Sep 12, 15, 22, 24, Oct 14, Nov 2, 4, 6, 13,
14, 16, 19, 21, 26, Dec 16, 18; 1725: DL, Jan 4, Feb 1, 4, 20, Mar 4, 15, 18,
31, Apr 2, 5, 7, 15, 16, 19, 28, 30, May 8, 21, Sep 11, 18, 25, 28, Oct 2, 7,
9, 12, 14, 15, 19, 20, 23, 27, 28, Nov 2, 4, 19, Dec 4, 6, 7, 9, 16, 22;
1726: DL, Jan 5, 11, 22, 24, 25, Feb 11, Mar 14, 17, 21, 24, 28, Apr 15, 20,
May 2, Sep 6, 15, 22, 24, Oct 13, 15, 18, 29, Nov 2, 4, 9, 12, 15, 19, 29,
Dec 7, 10, 17, 20, 21, 30; 1727: DL, Jan 26, Feb 18, 27, Mar 13, 20, 23, Apr
6, 8, 10, 12, 17, 19, 20, May 5, 24, Sep 12, 14, 16, 23, Oct 5, 6, 7, 12, 19,
20, 23, Nov 4, 9, 14, 18, 30, Dec 13; 1728: DL, Feb 16, 27, 29, Mar 2, 7, 14,
16, 18, 25, 28, Apr 4, 8, 11, 23, May 1, 2, 6, 7, 9, 10, 13, 20, 23, Sep 10,
12, 14, 21, 26, Oct 10, 17, 21, 23, 24, 31, Nov 7, 8, 14, 15, Dec 31; 1729:
DL, Jan 1, 2, 11, 13, 23, 27, 31, Feb 15, Mar 18, Sep 30, Oct 14, 16, 25, Nov
14, 25, Dec 1, 4, 5, 10, 13, 26, 29; 1730: DL, Jan 9, 24, Feb 23, Mar 19, Apr
2, 4, 6, 11, 13, 14, 15, 16, 18, 20, 23, May 4, 14, Sep 12, 15, 24, Oct 1, 3,
10, 28, Nov 16, 19, 21, 25, 26, 28, Dec 2, 4; 1731: DL, Jan 11, Mar 8, 18,
22, 25, 29, Apr 27, May 1, Sep 18, 23, Oct 5, 16, 26, Nov 9, 11, 23, 24, 25,
Dec 3, 7, 10, 17, 18, 22, 27, 28, 30; 1732: DL, Feb 2, 22, Mar 2, 6, 13, 16,
20, 21, 23, 27, 30, Apr 17, 18, 19, 20, 21, 22, 26, 27, 28, 29, May 4, 10,
12, Sep 8, 21, 23, Oct 17, 21, 28, 31, Nov 2, 4, 6, 8, 11, 14, 17, 18, 21,
Dec 22; 1733: DL, Feb 6, 12, 22, 26, Mar 5, 8, 10, 26, 28, 31, Apr 4, 9, 11,
16, 23, 24, 30, May 7, 24, Jun 4, 9, BFCGBH, Sep 4, DL, 22
Booth, John (tailor), 1789: DL, Jun 9; 1791: DLKING'S, Oct 1
Booth, John and Ursula Agnes, 1777: DL, May 2
Booth, Lower, 1753: BFGI, Sep 3, 4, 5
Booth, Miss (singer), 1715: DL, Jun 2, 17, 28, Jul 6, 19, Aug 5
Booth, Mrs (actor), 1741: BFH, Aug 22
Booth, Mrs Cockran Joseph (actor), 1776: CG, Nov 4; 1777: CG, Feb 5, May 5, 14;
1790: CG, Jun 8
Booth, Theatrical, 1722: SOU, Oct 3; 1761: SFT, Sep 21, 22
Booth, Tiled, 1729: BLA, Sep 30; 1743: SF, Sep 8; 1746: SOU, Sep 16, 25; 1747:
SF, Sep 14, 16, BHB, 26, SOU, Nov 16; 1748: SOU, Jul 4, 18, BHB, Oct 4, SOU,
31; 1749: SOU, Jan 2, 9, 26, Feb 20, SFGT, Sep 16, SOUGT, 22, 25, SOU, 28,
Oct 2, BHB, 3, SOU, 4, BHB, 5, SOU, 9, BHB, 10, 14, SOU, 16; 1751: SF, Sep 7,
9, 10, 11, 16, 17, 19; 1752: SFGT, Sep 18, 19, 20, 21, 22, SOU, 29, Nov 24;
1753: SFP, Sep 18, SFGT, 18, 19, 20, 21, SFP, 27; 1755: BFGT, Sep 3, 5, 6,
SFG, 18, 19, 20, 22; 1760: SF, Sep 13
Booth, Ursula Agnes, Mrs John (actor, singer, playwright), 1775: CG, Sep 22,
Nov 1, 3, 4, 13, Dec 1; 1776: CG, Jan 1, 5, May 15, DL, Nov 25, Dec 10; 1777:
DL, Jan 1, 4, Feb 24, Mar 13, 20, Apr 22, Sep 20; 1778: CG, Apr 27, DL, May
23, Oct 15, Nov 2, Dec 21; 1779: DL, Nov 3, Dec 27, 29; 1780: DL, May 5, 10,
Sep 23, Nov 8, Dec 6; 1781: DL, May 1, 16, Sep 18, 25, Oct 2, 12, 29, Nov 5,
13; 1782: DL, Mar 9, Apr 12, 25, May 14, 15, Sep 19, 24, Oct 16, Nov 26, Dec

26; <u>1783</u>: DL, Mar 3, May 12, 14, Sep 20, Oct 13, Dec 2, 19; <u>1784</u>: DL, Apr 19, 21, May 3, 21, Oct 18, Nov 9, 22; <u>1785</u>: DL, Jan 12, 20, Feb 2, Apr 14, 22, Sep 27, Oct 17, 26, Nov 3, Dec 26; <u>1786</u>: DL, Jan 14, 19, Feb 23, Mar 9, Sep 28, Oct 7, 27, Dec 5, 13, 28; <u>1787</u>: DL, Jan 11, Feb 10, Apr 13, Oct 15, 20, Nov 6, 21, Dec 11, 26; <u>1788</u>: DL, Jan 21, Feb 7, Mar 26, 31, Apr 14, May 30, Jun 10, Sep 13, 18, Oct 2, 9, 25, Nov 10, 17, 25, 26, 27, 29, Dec 11, 22; <u>1789</u>: DL, May 27, Jun 12, Sep 17, 19, 22, 24, Oct 1, 3, 8, 15, 24, Nov 24, Dec 5, 8; <u>1790</u>: DL, Feb 10, 15, 27, Mar 2, 22, Apr 16, May 12, 14, 15, Jun 1, Sep 11, 16, Oct 4, 7, 14, 18, 20, 23, 25, 27, Nov 30, Dec 7; <u>1791</u>: DL, Jan 25, Mar 22, 24, Apr 2, May 20, 26, HAY, Sep 16, DLKING'S, 22, Oct 1, 3, 10, 20, 25, 31, Nov 10, 12, 30, Dec 1; <u>1792</u>: DLKING'S, Jan 21, 25, 27, 28, Feb 8, Mar 26, Apr 12, 18, May 14, Jun 13, 15, DL, Sep 18, 25, 27, Oct 18, 25, Nov 10, 16, Dec 3, 7, 14, 17; <u>1793</u>: DL, Jan 5, 7, 14, 16, Feb 14, 25, Mar 5, 9, 11, Apr 5, 9, 17, HAY, Aug 12, Sep 21, 24, 26, 30, Oct 1, 8, 10, 22, 28, Nov 5, 16, 29, Dec 16; <u>1794</u>: HAY, Jan 2, Feb 11, 13, 20, DL, Apr 25, May 1, 8, 13, 16, 30, Jun 12, 14, 27, Jul 2, HAY, 8, 10, 12, 14, 19, 26, Aug 4, 12, 20, Sep 1, 3, 6, DL, 16, 18, 20, 23, 27, Oct 11, 14, 20, Nov 7, 29, Dec 5, 9, 10, 12, 30; <u>1795</u>: DL, Feb 6, 26, Apr 16, 22, 24, May 29, Jun 3, 6, HAY, 10, 11, 12, 24, Jul 1, 16, 22, 25, Aug 7, 10, 21, DL, Sep 19, 26, Oct 3, Nov 5, 6, 10, 14, 26, Dec 1, 2, 11, 18; <u>1796</u>: DL, Jan 6, 8, 11, 18, May 27, Jun 8, 13, HAY, 14, 17, 20, 29, 30, Jul 2, 5, 7, 11, 12, 26, Aug 3, 10, 17, Sep 5, DL, 20, 22, 24, Oct 8, 11, 15, 27, 28, Nov 1, 5, 9, 10, 22, Dec 5, 7, 20, 30; <u>1797</u>: DL, Jan 14, 17, Feb 1, 7, 16, Mar 6, Apr 19, 24, 27, 28, May 22, 23, HAY, Jun 13, 17, Jul 3, 4, 6, 15, Aug 15, 21, Sep 8; <u>1799</u>: DL, Oct 19

Boothby (actor), <u>1735</u>: LIF, Jul 23, Aug 1, 6, 22, 25, 29, YB/HAY, Sep 29, HAY, Dec 13, 17; <u>1736</u>: HAY, Apr 29, Jun 26

Boothby, Frances

--Marcelia; or, The Treacherous Friend, <u>1669</u>: BRIDGES, Aug 0; <u>1694</u>: DG, May 0

Bopins (singer), <u>1675</u>: ATCOURT, Feb 15

Bordeaux, <u>1791</u>: PAN, Apr 30; <u>1799</u>: KING'S, Mar 26

Bordoni, Faustina. See Bardoni, Faustina.

Borgard, Miss (spectator), <u>1759</u>: CG, Oct 22

Borghi, Anna Casentini, Sga Luigi (singer), <u>1791</u>: PAN, Mar 1, May 14, Jun 16, Dec 17, 31; <u>1792</u>: HAY, Feb 14, 28, Mar 27, 31, Apr 12; <u>1794</u>: KING'S, Jan 11, Feb 1, Mar 15, 18

Borghi, Luigi (composer), <u>1783</u>: KING'S, Mar 13

Boromeo (dancer), <u>1742</u>: DL, Sep 21, Oct 9, 25, Nov 8, 13, 17, 22, 26, 29, Dec 11, 31; <u>1743</u>: DL, Feb 11, Mar 8, Apr 7, 25, May 16

Borosini (Borseni), Francesco (singer), <u>1724</u>: KING'S, Oct 17, 31, Dec 1; <u>1725</u>: KING'S, Jan 2, Feb 13, Apr 10, May 11; <u>1746</u>: KING'S, Nov 4

Boroughs. See Burroughs.

Borrichius, Olaus (spectator), <u>1663</u>: BRIDGES, Jul 30

Borselli, Elisabetta, Sga Fausto (singer), <u>1789</u>: KING'S, Jan 10, Mar 24, May 9, 28, Jun 2; <u>1790</u>: HAY, Jan 7, Feb 2, 27, Apr 6, 29, May 27, 29

Borselli, Fausto (singer), <u>1789</u>: KING'S, Jan 10, Mar 24, May 9, 28, Jun 11; <u>1790</u>: HAY, Jan 7, Feb 2, 27, Mar 25, May 27, Jun 3, 10

Boscawen (actor), <u>1735</u>: YB, Mar 3, SOU, Apr 7

Boscawen, Admiral, <u>1750</u>: HAY, Oct 18

Boscawen, William (versifier), <u>1798</u>: CG, Feb 9

Bosch (beneficiary), <u>1741</u>: HIC, Mar 5; <u>1743</u>: LIF, Mar 15

Boschetti, Sga Mengis (singer), <u>1770</u>: KING'S, May 19; <u>1772</u>: KING'S, Feb 21

Boschi, Francesca Vanini, Sga Giuseppe Maria (singer), <u>1710</u>: QUEEN'S, Dec 6, 9; <u>1711</u>: QUEEN'S, Jan 10, Feb 24

Boschi, Giuseppe Maria (singer), <u>1710</u>: QUEEN'S, Nov 22; <u>1711</u>: QUEEN'S, Jan 10, Feb 24; <u>1720</u>: KING'S, Nov 19, Dec 28; <u>1721</u>: KING'S, Feb 1, Mar 28, Apr 15, May 20, Jun 14, Dec 9; <u>1722</u>: KING'S, Jan 10, Feb 22; <u>1723</u>: KING'S, Jan 12, Feb 19, Mar 30, May 14, Nov 27; <u>1724</u>: KING'S, Jan 14, Feb 20, Apr 18, May 21, Oct 31; <u>1725</u>: KING'S, Jan 2, Feb 13, Apr 10, May 11; <u>1726</u>: KING'S, Jan 15, Mar 12, May 5; <u>1727</u>: KING'S, Jan 7, 31, May 6, Oct 21, Nov 11; <u>1728</u>: KING'S, Feb 17, Apr 30

Boschi, Giuseppe Maria and Francesca Vanini (singers), <u>1711</u>: QUEEN'S, May 5

Boskotin (actor), <u>1732</u>: HAY, Nov 29

Bossi, Cesare (conductor, composer), <u>1796</u>: KING'S, Apr 21, Jun 2, Jul 7; <u>1797</u>: KING'S, Jan 17, Mar 28, Jun 15, Nov 28, Dec 20; <u>1798</u>: KING'S, Feb 6, Apr 26, Dec 26; <u>1799</u>: KING'S, Jan 29, Mar 26, Apr 18, DL, Jul 1; <u>1800</u>: KING'S, Jan 11, 28, May 8, 29, DL, Jun 2

Bossi, Mme Cesare (dancer), <u>1795</u>: KING'S, May 14, Jun 20; <u>1796</u>: KING'S, Feb 6, Mar 10, Apr 21, May 12, DL, 25, KING'S, Jun 2, Jul 7

Bostock (actor), <u>1742</u>: JS, May 31

Boston, <u>1779</u>: HAY, Jul 15

Boswell, James, <u>1763</u>: DL, Jan 19; <u>1772</u>: CG, Mar 5; <u>1775</u>: DL, Mar 27; <u>1789</u>: CG, Jun 16; <u>1790</u>: DL, Nov 17

Bosworth (payee), 1761: CG, Mar 10
Boteler (householder), 1745: GF, Mar 12
Boteler, Mrs. See Butler, Mrs.
Botelli (singer), 1717: HIC, Mar 20
Botheration. See Oulton, Walley Chamberlain.
Bott (house servant), 1786: CG, May 30; 1787: CG, May 28
Bottarelli, F
--Trionfo d'Amore, Il (opera), 1773: KING'S, Mar 9, 13
Bottarelli, Giovanni Gualberto (librettist), 1766: KING'S, Nov 25; 1768:
    KING'S, Mar 10; 1773: KING'S, Jan 19; 1779: KING'S, Mar 25
Botting, Roland (author), 1752: HAY, Dec 14
Bottle (song), 1792: CG, May 15
Bottle Conjurer Hoax, 1749: HAY, Jan 16
Bottle Conjurer Outdone, The; or, The Power of Magick, and the Escape of
    Harlequin (entertainment), 1749: SOU, Feb 20
Bottle Conjuror, 1749: DL, Jan 18; see also Nicholls, William
Bottomly, John (mercer), 1766: DL, Nov 7
Boucher (sub-treasurer), 1753: DL, May 4; 1754: DL, May 9; 1755: DL, Feb 20
Boucher, Mrs (ticket deliverer), 1750: DL, Feb 8; 1755: DL, Apr 30
Boucher, Thomas (actor, prompter), 1728: BFHM, Aug 24; 1730: GF, Jun 4; 1731:
    GF, Apr 27, Jun 2; 1732: GF, May 17; 1733: GF, May 22; 1734: GF, May 22;
    1736: GF, Apr 28; 1737: LIF, May 18; 1738: CG, May 18; 1739: CG, May 30;
    1740: CG, May 29; 1742: CG, May 11; 1743: CG, May 9
Bouchier (singer), 1693: ATCOURT, Apr 30
Boudet (dancer), 1726: HAY, Apr 14, 18, 22, 25, 27, May 6, 9
Boudet, Mlle (dancer), 1726: HAY, Apr 14, 25, 27, May 6, 9
Boudet, Mons and Mlle (dancer), 1726: HAY, Apr 13
Boudouin. See Baudouin.
Bouffer's Tavern, 1734: BLO, Jan 16
Boufon, Le; or, The Idiot (dance), 1740: DL, Nov 29, Dec 1, 2, 3, 16, 19, 23;
    1741: DL, Jan 8, 16, Feb 3, Apr 10, May 20, Oct 30, Nov 20, 23, 26, Dec 15,
    17, 30; 1742: DL, Jan 1, 4, 13, 20, Feb 8, 27, Mar 9, 25, 27, 29, 30, Apr 5,
    20, 21, 24, 26, May 20, 22, 24
Boufons du Cour (dance), 1742: CG, Nov 20, 22, 23, 24, 27, 29, 30, Dec 1, 4;
    1743: CG, Mar 5, 7, 22, Apr 15, 16, 25, May 2, 5
Bougier, Mlle (dancer), 1791: PAN, Feb 17, Mar 22
Boule, Phillip (scene painter), 1710: DL, Dec 30
Boulley, Maillet du (author), 1750: DL, Jan 1
Boultby, Mrs (actor), 1740: DL, May 5, CG, Oct 22, GF, Nov 27, Dec 8; 1741: GF,
    Feb 9; 1742: DL, Apr 28
Boulton (beneficiary), 1730: GF, Jun 18
Bouncing B Printing Office, 1782: HAY, Mar 18
Bounty (musician), 1675: ATCOURT, Feb 15
Bouquet (dance), 1793: CG, Apr 15, 18; 1795: CG, Feb 26, Nov 13, 14, 20; 1796:
    KING'S, Mar 1, 5, 8, 12, 15, 29, Apr 2, 5
Bouqueton (dancer), 1775: KING'S, Oct 31, Nov 7
Bourgeois Gentilhomme, Le. See Moliere.
Bourgeois, Mlle (dancer), 1793: KING'S, Feb 26
Bourgeoise (dance), 1742: CG, Nov 25
Bourk, Elizabeth, Mrs William (dancer), 1792: DLKING'S, Mar 19, DL, Dec 27
Bourk, Miss (dancer), 1790: DL, Oct 26; 1791: DLKING'S, Nov 5; 1792: DL, Nov
    21; 1794: DL, May 16, 30, Dec 20, 23; 1795: DL, May 6; 1796: DL, Oct 1, 29,
    Dec 26; 1797: DL, Jun 10
Bourk, William (dancer), 1785: DL, May 20; 1786: DL, Jun 6; 1787: DL, May 31;
    1788: DL, Dec 22; 1789: DL, May 22, Jun 9, Dec 26; 1790: DL, Jan 21, Apr 16,
    Jun 2, Oct 26, Dec 27; 1791: DLKING'S, Nov 5, Dec 31; 1792: DLKING'S, Mar 19,
    Apr 30, DL, Nov 21, Dec 27; 1794: DL, May 16, Jun 2, 9, Sep 27, Oct 9, 22,
    Nov 6; 1797: DL, Jun 15
Bourk, William and Miss (dancers), 1788: HAY, Apr 29
Bourlin, Antoine Jean. See Dumaniant.
Bourn, Barnard (actor), 1745: GF, Dec 19; 1746: GF, Mar 22
Bourne, Reuben
--Contented Cuckold, The; or, The Woman's Advocate (opera), 1691: NONE, Sep 0
Bournonville, Antoine (dancer), 1781: KING'S, Nov 17, 28; 1782: KING'S, Feb 2,
    21, Mar 7, 19, May 25
Bourrelier (house servant), 1786: CG, May 31; 1787: CG, May 19; 1788: CG, May
    15; 1789: CG, Jun 6; 1790: CG, May 29
Bourru Bienfaisant, Le. See Goldoni, Carlo.
Bousing, Antony Henry (renter), 1758: CG, Mar 6
Bousing, Mrs Antony Henry (renter), 1758: CG, Mar 6
Boute, Mrs. See Bowtell, Elizabeth Ridley.
Boutet de Monvel, Jacques Marie, 1792: DL, Oct 18; 1798: CG, Dec 11

--Raoul Sire De Crequi, 1792: DL, Oct 18
--Victimes Cloitrees, Les, 1798: CG, Dec 11
Bouton, Miss (actor), 1784: HAY, Feb 9
Boval (beneficiary), 1760: CG, Dec 9, 12
Boval (Bovile) (dancer), 1714: LIF, Dec 22, 28; 1715: LIF, Jan 7, 10, 14, 17,
   25, Feb 1, 3, 9, 26, Mar 1, 3, Apr 4, 19, 22, 25, 29, 30, May 2, 9, 10, 12,
   13, 24, Jun 7, DL, Oct 14, 24, 29, Nov 5, 17, 22, Dec 5, 19; 1716: DL, Jan
   14, 23, 26, Feb 18, Apr 9, 21, May 1, 14, Jun 6, Jul 12, 17, 26, Aug 16, Oct
   9, 18, 27, 29, Nov 3, 12, 14, 26, Dec 4, 7, 10, 13; 1717: DL, Jan 3, Feb 6,
   13, 19, Mar 2, 14, 28, Apr 4, May 16, 20, 29, Jun 6, LIF, Oct 25, Nov 1, 8,
   15, 22, Dec 6, 11; 1718: LIF, Jan 1, 3, 24, Mar 29, Apr 16; 1719: LIF, Jan 9,
   Apr 10, DL, Oct 12, 16, 19, Nov 23, 25; 1720: DL, Feb 5, 29, Mar 15, 29, Apr
   28, 29, May 6, 7, 9, 10, 12, 17, 19, 21, 23, 30, Jun 1, Sep 20, 27, Oct 13,
   22, 25, 31, Nov 23, 30, Dec 7, 14; 1721: DL, Feb 7, 23, Apr 10, 17, 25, 29,
   May 1, 5, 8, 9, 13, 16, 29, 31, Nov 13, 27, Dec 18, 22, 29; 1722: DL, Jan 10,
   19, Mar 10, Apr 5, 10, 12, 18, 19, May 1, 7, 8, 23, 29, Sep 27, Oct 9, 10,
   29; 1723: DL, Jan 29, Mar 21, 25, Apr 29, May 9, 13, 15, 21, 30, Jun 25, Jul
   12, Aug 2, 6, Nov 21, 22, 23, 26, Dec 31; 1724: DL, Jan 27, Feb 11, 17, Apr
   8, 11, 13, 29, May 2, 4, 8, 12, 18, Nov 14; 1725: DL, Feb 4, 20, Mar 31, Apr
   2, 16, 19, 28, 29, 30, May 1, Sep 25, 28, Oct 7, 12, 19, 25, Nov 16, 19, Dec
   6, 16; 1726: DL, Jan 25, Feb 11, Mar 21, Apr 15, 18, 19, 22, 23, 25, 26, 27,
   30, May 2, 3, 4, 6, 7, 11, 12, 13, 20, 23, Sep 13, 20, Oct 1, Nov 2, 15, Dec
   7, 12, 14, 17, 30; 1727: DL, Feb 10, 18, 27, Mar 23, Apr 8, 17, 18, 20, 21,
   25, 26, 29, May 3, 5, 10, 22, 24, Oct 5, 6, 12, 30, Nov 14, 21; 1728: DL, Feb
   27, Mar 16, 19, 28, 30, Apr 8, 24, 25, 30, May 2, 3, 6, 16, 23, Jun 13, Sep
   12, 17, Oct 10, 18, 21, 30, Nov 15; 1729: DL, Mar 13, 22, 24, Apr 19, May 28,
   Dec 26; 1730: DL, Jan 1, Apr 11, 13, 18, 23, 25, 29, May 4, 11, 19; 1733: DL,
   Oct 10, 12, Nov 13, Dec 5; 1734: DL/HAY, Mar 16, CG/LIF, Oct 2, Dec 19, 30;
   1735: CG/LIF, Feb 13, Jun 2
Bow Fair, 1748: HAY, Apr 18
Bow St Passage, 1760: CG, Sep 22; 1766: CG, Oct 3, 28, Nov 4, Dec 23; 1767: CG,
   Mar 26, Apr 24, 29; 1771: CG, Oct 24, 29, Nov 14; 1772: CG, Feb 1, Mar 30,
   May 13, Oct 5, 9, 23, Nov 12; 1773: CG, Mar 9, Apr 3, 28, Oct 20, 25, 29;
   1774: CG, Jan 7, May 6
Bow St, 1689: YB, Oct 17, Nov 11; 1690: GB, Oct 10; 1697: GB, Jan 7; 1729: BOS,
   Jan 21; 1732: DL, Sep 27, LIF/CG, Dec 7; 1736: CG, Mar 22, Nov 29; 1737: CG,
   Mar 12, DL, Apr 23; 1738: CG, Apr 7, DL, May 1; 1739: DL, Mar 26, CG, 27, DL,
   May 2; 1740: CG, Mar 27, DL, Apr 21, 26; 1741: DL, Jan 16, Feb 9, Apr 8;
   1742: CG, Mar 22, 29; 1743: DL, Mar 3, 10, 21, CG, Apr 2, DL, 13, HAY, 15;
   1744: HAY, Jan 21, Feb 6, CG, Apr 20, HAY, Jul 6; 1745: CG, Apr 2, 15; 1746:
   DL, Mar 1, CG, 13, DL, 13, CG, 18, Apr 4, DL, 28; 1747: DL, Feb 16, Mar 24,
   28, Apr 4; 1748: DL, Mar 10, 12, 15, 22, CG, Apr 14, 15, DL, 18, 27, 28;
   1749: DL, Mar 9, 11, 31, Apr 4, 13, 26; 1750: DL, Mar 10, 27, 29; 1751: CG,
   Mar 18, DL, Apr 18, 19, 24, 29; 1752: DL, Apr 11, 20; 1753: DL, Mar 26, Apr
   14, CG, 24; 1754: DL, Mar 27, Apr 16, 18, May 4; 1755: DL, Apr 3, 8, 14, 19,
   25, 26; 1756: DL, Apr 21; 1757: CG, Mar 21, DL, Apr 12, 13, CG, 26, DL, 26,
   27; 1758: CG, Jan 24, DL, Apr 21; 1760: CG, Apr 22; 1761: DL, Mar 30, Apr 1;
   1763: HAY, Aug 11; 1767: CG, Mar 24, Nov 30; 1768: CG, May 2, Jun 1, Oct 24;
   1772: MARLY, Jul 2; 1773: DL, Sep 18; 1774: CG, Feb 2, DL, Mar 23; 1776: CG,
   Feb 27, KING'S, Apr 16; 1777: CG, Apr 7, DL, 23, CG, May 5, 13, 20, HAY, Aug
   19; 1778: CG, Mar 30, DL, Apr 2, CG, 7, DL, 23, 25, CG, 25, May 1, DL, 5, CG,
   9, 11, 13, 16, 19, HAY, Aug 27, Sep 10; 1779: DL, Mar 23, CG, 27, Apr 7, 12,
   14, DL, May 3, 4, CG, 13, HAY, Sep 7; 1780: DL, Mar 16, CG, Apr 7, 10, 21,
   May 3, DL, 6, 10, HAY, Jul 27, Sep 5; 1781: CG, Apr 2, 3; 1782: CG, Apr 2,
   DL, 19, CG, Sep 23; 1783: CG, Apr 7, DL, May 12; 1784: CG, Mar 29; 1785: CG,
   Mar 12, 19, DL, Apr 18, CG, 25, May 11, HAY, Jul 26, Aug 19; 1786: CG, Apr 1,
   DL, May 3, 9, CG, 17, 24, DL, 25, HAY, Jul 21, 25, Aug 22; 1787: CG, Jan 23,
   HAY, Mar 12, CG, Apr 17, May 9, 11, DL, 22, HAY, Jul 31; 1788: CG, Mar 11,
   15, Apr 1, May 14; 1789: CG, Mar 31, Apr 14, May 26, Jun 3, 9, 10, 27; 1790:
   CG, Mar 27, Apr 6, 16, 22, DL, 23, CG, May 7, 13, 18, 20, DL, 27; 1791: CG,
   Apr 16, May 2, 6, 17, 18, 20, 24, 27, 31, Jun 4; 1792: CG, Mar 31, Apr 25,
   May 9, 11, 17, 19, DLKING'S, Jun 7, CG, Sep 17; 1793: CG, Mar 23, May 1, 10,
   16, Jun 10; 1794: CG, Apr 12, May 9, Jun 3, 11; 1795: CG, Mar 28, May 6, Jun
   12; 1796: CG, Mar 19, Apr 15, Sep 12, HAY, 16; 1797: CG, Apr 8, May 11, DL,
   Jun 1, CG, Dec 6; 1798: CG, Mar 31, May 9, DL, Jun 6, HAY, Sep 17; 1799: CG,
   Mar 16, DL, Apr 19, 25, CG, May 3, DL, 7, CG, Jun 7, Sep 16; 1800: CG, May 7,
   22
Bow wow wow (song), 1787: HAY, Apr 30
Bow, 1744: MEG, Sep 18
Bowan (actor), 1780: HAY, Sep 25
Bowcher. See Boucher.
Bowden, Wright (actor, singer), 1787: CG, Oct 18, Dec 22; 1788: CG, Jan 28, Feb

5, Apr 1, 15, May 22; <u>1794</u>: CG, May 2, Sep 22, Oct 3, 7, 10, 20, 21, 30, Nov
7; <u>1795</u>: CG, Mar 16, Apr 6, 24, 28, May 1, 6, 13, 16, 27, Jun 10, Sep 14, 21,
23, Nov 14, 27, 30, Dec 1, 5, 9, 21; <u>1796</u>: CG, Jan 4, 13, 23, Mar 14, 15, 17,
Apr 1, 9, 12, 29, 30, May 16, 17, 18, 20, 23, 26, 28, Sep 14, 17, 19, 21, 26,
30, Oct 3, 6, 7, 17, 21, 24, Nov 19, 24, Dec 26, 28; <u>1797</u>: CG, Jan 3, 10, Apr
19, May 2, 11, 18, 20, 23, 31
Bowen (actor), <u>1734</u>: JS, May 23; <u>1735</u>: HAY, Dec 13
Bowen, J (publisher), <u>1780</u>: CG, Feb 2, Sep 18; <u>1781</u>: DL, Feb 17
Bowen, Jemmy (the Boy) (singer), <u>1691</u>: NONE, Sep 0; <u>1695</u>: DL, Apr 1, Oct 0;
<u>1698</u>: DL, Mar 0; <u>1701</u>: HAW, Sep 15
Bowen, Mrs William (beneficiary), <u>1719</u>: DL, Apr 29, May 25; <u>1720</u>: DL, May 27;
<u>1722</u>: DL, May 28; <u>1723</u>: DL, Jun 4; <u>1725</u>: DL, May 24; <u>1726</u>: DL, Jun 3
Bowen (Bohen, Boin), William (actor), <u>1689</u>: DL, Apr 0, Nov 7, 20; <u>1690</u>: DL, Jan
0, Mar 0, DLORDG, 0, DL, Sep 0, NONE, 0, DL/IT, Oct 21, DL, Dec 0; <u>1691</u>: DL,
Jan 0, Mar 0, Apr 0, DG, May 0, NONE, Sep 0; <u>1692</u>: DL, Jan 0, Nov 0; <u>1693</u>:
DL, Feb 0, Mar 0, Apr 0, DG, May 0; <u>1694</u>: DL, Feb 0, Apr 0, DG, May 0, DL,
Sep 0; <u>1695</u>: DG, Apr 0, LIF, 30, DL, Nov 0, LIF, Dec 0; <u>1696</u>: DL, May 0, LIF,
Jun 0, DG, 0, LIF, 0, Nov 14, Dec 0; <u>1697</u>: LIF, Apr 0, May 0, Jun 0, Sep 0,
Nov 0; <u>1698</u>: LIF, Mar 0, Apr 0, May 0, YB, 28, Jun 7, DL/ORDG, Nov 0; <u>1699</u>:
LIF, Feb 0; <u>1700</u>: LIF, Jan 9, Mar 5, Sep 25; <u>1701</u>: LIF, Mar 6, DL, Jun 11,
Dec 0; <u>1702</u>: DL, Jan 0, 24, Dec 14; <u>1703</u>: DL, Mar 11; <u>1705</u>: QUEEN'S, Apr 26,
30, LIF/QUEN, Oct 17, LIF, 20, QUEEN'S, Nov 16, Dec 3, 5; <u>1706</u>: QUEEN'S, May
15, Jun 0, Jul 31, LIF/QUEN, Aug 16, QUEEN'S, Oct 30, Nov 22, Dec 2, 11, 13,
14, 27; <u>1707</u>: QUEEN'S, Jan 11, 13, 14, Mar 8, 27, Apr 30, Jul 18, 22, 30, Aug
19, DL/QUEEN, Oct 20, 23, 27, 29, Nov 1, 10, QUEEN'S, 22, DL/QUEEN, Dec 27;
<u>1708</u>: DL/QUEEN, Jan 1, DL, Feb 7, 26, Mar 8, 9, Apr 10, 17, 29, May 21, Jun
3, Oct 7, 9, 22, Dec 29, 31; <u>1709</u>: DL, Jan 17, 29, Feb 1, Mar 3, 15, 17, Apr
30, May 3, 17, 18, 25, Jun 1, QUEEN'S, Sep 24, 27, Oct 1, 8, 31, Nov 4, 8,
18, Dec 28; <u>1710</u>: QUEEN'S, Jan 19, Feb 1, 11, Apr 24, May 15, 16, Jun 1, 5,
Jul 19, Aug 16, DL/QUEEN, Oct 5, 7, Nov 4, 8, 11, 13, 14, 15, DL, 23, Dec 4,
7, 18, 30; <u>1711</u>: DL, Jan 18, Feb 22, DL/QUEEN, May 3, 11, 29, DL, 31, Sep 27,
Oct 10, 16, 26, 27, Nov 7, 27, 29; <u>1712</u>: DL, Jan 19, May 16, Jun 9, Aug 8,
Oct 13, Nov 4, 6, 26, Dec 29; <u>1713</u>: DL, Jan 10, 29, Feb 13, Jun 3, 17, Nov 9;
<u>1714</u>: DL, May 3, 14, 26, Jun 25, 29, Jul 20, Oct 22; <u>1715</u>: DL, Jan 6, 15, Feb
15, Mar 8, Apr 4, 30; <u>1716</u>: DL, Jan 7, Feb 9, 21, May 9, Oct 9, 12, 15, Dec
14; <u>1717</u>: DL, Jan 12, May 8, Jun 14, Aug 6, 9, Oct 28, Nov 25; <u>1718</u>: DL, Jan
27, Feb 19, LIF, Apr 18, DL, May 3, NONE, Jul 10; <u>1720</u>: DL, Oct 12
Bowen's Widow (beneficiary), <u>1721</u>: DL, May 25
Bowers (boxkeeper, pit doorkeeper), <u>1758</u>: DL, May 11; <u>1759</u>: DL, May 29; <u>1760</u>:
DL, May 15; <u>1761</u>: DL, May 27; <u>1762</u>: DL, May 24; <u>1763</u>: DL, May 18; <u>1764</u>: DL,
May 19; <u>1765</u>: DL, May 18; <u>1766</u>: DL, May 20; <u>1767</u>: DL, May 29, Jun 1; <u>1768</u>:
DL, May 27; <u>1769</u>: DL, May 20; <u>1770</u>: DL, Jun 4; <u>1771</u>: DL, May 29; <u>1772</u>: DL,
Jun 10; <u>1773</u>: DL, Jun 1
Bowers, Widow (actor), <u>1774</u>: DL, May 27
Bowford (dancer), <u>1733</u>: HAY, May 28
Bowington (actor), <u>1737</u>: LIF, Jun 15
Bowles, Miss (actor), <u>1779</u>: HAY, Oct 18
Bowles, Robert (actor), <u>1777</u>: CG, Sep 22, Oct 3, 10, Nov 7; <u>1778</u>: HAY, Jan 26,
CG, 28, HAY, Mar 23, 24, 31, Apr 9, 29, CG, May 11, 12, CHR, 25, 27, 29, Jun
1; <u>1780</u>: HAY, Aug 29
Bowley (actor), <u>1793</u>: DL, Jun 6; <u>1795</u>: DL, May 30; <u>1796</u>: DL, Jun 14; <u>1797</u>: DL,
Jun 14; <u>1798</u>: DL, Jun 15; <u>1799</u>: DL, Jul 4; <u>1800</u>: DL, Jun 17
Bowling Green, <u>1724</u>: SF, Aug 28, Sep 7; <u>1726</u>: SFLH, Sep 8; <u>1729</u>: SOU, Sep 23,
Oct 14; <u>1730</u>: SOU, May 18, Sep 24, Oct 8; <u>1731</u>: SFLH, Sep 8; <u>1732</u>: SOU, Oct
12, Dec 18, 26; <u>1733</u>: SOU, Oct 18; <u>1734</u>: SOU, Oct 7; <u>1735</u>: SOU, Apr 7, SFLT,
Sep 4, SFLP, 4; <u>1737</u>: SF, Sep 7; <u>1738</u>: SFL, Sep 5; <u>1740</u>: BF/WF/SF, Sep 8,
SOU, Oct 9; <u>1746</u>: SFY, Sep 8, SFW, 8, SFHP, 8, SOU, 16, 25, Oct 7, 21, Nov 3,
HAY, 27; <u>1747</u>: SF, Sep 9, 14; <u>1748</u>: SOU, Jan 19, Jul 18, SFP, Sep 7, SFLYYW,
7, SFBCBV, 7, 8, SFLYYW, 8, SOU, Sep 26, Oct 31; <u>1749</u>: SOU, Jan 2, 9, 26, Feb
20, BF/SFP, Sep 7, SF/SF, 7, SFP, 15, SFGT, 16, SOU, 18, SOUGT, 22, 25, SOU,
28, Oct 2, 9, 16; <u>1750</u>: SFYW, Sep 7, SFP, 7, SFYW, 8, SFP, 8, SFB, 8, 10,
SFP, 10, SF, 11, SFB, 12, SFP, 12, SFYW, 13, SFP, 13, SFY, 14; <u>1751</u>: SF, Sep
7, 9, 10, 11, 16, 17, 19; <u>1752</u>: SFGT, Sep 18, 19, 20, SFP, 21, SFGT, 21, SFP,
22, SFGT, 22, SFB, 22, SOU, 29, Nov 24; <u>1753</u>: SFP, Sep 18, SFGT, 18, 19, 20,
21, SFP, 27; <u>1754</u>: SFP, Sep 18, SFH, 19, HAY/SFB, 19, SFG, 21, SFP, 23, SFG,
24; <u>1755</u>: SOU, Jan 16, 20, SFG, Sep 18, 19, 20, 22; <u>1756</u>: SFW, Sep 18, SF,
18, 20, SFW, 20, SFB, 20, SF, 21, 22, 23, ACAD, Dec 15; <u>1757</u>: SF, Sep 17;
<u>1758</u>: SFW, Sep 18; <u>1759</u>: SFS, Sep 18; <u>1760</u>: SF, Sep 13, 18, 19, 20, 22; <u>1761</u>:
SFW, Sep 19, 21, SFT, 21, 22
Bowman (actor), <u>1792</u>: CII, Jan 16
Bowman (Boaaman, Boman) Jr (actor), <u>1712</u>: SML, Apr 11, May 21, Jun 11, 18; <u>1715</u>:
DL, Feb 4, Jun 17, Jul 1, Dec 6; <u>1716</u>: DL, Jun 8; <u>1717</u>: DL, May 31; <u>1719</u>: DL,

Jan 28; <u>1722</u>: HAY, Dec 17; <u>1729</u>: BFF, Aug 23; <u>1731</u>: GF, Jan 19; <u>1735</u>: GF, Mar
29; <u>1736</u>: CG, Jan 8, 19, Feb 18, Mar 27, LIF, 31, Apr 16, CG, May 14, 17,
BFHC, Aug 23, CG, Dec 2; <u>1737</u>: CG, Feb 1, 18, 26, Apr 14, 29, LIF, Aug 5, CG,
Nov 9; <u>1738</u>: CG, Jun 27, Jul 7, 11, 21, Aug 1; <u>1739</u>: CG, May 9; <u>1743</u>: SOU,
Feb 18, 25; <u>1744</u>: JS, Mar 16, MFHNT, May 1, MF, 3; <u>1758</u>: DL, Jun 22
Bowman, Elizabeth, Mrs John (actor), <u>1693</u>: DL, Mar 0, Apr 0; <u>1694</u>: DL, Apr 0,
DG, May 0; <u>1695</u>: LIF, Apr 30, Sep 0, Dec 0; <u>1696</u>: LIF, Mar 0, Apr 0, Nov 14,
Dec 0; <u>1697</u>: LIF, Feb 20, Apr 0, May 0, Jun 0, Nov 0, ATCOURT, 4; <u>1698</u>: LIF,
Mar 0, Nov 0; <u>1699</u>: LIF, May 0; <u>1700</u>: LIF, Jan 9, Feb 0, Mar 0, 5, Dec 0;
<u>1701</u>: LIF, Jan 0, Mar 0, DG, 21, LIF, Nov 0, Dec 0; <u>1703</u>: LIF, Jan 0, Mar 0,
Apr 28, Jun 11; <u>1704</u>: LIF, Jun 1, Nov 13; <u>1705</u>: QUEEN'S, Dec 27; <u>1706</u>:
QUEEN'S, Feb 21, Mar 7, Jun 0; <u>1707</u>: QUEEN'S, Jan 20, 25, Apr 1
Bowman, John (actor, singer), <u>1661</u>: ATCOURT, Apr 20; <u>1677</u>: DG, Sep 0; <u>1678</u>: DG,
Jan 0, Apr 5, Sep 0, Nov 0; <u>1679</u>: DG, Apr 0, Sep 0, Dec 0; <u>1680</u>: DG, Feb 0,
Jun 0, Sep 0; <u>1681</u>: DG, Mar 0; <u>1682</u>: DG, Jan 0, 23, Feb 9, Apr 0, DL, Nov 28;
<u>1683</u>: NONE, Sep 0, DL, Nov 12, Dec 0; <u>1685</u>: DLORDG, Jan 20, DL, Aug 0; <u>1686</u>:
DG, Mar 4, DL, Apr 0; <u>1688</u>: DG, Apr 0, DL, May 3; <u>1689</u>: DL, Mar 0, Apr 0, Nov
7, 20, Dec 4; <u>1690</u>: DLORDG, Jan 16, Mar 0, DL, 0, NONE, Sep 0, DL, Oct 0,
DL/IT, 21, DL, Nov 0, Dec 0; <u>1691</u>: DL, Jan 0, Apr 0, DG, May 0, NONE, Sep 0,
DL, Dec 0; <u>1692</u>: DL, Jan 0, Nov 0; <u>1693</u>: DL, Feb 0, Apr 0, ATCOURT, 30, DG,
May 0, NONE, Sep 0, DL, Oct 0; <u>1694</u>: DL, Mar 21, DG, May 0, NONE, Sep 0;
<u>1695</u>: LIF, Apr 30, Sep 0, Dec 0; <u>1696</u>: LIF, Mar 0, Apr 0, Jun 0, Nov 14, Dec
0; <u>1697</u>: LIF, Feb 20, Apr 0, May 0, Jun 0, Nov 0, ATCOURT, Nov 4; <u>1698</u>: LIF,
Jan 0, Mar 0, YB, May 10; <u>1699</u>: LIF, May 0; <u>1700</u>: LIF, Jan 9, Mar 0, 5, Apr
0, DL, Jul 9, LIF, Dec 0; <u>1701</u>: LIF, Jan 0, Mar 0, Apr 0, Jun 24, Nov 0;
<u>1702</u>: LIF, Jun 0, Dec 31; <u>1703</u>: LIF, Apr 28, May 0, Jun 14; <u>1704</u>: LIF, Jan
13, Feb 17, 24, Apr 29, Jun 1, Jul 27, Aug 1; <u>1705</u>: LIF, Jan 25, QUEEN'S, Nov
23; <u>1706</u>: QUEEN'S, Jan 3, Feb 11, 21, Apr 30, Oct 26, Dec 14, 16, 30; <u>1707</u>:
QUEEN'S, Jan 4, 14, 20, Feb 3, 15, 18, Mar 8, BH, 26, QUEEN'S, May 9, Jun 2,
10; <u>1708</u>: DL, Jun 17; <u>1709</u>: QUEEN'S, Sep 22, 27, Oct 25, 29, Nov 9, Dec 12;
<u>1710</u>: QUEEN'S, Apr 20, May 18, Jun 1, Aug 16, DL/QUEEN, Nov 14, 18, DL, 21;
<u>1711</u>: DL, Jan 16, Mar 17, DL/QUEEN, 24, DL, May 15, 18, Aug 31, Oct 9, Nov
24, Dec 13; <u>1712</u>: DL, Mar 17, Jun 2, Oct 8, 15, 28, Nov 28; <u>1713</u>: DL, Jan 5,
6, 29, Feb 19, Apr 14, Jun 17, 18, Nov 25, 27; <u>1714</u>: DL, Feb 2, May 17, 21;
<u>1715</u>: DL, Mar 14, 21, Apr 20, May 17, Dec 6; <u>1716</u>: DL, Feb 25, Mar 3, May 24,
Dec 17; <u>1717</u>: DL, Jan 9, 16, Feb 2, Mar 30, Apr 8, May 10, 11, 23, Jun 3, Aug
13, Oct 24, 25, 26, Nov 19; <u>1718</u>: DL, Feb 14, Mar 22, May 6, 9, Jul 8, Sep
25, Oct 4, 27, Dec 2, 19; <u>1719</u>: DL, Jan 28, May 8, Jun 2, 9, Oct 28, Nov 21;
<u>1720</u>: DL, May 13, Nov 29, Dec 17; <u>1721</u>: DL, Mar 2, 20, Apr 14, May 15, Jun
27, Aug 4, Oct 13, 14, Nov 3, Dec 28; <u>1722</u>: DL, Feb 10, 19, May 5, 26, Oct 6,
11, HAY, Dec 17, DL, 22; <u>1723</u>: HAY, Jan 31, DL, Feb 6, 9, HAY, 13, DL, May 8,
Jul 5, Aug 12, Oct 31, Nov 7; <u>1724</u>: DL, Feb 15, Apr 18, May 9; <u>1725</u>: DL, Jan
16, 27, Apr 20, 21, 24, May 7, Nov 1, 27; <u>1726</u>: DL, May 11, 16, 18, Oct 22,
Dec 17; <u>1727</u>: DL, Feb 4, 21, Mar 16, Apr 14, 17, 28, 29, May 10, Sep 7, 9,
Oct 7, Dec 5, 30; <u>1728</u>: DL, Apr 13, 29, May 11, Oct 5, 8, 28; <u>1729</u>: DL, Jan
15, 21, 25, Feb 22, 24, Apr 11, May 6, 7, 28, Sep 23, 27, Oct 7, 31, Nov 6,
29, Dec 27; <u>1730</u>: DL, Jan 3, 26, Apr 2, 27, May 6, Sep 19, 29, Oct 1, 17, 24,
Nov 30, Dec 1; <u>1731</u>: DL, Feb 8, Mar 29, May 5, 19, Jun 7, 11; <u>1732</u>: DL, Jan
15, Feb 11, 14, Apr 1, 17, May 5, Sep 21, 28, Oct 17, Nov 7, 13, Dec 6; <u>1733</u>:
DL, May 5, 10, DL/HAY, Oct 10, 12, 17, Nov 10, 28, Dec 5, 19; <u>1734</u>: DL/HAY,
Jan 17, HAY, Feb 1, DL/HAY, Apr 18, May 8, DL, 13, Sep 24, Oct 14, 24, 26,
Nov 8; <u>1735</u>: DL, Jan 23, Apr 11, May 17, Jun 11, Sep 11, 20, 23, 30, Oct 21,
25, 27; <u>1736</u>: DL, Mar 11, 23, May 18, BFHC, Aug 23, DL, Sep 9, Oct 9, 19, Nov
2, Dec 14, 20; <u>1737</u>: DL, May 7, 14, 18, Sep 20, 22, 24, Oct 1, 20; <u>1738</u>: DL,
Jan 11, 31, Apr 22, May 6, 26, Sep 16, 30, Oct 20, 26, 31, Nov 1, 20, Dec 19;
<u>1739</u>: DL, Mar 26
Bowman, Mrs (actor), <u>1716</u>: DL, Apr 2, 17, May 14, Jun 5, 19, Jul 3, 19, 24, 31,
Aug 9, 16, Oct 22; <u>1717</u>: DL, Feb 4, SH, Mar 27, DL, Oct 25, Nov 6; <u>1718</u>: DL,
Feb 6, Apr 14, May 7, 21, 28, Jun 27, Nov 26, 28; <u>1719</u>: DL, May 19, Jun 16,
Jul 3; <u>1720</u>: DL, May 14, Jun 11, Jul 26, SFLH, Sep 5; <u>1721</u>: DL, May 31, SFHL,
Sep 2; <u>1722</u>: RI, Aug 20, BFPMB, 25, SOU, Sep 25, HAY, Dec 17; <u>1723</u>: DL, Jun
28, Jul 12, 16, Aug 6; <u>1724</u>: DL, May 20, SF, Sep 2; <u>1725</u>: DL, Feb 20, May 17;
<u>1726</u>: DL, Feb 11, May 10, Nov 2; <u>1727</u>: DL, Nov 14; <u>1729</u>: DL, May 28; <u>1731</u>:
DL, Jun 7, Jul 23; <u>1733</u>: HAY, Mar 14
Bowness, Mrs (house servant), <u>1772</u>: DL, Mar 24
Bowtell (Bootel, Boute), Elizabeth Ridley, Mrs Barnaby (actor), <u>1662</u>: VERE, Jan
28; <u>1666</u>: BRIDGES, Dec 7; <u>1668</u>: BRIDGES, Jun 12; <u>1669</u>: BRIDGES, Jun 24; <u>1670</u>:
BRIDGES, Aug 0, BRI/COUR, Dec 0; <u>1671</u>: BRIDGE, Mar 0, Jun 0; <u>1672</u>: LIF, Apr
0, Jun 0, Nov 0; <u>1673</u>: LIF, Mar 0; <u>1674</u>: LIF, Mar 0, DL, May 16; <u>1675</u>: DL,
Jan 12, May 10, NONE, Sep 0; <u>1676</u>: DL, Dec 11; <u>1677</u>: DL, Jan 12, Mar 17, Jun
0, Oct 0, Dec 12; <u>1678</u>: DL, Feb 0, Mar 0; <u>1682</u>: DL, Nov 16; <u>1688</u>: DG, Apr 0,
DL, 0, May 3, NONE, Sep 0; <u>1689</u>: DL, Apr 0, NONE, Sep 0; <u>1690</u>: DL, Jan 0,

DLORDG, Mar 0; <u>1691</u>: NONE, Sep 0; <u>1695</u>: LIF, Sep 0, Dec 0; <u>1696</u>: LIF, Mar 0,
   Jun 0, Oct 0
Bowtell, Henry (actor), <u>1675</u>: ATCOURT, Feb 15
Bowyer, Mrs (singer), <u>1798</u>: DL, Nov 14, Dec 4, 29; <u>1799</u>: DL, Jan 19, May 24
Box (Secretary, Marine Society), <u>1757</u>: DL, May 11
Box-Lobby Challenge, The. See Cumberland, Richard.
Box-Lobby Loungers. See Stuart, Charles.
Boxing the Compass (song), <u>1798</u>: HAY, Aug 14; <u>1799</u>: CG, Apr 6, 16, 26, May 13,
   28, Jun 1, 3, 5; <u>1800</u>: CG, May 27
Boyack (actor), <u>1766</u>: HAY, May 19; <u>1768</u>: HAY, Dec 19; <u>1772</u>: HAY, Sep 21; <u>1775</u>:
   HAY, Feb 20, Nov 20; <u>1776</u>: HAY, Oct 7
Boyce (Bois), John (actor), <u>1701</u>: LIF, Mar 0; <u>1702</u>: DL, Dec 0; <u>1703</u>: DL, Mar
   11; <u>1710</u>: DL, Mar 25, GR, Aug 12, 24
Boyce, Mrs Thomas (dancer), <u>1790</u>: CG, Dec 20; <u>1791</u>: CG, Apr 25
Boyce, Samuel (prologuist), <u>1771</u>: CG, Dec 21
Boyce, Thomas (dancer, actor), <u>1788</u>: CG, Dec 26; <u>1789</u>: CG, May 28, Jun 8, 12,
   Sep 16, Nov 13, 30, Dec 3, 21; <u>1790</u>: CG, Jan 23, Apr 8, Jun 10, HAY, 25, CG,
   Oct 4, Nov 15, Dec 20; <u>1792</u>: CG, Dec 20, 26; <u>1793</u>: CG, Oct 28, Nov 19, Dec 19
Boyce (Boyse), Dr William (organist, composer, conductor), <u>1736</u>: DT, Apr 16;
   <u>1743</u>: DL, May 11, 16, NWLS, Nov 1; <u>1744</u>: CG, Mar 28; <u>1746</u>: CG, Mar 10, 13,
   Apr 7, GF, Dec 17; <u>1747</u>: ST, Apr 29; <u>1749</u>: DL, Dec 2, 13; <u>1750</u>: DL, Feb 23,
   Mar 15, Oct 1, 23, 30; <u>1751</u>: DL, Apr 10, May 4, Nov 11, 19; <u>1752</u>: CT/HAY, Jan
   7, CG, Mar 12, DL, Apr 25; <u>1753</u>: DL, Dec 1; <u>1754</u>: SOHO, Mar 26, CG, Apr 22,
   May 2; <u>1755</u>: CG, Dec 5; <u>1756</u>: DL, Apr 1; <u>1757</u>: DL, Apr 12, CG, 23; <u>1758</u>: DL,
   Feb 21, Mar 31; <u>1759</u>: DL, Mar 29, Apr 5, May 16, Dec 31; <u>1762</u>: CG, Dec 8;
   <u>1763</u>: CG, Oct 22; <u>1765</u>: MARLY, Aug 6; <u>1771</u>: DL, Dec 16; <u>1776</u>: DL, Mar 20, Nov
   16; <u>1777</u>: DL, Oct 28; <u>1779</u>: DL, Mar 19; <u>1782</u>: DL, Apr 20; <u>1783</u>: HAY, Aug 1;
   <u>1790</u>: CG, Mar 17; <u>1791</u>: CG, Mar 25, Apr 6, 13; <u>1792</u>: CG, Mar 7, 9, 14, 21,
   KING'S, 28, 30; <u>1793</u>: KING/HAY, Mar 6, CG, 6, KING/HAY, 13, CG, 20; <u>1794</u>: CG,
   Mar 14, 26, DL, Apr 2, 9, HAY, Aug 18; <u>1795</u>: CG, Mar 18; <u>1796</u>: CG, Feb 26;
   <u>1797</u>: CG, Mar 17, May 31; <u>1798</u>: CG, Mar 9; <u>1799</u>: CG, Feb 20, Mar 1, 13, Apr
   6; <u>1800</u>: CG, Mar 19
--David's Lamentation over Saul and Jonathan (musical), <u>1736</u>: DT, Apr 16; <u>1740</u>:
   HIC, Feb 22, 29, Mar 7, 14, 21, 27, Apr 2; <u>1741</u>: HIC, Mar 26
--Solomon (serenata), <u>1743</u>: NWLS, Nov 1; <u>1744</u>: CG, Mar 28, TB, Apr 17, HAY, 20;
   <u>1790</u>: CG, Mar 17; <u>1791</u>: CG, Apr 6, 13; <u>1792</u>: CG, Mar 9, KING'S, 30; <u>1793</u>:
   KING/HAY, Mar 6, CG, 6, KING/HAY, 13; <u>1794</u>: CG, Mar 14, 26, DL, Apr 2; <u>1795</u>:
   CG, Mar 18; <u>1796</u>: CG, Feb 26; <u>1797</u>: CG, Mar 17; <u>1798</u>: CG, Mar 9; <u>1799</u>: CG,
   Feb 20, Mar 1, 13; <u>1800</u>: CG, Mar 19
Boyce Jr, William (singer, double-bass player), <u>1789</u>: CG, Feb 27; <u>1790</u>: CG, Feb
   19; <u>1791</u>: CG, Mar 11, DLKING'S, Oct 15; <u>1792</u>: CG, Feb 24, DLKING'S, May 23;
   <u>1793</u>: CG, Feb 15; <u>1794</u>: CG, Mar 7, DL, May 16, 22, 23, Jun 18, 19, 23, 25,
   Nov 15, Dec 20; <u>1795</u>: DL, Feb 9, CG, 20, HAY, Jun 13, 20, Jul 31, DL, Oct 30,
   Nov 11, Dec 10; <u>1796</u>: DL, Jan 11, CG, Feb 12, DL, Mar 3, Apr 30, HAY, Jul 15,
   Aug 29; <u>1797</u>: CG, Mar 3, 15; <u>1798</u>: HAY, Jan 15, CG, Feb 23; <u>1799</u>: CG, Feb 8;
   <u>1800</u>: CG, Feb 28
Boyd, Hester (actor, singer), <u>1776</u>: DL, Oct 18, Nov 25, Dec 10, 28; <u>1777</u>: DL,
   Jan 1, 4
Boyd, Mrs (bookseller), <u>1742</u>: HAY, Jun 16
Boyer (actor), <u>1789</u>: DL, Nov 13, 14; <u>1790</u>: DL, Jan 8
Boyer, Abel, <u>1699</u>: DL, Dec 0; <u>1778</u>: CG, Mar 23
--Achilles; or, Iphigenia in Aulis, <u>1699</u>: DL, Dec 0
Boyes (actor), <u>1790</u>: DL, Apr 22
Boyes (coachmaker), <u>1777</u>: CG, Apr 28
Boyes, Daniel (beneficiary), <u>1735</u>: CG/LIF, May 14
Boyle, Charles, <u>1700</u>: LIF, Apr 0; <u>1701</u>: LIF, Dec 0
--As You Find It, <u>1703</u>: LIF, Apr 28
Boyle, John, Earl of Orrery, <u>1669</u>: LIF, Dec 14
Boyle, Juliana, Countess of Burlington, <u>1699</u>: LIF, Mar 0
Boyle, Richard, Earl of (actor), <u>1664</u>: LIF, Feb 8
Boyle, Richard, Earl of Burlington (author), <u>1670</u>: ATCOURT, Apr 6
Boyle, Roger, Earl of Orrery (Lord Brahals), <u>1664</u>: LIF, Aug 13, BRIDGES, Sep
   14, 28; <u>1665</u>: LIF, Apr 3, 6, NONE, May 4; <u>1666</u>: NONE, Jul 17, ATCOURT, Oct
   18; <u>1667</u>: BRIDGES, Oct 19, 23; <u>1668</u>: BRIDGES, Apr 1, LIF, Dec 8; <u>1669</u>: LIF,
   Apr 15, 16; <u>1701</u>: LIF, Dec 0
--Black Prince, The, <u>1666</u>: NONE, Jul 17; <u>1667</u>: BRIDGES, Oct 19, 23; <u>1668</u>:
   BRIDGES, Apr 1
--General, The (Altemira), <u>1664</u>: BRIDGES, Sep 14, 28, Oct 4, NONE, Nov 0; <u>1669</u>:
   BRIDGES, Apr 24; <u>1701</u>: LIF, Dec 0
--Guzman, <u>1669</u>: LIF, Apr 15, 16, Dec 14; <u>1692</u>: NONE, Sep 0
--Herod the Great, <u>1693</u>: NONE, Sep 0
--Mr Anthony, <u>1669</u>: LIF, Dec 14; <u>1689</u>: NONE, Sep 0

--Mustapha, <u>1665</u>: LIF, Apr 3, 4, 6; <u>1666</u>: ATCOURT, Oct 18, Nov 5; <u>1667</u>: LIF,
   Jan 5, NONE, Aug 10, LIF, Sep 4, BRIDGES, Oct 19, LIF, 22; <u>1668</u>: LIF, Feb 11;
   <u>1674</u>: NONE, Sep 0; <u>1686</u>: DLORDG, Oct 6; <u>1689</u>: NONE, Sep 0
--Tryphon, <u>1668</u>: LIF, Dec 8, 9, ATCOURT, 28
--Zoroastres, <u>1674</u>: NONE, Sep 0
Boys, Jeffrey (spectator), <u>1671</u>: LIF, Jan 9, NONE, Feb 3
Boyton, William (composer), <u>1789</u>: CG, May 22
Brabazon, Juliana (spectator), <u>1682</u>: DG, Aug 4
Braccioli, Grazio (librettist), <u>1733</u>: KING'S, Jan 27
Bracegirdle, Anne (actor), <u>1668</u>: NONE, Sep 0; <u>1676</u>: DG, Jun 8, Jul 3; <u>1680</u>: DG,
   Feb 0; <u>1685</u>: DL, Aug 0; <u>1688</u>: DL, Feb 0, May 3; <u>1689</u>: DL, Nov 20; <u>1690</u>: DL,
   Jan 0, DLORDG, 16, Mar 0, DL, 0, NONE, Sep 0, DL, 0, NONE, 0, DL, Oct 0,
   DL/IT, 21, DL, Nov 0, Dec 0; <u>1691</u>: DL, Jan 0, Mar 0, DG, May 0, NONE, Sep 0,
   DL, Dec 0; <u>1692</u>: DL, Jan 0, Feb 0, Mar 0, Apr 0, Jun 0, Nov 0, 8, Dec 9;
   <u>1693</u>: DL, Jan 16, Feb 0, Mar 0, Apr 0, DG, May 0, NONE, Sep 0, DL, Oct 0;
   <u>1694</u>: DL, Jan 0, Feb 0, Mar 21, Apr 0, DG, May 0; <u>1695</u>: LIF, Apr 30, Sep 0,
   Dec 0; <u>1696</u>: LIF, Feb 0, Apr 0, Jun 0, Nov 14; <u>1697</u>: LIF, Feb 20, Apr 0, May
   0, Jun 0, Nov 0; <u>1698</u>: LIF, Jan 0, Apr 0, May 0, Jun 0, NONE, Sep 0; <u>1699</u>:
   DLORLIF, Feb 20, LIF, Apr 0, May 0, Nov 7, Dec 0, 18; <u>1700</u>: LIF, Feb 0, Mar
   0, 5, Jul 5, Dec 0; <u>1701</u>: LIF, Jan 0, Mar 0, DG, 21, LIF, Apr 0, Dec 0; <u>1703</u>:
   LIF, Feb 0, Mar 0, Apr 28, May 0, 21; <u>1704</u>: LIF, Jan 13, ATCOURT, Feb 7, LIF,
   19, 24, ATCOURT, 28, LIF, Mar 30, ATCOURT, Apr 24, LIF, May 23, Nov 13, Dec
   4; <u>1705</u>: LIF/QUEN, Feb 22, QUEEN'S, Apr 9, LIF/QUEN, Oct 30, QUEEN'S, Nov 23;
   <u>1706</u>: QUEEN'S, Feb 21, Mar 7, 11, Jun 0, Oct 30, Nov 2, 9, 19, 20, 25, 29,
   Dec 2, 5, 6, 10, 11, 16, 30; <u>1707</u>: QUEEN'S, Jan 14, 20, 28, Feb 4, 18; <u>1709</u>:
   DL, Apr 7; <u>1748</u>: SFLYYW, Sep 12
Bracy (gallery keeper), <u>1677</u>: DL, Dec 12, 26
Braddy, Dr (author), <u>1702</u>: CC, May 21
Bradley (distiller), <u>1748</u>: NTW, Nov 16
Bradley, Mrs M (actor), <u>1772</u>: DL, Sep 22, Dec 26; <u>1777</u>: HAY, Oct 6
Bradney (actor), <u>1775</u>: HAY, Feb 2, Mar 23
Bradshaw (householder), <u>1742</u>: DL, Mar 16
Bradshaw (merchant), <u>1742</u>: DL, Feb 1, Apr 26
Bradshaw, Elizabeth (dancer), <u>1787</u>: DL, Jun 1
Bradshaw, Lucretia (actor, singer), <u>1696</u>: LIF, Apr 0; <u>1697</u>: LIF, Jun 0, Nov 0;
   <u>1700</u>: YB, May 8; <u>1703</u>: LIF, Nov 0; <u>1704</u>: LIF, Mar 25, ATCOURT, Apr 24, LIF,
   Aug 17, Oct 2; <u>1705</u>: LIF, Mar 1, Aug 1, LIF/QUEN, Oct 30; <u>1706</u>: QUEEN'S, Jan
   3, Mar 7, Nov 22, Dec 7, 11, 27; <u>1707</u>: QUEEN'S, Jan 3, Feb 14, 15, Mar 8, 27,
   Apr 1, 28, May 2, Jun 10, 20, 27, Jul 4, 10, 22, 26, Aug 1, 8, DL/QUEEN, Oct
   18, 20, 22, 23, 25, 31, Nov 1, QUEEN/DL, 8, DL/QUEEN, 10, 14, QUEEN'S, 22;
   <u>1708</u>: DL, Feb 4, 6, 14, 24, Mar 8, 15, 18, 25, 27, Apr 10, 15, 19, DL/QUEEN,
   21, DL, 29, DL/QUEEN, May 1, DL, 31, Jun 5, 11, 17, 19, 24, 26, Jul 1, 3, 10,
   13, 20, Aug 4, 28, Sep 4, 9, 11, 21, 23, 30, Oct 5, 9, 12, 13, 15, 21, 23,
   Dec 14, 21, 22, 28, 30, 31; <u>1709</u>: DL, Jan 3, 4, 10, 25, 26, 29, Mar 3, 17,
   21, 28, 31, Apr 5, 11, 14, 25, 26, 30, May 3, 17, Jun 2, Sep 6, Nov 23, 25,
   26, 28, 30, Dec 3, 6, 10, 17; <u>1710</u>: DL, Jan 3, 14, 18, 21, 26, 28, Feb 11,
   18, 25, YB, Mar 17, DL, 21, Apr 15, 21, 22, May 3, 23, 30, DL/QUEEN, Nov 4,
   6, 7, 8, 9, 16, DL, 21, 23, 27, 28, Dec 1, 7, 9, 14, 30; <u>1711</u>: DL, Jan 11,
   18, 20, 26, Feb 3, DL/QUEEN, 17, DL, 24, 27, Mar 17, 20, Apr 7, 21, DL/QUEEN,
   May 1, 3, DL, 8, DL/QUEEN, 11, DL, 18, DL/QUEEN, 29, DL, Jun 4, DL/QUEEN, 7,
   DL, 26, 29, Jul 10, 27, Aug 3, 17, 31, Sep 29, Oct 4, 10, 12, 16, 22, 24, 30,
   Nov 7, 27, Dec 18; <u>1712</u>: DL, May 3, 8, 12, 19, 29, Jun 2, 9, Jul 1, 4, 11,
   18, 29, Aug 1, 8, 12, Oct 6, 10, 14, 15, 16, 22, 23, Nov 3, 26, Dec 12, 27;
   <u>1713</u>: DL, Jan 5, 10, 19, Feb 13, Mar 28, May 11, 13, Jun 12, 17, 18, Oct 23,
   Nov 9, 23, 27; <u>1714</u>: DL, Mar 31, Apr 26, May 7, 17, 19, 28, Jun 29, Jul 13,
   20
Bradshaw, Mary, Mrs William (actor), <u>1743</u>: LIF, Jan 7, Feb 14, 17, SOU, 18,
   HAY, Apr 14, DL, Sep 17; <u>1744</u>: DL, Apr 9, May 8, 17, Sep 20, Oct 2, 6, Dec
   13; <u>1745</u>: DL, Jan 8, 26, Feb 11, Mar 12, 30, Apr 30, May 1, Oct 17, Nov 18,
   19, 30; <u>1746</u>: DL, Jan 2, May 1; <u>1752</u>: NWLS, Nov 16, 28, 30; <u>1753</u>: DL, Oct 9,
   Nov 14, 23, 26; <u>1754</u>: DL, Jul 2; <u>1755</u>: DL, Jan 15, Feb 18, Mar 20, Apr 15,
   25, Oct 7, 27, Nov 8, 15, Dec 1; <u>1756</u>: DL, Jan 21, Apr 10, 29, May 24, Sep
   25, Oct 13; <u>1757</u>: DL, Mar 24, May 9, 13, CG, 27, DL, Oct 29; <u>1758</u>: DL, Jan
   13, Apr 29, May 2, 12, Sep 16; <u>1759</u>: DL, Mar 24, May 4, 7, 11, 21, Oct 11,
   17, 31, Nov 9, 17, 22, Dec 1, 7; <u>1760</u>: DL, Jan 9, 24, Mar 20, 25, Apr 9, 22,
   28, May 7, Oct 2, 7, Nov 17, Dec 5, 29; <u>1761</u>: DL, Jan 10, Mar 23, Apr 3, 17,
   May 14, Sep 17, 19, Oct 7, 10, 23, 29, Nov 10, Dec 17, 28; <u>1762</u>: DL, Jan 5,
   7, 11, Feb 20, Mar 6, 15, 20, Apr 30, May 10, 17, 25, Sep 21, 25, Oct 5, 7,
   11, 12, Nov 2, 3, 12, 15, 16, Dec 1, 27; <u>1763</u>: DL, Jan 14, 15, 18, Feb 24,
   Mar 1, 14, 19, 21, Apr 30, Sep 17, 20, 27, 29, Oct 1, 21, Nov 2, 8, 9, Dec
   27, 28; <u>1764</u>: DL, Jan 3, 4, 18, 27, Mar 24, 26, Apr 30, Sep 15, 18, 25, Oct
   15, 17, 20, 25, Nov 8, 9, Dec 13, 26; <u>1765</u>: DL, Jan 3, 22, Feb 4, Mar 23, Apr

26, May 9, 17, 22, Sep 14, 17, 24, Oct 11; <u>1766</u>: DL, Jan 6, 9, 24, Mar 15,
Apr 12, 22, May 5, 6, 19, 21, 22, Sep 20, 25, 27, Oct 29, Nov 18, Dec 2, 10,
29; <u>1767</u>: DL, Jan 2, 24, Apr 6, 11, 22, May 8, 15, Sep 15, 16, 22, 24, 26,
Oct 9, 22, 23, Dec 5, 7, 26; <u>1768</u>: DL, Jan 9, 19, Mar 21, Apr 6, 14, May 2,
Sep 17, 20, 23, 26, 27, 28, Oct 4, 10, 11, 13, 19, 20, 25, 28, 31, Nov 17,
Dec 16, 30; <u>1769</u>: DL, Jan 27, Mar 14, 31, Apr 10, 18, 21, 28, May 1, Sep 21,
26, Oct 3, 4, 11, 13, 14, 21, 23, Nov 15, 16, 23, 29, Dec 6, 8, 16, 23; <u>1770</u>:
DL, Jan 3, 6, 16, 19, Feb 8, 21, Mar 22, Apr 3, May 3, 7, 11, 19, Sep 25, 27,
29, Oct 3, 4, 9, 13, 15, 19, 23, 25, 26, Nov 3, 13, 15, 16, 17, 19, 20, Dec
4, 6, 19; <u>1771</u>: DL, Jan 1, 2, 19, Mar 7, 11, 14, 21, 23, Apr 1, 5, 15, 17,
26, May 11, 27, Sep 21, 24, 28, Oct 1, 17, 19, 22, 26, 31, Nov 8, 14, 22, 25,
27, 28, Dec 3, 4, 26, 31; <u>1772</u>: DL, Jan 4, 9, 15, Feb 29, Mar 12, 24, Apr 2,
4, 6, 22, May 12, 13, 19, Jun 3, Sep 22, 29, Oct 6, 15, 20, 29, Nov 3, 6, 17,
27, Dec 8, 15, 21, 26; <u>1773</u>: DL, Jan 1, 9, 26, 29, Feb 4, 10, 25, 27, Mar 9,
Apr 1, 21, 23, May 13, 17, Sep 18, 23, 25, 28, Oct 2, 11, 13, 20, 25, 28, 30,
Nov 2, 9, 15, Dec 27, 31; <u>1774</u>: DL, Jan 5, 13, 18, 19, 22, Feb 2, 5, Mar 14,
15, 17, 22, Apr 19, May 3, 7, 9, 10, 20, Sep 20, 27, 29, Oct 1, 6, 8, 14, 20,
27, 28, Nov 1, 5, 16, 18, 29, 30, Dec 7; <u>1775</u>: DL, Jan 2, 18, 23, Mar 2, 18,
23, 28, Apr 8, 17, May 13, 20, Sep 26, 30, Oct 5, CG, 9, DL, 11, 31, Nov 6,
11, 18; <u>1776</u>: DL, Jan 3, Feb 1, 12, Mar 14, 21, 25, 28, Apr 8, 22, May 4, 6,
16, 23, Jun 3, Sep 21, Oct 9, 15, 18, 19, 30, Nov 7, 9, 29, Dec 18, 19; <u>1777</u>:
DL, Jan 1, Feb 24, Mar 13, 20, 31, Apr 21, 28, 29, CG, May 22, DL, 28, Sep
27, Oct 17, Nov 13, 24, Dec 3, 4, 11; <u>1778</u>: DL, Jan 2, 17, Feb 10, 24, Apr 9,
May 14, 23, 25, Sep 17, 22, 26, 29, Oct 1, 8, 15, 20, 28, 31, Nov 4, 25, Dec
21, 23; <u>1779</u>: DL, Jan 29, Mar 2, 11, 13, 15, 18, May 10, 15, 21, Sep 25, 30,
Oct 5, 21, 30, Nov 11, 19, 22, 24, Dec 20; <u>1780</u>: DL, Jan 11, 28, Apr 1, May
5, 10

Bradshaw, Miss (actor), <u>1785</u>: HAY, Feb 10
Bradshaw, William (boxkeeper), <u>1736</u>: DL, May 28; <u>1737</u>: DL, May 31; <u>1738</u>: DL,
   May 29; <u>1739</u>: DL, May 25; <u>1740</u>: DL, May 22; <u>1741</u>: DL, May 26, Sep 5; <u>1742</u>:
   DL, Mar 12, 15, 20, 22, 29, 30, Apr 1, 5, 20, 22, 24, 28, 30, May 18, Sep 11;
   <u>1743</u>: DL, May 20; <u>1744</u>: DL, May 17; <u>1745</u>: DL, May 1
Brady, L (payee), <u>1775</u>: DL, Jan 11
Brady, Master (dancer), <u>1785</u>: HAY, Feb 14
Brady, Nicholas
--Rape, The; or, The Innocent Impostor, <u>1692</u>: NONE, Jan 19, DL, Feb 0; <u>1729</u>:
   LIF, Nov 25, 26, 27, 28
Brady, Patrick (actor), <u>1779</u>: DL, Jan 11; <u>1787</u>: DL, Jun 4; <u>1788</u>: DL, Jun 5;
   <u>1790</u>: DL, May 6; <u>1795</u>: DL, Feb 12
Braganza. See Jephson, Robert.
Braggadocio, The; or, The Bawd Turn'd Puritan (play, anon), <u>1690</u>: NONE, Sep 0
Braghetti, Prospero (singer), <u>1793</u>: KING'S, Feb 5, 26, Apr 23, May 14, Jun 1;
   <u>1794</u>: KING'S, Jan 11, Feb 1, Mar 1, 18, Apr 1, 26, May 17, 29, Jun 5, Dec 6,
   20; <u>1795</u>: KING'S, Jan 10, 17, Feb 7, Mar 21, 28, Apr 30; <u>1796</u>: KING'S, Jan 5,
   19, Feb 9, 16, Apr 7, May 24, Jun 14; <u>1797</u>: KING'S, Jan 10, Feb 25, Jun 10,
   Nov 28, Dec 2, 12, 20; <u>1798</u>: KING'S, Jan 23, Feb 20, Mar 10, Apr 26, Dec 29;
   <u>1799</u>: KING'S, May 30; <u>1800</u>: KING'S, Feb 8, May 22, Jun 28
Brahals, Lord. See Boyle, Roger.
Braham, John (actor, singer), <u>1787</u>: CG, Apr 21, ROY, Jun 20; <u>1788</u>: CG, Jun 2,
   3, HAY, Aug 22; <u>1796</u>: DL, Apr 30, May 9, Jun 9, KING'S, Nov 26; <u>1797</u>: KING'S,
   Jan 10, Feb 14, CG, Mar 3, 10, 15, 17, 22, 24, 31, Apr 7, KING'S, 18, CG, Jun
   21
Bramstone (spectator), <u>1752</u>: DL, Dec 14
Bramwell, Georgiana (actor, singer), <u>1791</u>: DLKING'S, Oct 15; <u>1792</u>: DLKING'S,
   Mar 29, Apr 16, May 23, HAY, Jun 23, Jul 25, DL, Oct 4, 11, Nov 21, Dec 26;
   <u>1793</u>: DL, Mar 7, 21, May 31, HAY, Jun 17, Aug 3, 12, 16, Sep 2, 19, Oct 10,
   22, Nov 19, 30; <u>1794</u>: HAY, Feb 8, 24, Mar 13, DL, Apr 21, 26, 28, May 2, 8,
   16, Jun 9, Sep 23, 27, Oct 14, 27, 31, Nov 15, Dec 20; <u>1795</u>: DL, Jan 8, Feb
   6, 10, 12, 24, May 6, 30, Sep 17, Oct 30, Nov 11, 23, Dec 10; <u>1796</u>: DL, Jan
   11, 18, Mar 3, 12, Apr 30, Jun 7, 8, 10, 11, Sep 27, Oct 19, Nov 14; <u>1797</u>:
   DL, Jan 04
Brand, Hannah (actor, playwright), <u>1780</u>: HAY, Sep 25; <u>1792</u>: DLKING'S, Jan 18,
   Feb 2
--Huniades; or, The Siege of Belgrade (Agmunda), <u>1792</u>: DLKING'S, Jan 18, Feb 2
Brandenburgh House, <u>1799</u>: CG, Apr 19
Brandes, Ernst (German traveller), <u>1785</u>: DL, May 10
Brandes, Johann Christian, <u>1790</u>: CG, Nov 11
--Gasthoff, Der, <u>1790</u>: CG, Nov 11
--Trau, Schau, Wem, <u>1790</u>: CG, Nov 11
Brandi, Gaetano (oboist), <u>1798</u>: HAY, Jan 15
Brandon, James William (box-bookkeeper, housekeeper), <u>1775</u>: CG, May 27; <u>1776</u>:
   CG, May 21; <u>1777</u>: CG, May 23; <u>1778</u>: CG, May 6, 21, Sep 18; <u>1779</u>: CG, May 10,

Sep 20; <u>1780</u>: CG, May 8, Sep 18; <u>1781</u>: CG, May 14, Sep 17; <u>1782</u>: CG, May 13,
Sep 23; <u>1783</u>: CG, May 26, Sep 17; <u>1784</u>: CG, May 25, Sep 17; <u>1785</u>: CG, May 16,
Sep 19; <u>1786</u>: CG, May 25, 31, Sep 18; <u>1787</u>: CG, May 16, 30, Sep 17; <u>1788</u>: CG,
May 19, Sep 15; <u>1789</u>: CG, Feb 27, Jun 11, 16, Sep 14; <u>1790</u>: CG, Feb 19, May
31, Jun 8, 16, Sep 13; <u>1791</u>: CG, Mar 11, Jun 8, 9, Sep 12; <u>1792</u>: CG, Feb 24,
May 24, 29; <u>1793</u>: CG, Feb 15, Jun 3, Sep 16; <u>1794</u>: CG, Mar 7, Jun 9, 10, Sep
15; <u>1795</u>: CG, Feb 20, Jun 8, 10, Sep 14; <u>1796</u>: CG, Feb 12, May 26, 31, Sep
12, Oct 25, DL, Nov 29; <u>1797</u>: CG, Mar 3, May 16, Jun 1, 21, Sep 18; <u>1798</u>: CG,
Feb 9, 23, Jun 1, 11, Sep 17; <u>1799</u>: CG, Feb 8, Jun 3, 12, Sep 16; <u>1800</u>: CG,
Feb 28, May 29
Brandon, John (treasurer), <u>1798</u>: CG, May 29; <u>1799</u>: CG, May 29; <u>1800</u>: CG, Jun 3,
11
Brandon, Martha, Mrs Josiah John (fruit concessionaire), <u>1787</u>: CG, Dec 17;
<u>1788</u>: CG, May 30; <u>1797</u>: CG, Jun 7
Brangin, Rhoda (actor), <u>1779</u>: HAY, Oct 18, Dec 27; <u>1780</u>: HAY, Mar 28, Apr 5;
<u>1781</u>: CG, Oct 16; <u>1783</u>: CG, Oct 14; <u>1784</u>: CG, Apr 26, HAY, Jul 8, 19, 28, Aug
10, Sep 6, CG, Oct 12, Nov 11; <u>1785</u>: CG, Mar 29, May 7, 11, HAY, 28, 30, Jun
7, Aug 16, 31, CG, Sep 28, 30, Oct 17, 26, 31; <u>1786</u>: CG, Jan 5, Feb 1, 11,
16, Apr 18, 26, May 10, 11, HAY, Jun 14, 16, 19, 20, 29, Jul 8, 13, 19, 25,
Aug 3, 4, 17, CG, Sep 25, 27, Oct 16, 21, 28, Nov 15, Dec 21; <u>1787</u>: CG, Jan
2, 27, Feb 6, Mar 1, 15, HAY, Jun 16, 18, 20, 21, 23, 26, Jul 3, 7, Aug 7,
17, 21, 23, CG, Sep 19, Oct 3, 12, 17, 19, Dec 5, 27; <u>1788</u>: CG, Jan 5, Feb
23, Apr 21, 23, HAY, Jun 13, 18, 25, 28, Jul 3, 4, 24, Aug 9, 26, CG, Nov 6,
22, Dec 1; <u>1789</u>: CG, Jan 8, 15, 28, Apr 20, May 2, 15, HAY, Jun 22, 27, 30,
Jul 6, 15, Aug 10, Sep 8, CG, Oct 7, 14, Nov 5, 13, Dec 11, 26, 31; <u>1790</u>: CG,
Jan 20, Mar 13, Nov 22; <u>1791</u>: CG, Feb 16, Mar 14, Jun 13
Bransby, Astley (actor), <u>1744</u>: HAY, Apr 23; <u>1745</u>: DL, Jun 5, Oct 8, Nov 22, 30,
Dec 11, 26; <u>1746</u>: DL, Jan 8, 14, 16, 17, 24, Mar 10, Apr 4, 9, 10, 15, 16,
21, 23, 29, May 7, 14, 16, 19, Sep 23, 25, 30, Oct 23, 27, Nov 1, 7, Dec 2,
26, 29; <u>1747</u>: DL, Jan 2, 17, Feb 4, 7, Mar 3, 16, 17, 28, 30, Apr 11, 28, Sep
22, Oct 29, Nov 2, 6, Dec 5, 12, 16; <u>1748</u>: DL, Jan 6, 12, 18, Feb 3, Mar 19,
May 2, Sep 17, 22, 24, 27, 29, Oct 4, 13, 15, 19, 28, 29, Nov 9, 14, 29;
<u>1749</u>: DL, Apr 4, 29, May 16, CG, Sep 27, Oct 2, 4, 12, 18, 19, 23, 26, Nov 3,
8, Dec 26; <u>1750</u>: CG, Jan 16, Feb 5, Mar 1, Apr 3, May 1, Sep 28, Oct 17, 25,
26, Nov 8, 12, 22, 24, 29, 30, Dec 10; <u>1751</u>: DL, Jan 5, 12, CG, 17, Feb 23,
Mar 18, Apr 16, 22, May 16, Sep 23, 27, Oct 7, 9, 11, Nov 4, 6, 18, 22, 26,
Dec 5; <u>1752</u>: CG, Feb 6, Mar 16, 17, 30, Apr 30, May 4, Sep 20, 22, 25, Oct 2,
6, 12, 16, 18, 21, 24, 30, Nov 4, 7, 27, 28, Dec 5, 9, 11; <u>1753</u>: CG, Jan 8,
13, Feb 12, 21, Mar 10, 19, 24, May 7, 8, 18, DL, Sep 11, 13, 25, 27, 29, Oct
3, 4, 10, 20, 23, 25, Nov 5, 15, Dec 1; <u>1754</u>: DL, Mar 19, 30, Apr 16, 30, May
30, Sep 14, 19, 24, Oct 1, 3, 10, 11, 12, 14, 15, 16, 29, 30, Nov 4, 11, 22;
<u>1755</u>: DL, Feb 18, 22, Mar 4, 15, Apr 15, Sep 18, 23, Oct 2, 4, 8, 10, 13, 17,
23, 24, 28, Nov 1, 4, Dec 4, 6, 11, 18; <u>1756</u>: DL, Feb 24, Mar 27, 30, Apr 3,
10, May 18, Sep 21, 25, 30, Oct 2, 7, 9, 16, 19, 28, Nov 4, 12, 18, 19, 23,
Dec 3, 10, 11, 27; <u>1757</u>: DL, Jan 24, Feb 5, 22, Mar 7, Apr 11, 20, 26, May 2,
Sep 13, 22, 24, 27, 29, Oct 4, 7, 11, 15, 19, 20, 26, Nov 2, 4, 8, 10, 15,
19, 22, Dec 2, 3, 10; <u>1758</u>: DL, Jan 27, Feb 1, Mar 13, Apr 25, 27, May 2, 4,
23, Jun 1, 22, Sep 16, 21, 23, 26, 28, Oct 10, 12, 18, 19, 25, 30, Nov 4, 7,
14, 15, 16, 18, 24, 27, Dec 13, 18, 20; <u>1759</u>: DL, Jan 3, 17, Mar 20, 24, 31,
Apr 7, 17, 21, May 7, 14, 15, Jun 19, Jul 12, Sep 22, 25, 27, 29, Oct 9, 12,
17, 19, 22, 23, 25, 30, Nov 1, 5, 9, 10, 13, Dec 1, 7, 12, 31; <u>1760</u>: DL, Jan
1, Feb 8, 13, 21, Mar 17, 20, Apr 16, 24, 28, May 3, 7, Jul 29, Sep 23, 30,
Oct 3, 7, 11, 15, 18, 23, 24, 25, Nov 27, Dec 5, 17; <u>1761</u>: DL, Mar 26, Apr
17, 21, 23, 28, 29, May 1, 11, 28, Sep 5, 10, 14, 15, 19, 28, 30, Oct 1, 16,
20, 29, 31, Nov 9, 10, 21, 28, Dec 23; <u>1762</u>: DL, Feb 22, Mar 15, 20, Apr 21,
22, 30, May 7, 8, 10, 13, 19, Sep 21, 25, Oct 4, 5, 6, 7, 11, 12, 13, 14, 15,
20, 23, 28, 29, Nov 3, 4, 10, 17, 19, 26, Dec 6, 27; <u>1763</u>: DL, Jan 14, 17,
Feb 24, Mar 1, Apr 22, 29, Sep 17, 20, 22, Oct 8, 21, 24, 31, Nov 4, 9, 14,
22, 23, 29, 30, Dec 5, 28; <u>1764</u>: DL, Jan 4, 9, 13, 14, 18, 27, Feb 14, 18,
21, Mar 31, Apr 2, 10, 25, 30, May 2, Sep 15, 18, 20, 22, 25, 27, Oct 15, 17,
18, 19, 31, Nov 5, 9, 24, 27, Dec 18; <u>1765</u>: DL, Jan 2, 3, 14, 15, Mar 16, 19,
23, Apr 13, 15, 27, May 2, 18, 27, Sep 14, 17, 21, 24, Oct 2, 3, 14, 22, 25,
28, 31, Nov 11, 16, 25; <u>1766</u>: DL, Jan 6, 9, 13, 23, 24, Feb 13, Mar 15, 18,
20, 22, Apr 9, 22, 26, May 5, 10, 19, 20, 22, Sep 23, 25, 27, 30, Oct 8, 18,
29, Nov 4, 8, 24, Dec 2, 4, 6; <u>1767</u>: DL, Jan 24, Feb 7, Mar 21, 28, 30, 31,
Apr 11, May 8, 11, 22, 27, Sep 12, 15, 16, 17, 21, 26, Oct 9, 10, 21, 22, 29,
Nov 4, 5, 6, 19, 21, 23, 26, Dec 2, 15; <u>1768</u>: DL, Jan 9, 14, 16, 19, Mar 15,
17, 21, Apr 9, 14, 29, Sep 17, 20, 22, 23, 24, 26, 28, 29, Oct 4, 13, 15, 20,
31, Nov 4, 5; <u>1769</u>: DL, Jan 27, Mar 11, 16, Apr 10, 24, 25, May 1, Sep 16,
19, 21, Oct 3, 6, 7, 9, 10, 11, 13, 23, 26, Nov 13, 17, 18, 28, 29, Dec 16;
<u>1770</u>: DL, Jan 4, 19, Feb 7, 17, Mar 31, Apr 3, 7, 19, May 4, Sep 22, 29, Oct
2, 3, 9, 13, 17, 22, 23, 31, Nov 2, 3, 5, 10, 14, 16, 19, 20, Dec 13, 19;

1771: DL, Mar 11, 14, 21, Apr 2, 6, 13, 30, May 27, Sep 21, 26, 28, Oct 12, Nov 2, 4, 8, 9, 22, 23, 28, Dec 2, 3; 1772: DL, Jan 7, 11, 15, 20, Feb 6, Mar 24, 26, 28, Apr 7, 9, 25, May 4, 11, 13, HAY, 22, DL, 30, HAY, Jun 1, DL, 10, HAY, 29, Aug 10, DL, Sep 19, 22, 29, Oct 14, 16, 21, 28, 29, 31, Nov 4, 12, 16, 17, 20, 26, Dec 17, 18; 1773: DL, Jan 4, 13, 19, 21, Feb 2, 4, 10, 11, Mar 9, 30, Apr 3, May 6, 7, 10, 12, Sep 18, 21, Oct 2, 5, 23, 25, 30, Nov 2, 4, 20, 24, 25, 26, Dec 21; 1774: DL, Feb 2, 8, 15, Mar 12, 14, 17, 21, Apr 4, 28, May 2, 4, 10, 18, Sep 22, 24, 27, Oct 1, 4, 8, 12, 20, 24, 27, Nov 3, 4, 16, 17, 25, Dec 9, 26; 1775: DL, Apr 22, 24, 29, May 6, 10, 11, 12, 20, Sep 26, 28, Oct 3, 5, 17, 20, 21, 23, 31, Nov 1, 4, 20, 25, Dec 7, 29; 1776: DL, Jan 26, 27, Feb 20, Mar 11, 12, 14, 18, 25, 28, Apr 17, 19, May 1, 11, 13, 18, Sep 28, Oct 5, 8, 9, 12, 23, 25, 26, 29, Nov 4, 7, 25; 1777: DL, Jan 1, 4, 22, Feb 17, 20, Apr 11, 23, 29, HAY, May 30, Jul 11
Branson (house servant), 1768: CG, May 2; 1769: CG, Apr 24; 1770: CG, Apr 30; 1771: CG, May 14; 1772: DL, Jan 6, CG, Feb 18, May 19; 1773: CG, May 19; 1774: CG, May 10; 1775: CG, May 20; 1776: CG, Apr 29; 1777: CG, May 8; 1778: CG, May 7; 1779: CG, Apr 22; 1780: CG, May 5; 1781: CG, Apr 19; 1782: CG, May 17; 1783: CG, May 21
Branson, John (steward), 1743: KING'S, May 7
Branson, Mrs (actor), 1781: CG, Oct 16; 1784: CG, May 15
Brass Prophecy (entertainment), 1762: DL, Mar 30, Apr 19
Brassey (actor), 1728: HAY, May 8; 1748: BFLYY, Aug 24
Brathwaite (tailor), 1772: DL, Apr 29; 1774: DL, Dec 5
Brathwaite, Mrs (dancer), 1772: DL, Oct 10
Braun (composer), 1754: KING'S, Feb 28
Brave Betty was a maiden queen (song), 1798: CG, May 28, HAY, Aug 14; 1799: CG, Apr 6, May 3, Jun 3; see also Queen Bess
Brave Irishman, The. See Sheridan, Thomas.
Brave offspring of Ocean (song), 1798: CG, Apr 9
Bravoure des Femmes (dance), 1779: KING'S, Apr 15
Bravura Agitata (song), 1798: CG, Feb 28, Mar 30
Bravura Song (song), 1786: KING'S, Mar 21, Apr 6; 1789: CG, May 20; 1792: CG, Mar 7, May 22; 1793: CG, Feb 22; 1794: CG, Mar 14; 1796: CG, Mar 2; 1797: CG, May 11
Brawn (dancer), 1767: DL, Jan 24
Bray (dancer), 1693: NONE, Sep 0
Bray, Mrs (actor), 1727: BF, Aug 22
Break his bands of sleep asunder (song), 1790: DL, Mar 5; 1792: CG, Mar 7; 1794: CG, Mar 14
Bremner (music publisher), 1766: DL, Nov 21
Bremond, Sebastian (ballet master), 1674: ATCOURT, Feb 0
Brenoralt. See Suckling, Sir John.
Brent (actor), 1797: HAY, Jan 23, 26, May 10
Brent (singer), 1752: CG, Feb 26; 1763: CG, Oct 15
Brent, Charlotte (singer), 1756: DL, Dec 20; 1758: DL, Mar 3; 1759: CG, Feb 2, DL, Mar 23, CG, Apr 3, May 4, 12, Oct 10, 13, 22, Nov 3, 30; 1760: CG, Jan 18, Feb 14, 23, 29, Mar 17, 22, 27, Apr 21, 28, Sep 22, 24, 29, Nov 28, Dec 11, 22; 1761: KING'S, Mar 12, CG, 27, Apr 13, 23, May 25, Sep 7, 14, 16, 25, 26; 1762: CG, Feb 2, DL, 26, Mar 3, 5, CG, 20, 23, 30, Apr 1, 3, 24, CHAPEL, May 18, HAY, 20, RANELAGH, Jun 11, CG, Sep 29, Oct 1, 4, 8, Nov 1, 15, 23, 29, Dec 8; 1763: CG, Jan 24, Feb 24, Mar 22, Sep 21, Oct 8, 11, 22, Nov 3, 15, 22, Dec 12, 29; 1764: CHAPEL, Feb 29, CG, Mar 31, May 8, RANELAGH, Jun 13, CG, Oct 18, 23, 26, 27, Nov 7, 23, Dec 12; 1765: CG, Jan 31, KING'S, Feb 15, CG, Mar 11, 16, 28, 30, Apr 15, May 6, Oct 4, 7, 15, 22, 25, Nov 20, Dec 6; 1766: CG, Jan 8, Feb 8, Mar 22, CHAPEL, Apr 30, CG, May 8, Nov 12; 1785: HAY, Mar 15, CG, Apr 22
Brent, Mrs (actor), 1787: HAY, Jan 8; 1797: HAY, Jan 23, 26
Brerely (actor), 1777: HAY, May 1
Brereton (witness), 1692: DL, Dec 2
Brereton, Priscilla, Mrs William (actor), 1775: DL, Oct 17, 24; 1778: DL, Oct 6, 8, 28, Nov 9, 10, 14, 28, Dec 19; 1779: DL, Jan 23, Feb 3, Mar 15, Apr 10, 16, 19, 23, 28, May 1, 3, 7, 25, Sep 21, 23, 28, 30, Oct 7, 23, Nov 9, 17, 24, Dec 2, 9, 28, 29; 1780: DL, Jan 26, Feb 28, Mar 4, Apr 1, 19, Sep 23, 26, Oct 3, 10, 12, 14, 19, 21, 23, 28, Nov 3, 8, 9, 18, Dec 4, 8, 19; 1781: DL, Mar 10, Apr 24, May 5, Sep 15, 20, 27, 29, Oct 2, 16, 18, 25, 27, Nov 15, 21, Dec 14; 1782: DL, Jan 21, Feb 25, Mar 21, May 7, 10, 29, Sep 17, 20, 21, 26, Oct 3, 8, 10, 14, 26, 29, Nov 2, 12, 16, 22, Dec 5; 1783: DL, Jan 3, 15, Feb 12, Mar 3, 10, 20, Apr 7, 21, 23, 29, Sep 18, 23, Oct 7, 14, 18, 29, Nov 12, 21, 22, Dec 2, 29; 1784: DL, Jan 16, 17, Feb 14, Apr 19, 28, May 3, 10, 15, Sep 16, 18, 23, 28, 30, Oct 5, 7, 18, 21; 1785: DL, Jan 22, Mar 17, Apr 11, 14, 25, May 3, 11, 26, Sep 20, 24, 27, Oct 25, Nov 2, 7, 9, 11, 12, 18, 26, Dec 30; 1786: DL, Jan 4, 9, Feb 20, Jun 1, Sep 16, 21, 26, 30, Oct 5, 7, 16,

21, 30, Nov 15, 25, 29, Dec 26; <u>1787</u>: DL, Jan 13, 18, Mar 12, Apr 14, May 2, 21, 31, Sep 20, 25, Oct 2, 4, 9, 13, 30, Nov 13, 15, Dec 5, 7, 8, 27; <u>1788</u>: DL, Jan 4, 9, 11, Feb 25, Apr 29, May 26
Brereton, William (actor), <u>1768</u>: DL, Nov 10, 15; <u>1769</u>: DL, Apr 17, Oct 14, Dec 1, 12, 26; <u>1770</u>: DL, Jan 6, 19, May 2, 8, 15, Sep 22, 25, Oct 3, 17, Nov 9, 24, Dec 5; <u>1771</u>: DL, Mar 9, Apr 23, May 1, 8, 10, Sep 26, Oct 1, 15, 30, Nov 9, 11, 12, 22, Dec 4; <u>1772</u>: DL, Feb 22, Apr 20, 22, May 13, Sep 19, Oct 6, 8, Nov 9, 17, Dec 8, 22; <u>1773</u>: DL, Mar 23, Apr 26, May 6, 8, 15, Sep 21, Oct 2, 9, 13, 26, Nov 2, 4, 9, Dec 11, 15; <u>1774</u>: DL, Jan 19, Feb 2, 15, Mar 22, Apr 29, May 2, 20, 28, Sep 24, 27, 29, Oct 8, 12, 13, 20, Nov 1, 3, 4, 5, 7, 8, Dec 10; <u>1775</u>: DL, Jan 11, Feb 17, 23, Mar 2, 18, 21, 25, 30, Apr 3, 20, 29, May 3, 6, 10, 11, 12, 20, 27, Oct 20, 21, 25, 28, 31, Nov 1, 3, 4, 6, 7, 9, 20, 23, 28, Dec 18, 19, 26; <u>1776</u>: DL, Jan 3, 13, 20, 27, Feb 10, 12, 15, Mar 7, 18, 23, 28, Apr 8, 11, 17, 19, 22, May 3, CG, 22, DL, 22, Oct 1, 3, 5, 9, 10, 18, 26, 30, Nov 7, 9, 12, 16, 21, Dec 6, 10, 18, 28; <u>1777</u>: DL, Jan 29, Feb 17, 24, CG, May 24, DL, Sep 25, Oct 18, 28, 31, Nov 4, 13, 18, 29, Dec 3, 4, 11, 18; <u>1778</u>: DL, Jan 2, 5, 10, 24, Feb 10, Apr 21, 23, 27, May 21, CG, 22, DL, 23, Sep 24, 26, Oct 1, 8, 15, 20, 21, CG, 24, DL, 28, 31, Nov 4, 9, 10, 14, Dec 11, 21, 22; <u>1779</u>: DL, Jan 2, Feb 3, Apr 7, 10, 12, 16, 19, CG, May 19, DL, 25, Sep 23, 25, 28, 30, Oct 7, 23, Nov 9, 11, 15, 17, 18, 20, 24, Dec 2, 20, 27, 28, 29; <u>1780</u>: DL, Jan 1, 11, 18, 28, Feb 22, 28, Apr 4, 17, 19, 26, May 24, CG, 26, DL, Oct 2, 3, 5, 10, 11, 12, 17, 19, 20, 28, Nov 2, 3, 4, 6, 8, 9, 10, 13, 17, 27, Dec 4, 6, 8, 15; <u>1781</u>: DL, Jan 26, Feb 12, Mar 10, Apr 25, May 1, 5, 10, CG, 26, DL, Sep 20, 29, Oct 2, 4, 6, 19, 25, 27, Nov 5, 7, 15, 21; <u>1782</u>: DL, Jan 21, 22, Feb 25, Mar 16, 21, Apr 11, 15, 25, May 14, CG, 29, DL, Sep 17, 19, 20, 21, 28, Oct 1, 8, 14, 30, Nov 2, 12, 16, 22, 26, 29, Dec 5, 14, 19, 26; <u>1783</u>: DL, Jan 10, 15, 29, Feb 12, 18, 20, Mar 3, 20, Apr 10, 24, 28, 29, May 2, 12, CG, Jun 4, DL, Sep 20, 27, Oct 7, 14, 16, 17, 20, 21, Nov 3, 12, 20, 21, 22, Dec 2, 19, 22; <u>1784</u>: DL, Jan 3, 16, 17, 23, Feb 14, Apr 15, 19, 26, 28, May 3, CG, 29, DL, Sep 16, 23, 30, Oct 5, 19, 26, 28, Nov 4, 15, 16, 17, 19, 20, 22, 23, Dec 3; <u>1785</u>: DL, Jan 6, CG, 19, DL, 20, 22, Feb 2, Apr 12, 14, 25, 27, May 24, 26, Oct 25, 29, 31, Nov 2, 3; <u>1786</u>: CG, Jun 2; <u>1787</u>: CG, Jun 5; <u>1788</u>: CG, May 24; <u>1789</u>: CG, Jun 13
Brereton, William and Priscilla (actors), <u>1784</u>: DL, Oct 5; <u>1786</u>: DL, May 11
Brest, <u>1779</u>: CG, Apr 12
Bretagne (dance), <u>1738</u>: DL, May 25
Brethren farewell (song), <u>1789</u>: CG, Apr 3
Brett (singer), <u>1740</u>: CG, Oct 10; <u>1741</u>: CG, Jan 5, GF, Mar 3; <u>1743</u>: NWLS, Nov 1; <u>1744</u>: HAY, Nov 1, 5; <u>1745</u>: GF, Feb 14, 26, 28, Mar 5, 12, Apr 6, Nov 25, 26, 27, 28, 29, Dec 2, 3, 4, 6, 9, 10, 11, 13, 16, 17, 23, 26, 28; <u>1746</u>: GF, Jan 1, 2, 7, 9, 10, 13, 14, 22, Feb 25, HIC, Mar 10, GF, Dec 29; <u>1747</u>: GF, Jan 5, 9, 12, 16, 26, Feb 9, 16, 20, Mar 2, 10, 12, 14, 17, 23, 24, 26, 30, 31, Apr 2, 4, 7, 9, 11
Brett, Anne (actor), <u>1727</u>: DL, Nov 21; <u>1728</u>: DL, Feb 21, 27, Mar 19, Apr 8, 11, 24, May 3, 7, 8, 10, 22, Oct 18, 21, Nov 7, 8, 12; <u>1729</u>: DL, Jan 14, Mar 10, 15, 25, 27, Apr 8, 9, 10, 22, 23, 28, 30, May 1, 2, 7, Jun 13, 20, 24, Aug 7, Dec 8, 12; <u>1730</u>: DL, Apr 29, May 4, 15, Oct 28, Dec 3, 4; <u>1731</u>: DL, Apr 27, May 3, 5, 6, 7, 10, 19, Jun 7, Jul 23, Aug 6, 20, SF/BFFHH, 24, Sep 8, DL, Oct 16, 26, Nov 22, 25, Dec 15; <u>1732</u>: DL, Mar 4, 21, Apr 25, May 1, 3, 6, 8, 12, 25, 29, Jun 6, 23, 28, Jul 4, 7, BF, Aug 22, DL, Nov 7, 14, Dec 20; <u>1733</u>: DL, May 3, 18, BFCGBH, Aug 23, Sep 4, DL/HAY, Oct 5, 6, 12, 25, Nov 8, HAY, 19, DL/HAY, Dec 1, 28; <u>1734</u>: DL/HAY, Jan 7, 12, 23, 29, Feb 20, Mar 12, 19, Apr 26, May 3, JS, 24, HAY, Jun 5, 7, 17, 19, 21, 24, 28, Jul 19, 31, Aug 7, 14, 16, LIF, 20, HAY, 21, 22, DL, Sep 19, 24, 26, Oct 3, 8, 25, 26, Nov 1, 16, 19, Dec 11; <u>1735</u>: DL, Jan 20, 21, 28, Feb 18, Mar 3, 15, 25, Apr 7, 14, 16, 22, 25, May 2, 7, 8, 9, 14, 17, 20, 22, 29, Jun 5, HAY, 12, LIF, 19, DL, Jul 1, LIF, 11, 16, 23, Aug 1, 6, 22, 25, DL, Oct 1, 4, 7, 22, 31, Nov 15, 17, 20, 25, Dec 6, 18, 26; <u>1736</u>: DL, Jan 3, 6, 9, 12, Mar 22, 27, Apr 5, 6, 8, 13, May 7, 13, 14, 15, 18, 21, 22, HAY, Jun 29, Jul 7, DL, Sep 7, 23, 28, Oct 5, 12, 18, 19, 21, 23, 29, Nov 2, 10, Dec 14, 27, 31; <u>1737</u>: DL, Feb 14, Mar 2, 14, May 2, 3, 16, 17, 26, Sep 3, 17, Oct 8, 13, 20, 21, 27, Nov 1, 10, 17; <u>1738</u>: DL, Jan 19, 28, Apr 6, 10, 29, May 3, 8, 17, 22, 30
Brett, Elizabeth, Mrs Dawson (actor, dancer), <u>1722</u>: DL, Jan 5, May 3; <u>1723</u>: DL, May 24, Jun 6, 12, Jul 5, 12, 23, 26, Aug 6, 9, 12, 16, LIF, Nov 16, 28; <u>1724</u>: LIF, Feb 24, Mar 26, 28, Apr 14, 29, May 16, 27, 28, 29, Jun 1, 2, 3, Oct 27, Nov 6, 13; <u>1725</u>: DL, Feb 20, Apr 28, 29, May 1, Sep 28, Oct 19, 25, Nov 16, 19; <u>1726</u>: DL, Jan 11, Feb 2, 11, Mar 21, 24, 31, Apr 15, 19, 22, 23, 30, May 3, 4, 5, 6, 7, 9, 10, 11, 12, 13, 19, 20, 23, 25, Sep 13, 15, 20, 22, 29, Oct 1, 11, 15, 27, Nov 15, 23, 30, Dec 7, 12, 14, 29, 30; <u>1727</u>: DL, Jan 20, Feb 20, 27, Mar 23, Apr 6, 7, 8, 10, 12, 17, 18, 19, 20, 21, 22, 24, 25, 28, 29, May 1, 2, 3, 5, 8, 26, Sep 26, Oct 6, 12, 19, 20, 30, Nov 1, 9, 21; <u>1728</u>: DL, Feb 21, Mar 14, 16, 19, 21, Apr 4, May 1, 3, 6, 7, 8, 16, 17, 22;

1729: DL, Jan 31; 1735: DL, Apr 11, LIF, Aug 29; 1737: DL, Sep 1, 15, Oct 25,
   Nov 16; 1742: DL, Apr 28
Brett, Frances (actor), 1784: HAY, Aug 2, CG, Dec 27; 1785: HAY, Mar 15; 1786:
   CG, May 10, HAY, 12, Jun 19, Jul 29
Brett, Hannah, Mrs William (actor, singer), 1774: HAY, Jul 20, Aug 29, Sep 17;
   1778: HAY, Jun 11, 25, Aug 21, Sep 7; 1783: HAY, Jun 13, Jul 4, Aug 12, 13;
   1784: HAY, Jul 27; 1786: HAY, Jun 16, 17, 26, 30, Jul 7, 18
Brett, Master William (actor), 1782: HAY, Aug 17
Brett, William (singer, actor), 1774: HAY, Jun 27, Jul 6, 11, Sep 5; 1775: HAY,
   Jun 16, Jul 31, Aug 21, Sep 4; 1776: HAY, Jul 1, 8, Aug 2, 26, 27, Sep 2, 16;
   1778: HAY, Jun 3, 12, 25, Jul 9, 22, Aug 3, 7, 17, 21, Sep 7; 1782: HAY, Jul
   17, Aug 13, 17, 24, 30, Sep 14, 16, 18, CG, 25, 30, Oct 7, 9, 16, 22, 23, 30,
   Nov 2, 25, Dec 6, 14, 27, 31; 1783: CG, Mar 3, Apr 7, 25, May 6, 16, 17, 19,
   21, 23, 24, HAY, 31, Jun 2, 27, 30, Jul 4, 5, 8, 16, Aug 1, 26, CG, Sep 17,
   22, 24, Oct 1, 6, 8, 21, 24, 28, Nov 4, 8, 19, Dec 26; 1784: HAY, Jan 21, CG,
   31, Feb 13, 23, Mar 23, Apr 17, 24, 26, 27, May 1, 7, 10, 17, 25, HAY, 28,
   Jul 7, 24, 27, 28, 30, Aug 2, 10, 17, CG, Sep 22, Oct 1, 4, 8, 12, 25, 28,
   Nov 4, 11, Dec 27; 1785: CG, Jan 14, 21, Mar 7, 30, Apr 1, 15, 18, 22, May 4,
   HAY, Jun 3, 18, 28, Jul 13, 19, Aug 2, 8, 19, 26, CG, Sep 21, 23, Oct 10, 14,
   17, 21, Nov 2, 5, 14, Dec 5, 8, 9, 26; 1786: CG, Jan 6, 18, Feb 13, 23, Mar
   11, 14, 25, Apr 20, May 10, 22, HAY, Jun 9, 12, 13, 14, 17, 26, Jul 18, 25,
   Aug 10, 12, Sep 4
Brett, William and Frances (singer), 1785: HAY, Jul 19; 1786: CG, May 10, HAY,
   Jul 18
Brettagna Freggiata (song), 1789: KING'S, Apr 30
Brettingham, Robert (architect), 1793: KING'S, Feb 19
Breval, John, 1718: DL, Feb 19; 1723: DL, Jul 26
--Play is the Plot, The, 1718: DL, Feb 19, 20, 21, 24, 25, 27; 1723: DL, Jul 16
--Rape of Helen, The (ballad opera), 1733: LIF/CG, May 19
--Strollers, The, 1723: DL, Jul 16, 19, 23, Aug 9, Oct 24, 25; 1727: DL, Apr
   19, May 1, 3, 22, 24; 1728: DL, Apr 30, May 17, 20; 1729: DL, Apr 8, 9, 11,
   21, 25, May 7, Nov 28, Dec 5; 1730: DL, Jan 19, Sep 19, 29, Oct 8, Nov 12;
   1734: CG, May 7, 9, 16; 1736: HAY, Jul 13; 1739: CG, Sep 14, 15; 1741: DL,
   May 12
Brevio (composer), 1742: KING'S, Nov 2, Dec 4; 1749: KING'S, Mar 21
--Mandane (oratorio), 1742: KING'S, Dec 4, 7, 11, 14, 18, 21
Brew, J (printer), 1760: HAY, Dec 19
Brewer St, 1737: DL, Mar 17; 1744: HIC, May 16; 1746: HIC, Mar 10; 1749: HIC,
   Apr 21; 1750: HIC, May 18; 1751: HIC, May 23; 1753: HIC, Dec 31; 1754: HIC,
   Jan 2; 1760: HIC, Apr 29; 1762: HIC, Feb 12; 1773: HIC, May 18; 1792: HAY,
   Nov 26
Brewer, Anthony, 1679: NONE, Sep 0
--Lovesick King, The, 1679: NONE, Sep 0
--Perjured Nun, The, 1679: NONE, Sep 0
Brewer, George, 1794: HAY, Aug 9; 1796: HAY, Jun 11
--Bannian Day (farce), 1796: HAY, Jun 11, 13, 14, 15, 16, 18, 20, 27, Jul 13,
   18; 1797: HAY, Jun 16, Jul 4; 1798: HAY, Sep 7
--How to be Happy, 1794: HAY, Aug 9, 11, 14
Brewman (actor), 1789: KHS, Sep 16
Brewster (musician), 1771: GROTTO, Sep 9
Bribery on both Sides (farce, anon), 1784: CG, May 4
Brice (house servant), 1794: CG, Jun 16; 1795: CG, Jun 10; 1796: CG, May 21;
   1797: CG, Jun 2; 1798: CG, May 29; 1799: CG, May 21; 1800: CG, Jun 10
Brice, Miss (actor), 1782: HAY, Mar 21, May 6
Bricklayer, Miss (singer), 1756: DL, Nov 24, Dec 20; 1758: CG, Oct 9; 1767: CG,
   Feb 21, May 16, 20
Brida, Luigi (singer), 1794: KING'S, Dec 20; 1795: KING'S, Jan 27, Feb 20, Mar
   13, 21, 28, Apr 14, 30, May 26, 28, Jun 23, 30
Bride (actor, scene shifter), 1741: DL, Nov 11; 1743: DL, May 24; 1744: DL, May
   22; 1745: DL, May 9; 1746: DL, May 19; 1747: DL, May 14; 1749: DL, May 16;
   1750: DL, May 8; 1751: DL, May 9; 1753: DL, May 17; 1754: DL, May 21; 1755:
   DL, May 15; 1756: DL, May 18; 1757: DL, May 16; 1758: DL, May 15; 1759: DL,
   May 24; 1761: DL, May 21
Bride, Elizabeth (actor), 1755: DL, Nov 8; 1759: DL, Apr 5, May 21; 1760: DL,
   Apr 28, May 13, Jul 29, Oct 18; 1761: DL, Nov 28, Dec 11, 19; 1762: DL, Jan
   20, 25, Mar 15, 25, Apr 1, 28, Oct 25, 29, Dec 22; 1763: DL, Jan 19, Feb 3,
   Mar 14, Apr 19, May 31, Oct 8, 14, Nov 19, Dec 1; 1764: DL, Feb 18, Apr 27,
   Oct 19, Nov 5
Bridell, Jack (taverner), 1749: CG, Apr 28
Briden, 1669: BRIDGES, Jan 29, NONE, Feb 10
Bridewell, 1733: DL/HAY, Nov 16, HAY, 20; 1737: HAY, Mar 9; 1738: CG, Feb 13;
   1743: DL, Mar 7; 1752: TCJS, Aug 11; 1761: DL, Dec 14; 1776: CG, Feb 27

Bridge St Coffee House, 1751: DL, Dec 18
Bridges (actor), 1690: DL, Nov 0, Dec 0; 1692: DL, Nov 8
Bridges (actor), 1743: DL, Apr 7, 28, May 9, Sep 15, 17, 20, 24, 27, 29, Oct 1,
    4, 6, 11, 13, 15, 22, 25, 27, Nov 4, 8, 17, 18, 23, 24, Dec 1, 12, 19, 20;
    1744: DL, Jan 7, 27, Feb 21, Apr 2, 3, 17, 21, 25, Sep 15, 20, 27, 29, Oct 4,
    9, 13, 19, 20, 22, 24, 27, 30, Nov 2, 3, 6, 24, Dec 11; 1745: DL, Jan 4, Feb
    13, 20, Mar 18, 23, Apr 17, 19, 22, May 23, Jun 5, Sep 26, Oct 3, 5, 10, 12,
    19, Nov 20, 22, 28, Dec 10, 12, 13, 31; 1746: DL, Jan 14, 17, 18, 31, Apr 11,
    14, 15, 21, 23, Jun 11, Aug 6, 11, Sep 23, 25, 27, Oct 27, Nov 4, 5, 7, 21,
    Dec 15, 20, 26, 29; 1747: DL, Jan 2, 15, Feb 2, Mar 7, 12, 16, 23, 24, 28,
    Apr 23, 28, 29, CG, Nov 11, 16, 23, Dec 4, 9, 17, 19, 28; 1748: CG, Jan 2, 7,
    8, 9, 11, 12, 14, 15, 16, 19, 27, Mar 14, 24, 28, 31, Apr 16, 18, 21, 22, 27,
    May 4, BF, Aug 24, SFBCBV, Sep 7, CG, 21, 23, DL, Oct 8, 13, 19, 22, 27, 28,
    Nov 1, 2, 7, 14, 23, 28, Dec 17, 23, 28; 1749: DL, Jan 2, 13, 18, Apr 15, May
    8, 16, BFCB, Aug 23, DL, Sep 20, 21, 22, 28, Oct 3, 14, 17, Nov 16, 21, Dec
    7, 8, 9, 16, 18, 20, 29; 1750: DL, Jan 1, 6, 31, Mar 27, Apr 2, 18, 19, Sep
    8, 13, 15, 18, 25, Oct 22, 24, 26, 30, Nov 3, 7, 8, 13, 14, 28, Dec 19, 20,
    21; 1751: DL, Mar 18, Apr 20, May 1, 3
Bridges (actor), 1752: CG, May 11, 13; 1761: DL, Oct 17, Nov 4, Dec 30
Bridges St Theatre, 1668: BRIDGES, Sep 14
Bridges St, 1663: BRIDGES, May 7, LIF, 28, 29, VERE, Jun 1, BRIDGES, Jul 30;
    1664: NONE, Sep 0; 1666: NONE, Nov 29; 1667: NONE, Feb 12, LIF, Sep 16; 1669:
    NONE, Sep 0; 1671: BRIDGES, Aug 0; 1672: LIF, Feb 26, Mar 0, NONE, Sep 0;
    1717: DL, Jun 18; 1736: DL, Apr 6; 1738: DL, May 12; 1739: DL, Apr 5, May 9,
    15; 1740: DL, Apr 10, 28, May 2, 7; 1741: DL, Apr 1, 9, 24, May 1; 1744: CG,
    Apr 18, DL, May 4; 1747: DL, May 16; 1750: DL, Sep 8; 1752: DL, Apr 14, Nov
    21; 1754: DL, May 2; 1755: CG, Dec 19; 1770: DL, May 5; 1775: DL, Sep 23, 30;
    1777: DL, Apr 22, HAY, Aug 28; 1778: DL, May 4; 1779: DL, May 15; 1780: DL,
    May 10; 1784: CG, Apr 15; 1787: DL, Feb 3; 1788: HAY, Sep 30; 1790: DL, Apr
    5; 1791: DL, May 3; 1794: DL, Mar 12, HAY, 18; 1795: DL, Jun 3; 1797: DL, Sep
    19; 1799: HAY, Apr 17
Bridges-Cross-Burton-Vaughan Booth, 1748: BF, Aug 24, SFBCBV, Sep 7, 8, 9, 10,
    12, 13
Bridges, Mr and Mrs (actors), 1749: DL, Apr 13
Bridges, Mrs (actor), 1744: DL, Sep 15, 18, 20, Nov 1; 1745: DL, Feb 11, Sep
    19, 21, Oct 5, 10, 15, Nov 1, 14, 19, Dec 16; 1746: DL, Jan 14, Feb 24, Mar
    10, Apr 9, 11, 21, May 2, Aug 4, 11, Sep 23, Oct 2, 23, 27, Nov 1, 5, 22;
    1747: DL, Jan 2, 3, Mar 3, 12, 17, 21, 23; 1748: CG, Jan 1, 8, 15, 21, Mar 8,
    BF, Aug 24, SFBCBV, Sep 7, DL, Oct 19; 1749: DL, Jan 9, 13
Bridges, Thomas, 1771: HAY, Jul 24; 1775: HAY, Aug 21
--Dutchman, The, 1775: HAY, Aug 21, 23, 25, Sep 8
Bridgetower, George Augustus Polgreen (violinist), 1790: DL, Feb 19, 24, Mar
    24; 1792: KING'S, Feb 24, 29; 1795: CG, Feb 20, 27; 1796: CG, Feb 12; 1797:
    CG, Mar 3; 1798: CG, Feb 23; 1799: CG, Feb 8
Bridgman (actor), 1742: JS, May 31, Nov 8
Bridgman, Mrs (actor), 1794: CG, Oct 1
Bridgwater, Roger (actor), 1723: DL, Jun 12, Jul 5, Aug 12, Oct 15, 16, 24, Dec
    5; 1724: DL, Jan 15, May 12, RI, Jun 27, 29, Jul 4, 11, 13, 18, BFP, Aug 22,
    SF, Sep 5, DL, Dec 9; 1725: DL, Feb 1, Apr 21, May 1, BF, Aug 23, DL, Sep 28,
    Oct 19, Nov 3, 29; 1726: DL, Jan 12, Feb 2, 7, Apr 23, May 11, 20, 23, Sep
    15, Oct 1, 20, Nov 4, 9, 12, 19, 26, Dec 3, 12, 14; 1727: DL, Jan 25, Feb 11,
    21, Apr 19, 29, Sep 9, 21, Oct 6, 23, Nov 6, 9, 22, 30, Dec 4, 5, 9, 13, 30;
    1728: DL, Jan 4, 10, Feb 16, 24, Mar 9, Apr 1, 2, 13, 29, 30, May 1, 10, 17,
    20, 29, Sep 7, 14, 19, 21, Oct 15, 30, Nov 2, 7, 8; 1729: DL, Jan 1, 13, 20,
    21, 22, 25, 28, 29, Feb 3, 22, 24, 25, Apr 11, 23, 25, May 6, 7, 12, 28, Jun
    13, 20, 27, Jul 25, Sep 11, 23, Oct 7, 16, 31, Nov 4, 8, 12, 14, 18, 19, 21,
    22, 27, Dec 1, 3, 20, 26, 27; 1730: DL, Jan 3, 9, 21, 24, 26, Feb 28, Mar 21,
    30, Apr 14, 27, May 11, Sep 12, 15, 19, 29, Oct 1, 10, 20, 24, Nov 18, 23,
    30, Dec 2; 1731: DL, Jan 20, 27, Feb 8, 22, Mar 22, Apr 19, 26, May 7, 17,
    18, 19, Jun 7, 11, 22, Jul 6, 20, 23, Sep 18, 25, Oct 7, 9, 16, 21, Nov 1, 5,
    9, 15, 22, 23, Dec 1, 2, 3, 10, 17, 21, 22; 1732: DL, Feb 3, 14, Mar 14, Apr
    1, 17, May 3, 25, 29, Jun 1, Aug 4, 15, 17, 21, Sep 23, 28, Oct 5, 12, 17,
    21, 26, 28, Nov 4, 11, 13, 14, 21, Dec 6, 11, 14, 20; 1733: DL, Jan 16, 20,
    Feb 17, 22, Mar 8, 29, Apr 4, 11, 13, 19, 24, May 3, Sep 24, 28, Oct 1, 8,
    17, 24, 31, Nov 5, 14, 21, 23, 26, Dec 5, 11, 17, 21; 1734: DL, Jan 3, Feb
    11, Mar 7, LIF, Apr 15, DL/HAY, 20, DL, 23, LIF, 26, May 9, DL, 16, CG/LIF,
    Sep 30, Oct 14, 16, 18, Nov 12, 14, 28, Dec 5, 26; 1735: CG/LIF, Jan 6, 21,
    31, Feb 3, 13, 15, 22, LIF, Mar 3, CG/LIF, 13, 22, Apr 8, 10, LIF, 16,
    CG/LIF, 17, May 1, CG, 6, CG/LIF, 16, CG, Sep 12, 16, 17, Oct 10, 13, 17, 20,
    22, 31, Nov 1, 4, 7, 10, 15, 17, 22, 29, Dec 8, 15, 27, 31; 1736: CG, Jan 8,
    10, Feb 21, Mar 9, 20, 22, 23, 27, 29, Apr 6, 8, 13, 26, May 3, 17, 20, Sep
    15, 17, 20, 22, 24, 29, Oct 8, 11, 20, 22, 23, 30, Nov 1, 8, 11, 15, 22, 26,

Dec 2, 9, 20; <u>1737</u>: CG, Jan 10, 25, Feb 7, 14, 15, 26, Mar 26, 31, Apr 11,
14, 26, 28, May 16, Sep 16, 19, 21, 23, 26, 28, 30, Oct 3, 10, 14, 17, 19,
24, 27, 31, Nov 2, 18, 19; <u>1738</u>: CG, Jan 3, 6, 9, 13, 17, 18, 25, 31, Feb 6,
13, 16, 23, Mar 13, 18, 20, 25, Apr 5, 12, 17, 22, 25, May 18, Sep 15, 18,
20, 25, 27, 29, Oct 2, 4, 6, 11, 13, 14, 16, 18, 21, 23, 28, Nov 7, 9, 15,
17, 22, 24, 27, 28, 29, Dec 2, 4, 5, 7; <u>1739</u>: CG, Jan 15, Feb 10, 16, 24, 26,
Mar 3, 13, 27, Apr 7, May 1, 7, 17, 25, 29, Aug 2, 31, Sep 5, 7, 10, 12, 14,
15, 17, 28, Oct 4, 5, 8, 9, 10, 22, 25, Nov 2, 20, 22, 28, Dec 15, 21, 29;
<u>1740</u>: CG, Jan 10, 15, 17, Feb 6, Mar 11, Apr 14, 16, 30, May 2, 3, 5, 9, 23,
Jun 5, Sep 19, 22, 26, 29, Oct 3, 6, 8, 22, 23, 24, Nov 1, 6, 15, 20, Dec 5,
10, 13, 29; <u>1741</u>: CG, Jan 6, 7, 12, 21, 22, 23, 27, 28, 29, Feb 12, 16, Apr
1, 3, 9, 10, 11, 15, 17, 22, May 1, 11, 12, Sep 21, 23, 25, 28, Oct 5, 7, 8,
13, 15, 20, 21, 24, 31, Nov 7, 9, 11, 23, 26, Dec 1, 7, 11, 12, 17, 18; <u>1742</u>:
CG, Jan 2, Feb 4, Mar 13, 18, 27, Apr 24, May 4, 5, 7, Sep 29, Oct 1, 9, 13,
15, 16, 18, 19, Nov 8, 11, 13, 20, 22, 30, Dec 7, 15, 22; <u>1743</u>: CG, Feb 9,
Apr 9, Sep 21, 23, 28, 30, Oct 3, 5, 7, 12, 14, 17, 19, 24, 31, Nov 2, 17,
21, 30, Dec 3, 8, 17, 27, 31; <u>1744</u>: CG, Jan 4, 5, 7, 24, Feb 28, Mar 12, Apr
19, Sep 19, 24, 26, Oct 1, 10, 20, 24, 31, Nov 27, 28, Dec 13, 21, 28; <u>1745</u>:
CG, Jan 1, 7, 18, Feb 11, 15, Mar 11, Apr 17, 25, 26, May 10, 13, Sep 23, 25,
27, Oct 4, 7, 14, 16, Nov 4, 7, 11, 15, 18, 19, 23, Dec 2, 5, 6, 12, 13;
<u>1746</u>: CG, Jan 2, 11, 13, 25, Feb 3, 8, 24, Mar 15, Apr 1, 7, 21, 22, Jun 11,
16, 23, Sep 29, Oct 4, 6, 20, Nov 1, 3, 4, 6, 17, 24, Dec 19, 22, 26, 29;
<u>1747</u>: CG, Jan 9, 26, Feb 6, 12, Mar 7, Apr 20, May 11, Nov 13, 18, 23, Dec
15, 19, 28; <u>1748</u>: CG, Jan 8, 14, 21, 27, 29, Feb 3, 8, 10, 15, Mar 8, 14, 21,
Apr 16, 18, Oct 3, 7, 22, 25, Nov 9, 24, 28, Dec 9, 22; <u>1749</u>: CG, Jan 11, 13,
Mar 2, Apr 4, 5, 10, May 4, Sep 25, 29, Oct 16, 19, 23, 27, Nov 8, 11, 24,
Dec 26; <u>1750</u>: CG, Jan 16, 23, Feb 2, 22, 26, Mar 1, 13, Apr 2, 3, 5, 23, Sep
28, Oct 20, 23, Nov 22, 29, Dec 1; <u>1751</u>: CG, Feb 23, Apr 16, May 16, Sep 23,
25, Oct 7, Nov 14, 21, 26, Dec 14, 16, 26; <u>1752</u>: CG, Jan 18, 28, Mar 3, 30,
Sep 22, 25, Oct 4, 9, 21, 23, 31, Nov 1, 27, Dec 14, 19, 21; <u>1753</u>: CG, Jan
22, Feb 6, Mar 20, May 7, Sep 14, 21, 24, 26, Oct 10, 17, 22, 24, 31, Nov 7,
14, Dec 26; <u>1754</u>: CG, Mar 9, 26, Apr 17, HAY, Aug 20
Brief (actor), <u>1734</u>: HAY, Apr 17
Brief Remarks on the Original and Present State of the Drama (pamphlet), <u>1758</u>:
DL, Apr 14
Brigg (dancer), <u>1782</u>: DL, May 16; <u>1783</u>: DL, May 23; <u>1785</u>: DL, May 20; <u>1786</u>: DL,
Jun 6; <u>1787</u>: DL, May 31; <u>1788</u>: DL, Jun 3; <u>1790</u>: DL, Jun 2
Brigg, Mr and Mrs (dancers), <u>1790</u>: DL, Jun 2
Brigg, Mrs (actor, dancer), <u>1787</u>: DL, Jun 4; <u>1790</u>: DL, Oct 26; <u>1791</u>: DLKING'S,
Sep 27, Nov 5; <u>1792</u>: DL, Nov 21, Dec 27; <u>1794</u>: DL, May 16, 30, Dec 20, 23;
<u>1795</u>: DL, Feb 16, May 6, Oct 30; <u>1796</u>: DL, Jan 18, Mar 1, Oct 1, 29, Dec 26;
<u>1797</u>: DL, Jun 10; <u>1798</u>: DL, Jan 16, Feb 20, May 16, Oct 6, Nov 14, Dec 6;
<u>1799</u>: DL, Jan 19, Feb 5, Oct 14; <u>1800</u>: DL, Mar 11
Briggs (actor), <u>1781</u>: HAY, Mar 26
Briggs (house servant), <u>1784</u>: DL, May 15; <u>1800</u>: DL, Jun 13
Briggs, Miss (house servant), <u>1798</u>: DL, Jun 11; <u>1799</u>: DL, May 22
Bright (actor, singer), <u>1733</u>: MEG, Sep 28
Bright Author of my present Flame (song), <u>1741</u>: DL, Nov 14, 24, 27, Dec 3, 15;
<u>1742</u>: DL, Jan 5, 13, 18, 20, 29, Feb 3, 27, Mar 13, 16, 22
Bright Cynthia's power divinely great (song), <u>1695</u>: DL, Nov 0
Bright Phoebus (song), <u>1785</u>: DL, May 3, 11, 13, 25, 26; <u>1786</u>: DL, May 3; <u>1787</u>:
DL, May 18, 28; <u>1790</u>: DL, Apr 5
Bright Sol now darts (song), <u>1787</u>: CG, Oct 18
Bright, George (actor), <u>1679</u>: DG, Apr 0; <u>1680</u>: DG, Jun 0; <u>1681</u>: DG, Nov 0;
<u>1682</u>: DG, Jan 23, DL, Nov 28; <u>1683</u>: DG, May 31, NONE, Sep 0, DL, Dec 0; <u>1684</u>:
DL, Mar 0; <u>1688</u>: DL, May 3; <u>1689</u>: DL, Nov 20; <u>1690</u>: DL, Jan 0, DLORDG, Mar 0,
DL, Sep 0, NONE, 0, DL, Oct 0, DL/IT, 21, DL, Nov 0, Dec 0; <u>1691</u>: DL, Jan 0,
Mar 0, Apr 0, NONE, Sep 0, DL, Dec 0; <u>1692</u>: DL, Jan 0, Mar 0; <u>1693</u>: DL, Feb
0, Apr 0, DG, May 0; <u>1694</u>: DG, May 0, NONE, Jul 0, DL, Sep 0; <u>1695</u>: LIF, Dec
0; <u>1696</u>: LIF, Mar 0, Jun 0, Nov 14, Dec 0; <u>1697</u>: LIF, Apr 0, ATCOURT, Nov 4;
<u>1698</u>: LIF, Mar 0; <u>1699</u>: LIF, Dec 18; <u>1700</u>: LIF, Jan 9, Mar 5; <u>1701</u>: LIF, Jan
0; <u>1702</u>: LIF, Dec 31; <u>1705</u>: LIF, Aug 1, QUEEN'S, Dec 27; <u>1708</u>: DL, Jun 5
Bright, Lady Lucy (spectator), <u>1698</u>: DLORLIF, Mar 5, ROBERTS, 23
Bright, Mrs (actor), <u>1701</u>: LIF, Aug 0
Bright, Mrs (actor), <u>1750</u>: HAY, Feb 26, Mar 8, 13
Brilliants, The (interlude, anon), <u>1799</u>: CG, Jun 7
Bring out your cony-skins maids to me (song), <u>1686</u>: ATCOURT, Dec 1
Bring the laurels, bring the bays (song), <u>1790</u>: DL, Mar 17
Brinsley (actor), <u>1781</u>: HAY, Oct 16; <u>1782</u>: HAY, Jan 14
Briscall's Coffee House, <u>1758</u>: CG, Jul 6
Brisco, Samuel (publisher), <u>1698</u>: DLLIF, May 12
Bristol Theatre, <u>1771</u>: DL, Dec 11; <u>1772</u>: DL, Nov 26; <u>1786</u>: HAY, Jun 20

Bristol, Earl of. See Digby, George.
Bristol, Lady (spectator), 1719: RI, Jul 6; 1733: KING'S, Nov 3
Bristol, Lord (spectator), 1733: KING'S, Nov 3
Bristol, 1687: CITY, Oct 29; 1747: DL, Feb 9; 1761: DL, Apr 14; 1769: DL, Mar
    16, CG, Jul 3; 1774: HAY, Apr 4; 1776: DL, Sep 28; 1777: HAY, Sep 3; 1790:
    CG, Apr 6; 1796: CG, Dec 28; 1798: CG, May 12
Bristow, Mrs (singer), 1800: DL, Apr 29, May 3
Britain, The (dance), 1740: CG, May 5
Britain's best bulwarks (song), 1793: KING/HAY, Mar 13; 1795: HAY, Mar 4
Britain's Brave Tars!! See O'Keeffe, John.
Britain's Glory. See Benson, Robert.
Britain's Happiness. See Motteux, Peter Anthony.
Britain's Sons; or, Success to our Heroes (interlude), 1800: CG, May 22
Britan (pit keeper), 1677: DL, Dec 12, 26
Britannia (dance(, 1742: CG, Apr 1
Britannia (song), 1715: DL, Apr 7
Britannia. See Busby, Thomas; Lampe, John Frederick; Mallet, David.
Britannia; or, Love and Glory (masque), 1734: DL, Apr 29
Britannia; or, The Royal Lovers (play, anon), 1734: GF, Feb 11, Sep 25, Nov 18;
    1735: GF, Nov 6; 1736: LIF, Dec 7
Britannia's Triumph; or, The Contest of Love and Glory (entertainment), 1760:
    HAY, Feb 14, Apr 30, Sep 8
Britannicus. See D'Oyley, E.
Briten (actor), 1663: NONE, Sep 0
British Airs (song), 1795: CG, Apr 6
British Apollo (choir), 1709: SH, Nov 30
British Bacchanalian (dance), 1775: CG, May 12, 16
British Bucks (entertainment), 1761: CG, Mar 26
British Dance, Grand (dance), 1752: HAY, Dec 7; 1753: HAY, Apr 10; 1754: SFG,
    Sep 21
British Enchanters, The. See Granville, George.
British Fair (song), 1765: HAY, Aug 8
British Fortitude and Hibernian Friendship. See Cross, John Cartwright.
British Heroine, The. See Jackson, John.
British ladies (play), 1763: DL, Apr 29
British Loyalty; or, A Squeeze for St Paul's (entertainment), 1789: DL, Apr 30,
    HAY, Jun 17, KHS, Sep 16, WHF, Nov 11; 1790: DL, Apr 23, May 18; 1791: HAY,
    Oct 24; 1792: HAY, Oct 15
British Lying-in Hospital, 1756: CG, Dec 15; 1758: DL, Apr 5; 1759: KING'S, May
    2; 1764: DL, Dec 12; 1765: CG, Dec 17; 1768: KING'S, May 12, DL, Dec 16;
    1771: DL, Dec 21; 1776: DL, Dec 19
British March (music), 1798: CG, May 24
British Orphan, The. See Starke, Mariana.
British Roratory, The. See Smart, Christopher.
British Sailor, The. See Bernard, John.
British Salute (song), 1794: CG, May 9
British Soldier Triumphant (dance), 1788: HAY, Aug 13, 15, Sep 1, 12
British Tar's Triumph over M Soup-Maigre, The. See Yates, Richard.
British Volunteers (song), 1798: HAY, Aug 28, Sep 7
British Wives (song), 1771: GROTTO, Aug 30, Sep 3
Briton the Son of a Briton (song), 1763: CG, Apr 26
Briton, The. See Philips, Ambrose.
Britons never will be Slaves (song), 1745: DL, Oct 31, Nov 1
Britons Roused!; or, Citizen Soldiers (entertainment, anon), 1798: CG, May 16
Britons Strike Home (song), 1706: DL, Dec 19; 1707: DL, Apr 17; 1739: DL, Oct
    24, CG, 30, 31; 1741: CG, Apr 25, 30; 1744: CG, Mar 13, 15, 28, 29, 30, Apr
    2, DL, 9, CG, 12, 16, 17, DL, 23, CG, 30; 1745: DL, Dec 13; 1755: DL, Apr 2,
    3, CG, 9; 1756: CG, May 6; 1781: CG, May 1; 1791: CG, May 3, 16; 1792: CG,
    Apr 18; 1793: CG, Feb 15, KING/HAY, 15, CG, 20, 22, Mar 1, 6, 8, 13, 15, 20,
    22, Apr 24; 1794: CG, May 7; 1795: CG, Apr 24, May 31; 1797: CG, Apr 7, May
    31; 1798: CG, Feb 28, Mar 9; 1800: CG, Apr 23
Britons Strike Home; or, The Sailors' Rehearsal. See Phillips, Edward.
Britons, your country's gratitude behold (song), 1799: CG, Oct 7
Brittanicus. See Racine, Jean.
Britton, Mrs (actor), 1730: HAY, Jul 7, 17, TC, Aug 1; 1731: HAY, May 4
Brivio. See Brevio.
Brizzonie, Count Gaston di. See Torre di Rezzonico, Count Gaston della.
Broach, Mirza, Prince of (spectator), 1794: CG, Jun 4
Broad (boxkeeper), 1754: DL, May 20; 1755: DL, May 6; 1756: DL, May 10; 1757:
    DL, May 16; 1758: DL, May 15; 1760: DL, May 14; 1761: DL, May 14; 1762: DL,
    May 24; 1763: DL, May 18; 1764: DL, May 19; 1765: DL, May 18; 1766: DL, May
    20; 1768: DL, May 27; 1769: DL, May 20

Broad Court, 1747: DL, Mar 28; 1748: DL, Mar 15; 1749: DL, Mar 31, Apr 4; 1750:
    DL, Mar 27, 29; 1751: DL, Apr 18, 19; 1752: DL, Apr 11, 20; 1753: DL, Apr 14;
    1754: DL, Apr 18; 1755: DL, Apr 3, 19; 1757: DL, Apr 12; 1761: DL, Mar 30,
    Apr 1; 1768: CG, Oct 24; 1778: CG, Mar 30; 1779: CG, Mar 27, Apr 5, May 3;
    1780: CG, Mar 18, Apr 3; 1781: CG, Apr 2, 3, DL, May 16; 1782: CG, Apr 2;
    1783: CG, Apr 7; 1784: CG, Mar 29; 1785: CG, Mar 19, DL, Apr 25; 1786: DL,
    May 2, CG, 15, HAY, Jul 21; 1787: CG, May 11, HAY, Jul 31; 1788: CG, Apr 1,
    May 7, 14; 1789: CG, Apr 14, Jun 3, 9; 1790: CG, Apr 6; 1791: CG, May 2;
    1792: HAY, Oct 15; 1799: DL, Apr 25
Broad St, 1752: DL, Apr 20; 1785: DL, Apr 20; 1792: DLKING'S, Jun 7
Broad, Mrs (wardrobe keeper), 1760: CG, Sep 22
Broadhurst, Miss (singer), 1791: CG, Jan 15, Feb 10, DL, Mar 11, 23, Apr 1, 13,
    CG, 16, 30, May 12, 18, 27, Jun 3, 9, Sep 20, 23, 26, Oct 10, 20, Dec 26;
    1792: CG, Feb 28, Apr 12, 17, Sep 19, 20, 24, 28, Oct 3, 5, 8, 18, 19, 25,
    29, Nov 21, 24, 27, Dec 20, 31; 1793: CG, Jan 25, Feb 25, Apr 8, 9, 11, May
    4, 6, 21, Jun 8, 12
Broadway, 1790: DL, May 25
Brocke, Caspar Wilhelm von (commentator), 1733: LIF, Dec 29
Broderick (actor), 1771: HAY, Jan 28; 1776: HAY, Oct 7, CHR, 18
Broderip and Co (music publishers), 1799: CG, Jun 12
Broderip, Robert (composer), 1791: CG, May 18
Brodie (ironmonger), 1790: CG, Oct 4
Brogden (actor), 1730: BFOF, Aug 20
Brogden (beneficiary), 1757: DL, May 11
Broileau, two Mlles (actors), 1753: HAY, Mar 13
Broken Heart. See Ford, John.
Broken Heart, The (droll, anon), 1722: BFB, Aug 25
Broken Stock-Jobbers, The; or, Work for the Bailiffs (farce, anon), 1720: SOU,
    Oct 10
Brome, Sir Richard, 1662: VERE, Jul 7; 1677: DG, Feb 0; 1721: DL, Nov 17; 1770:
    DL, Oct 25
--Antipodes, 1661: VERE, Aug 26; 1662: VERE, Jul 7
--City Wit, The, 1661: LIF, Jul 6, 10
--Jovial Crew, The; or, The Merry Beggars, 1661: VERE, Jul 25, Aug 27, Nov 1;
    1662: VERE, Jan 21; 1669: BRIDGES, Jan 11; 1682: DL, Nov 16; 1683: DL, Dec 0;
    1685: NONE, Sep 0; 1689: ATCOURT, Nov 15; 1699: DL, Jun 29; 1702: DL, Aug 22;
    1704: DL, Mar 18, 20, Apr 17, Sep 11, Oct 2, Dec 28; 1705: DL, Dec 10; 1707:
    DL, Dec 30; 1708: DL/QUEEN, Jan 1, 2, 6, 20, Apr 7, DL, Oct 14; 1709: DL, Feb
    23; 1710: QUEEN'S, Jan 18, May 10; 1711: DL, Jan 19; 1712: DL, Jun 17; 1713:
    DL, Jun 19; 1714: DL, Oct 6, 8, 29; 1715: DL, Feb 17, Jun 6, Nov 4; 1716: DL,
    Apr 2, Oct 22; 1717: DL, Feb 4, Oct 30; 1718: DL, May 7, Nov 12; 1719: DL,
    Nov 6; 1720: DL, Aug 4, Dec 5; 1721: DL, Oct 16; 1722: DL, May 28; 1723: DL,
    Feb 5; 1724: DL, Feb 17; 1731: DL, Feb 8, 9, 10, 11, 12, 13, 15, 16, 18, Apr
    5, 28, 30, May 13, 19, Jul 20, 30, Sep 25, Nov 9, 16, 18, 22, Dec 16, 30;
    1732: DL, Mar 16; 1744: DL, Apr 9, 23; 1746: DL, Apr 15, 18; 1760: CG, Feb
    14, 15, 16, 18, 19, 23, Mar 1, 3, 4, 6, 8, 10, 11, 13, 29, Apr 7, 11, 16, 25,
    26, May 13, 28, Sep 22, Oct 2, 16, 24, Nov 17, Dec 8, 12, 26, 27; 1761: CG,
    Jan 5, 12, 19, 22, 26, Feb 23, Mar 14, 23, Apr 14, 23, 30, May 25, Sep 16,
    29, Oct 16, 29; 1762: CG, Jan 25, Feb 4, Mar 29, Apr 16, May 17, Sep 29, Oct
    22, Nov 23; 1763: CG, Jan 13, Apr 11, 30, May 16, Oct 11, Nov 17, Dec 21;
    1764: CG, Apr 3, 26, May 19, Oct 26; 1765: CG, Apr 10, 30, Nov 20; 1766: CG,
    Apr 11, May 9; 1767: CG, Jan 29, Mar 3, May 2; 1769: CG, May 10; 1770: DL,
    May 7, CG, 9, 25, DL, Oct 25, CG, Dec 13; 1771: CG, Jan 1, Feb 21, Mar 11,
    May 23; 1774: CG, Nov 1, 2, 4, Dec 28; 1775: CG, Feb 18, DL, Mar 23; 1776:
    CG, Oct 25, 28; 1777: CG, Jan 11, Feb 8, 13, 17, 27, Mar 3, 10, 13; 1780: CG,
    Mar 29, Apr 4, 6, 8, 11, 13, Dec 16; 1781: CG, Feb 10, 24, Oct 31, Nov 19,
    22, Dec 15; 1782: CG, Feb 12, 25; 1791: CG, Dec 15
--Northern Lass, The; or, The Nest of Fools, 1662: VERE, Apr 4; 1667: BRIDGES,
    Sep 14; 1669: BRIDGES, Jan 12; 1684: DL, Mar 0; 1699: NONE, Sep 0; 1704: DL,
    Nov 8, 9, 10, 13, 24, Dec 26; 1705: DL, Jan 12, Feb 3, 10, Jun 26, Oct 20,
    Nov 14, Dec 28; 1706: DL, Feb 4, 25, Mar 4, Apr 1, Jun 1, 22, QUEEN'S, Dec
    13; 1707: QUEEN'S, Jan 13, Feb 17, DL, Dec 2, 26; 1708: DL, Feb 26, Apr 14,
    Oct 22; 1709: DL, Feb 18; 1710: DL, Mar 25, Apr 18, DL/QUEEN, Nov 15; 1711:
    DL/QUEEN, Feb 13, DL, Dec 31; 1712: DL, Dec 15; 1713: DL, Feb 9, Dec 2; 1714:
    DL, Dec 8; 1716: DL, Apr 19, 23, May 25, Oct 31, Nov 28; 1717: DL, Jun 24,
    Nov 8; 1718: DL, May 22, Nov 19; 1719: DL, May 30, Oct 16; 1720: DL, Mar 29,
    Oct 7; 1721: DL, Feb 8, Nov 17; 1723: DL, Nov 22; 1730: DL, Nov 12; 1738: CG,
    Jan 18, 19
--Novella, The, 1669: BRIDGES, Jan 12
Bromfield (trunk maker), 1778: CG, May 19; 1779: CG, May 13
Bromfield, William (surgeon), 1752: CG, Nov 4; 1755: DL, Oct 13
Bromley, Master (musician), 1763: CG, Apr 11

Bromley, William (scene painter), 1799: CG, Dec 23
Brompton, 1781: DL, May 9; 1782: DL, May 1
Bromwich and Co (paper merchants), 1772: CG, Mar 3
Brone et Blonde (dance), 1733: BFMMO, Aug 23
Brook (beneficiary), 1723: LIF, May 28; 1743: LIF, Jun 3
Brook Green, 1798: CG, Apr 24
Brook St, 1743: CG, Feb 18, Mar 16; 1744: CG, Feb 10, KING'S, Oct 22, Nov 3;
   1745: KING'S, rket, 1701: MF, May 1; 1704: MFFB, May 1
Brook, J (printer), 1799: CG, Apr 16
Brook, Miss (actor), 1782: HAY, Jan 21
Brooke (prologuist), 1748: DL, Feb 13
Brooke, Edward (legal historian), 1792: HAY, Apr 16
Brooke, Frances, 1756: DL, May 4; 1770: HAY, Sep 3; 1781: CG, Jan 31; 1782: CG,
   Dec 31; 1788: CG, May 22, Nov 1
--Marian (farce), 1788: CG, May 22, 26, 29, Jun 5, 6, 9, Nov 1, 3, 14, 29, Dec
   4, 22; 1789: CG, Jan 15, 26, Feb 14, Mar 23, Apr 4, 18, May 9, 13, Jun 8, Nov
   21, Dec 10; 1790: CG, Apr 15, Jun 2; 1792: CG, Feb 25, Mar 1, 8, 20, 27, Apr
   24; 1793: CG, Nov 18, 21, 26; 1794: CG, Jan 24, Apr 7, Nov 5, 11, 15; 1795:
   CG, Nov 6, 11, Dec 12; 1798: CG, May 14; 1800: CG, May 17
--Rosina (opera), 1782: CG, Dec 31; 1783: CG, Jan 1, 4, 6, 9, 13, 15, 16, 17,
   29, 31, Feb 1, 4, 6, 8, 10, 19, 22, 26, 27, Mar 1, 4, 6, 8, 11, 13, 17, 18,
   20, 24, 25, 27, 29, Apr 3, 7, 10, 24, 29, May 8, Jun 6, Oct 3, 8, 13, 17, 23,
   27, Dec 1, 15; 1784: CG, Jan 27, Feb 11, 12, 18, 28, Mar 4, 13, 18, 22, 27,
   30, Apr 14, 21, May 1, 10, 25, 29, HAY, Aug 17, CG, Oct 28, Nov 11, 15, 22,
   26, Dec 9, 16, 21; 1785: CG, Feb 1, 5, 15, 24, Mar 8, DL, 28, CG, 30, DL, Apr
   6, 11, 18, 22, May 19, CG, 23, HAMM, Jun 24, Jul 11, HAY, Aug 2, 5, 9, Sep
   12, CG, 21, Oct 12, Nov 8, Dec 1; 1786: CG, Mar 2, 30, May 2, 12, HAMM, Jun
   9, HAY, Aug 10, CG, Nov 15, 29, Dec 14, 15; 1787: CG, Mar 10, 26, Apr 19, 30,
   May 8, Jun 7, Dec 21; 1788: CG, Jan 17, 28, Apr 25, 29, May 6, 20, 22, Oct
   13, Nov 1, 4, 19; 1789: CG, Jan 20, 27, Mar 17, Apr 2, DL, 21, CG, 22, DL,
   May 5, CG, 21, Nov 10, Dec 1; 1790: CG, Mar 27, Apr 19, May 24, Jun 11, Oct
   30; 1791: CG, May 12, 27; 1792: CG, Feb 28, Mar 3, 15, 24, 29, Apr 13, May 8,
   25, Jun 1, Dec 13, 15; 1793: CG, Apr 8, May 2, HAY, Aug 16, 17, 22, CG, Nov
   7; 1794: CG, Feb 1, HAY, 11, 13, 14, 18, 21, 26, Mar 4, 10, 18, 25, 29, Apr
   5, 8, CG, Jun 3, HAY, Jul 14, Aug 6, 16, CG, Sep 24, Oct 31; 1795: CG, Mar
   19, Jun 1, Sep 28, Nov 7; 1796: DL, May 27, CG, 28, HAY, Jul 2, 7, CG, Oct 5,
   Nov 3, 12; 1797: DL, May 23, HAY, Jul 15, Aug 16, 17, Sep 12; 1798: CG, May
   2, Jun 7, HAY, Aug 24, 29; 1799: CG, Jan 5, 8, 11, 12, 23, HAY, Jun 28, Jul
   1, CG, Sep 16; 1800: CG, Feb 8, DL, Jun 7, 12, HAY, Aug 23
--Siege of Sinope, The, 1781: CG, Jan 31, Feb 1, 2, 3, 5, 7, 9, 12, 16, 19
Brooke, Henry, 1739: DL, Mar 17; 1759: HAY, Sep 17; 1761: DL, Jan 3, 7, Dec 30;
   1763: DL, Nov 30; 1764: DL, Oct 24; 1768: DL, Dec 28; 1769: DL, Nov 21; 1788:
   HAY, Dec 22; 1789: KHS, Sep 16, WHF, Nov 9, 11
--Earl of Essex, The, 1761: DL, Jan 3, 5, 7, 14, 17, 21, 26, Feb 7, 21, 24, Dec
   30; 1763: DL, Apr 20, Oct 17, Nov 30; 1764: DL, Oct 24, Dec 26; 1767: DL, Oct
   26, Dec 28; 1768: DL, Apr 18, Dec 28; 1769: DL, Nov 21; 1770: HAY, Sep 3;
   1773: DL, Apr 27
--Galligantus, 1758: HAY, Dec 26, 28; 1759: HAY, Sep 17, 18, 20, 21, 25, 26,
   Oct 1, 3, 5, 10; 1760: DL, Apr 14
--Gustavus Vasa, 1739: DL, Mar 17
--Jack the Giant Queller, 1759: HAY, Sep 17
Brooke, John (actor), 1663: VERE, Mar 0
Brooke, Miss (actor), 1789: KHS, Sep 16, WHF, Nov 9, 11
Brooker, Miss (payee), 1773: DL, Dec 11
Brooker, Rebecca (actor, dancer), 1790: DL, Oct 26; 1791: DLKING'S, Nov 5;
   1792: DLKING'S, Mar 19, DL, Nov 21, Dec 23; 1794: DL, May 16, 30, Dec 20, 23;
   1795: DL, Feb 12, May 6, Oct 30; 1796: DL, Jan 18, Oct 1, 29, Nov 9, Dec 26;
   1798: DL, Jan 16, Feb 20, May 16, Oct 6, Nov 14, Dec 6; 1799: DL, Jan 19, Feb
   5, Jul 1, Oct 14, Dec 2; 1800: DL, Mar 11
Brookfield, 1707: BH, Mar 26; 1744: MF, May 4
Brookman (actor), 1763: HAY, Jun 9
Brooks (animal keeper), 1773: CG, Oct 28
Brooks and Mason (handbill publishers), 1749: DL, Nov 4
Brooks, J (engraver), 1750: DL, Sep 18
Brooks, James (house servant), 1742: DL, May 25; 1744: DL, May 22; 1745: DL,
   May 9; 1746: DL, May 19; 1747: DL, May 15; 1750: DL, Mar 3
Brooks Jr, Master (actor, dancer), 1737: DL, Oct 27, Nov 19; 1738: BFH, Aug 23,
   DL, Sep 23, Dec 4, 15; 1739: DL, May 30, Sep 26; 1741: DL, Oct 31
Brooks Sr, Master (actor), 1737: DL, Nov 19; 1738: DL, Dec 4
Brooks, Mrs (actor), 1786: HAY, Jul 19; 1787: HAY, May 16, DL, 30, HAY, Jul 20,
   21; 1788: HAY, Jun 18, 21, Jul 2, 3, 23, Aug 2, 18, 27; 1789: HAY, May 20,
   25, Jun 8, 15, 24, Jul 15, 30, Aug 5; 1790: HAY, Jun 14, 18, 26, Jul 7, Aug

7, 11, 13, 16, 25; <u>1791</u>: HAY, Jun 8, 13, 16, Jul 7, 9, Aug 9, 15, 31; <u>1792</u>:
HAY, Jun 15, 22, Jul 4, 16, Sep 6; <u>1793</u>: HAY, Jun 15, 21, Jul 19, Aug 7;
<u>1794</u>: HAY, Jul 10, 12, 14, 16
Brooks, Mrs (actor), <u>1798</u>: WRSG, Jun 8
Brooks, Mrs (charwoman), <u>1760</u>: CG, Sep 22; <u>1761</u>: CG, Apr 11
Brooks, Mrs (proprietor), <u>1775</u>: KING'S, Oct 31
Brooks's Club, <u>1789</u>: KING'S, Apr 21
Brooksbank, Miss (actor), <u>1785</u>: HAY, Jan 31
Brooksry, Mrs (milliner), <u>1755</u>: DL, Dec 16
Brookwell (musician), <u>1675</u>: ATCOURT, Feb 15
Broome, Cornet, <u>1767</u>: DL, Oct 27
Broomstick Solo (music), <u>1757</u>: CG, May 6
Broomstickado, Mynheer Von Poop Poop (actor), <u>1752</u>: CT, Feb 13; <u>1757</u>: HAY, Jun
28, Aug 31, Sep 2, 14, Oct 3; <u>1758</u>: HAY, May 18; <u>1760</u>: HAY, Feb 14, Sep 8
Brooth, Mrs (actor), <u>1740</u>: BFLP, Aug 23, SF, Sep 9
Broschi, Carlo (singer), <u>1734</u>: KING'S, Oct 29; <u>1735</u>: KING'S, Apr 8, Nov 25;
<u>1736</u>: KING'S, Jan 24, Nov 23; <u>1737</u>: KING'S, Jan 8, Feb 12, Apr 12, May 24;
see also Farinelli
Broschi, Riccardo (composer), <u>1734</u>: KING'S, Oct 29; <u>1737</u>: KING'S, Jan 8
Brothers, The. See Shirley, James; Young, Edward; Cumberland, Richard.
Brough (householder), <u>1791</u>: HAY, Mar 7
Broughton, Thomas (author), <u>1745</u>: KING'S, Jan 5
Broughton's Amphitheatre, <u>1745</u>: BRA, Jun 24
Brouncker (Bruncker), Lord Henry (spectator), <u>1666</u>: ATCOURT, Oct 18; <u>1667</u>:
BRIDGES, Jan 15, NONE, Feb 12, 16, LIF, Aug 20, BRIDGES, 22, Oct 29; <u>1668</u>:
LIF, Apr 3, 8, BRIDGES, 17, LIF, 29, BF, Sep 7, BRIDGES, 19
Brown (actor), <u>1724</u>: HAY, Feb 5, 20, SOU, Sep 24
Brown (actor), <u>1758</u>: HAY, Jan 12; <u>1763</u>: HAY, Sep 5; <u>1764</u>: HAY, Jun 13, 26, Jul
6, 13, 23, Aug 20, Sep 1
Brown (actor), <u>1770</u>: HAY, Nov 16; <u>1776</u>: HAY, Sep 23, CHR, Oct 7; <u>1779</u>: HAY, Mar
15, Dec 27; <u>1780</u>: HAY, Jan 3, Sep 25, Nov 13; <u>1781</u>: HAY, Mar 26, CII, Apr 9;
<u>1782</u>: HAY, Nov 25; <u>1783</u>: HAY, Dec 15; <u>1784</u>: HAY, Feb 9, Mar 8; <u>1785</u>: HAY, Apr
25, 26
Brown (actor), <u>1773</u>: CG, Nov 27; <u>1774</u>: CG, Apr 18, May 25
Brown (actor), <u>1798</u>: WRSG, Jun 8; <u>1799</u>: WRSG, May 17
Brown (actor, dancer, singer), <u>1748</u>: BFSY, Aug 24, SFP, Sep 7; <u>1749</u>: NWC, Nov
27; <u>1750</u>: HAY, Feb 16, SFP, Sep 7; <u>1751</u>: SF, Sep 9, 18
Brown (actor, singer), <u>1768</u>: CHAPEL, May 25, MARLY, Jul 28, Aug 4; <u>1769</u>: DL,
Mar 16, KING'S, Apr 5, MARLY, Aug 10, 17; <u>1770</u>: HAY, Mar 12, DL, 27, Jun 7;
<u>1771</u>: DL, Oct 15, Dec 4, 20; <u>1772</u>: DL, Apr 24, May 2, 18, 28, Oct 15; <u>1773</u>:
MARLY, Sep 3; <u>1776</u>: DL, Nov 25, Dec 10; <u>1777</u>: DL, Jan 1; <u>1788</u>: CG, Jan 5, 7,
15, 18, 21, Feb 23, Mar 1, 11, 15, 24, 28, Apr 8, 14, May 16; <u>1789</u>: CG, Jun
5; <u>1791</u>: HAY, Jul 30, Aug 31, DLKING'S, Oct 15; <u>1792</u>: DLKING'S, May 23, HAY,
Jun 23, Jul 25, DL, Oct 11, 18, Nov 21; <u>1793</u>: DL, Mar 7, 9, HAY, Jun 17, Aug
3, 12, 15, Oct 10, Nov 19; <u>1794</u>: HAY, Feb 24, CG, May 9, DL, 16, HAY, Jul 17,
18, 21, 24, Aug 27, DL, Oct 27, 31, Nov 15, Dec 20; <u>1795</u>: DL, Feb 9, HAY, Jun
13, 20, Jul 31, DL, Oct 30, Nov 11, Dec 10; <u>1796</u>: DL, Jan 8, 11, Mar 3, 12,
Apr 30, HAY, Jul 15, Aug 29; <u>1797</u>: HAY, Jun 23, Aug 14, 15, DL, Nov 8, Dec 9;
<u>1798</u>: DL, Jan 16, Feb 20, 24, HAY, Jun 30, Jul 21, Aug 11, DL, Oct 6, Nov 14,
26, Dec 4, 29; <u>1799</u>: DL, Jan 19, Feb 4, Mar 2, Apr 16, 23, 29, May 4, 24,
HAY, Jul 9, 13, 16, Aug 21, Sep 2
Brown (coal merchant), <u>1773</u>: CG, Nov 1
Brown (composer, musician) <u>1752</u>: JS, Mar 5; <u>1758</u>: SOHO, Apr 1, CHAPEL, Apr 27;
<u>1768</u>: KING'S, Feb 5
Brown (house servant), <u>1719</u>: LIF, Jun 3; <u>1720</u>: LIF, May 23
Brown (house servant), <u>1752</u>: CG, May 7; <u>1753</u>: CG, May 21
Brown (householder), <u>1746</u>: HIC, Mar 10
Brown Bear Tavern, <u>1745</u>: GF, Mar 18
Brown Beer of England (song), <u>1757</u>: HAY, Oct 3
Brown Jug (song), <u>1794</u>: CG, Jun 3
Brown, Abraham (violinist), <u>1740</u>: HIC, Mar 3; <u>1744</u>: SH, Feb 9; <u>1745</u>: CT, Jan
14, DT, Mar 14; <u>1746</u>: HIC, Mar 10
Brown, Ann (actor, singer), <u>1769</u>: CG, May 19, 25; <u>1771</u>: CG, Dec 23; <u>1772</u>: DL,
Oct 19, CG, 29, Nov 21; <u>1773</u>: CG, Feb 23, Apr 16, May 6, Oct 6, 20, 21, 23,
Nov 26, Dec 13, 16; <u>1774</u>: CG, Jan 3, 5, Feb 11, 17, Mar 12, Apr 13, 22, Sep
23, Oct 3, 7, 13, 14, 19, 20, 27, 29, Nov 1, 5, 19, Dec 23, 27; <u>1775</u>: DL, Mar
10, CG, 28, 30, Apr 4, May 2, 4, 5, 15, 26, Jun 1, Sep 20, 22, 25, 27, Oct
13, 17, 19, 31, Nov 9, 21, 24, Dec 16; <u>1776</u>: CG, Jan 3, Sep 25, 30, Oct 25,
Nov 9, 14, 26, Dec 2, 4, 27; <u>1777</u>: CG, Jan 3, 7, 13, 31, Feb 10, 25, Mar 31,
Apr 29, May 5, 9, Sep 22, 26, 29, Oct 3, 15, 17, 29, 30, Nov 3, 18; <u>1778</u>: CG,
Jan 29, Feb 4, 26, 28, Mar 23, Apr 25, May 6, Sep 18, 28, DL, 29, CG, Oct 2,
17, 23, 26, 27, Nov 23, Dec 19, DL, 23; <u>1779</u>: CG, Jan 4, 11, Feb 22, 23, Mar

20, 22, 27, Apr 10, May 6, 13, Sep 22, 24, Oct 1, 6, 8, 16, 18, 20, DL, 21, CG, Nov 12, 30, Dec 17, 18, 29; 1780: CG, Jan 7, 10, 11, Feb 1, 5, 8, 17, Mar 29, Apr 3, HAY, 5, CG, 7, 10, DL, Sep 21
Brown, Anthony
--Fatal Retirement, The, 1739: DL, Nov 12, 17
Brown, Henry (actor), 1753: DL, Feb 23
Brown, J (actor, singer), 1786: CG, Jan 31, Feb 1, 3, 16, Mar 16, May 9, 11, 30, Sep 18, 20, 25, Oct 6, 19, 21, 23, Nov 13, 15, 18, 22, 25, Dec 5, 12, 15, 26; 1787: CG, Jan 27, DL, Feb 17, CG, Mar 1, Apr 10, 11, 16, 17, 24, 27, May 15, 21, Sep 19, 24, 26, Oct 1, 12, 17, 18, 22, Nov 30, Dec 10, 17, 21, 26; 1789: CG, Jun 5
Brown, J and Mrs (actors), 1787: CG, May 18; 1788: CG, May 16
Brown, John (singer, actor) 1732: CR, Feb 23; 1733: HAY, Mar 20, 21, 26, MEG, Sep 28; 1736: BFHC, Aug 23
Brown, Dr John, 1754: DL, Dec 17; 1756: DL, Feb 27; 1763: CG, Mar 4, DL, Apr 27; 1767: KING'S, Jan 23; 1787: RLSN, Mar 28
--Athelstan, 1756: DL, Feb 27, 28, Mar 1, 4, 6, 9, 11, 15, 18
--Barbarossa; or, The Freedom of Algiers, 1754: DL, Dec 17, 18, 19, 20, 21, 23, 30, 31; 1755: DL, Jan 1, 2, 3, Feb 1, 4, 11, 15, May 27, Dec 23, 31; 1756: DL, Feb 27, Mar 9; 1758: DL, Apr 7; 1761: DL, Nov 21, 23; 1762: DL, Jan 13, Mar 8, Dec 6; 1763: DL, Jan 3, Nov 14; 1770: CG, Nov 1, 3, 6, 10, 13, 17, 24, Dec 1, 18; 1771: CG, Feb 7, Apr 4, 20, May 14, Oct 11, Nov 20, Dec 5; 1772: CG, Jan 23, Feb 29, May 30; 1776: CHR, Sep 27, Oct 9; 1779: CG, Feb 2, 8, 11; 1784: HAY, Sep 17, CG, Dec 13, 23; 1785: HAY, Apr 26; 1786: CG, Jan 4; 1787: RLSN, Mar 28; 1790: DL, May 18; 1798: CG, Jan 4
Brown, Miss (actor), 1759: HAY, Nov 10 ; 1767: SW, May 13
Brown, Miss (actor), 1778: CHR, Jun 3
Brown, Miss (actor), 1782: DL, Oct 26; 1791: HAY, Mar 7
Brown, Miss E (actor), 1798: DL, Nov 10
Brown, Mrs (actor), 1662: ATCOURT, Nov 1
Brown, Mrs (actor), 1707: DL/QUEEN, Nov 1
Brown, Mrs (actor), 1736: BFHC, Aug 23; 1746: GF, Dec 29; 1749: BFY, Aug 23; 1751: SF, Sep 9; 1764: HAY, Jul 16, 23, 30, Aug 20
Brown, Mrs (actor), 1790: HAY, Jun 16
Brown, Mrs (actor), 1798: HAY, Aug 28
Brown, Mrs (house servant), 1767: DL, Jan 17
Brown, Mrs (milliner), 1753: DL, Dec 11; 1756: HAY, Apr 1
Brown, Mrs (singer), 1797: HAY, Aug 15, 16
Brown, Mrs J (actor), 1786: CG, Jan 28, 31, Feb 3, 7, 13, 16, Mar 4, 14, 16, Apr 20, 21, Sep 20, 25, 29, Oct 6, 16, 19, 21, Nov 14, 15, 18, 22, 24, Dec 1, 6, 15; 1787: CG, Jan 26, 27, Mar 1, 12, 15, Apr 16, 26, May 18, 22, 23, HAY, Jun 20, 21, 22, Jul 3, 23, 25, Aug 28, 31, CG, Sep 26, Oct 1, 12, 18, 29; 1788: CG, Jan 2, 11, 15, Mar 1, 15, Apr 1, May 16
Brown, Sir Richard (Lord Mayor), 1660: CITY, Oct 29
Brown, Thomas (author), 1696: NONE, Sep 0
--Physick Lies a Bleeding; or, The Apothecary Turned Doctor, 1696: NONE, Sep 0
Brown, Thomas (beneficiary), 1744: HAY, Apr 26
Brown, Thomas (critic), 1699: BF, Aug 30, DLLIF, Sep 12
Brown, William (pickpocket), 1743: CG, May 6
Browne, (stationer), 1756: HAY, Mar 25
Browne, Sir Edward (spectator), 1662: VERE, Jan 1, REDBULL, May 26, VERE, Jun 2, NONE, Sep 0; 1666: NONE, Sep 0
Browne, Matthew Campbell (actor), 1787: HAY, May 18, 25, Jun 11, 13, 23, Jul 7, 19, 21, 25
Browne, Mrs (actor), 1736: LIF, Mar 24, CG, 27
Browne, Thomas (violinist), 1675: ATCOURT, Feb 15
Browning, Miss (dancer, singer), 1785: CG, Sep 23, Oct 17
Brownlow St, 1731: DL, Feb 10; 1733: DL, May 14; 1735: CG/LIF, Apr 24; 1736: CG, May 4; 1737: CG, Mar 26; 1738: DL, Mar 25; 1739: DL, Mar 17, CG, Apr 7, Dec 15; 1740: CG, Apr 14, 30; 1742: CG, Apr 30; 1746: DL, Apr 25; 1747: CG, May 7; 1748: CG, Mar 18; 1750: KING'S, Mar 13; 1751: CG, Apr 19, DL, 29; 1752: DL, Apr 14; 1754: DL, May 2; 1755: CG, Jan 8, Dec 16; 1756: DL, Apr 29, CG, Dec 15; 1758: DL, Apr 5; 1759: KING'S, May 2; 1764: DL, Dec 12; 1765: CG, Dec 17; 1768: KING'S, May 12, DL, Dec 16; 1771: DL, Dec 21; 1776: DL, Dec 19; 1777: DL, Apr 21, CG, May 14; 1780: CG, May 12
Brownsmith, John (actor, prompter, author), 1757: DL, Dec 22; 1758: DL, May 9, 17; 1759: DL, Jan 2, Feb 26, May 15, 21, 30; 1767: HAY, Jun 30, Jul 6, 22, Aug 10, Sep 18, DL, Nov 7; 1768: HAY, Jul 13, Sep 19; 1770: HAY, May 18, Sep 27, Oct 5, 29; 1778: HAY, Sep 8, 18; 1779: HAY, Aug 28, Oct 18
--Touchstone of Invention, The; or, The Soldier's Fortune, 1779: HAY, Oct 18
Browse (house servant), 1754: CG, May 18; 1755: CG, May 20; 1756: CG, May 24
Bruce, Mrs (dancer), 1705: LIF/QUEN, Sep 28, Oct 11, LIF, 12, LIF/QUEN, 17;

1706: QUEEN'S, Jan 2, 7, 9, 14, 22, 23, Apr 25, May 29, Jun 29
Bruce, Thomas, Earl of Ailesbury (spectator), 1691: DL, Jan 0
Brudenell, James, 5th Earl of Cardigan, 1797: KING'S, May 18
Brueys, David Augustin de
--Avocat Patelin, L', 1721: HAY, Dec 15; 1787: HAY, Aug 28
Brugier, Miss (dancer), 1799: CG, Apr 23, May 14
Bruman, Miss (actor), 1794: CG, Mar 7
Brumpton, 1750: DL, Jan 10
Brunette, Miss (actor), 1734: LIF, Oct 12, CG/LIF, Dec 30; 1735: LIF, Mar 3,
    CG/LIF, May 9, 27, GF/HAY, Jul 15, 18, Aug 1, HAY, 12, GF/HAY, 14, LIF, 25,
    HAY, 26, LIF, Sep 2, 5, CG, Oct 17, 20, Nov 6; 1736: CG, Jan 1, 23, LIF, Mar
    31, CG, May 8, 17, 20, Sep 24, Oct 8; 1737: CG, Jan 25, Feb 14, Apr 28, LIF,
    Jul 26, Aug 2, 5; 1738: CG, Jan 25, Feb 13, Apr 20, 22, Sep 20, 22, Oct 2,
    28, Nov 11, 13, 21; 1739: CG, Jan 1, May 1, 7, 17, 18, 25, 28, 29, Aug 21,
    Sep 5, 7, 10, 14, 21, 22, 25, Oct 1, 2, 4, Nov 10, 20, Dec 17; 1740: CG, Feb
    2, Mar 25, Apr 9, 14, 16, May 3, 7, 16, 21, Jun 5, Sep 19, 22, Oct 1, 8, 27,
    Nov 3; 1741: DL, May 28, Sep 8, 15, 17, Oct 23; 1742: DL, Mar 8, May 10, 12,
    22, Sep 11, LIF, Nov 24, 29, Dec 1, 6
Bruni, Domenico (singer), 1793: KING'S, Feb 5, Mar 12, 19, Jun 11
Brunoro (dancer), 1742: DL, Oct 9, 25, Nov 12, 13
Brunsdon, John (actor), 1774: HAY, Jan 24; 1778: CG, Sep 25, 28, Oct 14, Nov 4,
    21, Dec 1, 21; 1779: CG, Jan 22, 25, Feb 22, Apr 12, 15, 23, May 6, 21, Sep
    20, 27, Oct 6, 18, 20, 29, Nov 13, 19, 23, 25, 30; 1780: CG, Jan 18, Feb 2,
    26, Mar 14, 18, Apr 21, 25, 27, May 12, 17
Brunswick, Duke of, 1719: YB, Dec 19
Brunswick, Prince and Princess of, 1764: CG, Jan 19; 1767: CG, Apr 23, May 15;
    see also Prince; Princess
Brunswick, Prince of, 1764: DL, Jan 16, 20, 23; 1767: DL, May 28, RANELAGH, Jun
    1
Brunswick, Princess of, 1766: CG, Oct 23, Nov 20, Dec 18; 1767: CG, Jan 15, 29,
    Feb 19, DL, May 7; see also Princesses
Brunswick, Princess Caroline of, 1795: CG, Jun 6, Feb 27, Apr 6; see also
    Princesses
Brunton, Anne (actor), 1785: CG, Oct 17, 28, Nov 14, Dec 1; 1786: CG, Jan 31,
    Feb 23, Mar 6, 14, Apr 4, 8, 19, 26, Sep 27, Oct 2, 6, 21, 23, 26, 30, Nov
    27, Dec 4, 20; 1787: CG, Apr 11, 14, 17, May 21, Sep 24, 28, Oct 22, Nov 9,
    Dec 3, 15, 27; 1788: CG, Jan 14, Feb 4, Mar 10, 28, Apr 8, 11, 23, Sep 22,
    Oct 3, 27, Nov 1, 28, Dec 26, 29; 1789: CG, Feb 3, Apr 14, 20, 28, 30, May
    15, 19, 22, Jun 8, Sep 18, 25, Oct 6, 7, 23, Nov 23, 27, 30, Dec 7, 14, 21,
    26, 28, 31; 1790: CG, Jan 22, Feb 11, Mar 18, 22, May 5, 24, 31, Sep 13, 17,
    Oct 11, 18, Nov 1, 3, 27, 30, Dec 10, 20; 1791: CG, Jan 7, 12, Feb 4, Apr 5,
    11, 30, May 11, 14, Sep 12
Brunton, Elizabeth (actor), 1790: CG, May 5
Brunton, John (actor), 1774: CG, Apr 11, May 3; 1780: HAY, Jul 1; 1785: CG, Oct
    28, Dec 29; 1786: CG, Feb 23; 1789: CG, Jan 29
Bruodin (actor), 1749: BF/SFP, Aug 23, Sep 7, HAY, Oct 17
Brush, The (entertainment), 1790: DL, Apr 20, CG, 30
Brussels Court, 1729: HIC, May 21
Brussels Opera, 1711: GR, Sep 13; 1727: KING'S, Mar 23
Brussels Theatre, 1783: DL, Dec 4
Brussels, 1711: QUEEN'S, Mar 20
Bruton St, 1758: CG, Jan 12; 1790: DL, May 26
Brutus (play, anon), 1732: DL, Nov 17
Brutus of Alba; or, Augusta's Triumph. See Powell, George.
Brutus of Alba; or, The Enchanted Lovers. See Tate, Nahum.
Bryan (beneficiary), 1726: HAY, Mar 2
Bryan (composer), 1757: HAY, Oct 17; 1758: HAY, Jan 6, 25
Bryan (prompter), 1767: CG, May 11, 14; 1768: CG, Jan 9, May 2; 1773: CG, Feb
    18
Bryan, Michael (author), 1773: DL, Nov 8
Bryan, Mrs (beneficiary), 1724: HAY, Mar 9
Bryars, Mrs (boxkeeper), 1723: HAY, Apr 22
Brydges, Frank (actor), 1698: DLORLIF, Jul 13; 1699: DLLIF, Apr 22
Brydges, Henry (spectator), 1700: LIF, Mar 11
Brydges, James (author), 1697: DLDGLIF, Jan 22; 1698: DLORLIF, Feb 15; 1699:
    LIF, Dec 13; 1700: LIF, Mar 5; see also Chandos, Duke of
Bubb, Mrs (beneficiary), 1723: LIF, May 31
Buchanan (actor), 1724: HAY, Feb 20, SOU, Sep 24
Buchanan, Elizabeth, Mrs Charles (actor), 1727: LIF, Oct 21; 1728: HAY, Aug 9,
    BFHM, 24, LIF, Nov 20, Dec 7, 19, 31; 1729: LIF, Jan 13, 28, 31, Feb 3, 7,
    10, Mar 4, Apr 10, 28, Sep 12, 17, 26, Oct 3, Nov 8, 13, 22, 25; 1730: LIF,
    Apr 6, May 6, Sep 16, 21, Oct 14, 27, Nov 2, 23; 1731: LIF, Jan 13, Feb 3,

27, Mar 22, Apr 3, 23, May 10, 12, Sep 20, Oct 1, 6, Nov 2, 8, Dec 15, 29;
    1732: LIF, Jan 24, 28, Apr 21, 24, 29, May 15, 22, LIF/CG, Sep 25, Oct 9, 16,
    LIF, 18, LIF/CG, 21, 27, 30, Nov 1, 18, Dec 7; 1733: LIF/CG, Jan 1, 15, Feb
    5, 10, Mar 31, Apr 17, CG, May 1, 2, LIF/CG, 10, 21, 24, CG, Sep 15, 20, 22,
    Oct 2, 6, 11, 23, 25, DL/HAY, 27, CG, 27, 31, Nov 1, 9, 14, 21, 28, Dec 15,
    20, 31; 1734: CG, Jan 9, 18, Feb 14, Mar 5, 18, 28, Apr 16, 22, May 22,
    CG/LIF, Oct 14, 16, 18, 19, Nov 25, 28, Dec 6, 26; 1735: CG/LIF, Jan 21, Feb
    15, Mar 15, Apr 9, 10, 18, LIF, 19, CG, 25, CG/LIF, May 2, CG, 6, CG/LIF, 15,
    27, Jun 17, CG, Sep 17, 24, 29, Oct 3, 8, 17, 20, 22, Nov 1, 4, 10, 15, 22,
    29, Dec 8, 31; 1736: CG, Jan 8, 10, Feb 26, Mar 15, 18, 22, 27, 29, Apr 6,
    15, May 3, 17, Jun 14, Sep 15, 17, 20, 22, 24, 29, Oct 1, 13, 20, 22, Nov 1,
    29; 1737: CG, Jan 21
Bucheron, Le. See Guichard, Jean Francois.
Bucherons (dance), 1752: DL, Oct 17, 18, 21
Buchinger (musician), 1735: GF, Sep 29, Oct 10
Buchinger, Miss (dancer), 1761: HAY, Jun 23; 1763: HAY, Jul 20
Buck (mercer) 1767: DL, Feb 6
Buck, Lady Dorothy (speaks prologue), 1689: CHELSEA, Dec 0
Buck, Mrs (dresser), 1759: CG, Dec 8; 1760: CG, Sep 22
Buck, Timothy (actor, swordsman), 1715: LIF, Aug 31; 1717: LIF, Jun 12; 1722:
    LIF, Mar 15, May 16; 1724: SOU, Sep 24
Buck, William (actor), 1755: CG, Dec 3; 1756: CG, May 17, 21, Nov 22, Dec 10;
    1757: CG, Feb 19, May 6, 12, 19, 25, Oct 10, 19, Nov 5; 1758: CG, Apr 14, May
    8, Sep 25, Nov 13, 16, 21; 1759: CG, Feb 1, May 18, Sep 26, Nov 28, Dec 8,
    10, 31; 1760: CG, Feb 9, 11, 26, Apr 23, May 2, 14, Sep 22, Oct 17, Nov 18,
    Dec 5, 9; 1761: CG, Jan 28, Mar 30, May 5, Sep 14, Oct 13, Nov 13, Dec 11;
    1762: CG, Jan 2, 5, 7, Feb 22, Mar 9, 29, Apr 24, 28, May 12, 14, Sep 24, Oct
    2, 16, 21, 25, Nov 3, 26, Dec 4; 1763: CG, Feb 1, 14, Apr 27, May 11, 16, Sep
    23, 26, 28, Oct 7, 10, Nov 24, Dec 9, 26; 1764: CG, Jan 17, Feb 1, 15,
    Mar 8, May 21, Sep 21, Oct 5, 8, 11, 16, 17, 20, Nov 1, 3, 15, Dec 12, 21;
    1765: CG, Jan 8, 21, May 2, 10, 11, 20, Sep 23, Oct 8, 10, 14, 15, 17, 26,
    29, 30, Nov 18, 22, Dec 6, 9; 1766: CG, Apr 25, May 5, 6, Sep 22, 26, Oct 6,
    22, 25, 31, Nov 8, 18, 25, Dec 11, 13, 23; 1767: CG, Jan 1, 26, 28, 31, Feb
    28, Mar 21, Apr 24, 25, May 14
Buck's Lodge, The (interlude, anon), 1790: DL, May 14
Buckhurst, Lord. See Sackville, Charles.
Buckinger, Joseph (viola player), 1798: HAY, Jan 15
Buckingham Court, 1751: DL, Dec 18
Buckingham St, 1757: CG, Apr 15; 1779: DL, Mar 22; 1781: CG, Mar 31; 1782: CG,
    Mar 19; 1784: CG, Mar 23; 1785: CG, Mar 8; 1786: CG, Feb 25; 1797: CG, Jun 10
Buckingham, Duchess of. See Villiers, Mary.
Buckingham, Duke of. See Villiers, George.
Buckinghamshire, Countess of, 1792: DLKING'S, Apr 16
Buckle St, 1745: GF, Feb 26
Buckle thy Shoes at the Toes (song), 1735: GF, Oct 10
Buckley (actor, doorkeeper), 1742: DL, May 15, LIF, Dec 3, 6
Buckley. See Bulkley.
Bucknall (beneficiary), 1746: GF, Mar 18; 1747: GF, Mar 31
Bucks have at ye all; or, A Picture of a Playhouse (entertainment), 1760: DL,
    Mar 29; 1761: DL, Apr 1; 1762: DL, Mar 30, Apr 21; 1763: DL, Apr 5, HAY, Sep
    7; 1765: DL, Mar 30, Apr 20, May 7; 1766: DL, Apr 25, 29; 1767: DL, May 26,
    Jun 1; 1768: DL, Apr 18, 30, May 3, 30; 1769: DL, Apr 7, 15, 19; 1770: DL,
    Apr 3, 21, 27, May 4, 9, 17, 21, 28, 30, Jun 4, HAY, Sep 27; 1771: HAY, Jan
    28, Apr 1, DL, May 22, 28, HAY, Sep 20; 1772: DL, May 4, 25, Jun 5, HAY, Sep
    21; 1773: DL, Apr 27, May 12, 19, 31; 1774: DL, Mar 22, Apr 12, May 26; 1776:
    CG, Mar 30, HAY, Sep 17, 18, CHR, Oct 2, 14; 1777: DL, Apr 30, HAY, Aug 19;
    1778: HAY, Jan 26, DL, May 18, 19, CHR, Jun 22, HAY, Sep 10; 1779: DL, May
    21, HAY, Aug 10, 17, Sep 7; 1780: CII, Apr 19, DL, May 9, 20; 1781: HAY, Jan
    22, DL, Apr 2, May 16, 18; 1782: HAY, Mar 4, May 6; 1783: DL, May 2, 14;
    1784: DL, May 10, HAY, Aug 3, Nov 16; 1785: HAY, Jan 31, HAMM, Jul 15; 1786:
    HAMM, Jun 30; 1787: RLSN, Mar 27, 29, DL, May 14; 1788: CG, Mar 11, May 19;
    1789: CG, Mar 31, May 26, DL, Jun 13; 1790: CG, Apr 16, DL, 20; 1791: DL, May
    12, HAY, Oct 24; 1796: DL, Jun 2, 14; 1797: HAY, Jan 23; 1799: DL, Apr 25
Bucks of the Field (song), 1786: DL, May 5, 10
Bucks, Order of, 1766: CG, May 6; 1767: CG, May 19; 1772: DL, May 26; 1777:
    HAY, Feb 11; 1778: HAY, Mar 31; 1779: HAY, Dec 20
Budd (beneficiary), 1776: CG, May 21
Budd, Master (singer), 1750: NWC, Apr 16
Budd, Mrs (actor), 1697: LIF, Jun 0; 1701: LIF, Jan 0, Aug 0
Budgell, Anne (actor), 1741: DL, Oct 31, Nov 11; 1742: DL, May 25; 1744: DL,
    Feb 13, 21, Apr 2, 9, 28, 30, May 14, 16, Sep 22, 27, Oct 20, Nov 3; 1745:
    DL, Jan 16, Feb 2, 11, 12, Mar 18, Apr 29, 30; 1746: DL, Jan 29, Mar 10, 18,

Apr 17, 21, 22, GF, Dec 29, 31; 1747: GF, Jan 5, 12, 16, 22, 26, 29, Feb 5,
6, 9, 10, 16, 23, Mar 2, 5, 9, 12, 19, 23, 30, Apr 7, 9
Budgell, Eustace (poet laureate), 1737: HAY, Jan 14; 1744: DL, Feb 13
Buffalo Tavern, 1734: BFT, Aug 17, LIF, Oct 12; 1738: DL, Aug 19
Bugiani (dancer), 1753: CG, Apr 30; 1754: CG, Mar 30
Bugiani, Elizabeth (dancer), 1752: CG, Oct 10, 28, Dec 2, 4, 19; 1753: CG, Feb
6, 14, Mar 31, Apr 30, Dec 10; 1754: CG, Mar 2, 7, 14, 19, 25, 26, 30, Apr
29, May 22, KING'S, Nov 9; 1755: KING'S, Mar 18; 1756: KING'S, Mar 30, Apr 6
Buher (actor), 1683: DL, Dec 0
Builder's Prologue (entertainment), 1767: HAY, Jul 2, 3, 7, 9, 13, 17, 29
Bulkeley (Buckley), Henry (critic), 1676: DL, Dec 11
Bulkely (actor), 1743: LIF, Jan 14, Feb 14, Mar 24
Bulkley (musician), 1709: GO, Nov 21, SH, 30
Bulkley Jr (musician?), 1713: HAW, Jun 27
Bulkley (Buckley), George (violinist), 1771: CG, Nov 11; 1772: CG, Sep 21, DL,
Nov 26, Dec 18
Bulkley, Mary, Mrs George (actor, dancer), 1767: CG, Sep 17, 25, 26, Oct 5, 12,
29, 30, Nov 16, 17, 23, Dec 14; 1768: CG, Jan 1, 5, 7, 9, 13, 23, 29, Feb 27,
Apr 9, 22, Sep 19, 21, 27, Oct 4, Dec 9, 16; 1769: CG, Jan 12, Feb 3, 13, 18,
Mar 13, Apr 4, 7, 8, 11, 17, 21, 22, 27, May 1, 4, 8, 9, 11, 20, Sep 27, Oct
2, 7, 9, 17, 24, Nov 23, 29, Dec 1, 2, 29; 1770: CG, Feb 3, 12, 24, Apr 17,
18, 25, 28, May 1, DL, 4, CG, Sep 24, 28, Oct 5, 11, 13, 19, Nov 14, 15, 16,
17, 21, 30, Dec 21; 1771: CG, Jan 4, 12, 26, Apr 5, 6, 20, 24, 26, 27, Oct
19, 30, Nov 2, 7, 11, 19, 21, Dec 4, 23; 1772: CG, Jan 1, 14, 28, Mar 5, 19,
DL, 23, CG, 23, Apr 4, 9, May 1, 4, 9, 15, Sep 21, Oct 14, 29, Nov 14, Dec 5,
11, 26; 1773: CG, Jan 16, 29, Mar 15, 25, Apr 3, 16, 23, 24, May 3, 6, 15,
18, 22, 25, Nov 23, Dec 1, 3, 8, 10; 1774: CG, Jan 5, 29, Feb 11, 26, Mar 8,
Apr 12, 23, Sep 21, 26, 28, 30, Nov 4, 30, Dec 2, 12; 1775: CG, Jan 17, Feb
15, 17, 22, Mar 2, 4, Apr 1, 22, May 5, 6, 9, 11, 13, Sep 20, 22, 27, 29, Oct
9, 11, 23, Nov 1, 3, 10, 24, 30, Dec 2, 16; 1776: CG, Jan 24, 26, Feb 9, Apr
19, 27, 30, May 13, Sep 25, DL, Oct 3, CG, 16, Nov 15, 20, 26, Dec 5; 1777:
CG, Feb 5, May 13, 29, Oct 1, 15, 23, Dec 5, 10, 19, 20, 26; 1778: CG, Jan
15, 29, Feb 6, 13, 16, 25, Mar 9, 14, 24, DL, Apr 9, CG, 21, 22, May 19, Sep
18, Nov 21, Dec 8, DL, 11, CG, 15; 1779: CG, Jan 4, 6, 8, 9, 13, 19, 21, Apr
14, 21, 22, 23, 27, 28, May 5, DL, 14, CG, 15, 18, 19, 20, Sep 24, Oct 1, 4,
Nov 10, 11, 13, 16, 23, 25, 27, 30, Dec 1, 3, 11, 22; 1780: CG, Jan 7, Mar 4,
14, Apr 17, 21, 24, May 3, 24; 1782: HAY, Jun 6, 10, 20, 24, 29, Jul 16, Aug
9, 15, 22, DL, Sep 21, 28, Oct 5, 8, 14, 29, Nov 9, 12, 16, 29, Dec 11; 1783:
DL, Jan 29, CG, Feb 13, DL, Mar 20, Apr 24, 26, May 2, 12, HAY, 31, Jun 13,
16, 18, 30, Jul 5, Aug 13, 19, 26, 29, DL, Sep 27, Oct 21, 24, Nov 21; 1784:
DL, Jan 17, 28, Feb 3, Apr 21, May 3, HAY, Jun 1, 2, 17, Aug 19, 24; 1785:
HAY, Jun 17, 21, 29, Jul 23, Aug 2, 4, 23; 1786: HAY, Jun 13, 21, 28, 29, Jul
19, 24, Aug 12, 29; 1787: HAY, May 18, 25, Jun 11, 14, 22, 27, Jul 4, 7, 20,
27; 1788: HAY, Jun 10, 12, 17, 18, 19, 23, Jul 14, 29, 30, 31, Aug 4, 21, Sep
2, 13
Bull (actor), 1797: HAY, Dec 4
Bull (beneficiary), 1761: CG, Jan 6
Bull and Boat; or, Law! Law! Law! (entertainment), 1800: CG, May 10
Bull-and-Gate (public house), 1744: DL, May 17
Bullbrick, George (actor), 1750: DL, Dec 13; 1751: DL, May 13; 1752: DL, Apr
25; 1753: DL, May 11; 1754: DL, May 16; 1755: DL, May 5, Nov 8, 15; 1757: DL,
May 10
Bullock (imprisoned beneficiary), 1749: HAY, Oct 26
Bullock's Booth, 1719: BCA, Sep 24; 1720: BCA, Sep 23; 1722: BFB, Aug 25; 1728:
BFB, Aug 24; 1729: BFB, Aug 25; 1731: BFB, Aug 26; 1732: BFB, Aug 23; 1739:
BFB, Aug 23
Bullock-Leigh Booth, 1717: SFBL, Sep 9, SF, 20; 1718: SF, Sep 3
Bullock-Pack Booth, 1720: HOUN, Jun 13
Bullock-Widow Leigh Booth, 1719: BFBL, Aug 24; 1720: BFBL, Aug 23
Bullock, Ann, Mrs Hildebrand (dancer), 1715: LIF, May 9, 10, 12, 13, 24, Jun 3,
14, 23, Jul 8, KING'S, Aug 27, LIF, Sep 30, Oct 6, 13, 15, 19, 22, 26, 29,
31, Nov 2, 9, 10, 12, 15, 16, 18, 19, 22, 25, 26, 28, Dec 17, 21, 28; 1716:
LIF, Jan 3, 10, 19, 27, Feb 2, Apr 9, 30, May 7, 10, 18, 24, 31, Jun 1, 4,
12, Oct 22, 25, 26, 29, 30, 31, Nov 16, 22, 24, 28, 29, Dec 12, 17, 18, 21,
29; 1717: LIF, Jan 4, 7, 10, 11, 15, 17, 25, 31, Feb 2, Mar 2, 4, 18, 30, Apr
4, 8, 13, 25, 27, Oct 5, 7, 14, 21, 22, Nov 2, 5, 8, 15, 23, 25, Dec 6, 11,
12, 13, 26; 1718: LIF, Jan 1, 4, 7, 15, 21, Feb 20, Mar 1, 6, 8, 10, 18, 20,
Apr 15, 16, 24, May 3, 6, 15, 20, Jun 4, Sep 29, Oct 4, 14, 30, Nov 6, 8, 17,
18, 27, 29, Dec 4, 9, 22, 26, 29; 1719: LIF, Jan 9, 14, Feb 16, 24, Mar 10,
19, Apr 3, 7, 8, 10, 27, DL, Oct 14, 20, 30, Nov 3, 9, 16, 18, 23, 25, 27,
Dec 28; 1720: DL, Jan 12, Feb 1, 5, Mar 29, Apr 25, 29, May 5, 6, 9, 17, 20,
25, 27, Jun 1, 2, Sep 20, 22, 27, Oct 13, 22, 25, 31, Nov 8, 23, 30, Dec 7;

1721: DL, Feb 9, 23, Mar 23, Apr 10, 11, 12, 17, 29, May 1, 5, 9, 12, 17, 19,
23, 29, 31, Jun 6, Sep 14, 19; 1722: DL, Mar 27, 28, 31, Apr 5, 10, 12, 18,
26, 27, 28, 30, May 1, 4, 7, 8, 9, 11, 15, 17, 19, 22, 24, 25, 26, 28, 29,
30, Jul 6, Sep 27, Oct 5, 9, 10, 12, 29, 30, Dec 4, 27; 1723: DL, Jan 3, 18,
21, 29, Mar 21, 25, Apr 29, May 2, 8, 9, 13, 15, 16, 17, 18, 21, Oct 1, 3,
25, 28, Nov 1, 18, 20, 23, 26, Dec 31; 1724: DL, Jan 3, 27, Feb 4, 10, 17,
20, 27, Mar 9, 16, 26, Apr 7, 11, 13, 15, 18, 22, 29, May 2, 4, 8, 12, 14,
18; 1725: LIF, Mar 29, Apr 7, 10, 22, 30, May 1, 3, 4, 5, 6, 7, 10, 11, 12,
14, 17, 18, 21, 22, 24, 25, Oct 19, 22, Nov 22, 24, 29; 1726: LIF, Jan 3, 5,
Mar 31, Apr 18, 21, 22, 26, 27, May 2, 14, 18, 20, 23, 24, 30, Oct 5, 19, Nov
30; 1727: LIF, Jan 10, Feb 3, 9, Mar 11, 23, Apr 7, 21, 26, 27, May 3, 4, 15,
17, 18, 19, 22, Sep 13, Oct 17; 1728: LIF, Apr 22, 23, 24, May 6, 22, 30;
1729: LIF, Jan 13, Mar 20, Apr 12, 19, 22, 26, May 1, 6, 9, 13, 14, 15, 19,
20, 22, 23, BFB, Aug 25, LIF, Oct 28; 1730: LIF, Apr 10, 27, May 1, 11, 23,
27, 28, Jul 3, Dec 11; 1731: LIF, Jan 11, 19, Apr 3, 28, May 6, 21, BFB, Aug
26, LIF, Dec 14; 1732: LIF, Feb 9, Apr 22, May 3, 5, 8, 11, 15, 16, 17, 18,
BFB, Aug 23, GF, Oct 4, 5, 7, 10, 11, 16, 17, 18, 19, 23, 24, 26, 27, 28, 30,
Nov 2, 4, 6, 8, 11, 13, 14, 15, 17, 18, 21, 23, 24, 25, 27, 30, Dec 13, 15,
18; 1733: GF, Jan 10, Mar 1, 12, 26, Apr 10, 13, 16, 18, 20, May 4, 5, 7, 10,
11, 16, 18, 22, 23, Sep 12, 14, 17, 19, 20, 21, 25, 28, Oct 3, 11, 12, 15,
Nov 26, Dec 8, 10, 11, 14, 15, 17, 18, 19, 20, 21, 26, 27, 28; 1734: GF, Jan
2, 7, 8, 9, 10, 11, 12, 14, 18, 19, 22, 24, 26, 28, Feb 2, 5, Apr 18, 24, 26,
May 1, 3, 7, 8, 15, 16, 17, 20, 22, Sep 9, 11, 13, 16, 18, 20, Oct 14, Dec 2,
5, 6, 12; 1735: GF, Jan 13, 17, Mar 13, 17, 27, 29, Apr 17, 21, 22, 23, 24,
28, 30, May 1, 2, 5, Sep 10, 12, 24, Oct 3, 6, 10, 13, 15, Nov 3, 15, 19, 25,
Dec 1, 3, 4, 5, 6, 8, 9, 10, 11, 12, 13, 15; 1736: GF, Feb 4, 5, 6, 10, 11,
17, Mar 18, 20, 22, 25, 29, Apr 1, 6, 8, 12, 13, 17, 27, 28, 29, May 4, 5, 6,
10, LIF, Jun 18, Oct 5, Dec 3, 22; 1737: LIF, Jan 5, Mar 31, Apr 2; 1738: CG,
Dec 9; 1739: CG, Jan 6; 1740: GF, Oct 29; 1741: GF, Feb 14, Apr 6, 7, 16, Dec
28; 1742: GF, Jan 13, 14, Feb 8; 1747: SF, Sep 14; 1748: SFLYYW, Sep 7
Bullock, Charles (pallbearer), 1718: NONE, Jul 30
Bullock, Christopher (actor, dramatist), 1698: NONE, Sep 0; 1707: DL/QUEEN, Dec
31; 1708: DL, Jul 27, 29; 1709: DL, Apr 29, May 12, QUEEN'S, Sep 22, Oct 6,
17, 29; 1710: QUEEN'S, Jan 19, Mar 11, GR, Jun 21, 28, QUEEN'S, 29, GR, Jul
1, 6, 8, 12, DL/QUEEN, Nov 16, DL, Dec 1, 5, 7, 26; 1711: DL, Feb 3, 22, Mar
8, 17, May 8, 22, DL/QUEEN, 29, DL, 31, DL/QUEEN, Jun 5, DL, 29, Jul 3, 10,
27, Aug 3, 17, 31, Sep 25, 29, Oct 12, 13, 16, 22, Nov 3, 12, 23, 26, 29, Dec
31; 1712: DL, May 13, Jul 18, 22, Aug 8, Sep 30, Oct 15, 31, Nov 7, 26, Dec
12; 1713: DL, Jan 14, 29, Feb 9, May 12, Jun 5, 12, Sep 29, Dec 2; 1714: DL,
Jan 5, Mar 31, Apr 27, Jun 4, 14, 25, 29, Jul 13, 20, Nov 27; 1715: LIF, Jan
4, 7, 14, Feb 2, 3, Apr 23, 30, Jun 23, Aug 11, Sep 29, Oct 4, 5, 10, 11, 12,
24, Nov 29, 30, Dec 12; 1716: LIF, Jan 3, 4, 24, Mar 19, Apr 23, 27, Jul 4,
Aug 3, Oct 10, 20, Nov 5, 9, 26, Dec 4; 1717: LIF, Jan 8, 10, 28, Apr 6, May
2, 16, Jun 25, Jul 10, DL, Sep 28, LIF, Oct 15, 17, 24, 26, Nov 6, 11, 14,
20, 26, Dec 3, 7, 9, 12, 14; 1718: LIF, Feb 3, Apr 5, 19, 23, Jun 20, 30, Jul
4, Sep 26, 29, Oct 3, 6, 11, 15, 18, 31, Nov 11, 24; 1719: LIF, Jan 1, 3, 6,
16, 22, 27, Feb 7, 21, 28, Apr 2, May 27, Oct 2, 10, 13, 15, 17, 31, Nov 3,
5, 7, 12, 13, 17, 18, 19, 21, 23, 24, 26, Dec 5, 10; 1720: LIF, Jan 7, 11,
26, Feb 11, 22, 26, 29, Mar 28, Apr 26, May 10, 11, 17, 23, 30, Jun 9, Oct
11, 18, 22, 27, Nov 2, 3, 15, 18, 22, 29, Dec 1, 8, 17, 22, 26; 1721: LIF,
Jan 4, 10, 17, 24, 25, Feb 4, Mar 14, Apr 26, May 17, Sep 27, Oct 3, 5, 10,
12, 17, 19, 21, 24, 31, Nov 9, 13, 18, 25, Dec 2, 12, 18; 1722: LIF, Jan 9,
Mar 26, Apr 5; 1738: CG, Apr 7; 1748: CG, Jan 19; 1758: CG, Apr 3; 1778: HAY,
Dec 28; 1788: DL, Apr 21; 1789: DL, Dec 22
--Adventures of Half an Hour, The, 1716: LIF, Mar 19; 1724: HAY, Feb 20; 1756:
BFSI, Sep 3, 4, 6
--Cobler of Preston, The (Merry Cobler of Preston, The), 1716: LIF, Jan 24, 25,
26, 27, 31, Feb 1, 2, DL, 3, LIF, 3, 4, DL, 4, 6, 8, 9, 10, 14, LIF, 16, DL,
16, 18, 21, 23, 25, LIF, 27, DL, 27, LIF, Mar 1, 3, Apr 2, 5, DL, 5, 6, LIF,
14, 19, May 21, Jul 6, 13, 20, Aug 15, Oct 17, DL, 25, 26, LIF, Dec 28; 1717:
LIF, Jun 25, Jul 5, Oct 28, Dec 31; 1718: LIF, Feb 17, May 3, 29, Oct 28, Dec
8; 1719: LIF, Mar 17, Jun 11, Oct 27, Dec 30; 1720: LIF, Mar 31; 1721: LIF,
Jan 27, Nov 17; 1722: LIF, May 3; 1723: LIF, May 8; 1724: LIF, May 8, Nov 13;
1726: LIF, May 18, Aug 12, 16; 1730: LIF, May 7, GF, Jul 10, 13; 1731: GF,
Feb 8, 9, 11, 12, HAY, Mar 17, Apr 20, GF, May 15, 21, LIF, Oct 25; 1732:
LIF, May 11; 1735: YB, Sep 18; 1738: CG, Apr 7; 1741: JS, May 11; 1745: GF,
Apr 1, 26, May 2, MF, 10; 1759: CG, May 23
--Match in Newgate, A; or, The Vintner Tricked, 1704: LIF, Aug 1; 1705: LIF,
Oct 8
--Perjuror, The, 1717: LIF, Dec 12, 18, 19, 20, 21, 26, 28, 30; 1718: LIF, Jan
6, 9, 21, Feb 10, 22
--Slip, The, 1715: LIF, Feb 3, 5, 7, 10, 11, 15, 25, Mar 1, Apr 9, 30

113

--Traitor, The; or, The Tragedy of Amidea, 1698: NONE, Sep 0; 1699: DL, Oct 28; 1703: DL, Oct 19; 1704: DL, Oct 10; 1718: LIF, Oct 11, 13, 14, 27; 1719: LIF, Jan 5, Mar 21, May 29; 1720: LIF, Feb 11, Apr 27, Dec 1
--Woman Is a Riddle, A; or, The Way to Win a Widow, 1716: LIF, Dec 4, 5, 6, 7, 8, 10, 20, 26; 1717: LIF, Jan 4, 25, Mar 21, May 28, Nov 2, Dec 19; 1718: LIF, Mar 13, Nov 11, Dec 8; 1719: LIF, Apr 7, May 21, Nov 21, Dec 5; 1720: LIF, Feb 17, Dec 22; 1721: LIF, May 16, Jun 7; 1722: LIF, May 4, Oct 9; 1723: LIF, Feb 4; 1727: LIF, Apr 10, 18; 1731: GF, Oct 18, 20, 22, Dec 8; 1735: GF, Mar 10, Sep 24, 26, 29, Oct 1, 13, Nov 7; 1737: LIF, Jan 21, Feb 9; 1745: GF, Apr 1, 22; 1746: GF, Jan 20, Mar 11, Dec 22; 1748: CG, Jan 19, 23, 25; 1759: DL, Nov 9, 12, 14, 19; 1760: DL, Apr 23; 1761: DL, Apr 24, May 7; 1762: DL, May 10; 1766: HAY, Jul 31; 1770: DL, Apr 28; 1776: DL, Mar 12; 1778: HAY, Dec 28; 1780: CG, Apr 3; 1788: DL, Apr 21
--Woman's Revenge, A; or, A Match in Newgate, 1715: LIF, Oct 24, 25, 26, 27, Nov 12, 24, Dec 16, 29; 1716: LIF, Feb 3, Apr 14, Oct 19; 1717: LIF, Oct 30, Dec 12; 1718: LIF, Nov 6, 27; 1719: LIF, Jan 9, May 14, Oct 27, Nov 25, Dec 30; 1720: LIF, Mar 26, Jun 6; 1721: LIF, Jan 25, Feb 13; 1722: LIF, Apr 13, May 7, Oct 12; 1723: LIF, Oct 22, Dec 9; 1724: LIF, Jan 21, 31, May 25, Oct 20; 1725: LIF, Jan 18, Oct 22, Dec 28; 1726: LIF, Jan 28; 1727: LIF, Mar 9, Apr 8, 22, May 23, Nov 22, Dec 27; 1728: LIF, Oct 29, Dec 27; 1729: LIF, May 19, Oct 30, Dec 27; 1730: GF, Jan 5, LIF, 6, Feb 23, Mar 30, Apr 28, May 26, Oct 23, Nov 19; 1731: DL, Jan 1, LIF, 1, Feb 18, Mar 23, Dec 28; 1732: LIF, Jun 2; 1734: CG, Feb 5; 1736: CG, Dec 29; 1739: DL, Oct 29, 31; 1740: CG, Mar 1, 3, 6, 15, Apr 8; 1789: DL, Dec 20, 22
Bullock, Harriet (actor), 1727: LIF, Sep 29; 1731: BFB, Aug 26
Bullock, Henrietta Maria (dancer), 1719: LIF, Oct 5, 27; 1720: LIF, Feb 27, Mar 26, Apr 29, 30, May 11, 12, 19, 23, 24, 25, 30, Jun 6, Oct 4, Dec 6, 14, 26; 1721: LIF, Feb 21, Apr 26, 29, May 1, Dec 14; 1722: LIF, Mar 13, 29, Apr 6, 20, 24, May 2, 7, 8, 10, 16, 18, Jul 27, Oct 30, Nov 7, Dec 13; 1723: LIF, Feb 13, 19, May 18, 23, 24, 28, Oct 7, 16, Nov 2, 8, 19, 22, Dec 3, 9, 11, 12, 16; 1724: LIF, Jan 3
Bullock, Hildebrand (actor), 1712: SML, Jun 11; 1715: LIF, Feb 3, May 24, Jun 14, 23, Oct 24, 28; 1716: LIF, Jan 4, Apr 3, 11, 27, Jul 4; 1717: LIF, Nov 28, Dec 12; 1718: LIF, Jan 4, Apr 19, May 3, Jul 9, 24, Oct 3, Nov 24; 1719: LIF, Feb 7, 21, BFBL, Aug 24, LIF, Nov 20; 1720: LIF, Jan 7, 11, Mar 31, BFBL, Aug 23, LIF, Oct 18, Dec 8; 1721: LIF, Jan 31, Apr 1, 10, May 16, 23, 29, Oct 31, Nov 13; 1722: LIF, Mar 15, 30, 31, May 22, Oct 2, 30, Nov 27; 1723: LIF, Jan 10, Feb 1, 5, 9, 12, Mar 11, Apr 6, 16, Sep 28, Oct 14, 31, Dec 9, 11; 1724: LIF, Mar 26, May 5, 19, Jun 23, Jul 31, Sep 23, Oct 9; 1725: LIF, Apr 26, May 12, 18, 19, 21, 24, Oct 1, 11, Nov 30, Dec 3; 1726: LIF, May 2, 12, Jun 17, 24, Jul 15, 22, Aug 12, 19, Sep 14, 19, 28; 1727: LIF, Apr 19, Oct 26, 31, Dec 11; 1728: LIF, Jan 29, Apr 4, 24, 26, Jun 25, Aug 2, Sep 30, Nov 11; 1729: LIF, Jan 28, Feb 6, Apr 10, 17, 26, 30, May 7, 15, Oct 30, Nov 13, Dec 27; 1730: LIF, Jan 1, May 18, Sep 21, Oct 5, 23. Dec 4; 1731: LIF, Jan 11, Apr 26, May 21, 24, Sep 22, 27, Oct 1, 13, Dec 9; 1732: LIF, Feb 3, May 18, LIF/CG, Sep 25, 27, Oct 16, 30; 1733: LIF/CG, Jan 18, CG/LIF, 25, LIF/CG, Mar 30, CG, May 1, 2, 16, LIF/CG, 24, CG, Sep 25
Bullock, Jane, Mrs Christopher (actor), 1716: LIF, Apr 17; 1717: LIF, Jul 10, Oct 15, 17, 24, 26, 29, Nov 6, 9, 11, 14, 16, 19, 28, Dec 3, 7, 9, 10, 14, 28; 1718: LIF, Jan 2, Feb 1, 3, 18, Sep 26, 30, Oct 1, 3, 6, 8, 11, 15, 16, 18, 24, Nov 11, 13, 24, 25, Dec 2, 6, 8; 1719: LIF, Jan 3, 16, Feb 7, 28, Mar 12, Apr 11, 24, Oct 2, 5, 7, 10, 13, 15, 31, Nov 7, 12, 21, 26, Dec 10, 15; 1720: LIF, Jan 7, 8, 11, 26, Feb 11, 23, 26, 29, Mar 7, 28, May 19, 23, Jun 7, Nov 2, 3, 10, 15, 18, 19, 22, 29, Dec 1, 7, 17, 22, 27; 1721: LIF, Jan 4, 7, 10, 17, 19, 27, 28, Apr 17, 19, 20, 25, 27, May 5, 8, 10, Oct 14, 17, 19, 20, 24, 25, 26, 28, Nov 4, 9, 11, 13, 16, 18, 29, Dec 1, 11, 12, 16, 18; 1722: LIF, Jan 9, 13, Feb 2, 13, Mar 5, 10, 15, DL, Apr 20, LIF, May 4, 25, Sep 29, Oct 1, 2, 4, 6, 9, 11, 16, 18, 20, 22, 24, 26, 29, 31, Nov 5, 7, 8, 12, 14, 16, 17, 30, Dec 1, 7, 10, 14, 15, 21, 31; 1723: LIF, Jan 3, 11, 18, Feb 1, 16, 22, Mar 21, 28, Apr 16, 23, May 3, Dec 20; 1724: LIF, Sep 23, 28, Oct 7, 9, 12, 14, 17, 22, 23, 30, Nov 3, 4, 12, 17, 20, 24, 25; 1725: LIF, Jan 4, 11, 16, 19, Feb 27, Mar 11, 13, 31, Apr 5, 14, 17, 26, May 19, 20, Sep 29, Oct 1, 4, 11, 13, 15, 16, 19, 23, 25, 26, Nov 2, 3, 4, 6, 8, 9, 11, 12, 13, 17, 18, 23, 30, Dec 2, 3, 8, 15; 1726: LIF, Jan 14, Feb 19, Mar 19, 21, 24, Apr 2, 11, 22, 30, May 3, 4, 11, Sep 12, 14, 16, 19, 21, 23, 26, 28, 30, Oct 3, 12, 17, 24, Nov 2, 5, 8, 10, 11, 21, Dec 14; 1727: LIF, Jan 16, Feb 2, 7, 13, Apr 10, 17, 19, Jun 7, Sep 11, 15, 18, 20, 22, 25, 27, Oct 2, 9, 12, 26, 31, Nov 1, 9, 16, 17, Dec 14; 1728: LIF, Mar 9, 21, 25, 28, Apr 1, 4, 6, 26, 30, May 11, 18, 23, Sep 18, 30, Oct 1, 21, 23, Nov 11, 20, Dec 28, 31; 1729: LIF, Jan 16, 18, Feb 6, 22, Mar 3, 10, 27, Apr 8, 10, 11, 15, 16, 17, 24, 30, May 3, Sep 19, 24, 26, 29, Oct 6, 8, 10, 13, 15, 20, 22, 24, 29, 31, Nov 4, 7, 13, 14, 20, 25, Dec 15, 19; 1730: LIF, Jan 26, Apr 2, 20, 30, May

6, 7, 18, 20, 25, Jun 1, Sep 18, 23, 25, Oct 1, 5, 7, 12, 19, 26, 27, 30, 31,
Nov 3, 7, Dec 3, 4, 12, 14, 15; 1731: LIF, Jan 4, 8, 9, 20, 21, Mar 15, 29,
Apr 1, 26, May 1, 5, 10, 20, 25, 28, Jun 2, Sep 22, 27, 29, Oct 4, 11, 13,
15, 18, 20, 27, Nov 2, 6, 8, 12, 18, 25, Dec 1, 3, 6, 8, 9, 11; 1732: LIF,
Jan 7, 10, 18, 19, 26, 28, Feb 14, 15, 28, Mar 27, 30, Apr 10, 18, 24, 26,
27, May 1, 9, 12, LIF/CG, Oct 28, Nov 3, 7, 9, 11, 13, 14, 16, 17, 22, Dec 4,
14, 15, GF, 20, LIF/CG, 28; 1733: LIF/CG, Jan 1, 18, CG/LIF, 25, LIF/CG, 31,
Feb 1, 6, CG, 8, Mar 27, LIF/CG, 30, 31, Apr 2, 10, 11, 13, 30, CG, May 2,
LIF/CG, 7, 10, Jun 1, CG, 26, Jul 6, 31, Aug 2, 20, BFCGBH, 23, CG, Sep 25,
27, 29, Oct 4, 9, 16, 18, 19, 20, 23, 25, 26, 29, Nov 3, 8, 9, GF, 12, CG,
16, 26, 30, Dec 4, 8, 15, 17, 20; 1734: CG, Jan 9, 23, GF, Feb 11, CG, Mar
19, GF, Apr 19, CG, Sep 2, CG/LIF, 20, 23, 25, Oct 25, GF, 28, CG/LIF, 29,
Nov 11, 14, 21, 25, Dec 5, 26; 1735: CG/LIF, Jan 6, 17, 23, GF, 24, CG/LIF,
31, Feb 3, 4, 11, LIF, 12, CG/LIF, 13, LIF, Mar 3, GF, 6, CG/LIF, 13, 15, 29,
Apr 8, 9, 17, 18, 21, May 1, 15, CG, Sep 26, 29, Oct 10, 13, 15, 22, 29, 31,
Nov 6, 7, GF, 17, CG, Dec 15, GF, 17, CG, 22, 31; 1736: CG, Feb 10, GF, 20,
Mar 3, CG, 20, 22, Apr 13, LIF, May 5, CG, 13, 20, 24, Jun 14, LIF, Sep 30,
Oct 14, 21, Dec 7, 16; 1737: LIF, Feb 1; 1738: CG, Oct 4, 28, 30, Nov 18;
1739: CG, Jan 18, 20; 1740: GF, Dec 15; 1741: GF, Jan 27, Feb 19, Mar 12, Oct
9, 16
Bullock, Miss (dancer), 1778: CG, May 22
Bullock, Mrs William Sr (actor), 1697: DL, Jul 0
Bullock, William (actor), 1695: DL, Sep 0, DG, Nov 0; 1696: DL, Jan 0, Feb 0,
DG, Jun 0, DL, Nov 21; 1697: DL, Feb 0, May 8, 31, NONE, Sep 0; 1698: DL, Jun
0, DL/ORDG, Nov 0, DL, Dec 0; 1699: DLORLIF, Feb 20, DL, Apr 0, Nov 28; 1700:
DL, Jul 9, Dec 9; 1701: DL, Mar 1, May 31, Dec 0; 1702: DL, Jan 0, Feb 0, Nov
26, Dec 14; 1703: DL, Jan 27, Mar 11, Apr 10, Jun 4, 23, 30, BFPBS, Aug 23,
DL, Oct 28, Dec 2; 1704: DL, Jan 26, ATCOURT, Apr 24, DL, Jun 5, Dec 26;
1705: DL, Jan 18, Mar 29, Apr 23, Jun 12, 23, Oct 30, Nov 20; 1706: DL, Apr
0, 1, 8, BF, Aug 27, QUEEN'S, Nov 13, 14, 22, 25, Dec 2, 7, 13, 14, 27; 1707:
QUEEN'S, Jan 1, 4, 9, 13, 14, Feb 14, 15, 18, Mar 8, 27, 31, Apr 30, May 26,
Jun 10, 20, 25, 27, Jul 1, 4, 10, 22, 26, 30, Aug 12, DL/QUEEN, Oct 18, 20,
22, 23, 27, 28, 29, 31, Nov 1, 10, 11, 14, 18, Dec 27, 31; 1708: DL/QUEEN,
Jan 1, DL, Feb 4, 6, 26, Mar 8, 9, 15, 18, 27, Apr 10, 17, 26, Jun 5, 15, 19,
24, 26, Jul 1, 20, 29, Aug 4, 28, 31, Sep 3, 4, Oct 5, 12, 14, 15, 16, 18,
22, 25, 26, Dec 14, 18, 28, 30, 31; 1709: DL, Jan 1, 3, 4, 5, 11, 12, 13, 17,
18, 26, 27, Feb 1, 16, 19, Mar 3, 14, 15, 17, 31, Apr 11, 12, 14, 25, 30, May
3, 12, 17, QUEEN'S, Sep 22, 24, Oct 1, 6, 8, 11, 17, 22, 25, 28, 31, Nov 8,
11, 18, 19, Dec 12; 1710: QUEEN'S, Jan 5, 11, 14, 21, Feb 11, 18, Mar 4, 11,
Apr 17, 29, May 1, 6, 10, 15, 18, 24, 29, Jun 1, 5, GR, 15, QUEEN'S, 16, GR,
24, QUEEN'S, 29, Jul 19, DL/QUEEN, Oct 5, Nov 4, 6, 8, QUEEN'S, 10, DL/QUEEN,
13, 14, 15, 16, 17, 18, DL, 27, 28, Dec 1, 2, 4, 7, 12, 14, 15, 18, 22,
DL/QUEEN, 29; 1711: DL, Jan 9, 11, 15, 19, 20, 25, 26, DL/QUEEN, Feb 8, DL,
10, DL/QUEEN, 17, DL, Mar 3, 8, 17, Apr 7, 21, May 8, DL/QUEEN, 11, DL, 15,
18, 22, DL/QUEEN, 29, DL, 31, DL/QUEEN, Jun 22, DL, 26, 29, Jul 3, 10, 27,
Aug 3, 17, 31, Sep 22, 25, 29, Oct 4, 6, 10, 11, 12, 13, 16, 19, 20, 22, 24,
25, 26, 30, 31, Nov 1, 2, 6, 8, 23, 26, Dec 8, 10, 18, 21, 31; 1712: DL, Jan
19, May 13, Jun 2, 5, Jul 4, 11, 22, Aug 8, 26, Sep 23, 25, Oct 2, 6, 8, 10,
15, 16, 17, 20, 22, 30, Nov 3, 7, Dec 12, 30; 1713: DL, Jan 5, 6, 10, 12, 14,
29, Feb 9, 28, Mar 3, 16, May 12, 18, Jun 5, 12, 19, Oct 23, Nov 9, 16, 19,
23, 25, 27, Dec 2, 18; 1714: DL, Jan 28, Mar 31, Apr 27, May 10, 17, 21, 26,
28, Jun 2, 4, 18, 25, 29, Jul 13, 20, SF, Aug 31, DL, Oct 22, Nov 9, 15, 24,
Dec 6, 8, 16; 1715: LIF, Jan 4, 7, 14, Feb 2, 16, Mar 21, Apr 20, 30, May 3,
24, Jun 2, 7, 23, SF, Sep 15, LIF, 28, 29, Oct 4, 10, 12, 24, 28, Nov 30, Dec
12; 1716: LIF, Jan 4, 24, Mar 19, Apr 11, 17, 27, Jun 20, Jul 4, 6, Aug 3,
Oct 10, 17, 20, 22, Nov 5, 9, 13, Dec 4; 1717: LIF, Jan 22, 28, Feb 25, Mar
18, 28, May 18, Jun 25, Jul 10, NONE, Sep 12, LIF, Oct 15, 17, 21, 26, 28,
Nov 6, 11, 13, 26, 28, Dec 7, 14; 1718: LIF, Jan 2, 7, Feb 1, 3, 15, 27, Apr
5, Jun 30, RI, Jul 19, LIF, 24, NONE, 30, RI, Aug 2, 9, 11, 16, 23, NONE, 29,
SF, Sep 3, LIF, 26, 29, Oct 3, 11, 15, 28, 31, Nov 3, 11, 24, 26, Dec 10, 19,
30; 1719: LIF, Jan 31, Feb 7, 21, 28, Apr 21, DL, May 23, BFBL, Aug 24, B-L,
Sep 5, LIF, Oct 2, 5, 7, 10, 13, 15, 17, 29, Nov 3, 5, 13, 17, 18, 21, 23,
24, 26, Dec 28, 29; 1720: LIF, Jan 11, 26, Feb 11, Apr 26, BFBL, Aug 23, BCA,
Sep 23, LIF, Oct 1, 11, 13, 18, 22, Nov 10, 19, 22, 26, 29, Dec 1, 17, 22,
26; 1721: LIF, Jan 4, 19, 28, Feb 6, 9, Mar 11, Apr 1, 10, 17, May 25, Sep
27, Oct 3, 7, 12, 21, 25, 26, 31, Nov 9, 13, 18, 25, 29, Dec 11, 18, 27;
1722: LIF, Jan 9, 13, Feb 1, Mar 5, 8, 15, 29, 31, Apr 3, 13, May 4, 14, Jun
1, Jul 27, Sep 29, Oct 1, 2, 6, 9, 11, 12, 13, 16, 18, 19, 20, 22, 26, 29,
30, 31, Nov 7, 13, 14, 15, 17, 30, Dec 14, 15, 21; 1723: LIF, Jan 11, Feb 1,
Apr 6, 16, May 21, HA, Jul 22, LIF, Sep 28, 30, Oct 4, 7, 9, 10, 14, 18, 22,
24, 25, 29, 31, Nov 2, 12, 14, 16, 19, 28, Dec 11; 1724: LIF, Mar 16, 23, Apr
6, 29, May 19, 27, 28, Jun 23, Jul 14, 31, SF, Sep 2, LIF, 23, SOU, 24, LIF,

115

28, Oct 7, 9, 12, 22, 27, 30, Nov 3, 6, 11, 13, 18, 25, 26; 1725: LIF, Jan
11, 19, Mar 11, 29, 31, Apr 7, 10, 14, May 19, 20, 21, Sep 29, Oct 1, 11, 16,
19, 28, Nov 6, 8, 9, 12, 23, 24, 29, 30, Dec 2, 3, 7, 8, 15; 1726: LIF, Mar
21, Apr 11, 18, May 12, 25, Jun 17, 24, Jul 15, 22, Aug 2, 12, Sep 12, 14,
19, 21, 26, 28, Oct 17, 19, Nov 11, 21, 30; 1727: LIF, Jan 4, 9, Apr 10, May
9, 22, Sep 13, 15, 18, 27, Oct 9, 21, 26, 31, Nov 1, 17, Dec 14; 1728: LIF,
Jan 8, Mar 9, 28, Apr 23, 24, 26, May 11, 15, 20, 22, Jun 25, Jul 19, Aug 2,
BFB, 24, LIF, Sep 18, 30, Oct 1, Nov 1, 11, 19, 20, Dec 28, 31; 1729: LIF,
Jan 16, Feb 6, Apr 8, 10, 11, 15, 23, 30, May 3, 15, BFB, Aug 25, LIF, Sep
22, 24, 26, Oct 3, 8, SOU, 14, LIF, 22, 24, 29, 30, Nov 7, 13; 1730: LIF, Jan
1, Apr 2, May 7, 11, 15, 18, 25, RI, Jun 24, 27, Jul 16, LIF, Sep 21, 23, Oct
5, 23, Nov 6, 13; 1731: LIF, Jan 8, 9, 20, Apr 26, May 1, 10, 25, RI, Jul 8,
15, BFB, Aug 26, LIF, Nov 17, Dec 6, 8, 9; 1732: LIF, Jan 7, Apr 18, 24, 27,
May 8, RI, Aug 17, BFB, 23, CG/LIF, Sep 22, LIF/CG, 25, 27, Oct 6, 20; 1733:
CG/LIF, Jan 22, LIF/CG, Feb 1, Mar 30, Apr 2, 10, 11, BFCGBH, Aug 23, Sep 4,
CG, 22, 25, 29, Nov 30, Dec 3, 22; 1734: CG, Mar 28, Apr 20, May 9, RI, Jun
27, BFHBH, Aug 24, RI, Sep 26; 1736: LIF, Apr 16; 1739: CG, Jan 6, Apr 25,
BFB, Aug 23
Bullock Jr, William (actor), 1719: LIF, Feb 28; 1722: LIF, Jan 19, 29, HAY, Jun
28, LIF, Oct 19; 1724: LIF, Jun 23; 1725: LIF, Jan 4, 11, Apr 26, May 21, Dec
8; 1726: LIF, May 2, 26, Jul 5, 22, Aug 2, 19, Sep 14, 19, Dec 14; 1727: LIF,
Jan 4, 9, Feb 3, Apr 10, 19, 26, May 4, 15, 17, 22, Sep 11, 13, 15, 27, Oct
9, 21; 1729: BFB, Aug 25, LIF, Oct 30, GF, Nov 17, 18, 20, 21, 22, 24, Dec 1,
6, 9, 15, 20; 1730: GF, Jan 5, 9, 13, 19, 26, Feb 7, 9, 10, Mar 12, 17, 30,
Apr 2, 7, 10, 15, 28, May 26, Sep 16, 18, 21, 23, 25, 28, Oct 5, 9, 20, 21,
24, 30, 31, Nov 2, 10, 26, 30, Dec 1, 4, 7, 8, 21; 1731: GF, Jan 13, 20, 25,
Feb 8, 18, 22, 27, Mar 1, 8, 11, 13, 15, 16, 22, 23, Apr 27, May 7, 17, Jun
8, Oct 6, 8, 11, 13, 18, 25, 27, 29, Nov 1, 6, 8, 11 12, 16, 19, 20, 22, 24,
26, Dec 1, 13, 28; 1732: GF, Feb 21, 26, Mar 7, 20, 30, Apr 12, 17, 21, 24,
May 4, 10, RI, Aug 17, BFB, 23, GF, Oct 2, 4, 6, 7, 10, 11, 13, 14, 17, 24,
25, 26, 30, Nov 2, 3, 8, 27, Dec 1, 18; 1733: GF, Jan 24, Mar 27, Apr 6, 24,
May 7, 9, Jun 18
Bulls (actor), 1782: HAY, Nov 25
Bulls and Bears, The (farce, anon), 1715: DL, Dec 2, 3, 5
Bulmer (house servant), 1772: CG, Dec 29; 1774: CG, Feb 14
Bulstrode (magistrate), 1776: DL, Jan 1
Bulstrode, Sir Richard (spectator), 1670: DOVER, May 19
Bulteel, John
--Amorous Gallant, The; or, Love in Fashion, 1664: NONE, Sep 0; 1674: NONE, Sep
0
Bumper Squire Jones (song), 1742: DL, Mar 29, Apr 20, 21, 22, 23, 24, 26, 27,
May 3, 4, 18, 22, BFPY, Aug 25; 1743: DL, Apr 5, 7, 20, May 4, 5, 16, Nov 26;
1744: CG, Jan 19
Bumpkin (author), 1766: CG, Apr 4
Bunbury, Henry William (versifier), 1787: CG, Dec 26; 1788: HAY, Apr 29; 1789:
CG, Jun 8; 1791: DL, Mar 22; 1795: DL, Apr 16, CG, Nov 9
Bunbury's Representation of the Prince's Bow (entertainment), 1788: HAY, Apr 29
Buncombe, 1734: DL, Nov 27
Bundle of Prologues, A. See Garrick, David.
Bundle of Proverbs; or, Odds and Ends (song), 1799: CG, Apr 16, 18, May 3, 13,
Oct 7; 1800: CG, Apr 22, 26, May 27
Buona Figliuola Maritata, La. See Piccini, Niccolo.
Buona Figliuola, La. See Piccini, Niccolo.
Buonaiuti, Serafino (librettist), 1799: KING'S, May 14
Buononcini. See Bononcini.
Bur (actor), 1742: JS, Nov 8
Buranello (composer), 1761: KING'S, Jan 6; 1768: KING'S, Apr 21, Nov 5; 1769:
KING'S, Feb 14; see also Galuppi, Baldassare
Burbage (actor), 1794: DL, Oct 31
Burbero di Buon Cuore, Il. See Martin y Soler, Vicente.
Burden (singer, actor), 1784: HAY, Feb 23; 1793: HAY, Oct 10, Nov 19
Burden, Kitty (actor), 1760: HAY, Jun 28, CG, Sep 22, 24, Oct 13, 17, Nov 24,
29, Dec 18, 19; 1761: CG, Jan 3, 8, 10, Feb 17, 28, Mar 3, Apr 3, 17, May 8,
11, Sep 25, 28, Oct 3, 7, 12, 15, 20, 24, 31, Nov 2, 10, Dec 16; 1762: CG,
Jan 12, Mar 23, Apr 16, 17, 29, May 1, 19; 1765: HAY, Jul 15, 31, Aug 8, 30,
CG, Sep 27, Oct 14, Nov 19, Dec 12; 1766: CG, Feb 6, Apr 7, HAY, Jul 8, 15,
23, 31, KING'S, Aug 8, 18, HAY, 21, KING'S, Sep 5, 9, CG, Oct 8, 23, Nov 13,
Dec 6, 30; 1767: CG, Jan 3, Mar 17, May 8, HAY, Jun 8, 17, 22, 30, Jul 2, 8,
15, 22, 31, Aug 5, 21, Sep 18, 21; 1777: HAY, Sep 17, 18; 1778: CHR, May 25,
27, 29, Jun 1, 3, 8, 9, 18, 19, 22, 24; 1782: HAY, Nov 25
Burdon (singer), 1795: CG, Feb 20, Mar 11, 18; 1796: CG, Feb 17, 24; 1797: CG,
Mar 17

116

Bureau, Joseph G (musician), <u>1749</u>: HAY, Nov 10; <u>1750</u>: DL, May 22
Burford (actor), <u>1671</u>: DG, Nov 0; <u>1672</u>: DG, Aug 3
Burges (bricklayer, tenant), <u>1750</u>: DL, Jan 3; <u>1767</u>: DL, Feb 6, 7; <u>1772</u>: DL, Mar
    30; <u>1773</u>: DL, Mar 1; <u>1774</u>: DL, Jan 21; <u>1775</u>: DL, May 27; <u>1776</u>: DL, Apr 12
Burges, Alexander (hardware merchant), <u>1742</u>: GF, Jan 29
Burges, Elizabeth (actor), <u>1735</u>: YB, Mar 10, 12, May 19, HAY, Aug 4; <u>1736</u>: HAY,
    Feb 2, 16, Mar 5, LIF, 24, HAY, Apr 29, May 12; <u>1737</u>: LIF, Jan 10, HAY, Mar
    4; <u>1739</u>: CG, Sep 5, Oct 1, 10, Nov 10, 20; <u>1740</u>: CG, Jan 15, Mar 24, Apr 29,
    May 3, 7, Jun 5, Sep 19, 22, Nov 1, 7, 13; <u>1741</u>: CG, Jan 7, 21, Feb 17, 19,
    28, Mar 12, 17, May 4, 12, Sep 23, Oct 2, 21, 27
Burges, Sir James Bland (versifier), <u>1796</u>: DL, Apr 2
Burgess (musician), <u>1745</u>: DL, Apr 3
Burgess Jr, Henry (musician), <u>1738</u>: DL, Jan 26; <u>1739</u>: DL, Jan 17, May 3, 5, 22
Burgess, Master (actor), <u>1738</u>: DL, Oct 30; <u>1739</u>: DL, Feb 7, Oct 10
Burgess, Parson, <u>1699</u>: DLLIF, Sep 12
Burghall, J E (actor), <u>1778</u>: CG, Oct 5; <u>1779</u>: DL, Feb 8
Burgomaster (dance), <u>1779</u>: CG, Feb 16, 18, 22, May 21
Burgomaster and His Frow (dance), <u>1718</u>: LIF, Oct 30, Nov 3, 6; <u>1720</u>: LIF, Feb
    27; <u>1721</u>: LIF, May 4, DL, 17, 19; <u>1722</u>: DL, Mar 22, LIF, May 18; <u>1726</u>: LIF,
    Apr 20, May 26; <u>1738</u>: BFH, Aug 23, DL, Oct 26, 27
Burgomaster Tricked, The. See Booth, Barton.
Burgomaster's Daughter (dance), <u>1729</u>: DL, Dec 8
Burgon, Will, <u>1660</u>: MT, Nov 2
Burgoyne, Lieutenant-General John, <u>1769</u>: CG, Feb 18; <u>1772</u>: CG, Mar 5; <u>1774</u>: DL,
    Nov 5; <u>1775</u>: DL, Mar 18; <u>1780</u>: DL, Dec 27; <u>1782</u>: DL, Jan 21; <u>1786</u>: DL, Jan
    14, HAMM, Jul 10, DL, Oct 24; <u>1789</u>: DL, Apr 20, Oct 13; <u>1791</u>: DL, May 5;
    <u>1792</u>: DLKING'S, Apr 20
--Heiress, The, <u>1769</u>: CG, Feb 18; <u>1786</u>: DL, Jan 14, 16, 17, 19, 20, 21, 23, 24,
    25, 26, 27, 28, Feb 2, 3, 6, 7, 10, 14, 16, 22, 25, 28, Mar 7, 14, 23, 30,
    Apr 8, 21, 27, May 4, 12, 19, Jun 3, 8, HAMM, Jul 10, HAY, Aug 17, DL, Sep
    28, Oct 17, Nov 21, 30, Dec 23; <u>1787</u>: DL, Jan 8, 25, Feb 20, 27, Apr 11, 18,
    May 10, Jun 5, Oct 20, Nov 7, Dec 1; <u>1788</u>: DL, Jan 4, 25, Feb 1, 4, Apr 14,
    24, May 8, 12, Oct 9, 23, Nov 3, Dec 3; <u>1789</u>: DL, Apr 16, May 8, CG, 14, DL,
    15, 22, CG, Jun 13, DL, Sep 26, Oct 6, Nov 11, Dec 23; <u>1790</u>: DL, Apr 5, May
    4, 25, Sep 16, Nov 11; <u>1791</u>: DL, Feb 24, May 12, 25, DLKING'S, Nov 5, 21, 26,
    Dec 16, 21, 22, 30; <u>1792</u>: DLKING'S, May 24, Jun 16, DL, Oct 16, Dec 11, 18;
    <u>1793</u>: DL, Jan 11, 18; <u>1794</u>: DL, Jun 25, 26, Sep 20, Oct 30; <u>1795</u>: DL, Feb 3,
    Jun 4; <u>1796</u>: DL, Jan 19, Feb 18, Apr 26, Nov 1; <u>1797</u>: DL, Feb 23, Jun 16, Oct
    7, 14; <u>1798</u>: DL, Nov 5
--Lord of the Manor, The, <u>1780</u>: DL, Dec 27, 28, 29, 30; <u>1781</u>: DL, Jan 1, 3, 8,
    10, 11, 13, 15, 16, 18, 20, Feb 1, 7, 9, 14, 23, Mar 31, Apr 23, 30, Oct 6,
    11; <u>1782</u>: DL, Jan 21, Feb 4, 16, Apr 8, May 9; <u>1783</u>: DL, Nov 8, 18; <u>1784</u>: DL,
    May 7; <u>1786</u>: DL, Apr 4, 25, May 23; <u>1789</u>: DL, Apr 14; <u>1799</u>: DL, Apr 17
--Maid of the Oaks, The, <u>1774</u>: DL, Nov 5, 7, 8, 10, 12, 14, 15, 17, 18, CG, 19,
    DL, 22, 23, 25, 26, 30, Dec 5, 10, 14, 27, 28; <u>1775</u>: DL, Jan 5, 13, 19, Feb
    4, 16, 28, Mar 16, Apr 27, May 27, Nov 28, Dec 4, 6, 14, 15; <u>1776</u>: DL, Feb 5,
    6, 8, Mar 26, Apr 9, 20, Nov 7, 8, 11, 13, 15, 26; <u>1777</u>: DL, Feb 10, 13, 20;
    <u>1780</u>: DL, Feb 28, Mar 2; <u>1782</u>: DL, Jan 21, 23, 25, 28, Feb 1, 4, 6, 11, 14,
    19, 21, Mar 7, 23, Apr 9, 18, 29, May 17, HAY, Aug 15; <u>1783</u>: CG, Apr 25, May
    5, 22; <u>1784</u>: CG, Feb 13, 16, 20, 24, Mar 29, Apr 16, May 6; <u>1785</u>: CG, Jan 14,
    Feb 2, 3, May 5, Oct 10, Nov 7, 26; <u>1788</u>: CG, Feb 4, 11, May 22, 26, Jun 9,
    HAY, Jul 7, 11, 22, Sep 12; <u>1789</u>: CG, Mar 28, Apr 29; <u>1790</u>: CG, Feb 4, Nov
    19; <u>1791</u>: CG, Mar 3, 7; <u>1792</u>: CG, Mar 17, 22, Oct 18; <u>1793</u>: CG, Nov 12; <u>1794</u>:
    CG, Jan 27; <u>1796</u>: CG, Apr 20
--Richard Coeur de Lion, <u>1786</u>: DL, Oct 24, 25, 26, 27, 28, 30, 31, Nov 14, 15,
    16, 20, 21, 27, 28, 30, Dec 4, 11, 12, 14, 18, 20, 29; <u>1787</u>: DL, Jan 3, 6,
    10, 12, 18, 20, 25, 27, Feb 2, 6, 9, 13, 14, 20, 27, Mar 3, 13, 19, 26, 31,
    Apr 16, Nov 8, 17, 22, 28, 29, Dec 3; <u>1788</u>: DL, Mar 25, 27, Apr 1, 4, 9, 18,
    May 2, 15, Jun 7, 9, 13, Sep 23, Oct 6, 11, 18, 24, Nov 20, Dec 8; <u>1789</u>: DL,
    Jan 2, 16, 23, Mar 26, Apr 13, 22, May 18, 25, Oct 21, 26, Nov 2, 6, 9; <u>1791</u>:
    DLKING'S, Nov 16, 18, 23, 26, 29, Dec 1, 3, 6, 8, 9, 16, 19, 21, 23, 26, 29;
    <u>1792</u>: DLKING'S, Jan 23, Mar 8, 22, Apr 9, 13, 19, May 1, DL, Sep 29, Oct 13,
    Nov 5, 12, Dec 6, 10, 18; <u>1793</u>: DL, Jan 16, Feb 7, 28; <u>1796</u>: DL, Oct 19, 20,
    25, 27, 28, Nov 3, 8, 14, 22, 29, Dec 1, 6; <u>1797</u>: DL, Jan 5, 14, 17, 28, Mar
    28, Apr 20, 25, May 2, 25, Nov 8, 25, Dec 19
Burke (house servant), <u>1751</u>: DL, May 8; <u>1752</u>: DL, May 2
Burke, Edmund (Prime Minister), <u>1772</u>: CG, Mar 5
Burke, Mrs
--Ward of the Castle, The (opera), <u>1793</u>: CG, Oct 24, 25, 26
Burkett, Thomas (singer), <u>1776</u>: DL, Mar 23; <u>1780</u>: CG, Feb 17
Burkhead. See Birkhead, Matthew.
Burkinyoung. See Barkinyoung.

Burleigh, John (beneficiary), 1729: LIF, May 23
Burlesque Ballet (dance), 1754: HAY, Mar 30
Burlesque Cantata (entertainment), 1771: DL, May 4, 6, 11, 13
Burlesque Dance (dance), 1785: HAY, Aug 11
Burlesque Dance, Grand (dance), 1754: HAY, Apr 22
Burlesque Italian Medley Cantata (song), 1783: CG, May 6
Burlesque Ode (entertainment), 1755: HAY, Feb 10; 1768: MARLY, Jul 28, Aug 4
Burlesque Pas de Russe (dance), 1792: CG, Dec 20, 26; 1793: CG, Nov 19
Burletta of Orpheus (entertainment), 1786: HAY, Aug 29; 1796: HAY, Sep 5, 6
Burley, Widow (beneficiary), 1737: HAY, Feb 9
Burlington, Countess of. See Boyle, Juliana.
Burlington, Earl of. See Boyle, Richard.
Burlington, Lord (patron), 1715: GRT, Jul 23; 1735: KING'S, Mar 15; 1739: CG,
  Apr 10
Burn. See Byrn.
Burn (actor), 1779: DL, May 11, Sep 21
Burn my Wig (song), 1757: CG, Apr 18
Burn, Miss (dancer), 1759: HAY, Apr 18, KING'S, 21, HAY, May 10, MARLY, Aug 9,
  16, Sep 6, 7
Burn's, 1757: DL, May 3
Burnaby, William, 1700: DL, Oct 0; 1701: LIF, Jan 0, Mar 0, Apr 0; 1702: DL,
  Jan 0, May 0; 1703: LIF, Feb 0, Mar 0
--Ladies Visiting Day, The, 1701: LIF, Jan 0
--Love Betrayed; or, The Agreeable Disappointment, 1703: LIF, Feb 0; 1705: LIF,
  Mar 1
--Modish Husband, The, 1702: DL, Jan 0
--Reformed Wife, The; or, The Sickly Lady, 1700: DL, Mar 0; 1707: DL, Oct 31,
  Nov 3
Burnell (boxkeeper), 1719: LIF, May 19
Burnet, Richard (actor, dancer), 1728: DL, Nov 15; 1729: DL, Jun 13, 20, 27,
  BF, Aug 26; 1730: DL, Apr 23, BFOF, Aug 20, SFOF, Sep 9, DL, Oct 1, Dec 4;
  1731: DL, Jun 7, Aug 11, Oct 16; 1732: DL, May 12, Aug 1, Dec 26; 1733: DL,
  Mar 31, Oct 10, 24, Nov 13, Dec 5; 1734: DL, Feb 4, DL/HAY, Apr 26, DL, May
  15, HAY, 27
Burnett (actor), 1772: HAY, Dec 21; 1776: HAY, Oct 7; 1778: CHR, Jun 8, 10, 15,
  18, 19, 26; 1781: CII, Mar 15, 27, 30, Apr 5
Burnett, Miss (actor, singer), 1784: DL, Jan 7, 13, Sep 23, Nov 9, 22, 26;
  1785: DL, Jan 12, 20, Feb 2, Apr 14, May 19, HAY, Aug 8, DL, Sep 27, Oct 17,
  26, Dec 26; 1786: DL, Jan 6, Mar 6, 9, HAY, Jun 9, 16, 19, 29, Jul 13, 18,
  Aug 3, 10, 25; 1787: ROY, Jun 20; 1796: CG, Sep 19, Dec 19; 1797: CG, Mar 21,
  Apr 8, 25, 28, Jun 9, Sep 25, Oct 16, Nov 2, Dec 18; 1798: CG, Mar 19, 31,
  Apr 9, Sep 17, Oct 8, 15, 25, Nov 12, Dec 11, 15, 26; 1799: CG, Jan 29, Mar
  2, 25, Apr 13, 19, 23, May 28, Sep 30, Oct 7, 21, 24, Dec 27; 1800: CG, Jan
  7, 16, Feb 12, Mar 4, 25, May 1, Jun 2
Burnett, Mrs (actor), 1772: HAY, Dec 21
Burnett, Mrs (actor, singer), 1783: DL, Oct 13, Dec 2; 1784: DL, Jan 7, 13, Sep
  23, Nov 22; 1785: DL, Jan 12, 20, Feb 2, Apr 14, Sep 27, Oct 17, 26, Dec 26;
  1799: CG, Apr 3
Burney (harpsichordist), 1730: GF, May 12
Burney (Sr) (actor), 1718: LIF, Oct 30; 1729: GF, Nov 5, Dec 1, 19; 1730: GF,
  Feb 10, May 28, Jun 3, 19, BFPG, Aug 31, GF, Nov 11; 1731: GF, Feb 8, Mar 18
Burney, Dr Charles (musician, music historian), 1746: CG, Feb 14; 1750: DL, Dec
  13; 1770: DL, Mar 17, 26, May 4, RANELAGH, Jul 27, MARLY, Aug 28; 1772: CG,
  Apr 8; 1774: HAY, Feb 18; 1777: HAY, Jul 18; 1798: CG, Nov 7
--Cunning Man, The (musical), 1766: DL, Nov 21, 22, 25, 26, 27, Dec 1, 3, 5, 9,
  10, 11; 1767: DL, Jan 31, Feb 14, 17, 20, Mar 5, 19; 1768: DL, Feb 10, 18
Burney, Charles Rousseau (harpsichordist), 1766: DL, Dec 3; 1767: DL, Jan 1,
  15, Feb 12, 23, Mar 12, Apr 7, 25, 30, May 14, 23, Jun 3
Burney, Frances (playwright), 1776: CG, Oct 16; 1782: HAY, Jul 16
Burney, Thomas (dancer), 1726: LIF, May 9, Jul 22, 26, 29, Aug 2, 5, 9, 16, 19,
  23, Oct 12; 1727: DL, Oct 6, Nov 1; 1728: DL, Mar 30, Apr 30, May 9, Sep 19,
  Oct 10, 30, Nov 15; 1729: DL, May 8, 26, GF, Nov 25, Dec 2, 12, 15, 16, 17,
  19; 1730: GF, Jan 1, 3, 7, 20, 24, Feb 12, 23, Mar 2, 7, 9, 10, 14, 21, Apr
  1, 2, 3, 7, 10, 14, 16, 20, 24, May 13, 27, 28, Jun 1, 3, 4, 9, 12, 16, 19,
  30; 1731: GF, Dec 4, 6, 9, 11, 16, 17, 18, 20, 21, 22; 1732: GF, Jan 15, 25,
  26, 27, Feb 15, 17, 22, 24, 29, Mar 4, 25, 30, Apr 1, 12, 14, 15, 17, 19, 20,
  21, 24, 26, 27, 28
Burnley (house servant), 1732: LIF, May 18
Burns (actor), 1775: DL, May 27
Burnum (actor), 1729: HAY, Jan 10
Buroni, Sga (singer), 1777: KING'S, Dec 16
Burr, Mrs (singer), 1694: DLORDG, Feb 0

118

Burroughs (house servant), 1772: DL, Jun 10; 1774: DL, May 28; 1775: DL, May
    26; 1776: DL, May 22; 1778: DL, May 23; 1779: DL, May 28; 1780: DL, May 20;
    1781: DL, May 12
Burroughs, Mrs (actor), 1672: DG, Jul 4; 1673: DG, Mar 12
Burrows (house servant), 1746: GF, Feb 20
Burrows, James (actor), 1796: HAY, Sep 1, DL, 29; 1797: DL, May 18; 1799: CG,
    Jun 7
Burt (actor), 1745: GF, Oct 28, Nov 18
Burt, Nicholas (actor), 1659: NONE, Sep 0; 1660: NONE, Sep 0, COCKPIT, Oct 8,
    11, REDBULL, Nov 5, VERE, Dec 0, 3, 6, 8; 1661: NONE, Sep 0; 1662: VERE, Jan
    28; 1663: VERE, Mar 0, BRIDGES, May 7, NONE, Sep 0; 1664: NONE, Sep 0; 1665:
    BRIDGES, Jan 14, Apr 0; 1666: NONE, Sep 0, ATCOURT, Dec 10, BRIDGES, 27;
    1667: BRI/COUR, Feb 0, BRIDGES, Apr 16, 17, Oct 5, 19, Nov 2, Dec 11; 1668:
    BRIDGES, Jun 12, Sep 14, Nov 6, Dec 18; 1669: BRIDGES, Feb 6, Apr 17, May 6;
    1672: LIF, Nov 0; 1673: LIF, May 0; 1674: DL, May 16; 1675: DL, May 10; 1677:
    DL, Oct 0; 1678: DL, Mar 0
Burton, Edmund (actor), 1746: CG, Apr 30, Jun 11, GF, Oct 27, Nov 4, Dec 3, 16,
    18; 1747: GF, Mar 19, DL, Apr 20, HAY, 22, DL, 29, Nov 6, Dec 16, 26; 1748:
    DL, Jan 2, Apr 11, May 2, BF, Aug 24, SFBCBV, Sep 7; 1749: DL, Feb 6, Mar 6,
    Apr 29; 1750: DL, Jan 6, 15, Apr 23, Sep 28, Nov 14, Dec 3, 6, 14, 31; 1751:
    DL, Jan 5, 31, Feb 23, Mar 11, 18, Apr 29, May 10, 13, 17, Sep 7, 10, 12, 13,
    14, 18, Oct 10, 11, 22, 29, Nov 4, 28; 1752: DL, Jan 1, 16, 22, 28, Feb 6,
    13, Mar 14, Apr 14, 17, 18, 27, Sep 19, 21, Oct 5, 14, 16, 19, 23, 28, Nov 4,
    8, 25, 27, Dec 7, 8, 18; 1753: DL, Jan 8, 18, 24, Feb 7, 22, Mar 3, 19, 20,
    Apr 23, May 2, 4, 17, 21, 22, Sep 13, 18, 27, 29, Oct 3, 4, 9, 10, 12, 16,
    20, 23, 25, Nov 5, 14, 26, Dec 1, 22; 1754: DL, Jan 23, Feb 14, 18, 20, Mar
    18, 25, Apr 30, May 2, 13, 15, 20, Sep 14, 19, 24, 26, Oct 3, 5, 8, 26, Nov
    4, 11, 22, 30, Dec 9, 13; 1755: DL, Jan 21, 25, Feb 18, Mar 15, 18, 20, Apr
    8, 15, 25, May 6, 12, 19, Sep 13, 18, 20, 27, Oct 2, 4, 8, 10, 13, 17, 24,
    27, 28, Nov 4, 8, 15, Dec 5, 18; 1756: DL, Jan 2, 21, Feb 10, 24, 27, Mar 23,
    30, Apr 3, 10, 29, May 8, 10, 14, Sep 18, 23, 25, 30, Oct 2, 7, 9, 15, 16,
    21, 27, Nov 4, 6, 11, 12, 17, 18, Dec 10, 11, 27; 1757: DL, Jan 24, 27, Feb
    2, 5, Mar 24, Apr 11, 20, 26, 30, May 2, 6, 9, Sep 17, 20, 24, 29, Oct 4, 6,
    8, 11, 13, 15, 20, 25, 26, 27, Nov 4, 19, 22, Dec 3; 1758: DL, Jan 23, 28,
    Apr 5, 18, 22, May 2, 4, Jun 1, Sep 16, 19, 23, 26, 28, Oct 3, 7, 12, 17, 18,
    30, Nov 2, 4, 7, 8, 14, 16, Dec 13, 26, 28; 1759: DL, Jan 3, 6, 20, Feb 1,
    26, Mar 3, 20, 24, 31, Apr 7, 21, 27, May 7, 11, 14, 16, 18, 21, Jun 19, Jul
    12, Sep 25, 27, 29, Oct 2, 4, 9, 11, 12, 17, 19, 22, 23, 30, Nov 1, 3, 5, 13,
    22, 24, Dec 1, 12, 14, 31; 1760: DL, Jan 1, 11, Feb 8, 13, 21, Mar 17, 25,
    Apr 9, 28, 29, 30, May 3, 7, 8, 13, 16, Jun 19, Jul 29, Sep 20, 23, 30, Oct
    3, 7, 11, 15, 18, 22, 23, 24, 25, Nov 27, Dec 17, 30; 1761: DL, Feb 12, Mar
    28, Apr 1, 6, 17, 18, 20, 23, 24, 28, 29, May 1, 4, 11, 14, 25, Sep 8, 10,
    14, 15, 19, 28, 30, Oct 1, 7, 16, 17, 20, 24, 26, 29, 31, Nov 6, 9, 10, 17,
    28, Dec 29; 1762: DL, Jan 7, 15, 27, Feb 22, Mar 15, 20, Apr 21, 22, 28, May
    6, 7, 8, 15, 18, Sep 18, 28, Oct 1, 4, 6, 7, 8, 9, 11, 13, 14, 15, 23, 28,
    Nov 2, 3, 4, 10, 12, 16, 18, 19, 20, 27, Dec 10, 15, 22, 23, 27; 1763: DL,
    Jan 11, 14, 15, 17, 19, 22, Feb 28, Mar 1, 14, Apr 13, 20, May 7, 11, 17, Sep
    17, 20, 22, Oct 1, 8, 12, 17, 19, 21, 24, 31, Nov 1, 2, 9, 22, 23, 29, Dec
    14, 17, 26, 28; 1764: DL, Jan 7, 14, 18, 27, Feb 18, 21, Mar 3, 20, 27, 31,
    Apr 2, 25, May 1, 21, Sep 15, 18, 20, 22, 25, 27, Oct 4, 6, 13, 15, 17, 18,
    19, 20, 24, 31, Nov 9, 24, Dec 8, 13; 1765: DL, Jan 1, 2, 3, 8, 15, Feb 2, 5,
    6, 16, 26, Mar 16, 26, Apr 10, 13, 20, 22, May 3, Sep 14, 17, 19, 24, 26, Oct
    2, 12, 22, 23, 25, 28, 31, Nov 15, 16, Dec 20; 1766: DL, Jan 6, 9, 13, 17,
    22, Feb 13, Mar 18, 20, Apr 12, 14, 15, 16, May 2, 5, 19, 20, 22, Sep 23, 25,
    30, Oct 7, 8, 18, 29, 31, Nov 20, 24, Dec 2, 4, 6, 10; 1767: DL, Jan 24, Feb
    9, 21, Mar 21, 30, Apr 11, May 4, 8, 11, Jun 1, Sep 15, 16, 17, 18, 19, 21,
    23, 26, Oct 9, 10, 20, 21, 23, 26, 29, Nov 11, 19, 20, Dec 1, 7, 15; 1768:
    DL, Jan 14, 19, Mar 15, 19, Apr 12, 14, 26, 29, 30, Sep 17, 20, 22, 23, 26,
    29, Oct 4, 10, 11, 14, 15, 18, 25, 31, Nov 21; 1769: DL, Jan 24, 25, 27, Mar
    16, 29, Apr 3, 18, 25, May 1, Sep 19, 21, 23, 28, Oct 2, 3, 6, 7, 9, 11, 23,
    Nov 8, 9, 13, 16, 18, 22, 29, Dec 4, 23; 1770: DL, Jan 2, 4, 16, Mar 20, Apr
    3, 19, 26, May 4, 21, Sep 22, 29, Oct 3, 12, 16, 23, 31, Nov 1, 2, 3, 6, Dec
    4, 6; 1771: DL, Jan 2, 5, Mar 11, 21, Apr 2, 13, 15, 30, May 29, Sep 21, 26,
    28, Oct 17, 25, 29, Nov 28, Dec 2, 3, 23, 31; 1772: DL, Jan 7
Burton, Edmund and John (actors), 1766: DL, May 2
Burton, Elizabeth (actor), 1768: DL, Dec 1, 27; 1769: DL, Jan 18, May 10, Sep
    30, Oct 4; 1770: DL, Jan 6, Feb 27, Mar 22, May 12, 15, 22, HAY, Aug 13, DL,
    Nov 21, Dec 21, 22; 1771: DL, Mar 14, 23, Apr 6, 20, 26, 30
Burton, George (singer), 1749: DL, Apr 29, May 8; 1750: DL, Apr 30; 1751: DL,
    May 2; 1752: DL, Apr 20, 27; 1753: DL, May 4; 1754: DL, May 6; 1756: DL, Feb
    11; 1778: HAY, Sep 7; 1780: HAY, Apr 5; 1783: HAY, May 31
Burton, John (actor), 1762: DL, Oct 5, 28, Nov 3, 5, 17; 1763: DL, Jan 17, Apr

13, Sep 17, Oct 4, 24, Nov 29, Dec 5; <u>1764</u>: DL, Jan 18, Feb 20, 21, Mar 3, May 1, Sep 20, Oct 6, Nov 9, 13, 27; <u>1765</u>: DL, Feb 4, May 6, Oct 14, 18, Dec 7; <u>1766</u>: DL, Jan 20, 21, 24, Apr 12, 16, May 2, Sep 27, Oct 25; <u>1767</u>: DL, Jan 24, Feb 7, 9, May 6, 8, 11, Sep 17, 23, Dec 7, 10, 26; <u>1768</u>: DL, Mar 19, Apr 6, 29, May 26, 30, Sep 8, 17, 20, Oct 3, 6, 10, 31, Dec 7, 16; <u>1769</u>: DL, Jan 25, Mar 28, Apr 6, 12, 18, 21, Oct 2, 14, Nov 22, Dec 6, 8, CG, 14, 30; <u>1770</u>: DL, Feb 3, CG, Apr 20, DL, 26, May 4, 5, CG, Sep 24, 28, DL, Oct 5, 13, 29, Nov 3, 17, 23, 24, Dec 5, 6; <u>1771</u>: DL, Jan 2, Mar 7, 14, Apr 6, 17, 30, May 28, Nov 25, Dec 3, 4, 6, 14, 26; <u>1772</u>: DL, Jan 20, Mar 12, 28, Apr 4, 6, 25, May 4, 11, 12, 20, 22, Oct 1, 28, Nov 20, 27, 28, Dec 26; <u>1773</u>: DL, Jan 1, CG, 19, DL, Feb 4, CG, 6, 13, DL, 17, Apr 1, 3, 21, 23, May 1, 7, 24, Jun 2, MARLY, Sep 3, HAY, 18, DL, 25, Oct 11, 14, 20, CG, 20, DL, Nov 25, 26, Dec 16, 27, 30; <u>1774</u>: CG, Jan 14, DL, 19, 21, Feb 2, 7, 12, 24, Mar 12, 15, 21, Apr 8, 19, 25, May 2, 10, 11, 19, 28, Jun 2, HAY, Jul 15, 22, Aug 19, 24, 26, Sep 5, 6, 19, DL, 20, 27, Oct 5, CG, 11, DL, 12, 14, 20, 24, Nov 1, 3, 5, 11, 17, 18, 29, 30, Dec 7; <u>1775</u>: DL, Jan 2, 23, Mar 18, 28, Apr 17, May 6, 10, 11, 12, 15, 16, 20, Sep 26, 30, Oct 5, 11, 21, 26, 30, Nov 8, 10, 11, 16, 22, 25, Dec 11, 16; <u>1776</u>: DL, Jan 26, Feb 1, 12, Mar 21, 23, 25, 28, Apr 17, 24, May 1, 4, 8, 11, 13, 22, 23, Jun 3, HAY, 19, Jul 8, Sep 18, DL, 21, 26, Oct 9, 15, 18, 22, 25, Nov 5, 14, 21, 29, Dec 10, 14; <u>1777</u>: DL, Jan 1, 10, Feb 11, 20, 24, Mar 20, 31, Apr 7, 23, Jun 6, Sep 25, 27, Oct 31, Nov 10, Dec 3, 4, 13; <u>1778</u>: DL, Jan 1, 2, Feb 2, 10, 24, Apr 9, 20, 21, 27, May 2, 5, 21, 23, Sep 17, 19, 26, Oct 1, 3, 8, 15, 28, 31, Nov 4, 9, Dec 8, 21; <u>1779</u>: DL, Jan 8, 19, Mar 15, 16, 18, 22, 27, Apr 5, 16, 19, May 4, 10, 11, 18, 25, Sep 21, 25, 30, Oct 5, 7, 12, 30, Nov 5, 24, Dec 2, 27, 28, 29, 31; <u>1780</u>: DL, Jan 3, 11, 24, Apr 1, 3, 4, 14, 17, 21, 28, May 2, 4, 5, 10, 23, Sep 16, 19, 21, 23, 28, 30, Oct 3, 5, 11, 17, 25, 30, Nov 1, 2, 3, 8, 9, 18, 22, Dec 1, 4, 7; <u>1781</u>: DL, Jan 6, 16, Mar 19, 31, Apr 18, 24, May 1, 17, HAY, 30, Jul 28, DL, Sep 18, 25, 29, Oct 12, 15, 16, 18, 22, 24, CG, 27, DL, Dec 14, 31; <u>1782</u>: DL, Jan 3, Feb 2, CG, 18, DL, 25, 28, Mar 21, Apr 6, 15, 25, 27, May 3, 4, 7, 8, 14, 18, 29, HAY, Aug 17, DL, Sep 18, 19, 24, 28, Oct 3, 8, 10, 12, 26, 29, Nov 1, 5, 7, 14, 22, 23, 26, 30, Dec 26; <u>1783</u>: DL, Jan 3, 9, 24, Feb 12, Mar 3, 6, 20, 24, Apr 3, 7, 21, May 2, 12, 15, HAY, Jun 30, Aug 26, DL, Sep 16, 18, 25, 30, Oct 4, 7, 11, 13, 14, 18, 20, 31, Nov 8, 14, 18, 20, 24, 28, Dec 2, 13, 19, 29; <u>1784</u>: DL, Jan 7, 10, 13, 16, Mar 8, 29, Apr 16, 19, May 7, 10, 15, 18, Sep 16, 18, 21, 23, 25, Oct 11, 23, 26, Nov 1, 4, 23, Dec 10; <u>1785</u>: DL, Jan 11, 12, 13, 14, 20, Feb 8, 10, 21, Mar 17, Apr 1, 11, May 3, 9, 11, 12, 26, HAY, Jun 14, 16, 21, 23, 24, 29, 30, Jul 1, 9, 11, 13, 19, 21, 26, Aug 16, 19, 23, 31, Sep 2, DL, 20, 24, 27, Oct 6, 13, 26, Nov 2, 3, 9, 17, 26, Dec 1, 5, 26; <u>1786</u>: DL, Jan 16, Feb 18, Apr 6, 18, 26, 28, May 17, 22, 29, Jun 1, HAY, 12, 13, 17, 28, Jul 3, 7, 19, 21, 25, 28, Aug 4, 15, 29, Sep 11, DL, Oct 12, 27, 30, Nov 15, 18, 25, 29, Dec 26, 28; <u>1787</u>: DL, Jan 11, 13, 24, Mar 8, 29, Apr 9, 10, 13, 18, 27, May 3, 9, 21, 22, 28, HAY, Jun 18, 21, 27, 28, Jul 2, 19, 23, 25, Aug 4, 7, 24, Sep 8, DL, 18, 20, 25, 29, Oct 2, 26, Nov 3, 6, 21, 27, Dec 14, 22, 26; <u>1788</u>: DL, Jan 5, 21, 22, Feb 7, Mar 13, 31, Apr 10, 14, 25, 28, 30, May 1, 6, 19, 21, 22, 23, 30, Jun 2, HAY, 10, 11, 14, 19, 23, 26, 30, Jul 2, 10, Aug 4, 5, 9, 15, 25, 27, DL, Sep 13, 16, 18, 20, 27, 30, Oct 2, 7, 16, 22, 25, Nov 1, 8, 10, 17, 19, Dec 18; <u>1789</u>: DL, Jan 8, 10, 13, Feb 7, 21, 28, Mar 14, 17, Apr 15, May 5, 28, Jun 2, 5, 13, HAY, 19, 29, 30, Jul 3, 9, 30, 31, Aug 5, 10, 11, 27, 28, DL, Sep 12, 17, 19, 22, 24, Oct 1, 8, 15, 20, 24, Nov 4, 27, Dec 10, 23, 26; <u>1790</u>: DL, Jan 19, 26, 27, Feb 13, 18, 20, 23, Mar 2, 18, 22, May 14, 15, 18, 25, 26, Jun 3, HAY, 14, 15, 17, 19, 22, 26, 28, 30, Jul 5, 28, Aug 2, 7, 12, 31, Sep 4, 14, DL, 14, 16, Oct 2, 4, 7, 12, HAY, 13, DL, 16, 19, 20, 25, 26, 27, Nov 30, Dec 1, 14, 27; <u>1791</u>: DL, Jan 25, Feb 7, Mar 22, 24, 31, Apr 27, 29, 30, May 10, 11, 19, 20, HAY, Jun 6, 10, 13, 20, 23, 30, Jul 1, 4, 8, 14, 15, 20, 26, 30, Aug 5, 15, 16, 31, DLKING'S, Sep 27, 29, Oct 1, 3, 8, 13, 20, 25, 31, Nov 1, 2, 5, 7, 8, 10, 12, 30, Dec 1; <u>1792</u>: DLKING'S, Jan 9, Feb 11, 18, 23, 27, Apr 10, 11, 12, May 31, HAY, Jun 15, 18, 20, 23, 26, Jul 3, 9, 11, 14, 27, 31, DL, Sep 15, 18, 25, Oct 2, 4, 27, Nov 2, Dec 3, 4, 8, 10, 26, 27; <u>1793</u>: DL, Jan 16, Feb 16, 23, Mar 4, 7, 14, 16, Apr 5, 8, May 10, Jun 1, 4, HAY, 11, 21, 22, 24, 29, Jul 1, 5, 13, 25, Aug 3, 6, 14, 26, 28, Sep 10, 24, Oct 1, 7, 8, 15, 21, 22, 29, 30, Nov 5, 6, 16, Dec 10, 30; <u>1794</u>: HAY, Feb 8, 25, Mar 13, 17, DL, Apr 25, May 5, 6, 8, 16, 17, 30, Jun 4, 10, 14, HAY, Jul 8, 9, 10, 17, 18, 21, 22, Aug 4, 9, 11, 12, 13, 27, 29, Sep 1, 17, DL, 23, Oct 31, Dec 10, 12; <u>1795</u>: DL, Jan 13, 26, Feb 6, 12, Mar 16, Apr 24, May 29, 30, Jun 3, HAY, 9, 10, 11, 12, 13, 16, 24, 27, Jul 1, 4, 6, 8, 16, 18, 25, 30, 31, Aug 3, 20, 21, DL, Oct 27, Nov 5, 6, 14, 20, Dec 2, 10, 18, 19, 30; <u>1796</u>: DL, Jan 18, 22, Apr 18, 25, 29, May 11, Jun 8, HAY, 11, DL, 11, HAY, 13, DL, 13, HAY, 14, 17, 18, 20, 22, 25, 29, 30, Jul 5, 6, 7, 8, 9, 11, 15, 19, 21, 23, 26, Aug 12, 20

Burton, John (harpsichordist), <u>1749</u>: DL, Nov 24; <u>1757</u>: DL, Mar 25

Burton, Mrs (boxkeeper), 1722: DL, Apr 28; 1723: DL, May 7; 1724: DL, Apr 25;
  1725: DL, Apr 27; 1726: DL, Apr 30; 1727: DL, Apr 7; 1728: DL, May 14; 1729:
  DL, May 12; 1730: DL, May 14
Burton, Mrs Edmund (beneficiary), 1772: DL, May 11
Burton, Philippina (actor, author), 1770: HAY, Apr 27, Aug 8, 30, Sep 3, Nov 16
--Fashion Displayed, 1770: HAY, Apr 27, 30, May 9, Nov 16
Burton, William (actor, scene painter), 1794: CG, Sep 15, 24, Oct 14, 20, 30;
  1795: CG, Mar 19, 28, Apr 6, 8, May 14, 29, 30, Jun 16
Burtt (actor), 1784: HAY, Nov 16
Bury (beneficiary), 1720: DL, Jun 1; 1721: DL, May 29
Bury (singer), 1675: ATCOURT, Feb 15
Bury Fair. See Shadwell, Thomas.
Bury, Miss (dancer), 1789: HAY, May 22
Busby, Thomas (composer), 1786: HAY, Jul 7; 1799: HAY, Mar 29; 1800: CG, Jan
  16, Jun 16
--Britannia (oratorio), 1800: CG, Jun 16
--Prophecy, The (oratorio), 1799: HAY, Mar 29
Bush (actor), 1779: HAY, Jan 11
Bush (violinist), 1741: GF, Apr 2
Bushell (gallery keeper), 1769: CG, May 20, 23; 1770: CG, May 19, 24
Busiri, Overo il Trionfo D'Amore. See Pescetti, Giovanni Battista.
Busiris, King of Egypt. See Young, Edward.
Buss (beneficiary), 1750: DL, Feb 21
Bussy D'Ambois. See Chapman, George.
Bussy D'Ambois; or, The Husbands Revenge. See D'Urfey, Thomas.
Busy Body, The. See Centlivre, Susannah.
But bright Cecilia (song), 1789: CG, Mar 20; 1791: CG, Mar 25; 1792: CG, Mar 9,
  KING'S, 23, 30; 1793: CG, Feb 20; 1794: CG, Mar 26; 1797: CG, Mar 22; 1798:
  CG, Mar 28
But His Name Liveth (song), 1793: CG, Feb 15
But thanks be to God (song), 1793: KING/HAY, Feb 20; 1794: DL, Mar 19
But the waters overwhelmed (song), 1791: CG, Mar 23
But thou didst not leave his soul (song), 1790: CG, Mar 26; 1792: KING'S, Mar
  23; 1793: KING/HAY, Feb 20; 1794: DL, Mar 19; 1795: CG, Mar 20, 27; 1797: CG,
  Mar 3
But who may abide (song), 1793: KING/HAY, Feb 20; 1794: DL, Mar 19
Butcher (actor), 1724: BFP, Aug 22, SF, Sep 5; 1725: LIF, May 21, Oct 13
Butcher Row, 1728: LIF, May 11; 1732: LIF, Apr 27
Butcher Turned Gentleman, The (farce, anon), 1717: LIF, Mar 18, Apr 24; see
  also Footman Turned Gentleman, The
Butcher, Master (singer), 1746: SOU, Oct 27
Butcher, Mrs (actor), 1724: LIF, Aug 11, SF, Sep 5; 1725: LIF, Jan 4, 11, 15,
  Mar 13, Apr 5, 26, May 6, 17, Oct 4
Bute, Earl of (spectator), 1757: CG, Nov 25; 1761: DL, Jun 18
Bute, Lady (spectator), 1761: DL, Jul 27
Buthred. See Johnstone.
Butler (actor), 1770: HAY, Nov 21; 1774: HAY, Jan 24
Butler (beneficiary), 1720: LIF, May 27
Butler (beneficiary), 1748: NWSM, Dec 26
Butler (Boteler), Charlotte (actor, singer, dancer), 1675: ATCOURT, Feb 15;
  1680: DG, Feb 0, Jun 0; 1682: DG, Mar 0, Apr 0, Aug 10; 1683: DG, May 31, Jul
  0; 1684: DL, Mar 0, NONE, Aug 0; 1688: NONE, Sep 0; 1689: DL, Mar 0, Apr 0;
  1690: DL, Jan 0, DLORDG, Mar 0, DL, 0, Sep 0, NONE, 0, DL/IT, Oct 21, DL, Dec
  0; 1691: DL, Jan 0, DG, May 0, NONE, Sep 0, DL, Dec 0; 1692: DL, Jan 0, Feb
  0, Apr 0, DG, May 2
Butler (house servant), 1798: DL, Jun 9; 1799: DL, Jul 3
Butler, Elizabeth (actor), 1726: DL, Mar 24, Apr 15, 27, 29, May 11, 25, Sep 3,
  10, Oct 20, 27, Nov 26, Dec 14, 20; 1727: DL, Apr 14, 27, May 19, Sep 7, 16,
  19, 21, Oct 3, Nov 18, 21, Dec 4, 5; 1728: DL, Mar 9, May 2, 23, Sep 26, Oct
  8, 12; 1729: DL, Feb 15, 24, Mar 17, Apr 12, 14, 25, May 3, 14, Jun 13, Jul
  25, Sep 20, Oct 9, 23, 31, Nov 3, 19, Dec 13; 1730: DL, Mar 30, Apr 21, Sep
  17, Oct 10, 20, Nov 26, Dec 1; 1731: DL, Jan 20, Feb 22, Apr 1, 19, 23, May
  3, 7, 31, Jun 11, 22, Jul 23, Sep 21, 25, Oct 7, 9, 16, 21, 30, Nov 8, 13,
  15, 22, 24, Dec 17, 21, 22; 1732: DL, Feb 14, Apr 20, May 4, 5, Jun 9, Aug 4,
  15, 21, Sep 28, Oct 3, 10, 21, 26, Nov 7, 11, 13, 18, 23, Dec 6, 9, 14; 1733:
  DL, Jan 13, 22, 25, Feb 15, 17, 22, Mar 29, Apr 13, 19, 24, May 5, 29, Jun 4,
  DL/HAY, Sep 26, Oct 3, 5, 6, 8, 13, 17, 19, 20, 25, Nov 10, 23, 26, 27, Dec
  5, 12, 19, 22, HAY, 26; 1734: DL/HAY, Jan 12, 17, HAY, Feb 12, DL/HAY, Mar
  12, 23, 25, 30, Apr 2, DL, 4, 22, 29, DL/HAY, May 1, DL, 13, 16, 21, Sep 7,
  10, 14, 26, 28, Oct 8, 12, 17, 19, 21, 23, 26, Nov 8, 16, 20, Dec 6, 14, 19;
  1735: DL, Jan 13, 20, Feb 4, 10, 25, Mar 10, 13, Apr 14, 21, 23, 25, 28, May
  2, 10, Oct 1, 2, 7, 9, 11, 21, 23, 24, 25, 30, Nov 1, 3, 6, 10, 12, 17, 19,

20, 21, 26, Dec 6, 26; 1736: DL, Feb 5, Mar 4, 23, Apr 15, 29, May 4, 26, Sep 4, 7, 9, 18, 21, Oct 5, 21, 23, 25, 29, 30, Nov 1, 6, 8, 12, 13, 20, Dec 17, 23; 1737: DL, Jan 6, Feb 7, 28, Mar 1, 12, Apr 16, 27, May 2, Aug 30, Sep 3, 17, 24, 29, Oct 6, 24, 27, 31, Nov 11, 14, 16, 17, 19; 1738: DL, Jan 19, 31, Feb 10, Mar 2, 16, 21, Apr 21, 29, May 2, 3, 8, 13, 19, Sep 7, 9, 19, 21, 26, Oct 3, 20, 21, 24, 30, Nov 1, 2, 3, Dec 26; 1739: DL, Jan 3, 8, 15, 22, 26, Feb 3, 13, Mar 10, 13, 17, 27, Apr 12, 25, 28, 30, May 1, Sep 1, 4, 13, 15, 18, 20, 21, 24, Oct 6, 8, 10, 11, 13, 16, 18, 19, 22, 23, Nov 3, 8, 12, Dec 8, 14, 22; 1740: DL, Jan 5, 16, 19, Feb 7, 16, 23, Mar 11, 13, 17, 20, 27, Apr 16, 17, 22, 29, May 2, 20, 29, Sep 6, 9, 11, 23, 27, 30, Oct 4, 9, 11, 15, 23, 27, Nov 1, 6, 8, 11, 27, 29, Dec 6; 1741: DL, Mar 14, 31, Apr 4, 24, May 13, 14, 25, Jun 4, Sep 5, 8, 10, 12, 17, 19, Oct 6, 8, 10, 20, Nov 16, Dec 7, 14; 1742: DL, Jan 1, 22, Feb 11, 13, 15, Mar 8, 20, 29, 30, May 12, 19, LIF, Nov 24, Dec 1, 3, 13, 27, 30; 1743: LIF, Feb 2, 9, 17, 28, Mar 14, Apr 4
Butler, Elizabeth Preston, Duchess of Ormond, 1678: ATCOURT, Jan 18
Butler, James (actor), 1732: CR, Feb 23; 1733: DL, Jan 20; 1734: YB, Aug 28; 1739: KING'S, Jan 16
Butler, James, Duke of Ormond, 1667: LIF, Feb 4; 1668: LIF, May 11; 1671: ORMONDS, Feb 27; 1673: YH, May 5; 1676: DG, Nov 4; 1681: ATCOURT, Nov 15
Butler, John (gallery office keeper), 1786: KING'S, Dec 23; 1787: KING'S, Mar 17, Dec 8; 1788: KING'S, Apr 5
Butler, Lord John (spectator), 1667: LIF, Feb 4
Butler, Miss (singer), 1795: DL, Jun 4
Butler, Mrs (actor, singer), 1746: GF, Oct 27, 28, 31, Nov 4, 6, 7, 13, 14, Dec 27; 1748: BFP, Aug 24, DL, Sep 16; 1749: HAY, Apr 29, BFY, Aug 23; 1750: HAY, Feb 16
Butler, Mrs (householder), 1742: CG, Apr 20
Butler, Mrs William (actor, singer), 1786: DL, May 23; 1789: DL, Sep 24, Oct 13, Nov 13, 14, 17, Dec 26; 1790: DL, Jan 13; 1791: DLKING'S, Sep 27, Oct 15; 1792: DLKING'S, Feb 18, Mar 29, May 23, DL, Oct 11, Nov 21, Dec 26; 1793: DL, Mar 7; 1794: DL, Apr 21, 28, May 16, Jun 9, 24, HAY, Jul 17, 21, 24, 28, Aug 27, DL, Sep 27, Oct 22, 27, 31, Nov 15, Dec 20; 1795: DL, Feb 6, 12, May 6, HAY, Jun 13, 20, Jul 31, Sep 21, DL, Nov 11, 23, Dec 4, 10; 1796: DL, Jan 11, 18, Mar 3, 12, Apr 30, Jun 11, HAY, Jul 15, Aug 29, DL, Oct 19, Nov 9; 1797: DL, Jan 7, 20, Feb 9, May 24, Jun 10, HAY, 23, Aug 14, 15, 24, DL, Nov 8, Dec 9; 1798: DL, Feb 24, HAY, Jun 30, Jul 21, Aug 11, DL, Nov 14, Dec 4, 29; 1799: DL, Jan 19, May 24, HAY, Jul 9, Aug 21, DL, Oct 14, Nov 14, Dec 11, 28; 1800: DL, Jan 1, Mar 11, 13, Apr 29, May 3, Jun 12, HAY, Aug 14, 29
Butler, Philip (master carpenter), 1774: DL, Dec 3; 1775: DL, Sep 28; 1776: DL, May 4; 1777: DL, Apr 25; 1778: DL, May 11; 1779: DL, Jan 21, May 11, HAY, Oct 13, DL, Nov 5; 1780: DL, May 5; 1781: DL, May 4; 1782: DL, May 9, Sep 24; 1783: DL, May 20; 1784: DL, May 19; 1785: DL, May 17, Oct 1
Butler, Richard, Earl of Arran, 1664: BRIDGES, Sep 14; 1665: ATCOURT, Feb 2; 1678: ATCOURT, Jan 18; 1680: DGORDL, Feb 19; 1681: ATCOURT, Nov 15
Butler, Samuel (prologuist), 1668: ATCOURT, Oct 14
Butler, Thomas Stanley (composer), 1779: CG, Mar 20; 1780: CG, Feb 1
Butler, Thomas, Earl of Ossory, 1660: VERE, Dec 13
Butler, William (actor, dancer), 1780: DL, May 5; 1781: DL, May 4; 1782: DL, May 9; 1783: DL, May 20; 1784: DL, May 17; 1785: DL, May 17; 1794: DL, Jun 9, Sep 27, Nov 10, Dec 20; 1795: DL, Jun 6, Oct 30; 1796: DL, Jan 18, Apr 4, Oct 1, 19, 29, Nov 9, Dec 26
Butterfly (dance), 1770: DL, May 24; 1772: DL, Dec 4, 7, 30; 1780: DL, Sep 21, 26, Oct 5, 7, Dec 16; 1781: DL, Jan 15, Mar 6, Apr 24, 26, May 8, 10, 15, 17, 18, 23; 1783: DL, Apr 26, May 5, 7, 12, 16, 20
Butters, R (publisher), 1783: DL, Nov 22
Buttery, Miss (actor), 1781: CG, Dec 26; see also Cleland, Miss
Buxom Joan. See Willet, Thomas.
Buxom Lass (dance), 1735: CG/LIF, Apr 11
Buxton (actor), 1782: HAY, Mar 4
Buxton and Enderby (oil merchants), 1767: CG, Apr 27; 1771: CG, Dec 11; 1772: CG, Dec 28; 1773: CG, Feb 4, 17, Nov 1; 1774: CG, Jan 28, Apr 22
Buzaglio, Abraham (smith), 1767: CG, Dec 21; 1776: DL, Mar 16
Buzarglo (Barzago), Louis (scene painter), 1794: DL, Apr 21, Oct 28
By Jove I'll be free (song), 1748: NWSM, May 4
By sweet Music's powerful Note (song), 1798: CG, Apr 9
By the gaily circling Glass (song), 1800: CG, Jun 6
By these pigsnes eyes that stars do seem (song), 1693: DL, Apr 0
Byfield (organ builder), 1772: DL, Apr 9
Bynam, J (house servant), 1799: DL, Jul 2; 1800: DL, Jun 13
Byrd. See Bird.
Byrn (wigmaker), 1771: DL, Nov 18

Byrn, Eleanor (dancer), 1772: DL, May 5; 1774: DL, Apr 30; 1780: HAY, May 30;
  1781: HAY, Mar 26, May 30, Jun 1, 12, Jul 6, 23, Aug 8, 15; 1782: HAY, Jun 3,
  Aug 17, CG, Dec 6; 1783: CG, May 24, 26, HAY, Jun 5, 30, Jul 2, CG, Nov 19;
  1784: CG, Mar 18
Byrn, James (dancer), 1772: DL, May 5, Oct 10; 1774: DL, Apr 30, Jun 2; 1777:
  DL, Nov 10; 1778: HAY, Jun 8; 1779: HAY, Aug 27; 1780: HAY, May 30, Jun 5;
  1781: HAY, Mar 26, May 30, Jun 1, 12, Jul 6, 23, Aug 8, 10, 15; 1782: HAY,
  Jun 3, Aug 17, CG, Nov 29, Dec 6; 1783: CG, May 23, 24, 26, HAY, Jun 5, 20,
  30, Jul 2, 4, CG, Nov 19; 1784: CG, Apr 27, 28, May 21, Jun 10, HAY, Jul 13,
  Aug 26, CG, Oct 6, 22; 1785: CG, Mar 17, HAY, Jun 1, 27, Jul 6, 13, 28, Aug
  11, 31, CG, Sep 19, Oct 7, 10, Nov 10, 23; 1786: CG, Feb 24, Mar 4, HAY, Jun
  12, 19, 22, 30, Jul 3, 17, Aug 2, 12, Sep 4, CG, Oct 2, 6, Nov 14, Dec 12;
  1787: CG, Feb 9, 17, May 31, HAY, Jul 2, Aug 6, 14, 17, 21, CG, Sep 28; 1788:
  CG, Jan 24, 28, Feb 4, May 28, 30, HAY, Jun 10, 11, 27, Jul 7, Aug 5, 13, 15,
  Sep 4, CG, 15, Oct 1, 10, 22, Nov 7, Dec 26; 1789: CG, Feb 19, Mar 3, 16, 28,
  Apr 13, May 2, 7, 28, Jun 6, 8, 12, 13, HAY, Jul 16, 27, CG, Sep 16, 21, Oct
  2, 21, 24, Nov 13, 19, Dec 21, 31; 1790: CG, Jan 29, Feb 4, Mar 22, 23, Apr
  8, May 24, Jun 1, 4, 8, HAY, 19, 25, 26, Jul 1, 13, 16, CG, Oct 4, Nov 6, 15,
  23, Dec 20; 1791: CG, Jan 12, 15, Jun 6, HAY, 17, Jul 1, CG, Oct 20, 29, Nov
  2, 21, Dec 21, 22, 30; 1792: CG, Jan 11, 25, Feb 28, Apr 10, May 9, 10, 19,
  24, 28, Sep 20, Oct 8, 18, 25, 27, Nov 16, 24, Dec 20, 26; 1793: CG, Jan 16,
  Mar 11, 16, 23, Apr 15, May 3, 4, 10, 27, Sep 16, Oct 2, 12, 18, Nov 19, Dec
  19; 1794: CG, Feb 6, 12, 22, 25, Apr 7, 12, May 2, 9, 15, 23, 24, 26, Jun 6,
  Sep 26, Oct 1, 14, 20, 29, Nov 17, Dec 26; 1795: CG, Feb 19, 26, Mar 14, Apr
  6, 28, May 1, 6, 12, 13, 16, 29, Jun 6, Sep 21, Oct 2, 7, 8, 12, 23, 24, 26,
  29, Nov 13, 25, Dec 21; 1796: CG, Jan 4, Mar 15, Apr 8, 9, 12, 15, May 3, 10,
  Jun 7, Dec 19; 1797: CG, Mar 16; 1798: CG, Mar 19; 1799: CG, Mar 2; 1800: CG,
  Mar 4, May 27, Jun 13, DL, 13, CG, 13
--Governor, The; or, The Creolian Insurrection (ballet-pantomime), 1793: CG,
  Mar 11, 14, 16, 19, 21, Apr 1, 23
--Hercules and Omphale (ballet-pantomime), 1794: CG, Nov 17, 18, 19, 20, 21,
  22, 24, 25, 26, 27, 28, 29, Dec 1, 2, 3, 4, 5, 8, 9, 10, 11, 12, 13, 15, 16,
  17, 19, 20, 22, 23; 1795: CG, Jan 8, 9, 10, 16, 17, 23, 24, Mar 28, May 22,
  26, 28
--Nootka Sound; or, Britain Prepared (entertainment), 1790: CG, Jun 4, 5, 7, 9,
  10, 14, Oct 4
--Oscar and Malvina; or, The Hall of Fingal (ballet-pantomime), 1791: CG, Oct
  20, 21, 24, 26, 27, 28, 29, Nov 2, 3, 4, 10, 14, 17, 21, 22, 24, 28, Dec 1,
  5, 8, 12, 14, 19; 1792: CG, Jan 25, 28, 31, Feb 1, 9, 11, 15, 16, Mar 12, 19,
  Apr 9, 16, 23, 30, May 7, 14, 21, 31, Oct 25, 29, Nov 1, 5, 20, 26, Dec 6;
  1793: CG, Mar 4, Jun 6; 1794: CG, Feb 6, 7, 8, 10, 12, 17, Oct 14, 20, 22,
  Nov 3; 1795: CG, Mar 5, 9, 12, 14, 17, 23, 26, Oct 12, 21, 28, Nov 3, Dec 7,
  14, 16, 19; 1796: CG, Apr 16, 21, May 16, Jun 1; 1797: CG, Apr 8, May 22, 29,
  Nov 24; 1798: CG, Mar 19, 20, 22, 24, 26, 27, 29, Apr 19, May 5; 1799: CG,
  Mar 2, 4, 5, 9, 11, 12, 14; 1800: CG, Mar 4, 6, 8, 11, 15, Apr 25, Jun 5
--Provocation!, The (ballet-pantomime), 1790: CG, Oct 4, 5, 6, 8, 11, 12, 18,
  20, 22, 25, 26, 27, Nov 1, 3; 1791: CG, Jun 6; 1793: CG, May 27; 1795: CG,
  Oct 23, 26
--Shipwreck, The; or, French Ingratitude (Treachery and Ingratitude)
  (ballet-pantomime), 1790: CG, Oct 4; 1793: CG, May 27, 28, Jun 10; 1794: CG,
  Jun 3, 11; 1795: CG, Oct 23, 26, 31; 1796: CG, Feb 2, Jun 2
--Tythe Pig, The (ballet-pantomime), 1795: CG, May 12, 20, Jun 1, 3, 9, 11, 15
Byrn, James and Eleanor (dancers), 1774: HAY, Jun 10, 24; 1778: HAY, May 18,
  29, Jun 18, 24; 1779: HAY, May 31, Jun 2, 9, Jul 5, Aug 18; 1780: HAY, Jun
  15, Aug 4, Sep 2; 1781: HAY, Jul 6; 1782: HAY, Jun 6, Aug 9, 24; 1783: HAY,
  May 31, Jun 2, 4, 11, Aug 1
Byrn, Mrs (charwoman), 1760: CG, Sep 22
Byrne, Charles (giant), 1783: CG, May 23
Byrne, Miss (dancer), 1784: HAY, May 28, Aug 28; 1785: HAY, May 28, 31, Jun 1,
  23; 1786: HAY, Jun 19, 23, Jul 17; 1787: HAY, May 23
Byrne, Mrs (actor, dancer, singer), 1786: CG, Nov 13; 1787: CG, May 19, Dec 3,
  17; 1788: CG, Jan 7, 14, May 22, Sep 22, Dec 29; 1789: CG, Sep 14, 25, Oct
  12; 1790: CG, Feb 11, May 27, Sep 13, Oct 6, Nov 26, 27, Dec 20; 1791: CG,
  Sep 26, Oct 3, 10; 1792: CG, Jan 28; 1796: DL, Oct 1, 29, Nov 16, Dec 26;
  1797: DL, Jun 10; 1798: DL, Jan 16, Feb 20, May 16, Jun 2, Oct 6, Nov 14, Dec
  6; 1799: DL, Jan 19, Feb 5, Jul 2, Oct 14; 1800: DL, Mar 11, CG, May 27, Jun
  13
Byrne, Mrs (dancer), 1781: DL, May 18; 1782: DL, May 16
Byrne, P (printer), 1790: DL, Apr 16; 1800: CG, May 1
Byron, Frederick George (caricaturist), 1788: HAY, Apr 29

C, T (author), 1752: DL, Nov 18
Cabanel, Eliza and Harriot (dancer), 1796: KING'S, Jun 2; 1799: CG, May 25
Cabanel, Eliza or Harriot (dancer), 1796: KING'S, Jul 7, 12
Cabanel, Rodolpho (machinist), 1794: DL, Mar 12, Apr 21, Jun 9; 1795: DL, Feb
   12, May 6, Nov 23; 1796: DL, Jan 18, Nov 9, Dec 26
Cabell (dresser), 1760: CG, Sep 22
Cabinet of Fancy, The. See Stevens, George Alexander.
Cable (actor), 1761: CG, Feb 7
Cable, Mrs, 1767: CG, Jan 13
Cadell and Davies (publishers), 1798: DL, Jan 16
Cadell, Thomas (publisher), 1776: CG, Sep 25, KING'S, Nov 2, 5; 1777: KING'S,
   Jan 21, Mar 13, Apr 29, HAY, May 30, KING'S, Nov 4, 8, CG, Dec 10, KING'S,
   16; 1778: KING'S, Jan 20, Feb 7, Mar 3, Apr 2, 4, May 5, 30, HAY, Jun 25, Jul
   2, 30, Aug 3, DL, Nov 30, KING'S, Dec 22; 1779: KING'S, Apr 29, CG, May 6,
   HAY, 31, Jul 1, Aug 6, CG, Dec 9; 1780: CG, Feb 22, Apr 22, HAY, Jul 8, Aug
   5, 12; 1781: CG, Jan 31, DL, May 8, HAY, Jun 12, 16, KING'S, 23, HAY, Jul 9,
   18, Aug 22, Sep 4, CG, Nov 17, 28, Dec 26; 1782: HAY, Jun 4, Jul 2, 30, Aug
   17, CG, Nov 2, Dec 31; 1783: HAY, May 31, KING'S, Jun 3, HAY, 10, 30, Aug 1,
   12, 28; 1784: CG, Feb 10, Apr 17, HAY, May 28, 31, Jun 4, 17, 19, Aug 18, Sep
   2, 6; 1785: CG, May 12, HAY, 28, 30, 31, Jul 9, 20, CG, Dec 26; 1786: CG, Feb
   17, DL, Mar 9, 13, KING'S, 21, HAY, Jul 24, Aug 12, CG, Oct 21; 1787: HAY,
   Jun 22, Jul 2, Aug 17; 1788: KING'S, May 15, CG, 22, HAY, Aug 5, CG, Dec 13;
   1789: CG, Mar 16, HAY, May 18, KING'S, 28, CG, Sep 21, DL, Nov 7; 1790: CG,
   Jan 29, Mar 8, May 6, HAY, Jul 16, Sep 4, CG, Oct 19, Dec 20; 1791: CG, Feb
   26, Apr 5, Jun 3, HAY, Jul 30, CG, Oct 20, Dec 10; 1792: CG, Feb 2, 28, Apr
   17, Jun 2, Oct 25; 1793: DL, Apr 3, CG, Oct 24, HAY, Nov 23, Dec 26; 1794:
   CG, Feb 6; 1795: HAY, Jun 9, Jul 16; 1796: KING'S, May 5; 1799: DL, Jan 19
Cadell Jr, Thomas (publisher), 1799: DL, Mar 2; 1800: DL, Apr 29
Cadell, Thomas, and Davies, William (publishers), 1796: DL, Mar 12, Apr 20,
   HAY, Aug 29; 1798: CG, May 23, HAY, Jul 6; 1799: HAY, Jul 13
Cademan, Phillip (actor), 1662: LIF, Sep 30; 1663: LIF, Feb 23; 1664: LIF, Aug
   13, Nov 5; 1665: LIF, Apr 3; 1670: LIF, Sep 20, Nov 0; 1671: LIF, Mar 15, DG,
   Nov 0; 1672: DG, Jan 31, Jul 4; 1673: DG, Feb 18, Mar 12, May 0, Aug 9, 20;
   1676: DG, Aug 0
Cadmus et Hermione. See Quinalt, J B.
Caduta de Giganti, La. See Gluck, Christoph Willibald von.
Cady of Bagdad, The. See Portal, Abraham.
Caelia with mournful pleasure (song), 1698: NONE, Sep 0
Caelia. See Johnson, Charles.
Caernarvan, Marquis of (spectator), 1731: DL, Dec 8
Caernarvon Castle. See Rose, John.
Caesar and Urania (song), 1743: DL, Apr 15; 1747: DL, Apr 22; 1756: CG, Apr 19
Caesar Borgia, Son of Pope Alexander the Sixth. See Lee, Nathaniel.
Caesar in Egypt. See Cibber, Colley.
Caesarini (composer), 1712: QUEEN'S, Nov 12
Caffarelli, Gaetano Maioveno (singer), 1737: KING'S, Oct 29; 1738: KING'S, Jan
   3, CG, 18, KING'S, 28, Feb 25, Mar 14, Apr 15
Cagle. See Kaygill.
Caio Mario. See Piccini, Niccolo.
Caius Fabricius. See Handel, George Frederic.
Caius Marius. See Otway, Thomas.
Cajanus Sr, Mynheer (actor), 1734: GF, Apr 1
Cajanus, Daniel (giant, actor), 1734: DL, Feb 5, 26, 28, DL/HAY, Mar 2; see
   also Gargantua, Mynheer
Calabrian Peasants (dance), 1763: CG, Dec 22, 31; 1764: CG, Jan 2, 5, 7, 11,
   13, Feb 21, 22, 23, 25, 27, 28, 29, Mar 1, 2, 29, 31, Apr 2, 5, 7, 24, 30,
   May 7, 25, HAY, Aug 6, 15; 1765: CG, Nov 26, 29, 30
Calamita Di Cuori, La. See Galuppi, Baldassare.
Calcraft, John (renter), 1751: DL, Apr 23; 1758: CG, Mar 4; 1763: DL, Nov 19
Caldara, Antonio (composer), 1732: KING'S, May 23
--Lucius Papirius (opera), 1732: KING'S, May 23, 30, Jun 3, 6
Calderon (Spanish poet), 1662: LIF, Dec 23
Caldron, The; or, Pantomimical Olio (pantomime, anon), 1785: DL, Jan 20, 21,
   22, 24, 26, 28, 31, Feb 3, 5, 24, Mar 1, 14, May 5, 17, Sep 27, Oct 11, 18,
   24, Nov 7, 9, 14, 17; 1789: DL, Dec 26
Caleb Quotem and His Wife!; or, Paint, Poetry, and Putty. See Lee, Henry,
   Throw Physick to the Dogs!
Caledonia; or, The Pedlar Turned Merchant (play, anon), 1699: NONE, Sep 0
Caledonian Cottagers (dance), 1792: HAY, Oct 22
Caledonian Pas de Trois (dance), 1784: KING'S, Apr 15

Caledonian Reel (dance), 1783: KING'S, Nov 29; 1784: KING'S, Apr 15, CG, May
    11; 1785: KING'S, Mar 17, Apr 21, Jun 28
Caledonian Shepherds (dance), 1780: CG, Nov 6, 7, 15, 30; 1781: CG, Feb 7, 20,
    23, Sep 28, Oct 31, Nov 7
Caledonian Society, 1785: HAY, Jan 24
Caledonian Villagers (entertainment), 1782: HAY, Jan 21
Caledonian Wedding, The (dance), 1788: CG, Jun 3
Caley (hatter), 1771: DL, Dec 9
Caley, Master. See Cawley, Master.
Calfskin, Timothy (author), 1767: CG, Nov 12
Caligula. See Crowne, John.
Calisto. See Crowne, John.
Calkin (gallery doorkeeper), 1791: DL, May 31; 1792: DLKING'S, Jun 15; 1793:
    DL, Jun 6; 1795: DL, Jun 5; 1796: DL, Jun 15; 1797: DL, Jun 13; 1798: DL, Jun
    16; 1799: DL, Jul 3; 1800: DL, Jun 14
Call forth thy powers (song), 1794: DL, Apr 11
Call upon his name (song), 1792: KING'S, Mar 23, 28, 30
Callagan (gallery doorkeeper), 1800: CG, Jun 11
Callaway, Francis (beneficiary), 1752: CT/HAY, May 9
Callcott, John Wall (composer), 1789: DL, Apr 17; 1790: CG, Mar 8; 1792: CG,
    May 11; 1794: CG, May 23; 1795: CG, Apr 28, DL, May 2; 1796: HAY, Mar 28, CG,
    Apr 5; 1797: HAY, Jan 23; 1798: CG, May 28; 1799: HAY, Aug 21
Callois, Master (dancer), 1759: MARLY, Sep 6, 7; see also Cawley, Master
Callon (tailor), 1773: DL, Jan 21
Calms appear when storms are past (song), 1700: DL, Apr 29
Calori (Caroli), Angiola (singer), 1758: KING'S, Jan 10, Apr 6, Nov 11; 1759:
    KING'S, Jan 16, Nov 13; 1760: KING'S, Jan 15, Mar 1, SOHO, 13, HAY, 27,
    KING'S, Apr 17, HIC, 29, KING'S, May 15, 31, HAY, Jun 5, KING'S, Aug 25, Nov
    22, Dec 16; 1761: KING'S, Jan 6, SOHO, 28, KING'S, Feb 7, Apr 28; 1765:
    KING'S, Dec 3
Calphurnia. See Bononcini, Giovanni.
Calthorpe (Colthorp) (renter), 1747: DL, Apr 9; 1749: DL, Nov 16, Dec 27; 1750:
    DL, Mar 12, Apr 7; 1753: CG, Oct 24; 1767: DL, Jan 9, Apr 28; 1772: DL, Jan
    31, May 1, 2; 1773: DL, Jan 29; 1774: DL, Feb 4, May 20
Calvert, Benedict Leonard, 1699: LIF, Jan 5
Calvert, Charles (actor), 1784: HAY, Mar 22, Sep 17; 1786: HAY, Mar 6
Calvert, Charles, Lord Baltimore, 1699: LIF, Jan 5
Calvert, Mrs (beneficiary), 1757: CG, Dec 9
Calvesi, Teresa, Sga Vincenzo (singer), 1791: PAN, Mar 1, Apr 12, May 14, Jun
    16, Dec 17; 1792: HAY, Feb 14, 28, Mar 31, Apr 12
Calvesi, Vincenzo (singer), 1786: KING'S, Dec 23; 1787: KING'S, Jan 9, Feb 20,
    Mar 8, 29, Dec 8; 1788: KING'S, Jan 15, Feb 5, Mar 4, Apr 5, May 8, 15; 1791:
    PAN, Dec 31
Calypso and Telemachus. See Galliard, John Ernest.
Calypso. See Cumberland, Richard.
Camano, Mrs (actor), 1733: HAY, Jun 4
Camargo, Mme Cupis de (dancer), 1732: DL, Sep 23; 1750: DL, Sep 20, Oct 13, Nov
    7, 15, 17, 27, Dec 6, 12, 31; 1751: DL, Jan 2, 22, Feb 16, 23, Mar 12, 19,
    Apr 8, 9, 10, 20, 22, 24, 26, May 1, 11, 13, CG, Nov 11, Dec 4, 9, 10, 16;
    1752: CG, Jan 9, 16, Mar 30, Apr 15, 18, 22, Oct 19, 26, Nov 2, 14, Dec 7,
    26; 1753: CG, Mar 10, May 1, 5, Oct 8, 22, 24, 25, 30, Nov 7, 20, 26, Dec 4,
    15, 19, 21; 1754: CG, Feb 12, Apr 16, 24, 27, May 1, 4, Nov 23
Cambert, Robert (composer), 1674: ATCOURT, Feb 0
Camberwell, 1790: CG, May 5
Cambray (actor), 1787: CG, Oct 12, 22, 29, Nov 16; see also Fennell, James
Cambrian Quack (song), 1795: HAY, Mar 4
Cambridge, Charles Duke of (died), 1661: NONE, May 5
Cambridge, Lord (rebel), 1746: DL, Aug 4
Cambridge, University of, 1704: LIF, Jul 10
Cambro-Britons. See Boaden, James.
Cambro' Britons; or, Fishguard in an Uproar (interlude, anon), 1797: CG, May 31
Cambyses, King of Persia. See Settle, Elkanah.
Camden (actor), 1751: DL, Nov 29
Cameriera Accorta, La. See Galuppi, Baldassare.
Cameriera Astuta, La. See Storace, Stephen.
Cameron (actor), 1797: HAY, Dec 4
Cameron (boxkeeper), 1776: DL, May 20; 1777: DL, Jun 4; 1778: DL, May 26; 1779:
    DL, Jun 1; 1780: DL, May 25; 1781: DL, May 26; 1782: DL, May 31; 1784: DL,
    May 27; 1785: DL, May 26; 1786: DL, Jun 1; 1787: DL, Jun 7; 1788: DL, Jun 11;
    1789: DL, Jun 11; 1790: DL, Jun 4; 1791: DL, May 28; 1792: DLKING'S, Jun 14;
    1793: DL, Jun 5; 1795: DL, Jun 6; 1796: DL, Jun 13; 1797: DL, Jun 16; 1798:
    DL, Jun 14; 1800: DL, Jun 14

Camery (actor), 1777: HAY, Oct 9; 1778: DL, May 26
Camilla. See Haym, Nicolino Francesco.
Camille. See Marsollier des Vivetieres, Benoit Joseph.
Camille, Master (dancer), 1712: QUEEN'S, Mar 22
Camp Alarmed (dance), 1761: DL, Sep 25, 26, 28, 29, Oct 14, 16, 20, Nov 14, Dec
    5, 9; 1762: DL, Apr 24, May 3, 5, 14; 1763: DL, Mar 26, Apr 4, 9
Camp, The. See Sheridan, Richard Brinsley.
Campaign, The. See Jephson, Robert.
Campaigners, The. See D'Urfey, Thomas.
Campanini, Barbarina (Barbarini, Sga) (dancer), 1740: CG, Oct 25, 27, 30, Nov
    3, 13, 17, 21, 27, 28, Dec 2, 4, 5, 9, 11, 13, 16, 17, 20, 30; 1741: CG, Jan
    2, 3, 7, 8, 10, 17, 21, 28, 29, 31, Feb 2, 3, 6, 7, 12, 14, 17, 19, 23, 28,
    Mar 2, 5, 7, 9, 10, 12, 16, 17, 19, 30, 31, Apr 1, 2, 3, 6, 14, 15, 24, 29,
    Oct 24, 30, Nov 7; 1742: CG, Jan 11, 16, 20, 21, 25, Feb 6, 13, 22, Mar 4, 8,
    13, Apr 1, 5, 24, May 15, 20, 25, Jun 2, KING'S, Nov 2
Campbell (actor), 1732: HAY, Mar 2; 1736: HAY, Feb 11
Campbell, J (actor), 1793: CG, Nov 18, Dec 31; 1794: CG, Mar 17, 25, 27, May
    12, 14, 19, 22, 28, Jun 9, 10; 1796: CG, Apr 29, DL, Nov 3, Dec 16, 30; 1797:
    DL, Jan 10, 12, Feb 1, 3, 16, Mar 14, 20
Campbell, Miss (actor), 1779: HAY, Jan 11; 1780: HAY, Jan 17
Campbell, Miss (actor), 1799: HAY, Sep 10, DL, 21, Oct 29, 31; 1800: DL, Jun 12
Campbell, Mrs (actor), 1722: DL, May 24; 1723: DL, Feb 14, May 24, Jun 12, Jul
    5, Nov 6, 19, Dec 5; 1724: DL, Jan 15, Apr 29
Campbell, Mrs (actor), 1751: SF, Sep 17
Camperdown, 1797: DL, Oct 16, Nov 9; 1798: CG, Feb 28
Campi, F (composer), 1736: KING'S, Apr 13
Campioli, Antonio Gualandi (singer), 1731: KING'S, Dec 7; 1732: KING'S, Feb 15,
    Mar 25, May 23, Jun 10
Campion (actor), 1686: DLORDG, Dec 22
Campion, Maria Anne (actor), 1797: CG, Nov 20; 1798: CG, Oct 15; see also
    Spencer, Mrs
Campion, Mary Anne (actor, singer, dancer), 1698: DL, Mar 0, DL/ORDG, Nov 0;
    1700: DL, Jul 6; 1702: YB, Jul 2, DL, 7, Oct 23; 1703: DL, Jan 23, YB, 28,
    DL, Feb 1, 12, Apr 19, 27, May 13, 15, 28, Jun 22, Jul 1, Oct 8, 19, 21, 23,
    Nov 8, 10, Dec 14, 20, 31; 1704: DL, Jan 4, 7, 12, 18, LIF, Feb 1, DL, 22;
    1706: ATCOURT, Feb 5
Campioni (dancer), 1745: CG, Nov 9; 1746: CG, Apr 3; 1749: DL, Nov 27, Dec 2;
    1750: DL, Apr 7; 1754: DL, Oct 8, 19, 28, Dec 5; 1769: KING'S, Sep 5, Nov 7
Campioni, Sg and Sga (dancers), 1744: KING'S, Jan 3
Campioni, Sga (dancer), 1744: CG, Nov 17, Dec 8; 1745: CG, Jan 1, 8, 14, Feb
    11, Mar 11, 14, 18, 21, Apr 15, 18, 22, 23, 24, 25, May 3, 4, 8, 13, Nov 9,
    14, 23, Dec 14, 16, 17, 27; 1746: CG, Jan 7, 10, 22, 24, Feb 6, 7, 8, 10, 13,
    15, 18, 20, 22, 24, 25, Mar 6, 11, 13, 17, 18, 22, 31, Apr 2, 4, 7, 9, 11,
    14, 15, 17, 21, 25, 30, May 1, 13, Jun 11, Dec 31; 1747: CG, Jan 14, 21, Mar
    26, Apr 23, 29
Campistron, Jean Galbert de
--Alcibiade, 1722: HAY, Apr 9
--Jaloux de Sabuse, 1722: HAY, Mar 29
Campolini, Sga (singer), 1767: KING'S, Oct 27; 1768: KING'S, Mar 10
Can a Lover Pleasure find (song), 1792: CG, May 28
Can life be a blessing (song), 1679: DG, Apr 0; 1694: NONE, Sep 0
Can Love be controlled by Advice (song), 1742: GF, Apr 22, 29; 1748: CG, Mar 18
Can Luciamira's mistake (song), 1670: NONE, Sep 0
Cananetto (song), 1766: KING'S, Mar 13
Candidate, The. See Dent, John.
Candles snuffed to soft Musick (entertainment), 1751: CT, Dec 3
Candoni. See Cordoni.
Cane (publisher), 1790: HAY, Apr 6, 29, May 29
Canlets, Master (actor), 1785: DL, Nov 18
Canning, Elizabeth, 1754: HAY, Nov 8, 28
Canning, Mary Anne, Mrs George (actor), 1773: DL, Nov 6, 20; 1774: DL, Apr 12,
    18, 26, 28, May 7; 1775: DL, Mar 30, Apr 1; 1776: DL, Mar 23, Dec 14
Canning's Escape (play, anon), 1754: SFG, Sep 23, 24
Cannon Row, 1799: HAY, Apr 17
Cannon St, 1679: CS, Dec 17
Cannon Tavern, 1758: CG, Jul 6
Canon (song), 1779: HAY, Mar 17
Canons, 1767: CG, May 23
Canst thou for this (song), 1792: KING'S, Mar 14
Cantab (author), 1773: CG, Feb 2
Cantabile Song (song), 1767: KING'S, Mar 5
Cantabs, The. See Macnally, Leonard.

Cantata (song), 1706: DL, Apr 13; 1707: YB, Mar 26; 1710: YB, May 1; 1711: HDS, Apr 24; 1712: SH, Dec 30; 1713: QUEEN'S, Jun 20; 1714: HIC, Apr 28; 1716: LIF, Jan 27, DL, May 18, LIF, 24, Oct 10, 13, DL, Dec 31; 1718: LR, Dec 3; 1719: KING'S, Mar 21, LIF, Apr 3, 25, DL, Aug 4; 1721: KING'S, Jul 5; 1722: HAY, Jan 26, DL, Feb 28, KING'S, Mar 6; 1723: DL, Mar 20; 1724: LIF, Mar 19, Apr 25; 1725: LIF, May 3; 1727: LIF, Apr 5; 1729: HAY, Jan 28, GF, Dec 18; 1730: DL, Apr 28, Dec 3, GF, 19; 1732: GF, May 4, 15, 17, LIF, 17, GF, 23; 1733: HIC, Apr 20, CG, Jun 29; 1737: CG, Apr 21, 22, 28, May 5; 1738: CG, Apr 19, May 5, DL, 5, CG, 10; 1741: DL, Nov 13; 1742: DL, Mar 20; 1743: DL, Apr 20, May 11, 16; 1744: CG, Apr 12, 24, Nov 28, DL, Dec 26, 29, 31; 1745: DL, Jan 3, Mar 9, Apr 30, May 6, Jun 5; 1746: DL, Jan 14, 16, 17, 23, 24, 25, 28, Feb 7, 8, 10, 22, 24, 27, Apr 4, 7, 9, 10, CG, 12, DL, 17, 19, 21, 22, May 19, Nov 5, 28; 1747: DL, Mar 21, Apr 21, 30, Sep 19, 29; 1748: HAY, Sep 5; 1751: DL, Apr 10, CG, 23, Oct 19; 1752: DL, Mar 21, CT/HAY, 21, DL, Apr 25, CT/HAY, May 5, CG, Nov 3; 1753: CG, Jan 15, DL, Apr 26, Dec 20; 1754: HAY, Nov 28; 1755: KING'S, Mar 17, DL, Apr 2; 1756: CG, May 4, 13; 1757: CG, Jan 8, May 2, HAY, Aug 31, CG, Oct 31; 1758: DL, Mar 16, Nov 13, Dec 14; 1759: DL, Jan 11, Feb 14, Apr 24, Dec 7; 1760: DL, Feb 19, Oct 10, Dec 1, 15; 1761: DL, Apr 14, May 27, Sep 25; 1762: DL, Apr 14, 23, Nov 26; 1770: CG, Apr 26; 1773: CG, May 6; 1774: HAY, Jun 7; 1778: HAY, Apr 30; 1779: DL, Feb 26; 1791: KING'S, May 19; 1792: KING'S, Mar 23
Cantata of Alexis (song), 1731: GF, May 13
Cantata of Lydia (song), 1773: DL, May 10
Cantata of Vertumnus and Pomona (song), 1744: DL, Oct 2
Cantata on St Patrick's Day (song), 1727: HAY, Mar 17
Cantelo, Anne (actor), 1789: CG, Feb 27, Mar 6, 20, 27, Apr 3; 1790: CG, Feb 19, 24, 26, Mar 3, 17, 26
Cantelo, Hezekiah (bassoonist), 1794: CG, Mar 7; 1795: CG, Feb 20; 1796: CG, Feb 12; 1800: CG, Feb 28
Cantelo, Hezekiah and Thomas (bassoonist and oboist), 1797: CG, Mar 3; 1798: CG, Feb 23; 1799: CG, Feb 8
Canter (dancer), 1773: KING'S, Oct 23
Canter, James (scene painter), 1780: HAY, Sep 2
Canterbury Jests, The. See Ravenscroft, Edward.
Canterbury, Lord of, 1668: LIF, Dec 8
Canterbury, 1743: KING'S, Apr 19; 1796: DL, Jun 2, HAY, Aug 30
Cantrell (Chantrill), Miss (dancer, actor), 1736: DL, Feb 28, Mar 22, LIF, Apr 9; 1737: CG, Oct 3, 5, 12; 1738: CG, Feb 2, 3, 13, Mar 2, 7, 13, 16, 18, Apr 7, 19, 21, 24, 25, 27, May 6, 8, 10, 11, 12, 15, Oct 4, 20, 23, 26, 28, Nov 8, 13, 18, Dec 6; 1739: CG, Jan 3, 6, 8
Cantrell, Miss (singer), 1771: GROTTO, Jun 22, Aug 8, 22, 30, Sep 9
Cantrell, Mrs (actor, singer), 1716: LIF, Apr 27, Aug 3; 1717: LIF, Nov 28; 1718: LIF, Jan 20, Nov 11; 1724: LIF, Mar 23, Jun 3, Jul 14; 1728: BFHM, Aug 24; 1729: LIF, Apr 17, 23, May 5, 6, BF, Aug 26, LIF, Sep 19, Nov 4, 25, Dec 3, 15, 16; 1730: LIF, Jan 1, 2, 19, Mar 16, Apr 20, May 4, 14, 18, 25, Jul 3, Sep 21, Oct 7, Nov 10, 23, Dec 15; 1731: LIF, Apr 1, 3, 26, May 5, 6, 19, 20, Sep 20, 27, Oct 13, Nov 2, 18, Dec 1; 1732: LIF, Feb 21, Mar 20, 23, Apr 10, 18, 25, May 4, 9, LIF/CG, Sep 25, Oct 9, 16, Nov 18, 22, 24; 1733: LIF/CG, Feb 10, Mar 30, Apr 13, May 3, 19, CG, Jun 26, Jul 6, 27, Aug 2, 14, 20, SF/BFLH, 23, CG, Sep 20, Oct 6, 9, 11, 18, Nov 16, 21, 28, Dec 4; 1734: CG, Apr 19, May 6, 7, BFRLCH, Aug 24, DL, Sep 28, Oct 3, 5, 22, Nov 1; 1735: DL, Mar 3, 22, Apr 7, 28, May 2, 10, 14, GF/HAY, Jul 15, 18, 22, Aug 1, HAY, 12, GF/HAY, 14, 21, HAY, 26, DL, Sep 1, 18, 25, Oct 7, 11, 31, Nov 6, 10, 21, 25; 1736: DL, Jan 12, Feb 28, Mar 3, 27, 29, LIF, Apr 9, BFHC, Aug 23, CG, Oct 20, 22; 1737: CG, Feb 1, Sep 30, Oct 7
Caocormin, Sacheoutzim-Sinadab (Chinese visitor), 1735: LIF, Jun 19
Capdeville, Mlle (dancer), 1754: CG, Nov 26, 27, Dec 3; 1755: CG, Jan 4, Mar 15, 17, 18, Apr 15, 18, 21, 22, 25, 28, 30, Nov 1, Dec 17; 1756: CG, Jan 2, 21, 22, Feb 14, Mar 1, 2, 30, Apr 22, Oct 23; 1757: CG, Jan 28, Feb 16, Apr 29, 30, May 9, 19, Nov 5, 7, 29; 1758: CG, Feb 1, Apr 7, 8, 11, 12, 13, 14, 17, Oct 14, Nov 16, 23; 1759: CG, Apr 27, Oct 5, 15, Nov 21, 30; 1760: CG, Jan 12, 16, 18, Feb 12, 16, Mar 3, 18, Apr 12, 17, 18, Sep 22, Oct 20, 25, Dec 11, 15, 17, 18, 20, 22, 23, 31; 1761: CG, Jan 2, 8, 9, 10, 20, 21, 22, 24, Feb 2, 12, Mar 9, 30, Apr 1, 16, 21, 23, 29, May 1, 4, 8, 11, 13, 14, 20, 22, 25, Sep 16, 21, 23, 26, Oct 12, 13; 1762: CG, Jan 7, Feb 2, Mar 22, 27, Apr 19, 21, May 7, 12, 17; 1765: KING'S, Jan 5
Capdeville, Mlle, scholar of (dancer), 1756: CG, Apr 22
Cape (dresser), 1759: DL, May 28; 1760: DL, May 12; 1761: DL, May 20; 1774: DL, Apr 11
Cape Finisterre, 1747: DL, Nov 16
Cape St Vincent. See Sheridan, Richard Brinsley.
Cape St Vincent, 1797: HAY, May 10, KING'S, 18

Cape, Master (actor), 1761: DL, Dec 28; 1762: DL, May 18, Nov 5; 1763: DL, Oct
    4, Nov 23, 26; 1764: DL, May 23, 24, 29, Sep 22, Nov 13, Dec 26; 1765: DL,
    Mar 7, Dec 14; 1766: DL, Oct 28, 29; 1767: DL, May 1, 8, Sep 15, Dec 10;
    1768: DL, Apr 14, May 13, 23, Nov 9; 1769: DL, Jan 20, Apr 6, May 16, HAY,
    Aug 14, Sep 19, DL, 26, Oct 14; 1770: DL, Jan 6, 19, May 4, 28, Sep 25, Oct
    3, Nov 3; 1771: DL, Mar 7, Apr 17, Dec 4; 1772: DL, Apr 22, 25, May 25, Oct
    23, Dec 14, 26; 1773: DL, May 6, 10, Sep 25, Nov 9, Dec 11, 31; 1774: DL, Jan
    24, Mar 3; see also Everard, Edward Cape
Cape, Miss (entertainer), 1762: DL, Mar 29
Cape, Mrs (actor), 1772: DL, Jun 10
Capel Street Theatre, Dublin, 1778: CG, Mar 28
Capelletti, Giuseppe (composer), 1796: DL, Oct 29
Capitani (singer), 1763: HAY, Jun 9
Capitani, Master (dancer), 1760: HAY, Jun 5
Capitani, Polly (dancer), 1760: KING'S, May 31, HAY, Jun 2, 5, KING'S, Nov 22,
    Dec 16; 1761: KING'S, Jan 6, Feb 7, Mar 9, DL, Jun 16, Jul 2, 27, Sep 12, 14,
    Oct 17, Nov 13, Dec 28; 1762: DL, Feb 6, May 11, Oct 13; 1763: HAY, Jun 20,
    Jul 4, Aug 8; 1766: KING'S, Mar 13
Capochio and Dorinna. See Arne, Dr Thomas A.
Capon (actor), 1789: DL, Nov 13, 14; 1790: DL, Jan 8
Capon, Mary (dancer), 1767: CG, Apr 27, Sep 16; 1768: CG, Mar 12, Apr 16, Oct
    7; 1769: CG, Apr 8, May 16, 17, Nov 20, Dec 28, 29; 1770: CG, Jan 31, Apr 20,
    Oct 15; 1771: CG, Oct 11; 1772: CG, Apr 24; 1773: CG, Feb 6, Mar 16, Apr 24,
    Oct 14, 21, 28, Nov 3, 9, 25; 1774: CG, Jan 3, Feb 17, Apr 16, 27, May 10
Capon, William (scene designer), 1794: DL, Mar 12, Apr 21, Dec 20; 1795: DL,
    May 6; 1796: DL, Feb 27, Mar 12, Apr 2; 1798: DL, Dec 29; 1800: DL, Apr 29
Caporale (Caporali, Corporalli), Andrea Francisca (musician, composer), 1734:
    HIC, Mar 22, MR, Dec 13; 1735: YB, Feb 28, HIC, Apr 17; 1736: HIC, Jan 21,
    ST, Feb 11, CG, 19, LIF, Mar 8; 1737: ST, Mar 8, CT, May 2; 1740: HIC, Jan 4,
    Feb 1, 22, Mar 27, 28, Apr 11, 18, 25; 1741: HIC, Jan 16, HAY, Feb 3, HIC,
    19, 27, Mar 3, 6, HAY, 9, HIC, 13, KING'S, 14, HIC, 17, Apr 28; 1743: KING'S,
    Mar 30; 1744: KING'S, Mar 28, HAY, Apr 4, LIF, Dec 11; 1745: CT, Jan 14, HAY,
    Feb 14, Mar 23, CG, Apr 10
Cappelletti, Petronio (singer), 1791: KING'S, Jun 2, 25
Cappelletti, Teresa Poggi (singer), 1791: KING'S, Apr 26, May 12, 24, Jun 2
Capper, Miss (singer), 1799: CG, Feb 8, 15, 20, Mar 1, 6, 13, 15; 1800: CG, Feb
    28, Mar 5, 19
Capricci del Sesso, I. See Traetta, Tommaso, Le Serve Rivali.
Capriccio Drammatico, Il. See Cimarosa, Domenico.
Caprice Amoureux, Le. See Favart, Charles Simon.
Caprices de Galatee (dance), 1765: CG, Apr 18; 1781: KING'S, Mar 29, Apr 26,
    May 26, Jun 26; 1783: KING'S, May 1; 1789: KING'S, May 7, 12, 23, 26, 28, Jun
    13
Caprices de la Danse (dance), 1716: DL, Apr 11, 20, May 10; 1734: GF/HAY, Dec
    6; 1737: LIF, Jan 19; 1747: DL, Nov 2, 3, 7, 11; 1751: DL, Dec 12, 13, 14,
    20, 21; 1752: DL, Jan 1, 20; 1753: DL, Mar 31; 1790: HAY, Mar 25, Apr 6, 13,
    15
Caprices des Rebelles (dance), 1741: DL, Apr 7, 9, 14
Capricieuse (dance), 1734: DL, Nov 22; 1735: DL, Feb 5; 1791: KING'S, Jun 2, 6
Capricieux (dance), 1735: DL, Apr 25
Capricious Lady, The. See Pye, Henrietta; Cooke, William.
Capricious Lovers (dance), 1787: DL, Jun 1, HAY, Jul 6, DL, Sep 20, 29, Oct 26,
    Nov 24, Dec 12, 14; 1788: DL, Jan 26, Oct 13
Capricious Lovers, The. See Odingsells, Gabriel; Lloyd, Robert.
Captain, The. See Fletcher, John.
Captain, The; or, Town Miss (play, anon), 1677: DL, Apr 2
Captive King (song), 1793: CG, Mar 6, 8, 13, 20, 22
Captive of Spilburg, The. See Hoare, Prince.
Captive Prince, The; or, Love and Loyal (droll, anon), 1744: MF, May 3
Captive, The. See Bickerstaff, Isaac.
Captives, The. See Gay, John; Delap, John.
Captivity (song), 1793: KING/HAY, Feb 20, CG, 20, 27, Mar 1, 6, 8, 13, 20,
    KING/HAY, 20, CG, 22, May 27
Capuchin, The. See Foote, Samuel.
Capuchino, Sg and Sga (dancer), 1746: SFLY, Sep 8
Cara sei tu il mio bene (song), 1792: DLKING'S, Apr 19
Cara sposa (song), 1752: KING'S, Mar 24; 1769: HAY, Aug 25
Carabaldi (singer), 1773: KING'S, Oct 23
Caractacus. See Mason, William.
Caracteres de l'Amour (dance), 1734: CG, Mar 21, Apr 2, 17, 27, May 1, 6
Caracteres de la Danse (dance), 1725: LIF, Nov 27, Dec 3, 14; 1726: LIF, Apr
    18; 1727: LIF, Apr 14; 1731: LIF, Mar 25, Apr 5, DL, 19; 1734: HAY, Oct 30;

1735: HAY, Feb 17; 1736: DL, Apr 3; 1739: DL, Oct 23, 24; 1740: DL, Jan 12,
   Mar 10, 11, Apr 30, CG, May 13, DL, Oct 21, 22, 25; 1742: CG, Oct 25, Nov 4,
   6, 8, 9, 12, 16, 18, 23, 24, 25, 26, 27, 29, Dec 4, 6, 7, 8, 9, 10, 11, 13,
   14, 16, 18, 31; 1743: CG, Jan 3, 5, 7, 19, 21, Feb 14, Mar 7, 14, 22, Apr 5,
   6, 12, 13, 14, 19, 20, 25, 29, May 3, 5, 6, 9; 1746: DL, Apr 16; 1748: DL,
   Mar 24, Apr 29, May 3, 5; 1749: DL, Jan 10; 1751: CG, Apr 26, May 6, 7, 10,
   11; 1752: DL, Mar 16; 1762: DL, May 12; 1793: KING'S, Jan 26
Carara, Sga (singer), 1772: HAY, Apr 6; 1773: KING'S, Feb 5
Carata, Mahomet (the Turk) (equilibrist), 1749: BF/SFP, Aug 23, CG, Sep 29, Oct
   28, HAY, Nov 7, CG, Dec 23; 1751: SF, Sep 19
Carattaco. See Bach, Johann Sebastian.
Caravan at Rest, The (dance), 1796: KING'S, Jun 2, 7, 11, 14, 18, 28, Jul 5
Carbonelli (Carbenell), Giovanni Stephano (musician, composer), 1719: HIC, Feb
   13, LIF, Apr 16, DL, Oct 14; 1722: DL, Mar 14, Apr 26, May 16; 1723: DL, Apr
   30, May 15; 1724: DL, Apr 22; 1732: DL, Oct 12; 1733: HIC, Apr 20, LIF, May
   7; 1746: KING'S, Mar 25; 1748: KING'S, Apr 5; 1749: KING'S, Mar 21
Card Dance (dance), 1704: DL, Dec 20
Cardarelli, Sga (singer), 1775: KING'S, Oct 31, Dec 12; 1776: KING'S, Jan 9,
   Feb 3, 27, Mar 12, 28, Apr 23
Cardenas, Hamet Ben Hamet (ambassador), 1706: QUEEN'S, May 3, 15, DL, 21,
   LIF/QUEN, Aug 16, QUEEN'S, Oct 28, SH, Nov 6; 1707: QUEEN'S, Jul 3
Cardigan, Earl of. See Brudenell, James.
Cardigan, Earl of, 1725: LIF, Feb 24, 25
Cardigan, Wales, 1664: ATCOURT, Jan 0
Cardinal, The. See Shirley, James.
Cardinale (singer), 1789: KING'S, Jun 11
Cardmakers Arms Coffee House, 1744: HAY, Apr 23; 1745: GF, Feb 26
Cardon, Louis (harpist), 1785: DL, Feb 18, KING'S, Mar 12
Care labra (song), 1714: QUEEN'S, May 1
Care Paiple (song), 1746: KING'S, Mar 25
Careful Father, The; or, The Extravagant Son. See Prodigal Son, The.
Careless Husband, The. See Cibber, Colley.
Careless Lovers, The. See Ravenscroft, Edward.
Careless, Elizabeth (actor), 1728: HAY, Dec 30; 1730: HAY, Sep 18, SOU, 24;
   1731: GF, May 26; 1732: HAY, Apr 1; 1733: BFCGBH, Aug 23, Sep 4; 1741: JS,
   Oct 6, 27; 1743: JS, Mar 31, Apr 15; 1744: MFHNT, May 1, MF, Jun 7, 8
Cares of Love, The. See Chaves, A.
Cares of Lovers, The (song), 1693: NONE, Sep 0
Carestini (Carestino, Caristini), Giovanni (singer), 1733: KING'S, Oct 30, Nov
   13, Dec 4; 1734: KING'S, Jan 26, Mar 13, Apr 2, 27, May 18, CG/LIF, Nov 9;
   1735: CG, Jan 8, Mar 5, 28, Apr 1, 16; 1736: CG, Nov 27; 1739: HAY, Dec 1,
   15; 1740: HAY, Jan 22, Mar 15, May 10
Carey (actor), 1709: DL, Feb 5, May 3
Carey (householder), 1741: GF, Dec 2
Carey (singer), 1714: SH, Jan 28; 1715: DL, Aug 9; 1716: DL, May 25, 31, Jun 5,
   Aug 7
Carey (spectator), 1695: DLORLIF, Jun 22
Carey (violinist), 1754: DL, Feb 25
Carey St, 1743: LIF, Mar 22; 1748: DL, Apr 19; 1783: DL, Apr 26; 1784: DL, May
   12; 1785: DL, May 5; 1791: CG, Jun 4; 1795: HAY, Apr 22
Carey, George Saville (actor, author), 1771: DL, May 13; 1773: CG, Apr 27;
   1774: GRP, Jul 23; 1776: DL, Jun 1; 1780: HAY, Aug 2; 1784: HAY, Sep 17;
   1792: DLKING'S, May 29; 1800: CG, Apr 29
--Dupes of Fancy, The; or, Every Man his Hobby (farce), 1792: DLKING'S, May 29
--Noble Pedlar, The; or, The Fortune Hunter, 1770: MARLY, Aug 21; 1771: DL, May
   13
Carey, Henry (actor, author), 1722: LIF, Mar 15; 1724: DL, May 12; 1729: DL,
   Jun 20, Oct 27; 1730: DL, Apr 28, May 21, BFOF, Aug 20, DL, Dec 3; 1732: HAY,
   Mar 13, Apr 25, LIF, Nov 20, DL, Dec 1; 1733: DL, Jan 12, Oct 10, GF, Nov 12,
   DL/HAY, 24, GF, 28, DL, Dec 11, 29; 1734: DL/HAY, Feb 22; 1735: GF/HAY, Jul
   15, 18, 22, 29, Aug 1, 6, 8, 14, 21, GF, Sep 26, 29, Oct 1, 3, 6, 8, 10, 13,
   20, 22, 23, 24, Nov 3, 12, 13, 14, 15, Hay, Dec 17; 1736: GF, Mar 16, Apr 12,
   May 5; 1737: HAY, May 16; 1738: CG, Jan 24, DL, 26, CG, Mar 14, May 10, Dec
   9; 1739: CG, Jan 10, Dec 1; 1740: CG, Mar 18, Jun 5; 1742: CG, Apr 30; 1743:
   DL, Oct 4, CG, Nov 17; 1744: HAY, Oct 2; 1752: CG, Feb 6; 1758: CG, Apr 13;
   1773: CG, Nov 4; 1780: CG, Mar 27; 1785: CG, May 6; 1789: DL, Jun 3
--Amelia (musical), 1732: HAY, Mar 3, 13, 15, 20, 22, 24, 29, Apr 17, 21, 24,
   25, Dec 18, 23; 1743: HAY, Mar 24
--Betty; or, The Country Bumpkins, 1732: DL, Dec 1, 2, 4, 6, 7, 8, 9; 1733: DL,
   Jan 27
--Chrononhotonthologos, 1734: DL/HAY, Feb 22, 23, 25, 26, 28, Mar 2, 5, 7;
   1736: HAY, May 3; 1738: CG, Jul 21; 1742: DL, Apr 20, 29; 1743: JS, Feb 22;

1745: DL, Apr 30; 1746: GF, Mar 22; 1747: DL, Apr 11; 1748: NWSM, Dec 26;
1749: SOU, Oct 9; 1756: DL, Apr 29; 1759: DL, Feb 26; 1772: CG, Apr 21; 1779:
CG, May 3; 1780: CII, Apr 19; 1783: HAY, Aug 13, 19; 1788: HAY, Aug 27; 1789:
WHF, Nov 9; 1798: CG, Apr 11
--Contrivances, The; or, More Ways Than One, 1715: DL, Aug 9, 12, 16, 23; 1716:
DL, Apr 2, May 25; 1724: HAY, Jan 31, Feb 1, 4; 1729: DL, Jun 20, 24, 30, Aug
5, 7, 9, Sep 16, 18, Oct 7, 9, 11, 27, 31, Nov 11, Dec 15, 17; 1730: DL, Jan
3, 16, Feb 14, Apr 28, May 7, 12, 21, Sep 22, Oct 15, Nov 17, 20; 1731: DL,
Apr 22, May 5; 1732: DL, May 9, GF, 15, 17, DL, Oct 31, Nov 2, Dec 6; 1733:
DL, Jan 12; 1734: GF, Mar 18, LIF, Apr 15, 18, GF, 24, May 1, 8, 14, 15, HAY,
Jul 19, RI, Sep 12; 1735: GF, Mar 20, 29, Apr 21, Sep 15; 1736: DL, Mar 25,
Apr 5, 6, CG, 6, DL, 8, May 6, 15, 21, Oct 25; 1737: CG, Apr 26, DL, Sep 20,
22; 1738: CG, May 10, Jul 11; 1741: GF, Mar 7, 12, 16, Apr 8, 14, 28, May 7,
Sep 21, Oct 28, Nov 7; 1742: GF, Feb 8; 1746: DL, Jan 17, 22, Feb 10; 1747:
DL, Apr 29; 1752: CG, Feb 6, 7, Mar 7, 9, 12, 14, 16, 19, Apr 24, 25, 28, 29,
May 4, 5, 6, Sep 20, 22, 25, 27, Oct 12, 21, 28, Dec 5, 9, 18, 21, 22; 1753:
CG, Jan 8, Mar 22, Apr 10, May 5, 10, Sep 14, 19, 28, Nov 20, Dec 1, 6, 21;
1754: CG, May 6, 17, Sep 20, Oct 18, Nov 15, Dec 7, 20; 1755: CG, Jan 18, May
20, Oct 16, 18, 30, Nov 17, 25, 26, Dec 10; 1756: CG, Jan 15, 22, Feb 7, 24,
28, Apr 10, May 20, SW, Oct 9, CG, 25, Nov 24, Dec 17; 1757: CG, Feb 14, Sep
16, Nov 11, Dec 7; 1758: CG, Jan 10, 27, Feb 18, Mar 18, Apr 22, May 9, Nov
3, 7, 16, 21, 29, Dec 11, 21; 1759: CG, Jan 11, Feb 22, Apr 27, May 1, 25,
Oct 5, Dec 6; 1760: CG, May 19; 1761: CG, Mar 25, DL, Apr 3, 20, 23, CG, Oct
9, 23, Nov 10, 12, Dec 22; 1762: CG, Jan 13, Mar 25, Apr 17, May 5, DL, 13,
CG, 21, Sep 24, Oct 5, 21, DL, Nov 6, CG, Dec 22; 1763: CG, Sep 28, Oct 20;
1764: CG, Jan 12, DL, Apr 27, CG, May 22, Sep 28; 1765: CG, Sep 27; 1767: DL,
May 1, CG, 21; 1768: CG, Feb 1; 1769: HAY, Jun 5, 14, CG, Oct 14, Dec 2;
1771: HAY, Jul 10; 1772: HAY, Jul 10; 1773: CG, Apr 23, May 28, HAY, Jul 30,
Aug 2; 1785: CG, May 6, 28; 1786: CG, May 10
--Dragon of Wantly, The, 1737: HAY, May 10, 16, 17, 18, 19, CG, Oct 26, 27, 28,
29, 31, Nov 1, 2, 3, 4, 5, 7, 8, 9, 10, 11, 12, 14, 15, 16, 17, 18, 19; 1738:
CG, Jan 2, 3, 4, 5, 6, 7, 9, 10, 11, 12, 13, 14, 16, 18, 19, 20, 21, 23, 24,
25, 26, 27, 28, 31, Feb 1, 2, 3, 4, 6, 7, 8, 9, 10, 11, 14, 25, Mar 2, 7, 9,
14, 18, 25, Apr 6, 15, 20, 22, 29, May 10, DL, 16, BFH, Aug 23, CG, Sep 1,
15, 18, 20, 22, 27, 29, Oct 6, 13, 20, Nov 2, 11, 16, Dec 5, 9; 1739: CG, Feb
9, May 16, 17, Aug 29, 31, Sep 7, 10, 12, 19, 21, 28, Oct 23, Nov 10, 24, Dec
8; 1740: CG, Jan 4, 17, Feb 6, 7, Sep 19, Oct 31, Nov 8, 15, 25, Dec 12;
1741: CG, Apr 16, May 2, 4, Sep 30, Oct 22; 1742: CG, Mar 25, Apr 28, 30, May
12, 18; 1743: DL, Feb 2, 4, 8, Apr 7, 23, 28, May 5, 13; 1745: DL, Feb 15,
16, 18, 19, Mar 4, 5; 1746: CG, Apr 18; 1747: DL, Mar 7, 9, 10, 12, 14, 16,
17, 19, 21, 28, Apr 2, 6, 9, 22, Dec 3, 11, 21; 1748: DL, Jan 7, 16, Feb 5,
12, Mar 12, 17, Apr 16, 26, 29; 1751: CG, Apr 20, 22, 23, 29; 1752: CG, Apr
13; 1753: CG, Jan 6; 1755: CG, Apr 24, 28; 1756: CG, Apr 24; 1758: CG, Apr
13; 1762: CG, Mar 30, Apr 19, May 4, Nov 29, Dec 3; 1763: CG, Apr 8, 23, May
20; 1765: CG, Apr 26; 1767: CG, May 5, 11, 18, 19, 25, Oct 22, Nov 18, Dec 3;
1768: CG, Feb 11, Nov 25, Dec 2; 1769: CG, Sep 25, Oct 5, 13, 31; 1770: CG,
Jan 22, May 16; 1774: CG, Apr 7, 16, 21, May 3, 6, 16; 1782: CG, Mar 18, Apr
9, 19, 20
--Hanging and Marriage; or, The Dead Man's Wedding, 1722: LIF, Mar 15
--Happy Nuptials, The, 1733: GF, Nov 12, 13, 14, 15, 16, 17, 19, 22, 23, 24, 28
--Honest Yorkshireman, The (play), 1735: GF/HAY, Jul 15, 18, 22, 25, 29, Aug 1,
6, 8, 14, 21, BF, 23, GF, Sep 26, 29, Oct 1, 3, 6, 8, 10, 13, 20, 22, 23, 24,
Nov 3, 12, 13, 14, 15, 19, 25, 27, 28, 29, Dec 1, 2, 11, 12, 13, 15, HAY, 17;
1736: GF, Feb 3, 6, Mar 16, 30, Apr 12, 26, HAY, May 3, GF, 5, 6, RI, Jul 24,
LIF, Oct 5, 7; 1737: LIF, Jan 24, 25, Mar 26, 31, Apr 2, 11, 13, 15, 30, May
2, 4, 5, 7, 10, 18, Jun 15; 1738: CG, Mar 14, 16, Apr 4, 8, 12, 14, May 5,
12, 15, Jun 27, Jul 7, Aug 22, 29; 1739: CG, Jan 8, Mar 26, May 24, Nov 13,
15; 1740: CG, Jan 8, May 27, GF, Oct 20, 21, 22, 23, 29, 30, Nov 4, CG, 10;
1741: GF, Jan 22, NWC, Aug 22, GF, Sep 28, Nov 3, 4, 6, JS, 30; 1742: GF, Feb
19, CG, Mar 6, 15, UM, Apr 26, CG, May 1, 3, 4, 6, 10, 14, JS, Nov 8, LIF,
Dec 13, 15; 1743: NONE, Jan 31, LIF, Feb 17, JS, Mar 16, Apr 7; 1745: GF, Feb
4, Apr 24, May 3; 1754: CG, Apr 20; 1755: HAY, Sep 3; 1756: CG, Apr 6, 26,
May 14; 1757: CG, Mar 21; 1759: CG, Mar 19, Apr 21, May 8, Oct 1; 1760: CG,
Mar 17; 1776: CHR, Oct 4; 1785: HAMM, Jul 26, HAY, Aug 16; 1789: DL, Jun 3
--Lady Moore; or, The Dragoness (opera), 1755: CG, Apr 28, May 5, 8; 1756: CG,
Apr 24; 1758: CG, Apr 13
--Margery; or, A Worse Plague than the Dragon (Dragoness, The), 1738: CG, Dec
9, 12, 13, 14, 15, 16, 18, 19, 20, 21, 22; 1739: CG, Jan 5, 9, 10, Feb 10,
15, Mar 5, 8, Apr 28, May 5, Aug 31, Sep 21; 1740: CG, Jan 11; 1742: CG, Apr
30; 1758: CG, Apr 13
--Nancy; or, The Parting Lovers (True Blue; Love in Low Life; The Press Gang),
1739: CG, Dec 1, 14, 17, 18; 1740: CG, Jan 5, 15, Mar 18, Apr 16, 21, 28, May

2, 5, 9, 16, 29, Jun 5, BFHC, Aug 23, CG, Oct 1, 24, Nov 20, Dec 19, 22;
1741: CG, Jan 15, GF, Feb 6, 10, CG, 12, Mar 17, 30, JS, May 19; 1742: JS,
Jan 7, NWC, Dec 27; 1744: CG, Apr 19, HAY, Oct 2, 4, 6, 9; 1748: NWSM, Dec
26; 1755: CG, Apr 2, 3, 8, 11; 1756: CG, May 6; 1770: CG, Nov 12, 15, 17, 19,
21, 28, Dec 3, 4, 6, 20, 21; 1771: CG, Mar 4, Apr 4, 10, 18, 23, 25, 29, Nov
9, 11, Dec 14, 17, 18; 1772: CG, Jan 18, 24, 29, Mar 10, Apr 7, 21, May 2, 5,
22; 1773: CG, Apr 20, DL, May 11, CG, 11; 1774: CG, Mar 26, Apr 6, 8, 12, 21,
22, 30, May 3, 4, 16; 1775: CG, Apr 1, 8, 18; 1776: CG, Apr 9, 15, 16, 19,
Dec 23; 1777: CG, Mar 31, Apr 7, 8, 14, May 13; 1778: CG, Mar 30, Apr 4, 11,
21, 22, May 13, 23; 1779: CG, Apr 5, 6, May 4; 1780: CG, Mar·27, Apr 1, 3,
11, 12, Oct 2; 1781: CG, Apr 2, May 1, 22; 1786: CG, May 10; 1790: DL, May
11, 25; 1793: CG, Apr 11, 17; 1794: CG, Apr 23; 1795: CG, May 27
--Three Old Women Weatherwise (interlude), 1770: HAY, Mar 17, DL, May 11, 31
--Wedding Night, The, 1667: LIF, Mar 20, 21
Carey, Henry, friend of (musician), 1735: GF/HAY, Jul 15
Carey, Henry, scholar of (singer), 1735: GF/HAY, Jul 15, 18
Carey, Miss (actor), 1755: HAY, Aug 28, Sep 9, 11, 15
Carey, Mrs (singer), 1730: DL, Dec 3; 1743: CG, Nov 17
Carey's scholar (singer), 1714: SH, Jan 28
Cargill, Ann, Mrs R (actor), 1780: HAY, Aug 1, 10, 12, 21, 29, 30, 31, Sep 2,
DL, 21, 26, 28, Oct 7, 10; 1781: DL, Mar 10, Apr 18, 25, May 15, HAY, 30, Jun
26, Aug 8, 15, 17, 22, 28, Sep 8, 11, DL, 27, Oct 15, 29, Nov 15, 20, 24, Dec
13; 1782: DL, Jan 22, Apr 18, 20, May 16; 1784: HAY, Sep 17; 1788: CG, Apr 25
Carillon (music), 1790: DL, Mar 10
Carillon Sinfonia (music), 1790: CG, Feb 24
Carillon, Le (entertainment), 1718: LIF, Dec 30; 1719: LIF, Jan 15, KING'S, Mar
16
Carillon, Le; ou, L'Arlequin Dame Alison (farce, anon), 1720: KING'S, Jun 16;
1721: HAY, Jan 27, Feb 3; 1734: GF/HAY, Nov 22, Dec 2; 1735: GF/HAY, Feb 12,
Apr 7
Carlell, Lodowick, 1664: LIF, Mar 8; 1667: LIF, Feb 4
--Arviragus and Philicia, 1669: BRIDGES, Jan 12; 1672: NONE, Sep 0
--Deserving Favourite, The, 1669: BRIDGES, Jan 12
--Heraclius, 1663: NONE, Sep 0; 1664: ATCOURT, Jan 0, LIF, Mar 8; 1667: LIF,
Feb 4, Sep 5
--Osmond the Great Turk; or, The Noble Servant, 1669: BRIDGES, Jan 12
--Spartan Ladies, The, 1669: BRIDGES, Jan 12
Carleton (dancer),1729: HAY, Feb 25
Carleton Jr (lobby doorkeeper), 1770: DL, Jun 1; 1771: DL, May 30; 1772: DL,
Jun 9; 1773: DL, Jun 2; 1774: DL, May 28; 1775: DL, May 26; 1776: DL, May 22;
1777: DL, Jun 6; 1778: DL, May 25; 1779: DL, May 26; 1780: DL, May 20; 1781:
DL, May 24; 1782: DL, May 29, Oct 16; 1783: DL, May 28; 1784: DL, May 25;
1785: DL, May 27; 1786: DL, Jun 2; 1787: DL, Jun 8; 1788: DL, Jun 12; 1789:
DL, Jun 12; 1790: DL, Jun 5
Carleton Sr (house servant), 1766: DL, May 16; 1768: DL, May 24; 1770: DL, May
23; 1771: DL, May 21; 1772: DL, Jun 3; 1773: DL, May 28; 1775: DL, May 23;
1776: DL, May 18; 1777: DL, May 30; 1778: DL, May 22; 1779: DL, May 29; 1780:
DL, May 23; 1781: DL, May 25; 1782: DL, May 30
Carleton Sr and Jr (house servants), 1769: DL, May 16
Carleton Sr, Widow of (beneficiary), 1783: DL, May 29
Carleton, Mary (actor), 1664: LIF, Apr 15
Carleton, Miss (actor), 1784: HAY, Nov 16
Carleton, R
--Concealed Royalty, The; or, The May Queen, 1673: NONE, Sep 0
--Martial Queen, The, 1674: NONE, Sep 0
Carlini, Rosa (dancer), 1758: KING'S, Nov 11; 1759: KING'S, Jan 16, Mar 20
Carlisle St, 1738: GF, Jul 26; 1793: DL, May 30
Carlisle, James (actor, author), 1682: DL, Nov 16, 28; 1683: NONE, Sep 0, DL,
Dec 0; 1684: DL, Mar 0, Apr 0, DLORDG, Aug 0
--Fortune Hunters, The; or, Two Fools Well Met, 1689: DL, Mar 0; 1707: QUEEN'S,
Jun 10, Oct 11, DL/QUEEN, 31; 1708: DL/QUEEN, Jan 23; 1709: QUEEN'S, Oct 25;
1711: DL, May 15; 1717: LIF, Apr 29, May 1, 4; 1728: LIF, Mar 9, 11, Apr 22;
1729: LIF, Mar 15, Apr 11, May 13, Oct 22
Carlisle, Lord (correspondent), 1733: KING'S, Mar 17, 27
Carlisle, Mrs (actor), 1745: GF, Mar 9, 21, Apr 15, 18, 22
Carlton, Peter (actor), 1673: LIF, Dec 0; see also Charlton
Carlyle, Dr Alexander, 1749: CG, Feb 14
Carman (actor), 1766: CG, May 12
Carmarthen, Marquis of. See Osborne, Thomas.
Carmelite, The. See Cumberland, Richard.
Carmichael, Thomas (prompter), 1757: CG, Apr 30; 1758: CG, Apr 22
Carmignani, Sga (actor), 1763: HAY, Jun 9

Carmontelle, 1779: CG, Sep 27
--Poulet, Le, 1779: CG, Sep 27
Carnaby Market, 1756: HAY, Mar 25; 1787: HAY, Mar 12
Carnaby, James (actor), 1701: DL, May 12; 1705: DL, Mar 29, Jun 12, Sep 27;
    1707: DL, Oct 18, 23, 25; 1708: DL, Aug 28, 31, Sep 3; 1709: DL, Mar 17, May
    17, Sep 6; 1710: DL, Jan 14, Mar 14, 27, GR, Jul 22, 27, Aug 3; 1711:
    DL/QUEEN, May 25; 1712: DL, Jun 10; 1713: DL, Feb 19
Carnacchini, Emanuele (singer), 1765: KING'S, Dec 3
Carnan, Thomas (printer), 1751: DL, Mar 7
Carne, Elizabeth, Mrs John (house servant), 1769: CG, Jun 6; 1772: CG, May 4,
    Oct 19; 1773: CG, Apr 23, Oct 13; 1774: CG, Apr 12
Carne, John (house servant), 1760: CG, Sep 22
Carne, Miss (actor), 1781: HAY, Mar 26, Nov 12; 1782: HAY, Jan 21
Carne, Miss (dancer), 1799: CG, Oct 21; 1800: CG, Apr 29
Carnelys, John (actor), 1771: HAY, Jul 5
Carneval de Venice, Le (dance), 1757: HAY, Dec 26; 1758: HAY, Jan 6
Carnevale, Mme Pietro (singer), 1783: KING'S, Jan 7, Apr 29, Jun 3, 14; 1784:
    KING'S, Mar 18; 1792: CG, Apr 17
Carnevale, Pietro (deputy manager), 1786: KING'S, Jun 1; 1787: KING'S, Mar 1;
    1788: KING'S, May 29; 1789: KING'S, Feb 7
Carney (dancer), 1733: DL, Oct 24; 1734: DL, Feb 5, DL/HAY, Apr 26, DL, Oct 21;
    1735: DL, Nov 15; 1736: DL, Sep 7, Oct 12; 1738: DL, Jan 12, 24, Sep 23, Oct
    3, 30, Dec 15; 1739: DL, Feb 5, Mar 10, May 2, Sep 8, 13, 26, Oct 6, 10, 19,
    26, Nov 1, 22, 28, Dec 6, 11, 19; 1740: DL, Jan 5, Oct 13, 14, 15, 16, 27,
    31, Nov 17, Dec 4, 10, 19, 26; 1741: DL, Mar 17; 1742: GF, Mar 25, LIF, Nov
    24, 26, Dec 3, 13, 27; 1743: LIF, Jan 7, Feb 17, Mar 3, 8, 14, Apr 7; 1745:
    GF, Feb 4
Carnival Masquerade, A (entertainment), 1781: DL, Dec 20
Carnival of Venice, The. See Tickell, Richard.
Carnival, The. See Porter, Thomas.
Carnival, The; or, Harlequin Blunderer. See Charke, Charlotte.
Carnovale Di Venezia. See Guglielmi, Pietro.
Carny (house servant), 1745: CG, May 15; 1747: CG, May 22; 1748: CG, May 6;
    1749: CG, May 3
Caro spiegar vorrei (song), 1762: KING'S, Mar 1
Carolan, Turlogh (composer), 1782: CG, Nov 2; 1785: CG, May 12; 1786: CG, Oct
    16; 1787: CG, Mar 12; 1788: CG, Apr 1; 1789: CG, Mar 31, Sep 23; 1790: CG,
    May 6; 1793: CG, Apr 25; 1796: CG, Nov 5
Caroli, Angiola. See Calori, Angiola.
Caroline Elizabeth, Princess, 1727: DL, Nov 7; 1728: DL, Jan 27, KING'S, Feb
    17, LIF, 22, KING'S, Mar 9, 12, May 7, DL, Nov 20, Dec 11, 12, 19; 1729: DL,
    Jan 15, 16, Feb 5, Mar 13, Apr 15, 22, LIF, 29, Oct 22, Nov 11, DL, Dec 27,
    31; 1730: KING'S, May 23, RI, Oct 20, DL, Nov 26, KING'S, 28, DL, Dec 10,
    LIF, 16; 1731: LIF, Jan 14, DL, 21, Feb 25, LIF, Mar 11, DL, 30; 1732: DL,
    Feb 2; 1734: KING'S, Apr 2, DL/HAY, 18, GF/HAY, Oct 26, HAY, 28, GF/HAY, Nov
    6, Dec 5; 1735: GF/HAY, Jan 2, 9, HAY, 13, CG, Feb 20, LIF, 27, CG, Mar 12,
    Jul 2, Nov 8, DL, Dec 10; 1736: CG, Feb 23; 1757: CG, Dec 28, DL, 28, 29;
    1760: CG, Apr 26; see also Princesses
Caroline St, 1788: DL, Mar 13; 1789: CG, Feb 11; 1796: DL, Apr 18, May 23
Carousal (song), 1740: CG, Apr 16
Carpenter (actor), 1736: YB, Apr 26
Carpenter (dance), 1765: HAY, Jul 8, Aug 19, 21
Carpenter (printer), 1794: CG, Mar 25, HAY, Aug 18
Carpenter and Fruit Dealer (dance), 1764: DL, May 23, 24, HAY, Jun 26, Jul 27,
    Sep 5
Carpenter, Richard
--Pragmatical Jesuit New-levened, The, 1660: NONE, Sep 0
Carpenter, Robert (actor), 1774: HAY, Aug 10, 24, 26, 29, Sep 2, 5, 6, 12, 19,
    DL, 20, HAY, 30, DL, Oct 5, 11, 12, 14, 24, 27, 28, Nov 5, 21, 26, Dec 1;
    1775: DL, Jan 2, 23, Feb 4, 9, 20, 23, Mar 2, 18, 21, 23, Apr 17, 27, May 1,
    3, 13, 19, Sep 26, Oct 7, 11, 17, 21, Nov 6, 9, 10, 11, 18, 25, 28, Dec 7, 9,
    11; 1776: DL, Jan 27, Feb 1, 12, 15, Mar 14, 28, Apr 9, 10, 17, May 4, 11,
    18, Jun 5, Sep 21, 26, Oct 1, 15, 18, 19, Nov 25, Dec 10, 28, 31; 1777: DL,
    Jan 1, 4, 16, 28, 29, Feb 24, Mar 1, Apr 7, 18, 22, 25, May 9, 28, Sep 20,
    23, 27, Oct 18, Nov 10, 13; 1778: DL, Jan 1, 5, Feb 2, 10, 24, Mar 12, May
    11, 23, Sep 17, 24, Oct 1, 8, 10, 15, 20, Nov 2, 4, 20, Dec 21; 1779: DL, Apr
    7, May 8
Carpentier. See Charpentier.
Carpet Warehouse, 1778: CG, May 2; 1779: CG, Apr 28
Carpue (silk dyer), 1750: DL, Jan 4; 1767: DL, Apr 4; 1772: CG, Mar 3, DL, Jun
    10, CG, Dec 9; 1773: DL, Jun 2; 1774: CG, Apr 5, DL, Jun 2; 1775: DL, May 27;
    1776: DL, Jun 10

Carr and Co (merchants), 1749: DL, Nov 24
Carr, Mrs (dancer), 1741: SF, Sep 14
Carr, Oliver (actor), 1741: TC, Aug 4; 1742: JS, Apr 7, CG, Oct 14, 25, Nov 4,
    20, LIF, Dec 6, CG, 7; 1743: CG, Jan 5, May 2, 4, 11, DL, Sep 15, CG, 21, 28,
    Oct 10, 19, Nov 4, 19, Dec 8, 12; 1744: CG, Jan 11, Feb 3, Apr 25, 30, May
    14, Oct 3, 5, 8, 15, 24, 31, Nov 5, 9, Dec 6, 17, 21; 1745: CG, Feb 15, Apr
    4, 23, 26, 29, Sep 23, Oct 7, 14, 16, 31, Nov 4, 15, 28, Dec 10; 1746: CG,
    Jan 7, 11, 13, 23, Feb 4, 5, 6, 8, Mar 10, 13, 15, Apr 7, 15, Sep 29, Oct 1,
    4, 6, 20, 29, Nov 4, Dec 6; 1747: CG, Jan 20, Feb 2, Mar 17, Apr 24, May 12,
    15; 1750: SFYW, Sep 7; 1755: HAY, Sep 1, 3, 9, 11, 15
Carrignani, Giovanni (singer), 1763: KING'S, Feb 19
Carrissime (composer), 1772: CG, Apr 8
Carrogis, Louis. See Carmontelle.
Cartel, 1743: DL, Oct 6
Carter (actor), 1661: NONE, Sep 0
Carter (actor), 1746: SOU, Oct 16
Carter (scowrer), 1767: DL, Mar 19; 1772: DL, Jun 10; 1773: DL, Jun 2; 1774:
    DL, Jun 2, Oct 20; 1775: DL, May 27; 1776: DL, Mar 16, 25
Carter Lane, 1750: DL, Nov 28
Carter, Charles Thomas (composer), 1770: MARLY, Aug 21; 1775: DL, Feb 1, Mar
    18; 1777: DL, Mar 20; 1782: DL, May 18; 1783: DL, Feb 14, CG, 25, HAY, Aug 1;
    1787: DL, May 28; 1790: CG, Jun 3; 1792: CG, May 10, Oct 27; 1794: CG, May 2;
    1795: HAY, Mar 4, DL, May 19; 1797: CG, Jun 9, DL, 12
Carter, Miss (actor, singer), 1741: TC, Aug 4, JS, Nov 9; 1742: JS, Apr 7;
    1750: DL, Nov 23
Carter, Miss (singer), 1759: DL, Mar 23; 1764: HAY, Nov 13
Carter, Mrs (dresser), 1719: LIF, May 28
Carter, Mrs (scowrer), 1776: DL, Jun 10
Carter, Mrs (singer, dancer), 1728: HAY, Apr 3; 1729: HAY, Mar 27, May 7, 29;
    1730: LIF, Dec 15; 1731: LIF, Apr 3, 22, Nov 18; 1732: LIF/CG, Nov 24; 1736:
    LIF, Sep 28, Oct 21
Carter, Richard (musician), 1728: YB, Apr 12; 1736: GF, Apr 27; 1742: DL, Apr
    20; 1743: LIF, Mar 15
Carter, Thomas (singer), 1786: DL, Mar 3, 10, Apr 5
Carteret, Lady Jemima Montagu, 1666: ATCOURT, Oct 11
Carteret, Sir Philip (spectator), 1667: BRIDGES, Dec 30
Cartony (mercer), 1750: DL, Jan 20
Cartouche. See Legrand, Louis.
Cartwright, Anne, Mrs William (actor), 1785: HAY, Feb 10
Cartwright, George
--Heroic Lover, The; or, the Infanta of Spain, 1660: NONE, Sep 0
Cartwright, Master (dancer), 1759: CG, May 17
Cartwright, Mrs (actor), 1671: BRIDGES, Mar 0
Cartwright, Mrs (singer), 1772: MARLY, Aug 20, 25, 28, Sep 1, 7; 1775: DL, May
    24; 1776: DL, May 4, Oct 15; 1777: DL, Apr 21, May 15
Cartwright, Sir William, 1671: NONE, Jan 15
--Ordinary, The, 1671: NONE, Jan 15; 1672: DG, Sep 3; 1673: LIF, Apr 0
--Royal Slave, The, 1669: BRIDGES, Jan 12
Cartwright, William (actor), 1659: NONE, Sep 0; 1660: NONE, Sep 0, COCKPIT, Oct
    8, REDBULL, Nov 5, VERE, Dec 0, 3; 1661: NONE, Sep 0; 1663: VERE, Mar 0,
    NONE, Sep 0; 1665: BRIDGES, Jan 14, Apr 0; 1666: NONE, Sep 0, ATCOURT, Dec
    10; 1667: BRIDGES, Apr 16, Oct 5, 19, Nov 2; 1668: NONE, Sep 0, BRIDGES, 14,
    Nov 6, Dec 18; 1669: BRIDGES, Feb 6, Apr 17, May 6, LIF, 12, BRIDGES, Jun 24;
    1670: BRIDGES, Aug 0, BRI/COUR, Dec 0; 1671: LIF, Mar 9, BRIDGES, Jun 0, Dec
    7; 1672: LIF, Apr 0, Nov 0; 1673: LIF, May 0; 1674: DL, May 16; 1675: DL, Jan
    12, 25, Apr 23, May 10, NONE, Sep 0; 1676: DL, Jan 29, Sep 9, Dec 11; 1677:
    DL, Jan 12, May 5; 1681: DL, Jun 1; 1682: ATCOURT, Nov 15, DL, 16; 1685:
    DLORDG, Jan 20; 1710: DL, May 16; 1740: BF/WF/SF, Aug 23; 1746: GF, Mar 15,
    SOU, Sep 17, GF, Oct 31, Nov 3, 4, 6, 7, 13, 14, 18, 19, 20, 21, 26, 27, 28,
    Dec 3; 1748: CG, Mar 5; 1785: HAY, Feb 10
Caruso (musician), 1748: KING'S, Apr 26; 1756: DL, Aug 12
Caruso, Lodovico (composer), 1783: KING'S, Dec 16; 1792: CG, Mar 7
--Albergatrice Vivace, L' (opera), 1755: HAY, Feb 3, 17, 20; 1783: KING'S, Dec
    16
Carver, Robert (scene painter), 1771: DL, Sep 28, Nov 11; 1772: DL, Jun 10, Sep
    22; 1773: DL, Sep 25; 1774: DL, Sep 24, CG, Nov 19; 1775: CG, Apr 24; 1776:
    CG, Feb 26, Nov 14; 1777: CG, Nov 25; 1778: CG, Oct 14, 22; 1779: CG, Jan 4,
    Feb 27, Mar 20, Sep 22, Nov 30; 1780: CG, Apr 25, Dec 29; 1781: CG, May 7,
    28, Oct 1, DL, 19, CG, Dec 26; 1782: CG, Oct 10, Nov 2; 1783: CG, Sep 22, Dec
    23; 1784: CG, Jan 29, Sep 20, Dec 27; 1785: CG, Oct 13, Dec 20; 1786: CG, Dec
    26; 1787: CG, Nov 5, Dec 26; 1788: CG, Dec 26; 1789: CG, Dec 21; 1790: CG,
    Nov 15, Dec 20; 1799: CG, May 13

Cary St, 1737: LIF, May 5
Cary, Anthony, 6th Viscount Falkland, 1684: FALKLAND, Jul 25
Cary, Henry, 4th Viscount Falkland, 1667: LIF, Mar 21
--Marriage Night, The, 1663: LIF, Oct 0; 1667: LIF, Mar 20, 21
Cary, Mrs (actor), 1793: HAY, Oct 4, Nov 16, Dec 9; 1794: HAY, Feb 15
Cary's Coffee House, 1742: GF, Mar 25; 1744: HAY, Apr 23
Caryll, John, 1667: LIF, Mar 7
--English Princess, The; or, The Death of Richard III, 1667: LIF, Mar 7; 1672:
    NONE, Sep 0
--Sir Solomon Single; or, The Cautious Coxcomb, 1670: LIF, Apr 0, May 9, DOVER,
    19; 1671: ATCOURT, Nov 14; 1674: NONE, Sep 0; 1704: ATCOURT, Feb 28, LIF, Mar
    21, 23, 28, Apr 4, 17; 1705: DL, Jun 14, QUEEN'S, Dec 20; 1706: DL, Feb 23,
    QUEEN'S, Nov 11; 1707: DL, Mar 11, Oct 28; 1714: DL, Apr 3, 7, May 21, Oct
    12; 1719: DL, Jul 7, 31, Nov 9; 1720: DL, Jan 21
Casaia, Miss (dancer), 1766: HAY, Oct 27
Casali, Luigi (dancer), 1791: KING'S, Jun 2, 28, Jul 2, 9
Casanova, Mrs (dancer), 1727: KING'S, Apr 25
Casarini, Sga (singer), 1746: KING'S, Nov 4; 1747: KING'S, Apr 14, Nov 14;
    1748: HAY, Jan 12, KING'S, Feb 16, Mar 5, CG, 9, 23, KING'S, Apr 5, NWSM, May
    3
Cascina, La (pasticcio), 1763: KING'S, Jan 8, 10
Case of Authors Stated with Regard to Booksellers, the Stage, and the Public,
    The (criticism), 1758: NONE, Mar 1
Case of Charles Macklin (pamphlet), 1743: DL, Dec 7
Case of Mrs Clive Submitted to the Publick (pamphlet), 1744: CG, Oct 12
Case, Master (dancer), 1737: DL, Nov 19; 1738: DL, Dec 4
Caselli, Sga (singer), 1743: KING'S, Nov 15; 1744: KING'S, Jan 3, 31, Mar 28,
    Apr 3, 24
Casentini, Mad. See Borghi, Anna Casentini.
Caserta, 1797: KING'S, Apr 27
Casey (actor), 1748: BFSY, Aug 24
Casey, John (actor), 1767: CG, Nov 24, 30; 1768: CG, Jan 20, Apr 11, 13, 20,
    May 10, 31, HAY, Jun 8, 23, Jul 8, 13, 27, Aug 15, 19, 24, Sep 19; 1773: DL,
    Jan 12
Casey, Polly (singer), 1741: BFLW, Aug 22
Cash. See Coysh.
Cashell, Oliver (actor), 1739: DL, Sep 24, Oct 20, 29, Nov 5, 10, 15, 19, 20,
    28, Dec 11; 1740: DL, Jan 3, 19, Feb 19, Mar 13, May 2, 20, 30, Sep 23, Oct
    4, 13, 14, Nov 4, 10, 11, 19, 24, 26, 27, Dec 10, 15, 18, 19, 20; 1741: DL,
    Jan 15, Feb 14, Apr 3, 16, 29, May 13, CG, Sep 23, Oct 7, 10, 13, 15, 20, 21,
    30, 31, Nov 4, 11, 26, Dec 9, 17, 18; 1742: CG, Jan 19, Feb 25, Mar 13, 27,
    May 5, 7, Sep 22, Oct 1, 9, 11, 13, 18, 26, 27, Nov 4, 11, 15, 20, 25, Dec 7,
    11, 15, 21; 1743: CG, Jan 5, 18, Mar 15, Apr 27, May 4, Sep 21, 28, 30, Oct
    5, 10, 12, 28, Nov 4, 7, 19, 28, 30, Dec 3, 8, 12, 14, 16, 19, 27, 31; 1744:
    CG, Jan 5, 11, 14, 24, Feb 3, 28, Mar 3, 8, 12, Apr 19, 25, Sep 19, 24, 26,
    Oct 1, 5, 8, 10, 15, 16, 18, 20, 22, 24, 31, Nov 1, 5, 9, 12, 21, 30, Dec 5,
    6, 13, 17, 21, 26; 1745: CG, Jan 14, Feb 13, 15, Mar 11, 14, Apr 17, 20, 23,
    25, 26, DL, Jun 5, CG, Sep 23, 25, Oct 4, 7, 14, 16, 18, 31, Nov 4, 8, 15,
    16, 18, 22, 23, 25, 26, 28; 1746: CG, Jan 7, 11, 13, 25, Feb 3, 5, 8, Mar 3,
    10, 13, 15, Apr 1, 2, 3, 7, 23, Jun 9, 11, 13, 20, 23, 27, Sep 29, Oct 1, 4,
    13, 15, 20, 24, 27, 29, Nov 1, 3, 6, 13, 18, 24, 28, Dec 2, 6, 10, 17, 19,
    26, 29; 1747: CG, Jan 20, 29, Feb 2, 11, Mar 7, 17, 26, Apr 22, May 14, 20
Cashing. See Cushing.
Cason (dresser), 1760: CG, Sep 22
Cassani, Giuseppe (singer), 1708: DL/QUEEN, Feb 7; 1710: QUEEN'S, Jan 10, Mar
    23; 1711: QUEEN'S, Jan 10, Feb 24, Dec 12; 1712: QUEEN'S, Feb 27
Cassey (dance), 1754: HAY, Jul 4, 9, 11, Aug 29
Cast, my Love, thine eyes around (song), 1789: CG, Dec 21; 1790: CG, Jan 23,
    Nov 15; 1799: CG, May 13
Castalio. See Costollo.
Castelle (doorkeeper), 1794: CG, Jun 14; 1795: CG, Jun 10
Castelle, Mrs (actor, singer), 1793: CG, Oct 9, 24, 28, Nov 11, 28, Dec 7, 19;
    1794: CG, Jan 9, Feb 22, Mar 10, 31, Apr 24, Sep 29, Oct 22; 1795: CG, Jan
    31, Jun 6, Sep 14, 21, Oct 15, 19, Nov 4, 9, 16, 27, Dec 4, 18, 22; 1796: CG,
    Jan 1, Feb 2, Apr 2, 9, 20, 26, May 3, 16, Sep 12, 16, 19, 26, Oct 6, 7, Nov
    5, Dec 19, 27; 1797: CG, Jan 10, Feb 18, Mar 16, Apr 8, 25, 26, May 18, Jun
    9, Sep 25, Oct 16, 25, Nov 2, Dec 16, 18; 1798: CG, Feb 12, Mar 19, 31, Apr
    9, 17, May 12, Sep 17, Oct 8, Nov 12, Dec 11, 15, 26; 1799: CG, Mar 2, Apr 9,
    13, 23, May 28, Jun 7, Sep 18, 30, Oct 2, 7, 21, 24, Nov 11, 15, 18, Dec 10,
    23; 1800: CG, Jan 7, 16, Feb 7, 10, Mar 4, 25, May 1, HAY, Jul 2, 18, 28, 30,
    Aug 14
Castelli, Anna (singer), 1754: CG, Nov 18

Castephens (Castevens) (actor), 1775: HAY, May 24, Jul 7, 31, Sep 4, 16; 1776: CG, May 11; see also Stevens, William
Casti, Giovanni Battista (librettist), 1791: DL, May 3
--Grotta di Trofonio, La, 1791: DL, May 3
Castiglione (dancer), 1734: DL, Oct 28, Nov 1, Dec 21; 1735: DL, Jan 18, 21, 28, GF/HAY, Mar 28, May 1, GF, 23, Oct 6, 10, HAY, Dec 29; 1736: HAY, Jan 19, Feb 20, Apr 29
Castiglione, Master (dancer), 1771: HAY, Jun 14, 17, Jul 3, 5
Castle Coffee House, 1784: HAY, Jan 21
Castle Court, 1784: HAY, Jan 21
Castle of Andalusia, The. See O'Keeffe, John.
Castle of Montval, The. See Whalley, Thomas Sedgwick.
Castle of Sorrento, The. See Heartwell, Henry.
Castle of Wonders, The. See Andrews, Miles Peter, The Enchanted Castle.
Castle Spectre, The. See Lewis, Matthew Gregory.
Castle St, 1735: DL, May 30; 1739: DL, Apr 2; 1747: CG, May 11; 1748: CG, Apr 13; 1783: CG, May 10; 1784: CG, May 7; 1785: DL, Mar 31; 1787: DL, May 4; 1793: CG, May 23; 1795: DL, May 21, CG, 27; 1796: CG, May 12, DL, 13; 1797: DL, May 23; 1798: DL, May 24; 1799: DL, May 9; 1800: DL, Jun 3
Castle Tavern, 1723: CT, Dec 10; 1724: CT, Nov 24; 1733: LIF/CG, Apr 21; 1734: DL/HAY, May 4; 1735: CG/LIF, May 27; 1736: DL, May 14; 1737: CT, Feb 18; 1742: CG, Mar 1; 1743: LIF, Mar 14; 1744: CG, Apr 16; 1745: CT, Jan 14, HAY, Apr 1, CG, 23; 1746: DL, Apr 9; 1749: CG, Apr 28; 1751: CT, Mar 16, Dec 3, DL, 17; 1752: CT/HAY, Jan 7, 14, 21, 31, Feb 4, 6, 11, 18, CT, Mar 7
Castle Yard, 1736: HAY, Apr 6
Castle, Mrs (actor), 1734: LIF, Aug 20, HAY, 22
Castle, Richard (actor), 1757: CG, Nov 18; 1760: DL, Dec 12; 1761: DL, Feb 12, Apr 25, May 11, Jun 3, Sep 14, Nov 9, 14, 28, Dec 11, 23, 28; 1762: DL, Jan 27, Feb 10, Mar 18, 27, Apr 30, May 4, 14, Sep 21, 25, Oct 6, 7, 11, 12, 15, 18, Nov 3, 5, 10, 17, 19, 20, 23, Dec 6, 18; 1763: DL, Jan 15, 19, Apr 30, May 16, 18, 31, HAY, Jun 20, Jul 6, Aug 11, DL, Sep 17, 20, 27, Oct 4, 8, 19, 24, 28, Nov 5, 7, 9, 14, 28, 30, Dec 1, 5, 12, 15; 1764: DL, Jan 7, Feb 14, Mar 3, 20, Apr 12, May 18, HAY, Jul 6, 13, 16, 30, Aug 20, 29, DL, Sep 15, 20, 22, 25, 27, Oct 16, 17, Nov 14, Dec 19; 1765: DL, Sep 24, Oct 9, 30, Nov 16, 21, Dec 14; 1766: DL, Jan 6, 21, Apr 12, May 3, 14, 19, HAY, Jun 18, 26, Jul 1, 8, 31, KING'S, Aug 18, 20, 25, 29, Sep 13, DL, 23, 27, 30, Oct 4, 28, Nov 18, Dec 4; 1767: DL, Jan 24, Feb 19, Apr 28, May 28, HAY, 29, Jun 5, 17, 22, Jul 2, 15, Aug 5, 12, 25, 27, Sep 11, DL, 15, HAY, 16, DL, 23, 26, Oct 8, Nov 21; 1768: DL, Apr 4, 9, HAY, Jun 23, Jul 18, 27, Aug 24, DL, Sep 17, 26, Oct 1, 28, Nov 21; 1769: DL, Apr 3, 10, 12, 21, HAY, May 15, 29, Jul 12, 17, Aug 7, Sep 11, DL, 19, Oct 14, Nov 2; 1770: DL, Apr 26, HAY, May 16, 18, DL, 19, HAY, 23, 28, DL, 30, HAY, Jun 15, DL, Oct 3, 13, 17, 24, 29, Nov 3, 17, 24, 29; 1771: DL, Mar 7, Apr 2, 6, 17, HAY, May 15, 20, 29, Jun 5, 7, 14, 26, DL, Sep 26, 28; 1772: HAY, May 18, 22, 27, Jun 8, 15, 29, Aug 10, DL, Oct 1, 21; 1773: HAY, May 17, 26, 28, 31, Jun 18, Jul 2, Aug 11, 27, DL, Oct 5; 1774: DL, May 16, HAY, 30, Jun 6, Jul 4, 13
Castlemaine, Countess of. See Palmer, Barbara Villiers.
Castleman, Richard (treasurer), 1711: DL/QUEEN, Jun 12; 1712: DL, Jun 12; 1713: DL, Jun 1; 1714: DL, Jun 9; 1715: DL, Jun 2; 1716: DL, Jun 6; 1717: DL, May 15; 1718: DL, May 16; 1719: DL, May 4; 1720: DL, May 12; 1721: DL, May 9; 1722: DL, Apr 18; 1723: DL, May 21; 1724: DL, May 7; 1725: DL, May 3; 1726: DL, May 5; 1727: DL, May 8; 1728: DL, May 10; 1729: DL, May 2; 1730: DL, May 2; 1731: DL, Apr 29; 1732: DL, Apr 27; 1733: DL, Apr 27, Jun 9; 1734: DL/HAY, May 3; 1735: DL, May 9; 1736: DL, May 6; 1737: DL, May 10; 1738: DL, May 9; 1739: DL, May 5
Castlemayne, Countess of. See Palmer, Barbara Villiers.
Castles (house servant), 1734: DL, May 21
Castrucci (Castraccio), Pietro (musician, composer), 1715: GRT, Jul 23; 1716: HIC, Mar 14, 15, 21; 1717: HIC, Mar 13, 27, Apr 10; 1719: YB, Dec 19; 1720: YB, Feb 10, HIC, Jun 16; 1721: HIC, Apr 4; 1722: HIC, Feb 16, Mar 7; 1723: DL, Mar 20; 1724: HIC, Mar 18, 25, Apr 17, HAY, May 8; 1725: HIC, Mar 19; 1726: YB, Mar 30; 1727: YB, Mar 22; 1728: YB, Apr 10; 1729: HIC, Mar 28, Apr 16, 30; 1730: HIC, Feb 25; 1731: HIC, Feb 26; 1732: HIC, Feb 28; 1733: YB, Mar 8, LIF, May 7; 1736: HIC, Jan 21
Castrucci, Prospero (musician), 1729: HIC, Feb 25; 1733: SH, Mar 19
Casuist, a, 1751: HAY, Dec 27; 1752: CT/HAY, Jan 7, 14, 31, CT, Mar 7, CT/HAY, Apr 1, May 5
Cataclysm, The. See Ecclestone, Edward.
Cataline's Conspiracy. See Jonson, Ben.
Catalogue of Curiosities, Chiefly Theatrical, A (pamphlet), 1748: HAY, Jun 3
Catalogue of Plays (entertainment), 1729: WINH, Jul 19
Catalogue of Plays and Farces (song), 1794: CG, May 24

Catalonian Marriage (dance), 1763: CG, Mar 8, 10, 22, Apr 6, 13, 21, May 10, 13
Catalonian Peasants (dance), 1767: DL, May 18
Cataneo (music teacher), 1735: DL, Mar 3, CG/LIF, 24; 1762: KING'S, Apr 14
Catch (song), 1788: HAY, Aug 11; 1798: CG, Apr 9
Catch Club (song), 1770: Dl, Jun 7; 1771: DL, Apr 27; 1776: MARLY, May 23, 27,
   30
Catch Club, The (interlude, anon), 1788: HAY, Aug 22, 29; 1789: CG, Apr 21,
   HAY, Aug 10, 25; 1791: HAY, Aug 26
Catches and Glees (song), 1768: DL, Jun 21; 1770: HAY, Mar 12, DL, Jun 7,
   MARLY, Aug 21; 1771: DL, Apr 27, CG, Jun 6; 1772: HAY, Mar 16, DL, May 1, 13,
   19; 1774: HAY, Mar 15; 1775: HAY, Feb 16, Mar 9, May 1, Oct 30; 1776: HAY,
   Feb 22, Mar 5, Apr 18; 1779: CG, Apr 17; 1780: CG, Apr 18; 1781: HAY, Mar 26,
   CG, Apr 25, 27; 1782: CG, Apr 19; 1783: CG, May 6; 1784: DL, May 3; 1785: DL,
   Apr 18, HAY, Aug 19; 1786: HAY, Mar 6, DL, Apr 4; 1787: DL, Apr 9; 1789: CG,
   Apr 21, 29, HAY, Jun 23; 1791: CG, Apr 28, May 5, KING'S, 19; 1792: DLKING'S,
   Apr 10, 19, CG, May 11; 1794: CG, May 23; 1796: DL, May 27, Jun 3; 1799: CG,
   Apr 16
Cateman (householder), 1786: DL, May 24
Catenacci, Maria (singer), 1783: KING'S, Nov 29, Dec 16; 1784: KING'S, Jan 6,
   17, Feb 17, Mar 4, May 8, Jun 12; 1785: KING'S, Jan 4, 8, Feb 26, May 28, Jun
   14; 1786: KING'S, Feb 14, Mar 21, May 4
Caterina, Sga (wire dancer), 1756: SW, Oct 9
Cates (actor), 1746: CG, Jun 23
Catesby (actor), 1741: JS, Nov 9
Catherine and Petruchio. See Garrick, David.
Catherine St, 1735: DL, Apr 11; 1737: CG, Jan 17; 1744: DL, Apr 6, KING'S, Nov
   3, DL, 24; 1745: CT, Jan 14, DT, Mar 14; 1746: HIC, Mar 10; 1747: NONE, Mar
   27; 1748: DL, Mar 29; 1749: CG, Jan 17, DL, Mar 16; 1750: DL, Feb 9, 12, Mar
   26; 1751: DL, Feb 21, 28, Mar 8, Apr 12, May 1; 1752: CG, Feb 14, DL, 22, Apr
   13; 1753: DL, Dec 11; 1754: DL, Mar 30; 1757: DL, Apr 14, CG, 25; 1758: DL,
   Apr 11; 1766: DL, Sep 20; 1769: CG, Feb 25; 1776: DL, May 13; 1778: HAY, Aug
   25; 1779: DL, May 1, HAY, Aug 25; 1780: DL, Mar 14, HAY, Aug 29; 1782: DL,
   Apr 15; 1784: CG, May 1; 1785: DL, May 3; 1786: DL, May 8; 1787: DL, May 2,
   14; 1789: DL, May 27; 1791: HAY, Aug 5; 1792: CG, May 10; 1794: DL, Mar 12
Catley, Anne (actor, singer), 1762: CG, Oct 8, 22, Nov 1, 15; 1763: CG, Jan 24,
   26, Apr 26, MARLY, Jun 28; 1770: CG, Sep 24, Oct 2, 4, 23, Nov 8, 22, Dec 13,
   17; 1771: CG, Jan 19, 25, Mar 16, 18, 23, MARLY, Jul 30, Aug 3, 6, 8, 13, 15,
   17, 20, 22, 24, 27, 29, Sep 3, 5, 12; 1772: CG, Sep 30, Oct 7, 13, 17, Nov
   21, Dec 19, 23, DL, 26; 1773: CG, Feb 6, 26, Mar 3, 19, 27, Apr 13, Oct 16,
   21, 27, Nov 3, 6, 19, 26, Dec 16; 1774: CG, Jan 6, 7, 8, Feb 4, May 12, HAY,
   Jun 7, CG, Sep 28, Oct 3, 5, 15, 19, Nov 1, 10, 29, Dec 7, 23; 1775: CG, Jan
   21, Mar 21, 25, 28; 1776: CG, Sep 27, 30, Oct 7, 8, 9, 15, 23, 25, 30; 1777:
   CG, Jan 3, 25, Feb 25, Mar 10; 1780: CG, Feb 5, 8, 17, Mar 29, Apr 14, 15,
   27, May 11, Sep 20, 21, Oct 3, Nov 13, 15, Dec 9, 12, 16, 21, 23; 1781: CG,
   Jan 13, Feb 26, May 4, 5, Oct 16, 20, 23, 25, 30, 31; 1782: CG, Feb 14, 18,
   26, Mar 18, Apr 9, May 4, 28
Cato Burlesqued (play), 1719: RI, Jul 6
Cato of Utica. See Ozell, John.
Cato. See Addison, Joseph.
Cato, Marcus (author), 1789: KHS, Sep 16
Caton (boxkeeper), 1796: DL, Jun 15; 1797: DL, Jun 13; 1798: DL, Jun 9
Cator (renter), 1786: CG, Sep 29
Cattaneo, Marquis of (commentator), 1676: DG, Apr 30
Catton, Charles (scene painter), 1781: CG, Dec 26; 1782: CG, Oct 10; 1783: CG,
   Jan 18, Sep 22; 1785: CG, Sep 19; 1794: DL, Apr 21
Catton Jr, Charles (scene painter), 1785: CG, Dec 20
Catzoni, Sga. See Cuzzoni, Francesca.
Caulfield, John (actor, singer), 1795: DL, Feb 12, Oct 30, Nov 11, Dec 10;
   1796: DL, Jan 8, Mar 12, Apr 30, Sep 29, Oct 19, Nov 9; 1797: DL, Jan 7, May
   18, HAY, Jun 23, Aug 14, 15, 16, 24, 31, DL, Nov 8; 1798: HAY, Jun 30, Jul
   21, Aug 11, DL, Nov 14, Dec 4, 29, 31; 1799: DL, Mar 2, Apr 16, 23, 29, May
   24, HAY, Jul 9, 13, 16, Aug 21, Sep 2, 9, DL, Oct 14, Nov 14, Dec 11; 1800:
   DL, Jan 1, Mar 11, 13, Apr 29, HAY, Jul 2, Aug 14, 29, Sep 1, 11
Caulfield, Thomas (actor, singer), 1791: DLKING'S, Oct 15, 24, 31, Nov 4, 5, 7,
   16, 17, 25, 28; 1792: DLKING'S, Jan 13, 18, 21, 28, 31, Feb 11, 18, 23, Mar
   1, 6, 17, 19, 24, 29, 31, Apr 12, 14, 16, 17, 19, May 15, 19, 21, DL, Sep 25,
   Oct 4, 11, 13, 15, 31, Nov 2, 5, 6, 10, 21, Dec 10, 13, 26, 28, 31; 1793: DL,
   Jan 4, 7, 16, 22, Feb 5, 12, 16, 23, 26, Mar 7, 9, 18, Apr 9, 16, 22, 23, May
   4, 7, 10, 21, 22, 24, 29, Jun 1, 6, HAY, Aug 5, 12, Sep 19, 21, 24, 28, 30,
   Oct 1, 4, 5, 8, 10, 15, 21, 22, 24, Nov 4, 16, 19, 22, 23, 26, 29, Dec 10,
   16, 26, 30; 1794: HAY, Jan 1, 4, 13, 14, 17, 21, Feb 13, 20, 22, 24, Mar 13,
   27, 29, 31, Apr 3, DL, 21, 25, 29, May 1, 3, 15, 16, 23, Jun 6, 9, 14, 19,

27, HAY, Sep 17, DL, 23, 27, Oct 2, 4, 7, 9, 11, 14, 27, 28, 31, Nov 3, 14,
18, 29, Dec 9, 12, 16, 20, 23, 30; 1795: DL, Jan 12, 20, 26, Feb 2, 12, 17,
24, Mar 3, HAY, 4, DL, 14, 21, Apr 16, 22, 27, May 19, 26, 28, 29, Jun 1, 3,
HAY, 9, 10, 11, 13, 16, 17, 19, 20, Jul 4, 16, 22, 30, 31, Aug 3, 11, 22, 29,
Sep 1, 2, DL, 19, 26, 29, Oct 1, 5, 6, 8, 12, 15, 19, 21, 27, 30, Nov 6, 7,
11, 16, 19, 20, 23, 26, Dec 10, 11, 18, 19, 21, 23; 1796: DL, Jan 12, 18, Feb
15, 20, 29, Apr 2, 13, 18, 20, 25, 29, 30, May 2, 9, 13, 21, 23, 27, 30, Jun
7, HAY, 11, DL, 11, 13, HAY, 14, 15, 16, 17, 20, 22, 25, 29, Jul 2, 4, 5, 7,
8, 14, 15, 22, 23, 26, Aug 8, 11, 12, 13, 17, 18, 20, 23, 24, 29, 30, Sep 1,
7, 16, 17, DL, 24, 27, 29, Oct 3, 6, 10, 19, 22, 24, 25, 29, Nov 2, 5, 9, 10,
12, 15, 18, 23, 26, Dec 7, 9, 10, 26, 30; 1797: DL, Jan 12, 17, Feb 3, 9, 14,
16, 22, 23, Mar 6, 11, 20, Apr 6, 28, May 3, 8, 9, 12, 17, 19, 22, 27, Jun 6,
7, 9, 12, HAY, 12, DL, 14, HAY, 15, DL, 15, HAY, 16, 17, 19, 20, 22, 23, 26,
28, Jul 3, 4, 8, 10, 15, Aug 3, 5, 8, 9, 14, 15, 21, 22, 28, Sep 1, 4, 12,
14, DL, 28, 30, Oct 3, 5, 7, 17, 19, 28, 30, 31, Nov 2, 4, 6, 7, 8, 10, 11,
13, 15, 16, 17, 20, 21, 23, 24, 25, 27, Dec 8, 9, 16, 23; 1798: DL, Jan 9,
Feb 13, Mar 17, Apr 9, 14, May 11, 18, 21, 24, 30, Jun 6, 7, 12, HAY, 12, 13,
14, 15, 19, 20, 21, 23, 27, 29, 30, Jul 6, 13, 14, 21, 30, Aug 2, 4, 7, 11,
14, 20, 21, 23, 25, 27, 29, 30, Sep 3, 10, DL, 18, 20, 22, 25, 27, 29, Oct 4,
6, 8, 9, 11, 13, 16, 20, 27, Nov 3, 6, 14, 16, 26, Dec 3, 4, HAY, 17, DL, 19,
27; 1799: DL, Jan 8, 10, 11, 19, Feb 4, 9, 14, 23, 26, Mar 2, Apr 17, 19, May
1, 4, 6, 7, 8, 9, 20, 24, Jun 10, HAY, 18, 21, 22, 25, Jul 1, 2, DL, 4, HAY,
5, 6, 8, 9, 10, 12, 19, 20, 22, 23, 27, Aug 13, 21, 26, 28, Sep 16, DL, Oct
7, 8, 10, 12, 14, 15, 17, 21, 23, 26, 29, 30, 31, Nov 1, 7, 8, 12, 14, 21,
22, 25, 29, Dec 9, 11, 19; 1800: DL, Jan 4, 21, Feb 5, 12, 20, Mar 11, 27,
Apr 29, May 29, 30, Jun 2, 6, 11, HAY, 17, DL, 18, HAY, 19, 27, Jul 2, 7, 15,
Aug 7, 12, 14, 23, 26, 29, Sep 3
Caun, Susanna (actor), 1729: LIF, Jan 1
Caustin (house servant), 1746: DL, May 19
Caustin (mercer), 1750: DL, Jan 15
Causton (beneficiary), 1720: LIF, Jun 7
Cautherly (house servant), 1750: CG, May 7
Cautherly, Samuel (actor), 1755: DL, Apr 28, Oct 23, Nov 17; 1756: DL, May 5,
Sep 21, Dec 3; 1757: DL, Jan 18, Sep 13, Dec 22; 1760: DL, Oct 9, Dec 17;
1761: DL, Apr 29, May 8, Sep 26, Oct 31; 1762: DL, Nov 3; 1763: DL, Jan 17;
1765: DL, Sep 26, Nov 25; 1766: DL, Jan 6, Mar 20, Sep 23, 30, Oct 4, 7, 25,
Nov 8, 26, Dec 10, 15, 30; 1767: DL, Apr 11, 29, Jun 1, Sep 12, 17, 19, 25,
26, Oct 14, Nov 11, 16, 19, 27, Dec 21, 26; 1768: DL, Jan 19, 22, 23, Mar 15,
21, Apr 6, 12, 14, 25, May 30, Sep 8, 22, 23, 24, 27, 29, 30, Oct 4, 8, 20,
Nov 1, 17, Dec 1, 14, 16; 1769: DL, Jan 20, Feb 4, Mar 29, Apr 7, 10, CG, 22,
DL, May 1, Sep 16, 21, 26, 30, Oct 2, 3, 4, 5, 10, 14, 18, 21, 23, Nov 9, 13,
14, Dec 4, 12, 16, 19; 1770: DL, Jan 4, 19, Feb 8, Mar 3, Apr 3, 19, May 2,
15, 17, Sep 22, Oct 2, 3, 5, 15, 22, 23, 26, 29, Nov 6, 9, 13, 14, 20, 21,
23, Dec 17; 1771: DL, Jan 19, Mar 16, 21, Apr 2, 9, May 3, 23, 27, Sep 21,
24, 26, Oct 3, 5, 10, 12, 15, 17, 28, Nov 2, 4, 9, 11, 12, 22, 27, Dec 10,
30; 1772: DL, Jan 1, 4, Feb 21, Mar 28, Apr 22, 25, 28, May 14, 30, Jun 10,
Sep 19, 24, 26, Oct 6, 8, 14, 17, 23, Nov 3, 9, 16, Dec 22; 1773: DL, Jan 4,
26, Feb 4, Mar 30, Apr 16, 23, 29, May 10, 27, Jun 1, Sep 18, 21, 23, Oct 26,
28, 30, Nov 1, 25, Dec 10, 20, 21; 1774: DL, Feb 9, Mar 19, Apr 12, 19, 26,
May 10, 14, 28, Sep 17, 20, 22, 24, 27, Oct 5, 6, 14, 21, 28, Nov 16, Dec 1;
1775: DL, Jan 2, 11, Mar 9, 20, 23, 25, Apr 6, 8, CG, 24, DL, May 1, Sep 26
Cavalcade Espagnol, La (entertainment), 1719: KING'S, Mar 7; 1721: HAY, May 4
Cave of Trophonius, The. See Hoare, Prince.
Cavellos, Don Juan Bernalte de los (Spanish visitor), 1702: LIF, Dec 11
Cavendish Square, 1746: HIC, Mar 10; 1779: CG, May 8; 1782: KING'S, Mar 7, May
9, 23; 1783: CG, Feb 14; 1784: KING'S, Mar 4, CG, May 21; 1786: KING'S, Apr 6
Cavendish, Georgiana, Duchess of Devonshire, 1780: DL, May 24; 1798: HAY, Aug
23; 1800: DL, Apr 29, CG, Jun 12
Cavendish, Henry Lord (spectator), 1678: ATCOURT, Jan 18; 1697: LIF, Mar 4
Cavendish, Lady Rachel Russel (spectator), 1692: DL, Nov 9
Cavendish, Lord Charles (spectator), 1729: DL, Nov 1, Dec 27
Cavendish, Margaret, Duchess of Newcastle, 1667: LIF, Mar 28, 30, May 6
Cavendish, William, Duke of Newcastle, 1661: VERE, Oct 26, Dec 10; 1662: VERE,
Mar 11; 1667: LIF, Aug 15, 16; 1669: BRIDGES, Jan 29, Feb 2, NONE, 10; 1720:
DL, Jan 23
--Country Captain, The, 1661: VERE, Oct 26, LIF, Nov 25, VERE, 25, Dec 13;
1667: BRIDGES, May 18, Aug 14; 1668: BRIDGES, May 14; 1669: BRIDGES, Jan 12;
1689: NONE, Sep 0
--French Dancing Master, The, 1661: VERE, Dec 10; 1662: VERE, Mar 11, May 21
--Heiress, The, 1669: BRIDGES, Jan 29, NONE, 30, BRIDGES, Feb 1, 2
--Humourous Lovers, The, 1667: LIF, Mar 28, 30, May 6; 1676: NONE, Sep 0
--Triumphant Widow, The; or, The Medley of Humours, 1674: DG, Nov 26

--Variety, The, 1661: VERE, Dec 10; 1662: VERE, Mar 11; 1669: BRIDGES, Jan 12
Cavill (Gavill), Will (performer), 1671: NONE, Mar 31
Cawder (dresser), 1760: CG, Sep 22
Cawley (Caley), Master (actor, dancer), 1757: HAY, Jun 17, Jul 5, Oct 31; 1759:
    HAY, Apr 18, May 10, MARLY, Sep 6; see also Callois, Master
Cawston (house servant), 1796: DL, Jun 15; 1797: DL, Jun 13
Cawthorn, George (publisher), 1796: CG, Nov 19, DL, Dec 10; 1797: CG, May 9,
    DL, 15, Nov 9; 1798: CG, May 8, DL, Jun 6; 1799: HAY, Aug 21
Cawthorn, John (publisher), 1798: CG, Apr 24, HAY, Jun 12; 1800: CG, Apr 30,
    HAY, Sep 1
Cayley, Mary, Lady Marow (spectator), 1700: LIF, Mar 12, DL, 12
Cease, ah cease (song), 1789: DL, Mar 20; 1790: DL, Feb 24, Mar 12; 1791: DL,
    Apr 1, CG, 13; 1792: KING'S, Feb 29; 1794: DL, Mar 26
Cease, Cynthia, cease your fruitless tears (song), 1696: DG, Oct 0
Cease, Galatea (song), 1791: DL, Apr 1; 1792: KING'S, Feb 29; 1794: DL, Mar 26
Cease, gay Seducers (song), 1771: CG, Mar 16; 1782: CG, May 1
Cease, rude Boreas (song), 1794: CG, May 26; 1797: CG, May 22; see also Sea
    Storm; Storm, The
Cease thy Anguish (song), 1790: CG, Feb 26
Cease to Beauty (song), 1729: DL, Mar 26; 1791: DL, Apr 1; 1792: KING'S, Feb
    29; 1794: DL, Mar 26
Cease your funning (song), 1786: CG, Feb 21
Cecil Court, 1735: CAT, Jun 19; 1746: DL, Dec 30
Cecil St, 1738: DL, Mar 20; 1739: DL, Mar 13; 1740: DL, Mar 17; 1756: DL, Apr
    20; 1784: DL, May 3, Aug 20; 1785: DL, Apr 20
Cecil, Anne Cavendish, Lady Exeter (spectator), 1685: DLORDG, Dec 30
Cecil, James, 1st Marquis of Salisbury, 1792: DLKING'S, Jan 30; 1796: HAY, Sep
    16, 17; 1798: HAY, Mar 26, Sep 17; 1799: HAY, Sep 16; 1800: HAY, Sep 16
Cecilian Society, 1791: DL, Apr 13
Ceedo, Mrs. See Seedo, Mrs.
Ceffalo e Procri (opera), 1742: KING'S, May 18, 22, 25
Celadon and Florimel; or, The Happy Counterplot (play), 1796: DL, May 23
Celebrate this Festival (song), 1693: ATCOURT, Apr 30
Celebrated Story of Fryar Bacon, Fryar Bungy, the Brazen-Head, and Miles Their
    Man, 1732: BF, Aug 25
Celemene, pray tell me (song), 1695: DL, Nov 0
Celeste, Sga (singer), 1732: CRT, Nov 20; 1733: KING'S, Jan 27; see also
    Hempson, Celestina
Celestina. See Hempson, Celestina.
Celia has a thousand charms (song), 1695: DL, Oct 0; 1737: CG, Mar 26, Apr 21,
    May 2, 3, 6; 1742: DL, Feb 23, Mar 16, 18
Celia that I once was Blest by (song), 1739: DL, Jan 3, 6
Celiers, Mme (speaks epilogue), 1689: NONE, Sep 0
Celisia, Dorothea, 1771: DL, Jan 12
--Almida, 1771: DL, Jan 12, 14, 16, 18, 23, 25, 29, Feb 1, 4, 8, 25, Mar 4, Nov
    15
Celladon and Phyllis (dance), 1742: DL, May 25
Celotti (Celett, Celotte), Ziuliana (singer), 1705: LIF, Feb 9, YB, Apr 2;
    1706: YB, Mar 13; 1707: YB, Jan 22; 1712: HIC, Nov 13; 1713: SH, Mar 4; 1714:
    CA, Apr 19
Celson, Miss (singer), 1798: CG, Mar 14, 23, 28, 30
Centlivre, Susannah, Mrs Joseph, 1700: DL, Oct 0; 1702: LIF, Jun 0, Dec 31;
    1703: DL, Jun 4; 1705: LIF/QUEEN, Feb 22, DL, Nov 20; 1706: QUEEN'S, Nov 25;
    1709: DL, May 12, 21, QUEEN'S, Dec 12; 1710: DL, Mar 27, 30, Dec 30; 1712:
    DL, Jan 19; 1714: DL, Apr 27; 1716: DL, Dec 17; 1718: LIF, Feb 3; 1720: DL,
    Feb 20; 1721: LIF, Nov 29; 1722: LIF, Jan 3, DL, Oct 2; 1724: HAY, Mar 2;
    1735: DL, Jan 11, Feb 27, Oct 28, HAY, Dec 10; 1736: GF, Feb 21, DL, Dec 21;
    1738: DL, Feb 9, Sep 23, Oct 11; 1739: DL, Jan 13, 16, 18, Feb 7, CG, Sep 19,
    DL, Oct 15; 1740: CG, Oct 25, DL, Dec 9, CG, 27; 1741: CG, Sep 30, GF, Oct 5,
    DL, Dec 12; 1744: CG, Apr 21; 1756: DL, Oct 13; 1758: CG, Apr 3; 1762: CG,
    Apr 29; 1769: DL, Apr 10; 1779: DL, Apr 10; 1781: HAY, Oct 16; 1782: HAY, Jan
    21, Mar 21; 1784: HAY, Mar 8; 1789: CG, Apr 4; 1790: CG, Apr 21
--Angry Doctor and the Doubting Philosopher, The, 1703: DL, Jul 7
--Artifice, The, 1720: DL, Feb 20; 1722: DL, Oct 2, 3, 4; 1781: HAY, Oct 16
--Basset Table, The, 1705: DL, Nov 20, 21, 22, 23
--Beau's Duel; or, A Soldier for the Ladies, 1702: LIF, Jun 0, Oct 21; 1782:
    HAY, Jan 21; 1785: DL, Apr 11
--Bickerstaff's Burying, A; or, Work for the Upholders, 1710: DL, Mar 27, 28,
    30, May 11; 1711: DL, May 17
--Bold Stroke for a Wife, A, 1718: LIF, Feb 3, 4, 5, 6, 8, 10; 1728: LIF, Apr
    23, May 31, Jul 12, 16; 1729: LIF, Jan 29, SOU, Oct 14, GF, Nov 14, 15, Dec
    11; 1730: GF, Jan 8, May 11, Jun 16, Jul 10, Oct 20, Dec 17; 1731: GF, Jan

23, Feb 5, Apr 20, May 13, Jun 4, SOU, Sep 28, GF, Oct 29, Dec 15; <u>1732</u>: GF, Feb 2, HAY, Mar 23, Apr 4, GF, Oct 30, Nov 23; <u>1733</u>: GF, Mar 27, Oct 1, Dec 8; <u>1734</u>: GF, Feb 26, Apr 15, Sep 26, Oct 29; <u>1735</u>: GF, Jan 8, Mar 11, HAY, Dec 10; <u>1736</u>: HAY, Jul 14; <u>1737</u>: LIF, Feb 5, 10, 19, Apr 18; <u>1738</u>: CG, Jul 7; <u>1739</u>: DL, Jan 13, 16, 17, 18, Feb 7, Oct 15; <u>1740</u>: DL, Mar 22, GF, Oct 24, Nov 1, DL, 7, GF, Dec 26; <u>1741</u>: DL, Jan 24, Mar 5, GF, Apr 1, Oct 16; <u>1744</u>: GF, Dec 10, 17; <u>1745</u>: GF, Jan 25, Feb 25, Apr 16, Nov 14, Dec 30; <u>1746</u>: CG, Apr 28, GF, Nov 7, 17, CG, Dec 27, GF, 27; <u>1747</u>: GF, Mar 10; <u>1748</u>: SOU, Jan 19, NWC, Dec 26, DL, 26, 27; <u>1749</u>: DL, Mar 27, May 5, Dec 28; <u>1750</u>: DL, Apr 16, Dec 31; <u>1751</u>: DL, Jan 17, Apr 8, May 9, JS, Dec 16; <u>1752</u>: DL, Jan 1, May 5, Nov 27; <u>1753</u>: DL, Feb 2; <u>1754</u>: DL, Apr 19; <u>1757</u>: DL, May 2, 7; <u>1758</u>: CG, Apr 3, 6, 15, 18, May 6, 15, Nov 18, Dec 1, 27; <u>1759</u>: CG, Dec 14; <u>1760</u>: CG, May 19; <u>1761</u>: CG, Jan 6, DL, Apr 17, May 20, CG, Oct 14, DL, 29, Nov 13; <u>1762</u>: DL, Jan 1, CG, Feb 11, May 20, DL, 21, Dec 27, CG, 27; <u>1763</u>: CG, Jan 6, 27, Apr 5, May 2, Oct 19, Nov 9, Dec 7, DL, 28; <u>1764</u>: CG, Feb 21, Apr 25, DL, May 22, Sep 25, CG, Oct 16, Nov 9, Dec 28; <u>1765</u>: DL, Jan 22, Apr 9, CG, 25, Oct 26, Dec 27; <u>1766</u>: CG, Feb 27, Apr 12, DL, May 19, CG, Oct 25; <u>1767</u>: CG, Jan 6, Feb 26, Apr 2, Dec 26; <u>1768</u>: CG, Jan 21, Apr 7, Jun 3, Oct 10, Dec 26; <u>1769</u>: CG, Nov 3; <u>1770</u>: CG, May 18; <u>1771</u>: HAY, May 27, CG, Dec 28; <u>1772</u>: CG, Jan 4, 10; <u>1773</u>: CG, Dec 17; <u>1774</u>: CG, Dec 6, 14; <u>1776</u>: CHR, Sep 30; <u>1777</u>: DL, Apr 29, Jun 2, CHR, Jul 23; <u>1778</u>: HAY, Mar 31, CHR, Jun 18, CG, Oct 7, Nov 27; <u>1779</u>: CG, May 12, DL, 21, HAY, Oct 13, DL, Nov 22; <u>1780</u>: DL, Mar 29, May 17, Sep 19, Nov 25; <u>1781</u>: DL, May 25; <u>1782</u>: DL, Jan 19, Feb 23, Dec 7; <u>1783</u>: DL, Jan 27, Nov 13, Dec 26; <u>1784</u>: DL, Dec 28; <u>1785</u>: DL, May 25; <u>1786</u>: DL, Oct 25, Dec 22; <u>1787</u>: CG, Jan 2, May 31, Sep 19, Dec 29; <u>1788</u>: CG, Jun 4, Nov 28, Dec 2, 3; <u>1789</u>: CG, Feb 17, Mar 10; <u>1793</u>: HAY, Oct 26, 29, 31, Nov 7, 11, 13, 18, 26, Dec 26, 27; <u>1794</u>: HAY, Feb 19, Apr 7, Sep 17; <u>1795</u>: HAY, Jul 1, 8, 17, 28, Aug 6, 19; <u>1796</u>: HAY, Jul 9, 19, 28, Aug 19, DL, Oct 19, Dec 27; <u>1797</u>: DL, Feb 13, Jun 10, HAY, 24, Aug 10, DL, Sep 23, Dec 19; <u>1798</u>: DL, Jan 13, Feb 10, Jun 1, Oct 6, Nov 5, 14, Dec 14; <u>1799</u>: DL, Jan 29, Oct 8, 24, Nov 9; <u>1800</u>: DL, Jan 2, 22, Apr 15, May 8

--Busy Body, The, <u>1709</u>: DL, May 12, 13, 14, 16, 21, 28, Jun 4, QUEEN'S, Oct 11, 13, 15, IT, Nov 1, QUEEN'S, 1, DL, 26, Dec 8, QUEEN'S, 12, 14, 15, DL, 26; <u>1710</u>: DL, Jan 27, QUEEN'S, Apr 22, DL, May 16, GR, Aug 7, DL, Dec 12, 30; <u>1711</u>: DL, May 4, Oct 19; <u>1712</u>: SML, Jun 18, DL, Nov 24; <u>1713</u>: DL, Sep 24, Nov 20; <u>1714</u>: DL, Nov 5, LIF, Dec 22, 30; <u>1715</u>: LIF, Jan 14, Feb 21, Apr 7, DL, May 5, LIF, Sep 28, DL, Oct 17; <u>1716</u>: LIF, Jan 16, DL, Feb 20, LIF, Jun 12, DL, Oct 26, LIF, Nov 23; <u>1717</u>: LIF, Feb 6, May 22, DL, Oct 23, LIF, Nov 28; <u>1718</u>: LIF, Jan 18, Feb 4, May 1, RI, Jul 28, DL, Oct 29, LIF, Nov 8; <u>1719</u>: LIF, Feb 4, Apr 10, May 13, 19, Oct 5, DL, Nov 16, Dec 14; <u>1720</u>: DL, Mar 17, Oct 17, LIF, Nov 4; <u>1721</u>: LIF, Jan 3, Apr 17, Jun 6, Nov 29; <u>1722</u>: LIF, Jan 3, Mar 10, Apr 9, DL, 14, LIF, May 24, Oct 1, DL, 2, 3, SOU, 3, LIF, Dec 5; <u>1723</u>: DL, May 23, LIF, Oct 7, Dec 13; <u>1724</u>: LIF, Jan 13, Feb 14, May 9, RI, Jul 11, LIF, Oct 2, HAY, 13; <u>1725</u>: LIF, Jan 29, Feb 22, Mar 30, May 20, Oct 19; <u>1726</u>: LIF, Jan 26, Mar 15, May 14, Sep 16, SOU, 27; <u>1727</u>: LIF, Feb 4, Mar 2, May 26, Oct 4, Dec 6; <u>1728</u>: LIF, Apr 26, Nov 8; <u>1729</u>: LIF, May 3, Nov 7, GF, 8, Dec 6; <u>1730</u>: LIF, Jan 23, GF, Apr 27, May 22, RI, Jun 24, GF, 26, RI, Oct 20, DL, 28, GF, 31, LIF, Nov 16, DL, 16; <u>1731</u>: GF, Jan 9, LIF, 29, Apr 26, GF, May 11, DL, 31, LIF, Nov 9, GF, 19, DL, Dec 7; <u>1732</u>: LIF, Jan 11, DL, 19, LIF, Mar 4, GF, Apr 26, LIF, May 1, DL, 8, Sep 23, GF, Oct 10, LIF/CG, Nov 14, GF, 25, DL, Dec 22; <u>1733</u>: LIF/CG, Jan 20, DL, Apr 9, LIF/CG, May 8, DL, 24, CG, Sep 27, DL/HAY, Oct 19, Nov 16, DL, 21, Dec 1; <u>1734</u>: GF, Jan 10, DL/HAY, 28, DL, Feb 5, GF, 23, CG, Apr 1, May 7, GF, 9, CG, Sep 2, RI, 9, GF, 25; <u>1735</u>: GF, Jan 3, DL, 11, CG/LIF, 17, GF, Feb 4, LIF, 12, DL, 27, CG/LIF, Mar 24, DL, Oct 28; <u>1736</u>: CG, Feb 17, DL, 21, GF, 21, DL, Apr 27, LIF, May 5, CG, Nov 29, LIF, Dec 3, 8, DL, 21; <u>1737</u>: LIF, Mar 9, Apr 22, DL, May 16, CG, 19, DL, Sep 27, CG, Nov 14; <u>1738</u>: CG, Jan 27, DL, Feb 9, CG, May 11, DL, Sep 23, Oct 11, CG, Dec 12, DL, 28; <u>1739</u>: CG, Jan 31, May 10, DL, 31, CG, Sep 19, DL, Oct 3, CG, Dec 5; <u>1740</u>: CG, Jan 3, DL, 18, CG, Feb 19, Apr 22, May 3, DL, 26, CG, 27, DL, Sep 18, CG, Oct 13, GF, 17, CG, 25, GF, Nov 6, DL, Dec 9, CG, 27; <u>1741</u>: DL, Feb 3, Apr 11, GF, May 4, CG, 6, Sep 30, GF, Oct 5, CG, Nov 24, GF, Dec 1, DL, 12, 18, CG, 30; <u>1742</u>: DL, Jan 27, Feb 10, CG, 16, May 6, DL, Nov 19, LIF, 29; <u>1743</u>: DL, Jan 18, SOU, Feb 25, LIF, Jun 3, DL, Sep 20, CG, Oct 21; <u>1744</u>: CG, Apr 21, DL, Sep 29, GF, Nov 29, CG, 29, GF, Dec 4, DL, 14; <u>1745</u>: GF, Feb 9, CG, 12, May 15, DL, Oct 3, CG, Nov 13, GF, 18; <u>1746</u>: CG, Jan 23, DL, Mar 8, Aug 4, CG, Oct 8; <u>1747</u>: CG, Jan 21, Nov 11, Dec 23; <u>1748</u>: CG, Feb 3, Mar 7, DL, Sep 10, CG, Oct 27, JS, Dec 20; <u>1749</u>: DL, Jan 3, Feb 23, Mar 28, CG, Apr 25, DL, May 11, Sep 16, SOUGT, 25, SOU, 28, DL, Nov 23, CG, Dec 7, DL, 29; <u>1750</u>: CG, Feb 7, 14, DL, 17, CG, May 4, DL, Sep 25, CG, 26, DL, Nov 1, 2, Dec 29; <u>1751</u>: DL, Jan 14, May 4, CG, Dec 10; <u>1752</u>: CG, Apr 4; <u>1753</u>: DL, Jan 2, 5, May 17, Sep 22, Dec 29; <u>1754</u>: DL, May 7, Jul 2, Oct 22; <u>1755</u>: DL, Jan 28, Mar 20, Apr 17, HAY, Aug 21, 25; <u>1756</u>: DL, Sep 18, ACAD,

Dec 15, DL, 28; <u>1757</u>: DL, May 18, Oct 29, Dec 28; <u>1758</u>: HAY, Jan 25, DL, Dec
2, 4, 6, 7, 9, 12, 16, 22, 29; <u>1759</u>: DL, Jan 11, 15, Feb 2, Mar 1, CG, 22,
DL, 29, CG, 31, May 2, DL, 4, HAY, Sep 28, CG, Oct 3, Dec 13; <u>1760</u>: CG, Feb
6, DL, Mar 24, CG, Oct 13; <u>1761</u>: CG, Jan 16, Apr 22, 23, Jun 23, Oct 2; <u>1762</u>:
DL, Jan 11, 18, CG, Apr 17, DL, May 1, 24, CG, Oct 5, 7, 13, 15, 30, Nov 12,
24; <u>1763</u>: DL, Jan 18, CG, 19, Feb 15, Mar 17, Apr 6, 27, DL, May 11, CG, 20,
Sep 19, DL, 29, CG, Oct 29, DL, Nov 17, CG, Dec 8; <u>1764</u>: CG, Jan 7, Feb 18,
Mar 20, Apr 12, May 8, Sep 17, Oct 4, Nov 14, Dec 22; <u>1765</u>: CG, Feb 15, Mar
30, Apr 23, DL, May 22, HAY, Aug 8, CG, Oct 5, Nov 30; <u>1766</u>: CG, Jan 8, Feb
15, Apr 4, 19, DL, May 21, Sep 20, CG, Oct 28, Nov 22, Dec 19; <u>1767</u>: CG, Jan
8, Feb 13, Apr 4, 28, May 7, DL, 29, CG, Jun 9, HAY, Sep 7, CG, 19, Oct 27,
Dec 11; <u>1768</u>: CG, Jan 13, Feb 23, Mar 15, Apr 15, May 12, Sep 29, HAY, Oct 7,
CG, 20, Nov 25; <u>1769</u>: CG, Mar 4, Apr 27, Sep 20, Nov 7; <u>1770</u>: CG, Jan 23, May
23, HAY, Oct 5; <u>1771</u>: CG, May 3, HAY, 22, Sep 18, CG, Nov 16, 30; <u>1772</u>: CG,
Jan 2, 31, Mar 28, May 27, Sep 25, Oct 20, Dec 17; <u>1773</u>: CG, Jan 9, Feb 11,
May 21, Sep 20, Nov 11, 24, Dec 11; <u>1774</u>: CG, Jan 13, HAY, 24, CG, Apr 16,
May 4, Oct 27, Nov 23; <u>1775</u>: CG, Jan 10, Apr 19, May 26, HAY, Sep 19, CG, Oct
4; <u>1776</u>: CG, Apr 16, Oct 15; <u>1777</u>: CG, Jan 7, CHR, Jun 20; <u>1778</u>: CG, Jan 29,
Feb 19, May 21, CHR, Jun 3, CG, Oct 2, Nov 3; <u>1779</u>: CG, Jan 6, Apr 29, HAY,
Oct 18, CG, Nov 30; <u>1780</u>: CII, Mar 17, CG, May 23; <u>1781</u>: CG, Jan 10, 11, May
26; <u>1782</u>: CG, May 28, Sep 23; <u>1783</u>: DL, Jan 24, CG, May 14, Jun 4, DL, Sep
16, Nov 8; <u>1784</u>: DL, Jan 5, Feb 7, May 12, CG, 29, Dec 28; <u>1785</u>: HAMM, Jul
11, CG, Dec 22; <u>1790</u>: CG, Mar 27, Apr 14, 27, Dec 2, 4, 7, 16, 21; <u>1791</u>: CG,
Jan 1, HAY, Mar 7, CG, Jun 14, Sep 17; <u>1792</u>: HAY, Feb 20, CG, May 29, Sep 20;
<u>1793</u>: HAY, Oct 5, 12, 19, 25, Nov 1, 21; <u>1794</u>: CG, Nov 20; <u>1795</u>: CG, Apr 25,
Jun 4; <u>1796</u>: CG, Jun 6, HAY, Aug 9, 13; <u>1797</u>: CG, Jan 4, Oct 4; <u>1798</u>: CG, Jan
9, Feb 12, May 19; <u>1799</u>: CG, May 22; <u>1800</u>: CG, Jun 7
--Cruel Gift, The; or, The Royal Resentment, <u>1716</u>: DL, Dec 17, 18, 19, 20, 21,
22; <u>1717</u>: DL, May 3
--Gamester, The, <u>1705</u>: LIF/QUEN, Feb 22, Apr 27, May 23, LIF, S, Nov 19; <u>1706</u>:
QUEEN'S, Jan 14, Oct 31; <u>1709</u>: DL, Mar 17, 29, May 13, 16, 21, 28; <u>1710</u>: DL,
Feb 7, Mar 28, 30, May 23, GR, Jul 29, Aug 21; <u>1711</u>: DL/QUEEN, May 29, Jul
13; <u>1714</u>: DL, Jul 20, LIF, Dec 21, 29; <u>1715</u>: LIF, Feb 9, Jul 29; <u>1716</u>: LIF,
Jan 11, Apr 30, Nov 21; <u>1717</u>: LIF, Jun 25, Nov 18; <u>1718</u>: LIF, Jan 29, May 3,
RI, Aug 11; <u>1719</u>: LIF, May 25, Jun 11, Nov 3; <u>1720</u>: LIF, Apr 4; <u>1726</u>: LIF,
Aug 2, 5; <u>1727</u>: LIF, Oct 17, 20, Dec 12; <u>1728</u>: LIF, May 13; <u>1729</u>: GF, Nov 20,
27; <u>1730</u>: GF, Jan 16, Jul 17, Oct 24; <u>1731</u>: LIF, Apr 1, GF, 28, LIF, May 21;
<u>1732</u>: LIF, Jan 10; <u>1735</u>: CG/LIF, Mar 29, GF, Apr 9, 26, CG/LIF, May 20, GF,
Sep 22; <u>1736</u>: GF, Feb 26, LIF, Dec 10; <u>1737</u>: LIF, Feb 16; <u>1738</u>: CG, Jun 30,
Jul 7; <u>1740</u>: GF, Dec 29; <u>1741</u>: GF, Jan 31, CG, Feb 7, 9, 24, GF, Apr 20, CG,
30, GF, Oct 9, Dec 31; <u>1742</u>: JS, Jan 7, CG, Feb 22; <u>1743</u>: DL, Nov 26, Dec 30;
<u>1744</u>: DL, May 9, Oct 6, Nov 27, Dec 17; <u>1745</u>: DL, Mar 12, Oct 17; <u>1756</u>: DL,
Oct 12, 13; <u>1790</u>: CG, Apr 21
--Heiress, The; or, The Salamanca Doctor Out Plotted, <u>1702</u>: LIF, Dec 31
--Love at a Venture; or, The Rake Reclaimed, <u>1782</u>: HAY, Mar 21
--Love's Contrivance; or, Le Medecin Malgre Lui, <u>1703</u>: DL, Jun 4, 5, 7, 14, 22,
Jul 7, Oct 20; <u>1704</u>: DL, Jan 21, Feb 16, Mar 28, Apr 28, Jul 5; <u>1705</u>: DL, Jun
7; <u>1706</u>: DL, Feb 14; <u>1723</u>: DT, Nov 1, KAT, Dec 4, CT, 10, AVT, 31; <u>1724</u>: HT,
Mar 13, PY, Apr 20, LIF, Jul 14, 17; <u>1726</u>: LIF, Jun 17, 21
--Man's Bewitched, The; or, The Devil to Do About Her, <u>1709</u>: QUEEN'S, Dec 12,
14, 15; <u>1730</u>: GF, Apr 28, Jun 9, Jul 22; <u>1731</u>: GF, Apr 27; <u>1738</u>: BFP, Aug 23,
SFH, Sep 5; <u>1769</u>: DL, Apr 10; <u>1784</u>: HAY, Mar 8
--Marplot in Lisbon, <u>1755</u>: DL, Mar 20, Apr 5, 23; <u>1762</u>: CG, Apr 29, 30; <u>1772</u>:
DL, Apr 6
--Marplot, <u>1710</u>: DL, Dec 30; <u>1711</u>: DL, Jan 1, 2, 4, 5, 6, May 24; <u>1724</u>: HAY,
Feb 18
--Perjured Husband, The; or, The Adventures of Venice, <u>1700</u>: DL, Oct 0
--Perplexed Lovers, The, <u>1712</u>: DL, Jan 19, 21, 22
--Platonick Lady, The, <u>1706</u>: QUEEN'S, Nov 25, 26, 27, 28
--Stolen Heiress, The, <u>1779</u>: DL, Apr 10
--Wife Well Managed, A; or, Cuckoldom Prevented, <u>1724</u>: HAY, Mar 2; <u>1732</u>: TC,
Aug 17; <u>1789</u>: HAY, Aug 27
--Wonder, The; or, A Woman Keeps a Secret, <u>1714</u>: DL, Apr 27, 28, 29, May 1, 4,
6, Dec 16; <u>1733</u>: GF, Nov 14, 15, 16, 17, 19, 20, 21, 22, 23, 24, 26, 27, Dec
10, 11, 20; <u>1734</u>: GF, Jan 2, 8, 22, Feb 19, Mar 21, Apr 19, May 17, Sep 9,
Oct 5, CG/LIF, Nov 1, GF, Dec 11; <u>1735</u>: CG/LIF, Jan 1, GF, 28, Apr 10, 25,
Sep 17, Dec 4, 11; <u>1736</u>: GF, Mar 2, RI, Aug 21, LIF, Oct 9; <u>1737</u>: LIF, Jan 1,
Mar 26, Apr 29; <u>1741</u>: GF, Jan 28, Apr 29, Sep 21; <u>1742</u>: GF, Feb 18; <u>1744</u>: DL,
Jan 12; <u>1747</u>: GF, Apr 2; <u>1748</u>: CG, Apr 15; <u>1756</u>: CG, Mar 25, Apr 28, Oct 14,
DL, Nov 6, 8, CG, 8, DL, 10, 13, 15, 20, 25, 27, CG, 30, DL, Dec 2, 8; <u>1757</u>:
DL, Jan 6, 8, 14, CG, 19, DL, Feb 2, 18, Mar 28, Apr 15, 21, CG, May 13, DL,
26, Oct 13, Nov 18, Dec 13; <u>1758</u>: DL, Jan 25, Mar 18, Apr 20, May 26, Oct 7,

Nov 10; <u>1759</u>: DL, Jan 16, Feb 20, Mar 26, Jun 4, Nov 22, Dec 17; <u>1760</u>: DL, Jan 16, Mar 25, Apr 10; <u>1761</u>: CG, Feb 17, 19, 21, 24, Mar 2, 10, DL, 23, Apr 13, CG, 20, DL, May 4, CG, 18, Oct 7, DL, 7, 15, CG, Nov 7; <u>1762</u>: DL, Mar 23, CG, May 3, DL, 26, CG, Oct 1, DL, Nov 1, 2, Dec 29; <u>1763</u>: DL, Apr 5, May 19, CG, Oct 14, 15, DL, Nov 2, Dec 2; <u>1764</u>: CG, Jan 18, Oct 20, Dec 11, DL, 13; <u>1765</u>: DL, May 13, CG, 23, Oct 10, Dec 17; <u>1766</u>: CG, Apr 5, DL, Dec 10, 12, CG, 16; <u>1767</u>: CG, Nov 27, Dec 3, 18; <u>1768</u>: CG, Jan 14, 19, Apr 12, May 6, Jun 1, Oct 15, DL, 25, 28, Nov 2, 8, Dec 9, CG, 29; <u>1769</u>: DL, Jan 6, CG, Feb 4, Mar 30, Apr 8, DL, 24, Nov 16, Dec 9; <u>1770</u>: DL, Jan 24, CG, Apr 20, DL, Dec 4, 12; <u>1771</u>: DL, Dec 31; <u>1772</u>: DL, Mar 23, CG, Apr 25, DL, May 9, Dec 15; <u>1773</u>: DL, May 27; <u>1774</u>: DL, Jan 13, 21, Feb 14; <u>1775</u>: DL, Jan 18, 20, 25, May 25, CG, Oct 20, Dec 30; <u>1776</u>: CG, May 14, DL, 16, Jun 10, Dec 18; <u>1777</u>: CHR, Jun 27, DL, Dec 11; <u>1778</u>: CG, Apr 25, CHR, May 25; <u>1779</u>: CG, Jan 26, Nov 23; <u>1780</u>: DL, Nov 10; <u>1781</u>: CG, Jan 25, DL, Feb 10, May 9, Nov 7, 17; <u>1782</u>: CG, Jan 11, DL, Apr 29; <u>1783</u>: DL, Jan 10, May 9, Nov 20, Dec 3, HAY, 15; <u>1784</u>: DL, Feb 11, Mar 30, May 27, Nov 2, 22, CG, Dec 3; <u>1785</u>: DL, Apr 22, HAMM, Jun 17, DL, Oct 31; <u>1786</u>: DL, Jun 6, Oct 26, Dec 4, CG, 30; <u>1787</u>: DL, Jan 3, Feb 16, Oct 24; <u>1788</u>: DL, Jan 2, 7, 25, Mar 27, Apr 9, CG, Dec 31; <u>1789</u>: DL, Jan 1, Feb 2; <u>1791</u>: DLKING'S, Nov 29; <u>1792</u>: DL, Oct 31; <u>1793</u>: CG, May 8, HAY, Oct 24, Nov 11; <u>1794</u>: DL, Jun 17, Sep 18; <u>1795</u>: DL, Jan 24; <u>1797</u>: DL, Jan 10, Mar 30, Nov 2, Dec 5; <u>1798</u>: DL, Jun 2, Oct 20; <u>1799</u>: DL, Jan 25, Oct 17; <u>1800</u>: HAY, Feb 3

Cento (entertainment), <u>1781</u>: HAY, Aug 7, 17

Cephalus and Procris (masque), <u>1730</u>: DL, Oct 28, 29, 30, 31, Nov 2, 3, 4, 5, 6, 7, 9, 10, 11, 13, 14, Dec 4, 5, 7, 8, 9, 10, 15, 16, 17, 18, 19, 21, 22, 26, 28, 29, 30, 31; <u>1731</u>: DL, Jan 2, 4, 5, 6, 8, 9, 11, 12, 13, 14, 15, 16, 18, 19, 26, 28, 29, Feb 1, 2, 3, 4, 5, 6, 15, 16, 18, 19, 20, Mar 6, 9, 11, 13, 16, 30, Apr 3, 6, 10, 24, May 1, 4, 18, Oct 16, 23, 29, 30, Nov 4, 13, 17, 20, 29, Dec 27, 29; <u>1732</u>: DL, May 12, Dec 22, 26, 27, 28, 29, 30; <u>1733</u>: DL, Jan 1, 2, 3, 4, 5, 6, 8, 9, 10, 13, 17, 20, Nov 13, 14, 15, 16, 19, 21, 23, 24, Dec 11, 26, 27, 28, 29, 31; <u>1734</u>: DL, Jan 8, 9, 25, 26, Apr 23, May 15, Nov 1, 2, 4, 5, 6, 12, 20; <u>1735</u>: DL, May 14; <u>1740</u>: BFLP, Aug 23, SF, Sep 9

Cerail (Corail), Mlle (actor, dancer, singer), <u>1717</u>: KING'S, Mar 16, 21, Apr 11, LIF, 23, Nov 22, Dec 6, 11; <u>1718</u>: LIF, Jan 1, 3, HIC, Mar 26

Ceremonie Turque, La (entertainment), <u>1722</u>: HAY, Mar 26

Ceremony of Reception (entertainment), <u>1735</u>: HAY, Jan 13

Ceremony used in Shooting a Deserter (entertainment), <u>1799</u>: DL, Apr 25, Sep 24

Cermona Staccato Concerto (music), <u>1751</u>: CT, Dec 3

Cervetto, Giacobbe (violoncellist, composer), <u>1742</u>: DL, Nov 22, 23, Dec 18, 22, 28, 30; <u>1743</u>: DL, Jan 1, 3, 4, 5, 6, 25, May 5; <u>1744</u>: DL, May 8; <u>1747</u>: KING'S, Apr 14; <u>1750</u>: DL, Apr 23; <u>1753</u>: DL, Oct 20; <u>1761</u>: KING'S, Mar 12; <u>1763</u>: DL, Apr 27; <u>1769</u>: HAY, Apr 18; <u>1774</u>: KING'S, Feb 10; <u>1775</u>: KING'S, Mar 10, 17, 24, Apr 7; <u>1776</u>: KING'S, Feb 15; <u>1777</u>: CG, Feb 14, Mar 19; <u>1778</u>: KING'S, Apr 4; <u>1779</u>: DL, Feb 26, Mar 26

Cervetto, James (violoncellist), <u>1789</u>: KING'S, Jun 11; <u>1790</u>: HAY, Apr 29

Chabot Admiral of France. See Shirley, James.

Chabran, Charles (violinist), <u>1753</u>: KING'S, Apr 30

Chachi, Tomo (American Indian visitor), <u>1734</u>: LIF, Aug 20, CG, Sep 2, LIF, 6, CG/LIF, 23, LIF, Oct 1, DL, 4, GF, 5, HAY, 7, GF, 11, LIF, 12, DL, 14, GF, 17, CG/LIF, 25; <u>1738</u>: DL, Jan 31, Feb 21; see also American Princes, Indian Kings, American

Chaconne (dance), <u>1703</u>: LIF, Jun 14; <u>1704</u>: DL, Feb 10, Jul 1, LIF, Oct 16; <u>1705</u>: LIF/QUEN, Sep 28; <u>1706</u>: QUEEN'S, Jan 2, 7, 9, 14, 22, 23, Jun 13; <u>1710</u>: DL, Apr 12; <u>1715</u>: LIF, May 24, Nov 10; <u>1717</u>: DL, Oct 30, LIF, Nov 1, 5; <u>1718</u>: LIF, May 20, Jun 4, Nov 6; <u>1724</u>: LIF, May 5, Jun 3; <u>1725</u>: LIF, Apr 7, 26, May 3, 7, 10, 12, 17, 18, 21, 22, 25; <u>1726</u>: LIF, Mar 31, Apr 30, May 9, 11, 14, 23, 30, Jun 17, 21, Jul 1, 15, Aug 2, 5, 19, 23, Sep 19; <u>1727</u>: DL, Apr 25, May 1, LIF, 9, Sep 15; <u>1728</u>: LIF, Dec 12; <u>1729</u>: LIF, Mar 10, Apr 26; <u>1730</u>: DL, Apr 16, May 4, LIF, 21, 25, 28, Jun 1; <u>1731</u>: DL, Mar 25, LIF, May 5, 6, DL, 7; <u>1732</u>: DL, Apr 22, GF, Nov 4, 6, 8, 11, 17, 18, 24, DL, 25, GF, 27, Dec 13, 18; <u>1733</u>: GF, Mar 1, Apr 13, May 10, 18, Sep 14, 28; <u>1734</u>: GF, Jan 10, 19, 28, Sep 11, GF/HAY, Dec 27; <u>1739</u>: DL, May 19; <u>1741</u>: CG, Feb 7, Dec 30; <u>1742</u>: CG, Jan 4, 7, 25, Feb 4, 12, 13, 15, 20, 23, 26, Mar 1, 6, 15, 25, 27, 30, Apr 19, 22, 26, 28, DL, 29, CG, May 7; <u>1744</u>: CG, Nov 2, 9; <u>1772</u>: KING'S, Feb 29, Apr 7, 25, May 23; <u>1773</u>: KING'S, Jan 12, 15, 26, Feb 9, 20, 23, 27, Mar 16, Apr 20; <u>1774</u>: KING'S, Feb 22, Mar 12, 17, 24, Apr 9, 14, 19, May 10, 17, 28; <u>1775</u>: KING'S, Jan 17, Feb 7, 14, 21, Apr 4, 6, 8, May 11, 25, Jun 6; <u>1776</u>: KING'S, Apr 20, 25, May 4, Nov 30, Dec 17; <u>1777</u>: KING'S, Jan 11, DL, Apr 5, 14, 22, 25, KING'S, May 1, 15, Nov 4; <u>1779</u>: DL, May 17, KING'S, Nov 27, Dec 14; <u>1780</u>: KING'S, Apr 1; <u>1781</u>: KING'S, Feb 22; <u>1782</u>: KING'S, Feb 7; <u>1783</u>: KING'S, May 1

Chaconne des Characters, La (dance), <u>1753</u>: DL, Mar 31, Apr 24

Chaconne of Characters (dance), 1726: HAY, May 9; 1735: GF/HAY, Apr 7, HAY, May 26

Chaconne, Grand (dance), 1726: LIF, Apr 21; 1730: DL, Oct 10; 1772: KING'S, Apr 4, Jun 3; 1773: KING'S, Jan 12, 15, 19, 26, Mar 9, 16, 18, Apr 1, 17, 24, 27, 29, May 1, 3, 25, Jun 3, 12, 19, Nov 20, 23, 30, Dec 7; 1774: KING'S, Feb 12, Apr 19, May 5, Nov 8, Dec 3, 17; 1775: KING'S, Feb 7, 28, Mar 23, Apr 18, 22, 25, May 6, 16, 27, 30, Jun 6, 17, 24; 1776: KING'S, Feb 3, Apr 18, DL, May 3, KING'S, 30; 1777: KING'S, Feb 25; 1780: KING'S, Jan 22, Feb 19, Mar 9, 18, Apr 8, 22, May 2, 9, 12, 20, 25, 27, Jun 24, Dec 16, 19; 1781: KING'S, Jan 16, Mar 15, Apr 5, May 15, Jun 23; 1786: KING'S, Jan 24

Chalk, Miss Denny. See Chock, Dennis.

Chalmer, James (actor), 1783: CG, Oct 8, Nov 10, Dec 23; 1784: CG, Jan 29, Feb 18, Mar 16, 22, 23, Apr 13, May 12, 13, 15, 25, Sep 17, 20, 28, 29, Oct 11; 1785: CG, Apr 2, 8

Chalmers (prologuist), 1783: CG, Apr 26

Chalmers, Eleanor, Mrs James (actor), 1783: CG, Sep 19, Oct 1, 2, 6, 11, 14, 27, Dec 23; 1784: CG, Mar 30, Apr 1, 3, 13, May 7, 8, 26, Sep 17, Oct 4, Nov 12

Chalmers, William (scene painter), 1798: DL, Jan 16, Oct 6; 1799: DL, Jan 19, Oct 14

Chamber Horn (music), 1728: HIC, Mar 15, 20, LIF, 27

Chamber Horn Concerto (music), 1729: LIF, Mar 19

Chamber Organ (music), 1729: BFF, Aug 23

Chamberlain and Co (ironmongers), 1771: DL, Dec 12; 1772: DL, Jun 10

Chamberlaine, 1662: LI, Jan 3

Chamberlayne, William
--Wits Led by the Nose; or, A Poet's Revenge, 1676: NONE, Sep 0; 1677: DL, Jun 0

Chambermaid, The. See Phillips, Edward.

Chambers (actor), 1758: DL, Sep 16

Chambers (actor), 1777: DL, Nov 29; 1778: DL, Jan 5, 24, Mar 30, Apr 20, 23, May 5, 8, 16, Sep 19, 24, Oct 1, 3, 20, Dec 19; 1779: DL, Feb 8, Mar 16, Apr 12

Chambers, A A (actor, singer), 1788: HAY, Apr 29, Dec 22; 1789: HAY, May 18, Jun 1, 12, 17, 23, Aug 10, 11, 28, Sep 11

Chambers, Elizabeth, Mrs William (actor, singer), 1751: CG, Sep 27, Nov 16, 25, Dec 14; 1752: CG, Jan 6, Apr 25, May 4, 6, Sep 18, 20, Oct 6, 21, 30, Nov 29; 1753: CG, Apr 5, 12, 28, May 2, 9, Sep 10, 12, 14, Oct 10, 30, Nov 16; 1754: CG, Mar 25, Apr 6, 22, May 8, 13, 14, 15, 20, Sep 16, 20, 23, Oct 4, 11, Nov 2, 16, 20; 1755: CG, Jan 10, Apr 4, 9, Oct 16, 17, 20, 21, Nov 12, 17, Dec 2; 1756: CG, Mar 27, Apr 5, 6, 20, May 7, 20, Sep 22, Oct 1, 4, $, 25, 26, Nov 17, Dec 3, 6, 10; 1757: CG, Feb 16, 21, Mar 21, Apr 23, 26, 27, May 2, 11, 12, 13, 16, Sep 14, 16, 28, 30, Oct 8, 13, Dec 7, 10; 1758: CG, Feb 1, Mar 13, 29, Apr 5, 24, 25

Chambers, Harriet (actor), 1786: HAMM, Jul 12, 19, 24, 26; 1793: CG, Dec 18; 1794: CG, Jan 1, 3, 4, 21, 22, Feb 24, Mar 6, Apr 12, 30

Chambers, Isabella (singer, actor), 1722: HIC, Mar 8; 1723: HAY, Mar 13, DL, Apr 1, LIF, Oct 10, Nov 2, 16, 22, Dec 20; 1724: LIF, Mar 3, 16, 19, 23, 26, 28, Apr 6, 13, 23, 25, 30, May 4, 12, 30, Sep 30, Oct 9, Nov 12; 1725: LIF, Jan 21, Mar 13, 18, Apr 2, 5, 15, 16, 17, 20, 30, Oct 4, Nov 3, 13, 22, 30, Dec 2, 8; 1726: LIF, Jan 14, Mar 21, 31, Apr 13, May 4, 6, Sep 16, 23, 26, 30, Oct 5, 24, Nov 19, 26; 1727: LIF, Feb 13, Apr 5, Jun 7, Sep 22, 29, Oct 12, 26, Nov 7, 9, 17; 1728: LIF, Mar 25, 27, Apr 4, Sep 30, Oct 9, 14, 26, Nov 23; 1729: LIF, Jan 18, Mar 5, 12, 19, Apr 15, Oct 3, 10, 15, 28, Nov 1, 4; 1730: LIF, Jan 2, Mar 16, Apr 8, 15, 22, May 14; 1732: LIF, Nov 20; 1733: LIF, Feb 16, Mar 7; 1734: DL, Apr 15, GF, Sep 16, 18, 20, 25, Oct 16, 28, Nov 7, 8, 18, Dec 16; 1735: GF, Jan 24, Mar 6, 17, 27, 29, Apr 9, 10, 16, 17, 23, 24, 28, 29, May 2, 3, Oct 13, 15, Nov 3, 6, 13, 14, 17, 19, 25, Dec 4, 17; 1736: GF, Jan 3, Feb 4, 6, 17, 20, Mar 3, 22, 25, 29, Apr 1, 6, 8, 13, 17, 27, 29, May 4, LIF, Sep 28, Oct 21, Nov 16, 24, Dec 7, 16; 1737: LIF, Jan 10, Feb 1, Mar 21, 31, Apr 2, 12, 14, 21, 27, 28, May 5; 1738: CG, Nov 18; 1739: CG, Jan 20, Apr 27, Sep 22, Oct 3, 25, 26, Nov 13, Dec 4, 10; 1740: CG, Feb 12, Sep 26, Oct 10, Dec 16; 1741: CG, Jan 5, 21, Feb 17, 24, 28, Apr 8, 24

Chamouveau, Jean (actor, director of French company), 1661: ATCOURT, Dec 2

Champein, Stanislas (composer), 1797: DL, Feb 9

Champelon (beneficiary), 1706: QUEEN'S, Apr 20; 1707: QUEEN'S, May 21; 1708: QUEEN'S, May 20; 1709: QUEEN'S, May 4

Champetre Comique (dance), 1775: KING'S, Apr 22, 25, May 6, 16, 27, Jun 6, 17, 24

Champion (actor), 1738: SFL, Sep 5

Champion, Mrs (dancer), 1704: LIF, Mar 30

Champness (Chamnys), Samuel Thomas (actor, singer), 1744: CG, Mar 2; 1748: DL,

Nov 29; 1749: DL, May 9; 1750: DL, May 2; 1754: CHAPEL, May 15, HAY, 29;
1755: DL, Feb 3, May 9, Oct 8, 10, Nov 8, 15; 1756: DL, Feb 11, Apr 1, 2, 10,
May 3, 6, Oct 9, 16, Nov 24, Dec 20; 1757: CG, Mar 11, DL, Apr 12, May 7, Sep
17, Oct 4; 1758: DL, Feb 21, CG, 22, Mar 1, 3, DL, 29, 31, SOHO, Apr 1,
CHAPEL, 27, DL, May 2, 3, Jun 22, Sep 28, Oct 30, Nov 3; 1759: DL, Jan 3, Apr
5, CG, May 4, DL, 7, Jun 19, HAM, Aug 13, DL, Sep 25, Oct 12, Nov 24, Dec 1,
31; 1760: SOHO, Jan 18, CG, Feb 29, DL, May 5, 16, 29, Oct 11, 20, Nov 17,
Dec 13; 1761: DL, Jan 23, KING'S, Mar 12, DL, 30, Apr 13, 14, 29, May 11, 18,
Sep 8, 10, Oct 26, 31; 1762: DL, Feb 3, 26, Mar 3, 5, 6, Apr 23, RANELAGH,
Jun 11, DL, Sep 28, 29, Oct 7, 9, Nov 23; 1763: DL, Jan 17, Apr 9, 23, 27,
May 2, 14, Oct 28, 31, Nov 29, Dec 26; 1764: DL, Feb 24, CHAPEL, 29, DL, Mar
31, Apr 30, Sep 22, 25, Nov 2, HAY, 13, DL, 27; 1765: DL, Jan 22, Feb 11,
KING'S, 15, DL, Apr 22, 29, Sep 17, 24, Oct 28; 1766: DL, Feb 7, Apr 15, 23,
CHAPEL, 30, DL, Sep 30, Nov 21; 1767: DL, Jan 2, KING'S, 23, DL, 24, CG, Mar
6, DL, 21, May 5, CHAPEL, 13, HAY, 29, RANELAGH, Jun 1, DL, Sep 21, 22, HAB,
Dec 10; 1768: DL, Jan 14, KING'S, Feb 5, DL, 10, Apr 22, 27, CHAPEL, May 25,
DL, Sep 22, 27; 1769: HAY, Apr 18, DL, 22, May 1, Sep 30, Oct 2, 4, 14; 1770:
DL, Jan 4, Apr 30, HAY, May 4, DL, Sep 27, Oct 3, 25, 29, Nov 3, 14, Dec 13;
1771: DL, Mar 7, HAY, Apr 12, DL, 27, May 25, Oct 10; 1772: DL, Mar 28, Apr
2, 25, May 6, Sep 29, Oct 1, 20, Nov 12, Dec 30; 1773: DL, Feb 25, Apr 28,
May 10, Oct 9, 25, Dec 3, 27; 1774: DL, Jan 26, Feb 7, HAY, 18, 23, 25, DL,
Mar 19, CHAPEL, 30, DL, May 13; 1776: CG, Feb 23, CHAPEL, Apr 3; 1777: DL,
Feb 14; 1779: HAY, Mar 3, CG, Apr 17; 1780: CG, Apr 18; 1783: CG, May 6;
1789: CG, Feb 27; 1790: CG, Feb 19, 24, Mar 3; 1792: CG, Feb 24, Mar 9
Champness, Weldon (singer), 1758: CHAPEL, Apr 27
Champville, Gabriel-Leonard Herve du Bus de (actor), 1749: HAY, Nov 14; 1750:
DL, May 22
Chancellor, Lady, 1661: ATCOURT, Apr 20
Chancery Lane, 1715: CL, Jun 13; 1723: AVT, Dec 31; 1732: CL, Mar 15, 17, Apr
5; 1734: LIF, May 16; 1752: CG, Dec 12; 1764: CG, Mar 14
Chances, The. See Fletcher, John.
Chandos Anthems, 1776: DL, Mar 13; 1789: CG, Mar 20, DL, 25, CG, 27; 1790: CG,
Feb 24, Mar 17; 1791: DL, Mar 11, CG, 23; 1792: CG, Mar 9, KING'S, 14, 28;
1793: CG, Feb 15, KING/HAY, 27, Mar 13, CG, 13; 1794: CG, Mar 7, DL, 12, 21,
CG, 26; 1795: CG, Feb 20, 27; 1796: CG, Feb 26; 1797: CG, Mar 10, 22, 24;
1798: CG, Mar 9, 28; 1799: CG, Feb 8, Mar 1
Chandos St, 1675: WF, Jan 26, BANNSTER, Nov 25; 1732: LIF, Apr 25; 1733:
LIF/CG, Apr 23; 1735: CG/LIF, Apr 17; 1737: CG, Mar 24; 1738: CG, Mar 23;
1739: CG, Mar 22; 1740: CG, Mar 25; 1741: CG, Apr 2; 1755: DL, Apr 12
Chandos, Duke of (author), 1697: DLDGLIF, Jan 22; 1732: YB, Apr 20; 1767: CG,
May 23; 1772: DL, Mar 18; 1773: HAY, Mar 3; see also Brydges, James
Change of Crowns, The. See Howard, Edward.
Changeling, The. See Middleton, Thomas.
Changes, The. See Shirley, James.
Chanson a Boire (song), 1722: LIF, Mar 12; 1726: LIF, Apr 11, 20, 25; 1731:
LIF, Apr 8, 28; 1733: GF, Apr 13, CG, May 4, LIF/CG, 14, CG, Oct 20, Dec 18;
1734: CG, Apr 16, 18, May 13, GF, 14; 1736: CG, Apr 12, 27, May 4, 11, 14,
Nov 22, 23; 1737: CG, Jan 4, Apr 22, Nov 8; 1738: CG, Jan 23, Mar 7, Apr 11,
May 15; 1739: CG, Mar 5, May 24; 1741: CG, Oct 27, Nov 2
Chantrell, Mrs. See Cantrell, Mrs.
Chanu (householder), 1778: KING'S, Apr 30
Chapel Royal, 1674: DG, May 16; 1684: MS, Nov 22; 1731: ACA, Jan 14; 1760:
SOHO, Jan 18; 1773: HAY, Mar 3; 1790: CG, Feb 19; 1795: CG, Feb 27
Chapel St, 1777: CG, Apr 10
Chapelle, H (householder), 1757: CG, Mar 17; 1758: DL, Mar 7
Chaplet, The. See Mendez, Moses.
Chaplin, Sir Francis (Lord Mayor), 1677: CITY, Oct 29
Chaplin, Henry (actor, singer), 1774: CG, Oct 22, Dec 9; 1775: CG, Feb 21, May
2, HAY, 15, 17, 19, CG, 20, HAY, 24, 29, Jul 7, 31, Aug 16, Sep 4, 16, 19,
21, Oct 30; 1776: HAY, Sep 20, DL, 28, Oct 18, 25, Nov 4, 16, 25, Dec 10, 14,
28; 1777: DL, Jan 1, 4, Feb 8, 17, Mar 1, Apr 11, 22, May 8, 9, Sep 20, Oct
7, 17, 31, Nov 4, 18, 29, Dec 3, 18; 1778: DL, Jan 1, 5, 17, 24, Mar 16, 30,
Apr 20, 23, 27, May 23, Sep 22, 24, 26, Oct 1, 8, 15, 26, 27, Nov 2, 11, 18,
Dec 21; 1779: DL, Jan 8, Mar 13, 16, 22, Apr 12, 19, May 18, 19, Sep 18, 21,
25, 30, Oct 2, 5, 7, 16, 30, Nov 3, 8, Dec 4, 13, 20, 27; 1780: DL, Jan 12,
24, 28, Apr 3, 18, 21, 26, May 2, 5, 9, 10, 12, Sep 16, 19, 23, 28, 30, Oct
3, 5, 11, 17, 19, 23, 30, Nov 3, 4, 13, 27, 29, Dec 1, 4, 6, 15, 27; 1781:
DL, Jan 9, Mar 19, May 1, 15, 23, Sep 18, 25, Oct 12, 19, Nov 5, 13, Dec 13;
1782: DL, Jan 5, 17, Mar 16, Apr 6, 11, 23, 25, May 3, 7, 10, 15, 18, Sep 20,
24, 28, Oct 1, 5, 12, 24, 30, Nov 4, 8, 12, Dec 11, 14, 26; 1783: DL, Jan 29,
Feb 8, 18, Mar 6, 10, Apr 29, May 5, 12, 21, Sep 23, 25, 30, Oct 11, 13, 14,
17, 20, Nov 3, 8, 14, 18, 20, Dec 2, 10; 1784: DL, Jan 3, 7, 13, 17, Mar 6,

Apr 1, 14, 24, 26, 28, May 3, 7, 21, Sep 21, 23, Oct 19, 23, 26, 27, Nov 2,
5, 9, 15, 19, 20, 22, 26; <u>1785</u>: DL, Jan 12, 13, 14, 18, 19, 20, Feb 21, Mar
8, Apr 1, 11, 25, May 3, 9, 13, 24, Sep 17, 20, 27, Oct 6, 8, 15, 17, 20, 22,
26, Nov 1, 7, 8, 17, 18, 21, 22, Dec 1, 26; <u>1786</u>: DL, Jan 5, 6, 14, 16, 19,
Feb 18, Mar 9, 13, 27, 28, May 17, Sep 19, 23, 28, Oct 3, 5, 7, 10, 23, 24,
Nov 25, Dec 5, 19, 26; <u>1787</u>: DL, Jan 13, 23, 29, Feb 7, Mar 12, Apr 10, 13,
14, May 7, 9, 16, Jun 8, Sep 18, 25, Oct 2, 6, 18, 20, 26, 27, Nov 3, 5, 6,
8, 16, 21, 29, Dec 10, 11, 14, 26; <u>1788</u>: DL, Jan 1, 7, 16, 21, 31, Feb 7, Mar
3, 10, 29, Apr 11, 17, 18, 19, May 5, Jun 2, Sep 13, 20, 30, Oct 2, 4, 7, 9,
20, Nov 1, 4, 6, 10, 28, Dec 1, 4, 17; <u>1789</u>: DL, Jan 21, 31, Feb 16, 20, 26,
Mar 17, 21, May 11, 19, 22, 28, Jun 5, 9, 13
Chapman (actor), <u>1674</u>: LIF, Mar 0, NONE, Sep 0
Chapman (actor), <u>1775</u>: HAY, Sep 20
Chapman (dancer), <u>1799</u>: CG, Apr 13
Chapman (housekeeper), <u>1772</u>: DL, Mar 2, Jun 10
Chapman (musician), <u>1757</u>: CG, May 16; <u>1758</u>: CG, Apr 22; <u>1759</u>: CG, Apr 28; <u>1760</u>:
CG, Apr 12; <u>1761</u>: CG, Apr 17; <u>1762</u>: CG, May 8
Chapman (swordcutler), <u>1749</u>: CG, Apr 28
Chapman, Charlotte Jane (actor), <u>1788</u>: CG, Oct 22, Dec 19, 30; <u>1789</u>: CG, Feb
17, 21, Mar 5, Sep 30, Oct 30, Nov 2, 6, 19, 20, Dec 11, 14; <u>1790</u>: CG, Jan
13, Feb 11, Apr 7, May 26, 31, Sep 15, 17, Oct 15, 23, Nov 4, 6, Dec 10, 11;
<u>1791</u>: CG, Jan 3, 26, Feb 2, Mar 14, Apr 16, 28, 30, May 6, 10, 28, 31, Jun 1,
Sep 14, 20, Oct 7, 12, 13, 29, Nov 24, 26, 29; <u>1792</u>: CG, Jan 14, 17, Feb 2,
6, 7, 8, 23, Mar 6, 26, 31, Apr 12, 17, 18, 21, May 5, 15, 18, Sep 17, 19,
26, 28, Oct 3, 10, 24, 26, 27, 31, Nov 3, 6, 10, 14, Dec 5, 21; <u>1793</u>: CG, Feb
21, Apr 8, 11, 15, 18, 22, 23, May 8, 21, 23, 24, Jun 11, Sep 16, 18, 20, 25,
Oct 2, 5, 8, 14, 16, 17, 18, 19, 23, 29, Nov 1, 2, 9, Dec 6; <u>1794</u>: CG, Feb
18, 22, 24, Mar 6, 18, Apr 12, 23, 25, May 6, 13, 14, 16, 20, 21, 23, Sep 15,
26, Oct 3, 8, 15, 21, Nov 8, 12, 19, 21, Dec 6, 10, 31; <u>1795</u>: CG, Jan 23, 24,
29, Feb 3, 4, 6, 14, Mar 28, May 8, 13, 21, 25, 29, Jun 10, Sep 23, 25, 30,
Oct 2, 5, 16, 24, Nov 6, 27, Dec 4, 9, 28, 31; <u>1796</u>: CG, Jan 2, 5, 9, Mar 19,
29, Apr 13, 20, 22, 29, May 6, 21, Jun 2, Sep 14, 17, 23, 28, Oct 17, 20, 21,
Nov 5, 7, 19, Dec 8, 17, 19, 21; <u>1797</u>: CG, Jan 7, 10, Mar 4, 16, Apr 8, 29,
May 4, 6, 17, 31, Jun 2, 10, 13, 14, Sep 18, 20, 22, 25, 27, Oct 2, 11, 31,
Nov 4, 18, 23, Dec 8; <u>1798</u>: CG, Feb 6, Mar 20, 31, Apr 10, 13, 17, 28, May
12, 16, 22, Sep 17, 26, 28, Oct 1, 5, Nov 10, 21, 23; <u>1799</u>: CG, Jan 12, 23,
Apr 6, 10, 12, 16, 19, May 6, 15, 24, 28, 31, Jun 5, 7, HAY, 15, 19, 20, 27,
Jul 9, 23, Aug 13, CG, Sep 16, 20, 23, 25, Oct 16, 17, 18, 24, Nov 8, 14, Dec
10, 30; <u>1800</u>: CG, Jan 18, 29, Apr 5, May 12, 15, 27, 28, Jun 12, HAY, 13, 19,
Jul 15, Aug 2, 7, 12, 23, 27
Chapman, Frances R, Mrs George (actor, singer), <u>1798</u>: CG, Nov 1, 12, Dec 15,
26; <u>1799</u>: CG, Jan 29, Mar 2, 5, 9, 25, 27, Apr 2, 9, 13, 19, 23, May 4, 7,
13, 14, 15, 24, 28, Jun 7, Sep 20, 27, 30, Oct 7, 18, 24, 31, Nov 11, Dec 2,
10; <u>1800</u>: CG, Mar 4, 27, Apr 22, 26, 30, May 7, 17, 22, 27
Chapman, George, <u>1668</u>: LIF, Aug 20; <u>1751</u>: DL, Oct 22; <u>1776</u>: DL, Dec 28
--All Fools, <u>1668</u>: LIF, Aug 20
--Biron's Conspiracy, <u>1668</u>: LIF, Aug 20
--Bussy D'Ambois, <u>1660</u>: REDBULL, Aug 14; <u>1661</u>: VERE, Dec 30; <u>1669</u>: BRIDGES, Jan
12; <u>1674</u>: NONE, Sep 0
--Eastward Ho; or, The Prentices (with Ben Jonson and John Marston), <u>1751</u>: DL,
Oct 22, 29; <u>1763</u>: DL, Feb 1; <u>1775</u>: DL, Nov 9; <u>1776</u>: DL, Dec 28
--Revenge of Bussy D'Ambois, <u>1668</u>: LIF, Aug 20
--Widow's Tears, The, <u>1669</u>: BRIDGES, Jan 12
Chapman, Hannah, Mrs Thomas (actor), <u>1729</u>: BFB, Aug 25; <u>1730</u>: RI, Jul 16, LIF,
Nov 30; <u>1731</u>: RI, Jul 15, 22, BFB, Aug 26, LIF, Oct 4; <u>1732</u>: RI, Aug 17, BFB,
23, LIF/CG, Oct 4, 6, Nov 8, 14; <u>1733</u>: BFMMO, Aug 23, CG, Sep 27
Chapman, Henry (coachmaker), <u>1735</u>: CG/LIF, May 7
Chapman, Sir John (Lord Mayor), <u>1688</u>: CITY, Oct 28
Chapman, Mrs (householder), <u>1795</u>: CG, Jun 16
Chapman, Thomas (actor), <u>1723</u>: LIF, May 14, DL, Aug 16, SF, Sep 5, SOU, 25;
<u>1724</u>: LIF, May 15, RI, Jun 27, 29, Jul 4, 18, LIF, 21, SF, Sep 2; <u>1725</u>: LIF,
May 6, 21; <u>1726</u>: LIF, May 10, Jul 5, 22, Aug 2, 12, 19, Nov 2; <u>1727</u>: LIF, Sep
20, Oct 17, 19, 25, 31, Nov 16, Dec 8, 15, 16; <u>1728</u>: LIF, Jan 8, 17, 29, Mar
9, 21, 28, Apr 4, 6, 23, 24, 26, 29, May 6, 15, 16, 18, 22, 30, Sep 16, 18,
Oct 1, 7, 21, 23, Nov 1, 11, Dec 7, 28, 31; <u>1729</u>: LIF, Jan 13, 31, Feb 7, 10,
22, Mar 3, 4, 10, 27, Apr 15, 17, 23, 24, 26, May 3, 7, 13, BFB, Aug 25, LIF,
Sep 12, 17, 19, 22, 24, 26, Oct 3, 6, 8, 13, 20, 30, 31, Nov 7, 8, 14, 25;
<u>1730</u>: LIF, Jan 19, 26, Apr 2, 20, 29, 30, May 6, 7, 11, 13, 15, 20, 23, Jun
1, RI, 24, 27, Jul 16, BFLH, Aug 31, SFG, Sep 8, LIF, 16, 18, 21, 23, SOU,
24, LIF, Oct 5, 14, 19, 23, 26, 30, 31, Nov 2, 3, 6, 13, 23, Dec 3, 4, 30;
<u>1731</u>: LIF, Jan 4, 8, 9, 13, Feb 3, 27, Mar 15, 22, Apr 1, 3, 24, 26, May 1,
5, 10, 17, 25, Jun 2, RI, Jul 1, 8, 15, 22, BFB, Aug 26, LIF, Sep 17, 20, 22,

27, 29, Oct 1, 6, 11, 13, 25, 27, 30, Nov 2, 4, 8, 17, 25, Dec 3, 6, 8, 9,
11; 1732: LIF, Jan 10, 18, 19, 28, Feb 14, 15, 21, 28, Mar 2, 23, 25, 30, Apr
10, 17, 24, 26, 27, 29, May 1, 9, 22, RI, Aug 17, BFB, 23, CG/LIF, Sep 22,
LIF/CG, 25, 27, 29, Oct 2, 4, 6, 9, 11, 16, LIF, 18, LIF/CG, 23, 25, 27, 28,
30, Nov 1, 3, 4, 7, 9, 13, 14, 17, 18, 22, Dec 4, 7, CG/LIF, 16, LIF/CG, 26,
CG/LIF, 27; 1733: LIF/CG, Jan 1, 11, 15, 27, Feb 5, CG, 8, LIF/CG, 10, Mar
26, CG, 27, LIF/CG, 30, Apr 2, 3, CG, 4, LIF/CG, 10, 11, 12, 13, 17, 27, CG,
May 1, 2, LIF/CG, 7, 10, CG/LIF, 28, LIF/CG, Jun 1, RI, Aug 20, BFMMO, 23,
RI, Sep 10, CG, Oct 2, 4, 6, 9, 11, 16, 18, 19, 20, 25, 27, Nov 1, 3, 5, 8,
9, 10, 14, 16, 17, 19, 20, 21, 22, 26, 28, 30, Dec 1, 3, 4, 8, 15, 17, 20,
31; 1734: CG, Jan 5, 9, 16, 18, 23, Feb 14, Mar 5, 18, 28, Apr 6, 16, 30, May
7, 17, RI, Jun 27, BFRLCH, Aug 24, Sep 2, CG, 2, RI, 9, CG/LIF, 18, 20, 23,
25, RI, 26, CG/LIF, Oct 7, 9, LIF, 12, CG/LIF, 14, 16, 18, 19, 25, Nov 1, 7,
11, 21, 28, Dec 5, 26; 1735: CG/LIF, Jan 6, 17, 21, 23, 31, Feb 3, 4, 10, 11,
LIF, 12, CG/LIF, 13, 22, LIF, Mar 3, CG/LIF, 11, 29, Apr 9, 10, 11, 18, LIF,
19, CG/LIF, 21, CG, 25, CG/LIF, May 1, 2, 5, CG, 6, CG/LIF, 14, 15, 20, 26,
Jun 11, CG, Sep 12, 16, 17, 26, 29, Oct 3, 8, 10, 13, 15, 17, 20, 22, 24, 31,
Nov 6, 7, 8, 10, 12, 22, 29, Dec 8, 15, 31; 1736: CG, Feb 10, 26, Mar 15, 18,
20, 22, 27, 29, LIF, Apr 2, CG, 6, 8, HAY, 29, CG, 29, May 3, LIF, 5, CG, 13,
17, 20, BFHC, Aug 23, CG, Sep 29, Oct 1, 4, 6, 8, 11, 13, LIF, 18, CG, 22,
23, 25, Nov 1, 8, 11, 22, 25, 29, Dec 2, 6, 9, 20, 29; 1737: CG, Jan 10, 17,
DL, 19, CG, 21, 25, 28, Feb 3, 15, 26, Mar 10, 14, 17, 24, 28, Apr 11, 26,
May 16, 31, Sep 16, 19, 21, 23, 26, 30, Oct 3, 5, 10, 12, 17, 21, 24, 26, 28,
Nov 1, 2, 14, 18; 1738: CG, Jan 6, 9, 17, 18, 25, 31, Feb 6, 13, 16, 23, Mar
13, 18, 20, 25, Apr 7, 10, 22, May 18, Oct 2, 4, 9, 11, 13, 14, 20, 24, 26,
Nov 2, 7, 8, 11, 13, 15, 17, 20, 23, 24, 27, 28, 29, 30, Dec 2, 4, 5, 12, 15;
1739: CG, Jan 15, 23, 24, Feb 9, 10, 16, 20, 24, 26, Mar 13, 27, Apr 12, 25,
May 1, 2, 7, 25, Aug 2, BFHCL, 23, DL, Oct 3, 6, 11, 18, 19, 23, 26, 29, Nov
10, 19, Dec 8, 10, 20, 22; 1740: DL, Jan 16, Feb 4, Mar 17, 18, 20, Apr 16,
21, 25, May 6, 26, 29, BFHC, Aug 23, DL, Sep 9, 16, 18, 23, 25, Oct 4, 10,
11, 13, 23, 29, Nov 1, 6, 10, 19, 29, Dec 6, 15, 18, 19, 20; 1741: DL, Jan 6,
15, Feb 2, 14, 24, Apr 3, 8, 24, May 14, 25, BFH, Aug 22, CG, Sep 21, 25, 28,
30, Oct 2, 5, 8, 10, 13, 15, 21, 24, 26, 29, 31, Nov 7, 9, 11, Dec 11, 12,
21, 23, 30; 1742: CG, Jan 2, 8, 11, 19, 21, 23, 27, Feb 1, 3, 10, 27, Mar 20,
27, 29, Apr 22, 24, 28, May 1, 4, 5, 7, BFHC, Aug 25, CG, Sep 29, Oct 1, 4,
6, 13, 16, 25, 26, 27, 28, 29, Nov 3, 8, 15, 20, 22, 25, 30, Dec 21, 22;
1743: CG, Jan 18, Feb 9, Mar 15, 17, Apr 2, 4, 26, May 5, BFHC, Aug 23, CG,
Sep 21, 23, 26, 28, Oct 5, 7, 10, 14, 19, 21, 24, 26, 29, 31, Nov 2, 16, 17,
18, 21, 25, 30, Dec 8, 12, 16, 19, 31; 1744: CG, Jan 4, 5, 11, 14, 24, Feb
28, Mar 12, 13, 27, Apr 16, 19, May 14, Oct 3, 8, 10, 15, 20, 22, 24, 26, 27,
29, 31, Nov 1, 2, 7, 9, 22, 27, 28, 29, 30, Dec 5, 6, 10, 11, 17, 21; 1745:
CG, Jan 1, 2, 7, Feb 5, Apr 15, 20, 23, 25, 26, May 10, 13, 21, DL, Jun 5,
CG, Oct 2, 9, 11, 14, 16, 18, 29, Nov 7, 8, 9, 11, 13, 14, 18, 19, 22, 28,
30, Dec 12; 1746: CG, Jan 2, 11, 13, 18, 23, 25, Feb 3, 5, Mar 10, Apr 1, 2,
4, 7, 8, 15, 18, 22, 28, May 6, Jun 9, 11, 13, 16, 20, 23, 27, Oct 1, 3, 6,
8, 10, 13, 20, 27, 29, Nov 1, 3, 8, 11, 17, 18, 24, 26, Dec 2, 6, 10, 17, 19,
26, 27, 29; 1747: CG, Jan 17, 26, 29, 31, Feb 2, 3, 6, 11, Mar 17, DL, 19,
CG, 19, 21, Apr 7, 9, 20, May 20

Chapman, William (actor, singer), 1782: DL, Oct 3, 7, 26, Nov 5, Dec 26; 1783:
DL, Feb 7, Apr 26, May 2, 12, Sep 18, 25, Oct 4, 13, Nov 18, Dec 2, 5; 1784:
DL, Jan 3, 9, 13, Mar 30, Apr 12, May 12, 21, Sep 23, Nov 13; 1785: DL, Jan
6, 12, 20, Feb 2, Mar 28, Apr 11, 18, 20, 22, May 5, Sep 27, Oct 1, 13, Nov
18, Dec 19, 20, 26; 1786: DL, Apr 4, May 9; 1787: HAY, May 16, 23, 25, Jun
16, 18, 26, Jul 21, 27, Aug 3, Oct 14, 17, 21, Sep 3; 1788: HAY, Jun 10, 11,
12, 23, 26, 30, Jul 3, Aug 5, 11, 15, 22, 26, Sep 2, 3; 1789: HAY, May 18,
20, 25, 27, Jun 1, 3, 8, 10, 12, 17, 23, 25, 30, Jul 29, 30, 31, Aug 5, 10,
11, Sep 8, DL, 24; 1790: HAY, Jun 15, 16, 17, 19, 22, 25, 26, 28, 30, Jul 16,
19, Aug 6, 11, 12, 13, Sep 4, DL, Oct 4, 7, 11, HAY, 13, DL, 26, Nov 19, Dec
15, 27; 1791: DL, Jan 10, Feb 7, May 25, HAY, Jun 6, 8, 10, 17, 18, 20, 23,
25, 29, Jul 7, 8, 9, 30, Aug 16, 19, 24, 26, 31, DLKING'S, Sep 27, Oct 15,
25, 31, Nov 28
Chapotan
--Mariage d'Orphee et d'Eurydice, Le, 1661: COCKPIT, Aug 30
Chappuzeau, Jean (spectator), 1668: ATCOURT, Jan 13, LIF, Feb 11
Chapter Coffee House, 1744: DL, Apr 2; 1788: HAY, Sep 30
Chapter House, 1758: DL, Feb 3
Chapter of Accidents, The. See Lee, Sophia.
Chapter of Fashions (song), 1800: CG, Apr 22, Jun 2
Character of an excellent Actor, The (essay), 1743: DL, May 2
Character of Signora Cattina Venetia (entertainment), 1727: KING'S, Mar 16
Charadab-sina (Chinese mandarin), 1735: LIF, Jun 19
Charbonniers (dance), 1752: CG, Oct 28, Nov 11, 14, 30, Dec 6; 1753: CG, Jan 5,

8, 31, Feb 9, 16, Mar 6, 10, 13, Apr 3, 26, 28, May 3, 8; 1754: CG, Mar 7,
18, 28, Apr 2, 4, 20, 23; 1755: CG, May 6; 1760: CG, Dec 15, 16, 18, 20, 22;
1761: CG, Jan 6, 14, Feb 19, Mar 25, Apr 2, 6, 13, 20, May 6, 12, 18, Oct 12,
Nov 10; 1762: CG, Feb 10, 27, Mar 11, Apr 21, May 20
Chardin (actor), 1729: HAY, Feb 25, May 26, 29
Charing Cross, 1662: CC, Nov 10; 1667: CC, Mar 20, Oct 24; 1672: CC, Nov 11;
1687: CITY, Oct 29; 1693: BF, Aug 31; 1727: SG, Mar 8; 1738: GT, May 1; 1746:
DT, Mar 14; 1750: DL, Feb 21, Oct 1, Nov 28; 1751: DL, Mar 7, CG, Nov 19;
1752: DL, Dec 19; 1754: DL, Oct 25; 1756: DL, Jan 22, CG, Dec 8; 1757:
KING'S, Sep 20; 1758: CG, Jul 6; 1759: KING'S, May 8; 1762: KING'S, Jun 5;
1763: HAY, Sep 5; 1765: KING'S, Nov 23; 1768: KING'S, Nov 3; 1777: HAY, Feb
11; 1778: KING'S, Mar 19, 26, HAY, 31; 1779: KING'S, Apr 29; 1780: HAY, Aug
30; 1783: KING'S, May 20, HAY, Aug 27; 1784: HAY, Aug 26; 1785: DL, Mar 28;
1786: KING'S, Mar 23, DL, Apr 4; 1787: KING'S, Mar 29, CG, Apr 28; 1788:
KING'S, Feb 28, Mar 13, Apr 3, HAY, Aug 13; 1789: CG, Apr 21, KING'S, May 14,
HAY, Aug 25, 31; 1790: HAY, Sep 6; 1791: CG, Apr 28, HAY, Sep 5; 1792:
DLKING'S, Apr 19, HAY, Aug 22, Sep 10; 1793: DL, May 7; 1794: HAY, Aug 27;
1795: DL, May 19, HAY, Aug 18; 1796: DL, May 21, HAY, Sep 9; 1797: DL, May
27, HAY, Aug 3, Sep 11; 1798: HAY, Aug 18, Sep 10; 1799: HAY, Apr 17, Aug 10,
24, Sep 9; 1800: DL, Jun 2, HAY, Aug 2, Sep 8
Charitable Hospital, 1753: KING'S, May 12
Charity Boy, The. See Cross, John Cartwright.
Charke, Catharine Maria (actor), 1742: JS, Nov 22; 1744: MFHNT, May 1, MF, 3,
Jun 7, 27, HAY, Sep 29, Oct 11, Dec 17
Charke, Charlotte, Mrs Richard (actor, author), 1730: DL, Apr 8, 28; 1731: DL,
Jan 11, Feb 15, Apr 24, Jun 11, 22, Aug 18, Sep 23, Oct 16, Nov 1, Dec 17;
1732: DL, Feb 14, Apr 25, May 2, 12, Jun 9, Aug 1, 4, 15, 17, 21, BFMMO, 23,
DL, Oct 21, 26, Nov 21, 24, Dec 11, 18; 1733: DL, Jan 17, 26, 29, Mar 12, 28,
Apr 13, May 1, 7, BFCGBH, Aug 23, DL/HAY, Oct 5, 6, 15, 22, Nov 1, 9, 23, 28,
Dec 10, 17, 19, 20, 22, HAY, 26; 1734: DL/HAY, Jan 12, 17, Feb 22, Mar 30,
DL, Apr 15, 22, 23, DL/HAY, May 2, 3, DL, 13, 15, HAY, 21, LIF, 23, HAY, Jun
3, 5, 7, 12, 17, 19, 28, Jul 5, 10, 19, 26, 31, Aug 7, 14, 16, LIF, 20, HAY,
22, DL, Sep 19, Oct 3, 5, 17, Nov 2, 20; 1735: DL, Jan 22, Feb 18, Apr 14,
21, 23, LIF, Jun 19, DL, Jul 1, LIF, 11, 16, 23, 30, Aug 1, 6, 22, 25, 29,
Sep 2, 5, YB/HAY, 17, 24, YB, 26, YB/HAY, Oct 1, DL, Nov 18, 19, 20, Dec 26;
1736: HAY, Mar 5, 18, 19, Apr 5, 26, 29, May 3, 5, 27, Jun 26, Aug 2, BFFH,
23, SF, Sep 7, LIF, Oct 9, 23, 26, Nov 6, 9, 16, Dec 16, 20, 31; 1737: LIF,
Jan 10, Feb 12, 14, HAY, Mar 14, 21, Apr 13, May 3; 1740: BFFPT, Aug 23;
1742: BF, Aug 26, JS, Nov 22; 1743: JS, Mar 16; 1744: JS, Mar 28, MFHNT, May
1, MF, 3, Jun 6, 7, 8, 11, 27, HAY, Oct 4, Dec 26; 1745: HAY, Mar 4, GF, Nov
4, 5, 6, 8, 22, 23; 1755: HAY, Sep 4, 11, 15; 1756: BFGR, Sep 3; 1759: HAY,
Sep 28; 1760: DL, Apr 16
--Art of Management, The; or, Tragedy Expelled, 1735: YB/HAY, Sep 24, YB, 26,
YB/HAY, 29, Oct 1
--Carnival, The; or, Harlequin Blunderer, 1735: LIF, Sep 5, YB/HAY, 17
--Tit for Tat; or, The Comedy and Tragedy of War (puppet show), 1743: JS, Mar
16
Charke, Charlotte, Stake and Soup House, 1744: JS, Mar 28
Charke, Fisher Tench (dancer), 1729: LIF, Jan 1, BFF, Aug 23; see also Tench,
Fisher
Charke, Richard (musician), 1729: HAY, Jun 17, Jul 5, DL, 18, Aug 5, BFF, 23,
DL, Oct 2, 27, Dec 8, 10, 26; 1730: DL, Mar 30, Apr 24, 28, May 11, BFOF, Aug
20, DL, Oct 1; 1731: DL, Feb 8, Apr 1, 24, 26, May 19, Jun 7, 11, 25, Jul 20,
23, Aug 6, 11, Sep 25, 30, Oct 16, Nov 25; 1732: DL, Mar 21, Apr 25, May 8,
Sep 28, Nov 7, Dec 26; 1733: DL, Apr 4, May 7, DL/HAY, Oct 29, Nov 17; 1734:
DL/HAY, Mar 5, 30, HIC, Apr 5, DL/HAY, May 3, DL, 13, Sep 21; 1735: DL, Mar
24, Apr 29, May 17, Jun 5, LIF, Sep 5, DL, Nov 15; 1736: HAY, Jan 14, DL, Feb
9, 10, 11, 14, Apr 10, HIC, 19, DL, May 7, LIF, Jun 16, DL, Oct 28; 1737: DL,
Oct 27; 1744: HAY, Oct 20
Charles (actor), 1744: HAY, Sep 22, 25, 29, Oct 4, 18; 1755: HAY, Sep 1, 3, 9
Charles (dancer), 1740: GF, Dec 15; 1741: GF, Mar 3
Charles (Merry Trumpeter) (hornplayer, dancer, actor), 1729: SOU, Oct 14; 1730:
SOU, Oct 8; 1731: SOU, Sep 28; 1732: SOU, Oct 12; 1733: SOU, Oct 18
Charles (musician), 1733: DL/HAY, Oct 6, 20; 1734: DL, Apr 29, GF, Sep 9, 11,
13; 1735: HAY, Mar 26, ST, Apr 1, GF, May 15, Oct 10, ST, Nov 26; 1736: MR,
Feb 11; 1737: SH, Mar 11; 1738: DL, Mar 3; 1740: DL, May 21; 1744: HAY, Feb
20
Charles I, 1660: NONE, Aug 8; 1719: DL, Oct 29; 1745: MF, May 2; 1748: CG, Mar
5; 1792: DLKING'S, Jan 30; 1799: DL, Oct 7; see also Highness; King, the;
Majesty
Charles II, 1660: NONE, May 29, DC, Jun 0, CITY, Jul 5, ATCOURT, Aug 0, NONE,
8, VERE, Nov 9; 1661: ATCOURT, Apr 20; 1662: LI, Jan 3; 1663: ATCOURT, Feb 9,

Dec 10; 1664: ATCOURT, Jul 14, LIF, Aug 13; 1666: NONE, Nov 29; 1668:
ATCOURT, Dec 14; 1669: BRIDGES, Jun 24; 1677: DG, May 31; 1681: DG, Jan 0,
DL, Mar 0, NONE, Sep 0; 1682: DG, Jan 11, DL, 13, 14, DG, 19, DLORDG, Oct 24;
1683: NONE, Apr 0; 1684: DLORDG, Sep 29; 1685: NONE, Feb 6, DL, May 9, DG,
Jul 0; 1689: DLORDG, Nov 28; 1698: DL, Jul 9; 1701: DL, Aug 23; 1704: DL, Aug
2; 1705: QUEEN'S, Jun 8; 1708: DL, Jul 10; 1714: LIF, Dec 18; 1717: DL, Sep
28; 1720: LIF, Jan 11; 1723: HAY, Jan 28; 1739: DL, Mar 26; 1746: DL, May 2;
see also Highness; King, the; Majesty
Charles St, 1691: BG, Feb 26, Apr 2, 23, Sep 17, Oct 29, Nov 12; 1692: VENDU,
Mar 10; 1693: BG, Feb 3, Mar 23, Nov 30; 1694: BG, Jun 14, Oct 18, SMITH'S,
Nov 17, BG, 29; 1695: BG, Jun 10; 1734: YB, Dec 12; 1752: DL, Apr 8; 1755:
DL, Mar 15; 1757: CG, Mar 29; 1758: DL, Mar 3; 1759: DL, Mar 23; 1765: DL,
Apr 26; 1769: KING'S, Feb 24; 1784: DL, Apr 15, 16; 1785: DL, Apr 12; 1786:
DL, Apr 6, May 11; 1787: DL, Mar 29; 1788: DL, Apr 28; 1789: HAY, Jul 31;
1790: HAY, Apr 29; 1793: CG, May 24; 1794: CG, Apr 25; 1797: CG, May 31;
1800: DL, May 22
Charles, Master (actor), 1780: HAY, Nov 13
Charles, Master (dancer), 1748: KING'S, Nov 8; see also Poitier, Charles
Charlett, Arthur, 1700: LIF, Jan 28
Charlotte Augusta, Princess, 1797: DL, May 13; see also Princesses
Charlotte St, 1767: CG, Mar 30; 1777: DL, Apr 1, CG, 18, 23; 1778: DL, Apr 20,
CG, 21, 29; 1779: DL, Apr 12, CG, 17; 1780: DL, Apr 1, CG, 18; 1782: CG, Apr
17, 19; 1784: CG, Apr 14, 23, 24; 1786: DL, Apr 22; 1787: DL, Apr 17; 1788:
DL, Apr 29; 1790: DL, Apr 9; 1791: DL, May 7; 1792: DLKING'S, Apr 11, HAY,
Oct 15; 1793: DL, Apr 9; 1794: CG, May 2; 1795: CG, Apr 28, DL, 29; 1796: CG,
Apr 12, DL, May 6, 27; 1797: CG, May 2; 1798: CG, Apr 21; 1799: CG, Apr 6
Charlottenburg Festegiante. See Prussia, King of.
Charlton (actor), 1675: DL, May 10, Aug 0; 1676: DL, Dec 11; see also Carlton,
Peter
Charlton (boxkeeper), 1730: GF, Jun 18; 1731: GF, May 11
Charlton (violinist), 1798: HAY, Jan 15
Charmante Petite Fille (song), 1792: CG, Apr 25
Charming Clorinda (song), 1787: CG, Oct 18
Charming Warblers (song), 1729: HAY, May 12
Charms of a Camp (dance), 1784: CG, May 21, 25, 26, Oct 8, 13, 20, Nov 10;
1791: DL, May 25
Charms of my Peggy (song), 1791: CG, May 18
Charms of Polly Willis (song), 1745: CG, Mar 18, Apr 15
Charon, Mlle (dancer), 1755: DL, Nov 8, 15
Charpentier (Carpentier) (dancer), 1754: HAY, Aug 8
Charpentier (dance), 1754: HAY, Aug 6
Charpentier, Mrs (dancer), 1735: GF/HAY, May 12
Charter House, 1751: CHA, May 24
Charterhouse Scholars, 1723: CH, Aug 15
Chasse d'Amour (dance), 1798: KING'S, Jan 2, 16, Feb 10
Chasse de Diane (dance), 1740: DL, Dec 29; 1779: CG, May 21
Chasse, La (music), 1799: CG, Apr 19
Chasseur Royal (dance), 1732: DL, Feb 22, Mar 14, 16, 18, 30, Apr 1; 1735: DL,
Sep 18, Oct 27, 29, Nov 4, 5, 10, 15, Dec 1, 2, 6, 10, 16
Chasseurs (dance), 1743: DL, Feb 26, 28; 1765: HAY, Jul 8, 19, Aug 28; 1776:
KING'S, Nov 12, 16, 30; 1777: KING'S, Mar 15, Apr 12, 19, 26
Chasseurs Allemands (dance), 1752: CG, Dec 7, 8; 1753: CG, Jan 11, Apr 9, 25,
May 10, 17, 18
Chasseurs et Bergeres (dance), 1761: HAY, Jun 23, Jul 30, Aug 3, 6, 22
Chast Lucretia (song), 1736: HAY, Jan 14
Chaste Diana (song), 1757: HAY, Oct 21
Chastity thou cherub bright (song), 1790: CG, Mar 17
Chateauneuf (dancer), 1749: HAY, Nov 14; 1750: DL, May 22
Chateauneuf, Maria (actor, dancer), 1734: HAY, Oct 30, Nov 7, GF/HAY, 20, Dec
6, 26, 27, 28, 30; 1735: GF/HAY, Jan 2, Feb 5, HAY, 17; 1738: HAY, Oct 9;
1739: DL, Sep 13, 18, 20, 22, 25, 29, Oct 2, 3, 4, 6, 8, 11, 12, 13, 15, 18,
19, 23, 24, 26, 31, Nov 1, 7, 8, 9, 10, 14, 16, 19, 22, 23, 26, 28, Dec 8,
10, 12, 14, 15, 18, 19, 21, 22; 1740: DL, Jan 1, 3, 5, 7, 8, 11, 12, 14, 15,
29, 31, Feb 2, 4, 7, 9, 11, 12, 14, 15, 16, 18, 19, Mar 4, 6, 8, 10, 11, 13,
17, 18, 20, 22, 24, 27, Apr 7, 8, 9, 10, 14, 15, 16, 17, 18, 19, 21, 22, 24,
25, 26, 28, 29, 30, May 1, 2, 5, 6, 7, 8, 9, 12, 13, 14, 15, 16, 17, 19, 20,
21, 22, 23, 26, 29, Sep 6, 23, 25, 30, Oct 2, 4, 7, 9, 10, 13, 14, 18, 21,
22, 23, 24, 25, 27, 31, Nov 1, 7, 8, 10, 11, 12, 17, 27, 29, Dec 1, 2, 4, 10,
13, 19, 22, 29, 30; 1741: DL, Jan 2, 6, 8, 9, 12, 13, 21, 23, 24, 26, 28, Feb
3, 12, 14, 19, 24, Mar 2, 3, 5, 7, 9, 10, 12, 14, 17, 19, 21, 30, 31, Apr 1,
2, 4, 6, 7, 13, 14, 16, 17, 18, 20, 21, 22, 24, 27, 29, 30, May 1, 2, 4, 5,
6, 7, 9, 15, 20, 21, 22, 23, 26

Chatillion (dancer), <u>1735</u>: YB/HAY, Sep 17
Chatterley, Master J (dancer), <u>1799</u>: DL, Dec 2
Chatterley, Masters J and William Simmonds (dancers), <u>1799</u>: DL, Feb 5
Chatterley, Miss (actor, singer), <u>1791</u>: HAY, Sep 26, Oct 24; <u>1792</u>: CII, Jan 16,
     HAY, Feb 20, Oct 22; <u>1794</u>: DL, Apr 21, 28, May 16, Jun 9, 24, Jul 2, Sep 27,
     Oct 14, 22, 27, 31, Nov 15, Dec 20; <u>1795</u>: DL, Feb 6, 12, May 6, Oct 30, Nov
     10, 11, 23, Dec 4, 10; <u>1796</u>: DL, Jan 8, 11, 18, Mar 3, 12, Apr 30, Jun 7, 10,
     Oct 19, 24, Nov 9, Dec 2; <u>1798</u>: DL, Jun 5
Chatterley, Mrs Robert E (actor), <u>1796</u>: DL, Oct 19
Chatterley, Robert E (actor, call-boy), <u>1799</u>: DL, Feb 11
Chatterley, William Simmonds (actor, dancer), <u>1789</u>: DL, Dec 26; <u>1792</u>: DLKING'S,
     Mar 31, Jun 15, HAY, Jul 25, DL, Dec 27; <u>1793</u>: DL, Feb 23, Jun 6, HAY, Dec
     26; <u>1794</u>: HAY, Jan 4, DL, Apr 21, 29, May 24, Sep 23, Oct 11; <u>1795</u>: DL, Jun
     5, Sep 19, Nov 20; <u>1796</u>: DL, Apr 18, HAY, Jul 5, DL, Sep 24, Oct 1, Nov 9;
     <u>1797</u>: DL, Feb 9, 16, Mar 6, Apr 6, May 18, HAY, Aug 19, 21, DL, Sep 19, 21,
     Oct 7, 30, Dec 8; <u>1798</u>: DL, May 31, Jun 2, 5, HAY, 12, 15, DL, Sep 18, 25,
     Oct 16, Dec 3, 6, 21; <u>1799</u>: DL, Feb 11, May 7, 16, 24, HAY, Jul 6, 22, 23,
     DL, Oct 7, Dec 2, 11, 19; <u>1800</u>: DL, Jan 1, Jun 12
Chauncey, Dr, <u>1767</u>: HAY, May 29
Chaves, A, <u>1705</u>: LIF, Aug 1, 7
--Cares of Love, The; or, A Night's Adventure, <u>1705</u>: LIF, Aug 1, 3, 7
Chaworth, Lady G (commentator), <u>1675</u>: BF, Sep 3; <u>1676</u>: CITY, Oct 30; <u>1677</u>: DL,
     Jan 19
Che dirnen so (song), <u>1778</u>: KING'S, Apr 9
Che faro (song), <u>1790</u>: DL, Mar 24
Che Legge Spietata (song), <u>1762</u>: KING'S, May 11
Che quel Cor (song), <u>1748</u>: KING'S, Apr 5
Che vi par (song), <u>1792</u>: KING'S, Mar 28, 30
Cheap Experience (song), <u>1798</u>: HAY, Sep 17
Cheap Living. See Reynolds, Frederick.
Cheapside; or, All in the City (play, anon), <u>1783</u>: HAY, Sep 17
Cheapside, <u>1660</u>: CITY, Jul 5, Oct 29; <u>1662</u>: CITY, Oct 29; <u>1663</u>: CITY, Oct 29;
     <u>1681</u>: CITY, Oct 29; <u>1732</u>: TTT, Mar 3; <u>1734</u>: YB, Apr 24; <u>1745</u>: DT, Mar 14;
     <u>1746</u>: HIC, Mar 10; <u>1757</u>: DL, Apr 19; <u>1784</u>: HAY, Jan 21, Mar 3; <u>1794</u>: HAY, Jun
     2; <u>1799</u>: CG, Jun 12
Cheats of Harlequin, The (pantomime), <u>1720</u>: KING'S, Mar 10, 15
Cheats of Harlequin, The; or, The Farmer Outwitted. See Surel.
Cheats of Scapin, The. See Otway, Thomas.
Cheats, The. See Wilson, John.
Cheats, The; or, The Tavern Bilkers (pantomime), <u>1717</u>: LIF, Apr 22, 24, May 18,
     Dec 27; <u>1720</u>: LIF, Jan 1, 5, 23, Feb 3, 10, 24, May 3, 11, 14, Oct 4, Nov 4,
     Dec 17, 22; <u>1721</u>: LIF, Jan 3, 24, Feb 13, 20, Mar 14, 25, Apr 18, May 4, Oct
     10, 20, Nov 29, Dec 5, 12, 27; <u>1722</u>: LIF, Feb 6, 8, Oct 6, Nov 2, 12, Dec 13,
     26; <u>1723</u>: LIF, Feb 5, Apr 4, Oct 16; <u>1724</u>: LIF, Jul 14, 17, Oct 22; <u>1725</u>:
     LIF, Jan 18; <u>1726</u>: LIF, Jul 1, 5, 8, 12, Aug 9, Nov 16; <u>1727</u>: LIF, Dec 11;
     <u>1729</u>: LIF, Apr 22, May 21; <u>1731</u>: LIF, May 10; <u>1733</u>: LIF/CG, Jan 23, GF, May
     24
Checo. See Torinese, Checo.
Cheek, Thomas (author), <u>1691</u>: DL, Dec 0; <u>1695</u>: DL, Nov 0; <u>1699</u>: DL, Dec 0
Cheek's Apothecary, <u>1741</u>: DL, Feb 9
Cheer up my mates (song), <u>1667</u>: BRIDGES, Sep 25
Cheerily, Merrily; or, The Sailor's Life at Sea (song), <u>1792</u>: DLKING'S, May 29
Chelleri (bass viol player), <u>1725</u>: LIF, Apr 12
Chelsea Pensioner, The. See Dibdin, Charles.
Chelsea Quarters (song), <u>1797</u>: DL, Jun 12
Chelsea St, <u>1755</u>: DL, Mar 19
Chelsea, <u>1675</u>: NONE, Sep 0; <u>1689</u>: CHELSEA, Dec 0; <u>1733</u>: CHE, Jun 4; <u>1736</u>: CHE,
     May 24; <u>1739</u>: CG, Mar 27, CHE, May 8; <u>1756</u>: DL, Nov 12; <u>1791</u>: HAY, Aug 10;
     <u>1792</u>: CG, May 8, HAY, Aug 9
Cheney, Master (singer), <u>1770</u>: MARLY, Jun 16, Jul 19, 24, Aug 7, 16, Sep 11
Cheney, Miss (actor), <u>1763</u>: DL, Oct 1; <u>1764</u>: DL, Jan 13, Oct 20, 22; <u>1765</u>: DL,
     Apr 11, HAY, Jun 10
Chercheuse d'Esprit (dance), <u>1786</u>: KING'S, Dec 23
Chercheuse D'Esprit, La. See Favart, Charles Simon.
Cherokee Chiefs (visitors), <u>1730</u>: DL, Aug 19, LIF, Sep 28, Oct 1; <u>1734</u>: CG/LIF,
     Sep 30; <u>1762</u>: DL, Nov 23; <u>1790</u>: CG, Dec 17; see also American Princes; Indian
     Kings, American
Cherokee Chiefs, <u>1762</u>: HAY, Jul 20, 28; <u>1790</u>: CG, Nov 12, 16, 22, DL, 24, CG,
     Dec 11; see also American Princes; Indian Kings, American
Cherokee Nation, <u>1762</u>: DL, Nov 23; <u>1764</u>: DL, Oct 30
Cherokee, The. See Cobb, James.
Cherrier, Miss (dancer), <u>1708</u>: QUEEN'S, Jan 20

Cherrier, Rene (dancer), 1703: DL, Dec 14, LIF, 21; 1704: DL, Jan 4, 18, LIF,
    Feb 1, DL, 8, 10, 15, 22, 25, 26, 29, Mar 27, LIF, 30, DL, Apr 18, 22,
    ATCOURT, 24, DL, 25, 27, May 25, 31, Jun 9, 13, 21, 23, 29, Jul 1, Nov 11,
    23, 24, 25, 27, 29, Dec 1, 2, 6; 1705: DL, Jan 1, 8, 12, 15, 16, Feb 8, 12,
    Mar 3, 19, 31, Jun 9, 26, Jul 5, Sep 27, 29, Oct 13, Nov 5, 27, Dec 12, 17,
    19, 31; 1706: DL, Jan 5, 10, 11, 14, 21, 25, ATCOURT, Feb 5, DL, 19, 28, Mar
    5, 7, 9, 11, 12, 16, 25, 28, Apr 2, 13, Jun 28, Jul 5, DG, 9, Oct 30, Nov 1,
    DL/DG, 2, DL, 30, Dec 17, 27; 1707: DL, Jan 23, Feb 11, 13, Mar 3, 11, 25,
    Apr 3, May 24, Jun 2, Nov 22, 29, DL/QUEEN, Dec 9; 1708: QUEEN'S, Jan 20,
    DL/QUEEN, Feb 7, 10, 21
Chertsey, 1770: DL, Sep 22
Cherubini, Maria Luigi Carlo Zenobio Salvatore (composer), 1785: KING'S, Jan 8,
    Apr 2, 16; 1786: KING'S, Jan 24, Mar 30, May 4; 1787: KING'S, Jan 9; 1789:
    KING'S, Jan 24; 1794: DL, Jun 9, Sep 27; 1795: DL, Oct 1; 1797: DL, Feb 16;
    1800: DL, Jan 1
--Ifigenia in Aulide (opera), 1789: KING'S, Jan 24, 27, 31, Feb 7, 14, 21, Mar
    19, 28
--Demetrio (opera), 1785: KING'S, Jan 1, 4, 8, 15, 20, 22, 29, Feb 5, 12, 19,
    24; 1786: KING'S, Dec 23
--Finta Principessa, La (opera), 1785: KING'S, Apr 2, 5, 9, 12, 19, 26, May 3
--Giulio Sabino (opera), 1786: KING'S, Mar 30
Cheshire boy (dancer), 1724: DL, Oct 8, 14, 16; 1725: DL, Apr 3; 1726: DL, Jan
    6; 1737: HAY, May 5; see also Sant
Cheshire Cheese, 1699: DLLIF, Dec 25
Cheshire Comicks, The. See Johnson, Samuel.
Cheshire Round (dance), 1699: DLLIF, Sep 12; 1732: HAY, Mar 8
Cheshire, 1667: BF, Sep 4; 1729: HAY, Mar 29, May 2; 1730: HAY, Feb 23; 1741:
    HAY, Apr 11, May 15; 1743: CG, Apr 16
Chest Dance (dance), 1710: GR, Aug 5
Chester Theatre, 1788: CG, Sep 17; 1790: CG, Dec 2
Chester, 1737: HAY, May 5; 1773: HAY, Sep 18
Chesterfield, 5th Earl of. See Stanhope.
Chettle (actor, dancer, singer), 1740: GF, Oct 23, 24, 29, Nov 19, 20, 22, 24;
    1741: GF, Mar 19, Apr 2, 6, 13, 15, 16, 22, 28, JS, Jun 16, BFTY, Aug 22;
    1744: GF, Dec 3, 10, 26; 1745: GF, Feb 14, 20, Apr 15; 1746: GF, Feb 17;
    1747: BFC, Aug 22
Chettle (timber merchant), 1766: DL, Dec 26; 1772: DL, Jan 6, Jun 10; 1773: DL,
    Jan 21, Jun 2; 1774: DL, Jan 7, Jun 2, Dec 9; 1775: DL, May 27; 1776: DL, Jan
    26, Apr 11, Jun 10; 1777: DL, Nov 11
Chettle's Great Theatrical Booth, 1747: BFC, Aug 22
Chetwood, Anne, Mrs William Rufus (actor, dancer), 1738: DL, Sep 23, Oct 10,
    17, 21, 24, 30, Nov 11, Dec 11; 1739: DL, Feb 3, 7, May 2, Oct 10, 13, 16,
    25, 29, Nov 8, Dec 8, 10, 22; 1740: DL, Jan 8, 15, Apr 10, 22, 30, May 6, 20;
    1741: DL, May 5, Jun 4; 1742: LIF, Dec 28, 30; 1743: LIF, Jan 19, Feb 2, 14,
    28, Mar 14, 22, Apr 5, 8; 1744: DL, Jan 13, Mar 1, 28, Apr 9, May 5, 14, HAY,
    Sep 22, 25, Oct 4, 11, 18, 20, Dec 26; 1755: HAY, Sep 9, 11, 15
Chetwood, Richabella (actor), 1738: DL, May 17; 1739: DL, Apr 26, May 3, 25,
    28, Sep 6; 1744: HAY, Sep 29
Chetwood (Chetwin, Chetwynd), William Rufus (actor, prompter), 1703: LIF, May
    0; 1715: DL, Jun 10; 1716: DL, May 25; 1717: DL, May 10; 1718: DL, May 8;
    1719: DL, May 2, RI, Jul 6; 1720: DL, May 9; 1721: DL, May 8; 1722: LIF, Apr
    4; 1723: DL, May 15; 1724: DL, May 13, RI, Aug 3, SF, Sep 2; 1725: DL, May 5;
    1726: DL, May 4, Jun 3; 1727: DL, May 12; 1728: DL, May 17; 1729: DL, May 14;
    1730: DL, May 13; 1731: DL, May 4; 1732: DL, May 3; 1733: GF, Apr 13, May 24;
    1734: DL, May 15; 1735: DL, May 14; 1736: DL, May 13; 1737: DL, May 4; 1738:
    DL, May 17; 1739: DL, Mar 17; 1740: DL, Apr 30; 1741: CG, Jan 12, DL, May 5;
    1743: DL, Oct 6; 1749: DL, Mar 1; 1760: DL, Mar 20
--Emperor of China, The, 1731: SF/BFFHH, Aug 24, Sep 8
--Generous Free-Mason, The; or, The Constant Lady, 1730: BFOF, Aug 20, SFOF,
    Sep 9, HAY, Dec 28, 30; 1731: HAY, Jan 1, DL, May 3, BFYG, Aug 24; 1736: LIF,
    Jun 16; 1741: TC, Aug 4, NWC, 22
--Lover's Opera, The (opera), 1729: DL, May 14, 16, 26, 30, Jun 30, Oct 14, 16,
    21, 23, Nov 29, Dec 8, 11, 19; 1730: DL, Jan 5, Apr 8, 15, 17, 22, May 19,
    Oct 24, Nov 18, Dec 1; 1731: DL, Mar 25, Apr 21, 26, GF, Nov 5, 6, 8, 9, 10,
    11, 15, 16, 17, 18, 19, 20, 22, 25, 29, Dec 1, 2, 6, 7, 16, 18, 29, 30, 31;
    1732: GF, Jan 10, 11, 13, 15, 19, 22, Feb 18, 28, Mar 16, 25, Apr 11, 20, DL,
    May 1, GF, 2, 8, 19; 1733: GF, Jan 20, 22, 23, Feb 1, Apr 13, 30, Oct 19, 26,
    Nov 2; 1734: GF, Jan 2, 25, Feb 2, Mar 5, May 6, HAY, Jun 21, 24; 1735: GF,
    Mar 13, 17; 1736: GF, Feb 5, DL, Mar 22, GF, 22, DL, 29, GF, May 4; 1737:
    LIF, Mar 21, Apr 12, 18, 28, May 17; 1738: DL, Apr 26, May 25, 29; 1741: GF,
    Apr 10, DL, May 5; 1754: CG, Apr 22
--Mock Mason, The, 1733: GF, Apr 13

Chetwood, William Rufus and Anne (actor), 1739: DL, May 3
Chevalier a la Mode, Le. See D'Ancourt, Florent Carton.
Chevalier, Pierre (dancer), 1787: KING'S, Dec 8; 1788: KING'S, Jan 12, 29, Feb
  21, 26, Mar 15, Apr 3, 19, May 15
Chevrier (dancer), 1726: KING'S, Dec 17
Cheyne (carpenter), 1796: DL, Oct 8
Cheyne, Charles Lord (spectator), 1671: BRIDGES, Jan 25; 1673: ATCOURT, Jun 5
Chi nacque alle pene (song), 1748: CG, Feb 15
Chiampi. See Ciampi.
Chianova, Mrs (beneficiary), 1728: LIF, May 31
Chianti, Mrs. See Chimenti, Margherita.
Chichester, 1731: HAY, May 6; 1784: HAY, Aug 18
Chichly, Sir John (spectator), 1667: BRIDGES, Dec 11
Chico. See Torinese, Checo.
Child of Nature, The. See Inchbald, Elizabeth.
Child, Sir Francis (Lord Mayor), 1698: CITY, Oct 29
Child, Mrs (actor), 1781: HAY, Oct 16; 1782: HAY, Jan 14
Child's Coffee House, 1744: DL, Apr 2
Children in the Wood, The. See Morton, Thomas.
Children on the Ice (song), 1723: LIF, Oct 14
Children, The. See Hoare, Prince.
Chimenti (Chianti), Margherita (singer), 1736: KING'S, Nov 23, CG, 27; 1737:
  KING'S, Jan 8, Feb 12, Apr 12, May 24, Oct 29; 1738: KING'S, Jan 3, 28, Feb
  25, Mar 14, Apr 15; see also Droghierina, La
Chimera, The. See Odell, Thomas.
Chimes of the Times (song), 1729: YB, Apr 22, BFF, Aug 23; 1731: SF/BFFHH, Aug
  24, Sep 8
Chimney Corner, The. See Porter, Walsh.
Chimney Sweeper, The (ballad opera, anon), 1728: HAY, May 27; 1736: GF, Jan 29,
  31, Feb 2
Chimney Sweeper's Dialogue (song), 1702: LIF, Dec 29
Chimney-Sweepers, Little (beneficiaries), 1735: GF, Apr 9
China (horn player), 1724: HIC, Feb 26
China Hall Theatre, 1777: HAY, Feb 11, CHR, Jul 23; 1778: CHR, Jun 26; 1795:
  DL, Jan 22
China Terrace, 1800: CG, Jun 16
Chinese Dance (dance), 1742: CG, Nov 2; 1755: CG, Jan 4, 11, 18, 21, 23, 25,
  28, Apr 16
Chinese Festival, The (dance), 1755: DL, Nov 8, 10, 12, 13, 14, 15, 17, 18, Dec
  3; 1761: RANELAGH, Jun 12
Chinese Jerbs, 1770: RANELAGH, Oct 3
Chinese Mandarins (spectators), 1735: LIF, Jun 19; 1756: CG, Dec 21
Chinese Wedding (dance), 1764: KING'S, Nov 24
Chinnall (Chinnaw, Chinneau) (doorkeeper), 1764: DL, May 22; 1765: DL, May 21;
  1766: DL, May 16; 1767: DL, May 30; 1769: DL, May 17; 1770: DL, May 28; 1771:
  DL, May 25; 1772: DL, Jun 3
Chinois, Les; ou, Arlequin Major Ridicule (pantomime), 1718: LIF, Dec 19
Chinsani (Climsani), Sidi Mahomet (Tunisian ambassador), 1734: CG, Mar 28, GF,
  Apr 4, May 3
Chinzer (composer), 1751: KING'S, Apr 16
Chio mai vi polla (song), 1729: HIC, Apr 16
Chippendale, Mrs William (actor, singer), 1797: DL, Nov 8; 1798: DL, Oct 6, Nov
  14, Dec 4, 17, 29; 1799: DL, May 24, Oct 14, Nov 6, 14, Dec 11; 1800: DL, Jan
  1, Mar 11, 13, May 17
Chippendale, William (actor), 1793: HAY, Dec 26; 1795: DL, Jun 4; 1796: DL, Jun
  11, HAY, 22, 29, Jul 5, 12, Aug 8, 10, 18, 29, Sep 7; 1797: DL, Jun 10, HAY,
  13, 17, 20, 21, 24, 28, Jul 3, 10, 15, 18, Aug 1, 15; 1798: DL, May 19, Jun
  13, HAY, 13, 14, 16, 18, 21, 30, Jul 14, Aug 3, 4, 11, 15, 21, Sep 3, DL, 27,
  Nov 22, 29, Dec 4; 1799: DL, May 16, 24, HAY, Jun 18, 20, 22, 24, 25, 29, Jul
  2, 5, 9, 12, 13, 17, 23, 27, 30, Aug 5, 10, 13, 21, Sep 10, DL, 17, Oct 19,
  26, Nov 6, Dec 11; 1800: DL, Jan 3, 6, Feb 1, 19, Mar 3, Apr 15, 28, 29, May
  2, 3, 13, 29, Jun 11, 12, HAY, 13, 14, 16, 18, 19, 20, 21, 27, Jul 2, 3, 5,
  15, 16, 21, Aug 7, 8, 14, 15, 22, 23, 27, Sep 1
Chiri, Giovanni Battista (composer), 1764: HAY, Nov 13
Chiringhelli, Sga (dancer), 1774: DL, Apr 22
Chise, Mme (dancer), 1757: HAY, Jun 17
Chisholm (householder), 1743: CG, Apr 6
Chiswick, 1750: DL, Feb 13
Chit Chat. See Killigrew, Thomas.
Chit Chat; or, The Penance of Polygamy. See Walwyn, B.
Chitty (coal merchant), 1749: DL, Nov 8; 1766: DL, Nov 21
Chitty, Mrs (coal merchant), 1771: DL, Nov 15; 1772: DL, Jun 10, Nov 27; 1773:

DL, Jun 2, Oct 29; <u>1774</u>: DL, Jun 2, Oct 28; <u>1775</u>: DL, May 27, Nov 10; <u>1776</u>: DL, Jun 10

Choca, Mrs (actor), <u>1734</u>: MEG, Sep 30

Chock (Chalke), Miss Dennis (actor), <u>1695</u>: DL, Sep 0; <u>1696</u>: DG, Jun 0; <u>1697</u>: DG, Jun 0; <u>1698</u>: DL, Mar 0, Jun 0; <u>1699</u>: DL, Dec 0

Chock, Mrs (actor), <u>1671</u>: NONE, Sep 0

Chogia, Jusuf (Tunisian envoy), <u>1722</u>: LIF, May 4

Choice (song), <u>1755</u>: CG, Apr 15

Choice of Apollo, The. See Potter, John.

Choice of Harlequin, The. See Messink, James.

Choice of Hercules, The. See Handel, George Frederic.

Choice, The. See Murphy, Arthur.

Choleric Fathers, The. See Holcroft, Thomas.

Choleric Man, The. See Cumberland, Richard.

Chollet, Constance (dancer), <u>1771</u>: KING'S, Mar 9, 12

Cholmondeley, E (spectator), <u>1673</u>: NONE, Apr 21

Cholmondeley, Hugh Lord, <u>1699</u>: LIF, Apr 8

Choral Fund, <u>1798</u>: HAY, Jan 15; <u>1799</u>: HAY, Jan 24

Chorus, Grand (song), <u>1734</u>: ST, Mar 22; <u>1739</u>: DL, May 22, CG, Nov 1; <u>1746</u>: GF, May 1; <u>1770</u>: KING'S, Mar 8; <u>1771</u>: KING'S, Feb 28; <u>1773</u>: KING'S, Feb 2, Mar 9, Jun 19; <u>1779</u>: HAY, Mar 17; <u>1783</u>: HAY, Aug 12; <u>1785</u>: KING'S, Mar 17; <u>1788</u>: CG, Jan 14, DL, Feb 22

Chose (dancer), <u>1734</u>: DL, Sep 19, 24, 26, Oct 3, 5, 8, 10, 17; <u>1735</u>: DL, Jan 22

Christ Church, <u>1663</u>: BRIDGES, Nov 3

Christ, John (composer), <u>1785</u>: KING'S, May 12

Christ's Church College, <u>1748</u>: CG, Mar 5

Christian (beneficiary), <u>1734</u>: HA, Sep 11

Christian (dancer), <u>1750</u>: CG, Oct 30, Dec 21; <u>1751</u>: CG, Sep 30, Oct 28, Nov 11, Dec 13, 20; <u>1753</u>: DL, Oct 12, 13, Nov 26

Christian Hero, The. See Lillo, George.

Christian, Miss (actor), <u>1784</u>: HAY, Aug 6

Christian, Mrs (actor), <u>1732</u>: GF, Oct 6, 12, 14, 25, 30, Nov 17; <u>1733</u>: GF, Jan 1, 20, 24, Feb 5, Apr 4, 5, 16, 17, 25, 30, May 3, 23, HAY, 28, GF, 29

Christianity, <u>1775</u>: CG, Mar 18

Christie, J (publisher), <u>1789</u>: DL, Feb 7

Christmas (musician), <u>1675</u>: ATCOURT, Feb 15

Christmas Coffee House, <u>1750</u>: CG, Apr 2

Christmas Ordinary, The. See Richards, William.

Christmas Tale, A. See Garrick, David.

Chrononhotonthologos. See Carey, Henry.

Chronos, Chronos, mend thy pace (song), <u>1700</u>: DL, Apr 29

Chukatah (Cherokee chief), <u>1764</u>: DL, Oct 30; see also Cherokee Chiefs; American Princes; Indian Kings, American

Chumbley (doorkeeper), <u>1795</u>: DL, Jun 5; <u>1796</u>: DL, Jun 15; <u>1797</u>: DL, Jun 13; <u>1798</u>: DL, Jun 15; <u>1799</u>: DL, Jul 4; <u>1800</u>: DL, Jun 17

Church (actor), <u>1715</u>: LIF, Jun 2, 23

Church (actor, singer), <u>1770</u>: HAY, Oct 1, 29

Church (house servant), <u>1744</u>: DL, May 22

Church (performer on the Jew's harp), <u>1752</u>: CT/HAY, Mar 17; <u>1753</u>: HAY, Mar 29

Church Lane, <u>1745</u>: GF, Mar 12, 25; <u>1779</u>: HAY, May 10; <u>1791</u>: HAY, Aug 10; <u>1792</u>: CG, May 8, HAY, Aug 9

Church Music (music), <u>1732</u>: HIC, May 10

Church St, <u>1736</u>: CHE, May 24; <u>1788</u>: DL, Apr 24

Church, I B (charity patron), <u>1794</u>: DL, Jul 2

Church, John (singer), <u>1695</u>: DG, Apr 0; <u>1696</u>: DG, Oct 0; <u>1726</u>: IT, Feb 2

Churchill (duellist), <u>1679</u>: DG, Jun 21

Churchill, Charles (poet), <u>1749</u>: DL, Nov 1; <u>1761</u>: DL, Mar 14; <u>1763</u>: DL, Sep 17; <u>1769</u>: CG, Mar 16

Churchill, Miss (actor), <u>1782</u>: HAY, May 6

Churchman, William, <u>1757</u>: CG, Dec 22

Churchwarden I have been (song), <u>1794</u>: CG, May 26; see also Vestry Dinner

Churchyard Gate, <u>1747</u>: CG, Apr 20

Churton, Mrs (actor), <u>1792</u>: HAY, Feb 6, 20

Chute, John (correspondent), <u>1742</u>: KING'S, Apr 20

Chymical Counterfeits, The; or, Harlequin Worm Doctor (pantomime, anon), <u>1734</u>: GF, Dec 9, 10, 12, 13, 14, 17, 18, 19, 20, 21, 23, 26, 27, 28, 30, 31; <u>1735</u>: GF, Jan 1, 2, 3, 4, 6, 7, 8, 9, 10, 11, 13, 14, 15, 16, 17, 18, 20, Sep 17, 19, 22, 24; <u>1736</u>: GF, May 3, 13, LIF, Jul 1, 2, 7, 14, 16, 21; <u>1740</u>: GF, Nov 6, 7, 8, 10, 11, 12, 13, 14, 15, 17, 18, 19, 20, 21, 29, Dec 1, 2

Ciacchi (Ciocchi) (singer), <u>1746</u>: KING'S, Jan 7, 28, Mar 25, May 13, Nov 4; <u>1747</u>: KING'S, Apr 14, Nov 14; <u>1748</u>: HAY, Jan 12, KING'S, Apr 5

Ciampi (Chiampi), Lorenzo Vincenzio (composer), <u>1749</u>: KING'S, Mar 14, HAY, Nov

151

21; <u>1750</u>: KING'S, Feb 20, Apr 10; <u>1751</u>: KING'S, Apr 16; <u>1752</u>: KING'S, Mar 24; <u>1753</u>: KING'S, Apr 30; <u>1754</u>: KING'S, Jan 5, Feb 28, CG, Dec 9; <u>1755</u>: KING'S, Mar 17; <u>1761</u>: KING'S, Mar 12; <u>1762</u>: KING'S, Jan 11; <u>1763</u>: KING'S, Apr 25
--Adriano in Syria (opera), <u>1750</u>: KING'S, Feb 20, 24, Mar 3, 6, 10, 13, 27, Apr 3; <u>1765</u>: KING'S, Jan 26, 29, Feb 2, 5, 9, 16, 23
--Bertoldo (opera), <u>1762</u>: KING'S, Jan 11, 16, 19; <u>1764</u>: DL, Nov 28
--Didone (opera), <u>1754</u>: KING'S, Jan 5, 8, 12, 15, 19, 22, 26, Feb 19, Apr 2
--Famiglia de Bertholdi, La (opera), <u>1754</u>: CG, Dec 9, 16, 19, 23; <u>1755</u>: CG, Jan 3
--Honorius (opera), <u>1736</u>: KING'S, Apr 13
--Negligente, Il (opera), <u>1749</u>: HAY, Nov 21, 25, 2(, Dec 2, 5, 9, 12, 16; <u>1750</u>: KING'S, Mar 20, 24
--Tre Cicisbei Ridicoli, Li (opera), <u>1749</u>: KING'S, Mar 14, 18, Apr 1, CG, May 1, KING'S, 11, 27
--Trionfo di Camilla, Il (opera), <u>1750</u>: KING'S, Mar 31, Apr 7
Ciardini, Domenico (singer), <u>1762</u>: KING'S, Dec 4; <u>1763</u>: KING'S, Feb 19, Apr 25
Ciavartino (actor), <u>1754</u>: HAY/SFB, Sep 13
Cibber-Griffin-Bullock-Hallam Booth, <u>1733</u>: BFCGBH, Aug 23, Sep 4
Cibber, Colley (actor, author, manager), <u>1683</u>: NONE, Sep 0; <u>1685</u>: DL, May 9; <u>1690</u>: DL, Sep 0, Dec 0; <u>1691</u>: DL, Mar 0; <u>1692</u>: DL, Jan 0, Feb 0, 9, Mar 0; <u>1693</u>: DL, Apr 0; <u>1694</u>: DL, Jan 13, Mar 21, DG, May 0; <u>1695</u>: DL, Apr 1, DLANDLIF, May 0, DL, 0, Dec 0; <u>1696</u>: DL, Jan 0, Mar 0, Apr 0, Sep 0, Nov 21, DL/DL, Dec 0; <u>1697</u>: DL, Jan 0, Feb 0, May 8, 31, Jul 0, Sep 0; <u>1698</u>: DL, Jun 0; <u>1699</u>: DL, Dec 0; <u>1700</u>: DL, Feb 19, Apr 29, Nov 23, Dec 9; <u>1701</u>: DL, Apr 0, May 31, Jun 19, Dec 0; <u>1702</u>: DL, Jan 0, Feb 0, Oct 26, Nov 26, Dec 14; <u>1703</u>: DL, Mar 11, Apr 10, Jun 30, Oct 30, Dec 2; <u>1704</u>: LIF, Mar 30, DL, Apr 4, Oct 18, Dec 7, 26; <u>1705</u>: DL, Jan 18, Mar 29, QUEEN'S, Apr 9, DL, Oct 30, Dec 3; <u>1706</u>: DL, Mar 12, Apr 1, 8, DG, Jul 9, QUEEN'S, Nov 7, 9, 14, 22, 25, Dec 3, 7, 13, 16; <u>1707</u>: QUEEN'S, Jan 1, 13, 14, Feb 4, 15, 18, Mar 1, 8, 10, Apr 1, 30, May 9, DL/QUEEN, Oct 18, 22, 23, 27, 28, Nov 1, 10, 11, 15, 19, 20, QUEEN/DL, Dec 6, QUEEN'S, 13, 20, 22, DL/QUEEN, 26, 27, 29, 31; <u>1708</u>: DL/QUEEN, Jan 1, 2, 3, 6, QUEEN'S, 10, DL, 15, Feb 4, 7, 26, Mar 1, 16, 18, 27, Apr 10, 17, 22, 29, Jun 10, Oct 5, 7, 12, 14, 18, 19, 21, 22, 23, 26, Dec 14, 22, 30, 31; <u>1709</u>: DL, Jan 1, 3, 4, 5, 8, 10, 11, 12, 13, 14, 18, 26, 29, Feb 12, 19, Mar 3, 15, 17, 19, 24, 26, 31, Apr 14, May 7, QUEEN'S, Sep 22, 24, 29, Oct 1, 4, 6, 22, 31, Nov 8, 12, Dec 12; <u>1710</u>: QUEEN'S, Jan 11, 12, 14, 18, 19, 21, 26, Feb 11, 13, Mar 4, 27, Apr 13, May 15, 25, Jun 1, GR, 21, QUEEN'S, 22, 29, DL/QUEEN, Oct 4, 5, Nov 4, 6, QUEEN'S, 10, DL/QUEEN, 13, 15, 16, DL, 20, 28, 30, Dec 1, 4, 5, 14, 15, 18; <u>1711</u>: DL, Jan 15, 16, 18, 19, 25, Feb 10, 15, 19, 22, Mar 8, DL/QUEEN, 12, 15, DL, 19, Apr 7, Sep 25, 27, Oct 4, 10, 11, 13, 23, 26, Nov 1, 2, 5, 8, 10, 12, 26, 27, 29, Dec 3, 8, 21, 31; <u>1712</u>: DL, Sep 20, 30, Oct 6, 17, 23, 31, Nov 28, Dec 12, 27; <u>1713</u>: DL, Jan 29, Feb 9, 13, 19, 28, Mar 3, 9, Apr 14, May 11, Jun 23, Sep 29, Oct 23, Nov 9, 11, 18, 28, Dec 2, 18; <u>1714</u>: DL, Jan 5, Feb 2, Apr 26, May 26, 28, Oct 22, Nov 9, 24, 26, 27, Dec 8; <u>1715</u>: DL, Jan 5, 6, 15, Feb 22, Mar 12, 14, 28, Apr 20, May 17, 18, 20, 24, Oct 13, 22, Nov 5, 19, Dec 6, 12, 17, 20, 31; <u>1716</u>: DL, Jan 7, 11, 21, 23, 25, 26, Feb 9, 21, 23, Mar 10, May 9, Sep 29, Oct 4, 9, 12, 15, 16, 27, Nov 1, 2, 3, 12, 26, 29, Dec 4, 15; <u>1717</u>: DL, Jan 2, 16, 24, 26, 31, Feb 2, Mar 1, 14, Apr 11, May 2, Jun 24, Oct 3, 9, 10, 16, 21, 22, 26, 28, Nov 8, 18, 20, 23, 25, 27, 30, Dec 6, 21; <u>1718</u>: DL, Jan 20, 23, 27, Feb 14, 19, Mar 1, 8, 17, 22, 24, Apr 19, Sep 20, 25, Oct 2, 4, 7, 15, 17, 20, 21, 22, 25, 28, 31, Nov 18, 19, 24, 25, 26, Dec 2, 3, 10, 13, 16, 19; <u>1719</u>: DL, Jan 16, 24, Feb 14, Sep 12, 15, 17, 22, 29, Oct 3, 7, 9, 10, 13, 14, 16, 17, 23, 27, 28, Nov 3, 10, 11, 14, 17, 19, 20, 21, 26, Dec 2, 5, 11, 19; <u>1720</u>: DL, Jan 27, Feb 5, Mar 14, 19, Apr 21, May 27, Jun 2, Sep 10, 13, 15, 20, 24, 29, Oct 3, 4, 5, 7, 8, 13, 29, Nov 7, 10, 12, 15, 18, 29, Dec 1, 17; <u>1721</u>: DL, Jan 10, 13, 16, 17, 19, 23, Feb 3, 14, LIF, Mar 11, 13, DL, 23, LIF, 27, DL, Apr 13, 14, Sep 12, LIF, 27, Oct 7, DL, 12, 14, 18, 19, 20, 21, 23, 24, 25, 31, Nov 1, 7, 8, 11, 14, 15, 17, 18, 25, 28, Dec 9, 22, 28; <u>1722</u>: DL, Jan 4, 5, 9, 11, 13, Feb 8, 17, Apr 5, 26, 27, May 5, 14, 22, Sep 8, 18, 20, 22, 25, Oct 9, 10, 11, 13, 15, 16, 20, 22, 24, 26, 27, 31, Nov 1, 3, 7, LIF, 15, DL, Dec 4, 5, 7, 27; <u>1723</u>: DL, Jan 8, 9, 21, 28, Feb 15, Apr 1, 22, Jul 9, Sep 14, 17, 19, Oct 1, 9, 10, LIF, 10, DL, 19, 22, 23, 24, 26, 28, 31, Nov 1, 2, 6, 9, 14, 15, 16, 19, 21, 22, Dec 20; <u>1724</u>: DL, Feb 12, Apr 8, May 16, Sep 15, 17, 26, Oct 8, 10, 14, 22, 24, 28, Nov 3, 6, 7, 14, 19, 21, 27, 28, Dec 7, 9, 18, 22; <u>1725</u>: DL, Jan 4, 9, 27, Feb 3, 9, Apr 15, May 21, 31, Sep 4, 7, 9, 21, 25, 28, Oct 2, 7, 13, 15, 18, 23, 25, 27, Nov 2, 6, 8, 22, 27, 29, Dec 13; <u>1726</u>: DL, Jan 3, 5, 11, 22, Feb 18, Mar 17, Sep 3, 10, 15, 17, 22, 27, Oct 6, 11, 13, 15, 20, Nov 9, 25, 26, Dec 7, 12, 14, 17; <u>1727</u>: DL, Jan 3, 5, 25, 27, Feb 8, 9, 11, 21, Mar 7, Apr 8, 24, May 5, 8, 22, Sep 7, 9, 16, 19, 21, 26, Oct 5, 7, 14, 20, 26, Nov 9, 18, 21, 22, 27, Dec 1, 4, 30; <u>1728</u>: DL, Jan 2, 3, 5, 10, 20, Feb 14, 16, Mar 9, 14, Apr 2, May 10,

23, Sep 7, 12, 17, 26, 28, Oct 12, 18, 21, 23, 25, 28, 31, Nov 1, 7, 8, 12,
22, 27, 29, Dec 16; <u>1729</u>: DL, Jan 7, 8, 20, 22, 28, 29, 31, Feb 1, 3, 15, 22,
25, Mar 10, 15, May 14, Aug 16, Sep 11, 13, 16, 20, 23, 25, 30, Oct 2, 7, 9,
11, 14, 16, 23, Nov 1, 3, 6, 8, 14, 17, 18, 21, 22, 24, Dec 3, 13; <u>1730</u>: DL,
Jan 9, May 4, Sep 17, 22, 24, 29, Oct 1, 3, 10, 22, Nov 3, 19, 25, 26, 28,
Dec 1; <u>1731</u>: DL, Jan 8, 11, 12, Mar 8, 16, 22, 29, Apr 1, 8, GF, 23, 26, DL,
May 3, 10, Sep 21, 23, 25, 28, Oct 5, 7, 9, 14, 19, 26, 30, Nov 1, 8, 15, 24,
Dec 3, 6, 17, 18, 22; <u>1732</u>: DL, Jan 3, 7, 10, 15, 22, Feb 2, 10, 11, 14, Mar
23, Apr 17, 18, Sep 8, 30, Oct 3, 14, 19, 21, 24, 28, Nov 9, 13, 18, 21, 24,
Dec 6, 9, 14, 29; <u>1733</u>: DL, Jan 6, 12, 13, 19, Feb 17, 22, 26, Mar 5, 24, 29,
Apr 2, 4, 16, 17, 28, May 15, 23, 25, 28, 29, KING'S, Jun 2, DL, 4, DL/HAY,
Oct 5, 20; <u>1734</u>: HAY, Jun 28, DL, Oct 21, 31, Nov 14, 19, Dec 2, 5; <u>1735</u>: DL,
Jan 9, 25, 27, Feb 26, LIF, Jun 19, DL, Nov 19, KING'S, Dec 16, DL, 29; <u>1736</u>:
DL, Jan 8, Feb 18, CG, May 10, 18, DL, 27, Jun 23, Sep 11, Dec 17; <u>1737</u>: DL,
Feb 4, 8, HAY, Mar 2, DL, 3, 5, Apr 29, LIF, May 4, DL, Sep 6, Nov 8, 11;
<u>1738</u>: DL, Jan 3, Mar 18, CG, May 8, DL, 15, 25, Oct 13, 24; <u>1739</u>: DL, Jan 31,
Feb 6, CG, Aug 21, 09, Sep 14, Oct 2, 3, 8, 24, Nov 3, 7, Dec 12, 20; <u>1740</u>:
CG, Jan 8, 12, 24, Mar 24, DL, Apr 15, CG, 25, DL, May 16, CG, Sep 22, Oct 1,
6, 22, Nov 13, GF, Dec 6; <u>1741</u>: CG, Jan 12, 17, Feb 23, DL, May 7, JS, 19,
CG, Oct 2, DL, 20, Dec 3, GF, 9, CG, 14; <u>1742</u>: CG, Jan 4, Feb 3, 12, 26, DL,
Mar 20, LIF, Nov 24; <u>1743</u>: LIF, Feb 9; <u>1744</u>: DL, Jan 5, 13, 27; <u>1745</u>: HAY,
Jan 25, CG, Feb 15, 20, Mar 16, Oct 18, DL, 22, CG, Nov 16, Dec 10; <u>1746</u>: DL,
Mar 10, Nov 1, 28, CG, Dec 2; <u>1747</u>: DL, May 7; <u>1748</u>: CG, Mar 21; <u>1750</u>: DL,
Apr 23, CG, Oct 22, DL, Dec 24; <u>1751</u>: DL, Feb 27, Oct 4; <u>1752</u>: DL, Mar 9;
<u>1756</u>: CG, Mar 23, DL, 27; <u>1757</u>: CG, Jan 28, DL, Dec 10; <u>1758</u>: CG, Jan 12,
HAY, 12; <u>1760</u>: DL, Apr 16; <u>1765</u>: CG, Apr 19; <u>1766</u>: DL, Jan 30; <u>1768</u>: DL, Nov
17; <u>1771</u>: DL, Nov 27; <u>1772</u>: CG, Mar 21; <u>1773</u>: CG, Oct 9; <u>1774</u>: HAY, Sep 17;
<u>1778</u>: CG, Mar 14; <u>1784</u>: CG, Oct 6; <u>1788</u>: CG, Oct 29; <u>1791</u>: CG, May 2; <u>1792</u>:
DL, Oct 4; <u>1796</u>: DL, May 23
--Caesar in Egypt, <u>1724</u>: DL, Dec 9, 10, 11, 12, 14, 15
--Careless Husband, The, <u>1704</u>: DL, Dec 7, 8, 9, 11, 12, 13, 14, 15, 16, 21;
<u>1705</u>: DL, Jan 2, 9, 27, Feb 27, Mar 17, Jun 2, Oct 13, Nov 24; <u>1706</u>: DL, Feb
19, Apr 3, QUEEN'S, Nov 7, 12, 23, Dec 21; <u>1707</u>: QUEEN'S, Feb 11, Mar 10,
QUEEN/DL, Dec 6, QUEEN'S, 13, 15, QUEEN/DL, 30; <u>1708</u>: QUEEN/DL, Jan 21; <u>1709</u>:
DL, Jan 8, QUEEN'S, Nov 12; <u>1710</u>: QUEEN'S, Jun 13; <u>1711</u>: DL, Feb 19, Apr 27,
Oct 23; <u>1712</u>: DL, Jan 3, May 20, Sep 20, Oct 9; <u>1713</u>: DL, Feb 7, Nov 28;
<u>1714</u>: DL, Mar 8, Apr 5, Nov 13; <u>1715</u>: DL, Jan 11, LIF, Mar 19, DL, 31, May
24, Oct 22, Dec 8; <u>1716</u>: DL, Feb 4, Mar 24, Dec 15; <u>1717</u>: DL, Mar 14, Nov 23;
<u>1718</u>: DL, Jan 25, Mar 4, Apr 26, Nov 15; <u>1719</u>: DL, Jan 24, Apr 27, Oct 17;
<u>1720</u>: DL, Jan 28, Feb 27, Apr 26; <u>1721</u>: DL, Jan 10, Feb 4, Mar 25, Nov 11;
<u>1722</u>: DL, Jan 13, Mar 15, Apr 21, Sep 8, Nov 3; <u>1723</u>: DL, Mar 7, Apr 2, Nov
2, Dec 12; <u>1724</u>: DL, Mar 16, Apr 11, Oct 10, Nov 11; <u>1725</u>: DL, Jan 7, Mar 8,
Apr 28, Jun 3, Nov 6; <u>1726</u>: DL, Jan 8, Feb 26, Apr 25, Sep 27, Nov 8; <u>1727</u>:
DL, Jan 7, 14, Apr 19, Oct 14, Dec 2; <u>1728</u>: DL, Mar 21, Apr 26, Dec 7; <u>1729</u>:
DL, Feb 1, Apr 14, Nov 1, Dec 11; <u>1730</u>: GF, Mar 12, DL, Apr 4; <u>1731</u>: GF, Jan
13, 14, 15, 16, 18, Feb 13, Mar 8, Apr 26, Oct 6, Nov 3, Dec 14; <u>1732</u>: DL,
Jan 29, Feb 2, GF, 11, DL, Mar 6, Apr 13, GF, May 1, RI, Jul 22; <u>1733</u>: DL,
Mar 5, GF, 6, 29, DL, Apr 17, GF, May 23, DL/HAY, Oct 20, Dec 15; <u>1734</u>:
DL/HAY, Jan 3, GF, 11, DL/HAY, 29, GF, Feb 5, CG, 14, 15, GF, 28, DL/HAY, Mar
18, GF, 23, DL, Apr 23, LIF, 26, DL, 29, GF, May 13, DL, Nov 14; <u>1735</u>: GF,
Jan 20, DL, 31, GF, Feb 3, Mar 8, Apr 12, DL, 25, LIF, Jun 19, GF/HAY, Aug
14, GF, Nov 12; <u>1736</u>: HAY, Feb 16, DL, Apr 29, May 24; <u>1737</u>: LIF, Apr 2, 30;
<u>1738</u>: DL, May 2; <u>1739</u>: DL, Jan 15, Apr 9, CG, Aug 21, 29, Oct 2, Nov 7, Dec
17; <u>1740</u>: DL, Jan 5, CG, 8, Mar 24, DL, Apr 15, CG, 25, DL, May 16, Nov 8,
GF, 27, Dec 3, CG, 19; <u>1741</u>: GF, Feb 7, CG, Apr 18, GF, May 5, Oct 7; <u>1742</u>:
GF, Mar 15, 16, DL, 20, CG, Apr 1, DL, 22, GF, 26, CG, May 1, DL, Nov 22,
LIF, 24, 26; <u>1743</u>: LIF, Jan 19, Mar 3, Apr 8, DL, May 4; <u>1744</u>: DL, May 11,
MF, Jun 27, HAY, Sep 25, Oct 16, JS, Dec 10, HAY, 11; <u>1745</u>: DL, Jan 26, CG,
Feb 9, DL, 15, CG, 28, May 1, DL, 6, Oct 8, CG, Nov 12, Dec 4; <u>1746</u>: DL, Feb
12, CG, 22, DL, Mar 1, Apr 2, CG, 9, DL, Jun 6, Aug 8, Oct 25, GF, Dec 2, DL,
22; <u>1747</u>: GF, Feb 10, DL, 11; <u>1749</u>: CG, Feb 6, 21, Apr 14; <u>1750</u>: DL, Mar 19,
Apr 28, Oct 23; <u>1751</u>: DL, Apr 20, Sep 19; <u>1752</u>: DL, Jan 18, Feb 27, Apr 25,
Sep 23, Oct 17, Nov 21; <u>1753</u>: DL, Feb 27, May 11, Sep 20, Oct 17; <u>1754</u>: DL,
Jan 22, Apr 19, Sep 21, Dec 16; <u>1755</u>: CG, Jan 7, 17, DL, 18, Apr 28, Sep 16,
Nov 29; <u>1756</u>: DL, Oct 22, 23, 25, Nov 5, 22, Dec 7; <u>1757</u>: DL, Jan 1, 20, Feb
4, 8, Mar 17, Apr 29, Oct 7, Dec 10; <u>1758</u>: DL, Feb 11, May 10; <u>1759</u>: CG, Mar
24, DL, Apr 26, CG, May 24, DL, 30, Jun 28, Nov 2; <u>1760</u>: DL, Jan 2, May 14,
Oct 14; <u>1761</u>: CG, Apr 1, DL, 16, Sep 17, Dec 15; <u>1762</u>: DL, May 18, Sep 18,
CG, Oct 19; <u>1763</u>: CG, Apr 16, May 11, DL, Sep 24, Nov 28, CG, Dec 16; <u>1764</u>:
CG, May 3, DL, Sep 25, 29; <u>1765</u>: DL, Jan 11; <u>1767</u>: DL, May 16; <u>1770</u>: DL, Jan
25, 31, Oct 6; <u>1771</u>: DL, Nov 26; <u>1778</u>: CG, Feb 13, 17; <u>1781</u>: CG, Feb 8, 10,
Mar 29, May 12; <u>1784</u>: CG, Jan 23, 28, Feb 2, 6, 11, Mar 2, 25, Apr 3, 14, 29,

153

Jun 2; 1785: CG, Feb 8, 19, 26, Apr 28; 1787: DL, Mar 29, CG, 31, Apr 18;
1788: CG, Jan 9, Feb 21, Dec 19; 1789: CG, Feb 13, 20, DL, Dec 23; 1790: DL,
Jan 1, 8, Feb 5; 1791: DLKING'S, Dec 6; 1792: DL, Sep 29, CG, Nov 6, 9, 28
--Comical Lovers, The; or, Marriage a la Mode (Court Gallantry), 1707: QUEEN'S,
Feb 4, 5, 8, DL/QUEEN, 25, Nov 20; 1708: DL/QUEEN, Feb 21, May 19; 1709: DL,
Feb 12, QUEEN'S, Sep 29; 1710: QUEEN'S, Feb 6; 1711: DL, Feb 15; 1714: DL,
Oct 16, 18; 1715: DL, Jan 5, 21, Jun 3; 1717: DL, Apr 11; 1720: DL, Oct 8,
10, 11, Nov 9; 1721: DL, Apr 12; 1722: DL, Apr 27; 1746: DL, Mar 10, 11, 15,
Apr 1, 24, Nov 1; 1747: DL, May 7; 1752: DL, Feb 6, Mar 9, Apr 16; 1796: DL,
May 23
--Comical Resentment, The; or, Trick for Trick, 1759: CG, Mar 26
--Country Wake, The. See Doggett, Thomas, Hob.
--Damon and Phillida; or, Hymen's Triumph, 1729: DL, Aug 16, HAY, 19, BFR, 25,
DL, Oct 28, HAY, Nov 18, 20, 22, 26, 29, Dec 22, 23; 1730: HAY, Mar 11, 13,
18, 20, LIF, May 18, HAY, Jul 17, 18, 22, 23, 24, LIF, Sep 23, HAY, Nov 13,
18, GF, Dec 28, 29, 30, 31; 1731: GF, Jan 2, HAY, 4, GF, 4, 5, 6, HAY, 7, GF,
7, 8, HAY, 8, GF, 9, 11, 18, 21, 22, Feb 10, 13, Mar 2, 4, 9, HAY, 17, GF,
25, Apr 5, UM, 19, GF, 23, 29, May 7, 12, 17, 26, DL, Jun 7, GF, 8, DL, Jul
9, TCY, Aug 9, YB, 20, GF, Oct 11, 13, 15, 20, 22, 27, Nov 3, 12, 24, 26, 27,
30; 1732: GF, Jan 7, 8, Feb 10, Mar 18, HAY, Apr 4, GF, 10, LIF, 11, GF, 13,
LIF, 17, GF, May 1, HAY, 8, GF, 12, HAY, 15, WINH, 27, UM, Jun 19, DL, Nov 6,
13, HAY, 29; 1733: GF, Jan 27, Feb 2, Apr 19, DL, May 2, GF, 3, 21, Sep 28,
Oct 1, Nov 10, Dec 15, 20, 21; 1734: GF, Jan 11, 22, 29, Feb 6, Apr 18, CG,
May 8, GF, 10, Sep 18, LIF, Oct 1; 1735: GF, Mar 24, May 6, HAY, Aug 26, GF,
Sep 10, 12, Dec 8, 9, 10; 1736: GF, Feb 4, Mar 20, LIF, Apr 9, 14, GF, 29,
CG, 30, May 4, RI, Aug 14, DL, 26, 31, CG, Sep 20, 29, Nov 9, 23, Dec 13;
1737: CG, Jan 17, LIF, Mar 9, CG, 26, Apr 19, 25, LIF, 29, CG, May 3, 9, 17,
19, LIF, Jul 22, 26, CG, Sep 21, 23, Oct 5, DL, 11, 15, Nov 5, 11; 1738: DL,
Feb 18, Mar 13, May 27; 1739: DL, Jan 27, Feb 3, Mar 20, CG, 27, May 25, 30;
1740: CG, May 9, 19, GF, Nov 1; 1741: CG, May 12, 14, NWC, Aug 22, CG, Nov
30; 1744: HAY, Feb 15, CG, Mar 28, Apr 4, 20; 1745: CG, May 3, JS, Jun 4, GF,
Dec 16, 17, 23, 28; 1746: DL, Jan 3, 4, 6, GF, 6, DL, 7, 8, 9, 23, Feb 7, 20,
Mar 10, NWC, Sep 25, DL, Oct 14, 31, NWC, Dec 22; 1747: SF, Sep 14, CG, Dec
19; 1748: CG, Jan 2, DL, 6, CG, 9, 11, DL, 15, 25, Feb 10, CG, 25, Mar 24,
DL, Apr 15, CG, 28, DL, May 4, CG, Oct 14, 21, 28, Nov 7, 28, Dec 14; 1749:
CG, Jan 5, JS, Mar 15, CG, Apr 20, 25, 28, May 1, Sep 25, SOU, 28, CG, Oct 4,
Nov 1, 8; 1750: JS, Mar 28, CG, May 2, NWSM, Aug 20, CG, Sep 24, Oct 16, 20,
Nov 10; 1751: CG, Jan 14, 31, Apr 18, SF, Sep 16, CG, 23, Oct 9; 1752: CG,
Jan 28, May 2, Oct 6, Dec 18; 1753: CG, Sep 17, Nov 14; 1754: CG, Apr 18, Oct
7, 19; 1755: CG, Apr 15, Sep 29, Nov 12, 22, 24, Dec 3; 1756: CG, Jan 26, Feb
26, Oct 4, 8, DL, Nov 23, 29, Dec 15; 1757: CG, Jan 29, Sep 26, Dec 16; 1758:
CG, Sep 27; 1759: DL, Mar 20, 22, Sep 27, Oct 12; 1762: CG, Apr 26, May 7,
19, DL, 19; 1768: HAY, Aug 19, 22, 29, Sep 9, 15, 19, CG, Nov 26, DL, Dec 21,
23, 31; 1769: DL, Feb 3, CG, 18, DL, 23, CG, Oct 7, 9; 1770: CG, Feb 24, HAY,
Jul 20, 27, Aug 8, 13, Sep 11; 1773: HAY, May 28, Jun 18, Jul 12
--Double Gallant, The; or, The Sick Lady's Cure, 1707: QUEEN'S, Feb 4,
DL/QUEEN, Nov 1, 3, 4, 24; 1708: DL/QUEEN, Feb 16; 1712: DL, Dec 27, 29, 30;
1713: DL, Jan 3, 17, Feb 16, Apr 9, Nov 9; 1714: DL, Jan 13, May 14, Oct 22,
Dec 7; 1715: DL, May 7, Nov 14; 1716: DL, Jan 27, Nov 12; 1717: DL, Nov 27,
Dec 4; 1718: DL, Mar 3, May 22; 1719: DL, Oct 23, Dec 2; 1720: DL, Feb 12,
May 2; 1721: DL, Jan 13, Feb 27, May 1, Nov 28; 1722: DL, Feb 8, 17, Apr 5,
May 4, Oct 16, Dec 27; 1723: DL, Nov 14; 1724: DL, Jan 23, Mar 26, Oct 14,
Dec 2; 1725: DL, Mar 13, Oct 7, Dec 6; 1726: DL, Jan 27, Mar 15, Apr 20, Oct
6; 1727: DL, Feb 7, May 1, Oct 10; 1728: DL, Jan 5, Apr 23, Oct 25; 1729: DL,
Jan 23, Apr 30, Oct 2; 1730: DL, Jan 20, Apr 21; 1731: DL, Feb 19, GF, Mar
22, Apr 23, DL, May 3, Sep 28, Nov 30; 1732: DL, May 2, GF, 4, DL, Nov 24,
GF, 28; 1733: DL, Jan 9, Mar 15, GF, Apr 25, DL, May 1, DL/HAY, Oct 22, GF,
24, DL/HAY, Nov 13; 1734: DL/HAY, Jan 10, GF, May 7, DL, Nov 16, CG/LIF, 21,
Dec 30; 1735: GF, Jan 6, CG/LIF, Feb 14, GF, Mar 15, DL, Apr 19, CG/LIF, 21,
CG, Sep 26, DL, Nov 3, CG, 18, DL, Dec 10; 1736: CG, Feb 10, DL, 24, Apr 26,
CG, Oct 25, DL, Nov 1; 1737: CG, Jan 18, DL, Feb 2, CG, Apr 18, DL, 19, CG,
Oct 28, DL, Nov 11; 1738: CG, Feb 4, Apr 27, Oct 20, Dec 20; 1739: DL, Jan 8,
27, CG, Feb 21, May 11, Sep 22, DL, Oct 11, CG, Dec 20; 1740: CG, Jan 24, DL,
Feb 8, Mar 24, CG, Oct 1, DL, Nov 6, CG, 13, GF, Dec 1, CG, 6; 1741: CG, Feb
19, GF, Apr 14, CG, 20, DL, Dec 7; 1742: CG, Jan 19, DL, Feb 4, CG, Mar 20,
DL, 30, May 7, 8, CG, 14; 1743: CG, Mar 15, Apr 16, Oct 10; 1744: DL, May 1,
CG, 9, Dec 17; 1745: DL, Feb 11, CG, May 8, DL, Oct 15, CG, Dec 10; 1746: CG,
Mar 3, Apr 10, DL, May 14; 1747: CG, Feb 2; 1748: CG, Apr 29; 1749: CG, Apr
11, Nov 17; 1750: CG, May 2, DL, Dec 14, 17; 1751: DL, Feb 21, May 6; 1753:
CG, Feb 7, 9, 16, Mar 6, Apr 10, 26, May 15, Oct 5, DL, Nov 14; 1754: CG, Apr
30; 1755: CG, Dec 4, 9; 1756: CG, May 1, Oct 28, Dec 3; 1757: CG, Oct 20;
1758: CG, May 2; 1759: DL, Oct 11, 13, 18, 20, Dec 29; 1760: DL, May 19;

154

1761: DL, May 18, Oct 27; 1762: DL, Jan 22, Apr 24; 1763: DL, Mar 14, May 7;
1770: DL, Jan 16, Feb 15, Apr 21; 1772: DL, Apr 4, May 22; 1773: DL, Feb 18;
1774: DL, May 19; 1776: CG, Mar 19; 1779: DL, Apr 19; 1780: CG, Mar 18, Apr
19, May 8, Oct 10; 1781: CG, May 11, Sep 28; 1782: DL, Nov 12, Dec 28; 1783:
DL, Apr 7, May 7; 1784: DL, Jan 17, 21, Mar 16, CG, May 8; 1785: DL, Apr 25,
CG, Dec 7; 1786: CG, Sep 29; 1788: DL, Nov 8; 1791: CG, May 11; 1792:
DLKING'S, Apr 10; 1793: CG, Nov 1; 1795: CG, Apr 29; 1797: CG, Apr 8; 1798:
CG, Feb 2, 6
--Lady's Last Stake, The; or, The Wife's Resentment, 1707: QUEEN'S, Dec 13, 15,
16, 17, 19; 1708: DL, Feb 28; 1715: DL, Dec 17, 19; 1716: DL, Apr 7; 1719:
DL, Oct 6; 1720: DL, Mar 10; 1723: DL, Nov 9, 11; 1726: DL, Jan 22, Mar 7;
1730: DL, Oct 3, Nov 21; 1731: DL, Feb 6, Mar 18, May 6, Dec 18; 1732: LIF,
Apr 26; 1739: DL, Mar 13; 1740: DL, Apr 16; 1741: DL, Apr 24; 1742: DL, Apr
22; 1745: CG, Mar 14, 16, 23, 26, Apr 19, Nov 16, Dec 7, 20; 1746: CG, Apr 2,
DL, 10, CG, 30, DL, Dec 11; 1747: DL, Jan 21, CG, May 20; 1748: CG, Mar 24;
1751: DL, May 2; 1756: DL, Mar 27, Apr 30; 1760: DL, Apr 29, May 5; 1761: DL,
Apr 23; 1762: DL, Jan 15, May 5, Dec 10; 1771: DL, Apr 9; 1772: DL, Mar 30,
May 27; 1776: CG, Apr 30; 1778: CG, Mar 14, Apr 2, May 20; 1779: CG, Jan 13;
1786: CG, Mar 4
--Love in a Riddle, 1729: DL, Jan 7, 8
--Love Makes a Man; or, The Fop's Fortune, 1700: DL, Dec 9, 12, 13, 14, 18;
1701: DL, Jan 15, Jun 7, 13; 1702: DL, Oct 26; 1703: DL, Oct 6, Nov 16, Dec
17; 1704: DL, Feb 2, Mar 4, Oct 11, Dec 19; 1705: DL, Nov 2; 1706: DL, Jan
24, Dec 19, 30; 1707: DL, Feb 24, Oct 25, Nov 11; 1708: DL, Feb 4, Oct 12;
1709: DL, Jan 28, May 17, QUEEN'S, Oct 1, Nov 16; 1710: QUEEN'S, Jan 4, Feb
16, Apr 17, GR, Jun 15, DL/QUEEN, Nov 6; 1711: DL/QUEEN, Feb 1, Mar 12, May
11, DL, Oct 4, Dec 17; 1712: DL, May 5, Oct 6; 1713: DL, Mar 10, Nov 18;
1714: DL, Mar 9, Nov 24; 1715: DL, Jan 25, LIF, Apr 21, 30, Sep 29, DL, Nov
2, Dec 20; 1716: LIF, Jan 5, DL, Apr 5, LIF, May 4, DL, Oct 4, LIF, Nov 26;
1717: LIF, Feb 4, DL, 22, LIF, 25, May 30, DL, Jun 6, Oct 9, LIF, Nov 11, DL,
Dec 30; 1718: LIF, Feb 12, May 6, DL, 23, RI, Jul 26, LIF, Oct 6, Nov 20, DL,
22; 1719: DL, Apr 30, LIF, May 19, 29, Oct 10, DL, 27; 1720: LIF, Jan 4, Feb
24, DL, Mar 1, LIF, 29, May 7, DL, 26, CGR, Jun 22, DL, Oct 5, 27, LIF, Nov
29, Dec 28; 1721: LIF, May 11, DL, 31, LIF, Oct 3, DL, Nov 1; 1722: DL, Jan
22, Feb 15, LIF, 27, DL, Apr 12, LIF, 27, May 25, Oct 16, DL, 26; 1723: DL,
May 4, LIF, Oct 18, DL, Nov 15; 1724: LIF, Feb 1, Apr 7, DL, May 7, LIF, 18,
Oct 5, DL, Dec 18; 1725: LIF, May 3, DL, 12, Sep 28, LIF, Nov 23; 1726: LIF,
Feb 28, May 2, DL, Nov 9; 1727: DL, Jan 13, May 17; 1728: DL, Feb 14, LIF,
Mar 28, May 3; 1729: DL, Jan 20, Nov 21, GF, 24, 25, Dec 10; 1730: GF, Jan
12, Mar 5, Apr 9, DL, 30, LIF, May 7, RI, Jul 18, GF, Sep 16, Oct 28, HAY,
Nov 9, 11, LIF, Dec 8; 1731: GF, Jan 2, LIF, 9, GF, Feb 17, Apr 6, LIF, May
6, GF, 7, LIF, Dec 3, GF, 28; 1732: LIF, Feb 7, GF, 12, 14, LIF, Apr 19, GF,
24, SOU, Oct 12, GF, 17, LIF/CG, Nov 7, DL, Dec 1, 2, 14, GF, 18, 19; 1733:
DL, Jan 13, Mar 10, GF, 12, LIF/CG, May 7, DL, 23, RI, Aug 20, DL/HAY, Oct 5,
CG, Nov 26, DL, Dec 11, 31; 1734: GF, Jan 19, CG, Feb 7, GF, Apr 6, CG, May
2, GF, 6, CG/LIF, Sep 20, GF, Nov 6, DL, 20, CG/LIF, Dec 12; 1735: GF, Mar 1,
YB, 21, GF, Apr 22, DL, May 9, CG/LIF, 12, LIF, Aug 29, GF, Oct 6, DL, Nov
19; 1736: DL, Feb 18, CG, Mar 20, DL, May 27, LIF, Nov 6, DL, Dec 17, LIF,
30; 1737: DL, Mar 4, LIF, Apr 28, DL, May 27, Jun 11, Sep 29, Nov 8; 1738:
DL, Jan 3, CG, Apr 7, DL, May 25, CG, Oct 9, Nov 13, Dec 28; 1739: CG, Feb 7,
DL, Mar 10, 19, CG, 26, DL, May 4, CG, 18, Oct 3, DL, 18, 30, CG, Dec 12;
1740: DL, Jan 22, CG, 31, Apr 9, May 16, Oct 6, GF, Nov 18, DL, Dec 6, GF,
17; 1741: GF, Feb 5, CG, 23, Apr 16, GF, 22, DL, May 7, CG, Oct 2, DL, 20,
GF, 28, 29, 30, 31, Nov 3, 5, 28, CG, Dec 4, GF, 7, 9, DL, 11; 1742: GF, Jan
25, 26, CG, 27, GF, Feb 25, DL, Mar 2, GF, 25, DL, 25, CG, May 3, DL, 18, Oct
16, JS, Nov 9, 25, DL, Dec 8; 1743: DL, Jan 25, Apr 27, CG, May 5, DL, Sep
24, Nov 15; 1744: HAY, Nov 5, GF, Dec 18; 1745: CG, Jan 4, GF, 26, CG, Feb
13, GF, Apr 26, CG, May 6, Oct 11, GF, Nov 12, CG, 27; 1746: CG, Jan 20, GF,
29, CG, Apr 8, DL, 19, GF, Nov 28; 1747: CG, Feb 3, GF, Mar 31; 1748: CG, Jan
7, Mar 15, Apr 19, DL, Sep 22, CG, Dec 22; 1749: CG, Apr 12, DL, May 9, Nov
15, CG, Dec 8; 1750: CG, Feb 16; 1751: DL, Jan 5, 8; 1752: DL, Nov 8, CG, 23,
DL, Dec 6, 30; 1753: CG, Jan 25; 1754: CG, May 2, DL, Oct 12; 1755: DL, Jan
21, Dec 5; 1757: DL, May 7, CG, Nov 7; 1758: CG, Jan 18, Apr 27; 1759: CG,
May 7; 1760: CG, Apr 14, May 12; 1761: CG, Apr 27, Nov 6; 1762: CG, May 5,
DL, 7, Oct 28; 1763: CG, Jan 8, 11, 17, 20, Feb 22, Mar 19, Apr 26, May 24,
HAY, Sep 7, CG, 30, Oct 31; 1764: CG, Feb 10, DL, 21, CG, Apr 5, May 16, Sep
28, Dec 19; 1765: CG, Jan 29, May 10, Sep 27, Dec 14; 1766: CG, Mar 8, Apr
29, Oct 8, Nov 26; 1767: CG, Jan 20, Mar 26, May 21; 1768: CG, Dec 16, 28;
1769: CG, Apr 18, May 12, Oct 17; 1771: HAY, Aug 19, Sep 6, CG, Dec 4, 19;
1772: CG, Nov 12; 1774: CG, Dec 12, 30; 1775: CG, May 19; 1776: CG, Apr 19;
1778: CG, Feb 25, May 7, Nov 13, 21; 1779: CG, Nov 25; 1780: CG, Oct 13;
1784: DL, May 10; 1785: CG, May 6; 1786: CG, Jan 3; 1787: CG, Jan 11, 24;

1788: CG, Feb 14, Mar 24, 25, May 31, Dec 30; 1790: CG, Dec 10, 23, 29; 1792: CG, May 5, 12, DL, Oct 4, 6, 11, 24, Nov 8, CG, Dec 5; 1794: CG, May 14; 1795: CG, May 8; 1797: DL, Jun 12, HAY, Jul 10; 1798: DL, Dec 19, 26; 1799: DL, Jan 21, Oct 31, Nov 23, Dec 3; 1800: DL, Jan 6
--Love's Last Shift; or, The Fool in Fashion, 1696: DL, Jan 0, Dec 29; 1701: DL, May 30; 1703: DL, Jun 18, Oct 26, Dec 9; 1704: DL, Jan 11, Apr 1; 1705: DL, Apr 30, Oct 11; 1706: DL, Dec 5; 1707: DL/QUEEN, Oct 18, Nov 7; 1708: DL/QUEEN, Jan 19, DL, Dec 22; 1709: QUEEN'S, Oct 22; 1710: QUEEN'S, Jan 25; 1711: DL, Jan 15, Apr 19; 1712: DL, Feb 8; 1714: DL, Oct 14, Nov 4, 26; 1715: LIF, Apr 23, May 9, DL, 31, LIF, Oct 12, 31, DL, Dec 1; 1716: DL, Feb 2, Apr 12, LIF, May 21, 31, DL, Jun 6, LIF, Oct 4, DL, Nov 2; 1717: DL, Mar 19, Oct 21; 1718: DL, May 15, Nov 24; 1719: DL, Feb 2, May 5, Oct 14; 1720: DL, Mar 7, May 24, Nov 18; 1721: DL, Feb 6, Mar 13, LIF, Apr 27, May 18, DL, 22, LIF, Sep 27, DL, Nov 8, LIF, Dec 1; 1722: DL, Jan 11, Mar 8, LIF, May 10, Oct 11, DL, 31, LIF, Nov 27; 1723: DL, May 6, LIF, 13, DL, Nov 19; 1724: DL, Feb 27, Apr 16, Nov 27; 1725: LIF, Feb 6, Mar 13, DL, 31, May 4, LIF, Oct 23, DL, Nov 22; 1726: LIF, Feb 14, Apr 21, DL, May 4, Nov 2; 1727: DL, Jan 5, May 15; 1728: DL, Jan 3, Mar 28, May 9, Sep 17, Dec 10; 1729: LIF, Apr 10, DL, May 20, Nov 17; 1730: LIF, Apr 6, GF, 15, 25, DL, May 4, Oct 22, Dec 15; 1731: GF, Jan 20, 21, Apr 10, LIF, May 10, RI, Jul 15, LIF, Nov 8; 1732: LIF, Jan 13, Feb 4, Apr 11, RI, Aug 17, LIF/CG, Dec 2; 1733: GF, Mar 28, CG, May 2, GF, 7, Sep 27, CG, Oct 25, Dec 22; 1734: CG, Jan 31, GF, Mar 2, 30, CG, Apr 20, 27, CG/LIF, Sep 25; 1735: CG, Feb 24, CG/LIF, Mar 17, Apr 9, GF, 18, May 2, CG/LIF, Jun 17, CG, Sep 29, Dec 11; 1736: CG, Mar 5, DL, 13, 16, 18, 27, 30, CG, May 10, DL, Jun 23, Sep 11, CG, Oct 13, DL, Dec 13; 1737: DL, Feb 8, Mar 5, Apr 29, LIF, May 4, CG, 16, DL, Sep 6, CG, Oct 17; 1738: CG, Jan 4, DL, Mar 18, CG, May 8, DL, 15, CG, Oct 4, Dec 11; 1739: DL, Jan 22, CG, Feb 6, Apr 3, DL, 12, CG, May 23, DL, Sep 20, CG, Oct 8, Nov 15; 1740: CG, Jan 11, DL, Feb 4, Apr 24, May 5, CG, Oct 22, DL, Nov 14, GF, Dec 6, CG, 22; 1741: CG, Apr 22, GF, 30, DL, May 14, Sep 12, Oct 6, CG, Dec 1; 1742: CG, Feb 26, Apr 20, DL, Sep 28, CG, Oct 16; 1743: CG, Jan 3, Apr 14, DL, May 16; 1744: CG, Jan 4, May 7, DL, Nov 2, 19; 1745: CG, Jan 7, DL, Feb 14, GF, Mar 30, CG, Apr 27, Oct 9, Nov 21, DL, Dec 11; 1746: DL, Apr 17, CG, 24, DL, Dec 29; 1747: CG, Jan 31, May 15; 1748: CG, Jan 2, Feb 2; 1749: CG, Apr 21, DL, Dec 9, 14; 1750: DL, Jan 26, May 8, Sep 13, 15, Dec 17; 1751: DL, Jan 16, 19, Feb 15, May 10, Sep 13, 14, Dec 30; 1752: DL, Mar 2, Apr 30, Dec 18, 21, 22; 1753: DL, Jan 1, 12; 1754: DL, Mar 23, CG, Oct 29; 1756: DL, May 5; 1763: CG, Feb 14, 19, 26, Mar 26, Apr 8, 23, Oct 12, Nov 14; 1764: CG, Feb 14, May 24, Oct 12; 1765: CG, Jan 3, Nov 28; 1766: CG, Feb 22, DL, Apr 25, CG, 26, Oct 14, Nov 29; 1767: CG, May 8; 1772: CG, Jan 15, 17, 22; 1773: CG, Jan 14
--Myrtillo (masque), 1715: DL, Nov 5, 7, 15, 21, 22, 25, Dec 1, 21; 1716: DL, Jan 4, Feb 2, 20; 1730: LIF, Apr 23
--Nonjuror, The, 1717: DL, Dec 6, 7, 9, 10, 11, 12, 13, 14, 16, 17, 18, 19, 20, LIF, 21, DL, 21, 26, 27, LIF, 28; 1718: DL, Jan 1, 16, 17, Feb 7, 17, Mar 10, Apr 16, RI, Aug 18, DL, Oct 18; 1734: HAY, Jun 28, Jul 1; 1741: JS, May 19; 1743: LIF, Feb 9, 10, 28; 1745: CG, Oct 18, 21, DL, 22, CG, 23, DL, 24, CG, 25, DL, 26, 28, CG, 28, DL, 29, 30, CG, 30, DL, 31, CG, Nov 6, DL, 7, 13, Dec 4, 23; 1746: CG, Jan 15, DL, 22, Feb 15, CG, Dec 2; 1747: CG, Jan 19; 1750: CG, Jan 4, 9, Apr 27; 1753: DL, Feb 6, Apr 24, Sep 15, Nov 23; 1754: DL, Feb 12, CG, Oct 21, 22, 23, Nov 19; 1755: CG, Jan 2, 25, Apr 30, Sep 29, Oct 28, Dec 10; 1756: CG, Feb 25, Oct 12, Dec 9; 1757: CG, Jan 22, Oct 27; 1759: CG, Nov 26; 1768: DL, Nov 17; 1771: DL, Nov 27; 1773: CG, Oct 9; 1784: CG, Oct 6; 1785: CG, Oct 29
--Papal Tyranny in the Reign of King John, 1745: CG, Feb 15, 16, 18, 19, 20, DL, 20, CG, 21, 22, 23, 25, 26, Mar 6, Apr 4; 1746: CG, Feb 8
--Perolla and Izadora, 1705: DL, Dec 3, 4, 5, 6, 7, 8; 1706: DL, Jan 2
--Provoked Husband, The; or, A Journey to London, 1728: DL, Jan 10, 11, 12, 13, 15, 16, 17, 18, 19, 20, 22, 23, 24, 25, 26, 27, 29, 31, Feb 1, 2, 3, 5, 6, 7, 8, LIF, 8, DL, 9, 10, 12, 16, 22, 23, 24, Mar 4, 16, Apr 11, 30, May 3, 24, Jun 6, 13, Sep 7, 24, Oct 19, Nov 11; 1729: DL, Jan 18, Mar 20, Apr 15, 26, Sep 11, Oct 18, Dec 6; 1730: DL, Jan 17, GF, Feb 9, 12, DL, 14, GF, 17, Mar 14, 16, DL, 16, GF, Apr 1, DL, 11, GF, Jul 6, RI, 16, GF, Sep 23, Oct 16, Nov 17, HAY, 27, GF, Dec 15, 19; 1731: GF, Jan 12, Feb 10, HAY, 10, GF, Mar 9, HAY, May 7, GF, Oct 13, DL, Nov 1, 2, LIF, 2, DL, 3, LIF, 3, GF, 9, DL, Dec 4, LIF, 22, GF, 29; 1732: DL, Jan 22, GF, Feb 17, Mar 13, LIF, 23, DL, 27, GF, Apr 15, DL, 19, LIF, 21, GF, May 17, DL, Oct 7, LIF/CG, 16, GF, 25, 28, Nov 10, 29, Dec 27; 1733: LIF/CG, Jan 19, GF, Feb 15, 26, DL, Mar 29, LIF/CG, 31, DL, Apr 2, 7, GF, 16, DL, 20, GF, May 16, DL, 25, HAY, 28, CG, Sep 20, GF, 21, DL/HAY, Oct 13, Nov 7, GF, 7, HAY, 19, CG, 22, DL/HAY, Dec 18; 1734: CG, Jan 15, DL, Mar 4, GF, 7, 12, DL/HAY, 23, DL/LIF, Apr 1, GF, May 1, CG, 6, DL/HAY, 22, HAY, Jun 7, 14, 26, Jul 10, LIF, Aug 20, CG/LIF, Oct 16, DL, 21, GF, Nov 12, CG/LIF, Dec 31; 1735: CG/LIF, Jan 13, DL, 25, GF, Feb 17,

CG/LIF, Mar 20, GF, 22, May 6, CG, 6, DL, 23, LIF, Jul 16, GF/HAY, 18, Aug 8,
CG, Sep 17, GF, Nov 3, CG, 24; 1736: CG, Jan 5, Feb 7, GF, 17, CG, Mar 23,
DL, Apr 15, May 18, CG, Jun 8, LIF, 8, HAY, 29, Jul 7, 13, CG, Sep 17, LIF,
Oct 26, CG, Dec 6; 1737: DL, May 5, CG, 9, Oct 3, Nov 16; 1738: CG, Jan 11,
DL, Feb 2, CG, Apr 6, Sep 27, Nov 8, Dec 30; 1739: CG, Mar 20, DL, 27, May 3,
26, CG, Sep 14, Oct 24, Nov 3; 1740: CG, Jan 12, Apr 16, DL, May 6, CG, Sep
22, Oct 28, GF, 31, CG, Dec 12; 1741: CG, Jan 17, DL, Feb 2, 7, CG, Apr 2,
GF, 23, DL, May 28, Sep 15, GF, 25, CG, 28, DL, Oct 31, CG, Nov 19, 20, 21,
Dec 23; 1742: CG, Jan 13, 28, GF, 29, CG, Mar 6, GF, Apr 20, CG, 28, DL, May
17, Oct 27, Nov 8; 1743: CG, Feb 9, Mar 21, LIF, Apr 5, CG, 21, Sep 23, Nov
24; 1744: CG, Jan 31, DL, Mar 12, 17, 28, 30, CG, Apr 10, DL, 16, CG, Sep 21,
DL, Nov 1, 14, Dec 12; 1745: DL, Jan 7, GF, Mar 11, DL, 16, GF, 30, DL, Apr
18, GF, 25, CG, May 10, DL, Jun 5, Sep 21, GF, Nov 4, CG, 8, DL, 19, Dec 16;
1746: CG, Jan 10, GF, 10, DL, 25, CG, Apr 12, DL, May 12, Jun 13, CG, Oct 1,
GF, Nov 18, CG, Dec 3; 1747: DL, Jan 3, 5, 6, 8, 10, 12, 13, 23, 28, 31, Feb
20, GF, 25, DL, 25, Mar 21, Apr 6, 25, May 6, 18, CG, 19, DL, Sep 24, SOU,
Oct 5, DL, 26, Nov 9; 1748: CG, Jan 15, DL, 22, CG, Feb 20, DL, Mar 26, CG,
Apr 12, DL, Oct 1, SOU, 10, CG, Nov 3, DL, 12, CG, 18, Dec 14; 1749: CG, Jan
5, DL, 11, Apr 13, CG, 17, Sep 29, DL, Oct 10, Nov 10, CG, 25, DL, Dec 23;
1750: CG, Jan 11, DL, 22, 23, Feb 13, Apr 17, CG, Oct 27, Nov 20, Dec 31;
1751: CG, Jan 24, Mar 5, Apr 26, DL, May 1, Nov 5, 7, 12, CG, 25, 28, 29, 30,
Dec 2; 1752: CG, Jan 9, DL, Feb 4, CG, Apr 8, DL, May 1, CG, Oct 14, 28, DL,
Dec 19, 27; 1753: CG, Jan 19, Feb 10, DL, Mar 2, CG, Apr 9, DL, 24, CG, May
3, Sep 10, DL, Oct 20, CG, Nov 8, Dec 4; 1754: DL, Jan 19, CG, Apr 27, DL,
May 18, CG, Oct 16, 28, 31, Nov 9; 1755: CG, Jan 13, Feb 17, Apr 7, DL, May
6, CG, 9, HAY, Aug 25, CG, Oct 21, Nov 29; 1756: CG, Jan 29, Mar 29, May 8,
DL, 14, Oct 21, CG, Nov 13, Dec 20; 1757: CG, Feb 18, DL, Apr 2, 14, CG, 15,
May 25, Sep 26, Oct 26; 1758: CG, Jan 14, Apr 5, DL, 18, CG, Oct 24, Nov 25;
1759: CG, Jan 20, Feb 10, DL, Mar 20, CG, Apr 3, DL, 27, CG, May 15, Oct 1,
Nov 24, Dec 22; 1760: CG, Feb 25, May 1, 23, DL, Jun 19, CG, Oct 8, DL, 22,
CG, Dec 1; 1761: CG, Apr 7, Sep 18; 1762: CG, Nov 16, Dec 28; 1763: CG, Oct
24; 1764: DL, Mar 3, 6, 10, Apr 3, May 1, 3, 15, 29, Oct 6, 11, Nov 15, Dec
10; 1765: DL, Feb 5, Mar 12, Apr 19, May 27, CG, Oct 11, DL, 18; 1766: DL,
Apr 15, KING'S, Aug 27, Sep 1, 11; 1767: DL, Feb 9, May 6, 19, HAY, Jul 22,
27, DL, Sep 18, Oct 6, CG, Nov 10; 1768: DL, Jan 2, CG, Apr 7, DL, 9, 30, CG,
May 30, Sep 30, DL, Nov 21; 1769: DL, Jan 4, 13, CG, Feb 13, DL, Apr 8, CG,
14, May 11, DL, Oct 16, Nov 2, CG, 29, DL, Dec 18; 1770: CG, Jan 2, DL, 17,
CG, 31, DL, Feb 27, May 7, 26, CG, Oct 13, DL, 16, Nov 2, CG, Dec 7, 11, 15;
1771: CG, Jan 3, 11, 22, Feb 11, Apr 2, DL, May 7, CG, 15, HAY, Sep 19, CG,
Oct 4, DL, 25, Nov 30; 1772: CG, Jan 14, Nov 14, DL, 28, Dec 19; 1773: CG,
Apr 24, Dec 1, DL, 16; 1774: CG, Jan 4, May 18, DL, Nov 11, CG, 12, DL, Dec
17; 1775: CG, May 6, DL, Oct 26; 1776: CG, Jan 25, Oct 12, Nov 5, CG, 7, 29,
DL, Dec 19; 1777: DL, Mar 20, Apr 5, May 8, 28, HAY, Sep 19; 1778: HAY, Aug
21, 25, 26, 29, Sep 12, 18, CG, 30, Oct 30; 1779: CG, Jan 5, Apr 8, DL, Nov
5; 1780: DL, Jan 20, Apr 15, Oct 26, Dec 9; 1781: CG, Apr 21; 1782: CG, Jan
18, DL, 26, Feb 2, 7, 19, Mar 11, May 30, Sep 18, Nov 9, Dec 13, 30; 1783:
DL, Jan 21; 1784: DL, Feb 3, Sep 18, Oct 29; 1785: DL, Jan 8, May 20, Dec 7;
1786: CG, Feb 4, 8, May 27, DL, Jun 2, HAY, Jul 19, 22, HAMM, 24, HAY, Aug 9,
Sep 5; 1787: CG, Jan 26, Feb 7, 12, DL, May 30, Dec 6; 1788: CG, Jan 11, DL,
16, 23, Oct 20; 1789: DL, May 19, Sep 15, 17; 1790: CG, Dec 17; 1791: CG, Jan
4, 5, 11, 22, 28, Feb 12, Oct 27, DLKING'S, Dec 1, 8, CG, 29; 1792: CG, Sep
21, Dec 8; 1793: CG, Oct 22; 1794: DL, Sep 23, 27, CG, Oct 14, 17, Nov 1;
1795: DL, Jan 23, CG, Apr 27, Oct 15, DL, Dec 2; 1796: DL, Jan 4, Nov 22, Dec
22; 1797: DL, Jan 25, CG, Feb 20, DL, Mar 16; 1798: CG, Sep 28; 1799: HAY,
Jan 28
--Refusal, The; or, The Lady's Philosophy, 1721: DL, Feb 14, 15, 16, 17, 18,
    20; 1746: DL, Nov 28, 29, Dec 1, 3, 4, 6, 8, 19; 1747: DL, Feb 28, Apr 21,
    Sep 19, 29, Oct 1, 28; 1748: DL, Jan 23, Apr 22; 1750: CG, Oct 22, 30, 31,
    Nov 3, 9; 1751: CG, Jan 10, Feb 5, May 11, Oct 19, Dec 20; 1752: CG, Jan 14,
    Mar 21, Apr 25, Nov 3, Dec 5; 1753: CG, Jan 15, May 1, DL, Dec 20; 1757: CG,
    Jan 8, 10, Mar 12, May 2, Oct 31; 1758: CG, Jan 19; 1759: DL, Dec 19, 21, 27;
    1760: DL, Jan 17, 18; 1761: CG, Jan 2, 14, 20, Feb 28, Apr 15, DL, 24; 1763:
    CG, Apr 12; 1766: CG, Apr 2; 1769: CG, Apr 1; 1770: CG, Jan 6, 27; 1772: CG,
    Apr 22; 1775: CG, Oct 24; 1777: CG, Jan 2
--Rival Fools, The; or, Wit at Several Weapons, 1709: DL, Jan 11, 12, 13, 14,
    24; 1722: DL, Jan 4, 5; 1774: HAY, Sep 17
--Rival Queans, The; or, The Life and Death of Alexander the Little (
    burlesque), 1710: QUEEN'S, Jun 29; 1719: LIF, Jun 24, 25; 1738: DL, May 17;
    1765: CG, Apr 19; 1780: CG, Apr 19, 20; 1791: CG, May 2
--School Boy, The; or, The Comical Rivals, 1702: DL, Oct 26; 1703: DG, Apr 30,
    DL, Jul 7; 1704: DL, Feb 16, Mar 28, Oct 4, 27, Dec 4; 1705: DL, Oct 27;
    1710: QUEEN'S, Feb 13, 17, 27, Mar 2, May 16, DL, Dec 4; 1711: DL, Dec 21;

157

1712: DL, Jan 5, May 16, Oct 17, Dec 5; 1713: DL, Oct 28, Nov 6; 1714: DL, Jan 12, Apr 8; 1715: DL, Mar 17, May 10, Oct 27; 1716: DL, May 18; 1717: DL, Jan 4; 1719: DL, Oct 28; 1722: SOU, Sep 25; 1723: HAY, Apr 22, DL, Jul 2, 9, 26; 1724: DL, May 12, 19, Oct 20, Nov 16; 1725: DL, Apr 20; 1727: DL, Apr 29; 1728: HAY, Nov 5, 6; 1729: DL, May 12; 1730: LIF, Mar 31, Apr 7, 9, 11, 14, 16, 18, 30, May 5, Jun 3, 8, Dec 18; 1731: LIF, Mar 25, May 5, 26, Oct 20; 1732: LIF, Apr 12, LIF/CG, Sep 27, Nov 14; 1733: LIF/CG, Feb 5, Apr 16; 1734: CG, May 3, LIF, 23; 1735: CG/LIF, Jan 17, May 9, 13, 16, 27, LIF, Jun 12; 1736: CG, May 1, 13; 1737: CG, Jan 7, 21; 1739: CG, May 11; 1740: CG, Mar 20, DL, Apr 19, CG, May 5, 7, Oct 23, Nov 1, 19; 1741: CG, Oct 27, Nov 2, Dec 11; 1742: CG, Feb 16, GF, 22, 24, 25, 26, CG, Mar 1, GF, 18, CG, Apr 21, GF, 22, JS, May 3, CG, Nov 19, Dec 3, LIF, 22; 1743: DL, Mar 21, 22, Apr 14, CG, May 4, 5, DL, Oct 4, 6, 8, CG, 21, 24, DL, 25, 28, Nov 14, CG, 24, Dec 6; 1744: DL, Apr 2, CG, Oct 5, DL, Nov 24; 1745: CG, Jan 3, JS, Mar 26, CG, Apr 15, May 14, 15, DL, Jun 5, CG, Nov 2, 11; 1746: GF, Feb 27, Mar 4, CG, May 2, Oct 3, GF, Dec 2, 3, 4, 8, 11, 12, 18, JS, 29, GF, 31; 1747: GF, Feb 3, 12, 13, DL, Mar 30; 1748: DL, Apr 14, Oct 8, 26, Nov 3, Dec 6, 20; 1750: HAY, Mar 15, DL, Apr 19; 1754: CG, Oct 15, 16, 22, Nov 4, 23, Dec 30; 1755: CG, Apr 17, 18, May 9, Oct 27, Dec 16; 1756: CG, Feb 12, Mar 2, Nov 17; 1757: CG, Mar 31, DL, May 27, CG, 27; 1758: CG, Feb 21, May 4, Dec 9, 16; 1759: CG, Jan 2, Feb 26, Oct 22, 29, Nov 14; 1761: CG, May 11; 1763: DL, Mar 26; 1767: HAY, Aug 7, 17, 24, 31; 1768: HAY, Jul 25, 29; 1774: DL, Mar 22; 1785: DL, Mar 30
--She Would and She Would Not; or, The Kind Impostor, 1702: DL, Nov 26; 1707: DL, Mar 25, Apr 29; 1714: DL, Apr 10, 13, 15, 21, May 10, Jun 9, Sep 30, Nov 8; 1715: DL, Jan 13, Mar 29, May 20, Oct 24; 1716: DL, Jan 23, Nov 26; 1717: DL, Nov 11; 1719: DL, Mar 31, Apr 25; 1720: DL, Feb 5, May 16, CGR, Jun 22, DL, Oct 3, Nov 25; 1721: DL, May 17; 1722: DL, Apr 10, Oct 30; 1723: DL, Feb 11; 1726: DL, Mar 17; 1727: DL, May 5; 1728: DL, Mar 19, 23, May 10, 22, Nov 7; 1729: DL, Nov 14; 1731: LIF, Nov 25, 27, 29, 30, DL, Dec 3, GF, 21, 22; 1732: DL, Jan 5, LIF, Feb 22, GF, Apr 10, LIF, May 5, LIF/CG, Oct 23; 1733: LIF/CG, Feb 1, Apr 30, Jun 1, CG, Oct 19, Dec 6; 1734: CG, Feb 22, Apr 30; 1735: CG/LIF, Feb 4, LIF, Apr 16, CG, Oct 24, Dec 22; 1736: CG, May 18; 1737: CG, Jan 17, HAY, Mar 2, CG, Oct 12; 1738: CG, Apr 26, Oct 26, DL, Nov 14, 15, 16, 28; 1739: DL, May 11, Nov 16; 1740: DL, Feb 1, CG, May 2; 1742: CG, Feb 3, 6, Mar 22, Apr 30, May 17; 1743: HAY, Apr 25, CG, Nov 16, Dec 6; 1744: CG, May 4, Oct 3; 1745: CG, Nov 14; 1746: GF, Jan 6, 7, CG, 8, Feb 11, Mar 18, Apr 29, Oct 10; 1747: CG, Jan 15, Feb 4, Apr 24; 1748: DL, Jan 18, 19, Feb 9, Apr 12, Sep 17; 1749: CG, Apr 19, DL, 28; 1750: CG, Dec 10, 12, 14, 19; 1751: CG, May 4; 1752: CG, Jan 3, 20, May 2, Oct 19, Nov 25; 1753: CG, Jan 18, May 17, Oct 1, Nov 13, Dec 29; 1754: CG, Apr 16, Oct 7, Dec 17; 1755: CG, Feb 10, Nov 21; 1756: CG, May 18; 1757: CG, Oct 22, 24, 25, Nov 29; 1758: HAY, Jan 12, 16, CG, 17; 1759: CG, Jan 4, Dec 17; 1763: CG, Mar 21, Apr 20, Oct 21, Dec 6; 1764: CG, Feb 7, Oct 10, DL, 22, 30, Dec 20; 1765: CG, Jan 18, May 8, Dec 3; 1766: CG, Mar 6, Apr 24, Oct 16, Dec 11; 1767: CG, Jan 27, May 22; 1768: CG, May 11, Sep 23, Oct 11; 1769: CG, Jan 4, Oct 3; 1770: CG, Feb 7; 1772: CG, Feb 22, Mar 3, Dec 22; 1773: CG, Jan 5; 1774: CG, Jan 15, May 19, Nov 3; 1775: CG, Jan 5, 19, Apr 17, 27, DL, Nov 23, Dec 22; 1776: DL, May 15; 1778: CG, Feb 6, 11, 18, Sep 18; 1782: DL, Jan 22, 24; 1783: KING'S, Mar 13, CG, Sep 26, Oct 1; 1784: CG, Jan 6, May 25; 1786: CG, Jan 14, DL, Mar 20, 27, Apr 3, 19, 28, May 2, Oct 10; 1787: DL, Jan 1, 12, 31, Feb 15, Mar 1, 26, Apr 27, May 22, Oct 22, 24; 1788: DL, Apr 11, Oct 22, Dec 31; 1789: DL, Jan 21, Feb 26, Mar 16, Apr 30, Jun 5; 1790: DL, Feb 18, Apr 6, 12, May 5, CG, Jul 16, DL, Oct 25, Nov 25, Dec 28; 1791: DL, Mar 2, May 6, HAY, Jul 26, DLKING'S, Oct 20, Nov 1, Dec 26; 1792: DLKING'S, Mar 12, Apr 26, May 29, Jun 5; 1793: DL, Mar 7, May 6; 1794: HAY, Aug 13; 1795: DL, Apr 22, May 26, Nov 7, Dec 17; 1796: DL, Feb 22, Mar 7, 30, May 26; 1797: DL, May 24, Jun 1, Sep 28; 1799: DL, Feb 9, Apr 19; 1800: DL, Apr 18, 28, May 15, Jun 3
--Venus and Adonis (masque), 1715: DL, Mar 12, 15, 22, 24, 29, 31, Apr 7, 18, 28, May 6, 23, Oct 20, 29, Nov 1, 10, 17, 18, Dec 8, 15, 26, 27; 1716: DL, Jan 6, 19, Apr 3, May 2; 1718: LIF, Nov 18, 20, 22, 29, Dec 2, 6, 22, 27, 31; 1719: LIF, Jan 5, 14, Feb 17, Mar 7; 1725: LIF, Mar 15, Apr 2, 12; 1730: LIF, Mar 16; 1748: CG, Mar 21, Apr 15
--Woman's Wit; or, The Lady in Fashion, 1697: DL, Jan 0
--Xerxes, 1699: LIF, Feb 0
--Ximena; or, The Heroic Daughter, 1699: DL, Dec 0; 1700: DL, Dec 13; 1702: DL, Nov 26; 1712: DL, Nov 28, 29, Dec 1, 2, 3, 4; 1713: DL, Jan 15, Mar 2; 1718: DL, Oct 31, Nov 1, 3, 11; 1772: CG, Mar 21
Cibber, Jane, Mrs Theophilus (actor, singer), 1725: DL, Sep 16, Oct 2, 7, 16, 23, Nov 2, 8, Dec 9; 1726: DL, Jan 11, 22, Feb 2, Mar 17, Apr 15, Sep 6, 13, 15, Oct 6, 13, 27, Nov 26, Dec 3; 1727: DL, Feb 10, 23, Apr 19, 22, 24, May 5, 8, Sep 26, Oct 23, Nov 1, 9, 18, 22, Dec 9; 1728: DL, Jan 5, 10, Apr 1, 2, 11, 13, May 10, 20, 23, Sep 7, 12, 19, Oct 15, 22, 25, Nov 7; 1729: DL, Jan

1, 2, 7, 13, 20, 22, 24, 25, 29, Feb 15, 17, 24, 25, Apr 15, 16, May 1, 8,
14, Jun 13, 27, Sep 11, 13, Oct 2, 9, 30, Nov 3, 4, 7, 8, 12, 14, 18, 19, 21,
22, Dec 1, 5, 8, 13, 20; 1730: DL, Jan 19, 21, 26, Feb 28, Mar 19, 21, Apr
14, 20, May 1, 11, Sep 17, 26, Oct 3, 8, 20, 28, Nov 18, 25, 26, 30, Dec 2,
4; 1731: DL, Jan 20, 27, Feb 8, Apr 5, 8, May 3, 13, 31, Jun 11, 22, Jul 20,
Sep 21, 25, 28, 30, Oct 16, 19, Nov 1, 5, 9, 24, Dec 2, 3, 7, 10, 16, 18, 21,
22, 29; 1732: DL, Jan 10, Feb 2, 10, 14, Mar 14, 23, Apr 13, 28, Sep 23, 30,
Oct 5, 28, Nov 14, 18, 24, Dec 11, 14; 1733: DL, Jan 25; 1739: CG, Aug 2;
1742: DL, Apr 28
Cibber, Jenny (actor), 1741: DL, Dec 19; 1742: DL, Mar 20, Apr 28, May 31, Oct
5, 7, 13, 16, Dec 7, LIF, 27; 1743: LIF, Mar 14; 1744: HAY, Aug 28, Sep 5,
11, 22, 27, 29, Oct 4, 11, 18, 20, Nov 8, Dec 17, 26; 1745: CG, Feb 15; 1750:
DL, Oct 18, 19, 23
Cibber, Jenny and Betty (beneficiaries), 1739: CG, Aug 2
Cibber, Katherine, Mrs Colley (actor), 1693: NONE, Sep 0; 1694: DL, Feb 0, DG,
May 0, NONE, Sep 0; 1695: DL, Dec 0; 1696: DL, Jan 0, Mar 0; 1697: DL, Jan 0,
NONE, Sep 0, DL, 0
Cibber, Susannah Maria, Mrs Theophilus (actor, singer, author), 1734: DL/HAY,
Apr 26, DL, 29, DL/HAY, May 3, DL, 13, Oct 5, 25, Dec 12; 1735: DL, Nov 12;
1736: DL, Jan 12, Feb 9, Mar 13, 23, Apr 13, Aug 26, Sep 11, Oct 5, Nov 22;
1737: DL, Jan 14, Mar 7, 10, 14, 15, 22, Apr 20, Sep 1, 6, 8, 17, Oct 6, 19,
Nov 1, 4, 12; 1738: DL, Jan 11, Mar 4, 16, 21, Apr 6, 12; 1742: CG, Sep 22,
29, Oct 1, 4, 6, 11, 13, 15, 16, 21, Nov 3, 13, 15, 25, 29, Dec 15; 1743: CG,
Jan 5, Feb 18, 23, Mar 14, 23, DL, Oct 15; 1744: CG, Feb 24, KING'S, Jun 9,
DL, Oct 17, 20, 23, 25, 27, Nov 2, KING'S, 3, DL, 5, 6; 1745: KING'S, Jan 5,
9, 12, DL, 14, Feb 6, 13, 14, 20, KING'S, Mar 1, DL, 7, 16, 18, Sep 26, 28,
Oct 24, Dec 9, CG, 9, 14, 21; 1746: DL, Jan 20, Apr 10, 12, CG, Nov 11, 14,
17, 19, 28, Dec 1, 4, 5, DL, 5, CG, 11, 17; 1747: CG, Jan 2, 12, 20, Feb 10,
11, 26, 28, Mar 7, 19, DL, 19, CG, 31, Apr 4, 9, 21, 27, DL, Oct 20, 22, 30,
Nov 4, 7, 10, 13, 18, Dec 11, 12; 1748: DL, Jan 2, 20, Feb 1, 13, 16, Mar 5,
7, 10, Oct 4, 6, 8, 11, 15, 18, 22, Nov 2, 4, 8, 11, 29, Dec 10; 1749: DL,
Jan 9, 20, Feb 1, 6, Mar 7, 29, Apr 5, 8, 14, May 16, Sep 16, CG, Oct 4, DL,
5; 1750: DL, Sep 8, CG, 28, DL, Oct 1, 2, 12, CG, 17, 19, 23, 25, 26, Nov 1,
Dec 1, 7, 13, 18, 19; 1751: CG, Jan 19, Feb 16, 23, 26, DL, Mar 16, CG, 16,
May 2, 10, DL, Oct 7, CG, 7, 9, 11, 17, 21, 23, 25, 26, Nov 4, 18, 25, 28,
Dec 2, 5, 16, DL, 30; 1752: CG, Jan 18, Feb 8, Mar 2, 7, 17, 18, 20, 23, Apr
15, 24, Oct 21, 24, 27, 30, 31, Nov 4, 10, 22, 28, Dec 9, 12, 21; 1753: CG,
Jan 8, Feb 21, Mar 10, 20, 26, Apr 9, 27, DL, Oct 2, 4, CG, 10, DL, 12, 16,
25, 30, 31, CG, Nov 1, DL, 15, 26, Dec 1, 22; 1754: DL, Jan 23, Feb 25, Mar
16, 23, 25, Oct 5, 11, 16, 21, 29, Nov 6, 7, 30, Dec 4, 17; 1755: DL, Jan 17,
22, Feb 22, CG, Mar 6, DL, 11, CG, 12, DL, 14, 15, 17, 18, 20, Apr 8, May 23,
Sep 27, Oct 4, 8, 13, 24, 27, 31, Nov 6, 17, Dec 13, 23; 1756: DL, Jan 7, 10,
12, 21, Feb 10, 12, 14, 27, Mar 22, 25, Apr 6, 8, 28, Nov 11, 16, 19, 23, 24,
Dec 7, 9, 17; 1757: DL, Jan 18, 19, 24, 27, Feb 28, Mar 3, 21, 24, Apr 21,
26, May 3, 6, Sep 22, 24, Oct 1, 6, 11, 12, 25, Nov 1, 10, 15, Dec 2, 3, 5,
22; 1758: DL, Feb 13, 18, 21, 25, Mar 7, 11, 14, 30, Apr 7, 25, Jun 1, Oct
10, 13, 14, 25, Nov 2, 3, 8, 15, 18; 1759: DL, Jan 20, Feb 1, 23, Mar 3, 19,
24, Apr 3, 17, May 31, Oct 2, 11, 17, 24, 26, Nov 3, 10, 24, 27, Dec 1, 20;
1760: DL, Feb 21, 23, Mar 4, 17, 22, Apr 10, 11, 14, May 10, 27, Dec 30;
1761: DL, Jan 2, 8, 10, 23, Feb 5, Mar 9, 23, 28, Apr 20, May 28, Jun 3, Sep
8, 10, 15, 18, 23, 29, Oct 7, 17, 27, Nov 21, Dec 17, 23; 1762: DL, Jan 27,
Feb 10, Mar 18, Sep 28, 29, Oct 6, 9, 12, 16, 20, Nov 1, 2, 17, 19, 27; 1763:
DL, Jan 11, 19, Mar 14, 15, 19, 21, Apr 29, May 6; 1764: DL, Oct 23, 26, 31,
Nov 8, 17, Dec 8, 12, 13, 19; 1765: DL, Jan 2, 14, 23, Feb 6, Mar 7, 11, CG,
26, DL, 29, Apr 25, Dec 2, 5, 13; 1766: DL, Jan 30, Feb 6, Mar 11
--Oracle, The, 1752: CG, Feb 8, Mar 17, 18, 20, 23, Apr 6, 10, 17, 20; 1753:
CG, Mar 10, 17, 20, DL, 24, CG, 29, May 2, DL, 7; 1754: DL, May 10; 1755: DL,
Dec 18, 20, 30; 1756: DL, Jan 7, 13, May 6, 14, 17, Sep 25; 1757: DL, May 6;
1758: DL, May 12, 16, 18, Jun 22, Dec 7; 1759: DL, Feb 2, Mar 1; 1765: CG,
Mar 26, May 3; 1795: WLWS, Jun 19
Cibber, Theophilus (actor, author), 1720: DL, Dec 17; 1721: DL, May 20; 1722:
DL, May 14, Sep 15, Oct 13, Dec 11; 1723: DL, Jan 7, 9, May 16, Jun 12, Jul
5, Aug 12, 16, Sep 14, 28, Oct 2, 3, 10, 16, 24, Nov 16; 1724: DL, Apr 29,
Sep 24, 29, Nov 21, 27, Dec 7, 9; 1725: DL, Jan 4, Feb 20, Mar 15, Apr 22,
28, 30, May 11, BF, Aug 23, DL, Sep 11, 14, 16, 25, Oct 27, Nov 2, 22, Dec
22; 1726: DL, Feb 11, 21, Mar 17, Apr 15, May 7, 23, Jun 3, Sep 13, 17, 29,
Oct 1, 13, 20, Nov 2, 12, Dec 20, 30; 1727: DL, Jan 20, 27, Feb 21, 27, Apr
8, 19, May 5, 15, Sep 16, 23, 30, Oct 5, 6, 12, Nov 14, 18, Dec 5, 13; 1728:
DL, Mar 9, 28, Apr 11, May 10, 17, 20, 23, 29, 31, Sep 14, 17, 19, 21, Oct 3,
18, 21, 30, Nov 7; 1729: DL, Jan 11, Feb 3, 15, 24, Mar 15, 17, 27, 29, Apr
15, 23, May 3, 6, 7, 12, 14, Jun 13, 20, 27, Jul 25, Aug 5, 9, Sep 23, 30,
Oct 22, 27, 31, Nov 5, 8, 14, 17, 27, Dec 2, 3, 5, 8, 13; 1730: DL, Jan 24,

Mar 30, Apr 20, May 11, Sep 12, 17, 19, 29, Oct 1, 3, 8, 20, 22, 28, Nov 16,
18, 25, 26, 28, 30, Dec 1, 2, 4, 30; 1731: DL, Jan 11, 20, Mar 15, 16, Apr 1,
5, 21, 24, 29, May 1, 4, 7, 8, 10, 17, 18, 19, Jun 11, 22, Jul 20, 23, Aug 6,
11, 18, Sep 18, 23, 25, 28, 30, Oct 7, 9, 14, 16, 19, 21, 30, Nov 5, 6, 8, 9,
15, 22, 24, 25, Dec 2, 3, 7, 10, 18; 1732: DL, Jan 1, 5, 10, 15, 20, Feb 1,
3, 10, 14, Mar 14, 20, 21, 23, 30, Apr 17, 25, 27, 28, May 3, 4, 5, 9, 12,
Jun 1, 9, 23, Jul 28, Aug 4, 21, 22, Sep 8, 19, 23, 28, 30, Oct 3, 5, 10, 12,
17, 19, 26, 28, 31, Nov 4, 7, 9, 11, 13, 14, 18, Dec 4, 11; 1733: DL, Jan 19,
Feb 17, 26, Mar 5, 10, 12, 26, 28, 31, Apr 13, 19, 23, 24, 30, May 1, 3, 7,
9, KING'S, Jun 2, DL, 4, 9, BFCGBH, Aug 23, Sep 4, RI, Sep 10, DL/HAY, 26,
Oct 5, 6, 10, 12, 13, 17, 20, 22, 27, Nov 1, 5, 10, 12, 14, 23, 28, Dec 5,
17, 20, 22, HAY, 26; 1734: DL/HAY, Jan 12, 17, HAY, Feb 12, DL/HAY, Mar 12,
23, 25, 30, Apr 1, 2, 17, 18, 20, DL, 22, DL/HAY, 26, DL, 29, DL/HAY, May 1,
4, DL, 13, 15, LIF, 23, 29, RI, Sep 2, DL, 7, 10, 14, 19, 24, 28, Oct 5, 8,
14, 17, 19, 21, 24, 25, 26, 29, Nov 1, 4, 8, 16, 18, 20, 22, 25, Dec 6, 12,
14, 19; 1735: DL, Jan 11, 13, 20, 23, 28, Feb 4, 10, 24, Mar 6, 10, 17, 22,
29, Apr 11, 14, 23, 25, 28, May 13, 14, Jun 3, Jul 1, GF/HAY, 15, LIF, Aug 1,
GF/HAY, 8, DL, Sep 1, 4, 6, 9, 15, 20, 23, 27, Oct 11, 21, 23, 24, 25, 27,
28, 30, Nov 1, 3, 4, 6, 7, 12, 15, 19, 20, 21, 24, Dec 6, 26; 1736: DL, Jan
3, 12, 27, Feb 5, 9, 20, Mar 11, 13, 18, 23, 27, 30, LIF, Apr 14, DL, 15, 29,
30, May 4, 18, 25, 26, Aug 26, Sep 4, 7, 9, 11, 18, 21, 23, 28, Oct 5, 7, 9,
12, 13, 16, 19, 22, 23, 27, 30, Nov 1, 4, 6, 12, 15, 20, 22, Dec 14, 17, 20,
21; 1737: DL, Jan 6, 10, 14, 17, 26, 29, Feb 5, 19, 28, Mar 1, 7, 10, 19, 21,
22, Apr 12, 15, 20, 23, 27, May 7, Aug 30, Sep 3, 6, 8, 13, 27, 29, Oct 1, 8,
11, 13, 20, 21, 24, 27, 31, Nov 1, 11, 12, 15, 16; 1738: DL, Jan 5, 11, 14,
19, 26, Feb 16, 23, 28, Mar 2, 4, 16, 21, Apr 6, 17, May 6, Sep 9, 12, 14,
16, 19, 21, 23, 26, 28, 30, Oct 3, 12, 13, 17, 18; 1739: DL, Jan 4, 8, 9, 11,
12, 15, 16, 18, 19, 22, 26, 31, Feb 1, 3, 12, 23, Mar 8, 10, 13, 20, 26, May
17, CG, Aug 2, 10, 21, 31, Sep 5, 7, 12, 14, 19, 22, 25, 28, Oct 1, 2, 3, 8,
10, Nov 2, 3, 5, 6, 9, 10, 20, Dec 1, 6; 1740: CG, Jan 17, Feb 7, Mar 10, 11,
18, 20, 25, Apr 29, May 5, 12, 23, 27, Jun 5, Sep 15, 19, 22, 24, 29, Oct 1,
6, 22, 23, 25, 27, Nov 1, 4, 6, Dec 6, 10, 18, 29; 1741: CG, Jan 12, 14, Feb
14, Mar 2, 9, 16, 30, Apr 3, 18, 22, 23, 24, May 1, 11, DL, Sep 5, 8, 12, Oct
6, 8, 15, 20, 21, Nov 4, 16, 21, Dec 3, 7, 8, 12, 19; 1742: DL, Jan 4, 14,
22, 26, Feb 5, 12, 13, 24, Mar 8, 9, 20, 22, 27, 29, 30, Apr 5, 28, LIF, Nov
24, 29, Dec 1, 3, 6, 13, 22, 27, 28, 30; 1743: LIF, Jan 10, Feb 2, 9, 11, 17,
28, Mar 14, 22, 24, Apr 8, 9, 11, DL, May 6, Oct 4, 18, Nov 12, 15, 22, 23,
Dec 1, 12, 16; 1744: DL, Feb 4, 6, Mar 12, 28, Apr 23, May 11, HAY, Aug 28,
Sep 11, 22, 25, 27, 29, Oct 4, 11, 16, 18, 20, 22, Nov 8, 10, DL, 19, HAY,
Dec 17; 1745: CG, Jan 2, 4, 7, 18, 23, Feb 1, 9, 15, 18, DL, 20, CG, Mar 14,
18, 21, Apr 1, 2, 4, 17, 20, 25, Nov 9, 12, 16, 18, 21, 22, 23, 25, 27, 28,
Dec 2, 5, 6, 10, 13; 1746: CG, Jan 2, 13, 25, Feb 6, 8, Mar 10, 18, DL, 31,
Apr 2, 7, 10, May 2, Jun 6, 9, Aug 4, 6, Sep 25, 27, Oct 2, 25, 27, Nov 5,
22, CG, 24, DL, 28, Dec 11, 20, 29; 1747: DL, Jan 2, 15, Feb 18, Mar 23, CG,
Nov 11, 13, 16, DL, 17, CG, 18, 24, 25, Dec 9, 15, 17; 1748: CG, Jan 2, 7, 8,
9, 14, 15, 16, 19, 29, Feb 5, Mar 8, 14, 24, 28, Apr 11, 13, 14, 21, 26, 28,
29, Sep 21, 23, 30, DL, Dec 10, CG, 22; 1749: CG, Jan 2, 3, 25, Feb 6, Mar 2,
4, 9, 29, Apr 5, 7, 10, 11, 15, 17, 18, 19, 21, 25, May 4; 1750: DL, Sep 25,
Oct 1; 1752: DL, Feb 17; 1753: DL, Feb 6; 1754: CG, Feb 12, DL, Jul 2, CG,
Oct 22, 29, Nov 1, 2, 6, Dec 30; 1755: CG, Jan 7, DL, Mar 22, CG, Apr 2, 4,
HAY, Aug 21, 25, 28, Sep 1, 4, 9, 11, 15; 1756: HAY, Jan 14, 19, LRRH, 28, ,
Feb 4, LRRH/PCR, 11, NWGF, Mar 18, DL, Apr 26, ACAD, Dec 15; 1757: CG, May
25, HAY, Jun 15, Jul 5, Aug 11, 22, 31, Sep 2, 8, 13, 14, 23, 28, Oct 3, 12,
Dec 24; 1758: HAY, Jan 12, 16, 18, 25, Mar 6, CG, Jul 6, DL, Oct 27
--Apollo and Daphne (entertainment), 1723: DL, Aug 12, 13, 14
--Comical Humours of Sir John Falstaff, Justice Shallow, Ancient Pistol, and
    Others, 1733: BFCGBH, Sep 4
--Damon and Daphne, 1733: DL, May 7
--Dissertation, A (lecture), 1756: HAY, Jan 14, 19, LRRH, 28, 31, Feb 4,
    LRRH/PCR, 18, PCR, 21, LRRH/PCR, 25, NWGF, Mar 08
--Harlot's Progress, The; or, The Ridotto Al'Fresco, 1733: DL, Mar 31, Apr 3,
    5, 7, 10, 12, 14, 17, 20, 21, 26, 28, May 4, 8, 11, 16, 17, 25, 28, TC, Jul
    30, BFCGBH, Aug 23, Sep 4, SF, 10, MEG, 28, DL, Oct 24, 26, 27, 29, Nov 2, 5,
    6, 9, 26, 27, 28, 29, 30, Dec 3, 8, 13, 14, 17, 21; 1734: DL, Jan 1, 4, 10,
    18, 19, 23, 28, Mar 4, DL/HAY, Apr 26, 30, May 2, 17, DL, Oct 21, 22, 23, 25,
    26; 1735: DL, Nov 15, 21; 1736: DL, Sep 7, 9, 11, 14, 16, 25, Oct 12; 1737:
    DL, Apr 29, Oct 27, 28, 29, 31, Nov 1, 2, 3, 7, 8; 1738: DL, Jan 12, May 8,
    Sep 23, 26, 28, 30, Oct 21, 23, 25, 26, Dec 8, 9, 11, 15; 1739: DL, Feb 5, 6,
    26, Apr 28, Sep 26, 29, Oct 1, 2, 4, 15, Nov 19, Dec 11, 19, 20, 26, 29;
    1741: DL, Oct 31, Nov 4, 5; 1742: DL, Feb 16; 1743: TCY, Aug 4; 1744: DL, Apr
    6; 1746: GF, May 1, SOU, Oct 16, 29; 1749: BF/SFP, Aug 23, 24, 25, 26, Sep 7,
    8, 9, 11, 12

--Historical Tragedy of the Civil War, An, 1723: DL, Jul 5
--Humourists, The, 1754: DL, Jul 2
--Lover, The, 1731: DL, Jan 20, 21, 22, 23, 25, 26, 28, 29, Apr 5
--Patie and Peggy; or, The Fair Foundling, 1730: DL, Apr 20, Nov 25, 26, 30,
    Dec 2; 1731: DL, Apr 23, May 31; 1735: GF, Nov 26
Cibber's Academy, 1744: HAY, Nov 1, 5
Cibber's Histrionic Academy, 1756: ACAD, Dec 15
Cibber's scholars (actors), 1756: ACAD, Dec 15
Cicero's Head (print shop), 1738: CG, Aug 22; 1756: DL, Jan 23
Cicilia and Clarinda. See Killigrew, Thomas.
Cicisbea alla Moda, La. See Galuppi, Baldassare.
Cid, Il. See Sacchini, Antonio Maria Gasparo.
Cid, Le. See Corneille, Pierre.
Cieco Amor (song), 1714: QUEEN'S, May 1
Ciface. See Grossi, Giovanni Francesco.
Cifeccio. See Grossi, Giovanni Francesco.
Cifra, La. See Salieri, Antonio.
Cimadoro, Giambattista (composer, pianist), 1795: KING'S, May 14; 1797: KING'S,
    Jun 8; 1800: CG, Mar 7
--Ati e Cibele (masque), 1795: KING'S, May 14
--Pimmaglione (opera), 1797: KING'S, Jun 8
Cimarosa, Domenico (composer), 1785: KING'S, Jan 25; 1787: KING'S, Jan 9; 1788:
    KING'S, Jan 15, May 8, CG, Dec 13; 1789: KING'S, Mar 24, CG, Nov 24; 1790:
    HAY, Jan 7, CG, May 6, Oct 19; 1791: CG, Oct 3; 1792: HAY, Feb 14, DLKING'S,
    May 23; 1793: KING'S, Mar 19; 1794: KING'S, Jan 11, Mar 1, May 15; 1795:
    KING'S, Feb 27; 1796: KING'S, Feb 16; 1798: KING'S, Apr 10; 1799: KING'S, Apr
    9
--Capriccio Drammatico, Il (opera), 1794: KING'S, Mar 1, 8, 18, 22, 25, 29, Apr
    1, 29; 1798: KING'S, Apr 10, 14, May 1, 15, 22, Jul 10; 1800: KING'S, May 13,
    17, 20, 29, 30, Jun 3, 10, 19, Jul 1, 8, 15, 22
--Giannina e Bernardone (opera), 1787: KING'S, Jan 9, 13, 16, 20, 23, 27, Feb
    3, 27, Mar 13
--Locandiera, La (L'Italiana in Londra) (opera), 1788: KING'S, Jan 15, 19, 22,
    26, 29, Feb 12, 19
--Matrimonio Segreto, Il (opera), 1794: KING'S, Jan 11, 14, 18, 21, 25, 28;
    1798: KING'S, Apr 21, 24, 28, May 1, 15, 22, Jul 10; 1799: KING'S, Apr 6, 9,
    13, 18, 20
--Ninetta; o, Chi dell' Altrui si veste, presto si spoglia (opera), 1790: HAY,
    Jan 7, 9, 12, 16, 19, 23, 26, 29, Feb 23, Mar 16, May 20
--Olimpiade, L' (opera), 1783: KING'S, Mar 6, 15, Apr 10, May 1, 8, 31, Jun 6,
    28; 1788: KING'S, May 8, 13, 17, 20, 24, 29, Jun 7, 14, 17, 21; 1789: KING'S,
    Apr 2, 4, 14, 18, 25, 28, 30, May 5, 7, 19, 26
--Pittore Parigino, Il (opera), 1785: KING'S, Jan 25, Feb 1, 8, 15, Mar 8, 15,
    May 10
--Traci Amanti, I (opera), 1796: KING'S, Feb 16, 20, 23, 27, Mar 1, 8, 29
--Trame Deluse, Le (opera), 1792: HAY, Feb 14, 16, 18, 21, 25, Apr 21, May 5
--Villana Riconosciuta, La (opera), 1789: KING'S, Mar 24, 31, May 5
Cimene. See Bertoni, Fernando Giuseppe.
Cinna. See Bianchi Jr, Francesco.
Cinna; ou, La Clemence d'Auguste (opera, anon), 1722: HAY, Feb 22
Cinna's Conspiracy (play, anon), 1713: DL, Feb 19, 21, 23
Cinthia and Endimion. See D'Urfey, Thomas.
Cintio (beneficiary), 1727: KING'S, Mar 2
Ciperini (singer), 1759: BFS, Sep 3
Ciprandi, Ercole (singer), 1754: KING'S, Nov 9; 1755: KING'S, Mar 17; 1764:
    KING'S, Nov 24; 1765: KING'S, Jan 26, Mar 28; 1766: KING'S, Jan 25, Apr 10
Cipriani, Giovanni Battista (scene painter), 1772: CG, Jan 4, 20, Dec 1; 1779:
    CG, Nov 30; 1781: CG, May 1, 7, Dec 26; 1782: CG, Oct 10; 1783: CG, Sep 22
Cipriani, Lorenzo Angelo (singer), 1791: PAN, Mar 1, Jun 16, Dec 17; 1792: HAY,
    Feb 14, 28, Mar 31, Apr 12, May 15; 1795: KING'S, Jan 10, 27, Feb 7, CG, Apr
    6, KING'S, 14, May 26
Circe. See Davenant, Charles.
Ciro Riconosciuto, Il. See Cocchi, Gioacchino.
Cirri, Giovanni Battista (composer), 1764: CG, Jun 5; 1770: KING'S, Feb 2, Jun
    12; 1771: KING'S, Mar 21; 1772: CG, Mar 20, HAY, 23, CG, 25, Apr 3, 8; 1774:
    DL, Feb 23, HAY, 23, Mar 9
Cistre (music), 1788: KING'S, May 22
Cities Loyalty Display'd, The (pamphlet), 1661: NONE, Apr 22
Citizen, The. See Murphy, Arthur.
City Apprentice Turn'd Beau, The; or, Love in a Hamper (farce), 1731: HAY, Jun
    2
City Association, The; or, The National Spirit Rous'd (play, anon), 1780: HAY,

161

City Bride, The. See Harris, Joseph.
City Heiress, The. See Behn, Aphra.
City Lady, The. See Dilke, Thomas.
City Madam, The. See Massinger, Phillip.
City Market, 1663: BF, Aug 25
City Marshall, 1762: BFY, Sep 3
City Match, The. See Mayne, Jasper.
City Music, 1659: NONE, Dec 18
City Night-Cap, The. See Davenport, Robert.
City Nymphs, The. See Steele, Sir Richard.
City Politiques, The. See Crowne, John.
City Ramble, The; or, A Playhouse Wedding. See Settle, Elkanah.
City Ramble, The; or, The Humours of the Counter. See Knipe, Captain Charles.
City Revels (dance), 1750: DL, Oct 29
City Road, 1771: DL, Dec 17; 1773: CG, Dec 18; 1782: DL, Dec 19
City Wit, The. See Brome, Sir Richard.
City Wives' Confederacy, The. See Vanbrugh, Sir John.
Civil War of England, 1773: HAY, Aug 13
Cizo (singer), 1790: DL, Feb 24, Mar 10, 17
Clagget (Clogget), Walter (musician, composer), 1760: HAY, Sep 8; 1761: HAY,
    Feb 26; 1768: DL, May 30; 1787: CG, Dec 26
Clairon, Mme (actor), 1760: DL, Mar 17
Clamakin (Clamchin), Mrs (dancer), 1730: LIF, Dec 15; 1731: LIF, Apr 22
Clancy, Dr (blind beneficiary), 1744: DL, Apr 2
Clandestine Marriage, The. See Garrick, David.
Clanfield (pyrotechnist), 1773: DL, Nov 19; 1776: DL, May 20
Clapham, Mrs (actor), 1786: HAY, Mar 6
Clapham, 1746: SOU, Nov 3
Clapton, 1722: CLA, May 4
Claracilla. See Killigrew, Thomas.
Clare Court, 1778: DL, May 4; 1782: CG, Apr 27
Clare Market, 1724: BT, Jan 29; 1737: CG, Mar 10, DL, 29; 1739: DL, May 1;
    1746: DL, Mar 1; 1778: HAY, Mar 24, Apr 29, Aug 21; 1782: DL, May 8; 1785:
    HAY, Mar 15; 1790: DL, May 27; 1791: DL, May 20; 1792: DLKING'S, Jun 7
Clare St, 1737: CG, Mar 10, DL, 29; 1741: DL, Apr 17; 1790: DL, May 27; 1791:
    DL, May 20
Clare's Academy, 1726: CLAR, Nov 14
Claremont, William (actor), 1793: CG, Sep 18, 23, Oct 2, 7, 10, 25, 31, Nov 14,
    18, Dec 18; 1794: CG, Mar 11, 25, 27, Apr 10, 24, 29, May 19, 22, 31, Jun 2,
    4, 5, Sep 15, 17, 19, 29, Oct 6, 7, 8, 15, 20, 23, 30, Nov 8, 12; 1795: CG,
    Feb 21, Mar 16, 28, Apr 23, 29, May 6, 7, 14, 25, Jun 3, 4, 10, Sep 14, 21,
    Oct 2, 16, 19, 22, 23, Nov 6, 7, 27, Dec 7, 9, 23, 26, 30; 1796: CG, Jan 2,
    8, 13, Mar 15, 30, Apr 5, 19, 22, May 3, 12, 20, 23, Sep 12, 19, 23, 26, 30,
    Oct 20, 24, Nov 5, 19, 21, 24, Dec 17, 19, 31; 1797: CG, Jan 2, 10, Feb 18,
    23, Apr 8, May 6, 9, 11, 16, 18, Jun 10, Sep 18, 20, 25, 29, Oct 2, 6, 11,
    12, 20, 24, 25, Nov 1, 2, 3, 7, 10, 13, 15, 20, Dec 19, 27, 28; 1798: CG, Jan
    5, Feb 9, 12, 14, 20, Mar 31, Apr 11, May 23, 24, 29, 30, Sep 17, 26, 28, Oct
    5, 8, 30, 31, Nov 1, 5, 9, 10, 12, Dec 18, 26; 1799: CG, Jan 3, 25, 29, Mar
    16, 25, Apr 2, 5, 6, 9, 12, 26, May 4, 6, 13, 15, 16, 17, 24, 28, Jun 1, 7,
    Sep 18, 20, 23, 27, Oct 2, 4, 7, 11, 14, 16, 18, 21, 24, 25, 29, Nov 7, 8, 9,
    11, 14, 30, Dec 2, 9, 10, 23, 30; 1800: CG, Jan 8, 11, 13, 16, 20, 21, 27,
    29, Feb 5, Mar 27, Apr 5, 30, May 1, 2, 13, 17, 23, 27, 29, 30, Jun 2, 7, 12
Clarence, William, Duke of, 1791: HAY, Mar 7; 1794: DL, Jul 2; 1797: HAY, May
    10, KING'S, 18, CG, Jun 14, DL, Oct 27; 1799: HAY, Jan 24; 1800: CG, Jun 12
Clarendon, Earl of. See Hyde, Edward.
Clarendon, Miss (actor), 1742: JS, Nov 8
Clarendon's Warehouse, 1751: DL, Mar 16
Clarges, Sir Thomas (author), 1664: ATCOURT, Jan 0
Claridge, John (lobby doorkeeper, supernumerary), 1767: CG, May 9; 1768: CG,
    Jun 3, 4; 1769: CG, May 19, 22; 1770: CG, May 18, 21; 1771: CG, May 27, Nov
    13; 1772: CG, Jan 2, Mar 9, 26, May 29, 30, Nov 3; 1773: CG, May 22; 1774:
    CG, May 7; 1775: CG, May 30; 1776: CG, May 21; 1777: CG, May 23; 1778: CG,
    May 21; 1779: CG, May 15; 1780: CG, May 24; 1781: CG, May 25; 1782: CG, May
    28; 1783: CG, May 31; 1784: CG, May 22; 1786: CG, Jun 2; 1787: CG, May 31;
    1788: CG, May 24; 1789: CG, Jun 16; 1790: CG, Jun 12
Clarinet (music), 1737: SH, Mar 11; 1762: RANELAGH, Jun 16; 1792: CG, Mar 14
Clarinet and Bassoon Concertante (music), 1784: HAY, Aug 5
Clarinet and French Horn Concerto (music), 1760: HAY, Feb 15
Clarinet Concerto (music), 1727: YB, Apr 26; 1751: HAY, Dec 30; 1752: CT/HAY,
    Jan 7; 1773: HAY, Feb 26, Mar 3, 5, 17, 24, 26; 1774: KING'S, Feb 10, PANT,
    Apr 4; 1775: HAY, Feb 16, Mar 9; 1783: DL, Mar 21; 1784: DL, Mar 19, HAY, Aug

3; 1797: CG, Mar 17; 1799: CG, May 18; 1800: CG, Apr 2
Clark (actor), 1731: SF/BFMMO, Sep 8
Clark (singer), 1792: CG, Feb 28; 1793: KING/HAY, Mar 13, 15; 1799: DL, Feb 4,
   Mar 2, Apr 16, 23, 29, May 24, Dec 11, 28; 1800: DL, Apr 29, May 3
Clark, Blanchville, 1773: CG, Apr 19
Clark, Master (dancer), 1730: SFOF, Sep 9
Clark, Misses (actor, singer), 1736: CG, Apr 6, HAY, Jun 29, Jul 7, SF, Sep 7;
   1737: CG, Apr 26; 1742: JS, Nov 8; 1743: BFGA, Aug 23
Clark, Mrs (house servant), 1789: CG, Jun 6
Clark, Thomas (actor) 1674: DL, May 16; 1675: DL, Apr 30, Aug 0, NONE, Sep 0;
   1676: DL, Jan 29, Dec 11; 1677: DL, Mar 0, 17, May 5, Oct 0, Dec 12; 1678:
   DL, Feb 0, Mar 0; 1680: DL, Feb 0, Mar 0; 1681: DL, May 0, Oct 0; 1682: DL,
   Feb 4, Mar 11, Nov 16; 1691: NONE, Sep 0
Clark's School, 1698: CLARK'S, Apr 1
Clarke (actor), 1743: DL, Jan 27, Feb 2, SF, Sep 8; 1744: HAY, May 10; 1750:
   SFYW, Sep 7
Clarke (actor), 1778: HAY, Dec 28; 1779: HAY, Feb 22; 1786: HAMM, Jun 5; 1788:
   HAY, Aug 5; 1790: HAY, Sep 29
Clarke (beneficiary), 1725: LIF, May 22; 1726: LIF, May 26
Clarke (beneficiary), 1787: CG, May 19; 1788: CG, May 31; 1790: CG, Jun 8;
   1794: CG, Jun 16; 1795: CG, Jun 4; 1796: CG, Jun 4; 1797: CG, Jun 21
Clarke (dancer) 1772: HAY, Dec 21
Clarke (dancer), 1704: LIF, Jun 8
Clarke (dancer), 1726: LIF, Jul 19, DL, Oct 1, Nov 2, Dec 30; 1727: DL, Feb 27,
   Apr 13, Oct 6, Nov 14; 1728: DL, Mar 19
Clarke (house servant), 1760: CG, May 19; 1761: CG, May 15
Clarke (singer), 1729: DL, Mar 26, Jun 20, Jul 29
Clarke (upholsterer), 1747: DL, Mar 17; 1748: DL, Mar 26; 1749: DL, Mar 30;
   1750: CG, Mar 31
Clarke, C (publisher), 1794: KING'S, Jan 11, Feb 1, Mar 1, 18, Apr 26, May 17,
   29, Jun 5, Dec 6; 1795: KING'S, Jan 10, Feb 7, Mar 21, May 14; 1796: KING'S,
   Jan 5; 1798: KING'S, Apr 10; 1799: KING'S, Mar 26, Jun 25; 1800: KING'S, May
   13
Clarke, Jeremiah (actor), 1677: DG, Feb 12; 1696: DG, Jun 0; 1697: DG, Jun 0,
   SH, Nov 22, HIC, Dec 9, YB, 16; 1698: DL/ORDG, Nov 0; 1703: LIF, Dec 21;
   1705: DL, Jun 26; 1706: YB, Dec 20; 1710: DL, May 26
Clarke, John Woodruffe (actor), 1797: CG, Sep 18, 25, 27, Oct 2, 4, 6, 11, 12,
   13, 23, 24, 26, 31, Nov 1, 2, 3, 8, 13, 15, 18, 20, 21, 22, DL, 25, CG, 29,
   Dec 5, 8, 18; 1798: CG, Jan 4, 5, Feb 9, 13, 20, Mar 17, 20, 22, 31, Apr 10,
   11, 13, 18, 19, 20, 23, 27, 28, May 7, 10, 15, 23, 24, 28, 30, Jun 5, 7, 11,
   Sep 17, 21, 26, 28, Oct 1, 3, 5, 8, 15, 31, Nov 1, 6, 7, 10, 12, 17, 22, Dec
   11, 22, 26; 1799: CG, Jan 5, 14, 17, 28, Mar 5, 25, Apr 5, 12, 16, 19, May 3,
   4, 6, 15, 22, CG, 25, 31, Jun 1, 8, 12, HAY, 17, 18, 19, 20, 21, 22, 24, 25,
   28, 29, Jul 2, 12, 20, 23, 26, 27, Aug 6, 10, 21, 26, 28, Sep 16, DL, 17, 19,
   24, 26, 28, Oct 1, 14, Nov 14, 20, Dec 17, 26; 1800: DL, Jan 1, 2, 24, Feb 4,
   7, 14, Mar 4, 11, 13, 27, Apr 14, 15, 17, May 13, 30, Jun 7, CG, 13, DL, 16
Clarke, Mary Anne (actor), 1792: HAY, Feb 20
Clarke, Master (dancer), 1781: HAY, Aug 8; 1783: HAY, Jun 5, Jul 4
Clarke, Master (singer), 1785: DL, Apr 18; 1786: DL, Apr 4; 1787: DL, Feb 1,
   Apr 9, Nov 5
Clarke, Matthew (actor) 1755: CG, Oct 30, Nov 1, 26, 29, Dec 10, 15; 1756: CG,
   Feb 5, 19, Mar 23, Apr 29, Nov 1, 17; 1757: CG, Feb 9, 19, Apr 25, Oct 14,
   19, Nov 18, 23; 1758: HAY, Jan 12, 18, CG, 27, Feb 1, Mar 11, Apr 3, 10, 14,
   Sep 20, 27, Oct 4, 6, 14, Nov 13, 16, 18, 23, Dec 2; 1759: CG, Jan 11, Feb 1,
   15, Mar 22, Apr 18, 20, DL, May 31, CG, Sep 24, Oct 3, Nov 28, 30, Dec 7, 14,
   15, 27, 28; 1760: CG, Jan 14, 18, Feb 14, Mar 6, 20, 24, Apr 9, 18, May 7,
   Sep 22, Oct 10, 13, 20, 23, Nov 18, Dec 2, 9, 11, 31; 1761: CG, Jan 6, 7, 10,
   Mar 3, 5, 30, Apr 2, 6, 21, 30, May 21, Sep 11, 14, 16, 21, 26, 28, 30, Oct
   2, 3, 6, 14, 21, 23, 26, Nov 9, 13, Dec 11, 28, 30; 1762: CG, Feb 3, 15, Mar
   2, 13, 20, 23, Apr 13, 26, Sep 29, Oct 2, 5, 6, 8, 9, 11, 16, Nov 1, 8, 15,
   16, Dec 27; 1763: CG, Jan 14, Feb 14, Apr 13, 15, May 9, Sep 19, Oct 3, 8,
   11, 12, 17, 19, 24, 26, Nov 15, Dec 26; 1764: CG, Jan 9, 14, 28, Feb 9, 13,
   15, Mar 27, Apr 10, 12, May 7, 9, 11, 21, Sep 17, 24, Oct 1, 3, 8, 12, 15,
   16, 18, 22, 26, 29, Nov 7, 30, Dec 7, 21; 1765: CG, Feb 15, 18, Mar 26, Apr
   9, 11, 12, Sep 23, Oct 3, 5, 9, 11, 14, 16; 1766: CG, Jan 31, Feb 5, 10, 15,
   22, 27, Mar 4, 10, 15, 17, 20, 31, Apr 1, 11, May 6, 13, 16, Sep 22, 26, Oct
   6, 14, 31, Nov 10, 19, 21, 22, 27, 28, Dec 4, 6, 10, 27; 1767: CG, Jan 1, 6,
   29, Feb 14, Mar 2, 23, 28, 31, Apr 6, 11, 22, 24, 25, May 11, Sep 14, 19, 21,
   22, 23, Oct 6, 16, 19, 29, 30, Nov 7, 10, 18, 23, Dec 5, 26, 28; 1768: CG,
   Jan 20, 25, 29, Feb 20, 23, Mar 17, Apr 13, 18, 20, 21, Sep 20, 22, 27, 28,
   30, Oct 5, 17, 26, Nov 4, 17, 24, Dec 3; 1769: CG, Feb 18, Mar 13, 28, 29,
   Apr 4, 6, 12, May 3, 5, Sep 22, Oct 4, 24, 26, Nov 1, 29, Dec 1, 2, 19; 1770:

CG, Jan 11, 19, 26, 31, Feb 2, 3, 12, 16, 24, Mar 24, 27, 29, Apr 19, 25, 28,
30, May 8, 22, Sep 26, 28, Oct 5, 8, 11, 13, 16, 19, 23, 25, 29, Nov 1, 29,
Dec 4, 12, 15; 1771: CG, Jan 12, 26, 28, Mar 12, Apr 3, 5, 8, 9, 24, Oct 4,
9, 11, 15, 18, 19, 22, Nov 5, 11, 26, Dec 11, 21, 30; 1772: CG, Jan 1, 15,
27, Mar 21, DL, 23, CG, 24, 30, Apr 6, 7, 21, May 4, 8, 11, Sep 28, Oct 5,
Nov 6, 21, Dec 3, 14; 1773: CG, Jan 6, 7, 14, 16, 25, Mar 22, 30, Apr 3, 16,
17, 27, 28, May 1, 3, 4, 22, Oct 4, 5, 8, 11, 15, 21, 23, Nov 12, 18, 27, Dec
1, 4, 9, 11, 21, 27; 1774: CG, Jan 3, 10, 13, 26, Feb 11, 26, Mar 14, 15, 21,
Apr 11, 19, May 18, Sep 19, Oct 3, 4, 7, 11, 13, 17, 24, 25, 29, Nov 12, 14,
19, 24, 25, Dec 2, 9, 17, 27; 1775: CG, Jan 3, Feb 24, Mar 18, 20, Apr 1, 8,
19, 22, May 17, 18, 20, Sep 20, 22, 25, Oct 6, 19, 21, 28, 30, Nov 9, 13, 14,
24, Dec 1, 2, 8, 16, 29; 1776: CG, Jan 1, 5, Feb 9, 22, 27, Mar 5, Apr 9, 15,
May 8, 10, 13, Oct 7, 8, 17, 29, 31, Nov 1, 4, 7, 11, 12, 25, 26, 28, Dec 2,
5, 6, 17, 18, 26; 1777: CG, Jan 7, 17, Feb 5, Apr 7, 8, 14, May 5, Sep 29,
Oct 6, 8, 16, Nov 13, 27, Dec 3; 1778: CG, Jan 20, Feb 28, Mar 2, 7, 30, Apr
4, 7, 11, 22, May 5, 6, 11, Sep 21, 23, 28, 30, Oct 5, 12, 16, 24, 26, 28,
31, Nov 10, Dec 3, 8, 11, 26; 1779: CG, Jan 11, 14, Feb 2, 22, 23, Mar 9, 22,
Apr 13, May 6, Sep 20, 24, 27, Oct 1, 4, 11, 13, 18, 23, Nov 1, 6, 8, 11, 19,
22, Dec 1, 9; 1780: CG, Jan 12, 17, Apr 12, 27, May 3, 24, Jun 1, Sep 18, Oct
2, 4, 6, 9, 11, 18, 23, 26, 30, Nov 2, 24, 25, 27, Dec 27; 1781: CG, Jan 31,
Feb 15, Apr 23, May 10, Sep 24, Oct 5, 23, 31, Nov 8, Dec 10, 11, 17, 20;
1782: CG, Jan 4, 7, 18, 22, Feb 4, 5, Mar 19, Apr 16, DL, 17, CG, 20, May 2,
20, Sep 27, Oct 7, 14, 19, 23, 29, Nov 1, 18, 27, 30, Dec 2, 12, 27, 30, 31;
1783: CG, Jan 1, 27, Mar 29, 31, Apr 5, 25, May 2, Sep 22, Oct 3, 6, 9, 13,
17, 20, Nov 8, 10, Dec 5, 11; 1784: CG, Jan 16, DL, 22, CG, 29, 31, Feb 5,
13, 23, Mar 1, 20, 22, Apr 21, May 17, 26, Sep 17, 20, 29, Oct 1, 4, 11, 18,
25, 28, 30, Nov 10, Dec 13; 1785: CG, Jan 14, 19, Feb 4, 14, Apr 8, May 4, 7,
HAY, Jul 13, CG, Sep 21, 23, 26, 28; 1786: CG, May 6
Clarke, Miss (actor), 1785: HAY, Jan 31, Apr 25
Clarke, Miss (house servant), 1798: DL, Jun 11; 1799: DL, May 22
Clarke, Miss (singer), 1744: MFDSB, May 1
Clarke, Mr and Mrs (actor), 1731: YB, Aug 20
Clarke, Mrs (actor), 1786: HAMM, Jun 28, Jul 7, 10, 19, 24, 26
Clarke, Mrs (actor, singer), 1727: LIF, Oct 17; 1728: LIF, Jan 29, Apr 6, HAY,
May 8, LIF, 23; 1729: HAY, Jan 2, Feb 25, May 26, 29, Jun 14, Jul 26, BFR,
Aug 25, BFB, 25, GF, Nov 5, 11, HAY, 12, GF, 17, 20, 24, Dec 20; 1730: HAY,
Mar 11, 12, Apr 8, 20, 30, May 1, LIF, 23, BFR, Aug 22, Sep 4, SFP, 9, SF,
14, HAY, Oct 21, Nov 16, Dec 28; 1731: HAY, Mar 10, Apr 22, YB, Aug 20; 1732:
HAY, Mar 8, 17, 23, BFMMO, Aug 23; 1733: BFMMO, Aug 23, DL/HAY, Oct 19, Nov
24, 26, Dec 27; 1734: DL/HAY, Feb 22, BFFO, Aug 24; 1735: TC, May 28; 1744:
HAY, Sep 29, Oct 11; 1746: JS, Dec 29; 1747: HAY, Mar 24, SF, Sep 24
Clarke, Mrs (actor, singer, dancer), 1695: DL, Sep 0; 1703: LIF, Jun 11; 1704:
LIF, Mar 23, Jul 4, Aug 9; 1705: LIF, Jan 25; 1715: LIF, Jun 23; 1722: HAY,
Jun 28; 1723: BUH, Jan 11
Clarke, Nathaniel (actor, dancer), 1728: LIF, Jan 29, DL, May 20, LIF, Jun 25,
Jul 2, HAY, Aug 9, BFHM, 24, LIF, Dec 28; 1729: LIF, Apr 23, 30, May 6, 7,
12, DL, Jun 20, BF, Aug 26, LIF, Sep 19, Dec 27; 1730: LIF, May 15, 20, 23,
Oct 7, 23; 1731: LIF, Jan 8, 13, May 21, YB, Aug 20, SOU, Sep 28, LIF, Oct
13, Dec 8; 1732: LIF, Feb 21, LIF/CG, Sep 25, CG/LIF, Dec 16; 1733: LIF/CG,
Jan 18, Mar 30, CG, May 1, CG/LIF, 28, CG, Jul 6, 27, Aug 2, 14, BFMMO, 23,
CG, Dec 1; 1734: CG, Mar 28, BFHBH, Aug 24, BFRLCH, 24, Sep 2, CG/LIF, 27,
Nov 21; 1735: CG/LIF, Mar 11, TC, May 28, CG, Sep 26, Oct 1, 13; 1736: CG,
Mar 18, 27, LIF, Apr 16, CG, May 17, BFHC, Aug 23, CG, Oct 25; 1737: CG, Feb
26, Mar 15, 24, May 13, LIF, Aug 2, CG, Sep 16; 1738: CG, Feb 4, Mar 25, May
3, Jun 30, Jul 11, Aug 29, Oct 20, Nov 29; 1739: CG, Feb 10, May 7, 11, Aug
2, 21, Sep 5, 22, 28, Oct 22, 25; 1740: CG, Jan 15, Mar 11, Apr 21, 28, May
9, 29, Oct 1, Nov 1, Dec 29; 1741: CG, Jan 27, Feb 7, 19, Mar 5, 7, Apr 3,
11, 30, May 4, 12, Sep 25, Oct 13; 1742: CG, Jan 2, Feb 22, May 5
Clarke, W (publisher), 1788: DL, Mar 29
Clarkson (actor), 1750: HAY, Jul 26
Clarkson (pit office keeper), 1723: LIF, Jun 3; 1724: LIF, May 22; 1725: LIF,
May 10
Clary, Mme (dancer), 1757: HAY, Dec 26
Clatterbane (musician), 1774: HAY, Mar 15
Clauchette, La (dance), 1772: KING'S, Jun 11, 20
Claudio (musician), 1714: HIC, May 5; 1715: GRT, May 17; 1716: LIF, Jan 27;
1718: HIC, Mar 19, LIF, Nov 6, 27; 1723: DL, Mar 20; 1724: HIC, Apr 20; 1729:
HIC, Feb 18; see also Rogier, Claudio
Claudio (violinist), 1758: CHAPEL, Apr 27
Clauigney (actor), 1721: HAY, Apr 28
Clauigney, Mrs (actor), 1721: HAY, Apr 28
Clavigo. See Goethe, Johann Wolfgang von.

Claxton (dancer), 1703: DL, Feb 3, 12, DG, Apr 30, DL, Jun 16, 18, Oct 9, Dec
    27, 31; 1704: DL, Jan 11, Oct 20; 1705: DL, Jan 8, Dec 17; 1706: DL, Jan 21;
    1707: YB, Nov 19
Claxton Jr (composer), 1707: YB, Nov 19
Clay (cabinet maker), 1777: HAY, Sep 18
Clayton, Master (dancer), 1763: HAY, Aug 5
Clayton, Mrs (spectator), 1716: DL, Apr 9
Clayton, Sir Robert (Lord Mayor), 1679: CITY, Oct 29
Clayton, Thomas (composer), 1705: DL, Jan 16; 1707: DL, Feb 1, Mar 4; 1710: YB,
    May 3; 1711: YB, May 24, Jul 16, QUEEN'S, Dec 26; 1712: DL, Jan 18; 1716:
    HIC, Dec 13; 1718: LIF, Nov 15
--Arsinoe (opera), 1705: DL, Jan 16, 25, Feb 1, SJP, 6, DL, Mar 5, 8, 13, 20,
    27, Apr 12, 19, May 12, 31, Jun 7, 21, 28, Jul 10, Oct 27, Nov 17, 19, 27,
    30, Dec 11, 18; 1706: DL, Jan 23, Feb 14, 21, 28, Mar 9, Jun 14, 25, 28, DG,
    Jul 9, Aug 8; 1707: DL, Feb 18, 22, Mar 1; 1710: YB, May 3; 1711: YB, May 24;
    1716: HIC, Dec 13
Clayton, William (musician), 1675: ATCOURT, Feb 15
Clear Stage and no Favour, A; or, Tragedy and Comedy at War (poem), 1742: DL,
    Dec 1
Clear, Richard (carver), 1659: CITY, Oct 29; 1660: CITY, Oct 29; 1662: THAMES,
    Aug 23
Cleartes (opera), 1716: KING'S, Apr 18, 21, 25, 28, May 5, 12, Jun 6, 13, 30,
    Dec 8, 15, 22; 1717: KING'S, Mar 30, Jun 1
Cleater, Mrs (dresser), 1746: CG, Nov 19
Cleavely, Price (singer), 1732: CR, Feb 23
Cleaver, Mrs (householder), 1799: HAY, Apr 17
Clegg, John (musician), 1723: HAY, May 24; 1724: LIF, Apr 13, HAY, May 8; 1735:
    HIC, Apr 17; 1736: ST, Feb 11, LIF, Mar 8; 1737: ST, Mar 8; 1741: HAY, Feb 3,
    KING'S, Mar 14
Cleland, Miss (actor), 1781: CG, Dec 26; 1782: CG, Jan 1, Sep 27, Oct 16, 22,
    Dec 20, 30; 1783: CG, Jan 1, Feb 19, Mar 31; see also Buttery, Miss
Clement, Franz (violinist), 1791: DL, Mar 11, 23, 30, Apr 6, 13, 15, KING'S,
    May 19
Clement's Inn, 1722: MBS, Mar 26; 1740: DL, Feb 18; 1770: CG, Oct 23; 1786: DL,
    May 22; 1797: CG, May 17, HAY, Aug 8; 1798: CG, Apr 20, DL, May 15, 23, HAY,
    Aug 14, 16; 1799: CG, Apr 16, DL, May 4; 1800: CG, Apr 22, DL, May 29
Clementi, Muzio (pianist, composer), 1784: KING'S, Mar 4; 1789: KING'S, Jun 11;
    1790: CG, Feb 24; 1793: CG, May 21; 1795: HAY, Mar 4
Clementina. See Kelly, Hugh.
Clementina, Sga (singer), 1763: DL, Apr 27; see also Cremonini, Clementina
Clementine (singer), 1699: DL, Apr 15, LIF, May 0
Clemenza di Scipione, La. See Bach, Johann Christian.
Clemenza di Tito, La. See Cocchi, Gioacchino.
Clench. See Clinch.
Clendining, Elizabeth, Mrs William (actor, singer), 1792: CG, Nov 3, 27, Dec
    13, 22; 1793: CG, Jan 9, 25, Feb 25, Mar 13, 20, 23, Apr 4, 11, 15, 17, 25,
    May 1, 4, 6, 11, 15, 16, 24, Sep 16, 18, 23, 30, Oct 5, 7, 8, 9, 15, 24, 29,
    Nov 5, 22; 1794: CG, Feb 3, 22, Mar 6, Apr 29, May 23, 26, Jun 3, Sep 15, 22,
    26, 29, Oct 1, 7, 20, 21, 29, Nov 22, Dec 30; 1795: CG, Jan 2, 29, Mar 17,
    19, Apr 6, 8, 9, 23, 24, May 6, 14, 21, Jun 6, 10, Sep 21, 28, Oct 7, 8, 14,
    15, 19, Nov 27, 30, Dec 7, 21; 1796: CG, Jan 4, 13, Mar 14, 15, Apr 5, 9, 12,
    15, 22, May 10, 11, 16, 18, 23, 24, Sep 12, 14, 19, 23, 26, Oct 6, 7, 20, 24,
    Nov 5; 1797: CG, Jan 7, 10, Feb 18, Apr 19, 25, 26, May 11, 17, 18, 23, 24,
    Jun 8, Sep 25, 29, Oct 2, 4, 11, Nov 2, 10, 18, 24, Dec 16, 26; 1798: CG, Jan
    1, Feb 12, Apr 9, 10, 16, May 1, 24, Jun 6
Clendining, Miss (actor), 1798: CG, May 24
Cleomenes, The Spartan Hero. See Dryden, John.
Cleone. See Dodsley, Robert.
Cleonice (opera), 1763: KING'S, Nov 26, 29, Dec 3, 6, 10
Cleonice, Princess of Bithynia. See Hoole, John.
Cleora. See Aston, Anthony.
Clerici, Roberto (scene painter), 1716: KING'S, May 15; 1719: KING'S, Mar 21;
    1720: KING'S, Apr 2
Clerk. See Clarke.
Clerk, Miss (actor), 1787: HAY, Mar 12
Clerke. See Clarke.
Clerke, Dr (spectator), 1662: LIF, Oct 18; 1663: ATCOURT, Feb 23; 1667: NONE,
    Feb 13
Clerke, Mrs (spectator), 1664: BRIDGES, Aug 18
Clerkenwell Charity School, 1712: CLKCS, Feb 6
Clerkenwell, 1661: REDBULL, Mar 23; 1711: CLK, Feb 6; 1741: NWC, Aug 22; 1743:
    LIF, Apr 7; 1744: DL, May 11; 1746: NWC, Sep 15; 1748: NWC, Nov 21, Dec 26,

29; <u>1749</u>: NWC, Nov 27; <u>1751</u>: NWC, Dec 26
Cleveland (dancer), <u>1728</u>: HAY, Oct 15
Cleveland, Thomas (actor), <u>1792</u>: HAY, Aug 6, 9
Cliefden, <u>1743</u>: NONE, Jul 13; <u>1745</u>: DL, Mar 20; <u>1751</u>: DL, Feb 23, Mar 8
Cliff, Mrs (householder), <u>1745</u>: GF, Feb 26
Clifford (actor), <u>1781</u>: CII, Mar 27, 30, Apr 5, 9
Clifford, Henry (actor), <u>1796</u>: HAY, Feb 22, Mar 28
Clifford, Mrs (actor), <u>1779</u>: HAY, Mar 15; <u>1781</u>: CII, Mar 27, Apr 5, 9
Clifford, Mrs (spectator), <u>1661</u>: VERE, Oct 9
Clifford's Inn, <u>1723</u>: BHT, Dec 23; <u>1798</u>: CG, May 22; <u>1799</u>: CG, May 25; <u>1800</u>:
  CG, May 30
Climsani, Sidi Mahomet. See Chinsani, Sidi Mahomet.
Clinch (Clench, Clynch) (entertainer), <u>1699</u>: DLLIF, Sep 12; <u>1702</u>: DL, Aug 22;
  <u>1703</u>: DL, Jun 18; <u>1704</u>: DL, Jun 5, 7; <u>1710</u>: DL, May 26
Clinch, Lawrence (actor), <u>1772</u>: DL, Oct 16, 17, 28, 29, 31, Nov 21, Dec 26;
  <u>1773</u>: DL, Jan 16, 27, Feb 27, Apr 28, Nov 13; <u>1774</u>: DL, Mar 26, Apr 23, May
  27, CG, Oct 1, 4, 11, 20, 22, 31, Dec 26; <u>1775</u>: CG, Jan 7, 28, May 2, Jun 1,
  Sep 25, Oct 13, 17, 25, 28, Nov 1, 4, 13, 17, Dec 1; <u>1776</u>: CG, Jan 1, Apr 22;
  <u>1782</u>: HAY, Sep 21
Clinford (actor), <u>1792</u>: HAY, Oct 15
Clingo (pit doorkeeper), <u>1760</u>: CG, May 19, Sep 22; <u>1761</u>: CG, May 15; <u>1763</u>: CG,
  May 26
Clinton, Master (dancer), <u>1763</u>: HAY, Aug 11, 15, 22, 24, Sep 3, 5, 7, DL, Oct
  14, Nov 10, 23, 26; <u>1764</u>: DL, Jan 13, Feb 24, May 23, HAY, Jun 26, 28, 29,
  Jul 10, 23, 27, 30, Aug 24, Sep 1; <u>1765</u>: HAY, Jun 10, 19, Jul 8, 19, Aug 7,
  8, 9, 21, 28, Sep 2, 9
Clio, Hannah (author), <u>1761</u>: DL, Jun 18
Clitherow, Benjamin (pyrotechnist), <u>1754</u>: SFH, Sep 19
Clive, Catherine Raftor (actor, singer), <u>1732</u>: DL, Jan 14; <u>1733</u>: DL, Feb 10,
  Oct 5, 10, 12, 19, 22, 24, Nov 7, 13, 21, 26, Dec 5, 11, 14, 19, 26, 29;
  <u>1734</u>: DL, Jan 8, 15, 19, 28, Feb 4, 11, DL/LIF, Mar 11, DL/HAY, 16, 18, 23,
  25, LIF, Apr 4, 15, 18, DL, 22, 23, DL/HAY, 26, 27, DL, 29, LIF, May 9, DL,
  13, 15, 16, DL/HAY, 23, LIF, 29, DL, Sep 7, 14, Oct 5, 8, 9, 10, 19, 21, 22,
  25, 29, Nov 1, 7, 13, 18, 22, Dec 12; <u>1735</u>: DL, Jan 6, 11, 13, 23, Feb 4, 5,
  25, Mar 1, 6, 10, 13, 17, 22, 24, 29, Apr 11, 15, 16, 21, 23, 25, May 5, 6,
  14, Jun 3, Sep 1, 4, 6, 9, 15, 27, 30, Oct 2, 9, 11, 21, 23, 24, 28, 31, Nov
  1, 3, 15, 17, 22, 27, Dec 5, 6, 26; <u>1736</u>: DL, Jan 3, 12, 27, Feb 9, 20, 26,
  28, Mar 3, 23, 25, 27, Apr 1, 6, 12, 15, 22, 29, May 3, 4, 14, 22, 25, Aug
  26, Sep 4, 7, 9, 16, 18, 23, 28, Oct 2, 12, 13, 16, 18, 20, 21, 25, 30, Nov
  1, 2, 6, 8, 12, 13, 15, 19, 22, 23, Dec 7, 21, 31; <u>1737</u>: DL, Feb 10, 19, 28,
  Mar 1, 5, 12, 15, 19, 21, 22, Apr 12, 15, 23, 29, May 3, 5, 6, 7, 19, 27, Aug
  30, Sep 1, 3, 6, 8, 15, 17, 20, 24, 27, Oct 8, 11, 21, 22, 24, 25, 27, 31,
  Nov 11, 12, 14, 15, 17; <u>1738</u>: DL, Jan 5, 14, 25, 26, 27, 31, Feb 2, 16, 23,
  Mar 2, 3, 4, 20, 21, 25, Apr 14, 17, 22, 27, 29, May 2, 8, 13, 31, Sep 7, 9,
  12, 19, 21, 23, 26, 28, Oct 17, 18, 20, 21, 24, 25, 26, Nov 2, 3, 8, 11, 14,
  25, 30, Dec 6, 7, 9; <u>1739</u>: DL, Jan 1, 8, 13, 15, 18, 22, 27, Feb 1, 3, Mar 1,
  13, 26, 27, 31, Apr 24, 25, 27, 28, 30, May 1, 15, 18, 19, 28, Sep 1, 4, 6,
  11, 15, 18, 20, 22, 26, 27, Oct 3, 4, 6, 9, 11, 15, 16, 19, 22, 23, 25, 26,
  27, Nov 7, 8, 10, 12, 15, 16, 20, 23, 28, Dec 4, 8, 10, 15, 17, 22, 26, 31;
  <u>1740</u>: DL, Jan 5, 10, 16, Feb 7, Mar 8, 11, 17, 20, 25, 29, Apr 8, 12, 15, 16,
  17, 18, 21, 23, 24, 29, 30, May 1, 9, 12, 13, 14, 20, 26, 29, Sep 6, 9, 11,
  13, 18, 20, 25, 27, 30, Oct 9, 17, 23, 28, Nov 1, 6, 7, 8, 11, 13, 19, 24,
  26, 27, 28, 29, Dec 3, 10, 15, 20; <u>1741</u>: DL, Jan 15, Feb 2, 10, 14, Mar 14,
  17, 24, 30, 31, Apr 3, 4, 6, 16, 24, 29, May 5, 14, 15, 22, 25, 27, Sep 5, 8,
  10, 12, 15, 17, 19, 22, 24, Oct 6, 8, 10, 12, 15, 21, 23, Nov 2, 20, Dec 16,
  21; <u>1742</u>: DL, Jan 4, 20, 27, Feb 4, 11, Mar 8, 12, 20, 22, 27, 29, 30, Apr 5,
  6, 8, 17, 20, 22, 28, 30, May 1, 6, 17, 19, Sep 11, 14, 16, 18, 21, 25, 28,
  30, Oct 2, 12, 18, 27, Nov 1, 3, 8, 12, 16, 19, 22; <u>1743</u>: DL, Jan 11, 17, Feb
  9, 11, 12, CG, 18, 23, DL, Mar 3, 7, 8, 19, CG, 23, DL, Apr 7, 19, May 6,
  LIF, Jun 3, DL, Sep 13, Oct 15, CG, Nov 17, Dec 7, 9, 13, 14, 16, 20, 23, 26;
  <u>1744</u>: CG, Jan 3, 4, 5, 7, 18, 19, Feb 9, 14, 24, Mar 3, 8, 12, 13, CR, 21,
  CG, 28, Apr 2, 13, 18, 19, 21, 28, May 9, Oct 12, HAY, 22, Nov 2, DL, 19, CG,
  27, 30, Dec 3, 5, 10, 11, 12, 17, 19, 22, 29, 31; <u>1745</u>: CG, Jan 1, 2, 7, 11,
  14, 18, Feb 1, 9, 11, 12, 15, Mar 6, 14, 18, 25, Apr 2, 3, 4, 15, 20, 22, 23,
  26, 29, 30, May 3, 29, DL, Nov 23, 25, 26, 27, 28, 29, 30, Dec 5, 9, 10, 11,
  16, 17, 20, 30; <u>1746</u>: DL, Jan 3, 4, 10, 14, 17, 31, Feb 6, 24, Mar 1, 3, 8,
  10, 13, 17, 18, Apr 4, 8, 10, 14, 15, 21, May 12, Jun 6, Sep 23, 25, 27, 30,
  Oct 14, 23, 27, Nov 1, 5, 22, 28, Dec 11, 15, 20, 22, 30; <u>1747</u>: DL, Jan 2,
  10, 21, SOU, 21, DL, 24, Feb 28, Mar 7, 12, 19, 24, 30, Apr 4, 10, 22, 23,
  28, May 5, 7, 12, 16, Sep 15, 17, 19, 22, 24, Oct 1, 23, 24, Nov 2, 6, 7, 10,
  13, 14, 25, 27, Dec 3, 11, 23, 26, 31; <u>1748</u>: DL, Jan 6, 12, 18, 20, 27, Feb
  1, 3, Mar 8, 21, 24, Apr 20, 27, Sep 10, 13, 15, 17, 20, 24, Oct 1, 4, 6, 15,

18, 21, Nov 3, 9, 14, 23, 28, Dec 10, 21, 26, 28; 1749: DL, Jan 2, 18, 25,
Feb 20, 21, Mar 13, 30, Apr 10, May 1, 16, Sep 16, 19, 20, 21, 22, 26, 28,
Oct 3, 10, 11, 17, 23, 24, 26, 28, Nov 9, 21, 27, 28, Dec 2, 7, 9, 18, 28,
30; 1750: DL, Jan 1, 4, 6, 18, 22, 29, Feb 10, 15, Mar 15, 17, 19, 27, Sep 8,
11, 13, 15, 18, 20, 25, 27, Oct 1, 11, 13, 15, 16, 17, 18, 19, 20, 22, 23,
26, 30, 31, Nov 2, 12, 13, 15, 24, Dec 11, 13, 14, 18, 26, 31; 1751: DL, Jan
7, 12, Feb 23, Mar 12, 16, 19, Sep 10, 12, 13, 14, 17, 18, 19, 21, 24, 28,
Oct 1, 3, 4, 11, 17, 29, Nov 16, 19, Dec 5, 14; 1752: DL, Jan 1, 6, 28, Feb
6, Mar 9, Apr 21, Sep 16, 19, 23, Oct 3, 7, 10, 14, 16, 21, 23, 26, 30, Nov
25, 27, 28, Dec 18; 1753: DL, Jan 2, 3, 8, 13, 22, Mar 10, 20, 22, Apr 3, 5,
27, May 4, 17, Sep 8, 11, 13, 15, 20, 22, Oct 3, 12, 18, 19, 23, 30, 31, Nov
6, 7, 8, 14, Dec 20; 1754: DL, Jan 7, 16, Feb 1, 25, Mar 23, Apr 16, Jul 2,
Sep 14, 17, 19, 21, Oct 3, 5, 12, 14, 15, 18, 22, 23, 25, Nov 7; 1755: DL,
Jan 6, 15, 17, Feb 18, CG, Mar 12, DL, 13, 17, Apr 19, Sep 16, 18, 20, 23,
27, 30, Oct 3, 9, 24, 27, Nov 12, 13, 22, 28, Dec 1; 1756: DL, Jan 2, 3, 21,
Mar 23, 27, 30, Apr 3, 6, May 5, 12, 18, 24, Oct 5, 7, 12, 16, 19, 23, 29,
Nov 1, 2, 6, 11, 13, 24, Dec 15; 1757: DL, Jan 3, 26, Feb 5, Mar 28, Apr 11,
13, 20, 21, Sep 10, 27, 29, Oct 6, 7, 12, 13, 15, 18, 24, Nov 2, 15, 19;
1758: DL, Jan 24, Feb 4, 9, 11, 20, Mar 16, 29, 30, Apr 3, May 2, 4, 17, Jun
22, Sep 16, 23, 30, Oct 7, 12, 14, Nov 1, 3, 8, 13, 14, 15, 17, 24, Dec 18,
19, 28, 29; 1759: DL, Jan 17, 20, Feb 3, Mar 26, Apr 19, 26, May 7, Sep 22,
Oct 2, 16, 25, 26, 27, 31, Nov 2, 8, 17, 22, 23, 30, Dec 12, 19; 1760: DL,
Jan 10, 24, Mar 20, 24, 29, Apr 9, 11, 29, May 7, 19, Sep 23, 30, Oct 7, 8,
10, 14, 22, Nov 17, 22, Dec 2, 22, 30; 1761: DL, Jan 10, 12, Feb 12, Mar 23,
26, Apr 1, 2, 13, 15, 21, May 8, 11, 18, Sep 5, 8, 10, 17, 18, 23, 25, 28,
Oct 7, 10, 14, 21, 24, Nov 23, Dec 14, 17; 1762: DL, Jan 7, 11, 15, 20, 27,
29, Feb 10, 20, Mar 20, 22, Apr 22, Sep 18, 21, 29, Oct 2, 4, 8, 9, 14, Nov
2, 10, 11, 12, 26, Dec 1, 10; 1763: DL, Jan 7, 14, 17, 18, 22, Mar 19, 21,
May 2, 7, 9, 14, Sep 17, 24, 29, Oct 1, 12, 13, 15, 29, Nov 1, 2, 8, 19, 30,
Dec 10, 14; 1764: DL, Jan 3, 9, 14, 23, Mar 24, 27, Apr 2, Sep 15, 29, Oct 4,
13, 18, 20, 26, Nov 7, 8, 28, Dec 13, 18; 1765: DL, Jan 18, 24, Mar 2, 18,
19, Apr 15, May 11, 17, Sep 14, 19, 21, Oct 11, 23, 30, 31, Nov 22, Dec 7;
1766: DL, Jan 23, 28, Feb 15, 20, Mar 17, May 10, 16, Oct 7, 9, 17, 18, Nov
17, 20, Dec 10, 15; 1767: DL, Jan 24, Feb 17, 19, Mar 21, 23, Apr 7, 22, May
4, 16, Sep 12, 19, Oct 8, 14, 23, Nov 20, 23, 28, Dec 5; 1768: DL, Mar 17,
Apr 6, Sep 24, 28, Oct 1, 5, 18, 19, 25, Dec 20; 1769: DL, Feb 4, Mar 29, Apr
19, 24; 1772: CG, Jan 7; 1782: CG, Dec 3
--Every Woman in Her Humour, 1760: DL, Mar 20
--Faithful Irish Woman, The, 1765: DL, Mar 18
--Island of Slaves, The, 1761: DL, Mar 26
--Rehearsal, The; or, Bayes in Petticoats, 1750: DL, Mar 15, Apr 3, 26, 27;
1751: DL, Mar 12, 19, May 31; 1753: DL, Mar 22, Apr 3, May 4, Oct 31; 1755:
DL, Apr 19; 1762: DL, Mar 22, May 10
--Sketch of a Fine Lady's Return from a Rout, 1763: DL, Mar 21
Clochette (dance), 1777: KING'S, Mar 15, Apr 19, 22, 26, May 6, 27, 31, Jun 3,
10, 17, 24, 28, Jul 5, Nov 15, 18, 29, Dec 9, 13; 1778: KING'S, Jan 17, 20,
27, Jun 9, 20
Clock-Case, The; or, Female Curiosity (interlude, anon), 1777: CG, May 2
Clodio. See Claudio.
Clogget. See Clagget.
Close in a hollow silent cave (song), 1678: DG, Jun 0
Closson (Cloesong) (actor, dancer, bird imitator), 1740: TCLP, Aug 4, BFLP, 23,
SF, Sep 9; 1755: BFGT, Sep 5
Closson, Mlle (dancer), 1740: BFLP, Aug 23
Clothworkers, Society of, 1677: CITY, Oct 29
Clothworkers, 1694: CITY, Oct 29
Clotilda. See Conti, Francesco.
Clough, Chevalier (composer), 1782: DL, May 10
Clough, Mrs (actor), 1670: LIF, Sep 20; 1671: LIF, Mar 6; 1673: DG, Mar 12, May
0
Clough, Thomas (actor), 1741: BFH, Aug 22, GF, Sep 14, 16, 30, Oct 2, 9, Nov 4,
9, Dec 23; 1742: GF, Jan 5, 23, Feb 3, LIF, Dec 6, 13, 27, 28; 1743: LIF, Jan
7, 14, Feb 14, 17, HAY, Apr 14, BFYWR, Aug 23, SF, Sep 8; 1749: BFCB, Aug 23;
1752: DL, Oct 11, 19, Nov 8, 30, Dec 8; 1753: DL, Apr 25, May 16, 18, 21, Sep
11, 25, Oct 9, 20, Nov 1, 14, 19, Dec 26; 1754: DL, Jan 7, Feb 9, 14, May 6,
Jul 2, Sep 14, 17, 19, Oct 12, 18, Nov 7, 11, 22, Dec 5, 13; 1755: DL, Feb
22, Apr 25, Oct 3, 7, 13, 17, 25, 31, Nov 8, 15, 22, 26; 1756: DL, Jan 21,
Apr 3, 29, May 1, 11, 18, Sep 28, Oct 18, 23, 29, Nov 6, 12, 18, 19, Dec 27;
1757: DL, Mar 24, Apr 27, May 9, 10, CG, 27, DL, Sep 29, Oct 7, 18, Nov 30,
Dec 27; 1758: DL, May 2, 17, Nov 16, 17, 27, Dec 28; 1759: DL, Jan 6, 17, 31,
Apr 7, May 11, 16, 18, 22, Sep 22, 29, Oct 9, 22, 30, 31, Nov 19, Dec 1, 31;
1760: DL, Mar 4, Apr 22, 28, 29, May 6, 8, 16, Oct 3, 11, 15, Dec 29; 1761:

DL, Feb 12, May 1, 8, Sep 10, 14, Oct 14, Nov 5, 9, 25, Dec 22, 28; 1762: DL, Jan 20, 23, Mar 1, Apr 1, 30, May 7, 12, 17, 26, Sep 25, Oct 7, 8, 15, 25, 28, Nov 3, 5, 10, 18, 23, Dec 28; 1763: DL, Jan 8, 15, Feb 24, May 7, 9, Sep 22, Oct 4, 12, 14, 17, 28, 31, Nov 9, 19, 23, 26, 30, Dec 17, 26; 1764: DL, Jan 4, 27, Feb 21, Mar 3, Apr 14, May 11, 14, Sep 20, 22, 25, Oct 4, 6, 13, 15, 17, 20, Nov 13; 1765: DL, Jan 18, 22, Apr 13, May 14, Sep 19, 24, Oct 5, Nov 16; 1766: DL, Jan 9, 24, 29, Apr 16, May 3, 9; 1767: DL, Jan 22, 24, Feb 5, Sep 17; 1768: DL, Sep 26, Oct 20, 28, 31; 1769: DL, Mar 16, May 12, Oct 2, 9, 14, 21, 23, Nov 14, Dec 16; 1770: DL, Jan 19, May 22, Oct 3, 4

Clown's Dance (dance), 1706: QUEEN'S, Jun 13; 1714: DL, Nov 11; 1725: LIF, Jan 4; 1729: DL, Apr 25, May 2; 1731: LIF, May 5, Jun 7; 1733: LIF/CG, Apr 30, May 3, CG, 4, DL/HAY, Dec 19; 1734: DL/HAY, Jan 1, 10, Mar 26; 1735: DL, Apr 22, 28, May 1, 5, 6, 8, 22, 23; 1736: CG, Jan 9, 19, Mar 25, 27, Apr 27, May 6, Sep 17, 29, Oct 4, 6, 27, Nov 23; 1737: CG, Jan 17, Mar 10, 24, Apr 12, 14, LIF, 18, 21, CG, 22, LIF, 25, CG, 25, LIF, 27, 28, 30, May 5, 6, 17, 18; 1738: CG, Mar 14, Apr 22; 1752: CG, May 4; 1753: CG, May 9, 15, 21; 1754: DL, May 7; 1755: HAY, Sep 3; 1756: CG, May 1; 1757: CG, May 2, 12, DL, 23; 1758: CG, Apr 21; 1759: CG, Apr 30; 1760: CG, May 5, 7, 8, 14; 1761: CG, Apr 27; 1771: DL, May 15

Clown's Stratagem, The; or, A New Way to get a Wife (entertainment), 1730: DL, May 18, 21

Clowns' Contention, The (entertainment), 1722: LIF, May 17

Club of Fortune Hunters, The. See Macklin, Charles.

Clun, Walter (actor), 1659: NONE, Sep 0; 1660: NONE, Sep 0, COCKPIT, Oct 8, 11, REDBULL, Nov 5, VERE, 8, Dec 0, 8; 1661: VERE, Aug 10, NONE, Sep 0; 1662: VERE, Jan 28; 1663: VERE, Mar 0, BRIDGES, May 7, 8, NONE, Sep 0; 1664: BRIDGES, Aug 3; 1669: BRIDGES, Jan 11, Feb 6, Apr 17

Clutterbuck, James (financier), 1749: DL, May 16, Nov 24; 1750: DL, Jan 4; 1753: DL, Sep 8; 1767: DL, May 1, 22; 1771: DL, Oct 18; 1772: DL, May 8, 23, 30, Jun 10, Oct 30; 1773: DL, Apr 24, 30, Jun 2, Dec 3; 1774: DL, Jun 2, Nov 11; 1775: DL, May 20, 27; 1776: DL, Jun 10

Clynch. See Clinch.

Clyton (speaks epilogue), 1684: DL, Sep 0

Coach and Horses Inn, 1792: HAY, Oct 15

Coakayne, Miss. See Cokayne, Mary.

Coal Hole Tavern, 1747: RL, Jan 27

Coalition. See Macnally, Leonard.

Coates (doorkeeper), 1794: CG, Jun 10; 1795: CG, May 30; 1796: CG, Jun 6; 1797: CG, May 25; 1798: DL, Jun 2, CG, 5; 1799: CG, May 21; 1800: CG, Jun 10

Coates, Elizabeth (actor), 1797: CG, Sep 22, Oct 4, 28, Dec 8; 1798: CG, Mar 31, Sep 21, 26

Coates, Mrs (singer, actor), 1797: DL, Oct 12, Nov 8; 1798: DL, Apr 30, May 11, Nov 14, 29, Dec 4, 13, 14, HAY, 17, DL, 29; 1799: DL, Jan 19, Feb 26, Apr 22, May 3, 24, 29, Sep 24, Oct 14, 19, Nov 6, 14, Dec 7, 11, 12, 28; 1800: DL, Jan 1, 2, 25, Feb 6, Mar 11, 13, Apr 30, May 10, 13, 17, Jun 9, HAY, Jul 2, Aug 14

Coats, Miss (singer), 1779: DL, Nov 3, Dec 27; 1780: DL, Sep 23, Dec 12

Cobb, James, 1779: DL, Apr 5; 1780: HAY, Aug 12, 26; 1781: CG, Apr 28, HAY, Aug 22; 1785: DL, Apr 27, Sep 22, Dec 8, 26; 1786: DL, Feb 18, Nov 25; 1787: DL, Jan 13, Apr 25, HAY, Aug 7, DL, Dec 20; 1788: DL, Feb 1, 25, Oct 25; 1789: DL, Nov 24; 1790: DL, Jan 14; 1791: DL, Jan 1, DLKING'S, Sep 22; 1792: DLKING'S, Mar 17, DL, Nov 21; 1793: DL, May 7; 1794: DL, Jul 2, Dec 20; 1796: DL, Feb 20; 1798: CG, Nov 12; 1800: CG, May 1

--Algerine Slave, The, 1785: DL, Dec 8; 1792: DLKING'S, Mar 17

--Cherokee, The (opera), 1794: DL, Nov 13, 19, 20, 25, 26, 28, Dec 1, 2, 5, 8, 9, 10, 11, 12, 13, 15, 16, 17, 18, 19, 20, 22, 23, 26, 27, 29, 31; 1795: DL, Jan 2, 3, 5, 7, 9, 14, 16, 19, 21, Feb 5, 9, 19, 26, Oct 30; 1798: DL, Jun 12

--Contract, The; or, The Female Captain, 1779: DL, Apr 5; 1780: HAY, Aug 26, 28

--Doctor and the Apothecary, The (farce), 1788: DL, Oct 25, 27, 30, 31, Nov 3, 5, 6, 11, 12, 15, 18, 22, 26, 27, Dec 11, 13, 16, 27; 1789: DL, Jan 13, 28, 31, Feb 4, 24, Mar 10, 14, 24, Apr 23, May 8, 13, 21, Jun 9, Oct 22, 24; 1790: DL, May 4, 28; 1791: DLKING'S, Nov 12, 15, 21, 24, Dec 5, 13, 28; 1702: DLKING'S, Jan 4, Feb 8, May 2, 14, 31, Jun 13, DL, Dec 14; 1795: DL, Dec 18, 28; 1796: DL, Jan 4, 13, Mar 5, 15, Apr 1, 5, Nov 18, Dec 3, 5; 1797: DL, May 20, Oct 23; 1798: DL, Jan 1

--English Readings (farce), 1787: HAY, Aug 7, 11, 13, 22, 23, 25

--First Floor, The (farce), 1787: DL, Jan 9, 13, 15, 16, 17, 19, 22, 23, 24, 25, 26, 31, Feb 1, 3, 5, 12, 16, 22, 26, Mar 6, 10, 15, Apr 12, 14, 20, May 19, 29, Jun 2, 9, Sep 18, 25, 27, Oct 18, Nov 15, Dec 11, 15, 20, 21; 1788: DL, Jan 17, Feb 14, Mar 4, Apr 5, 12, May 27, Jun 6, 11, Sep 30, Nov 26; 1789: DL, Feb 19, Jun 10, Sep 12, Oct 13, Dec 3; 1790: DL, Jun 2; 1791: DLKING'S, Nov 10, Dec 14; 1792: DLKING'S, Jan 3, 19, Feb 10, Apr 28, May 19,

Jun 6, 16, DL, Dec 3; <u>1793</u>: DL, Feb 8, Jun 6, HAY, Sep 21, Oct 7, 18, Nov 14,
26; <u>1794</u>: HAY, Feb 17; <u>1795</u>: DL, Dec 19; <u>1796</u>: DL, Jan 8, May 4; <u>1797</u>: DL,
Apr 27; <u>1798</u>: DL, Jan 9; <u>1799</u>: DL, Jun 10, Nov 12; <u>1800</u>: DL, Jan 4, 25, Apr 3
--Fortune's Wheel (farce), <u>1793</u>: DL, May 7
--Glorious First of June, The. See Sheridan, Richard Brinsley.
--Haunted Tower, The (opera), <u>1789</u>: DL, Nov 24, 25, 26, 28, Dec 1, 3, 4, 5, 8,
10, 11, 12, 15, 16, 17, 19, 22, 29, 31; <u>1790</u>: DL, Jan 2, 5, 7, 9, 12, 14, 16,
19, 21, 23, 26, 28, 29, Feb 1, 2, 4, 6, 9, 11, 13, 16, 20, 25, Mar 4, 11, 15,
18, 25, Apr 8, 13, 15, 19, 22, 27, 29, May 6, 13, Sep 11, Oct 2, 5, 9, 16,
19, 26, 30, Nov 2, 6, 9, 13, 20, 27, Dec 4, 11, 15, 18, 22, 27; <u>1791</u>: DL, Jan
4, Mar 4, 8, 24, Apr 5, 11, 30, May 7, 17, 23, Jun 2, DLKING'S, Sep 22, 24,
Oct 8, 18; <u>1792</u>: DLKING'S, Jun 4, 8, 12, DL, Sep 18, 19, Oct 2, 8, Nov 6;
<u>1793</u>: DL, Feb 1, 7, 21, May 31, HAY, Dec 16, 20, 28; <u>1794</u>: HAY, Jan 3, 13,
24, Feb 6, Mar 24, Apr 1, DL, Oct 18, 20; <u>1796</u>: DL, Jun 9; <u>1797</u>: DL, May 22,
Jun 6, Oct 17, 19, Nov 6, Dec 6; <u>1798</u>: DL, Jun 14; <u>1800</u>: DL, May 14, 23, Jun
3, 4, 14
--Humourist, The; or, Who's Who? (farce), <u>1785</u>: DL, Apr 27, 28, 29, 30, May 2,
4, 7, 14, 18, Sep 22, Oct 1, 8, 25, Nov 5, 11, 19, 26, Dec 10, 15, 17; <u>1786</u>:
DL, Feb 8, 15, Mar 9, Apr 1, 22, May 8, 23, Jun 6, Sep 19, Oct 9, Nov 21, Dec
13; <u>1787</u>: DL, Apr 25, May 10, 23, Jun 4, Oct 30, Nov 30, Dec 11, 19; <u>1788</u>:
DL, Jan 31, Feb 1, 23, 28, Apr 30, May 9, 28, Jun 10, Sep 27, Nov 4, 12, 25;
<u>1789</u>: DL, Oct 22, 31, Nov 25, Dec 4; <u>1790</u>: DL, Apr 12, May 29; <u>1791</u>: DL, Mar
4, DLKING'S, Oct 18, Nov 4, 18, Dec 12; <u>1792</u>: DLKING'S, Jan 2, 10, 16, 27,
Feb 2, Mar 1, Apr 18, May 7, DL, Nov 16, 19, 30; <u>1793</u>: DL, Feb 1, 2, Mar 5,
Jun 3, HAY, Sep 26, Oct 11, 15, Nov 15; <u>1794</u>: HAY, Jan 17; <u>1795</u>: DL, Sep 29,
Dec 12; <u>1796</u>: DL, Jan 6, Mar 14, Dec 7; <u>1797</u>: DL, Mar 30, Apr 21, May 5, Sep
26, 28, Nov 6, 22, Dec 16; <u>1798</u>: DL, Oct 8, Nov 29, Dec 12; <u>1799</u>: DL, Jan 11,
Apr 4, May 29, Jun 7, 22, Nov 1, 14, Dec 4, 5, 23; <u>1800</u>: DL, Jan 13, 17, May
15
--Kensington Gardens; or, The Walking Jockey (interlude), <u>1781</u>: HAY, Aug 22,
24, 31
--Love in the East; or, Adventures of Twelve Hours (opera), <u>1788</u>: DL, Feb 25,
26, 28, Mar 3, 6, 11, 26, 28, Apr 10
--Paul and Virginia (farce), <u>1800</u>: CG, Apr 28, May 1, 3, 5, 8, 9, 12, 14, 16,
19, 21, 26, Jun 9, 12
--Pirates, The (opera), <u>1792</u>: DL, Nov 21, 22, 23, 24, 26, 27, 28, 29, 30, Dec
1, 3, 4, 6, 7, 8, 10, 14, 22, 29; <u>1793</u>: DL, Jan 1, 3, 5, 8, 12, 15, 19, 22,
Feb 4, 11, 21, Mar 11, Apr 8, 18, May 20, 27, Jun 3; <u>1794</u>: DL, May 9, 14, 15,
16, 23, 30, Oct 25, 27, Nov 17, 25; <u>1795</u>: DL, Nov 11; <u>1796</u>: DL, Jan 8, May
25; <u>1797</u>: DL, Jun 6; <u>1798</u>: DL, May 23; <u>1799</u>: DL, Apr 19
--Poor Old Drury!!!, <u>1791</u>: DLKING'S, Sep 22, 24, 27, 29, Oct 1, 3, 4, 6, 8, 10,
11, 13, Nov 28, 29, Dec 20, 23
--Ramah Droog; or, Wine does Wonders (opera), <u>1798</u>: CG, Nov 12, 13, 14, 15, 16,
19, 21, 23, 26, 28, 30, Dec 3, 4, 6, 13, 20, 26, 28, 31; <u>1799</u>: CG, Jan 4, 7,
10, 15, 21, Feb 2, 19, 23, 28, Mar 7, 25, 26, Apr 1, 5, 22, May 27, Jun 10,
Oct 23, 24, 30; <u>1800</u>: CG, Feb 4, Mar 10, 13, May 24
--Shepherdess of Cheapside, The (farce), <u>1796</u>: DL, Feb 20, 25
--Siege of Belgrade, The (opera), <u>1789</u>: DL, Nov 24; <u>1791</u>: DL, Jan 1, 3, 5, 7,
8, 10, 11, 12, 13, 14, 15, 18, 19, 21, 22, 25, 26, 28, 29, Feb 1, 4, 5, 7, 8,
10, 12, 15, 18, 19, 21, 22, 26, Mar 1, 5, 12, 15, 19, 26, Apr 2, 9, 16, 25,
May 2, 9, 21, 27, Jun 3, DLKING'S, Sep 29, Oct 13, 17, 24; <u>1792</u>: DLKING'S,
May 30, Jun 6, 9, DL, Oct 6, 9, 15, 27, Nov 3; <u>1793</u>: DL, Apr 1, May 16, 29,
Jun 6; <u>1794</u>: DL, May 1, 2, 3, 6, 20, 27, Oct 4, Nov 1, 3, Dec 1, 15; <u>1795</u>:
DL, Oct 6, Nov 4, Dec 16; <u>1796</u>: DL, Jan 6, 12, May 25, Nov 10, 25; <u>1797</u>: DL,
Jan 4, 13, Feb 2, Mar 4, 27, Jun 5, Nov 20, Dec 12; <u>1798</u>: DL, Jun 9; <u>1799</u>:
DL, May 8; <u>1800</u>: DL, Jun 6
--Strangers at Home, The (opera), <u>1785</u>: DL, Dec 8, 9, 10, 12, 13, 15, 17, 20,
22, 23, 31; <u>1786</u>: DL, Jan 4, 12, Feb 4, 13, 21, Mar 18, May 2, 16, Sep 23,
Dec 1; <u>1787</u>: DL, Apr 25; <u>1789</u>: DL, Feb 18, Mar 5, 9, Apr 17, May 14; <u>1790</u>:
DL, May 31; <u>1791</u>: DL, May 19; <u>1792</u>: DLKING'S, Mar 17; <u>1799</u>: DL, Apr 19; <u>1800</u>:
DL, May 29
--Wedding Night, The (farce), <u>1780</u>: HAY, Aug 3, 12, 14
--Who'd Have Thought It! (farce), <u>1781</u>: CG, Apr 28, May 9, HAY, Jul 6
Cobham, Charles (violinist), <u>1794</u>: CG, Mar 7; <u>1796</u>: CG, Feb 12; <u>1797</u>: CG, Mar
3; <u>1798</u>: CG, Feb 23; <u>1799</u>: CG, Feb 8; <u>1800</u>: CG, Feb 28
Cobler of Castle Dormot (dance), <u>1788</u>: CG, May 30
Cobler of Castlebury, The. See Stuart, Charles.
Cobler of Preston, The. See Bullock, Christopher.
Cobler, The (dance), <u>1733</u>: LIF/CG, May 14
Cobler, The. See Dibdin, Charles.
Cobler's Jealous Wife (dance), <u>1727</u>: DL, Apr 21, May 5, 8, 15, 22, Oct 30, Nov
21

Cobler's Lamentation (Cobler's Tragical End at Last) (song), 1728: LIF, Mar 28,
    Apr 1, 6, 23, 30, May 2, 3, 23, 29, HAY, Jul 22, Aug 12; 1744: CG, Mar 14
Cobler's Opera, The. See Ryan, Lacy.
Cobler's Song (song), 1795: DL, May 19
Cobston, William (beneficiary), 1719: LIF, Dec 23
Cocchi, Gioacchino (composer), 1749: KING'S, Feb 28, Mar 21; 1750: KING'S, Apr
    10; 1753: CG, Dec 17; 1755: KING'S, Mar 17; 1757: KING'S, Mar 24; 1758:
    KING'S, Jan 10, Mar 14, Apr 6, Nov 11; 1759: KING'S, Jan 16, Nov 13; 1760:
    KING'S, Jan 15, Nov 22, Dec 16; 1761: KING'S, Jan 6, Feb 7; 1762: KING'S, Apr
    3, May 11; 1765: KING'S, Dec 3; 1771: KING'S, Feb 9
--Amanti Gelosi, Gli (opera), 1753: CG, Dec 17, 19, 20, 29, 31; 1754: CG, Jan
    2, 4, 7, 9, 11, 14, 15, 16, 18, 28, Feb 8, 21, 22, Mar 11, BFSIY, Sep 3, 4,
    5, 6; 1756: CG, Feb 2
--Ciro Riconosciuto, Il (opera), 1759: KING'S, Jan 16, 20, Feb 3, 6, 10, 13,
    17, 24, 27, Mar 3, 10, 13, 17, 20, 24, 31, Apr 7, 17, May 2, 22; 1760:
    KING'S, Mar 24
--Clemenza Di Tito, La (opera), 1760: KING'S, Jan 15, 19, 22, 26, Feb 2, 9, 16,
    19, 23, 25, May 8, 17; 1765: KING'S, Dec 3, 10, 14, 17, 21, 28; 1766: KING'S,
    Jan 7, 11, 18; 1796: DL, Nov 15
--Erginda Regina Di Livadia (opera), 1760: KING'S, May 31, Jun 3, 7
--Famiglia in Scompiglio, La; or, The Family in Uproar (opera), 1762: KING'S,
    Apr 3, 12, 19, 26, May 1, 18
--Issipile (opera), 1758: KING'S, Mar 14, 18, Apr 1, 8, 15, 22
--Maestra, La (opera), 1749: KING'S, Feb 28
--Semiramide Reconosciuta, La (opera), 1771: KING'S, Feb 2, 9, 12, 16
--Speranze della Terra, Le (musical), 1761: KING'S, Sep 19
--Tempio della Gloria, Il (opera), 1759: KING'S, Feb 20
--Tito Manlio (opera), 1761: KING'S, Feb 7, 14, 21, 28
--Zenobia (opera), 1758: KING'S, Jan 10, 14, 17, 21, 28, 31, Feb 4, 11, 18, Mar
    11, Apr 29
Cocher Suppose, Le. See Hauteroche, Noel le Breton, Sieur de.
Cochinino (musician), 1754: HAY/SFB, Sep 13
Cochois (Cochoy), Francis H (actor), 1734: HAY, Nov 7, GF/HAY, Dec 9, 27; 1735:
    GF/HAY, Mar 21, HAY, Apr 16
Cochois, Michel (actor), 1719: LIF, Jan 13; 1734: GF/HAY, Nov 20, HAY, Dec 13,
    GF/HAY, 27, 30; 1735: GF/HAY, Jan 8, Feb 6, HAY, Mar 19, GF/HAY, Apr 25, HAY,
    May 9, GF, 23
Cochois, Mrs Michel (actor), 1719: LIF, Jan 13; 1734: GF/HAY, Dec 30; 1735:
    GF/HAY, Jan 8, Feb 6, HAY, Mar 19, Apr 16, May 9, GF, 23
Cock and Bottle Tavern, 1787: HAY, Mar 12
Cock and Magpie Tavern, 1785: HAMM, Jul 25; 1786: HAMM, Jun 30, Aug 5
Cock and Turk's Head Tavern, 1750: CG, Apr 5; 1752: CG, Mar 30
Cock Coffee House, 1754: DL, Dec 16
Cock Lane Ghost, 1762: DL, Jan 29; 1772: CG, Jan 31
Cock Tavern, 1780: CII, Apr 19
Cockburn (actor), 1784: HAY, Feb 9; 1785: HAY, Jan 24
Cockney brogue, 1767: CG, Nov 28
Cockney Hunt, The; or, Easter Monday's Chase through Epping Forest (e
    ntertainment), 1786: DL, Apr 17
Cockspur St, 1769: KING'S, Feb 24; 1776: CG, Oct 23; 1778: KING'S, Mar 26;
    1799: DL, May 7, HAY, Aug 24
Cockye, Miss (actor), 1685: DLORDG, Jan 20
Cocoa-Tree Coffee House, 1758: DL, Mar 10
Cocu Battu et Content, Le (play), 1721: HAY, Jan 6; 1725: HAY, Jan 6, Mar 4
Cocu Imaginaire, Le. See Moliere.
Codgerino, Sg and Sga (dancers), 1752: SFB, Sep 22
Codrile (dance), 1790: DL, Jun 2
Codrington (versifier), 1789: HAY, Aug 5
Codrington, Colonel (sponsor), 1699: LIF, Nov 26, Dec 0; 1700: LIF, Apr 0
Coe (pit office keeper), 1718: LIF, May 6; 1719: LIF, May 11; 1720: LIF, May
    19; 1721: LIF, May 17; 1722: LIF, May 18, SOU, Oct 3; 1723: SOU, Feb 18, LIF,
    May 28
Coffee House Politician, The. See Fielding, Henry.
Coffee House, The. See Miller, James.
Coffey, Charles, 1729: HAY, May 29, DL, Jun 13, SF, Sep 8; 1730: HAY, Jan 21,
    Apr 27; 1731: DL, Aug 6; 1733: DL, Jan 29; 1735: DL, May 6; 1736: DL, May 29
--Beggar's Wedding, The, 1729: HAY, May 29, 30, 31, Jun 3, 4, 5, 6, 10, 11, 12,
    13, 14, 17, 18, 19, 21, 24, 25, 26, 27, 28, Jul 1, 2, 5, 9, 10, 12, 16, 19,
    23, 28, Aug 6, 8, 13, DL, 16, BFF, 23, BFR, 25, SF, Sep 8, 12, 15, DL, 23,
    27, BLA, 30, DL, Oct 2, 4, Nov 18, HAY, 22, Dec 23, DL, 27; 1730: DL, Jan 17,
    Apr 6, 14, 18, HAY, 29, 30, Jul 28, DL, Oct 13, HAY, 26, DL, Nov 16, HAY, Dec
    14; 1731: DL, Dec 22; 1733: HAY, May 12; 1734: HAY, Jul 5, 8, 19; 1735: GF,

Apr 22; <u>1737</u>: NWLS, May 30; <u>1738</u>: CG, Apr 18, 19, 28, May 3, 11, 16, 18;
<u>1739</u>: CG, Apr 23, DL, 30; <u>1750</u>: CG, Oct 19, Nov 8, 12; <u>1763</u>: DL, Feb 26, Mar
1, Apr 22, May 13, 16; see also Coffey, Charles, Phebe
--Boarding School Romps, The; or, The Sham Captain, <u>1733</u>: DL, Jan 29, 31, Feb
1, 2
--Devil to Pay, The; or, The Wives Metamorphosed, <u>1731</u>: DL, Ju 26, 28, Nov 3,
5, 6, 8, 10, 11, 15, 23, 24, 30, Dec 2, 3, GF, 8, DL, 8, GF, 9, 10, 11, 13,
14, DL, 14, 15, GF, 15, DL, 17, GF, 17, DL, 18, 20, GF, 27, 28, DL, 31; <u>1732</u>:
GF, Jan 1, 5, 6, 12, 14, DL, 14, 15, 17, GF, 17, 18, DL, 19, 24, GF, 24, 29,
Feb 1, 11, 17, DL, 28, 29, GF, Mar 2, 4, DL, 9, 11, 13, 20, 23, 27, GF, 27,
DL, 30, GF, 30, HAY, 31, DL, Apr 1, GF, 1, DL, 12, 13, 14, GF, 15, DL, 15,
18, 19, GF, 19, DL, 20, 24, 25, 26, GF, 26, DL, 27, GF, 28, DL, 28, May 3, 4,
GF, 9, DL, 10, 17, GF, 22, DL, 29, Jun 6, 9, Oct 14, 21, 26, Nov 4, 8, 10;
<u>1733</u>: DL, Jan 11, 15, 16, 22, 24, 26, Feb 1, Mar 5, GF, 8, DL, 12, GF, 12,
17, 27, 29, DL, 29, Apr 2, GF, 5, LIF/CG, 13, GF, 16, LIF/CG, 17, 19, GF, 20,
HAY, 23, LIF/CG, 23, 30, GF, May 8, LIF/CG, 8, DL, 10, CG, 11, DL, 15,
LIF/CG, 18, GF, 18, DL, 23, CG, Jul 6, 10, Aug 3, DL, Sep 24, DL/HAY, 26, DL,
26, 28, DL/HAY, 28, CG, 29, DL/HAY, Oct 1, 5, 8, GF, 11, 18, DL/HAY, 19, GF,
22, 24, DL/HAY, 24, Nov 23, GF, 26, DL/HAY, 28, Dec 1, DL, 7, GF, 10, 11, 17,
19, 26; <u>1734</u>: DL/HAY, Jan 3, DL, 4, DL/HAY, 5, 7, GF, 10, 24, DL/HAY, Feb 4,
6, Mar 16, GF, 19, DL/HAY, 19, 26, JS, Apr 22, 29, DL/HAY, May 8, LIF, 9, GF,
13, 16, DL/HAY, 22, 23, JS, 24, 29, HAY, Jun 5, 12, Aug 7, 12, 14, DL, Sep
14, 17, CG/LIF, 23, 25, DL, 26, Oct 24, CG/LIF, 31, DL, Nov 7, Dec 9, 10;
<u>1735</u>: DL, Feb 13, 14, 15, 20, 24, YB, Mar 12, DL, 13, GF, Apr 9, DL, 18, 28,
GF, 29, CG/LIF, 29, DL, May 1, GF, 1, DL, 6, GF, 15, CG/LIF, 19, DL, 20, 23,
29, 30, LIF, Jun 19, Jul 11, DL, Sep 4, CG, 12, 19, DL, 25, CG, Oct 15, DL,
Nov 6, 19, GF, Dec 6, DL, 20, 31; <u>1736</u>: DL, Jan 9, 10, CG, Feb 24, DL, 25,
27, CG, Mar 16, 25, Apr 13, LIF, 20, YB, 26, CG, May 3, LIF, 5, CG, 8, DL, 8,
GF, 10, DL, 17, LIF, 19, DL, 20, CG, 20, 25, DL, 27, RI, Aug 21, CG, Sep 15,
DL, 23, 30, CG, Oct 4, DL, 22, 30, Nov 10, CG, 11, DL, Dec 14; <u>1737</u>: DL, Mar
12, 17, CG, Apr 12, 15, DL, 16, 19, LIF, 21, DL, 30, CG, May 6, DL, 9, 12,
CG, 13, DL, 21, CG, 23, DL, 26, Aug 30, Sep 1, 3, 6, 13, 15, 17, 24, 27,
Oct 1, 4, 8, 20, Nov 4, 12; <u>1738</u>: DL, Jan 20, CG, Apr 17, DL, 21, 24, 27, May
6, 11, 18, 19, 23, CG, Jun 30, Aug 30, DL, Sep 9, Oct 11, CG, 26, DL, Dec 14,
18, 28, 30; <u>1739</u>: DL, Jan 2, 9, 22, 29, Mar 12, 13, 17, 27, Apr 3, CG, 30,
DL, May 7, CG, 15, DL, 16, 22, Sep 1, 4, 14, CG, Oct 2, DL, 9, CG, Nov 9;
<u>1740</u>: DL, Mar 17, 25, 27, Apr 9, 16, 22, CG, 23, DL, 24, May 12, CG, 12, DL,
13, 15, 20, Sep 11, 13, 16, 18, 20, 23, 25, 30, Oct 4, 10, 11, 13, 21, 25,
31, Nov 5, 8, 13, Dec 3, GF, 6, 8, 9, DL, 9, 12, 19; <u>1741</u>: DL, Jan 16, CG,
27, GF, 29, Feb 5, DL, 9, Mar 30, 31, Apr 2, 6, 13, CG, 13, DL, 14, 18, GF,
22, DL, 24, CG, 25, GF, May 1, CG, 5, DL, 7, 26, Sep 10, 12, GF, 16, JS, 29,
DL, Oct 6, 8, 10, 20, GF, Dec 14, 21, 28, 29; <u>1742</u>: GF, Jan 1, 4, DL, 28, Feb
5, GF, 13, DL, Mar 2, 16, 27, Apr 21, 22, GF, May 3, DL, 11, Sep 14, 18, JS,
Nov 22, DL, Dec 15, 29; <u>1743</u>: DL, Jan 1, LIF, 7, 10, DL, 17, 27, Feb 9, LIF,
9, 11, Mar 3, DL, 12, LIF, 21, Apr 5, 6, 7, 8, 13, DL, 20, 22, May 7, CG, Oct
5, 7, 12, 14, 29, Nov 2, 5, 21; <u>1744</u>: CG, Jan 3, 11, 12, 16, 19, Mar 8, 29,
DL, Apr 17, CG, 23, DL, 28, May 4, 5, 8, CG, 10, DL, 14, 17, 22, CG, Sep 26,
DL, 27, CG, 28, DL, 29, Oct 4, 6, CG, 16, Dec 11, DL, 19; <u>1745</u>: CG, Jan 8,
DL, 25, 26, GF, Feb 4, 26, Mar 9, 11, 12, CG, 14, 18, GF, Apr 6, CG, 18, GF,
22, 25, CG, May 2, 8, Oct 2, 14, GF, 28, 29, 30, CG, Nov 9, DL, 25, 26, Dec
5, 9, CG, 30; 17Apr 8, DL, 21, May 28, Dec 14; <u>1796</u>: DL, Mar 8, 46: GF, Jan
3, DL, 25, HIC, Feb 3, DL, 12, GF, 13, DL, 22, GF, 24, DL, Mar 1, GF, 15, DL,
Apr 4, Sep 27, Oct 2, 4, 18, NWC, 20, SOU, 21, DL, 25, 28, Nov 19; <u>1747</u>: GF,
Jan 12, 13, DL, 15, GF, 21, Feb 2, 9, DL, 28, CG, Mar 23, GF, Apr 9, DL, May
4, CG, 5, DL, Sep 24, Oct 20, Nov 14, CG, Dec 17, DL, 23; <u>1748</u>: DL, Feb 1,
CG, 11, 15, 29, DL, Mar 24, May 5, Sep 20, 22, CG, 28, DL, Oct 1, CG, 12,
SOU, 12, CG, 22, DL, Nov 5, 11, CG, 12, Dec 8, DL, 12, 19; <u>1749</u>: SOU, Jan 9,
DL, 19, 31, CG, Mar 4, DL, 9, CG, 13, DL, 30, Apr 12, CG, 21, 29, DL, May 6,
9, Sep 22, SOUGT, 25, CG, 27, DL, 30, CG, Oct 9, 14, DL, 14, 31, CG, Nov 16,
DL, 25, NWC, 27; <u>1750</u>: DL, Feb 7, 23, CG, Apr 3, DL, Sep 13, CG, 26, Oct 22,
27, Nov 13, DL, 16, CG, Dec 6; <u>1751</u>: CG, Jan 15, Feb 9, Mar 21, Apr 8, DL,
10, CG, 16, 19, 27, May 7, 13, DL, Sep 19, CG, 25, DL, 27, CG, Oct 11, DL,
21, 25, CG, Nov 8, DL, Dec 6; <u>1752</u>: CG, Jan 21, May 13, DL, Sep 16, CG, 29,
DL, Oct 5, Nov 24, NWLS, 28, 30, DL, Dec 8, 12, CG, 23; <u>1753</u>: CG, Apr 7, 9,
DL, 14, CG, 27, May 8, 11, DL, Sep 15, CG, 24, DL, Oct 25, Nov 10, 28, CG,
Dec 4, DL, 11; <u>1754</u>: DL, Feb 11, Mar 28, CG, Apr 27, May 8, 9, DL, 22, CG,
Sep 18, DL, 19, 24, CG, Oct 21, DL, Nov 2, Dec 16; <u>1755</u>: DL, Jan 31, Apr 10,
11, 18, 22, HAY, Sep 9, DL, 20, CG, Oct 1, DL, 14, 28, CG, Nov 8, 21, DL, 24,
CG, Dec 13, DL, 16, CG, 18; <u>1756</u>: CG, Jan 2, DL, Feb 9, Apr 20, May 1, 20,
Oct 12, 20, Nov 6, CG, 8, 19; <u>1757</u>: CG, Jan 14, DL, Mar 7, 12, CG, Apr 30,
May 9, DL, Sep 27, Oct 11, Nov 1, CG, 18, Dec 9, 20; <u>1758</u>: CG, Feb 14, DL,
Apr 5, CG, 11, DL, 20, 21, CG, Sep 18, DL, 23, Oct 6, CG, 26; <u>1759</u>: CG, Jan

9, DL, Feb 5, Mar 13, CG, May 11, Sep 24, Dec 18; 1760: CG, May 16, Oct 6, 10, DL, Nov 22, 26; 1761: DL, Jan 27, CG, Apr 24, 29, May 15, Sep 9, DL, 18; 1762: CG, Apr 21, May 8, 13, Sep 22, DL, Oct 4, 13, 14, CG, 20, DL, Dec 23; 1763: DL, Jan 11, Apr 8, 12, 30, CG, May 7, Sep 19, DL, Oct 15; 1764: DL, Mar 22, Apr 24, CG, May 14, Sep 17, Oct 10, DL, Nov 7; 1765: DL, Jan 12, 21, Apr 10, CG, May 8, Sep 16, DL, Nov 22, 25; 1766: CG, Jan 23, DL, Apr 26, 28, May 7, 13, CG, 14, DL, 20, 22, Sep 20, Oct 10; 1767: DL, Feb 3, Mar 2, 7, Apr 2, CG, May 22, 23, Sep 15, DL, 25, Dec 3; 1768: DL, Feb 8, Mar 22, 26, CG, Apr 23, HAY, Jun 29, Jul 1, CG, Oct 11; 1769: DL, Jan 6, Feb 4, CG, Apr 8, 25, May 6, 12, DL, 18, HAY, 22, CG, Sep 30, Dec 6; 1770: DL, Feb 13, CG, May 15, HAY, Jun 27, DL, Sep 22, 27; 1771: DL, Jan 15, 28, Feb 6, 26, Apr 18, CG, 30, HAY, Jul 1, CG, Sep 27, Nov 6, Dec 12; 1772: DL, Feb 4, Mar 9, CG, May 29, DL, Jun 2, Oct 14, Dec 11; 1773: CG, Mar 27, Sep 20, DL, Nov 24; 1774: DL, Mar 1, HAY, Jul 6, 20, Aug 1, 29, DL, Oct 20; 1775: HAY, Feb 2, Jun 16, Jul 3, 10, Sep 12, DL, Dec 5; 1776: DL, May 27, Jun 8, HAY, Jul 1, CHR, Sep 30; 1777: CG, Apr 22, DL, May 19, 24, Jun 4, CHR, Jul 2, DL, Sep 25; 1778: DL, May 23, CHR, Jun 3; 1779: DL, Apr 9, HAY, Nov 8; 1781: DL, May 11; 1782: CG, Feb 14, May 28, HAY, Sep 16; 1785: CG, Apr 11; 1787: CG, Mar 1, Jun 9; 1788: DL, Dec 17, 19, 23, 26, 31; 1789: DL, Jan 21, Feb 9, 26, Mar 9, 16, Apr 17, 27, May 4, 14, 29, Jun 13, HAY, Aug 5; 1790: DL, Mar 2, 9, Apr 9, 27, May 1, 21, Oct 20, Dec 16; 1791: DL, Jan 8, 21, Feb 8, 17, Mar 2, 26, Apr 26, May 6, Jun 1, DLKING'S, Sep 24, Oct 18, 26, Nov 3, 7, Dec 17, 30; 1792: DLKING'S, Jan 13, 26, Feb 15, 25, Mar 15, 24, 31, Apr 25, May 15; 1793: DL, Apr 1, 22, 25, May 14, 24; 1794: DL, Oct 30, Nov 15, Dec 9; 1795: DL, Jan 6, 16, CG, 23, Aug 6, 16, 20, SF, Sep 8, DL, Oct 2, 5, 7, 9, 12, 14, 19, 21, 31, May 2, 21, HAY, Jul 15, Aug 27, DL, Oct 24, 31, Nov 23, 30, Dec 8; 1797: DL, May 29, Jun 6, CG, 13, DL, Oct 5, Nov 16; 1798: DL, Mar 31, Apr 23, May 5, Jun 15; 1799: DL, Feb 19, 25, Apr 2; 1800: CG, Mar 17, DL, 24, Apr 26, 30, May 19, Jun 4
--Female Parson, The; or, Beau in the Suds, 1730: HAY, Apr 27, 29, 30
--Merry Cobler, The (farce), 1735: May 6
--Phebe (Phoebe); or, The Beggar's Wedding, 1729: DL, Jun 13, 18, 20, 24, 27, Jul 4, 8, 11, 15, 29, Aug 7, Dec 30; 1730: DL, Apr 27, May 6, GF, Jun 23, 26, Jul 2, 24, Oct 14, 15, 31, Nov 2, 19, 30; 1731: GF, Jan 16, DL, Apr 19, May 10, Jul 6, TC, Aug 12, 13, 14, 16, 17, 18, 19, GF, Dec 20, 21, 22; 1732: GF, Jan 27, 28, DL, Feb 2; 1734: GF, Mar 25, Apr 26, May 17; 1736: DL, Oct 20; 1737: DL, Mar 5; 1739: DL, Dec 22; 1746: CG, Feb 24, 25, 27, Mar 1, 3, 4, 6, 10, 15, 17, Apr 2, 8, 9, 12, 24, 29; 1747: CG, Mar 7, 12, 14, 19, May 4, 6, 12, 15, 16, 19; 1748: CG, Apr 18; 1749: CG, Apr 4, 5, 11, Sep 29, Oct 2, 13, Nov 17, 18; 1750: CG, Mar 19, 31, Apr 17, 25; 1755: SOHO, Jan 16; 1761: CG, Apr 20; 1763: DL, Feb 24; 1775: DL, Apr 17; see also Coffey, Charles, The Beggar's Wedding
Cogan, John (actor), 1664: LIF, Aug 13; 1672: DG, Jan 31; 1676: DG, Aug 0
Coggia (Coja), Sidi Usuph (Tunisian envoy), 1733: DL/HAY, Nov 1; 1734: CG, Mar 28
Coggs (chandler), 1767: DL, Jan 7
Cohen (musician), 1770: MARLY, Sep 11
Coin (dancer), 1715: DL, Apr 9
Coinde (ballet master), 1789: KING'S, Mar 3, CG, Jul 2
Cointe. See LeCointe.
Cointrie, Mad. See DeLaCointrie, Mme.
Coish. See Coysh.
Coja, Jousef. See Coggia, Sidi Usuph.
Cokayne (Cockayne), Mary (actor), 1753: CG, Oct 5, 20, 22; 1754: CG, May 4, 13, Sep 25, Oct 9, Nov 30; 1755: CG, May 9; 1756: CG, Dec 10; 1757: CG, Apr 13, Oct 10, 13; 1758: CG, May 8, Oct 9; 1759: CG, May 18, Oct 10; 1760: CG, Apr 12, Sep 22, 24; 1761: DL, Jun 15, Jul 2, Aug 8, CG, Sep 23, Oct 31; 1762: CG, Mar 27, 29, May 13, Oct 4; 1763: CG, May 14, 25, Oct 10, 25, 26; 1764: CG, Feb 18, Mar 24, Apr 28, May 5, 16, 18, Sep 24, Oct 1, Dec 29; 1765: CG, May 15, Oct 4, 12, Nov 12; 1766: CG, Apr 15, 26, May 15, Oct 15, Nov 12; 1767: CG, Jan 31, May 18, Sep 18; 1768: CG, Feb 27, May 27, Oct 26; 1769: CG, Oct 20, Dec 29; 1770: CG, Mar 22, 31, May 5, Sep 26, HAY, 27, CG, Oct 18, Dec 31; 1771: CG, Apr 29, Sep 28, Oct 15; 1775: HAY, Feb 2
Cokayne, Sir Aston, 1748: CG, Mar 5
--Trappolin, The Supposed Prince, 1661: NONE, Sep 0; 1674: NONE, Sep 0
Coke, Elizabeth (correspondent), 1704: ATCOURT, Feb 28
Coke, John (spectator), 1697: LIF, Feb 20, Mar 13
Coke, Thomas (spectator), 1696: NONE, Jan 21, Apr 2, LIF, Nov 19; 1697: LIF, Mar 13; 1700: LIF, Mar 11, DL, 13; 1704: ATCOURT, Feb 28, LIF, Jun 26
Coker (actor), 1715: LIF, Feb 3, Jun 23, Oct 5, 11, 28; 1716: LIF, Jan 24, Apr 3, 11, 27, May 18, Jul 4; 1717: LIF, May 16; 1718: LIF, May 15; 1719: LIF, Dec 10; 1720: LIF, Jan 11, May 24, BFBL, Aug 23; 1721: LIF, May 19
Coker (dancer), 1733: HAY, Mar 19

Coker, Mrs (actor), 1731: SFLH, Sep 8, SF, 8; 1736: SF, Sep 7; 1739: BFH, Aug
   23
Colborne, John (boxkeeper), 1781: CG, May 23; 1782: CG, May 24; 1783: CG, Jun
   3; 1784: CG, May 28
Cold Bath Fields, 1738: CG, Jan 24; 1743: CG, Nov 17
Cole (billsticker), 1760: CG, Sep 22; 1761: CG, May 15
Cole (boxkeeper), 1795: DL, Jun 5; 1796: DL, Jun 13; 1797: DL, Jun 16; 1798:
   DL, Jun 14
Cole (harpsichordist), 1720: LIF, Mar 12; 1721: LIF, Mar 18
Cole (house servant), 1749: DL, Nov 24
Cole (turner), 1766: DL, Dec 26; 1767: DL, Feb 27; 1771: DL, Dec 12; 1772: DL,
   Jun 10; 1773: DL, Jan 21, Jun 2, Nov 19; 1774: DL, Jan 7, Jun 2, Oct 20, Nov
   25; 1775: DL, May 27
Cole, E D (actor, dancer, prompter), 1707: DL, Oct 25; 1710: DL, Mar 14, 27,
   Apr 21, GR, Jul 27, Aug 3, 12, 28, Sep 11, 30; 1715: DL, Aug 9; 1720: DL, Dec
   17; 1732: HAY, Feb 16, Mar 2, 17, 23, 31, May 8, 10, 15, BF, Aug 22; 1733:
   GF, Jan 27, Apr 12, May 3, CG, Jul 6, 27, Aug 2, 14, 20; 1734: HAY, Jun 5,
   24, YB, Jul 8, HAY, Aug 14, DL, Nov 8; 1735: DL, Jan 22, YB, Mar 21, DL, May
   10, Jul 1, GF/HAY, 15, 22, LIF, Aug 1, HAY, 12, GF/HAY, 21, HAY,
   26, DL, Oct 7, Nov 15, 20; 1736: DL, Jan 3, LIF, Apr 14, DL, Sep 7, 28, Oct
   12, Nov 15, Dec 6, 11, 31; 1737: DL, May 17, Oct 13, 21, 25, 27, Nov 1; 1738:
   DL, Mar 18, May 17, 26, Sep 23, Oct 16, Dec 15; 1739: DL, Jan 1, May 28, Sep
   6, 18, 26, Oct 15, Nov 15, Dec 10, 11; 1740: DL, May 23; 1741: GF, Apr 21
Cole, Miss (actor, singer, dancer), 1733: GF, Jan 8, 15, Feb 1, Mar 3, Apr 11,
   13, 19, 24, May 4, 11, 14, 23, 24, HAY, 28, BFCGBH, Aug 23, GF, Sep 24, Oct
   31, Nov 8; 1734: GF, Feb 11, Mar 18, May 8, DL, Oct 19, 26; 1735: DL, Apr 11,
   May 22, 29, GF/HAY, Aug 1, HAY, 12, DL, Oct 23, 25, Nov 21; 1736: DL, Feb 28,
   Mar 11, 27, May 6, 20, HAY, Jun 29, DL, Sep 18, Oct 9, 25, Nov 12, 13, 23,
   Dec 4, 20; 1737: DL, Jan 6, Feb 10, Mar 15, Apr 12, May 20, Sep 1, 20, Oct 1,
   20, 22, 24, Nov 19; 1738: DL, Apr 14, May 3, 16, 18, BFH, Aug 23, DL, Sep 16,
   30, Oct 19, 30, Dec 4, 7; 1739: DL, Feb 7, Apr 28, May 16, Oct 5, 10, 13, 17,
   26, Nov 20, Dec 26; 1740: DL, Feb 7, Mar 20, Apr 17, May 9, Sep 16, Oct 7,
   14, 15, Nov 28, Dec 26; 1741: GF, Apr 21, DL, May 23, Oct 6, 8, Nov 21; 1742:
   DL, Mar 29, Apr 20, 30, May 25, 26; 1743: HAY, Mar 23, DL, Nov 18, 29, Dec 6;
   1744: DL, Jan 7, Apr 28, 30, May 14, 16, 22, Sep 18, Oct 19, 30, Dec 26;
   1745: DL, Jan 12, 17, Apr 30, May 8, Oct 8, 12, Nov 18, 19, 30, Dec 11, 13,
   16; 1746: DL, Jan 8, 25, Mar 13, Apr 11, 23, Sep 23, 30, Oct 11, Nov 1, 7,
   Dec 26, JS, 29; 1747: DL, Jan 15, Feb 2, Mar 3, 7, 16, Nov 2, 6, 13, 16, 18,
   Dec 5; 1748: DL, Jan 2, 20, Mar 19, Apr 28, Sep 10, 27, 29, Oct 1, 6, 11, 27,
   28, Nov 2, 3, 14, Dec 26; 1749: DL, Jan 9, Feb 21, 23, Mar 31, Apr 29, May
   12, Sep 16, 19, 21, 22, 26, 28, Oct 10, 26, Nov 9, 16, 27, 28, 29, Dec 2, 8,
   12, 20, 26, 28; 1750: DL, Jan 1, 19, Feb 7, 10, 15, 24, Mar 15, 22, 29, 31,
   Apr 2, 9, 17, 19, 25, 27
Cole, Mrs (actor), 1696: DL, Mar 0, May 0
Cole, William (beneficiary), 1756: CG, Dec 23
Coleman (actor), 1749: SOU, Jan 2; 1750: SFYW, Sep 7
Coleman St, 1759: DL, Apr 16
Coleman, Dr (musician), 1660: NONE, May 29; 1675: ATCOURT, Feb 15
Coleman, Mrs (tailor), 1750: DL, Feb 6; 1754: DL, Mar 28; 1755: DL, Apr 2;
   1760: CG, Jan 26
Coles (house servant), 1760: CG, May 19
Colin and his Rival Lasses (dance), 1757: HAY, Aug 19, Sep 2, 28
Colin and Phebe (dance), 1758: HAY, Mar 6
Colin and Phebe (song), 1745: DL, Sep 21, 24, 26, 28, Nov 11; 1746: DL, Mar 17,
   Apr 18, 19, 22, 28
Colin cured of roving (song), 1785: HAY, Aug 2; 1786: DL, Apr 25, May 10
Colin Maillard. See D'Ancourt, Florent Carton.
Colin's Nosegay (dance), 1786: HAY, Aug 2, Sep 2
Colista (composer), 1708: SH, Feb 4
Collard (dancer), 1736: HAY, Jan 19, Apr 29
Collection of the Dresses of Different Nations, Antient and Modern, A (book),
   1757: DL, Jan 1
College (Colledge) (tailor), 1773: CG, Apr 13
College of Physicians, 1768: CG, Mar 15
Colles, Hester, Mrs Joseph (actor), 1777: HAY, Jun 19, Jul 18, 24, Aug 9, 14,
   15, 25, 29, Sep 3, 19, DL, Oct 31, Nov 10, 13, 24, 29, Dec 13, 15, 29; 1778:
   DL, Jan 22, 24, Feb 10, 24, Mar 9, Apr 23, May 5, 16, Sep 17, 19, 29, Oct 1,
   3, 20, Nov 4; 1779: DL, Jan 2, Mar 22, May 11, 19, Sep 18, Dec 2, 8; 1780:
   DL, Apr 3, 19, May 6, 10, 25
Collet (actor), 1729: GF, Oct 31, Nov 3, 4, 5, 6, 7, 8, 10, 11, 14, 17, 20, 21,
   24, Dec 1, 3, 9, 20; 1730: GF, Jan 5, 9, 13, 19, 26, 31, Feb 7, 9, Mar 17,
   30, Apr 2, 6, 7, 15, 17, 28, May 14, 28, Jun 5, 8, 9, 16, Jul 1, 6, 8,

BFPG/TC, Aug 1, BFPG, 20, GF, Sep 16, 18, 21, 23, 25, 28, 30, Oct 2, 5, 20,
21, 24, 30, 31, Nov 2, 6, 10, 11, 26, 27, 30, Dec 1, 3, 7, 8, 16, 21; 1731:
GF, Jan 20, Feb 18, 22, 27, Mar 1, 2, 13, 15, 22, Apr 8, 27, May 7, 14, 20,
Jun 1, 2, TC, Aug 4, 12, GF, Oct 8, 11, 13, 18, 25, 29, Nov 1, 6, 8, 11, 12,
16, 19, 20, 22, Dec 1, 6, 28; 1732: GF, Feb 2, 26, Apr 10, 12, 26, 27, May
11, Oct 2, 6, 10, 17, 24, 25, 26, Nov 2, 3, Dec 1, 18; 1733: GF, Jan 19, 24,
27, Feb 5, 13, Mar 28, Apr 27, May 9, 15, Sep 10, 12, 17, 25, 27, 28, Oct 4,
17, 22, 24, Dec 26
Collet (actor), 1770: HAY, Nov 21; 1771: HAY, May 17, 20, 27, Jun 5, 10, Aug
28, Sep 16
Collet, Ann (mercer), 1767: DL, May 27
Collet, Catherine (actor, singer, dancer), 1766: DL, May 5; 1767: DL, Jan 2,
Apr 11, 29, May 8, Sep 15, 17, 22, 26; 1768: DL, Jan 9, May 5, Aug 18, Sep
27, 29, Oct 11, 21; 1769: DL, Oct 4, Nov 13, 24, Dec 16, 30; 1770: DL, Jan
19, May 30, Oct 17, Nov 29; 1771: DL, Apr 2, 6, Oct 15, Dec 9; 1772: DL, Feb
21, Mar 26, Jun 10, Oct 21, Nov 12, Dec 2, 26; 1773: DL, May 10, Sep 25;
1774: DL, Mar 14; 1775: DL, Mar 20; 1776: DL, Oct 1, 18, Nov 25, Dec 5, 10;
1777: DL, Jan 1, 4, Mar 20, Apr 21, 22, May 9, 28, Sep 20, Oct 2, 23, Nov 10,
24, Dec 4, 13, 15; 1778: DL, Jan 1, 5, 17, 22, 23, 28, Mar 9, Apr 11, 30, May
16, 23, Sep 17, 24, 29, Oct 8, 10, 13, 19, 27, Nov 2, 6, 18, Dec 23; 1779:
DL, Jan 1, 8, 29, Mar 13, 15, 18, Apr 12, May 11, Jun 1, Sep 18, 21, 30, Oct
2, 5, 19, 21, 25, 26, 30, Nov 3, 13, 19, 27, Dec 2, 22, 27; 1780: DL, Jan 3,
21, Feb 28, Apr 26, May 5, 9, 10, Sep 16, 19, 21, 23, 26, 30, Oct 3, 7, 10,
11, 12, 17, 25, 26, 30, Nov 3, 23, 28, Dec 1, 6; 1781: DL, Jan 8, 22, 24, 29,
Apr 21, May 1, 8, 16, Sep 15, 20, 22, 25, 29, Oct 12, 13, 15, 19, 29, 30, Nov
5, 13, 20, 29, Dec 27; 1782: DL, Jan 3, 26, Mar 16, Apr 3, 12, 18, 25, May 3,
14, 29, Sep 17, 18, 19, 20, 28, Oct 3, 10, 16, 26, Nov 4, 5, 6, 22, 30, Dec
6, 26; 1783: DL, Feb 22, Mar 6, 17, 20, 24, Apr 28, May 8, 10; 1787: DL, Feb
22, Apr 20, 25, May 11, 22, Jun 2, Sep 27, Oct 4, Nov 3, 21, Dec 17, 19;
1788: DL, Jan 22, 28, Feb 25, Apr 28, May 2, Jun 2, HAY, 11, 23, Jul 2, 4,
14, Aug 4, 13, 15, 18, 25, 27, 29, DL, Oct 9, 14, 16, 23, Nov 17, 18, Dec 23;
1789: DL, Jan 27, 31, May 11
Collet, Mrs (actor, singer), 1771: HAY, May 17, 20, 22, 23, 27, DL, 27, HAY,
29, 31, Jun 10, 12, 26, Jul 1, 3, Aug 28, Sep 16, 19, 20
Collet, Mrs, 1775: DL, Nov 4
Collet, Richard (musician), 1737: HIC, Mar 24
Collet, Richard or Thomas (musician), 1737: HIC, Mar 24, CT, May 2; 1741: HIC,
Feb 5, HAY, 26, DL, Apr 16; 1748: HAY, Jan 29; 1758: CHAPEL, Apr 27; 1765:
MARLY, Aug 6; 1767: DL, Feb 28
Collet, Thomas (musician), 1743: LIF, Mar 15
Colley (house servant), 1775: CG, May 27; 1776: CG, May 22; 1777: CG, May 24;
1778: CG, May 22; 1779: CG, May 19; 1780: CG, May 26; 1781: CG, May 26; 1782:
CG, May 29; 1783:CG, Jun 4; 1784: CG, May 29
Collier (actor), 1731: SFGT, Sep 8
Collier, Sir George, 1776: DL, Dec 5; 1789: CG, Mar 16
--Death of Captain Cook, The (ballet-pantomime), 1789: CG, Mar 16, 17, 19, 21,
23, 24, 26, 30, Apr 2, 13, 16, 17, 18, 22, 23, 25, 27, May 1, 4, 7, 13, 16,
18, 25, Jun 1, 5, 12, 18, Sep 21, 23, Oct 5, 12, 17, 26, Nov 3, 10, 21, 24,
Dec 7, 12, 18; 1790: CG, Feb 23, Mar 4, 9, 15, Apr 5, 24, 26, May 25, Nov 6,
10, 16; 1791: CG, May 30, Jun 15; 1794: CG, May 15, 19, 27; 1795: CG, Oct 29,
Nov 2; 1796: CG, May 4; 1799: CG, Oct 21, 23, 26, 28; 1800: CG, May 17
--Selima and Azor, 1776: DL, Dec 4, 5, 6, 7, 9, 10, 11, 12, 16, 18, 21, 23, 28,
30, 31; 1777: DL, Jan 14, 17, 21, 27, 31, Feb 6, 7, 11, 15, 17, 22, Mar 6,
Oct 23, 28; 1778: DL, Feb 10, 25, 28, Mar 7, 26, Apr 6, 9, Oct 13; 1779: DL,
Jan 4, Oct 26, Nov 17, 25, Dec 21; 1780: DL, Apr 1, 4, 26, Oct 3, 14; 1788:
DL, Jan 28, 29, Feb 1, 4, 7, 12, 19, Mar 1, 31, Oct 14, 28, Nov 17; 1789: DL,
Jan 3, 17, Feb 5, 14, Oct 8, 10; 1792: DLKING'S, Mar 10, 26, Apr 21
Collier, Jeremy (critic), 1697: IT, Nov 1; 1698: DL, Jun 0; 1699: DLLIF, Sep
12; 1702: SH, May 7; 1703: DL, Nov 27
Collier, Rev William (prologuist), 1781: CG, Jan 31
Collier, William (director of opera company), 1710: QUEEN'S, Nov 22
Colliers (dance), 1756: DL, Nov 22, 23; 1760: DL, Oct 24, 25, CG, 25, DL, Nov
24, 25, 26, Dec 3, 9
Colline (actor), 1744: DL, Nov 7
Collings (actor), 1792: HAY, Feb 6
Collings (scene painter), 1794: DL, May 3
Collins (actor), 1771: HAY, Apr 15, 24, May 17
Collins (supernumerary, doorkeeper), 1779: DL, May 18; 1780: DL, May 10; 1781:
DL, May 5; 1782: DL, Apr 27
Collins, Clementina (actor), 1785: DL, Apr 26, Oct 26, 31, Nov 18, Dec 1; 1786:
DL, Jan 19, Mar 4, 27, May 9, Sep 19, Oct 10, 26, 30, Nov 18, Dec 6, 26;
1787: DL, Jan 13, Feb 7, Mar 29, Apr 17, May 3, CG, 22, DL, Sep 18, 25, Oct

24, 26, Nov 24, 27, Dec 5, 26; 1788: DL, Jan 5, Mar 29, Apr 11, 14, 21, 28,
May 7, 21, 30, Sep 27, 30, Oct 2, 4, 9, 13, 14, 18, 21, 22, Nov 4, 29, Dec 6,
17, 22; 1789: DL, Jan 1, 13, Feb 21, 28, May 22, Jun 5, 12, 13, Sep 12, 15,
17, 19, Oct 1, 17, 22, 28, 31, Nov 24, Dec 5, 8, 10, 17; 1790: DL, Jan 19,
Feb 11, 18, Mar 18, 23, May 18, Jun 1, CG, 16, DL, Sep 11, Oct 2, 5, 7, 9,
25, 26, 27, Nov 3, 4, Dec 14; 1791: DL, Jan 10, 25, Feb 1, 15, 25, Apr 28,
30, May 11, 19, 31, DLKING'S, Sep 27, 29, Oct 3, 8, 24, 31, Nov 1, 2, 4, 5,
10, 11, 15, 22, 29, Dec 1; 1792: DLKING'S, Jan 5, 6, 7, 9, 18, Feb 7, Mar 1,
26, 29, May 8, 23, 29, Jun 13, 14, 15, 16, DL, Sep 15, 19, 25, Oct 9, 18, 31,
Nov 3, 16, 26, Dec 3, 4, 11, 13, 21, 27; 1793: DL, Jan 1, 21, 31, Feb 8, 12,
21, 25, Mar 4, 5, 7, 9, Apr 22, May 1, 3, 7, 10, 22; 1794: DL, Apr 25, 26,
May 1, 3, Jun 6, 14, 16, 17, 20, 23, 25, 26, 28, Jul 7, Sep 18, 20, 27, Oct
4, 25, 29, Nov 3, 15, 29, Dec 9, 12; 1795: DL, Jan 8, 9, 15, 23, 27, Feb 12,
Mar 10, 14, May 2, 6, 20, 26, 29, 30, Jun 6
Collins, J (actor), 1782: HAY, Aug 17
Collins, John (actor), 1792: CG, May 15; 1794: CG, May 26
Collins, Mrs (actor), 1771: HAY, Apr 15, Jun 26, Jul 8, 24, Aug 26, Sep 2, 18
Collins, Mrs J (actor), 1790: CG, Jul 16
Collins, Mrs William (beneficiary), 1763: CG, May 14
Collins, Widow (beneficiary), 1783: DL, May 26
Collins, William (actor, dancer), 1741: TC, Aug 4; 1743: BFYWR, Aug 23, DL, Oct
27, Nov 23, 26, 29; 1744: DL, Jan 12, Feb 1, 16, Mar 10, 12, Apr 2, 9, 10,
20, 28, May 1, 8, 9, 16, 22, 24, Sep 18, 22, Oct 6, 17, 30, Nov 10, 16, Dec
12; 1745: DL, Jan 4, 8, Feb 11, Apr 17, May 1, 8, 9, Sep 28, Oct 5, 12, 15,
17, Nov 14, 19, 26, Dec 30; 1746: DL, Jan 3, 14, 17, 24, Mar 3, 17, 18, Apr
4, 9, 11, 19, 23, 25, May 9, Sep 23, Oct 2, 14, Nov 5, Dec 11, 26; 1747: DL,
Jan 2, 15, Feb 10, Mar 28, 31, Apr 28, 29, May 5, 8, CG, Oct 31, Nov 11, 13,
16, 18, 23, Dec 9, 17, 19; 1748: CG, Jan 7, 12, 14, 19, 21, 27, Feb 1, 10,
23, Mar 8, 14, 28, Apr 11, 13, 15, 21, 22, 27, 29, May 2, 3, Oct 7, 14, 17,
27, 29, Nov 3, 9, 15, 16, 24, 28, Dec 20, 22; 1749: CG, Jan 2, 25, Mar 2, 4,
9, 29, 30, Apr 5, 11, 25, May 4, Sep 25, 29, Oct 11, 12, 16, 18, 19, 23, 26,
27, 30, Nov 3, 8, 9, 17, 18, 21, 24, Dec 7, 8, 29; 1750: CG, Jan 18, Feb 22,
Mar 1, 17, Apr 26, May 2, Sep 24, 26, 28, Oct 13, 15, 16, 22, 23, 24, 27, 29,
Nov 6, 8, 12, 22, 24, Dec 10; 1751: CG, Apr 16, 22, 26, May 3, 6, 7, 8, 16,
Sep 23, 25, Oct 7, 8, 11, 29, Nov 6, 16, 18, 26, 28, Dec 10, 14; 1752: CG,
Jan 3, 6, 29, Feb 6, Mar 12, 16, 17, Apr 4, 27, 28, 30, May 4, 5, Sep 20, 25,
Oct 2, 4, 6, 9, 11, 14, 19, 21, 23, 30, 31, Nov 1, 7, 9, 23, Dec 5, 11, 13;
1753: CG, Jan 8, 22, Feb 7, 12, Mar 19, 24, Apr 5, May 7, 8, 11, 14, Sep 10,
14, 17, 24, 26, Oct 1, 3, 5, 10, 22, 24, 31, Nov 1, 7, 9, Dec 11; 1754: CG,
Mar 9, 26, Apr 6, 20, 24, 25, 30, May 2, 7, 9, 13, 15, Sep 16, 20, 23, 25,
27, 30, Oct 2, 4, 7, 9, 11, 16, Nov 16, 20, Dec 10, 13, 30; 1755: CG, Jan 4,
16, 28, Feb 8, Mar 22, Apr 21, May 1, 6, 15, Sep 29, Oct 3, 6, 8, 10, 14, 16,
18, 20, 21, 22, Nov 10, 12, 13, 17, 21, Dec 4, 5; 1756: CG, Jan 6, Mar 25,
Apr 3, 6, 20, 29, May 6, 17, Sep 20, 22, 24, 27, 29, Oct 1, 4, 6, 14, 19, 20,
21, 22, 25, 26, Dec 17, 20, 21, 27; 1757: CG, Jan 1, 4, 6, 13, 19, 20, 25,
Feb 9, 16, 19, Mar 21, Apr 26, May 3, 16, Sep 16, 21, 23, 26, 28, 30, Oct 5,
8, 10, 12, 13, 14, 15, 19, 20, 22, Nov 2, 3, 7, 9, 14, 18, 23, Dec 7, 10;
1758: CG, Feb 1, Mar 11, 14, Apr 14, 27, Sep 20, 22, 25, 27, Oct 2, 4, 9, 13,
20, 24, 30, Nov 1, 2, 3, 9, 13, 16, 18, 21, 23, 27; 1759: CG, Jan 4, Mar 17,
19, 22, 27, Apr 7, 28, May 2, 3, 7, 8, Sep 24, 26, 28, Oct 1, 3, 5, 10, Nov
28, 30, Dec 6, 8, 10, 14, 18, 31; 1760: CG, Jan 14, 31, Feb 14, Mar 17, 18,
Apr 8, 9, 17, 18, 24, 29, May 2, 7, 12, 14, Sep 22, 24, 29, Oct 1, 8, 10, 13,
14, 17, 20, 25, Nov 24, 29, Dec 18; 1761: CG, Jan 6, 7, 10, 23, Feb 17, Apr
2, 10, 24, 27, May 8, 11, 15, Sep 7, 11, 14, 18, 21, Oct 2, 5, 7, 9, 10, 13,
14, 15, 20, 22, 26, Nov 2, 6, 9, 10, Dec 11; 1762: CG, Feb 15, 22, Apr 26,
29, May 6, 11, Sep 24, 27, 30, Oct 1, 2, 4, 8, 11, 13, 14, 20, 21, Nov 16,
Dec 8; 1763: CG, Jan 18
Collins, William (poet), 1781: CG, Mar 23, 31; 1785: HAY, Apr 26; 1790: CG, Apr
30, HAY, Sep 29; 1793: CG, Apr 17; 1794: HAY, Aug 30; 1795: DL, Apr 14, CG,
24, DL, May 30, WLWS, Jun 19; 1796: CG, Mar 14, HAY, 28, DL, Apr 12, HAY, 27,
Sep 16; 1797: HAY, Aug 22, Sep 18; 1798: CG, Apr 18, DL, Jun 15; 1799: DL,
May 16, CG, Jun 12; 1800: CG, Apr 19
Collonna, Pompeo (composer), 1732: HIC, Mar 31
Colman, Francis (actor, author), 1734: KING'S, Jan 26
Colman the elder, George (author, manager), 1760: DL, Dec 5; 1761: DL, Feb 12;
1763: DL, Oct 8, 18, Nov 4, 23, 26, Dec 24; 1765: CG, Dec 3; 1766: DL, Mar 4,
Dec 13; 1767: DL, Feb 21, 27, Mar 3, CG, Jun 9, Nov 7, 10, 12, 17, 23, 26,
Dec 9; 1768: CG, Feb 20, Mar 1, Nov 5, 26; 1769: CG, Feb 18, Oct 7, 14; 1770:
CG, Nov 22, Dec 26; 1771: CG, Feb 23, HAY, Jun 26, CG, Nov 12, 30; 1772: CG,
Jan 25, 27, Feb 18, Oct 17, Nov 21; 1773: CG, Jan 1, 6, 11, 13, DL, Feb 1,
CG, 3, Mar 6, Oct 27, 28, 30, Nov 20, Dec 16; 1774: CG, Jan 29, Feb 24, Apr
9, May 26, Nov 24; 1775: DL, May 1; 1776: DL, Jan 13, Mar 7, Apr 24, HAY, Aug

28, Sep 16, DL, 21, Nov 11; 1777: DL, May 8, HAY, 15, Jun 19, Jul 18, Aug 30,
DL, Oct 31; 1778: HAY, May 18, Jun 11, Jul 2, 11, 30; 1779: DL, Jan 2, HAY,
May 31, Jun 10, 19, Jul 20, Aug 31; 1780: HAY, Mar 1, DL, Apr 19, HAY, May
30, Jun 7, Aug 5, Sep 2, DL, Oct 20; 1781: DL, May 8, HAY, 30, Aug 8, DL, Oct
6; 1782: CG, Mar 16, Apr 1, HAY, Jun 3, 29, Jul 16, Aug 5, 17, DL, Oct 1;
1783: CG, Jan 17, HAY, May 31, Jun 5, 30, Jul 5, 26, Aug 12, 28; 1784: HAY,
Mar 22, CG, Apr 26, May 7, HAY, 31, Jun 2, 17, 19, Jul 12, Aug 18, 26, Sep 2,
13, DL, Oct 9, 26; 1785: DL, Jan 27, HAMM, Jul 6, HAY, Aug 4, 10, DL, Oct 6;
1786: CG, May 20, HAY, Jun 9, Jul 24, Aug 29; 1787: CG, Jan 27, RLSN, Mar 29,
HAY, May 16, Jul 7, Aug 28, DL, Nov 6; 1788: CG, Mar 26, DL, Apr 21, May 7,
CG, 12, HAY, Aug 9, 18, 20; 1789: HAY, Feb 23, CG, Apr 20, DL, 30, HAY, May
18, Jun 22, CG, Nov 20; 1790: HAY, Oct 13, DL, Nov 2; 1791: HAY, Aug 31,
DLKING'S, Oct 10; 1792: DL, Oct 15; 1793: DL, May 17, HAY, Sep 19; 1794: DL,
May 17, CG, 30; 1795: DL, May 29; 1796: HAY, Feb 22, DL, Jun 6, Oct 17; 1797:
DL, May 1, Nov 20; 1798: DL, Sep 25; see also Novestris
--Achilles in Petticoats, 1773: CG, Dec 16, 17, 20, 22, 29, 30; 1774: CG, Jan
10, Feb 4, 15, Mar 1
--Blade Bone, The; or, Agreeable Companion (or, Harlequin's Frolic) (
interlude), 1788: HAY, Aug 20; 1789: DL, Apr 30
--Clandestine Marriage, The. See Garrick, David.
--Deuce is in Him, The, 1763: DL, Nov 4, 5, 7, 8, 9, 10, 11, 12, 14, 15, 16,
17, 18, 19, 21, 25, Dec 17, 21; 1764: DL, Feb 8, 10, 18, 22, 28, Mar 13, 20,
Apr 10, Nov 14, 17, 21, 27, Dec 12, 14, 17; 1765: DL, Jan 9, Feb 23, Mar 30,
Apr 12, May 2, 4, 18, 22, Sep 19, Oct 1; 1766: DL, Mar 22, Apr 17, 23, May 5,
12, Oct 21, 27, Dec 10, 12, 16; 1767: DL, Feb 18, Mar 14, 30, Apr 6, Dec 19;
1768: DL, Jan 13, 27, Feb 29, May 4, 11, Oct 15; 1769: DL, Feb 14, Apr 14,
May 19; 1770: DL, Dec 29; 1771: CG, Apr 20, 23, May 10, DL, 22, HAY, Jul 8,
DL, Oct 24, CG, Nov 2; 1772: DL, Jan 28, May 7, CG, 27, Sep 21, Nov 6, 17,
25; 1773: DL, Mar 23, CG, Apr 13, DL, Oct 18, CG, Dec 8, DL, 28; 1774: DL,
Jan 11, CG, 12, Sep 28, DL, Nov 10; 1775: DL, Jan 25, Feb 28, CG, Sep 27, Dec
22; 1776: CG, Jan 17, Feb 22, DL, 22, May 21, 30; 1777: HAY, Feb 11, May 1,
CG, 29, HAY, Jun 27, DL, Nov 29; 1778: DL, Jan 17, HAY, Mar 24; 1779: DL, Oct
21, Dec 18; 1780: CII, Mar 17; 1781: DL, Feb 17; 1782: CG, Nov 14; 1783: DL,
Oct 24; 1784: CG, May 13, DL, Dec 11; 1785: DL, May 27, HAY, Jul 22, 23, Aug
18; 1789: WHF, Nov 11; 1790: DL, Feb 11, Mar 4, 15, Apr 28, HAY, Aug 10, 23,
Sep 2, DL, 11, Nov 10, Dec 7; 1791: DL, Jan 1, Apr 4; 1793: DL, Feb 21; 1797:
DL, May 1
--Election of the Managers, The (prelude), 1784: HAY, May 28, Jun 2, 3, 4, 5,
7, 8, 10, 11, 12, 16
--English Merchant, The, 1767: DL, Feb 2, 21, 23, 24, 25, 26, 27, 28, Mar 2, 3,
5, 7, 9, 12, 14, 17, 26, Sep 23, Oct 5, CG, 5, 7; 1768: DL, May 3, 13, 23;
1769: CG, Jan 28, Feb 6, DL, Apr 5, CG, 21, Nov 15; 1770: CG, Feb 21; 1771:
CG, Jan 4, 10, Nov 21; 1772: CG, Feb 26; 1777: HAY, May 15, Jul 14; 1779:
HAY, Jul 16, Aug 14; 1781: HAY, Jul 18, 20, 26, Aug 3, Sep 1, 3, 4; 1782:
HAY, Jun 15, Jul 2, 6, Aug 22, 31; 1783: HAY, Aug 27; 1784: HAY, Mar 22, Jun
2, Jul 9; 1785: HAY, Jun 17, Jul 8, 18, Sep 14; 1786: HAY, Jun 21, Jul 15,
28; 1787: HAY, Jun 14, Jul 2, 17, Aug 20; 1788: HAY, Jun 28, Jul 14, Aug 4;
1789: HAY, May 18, 22; 1790: HAY, Jun 16
--Fairy Prince, The, 1771: CG, Nov 9, 11, 12, 13, 14, 15, 16, 18, 19, 20, 21,
22, 23, 25, 26, 27, 28, 29, 30, Dec 2, 3, 4, 5, 6, 9, 23; 1772: CG, Jan 6, 7,
8, 9, 10, 14, 17, 20, 22, 27, 28, Feb 22, Apr 11, May 28, Oct 29
--Fairy Tale, A, 1761: DL, Jan 31; 1763: DL, Nov 26, 28, 29, Dec 6, 16, 19, 22,
23; 1764: DL, Feb 9, 10, 13, 15, Mar 3, 6, Apr 7, 28, May 5, 8, 15, 17, 23,
Sep 22, 27, Oct 6, 11, 15, 17, 27, Nov 14; 1765: DL, Jan 26, 28, 31, Mar 2 ,
Apr 17, Dec 14, 18; 1766: DL, Feb 11, 18, Apr 9, 12, May 14, 19, Oct 28, 31;
1767: DL, Apr 28; 1777: HAY, Jul 18, 21, 22, 23, 29, Aug 15, 25, Sep 5
--Female Chevalier, The, 1778: HAY, May 18, 21, 25, Jun 1, 5, 18, 30
--Genius of Nonsense, The (pantomime), 1780: HAY, Sep 2, 4, 6, 7, 8, 9, 11, 12,
13, 14, 15; 1781: HAY, May 30, 31, Jun 4, 5, 8, 11, 14, 22, 25, 29, Jul 2, 5,
14, 21, 24, 28, 30, Aug 4; 1782: HAY, Jun 18, 19, 24, 27, Jul 24, 29, 30;
1783: HAY, Jun 7, 10, 11, 14, 16, 23, Aug 20; 1784: HAY, Jul 19, 30, Aug 9,
13, 19, 30, Sep 2; 1785: HAY, Aug 19; 1789: DL, Apr 30
--Jealous Wife, The, 1761: DL, Feb 12, 14, 16, 17, 19, 21, 23, 26, 28, Mar 2,
3, 7, 10, 12, 25, 31, Apr 8, May 12, 19, Jun 1, Oct 24, 30, Nov 5, 11, Dec
22; 1762: DL, Jan 26, CG, Mar 20, DL, 22, CG, 25, DL, Apr 19, CG, 23, DL, 28,
29, CG, May 1, DL, 15, Oct 8, CG, Nov 8, DL, Dec 7; 1763: DL, Mar 24, Apr 14,
May 26, Sep 17, Oct 12, Nov 12, 26, Dec 20; 1764: DL, Jan 11, Feb 3, 25, CG,
May 11, DL, 19, Oct 2, 13, Nov 1, 20, Dec 15; 1765: DL, Jan 17, Feb 14, Apr
29, Sep 19, Oct 10; 1766: DL, Jan 16, Apr 23, Oct 7, Dec 1; 1767: DL, Jan 22,
Feb 12, 17, May 1, Sep 19, Oct 7, CG, 31, DL, Nov 18; 1768: CG, Jan 16, DL,
22, CG, 28, DL, Apr 5, CG, May 3, DL, 10; 1769: DL, Mar 29, CG, Apr 4, DL,
25, Dec 4; 1770: CG, Apr 26, DL, May 10, Nov 6; 1771: CG, Feb 9, 19, Apr 17,

176

DL, 22, May 22, CG, Oct 14, 16, Nov 15; 1772: CG, Feb 27, DL, Jun 10; 1773:
CG, Jan 28, Feb 3, DL, Mar 30, CG, Dec 23; 1774: DL, May 18, CG, Oct 21;
1775: CG, Oct 13; 1776: DL, Jan 27, Apr 23, HAY, May 2, CG, 21; 1777: DL, Jan
28, 29, Apr 23, Sep 23; 1778: HAY, Mar 23, DL, May 16; 1779: DL, Jan 23, Mar
1, Apr 24, HAY, Jun 18, 21, 23, 29, Aug 10; 1780: CG, Oct 31, Nov 7; 1782:
DL, Apr 30, CG, May 3; 1783: CG, May 20; 1784: DL, May 5, Sep 28; 1785: DL,
Jan 8, Feb 8, HAY, Jun 29, Jul 4, 16, Aug 3, Sep 5, DL, 27; 1786: DL, Jan 7,
May 26, HAY, Jul 3, Sep 11, 13, DL, 30; 1787: DL, Jan 17, Jun 6, HAY, 28, Jul
21, DL, Dec 7; 1788: DL, Jan 11, Apr 3, HAY, 9, CG, 23, HAY, 29, CG, May 23,
DL, Jun 3, Sep 25, Nov 14, CG, Dec 27; 1789: DL, Feb 19, Jun 2, Sep 29; 1792:
DLKING'S, Feb 8, Apr 28, May 5; 1793: DL, Mar 12, May 17; 1794: CG, Apr 7,
23, Jun 9; 1795: CG, Apr 22; 1797: CG, Nov 11, 14, 22; 1798: CG, Jan 25, May
1, HAY, Dec 17; 1799: DL, Feb 26, HAY, Jun 22, 27, Jul 5
--Man and Wife; or, The Shakespeare Jubilee, 1769: CG, Oct 7, 9, 10, 11, 12,
13, 14, 16, 19, 21, 25, 27, 31, Nov 2, 21; 1770: CG, Jan 24, 26, Mar 15, 17,
19, 22, 24, 26, Apr 26, May 2; 1771: CG, Dec 23; 1772: CG, Jan 11, 13, 16,
18, 23, 29, Mar 14, 21, Apr 6, 11, Oct 29, Nov 10, 17, Dec 2; 1773: CG, Jan
26, Feb 9, Mar 1, Apr 3, 19, 26, 30, May 3, 14, Oct 21; 1777: CG, Dec 20;
1778: HAY, May 29, Jun 1, 5, 18, 30, Aug 13, 15; 1779: HAY, Jun 2, Jul 29;
1783: HAY, Jun 18, 21, 25, Jul 3, 16, 19; 1784: CG, May 7, HAY, Jun 28
--Man of Business, The, 1774: CG, Jan 27, 29, Feb 1, 2, 3, 4, 8, 15, 17, 18,
19, 21, 22, 24, 28, Mar 8, 24, Apr 14, 27
--Manager in Distress, The (prelude), 1780: HAY, May 30, Jun 2, 3, 5, 6, 7, 9,
10, 12, 14, 17, 22, 23, 28, Jul 5, 11, 14, 17, 19, 21, 25, 28, 31, Aug 22,
26; 1781: HAY, Aug 22, 28, Sep 15; 1782: HAY, Aug 27, Sep 3, 10, 14; 1783:
HAY, Aug 22; 1784: HAY, Mar 22, Jul 28, Aug 26; 1785: DL, Apr 20, HAY, Jun 1,
2, Jul 20, Aug 1, Sep 7; 1786: HAY, Jun 29, Jul 8, Sep 14; 1787: HAY, Jun 23,
Jul 5, 6; 1789: HAY, May 29, Jun 3, 8, 12, 22, 27, Jul 11, Aug 15, 22; 1790:
HAY, Jul 5, 7, 9; 1791: HAY, Aug 18, 20, 23, 27, 30, Sep 3, 16; 1796: HAY,
Sep 17
--Mother Shipton; or, The Harlequin Gladiator (pantomime), 1770: CG, Dec 26,
27, 28, 29, 31; 1771: CG, Jan 1, 2, 3, 4, 5, 7, 8, 9, 10, 11, 12, 14, 15, 16,
17, 18, 19, 21, 22, 23, 24, 25, 26, 28, 29, 31, Feb 1, 2, 4, 5, 6, 7, 8, 9,
11, 12, 14, 16, 18, 19, 21, Mar 11, 21, Apr 1, 11, 15, 26, May 2, 3, 14, 20,
30, Oct 15, 17, 19, 21, 28, Nov 13, Dec 26, 27, 28, 30, 31; 1772: CG, Jan 1,
2, 3, 4, Feb 24, 25, 26, 27, 28, 29, Mar 2, 3, 7, 9, 12, 16, 17, 19, 23, 26,
Apr 20, 27, May 7, 8, 9, 18, 30, Oct 16, 21, 23, 26, Nov 2, 3; 1773: CG, Oct
28; 1774: CG, Apr 11, 14, 28, May 4, 9, 23, 24; 1776: CG, Apr 27; 1777: CG,
Apr 23; 1778: CG, Feb 23, 24, 25, 26, 28, Mar 2, 3, 7, 10, 12, 17, 26, Apr 6,
20, 29, May 12, 15, 18, 21; 1780: CG, Apr 7; 1785: HAMM, Jul 15; 1789: CG,
Dec 21; 1790: CG, Nov 15
--Musical Lady, The, 1762: DL, Mar 6, 8, 9, 11, 13, 16, Apr 19, 24, 27, May 3,
14, Sep 25, 29, 30, Oct 9, 20, Nov 16, Dec 15, 17; 1763: DL, Feb 19, Mar 19,
Apr 18, 25, May 4, 9, 11, 20, Sep 27, Oct 27; 1764: DL, Apr 3, 9, May 2, 19,
Sep 18, Oct 23, Dec 22; 1765: DL, Jan 5, 19, CG, Apr 24, DL, May 3, 17, 21,
Sep 17, Oct 15, Dec 13; 1766: DL, Apr 4, 29, Dec 29; 1767: DL, Jan 3, 16, 17,
Mar 12, 16, 17, May 28, 30, Jun 1, CG, Dec 8; 1768: CG, Feb 2, Mar 17, Apr
25, May 6, 13, DL, Oct 25, CG, Dec 21; 1769: CG, Jan 17, 24, Dec 20; 1770:
CG, Mar 6, DL, Dec 6, 15; 1771: DL, Jan 26, Mar 2, Apr 25, Dec 4, 10; 1773:
DL, Jan 29, Feb 17, CG, May 10, Sep 22, Nov 10, DL, Dec 31; 1775: CG, Dec 23;
1776: CG, Feb 10; 1784: CG, Sep 24, 29, Oct 1, 6, 25; 1785: CG, Apr 6; 1787:
HAY, Apr 30
--New Brooms! (prelude), 1776: DL, Sep 21, 24, 26, 28, Oct 1, 8, 9, 10
--Oxonian in Town, The, 1767: CG, Oct 13, Nov 7, 9, 10, 11, 12, 13, 14, 16, 17,
23, 25, 26, 28, 30, Dec 5, 19, 23, 28; 1768: CG, Jan 20, 27, Feb 13, 20, Mar
7, 9, Sep 28, Oct 5, 26, Nov 15, 23, 30, Dec 20; 1769: CG, Jan 6, Mar 9, 11,
31, Apr 17, May 15, 25, Oct 18, Nov 21; 1770: CG, Apr 3, 19, May 11; 1772:
CG, Jan 21
--Polly Honeycomb, 1760: DL, Dec 5, 6, 8, 9, 11, 12, 17, 20, 31; 1761: DL, Jan
2, 3, 8, 9, 19, 20, 22, 23, 26, Feb 24, Mar 23, 25, 30, Apr 7, 28, May 6, 12,
13, 16, 21, 27, Jun 3, Sep 19, 26, Oct 6, 13, Nov 12, Dec 1, 23; 1762: DL,
Jan 9, Feb 13, 16, 27, Apr 15, May 1, HAY, Aug 30, Sep 2, 6, 8, DL, Oct 12,
CG, 14, 18, 25, 27, DL, Nov 15, Dec 31; 1763: DL, Feb 1, 17, Mar 12, Apr 16,
May 5, CG, 6, DL, 12, CG, 24, DL, Sep 20, Oct 10, 22, Nov 24; 1764: DL, Feb
16, Mar 17, Apr 10, 23, May 18, Sep 15, Oct 9, Nov 12, Dec 8; 1765: DL, Jan
2, 16, Feb 9, 14, Apr 24, May 16, 27, HAY, Jul 31, Aug 16, DL, Sep 14, Oct 2,
CG, 19, 22, 25; 1766: CG, Feb 1, DL, Sep 25, Oct 11, Dec 4, 13; 1770: DL, Dec
19; 1771: DL, Jan 3, 24, Feb 11, Dec 3; 1773: DL, Feb 10, CG, May 19, DL, Oct
2, Dec 11; 1775: DL, May 20; 1776: DL, Nov 7, CG, 19, Dec 6, 11; 1777: HAY,
Jun 16, 19, 20, CHR, 23, HAY, 26, Aug 2, 27; 1778: HAY, Jun 3, Jul 13, CG,
Oct 5; 1779: DL, Mar 11, HAY, Jul 5, 10, Aug 2; 1780: HAY, Jun 5, 14; 1784:
HAY, Jun 28; 1787: HAY, Jun 13, 16; 1789: HAY, Aug 1; 1790: DL, Feb 27, Mar

6, 16, Oct 25; 1793: HAY, Aug 2, 26
--Portrait, The (burletta), 1770: CG, Nov 22, 23, 24, 26, 27, 29, 30, Dec 1, 5, 10, 14; 1771: CG, Mar 5, 9, 18; 1774: CG, Feb 17, 19, 22; 1777: HAY, Jul 24, 28, Aug 1, 6, 11, 13, 15, 29, Sep 9, 13; 1778: HAY, Jul 22, 24, 30; 1789: HAY, Jul 31
--Preludio, A, 1781: HAY, Aug 8, 9, 10, 11, 13, 14, 16, 18, 20, 23, 27, 29, 30, Sep 1, 6, 8, 11, 14; 1782: HAY, Jun 3, 5, 7, 14, 17, 25, Jul 27; 1783: HAY, Jun 20
--Separate Maintenance, The, 1779: HAY, Aug 31, Sep 1, 2, 3, 6, 8, 9, 10, 13, 14, 15, 16; 1780: HAY, Jun 13, 16, 21, 28, Jul 4, 7, 13, 18, 26, Aug 3, Sep 12; 1781: HAY, May 31, Jun 5, 14, 15, 21, 22, 28, Jul 12, 21, 27, Sep 4, 5; 1782: HAY, Jun 20, 22, 28, Jul 9, Aug 21, 29; 1783: HAY, Jun 13, 27, Aug 12, 28, Sep 10; 1784: HAY, May 29, Jun 12; 1785: HAY, Jun 7, Jul 1; 1786: HAY, Jun 16; 1787: HAY, Jun 18, 30
--Sheep Shearing, The; or, Florizel and Perdita (pastoral), 1777: HAY, Jul 18, 21; 1783: HAY, Aug 20, 27
--Spanish Barber, The; or, The Fruitless Precaution (opera), 1777: HAY, Aug 30, Sep 1, 2, 4, 8, 11, 16; 1778: HAY, Jun 11, 12, 16, 17, 23, 24, 29, Jul 6, 21, 23, 25, Aug 1, 11, 24, Sep 3, 8, 11; 1779: HAY, Jun 2, 9, 11, 17, 19, 24, 26, 30, Jul 9, 15, 30, Aug 6, 20, 26, Sep 4, 17; 1780: HAY, Jun 23, 24, 27, Jul 5, 11, 17, 25, Aug 1, 8, Sep 7, 15; 1781: HAY, May 30, 31, Jun 11, 18, 25, Jul 3, 24, Sep 12, 15; 1782: HAY, Jun 13, 17, 26, 28, Jul 13, 20, 24, Aug 2, 16, 27, Sep 3, 10; 1783: HAY, Jun 3, 12, 17, 26, Jul 17, 24, Aug 1, 18, Sep 8; 1784: HAY, May 28, Jun 3, 9, 15, Jul 1, 5, 13, 22, 28, Aug 28, Sep 8; 1785: HAY, Jun 3, 23, Jul 6, Aug 19; 1786: HAY, Jun 12, 30, Aug 10, 18, Sep 7, 14; 1787: HAY, Jun 13, Jul 6, Aug 7; 1788: DL, Apr 21, HAY, Jun 26, Jul 8, Aug 13, 30; 1789: HAY, Jul 8, 9, 31; 1790: HAY, Jun 30, Jul 12, Aug 13, 21, 28, Sep 2, 9, Oct 13; 1791: HAY, Jun 6, 14, Jul 1, Sep 14, 16; 1792: HAY, Jun 22, Jul 18, Aug 16; 1793: HAY, Jun 11, 25; 1794: HAY, Jul 25, 30; 1795: DL, Nov 16, 18, 19, Dec 1, 8, 15, 22, 29; 1796: HAY, Jun 20, 27, Jul 14, Aug 9; 1797: HAY, Jun 26, Jul 4; 1798: HAY, Jun 21, Jul 10, 17; 1799: HAY, Jul 10
--Spleen, The; or, Islington Spa, 1776: DL, Feb 24, Mar 2, 7, 9, 16, Apr 11, 13, 16, 24, May 9, 13
--Suicide, The, 1778: HAY, Jul 11, 13, 15, 17, 20, 22, 24, 27, 29, Aug 4, 7, 13, 19, 28, Sep 1, 10, 12, 15, 16; 1779: HAY, Jun 10, 14, 16, 22, 28, Jul 13, 24, Aug 11, 23, 30, Sep 17; 1780: HAY, May 30, Jun 6, 23, Jul 8, 21, 31, Sep 6, 13; 1781: HAY, Jun 8, 19, Jul 5, 16, Sep 10, 13; 1782: HAY, Jun 6, 8, 18, 27, Jul 4, 25, Aug 20, Sep 5; 1783: HAY, May 31, Jun 19, Aug 23, Sep 3, 5; 1784: HAY, Jun 1, 11; 1785: HAY, Jun 21, Jul 5, 30, Sep 1; 1786: HAY, Jun 28, Sep 11; 1787: HAY, Jun 27, Jul 5, 30; 1788: HAY, Jun 10, 14, Sep 2, 11; 1789: HAY, Jun 19, 23, Jul 3, Aug 7; 1790: HAY, Jun 19, 25, Jul 14, Aug 10, 27, Sep 7; 1792: HAY, Jun 20, 30, Jul 7, 19, Aug 13; 1794: HAY, Jul 9, 15; 1795: DL, Dec 30
--Tit for Tat, 1786: HAY, Aug 29, 31, Sep 2, 5, 6, 9, 12, 15; 1787: HAY, Jul 20, 24, Aug 1, 14, 25, 30; 1788: DL, May 7, CG, 12, HAY, Jun 18, Jul 23, Aug 5, 8; 1789: HAY, Jun 15, Jul 1; 1790: DL, Apr 30, Jun 5, HAY, Jul 7, Aug 30, Sep 3; 1793: DL, Jan 3, 8, 12, Feb 4, 14, HAY, Jul 19, 25, Aug 24; 1794: HAY, Jul 16, 25, Aug 7, 15, DL, Oct 20, Dec 27; 1795: DL, Jan 20, May 6, HAY, Jul 16, 29; 1796: DL, Jun 14, HAY, Jul 6, Aug 4; 1797: HAY, Jun 13; 1798: HAY, Aug 31
--Village Lawyer, The (farce), 1787: HAY, Aug 28, 30, 31, Sep 4, 10, 12; 1788: HAY, Jun 16, 25, Jul 9, 15, 21, Aug 1, 22, 28; 1789: HAY, Jul 4, 23, 28; 1790: HAY, Jul 22, 30, Aug 6, 17, 21, 27, Sep 3; 1791: HAY, Jun 10, 21, 27, Jul 6, 19, 22, 25, Aug 2, 19, 22, Sep 5, 10; 1792: HAY, Jun 19, 27, Jul 20, 24, 31, Aug 10, 14, 18, 22, Sep 1; 1793: HAY, Jun 13, 20, Jul 3, 15, 20, 25, 29, Aug 13, 30, Sep 4, 7, 14; 1794: HAY, Jul 22, 26, Aug 26, Sep 4, 11; 1795: HAY, Jun 18, 25, Jul 7, 23, 24, Aug 11, 28, DL, Oct 6, 10, 28, Nov 4, 11, 20, Dec 16; 1796: HAY, Jul 6, 11, 22, 29, Aug 1, 20, Sep 9, 15; 1797: HAY, Sep 11, 14, 15; 1798: HAY, Jun 20, 29, Jul 11, 19, Aug 1, 22, Sep 11; 1799: DL, Apr 18, HAY, Jun 15, 21, Jul 27; 1800: HAY, Jul 12, 26, Aug 7, Sep 13
--Young Actor, The (interlude), 1781: DL, May 8, HAY, Aug 17
Colman the younger, George (manager, dramatist), 1781: HAY, Sep 8; 1782: HAY, Aug 16; 1784: HAY, Jun 19; 1785: HAY, Jul 9; 1786: CG, May 11; 1787: HAY, Aug 4; 1788: HAY, Jul 10, Aug 9; 1789: DL, Apr 30, HAY, Jul 11, Aug 11; 1790: HAY, Jun 14, Aug 13; 1791: CG, Apr 16, DL, Jun 4, HAY, Jul 30, Aug 24; 1792: DLKING'S, Mar 29, HAY, Jun 15, Aug 23, Sep 5; 1793: DL, Apr 3, 8, HAY, Jun 29, Aug 3; 1794: HAY, Jan 14, Feb 22, DL, Apr 21, CG, 29, HAY, Sep 17, DL, Oct 28; 1795: DL, Apr 16, CG, May 14, HAY, Jun 9; 1796: DL, Mar 12, Apr 13, CG, 26, HAY, Jul 7, 23; 1797: DL, Apr 28, CG, May 16, HAY, Jul 15, Sep 16, CG, Oct 6, Dec 12; 1798: DL, Jan 16, CG, Apr 24, HAY, Jun 14, Jul 6, 21; 1799: DL, Jan 19, Mar 2, CG, 14, DL, Apr 19, CG, 23, 30, HAY, Jun 24, Jul 13, CG, Oct 31; 1800: HAY, Jun 13, Sep 1

--Battle of Hexham, The; or, Days of Old, <u>1789</u>: HAY, Aug 8, 11, 13, 14, 15, 17,
  19, 21, 22, 24, 26, 29, 31, Sep 3, 5, 7, 8, 9, 10, 12, 14, 15; <u>1790</u>: HAY, Jun
  15, 21, 25, 28, Jul 3, 6, 10, 13, 17, 20, 24, 29, Aug 2, 31, Sep 6, 10, 13,
  15; <u>1791</u>: HAY, Jun 8, 16, 24, Jul 4, 8, 15, 21, 28, Aug 16, 26, Sep 1, 7;
  <u>1792</u>: HAY, Jun 18, 19, 21, 28, Jul 5, 12, 20, 24, 30, Aug 11, 17, 21, 31, Sep
  3, 11; <u>1793</u>: HAY, Jun 12, 22, Jul 3, 17, 22, 27, Aug 20, Sep 7; <u>1794</u>: HAY,
  Jul 18, Sep 2; <u>1795</u>: CG, May 14, HAY, Jun 9, Jul 18, CG, Dec 7, 18; <u>1796</u>:
  HAY, Jun 13, 29, Jul 20; <u>1797</u>: HAY, Jun 19, 27, 30, Jul 7, 11, Aug 3; <u>1798</u>:
  HAY, Jun 12, Jul 6; <u>1799</u>: HAY, Jul 23, Aug 19
--Blue Beard; or, Female Curiosity, <u>1798</u>: DL, Jan 16, 17, 18, 19, 20, 23, 24,
  25, 26, 27, 31, Feb 1, 3, 6, 7, 8, 9, 10, 13, 14, 15, 16, 17, 20, 22, 24, 27,
  Mar 1, 3, 6, 8, 10, 13, 17, 20, 26, 27, 29, Apr 10, 11, 12, 16, 17, 19, 20,
  24, 26, 27, May 1, 3, 4, 9, 14, 15, 16, 17, 22, 25, 28, 30, Jun 4, 5, 7, 12,
  Oct 6, 9, 11, 13, 22, 25, 30, Nov 5, 9, 12, 26, 27, Dec 3, 10, 13, 17, 26,
  27, 31; <u>1799</u>: DL, Jan 2, 3, 4, 7, 8, Apr 15, 16, 19, 20, 23, 26, 29, 30, May
  2, 6, 10, 13, 14, 30, Oct 14, 15, 17, 19, 21, 22, 28, 29, Nov 1, 4, 5, 9, 11,
  20, 23, 26, Dec 2, 6, 9, 26, 27, 30; <u>1800</u>: DL, Mar 6, 8, 10
--Blue Devils (farce), <u>1798</u>: CG, Apr 24, HAY, Jun 12, 13, 27, Jul 3, 14, 23,
  Aug 16, Sep 8; <u>1799</u>: HAY, Jul 10, 11, 13, 16, 24, Sep 4; <u>1800</u>: HAY, Jun 14,
  Jul 2, 26, Aug 21, Sep 9
--Family Party, The (farce), <u>1789</u>: HAY, Jul 11, 14, 17, 22, Aug 4, 7, 18
--Female Dramatist, The (farce), <u>1782</u>: HAY, Aug 16
--Feudal Times; or, The Banquet Gallery, <u>1799</u>: DL, Jan 19, 21, 22, 23, 24, 25,
  26, 28, 29, 31, Feb 1, 2, 4, 7, 9, 11, 14, 16, 18, 19, 21, 23, 25, 26, 28,
  Mar 2, 4, 5, 11, 12, 14, 16, 25, 26, 27, 28, Apr 1, 9, 17
--Heir at Law, The, <u>1797</u>: HAY, Jul 15, 17, 18, 19, 20, 21, 22, 24, 25, 26, 27,
  28, 29, 31, Aug 2, 4, 5, 7, 11, 17, 21, 25, Sep 1, 5, 11, 13, 15, 16, CG, Dec
  12, 20; <u>1798</u>: CG, Feb 7, Mar 1, Apr 24, May 8, HAY, Jun 14, 22, 28, Jul 4,
  12, 18, Aug 6, 10, 18, 24, 31, Sep 8, 13; <u>1799</u>: CG, Mar 14, HAY, Jun 24, Jul
  1, 8, 15, 22, 29, Aug 5, 12, 19, 29, Sep 3, 11; <u>1800</u>: CG, Apr 26, May 6, HAY,
  Jun 13, 20, 27, 30, Jul 8, 24, Aug 5, 26, Sep 8
--Inkle and Yarico (opera), <u>1787</u>: HAY, Aug 4, 6, 8, 11, 13, 15, 18, 24, 27, 30,
  31, Sep 1, 3, 4, 8, 10, 11, 12, 13, 14, 15; <u>1788</u>: CG, Mar 26, HAY, Jun 23,
  27, Jul 1, 3, 5, 9, 16, 21, 25, 28, Aug 1, 15, 18, 26, 29, Sep 3, 8, 10, 12,
  15, CG, Oct 22, 25, 31, Nov 5, 17, 24, Dec 5; <u>1789</u>: CG, Jan 1, 26, 29, 31,
  Feb 7, 17, 21, 28, Mar 10, 21, 30, Apr 16, 25, May 1, 6, 16, DL, 28, CG, Jun
  1, DL, 8, CG, 18, HAY, 25, Jul 6, 9, 13, 14, 22, 25, 29, Aug 7, 12, 28, Sep
  2, KHS, 16, CG, Oct 13, Nov 3, DL, 4, WHF, 9, CG, Dec 22; <u>1790</u>: CG, Jan 12,
  23, Apr 8, HAY, Jun 28, Jul 1, 8, 26, Aug 4, 17, 19, 23, 25, Sep 1, 8, 14;
  <u>1791</u>: CG, Apr 28, May 17, 28, HAY, Jun 10, 21, Jul 6, 19, Aug 5, 10, CG, Nov
  2, DLKING'S, 2, CG, 9, Dec 2, 23; <u>1792</u>: CII, Jan 16, DLKING'S, Mar 19, CG,
  Apr 25, May 28, HAY, Jul 3, 17, 31, Sep 1, CG, 26; <u>1793</u>: CG, Apr 25, May 16,
  Jun 8, HAY, 13, 20, Jul 22, 23, Aug 1, Sep 7, Oct 4, 10, Dec 9, CG, 17; <u>1794</u>:
  CG, Jun 12, 14, HAY, Jul 11, 16, Aug 2, 12, 23, Sep 6, 13, CG, Dec 30; <u>1795</u>:
  CG, May 16, HAY, Jun 15, Jul 13, Aug 12; <u>1796</u>: CG, Apr 15, May 18, HAY, Jul
  21, Aug 17, 27; <u>1797</u>: CG, May 9, 23, HAY, Jun 21, 29; <u>1798</u>: CG, Apr 18, 24,
  May 9, Jun 1, HAY, 16, Aug 28, CG, Sep 26; <u>1799</u>: CG, Mar 5, May 13, Jun 5,
  HAY, 20, 26, CG, Dec 16; <u>1800</u>: CG, Jan 6, Apr 23, HAY, Jun 16, 21, Aug 2, Sep
  4
--Iron Chest, The, <u>1796</u>: DL, Mar 12, 17, 19, 28, 29, May 25, HAY, Aug 29, 31,
  Sep 2, 3, 5, 6, 8, 9, 10, 12, 13, 14, 15; <u>1797</u>: HAY, Aug 14, 22, 31; <u>1798</u>:
  HAY, Jul 16, 30, Aug 9, 16, Sep 11; <u>1799</u>: CG, Apr 23, May 18, HAY, Jul 27,
  Aug 15, 22, Sep 5, 13, 16; <u>1800</u>: HAY, Jul 31, Aug 7
--Mountaineers, The, <u>1793</u>: HAY, Aug 3, 5, 7, 8, 9, 10, 14, 15, 16, 17, 19, 21,
  22, 23, 26, 28, 29, 31, Sep 2, 4, 5, 6, 9, 11, 13, 14, 19, 26, Oct 2, 7, 14,
  16, 23, 30, Nov 2, 6, 9, 14, 15; <u>1794</u>: HAY, Jul 21, 23, 28, 31, Aug 21, 28,
  Sep 8, 10, 13, DL, Oct 7, 13, 21, 22, 30, 31, Nov 10, 24, Dec 8; <u>1795</u>: DL,
  Jan 12, 26, Feb 2, 23, HAY, Jul 31, Aug 10, 15, 20, DL, Oct 27; <u>1796</u>: DL, Jan
  11, 21, Mar 3, May 21, Jun 7, HAY, 25, 28, Jul 1, Aug 12, 15, 22, Sep 16, CG,
  Oct 6, DL, Nov 26; <u>1797</u>: DL, Mar 27, HAY, Aug 9, 12; <u>1798</u>: DL, Jun 7, HAY,
  20, Jul 3, 17, Sep 6; <u>1799</u>: HAY, Jul 12, Aug 20; <u>1800</u>: DL, Jun 11, HAY, 24,
  Aug 23, 30
--My Nightgown and Slippers (interlude), <u>1797</u>: DL, Apr 28; <u>1799</u>: DL, Apr 19
--New Hay at the Old Market (prelude), <u>1795</u>: HAY, Jun 9, 10, 11, 12, 13, 16,
  17, 18, 19, 24, 27, 29, Jul 2, 4, 10, 11, 15, 17, 21, 25, 29, Aug 1, 10, 12,
  14, 19, 24, 31, Sep 7, 11, 14, 15; <u>1796</u>: DL, Apr 13, Jun 7, HAY, Jul 7
--Poor Old Hay-Market; or, Two Sides of the Gutter!!!, <u>1792</u>: HAY, Jun 15, 18,
  19, 20, 21, 25, 28, Jul 5, 7
--Review, The; or, The Wags of Windsor (farce), <u>1798</u>: HAY, Jul 6; <u>1800</u>: HAY,
  Sep 1, 2, 4, 5, 6, 9, 10, 11, 12, 13
--Surrender of Calais, The, <u>1791</u>: HAY, Jul 30, Aug 1, 3, 4, 6, 8, 9, 11, 15,
  17, 18, 20, 22, 23, 25, 27, 29, 31, Sep 2, 3, 5, 6, 8, 9, 10, 12, 13, 15;

1792: DLKING'S, Mar 29, Apr 11, HAY, Jun 23, 25, 26, 29, Jul 2, 6, 13, 21,
   27, Aug 3, 8, 14, 20, 28, Sep 1, 10, 13; 1793: HAY, Jun 17, 24, 28, Jul 8,
   20, 29, Aug 13, 27; 1794: HAY, Jul 17, 24, Aug 22, 30; 1795: HAY, Jun 13, 19,
   Jul 24, Aug 13, 26, DL, Dec 10; 1796: HAY, Jul 15, 22, Aug 5, 20, 26; 1797:
   HAY, Jun 23, 28, Jul 5, 14, Aug 1, 24, Sep 7; 1798: HAY, Jul 14, 19, Aug 1,
   DL, Dec 4; 1799: HAY, Jul 2, 26, Aug 24, Sep 10; 1800: HAY, Jun 19, 26
--Sylvester Daggerwood (interlude), 1795: HAY, Jun 9; 1796: DL, Apr 13, HAY,
   Jul 7, 16, 25, Aug 2, 10, 17, Sep 2, 5, 9, 16; 1797: DL, Feb 21, Mar 7, 9,
   May 8, 10, 17, 22, 27, Jun 1, 2, 7, HAY, Aug 14, Sep 1, 2, 6, 11, 15, 16, DL,
   Nov 13, Dec 23; 1798: DL, Apr 27, 30, May 11, 15, 18, Jun 1, 5, 7, WRSG, 8,
   DL, 13, HAY, Aug 6, DL, Dec 11, HAY, 17; 1799: DL, Apr 18, May 7, 9, Jun 1;
   1800: DL, Apr 28, May 30, Jun 10
--Two to One (opera), 1784: HAY, Jun 19, 21, 22, 23, 25, 26, 28, 30, Jul 2, 8,
   10, 15, 17, 21, 23, 26, 31, Aug 14, 25, Sep 15; 1785: HAY, May 28, Jun 8, 22,
   Aug 1, 11; 1786: HAY, Jul 12, 15, Aug 3, Sep 1; 1787: HAY, Jun 20, Jul 3, Aug
   2; 1789: HAY, Jun 29, Jul 10; 1791: HAY, Jul 22; 1792: HAY, Jul 23
--Ut Pictura Poesis!; or, The Enraged Musician, 1789: HAY, May 18, 20, 22, 25,
   27, 29, Jun 1, 3, 8, 12, 15, 19, 23, Jul 17, 24, 28, Sep 4
--Ways and Means; or, A Trip to Dover, 1788: HAY, Jul 10, 12, 15, 17, 19, 22,
   26, Aug 2, 7; 1790: HAY, Jun 18, 24, Jul 2, 9, 14, 28, Aug 6, 18; 1791: HAY,
   Jun 18; 1792: HAY, Aug 9; 1793: HAY, Jun 14, 19, 26, Jul 30, Oct 8, 17, Nov
   22, 28, Dec 4, 12, 18; 1794: HAY, Jan 7, 10, Feb 5, 12, Sep 1, 9; 1795: HAY,
   Jun 12, 17, Jul 3, 30, Aug 5, Sep 1; 1796: HAY, Jul 7, 16, Aug 2, 25; 1797:
   HAY, Jan 23; 1798: DL, Jun 12, HAY, Aug 3, 8, Sep 1, 12; 1799: HAY, Jun 25,
   Jul 13; 1800: HAY, Feb 3, Jul 5
Colomba, Giovanni Battista Innocenzo (machinist, scene painter), 1773: KING'S,
   Oct 23; 1774: KING'S, Nov 8; 1775: KING'S, Feb 7, Nov 7; 1777: KING'S, Jan 21
Colombati, Elisabetta (singer), 1794: KING'S, Mar 1, 18, Apr 26, May 17, 29,
   Dec 6, 20; 1795: KING'S, Jan 10, 17, 24, 27, Feb 7, Mar 21, May 14, 26, Jun
   2, 23, Dec 12; 1796: KING'S, Jan 5, Feb 9, Mar 10; 1797: KING'S, Dec 9; 1798:
   KING'S, Jan 23, Mar 10, 22, Apr 10, 21
Colombe, Emilie (dancer), 1789: KING'S, Jan 10, Mar 3, 17, 19, 31, Apr 28, May
   26, Jun 16, CG, 30
Colombine Avocat, Pour et Contre. See Fatouville, Nolant de.
Colombine Courtezan. See Cupid and Psyche.
Colombine Docteur Au Droit (play), 1725: HAY, Feb 3
Colombine Fille Scavante et Marinete Captaine d'Infanterie, 1718: LIF, Dec 17;
   1726: HAY, Apr 14
Colonie, La. See Saint-Foix, Germain Francois Poulain de.
Coltellini, Marco (librettist), 1774: KING'S, Jan 15; 1783: KING'S, Apr 29
Colthorp. See Calthorpe.
Columbus. See Morton, Thomas.
Colvill (singer), 1779: HAY, Dec 27
Comanni (dancer), 1734: CG, Jan 25
Combes. See Coombs.
Come, all the youths whose hearts have bled (song), 1680: DG, Feb 0
Come all with moving songs (song), 1696: LIF, Nov 14
Come, all ye shepherds (song), 1698: DL, Mar 0
Come, all you Nymphs of Cynthia's Train (song), 1697: DG, Jun 0
Come and Listen to my Ditty (music), 1737: HIC, Apr 1
Come and trip it (song), 1791: CG, Mar 18; 1792: CG, Mar 14, 21; 1793: CG, Mar
   20; 1794: CG, Mar 21, DL, Apr 9; 1796: CG, Feb 17
Come, Blooming Boy (song), 1761: KING'S, Mar 12
Come, but keep (song), 1791: CG, Mar 30; 1794: CG, Mar 21, DL, Apr 9
Come buy my earthenware (song), 1798: CG, Apr 9
Come cheer up, my lads (song), 1797: CG, Oct 16
Come, come, all noble souls (song), 1789: CG, May 5, HAY, Aug 25; 1791: CG, May
   18; 1798: CG, Mar 9; 1799: CG, Mar 1
Come, come, my good shepherds (song), 1783: CG, May 19; 1785: HAY, Jan 24;
   1787: CG, May 21; 1788: CG, Apr 11, May 3; 1790: CG, Feb 11; 1792: CG, May 11
Come, ever smiling liberty (song), 1747: CG, May 4; 1748: CG, Mar 8, 28, 31,
   KING'S, Apr 5, CG, 21, 27, HAY, Dec 9; 1789: CG, Mar 27; 1790: CG, Feb 26,
   Mar 19; 1791: CG, Mar 23; 1794: CG, Mar 26, DL, Apr 9; 1796: CG, Feb 26;
   1797: CG, Mar 31; 1798: CG, Mar 30; 1799: CG, Mar 1, 15; 1800: CG, Mar 5
Come, every jovial fellow (song), 1796: CG, May 16, Jun 1; 1797: CG, May 22;
   1798: CG, Mar 19; 1799: CG, Mar 2, 4; 1800: CG, Mar 4, 8, Jun 5
Come, gentle eve (song), 1793: KING/HAY, Mar 13
Come Hodge, come Robin (song), 1696: LIF, Apr 0
Come, honest Friends (song), 1780: CG, Apr 10; 1781: CG, Apr 3, 25, 27; 1783:
   HAY, Aug 1
Come if you dare (song), 1798: CG, Feb 28; 1799: CG, Mar 1; 1800: CG, Mar 21
Come, Jug my honey, let's to bed (song), 1684: DLORDG, Dec 0

Come, let us all a Maying go (song), 1792: CG, May 11
Come, let us prepare (song), 1735: DL, May 13; 1736: DL, May 4; 1737: DL, May
   7; 1738: CG, May 1; 1739: DL, May 15, 28; 1747: DL, May 16
Come, let us Trip (song), 1746: CG, Apr 29
Come, painter, with thy happiest flight (song), 1790: CG, Nov 23; 1791: CG, Sep
   19; 1793: CG, May 21; 1794: CG, Apr 12, Oct 29; 1795: CG, Oct 7; 1797: CG,
   Oct 2; 1799: CG, Dec 9
Come, pass the Box (song), 1796: CG, Mar 15, Oct 24
Come, pensive nun (song), 1791: CG, Mar 18; 1794: CG, Mar 21, DL, Apr 9
Come potesti ob Dio (music), 1741: HIC, Apr 24
Come, rather goddess (song), 1791: CG, Mar 18; 1794: CG, Mar 21, DL, Apr 9
Come, Roger and Nell (song), 1789: CG, Dec 21; 1790: CG, Jan 23, May 31, Nov 15
Come, Rosalind, O Come and See (song), 1746: GF, Feb 18, CG, Apr 12
Come, Strephon, Phyllis come let's troth (song), 1697: DG, Jun 0
Come, thou goddess (song), 1790: DL, Mar 10, CG, 17, 26; 1791: CG, Mar 18;
   1793: CG, Mar 20; 1794: CG, Mar 21, DL, Apr 9
Come, Thyrsis, come (song), 1695: LIF, Dec 0
Come unto him (song), 1790: DL, Mar 17, 24; 1793: KING/HAY, Feb 20; 1794: DL,
   Mar 19
Come unto these yellow sands (song), 1793: KING/HAY, Feb 15, 27
Come, ye smiling hours (song), 1789: CG, Apr 3; 1790: CG, Mar 17
Come, ye Sons of Art (song), 1694: ATCOURT, Apr 30
Come, ye who from your souls (song), 1794: CG, Jun 4
Comedia in Comedia, La. See Rinaldo da Capua.
Comediante Fatta Cantatrice, La (burletta), 1756: CG, Jan 12, 16
Comediens Esclaves, Les (play), 1735: GF/HAY, Apr 14
Comedy of Errors, The. See Shakespeare, William.
Comedy Within a Comedy, A; or, The Foppish Merchant Turned Comedian (play),
   1727: KING'S, Mar 2
Comer, Mrs (householder), 1745: GF, Feb 4
Comerford, (actor), 1793: HAY, Jun 29, Jul 6, Aug 3, 5, 14, Oct 10, Dec 26;
   1794: HAY, Jan 17, 29, Feb 22
Comerford, Henry (actor), 1776: CHR, Sep 23, 25, 27, 30, Oct 2, 4, 7, 9, 11,
   14, 16, 18; 1777: HAY, Feb 11, May 1
Comet, The. See Bellamy, Thomas.
Comfort ye my people (song), 1790: CG, Mar 26; 1793: KING/HAY, Feb 20; 1794:
   DL, Mar 19; 1795: CG, Mar 20, 27; 1797: CG, Mar 3; 1798: CG, Mar 30; 1799:
   CG, Feb 13
Comic Air (song), 1776: CHR, Sep 23; 1782: DL, May 10
Comic Allemande (dance), 1785: HAY, Feb 21, 28
Comic Ballet (dance), 1734: DL, Nov 20; 1736: CG, Feb 26, Apr 1, 17, 30, May 4,
   18, 24; 1738: BFP, Aug 23; 1739: CF, Sep 12, 15, 28, Oct 30, Nov 6, 7, 8, 9,
   10, 13, 14, 20, 21, 23, 24, 26, 28, Dec 3, 6, 8, 12, 14, 18, 19, 21, 29;
   1740: CG, Jan 4, 5, 8, 15, 17, Feb 2, 6, 7, Mar 10, 20, 24, 27, Apr 9, 14,
   16, 18, 28, May 12, 23, Jun 5, Sep 29, Oct 3, GF, 29, CG, 31, Nov 3, 7, DL,
   12, CG, 13, 15, DL, 17, CG, 18, 19, 20, DL, Dec 2, CG, 19, 22; 1741: CG, Mar
   2, 12, 16, 30; 1742: DL, Nov 22, LIF, Dec 3, 6, 13; 1743: LIF, Jan 7, Feb 11,
   CG, Apr 25; 1746: CG, Mar 13, 18, Apr 3, 4; 1753: CG, Oct 30; 1754: CG, Jan
   12; 1758: CG, Apr 24, 28, 29, May 2, 3; 1770: CG, Oct 11; 1772: KING'S, Mar
   12; 1777: KING'S, Feb 4, 22, 25, Mar 13, May 20; 1783: DL, Dec 4, 5, 9; 1784:
   DL, Jan 22, May 18
Comic Ballet, Grand (dance), 1734: DL, Dec 26; 1735: DL, Jan 1; 1741: DL, Apr
   29; 1743: CG, Apr 7, 9, 12, 14, May 3, 6, 9, 11; 1746: CG, Feb 24, 27, Mar 1,
   3; 1751: CG, Dec 16; 1752: CG, Jan 27, Feb 3, 4, 6, Mar 17, Apr 3, 8, 10, 17,
   18, 20, 22, 25, May 4
Comic Concert (dance), 1788: DL, Jun 5
Comic Dance (dance), 1700: LIF, Jul 5; 1702: DL, Jun 9; 1703: YB, Feb 5, DL,
   Oct 15, LIF, 25, DL, Nov 1, 5, 11, 27; 1704: LIF, Jul 14; 1705: LIF, Jan 25,
   DL, Jun 28; 1706: QUEEN'S, Jan 17, Mar 11, 25, Apr 3, 20, 26, Jun 13, 29;
   1707: DL, Jun 4, HA, Aug 1; 1708: DL, Jan 3; 1710: DL, Feb 4, Jun 2; 1712:
   DL, May 29, Jun 17; 1715: DL, Nov 10, 19, 21, 23, Dec 21; 1716: LIF, Apr 5;
   1717: LIF, Jan 4, DL, Apr 9, May 6, LIF, 13, Jul 5, Oct 18, Nov 1, DL, 18,
   LIF, Dec 11; 1718: DL, Apr 22, LIF, 24, DL, 28, LIF, 30, DL, May 6, LIF, 15,
   DL, 20, 23, Jun 4, DL, Aug 12, Oct 8; 1719: DL, Jan 8, Apr 14, B-L, Sep 5;
   1720: LIF, Mar 8, DL, Oct 17; 1721: DL, May 16; 1722: DL, Mar 10; 1724: DL,
   May 12, 14, Oct 8, Dec 21; 1725: LIF, Mar 29, DL, May 10, 12; 1726: DL, Jan
   5, HAY, Apr 14; 1727: DL, May 5, 17; 1728: DL, May 10, 22; 1729: LIF, May 9,
   14, 19, DL, Nov 21; 1730: LIF, Apr 25, May 1, 7, DL, 18, 19, 27, Oct 10;
   1731: DL, Mar 25, LIF, May 19, 25, Jun 2, GF, Oct 29, Nov 1, LIF, 12, Dec 7;
   1732: LIF, Mar 9, DL, 16, LIF, Apr 22, LIF/CG, Dec 8, 9, 12, CG/LIF, 16, 19;
   1733: LIF/CG, Jan 23, CG, 24, LIF/CG, 29, Feb 1, Mar 12, DL, 15, LIF/CG, 28,
   31, Apr 10, 16, 17, BFCGBH, Sep 4, DL/HAY, Oct 13, 15, GF, Dec 27, 28, 29;

1734: DL, Apr 25, DL/HAY, May 4, DL, 16, Nov 4, 11, 15; 1735: DL, Jul 1, Sep 30, Nov 19, CG, 22, 24, Dec 12, DL, 17, CG, 18; 1736: CG, Jan 2, Mar 20, Apr 8, DL, 15, CG, May 8, 11, 14, DL, 15, CG, 17, 18, DL, Oct 23, 25, CG, Nov 9, 11, Dec 13; 1737: CG, Jan 7, 17, 24, Mar 7, 15, 17, 19, 26, 28, Apr 12, 15, 25, 26, 28, 29, May 5, 9, 12, Oct 3, 5, 12, DL, Nov 2, 7; 1738: CG, Feb 10, Mar 16, Apr 4, 7, 19, 21, 24, 25, 27, 29, May 2, 6, 8, 10, 11, 12, 15, DL, 22, 23, CG, Oct 20, 23, 26, Nov 2, 8, 13, Dec 6, 11; 1739: CG, Jan 3, 6, 8, 15, Mar 13, 15, 19, 22, 26, 27, Apr 2, DL, 3, CG, 7, 30, May 4, 7, 9, 11, DL, 12, CG, 18, DL, 30, CG, Aug 21, Sep 5, Oct 2, Nov 1; 1740: CG, May 7, 9, 14, 29, GF, Oct 24, 29, Nov 10, 13, 17, 18, 27, Dec 1, 12; 1741: CG, Apr 7, 8, 9, 23, 25, 27, 30, May 1, 2, 4, 5, DL, 7, CG, 7, GF, Oct 7, CG, Dec 9, 11, 16; 1742: CG, Apr 5, 19, 21, 27, 28, 30, May 3, DL, 3, CG, 5, 10, 11, 12, 17, 18, Oct 1, 4, LIF, Nov 26, 29, Dec 3, 13; 1743: DL, Apr 7, CG, 21; 1744: DL, Apr 4, May 23; 1745: DL, Mar 11, CG, Apr 18, 23, 26, 27, 30, May 1, 2; 1746: GF, Feb 17; 1747: GF, Feb 16, DL, Mar 21, Apr 10, 21, CG, 23, DL, 30; 1748: DL, Mar 14, Apr 16, 18, 21, May 6, 11, 16, 18, CG, Dec 20, 27; 1749: CG, Mar 13, Apr 5, 10, 11, 14, 18, 19, 21, 24, 25, May 3, DL, Oct 18, 20, 23, 30, Dec 7, 26, 27, 28; 1750: DL, Jan 5, 19, Feb 12, 21, 22, Mar 13, 22, 26, Apr 23, May 3, 8, 10, Nov 17, 19, 20, 22, 24, 27, 28, Dec 1, 6, 14, 17, 19, 31; 1751: DL, Jan 1, 4, 18, May 4, 8, 9, 13, 14, Sep 21, Oct 15, 18, Nov 23, Dec 20; 1752: DL, Jan 20, 21, Feb 5, Apr 16, 23, 27, May 1, 2, 4, 5, Sep 19, Oct 10, Nov 25, 27; 1753: DL, Apr 2, 3, 5, 7, May 14, 15, 16, 17, Oct 3; 1754: DL, Feb 7, 16, Mar 12, CG, May 1; 1755: DL, Feb 3, Apr 1, 3, 10, CG, 15, 16, 18, 21, 22, DL, 22, 24, CG, 24, 25, 26, 28, 29, 30, DL, Sep 30, Oct 2, 9, 14; 1756: DL, Feb 4, 5, 7, 14, 21, 24, Mar 2, 8, 13, Apr 10; 1757: CG, Feb 16, DL, Mar 21, May 2, 7, 9, 19, 26, HAY, Aug 27, 29; 1758: DL, Apr 10, CG, 17, 18, 20, 22, May 8, 9, 10, 11, 12; 1759: DL, Apr 7, May 17, MARLY, Aug 9, 16, CG, Nov 13; 1760: CG, Jan 4, 8, 12, Feb 12, 16, Mar 18, 22, DL, Apr 17, CG, 21, 22, 24, DL, May 2, CG, 12, 15, DL, 17, CG, 19, DL, 27, 29; 1761: CG, Jan 24, 27, DL, Mar 7, CG, 27, 30, Apr 1, DL, 10, CG, 16, DL, 18, CG, 21, 23, 29, May 1, 4, 5, , 13, 14, DL, 15, Sep 19, SFT, 21, DL, Oct 17; 1762: CG, Apr 23, DL, 28, May 4, 5, 6, 11, 22, Dec 10, 13, 15, 17; 1763: DL, Jan 14, CG, Feb 24, Apr 7, 9, 14, 16, 18, 21, 26, 27, 28, 30, May 3, 4, 7, 10, 13, 19, 24, HAY, Aug 15, 24, Sep 7; 1764: CG, May 1, HAY, Sep 5, 11, DL, Dec 13, 14, 19, 20; 1765: DL, Jan 28, 29, 31, Feb 15, 18, 21, 25, May 15, 16, 18, 21, 22, HAY, Jun 10, 14, 17; 1766: DL, Feb 7, 18, Apr 14, 17, 18, CG, 21, DL, May 3, 7, 16, 19, 20, 21, HAY, Jul 31; 1767: DL, Mar 2, 3, 24, Apr 24, 30, May 1, HAY, Jul 8, 15, Sep 21, CG, Oct 21, 22, 24, 27, 28, Nov 6, 7, 10, DL, 16, CG, 17, 26, 30, Dec 1, 3, 8, 10, 14, 17; 1768: CG, Jan 1, 2, DL, 11, CG, 12, DL, 16, CG, 19, DL, 21, CG, 22, 25, DL, 27, Feb 12, CG, 15, 18, Mar 12, Apr 7, 16, DL, 30, CG, May 27, 28, Oct 7, 22, 25, DL, Nov 5, CG, 15, DL, Dec 10, 15, 27, 31; 1769: DL, Jan 6, 7, CG, 10, DL, 23, 24, 27, Feb 1, 7, 11, 13, 16, 18, 20, 21, Mar 11, 13, 14, 18, 30, 31, Apr 3, 7, 8, 10, 13, 15, 17, 18, 19, 22, 27, 28, May 3, 4, 6, 8, 15, CG, Sep 18, DL, 26, Oct 13, CG, 16, DL, 31, CG, Nov 20, DL, Dec 22; 1770: DL, Jan 18, Feb 19, Mar 12, 20, 22, 26, Apr 7, 16, 19, CG, 20, DL, 21, 25, May 10, 11, 19, Sep 22, Oct 2, CG, 10, 13, 16, 17, 23, DL, 25, CG, 25, 27, DL, 30, CG, Nov 1, DL, 3, CG, 7, DL, 14, CG, 20, DL, 22, CG, 26, DL, Dec 1, 8, 10, 21; 1771: DL, Jan 5, 15, CG, Feb 25, DL, Mar 4, 18, 23, Apr 1, 2, 9, 10, 12, CG, 13, DL, 13, 16, CG, 17, DL, 19, CG, 19, DL, 20, CG, 23, DL, 29, CG, 30, DL, May 1, 6, 7, CG, 10, DL, 13, CG, 13, DL, 14, CG, 16, 22, 23, KING'S, Jun 1, HAY, 17, DL, Sep 21, 26, Oct 1, 3, CG, 9, DL, 16, 18, 22, 24, CG, 31, DL, Nov 1, 2, 8, CG, Dec 23; 1772: CG, Jan 1, 9, 15, 16, 18, 20, 22, 23, Mar 14, 21, DL, 26, 31, Apr 23, 24, CG, May 9, 12, 13, DL, 18, Sep 22, 24, Nov 6, 13, 17, 24, Dec 11, 15; 1773: DL, Jan 4, 29, Feb 5, 8, 9, 22, Mar 18, 20, 23, 25, Apr 15, 22, CG, 26, DL, 27, 29, 30, May 1; 1774: KING'S, Mar 17, CG, Apr 27, May 17, 20, Dec 7; 1775: DL, Apr 28, CG, 29, May 6, 13, 29, Nov 18, DL, Dec 19; 1776: DL, Apr 15, May 1, 8, Dec 17; 1777: CG, Apr 25, May 23, DL, Jun 4, Oct 17; 1778: CG, May 2; 1779: CG, Apr 28; 1780: DL, Oct 2; 1785: HAY, Feb 14, DL, Mar 7; 1793: DL, Jun 7, 10
Comic Dance in the Footing Manner (dance), 1732: LIF, May 9
Comic Dance of the Old Woman (dance), 1741: CG, Mar 7
Comic Dance, Grand (dance), 1716: LIF, Nov 15, 17, 19, 29, Dec 8, 10, 11, 20, 27, 28; 1717: LIF, Jan 1, Mar 12, 21, 23, 25, Apr 8, Jun 7; 1718: LIF, Jan 4, Mar 8, Apr 28; 1728: LIF, Apr 30; 1731: LIF, Nov 8; 1732: LIF, May 5; 1737: CG, Mar 24; 1742: DL, Nov 17, 19, 22, 24, 25, 30, Dec 1, 3, 6, 8; 1744: DL, Dec 17; 1745: DL, Sep 26, 28, Oct 1, 3, 5, 10, 19, 24, 26, 31, Nov 7, 19, 26, 28, Dec 16; 1747: DL, Feb 16, Apr 2; 1752: SFB, Sep 22
Comic Dialogue (entertainment), 1704: DL, Jan 18, LIF, Feb 19, Jul 10; 1705: DL, Jun 26; 1706: QUEEN'S, Apr 20, 30; 1709: HA, Sep 19; 1710: DL, Apr 1, QUEEN'S, Jul 13; 1714: DL, Jun 11; 1718: GLOBE, Dec 3; 1759: DL, Mar 29
Comic Duet (song), 1791: KING'S, May 19
Comic Entertainment (entertainment), 1703: DL, Oct 12, Nov 23; 1710: GR, Aug

182

14; <u>1711</u>: GR, Sep 3; <u>1715</u>: DL, Oct 19; <u>1720</u>: LIF, May 3; <u>1754</u>: CG, Dec 3;
   <u>1755</u>: CG, Jan 4, 15, 18, 25, Mar 17, 18, Apr 15
Comic Epilogue (entertainment), <u>1757</u>: HAY, Aug 31, Sep 2, 8, 16, 28
Comic Interlude (song), <u>1741</u>: CG, May 15
Comic Lecture (entertainment), <u>1755</u>: HAY, Apr 12, 14, 16; <u>1757</u>: HAY, Aug 11,
   31, Sep 2, 8, 28, Oct 3, 12; <u>1759</u>: HAY, Nov 9; <u>1760</u>: HAY, Sep 9; <u>1761</u>: CG,
   Mar 26
Comic Medley (entertainment), <u>1773</u>: HAY, Sep 18
Comic Medley Overture (music), <u>1734</u>: DL/HAY, Mar 30, May 3, DL, 13, 16; <u>1736</u>:
   DL, Oct 28, Dec 20; <u>1737</u>: DL, Mar 14, HIC, Apr 1, DL, 13, 29; <u>1757</u>: HAY, Aug
   11, 22, 24
Comic Minuet (dance), <u>1755</u>: CG, Apr 16
Comic Mirror. See Dibdin, Charles.
Comic Oration (entertainment), <u>1757</u>: HAY, Sep 16, 28
Comic Pantomime Dance (dance), <u>1735</u>: GF/HAY, Mar 28; <u>1740</u>: DL, Apr 18, 26
Comic Pantomime Entertainment (entertainment), <u>1742</u>: GF, Jan 15
Comic Peasant Dance (dance), <u>1738</u>: TC, Aug 7, SFH, Sep 5
Comic Prologue (entertainment), <u>1664</u>: LIF, Sep 10
Comic Sketch of the Times (entertainment), <u>1785</u>: HAY, Jan 31; <u>1792</u>: HAY, Feb 20
Comic Song (song), <u>1706</u>: QUEEN'S, Apr 20, 26, 30, May 2, 15, LIF/QUEN, Aug 16;
   <u>1716</u>: GLOBE, Dec 28; <u>1717</u>: DL, May 14, 27; <u>1723</u>: DT, Nov 12, KAT, Dec 4;
   <u>1724</u>: HT, Mar 13, PY, Apr 20, CT, Nov 24; <u>1730</u>: DL, May 21; <u>1731</u>: HAY, Mar
   19; <u>1760</u>: SF, Sep 18; <u>1789</u>: CG, May 19; <u>1790</u>: CG, Nov 23; <u>1791</u>: CG, Sep 19;
   <u>1792</u>: CG, May 19; <u>1793</u>: CG, May 24, Jun 3; <u>1794</u>: CG, Apr 12, May 10, 13;
   <u>1798</u>: CG, May 25; <u>1799</u>: WRSG, May 17, CG, Jun 5; <u>1800</u>: CG, May 6
Comic Wedding Dance, Grand (dance), <u>1717</u>: LIF, Jan 14, 21, 31, Mar 11, Apr 27,
   May 16; <u>1718</u>: LIF, Dec 26
Comical Adventures of Master Billy Softhead, His Mother, and Sister Sally, The
   (farce), <u>1717</u>: SFBL, Sep 9
Comical Courtship; or, The Battle Royal (play, anon), <u>1778</u>: CHR, Jun 15, 26
Comical Dialogue (song), <u>1720</u>: SOU, Oct 3
Comical Disappointment, The; or, The Miser Outwitted (entertainment), <u>1736</u>:
   HAY, Jul 14
Comical Distresses of Pierot, The (entertainment), <u>1729</u>: DL, Dec 10
Comical Gallant, The. See Dennis, John.
Comical Humours and Adventures of Trusty (farce, anon), <u>1748</u>: BFLYY, Aug 24;
   <u>1755</u>: SFG, Sep 18
Comical Humours of Anthony Noodle, His Man Weazle, and Captain Blunderbuss, The
   (droll, anon), <u>1717</u>: TC, Aug 5, 6, 7, 8, 9, 10, 12, 13; <u>1719</u>: BFPM, Aug 24;
   <u>1727</u>: BF, Aug 21
Comical Humours of Cimon and Mopsus, The (droll), <u>1731</u>: UM, Apr 19
Comical Humours of Mopsey and Collin (entertainment), <u>1722</u>: SFM, Sep 5
Comical Humours of Sir John Falstaff, Justice Shallow, Ancient Pistol, and
   Others. See Cibber, Theophilus.
Comical Humours of Squire Pancho, <u>1744</u>: MFDSB, May 1
Comical Humours of Toby Stag, the Huntsman, and a Merry Poet, The (droll),
   <u>1723</u>: BFL, Aug 22
Comical Lovers, The. See Cibber, Colley.
Comical Resentment, The. See Cibber, Colley.
Comical Revenge, The. See Etherege, Sir George.
Comical Revenge, The; or, A Doctor in Spight of his Teeth (ballad opera), <u>1732</u>:
   DL, May 2, 12
Comical Transformation, The. See Jevon, Thomas, The Devil of a Wife.
Commano, Giovanni Giuseppe (singer), <u>1730</u>: KING'S, Nov 3; <u>1731</u>: KING'S, Feb 2,
   Apr 6; <u>1732</u>: HAY, Nov 16
Commissary, The. See Foote, Samuel.
Commissioners, <u>1682</u>: DL, Feb 4, 6
Committee, The. See Howard, Sir Robert.
Commonwealth of Women, A. See D'Urfey, Thomas.
Como, Antonio (dancer), <u>1770</u>: KING'S, May 19; <u>1771</u>: KING'S, Jun 1; <u>1773</u>: DL,
   Sep 30, Oct 2, 9, Nov 25, Dec 27; <u>1774</u>: DL, Apr 12, 22, May 20, Oct 1, 5, 14,
   18, 27, Nov 5, Dec 26; <u>1775</u>: DL, Apr 3, 22, May 8, 25, Sep 26, Oct 20, Nov
   28, Dec 11, 12; <u>1776</u>: DL, Feb 27, Mar 2, 19, May 3, 18, Jun 3
Como, Sga Antonio (dancer), <u>1775</u>: DL, Mar 16, Apr 3, May 8
Comondain calza altronda (song), <u>1726</u>: DL, Apr 28
Compiangermi non sai (song), <u>1754</u>: KING'S, Feb 28
Complaint (song), <u>1798</u>: DL, May 7
Complaisant, Le. See Pont-de-Veyle, Antoine de Feriol, comte de.
Compromise, The. See Sturmy, John.
Compton St, <u>1740</u>: DL, May 5
Compton, Lady Elizabeth (correspondent), <u>1734</u>: DL, Nov 27
Comte D'Albert et sa Suite, Le. See Sedaine, Michel Jean.

Comus. See Milton, John.
Con un moro orrendore strano (song), 1792: KING'S, Mar 14, 21
Conant, N (printer), 1779: HAY, Jul 17; 1780: HAY, Jul 15
Concanen, Matthew (author), 1731: DL, Feb 8
Concealed Royalty, The. See Carleton, R.
Concerto Spirituale (music), 1750: DL, Mar 16, Apr 11; 1756: DL, Apr 2; 1758:
     DL, Mar 10; 1759: CG, May 4; 1772: CG, Mar 27, Apr 8, 10; 1773: HAY, Mar 3,
     17; 1776: CG, Mar 6, 15
Condell, Charlotte (actor), 1755: CG, Apr 30; 1756: CG, Mar 23, May 19, Nov 1,
     Dec 15; 1757: CG, Feb 21, Apr 25, 30, Oct 3, 7, Nov 7, 26; 1758: CG, Feb 1,
     11, Mar 11, 14, Apr 3, 8, 10
Condell, Henry (musician), 1771: CG, May 23; 1773: CG, May 25
Condell, John (boxkeeper, fruit concessionaire), 1748: CG, May 5; 1749: CG, Apr
     29; 1750: CG, May 4; 1751: CG, May 13; 1752: CG, May 6; 1753: CG, May 17;
     1754: CG, May 20; 1755: CG, May 16; 1756: CG, May 20; 1757: CG, May 17; 1758:
     CG, May 10; 1759: CG, May 23; 1760: CG, May 16, 23, Sep 22; 1761: CG, May 13,
     Nov 26; 1763: CG, May 24; 1764: CG, May 23; 1765: CG, May 23; 1766: CG, May
     14, Nov 27, DL, Dec 9; 1767: CG, Jan 14, DL, Feb 20, CG, Mar 12, May 11, 21,
     22, DL, 25, CG, Nov 14; 1768: CG, Jan 7, Mar 10, May 25, Jun 1, 4, Nov 14;
     1769: CG, Jan 5, Mar 7, May 16, 18, Nov 14; 1770: CG, Jan 10, Mar 5, May 23,
     25; 1771: CG, May 23, Nov 27, DL, Dec 10; 1772: CG, Jan 31, DL, Mar 7, CG,
     31, May 26, DL, Jun 10, CG, Nov 26, DL, Dec 17; 1773: CG, Feb 1, DL, Mar 1,
     CG, Apr 1, May 25, DL, 27, CG, 31, Nov 26, DL, Dec 7; 1774: CG, Jan 15, DL,
     Feb 22, Mar 23, CG, 24, DL, May 10, CG, 17, DL, Dec 14; 1775: DL, Feb 22, May
     22, CG, 23, DL, Dec 13; 1776: DL, Feb 29, CG, May 17, DL, Jun 1, CG, Dec 11;
     1777: CG, May 21; 1778: CG, May 19; 1779: CG, May 13
Condell Jr, John (boxkeeper), 1780: CG, May 20; 1781: CG, May 23; 1782: CG, May
     24; 1783: CG, Jun 3; 1784: CG, May 28
Conduit St, 1799: CG, May 24; 1800: CG, May 17
Confederacy, The. See Vanbrugh, Sir John, The City Wives' Confederacy.
Confederates, The; or, The First Happy Day of the Island Princess (poem), 1698:
     DL/ORDG, Nov 0; 1699: DLORLIF, Feb 20
Confession (song), 1736: CG, Apr 12, May 3, 11
Conforto (Conforti), Nicolo (composer), 1753: KING'S, Apr 30; 1755: KING'S, Mar
     17; 1757: KING'S, Mar 8
--Antigono (opera), 1757: KING'S, Mar 8, 12, 15, 19, 22, 26, 29, Apr 2, 16, 19,
     23
Confusione nata dalla Somiglianza, La. See Portogallo, Marcos Antonio, I Due
Gobbi.
Congreve, William, 1693: DL, Feb 0, Mar 0, Apr 0, NONE, Sep 0, DLORDG, Nov 0,
     NONE, Dec 12; 1694: DL, Jan 0, 13, NONE, Mar 22; 1695: LIF, Apr 30, Aug 0,
     DL, Nov 0; 1696: LIF, Feb 0; 1697: ATCOURT, Feb 6, LIF, 20, Mar 13, DL, Sep
     0; 1698: LIF, Mar 0, DLLIF, May 12; 1699: LIF, Mar 4, DLLIF, Dec 25; 1700:
     LIF, Mar 5, 12; 1701: DG, Mar 21; 1703: DL, Nov 6; 1704: ATCOURT, Feb 7, LIF,
     Mar 30; 1705: DL, Jan 15, QUEEN'S, Apr 9; 1709: DL, Apr 7; 1718: DL, Jan 8,
     9, 28, Feb 14, Apr 18, LIF, Oct 18, 20, DL, Dec 19; 1719: DL, Jan 9, 11, Feb
     10, Mar 3, Apr 1, May 12, Nov 10, Dec 8; 1720: DL, Jan 20, LIF, Mar 10, DL,
     Nov 26; 1721: DL, Mar 6, Apr 14, Nov 24, Dec 29; 1722: LIF, Jan 8, 13, 18,
     DL, Mar 5, 6, Apr 17, LIF, 20, DL, Oct 23, LIF, 24, DL, Nov 28, Dec 19; 1723:
     DL, Jan 5, 22, 25, Apr 1, May 17, Oct 1, 15, Dec 20; 1724: LIF, Mar 23, May
     28, DL, Nov 7; 1725: DL, Jan 27, Apr 12, 20, LIF, May 17, DL, Sep 7, LIF, Nov
     2, DL, 16, 27; 1726: DL, Jan 25, May 3, LIF, 4, DL, 9, LIF, 10, DL, 17, 18,
     LIF, 26, DL, Sep 10, Oct 11, Dec 17; 1727: DL, Feb 4, Mar 20, 23, May 2, Sep
     26, Oct 6, 7, Dec 6, 7, 8; 1728: DL, Feb 21, 28, Apr 6, 9, Sep 12, 26, Oct 5,
     28, Dec 19, 31, LIF, 31; 1729: DL, Jan 4, 24, Mar 10, LIF, 10, DL, 17, 22,
     LIF, Apr 12, DL, 29, May 21, Sep 13, 27, Oct 9, Nov 6, Dec 12, 15, 19; 1730:
     DL, Jan 5, 8, LIF, 13, DL, Feb 26, Apr 6, LIF, 13, DL, 18, LIF, 25, DL, May
     1, Sep 17, 19, LIF, Oct 19, Nov 17; 1731: DL, Jan 14, LIF, 19, Feb 26, DL,
     Mar 29, Apr 8, 22, May 5, Sep 25; 1732: LIF, Jan 19, DL, Feb 11, LIF, Mar 20,
     GF, Apr 1, DL, 1, 12, LIF, 28, May 9, GF, Oct 2, DL, 28, 31, Nov 2, 6,
     LIF/CG, 22, DL, Dec 6, LIF/CG, 7, DL, 8, LIF/CG, 8; 1733: DL, Jan 4, 12, Feb
     1, LIF/CG, 2, Apr 23, DL, 24, LIF/CG, 27, GF, May 8, 10, DL/HAY, Sep 26, Oct
     1, CG, 6, 9, DL/HAY, 24, 25, CG, Nov 16, DL/HAY, 24, Dec 5, 6; 1734: DL/HAY,
     Jan 22, 23, Feb 8, Mar 4, CG, 11, DL/HAY, 26, DL, Apr 4, CG, 22, DL/HAY, 30,
     May 23, DL, Sep 28, Oct 3, CG/LIF, 7, DL, 30, Nov 19, CG/LIF, Dec 6, DL, 12,
     16; 1735: DL, Jan 1, 20, Feb 15, Mar 20, CG/LIF, 25, DL, Apr 18, May 20, Sep
     4, 25, CG, Oct 8, DL, 11, 14, 16, 18, 20, 29, Nov 8, 12, 26, 28, Dec 2, 3,
     12, CG, 17, 18; 1736: DL, Jan 28, 29, Feb 5, 17, Mar 5, CG, Apr 5, DL, May 7,
     CG, 8, DL, 14, CG, Oct 1, DL, 30, Nov 3, 6, 11, 25, Dec 6, 10; 1737: CG, Jan
     10, DL, Feb 22, 24, May 2, Aug 30, Sep 15, CG, Oct 19, 21, DL, 31, Nov 2;
     1738: DL, Jan 10, CG, 21, 24, DL, Feb 14, Apr 13, May 8, 26, Sep 19, Oct 17,
     CG, Nov 11, Dec 8, DL, 26, 30; 1739: CG, Sep 12, 17, 25, Nov 27; 1740: CG,

184

Feb 7, DL, Mar 17, CG, Apr 29, Sep 29; <u>1741</u>: CG, Sep 25; <u>1742</u>: GF, Jan 5, 20,
28, DL, Mar 12, CG, Oct 6, 19, 28, DL, Nov 1; <u>1743</u>: LIF, Feb 17; <u>1744</u>: CG,
Feb 10, DL, Apr 23, CG, Dec 11; <u>1745</u>: CG, Oct 2; <u>1747</u>: HAY, Apr 22; <u>1748</u>: DL,
Apr 20; <u>1749</u>: CG, Apr 7; <u>1750</u>: DL, Nov 13; <u>1751</u>: HAY, Feb 5; <u>1754</u>: HAY, Jan
31; <u>1759</u>: CG, Nov 30; <u>1767</u>: HAY, Aug 14; <u>1771</u>: CG, Jun 6; <u>1774</u>: DL, Dec 19;
<u>1775</u>: DL, Oct 7; <u>1776</u>: CG, Mar 5, DL, Nov 29; <u>1782</u>: CG, Mar 19; <u>1789</u>: CG, Dec
18; <u>1792</u>: HAY, Nov 26
--Double Dealer, The, <u>1693</u>: DL, Oct 0, DLORDG, Nov 0, NONE, Dec 12; <u>1694</u>: DG,
Jan 10, DL, 13, NONE, Mar 22; <u>1698</u>: DLLIF, May 12; <u>1699</u>: LIF, Mar 4; <u>1703</u>:
LIF, Nov 29; <u>1718</u>: LIF, Oct 18, 20, Nov 18, Dec 4; <u>1720</u>: LIF, Mar 7, 10, May
11, Nov 2, 25; <u>1721</u>: LIF, May 2, Dec 12; <u>1722</u>: LIF, Jan 8, Apr 20, Oct 24;
<u>1723</u>: LIF, Apr 4; <u>1724</u>: LIF, Jan 20, Feb 8, 22, Apr 13, Jun 3; <u>1725</u>: LIF, Jan
5, 16, Nov 2; <u>1726</u>: LIF, Feb 9, 26, May 10, Oct 10, Dec 9; <u>1727</u>: LIF, Apr 19;
<u>1728</u>: LIF, Jan 5, Apr 4; <u>1729</u>: LIF, Jan 25, Mar 10, Apr 12, Oct 25; <u>1730</u>:
LIF, Jan 13, Apr 25, Oct 19; <u>1731</u>: LIF, Jan 19, Feb 26, Nov 6; <u>1732</u>: LIF, Jan
19, Apr 28; <u>1733</u>: CG, Feb 8, Nov 16; <u>1735</u>: DL, Oct 11, 14, 16, 18, 20, 29,
Nov 8, 11, 28, Dec 12; <u>1736</u>: DL, Jan 29, Mar 22, Apr 8, CG, 13, DL, May 14,
Nov 6, 25; <u>1737</u>: DL, Feb 4, May 10, Oct 31; <u>1738</u>: DL, Jan 10, Feb 14, May 10,
Sep 19, Oct 28; <u>1739</u>: DL, Jan 11, CG, Feb 26, 27, 28, May 3, DL, 15, CG, Sep
12, DL, Oct 19, CG, Nov 24, DL, Dec 19; <u>1740</u>: DL, Feb 9, CG, May 14, 20, Sep
29; <u>1741</u>: CG, Apr 8, Nov 23, 28, Dec 21; <u>1742</u>: CG, Mar 16, DL, 29, CG, Oct
19, Nov 17; <u>1744</u>: CG, Jan 7, DL, Apr 23; <u>1745</u>: CG, Jan 18, Mar 4, 9, May 21,
Dec 6; <u>1746</u>: CG, Jan 17, Dec 22; <u>1747</u>: CG, Mar 5, 31, May 6; <u>1748</u>: DL, Dec
21; <u>1749</u>: DL, Jan 18, CG, Apr 5, Oct 16, 31, DL, Nov 27, CG, Dec 13; <u>1750</u>:
CG, Jan 22, Apr 19, Oct 20; <u>1751</u>: CG, Jan 28, Nov 21; <u>1752</u>: CG, Jan 13, Mar
2, Apr 16, Dec 19; <u>1754</u>: CG, Nov 28, Dec 4; <u>1755</u>: CG, Jan 18, May 16, Nov 7;
<u>1756</u>: CG, Mar 1, 4, Oct 18, DL, 29, Nov 1, CG, Dec 8; <u>1757</u>: CG, Jan 17, DL,
Feb 19, May 4, Oct 18; <u>1758</u>: CG, Oct 26, DL, Nov 17; <u>1759</u>: CG, Mar 6, May 25;
<u>1761</u>: DL, Oct 14; <u>1773</u>: DL, Mar 23, Apr 14; <u>1776</u>: CG, Mar 5, HAY, Sep 2, 12,
CG, Dec 17; <u>1782</u>: CG, Mar 19, Apr 16, May 25; <u>1784</u>: DL, Dec 3, 8, 16; <u>1785</u>:
DL, Jan 3, 26, Feb 5, Apr 4, May 12; <u>1787</u>: DL, Nov 29, Dec 21; <u>1788</u>: DL, May
30
--Judgment of Paris, The (masque), <u>1701</u>: DG, Mar 21, 28, May 6; <u>1702</u>: DL, Dec
29; <u>1704</u>: DL, Jan 18, LIF, Feb 1; <u>1705</u>: LIF, Mar 10; <u>1706</u>: QUEEN'S, Mar 11,
Apr 15; <u>1742</u>: DL, Mar 12, 19, Apr 17, Oct 19; <u>1746</u>: DL, Apr 12; <u>1748</u>: DL, Apr
20; <u>1750</u>: CG, Apr 5, 19; <u>1751</u>: HAY, Feb 5; <u>1759</u>: CG, Apr 3, Nov 30, Dec 4;
<u>1760</u>: RANELAGH, Jun 18; <u>1761</u>: RANELAGH, Jun 12; <u>1768</u>: HAY, Aug 24, 26, 31,
Sep 2, 5; <u>1771</u>: CG, Jun 6
--Love for Love, <u>1695</u>: LIF, Apr 30, May 1, 2, 3, 4, 6, 7, 8, 9, 10, 11, 13, 14;
<u>1696</u>: NONE, Apr 3; <u>1697</u>: ATCOURT, Feb 6, IT, Nov 1; <u>1700</u>: LIF, Jun 28; <u>1704</u>:
LIF, Apr 26, Jun 1; <u>1705</u>: QUEEN'S, Jun 25, 27, 29, Nov 22; <u>1706</u>: QUEEN'S, Jan
8, 9; <u>1708</u>: DL, Feb 7, Mar 1, 2, 20, Jun 10, Oct 7; <u>1709</u>: DL, Mar 12, Apr 7,
16, QUEEN'S, Sep 24, Oct 18, Dec 1, DL, 3, 5, QUEEN'S, 28; <u>1710</u>: QUEEN'S, Jan
16, DL, Apr 20, Jun 6, DL/QUEEN, Oct 5, Nov 9; <u>1711</u>: DL/QUEEN, Feb 12, Mar
15, Apr 12, May 25, DL, Sep 27, Dec 6; <u>1712</u>: DL, Jan 31, Apr 22, May 19, Nov
27; <u>1713</u>: DL, Jan 2, Feb 13, Mar 7, May 25, Oct 12; <u>1714</u>: DL, Mar 11, May 26,
Oct 1, Nov 30; <u>1715</u>: LIF, Jan 12, Feb 2, DL, Mar 8, Apr 9, LIF, May 10, DL,
Oct 28; <u>1716</u>: DL, Jan 9, Mar 20, LIF, Apr 9, DL, May 9, LIF, Jun 6, Aug 10,
DL, Oct 9, LIF, Dec 3, DL, 7; <u>1717</u>: DL, Mar 11, 25, LIF, May 10, DL, Nov 25;
<u>1718</u>: DL, Feb 11, LIF, 22, Mar 18, DL, Apr 3, LIF, 16, DL, 29, RI, Aug 9, DL,
Oct 15, HC, 16, LIF, 30, DL, Dec 22; <u>1719</u>: DL, Apr 11, LIF, May 7, DL, 27,
Sep 17, LIF, Nov 13, DL, 30, LIF, Dec 15; <u>1720</u>: DL, Feb 4, May 10, SOU, Oct
3, DL, 4, Dec 2; <u>1721</u>: DL, Feb 2, Apr 27, May 23, Sep 12, Nov 24, Dec 29;
<u>1722</u>: DL, Mar 6, Apr 18, May 25, Sep 18, Nov 28; <u>1723</u>: DL, Jan 22, Mar 16,
May 17, HA, Jul 22, DL, Sep 17, Nov 25, DT, 26, Dec 6, DL, 16; <u>1724</u>: DL, Jan
9, BPT, Mar 18, DL, Apr 30, Sep 15, Nov 25; <u>1725</u>: DL, Feb 8, May 6, Sep 9,
Nov 19; <u>1726</u>: DL, Mar 1, May 9, Oct 11, Dec 2; <u>1727</u>: DL, Feb 10, Apr 12, Sep
26, Dec 8; <u>1728</u>: DL, Feb 15, May 6, Sep 12, Dec 5; <u>1729</u>: DL, Jan 4, Mar 10,
May 21, Sep 13, GF, Nov 5, 18, Dec 5, DL, 19; <u>1730</u>: GF, Jan 22, Feb 14, Apr
10, DL, 18, May 1, 12, GF, 18, RI, Aug 6, GF, Sep 28, Nov 23, Dec 14; <u>1731</u>:
GF, Feb 8, HAY, 26, GF, Apr 5, DL, 8, 22, GF, Jun 8, Nov 11; <u>1732</u>: GF, Jan
20, 21, 24, 25, Mar 16, May 10, DL, Oct 28, 31, Nov 2, GF, 3, DL, 6, 25, 27,
Dec 29; <u>1733</u>: DL, Jan 12, GF, 20, DL, Apr 24, GF, May 8, DL, 21, DL/HAY, Sep
26, 28, Oct 1, GF, 22, DL/HAY, 24, Nov 15, 24; <u>1734</u>: BLO, Jan 16, GF, 24, IT,
Feb 2, DL/HAY, 4, Mar 4, GF, 14, DL, Apr 4, GF, 27, DL/HAY, May 23, DL, Sep
7, HAY, Oct 7, GF, 7, DL, 30, GF, Dec 20; <u>1735</u>: DL, Jan 1, GF, Feb 7, 20, DL,
Mar 20, May 20, RI, Aug 16, DL, Sep 4, GF, Nov 10, DL, 26; <u>1736</u>: GF, Feb 6,
DL, 17, Apr 3, GF, May 6, DL, 7, LIF, Oct 23, DL, 30, Dec 10; <u>1737</u>: HAY, Mar
7, DL, 26, May 13, Aug 30, Nov 2; <u>1738</u>: DL, Apr 13, May 26, Nov 3, Dec 30;
<u>1739</u>: DL, Feb 23, Apr 3, CG, May 2, DL, 30, Sep 4, Oct 26, Nov 22; <u>1740</u>: DL,
Jan 16, Feb 6, Mar 4, CG, 25, DL, Apr 21, CG, May 3, DL, 21, Sep 9, GF, Oct
28, Nov 21, DL, Dec 12; <u>1741</u>: DL, Jan 16, Apr 28, GF, May 1, DL, 25, Sep 5,

GF, 16, DL, Oct 27, Nov 6, GF, Dec 30; 1742: DL, Jan 19, CG, Mar 27, DL, Apr
21, UM, 26, GF, May 6, DL, 25, Sep 18, Nov 6; 1743: DL, Jan 1, LIF, Feb 17,
SOU, 18, LIF, Apr 11, DL, May 11, Sep 17, Nov 14, Dec 21; 1744: DL, May 5,
Sep 15, GF, Dec 19, 27; 1745: DL, Jan 8, GF, 23, 28, DL, 29, Feb 18, GF, Mar
19, DL, May 1, Oct 10, GF, Nov 21, CG, 25, DL, Dec 30; 1746: DL, Jan 16, GF,
Feb 3, DL, 20, CG, Apr 18, DL, Oct 27, 30, GF, Nov 3, 6, DL, Dec 4; 1747: DL,
May 14; 1748: DL, Jan 12, Feb 12, CG, Mar 26, DL, May 6, Sep 20, Oct 27;
1749: DL, Jan 4, Feb 4, Sep 20, Nov 17; 1750: DL, Jan 18, Oct 26; 1751: DL,
Sep 17; 1753: DL, Jan 22, Feb 19, May 16; 1754: DL, Jan 16, 18, 21, 25, Feb
15, CG, May 13, DL, 14; 1755: DL, Jan 15, CG, Feb 8, 15, Apr 24, DL, May 15,
CG, Oct 10, Nov 25, DL, Dec 1; 1756: CG, Jan 2, Feb 27, May 4, DL, 24, CG,
Oct 21, Nov 19, 25; 1757: CG, Jan 20, May 9, Oct 12, Dec 19; 1758: CG, May 9,
Oct 13, Nov 27; 1759: CG, May 23, Dec 18; 1760: DL, Apr 9, 18, May 12, CG,
Oct 14, Dec 19, 20; 1761: CG, Oct 26; 1762: DL, Jan 7, May 3, CG, 21, DL, Nov
12; 1763: DL, May 16, Oct 1, 6, Nov 3, 11; 1764: DL, Jan 17, CG, Feb 9, Oct
3, DL, 20, CG, Nov 20, 22, DL, Dec 27; 1765: CG, Jan 22, May 17, Nov 1, 14,
19; 1766: CG, Dec 6; 1767: CG, Mar 5; 1769: DL, Dec 23; 1770: DL, Jan 20, Feb
26, May 14, Jun 5, Nov 15; 1771: DL, Nov 14; 1773: CG, May 6; 1774: CG, Apr
5, May 6, 14; 1775: CG, May 9; 1776: CG, Apr 27, Nov 15, DL, 29, Dec 3, 5, 9;
1777: DL, Jan 14, 27, Feb 6, Mar 22, Apr 3; 1778: DL, Mar 5, 19, Apr 6, Oct
13, Nov 7, 21; 1779: DL, Jan 2, Mar 9, Oct 12; 1780: DL, Jan 5, Mar 14, HAY,
Sep 5, DL, Nov 28, Dec 7; 1781: DL, Jan 12, Nov 6; 1783: DL, May 5, Nov 25,
28; 1784: DL, Mar 20, May 24; 1786: CG, Jan 28, Nov 15, DL, Dec 11, 18, 21,
CG, 28; 1787: DL, Jan 3, CG, 5, DL, Feb 6, 9, 14, Mar 10, Apr 23, May 8, Oct
15, Nov 14; 1788: DL, Oct 11, 30, Dec 8, 15; 1789: DL, Feb 23, Apr 13, May 5,
Jun 3, Oct 3, Nov 6; 1790: DL, Feb 23, Apr 23, May 8, Oct 12; 1791: DL, Apr
12, May 11, Jun 1, DLKING'S, Oct 25, Dec 19; 1792: DLKING'S, Apr 19; 1793:
DL, Apr 25; 1794: DL, Nov 3, 6, 7, 21, 28; 1795: DL, Jan 8, Apr 23, Nov 5;
1796: DL, Jan 7, Mar 8, Apr 7, Oct 15, Nov 14; 1797: CG, Jun 13, DL, Nov 28;
1799: DL, Apr 8, 16, Oct 22; 1800: DL, Mar 22, Apr 3, Jun 17
--Mourning Bride, The, 1697: LIF, Feb 20, 22, 23, 24, 25, 27, Mar 1, 2, 3, 4,
6, 8, 9, 13; 1700: LIF, Feb 27; 1707: QUEEN'S, May 28; 1708: DL, Mar 25;
1710: DL, Jan 18; 1712: DL, Mar 8, May 8, Nov 18; 1713: DL, Nov 17; 1716: DL,
Dec 12; 1719: DL, Jan 9, 11, 13, 14, 15, Feb 10, Apr 1, Dec 8; 1720: DL, Jan
20, Nov 26; 1721: DL, Mar 20; 1722: DL, Apr 17, Oct 23, Dec 19; 1723: DL, May
3, Oct 15; 1724: DL, Jan 13, Mar 3, Oct 9, Dec 17; 1725: DL, Feb 23, 25, Apr
20, Oct 19; 1726: DL, Jan 7, Feb 22, Mar 29, May 18; 1727: DL, Feb 4, Mar 23,
May 2, Oct 6; 1728: DL, Oct 5, Dec 31; 1729: DL, Sep 27, Dec 15; 1730: DL,
Jan 8, Feb 26, May 15, Sep 19, Nov 7; 1731: DL, Apr 10, GF, Dec 9, 11, 16;
1732: DL, Apr 1, GF, 1, DL, Sep 16, GF, Oct 18, 19, 20, 21, 23, Nov 1, Dec
21; 1733: GF, Feb 3, 13, Apr 5, May 5, Sep 14, Nov 13, 28; 1734: GF, Jan 26,
Mar 26, CG, Apr 22, May 17, DL, Sep 28, Oct 1, Nov 19, GF, 22, DL, Dec 12;
1735: DL, Nov 12, Dec 3, CG, 17; 1736: CG, Jan 28, DL, Nov 11; 1737: DL, Feb
24, Mar 9, CG, 31, DL, May 2, CG, Oct 19; 1738: CG, Jan 21, DL, Feb 10, CG,
Apr 19, DL, 26, CG, Oct 28, DL, Nov 1; 1739: CG, Feb 2; 1740: DL, May 2, GF,
Nov 12; 1741: CG, Jan 28, Feb 5, Dec 17; 1742: CG, Apr 10; 1743: DL, Oct 15;
1750: HAY, Feb 22, CG, Apr 3, DL, Dec 3, 4, 5, 7, 8, 10, 11, 12, 15, 20;
1751: DL, Feb 19, Apr 15, 30; 1752: DL, Feb 5, Mar 7, Apr 11; 1753: DL, Mar
10, 22, May 22; 1755: DL, Jan 25, 27, 29, CG, Feb 13, 20, 22, Mar 1, DL, 22,
Apr 23, CG, 28, DL, May 21, Sep 20, 30, Oct 21, Nov 25; 1756: DL, Jan 3, 9,
CG, Mar 30, May 3, DL, 7, Nov 17, Dec 6; 1757: CG, Jan 14, DL, 25, Feb 9, Mar
29, CG, 31, DL, May 12, Sep 20, CG, Oct 21, Dec 2, DL, 26; 1758: DL, Jan 10,
16, May 1, 9, Sep 19, Dec 11; 1759: CG, Jan 12, DL, Mar 10, May 29, Oct 4,
31; 1760: CG, Jan 4, DL, Apr 30; 1761: DL, Jan 28, May 6, Sep 21, CG, Oct 23,
DL, Nov 14; 1762: DL, Mar 6, Nov 1; 1763: DL, Feb 28, CG, Oct 17, DL, Nov 7;
1764: CG, Feb 6, Mar 13, Oct 15, Nov 19; 1765: DL, Feb 4, Mar 16, CG, Oct 23,
DL, Dec 6, 27; 1766: DL, Jan 20; 1767: CG, Mar 2, Sep 21, DL, Nov 24; 1768:
DL, Apr 23, CG, May 27, DL, Sep 26; 1769: DL, Jan 20, Oct 21, 30; 1770: DL,
Jan 22, Oct 8, 11, HAY, Dec 19; 1771: DL, Apr 29, Sep 28; 1772: DL, Apr 11,
May 19, Oct 24; 1773: DL, Jan 16, May 11, Nov 13, 29; 1775: DL, May 1, Nov
21, Dec 30; 1776: CHR, Oct 14, CG, Dec 18; 1778: DL, Nov 16; 1779: DL, Jan
16; 1780: DL, Nov 1; 1781: CG, May 14, Dec 20, 29; 1782: CG, Mar 18, Apr 15,
Dec 2; 1783: CG, Jan 15, DL, Mar 18, May 22, 24, Jun 2, Oct 24; 1784: CG, Feb
5, DL, 21, Apr 17; 1785: DL, Jan 14, Feb 24, Apr 26, Sep 24; 1786: CG, Apr
19, May 4, Oct 30; 1787: DL, May 19, CG, 30; 1788: CG, Mar 10, May 27, Dec
26; 1789: DL, Jan 6, CG, Jun 6; 1791: DL, May 14; 1792: HAY, Nov 26; 1793:
DL, Feb 5, CG, Mar 4, DL, May 28; 1794: DL, Nov 28, 29; 1795: DL, Oct 12;
1796: DL, Feb 22, HAY, 22, DL, Dec 9; 1799: DL, May 20
--Old Batchelor, The, 1693: DL, Mar 0, NONE, Sep 0; 1694: NONE, Mar 22,
ATCOURT, Apr 16; 1695: DLANDLIF, May 0; 1696: NONE, Sep 0; 1700: DL, Nov 8;
1701: DL, Mar 25; 1702: DL, Nov 19; 1703: DL, Jul 7, Oct 13, Nov 18; 1704:
DL, Sep 26, Oct 26; 1705: DL, Jan 15, Oct 22, Dec 11; 1706: DL, Jan 14, Feb

28; <u>1708</u>: DL, Mar 15, Dec 30; <u>1709</u>: DL, Apr 28, QUEEN'S, Dec 8; <u>1710</u>: QUEEN'S, Mar 9, Jul 6, DL, Nov 27; <u>1711</u>: DL, May 5, Oct 24; <u>1712</u>: DL, May 13, Oct 10, Dec 17; <u>1713</u>: DL, Apr 10, Oct 5, Dec 30; <u>1714</u>: DL, May 28, Sep 23, Nov 11; <u>1715</u>: LIF, Jan 4, DL, 8, LIF, Feb 4, DL, 16, LIF, Mar 12, Apr 2, DL, Oct 14, LIF, Nov 7, DL, 8; <u>1716</u>: LIF, Jan 23, DL, Feb 27, Apr 20, LIF, Jun 5, DL, Oct 12, LIF, Nov 29; <u>1717</u>: DL, Jan 28, Apr 25, LIF, Oct 15, DL, Nov 15, LIF, 23; <u>1718</u>: LIF, Jan 23, DL, 27, Apr 30, May 3, Oct 28; <u>1719</u>: DL, Jan 26, Apr 14, LIF, 29, DL, May 19, Oct 1, Dec 10; <u>1720</u>: DL, Feb 2, Jun 2, Sep 13, Nov 8, SOU, 28, DL, Dec 14; <u>1721</u>: DL, Mar 7, Apr 29, Oct 12, Dec 7; <u>1722</u>: LIF, Jan 13, 15, 18, 31, Apr 10, DL, 25, LIF, May 18, DL, Sep 20, LIF, Nov 7, Dec 19; <u>1723</u>: DL, Jan 2, Apr 19, Oct 1, DT, Nov 1, KAT, Dec 4, CT, 10, DL, 18, AVT, 31; <u>1724</u>: DL, Mar 2, HT, 13, LIF, 21, 23, PY, Apr 20, DL, May 20, LIF, 28, DL, Sep 17, Oct 23; <u>1725</u>: LIF, Jan 4, DL, Feb 22, LIF, May 17, DL, 19, Sep 7, Nov 16, LIF, Dec 1; <u>1726</u>: LIF, Feb 7, DL, 14, May 3, LIF, 4, 26, DL, Sep 10, LIF, Nov 7, DL, 7; <u>1727</u>: DL, Jan 3, Sep 19, LIF, Nov 20, DL, Dec 6; <u>1728</u>: DL, Feb 21, Apr 9, LIF, May 11, DL, Sep 26, Nov 27, LIF, Dec 31; <u>1729</u>: DL, Jan 24, Mar 17, LIF, Apr 14, Sep 24, DL, Oct 9, GF, Nov 17, DL, Dec 12, GF, 19; <u>1730</u>: GF, Feb 16, LIF, Apr 13, GF, Jun 1, DL, Sep 17, Nov 9, LIF, 17, GF, Dec 1; <u>1731</u>: DL, Jan 12, GF, 19, LIF, Feb 23, May 5, DL, Sep 25, LIF, Nov 20, GF, 20, DL, 25; <u>1732</u>: DL, Jan 7, GF, 27, 28, LIF, Feb 24, Mar 20, May 9, DL, Oct 3, GF, 6, Nov 13, 14, 20, LIF/CG, 22, DL, Dec 8; <u>1733</u>: GF, Jan 12, LIF/CG, Feb 2, DL, 6, LIF/CG, Apr 27, DL, 27, GF, May 10, Sep 17, CG, Oct 9, DL/HAY, 25; <u>1734</u>: BLO, Jan 16, CG, 17, GF, 28, DL/HAY, Feb 8, DL, Oct 3, GF, Nov 1, DL, Dec 16; <u>1735</u>: GF, Jan 11, Feb 18, DL, 26, CG/LIF, May 1, DL, Sep 25, CG, Nov 7, GF, 21, DL, Dec 2; <u>1736</u>: DL, Jan 28, GF, Feb 11, DL, Mar 5, CG, May 24, DL, Nov 3, YB, Dec 1, DL, 6; <u>1737</u>: LIF, Jan 4, CG, 10, DL, Feb 22, Sep 15; <u>1738</u>: DL, May 16, CG, 18, DL, Oct 17, CG, Nov 28; <u>1739</u>: CG, Jan 16, DL, May 12, CG, Sep 17, DL, Oct 25, Nov 1; <u>1740</u>: DL, Feb 2, Mar 18, Sep 25, GF, Oct 21, DL, Nov 17; <u>1741</u>: CG, Jan 12, 13, 14, 19, Mar 10, Apr 11, 15, GF, 28, CG, Sep 25, Nov 30; <u>1742</u>: GF, Jan 5, 6, 7, 8, 9, 11, CG, 11, GF, 12, 13, 20, Feb 24, DL, Mar 27, May 10, GF, 10, 18, CG, Oct 6, DL, Nov 1, CG, 12, DL, 13, Dec 3, CG, 9, LIF, 30; <u>1743</u>: LIF, Jan 17, Feb 28, Apr 9, DL, 11, 22, CG, May 2, DL, 9, CG, Nov 21, DL, Dec 1, CG, 21; <u>1744</u>: DL, Jan 5, CG, Mar 28, DL, Apr 4, CG, 28, Nov 7; <u>1745</u>: CG, Jan 11, GF, 15, 16, DL, Apr 19, CG, May 3, DL, Sep 24, GF, Nov 19, 20, CG, Dec 12; <u>1746</u>: DL, Jan 28, GF, Feb 18, CG, Nov 26; <u>1747</u>: CG, Mar 2, HAY, Apr 22, CG, Dec 15; <u>1748</u>: CG, Feb 1, May 5, Sep 30, Nov 21; <u>1749</u>: CG, Oct 6, Nov 29; <u>1750</u>: CG, Nov 19; <u>1752</u>: CG, Dec 14; <u>1753</u>: CG, Jan 31, Oct 17, DL, 24, 27, 29, 30, Nov 2, 12, 30, Dec 15; <u>1754</u>: DL, Jan 29, Feb 22, CG, Oct 14, Nov 12; <u>1755</u>: CG, May 12; <u>1756</u>: CG, Feb 9, DL, Oct 14; <u>1758</u>: DL, Oct 27; <u>1760</u>: CG, Apr 29; <u>1762</u>: CG, Apr 21; <u>1766</u>: HAY, Aug 21; <u>1767</u>: HAY, Aug 14; <u>1769</u>: HAY, Aug 25, 28; <u>1770</u>: HAY, Aug 24, Sep 7, 14; <u>1771</u>: HAY, Sep 2; <u>1772</u>: HAY, Sep 8; <u>1775</u>: HAY, Sep 18; <u>1776</u>: DL, Nov 19, 20, 22, 27, 30, Dec 4, 7, 11; <u>1777</u>: DL, Feb 11, Apr 12, Oct 9; <u>1778</u>: DL, May 18, Nov 20, 28; <u>1780</u>: DL, Feb 26, Mar 4, Dec 19; <u>1781</u>: DL, Jan 27, May 22; <u>1782</u>: DL, Apr 10, May 10; <u>1789</u>: CG, Mar 5, 12

--Squire Trelooby, <u>1704</u>: LIF, Mar 30, May 23, Jun 6; <u>1706</u>: QUEEN'S, Jan 28, 29, 31, Feb 1, 4, 18, Apr 22

--Way of the World, The, <u>1699</u>: DLLIF, Dec 25; <u>1700</u>: LIF, Mar 5, 6, 7, 9, 11, 12; <u>1705</u>: QUEEN'S, Dec 17; <u>1715</u>: LIF, Apr 28, May 17; <u>1718</u>: DL, Jan 8, 9, 10, 14, 28, Feb 14, Mar 18, Apr 18, Dec 19; <u>1719</u>: DL, Mar 3, May 12, Nov 10; <u>1721</u>: DL, Mar 6, Apr 14; <u>1722</u>: DL, Mar 5; <u>1723</u>: DL, Jan 5, 25, Apr 1, Dec 20; <u>1724</u>: DL, Feb 5, May 2, Nov 7; <u>1725</u>: DL, Jan 27, Apr 12, May 13, Nov 27; <u>1726</u>: DL, Jan 25, Apr 12, Dec 17; <u>1727</u>: DL, Mar 20, Apr 28, Jun 2, Oct 7, Dec 7; <u>1728</u>: DL, Feb 28, Apr 6, Oct 28, Dec 19; <u>1729</u>: DL, Feb 10, Mar 22, Apr 29, Nov 6; <u>1730</u>: DL, Jan 5, Apr 6; <u>1731</u>: DL, Jan 14, Feb 20, Mar 29, May 5; <u>1732</u>: DL, Jan 8, Feb 11, Apr 12, Dec 6, 7, LIF/CG, 7, 8, 9; <u>1733</u>: DL, Jan 4, Feb 1, LIF/CG, Apr 23, CG, Oct 6, DL/HAY, Dec 5, 6; <u>1734</u>: DL/HAY, Jan 22, 23, CG, Mar 11, DL/HAY, 26, Apr 30, CG/LIF, Oct 7, Dec 6; <u>1735</u>: DL, Jan 20, Feb 15, CG/LIF, Mar 25, DL, Apr 18, CG/LIF, May 2, CG, Oct 8, Nov 21, Dec 18; <u>1736</u>: CG, Jan 31, DL, Feb 5, CG, Apr 5, May 8, Oct 1, Nov 9; <u>1737</u>: CG, Mar 12, DL, Apr 27, CG, May 17, Oct 21; <u>1738</u>: CG, Jan 24, May 1, DL, 8, CG, Nov 11, Dec 8, DL, 26; <u>1739</u>: CG, Jan 19, Sep 25, Nov 27, Dec 8; <u>1740</u>: CG, Feb 7, DL, Mar 17, CG, Apr 29, Oct 27; <u>1741</u>: CG, Mar 2, Apr 27; <u>1742</u>: CG, Jan 23, 25, GF, 27, 28, Mar 1, CG, 4, Apr 8, GF, 27, CG, May 13, Jun 2, Oct 28, Dec 17; <u>1743</u>: CG, Sep 26; <u>1744</u>: DL, May 14, CG, Dec 11; <u>1745</u>: CG, Mar 21, Oct 2; <u>1746</u>: CG, Feb 24, GF, Mar 20, CG, Dec 10; <u>1747</u>: CG, Jan 24, May 11; <u>1748</u>: CG, Apr 26; <u>1749</u>: CG, Apr 7, 26, 29; <u>1750</u>: DL, Nov 13, 14, 15, 17, 20, 22, Dec 1, 6, 21; <u>1751</u>: DL, Jan 2, 10, Feb 1, Apr 26, 27, CG, May 9, DL, Sep 21, CG, Oct 22, DL, 28, CG, Nov 19, 23, Dec 20; <u>1752</u>: DL, Jan 20, Feb 5, CG, 29, Apr 11, DL, 23, Oct 10, CG, Nov 16; <u>1753</u>: DL, Jan 20, 31, Feb 21, Apr 28, CG, May 15, Oct 8, DL, 18, CG, Nov 19; <u>1754</u>: DL, Jan 3, May 16, CG, Sep 18, DL, Oct 23, CG, Nov 25; <u>1755</u>: CG, Jan 9, DL, 23, CG, Feb 13, Mar 4, May 1, DL, 8, CG, Oct

1, Nov 8, Dec 23; 1756: CG, Oct 1, Nov 12; 1757: CG, Jan 12, May 11, Sep 14,
Nov 15; 1758: DL, Mar 16, Apr 6, CG, Sep 18, DL, Nov 13, Dec 14; 1759: DL,
Jan 11, CG, Feb 8, DL, 14, Apr 24, May 24, Oct 16, Dec 7; 1760: DL, Jan 8,
Feb 19, CG, May 8, DL, Oct 10, Dec 15; 1761: DL, May 27, Sep 25; 1762: DL,
Apr 14, 21, Nov 26; 1764: DL, Jan 9, CG, Nov 20, 24, Dec 1, 6, DL, 18; 1765:
CG, Jan 19, DL, Feb 7, CG, Mar 18, Apr 17, DL, May 20, CG, Sep 25, Dec 7;
1766: DL, May 10, CG, Dec 19, 30; 1767: CG, Feb 27, May 18; 1768: DL, Mar 17,
CG, May 26; 1771: DL, Mar 18, Apr 12; 1772: CG, Apr 4; 1774: DL, Mar 15;
1775: DL, Oct 7, 27; 1776: CG, Nov 2, 26, DL, Dec 31; 1777: DL, Jan 2, 9, 24,
Apr 7, 19; 1778: DL, Jan 23, May 27, Oct 19, Nov 3; 1779: DL, Mar 27, May 1,
Oct 19, Nov 4, Dec 17; 1780: DL, Mar 6, 16, Apr 13, Oct 31, Dec 20; 1781: DL,
Jan 22, Feb 8, May 7, Oct 13; 1782: DL, Jan 9, Feb 6, Apr 1, 24, May 13, CG,
Dec 6, 10, 20; 1784: DL, Jan 28, Feb 12, Apr 12, May 18, CG, Nov 11; 1785:
DL, Apr 20; 1786: DL, May 25; 1787: DL, May 23; 1788: DL, May 14, Nov 12;
1789: DL, May 7, Sep 15, CG, Dec 18; 1790: CG, Jan 13, 20; 1797: CG, Oct 28,
Nov 7; 1798: CG, Jan 31
Coninsby, Gilbert (singer), 1675: ATCOURT, Feb 15
Conjugal Frolic (dance), 1788: DL, Feb 21, Mar 13, May 6, Sep 16
Conjuror, The. See Andrews, Miles Peter.
Connard, Miss (singer), 1794: HAMM, Mar 24
Connell, E (singer, actor), 1784: HAY, Dec 13; 1785: HAY, Jan 31, Feb 10, Mar
15; 1786: HAY, Mar 6
Connell, Maria, Mrs E (actor), 1785: HAY, Mar 15
Connell, Master (actor), 1745: DL, Jan 31, Apr 3; 1746: DL, Apr 12; 1747: DL,
Jan 13
Connelley, Miss (house servant), 1724: LIF, May 29
Connelly (draper), 1774: CG, Jan 18
Connelly, Miss (dancer), 1799: DL, Feb 5
Conner (innkeeper), 1773: CG, Feb 11
Conner, Patrick (publisher), 1793: DL, Mar 11, HAY, Aug 30, Sep 30
Connexion of the Indian Emperour to the Indian Queen, The (pamphlet), 1665:
BRIDGES, Apr 0
Connoisseur, The. See Connolly, Joseph.
Connolly (author), 1736: DL, Feb 20
Connolly (tavern keeper), 1784: HAY, Mar 8
Connolly, Joseph
--Connoisseur, The; or, Every Man in his Folly, 1736: DL, Feb 20, Mar 2, 4
Connor (actor), 1788: HAY, Apr 9
Connor (tavern keeper), 1741: DL, Mar 24; 1743: CG, May 11; 1744: CG, May 14;
1745: CG, May 15
Conquest is not to bestow (song), 1800: CG, Mar 5
Conquest of China by the Tartars, The. See Settle, Elkanah.
Conquest of Granada, The. See Dryden, John.
Conquest of Spain, The. See Pix, Mary.
Conquest of St Eustatia, The (interlude, anon), 1781: DL, Mar 31
Conquesta Del Massico, La. See Vento, Mathias.
Conquista del Vello D'Oro, La. See Pescetti, G. B.
Conscious Lovers, The. See Steele, Sir Richard.
Consequences of Industry and Idleness, The; or, The Apprentice's Guide (droll,
anon), 1748: BFSY, Aug 24
Consider Fond Shepherd (song), 1748: CG, Apr 20; 1784: DL, Mar 5; 1787: DL, Mar
7; 1790: CG, Mar 26; 1791: DL, Apr 1, CG, 13; 1792: KING'S, Feb 29, Mar 30;
1794: DL, Mar 26
Consiglio Imprudente, Il. See Bianchi, Francesco.
Consolati o Bella (song), 1734: DL/HAY, Jan 5
Conspiracy Discovered, The; or, French Policy Defeated (entertainment), 1746:
DL, Aug 4, 6, 8, 11
Conspiracy, The. See Jephson, Robert.
Conspiracy, The; or, The Change of Government. See Whitaker, William.
Constable (house servant), 1768: CG, Jun 3; 1776: CG, May 21
Constance, Mlle (dancer), 1784: CG, Apr 17, HAY, May 10
Constant Couple, The. See Farquhar, George.
Constant Couple, The; or, The Fop Bit (farce, anon), 1746: SFHP, Sep 8; 1750:
SFP, Sep 7, 8, 10, 12, 13
Constant Lovers (dance), 1734: BFHBH, Aug 24
Constant Lovers, The; or, The False Friend (droll), 1719: BFBL, Aug 24
Constant Lovers, The; With the Comical Humours of Mons Ragout (droll), 1734:
BFFO, Aug 24
Constant Lovers, The; With the Humours of Sir Timothy Little Wit and His Man
Trip (droll), 1714: SF, Aug 31
Constant Maid (song), 1733: GF, Apr 23
Constant Maid, The. See Shirley, James.

Constant Nymph, The; or, The Rambling Shepheard (play, anon), 1677: DG, Jul 0
Constant Quaker, The; or, The Humours of the Navy (Wapping) (play), 1748: BFH,
    Aug 24; 1755: BFGT, Sep 3, 5, 6
Constante et Alcidonis (dance), 1798: KING'S, Feb 6, 10, Mar 6, May 8
Constantine the Great. See Lee, Nathaniel; Francis, Dr Philip.
Constantini (dancer), 1741: DL, Oct 21, Nov 11, 28, Dec 14, 18; 1742: DL, Jan
    6, Feb 24, Mar 13
Constantini, Sga (dancer), 1726: KING'S, Mar 12, Dec 17; 1727: KING'S, Mar 16,
    Apr 25
Constantinople, Emperor of, 1733: DL, Nov 26
Constantinople, 1703: DG, Apr 30; 1710: DL, Feb 2; 1747: BFH, Aug 22
Constitution of the French and British Theatres (lecture), 1754: HAY, Dec 23
Constitution Song (song), 1785: HAY, Jan 24
Consultation, The (play, anon), 1705: QUEEN'S, Apr 24, 25
Contadina in Corte, La. See Sacchini, Antonio Maria Gasparo.
Contadine Bizzarre, Le. See Piccini, Niccolo.
Contadini Bizzarri, I. See Sarti, Giuseppe.
Contair, Mme. See DeLaCointrie, Mme.
Conte de Warwick, Le. See LaHarpe, Jean Francois de.
Conte Ridicolo, Il. See Paisiello, Giovanni.
Conte, Prince of, 1770: DL, Mar 14
Contending Deities, The. See Prelleur.
Contented Colonel, The. See Suckling, Sir John, Brenoralt.
Contented Cuckold, The (play), 1763: HAY, Sep 5
Contented Cuckold, The; or, The Woman's Advocate. See Bourne, Reuben.
Contented Farmer (song), 1729: BFF, Aug 23
Contented Man (song), 1743: CG, Apr 15
Contented Mind (song), 1737: CG, Apr 19
Contention of Wit and Wealth, The (entertainment), 1773: CG, Mar 20
Contento in Grembo a Morte (song), 1749: KING'S, Mar 21
Contessina, La. See Gassman, Florian Leopold.
Contest of Love and Glory, The. See Britannia's Triumph.
Conti, Anna (dancer), 1754: KING'S, Nov 9
Conti, Francisco (musician), 1707: HIC, Apr 2; 1709: QUEEN'S, Mar 2
--Clotilda, 1709: QUEEN'S, Mar 2, 5, 12, 15, 19, 24, 26, Apr 2; 1711: QUEEN'S,
    May 16, 19, 23; 1713: QUEEN'S, Apr 25
Conti, Gioachino (singer), 1736: CG, May 5, 12, Nov 6, Dec 8; 1737: CG, Jan 12,
    Feb 16, May 18; 1750: DL, Apr 11; see also Gizziello
Conti, Vincenzo (scene painter), 1766: KING'S, Nov 25; 1768: KING'S, Mar 10
Contini, Giovanna (singer), 1742: KING'S, Nov 2, Dec 4; 1743: KING'S, Jan 1,
    Feb 22, Apr 5
Contract, The. See Francklin, Dr Thomas.
Contract, The; or, The Biter Bit, (ballad farce, anon), 1736: HAY, Jan 21
Contract, The; or, The Female Captain. See Cobb, James.
Contrast, The. See Hoadley, John.
Contrast, The; or, The Jew and Married Courtezan. See Waldron, Francis
    Godolphin.
Contri, Mlle. See DeLaCointrie, Mme.
Contrite Comedian's Confession (verse), 1750: DL, Oct 1
Contrivances, The. See Carey, Henry.
Converts, The. See S, J.
Convezzo luinghiero (song), 1713: QUEEN'S, Apr 25
Convitato di Pietra (dance), 1785: KING'S, Mar 12, 29, Apr 5, 7, 14, 28, May 10
Convitato di Pietra, Il (entertainment), 1726: KING'S, Dec 21
Convito degli Dei, Il (dance), 1785: KING'S, Feb 5, 12
Convito, Il. See Bertoni, Francesco Giuseppe.
Conway, Edward Viscount, 1666: NONE, Jul 17
Conway, Henry Seymour, 1789: DL, Apr 20; 1795: DL, Apr 17
--False Appearances, 1789: DL, Apr 20, 22, 25, May 1, 12, 16
Conwy (actor), 1797: HAY, May 10
Conyers (Convers) (singer), 1744: MFDSB, May 1; 1746: DL, Aug 11
Conyngham, Lord, 1764: KING'S, Jan 21
Cook (beneficiary), 1732: LIF, Feb 25
Cook (boxkeeper), 1717: DL, Jun 3; 1718: DL, Jun 4; 1719: DL, May 30; 1720: DL,
    Jun 2; 1721: DL, Jun 6; 1722: DL, May 30; 1723: DL, May 31; 1724: DL, May 19;
    1725: DL, May 21; 1726: DL, May 25; 1727: DL, May 26; 1728: DL, May 31; 1729:
    DL, May 20; 1730: DL, May 27
Cook (dancer), 1716: LIF, Oct 19, 29, 30, Nov 15, 28, Dec 18, 29; 1717: LIF,
    Jan 4, 14, 31, Mar 2, 19, Apr 8, 25, May 13, 16, 28, Jun 7, Oct 5, 7, 14, 29,
    31, Nov 8, 9, 12, 15, 22, Dec 6, 9, 11, 13, 27; 1718: LIF, Jan 1, 2, 3, 4,
    15, 20, 21, 24, 27, Feb 4, Mar 8, 10, TEC, 19, LIF, 29, Apr 15, 16, 30, May
    15, 20, RI, Jul 26, 28, LIF, Aug 6, Nov 13, 24, 29, Dec 1, 8; 1719: LIF, Jan

9, Apr 10, May 7, 29, Jun 25; 1720: LIF, Nov 18, Dec 6, 14, 26; 1721: LIF,
  Feb 1, 21, 28, Apr 26, 29, May 1
Cook (musician), 1735: HIC, Feb 21; 1737: HIC, Apr 7
Cook (singer), 1794: DL, May 16, Oct 27, Nov 15, Dec 20; 1795: DL, Feb 9, Oct
  30, Nov 11, Dec 10; 1796: DL, Jan 8, Mar 12, Apr 30, May 4, Oct 19, Nov 9;
  1798: DL, Jan 16, Feb 1; 1799: DL, Jan 19, 23, Feb 4, Mar 2, Apr 16, 23, 29,
  May 24, Oct 14, Nov 14, Dec 11; 1800: DL, Jan 1, Mar 11, Apr 29
Cook (singer, violinist), 1694: NONE, Sep 0; 1696: DL, Apr 0; 1703: LIF, Apr
  28, HA, Aug 21, LIF, Oct 25, YB, Dec 11; 1704: LIF, Feb 11, Apr 29, Jun 8,
  Jul 4, 10, 24, 27, Aug 9, Oct 16; 1705: DL, Jan 16, HAW, Aug 18, LIF/QUEN,
  Sep 28, Oct 11, 17; 1706: QUEEN'S, Jan 2, 17, LIF/QUEN, 25, QUEEN'S, Mar 7,
  Apr 20, 30, LIF/QUEN, Jul 6; 1708: QUEEN'S, Dec 14; 1709: SH, Aug 25, HA, Sep
  3; 1710: SH, Mar 22, YB, Apr 17; 1712: B&S, Nov 24; 1715: LIF, Jan 25, Feb 9,
  28, Mar 3, 21, 24, 31, Apr 2, 4, 19, May 2, Jun 3, 14, Aug 10, 11, 23, Oct 6,
  18; 1716: LIF, Mar 10, Apr 11, May 2
Cook (spectator), 1699: DLLIF, Apr 22
Cook in the Coal Hole, The (song), 1784: HAY, Aug 24; 1785: CG, Apr 11
Cook Jr (dancer), 1717: LIF, Nov 8, 15, 22, Dec 6; 1718: LIF, Jan 1, 2, 3, 15,
  24, Mar 29, Apr 15, 16, RI, Jul 26; 1719: LIF, Apr 29, May 13, 21, 25, 28
Cook, Captain James (mariner), 1785: CG, Dec 26; 1786: CG, Oct 9; 1788: CG, Mar
  24; 1799: CG, Oct 21
Cook, Mary (actor, singer), 1715: LIF, Jan 17, 25; 1716: LIF, Apr 27; 1717:
  LIF, May 15; 1718: LIF, Apr 30; 1719: LIF, May 18, Oct 2; 1720: LIF, Feb 23,
  Apr 26, Jun 7, BFBL, Aug 23; 1721: LIF, May 9, SFHL, Sep 2; 1722: LIF, May
  16; 1725: LIF, May 17, BF, Aug 23, LIF, Oct 16; 1726: LIF, Jul 5, Aug 19;
  1727: LIF, Apr 19, May 4, 17, Dec 11; 1728: LIF, Apr 23, 24, May 22, Jul 2;
  1729: LIF, Apr 19, May 13; 1732: LIF, Feb 14, May 31, LIF/CG, Oct 28, Dec 26;
  1733: LIF/CG, Mar 26, 30, CG, Oct 16, 29; 1734: CG, Jan 23, May 3, CG/LIF,
  Oct 29; 1735: CG/LIF, Jan 23, May 16, CG, Oct 29; 1736: CG, Oct 29; 1737: CG,
  Oct 29, Nov 17; 1738: CG, Oct 30; 1739: CG, Jan 22, Oct 29; 1740: CG, May 7;
  1745: CG, Mar 19
Cook, Mrs (actor), 1730: LIF, May 23
Cook, Mrs (actor), 1748: HAY, Mar 30
Cook, Mrs (dancer), 1763: CG, Jan 26, Feb 3
Cook, Widow (boxkeeper), 1731: DL, May 13; 1732: DL, May 10; 1733: DL, May 23;
  1737: DL, May 30
Cook's Court, 1718: NONE, Jul 30
Cooke (actor), 1762: CG, Apr 29, HAY, Oct 25
Cooke (actor), 1782: HAY, Dec 30; 1784: HAY, Feb 23
Cooke (equilibrist), 1751: SF, Sep 7, 16, 19
Cooke (musician), 1719: HIC, Feb 18
Cooke (printer), 1758: DL, Sep 16
Cooke (singer), 1796: CG, Oct 6; 1797: CG, Feb 18
Cooke, Dr Benjamin (musician, composer), 1758: SOHO, Apr 1; 1761: CG, Jun 23;
  1773: DL, Oct 21; 1774: DL, Jan 26, Mar 26, May 27, Nov 23; 1776: DL, Jan 15,
  Mar 28; 1786: DL, Mar 9; 1787: DL, Feb 1; 1791: CG, May 31, Jun 6
Cooke, Dr Benjamin, scholars of (singers), 1771: DL, Nov 12, Dec 4; 1772: DL,
  Mar 3, Dec 11; 1773: DL, May 25
Cooke, Edward
--Love's Triumph; or, The Royal Union, 1677: NONE, Sep 0
Cooke, George Frederic (actor), 1778: HAY, Apr 9, 29, 30, CHR, May 25, 27, 29,
  Jun 1, 3, 8, 9, 10, 15, 18, 19, 22, 24, 26, Jul 30; 1779: HAY, Feb 22, May 10
Cooke, Captain Henry, 1667: NONE, Feb 13
Cooke, James (actor, singer), 1791: DL, Jan 1, 18, DLKING'S, Nov 5, 7, 16, 25,
  28, Dec 14, 31; 1792: DLKING'S, Jan 18, 21, 28, Feb 18, Mar 6, 10, 17, 19,
  29, Apr 16, May 23, Jun 13, DL, Sep 25, Oct 4, 11, 13, 18, Nov 2, 3, 21, 29,
  Dec 10, 13, 26; 1793: DL, Jan 7, 16, 22, 23, Feb 16, 26, Mar 5, May 10, 24,
  31, Jun 1, HAY, 11, 12, 13, 17, 21, 29, Jul 5, Aug 3, 12, 16, Sep 2, 19, 21,
  24, 26, Oct 1, 4, 5, 8, 10, 15, 18, 21, 29, Nov 6, 16, 19, Dec 9, 10, 16, 19,
  23, 26, 28, 30; 1794: HAY, Jan 4, 13, 14, Feb 6, 8, 11, 20, 22, 24, Mar 31,
  DL, Apr 21, 25, May 16, 19, 22, 23, 30, Jun 9, 14, 18, 21, 23, 24, HAY, Jul
  8, 9, 10, 11, 14, 17, 18, 19, 21, 24, 25, Aug 4, 11, 13, 20, 27, 29, Sep 2,
  3, 4, 15, 17, DL, 23, 27, Oct 7, 14, 27, Nov 15, 22, Dec 20; 1795: DL, Jan
  21, 24, 27, 29, 31, Feb 2, 3, 5, 6, Mar 10, 14, May 6, 28, Jun 4, HAY, 9, 10,
  11, 13, 15, 20, Jul 1, 4, 8, 16, 22, 25, 31, Aug 20, 21, 27, 29, Sep 2, DL,
  19, 22, 24, 29, Oct 1, 6, 21, 26, 30, Nov 6, 11, 16, 19, 20, 23, 26, Dec 4,
  10, 18; 1796: DL, Jan 18, Mar 12, Apr 2, 30, May 9, 13, 27, Jun 4, 10, 13,
  Sep 24, Oct 10, 19, 24, Nov 5, 9, 10, 18, 26, Dec 16, 26; 1797: DL, Jan 7,
  12, 17, 20, Feb 3, 7, 9, 17, 22, 28, Mar 14, 18, 25, Apr 17, 20, 28, 29, May
  2, 23, 24, Jun 7, 12, Oct 5
Cooke, John, 1667: LIF, Sep 12
--Tu Quoque; or, The City Gallant, 1661: LIF, Jul 3, 6, 11; 1667: LIF, Sep 12,

190

16, Dec 16
Cooke, Mrs (beneficiary), 1757: DL, May 9
Cooke Jr, Phillip (dancer), 1739: CG, Jan 16, Apr 7, DL, Dec 10; 1740: DL, Apr
  8, 11, May 15; 1742: CG, Oct 23, 25, Nov 8, 9, Dec 7, 10, 11, 13, 14, 16, 17,
  18; 1743: CG, Feb 4, 9, 10, 17, 21, Mar 22, 24, Apr 2, 5, 12, 13, May 4, 20;
  1744: CG, Feb 9, 11, 14, Mar 3, 8, 28, 30, Apr 2, 4, 6, 16, 17, 23, 27, 30,
  May 7, 10, 11, 14, Oct 10, 22, Nov 2, 9, 17, Dec 6, 8, 14, DL, 19; 1745: CG,
  Jan 1, 3, 8, 14, 25, Feb 11, Mar 11, 14, 18, 21, 28, Apr 2, 4, 15, 22, 23,
  24, 25, 26, May 3, 4, 6, 7, 8, 10, 13, 14, Sep 30, Oct 2, 4, 7, 9, 14, 16,
  18, 23, 25, 29, Nov 6, 9, 14, 20, 23, Dec 14, 16, 17; 1746: CG, Jan 14, 22,
  24, 29, Feb 3, 4, 6, 7, 8, 10, 13, 15, 18, 20, 22, 24, 25, Mar 1, 6, 10, 11,
  13, 15, 17, 18, 22, 31, Apr 2, 3, 4, 7, 9, 15, 17, 18, 21, 23, 25, 26, 30,
  May 1, 13, Jun 9, 11, 13, 16, 20, 23; 1747: DL, Jan 21, 22, 24, 31, Feb 4, 7,
  11, 16, 18, 20, Mar 17, Sep 29, Oct 1, 17, 23, 27, 29, Nov 2, 13, 16, 17, 23,
  28, Dec 3, 26; 1748: DL, Jan 8, 14, 18, Feb 3, 9, 12, 27, Mar 5, 7, 10, 12,
  17, 24, 26, 29, 31, Apr 2, 15, 19, 20, 23, 25, Oct 19, 27, Nov 3, 7, 12, 29,
  30, Dec 3, 21, 26; 1749: DL, Jan 7, 9, 10, 18, Feb 21, Mar 7, 9, 11, 13, 14,
  30, Apr 5, 8, 12, 14, May 6, 13, 16; 1750: CG, Jan 31, Mar 29, 31, Apr 5, 17,
  18, 20, 21, 23, 24, Sep 26, Dec 21; 1751: CG, Jan 17, Mar 19, Apr 12, 17, 18,
  Sep 25, Oct 9, 21, 28, Nov 11, 19, 20; 1752: CG, Jan 23, Mar 19, Apr 13, Oct
  26, Nov 2, 13, 27, Dec 7, 8, 16, 18; 1753: CG, Feb 6, Mar 29, Apr 9, 30, May
  5, 9, Oct 18, 20, 25, Nov 3; 1754: CG, Jan 5, DL, 26, CG, Apr 4, 25, May 6
Cooke Sr, Phillip (dancing master), 1739: CG, Jan 16, DL, Nov 28; 1740: DL, Jan
  5, 15, Feb 13, Apr 29, May 7, 18
Cooke, Sir Robert, 1668: BRIDGES, May 30
Cooke, Sarah (actor), 1671: NONE, Sep 0; 1674: NONE, Sep 0; 1677: DL, Mar 0;
  1678: DL, Feb 0; 1680: DL, Dec 0; 1681: DL, May 0, Oct 0; 1682: DL, Feb 4,
  NONE, Sep 0, ATCOURT, Nov 15, DL, 16, 28; 1683: NONE, Sep 0, DL, Nov 12, Dec
  0; 1684: ATCOURT, Feb 11, DL, Apr 0, NONE, Aug 0; 1685: DLORDG, Jan 20, DL,
  Aug 0; 1686: DL, Jan 0, DG, Mar 4, DL, Apr 0; 1687: DG, Mar 0, ATCOURT, Apr
  25; 1688: DL, Apr 0
Cooke, Thomas, 1730: HAY, Nov 30; 1731: DL, Aug 18; 1737: DL, May 17; 1743: DL,
  Dec 19
--Battle of the Books, The, 1731: HAY, Jan 14
--Battle of the Poets, The; or, The Contention for the Laureat, 1730: HAY, Nov
  30, Dec 4, 7, 14, 23, 30
--Eunuch, The; or, The Darby Captain (farce), 1737: DL, May 17
--Love's the Cause and Cure of Grief; or, The Innocent Murderer, 1743: DL, Dec
  14, 19
--Triumphs of Love and Honour, The, 1731: DL, Jul 23, Aug 18
Cooke, William, 1783: CG, Jan 17
--Capricious Lady, The, 1783: CG, Jan 17, 20, 22, 24, Feb 7, 12, 21; 1784: CG,
  Feb 13, 16; 1785: CG, May 26; 1788: CG, Feb 25
Cooling, 1669: ATCOURT, Feb 15
Coombe, Harvey Christian (alderman), 1794: DL, Jul 2; 1797: DL, Oct 27
Coombs (Combes) (actor, property man), 1789: CG, Jun 16; 1790: CG, May 29;
  1791: CG, Jun 2; 1792: CG, Mar 31, May 10, 25; 1793: CG, Mar 11, Apr 8; 1794:
  CG, Jun 12; 1795: CG, May 1, Jun 17, Oct 8, Nov 16, Dec 9; 1796: CG, Jan 23,
  Jun 4, Oct 14; 1797: CG, Jun 7, Nov 24; 1798: CG, Mar 31, Apr 9, May 19, Oct
  3; 1799: CG, May 28, Jun 8, Oct 2, 21; 1800: CG, Apr 5
Coombs, Miss (actor), 1795: CG, Nov 16; 1799: CG, Mar 25, Apr 13, Dec 23; 1800:
  CG, Jan 23
Cooper (actor), 1785: HAY, Jan 31; 1787: HAY, Mar 12; 1788: HAY, Apr 9, 29, Sep
  30; 1794: HAMM, Mar 24; 1799: OCH, May 15
Cooper (boxkeeper), 1730: DL, May 7; 1731: DL, May 13; 1732: DL, May 10; 1733:
  DL, May 23; 1734: DL/HAY, May 22; 1735: DL, May 29; 1736: DL, May 27; 1737:
  DL, May 31; 1739: DL, May 26; 1740: DL, May 19; 1742: CG, May 14; 1744: CG,
  May 11; 1745: CG, May 14; 1746: CG, May 6
Cooper and His Wife (dance), 1715: DL, May 31
Cooper Outwitted, The; or, Harlequin Happy (pantomime), 1742: DL, Apr 26
Cooper, Anthony Ashley, Lord Shaftesbury, 1677: DG, Nov 17; 1683: DLORDG, Feb
  0; 1747: CG, Apr 1
Cooper, Elizabeth, 1735: CG/LIF, Feb 22; 1736: HAY, May 17
--Nobleman, The; or, Family Quarrel, 1736: HAY, May 17, 18, 19
--Rival Widows, The; or, The Fair Libertine, 1735: CG/LIF, Feb 22, 25, 27, Mar
  1, 4, 6
Cooper, M (printer), 1747: CG, Mar 19; 1749: DL, Feb 15; 1750: DL, Jan 4, Mar
  5; 1752: DL, Nov 27; 1756: DL, Mar 9; 1759: DL, May 1; 1766: CG, Nov 5, Dec
  5; 1767: CG, Jan 5, DL, Feb 10, CG, 16, Mar 9, 14, Apr 11, May 11, DL, 15;
  1771: CG, Oct 11, Nov 6, Dec 10; 1772: CG, Jan 16, Feb 6, Mar 14, Apr 4, May
  26, Oct 13, Nov 4, Dec 8; 1773: CG, Jan 7, Feb 5, Mar 11, Oct 15, Nov 3, Dec
  2; 1774: CG, Feb 8, Mar 10, Apr 7, May 9; 1776: CG, Nov 14; 1780: CG, May 29;

        1781: CG, May 28; 1784: CG, Jun 2; 1787: CG, Nov 8
Cooper, Miss (dancer), 1785: HAY, Apr 15
Cooper, Mrs (actor), 1722: HAY, Dec 17; 1734: DL, Jan 3, Feb 4, LIF, Apr 26
Cooper, Mrs (house servant), 1775: DL, Dec 9
Cooper, The. See Arne, Dr Thomas A.
Cooper, Thomas Apthorpe (actor), 1795: CG, Oct 19, Nov 2, 6, 30
Coopers (dance), 1765: DL, Feb 15, 18, 21, 25, 28, Mar 4; 1776: HAY, Jun 26,
    28, Jul 1, 3; 1777: CG, Apr 25; 1778: DL, Dec 11, 17, 28; 1779: DL, Jan 1,
    11, 14, 22, May 14; 1780: DL, Feb 24, May 24
Coote, J (printer), 1759: CG, Mar 28
Cope, Sir John (spectator), 1697: LIF, Mar 9
Cope, Mrs (dancer), 1770: HAY, Oct 5
Copeland, Mrs (actor), 1729: LIF, Dec 16
Coper (singer), 1695: LIF, Dec 0
Copin, Elizabeth (actor, dancer), 1745: DL, Sep 26, Oct 1, Dec 27; 1746: DL,
    Sep 30, Nov 21; 1747: DL, Mar 19, CG, Nov 13, Dec 17, 23; 1748: CG, Jan 7,
    15, 16, 19, Feb 10, Mar 28, Apr 13, Sep 26, 28, 30, Nov 9, 15, 26; 1749: CG,
    Mar 29, Apr 7, 15, 17; 1755: CG, Jan 13, 22, Feb 6, Mar 6, Apr 3, 16, May 6,
    Oct 3, 16, 18, 21, Nov 10; 1756: CG, Feb 24, Sep 24, Oct 20, 22, Nov 9, 13,
    Dec 10; 1757: CG, Feb 9, 12, 19, Sep 21, 26, Oct 14, Nov 9, 23; 1758: CG, Sep
    22, 27, Oct 20, 24, Nov 9, 13; 1759: CG, Mar 27, Sep 24, 26, 28, Oct 1, 5,
    10, 22, Dec 6; 1760: CG, Mar 18, Apr 9, Sep 22, 24, Oct 8, 20; 1761: CG, Mar
    25, May 11, Sep 7, 11, 18, Oct 5; 1762: CG, Apr 27, May 13, Oct 4, 11, 14,
    Nov 16; 1763: CG, Oct 8, 26, Nov 18, 22; 1764: CG, Jan 5, 26, Mar 27, Oct 18;
    1765: CG, Jan 8, Oct 12, 15, 19; 1766: CG, Dec 2, 20; 1767: CG, Sep 26, Oct
    5, 9; 1768: CG, Jan 6, Feb 25, Sep 20, Oct 22, Nov 16; 1769: CG, Jan 23, Oct
    2, 7; 1770: CG, Apr 25, Nov 16, Dec 26; 1771: CG, Jan 1, 15; 1772: CG, May
    20; 1773: CG, May 19
Copland (house servant), 1789: CG, Jun 13; 1790: CG, Jun 8; 1791: CG, Jun 9
Coply, Sir Godfrey (spectator), 1700: LIF, Mar 5, 11, DL, 13, DLORLIF, Apr 18
Coppola, Giuseppe (singer), 1777: KING'S, Nov 4, 8, Dec 16; 1778: KING'S, Jan
    20, Feb 7, Mar 3, Apr 2, 4, May 5, 30, Nov 28, Dec 22; 1779: KING'S, Mar 25,
    Apr 29, May 15, 29, Jul 3
Coq du Village (dance), 1784: KING'S, Feb 26, Mar 2, 9, 20, 30, Apr 22, Jun 1,
    5, 19
Coq du Village, Le. See Favart, Charles Simon.
Coquet, The. See Molloy, Charles.
Coquet's Surrender, The; or, The Humorous Punster (play, anon), 1732: HAY, May
    15
Coquette (dance), 1732: DL, Apr 18; 1733: GF, Dec 18, 28; 1734: GF, Jan 7, 9,
    11, 12, 18, 22
Coquette et Jaloux (dance), 1734: DL, Dec 2; 1735: DL, Jan 8
Coquette Francoise (dance), 1734: CG/LIF, Dec 14, 26; 1735: CG/LIF, Jan 17, Mar
    15, 20, 25, Apr 11
Coquette Quaker (dance), 1779: CG, Nov 9, 11, Dec 29
Coquette sans la Savoir, La. See Favart, Charles Simon.
Coquette Shepherdess (dance), 1722: DL, Mar 15; 1727: DL, Mar 20, Apr 19, 20;
    1728: DL, Apr 11
Coquette, The. See Galuppi, Baldassare.
Coquette, The; or, The Mistakes of the Heart. See Hitchcock, Robert.
Coradini, Sga (dancer), 1767: KING'S, Oct 27
Corail, Mlle. See Cerail, Mlle.
Corar, Mrs. See Currer, Elizabeth.
Corbally, Miss (actor), 1732: RIW/HAY, Sep 4
Corbeta, Francisco (guitarist), 1675: ATCOURT, Feb 15
Corbett (actor), 1780: HAY, Nov 13
Corbett (singer), 1748: JS, May 30
Corbett (spectator), 1668: LIF, Jan 6, Mar 26
Corbett, C (printer), 1747: DL, Mar 19; 1748: DL, Dec 10; 1750: DL, Oct 1
Corbett, Mary (actor), 1667: BRIDGES, Aug 12; 1672: BRIDGES, Jan 0; 1675: DL,
    Jan 12, Aug 0, Nov 17; 1676: DL, Jan 29, ATCOURT, May 29; 1678: DL, Feb 0,
    Mar 0; 1681: DL, May 0, Oct 0
Corbett, William (musician, composer), 1699: YB, Mar 17; 1704: YB, Mar 29, May
    18, LIF, Jun 8; 1705: YB, Feb 13; 1706: YB, Mar 18; 1707: YB, Mar 19, 26;
    1711: HDS, Apr 24; 1713: HIC, Mar 25, Apr 9; 1714: HIC, Apr 28; 1715: GRT,
    Apr 26; 1724: HAY, Mar 18; 1728: HIC, Mar 20; 1734: YB, Mar 8, Apr 5
Corbyn, Master (dancer), 1785: HAY, Dec 26
Cordans, Bartholmeo (composer)
--Ormisda (opera), 1730: KING'S, Apr 4, 7, 11, 14, 18, 21, 25, 28, May 2, 5, 9,
    12, 14, Jun 9, Nov 24, 28, Dec 1, 5, 8; 1732: LIF, Apr 19
Cordelier (dance), 1731: LIF, May 10
Cordoni (Candoni) (musician), 1760: SOHO, Mar 13, HAY, 27, HIC, Apr 29

Corelli, Michael Arcangelo (composer), 1703: DL, Feb 11, Nov 10, Dec 22; 1704:
    DL, Feb 4; 1705: DL, Nov 8; 1707: YB, Apr 18, May 23; 1708: SH, Feb 4, Mar
    26; 1709: SH, Nov 30; 1713: CA, Mar 20; 1714: HIC, Apr 28; 1719: DL, Oct 14;
    1722: DL, Mar 14, HAY, May 11; 1723: DL, Mar 20, May 15; 1724: HIC, Mar 25;
    1725: DL, May 6, 10, 19; 1726: YB, Mar 30, DL, May 4, 5, 23; 1727: YB, Mar
    22, DL, May 1, 8, 12; 1728: YB, Apr 10, DL, May 17; 1729: DL, Feb 26, HIC,
    Apr 16, DL, 23, HIC, 30; 1730: HIC, Feb 25, DL, May 18; 1731: HIC, Feb 4, 26;
    1732: HIC, Feb 28, LIF, Mar 10, CL, 17, HIC, 31, DL, May 3; 1733: DL, Apr 4,
    GF, 25, HIC, 27, DL/HAY, Oct 6, HAY, Nov 19, DL/HAY, Dec 20, DL, 31; 1734:
    DL/HAY, Jan 26, HIC, Mar 20, GF, May 8, HA, Sep 11; 1737: HIC, Apr 1, DL, May
    4, 27; 1739: DL, May 22; 1741: DL, Apr 4; 1789: DL, Feb 27, Mar 20; 1793: CG,
    Mar 8; 1794: CG, Mar 28, Apr 4; 1795: KING'S, Mar 13; 1797: CG, Apr 5
--1st Concerto, 1725: DL, May 19; 1726: YB, Mar 30, DL, May 4; 1728: YB, Apr
    10; 1731: HIC, Feb 26; 1732: HIC, Feb 28; 1733: DL/HAY, Oct 6, Nov 19; 1737:
    HIC, Apr 1, DL, May 27; 1739: DL, May 22
--2nd Concerto, 1725: DL, May 10
--4th Concerto, 1770: MARLY, Sep 4
--5th Concerto, 1727: DL, May 1
--7th Concerto, 1732: CL, Mar 17
--8th Concerto, 1722: DL, Mar 14; 1723: DL, May 15; 1725: DL, May 6; 1726: YB,
    Mar 30, DL, May 5, 23; 1727: DL, May 1, 8; 1728: YB, Apr 10, DL, May 17;
    1729: HIC, Apr 16; 1731: HIC, Feb 26; 1732: HIC, Feb 28, DL, May 3; 1734:
    DL/HAY, Jan 26, GF, May 8; 1737: HIC, Apr 1; 1793: CG, Mar 8; 1794: CG, Mar
    28, Apr 4; 1795: KING'S, Mar 13, CG, 20; 1797: CG, Apr 5
Corer, Mrs. See Currer, Elizabeth.
Corer St, 1737: LIF, Apr 2
Corey, John (actor, author), 1701: LIF, Aug 0, Nov 0, Dec 0; 1702: LIF, Jun 0;
    1703: LIF, Nov 0; 1704: LIF, Jan 13, Jul 4, Oct 2, Nov 13; 1705: LIF/QUEN,
    Feb 22, LIF, Aug 1, QUEEN'S, Nov 23; 1706: QUEEN'S, Jan 3, Feb 11, Jun 0, Dec
    16; 1707: QUEEN'S, Apr 21, Jun 25, 27, Jul 10, 22, 26, DL/QUEEN, Dec 27;
    1708: DL/QUEEN, Jan 1, DL, Feb 9, Apr 15, 19, 22, May 31, Jun 11, DL/QUEEN,
    22, DL, 24, 26, Jul 1, 10, 27, 29, Sep 4, 18, 21, Oct 9, Dec 21; 1709: DL,
    Jan 6, Feb 25, Mar 17, Apr 11, May 2, 18, Jun 2, Nov 23, 24, 25, 30, Dec 10;
    1710: DL, Jan 3, 14, 18, Feb 1, 16, 25, Mar 7, 11, 14, GR, Jun 15, 21, 24,
    28, Jul 1, 6, 8, 10, 12, 15, 20, Aug 3, 7, 12, 24, 26, 28, Sep 1; 1711: DL,
    Feb 3, Mar 20, May 18, 24; 1712: DL, May 30, Nov 7; 1713: DL, Jun 5; 1714:
    DL, May 17, 21, Jun 2; 1715: LIF, Jan 3, 7, Feb 3, 5, Mar 26, Jun 14, Oct 4,
    7, 11, Dec 12; 1716: LIF, Feb 21, May 2, Jul 11, Aug 3, Nov 9, 10, 13, Dec 1;
    1717: LIF, Jan 8, 22, 28, Mar 11, Apr 24, Oct 15, 26, Nov 14, 16, 19, 26, Dec
    10; 1718: LIF, Jan 7, 11, Feb 18, Mar 1, Apr 23, NONE, Jul 30, LIF, Sep 26,
    30, Oct 1, 16, 18, Nov 13; 1719: LIF, Jan 16, Feb 21, Apr 1, DL, Jun 26, Nov
    11, Dec 11; 1720: DL, May 11, 30, Dec 17; 1721: DL, May 11, Jun 20, Aug 4,
    BF/SF, Sep 2, DL, Nov 30; 1722: DL, Jan 6, 26, Mar 31, May 18, Oct 11, Dec
    22; 1723: DL, Jan 9, May 10, 20, Dec 5, 30; 1724: DL, Apr 18, May 4, 14, SF,
    Sep 2, DL, Dec 3; 1725: DL, Feb 1, Apr 26, May 11, Jun 18, Sep 30, Oct 5, 16,
    21, Nov 29; 1726: DL, Apr 29, May 12, 23, Oct 22, Nov 26, Dec 3, 12; 1727:
    DL, Apr 19, 26, 27, May 12, BF, Aug 21, DL, Dec 13, 30; 1728: DL, Jan 4, Apr
    1, 13, 29, May 1, 6, 8, 17, 29, Sep 14, Oct 5, 12, 15; 1729: DL, Jan 15, 21,
    25, Feb 22, Apr 23, 30, May 3, 6, 7, 28, Jun 27, Jul 25, Sep 20, 23, 27, Oct
    7, 25, Nov 4, 27, Dec 27; 1730: DL, Jan 3, 26, Apr 27, Sep 19, 26, 29, Oct 1,
    24, Nov 25, 30, Dec 1, 11; 1731: DL, Jan 27, Feb 22, Apr 3, 27, May 17, 19,
    Nov 5, Dec 21; 1732: DL, Apr 1, 11, 17, 24, 25, May 5, Sep 21, 28, Oct 17,
    GF, Nov 18; 1733: GF, Jan 18, Feb 19, DL, Sep 28, Nov 2, 5, 13, 14, Dec 17;
    1734: DL, Jan 31, May 13, DL/HAY, 24, DL, Oct 9, 14, Nov 8; 1735: DL, Jan 8,
    28, Apr 11
--Metamorphosis, The; or, The Old Lover Outwitted, 1704: LIF, Oct 2; 1728: HAY,
    Oct 15, 17; 1729: HAY, Mar 12
Corey, Katherine Mitchell (actor), 1661: VERE, Dec 16; 1663: VERE, Mar 0; 1664:
    BRIDGES, Aug 3, Nov 0; 1665: BRIDGES, Jan 14; 1666: ATCOURT, Dec 10, BRIDGES,
    27; 1667: BRI/COUR, Feb 0, BRIDGES, Apr 16, 17, Oct 19; 1668: BRIDGES, Nov 6,
    Dec 18; 1669: BRIDGES, Apr 17, May 6; 1670: BRIDGES, Aug 0; 1671: BRIDGES,
    Mar 0, Jun 0; 1673: LIF, Mar 0, May 0; 1674: LIF, Mar 0, DL, May 16; 1675:
    DL, Jan 12, Apr 23, NONE, Sep 0; 1676: DL, Dec 11; 1677: DL, Mar 17, May 5,
    Dec 12; 1678: DL, Mar 0; 1682: DL, Feb 4, Nov 16; 1683: DG, May 31; 1684: DL,
    Mar 0, Apr 0; 1685: DLORDG, Jan 20, DG, Jul 0, DL, Aug 0; 1686: DL, Jan 0;
    1687: DG, Mar 0; 1688: DL, May 3; 1689: DL, Apr 0, Nov 20; 1690: DL, Jan 0,
    Mar 0, NONE, Sep 0, DL, Oct 0, DL/IT, 21, DL, Dec 0; 1691: DL, Jan 0, Mar 0,
    Apr 0, NONE, Sep 0, DL, Dec 0; 1692: DL, Jan 0, Mar 0
Corey, Mrs (householder), 1737: LIF, Apr 2
Corfe (singer), 1736: LIF, Sep 28, Oct 21, Dec 7, 17, 31; 1740: LIF, Mar 26;
    1744: KING'S, Nov 3; see also Corse
Corfe, Arthur Thomas (pianist), 1792: KING'S, Feb 24, Mar 14, CG, May 11

Cori, Angelo (composer), 1735: KING'S, Apr 8
Corinna, I excuse thy face (song), 1691: DL, Dec 0
Corinna in the bloom of youth (song), 1690: DL, Dec 0
Coriolanus. See Shakespeare, William; Thomson, James; Ariosti, Attilio.
Coriolanus; or, The Roman Matron. See Kemble, John Philip.
Coritong, Hodge Brean (Tripoline ambassador), 1744: CG, Mar 15
Cork Theatre, 1768: DL, Nov 23
Corker, John, 1774: CG, Jan 11
Cormeo, Il (song), 1746: KING'S, Mar 25
Corn Thrashers (dance), 1777: DL, Apr 19, May 15
Cornacchini, Emanuele (singer), 1759: KING'S, Nov 13; 1760: KING'S, Jan 15, Feb
    16, 25, Mar 1, Apr 17, May 31
Cornbury, Viscount, 1665: NONE, Feb 9
Corne (actor), 1782: HAY, Dec 30
Corneille (harpsichordist), 1675: ATCOURT, Feb 15
Corneille, Pierre, 1660: NONE, Sep 0; 1662: COCKPIT, Jan 20, ATCOURT, Dec 1;
    1664: LIF, Mar 8, BRIDGES, May 2; 1666: LIF, Dec 0; 1668: ATCOURT, Feb 4,
    NONE, Sep 0; 1718: DL, Oct 31, Nov 1; 1722: HAY, Jan 15, 22, Feb 12, Apr 2;
    1734: HAY, Nov 25; 1772: CG, Mar 21
--Cid, Le, 1718: DL, Oct 31, Nov 1; 1722: HAY, Jan 15; 1734: HAY, Nov 25
--Horaces, Les, 1722: HAY, Apr 2
--Menteur, Le, 1722: HAY, Jan 22
--Mistaken Beauty; or, The Lyar, 1660: NONE, Sep 0; 1667: BRIDGES, Nov 28;
    1684: DL, Sep 0
--Rodogune, 1722: HAY, Feb 12
--Valiant Cid, The, 1662: ATCOURT, Dec 1; 1666: LIF, Dec 0; 1675: DG, Dec 0
Corneille's Horace and the Roman Father Compared (book), 1750: DL, Mar 1
Cornelia. See Berkeley, William.
Cornelys, John (actor), 1771: HAY, May 20, 23, 31, Jun 5, 7, Jul 3, 10, 24, Aug
    19, 26, Sep 9; 1791: HAY, Jun 13, Aug 9, 13
Cornelys, Margaret, Mrs John (actor), 1795: CG, Jan 31, May 2
Cornelys, Miss (actor), 1794: CG, Sep 15, 24, Oct 7, 14, 23; 1795: CG, Jan 28,
    29, Mar 28, Apr 22, 25, 29, May 1, 29, Jun 16
Cornelys, Teresa (actor, proprietor), 1746: KING'S, Jan 7; 1765: KING'S, Feb
    15; 1769: KING'S, Jun 6; 1771: CG, Jun 6
Cornet (dancer), 1727: KING'S, Mar 16
Cornhill, 1690: HUGHS, Jan 8; 1718: LIF, Apr 18; 1732: GV, Feb 10; 1737: ST,
    Mar 8; 1742: GF, Jan 29, Mar 18, Apr 22; 1743: DL, Apr 29; 1744: DL, Apr 2,
    Dec 12; 1745: DL, Apr 1; 1746: GF, Jan 15, 22, HIC, Mar 10, CG, 13, May 2;
    1748: DL, Mar 12, Apr 23, May 2; 1749: DL, Apr 5; 1750: DL, Jan 11, Feb 22,
    Mar 22, Nov 28; 1751: DL, Mar 14, Dec 17, 18; 1752: DL, Apr 10, Nov 15, Dec
    19, 22; 1753: DL, May 22; 1756: CG, Dec 8; 1757: DL, Dec 21; 1758: CG, Jul 6;
    1759: DL, Mar 30, CG, May 8; 1763: DL, Apr 27; 1772: CG, May 6; 1777: HAY,
    Oct 13; 1782: HAY, Mar 18; 1784: HAY, Jan 21
Cornish Comedy, The. See Powell, George.
Cornish Hero, The; or, Jack the Giant Killer (interlude), 1725: LIF, Apr 16
Cornish Squire, The. See Ralph, James.
Cornish, James (oboist), 1794: CG, Mar 7; 1795: HAY, Mar 4; 1796: CG, Feb 12;
    1797: CG, Mar 3; 1798: CG, Feb 23; 1799: CG, Feb 8; 1800: CG, Feb 28
Corno Obligato (music), 1793: CG, Mar 20; 1794: CG, Mar 21
Cornwall, 1755: HAY, Sep 4
Cornwallis (rioter), 1721: LIF, Feb 1
Cornwallis, Henrietta (actor), 1668: ATCOURT, Jan 13, Feb 4
Coronation Anthems, The (music), 1735: SH, Mar 28; 1736: YB, Mar 4, SH, Apr 16;
    1737: CT, May 2; 1742: GF, Apr 29; 1755: HAY, Dec 15; 1758: HAY, Feb 2; 1762:
    CG, Mar 3, 24, KING'S, May 11, CHAPEL, 18, RANELAGH, Jun 16, HAY, Sep 1;
    1763: CG, Feb 23; 1764: HAY, Nov 13; 1765: CG, Feb 27; 1766: CG, Feb 19;
    1767: RANELAGH, Jun 1; 1768: CG, Feb 24; 1770: DL, Mar 14, 28; 1771: DL, Feb
    27, Mar 15; 1772: DL, Mar 6, 25; 1773: DL, Mar 10; 1774: DL, Feb 25; 1775:
    DL, Mar 17, 22, KING'S, 24; 1776: DL, Mar 1, 15; 1777: DL, Feb 14, Mar 14,
    CG, 19, 21; 1778: DL, Mar 13, 27; 1781: DL, Mar 30; 1782: DL, Mar 1; 1783:
    DL, Mar 14, 28; 1784: DL, Feb 27, Mar 12, 26; 1785: DL, Feb 23; 1786: DL, Mar
    10; 1789: CG, Mar 6; 1790: DL, Feb 19, CG, 19, DL, 26, CG, Mar 3, 17; 1791:
    DL, Mar 11, CG, 11, DL, 23, CG, 23; 1792: KING'S, Feb 24, CG, 29, KING'S, 29,
    CG, Mar 9, KING'S, 14, CG, 28, KING'S, 28, 30; 1793: KING/HAY, Feb 15, CG,
    15, KING/HAY, 15, CG, 15, 22, Mar 8, 13; 1794: CG, Mar 7, DL, 12, 14, CG, 21,
    DL, Apr 2, 10, KING'S, May 15; 1795: CG, Feb 20, KING'S, Mar 13, CG, 18;
    1796: CG, Mar 16; 1797: CG, Mar 17, 24; 1798: CG, Mar 2; 1799: CG, Feb 15;
    1800: CG, Feb 28, Apr 4
Coronation Ode (song), 1761: DL, Mar 30
Coronation of Queen Elizabeth, The, 1680: BF/SF, Aug 0
Coronation, The (procession), 1752: DL, Sep 26; 1761: DL, Sep 30, Oct 2, 3, 5,

6, 8, 9, 10, 12, 14, 16, 17, 20, 23, 29, Nov 2, CG, 6, DL, 9, 11, CG, 12, 13,
DL, 13, CG, 13, 14, 16, DL, 17, CG, 17, DL, 17, 18, CG, 18, DL, 19, CG, 19,
20, DL, 20, 21, CG, 21, DL, 23, CG, 23, 24, 25, 26, 27, 28, 30, Dec 1, 2, 3,
DL, 4, CG, 4, 5, 7, 8, 9, 11, 12, 14, 15, 17, 18, 19, 21, 23, 26, 28, 29, 30,
31; _1762_: CG, Jan 1, 2, 4, 5, 6, 8, 9, 11, 14, 16, 18, 19, 20, 21, 23, 26,
27, Feb 8, 10, 13, 16, 20, 27, Mar 6, 11, 16, 18, Apr 12, May 10, 18, 24, Oct
2, 9, 16, 23, Nov 26, Dec 31; _1766_: CG, Sep 22, 24, 26, 29, Oct 1, 3, 6, 7,
9, 11, 13, 17, 20, 24, 27, 31, Nov 3, 5, 10, 17, Dec 26, 27, 29; _1767_: CG,
Apr 23, May 27, 28, Sep 22, 23, 24, Dec 29; _1768_: CG, Sep 22, Oct 19, Nov 4,
22; _1769_: CG, Sep 22, Oct 4, 28; _1770_: CG, Jan 1
Coronell (beneficiary), _1757_: CG, Nov 22
Coror, Mrs. See Currer, Elizabeth.
Corpora (musician), _1722_: HAY, Jan 26
Corporalli. See Caporale.
Corrar, Mrs. See Currer, Elizabeth.
Corri, Domenico (composer), _1774_: KING'S, Dec 3; _1788_: CG, Nov 6; _1789_: CG, Sep
28; _1800_: CG, Mar 21
Corri, Sga (actor), _1775_: DL, Mar 10, KING'S, 24
Corria, Antonio (composer), _1717_: CORH, Apr 26
Corse (singer), _1730_: BFPG/TC, Aug 1, GF, Nov 6; _1731_: GF, May 13; _1733_: LIF,
Mar 7, DL/HAY, Oct 29, Nov 24, 26; _1734_: DL/HAY, Jan 28; see also Corfe
Corse, Joseph (singer), _1775_: DL, Mar 10
Corsican Sailors' Punch House (dance), _1771_: CG, Apr 12, 20, 26, May 6, Sep 30,
Oct 11, 16, 24, 29, Dec 20; _1772_: CG, Sep 30, Oct 7, 22, Dec 18; _1773_: CG,
Oct 13; _1774_: CG, Jan 7, Mar 19, Apr 9
Cortegiano (dance), _1735_: HAY, Dec 29
Cory, Thomas (actor), _1798_: DL, Nov 17, Dec 4, 15, 27; _1799_: DL, Jan 19, Feb 5,
Mar 2, Apr 20, May 7, 24, Jul 3, Sep 17, Oct 3, Dec 11, 30; _1800_: DL, Jan 1,
25, Feb 4, 7, 14, Mar 11, Apr 29, May 29, Jun 11, 18
Cory, William (actor), _1675_: DL, Aug 0
Corye, John
--Cure for Jealousy, A, _1699_: LIF, Dec 0
--Generous Enemies, The; or, The Ridiculous Lovers, _1671_: BRIDGES, Jun 0; _1695_:
NONE, Sep 0
Cosa Rara, La. See Martin y Soler, Vicente.
Cosacco (dance), _1767_: KING'S, May 14
Cosh. See Coysh.
Cosroe (pasticcio), _1770_: KING'S, Nov 24, Dec 1, 4, 8; _1771_: KING'S, Jan 5, Mar
12
Cossac Jaloux (dance), _1787_: KING'S, May 17, 19
Cossack (dance), _1760_: CG, Oct 10, 14; _1761_: DL, Oct 20; _1762_: CG, Apr 27, May
8, 10, 14, 19; _1784_: KING'S, Feb 7; _1785_: KING'S, Mar 17
Cossaque (dance), _1780_: KING'S, Apr 20
Cossaque et Pas Russe (dance), _1791_: DL, May 20, 25
Cossins, W (witness), _1735_: GF/HAY, Mar 18, Apr 25
Costa, Gioacchino (singer), _1790_: HAY, Jan 7, Feb 2, 27, Apr 6, 29, May 27, 29
Costain (dresser), _1766_: DL, Dec 17; _1767_: DL, Jan 27; _1771_: DL, Dec 7; _1773_:
DL, Jan 18; _1774_: DL, Mar 19
Costanza Di Rosinella, La. See Guglielmi, Pietro.
Costanza, Sga (dancer), _1742_: DL, Sep 21, Oct 9, 25, Nov 12, 13, 29; _1743_: DL,
May 16
Costello, Miss (actor), _1780_: HAY, Apr 5
Costin (boxkeeper), _1747_: DL, May 11; _1750_: DL, May 10; _1755_: DL, May 6; _1758_:
DL, May 9; _1760_: DL, May 6; _1769_: DL, May 12; _1770_: DL, May 18; _1771_: DL, May
27; _1772_: DL, May 25
Costo (actor), _1750_: HAY, Feb 9, 16, 26, Mar 13
Costollo (Castalio, Costello, Costelow), Patrick (actor), _1745_: SMMF, Feb 28;
_1746_: SOU, Oct 27; _1747_: GF, Feb 23, Mar 9, 16, 23, HAY, Apr 22; _1748_: NWC,
Apr 4, BFSY, Aug 24; _1749_: NWLS, Feb 27, HAY, Apr 3, May 15, BFC, Aug 23, DL,
Oct 18, Dec 12, 20, 27; _1750_: DL, Apr 30, Sep 22, Oct 22, 30; _1751_: DL, Jan
21, 26, May 1, Sep 12, 24, Oct 16, Nov 29, Dec 26; _1752_: DL, Jan 11, 21, 23,
Apr 1, 3, 4, 6, 21, May 2; _1754_: DL, Feb 9, CG, Mar 28, Oct 14, Nov 1, 12,
29, Dec 10, 13, 30; _1755_: CG, Jan 8, 14, Mar 18, Apr 7, 30, May 3, 12, Oct
11, 16, Nov 13, 21, Dec 11; _1756_: CG, Jan 6, Feb 3, 13, Mar 22, 27, 30, Apr
1, May 7, 26, Sep 20, Oct 4, 11, 16, 19, 22, 29, Nov 8, 9, 10, 22, 23, 24,
Dec 6, 7, 8, 10, 20, 21; _1757_: CG, Jan 6, 28, DL, Apr 2, CG, May 4, 17, Sep
16, 21, 23, Oct 17, 22, Nov 2, Dec 14; _1758_: CG, Jan 28, Feb 1, Mar 13, 14,
28, 29, Apr 3, 13, 14, 24, 25, 27, Sep 22, 25, Oct 20, Nov 2, 18, 23; _1759_:
CG, Jan 4, Mar 3, 17, 20, 24, 27, 31, Apr 28, May 7, 14, 24, Sep 26, 28, Oct
3, 15, 30, Nov 7, 8, 30, Dec 31; _1760_: CG, Jan 9, 16, 31, Feb 14, Apr 17, 18,
May 1, 2, 5, 19, 23, Sep 22, Oct 11, 13, 17, 25; _1761_: CG, Jan 6, Apr 2, 17,
21, May 8, Sep 23, 26, Oct 2, 10, 14, 17, Nov 2, 6, Dec 11; _1762_: CG, Mar 22,

195

Apr 30, May 11, Sep 27, Oct 2, 5, 19, 20, 21, 25, Nov 3, 15, Dec 27; 1763:
CG, Apr 15, 25, 30, May 11, 16, Sep 19, 23, 28, Oct 7, 10, 19, Nov 10, 26;
1764: CG, Jan 5, 9, Feb 1, 11, 17, Mar 27, 29, May 1, 21, Sep 17, 19, 21, 28,
Oct 5, 10, 12, 16, 17, Nov 1, 15, 16, Dec 29; 1765: CG, Feb 18, Apr 26, 30,
May 11, HAY, Jun 10, Jul 31, Aug 8, 9, 21, 30, Sep 11, CG, 18, 20, 27, Oct 2,
3, 5, 8, 12, 14, 26, 30, Nov 22, Dec 3, 6, 26; 1766: CG, Jan 31, Apr 29
Cotes (singer), 1767: CG, Nov 4
Cotillon (dance), 1717: LIF, Dec 11; 1723: DL, May 16; 1726: HAY, May 9; 1768:
DL, Apr 6, 26, 30; 1771: DL, Apr 22, CG, May 17; 1772: CG, May 16; 1773: CG,
May 26; 1774: CG, May 18, 20; 1775: CG, May 26; 1782: CG, Apr 2, 27
Cotshal (actor), 1758: HAY, Jan 16, 18
Cottage Maid, The (entertainment), 1791: CG, Jun 3
Cottage on the lawn (song), 1778: CG, May 11; 1779: CG, Sep 27
Cottagers, The. See Goodenough, Richard Josceline; Ross, Anne.
Cotten (house servant), 1750: CG, Jan 3
Cotterel, Miss (actor), 1750: HAY, Feb 16
Cottin (Cottine) (dancer), 1700: DL, Jul 6; 1702: DL, Oct 20; 1704: DL, Aug 15,
Nov 13; 1705: DL, Dec 17
Cottington, Elizabeth (correspondent), 1669: BRIDGES, Jun 24
Cotton (actor), 1782: HAY, Jan 14
Cotzoni, Mme. See Cuzzoni, Francesca.
Could a Man be Secure (song), 1790: DL, May 20; 1791: DL, May 6; 1792:
DLKING'S, Apr 10
Coulon, Anne Jacqueline (dancer), 1787: KING'S, Dec 8; 1788: KING'S, Jan 12,
15, 29, Feb 21, 28, Mar 13, Apr 3, 19, May 29, 31
Coulon, Eugene (dancer), 1787: KING'S, Dec 8; 1788: KING'S, Jan 12, 29, Feb 21,
28, Mar 13, 15, May 15
Council of State, 1660: NONE, Apr 23
Count of Burgundy, The. See Pope, Alexander.
Count of Narbonne, The. See Jephson, Robert.
Counterfeit Bridegroom, The. See Middleton, Thomas.
Counterfeit Heiress, The. See D'Urfey, Thomas.
Counterfeits, The (play, anon), 1764: DL, Mar 26
Counterfeits, The. See Leanerd, John.
Countess of Salisbury, The. See Hartson, Hall.
Country Amusements (dance), 1750: DL, Nov 2, 3, 5, 6, 9, 10, 12, 14, 15, 17,
20, 22, 24, Dec 17, 21; 1753: DL, Apr 12, 14, 25, 26, 27, 30, May 22; 1754:
DL, Apr 16, 26, May 2, 7, 10, 24, 30
Country and Town (song), 1798: DL, Jun 8
Country Attorney, The. See Cumberland, Richard.
Country Captain, The. See Cavendish, William.
Country Clergyman, The (monologue), 1795: HAY, Mar 4
Country Club (song), 1798: DL, May 7; 1799: DL, Apr 8, 24, May 9, HAY, Aug 17
Country Coquet, The; or, Miss in her Breeches (ballad opera, anon), 1755: DL,
Nov 18
Country Dance (dance), 1713: SH, Feb 23; 1725: HAY, Apr 14; 1726: DL, Apr 21;
1729: DL, Aug 7; 1731: DL, Aug 20; 1734: HAY, Jun 21, 24, 28; 1739: CG, Sep
14; 1748: HAY, Jan 25; 1749: HAY, Feb 23, CG, Apr 7, HAY, 8, 11, 12, 15, 20,
22, 28, May 1, 6, 10; 1750: DL, Mar 17, May 21; 1751: NWC, Dec 26; 1753: DL,
Mar 26; 1755: HAY, Aug 21, 25; 1758: CG, Oct 9; 1759: CG, Jan 29, 31, Feb 5,
Mar 20, DL, Jun 19, CG, Oct 10, 12, 23, Nov 2; 1760: CG, Jan 8, Mar 24, Apr
10, 28, Sep 24; 1761: CG, May 18, DL, Sep 12; 1762: DL, Sep 25; 1763: CG, Apr
18, DL, Sep 27; 1764: DL, Sep 18; 1765: DL, Sep 17; 1766: DL, Oct 23, Dec 29;
1767: DL, May 30, Sep 16; 1768: DL, Sep 20, Oct 25; 1769: HAY, Jul 12, Aug 9,
29; 1770: DL, Dec 6; 1771: DL, Dec 4; 1773: DL, Jan 29, KING'S, Apr 27, May
28, Jun 8, DL, Dec 31; 1776: DL, Sep 26, CG, 27, DL, Oct 31, CG, Dec 5; 1777:
KING'S, Feb 4, HAY, Aug 12, DL, Oct 2, CG, 15; 1778: DL, Feb 10, HAY, Apr 29,
DL, Nov 4; 1779: CG, Apr 28, DL, May 10, Oct 25, CG, Dec 31; 1780: DL, Apr 1,
HAY, Jul 27, DL, Sep 21, 26; 1781: DL, Sep 15; 1782: DL, Apr 15, May 4, Oct
3; 1783: DL, Jan 31, Sep 25, Oct 9; 1784: DL, May 22, Oct 14; 1787: DL, May
11, Sep 27, Dec 12; 1792: DLKING'S, May 17
Country Dance and Scotch Reel (dance), 1797: DL, Jun 10
Country Dance on one Drum (music), 1743: JS, Jan 5
Country Dialogue (song), 1704: LIF, Jul 24; 1705: LIF, Jan 25; 1715: DL, Jun 6
Country Diversions (dance), 1781: KING'S, Feb 22
Country Farmer, The; or, Trick upon Trick (play), 1738: SFL, Sep 5
Country Farmer's Daughter (dance), 1702: DL, Dec 8; 1703: DL, Feb 12; 1704: DL,
Aug 16, Oct 20; 1705: DL, Jan 1, LIF/QUEN, Oct 11
Country Frenchman and his Wife (dance), 1704: DL, Jun 7
Country Gallant (dance), 1780: KING'S, Nov 25, 28, Dec 2, 9, 12
Country Gentleman, The. See Howard, Sir Robert.
Country Girl, The (dance), 1724: LIF, May 29, Jun 2, 3

Country Girl, The. See Garrick, David.
Country House, The. See Vanbrugh, Sir John.
Country Innocence, The. See Leanerd, John; Fletcher, John, The Maid in the
  Mill.
Country Knight, The (play, anon), 1675: DG, Mar 19; 1676: DG, Jan 10
Country Lad and Lass (dance), 1716: DL, May 31; 1718: DL, May 27; 1720: DL, Nov
  22
Country Lass (dance), 1724: LIF, Jun 1; 1727: DL, May 3; 1732: GF, Mar 30, DL,
  Nov 14; 1757: CG, May 12, 13, 16, 25, 27, HAY, Sep 8; 1758: CG, Apr 29
Country Lasses, The. See Johnson, Charles.
Country Macaroni Assembly (dance), 1775: CG, May 12, 16
Country Mad-Cap in London, The. See Arne, Dr Thomas A.
Country Mad-Cap, The; or, Miss Lucy in Town (farce, anon), 1777: CG, Apr 14,
  17, 25, May 6, 14; 1778: CG, May 22; 1782: CG, Apr 17, 19, 25, Nov 6, 15, Dec
  7; 1783: CG, May 31, Oct 11, Nov 11, Dec 6; 1786: CG, May 9, 17; 1788: CG,
  Jun 3
Country Maid (dance), 1721: DL, May 19; 1723: DL, May 15, Nov 21
Country Man and Woman (dance), 1714: DL, Jul 13, 16; 1717: DL, Aug 6
Country Revel, The. See Aubrey, John.
Country Revels (dance), 1733: DL, Apr 16, May 7
Country Revels, The (pantomime, anon), 1732: DL, Nov 17, 18, 20, 21, 22, 23,
  24, 25, 27, 28, Dec 13, 14, 15, 16, 18, 19, 20; 1733: DL, May 24
Country Squabble (dance), 1783: HAY, Jul 2, Aug 8; 1784: HAY, Apr 30, May 10
Country Wake Dance (dance), 1748: NWC, Apr 4; 1779: HAY, Jun 9, 10, Jul 29, Aug
  27; 1780: HAY, Aug 24
Country Wake, The. See Doggett, Thomas, Hob.
Country Wedding (dance), 1735: HAY, Apr 11
Country Wedding (song), 1757: DL, Mar 31; 1759: CG, Apr 23, 30, May 7
Country Wedding and Skimmington, The. See Hawker, Essex.
Country Wedding, The; or, The Cockneys Bit (play), 1749: HAY, May 16; 1750:
  HAY, Apr 17
Country Wedding, The; or, The Roving Shepherd (play), 1738: BFP, Aug 23
Country Wife, The. See Wycherley, William.
Country Wit, The. See Crowne, John.
Countryman and Harlequin (dance), 1715: LIF, Apr 23
Countryman Deceived (dance), 1781: DL, Jan 2, 24
Countryman Metamorphosed (dance), 1770: CG, Oct 10, 11, 13
Countryman or Clown, The (play, anon), 1659: MT, Nov 0; 1660: MT, Feb 0
Coup de Grace, The; or, The Death of Harlequin (play), 1754: HAY, Mar 4, 7, 9,
  11
Couronnement de Zemire (dance), 1779: KING'S, Feb 23, Mar 2
Course of Comic Lectures, A. See Stevens, George Alexander.
Court (singer), 1761: CG, Oct 13
Court Cards' Dance (dance), 1735: GF, Oct 15, 20, 22, 23, 24
Court Gallantry; or, Marriage a la Mode. See Cibber, Colley, The Comical
  Lovers.
Court me not to scenes of pleasure (song), 1791: CG, Dec 10
Court Minuet (dance), 1776: CG, May 3; 1777: DL, Apr 3, May 2; 1793: KING'S,
  Jun 11
Court of Alexander, The. See Stevens, George Alexander.
Court of Apollo, The (interlude, anon), 1790: DL, May 20; 1791: DL, May 18;
  1792: DLKING'S, Apr 10
Court of Chancery, 1733: DL, Jun 9
Court of Common Council, 1700: BF, Jun 25
Court of Common Pleas, 1700: DLANDLIF, Jun 14; 1768: DL, Nov 23
Court of Comus (song), 1753: CG, Apr 5
Court Secret, The. See Shirley, James.
Courteen (householder), 1749: DL, Apr 13
Courteen's Coffee House, 1748: DL, Apr 18
Courtenay, John (versifier), 1787: DL, Apr 14, Dec 11
Courtenay, Miss (actor), 1777: CG, Nov 18
Courteville, Raphael (Ralph) (composer), 1695: DL, Nov 0, DG, 0, DL, 0
Courteville Jr, Raphael (organist), 1720: YB, Apr 1
Courti, Giacomo (beneficiary), 1712: OSG, Apr 9
Courtney (actor, singer), 1773: HAY, May 24, 31, Jun 14, 16, 18, 28, Jul 2, 21,
  26, 28, Aug 4, 11, 13, 27, 30, Sep 14, 15, 18, DL, Oct 9, Nov 2, 25, Dec 27;
  1774: DL, Jan 11, 15, 19, Feb 9, Mar 22, Apr 8, 15, HAY, May 16, 30, DL, Jun
  2, HAY, 8, 13, 15, 17, 24, 27, Jul 6, 15, 25, Aug 10, 19, 24, 29, DL, Nov 25;
  1775: DL, May 27; 1778: DL, Jan 2, Feb 10, Mar 31
Courtney (singer, dancer), 1749: CG, May 4; 1751: CG, Apr 16; 1752: CG, Oct 10;
  1758: CHAPEL, Apr 27; 1759: CG, Dec 10; 1760: CG, Jan 18, May 3, DL, Oct 20;
  1761: DL, May 29; 1762: DL, May 17

Courtney, Denis (bagpiper), 1791: CG, May 20, Oct 24, Dec 19; 1792: CG, May 28, 31, Oct 25; 1794: CG, Feb 6, May 26, HAY, Jun 2, CG, 11
Courts (singer), 1760: CG, Jan 18, Dec 11; 1761: CG, Sep 26; 1762: CG, Jan 28; 1764: CG, Jan 4
Courtship a la Mode. See Crauford, David.
Cousins (hairdresser), 1767: CG, Feb 19
Cousser, Sigismond (composer), 1705: LIF, Feb 9
Coustos (singer), 1747: DL, May 16; 1749: HAY, Apr 29, May 29, 31
Coutts, Miss (actor), 1779: HAY, Jan 11
Covent Garden Parish, 1773: DL, Jun 2; 1774: DL, May 30, Jun 2, Dec 6; 1775: DL, Apr 3; 1776: DL, May 3, 10; 1784: CG, Feb 18
Covent Garden Piazza, 1779: CG, Apr 28
Covent Garden Theatre. See Macklin, Charles.
Covent Garden Tragedy, The. See Fielding, Henry.
Coventry St, 1784: HAY, Jan 21
Coventry, Sir William (spectator), 1667: BRIDGES, Apr 15; 1669: BRIDGES, Jan 13, Feb 27, Mar 4, 6
Cow Keepers (dance), 1760: DL, Feb 11, Mar 13, 17, 20, 27, 29, Apr 17, 21, 23, May 1, 2, 5, 6, 7, 26, 29, 31, Oct 8, 9, Nov 28, Dec 22; 1761: DL, Jan 9, Mar 2, 23, 26, Apr 7, Oct 14, Dec 15; 1762: DL, May 10, 12, 15, 25, 26; 1763: DL, Mar 15, 21, May 4; 1764: DL, May 4, 9, 15, 29; 1768: DL, Apr 26, 30; 1770: HAY, May 21, 23, 28, 30, Jun 1, 5, 8, 18, 20, 22, 25, 27, Jul 27, 30, Aug 1, 6, 27, 29, 30, 31, Sep 1, 12, 13, 14, 15; 1771: HAY, May 15, 27, Jun 19, 24, Jul 17, 29, Aug 12; 1778: DL, Sep 26
Cow Lane, 1727: BF, Aug 23; 1733: BFYY, Aug 23; 1742: BFG, Aug 25; 1749: BF/SFP, Aug 23; 1761: BFY, Aug 31; 1762: BFY, Sep 3; 1772: DL, Mar 17
Cowcher (actor), 1781: HAY, Mar 26
Cowcieroy (householder), 1782: HAY, Jan 14
Cowley (actor), 1760: CG, Dec 23; 1761: CG, Jun 23
Cowley, Abraham, 1661: LIF, Dec 16; 1680: EVEHYN, Sep 23; 1702: LIF, Oct 5; 1712: DL, Aug 1; 1723: LIF, Jan 3, 4, 9, Mar 28, Apr 22, Nov 1; 1731: GF, Jun 9; 1737: CG, Apr 18
--Cutter of Coleman Street, The, 1661: LIF, Dec 16, 17, 18, 19, 20, 21; 1662: NONE, Sep 0; 1668: LIF, Aug 5; 1669: ATCOURT, Feb 1; 1672: DG, Feb 5, Nov 0; 1675: DG, Jan 8; 1676: DG, Sep 12; 1677: DG, May 31; 1691: NONE, Sep 0; 1702: LIF, Oct 5; 1712: DL, Aug 1, 5, 12; 1713: DL, Jun 15; 1723: LIF, Jan 3, 4, 5, 9, 17, Mar 28, Apr 22, May 30, Nov 1; 1724: LIF, Jan 9
--Guardian, The, 1669: BRIDGES, Jan 12
Cowley, Hannah, 1776: DL, Feb 15; 1779: CG, Jan 4, DL, Apr 10, HAY, Jul 31; 1780: CG, Feb 22, DL, Apr 4; 1781: CG, Feb 24, Mar 24; 1782: CG, Feb 9; 1783: CG, Feb 25, Dec 6; 1786: HAMM, Jul 19, DL, Nov 25; 1788: DL, Jan 31; 1791: CG, Dec 3; 1794: CG, Dec 6
--Albina, Countess Raimond, 1779: HAY, Jul 31, Aug 2, 3, 9, 16, 19, 28, Sep 11
--Belle's Stratagem, The, 1780: CG, Feb 22, 24, 26, 28, 29, Mar 2, 4, 6, 7, 9, 11, 13, 16, 28, 30, 31, Apr 4, 6, 8, 13, 15, 20, 26, May 2, 9, 15, 22, 29, Nov 8, 11, 13, 17, 21, Dec 9, 16, 23; 1781: CG, Jan 6, 19, 26, 27, Feb 6, 22, Mar 1, 6, 13, 27, Apr 3, 7, 27, May 18, Sep 19, Oct 26, Nov 13, Dec 6, 21; 1782: CG, Jan 15, 29, Apr 19, May 10, Oct 18, Dec 17; 1783: CG, Mar 25, Apr 12, May 6, 30; 1784: CG, Jan 14, May 15, Sep 24, Dec 21; 1786: HAMM, Jul 26, CG, Sep 18, 22; 1787: CG, May 4, Nov 22, Dec 20; 1788: CG, Mar 13, Oct 15, Dec 9; 1789: CG, Jun 10, Oct 17; 1790: CG, Jan 23, DL, Mar 22, Apr 7, May 27, Jun 5, CG, Sep 15; 1791: CG, Feb 15, 21, DL, May 10, 26, CG, Jun 3; 1792: CG, Feb 6, DLKING'S, May 17, Jun 5, CG, Oct 17, DL, Dec 10; 1793: DL, Jan 8, Mar 21, CG, Oct 10; 1794: CG, Feb 10, May 24; 1795: CG, Jan 24; 1796: DL, May 13, 30, Jun 9, Oct 20, 25, Nov 16; 1797: DL, May 19, CG, Jun 10, DL, Nov 10, 14; 1798: DL, Feb 22; 1799: DL, Jan 11, 26, Feb 9, May 9, Jul 2, Oct 29, Nov 20; 1800: DL, Jan 1, CG, Mar 27, Jun 12, DL, 16
--Bold Stroke for a Husband, A, 1772: CG, Dec 28; 1783: CG, Feb 22, 25, 26, 27, 28, Mar 1, 3, 6, 10, 13, 17, 20, 24, 27, Apr 3, 10, 24, May 8, 15, Oct 17, 31, Nov 1, 7, 12, 28; 1784: CG, May 21; 1786: CG, May 26, HAMM, Jul 19; 1795: CG, May 29
--Day in Turkey, A; or, The Russian Slaves (opera), 1791: CG, Dec 3, 5, 6, 9, 30; 1792: CG, Jan 2, 5, 10, 13, 16, 20, 27, Feb 1, Apr 14, May 25; 1794: CG, Jan 14, Feb 3, 17, Mar 11
--Fate of Sparta, The; or, The Rival Kings, 1788: DL, Jan 31, Feb 2, 5, 9, 12, 14, 16, 19, 23
--More Ways than One to Win Her, 1745: GF, Mar 7, Apr 23, 24; 1783: CG, Dec 6, 8, 9, 10, 12, 13, 15, 17, 19, 22; 1784: CG, Jan 15, 17, 20, Feb 3, May 18; 1789: CG, May 19
--Runaway, The, 1776: DL, Feb 13, 15, 16, 17, 19, 20, 22, 26, 27, 29, Mar 4, 5, 9, 16, 30, Apr 11, 13, 18, May 24, Oct 1, Nov 1; 1777: DL, Apr 18, May 6; 1778: DL, Jan 10, Apr 28, May 22, Nov 14; 1779: DL, Nov 17; 1780: DL, Jan 7,

Feb 26, Apr 14, May 16; <u>1781</u>: DL, May 5, Oct 27; <u>1782</u>: DL, Jan 5, May 3, Nov
2; <u>1783</u>: DL, May 20; <u>1789</u>: DL, Jun 4; <u>1790</u>: DL, Jun 1; <u>1791</u>: DL, May 31
--School for Grey-Beards, A; or, The Mourning Bride, <u>1786</u>: DL, Nov 25, 27, Dec
4, 7, 8, 12, 14, 16, 22, 29; <u>1787</u>: DL, Mar 3, 5, 6
--School of Eloquence, The (interlude), <u>1780</u>: DL, Apr 4
--Second Thoughts are Best, <u>1781</u>: CG, Feb 24, Mar 24
--Town before You, The, <u>1794</u>: CG, Dec 6, 8, 9, 10, 18, 19, 22; <u>1795</u>: CG, Jan
13, 16, 20, 22, 27
--Which is the Man?, <u>1782</u>: CG, Feb 9, 11, 12, 14, 16, 18, 19, 21, 23, 25, 28,
Mar 2, 4, 7, 9, 11, 12, 23, Apr 3, 6, 13, May 8, 16, Oct 8, 26, Nov 26; <u>1783</u>:
CG, Apr 8; <u>1784</u>: CG, Mar 16, Apr 24; <u>1785</u>: CG, May 13, 28; <u>1786</u>: CG, Feb 16;
<u>1787</u>: CG, Nov 28; <u>1788</u>: CG, Oct 17; <u>1790</u>: CG, Apr 27; <u>1791</u>: CG, May 24
--Who's the Dupe? (farce), <u>1779</u>: DL, Apr 10, 17, 20, 21, 23, 26, 27, May 6, 10,
13, 14, 20, 24, 27, Jun 3, Dec 9, 11, 15, 28, 30; <u>1780</u>: DL, Feb 5, Mar 11,
Apr 11, 22, 28, May 20, 23, Sep 26, Oct 18, Nov 17; <u>1781</u>: DL, Jan 24, Apr 21,
27, May 10, 16, 23, Sep 15, Oct 19; <u>1782</u>: HAY, Aug 6, DL, Sep 17, Oct 22, Nov
8; <u>1783</u>: DL, Feb 10, 17, Mar 15, Apr 8, 12, May 2, 21, HAY, Jun 24, DL, Oct
29, Nov 11, Dec 18, 31; <u>1784</u>: DL, Feb 6, Apr 13, 17, 29, May 17, 26, HAY, Jun
26, 30, Jul 10, Aug 7, DL, Oct 21, Dec 7, 15; <u>1785</u>: DL, Feb 12, Mar 5, Apr
16, May 11; <u>1786</u>: DL, Feb 20, May 3, 11, 20, Sep 21, Oct 16, Nov 24; <u>1787</u>:
DL, Apr 17, 26, May 5, 14, 31, Dec 5, 8; <u>1788</u>: DL, Mar 15, Apr 7, Oct 21,
HAY, Dec 22; <u>1789</u>: DL, Mar 5, 21, Jun 6, Oct 17, Nov 4, 28, Dec 8, 16; <u>1790</u>:
DL, Apr 22, HAY, Aug 25, Sep 6, 11, 15; <u>1791</u>: DL, Feb 15, Apr 30, HAY, Jun 8,
Aug 26, Sep 12, 15, DLKING'S, Oct 24; <u>1792</u>: DLKING'S, May 22, HAY, Aug 15,
DL, Oct 8, HAY, 15; <u>1793</u>: DL, Jan 1, HAY, Jun 15, Jul 12, 22, 24, Aug 28, Sep
5, 6, 19, 28, Oct 16, 26, Nov 19; <u>1794</u>: HAMM, Mar 24; <u>1795</u>: DL, Jan 1, 2, CG,
May 8; <u>1796</u>: HAY, Mar 28, DL, Oct 13, 29, Nov 26; <u>1797</u>: DL, Jan 5, Apr 22,
Dec 9; <u>1798</u>: DL, Jan 12; <u>1800</u>: DL, May 1
--World as it Goes, The; or, A Party at Montpelier (farce), <u>1781</u>: CG, Feb 24,
Mar 24
Cowley, Mrs (beneficiary), <u>1733</u>: HAY, Mar 19
Cowper, Mrs (actor), <u>1749</u>: CG, Apr 11, 12, 25; <u>1753</u>: DL, Oct 9, 10, 13, 24, Nov
14, 15, 16, 26; <u>1754</u>: DL, Jan 7, Mar 25, Apr 20, May 4; <u>1755</u>: DL, Oct 10, 13,
24, 31, Dec 4; <u>1756</u>: DL, Apr 30, May 5, 10, 18, Oct 14, 16, 28, Nov 12; <u>1757</u>:
DL, Jan 24, May 5
Cowslade, Miss (actor), <u>1755</u>: HAY, Sep 9, 11, 15
Cox (actor), <u>1741</u>: JS, Nov 30
Cox (actor), <u>1788</u>: DL, Nov 17, 28, Dec 6, 22; <u>1789</u>: DL, May 22, 28; <u>1792</u>: HAY,
Oct 15, Nov 26
Cox (dancer), <u>1732</u>: DL, Dec 14, 26; <u>1735</u>: DL, May 14, Jul 1; <u>1736</u>: LIF, Mar 31,
Dec 16, 31
Cox (house servant), <u>1730</u>: GF, Jun 29
Cox (undertaker), <u>1774</u>: CG, Feb 14
Cox-Heath, <u>1781</u>: DL, Sep 25
Cox, E (publisher), <u>1779</u>: KING'S, Dec 14; <u>1780</u>: KING'S, May 9; <u>1781</u>: KING'S,
Feb 22, Mar 8, 29, Apr 5, Jun 5, Nov 17; <u>1782</u>: KING'S, Jan 12, Mar 2, 7, 16;
<u>1785</u>: KING'S, Jan 25; <u>1792</u>: DL, Nov 21; <u>1794</u>: DL, Dec 20; <u>1796</u>: DL, Feb 20
Cox, Elizabeth (actor), <u>1671</u>: BRIDGES, Mar 0; <u>1672</u>: LIF, Apr 0, Nov 0; <u>1674</u>:
LIF, Mar 0, DL, May 16; <u>1675</u>: DL, Jan 25, Apr 23, NONE, Sep 0, DL, Nov 17;
<u>1676</u>: ATCOURT, May 29; <u>1681</u>: DL, Oct 0; <u>1682</u>: DL, Mar 11
Cox, Gabriel (master carpenter), <u>1782</u>: CG, May 28; <u>1783</u>: CG, May 31; <u>1784</u>: CG,
May 22; <u>1786</u>: CG, May 31; <u>1787</u>: CG, May 28; <u>1788</u>: CG, May 28, Sep 22; <u>1789</u>:
CG, Jun 12, Sep 28; <u>1790</u>: CG, Jun 3, Sep 29; <u>1791</u>: CG, Jun 10, Sep 17; <u>1792</u>:
CG, May 30
Cox, H S (actor), <u>1751</u>: DL, Nov 26
Cox, John? (singer), <u>1754</u>: CHAPEL, May 15; <u>1757</u>: DL, Mar 25; <u>1758</u>: CHAPEL, Apr
27; <u>1762</u>: HIC, Feb 12
Cox, Miss (actor), <u>1795</u>: CG, Nov 16; <u>1798</u>: CG, Mar 19; <u>1799</u>: CG, Jan 29, Mar 2,
25, Apr 13, Jun 12, Sep 20, Oct 9, 21, Nov 14, Dec 23; <u>1800</u>: CG, Jan 16, Feb
10, Mar 4, 25, 27, Apr 5, 29, May 27, Jun 2, 7
Cox, Mrs (actor, singer), <u>1781</u>: HAY, Nov 12; <u>1782</u>: HAY, Nov 25
Cox, Mrs (householder), <u>1747</u>: CG, May 11
Cox, Mrs (singer), <u>1760</u>: DL, Apr 14
Cox, Susannah (actor), <u>1703</u>: DL, Jun 23, Dec 2; <u>1704</u>: DL, Jan 26, Jul 1; <u>1705</u>:
DL, Jun 12, Jul 25; <u>1707</u>: DL, Oct 18, 23, 25; <u>1708</u>: DL, May 31, Jun 26, Aug
28, 31, Sep 4; <u>1709</u>: DL, Mar 17, May 19, 31, Nov 23, 26, 30; <u>1710</u>: DL, Jan
18, 31, Feb 25, Mar 11, 14, 27, Dec 30; <u>1711</u>: DL, Feb 10, May 15, Aug 3, Oct
12, Dec 8; <u>1712</u>: DL, Mar 17, May 26, Oct 28, Nov 7; <u>1713</u>: DL, Feb 19, Jun 12;
<u>1714</u>: DL, Mar 31, Apr 27, May 26, Jun 18; <u>1715</u>: DL, May 7, Jul 1
Coxcomb, The. See Fletcher, John.
Coxcombs, The. See Gentleman, Francis.
Coyle, Miles (viola player), <u>1797</u>: CG, Mar 3; <u>1798</u>: CG, Feb 23

Coysh (Cash, Coish, Cosh), John (actor), 1671: NONE, Sep 0; 1673: LIF, Mar 0,
  Dec 0; 1674: LIF, Mar 0, DL, May 16, NONE, Sep 0; 1675: DL, Aug 0; 1677: DL,
  Mar 0, 17, Jun 0, Dec 12; 1678: DL, Feb 0, Mar 0; 1681: DL, Oct 0; 1682: BF,
  Aug 24
Coysh, Miss (actor), 1682: DL, Mar 11
Coysh, Mrs John (actor), 1671: NONE, Sep 0; 1675: DL, Apr 30
Cozeners, The. See Foote, Samuel.
Cradock (will executor), 1750: CG, Feb 2; see also Hughes
Cradock, Joseph, 1771: CG, Dec 11; 1772: CG, Jan 24
--Zobeide, 1771: CG, Dec 11, 12, 13, 14, 16; 1772: CG, Jan 13, 16, 18, 21, 24,
  28, Feb 1, 6, Mar 10
Craford, Mrs. See Crawford, Mrs.
Craftsman, The. See Mottley, John.
Cragg, James (actor), 1704: LIF, Jun 26
Craggs (actor), 1744: HAY, Apr 6, May 10
Craig, Master (singer), 1792: CG, Feb 28
Craig's Court, 1750: DL, Oct 1
Cramer, Franz (conductor), 1800: CG, Jun 16
Cramer, Wilhelm (conductor, violinist), 1773: HAY, Apr 19; 1774: KING'S, Feb
  10; 1775: KING'S, Jan 26, Mar 8, 10, 17, 22, 24, 29, 31, Apr 5, 7; 1778:
  KING'S, Mar 5, Apr 4; 1779: DL, Feb 19, KING'S, Mar 11, DL, 26; 1780: DL, Feb
  11, KING'S, May 31; 1781: DL, Mar 2, KING'S, Jun 14; 1788: KING'S, Jan 12,
  Feb 21, May 29; 1789: KING'S, Jun 11; 1790: HAY, Apr 29; 1792: HAY, Feb 28;
  1794: KING'S, Apr 26, May 15; 1795: KING'S, Feb 20; 1799: HAY, Mar 29
Cranbourn Alley, 1735: DL, May 30; 1739: DL, Apr 2; 1742: GF, Apr 8; 1748: DL,
  Apr 12; 1749: DL, Apr 7; 1751: DL, Apr 20; 1752: DL, Apr 1
Cranbourn St, 1747: CG, May 11
Crane Court, 1732: FS, Nov 30
Crane, John (house servant), 1761: CG, May 15
Cranfield (actor, dancer), 1780: CG, May 17; 1782: CG, Apr 27; 1783: CG, Apr
  22, May 23; 1788: CG, May 12; 1789: CG, Mar 16, May 28, Jun 8, Sep 16, 21,
  Nov 13; 1790: CG, Oct 4, Nov 6, Dec 20; 1791: CG, May 3, Jun 6, Oct 20, 24;
  1792: CG, Oct 25, Dec 26; 1793: CG, Apr 8, May 27, Dec 19; 1794: CG, Feb 6,
  May 7, 15, 26, Oct 14; 1795: CG, Mar 14, May 12, Oct 12, 23, 29, Nov 16, Dec
  21; 1796: CG, Jan 4, Mar 15, May 10, Oct 13, Dec 19; 1797: CG, Feb 18, Mar
  16, Apr 8, 27, May 3, 15, 18, 22, Jun 9, Oct 12, Dec 26; 1798: CG, Oct 25;
  1800: DL, May 14
Cranfield, Frances, Countess of Dorset, 1667: LIF, Nov 7
Cranfield, Louisa (actor, singer), 1775: CG, May 4; 1776: CG, May 4, 11; 1777:
  CHR, Jun 18, 23, Jul 2, CG, Nov 25; 1778: CG, Oct 22; 1779: CG, Nov 30; 1780:
  CG, Jan 10, May 3, 6; 1781: CG, Oct 16, 22; 1784: CG, Sep 24, Oct 25, Nov 12;
  1785: CG, Sep 23, 30, Oct 17, Nov 14, Dec 26; 1786: CG, Jan 18, May 23, Oct
  9, 21, 23, Nov 18; 1787: CG, Jan 31, May 28
Cranfield, Miss (dancer), 1798: CG, Mar 19, Apr 30, Jun 4; 1799: CG, Jan 29;
  1800: DL, Jun 2
Cranfield, Mrs (dancer), 1790: CG, Dec 20; 1793: CG, Mar 11, Dec 19; 1795: CG,
  Nov 9, 16
Cranfield, T (dancer), 1796: CG, Mar 15; 1797: CG, May 26; 1798: CG, Mar 19,
  Dec 11; 1799: CG, Jan 29, Mar 2, 25, Dec 23; 1800: CG, Mar 4
Cranford, Miss (actor, singer), 1784: DL, Jan 7, 13, Sep 23, Nov 22; 1785: DL,
  Jan 20, Feb 2, Apr 14, HAMM, Jun 17, 27, Jul 1, 2, 4, 6, 15, 22, 25, DL, Sep
  27, Oct 17, 26, Dec 26, 29; 1786: DL, Feb 23, May 27, HAY, Jun 16, Jul 7, 18,
  DL, Sep 28, Oct 7, 24, Dec 5; 1787: HAY, Jul 21, DL, Nov 8, 21, Dec 26; 1788:
  DL, Feb 21, Mar 26, HAY, Jun 11, 12, DL, Oct 20, Nov 10, Dec 4; 1789: DL, Jun
  9, HAY, Aug 11
Cranke
--True Briton, The (opera), 1782: DL, Apr 17
Crapignant; or, The French Lawyer (farce, anon), 1719: LIF: Feb 5
Crauford, David, 1700: DL, Jul 9; 1704: LIF, Mar 25
--Courtship a la Mode, 1700: DL, Jul 9
--Love at First Sight, 1704: LIF, Mar 25
Craven (actor), 1749: NWLS, Feb 27, HAY, Apr 29, May 26
Craven Buildings, 1735: CG/LIF, Mar 22; 1737: DL, May 3; 1738: DL, May 5; 1739:
  DL, Mar 22, Apr 10, 28; 1740: DL, Mar 20, Apr 19; 1742: DL, Mar 12, CG, 25;
  1745: DL, Mar 14; 1746: DL, Mar 18; 1747: DL, Mar 14; 1748: CG, Mar 8; 1777:
  DL, Apr 21, May 6; 1779: DL, May 15, 17; 1782: DL, May 9; 1783: DL, May 5;
  1786: DL, May 23
Craven St, 1777: CG, Dec 19; 1798: DL, May 21; 1799: DL, May 1; 1800: DL, May
  19
Craven, Elizabeth Baroness, 1780: DL, May 24; 1781: HAY, Jul 18; see also
  Anspach, Margravine of
--Miniature Picture, The, 1780: DL, May 24, 26, 27, 31; 1799: DL, May 24

--Princess of Georgia, The, <u>1799</u>: CG, Apr 19
--Silver Tankard, The; or, The Point at Portsmouth (farce), <u>1781</u>: HAY, Jul 18,
 20, 23, 25, 27, Aug 1
Craven, Miss (actor), <u>1773</u>: HAY, May 17, 19, Jun 14, 18, Jul 28, Aug 11, 27,
 Sep 3
Craven, William, Baron, <u>1661</u>: LIF, Aug 17
Craven, William, 6th Baron, <u>1780</u>: DL, May 24
Crawford, Ann, Mrs Thomas (actor), <u>1778</u>: CG, Oct 24, 28, 31, Nov 4, 19, Dec 3,
 11, 17; <u>1779</u>: CG, Jan 11, 14, 26, 29, Feb 12, Mar 4, 9, 22, Apr 6, 8; <u>1780</u>:
 HAY, Jun 2, 14, 26, Jul 6, 24, 31, Aug 11, 14, DL, Oct 5, 11, 17, 26, Nov 1,
 4, 10, 13, 27, 29, Dec 4, 6, 15; <u>1781</u>: DL, Jan 6, 9, Feb 12, 17, Mar 1, 3,
 19, 27, Apr 18, May 19, Oct 11; <u>1783</u>: CG, Nov 13, 22, 27, Dec 1, 11, 18, DL,
 22; <u>1784</u>: CG, Jan 3, 16, 22, 31, Feb 5, 9, 19, 23, Mar 1, 4, 20, Apr 12, 15,
 Nov 29, Dec 13; <u>1785</u>: CG, Jan 19, Mar 3, 15, Apr 12; <u>1788</u>: CG, Apr 25; <u>1789</u>:
 CG, May 15; <u>1790</u>: CG, Apr 29, HAY, Aug 18; <u>1791</u>: CG, May 10; <u>1797</u>: CG, Oct
 23, Nov 29, Dec 27; <u>1798</u>: CG, Jan 5, Apr 16; <u>1799</u>: HAY, Feb 25
Crawford, Miss (actor), <u>1771</u>: HAY, Jan 28
Crawford, Mrs (dancer), <u>1760</u>: CG, Sep 22, Dec 11; <u>1761</u>: CG, Mar 9, Apr 11, 24,
 May 25
Crawford, Peter (treasurer), <u>1749</u>: KING'S, May 20; <u>1755</u>: KING'S, Nov 11; <u>1757</u>:
 KING'S, Sep 20; <u>1762</u>: KING'S, Apr 14, Jun 5, Nov 13; <u>1763</u>: KING'S, Feb 21,
 May 31; <u>1765</u>: KING'S, Nov 23; <u>1767</u>: KING'S, May 9; <u>1769</u>: KING'S, Sep 5; <u>1772</u>:
 KING'S, Nov 14; <u>1773</u>: KING'S, Apr 19; <u>1775</u>: KING'S, Oct 31; <u>1782</u>: KING'S, May
 2
Crawford, Thomas (actor), <u>1779</u>: CG, Mar 22, Apr 20; <u>1780</u>: HAY, Jul 24, DL, Nov
 29; <u>1781</u>: DL, Jan 9, Mar 19, Apr 18, May 19
Crawford, Tom (beneficiary), <u>1728</u>: LIF, May 11
Crawley Pink (ship), <u>1743</u>: CG, Oct 28
Crazy Jane (song), <u>1799</u>: HAY, Aug 24, 27, Sep 2, 9, 16; <u>1800</u>: DL, May 30, Jun
 5, 9, 10, 16, 17, 18
Crazy Kate (song), <u>1788</u>: HAY, Apr 29
Creation of the World; or, Paradise Lost (droll), <u>1695</u>: SF, Sep 0
Creation, The. See Haydn, Franz Joseph.
Crebillon, Prosper, <u>1722</u>: HAY, Jan 18
--Astre and Thieste, <u>1722</u>: HAY, Jan 18
--Rhadamisthe et Zenobie, <u>1721</u>: HAY, Dec 28; <u>1722</u>: HAY, Jan 6, 18
Credulous Husband, The; or, The Intriguing Wife (farce), <u>1747</u>: HAY, Apr 22;
 <u>1754</u>: BFYJN, Sep 3, 4, 5, 6; <u>1766</u>: HAY, Aug 21
Creed (singer), <u>1794</u>: DL, Oct 31; <u>1795</u>: DL, Feb 12
Creed, John (spectator), <u>1660</u>: COCKPIT, Aug 18, Oct 11; <u>1661</u>: SALSBURY, Feb 9,
 Mar 19, Apr 6, ATCOURT, 20, VERE, 27; <u>1662</u>: ATCOURT, Nov 10, 17; <u>1663</u>:
 ATCOURT, Jan 5, LIF, 17, Feb 23, CITY, Oct 29; <u>1664</u>: LIF, Aug 13, BF, Sep 7,
 BRIDGES, 28; <u>1665</u>: LIF, Apr 3; <u>1666</u>: BRIDGES, Dec 27; <u>1667</u>: LIF, Jul 20,
 BRIDGES, Oct 18; <u>1668</u>: LIF, May 5, BRIDGES, Jun 22
Creighton, Mrs (renter), <u>1758</u>: CG, Jan 6, Feb 23
Creitsmar, Mrs (spectator), <u>1695</u>: DLORLIF, Dec 9
Cremona Opera, <u>1782</u>: KING'S, Jan 12
Cremonini, Clementina (singer), <u>1763</u>: KING'S, Feb 19, Apr 25, HAY, Jun 9; <u>1764</u>:
 DL, Feb 24, Apr 5, CG, Jun 5, DL, Nov 2, 12, KING'S, 24, DL, 30; <u>1765</u>:
 KING'S, Jan 26, Mar 28; see also Clementina, Sga
Cremonini, Domenico (singer), <u>1784</u>: KING'S, Dec 18; <u>1785</u>: KING'S, Jan 8, 25,
 Feb 26, Apr 2, 16; <u>1786</u>: KING'S, Jun 17, Dec 23; <u>1787</u>: KING'S, Jan 9, Feb 17,
 Mar 8, 29, Apr 17, May 29, Jun 16
Crescentini, Girolamo (singer), <u>1785</u>: KING'S, Jan 8, Feb 24, 26, Apr 16, 21
Creso (opera, anon), <u>1777</u>: KING'S, Nov 8, 15, 22, 29, Dec 6, 13, 20; <u>1778</u>:
 KING'S, Jan 3, 10, 17, 24, 31, Mar 5, 19, 24, Jun 13; <u>1781</u>: KING'S, Jun 23;
 <u>1791</u>: CG, Apr 6
Creso. See Sacchini, Antonio Maria Gasparo.
Crespi (Crispi), Sga (dancer), <u>1770</u>: KING'S, May 19; <u>1772</u>: KING'S, Apr 28, May
 5, 9, 12, 16, 23, 28, Jun 9, 11, Nov 21, Dec 8; <u>1773</u>: KING'S, Jan 2, 5, Feb
 20, 27, Mar 9, 16, 18, 23, 30, Apr 1, 17, 24, Jun 19, DL, Sep 30, Oct 2, 9,
 Nov 25, Dec 27; <u>1774</u>: DL, Apr 12, 22, Oct 5, 14, Nov 5, Dec 26; <u>1775</u>: DL, Mar
 16, Apr 22, May 8, 25, Sep 26, Oct 20, Nov 28, Dec 12, 19; <u>1776</u>: DL, Feb 27,
 Mar 2, 19, May 3, 18, Jun 3, 10, Oct 9, 24, Nov 6, 7, Dec 4, 18; <u>1777</u>: DL,
 Feb 10, Apr 5, 22; <u>1778</u>: DL, Jan 28, Mar 24, Oct 3, Nov 2, Dec 11; <u>1779</u>: DL,
 May 14, 17, Sep 28, Nov 3, 20, 26, Dec 10, 17; <u>1780</u>: DL, Feb 24, 28, Mar 13,
 KING'S, Apr 22, DL, May 2, KING'S, Nov 25, Dec 2, 16; <u>1781</u>: DL, Jan 2,
 KING'S, 13, DL, 18, KING'S, 23, DL, 31, KING'S, Feb 22, DL, Mar 12, Apr 30,
 May 14, KING'S, Jun 5, Jul 3, Nov 17, 20, 28, Dec 11; <u>1782</u>: KING'S, Feb 2,
 23, Mar 19, Apr 11, May 2, 9, 25, Nov 14, 30, Dec 12, 19, 31; <u>1783</u>: KING'S,
 Jan 11, Feb 15, Mar 13, Apr 10, 24, May 1, 31, Jun 28; <u>1786</u>: KING'S, Jan 24,
 Feb 18, Mar 11, May 23, Jun 6

Crespi, Sg and Sga (dancer), 1775: DL, May 8
Crespigny, Mrs (theatre proprietor), 1790: CG, May 5
Cressea, Mrs (impressaria), 1698: YB, Jun 1
Cresswell (actor), 1780: CII, Feb 29
Cresswell, John (machinist), 1796: CG, May 30, Nov 5, Dec 19; 1797: CG, Mar 16,
    May 29, Oct 2, Nov 24, Dec 26; 1798: CG, Feb 12, Apr 9, May 18, 23, Nov 12;
    1799: CG, Jan 29, Jun 6, Oct 7, Dec 23; 1800: CG, Jun 7
Creswick (actor), 1758: DL, Apr 22, CG, Sep 29; 1759: CG, Feb 27, Apr 30, May
    5, 21; 1760: CG, Mar 18, May 8, 12, 14, Sep 22, Oct 1, Dec 19; 1761: CG, Feb
    28, Mar 30, Apr 1, 6, 27, May 8, Sep 30, Oct 10, Nov 6; 1773: HAY, Sep 16,
    18; 1776: HAY, May 2; 1778: HAY, Mar 23, Apr 30; 1779: HAY, Dec 20
Creta, Joachim Frederic (horn player), 1729: LIF, Jan 16
Creusa in Delfo. See Rauzzini, Venanzio.
Creusa, Queen of Athens. See Whitehead, William.
Crew, Sir Thomas (spectator), 1660: VERE, Dec 4; 1667: NONE, Jul 13
Crewe (actor), 1792: HAY, Apr 16
Cricketters (dance), 1778: CG, Jan 28, 29, May 2
Cridland (boxkeeper), 1762: DL, May 21; 1763: DL, May 16; 1764: DL, May 18;
    1765: DL, May 20; 1766: DL, May 16; 1767: DL, May 30; 1768: DL, May 25; 1769:
    DL, May 22; 1770: DL, Jun 1; 1771: DL, May 30; 1772: DL, Jun 9; 1773: DL, Jun
    1
Crier, The (song), 1799: HAY, Sep 16
Cries of Dublin (entertainment), 1748: SOU, Oct 24; 1749: SOU, Jan 26; 1756:
    CG, Apr 23, May 17
Cries of Edinburgh (entertaineent), 1763: HAY, May 3; 1765: HAY, May 16; 1768:
    HAY, Dec 19; 1772: HAY, Sep 21; 1775: HAY, Feb 20; 1776: HAY, Oct 7; 1782:
    HAY, Apr 9; 1785: HAY, Jan 24; 1791: HAY, Sep 26, Dec 12; 1792: HAY, Oct 22
Cries of London (London Cries) (entertainment), 1741: CG, Apr 16; 1742: CG, Apr
    28, May 3, 4, 5, 6, 14; 1754: CG, Apr 17; 1755: CG, Apr 10, May 5; 1756: CG,
    Mar 25, Sep 27; 1757: CG, Apr 18, Sep 28; 1758: CG, Apr 3, BFYS, Sep 6; 1759:
    CG, Mar 22; 1760: CG, Mar 20, May 2; 1761: CG, Mar 26, May 4, 8; 1762: CG,
    Feb 22; 1763: CG, Apr 5; 1764: CG, Feb 1, Mar 27, Apr 27, DL, May 12, CG, Nov
    29; 1765: HAY, Jul 29; 1766: CG, Mar 18, DL, Apr 2, 5, CG, 7, 15, 21, 26, DL,
    28, May 6, 12, CG, Dec 20; 1767: CG, Mar 24, DL, Apr 20, 21, May 2, 5; 1768:
    CG, Mar 21; 1769: CG, Mar 16, DL, Apr 8, CG, May 1; 1770: CG, Mar 26; 1771:
    CG, Mar 18, Apr 2, May 4; 1772: CG, Mar 28; 1773: CG, Mar 23, Apr 23; 1774:
    CG, Apr 23; 1775: CG, Mar 28; 1776: CG, May 10, HAY, Sep 16, 18, 20, 23;
    1778: CHR, Jun 24
Cripplegate, 1723: CT, Dec 10; 1724: CT, Nov 24
Crisis, The. See Holcroft, Thomas.
Crisp, Charles (actor), 1799: OCH, May 15
Crisp, Henry, 1754: DL, Feb 25
--Virginia, 1754: DL, Feb 25, 26, 28, Mar 2, 4, 5, 7, 9, 11, 12, Apr 2; 1755:
    DL, Apr 18
Crisp, John (actor), 1799: OCH, May 15
Crisp, Miss (actor), 1799: OCH, May 15
Crisp, Mrs (actor), 1787: HAY, Mar 12
Crisp, Samuel (actor), 1741: GF, Feb 10, 14, 19, Mar 3, 7, Apr 7
Crispi, Sga. See Crespi, Sga.
Crispin and Crispianus; or, A Shoemaker a Prince (droll), 1699: BF, Aug 30;
    1702: MF, May 5
Crispin Rival de Son Maitre (farce), 1721: HAY, Dec 5; 1722: HAY, Jan 23, Mar
    12
Crispin St, 1776: STRAND, Jan 23
Crispus. See Bononcini, Giovanni.
Critic, The. See Sheridan, Richard Brinsley.
Critical Balance of the Performers, A (pamphlet), 1765: DL, Sep 14
Critical Remarks on the Tragedy of Athelstan (pamphlet), 1756: DL, Mar 9
Critical Strictures on the New Tragedy of Elvira (article), 1763: DL, Jan 19
Criticism on Mahomet and Irene, A (pamphlet), 1749: DL, Feb 23
Croaker, Alley (singer), 1759: BFS, Sep 3
Croce, Elena (singer), 1716: KING'S, Jun 6, 13; see also Viviani, Sga
Croesus. See Haym, Nicolino Francesco.
Croft, Sir Arthur (renter), 1758: CG, Feb 23
Croft, John (renter), 1758: CG, Feb 23
Croft, William (composer), 1697: LIF, May 0; 1726: IT, Feb 2
Crofts (actor), 1740: GF, Oct 21, 22, 24, Nov 4, 7, 22, 24, 29, Dec 8, 10, 15;
    1741: GF, Jan 15, 20, 27, 29, Feb 2, 10, 16, 19, Mar 3, 16, Apr 15, 17, 29,
    BFTY, Aug 22, GF, Sep 16, 18, 21, 30, Oct 2, 9, 16, 19, 28, Nov 4, 9, 27, Dec
    16
Crofts, Henry (actor), 1771: DL, Dec 4; 1772: DL, Feb 21, May 7
Crofts, Mrs (actor), 1680: DG, Nov 1; 1681: DG, Jan 0

Crokatt (bookseller), 1728: LIF, Dec 31
Crokatt, Mrs (beneficiary), 1750: DL, Feb 22
Crokett, Mrs (haberdasher), 1751: CG, Nov 19
Cromarty, Lord (rebel), 1746: DL, Aug 4
Cromwell, Henry (correspondent), 17111: DL, Nov 20
Cromwell, Lady Mary (spectator), 1663: BRIDGES, Jun 12
Cromwell, Oliver, 1668: BRI/COUR, Dec 2
Cromwell's Conspiracy (play, anon), 1660: NONE, Aug 8
Crook, Miss (actor), 1747: DL, May 13, Oct 29
Crooked Billet (householder), 1742: HAY, Jun 16
Crookhaven, 1750: DL, Feb 24
Croome's auditorium, 1667: BF, Sep 4
Cropley (draper), 1771: DL, Nov 14, Dec 12; 1772: DL, Jan 6, 7, Jun 10, Dec 8;
    1773: DL, Jan 21, Mar 1, Jun 2, Nov 5, 19; 1774: DL, Jan 21, Jun 2, Nov 18,
    Dec 9; 1775: DL, Jan 10, May 27
Cropponi (actor, dancer), 1733: DL/HAY, Oct 29; 1734: DL/HAY, Jan 28
Crosby (house servant), 1786: CG, Jun 1
Crosby Square, 1705: HDR, Jan 2
Crosby, John (actor), 1662: ATCOURT, Nov 1; 1670: LIF, Jan 0, Sep 20, Nov 0;
    1671: LIF, Jan 10, Mar 6, Jun 0, Sep 0, DG, Nov 0; 1672: DG, Jul 4, Aug 3,
    Nov 4; 1673: DG, May 0, Jul 3; 1674: DG, Nov 9; 1675: DG, Sep 0, NONE, 0;
    1676: DG, Jun 8, Jul 3, Aug 0, Dec 0; 1677: DG, Feb 12, Mar 24, Jun 0, Sep 0;
    1678: DG, Jan 17, Jun 0, Sep 0, Nov 0; 1679: DG, Mar 0, Apr 0
Crosby, Miss (singer), 1800: CG, Feb 28, Mar 5, 19
Crosdill (Crusdile), John (violoncellist), 1770: CG, Mar 30; 1773: KING'S, Feb
    5, HAY, Mar 26, KING'S, Apr 12, HAY, 19; 1774: HIC, May 9; 1775: KING'S, Jan
    26, Mar 8, 22, 29, Apr 5; 1779: DL, Mar 19, 26; 1782: DL, Feb 15, Mar 1;
    1784: DL, Mar 5
Cross (actor), 1772: HAY, Dec 21; 1782: HAY, Nov 25; 1783: HAY, Dec 15; 1784:
    HAY, Feb 23, Mar 8, Nov 16, Dec 13; 1785: HAY, Jan 31, Mar 15, Apr 25, 26
Cross Court, 1778: CG, May 19; 1779: CG, May 13; 1796: HAY, Sep 16; 1798: HAY,
    Sep 17; 1800: HAY, Jun 13
Cross Daggers Tavern, 1697: BF, Aug 24; 1698: BF, Aug 25; 1700: BF, Aug 0;
    1701: MF, May 1, BF, Aug 25; 1702: BFBF, Aug 24; 1705: BF, Aug 27
Cross Partners. See Inchbald, Elizabeth.
Cross Purposes. See O'Brien, William.
Cross St, 1720: CGR, Jun 22; 1721: GG, Mar 22; 1743: CG, Nov 17; 1760: HAY, Aug
    15; 1774: DL, Mar 23
Cross-Bridges' Booth, 1749: BFCB, Aug 23, 24, 25, 26, 28
Cross, Frances, Mrs Richard (actor, singer), 1735: DL, Feb 4, 5, 15, 17, 20,
    25, Mar 6, 10, 24, Apr 11, 14, 19, 22, 26, 28, May 1, 2, 6, 7, 14, 23, LIF,
    Jun 12, 19, GF/HAY, Jul 15, 18, 22, Aug 14, 21, DL, Sep 4, 6, 9, 11, 13, 15,
    18, 25, 30, Oct 4, 7, 9, Nov 3, 6, 7, 10, 12, 20, 21, 29, Dec 6; 1736: DL,
    Jan 3, Feb 5, 9, 20, 28, Mar 11, 13, 23, Apr 12, 15, May 25, Aug 26, Sep 11,
    14, 16, 18, 23, Oct 7, 9, 12, 22, 23, 25, 29, Nov 2, 3, 8, 13, 15, 19, 22,
    23, Dec 7; 1737: DL, Jan 6, 29, Feb 1, 2, 5, 8, 21, Mar 12, Apr 12, 27, May
    5; 1738: DL, Sep 16, 28, Oct 18, 26, 27, Nov 2, 17, 21, 25, Dec 9; 1739: DL,
    Jan 3, 13, 26, Feb 3, 12, Mar 8, 22, 27, Apr 12, May 14, 18, 28, CG, Sep 7,
    12, 17, 25, Oct 10, DL, 13, CG, 22, 25, 29, Nov 1, 3, 6, 10, Dec 4; 1740: CG,
    Jan 12, Feb 6, 7, Apr 14, 28, May 14, 23, Jun 5, BFHC, Aug 23, CG, Sep 19,
    29, Oct 8, 27, Nov 21, Dec 10, 29; 1741: CG, Jan 23, 28, 29, Feb 17, Apr 30,
    May 4, 12, BFH, Aug 22, DL, Oct 21, Nov 6, 21, Dec 7, 12, 14, 23; 1742: DL,
    Jan 4, 22, Feb 13, Mar 8, 22, 27, Apr 5, 20, May 28, Sep 16, 18, 25, 30, Oct
    2, 7, 9, 12, 16, 18, 26, 27, 30, Nov 1, 8, 12, Dec 14, 22; 1743: DL, Jan 27,
    28, Feb 10, 17, SOU, Mar 30, DL, Apr 15, 29, May 26, TCD/BFTD, Aug 4, DL, Sep
    15, 17, 20, 22, 24, 29, Oct 1, 4, 13, 20, 25, Nov 8, 12, 17, 23, 29, Dec 1,
    6, 12, 16; 1744: DL, Jan 27, Apr 10, 17, 23, May 1, 14, 22, Sep 15, 18, 27,
    29, Oct 9, 17, 19, 24, Nov 1, 6, 16, 24, Dec 11; 1745: DL, Jan 4, 22, Feb 11,
    13, 20, Apr 19, Jun 5, Nov 6, 11, 22, Dec 13, 20; 1746: DL, Jan 14, 25, Feb
    13, Mar 10, 13, 17, Apr 7, 14, 21, May 2, 9, Jun 11, 13, Aug 4, 6, 8, 11, Sep
    27, Nov 1, 5, Dec 2, 4, 9, 11, 12, 26, 30; 1747: DL, Jan 15, 20, Mar 23, 31,
    Apr 20, 28, May 12, Sep 24, Oct 1, 15, 17, 24, 30, Nov 7, Dec 23; 1748: BF,
    Aug 24, SFBCBV, Sep 7, DL, 15, 20, Oct 1, 6, 8, 15, 29, Nov 7, 11; 1749: DL,
    Jan 13, BFCB, Aug 23, DL, Oct 10, 13, 14, 18, 30, Nov 9, 21, 28; 1750: DL,
    Apr 3, May 2, 3, Sep 21, 27, Oct 22, 29, Nov 1, 12, 14, 24; 1751: DL, Jan 16,
    Feb 1, 2, 18, Apr 25, May 1, Sep 12, 13, Oct 2, 3, 17, 26, 29, Nov 2, 7, 16,
    29; 1752: DL, Mar 9, 10, Apr 3, 4, 15, Sep 16, 28, Oct 7, 14, 21, 25, 26, Nov
    3, 17, 30, Dec 18, 19, 20; 1753: DL, Jan 2, 3, Apr 14, 25, May 3, Sep 8, 11,
    22, 29, Oct 12, 20, Nov 1, 6, 7, 26; 1754: DL, Feb 9, Mar 26, May 24, Jul 2,
    Sep 14, Oct 3, 5, 14, 22; 1755: DL, Jan 17, 22, Apr 15, May 6, Sep 23, 27,
    Oct 2, 27, 31, Nov 22; 1756: DL, Feb 24, Mar 23, Apr 10, May 14, 18, Sep 18,
    Oct 5, 7, 21, Nov 2, 11; 1757: DL, Mar 24, Apr 11, Sep 10, Oct 6, 12, 26, 29,

Nov 22, Dec 3; <u>1758</u>: DL, Apr 18, May 17, Jun 22, Oct 14, 18, Nov 1, 24, Dec
8, 22; <u>1759</u>: DL, Jan 17, 20, Mar 20, 31, Apr 7, May 4, 7, 11, Jun 19, Sep 25,
27, Oct 2, 26, 27, Nov 13; <u>1760</u>: DL, Apr 24, 25, May 8, Jun 19, Jul 29, Sep
20, 23, Oct 22, 23, Nov 17, Dec 2, 30; <u>1761</u>: DL, Apr 20, May 4, Sep 5, 8, 10,
19, 23, Oct 10; <u>1762</u>: DL, Jan 20, Mar 15, Apr 1, May 7, 19, Sep 28, 29, Oct
13, 23, 25, Dec 1, 15; <u>1763</u>: DL, Apr 30, May 31, Sep 22, Oct 14, 31, Nov 8,
19, Dec 14; <u>1764</u>: DL, Feb 18, Mar 3, Apr 28, Sep 18, 22, Oct 4, 6; <u>1765</u>: DL,
Jan 18, 23, 24, May 15, 17, 20, 22, Sep 17, Oct 18, 23, Dec 5; <u>1766</u>: DL, Jan
29, May 7, 20, 21, Sep 30, Oct 10, Nov 20; <u>1767</u>: DL, Jan 24, Feb 9, Apr 22,
May 22, Sep 18, 21, 23, 25, Nov 11, 20, Dec 1; <u>1768</u>: DL, Apr 14, May 10, Sep
8, Oct 15, 18, Nov 1, 21, Dec 14; <u>1769</u>: DL, Jan 9, Apr 12, May 3, Oct 2, 6,
Nov 2, 8; <u>1770</u>: DL, Feb 8, Apr 3, May 22, Oct 12, 16, 29, Nov 3, Dec 17;
<u>1771</u>: DL, Mar 12, 21, May 17, Oct 10, 25, 29, Nov 11, 28; <u>1772</u>: DL, Feb 17,
Mar 21, May 13, 14, 25, Oct 1, 17, Nov 28; <u>1773</u>: DL, Jan 19, Feb 11, Apr 3,
May 21, Nov 24, Dec 16, 20; <u>1774</u>: DL, May 16, Nov 3, 11; <u>1775</u>: DL, Apr 8, May
10, 17, Oct 20, 21, 26; <u>1776</u>: DL, May 8, 22, 24, Nov 5; <u>1777</u>: DL, Apr 30
Cross, John Cartwright (actor, author), <u>1790</u>: CG, Oct 4, 6, 19, 20, 30, Nov 4,
6, 11, 15, 23, Dec 11, 20; <u>1791</u>: CG, Jan 3, Feb 4, 16, Apr 11, 16, May 11,
DL, 11, CG, 26, Jun 6, Oct 6, 10, 12, Nov 24, Dec 3, 10, 13, 21, 22; <u>1792</u>:
CG, Feb 2, 18, Mar 26, 31, May 4, 10, 11, 12, Sep 19, Oct 8, 10, 12, 19, 24,
27, 29, Nov 3, 24; <u>1793</u>: CG, Mar 23, May 4, Nov 11, Dec 7; <u>1794</u>: CG, Jan 14,
HAY, Feb 8, CG, Apr 29, May 2, 13, 26, 28, HAY, Jul 9, 17, 21, 26, Aug 16,
20, 23, Sep 3, CG, 15, Oct 20, 23, 29, 30, Dec 6; <u>1795</u>: CG, Mar 19, Apr 28,
HAY, Jun 9, 11, 13, 15, 20, Jul 16, 22, 31, Aug 3, 19, 20, 21, 27, 29, Sep 2,
CG, 30, Oct 2, 7, 8, 9, 16, 19, 24, Nov 27, Dec 7, 9; <u>1796</u>: CG, Jan 23, Mar
30, Apr 6, 14, 15, May 5, Jun 3, DL, Nov 5; <u>1797</u>: CG, May 11, Nov 13, 24, Dec
26; <u>1798</u>: CG, Feb 12, Mar 31, Apr 9, May 1, Oct 15; <u>1799</u>: CG, Jun 1
--Apparition, The, <u>1794</u>: HAY, Sep 3, 4; <u>1795</u>: HAY, Aug 25
--British Fortitude and Hibernian Friendship; or, An Escape from France
(interlude), <u>1794</u>: CG, Apr 29, May 1, 3, 12, 13, 17, 30, Jun 11; <u>1795</u>: CG,
May 25; <u>1796</u>: CG, Apr 5, 19, May 13; <u>1797</u>: CG, May 9, 10, 12; <u>1798</u>: CG, Apr
17, May 14, Jun 6; <u>1799</u>: CG, Mar 5, Apr 26
--Charity Boy, The, <u>1796</u>: HAY, Aug 29, DL, Nov 5, 7
--Genoese Pirate, The; or, Black-Beard (ballet-pantomime), <u>1798</u>: CG, Oct 15,
18, 22
--Harlequin and Quixotte; or, The Magic Arm (pantomime), <u>1797</u>: CG, Dec 26, 27,
28, 29, 30; <u>1798</u>: CG, Jan 1, 2, 3, 4, 5, 6, 8, 9, 10, 11, 12, 13, 15, 16, 17,
18, 19, 20, 22, 23, 24, 25, 26, 29, Feb 2
--Harlequin's Return (pantomime), <u>1798</u>: CG, Apr 9, 10, 12, 13, 14, 26
--Joan of Arc; or, The Maid of Orleans (ballet-pantomime), <u>1798</u>: CG, Feb 10,
12, 13, 14, 15, 16, 17, 19, 24, 26, 27, Mar 1, 3, 5, 6, 10, 12
--Naples Bay; or, The British Seamen at Anchor (interlude), <u>1794</u>: CG, May 2, 28
--New Divertisement, The (interlude), <u>1794</u>: CG, May 26
--Point at Herqui, The; or, British Bravery Triumphant (interlude), <u>1796</u>: CG,
Apr 15, 22, May 3, 18, Jun 1
--Purse, The; or, Benevolent Tar (musical), <u>1794</u>: HAY, Feb 5, 8, 11, 12, 13,
14, 19, Mar 1, 8, 17, 24, 31, Aug 22, Sep 10, 12, 17; <u>1795</u>: HAY, Aug 18, 26,
DL, Dec 30; <u>1796</u>: DL, May 30, Jun 8, HAY, 15, 17, 27, Jul 4, 9, 19, 25, 30,
Aug 10, 31; <u>1797</u>: DL, Feb 16, 21, Mar 9, Apr 19, May 6, 27, Jun 8, HAY, 26,
Jul 5, 14, 17, 29, Aug 1, Sep 5, 7; <u>1798</u>: HAY, Jun 15, Aug 3, 20, 29, Sep 3;
<u>1799</u>: DL, May 31, Jun 15, HAY, 19, DL, 24, 27, HAY, Jul 6, 10, 18, 22, 30,
Aug 21, Sep 3, DL, Dec 19; <u>1800</u>: DL, Apr 29
--Raft, The; or, Both Sides of the Water (interlude), <u>1798</u>: CG, Mar 31, Apr 9,
10, 12, 13, 14, 16, 26, May 2, 21, 31
--Round Tower, The; or, The Chieftains of Ireland (ballet-pantomime), <u>1797</u>: CG,
Nov 24, 25, 27, 28, 29, 30, Dec 1, 2, 4, 5, 6, 7, 8, 9, 11, 12, 13, 14, 15,
16, 22; <u>1798</u>: CG, Jan 27, Feb 19, 24, Jun 6; <u>1799</u>: CG, Jun 6
--Surrender of Trinidad, The; or, Safe Moored at Last (entertainment), <u>1797</u>:
CG, May 11
--They've Bit the Old One; or, The Scheming Butler (interlude), <u>1798</u>: CG, May 1
--Way to Get Un-Married, The (interlude), <u>1796</u>: CG, Mar 30, May 6, 11, Jun 2
Cross, Letitia (actor, dancer, singer), <u>1694</u>: NONE, Sep 0; <u>1695</u>: DG, Apr 0, DL,
Sep 0, NONE, 0, DL, Oct 0, DG, Nov 0, DL, 0; <u>1696</u>: DL, Jan 0, Feb 0, Mar 0,
May 0, DG, Jun 0, Aug 0, DL, Sep 0, DG, Oct 0, DL, Nov 21; <u>1697</u>: DL, Jan 0,
Feb 0, DG, Jun 0, DL, Sep 0; <u>1698</u>: DL, Feb 0, Mar 0, May 0; <u>1704</u>: DL, Dec 16;
<u>1705</u>: DL, Jan 2, 16, Feb 8, Mar 19, Apr 23, May 18, Jun 9, 16, 26, 28, Jul 3,
5, 18, Sep 25, Oct 2, 13, 16, Nov 20; <u>1706</u>: DL, Jan 11, 14, 21, 24, 25, Mar
7, 11, 16, 26, Apr 1, 2, Jun 11, 18, 22, DL/DG, Nov 2; <u>1707</u>: DL, Jan 1, 27,
Feb 11, Apr 14, DL/QUEEN, Oct 22, Nov 1, 11, 18, 20, QUEEN'S, Dec 13; <u>1708</u>:
DL/QUEEN, Jan 1, DL, May 21, DL/QUEEN, 27, DL, Oct 14, 26; <u>1709</u>: DL, Jan 27,
Feb 12, Apr 28, May 12, QUEEN'S, Sep 24, Oct 11, Nov 4, 15, Dec 12; <u>1710</u>:
QUEEN'S, Jan 5, 10, 18, 19, 21, Apr 22; <u>1715</u>: LIF, Jan 4, 7, 14, 25, Feb 5,

16, Apr 28, Jun 23, Jul 5, 14, Aug 3, 10, 11, 23, Sep 28, Oct 10, 11, 12, 24, 26, 28, 29, 31, Nov 1, 4, 9, 10, 12, 15, 16, 17, 18, 19, 21, 23, 25, 26, 29, Dec 12, 28, 30; 1716: LIF, Jan 3, 6, 11, 19, Feb 6, 7, 16, 21, 27, 28, Mar 10, 22, 24, Apr 5, 6, 9, 30, May 2, 11, 18, 24, 31, Jun 1, 12, 20, Jul 13, 18, 25, Aug 3, Nov 9, 10, 12, 13, 14, 22, 28, 29, Dec 4, 13; 1717: LIF, Jan 1, 8, 10, 14, 15, 22, 28, 31, Mar 19, 21, May 23; 1720: LIF, Oct 4, 13, 18, 22, Nov 15, 18, 25, Dec 22, 26, 28; 1721: LIF, Jan 7, 25, Feb 6, 9, 21, Mar 23, Apr 1, 17, 19, 29, May 1, 5, Sep 27, Oct 19, 21, Dec 1; 1722: LIF, Mar 29, 31, Apr 9, 19, May 4, Jul 25, Oct 1, 9, 11, 13, 19, Nov 7, 12, Dec 13; 1723: LIF, Jan 2, Feb 13, 15, 19, Apr 18, May 23, 24, 28, Nov 12, 28, Dec 2, 20; 1724: LIF, Mar 14, 23, 24, Apr 7, 22, 28, May 13, 30, Jun 3, Sep 30; 1725: LIF, Apr 22; 1732: HAY, May 8

Cross, Mrs (singer, actor), 1790: CG, Oct 6, 15, Nov 26; 1791: CG, Mar 14, May 19, Jun 3, Sep 14, 21, 26, 30, Oct 3, 10, Dec 10, 22; 1792: CG, Feb 14, 28, Apr 10, 12, May 10, Sep 19, Oct 3, 8, 19, 27, 29, Nov 3, Dec 26, 31; 1793: CG, Apr 9, May 10, Jun 11

Cross, Richard (actor, dancer, prompter), 1729: HAY, Nov 12; 1730: HAY, Oct 21, Nov 30, Dec 28; 1731: HAY, Jan 18, Feb 3, May 12, TCY, Aug 9, SF/BFFHH, 24, SFGT, Sep 8, DL, Nov 25; 1732: HAY, Feb 16, Mar 2, 17, DL, 21, HAY, 23, Apr 27, DL, May 6, HAY, 8, 15, WINH, 27, DL, Aug 1, 17, BFMMO, 23; 1733: BFCGBH, Aug 23, Sep 4, DL/HAY, Nov 27; 1734: DL/HAY, Feb 22, Mar 30, DL, Apr 15, DL/HAY, 16, 17, 18, 20, DL, May 13, 16, 21, DL/HAY, 24, HAY, 27, RI, Jun 27, Sep 12, DL, 14, 24, 28, Oct 5, HAY, 7, DL, 9, 10, 14, 17, 21, 23, 26, Nov 1, 8, 22, 23; 1735: DL, Jan 25, 28, 29, Feb 25, Mar 6, 10, Apr 28, May 14, 20, Jun 9, LIF, 12, 19, DL, Jul 1, GF/HAY, 15, 18, 22, Aug 1, LIF, 1, HAY, 12, GF/HAY, 14, 21, DL, Sep 6, 9, 11, 30, Oct 2, 9, 21, 24, 25, 27, 28, Nov 6, 12, 21, 22, Dec 13, 26; 1736: DL, Jan 3, 12, Feb 20, 28, Mar 3, 25, 27, Apr 15, May 25, Aug 26, Sep 7, 9, Oct 18, 19, 20, Nov 2, 8, 13, 15, 22, Dec 18, 31; 1737: DL, Jan 6, 29, Feb 10, Mar 17, May 5, 27, Sep 3, 6, 20, 22, 29, Oct 1, 11, 27; 1738: DL, Jan 11, 19, 31, Feb 16, Mar 21, Apr 13, May 3, 6, 10, 13, 17, 29, Sep 9, 14, 16, 28, 30, Oct 18, 20, 21, 26, 28, 31, Nov 3, 4, 20, 23, 30, Dec 6; 1739: DL, Jan 3, 16, Feb 3, Mar 10, 22, 24, 27, Apr 3, 5, 10, 25, May 18, 19, CG, Dec 8; 1740: BFHC, Aug 23; 1741: CG, May 4, DL, Jun 4, TC, Aug 4, BFH, 22, DL, Sep 17; 1742: DL, Feb 9, 15, Apr 8, 19, 20, 21, 24, 29, 30, May 3, 4, 6, 7, 8, 27, Sep 14, Oct 18, 20, 22, 27; 1743: DL, Feb 11, Mar 21, Apr 4, 6, 7, 15, 16, May 2, 14, 24, Sep 15, 17, 22, 24, 27, Oct 1, 4, 6, 13, 15, 25, Nov 5, 12, 17, 18, 26, 29, Dec 16, 21; 1744: DL, Jan 7, 17, Apr 9, 10, 21, May 4, 9, 14, 16, Sep 18, Oct 6, 19, 30, Nov 2, 6, 17, 24, Dec 11; 1745: DL, Apr 22, 30; 1746: DL, Apr 7, 14, 21, 25, Aug 6, 8, 11, SOU, Oct 16; 1747: DL, Jan 24, GF, Mar 16, DL, Apr 20, May 1, 14; 1748: BF, Aug 24, SFBCBV, Sep 7, DL, Nov 7; 1749: DL, May 1, BFCB, Aug 23, DL, Oct 14; 1750: DL, Jan 26, Mar 15, Apr 19, May 4, HAY, Jul 26, DL, Sep 8, 13, 15, Nov 14; 1751: DL, Jan 14, Feb 18, 21, Mar 16; 1752: DL, Jan 11, Apr 30, May 8, Oct 21; 1753: DL, Mar 22; 1754: DL, Jul 2; 1759: DL, Dec 12; 1760: DL, Jan 23, Feb 20

--Henpecked Captain, The, 1749: DL, Apr 29, May 1

Cross, Richard (actor, dancer, violinist), 1748: DL, Mar 19, BF, Aug 24, DL, Oct 28, 29, Nov 29; 1749: BFCB, Aug 23, DL, Oct 17; 1750: DL, Jan 19, 22, Feb 12, Apr 23, Sep 28, Nov 13; 1751: DL, May 13, Sep 14, Oct 29; 1752: DL, Jan 11, Oct 16, Nov 27; 1753: DL, May 5; 1754: DL, Jul 2; 1755: HAY, Dec 15; 1757: DL, Apr 28, CG, May 27

Cross, Richard (actor, prompter), 1700: DL, Dec 9; 1703: DL, Mar 11; 1705: DL, Jan 18, Mar 29, Jun 12; 1707: QUEEN'S, Jan 4, 13, 14, Feb 18, Jun 18, Jul 1, 10, 22, 26, 30, Aug 12, DL/QUEEN, Oct 22, 29, Nov 1; 1708: DL/QUEEN, Jan 1, DL, Feb 4, 13, 24, Mar 13, 16, 18, Apr 29, Jun 11, 19, 24, 26, Jul 20, 29, Aug 31, Sep 4, 9, 14, 16, 18, Oct 25, Dec 20; 1709: DL, Apr 25, 28, May 17, QUEEN'S, Sep 27, Oct 1, 25, 31, Nov 4, 9, 18, Dec 12; 1710: QUEEN'S, May 1, 16, 24, GR, Jun 15, QUEEN'S, Aug 16, DL/QUEEN, Oct 7, Nov 6, DL, Dec 11, 18; 1711: DL, May 22, Jul 3, 10, 27, Aug 24, 31, Oct 22, 26; 1712: DL, Jan 1, Jun 10, Jul 11, Nov 4; 1713: DL, Jan 19, 29, Mar 16, Nov 16; 1714: DL, May 17, Jun 2, 25, Jul 13, Oct 22, Dec 8; 1715: DL, Jan 3, Feb 4, 23, 25, Jun 6, 28, Jul 6, Aug 9; 1716: DL, May 11, Jul 12, Oct 6, 29; 1717: DL, May 10, 17, Jun 3, 6, 10, 24, Jul 2, 16, Aug 6, Oct 9, 24, 28, Nov 19; 1718: DL, May 15, 22, Jun 11, Aug 1, Oct 27, Nov 19; 1719: DL, Jan 28, Oct 16, 27, 28, 30, Nov 11; 1720: DL, Jan 13, May 19, 20, Sep 22, Oct 5, 7, 12, Nov 22, Dec 6, 8; 1721: DL, May 24, Jun 20, Aug 18, Oct 6, 10, 13, Nov 1, 17, 25, Dec 1; 1722: DL, May 16, Dec 3; 1723: DL, May 20, 29, Oct 30, Nov 12, 15, 22; 1724: DL, Apr 18, 29, May 5, Nov 16

Cross, Richard and Frances (actors), 1740: CG, Apr 14; 1759: DL, May 4

Cross, Thomas (numberer), 1717: LIF, May 17, Jun 12; 1718: LIF, May 20; 1719: LIF, Apr 1; 1720: LIF, Apr 20; 1721: LIF, May 11; 1722: LIF, May 3; 1723: LIF, May 6; 1724: LIF, Apr 30; 1726: LIF, Apr 29

205

Cross, Thomas (publisher), 1696: DL, May 0; 1698: NONE, Sep 0
Cross, Thomas (treasurer), 1664: MT, Nov 1
Crosse, Widow (beneficiary), 1739: CG, Dec 12
Crossfield (singer), 1698: DL/ORDG, Nov 0
Crossman, Mrs John (actor), 1797: DL, Feb 7, Mar 6
Crotchet Lodge. See Hurlstone, Thomas.
Crouch (actor), 1743: JS, Feb 2
Crouch, Anna Maria, Mrs Rawlings Edward (actor, singer), 1785: DL, Oct 1, 11,
    13, 15, 17, 20, 26, 27, Nov 1, 11, 18, Dec 8; 1786: DL, Jan 6, 14, Apr 4, 18,
    24, 26, May 15, Sep 23, 28, Oct 7, 9, 21, 24, Nov 18, 25, Dec 5, 6, 21, 28;
    1787: DL, Jan 26, Feb 23, Mar 7, 8, 30, 31, Apr 18, 20, 23, 27, May 11, 22,
    Sep 27, Oct 4, 16, 20, 22, 25, Nov 3, 8, 10, 12, 13, Dec 17, 19; 1788: DL,
    Jan 22, 26, 28, Feb 8, 20, 22, 25, Mar 5, 27, Apr 4, 7, 8, CG, 25, DL, May 1,
    6, 8, 23, 30, Sep 20, Oct 4, 9, 14, 16, 23, 25, Nov 1, 25, Dec 16, 23; 1789:
    DL, Jan 8, Feb 18, 27, Mar 6, 9, 18, 20, 25, 26, Apr 14, 17, 20, CG, May 15,
    DL, 19, 23, 27, 28, Jun 3, Sep 24, 26, Oct 10, 13, 15, 22, 24, 26, 28, Nov 4,
    13, 24, Dec 7, 12, 15; 1790: DL, Feb 10, 19, 24, 26, Mar 5, 10, 17, 19, Apr
    5, 9, 16, May 11, 12, 25, 31, Jun 1, CG, 16, DL, Sep 11, 16, Oct 4, 11, Nov
    19, 30, Dec 8; 1791: DL, Jan 1, Feb 10, 17, Mar 3, 16, 23, 24, 25, Apr 1, 13,
    26, 28, May 3, 19, 21, DLKING'S, Sep 22, 27, 29, Oct 15, 25, 29, Nov 2, 5, 9,
    12, 16, 17, 23, 26, 28, 29, 30, Dec 7, 31; 1792: DLKING'S, Jan 26, 27,
    KING'S, Feb 24, 29, Mar 7, DLKING'S, 10, KING'S, 14, DLKING'S, 17, KING'S,
    21, 23, DLKING'S, 26, 27, KING'S, 28, 30, DLKING'S, May 8, 23, DL, Sep 27,
    Oct 9, 11, 13, 16, 18, Nov 10, 21, Dec 14; 1793: DL, Jan 2, 23, CG, Feb 15,
    20, 27, Mar 1, 6, DL, 7, CG, 8, 13, 20, KING/HAY, 20, CG, 22, DL, Apr 8, CG,
    25, DL, May 7, 10; 1794: DL, Mar 12, 19, 26, Apr 2, 4, 9, 10, 11, 21, 26, May
    1, 3, 9, 16, 17, 19, Jun 9, 26, Sep 27, Oct 6, 7, 27, 30, Nov 3, Dec 20;
    1795: DL, Apr 7, May 4, 6, Sep 29, Oct 1, 6, 30, Nov 11, Dec 18; 1796: DL,
    Apr 26, May 25, Sep 22, Oct 10, 19, Nov 1, 10, Dec 5; 1797: DL, Feb 7, 9, 16,
    22, May 17, Sep 23, Oct 14, 23, Nov 7, 8, 20, 24, Dec 9; 1798: DL, Jan 16,
    Feb 13, 20, Sep 27, Oct 6, 16, Nov 14, 26; 1799: DL, Jan 19, Feb 23, Mar 2,
    Apr 2, 15, 25, May 4, 8, 24, Jun 28, Sep 24, Oct 14, Nov 14, 16, Dec 11, 30;
    1800: DL, Apr 14, 29, May 13, 14, Jun 6
Crouch, William (composer), 1789: CG, Feb 24
Crow St Theatre, Dublin, 1762: CG, Apr 29; 1776: CG, Dec 6; 1777: CG, May 7,
    HAY, Jun 11, DL, Oct 2, CG, 16, Nov 7, DL, 8; 1778: CG, Jan 12, HAY, Feb 9,
    CG, May 5; 1780: CG, Feb 17, May 4, HAY, Jul 6; 1781: HAY, Jun 26, DL, Oct
    11; 1782: DL, Apr 11, May 18; 1783: CG, Apr 7; 1785: HAY, Feb 12, Jun 9;
    1786: DL, Jan 24; 1788: CG, May 16, HAY, Jul 24; 1789: CG, Jun 2, Sep 14, 23;
    1790: CG, Mar 22, HAY, Jun 26; 1793: HAY, Nov 5; 1795: CG, Jan 31, Oct 22;
    1798: CG, Oct 15
Crow, Miss (actor), 1796: HAY, Feb 22
Crowe, Jane, Mrs William (dancer), 1792: CG, Dec 26; 1793: CG, Mar 11, Dec 19;
    1795: CG, Nov 9, 16; 1796: CG, Apr 9; 1798: CG, Mar 19; 1799: CG, Jan 29, Mar
    2, 25, Apr 13
Crowe, William (dancer), 1796: CG, Mar 15
Crowing of the Cock (entertainment), 1733: HAY, Jun 4
Crowley's Show, 1695: SF, Sep 0
Crown and Anchor Tavern, 1734: CR, Nov 27; 1737: CR, Apr 29; 1743: CR, Feb 24;
    1745: CG, Mar 6; 1751: DL, May 2; 1762: CG, May 6; 1773: CR, Apr 14, 21, 30;
    1775: HAY, Feb 2; 1797: CG, Jun 21
Crown and Cushion Tavern, 1746: DL, Apr 12
Crown and Scepters Tavern, 1735: DL, Mar 29
Crown and W Tavern, 1758: CG, Jul 6
Crown Court, 1736: CG, May 3; 1737: DL, May 7; 1742: DL, Apr 24; 1743: DL, Apr
    9; 1752: DL, Apr 15; 1753: DL, Apr 27; 1754: DL, Apr 17; 1755: DL, Apr 26;
    1757: CG, Mar 29, DL, Apr 28; 1759: DL, Jul 12; 1762: CG, Apr 3; 1777: CG,
    May 13; 1778: CG, May 11, 13; 1780: CG, May 3; 1786: DL, May 3, 24; 1792: CG,
    May 19; 1793: CG, Jun 10
Crown Inn, 1755: DL, Dec 16; 1757: CG, Mar 31; 1780: CII, Apr 19
Crown St, 1782: CG, May 3, DL, 10
Crown Tavern, 1697: BF, Aug 24; 1699: BF, Aug 23; 1700: BF, Aug 0; 1701: BF,
    Aug 25; 1702: BFBF, Aug 24; 1728: CRT, Dec 18; 1731: CRT, Mar 10; 1739: CRT,
    Jan 18; 1740: BFFPT, Aug 23; 1744: HAY, Apr 23; 1745: DL, Mar 20, Apr 3, 16;
    1756: CRT, Oct 28; 1757: CRT, Feb 7
Crown with festal pomp (song), 1790: CG, Mar 3
Crowne, John, 1675: DG, Mar 19; 1682: NONE, Jun 26; 1683: DL, Jan 19; 1685:
    NONE, Feb 6, DL, May 9; 1688: DLORDG, Jan 9, DL, Apr 0; 1692: NONE, May 14,
    DL, Jun 0, DLORDG, Aug 24; 1693: DLORDG, Nov 0; 1694: DL, Apr 0; 1698: NONE,
    Sep 0; 1712: DL, Jul 11, 15; 1716: DL, Jul 17; 1717: DL, Feb 18, LIF, Jul 10,
    12, DL, Nov 6; 1718: LIF, Feb 24, DL, Mar 11, Nov 21; 1721: DL, Nov 7; 1736:
    DL, Jan 2; 1790: HAY, Aug 6

--Ambitious Statesman, The; or, The Loyal Favourite, 1679: DL, Mar 0; 1680: NONE, Sep 0
--Andromache, 1674: DG, Aug 0
--Caligula, 1698: DL, Mar 0
--Calisto; or, The Chaste Nimph, 1674: DL, Mar 30, NONE, Sep 22, ATCOURT, Dec 15, 22; 1675: ATCOURT, Jan 25, Feb 2, 15, 16, 22, Apr 23
--City Politiques, The, 1682: NONE, Jun 26; 1683: DL, Jan 19; 1685: ATCOURT, Nov 16; 1705: LIF, Aug 14, Sep 12, LIF/QUEN, 28, Oct 11; 1712: DL, Jul 11, 15; 1717: LIF, Jul 10, 12, 17, Oct 29, Dec 2; 1718: LIF, Feb 24
--Country Wit, The; or, Sir Mannerly Shallow, 1675: DG, Mar 19; 1676: DG, Jan 10, Sep 21; 1692: NONE, Sep 0; 1697: NONE, Sep 0; 1703: LIF, Sep 28; 1704: LIF, Feb 2, Oct 16; 1707: QUEEN'S, Dec 20, 22; 1708: QUEEN'S, Jan 9, DL, Feb 6, Jul 13, Dec 28; 1709: DL, Dec 6; 1710: DL, Jan 10; 1716: DL, Jul 12, 17, 26, Oct 29; 1717: DL, Feb 18, Nov 6, 22; 1718: DL, Mar 11, Jun 4, Nov 21; 1721: DL, Jul 28; 1727: DL, Jan 20, 23, May 23
--Darius, King of Persia, 1688: DL, Apr 0
--Destruction of Jerusalem, The, 1677: DL, Jan 12, 18; 1682: DL, Jan 13; 1685: DLORDG, Jan 13; 1692: NONE, Sep 0; 1696: NONE, Sep 0; 1712: DL, Jul 1
--English Friar, The; or, The Town Sparks, 1690: DLORDG, Mar 0
--History of Charles VIII of France, The, 1671: DG, Nov 0; 1672: DG, May 17, NONE, Sep 17; 1679: NONE, Sep 0
--Juliana; or, The Princess of Poland, 1671: LIF, Jun 0
--Justice Busy; or, The Gentleman Quack, 1698: NONE, Sep 0
--Married Beau, The; or, The Curious Impertinent, 1694: DL, Apr 0
--Misery of Civil War, The, 1680: DG, Feb 0; 1681: NONE, Sep 0
--Regulus, 1692: NONE, May 14, DL, Jun 0, DLORDG, Jul 20, Aug 24
--Sir Courtly Nice; or, It Cannot Be, 1683: DL, Jan 19; 1685: NONE, Feb 6, DL, May 9, 11, DG, Jul 0, ATCOURT, Nov 9; 1686: DLORDG, May 10, ATCOURT, Nov 3; 1687: DLORDG, Jan 11; 1688: DLORDG, Jan 9; 1689: DLORDG, May 31; 1690: ATCOURT, Apr 30; 1692: NONE, Sep 0; 1699: NONE, Sep 0; 1703: LIF, Sep 21, DL, Oct 30; 1704: LIF, Feb 4, DL, Oct 24; 1705: DL, Jan 6, Mar 3, LIF, Jul 27, DL, Oct 17, Dec 17; 1706: QUEEN'S, Nov 22; 1707: QUEEN'S, Jan 17, DL/QUEEN, Oct 23; 1708: DL/QUEEN, Feb 2, DL, Oct 5; 1709: DL, Feb 4, QUEEN'S, Oct 6, Dec 21; 1710: GR, Jun 28, Sep 7, DL/QUEEN, Nov 16; 1711: DL/QUEEN, May 26, DL, Nov 26; 1712: DL, Dec 12; 1713: DL, Mar 24, Oct 23; 1714: DL, Apr 2; 1715: DL, Jan 29, Mar 22, Oct 19; 1716: DL, Jan 16, 19, Apr 11, 27, Jun 9, Jul 17, Oct 29, Nov 29; 1717: DL, Feb 18, Mar 1, 25, May 16, LIF, Jul 10, 12, DL, Oct 3, Nov 6; 1718: DL, Jan 3, Mar 11, Jun 6, HC, Oct 6, DL, 7, Nov 21, Dec 29; 1719: DL, Apr 22, 25, Sep 15, Nov 27; 1720: DL, Oct 13, Nov 30; 1721: DL, May 11, Nov 7; 1722: DL, Jan 31, May 11, Oct 20; 1723: DL, Jan 3, May 16, Oct 24, Nov 20; 1724: DL, Jan 10, HAY, 20, Feb 5, DL, Oct 24, Dec 4; 1725: DL, Mar 20, Sep 21, Dec 31; 1726: DL, Feb 11, May 25, Oct 1; 1727: DL, Jan 4, Mar 7, May 19, Nov 21; 1728: DL, Nov 29; 1729: DL, Mar 6, Oct 23; 1730: DL, Feb 23; 1731: GF, Feb 18, DL, Apr 1, Nov 8, Dec 20; 1732: DL, Feb 1, Sep 12, Dec 9; 1735: DL, Jan 9, 10, Dec 29; 1736: DL, Jan 2; 1743: LIF, Mar 24; 1744: DL, Apr 17, 28; 1746: CG, Jan 25, 27, 28, 29, 31, Feb 1, 7, 27, Apr 4, DL, 14, 26, CG, May 13, DL, Sep 27, CG, Nov 24; 1747: CG, Jan 23, May 4; 1749: CG, Apr 10; 1751: DL, Oct 10, 17, 18; 1753: DL, Nov 6, Dec 14; 1758: CG, Jul 6, DL, Nov 24; 1760: CG, Apr 24, May 15; 1764: CG, Mar 27, Apr 27; 1770: CG, Apr 25; 1781: CG, Apr 28; 1790: HAY, Aug 6
--Sir Thomas Callico; or, The Mock Nabob, 1758: CG, Jul 6
Crowned with conquest (song), 1783: CG, Nov 8, 21; 1784: CG, Jan 2
Crowns of Sweet Roses (song), 1737: CG, Mar 17
Crowther (actor), 1782: HAY, Nov 25
Croza (Crosa), Dr John Francis (director), 1748: KING'S, Nov 8; 1749: KING'S, Feb 18, 28, Apr 29, May 20; 1750: KING'S, Apr 7, May 16
Crozier, Miss (singer, dancer), 1742: SF, Sep 16
Crudel perche finora (song), 1789: KING'S, May 9
Crudge, Alexander (doorkeeper), 1753: CG, Apr 24, May 21; 1754: CG, May 4, Sep 16; 1755: CG, May 8, Dec 19; 1756: CG, May 21, Sep 20, Dec 8, 15; 1757: CG, Mar 22, 29, 31, Apr 13, 25, 26, May 10, 27, Sep 16; 1758: CG, Apr 27, Sep 18
Crudo Amore (song), 1750: KING'S, Apr 10
Cruel fate (song), 1791: CG, May 18
Cruel Gift, The. See Centlivre, Susannah.
Cruel Uncle, The; or, Usurping Monarch (play), 1743: BFYWR, Aug 23
Crusade, The. See Reynolds, Frederick.
Crusdile. See Crosdill.
Crutch Dance (dance), 1776: CG, Oct 25; 1780: CG, Mar 29, Dec 16; 1781: CG, Oct 31; 1783: DL, May 12, Dec 2; 1785: DL, Jan 12; 1790: CG, Jun 1; 1791: CG, Dec 15
Crutched-Fryars, 1739: CG, Jan 8
Cruttwell, R (publisher), 1777: HAY, Oct 9

Cry out and shout (song), 1792: KING'S, Mar 23, 28, 30
Cryer's Chaunt (song), 1796: CG, Jan 4
Cubit and Son (musicians), 1798: HAY, Jan 15
Cubitt (tinman), 1771: DL, Nov 6, Dec 12; 1772: DL, Jun 10, Dec 8; 1773: DL,
    Jun 2, Nov 19; 1774: DL, Jun 2, Oct 20; 1775: DL, Feb 23, May 27, Dec 2, 8;
    1776: DL, Jan 5, Mar 25, Apr 11, May 11, Jun 10
Cubitt, William (actor, singer), 1775: DL, Oct 5, 11, 17, 24, 28, Nov 1, 9, 11,
    17, 22, 28, Dec 7, 11; 1776: DL, Feb 1, 15, Mar 14, Apr 9, May 22, Jun 1;
    1781: CG, Jan 1, Apr 28, 30, May 3, 4, 7, 12; 1784: CG, Sep 20, 21, 27, 29,
    Oct 4, 8, 11, 12, 18, 25, 27, Nov 4, 6, 12, 13, 16, 25, Dec 4; 1785: CG, Jan
    8, 19, 21, Feb 21, 28, Mar 5, 8, 29, 30, Apr 25, May 6, 7, 11, 12, 26, Sep
    19, 21, 23, 26, 28, Oct 3, 5, 17, 19, 21, 27, Nov 1, 2, 9, 14, 19, 21, 22,
    29, Dec 9; 1786: CG, Jan 7, 18, Feb 7, 11, 16, 17, 25, Mar 4, 6, 14, 25, Apr
    1, 18, 19, 20, 24, May 6, 9, 15, 23, 30, Sep 18, 20, 25, Oct 6, 16, 21, 23,
    25, 26, 30, Nov 13, 14, 22, 23, 24, 25, 29, 30, Dec 5, 8, 26; 1787: CG, Jan
    4, 11, Feb 6, 10, 20, Mar 5, 12, 26, 31, Apr 10, 11, 13, 16, 24, 25, 27, 30,
    May 5, 9, 14, 21, 25, Sep 17, 19, 21, 24, Oct 1, 5, 10, 12, 17, 18, 19, 22,
    29, Nov 5, 7, 19, 26, 30, Dec 3, 10, 14, 21, 26; 1788: CG, Jan 5, 14, 21, 28,
    Feb 4, 5, 14, 25, Mar 1, 10, 24, 26, 29, Apr 1, 29, May 13, Jun 4, Sep 22,
    24, 29, Oct 1, 3, 8, 13, 17, 21, Nov 6, 10, 12, 20, 26, Dec 1, 15, 23, 26,
    27, 29, 30; 1789: CG, Jan 20, 21, Feb 16, Mar 3, 5, 14, 28, Apr 4, 14, 21,
    30, May 2, 5, 27, Jun 2, 5, 8, 12, 16, Sep 14, 16, 23, 25, 28, 30, Oct 2, 7,
    9, 12, 16, 21, 24, 28, Nov 6, 12, 14, 16, 19, 20, Dec 2, 21; 1790: CG, Jan
    19, Feb 4, 8, 11, 23, 25, Mar 27, Apr 12, 14, 20, 21, 24, May 6, 7, 15, 21,
    Jun 10, HAY, 15, 16, 18, 19, 22, 25, 26, Jul 16, Aug 2, 13, Sep 4, CG, 13,
    15, 29, Oct 1, 4, 5, 6, 8, 13, 18, 19, 20, 23, 25, Nov 4, 8, 11, 15, 16, 19,
    23, 25, 27, Dec 6, 8, 20, 28; 1791: CG, Jan 15, 26, Feb 11, Mar 5, 14, Apr
    11, 16, 28, 30, May 2, 3, 5, 6, 11, 16, 19, 27, Jun 1, 6, 10, HAY, 24, 29,
    Jul 1, 12, 15, 30, Aug 5, 10, 16, 19, 24, 26, Sep 2, 5, 8, 12, CG, 16, 17,
    19, 20, 21, 23, 26, 28, 30, Oct 3, 5, 10, 12, 17, 20, 21, 24, Nov 7, 25, Dec
    3; 1792: CG, Feb 2, 28, Mar 10, Apr 10, 12, May 2, 7, 15, 18, 22, 30, Jun 2,
    HAY, 15, 18, 20, 22, 23, 27, Jul 20, 25, 31, Aug 6, 9, 15, 22, Sep 6, CG, 20,
    Oct 1, 3, 5, 8, 10, 12, 15, 18, 24, 29, 31, Nov 5, 8, 14, Dec 1, 20, 22;
    1793: CG, Jan 2, 9, 19, Feb 14, 25, Mar 23, Apr 3, 4, 15, 18, 24, 30, May 8,
    21, 24, Jun 5, 12, Sep 16, 17, 18, 20, 23, 25, 27, 30, Oct 3, 4, 5, 7, 8, 11,
    12, 14, 15, 16, 18, 24, 29, 30, 31, Nov 1, 5, 12, 13, 15, 16, 23, 30, Dec 9,
    18, 19; 1794: CG, Jan 14, 22, Feb 1, 24, Mar 6, Apr 10, 12, 25, 29, May 2, 6,
    16, 22, 27, Jun 6; 1798: CG, May 15
Cuckold in Conceit, The. See Vanbrugh, Sir John.
Cuckolds-Haven. See Tate, Nahum.
Cuckoo Concerto (music), 1724: YB, Mar 27; 1731: DL, Jul 23, 27, Aug 3, 11, 20;
    1733: DL/HAY, Oct 20, HAY, Nov 19; 1734: DL/HAY, Jan 4, 10, 26, GF, May 1,
    13; 1735: DL, May 13, LIF, Jun 12
Cuckoo Dance (dance), 1742: DL, Apr 8; 1761: DL, Feb 12, 14, 16, 17, 19, 21,
    Mar 3; 1763: DL, Nov 10, 12, 17
Cuckoo on the Violin (music), 1735: HAY, Oct 24
Cuckoo Overture (music), 1757: HAY, Sep 8
Cuckoo Solo (song), 1736: LIF, Apr 16
Cuckoo Song (song), 1741: JS, Feb 20; 1770: DL, May 9; 1773: DL, Apr 19, Nov 2;
    1774: DL, Oct 1, CG, Dec 20; 1776: CG, Feb 5, Nov 12; 1778: CG, Feb 24; 1780:
    DL, Oct 5; 1782: DL, Apr 11, Sep 28; 1783: CG, May 17, HAY, Jul 4, DL, Oct
    16; 1784: CG, Sep 17, DL, Oct 26; 1786: CG, Feb 7, DL, 18; 1787: DL, May 29;
    1788: DL, Dec 17; 1789: DL, Sep 22, CG, Nov 20; 1790: CG, Oct 20, DL, 27;
    1791: DLKING'S, Oct 3, CG, 6; 1792: CG, Oct 10; 1793: DL, Mar 4; 1797: DL,
    May 12
Cudgell'd Husband (dance), 1763: CG, Nov 1, 2, 3, 10, 11, 23, 25; 1764: CG, May
    2, 5, 9, 11, 18
Cudworth (actor), 1689: DL, Nov 20; 1690: DL, Dec 0
Cue (Kew, Q), Nathaniel (actor), 1671: NONE, Sep 0; 1673: LIF, Dec 0; 1677: DL,
    Jun 0; 1678: DL, Feb 0
Cuerton (dancer), 1800: CG, May 23
Cuirande Enchantee, La (entertainment), 1725: HAY, Feb 5
Culte d'Amour (dance), 1777: KING'S, May 8
Culver (singer), 1772: MARLY, Aug 20, Sep 1, 7
Cumberland Corn Thrashers (dance), 1773: CG, Apr 24, May 28
Cumberland, Duke of, 1732: LIF, Jan 5, DL, Mar 16; 1746: KING'S, Jan 7, DL, Apr
    29, HAY, 30, DL, May 2, BF, Aug 23, SFHP, Sep 8, JS, Oct 2
Cumberland, Ernest Augustus, Duke of, 1800: CG, Jun 12
Cumberland, Henry Frederick, Duke of, 1790: NONE, Sep 18, HAY, Oct 13
Cumberland, Richard, 1761: DL, Jun 18, Jul 27; 1765: CG, Dec 6; 1766: CG, Jan
    29; 1767: CG, Mar 16, RANELAGH, Jun 1; 1768: CG, Apr 12; 1769: CG, Dec 2, 21;
    1771: DL, Jan 19, HAY, Jun 26, DL, Dec 4, 14; 1772: DL, Jan 20, 22, 25, 29;

1773: CG, Oct 15, Dec 23; 1774: DL, Feb 9, Dec 17, 19; 1777: CG, Feb 1, DL, Dec 18, CG, 19; 1778: CG, Jan 15, DL, 24; 1779: CG, Mar 20, Oct 13, Nov 10; 1780: CG, Feb 1, CII, 29; 1782: CG, Apr 20; 1783: CG, Jan 28, Feb 8; 1784: DL, Sep 30, Dec 2, 22; 1785: CG, Mar 8; 1786: HAMM, Aug 5; 1787: CG, Apr 25, HAY, Jul 7, DL, Nov 10; 1789: DL, Jan 26, CG, May 8; 1791: CG, May 2; 1792: CG, Sep 17; 1793: CG, Apr 4; 1794: HAY, Feb 22, DL, May 8, Jun 10, Oct 28; 1795: DL, Feb 28, CG, May 2, DL, 12, Oct 20; 1796: CG, Jan 6, 13, HAY, Jul 23; 1797: DL, May 8, CG, 18, DL, 29, CG, Oct 12, DL, 27, CG, Nov 23; 1798: CG, Apr 30, Oct 25, DL, Dec 5, 7; 1800: CG, Jan 16, DL, May 10
--Amelia, 1768: CG, Apr 12, 20, 21, 28, May 9; 1771: DL, Dec 14, 16
--Arab, The (Alcanor), 1785: CG, Mar 8
--Armourer, The (opera), 1793: CG, Apr 4, 5, 6
--Battle of Hastings, The, 1778: DL, Jan 24, 26, 27, 29, 31, Feb 2, 3, 4, 5, 9, 12, Mar 2, Apr 28, Oct 1
--Box-Lobby Challenge, The, 1794: HAY, Feb 22, 24, 26, 27, Mar 1, 3, 6, 8, 11, 15, 20, 27
--Brothers, The, 1769: CG, Nov 25, Dec 2, 4, 5, 6, 7, 8, 9, 11, 12, 13, 14, 16, 18, 23; 1770: CG, Jan 9, 16, 23, 25, Feb 3, 10, 20, Mar 3, May 24, Oct 19, 24, 31, Nov 28, Dec 5; 1771: CG, Jan 9, Feb 6, Apr 1, May 8, HAY, Jun 10, 24, Jul 24, CG, Oct 19, Nov 22, Dec 27; 1772: CG, May 16; 1774: DL, Mar 22; 1775: DL, Feb 23, May 8, Sep 23; 1778: CG, Jan 15, DL, Mar 30; 1779: HAY, Nov 8; 1786: CG, May 17; 1787: CG, Apr 25, May 11, Oct 10; 1788: CG, May 30; 1789: CG, Jun 16; 1791: CG, May 2
--Calypso, 1779: CG, Mar 20, 23, 25, Apr 22
--Carmelite, The, 1784: DL, Dec 2, 4, 7, 9, 11, 14, 15, 18; 1785: DL, Jan 7, 12, 19, Mar 1, 19, Oct 13, 27; 1787: DL, Nov 20
--Choleric Man, The, 1774: DL, Dec 19, 20, 21, 22, 23, 27, 30; 1775: DL, Jan 12, 14, 17, 27, Feb 8, 14, 15
--Country Attorney, The, 1787: HAY, Jul 7, 9, 10, 12, 14, 16, Aug 22; 1789: CG, May 8
--Days of Yore, The, 1796: CG, Jan 13, 14, 15, 20, Feb 2, Mar 14, May 18; 1797: CG, May 24
--Dependent, The, 1795: DL, Oct 20
--Don Pedro, 1796: HAY, Jul 23, 25, 27, 29, Aug 1
--Duke of Milan, The, 1779: CG, Nov 10, 12, 15
--Eccentric Lover, The, 1798: CG, Apr 30, May 2
--False Impressions, 1797: CG, Nov 23, 24, 25, 27, 28, 30, Dec 1, 2, 4, 6, 7, 9, 11, 13, 15, 21; 1798: CG, Jan 2, 6, Feb 7, Mar 29, Apr 20
--Fashionable Lover, The, 1772: DL, Jan 20, 21, 22, 23, 24, 25, 27, 28, 29, 31, Feb 3, 4, 6, 8, 17, 18, 20, 22, 25, Mar 17, 19, May 23, Oct 28; 1773: DL, Feb 1, Apr 13, May 18, Nov 26, Dec 1; 1774: DL, Apr 15; 1775: DL, May 6; 1778: CHR, Jun 22; 1786: CG, May 9, 17; 1795: CG, May 2
--First Love, 1795: DL, May 12, 13, 14, 16, 22, 25, Jun 1, 8, Sep 17, Oct 10, 17, 24, 31, Nov 21, 28, Dec 5, 12, 19, 31; 1796: DL, Jan 9, 28, Feb 23, Mar 15, 17, Apr 5, May 5, 31, Oct 4, Nov 18; 1797: DL, Jun 2; 1798: DL, Mar 8, Jun 16
--Impostors, The, 1789: DL, Jan 26, 28, Feb 4, 5, 6, 9, 11
--Jew, The, 1794: DL, Apr 24, 26, 28, 29, 30, May 2, 5, 6, 7, 8, 9, 10, 13, 15, 17, 21, 24, 28, 31, Jun 3, 5, HAY, Sep 3, DL, 16, 25, Oct 2, 9, 13, 16, 23, Nov 6, 13, 20, 27, Dec 4, 11, 18; 1795: DL, Jan 1, 3, 10, 17, Feb 4, 14, May 1, Jun 5, HAY, Jul 25, Aug 1, 8, 20, DL, Oct 3; 1796: DL, Jan 16, Mar 15, HAY, Jun 30, Jul 2, Sep 17, CG, 21, 28, Oct 3, DL, 11, CG, 12, DL, 18, CG, Nov 16, DL, Dec 10; 1797: DL, May 8, CG, 19, DL, Jun 13, HAY, Sep 8; 1798: DL, Feb 3, HAY, Mar 26, DL, Oct 30, Nov 9; 1799: DL, Jan 24, HAY, Jul 6, 11, 18, 25, Sep 7, DL, Nov 2; 1800: HAY, Jun 14, 28, Jul 9, 30, Sep 6
--Joanna, 1800: CG, Jan 16, 17, 18, 20, 21, 23, DL, 23, CG, 24, 25, 27, 28, 31, Feb 1, 5, 7
--Last of the Family, The, 1797: DL, May 8, 10, 11, 13, 26
--Mysterious Husband, The, 1783: CG, Jan 28, 29, 31, Feb 1, 3, 4, 6, 8, Mar 4, 8, 11, 18, May 10, 31, Nov 24; 1796: CG, Jan 4, 6
--Natural Son, The, 1784: DL, Dec 22, 23, 29, 30, 31; 1785: DL, Jan 1, 28, Feb 3, 17, 24, 28, Mar 10, Oct 4, Dec 27; 1786: HAMM, Aug 5; 1787: DL, Jan 24, May 25; 1794: DL, May 17, 19, Jun 2, 4, 10, 13, 21; 1795: DL, Feb 12
--New Occasional Prelude, A (prelude), 1792: CG, Sep 17, 19
--Note of Hand, The; or, A Trip to Newcastle, 1774: DL, Feb 9, 10, 11, 14, 21, 24, 26, Mar 3, 5, 7, 8, 24, Apr 7, May 11, 13, Sep 20, Oct 22, 28, Nov 14; 1775: DL, Mar 13, May 22, Sep 26; 1776: DL, Sep 26; 1778: DL, Feb 2, 6
--School for Widows, A, 1787: HAY, Jul 7; 1789: CG, May 8, 9, 11
--Summer's Tale, The (musical), 1765: CG, Dec 2, 6, 9, 11, 13, 16; 1766: CG, Jan 8, 18, 20, 22, 24, 27, 29; 1768: CG, Apr 12, 28; 1769: CG, Dec 2; 1771: DL, Dec 14
--Village Fete, The (interlude), 1797: CG, May 18, 19, 22, 26

--Walloons, The, <u>1782</u>: CG, Apr 20, 22, 25, May 2, 7, 9, Oct 4, 11, 15; <u>1783</u>: CG, Feb 8
--West Indian, The, <u>1771</u>: DL, Jan 19, 21, 22, 24, 26, 28, 31, Feb 2, 5, 6, 7, 9, 11, 12, 14, 16, 18, 19, 23, 25, 26, Mar 2, 7, Apr 11, HAY, 15, DL, 18, 25, May 2, 9, 16, HAY, Aug 26, Sep 9, DL, 24, Oct 9, 21, Nov 1, 16, 29, Dec 7; <u>1772</u>: DL, Jan 4, 17, 20, Feb 7, 24, Mar 24, Apr 20, 28, May 16, Jun 1, Sep 26, Oct 14, Nov 25, Dec 9; <u>1773</u>: DL, Jan 7, 28, Feb 12, Mar 15, Apr 15, May 7, Jun 1, Sep 23, Oct 7, CG, 15, 16, 19, 20, 29, Nov 26, DL, Dec 18; <u>1774</u>: CG, Jan 11, DL, 29, Apr 11, May 9, CG, 17, DL, Oct 14, CG, 14, Nov 25, 30, DL, Dec 19, CG, 23; <u>1775</u>: DL, Mar 6, May 19, CG, 24, Sep 22, Dec 22; <u>1776</u>: DL, Apr 8, CG, May 22, DL, Oct 30, Dec 23; <u>1777</u>: CG, Feb 5, May 12, 23, Dec 19; <u>1778</u>: DL, Oct 8, Dec 16; <u>1779</u>: DL, Mar 2, 11, Apr 20, CG, May 15, DL, Sep 30, CG, Dec 1, HAY, 20; <u>1780</u>: CG, Jan 13, DL, Feb 5, CII, 29, DL, Apr 8, CG, May 20, DL, Oct 12, CG, Nov 27; <u>1781</u>: DL, May 15, CG, 25, DL, Oct 2; <u>1782</u>: DL, Feb 1, Apr 20, May 15; <u>1783</u>: DL, Jan 15, Feb 5, May 29, Nov 12, Dec 11; <u>1784</u>: DL, Jan 20, Sep 16; <u>1785</u>: DL, May 19, CG, Oct 5, 13; <u>1786</u>: DL, Jan 4, CG, Feb 22; <u>1787</u>: DL, Feb 19, HAY, Mar 12, DL, May 31, CG, Nov 14, DL, Dec 8; <u>1788</u>: DL, Jan 18, CG, 23, DL, Jun 5, CG, Sep 17, DL, Oct 25, Nov 15, 27; <u>1789</u>: DL, Jan 5, 20, 28, Jun 11, Sep 19, Nov 18; <u>1790</u>: DL, May 8, Jun 2, Dec 3; <u>1793</u>: DL, Jun 5; <u>1794</u>: CG, Jan 3; <u>1797</u>: CG, Oct 21; <u>1800</u>: CG, Jan 29
--Wheel of Fortune, The, <u>1795</u>: DL, Feb 14, 26, 28, Mar 2, 5, 9, 12, 16, 19, 23, 26, 28, Apr 6, 8, 9, 10, 13, 21, May 5, 9, Sep 22, Oct 1, 13, Nov 18; <u>1796</u>: DL, Jan 14, Feb 8, Apr 8, Sep 29, Nov 11, Dec 8; <u>1797</u>: DL, Jan 18, Feb 10, Apr 18, May 30, Sep 30, Nov 8, Dec 7; <u>1798</u>: DL, Jan 6, 12, Feb 16, Oct 9, 25, Nov 12, 20, Dec 13; <u>1799</u>: DL, Jan 22, Sep 24, Nov 1, 30; <u>1800</u>: DL, Jan 23, May 1
--Widow of Delphi; or, The Descent of the Deities (opera), <u>1780</u>: CG, Feb 1, 2, 3, 7, 10, 14, 15
--Word for Nature, A, <u>1798</u>: DL, Dec 5, 6, 7, 8, 10
Cumberland, William, Duke of, <u>1748</u>: HAY, Dec 9; <u>1752</u>: DL, Jan 2; <u>1765</u>: DL, Nov 1, CG, 1; <u>1766</u>: CG, Nov 20; <u>1767</u>: CG, Jan 6, DL, 9, CG, 15, 29, Feb 27; <u>1768</u>: CG, Jan 2, Dec 30; <u>1770</u>: CG, Jan 19; <u>1773</u>: CG, Jan 8, Feb 18; <u>1774</u>: CG, Jan 14; see also Dukes
Cummins (bookseller), <u>1746</u>: CG, Jan 24
Cummins (house servant), <u>1773</u>: CG, Jan 8, Feb 18
Cumyns, Mrs (versifier), <u>1785</u>: CG, Apr 25
Cunha, Don Luis da (Portuguese ambassador), <u>1703</u>: LIF, Jun 14; <u>1716</u>: DL, Jun 6
Cunning Isaac's Escape from the Duenna (entertainment), <u>1778</u>: CG, Apr 27
Cunning Love (dance), <u>1771</u>: DL, Feb 4, Mar 16, 19, Apr 3, 5, 30
Cunning Man, The. See Burney, Dr Charles.
Cunningham (actor, dancer, singer), <u>1733</u>: DL, Feb 12, Mar 31, May 7, 21, CG, Jul 10, BFMMO, Aug 23, DL, Nov 26; <u>1734</u>: GF, Jan 14, DL, 29, GF, Nov 4; <u>1735</u>: GF, Jan 24, Mar 6; <u>1736</u>: HAY, Jan 19; <u>1744</u>: JS, Mar 2, MF, Jun 7; <u>1745</u>: GF, Apr 15; <u>1746</u>: GF, Mar 20, SOU, Oct 7, 16, 20, 27; <u>1747</u>: JS, Apr 1, SF, Sep 14; <u>1748</u>: DL, Feb 16, 25, BFH, Aug 24, SFLYYW, Sep 7, BHB, Oct 1
Cunningham (linen draper), <u>1731</u>: DL, Jan 27
Cunningham, John, <u>1747</u>: SMMF, Aug 28
--Love in a Mist, <u>1747</u>: SMMF, Aug 28; <u>1748</u>: HAY, Apr 20, JS, Dec 26
Cuper's Gardens, <u>1754</u>: SFH, Sep 19
Cupid and Bacchus. See Purcell, Henry.
Cupid and Psyche (dance), <u>1797</u>: DL, May 22, CG, Jun 14, 21, Oct 28, 31, Nov 4, 7
Cupid and Psyche; or, Colombine Courtezan (Harlequin Restored) (pantomime, anon), <u>1734</u>: DL, Feb 4, 5, 6, 7, 8, 9, 11, 12, 14, 15, 16, 18, 19, 20, 21, 22, 23, 25, 26, 28, Mar 2, Apr 15, DL/HAY, 16, 17, 19, 20, 24, May 24, DL, Oct 5, 10, 12, 14, 15, 16, 17, 19, Nov 22, 23, 30, Dec 3, 6, 19, 20, 21, 26, 27, 28, 30, 31; <u>1735</u>: DL, Jan 1, 2, 3, 4, 11, Feb 5, 7, 8, Apr 15, 19, 25, May 2, Sep 1, 13, 18, 20, 23, Oct 2, 4, 27, Nov 4, 5, 10, Dec 6, 9, 10, 15, 16, 26, 27; <u>1736</u>: DL, Jan 7, May 3, 13, 14, 19, 31, Sep 4; <u>1738</u>: DL, Sep 12, 14, 16, 19, Oct 17, 18, 19, 20, 28, Nov 30, Dec 1, 2; <u>1739</u>: DL, Jan 8, 11, 12, 13, Mar 1, 2, 5, 6, May 18, BF, Aug 27, SF, Sep 8, DL, 27, 28, Oct 3, Nov 14, 16, Dec 15; <u>1740</u>: DL, Apr 18; <u>1744</u>: DL, Jan 5, 7, 9, 10, 11, 13, 14, 16, 26, 27, 28, 31, Oct 24, 25, 27, Nov 3, 15, 16; <u>1749</u>: SOU, Feb 13, CG, Apr 12; <u>1754</u>: CG, May 1; <u>1757</u>: CG, Apr 27
Cupid make your virgins tender (song), <u>1697</u>: NONE, Sep 0
Cupid Recruiting (dance), <u>1780</u>: CG, Apr 17, 24, 29, May 18; <u>1791</u>: DL, May 25
Cupid, <u>1751</u>: HAY, Dec 27; <u>1752</u>: CT/HAY, Jan 7; see also Hallet, Benjamin
Cupid's Friendship. See Yarrow, Joseph.
Cupid's Power I Despise (song), <u>1748</u>: CG, Mar 31
Cupid's Remonstrance (entertainment), <u>1772</u>: DL, Apr 27, 29
Cupid's Revenge. See Fletcher, John; Gentleman, Francis.
Cupids' Dance (dance), <u>1778</u>: DL, Jan 17, Dec 23; <u>1779</u>: DL, Mar 23, Oct 21;

1780: DL, Sep 28; 1784: CG, Mar 27, DL, Nov 26; 1786: DL, Jan 6, Mar 20
Curco (singer), 1694: NONE, Sep 0; 1695: LIF, Dec 0
Cure for a Coxcomb, A; or, The Beau Bedeviled (play, anon), 1792: CG, May 15
Cure for a Cuckold, A. See Webster, John.
Cure for a Scold, A. See Worsdale, James.
Cure for a Scolding Wife, A (entertainment), 1786: HAY, Aug 25
Cure for all Grief (song), 1744: CG, Apr 17
Cure for Dotage, A (musical), 1771: MARLY, Aug 3, 6
Cure for Jealousy, A. See Corye, John.
Cure for the Heart Ache, A. See Morton, Thomas.
Cure of Saul, The. See Arnold, Dr Samuel.
Cure of the Spleen. See Shuter, Edward.
Curioni, Rosa (singer), 1754: KING'S, Nov 9; 1755: DL, Feb 3, KING'S, Mar 17,
    Apr 10; 1756: DL, Feb 11; 1761: KING'S, Oct 13, Nov 10; 1762: KING'S, May 11
Curiosities in the Tower of London (entertainment), 1784: CG, Apr 26, HAY, Aug
    24; 1785: CG, Apr 11, HAY, Aug 23; 1787: CG, Apr 10; 1788: CG, Apr 11, May
    12, 19; 1789: CG, May 14
Curiosity. See Trapp, Joseph.
Curioso Indiscreto, Il. See Anfossi, Pasquale.
Curler, Mrs. See Cuyler, Margaret.
Curona (singer), 1734: CR, Nov 27
Currer (Corar, Corer, Corrar), Elizabeth (actor), 1675: DG, May 28; 1676: DG,
    Jan 10, Mar 0, May 25; 1677: DG, Sep 0; 1678: DG, Jan 17, Jun 0; 1679: DG,
    Mar 0, Sep 0, Dec 0; 1680: DG, Feb 0; 1681: DG, Jan 0, Nov 0, DG/IT, 22;
    1682: DG, Jan 0, Feb 9, Apr 0; 1683: DG, May 31, Jul 0; 1684: DLORDG, Aug 0;
    1689: DL, Nov 20
Currey, Francis (feather merchant), 1767: CG, Feb 2
Curryer (Currier) (pit office keeper), 1745: DL, May 6; 1746: DL, May 7; 1747:
    DL, May 12
Curse upon the fruitless maid, A (song), 1699: NONE, Sep 0
Curteen (Curten) (boxkeeper), 1773: CG, May 22; 1774: CG, May 14; 1775: CG, May
    27; 1776: CG, May 17; 1777: CG, May 21; 1778: CG, May 19; 1779: CG, May 13;
    1780: CG, May 20; 1781: CG, May 23; 1782: CG, May 24; 1783: CG, Jun 3; 1784:
    CG, May 28; 1786: CG, May 31; 1787: CG, May 19; 1788: CG, May 15; 1789: CG,
    Jun 6; 1790: CG, May 29; 1791: CG, Jun 2; 1792: CG, May 29; 1794: CG, May 31;
    1795: CG, May 30; 1797: CG, Jun 6; 1798: CG, Jun 5
Curtet (Curtat, Curtete), Pierre (dancer), 1762: DL, Nov 23; 1764: CG, Jan 14,
    16; 1765: CG, May 22, Oct 28; 1766: CG, Oct 25, Nov 18; 1767: CG, Apr 27, May
    9, Oct 17; 1768: CG, May 25; 1769: CG, May 17; 1770: CG, Mar 23, May 25;
    1771: CG, May 17; 1772: CG, Apr 20, May 16; 1773: CG, Apr 15, 24, May 26;
    1774: CG, May 18, 20
Curties (actor, singer), 1794: CG, Oct 15, Nov 6; 1795: CG, Sep 14, Oct 16, 30,
    Nov 7, 16, Dec 9; 1796: CG, Jan 23, 25, Feb 1, 18, Mar 15, Apr 9, Sep 16, 21,
    26, Oct 7, 29, Nov 5, 19, 25, Dec 9, 19, 26, 29; 1797: CG, Jan 25, Feb 18,
    Mar 4, 7, Apr 8, 25, May 18, 23, Jun 2, Sep 18, Nov 4, 23, Dec 19, 26; 1798:
    CG, Feb 9, 12, 13, Mar 27, 29, 31, Apr 9, 11, 20, 21, 30, Jun 5, Sep 17, Oct
    11, 15, Nov 12, Dec 8, 11, 26; 1799: CG, Jan 12, 14, 16, 29, Feb 19, Mar 16,
    Apr 2, 9, 13, 23, 27, May 4, 15, 28, Jun 7, Sep 25, 30, Oct 14, 21, 24, 31,
    Nov 7, 12, 30, Dec 2; 1800: CG, Jan 16, Feb 3, 8, 10, Mar 25, 27, Apr 5, 23,
    28, 29, May 1, 7, 12, 13, 27, Jun 2
Curtis (actor), 1777: HAY, Oct 9; 1779: HAY, Mar 15; 1786: HAMM, Jun 5, 7, 28,
    30, HAY, Dec 18; 1787: HAY, Apr 30; 1788: HAY, Apr 9, Dec 22
Curtis (bondsman), 1771: DL, Dec 17
Curtius, Quintus (author), 1769: CG, Dec 15
Curtz (Curz), Mlle (dancer), 1770: KING'S, May 19; 1772: KING'S, Jun 11
Cushing, John (actor), 1741: TC, Aug 4; 1742: JS, Apr 7; 1743: MF, May 9, SF,
    Sep 8; 1744: GF, Dec 4, 10, 11, 12, 26; 1745: GF, Feb 4, 14, Mar 7, 18, Oct
    28, 31, Nov 11, 13, 14, 18, 19, 22, 23, 25, 26, 27, 28, Dec 2, 4, 6, 9, 11,
    13, 16, 19, 27; 1746: GF, Jan 1, 2, 3, 6, 13, 15, 17, 20, 27, 31, Feb 3, 11,
    Mar 3, 10, 20, May 1, BFWF, Aug 25, SFW, Sep 8, NWMF, Oct 6, SOU, 7, 16, 20,
    GF, 27, 28, 29, 31, Nov 4, 6, 7, 13, 14, 18, 19, 20, 21, 26, 28, Dec 1, 3, 5,
    9, 10, 11, 12, 15, 17, 18; 1747: GF, Jan 2, 5, 9, 16, 22, 26, 29, Feb 2, 3,
    5, 6, 16, Mar 2, 5, 9, 10, 16, 24, 26, 30, Apr 2, HAY, 22; 1748: CG, Jan 14,
    Mar 8, 14, 28, HAY, 30, NWC, Apr 4, CG, Sep 23, 26, Oct 3, 14, 27, Nov 21,
    26, Dec 17, 26; 1749: CG, Jan 2, 10, 25, Mar 2, 4, 9, 29, 30, 31, Apr 11, 19,
    24, May 4, BFC, Aug 23, SOUGT, Sep 22, CG, 27, Oct 2, 4, 6, 11, 12, 16, 18,
    20, 23, 25, 30, Nov 1, 8, 17, 21, Dec 8, 27; 1750: CG, Jan 24, Mar 1, 27, Apr
    17, 26, Oct 12, 13, 15, 18, 22, 29, Nov 8, 19, 22, 28, 29, Dec 4, 8; 1751:
    CG, Jan 11, 17, Mar 5, 18, Apr 16, May 8, 9, 16, Sep 23, 27, Oct 7, 19, 22,
    29, Nov 7, 11, 16, 22, 26, Dec 14; 1752: CG, Jan 6, 29, Mar 16, 17, 30, Apr
    10, May 4, Sep 20, 22, 25, Oct 2, 9, 18, 21, Nov 9, 13, 16, 23, 28, Dec 5, 7,
    8, 11, 14, 20; 1753: CG, Jan 17, 22, Feb 7, Mar 19, Apr 5, May 7, 8, 14, 18,

Sep 10, 12, 14, 21, Oct 3, 5, 8, 10, 17, 24, 30, 31, Nov 9, 26; <u>1754</u>: CG, Mar 9, Apr 20, May 2, 7, 13, Sep 16, 18, 20, 30, Oct 4, 9, 14, 15, 23, 24, Nov 14, 16, 20, 29, Dec 10, 30; <u>1755</u>: CG, Jan 10, 28, Feb 20, Mar 18, Apr 16, 18, 30, May 15, Oct 1, 6, 17, 18, 20, 21, 22, 31, Nov 4, 10, 12, 17, Dec 3, 4, 11; <u>1756</u>: CG, Jan 6, 15, Feb 3, 9, 19, Mar 30, Apr 1, 20, 29, May 11, 13, Sep 20, 22, 29, Oct 1, 4, 6, 11, 19, 20, 25, 28, Nov 4, 9, 11, 17, 24, Dec 1, 2, 10, 20; <u>1757</u>: CG, Jan 10, 14, 27, 28, Feb 9, 16, Apr 13, May 12, Sep 14, 16, 21, 23, 28, Oct 5, 8, 13, 14, 17, 20, 21, 28, 31, Nov 4, 5, 7, 9, 11, 29, Dec 7, 10, 14, 20, 21; <u>1758</u>: CG, Mar 11, Apr 3, 14, 17, May 4, Sep 18, 20, 22, 25, Oct 4, 9, 27, 30, Nov 1, 4, 9, 13; <u>1759</u>: CG, Jan 12, Feb 1; <u>1762</u>: CG, Jan 28, Mar 13, Apr 16, 21, Nov 1, Dec 28; <u>1763</u>: CG, Jan 8, Feb 1, 14, Apr 12, 25, May 23, Sep 28, 30, Oct 8, 12, 15, 24, Nov 10, 18, 26, Dec 9; <u>1764</u>: CG, Jan 9, 14, 25, Mar 8, 20, Apr 10, Sep 26, 28, Oct 11, 24, Nov 3, 5, 15, 16, 27; <u>1765</u>: CG, Jan 3, 8, 21, Feb 18, Apr 9, Sep 20, 23, 27, Oct 8, 9, 11, 15, 17, 30, Nov 22, 27, 28, Dec 26; <u>1766</u>: CG, Jan 9, 31, Feb 6, Sep 22, Oct 6, 14, 17, 18, 22, Nov 4, 8, 12, 19, Dec 6, 11, 13, 23, 27; <u>1767</u>: CG, Jan 1, 29, 31, Feb 28, Apr 6, 24, 25, May 18, Sep 14, 17, 18, 19, Oct 8, Nov 7, 28, Dec 14; <u>1768</u>: CG, Jan 18, 29, Feb 20, Mar 24, Apr 20, 22, 25, May 7, 27, Sep 21, 27, Oct 4, Nov 8, 9, 17, Dec 16, 22; <u>1769</u>: CG, Jan 2, Feb 18, Sep 25, 27, Oct 2, 5, 14, Nov 17, Dec 1, 19, 29; <u>1770</u>: CG, Jan 1, 3, 18, 24, 27, Mar 20, Apr 24, 25, 28, May 21, Sep 24, Oct 1, 11, 15, 29, Nov 17, Dec 21; <u>1771</u>: CG, Jan 26, Sep 30, Oct 19, 30, Nov 7, 19, Dec 4, 6, 14, 16, 30; <u>1772</u>: CG, Feb 25, Mar 23, Sep 21, 28, Oct 14, 16, Nov 12, Dec 11, 26; <u>1773</u>: CG, Jan 25, Apr 23, 24, 27, May 4, 6, 28, Sep 27, Oct 6, 28, Nov 9, 20, 23, Dec 3, 18, 23; <u>1774</u>: CG, Jan 26, 29, Feb 14, 24, Mar 15, Apr 5, 11, May 18, Sep 19, 23, 26, 30, Oct 11, 20, 26, 27, Nov 8, 19, Dec 12, 27; <u>1775</u>: CG, Feb 23, Mar 30, Apr 28, May 8, 17, Sep 29, Oct 4, 13, Nov 22, Dec 21; <u>1776</u>: CG, Jan 15, Mar 28, Apr 19, 27, 29, 30, May 10, Sep 23, Oct 11, Nov 2, 15; <u>1777</u>: CG, May 2, 15, Sep 22, 29, Oct 1, 15, Nov 19; <u>1778</u>: CG, Jan 20, 29, Feb 11, 23, 25, May 5, 11, 14, Oct 2, 14, 23, Nov 21, Dec 1, 21; <u>1779</u>: CG, Apr 24, May 21, Oct 20, Nov 9, 13, 25, 30, Dec 31; <u>1780</u>: CG, Feb 2, May 17, Sep 20, Oct 6, 19, Nov 1; <u>1781</u>: CG, Jan 10, Dec 5, 8; <u>1782</u>: CG, Mar 19, May 6, 28

Cushing, John and Mrs (actor), <u>1746</u>: GF, Mar 10
Cushing, Mrs John (actor, singer), <u>1743</u>: MF, May 9, SF, Sep 8; <u>1744</u>: GF, Dec 3, 11, 26; <u>1745</u>: GF, Feb 14, Mar 7, 26, Oct 28, Nov 4, 11, 13, 18, 19, 25, 26, 27, Dec 2, 4, 9, 13; <u>1746</u>: GF, Jan 1, 3, 6, 13, 15, 17, 20, 27, Feb 3, 11, 17, Mar 10, BFWF, Aug 25, SFW, Sep 8, NWMF, Oct 6, SOU, 16, GF, Nov 18, 19, 26, 27, 28, Dec 1, 3, 5, 10, 11, 12, 17, 18, 22; <u>1747</u>: GF, Jan 5, 9, 16, 19, 22, Feb 2, Mar 2, 5, 9, 30, Apr 2; <u>1749</u>: NWLS, Feb 27, HAY, Apr 29, May 29, BFC, Aug 23, SOUGT, Sep 22, CG, 29; <u>1751</u>: CG, Feb 6, May 9, Sep 27, 30, Oct 12

Cushing's Booth, <u>1749</u>: BFC, Aug 23, 24, 25, 26, 28
Cussans, John P (actor), <u>1798</u>: HAY, Mar 26
Cussans, Mrs (actor), <u>1799</u>: CG, Nov 11
Custom of the Country, The. See Fletcher, John.
Custonelli, Sga (singer), <u>1752</u>: CT/HAY, May 9
Cuthbert (actor), <u>1743</u>: BFYWR, Aug 23; <u>1748</u>: SFLYYW, Sep 7, BHB, Oct 1
Cuthbert (machinist), <u>1798</u>: CG, Nov 12
Cuthbert, Mrs (actor), <u>1743</u>: BFYWR, Aug 23; <u>1744</u>: JS, Dec 10
Cuthbert, Thomas (violinist), <u>1711</u>: SH, Apr 11, May 9, RIW, Jul 21; <u>1712</u>: SH, May 14
Cuthbertson, Catherine, <u>1793</u>: DL, Feb 25
--Anna, <u>1793</u>: DL, Feb 25, 28
Cutter Lane, <u>1757</u>: DL, Apr 19
Cutter of Coleman Street, The. See Cowley, Abraham; Garrick, David, The Guardian.
Cuttin, Master (singer), <u>1732</u>: GF, Nov 28, 30, Dec 15, 22, 27, 29; <u>1733</u>: GF, Apr 23; <u>1735</u>: GF, May 6
Cuyler (Curler), Margaret (actor), <u>1777</u>: DL, Jan 4, Apr 24, Sep 20, Oct 17; <u>1778</u>: DL, Sep 22, Oct 15, Nov 2; <u>1779</u>: DL, Mar 16, HAY, May 31, Jul 2, Aug 17, 24, 31, DL, Nov 3, 6, Dec 20; <u>1780</u>: DL, May 10, HAY, 30, Jun 2, 9, 13, 26, Jul 1, 10, Aug 5, 26, Sep 5, DL, 23, Oct 2, 17; <u>1781</u>: DL, May 8, HAY, Jun 1, 7, 16, 22, Jul 23, Aug 22; <u>1782</u>: HAY, Jun 4, 10, 11, 20, Aug 13; <u>1783</u>: HAY, Jun 4, 6, 13, 16; <u>1784</u>: HAY, Mar 22, May 29, Jun 22, 25, Jul 6, 20, Sep 17; <u>1785</u>: HAY, May 28, Jun 6, 7, 15, Jul 21, 26, DL, Nov 18, Dec 26; <u>1786</u>: HAY, Jun 15, 16, Jul 8, 21, 27, Aug 10, 12, DL, Nov 25, Dec 14; <u>1787</u>: DL, Feb 15, HAY, Jun 11, 18, 20, Jul 4, 7, Aug 1, 4, 17, DL, Nov 1, 10, Dec 26; <u>1788</u>: DL, Jan 21, May 7, 14, HAY, Jun 12, 17, 18, 23, Jul 3, 24, DL, Sep 18; <u>1789</u>: HAY, Jun 17, 24, Jul 6, Sep 8; <u>1790</u>: DL, Feb 18, HAY, Jun 15, 16, 17, 25, Jul 5, Aug 16, DL, Sep 30; <u>1791</u>: HAY, Jun 13, 17, 18, 20, 23, Jul 8, Aug 10, 18, DLKING'S, Nov 14; <u>1792</u>: DLKING'S, Mar 1, 6, HAY, Aug 6, 22, Sep 5; <u>1793</u>: DL, Feb 12, 16, Apr 1, HAY, Jun 14, 22, 29, Aug 12, Sep 28, Oct 29; <u>1794</u>: HAY,

Jan 27, Jul 8, 11, 22, Sep 17, DL, Oct 27; 1795: DL, Feb 12, May 6, HAY, Jun
16, Jul 1, DL, Nov 20; 1796: DL, Jan 18, Apr 25, May 23, HAY, Jun 11, Jul 9,
Sep 17; 1797: DL, Feb 1, Mar 6, HAY, Jun 12, DL, 14, HAY, 24, Aug 14; 1798:
DL, Jun 1, HAY, 13, 15, DL, Nov 29, HAY, Dec 17; 1799: DL, Apr 22, HAY, Jun
15, Aug 10, DL, Oct 19, 24, Dec 7, 12; 1800: DL, Feb 6, Apr 1
Cuzzoni (Catzoni, Cotzoni), Francesca (singer), 1723: KING'S, Jan 12, 15, EBH,
18, KING'S, Feb 19, Mar 2, 26, 30, May 14, Nov 27; 1724: KING'S, Jan 14, Feb
20, Apr 18, May 21, Oct 31, Dec 1; 1725: KING'S, Feb 13, Apr 10, May 11;
1726: KING'S, Jan 15, Feb 5, Mar 12, May 5; 1727: KING'S, Jan 7, 31, May 6,
Jun 6, Jul 0, Oct 21, Nov 11, CR, 22; 1728: KING'S, Feb 17; 1729: HIC, Apr
16; 1733: HIC, Jun 15; 1734: LIF, Apr 20, May 11, KING'S, Oct 29; 1735:
KING'S, Feb 1, CRT, Mar 24, KING'S, Apr 8, May 3, Nov 25; 1736: KING'S, Jan
24, Apr 13; 1747: KING'S, Nov 12; 1750: HIC, May 18; 1751: KING'S, Apr 16,
HAY, 27, DL, May 1, HIC, 23; 1754: KING'S, Mar 12
Cyclopedia, The. See Hoper, Mrs.
Cyclops Dance (dance), 1704: DL, Jun 21; 1756: DL, Dec 27
Cymbal Concerto (music), 1752: CG, Jan 6
Cymbal Solo (music), 1752: CT/HAY, Feb 4, 6
Cymbalo (music), 1752: CT/HAY, Mar 12
Cymbalo Concerto (music), 1752: CT/HAY, Jan 14, May 5
Cymbalo Solo (music), 1752: CT/HAY, Apr 1, May 5
Cymbalo Voluntary (music), 1752: CT/HAY, Jan 21; 1757: HAY, Sep 5, 8
Cymbeline. See Shakespeare, William.
Cymber, Miss (actor), 1747: HAY, Mar 24, Apr 20
Cymon (opera, anon), 1790: CG, Mar 22, Apr 9, 29, Oct 1, 26, Nov 20; 1791: CG,
Feb 14, Sep 21; 1793: CG, Dec 9, 13; 1794: CG, Oct 23; 1795: CG, Sep 21, Nov
20; 1796: CG, May 27, Nov 24, Dec 16; 1798: CG, May 7; 1799: CG, Jan 17, 19,
May 21, Dec 4
Cymon (play). See Garrick, David.
Cymon and Iphigenia (song), 1753: DL, Mar 27; 1755: DL, Mar 13, 15; 1756: DL,
Mar 30; 1758: DL, Mar 11, 16; 1767: CG, May 5; 1768: CG, May 11; 1775: HAY,
May 1
Cynic, The; or, The Force of Virtue (play, anon), 1731: GF, Feb 22, 23, 24
Cynthia frowns when e're I woo her (song), 1693: DL, Oct 0
Cynthia's Revels. See Jonson, Ben.
Cyrus the Great. See Banks, John.
Cyrus. See Hoole, John.
Cyrus; or, Odio ed Amore. See Rolli, Paolo Antonio.
Cytherea. See Smith, John.
Czar of Muscovy, The. See Pix, Mary.
Czar, The. See O'Keeffe, John

D Jr (property man), 1767: DL, Jan 24
D, J (author), 1759: HAY, Oct 3
Da forte morir sapro (song), 1791: DL, Apr 1, 6, 15
Dabell (actor), 1772: HAY, Jun 12
Daborne, Robert
--Poor Man's Comfort, The, 1661: REDBULL, May 28, LIF, Jul 10
Dace (dancer), 1735: DL, Mar 3
Dacres (actor), 1661: LIF, Aug 24, Dec 16
Dagge, Henry (manager), 1773: CG, Mar 6
Dagley (silversmith), 1736: DL, May 14
Daglish, Master (actor), 1790: DL, Dec 7
Daglish, Thomas (music copyist), 1780: DL, Apr 26; 1781: DL, May 11; 1782: DL,
May 16; 1783: DL, May 23, Sep 27; 1784: DL, May 24; 1785: DL, May 23; 1786:
DL, May 29; 1787: DL, Jun 8; 1788: DL, Jun 6; 1789: DL, Jun 10, Sep 17; 1790:
DL, Jun 2; 1791: DL, May 31; 1792: DLKING'S, Jun 13; 1796: DL, Jun 10; 1797:
DL, Jun 15
Dahuron, Francis (flutist), 1719: HIC, Feb 13, May 7; 1741: HAY, Feb 3
Daigueville (Dagueville, Daigville, D'Egville), Fanny (dancer), 1779: CG, May
8, 21; 1780: CG, Jan 8, May 16; 1788: DL, Jun 5; 1790: DL, Jun 1; 1791: DL,
May 20, 25, DLKING'S, Dec 31; 1792: DLKING'S, Jun 7; 1795: DL, Feb 12, May 6,
26; 1798: DL, May 9; 1800: CG, May 2
Daigueville, Fanny and Lewis (dancers), 1800: CG, May 2
Daigueville, Fanny and Sophia (dancers), 1792: DL, Nov 21, Dec 27; 1793: DL,
Mar 7; 1794: DL, May 16, Oct 27; 1800: DL, May 14
Daigueville, Fanny, George and James Harvey (dancers), 1788: DL, Jun 5; 1791:
DL, May 25
Daigueville, George (dancer), 1787: HAY, Aug 7; 1791: DL, Apr 29, May 24,

DLKING'S, Dec 31; 1792: DLKING'S, Jun 7, HAY, Jul 25, DL, Nov 21; 1794: DL, May 16, Jun 9, 12, 25, Jul 4, Sep 27, Oct 27, Nov 10, Dec 20; 1795: DL, Jan 5, Feb 6, 12, 24, May 6, 20, 26
Daigueville, James Harvey (dancer), 1776: CG, May 3; 1777: CG, Oct 1, Nov 11; 1778: CG, May 22, Nov 10, 25, 27; 1779: CG, May 3, DL, 14, CG, 21, Nov 23; 1780: CG, Jan 8, May 18; 1781: DL, May 11; 1783: KING'S, Mar 13, Apr 12; 1786: KING'S, Feb 18, Apr 27, HAY, Jun 14, 21, Aug 12, Sep 4; 1787: HAY, Jul 30, Aug 7, 14, 17, 21; 1788: DL, Apr 14; 1791: PAN, Mar 22; 1794: DL, Jul 2, Oct 31; 1795: DL, Feb 12, Mar 12, May 20, Jun 1; 1799: KING'S, Mar 26, May 2, DL, 8
--Alexander the Great; or, The Conquest of Persia (pantomime), 1795: DL, Feb 11, 12, 13, 14, 16, 17, 19, 21, 23, 24, 26, 28, Mar 2, 3, 5, 7, 9, 10, 12, 14, 16, 17, 19, 21, 23, 24, 26, 28, Apr 6, 7, 8, 9, 10, 11, 13, 15, 23, May 20
Daigueville, James Harvey and Fanny (dancers), 1780: CG, May 18; 1795: DL, Jun 1
Daigueville, James Harvey and George (dancers), 1786: HAY, Jul 6, Sep 1, DL, Oct 24; 1787: DL, Jan 13, Jun 1, Sep 20, Nov 8; 1788: DL, Jun 5; 1791: DL, May 25
Daigueville, Lewis (dancer), 1792: HAY, Jul 25, DL, Oct 13; 1794: DL, May 16, Oct 27; 1800: CG, May 2
Daigueville, Lewis and Sophia (dancers), 1793: DL, Jun 4
Daigueville, Mrs Peter (dancer), 1769: DL, Sep 23, Oct 4, Nov 20; 1770: DL, Dec 1, 7, 11, 13; 1771: DL, Jan 15, Apr 22; 1772: DL, Apr 24, Nov 12; 1773: DL, Mar 27, Apr 22, May 4; 1775: CG, May 8, 12; 1781: HAY, Aug 8; 1782: HAY, Jun 3, Jul 6; 1783: HAY, Jun 5, 30, Jul 2; 1784: HAY, Apr 30, May 10, Aug 26; 1785: KING'S, Jan 11, HAY, Feb 14, 21, Mar 10, Apr 15, Aug 11; 1797: CG, Nov 4; 1799: KING'S, Mar 26, May 2, DL, 8, CG, Dec 23; 1800: KING'S, Jan 11, 28, Feb 1, 11, 18, DL, Jun 2
Daigueville, Peter (dancer), 1768: DL, Nov 1, 2, 3, 16, 21, Dec 5, 10; 1769: DL, Jan 16, 18, 24, Sep 26, 30, Oct 14, 26, Nov 16, 20; 1770: DL, Jan 4, Apr 25, 27, 28, May 24, 30, Jun 4, Sep 22, 25, Oct 3, 4, 10, 25, Nov 3, 14, 19, Dec 7, 13; 1771: DL, Jan 15, Feb 4, Mar 4, 7, 12, HAY, Apr 6, DL, 22, May 1, 16, 24, Sep 21, Oct 26, Nov 18, Dec 4, 26; 1772: DL, Mar 17, 21, 26, Apr 24, 25, Jun 9, Sep 22, Oct 3, Nov 12, 21, Dec 4, 26; 1773: DL, Feb 25, Mar 25, 27, Apr 1, 22, May 4, 5, 10, Jun 2, Sep 25, Oct 21; 1774: DL, Feb 24, KING'S, Apr 28, CG, Oct 7, 15, Nov 19, Dec 1, 14, 16, 20, 27; 1775: CG, Jan 24, Mar 30, May 12, 17, 18, Sep 25, Oct 13, 18, 24, 26, Nov 9, 18, 21, Dec 7, 26; 1776: CG, Feb 5, Mar 4, 12, 25, Apr 13, May 3, 4, 6; 1777: CG, Apr 28, Oct 1, Nov 3, 11, 21, 25; 1778: CG, Jan 28, Feb 24, Apr 20, 21, May 9, Oct 14, 16, 22, 23, Nov 23, 25, Dec 12; 1779: CG, Jan 4, Mar 20, Apr 19, May 3, DL, 14, CG, 21, Sep 22, Oct 6, 8, 22, Nov 9, 23, Dec 17, 29; 1780: CG, Apr 17, May 6, 8, 16, 18; 1782: KING'S, Dec 12; 1783: KING'S, Feb 15, Mar 11; 1786: KING'S, Jan 24, Feb 18, Mar 23, Apr 1, 27; 1788: HAY, Aug 5; 1790: DL, Oct 26; 1791: PAN, Mar 19, 24, May 9, 17, DL, 20, PAN, Dec 17; 1792: HAY, Feb 14, Mar 10, Apr 14, Jul 25, DL, Nov 21; 1793: KING'S, Feb 26, Apr 6, 23, Jun 1, DL, 3, 7; 1794: KING'S, Apr 1, DL, May 16, KING'S, 31, DL, Jul 2, Oct 27, KING'S, Dec 6; 1797: DL, Nov 10; 1799: KING'S, Mar 26, Apr 18, May 2, DL, 8, KING'S, Jun 17; 1800: KING'S, Jan 11, 28, Feb 11, 25, Mar 4, 22, Apr 15, CG, May 2, DL, 14, KING'S, 29, Jun 21, Jul 19
Daigueville, Peter and Mrs (dancers), 1769: DL, Nov 23, Dec 28; 1770: DL, Jan 18; 1772: DL, Jun 6, 9
Daigueville, Sophia (dancer), 1792: DLKING'S, Jun 7, HAY, Jul 25, DL, Oct 13; 1795: DL, Feb 12, May 6
Daigueville, Sophia and George (dancers), 1795: DL, Jun 1
Daigueville's scholars (dancers), 1771: KING'S, Mar 12, DL, Apr 22, Nov 18; 1772: DL, Jan 11, Mar 21; 1773: DL, Apr 19, 22, May 6, 13; 1774: KING'S, Mar 24; 1775: CG, May 12; 1778: CG, May 9
Daiguevilles, Fanny, George, James Harvey, Lewis, and Sophia (dancers), 1792: DL, Dec 27
Daiguevilles, the young (dancers), 1787: DL, Jun 1, HAY, 13, 29, Jul 2, 6; 1788: DL, Feb 21, Sep 16, 23, Oct 4, 13, Nov 13; 1789: DL, Jan 17, May 19, 27, Oct 26, Nov 21, Dec 4, 9, 26; 1790: DL, Jan 23, Mar 8, 23, Apr 5, May 18, Jun 1, Dec 27; 1791: DL, May 20, 25, DLKING'S, Nov 16; 1792: DLKING'S, Jun 7, DL, Nov 2; 1793: DL, Jun 7
Dailey (jeweler), 1738: DL, May 12
Dailey, Mrs. See Daly, Mrs.
Daily, Mrs (actor), 1763: HAY, Jun 20
Daincourt, Lord. See Leke, Robert.
Dakers, Andrew (painter), 1659: CITY, Oct 29
Dal Labro (song), 1750: KING'S, Apr 10
Dal suo gentil sembiante (song), 1754: KING'S, Feb 28

Dalby (house servant), 1786: CG, Jun 1; 1787: CG, May 31; 1788: CG, May 24;
    1789: CG, Jun 6; 1790: CG, Jun 8
Dale (watchmaker), 1751: DL, Apr 29
Dale (watchmaker), 1754: DL, Apr 18
Dale, Thomas (physician), 1792: HAY, Apr 16
Dale, William (boxkeeper), 1777: DL, Jun 4; 1778: DL, May 19; 1779: DL, May 25;
    1780: DL, May 9; 1781: DL, May 18; 1782: DL, May 16; 1783: DL, May 23; 1784:
    DL, May 24; 1785: CG, Apr 25, DL, May 23; 1786: DL, May 26; 1787: DL, Jun 1;
    1788: DL, Jun 5; 1789: DL, Jun 9; 1790: DL, Jun 1; 1791: DL, May 25; 1792:
    DLKING'S, Jun 7; 1793: DL, Jun 3; 1795: DL, Jun 1; 1796: DL, Jun 11; 1797:
    DL, Jun 10; 1798: DL, Jun 13; 1799: DL, Jul 2; 1800: DL, Jun 13
Dale Jr, William (boxkeeper), 1788: DL, Jun 6; 1789: DL, Jun 10; 1796: DL, Jun
    15; 1797: DL, Jun 15; 1798: DL, Jun 9; 1799: DL, Jul 3; 1800: DL, Jun 14
Daley (sadler), 1776: DL, Jun 10
Dalkeith, Lady, 1711: QUEEN'S, Apr 25
Dall, Miss (actor, singer), 1790: CG, Feb 19, 24, 26, Mar 3, 17, 19, 26; 1791:
    CG, Feb 26, Mar 10, May 14, 20; 1792: CG, May 10, Oct 19, 27; 1793: CG, Mar
    1, HAY, Jun 12, 13, 17, Jul 9, 15, Aug 3, 6, 12, 16, 27, Sep 2
Dall, Nicholas Thomas (scene painter), 1757: CG, Sep 16, Dec 31; 1759: CG, Sep
    28; 1760: CG, Feb 2, 23, Sep 22, Dec 6; 1761: CG, Oct 3; 1768: CG, Mar 15;
    1769: CG, Oct 27; 1770: CG, Jan 27; 1771: CG, Dec 7; 1772: CG, Jan 31, Nov
    24, Dec 17; 1773: CG, Feb 10, Mar 27, Dec 3; 1774: CG, Feb 11, Mar 22, Nov
    19; 1775: CG, Apr 24, Dec 26; 1776: CG, Feb 26, Nov 12, 14, Dec 6, 26; 1777:
    CG, May 3; 1789: CG, Dec 21; 1790: CG, Nov 15; 1796: CG, Mar 15, Oct 24;
    1799: CG, May 13
Dall'Abaco, Giuseppe Marie Clement (violoncellist), 1736: HIC, Apr 15
Dallainval, L J C
--Embarras des Richesses, L', 1734: GF/HAY, Oct 26, HAY, Nov 25, GF/HAY, Dec 5,
    26; 1735: GF/HAY, Jan 21, Feb 28, Mar 18, HAY, 22, GF/HAY, May 1, 12, GF, 23;
    1738: HAY, Oct 9
Dallon (house servant), 1759: CG, Dec 22; 1760: CG, Apr 15
Dalmaine (embroiderer), 1750: DL, Apr 23; 1774: DL, Jun 2
Dalrymple, Mrs (house servant), 1782: CG, May 10; 1783: CG, May 28
Dalton (ticket taker), 1761: DL, May 25; 1762: DL, May 21; 1763: DL, May 16
Dalton, Dr John (author), 1738: DL, Mar 4; 1748: CG, Dec 10
Dalton, Miss (actor), 1791: HAY, Dec 26
Daly (actor), 1732: RIW/HAY, Sep 4
Daly (actor), 1779: HAY, Oct 13
Daly (Dailey), Mrs (actor), 1763: DL, Mar 24, HAY, Jun 27, Aug 1, Sep 5, 7
Daly, Richard (actor), 1779: CG, Mar 4, Apr 8, 20
Dalyrac, Nicolas (composer), 1787: CG, Apr 24; 1790: CG, Mar 8
Dama Demonio, e la Serva Diavolo, La (opera), 1727: KING'S, Apr 8
Dama Pastorella, La. See Salieri, Antonio, La Sifra.
Damaria (payee), 1775: DL, Nov 15
Damascene, Alexander (singer, composer), 1684: DLORDG, Aug 0; 1693: ATCOURT,
    Apr 30; 1694: ATCOURT, Apr 30
Dame Bienfaisante, La (dance), 1783: KING'S, May 8
Dame Dobson. See Ravenscroft, Edward.
Dame Gigogne (dance), 1726: LIF, Jul 5
Dame Invisible, La. See Hauteroche, Noel le Breton, Sieur de.
Dame of Honour (song), 1706: QUEEN'S, Apr 15, BF, Aug 27; 1715: DL, May 24, Jun
    2; 1722: RI, Aug 20; 1723: DL, Jul 26; 1724: RI, Jun 22
Dame Ragonde (dance), 1716: LIF, Oct 19; 1738: CG, Apr 10
Dame Ragonde and her eight Children (dance), 1702: DL, Aug 20; 1717: DL, Nov 12
Dame Ragonde and her Family (dance), 1716: DL, May 16, Oct 18
Dame Ragonde and her Two Sons (dance), 1725: LIF, May 3, 6
Damer, Anne Seymour, Mrs John (sculptor), 1780: DL, May 24; 1793: HAY, Dec 2
Damnation. See Stuart, Charles.
Damoiselles a la Mode, The. See Flecknoe, Richard.
Damon and Chloe (song), 1754: DL, May 15
Damon and Clora (song), 1779: HAY, Oct 18
Damon and Daphne. See Cibber, Theophilus.
Damon and Musidora (dance), 1782: CG, Dec 31; 1783: CG, Feb 13, Apr 30, Oct 1;
    1784: CG, Mar 11; 1785: CG, Apr 9
Damon and Phillida (dance), 1736: DL, Apr 30, May 6, 11, 21
Damon and Phillida. See Cibber, Colley.
Damon if you wilt believe me (song), 1684: DLORDG, Aug 0
Damon, let a friend (song), 1694: DG, May 0
Damport, Betty. See Davenport, Elizabeth.
Danby, Charles (actor, singer), 1776: DL, Nov 25; 1781: DL, Oct 19; 1785: DL,
    Apr 29, May 6, 19, Oct 26, 29; 1786: DL, Jan 6, Mar 9, May 25, Oct 7, Dec 5;
    1787: DL, Feb 1, Nov 3, 5; 1788: DL, May 1, Oct 16, 20, Nov 17, Dec 4; 1789:

215

DL, Jan 27, Oct 13, 28, Nov 13, 14, Dec 26; 1790: DL, Jan 8, Apr 16, 23, May 14, 15, 18, Oct 11, 26; 1791: DLKING'S, Sep 27, Oct 15, Nov 2, 5, 9, 16, 25, 28; 1792: DLKING'S, Feb 18, Mar 29, May 23, DL, Oct 11, 13, 18, Nov 21, Dec 13, 26; 1793: DL, Mar 7, May 10; 1794: DL, Apr 21, 28, May 1, 16, 23, Jun 9, 12, Sep 27, Oct 14, 27, 31, Nov 15, Dec 20, 29; 1795: DL, Jan 8, May 6, Oct 1, 30, Nov 11, 23, Dec 4, 10; 1796: DL, Jan 18, Mar 12, Apr 30; 1797: DL, Nov 8, Dec 9; 1798: DL, Jan 16, Feb 20, Oct 6, 11, Nov 14, 26, Dec 4, 29; 1799: DL, Jan 19, Feb 4, Mar 2, Apr 16, 23, 29, May 4, 24, Jun 28, Oct 12, 14, Nov 14, Dec 11; 1800: DL, Jan 1, Mar 11, Apr 29, May 10, Jun 5
Danby, John (singer, composer), 1776: DL, Nov 25; 1780: DL, Nov 23; 1783: DL, Oct 13; 1784: DL, May 12; 1785: DL, Apr 22, May 5, 19; 1786: DL, May 5, 25, Dec 6; 1787: DL, May 30, Nov 6; 1788: DL, May 30; 1792: CG, May 11
Danby, Lord, 1728: HAY, Feb 16
Danby, Master (singer), 1792: HAY, Jul 25; 1799: DL, May 24, Oct 12, 14, Nov 14, Dec 11; 1800: DL, Jan 1, Mar 11, Apr 29
Dance a la Ronde (dance), 1749: HAY, May 2, 11, 13, 29, 31; 1750: HAY, Feb 16
Dance by a Switzer (dance), 1710: GR, Aug 5
Dance du Village, La (dance), 1755: HAY, Sep 1, 9, 11, 15
Dance in Fetters (dance), 1791: HAY, Dec 12
Dance in Imitation of Mlle D'Subligny (dance), 1703: DG, Apr 30, DL, Nov 9; 1704: DL, Aug 15
Dance, George (composer), 1798: CG, Oct 24
Dance, Grand (dance), 1704: DL, Jan 4; 1705: QUEEN'S, Apr 26, Nov 17, Dec 12, LIF/QUEN, 26; 1716: LIF, May 10; 1717: LIF, Apr 25; 1718: LIF, May 6; 1724: DL, Nov 14; 1725: LIF, Mar 13; 1726: LIF, Mar 21, Apr 30, May 2, 10; 1728: LIF, May 6; 1729: LIF, Mar 20; 1730: DL, Apr 14, LIF, 27, DL, 29, May 19; 1731: LIF, May 3, 5; 1733: HAY, Mar 16; 1735: HAY, Apr 11, GF/HAY, May 2, Jun 2; 1738: CG, Mar 23, DL, Nov 30, Dec 7, 20; 1739: DL, Jan 6; 1740: CG, Apr 23; 1741: DL, May 4, TC, Aug 4; 1742: LIF, Dec 6; 1743: DL, Nov 8; 1744: DL, Dec 17, 19, 20, 26, 27, 28; 1745: DL, Jan 1, 8, 10, 11, 16, 22, 29, Feb 5, 6, 9, Mar 11, Apr 6, 26, Oct 8, 17; 1746: DL, Feb 6, 7, 20, 24, 27, Apr 3; 1748: KING'S, Nov 8, 12; 1750: DL, Nov 2; 1753: HAY, Mar 31; 1758: DL, Apr 24; 1759: DL, May 9, 11, 14; 1760: HAY, Mar 27; 1762: HAY, Mar 16; 1766: DL, Feb 3; 1772: KING'S, Nov 21, Dec 5, 8; 1775: DL, May 8; 1777: DL, Apr 25, 26, May 1, 2, 3, 6; 1778: DL, Nov 2, 27, Dec 23; 1779: DL, May 5, 17; 1780: DL, Feb 28, Mar 13; 1782: CG, Mar 19, Dec 20; 1784: CG, Mar 6, Oct 27; 1785: CG, Feb 12, Nov 23, Dec 7; 1786: CG, Feb 2, Mar 11, Apr 24, May 11; 1787: CG, Feb 9, DL, 15; 1788: DL, Sep 18; 1789: CG, Feb 19, Apr 2, Nov 19; 1790: DL, Feb 18, CG, May 24, DL, Sep 30; 1791: DLKING'S, Nov 14; 1795: CG, Jun 6; 1796: CG, Mar 15, Jun 7
Dance, James (actor, author), 1741: GF, Nov 9; 1745: GF, Jan 7, Feb 7, Mar 12, 14, 23, 26, 28, Apr 17; 1746: CG, May 2, DL, 9; 1747: GF, Mar 23; 1748: CG, Oct 17; see also Love, James
--Hermit, The; or, Harlequin at Rhodes, 1766: DL, Jan 6, 7, 8, 9, 10, 11, 13, 14, 15, 16, 17, 18, 20, 21, 22, 24, 25, 27, 28, 29, Feb 1, 3, 4, 5, 6, 7, 8, 10, 15, Sep 27, Oct 2, 4, 7, 8, 9, 11, 14, 16, 20, 22, 24, Nov 13, 17; 1767: DL, Sep 23, 24; 1768: DL, Apr 18; 1769: DL, Apr 12, 21, 26, May 5
--Ladies' Frolick, The, 1770: DL, May 7, Oct 25, 27, Nov 13, 20; 1771: DL, Jan 31, Feb 2, 23, May 21, 25, 30; 1774: DL, Apr 15, 21, May 16, 23; 1775: DL, Mar 23, Apr 3; 1783: DL, May 12, Dec 2, 12; 1784: DL, Apr 17, May 1; 1785: DL, Jan 12; 1790: CG, Jun 1
--Pamela, 1741: GF, Sep 22, Nov 9, 10, 11, 12, 13, 14, 16, 17, 18, 19, 20, 21, 24, 27, Dec 4, 9, 14, 18, HAY, 28; 1742: GF, Feb 26
--Witches, The; or, A Trip to Naples, 1771: DL, Dec 26, 27, 28, 30; 1772: DL, Jan 1, 2, 4, 6, 7, 9, 10, 13, 15, 17, Feb 3, 6, 7, 8, 18, 19, 20, 25, Mar 3, 16, 17, Apr 27, May 23, Oct 3, 8, 30, Nov 4, 9, 16, Dec 3, 9, 14; 1789: DL, Dec 26
--Witches, The; or, Harlequin Cherokee, 1715: DL, Jul 8; 1762: DL, Nov 23, 24, 25, 26, 27, 29, 30, Dec 1, 2, 3, 4, 6, 7, 8, 9, 10, 11, 13, 14, 16, 20, 21, 22, 23, 27, 28, 29, 30; 1763: DL, Jan 1, 8, 10, 14, Feb 2, 21, 28, Mar 5, 14, 22, Apr 7, 15, 21, May 6, 10, 26, Oct 28, 31, Nov 1, 2, 3; 1764: DL, May 12, 24, 29, Sep 25, 29, Oct 4, 13, 16, 18, 19, 30; 1765: DL, Apr 13, 16, 18, May 11, 23, Sep 24, 26, 28, Oct 3, 11; 1766: DL, Mar 31
Dance, James and Mrs (actors), 1767: DL, Jan 24
Dancer, Ann, Mrs William (actor), 1766: HAY, Jul 12, KING'S, Aug 8, 13, 18, 25, 27, Sep 5, 9, 13, 15, 19; 1767: HAY, Jun 22, 26, 30, Jul 6, 8, 15, 22, 31, Aug 5, 10, 14, 21, 26, 28, 31, DL, Sep 12, HAY, 16, 18, 21, DL, Oct 14, CG, 16, DL, 21, 22, 27, 29, Nov 5, 11, 20, 21, 24, 26, Dec 1, 15, 22; 1768: DL, Jan 2, 6, 14, 23, Feb 6, 27, Mar 15, 21, 24, Apr 27, May 12, Sep 22; 1777: CG, Oct 16
Dancer, John Wimperis (actor, singer), 1769: HAY, Sep 19; 1770: HAY, May 9, 16, 18, 23, 25, 28, 30, Jun 1, 5, 18, 22, 27, Jul 9, Aug 1, 8, 22, 31, Sep 3, 13,

27, Oct 1, 5; 1771: HAY, May 15, 17, 20, 22, 23, 27, 29, 31, Jun 5, 7, 10,
21, 26, Jul 5, 10, 12, Aug 19, 26, 28, Sep 16, 18, 19, 20; 1772: HAY, May 20,
22, 27, Jun 8, 15, Jul 3, 6, 10, 15, Aug 4, 10, Sep 8, 17, 18; 1776: CHR, Sep
23, 25, 27, Oct 2, 4, 7, 9, 11, 14, 16, 18; 1782: HAY, Mar 21
Dancer, John, 1659: NONE, Sep 0
--Aminta (pastoral), 1659: NONE, Sep 0
Dancer, Miss (actor), 1783: HAY, Sep 17; 1787: DL, May 3, Jun 1; 1788: HAY, Sep
30
Dancer, William (actor), 1749: HAY, May 19; 1750: NWC, Apr 16
Dancers Damned, The; or The Devil to Pay at the Old House, 1755: DL, Nov 12, 14
Dances upon the Head of a Mast (dance), 1701: BF, Aug 25
Dancey (Dansey), Miss (dancer, actor), 1731: BFB, Aug 26; 1732: HAY, Feb 16,
Mar 2, 17, Apr 27; 1733: DL/HAY, Dec 27; 1734: DL/HAY, Jan 12, Feb 22,
BFRLCH, Aug 24; 1735: DL, Jan 11, May 2, LIF, Jun 12, DL, Oct 28; 1736: DL,
May 20, 26, CG, Nov 3, 26; 1737: CG, Feb 14, BF, Aug 23; 1738: CG, Feb 13,
16, Apr 18, 27, May 10, Jun 30, Jul 11, Oct 30, Nov 18, 21, 27, Dec 4; 1739:
CG, Jan 1, 8, 20, Mar 20, May 9, 17, Sep 10, 22, Oct 3, Dec 4, 6; 1740: CG,
Jan 10
Dancey, Mrs (dancer, actor), 1732: HAY, Feb 16; 1733: BFCGBH, Sep 4, DL/HAY,
Nov 26; 1734: DL, Oct 21; 1735: DL, May 6, Oct 7, Nov 20; 1736: BFFH, Aug 23;
1737: CG, Apr 11, BF, Aug 23, SF, Sep 7, CG, Oct 5; 1738: CG, Aug 29; 1739:
CG, Feb 9, May 9
Dancing Academy (dance), 1762: CG, Apr 23; 1771: CG, Apr 12
Dancing Dogs, 1707: MF, May 13; 1718: RI, Aug 30, SF, Sep 6
D'Ancourt, Florent Carton, 1749: CG, Mar 29; 1780: HAY, Apr 5
--Chevalier a la Mode, Le, 1722: HAY, Apr 5
--Colin Maillard, 1722: HAY, Apr 9
--Ete des Coquettes, L', 1722: HAY, Jan 18, Feb 19
--Mary Retrouve, Le, 1721: HAY, Jan 13, Apr 10
--Vacances des Procureurs, Les, 1721: HAY, Jan 26, Feb 23; 1722: HAY, Jan 9;
1725: HAY, Feb 8, Mar 11
Dandham, Miss (dancer), 1733: GF, Oct 29
Dandrige (householder), 1741: DL, Mar 14
Daney (house servant), 1766: DL, May 19
D'Anfoy (dancer), 1730: GF, Mar 10, 14
Danger is over, The (song), 1694: DL, Feb 0
Dangerfield (boxkeeper), 1792: DLKING'S, Jun 15; 1793: DL, Jun 6; 1795: DL, Jun
6; 1796: DL, Jun 13; 1797: DL, Jun 16; 1798: DL, Jun 14
Dangeville (dancer), 1720: KING'S, Mar 24, 26, LIF, Apr 4, KING'S, 26, 29, May
6, 9, 10, 27, 31
Daniel (actor), 1782: HAY, Mar 4; 1787: HAY, Jan 8
Daniel-Malone-James Booth, 1743: TCD/BFTD, Aug 4
Daniel-Smith Booth, 1744: MFDSB, May 1
Daniel, Mary, Mrs William (actor, dancer), 1742: DL, Dec 27; 1743: JS, Feb 22,
TCD/BFTD, Aug 4; 1744: JS, Mar 16, HAY, Apr 23, GF, Dec 4, 10, 26; 1745: GF,
Feb 14, 26, Mar 30, Apr 24, JS, Dec 26; 1746: CG, Apr 22, Jun 16, 23; 1747:
CG, May 12, Dec 17; 1748: CG, Mar 28, HAY, Apr 30, May 2, BFLYY, Aug 24,
SFLYYW, Sep 7, BHB, Oct 1, HAY, Nov 14, JS, Dec 20, NWC, 26, JS, 26; 1749:
SOU, Jan 2, HAY, Apr 29, BFCB, Aug 23; 1750: HAY, Feb 16
Daniel, William (actor), 1736: SF, Sep 7; 1743: JS, Mar 16, TCD/BFTD, Aug 4;
1744: JS, Mar 16, GF, Dec 26; 1745: GF, Feb 14, Mar 30, Apr 15; 1746: SFW,
Sep 8, SOU, Oct 21; 1748: SOU, Oct 31, JS, Dec 20, NWC, 26; 1749: SOU, Feb
13, JS, Mar 27, HAY, Apr 29; 1750: HAY, Feb 16
Daniel, William and Mary (actors), 1748: HAY, Nov 14
Daniell, Thomas (landscape painter), 1798: CG, Nov 12
Daniels, Alicia (actor), 1791: DL, May 26, DLKING'S, Oct 3, 15; 1792: DLKING'S,
Apr 10
Daniels, Miss (dancer, singer), 1795: DL, Feb 12; 1796: DL, Oct 1, 29; 1798:
DL, Jan 16, Feb 20, May 16, Oct 6, Nov 14, Dec 6; 1799: DL, Jan 19, Feb 5,
Oct 14, Nov 11, Dec 2; 1800: DL, Mar 6, 10
Danish Envoy, 1703: DL, Jun 22
Danish King, 1768: CG, Oct 10
Danish Song, 1715: SH, Jun 30
Danish Woman and her Company, 1698: BF, Aug 25
Dannell (actor), 1784: HAY, Nov 16
Danny (house servant), 1759: DL, May 22; 1765: DL, May 22
Danoyer. See Denoyer.
Danse des Sabots (dance), 1785: KING'S, Jun 9, 14
Danzi, Francesca (singer), 1777: KING'S, Nov 8; 1778: KING'S, Feb 7, Mar 19,
Apr 4, May 30, Jun 13, 20
Daphne and Amintor. See Bickerstaffe, Isaac.
DaPonte, Lorenzo (librettist, impresario), 1794: KING'S, Feb 1, Mar 1, Jun 23;

217

1795: KING'S, Jan 27, May 26, 28; 1796: KING'S, May 24, Jun 14, Jul 23, Dec 20; 1797: KING'S, Jan 10, Feb 25, Mar 11, Jun 8, 10, Dec 12; 1798: KING'S, Feb 20, Mar 10, Dec 8; 1799: KING'S, Jan 22, May 14; 1800: KING'S, Feb 8, Mar 18, Jun 28

Darastanti, Sga. See Durastanti, Margherita.

D'Arblay, Frances, 1795: DL, Mar 21

--Edwy and Elgiva, 1795: DL, Jan 5, Mar 5, 7, 10, 12, 14, 16, 19, 21

Darby (house servant), 1760: CG, May 19; 1762: CG, May 21

Darby, Lord. See Osborne, Thomas.

D'Arcy (actor, singer), 1798: HAY, Jun 23, Jul 10, 13, 21, Aug 11, 21, 23, 28, Sep 17

D'Arcy, Miss (actor), 1770: CG, Dec 7; 1771: CG, Jan 29, Feb 11, Apr 16, Sep 27, Oct 4

Darius. See Ariosti, Attilio.

Darius, King of Persia (droll, anon), 1722: BFLSH, Aug 25; 1723: MO, Apr 15

Darius, King of Persia. See Crowne, John.

Darius, King of Persia; or, The Noble Englishman (farce, anon), 1741: BFLW, Aug 22

Darley (printer), 1772: CG, Dec 28

Darley, William (actor, singer), 1781: CG, Sep 24, Nov 12, Dec 17, 26; 1782: CG, Feb 19, Mar 14, 16, 18, Apr 30, May 6, 8, 17, 20, 27, HAY, Jun 12, 18, Aug 17, Sep 18, CG, Oct 7, 11, 22, Nov 18, 25, Dec 27; 1783: CG, May 19, 23, 24, 28, Sep 22, Oct 6, 14, Nov 8; 1784: CG, Jan 29, Feb 7, 17, Mar 27, Apr 17, 26, May 24, 26, Sep 17, 20, Oct 4, 12, 18, 25, Nov 6, 12, 16, Dec 6, 27; 1785: CG, Mar 7, 30, Apr 1, 6, 12, 22, 25, May 4, 7, 11, 12, 26, Sep 23, 30, Oct 3, 14, 17, 21, Nov 4, 14, 21, Dec 5, 26; 1786: CG, Jan 6, 18, Feb 7, Mar 14, 18, 25, Apr 19, May 6, 9, 22, 27, 31, Oct 9, 16, 21, 23, 26, Nov 17, 22, 23, 24, 30, Dec 5, 23, 26; 1787: CG, Jan 13, Feb 9, Mar 12, 31, Apr 10, 24, 27, May 9, 12, 21, 24, Sep 19, 21, 24, 26, Oct 1, 3, 5, 18, 22, 31, Nov 7, Dec 3, 6; 1788: CG, Jan 14, 28, Feb 5, Mar 24, 26, 29, Apr 1, 11, 30, May 16, 21, 22, Sep 17, 22, 24, 29, Oct 3, 8, 16, 17, 21, 22, Nov 1, Dec 15, 26, 29; 1789: CG, Jan 3, 20, Feb 14, 19, 24, Mar 3, 14, 16, Apr 15, 21, May 5, 28, 29, Jun 8, 10, 11, Sep 14, 16, 18, 21, Oct 12, 13, 16, 21, 23, 24, 30, Nov 14, 21, Dec 3, 12, 21; 1790: CG, Jan 23, Mar 8, 22, 27, Apr 6, 12, 21, May 5, 6, 7, 24, Jun 1, 4; 1791: CG, Sep 12, 16, 19, 20, 23, 26, 28, 30, Oct 3, 10, 20, Nov 1, 2, 7, 19, 25, Dec 10, 15, 22; 1792: CG, Feb 23, 25, 28, Mar 13, Apr 12, 18, May 11, 15, 19, 22, 23, Sep 19, 20, 21, 26, 28, Oct 5, 8, 19, 25, 29, Dec 20, 26; 1793: CG, Jan 9, Mar 23, Apr 9, 10, 11, 24, May 3, 10, 11, 15, 21, Jun 5, 12

Darling (actor), 1785: HAY, Apr 25

Darlington, Countess of, (spectator), 1723: KING'S, Feb 23

Darraugh, George, 1743: BFFP, Aug 23

Darrel, 1762: DL, Nov 26

Dartmouth St, 1793: DL, Jun 1

Dartmouth, Lady, 1732: BLA, Jun 24

Dashwood (doorkeeper), 1800: DL, Jun 14

D'Auberval (Doberval, Duberval), Jean (dancer), 1764: KING'S, Jan 24, Feb 7, 14, 21, Mar 20, 29, 31, Apr 14; 1783: KING'S, Dec 6; 1784: KING'S, Jan 17, Feb 3, 7, 26, Mar 6, 11, 18, 25, Apr 24, May 13; 1788: KING'S, May 29; 1791: PAN, Feb 17, Mar 19, 24, Apr 30, May 3, 9, Dec 17, 31; 1792: HAY, Feb 14, Mar 10, Apr 14; 1795: DL, May 20; 1799: KING'S, Mar 26, Apr 18; 1800: KING'S, Jan 11

D'Auberval, Mme Jean (dancer), 1783: KING'S, Dec 6; 1791: PAN, Feb 17, Mar 22, 24, May 9, 17, Jun 10, Dec 17; 1792: HAY, Feb 14, Mar 10, Apr 14; see also Theodore, Mme

Daughter of Gods (song), 1791: CG, Mar 23

D'Aumont, Duke (French ambassador), 1713: SH, May 15, DL, Jun 3, Sep 24, Oct 15

Dauphin Minuet (dance), 1772: DL, Mar 17; 1773: DL, Apr 24

Dause, Mrs (dancer), 1760: CG, Sep 22

D'Auvigne (ballet master), 1773: KING'S, Feb 2

Davenant, Charles (proprietor, author), 1671: DG, Nov 9; 1682: DG, Nov 9; 1698: DL, May 3

--Circe (opera), 1677: DG, May 12; 1682: DG, Jan 19, Jun 10; 1684: NONE, Sep 0; 1689: DG, Jun 13; 1690: ATCOURT, Nov 7; 1698: NONE, Sep 0; 1701: LIF, Jun 24; 1704: LIF, Jul 14; 1706: LIF/QUEN, Apr 1; 1719: LIF, Apr 11, 13, 14, 15, 21, 24, May 18

Davenant, Dr (spectator), 1697: LIF, Feb 27, DLORLIF, Sep 15; 1700: DLORLIF, Jan 23

Davenant, Lady, 1671: DG, Nov 9

Davenant, Thomas (manager), 1692: NONE, Jan 19; 1693: DL, Mar 0

Davenant, Sir William (manager, playwright), 1660: COCKPIT, Oct 8, REDBULL, Nov 5, SALSBURY, 15, VERE, 19, SALSBURY, Dec 12; 1661: LIF, Jun 28, Jul 2, Aug

24, LIF/MT, Nov 1; 1662: LIF, Feb 15; 1663: NONE, Mar 0, May 0, LIF, Jul 22,
Oct 24, Dec 10, 22; 1664: ATCOURT, Jan 0, LIF, Sep 10, Nov 5; 1665: LIF, Apr
3; 1666: ATCOURT, Dec 17, LIF, 28; 1667: LIF, Jan 7, NONE, Feb 13, LIF, Apr
19, NONE, Sep 0, LIF, 12, Oct 16, Nov 6, 7; 1668: LIF, Jan 6, Mar 26,
BRIDGES, Apr 7, LIF, 8, Aug 31; 1671: DG, Nov 9; 1675: DLORDG, Dec 2; 1706:
QUEEN'S, Jul 31; 1712: DL, Jan 7, 11, Nov 5; 1718: DL, Jun 11, Aug 1; 1721:
DL, Aug 22; 1722: DL, Jan 3; 1723: DL, Jan 7, Jun 6; 1724: DL, Jan 7, Oct 30;
1725: DL, Oct 30; 1726: LIF, Jul 15, Aug 19; 1727: DL, Jan 24, May 22, Dec
29; 1729: DL, May 28, Oct 30; 1730: DL, Nov 30; 1731: DL, Jun 7, Dec 2; 1732:
DL, Dec 26; 1733: DL, Jan 24; 1737: DL, Feb 10, Apr 11, 14, 25; 1745: GF, Feb
14, Apr 15, Dec 4; 1747: GF, Jan 16; 1750: DL, Jan 1; 1775: CG, Nov 3
--Law against Lovers, The, 1662: LIF, Feb 15, 18, ATCOURT, Dec 17
--Love and Danger; or, The Mistaken Jealousy, 1692: NONE, Sep 0; 1703: DL, Nov
6, 8, 17
--Love and Honour, 1661: LIF/MT, Oct 21, 23, 25, Nov 1, 11; 1674: DG, Sep 0
--Man's the Master, The, 1668: LIF, Mar 26, Apr 3, 23, May 7; 1673: DG, Aug 9;
1726: LIF, Jul 15, 19; 1775: CG, Nov 3, 11, 15, Dec 28; 1786: HAY, Aug 29
--Playhouse To Be Let, The, 1663: NONE, May 0, LIF, Aug 0; 1706: QUEEN'S, Jul
31
--Rivals, The, 1664: LIF, Sep 10, Dec 2; 1665: LIF, Jan 6; 1667: LIF, Nov 19
--Siege of Rhodes, The, 1661: LIF, Jun 28, Jul 1, 2, 3, 5, 8, 10, Nov 15; 1662:
LIF, May 20, Dec 27; 1663: NONE, Mar 0; 1667: NONE, Feb 13, LIF, May 21
--Siege of Rhodes, Part II, The, 1661: LIF, Jun 29, Jul 2, 4, 6, 9, 11, Nov 15;
1662: LIF, Jan 9, May 20, Dec 27; 1677: DG, Feb 24
--Unfortunate (Ungrateful) Lovers, The, 1659: NONE, Sep 0; 1660: REDBULL, Aug
14, VERE, Nov 19; 1664: LIF, Mar 7; 1667: LIF, Sep 11; 1668: LIF, Apr 8, Dec
3; 1674: DG, Oct 0
--Wits, The, 1661: LIF, Aug 15, 16, 17, 19, 20, 21, 22, 23, 24; 1667: LIF, Apr
18, 20, ATCOURT, May 2; 1669: LIF, Jan 18; 1672: DG, Aug 21; 1726: LIF, Aug
19
Davencourt (dancer), 1705: QUEEN'S, Dec 12
Davenett (house servant), 1789: CG, Jun 5
Davenett, Harriett (actor, dancer, singer), 1778: DL, Sep 24; 1779: DL, Mar 13,
Sep 25, 28, Oct 7, 30, Nov 1, Dec 27; 1780: DL, Jan 11, 20, Apr 15, 17, 26,
CG, Sep 25, DL, Oct 23; 1781: CG, Jan 25, Feb 24, Mar 8, 24, Apr 30, May 3,
10, Oct 5, 16, Dec 5, 17; 1782: CG, Jan 11, 18, 22, Feb 9, 21, Apr 1, 9, 10,
23, 27, May 8, 27, 29, DL, Jun 1, CG, Oct 3, 8, 19, 22, Nov 18; 1783: CG, Jan
3, Feb 25, Apr 7, 22, May 3, 17, 20, 26, 28, Sep 24, Oct 2, 6, 16, 27, 31,
Nov 8; 1784: CG, Jan 5, 9, 14, 29, Feb 12, 18, 20, Mar 16, May 1, 7, 15, 21,
28, Sep 20, Oct 4, 8, 12, 22, 25, 28, Dec 2; 1785: CG, Jan 14, 21, Apr 6, 13,
25, May 13, Sep 23, Oct 7, 10, 17, 22, Nov 2, 14, Dec 13, 14, 15, 26; 1786:
CG, Jan 18, Feb 16, Mar 23, 27, May 3, 4, 15, 18, 20, 24, 26, DL, Jun 7, CG,
Oct 6, 23, Nov 13, Dec 15, 21; 1787: CG, Jan 2, Mar 1, Apr 10, 11, May 28,
Sep 19, 24, Oct 1, 22, Nov 14, Dec 3, 21, 26; 1788: CG, Jan 18, Feb 26, Apr
21, May 27, Sep 17, 22, 29, Nov 21, 26, 28, Dec 26, 29; 1789: CG, Apr 30, May
6, Sep 14, Oct 12, Nov 12, 13, 19, Dec 2; 1790: CG, Mar 27, May 7, 27, 31,
Jun 16, Sep 13, 15, 29, Oct 6, Nov 26; 1791: CG, Apr 11, 30, May 10, 24, 26,
Jun 3, Sep 21, 26, Oct 3, 10, Dec 21, 22; 1792: CG, Jan 16, 19, Feb 28, Mar
31, May 10, 22, Sep 20, Oct 8, 19, 29; 1793: CG, Sep 30, Oct 7, Nov 11, Dec
9, 27; 1794: CG, Apr 30; 1798: CG, Mar 19
Davenport (actor), 1770: HAY, Oct 29
Davenport (dancer), 1729: BFR, Aug 25, HAY, Dec 27; 1730: HAY, Mar 20, 30, Apr
20, Jun 27, Jul 17, SFP, Sep 9, SF, 14, HAY, Oct 21, Nov 16, Dec 28; 1731:
HAY, Jan 18, Feb 3, 26, Mar 5, 19, 24, Apr 22, May 12, 13; 1732: HAY, Mar 8,
May 12, BFMMO, Aug 23, DL, Sep 23, 28, Oct 19, Nov 17, Dec 22, 26; 1733: DL,
Feb 12, Mar 26, 31, Apr 16, 20, May 7, 14, CG, Aug 9, 14, 16, 17, 21, BFMMO,
23, DL, Oct 10, 12, 24, Nov 13, 26, 27, Dec 5; 1734: DL, Jan 1, Feb 4, Mar 7,
DL/LIF, 11, DL/HAY, 12, 16, 18, DL/LIF, Apr 1, DL/HAY, 1, DL, 15, DL/HAY, 26,
DL, 29, DL/HAY, May 1, 8, DL, 15, 16, DL/HAY, 22, 23, HAY, 27, LIF, 29, HAY,
Jun 19, 21, 24, 28, Jul 10, 19, 31, Aug 7, 14, 16, LIF, 20, HAY, 21, BFFO,
24, DL, Sep 7, 10, 19, 24, 26, Oct 3, 5, 8, 10, 17, 21, 22, 25, 28, Nov 1,
16, 22, Dec 9, 11, 12, 17, 21; 1735: DL, Jan 17, 18, 21, 28, Feb 5, 13, 14,
18, Mar 3, 15, 25, Apr 7, 11, 25, May 14, 17, Jun 5, Jul 1, LIF, 11, GF/HAY,
18, 22, DL, Sep 15, Oct 1, 7, 22, 31, Nov 13, 15, 17, 20, 25, Dec 6, 18;
1736: DL, Jan 3, Feb 28, Mar 22, 27, Apr 6, 30, May 14, 15, 21, LIF, Jun 16,
CG, Nov 26; 1737: CG, Feb 14; 1738: CG, May 4; 1739: CG, May 21, DL, Oct 10,
Nov 28; 1740: DL, Feb 13, Apr 11, GF, Oct 29, Nov 13, 17, 18, 27, Dec 1, 15;
1741: DL, May 14, CG, Oct 17, Nov 26, 30; 1742: CG, Jan 8, Feb 22, Mar 9;
1744: DL, May 23; 1747: DL, Jan 24
Davenport, Elizabeth (actor), 1664: BRIDGES, Nov 0; 1667: BRI/COUR, Feb 0,
BRIDGES, Oct 19; 1675: DL, Apr 30
Davenport, Frances (actor), 1664: BRIDGES, Nov 0; 1667: BRI/COUR, Feb 0,

BRIDGES, Oct 19; <u>1668</u>: BRIDGES, Apr 7

Davenport, George Gosling (actor), <u>1794</u>: CG, Sep 19, Oct 7, 8, 20, 23, 30, Nov 6, 24; <u>1795</u>: CG, Jan 8, 31, Feb 3, 5, Mar 19, Apr 8, 29, May 14, 19, Jun 2, 4, 6, 13, 15, Sep 14, 18, 21, 23, 30, Oct 7, 8, 9, 16, 19, 22, 24, Nov 7, 9, 16, 25, 27, Dec 2, 5, 7, 9, 21, 22, 29; <u>1796</u>: CG, Jan 13, 23, Mar 14, 15, 30, Apr 19, 29, May 4, 12, Jun 7, Sep 12, 16, 17, 19, 26, 30, Oct 5, 6, 13, 14, 18, 20, 21, 25, Nov 19, 21, 24, Dec 9, 17, 19, 27, 31; <u>1797</u>: CG, Feb 18, Apr 8, 19, May 22, HAY, Jun 12, CG, 13, HAY, 17, 20, 21, 22, 23, 24, 29, Jul 6, 10, Aug 3, 9, 28, 31, Sep 2, 9, 12, CG, 18, 25, 29, Oct 2, 6, 11, 20, 25, Nov 2, 3, 7, 8, 9, 13, 15, 20, 23, 29, Dec 23, 27, 28; <u>1798</u>: CG, Feb 6, 9, 13, Mar 31, Apr 11, 19, 27, May 8, 15, 16, 28, 30, Jun 4, HAY, 12, 13, 16, 20, 21, 27, Jul 14, 21, Aug 6, 7, 11, 14, 21, 29, Sep 3, 10, CG, 17, 19, 26, 28, Oct 3, 8, 11, 22, 30, Nov 1, 6, 9, 10, 17, 20, 21; <u>1799</u>: CG, Jan 24, 25, 26, Apr 12, 16, 30, May 6, 15, Jun 7, HAY, 15, 19, 20, 22, 24, 25, 27, 29, Jul 2, 5, 16, 17, 20, 26, Aug 10, 15, 17, 20, 21, Sep 10, CG, 18, 20, 23, 25, 27, 30, Oct 2, 4, 7, 10, 11, 25, 29, 31, Nov 8, 9, 13, 14, 30, Dec 7, 30; <u>1800</u>: CG, Jan 16, 21, 27, Feb 8, 19, Mar 27, Apr 5, 30, May 2, 13, 23, 30, HAY, Jun 13, 14, 16, 17, 19, 20, 21, 27, 28, Jul 5, 26, Aug 7, 12, 20, 23, 27, 29, Sep 3, 4, 5

Davenport, George Gosling and Mary Ann (actors), <u>1797</u>: CG, Oct 11

Davenport, Hester (actor), <u>1661</u>: LIF, Jun 28, Aug 15, 24, LIF/MT, Oct 21; <u>1662</u>: LIF, Jan 9, Feb 18, Apr 2, May 20, ATCOURT, Dec 1, LIF, 27; <u>1663</u>: LIF, Jan 1, 8; <u>1665</u>: LIF, Apr 3

Davenport, J (publisher), <u>1797</u>: KING'S, Apr 27, Dec 9; <u>1800</u>: KING'S, Apr 24

Davenport, Mary Ann, Mrs George Gosling (actor, dancer), <u>1794</u>: CG, Sep 24, Oct 14, 20, 21, Dec 8, 9, 31; <u>1795</u>: CG, Jan 23, 29, Feb 14, Mar 28, Apr 8, 23, 28, 29, May 1, 13, 29, Jun 13, 16, Sep 14, 16, 18, 21, 28, Oct 2, 5, 14, 15, 19, 24, 30, Nov 7, 9, 14, 18, 23, 30, Dec 5, 9, 15, 29; <u>1796</u>: CG, Jan 2, 9, 23, Mar 14, 19, Apr 1, 5, 20, 29, May 10, 20, 23, 27, Jun 7, Sep 14, 16, 17, 19, 21, 26, Oct 5, 17, 20, 29, Nov 7, 24, Dec 13, 15, 26, 27; <u>1797</u>: CG, Feb 18, 20, 27, Apr 29, May 9, 16, 17, 23, Jun 2, 12, HAY, 12, 13, 20, 24, 28, 29, Jul 13, 15, Aug 8, 23, 24, Sep 8, 11, CG, 18, 20, 27, 29, Oct 11, 20, 21, 25, 28, Nov 2, 7, 8, 11, 15, 18, 20, 22, 23, Dec 12, 19, 23; <u>1798</u>: CG, Jan 9, Feb 9, 20, Mar 17, Apr 13, 21, 27, May 1, 7, 8, 10, 16, 19, 22, 24, 31, Jun 7, HAY, 13, 14, 15, 18, 20, 21, 27, 28, 30, Jul 5, 6, 17, Aug 3, 4, 11, 14, 29, Sep 10, CG, 17, 19, 21, 28, Oct 3, 8, 11, 31, Nov 5, 21, Dec 29; <u>1799</u>: CG, Jan 5, 12, 17, 25, 28, Mar 14, Apr 8, 12, 16, 26, 27, 30, May 4, 24, 25, 31, HAY, Jun 15, 17, 18, 20, 21, 24, 25, 26, 28, Jul 6, 9, 16, 30, Aug 5, 10, 17, CG, Sep 16, 18, 25, 30, Oct 4, 7, 10, 16, 17, 18, 21, 25, 31, Nov 11, 30, Dec 4, 7, 30; <u>1800</u>: CG, Jan 29, Feb 8, 19, Apr 5, 15, 26, May 10, 12, 17, 20, Jun 12, HAY, 13, 14, 18, 21, 28, Jul 1, 5, 7, 15, 26, Aug 8, 12, 23, Sep 3, 13

Davenport, Miss (actor), <u>1734</u>: DL/HAY, Apr 26

Davenport, Mr and Mrs (dancers), <u>1734</u>: DL, Jan 14, 16, 22, LIF, May 9, DL, 16, DL/HAY, 22, LIF, 23, DL/HAY, 23, HAY, 27, JS, 31; <u>1735</u>: GF/HAY, Jul 18, 22, Aug 14; <u>1736</u>: DL, May 15, 25, 27, 28; <u>1740</u>: GF, Dec 2, 3, 5, 12

Davenport, Mrs (actor, dancer), <u>1733</u>: DL, Oct 12, 24, Nov 13, 21, 27, Dec 5, 11; <u>1734</u>: DL, Jan 1, Feb 4, Mar 7, DL/HAY, 12, 16, 18, DL/LIF, Apr 1, DL/HAY, 1, 2, DL, 15, DL/HAY, 26, DL, 29, DL/HAY, May 8, DL, 15, DL/HAY, 17, LIF, 23, BFFO, Aug 24, DL, Sep 19, Oct 5, 10, 17, 21, Nov 1, Dec 12, 21; <u>1735</u>: DL, Jan 18, 21, Feb 18, Mar 3, 15, 25, Apr 7, 11, 26, May 14, 17, Jun 5, LIF, 12, Jul 11, GF/HAY, 18, DL, Sep 15, Oct 1, 7, 22, Nov 15, 17, 20, 25, Dec 6, 18; <u>1736</u>: DL, Jan 3, Feb 28, Mar 27, LIF, Jun 16, DL, Sep 7; <u>1739</u>: DL, Oct 10, Nov 22, 28; <u>1740</u>: DL, Jan 15, Feb 13, GF, Oct 29, Dec 15

Davenport, Robert, <u>1690</u>: DL, Nov 0
--City Night-Cap, The, <u>1660</u>: NONE, Sep 0
--Politic Queen, The, <u>1690</u>: DL, Nov 0

David and Jonathan. See Barbandt, Charles.

David St, <u>1733</u>: LIF/CG, Apr 24; <u>1739</u>: DL, May 4; <u>1742</u>: DL, Apr 29; <u>1743</u>: DL, Apr 15; <u>1747</u>: DL, Apr 28

David. See Porpora, Nicola.

David, Jacques Louis (painter), <u>1786</u>: CG, Oct 16; <u>1797</u>: KING'S, Nov 28

David's Lamentation. See Boyce, Dr William.

Davide, Giacomo (singer), <u>1791</u>: KING'S, Feb 23, Mar 10, Apr 16, 26, May 12, 19, 23, 24, Jun 2

Davidson, J (printer), <u>1745</u>: DL, Apr 1; <u>1749</u>: CG, Jan 17

Davidson, Mrs (actor), <u>1723</u>: DL, Jun 12

Davies. See Davis.

Davies (actor), <u>1784</u>: HAY, Mar 8

Davies (dancer), <u>1796</u>: CG, Dec 19; <u>1799</u>: CG, Jan 29, Mar 25

Davies St, <u>1777</u>: CG, May 22; <u>1778</u>: CG, May 20; <u>1779</u>: CG, May 18; <u>1780</u>: CG, May 19

Davies, Anna (actor), <u>1786</u>: HAY, Jul 28; <u>1788</u>: DL, Jun 5; <u>1789</u>: DL, Jun 9
Davies, Cecilia (Inglesina) (singer), <u>1759</u>: DL, Dec 7; <u>1760</u>: DL, Oct 7; <u>1761</u>:
   DL, May 19; <u>1765</u>: MARLY, Aug 6; <u>1766</u>: MARLY, Sep 26; <u>1767</u>: MARLY, Sep 18;
   <u>1773</u>: KING'S, Oct 23, Nov 20, 27, Dec 18; <u>1774</u>: KING'S, Jan 29, Feb 5, 10,
   24, Mar 8, CHAPEL, 26, 30, KING'S, Apr 19, 28, May 17, Jun 3; <u>1775</u>: CHAPEL,
   Nov 23; <u>1776</u>: HAY, Sep 20, KING'S, Nov 5; <u>1777</u>: KING'S, Jan 21, Mar 1, 13,
   15, 20, May 3, 24; <u>1791</u>: DL, Mar 11, 23, Apr 1, 6, 13, 15
Davies, Elizabeth (actor, singer), <u>1762</u>: CG, Sep 22, Oct 21, Nov 1, 15, 16, Dec
   8; <u>1763</u>: CG, Jan 14, Feb 14, May 7, Sep 19, 23, Oct 3, 8, 14, 22, 24, Nov 3,
   22; <u>1764</u>: CG, Jan 3
Davies, Elizabeth, Mrs William (actor), <u>1770</u>: DL, Sep 29, Oct 9, 27, 29, Nov
   22; <u>1771</u>: DL, Apr 6, Sep 28, Oct 1, 12, 25; <u>1772</u>: DL, Mar 7, 10, 12, 19, 21,
   26, Apr 2, 9, 20, 25, Sep 22, 29, Oct 6, 20, 21, Nov 16, 27, 28, Dec 2; <u>1773</u>:
   DL, Jan 9, 19, Feb 18, Mar 9, Apr 19, 23, Oct 2, 13, 18, 20, 25, 26, Nov 2,
   9, 24, Dec 16, 21; <u>1774</u>: DL, Jan 4, 10, 14, 19, Feb 2, Mar 14, 17, 22, Apr
   25, May 3, 14, Sep 24, 29, Oct 1, 20, Nov 1, 3, 10, 11, 18, Dec 2; <u>1775</u>: DL,
   Jan 23, Feb 23, Mar 2, 28, Apr 8, 17, 19, 21, May 1, 12, 13, Sep 23, 26, 30,
   Oct 5, 7, 20, 26, 28, Nov 20, 23, 25, Dec 26, 29; <u>1776</u>: DL, Jan 13, Feb 22,
   Mar 7, 12, 14, 18, 25, Apr 22, 24, May 11, 23, CHR, Sep 23, 25, DL, Oct 3, 5,
   9, CHR, 16, DL, Nov 5, 9, 12, 16, 25, Dec 10; <u>1777</u>: DL, Jan 1, Mar 20, Apr 3,
   9, 18, 21, 22, 28, May 8, 9, HAY, 15, DL, Jun 6, HAY, 19, 27, Jul 15, Aug 7,
   12, 19, Sep 3, 19, DL, 25, 27, Oct 14, 31, Nov 8, 14, 24, 29, Dec 3, 13;
   <u>1778</u>: DL, Jan 8, 10, 17, May 5, 21, Sep 29, Oct 1, 3, 17, 21, Nov 9, Dec 11,
   21, 23; <u>1779</u>: DL, Jan 7, Apr 19, 23, May 1, 10, Sep 23, 25, Oct 21, Nov 5,
   24, Dec 8, HAY, 27, DL, 28; <u>1780</u>: DL, Jan 7, Apr 1, May 24, 25
Davies, Hugh (actor), <u>1742</u>: GF, Jan 19; <u>1743</u>: DL, Oct 6, Nov 5
Davies, Marianne (singer), <u>1757</u>: CG, Apr 22
Davies, Master (dancer), <u>1779</u>: CG, May 4
Davies, Miss (singer), <u>1794</u>: DL, Jun 9, 24, Sep 27, Oct 6, Nov 6, Dec 20; <u>1795</u>:
   DL, Jan 1, 19, Feb 24
Davies, Rowland (spectator), <u>1689</u>: DG, Jun 13
Davies, Susannah, Mrs Thomas (actor), <u>1752</u>: DL, Sep 23, 30, Oct 11, 19, 21, Nov
   4, 8, 16, 22, 28, 30, Dec 7; <u>1753</u>: DL, Jan 13, 16, Feb 6, Apr 3, 25, 26, May
   25, Sep 8, 11, 15, 20, 25, 27, Oct 13, 24, 31, Nov 1, 5, 8, 26, Dec 26; <u>1754</u>:
   DL, Feb 1, 21, Mar 19, Apr 24, Sep 14, 17, 21, 26, Oct 1, 3, 12, 18, 22, 30,
   Nov 4, 6, 11, 22, Dec 7; <u>1755</u>: DL, Jan 6, 22, Mar 4, 20, Apr 3, 8, 11, Sep
   13, 16, 25, Oct 2, 7, 23, 31, Nov 1, 4, 12, 22, 26, Dec 4, 5, 6; <u>1756</u>: DL,
   Jan 1, 12, Feb 10, 24, Mar 25, 27, 30, Apr 22, May 1, 18, 19, Sep 18, 21, 23,
   28, Oct 5, 7, 14, 19, 28, 29, Nov 4, 6, 23, Dec 9, 10, 11, 27; <u>1757</u>: DL, Jan
   3, 27, Mar 22, 28, Apr 25, 29, May 23, Sep 13, 15, Oct 8, 13, 18, 19, 25, 26,
   29, Nov 4, 8, 22, Dec 27; <u>1758</u>: DL, Jan 28, Feb 20, 27, Mar 16, Apr 27, May
   2, 15, 17, Sep 23, Oct 3, 7, 12, 18, 21, 27, Nov 1, 4, 8, 10, 13, 17, 23;
   <u>1759</u>: DL, Jan 6, 17, Mar 31, Apr 7, May 11, 14, 16, Sep 22, 27, Oct 5, 16,
   19, 23, 26, 27, Nov 3, 5, 13, 22, Dec 31; <u>1760</u>: DL, Jan 19, Feb 15, Mar 20,
   24, Apr 11, 24, May 8, 16, Jun 3, Sep 30, Oct 8, 9, 10, 23, 24, Nov 18, 20,
   21, 27, Dec 13; <u>1761</u>: DL, Jan 10, 23, Mar 23, 26, Apr 28, May 25, Sep 12, 19,
   25, 26, 29, Oct 1, 6, 7, 10, 14, 20, Nov 4, 6, 18, Dec 17; <u>1762</u>: DL, Jan 11,
   20, Mar 20, Apr 19, May 7, Sep 30, Oct 4, 5, 13, 23, 28, Nov 2, 4, 26, 27,
   Dec 1, 11; <u>1763</u>: DL, Jan 18, Mar 1, 15, 19, Apr 6, 19, May 17, 31, Sep 22,
   29, Oct 24, Nov 2, 4, 8, 19, Dec 26; <u>1764</u>: DL, Jan 3, 7, 9, 13, 25, 27, Feb
   15, Mar 27, Apr 12, 14, 24, 25; <u>1778</u>: DL, May 27
Davies, Thomas (actor, printer, bookseller), <u>1736</u>: HAY, May 27; <u>1737</u>: HAY, Mar
   21, Apr 13, LIF, Sep 7; <u>1746</u>: CG, Jan 24, DL, Apr 29, CG, Oct 20, 24, 31, Dec
   8; <u>1747</u>: CG, Jan 1, Mar 3, May 11; <u>1752</u>: DL, Oct 16, 26, Dec 7, 19; <u>1753</u>: DL,
   Jan 11, 20, 23, Feb 7, Apr 26, Oct 3, 6, 16, 20, Dec 1, 20, 22; <u>1754</u>: DL, Jan
   12, 23, Feb 25, Mar 30, Apr 24, Sep 24, Oct 10, 16, 25, Nov 11, 30, Dec 9,
   17; <u>1755</u>: DL, Feb 22, Apr 8, 11, 15, May 2, 6, 8, 13, 21, HAY, Sep 11, 15,
   CG, 29, DL, Oct 3, 4, 10, CG, 17, DL, 23, CG, 24, Nov 1, DL, 6, CG, 8, 15,
   22, 29, Dec 5, 13, DL, 18, 23; <u>1756</u>: DL, Jan 21, Feb 10, 24, 27, Apr 23, May
   24, Sep 21, 25, 30, Oct 16, 29, Nov 19, Dec 11; <u>1757</u>: DL, Jan 11, 18, 27, Mar
   19, 21, Apr 25, 30, May 24, Sep 13, 22, 24, 27, Oct 4, 18, 25, Nov 1, 22, Dec
   2, 3, 8; <u>1758</u>: DL, Jan 19, Feb 4, 21, Mar 11, Apr 20, Sep 21, 26, Oct 7, 10,
   12, 18, 30, Nov 2, 3, 8, 15, 17, 18, Dec 18, 23; <u>1759</u>: DL, Jan 3, Feb 15, 21,
   Mar 3, 10, 22, Apr 19, 20, 21, May 17, Sep 29, Oct 4, 5, 12, 17, 19, 22, 23,
   Nov 3, 10, 24, 30, Dec 12, 19, 20, 31; <u>1760</u>: DL, Jan 11, Feb 13, 21, Apr 11,
   Jun 19, Sep 30, Oct 8, 9, 17, 18, Nov 27, Dec 17; <u>1761</u>: DL, Jan 3, 8, 23, 28,
   31, CG, Mar 25, DL, Apr 18, 29, May 1, 25, 28, 29, Jul 2, Aug 8, Sep 12, 15,
   18, 21, 24, 26, 29, 30, Oct 1, 14, 26, 31, Nov 6, 21, 28, Dec 11, 23, 30;
   <u>1762</u>: DL, Jan 27, CG, Feb 3, DL, Mar 25, CG, Apr 19, DL, 19, 22, 30; <u>1763</u>:
   HAY, Aug 1, DL, Sep 17; <u>1767</u>: DL, Oct 22; <u>1778</u>: DL, May 27
Davies, Thomas (author), <u>1704</u>: LIF, Dec 4; <u>1720</u>: LIF, Oct 22; <u>1725</u>: DL, Apr 5;
   <u>1728</u>: DL, Jan 10

Davies, Sir Thomas (Lord Mayor), 1676: CITY, Oct 30
Davies, Thomas and Susannah (actors), 1754: DL, Apr 24; 1756: DL, Apr 23; 1757:
  DL, Apr 25; 1758: DL, Apr 20; 1759: DL, Apr 20; 1760: DL, Apr 11; 1761: DL,
  Apr 7; 1762: DL, Apr 19; 1775: DL, May 4; 1776: DL, Apr 30
Davies, William (actor, singer), 1770: DL, Sep 25, 29, Oct 9, 25, 29, Nov 1,
  13, 24, Dec 4, 5, 20, 22; 1771: HAY, Jan 28, DL, Feb 9, Mar 16, Apr 1, May 8,
  14, HAY, 15, DL, 27, HAY, Jun 14, 26, DL, Sep 24, Oct 10, 15, 22, Nov 2, Dec
  4, 6, 10, 14, CG, 17, DL, 20, 21; 1772: DL, Jan 1, 14, Feb 5, 26, 27, Mar 12,
  21, 23, 26, 28, Apr 6, 25, CG, May 1, DL, 18, 20, Jun 10, HAY, 10, Jul 3, DL,
  Sep 29, Oct 1, 8, 13, 24, Nov 3, 6, Dec 5, 7, 8, 15, 16, 17, 18, 30; 1773:
  DL, Jan 23, Feb 1, Mar 27, 29, Apr 23, May 10, 11, 12, 17, Jun 1, 2, HAY, Sep
  18, 20, DL, 30, Oct 5, 8, 19, 25, Nov 9, 13, Dec 3, 8, 10, 27; 1774: DL, Jan
  10, Feb 2, 8, 19, Mar 15, 19, 22, Apr 15, 21, CG, 23, DL, 29, May 3, CG, 11,
  DL, 27, Sep 20, 22, 29, HAY, 30, DL, Oct 1, 4, 8, 19, 21, 27, Nov 4, 5, 7, 8,
  16, 18, CG, 24, DL, 29, CG, 29, DL, Dec 2, 22; 1775: DL, Jan 2, 11, 23, Feb
  17, 23, Mar 18, 23, 25, Apr 19, CG, 22, DL, 22, 29, May 1, CG, 2, DL, 4, 13,
  HAY, 26, DL, 27, HAY, Jun 5, Jul 19, Aug 30, DL, Sep 23, 26, 28, 30, Oct 3,
  10, 11, 12, 17, 23, Nov 1, 3, 4, 18, 21, CG, 21, DL, 24, 25, CG, 27, DL, 27,
  28, CG, 28, DL, Dec 5, 7, CG, 9, DL, 16, 26; 1776: DL, Jan 13, 31, Feb 1, 3,
  Mar 16, 25, 28, Apr 9, 10, 12, 15, 22, 26, 30, May 20, 22, Jun 8, 10, HAY,
  Sep 17, DL, 21, 24, 26, Oct 5, 10, 12, 19, 23, 26, Nov 7, 9, 21, 25, Dec 10,
  14; 1777: DL, Jan 1, 14, Feb 17, Apr 1, 5, 11, 18, 22, 28, 30, May 2, 3, 9,
  HAY, 15, DL, 28, Jun 6, HAY, 11, 19, 26, Jul 3, 15, 24, Aug 7, 12, 14, 19,
  29, Sep 3, 10, 19, DL, 20, 23, 27, 30, Oct 2, 7, 17, 18, 31, Nov 13, 18, 19,
  22, 29, Dec 13; 1778: DL, Jan 5, 8, Feb 19, Mar 16, 30, Apr 20, 27, May 2, 5,
  21, 23, Sep 19, 24, 26, Oct 1, 3, 15, 16, 20, 22, 26, Nov 9, 10, 16, 27, Dec
  1, 18; 1779: DL, Apr 12, Sep 18, 25, Oct 7, 9, 23, 25, Nov 1, 12, 19, 27, CG,
  Dec 17, 18, DL, 27, 28; 1780: DL, Feb 28, 29, Mar 4, Apr 3, 14, 17, 18, 21,
  26, 29, May 4, 9, 10, CG, Oct 3, 30, Nov 13, 24, Dec 16; 1781: CG, Jan 8, 31,
  Feb 15, Apr 2, 3, DL, 18, CG, 25, 28, May 2, 4, 5, 7, 9, 12, 16, Sep 21, 24,
  Oct 3, 24, 27, 30, 31, Nov 2, 12, 24, 28; 1782: CG, Feb 23, Mar 21, Apr 10,
  30, May 6, 11, 17, 22, 27, 28, HAY, Aug 5, Sep 16, 21, CG, 25, 27, 30, Oct 2,
  7, 9, 14, 17, 18, 21, 29, Nov 1, 2, 4, 8, 16, 18, 19, 22, 25, DL, 29, CG, 30,
  Dec 2, 6, 12, 14, 19, 27, 30, 31; 1783: CG, Jan 1, 17, 23, 27, Feb 19, Mar
  29, Apr 7, DL, 10, CG, 22, 23, 25, 26, May 7, 9, 10, 12, 16, 19, 29, 30, HAY,
  Jun 18, Aug 15, 22, CG, Sep 17, 19, 22, 24, 26, Oct 2, 3, 6, 8, 9, 13, 16,
  17, 20, 24, 28, Nov 4, 8, 10, 27, Dec 5; 1784: CG, Jan 3, 7, 9, 13, 14, 16,
  24, 29, 31, Feb 4, 5, 7, 9, 10, 13, 23, Mar 6, 20, 22, 23, Apr 17, 24, 26,
  May 7, 11, 12, 17, 19, 25, 26, HAY, 28, CG, Jun 2, HAY, 4, 5, CG, 10, HAY,
  14, 16, 19, 25, Jul 7, 13, 15, 19, 24, 28, 30, Aug 2, 5, 17, 18, 20, 24, 26,
  Sep 13, 14, CG, 17, 20, 21, 22, 24, 27, 28, 29, Oct 4, 8, 11, 12, 18, 25, 27,
  28, 29, 30, Nov 3, 4, 6, 10, 16, 20, 25, 29, 30, Dec 1, DL, 2, CG, 13, 17,
  22, 27, 28; 1785: CG, Jan 8, 14, 19, 21, Feb 7, 21, 28, Mar 7, 29, 30, Apr 1,
  8, 11, 12, 18, 22, May 4, 6, 12, 18, 26, HAY, 28, 30, 31, Jun 2, 9, 18, 24,
  Jul 2, 21, Aug 16, 19, 23, 26, Sep 2, CG, 19, 21, 23, 26, 28, 30, Oct 3, 7,
  10, 12, 14, 17, 20, 21, 27, 28, Nov 2, 3, 4, 7, 9, 14, 19, 21, 22, 23, 29,
  Dec 8, 9, 10, 14, 16, 22, 26; 1786: CG, Jan 3, 5, 6, 14, 18, 28, 31, Feb 7,
  17, 18, 23, 25, Mar 6, 7, 14, Apr 4, 18, 19, 20, 26, May 3, 5, 9, 10, 11, 13,
  15, 20, 22, 24, 26, HAY, Jun 9, 14, 19, 20, 22, 26, 28, 29, Jul 11, 12, 13,
  18, 21, 25, Aug 10, 12, 15, 25, 29, Sep 9, CG, 18, 20, 27, Oct 6, 9, 12, 16,
  18, 21, 23, 25, 26, 30, 31, Nov 13, 14, 15, 22, 23, 24, 25, 27, 28, 30, Dec
  1, 5, 7, 12, 13, 26; 1787: CG, Jan 2, 4, 8, 11, 27, 31, Feb 9, 10, 20, Mar
  12, 26, 27, 31, Apr 11, 14, 16, 17, 25, 27, May 11, 14, 21, 23, HAY, Jun 14,
  16, 18, 20, 21, 22, 25, 27, 28, Jul 2, 13, 19, 20, 21, 25, Aug 3, 4, 10, 14,
  17, 21, 28, 29, CG, Sep 17, 19, 21, 24, 26, 28, Oct 1, 3, 5, 10, 12, 17, 19,
  22, 29, 31, Nov 2, 5, 7, 16, 19, 20, 22, 23, 30, Dec 3, 21, 22, 27; 1788: CG,
  Jan 2, 3, 5, 10, 14, 29, Feb 4, 9, 14, 23, 25, Mar 1, 10, 11, 15, 24, 26, 29,
  Apr 1, 2, 8, 15, 26, 30, HAY, Jun 10, 12, 13, 16, 18, 19, 20, Jul 1, 7, 10,
  24, Aug 2, 4, 13, 15, 22, 25, 29, Sep 3, 9, CG, 15, 17, 19, 22, 24, 26, Oct
  1, 3, 8, 10, 13, 15, 16, 17, 18, 21, 22, 24, 29, Nov 6, 20, 21, 28, Dec 15,
  26, 29, 30; 1789: CG, Jan 20, 21, Feb 11, 19, 21, Mar 28, Apr 14, 20, 21, 28,
  May 2, 5, 8, 22, 26, 29, Jun 5, 8, 12, 16, 18, HAY, 19, 22, 25, 26, 27, 29,
  Jul 3, 11, 29, 31, Aug 5, 10, 11, Sep 14, CG, 14, 16, 18, 23, 25, 28, Oct 2,
  7, 12, 13, 16, 20, 21, 23, 28, 30, 31, Nov 2, 12, 13, 16, 19, 20, 23, Dec 2,
  10, 21, 26, 31; 1790: CG, Jan 22, 23, 29, Feb 4, 25, Mar 27, Apr 12, 14, 20,
  21, 24, May 1, 3, 6, 7, 11, 13, 18, 24, 26, 31, Jun 1, 4, HAY, 15, 16, 18,
  22, 28, Jul 5, 16, Aug 13, 20, Sep 4, CG, 13, 15, 17, Oct 1, 5, 6, 8, 11, 12,
  13, 18, 19, 20, 23, Nov 1, 3, 4, 8, 11, 12, 13, 15, 19, 23, Dec 6, 8, 10, 11,
  20, 28; 1791: CG, Jan 3, 12, 14, 15, Feb 2, 11, 16, Mar 5, Apr 5, 28, 30, May
  2, 5, 6, 10, 16, 18, 31, Jun 1, 6, HAY, 16, 17, 18, 20, 21, 30, Jul 15, 22,
  30, Aug 10, 13, 16, 24, 26, 27, 30, Sep 2, 5, 8, CG, 14, 16, 17, 23, 26, Oct
  3, 6, 10, 17, 19, 21, 24, Nov 2, 4, 5, 7, 15, 19, 24, 25, Dec 3, 15, 21, 22;

1792: CG, Jan 14, Feb 6, 23, 28, Mar 22, 31, Apr 10, 12, 17, 18, May 5, 15,
18, 19, 22, 30, Jun 2, HAY, 15, 18, 20, 27, Jul 3, 9, 16, 23, Aug 2, 6, 9,
22, 31, CG, Sep 20, 24, 26, 28, Oct 1, 3, 5, 8, 10, 12, 15, 17, 18, 24, 26,
29, Nov 5, 12, 14, Dec 5, 13, 20; 1793: CG, Jan 2, 3, 14, 25, Mar 4, Apr 8,
11, 15, 24, May 11, 15, 24, Jun 5, HAY, 11, 12, 13, 14, 17, Jul 15, Aug 3, 6,
12, 16, 20, 27, Sep 2, CG, 17, 18, 20, 23, 30, Oct 1, 2, 4, 5, 7, 8, 9, 10,
14, 16, 21, 29, 30, Nov 1, 2, 7, 11, 12, 16, 18, 19, Dec 6, 17, 18, 19, 20,
28, 30; 1794: CG, Jan 6, 22, Feb 1, Mar 6, 17, Apr 23, 25, 29, May 1, 2, 6,
14, HAY, Jul 8, 11, 14, 17, 18, 21, 22, 26, 29, Aug 1, 4, 12, 18, 20, 25, 27,
Sep 1, CG, 15, 17, 19, 22, 24, 29, Oct 1, 7, 10, 15, 20, 30, Nov 11, 12, Dec
30; 1795: CG, Jan 14, 19, Feb 3, 4, 17, 21, Mar 17, 28, Apr 24, 29, May 8,
14, 27, 29, Jun 1, HAY, 9, 11, 12, CG, 13, HAY, 15, 16, 19, 22, 23, Jul 1, 3,
6, 20, 31, Aug 3, 18, 21, 29, Sep 21; 1796: HAY, Jun 11, 13, 14, 15, 16, 17,
22, 25, Jul 2, 5, 6, 7, 15, 21, 23, Aug 3, 8, 11, 18, 29, Sep 3, 5, 7, 17;
1797: CG, May 26, HAY, Jun 12, 13, 16, 19, 21, 23, 28, Jul 6, 10, 14, 15, Aug
9, 14, 19, 23, 24, 28, Sep 1, 13, CG, Dec 26; 1798: CG, Feb 2, HAY, Jun 12,
14, 15, 16, 18, 20, 28, Jul 14, 16, 21, Aug 3, 4, 21, 29, 31, Sep 3, 7; 1799:
DL, Jan 19, HAY, Jun 15, 17, 18, 19, 20, 25, 28, Jul 2, DL, 5, HAY, 12, 13,
20, 23, 27, Aug 21; Sep 2
Davies, William (publisher), 1790: CG, Jan 29; 1795: HAY, Jun 5, Jul 16; 1799:
DL, Mar 2; 1800: DL, Apr 29
Davis. See Davies.
Davis (actor), 1696: LIF, Mar 0
Davis (actor), 1722: LIF, Dec 15; 1723: LIF, May 10
Davis (actor), 1758: HAY, Jan 18, 25
Davis (actor), 1780: CII, Mar 6, Apr 19
Davis (dancer), 1736: LIF, Oct 9; 1739: CG, Dec 10; 1740: CG, Feb 12, Oct 10;
1741: CG, Jan 5, Feb 24, BFH, Aug 22, CG, Oct 24, Nov 7; 1742: BF, Aug 25,
NWC, Dec 27; 1743: BFHC, Aug 23; 1746: BF, Aug 23, CG, Dec 5; 1749: JS, Mar
28, CG, May 3, Nov 23; 1750: CG, Mar 15, May 10, Oct 29; 1751: CG, Sep 30
Davis (singer, actor), 1733: HAY, Jun 4, DL/HAY, Oct 29; 1734: DL/HAY, Feb 22;
1735: GF/HAY, Mar 21; 1737: HAY, Mar 14
Davis (violinist), 1761: CG, Oct 13
Davis, Elizabeth, Mrs Thomas Dibble (the first) (actor), 1768: HAY, Jun 8
Davis, John (actor), 1797: DL, Nov 4, 9, 11, 17, 18, Dec 14; 1798: DL, Jan 16,
Jun 6
Davis, John (singer), 1703: LIF, Apr 28, HA, Aug 21, LIF, Oct 25; 1704: LIF,
Feb 11, Apr 29, Jun 8, Jul 4, 10, 24; 1705: LIF, Jan 25, HAW, Aug 18
Davis, Katherine (actor), 1681: DG, Nov 0; 1691: DL, Jan 0
Davis, Lockyer (printer), 1756: DL, Mar 9
Davis, Mary (Moll) (actor, dancer, singer), 1662: LIF, Feb 18; 1663: LIF, Feb
23, Oct 0, ATCOURT, Dec 10; 1664: LIF, Mar 0, 8, NONE, Apr 27, LIF, Aug 13;
1665: LIF, Apr 3; 1667: LIF, Mar 7, Aug 5, 15, Nov 7; 1668: BRIDGES, Jan 11,
ATCOURT, 13, LIF, Feb 6, BRIDGES, Apr 7, ATCOURT, May 29, LIF, 31, Dec 21;
1669: LIF, Jan 21; 1675: ATCOURT, Feb 15; 1681: NONE, Sep 0
Davis, Master (dancer), 1792: CG, Feb 28
Davis, Miss (actor), 1788: DL, Dec 17; 1789: DL, Jun 13
Davis, Miss (actor, dancer), 1739: CG, Dec 10; 1740: CG, Feb 12, May 7, Oct 10,
Nov 1; 1741: CG, Jan 5, 21, Feb 17, 24, 28, Apr 24, May 11, BFH, Aug 22, CG,
Oct 24, Nov 7, Dec 28; 1742: CG, May 14, Oct 9, 16; 1743: CG, Jan 1, SOU, Feb
18, CG, Mar 1; 1749: HAY, Apr 29, May 29, BFCB, Aug 23; 1750: HAY, Feb 9, 16,
CG, Nov 19, Dec 27; 1751: CG, Jan 7, Apr 16, May 14, Sep 30, Oct 12, 28, Nov
6; 1752: CG, May 2, Oct 10, 18, Nov 7; 1753: CG, May 2, Sep 12, Dec 22; 1754:
CG, Sep 16; 1755: CG, Jan 20, HAY, Sep 1, 3, 9, 11, 15, CG, Oct 17; 1756: CG,
May 1, Sep 22, Oct 28; 1757: CG, Oct 13, 20; 1758: CG, Oct 9; 1759: CG, Oct
10; 1760: CG, Jan 18, Apr 12, Sep 22, Dec 11; 1761: CG, Mar 25, Apr 11, Sep
26, Oct 5; 1762: CG, Mar 27, Oct 4, 8, 14; 1763: CG, May 7, Oct 26, Nov 15;
1764: CG, Mar 24
Davis, Miss (beneficiary), 1741: JS, Dec 28
Davis, Mrs (actor), 1741: CG, Apr 17, TC, Aug 4
Davis, Mrs (singer), 1726: LIF, May 6; 1727: YB, Apr 26; 1732: KING'S, May 2,
Jun 10
Davis, Mrs K (dancer), 1790: DL, Oct 26; 1792: DLKING'S, Mar 19
Davis, Mrs Thomas Dibble (the fifth) (actor), 1792: CG, Mar 10, 31, May 15, 30,
Oct 1, 5, 12, 29, Dec 8, 31; 1793: CG, Jan 2, 25, Apr 11, 15, 18, 20, May 27,
Jun 1, 6
Davis, Sarah, Mrs William (actor, singer), 1789: DL, Sep 24, Nov 13, 14, Dec
26; 1790: DL, Jan 13, Oct 11; 1791: DL, May 26, DLKING'S, Oct 15, Nov 5, 16;
1792: DLKING'S, Mar 6, May 23
Davis, Thomas Dibble (actor, manager), 1758: CG, Oct 20, 23, 31, Nov 2, 4, 14,
16, 21, 23, Dec 18; 1759: CG, Jan 4, 12, Feb 1, Mar 3, CG, 19, 20, Apr 5, May
3, 7, 8, 11, 14, 17, Sep 26, Oct 15, Nov 5, 30, Dec 5; 1760: CG, Jan 4, 9,

223

14, 24, Mar 17, 25, Apr 18, May 2, 5, 7, 12, HAY, Jun 28, CG, Sep 22, Oct 11,
17, 18, Nov 18, 24, Dec 9, 18; 1761: CG, Jan 8, 10, 28, Mar 3, 26, 30, Apr
13, 17, 27, May 5, 11, DL, Jun 15, Jul 2, 21, 27, CG, Sep 14, 21, 23, 25, 26,
Oct 5, 17, 20, 23, 31, Nov 4, 6, 10, 13, Dec 11, 22; 1762: CG, Jan 2, 5, Feb
15, 25, Mar 23, 27, Apr 24, 27, May 1, 7, HAY, Sep 7, CG, 20, 22, 24, 27, Oct
2, 6, 9, 12, 13, 14, 16, 20, Nov 3, 29, Dec 8, 10; 1763: CG, Jan 8, 28, Feb
14, Apr 25, May 9, 11, 16, HAY, Jun 20, 27, Jul 6, 18, Sep 5, 7, CG, 21, 26,
30, Oct 7, 17, 20, 21, 26, Nov 4, 10, 23, Dec 26; 1764: CG, Jan 5, Feb 1, 11,
13, 15, 17, Mar 8, 29, May 15, 18, HAY, Jun 13, 26, Jul 6, 13, 16, 30, Aug 8,
20, Sep 1, CG, 19, 21, 24, 26, 28, Oct 5, 8, 10, 11, 15, 16, 17, 19, 22, 30,
Nov 5, Dec 21, 29; 1765: CG, Jan 14, 21, Feb 18, Mar 26, Apr 19, May 10, 11,
HAY, Jun 10, 24, Jul 15, 17, 31, Aug 8, 9, 21, 30, Sep 11, CG, 18, 27, 30,
Oct 3, 4, 5, 7, 9, 12, 14, 16, 22, 23, 28, 30, Nov 22, 27, Dec 3, 19, 20;
1766: CG, Jan 31, Mar 10, 31, Apr 14, 18, 21, 25, 26, 29, May 6, HAY, Jun 18,
26, Jul 1, 3, 8, 15, 18, 31, KING'S, Aug 8, 13, 18, 20, HAY, 21, KING'S, 25,
27, 29, HAY, Sep 2, KING'S, 13, 19, CG, 22, 26, Oct 6, 15, 16, 31, Nov 4, 8,
10, 19, 26, 27, Dec 4, 10, 13; 1767: CG, Jan 26, Feb 28, Mar 2, 17, 23, 28,
Apr 25, May 7, 19, HAY, 29, Jun 4, 5, 8, CG, 9, HAY, 10, 12, 15, 17, 22, 30,
Jul 2, 6, 8, 31, Aug 5, 7, 10, 12, 14, 27, 28, Sep 4, 7, CG, 14, 21, 22, 23,
25, Oct 16, Nov 4, 7, 18, 20, 23, Dec 5, 8, 14; 1768: CG, Feb 20, 25, 27, 29,
Mar 5, Apr 13, 20, 25, May 4, 11, 13, HAY, Jun 8, 17, 22, 23, Jul 8, 13, 18,
25, 27, Aug 15, 24, CG, Sep 19, 22, 23, 26, 28, HAY, Oct 7, CG, 22, 24, 25,
Nov 4, 17, 26, Dec 3, 16; 1769: CG, Jan 2, Mar 29, Apr 12, 17, 26, May 3, 4,
5, 6, HAY, 15, 24, 29, Jun 2, 5, 9, 16, 21, Jul 12, 17, 24, CG, Sep 18, HAY,
19, CG, 22, 29, Oct 3, 4, 6, 7, 17, 24, 26, Nov 1, 4, 17, 27, Dec 29; 1770:
CG, Feb 17, 24, Mar 8, 24, Apr 2, 24, 28, May 7, 12, 14, 23, HAY, Sep 27, Oct
1, 15, 29; 1771: HAY, May 15, 20, 31, Jun 5, 26, Jul 3, Aug 19, Sep 18, CG,
Nov 25, Dec 4, 10, 11, 23; 1772: CG, Jan 25, Feb 1, 4, 22, Mar 24, Apr 21,
May 8, 11, HAY, 18, CG, 20, HAY, 22, 27, 29, Jun 1, 8, 29, Aug 10, Sep 17,
CG, 21, 25, 28, Oct 5, 12, 23, 26, Nov 2, 4, 6, Dec 3, 22; 1773: CG, Jan 29,
Mar 15, Apr 15, 23, 27, 28, May 4, 8, HAY, 17, 19, CG, 20, HAY, 26, 28, 31,
Jun 11, 18, 28, Jul 2, 12, 21, Aug 11, 27, Sep 3, 16, CG, 22, DL, 28, CG, Oct
4, 11, 18, 22, 25, Nov 4, 27, Dec 4; 1774: CG, Jan 3, 15, 29, Feb 14, 24, 28,
Mar 14, 15, Apr 7, 21, 30, May 7, HAY, 16, 30, Jun 1, 3, 6, 10, 17, 27, Aug
19, CG, Sep 19, 23, Oct 11, 20, 22, Nov 8, Dec 12, 15, 17; 1775: CG, Apr 8,
22, HAY, May 17, CG, 19, 20, HAY, 22, 26, Jun 7, 12, 28, Jul 7, 14, 28, Sep
1, 13, 16, CG, 29, Nov 4, 30, Dec 1, 21; 1776: CG, Feb 13, May 10, 11, HAY,
20, CG, 21, HAY, 22, CG, 30, DL, Jun 10, HAY, 28, Jul 5, 10, 17, 29, Aug 2,
12, Sep 16, 18, CG, Oct 11, 24, 31, Nov 13, 14, 25, Dec 2, 19; 1777: CG, Jan
8, 15, Mar 3, Apr 16, HAY, May 28, 30, Jun 6, 11, 19, 30, Jul 7, 15, 18, 24,
30, Aug 7, 14, 25, 29, Sep 15, 16, 17, 19, Oct 9, CG, Nov 19; 1778: CG, Jan
28, HAY, May 18, 21, Jun 1, 8, 19, Jul 2, 11, 30, Aug 6, 20, 27, Sep 17, 18,
Dec 28; 1779: HAY, May 31, Jun 10, 22, 25, Aug 13, 24, 27, Sep 17, Oct 18,
Dec 27; 1780: HAY, Apr 5, May 30, Jun 2, 5, 14, 23, 26, 29, Jul 1, 6, 10, 24,
29, Aug 5, 12, 14, 17, 24, Sep 8, 11, CG, Nov 15; 1781: HAY, Jun 7, 16, Jul
18, 23, Aug 7, Sep 1, Nov 12, CG, Dec 5; 1782: HAY, Jan 21, Jun 4, 8, 11, 12,
Aug 9, 13, 17, 27, Sep 18; 1783: HAY, Jun 4, 30, Jul 5, Aug 28; 1784: HAY,
Feb 23; 1785: ARME, Aug 16; 1788: HAY, Sep 30
Davis, Widow (beneficiary), 1734: GF, May 2
Davison, Mary (actor), 1723: DL, Jul 5, Aug 12, 16; 1724: DL, May 20, RI, Jul
   4; 1725: DL, May 17
Davison, William (informant), 1749: HAY, Nov 17
Davy, John (composer), 1800: CG, May 20, Jun 5, HAY, Aug 14
Davy, Master (dancer), 1741: GF, Apr 9
Davys, Mary, 1716: LIF, Apr 27
--Northern Heiress, The; or, The Humours of York, 1716: LIF, Apr 27, 28, May 1
Daw, Miss (dancer), 1760: CG, Dec 11; 1761: CG, Jan 12, Mar 9, Apr 17, Sep 16,
   21, 26; 1762: CG, Jan 28, Apr 17; 1763: CG, Jan 26, May 13, 26, Oct 12, Nov
   22, Dec 8, 28; 1764: CG, Apr 25, May 22, Oct 18, 27, Nov 3; 1765: CG, May 22,
   Oct 7; 1766: CG, May 3, Nov 15, 18; 1767: CG, Mar 24, 28, Apr 27
Dawes (singer), 1792: CG, Feb 28
Dawes, Mrs (actor), 1777: CHR, Jun 18, 25; 1778: HAY, Apr 29, 30; 1779: CG, Apr
   19
Dawson (actor), 1733: GF, Sep 25, CG, Oct 11, Dec 20; 1734: CG, Mar 28, BFRLCH,
   Aug 24; 1748: DL, Apr 13
Dawson (actor), 1787: HAY, Mar 26; 1789: HAY, Feb 23; 1792: HAY, Feb 6; 1797:
   HAY, Dec 4
Dawson, Miss (actor), 1782: HAY, Jan 21
Dawson, Nancy (dancer), 1758: CG, Feb 1, Apr 22, 28, May 2, Oct 14, Nov 16, 23;
   1759: CG, May 16, Oct 12, Nov 13; 1760: CG, Jan 8, 16, Mar 20, 24, Apr 7, 10,
   16, 23, 29, 30, DL, Sep 23, Oct 8, 11, 24, Dec 13; 1761: DL, Mar 26, Apr 16,
   23, Sep 5, 10, Oct 14, Nov 3, 28, 30, Dec 15, 17, 19, 22; 1762: DL, Feb 3,

May 1, 20, 24, BFY, Sep 3, DL, 21, Oct 15; <u>1763</u>: DL, Feb 24, Mar 15, Apr 25, 26, May 4, Sep 17, 22, Nov 2, Dec 26, 28; <u>1764</u>: DL, May 10

Dawson, Richard (house servant), <u>1752</u>: DL, May 4; <u>1753</u>: KING'S, Apr 30, DL, May 17; <u>1758</u>: KING'S, Apr 6; <u>1759</u>: CG, Feb 2

Dawson's Tavern, <u>1745</u>: GF, Mar 18

Day (dancer), <u>1742</u>: JS, May 31

Day (dresser), <u>1746</u>: CG, Nov 12; <u>1747</u>: CG, Jan 21

Day (turner), <u>1760</u>: CG, Feb 16; <u>1761</u>: CG, Apr 11

Day after the Wedding (entertainment), <u>1720</u>: KING'S, Mar 8

Day at Rome, A. See Smith, Charles.

Day in Turkey, A. See Cowley, Hannah.

Day is come, I see it rise, The (song), <u>1673</u>: LIF, May 0

Day of Taste, A; or, London Raree Show (entertainment), <u>1760</u>: CG, Mar 20, Apr 16, 29; <u>1761</u>: CG, Apr 22

Day of Thy Birth (song), <u>1789</u>: DL, Mar 25

Day, John, <u>1668</u>: LIF, Aug 20

--Humour Out of Breath, <u>1668</u>: LIF, Aug 20

Day, Mrs (actor), <u>1788</u>: HAY, Apr 29, Dec 22; <u>1791</u>: HAY, Mar 7

Day, Mrs (seamstress), <u>1773</u>: CG, Dec 27

Day, The (entertainment), <u>1787</u>: HAY, Aug 14, 21

Dayes, Mary (actor, singer), <u>1772</u>: CG, May 2; <u>1773</u>: CG, Oct 27; <u>1774</u>: CG, Mar 12, Apr 7, 12, 22, Sep 23, Oct 4, 11, 13, 15, Nov 1, 19, 24, Dec 20, 27; <u>1775</u>: CG, Jan 7, Feb 11, Mar 2, 30, Apr 4, 8, 22, 28, May 16, Sep 25, 27, Oct 6, 13, 16, 17, 18, 19, Nov 13, 22, Dec 1, 15, 16; <u>1776</u>: CG, Jan 15, Feb 5, 17, 22, Mar 16, 19, 30, Apr 9, 13, 16, 23, 26, 29, May 6, 18, 22, Sep 23, Oct 2, 7, 9, 15, 16, 25, 29, 31, Nov 14, 25, 30, Dec 2, 4, 23, 27; <u>1777</u>: CG, Jan 7, 25, Feb 22, 25, 27, Mar 18, Apr 7, 24, May 13, Sep 22, 26, 29, Oct 10, 15, 16, 21, 30, 31, Nov 12, 25, 27, 29, Dec 3, 15, 20; <u>1778</u>: CG, Jan 8, 15, 20, Feb 2, 4, 16, 24, 26, Mar 30, 31, Apr 4, 6, 7, 9, 24, May 12, 14, Sep 28

Days of Yore, The. See Cumberland, Richard.

Days we now possess, The (song), <u>1795</u>: CG, May 14, 21, 27

D'Blainville (dancer), <u>1733</u>: GF, Apr 20

De Lascia un tell desio (song), <u>1735</u>: DL, Apr 29

De mi Cara (song), <u>1727</u>: LIF, May 4, 8

De Montfort. See Baillie, Joanna.

Dead Alive, The. See O'Keeffe, John.

Dead is the dream (song), <u>1793</u>: CG, Mar 20, 22

Dead March (music), <u>1739</u>: DL, Apr 30; <u>1741</u>: HIC, Feb 5, HAY, 26; <u>1786</u>: DL, Mar 10; <u>1789</u>: CG, Mar 6, DL, 18, CG, 27; <u>1790</u>: DL, Feb 24, 26, CG, 26, DL, Mar 17, CG, 19; <u>1791</u>: DL, Mar 23, CG, 23, 25; <u>1792</u>: KING'S, Feb 24, CG, Mar 2, KING'S, 30; <u>1793</u>: CG, Feb 15, KING/HAY, 22; <u>1794</u>: CG, Mar 7, DL, Apr 4, 10, 11; <u>1795</u>: CG, Feb 20, Mar 25, May 6; <u>1796</u>: CG, Feb 24, Mar 16; <u>1797</u>: CG, Mar 10; <u>1798</u>: CG, Mar 9; <u>1799</u>: CG, Feb 8, DL, Apr 25, Sep 24; <u>1800</u>: CG, Feb 28, Mar 21

Dead shall live, The (song), <u>1791</u>: CG, Mar 25; <u>1792</u>: CG, Mar 9; <u>1793</u>: CG, Feb 20; <u>1794</u>: CG, Mar 26, Apr 11; <u>1797</u>: CG, Mar 22; <u>1798</u>: CG, Mar 28

Deaf Indeed. See Topham, Edward.

Deaf Lover, The. See Pilon, Frederick.

Deal, <u>1799</u>: DL, Oct 3

DeAmicis, Anna Lucia, Sga Domenico (singer, dancer), <u>1763</u>: KING'S, Feb 19, Mar 24, Apr 21, 25, HAY, Jun 9

Dean (householder), <u>1763</u>: CG, Mar 19

Dean St, <u>1737</u>: LIF, Apr 27; <u>1746</u>: DT, Mar 14; <u>1754</u>: SOHO, Mar 26, 28, KING'S, Apr 2; <u>1755</u>: SOHO, Jan 16, Mar 11; <u>1756</u>: SOHO, Feb 2, Mar 16; <u>1757</u>: SOHO, Feb 1, Mar 14; <u>1758</u>: SOHO, Mar 31, Apr 1; <u>1759</u>: SOHO, Mar 1; <u>1760</u>: SOHO, Jan 18, Feb 14; <u>1761</u>: SOHO, Jan 21, 28, Apr 15; <u>1762</u>: SOHO, Feb 9, CG, Mar 22, SOHO, Apr 21; <u>1763</u>: SOHO, Feb 4; <u>1774</u>: DL, Feb 24; <u>1785</u>: KING'S, May 19; <u>1787</u>: CG, Mar 27

Dean, J (publisher), <u>1684</u>: DL, Mar 27

Dean Jr, Thomas (musician), <u>1707</u>: YB, Apr 18; <u>1708</u>: SH, Feb 4

Dean Sr, Thomas (musician), <u>1701</u>: YB, Mar 26, HAW, Jul 27; <u>1702</u>: HAW, May 11, Jun 1; <u>1703</u>: HA, May 18; <u>1704</u>: YB, Mar 24, LIF, Jul 14; <u>1707</u>: YB, Mar 26, Apr 18, Dec 17; <u>1708</u>: SH, Feb 4, Mar 26; <u>1709</u>: HA, Jul 30, Sep 3, GO, Nov 21, SH, 30; <u>1710</u>: SH, Mar 22, YB, Apr 17; <u>1711</u>: SH, Apr 26

Dean's Yard, <u>1743</u>: WS, Nov 25; <u>1785</u>: CG, Apr 22; <u>1786</u>: CG, May 13; <u>1787</u>: CG, May 4; <u>1796</u>: CG, Jun 7; <u>1797</u>: CG, May 31; <u>1798</u>: CG, May 30

Dear is my little native vale (song), <u>1793</u>: KING/HAY, Mar 6, 13

Dear Mary adieu (song), <u>1794</u>: CG, May 21; <u>1799</u>: CG, Mar 16, Apr 18; see also Farewell to Old England

Dear Pretty Maid (song), <u>1729</u>: HAY, Feb 11

Dear Pretty Youth (song), <u>1694</u>: NONE, Sep 0; <u>1707</u>: DL, Jan 1; <u>1723</u>: DL, Jun 6; <u>1729</u>: DL, Oct 30; <u>1733</u>: DL, Nov 26; <u>1734</u>: DL, May 15, Oct 22; <u>1735</u>: DL, Oct

31; <u>1739</u>: DL, Dec 26; <u>1741</u>: DL, May 15
Dear Yanco say, and true he say (song), <u>1790</u>: CG, Nov 23; <u>1791</u>: CG, Sep 19;
   <u>1793</u>: CG, May 21; <u>1794</u>: CG, Apr 12, Oct 29; <u>1795</u>: CG, Oct 7; <u>1797</u>: CG, Oct 2;
   <u>1799</u>: CG, Dec 9; see also Indian Song
Dease (actor), <u>1732</u>: RIW/HAY, Sep 4
Death (nickname, pugilist), <u>1788</u>: CG, Dec 30
Death and Renovation of the Elk (song), <u>1795</u>: CG, Nov 16
Death and Revival of Harlequin, The (pantomime, anon), <u>1780</u>: CII, Mar 6; <u>1785</u>:
   HAMM, Jun 27, Jul 4, 6
Death of a Stag (song), <u>1724</u>: DL, May 12; <u>1780</u>: CG, Apr 10, HAY, Jul 27; <u>1781</u>:
   CG, Apr 3, May 4; <u>1782</u>: CG, May 4, 6
Death of Abel, The. See Piccini, Niccolo.
Death of Captain Cook, The. See Collier, Sir George.
Death of Captain Faulknor, The. See Pearce, William.
Death of Hannibal, The. See Theobald, Lewis.
Death of King Henry VI, The (interlude), <u>1702</u>: DL, Oct 26
Death of the Wild Boar (dance), <u>1741</u>: DL, Feb 12
Death of the Wild Goat (dance), <u>1742</u>: GF, Jan 14, Apr 24, May 27
Death, Thomas (actor), <u>1763</u>: HAY, Jun 20, Jul 6, 18, Aug 1, 5; <u>1764</u>: HAY, Jun
   13, 26, Jul 6, 13, 16, 23, Aug 20, 31, Sep 1; <u>1770</u>: HAY, Sep 27; <u>1777</u>: CG,
   Oct 8, 13, 21, Nov 4; <u>1778</u>: CG, Jan 15, 20, Feb 25, Apr 27; <u>1788</u>: HAY, Sep 30
Deb. See Willett, Deborah.
Debating Catch (song), <u>1799</u>: CG, Jun 7
Debauchee, The. See Behn, Aphra.
Debauchees, The. See Fielding, Henry.
DeBlois (dancer), <u>1732</u>: TC, Aug 4
Debon, Mme (singer, dancer), <u>1742</u>: SF, Sep 16
Debora and Sisara. See Guglielmi, Pietro.
Deborah. See Handel, George Frederic.
Deborah; or, A Wife For You All. See Fielding, Henry.
Debourg. See Dubourg.
DeBreame, Maxent (oboist), <u>1675</u>: ATCOURT, Feb 15
Debrett, J (publisher), <u>1786</u>: DL, Jan 14, Oct 24; <u>1787</u>: DL, May 3; <u>1788</u>: HAY,
   Aug 9; <u>1789</u>: DL, Mar 21, CG, Apr 14, DL, 20, May 1, HAY, 25, Jun 30, Jul 11,
   Aug 5, CG, Oct 2, DL, Nov 13; <u>1790</u>: HAY, Aug 11, DL, Nov 3; <u>1791</u>: CG, Jan 14;
   <u>1792</u>: CG, Feb 18, DLKING'S, Apr 20, CG, May 10, HAY, Jul 7, 25, CG, Oct 27;
   <u>1793</u>: CG, May 3, HAY, Jun 29, Aug 3, Sep 19, 21, CG, Nov 23; <u>1794</u>: HAY, Feb
   22, CG, 22, DL, Dec 12
DeBroc (DeBroke) (dancer, acrobat), <u>1720</u>: KING'S, Apr 26; <u>1734</u>: BFHBH, Aug 24;
   <u>1743</u>: TCD/BFTD, Aug 23
Debrose (draper), <u>1766</u>: DL, Dec 26; <u>1767</u>: DL, Jan 23
DeCamp (dancer), <u>1727</u>: KING'S, Mar 23
DeCamp, Adelaide (actor, dancer), <u>1792</u>: DL, Dec 27; <u>1799</u>: CG, May 7
DeCamp, Maria Theresa (actor, dancer, singer), <u>1783</u>: KING'S, May 1; <u>1784</u>:
   KING'S, Feb 3, 26, Mar 11; <u>1786</u>: KING'S, Mar 23, Apr 6, 27, HAY, Jun 14, 21,
   Jul 6, Aug 12, Sep 1, 4, 6, Feb 3, 26, Mar 11; <u>1786</u>: KING'S, Mar 23, Apr 6,
   27, HAY, Jun 14, 21, Jul 6, Aug 12, Sep 1, 4, 6, Feb 3, 26, Mar 11; <u>1786</u>:
   KING'S, Mar 23, Apr 6, 27, HAY, Jun 14, 21, Jul 6, Aug 12, Sep 1, 4, 6, Feb
   3, 26, Mar 11; <u>1786</u>: KING'S, Mar 23, Apr 6, 27, HAY, Jun 14, 21, Jul 6, Aug
   12, Sep 1, 4, 6, Feb 3, 26, Mar 11; <u>1786</u>: KING'S, Mar 23, Apr 6, 27, HAY, Jun
   14, 21, Jul 6, Aug 12, Sep 1, 4, 6, Feb 3, 26, Mar 11; <u>1786</u>: KING'S, Mar 23,
   Apr 6, 27, HAY, Jun 14, 21, Jul 6, Aug 12, Sep 1, 4, 6, Feb 3, 26, Mar 11;
   <u>1786</u>: KING'S, Mar 23, Apr 6, 27, HAY, Jun 14, 21, Jul 6, Aug 12, Sep 1, 4, 6,
   Feb 3, 26, Mar 11; <u>1786</u>: KING'S, Mar 23, Apr 6, 27, HAY, Jun 14, 21, Jul 6,
   Aug 12, Sep 1, 4, 6, DL, Oct 24; <u>1787</u>: DL, Jan 13, Feb 7, Jun 1, HAY, 13, 29,
   Jul 2, 6, 30, Aug 7, 14, 17, 21, DL, Sep 20, Nov 8; <u>1788</u>: DL, Feb 21, Jun 5,
   7, HAY, Jul 7, Aug 5, 13, 15, DL, Sep 16, 23, Oct 4, 13, Nov 13; <u>1789</u>: DL,
   Jan 17, May 19, 22, 27, HAY, Jul 8, 27, DL, Oct 26, Nov 21, Dec 4, 9, 26;
   <u>1790</u>: DL, Jan 23, Mar 8, Apr 5, May 15, 18, Jun 1, HAY, 25, DL, Oct 21, 26,
   27, Dec 27; <u>1791</u>: DL, Mar 24, Apr 29, May 3, 20, 24, 25, HAY, Jun 17, Jul 1,
   30, Aug 24, 31, Sep 13, DLKING'S, 27, Oct 3, 15, Nov 5, 14, 16, Dec 2, 10,
   31; <u>1792</u>: DLKING'S, Jan 28, Feb 18, Mar 1, 19, 29, Apr 16, May 23, Jun 7, 13,
   HAY, 23, 27, Jul 25, 28, Aug 2, 6, 14, 15, 20, 28, Sep 1, 10, 14, DL, 18, 20,
   27, Oct 18, Nov 2, 5, 10, 21, 27, Dec 13, 17, 22, 26; <u>1793</u>: DL, Jan 10, 23,
   Feb 4, 7, Mar 2, 7, 21, Apr 1, 29, May 9, 10, 13, 15, 21, Jun 1, 3, 10, HAY,
   11, 14, 17, 22, Jul 23, 24, Aug 3, 6, 12, 16, 20, 23, 30, Sep 2, 4, 6, 9, 19,
   21, 30, Oct 1, 4, 7, 10, 15, 22, 24, Nov 5, 16, 19, 29, 30, Dec 10, 16, 19,
   26; <u>1794</u>: HAY, Jan 4, 7, 9, 11, 13, 27, 28, Feb 8, 20, 22, DL, May 14, 16,
   Jun 6, 9, 17, Jul 2, HAY, 8, 11, 12, 17, 18, 19, 21, 22, 24, 26, 29, Aug 9,
   12, 18, 20, 27, 28, 30, Sep 1, 3, 6, 13, DL, 16, 18, 20, 23, 27, Oct 14, 18,
   20, 31, Nov 29, Dec 12; <u>1795</u>: DL, Jan 2, 19, Feb 6, 10, Mar 26, Apr 7, 16,
   May 1, 9, 18, 20, 27, Jun 3, HAY, 9, 10, 11, 13, 15, 16, 24, Jul 6, 16, 22,

31, Aug 10, 11, 21, 25, 29, Sep 1, DL, 17, 22, 24, 26, 29, Oct 1, 15, Nov 7,
12, 19, 23, Dec 2, 7, 10; 1796: DL, Jan 1, 8, 11, 15, 18, Mar 3, 5, 7, 12,
Apr 1, 13, 25, 28, May 13, 17, 23, 25, 27, Jun 1, 2, 7, 8, 10, 13, HAY, 13,
14, 20, 24, 25, 28, Jul 5, 6, 8, 11, 12, 15, 21, 23, 26, 27, Aug 8, 13, 17,
23, 29, DL, Sep 20, 22, 27, 29, Oct 1, 6, 10, 19, 27, Nov 5, 9, 10, 28, Dec
2, 6, 10, 16, 20, 21; 1797: DL, Jan 7, 10, 12, 14, 20, Feb 2, 7, 9, 23, 28,
Mar 2, 6, May 12, 15, 22, 23, Jun 1, 6, 7, HAY, 12, 13, 15, 16, 20, 21, 22,
23, 26, 28, 30, Jul 3, 4, 8, 10, 15, Aug 5, 8, 9, 10, 14, 15, 24, 28, Sep 4,
9, 11, DL, 21, Oct 3, 7, 19, 21, 31, Nov 2, 7, 8, 20, 24, Dec 9, 11, 23;
1798: DL, Jan 16, 25, Feb 20, May 7, 24, 30, 31, Jun 6, 7, HAY, 12, 13, 15,
16, 18, 20, 21, 22, 23, 27, 29, 30, Jul 5, 10, 14, 16, 20, 21, 30, Aug 4, 21,
23, 29, 30, 31, Sep 10, DL, 18, 22, 27, Oct 6, 13, 15, 16, 20, Nov 3, 13, 22,
26, 29, Dec 4, 21; 1799: DL, Apr 3, 5, 8, 17, 19, 22, May 2, 3, 4, 7, 8, 24,
HAY, Jun 17, DL, 28, HAY, Jul 2, 4, 8, 9, 10, 12, 13, 19, 20, 27, 30, Aug 10,
13, 17, 21, 26, 27, 28, DL, Sep 17, 21, Oct 3, 14, 17, 19, Nov 2, 6, 7, 8,
14, 16, Dec 2, 11, 17; 1800: DL, Jan 1, 11, 18, 21, Feb 1, 6, 7, Mar 11, Apr
23, 25, 28, 29, May 14, 21, 23, 29, 30, Jun 3, 7, 11, HAY, 14, 17, 18, 19,
20, Jul 2, 15, 29, 30, Aug 7, 8, 12, 14, 19, 23, 26, 29, Sep 1
--First Faults, 1799: DL, May 3
DeCamp, Sophia (dancer), 1777: KING'S, Apr 12, May 1, 8, 20, 24, Jun 24; 1797:
DL, Mar 6
DeCamp, Vincent (actor, singer), 1777: CG, Feb 28; 1779: HAY, Mar 17; 1792: DL,
Nov 5, Dec 26; 1793: DL, Feb 12, HAY, Aug 6, Sep 24, 30; 1794: HAY, Jan 9,
DL, Apr 21, May 19, HAY, Aug 27, Sep 6, DL, Oct 7, Dec 20; 1795: DL, Jan 19,
Feb 2, May 6, HAY, Aug 10, DL, Sep 29, Oct 27, 30, Nov 11, 23, Dec 4, 10;
1796: DL, Jan 18, Feb 27, Mar 12, Apr 2, 4, 30; 1799: DL, Nov 13, Dec 17;
1800: DL, Feb 12, Mar 13, May 12, Jun 18
Decastro, James (actor, entertainer), 1776: HAY, Sep 18; 1777: HAY, Oct 9;
1779: HAY, Oct 18, Dec 20; 1784: HAY, Dec 13; 1785: HAY, Feb 12; 1786: HAY,
Mar 6; 1787: HAY, Jan 8
Deceiver Deceived, The. See Pix, Mary.
Deception (play, anon), 1784: DL, Oct 28, 29
Deceptions with Cards (entertainment), 1785: HAY, Feb 21
Dechaliers, Mrs. See Deschalliez, Louise.
Decius and Paulina (masque), 1718: LIF, Mar 22
Declamation. See Aston, Anthony.
Declare his honour (song), 1790: CG, Mar 3; 1792: CG, Mar 9
Decoy, The. See Potter, Henry.
Deeble (singer), 1767: DL, May 9
Deeper and deeper still (song), 1790: CG, Mar 3; 1791: DL, Mar 25; 1792:
KING'S, Mar 23, 30; 1793: CG, Mar 8; 1794: DL, Mar 12, 14; 1795: CG, Mar 13,
27; 1797: CG, Mar 10; 1799: CG, Feb 8, 20; 1800: CG, Mar 5
Deering, Charles, 1682: DG, Apr 27; 1685: DG, Jun 10; 1709: QUEEN'S, Jan 19,
Mar 17
Deering, Sir Edward, 1664: ATCOURT, Jan 0, BRIDGES, Sep 14; 1679: BF, Sep 3;
1682: DG, Apr 27
DeFabrice, 1721: KING'S, Apr 15; 1723: KING'S, Jan 15
Defeat of Apollo, The; or, Harlequin Triumphant (entertainment), 1737: HAY, Jan
8, 14, 15, 17, 21, 26
Defence of Mr Garrick in Answer to the Letter Writer, A (pamphlet), 1759: DL,
Nov 1
Defenne, Mrs (French boarding-school), 1728: MDS, Apr 3
DeFesch (Fesch), Mrs (singer), 1732: HIC, May 10
DeFesch, William (musician, composer), 1732: HIC, Mar 13, May 10; 1733: LIF,
Feb 16, DT, May 30; 1734: YB, Apr 8; 1735: HAY, Mar 26; 1740: CR, Feb 29;
1744: CR, Mar 21; 1745: CG, Mar 6, 20; 1746: CG, Feb 14, DL, Apr 8; 1754: DL,
Mar 23; 1755: DL, Mar 17
--Joseph (opera), 1745: CG, Mar 6, 20, Apr 3
--Judith (oratorio), 1733: LIF, Feb 8, 16, 21; 1740: CR, Feb 29
--London Prentice, The (operetta), 1754: DL, Mar 23, May 14; 1755: DL, Mar 17
--Love and Friendship (serenata), 1744: CR, Mar 21; 1745: CG, Mar 6, 14; 1746:
DL, Apr 8
DeFompre (dancer, actor), 1725: HAY, Mar 8; 1736: CG, Apr 8
DeFrano, Mlle (dancer), 1737: BF, Aug 23, SF, Sep 7
Degar. See Delagarde.
Deghi che io son fedele (song), 1758: KING'S, Apr 6
DeGiardini, Felice (musician, composer), 1750: HIC, May 18; 1751: DL, May 1;
1752: KING'S, Mar 24; 1753: HAY, Apr 2; 1754: DL, Mar 27, KING'S, Apr 25, CG,
May 23; 1755: DL, Mar 12, 14; 1756: KING'S, Feb 17, DL, Apr 2; 1757: DL, Mar
23, KING'S, 24, DL, 25, KING'S, Apr 30, Jun 18; 1758: DL, Mar 10; 1759: CG,
May 4; 1760: CG, Feb 27, 29, KING'S, Apr 15, 17, May 15; 1761: CG, Feb 6;
1762: CG, Feb 26, CHAPEL, May 18, KING'S, Nov 13, CG, Dec 8; 1763: KING'S,

Mar 5, DL, Apr 27, HAY, Jun 9, CG, Oct 22, KING'S, Nov 26, Dec 10; 1764:
KING'S, Jan 21, 24, CHAPEL, Feb 29, KING'S, May 5; 1765: KING'S, Feb 15, Mar
7; 1767: CHAPEL, May 13; 1768: CHAPEL, May 25; 1769: HAY, Feb 10, 15, Mar 10,
KING'S, Apr 5; 1770: CG, Mar 2, 7, 30, HAY, May 4; 1771: HAY, Apr 17, CHAPEL,
27, MARLY, Sep 3; 1774: CHAPEL, Mar 26, 30; 1776: CHAPEL, Apr 3, KING'S, Nov
2, 5, Dec 14; 1777: KING'S, Feb 4, Mar 1, Apr 1, 29; 1779: CG, Feb 23; 1781:
DL, May 19, KING'S, Jun 5; 1782: KING'S, Apr 18, CG, Nov 2, KING'S, 2; 1789:
CG, Mar 31; 1790: HAY, Jan 7, Feb 2; 1792: CG, Nov 24; 1794: CG, Mar 14, Apr
11, May 2; 1795: CG, Mar 4, 13, 25
--Antigona (opera), 1760: KING'S, Apr 17, 26, May 3, 10, 15; 1765: KING'S, Mar
28
--Enea e Lavinia (opera), 1764: KING'S, May 5, 8, 12, 19, 26, 29, Jun 12, HAY,
16
--Padre e Il Figlio Rivali, Il (opera), 1770: KING'S, Feb 6, 13, 20
--Rosmira (opera), 1757: KING'S, Apr 30, May 3, 7, 14, 17, 21, 24, Jun 18
--3rd Concerto, 1795: CG, Mar 4; 1796: CG, Feb 19
--6th Concerto, 1795: CG, Mar 13
DeGiovanni, Pasquale (singer), 1796: KING'S, Jan 5, Feb 9, Apr 16, May 24, Jun
14, Dec 6, 20; 1797: KING'S, Jan 7, 10, Jun 8, Nov 28, Dec 2, 12; 1798:
KING'S, Feb 20, Mar 22, Apr 10, 26, Dec 8, 29; 1799: KING'S, Jan 22, May 30;
1800: KING'S, Feb 8, 18, Mar 18, Apr 15, Jun 17
Degotti (scene painter), 1797: KING'S, Nov 28
Degrang (singer), 1675: ATCOURT, Feb 15
DeGremont, Mlle (beneficiary), 1720: KING'S, Jun 20
DeGrimbergue (French manager), 1720: KING'S, Apr 29, Jun 13
D'Egville. See Daigueville.
DeHenney, Mme (dancer), 1753: CG, May 14
DeHondre (bookseller), 1769: CG, Feb 25
Dehors Trompeurs, Les. See Boissy, Louis de.
Deidamia. See Handel, George Frederic.
Deincourt, Lord. See Leke, Robert.
DeJardin (dancer), 1750: CG, Jan 8, 9, 31
Dejaure, Jean Elie Bedeno (author), 1794: DL, Jun 9
Dejeuner Espagnol (dance), 1783: KING'S, May 1
Dekker, Thomas
--Hannibal, 1672: DG, Mar 9
--Virgin Martyr, The (with Phillip Massinger), 1661: VERE, Feb 16; 1662: VERE,
Jan 10; 1668: BRIDGES, Feb 27, Mar 2, May 6, 7
Del Cara amabil Volto (song), 1758: KING'S, Apr 6
Del fallo ful camin (song), 1713: QUEEN'S, Apr 25; 1714: QUEEN'S, May 1
Del mi Minaccia (song), 1741: HIC, Apr 24
Del Minacciar del Vento (song), 1745: CG, Apr 10
Delaboyde (beneficiary), 1746: DL, Apr 30
DelaBrune, Mlle (dancer), 1738: SFH, Sep 5
DelaChapelle (dancer), 1791: PAN, Dec 31; 1792: HAY, Feb 14, Mar 10, Apr 14
DeLaCointrie (dancer), 1751: CG, Dec 20; 1752: CG, Dec 7
DeLaCointrie (L'Cointri, Contair), Mme (dancer), 1749: CG, Apr 15, 21, 24, DL,
Oct 11, Nov 9; 1750: DL, Jan 18, Mar 17, Apr 5, 20, 27, 28, CG, Dec 21, 26;
1751: CG, Apr 25, May 4, Oct 28
DelaCour (scene painter), 1740: HAY, May 10
Del'Acqua, Teresa (singer), 1790: HAY, Mar 25, May 27
DelaCroix, Mlle (dancer), 1791: KING'S, Jun 28; 1797: CG, Mar 16, Jun 7, Oct 9,
21; 1799: CG, Apr 20
Delagarde (Leguard, Degar) (dancer), 1705: QUEEN'S, Dec 12; 1706: QUEEN'S, Apr
25, May 29, Jun 13, 29, LIF/QUEN, Jul 6; 1707: DL, Feb 13, Oct 21, Nov 3, 4,
6, 11, 28, 29, DL/QUEEN, Dec 9, DL, 17; 1708: DL, Jan 3, DL/QUEEN, Feb 21;
1710: DL, Jan 26; 1711: QUEEN'S, Apr 7; 1712: DL, May 2; 1715: LIF, Jan 1, 6,
13, 20, 25, Feb 22, Mar 5, 10, 15, 26, Apr 2, 4, 18, 25, 28, 29, May 2, 9,
10, 12, 13, 24, Jun 3, 14, 23, Jul 8, KING'S, Aug 27, LIF, Sep 30, Oct 6, 13,
15, 19, 22, 26, 29, 31, Nov 2, 9, 10, 12, 15, 16, 18, 19, 22, 25, 26, 28, Dec
17, 21, 28, 30; 1716: LIF, Jan 3, 10, 19, 27, Feb 2, 27, Apr 5, 9, 30, May 7,
10, 18, 24, 31, Jun 1, 4, 12, Oct 22, 25, 26, 29, 30, 31; 1718: LIF, Oct 3,
4, 8, 14, 24, 30, Nov 6, 8, 13, 17, 18, 27, 29, Dec 4, 8, 9, 22, 26; 1719:
LIF, Jan 2, 14, Feb 16, 24, Apr 7, 27; 1721: DL, May 17; 1724: LIF, May 5;
1726: LIF, Nov 26; 1727: LIF, Nov 17; 1729: LIF, Jan 18, Apr 8, Nov 4; 1730:
LIF, Jan 2, Apr 10, 25, May 13, 21, 28, Nov 7, Dec 15; 1731: LIF, Jan 18, May
20, Oct 4, Nov 18, Dec 1; 1732: LIF, Apr 22, LIF/CG, Nov 8, 24, Dec 9; 1733:
LIF/CG, Jan 23, Feb 5, Mar 12, CG, 27, LIF/CG, 28, 29, Apr 2, 12, 18, 23, 24,
CG, May 1, LIF/CG, 7, 8, 10, CG, 16, 17, LIF/CG, 18, 21, CG/LIF, 28, LIF/CG,
29, Jun 1, CG, 26, 29, Aug 14, 17, 21, Sep 22, 25, 27, Oct 4, 6, 11, 18, Nov
1, 12, Dec 4, 11, 28; 1734: CG, Jan 1, 14, 17, 25, Feb 26, Mar 11, 16, Apr 1,
27, May 1, 7, 9, 10, 14, 15, 16, 17, CG/LIF, Sep 20, Oct 2, 31, Nov 29, Dec

5, 12, 14, 19, 30; <u>1735</u>: CG/LIF, Jan 1, 13, 14, 17, Feb 3, 13, 22, Mar 11,
   15, Apr 14, 17, May 5, CG, 8, CG/LIF, 16, 19, Jun 2, CG, Nov 6, 15, 28, Dec
   2, 27; <u>1736</u>: CG, Jan 23, Mar 2, 6, Apr 29, Sep 29
Delagarde, Charles (Jr) (dancer), <u>1728</u>: LIF, Oct 9; <u>1729</u>: LIF, Jan 16, 18, Feb
   6, Oct 24, Nov 4; <u>1730</u>: LIF, Sep 25, Oct 9, Nov 7; <u>1731</u>: LIF, Sep 27, Oct 4,
   Nov 6, 13; <u>1732</u>: GF, Jan 15, LIF/CG, Oct 4, 30, Nov 8, CG/LIF, Dec 19,
   LIF/CG, 27; <u>1733</u>: LIF/CG, Jan 16, Apr 16, CG, Oct 13, Dec 7; <u>1734</u>: CG, Apr 1
Delagarde, Charles and J (dancers), <u>1718</u>: LIF, Oct 18, 23, 24, 28, 30, Nov 4,
   6, 8, 18, 27, 29, Dec 4, 29; <u>1719</u>: LIF, Jan 2, 3, 5, 9, 13, 14, Feb 16, 24,
   Apr 3, 7, 9, 27, 29, 30, May 7, 13, 19, 21, 25, 26, 28, 29, Jun 3; <u>1720</u>: LIF,
   Jan 15, 20, Feb 24, Mar 8, Apr 28, May 10, 12
Delagarde, J (dancer), <u>1732</u>: GF, Dec 20; <u>1733</u>: GF, Jan 10, 23, Feb 2, 12, Mar
   1, 12, Apr 6, 17, 18, 20, 24, 25, 27, 30, May 3, 5, 11, 15, 16, 23, Sep 12,
   28, Oct 1, 9, 15, 16, 18, 19, 24, 26, 31, Nov 2, 12, 29, Dec 8, 11, 15, 19,
   28; <u>1734</u>: GF, Jan 8, 11, 14, 28, 31, Feb 5, Mar 11, Apr 19, May 1, 6, 7, 8,
   13, 22, Oct 14, 28, Nov 18, Dec 28; <u>1735</u>: GF, Jan 6, 7, 24, Mar 6, 17, 29,
   Apr 9, 10, 16, 17, 21, May 3, Sep 10, 26, Oct 3, Nov 6, 12, 14, 17, 25, 29,
   Dec 10, 13, 15, 17; <u>1736</u>: GF, Feb 20, Mar 3, Apr 12, 13, 17, 28, May 6, LIF,
   Sep 30, Oct 14, 21, Nov 9, 13, 18, 27, Dec 3, 7, 16; <u>1737</u>: LIF, Feb 1, Mar
   21, Apr 12, 14, 18, 25, 27, 29, 30, May 2, 5, 6, 7, 18, Jun 15; <u>1739</u>: CG, Jan
   15, 16, 20, Mar 2, May 9, Sep 22, Oct 3, 15, Dec 4, 10; <u>1740</u>: CG, Feb 12, Mar
   25, Apr 29, Sep 26, Oct 10, 22, 29, Dec 29; <u>1741</u>: CG, Jan 5, 21, Feb 17, 24,
   28, Apr 2, 23, 25, 27, May 4, 5, 8, 11, 14, Sep 28, Oct 17, 24, 27, Nov 26,
   Dec 15, 28, 30; <u>1742</u>: CG, Jan 8, 21, 25, 26, Feb 22, Mar 9, Apr 27, 30, May
   5, 10, Sep 29, Oct 1, 9, 15, 16, 25, Nov 2, Dec 21; <u>1743</u>: CG, Jan 8, Feb 4,
   Mar 8, Apr 18, 21, Oct 3, Dec 20, 26; <u>1744</u>: CG, Jan 14, Feb 14, Mar 3, Apr 6,
   24, Oct 10, 22, 31, Dec 8; <u>1745</u>: CG, Jan 1, 14, 25, May 2, 6, 7, Oct 29, Nov
   14, 23, Dec 27; <u>1746</u>: CG, Apr 30, May 13, Jun 13, Dec 19, 31; <u>1747</u>: CG, May
   13, Dec 26; <u>1748</u>: CG, Mar 3, 14, 28, Apr 12, Oct 27; <u>1749</u>: CG, Mar 9, Apr 19,
   Nov 23; <u>1750</u>: CG, Apr 17, Oct 29, 30
Delagarde, J and Mrs (dancers), <u>1743</u>: CG, Apr 18
Delagarde, Mrs (dancer), <u>1710</u>: DL, Jan 26; <u>1711</u>: QUEEN'S, Apr 7
Delagarde, Mrs J (actor, dancer), <u>1741</u>: CG, Mar 30, 31, Apr 3, 6, 7, 8, 9;
   <u>1742</u>: DL, Apr 23, CG, Oct 1, 6, 15, 25, Nov 2, 23, 25, Dec 21; <u>1743</u>: CG, Mar
   8, Apr 9, 18, Sep 26, 30, Oct 3, 26, Nov 24, Dec 17, 20, 26; <u>1744</u>: CG, Jan
   14, Feb 13, Mar 3, 15, Apr 14, 16, 24, Oct 10, 12, 22, 31, Dec 8; <u>1745</u>: CG,
   Jan 1, 14, 25, Mar 28, Apr 2, 19, May 2, 4, 7, Nov 14, Dec 27; <u>1746</u>: CG, Apr
   15; <u>1748</u>: CG, Mar 3, Apr 19, 20, Oct 27; <u>1750</u>: CG, Apr 28, Dec 21, 26; <u>1751</u>:
   CG, Apr 25, Dec 4, 5
Delagarde's scholar (dancer), <u>1707</u>: DL, Oct 21, Nov 3
Del'Agata, Michael (dancer), <u>1762</u>: DL, Oct 9; <u>1763</u>: DL, Jan 3, Feb 24
Delago, King of, <u>1721</u>: DL, Apr 27, May 2, LIF, 3, DL, 26
DeLaGrange (dancer), <u>1738</u>: TC, Aug 7, BFP, 23, SFH, Sep 5
DeLaGrange, Mlle (dancer), <u>1738</u>: TC, Aug 7, BFP, 23, SFH, Sep 5
DeLaGrange, Prince (spectator), <u>1662</u>: LI, Jan 3
DeLaHay (dancer), <u>1707</u>: HA, Aug 1
DeLaHay (dancer), <u>1736</u>: HAY, Feb 20; <u>1738</u>: TC, Aug 7, SFH, Sep 5
Delahay St, <u>1784</u>: HAY, Jul 24; <u>1785</u>: HAY, Feb 24; <u>1786</u>: HAY, Jul 14; <u>1787</u>: HAY,
   Jul 25
Delahoy (dancer), <u>1799</u>: CG, Jan 29
Delahyde (musician), <u>1747</u>: DL, May 12
Delaistre (Delater) (dancer), <u>1755</u>: DL, Nov 8, 15; <u>1756</u>: DL, Jan 8; <u>1757</u>: DL,
   Oct 20, 29, Nov 26, Dec 17, 23; <u>1758</u>: DL, Apr 15, 19, 27, May 26, CG, Nov 16,
   23; <u>1759</u>: CG, Mar 24, Apr 27, May 16
DelaMagre. See Delamaine.
Delamaine (DelaMagre, Delemayne), Henry (dancer), <u>1733</u>: GF, Sep 10; <u>1735</u>: DL,
   Sep 15, Oct 1, 22, Nov 17; <u>1736</u>: DL, Feb 28, Mar 25, 27, 29, Apr 8, 16, 27,
   28, May 4, 15, 20, LIF, Nov 9, 16, 22, 23, 26; <u>1737</u>: CG, Oct 26; <u>1741</u>: DL,
   Oct 31, Nov 14, 28, Dec 14, 18; <u>1742</u>: DL, Jan 6, Feb 18, 25, CG, Mar 9, 15,
   Oct 25, Dec 10; <u>1743</u>: CG, Jan 19, Mar 5, LIF, 22, CG, Apr 2, 6, 22; <u>1749</u>: CG,
   Sep 25
DeLaMotte, Houdart. See LaMotte, Houdart de.
DelaNash, Mlle, <u>1748</u>: HAY, Apr 21
Delane, Dennis (actor), <u>1731</u>: GF, Nov 24, 26, 27, Dec 3, 7, 9, 13, 20, 30;
   <u>1732</u>: GF, Jan 29, Feb 17, 21, 26, Mar 20, 27, 28, Apr 1, 12, 27, Oct 2, 4, 5,
   9, 12, 13, 18, 24, 25, 26, Nov 4, 18, 27, Dec 1, 29; <u>1733</u>: GF, Jan 1, 8, 17,
   18, Feb 12, 19, 20, Mar 15, 17, 28, 30, Apr 2, 11, 17, 19, May 5, 9, 29, Sep
   10, 12, 14, 19, 20, 21, 24, 25, 28, Oct 3, 4, 5, 9, 15, 18, 25, Nov 5, 8, 10,
   13, 14, 29, Dec 10, 18; <u>1734</u>: GF, Jan 3, 14, 31, Mar 5, 11, 19, Apr 6, 19,
   26, May 8, 15, 16, Sep 9, 11, 13, 16, 18, 20, Oct 16, 21, 23, Nov 4, 6, 7,
   11, 12, 18, 22, 25, 27, 29, Dec 2, 6, 12, 16; <u>1735</u>: GF, Jan 1, 4, 13, Feb 5,
   6, 8, 25, Mar 20, 29, Apr 14, 16, 22, CG, Oct 25, Nov 1, 4, 8, 10, 15, 17,

22, 28, Dec 15, 31; <u>1736</u>: GF, Jan 3, CG, 8, 10, 17, Feb 21, Mar 2, 9, 15, 18,
Apr 8, 29, May 13, Sep 15, 20, 22, 27, 29, Oct 4, 6, 11, 15, 20, 22, 23, 30,
Nov 1, 4, 8, 15, 25, 26, Dec 2, 9; <u>1737</u>: CG, Feb 7, 14, 15, 24, 26, Mar 14,
17, 24, 31, May 3, 31, Sep 16, 19, 23, 28, 30, Oct 7, 10, 14, 19, 22, 24, 26,
27, 31, Nov 1, 4, 15, 19; <u>1738</u>: CG, Jan 3, 13, 17, 25, 26, Feb 6, 13, 16, 23,
Mar 13, 14, 18, 20, 25, Apr 7, 10, 12, 17, 24, Jul 21, Sep 15, 18, 20, 25,
29, Oct 6, 9, 11, 14, 16, 18, 21, 23, 24, 28, 31, Nov 2, 4, 9, 18, 22, 23,
24, 29, 30, Dec 2, 4, 5, 7; <u>1739</u>: CG, Jan 4, 17, Feb 10, 16, 24, Mar 3, 13,
20, Sep 10, 15, 21, 27, 29, Oct 3, 4, 6, 9, 10, 22, 23, 25, Nov 1, 2, 5, 6,
9, 10, 17, 22, 28, Dec 4, 6, 10, 21, 29; <u>1740</u>: CG, Jan 15, 17, Mar 11, 25,
May 16, Sep 19, 26, Oct 6, 23, 24, 31, Nov 4, 7, 20, GF, 22, CG, Dec 4, 5,
13; <u>1741</u>: CG, Jan 7, 15, 22, 23, 27, 28, Feb 12, 17, 26, Mar 9, 12, 30, Apr
1, 2, 9, 24, May 12, DL, Sep 10, 19, Oct 8, 12, Nov 2, 4, 16, 21, Dec 8, 14,
19; <u>1742</u>: DL, Jan 4, 25, Feb 3, 11, 16, Mar 2, 8, 15, 20, 27, Apr 5, 27, 28,
May 17, Sep 11, 16, Oct 12, 18, Nov 1, 3, 4, 16, 22, Dec 8, 22; <u>1743</u>: DL, Jan
11, 27, 28, Feb 4, 11, 17, Mar 3, 14, 24, Apr 29, May 2, 6, Sep 24, 27, 29,
Oct 6, 8, 11, 13, 15, 25, 27, Nov 4, 8, 12, 17, 18, 23, 24, 29, Dec 12, 15,
19, 20; <u>1744</u>: DL, Jan 12, 27, CG, Feb 10, DL, 21, Mar 12, 13, 30, Apr 2, 25,
28, May 4, 11, 22, Sep 27, Oct 4, 13, 17, 20, 22, 23, 27, Nov 1, 5, 7, 8, 16,
24, Dec 11, 19, 28; <u>1745</u>: DL, Jan 4, 14, 26, Feb 7, 20, Mar 11, 18, May 9,
Sep 19, 21, Oct 1, 5, 8, 12, 19, Nov 1, 4, 9, 11, 14, 20, 23, 26, Dec 12, 17;
<u>1746</u>: DL, Jan 14, 18, 29, 31, Mar 10, 15, 18, Apr 12, 21, 23, Sep 23, Oct 2,
4, 23, 25, Nov 1, 4, 5, 7, 15, 28, Dec 15, 26; <u>1747</u>: DL, Jan 3, 24, Feb 16,
Mar 7, 16, 19, 24, 28, 30, Apr 20, 23, 27, May 1, 5, Sep 15, 19, 22, 24, Oct
15, 20, 24, Nov 4, 6, 10, 13, 18, Dec 16; <u>1748</u>: DL, Jan 2, 20, Mar 10, 15,
19, Apr 28, CG, Oct 17, 21, 24, Nov 1, 3, 4, 15, 24, 28, Dec 1, 2, 9, DL, 10,
CG, 21, 22, 26; <u>1749</u>: CG, Jan 13, Feb 6, Mar 2, 4, 6, 13, 14, May 4, Sep 27,
29, Oct 2, 9, 12, 19, 26, 27, Nov 2, 3, 4, 8, 21, 23, 24, Dec 8, 16; <u>1750</u>:
CG, Jan 16, 31, Feb 2, 20, 22, Mar 12, 17, 31, DL, Apr 2
Delane, Miss (actor), <u>1734</u>: GF, May 3
Delany, Mrs (spectator), <u>1744</u>: CG, Feb 10, 24, Mar 21
DeLanza (composer), <u>1800</u>: DL, Jun 3
Delap, John, <u>1781</u>: DL, Feb 17; <u>1786</u>: DL, Mar 9
--Captives, The, <u>1786</u>: DL, Mar 9, 11, 13
--Hecuba, <u>1761</u>: DL, Dec 11, 12, 14, 15, 19; <u>1762</u>: DL, Jan 8
--Royal Suppliants, The, <u>1781</u>: DL, Feb 17, 19, 20, 22, 24, 27, Mar 1, 3, 17,
20, 29, Apr 20
Delascey (dancer), <u>1757</u>: HAY, Dec 26
Delassements Militaires, Les (dance), <u>1797</u>: KING'S, Jan 17, 24, 31, Feb 7, 11,
Apr 1, DL, May 22, KING'S, 27, Jul 15, 22, CG, Oct 21, 24, 28, 31, Nov 4, 7
Delater. See Delaistre.
Delaval, E (actor), <u>1751</u>: DL, Mar 7
Delaval, E and John (actors), <u>1751</u>: DL, Mar 7
Delaval, E, John and Sir Francis (actors), <u>1755</u>: DL, Mar 4
Delaval, Sir Francis (actor), <u>1751</u>: DL, Mar 7; <u>1752</u>: DL, Jan 24; <u>1753</u>: CG, Mar
24
Delaval, John (actor), <u>1751</u>: DL, Mar 7
Delaval, Mlle (dancer), <u>1704</u>: LIF, Dec 12; <u>1705</u>: LIF, Jan 9, 13, Feb 20,
LIF/QUEN, Mar 3, LIF, 10, 31, QUEEN'S, Apr 23, 26
Delaval, Mme (harpist), <u>1796</u>: CG, Feb 12, 17, 24, Mar 2, 11, 16
Delawn (dancer), <u>1734</u>: YB, Aug 28
DelCampo, Thomazio Alegro (acrobat), <u>1718</u>: AC, Sep 24
DelCaro, Sga (dancer), <u>1790</u>: HAY, Jan 7, Feb 6, 13, Apr 6, 15, May 4, 20, 27;
<u>1794</u>: KING'S, Jan 11, Mar 1, 4, Apr 1, May 31, DL, Jul 2, KING'S, Dec 6, 20;
<u>1795</u>: KING'S, Jan 20, Mar 26, May 14, 16, 28, Jun 20; <u>1796</u>: KING'S, Jan 9,
Feb 6, DL, Oct 1, 29, Dec 14; <u>1797</u>: DL, Feb 22, Mar 6, May 13, Jun 10, HAY,
Aug 3, DL, Nov 9; <u>1798</u>: DL, Mar 24, May 11, 16, 21, 24, 31, Jun 18, Sep 15,
Nov 14, Dec 6; <u>1799</u>: DL, Feb 5, May 2, CG, 14, DL, Jul 1, Nov 27, Dec 2;
<u>1800</u>: DL, Mar 8, May 29, Jun 2
Delectante (correspondent), <u>1769</u>: KING'S, Feb 24
Del'Epine, Francesca Margherita (singer), <u>1703</u>: LIF, Jun 8, 11; <u>1704</u>: DL, Jan
29, Feb 5, 12, 19, 26, Apr 22, 29, May 31, CC, Jun 7, DL, 21, Jul 5, Dec 30;
<u>1705</u>: DL, Jan 4, Mar 10, Oct 24, Nov 6, Dec 1, 15; <u>1706</u>: DL, Jan 12, ATCOURT,
Feb 5, DL, 16, 23, Apr 13; <u>1707</u>: DL, Jan 9, Feb 4, Nov 15; <u>1708</u>: QUEEN'S, Feb
26, Apr 10; <u>1709</u>: QUEEN'S, Feb 12, Mar 2, Apr 9; <u>1710</u>: QUEEN'S, Jan 10, Mar
23, Apr 21, PCGR, Jun 14; <u>1711</u>: QUEEN'S, Apr 14, May 12, Dec 5, 12; <u>1712</u>:
QUEEN'S, Jan 23, Feb 27, Nov 22; <u>1713</u>: QUEEN'S, Jan 10, Feb 26; <u>1714</u>:
QUEEN'S, Jan 9, KING'S, Oct 23, Nov 16; <u>1715</u>: DL, Mar 12, Apr 7, 20, KING'S,
Aug 27, DL, Nov 5, 7, 10; <u>1716</u>: DL, Apr 17; <u>1717</u>: LIF, Feb 27, Jun 1; <u>1718</u>:
LIF, Nov 18, Dec 9; <u>1719</u>: LIF, Apr 16; <u>1720</u>: DL, May 17, KING'S, Jun 18, 22,
25; see also Margarita, Sga
Del'Epine, Manina (singer), <u>1714</u>: QUEEN'S, Apr 3; see also Manina, Sga

Delfevre, Mme (dancer), <u>1786</u>: KING'S, Dec 23; <u>1787</u>: KING'S, Jan 6, 20, Feb 13,
   Mar 13
Delia (song), <u>1766</u>: CG, Apr 18
Delia tired Strephon with her flame (song), <u>1700</u>: LIF, Mar 0
Delicati, Luigi (singer), <u>1789</u>: KING'S, Jan 10, Mar 24, Jun 11
Delicati, Margherita (singer), <u>1789</u>: KING'S, Jan 10, Feb 28, Mar 21, 24, Jun 11
Deligny, Louise (dancer), <u>1791</u>: PAN, Feb 17, Mar 19, 22, May 9, 17
Delisle (actor, dancer), <u>1734</u>: GF/HAY, Dec 2, 27; <u>1735</u>: GF/HAY, Jan 8, 9, HAY,
   Apr 16, GF/HAY, 25, May 1, 2, GF, 23, GF/HAY, Jun 2; <u>1736</u>: CG, Mar 23
DeLisle (dancer), <u>1675</u>: ATCOURT, Feb 15
DeLisle, Mlle (actor), <u>1720</u>: KING'S, Mar 22, LIF, Apr 4, KING'S, 26, May 10,
   27; <u>1721</u>: HAY, Feb 9, 10, 25
DeLisle, Mlle (dancer), <u>1735</u>: CG, Nov 22, 24, Dec 12, 18; <u>1736</u>: CG, Jan 2, 9,
   12, Feb 23, Mar 2, 6, 20, 22, 29, 30, Apr 1, 5, 10, 15, 17, May 1, LIF, 5,
   CG, 6, 10, 11, 17, 18, LIF, 19, CG, 25, 31, Jun 4
DeLissale (house servant), <u>1742</u>: CG, Feb 8
DeLiury, Mlle (actor), <u>1720</u>: KING'S, Jun 20
Dell (horn player), <u>1760</u>: CG, Nov 28
Dell, Henry
--Frenchified Lady, The, <u>1756</u>: CG, Mar 23, Apr 8, 30; <u>1757</u>: CG, Jan 28, Feb 1,
   8, 10, 12, 16, 24, Mar 24, 28, Apr 16; <u>1758</u>: DL, Mar 11, May 1; <u>1762</u>: CG, Mar
   27; <u>1760</u>: DL, Apr 11; <u>1770</u>: DL, Mar 24; <u>1773</u>: DL, Mar 27
Dellarundo, Fonidoso (author), <u>1772</u>: HAY, Sep 17
Delony (guitarist), <u>1675</u>: ATCOURT, Feb 15
Delorme, Mlle (dancer, actor), <u>1730</u>: DL, Apr 13, 14, 23, 24, 27, 29, 30, May 1,
   2, 4, 11, 15, 19, 27, HAY, Jul 28, BFOF, Aug 20, DL, Sep 15, 17, 24, Oct 8,
   10, 22, 28, Nov 19, Dec 4; <u>1731</u>: DL, Oct 16, Nov 25, Dec 15, 28; <u>1732</u>: DL,
   Feb 22, Mar 21, Apr 17, 21, 22, 26, 27, 28, May 2, 3, 6, 12, 29, Jun 6, Aug
   1, Nov 8, 17, Dec 14, 26; <u>1733</u>: DL, Jan 23, Feb 12, Mar 26, 31, Apr 16, 20,
   May 5, 7, BF, Aug 23, DL, Oct 10, 12, 19, 24, Nov 13, 27, Dec 5, 7, 11, 13;
   <u>1734</u>: DL, Jan 1, Feb 4, Mar 7, DL/HAY, 18, Apr 1, DL/LIF, 1, DL/HAY, 2, DL,
   15, DL/HAY, 26, DL, 29, May 15, CG/LIF, Dec 30; <u>1735</u>: CG/LIF, Jan 17, Feb 3,
   13, 22, Mar 11, 15, Apr 14, 17, 24, May 9, 16, 20, CG, Sep 26, Oct 3, 13, 17,
   Nov 6, 11, Dec 18; <u>1736</u>: CG, Jan 1, 5, 9, 10, 23, Feb 23, 26, Mar 6, 11, Apr
   8, May 6, 8, 11, BFHC, Aug 23, CG, Sep 22, 29, Oct 4, 6, 8, 27, Nov 3, 9, 23,
   26; <u>1737</u>: CG, Jan 28, Feb 14, Mar 7, 24, 28, Apr 15, May 12
Delosne de Monchesney
--Phenix, Le; ou, Arlequin Ambassadeur de Colombine Becha, <u>1721</u>: HAY, Mar 16
DeLoutherbourg, Philip James (scene painter), <u>1773</u>: DL, Mar 20, Apr 22, Jun 2,
   Oct 9, 30, Nov 25, Dec 15, 27; <u>1774</u>: DL, Jan 17, Feb 15, 21, Mar 15, Apr 15,
   May 16, Sep 24, Oct 14, 15, Nov 5; <u>1775</u>: DL, Oct 18, Nov 11; <u>1776</u>: DL, Feb 9,
   Oct 18, Nov 7, Dec 5; <u>1777</u>: DL, Jan 4, Oct 31; <u>1778</u>: DL, Jan 1, 2, Oct 8, 15,
   31; <u>1779</u>: DL, Jan 8, Mar 11, Sep 30, Oct 5, 30, Nov 6, 27, Dec 13; <u>1780</u>: DL,
   Jan 3, May 5, Sep 19, 30, Dec 27; <u>1781</u>: DL, Jan 29, CG, May 7, DL, Sep 20,
   Nov 29, Dec 13; <u>1785</u>: CG, Dec 20; <u>1788</u>: CG, Mar 24; <u>1799</u>: DL, May 24
Delpini, Carlo Antonio (dancer), <u>1776</u>: CG, Dec 26, 27; <u>1777</u>: CG, Jan 9, Apr 23,
   Oct 1, Nov 25; <u>1778</u>: CG, May 6, Oct 14, 22; <u>1779</u>: CG, Jan 4, Apr 23, Oct 6,
   DL, 30, Dec 10, 17; <u>1780</u>: DL, Jan 3, Feb 28, CG, Apr 7, DL, 24, May 2, 5, CG,
   6, DL, 9, Sep 19, 30, Oct 30; <u>1781</u>: DL, Jan 2, 18, 29, KING'S, Feb 22, DL,
   Mar 12, Apr 25, May 14, HAY, 30, KING'S, Jul 3, HAY, Aug 8, 31, DL, Oct 2,
   12; <u>1782</u>: DL, Jan 3, 5, May 10, CG, 11, 14, DL, 15, HAY, Jun 3, 18, Aug 17,
   DL, Sep 20, Nov 4, 11, Dec 26; <u>1783</u>: HAY, Jun 5, 7, 20, 30, Jul 2, Aug 29;
   <u>1784</u>: HAY, Apr 30, May 10, Jul 19, Aug 26; <u>1785</u>: HAY, Feb 7, 14, 21, 28, Mar
   7, 10, 14, Apr 11, 15, 18, 29, Jul 13, Aug 11, 19, 31, CG, Dec 26; <u>1786</u>: CG,
   Feb 24; <u>1788</u>: HAY, Apr 29, CG, Dec 26; <u>1789</u>: CG, Mar 16, 26, Apr 25, May 28,
   Sep 16, 21, Nov 13, Dec 21; <u>1790</u>: CG, Jan 23, May 26; <u>1791</u>: CG, Dec 21; <u>1793</u>:
   HAY, Oct 10, Dec 26, 31; <u>1794</u>: HAY, Jan 7; <u>1796</u>: CG, Mar 15, Nov 5, Dec 19;
   <u>1797</u>: CG, Feb 18, Mar 20, May 26, Jun 1, 9; <u>1798</u>: HAY, Sep 17; <u>1799</u>: CG, Oct
   21, Dec 23; <u>1800</u>: CG, Feb 10, Apr 29, 30, Jun 2, 6
--Blue Beard; or, The Flight of Harlequin (pantomime), <u>1791</u>: CG, Dec 21, 22,
   23, 26, 27, 28, 29, 30, 31; <u>1792</u>: CG, Jan 2, 3, 4, 5, 6, 7, 9, 10, 11, 12,
   13, 14, 16, 17, 18, 19, 20, 21, 23, 27, Feb 6, 17, 18, Oct 8, 15, 22
--Don John (pantomime), <u>1789</u>: DL, May 22, CG, 28, Jun 1, 6, 15, 18, Sep 16, Nov
   2, WHF, 11; <u>1790</u>: DL, Oct 26, 30, Nov 1, 6, 9, 17, 26, Dec 1, 23; <u>1791</u>: DL,
   Feb 12, 18, Mar 5, 12, 19, Apr 16, 27, DLKING'S, Nov 5, 9, 25, Dec 2, 20, 27;
   <u>1796</u>: DL, Jun 7; <u>1797</u>: DL, May 19; <u>1798</u>: DL, May 11, Jun 13; <u>1799</u>: DL, May
   21; <u>1800</u>: CG, Jun 2
--Here and There and Every Where (pantomime), <u>1785</u>: HAY, Aug 31, Sep 1, 5, 7,
   9, 12, 14, 15, 16; <u>1786</u>: HAY, Jul 3, 5, 10, 17, 31, Sep 4
Delpini, Mrs Carlo Antonio (actor), <u>1788</u>: HAY, Apr 29; <u>1789</u>: CG, May 28; <u>1790</u>:
   CG, May 26; <u>1797</u>: CG, Jun 9
Deluge, The. See Ecclestone, Edward.

Delune, Mrs (dancer), 1744: CG, Feb 11
Demagny, Widow (beneficiary), 1737: LIF, Jun 15
Demaimbray (Demembray) (machinist), 1742: DL, May 8; 1743: DL, May 2; 1744: DL,
   May 5
DeMajo (singer), 1766: KING'S, Mar 13
Demar (dancer), 1736: HAY, Feb 20
Demaria (dancer), 1773: DL, Oct 2
Demaria, J (scene painter), 1794: DL, Jun 9; 1799: DL, May 24, Dec 11
Demera, Sga (singer), 1771: KING'S, Mar 14
Demetrio (opera), 1757: KING'S, Nov 8, 12, 15, 19, 22, 26, 29, Dec 3, 6, 10,
   13, 17, 23; 1758: KING'S, Jan 7, Feb 25, 28, Mar 7, Apr 26, May 2, 12, 27,
   Jun 5, Dec 16, 23, 30; 1759: KING'S, Jan 4, Mar 5, Apr 3; 1760: CG, Mar 27;
   1761: KING'S, Apr 28; 1762: KING'S, Mar 1
Demetrio. See Lampugnani, Giovanni Battista; Guglielmi, Pietro; Cherubini,
   Maria Lorenzo.
Demetrius. See Pescetti, Giovanni Battista.
Demi-Character Dance (dance), 1753: DL, Nov 1, 3, 5; 1771: HAY, Apr 24; 1796:
   KING'S, Mar 1
DeMira, Sga (singer), 1793: KING'S, Feb 26, Apr 23, May 14, Jun 8; 1794:
   KING'S, Feb 1, Mar 1, 18, Jun 5; 1800: KING'S, Feb 18
DeMirail. See Dumirail.
Democrite Amoureux. See Regnard, Jean Francois.
Demofoonte. See Duni, Egidio; Jomelli, Niccolo; Vento, Mathias; Bertoni,
   Fernando Giuseppe.
Demons' Dance (dance), 1778: DL, Jan 17, Dec 23; 1779: DL, Mar 23, Oct 21;
   1780: DL, Sep 28; 1782: DL, Apr 18, May 2; 1784: CG, Mar 27, DL, Nov 26;
   1786: DL, Jan 6
Denbigh, Isabella Countess of (correspondent), 1744: KING'S, Jun 22
Denbigh, Lady. See Firebrace, Hester.
Denby (flutist), 1709: HA, Sep 3
Denham (bookseller), 1782: HAY, Mar 18
Denham, Sir John, 1660: ATCOURT, Nov 19; 1663: VERE, Mar 0; 1668: ATCOURT, Feb
   4; 1676: DL, Dec 11
--Sophy, The, 1660: SALSBURY, Dec 12; 1670: LIF, Jan 12; 1674: DG, Oct 0
Denham, Miss (dancer), 1757: HAY, Jul 5
Denham, Robert (singer), 1732: CR, Feb 23
Denis, Miss B (dancer), 1800: DL, May 14, Jun 2
Denis, Miss E (dancer), 1800: DL, May 14, Jun 2
Denman, William (actor, singer), 1792: DLKING'S, May 23; 1794: DL, May 22, Jun
   2, 12, Oct 31, Nov 15, Dec 20; 1795: DL, Feb 9, Oct 30, Nov 11, Dec 10; 1796:
   DL, Jan 8, 11, Mar 3, 12, Apr 30, Sep 29, Oct 19, 27, Nov 5, 9, 26, Dec 26;
   1797: DL, Jan 7, 12, HAY, 23, DL, Feb 3, 22, Mar 6, May 18, Jun 12, Nov 8;
   1798: DL, Jan 16, Feb 20, Oct 6, Nov 14, 26, Dec 4, 29, 31; 1799: DL, Jan 19,
   28, CG, Feb 8, Mar 13, Sep 30, Oct 7, Nov 14, Dec 5, 16, 23; 1800: CG, Jan
   16, Feb 10, 28, Mar 4, 5, 19, 25, Apr 2, 5, 26, May 1, 2, 6, 17, 30, Jun 3,
   10, 16
Denmark, King of, 1768: DL, Aug 18, Sep 8, HAY, 19, CG, 20, DL, 22, 29, Oct 1,
   CG, 1, DL, 6, 11, CG, 12, DL, 14, Nov 9
Denmark, Prince and Princess of, 1687: CITY, Oct 29; 1689: CITY, Oct 29; 1692:
   DLORDG, Jul 14; 1700: DG, Jan 3
Denmark, Prince George of, 1708: DL, Oct 28
Denmark, Prince of, 1662: CITY, Oct 29; 1687: CITY, Oct 29
Denmark, Princess of, 1691: YB, Apr 13; 1697: ATCOURT, Feb 6
Denner (violinist), 1758: CHAPEL, Apr 27
Dennis (actor), 1779: HAY, Dec 20
Dennis (singer), 1755: BF, Sep 3
Dennis, John, 1660: VERE, Nov 9; 1661: LIF, Dec 16; 1676: DG, Mar 11, DL, Dec
   11; 1683: DL, Jan 19; 1685: NONE, Feb 6; 1697: DL, May 8, NONE, Sep 0; 1698:
   NONE, Sep 0, LIF, Nov 0; 1699: LIF, Nov 26, Dec 0; 1702: DL, May 0, Dec 0;
   1704: LIF, Feb 24; 1705: DL, Feb 16; 1709: DL, Feb 5; 1719: NONE, Mar 26, DL,
   Nov 11, 12, 13; 1725: LIF, Jan 4; 1731: LIF, Jan 4; 1733: DL/HAY, Dec 18
--Appius and Virginia, 1709: DL, Feb 5, 7, 8, 9
--Comical Gallant, The; or, The Amours of Sir John Falstaffe, 1660: VERE, Nov
   9; 1661: LIF, Dec 16; 1702: DL, May 0
--Gibraltar; or, The Spanish Adventure, 1705: DL, Feb 13, 16, 20
--Invader of His Country. See Shakespeare, William, Coriolanus.
--Iphigenia, 1699: LIF, Nov 26, DL, Dec 0, LIF, 0, DL, 14
--Liberty Asserted; or, French Perfidy Displayed, 1704: LIF, Feb 24, 25, 26,
   29, Mar 2, 4, 6, 9, 11, 16, 27; 1707: QUEEN'S, May 2; 1746: CG, Apr 23, 25
--Plot and no Plot, A; or, Jacobite Credulity, 1697: DL, May 8; 1746: CG, Apr
   23
--Rinaldo and Armida, 1698: DL/ORDG, Nov 0, LIF, 0, DL, Dec 0; 1699: LIF, Jan

5; <u>1705</u>: QUEEN'S, Apr 26
--Victim, The; or, Achilles and Iphigenia in Aulis, <u>1699</u>: DL, Dec 0
Dennis, Mr and Mrs (singer, dancer), <u>1752</u>: SOU, Sep 29
Dennis, Mrs (singer), <u>1720</u>: YB, Feb 15, KING'S, Apr 2
Dennis, Mrs (singer), <u>1755</u>: BF, Sep 3
Dennis, <u>1772</u>: DL, Dec 17
Dennison (dancer), <u>1750</u>: CG, Apr 18; <u>1751</u>: CG, May 1, Sep 30, Oct 2, Nov 11,
   Dec 13; <u>1752</u>: CG, Jan 16, Apr 15, Oct 10, Dec 7; <u>1753</u>: DL, Oct 17, Nov 17,
   21, 23, Dec 19, 26; <u>1754</u>: DL, Jan 7, 28, Apr 4, May 4, Oct 3, 11; <u>1755</u>: DL,
   Apr 24, 29, Sep 30, Oct 8, Nov 8, 22
Dennison, Mr and Mrs (dancer), <u>1752</u>: SFP, Sep 21
Denny (doorkeeper), <u>1758</u>: DL, May 17; <u>1760</u>: DL, May 6; <u>1768</u>: DL, May 30
Denny, Miss (dancer), <u>1799</u>: CG, Jan 29
Dennychock, Miss. See Chock, Dennis.
Denoyer (Danoyer, Desnoye) (dancer), <u>1721</u>: DL, Jan 11, 18, Mar 13, 30, Apr 11,
   12, 14, 17, May 1, 5, 8, 9, 10, 12, 16, 18, 24, 29, Sep 19, Oct 16, 18, Nov
   13, Dec 18, 20, 22; <u>1722</u>: DL, Jan 8, 10, 19, 24, Mar 10, 28, Apr 5, 9, 18,
   19, 24, 26, 27, 28, 30, May 2, 4, 5, 15, 23, 24, 28, 29; <u>1731</u>: DL, Dec 22,
   27, 28, 30; <u>1732</u>: DL, Feb 2, 22, Mar 2, 6, 13, 16, 23, 27, 30; <u>1733</u>: DL, Feb
   12, 22, 26, Mar 5, 8, 10, 15, 26, 28, 31; <u>1734</u>: DL, Nov 4, 5, 11, 15, 23, Dec
   2, 12; <u>1735</u>: DL, Jan 8, 9, 18, 23, Feb 4, 15, 18, 27, Mar 3, 10, 13, 17, 20,
   22, 24, 25, 27, 29, Apr 7, CG/LIF, 24, DL, 25, May 7, Sep 15, 18, Oct 1, 27,
   28, 29, Nov 3, 4, 5, 8, 10, 15, 19, 27, 28, Dec 1, 2, 3, 6, 10, 16, 22, 31;
   <u>1736</u>: DL, Jan 2, 3, 29, Feb 2, 5, 9, 10, 11, 13, 14, 21, 28, Mar 3, 23, 27,
   Apr 3, 10, May 5, 8, 19, Oct 26, 28, Nov 1, 4, 9, 11, 13, 16, 22, Dec 3, 11,
   23, 30; <u>1737</u>: DL, Jan 4, 29, Feb 5, 16, Mar 5, 7, 10, 12, 14, 15, 22, Apr 23,
   26, 30; <u>1738</u>: DL, Jan 11, 13, 21, Feb 1, 3, 6, 9, 23, Mar 4, 13, 14, 16, Apr
   29, May 1, 6, 10, 12, 18, Dec 8, 11; <u>1739</u>: DL, Jan 13, 16, Feb 28, Mar 3, 8,
   10, 12, 13, Apr 2, 9, 12, 24, 25, 27, May 1, 2, 15, Oct 19, 26, Nov 1, 7, 8,
   9, 10, 14, 22, 23, 28, Dec 8, 10, 12, 22; <u>1740</u>: DL, Jan 12, 15, 29, Mar 13,
   17, 20, 22, 24, 27, Apr 8, 9, 10, 14, 15, 16, 17, 18, 21, 22, 24, 25, 26, 29,
   30, May 1, CG, Oct 25, 27, 30, Nov 3, 17, 21, 27, 28, Dec 2, 4, 5, 9, 11, 13,
   16, 17, 20, 30; <u>1741</u>: CG, Jan 2, 3, 8, 17, 21, 28, 29, 31, Feb 3, 6, 7, 12,
   14, 17, 19, 23, 28, Mar 2, 5, 7, 9, 10, 16, 19, 30, 31, Apr 3, 6, 14, 15, 29;
   <u>1742</u>: CG, Jan 11, 21, 25, Feb 6, 22, Mar 4, 8, 13, Apr 1, 5
Denoyer's apprentice (dancer), <u>1732</u>: GF, Oct 13; <u>1735</u>: DL, Mar 17, 24; <u>1736</u>:
   DL, Feb 21, Apr 3, 15, LIF, 20, DL, May 8, 19, 21, 22, 27, 28, Jun 23, Oct
   16; <u>1737</u>: DL, Feb 22, Mar 5, 14, 19, 21, 22, May 4, 5, 9, 14, 16, 18, 24, 25,
   26, 27, 30, 31, Jun 11
Dent (householder), <u>1782</u>: CG, Apr 29
Dent, John, <u>1782</u>: HAY, Aug 5, DL, Nov 5; <u>1783</u>: HAY, Aug 13; <u>1785</u>: CG, May 7;
   <u>1787</u>: DL, May 8; <u>1795</u>: CG, Apr 8
--Candidate, The, <u>1782</u>: HAY, Aug 5, 8, 10, 12, 14
--Lawyer's Panic, The; or, Westminster Hall in an Uproar (prelude), <u>1785</u>: CG,
   May 7, 11, HAY, Aug 16; <u>1786</u>: HAY, Aug 4
--Receipt Tax, The (farce), <u>1783</u>: HAY, Aug 13, 15, 20
--Telegraph!, The; or, A New Way of Knowing Things (prelude), <u>1795</u>: CG, Apr 8
--Too Civil by Half (farce), <u>1782</u>: DL, Nov 5, 6, 7, 9, 12, 15, 18, 19, 21, 22,
   26, 28, Dec 10, 19; <u>1783</u>: DL, Jan 2, Feb 4, 13, 21, 26, Mar 11, May 3, 19;
   <u>1784</u>: DL, Jan 3, 6, 29, Mar 27, Apr 15, 21, May 4, Nov 13; <u>1785</u>: DL, Feb 19,
   Apr 21, Oct 13, Nov 22; <u>1786</u>: DL, Nov 18; <u>1787</u>: DL, May 8, 16, 30; <u>1788</u>: DL,
   May 6
Denton, Mrs (actor), <u>1749</u>: HAY, May 26; <u>1767</u>: HAY, Jul 2, 8, 22
Dents, De Long (dancer), <u>1723</u>: BFPJ, Aug 22, RI, Sep 2
Dents, De Long, two children of (dancer), <u>1723</u>: BFPJ, Aug 22, RI, Sep 2
Denys, Miss (dancer), <u>1798</u>: DL, May 9
D'Eon de Beaumont, Charles Genevieve (La Chevaliere) (fencer), <u>1793</u>: DL, May 30
DePaoli, Gaetano (singer), <u>1795</u>: KING'S, Jun 23
Depar (musician), <u>1703</u>: RIW, Aug 12
Dependent, The. See Cumberland, Richard.
Depit Amoureux (dance), <u>1736</u>: CG, May 11
Deport (wigmaker), <u>1749</u>: DL, Nov 3
Deposing and Death of Queen Gin, The (interlude), <u>1736</u>: HAY, Aug 2
Deppo Lombre (song), <u>1728</u>: HAY, Aug 9
Deptford, <u>1731</u>: LIF, Jun 7; <u>1776</u>: CHR, Sep 25, Oct 14; <u>1778</u>: CHR, May 25
Depths have covered them (song), <u>1794</u>: DL, Apr 9
Derby (office keeper), <u>1758</u>: CG, May 12; <u>1759</u>: CG, May 25; <u>1760</u>: CG, Sep 22;
   <u>1761</u>: CG, May 15
Derby, Countess of. See Stanley, Dorothea.
Derham, Miss. See Durham, Miss.
Dermot and Kathlane; or, The Irish Wedding (dance), <u>1793</u>: CG, Oct 18, 22, 26,
   29, Nov 1, 2, 16, Dec 6, 10, 11, 13, 14, 16, 17, 18; <u>1794</u>: CG, Feb 14, 19,

Apr 24, 30, May 16, 31, Jun 16, 17; <u>1795</u>: CG, Feb 19, 21, 24, 28, Jun 4;
   <u>1796</u>: CG, Apr 8
Deroissi, Miss (dancer), <u>1763</u>: CG, May 7
DeRoy, Pierre (scene painter), <u>1775</u>: DL, Nov 11
Derrick, Samuel (author), <u>1752</u>: CG, Mar 6; <u>1756</u>: CG, Dec 17
Desbarques (DeBargues, DuBargues) (dancer), <u>1705</u>: LIF/QUEN, Nov 6, QUEEN'S, 15,
   17, 20, LIF/QUEN, Dec 4, QUEEN'S, 8, 12, LIF/QUEN, 26; <u>1706</u>: QUEEN'S, Jan 2,
   7, 9, 14, 22, 23, Feb 2, 9, Mar 4, 11, Apr 3, LIF/QUEN, 11, QUEEN'S, 20, 25,
   30, May 15, Jun 13, DL, Dec 3, 7, 17, 27; <u>1707</u>: DL, Jan 13, 16, 23, Feb 13,
   20, Mar 8, 11, Apr 3, May 24, DL/QUEEN, Dec 9; <u>1708</u>: QUEEN'S, Jan 20,
   DL/QUEEN, Feb 7, 10, 21
Desbarques, Mrs (dancer), <u>1708</u>: DL/QUEEN, Feb 7, 10, 21
Descent of the Heathen Gods, The; or, Cuckoldom no Scandal (droll), <u>1749</u>: BFY,
   Aug 23, 24, 25, BFYT, 26, BFY, 28
Deschalliez (DeSchallier, Dechaliers), Louise (dancer), <u>1720</u>: KING'S, Apr 26,
   May 3, 9, 10, 27, Jun 17; <u>1721</u>: HAY, Feb 21, 27, Mar 6, LIF, Apr 27
Description of a Cockney (song), <u>1795</u>: CG, May 6
Description of a Fair (song), <u>1789</u>: HAY, Aug 25
Description of a Storm (entertainment), <u>1772</u>: HAY, Dec 21
Desdechina, Sga (dancer), <u>1749</u>: CG, Jan 11
Desert Island, The. See Murphy, Arthur.
Deserted Daughter, The. See Holcroft, Thomas.
Deserter of Naples, The; or, Royal Clemency (pantomime, anon), <u>1788</u>: DL, Jun 2;
   <u>1791</u>: DL, Mar 24; <u>1792</u>: DLKING'S, May 22; <u>1793</u>: HAY, Oct 10, 11, 12; <u>1800</u>:
   CG, Apr 29, May 27, Jun 6
Deserter, The (Deserteur, Le; ou, La Clemence Royale) (dance), <u>1784</u>: KING'S,
   May 13, 20, 22, 25, Jun 1, 3, 8, 10, 12, 15, 17, 19, 22, 26, 29, Jul 3; <u>1785</u>:
   KING'S, Jan 11, 22, Feb 5, HAY, 7, 14, KING'S, 15, HAY, 21, KING'S, 26, HAY,
   28, Mar 7, KING'S, 8, HAY, 10, 14, Apr 11, 15, 18, 20, KING'S, 21, 26, HAY,
   29, KING'S, May 3, 7, Jun 14, 18, Jul 2, HAY, Aug 11, Sep 12; <u>1786</u>: CG, Feb
   24; <u>1788</u>: KING'S, May 29, Jun 10, 14, 17, 19, 21; <u>1789</u>: CG, Nov 13, 25, Dec
   4, 18; <u>1790</u>: CG, Feb 4, 13; <u>1791</u>: PAN, Mar 24, 26, 29, Apr 9, 28, Jun 18;
   <u>1795</u>: DL, May 20, 22; <u>1798</u>: KING'S, Jun 14, 16, 19, 23, Jul 3, 7, 28, Aug 4;
   <u>1799</u>: KING'S, Feb 12, Jul 9, 13, 20; <u>1800</u>: HAY, Jul 15
Deserter, The. See Dibdin, Charles.
Desertore, Il (dance), <u>1779</u>: KING'S, Dec 14, 21; <u>1780</u>: KING'S, Feb 8, 15, Apr
   1, 4, 11, 13
Deserving Favorite, The. See Carlell, Lodowick.
Deshaln (beneficiary), <u>1737</u>: LIF, May 10
Deshayes (dancer), <u>1735</u>: HAY, Apr 16, May 9, GF, May 23
DesHayes, Andre J J (dancer), <u>1800</u>: KING'S, Jan 11, 28, Mar 1, 4, Apr 15, DL,
   May 14, KING'S, 29, Jun 24, 28
Desormes (actor), <u>1749</u>: HAY, Nov 14; <u>1750</u>: DL, May 22
Despairing Shepherd (song), <u>1733</u>: GF, May 22
Desse (dancer), <u>1735</u>: CG, Sep 26, Oct 3, 13, 17, Nov 6, 11, 15, 28, Dec 2, 18;
   <u>1736</u>: CG, Jan 1, 9, 10, 21, 23, Feb 23, 26, Mar 2, 6, 11, Apr 28, 29, May 6,
   11, Sep 22, Oct 4, 6, 8, 20, 27, Nov 3, 9, 23, 26, Dec 28; <u>1737</u>: CG, Jan 28,
   Feb 14, Mar 7, 24, 28, Apr 15, May 12, Oct 7; <u>1738</u>: CG, Feb 2, 3, 13, Mar 2,
   7, 13, 16, 18, Apr 18, 26, Oct 4, 26, 28, 30, Nov 18; <u>1739</u>: CG, Feb 24, Mar
   22, 26, 27, Apr 3, 24, 25, 27, 30, May 1, 2, 4, 8, 9, 11, 14, 16, 17, 18, 21,
   23, 24, 25, 28, 29, 30, Sep 5, 7, 10, 12, 15, 17, 19, 22, Oct 2, 3, 15, Nov
   1, 8, 9, 14, 15, 16, 20, 21, 23, 28, Dec 4, 6, 10, 13; <u>1740</u>: CG, Jan 8, Feb
   12, Mar 10, 20, 25, 27, Apr 14, May 5, 9, 14, 19, 21, 23, 27, 29, DL, Oct 10,
   13, 15, 16, 22, 23, 24, 25, 27, 31, Nov 13, 14, 15, 17, 18, 22, 25, 26, Dec
   4, 13, 19; <u>1741</u>: DL, Jan 20, 23, 26, 29, CG, Mar 5, DL, Apr 11, 13, 17, 20,
   25, 30, May 7, 18, 20, Oct 12, 15, 17, 19, 20, 21, 27, Nov 11, 20, Dec 4;
   <u>1742</u>: DL, Jan 6, Feb 18, Mar 8, 13, Apr 29, Sep 21; <u>1743</u>: DL, Feb 4, 11, Mar
   8, May 2, 4, 14, Oct 13, 15, Nov 19, 23, 26; <u>1744</u>: DL, Jan 19, Feb 1, 3, Apr
   9, May 5, Oct 2, 17, 19; <u>1745</u>: DL, Apr 27, Dec 17; <u>1746</u>: DL, Jan 31, Feb 6,
   Mar 3, 10, Apr 2, 24, 25, Jun 6, 9, 11, 13, CG, Dec 19; <u>1747</u>: CG, Jan 9, May
   7, Dec 26; <u>1748</u>: CG, Mar 3, 14, Apr 18, Oct 27; <u>1749</u>: CG, Mar 9, Apr 24, Nov
   23; <u>1750</u>: CG, Jan 8, Apr 25, 28, Oct 29, Dec 21, 26; <u>1751</u>: CG, Jan 17, Apr
   25, May 9, Sep 30, Oct 28, Nov 11; <u>1752</u>: CG, Jan 16, Apr 25, Oct 10, Dec 7;
   <u>1753</u>: CG, May 10; <u>1754</u>: CG, May 14; <u>1755</u>: CG, May 6; <u>1756</u>: CG, May 11; <u>1757</u>:
   CG, May 12, Dec 10; <u>1758</u>: CG, Feb 1, Mar 7, May 4, Oct 14, Nov 16, 23; <u>1759</u>:
   CG, May 21, Dec 10; <u>1760</u>: CG, Jan 16, 18, Apr 17, May 8, Sep 22, Oct 20, Dec
   11; <u>1761</u>: CG, Jan 22, Mar 9, Apr 2, May 8, 20, Sep 16, 21, 29; <u>1773</u>: CG, Jan
   5
Desse Jr (dancer), <u>1761</u>: CG, Mar 9, May 8
D'Esser (dancer), <u>1748</u>: SFP, Sep 7
Dessessars (actor), <u>1734</u>: GF/HAY, Nov 20, Dec 2, 9, HAY, 13, 20, 23, GF/HAY,
   27, 30; <u>1735</u>: GF/HAY, Jan 9, HAY, 13, GF/HAY, 16, Feb 5, Mar 10, HAY, 19, Apr

16, May 9, GF, 23

Dessessars, Mrs (actor), 1734: GF/HAY, Nov 20, HAY, Dec 13, 23; 1735: HAY, Jan 13, GF/HAY, Mar 10

Destouches, 1722: HAY, Feb 17; 1766: CG, Apr 26; 1776: HAY, Jun 12; 1777: CG, Feb 22; 1780: DL, Nov 22; 1781: HAY, Nov 12; 1789: HAY, Jul 15; 1790: DL, Nov 17; 1791: CG, Feb 4, HAY, Jul 9; 1792: HAY, Aug 23; see also Nericault, Philippe

--Amour Use, L', 1776: HAY, Jun 12; 1792: HAY, Aug 23

--Dissipateur, Le; ou, L'Honnete Friponne, 1780: DL, Nov 22; 1781: HAY, Nov 12; 1790: DL, Nov 17; 1791: HAY, Jul 9

--Glorieux, Le, 1791: CG, Feb 4

--Ingrat, L', 1722: HAY, Feb 17

--Irresolu, L', 1777: CG, Feb 22

--Philosophe Marie, Le, 1789: HAY, Jul 15

Destra ti chiedo (song), 1757: KING'S, Mar 24

Destrade (dancer), 1740: CG, Oct 10; 1741: CG, Jan 5, Feb 28, Apr 22, 27, Sep 28, Oct 17, Nov 26, Dec 15, 22; 1742: CG, Jan 8, 21, 25, 26, Feb 22, Mar 9, Apr 23, Sep 29, Oct 1, 9, 15, 16, Nov 2, Dec 21; 1743: CG, Jan 8, Feb 4, 26, Mar 8, Apr 16, Dec 20, 26; 1744: CG, Jan 14, Feb 14, Mar 3, Apr 6, 14, 19, Oct 10, 22, 31, Dec 8; 1745: CG, Jan 1, 14, Apr 16, 25, May 2, 7, Oct 29, Nov 14, 18, 23, Dec 27; 1746: CG, Apr 8, 17, May 13, Jun 13, Dec 19, 31; 1754: CG, Mar 20

Destrir al arme uiate (song), 1763: KING'S, Apr 25

Destrir che all' armi usato (song), 1755: KING'S, Mar 17

Destruction of Jerusalem, The. See Crowne, John.

Destruction of Troy, The. See Banks, John.

DeSureis, Jean (French actor), 1688: ATCOURT, Sep 29

Detection, The; or, A Sketch of the Times (play, anon), 1780: HAY, Nov 13

Dettingen Te Deum. See Handel, George Frederic.

Dettingen, Song upon the Victory at (song), 1743: BFYWR, Aug 23; 1773: HAY, Mar 3

Deuce is in Him, The. See Colman the elder, George.

Deuil Comique, Le (farce), 1725: HAY, Mar 1

Deuil de Maistre Andre, Le (farce), 1726: HAY, Apr 13

Deuil, Le. See Hauteroche, Noel le Breton, Sieur de

Deutsche Hausvater, Der. See Gemmingen, Otto Heinrich Freiherr von.

Deux Arlequins, Les. See Noble, Eustace le.

Deux Jumelles (dance), 1799: KING'S, Jan 29, Feb 2

Deux Octaves, Les (play), 1725: HAY, Jan 11

Deux Pierrots, Les (farce), 1721: HAY, Mar 20; 1726: HAY, Apr 27

Deux Soeurs (dance), 1776: KING'S, Feb 3, 6, 10, 13, 24, 29, Mar 2, 5, 7, 9, 14, 16, 23, 28, 30, Apr 13, Jun 11, 15, 22

Deux Solitaires (dance), 1786: KING'S, May 23, Jun 15, 22, 27, Jul 8

DeVaul. See Duval.

Devaynes, W (charity patron), 1794: DL, Jul 2

DeVeil, Colonel Thomas (Justice), 1737: DL, Feb 21, Mar 5; 1738: HAY, Oct 9; 1743: DL, Mar 7; 1744: HAY, Nov 1, 8; 1748: DL, Dec 10; 1750: DL, Oct 1

D'Evelyn, Miss (actor, singer), 1797: DL, Jan 19, Feb 22, 27, Apr 17, May 3, 17, 19, Jun 7; 1798: CG, Feb 12, 13

Deveraux Court, 1752: DL, Mar 17; 1754: CG, Jan 29

DeVere, Aubrey, Earl of Oxford, 1661: LIF/MT, Oct 21; 1662: LIF, Jan 9, May 20; 1664: LIF, Aug 13; 1666: ATCOURT, Oct 18; 1691: DLORDG, Mar 17

DeVerneuil (actor), 1734: GF/HAY, Nov 20

Device, The; or, The Deaf Doctor. See Pilon, Frederick.

Device, The; or, The Marriage-Office. See Richards.

Devil he pulled off his jacket of flame, The (song), 1699: DL, May 0

Devil in a Wood, The. See Phillips, Edward.

Devil in the Wine-Cellar, The. See Hill, Aaron, The Walking Statue.

Devil is an Ass, The. See Jonson, Ben.

Devil of a Duke, The. See Drury, Robert.

Devil of a Lover, A. See Moultrie, George.

Devil of a Wife, A (droll), 1699: BF, Aug 23

Devil of a Wife, The. See Jevon, Thomas.

Devil take the war that hurried Willy from me (song), 1695: NONE, Sep 0

Devil to Pay, The. See Coffey, Charles.

Devil upon Crutches in England, The; or, Night Scenes in England (pamphlet), 1754: DL, Dec 4

Devil upon Two Sticks, The (entertainment), 1729: DL, Oct 25

Devil upon Two Sticks, The. See Foote, Samuel.

Devil's Tavern, 1731: DT, Apr 23; 1734: TB, Jan 26; 1735: TB, Apr 24; 1736: DT, Apr 16; 1737: DT, Mar 7; 1774: DL, Jan 19, Mar 9

DeVilliers. See Villiers.

Devils' Dance (dance), 1727: DL, May 22; 1739: DL, Dec 26; 1740: DL, Jan 4
Devils' Masque (dance), 1729: DL, May 28
Devin du Village (dance), 1777: KING'S, Nov 4, 8, 15, 18, 29, Dec 9, 13, 20,
   23; 1778: KING'S, Jan 3, Feb 3, 10, 24, Mar 3, 10, 17, 24
Devin du Village. See Rousseau, Jean Jacques.
Devisse (dancer), 1750: DL, Oct 31, Nov 1, 2, 3, 27, Dec 11, 18, 20, 22; 1751:
   DL, Jan 11, 12, 14, 17, 19, 22, 23, 24, 25, 29, Feb 14, 18, 19, 21, 23, Mar
   11, 12, 14, 18, 19, Apr 8, 9, 10, 11, 12, 15, 16, 17, 18, 23, 24, 25, 29, 30,
   May 2, 17, 18, 22; 1752: SFB, Sep 22, DL, Oct 3, 17, 25, 26, 30, Nov 2, 25,
   28, Dec 1, 8, 19, 21; 1753: DL, Jan 1, 5, 15, 24, Feb 19, Mar 20, 22, 24, 26,
   29, 31, Apr 2, 12, 24, May 7, 8, Sep 22, 29, Oct 3, 20, Nov 10, 14, 17, 26,
   Dec 19, 26; 1754: DL, Jan 7, 26, 31, Feb 11, 23, Mar 12, 16, 18, 19, 23, 26,
   30, Apr 1, 6, 16, 17, 26, May 30, Jul 2
Devo. See Devoto.
DeVoltore (acrobat), 1734: BFHBH, Aug 24
Devonshire girl (dancer), 1702: DL, Dec 8; 1703: DL, Feb 3, 12, Mar 13, Apr 19,
   DG, 30, DL, Oct 9, 15, 16, 25, 26, Nov 1, 5, 9, 10, 16, 29, Dec 13, 14, 27,
   31; 1704: DL, Jan 4, 11, 24, Feb 15, 22, 26, 29, Mar 14, 27, 30, Apr 3, 22,
   27, May 25, Aug 15, 16, Oct 20; 1706: ATCOURT, Feb 5
Devonshire Minuet (dance), 1781: KING'S, Apr 26, DL, May 17, 22, 26, Sep 15,
   Nov 22, 24; 1782: DL, Apr 27, CG, May 25, DL, Oct 3, 17, 31, Nov 12, 22, CG,
   29, Dec 6, DL, 7, CG, 14, 20; 1783: DL, Feb 10, Mar 1, CG, May 24, DL, 30,
   31, CG, Jun 4; 1784: DL, Jan 3; 1785: HAY, Apr 29; 1791: KING'S, Jun 2, 10
Devonshire Reel (dance), 1788: DL, Jun 5
Devonshire St, 1740: DL, May 15; 1782: CG, May 1
Devonshire, Duchess of. See Cavendish, Georgiana.
Devonshire, 1765: MARLY, Oct 5
Devoto (house servant), 1778: DL, May 23; 1779: DL, May 28; 1780: DL, May 23;
   1781: DL, May 12; 1782: DL, Apr 27; 1783: DL, May 26; 1784: DL, May 22
Devoto (Devo, Devolto), Anthony (puppet master), 1671: NONE, Feb 3; 1672: NONE,
   Jan 9, CC, Nov 11
--Dutch Cruelties at Amboyna, The, 1672: CC, Nov 11
Devoto, John (scene painter), 1723: DL, Sep 24; 1726: DL, Dec 30; 1728: DL, Nov
   15; 1731: DL, Nov 15; 1735: GF, Jan 24; 1736: GF, Jan 27; 1741: GF, Mar 3;
   1746: GF, Jan 29, Feb 3
Devoto, Miss (actor), 1746: GF, Jan 29
Dewes, Mrs (correspondent), 1744: CG, Feb 10, 24
Dexter, John (actor), 1751: DL, Oct 22, 23, Nov 25, 28; 1752: DL, Feb 6, 17,
   Mar 17, Oct 5, Nov 8, 28, Dec 2, 7; 1753: DL, Jan 8, Feb 6, 22, Apr 3
Dezede, N (composer), 1794: CG, Nov 17
D'Herbage (actor), 1736: HAY, Apr 29
D'Hervigni (Hervigni), Mlle (dancer), 1735: CG, Dec 31; 1736: CG, Jan 1, 2, 7,
   9, 23, Feb 23, 26, Mar 25, 27, 29, Apr 1, 6, 8, 10, 15, 26, 27, 29, May 6, 8,
   11, 13
Di Lor Mio (song), 1736: DL, Dec 15, 16
Di luci adourno (song), 1713: QUEEN'S, Apr 25
Di Nobil Alma (song), 1761: KING'S, Mar 12
Di quanto Cor le pene (song), 1763: KING'S, Apr 25
Di questo Cor Fedele (song), 1749: KING'S, Mar 21
Di se senti (music), 1713: QUEEN'S, Apr 25
Dial (lodgings), 1743: CG, Apr 27; 1744: CG, Apr 25
Dial and Crown Tavern, 1739: DL, Apr 2
Dialogue between a Courtier and a Farmer's Wife (song), 1734: CG, Mar 18, 28
Dialogue between a Drunken Rake and a Town Miss (song), 1712: DL, Aug 5
Dialogue between a Drunken Smith and his Wife (song), 1715: LIF, Jun 3
Dialogue between a Frenchwoman and Dutchwoman (song), 1706: QUEEN'S, Jun 29;
   1719: LIF, Oct 10
Dialogue between a Milkmaid and Gentleman (song), 1729: DL, Jun 24
Dialogue between a Rake and a Widow (song), 1727: LIF, Mar 13; 1729: DL, Jun
   24; 1741: GF, Apr 16
Dialogue between a Rake and Country Maid (song), 1723: DL, Aug 2, 9; 1740: DL,
   May 13
Dialogue between a Town Miss and a Drunken Soldier (song), 1705: LIF, Jan 25,
   LIF/QUEN, Oct 17; 1706: QUEEN'S, Jan 17
Dialogue between Cupid and Bacchus (song), 1707: DL, Jan 1
Dialogue between English and Paris Gazetteers on the Victory at Ramilly (song),
   1707: DL, Jan 7
Dialogue between Honour Faction and Peace (song), 1713: CA, Mar 20
Dialogue between Macheath and Polly (song), 1728: HAY, Aug 9, 12
Dialogue between the two Mad Lovers (entertainment), 1700: DL, Jul 6
Dialogue between two Beaus and two Coquet Ladies (song), 1702: DL, Oct 23
Dialogue Epilogue (entertainment), 1762: CG, Apr 21

Dialogue Epilogue between Tom Jarvis and his Horse (entertainment), 1754: CG, Apr 6
Dialogue in Green Room, or Disturbances in Pit (pamphlet), 1763: DL, Feb 10
Dialogue in the Shades (entertainment), 1785: HAY, Apr 26
Dialogue No Never (song), 1754: CG, Apr 22
Dialogue of Jack and Jenny (song), 1749: CG, Apr 25
Dialogue of Jenny and Kate (song), 1759: DL, Apr 2
Dialogue Prologue (entertainment), 1753: CG, Mar 24
Dialogue upon Himself, A (entertainment), 1759: CG, Mar 22
Diamond Cut Diamond. See Hook Jr, James.
Diamond. See Dimond.
Diana (song), 1777: CG, May 29
Diana and Acteon. See Roger.
Diana and Endymion. See Pescetti, Giovanni Battista.
Diana on Mount Latmos. See Ariosti, Attilio.
Diana, Sga (actor), 1727: KING'S, Feb 9
Diana, Sga (singer), 1715: GRT, May 9
Diana's Chase (song), 1775: HAY, Feb 16; 1786: CG, Apr 21
Diana's Madness; or, Fatime, a Favourite Slave in the Seraglio (entertainment),
    1726: KING'S, Nov 5
Diane a la Chasse (dance), 1740: DL, Dec 29, 30; 1741: DL, Jan 2, 3, 10, 12,
    14, 17, 20, 26, Feb 14
Diane et Endymion (dance), 1776: KING'S, Mar 12, 19, 26, Apr 20, 23, 27, 30,
    May 4, 7, 11, 14, 18, 30, Jun 6, 11, 15, 18, 22, 29; 1799: KING'S, Feb 19
Dias, Don Joseph (Moroccan ambassador), 1708: DL, Oct 9; 1709: DL, Jun 1
DiAspino, Don Diego (singer), 1744: HAY, Jan 19; 1745: HAY, Feb 14
Diavolino (musician), 1754: HAY/SFB, Sep 13
Dibble, Robert (actor, singer), 1793: HAY, Aug 3, 12, 15, Nov 19; 1794: HAY,
    Jul 17, 18, 21, 24, Aug 27; 1795: HAY, Jun 13, 20, Jul 31, DL, Oct 30, Nov
    11, Dec 10; 1796: DL, Jan 8, Mar 12, Apr 30, HAY, Jul 15, Aug 29, DL, Sep 29,
    Oct 19; 1797: DL, Jan 7, May 18, HAY, Jun 23, Aug 14, 15, 16, 31, DL, Nov 8;
    1798: DL, Jan 16, Feb 1, HAY, Jun 30, Jul 21, Aug 11; 1799: DL, Jan 19, 28,
    HAY, Jul 9, 13, Aug 21, Sep 2, 9, DL, Nov 14; 1800: DL, Jan 1, Mar 11, 13,
    HAY, Jun 14, Jul 2, 21, Aug 14, 29, Sep 1, 11
Dibdin, Ann, Mrs Thomas John (actor), 1799: CG, Sep 18, Oct 29, Dec 16; 1800:
    CG, Feb 4, 8, 19, Mar 17, 25, May 13, 27, 28, Jun 2, 4
Dibdin, Charles (dramatist, songwriter, composer), 1760: CG, Dec 5, 11; 1761:
    CG, Apr 17, Sep 26, Oct 13, Nov 11, 13; 1762: CG, Jan 28, May 13, Oct 8, Nov
    1, 15; 1763: CG, May 7, 17, Oct 3, 14, Nov 15, Dec 29; 1764: CG, Jan 3, 14,
    Feb 22, May 21, Sep 21, Oct 1, 18, Nov 5, 7, Dec 26; 1765: CG, Jan 31, Feb
    15, Apr 12, 24, May 1, 11, 13, Oct 3, 7, 9, 12, 14, 22, 29; 1766: CG, Feb 5,
    Apr 30, Oct 10, 14, 21, 25, Nov 18, 21, Dec 3, 29; 1767: CG, Jan 29, Feb 14,
    21, Apr 21, 27, May 7, 16, 23, Sep 14, 19, 25, Oct 5, 8, 9, 17, 27, 30, Nov
    4, 10, 16, 18; 1768: CG, Mar 22, May 5, 13, 24, DL, Sep 8, 22, Oct 3, Dec 21;
    1769: DL, Mar 31, Apr 11, 27, HAY, Jun 21, Aug 31, DL, Sep 23, Oct 14; 1770:
    DL, Jan 4, Apr 25, May 8, RANELAGH, 28, Jul 20, MARLY, Aug 28, DL, Sep 25,
    Oct 2, 3, 29, Nov 1, 3, Dec 7; 1771: DL, Jan 18, Mar 7, Apr 12, HAY, Jun 5,
    Jul 24, DL, Oct 1, 22, 28; 1772: DL, Mar 3, 17, 18, Apr 24, May 1, 13, 19,
    Sep 26, 29, Nov 6, Dec 2, 23, 26; 1773: DL, Feb 1, 27, Mar 4, Apr 14, May 13,
    HAY, Aug 11, MARLY, 25, HAY, Sep 20, DL, 28, 30, Oct 16, 25, Nov 2, Dec 18,
    27, 28, 31; 1774: DL, Jan 8, Apr 5, 8, HAY, Aug 8, 10, 19, DL, Sep 20, 24,
    Oct 11, Nov 21, 25, Dec 1, 9, 20; 1775: DL, Feb 1, Apr 18, May 2, 3, 27, Dec
    12, 27; 1776: HAY, Aug 26, DL, Oct 18, CG, Nov 14, 25; 1777: DL, Mar 8, HAY,
    Jul 18, DL, Oct 7; 1778: CG, Feb 4, DL, Apr 27, HAY, Aug 3, CG, Sep 18, Oct
    2, DL, 6, CG, 14; 1779: CG, Jan 4, DL, Apr 19, CG, May 6, HAY, Jul 1, CG, Oct
    6, DL, 19, CG, 20, Nov 30; 1780: CG, Jan 18, HAY, Mar 1, DL, Apr 13, Oct 12,
    CG, Nov 25, DL, Dec 12, CG, 29; 1781: CG, Sep 17, Oct 1, 27; 1782: HAY, Jul
    2; 1783: CG, May 19, HAY, Aug 1; 1785: DL, Feb 8, Nov 18; 1786: DL, Dec 21;
    1787: HAY, May 16; 1788: DL, May 8; 1789: CG, May 6, DL, 15, 28, CG, Jun 8,
    DL, Sep 22, CG, Dec 21; 1790: CG, Apr 30, DL, May 20, CG, Oct 4, Nov 15, 23;
    1791: CG, May 2, 17, DL, 17, CG, 18, Jun 6, Sep 19; 1792: DLKING'S, May 1,
    CG, 15, 19, 28, Dec 20; 1793: CG, Mar 11, May 21, Oct 2, Nov 15; 1794: CG,
    Apr 12, May 2, 26, Jun 4, HAY, Sep 17, CG, Oct 29; 1795: CG, Jan 12, Apr 28,
    DL, May 19, Jun 2, CG, Oct 7, 26; 1796: DL, Apr 13, Jun 3, HAY, Aug 23, Sep
    1; 1797: CG, May 17, DL, Jun 7, 8, HAY, Aug 10, CG, Oct 2, DL, Nov 10; 1798:
    CG, Apr 20, DL, May 7, CG, 28, HAY, Sep 17, CG, Oct 25; 1799: CG, Jan 29, DL,
    Apr 8, CG, May 3, 13, Jun 4; 1800: CG, May 7, Jun 11
--Annette and Lubin (opera), 1778: CG, Oct 2, 5, 7, 9, 12, 21, 30; 1779: CG,
    Apr 19, 21; 1786: CG, May 9, 15, 17; 1787: CG, Apr 16, 28, May 3; 1788: CG,
    Mar 11; 1789: CG, Apr 30, May 16, 25, Jun 5; 1790: CG, Apr 21, Jun 4, Nov 16;
    1793: CG, Nov 13; 1794: CG, Jun 2; 1796: CG, Sep 23; 1797: CG, May 13
--Chelsea Pensioner, The (opera), 1779: CG, May 6, 11, 14, 17

--Cobler, The; or, A Wife of Ten Thousand (musical), 1774: DL, Dec 9, 12, 13, 14, 15, 20, 27, 28, 31; 1775: DL, Jan 10, 18, 21

--Comic Mirror, 1780: HAY, Mar 1

--Deserter, The (farce), 1773: DL, Nov 2, 4, 5, 8, 11, 13, 16, 19, 29, Dec 2, 13, 30; 1774: DL, Jan 12, Apr 5, 11, 18, May 6, Oct 11, 17, 24, Nov 21, Dec 1, 6, 7, 30; 1775: DL, Jan 6, Feb 20, Mar 28, Apr 18, 20, 25, 27, May 2, Oct 7, Nov 16, 27, Dec 1; 1776: DL, Jan 29, Feb 16, 26, Mar 11, May 8, 15, 23, Jun 1; 1777: DL, Mar 1, 4, 11, 15, Apr 21, 30, May 9, 15, 22, Jun 3, Sep 23, Nov 7, Dec 5, 30; 1778: DL, Jan 28, Mar 14, May 16, Oct 10, Dec 18, 31; 1779: DL, May 12, Dec 22; 1780: HAY, Aug 10, DL, Nov 28; 1781: DL, Apr 18, May 2, 18; 1782: CG, Apr 30, May 1; 1783: DL, May 20, 29; 1784: DL, Jan 31, Mar 6, 25, HAY, Aug 24, DL, Nov 16, Dec 29; 1785: CG, Apr 25, DL, May 16, CG, 18, HAY, Aug 23, DL, Oct 15, Nov 8; 1786: CG, May 6, 22, DL, 25, Jun 1; 1787: CG, Apr 10, 20, DL, May 22, CG, 28, DL, Jun 1, CG, Sep 19, DL, Dec 17, 18, 21, 22; 1788: DL, Jan 1, 21, Feb 5, 16, Mar 8, Apr 23, CG, May 17, DL, 21, CG, Jun 4, Sep 29, DL, Nov 1, 21, Dec 2, 12; 1789: DL, Jan 6, Feb 10, Mar 17, 28, KING'S, Apr 2, CG, May 28, DL, Jun 2, 9, Oct 15, 29, CG, Nov 16; 1790: DL, May 7, CG, Sep 15, DL, Nov 30; 1791: DL, May 20, DLKING'S, Oct 25, Nov 8; 1792: DLKING'S, Mar 6, 20, Apr 14, CG, May 22; 1793: CG, Oct 18; 1794: CG, May 29; 1795: CG, Sep 25; 1796: DL, May 11, Sep 22, Oct 8, 15; 1797: DL, Feb 1, Sep 23, Dec 13, 28; 1798: DL, Jan 13; 1799: DL, Apr 25, 27, May 16, 21, Sep 24, Oct 23, Nov 2, 21, 30, Dec 14; 1800: DL, Apr 21, May 21

--Gipsies, The (opera), 1778: HAY, Aug 3, 4, 5, 10, 12, 20

--Hannah Hewit; or, The Female Crusoe (farce), 1798: DL, May 7

--Harlequin Freemason (pantomime), 1780: CG, Dec 28, 29, 30; 1781: CG, Jan 1, 2, 3, 4, 5, 6, 8, 9, 10, 11, 12, 13, 15, 16, 17, 18, 19, 20, 22, 23, 24, 25, 26, 27, 29, 31, Feb 1, 2, 3, 5, 6, 9, 12, 15, 16, 17, 19, Mar 1, 5, 6, 12, 17, 19, 22, 27, 29, Apr 5, 16, May 3, 17, 28, Oct 1, 3, 5, 8, 10, 11, 15, 17, 18, Dec 3, 10; 1789: CG, Dec 21; 1790: CG, Nov 15; 1793: CG, Oct 2; 1799: CG, May 13

--Harvest Home (opera), 1787: HAY, May 16, 18, 21, 25, Jun 11, 19, Jul 7

--Islanders, The (opera), 1780: CG, Nov 25, 28, 29, Dec 1, 2, 4, 5, 6, 8, 11, 13, 15, 20; 1781: CG, Jan 11, 16, 20, 23, Feb 15, 23, Mar 17, Apr 19, Sep 17

--Jupiter and Alcmena (burletta), 1781: CG, Oct 27, 29

--Liberty Hall; or, The Test of Good Fellowship (opera), 1785: DL, Feb 8, 10, 14, 17, 24, 28, Mar 3, 8, 14, 29, Apr 9

--Loyal Effusion, A (interlude), 1794: CG, Jun 4, 9, 13, 18

--Maid the Mistress, 1770: RANELAGH, May 28, Jun 27, Jul 4, 13

--Marriage Act, The, 1780: CG, Nov 25; 1781: CG, Sep 17, 19, 24, 28

--Metamorphoses, The, 1776: HAY, Aug 26, 27, 28, 30

--Mirror, The; or, Harlequin Every-where (pantomime), 1779: CG, Nov 30, Dec 1, 2, 3, 4, 6, 7, 8, 9, 10, 11, 13, 14, 15, 16, 17, 27, 28, 29, 30, 31; 1780: CG, Jan 1, 3, 4, 5, 6, 10, 11, 12, 17, 22, 24, 26, 29, Feb 19, Mar 6, 13, 28; 1781: CG, May 7; 1793: CG, Dec 19

--None are so Blind as Those Who Won't See (farce), 1782: HAY, Jul 2, 3, 4, 8, 9, 16, 19

--Oddities, The (entertainment), 1790: CG, Nov 23

--Pasquin's Budget; or, A Peep at the World (puppet show), 1780: HAY, Mar 1

--Poor Vulcan (burletta), 1778: CG, Feb 4, 5, 7, 10, 11, 12, 13, 16, 17, 18, 19, 21, Mar 5, 14, 21, 23, Apr 2, 7, 11, 21, 25, May 11, 16, Sep 28, Oct 28, Nov 13, Dec 3, 17; 1779: CG, Jan 1; 1780: CG, Apr 3, 12; 1781: CG, Mar 31, Apr 27, May 15, Nov 12, 13; 1783: CG, Mar 3, May 30; 1784: CG, May 7, 28; 1785: CG, Dec 3, 5, 6; 1786: CG, Feb 3, 6, May 30, Nov 22, Dec 22; 1787: CG, Sep 26; 1788: CG, Apr 12, May 7, Jun 2, Oct 8; 1789: CG, May 27, Jun 3, Sep 18; 1790: CG, Feb 9, Apr 24; 1799: CG, May 7

--Quaker, The (musical), 1775: DL, May 3; 1777: DL, Oct 7, 9, 11, 14, 16, 17, 18, 21, 22, 24, 25, 30, Nov 1, 6, 21, 28, Dec 2, 10; 1778: DL, Jan 15, 21, 29, Feb 7, 16, 26, Mar 3, 10, 31, Apr 22, 25, May 7, HAY, Aug 21, DL, Oct 6, Nov 19, Dec 1, 12, 17; 1779: DL, Mar 4, Apr 28, May 4, 15, 21, 25, Oct 19, Nov 18, Dec 6; 1780: DL, Mar 13, Apr 7, May 6, 23, HAY, Aug 17, 23, DL, Oct 12, 31, Dec 2; 1781: CII, Mar 30, DL, May 12, 22, Nov 29; 1782: DL, Feb 19, 25, Apr 27, CG, Dec 14, 17; 1783: CG, Feb 25, DL, Mar 20, 22, CG, Apr 5, DL, 22, CG, May 17, HAY, Jul 8, DL, Sep 16, CG, 24, DL, 30, Nov 7, CG, 26, DL, 26; 1784: DL, Feb 17, Apr 22, Sep 30, Oct 16, 27, Dec 4; 1785: HAY, Feb 12, DL, Apr 2, HAMM, Jun 27, DL, Sep 17, Oct 22, Nov 12, 26; 1786: DL, Jan 14, CG, May 24, HAY, Jun 17, Jul 19, 24, DL, Oct 19; 1787: DL, Apr 9, Jun 8, Sep 18; 1788: HAY, Aug 4; 1789: CG, May 6, 22, Jun 10, HAY, Aug 28, DL, Dec 23; 1790: DL, May 19, 25, Jun 3, CG, 16; 1791: CG, Apr 30; 1792: DLKING'S, Feb 11, 21, May 5, 11, Jun 14; 1793: DL, Jun 10, HAY, Oct 21, CG, Nov 22, Dec 12; 1794: HAY, Feb 5, 8, 12, 22, Mar 22, DL, May 7, 8, 10, Jun 2; 1795: DL, Jan 29, May 30; 1796: HAY, Jul 12, 23; 1797: DL, Dec 20; 1798: DL, Feb 12

--Rose and Colin (opera), 1778: CG, Sep 18, 21, 23, 25, 30, Oct 24, 31, Dec 11,

19; <u>1779</u>: CG, Apr 7, 14, 26; <u>1782</u>: HAY, Aug 30; <u>1783</u>: CG, Oct 15; <u>1784</u>: CG,
Apr 27, May 4, 8; <u>1787</u>: CG, May 21; <u>1789</u>: CG, Jan 3; <u>1790</u>: CG, May 7, Nov 25,
Dec 14, 15; <u>1791</u>: CG, Jan 7, May 16, Oct 5, 29; <u>1793</u>: CG, Oct 16, Nov 15, Dec
16; <u>1794</u>: CG, May 28; <u>1795</u>: CG, Sep 16, Oct 23; <u>1797</u>: CG, Nov 11; <u>1798</u>: CG,
Mar 3, 5, 6, 10, 13
--Seraglio, The (with Edward Thompson) (opera), <u>1776</u>: CG, Nov 14, 15, 18, 21,
23, 25, 26, 28, Dec 17, 18
--Shepherd's Artifice, The, <u>1764</u>: CG, May 21; <u>1765</u>: CG, Apr 12, May 13
--Shepherdess of the Alps, The (opera), <u>1780</u>: CG, Jan 18, 19, 20
--Touchstone, The; or, Harlequin Traveller (pantomime), <u>1779</u>: CG, Jan 4, 5, 6,
7, 8, 9, 11, 12, 13, 14, 15, 16, 18, 19, 20, 21, 22, 23, 26, 27, 28, 29, Feb
1, 2, 3, 4, 5, 6, 8, 9, 15, 20, Mar 9, 11, 15, 16, 18, Apr 7, 12, 15, 17, 19,
May 10, 24, Oct 6, 8, 11, 15, 16, 18, Nov 4, 5, 6, 10, 16, Dec 20; <u>1780</u>: CG,
Mar 27, Apr 1, 7, 17, Nov 15, 18, 20; <u>1781</u>: CG, Apr 20, May 12, 16, Nov 2, 3,
5, 7, 9, 16, 21; <u>1782</u>: CG, May 11, 14, 15, 21; <u>1789</u>: CG, Nov 30, Dec 3, 4
--Waterman, The; or, The First of August (or, The Rowing Match) (opera), <u>1774</u>:
HAY, Aug 8, 10, 12, 15, 17, 19, 22, 26, 31, Sep 7, 9, 13, 15, 16, 19; <u>1775</u>:
HAY, May 31, Jun 2, 5, 7, 12, 19, 26, 30, Jul 5, 17, 24, 28, Aug 4, 18, 28,
Sep 7, 11; <u>1776</u>: DL, Apr 12, 20, 25, 26, May 10, 16, Jun 10, HAY, Sep 2, 4,
10, 12, DL, Oct 5, 15, Nov 13, Dec 19; <u>1777</u>: DL, Feb 24, May 14, 27, Jun 2,
HAY, Jul 15, Aug 28, Sep 12, 16, DL, Nov 19, 26, Dec 9, 20; <u>1778</u>: DL, Jan 13,
27, Feb 13, Apr 28, May 8, 19, 21, HAY, Jun 11, 24, 29, Jul 6, 15, 29, Aug 1,
DL, Oct 22, Nov 24; <u>1779</u>: HAY, Aug 17; <u>1780</u>: DL, Apr 29; <u>1781</u>: CG, Feb 15,
HAY, Aug 7, DL, Dec 6; <u>1782</u>: HAY, Jul 25, Aug 1; <u>1783</u>: CG, Feb 3, May 29,
HAY, Jul 28; <u>1785</u>: DL, Jan 17, May 25, HAMM, Jul 4, 8, DL, Oct 27, Nov 29;
<u>1786</u>: DL, May 29, Dec 6; <u>1788</u>: DL, May 8, 17, Jun 12, Sep 13; <u>1789</u>: DL, Feb
7, Mar 3, 10; <u>1792</u>: DLKING'S, Feb 7, DL, Sep 29; <u>1794</u>: CG, Jun 11; <u>1797</u>: CG,
Jun 5, 10, 12; <u>1798</u>: CG, Apr 20, Jun 2, WRSG, 8
--Wedding Ring, The (musical), <u>1773</u>: DL, Feb 1, 2, 3, 4, 5, 8, 10, 18, Mar 4,
6, 11, 22, Apr 14, May 5, 26, Sep 23, 30, Oct 19, Nov 19, Dec 15; <u>1774</u>: DL,
Mar 24, Apr 26, May 28, Oct 1
--Wives Revenged, The (opera), <u>1778</u>: CG, Sep 18, 21, 23, 25, 30, Oct 7, 12, 21,
30, 31, Dec 11, 23; <u>1779</u>: CG, May 1; <u>1780</u>: CG, Apr 7, 27; <u>1783</u>: CG, Nov 1;
<u>1784</u>: CG, May 7; <u>1790</u>: CG, May 11, Jun 12, Nov 3, 10, 24, Dec 8; <u>1791</u>: CG,
May 9, 30, Jun 10; <u>1792</u>: CG, Apr 18; <u>1795</u>: CG, Oct 23, 31, Nov 5
Dibdin, Charles Isaac Mungo (machinist), <u>1799</u>: CG, Dec 23
Dibdin, Miss (dancer), <u>1799</u>: CG, Jan 29, Mar 2, 25, Apr 13, Oct 7, 21, 28;
<u>1800</u>: CG, Jan 23, Mar 4, May 1, 27, HAY, Jul 2
Dibdin, Thomas John (actor, dramatist, songwriter), <u>1798</u>: CG, Oct 19, 25, 31,
Nov 23, Dec 11, 13; <u>1799</u>: CG, Jan 29, Mar 16, Apr 8, 16, May 4, 7, Sep 16,
Oct 7, Dec 23; <u>1800</u>: DL, Feb 1, CG, 19, Mar 25, Apr 5, 22, May 12, 23, 28,
Jun 5
--Birth Day, The, <u>1799</u>: CG, Apr 8, 10, 11, 13, 17, 18, 20, 24, 25, May 4, 8,
16, 23, Jun 10, Oct 21, 23, Nov 20; <u>1800</u>: CG, Jan 4, 9, 14, 22, Feb 6, Mar
17, May 15, Jun 6, 12, HAY, Sep 3, 9
--Five Thousand a Year, <u>1799</u>: CG, Mar 16, 25, 27, 29, Apr 2, 3, 4; <u>1800</u>: CG,
Jun 2
--Hermione, The; or, Valour's Triumph (interlude), <u>1800</u>: CG, Apr 5, 14, 22, May
28, 29
--Horse and the Widow, The (farce), <u>1799</u>: CG, May 4, 8, 9, 16, 23, 30, Jun 5,
Oct 18; <u>1800</u>: CG, Jan 4, 9, 14, 22, May 12, 14, 16
--Jew and the Doctor, The (farce), <u>1798</u>: CG, Nov 23, 24, 26, 27, 28, 29, 30,
Dec 1, 3, 4, 5, 6, 7, 10, 13, 20, 26, 28, 31; <u>1799</u>: CG, Jan 4, 7, 10, 15, 21,
Feb 2, Mar 7, Apr 10, 20, 25, May 23, Jun 12, HAY, 27, Jul 4, Aug 15, 19, Sep
4, 10, CG, Oct 23, 24, 30, Dec 16, 18; <u>1800</u>: CG, Feb 14, Mar 10, Apr 15, May
7, HAY, Jun 13, 23, Jul 2, 29, Aug 16
--Liberal Opinions, <u>1800</u>: CG, May 12, 14, 16, 21
--Magic Oak, The; or, Harlequin Woodcutter (pantomime), <u>1799</u>: CG, Jan 24, 25,
29, 31, Feb 1, 4, 5, 7, 9, 11, 12, 14, 16, 18, 19, 21, 23, 25, 26, 28, Mar 7,
25, 26, 27, 28, 29, 30, Apr 1, 4, 5, 8, 11, 29, May 2, 6
--Mouth of the Nile, The (interlude), <u>1798</u>: CG, Oct 25, 29, 30, 31, Nov 5, 6,
7, 8, 9, 10, 17, 20, 22, 24, 29, Dec 1, 7, 26, 28, 31; <u>1799</u>: CG, Jan 4, 7, 9,
10, 15, 21, Feb 2, Mar 7, Apr 3, Nov 9, 11; <u>1800</u>: CG, May 23
--Naval Pillar, The (interlude), <u>1799</u>: CG, Oct 7, 9, 10, 11, 14, 16, 21, 23,
26, 29, Nov 4, 7
--Of Age To-morrow (farce), <u>1800</u>: DL, Feb 1, 3, 4, 5, 7, 13, 14, 15, 17, 18,
19, 20, 21, 22, 24, 25, 27, Mar 1, 3, 4, 8, 22, 25, 29, Apr 16, 18, 19, 22,
23, May 3, 5, 7, 9, 20, 26, Jun 2, 6, 9, 13
--St David's Day (farce), <u>1800</u>: CG, Mar 25, 29, 31, Apr 1, 3, 14, 16, 18, 21,
May 15, 21, 28, Jun 6
--Sunshine after Rain (farce), <u>1799</u>: CG, Apr 16
--Tagg in Tribulation! (farce), <u>1799</u>: CG, May 7

--True Friends (farce), 1800: CG, Feb 17, 19, 20, 21, 22, 25
--Volcano, The; or, The Rival Harlequins (pantomime), 1799: CG, Dec 23, 26, 27, 28, 30, 31; 1800: CG, Jan 1, 2, 3, 4, 6, 7, 8, 9, 10, 11, 13, 14, 15, 20, 21, 22, 23, 24, 25, 27, 28, 31, Feb 1
Dick (tailor), 1790: CG, Oct 15; 1791: CG, Oct 20; 1794: CG, Jun 4, Sep 22, Nov 17, Dec 26; 1795: CG, Apr 6, Jun 4, Dec 21; 1796: CG, Mar 15, Jun 3, Nov 5, Dec 19; 1797: CG, Mar 16, Nov 24, Dec 26; 1798: CG, Feb 12, May 18, Nov 12, Dec 11; 1799: CG, Jan 29, Apr 19, May 17, Jun 6, Dec 23; 1800: CG, Jan 16, Jun 3
Dick, Mrs (house servant), 1797: CG, May 18
Dickenson (oboist), 1798: HAY, Jan 15
Dickenson, B (printer), 1749: HAY, Feb 10; 1750: DL, Feb 21
Dickenson, Mrs (boxkeeper), 1747: DL, Apr 29
Dickins (actor), 1705: LIF/QUEEN, Feb 22, QUEEN'S, Nov 23; 1706: QUEEN'S, Jan 3
Dickinson, John (gallery office keeper), 1745: DL, May 1; 1746: DL, Apr 19; 1747: DL, Apr 29; 1748: DL, May 4; 1749: DL, May 2; 1750: DL, May 2; 1752: DL, Apr 23; 1753: DL, May 9; 1754: DL, May 13; 1755: DL, May 2; 1756: DL, May 6; 1757: DL, May 12; 1758: DL, May 5; 1759: DL, May 17; 1760: DL, May 9; 1761: DL, May 18; 1762: DL, May 19; 1763: DL, May 11; 1764: DL, May 16; 1765: DL, May 13; 1766: DL, May 12; 1767: DL, May 20, 22; 1768: DL, May 9; 1769: DL, May 10; 1770: DL, May 21; 1771: DL, May 22; 1772: DL, May 27; 1773: DL, May 25; 1774: DL, May 23; 1775: DL, May 22; 1776: DL, May 15; 1777: DL, May 28; 1778: DL, May 21; 1779: DL, May 26
Dickson. See Dixon.
Dico su questa sponda (song), 1729: HIC, Apr 30
Did You Ever See The Like? (entertainment), 1730: DL, Dec 3
Diddle, Sir Dilberry, 1747: HAY, Apr 25
Didelot, Charles Louis (dancer, choreographer), 1787: KING'S, Dec 8; 1788: KING'S, Jan 12, 15, 29, Feb 21, 28, Mar 13, 15, Apr 3, 19, May 15, 22, 29, 31; 1789: KING'S, Jan 10, 31, Feb 10, Mar 3, 17, 31, Apr 28, May 26, Jun 13, 15; 1791: PAN, Feb 17, Mar 19, 22, May 9, 17, Jun 10; 1796: KING'S, Feb 20, Mar 1, 5, 8, 10, Apr 2, 21, May 12, DL, 25, KING'S, Jun 2, Jul 2, 7, 16, 23, Nov 26, Dec 6, 13; 1797: KING'S, Jan 10, 17, Feb 7, Mar 11, 28, Apr 6, 8, 25, DL, May 22, KING'S, 25, CG, Jun 14, KING'S, 15, 17, CG, Oct 21, 28, Nov 4, KING'S, 28, Dec 20; 1798: KING'S, Jan 2, Feb 6, Mar 22, 31, Apr 19, 26, DL, May 9, KING'S, 10, CG, Jun 11, KING'S, 14, Dec 8; 1799: KING'S, Mar 26, Apr 18, May 2, DL, 8; 1800: KING'S, Jan 11, 28, Mar 1, 4, Apr 15, May 8, DL, 14, KING'S, 29, Jun 19, 24, 28
Didelot, Charles Louis and Marie Rose (dancers), 1800: KING'S, Jun 19
Didelot, Marie Rose, Mme Charles Louis (Mme Rose) (dancer), 1791: PAN, Feb 17, 26; 1796: KING'S, Feb 20, Mar 1, 5, 8, 10, Apr 2, 21, May 12, DL, 25, KING'S, Jun 2, Jul 2, 7, 16, 23, Nov 26, Dec 6, 13; 1797: KING'S, Jan 10, 17, Feb 7, Mar 11, 28, Apr 6, 25, DL, May 22, KING'S, 25, CG, Jun 14, KING'S, 17, CG, Oct 21, Nov 4, KING'S, 28, Dec 20; 1798: KING'S, Jan 2, Feb 6, Mar 22, Apr 19, May 10, Jun 26, Dec 8; 1799: KING'S, Mar 26, Apr 18, May 2, DL, 8; 1800: KING'S, Jan 11, 28, Feb 1, 11, 18, Mar 4, 22, Apr 15, Jun 19, 28, Jul 12
Diderot, Denis, 1780: HAY, Aug 5; 1786: DL, Jan 14
--Pere de Famille, Le, 1780: HAY, Aug 5; 1786: DL, Jan 14
Didier, Abraham J (actor), 1764: DL, Oct 2, 22, Nov 28; 1765: DL, Mar 2, Apr 30; 1771: HAY, May 17, 23, 29, 31, Jun 10, 14, 26, Jul 8, Aug 26, Sep 2, 16; 1772: DL, Mar 23; 1786: CG, Dec 13
Didier, Margaret, Mrs Abraham J (actor), 1771: HAY, May 15, 17, 20, 22, 23, 27, 29, Jun 3, 5, 7, 10, 12, 21, Jul 1, 5, 8, 10, 15, 24, Aug 19, 26, Sep 2, 16, 18; 1772: DL, Mar 23
Dido. See Handel, George Frederic; Hasse, Johann Adolph; Hook, James.
Dido and Aeneas. See Tate, Nahum; Pepusch, John Christopher; Arne, Dr Thomas A.
Dido, The Queen of Carthage. See Reed, Joseph.
Didone. See Ciampi, Lorenzo; Sacchini, Antonio Maria Gasparo; Paisiello, Giovanni.
Didone Abbandonata da Enea. See Sani, Domenico.
Didone Abbandonata. See Anfossi, Pasquale.
Didone Abbandonata, La. See Perez, Davide.
Diego und Leonore. See Unzer, Johann Christoph.
Dietrich, Christian (brass player), 1758: CHAPEL, Apr 27
Dietrichsen, F (publisher), 1795: KING'S, May 26
Dieupart (Dupar), Charles (musician, composer), 1703: DL, Feb 14; 1704: DL, Feb 22, YB, May 18; 1707: YB, May 23; 1711: QUEEN'S, Dec 26; 1712: DL, Jan 18; 1722: DL, Mar 14, May 11; 1723: DL, May 15; 1726: DL, May 4; 1734: HA, Sep 11
Difesa D'Amore, La (serenata), 1775: KING'S, May 6, 13, 20, 27, Jun 10, 24
Difference of Nations (dance), 1733: GF, Mar 12, 13, 17, 27, 30, 31, Apr 2, 6, 9, 13, 18, 27, May 9, 21, 23

Different Widows, The. See Pix, Mary.
Digby (actor, singer), <u>1781</u>: HAY, Jan 22
Digby, George, Earl of Bristol, <u>1663</u>: LIF, Jan 8; <u>1664</u>: LIF, Jul 20, NONE, Nov
    0
--Elvira; or, The Worst Not Always True, <u>1664</u>: NONE, Nov 0; <u>1666</u>: NONE, Sep 0
--Worse and Worse, <u>1664</u>: LIF, Jul 20; <u>1666</u>: ATCOURT, Nov 26
Digges, John Dudley West (actor), <u>1777</u>: HAY, Aug 14, 29, Sep 10, 19, Oct 6;
    <u>1778</u>: HAY, Jun 19, Jul 30, Aug 21, Sep 2, 7, 17, 18, CG, 25, 28, 30, Oct 16,
    22, Nov 10; <u>1779</u>: CG, Jan 18, 19, Feb 12, Apr 6, HAY, May 31, Jun 18, Jul 31,
    Aug 18, 24; <u>1780</u>: HAY, Jun 2, 26, Jul 10, Aug 22, 24; <u>1781</u>: HAY, Jun 4, 16,
    Jul 9, Aug 1, 7
Diggs, Mrs (beneficiary), <u>1727</u>: LIF, Apr 28
Diggs, Richard (actor), <u>1715</u>: DL, Dec 6; <u>1717</u>: DL, May 30, SF, Sep 9; <u>1718</u>: DL,
    Jan 31, LIF, Apr 19, 29, Jun 20, 30, Sep 29, Oct 3, 4, 11, 16, Nov 24, 25;
    <u>1719</u>: LIF, Apr 29, Oct 15, Nov 7, 12, 17, 18, 19, Dec 10; <u>1720</u>: LIF, Jan 7,
    11, Feb 11, 23, 29, Apr 28, BFBL, Aug 23, LIF, Oct 18, Nov 1, 10, 22, Dec 8,
    31; <u>1721</u>: LIF, Mar 4, Apr 13, 25, Oct 17, Nov 4, 13, 15, 18, 24, 27, 28, Dec
    2, 18; <u>1722</u>: LIF, Jan 22, Mar 28, 30, Apr 11, 13, May 15, 17, Jun 1, 2, 13,
    Oct 12, 19, 22, 27, 30, 31, Nov 3, 8, 17, 22, Dec 10, 14, 15, 21, 31; <u>1723</u>:
    LIF, Jan 2, 11, 18, Feb 15, 22, Mar 30, Apr 19, 30, May 3, Sep 28, Oct 2, 4,
    18, 22, Nov 7, 12, 18, 21, 26, 28, Dec 2, 7; <u>1724</u>: LIF, Feb 24, Mar 16, 19,
    26, 28, Apr 14, 23, 28, May 19, 27, 29, Sep 23, Oct 7, 22, 23, 27, 30, Nov
    12, 13, 17, 18, 20, 24, 26; <u>1725</u>: LIF, Jan 14, Feb 27, Mar 13, 29, 31, Apr 7,
    23, 26, May 21, Sep 24, 29, Oct 1, 4, 11, 15, 23, 26, 28, Nov 9, 12, 18, 23,
    24, 29, 30, Dec 6, 7; <u>1726</u>: LIF, Feb 19, Mar 24, Apr 27, May 4, 18, Sep 12,
    19, 28, Oct 3, 12, 17, 19, Nov 8, 18; <u>1727</u>: LIF, Jan 4, 9, 16, Apr 3, 12
Dighton (actor), <u>1733</u>: HAY, Feb 20; <u>1741</u>: GF, Dec 30; <u>1742</u>: GF, Jan 1, 2, 11,
    Feb 18, 24, Mar 23, Apr 8, 21, 24, May 10, 19, LIF, Dec 1, 6, 13, 22, 27, 30;
    <u>1743</u>: LIF, Jan 10, 14, Feb 11, 14, 17, Mar 24
Dighton, Robert (actor, singer), <u>1781</u>: HAY, Mar 26, CG, May 5; <u>1784</u>: CG, Apr
    28, HAY, Dec 13; <u>1785</u>: HAY, Feb 12, Mar 15; <u>1788</u>: HAY, Apr 9; <u>1800</u>: CG, May
    28, Jun 13
Dignam (house servant), <u>1743</u>: LIF, Apr 6
Dignum, Charles (actor, singer), <u>1784</u>: DL, Oct 14, Nov 26, Dec 18, 20, 27;
    <u>1785</u>: DL, Feb 2, Mar 28, Apr 8, 11, 18, 22, May 3, 11, 13, 19, 25, 26, Oct 1,
    11, 20, Nov 18, Dec 8; <u>1786</u>: DL, Jan 5, 6, Mar 9, Apr 4, 24, May 3, 5, 10,
    22, 25, Sep 23, Oct 9, Dec 26; <u>1787</u>: DL, Jan 19, 26, Feb 1, 15, 23, Mar 7,
    Apr 9, 23, May 18, 28, Sep 25, 27, Oct 4, 13, 22, 25, Nov 1, 3, 5, 8, 21, 23;
    <u>1788</u>: DL, Jan 16, 22, 26, Feb 8, 22, 25, Mar 5, 24, Apr 3, 7, May 1, 6, 8,
    23, 24, 26, 30, Jun 3, 11, Sep 13, 18, 20, 23, Oct 13, 16, 23, Nov 10, 17,
    18; <u>1789</u>: DL, Feb 18, 26, 27, Mar 9, 18, 20, 25, Apr 2, 14, 17, 21, May 19,
    22, 27, 28, Sep 15, 19, 26, Oct 1, 13, 22, 24, 26, 27, Nov 4, 24, Dec 3, 9,
    23, 26; <u>1790</u>: DL, Jan 15, Feb 18, 19, 24, 26, Mar 2, 10, 13, 17, 23, Apr 5,
    16, 20, 23, May 4, 11, 14, 15, 18, 19, 20, 25, 27, 28, 31, Jun 1, 3, Sep 11,
    30, Oct 4, 7, 11, 19, 20, 26, 27, Dec 8, 11, 22; <u>1791</u>: DL, Jan 1, 11, Feb 10,
    Mar 11, 23, 25, Apr 1, 13, May 3, 6, 17, 18, 19, 26, DLKING'S, Sep 22, 24,
    27, 29, Oct 3, 4, 15, 26, 29, 31, Nov 2, 5, 9, 14, 16, 17, 30, Dec 31; <u>1792</u>:
    DLKING'S, Jan 7, 11, 18, Feb 8, 11, 18, KING'S, 24, 29, DLKING'S, Mar 1, 6,
    10, KING'S, 14, DLKING'S, 17, KING'S, 23, 28, 30, DLKING'S, Apr 10, 19, May
    23, 29, DL, Sep 15, 18, 20, 25, 27, 29, Oct 9, 18, Nov 2, 5, 10, 21, 29, Dec
    13, 26, 27; <u>1793</u>: DL, Jan 22, 31, Feb 6, 12, KING/HAY, 15, DL, 16, KING/HAY,
    20, 22, DL, Mar 4, 5, KING/HAY, 6, DL, 7, KING/HAY, 13, 15, 20, DL, Apr 1, 8,
    22, 29, May 7, 10, 21, 24, Jun 10, HAY, Sep 19, 24, 30, Oct 1, 4, 18, 22, Nov
    5, 19, 30, Dec 14, 16, 23, 26; <u>1794</u>: HAY, Jan 4, 21, 27, 31, Feb 8, 11, 24,
    DL, Mar 12, 19, 21, 26, Apr 4, 9, 10, 11, 21, 25, 26, 28, 29, May 1, 3, 7, 8,
    16, 19, Jun 9, 19, HAY, Sep 17, DL, 23, 27, Oct 7, 14, 16, 20, 27, 29, 31,
    Nov 3, 12, 15, Dec 9, 20, 30; <u>1795</u>: DL, Jan 7, 22, 26, 28, 31, Feb 2, 17, Mar
    10, 14, Apr 16, May 2, 4, 6, 9, 18, 19, 27, 28, 29, 30, Jun 2, 3, Sep 17, 26,
    29, Oct 1, 6, 15, 27, 30, Nov 6, 11, 12, 20, 23, Dec 2, 7, 11, 14, 18, 30;
    <u>1796</u>: DL, Jan 18, Mar 12, Apr 2, 13, 25, 30, May 5, 11, 25, 27, Jun 1, 3, 7,
    8, HAY, Jul 7, DL, Sep 27, 29, Oct 3, 10, 24, Nov 5, 10, 26, Dec 10, 16;
    <u>1797</u>: DL, Jan 7, 12, 20, Feb 9, 11, 16, 22, Mar 6, 7, 14, 28, Apr 25, 29, May
    12, 19, 22, 23, Jun 7, 8, 14, CG, 21, DL, Sep 19, 26, Oct 5, 7, 16, 19, 31,
    Nov 4, 7, 8, 9, 17, 20, 21, 24, 27, Dec 2, 9, 20; <u>1798</u>: DL, Jan 16, Feb 20,
    May 7, 11, 18, 21, 23, 24, 31, Jun 6, 7, 8, Sep 18, 27, 29, Oct 2, 11, 16,
    Nov 3, 13, 26, Dec 3, 21; <u>1799</u>: DL, Jan 8, 19, Feb 14, 16, 19, Apr 22, May 4,
    8, 17, 24, 31, Jun 4, 28, Sep 19, 26, Oct 1, 3, 12, 14, Nov 7, 14, Dec 11,
    19; <u>1800</u>: CG, Feb 28, Mar 5, DL, 11, CG, 14, 19, DL, 24, Apr 1, 14, 21, 29,
    May 10, 13, 16, 19, 23, 29, Jun 3, 4, 6, 7, 10, 11
Dilettante, Il. See Hook, James.
Dilke, Thomas (Dilks, Captain), <u>1695</u>: LIF, Dec 0
--City Lady, The; or, Folly Reclaimed, <u>1696</u>: LIF, Dec 0

--Lover's Luck, The, 1695: LIF, Dec 0
--Pretenders, The; or, The Town Unmasked, 1698: LIF, Mar 0
Dille che d'altra Face (song), 1750: KING'S, Apr 10
Dilly, Charles (publisher), 1782: CG, Feb 9; 1783: CG, Jan 28; 1784: DL, Dec 2,
    22; 1786: HAY, Aug 29; 1787: DL, Jan 13, Apr 14, HAY, Aug 7, DL, Dec 11;
    1788: DL, Oct 25; 1789: DL, Jan 26; 1790: DL, Mar 18; 1793: CG, Apr 4; 1794:
    DL, May 8; 1795: DL, Feb 28, May 1, 12; 1796: CG, Jan 13, DL, Apr 13; 1797:
    CG, Nov 23
Dilly, Edward and Charles (publishers), 1778: DL, Jan 24, CG, Nov 23
Dimmi tre Dei morir (song), 1726: DL, Apr 28
Dimmock (Dymuck) (doorkeeper, billsticker), 1758: CG, May 12; 1759: CG, May 25;
    1760: CG, May 19, Sep 22; 1761: CG, May 15; 1762: CG, May 21
Dimmock, Young (actor), 1739: DL, Oct 15, Dec 11
Dimond (Diamond), William Wyatt (actor, manager), 1772: DL, Oct 1, 10, 31, Nov
    21, Dec 16; 1773: DL, Jan 2, 13, 15, 30, May 14, Nov 9, Dec 27; 1774: DL, Jan
    19, Feb 2, Mar 19, 26, Apr 25, May 5, 7; 1775: HAY, Jul 7; 1778: HAY, Sep 17;
    1779: HAY, Jun 18, Jul 16, 31, Aug 10, 17, 18, 31; 1784: HAY, Nov 16; 1785:
    HAY, Jan 31; 1786: HAY, Mar 6; 1789: CG, May 22; 1790: HAY, Sep 29; 1798: CG,
    May 12
Dine (Dyne), Richard (singer), 1776: DL, Mar 6, 22, CHAPEL, Apr 2
Dingdong (musician), 1774: HAY, Mar 15
Dingle (actor), 1661: NONE, Sep 0
Dioclesian. See Dryden, John, The Prophetess.
Dione. See Lampe, John Frederick.
Dirge (song), 1754: HAY, Aug 8; 1755: CG, Oct 29; 1783: CG, Sep 22; 1788: DL,
    Nov 17; 1789: CG, Sep 14, Nov 9; 1793: CG, Oct 9; 1794: CG, Sep 29; 1795: CG,
    Oct 19; 1796: DL, Apr 25, 28, CG, Sep 12, 19; 1797: CG, Sep 25; 1798: CG, Apr
    28, Sep 17, 24; 1799: CG, May 10
Dirge from Romeo and Juliet, 1750: DL, Oct 1, 1765: CG, Oct 7; 1767: CG, Sep
    25; 1773: CG, Oct 25; 1776: CG, Oct 7; 1777: CG, Sep 29; 1778: CHR, Jun 10,
    CG, Oct 26; 1779: CG, Nov 8; 1780: CII, Mar 13; 1781: CG, Sep 24; 1782: CG,
    Oct 7; 1783: CG, Sep 22, Oct 27; 1784: CG, Jan 19, Apr 12, Oct 25, Nov 8, 19,
    26; 1785: CG, Mar 28, Nov 14, 21; 1786: CG, Oct 23, Dec 11; 1787: RLSN, Mar
    31, CG, Sep 24; 1788: CG, Sep 22; 1789: CG, Sep 14, Nov 9; 1790: CG, Sep 13;
    1791: CG, Sep 26; 1792: CG, Jan 16, Oct 8, 22; 1793: CG, Oct 7; 1794: CG, Oct
    20; 1795: CG, Sep 21; 1796: CG, May 17, HAY, Sep 7; 1797: CG, Nov 2; 1798:
    CG, Jan 1; 1799: CG, Oct 7, Nov 18, Dec 9
Dirti ben Mio (song), 1745: CG, Apr 10
Disabye (musician), 1713: SH, May 12
Disappointed Marriage, The. See Behn, Aphra.
Disappointment, The (play, anon), 1734: YB, Jul 8
Disappointment, The; or, The Mother in Fashion. See Southerne, Thomas.
Disaster of Bet Bouncer (entertainment), 1792: CG, Apr 10
Disbanded Officer, The. See Johnstone, James.
Disciolta da pene (song), 1757: KING'S, Mar 24
Disconsolate Sailor (song), 1793: CG, May 24; 1797: CG, May 24; see also When
    my Money was gone
Discordia Conjugale, La. See Paisiello, Giovanni.
Discovery, The. See Sheridan, Frances.
Disdainful of danger (song), 1790: DL, Mar 10, CG, 26; 1791: CG, Mar 25; 1792:
    CG, Mar 16; 1793: CG, Feb 20; 1794: CG, Mar 21, DL, Apr 4; 1796: CG, Mar 16;
    1797: CG, Mar 31; 1799: CG, Mar 15; 1800: CG, Feb 28
Disertore, Il. See Guglielmi, Pietro; Tarchi, Angelo.
Disfatta di Dario, La (pastiche), 1762: KING'S, Mar 20, 27, Apr 17, 24, May 1,
    8
Disgraces D'Arlequin, Les (pantomime, anon), 1721: HAY, Apr 18; 1726: KING'S,
    Nov 30
Dish of All Sorts (entertainment), 1759: CG, Mar 22, Apr 17; 1762: CG, Mar 29,
    May 3; 1763: CG, May 18; 1798: HAY, Aug 14
Disinterested Love. See Hull, Thomas.
Disney (Dizny), Thomas (actor), 1671: NONE, Sep 0; 1678: DL, Feb 0; 1681: DL,
    May 0; 1682: DL, Mar 11; 1695: DG, Apr 0, DL, Sep 0, Oct 0; 1696: DL, Feb 0,
    May 0, Jul 0; 1697: DL, Feb 0, DG, Jun 0, DL, Jul 0; 1698: DL, Mar 0
Dispensary for the Infant Poor, 1772: CG, Dec 19; 1773: DL, Dec 21; 1777: DL,
    Dec 30
Dispensary, The. See Garth, Sir Samuel.
Disperata in Van m'affano (song), 1762: KING'S, May 11
Dispute between the Managers and Their Actors Adjusted, The (book), 1744: DL,
    Oct 2
Disputes between the Director of DL and the Pit Potentates, The (pamphlet),
    1744: DL, Nov 19
Dissembled Wanton, The. See Welstead, Leonard.

Dissertation on Comedy, A (entertainment), 1750: DL, Jan 1
Dissertation on Hobby Horses (entertainment), 1774: HAY, Sep 17; 1787: CG, May
  18; 1789: HAY, Jul 31; 1790: CG, May 11; 1791: CG, May 24, Jun 4; 1798: HAY,
  Sep 7
Dissertation on Macaronies (entertainment), 1773: DL, Apr 28, May 15, 18; 1781:
  CII, Apr 5; 1788: CG, Apr 26; 1790: CG, May 7
Dissertation on The Famous Beggar's Opera (song), 1729: FLR, Nov 29
Dissertation upon Law (entertainment), 1790: CG, Apr 7; 1791: HAY, Mar 7
Dissertation, A. See Cibber, Theophilus.
Dissipateur, Le. See Destouches.
Dissipation. See Andrews, Miles Peter.
Distracted I Turn (song), 1742: DL, Oct 19; 1743: DL, Apr 11
Distressed Baronet, The. See Stuart, Charles.
Distressed Beauty; or, The London Apprentice (entertainment, anon), 1722: RI,
  Aug 20, BFPMB, 25, SF, Sep 5, 22, 24
Distressed Bride, The (play), 1722: LIF, Dec 17, 18
Distressed Innocence. See Settle, Elkanah.
Distressed Lovers (dance), 1782: DL, Feb 19, 23
Distressed Merchant, The; or, The Jew of Venice (droll), 1754: SFP, Sep 18, 19,
  20, 21, 23, 24
Distressed Mother, The. See Philips, Ambrose.
Distressed Sailor, The; or, The Comical Humours of the Wapping Landlady (play),
  1753: BFGI, Sep 3, 4, 5, SFGT, 18, 19, 20, 21
Distressed Wife, The. See Gay, John.
Ditcher (doorkeeper), 1800: DL, Jun 14
Dite che fa (song), 1786: DL, Mar 10
Ditters. See Dittersdorf, von.
Dittersdorf, Carl Ditters von (composer), 1788: DL, Oct 25; 1792: CG, Apr 17;
  1794: DL, Dec 20; 1795: DL, Oct 30
Diversion a la Mode (dance), 1782: CG, Nov 29, Dec 6, 11, 14, 20; 1783: CG, May
  24, Jun 4
Diversions of the Morning, The. See Foote, Samuel.
Divertimento Napolitano (dance), 1759: KING'S, May 22
Diverting Song (song), 1731: GF, Jan 13
Divertissement (entertainment), 1776: KING'S, Feb 6, 10, 17, DL, Mar 19,
  KING'S, Apr 18; 1777: KING'S, May 1; 1778: KING'S, Feb 7, 24, Mar 21, 24, 28,
  Apr 4, 11, 28, May 26, Jun 2, 9; 1779: KING'S, May 29, Jun 5; 1782: KING'S,
  Nov 2, 5, 9, 14, 19, 30, Dec 10, 12, 17, 19, 28, 31; 1783: KING'S, Jan 11,
  25, 28, Feb 4, 18, Mar 4, 6, 11, 27, Apr 5, 12, 26, Nov 29, Dec 16; 1784:
  KING'S, Feb 7, 14, 17, Mar 2, Apr 15, 20, 24, May 1, 8, 11, 15, CG, 21,
  KING'S, 22, Jun 12, 15, 26, Dec 18; 1785: KING'S, Jan 1, 11, 15, 22, Feb 24,
  Mar 3, 8, 12, 17, 29, Apr 26, May 10, 28, HAY, Jun 1, KING'S, 18, 28; 1786:
  KING'S, Feb 21, 25, Mar 11, 16, 21, Apr 1, 4, 6, HAY, Jun 19, KING'S, Dec 23;
  1787: KING'S, Jan 6, 16, 20, Feb 13, Mar 10, 13, 29, Apr 17, 28, May 1, 19,
  Jun 5, 16, 19, Dec 8; 1788: KING'S, Jan 3, CG, 24, KING'S, 29, CG, Mar 1, Apr
  14, KING'S, May 29, CG, Oct 1, Nov 12; 1789: KING'S, Jan 10, CG, 26, KING'S,
  31, Feb 7, 10, 14, Mar 3, 10, 17, 21, 31, May 28, Jun 6, 9, 11, 15, 16, CG,
  27, 30, Jul 11, Oct 2, 20, Nov 20, Dec 1; 1790: HAY, Jan 7, CG, 16, HAY, Feb
  6, May 11, 13, 15, 18, 27, 28, 29, Jun 1, 3, CG, Jul 6, 10, 17, Nov 23, 24,
  25, 26, 27, 29, 30, Dec 1, 3, 9, 13, 18; 1791: CG, Jan 12, 14, 19, 26, Feb 2,
  9, 16, PAN, 17, CG, 23, PAN, 26, KING'S, Mar 10, PAN, 19, 22, KING'S, 26,
  PAN, 26, KING'S, 31, Apr 11, 12, 26, CG, 27, KING'S, May 3, PAN, 10, KING'S,
  10, PAN, 14, 17, KING'S, 19, 23, CG, 25, PAN, 31, Jun 2, KING'S, 4, PAN, 10,
  16, KING'S, 17, 28, Jul 9, CG, Sep 19, 26, Nov 18, 30, Dec 9; 1792: HAY, Feb
  14, CG, Mar 5, HAY, 17, 24, CG, Apr 10, HAY, 14, 17, CG, 20, 25, May 19, 28,
  Nov 24; 1793: CG, Jan 16, KING'S, 26, Feb 5, 16, Mar 5, 19, May 7, CG, 21,
  KING'S, Jun 4, 8, 18; 1794: KING'S, Jan 11, 18, Feb 1, 11, Mar 4, 11, 22, Apr
  1, CG, 12, KING'S, 26, CG, May 10, KING'S, 31, Jun 3, 24, CG, Oct 29, KING'S,
  Dec 6, 20; 1795: KING'S, Jan 10, 20, 27, Feb 28, Mar 3, 24, 26, Apr 7, 11,
  May 22, 26, CG, Jun 5, Oct 7, Nov 4, 5; 1796: KING'S, Feb 9, 16, 20, Mar 8,
  10, 12, 15, CG, Apr 8, KING'S, 12, May 17, 28; 1797: KING'S, Jan 3, 7, 10,
  Apr 8, CG, Oct 2, 13, 28, Nov 9, Dec 18; 1798: KING'S, Apr 19, 21, CG, 28,
  May 11; 1799: CG, Mar 16, 25, KING'S, 26, CG, 27, KING'S, 30, CG, Apr 10, 13,
  17, 18, KING'S, May 4, CG, Jun 8, KING'S, 11, CG, Dec 9; 1800: KING'S, Jan
  11, 28, Feb 1, 4, 8, 11, CG, 15, KING'S, Mar 8, May 8, 13, Jul 29
Divertissement Asiatique (dance), 1787: KING'S, Jun 14, 16, 19
Divertissement Ballet (dance), 1800: DL, Jun 2
Divertissement Bayadaire (dance), 1800: KING'S, May 29, 30
Divertissement Dance (dance), 1781: KING'S, Nov 17, 20, 24, 28, Dec 11; 1782:
  KING'S, Jan 1, 10, 12, 26, 29, 31, Feb 5, 7, 9, 14, 16, 19, 21, 26, 28, Mar
  2, 7, 9, 12, 14, 16, 21, 23, Apr 13, 20, May 14, 25, Jun 1, 15
Divertissement Serieux (dance), 1786: KING'S, Jan 24

243

Divertissement Villageois (dance), 1786: KING'S, Jan 24, Feb 18, 25, Mar 11,
16, 21, 23
Dives, 1759: CG, Oct 22, DL, 27; 1760: CG, Oct 16
Divine Astrea hither flew to Cynthia's brighter Throne (song), 1697: DG, Jun 0
Divine Comedian, The. See Tuke, Richard.
Divine Dialogues. See Lesly, George.
Divorce du Mariage, Le. See Regnard, Jean Francois.
Divorce, Le. See Regnard, Jean Francois.
Divorce, Le; ou, Arlequin Fourbe et Demi (pantomime), 1718: LIF, Dec 30; 1719:
LIF, Jan 15, KING'S, Feb 12; 1720: KING'S, Jun 16; 1721: HAY, Jan 17
Divorce, The. See Hook, James; Jackman, Isaac.
Dixit Dominus (song), 1772: CG, Apr 8, 10; 1773: HAY, Mar 17; 1789: DL, Mar 25
Dixon (doorkeeper), 1763: CG, May 26; 1768: CG, May 28, 30; 1769: CG, May 20,
23; 1770: CG, May 19, 23; 1771: CG, May 27
Dixon (upholsterer), 1798: HAY, Aug 18
Dixon, Clara Ann (singer, actor), 1799: DL, Apr 15; 1800: KING'S, Jan 11, Feb
8, DL, Jun 6
Dixon, James (actor), 1661: LIF, Aug 24
Dixon, William (singer), 1792: CG, Feb 28; 1794: DL, May 16, Jun 25, Oct 27,
Nov 15, Dec 20; 1795: DL, Feb 9, Oct 30, Nov 11, Dec 10; 1796: DL, Jan 8
D'Maas (composer), 1771: CG, Mar 1
D'Noble (author), 1725: HAY, May 7
Doating Lovers, The. See Hamilton, Newburgh.
Doberval. See D'Auberval.
Dobosch (furrier), 1772: CG, Nov 27; 1774: CG, Mar 22
Dobson (actor), 1792: HAY, Oct 15
Dobson (pipemaker), 1774: DL, Feb 22
Dockyard, The (dance), 1779: CG, Sep 22, 24, 27, 29, Oct 1, Nov 15, 20, 23, Dec
4, 17, 21, 23; 1780: CG, Jan 8, 28
Doctor against His Will, The. See Moliere.
Doctor and the Apothecary, The. See Cobb, James.
Doctor Faustus. See Marlowe, Christopher.
Doctor Last in his Chariot, The. See Bickerstaffe, Isaac.
Doctor Last's Examination (interlude, anon), 1780: DL, Apr 29; 1782: HAY, Dec
30; 1787: RLSN, Mar 31, HAY, Aug 14, 21; 1790: DL, May 4; 1795: CG, May 29;
1796: CG, Jun 2
Doctor's Commons Coffee House, 1750: DL, Feb 21
Doctor's Commons, 1780: DL, Mar 31; 1788: HAY, Sep 30
Doctrine of an Israelite (song), 1790: CG, Apr 30
Dodd, A (printer), 1749: DL, Jan 20; 1750: DL, Feb 26, Mar 6
Dodd, Benjamin (printer, publisher), 1744: DL, Mar 1; 1758: CG, Feb 10; 1759:
CG, Mar 23; 1764: CG, Mar 14, Apr 6, 13
Dodd, James Solas, 1779: CG, Apr 30
--Gallic Gratitude; or, The Frenchman in India (The Funeral Pile) (farce),
1779: CG, Apr 30, May 19
Dodd, James William (actor), 1765: DL, Oct 3, 10, 22, 24, Nov 16, Dec 7, 14,
16, 21; 1766: DL, Jan 6, 13, 20, 21, 23, 24, 29, Feb 13, Mar 22, Apr 1, 12,
14, 16, 18, 25, May 21, 22, Sep 20, 23, 25, Oct 7, 9, 17, 18, 21, 23, 25, 29,
31, Nov 7, 20, 28, Dec 6, 15, 29; 1767: DL, Jan 24, Mar 21, Apr 21, 22, 27,
29, May 1, 16, 18, 28, HAY, 29, DL, Sep 15, 18, 19, 26, Oct 9, 14, 15, 20,
21, 23, 29, Nov 6, 16, 23, Dec 5, 22; 1768: DL, Jan 9, Feb 20, Mar 10, Apr
11, 16, 18, May 7, Sep 17, 23, 26, 27, 28, 30, Oct 6, 10, 19, 25, 31, Nov 21,
Dec 1, 14, 16, 21; 1769: DL, Jan 27, Feb 4, 13, Mar 29, Apr 3, 24, 28, May 1,
15, Sep 16, 19, 21, 23, 30, Oct 2, 5, 7, 14, Dec 19, 20, 22, 23, 28; 1770:
DL, Jan 13, 17, 25, Feb 7, 8, Mar 13, 22, 27, Apr 3, 21, May 2, 7, 10, 15,
21, 24, 29, Jun 7, Sep 22, 29, Oct 3, 5, 6, 13, 16, 19, 22, 25, 26, 29, 31,
Nov 6, 10, 15, 16, 21, 23, 28, Dec 6, 19, 22, 28; 1771: DL, Jan 22, Feb 21,
Mar 21, 23, Apr 2, 15, 26, May 13, 22, Sep 21, 26, 28, Oct 3, 8, 10, 17, 19,
25, 28, 31, Nov 1, 6, 8, 9, 14, 23, 25, 26, Dec 3, 4, 10, 11, 30; 1772: DL,
Jan 1, 7, 11, 15, 20, Feb 27, Mar 23, Apr 6, May 13, 27, Jun 10, Sep 19, 22,
24, 29, Oct 1, 8, 15, 23, 28, 30, 31, Nov 27, 28, Dec 2, 7, 29; 1773: DL, Jan
4, 9, 29, Feb 2, 10, 23, 27, Mar 9, 23, 30, Apr 1, 23, 30, May 24, 27, Sep
21, 25, Oct 2, 20, 25, Nov 1, 9, 20, 26, Dec 10, 16, 17, 21, 27, 31; 1774:
DL, Jan 5, 10, 22, 26, Feb 2, 9, 24, Mar 3, 15, 17, 22, 26, Apr 7, 15, 27,
May 3, 9, 10, 14, 18, Sep 17, 20, 22, 27, 29, Oct 5, 26, Nov 5, 7, 11, 22,
Dec 1, 2; 1775: DL, Jan 11, 23, Feb 1, 23, Mar 2, 18, 23, 28, Apr 4, 8, 19,
22, May 6, 12, 20, Sep 23, 26, 30, Oct 3, 10, 17, 21, 24, 26, 27, Nov 1, 9,
20, 28, Dec 16, 18, 23, 29; 1776: DL, Jan 20, 27, Feb 10, Mar 14, 18, 21, 26,
28, Apr 10, 22, 25, 26, May 16, 20, 22, 23, Jun 3, 10, Sep 21, 26, Oct 5, 9,
10, 18, 26, Nov 5, 6, 7, 9, 19, 28, 29, Dec 5, 10, 14, 28; 1777: DL, Jan 1,
14, 16, 28, Feb 24, Mar 17, 20, 31, Apr 3, 11, May 8, Sep 23, Oct 2, 14, 18,
22, 23, 29, 31, Nov 14, Dec 4, 26; 1778: DL, Jan 2, 8, 17, Feb 19, 24, Mar

244

12, 30, Apr 6, 30, May 1, 2, 23, Sep 17, 19, Oct 3, 6, 13, 15, 17, 28, Nov
10, 20, 30, Dec 19, 21, 23; 1779: DL, Jan 2, 7, 23, Feb 3, Mar 11, 13, 15,
18, 27, CG, Apr 21, DL, 28, May 5, 19, Sep 21, Oct 16, 21, 23, 26, 30, Nov 5,
6, 9, 18, 19, 24, Dec 4, 8, 17, 27, 31; 1780: DL, Jan 5, 11, Feb 3, 22, 28,
Apr 1, 3, 5, 18, 19, 26, May 4, 10, Sep 16, 21, 28, Oct 3, 5, 14, 20, 23, 26,
28, Nov 2, 3, 17, 22, 25, Dec 4, 27; 1781: DL, Mar 19, Apr 3, 21, 24, May 1,
8, 10, Sep 22, 25, 27, 29, Oct 6, 12, 18, 25, 26, 29, Dec 13, 31; 1782: DL,
Jan 1, 9, 21, 26, Mar 21, Apr 6, 12, 18, 23, 25, 30, May 7, 11, 18, Sep 18,
19, 20, 21, 26, Oct 1, 5, 8, 12, 16, 18, 29, Nov 22, Dec 5, 11; 1783: DL, Jan
3, 29, Apr 28, May 2, 5, 12, Sep 20, 25, 27, Oct 2, 18, 22, 30, 31, Nov 18,
20, 21, 28, Dec 2, 5, 12; 1784: DL, Jan 3, 10, 16, Feb 14, Mar 8, 22, 29, Apr
1, 12, 14, 21, 28, May 3, 5, 18, 21, Sep 18, 21, 23, 28, Oct 11, 14, 18, 26,
28, Nov 1, 4, 12, 19, 23, 26, Dec 3; 1785: DL, Jan 6, 12, 13, 22, Feb 2, 8,
21, Mar 8, 30, Apr 11, 18, 26, May 3, 6, 11, Sep 17, 20, 27, Oct 6, 18, Nov
1, 11, 15, 18, 21, 26, Dec 7, 29; 1786: DL, Jan 6, 7, 9, Feb 23, Apr 4, 6,
17, 18, 28, May 29, Jun 1, Sep 16, 21, 23, 26, 28, 30, Oct 12, 21, 24, Nov
15, Dec 11; 1787: DL, Jan 12, 18, 23, 29, Apr 10, 18, 20, May 9, 14, 21, 30,
Jun 1, Sep 20, 22, 25, Dec 19, 28; 1788: DL, Jan 2, 5, 28, Feb 26, Mar 6, 10,
28, 31, Apr 3, 8, May 1, 19, 21, 23, 30, Jun 6, Sep 16, 23, 25, 27, Oct 4,
11, 13, 14, 20, 25, Nov 12, 17, 21, 26; 1789: DL, Apr 14, 15, May 7, 23, 27,
Jun 1, 3, Sep 15, 17, 29, Oct 3, 10, 22, Nov 5, 21, 30, Dec 5; 1790: DL, Jan
1, 15, Feb 8, 10, 13, 15, Mar 1, 13, Apr 6, 14, Jun 1, CG, 16, DL, Sep 14,
Oct 7, 12, 18, 27, Nov 1, 2, 3, 4, 10, 13, 17, Dec 1; 1791: DL, Jan 25, Mar
28, Apr 26, 27, May 20, DLKING'S, Sep 27, Oct 1, 4, 6, 10, 25, Nov 4, 8, 11,
30, Dec 1, 6; 1792: DLKING'S, Feb 8, 14, Mar 26, Apr 9, 20, 21, May 4, Jun 4,
13, 15, DL, Sep 15, 22, 29, Oct 2, 4, 13, 15, 18, 20, Dec 28; 1793: DL, Jan
9, Feb 28, Mar 5, 12, Apr 17, 20, 25, 29, May 24, Jun 1; 1794: DL, Apr 21,
29, May 5, 17, 19, Jun 16, 19, 25, Jul 2, Sep 27, Oct 7, 22, Nov 5, 7, 12,
14, 18, Dec 5, 12, 13; 1795: DL, Jan 5, Mar 10, Apr 17, 22, May 9, 26, Sep
26, 29, Oct 22, Nov 3, 5, 7, 10, 19, 26, Dec 2, 7, 11; 1796: DL, Jan 23, Feb
1, 27, 29, Mar 12, 19, 28, Apr 13, 25, 29, May 3, Jun 4, 6, 8, 13
Dodd, Martha, Mrs James William (actor), 1766: DL, Jan 29, Apr 25
Dodimear (dancer), 1793: CG, Mar 11
Dodsley, James (printer), 1776: DL, Dec 14; 1779: DL, Apr 10; 1782: CG, Dec 14;
    1790: DL, May 7
Dodsley, Robert (author, printer, bookseller), 1735: CG/LIF, Feb 3; 1737: DL,
    Jan 29, Feb 2; 1738: DL, Feb 23; 1741: DL, Apr 3; 1744: CG, Apr 18; 1745: DL,
    Apr 1; 1747: DL, Oct 24; 1749: CG, Jan 17, DL, Feb 9, 15, 21; 1750: DL, Mar
    5, 28, Apr 4, 23; 1751: DL, Feb 5; 1752: CG, Mar 18; 1753: DL, Feb 9, 19, CG,
    23, DL, Mar 6; 1754: CG, Jan 24, 29; 1756: DL, Jan 22; 1758: DL, Mar 2, 7,
    CG, Dec 2
--Blind Beggar of Bethnal Green, The, 1741: DL, Apr 3; 1749: BFYT, Aug 23, 24,
    25, 26, 28
--Cleone, 1758: CG, Dec 2, 4, 5, 6, 7, 8, 9, 12, 13, 14, 15, 16, 23, 30; 1759:
    CG, Feb 6, 24, Apr 2, HAY, 18, CG, May 9, HAY, 10; 1761: CG, Apr 21, May 2,
    Oct 6, 9, Nov 3; 1764: CG, Dec 7, 10; 1766: CG, Feb 5; 1767: CG, Mar 31;
    1785: HAY, Apr 8; 1786: DL, Nov 22, 24
--King and the Miller of Mansfield, The (Miller of Mansfield, The), 1737: DL,
    Jan 29, Feb 1, 2, 3, 4, 5, 7, 8, 9, 10, 11, 12, 14, 15, 16, 17, 18, 21, 22,
    26, HAY, Mar 2, DL, 14, 17, 21, CG, 21, DL, 22, 24, 28, 31, Apr 2, 13, 25,
    May 5, 16, 19, 23, Jun 11; 1738: DL, Jan 18, 19, 21, 23, Feb 6, 21, 23, Mar
    16, 18, 25, Apr 13, May 1, 5, 9, 12, 26, 30; 1739: DL, Jan 16, 17, 19, 20,
    Feb 1, 9, Apr 5, 7, 9, 10, 26, May 25, 26, 30, 31; 1740: DL, Jan 8, 10, 11,
    14, Mar 4, 6, May 2, 5, 19, 21, 30, Sep 9, Oct 2, 20, 24, GF, 25, 27, 28, DL,
    Nov 22; 1741: DL, Feb 24, Mar 7, CG, 9, 12, 16, DL, Apr 4, CG, 8, DL, 17, 22,
    CG, 27, DL, 28, CG, 30, May 1, DL, 2, CG, 8, DL, 9, CG, 11, DL, 27, Sep 17,
    19, Oct 9, CG, Dec 9, JS, 28; 1742: CG, Mar 18, Apr 20, DL, 23, CG, 26, DL,
    28, 29, 30, May 1, 3, 4, CG, 5, DL, 8, CG, 11, DL, 13, 17, CG, 17, DL, 24,
    25, 27, Sep 25; 1743: DL, Jan 4, 6, CG, May 2, DL, 23, 24, 26; 1744: JS, Mar
    20, MF, Jun 27, HAY, Oct 13, 16; 1745: NWMF, Feb 7, SMMF, 28, GF, Mar 30, Apr
    2, 17, MF, May 6, DL, 8; 1746: GF, Jan 10, 13, JS, Oct 2, CG, 13, 15, 17, Nov
    8, 10, 18; 1747: GF, Feb 16, 18, DL, Apr 20; 1748: DL, May 2, 3, SOU, Jul 4,
    DL, Oct 18, SOU, 24, DL, 25, Nov 9, 22, Dec 7, 13, JS, 20; 1749: DL, Jan 27,
    JS, Mar 27, CG, Apr 17, 18, 22, May 3, DL, 5, Sep 26, CG, Oct 6, 11; 1750:
    DL, Feb 22, CG, Nov 17, 21, 24, 26, 27, Dec 5, 10, 22; 1751: CG, Jan 3, 12,
    Feb 4, 16, Apr 11, May 4, 14, DL, Sep 17, 26, CG, 27, Oct 17, 25, Dec 16;
    1752: CG, Feb 3, DL, Dec 18, 22; 1753: CG, Oct 5, 8, 20, Nov 15, Dec 8; 1754:
    DL, May 13, 15, 16, 18, 20, 30, Sep 14, CG, Oct 9, Nov 9; 1755: DL, Apr 24,
    CG, May 7, DL, Sep 18, Oct 2, 7, 17, CG, Nov 11, DL, 21, Dec 6, 19; 1756: CG,
    Jan 3, 28, May 8, Sep 20, DL, 23, Oct 11, Nov 18, Dec 2, CG, 13; 1757: DL,
    May 17, 19, Sep 17, CG, Dec 6; 1758: DL, Apr 10, CG, May 8, DL, 15, 17, CG,
    Sep 25, DL, 28, Oct 14, CG, Dec 7, 22; 1759: CG, Sep 26; 1760: CG, Apr 19,

22, DL, May 16, Jul 29; 1761: DL, May 14, 25; 1762: DL, May 18; 1763: CG, May
14; 1764: CG, May 18; 1765: CG, Oct 4; 1768: CG, Feb 25, Oct 22, DL, 28;
1769: CG, Jan 16, 23, Sep 18; 1770: DL, Feb 21, Jun 1, HAY, Nov 21, DL, 24,
Dec 13; 1771: HAY, Mar 4, Apr 6, DL, Nov 28; 1772: DL, Feb 5, Dec 21; 1774:
DL, Jan 18, HAY, Apr 4, DL, May 26, Oct 8, Nov 5; 1775: DL, Sep 23; 1776:
CHR, Sep 27; 1779: DL, Mar 13, 20, May 29; 1781: CII, Apr 5; 1786: HAMM, Jun
28; 1787: RLSN, Mar 27; 1788: DL, Mar 29, Apr 22, 26, HAY, Aug 26, DL, Nov
29; 1789: DL, Nov 24; 1792: DLKING'S, Jan 7, 14, May 23; 1794: DL, May 3
--Sir John Cockle at Court (farce), 1738: DL, Feb 23, 25, 27, 28, Apr 29, May
2; 1741: HAY, Dec 28; 1787: HAY, Aug 28
--Toy Shop, The, 1735: CG/LIF, Feb 3, 4, 6, 7, 8, 10, 11, Mar 6, 13, 15, 18,
24, 25, 29, Apr 9, 10, 14, 17, LIF, 19, CG/LIF, 21, 23, GF, 30, LIF, 30,
CG/LIF, May 1, GF, 2, CG/LIF, 2, CG, 6, CG/LIF, 7, 12, 14, 20, CG, Sep 16,
17, Dec 2; 1736: CG, Jan 9, Oct 6, 20; 1737: CG, Jan 24, DL, Feb 3, 5, 7, 8,
10, 16, 17, 18, 21, 22, 26, CG, Mar 12, DL, 14, 17, CG, 21, DL, 21, Apr 2,
13, 25, CG, May 2, DL, 5, 16, 23, CG, Sep 30; 1738: DL, Jan 19, 21, 23, Feb
6, Mar 16, 18, CG, 20, Oct 24, Nov 8; 1739: DL, Jan 16, 19, CG, Nov 6, Dec
13; 1741: DL, Apr 8, 9, HAY, Dec 28; 1743: CG, Mar 17, 21, Apr 27; 1757: DL,
May 9, 10, 14, 16, 18; 1758: DL, Apr 22; 1785: DL, Apr 25; 1789: DL, May 11,
19; 1790: DL, May 7
--Triumph of Peace, The (masque), 1749: DL, Feb 21, 23, 25, 27, 28, Mar 2, 4,
6, 27, 28, May 1
Dodsley, Robert and James (printers), 1742: GF, Apr 22; 1750: DL, Feb 27; 1757:
CG, Mar 17, DL, Apr 23; 1758: DL, Jan 26
Dodson (actor), 1731: GF, May 14; 1734: MEG, Sep 30
Dodson, Miss (actor, singer), 1740: CG, Nov 18; 1741: CG, Feb 7, 28, Mar 9, Apr
17, 30, BFH, Aug 22, CG, Oct 24, Nov 7, Dec 9; 1742: CG, Feb 22, May 11, Dec
21, 29; 1743: BFHC, Aug 23; 1749: NWSM, May 10, 15
Doe, John (house servant), 1768: CG, Mar 26, Apr 4, May 28, 30; 1769: CG, May
20, 22; 1770: CG, May 18, 21; 1771: CG, May 27, Oct 23, Nov 13; 1772: CG, Jan
2, Mar 9, 26, May 23, 30, Oct 24, Nov 3; 1773: CG, May 22, Oct 15; 1774: CG,
Apr 7, May 7; 1775: CG, May 30; 1776: CG, May 21, Nov 25; 1777: CG, May 23;
1778: CG, May 21; 1779: CG, May 15; 1780: CG, May 24; 1781: CG, May 25; 1782:
CG, May 28; 1783: CG, May 31; 1784: CG, May 22; 1786: CG, Jun 1; 1787: CG,
May 30; 1788: CG, May 31; 1789: CG, Jun 16; 1790: CG, Jun 12; 1791: CG, Jun
14; 1792: CG, May 29; 1794: CG, Jun 4; 1795: CG, Jun 4; 1796: CG, Jun 3;
1797: CG, May 25; 1798: CG, May 29; 1799: CG, May 17; 1800: CG, Jun 7
Doe, Miss (actor), 1772: CG, Mar 30
Dog Tavern, 1723: DT, Nov 1; 1724: DT, Dec 2; 1750: DL, Feb 21
Doget. See Doggett.
Doget (actor), 1748: BFSY, Aug 24
Doggett (actor), 1791: HAY, Dec 26
Doggett, Thomas (actor, author), 1691: DL, Jan 0; 1692: DL, Jan 0, Jun 0, Nov
0, 8; 1693: DL, Feb 0, Mar 0, Apr 0, DG, May 0, NONE, 9, Sep 0, DL, Oct 0;
1694: DL, Jan 0, Feb 0, DLORDG, 0, DL, Apr 0, DG, May 0, DL, Sep 0; 1695:
LIF, Apr 30, DLANDLIF, May 0, LIF, Sep 0, Dec 0; 1696: LIF, Apr 0, NONE, 3,
Oct 26, DL, Nov 21, Dec 0, DL/DL, 0; 1697: DL, Jan 0, Feb 0, May 8; 1699: BF,
Aug 23, LIF, Dec 18; 1701: LIF, Jan 0, DG, Apr 11, May 6, Jun 3, LIF, 24;
1702: LIF, Dec 31; 1703: LIF, Feb 0, 11, Apr 28, BFPD, Aug 23; 1704: DL, Jan
18, LIF, Feb 2, 11, 19, ATCOURT, 28, LIF, Mar 30, Apr 20, 22, ATCOURT, 24,
LIF, 26, 29, Jul 27; 1705: DL, Jan 10, 15, 31, Mar 15, LIF/QUEN, Oct 30,
QUEEN'S, Nov 12, 17, Dec 27; 1706: QUEEN'S, Jan 8, Apr 20, 30; 1708: DL, Mar
1, 2, DL/QUEEN, 6, DL, 8, 15, 27; 1709: DL, Apr 7, QUEEN'S, Sep 24, Oct 1, 8,
11, 31, Nov 12, 15, 18, 19, Dec 8, 12; 1710: QUEEN'S, Jan 5, 10, 14, 16, Feb
1, 11, 18, Mar 11, 16, Apr 11, Jul 6, 13, 21, 26, DL/QUEEN, Oct 5, 7, Nov 14,
18, DL, 20, 23, 27, Dec 5, 18, 21, 30; 1711: DL, Jan 9, 20, 25, Feb 3, Mar
19, Apr 7, Sep 22, 27, 29, Oct 6, 11, 13, 20, 24, 26, Nov 7, 9, 12; 1712: DL,
Jun 12, Sep 23, 25, Oct 10, 30, Nov 27, Dec 6, 19; 1713: DL, Jan 10, 29, Feb
28, Oct 12, 15, 21, Nov 11, 19; 1717: DL, Mar 18, 25, Apr 1; 1721: DL, Sep
20; 1730: BFPG/TC, Aug 1, 24; 1734: DL, Sep 28
--Hob; or, The Country Wake, 1696: LIF, Apr 0, NONE, Sep 0; 1710: QUEEN'S, Feb
18; 1711: DL, Oct 6, 8, 13, 15, 23, 25, Nov 3, 30, Dec 13, 15, 18, 27; 1712:
DL, Feb 7, 14, Mar 13, Apr 10, 26, May 17, Sep 23, Oct 2, 9, 16, 31, Dec 18,
31; 1713: DL, Jan 9, Mar 17, 28, Apr 11, Oct 6, 21, Nov 10, 20; 1715: DL, Jan
11, 14, 17, 28, LIF, Feb 4, 10, 11, 15, 25, Mar 1, 12, Apr 7, 18, DL, 19, 30,
LIF, May 10, Jun 2, DL, 6, Aug 2, LIF, Oct 3, 17, Nov 2, Dec 29; 1716: LIF,
Mar 22, Apr 9, DL, May 3, 24, 30, Jun 28, Jul 10, Dec 11; 1717: LIF, Jan 8,
DL, Apr 1, LIF, 23, May 24, DL, Jun 7, Jul 2, LIF, Oct 30, Nov 5, DL, 7, LIF,
Dec 21; 1718: LIF, Jan 6, DL, Feb 6, LIF, Mar 15, 31, DL, May 20, LIF, 27,
DL, 29, Jun 13, LIF, Jul 9, DL, 25, LIF, Aug 6, RI, 16, 23, Oct 9, DL, 27,
Nov 7, LIF, Dec 1, 26; 1719: LIF, Mar 31, May 14, DL, 18, LIF, 25, 29, Oct
20, Dec 3; 1720: DL, Jan 4, LIF, 5, 11, DL, 19, LIF, Mar 8, 31, DL, Apr 19,

LIF, 22, May 4, DL, 14, 18, 27, LIF, Jun 8, Oct 31, Dec 27; 1721: LIF, Feb
15, 28, DL, Jun 6, LIF, Oct 25, Dec 27; 1722: LIF, Apr 9, DL, May 2, 7, 17,
LIF, 24, SF, Sep 24, LIF, Oct 12, Dec 27; 1723: LIF, Feb 13, DL, Mar 30, Apr
16, LIF, May 2, 6, 20, DL, 25, Jul 2, 9, SOU, Sep 25, LIF, Oct 9, DL, 18, DT,
Nov 1, 26, Dec 6, LIF, 9, CT, 10; 1724: DL, Jan 13, BPT, Mar 18, LIF, May 7,
DL, 16, LIF, 25, RI, Jul 4, HAY, Oct 13, DL, 21, 24, LIF, Nov 11, 18, DL, Dec
8; 1725: LIF, Jan 18, May 14, DL, 19, LIF, 19, DL, Oct 26, Nov 25, Dec 9, 29;
1726: DL, Jan 4, Apr 22, May 16, 23; 1727: DL, May 4, Oct 20; 1728: LIF, Apr
1, 22, 30, DL, May 17; 1729: LIF, Apr 17, DL, May 9, RI, Jul 26, DL, Dec 31;
1730: GF, Jan 5; 1731: DL, May 17, Jun 9, Jul 13, Aug 3, Sep 28; 1734: BLO,
Jan 16, DL, Sep 28; 1739: CG, Nov 7; 1745: GF, May 1; 1760: CG, Mar 18
--Mad Tom of Bedlam; or, The Distressed Lovers, 1730: BFPG/TC, Aug 1, 24
D'Ogni Amator (song), 1748: KING'S, Apr 5
Doisson, Raymond, 1719: LIF, Jan 27
--Baron de la Crasse, Le; or, My Lord Sloven, 1719: LIF, Jan 27; 1720: KING'S,
May 31; 1721: HAY, Feb 2; 1734: HAY, Dec 16; 1735: HAY, Jan 3, GF/HAY, Mar 17
Doktor und Apotheker. See Stephanie, Gottlieb.
Dolcezze dell' Amor (song), 1750: KING'S, Apr 10
Doldrum, The. See O'Keeffe, John.
Dolly's (dining place), 1767: CG, Sep 17
Dolmain. See Dalmaine.
Domine Probasti (anthem), 1702: CC, May 21
Dominic (scene painter), 1726: DL, Dec 30
Dominique, Mme (dancer), 1748: BFH, Aug 24
Domitilla, Miriamne (dancer), 1741: CG, Oct 24, 30, Nov 7; 1742: CG, Jan 21,
25, Feb 6, 10, Apr 5, May 1, Dec 9, 18, 21; 1743: CG, Apr 8, Dec 20; 1744:
CG, Jan 14, Feb 14, Mar 3, 15, 28, Apr 4, 9, 16, 23, May 10
Don Calascione. See Barlocci, G.
Don Carlos. See Otway, Thomas.
Don Giovanni. See Gazzaniga, Giuseppe.
Don Japhet D'Armenie (farce), 1721: HAY, Dec 21
Don Jerome's Trip to England (entertainment), 1778: CG, May 8
Don John. See Shadwell, Thomas; Delpini, Carlo.
Don Juan; or, The Libertine Destroyed (dance), 1785: KING'S, Apr 7, 15, 18, 20,
29, May 28, Jun 9
Don Juan; or, The Libertine Destroyed (pantomime), 1782: DL, May 10
Don Pasquin D'Avalos (play, anon), 1721: HAY, Dec 18; 1725: HAY, Jan 13; 1735:
GF/HAY, Apr 7
Don Pedro. See Cumberland, Richard.
Don Quixote (entertainment), 1769: SW, Mar 27
Don Quixote (play). See D'Urfey, Thomas; Arnold, Dr Samuel; Piguenit, D J.
Don Quixote in England. See Fielding, Henry.
Don Saverio. See Arne, Dr Thomas A.
Don Sebastian. See Dryden, John.
Don Trustullo. See Jomelli, Niccolo.
Dona, Count (spectator), 1668: ATCOURT, Feb 4
Donadieu, Miss (singer), 1775: HAY, May 1
Donaldson (actor), 1772: HAY, Dec 21
Donaldson, Mrs (singer), 1755: CG, Apr 2
Donell (haberdasher), 1750: DL, Jan 31
Donna di Spirito, La. See Piccini, Niccolo.
Donna Piu Constante Dell' Humo, La (entertainment), 1727: KING'S, Feb 9
Donne donne chi vi crede (song), 1792: DLKING'S, Apr 19
Donne Vindicate, Le. See Piccini, Niccolo.
Donovan, Master (actor), 1739: DL, Oct 10; 1740: DL, Oct 14, Dec 26
Door (merchant), 1773: CG, Jan 8; 1774: CG, Feb 14
Doorsming (singer), 1748: HAY, Sep 5
Doppo L'Orrore (song), 1770: DL, Mar 14
Dorastus and Fawnia; or, The Royal Shepherd and Shepherdess (droll), 1703: BFP,
Aug 23; 1729: BFB, Aug 25; 1749: NWSM, May 10, 15
Dore, Mrs (actor), 1785: HAY, Apr 25
Dorell, Miss (actor), 1797: DL, Jun 2
Dorey's Boarding School, 1733: CHE, May 9
Dorien (actor), 1773: MARLY, Sep 3
Dorion Jr (actor, singer), 1791: DLKING'S, Oct 15; 1792: DLKING'S, May 23, HAY,
Jun 23, DL, Oct 11, 18, Nov 21; 1793: DL, Mar 7, 9, HAY, Jul 20, Aug 3, 12,
16, Sep 2, 19, Oct 10, Nov 19; 1794: HAY, Feb 24, DL, May 16, 22, Jun 2, 9,
12, 23, HAY, Jul 17, 18, 21, 24, DL, Sep 27, Oct 27, 31, Nov 15, Dec 20;
1795: DL, Jan 19, Feb 3, HAY, Jul 31
Dorion, Fierman Joseph (actor, singer, music copyist), 1781: HAY, Aug 8; 1782:
HAY, Jun 3, Aug 17; 1789: HAY, Aug 11, DL, Nov 13, 14; 1790: DL, Jan 8, HAY,

Jul 16; 1791: HAY, Jul 30, Aug 31, DLKING'S, Oct 15, Nov 16; 1792: DLKING'S, Mar 29, May 23, DL, Oct 11, 13, Nov 21; 1793: DL, Mar 7, HAY, Jun 17, Aug 12, 16, Sep 2, 19, Oct 10, Nov 19; 1794: HAY, Feb 24, DL, Mar 28, May 16, Jun 9, 25, 27, HAY, Aug 27, DL, Sep 27, Oct 27, 31, Nov 15, Dec 20; 1795: DL, Feb 9, 24, HAY, Jun 13, 20; 1798: CG, Mar 28
Dorival, Anne Marguerite (dancer), 1784: KING'S, Dec 18; 1785: KING'S, Jan 1, 11, 22, Feb 5, 12, 26, Mar 3, 12, 17, Apr 7, 21, May 12, 24, Jun 9, 18, 21; 1790: HAY, Jan 7, Feb 6, 27, Apr 6, 15, May 4, 11, 20, 25, 27, 29, Jun 1; 1791: KING'S, Mar 26, 31, Apr 12, May 19, Jun 6, 10, 25, 28, Jul 9
Dorman (coal merchant), 1771: DL, Oct 28; 1772: DL, Jun 10, Oct 19; 1773: DL, Jun 2; 1774: DL, Feb 22
Dorman, Elizabeth, Mrs Ridley (actor, singer), 1762: DL, Nov 23; 1763: DL, Feb 24, Apr 23, Oct 28; 1764: DL, Jan 24, Feb 24, 27, Apr 12, 26, 28, Sep 25, Oct 29; 1765: DL, Feb 15, Apr 22, 23, Sep 24; 1766: DL, Feb 7, Apr 12, 30, CG, May 3, DL, 3; 1767: DL, Jan 2, May 13, Sep 21, 22, 26, Nov 7, 18, Dec 26; 1768: DL, Jan 14, Mar 15, Apr 22, 27, May 4, Sep 8, 20, 22, 27, Oct 3, HAY, 7, DL, 10; 1769: DL, Mar 16, 28, Apr 7, 28, May 1, KING'S, Jun 1, DL, Sep 23, Oct 2, 9; 1770: DL, Jan 4, Feb 8, May 7, 11, Jun 7, MARLY, Aug 21, DL, Sep 27, Oct 2, 13, 25, 29, Nov 14, 17, 19, 21, 24, Dec 7, 13; 1771: DL, Jan 1, 18, Apr 9, May 8, 13, 25, GROTTO, Jun 22, Aug 8, DL, Oct 1, 10, 21, Dec 2, 6, 26; 1772: DL, Apr 22, 25
--Sir Roger deCoverley; or, The Merry Christmas (entertainment), 1740: CG, Nov 18; 1746: DL, Dec 30
Dorman, Joseph, 1736: HAY, Apr 26; 1746: DL, Dec 30
--Female Rake, The; or, Modern Fine Lady, 1736: HAY, Apr 26
Dorman, Ridley (violinist), 1767: DL, Jun 1; 1774: DL, Jun 2
Dormen (house servant), 1740: CG, Nov 18
Dormer. See Dorman.
Dorney, Richard (violinist), 1675: ATCOURT, Feb 15
Dorset Court, 1660: DC, Jun 0
Dorset St, 1787: CG, Jun 15
Dorset, Countess of. See Sackville, Mary Compton.
Dorset, Earl of. See Sackville, Charles.
Dorset, Earl of, 1718: LIF, Jun 25; 1751: DL, Nov 29
Dorset, Lady. See Cranfield, Frances.
Dorset, Sons of Lord, 1728: HAY, Feb 16
Dorsetshire, 1796: DL, Apr 2
Dorta, Rachele (singer), 1784: KING'S, Jan 6, Feb 24, Mar 25, Apr 15, Jun 10, 12, Dec 18; 1785: KING'S, Jan 4, 8, 29, Mar 17, Apr 2, 28; see also Giorgi, Rachele Dorta
Dorta, Rosina (singer), 1784: KING'S, Feb 24, Apr 15
Dorus and Cleora (song), 1757: HAY, Oct 17
Dorvigny, 1782: HAY, Jul 2; 1784: CG, Jun 14; 1785: CG, May 6
--Aveugle Pretendu, L', 1782: HAY, Jul 2
--Fete de Campagne, La; ou, L'Intendant Comedien malgre Lui, 1784: CG, Jun 14; 1785: CG, May 6
Dorville's Row, 1785: HAMM, Jul 15; 1786: HAMM, Jun 5, Jul 7, 24, Aug 5
Dosel (doorkeeper), 1789: CG, Jun 16; 1790: CG, May 27, Jun 12; 1791: CG, Jun 14; 1792: CG, Jun 1; 1794: CG, Jun 17; 1795: CG, Jun 17; 1796: CG, Jun 6
Doser (beneficiary), 1789: CG, Jun 13
Dossie, Robert, 1768: HAY, Jul 8
--Statesman Foiled, The, 1768: HAY, Jul 8, 13, 18, 22
Dotage; or, The Natural Mistake (dance), 1786: CG, Nov 14, 16, 17; see also Hibernian Dotage
Dotti, Anna (singer), 1724: KING'S, Oct 31, Dec 1; 1725: KING'S, Feb 13, Apr 10; 1726: KING'S, Jan 15, May 5; 1727: KING'S, Jan 7, 31, May 6
Dottore, Il (musical), 1770: KING'S, Jan 6
Double Amour, The. See Stewart, Thomas.
Double Bass (music), 1732: LIF, Feb 25
Double beat (song), 1794: CG, Mar 26; 1798: CG, Mar 14
Double Curtell, Flute and Bells (entertainment), 1702: DL, Aug 22; 1703: DL, Jun 18; 1704: DL, Jun 5
Double Dealer, The. See Congreve, William.
Double Deceit, The. See Popple, William.
Double Deception, The. See Richardson, Elizabeth.
Double Disappointment, The. See Mendez, Moses.
Double Disguise, The. See Hook, Harriet Horncastle.
Double Distress, The. See Pix, Mary.
Double Epreuve (dance), 1799: KING'S, Jun 8, 17, 22, 29, Jul 2, 9, 13, 20
Double Face (dance), 1734: HAY, Nov 7
Double Falsehood, The. See Theobald, Lewis.
Double Festival (dance), 1776: DL, Nov 7, 26, Dec 18; 1777: DL, Jan 4, 6, 17,

Feb 10, 13, 15, 18, Mar 1, Sep 20
Double Gallant, The. See Cibber, Colley.
Double Hornpipe (dance), 1763: DL, May 4, 9, 11, 13, 31, HAY, Jun 20; 1764: CG,
   May 1, DL, 14, 19, 21, CG, 22, DL, 23, 24, 29; 1765: DL, May 2, 11, 13, 14,
   15, 18, 21; 1766: CG, Apr 21, DL, May 9, 10, 20; 1767: DL, Apr 4, CG, 27, May
   2, 4, 5, 7, 11, DL, 11, CG, 12, 13, 14, DL, 15, CG, 18, DL, 19, CG, 19, DL,
   20, CG, 20, 21, DL, 22, CG, 22, 25, DL, 25, CG, 26, 28, DL, 30, Jun 1; 1768:
   CG, May 3, 6, 7, DL, 9, CG, 10, DL, 13, 23, 24, 25, HAY, Aug 1, 19, Sep 7,
   13; 1769: CG, Apr 8, 11, 12, 13, 19, 21, 24, DL, 25, CG, May 3, 12, DL, 16,
   20, HAY, Jul 12, Aug 9, 29; 1770: CG, Apr 24, 27, DL, May 4, CG, 12, 25, HAY,
   Jul 4, 16, Aug 1, Sep 5; 1771: CG, Apr 22, May 1, 7, 8, 11, 15, 17, 28, HAY,
   Jun 17, 26, Jul 12, 17, 24, Aug 19, Sep 20; 1772: CG, Apr 24, DL, May 5, Jun
   3; CG, Sep 21, 23, Oct 9, 13, 15; 1773: CG, Feb 18, 27, Apr 17, May 14, HAY,
   19, Jun 14, 16, 30, Jul 9, CG, Sep 29, Oct 1, 5, 14, Dec 6; 1774: CG, Apr 12,
   May 11, 13; 1775: CG, May 3, 8, 11; 1777: CG, May 9; 1778: DL, May 8; 1779:
   DL, Apr 17, May 29; 1783: DL, May 2; 1785: DL, May 17, HAMM, Jul 22; 1787:
   CG, May 19; 1788: HAY, Apr 29; 1790: HAY, Jul 13, 23, Aug 10, 11, 21, Sep 10;
   1795: CG, May 29, Jun 9
Double Inconstance, La. See Marivaux, Pierre Carlet de Chamblain de.
Double Jealousy (dance), 1736: DL, Mar 27, Apr 1, 13, May 13, 15, Sep 7, 11,
   21, 23, 28; 1738: DL, Nov 8, 27, Dec 15, 30; 1739: DL, Jan 5
Double Mandolin Concerto (music), 1773: CG, Apr 27
Double Marriage, The. See Fletcher, John.
Double Mistake, The. See Griffith, Elizabeth.
Double Mistress, The. See Manley, Mary.
Double Surprise (dance), 1781: CG, Dec 19, 22; 1782: CG, Feb 25
Double Traitor Roasted, The (opera), 1748: WH, Jan 1
Doubtful Heir, The. See Shirley, James.
Douglas (actor), 1770: HAY, Dec 19
Douglas (house servant), 1787: DL, Jun 4; 1788: DL, Jun 6; 1797: DL, Jun 15;
   1800: DL, Jun 14
Douglas. See Home, John.
Douglas, George, Lord Dunbarton, 1684: DLORDG, Oct 29
Douglas, Miss (actor), 1777: HAY, Apr 22
Douglas, William (trumpeter), 1720: HIC, Feb 23; 1721: HIC, Mar 15; 1722: HIC,
   Feb 16; 1723: HIC, Mar 6; 1724: HIC, Feb 26; 1745: HAY, Feb 20
Douglas, William, Marquis and Duke of Queensberry, 1682: DLORDG, Jul 18
Dove (surgeon), 1749: DL, Mar 18
Dove sei amato bene (song), 1770: DL, Mar 14, 16; 1786: DL, Mar 10, 29; 1787:
   KING'S, Mar 1; 1790: DL, Mar 5; 1795: KING'S, Mar 13
Dove sei et non e si vago e Bello (song), 1726: LIF, Mar 28
Dove Spiega (song), 1738: DL, May 15
Dove, Elizabeth, Mrs Michael (actor, dancer), 1731: HAY, Mar 24; 1732: HAY, Mar
   17; 1733: GF, Oct 17, Dec 26, 28, 31; 1734: GF, Jan 8, 28, Feb 11, Oct 28,
   Dec 9; 1735: GF, Jan 10, 13, 24, Feb 4, Mar 6, Sep 17, Oct 15, Nov 17, Dec
   17; 1736: GF, Feb 17, 20, Mar 3, LIF, Sep 30, Oct 9, 21, Dec 7, 16, 17, 31;
   1738: TC, Aug 7, BFP, 23, SFH, Sep 5; 1739: BFH, Aug 23; 1740: BFH, Aug 23;
   1741: SF, Sep 14; 1742: BFPY, Aug 25, SF, Sep 8, SOU, 27; 1743: TCD/BFTD, Aug
   23; 1744: GF, Dec 26; 1745: GF, Mar 11, Nov 4, 11, 19, 28; 1746: GF, Jan 13,
   Feb 7, 17, 25, Oct 31, Nov 6, 18, 19, 21, Dec 3, 5, 29; 1747: GF, Feb 2, Mar
   2, CG, Nov 16
Dove, Michael (actor, dancer), 1729: HAY, Feb 11, 25, Mar 29, May 7, 26, 29,
   Jun 14, 17, 26, Jul 23, DL, Aug 16, BFR, 25, SF, Sep 8, HAY, Nov 12, Dec 18;
   1730: HAY, Jan 16, 21, Feb 12, Mar 5, 11, 20, 30, Apr 20, 24, May 1, Jun 23,
   27, Jul 17, TC, Aug 1, 11, BFR, 22, Sep 4, SFP, 9, SF, 14, HAY, 18, Nov 16;
   1731: HAY, Jan 15, 18, Mar 17, Apr 22, May 12, 13, TCY, Aug 9; 1732: HAY, Feb
   16, Mar 10, Apr 27, May 8, 10, TC, Aug 4; 1733: GF, Jan 13, 26, Mar 5, Apr
   11, May 16, HAY, 28, GF, Sep 24, Oct 17, 25, Nov 10, Dec 14, 26; 1734: GF,
   Feb 11, Apr 19, May 16, Sep 25, Oct 14, Nov 18, Dec 9; 1735: GF, Jan 13, 18,
   25, Feb 17, Mar 6, May 1, 2, 3, 5, 6, GF/HAY, Jul 22, HAY, Aug 4, 12, GF/HAY,
   21, HAY, 26, LIF, 29, GF, Sep 12, 17, 19, 26, Oct 15, Nov 3, 6, 11, 17, Dec
   8; 1736: GF, Feb 4, 9, 20, Mar 3, 18, Apr 28, LIF, Jul 1, Oct 5, 9, 21, 26,
   Nov 6, 11, 13, 16, 18, 20, Dec 7, 11, 16, 31; 1737: LIF, Jan 20, HAY, Feb 25;
   1738: TC, Aug 7, CG, 22, SFH, Sep 5, CG, Dec 18; 1739: CG, Jan 22, Apr 25,
   26, May 4, 21, BFH, Aug 23; 1740: BFH, Aug 23; 1741: GF, Mar 3, Apr 22; 1742:
   BFPY, Aug 25, SOU, Sep 27, LIF, Dec 1, 3, 27; 1743: LIF, Jan 14, Feb 14, 17,
   Apr 5, 7, TCD/BFTD, Aug 23, DL, Sep 24; 1744: GF, Dec 3, 26; 1745: GF, Feb
   14, Mar 7, 11, Oct 28, Nov 11, 12, 14, 23, 27, Dec 2, 4, 9; 1746: GF, Jan 1,
   2, 3, 13, 31, Feb 17, Mar 4, Oct 28, 29, Nov 4, 6, 7, 13, 14, 19, 20, 21, 26,
   28, Dec 3, 5, 9, 10, 11, 15, 17, 22; 1747: GF, Jan 5, 9, 16, 26, Feb 2, 9,
   Apr 9
Dove, Michael and Elizabeth (actors), 1746: GF, Feb 17; 1747: GF, Apr 9

Dover St, 1779: KING'S, Apr 15; 1780: KING'S, Apr 13, 20; 1781: KING'S, Apr 26;
    1782: KING'S, Apr 30
Dover, John
--Mall, The; or, The Modish Lovers, 1674: LIF, Jan 0, Mar 0
--Roman Generals, The; or, The Distressed Ladies, 1667: NONE, Sep 0
Dover, 1670: LIF, Apr 0, BRIDGES, May 0, DOVER, 11, 19, BRI/COUR, Dec 0; 1681:
    DL, May 0; 1749: CG, Dec 21
Dovoto. See Devoto.
Dow, Alexander, 1768: DL, Dec 17; 1774: DL, Feb 19, 22
--Sethona, 1774: DL, Feb 19, 21, 22, 24, 26, 28, Mar 3, 5, 8
--Zingis, 1768: DL, Dec 17, 19, 21, 22, 23; 1769: DL, Jan 3, 5, 9, 11, 14, 16,
    21, 31, Nov 27
Dowager, Princess, 1767: CG, Jan 15, DL, 15; 1768: CG, Jan 2; 1769: CG, Jan 6;
    see also Princesses
Dowgate, 1702: PR, Jun 30
Dowglas. See Douglas.
Down (house servant), 1731: GF, May 14
Down with this love (song), 1673: LIF, Mar 0
Downes (actor), 1729: HAY, Apr 22, May 2, 7, BF, Aug 26
Downes, J (publisher), 1795: CG, Apr 8
Downes, John (actor), 1661: LIF, Jun 28
Downes, John (prompter), 1704: ATCOURT, Feb 7, 28, Apr 24; 1705: QUEEN'S, Apr
    9, May 0, LIF/QUEN, Oct 30, QUEEN'S, Nov 23; 1706: ATCOURT, Feb 5
Downing, George, 1772: DL, Apr 25; 1780: CG, Apr 19
--Humours of the Turf, The, 1772: DL, Apr 25, May 4, 6, 20
--Volunteers, The; or, Taylors to Arms! (prelude), 1780: CG, Apr 19, 28
Dowson (actor), 1777: HAY, Oct 9, 13
Dowson, Ann (singer), 1771: GROTTO, Jun 22, Aug 8, 30, Sep 3, 9
Dowton, William (actor), 1796: DL, Oct 11, 27, Nov 21, 22, Dec 10; 1797: DL,
    Jan 12, Feb 1, Mar 9, Apr 24, 25, May 8, 12, 17, 22, 23, 25, Jun 6, 12, Oct
    3, 12, 14, 17, 19, 21, 31, Nov 7, 13, 17, 25, 27, Dec 14; 1798: DL, Jan 20,
    23, 24, Feb 13, 14, 16, May 19, 24, Jun 5, 6, 15, Sep 22, 29, Oct 4, 11, Nov
    3, 10, 12, 20, 22, 29, Dec 5, HAY, 17, DL, 19, 21; 1799: DL, Feb 4, 19, 23,
    26, Mar 2, Apr 8, May 3, 24, Jun 18, Jul 1, Sep 17, 19, 21, 28, Oct 5, 12,
    19, 31, Nov 1, 7, 16, 27, Dec 2, 11, 17; 1800: DL, Apr 29, May 12, 14, 21
Doyle (house servant), 1800: DL, Jun 13
Doyle, John (actor, singer), 1778: CG, Nov 23; 1779: CG, Feb 8, 13, Oct 8, 11,
    18, Nov 8, 30, Dec 29; 1780: CG, Feb 8, Apr 10, 27, Sep 22, Oct 23, Nov 15;
    1781: CG, Apr 3, 23, 25, May 16, Sep 24, Oct 19, Nov 2, 7, 12, Dec 17, 26;
    1782: CG, May 6, 11, 14, 20, Sep 30, Oct 7, 22, Nov 18, 25, Dec 27; 1783: CG,
    May 19, 24, Sep 17, 22, Oct 6, 14, Nov 8, 21, Dec 18; 1784: CG, Jan 19, 29,
    Apr 26, May 11, Sep 20, 22, Oct 4, 12, 18, 25, Dec 13, 27; 1785: CG, May 4,
    7, 12, 26, Sep 30, Oct 17, 21, Nov 4, 14, Dec 5, 8, 26; 1786: CG, Jan 18, Feb
    21, May 30; 1787: CG, Sep 24, 26, Oct 1, 18, 22, Dec 3; 1788: CG, Oct 21, Dec
    29; 1789: CG, Jun 2
Doyle, Mrs (house servant), 1789: CG, Jun 6
D'oyley, E
--Britannicus; or, The Man of Honour, 1694: NONE, Sep 0
Dozen at the Gangway (song), 1794: CG, May 9
Dr Bobadil's Monody (pamphlet), 1752: DL, Dec 23
Draghi, Giovanni Baptista (Signior Joanni, Signor Baptist) (composer), 1667:
    NONE, Feb 12; 1668: ATCOURT, Sep 28; 1675: DG, Feb 27; 1682: DG, Apr 0, Aug
    10; 1684: FALKLAND, Jul 25, DLORDG, Aug 0; 1687: MS, Nov 22; 1688: DL, Feb 0;
    1696: LIF, Mar 0; 1697: YB, Feb 24; 1698: YB, Mar 30; 1701: YB, Mar 24
Dragon (performing dog), 1775: CG, Jan 6, DL, Feb 1
Dragon de Moscovie, Le (play), 1719: KING'S, Mar 16; 1720: KING'S, May 20;
    1721: HAY, Jan 20; 1725: HAY, Apr 14
Dragon of Wantly, The. See Carey, Henry.
Draidens. See Dryden.
Drake (upholsterer), 1663: IT, Nov 2
Drake, J
--Sham Lawyer, The; or, The Lucky Extravagant, 1697: DL, May 31
Drake, Miss (dancer, singer), 1798: DL, Oct 6, Nov 14, Dec 6; 1799: DL, Jan 19,
    Feb 5, Oct 14; 1800: DL, Mar 11, HAY, Jul 2
Dramatic Cento, A (entertainment), 1796: DL, May 25
Dramatic Congress, The (pamphlet), 1743: DL, Oct 6
Dramatic Execution of Agis, The (pamphlet), 1758: DL, Mar 13
Dramatic Lecture (lecture), 1749: BBT, Mar 1
Dramatic Oglio (entertainment), 1782: DL, Sep 17
Dramatic Puffers, The. See Bate, Henry.
Dramatic Time-Piece (pamphlet), 1767: DL, Nov 7
Dramatic Turtle (entertainment), 1760: BFG, Sep 3

Dramaticus (author), 1773: DL, Mar 22
Dramatist, The. See Reynolds, Frederick.
Draper (singer), 1776: CHAPEL, Apr 2
Draper, Matthew, 1731: HAY, Jan 20
--Spendthrift, The, 1731: HAY, Jan 20, 25, 27, Feb 4, Mar 5
Draper, Miss (singer), 1776: DL, Mar 1; 1777: DL, Feb 14; 1778: DL, Mar 6, 27;
   1779: DL, Feb 19, Mar 12; 1780: DL, Feb 11; 1781: DL, Mar 2, 30; 1782: DL,
   Feb 15
Draper, S (bookseller, publisher), 1747: CG, Mar 7; 1749: CG, Mar 3; 1750: DL,
   Oct 11; 1756: DL, Jan 31
Draper's Hall, 1660: DH, Mar 28; 1696: DL, Feb 0
Drapers, Company of, 1675: CITY, Oct 29; 1676: CITY, Oct 30; 1679: CITY, Oct
   29; 1684: CITY, Oct 29; 1691: CITY, Oct 29
Dreamer Awake, The. See Eyre, Edmund John.
Dressler, John (trombonist), 1792: KING'S, Feb 24, Mar 14; 1793: KING/HAY, Feb
   15; 1796: CG, Feb 12; 1797: CG, Mar 3; 1798: HAY, Jan 15, CG, Feb 23; 1799:
   CG, Feb 8; 1800: CG, Feb 28
Drew (actor), 1722: HAY, Dec 17; 1723: HAY, Jan 31, Feb 13, Mar 14, Apr 15, 22,
   HA, Jul 22
Dreyden. See Dryden.
Dridge (actor), 1740: DL, Oct 27
Drinking Song (song), 1731: LIF, May 17; 1732: GF, May 15; 1796: CG, Mar 15, 17
Driscol (wigmaker), 1755: DL, Apr 19
Driscoll (house servant), 1746: CG, May 7; 1747: CG, May 19; 1748: CG, May 5;
   1749: CG, May 3; 1750: CG, May 7; 1751: CG, May 14; 1752: CG, May 7; 1753:
   CG, May 21; 1754: CG, May 18; 1755: CG, May 20; 1756: CG, May 24
Droghierina, La (singer), 1737: KING'S, Jan 8, Feb 12, Apr 12, May 24, Oct 29;
   1738: KING'S, Jan 3, 28, Mar 14; see also Chimenti, Margherita
Drollelo, Mynheer (dancer), 1746: SFLY, Sep 8
Dromat (Droma), Mlle (dancer), 1793: KING'S, Feb 26; 1795: CG, Apr 6
Drouville (dancer), 1771: KING'S, Jun 1, CG, Nov 4; 1773: HAY, Jun 16
Drowsy Cobler (dance), 1749: BFY, Aug 23
Druid's Song, The (song), 1704: DL, Jan 4
Druids, The. See Fisher, John Abraham.
Drummer, The. See Addison, Joseph.
Drummond, Andrew (banker), 1738: KING'S, May 23; 1756: SFB, Sep 20; 1757:
   KING'S, Sep 20; 1759: KING'S, May 8; 1762: KING'S, Jun 5, Nov 13; 1765:
   KING'S, Nov 23; 1766: KING'S, Oct 21; 1768: KING'S, Nov 3; 1772: KING'S, Nov
   14; 1783: KING'S, May 20
Drummond, John (correspondent), 1682: DLORDG, Jul 18
Drums Demolished. See Bickerstaff's Unburied Dead.
Drunken Beau and a Chimney Sweeper (dance), 1704: LIF, Jul 27
Drunken Buck (entertainment), 1776: CHR, Oct 9
Drunken Dance (dance), 1718: LIF, Dec 5, 12; 1719: KING'S, Mar 17; 1720: DL,
   Aug 16
Drunken French Peasant (dance), 1724: LIF, Apr 10
Drunken Man (dance), 1716: LIF, Dec 11, 20, GLOBE, 28; 1717: GLOBE, Jan 18;
   1719: BCA, Sep 24, LIF, Dec 28; 1720: LIF, May 10, 11, 12, 24, BCA, Sep 23,
   SOU, Oct 10; 1721: LIF, May 18, HAY, Jul 14; 1722: DL, May 3, Jul 6, RI, 23,
   Aug 20; 1723: DL, May 30, HA, Jul 8, DL, 26, 30, Aug 6, DT, Nov 12, KAT, Dec
   4, DT, 6; 1724: BPT, Mar 11, HT, 13, BPT, 18, DL, Apr 28, RI, Jun 22, Aug 3,
   BFL, 22; 1725: DL, May 19; 1727: DL, Apr 24, May 15; 1728: DL, Apr 29, May
   10, 22, 29; 1730: BFPG/TC, Aug 1, 24; 1731: DL, Apr 8, LIF, May 28; 1732:
   LIF, Apr 14, 17, May 4, 5, 17, WINH, 27; 1733: LIF/CG, Apr 2, 17; 1734: TB,
   Jan 26, CG, Apr 19, HA, Sep 2, RI, 26, LIF, Oct 12; 1736: LIF, Mar 31, DL,
   Apr 6, May 3; 1737: CG, Apr 12, May 6, 31; 1738: CG, Jan 17; 1740: CG, Jun 5;
   1742: JS, May 31; 1756: CG, Mar 25, May 20; 1758: CG, Apr 3; 1762: CG, Apr
   16, 28, 30, May 11, DL, 17, HAY, Oct 25; 1763: HAY, Sep 7; 1764: CG, May 7,
   DL, 11; 1770: CG, May 10; 1774: DL, Apr 27, CG, May 2, DL, 3, 5, HAY, Aug 19;
   1775: DL, Apr 24, CG, May 9; 1779: HAY, May 10; 1788: HAY, Dec 22; 1790: HAY,
   Sep 29; 1791: HAY, Dec 26
Drunken Miller (dance), 1723: LIF, May 3
Drunken Newswriter (entertainment), 1770: HAY, Oct 1; 1771: HAY, Mar 11, Apr 1
Drunken Peasant (dance), 1715: DL, Apr 9; 1725: DL, Nov 3; 1729: DL, Mar 13,
   27, Apr 25, May 2; 1733: DL, Mar 10, Apr 4, 24, May 2, 5, 9, 18, 21, 24, Sep
   26, DL/HAY, Oct 12, DL, 17, DL/HAY, 19, 24, DL, 27, Nov 2, GF, 6, 8, DL/HAY,
   14, DL, Dec 7, 31; 1734: GF, Jan 7, DL, 31, DL/HAY, Mar 12, 28, Apr 1, 6, DL,
   29, DL/HAY, May 1, DL, Sep 10, 12, Oct 8, 26, Nov 7, 16, 19, Dec 4, 9; 1735:
   DL, Jan 16, 17, 29, Feb 4, 6, 13, 15, Mar 29, Apr 11, 14, 18, 21, 25, May 1,
   5, 6, 9, 14, 23, Jun 3, 11, Jul 1, Nov 3, 6, 12, Dec 22; 1736: DL, Jan 3, 5,
   Mar 20, 22, 23, 29, Apr 12, 30, May 3, 25, Jun 2, Aug 31, Sep 25, 28, 30, Oct
   2, 16, 22, 30, Nov 1, 8; 1737: DL, Feb 5, 8, 18, 22, Mar 14, Apr 13, 19, 26,

251

29, May 2, 4, Nov 11, 12, 14, 15; 1738: DL, Jan 24, 27, 28, Feb 3, 6, 11, 14, 21, Apr 13, 14, 17, 21, May 3, 5, 6, 9, 10, 11, 15, 17, 26, 27, 29, 30, Oct 5, 7, 16, 21, 26, Nov 29, 30; 1739: TC, Aug 8, CG, 10, 21, BF, 27, SF, Sep 8, DL, Nov 13, 20, 21, Dec 7, 14, 21, 28; 1740: DL, Jan 3, 8, 11, 14, Feb 5, 8, 11, 18, Mar 4, 6, 8, 10, 18, Apr 7, 11, 19, 30, May 2, 8, 14, 19, 20, 22, 26, 28, BFLP, Aug 23, SF, Sep 9, SOU, Oct 9, CG, 23, GF, 23, 24, CG, 31, Nov 7, 18, GF, 19, CG, 19, GF, 20, 22, 24; 1741: GF, Mar 19, Apr 2, 6, 13, 15, 16, 22, 28, CG, May 12, JS, Jun 16, DL, Oct 29, Nov 21, Dec 1, 3, 26; 1742: DL, Jan 2, Feb 6, 19, Mar 2, Apr 6, 20, 24, 26, 27, GF, 29, DL, May 15, 22, CG, Sep 29; 1743: JS, Mar 23, Apr 25; 1744: GF, Dec 10; 1746: GF, Feb 10, 17, May 1, SFHP, Sep 8, GF, Oct 27, SOU, 27; 1747: GF, Mar 10, SOU, Oct 5; 1748: CG, Mar 28, Apr 20, HAY, Sep 5; 1749: CG, Apr 3, 17, 29, DL, May 9; 1750: DL, May 2; 1751: CG, May 6, 7; 1752: CG, Apr 29, 30, May 2, 4, 6, 7, 8; 1753: CG, May 3, 5, 9, 15, 21; 1754: CG, Apr 30, DL, May 7; 1755: CG, Apr 16, DL, May 15, HAY, Aug 21, Sep 3; 1756: CG, May 1, DL, 6, CG, 13; 1757: CG, May 2, 12, 13, DL, 23; 1758: CG, Apr 21, May 2; 1759: CG, Apr 30, May 1, 15; 1760: CG, Apr 28, May 5, 7, 8, 14; 1761: CG, Apr 27; 1762: CG, Dec 31; 1763: CG, Apr 27, May 11; 1764: CG, Apr 27; 1765: CG, Apr 29, May 8; 1766: CG, Apr 21, May 2; 1767: CG, May 1; 1771: DL, May 15; 1772: CG, May 14, DL, 26; 1773: DL, May 17, 21; 1785: HAMM, Jul 26

Drunken Peasant and Clown (dance), 1740: GF, Dec 4, 5

Drunken Sailor Reclaimed (dance), 1786: CG, Mar 4, Apr 24, May 2, 9, Dec 12, 19; 1787: CG, May 16

Drunken Songs (song), 1732: LIF, May 4

Drunken Swiss (dance), 1723: LIF, Nov 16, 19, 27, Dec 9, HAY, 26, 30; 1735: CG, Oct 31; 1762: DL, Apr 24; 1789: DL, May 7; 1793: CG, Oct 15, Nov 12, 21

Drunken Tyrolese (dance), 1746: CG, Feb 27, Mar 1, 3, 6, 10, 20, 22, 31, Apr 1, 2, 5, 8, 9, 11, 12, 16, 19, 26, 29, 30

Drury Lane Playhouse Broke Open, 1747: DL, Oct 3

Drury, Robert (author, actor), 1732: DL, Aug 17; 1733: GF, Mar 5, CG, Aug 14; 1734: YB, Nov 19, 29; 1736: HAY, Feb 2, May 12

--Devil of a Duke, The; or, Trapolin's Vagaries (Conjuror's Bastard, The), 1732: DL, Aug 17, Sep 23, 26, Oct 19, Nov 15; 1741: BFH, Aug 22

--Fancied Queen, The, 1733: CG, Aug 14, 16

--Mad Captain, The, 1733: GF, Mar 3, 5, 6, 10, 13, 26, Apr 9, May 5, Nov 7, 8, 9, Dec 27; 1734: GF, Jan 1, 23, Apr 27, YB, Nov 19

--Rival Milliners, The; or, The Humours of Covent-Garden (or, A Medley of Suitors), 1736: HAY, Jan 19, 20, Feb 2, LIF, Mar 3, 24, HAY, May 12, Jul 30; 1737: HAY, Jan 21, Feb 9, 14, Mar 4; 1779: HAY, Dec 27

Drury, T (author), 1736: HAY, Jan 19

Dryads and Sylvans (song), 1790: CG, Mar 3

Dryden (Draidens, Dreyden), John, 1660: NONE, Sep 0; 1661: LIF, Dec 16; 1666: NONE, Sep 0; 1667: BRI/COUR, Mar 2, 14, BRIDGES, Apr 0, LIF, Aug 15, 16, Nov 7; 1668: LIF, Jan 6, Feb 22, BRIDGES, Jun 19, 22, Sep 15; 1669: BRIDGES, Jun 24; 1670: BRI/COUR, Dec 0; 1671: BRIDGES, Jan 2, Dec 7; 1672: LIF, Feb 26, Jun 0, NONE, Sep 0; 1673: NONE, Jul 0; 1674: LIF, Mar 0, DL, 26, OXFORD, Jul 0; 1676: DG, Mar 11, NONE, Sep 0; 1677: DL, Jul 0, Dec 12; 1678: DL, Feb 0, DG, Mar 11, 21, Sep 0; 1680: DG, Jan 0, NONE, Sep 0; 1681: DL, Mar 0, May 0, Oct 0; 1682: DL, Feb 4, DG, Apr 21, May 31, DLORDG, Jul 18, DL, Nov 16, 28; 1683: DL, Nov 12; 1684: DL, Apr 0, DLORDG, May 24, NONE, Aug 0; 1685: DLORDG, Jan 1, DG, Jun 3; 1687: IT, Feb 2, NONE, 16; 1689: DL, Nov 20; 1690: DG, Jun 0, DL/IT, Oct 21, DL, Dec 0; 1691: DG, May 0, NONE, Aug 13; 1692: DG, Jan 7, NONE, 19, Feb 12, Mar 28, DL, Apr 0, NONE, 9, DL, Nov 8; 1693: DL, Mar 0, Apr 0, NONE, May 9, DL, Oct 0, DLORDG, Nov 0, NONE, Dec 12; 1694: DG, Jan 10, NONE, 11, Mar 22; 1695: WS, Dec 0; 1696: LIF, Feb 0, NONE, Mar 26; 1697: NONE, Sep 0, 3, SH, Nov 22, NONE, Dec 0; 1698: DL, Feb 0; 1699: DLORLIF, Feb 20, LIF, Mar 4, Nov 7, 26, Dec 0, DL, 0, 14; 1700: LIF, Mar 12, Apr 0, NONE, 11, DL, 29, DLLIF, May 13; 1701: LIF, Jan 0; 1704: DL, Apr 20, Jul 11, Aug 18, Sep 19; 1705: DL, Apr 21, May 16, 18, QUEEN'S, 24, LIF, Jul 20; 1707: QUEEN'S, May 21, Jul 26; 1709: DL, Jan 7; 1710: GR, Sep 28; 1711: YB, May 24, Jul 16; 1712: DL, Jan 7, 11, Nov 5; 1713: DL, Oct 14, 16, Nov 7; 1714: DL, Jan 22, Apr 14, Jun 14; 1715: DL, Jul 6; 1716: DL, May 18, 30, Jul 3, 5, HIC, Dec 13; 1717: LIF, Apr 11, DL, May 4, Jul 2, Oct 14, 18; 1718: DL, Jun 11, Aug 1, Dec 3, 4, 27; 1719: DL, Oct 30, Dec 30; 1720: DL, Apr 22, Jun 17, Sep 22, LIF, Nov 11, DL, Dec 9; 1721: LIF, Feb 18, DL, May 18, Aug 8, 22, Sep 21, Oct 6, LIF, Nov 9, DL, 10, Dec 11, 12, 21; 1722: DL, Jan 3, Apr 19, 27, May 15, Jul 6, Oct 27, LIF, Nov 8, 24; 1723: LIF, Jan 1, DL, 7, 26, LIF, 26, DL, Mar 11, LIF, May 10, 29, DL, Jun 6, LIF, Sep 28, DL, Oct 26, LIF, Dec 17; 1724: DL, Jan 7, Feb 1, Apr 28, RI, Jul 18, LIF, 24, Sep 23, DL, Oct 30, LIF, Nov 19, 28, DL, Dec 8; 1725: LIF, Apr 14, Oct 11, DL, 14, 30; 1726: LIF, Apr 14, Sep 28, Dec 30; 1727: DL, Jan 24, Feb 23, 28, May 22, LIF, Oct 31, DL, Nov 1, Dec 29; 1728: LIF, Jan 1, DL, Apr 22, LIF, Nov 11; 1729: DL, May 28,

LIF, Oct 13, DL, 30, Nov 13, 28, Dec 26; <u>1730</u>: DL, May 14, LIF, Oct 5, DL, Nov 30, HAY, Dec 2; <u>1731</u>: DL, Apr 3, LIF, 24, DL, Jun 7, Dec 2; <u>1732</u>: LIF, Apr 24, GF, Oct 2, DL, Dec 26; <u>1733</u>: DL, Jan 24, DL/HAY, Dec 12, CG, 20; <u>1734</u>: CG, Jan 7, DL/HAY, 9, DL, Sep 12, 30, Dec 19; <u>1735</u>: DL, Jan 2, GF, 2, DL, 22, May 5, Sep 30, Oct 4, CG, Nov 10, 11, DL, 25, CG, Dec 12, GF, 17; <u>1736</u>: DL, Feb 4, CG, 19, Mar 3, GF, 15, 16, 30, Apr 26, LIF, Sep 28, 30, Oct 2, DL, Nov 2, 29; <u>1737</u>: DL, Feb 10, HAY, Mar 3, CG, 16, 30, DL, Apr 11, 14, 25, CG, Jun 25, DL, Sep 20; <u>1738</u>: DL, Mar 16, Apr 14, CG, 17, Oct 16, DL, 26, Nov 30, Dec 8, CG, 13; <u>1739</u>: DL, Jan 2, 3, 5, 6, 29, KING'S, Feb 17, Mar 20, DL, May 5, CG, Dec 10; <u>1740</u>: DL, Jan 3, Mar 8, LIF, 28, DL, Nov 19, CG, Dec 11, 17; <u>1741</u>: CG, Jan 3, Feb 12, LIF, Apr 8; <u>1742</u>: DL, Mar 12; <u>1743</u>: CG, Nov 30; <u>1744</u>: CG, Mar 12, 15, Sep 19; <u>1745</u>: DL, Jan 17, GF, Feb 14, Apr 15, Dec 4; <u>1746</u>: CG, Mar 10, DL, 10, CG, 13, DL, Nov 1; <u>1747</u>: GF, Jan 16, DL, Apr 28, May 7, Oct 3, Dec 26; <u>1750</u>: DL, Jan 1, 2, Oct 23, 30; <u>1751</u>: SF, Sep 9; <u>1752</u>: DL, Mar 9, 21, 31, Apr 21, Dec 5, 7; <u>1755</u>: CG, Jan 10, DL, Feb 3; <u>1756</u>: DL, Feb 11, CG, Mar 23, DL, Dec 21; <u>1757</u>: CG, Jan 28; <u>1762</u>: DL, Feb 26, CG, Mar 3; <u>1763</u>: DL, Mar 12; <u>1764</u>: CG, Mar 30; <u>1769</u>: HAY, Jun 21; <u>1770</u>: DL, Dec 13; <u>1771</u>: DL, Mar 16, CG, Nov 12; <u>1772</u>: DL, Mar 6, 18; <u>1774</u>: CG, Mar 22, Apr 7; <u>1776</u>: HAY, Apr 18; <u>1777</u>: CG, Apr 7; <u>1778</u>: DL, Apr 3; <u>1780</u>: HAY, Aug 22; <u>1781</u>: HAY, Jun 4, CG, Oct 27; <u>1782</u>: HAY, Jun 24; <u>1784</u>: DL, Nov 22; <u>1787</u>: HAY, May 16, DL, Oct 26; <u>1789</u>: HAY, May 20, DL, Oct 13; <u>1790</u>: DL, Mar 19, Oct 11, CG, Nov 1; <u>1791</u>: DLKING'S, Nov 9; <u>1792</u>: HAY, Aug 31, DL, Dec 13; <u>1793</u>: CG, Feb 20, HAY, Nov 19; <u>1794</u>: CG, Mar 14, May 26; <u>1795</u>: CG, Apr 24; <u>1796</u>: CG, Feb 12, DL, May 23; <u>1797</u>: DL, Feb 22, Dec 9; <u>1799</u>: DL, May 4, Nov 14; <u>1800</u>: KING'S, Apr 15
--Albion and Albanius (opera), <u>1685</u>: DG, Jun 3, 10, 13, Jul 0; <u>1687</u>: DG, Mar 15; <u>1690</u>: NONE, Sep 0
--Alexander's Feast (ode), <u>1697</u>: SH, Nov 22; <u>1711</u>: YB, May 24, Jul 16; <u>1716</u>: HIC, Dec 13; <u>1736</u>: CG, Feb 19, 25, Mar 3, 12, 17; <u>1737</u>: CG, Mar 16, 18, 30, Apr 5, Jun 25; <u>1739</u>: CRT, Jan 18, KING'S, Feb 17, 24, Mar 20, DL, Apr 3, 10, CG, 26, DL, May 22, LIF, Nov 22, 27; <u>1741</u>: DL, May 28; <u>1742</u>: DL, Mar 12, 19, Apr 17, GF, 22; <u>1745</u>: CG, Apr 27; <u>1748</u>: KING'S, Apr 5; <u>1751</u>: CG, Mar 1, 6, 8, 13, Apr 23; <u>1753</u>: KING'S, Mar 2, CG, 9, 12, 14; <u>1754</u>: HAY, Feb 11; <u>1755</u>: HAY, Feb 10, CG, 14, 19, HAY, Apr 18; <u>1756</u>: SOHO, Mar 16; <u>1762</u>: DL, Feb 26, CG, Mar 3, DL, 3, CG, 24, HAY, Sep 1; <u>1763</u>: CG, Feb 23, Mar 11, MARLY, Jun 28; <u>1765</u>: CG, Feb 27; <u>1766</u>: CG, Feb 19, 21, Mar 7; <u>1767</u>: RANELAGH, Jun 1; <u>1768</u>: CG, Feb 24; <u>1770</u>: DL, Mar 14, 28; <u>1771</u>: DL, Feb 27, Mar 15; <u>1772</u>: DL, Mar 6, 25; <u>1773</u>: DL, Mar 10; <u>1774</u>: DL, Feb 25; <u>1775</u>: DL, Mar 17, KING'S, 24, 31; <u>1776</u>: DL, Mar 1, 15, HAY, Apr 18; <u>1777</u>: DL, Feb 14; <u>1778</u>: DL, Mar 18, Apr 3; <u>1779</u>: DL, Mar 12, 19; <u>1780</u>: DL, Feb 11; <u>1781</u>: DL, Mar 2, 28; <u>1782</u>: DL, Mar 1, 15; <u>1783</u>: DL, Mar 28, Apr 4; <u>1784</u>: DL, Mar 12, 26, CG, Apr 27; <u>1785</u>: DL, Feb 25; <u>1788</u>: DL, Feb 20; <u>1789</u>: CG, Mar 20, Apr 3; <u>1790</u>: DL, Feb 24, CG, Mar 3, DL, 5, CG, 8, DL, 17, 19, CG, 19, 26; <u>1791</u>: DL, Mar 11, CG, 25, Apr 13; <u>1792</u>: KING'S, Feb 29, CG, Mar 7, KING'S, 7, 14, 23, CG, 23, KING'S, 28, 30; <u>1793</u>: KING/HAY, Feb 15, CG, 20, KING/HAY, Mar 6, CG, 8, 20; <u>1794</u>: CG, Mar 14, DL, 26, Apr 9, 11; <u>1795</u>: CG, Feb 27, Apr 24; <u>1796</u>: CG, Feb 12, Apr 1, May 17; <u>1797</u>: CG, Mar 15; <u>1798</u>: CG, Mar 28; <u>1799</u>: CG, Feb 8, Mar 1, 15, May 15, 23, 31; <u>1800</u>: CG, Mar 14, KING'S, Apr 15
--All for Love; or, The World Well Lost, <u>1677</u>: DL, Jul 0, Dec 12; <u>1684</u>: NONE, Aug 0; <u>1686</u>: ATCOURT, Jan 20; <u>1691</u>: NONE, Sep 0; <u>1692</u>: NONE, Feb 12; <u>1694</u>: DG, May 9; <u>1695</u>: NONE, Sep 0; <u>1698</u>: NONE, Sep 0; <u>1701</u>: DL, Jan 7; <u>1704</u>: ATCOURT, Feb 7, LIF, May 20; <u>1705</u>: LIF, Feb 8, QUEEN'S, Dec 12; <u>1709</u>: DL, May 2; <u>1718</u>: DL, Dec 3, 4, 5, 6, 8, 9, 17, 27; <u>1719</u>: DL, Jan 23, NONE, Mar 26, DL, Apr 20, Nov 17; <u>1720</u>: DL, Feb 6, Mar 8, May 18; <u>1721</u>: DL, Jan 19, Feb 25, Mar 27, Oct 19; <u>1722</u>: DL, Apr 19, Oct 27; <u>1723</u>: DL, Jan 26, Oct 26; <u>1724</u>: DL, Feb 1, Mar 9, Nov 14; <u>1725</u>: DL, Feb 4, Apr 19, Nov 20; <u>1726</u>: DL, Mar 5, Apr 2; <u>1727</u>: DL, Oct 21; <u>1728</u>: DL, Nov 9, Dec 21; <u>1729</u>: DL, Mar 15; <u>1730</u>: HAY, Dec 2; <u>1731</u>: DL, Apr 3; <u>1732</u>: GF, Oct 2; <u>1734</u>: DL/HAY, Apr 2, DL, Dec 19, 20, 21; <u>1735</u>: DL, Jan 22, May 5; <u>1736</u>: CG, Jan 10, 12, 13, Mar 11, Apr 10, Sep 22, Dec 4; <u>1737</u>: CG, Jan 1, HAY, Feb 11, CG, 28, Mar 26, Oct 14; <u>1738</u>: CG, Jan 14, DL, Mar 16, CG, Sep 29; <u>1739</u>: CG, Jan 13, Mar 22, Oct 9; <u>1741</u>: CG, Feb 12; <u>1744</u>: DL, Dec 3; <u>1746</u>: DL, Mar 18; <u>1747</u>: DL, Jan 31, Feb 2, 3, 5, 10, 12, 13, 14, 19, 21, Apr 27; <u>1750</u>: CG, Mar 12, DL, Apr 2, 26; <u>1751</u>: CG, Jan 3, 4, 5, 8, 9, Feb 13, 26, Apr 15, May 7; <u>1753</u>: CG, Mar 10; <u>1754</u>: CG, Apr 20; <u>1755</u>: CG, Apr 17, Nov 22, 24; <u>1756</u>: CG, Feb 4, 27, Nov 29; <u>1757</u>: CG, Apr 21; <u>1758</u>: CG, Mar 9; <u>1765</u>: CG, Apr 11, May 22; <u>1766</u>: CG, Mar 17, DL, 22, Apr 26; <u>1767</u>: CG, May 11; <u>1768</u>: DL, Mar 21, CG, Apr 13; <u>1770</u>: CG, May 25; <u>1771</u>: DL, Mar 23; <u>1772</u>: DL, Dec 17; <u>1773</u>: DL, Jan 8, 12, 27, CG, Apr 28, Dec 4, 29; <u>1774</u>: DL, Apr 4, 28; <u>1775</u>: DL, May 12; <u>1776</u>: DL, Mar 18, CG, Oct 24; <u>1778</u>: DL, Apr 23; <u>1779</u>: CG, Jan 19, Feb 5; <u>1780</u>: DL, Nov 13, Dec 18; <u>1781</u>: CG, May 7; <u>1784</u>: CG, Feb 23; <u>1788</u>: DL, May 5; <u>1790</u>: CG, May 24, Nov 1
--Amboyna, <u>1673</u>: LIF, May 0; <u>1690</u>: NONE, Sep 0

--Amphitryon; or, The Two Sosias, 1690: ATCOURT, Apr 30, DL, Oct 0, DL/IT, 21,
Nov 1; 1693: NONE, Sep 0; 1705: DL, May 16, 18, QUEEN'S, 24, LIF, Jul 20;
1706: DL, Jan 25, Mar 11; 1707: QUEEN'S, May 21, Jun 2; 1708: DL, Feb 3, 13,
Sep 16; 1709: DL, Mar 2, QUEEN'S, Nov 9, DL, Dec 7; 1710: DL, Dec 11; 1712:
DL, Feb 18, Oct 27; 1713: DL, Jan 19, Nov 6; 1716: DL, May 18; 1717: DL, Feb
13, May 22; 1719: DL, May 11, Oct 30, Dec 30; 1720: DL, Apr 22, Sep 22, Dec
9; 1721: DL, May 18, Oct 6; 1722: DL, Feb 2, May 15; 1724: DL, Mar 17, Apr
28, Dec 8; 1725: DL, Oct 14; 1726: DL, Jan 10, Nov 10; 1727: DL, Feb 6; 1728:
DL, Mar 12, Nov 18; 1729: DL, Nov 28; 1730: DL, Apr 29, Oct 6, Dec 7; 1731:
DL, Feb 2, May 8, Nov 10; 1732: DL, Jan 25, Mar 28, Sep 26; 1733: DL/HAY, Dec
12; 1734: DL/HAY, Jan 9, DL, Sep 12, 30; 1735: DL, Oct 4, Nov 25; 1736: DL,
Apr 6, May 11, Nov 23; 1739: DL, Jan 3, 5, 6, 29, Oct 8, Dec 12; 1740: DL,
Feb 5, May 12; 1741: DL, Mar 31; 1746: DL, Apr 18; 1747: DL, Apr 28; 1756:
DL, Dec 15, 16, 17, 21, 22, 23; 1757: DL, Jan 5, 15, Feb 14, Mar 15, Apr 22;
1758: DL, Jan 24, Apr 15, 19, May 8; 1759: DL, Nov 17; 1762: DL, Feb 20;
1769: DL, Nov 23, 25, 27, 30, Dec 7, 21; 1770: DL, Jan 12, Feb 1, 22, Mar 19,
Apr 28, Oct 4; 1771: DL, Oct 26; 1773: DL, Feb 25, CG, Mar 20, DL, May 28;
1774: DL, May 20; 1776: CG, May 6; 1777: CG, Apr 28; 1778: CG, May 18; 1779:
CG, May 10; 1780: CG, Apr 12, 24; 1781: CG, Oct 27; 1784: DL, May 17; 1792:
HAY, Aug 31
--Assignation, The; or, Love in a Nunnery, 1672: LIF, Nov 0; 1677: NONE, Sep 0;
1691: NONE, Sep 0; 1695: NONE, Sep 0; 1716: DL, Jul 3, 5; 1743: CG, Nov 30,
Dec 1
--Aurengzebe; or, The Great Mogul, 1675: DL, Nov 17, 20; 1676: ATCOURT, May 29;
1684: NONE, Sep 0; 1690: NONE, Sep 0; 1691: NONE, Sep 0; 1693: NONE, Sep 0;
1698: NONE, Sep 0; 1705: LIF/QUEN, Nov 10; 1706: QUEEN'S, Apr 25; 1707:
QUEEN'S, Feb 1; 1708: DL, Feb 19; 1709: DL, Apr 2, 7, Nov 23, Dec 13, 20;
1710: DL, Apr 25, GR, Sep 28; 1711: DL, Feb 24, Nov 24, Dec 7; 1712: DL, Oct
28; 1713: DL, May 16, Dec 15; 1716: LIF, Jul 11, Aug 17, Nov 1, Dec 1; 1717:
LIF, Feb 5, Dec 10; 1718: LIF, Feb 13; 1721: DL, Dec 11, 12, 13, 14, 21;
1723: DL, Mar 11; 1727: DL, Feb 23, 28; 1729: DL, Nov 19, 20; 1743: JS, Mar
23; 1774: CG, Apr 7
--Cleomenes, The Spartan Hero, 1675: DG, Feb 27; 1691: NONE, Aug 13; 1692:
NONE, Feb 12, Mar 28, DL, Apr 0, NONE, 9; 1695: WS, Dec 0; 1721: DL, Aug 8
--Conquest of Granada, The; or, Almanzor and Almahide, 1670: BRI/COUR, Dec 0;
1671: BRIDGES, Jan 2, BRI/COUR, 3, 10, 26, 31, Feb 10, 11; 1675: DL, Dec 21;
1676: NONE, Sep 0; 1677: NONE, Sep 0; 1684: NONE, Aug 0; 1686: NONE, Sep 0;
1694: NONE, Sep 0; 1698: DL, Feb 0; 1704: DL, Apr 20; 1706: DL, Apr 27; 1709:
DL, Mar 5
--Don Sebastian, 1689: DL, Dec 4; 1691: NONE, Sep 0; 1697: DL, May 26, NONE,
Sep 0; 1698: DL, Feb 0; 1705: LIF, Mar 10; 1706: QUEEN'S, Jan 12, 17, Feb 9;
1707: QUEEN'S, Mar 6; 1709: DL, Apr 9; 1711: GR, Aug 2, 16; 1712: DL, May 27;
1716: LIF, Nov 17, 19, 20; 1717: LIF, Jan 28, Feb 28; 1718: LIF, Mar 6, Apr
28, Sep 26; 1719: LIF, Mar 19, May 6; 1720: LIF, Apr 26; 1721: LIF, Mar 23,
May 9, Nov 9; 1724: LIF, Apr 29; 1725: LIF, Apr 14; 1732: LIF, Apr 24; 1743:
JS, Jan 5; 1744: CG, Mar 12, 15, 17, Apr 9, May 21, 30, Sep 19, Oct 27; 1745:
CG, Jan 24, Mar 18, Apr 15; 1746: CG, Nov 1; 1747: CG, Jan 14, Apr 22, 23;
1749: CG, Jan 11, Apr 3; 1750: CG, Apr 23; 1752: DL, Dec 5, 7, 11, 15; 1753:
DL, Jan 6, 10, 25; 1769: HAY, Jun 21; 1771: DL, Mar 16; 1774: CG, Mar 22, May
16; 1794: CG, May 26
--Duke of Guise, The; or, The Massacre at Paris (with Nathaniel Lee), 1682:
DLORDG, Jul 18, DL, Nov 28, 29, 30, Dec 1; 1684: DLORDG, May 24; 1686: NONE,
Sep 0; 1689: DL, Nov 7; 1697: NONE, Sep 0; 1698: NONE, Sep 0; 1716: DL, Aug
9, 14, 21, Oct 30; 1745: GF, Oct 28, 29, 30, CG, 31, GF, 31, CG, Nov 1, GF,
1, CG, 2
--England's Deliverance from Popish Conspirators, 1696: NONE, Mar 26
--Evening's Love, An; or, The Mock Astrologer, 1668: BRIDGES, Jun 12, 13, 15,
16, 17, 18, 19, 20, 22; 1669: BRIDGES, Mar 8; 1671: NONE, Sep 0; 1674: NONE,
Sep 0; 1682: DL, Nov 16; 1686: ATCOURT, Feb 16, DLORDG, Oct 13; 1690: NONE,
Sep 0; 1705: DL, Apr 21, Jun 9, Oct 9; 1706: DL, Jan 19; 1713: DL, Oct 14,
16, Nov 7; 1714: DL, Jan 22; 1716: DL, May 30; 1717: DL, Oct 18
--Indian Emperor, The; or, The Conquest of Mexico by the Spaniards, 1665:
BRIDGES, Apr 0; 1667: BRIDGES, Jan 15, 22, Aug 22, Nov 11; 1668: ATCOURT, Jan
13, BRIDGES, 20, Mar 28, Apr 21, Jun 20; 1669: NONE, Sep 0; 1671: BRIDGES,
Jan 2; 1674: DL, May 12, NONE, Sep 0, DL, Nov 10; 1680: NONE, Sep 0; 1685:
NONE, Sep 0; 1691: DLORDG, Dec 0; 1692: DL, Nov 30; 1693: NONE, Sep 0; 1695:
NONE, Sep 0; 1702: LIF, Dec 11; 1705: QUEEN'S, Apr 14, Jun 9, LIF/QUEN, Nov
7; 1707: QUEEN'S, Jan 25, Feb 13, Mar 3, QUEEN/DL, Nov 8, Dec 3; 1708:
QUEEN/DL, Mar 4, DL, Sep 30; 1709: DL, Jan 7, Feb 25, QUEEN'S, Dec 3, 10;
1710: QUEEN'S, Mar 13; 1711: DL, Jan 27, Apr 17, Nov 3; 1712: DL, Jun 19, Oct
21; 1713: DL, Jan 13, Mar 21, Oct 10; 1714: DL, Jun 14, Oct 5; 1715: LIF, Jan
19, Feb 5, 22, Nov 8; 1717: LIF, Jan 8, Mar 18, Nov 14; 1718: DL, Jan 4, 6,

15, Apr 22, Nov 6; <u>1720</u>: LIF, May 17; <u>1721</u>: LIF, Apr 19, May 26, DL, Nov 10,
Dec 6; <u>1724</u>: LIF, Jul 21, 24; <u>1729</u>: DL, Nov 12, 13, Dec 26; <u>1730</u>: DL, May 14,
Nov 13; <u>1731</u>: DL, Jan 27, May 12, Dec 21; <u>1732</u>: DL, Jan 27, SJP, Apr 26, 27;
<u>1733</u>: DL, Jan 20; <u>1734</u>: GF, Jan 14, 15, 16, 17, Feb 8, YB, Nov 25; <u>1735</u>: GF,
Mar 20; <u>1736</u>: GF, Apr 8, May 10, LIF, Dec 20, 21; <u>1737</u>: LIF, May 7
--Indian Queen, The (with Sir Robert Howard), <u>1664</u>: BRIDGES, Jan 25, 26, 27,
28, 29, Feb 1, 2, 3, 4, 5, NONE, Sep 0; <u>1665</u>: BRIDGES, Apr 0; <u>1668</u>: BRIDGES,
Jun 27; <u>1691</u>: NONE, Sep 0; <u>1695</u>: DG, Apr 0; <u>1696</u>: DG, Apr 29; <u>1697</u>: DG, Mar
13, DL, Jun 5, DLORDG, Dec 18; <u>1701</u>: DL, Jan 11; <u>1704</u>: DL, Mar 28; <u>1705</u>: DL,
Dec 26; <u>1706</u>: DL, Apr 2, 4; <u>1711</u>: SH, Apr 11, May 9; <u>1715</u>: DL, Jul 19, 22,
29; <u>1752</u>: DL, Mar 21
--Kind Keeper, The; or, Mr Limberham, <u>1677</u>: DL, Jul 0; <u>1678</u>: DG, Mar 11; <u>1689</u>:
NONE, Sep 0; <u>1690</u>: NONE, Sep 0
--King Arthur; or, The British Worthy, <u>1691</u>: DG, May 0, Dec 0; <u>1692</u>: DL, Jan 0,
DG, 7, May 2; <u>1694</u>: NONE, Sep 0; <u>1698</u>: DL, Feb 0, DG, 7, 25, Mar 19; <u>1701</u>:
DL, Jan 29, Feb 1, Apr 8; <u>1704</u>: DL, Jan 4, Mar 28; <u>1705</u>: DL, Apr 30, Jun 5,
16, 30; <u>1706</u>: DL, Mar 2, 12; <u>1711</u>: SH, Apr 11, May 9; <u>1715</u>: LIF, Jan 25, Oct
6; <u>1716</u>: LIF, May 10, 22; <u>1735</u>: GF, Dec 17, 18, 19, 20, 22, 23, 26, 27, 29,
30, 31; <u>1736</u>: GF, Jan 1, 2, 3, 5, 6, 7, 8, 9, 10, 12, 13, 14, 15, 16, 17, 19,
20, 21, 22, 23, 24, 26, 27, 28, Feb 12, 13, Mar 15, 16, 29, 30, Apr 8, 26,
LIF, Sep 28, 30, Oct 2, Dec 27, 28, 29; <u>1741</u>: GF, Feb 19, 21, 23, 24; <u>1770</u>:
DL, Dec 11, 13, 14, 15, 17, 19, 20, 22, 26, 27, 29, 31; <u>1771</u>: DL, Jan 2, 3,
7, 9, 11, 17, Feb 21, 28, Mar 5, Apr 4; <u>1772</u>: DL, Mar 21, 31, Apr 23, Nov 12,
14, Dec 5; <u>1773</u>: DL, Apr 28, May 25; <u>1781</u>: DL, Oct 19, 22, 24, 26, 31, Nov 8,
10, 16, 22, Dec 11; <u>1782</u>: DL, Jan 1, 29; <u>1784</u>: DL, Nov 22; <u>1793</u>: KING/HAY,
Mar 6
--Love Triumphant; or, Nature Will Prevail, <u>1693</u>: NONE, Dec 12; <u>1694</u>: DL, Jan
0, DG, 10, NONE, Mar 22
--Marriage a la Mode, <u>1672</u>: LIF, Apr 0; <u>1674</u>: DL, Apr 23; <u>1675</u>: DL, Jun 19;
<u>1683</u>: NONE, Sep 0; <u>1690</u>: NONE, Sep 0; <u>1697</u>: DL, Jun 18, NONE, Sep 0; <u>1698</u>:
DL, Feb 0; <u>1700</u>: DL, Nov 29; <u>1703</u>: DL, Feb 1, 11; <u>1745</u>: DL, Jan 17
--Mistaken Husband, The, <u>1674</u>: LIF, Mar 0
--Ode on St Cecilia's Day (musical poem), <u>1687</u>: MS, Nov 22; <u>1691</u>: SH, Nov 23;
<u>1692</u>: SH, Nov 22; <u>1697</u>: NONE, Sep 3, SH, Nov 22; <u>1703</u>: YB, Mar 19; <u>1739</u>: LIF,
Nov 22, 27, Dec 13, 20; <u>1740</u>: LIF, Feb 21, Mar 28; <u>1741</u>: HAY, Feb 26, LIF,
28, Mar 11, Apr 8; <u>1754</u>: CG, May 23; <u>1755</u>: CG, Feb 21; <u>1764</u>: CG, Mar 9, 30;
<u>1767</u>: CG, Mar 27; <u>1768</u>: CG, Mar 11; <u>1769</u>: HAY, Feb 2; <u>1770</u>: DL, Mar 16; <u>1772</u>:
DL, Mar 6, 18; <u>1773</u>: DL, Mar 5; <u>1776</u>: HAY, Apr 18; <u>1777</u>: DL, Feb 28; <u>1778</u>:
DL, Mar 6, Apr 3; <u>1780</u>: DL, Feb 11, Mar 10; <u>1781</u>: DL, Mar 2; <u>1782</u>: DL, Feb
22; <u>1783</u>: DL, Mar 7, 21, Apr 4; <u>1784</u>: DL, Mar 5, CG, Apr 27; <u>1785</u>: DL, Feb
18; <u>1789</u>: CG, Mar 6, 20; <u>1790</u>: CG, Mar 3, 17; <u>1791</u>: CG, Mar 25, DL, Apr 1;
<u>1792</u>: CG, Mar 9, KING'S, 23, 30; <u>1793</u>: KING/HAY, Feb 15, CG, 20, Mar 8, 13,
22; <u>1794</u>: CG, Mar 12, DL, 12, 21, CG, 26, Apr 11; <u>1795</u>: CG, Mar 4, Apr 29;
<u>1796</u>: CG, Feb 26, Mar 16; <u>1797</u>: CG, Mar 22, 31; <u>1798</u>: CG, Mar 14, 28; <u>1799</u>:
CG, Feb 8, 22; <u>1800</u>: CG, Feb 28, Mar 19
--Oedipus, King of Thebes (with Nathaniel Lee), <u>1678</u>: DG, Sep 0; <u>1681</u>: NONE,
Sep 0; <u>1686</u>: NONE, Sep 0; <u>1691</u>: NONE, Sep 0; <u>1692</u>: DLORDG, Oct 13; <u>1696</u>: LIF,
Jul 0; <u>1698</u>: DL, Nov 26; <u>1702</u>: LIF, Jun 22; <u>1704</u>: LIF, Feb 8; <u>1705</u>: DL, Jan
11, Feb 14; <u>1706</u>: LIF/QUEN, Apr 11, QUEEN'S, Jun 13; <u>1707</u>: DL, Nov 22, Dec 4;
<u>1708</u>: DL, Jan 10, Oct 23; <u>1710</u>: DL, Jan 14, Mar 16, GR, Aug 3, 31; <u>1711</u>: DL,
May 18; <u>1712</u>: DL, Jun 2; <u>1713</u>: DL, Jan 5, Nov 27; <u>1715</u>: LIF, Nov 1, 16; <u>1716</u>:
LIF, Oct 23; <u>1717</u>: LIF, Jan 22, May 15; <u>1722</u>: LIF, Nov 8, 9, 10, 13, 24, DL,
Dec 12; <u>1723</u>: LIF, Jan 1, 26, Apr 6, May 10, Sep 28, Dec 17; <u>1724</u>: HAY, Feb
13, LIF, Apr 27, Sep 23, SOU, 24, LIF, Nov 19; <u>1725</u>: LIF, Oct 11; <u>1726</u>: LIF,
Apr 14, Sep 28, Dec 30; <u>1727</u>: LIF, Oct 31; <u>1728</u>: LIF, Jan 1, Nov 11; <u>1729</u>:
LIF, Oct 13; <u>1730</u>: LIF, Oct 5; <u>1731</u>: LIF, Apr 24, Dec 9; <u>1734</u>: GF, Dec 16,
17, 18, 19, 30; <u>1735</u>: GF, Jan 16, CG, Nov 10, 11, Dec 12; <u>1736</u>: CG, Mar 2,
Nov 1; <u>1737</u>: CG, Jan 11; <u>1738</u>: CG, Mar 25; <u>1739</u>: CG, Feb 10; <u>1740</u>: CG, Jan
15, DL, Nov 19, 20, 21; <u>1744</u>: DL, Apr 2; <u>1755</u>: CG, Jan 10, 11, 13, 15
--Rival Ladies, The, <u>1664</u>: BRIDGES, Jun 0, Aug 4; <u>1674</u>: NONE, Sep 0; <u>1692</u>:
NONE, Sep 0
--Secret Love; or, The Maiden Queen, <u>1666</u>: NONE, Sep 0; <u>1667</u>: BRI/COUR, Feb 0,
Mar 2, 4, 5, 14, 25, BRIDGES, Apr 0, BRI/COUR, 18, May 24, Aug 23; <u>1668</u>:
BRIDGES, Jan 4, 24, ATCOURT, 27, BRIDGES, Jun 20; <u>1669</u>: BRIDGES, Jan 1, 13,
IT, Nov 1; <u>1672</u>: LIF, Jun 0; <u>1676</u>: DL, Dec 5; <u>1678</u>: NONE, Sep 0; <u>1686</u>:
DLORDG, Dec 14, ATCOURT, 15; <u>1690</u>: NONE, Sep 0; <u>1697</u>: NONE, Sep 0; <u>1698</u>: DL,
Feb 0; <u>1699</u>: NONE, Sep 0; <u>1704</u>: DL, Jul 11, Sep 19, Nov 6; <u>1705</u>: DL, Feb 8,
9, 17, Mar 10, Jul 3; <u>1706</u>: DL, Feb 9, 16, Mar 26
--Secular Masque, The, <u>1746</u>: CG, Mar 10, 13; <u>1750</u>: DL, Oct 23, 30, 31, Nov 9,
10
--Sir Martin Marall; or, Feigned Innocence, <u>1667</u>: LIF, Aug 15, 16, 17, 19, 20,
21, Sep 28, Oct 4, 14, Nov 5; <u>1668</u>: LIF, Jan 1, 8, ATCOURT, Feb 3, LIF, Apr

18, 25, May 22, ATCOURT, Nov 16; 1669: LIF, Apr 24; 1670: IT, Nov 1; 1671:
DG, Nov 9, 10, 11, 13; 1672: DG, Jul 4, Aug 31; 1673: DG, Oct 21; 1675: DG,
Jan 21, 22; 1677: NONE, Sep 0; 1686: ATCOURT, Oct 20; 1690: NONE, Sep 0;
1696: NONE, Sep 0; 1704: DL, Aug 18, Oct 4, Dec 4; 1707: QUEEN'S, Jul 8, 26;
1708: DL, Jun 24; 1710: DL, Jan 25, QUEEN'S, Jun 16, DL, Dec 4; 1711: DL, Jul
20, Dec 21; 1712: DL, Aug 5, Oct 17; 1713: DL, Dec 7; 1714: DL, Oct 19; 1715:
DL, Jul 6; 1717: DL, Jul 2; 1719: DL, Apr 13, Nov 2; 1720: DL, Jun 17; 1721:
DL, Aug 15; 1722: DL, Jul 6; 1727: DL, Nov 1; 1728: DL, Apr 22
--Spanish Fryar, The; or, The Double Discovery, 1680: DG, Nov 1; 1681: DG, Mar
8; 1684: DLORDG, Nov 29; 1685: NONE, Sep 0; 1686: DLORDG, Dec 8; 1687: IT,
Feb 2; 1689: DLORDG, May 28, NONE, Sep 0; 1693: NONE, May 9, Sep 0, DLORDG,
Nov 0; 1698: IT, Feb 2; 1703: DL, Nov 4; 1704: DL, Mar 30, LIF, Apr 29, Jun
24, DL, Oct 18, 19, Nov 16, Dec 18; 1705: DL, Feb 12, May 22, Oct 5, QUEEN'S,
Dec 3; 1706: QUEEN'S, Jan 8, 26, Oct 15, Nov 13; 1707: QUEEN'S, Jan 29, Mar
18, Oct 16, DL, Nov 8; 1708: DL, Jan 9, DL/QUEEN, 28, DL, Feb 23, Oct 2;
1709: DL, Jan 21, QUEEN'S, Oct 21, DL, Nov 24; 1710: DL, Feb 9, 16, QUEEN'S,
Apr 14, DL/QUEEN, Nov 7; 1711: DL/QUEEN, Feb 26, DL, Oct 9; 1712: DL, Jan 12,
Apr 10, May 15, SML, Jun 11, DL, Oct 8; 1713: DL, Feb 11, Nov 4, 30; 1714:
DL, Apr 14, Oct 4, Nov 15; 1715: DL, Jan 3, LIF, 15, DL, Feb 3, May 4, LIF,
Oct 4, DL, Nov 9; 1716: LIF, Feb 1, DL, 13, May 10, LIF, 11, DL, Oct 11, LIF,
Nov 13, DL, Dec 31; 1717: LIF, Feb 1, 7, GLOBE, Mar 2, DL, 30, May 4, Oct 14,
Nov 26; 1718: LIF, Feb 15, DL, 18, May 6, RI, Jul 19, LIF, Oct 1, DL, 8, LIF,
Nov 3; 1719: DL, Jan 8, LIF, Mar 12, DL, Apr 8, LIF, Oct 7, DL, 21, Dec 7,
LIF, 31; 1720: DL, Mar 21, LIF, Apr 20, DL, Jun 1, LIF, Oct 13, DL, Nov 1,
Dec 27; 1721: LIF, Jan 21, DL, May 2, LIF, 8, DL, Sep 21; 1722: DL, Jan 1,
Mar 3, LIF, 15, May 17, DL, Sep 13, LIF, Dec 10, DL, 31; 1723: LIF, Feb 7,
May 29, DL, 30, Sep 26, DT, Nov 1, LIF, Dec 2, KAT, 4, AVT, 31; 1724: LIF,
Jan 2, DL, 14, LIF, Feb 12, HT, Mar 13, LIF, Apr 10, PY, 20, LIF, May 2, RI,
Jul 18, DL, Sep 22, LIF, Nov 20, CT, 24, DL, Dec 30; 1725: LIF, Apr 15, DL,
29, Sep 23, LIF, Nov 18, DL, Dec 7, HAY, 27; 1726: LIF, Feb 10, May 16, DL,
17, LIF, Oct 12, DL, Dec 21; 1727: DL, Sep 9, 12, LIF, Dec 18; 1728: DL, May
31, HAY, Aug 9, 12, Sep 6, Oct 26, DL, Nov 14; 1729: LIF, Feb 5, HAY, Mar 19,
LIF, Oct 20, GF, Nov 10, DL, 25, GF, 28; 1730: LIF, Jan 29, GF, Mar 7, DL,
Apr 2, GF, Jun 4, RI, 27, GF, Oct 2, LIF, Nov 3, GF, 20; 1731: GF, Jan 5, DL,
15, HAY, 18, Mar 12, LIF, Oct 11, GF, Nov 15, Dec 3, DL, 14; 1732: LIF, Jan
17, GF, Feb 4, 8, HAY, May 10, GF, 23, DL, Sep 21, GF, Oct 12, Nov 24,
LIF/CG, Dec 4, GF, 16; 1733: GF, Jan 16, 27, Apr 17, LIF/CG, May 21, DL, Sep
28, Oct 19, CG, Nov 9, GF, Dec 18; 1734: GF, Jan 12, BLO, 16, GF, Feb 13, Apr
2, YB, 24, GF, May 2, CG, 9, RI, Sep 12, DL, Oct 9, GF, 23; 1735: GF, Jan 2,
DL, 2, GF, Apr 16, CG, May 8, DL, Sep 30, GF, Oct 27, 28, 29, 30, 31, Nov 13,
HAY, Dec 29; 1736: GF, Feb 4, DL, 4, GF, Mar 8, DL, Nov 2, LIF, 26, DL, 29,
LIF, Dec 31; 1737: LIF, Feb 17, Apr 14, CG, May 3, DL, 9, Sep 20; 1738: DL,
Apr 14, CG, 17, Oct 16, DL, 26, Dec 8, CG, 13; 1739: DL, Jan 2, CG, 6, DL,
Apr 7, CG, May 29, DL, Oct 9, Dec 18; 1740: DL, Jan 31, May 28, GF, Oct 27,
Nov 22, CG, Dec 5, 11, 17, GF, 19; 1741: CG, Jan 3, 8, GF, 22, CG, 26, GF,
Feb 12, CG, Mar 17, Apr 28, GF, Sep 18, CG, 23, Oct 27, JS, Nov 9, DL, Dec
16; 1742: GF, Jan 2, CG, 16, DL, 20, CG, Mar 15, Oct 11, Nov 2, Dec 31; 1743:
DL, Jan 11, CG, Feb 11, 28, DL, Mar 10, CG, Apr 6, Oct 12, DL, 27, CG, Dec
20; 1744: CG, Jan 16, Apr 14, DL, Oct 13, CG, Nov 21, GF, Dec 31; 1745: GF,
Jan 31, DL, 31, CG, Apr 29, Oct 7, DL, Nov 20, GF, 26; 1746: SOU, Oct 31, GF,
Nov 20; 1747: CG, Mar 7, Apr 6, 25, SOU, 27; 1748: CG, Jan 14, Mar 19, JS,
May 30, CG, Sep 28, Nov 1; 1749: CG, Apr 4, Oct 9, Nov 21, Dec 1; 1751: SF,
Sep 9; 1755: CG, Apr 8, May 13, Oct 27; 1756: CG, Oct 23, Dec 4; 1757: CG,
Jan 15, DL, Feb 22, 26, CG, Dec 1, 3; 1758: CG, Jan 9, DL, Feb 1, CG, Apr 29,
Nov 7, DL, 14; 1759: CG, Mar 26, May 16; 1760: CG, Feb 28; 1761: CG, Mar 5,
Apr 11, DL, May 11, CG, 13, Oct 3; 1762: CG, Mar 1, DL, Nov 17, 24; 1763: CG,
Jan 14, DL, Feb 21, Mar 22, Dec 5; 1764: DL, Feb 9, CG, Nov 30; 1768: HAY,
Aug 19; 1774: CG, Apr 19; 1775: HAY, Sep 4, 12; 1777: CG, Apr 7; 1778: HAY,
Jan 26, DL, Dec 22, 26, 30; 1779: DL, Jan 4, 15, 27, Mar 6, Apr 5, May 11;
1780: HAY, Aug 22, 26, Sep 4, CG, Dec 12, 18, 21; 1781: CG, Apr 30, HAY, Jun
4, 18, Jul 2, CG, Dec 18; 1782: HAY, Jun 24; 1783: CG, Oct 15; 1784: HAY, Apr
30; 1785: HAMM, Jul 15; 1787: HAY, May 16, 23; 1789: HAY, May 20
--State of Innocence, The, 1673: NONE, Sep 0
--Tyrannic Love; or, The Royal Martyr, 1669: BRIDGES, Jun 24; 1676: DL, May 18,
NONE, Sep 0; 1685: NONE, Sep 0; 1694: NONE, Sep 0
--Virgin Queen, The, 1667: BRI/COUR, Mar 14
--Wild Gallant, The, 1663: VERE, Feb 5, ATCOURT, 23; 1667: BRIDGES, Apr 0;
1668: NONE, Sep 0; 1683: NONE, Sep 0; 1693: NONE, Sep 0
Dryden Jr, John
--Husband His Own Cuckold, The, 1696: LIF, Feb 0
DuBargues. See Desbargues.
DuBec, Jean, Abbot of Mortimer (author), 1750: CG, Nov 5

DuBellamy, Charles Clementine (actor, singer), 1766: KING'S, Sep 13, CG, Nov
12, 18, 21, Dec 3, 9; 1767: CG, Feb 14, 21, Mar 3, 17, Apr 23, 25, May 5, 20,
28, HAY, Aug 14, CG, Sep 14, 16, 25, Oct 5, 7, 8, 14, 16, 17, 20, 22, 23, 27,
30, Nov 4, 7, 17, 18, Dec 4, 5, 31; 1768: CG, Jan 20, Apr 20, 22, 29, May 2,
11, Sep 19, 20, 21, 26, 28, Oct 5, 10, 11, 14, 17, 22, Nov 4, 9, Dec 26;
1769: CG, Jan 7, 14, Apr 7, 12, 17, May 2, HAY, 15, 19, 22, 26, Jun 5, 21,
Jul 21, Aug 2, 7, 11, 14, 25, 28, 30, Sep 11, CG, 22, 25, 27, 29, Oct 3, 6,
7, 10, 18, 20, 27, Nov 6, 24, Dec 5, 19; 1770: CG, Jan 3, 18, 20, 23, 25, 27,
Feb 9, 24, Mar 8, 29, Apr 3, 7, May 1, 9, HAY, 18, 21, 23, Jun 5, 27, Jul 20,
Aug 1, 8, 24, 31, Sep 20, CG, 24, 28, Oct 1, 5, 8, 16, 17, 23, 25, 29, Nov 2,
5, 8, 14, Dec 13, 26; 1771: CG, Jan 1, 25, Feb 21, Mar 14, Apr 6, 12, 24, 30,
May 1, 23, 25, 30, Oct 15, 18, 21, 25, 30, Nov 2, 4, 5, 8, 9, 11, 12, 21, Dec
9, 23; 1772: CG, Jan 21, 27, 31, Feb 3, 7, 17, Apr 23, May 4, 6, 29, Sep 21,
23, Oct 7, 17, 30, Nov 2, 4, 6, 14, 28, Dec 15, 19, 26; 1773: CG, Jan 6, Feb
6, Mar 15, 22, 27, Apr 3, 13, May 6, 11, HAY, 17, CG, 22, HAY, 24, CG, 28,
HAY, 28, Jun 4, Jul 2, 5, 30, Aug 11, 16, 20, 27, Sep 17, CG, 22, 27, Oct 6,
16, 22, 23, Nov 4, 6, 26, 30, Dec 7, 8, 13, 16; 1774: CG, Jan 29, Feb 7, 11,
12, Mar 19, HAY, Apr 4, CG, 7, 9, 26, May 14, DL, Jun 2, MARLY, 16, 30, Jul
6, 23, 28, Aug 1, 18, Sep 3, CG, 19, 21, 23, 26, 28, Oct 7, 11, 13, 15, 19,
21, Nov 1, 8, 19, 29, Dec 27; 1775: CG, Mar 30, Apr 4, DL, 21, CG, May 4, 10,
HAY, 17, CG, 20, 23, 27, 29, Sep 20, HAY, 21, CG, 25, 27, 29, Oct 11, 13, 18,
19, 23, Nov 4, 21, Dec 26; 1776: CG, Jan 5, Feb 12, 26, Mar 16, 25, Apr 16,
May 7, 18; 1777: HAY, Jun 9, 11, 19, 27, Jul 18, 28, Aug 12, 22, 25, 30, Sep
3; 1780: HAY, May 30, Jun 3, 24, Jul 8, 14, 27, Aug 12, 24, 29, 31, DL, Sep
26, Oct 7, 10, 17, Nov 9, 10, 11, 23, Dec 27; 1781: DL, Jan 6, Apr 23, 25,
May 9, 15, Sep 15, 25, 27, Oct 6, 11, 12, 19, 29, Nov 20, Dec 13; 1782: CG,
Mar 18, DL, Apr 11, 17, May 1, 7, 8, 16, 18
DuBellamy, Charles Clementine and Frances Maria (actors), 1768: CG, May 11;
1769: CG, May 2; 1770: CG, May 9; 1771: CG, May 1; 1772: CG, May 6; 1773: CG,
May 6
DuBellamy, Frances Maria, Mrs Charles Clementine (actor, singer), 1766: CG, Nov
7; 1767: CG, Jan 23, 26, Jun 9, Sep 14, 23, Oct 19, 22, 30, Nov 20; 1768: CG,
Jan 1, Feb 20, Apr 13, May 10, 11, Oct 12, 25, 26, Nov 17, 19, Dec 16; 1769:
CG, Apr 15, 22, 24, 27, May 2, HAY, Jul 17, Aug 7, 14, 16, 25, Sep 11, CG,
Oct 17, 18, Nov 1; 1770: CG, Feb 24, Dec 5; 1771: CG, Apr 10, 23, May 1, 4,
Oct 19; 1772: CG, Jan 3, May 5, 6, 8, 16, 19; 1773: HAY, May 26
Duberval. See D'Auberval.
Dublin Maggot (dance), 1737: DL, Mar 12, Apr 19
Dublin Theatre, 1704: LIF, Aug 17; 1710: QUEEN'S, Mar 16; 1725: LIF, Oct 25;
1729: GF, Oct 31, Nov 4; 1730: DL, Apr 30, HAY, Jun 27; 1739: CG, Apr 5, 12;
1742: DL, Mar 8, GF, May 12, DL, Sep 18, LIF, Dec 28; 1743: DL, Apr 7; 1744:
CG, Feb 28, HAY, Sep 19; 1747: DL, Apr 29; 1748: DL, Apr 2, JS, Dec 26; 1749:
DL, Sep 23; 1750: DL, Nov 3; 1752: HAY, Mar 12, CG, Apr 18, Sep 25; 1753: DL,
Apr 12; 1763: DL, Sep 27; 1768: CG, May 30; 1769: CG, Apr 22, Dec 1; 1770:
DL, Oct 16, CG, Nov 2; 1773: CG, Oct 15; 1774: CG, Apr 12; 1777: HAY, Aug 29,
Sep 13; 1779: HAY, May 10; 1780: HAY, Jan 3, Mar 28; 1782: HAY, Jan 14; 1783:
HAY, May 31, CG, Sep 17, HAY, 17, CG, 24, DL, 30, CG, Oct 2; 1784: HAY, Sep
17, CG, 22; 1791: HAY, Jun 13; 1793: CG, Sep 23; 1794: HAY, Jun 2, CG, Sep
19, 24; 1796: CG, Sep 17, Oct 6; 1797: DL, May 27, CG, Sep 22, Oct 13; 1798:
HAY, Sep 3, CG, 19, Oct 15, Nov 1; 1799: DL, Apr 27, Sep 26, CG, Oct 14, Nov
7; 1800: DL, Feb 22
Dublin, 1663: NONE, May 0; 1702: DL, Oct 20, Nov 13; 1723: LIF, Oct 2; 1726:
LIF, Jul 5; 1731: GF, Nov 15; 1732: GF, Apr 10, RIW/HAY, Sep 4, GF, Oct 4,
Nov 25; 1736: CG, Oct 27; 1741: BFLW, Aug 22, KING'S, Nov 21; 1742: DL, Mar
22, Apr 5, CG, 29; 1743: DL, Apr 7, 28, Oct 4, 8; 1744: NONE, Jun 5, HAY, Sep
25, Oct 4; 1745: DL, Sep 19, 24; 1746: DL, Apr 29, Oct 4, CG, 15, DL, Nov 10;
1747: DL, Jan 3, SMMF, Aug 28; 1748: CG, Sep 22, HAY, Dec 5, 12; 1749: DL,
Mar 9, Apr 15, CG, Oct 23, 27; 1750: DL, Feb 24, Sep 25, Nov 3, 8; 1751: DL,
Sep 13; 1752: DL, Mar 12, CG, Sep 18, DL, 23, CG, 29; 1753: DL, Feb 1; 1754:
CG, Oct 11; 1757: DL, Oct 8; 1758: DL, Oct 27; 1759: CG, Mar 28, DL, Oct 2,
6, HAY, Nov 9; 1761: DL, Jan 3, CG, Jun 23, DL, Dec 11; 1764: DL, Sep 18, Oct
29, KING'S, Nov 27; 1765: DL, May 17; 1766: HAY, Jul 12, KING'S, Aug 8; 1767:
DL, Jun 3, HAY, 8, CG, Nov 28; 1768: DL, Nov 11; 1769: HAY, May 15, 29, Sep
19; 1770: DL, Mar 26, Oct 8, CG, Nov 8; 1771: DL, Mar 12, HAY, Jun 5, Sep 19;
1772: CG, Jan 25; 1774: HAY, May 16, CG, Oct 20; 1775: HAY, Jul 7; 1776: HAY,
May 2; 1777: DL, May 8; 1778: CG, Feb 17, DL, Mar 16, CG, 28; 1781: HAY, Jun
16, Nov 12; 1782: HAY, Nov 25; 1783: HAY, Aug 28; 1784: HAY, Jul 6, Aug 21,
DL, Oct 5, CG, Nov 16; 1785: DL, Dec 26; 1787: CG, Jun 15, Dec 15; 1788: CG,
Mar 11, DL, 13, CG, Apr 29; 1789: DL, Nov 24, Dec 10; 1790: DL, Mar 22, Apr
16; 1791: DL, Jan 1, CG, Apr 16; 1792: CG, Mar 26, Sep 26; 1793: DL, Mar 11,
CG, May 3, HAY, Aug 30, Sep 30, CG, Oct 9; 1794: CG, Sep 15; 1796: DL, Nov 2,
15; 1797: CG, Mar 3, Nov 20

DuBois (beneficiary), 1730: LIF, Apr 24
Dubois, Jean Baptiste (actor, dancer), 1789: DL, Dec 26; 1790: DL, Oct 26, 27;
    1791: DL, Jan 1, Feb 7, 8, 11; 1792: DL, Nov 21; 1793: DL, Jan 23; 1794: DL,
    Dec 12, 20; 1795: DL, Feb 12, Oct 30; 1796: DL, Jan 18, 26, Mar 17, Apr 4,
    Oct 20, 29, Nov 9; 1798: DL, Dec 6
Dubois, Lady Dorothea (author), 1770: MARLY, Sep 20; 1773: MARLY, Aug 27
Dubourg (Debourg), Matthew (violinist, composer), 1715: LIF, Apr 7, GRT, 28,
    LIF, May 13; 1716: HIC, Apr 19; 1717: HIC, Mar 22, Apr 3, May 3, SH, 10, DL,
    22, SH, Dec 23; 1718: HIC, Jan 17, TEC, Mar 12, SH, Dec 23; 1719: HIC, Feb
    18; 1720: HIC, Feb 23, YB, Apr 1, DL, 8; 1721: YB, Feb 6, HIC, Mar 1, 3, 15,
    HAY, Aug 2; 1727: YB, Jun 1, CR, Nov 22; 1728: HIC, May 15; 1736: CG, May 15;
    1743: CG, Mar 2, 18, 23, 25, 29, 31; 1749: HIC, Apr 21; 1750: KING'S, Apr 10;
    1751: KING'S, Apr 16; 1752: DL, Dec 2; 1754: KING'S, Feb 28; 1755: KING'S,
    Mar 17; 1756: KING'S, Apr 5; 1758: KING'S, Apr 6; 1759: CG, Feb 2; 1761:
    KING'S, Mar 12
Dubresney, Charles Riviere
--Opera de Compagne Precede du Grondeur, L', 1721: HAY, Feb 21
DuBreuil (DuBrill) (dancer), 1711: QUEEN'S, Mar 20, GR, Sep 13; 1722: HAY, Feb
    26
DuBreuil, Mrs (dancer), 1722: HAY, Feb 26
Dubuisson (actor, dancer), 1734: GF/HAY, Dec 2, HAY, 13, 23, GF/HAY, 27, 30;
    1735: GF/HAY, Jan 8, 9, HAY, 13, GF/HAY, 16, Feb 5, HAY, Apr 16, GF/HAY, May
    1, GF, 23; 1741: CG, Nov 11, 21, Dec 9, 30; 1742: CG, Jan 25, Feb 6, 10, 13,
    Apr 21
Duca d'Atene, Il. See Bertoni, Fernando Giuseppe.
Duchesne (dancer), 1791: PAN, Feb 17, 26
Duchesne, Mme (dancer), 1791: PAN, Feb 17
Duchess of Malfi, The. See Webster, John.
Duchess of Newcastle, The (spectator), 1667: LIF, Mar 28
Duchess, 1661: LIF, Aug 15, VERE, 27; 1663: ATCOURT, Jan 5; 1666: ATCOURT, Oct
    29; 1676: CITY, Oct 30; 1687: CITY, Oct 29; 1733: CG, Apr 4
Duck (gallery doorkeeper), 1737: CG, May 19; 1738: CG, May 16; 1741: CG, May 7;
    1742: CG, May 11; 1743: CG, May 6; 1744: CG, May 14
Duck Lane, 1749: BFHG, Aug 23
Dudley (bookseller), 1744: DL, Dec 13
Dudley (house servant), 1800: DL, Jun 14
Dudley, Sir Henry Bate (dramatist), 1778: HAY, Aug 17; 1782: CG, Feb 9; 1791:
    CG, Mar 8; see also Bate, Henry
Dudley, Miss (actor), 1778: HAY, Dec 28; 1779: HAY, Mar 15, Oct 18; 1780: HAY,
    Jan 3, Mar 28; 1783: HAY, Sep 17
Due Castellani Burlati, I. See Fabrizi, Vincenzo.
Due Contesse, Le. See Paisiello, Giovanni.
Due Fratelli Rivali, I. See Winter, Peter von.
Due Gobbi, I. See Portogallo, Marcos Antonio.
Due pupille (song), 1714: QUEEN'S, May 1
Due Svizzeri, I. See Ferrari, Giacomo Gotifredo.
Duel, The. See O'Brien, William.
Duellist, The. See Kenrick, Dr William.
Duenna, The. See Sheridan, Richard Brinsley.
Duetto Jovial (song), 1742: CG, Apr 22
Duff (dancer), 1720: LIF, Dec 26
Duffett, Thomas, 1673: LIF, Dec 0, DG, 6; 1674: LIF, Jan 0, Mar 0, NONE, Sep 0;
    1675: DL, Jul 0, Aug 0
--Amorous Old Woman, The, 1674: LIF, Mar 0; 1683: NONE, Sep 0
--Beauties Triumph, 1675: NONE, Sep 0
--Mock Tempest, The; or, The Enchanted Castle, 1674: DL, Nov 19; 1682: DL, Mar
    2
--Psyche Debauched, 1675: DL, Aug 0, 27
--Spanish Rogue, The, 1673: LIF, Mar 0, DG, 12
Duffey, Peter (actor, singer), 1789: CG, Sep 23, 25, Oct 12, 21, 28, 31, Nov 9,
    14, Dec 12, 21; 1790: CG, Jan 13, 23, Apr 21, May 5, 24, Jun 3
Duffield (Duffill), Caesar (musician), 1675: ATCOURT, Feb 15
Duffield, John (dancer), 1720: LIF, Jan 23, May 11, Dec 22, 26, 28; 1721: LIF,
    May 1, Oct 10
Duffield's Old Wells Theatre, 1707: HA, Aug 1
Dufort, Louis de, Lord Feversham, 1697: STRAND, Jun 17
Dufour (dancer), 1760: CG, Sep 22; 1761: CG, Mar 9, Apr 11, Sep 21; 1762: CG,
    May 13; 1763: CG, Jan 26
Dufour, Camilla (actor, singer), 1797: DL, Oct 19, Dec 9; 1798: CG, Feb 23, Mar
    2, 9, 14, 28, 30; 1799: DL, May 24, Jun 28
Dugay (dancer), 1741: GF, Oct 7, 9, 12
Dugdale (actor), 1779: HAY, Oct 18

Duge, M (acrobat), <u>1745</u>: GF: Apr 15, 16
Dugrande (dancer), <u>1743</u>: CG, Jan 8
Duibuisson. See Dubuisson.
Duill, Catherine Mary, Mrs John Lewis (actor), <u>1786</u>: CG, May 13
Dujoncel (dancer), <u>1749</u>: HAY, Nov 14; <u>1750</u>: DL, May 22
Duke (actor), <u>1660</u>: REDBULL, Nov 5; <u>1680</u>: DG, Dec 8; see also Watson, Marmaduke
Duke and no Duke, A. See Tate, Nahum.
Duke of Clarence Coffee House, <u>1792</u>: HAY, Oct 15; <u>1795</u>: HAY, Apr 22
Duke of Guise, The. See Dryden, John.
Duke of Lerma. See Howard, Sir Robert.
Duke of Milan. See Massinger, Phillip.
Duke of Milan, The. See Cumberland, Richard.
Duke St, <u>1733</u>: HAY, Mar 29; <u>1737</u>: LIF, Mar 26; <u>1738</u>: DL, Apr 26; <u>1739</u>: DL, Apr
    30; <u>1740</u>: DL, Mar 27; <u>1741</u>: DL, Mar 30; <u>1742</u>: DL, Feb 1, 24, Mar 16; <u>1743</u>:
    NONE, Jan 31, DL, Mar 24; <u>1748</u>: DL, Apr 20; <u>1755</u>: KING'S, Apr 17; <u>1756</u>:
    KING'S, Apr 29, DL, Dec 18; <u>1757</u>: CG, Mar 22, DL, May 11, CG, Dec 2; <u>1759</u>:
    CG, Dec 21; <u>1761</u>: CG, Dec 22; <u>1762</u>: KING'S, Apr 29; <u>1786</u>: DL, May 1; <u>1791</u>:
    PAN, Jun 2; <u>1797</u>: CG, Jun 13
Duke, Richard (poet), <u>1680</u>: DG, Dec 8; <u>1683</u>: DG, Jul 0
Duke, the, <u>1661</u>: LIF, Aug 15, VERE, 27; <u>1662</u>: LI, Jan 3; <u>1663</u>: ATCOURT, Jan 5,
    LIF, Dec 22; <u>1666</u>: ATCOURT, Oct 29; <u>1667</u>: LIF, May 6; <u>1670</u>: DOVER, May 11;
    <u>1676</u>: CITY, Oct 30; <u>1727</u>: WS, Dec 14; <u>1729</u>: DL, Mar 13, RI, Aug 6, BFR, Aug
    25, DL, Oct 28; <u>1730</u>: WS, Jan 15, LIF, Feb 19, KING'S, Mar 31, LIF, Apr 9,
    DL, 30, LIF, Dec 3, DL, 17; <u>1731</u>: KING'S, Feb 20, Apr 10, DL, 19, KING'S, 20,
    DL, May 1, HC, Oct 18, LIF, Nov 18, DL, Dec 22; <u>1732</u>: LIF, Jan 5, Mar 27,
    SJP, Apr 27, RI, Jul 22, GF, Oct 11, LIF/CG, 28, KING'S, Dec 12, DL, 14,
    KING'S, 19, CG/LIF, 21, DL, 27, KING'S, 30; <u>1733</u>: LIF/CG, Jan 23, KING'S, 27,
    DL, Feb 27, HAY, Jun 4, DL, Oct 27; <u>1734</u>: KING'S, Jan 12, Feb 2, IT, 2, DL,
    Mar 7, LIF, Jun 15, DL, Sep 19, GF/HAY, Nov 6, HAY, 14, DL, 18, GF/HAY, 22,
    Dec 18; <u>1735</u>: GF/HAY, Jan 9, HAY, Feb 10, CG, 20, HAY, Mar 27, GF/HAY, Apr
    21, HAY, 28, GF/HAY, May 15, CG, Jul 2, DL, Sep 15, Oct 1, 29, Nov 8, CG, 8,
    19, DL, 26, Dec 10, 31; <u>1736</u>: DL, Jan 8, KING'S, 27, CG, 29, Feb 5, DL, 11,
    CG, 19, 23, 26, Apr 8, May 12, 15, 19, NONE, Sep 7, DL, Nov 4, CG, 13, Dec 8;
    <u>1737</u>: KING'S, May 31, CG, Jun 1; <u>1738</u>: CG, Mar 23, DL, Apr 12, Oct 17, 24,
    28, Nov 3, 10, 21, 24, 27; <u>1739</u>: CG, Jan 11, KING'S, 16, CG, 20, Mar 22, DL,
    Sep 20, 25, CG, Nov 3, 10, 24, Dec 1, LIF, 13, CG, 21, 22; <u>1740</u>: CG, Oct 25,
    Nov 13, 27, Dec 4, 11; <u>1741</u>: DL, Jan 24, Mar 19, 31, CG, Apr 2, DL, 6, Dec 2;
    <u>1742</u>: DL, Jan 13, 20, Feb 4, 10, 16, 18, 24, Mar 11, 25, May 11, 31, Sep 23,
    Oct 9, 20, Nov 4, 16, 24, Dec 8, 16, 31; <u>1743</u>: DL, Jan 5, 19, 26, Feb 9, Mar
    1, Apr 6, 12; <u>1744</u>: CG, Jan 19, Mar 30; <u>1746</u>: GF, May 1, CG, Oct 31, Nov 7,
    10, 12, 25; <u>1747</u>: CG, Jan 2, 13, 14, 27; <u>1750</u>: DL, Jan 11, CG, Feb 14, DL,
    Mar 10; <u>1751</u>: DL, Oct 28; <u>1754</u>: CG, Jan 28
Dukes (dancer), <u>1730</u>: GF, Apr 3, 14, 16, 28, May 28, Jul 6, 27, Nov 11; <u>1731</u>:
    GF, Oct 25; <u>1734</u>: CG, Jan 14, 25, Feb 26, Mar 16, Apr 1, 27, May 1, 7, 8,
    CG/LIF, Sep 25, Oct 2, 31, Nov 29, Dec 19, 30; <u>1735</u>: CG/LIF, Feb 13, 22, Apr
    14, 17, May 2, 5, CG, 6, 8, CG/LIF, 9, 12, 13, 15, 16, 19, 20, 22, 26, 27,
    Jun 2, DL, Oct 22, Nov 15, 17, 20, 25, Dec 6, 18; <u>1736</u>: DL, Jan 3, Feb 28,
    Mar 22, 27, GF, May 6, DL, Sep 7, 9, Oct 5, 12, Nov 2, 13; <u>1737</u>: DL, Feb 10,
    May 3, 13; <u>1742</u>: GF, Apr 20; <u>1743</u>: LIF, Mar 3; <u>1744</u>: MF, May 3, HAY, 10
Dukes Court, <u>1744</u>: CG, Jan 19; <u>1746</u>: CG, Mar 13; <u>1748</u>: DL, Mar 12, Apr 14, 27;
    <u>1749</u>: DL, Mar 11, Apr 26; <u>1750</u>: CG, Apr 5; <u>1751</u>: DL, Apr 29; <u>1753</u>: DL, Apr
    14; <u>1754</u>: DL, Apr 16; <u>1755</u>: DL, Apr 14, 26; <u>1756</u>: DL, Apr 21; <u>1757</u>: DL, Apr
    27; <u>1758</u>: DL, Apr 21; <u>1777</u>: DL, Apr 23, CG, May 20; <u>1778</u>: DL, May 5, CG, 16,
    19; <u>1779</u>: DL, May 4; <u>1785</u>: CG, Apr 22; <u>1786</u>: DL, May 9, CG, 13; <u>1787</u>: CG, May
    4, DL, 22; <u>1791</u>: CG, Mar 11; <u>1792</u>: CG, Feb 24; <u>1793</u>: CG, Feb 15, May 24;
    <u>1794</u>: CG, Mar 7; <u>1796</u>: CG, Jun 7; <u>1797</u>: CG, May 31; <u>1798</u>: CG, May 30
Dukes of Cumberland and Gloucester, <u>1767</u>: CG, Feb 19
Dukes of Cumberland and York, <u>1766</u>: CG, Oct 23
Dukes of Gloucester and York, <u>1767</u>: DL, Jan 2
Dukes of Montague and Richmond, <u>1726</u>: KING'S, Sep 21
Dulau, A (publisher), <u>1797</u>: KING'S, Apr 6
Dulce Domum (song), <u>1799</u>: CG, Mar 13, 15
Dulisse (Dulies), Mlle (dancer), <u>1757</u>: HAY, Jul 1, 5, Aug 22, 31, Sep 14, Oct
    12, 17; <u>1758</u>: HAY, Jan 25, Mar 13, May 18; <u>1759</u>: CG, May 16
Dulisse, Mme (dancer), <u>1757</u>: HAY, Sep 2, 8, 14, 28, Oct 3, 17, Dec 26; <u>1758</u>:
    HAY, Jan 27, CG, Oct 14, Nov 16, 23
Dulm (dancer), <u>1767</u>: HAY, Jul 31
Dulondel (actor), <u>1720</u>: KING'S, Jun 20
Dumai, D (dancer), <u>1756</u>: CG, May 11, 18; <u>1757</u>: CG, Dec 10; <u>1758</u>: CG, Apr 28,
    May 2, 8, Oct 14, Nov 16, 23; <u>1759</u>: CG, May 18, Dec 10; <u>1760</u>: CG, Jan 16, 18,
    Apr 12, 17, Sep 22, Oct 20, Dec 11; <u>1761</u>: CG, Mar 9, Apr 2, 11, Sep 16, 21,
    26; <u>1762</u>: CG, Apr 17, May 11; <u>1763</u>: CG, Jan 26, May 7, 13, Dec 29; <u>1764</u>: CG,

Jan 14, May 22, Sep 21, Oct 27; 1765: CG, May 9, 20, Oct 28; 1766: CG, Apr 25, May 9, Oct 25, Nov 18, 20; 1767: CG, May 20, Oct 17; 1768: CG, May 31, Jun 4; 1769: CG, May 17, 20, Nov 4; 1770: CG, May 25, Oct 1; 1771: CG, May 17; 1772: CG, Apr 20, May 16, 23; 1773: CG, Apr 24, May 26; 1774: CG, May 18, 20; 1775: CG, May 26; 1776: CG, Feb 20, May 15, Oct 4, 7, Nov 25; 1777: CG, May 20, Sep 29; 1778: CG, May 16, Oct 26; 1779: CG, May 8, Nov 8; 1780: CG, May 16; 1781: CG, May 18; 1782: CG, Apr 2, 9, May 25; 1783: CG, Apr 22, May 23

Dumaniant, 1787: CG, May 22; 1788: CG, Mar 1; 1791: DL, May 11
--Guerre Ouverte; ou, Ruse Contre Ruse, 1787: CG, May 22
--Intrigants, Les; ou, Assaut de Fourberies, 1788: CG, Mar 1
--Nuit aux Aventures, La; ou, Les Deux Morts Vivants, 1791: DL, May 11
Dumb Cake, The. See Wewitzer, Ralph.
Dumb Farce, The. See Thurmond, John.
Dumb Lady, The. See Lacy, John.
Dumirail (DeMirail) (dancer), 1674: DL, Mar 30; 1709: QUEEN'S, Feb 5; 1717: LIF, Apr 23
Dumirail's scholar (dancer), 1717: KING'S, Mar 21
Dumont (dancer), 1741: DL, Oct 12, 15, 17, 19, 21, 27, Nov 11, 28, Dec 4, 14, 18; 1742: DL, Jan 6, CG, Oct 6, 9, 15, 25, Nov 2, 25, Dec 21; 1743: CG, Jan 8, Feb 4, Mar 8, 19; 1749: CG, Nov 23; 1750: CG, Oct 29
Dumont, Mlle (dancer), 1781: KING'S, Nov 17, 20, 24; 1782: KING'S, Mar 9
Dumont, Mme (actor), 1725: HAY, Mar 29
Dumont, Mme (dancer), 1748: CG, Mar 3, Apr 12, 28, Oct 27
Dumont, Mrs (beneficiary), 1747: CG, May 12
Dumoulin (dancer), 1732: DL, Sep 23
Dunant (actor), 1799: OCH, May 15
Dunbar (boxkeeper), 1744: DL, May 22; 1745: DL, May 9; 1746: DL, May 3; 1747: DL, May 8; 1748: DL, May 16; 1749: DL, May 11; 1750: DL, May 8; 1751: DL, May 8; 1752: DL, May 4; 1753: DL, May 14; 1754: DL, May 20; 1755: DL, May 12; 1756: DL, May 13; 1757: DL, May 16; 1758: DL, May 15; 1759: DL, May 24; 1760: DL, May 14; 1761: DL, May 14
Dunbar, Widow (beneficiary), 1762: DL, May 21
Dunbarton, Lord. See Douglas, George.
Dunblaine, Viscount. See Osborne, Peregrine.
Duncalfe, Henry (musician), 1732: GV, Feb 10
Duncan, Adam, Admiral Lord Viscount, 1797: DL, Oct 16, 27, Nov 9; 1798: CG, Feb 28
Duncan, Mrs Timothy (actor), 1788: CG, Sep 17
Duncan, Timothy (actor), 1788: CG, Sep 17; 1797: HAY, Dec 4, CG, 19
Duncan, Timothy and Mrs (actors), 1788: CG, Sep 17
Duncomb, Sir J, 1669: BRIDGES, Mar 6
Duncombe, William, 1734: DL, Nov 25; 1744: DL, Jan 2
--Junius Brutus, 1731: SS, Nov 8; 1734: DL, Nov 25, 26, 27, 28, 29, 30, Dec 2; 1735: DL, Feb 24
Duni, Egidio Romoaldo (composer), 1785: CG, May 12; 1786: CG, Oct 16; 1787: CG, Mar 12; 1790: CG, May 6
--Demofoonte (opera), 1737: KING'S, May 24
Dunlap, William, 1799: CG, May 18
--Tell Truth and Shame the Devil (farce), 1799: CG, May 18
Dunning (actor), 1747: RL, Jan 27; 1748: HAY, Feb 29
Dunstall-Vaughan-Warner Booth, 1758: BFDVW, Sep 2, 4, 5, 6
Dunstall, John (actor), 1740: GF, Oct 20, 21, 22, 23, 24, 25, 27, 28, 30, 31, Nov 4, 6, 15, 18, 19, 22, 25, 28, 29, Dec 1, 4, 5, 6, 8, 10, 12, 15; 1741: GF, Jan 15, 20, 27, 28, Feb 10, 12, 14, 16, 19, Mar 3, 7, 16, 19, Apr 15, 17, 27, 30, BFTY, Aug 22, GF, Sep 14, 16, 18, 21, 25, 28, Oct 2, 9, 16, 19, 23, 28, Nov 9, Dec 9, 16, 26; 1742: GF, Jan 1, 18, 27, Feb 3, Mar 27, Apr 6, May 3, 21, LIF, Nov 29, Dec 1, 3, 6, 13, 22, 27, 28, 30; 1743: LIF, Jan 7, 14, Feb 2, 14, 17, SOU, 18, 25, LIF, 28, Mar 24, Apr 8, HAY, 14, CG, Sep 21, Oct 5, 10, 17, Nov 7, 25, Dec 9; 1744: DL, Jan 12, 27, Feb 13, Apr 2, 9, CG, 26, DL, May 1, 5, 14, 16, 22, Sep 25, CG, 26, Oct 3, 10, Nov 8, Dec 6, 12, 17; 1745: CG, Mar 18, 21, Apr 4, 20, May 1, 2, 13, Sep 30, Oct 2, 7, Nov 15, 22, Dec 5, 10, 13, 21; 1746: CG, Jan 2, 9, Mar 18, 20, Apr 23, 28, 29, May 7, Oct 1, 4, 6, Nov 6, Dec 11, 27; 1747: CG, Jan 29, Feb 2, May 11, Oct 31, Nov 13, 23, Dec 17, 19, 28; 1748: CG, Jan 7, 8, 12, 14, 15, 21, 27, Feb 10, 11, 23, Mar 8, 14, 28, Apr 11, 13, 15, 20, 22, 27, 29, Sep 23, 26, 28, Oct 10, 14, 17, Nov 3, 15, 16, 24, Dec 21, 22, 23, 26; 1749: CG, Jan 11, 25, Mar 2, 4, 29, Apr 7, 10, 11, May 4, Sep 25, 27, 29, Oct 2, 11, 12, 16, 18, 19, 20, 25, 26, Nov 1, 3, 8, 9, 17, 21, Dec 8, 27; 1750: CG, Jan 24, Feb 19, 22, Mar 1, 17, 27, Apr 23, 26, 28, Sep 24, 26, 28, Oct 12, 13, 15, 17, 22, 25, 26, Nov 3, 6, 8, 12, 19, 20, 22, 24, 28, 29, Dec 21; 1751: CG, Apr 11, 15, 16, 22, 24, 27, May 2, 8, 14, Sep 23, 25, 27, 28, Oct 7, 11, 18, 19, 26, Nov 7, 11,

13, 14, 18, 22, 28, Dec 14; <u>1752</u>: CG, Jan 6, 29, Feb 6, Mar 16, 17, 30, Apr
28, 30, May 4, Sep 18, 20, 22, 29, Oct 2, 4, 6, 9, 10, 14, 21, 30, Nov 1, 3,
23, 27, 28, Dec 5, 8, 11, 13; <u>1753</u>: CG, Jan 8, 22, Feb 7, 12, Mar 19, 24, May
7, 8, 18, Sep 10, 12, 14, 17, 21, 24, 26, Oct 1, 3, 5, 10, 17, 22, 24, 25,
31, Nov 1, 2, 7, 12, 26, Dec 5; <u>1754</u>: CG, Mar 9, 18, Apr 17, 20, 22, 24, 29,
May 2, 7, 13, 15, Sep 16, 18, 20, 25, 30, Oct 2, 7, 9, 11, 15, 16, 17, 23,
Nov 12, 13, 16, 20, Dec 10, 13, 30; <u>1755</u>: CG, Jan 8, 28, Feb 8, Apr 2, 10,
May 3, 15, Sep 29, Oct 1, 3, 6, 8, 10, 11, 14, 16, 17, 18, 20, 21, 22, 23,
27, 31, Nov 3, 5, 13, 15, 17, Dec 3, 4, 11; <u>1756</u>: CG, Jan 6, Feb 3, Mar 27,
Apr 1, 5, 6, May 6, 7, 17, Oct 4, 6, 8, 11, 16, 19, 20, 21, 25, 28, Nov 3, 8,
13, 16, 17, 22, 29, Dec 1, 7, 10, 30; <u>1757</u>: CG, Jan 8, 27, 28, Feb 9, Mar 21,
Apr 27, May 6, 16, 25, Sep 14, 16, 21, 26, Oct 5, 10, 12, 13, 14, 15, 17, 20,
28, 31, Nov 2, 5, 7, 11, 18, 24, Dec 7, 8, 10, 14; <u>1758</u>: CG, Jan 20, Feb 1,
21, Mar 11, 14, 29, 30, Apr 3, 14, 28, Sep 18, 22, 27, Oct 4, 9, 13, 24, 30,
Nov 1, 2, 3, 4, 13, 18, 20, 21, 23, 27, Dec 9; <u>1759</u>: CG, Jan 29, Feb 1, 26,
Mar 3, 5, 17, 19, 20, 26, Apr 7, 20, 28, May 1, 3, 7, 8, 11, 21, 24, Sep 24,
Oct 1, 3, 5, 8, 10, 22, 30, Nov 23, 28, 30, Dec 6, 10, 18, 31; <u>1760</u>: CG, Jan
9, 31, Feb 14, Mar 8, 17, 18, 20, 24, Apr 8, 9, 17, 18, 21, 24, May 5, 8, 12,
19, 23, Sep 22, 24, 29, Oct 1, 6, 8, 10, 14, 25, Nov 22, 24, Dec 18, 19;
<u>1761</u>: CG, Jan 2, 6, 7, 8, Apr 1, 2, 17, 20, 27, May 8, 11, Sep 7, 9, 14, 16,
18, 25, Oct 3, 9, 13, 14, 17, 20, 26, Nov 2, 6, 9, 10, 17, Dec 11; <u>1762</u>: CG,
Jan 7, 28, Feb 15, Mar 1, 13, 20, 29, Apr 21, 24, 26, May 11, Sep 20, 22, 24,
29, Oct 2, 4, 6, 13, 14, 16, 21, 25, 28, Nov 3, 8, 12, 15, 16, Dec 8, 27;
<u>1763</u>: CG, Jan 8, 14, Feb 1, 14, Mar 21, Apr 12, 18, May 9, Sep 19, 21, 23,
26, 28, 30, Oct 10, 11, 12, 19, 21, 22, 24, 26, Nov 2, 3, 15, 18, 22, 23, 26,
Dec 2, 8, 9; <u>1764</u>: CG, Jan 21, 26, Feb 9, 11, 15, 22, Mar 20, 27, 29, Apr 5,
10, 28, May 3, 11, 15, 21, DL, 21, CG, Sep 17, 19, 24, 26, 28, Oct 1, 3, 5,
10, 11, 12, 16, 23, Nov 1, 3, 8, 9, 15, 16, 30, Dec 12; <u>1765</u>: CG, Jan 8, Feb
18, Apr 9, 10, 19, 23, May 2, 9, 11, Sep 16, 18, 20, 23, 25, 27, 30, Oct 2,
4, 5, 8, 11, 14, 15, 16, 17, 19, 26, 31, Nov 12, 19, 20, 21, 22, 27, 28, Dec
3, 6, 12, 21, 26; <u>1766</u>: CG, Jan 7, 9, 31, Feb 5, Mar 15, Apr 2, 7, 8, 15, 25,
26, DL, May 22, CG, Sep 22, Oct 6, 8, 14, 15, 16, 18, 22, 23, 25, 28, 29, 30,
Nov 14, 25, 27, Dec 6, 20, 23; <u>1767</u>: CG, Jan 10, 28, 29, Feb 19, 21, 27, 28,
Mar 16, Apr 6, 25, 28, May 19, 21, 22, Sep 14, 15, 17, 18, 19, 21, 22, 26,
Oct 8, 13, 16, 27, 31, Nov 6, 10, 17, 23, 28, Dec 14, 26; <u>1768</u>: CG, Jan 9,
20, 29, Feb 1, 5, 25, 27, Mar 10, Apr 19, 20, 25, 29, May 5, 6, 11, Sep 19,
21, 23, 24, 29, 30, Oct 4, 6, 7, 10, 11, 12, 14, 15, 17, 22, Nov 4, 16, 26,
Dec 16, 19, 23; <u>1769</u>: CG, Jan 2, Feb 16, Mar 6, 16, Apr 1, 4, 12, 14, 17, 22,
May 2, 5, 23, 25, Sep 18, 20, 22, 27, 29, 30, Oct 3, 6, 7, 11, 12, 14, 17,
24, 27, Nov 3, 11, 17, 27, 29, Dec 1, 2, 20, 29; <u>1770</u>: CG, Jan 3, 8, 16, 18,
27, Feb 3, 5, 12, 23, Mar 20, 31, Apr 5, 20, 25, 26, May 7, 9, 10, Sep 26,
Oct 2, 8, 11, 13, 19, 25, Nov 2, 8, 14, 16, 17, 23, 30, Dec 3, 13, 17; <u>1771</u>:
CG, Jan 12, 25, 26, Feb 9, Apr 3, 6, 10, 17, 23, 30, May 3, 16, 22, Sep 23,
25, 27, DL, Oct 1, CG, 2, 4, 9, 11, 14, 19, 22, 28, Nov 1, 7, 8, 11, 16, Dec
4, 9, 18, 23; <u>1772</u>: CG, Jan 4, 15, 27, Feb 8, 17, 22, 24, 25, Mar 23, 24, 30,
31, Apr 4, 22, DL, 24, CG, 25, 28, Sep 23, 25, 28, 30, Oct 9, 12, 13, 14, 29,
30, Nov 10, 14, 17, 21, 30, Dec 17, 19, 22, 28; <u>1773</u>: CG, Jan 4, 6, 14, 28,
Mar 22, 27, DL, Apr 13, CG, 17, 23, 27, May 3, 4, 6, 19, Sep 20, 24, 29, Oct
1, 5, 6, 15, 18, 21, 23, 27, Nov 9, 23, 25, Dec 1, 7, 16, 17, 23; <u>1774</u>: CG,
Jan 5, 15, Feb 15, 28, Mar 12, 22, Apr 5, 6, 11, 12, 14, 19, 23, Sep 28, Oct
5, 11, 14, 20, 21, 27, Nov 1, 2, 3, 12, 29, Dec 2, 6, 12, 26, 27; <u>1775</u>: CG,
Jan 3, 17, 21, Feb 23, Mar 30, Apr 1, 19, 28, May 2, 4, 9, 17, 18, Jun 1, Sep
20, 22, 25, Oct 4, 6, 13, 16, 19, 20, 24, 31, Nov 3, 16, 22, 24, Dec 2, 5, 7,
16, 29; <u>1776</u>: CG, Apr 19, 23, 27, May 10, 13, Sep 23, 27, 30, Oct 9, 15, 17,
24, 25, 29, 31, Nov 2, 7, 8, 14, 15, 26, Dec 2, 26, 27; <u>1777</u>: CG, Jan 2, 3,
8, 25, DL, 28, CG, Feb 5, Mar 17, Apr 7, 22, 29, Sep 22, 26, 29, Oct 3, 15,
16, 17, Nov 3, 17, 20, Dec 19, 20; <u>1778</u>: CG, Jan 20, 29, Feb 11, 25, 28, Mar
30, Apr 25, 28, May 6, 9, 11, HAY, Aug 27, CG, Sep 18, 21, 30, Oct 2, 7, 9,
12, 15, 17, 21, 23, Nov 21, Dec 2, 19, 21

Dunstall, John and Mary (actors), <u>1741</u>: GF, Apr 10; <u>1743</u>: LIF, Mar 24; <u>1748</u>:
CG, Apr 13
Dunstall, Mary, Mrs John (actor, singer), <u>1740</u>: GF, Oct 22, 25, 27, 28, 31, Nov
15, 17, 21, 25, 26, 29, Dec 1, 5, 6, 12, 15; <u>1741</u>: GF, Jan 15, 20, 27, 28,
Feb 2, 10, 14, 19, Mar 3, 7, 19, Apr 10, 15, 22, 29, BFTY, Aug 22, GF, Sep
16, 21, 25, 28, 30, Oct 2, 5, 9, 16, 23, Nov 4, 9, 27, 30, Dec 2, 16, 17, 26,
29; <u>1742</u>: GF, Jan 1, 5, 18, 19, 25, Feb 3, 19, Apr 6, 21, 27, LIF, Nov 24,
JS, 25, LIF, 29, Dec 3, 6, 13, 22, 27, 28, 30; <u>1743</u>: LIF, Jan 14, 21, Feb 2,
14, 17, SOU, 18, 25, LIF, 28, Mar 24, Apr 5, 7, 8, HAY, 14, CG, Oct 5, 10,
17, 21, 29, Nov 2, 7, 16, 30, Dec 16; <u>1744</u>: DL, Jan 12, Feb 13, 28, Mar 12,
Apr 6, 17, May 4, 5, 16, CG, 16, DL, 22, Sep 22, CG, 26, Oct 3, 22, 29, Nov
9, 24, Dec 5; <u>1745</u>: CG, Feb 14, Apr 4, 22, 26, May 2, 10, 13, Oct 2, 7, 29,
Nov 8, 14, 20, 22, 29, Dec 5, 10, 13, 14; <u>1746</u>: CG, Jan 7, 13, Feb 6, 17, 24,

Mar 8, 10, 11, 18, Apr 3, Sep 29, Oct 1, 6, 10, 15, 29, Dec 11, 29; 1747: CG,
   Feb 27, Mar 7, 10, Apr 24, May 11, Oct 31, Nov 13, 25, Dec 9, 15, 17, 26;
   1748: CG, Jan 1, 15, 21, 26, 29, Feb 13, Mar 3, 8, 28, Apr 11, 13, 15, 18,
   20, 27, Sep 21, 23, 26, 28, 30, Oct 7, 14; 1749: CG, Jan 26, Mar 2, 4, 14,
   Apr 5, 7, 10, 11, May 4, Sep 27, 29, Oct 6, 18, 20, 30, Nov 1, 8, 21; 1750:
   CG, Feb 7, 22, Mar 1, 19, 27, 31, Apr 19, 26, May 3, Sep 26, Oct 12, 27, 29,
   Nov 3; 1751: CG, Mar 12, Apr 29, May 2, 8, 11, 14, Sep 23, 27, Oct 19, 22,
   26, 29, Nov 6, 19, 28; 1752: CG, Jan 6, 29, Apr 28, 30, Sep 18, Oct 9, 14,
   Nov 2, 3, 9, 16, 28, Dec 28; 1753: CG, Feb 16, May 3, 8, Sep 10, 12, Oct 3,
   5, 8, 31, Nov 1, 9, Dec 7, 15; 1754: CG, May 7, Sep 16, 18, 27, 30, Oct 16,
   Nov 5, Dec 2, 13; 1755: CG, Mar 17, May 3, Oct 6, 17, Nov 10, 13; 1756: CG,
   Apr 1, Sep 22, 29, Nov 9; 1757: CG, Apr 13, May 6, 19, Sep 28, Oct 13; 1758:
   CG, Mar 30
Dunstan, Sir Jeffery (actor), 1782: HAY, Dec 30
Dunstone, Mrs (actor), 1735: HAY, Aug 4
Dunton, John
--Visions of the Soul, The, 1691: NONE, Sep 0
Dupar. See Dieupart.
DuParc, Elizabetta (singer), 1736: KING'S, Nov 23; 1737: KING'S, Jan 8, Feb 12,
   Apr 12, May 24, Oct 29; 1738: KING'S, Jan 3, 28, Mar 14; 1744: CG, Feb 10
Dupe, The. See Sheridan, Frances.
Duperier, Francois (actor, manager), 1684: ATCOURT, Jun 10, Oct 29
Dupes of Fancy, The. See Carey, George Saville.
Duplessis (Duplessy), Lewis (dancer), 1725: LIF, Apr 17, May 26, DL, Nov 19,
   Dec 6; 1726: DL, Feb 11, Mar 31, Apr 15, 23, 26, 27, 30, May 2, 4, 13, Jun 3,
   Oct 1, 27, Nov 2, 15, 23, 30, Dec 7, 14, 30; 1727: DL, Feb 27, Mar 23, Apr
   12, 20, 25, May 2, 17, 26; Nov 14
Duplicity. See Holcroft, Thomas.
Duplin, Lord (actor), 1720: HIC, Feb 2
Duport, Jean Pierre (violoncellist), 1770: KING'S, Mar 1, 8, DL, 14, 16, 21,
   KING'S, 22, DL, 28, KING'S, 29, DL, Apr 6, HAY, May 3, 4; 1771: KING'S, Jan
   10, Feb 8, DL, 15, HAY, Apr 12; 1772: KING'S, Feb 21, DL, Mar 6, CG, 11, HAY,
   30, CG, Apr 10, HAY, 27
Duport, Miss (singer), 1770: KING'S, Mar 8
Dupre (dancer, choreographer), 1714: LIF, Dec 22, 28; 1715: LIF, Jan 7, 10, 12,
   14, 17, 25, Feb 1, 3, 5, 9, 26, Mar 1, 3, 10, 21, 22, Apr 4, 7, 19, 22, 25,
   30, May 2, 10, 12, 24, Jun 7, 14, DL, Oct 14, 19, 24, 29, Nov 5, 17, 19, 22,
   Dec 5, 19; 1716: DL, Jan 14, 23, 26, Feb 18, Mar 8, Apr 9, 10, 21, 26, May 1,
   14, 25, 31, Jun 6, Oct 9, 18, 27, 29, Nov 3, 12, 14, 26, Dec 4, 7, 10, 13;
   1717: DL, Jan 3, Feb 6, 13, 19, Mar 2, 7, 14, 19, 28, Apr 4, May 16, 20, 29,
   Jun 6, LIF, Oct 25, Nov 1, 8, 15, 22, Dec 6, 11, 13, 27; 1718: LIF, Jan 3,
   10, 15, 24, Feb 14, Apr 16; 1719: LIF, Jan 9, Mar 10, Apr 10; 1720: LIF, Nov
   18, 19, 25, Dec 6, 14, 20, 26; 1721: LIF, Jan 7, Feb 1, 21, 28, Apr 19, 26,
   29, May 1; 1723: LIF, Apr 27, Oct 7, 16, 19, Nov 2, 8, 19, 22, Dec 3, 9, 11,
   12, 16, 20; 1724: LIF, Jan 3, 4, Mar 23, 28, Apr 6, 7, 8, 21, 22, 23, 24, 27,
   28, May 2, 4, 5, 8, 12, 13, 19, 22, Sep 25, 28, 30, Oct 5, 9, 12, Nov 3, 10,
   13, 18; 1725: LIF, Jan 21, Mar 13, 29, 31, Apr 14, 15, 17, 20, 21, 22, 23,
   Oct 4, 21, Nov 3, 13, 22, 29, 30, Dec 2, 8; 1726: LIF, Jan 3, 14, Mar 21, Apr
   18, 21, 22, 30, May 14, 23, Sep 16, 19, 23, 26, 30, Oct 5, 24, 29, Nov 9, 21,
   Dec 3; 1727: LIF, Feb 13, Mar 20, Apr 21, 27, May 8, Sep 20, 22, 27, 29, Oct
   12, 25, 27, Nov 7, 9, 17, Dec 19; 1728: LIF, Apr 22, 30, May 6, Sep 30, Oct
   9, 14, 23, 26, Nov 23; 1729: LIF, Jan 18, 31, Feb 6, Mar 20, 27, Apr 8, 12,
   19, 22, 26, May 8, Oct 3, 10, 15, 22, 24, 28, Nov 1, 4; 1730: LIF, Jan 2, Apr
   10, 24, May 14, Sep 21, 25, Oct 1, 9, 27, Nov 7, Dec 11, 15, 30; 1731: LIF,
   Apr 3, 5, 28, May 3, 5, 6, 20, Sep 27, Oct 4, 11, 15, Nov 2, 6, 13, 18, 25,
   Dec 1, 14; 1732: LIF, Apr 22, May 5, LIF/CG, Oct 4, 13, 30, Nov 8, 24, Dec
   27; 1733: LIF/CG, Jan 16, 23, Feb 5, Mar 12, 28, 29, Apr 2, 12, 24, 30, CG,
   May 1, LIF/CG, 3, 7, 8, GF, 14, CG, 16, CG/LIF, 28, LIF/CG, 29, CG, Oct 11,
   13, Nov 24, Dec 7; 1734: CG, Jan 1, 14, 25, Feb 26, Apr 27, May 1, 7, 8;
   1735: CG, Dec 1
Dupre (house servant), 1780: DL, May 17
Dupre (lute player), 1679: SLINGSBY, Nov 20; 1704: YB, Nov 8
Dupre (singer), 1754: CHAPEL, May 15
Dupre Jr (dancer), 1715: DL, Oct 14, 24, 29, Nov 5, 17, 22, Dec 5, 19; 1716:
   DL, Jan 14, 23, 26, Feb 18, Apr 9, 21, May 1, 14, 25, Jun 6, Oct 9, 18, 27,
   29, Nov 3, 12, 14, 26, Dec 4, 7, 10, 13; 1717: DL, Jan 3, Feb 6, 13, Mar 28,
   Apr 4, May 16, 20, 29, Jun 6
Dupre, Eleonore (dancer), 1776: DL, Nov 7, 15, Dec 18; 1777: DL, Jan 4, 9, Feb
   10, Apr 14, Sep 20, Oct 2; 1778: DL, Jan 17
Dupre, James (dancer), 1725: LIF, Oct 4, Nov 13, 30, Dec 2; 1726: LIF, Jan 14,
   Apr 21, 30, Sep 23, 26, 30, Oct 3, 5, 24, 29, Nov 9, 14, 21, Dec 3; 1727:
   LIF, Feb 13, Sep 20, 29, Oct 27, Nov 7, 9, 17, Dec 19; 1728: LIF, Apr 22, May

11, 15, Sep 30, Oct 9, 14; 1729: LIF, Jan 16, 18, 31, Feb 6, Apr 8, May 8, Oct 3, 22, 24, 28, Nov 1, 4; 1730: LIF, Jan 2, Apr 24, 27, May 14, Sep 21, Oct 9, 27, Nov 7, Dec 11, 15, 30; 1731: LIF, Apr 3, May 6, 20, Sep 27, Oct 4, 11, Nov 6, 13, 18, Dec 1; 1732: LIF, Apr 22, May 5, LIF/CG, Oct 4, 30, Nov 24, Dec 8, 9, 26, 27; 1733: LIF/CG, May 3, 14, CG, Oct 11, 13, Dec 7; 1734: CG, Jan 1, Apr 1, May 6, CG/LIF, Oct 2, Nov 29, Dec 19, 30; 1735: CG/LIF, Jan 1, Feb 22, Apr 17, May 9, 19, Jun 2, CG, Sep 26, Oct 3, 17; 1736: CG, Jan 1, 9, 10, 23, Feb 23, Mar 6, 11, May 6, 8, 11, Jun 4, Sep 22, Oct 8, Nov 3, 9, 26, Dec 28; 1737: CG, Jan 28, Feb 14, Mar 7, Apr 25, May 12, 13, DL, 13, CG, Oct 7; 1738: CG, Feb 13, Mar 16, Apr 25, 26, Oct 4, 28, 30, Nov 18, Dec 9; 1739: CG, Jan 15, 16, 20, Feb 15, Mar 2, 5, May 5, 8, 21, Sep 22, Oct 3, Dec 4; 1740: CG, Feb 12, May 5, Sep 26, Oct 10, 22, 29, Dec 29; 1741: CG, Jan 5, 21, Feb 10, 17, 24, 28, Apr 22, 24, 27, Sep 28, Oct 17, 24, Nov 26, Dec 15, 28, 30; 1742: CG, Jan 8, 21, 25, 26, Feb 22, Apr 29, Sep 29, Oct 1, 9, 16, Dec 21, 28; 1743: CG, Jan 8, Feb 4, Mar 8, Apr 28, Dec 20, 26; 1744: CG, Jan 14, Feb 14, Mar 3, Apr 6, 26, Oct 22, 31, Dec 8; 1745: CG, Jan 1, 14, May 2, Oct 29, Nov 14, 23, Dec 27; 1746: CG, Apr 17, 22, May 13, Jun 13, Dec 19, 31; 1747: CG, May 4, Dec 26; 1748: CG, Mar 3, Apr 28; 1749: CG, Mar 9, Apr 24, Nov 23; 1750: CG, May 1, Oct 29, 30; 1751: CG, May 9
Dupre, Mrs (dancer), 1736: CG, Dec 13; 1738: CG, Jan 20; 1739: CG, May 9, Nov 13; 1740: CG, Dec 12; 1742: CG, Dec 22; 1744: CG, Apr 7; 1748: CG, Apr 26; 1749: CG, Apr 22; 1750: CG, Apr 27; 1751: CG, May 4; 1753: CG, May 5; 1755: DL, Oct 8; 1761: CG, Apr 17
Dupre's scholar (dancer), 1725: LIF, Oct 26; 1726: LIF, May 11
Dupree, Miss (harpist), 1797: CG, Mar 10
Dupret (choreographer), 1800: DL, Jun 2
Duprez (dancer), 1781: DL, May 5; 1782: DL, Jan 4, Apr 27, May 10, 17
Dupuis (Dupuy) (dancer), 1757: HAY, Dec 26; 1758: DL, Nov 2, 3; 1759: DL, Apr 18
Dupuis, Thomas Sanders (organist), 1761: SOHO, Jan 21; 1762: DL, Mar 26, 31
DuQua, Mrs (actor), 1697: LIF, Jun 0
Duquesney Jr (dancer), 1784: HAY, Apr 30, May 10; 1786: KING'S, Jan 24, Feb 18, Mar 11, Apr 1, 27
Duquesney, Jacques Alexandre (dancer), 1762: CG, Oct 23; 1763: CG, Jan 1, 26, 27, Mar 8, 12, 19, 26, Apr 7, 21, May 7, 10, 13, Sep 21, Oct 12, 14, Nov 1, 15, 30; 1764: CG, Jan 14, 20, Mar 20, 29, Apr 2, 10, May 1, 2, 5, 21, 22, Oct 3, 18, Nov 1, 5, 7, Dec 12; 1765: CG, Jan 31, Apr 9, 18; 1766: DL, Nov 11, 21, 29, Dec 2; 1767: DL, Jan 2, 24, Mar 2, 3, 17, 24, Apr 24, 27, 30, May 18, Sep 21, 22, 26, Nov 16; 1768: DL, Jan 16, Feb 4, 10, Apr 6, 30, HAY, May 30, Jul 27, Sep 13; 1785: HAY, Feb 14, 21, Mar 10, Apr 15, 29, KING'S, Jun 18, 25; 1786: KING'S, Feb 25, Mar 21, 23, May 23; 1789: KING'S, Jan 10, 31, Mar 3, 17, 31, May 26, Jun 15; 1790: HAY, Jan 7, Feb 6, 13, Apr 6, 15, May 4, 27; 1791: PAN, Feb 17, May 28
Durac (actor), 1725: HAY, Apr 19
Duranci (actor), 1791: DLKING'S, Dec 31; 1792: DLKING'S, Mar 19, Apr 30
Durancy (actor), 1749: HAY, Nov 14
Durancy, Francoise Marie (actor), 1749: HAY, Nov 14
Durancy, Mons and Francoise Marie (actors), 1750: DL, May 22
Durand, Mlle (dancer), 1791: PAN, Feb 17, 26, Mar 22
Duras, Louis de, Marquis of Blanfort, 1665: ATCOURT, Feb 2
Durastanti, Margherita (singer), 1720: KING'S, Apr 2, 27, May 30, Nov 19, Dec 28; 1721: KING'S, Feb 1, Mar 28, Apr 15, May 20, Jun 14, Jul 5; 1723: KING'S, Jan 12, Feb 19, Mar 12, 30, May 14, Nov 27; 1724: KING'S, Jan 14, Feb 20, Mar 17, Apr 18, May 21; 1733: KING'S, Oct 30, Nov 3, 13, Dec 4; 1734: KING'S, Jan 26, Mar 13, 28, Apr 2, 27, May 18
D'Urfey, Thomas, 1674: NONE, Sep 0; 1676: DG, Nov 4, DL, 18; 1680: DG, Jun 0; 1681: DL, Oct 0; 1682: DL, Mar 0; 1684: DG, Jun 0, DLORDG, Dec 0; 1689: NONE, Sep 0; 1690: MTH, Mar 27, ATCOURT, Apr 30, NONE, Sep 0, DL, Dec 0; 1691: DL, Jan 0, ATCOURT, 1, SH, Nov 23; 1692: DL, Jan 0, NONE, 19, DL, Nov 0; 1693: DL, Mar 0, Apr 0, DLORDG, Oct 0, Nov 0; 1694: DG, May 0; 1695: NONE, Sep 0, DL, 0, Oct 0, Nov 0, DG, 0; 1696: DL, May 0, Dec 0; 1697: LIF, Nov 0; 1698: DLLIF, May 12; 1700: LIF, Jul 5; 1701: DL, May 31; 1703: DL, Feb 3, Mar 11; 1706: QUEEN'S, Apr 5, DL, 8; 1709: DL, May 5; 1713: DL, Jun 15; 1714: DL, Jun 7; 1715: DL, Jun 3; 1716: DL, May 29; 1717: DL, May 27; 1724: LIF, Jul 31; 1739: CG, May 17; 1762: CG, Apr 16; 1785: CG, Mar 29
--Banditti, The; or, A Ladies Distress, 1686: DL, Jan 0
--Bath, The; or, The Western Lass, 1701: DL, May 31, Jun 9; 1702: DL, Dec 8
--Bussy D'Ambois; or, The Husband's Revenge, 1691: DL, Mar 0; 1698: NONE, Sep 0
--Campaigners, The; or, The Pleasant Adventures at Brussels, 1698: DL, Jun 0; 1749: DL, May 1
--Cinthia and Endimion; or, The Loves of the Deities, 1696: DL, Dec 0; 1697: DL, Apr 5

--Commonwealth of Women, A, 1685: DL, Aug 0
--Counterfeit Heiress, The; or, The Boarding School, 1762: CG, Apr 16
--Don Quixote, 1693: DLORDG, Oct 0, Nov 0; 1694: DG, May 0; 1695: DG, Nov 0;
1698: DLLIF, May 12; 1700: LIF, Jul 5; 1702: DL, Nov 19; 1703: LIF, Jun 14;
1704: LIF, Apr 29, Aug 9; 1705: QUEEN'S, Apr 30; 1706: LIF/QUEN, Aug 16;
1710: QUEEN'S, Feb 1; 1711: GR, Aug 13, 18; 1712: DL, Jun 9; 1713: DL, Jun
17; 1720: LIF, May 5; 1722: LIF, Mar 31, Apr 24, May 29, Oct 26; 1723: LIF,
Jan 2, Oct 4, Dec 16; 1724: LIF, Jan 27, May 5, Jun 5; 1733: GF, Dec 28, 29,
31; 1734: GF, Jan 1
--Don Quixote, Part II, 1694: DG, May 0; 1710: DL, Feb 4, 6, 17; 1715: LIF, May
2, 5, Jun 6, Oct 11, Dec 28; 1716: LIF, Jan 26, Apr 3, 25, DL, Jul 24; 1717:
LIF, Mar 1, Nov 9, 25; 1718: LIF, Jan 25, Apr 24, Nov 10; 1720: LIF, Oct 4;
1721: LIF, Feb 20, May 4; 1728: LIF, Apr 24; 1729: LIF, Dec 26; 1730: LIF,
May 23; 1785: CG, Mar 29
--Don Quixote, Part III, 1695: DG, Nov 0
--Fond Husband, The; or, The Plotting Sisters, 1677: DG, May 31, Jun 8, DL, Jul
0, NONE, Sep 0; 1680: DG, Jun 0; 1684: IT, Nov 1; 1687: ATCOURT, Jan 3; 1704:
DL, Jun 21, Jul 28; 1707: QUEEN'S, Jun 20, Jul 25; 1709: DL, Feb 16; 1710:
QUEEN'S, May 6, GR, Aug 10, 17, 29; 1713: DL, Jun 15; 1715: LIF, Oct 21, 28;
1716: LIF, Jan 18; 1726: LIF, Jun 24, 28, Jul 1, 29, Aug 23, Nov 30, Dec 26;
1727: LIF, Mar 14, Apr 13, Dec 4; 1728: LIF, Aug 2; 1729: LIF, May 15; 1732:
LIF, Feb 14, Mar 27, May 2, 31, LIF/CG, Oct 28; 1734: GF, Nov 13, 14, 15, 16,
19, 20, 21, 28, Dec 10, 26, 27, 28; 1735: CG/LIF, Jan 6, 7, GF, 15, Feb 14,
CG/LIF, Apr 7, Jun 2, CG, Nov 12, GF, 14; 1736: GF, Feb 24, May 4; 1737: LIF,
Mar 29; 1740: DL, Nov 29; 1744: JS, Mar 16
--Fool Turned Critick, The, 1676: DL, Nov 18
--Fool's Preferment; or, The Three Dukes of Dunstable, 1688: DG, Apr 0; 1703:
DL, Jul 16
--Injured Princess, The; or, The Fatal Wager, 1682: DL, Mar 0; 1703: LIF, Sep
28
--Intrigues at Versailles, The; or, A Jilt in all Humours, 1697: LIF, May 0
--Love for Money; or, The Boarding School, 1691: DL, Jan 0; 1692: NONE, Mar 11;
1695: NONE, Sep 0; 1707: DL, Apr 14; 1708: DL, May 21; 1718: DL, Jul 11, 15,
29, Aug 8, HC, Oct 13, DL, 14, Nov 14; 1720: DL, Jul 7, 12; 1721: DL, May 29;
1725: DL, Apr 21
--Madam Fickle; or, The Witty False One, 1676: DG, Nov 4; 1681: NONE, Sep 0;
1690: NONE, Sep 0; 1704: LIF, Jul 24; 1711: DL, Sep 29, Oct 1
--Marriage Hater Matched, The, 1692: DL, Jan 0, NONE, Mar 11, Sep 0; 1699: DL,
Dec 14; 1700: DL, Dec 28; 1704: DL, Jun 23; 1708: DL, Mar 8; 1709: DL, Apr
30; 1715: LIF, May 18
--Massaniello; or, A Fisherman a Prince, 1699: DL, May 0; 1724: LIF, Jul 31,
Aug 4, 7, 21; 1725: LIF, Mar 29, Apr 24, May 21
--Modern Prophets, The; or, New Wit For A Husband, 1709: DL, May 3, 4, 5
--Old Mode and the New, The; or, Country Miss with her Fourbeloe, 1703: DL, Mar
11, 13
--Richmond Heiress, The; or, A Woman Once in the Right, 1693: DL, Apr 0,
DLORDG, Oct 0, Nov 0; 1714: DL, Mar 2, Jun 7
--Royalist, The, 1682: DG, Jan 23, 24, 25, May 31
--Siege of Memphis, The; or, The Ambitious Queen, 1676: DL, Sep 0
--Sir Barnaby Whigg; or, No Wit like a Woman's, 1681: DL, Oct 0
--Squire Oldsapp; or, The Night-Adventurers, 1678: DG, Jun 0
--Trick for Trick; or, The Debauched Hypocrite, 1678: DL, Mar 0
--Virtuous Wife, The; or, Good Luck at Last, 1679: DG, Sep 0, Oct 0; 1705:
QUEEN'S, Jun 18, 20, 22
--Wife for Any Man, A, 1695: NONE, Sep 0
--Wonders in the Sun, The; or, The Kingdom of the Birds, 1706: QUEEN'S, Apr 5,
6, 8, 9, 10, 26, 30, May 2, 15
Durham (Derham), Miss (dancer), 1757: HAY, Jun 17, Aug 22, 27, Sep 2, 8, 14,
Dec 26; 1758: HAY, Jun 1
Durham, T (printer), 1755: CG, Mar 13
Durham, 1793: CG, Feb 15
Durravan, Malachy (actor), 1779: HAY, Feb 22
DuRuel (dancer), 1703: DL, Jan 2, 23, Feb 18, Apr 19, 27, May 13, 15, 25, Jun
12, 14, 16, 19, 22, 30, Jul 1, Oct 19, Nov 2, 10, Dec 14, 16, 20, LIF, 21,
DL, 22, 31; 1704: DL, Jan 4, 7, 12, 13, 15, 18, 24, LIF, Feb 1, DL, 1, 3, 4,
8, 9, 16, 22, 26, 29, Mar 14, 20, LIF, 30, DL, Apr 3, 20, 22, ATCOURT, 24,
DL, 25, May 19, 25, 31, Jun 5, 7, 9, 13, 21, 23, 29, Oct 14, Nov 11, 18, 30;
1705: DL, Jan 15, 16, 26, SJP, Feb 6, DL, 7, 8, 10, 12, 24, Mar 1, 3, 31, Nov
24, Dec 1, 6, 8, 18, 19, 27, 31; 1706: DL, Jan 3, 5, 10, 11, ATCOURT, Feb 5,
DL, 19, Mar 5, 11, 12, 14, 16, 28, Apr 1, 3, 13, Dec 18, 19, 21, 27; 1707:
DL, Jan 13, 16, 23, Feb 11, 13, 20, 24, Mar 3, 11, Apr 3, May 24
DuRuel, Mrs (dancer), 1704: DL, Apr 20, 22, ATCOURT, 24, DL, 25, Jun 7, 13, 21,

29, Jul 1, Oct 14, 23, Nov 11, 18, Dec 1, 2, 6; 1705: DL, Jan 16, SJP, Feb 6, DL, 7, 10, 24, Mar 1, 3, 31, Nov 24, Dec 1, 6, 8, 18, 27, 31; 1706: DL, Jan 3, 5, 10, 11, ATCOURT, Feb 5, DL, 19, Mar 5, 12, 28, Apr 2, 3, 13

DuRuel's scholar (dancer), 1712: SH, Dec 8

Dussek, Jan Ladislav (pianist), 1790: DL, Mar 3; 1793: KING/HAY, Feb 15, 22, CG, Mar 15; 1796: CG, Feb 12, 19; 1797: CG, Mar 15, 22, 24, HAY, Aug 3; 1798: CG, Mar 2, 9, 14, 16, DL, Nov 14; 1799: DL, Jan 19, CG, Feb 13, Mar 6, DL, May 24, Dec 11; 1800: CG, Mar 21

Dussek, Sophia, Mrs Jan Ladislav (singer, harpist), 1793: CG, Mar 8; 1795: KING'S, Feb 27; 1800: CG, Feb 28, Mar 5, 7, 19, 21, 26, Apr 2

Dust Cart (song), 1753: HAY, Apr 10

Dusty Miller (dance), 1729: LIF, Apr 19, 22, BFF, Aug 23

Dutch Ambassador, 1667: ATCOURT, Nov 15

Dutch and Scotch Contention, The; or, Love and Jealousy (entertainment), 1729: LIF, Oct 22, 24, 31, Nov 13, Dec 1, 29, 30; 1730: LIF, Jan 26, Apr 6, Oct 27, Nov 2, Dec 2; 1731: LIF, Jan 8, 20, Mar 29, Oct 11, 18, Nov 8, 12, Dec 3, 17; 1732: LIF, Jan 19

Dutch Boor (dance), 1717: DL, Apr 24; 1724: LIF, May 5, 20, 27, Jun 1; 1725: LIF, May 7; 1726: LIF, Apr 15; 1734: GF, Mar 18, May 6

Dutch Burgomaster and His Frow (dance), 1718: LIF, Dec 26; 1720: LIF, Jan 23; 1725: LIF, May 14, 20, 25; 1728: LIF, May 18

Dutch Children (actors), 1745: HAY, Mar 2, 5, 6

Dutch Clown (dance), 1730: LIF, Apr 8

Dutch Cruelties at Amboyna, The. See Devoto, Anthony.

Dutch Dance (dance), 1730: DL, Apr 14; 1733: DL, Nov 21, 23; 1734: DL/LIF, Mar 11; 1739: DL, Apr 10, May 26; 1741: GF, Jan 20, DL, Nov 14, 21, 24, 27, Dec 2, 5, 10, 12, 19, 23, 26, 29, 31; 1742: DL, Jan 2, 8, 16, 23, Feb 5, 6, 13, 20, Mar 23, 27, Apr 22, 27, May 1, 17, 24, 27; 1747: DL, Nov 28, Dec 2, 3, 9, 10, 12, 15; 1748: DL, Jan 1, 7, 12, 19, 26, 28, Feb 11, 12, Mar 3, 8, 14, 24, 26, NWC, Apr 4, DL, 12, 14, 16, 21, 22, 26, May 3, 11, 17, 25, Dec 3, 16, 29; 1749: DL, Jan 17, Apr 1, 8, 10; 1750: CG, Mar 19, 31, Apr 3, 23, 24; 1752: DL, Nov 25, 27, Dec 2, 5, 11; 1753: DL, Apr 26, 30, May 11, Sep 20, CG, Oct 18, 30, Nov 3, DL, 17, 19, CG, 19, DL, 20, Dec 11, 21; 1754: DL, Mar 26, CG, Apr 23, 25, May 1, 2, 9, 13, 15, 17, 20; 1757: CG, Apr 22, HAY, Jun 17, Nov 7; 1758: CG, Apr 11, May 4, 5; 1759: DL, May 15, Jun 19, 28, Jul 12, Dec 12; 1760: DL, Jun 19, Jul 29; 1761: DL, Sep 25, 26, 28, 29, Oct 7, 12, Dec 2, 14; 1762: CG, Feb 2, 5, 9, 12, 16, 19, 23, DL, Mar 22, CG, Apr 1, 14, DL, May 19, Sep 21; 1763: DL, Mar 22, 24, Apr 12, 14, 25, 30, May 23; 1764: DL, May 2, 11, 14; 1765: DL, Feb 13, Nov 20, 25; 1769: CG, Nov 11, 16, Dec 30; 1770: CG, Jan 17, Feb 15, 23, Mar 26, May 2, 4, 17, 19; 1771: HAY, Apr 6; 1772: KING'S, May 14, 16, 26, Jun 9; 1773: CG, Dec 30; 1774: CG, Jan 8

Dutch Dance, Grand (dance), 1751: CG, Oct 21, 25, Nov 18; 1752: CG, Jan 25, Mar 7, 9, 16, 19, 30, Apr 3, 13, 22

Dutch dancer, 1679: BF, Sep 3

Dutch Lasses (dance), 1720: DL, Jul 14, Oct 25

Dutch Lover, The. See Behn, Aphra.

Dutch Milkmaid (dance), 1767: CG, Nov 14, 16, 18, 21, 25, 28, Dec 2, 5, 17, 19, 28; 1768: CG, Jan 1, Feb 29, Apr 16, 25, Sep 28, Oct 3, 28, Nov 3; 1770: CG, Jan 24, Feb 15, Sep 24, Oct 2; 1771: CG, May 24, Sep 23; 1772: CG, Jan 11, Sep 25, Oct 16, Nov 10; 1773: CG, Jan 23, 26, Feb 9, 17

Dutch Peasant (dance), 1757: CG, May 12, 16, 25, 27, HAY, Sep 8

Dutch performers, 1698: SF, Sep 17; 1722: SF, Sep 22

Dutch Quaker (dance), 1781: DL, Mar 12, 19, Apr 30, May 14

Dutch Sailor (dance), 1732: HAY, Mar 23; 1750: DL, May 1; 1757: CG, May 25, 27

Dutch Skating Dance (dance), 1771: KING'S, May 23

Dutch Skipper (dance), 1704: DL, Jan 13, Jun 7; 1706: DL, Jun 25; 1707: DL, Mar 25; 1710: DL, Feb 14, GR, Jul 27, Aug 7; 1711: DL, May 21; 1712: DL, May 30, Jun 10, 12, GR, Jul 19, SH, Dec 8; 1713: DL, Jun 12, 19; 1715: LIF, Jan 6, 20, DL, Feb 28, LIF, Apr 2, 18, 28, May 2, 24, Jun 3, Jul 5, Aug 11, 23, KING'S, 27, LIF, Oct 10, 12, 19, 22, DL, 28, LIF, Nov 19; 1716: LIF, Apr 9, May 18, DL, 18, LIF, Jun 8, 20, Nov 1, 5, 10, 12, 14, 19, 30, Dec 22; 1717: LIF, Jan 11, Feb 1, Mar 21, 30, Apr 8, May 16, 20, Jun 7, Nov 5, 23, 25, Dec 10, 26; 1718: LIF, Jan 1, 4, Feb 11, Mar 8, 18, 20, Apr 24, May 3, 6, Jun 4, Oct 3, 14, Nov 27; 1719: LIF, Apr 7, DL, May 12, Oct 14; 1720: LIF, May 19; 1722: LIF, Jan 1, Apr 28; 1723: DL, May 16, LIF, 23, 24, BFPJ, Aug 22; 1724: DL, Mar 26; 1726: DL, Apr 21, 29, May 5, LIF, Jun 24; 1727: LIF, Jan 31, May 8; 1729: LIF, Apr 19, May 1, 14, 19, HAY, Dec 27; 1730: GF, Jan 1, 3, Mar 9, HAY, 20, GF, Apr 20, May 13, Jun 1, 12, HAY, 27, BFPG/TC, Aug 1, 24; 1731: GF, May 13, 17; 1732: HAY, May 12, BFB, Aug 23, GF, Oct 10, 11, 16, 27; 1733: HAY, Mar 14, 20, 22, 26, Apr 18, 23, CG, May 4, GF, 8, CG, 17, HAY, 26, GF, Sep 17, 20, 25, Oct 12, DL, 31, GF, Nov 26, Dec 10, 11, 18, 20, 21, 26, 27, 28; 1734: GF, Jan 2, 8, 9, 10, 18, 19, 22, Feb 2, Apr 18, May 7, 15, 16, 17,

20, JS, 31, GF, Sep 18, Dec 5; 1735: GF, Apr 22, 30, Dec 3, 4, 5, 6, 8, 9,
11, 13; 1736: GF, Feb 6, 11, 17, Mar 18, 20, 22, 25, Apr 1, 6, 8, 12, 13, 17,
May 10; 1742: GF, May 10, CG, Oct 25, Nov 8, 12, 19, 24, Dec 1, 3, 6, 8, 9,
15, 16, 17, 20, 22, NWC, 27, CG, 30; 1743: CG, Jan 17, 24, Feb 2, 3, 14, 24,
28, Mar 14, Apr 4, 14, 20, 27, 29, May 2, 3, 5, 11, 23; 1757: HAY, Oct 17;
1759: CG, Oct 17, 23, Nov 2, Dec 5, 18; 1760: CG, Mar 20, 25, Apr 10, 25, May
8; 1763: CG, Jan 1, 3, 4, 11, 19, 27, Feb 2, 4, 5, 14, Mar 5, 7, 10, 22, Apr
5, 12, May 26; 1764: CG, May 5, 9, 10, 12, 14
Dutch Story (entertainment), 1762: HAY, Oct 25
Dutch woman (actor), 1677: BF, Aug 30
Dutchess of Monmouth, with his Play of the Noble, Fair, and Virtuous Emilia,
The (poem), 1671: NONE, Sep 0
Dutchman (dance), 1764: HAY, Jul 23; 1765: HAY, Jul 19, Aug 7, 8, 9, 19, 21
Dutchman and His Frow (dance), 1722: LIF, Apr 24, May 23, RI, Aug 20; 1729: DL,
Dec 8; 1730: GF, Jan 17, 20, DL, Apr 25, 29, May 2, 13, 19, Sep 17; 1731: DL,
Apr 27; 1733: CG, Mar 27, DL, May 14, CG, 16; 1734: DL/HAY, Mar 18, 25, DL,
Apr 22, DL/HAY, May 3, DL, 21, DL/HAY, 22, 23, DL, Sep 26, Oct 9, 10, 12, 14,
15, 16, Nov 16, 19, Dec 11; 1735: DL, Jan 20, 21, 28, Feb 14, Apr 11, 14, 16,
22, 25, May 2, 7, 8, 9, 20, 22, 29, Oct 4, Dec 18, 26; 1736: DL, Jan 6, 9,
Apr 5, 6, 8, 29, May 7, 18, 22, Oct 18, 19, 21, 29, Nov 10, LIF, Dec 3, DL,
14, LIF, 22; 1737: LIF, Jan 5, DL, Mar 14, LIF, 31, Apr 2, DL, May 2
Dutchman and Provincials (dance), 1764: HAY, Jul 10, Aug 15
Dutchman, The. See Bridges, Thomas.
Dutchwoman (dance), 1730: DL, Apr 24; 1732: HAY, Feb 16, DL, May 2, Oct 26, Nov
7, 14; 1733: DL, Mar 15, Apr 4, 30, May 9, 18; 1734: DL/HAY, Mar 19, Apr 1,
DL, 4
Dutchwoman's Booth, 1682: BF, Aug 24; 1701: BF, Aug 25
Dutchwoman's Company of Rope Dancers, 1700: BF, Aug 0
Dutiful Deception, The (play, anon), 1778: CG, Apr 22, May 8, 14, Oct 24
Dutton (actor), 1730: BFR, Aug 22, SFP, Sep 9
Dutton, Frederick (actor), 1781: HAY, Nov 12; 1784: HAY, Mar 22; 1785: HAY, Mar
15; 1800: DL, Jun 5
Dutton, Mrs (actor), 1730: SFP, Sep 9
Dutton, Thomas (lyricist), 1800: CG, May 17, Jun 16
Duval (dancer), 1764: KING'S, Mar 10, 20, 29, 31; 1767: SW, May 13
Duval (DeVaul) (dancer), 1742: CG, Sep 29, Oct 9
Duval, Alexandre Vincent Pineu, 1799: HAY, Jul 13
--Prisonnier, Le; ou, La Ressemblance, 1799: HAY, Jul 13
Duval, Mlle (dancer), 1740: DL, Dec 26; 1741: DL, Jan 1, 7, 9, 15, 20, 26, 29,
Feb 7, BFH, Aug 22, GF, Sep 28, Oct 9, 16, 19; 1744: CG, Oct 10, Nov 27, Dec
8; 1745: CG, Jan 1, 14, 25, Apr 16, Nov 23, 25
Dwarf Dance (dance), 1786: HAY, Mar 6
Dyamond (acrobat), 1660: CITY, Oct 29
Dyas (actor), 1723: HAY, Dec 12
Dyell (actor), 1776: HAY, Sep 18
Dyer (actor), 1732: LIF/CG, Nov 14, Dec 26, 28; 1733: LIF/CG, Mar 26, CG, May
1, LIF/CG, 7, 10, CG, Sep 27, 29, Oct 11; 1734: HAY, Oct 7, GR, Nov 4
Dyer (dancer), 1675: ATCOURT, Feb 15
Dyer, Harriet, Mrs Michael (actor), 1749: CG, Nov 3; 1751: CG, Apr 15, Nov 13,
Dec 14; 1752: CG, Jan 6, Oct 10, Nov 1, 23, 28; 1753: CG, Feb 7, Oct 3, 5,
24, 31, Nov 1, 2, 12; 1754: CG, Apr 17, May 2, Sep 30, Oct 9, Nov 1, 14, Dec
13; 1755: CG, Feb 18, Apr 23, Oct 16, 18, 22, Nov 13, Dec 3; 1756: CG, Mar
27, Apr 28, May 7, Oct 8, 20, 21, 22, Dec 7; 1757: CG, Apr 27, May 3, 13, 18,
Sep 21, Oct 12; 1758: CG, Apr 13, 19, Sep 22, Oct 6; 1759: CG, Feb 1, Mar 27,
Apr 28, May 7, Sep 28, Nov 5, Dec 6, 10, 28; 1760: CG, Jan 16, Apr 12, 23,
May 1, 12, 14, Sep 22, Oct 15, 20, 25, Nov 18; 1761: CG, Jan 7, Apr 27, May
7, 8, 25, Sep 16, Nov 2, 6, 9; 1762: CG, Apr 28, May 1, 13, Dec 22; 1763: CG,
Jan 26, Feb 14, Apr 20, 27, Oct 12, 14, Nov 7; 1764: CG, Jan 14, 27, Mar 13,
Apr 27, May 5, Sep 28, Oct 5, 12, 18, 20, Nov 5; 1765: CG, Apr 9, May 10, Oct
2, 9, 28, Nov 28; 1766: CG, Oct 14, 25, Nov 25; 1767: CG, Jan 29, Sep 19, 26,
Oct 5, 9, 17, Nov 6, 10; 1768: CG, Jan 6, Mar 15, 24, Apr 30, Sep 20, 24, Oct
6, HAY, 7, CG, 24, Nov 8, 16, Dec 22, 26; 1769: CG, Jan 19, Feb 13, 28, Apr
4, 20, May 11, 19, HAY, Jul 12, Aug 2, 14, 16, 25, 31, Sep 11, 12, CG, 30,
Oct 2, 5, 23, Nov 4; 1770: CG, Jan 27, Mar 31, HAY, Aug 8, 24, Sep 13, CG,
Oct 1, HAY, 1, CG, 15, 17, Nov 12, 16, 23; 1771: CG, Apr 22, May 1, 21, Nov
4; 1772: CG, Jan 31, Feb 17, 25, 27, Mar 23, Nov 30; 1773: CG, Feb 6, May 6,
18, HAY, Sep 16
Dyer, James (dancer), 1770: CG, Jan 6, May 23
Dyer, Michael (actor), 1749: CG, Oct 27, Nov 1, 17, 21, Dec 7, 8, 27; 1750: CG,
Jan 4, 16, Feb 22, Mar 1, 26, Apr 20, Sep 24, 28, Oct 13, 17, 18, 20, 23, 24,
25, 27, 31, Nov 12, 19, 28, 29, Dec 21; 1751: CG, Jan 3, Feb 16, 23, Mar 16,
Apr 11, 15, 24, May 2, 9, 16, Sep 23, Oct 7, 8, 9, 11, 17, 19, 21, 22, 26,

Nov 11, 12, DL, 12, CG, 13, 16, 21, 26, 28, Dec 14; <u>1752</u>: CG, Jan 6, 18, Mar
17, 23, 30, Apr 24, 28, May 4, Sep 25, 29, Oct 6, 9, 10, 11, 12, 14, 16, 21,
24, 27, 31, Nov 1, 3, 16, 22, 23, 28, Dec 8, 11, 12, 13, 19; <u>1753</u>: CG, Feb 7,
Mar 10, 20, 29, Sep 10, 14, 17, 26, Oct 5, 8, 10, 24, 25, 27, 30, 31, Nov 2,
7, 22, 26, 30; <u>1754</u>: CG, Feb 12, Mar 26, Apr 2, 6, 17, 20, May 2, 13, 15, Sep
18, 20, 23, 30, Oct 2, 4, 11, 15, 16, 18, 22, 24, 29, Nov 6, 20, 27, 28, Dec
13, 30; <u>1755</u>: CG, Jan 14, Feb 8, 18, 20, 24, Mar 18, 22, Apr 4, 11, May 7,
14, Sep 29, Oct 1, 3, 6, 8, 10, 11, 17, 20, 21, 23, 30, 31, Nov 4, 7, 12, 13,
22, 26, Dec 3, 4, 5, 11, 12; <u>1756</u>: CG, Jan 6, 15, Mar 18, 22, 23, 25, 30, Apr
1, 8, 20, 29, Sep 24, 27, Oct 1, 4, 11, 12, 13, 14, 18, 19, 21, 25, 26, 28,
Nov 11, 13, 16, 29, Dec 1, 7; <u>1757</u>: CG, Jan 8, 14, 27, Feb 9, 16, 19, 21, Apr
13, May 16, Sep 14, 16, 26, 28, 30, Oct 3, 8, 12, 14, 19, 20, 21, 27, 28, 31,
Nov 2, 5, 7, 11, 14, 16, 23, 26, Dec 7, 14, 20; <u>1758</u>: CG, Jan 11, 27, Mar 9,
11, 27, Apr 3, 4, 7, 12, 17, Sep 18, 20, 27, 29, Oct 2, 6, 13, 16, 20, 23,
24, 26, 30, Nov 1, 13, 14, 16, 18, Dec 2; <u>1759</u>: CG, Jan 4, 11, 12, Feb 1, 15,
Mar 5, 17, 26, 29, Apr 20, 28, May 3, 7, 11, Sep 24, Oct 1, 3, 5, 11, Nov 23,
26, Dec 7, 8, 12, 14, 17, 18, 19, 21, 22, 28, 31; <u>1760</u>: CG, Jan 4, 14, 18,
Feb 14, Mar 18, 24, 25, Apr 8, 17, 24, May 2, 7, 8, 12, Sep 22, 29, Oct 1, 8,
13, 14, 15, 18, 20, 23, 25, Nov 18, 22, 24, 29, Dec 9, 11, 18; <u>1761</u>: CG, Jan
2, 6, 10, 23, Feb 17, Mar 3, 26, 30, Apr 6, 21, 27, May 14, 21, 25, Sep 11,
16, 18, 21, 25, 26, 28, 30, Oct 3, 6, 7, 10, 12, 13, 14, 19, 22, 23, 24, 26,
31, Nov 2, 4, 6, 13, Dec 11, 22, 28, 30; <u>1762</u>: CG, Jan 22, 28, Feb 15, 22,
Mar 13, 20, 23, 27, Apr 19, 21, 30, May 11, 13, Sep 22, 27, 29, 30, Oct 1, 2,
6, 9, 11, 12, 14, 16, 25, Nov 1, 5, 8, 15, 16, Dec 8, 27; <u>1763</u>: CG, Jan 28,
Feb 14, Apr 5, 12, 20, 25, May 6, 9, Sep 23, 28, Oct 5, 8, 10, 11, 12, 14,
15, 19, 20, 22, 24, Nov 3, 4, 26, Dec 26; <u>1764</u>: CG, Jan 9, 14, 26, 28, Feb 1,
9, 15, Mar 24, 29, Apr 3, 4, 10, May 9, 11, Sep 19, Oct 1, 3, 8, 12, 16, 20,
23, 24, 26, 30, Nov 1, 5, 8, 15, 16, 29, Dec 7, 12; <u>1765</u>: CG, Jan 14, Mar 26,
Apr 9, 10, 11, 16, 19, 24, May 6, 7, Sep 18, 20, 25, 30, Oct 4, 8, 9, 10, 11,
19, 26, 28, 31, Nov 12, 13, 19, 20, 22, 25, 28, Dec 6, 26; <u>1766</u>: CG, Jan 9,
Feb 5, 25, Mar 15, 17, 20, Apr 1, 2, 7, 14, 18, May 16, Sep 22, 26, Oct 6, 8,
14, 18, 22, 25, 30, Nov 4, 7, 18, Dec 6, 9, 16, 30; <u>1767</u>: CG, Jan 1, 10, 29,
Feb 19, 28, Mar 23, 28, 31, Apr 6, 11, 20, May 5, 11, 23, Sep 14, 17, 18, 19,
22, 23, Oct 6, 22, 31, Nov 7, 10, 26, 28, Dec 5, 8, 26, 29; <u>1768</u>: CG, Jan 9,
Feb 25, Apr 9, 12, 13, 19, 25, May 5, Sep 19, 21, 22, 24, 27, 30, Oct 7, 10,
12, 25, 27, Dec 12, 21; <u>1769</u>: CG, Jan 2, Mar 16, 27, Apr 1, 4, 7, 12, 22, May
3, 11, Sep 18, 22, 27, 29, Oct 2, 7, 27, Nov 1, 3, 17, 23, 27, 29, Dec 1, 2,
20, 28; <u>1770</u>: CG, Jan 6, Feb 3, 23, 26, Mar 20, 24, 27, Apr 3, 20, 26, May 9,
Sep 24, 26, 28, Oct 2, 11, 13, 19, 25, Nov 2, 8, 15, 16, 17, 23, 30, Dec 3,
13, 21; <u>1771</u>: CG, Jan 25, 28, Feb 9, Apr 2, 3, 6, 30, Sep 23, 25, Oct 4, 14,
19, 22, 25, 30, Nov 1, 2, 7, 8, 19, Dec 21; <u>1772</u>: CG, Jan 4, DL, Mar 23, CG,
31, Apr 4, 22, May 14, Sep 21, 23, Oct 14, 19, 26, 27, Nov 6, 14, Dec 4, 5,
28; <u>1773</u>: CG, Jan 6, Feb 10, 19, Apr 13, May 6, 10, 11, 19, 22, 24, Sep 22,
24, 29, Oct 5, 8, 18, Nov 23, Dec 1, 3, 4, 9, 16, 17, 23; <u>1774</u>: CG, Jan 29,
Feb 7, Apr 5, 9, 14
Dyer, Michael and Harriet (actors), <u>1749</u>: CG, Oct 23
Dyer, Mrs (actor), <u>1733</u>: DL, Dec 7; <u>1734</u>: HAY, May 27
Dyer, Mrs (singer), <u>1692</u>: DG, May 2, DL, Nov 8; <u>1693</u>: DL, Feb 0
Dying and Skeleton Scene, The (entertainment), <u>1797</u>: CG, Jun 9
Dying Scene (entertainment), <u>1785</u>: HAY, Feb 12
Dyke (actor), <u>1661</u>: NONE, Sep 0
Dyke, John (actor, dancer, <u>1797</u>: CG, May 26, Sep 18, Oct 9, Nov 11, 20, 21, 24,
Dec 26; <u>1798</u>: CG, Feb 12, Mar 19, 20, 31, Apr 9, 23, May 12, 19, 28, Jun 2,
Sep 17, 21, Oct 8, 10, 11, 15, 25, Dec 11, 15; <u>1799</u>: CG, Jan 26, 29, Mar 2,
4, 25, Apr 2, 13, 19, May 13, 14, 20, 21, 28, Jun 4, 6, Sep 18, 30, Oct 2, 7,
10, 21, 26, 28, Nov 18
Dykes (boxkeeper), <u>1723</u>: HAY, Mar 14; <u>1725</u>: HAY, Apr 16
Dymuck. See Dimmock.
Dyne. See Dine.
Dyne, John (composer), <u>1791</u>: DL, May 18
Dynion (actor), <u>1661</u>: NONE, Sep 0

E Maggiore degn' altro Dolore (song), <u>1754</u>: KING'S, Feb 28
E vano ognipensiero (song), <u>1713</u>: QUEEN'S, Apr 25; <u>1714</u>: QUEEN'S, May 1
Each joy in thee possessing (song), <u>1787</u>: DL, May 11
Eagan. See Egan.
Eagle and Child Tavern, <u>1750</u>: DL, Nov 28
Eagle Court, <u>1736</u>: DL, Apr 30
Eagle Inn, <u>1789</u>: KHS, Sep 16

Eagle, Master (actor), 1740: DL, Oct 15, Dec 26
Eagles (musician), 1675: ATCOURT, Feb 15
Eaglesfield (dancing master), 1700: DL, Jul 6
Ealy. See Eley.
Earl of Essex (puppetry), 1717: BF, Aug 24
Earl of Essex, The. See Banks, John, The Unhappy Favourite.
Earl of Essex, The. See Jones, Henry; Brooke, Henry.
Earl of Warwick, The. See Francklin, Dr Thomas.
Earl of Warwick, The; or, The British Exile. See Tolson, Francis.
Earle, Colonel, 1692: DL, Dec 9
Earle, William Benson (singer), 1796: DL, Oct 19; 1797: DL, Jan 7
Early Horn (song), 1737: LIF, Mar 21, Apr 29, May 17; 1738: DL, May 3, 5, 12;
    1739: DL, Sep 1, Oct 9; 1740: DL, Mar 27, Apr 22, Sep 11, Oct 2, 23, Nov 1,
    GF, Dec 6; 1741: DL, Sep 10, Oct 24, 31, Dec 5, 7, 9, 12, 14, 18, 26, 28, 31;
    1742: DL, Jan 5, 14, 27, Mar 1, 6, 23, 30, Apr 26, Sep 14, 21, Nov 1; 1743:
    DL, Mar 15, JS, 23; 1745: DL, Apr 17, 29, May 1, 13; 1746: DL, Sep 27; 1747:
    GF, Mar 24, DL, May 7; 1748: CG, Sep 28, JS, Dec 26; 1749: CG, Mar 4; 1753:
    CG, May 11, Sep 24; 1754: CG, Sep 18; 1763: DL, Oct 15; 1764: DL, Nov 7;
    1765: DL, Nov 22; 1769: CG, Apr 25, HAY, May 22; 1776: DL, Jun 8; 1777: CG,
    Apr 22, CHR, Jun 27; 1781: CG, May 7, DL, 23; 1782: CG, Apr 9, May 4; 1783:
    CG, Apr 22; 1787: HAY, Aug 14, 21; 1797: DL, Jun 6
East Harding St, 1784: HAY, Feb 9
East Indian, The (play, anon), 1782: HAY, Jul 16, 17, 19, 23, 26, 29, Aug 1, 5,
    10, 17
East Indian, The. See Lewis, Matthew Gregory.
East Indies, 1684: BFORSF, Sep 6
East Place, 1788: DL, May 7; 1789: DL, May 22; 1790: DL, May 14; 1791: DL, May
    12, HAY, Sep 16
East St, 1754: DL, Mar 28; 1755: DL, Apr 2
Eastcheap, 1749: CG, Apr 28
Eastcourt. See Estcourt.
Easter Monday; or, Description of the Cockney Hunt (entertainment), 1792:
    DLKING'S, Apr 9
Easter Pastimes (prelude, anon), 1790: DL, Apr 5, 7
Eastgate (hosier), 1757: CG, Apr 13
Eastland, Edward (actor), 1674: LIF, Mar 0
Eastland, Mrs (actor), 1661: NONE, Sep 0; 1669: BRIDGES, Jun 24; 1670:
    BRI/COUR, Dec 0
Eastward Ho. See Chapman, George.
Eaton (tailor), 1772: DL, Dec 14
Eaton St, 1782: CG, Apr 24; 1795: DL, May 29; 1796: DL, Jun 2, HAY, Sep 17
Eaton, Jer (actor, dancer), 1716: LIF, Dec 4; 1717: LIF, May 28; 1726: SFSE,
    Sep 8; 1728: LIF, Jan 29, Jul 2, 12, Aug 2; 1729: LIF, Jan 18, BLA, Sep 30,
    GF, Nov 8, 14, 25, Dec 2, 12, 15, 16, 17, 19, 20; 1730: GF, Jan 1, 3, 5, 20,
    24, Feb 6, 7, 12, Mar 7, 10, 14, 21, Apr 1, 2, 3, 7, 8, 10, 14, 24, 28, May
    13, 19, 26, 27, 28, Jun 1, 3, 4, 12, 16, 17, 19, 29, 30, Jul 6, 10, 17,
    BFPG/TC, Aug 1, GF, Sep 18, SOU, 24, GF, 30, Oct 21, 23, 30, Nov 6, 11; 1731:
    SF, Sep 8, GF, Oct 8, 11, 18, 20, 25, 26, 27, 29, Nov 1, 3, 4
Eaton, Mrs (actor), 1736: HAY, Apr 26
Eaux de Merlin, Les (pantomime), 1721: HAY, Dec 12
Eaves (house servant), 1786: CG, May 27
Eberardi, Teresa (singer), 1760: KING'S, Nov 22, Dec 16; 1761: KING'S, Jan 6,
    SOHO, 21, KING'S, Feb 7, DL, 27, KING'S, Apr 28, Oct 13, Nov 10; 1762:
    KING'S, May 11
Eberlin (Ebelin) (scene painter), 1726: DL, Dec 30; 1732: HIC, Mar 6
Ebral (apothecary), 1744: CG, Apr 18
Eccentric Lover, The. See Cumberland, Richard.
Eccles, Henry (musician), 1705: HDR, Jan 2
Eccles, John (composer), 1690: DL, Dec 0; 1691: NONE, Sep 0; 1693: DL, Apr 0,
    NONE, Sep 0; 1694: DL, Jan 0, Feb 0, DLORDG, 0, DL, Mar 21, Apr 0, DG, May 0,
    NONE, Sep 0; 1695: LIF, Apr 30, Aug 0, Sep 0, Dec 0; 1696: LIF, Mar 0, Apr 0,
    Jun 0, Nov 14, Dec 0; 1697: LIF, Jun 0, Nov 0, ATCOURT, 4; 1698: LIF, Mar 0,
    NONE, Sep 0, LIF, Nov 0; 1700: LIF, Mar 0, ATCOURT, Nov 4; 1701: DG, Mar 21;
    1702: HAW, Jul 27; 1704: LIF, Jul 24; 1705: LIF, Jan 25, RIW, Jul 14, HAW,
    Aug 18, LIF/QUEN, Sep 28; 1706: QUEEN'S, Mar 11, Apr 15; 1713: SH, May 15;
    1715: LIF, Nov 22; 1723: DL, Jul 16, 30, Aug 6, 16; 1724: DL, May 5, 6; 1725:
    DL, May 17; 1726: DL, May 17
Eccles, Miss (actor), 1787: HAY, Jul 19
Eccles, Solomon (composer), 1693: DL, Apr 0
Ecclestone, Edward
--Cataclysm, The; or, General Deluge of the World (opera), 1684: NONE, Sep 0
--Deluge, The; or, The Destruction of the World (opera), 1689: NONE, Sep 0

--Noah's Flood; or, The Destruction of the World, 1678: NONE, Sep 0; 1684:
    NONE, Sep 0; 1695: SF, Sep 0
Echard (translator), 1717: DL, Jul 9, 11
Echells (actor), 1778: HAY, Jan 26
Echo (music), 1704: DL, Feb 9; 1705: DL, Jan 15, Dec 19; 1706: DL, Jan 3
Echo Flute (music), 1713: HIC, Mar 25; 1715: DL, Apr 28, Nov 2; 1719: DL, May 9
Echo Flute Solo (music), 1715: DL, Jun 2
Echo Flute, Hautboy, German Flute and Trumpet (music), 1714: HIC, Apr 28
Echo of Anacreon (song), 1760: HAY, Sep 8
Echo Song (song), 1740: DL, Apr 25, May 7; 1741: DL, Apr 13, May 22
Eclogue, An; or, Representation in Four Parts (music), 1659: NONE, Dec 18
Ecole de Jaloux, L'. See Montfleury, Antoine.
Ecole des Femmes, L'. See Moliere.
Ecole des Maris, L'. See Moliere.
Ecosseisse, L'. See Voltaire.
Eddis (doorkeeper), 1768: CG, Jun 1; 1769: CG, May 16, 20
Eddleston (doorkeeper), 1776: DL, May 22; 1777: DL, Jun 6
Eddleston, Widow (beneficiary), 1778: DL, May 22
Eden (actor), 1750: HAY, Apr 17
Eden (actor), 1782: HAY, Mar 4
Edgar and Emmeline. See Hawkesworth, John.
Edgar. See Rymer, Thomas.
Edge, Miss (actor), 1793: CG, Mar 4
Edgerton, Miss. See Egerton, Mrs.
Edgeware Road, 1796: CG, May 25
Edinburgh Buck (entertainment), 1784: HAY, Feb 9
Edinburgh Coffee House, 1758: HAY, Jan 27; 1777: HAY, Oct 13; 1782: HAY, Mar 18
Edinburgh Theatre, 1740: DL, May 28; 1770: HAY, May 21; 1774: DL, Jan 29; 1775:
    HAY, Feb 20; 1776: CG, May 8, CHR, Sep 25, DL, Nov 25; 1777: CG, May 29;
    1778: HAY, Jun 1, CHR, 10, HAY, Jul 1; 1779: DL, Oct 12; 1780: HAY, Jan 17,
    Sep 25, Nov 13; 1781: HAY, Jan 22, CG, Dec 26; 1782: CG, Apr 30; 1783: DL,
    Feb 18, HAY, Jun 6, Sep 17, DL, Oct 18, HAY, Dec 15; 1785: HAY, Apr 26; 1786:
    HAY, Mar 6; 1787: HAY, May 16, 18, DL, Oct 2, CG, 12; 1788: HAY, Jul 2; 1789:
    CG, Oct 16; 1790: CG, Oct 20; 1793: CG, Sep 20; 1794: HAY, Jun 2; 1797: CG,
    Jun 21, DL, Sep 21, CG, Oct 23, DL, 26, Dec 5, 13; 1798: CG, Apr 28; 1799:
    HAY, Jun 15, DL, Nov 13, CG, Dec 9; 1800: CG, Apr 29
Edinburgh, 1680: DL, Feb 0; 1733: DL, Oct 1; 1744: JS, Mar 2, HAY, Dec 26;
    1748: DL, Apr 23, HAY, Dec 5, 12; 1757: CG, Mar 12, 14; 1761: DL, Nov 14;
    1768: HAY, Feb 22; 1769: CG, Mar 11, DL, Oct 6; 1770: CG, Sep 24; 1771: HAY,
    May 17; 1774: HAY, Jan 24, May 30; 1776: HAY, Oct 7; 1777: HAY, Sep 10, 19;
    1778: CG, Feb 17, CHR, Jul 30; 1780: HAY, Aug 24; 1783: CG, May 31; 1786: CG,
    Sep 25; 1789: CG, Dec 5; 1790: CG, Dec 20; 1791: CG, May 18; 1792: CG, Oct 8,
    Nov 2; 1794: HAY, Jul 25; 1795: HAY, Aug 3; 1798: CG, Apr 28
Edlin (spectator), 1662: LIF, Apr 2
Edmead, Elizabeth (actor), 1799: DL, Feb 26
Edmonds (boxkeeper), 1754: HAY/SFB, Sep 17
Edmonds (house servant), 1798: DL, Jun 16; 1799: DL, Jul 2; 1800: DL, Jun 13
Edward and Eleonora. See Thomson, James.
Edward III. See Mountfort, William.
Edward the Black Prince. See Boyle, Roger, The Black Prince; Shirley, William.
Edward, Miss (actor), 1724: SOU, Sep 24
Edward, Mrs (actor), 1797: HAY, Aug 14, 31; 1798: HAY, Jul 21, Aug 11; 1799:
    HAY, Aug 21
Edward, Mrs (actor, singer), 1797: HAY, Jun 12, 15, 17, 19, 21, 23, Jul 3, 10,
    Aug 5, 9, 15, 23; 1798: HAY, Jun 12, 13, 16, 18, 19, 20, 21, 23, 30, Jul 6,
    10, 13, 14, 16, Aug 2, 15, 21, 23, 30, Sep 3, 12, 14, 17; 1799: HAY, Jun 15,
    17, 20, 24, 25, Jul 5, 9, 19, 23, Aug 10, 17, 26
Edward, Prince, 1743: CG, Apr 26; 1744: CG, Feb 1, May 10; 1745: HAY, Mar 5,
    CG, 11, 28, May 4; 1746: CG, Nov 28; 1747: CG, May 14; 1748: CG, Oct 25, Nov
    10, Dec 21; 1749: LEI, Jan 7, CG, Feb 9, 27, May 4, Dec 16; 1750: CG, Mar 12;
    1751: DL, Oct 28; 1752: CG, Feb 8, Dec 30; 1754: DL, Jan 31, Dec 12; 1755:
    CG, Dec 18, DL, 31; 1756: DL, Jan 9, Mar 4; 1757: CG, Nov 5; 1758: CG, Jan
    28, Feb 4, MARLY, Jul 4; 1760: CG, Feb 5; 1767: DL, Sep 28, CG, 28; see also
    Highness; Princes
Edwards (actor), 1770: HAY, Nov 16; 1771: HAY, Apr 15
Edwards (actor, dancer), 1737: LIF, Feb 1; 1739: DL, May 19; 1740: DL, May 8;
    1741: DL, May 28; 1742: DL, May 25, NWC, Dec 27; 1743: DL, May 12; 1744:
    MFHNT, May 1, MF, 3, DL, 15; 1745: DL, May 9; 1746: GF, Oct 29, JS, Dec 29;
    1747: GF, Jan 2; 1750: HAY, Feb 9, 16, DL, 23, HAY, 26, Mar 13, JS, 28
Edwards (boxkeeper), 1792: DLKING'S, Jun 15; 1793: DL, Jun 6; 1794: DL, Apr 21;
    1795: DL, Jun 6; 1796: DL, Jun 13; 1797: DL, Jun 16; 1798: DL, Jun 14; 1799:
    DL, Jul 4

Edwards (harpist), 1782: CG, Apr 27
Edwards (house servant), 1786: CG, May 27; 1787: CG, May 30
Edwards (singer), 1693: ATCOURT, Apr 30; 1695: DL, Sep 0; 1696: DL, Feb 0, DG,
    Oct 0
Edwards (singer), 1777: DL, Feb 21; 1778: DL, Jan 5, HAY, Mar 24, DL, 31; 1779:
    DL, Nov 27, Dec 27; 1780: DL, Dec 6; 1781: DL, May 1, 10, 18; 1785: HAY, Feb
    10
Edwards and Co (mercers), 1789: CG, Oct 6
Edwards, James (Lord Mayor), 1673: NONE, Apr 21; 1678: CITY, Oct 29
Edwards, James (publisher), 1778: HAY, Jun 10
Edwards, John (boxkeeper), 1797: DL, Jun 15; 1798: DL, Jun 15; 1800: DL, Jun 17
Edwards, Miss (actor), 1768: HAY, May 30, Jun 6, 27, Jul 8, 27, Aug 19, 24, Sep
    19; 1769: HAY, Feb 2
Edwards, Miss (actor), 1792: HAY, Oct 15
Edwards, Miss (actor, singer), 1737: DL, Nov 19; 1738: DL, Jan 6, May 16, BFH,
    Aug 23, DL, Oct 30; 1739: DL, Feb 7; 1740: DL, Mar 8, 17, 25, 29, Apr 19, May
    9, 12, 14, 22, Oct 14, LIF, Nov 22, DL, Dec 26; 1741: LIF, Jan 10, DL, Mar
    14, 24, Apr 24; 1742: DL, Mar 8, 12; 1743: CG, Feb 18, DL, Mar 8, 14, CG, 23,
    DL, May 6; 1744: CG, Mar 13, CR, 21, CG, Apr 2, 28, HAY, Dec 11; 1745: CG,
    Mar 6, 14, Apr 3, 20, May 29, DL, Nov 30, Dec 17; 1746: DL, Jan 4, 31, Feb 6,
    24, Mar 1, 3, 10, 13, 17, 18, 22, Apr 8, 9, 15, 18, 19, 21, 22, 23, 25, 28
Edwards, Mrs (actor), 1735: HAY, Dec 29
Edwards, Mrs (actor), 1779: HAY, Oct 13
Edwards, Mrs (actor), 1786: HAY, Jul 7; 1787: HAY, May 16, Jul 16, 21, Aug 14,
    21, 31; 1788: HAY, Jun 12, 16, Jul 16, Aug 4, Sep 3; 1789: DL, Mar 9, 30, Apr
    14, May 19, 22, 28, Jun 3, HAY, 25, Jul 4, 30, Aug 5, 11, 27, 28, 29, DL, Sep
    24, 26, Oct 13, 27, Nov 4, 13, Dec 7, 23, 26; 1790: DL, Jan 6, Feb 11, Mar 6,
    22, May 31, HAY, Jun 15, 26, 28, Jul 5, 16, 22, Aug 6, 13, DL, Sep 16, Oct
    11, 26, Dec 8; 1791: DL, Feb 8, Apr 27, May 19, HAY, Jun 8, 10, 13, Jul 9,
    30, Aug 19, 31, DLKING'S, Sep 22, 27, 29, Oct 1, 3, 6, 29, Nov 2, 5, 8, 9,
    30; 1792: DLKING'S, Jan 9, Feb 11, 18, Mar 17, 29, Apr 10, Jun 13, DL, Sep
    19, Nov 17, 27, Dec 13, 26; 1793: DL, Jan 5, Feb 25, 28, Mar 4, 12, Apr 5, 8,
    22, May 9, 13, 21, Jun 10
Edwards, Sampson ("The Merry Cobbler of Haymarket") (correspondent), 1752: DL,
    Dec 9, 22
Edwards, Thomas (actor, author), 1728: LIF, Feb 21, HAY, May 8; 1729: LIF, Dec
    3; 1741: DL, Jan 31
Edwards, Widow, 1746: CG, Dec 22
Edwin (spectator), 1700: LIF, Mar 9
Edwin and Angelina (entertainment), 1788: HAY, Aug 13
Edwin and Emma (entertainment), 1789: WHF, Nov 9
Edwin. See Jeffreys, George.
Edwin, D (Master) (actor), 1784: DL, Apr 30, HAY, Aug 5
Edwin, Elizabeth Rebecca, Mrs John Jr (actor), 1792: HAY, Jun 20
Edwin, John (actor, entertainer, singer), 1776: HAY, Jun 19, Jul 1, 5, 8, 10,
    Aug 2, 19, Sep 2; 1777: HAY, Jun 9, 11, 26, Jul 7, 15, 18, 24, 30, Aug 9, 12,
    22, 25, 30, Oct 6; 1778: HAY, Jun 11, 12, 25, Jul 9, 11, 22, Aug 3, 7, 17,
    Sep 7; 1779: HAY, Jun 2, 7, 9, 10, 12, 17, Jul 1, 17, Aug 14, 17, 31, CG, Sep
    24, 27, Oct 1, 13, 16, 23, Nov 4, 13, 30, Dec 31; 1780: CG, Jan 7, 18, Feb 1,
    22, 26, Apr 21, 22, 25, HAY, May 30, Jun 3, 5, 6, 13, 15, 17, 24, 28, 29, Jul
    8, 10, 15, 29, Aug 5, 10, 11, 17, 22, 24, 29, 31, Sep 2, 5, 11, CG, Oct 2, 3,
    19, 21, Nov 1, 4, 25; 1781: CG, Jan 18, Feb 15, 24, Mar 3, 24, Apr 2, 18, 25,
    28, 30, HAY, May 30, Jun 1, 4, 5, 7, 9, 12, 16, 19, 21, 26, Jul 9, 23, 28,
    Aug 7, 8, 17, 22, 24, 28, 29, Sep 4, CG, 17, Oct 13, 19, 25, 27, 30, Nov 24,
    28, Dec 5, 8, 11, 26; 1782: CG, Feb 2, 4, 6, 9, 14, 21, Mar 16, 18, Apr 1, 4,
    10, 20, 23, 24, May 6, 7, 14, 17, HAY, Jun 3, 4, 6, 10, 12, 13, 18, 20, 24,
    Jul 5, 17, 25, 30, Aug 9, 15, 16, 17, 24, 27, 28, Sep 3, CG, 23, 25, 27, 30,
    Oct 3, 4, 9, 16, 17, 23, Nov 2, 4, 19, 25, Dec 14; 1783: CG, Jan 4, Feb 3,
    14, 19, 25, Apr 7, 23, 25, 26, 28, May 3, 7, 9, 19, 21, 26, 29, HAY, 31, Jun
    2, 3, 5, 6, 7, 10, 13, 16, 20, 30, Jul 4, 5, 8, 26, 28, Aug 1, 13, 20, 26,
    29, Sep 9, CG, 17, 19, 24, 26, Oct 1, 2, 9, 11, 16, 17, 24, 28, 31, Nov 4, 8,
    19, Dec 6, 23; 1784: CG, Jan 9, 13, 14, 29, Feb 13, 18, Mar 27, Apr 13, 17,
    24, 26, 27, May 1, 4, 7, 10, 19, 25, 26, HAY, 28, 29, Jun 1, 2, 4, CG, 10,
    HAY, 10, 14, 19, Jul 7, 19, 20, 24, 27, 30, Aug 2, 10, 17, 20, 21, 24, 26,
    Sep 6, CG, 20, 21, 22, 29, Oct 6, 8, 12, 18, Nov 6, 13, 16, 20, 25, Dec 3, 4,
    14, 22; 1785: CG, Jan 14, 21, 29, Feb 7, HAY, 10, CG, 15, Mar 12, 19, 29, 30,
    Apr 1, 2, 5, 11, 12, 18, 22, 25, May 4, 7, 12, 16, 17, HAY, 28, 30, 31, Jun
    2, 3, 6, 7, 9, 16, 21, 28, Jul 9, 11, 13, 19, 26, 28, Aug 16, 19, 23, 26, Sep
    16, CG, Oct 7, 10, 14, 20, 21, 22, 26, 29, Nov 1, 2, 3, 4, 10, 14, 21, 22,
    Dec 23, 26, 28, 30; 1786: CG, Jan 7, 14, 20, 28, 31, Feb 4, 17, Mar 2, 7, 18,
    Apr 1, 4, 18, 20, 24, May 3, 6, 9, 11, 15, 22, 24, 26, HAY, Jun 9, 10, 12,
    13, 14, 15, 16, 17, 19, 20, 26, 28, 29, Jul 12, 14, 25, Aug 12, 15, 25, 29,

Sep 4, 9, CG, 18, 22, Oct 9, 16, 21, 31, Nov 18, 22, 23, 24, 25, 29, 30, Dec
1, 5, 6, 18; 1787: CG, Jan 26, 27, Feb 6, 13, 20, Mar 1, 12, 26, Apr 10, 11,
16, 17, 28, May 9, 11, 21, 22, HAY, Jun 13, 14, 16, 18, 20, 21, 25, 27, Jul
2, 3, 4, 19, 23, 25, 27, Aug 4, 10, 14, 17, 21, 28, 29, CG, Sep 17, 19, 21,
24, 26, Oct 1, 5, 10, 11, 17, 18, 31, Nov 5, 7, 8, 19, 22, 23, Dec 5, 22;
1788: CG, Jan 4, 11, 28, 29, Feb 4, 9, 23, Mar 1, 24, 26, 29, Apr 1, 2, 11,
23, 25, 26, 29, May 12, 19, Jun 3, HAY, 10, 11, 12, 13, 16, 19, 20, 23, 26,
30, Jul 2, 4, 7, Aug 2, 16, 22, 25, 27, Sep 3, 4, CG, 15, HAY, 15, CG, 17,
19, 22, 24, 26, 29, Oct 1, 3, 7, 8, 17, 21, 22, 24, 28, Nov 6, 12, 17, 18,
27, Dec 1, 13, 15, 27; 1789: CG, Jan 2, 8, 20, 28, Feb 3, 6, 21, 24, Mar 28,
31, Apr 4, 15, 20, 21, 30, May 2, 5, 6, 14, 15, 19, 20, 22, Jun 8, 12, HAY,
19, 22, 24, 25, 26, 27, 29, Jul 3, 4, 31, Aug 5, 10, 11, 25, 27, CG, Sep 14,
23, 25, 28, Oct 2, 6, 7, 9, 13, 16, 20, 21, 23, 24, 27, 28, 30, 31, Nov 2, 5,
11, 14, 16, 21, Dec 2, 12, 21; 1790: CG, Jan 22, Feb 4, 6, 25, Mar 8, 18, 22,
Apr 7, 12, 21, May 6, 24, 31, DL, Jun 2, HAY, 15, 16, 22, 23, 25, 28, Jul 5,
Aug 2; 1791: CG, Apr 28
Edwin, John Jr (actor), 1777: HAY, May 15, Jul 18, Aug 7; 1778: HAY, Jul 30;
   1779: HAY, May 31, Aug 17; 1780: CG, Apr 22, HAY, Jul 1, 10, Sep 2, CG, Oct
   3; 1781: CG, Apr 30, HAY, May 30, Jun 16, Aug 8, 22, 24, CG, Oct 30, Dec 18;
   1782: HAY, Jun 3, 18, CG, Sep 27; 1783: CG, Apr 7, HAY, Jun 5, 7, 26, Sep 26;
   1784: DL, May 11, HAY, Jul 19, CG, Nov 6; 1787: HAY, Aug 17; 1788: CG, Mar
   26, HAY, Aug 15, Sep 15; 1789: HAY, May 18, Jun 1, 5, 10; 1791: HAY, Jun 8,
   Jul 20, 22; 1792: HAY, Jun 18, 20, Jul 23, 27, Aug 2, 9, 17, 20, 22, Sep 1
Edwin, Sarah (actor), 1791: DLKING'S, Dec 31; 1792: DLKING'S, May 23, DL, Nov
   21, Dec 22; 1793: DL, Jan 19
Edwin, Sarah, Mrs John (actor), 1781: HAY, Jul 9, Aug 24; 1783: HAY, Aug 13,
   26; 1784: HAY, Aug 10, 24; 1785: HAY, Aug 23; 1786: HAY, Jun 20, 26, Jul 3,
   7, 11, 18, Aug 25; 1787: HAY, Jun 16, 21, Jul 3, 13, 31, Aug 10, 28; 1788:
   HAY, Jun 16, Jul 4, Aug 9, 13, 27; 1789: HAY, May 25, 27, 29, Jun 26, DL, Nov
   13, 20, Dec 26; 1790: DL, Jan 22, Feb 5; 1791: DL, May 26, HAY, Jun 16, 23,
   Jul 15, 30, Aug 16, 31, DLKING'S, Oct 15; 1792: DLKING'S, Feb 18, Mar 29, Jun
   13, HAY, 15, 18, 23, 25, 29, Jul 14, 25, Aug 9, 22, DL, Oct 11, 13, Nov 21,
   Dec 26; 1793: DL, Jan 16, Mar 7, Apr 8, May 31, HAY, Jun 12, 17, Aug 3, 7,
   12, 16, Sep 2, 19, 21, 28, Oct 10, 28, Nov 19
Edwy and Elgiva. See D'Arblay, Frances.
Edzard, Mrs (actor), 1723: LIF, May 22; 1724: LIF, May 25
Egan, Miss (dancer), 1764: DL, Jan 24, May 14; 1767: DL, Jan 24, May 11; 1768:
   DL, Apr 26; 1769: DL, May 17
Egan, Mrs William (tailor), 1786: CG, Jun 2; 1787: CG, Jun 5; 1795: CG, Apr 6,
   Jun 4, Dec 21; 1796: CG, Mar 15, May 23, Nov 5, Dec 19; 1797: CG, Mar 16, May
   18, Nov 24, Dec 26; 1798: CG, Feb 12, HAY, Jul 21, CG, Nov 12, Dec 11; 1799:
   CG, Jan 29, Apr 19, May 22, Jun 6, Dec 23; 1800: CG, Jan 16, May 23, HAY, Jul
   2
Egan, William (actor), 1767: DL, Jan 24; 1775: HAY, May 15, 17, 19, 22, 29, Jun
   5, Jul 17, Aug 16, Sep 4; 1776: HAY, Jul 1, 3, 8, 10, 12, 24; 1777: HAY, May
   15, 28, 30, Jun 6, 11, 19, 26, 30, Jul 7, 15, 18, 24, Aug 7, 9, 14, 18, 25,
   29, 30, Sep 9, 10; 1778: HAY, Jun 1, 8, 11, 19, Jul 2, 11, 30, Aug 27, Sep 2,
   7, CG, Oct 21, Nov 4, 23, Dec 26; 1779: CG, Jan 1, 11, 18, 22, Apr 24, 26,
   30, May 12, 19, HAY, 31, Jun 2, 4, 10, 18, Jul 16, 17, 31, Aug 6, 13, 17, 18,
   24, Sep 8, CG, 20, Oct 6, 8, 20, Nov 16, 23; 1780: CG, Jan 17, Apr 21, 25,
   May 12, 24, HAY, 30, Jun 6, 9, 14, 23, 24, Jul 1, 10, 15, 24, Aug 14, 17, 24,
   Sep 2, 11, CG, 18, Oct 2, 19, 31, Nov 15, 22; 1781: CG, Feb 24, Mar 8, Apr
   30, May 12, 16, HAY, 30, Jun 11, 16, 21, Jul 9, 18, 23, Aug 7, 22, 24, 29,
   Sep 4, 12, CG, Nov 2, 8, 21, 24, Dec 5, 11, 26; 1782: CG, Jan 4, Mar 16, Apr
   1, May 3, 17, 20, HAY, Jun 4, 6, 10, 11, 12, 13, Jul 16, Aug 17, 27, CG, Oct
   16, 17, Dec 9, 31; 1783: CG, Mar 29, May 20, 21, HAY, 31, Jun 2, 3, 5, 6, 7,
   18, 30, Jul 4, Aug 13, 19, 22, 26, 27, 28, 29; 1784: HAY, May 28, 29, Jun 1,
   2, 14, Jul 12, 13, 14, 19, 28, Aug 6, 17, 19, 24, Sep 13, CG, 21, 22, Oct 11,
   12, 28, Nov 4, 16, 17, Dec 29; 1785: CG, Jan 21, 24
Egan, William Jr (actor), 1788: CG, May 17; 1789: CG, Jun 16, Sep 25, Oct 12,
   Nov 2, 6, 10, 16, Dec 14, 29; 1790: CG, Jan 22, 29, Mar 8, 13, 22, Apr 14,
   24, Jun 12, 16; 1791: CG, Jun 2; 1792: CG, May 12; 1794: CG, Jun 4; 1798: CG,
   May 18
Egeirophadron, An (interlude, anon), 1799: CG, May 13, Jun 6
Egerson, Mrs (actor), 1800: CG, May 20
Egerton (actor), 1734: YB, Aug 28
Egerton, Daniel (actor), 1792: CII, Jan 16, HAY, Oct 15; 1796: HAY, Sep 28;
   1797: HAY, Jan 23, 26, CG, Jun 5, HAY, Sep 18; 1798: HAY, Mar 26, CG, Apr 28,
   HAY, Sep 6
Egerton, F Ambrose, 1774: DL, Apr 5
Egerton, Mrs (actor), 1727: LIF, Sep 13; 1728: LIF, Jul 19; 1729: DL, May 12;
   1734: HAY, Apr 5, 17, May 27, Jul 19, 26, 31, Aug 16, LIF, Oct 1; 1735: LIF,

Jun 19, Jul 16, GF/HAY, Aug 1, 8, HAY, 12, GF/HAY, 14, 21, HAY, 26; 1736:
HAY, Jan 14, 19, Mar 5, LIF, 24, HAY, Apr 29, Jul 30; 1737: LIF, Jun 15, Sep
7; 1740: DL, Feb 13, Sep 9, 13, 20, 30, Oct 2, 23, Nov 13, 29, Dec 20; 1741:
DL, Feb 2, May 12, 21, BFLW, Aug 22, DL, Sep 5, 15, 17, 22, Oct 6, 15, Dec 7;
1742: DL, Jan 6, Apr 24; 1743: DL, Sep 17, 20, 22, Oct 4, 11, 13, 22, Nov 8,
12, 18, 26; 1744: DL, Mar 12, Apr 10, May 1; 1745: DL, May 7; 1758: DL, Jun
22

Egerton, Mrs (actor), 1792: HAY, Oct 15; 1797: HAY, Jan 26; 1798: HAY, Mar 26
Egerton, Mrs F Ambrose (actor) 1770: DL, Oct 16, Nov 6, 16; 1771: DL, Jan 4,
    19, Mar 18, Apr 29, Sep 24, Oct 21, Nov 11, 12, 13, 14, 22, 23, Dec 10, 23,
    26, 30; 1772: DL, Jan 1, 3, 4, 7, 20, Feb 25, Mar 10, 21, 23, 30, Apr 4, 21,
    29, May 20, HAY, 20, Jun 1, 29, Aug 4, DL, Sep 19, 26, Oct 3, 6, 8, 14, 28,
    Nov 9, 20, 27, 30, Dec 30; 1773: DL, Jan 1, Feb 2, 18, Mar 23, 30, Apr 17,
    23, 27, 30, HAY, May 17, Jun 7, Jul 16
Egerton, T and J (publishers), 1783: CG, Nov 8; 1785: CG, Apr 12; 1788: DL, Nov
    28; 1790: DL, Mar 8; 1793: CG, Feb 25
Egizzielli (singer), 1736: CG, May 12
Egleton (actor), 1717: LIF, Dec 12; 1718: LIF, Apr 19, May 3, Oct 11; 1719:
    LIF, Jan 16, Feb 7, May 7, Oct 7, 31, Nov 5, 7, 16, 17, 26, Dec 10, 18; 1720:
    LIF, Jan 7, 11, 21, 26, Feb 9, 11, 23, 29, Mar 15, 28, Apr 26, SFLH, Sep 5,
    LIF, Oct 1, 13, 22, Nov 10, 18, 22, 25, Dec 8, 31; 1721: LIF, Jan 4, 19, Feb
    1, 9, Mar 4, 11, 13, 27, Apr 1, 12, 13, May 10, 29, Sep 23, Oct 7, 12, 21,
    24, 26, 28, Nov 7, 13, 14, 16, 18, 24, 25, 27, 28, Dec 2, 11, 12, 18; 1722:
    LIF, Jan 13, 22, Feb 2, 13, Mar 5, 15, 29, 31, Apr 13, 20, May 4, 10, 25, 29,
    Oct 2, 4, 6, 9, 11, 12, 13, 16, 19, 20, 22, 23, 24, 26, 27, 29, 31, Nov 1, 2,
    3, 8, 12, 14, 16, 17, 22, 29, Dec 14, 21, 31; 1723: LIF, Jan 3, 11, Feb 1, 9,
    22, Mar 30, Apr 18, 23, May 3, 29, 31, BFPJ, Aug 22, SF, Sep 5, SOU, 25, LIF,
    28, Oct 2, 4, 7, 10, 14, 18, 22, 24, 25, 29, Nov 1, 12, 14, 16, 18, 21, 26,
    28, Dec 2, 7; 1724: LIF, Mar 16, Apr 6, 14, 22, 28, 29, May 15, 19, 27, 29,
    Jun 3, Sep 23, Oct 7, 12, 14, 22, 27, 30, Nov 6, 11, 12, 17, 18, 24, 25, 26;
    1725: LIF, Jan 11, 16, Feb 27, Mar 13, 29, 31, Apr 5, 14, May 17, 19, 20, Sep
    24, 29, Oct 1, 4, 11, 13, 15, 19, 23, 26, 28, Nov 2, 6, 9, 11, 12, 23, 29,
    Dec 3, 6, 8, 16; 1726: LIF, Mar 19, 24, Apr 11, 20, May 3, 4, 11, 12, SFSE,
    Sep 8, LIF, 14, SOU, 27
Egleton, Mr and Mrs (actors), 1723: LIF, Apr 4; 1724: LIF, Apr 6; 1725: LIF,
    Apr 7
Egleton, Mrs (actor, author), 1721: LIF, Sep 27, 29, Oct 3, 5, 7, 19, 20, 21,
    25, 28, Nov 9, 11, 13, 18, 28, 29, Dec 11, 12, 16, 18; 1722: LIF, Jan 13, 22,
    Feb 2, Mar 5, 15, 31, Apr 13, May 4, Sep 29, Oct 1, 2, 4, 6, 9, 11, 12, 19,
    22, 24, 26, 29, 31, Nov 1, 7, 12, 14, 17, Dec 7, 14, 15, 21, 31; 1723: LIF,
    Jan 3, Feb 1, 22, Mar 25, 30, Apr 16, BFPJ, Aug 22, SF, Sep 5, SOU, 25, LIF,
    Oct 2, 4, 7, 9, 14, 19, 22, 24, 25, 29, Nov 1, 12, 16, 18, 26, 28, Dec 7;
    1724: LIF, Mar 16, 19, 23, Apr 6, 22, 28, 29, May 5, 27, Jun 3, Sep 25, Oct
    12, 14, 22, 23, 27, 30, Nov 6, 11, 12, 17, 18, 25; 1725: LIF, Jan 4, 16, 19,
    Feb 27, Mar 11, 13, 31, Apr 5, 7, 14, 26, 28, May 19, 20, Oct 19, 21, 23, 26,
    Nov 2, 6, 9, 11, 12, 17, 29, Dec 6, 7, 8, 16; 1726: LIF, Jan 5, 7, Mar 21,
    24, Apr 20, 27, May 4, 11, Sep 14, 21, Oct 17, 24, 29, Nov 8, 10, 11, Dec 14;
    1727: LIF, Jan 9, Feb 7, Apr 26, 28, May 3, 9, 22, Sep 15, 18, 20, 25, 27,
    Oct 2, 17, 27, Nov 1, Dec 11, 14; 1728: LIF, Jan 8, 29, Mar 9, 21, 25, Apr 1,
    4, 6, 24, 26, May 11, Sep 18, Oct 7, Nov 19, Dec 28, 31; 1729: LIF, Jan 16,
    Feb 10, 22, Mar 10, 17, Apr 10, 11, 15, 16, 17, 19, 23, 24, 30, May 3, 6,
    BFF, Aug 23, LIF, Sep 19, 24, 26, 29, Oct 3, 8, 10, 22, 29, 30, 31, Nov 7,
    14, Dec 3; 1730: LIF, Jan 19, 26, Apr 2, 13, 20, 30, May 6, 11, 14, 15, 18,
    23, 25, Jul 3, TC, Aug 1, 11, BFLH, 31, SFLH, Sep 8, SFG, 8, LIF, 21, 23, Oct
    7, 12, 14, 19, 23, 26, 30, 31, Nov 6, 10, Dec 3; 1731: LIF, Jan 8, 20, 21,
    Mar 22, Apr 1, 23, 26, 29, May 1, 5, 6, 10, 13, 21, SF/BFFHH, Aug 24, Sep 8,
    LIF, 17, 22, 27, 29, Oct 1, 13, 18, 30, Nov 2, 8, 12, 25, Dec 8; 1732: LIF,
    Jan 7, 10, 18, 19, 26, 28, Feb 15, 21, Mar 20, 23, 30, Apr 18, 22, 24, 27,
    May 1, 2, 9, LIF/CG, Sep 25, 27, Oct 2, 6, 11, 16, 20, 23, Nov 1, 3, 9, 14,
    17, 22, Dec 7, 14, 15, CG/LIF, 16; 1733: LIF/CG, Jan 15, 18, CG, Feb 8,
    LIF/CG, 10, Apr 10, 11, CG, May 2, 4, LIF/CG, 8, 10, 18, 19, 21, Jun 1
--Maggot, The (ballad opera), 1732: LIF, Apr 18
Egmont, Earl of (spectator), 1733: HAY, Jun 6; 1734: KING'S, Jan 29, Feb 12,
    LIF, Mar 12, KING'S, Apr 2; 1735: CG, Mar 12, May 14; 1736: CG, Feb 19; 1744:
    CG, Mar 21
Egyptian Festival, The. See Franklin, Andrew.
Egyptiens (dance), 1741: DL, Feb 9, 14, 16, Mar 3, Apr 21, 29; 1742: DL, Feb
    24, 26, Mar 1, 6, 13
Eichner, Ernst (musician), 1773: HAY, Apr 19
Eiffert, Phillip (musician), 1776: KING'S, Jun 8
Eisent (musician), 1766: KING'S, Apr 10
Elcock, Mrs (actor), 1785: HAY, Mar 15

Elder 'Prentice's Song (song), 1735: HAY, Aug 4
Elder Brother, The. See Fletcher, John.
Elders, The. See Man, Henry.
Elderton. See Elrington.
Eldred (singer), 1695: DL, Sep 0; 1696: LIF, Mar 0, Jun 0
Eldred. See Jackson, John.
Eleardi, Sga (singer), 1760: KING'S, Aug 25
Election of the Managers, The. See Colman the elder, George.
Election, The. See Andrews, Miles Peter; Urquhart, David Henry.
Election, The; or, Bribes on Both Sides. See Fielding, Henry.
Electra. See Francklin, Dr Thomas.
Electrical Catch (song), 1784: HAY, Jul 30
Elegy (song), 1784: DL, Apr 12; 1794: CG, Oct 20; 1795: CG, Jan 5, Sep 21;
    1796: CG, May 17, Sep 19
Elegy, The (prose), 1769: HAY, Feb 2
Eleventh of June, The. See O'Keeffe, John.
Eley (Ealy), Christoph Friedrich (clarinetist), 1793: CG, Dec 19; 1794: DL, Mar
    14, CG, Nov 17; 1795: HAY, Mar 4; 1799: CG, Jan 29
Elford, Mrs (dancer), 1700: LIF, Jul 5; 1701: LIF, Oct 21; 1702: LIF, Dec 11;
    1703: LIF, Feb 11, Apr 28, Jun 1, 5, 8, 11, 14, DL, Dec 14, LIF, 21; 1704:
    DL, Jan 4, 18, LIF, Feb 1, DL, 22, LIF, Mar 30; 1705: LIF, Jan 9, DL, 16,
    LIF, Feb 20, Mar 1, LIF/QUEN, 3, LIF, 10, 31, QUEEN'S, Apr 23, 26, LIF, Sep
    12, LIF/QUEN, Oct 11, QUEEN'S, Nov 12, 15, 17, 20, Dec 12, LIF/QUEN, 26;
    1706: QUEEN'S, Jan 2, 7, 9, 14, 22, Feb 2, ATCOURT, 5, QUEEN'S, 9, Mar 4, 11,
    Apr 3, LIF/QUEN, 11, QUEEN'S, 20, 25, 30, May 15, 29, Jun 13
Elford, Mrs, scholar of (dancer), 1705: LIF, Aug 7
Elford, Richard (singer), 1703: YB, Mar 19, RIW, Aug 12; 1705: LIF/QUEN, Sep 28
Elfrid. See Hill, Aaron.
Elfrida. See Mason, William; Paisiello, Giovanni.
Elhossemy, Muley Ismael Ben Shreif (Moroccan emperor), 1709: DL, Jun 1
Eliot's St James Coffee House, 1711: YB, May 24
Elisa (dance), 1798: KING'S, May 10, 15, 19, Jun 26, Dec 26; 1799: KING'S, Jan
    15
Elisa. See Haym, Nicolino Francesco.
Elisee, Pere (physician), 1798: KING'S, Dec 15
Elisi, Filipo (singer), 1760: KING'S, Aug 25, Dec 16; 1761: KING'S, Feb 7, Oct
    13; 1762: KING'S, Mar 1, May 1, 11; 1765: KING'S, Nov 23; 1766: KING'S, Jan
    25, Mar 13, Apr 10
Eliza. See Arne, Dr Thomas A.
Elizabeth I, 1799: DL, Oct 7
Elizabeth, Princess, 1680: ATCOURT, Feb 20, 27; 1747: CG, May 14; 1748: CG, Nov
    10, Dec 21; 1749: LEI, Jan 7, CG, Feb 9, 27, May 4, Dec 16; 1750: CG, Mar 12;
    1752: CG, Dec 30; 1757: CG, Nov 5; 1758: CG, Jan 28, Feb 4; 1759: HAY, Sep
    17; see also Princesses
Ellard, Thomas (actor), 1767: HAY, Jul 15, 24
Ellen a Roon (song), 1742: DL, Mar 8, 22, Apr 5, 6, 20, May 1, 17; 1745: CG,
    Mar 14, Apr 26; 1748: DL, Mar 21, CG, 24, Apr 21, 28, SOU, Oct 24; 1752: CG,
    Apr 13; 1755: CG, Apr 2; 1757: DL, Mar 28, CG, Apr 22, DL, May 14; 1760: CG,
    Mar 17; 1761: CG, Mar 25; 1772: CG, Apr 29, May 5, 15, 25; 1774: CG, Dec 23;
    1775: HAY, Feb 2; 1780: CG, Mar 29, DL, Apr 18
Ellen a Roon on the German Flute (music), 1756: CG, Mar 23
Elliot (actor), 1715: LIF, Feb 3
Elliot (actor), 1779: CG, Dec 16; 1784: DL, Aug 20
Elliot (actor, singer), 1799: DL, Feb 4, Mar 2, May 24, HAY, Aug 28, DL, Oct
    14, Nov 14, Dec 11, 28; 1800: DL, Jan 1, Mar 11, 13, Apr 29, May 3
Elliot (house servant), 1747: DL, May 18, CG, 22; 1748: CG, May 6; 1749: CG,
    May 3; 1750: CG, May 7; 1752: CG, May 7; 1755: CG, May 20; 1756: CG, May 24;
    1757: CG, May 20; 1758: CG, May 12; 1759: CG, May 25; 1767: CG, Mar 16; 1772:
    DL, Jan 14
Elliot, Anne (actor), 1761: DL, Jul 2, 4, 9, 27, Aug 5; 1762: HAY, Aug 10, 30,
    Sep 2, 6, 7, 20, 30, Oct 14, 19, Nov 12, 15; 1763: CG, Feb 1, Apr 16, 25,
    May 11, Sep 21, 23, 28, Oct 5, 15, 18, 26, Nov 26, Dec 16; 1764: CG, Jan 2,
    9, Feb 9, Mar 20, 27, Apr 30, Sep 24, Oct 1, 3, 11, 16, Nov 15, 16; 1765: CG,
    Jan 10, Mar 14, Apr 17, 30; 1766: DL, Mar 20, CG, Oct 8, Nov 7, 27, Dec 6,
    30; 1767: CG, Jan 2, 10, 13, 20, Feb 18, 28, Mar 24; 1769: CG, Dec 7
Elliot, Master (actor, singer), 1795: CG, Feb 20, Mar 11, 25; 1796: CG, Feb 12,
    17, Mar 16; 1797: CG, Mar 3, 10, 31, Apr 7, DL, Oct 3, 7; 1798: CG, Feb 23,
    Mar 2, 9, 14, 28, 30; 1799: HAY, Jan 24, CG, Feb 8, 13, 15, Mar 6, 15, HAY,
    29; 1800: CG, Feb 28, Mar 14, 19, 21, 26, Jun 16
Elliot, Mrs (actor), 1780: DL, Jan 20
Elliot, Mrs (beneficiary), 1723: LIF, Jun 3
Ellis (scowrer), 1767: CG, Feb 19; 1768: CG, May 28, Jun 2; 1769: CG, May 20,

25; <u>1770</u>: CG, May 19, 24; <u>1771</u>: CG, May 27
Ellis and Scott, <u>1782</u>: HAY, Jan 14
Elliston, Robert William (actor), <u>1796</u>: HAY, Jun 25, 30, Aug 29, Sep 7, 16, CG,
   21, Oct 3, 12, 26, Nov 24; <u>1797</u>: HAY, Aug 9, 14, 19, 28, Sep 4, 8
Ellwick (musical instrument maker), <u>1794</u>: HAY, Jun 2
Ellys, John (painter), <u>1732</u>: DL, Oct 31; <u>1733</u>: DL, Jun 4, 9
Elmerick. See Lillo, George.
Elmsley, Peter (publisher), <u>1796</u>: HAY, Mar 28
Elmy, Mary (actor), <u>1734</u>: DL, Jan 31, Feb 4, 11, DL/LIF, Mar 11, DL, Apr 15,
   DL/LIF, May 3, DL, 13, BFHBH, Aug 24; <u>1735</u>: DL, May 20; <u>1736</u>: HAY, Feb 11,
   Jun 26; <u>1737</u>: CG, Apr 11, LIF, Aug 2; <u>1738</u>: CG, May 18; <u>1744</u>: HAY, Oct 4;
   <u>1745</u>: DL, Feb 11; <u>1747</u>: DL, Jan 3, 24, Mar 12, 23, 24, Apr 4, Sep 24, 26, Oct
   3, Nov 4, 6, 17, Dec 4, 5; <u>1748</u>: DL, Feb 1, Apr 2, Sep 13, 20, 22, 27, Oct 1,
   22, Nov 4, 11, 14; <u>1749</u>: DL, Jan 13, Mar 7, Apr 3, 29, May 16, Sep 19, 20,
   28, Oct 10, 11, 18, 21, 26, Nov 2, 4, 15, 21, 28, Dec 16; <u>1750</u>: DL, Feb 6,
   Apr 2, CG, Oct 16, 27, Nov 5, 19, Dec 21; <u>1751</u>: CG, Jan 1, 3, Feb 23, Mar 16,
   Apr 12, 19, 22, May 7, 9, Oct 11, 19, 21, 22, Nov 4, 21, 28; <u>1752</u>: CG, Jan
   28, Mar 17, 23, Apr 6, 24, Oct 4, 12, 14, Nov 4, 16, 22, 28, Dec 12, 14;
   <u>1753</u>: CG, Feb 6, Mar 10, Apr 12, Sep 10, 24, Oct 8, 17, 27, DL, 30, CG, 30,
   Nov 5, 7, 30; <u>1754</u>: CG, Apr 20, 24, May 13, Sep 18, 27, Oct 14, 16, 22, 24,
   Nov 4, 6, Dec 4; <u>1755</u>: CG, Jan 7, Feb 8, Mar 6, Apr 17, May 7, Sep 29, Oct 1,
   10, 21, 30, Dec 11; <u>1756</u>: CG, Feb 9, Apr 26, Oct 1, 12, 21, Nov 13, 29; <u>1757</u>:
   CG, Jan 27, Feb 19, 21, Apr 21, Sep 14, 26, Oct 8, 12, 15, 19, 20, 27, Nov
   11, 16, Dec 5; <u>1758</u>: CG, Jan 27, Mar 9, Apr 12, 14, 17, Sep 18, Oct 13, 24,
   30, Nov 16, Dec 2, 21; <u>1759</u>: CG, Jan 11, Mar 24, Apr 24, May 11, 25, Oct 1,
   Nov 26, Dec 12, 18, 22; <u>1760</u>: CG, Jan 14, Mar 18, Apr 21, 29, May 8, Sep 22,
   Oct 1, 8, 14, Dec 9; <u>1761</u>: CG, Mar 26, 30, Apr 1, 13, 21, May 7, Sep 18, Oct
   6, 10, 19, 26, 31, Dec 28, 30; <u>1762</u>: CG, Mar 16, Apr 29
Eloisa. See Reynolds, Frederick.
Elopement, The (dance), <u>1790</u>: DL, Mar 8
Elopement, The. See Havard, William; Messink, James.
Elpidia. See Vinci, Leonardo.
Elrington Jr (beneficiary), <u>1717</u>: LIF, May 15
Elrington, Miss (singer), <u>1781</u>: CG, Dec 17; <u>1782</u>: CG, May 10, 27
Elrington, Mrs (actor), <u>1750</u>: CG, Apr 25
Elrington, Richard (actor), <u>1750</u>: CG, May 7, Oct 25, 26, Nov 12, 22, 24, 29;
   <u>1751</u>: CG, Feb 8, 15, 23, Mar 12, Apr 16, May 9
Elrington, Thomas (actor), <u>1709</u>: DL, Dec 2, 15; <u>1710</u>: DL, Jan 14, 31, Feb 1,
   11, 25, Mar 7, 14, May 23, 26, GR, Jun 15, 21, 24, Jul 1, 6, 8, 10, 12, 15,
   20, 22, 27, 29, Aug 3, 7, 10, 19, 24, 28, Sep 9, 28, 30; <u>1711</u>: DL, Mar 10,
   Apr 7, May 18, DL/QUEEN, 29, DL, Aug 3, 17, 24, 31, Oct 4, 12, 13, 18, 20,
   Nov 12; <u>1712</u>: DL, May 27, Jun 5, Nov 28; <u>1715</u>: DL, Jan 24, 26, Feb 3, 12, 19,
   21, Mar 21, Apr 20; <u>1716</u>: LIF, Oct 6, 13, 15, 18, 20, 23, 25, 27, Nov 1, 3,
   9, 13, 17, 26, 27, Dec 4; <u>1717</u>: LIF, Jan 8, Feb 11, Mar 11, 16, 25, 28, Apr
   23; <u>1718</u>: DL, Sep 27, Oct 8, Nov 5, 27, Dec 2; <u>1719</u>: DL, Jan 9, 16, 28, Mar
   7, 12; <u>1726</u>: DL, May 7; <u>1728</u>: DL, Sep 10, 14, 19, 21, Oct 1, 5, 8, 12, 15,
   18, 22, Nov 2, 9, 14, 26, 28, Dec 6, 14, 17, 28; <u>1729</u>: DL, Jan 11, Mar 29
Elsam, Mrs (actor), <u>1716</u>: LIF, Dec 4; <u>1717</u>: LIF, May 15; <u>1718</u>: LIF, Jan 4, Apr
   30, May 13, Jun 20, Jul 24, RI, Aug 2, 9, 11, LIF, Nov 11; <u>1719</u>: LIF, May 25,
   Dec 15; <u>1720</u>: LIF, Jan 11, Feb 17, Mar 15, May 24, Dec 22; <u>1721</u>: LIF, May 15,
   29, SF, Sep 8; <u>1726</u>: SFSE, Sep 8; <u>1728</u>: HAY, Oct 15; <u>1730</u>: HAY, Sep 18, SOU,
   24
Elvira. See Mallet, David.
Elvira; or, The Worst Not Always True. See Digby, George.
Elwood, (staymaker), <u>1745</u>: CG, Apr 26
Embarkation (song), <u>1799</u>: CG, Oct 7
Embarkation, The. See Franklin, Andrew.
Embarkment for Cytherea (dance), <u>1778</u>: CG, Nov 25, 27, 30, Dec 23; <u>1779</u>: CG,
   May 2 , Oct 22; <u>1780</u>: CG, May 18
Embarquement pour Cythere, L' (dance), <u>1789</u>: KING'S, Jan 10, CG, Jun 27
Embarras des Richesses, L'. See Dallainval, L J C.
Embarras du choix, L' (dance), <u>1774</u>: KING'S, May 5, 12, 17, 28, Jun 3
Emberton (stage doorkeeper), <u>1746</u>: DL, May 9; <u>1747</u>: DL, May 8
Emery, John (actor), <u>1798</u>: CG, Sep 21, Oct 3, 5, 24, 25, 29, Nov 1, 7, 9, 12,
   14, 21, 22, 23, Dec 11, 14, 22, 26; <u>1799</u>: CG, Jan 12, 14, 29, 31, Mar 16, Apr
   2, 6, 18, 23, 26, 27, 30, May 3, 4, 14, 15, 25, 28, 31, Jun 1, Sep 20, 25,
   27, 30, Oct 2, 7, 11, 16, 18, 24, 25, 31, Nov 9, 11, Dec 2, 9, 23, 30; <u>1800</u>:
   CG, Jan 11, 16, 22, 29, Feb 4, 19, Apr 5, 15, 17, 22, 24, 26, 30, May 1, 2,
   10, 12, 17, 28, 30, HAY, Jun 13, 14, 16, Jul 1, 2, 7, 15, 26, Aug 7, 14, 15,
   29, Sep 1, 3, 5, 6
Emery, Widow (beneficiary), <u>1774</u>: CG, May 7; <u>1776</u>: CG, May 4; <u>1778</u>: CG, May 14
Emilia Galotti. See Berington, Joseph.

Emilia. See Flecknoe, Richard.
Emmet (doorkeeper), 1744: CG, May 11; 1745: CG, May 14; 1746: CG, May 6; 1747:
  CG, May 19; 1748: CG, May 5
Emperor of China, The. See Chetwood, William Rufus.
Emperor of the East, The. See Massinger, Phillip.
Emperor of the Moon, The. See Behn, Aphra.
Emperor's Cossack (dance), 1782: KING'S, Jan 29, Feb 2, Mar 14
Empio Rigor del Fato, L' (song), 1729: HIC, Apr 16; 1733: DL/HAY, Oct 6, HAY,
  Nov 19; 1734: DL/HAY, Jan 4, HAY, Aug 21, 22
Empress of Morocco, The. See Settle, Elkanah.
Encampment (dance), 1764: KING'S, Jan 24, Feb 14
Enchanted Castle, The. See Andrews, Miles Peter.
Enchanted Garden, The (dance), 1740: DL, Dec 13, 15, 16, 18, 26; 1741: DL, Jan
  8, 13, 27, Feb 3
Enchanted Island of Arcadia (pantomime), 1726: KING'S, Oct 21, 25
Enchanted Peasant (dance), 1761: DL, Jan 24, 26, Feb 26, 28
Enchanted Wood, The. See Francis.
Enchanter, The (opera), 1729: BOS, Jan 21, 22, 25, 31, Feb 1
Enchanter, The; or, Love and Magic. See Garrick, David.
Enchantress (dance), 1775: CG, Feb 1, 8, 13, Apr 29, May 10, 20, 24, 26, 29;
  1776: CG, Oct 31, Nov 6; 1777: CG, Nov 4, 18
Enderby (oil merchant), 1776: CG, Dec 27; 1780: CG, May 29; 1786: CG, Feb 8;
  1791: CG, Feb 22; 1797: CG, Feb 17; 1798: CG, Nov 10
Endimion, the Man in a Moon, a Masque (masque, anon), 1697: DL, Sep 0
Endimione. See Bach, Johann Christian.
Endless pleasure (song), 1754: KING'S, Feb 28
Enea e Lavinia. See DeGiardini, Felice; Sacchini, Antonio Maria Gasparo.
Enee et Didon (dance), 1798: KING'S, Apr 19
Enfant Prodigue, L'; or, The Prodigal Son (play, anon), 1719: KING'S, Mar 19;
  1739: CHE, May 8
Enfants Jardiniers Suedois (dance), 1742: DL, Apr 3, 10, 19, May 7
England in Miniature (song), 1729: HAY, Jun 6
England Preserved. See Watson, George.
England Triumphant; or, The British General (play, anon), 1756: BFGR, Sep 3
England's deliverance from Popish Conspirators. See Dryden, John.
England's Glory (interlude, anon), 1797: CG, Oct 18, 20, 23, 24, 26, 28, 31,
  Nov 1, 4, 7, 9
England's Glory; or, The British Tars at Spithead (interlude, anon), 1795: CG,
  May 16
Englefield Green, 1776: DL, Dec 10
English Ballad (song), 1728: LIF, Mar 18, 27, Apr 22, Jul 12; 1729: HAY, Mar 7,
  29; 1730: LIF, Apr 22
English Ballet (dance), 1739: CG, Sep 14; 1754: HAY, Mar 11
English Cantata (song), 1706: DL, Apr 13, Jun 1; 1715: DL, Apr 7, Nov 23; 1716:
  DL, Jan 23, Apr 12, Nov 26; 1724: KING'S, Mar 17; 1727: YB, Apr 26; 1731:
  LIF, Apr 29, May 17; 1733: DL, Oct 10, Dec 11; 1734: LIF, Apr 18, CG, 25, May
  1; 1735: GF/HAY, Jul 18, DL, Dec 26; 1736: GF, Apr 17; 1737: DL, Oct 18;
  1739: CG, Apr 26
English Cantata, Mock (song), 1757: CG, May 6
English Captain (song), 1740: DL, Apr 17, 18, 19, 21, 22, 24, 25, 28
English children (dancers), 1747: CG, May 4, 6, 12
English Clown (dance), 1719: DL, May 4, 11; 1720: DL, Apr 5; 1721: DL, Apr 10;
  1729: DL, Apr 28; 1735: DL, Apr 18, 21
English Dialogue (song), 1693: YB, Jun 17; 1724: BPT, Feb 21; 1733: DL, Feb 26;
  1735: DL, Jan 23
English Duetto (song), 1725: SH, Apr 30
English Epilogue (entertainment), 1749: HAY, Jun 24
English Friar, The. See Crowne, John.
English Gardeners (dance), 1769: DL, Dec 6, 12, 14, 20; 1770: DL, Jan 4, Apr
  20, 27, May 9, 17
English gentry, 1677: ATCOURT, May 29; 1776: KING'S, Mar 30
English habits, 1762: DL, Nov 3; 1767: DL, Nov 5; 1776: KING'S, Jan 13, CG, Mar
  23
English Hero's Welcome Home (song), 1746: CG, Jan 8
English Horn (music), 1795: KING'S, Jun 16
English Lawyer, The. See Ravenscroft, Edward.
English Maggot (dance), 1731: DL, Jan 23, Apr 5, 22, 26, May 3, 5, 6, 7, 17,
  19, Nov 11, Dec 28; 1732: DL, May 29, Jun 6, 23, 28, Jul 4, 7, Oct 21, Nov 7;
  1733: DL, Jan 23, Apr 30, May 5, 18, Sep 26, Nov 23; 1734: DL, Jan 22,
  DL/LIF, Mar 11, DL/HAY, 19, 23, 26, 28, 30, DL/LIF, Apr 1, LIF, 15, CG, 19,
  DL, 22, 25, DL/HAY, 26, 27, DL, 2(, DL/HAY, May 1, DL/LIF, 3, DL/HAY, 8, DL,
  13, 21, DL/HAY, 22, 23, LIF, 29, DL, Dec 26, 31; 1735: DL, Jan 17, 18, 21,

28, Feb 3, CG/LIF, Apr 14, DL, 18, 29, May 6, 8, 9, 13, 20, 22, 23, 29, 30,
Jun 3, 11, Sep 25, Oct 1, 4, Nov 6, 12, 25, GF, Dec 10, 15, DL, 18, 27; 1736:
DL, Jan 3, 5, 6, 7, 9, Feb 2, 4, 14, 17, 18, 21, 24, 25, 27, Mar 11, 20, 22,
GF, 22, DL, 23, 25, GF, 25, 29, DL, 29, Apr 1, 5, 6, GF, 6, DL, 12, 13, 15,
16, GF, 27, DL, 27, GF, 28, 29, DL, 29, May 4, GF, 5, DL, 6, 7, 18, 20, 21,
22, 25, 27, 28, Jun 2, Oct 22, 25, 28, 29, 30, Nov 2, 3, 6, 8, 10, 12, 17,
20, Dec 9, 10, 17, 22;1737: DL, Jan 5, Feb 18, Mar 2, 4, 15, 19, 21, Apr 13,
19, 26, 30, May 2, 4, 5, 6, 7, 11, 14, 16, 18, 20, 24, 25, 26, 27, 30, 31;
1738: DL, May 1, 8, 12; 1739: DL, May 9; 1742: BFHC, Aug 25
English Medley (dance), 1730: DL, Apr 4, 11
English Merchant, The. See Colman the elder, George.
English Mirror, The. See Shuter, Edward.
English Monarchy, 1674: NONE, Dec 14
English Monsieur, The. See Howard, James.
English Music (music), 1701: DG, May 21
English Music Consort (music), 1702: CC, Apr 25
English nobility, 1723: KING'S, Feb 9; 1776: KING'S, Mar 30
English Opera Song (song), 1731: GF, Jan 13
English Peace Song (song), 1667: ATCOURT, Oct 1
English Peasant (dance), 1733: GF, Apr 20; 1734: GF, Jan 24
English Peasant's Pursuit (dance), 1735: HAY, Jun 12
English Princess, The. See Caryll, John.
English Puppet Theatre, 1662: ATCOURT, Oct 8; 1667: CC, Oct 24
English Readings. See Cobb, James.
English Rogue, The. See Thomson, Thomas.
English Sailor (dance), 1743: LIF, Jan 7
English Sailor and Mistress (dance), 1739: CG, Oct 31
English Sailor at Marseilles (dance), 1765: HAY, Aug 7, 8, 9, 28, Sep 9
English Sailors in America, The (entertainment), 1760: CG, Mar 20, Apr 16
English Serenata (song), 1744: CR, Mar 21
English slaves, 1700: LIF, Jun 28
English Song (song), 1667: ATCOURT, Oct 1; 1693: YB, Jun 17; 1701: RIW, Aug 11;
1703: YB, Jan 28, DL, Feb 11, Nov 30, Dec 14, LIF, 21; 1704: DL, Jan 4, 18,
LIF, Feb 1, DL, 22, LIF, Mar 7, DL, 14, YB, Apr 20, DL, May 31, CC, Jun 7,
DL, 21, Jul 5, YB, Nov 16, Dec 30; 1705: DL, Jan 4, 16, Apr 13, 18, Jun 16,
23, Oct 24, QUEEN'S, Nov 17, DL, Dec 1, 15; 1706: DL, Jan 12, 29, Feb 16, 23,
Apr 13, DL/DG, Nov 21, DL, Dec 5; 1707: DL, Feb 4, YB, Mar 5, Apr 4; 1710:
YB, Apr 17, QUEEN'S, Jul 13, Aug 16; 1712: GR, May 19; 1715: LIF, Feb 26, 28,
SH, May 2, LIF, 5; 1716: HIC, Mar 21, DL, May 25; 1717: LIF, Nov 26; 1718:
YB, Mar 5, LIF, Oct 11; 1720: LIF, May 23; 1721: LIF, Dec 7, 18, 19, 20;
1723: DL, Apr 1, LIF, May 3, Oct 10, HAY, Dec 12; 1724: BPT, Feb 21, LIF, Mar
16, 26, DL, May 22, LIF, Jun 4, DL, Oct 14, LIF, 22, Nov 12; 1725: LIF, Mar
13, DL, Apr 22, SH, 30; 1726: DL, Jan 8, 18, HAY, Feb 24, LIF, Mar 31, Apr
29, May 6; 1727: LIF, Jan 9, May 17; 1728: LIF, Mar 9, HAY, Apr 3; 1729: FLR,
Dec 1; 1730: GF, Apr 14, Jun 16; 1731: LG, Mar 8, CRT, 10, DL, Apr 22, GF,
Jun 1, 3, Oct 6, DL, Nov 1; 1732: HIC, Mar 27, DL, Apr 25, SF, May 19, HAY,
Jun 1, DL, Nov 14; 1733: DL, May 9, CG, 16; 1734: GF, Sep 9, 16, 18; 1735:
HAY, Mar 22, GF, Apr 16, 28; 1736: GF, Apr 6; 1737: CG, Mar 26, HIC, Apr 1,
CG, May 5, LIF, Sep 7; 1738: DL, Mar 3; 1742: DL, Mar 8; 1743: IT, Dec 26;
1744: SH, Feb 9; 1748: CG, Feb 13, Mar 14; 1757: HAY, Aug 17, Sep 5, 14;
1771: CG, Mar 13
English Tars in America, The; or, The Good Woman Without a Head (play), 1761:
CG, Mar 30
English verse, 1745: DL, Mar 28
Englishman in Paris, The. See Foote, Samuel.
Englishman Returned from Paris, The. See Murphy, Arthur.
Enoe (house servant), 1780: DL, May 17; 1781: DL, May 26; 1782: DL, May 30;
1783: DL, May 29
Enoe, Mrs (house servant), 1784: DL, May 15
Enraged Musician, The (print), 1789: HAY, May 18
Enrico. See Galuppi, Baldassare.
Enter (beneficiary), 1733: HIC, Mar 21
Entered Prentice's Song (song), 1734: DL/HAY, May 4; 1736: DL, May 4; 1741: GF,
Apr 29
Enthusiast, The; or, The Spiritual Mountebank (droll), 1744: HAY, Jul 10
Enthusiastic Song (song), 1698: DL/ORDG, Nov 0; 1702: DL, Nov 14; 1704: DL, Jul
1; 1706: DL, Jan 10, Dec 10; 1708: DL, Jan 3; 1721: LIF, Apr 20; 1722: LIF,
Mar 8, May 14, Oct 30; 1723: LIF, Nov 2; 1724: LIF, Oct 9; 1725: LIF, Nov 30;
1726: LIF, Apr 18, May 30, Nov 21; 1727: LIF, Oct 26; 1729: LIF, Oct 24;
1739: CG, Dec 10
Entree (dance), 1772: KING'S, Mar 3; 1773: KING'S, Mar 18; 1775: KING'S, Jan 7;
1777: KING'S, Apr 12

Entree de Flore, L' (dance), 1748: DL, Oct 27, 31, Nov 1, 3, 11, 12, 16, 17,
  19, 21, 23, 25, 28, Dec 16; 1749: DL, Mar 14, 20, Apr 11, Oct 24; 1750: DL,
  Mar 24, 26, Apr 23, 27; 1751: DL, Oct 15, 17, 19, 23, 24, 30, Nov 25, 29, Dec
  11; 1752: DL, Apr 16, Nov 6, 16, 22, Dec 11, 15, 18; 1753: DL, Feb 6, 26, Mar
  24, Apr 2, 3, 5, 9, Nov 23, 27, Dec 11, 13
Entremets, An (entertainment, anon), 1797: CG, May 16
Envious Statesman, The; or, The Forced Physician (entertainment), 1732: BF, Aug
  16, 22
Ephesian Duke; or, Blunder upon Blunder, yet All's Right at Last (play), 1743:
  BFFP, Aug 23
Ephesian Matron, The. See Johnson, Charles; Bickerstaff, Isaac.
Epi-congee (dance), 1757: HAY, Sep 14
Epilogue of Nobody (entertainment), 1753: DL, Feb 6
Epilogue of Thanks (song), 1751: CG, Apr 24
Epilogue on Jealousies (entertainment), 1798: CG, May 1; 1799: HAY, Jun 22
Epilogue on Lying (entertainment), 1757: DL, May 3, 23
Epilogue on Modern Taste (entertainment), 1769: CG, Mar 16
Epilogue on the Furor Dramatica (entertainment), 1787: RLSN, Mar 29
Epilogue Riding on an Ass. See Haynes, Joseph.
Epilogue Song (song), 1776: CG, May 8, DL, Dec 14; 1778: HAY, Feb 9, Apr 9, DL,
  May 2, CHR, Jun 24, DL, Sep 19, Nov 10; 1779: DL, Oct 23; 1782: DL, Apr 6,
  HAY, Aug 15, DL, Sep 21; 1783: CG, May 7, DL, Oct 31, HAY, Dec 15; 1784: DL,
  May 3, Sep 21, HAY, Dec 13; 1785: HAY, Apr 26, DL, Nov 11; 1786: DL, Apr 28,
  May 9; 1790: DL, Jun 5, Nov 3; 1791: DLKING'S, Nov 4; 1792: DLKING'S, Jun 4,
  DL, Oct 2; 1793: DL, May 1, 24; 1794: DL, May 5; 1795: CG, Jun 6; 1799: DL,
  Feb 23, Nov 27
Epilogue to Music (song), 1750: CG, Mar 29
Epilogue to the Court (entertainment), 1659: NONE, Sep 0
Epilogue to the Duchess (entertainment), 1668: ATCOURT, Oct 14
Epilogue to the Town (song), 1742: CG, Apr 22
Epilogue to the University of Oxford (entertainment), 1674: OXFORD, Jul 0
Epilogue upon an Elephant (entertainment), 1704: MFFB, May 1
Epilogue upon Epilogues (entertainment), 1764: DL, May 17
Epilogue upon Two Prologues (entertainment), 1750: DL, Oct 18, 19, 22
Epithalamium (song), 1771: CG, Dec 11, 12; 1775: DL, Feb 1; 1778: CG, Mar 30,
  DL, Oct 27; 1779: DL, Dec 14; 1781: DL, Nov 27, 29; 1782: DL, Oct 10, Nov 6,
  CG, Dec 14; 1783: DL, Mar 15, Oct 8; 1784: CG, Mar 20, HAY, Aug 5, DL, Oct
  12; 1786: CG, Jan 2, DL, Feb 23, CG, Mar 14, 25, DL, Oct 12, CG, 26; 1787:
  DL, Oct 11; 1788: DL, Oct 28; 1789: CG, Jun 8, Dec 21; 1790: DL, Dec 7; 1791:
  CG, Feb 11; 1792: DLKING'S, Jan 21, DL, Dec 17; 1794: DL, Oct 11; 1795: DL,
  Sep 19, Nov 2; 1796: DL, Sep 24, Nov 19; 1797: DL, Oct 30; 1798: DL, Dec 3;
  1799: DL, Mar 26, Nov 22
Epithalamium, Grand (entertainment), 1736: DL, Apr 22
Epouses Persanes, Les (dance), 1777: KING'S, Jan 21, Feb 1, 22, 25, Mar 8, Apr
  29; 1783: KING'S, Feb 15, 18, 22, 25, 27, Mar 1, 11
Epouvantes de Scaramouche et Arlequin Juge Comique, Les (pantomime), 1725: HAY,
  Apr 12
Epoux du Tempe (dance), 1793: KING'S, Jan 26, Feb 5, 16, 26, Apr 23, Jun 1
Epreuve Reciproque, L' (play), 1722: HAY, Jan 22, Feb 6, Mar 5
Epreuve Villageoise, L'. See Gretry, Andre Ernest Modeste.
Epsom Races, 1734: DL/HAY, May 2
Epsom Wells. See Shadwell, Thomas.
Equilibres on Slack Rope (entertainment), 1747: BFH, Aug 22; 1749: SFP, Sep 15,
  SOU, 18; 1750: NWSM, May 10
Equilibres on the wire (entertainment), 1751: SF, Sep 7, 16, 19; 1753: BFGI,
  Sep 3, 4, SFGT, 18; 1757: HAY, Oct 17, 31, Nov 2, Dec 26; 1760: CG, Apr 19,
  HAY, Jun 2
Equivalent, The (song), 1795: CG, Apr 24
Era stupido a pensolo (song), 1762: KING'S, Mar 1
Erard (actor), 1736: CG, Feb 19
Erginda Regina Di Livadia. See Cocchi, Gioacchino.
Erifile. See Sacchini, Antonio Maria Gasparo.
Erminia. See Bononcini, Giovanni.
Erminia; or, The Fair and Vertuous Lady. See Flecknoe, Richard.
Ernelinda. See Heidegger, John James.
Ernly, Sir Edward (spectator), 1699: DLLIF, Apr 22
Eroe Cinese, L'. See Galuppi, Baldassare; Rauzzini, Venanzio.
Errington (actor), 1775: HAY, Mar 23
Errore di Solomone, L'. See Veracini, Francis.
Errors of the Press (entertainment), 1796: CG, May 17
Erskine, Thomas Alexander, 6th Earl of Kelly, 1782: CG, Nov 25; 1783: CG, Jan
  18

Erskine, Thomas, 1794: DL, Jul 2
Erwin (beneficiary), 1737: DL, May 30
Erwin, Mrs (singer), 1699: DL, Dec 0; 1700: DL, Mar 0, Apr 29
Esbury (dresser), 1760: CG, Sep 22
Escape into Prison, An (farce), 1791: DL, May 11; 1797: CG, Nov 10, 13, 14
Escape, The (interlude, anon), 1798: DL, May 21
Escapes of Harlequin by Sea and Land, The; or, Colombine Made Happy At Last
    (pantomime), 1739: BFB, Aug 23; 1745: MF, May 6, NWMF, 13
Escapes of Harlequin, The (pantomime), 1722: DL, Jan 10, 11, 12, 15, 17, 18,
    31, Feb 6, Apr 4, Oct 20, Dec 1, 21; 1723: DL, Apr 15, May 13, 27, Oct 9, 23,
    Nov 7, 23; 1724: DL, Feb 3, May 2; 1725: DL, Oct 19, 22; 1728: HAY, Jun 20
Escapes of Harlequin, The. See Thurmond, John.
Escapes of Harlequin, The; or, Fribble Tricked (pantomime), 1754: SFP, Sep 18,
    19, 20, 21, 23, 24
Escoelil, Mlle (dancer), 1775: KING'S, Oct 31
Espiegle Soubrette, L' (dance), 1794: KING'S, Dec 20; 1795: KING'S, Jan 10, 24,
    27, Mar 24
Essay of different Kinds of Harmony (music), 1734: YB, Apr 5
Essay on Acting, An, 1744: DL, Jan 2, 7
Essay on Tragedy, with a Critical Examen of Mahomet and Irene (criticism),
    1749: DL, Feb 15
Essay Upon the Present State of the Theatre in France, England, and Italy, An
    (book), 1760: DL, Jan 1
Esser, Miss (singer, musician), 1771: MARLY, Jun 27, Jul 6, 13, 18, 20, 27, Aug
    13, 17, 22, 24, Sep 3, 5, 17
Essex (actor), 1697: DL, Jul 0
Essex (actor), 1782: HAY, Mar 4, Nov 25; 1786: HAMM, Jul 19, 26
Essex (dancer), 1702: DL, Aug 20; 1703: YB, Feb 5, DL, Nov 5
Essex (dancer, actor), 1724: DL, Sep 26, Oct 16, Nov 2, 14, 23, Dec 7; 1725:
    DL, Jan 25, Feb 20, Apr 7, 21; 1726: LIF, May 9, DL, Sep 22, Oct 1, 6, 27,
    Nov 23, 30, Dec 10, 12, 14, 30; 1727: DL, Feb 8, 27, Apr 12, 18, 20, 21, 25,
    28, 29, May 1, 2, 3, 5, 10, 15, 22, 26, Sep 26, Oct 7, 12, 19, 30, Nov 1, 14,
    18, 21; 1728: DL, Jan 5, Feb 29, Mar 16, 19, 21, 30, Apr 4, 23, 24, 30, May
    1, 6, 9, 10, 15, 16, Jun 13, Sep 12, 17, 19, 26, Oct 10, 18, 24, 31, Nov 7,
    8, 12, 15; 1729: DL, Jan 14, 27, 31, Mar 10, 18, 22, 24, 25, 27, Apr 10, 17,
    19, 22, 30, May 1, 2, 14, 26, 28, Oct 9, Nov 3, Dec 12; 1730: DL, Jan 1, Apr
    10, 13, 14, 15, 16, 18, 22, 23, 24, 27, 29, 30, May 1, 4, 11, 15, 19, Sep 17,
    Oct 8, 10, 28, Nov 19, 30, Dec 3, 4; 1731: DL, Jan 27, Mar 22, Apr 1, 6, 19,
    May 7, Oct 16, 26, Nov 11, 22, 25, Dec 15, 28; 1732: DL, Feb 2, 22, Mar 4,
    21, Apr 17, 19, 21, 22, 24, 26, 28, 29, May 1, 2, 3, 6, 10, 12, Sep 23, 28,
    Oct 19, Nov 8, 17, Dec 22; 1733: DL, Jan 23, 25, Feb 2, 26, Mar 5, 26, 28,
    29, 31, Apr 16, 24, May 1, 2, 3, 7, 9, 14, 18, 21, DL/HAY, Oct 6, 25, 27, Nov
    8, 12, 17, HAY, 19, DL/HAY, 23, 24, 26, 28, Dec 1, 3, HAY, 13, DL/HAY, 20,
    28, 31; 1734: DL/HAY, Jan 1, 2, 7, 10, 12, 16, 23, 29, Feb 4, 6, 20, Mar 4,
    9, 12, 16, 18, 19, Apr 1, 2, DL, 15, 22, DL/HAY, 26, 27, DL, 29, DL/HAY, May
    1, 22, 23, LIF, 29, DL, Sep 7, 10, 19, 24, 26, Oct 3, 5, 8, 10, 17, 21, 25,
    Nov 1, 7, 15, 16, 22, Dec 4, 9, 11, 17, 19, 21, 28, 31; 1735: DL, Jan 1, 11,
    16, 17, 18, 21, 23, 25, 28, Feb 3, 4, 13, 14, 18, Mar 3, 10, Apr 22, 28, May
    14, Jun 5, Sep 1, Oct 1, 7, 27, Nov 3, 12, 15, 17, 22, 25, 28, Dec 2, 4, 6,
    10, 12, 16, 17, 18, 26, 31; 1736: DL, Jan 3, 8, Feb 2, 4, GF, 7, DL, 11, 12,
    13, 14, 28, Mar 3, 11, 20, 22, 23, 25, 27, 29, Apr 5, 6, 8, 10, 12, 15, 17,
    26, 28, 29, 30, May 4, 6, 11, 14, 18, 20, 21, 22, 25, Jun 2, 23, Aug 26, 31,
    Sep 7, 11, 16, Oct 2, 5, 12, 15, 16, 18, 19, 21, 22, 23, 26, 28, 29, Nov 1,
    2, 3, 5, 6, 8, 9, 11, 12, 13, 15, 17, 23; 1737: DL, Apr 23; 1738: DL, May 1;
    1739: DL, May 2; 1740: DL, Apr 26, Nov 12, 17, Dec 2; 1741: DL, Apr 18; 1743:
    CG, Apr 5; 1746: CG, Apr 17
Essex Buildings, 1678: EB, Nov 22, 25; 1679: EB, Jan 9
Essex, Miss (actor), 1776: HAY, Jun 12, 26, Sep 18, 20, 23, Oct 7, DL, Nov 19;
    1777: CHR, Jun 20, 23, 25, 27, 30, Jul 2, 21, 23, HAY, Oct 9
Essex, Miss J (actor), 1776: HAY, Sep 18, 23
Essex, Mrs (actor), 1696: DL, Sep 0
Essex, 1718: DL, Apr 25; 1743: DL, May 16; 1758: CG, May 3
Estcourt (Eastcourt), Richard (actor), 1703: DL, Apr 10; 1704: DL, Oct 18, 19,
    21, 24, 26, 28, IF, Nov 1, DL, 4, 8, 11, 14, 18, 25, Dec 20; 1705: DL, Jan
    10, 18, Feb 15, Mar 15, 29, Apr 23, Jun 12, 14, Sep 29, Nov 20, Dec 15; 1706:
    DL, Jan 28, Feb 23, Mar 5, 27, 30, Apr 1, 8, DG, Jul 9, DL/DG, Nov 21, DL,
    Dec 3, 7; 1707: DL, Jan 1, Feb 20, Mar 11, 17, 25, Apr 3, 14, 17, Oct 18, 21,
    23, 28, Nov 4, 8, 18, 20, Dec 2, 11, 19; 1708: DL, Jan 7, 15, Feb 3,
    DL/QUEEN, 5, DL, 7, 12, DL/QUEEN, Mar 6, DL, 15, 16, 18, DL/QUEEN, 23, Apr 6,
    8, 21, DL, 22, May 21, Oct 7, 15, 19, 22; 1709: DL, Jan 4, 5, 18, 21, 22, 27,
    Feb 19, Mar 2, 8, 10, 31, Apr 9, 14, 28, May 12, 18, Jun 2, QUEEN'S, Sep 22,
    24, Oct 6, 11, 21, 29, 31, Nov 8, 9, 15, 18, Dec 12; 1710: QUEEN'S, Jan 5,

278

11, 12, 14, Feb 9, Apr 10, Jun 29, Jul 13, DL/QUEEN, Oct 4, 5, Nov 4, 7,
QUEEN'S, 10, DL, Dec 2, 11, 12, 14, 18, 21; 1711: DL, Jan 11, Feb 10,
DL/QUEEN, 13, DL, Mar 5, 6, Apr 3, DL/QUEEN, 30, Jun 7, DL, Sep 25, 27, Oct
9, 17, 19, 24, 26, Nov 1, 6, 8, 9, Dec 8, 10, 31; 1712: DL, Apr 22, Jun 12;
1717: LIF, Oct 17, Nov 1, Dec 7; 1718: LIF, Feb 17; 1722: LIF, Mar 5
--Fair Example, The; or, The Modish Citizens, 1703: DL, Apr 10, 12, 13, Nov 16,
26; 1717: LIF, Oct 17, 19, Nov 1, Dec 7; 1718: LIF, Jan 9, Feb 17, Apr 30,
Oct 15
--Prunella, 1708: DL, Feb 12
Este, Mrs (actor), 1735: DL, Jul 1, GF/HAY, Aug 14, HAY, 26; 1746: GF, Mar 22
Este, William (actor), 1734: DL/HAY, Apr 26, 27, May 17, LIF, 23, JS, 29, HAY,
Jun 5, 14, 17, 19, 21, 28, Jul 19, 26, LIF, Aug 20, HAY, 22, BFHBH, 24, DL,
Sep 24, 28, Oct 5, HAY, 7, DL, 10, 21, Nov 1, 8, Dec 6; 1735: DL, Jan 6, 11,
22, 23, 28, Feb 4, 25, Mar 6, 10, Apr 26, May 14, LIF, Jun 12, GF/HAY, Jul
15, 18, 22, Aug 1, HAY, 12, GF/HAY, 14, 21, HAY, 26, DL, Sep 9, 11, 15, 30,
Oct 31, Nov 1, 6, 12, 13, 15, 21, 22, Dec 6; 1736: DL, Jan 1, 3, 12, Feb 16,
28, LIF, Apr 9, DL, May 25, LIF, Jun 16, DL, 23, Aug 26, Sep 4, 7, 23, Oct 5,
9, 12, 13, 18, 19, 20, 25, 27, 29, Nov 3, 15, 22, Dec 7, 20, 30, 31; 1737:
DL, Jan 6, 14, 29, Feb 5, 10, 19, Apr 2, 11, 29, May 4, 17, 19, 21, 27
Esten, Harriet Pye, Mrs James (actor), 1790: CG, Oct 20, 23, 27, Nov 19, 23,
Dec 6, 17, 31; 1791: CG, Feb 11, 12, 15, Oct 3, 6, 13, 17, 20, 21, 27, 28,
Nov 5, Dec 3; 1792: CG, Jan 14, Feb 8, Mar 22, 31, Apr 14, 28, HAY, Aug 28,
CG, Sep 17, 21, 24, Oct 3, 8, 10, 12, 18, 24, 26, Nov 5, 7, 28, Dec 1; 1793:
CG, Jan 21, 29, Feb 4, 21, Apr 8, 15, 17, 18, 20, May 8, 23, Jun 10, 11, Sep
18, Oct 1, 2, 4, 5, 7, 8, 11, 17, 18, 22, 25, 29, Nov 1, 12, 23, Dec 30;
1794: CG, Jan 6, 14, Feb 5, 24; 1795: CG, Apr 29
Esther. See Handel, George Frederic.
Ete des Coquettes, L'. See D'Ancourt, Florent Carton.
Etearco (opera), 1711: QUEEN'S, Jan 10, 13, 17, 20, 24, 27, 31
Eternal God (song), 1792: KING'S, Mar 28
Ethelinda. See Rowe, Nicholas, The Royal Convert.
Etherege (Etheridge), Sir George, 1668: LIF, Feb 6; 1671: DG, Nov 9; 1676:
NONE, Sep 0; 1684: DLORDG, Aug 0; 1685: ATCOURT, Nov 30; 1687: NONE, Feb 16,
DL, May 12; 1704: DL, May 31; 1705: DL, Jan 10, 13, 24, Jul 5; 1706: QUEEN'S,
Dec 5, 14; 1707: QUEEN'S, Jan 9, 18, DL/QUEEN, Nov 18; 1709: DL, May 18,
QUEEN'S, Nov 15; 1711: DL, Apr 20, Jun 4, GR, Sep 13, DL, Nov 9, 29; 1712:
DL, Feb 9, 21, Oct 30, Dec 13; 1713: DL, Mar 5, 12, May 27, Nov 19, Dec 5,
12; 1714: DL, Jan 21, Nov 2; 1716: DL, Apr 26, 28, Dec 5, 14; 1717: DL, May
6, Nov 13; 1719: DL, Nov 18; 1720: DL, Sep 29, Nov 11; 1721: DL, Nov 25;
1722: DL, Jan 27, Mar 17, Oct 13; 1723: DL, Feb 28; 1724: DL, Nov 21; 1725:
DL, Jan 23, Apr 7, May 8, Nov 2; 1726: DL, Jan 29, LIF, Mar 21, DL, Apr 15,
LIF, 29, DL, Oct 13, Nov 26, 28, Dec 10, 16; 1727: LIF, May 9, DL, Nov 18,
LIF, Dec 14; 1728: DL, Apr 25; 1729: DL, Feb 15, Nov 26, Dec 5; 1732: DL, Apr
28, Nov 18; 1733: DL, Jan 11, 23, CG, Dec 8, 10, 11, 14, 29; 1734: CG, Jan
24, Feb 16, Mar 25, Apr 17, May 1, CG/LIF, Oct 25, Dec 16; 1735: DL, Jan 27,
CG/LIF, Mar 10, May 22; 1738: DL, Mar 21, Apr 24; 1739: DL, Feb 3, 6, 12, CG,
Nov 10, 12, 16; 1740: CG, Jan 22; 1742: DL, Mar 8; 1750: CG, Dec 21
--Comical Revenge, The; or, Love in a Tub, 1664: LIF, Mar 0, NONE, Apr 27;
1665: LIF, Jan 4; 1666: ATCOURT, Oct 29; 1667: LIF, Apr 9, Aug 15, Dec 28;
1668: NONE, Feb 0, LIF, 6, Apr 29; 1669: IT, Feb 2, LIF, Mar 30; 1671: DG,
Nov 13, 14, 15; 1672: DG, Aug 17; 1688: NONE, Sep 0; 1689: NONE, Sep 0; 1695:
DLORLIF, Dec 9; 1696: NONE, Sep 0; 1704: LIF, Jan 26, Feb 21, DL, May 31;
1705: DL, Jan 10, 13, 24, Mar 12, Apr 18, Oct 12; 1706: QUEEN'S, Dec 14;
1708: DL, Jan 7; 1709: DL, May 18; 1712: DL, Feb 21, 22, Jun 12; 1713: DL,
Jan 10, May 27, Dec 5; 1714: DL, Dec 2; 1715: LIF, Apr 26; 1716: DL, Apr 9,
Dec 14; 1720: DL, Sep 29, 30; 1726: DL, Nov 26, 28, Dec 16
--Love in a Tubb, 1665: LIF, Jan 4; 1668: LIF, Apr 29; 1671: DG, Nov 13
--Man of Mode, The; or, Sir Fopling Flutter, 1676: DG, Mar 11, Apr 18, 30, Oct
16; 1679: BRUSSELS, Oct 3; 1680: ATCOURT, Feb 17; 1683: NONE, Sep 0; 1685:
ATCOURT, Nov 30; 1692: NONE, Mar 11, Sep 0; 1698: NONE, Sep 0; 1704: LIF, Apr
8; 1705: LIF, Jan 9, Feb 9, QUEEN'S, Jun 4, LIF/QUEN, Nov 9; 1706: DL, Jan 5,
7, 26, Feb 19, QUEEN'S, Nov 9, 16; 1707: QUEEN'S, Jan 18; 1708: DL, Mar 2,
Apr 29; 1709: DL, Jan 29; 1710: QUEEN'S, Jan 19; 1711: DL, Feb 22, Mar 1, Apr
20, Jun 4, Nov 29; 1713: DL, Jan 22, Mar 5, Dec 12; 1714: DL, Jan 21, Apr 30,
Nov 27; 1715: DL, Feb 8, Apr 4, Nov 19; 1716: DL, Mar 5, Apr 28, Nov 22;
1717: DL, Jan 26, Apr 6; 1718: DL, Jan 18, Mar 25, Dec 13; 1719: DL, Feb 6,
Apr 6, Oct 3; 1720: DL, Feb 2, Mar 3, May 5; 1721: DL, Jan 2, 23, Apr 25, Nov
25; 1722: DL, Jan 27, Mar 12, 17, Oct 13, Dec 8; 1723: DL, Feb 28, Nov 16;
1724: DL, Jan 25, Mar 23, Apr 29, Nov 21; 1725: DL, Jan 23, Apr 7, Nov 2;
1726: DL, Jan 29, Apr 15, Oct 13, Dec 10; 1727: DL, May 3, Nov 18; 1728: DL,
Feb 29, Apr 25, Nov 30; 1729: DL, Feb 15, Apr 12, Dec 13; 1730: DL, Apr 10,
Nov 26; 1731: DL, Jan 9, Apr 28, Nov 24, Dec 30; 1732: DL, Mar 13, Apr 20,

28, Nov 18; 1733: DL, Jan 11, 23, Apr 16; 1735: DL, Jan 27; 1738: DL, Mar 21,
   Apr 24; 1739: DL, Feb 3, 6, 12, May 2, CG, Nov 10, 12, 16; 1740: CG, Jan 22;
   1742: DL, Mar 8, Apr 6, May 27; 1746: CG, Feb 6, 13, Mar 1; 1747: DL, Mar 23;
   1749: CG, Mar 29, Apr 22; 1753: DL, Nov 26, 29, Dec 19, 31; 1754: DL, Feb 19,
   Apr 26; 1755: DL, Jan 22, Apr 25, Oct 31; 1766: CG, Mar 15
--She Would if She Could, 1668: LIF, Feb 6, 25, Mar 7, Apr 20, ATCOURT, May 29;
   1669: LIF, Feb 1; 1670: LIF, Jun 20; 1674: DG, Dec 30; 1676: DG, Feb 0; 1680:
   DL, Jan 27, ATCOURT, Feb 27; 1692: NONE, Sep 0; 1698: NONE, Sep 0; 1704: LIF,
   Apr 22; 1705: DL, Mar 15, 19, Jul 5, Oct 2, QUEEN'S, Dec 7; 1706: DL, Jan 12,
   QUEEN'S, Oct 18, Dec 5; 1707: QUEEN'S, Jan 9, DL/QUEEN, Nov 18; 1708:
   DL/QUEEN, Mar 6; 1709: QUEEN'S, Nov 15; 1710: DL, Dec 21; 1711: DL, Mar 19,
   GR, Sep 13, DL, Nov 9; 1712: DL, Feb 9, Oct 30, Dec 13; 1713: DL, Mar 12, May
   19, Nov 19; 1714: DL, Nov 2; 1716: DL, Apr 26, Dec 5; 1717: DL, May 6, Nov
   13; 1719: DL, May 25, Nov 18; 1720: DL, Nov 11; 1725: DL, May 8; 1726: LIF,
   Mar 21, 22, 29, Apr 29, Oct 14; 1727: LIF, May 9, Dec 14; 1729: DL, Nov 26,
   Dec 5; 1732: DL, Apr 28; 1733: CG, Dec 8, 10, 11, 12, 13, 14, 29; 1734: CG,
   Jan 24, Feb 16, Mar 25, Apr 17, May 1, CG/LIF, Oct 25, Dec 16; 1735: CG/LIF,
   Mar 10, May 22, CG, Nov 6; 1736: CG, Feb 6; 1742: CG, Feb 27, Mar 9, Apr 5;
   1750: CG, Dec 21; 1751: CG, Jan 7
Etherington (house servant), 1760: CG, Sep 22
Etherington, Christopher (publisher), 1789: KING'S, Jan 10, 24
Ethiopians' Dance (dance), 1728: DL, May 9, 15, Oct 10; 1730: LIF, Apr 24;
   1732: LIF, Apr 26; 1739: DL, Jan 20, 24, Mar 13, 17, 20, Apr 2, May 7, 10,
   15, 23, 26, 31, Sep 14, Oct 16; 1740: DL, Nov 26
Ethiopians' Dance, Grand (dance), 1732: LIF, Apr 25; 1739: DL, Jan 16
Etiquette (entertainment), 1784: HAY, Sep 17
Eton School, 1732: LIF, Mar 7
Etourdi, L'. See Moliere.
Eudora. See Hayley, William.
Eugene, Prince, 1710: QUEEN'S, Jul 13; 1712: QUEEN'S, Jan 9, TGB, Feb 4
Eugenia. See Francis, Philip.
Eulogium on Money (entertainment), 1793: CG, Apr 8
Eumene (pastiche), 1765: KING'S, Nov 23, 26, 29; 1766: KING'S, Mar 13
Eunuch, French (singer), 1668: BRIDGES, Oct 12, 14
Eunuch, The. See Heminge, William; Terence.
Eunuch, The; or, The Darby Captain. See Cooke, Thomas.
Eunuch's Dialogue (song), 1705: DL, Jun 9; 1706: DL, Jan 14, Mar 11
Eunuchs of the Seraglio (dance), 1729: DL, Oct 30
Euphrates Lodge, 1769: DL, Apr 15
Euriso. See Sacchini, Antonio Maria Gasparo.
Euristeo. See Galuppi, Baldassare.
Europa Tavern, 1776: CHR, Oct 18
Europe's Revels for the Peace (masque), 1697: ATCOURT, Nov 4; 1706: QUEEN'S,
   Jan 28, 29, 31, Feb 1, 4, Mar 25, 27
European in America (dance), 1771: DL, Apr 22; 1772: DL, Apr 24
Eurydice Hissed. See Fielding, Henry.
Eurydice. See Mallet, David.
Eurydice; or, The Devil Henpecked. See Fielding, Henry.
Eurypides, 1699: LIF, Nov 26
--Haraclidae, 1781: DL, Feb 17
Euthyme et Eucharis (dance), 1788: KING'S, Mar 13, 15, 29, Apr 3, 10
Evan (bookseller), 1794: HAY, Jun 2
Evan (householder), 1754: DL, Apr 24
Evans (acrobat), 1703: DL, Apr 27, DG, 30; 1705: LIF/QUEN, Oct 11
Evans (actor), 1710: QUEEN'S, Mar 16, Apr 14, May 4; 1715: DL, Jan 22, 26, Feb
   3, 12, Mar 21, 28, Apr 19; 1718: LIF, Sep 26, 29, 30, Oct 1, 3, 4, 8, 16, Nov
   4; 1723: DL, Aug 12, 16
Evans (actor), 1730: DL, Oct 28, Dec 4; 1731: DL, Jun 7, Jul 23, SF/BFMMO, Aug
   26, DL, Oct 16, Nov 25; 1732: DL, Mar 21, May 6, 12, GF, Dec 20; 1733: GF,
   Jan 10, 13, Apr 6, 20, May 11, 24, Sep 24, Oct 25, Nov 12, 29, Dec 28; 1734:
   GF, Jan 14, 31, Feb 11, Mar 11, Apr 19, May 8; 1735: GF/HAY, Apr 25
Evans (actor), 1770: HAY, Dec 19; 1777: HAY, Oct 9; 1778: HAY, Dec 28
Evans (actor), 1797: HAY, Jan 23
Evans (boxkeeper), 1736: CG, May 27; 1737: CG, May 9; 1738: CG, May 11; 1739:
   CG, May 15, DL, 28; 1740: CG, May 16; 1741: CG, May 11; 1742: JS, Jan 25, CG,
   May 10, JS, 31, CG, Nov 25; 1743: CG, Apr 26, May 5; 1744: CG, May 9; 1745:
   CG, May 13; 1746: CG, May 5; 1747: CG, May 20; 1748: CG, May 2; 1749: CG, May
   1; 1750: CG, May 4; 1751: CG, May 11; 1752: CG, May 8; 1753: DL, Apr 26, CG,
   May 15; 1754: CG, May 17; 1755: CG, May 15; 1756: CG, May 20; 1757: CG, May
   18; 1758: CG, May 10; 1759: CG, May 23; 1760: CG, May 15, Sep 22; 1761: CG,
   May 14; 1762: CG, May 19; 1763: CG, May 25; 1764: CG, May 24; 1765: CG, May
   24; 1771: CG, May 23, Sep 28, Oct 24; 1772: CG, Apr 22, May 26; 1773: CG, Jan

29, May 25, Dec 17; 1774: CG, Apr 20, May 17, Nov 1; 1775: CG, May 23; 1776:
CG, May 17; 1777: CG, May 21; 1778: CG, May 19; 1779: CG, May 13; 1780: CG,
May 20
Evans (wire walker), 1753: BFGI, Sep 3, 4
Evans, Benjamin (actor), 1793: HAY, Dec 26; 1794: DL, Apr 21, 28, May 1, 6, 8,
30, Jun 9, Jul 4, Sep 27, Nov 1, 5, 10, 15, 19, 29, Dec 6, 9, 20; 1795: DL,
Jan 3, 5, 6, 12, 22, 26, 28, Feb 3, 6, 10, 12, 28, Mar 2, 10, 21, Apr 17, 21,
May 6, 30, Jun 4, Sep 22, 24, Oct 1, 10, 20, 30, Nov 6, 10, 11, 20, 21, 23,
26, Dec 2, 4, 12, 18; 1796: DL, Jan 18, 23, Feb 20, 27, Mar 12, Apr 2, 25,
30, May 9, 24, Jun 4, 11, 13, 14, Sep 22, 27, 29, Oct 19, 24, 25, Nov 2, 9,
10, 15, 18, 22, 26, 28, Dec 5, 6, 9, 10, 16, 26; 1797: DL, Jan 7, 10, 20, 24,
27, Feb 1, 7, 9, 16, 17, Mar 16, Apr 19, 24, 27, May 5, 15, 16, 18, 24, 26,
CG, Jun 21, DL, Sep 23, 26, Oct 5, 9, 12, 21, 24, 28, 30, 31, Nov 4, 6, 7, 9,
11, 17, 23, 24, 25, Dec 2, 9, 20, 21; 1798: DL, Jan 16, 24, 25, 26, Feb 1,
13, 24, Mar 8, 17, 24, 26, May 30, Jun 7, CG, 11, DL, 13, Sep 18, 20, Oct 4,
6, 8, 20, Nov 10, 13, 14, 26, 28, 29, Dec 4, 5, 11, 21, 29; 1799: DL, Jan 2,
8, 19, Feb 4, 9, Mar 2, 11, Apr 22, May 1, 9, 20, 24, Sep 19, Oct 12, 14, 17,
19, 26, 31, Nov 6, 8, 14, 16, 25, Dec 5, 11; 1800: DL, Jan 1, 4, Feb 12, Mar
11, Apr 29, May 10, Jun 4, 11, 12, 18
Evans, Erasmus (actor), 1697: DL, Sep 0; 1698: DL, Feb 0, Mar 0, Jun 0,
DL/ORDG, Nov 0; 1699: DL, Dec 0
Evans, Evan (harpist), 1758: DL, Mar 29; 1759: CG, May 5; 1760: CG, Mar 17, May
6, 7; 1761: CG, May 6; 1762: CG, May 4; 1771: CG, Apr 24; 1776: CG, Apr 22
Evans, Master (actor), 1755: DL, Feb 3
Evans, Mrs (actor), 1678: DG, Sep 0
Evans, Mrs (dancer), 1703: LIF, Dec 21; 1704: LIF, Mar 23, Jun 8, 26, Jul 4,
10, 27, Aug 9, Oct 16; 1705: DL, Nov 23, 27, Dec 6, 12, 18, 29, 31; 1706: DL,
Jan 2, 3, 10, 11, Mar 7, 11, 14, 16, 25, Apr 2, 3, Jun 20, 22, DG, Jul 9,
DL/DG, Nov 2, DL, 30, Dec 7; 1707: DL, Jan 13, 23, Feb 11, 24, Mar 11, Nov
22, 28, DL/QUEEN, Dec 9, DL, 17, 27; 1708: DL, Jan 3, 9, DL/QUEEN, Feb 7, 21
Evans, Mrs (dancer), 1734: GF, Jan 8, 28
Evans, Susannah (actor), 1761: CG, Apr 2, 20, Dec 28, 30; 1762: CG, Jan 5, 7,
Mar 27, Oct 4, 9; 1763: CG, May 11, Sep 30, Oct 7, Nov 29, Dec 9, 26; 1764:
CG, Jan 5, Feb 1, Sep 21, Oct 5, 8, 11, Nov 3; 1765: CG, Apr 30, May 11, Oct
3, 12, 15; 1766: CG, Apr 15, Oct 18; 1767: CG, Jan 1, Oct 8, Nov 28; 1768:
CG, Feb 25, Sep 27, 28; 1769: CG, Feb 27, Oct 2; 1770: CG, Apr 24, Dec 26;
1771: CG, Jan 1, 15, Dec 4; 1772: CG, May 20; 1773: CG, Apr 23; 1774: CG, Sep
23
Evans, Susannah (dancer), 1699: STJAMES, Sep 0, DLLIF, Dec 25; 1700: LIF, Jul 5
Evans, Thomas (publisher), 1773: CG, Nov 27; 1776: DL, Jun 1, CG, Nov 14; 1778:
HAY, Aug 17; 1779: DL, Feb 8, CG, 22, Mar 20, HAY, Jun 12; 1782: HAY, Jun 11;
1783: CG, Feb 25, DL, Mar 24, CG, Oct 21, DL, Dec 5, CG, 6
Evans, Thomas (subtreasurer), 1764: DL, May 9; 1765: DL, May 10; 1766: DL, May
5, Nov 5; 1767: DL, Jan 15, May 12, 27; 1768: DL, May 3; 1769: DL, May 5;
1770: DL, May 10; 1771: DL, May 13, Nov 1; 1772: DL, Mar 18, Jun 10, Nov 4;
1773: DL, Jun 2, Nov 5; 1774: DL, Jun 2, Nov 11; 1775: DL, May 27, Nov 24;
1776: DL, Feb 9, Mar 25, Jun 10
Evants, Mrs (actor), 1782: CG, Oct 23, 25
Evatt, Robert (actor), 1787: CG, Oct 29; 1788: CG, Jan 9, Feb 5, Mar 3, Apr 5,
15, 23, 29, 30, May 15, 16, 19, 27, 30, Oct 3, 22, Nov 7, 22, 28, Dec 1, 19,
26; 1789: CG, Jan 10, 21, 28, 31, Feb 3, 6, 11, Mar 16, Apr 14, 20, 28, 30,
May 8, 15, 16, 27, Jun 5, Sep 16, 21, 23, 25, Oct 2, 7, 9, 13, 31, Nov 7, 11,
12, 16, 20, 27, 30, Dec 11, 21, 29, 31; 1790: CG, Jan 4, Mar 13, 22, 27, Apr
14, May 1, 5, 27, HAY, Jun 15, 17, 18, 19, 22, 28, Jul 5, 16, 19, Aug 2, 6,
10, 11, 12, 13, Sep 4, 11, CG, 13, 29, Oct 1, 4, 5, 11, 13, 18, 20, 25, Nov
1, 4, 6, 11, 15, 16, Dec 6, 28, 31; 1791: CG, Jan 12, 14, Feb 4, Apr 5, 16,
28, May 2, 3, 20, 26, HAY, Jun 10, CG, 13, HAY, 16, 20, 25, Jul 7, 9, 14, 15,
26, 30, Aug 10, 13, 16, 18, 24, 31, Sep 1, 2, 12, CG, 19, 21, 23, 26, 30, Oct
3, 6, 12, 13, 17, 24, Nov 9, Dec 2, 3, 15, 21, 26, 30; 1792: CG, Feb 13, 18,
Mar 31, Apr 12, 18, May 5, 12, 15, 18, 30, HAY, Jun 15, 18, 19, 20, 23, 26,
29, Jul 3, 7, 11, 16, 19, Aug 6, 9, 15, 17, Sep 4, 5, 6, CG, 24, 26, Oct 8,
10, 15, 24, Nov 3, 5, 12, 28, Dec 1, 5, 27; 1793: CG, Jan 7, 9, 29, Mar 4,
11, Apr 4, 8, 11, 15, May 10, 27, Jun 10, HAY, 12, 13, 14, 15, 17, 21, 22,
25, 26, 29, Jul 5, 13, 19, 25, 27, Aug 3, 5, 6, 14, Sep 2, 7, CG, 16, 25, 27,
Oct 2, 4, 7, 8, 9, 11, 14, 29, 30, Nov 8, 13, 18, 23, Dec 5, 9, 17, 18, 19,
30; 1794: CG, Jan 14, 20, 24, Feb 4, 18, 26, Mar 11, 27, Jun 14
Evelina. See Sacchini, Antonio Maria Gasparo.
Evelyn, John (author), 1662: NONE, Dec 15; 1664: LIF, Mar 0; 1665: NONE, Feb 9,
LIF, Apr 4; 1669: BRIDGES, Feb 15; 1670: BRI/COUR, Dec 0; 1671: BRIDGES, Dec
7; 1674: NONE, Sep 22, ATCOURT, Dec 15, 22; 1675: ATCOURT, Feb 15, NONE, Dec
23; 1694: DL, Jan 0
Evelyn, Master (actor), 1749: LEI, Jan 7

Evelyn, Mrs John (spectator), 1668: BRIDGES, Dec 18; 1669: BRIDGES, Jan 16, 29, NONE, Feb 10; 1670: BRI/COUR, Dec 0
Even so in Christ shall all be made alive (song), 1793: KING/HAY, Feb 20; 1794: DL, Mar 19
Evenel (actor), 1742: BFPY, Aug 25
Evenements Impreyues (dance), 1776: KING'S, Jan 9, 20, 23, Feb 10
Evenements Imprevus. See Gretry, Andre Ernest Modeste.
Evening's Adventure, An; or, A Night's Intrigue (play, anon), 1679: NONE, Sep 0
Evening's Love, An. See Dryden, John.
Everard, Ann, Mrs Edward Cape (actor), 1778: HAY, Mar 23, Sep 18; 1779: HAY, Mar 8; 1791: HAY, Mar 7
Everard, Edward Cape (actor), 1773: DL, Dec 31; 1774: DL, Feb 2, 9, Mar 3, Apr 5, 21, 25, HAY, May 16, 30, Jun 1, 8, 13, 24, Jul 6, 15, 25, Aug 24, 26, Sep 5, 12, 21, 30, DL, Oct 19, Dec 9, 19; 1775: DL, Jan 2, 23, Feb 18, Mar 23, 25, Apr 17, May 8, 13, HAY, 15, DL, 16, HAY, 17, 19, 22, 26, DL, 27, HAY, 29, Jun 5, 7, Jul 7, 21, 31, Aug 2, 7, 9, Sep 4, 18, 19, 20, 21, DL, 26, Oct 11, 24, Nov 3, 9, 14, Dec 7; 1776: DL, Jan 27, Feb 6, 15, Mar 7, 23, May 4, 7, 11, 22, 23, Jun 1, 10, Sep 21, Oct 9, 15, Dec 31; 1777: DL, Jan 1, 28, Feb 24, Mar 20, Apr 7, May 2; 1778: HAY, Mar 23, CHR, Jun 1, 3, 8, 9, 10, 15, 18, 19, 22, 24, Jul 30, HAY, Sep 18, Dec 28; 1779: HAY, Feb 22, Mar 8; 1791: HAY, Mar 7; 1795: HAY, Apr 22; see also Cape, Master
Everett (singer), 1796: CG, Oct 6; 1797: CG, Feb 18, Apr 25, Dec 26; 1798: CG, Nov 12, Dec 11, 26; 1799: CG, Jan 14, 21, Apr 2, 13, 23, May 4, Oct 24; 1800: CG, Jan 16, Feb 10
Eversman (Eversmond) (musician), 1724: HIC, Mar 18, LIF, 19, Apr 25; 1728: LIF, May 3; 1729: YB, Mar 28; 1730: LIF, May 15; 1731: YB, Mar 12, LIF, May 12; 1732: LIF, May 10, GF, Nov 30; 1733: GF, Jan 18, 19, Feb 2, Apr 25, May 15, 18, 24; 1734: GF, Mar 25, Apr 18, May 1, 13; 1735: GF, Jan 24, Apr 23, 29; 1736: GF, Apr 27, ST, Dec 17
Every Body Mistaken. See Taverner, William.
Every day will I give thanks (song), 1789: CG, Mar 27; 1790: CG, Feb 24; 1791: DL, Mar 11; 1792: CG, Mar 9, KING'S, 28, 30; 1793: CG, Mar 13, KING/HAY, 13; 1794: DL, Mar 21, CG, 26; 1795: CG, Feb 27; 1796: CG, Feb 26; 1797: CG, Mar 22; 1798: CG, Mar 28; 1799: CG, Mar 1; 1800: CG, Mar 5
Every Man in His Humour. See Jonson, Ben.
Every Man out of His Humour. See Jonson, Ben.
Every One has His Fault. See Inchbald, Elizabeth.
Every Valley (song), 1790: CG, Mar 26; 1793: KING/HAY, Feb 20; 1794: DL, Mar 19; 1795: CG, Mar 27; 1798: CG, Mar 30
Every Woman in Her Humour. See Clive, Catherine.
Eves (dancer), 1774: CG, Apr 15; 1780: CG, May 23; 1782: CG, May 10; 1784: CG, May 11
Evil Spirits' Dance (dance), 1777: DL, Dec 4
Evison, Miss (actor), 1779: HAY, Dec 27
Ewart, Simon (patentee), 1776: DL, Jan 19
Ewin, Mrs (haberdasher), 1747: CG, Jan 29
Examination of a Stage Candidate (entertainment), 1784: HAY, Sep 17
Examination of Doctor Last before the College of Physicians (entertainment), 1780: CII, Apr 19
Excell, James (actor), 1730: DL, May 13, GF, Jul 17, BFOF, Aug 20, SFOF, Sep 9, HAY, 18, DL, Oct 28, Dec 4; 1731: DL, Feb 8, May 8, Jul 20, 23, TC, Aug 4, 5, 6, 7, 9, 10, DL, 11, TC, 12, 13, 16, 17, 18, 19, SF/BFFHH, 24, Sep 8, DL, 25, GF, Nov 5, SUN, 30; 1732: GF, Feb 2, Mar 7, Apr 17, 19, 21, 27, 28, May 1, 2, 4, 10, 12, 15, 17, 18, 23, Nov 3, Dec 20; 1733: GF, Jan 24, Feb 5, Mar 17, Apr 13, 19, May 7, 14, 16, 18, 21, 22, BFMMO, Aug 23, GF, Oct 17, Dec 26; 1734: GF, Jan 31, Feb 11, Mar 18, ST, 22, GF, Apr 1, 19, May 1, 14, SFG, Sep 7, GF, 25, Oct 17, Nov 18; 1735: GF, Jan 24, Mar 6, Apr 21, 23, May 3; 1741: GF, Apr 29
Exchange Alley, 1723: KING'S, Mar 2; 1728: CRT, Dec 18; 1731: WINH, Jun 21; 1749: CG, Apr 28; 1752: DL, Apr 22; 1754: CG, Jan 29; 1756: DL, Nov 12; 1759: CG, May 8
Exchequer Eating-House, 1724: PY, Apr 20
Excise Bill, 1733: HAY, Mar 22; 1737: HAY, Apr 18
Excise Office Coffee House, 1782: HAY, Jan 14
Excise-Man, The. See Knapp, Henry.
Exciseman Tricked, The. See Stewart, James.
Excommunicated Prince, The. See Bedloe, Captain William.
Exeter Court, 1739: CG, Mar 13
Exeter Exchange, 1690: EC, Feb 24; 1743: HAY, Mar 23
Exeter Music Meeting, 1700: EC, Mar 1, 15
Exeter St, 1739: DL, May 11; 1748: DL, Apr 14
Exeter Theatre, 1781: HAY, Jun 1; 1790: CG, Oct 19

Exeter, Lady. See Cecil, Anne Cavendish.
Exeter, 1703: DG, Apr 30; 1750: DL, Mar 22; 1772: DL, Apr 20; 1789: HAY, Aug 5,
    DL, Sep 22
Exhibition of Strength (entertainment), 1734: DL/HAY, Mar 2, HIC, Jul 10, LIF,
    Sep 6; 1735: HAY, Mar 22
Exhibition of Theatrical Portraits (entertainment), 1798: CG, May 25
Exordium (entertainment), 1795: HAY, Mar 4; 1798: CG, Apr 11
Experiment, The. See Stuart, Charles.
Exposure, The (play, anon), 1663: BRIDGES, Nov 0
Eyferd (musician), 1758: CHAPEL, Apr 27
Eyre (beneficiary), 1723: HAY, Feb 13
Eyre, Anthony, 1676: NONE, Sep 0
Eyre, Edmund John (actor, playwright), 1791: CG, May 6, 28
--Dreamer Awake, The; or, The Pugilist Matched, 1791: CG, May 6, 28
Eyres (actor), 1733: GF, Dec 26; 1734: GF, Jan 8, 9, Oct 16; 1735: GF, Jan 10
Ezio. See Hasse, Johann Adolph; Bertoni, Fernando Giuseppe; Handel, George
    Frederic.

F, E (author of pamphlet), 1747: DL, Oct 17
F, H (author), 1761: CG, Feb 2
Fa la la (song), 1796: CG, Apr 5, 19; 1799: CG, Apr 26
Fabian, Mrs (actor), 1781: CII, Mar 15
Fabian, R, 1735: DL, May 10
--Trick for Trick (farce), 1735: DL, May 10; 1741: GF, Oct 2, 5, 7
Fabiani, Michele (dancer), 1786: KING'S, Mar 11, 16, 23, Apr 1, 27, May 23, Jun
    1
Fable of the Iron and the Earthen Pot, The (poem), 1743: DL, Dec 14
Fabres, Mlle (dancer, actor), 1742: CG, Jan 8, 21, Feb 22, May 11, DL, Sep 21;
    1743: DL, Feb 4, 11, CG, Dec 20; 1744: CG, Jan 14, Feb 11, 14, Mar 3, Apr 6,
    26
Fabri, Annibale Pio (singer), 1729: KING'S, Dec 2; 1730: KING'S, Feb 24, Apr 4,
    May 19, Nov 3; 1731: KING'S, Feb 2, Apr 6
Fabrizi, Vincenzo (composer), 1790: HAY, Feb 2
--Due Castellani Burlati, I (opera), 1790: HAY, Feb 2, 6, 9, 13, 16, 20, 23
Fabrizzi, Orsola (singer), 1796: KING'S, Feb 16, Mar 15, 29, Apr 16, May 5, Jun
    14, Dec 6, 20; 1797: KING'S, Jan 7, Apr 18, Jun 8, Jul 18
Facheaux, Les. See Moliere.
Factious Citizen, The; or, The Melancholy Visioner. See Mr Turbulent.
Faggot Binders (dance), 1758: HAY, Mar 6, 16, DL, Jun 1, 22; 1764: DL, Feb 24,
    27, Mar 1, 2, 5, 8, 12, Apr 2, 5, 14, May 1
Faini, Anna Maria (singer), 1737: KING'S, Jan 1, 25, Feb 19, Mar 26
Fair American, The. See Pilon, Frederick.
Fair amoret is gone astray (song), 1698: LIF, Mar 0
Fair and Comely is my Love (song), 1750: KING'S, Apr 10
Fair Bride, The. See Yates, Richard.
Fair Captive, The. See Haywood, Eliza.
Fair Circassian, The. See Pratt, Samuel Jackson.
Fair Example, The. See Estcourt, Richard.
Fair Hypocrite, The. See Galliard, John Ernest.
Fair in an Uproar; or, A Prologue to the Dancing-Dogs, The (pamphlet), 1707:
    BF, Aug 30
Fair Iris (song), 1703: DL, Jul 1; 1706: DL, Mar 26
Fair Kitty (song), 1757: CG, May 2
Fair Lunatick, The (droll), 1749: BFCB, Aug 23, 24, 25, 26, 28
Fair Maid of the Inn, The. See Fletcher, John.
Fair Maid of the West, The. See Heywood, Thomas.
Fair Monitor (song), 1758: DL, Mar 18
Fair Orphan, The (play), 1774: HAY, Sep 17
Fair Penitent, The. See Rowe, Nicholas.
Fair Quaker of Deal, The. See Shadwell, Charles.
Fair Refugee, The; or, The Rival Jews (play, anon), 1785: HAY, Feb 10
Fair Rosale (song), 1792: KING'S, Mar 14, 28, 30; 1793: KING/HAY, Feb 15, DL,
    May 24; 1794: DL, Mar 21, Apr 4; 1795: DL, May 27
Fair Rosamond (droll, anon), 1734: BFHBH, Aug 24; 1736: BFHC, Aug 23; 1741:
    BFH, Aug 22
Fair Rosamond. See Addison, Joseph, Rosamond.
Fair, The. See Rich, John.
Fairbank, Henry (actor, dancer), 1697: DL, Jul 0; 1698: DL, Jun 0, Dec 0; 1699:
    DL, Dec 0; 1700: DL, Mar 0, Jul 9, Oct 0; 1701: DL, Feb 4, Apr 0, Dec 0;

1702: DL, Oct 30, Nov 0, Dec 14; 1703: DL, Mar 11, LIF, Apr 28, Jun 14, DL, Jul 1; 1704: DL, Jan 7, May 0; 1705: DL, Jan 18, Mar 29, Jun 12, 26; 1706: DL, Apr 0, 8, QUEEN'S, 20, Nov 14, Dec 2, 28; 1707: QUEEN'S, Jan 1, 4, Feb 10, 14, Jun 2, 20, 25, Jul 1, 4, 22, 30, Aug 1, 12, Oct 21, DL/QUEEN, 22, 28, 29, 31, Nov 1, 14, Dec 31; 1708: DL/QUEEN, Jan 1, DL, Feb 6, Mar 15, 16, DL/QUEEN, Apr 6, DL, 15, 17, 19, Jun 11, 17, 19, 26, Jul 20, 29, Aug 4, 31, Sep 3, 4, 14, 16, 28, Oct 5, 25, Dec 18, 20, 21, 28, 29, 30; 1709: DL, Jan 18, Apr 25, 27, May 3, 6, 10, 17, Jun 2, Nov 24; 1710: DL, Mar 18, GR, Aug 24; 1717: DL, Oct 10; 1718: DL, Apr 28, May 6, 30, Jun 13, Jul 18, Nov 7; 1724: DL, Dec 18

Fairbrother, Robert (actor, dancer), 1784: HAY, Dec 13; 1788: DL, Dec 22; 1789: DL, May 22, Nov 13, 14, Dec 22, 26; 1790: DL, Jan 8, Mar 8, May 15, Oct 11, 14, 26, Dec 23, 27; 1791: DL, Feb 7, 11, Apr 27, DLKING'S, Nov 5, Dec 31; 1792: DLKING'S, Mar 19, DL, Nov 21; 1793: DL, Jan 23; 1794: DL, May 22, Jun 9, Sep 27, Oct 23, Dec 20; 1795: DL, Feb 12, May 6, 20, Oct 30; 1796: DL, Jan 18, Apr 13, Jun 7

Fairclough (singer), 1798: CG, Nov 12, Dec 11; 1799: CG, Mar 26, Apr 22, May 4; 1800: CG, Jan 16

Fairest Isles (song), 1793: KING/HAY, Mar 6

Fairest nymph that ever blessed our Shore (song), 1696: DG, Aug 0

Fairies Sporting (song), 1787: HAY, Aug 14, 21

Fairies, The. See Garrick, David.

Fairies' Ballet (dance), 1779: KING'S, Feb 23, Mar 2, Apr 15, May 13, 15, 21, Jun 29

Fairies' Dance (dance), 1768: CG, Apr 8

Fairlamb, Miss (actor), 1770: HAY, Oct 1, 5, Nov 16, 21, Dec 14, 19; 1771: HAY, Mar 4, Apr 15, 20

Fairy Favour, The. See Hull, Thomas.

Fairy Favour, The; or, Harlequin Animated. See Johnston, Roger.

Fairy Festival, The. See Rose, John.

Fairy Music (music), 1769: CG, Oct 7

Fairy Prince, The. See Colman the elder, George.

Fairy Queen, The. See Settle, Elkanah.

Fairy Queen, The; or, Harlequin Turn'd Enchanter (dance), 1730: DL, May 15

Fairy Song (song), 1732: HAY, May 15

Fairy Tale, A. See Colman the elder, George.

Fairy, The; or, Harlequin in the Shades (pantomime), 1755: BF, Sep 6

Faithful Bride of Granada, The. See Taverner, William.

Faithful Couple, The; or, The Royal Shepherdess (droll), 1722: SFM, Sep 5

Faithful General, The (play, anon), 1706: QUEEN'S, Jan 3, 4, 5

Faithful Irish Woman, The. See Clive, Catherine.

Faithful Lovers (dance), 1739: CG, Nov 1, 9, 15, 16, 20, 21, 23, 28, Dec 6, 13; 1740: CG, Jan 8, May 5

Faithful Mariner (song), 1722: LIF, Mar 12

Faithful Shepherd (dance), 1735: CG/LIF, Feb 22, Mar 6, Apr 17, 21, CG, Oct 3, 15, 28, Nov 13, 19, 28, Dec 2; 1736: CG, May 6, 11

Faithful Shepherd, The. See Fanshaw, R.

Faithful Shepherd, The. See Handel, George Frederic, Pastor Fido.

Faithful Shepherdess, The. See Fletcher, John.

Faithful Virgins, The (play, anon), 1663: LIF, Jun 0

Faithful Wife, The (farce), 1726: KING'S, Sep 28

Fal de ral tit (song), 1782: HAY, Aug 17; 1783: HAY, Jun 30; 1785: HAY, Jul 13; 1786: HAY, Sep 4

Fal Lal (song), 1798: DL, Jun 12

Falconbridge, Lord. See Belasyse, Thomas.

Falkland, Lord. See Cary.

Falkner, Anna Maria (singer), 1745: CG, Nov 23; 1746: CG, Jan 8, Mar 20, Apr 25, 29; 1748: CG, Feb 13, 15, 20, Mar 3, 14, 28, 31, Apr 6, 14, 18, 21, 27, Sep 26, Oct 27, Dec 10, 26, 27; 1749: CG, Mar 9, 14, 29, 31, Apr 4, 14, 25, May 4, Oct 12, 20, Nov 23; 1750: CG, Mar 19, 27, 29, Apr 5, 19, 24, 25, 26, 27, 30, MARLY, Aug 16, CG, Oct 12, 29, Nov 8, Dec 26; 1751: CG, Mar 1, 21, Apr 8, 12, 16, 20, 23, 24, Sep 30, Dec 4; 1752: CG, Mar 17, Apr 3, 18; 1755: CG, Apr 2

Falkner, Miss E (dancer), 1748: CG, Apr 21

Fall of Bob, Alias Gin, The (play, anon), 1737: HAY, Jan 6, 14, 15, 17

Fall of Egypt, The. See Hawkesworth, John.

Fall of Martinico, The; or, Britannia Triumphant (prelude, anon), 1794: CG, May 24

Fall of Milan, The (play, anon), 1724: HAY, Feb 24

Fall of Mortimer, The. See Mountfort, William.

Fall of Phaeton, The (droll), 1733: SF/BFLH, Aug 23, Sep 10

Fall of Phaeton, The; With Harlequin a Captive. See Pritchard, William.

Fall of Saguntum, The. See Frowde, Philip.
Fall of the Earl of Essex, The. See Ralph, James.
Fallaci Apparenze, Le (opera), 1792: HAY, Mar 31
Fallen is the foe (song), 1789: CG, Mar 27; 1790: DL, Mar 10; 1791: DL, Mar 11,
    CG, 23; 1792: KING'S, Feb 29, CG, Mar 2; 1793: CG, Feb 15, KING/HAY, Mar 13;
    1794: CG, Mar 7, DL, 12, Apr 11; 1795: CG, Feb 20, KING'S, Mar 13, CG, 27;
    1796: CG, Feb 24; 1797: CG, Mar 10; 1798: CG, Mar 30; 1799: CG, Feb 15; 1800:
    CG, Mar 5
Falling Out of Lovers is the Renewing of Love, The (farce), 1710: GR, Aug 31
Falsa Imagine (song), 1734: HIC, Jul 10; 1751: KING'S, Apr 16
False and True. See Moultrie, George.
False Appearances. See Conway, Henry Seymour.
False Colours. See Morris, Edward.
False Concord. See Townley, James.
False Count, The. See Behn, Aphra.
False Delicacy, The. See Kelly, Hugh.
False Friend, The. See Vanbrugh, Sir John.
False Friend, The; or, The Fate of Disobedience. See Pix, Mary.
False Impressions. See Cumberland, Richard.
False One, The. See Fletcher, John.
False Shame; or, The White Hypocrite. See Mackenzie, Henry, The Force of
    Fashion.
Falstaff's Wedding. See Kenrick, Dr William.
Falwood (beneficiary), 1745: DL, May 8
Fame. See Lacy, James.
Famiglia de Bertholdi, La. See Ciampi, Lorenzo.
Famiglia in Scompiglio, La. See Cocchi, Gioacchino.
Family Compact, The. See Rose, John.
Family Distress. See Neuman, Henry.
Family Party, The. See Colman the younger, George.
Famme Matresse, Le. See Femme Maitresse.
Famous Sea Fight at La Hogue (song), 1745: CG, Mar 28
Famous Tragedy of the Life and Death of Mrs Rump (play, anon), 1660: NONE, May
    29
Fancied Queen, The. See Drury, Robert.
Fancy's Festival (song), 1795: HAY, Mar 4
Fandango (dance), 1783: KING'S, Apr 10, 26, May 1, 8, CG, 9; 1785: KING'S, Jan
    1, Feb 24; 1789: DL, May 22; 1795: KING'S, May 28
Fandango Overture (music), 1778: HAY, Jun 11; 1779: HAY, Jun 2; 1780: HAY, Jun
    24
Fane, Sir Francis, 1684: ATCOURT, Feb 11
--Love in the Dark; or, The Man of Business, 1675: DL, May 10
--Sacrifice, The, 1685: NONE, Sep 0
Fanfaron, 1748: DL, Apr 12
Fanny, Miss (author), 1772: CG, Jan 31
Fanshaw, R
--Faithful Shepherd, The, 1668: NURSERY, Feb 25, LIF, Aug 20
Fantaisies de la Danse (dance), 1750: DL, Apr 28, May 1
Fantastic Dance (dance), 1777: DL, Jan 4
Fantastic Spirits' Dance (dance), 1737: DL, Apr 11; 1739: DL, Dec 26; 1750: DL,
    Jan 1; 1756: DL, Feb 13; 1760: DL, Dec 11; 1762: DL, Oct 30; 1763: DL, Nov
    15; 1765: DL, May 1; 1767: DL, Apr 4; 1777: DL, Sep 20; 1778: DL, Nov 2;
    1779: DL, Nov 3; 1780: DL, Mar 13, Apr 24, Sep 23, Dec 12; 1781: DL, Nov 13;
    1784: DL, Nov 9; 1785: DL, Oct 17; 1786: DL, Dec 5
Fantastic Spirits' Dance, Grand (dance), 1747: DL, Dec 26; 1757: DL, Oct 20;
    1758: DL, Oct 24; 1762: DL, Mar 1; 1767: DL, Apr 4; 1768: DL, Apr 22; 1769:
    DL, Mar 16, Oct 9; 1770: DL, Nov 19; 1771: DL, Dec 2; 1773: DL, May 12; 1774:
    DL, Apr 4, Dec 26; 1776: DL, May 18
Fantocini, 1770: GRP, Dec 10
Faramondo (opera), 1738: KING'S, Jan 3, 7, 10, 14, 17, 21, 24, May 16
Farewell Address (entertainment), 1792: HAY, Sep 5
Farewell each Tonish Life (song), 1792: CG, May 15
Farewell Folly. See Motteux, Peter Anthony.
Farewell for the Present Season (entertainment), 1797: DL, May 1
Farewell to old England dear Mary adieu (song), 1793: CG, May 27, 28, Jun 10;
    1798: CG, May 28, 30; see also Dear Mary adieu
Farewell ungrateful traitor (song), 1680: DG, Nov 1
Farewell ye limpid springs (song), 1761: KING'S, Mar 12; 1789: CG, Mar 20, DL,
    25; 1790: CG, Feb 24, DL, Mar 10; 1791: CG, Mar 11, DL, 25; 1792: CG, Mar 2;
    1793: CG, Feb 15, KING/HAY, 27; 1794: CG, Mar 7; 1795: CG, Mar 13; 1796: CG,
    Feb 24; 1797: CG, Mar 17; 1798: CG, Mar 9; 1799: CG, Feb 8; 1800: CG, Mar 5
Farili bo boo (song), 1791: CG, May 18

Farinella, Sga (actor), 1774: KING'S, Nov 8, Dec 3, 13; 1775: KING'S, Jan 14,
    Feb 7, Mar 7, 30, May 6, 23
Farinelli (singer), 1734: KING'S, Oct 29, Nov 2, 5, CR, 27, PM, 29; 1735:
    KING'S, Feb 1, Mar 15, CRT, 24, KING'S, Apr 8, May 3, Nov 25, Dec 16, 20;
    1736: KING'S, Jan 24, Mar 27, Apr 13, Nov 23, CG, 27; 1737: KING'S, Jan 8,
    Feb 12, Apr 12, 26, HAY, May 16, KING'S, 24, Jun 14; 1738: HAY, Mar 3, DL,
    Apr 12; 1741: DL, Oct 15, 24, Dec 3; 1742: DL, Feb 3; 1745: DL, Mar 16; 1747:
    KING'S, Nov 12; 1753: HAY, Mar 13; 1782: KING'S, Jan 12; 1784: KING'S, May 8;
    see also Broschi, Carlo
Farlee, Elizabeth (actor), 1671: BRIDGES, Mar 0; 1677: DL, Jun 0; 1678: DL, Feb
    0, Mar 0
Farley, Charles (actor, author), 1784: CG, Oct 11; 1785: CG, Feb 4, Apr 18,
    HAY, Aug 31, CG, Sep 21; 1786: HAY, Jul 21, 24, CG, Sep 20; 1787: HAY, Jun
    22, Aug 4; 1788: CG, Jun 4, HAY, 23, Aug 5, 9, 16, Sep 3, CG, Oct 22, Dec 26;
    1789: CG, May 28, Jun 5, 8, 13, Oct 13, 31, Nov 19, Dec 10, 21, 31; 1790: CG,
    Jan 22, 23, Feb 25, Mar 8, 27, Apr 29, May 11, 27, HAY, Jun 22, 23, Jul 22,
    Aug 6, 12, 13, Sep 4, CG, 13, 29, Oct 1, 4, 5, 8, 12, 18, Nov 4, 6, 11, 12,
    15, 18, Dec 15, 16, 20; 1791: CG, Jan 12, Feb 4, Mar 12, Apr 16, 28, May 3,
    20, 26, Jun 6, HAY, 16, 20, 21, 23, Jul 7, 22, Aug 2, 5, 13, 24, Sep 3, CG,
    17, 21, 28, 30, Oct 12, 20, 24, Nov 1, 2, 5, 9, Dec 3, 21, 22; 1792: CG, Jan
    25, 28, 31, Feb 8, 18, Mar 6, 31, May 5, HAY, Jun 15, 19, 20, 23, 29, Jul 7,
    11, 14, 23, Aug 6, 9, 22, 23, 30, Sep 1, 15, CG, 19, Oct 8, 10, 12, 15, 24,
    25, 26, 27, Nov 3, 14, Dec 1, 20, 26; 1793: CG, Jan 29, 31, Mar 11, 16, Apr
    8, May 4, 10, 27, Jun 12, Sep 16, 20, Oct 1, 2, 9, 16, 17, 21, 29, Nov 11,
    19, 23, Dec 9, 17, 19; 1794: CG, Jan 2, 14, 21, Feb 5, 6, 22, Apr 29, May 26,
    28, Jun 13, Sep 15, 19, 22, 24, Oct 1, 3, 7, 14, 21, 30, Dec 26; 1795: CG,
    Jan 29, Feb 6, 14, Mar 14, 16, 19, 28, Apr 6, 8, 23, 25, May 1, 12, 25, 29,
    Jun 4, 8, 12, Sep 14, 18, 21, 23, 30, Oct 2, 8, 12, 16, 19, 23, 24, Nov 3, 7,
    9, 13, 16, 18, 27, Dec 4, 5, 7, 9, 15, 21; 1796: CG, Jan 4, 8, 23, Mar 14,
    15, 30, Apr 1, 5, 25, 29, May 3, 18, 21, 23, 30, Jun 6, 7, Sep 12, 14, 16,
    17, 19, 23, 26, Oct 3, 5, 6, 7, 10, 14, 20, 21, 24, 29, Nov 7, 19, 21, Dec 1,
    7, 9, 15, 21, 26; 1797: CG, Jan 4, 10, Feb 13, 18, 22, 23, Mar 16, Apr 8, 19,
    25, May 17, 22, 27, 29, 31, Jun 2, 7, 13, Sep 18, 20, 22, 25, 27, 29, Oct 2,
    4, 6, 9, 11, 16, Nov 20, 21, 22, Dec 8, 16, 23; 1798: CG, Jan 11, Feb 5, 6,
    9, 12, 22, Mar 17, 19, 20, 27, 31, Apr 16, 19, 21, 28, 30, May 1, 7, 12, 15,
    16, 23, 24, 28, 31, Jun 4, Sep 17, 19, 21, Oct 1, 3, 5, 8, 15, 25, 30, 31,
    Nov 5, 10, 12, 14, 20, 21, 23, Dec 11, 26; 1799: CG, Jan 22, 28, 29, Mar 2,
    16, 25, Apr 6, 13, 27, 30, May 4, 13, 14, 15, 22, 24, 28, 31, Jun 5, 6, 7,
    Sep 27, 30, Oct 7, 16, 17, 18, 21, 24, 29, 31, Nov 9, 11, 14, Dec 2, 7, 10,
    23, 30; 1800: CG, Jan 16, Feb 10, Mar 4, 27, Apr 5, 22, 23, 30, May 10, 12,
    15, 20, 27, 29, Jun 2, 7, 12, HAY, 13, 16, 19, 27, Jul 2, 5, 7, Aug 12, 14,
    26, 27, Sep 1
--Raymond and Agnes; or, The Castle of Lindenbergh (ballet-pantomime), 1797:
    CG, Mar 13, 16, 18, 20, 21, 23, 25, 27, 28, 30, Apr 1, 3, 4, 6, 21, 22, 27,
    28, May 1, 3, 5, 15, Jun 1, Oct 9, 12; 1798: CG, Apr 23, 25, 30, May 2, 7,
    10, Jun 4; 1799: CG, Apr 13, 15, 17, 18, 20, 22, 24, 25, May 9, 27; 1800: CG,
    Feb 10, 12, 13, 17, 24, Mar 3, 4, 17, 20, 24, Apr 28, May 1
Farm House, The. See Kemble, John Philip.
Farm Yard (entertainment), 1797: CG, Jun 9
Farmer Tricked, The; or, Harlequin Happy (play), 1757: HAY, Oct 31, Nov 2, 4,
    7, 9; 1763: DL, Apr 30
Farmer, Jane (actor), 1787: HAY, Aug 29; 1788: HAY, Sep 9, DL, Nov 17, 25, Dec
    1, 29; 1789: DL, Jan 19, Feb 7, 16, Mar 21, Apr 21, May 19, Sep 12
Farmer, Jo (musician), 1675: ATCOURT, Feb 15
Farmer, Master (singer), 1784: HAY, Mar 24
Farmer, The. See O'Keeffe, John.
Farmer, Thomas (composer), 1672: DG, Jul 4; 1675: ATCOURT, Feb 15; 1678: DG,
    Jan 17; 1679: DG, Apr 0, May 0, Sep 0; 1680: DG, Jun 0, Sep 0; 1681: DG, Jan
    0, ATCOURT, Nov 15; 1683: DL, Nov 12; 1684: DLORDG, Dec 0
Farmer's Blunder (entertainment), 1778: HAY, Mar 31; 1783: HAY, Sep 17, Dec 15
Farmer's Dance (dance), 1748: NWC, Apr 4
Farmer's Return from London, The. See Garrick, David.
Farmer's Son, The; or, The Maiden's Second Slip (pastoral ballad, anon), 1733:
    HAY, Mar 14, 27
Farmers and Their Wives (dance), 1723: DL, Aug 2, 6
Farnace. See Perez, Davide.
Farnel (householder), 1741: DL, Apr 1, 9
Farnell (householder), 1740: DL, Apr 10
Farnese, Luiggia (singer), 1776: KING'S, Nov 2, 5; 1777: KING'S, Jan 21, Feb 4,
    Mar 1, 13, 20, Apr 1, 17, 29, May 24
Farnese, Marianna (singer), 1777: KING'S, Jan 21, Mar 15, 20, May 20, 24
Farquhar, George (author), 1700: DL, Feb 19, Jul 9; 1701: DL, Apr 0; 1702: DL,

Feb 0, Nov 0, Dec 0, 14; 1704: LIF, Feb 2; 1706: DL, Apr 8, QUEEN'S, Nov 25;
1707: QUEEN'S, Mar 8; 1712: DL, Jul 22, 25; 1716: LIF, Nov 3, 5, 6, 7, 16,
Dec 18, 19; 1717: LIF, Oct 22, Nov 6; 1718: LIF, Apr 29; 1719: LIF, Oct 15;
1720: LIF, May 24; 1721: DL, Oct 24, LIF, Nov 18, 20, 21, Dec 15; 1722: DL,
Jan 18; 1723: DL, Oct 16, 17, Nov 13; 1724: HAY, Feb 27, LIF, Jun 23, 26, Jul
29; 1725: DL, Nov 29, 30, Dec 1, 2, LIF, 3, DL, 17; 1726: DL, Jan 20, Apr 19,
May 19, Dec 12; 1727: DL, Feb 8; 1728: DL, Jan 2, LIF, Apr 6, DL, May 7, LIF,
22, DL, Nov 12; 1729: LIF, Apr 15, DL, May 16, LIF, 22, Oct 8, DL, Nov 24;
1730: LIF, Mar 17; 1731: LIF, May 1; 1732: LIF/CG, Sep 25, Dec 28; 1733:
LIF/CG, Mar 29, 30, 31, Apr 11, 20, CG, May 2, DL/HAY, Oct 27, Nov 1; 1734:
DL/HAY, Jan 11, DL, Nov 22, Dec 14; 1735: DL, Apr 22, GF/HAY, Jul 22, 29, Aug
21, HAY, Sep 29, Oct 24; 1736: DL, Jan 3, 5, 6, 7, 9, HAY, 14, DL, Feb 2, 7,
HAY, 19, DL, Apr 5, May 25, Nov 15, 20, Dec 22; 1737: LIF, Jan 19, DL, Feb
16, Apr 2, May 14, 26, 31, LIF, Jun 15, CG, Nov 18; 1738: CG, Feb 1, DL, Apr
17, May 9, CG, Aug 29, DL, Sep 28, Oct 18, Nov 18, Dec 21; 1739: DL, Jan 9,
CG, Sep 7; 1740: CG, Nov 6, 8, 10, 11, 19, GF, 29, CG, Dec 30; 1741: CG, Feb
14, Apr 1, 10; 1742: LIF, Dec 13; 1750: HAY, Feb 9, DL, Dec 19; 1753: CG, Nov
26; 1754: CG, Oct 15; 1755: CG, Oct 31; 1756: HAY, Jun 8, CG, Dec 1; 1757:
CG, Oct 28; 1758: DL, Oct 3; 1781: HAY, Mar 26; 1787: CG, Apr 16; 1789: DL,
Jan 26
--Beaux' Stratagem, The (Stratagem, The), 1707: QUEEN'S, Mar 8, 11, 13, 15, 17,
20, 29, 31, Apr 5, 15, DL, 17, QUEEN'S, 29, Jun 5, Oct 14, DL/QUEEN, Nov 10,
Dec 2; 1708: DL/QUEEN, Jan 28, Feb 17, Apr 8, May 20, DL, Oct 8; 1709: DL,
Mar 3, Apr 16, May 25, Jun 1, QUEEN'S, Nov 8, Dec 19; 1710: QUEEN'S, May 3,
DL/QUEEN, Nov 4; 1711: DL/QUEEN, Jan 8, Feb 20, Apr 2, Jun 5, DL, Oct 10;
1712: DL, Jan 28, May 2, SML, Jun 11, DL, Oct 16, Nov 6; 1713: DL, Jan 21,
Nov 23; 1714: DL, Mar 18, May 31, Sep 29, Dec 31; 1715: DL, Apr 19, Oct 15,
Dec 14; 1716: DL, Feb 21, Apr 10, Oct 15; 1717: DL, Jan 7, Mar 12, Jun 7, Oct
28; 1718: DL, Jan 22, Apr 15, May 21, HC, Sep 23, DL, 24, Dec 16; 1719: DL,
Feb 7, Apr 23, Oct 9, Dec 4; 1720: DL, Feb 10, 16, May 6, Nov 7, Dec 12;
1721: DL, Apr 15, HAY, Jul 14, DL, Oct 2, LIF, Nov 18, 20, 21, Dec 15, DL,
27; 1722: LIF, Jan 17, DL, Mar 28, LIF, May 23, DL, Oct 8, LIF, 31, Nov 23;
1723: DL, Jan 21, HAY, Mar 14, DL, May 2, LIF, Jun 28, DL, Oct 9, LIF, Dec 6, DL,
11; 1724: LIF, Jan 11, Feb 15, Mar 16, BPT, 18, LIF, Apr 8, DL, 10, LIF, May
1, 30, RI, Jun 29, LIF, Sep 25, DL, Oct 8, Dec 21; 1725: LIF, Feb 2, DL, 11,
LIF, 18, Mar 31, Apr 19, DL, 23, LIF, May 7, Sep 29, DL, Oct 18, LIF, Nov 25,
DL, Dec 21; 1726: LIF, Feb 1, DL, 18, LIF, Mar 8, HAY, 31, Apr 12, DL, 23,
LIF, 27, May 19, Sep 12, DL, Oct 4, LIF, Nov 17, DL, Dec 7; 1727: LIF, Jan
31, Apr 26, DL, May 26, LIF, Jun 7, Sep 15, DL, 28, LIF, Nov 11, Dec 2; 1728:
DL, Mar 14, LIF, Apr 29, DL, May 15, LIF, Sep 18, DL, Oct 31, LIF, Dec 20,
DL, 20; 1729: LIF, Jan 28, DL, Feb 17, LIF, Mar 17, HAY, Apr 8, DL, 9, LIF,
May 1, 27, Sep 26, DL, Oct 24, GF, Nov 3, DL, 7, GF, 13, FLR, Dec 1, GF, 15,
17; 1730: LIF, Jan 24, HAY, Feb 4, 6, GF, Mar 2, HAY, 5, LIF, 21, GF, Apr 17,
LIF, 24, DL, 25, LIF, May 27, GF, 29, HAY, Sep 18, GF, 21, LIF, 23, SOU, 24,
GF, Oct 26, DL, 27, Nov 3, LIF, 18, GF, Dec 12, DL, 30; 1731: HAY, Jan 15,
GF, Feb 11, LIF, Mar 6, HAY, 10, DL, Apr 21, GF, May 10, LIF, 24, GF, 26, YB,
Aug 20, LIF, Sep 22, GF, Oct 8, DL, Nov 6, GF, 27, LIF, Dec 7; 1732: DL, Jan
3, LIF, 5, Feb 17, GF, Mar 23, HAY, Apr 1, LIF, 14, DL, 26, LIF, May 17, GF,
18, LIF/CG, Sep 27, GF, Oct 4, DL, 12, GF, Nov 17, DL, 20, LIF/CG, 21, GF,
30; 1733: DL, Jan 16, LIF/CG, Feb 6, DL, 8, GF, Mar 13, HAY, 19, GF, Apr 20,
HAY, May 26, CG, Sep 25, DL, Oct 5, GF, 18; 1734: BLO, Jan 16, CG, 16, GF,
18, DL, Feb 7, 28, Apr 25, CG, 26, LIF, May 17, GF, 20, HAY, 27, Jun 24, Aug
16, HA, Sep 2, CG/LIF, 23, GF, Oct 1, 31, CG/LIF, Nov 12; 1735: GF, Jan 27,
Feb 25, CG/LIF, Mar 18, LIF, Apr 30, DL, May 14, HAY, Aug 26, CG, Sep 16, GF,
Nov 20, CG, Dec 2, HAY, 23; 1736: CG, Feb 28, GF, Apr 6, CG, May 27, LIF, Jun
16, HAY, Jul 29, RI, Aug 28, CG, Oct 8, LIF, Nov 24, CG, Dec 13; 1737: HAY,
Mar 5, DL, Apr 12, LIF, 12, DL, May 14, Oct 11, CG, Nov 18; 1738: CG, Feb 1,
Apr 21, DL, May 9, Sep 28, CG, Nov 7, DL, 27; 1739: CG, Jan 3, Feb 23, DL,
Mar 12, CG, May 1, DL, 22, Sep 11, Nov 13, CG, Dec 15; 1740: CG, Jan 25, DL,
May 8, CG, 21, DL, Sep 13, GF, Oct 15, 16, Nov 8, DL, Dec 1; 1741: GF, Jan
20, CG, 21, GF, Feb 16, CG, Apr 6, GF, 9, CG, May 8, DL, 22, Sep 22, GF, 30,
JS, Oct 6, CG, Nov 9, DL, Dec 9; 1742: CG, Jan 26, GF, Feb 2, DL, 3, CG, 10,
Apr 6, DL, 10, May 8, Oct 14, CG, Nov 30, DL, Dec 22, 23, 28, LIF, 28, DL,
31; 1743: DL, Jan 12, 26, Feb 7, 8, Mar 1, LIF, 15, JS, 31, DL, Apr 13, HAY,
15, DL, May 26, Oct 11, CG, 31, DL, Dec 22; 1744: DL, Feb 9, HAY, May 16, MF,
Jun 7, DL, Sep 20, Nov 7, CG, 27, DL, Dec 1, 29, 31; 1745: DL, Jan 3, GF, 18,
DL, 19, NWMF, Feb 7, DL, 9, Mar 30, Apr 22, GF, 23, DL, Sep 19, CG, Nov 7,
GF, 13, DL, 16, GF, Dec 23; 1746: GF, Feb 24, DL, Mar 4, GF, 15, CG, Apr 5,
DL, Jun 9, CG, 23, NWSM, Jul 28, DL, Aug 6, SOU, Oct 16, 21, DL, 23, GF, 31,
CG, Nov 3, 12, 25, HAY, 27; 1747: DL, Jan 26, CG, Apr 2, DL, May 18, Oct 15,
Nov 3, Dec 1; 1748: CG, Jan 8, DL, 25, Mar 29, HAY, 30, CG, May 6, Oct 7, DL,
Nov 11, NTW, 16, HAY, 22, CG, Dec 2; 1749: DL, Jan 17, Mar 18, Apr 8, CG, 26,

28, SOU, Oct 4, DL, 18, Nov 11, CG, 24; 1750: DL, Mar 17, 31, Apr 18, 21, CG,
28, DL, Sep 21, Oct 17, Dec 19; 1751: DL, Jan 18, 22, Apr 10, May 18, CG, Sep
25, DL, Oct 2, Nov 6, NWC, Dec 26; 1752: DL, Jan 9, CG, Feb 17, Mar 31, DL,
Apr 17, CG, May 6, DL, Sep 28, CG, Oct 23, DL, Nov 6, 23, SOU, 24; 1753: DL,
Jan 26, Apr 12, Sep 29, Nov 27; 1754: DL, Jan 10, Feb 21, Mar 26, CG, May 15,
DL, 30, Oct 3, KS, 7; 1755: DL, Jan 20, Apr 2, CG, 2, May 6, DL, Oct 2, CG,
24, DL, Nov 21; 1756: DL, Mar 23, Apr 23, CG, 27, May 19, Sep 29, DL, Oct 7,
CG, Nov 27, Dec 15; 1757: CG, Jan 21, DL, Mar 12, Apr 12, CG, 30, Oct 7, DL,
26, CG, Dec 23; 1758: DL, Feb 16, CG, Apr 8, Oct 25, Nov 29; 1759: CG, Jan
15, Feb 23, Mar 12, DL, Apr 7, CG, 27, DL, Sep 27, Nov 16, CG, Dec 20, 29;
1760: DL, Jan 15, CG, 15, DL, Mar 29, CG, May 6, Oct 6, DL, 23, CG, Nov 21;
1761: DL, Jan 6, Apr 4, 10, CG, 28, DL, May 2, 15, HAY, Jun 23, 27, 30, Jul
2, 4, 6, 7, 8, 9, 11, 13, 21, Aug 5, CG, Sep 9, DL, 19; 1762: CG, Mar 2, DL,
30, Apr 26, CG, 28, DL, May 19, CG, Sep 20, DL, Oct 13, CG, Nov 11, DL, 22;
1763: DL, Apr 12, May 13, HAY, Sep 5, DL, 22, CG, Oct 18, DL, Nov 10, Dec 12,
27; 1764: CG, Jan 24, Mar 10, Apr 30, DL, Sep 18, CG, Oct 25, DL, Nov 12;
1765: CG, Jan 10, Apr 18, Sep 16, Dec 28; 1766: DL, May 20, HAY, Aug 21, CG,
Nov 11; 1767: CG, Jan 2, Mar 14, HAY, Jun 17, CG, Nov 17, DL, Dec 1, 3, 14,
16; 1768: DL, Jan 16, CG, Apr 22, DL, May 6, 12, HAY, Jun 23, Jul 22, CG, Oct
14, DL, 15, Dec 31; 1769: CG, Jan 12, Apr 20, DL, May 18, HAY, Jun 5, DL, Oct
6, CG, Dec 22; 1770: CG, Feb 8, DL, 13, CG, May 26, HAY, Jul 25, Sep 27, CG,
Oct 27, DL, Nov 3, 8; 1771: CG, Jan 29, Feb 4, Apr 1, May 16, Sep 27, Nov 18,
DL, 28; 1772: CG, Jan 20, Mar 12, DL, Apr 21, CG, May 26, Oct 16, Dec 19;
1773: DL, Jan 19, 29, CG, Feb 18, 27, DL, Apr 17, CG, May 27, DL, Nov 24, Dec
9, 15; 1774: CG, Jan 5, Feb 12, May 20, HAY, Sep 19, DL, Nov 3, 29; 1775: CG,
May 4, DL, 5, HAY, Sep 16, DL, Oct 20, CG, Nov 24, DL, Dec 1, 23; 1776: DL,
May 7, HAY, Sep 23, CG, Nov 26; 1778: CG, Feb 28, May 19, DL, Dec 11; 1779:
CG, Jan 11, Apr 23, May 19, HAY, Aug 17, DL, Sep 28, Dec 9, 10; 1780: DL, Jan
18, Mar 18, 31, CII, Apr 5, DL, 15, CG, May 24, HAY, Jun 9, 10, Aug 11, CG,
Sep 18, DL, Dec 8; 1781: DL, Nov 21; 1782: DL, Jan 4, CG, 4, May 29, DL, 31,
Dec 5, 9; 1783: DL, Dec 2; 1784: DL, Jan 14, Mar 23, Sep 23; 1785: CG, Nov
19, 30; 1786: CG, Feb 10, May 6, Jun 2; 1787: CG, Jan 4, DL, 18, Feb 13,
RLSN, Mar 30, DL, Sep 20, CG, Oct 19; 1788: DL, Jan 4, CG, 17, Feb 7, Mar 31,
DL, May 26, HAY, Jul 24, Sep 4, CG, 24, Nov 4; 1789: DL, Jan 7, 26, CG, Sep
16, DL, Nov 21; 1790: CG, May 27, DL, 29, CG, Dec 28; 1792: DLKING'S, Jun 15,
DL, Oct 18, Nov 19, Dec 20; 1793: DL, Jun 7, CG, Sep 27, Dec 28; 1794: CG,
Jan 25, Jun 14, DL, 16, CG, Sep 19; 1795: CG, Jan 3; 1796: DL, Oct 27, CG,
Dec 31; 1797: CG, Dec 22, 28; 1798: CG, Mar 22, May 5, DL, Oct 13; 1799: CG,
Oct 11; 1800: CG, Jan 7
--Constant Couple, The; or, A Trip to the Jubilee, 1699: DL, Nov 28, Dec 0,
LIF, 0, DL, 0; 1700: DL, Feb 13, Jun 15, Jul 13, Oct 26; 1701: DL, Jan 25;
1702: DL, Oct 23; 1703: DL, Feb 3, Oct 28, Nov 19, Dec 20; 1704: DL, Jan 24,
May 25, Oct 12, Dec 30; 1705: DL, Nov 7; 1707: QUEEN'S, Mar 27, Apr 19,
DL/QUEEN, Oct 20; 1708: DL/QUEEN, May 25; 1709: DL, Mar 14, May 24, QUEEN'S,
Oct 28; 1710: QUEEN'S, Feb 27, May 8, Jul 21; 1711: DL, Jan 26; 1712: DL, May
6, Oct 22; 1713: DL, Jan 7, Apr 6, Oct 22; 1714: DL, May 24, Oct 11, Nov 23;
1715: DL, Jan 18, Mar 5, Apr 30, Jun 2, Oct 20, Dec 21; 1716: DL, Mar 8, May
14, Jun 15, Oct 19; 1717: DL, Jan 10, Apr 9, May 17, Jun 14; 1718: DL, Feb 5,
Apr 21, May 14, HC, Oct 9, DL, 10, Dec 12; 1719: DL, Feb 4, May 14, Sep 24,
Dec 1; 1720: DL, Jan 19, May 23, Oct 15; 1721: DL, Jan 20, Feb 9, Mar 9, May
5, Sep 28, Dec 4; 1722: DL, Jan 18, Mar 29, Apr 28; 1723: DL, Jan 17, Apr 18;
1724: DL, Nov 26, Dec 16; 1725: DL, Jan 18, Feb 5, Mar 4, May 27, Oct 9, Dec
4; 1726: DL, Feb 5, Mar 14, Sep 24, Dec 1; 1727: DL, Apr 6, Sep 14, Nov 20;
1728: DL, Mar 2, Oct 17, Dec 12; 1729: DL, Mar 27, Dec 4, GF, 20, 22, 26, 27,
29, 30, 31; 1730: GF, Jan 1, 2, 3, Feb 6, DL, 10, GF, Mar 10, Apr 14, May 13,
Jun 12, 25, Jul 14, 30, Sep 30, Oct 23, DL, Nov 14, GF, 28, Dec 31; 1731: GF,
Feb 20, Mar 11, LIF, 22, 27, GF, 30, Apr 22, LIF, 29, DL, May 1, GF, 5, LIF,
13, RI, Jul 1, LIF, Oct 1, GF, 11, Nov 17, DL, 20, Dec 8, GF, 18; 1732: LIF,
Jan 8, GF, Feb 5, DL, Mar 20, LIF, Apr 17, GF, 19, May 22, DL, Oct 24, GF,
26, LIF/CG, Nov 1, GF, 9, Dec 15; 1733: GF, Jan 13, LIF/CG, 27, GF, Feb 17,
LIF/CG, Mar 12, DL, 28, GF, Apr 13, LIF/CG, 18, GF, May 9, Sep 12, DL/HAY,
Oct 27, CG, Nov 1, GF, 12; 1734: GF, Feb 11, Mar 16, DL/HAY, 28, CG, Apr 16,
GF, 17, Sep 13, Oct 28, DL, Nov 22; 1735: CG/LIF, Jan 21, GF, Feb 12, DL, Mar
27, CG/LIF, Apr 11, GF, 21, DL, 22, GF, May 3, RI, Jun 28, GF, Sep 12, CG,
Nov 29, GF, Dec 6; 1736: GF, Feb 10, CG, 16, May 4, LIF, Oct 12, CG, Nov 11,
LIF, Dec 11; 1737: LIF, Jan 5, Feb 25, May 5, CG, 20; 1738: CG, Jan 9, Mar
14, May 12, Oct 13, Dec 16; 1739: CG, Feb 17, DL, Mar 22, CG, Apr 7, Sep 28,
Nov 13, DL, 21; 1740: CG, Jan 29, DL, Apr 9, CG, Nov 1, GF, 13, CG, 21, 22,
24, 25, 26, 27, 28, 29, Dec 1, 2, 9, 20, 29; 1741: CG, Jan 9, 24, GF, Mar 5,
CG, Apr 3, GF, May 7, DL, Sep 8, GF, 14, CG, Nov 7, GF, Dec 22; 1742: DL, Jan
4, 5, 7, 11, 13, 14, 18, 21, GF, Feb 1, Mar 4, DL, Oct 12, Nov 17, Dec 18;
1743: JS, Feb 22, DL, Mar 17, 19, LIF, 22, DL, 26, LIF, Apr 13, DL, Oct 13,

Nov 1, 19, Dec 14; <u>1744</u>: DL, Jan 4, Feb 2, May 9, Sep 18, Nov 8, Dec 5; <u>1745</u>:
DL, Jan 17, GF, Feb 26, Apr 24, DL, May 10, Nov 1, 2, Dec 7, 28; <u>1746</u>: GF,
Feb 27, DL, Mar 3, Apr 28, Oct 2, Dec 12; <u>1747</u>: JS, Feb 3, GF, 5, DL, 18, GF,
24, Mar 24, HAY, May 28, DL, Oct 24, Nov 21, 23; <u>1748</u>: DL, Jan 28, Apr 14,
SOU, Aug 1; <u>1749</u>: CG, Mar 4, 30, Apr 19, 26, Nov 21, 22, DL, Dec 12, 13, CG,
30; <u>1750</u>: CG, Jan 2, DL, May 2, CG, 10, Oct 13, Nov 17; <u>1751</u>: CG, Jan 16, DL,
26, CG, Apr 29; <u>1752</u>: DL, Apr 3; <u>1753</u>: DL, Apr 25, Nov 1; <u>1754</u>: DL, May 22,
CG, Nov 1, 13, Dec 7; <u>1755</u>: CG, Jan 20, 22, Mar 17, May 22, Oct 16, Nov 20,
27; <u>1756</u>: CG, Jan 27, Feb 18, Mar 15, Apr 23, May 26, Oct 22, Dec 2; <u>1757</u>:
CG, Jan 13, Mar 29; <u>1759</u>: CG, Mar 27, May 18, Sep 28; <u>1761</u>: CG, Apr 1; <u>1762</u>:
DL, Apr 1, 21, May 12, Oct 25, Nov 29; <u>1763</u>: CG, Apr 15, DL, May 18, Oct 14;
<u>1764</u>: DL, Feb 23; <u>1766</u>: DL, Jan 29; <u>1771</u>: DL, Mar 12, 23; <u>1772</u>: DL, Mar 21,
Apr 23; <u>1776</u>: DL, May 8; <u>1779</u>: DL, Apr 16; <u>1782</u>: HAY, Jan 14; <u>1785</u>: CG, Mar
29, Sep 28, Dec 23, 31; <u>1786</u>: CG, May 18; <u>1788</u>: DL, Mar 31, May 2, 16, 31,
Jun 13, Sep 18, 25, Oct 13, 27, Nov 26, Dec 19; <u>1789</u>: DL, Jan 5, 14, Feb 13,
Mar 2, 23, May 4, 20, 29, HAY, Jul 30, Aug 3, Sep 1, 11, CG, 30, DL, Oct 8,
CG, 9, 30, DL, Nov 20; <u>1790</u>: DL, Feb 12, Mar 16, Oct 4, Dec 10; <u>1792</u>:
DLKING'S, Jun 13; <u>1793</u>: HAY, Nov 5, Dec 5, 17; <u>1794</u>: HAY, Jan 1; <u>1795</u>: DL,
May 29
--Inconstant, The; or, The Way to Win Him, <u>1699</u>: DL, Nov 28; <u>1702</u>: DL, Feb 0;
<u>1716</u>: LIF, Dec 18, 19, 31; <u>1723</u>: DL, Oct 16, 17, Nov 13; <u>1729</u>: GF, Dec 3, 18;
<u>1730</u>: GF, Jan 6, HAY, Nov 13, GF, Dec 7; <u>1731</u>: GF, Jan 4, Mar 1, 2, Nov 22;
<u>1732</u>: GF, May 15, Oct 14; <u>1733</u>: GF, Oct 25; <u>1734</u>: GF, Mar 28, Oct 14; <u>1735</u>:
GF, Feb 1, May 5, HAY, Dec 17; <u>1736</u>: HAY, Feb 19, CG, Apr 6, May 11, GF, 13,
LIF, Nov 9, 11; <u>1737</u>: LIF, Jan 20; <u>1739</u>: DL, Apr 10, 14; <u>1740</u>: GF, Nov 19;
<u>1742</u>: GF, Mar 22, Apr 29; <u>1744</u>: DL, Oct 11, Dec 7, 21; <u>1745</u>: DL, Nov 18;
<u>1751</u>: DL, Mar 12, 19, HAY, Nov 21, DL, Dec 14; <u>1752</u>: DL, Mar 21; <u>1753</u>: DL,
Apr 3, CG, Nov 26, 27, Dec 1; <u>1754</u>: DL, Feb 1, 4, 7, 16, Mar 14, May 13, Sep
17, CG, Oct 15, DL, Dec 10; <u>1755</u>: DL, Jan 7, CG, 31, DL, Apr 24, CG, Oct 31,
DL, Nov 12; <u>1756</u>: CG, Dec 1; <u>1757</u>: DL, Jan 3, CG, 26, DL, May 5, CG, Oct 28,
Dec 13; <u>1758</u>: DL, Feb 20, Apr 27, 29; <u>1759</u>: CG, Mar 5; <u>1761</u>: DL, Mar 26;
<u>1763</u>: CG, Feb 1, 9, Mar 3, May 16, 25, Sep 28, Oct 25, Dec 10; <u>1764</u>: CG, Feb
3, DL, 25, CG, Oct 11, Nov 20; <u>1765</u>: CG, May 9, Oct 17, Dec 21; <u>1766</u>: CG, Dec
23; <u>1768</u>: CG, May 27, Dec 22; <u>1769</u>: CG, Jan 25, Oct 5; <u>1770</u>: CG, May 19;
<u>1771</u>: CG, Dec 6; <u>1772</u>: CG, Feb 25, May 29, Nov 12; <u>1773</u>: CG, May 25, Dec 18;
<u>1774</u>: CG, Jan 18, May 14; <u>1779</u>: CG, Nov 4; <u>1780</u>: DL, Apr 3, 25; <u>1787</u>: CG, Dec
10, 14; <u>1789</u>: DL, Nov 5, 13, 20; <u>1790</u>: DL, Jan 13, 27, May 20, Nov 4; <u>1791</u>:
DLKING'S, Nov 11, 16, Dec 15, 29; <u>1792</u>: DLKING'S, Feb 8, DL, Sep 29, Nov 20,
Dec 6, 19; <u>1794</u>: DL, Apr 28, 29, Jun 9; <u>1795</u>: DL, Jan 19, 20, Feb 13; <u>1796</u>:
DL, Feb 29, Mar 31; <u>1797</u>: DL, Apr 6; <u>1798</u>: DL, May 7; <u>1799</u>: DL, Apr 27, May
18; <u>1800</u>: DL, May 12, Jun 7
--Love and a Bottle, <u>1698</u>: DL, Dec 0; <u>1712</u>: DL, Jul 22, 25; <u>1724</u>: HAY, Feb 27,
LIF, Jun 23, 26, 30, Jul 29, Aug 20, Nov 25; <u>1725</u>: LIF, Apr 22, May 24, Dec
3; <u>1728</u>: LIF, Apr 6, May 22; <u>1733</u>: LIF/CG, Mar 30; <u>1735</u>: NONE, Sep 11, HAY,
29, Oct 24; <u>1738</u>: CG, Aug 29; <u>1740</u>: GF, Dec 12, 15, 16; <u>1781</u>: HAY, Mar 26
--Recruiting Officer, The, <u>1706</u>: DL, Apr 8, 9, 10, 12, 13, 15, 17, 20, Jun 6,
11, 20, DG, Oct 24, Nov 1, QUEEN'S, 14, 18, DL, 30, QUEEN'S, 30, DL, Dec 7,
QUEEN'S, 19, 28; <u>1707</u>: DL, Jan 2, 16, QUEEN'S, Feb 10, DL, 20, QUEEN'S, 24,
DL, Mar 3, 6, QUEEN'S, 8, 11, 13, DL, 17, 27, QUEEN'S, 31, Apr 5, 17, DL, 17,
May 29, QUEEN'S, Jun 5, Oct 13, DL, 18, 21, Nov 1, 26, Dec 19, DL/QUEEN, 31;
<u>1708</u>: DL, Jan 16, DL/QUEEN, Apr 6, DL, Sep 7; <u>1709</u>: DL, Jan 5, Feb 24, Mar 7,
Apr 12, May 6, 25, Sep 6, QUEEN'S, 22, Oct 24, Dec 7, DL, 15, QUEEN'S, 29;
<u>1710</u>: QUEEN'S, Mar 16, DL, May 10, QUEEN'S, Jul 13, GR, 27, DL/QUEEN, Oct 4,
Dec 29; <u>1711</u>: DL/QUEEN, Feb 5, Mar 24, DL, Apr 3, GR, Jul 23, 28, DL, Sep 25;
<u>1712</u>: DL, Feb 2, Jun 10, SML, Jul 9, DL, Sep 30, Nov 14; <u>1713</u>: DL, Jan 12,
Oct 26; <u>1714</u>: DL, Jan 4, Sep 21, Dec 14, LIF, 18, 20, 31; <u>1715</u>: DL, Jan 26,
LIF, Feb 24, Apr 28, Jun 1, Aug 10, Oct 10, Nov 14; <u>1716</u>: DL, Jan 11, LIF,
Feb 2, Apr 20, Oct 15; <u>1717</u>: DL, Jan 2, LIF, Feb 8, DL, May 29, LIF, Jun 5,
SF, Sep 25, LIF, Oct 14, DL, Nov 18, LIF, Dec 6; <u>1718</u>: LIF, May 27, DL, 29,
AC, Sep 24, LIF, 29, DL, Oct 20; <u>1719</u>: DL, Jan 2, Sep 22, LIF, Nov 18, Dec 8;
<u>1720</u>: DL, Feb 8, LIF, May 10, DL, 21, Sep 20, BCA, 23, LIF, Oct 18, DL, Nov
14; <u>1721</u>: LIF, Feb 8, DL, Mar 21, LIF, May 23, Oct 12, DL, 24; <u>1722</u>: DL, May
3, LIF, 8, Jun 27, Jul 19, SOU, Sep 26, LIF, Oct 2, DL, Dec 4; <u>1723</u>: LIF, Feb
15, DL, Mar 18, HAY, Apr 15, LIF, May 22, Oct 25; <u>1724</u>: LIF, Jan 17, Feb 17,
DL, Mar 10, LIF, Apr 11, DL, May 16, LIF, Jun 1, Sep 30, DL, Nov 20; <u>1725</u>:
LIF, Jan 25, DL, Mar 2, LIF, May 5, DL, 21, LIF, Oct 13, Dec 13, DL, 13;
<u>1726</u>: LIF, Jan 20, DL, Feb 16, LIF, Mar 28, May 12, DL, 19, LIF, Sep 14;
<u>1727</u>: LIF, Feb 3, DL, 8, LIF, Mar 11, May 10, Sep 27, Dec 15; <u>1728</u>: DL, Jan
2, May 7, LIF, 8, DL, Nov 12, Dec 27; <u>1729</u>: HAY, Jan 31, Mar 28, LIF, Apr 15,
DL, May 16, LIF, 22, SOU, Sep 23, LIF, Oct 8, GF, 31, Nov 1, DL, 24, GF, Dec
9; <u>1730</u>: LIF, Jan 22, GF, Feb 7, LIF, Mar 12, 17, GF, Apr 8, LIF, May 1, GF,
19, HAY, Jun 4, GF, 29, Jul 24, Sep 18, LIF, Oct 2, SOU, 8, RI, 27, DL, Nov

6, GF, 19, LIF, Dec 10, GF, 16; <u>1731</u>: LIF, Feb 16, Mar 15, GF, 20, LIF, May
1, GF, 15, HC, Oct 18, DL, 19, GF, Nov 6, LIF, Dec 4; <u>1732</u>: GF, Feb 9, HAY,
Mar 31, Apr 6, LIF, 27, HAY, 27, LIF/CG, Sep 25, GF, Oct 7, 31, Nov 15, SOU,
Dec 26, LIF/CG, 28; <u>1733</u>: HAY, Feb 21, Mar 14, LIF/CG, Apr 11, HAY, 18, GF,
May 4, CHE, Jun 4, CG, Oct 4, GF, 12, DL, 31, DL/HAY, Nov 1; <u>1734</u>: DL/HAY,
Jan 11, GF, Feb 2, CG, Mar 4, GF, Apr 4, Sep 27, LIF, Oct 12, CG/LIF, Dec 5,
DL, 14, GF, 31; <u>1735</u>: GF, Jan 7, 25, LIF, Mar 3, SOU, Apr 7, GF, 8, CG, Oct
13, DL, 30, GF, Nov 24, HAY, Dec 13; <u>1736</u>: DL, Feb 7, GF, 25, CG, Mar 22,
LIF, Apr 19, CG, May 20, Sep 24, LIF, Nov 13, DL, 20, LIF, Dec 16, DL, 22;
<u>1737</u>: LIF, Jan 19, HAY, Feb 17, DL, May 26, 31, LIF, Jun 15; <u>1738</u>: CG, Apr
22, Oct 2, Dec 18; <u>1739</u>: CG, Apr 24, Sep 7, Dec 13, DL, 22; <u>1740</u>: DL, Jan 11,
CG, Feb 2, DL, Apr 10, CG, May 19, DL, 29, Sep 23, GF, Oct 22, CG, Nov 6, 8,
10, 11, 19, GF, 29, CG, Dec 30; <u>1741</u>: CG, Feb 14, Apr 10, GF, 16, CG, May 11,
DL, Sep 8, CG, 21, JS, 29, GF, Oct 12, DL, 22, Dec 5, 15, CG, 16; <u>1742</u>: GF,
Jan 1, 14, CG, 14, DL, Feb 2, 8, Mar 1, CG, 30, GF, Apr 6, DL, 26, May 10,
CG, 18, DL, Oct 2, 19, 29, LIF, Dec 13, 15, DL, 15, LIF, 17, 20, 22; <u>1743</u>:
DL, Jan 24, LIF, Mar 21, SOU, 30, DL, Apr 23, JS, 25, DL, May 5, Sep 15, Nov
3, 22, Dec 7; <u>1744</u>: DL, Jan 17, Feb 6, Apr 6, 19, HAY, 23, DL, May 23, MF,
Jun 8, HAY, Sep 27, DL, Oct 9, Nov 12, GF, 26, 30, DL, Dec 18, GF, 26; <u>1745</u>:
DL, Jan 21, SMMF, Feb 11, DL, Apr 4, 29, GF, 29, CG, May 13, SMMF, Jul 11,
DL, Sep 26, GF, Nov 5, DL, 7, CG, Dec 5, DL, 5, 9; <u>1746</u>: GF, Jan 2, DL, Feb
6, GF, 17, Mar 17, HAY, Apr 30, CG, May 6, DL, Jun 11, CG, Oct 6, NWC, 20,
GF, 28, SOU, Nov 3, DL, 21, GF, 27; <u>1747</u>: CG, Jan 28, GF, Feb 3, CG, May 22,
SMMF, Jul 20, SF, Sep 16, CG, Nov 13, DL, 16, Dec 2; <u>1748</u>: CG, Feb 13, Mar
18, DL, 28, CG, 31, NWC, Apr 4, CG, Sep 23, DL, Nov 1; <u>1749</u>: CG, Jan 3, SOU,
9, JS, Mar 27, SOU, Sep 28, BHB, Oct 10, 14, CG, Nov 1, Dec 5; <u>1750</u>: HAY, Feb
2, 9, Apr 9, CG, May 1, DL, Nov 3, Dec 28; <u>1751</u>: DL, Jan 23, Feb 14, Apr 9,
May 8, SF, Sep 19, CG, 23; <u>1752</u>: CG, Feb 18, Apr 7, DL, 20, 27, SOU, Sep 29,
CG, Oct 9, NWLS, Nov 30, DL, Dec 29; <u>1753</u>: CG, Feb 2, May 21, DL, Oct 9, CG,
31, DL, Dec 11; <u>1754</u>: DL, Jan 19, Feb 5, 13, CG, May 4, DL, Sep 26, 28, Oct
17, Dec 5, CG, 13; <u>1755</u>: CG, Feb 3, DL, Apr 29, HAY, Sep 9, DL, 13, CG, Nov
13, Dec 16; <u>1756</u>: CG, Feb 10, 23, Apr 1, 24, DL, May 17, CG, Dec 7, DL, 27;
<u>1757</u>: CG, Apr 26, DL, May 19, Oct 8, CG, Nov 2; <u>1758</u>: DL, May 16, Oct 3, 5,
Nov 27; <u>1759</u>: DL, Feb 12, CG, Apr 28, DL, May 15, Sep 22; <u>1760</u>: DL, May 21,
CG, Oct 25; <u>1761</u>: CG, May 8, Nov 2; <u>1762</u>: CG, Mar 9, May 19, Oct 21, Nov 6,
Dec 22; <u>1763</u>: CG, Feb 3, May 14, Sep 23, Nov 7; <u>1764</u>: DL, Jan 13, 20, CG, 27,
May 5, Oct 5, Dec 20; <u>1765</u>: DL, May 18, CG, Oct 2, 29; <u>1766</u>: CG, Nov 25;
<u>1767</u>: CG, Jan 3, Mar 19, Nov 6, DL, 26, Dec 2; <u>1768</u>: CG, Jan 7, May 28, Oct
6, 27; <u>1769</u>: CG, May 6, Sep 30, Nov 14; <u>1770</u>: CG, Nov 23; <u>1771</u>: CG, Jan 19,
DL, Nov 2, CG, 28, Dec 9; <u>1772</u>: CG, Feb 5, Oct 30; <u>1773</u>: CG, Jan 22, Feb 17,
Dec 7; <u>1774</u>: CG, May 24; <u>1775</u>: DL, Apr 21, May 16; <u>1776</u>: DL, Apr 24, CG, Sep
23, CHR, Oct 18; <u>1777</u>: CG, May 24, Sep 22, Dec 9; <u>1778</u>: CG, Oct 14, 15; <u>1781</u>:
CII, Mar 15, DL, Apr 18; <u>1783</u>: CG, Sep 19; <u>1785</u>: DL, May 3; <u>1786</u>: DL, Jun 1;
<u>1788</u>: CG, Jan 29, Feb 19, 28, Mar 27, Sep 19, Nov 14; <u>1789</u>: CG, Jan 5, Jun 9;
<u>1790</u>: CG, Feb 25, May 29, Oct 8, Dec 27; <u>1791</u>: DL, Apr 27, May 18, CG, Jun
10, DLKING'S, Nov 8; <u>1792</u>: CG, Nov 14, 16; <u>1793</u>: CG, Apr 11, DL, Jun 1, HAY,
Nov 16, 20, 30, Dec 7, 17; <u>1794</u>: HAY, Jan 2, 11, Feb 5, Mar 17; <u>1795</u>: HAY,
Jul 22, Aug 14, DL, Nov 26; <u>1796</u>: DL, Jan 2, CG, May 21, HAY, Jul 26; <u>1797</u>:
DL, Jun 7, HAY, Jul 3; <u>1798</u>: CG, Oct 5
--Sir Harry Wildair, <u>1701</u>: DL, Apr 0, May 2, 3, 28; <u>1737</u>: LIF, Feb 1, 2, 3, 4,
Mar 15
--Stage Coach, The, <u>1704</u>: LIF, Feb 2, Apr 29, Oct 16; <u>1705</u>: QUEEN'S, Nov 16;
<u>1707</u>: QUEEN'S, Apr 14, May 26; <u>1709</u>: DL, May 17, 19, 24, 31, Jun 1, QUEEN'S,
Oct 1, 4, 8, Nov 5, Dec 5, DL, 8, QUEEN'S, 26; <u>1710</u>: DL, Feb 9, QUEEN'S, Apr
11, Jul 21, GR, Sep 23, DL/QUEEN, Oct 7; <u>1711</u>: DL, May 10, Jun 26, Jul 20;
<u>1712</u>: DL, May 3, 13, Jun 17, Aug 5, Oct 24; <u>1713</u>: DL, Jan 28, Jun 1, 19, Dec
7; <u>1714</u>: DL, Jan 18, Oct 19, Dec 10; <u>1715</u>: LIF, Jan 6, SH, Mar 1, LIF, Nov 3,
8; <u>1716</u>: DL, Jul 5, Aug 14, 21, Oct 23, 30; <u>1717</u>: DL, May 23, Jun 3, Aug 13,
16, 20, 23, LIF, Nov 23; <u>1718</u>: LIF, Feb 24, DL, May 13, Jul 8, RI, 19, DL,
22, RI, 28, DL, Aug 22; <u>1719</u>: DL, May 19, LIF, 19, DL, Jul 28, Aug 11, RI,
Sep 5, LIF, Nov 25; <u>1720</u>: LIF, Mar 26, DL, Apr 29, May 20, 25, Jun 14, Aug 2,
20, Dec 7; <u>1721</u>: DL, Jun 27; <u>1722</u>: DL, May 25; <u>1723</u>: HAY, Jan 10, DL, May 3,
29, Jun 28, HA, Jul 8, 9, DL, 12; <u>1724</u>: DL, Feb 6, May 14, 20, RI, Aug 3, DL,
Oct 19; <u>1725</u>: DL, May 14, 21; <u>1726</u>: DL, Apr 23, May 7, 12, 20; <u>1727</u>: DL, Apr
24, May 15; <u>1728</u>: DL, Apr 22; <u>1729</u>: DL, Apr 14; <u>1730</u>: DL, Jan 8, GF, Jul 17;
<u>1731</u>: GF, Feb 22, 23, 24, 27, Mar 6, 11, 16, 23, 30, Apr 6, 19, 28; <u>1732</u>: GF,
Apr 27, May 3, 5; <u>1733</u>: LIF/CG, Mar 29, 31, Apr 20, 24, CG, May 2; <u>1734</u>: GF,
May 7, 20, RI, Sep 2; <u>1736</u>: LIF, Apr 29; <u>1739</u>: CG, Apr 3, 26, May 14, 23, 29;
<u>1740</u>: CG, Mar 24, May 2, 13; <u>1744</u>: GF, Dec 22; <u>1745</u>: GF, Jan 2, 3, 4, 15, 16,
17, Feb 7, 8, 9, Nov 5, 7, DL, Dec 30, 31; <u>1746</u>: DL, Jan 1, 13, 15, 16, GF,
24, DL, 24, 28, GF, 29, DL, Feb 8, 13, GF, Nov 19, 20, 21, 24, 25; <u>1747</u>: DL,
Mar 3; <u>1750</u>: CG, Mar 17, 20, May 4, Nov 6; <u>1751</u>: CG, Jan 4, Feb 18; <u>1764</u>: DL,

May 11; 1787: CG, Apr 16
--Twin Rivals, The, 1702: DL, Dec 14; 1716: LIF, Nov 3, 5, 6, 7, 16, Dec 11,
15; 1717: LIF, Jan 21, Mar 14, Apr 6, May 23, Oct 22, Nov 6; 1718: LIF, Jan
15, Apr 29; 1719: LIF, Apr 27, Oct 15, Nov 20; 1720: LIF, May 24, Nov 22;
1721: LIF, Jan 18; 1725: DL, Nov 29, 30, Dec 1, 2, 17; 1726: DL, Jan 20, Apr
19, Dec 12; 1735: GF/HAY, Jul 22, 25, 29, Aug 21; 1736: DL, Jan 3, 5, 6, 7,
9, HAY, 14, DL, Feb 2, 3, Apr 5, May 25, Nov 15; 1737: HAY, Feb 9, DL, 16,
Apr 2, May 11; 1738: DL, Apr 17, Oct 18, Nov 18, Dec 21; 1739: DL, Jan 9, CG,
Apr 12, 30, DL, May 8, 18, Sep 22, Dec 21; 1740: DL, Jan 28, CG, May 5, DL,
Nov 13; 1741: DL, Apr 1, CG, May 1, DL, Oct 21, Dec 17; 1742: JS, May 3;
1743: DL, Jan 28, May 24, Nov 23; 1745: DL, Jan 4, GF, Feb 28, Mar 2, Apr 20,
Nov 11; 1746: CG, Jan 2, 3, DL, 14, CG, Mar 11, DL, Nov 5, GF, 19; 1747: CG,
Jan 29, Feb 5, May 16; 1749: CG, Nov 23, Dec 11; 1750: CG, Jan 25, Feb 12,
Dec 14; 1752: CG, Apr 30; 1753: CG, Jan 2, Feb 12, Nov 1; 1755: CG, Jan 4,
29; 1757: CG, Feb 9, 15, 17, May 6, Oct 14, Nov 10, Dec 8; 1758: DL, Oct 18,
20, CG, Nov 13; 1759: CG, Mar 13, Oct 5, 8, Dec 27; 1769: CG, Dec 1, 28;
1770: CG, Jan 4, Feb 2, May 19, Oct 11; 1771: DL, Apr 5; 1778: CG, Oct 21,
Nov 6, 13; 1779: CG, Nov 16
Farquhar, George, children of, 1717: DL, May 29
Farquhar, Miss (actor), 1750: DL, Dec 19; 1756: HAY, Jun 8; 1757: DL, May 13;
1758: DL, Dec 23
Farr (actor), 1685: DL, Aug 0
Farrell (actor), 1781: CII, Mar 27, 30, Apr 5, 9; 1783: HAY, Dec 15; 1784: HAY,
Mar 8
Farrell, Margaret (actor), 1771: HAY, Jun 5, Sep 2; 1773: CG, Nov 5; 1775: HAY,
May 1; 1776: HAY, Feb 22, CG, Mar 16, Dec 6, 27; 1777: CG, Jan 7, 25, Feb 25,
28, Mar 14, 17, 19, May 5, 13, 14, 29, Oct 17, 30, Nov 18, Dec 3, 19; 1778:
CG, Jan 8, 31, DL, Mar 6, 18, 27, Apr 1, CG, 25, May 1, 9, 11, DL, Sep 17,
CG, 18, Oct 2, 16, 17, 22, Nov 4, 23; 1779: CG, Jan 4, 22, 26, 27, DL, Apr 6
Farrell, Thomas (actor), 1769: HAY, May 15, 22, 24, 26, 29, Jun 5, Jul 12, Sep
1, 6, 11, 19; 1770: HAY, May 16, 18, 23, 30, Jun 18, 22, 25, 27, Jul 9, 20,
25, Aug 1, 8, 22, 24, 31, Sep 13, 20, Oct 1; 1771: HAY, May 15, 17, 20, 22,
23, 27, 29, 31, Jun 5, 7, 10, 14, 21, Jul 1, 3, 5, 10, 24, Aug 28, Sep 18;
1772: HAY, May 18, 27, Jun 1, 5, 8, 15, 29, Jul 3, 10, Aug 10, Sep 17, 18
Farren, Elizabeth (actor), Jun 9, 30, Aug 12, 18, 30, Sep 16; 1778: HAY, Jun
11, Jul 1, 11, Aug 21, Sep 2, 16, 18, CG, 23, 30, DL, Oct 8, CG, 9, DL, 15,
CG, 22, DL, 31, Dec 21; 1779: DL, Feb 3, 20, Mar 13, Apr 9, 21, 28, May 1, 6,
10, 21, HAY, Jun 2, 10, Aug 17, 18, 31, Sep 16, DL, 30, Oct 12, 16, Nov 5,
CG, 6, DL, 9, 17, 18, 22, 29, Dec 2; 1780: DL, Jan 26, Feb 22, Mar 4, Apr 3,
5, May 20, 24, HAY, 30, Jun 13, 23, 24, Aug 5, 22, 24, 25, Sep 5, DL, 19, 21,
Oct 12, 19, 20, 28, 31, Nov 2, 17, 22, Dec 7, 19, 27; 1781: DL, Jan 3, Feb
17, Mar 28, Apr 17, 23, 24, May 1, 5, 8, 9, CG, 12, DL, 17, HAY, 30, Jun 4,
5, 7, Jul 18, Aug 21, 24, Sep 12, DL, Oct 2, 6, 13, 18, 19, 25, 26, 27, 29,
Nov 6, 7, 10, 27; 1782: DL, Jan 19, 26, Feb 25, Mar 21, Apr 8, 15, 23, 24,
25, May 7, 8, 10, 11, 14, Sep 18, 19, 20, 21, 24, 26, Oct 1, 5, 8, 14, 18,
29, Nov 2, 7, 12, 26, Dec 5, 7, 19; 1783: DL, Jan 3, 10, 15, 24, 29, Mar 20,
Apr 28, 29, May 5, 12, Sep 16, 20, Oct 7, 18, 22, Nov 12, 13, 20, 21, 27, 28,
Dec 2, 19; 1784: DL, Jan 10, 17, 28, Feb 3, 14, Apr 19, 21, May 5, 17, HAY,
29, Jun 2, Jul 8, 20, Aug 19, Sep 2, DL, 16, 18, 23, 28, Oct 11, 18, 26, 28,
Nov 4, 11, 22, 25, Dec 3, 10, 22, 28; 1785: DL, Jan 20, 22, Mar 19, Apr 11,
18, 20, 25, May 6, 11, 24, HAY, Jun 4, 6, 7, 17, Jul 26, Aug 4, Sep 2, DL,
20, 27, Oct 4, 6, 26, 31, Nov 3, 5, 26, Dec 2, 5, 7, 29; 1786: DL, Jan 4, 9,
10, 14, Apr 1, 26, May 10, 17, 25, HAY, Jun 13, 15, 16, 21, 23, Jul 3, 13,
24, Aug 17, 29, DL, Sep 16, 26, 28, 30, Oct 7, 12, 24, 25, 26, 27, 28, Nov
14, 25, Dec 11, 21, 29; 1787: DL, Jan 18, 24, Mar 12, 24, 26, 29, May 21, 23,
HAY, Jun 11, 14, 18, 22, 23, 28, Jul 4, 7, Aug 17, 21, DL, Sep 20, Oct 2, 13,
15, 20, 24, Nov 6, 10, 29, Dec 6, 7, 28; 1788: DL, Jan 2, 16, 25, Mar 26, Apr
21, 28, 30, May 1, 6, 7, 14, 21, 22, HAY, Jun 12, 17, 19, Jul 14, Aug 9, 13,
25, 29, DL, Sep 13, 23, 25, 27, Oct 9, 11, 20, Nov 5, 8, 12, 19, Dec 18;
1789: DL, Jan 1, 13, Apr 20, May 1, 27, Sep 15, 22, 26, 29, Oct 3, 10, 13,
20, 21, 24, 28, Nov 3, 5, 7, 27, Dec 2; 1790: DL, Jan 1, Feb 15, Mar 2, Apr
14, 17, May 14, 18, Sep 16, Oct 9, 11, 12, 16, 18, 20, Nov 1, 2, 4, 5, 10,
Dec 1; 1791: DL, Jan 17, Apr 28, May 5, 10, 20, Jun 4, DLKING'S, Sep 27, Oct
1, 4, 10, 13, 20, 25, Nov 5, 9, 11, 29, Dec 1, 6; 1792: DLKING'S, Jan 18, Apr
10, 20, DL, Sep 15, 20, 22, 29, Oct 13, 15, 16, 20, 27, 31, Nov 2, Dec 7;
1793: DL, Jan 2, 16, Feb 14, Mar 14, Apr 3, 17, 22, 25, May 1; 1794: DL, Apr
21, 25, 29, May 1, 3, 6, 7, 8, 9, 17, Jun 2, 10, 14, 17, Nov 5, 6, 7, 12, 20,
27, Dec 5, 10, 19; 1795: DL, Jan 16, 20, 23, 24, Feb 3, 9, 12, 28, Apr 17,
24, May 12, Jun 4, Sep 17, 22, CG, 25, DL, 26, Oct 3, 20, 22, 30, Nov 5, 10,
14, Dec 2, 9; 1796: DL, Jan 23, Feb 1, 29, Mar 12, 15, 29, Apr 26, May 12,
23, Jun 6, Sep 27, 29, Oct 4, 8, 10, 11, 15, 17, 28, Nov 1, 8, 22, 29, Dec 6,
20, 29; 1797: DL, Jan 10, 12, 14, 17, 27, Feb 1, 2, 7, 22, Apr 6, 8, 18, May

Farren, Mary (actor), 1778: DL, Nov 16, CG, Dec 7, DL, 14, 22; 1780: DL, Apr
22, Nov 17, Dec 2, 5; 1781: DL, Jan 26, Apr 3, 18; 1788: HAY, Jul 2; 1795:
CG, May 13
Farren, Peggy (actor), 1777: HAY, May 15, Jul 18
Farren, William (actor), 1768: CG, Oct 24; 1773: HAY, Sep 16, 18; 1774: HAY,
Jan 24; 1775: DL, Mar 20, Nov 4, 18, Dec 29; 1776: DL, Jan 9, 19, Mar 11, 16,
28, May 18, 22, Sep 24, 26, Oct 3, 10, 19, 26, 29, Nov 4, 6, 19, 25, 30, Dec
10, 14, 28; 1777: DL, Jan 1, 4, 28, Feb 17, Apr 7, 17, 28, May 8, 15, Sep 20,
23, 30, Oct 7, 9, 14, 17, 22, 31, Nov 4, 8, 14, 18, 27, 29, Dec 3, 15, 18;
1778: DL, Jan 2, 5, 24, Feb 2, 10, 24, Mar 31, Apr 23, May 4, Sep 17, 19, 22,
29, Oct 6, 15, CG, 16, DL, 28, Nov 7, 21, 28, CG, Dec 7, 8, DL, 15, 19, 22;
1779: CG, Jan 19, DL, 23, Feb 6, 8, 20, Mar 16, 25, Apr 5, CG, 6, DL, 28, May
1, 6, Sep 18, 21, CG, Oct 4, DL, 12, 30, Nov 11, 22, 24, Dec 20; 1780: DL,
Jan 11, 24, 26, Mar 4, Apr 3, 5, 6, 12, 22, May 10, Sep 16, 19, 21, 23, Oct
2, 3, 5, 10, 14, 23, 31, Nov 1, 3, 4, 9, 13, 27, Dec 4, 6, 7, 19; 1781: DL,
Jan 9, Feb 17, Mar 27, Apr 18, May 11, 17, Sep 18, 25, 27, 29, Oct 12, 16,
19, 26, 29, Nov 5, 6, 13, 27; 1782: DL, Jan 19, Mar 16, Apr 23, 30, May 7,
10, 29, Sep 24, 26, Oct 1, 3, 10, 18, 30, Nov 12, 16, 22, Dec 7, 26; 1783:
DL, Jan 3, Feb 18, 22, Mar 10, 17, 18, Apr 7, 21, 24, 29, May 5, Sep 23, 30,
Oct 7, 8, 14, 18, 20, 22, 24, Nov 13, 28, Dec 10, 12, 22, 29; 1784: DL, Jan
1, 3, 16, 17, 22, 23, Feb 14, Mar 6, Apr 12, 19, 24, 26, May 5, 21, CG, Sep
27, Oct 1, 4, 6, 11, 18, 30, Nov 4, 11, 29, Dec 3, 27; 1785: CG, Jan 21, DL,
Feb 2, CG, 4, 7, 15, 21, 28, Mar 7, 8, Apr 2, 8, 11, 12, 13, 22, May 4, 18,
HAY, Aug 4, CG, Sep 21, 23, 26, Oct 5, 12, 17, 28, 29, Nov 2, 7, Dec 1, 7, 9,
20, 26; 1786: CG, Jan 2, 4, 6, 18, 20, 28, Feb 4, 18, 23, Mar 6, 14, Apr 8,
18, 24, 26, May 3, 5, 13, 15, Sep 18, 20, 25, 27, 29, Oct 2, 4, 12, 21, 25,
26, Nov 15, 18, 22, 27, 29, Dec 4, 13, 18, 20, 27, 30; 1787: CG, Jan 4, 8,
15, 26, Feb 10, Mar 15, 26, 27, 31, Apr 11, 16, 25, 27, 30, May 23, Sep 17,
26, 28, Oct 1, 5, 10, 17, 19, 22, 31, Nov 5, 7, 9, 14, 19, 22, 28, 30, Dec 3,
5, 15, 27, 28; 1788: CG, Jan 2, 3, 9, 10, 11, 14, 21, Feb 4, 14, 25, Mar 15,
26, Apr 8, 23, May 12, Sep 17, 24, Oct 3, 8, 10, 15, 17, 18, 27, Nov 1, 10,
12, 28, Dec 19, 27, 29, 30, 31; 1789: CG, Jan 8, 10, 15, 20, 21, 28, Feb 21,
Mar 5, 28, Apr 15, 20, 28, May 8, 14, 19, 26, Jun 8, 16, Sep 16, 18, 25, 30,
Oct 6, 9, 12, Nov 2, 5, 6, 7, 10, 16, 27, 30, Dec 2, 5, 11, 14, 21, 26, 31;
1790: CG, Jan 13, 22, 23, 29, Feb 11, Mar 22, Apr 20, 27, May 5, 11, 18, 24,
Sep 15, 17, Oct 4, 6, 13, 15, 18, 23, 27, Nov 1, 4, 11, 23, Dec 6, 17, 28,
31; 1791: CG, Jan 3, 7, 12, Feb 4, 11, Apr 5, May 2, 10, 11, 18, 19, 27, HAY,
Jul 30, CG, Sep 16, 19, 21, 23, Oct 3, 7, 10, 13, 17, 20, 24, 27, 28, Nov 5,
24, 29, Dec 2, 3, 21, 26; 1792: CG, Feb 6, Mar 26, 31, Apr 10, 12, 18, May 2,
19, Sep 21, 24, 28, Oct 12, 15, 17, 24, 26, 29, Nov 3, 5, 7, 10, 12, 24, 28,
Dec 1, 20; 1793: CG, Jan 21, 29, Mar 4, Apr 8, 18, 24, May 8, 24, Sep 18, 20,
27, 30, Oct 1, 2, 4, 5, 8, 9, 10, 11, 14, 22, 23, 29, Nov 1, 18, Dec 5, 30;
1794: CG, Jan 3, 13, 14, Feb 18, 24, Mar 17, 25, Apr 12, May 6, 13, 14, 19,
30, Jun 5, 13, DL, 19, CG, Sep 15, 19, 22, 29, Oct 1, 6, 7, 14, 15, 20, 30,
Nov 8, 12, 22, Dec 31; 1795: CG, Jan 6, 24, 29, Feb 6, 21, Mar 28, Apr 6, 8,
23, 24, May 13
Farrer, Mrs (actor), 1788: HAY, Dec 22; 1789: HAY, Feb 23
Farrier Nicked, The; or, The Exalted Cuckold (pantomime), 1734: BFRLCH, Sep 2
Farringdon Ward, 1724: DT, Dec 2
Farrington and Scarr (mercers), 1767: CG, Feb 17; 1772: CG, Dec 3; 1773: CG,
Jan 15; 1774: CG, Jan 27, May 25
Fashion Displayed. See Burton, Philippina.
Fashionable Lady, The. See Ralph, James.
Fashionable Levities. See Macnally, Leonard.
Fashionable Love; or, The Happy British Tar (interlude, anon), 1778: HAY, Dec
28
Fashionable Lover, The. See Cumberland, Richard.
Fashionable Lover, The; or, Wit In Necessity (play, anon), 1706: DL, Apr 0
Fashionable Wife, The; or, The Female Gallant (play, anon), 1782: HAY, May 6
Fashions (musician), 1675: ATCOURT, Feb 15
Fast Asleep. See Birch, Samuel.
Fat Dolly (song), 1795: CG, May 1; 1796: CG, May 16; 1797: CG, May 2; 1798: CG,
Apr 24, Jun 6; 1799: CG, May 3; 1800: CG, Apr 15, May 15
Fat Farmer and his Family (dance), 1736: DL, Apr 6, 8
Fatal Constancy, The. See Jacob, Hilderbrand.
Fatal Contract, The. See Heminge, William.
Fatal Curiosity, The. See Lillo, George.
Fatal Discovery, The. See Home, John.
Fatal Discovery, The; or, Love in Ruins (play, anon), 1670: BRI/COUR, Dec 0;
1697: NONE, Sep 0; 1698: DL, Feb 0
Fatal Dowry, The. See Field, Nathan.

Fatal Extravagance, The. See Mitchell, Joseph; Hill, Aaron.
Fatal Falsehood. See Hewitt, John; More, Hannah.
Fatal Friendship. See Trotter, Catherine.
Fatal Interview, The. See Hull, Thomas.
Fatal Jealousy, The. See Payne, Henry Nevil.
Fatal Legacy, The. See Robe, Jane.
Fatal Love; or, The Degenerate Brother. See Wandesford, Sir Osborne Sidney.
Fatal Love; or, The Forced Inconstancy. See Settle, Elkanah.
Fatal Marriage, The. See Southerne, Thomas.
Fatal Mistake, A. See Haynes, Joseph.
Fatal Retirement, The. See Brown, Anthony.
Fatal Secret, The. See Theobald, Lewis.
Fatal Villainy, The. See Walker, Thomas.
Fatal Vision, The. See Hill, Aaron.
Fate of Capua, The. See Southerne, Thomas.
Fate of Sparta, The. See Cowley, Hannah.
Fate of Villainy, The; or, Virtue Triumphant (play), 1746: SFW, Sep 8
Father Girard the Sorcerer; or, The Amours of Harlequin and Miss Cadiere
    (farce, anon), 1732: GF, Feb 2, 3, 4, 5, 7, 8, 9, 12, 14, 15, 16
Father Mother and Suke (song), 1794: CG, May 26
Father of Heaven (song), 1751: KING'S, Apr 16; 1752: KING'S, Mar 24; 1797: CG,
    Mar 31
Father's Own Son. See Fletcher, John, Monsieur Thomas.
Fathers, The. See Fielding, Henry.
Fatouville, Nolant de, 1790: HAY, Jun 26
--Arlequin Empereur de la Lune; or, Harlequin Emperor in the Moon (farce),
    1719: KING'S, Mar 7, 10, 12; 1721: HAY, May 4; 1725: HAY, Apr 9, 28; 1735:
    HAY, Jan 27, 29, Feb 1, 3, GF/HAY, 13
--Arlequin Lawyer; ou, Grapignan (farce), 1719: LIF, Jan 20, Feb 5; 1721: HAY,
    Feb 13
--Arlequin Protee (farce), 1721: HAY, Apr 28; 1725: HAY, Jan 4; 1726: HAY, May
    2
--Colombine Avocat, Pour et Contre, 1718: LIF, Dec 3, 5; 1721: HAY, Jan 5
--Fille Scavante, La, 1725: HAY, Jan 29
--Precaution Inutile, La, 1790: HAY, Jun 26
Faucon, Le. See Lisle de la Drevetiere, L F.
Faulcon Court. See Lisle de la Drevetiere, L F.
Faulkener, Miss. See Falkner, Anna Maria.
Faulkner (Irish printer), 1767: HAY, Aug 25
Faulkner, Samuel (actor), 1796: DL, Dec 21; 1797: HAY, Feb 9; 1799: CG, Jun 12,
    HAY, Aug 22
Faulknor, Captain Robert (naval officer), 1795: CG, May 6
Faune Infidele (dance), 1793: KING'S, Apr 2, 6, 9, 20, 30
Faunes Vainques (dance), 1774: KING'S, May 12
Fausan (dancer), 1740: DL, Nov 29, Dec 1, 2, 13, 22, 23, 29, 30; 1741: DL, Jan
    2, 8, 16, 17, 20, 22, 24, 26, 27, 28, 31, Feb 3, 6, 9, 10, 12, 14, 17, 19,
    Mar 2, 3, 5, 9, 12, 16, 19, Apr 10, 11, 15, 21, 23, 25, May 11, 18, 20, TC,
    Aug 4, DL, Nov 28, Dec 14, 18, 21; 1742: DL, Feb 1, Mar 13
Fausan, Sg and Sga (dancers), 1741: DL, Oct 21, 27, 30, Nov 3, 10, Dec 18, 22;
    1742: DL, Jan 6, 23, 25, Feb 1, 8, 12, 24, Mar 4, 13, 29; 1743: HAY, Mar 23
Fausan, Sga (dancer), 1740: DL, Nov 29, Dec 1, 2, 13, 22, 23, 29, 30; 1741: DL,
    Jan 2, 8, 16, 17, 20, 22, 24, 26, 27, 28, 31, Feb 3, 6, 9, 10, 12, 14, 17,
    19, Mar 2, 3, 5, 9, 12, 16, 19, Apr 10, 11, 15, 21, 23, 25, 29, 30, May 11,
    18, 20, TC, Aug 4, DL, Nov 28, Dec 14, 18, 21; 1742: DL, Feb 24
Fausse Coquette, La. See Biancolelli, Louis.
Fausse Inconstance, La. See Beauharnais, Fanny de.
Fausse Suivante, La. See Marivaux, Pierre Carlet de Chamblain de.
Faustina, Sga (singer), 1724: HAY, Mar 18; 1725: LIF, Mar 18; 1726: KING'S, May
    5; 1727: KING'S, Jan 7, Mar 7, 18, Apr 15, Jun 6, Jul 0, CR, Nov 22; 1728:
    KING'S, Feb 17, Jun 11; 1729: HIC, Apr 16; 1747: KING'S, Nov 12; 1754:
    KING'S, Mar 12; see also Bardoni, Faustina
Faustina's Answer to Senesino's Epistle (poem), 1727: KING'S, Mar 18
Faux (composer), 1731: ACA, Jan 14
Faux, John (doorkeeper), 1793: DL, Jun 6; 1795: DL, Jun 5; 1796: DL, Jun 15;
    1797: DL, Jun 13; 1798: DL, Jun 9; 1799: DL, Jul 2; 1800: DL, Jun 13
Favart, Charles Simon, 1764: DL, Nov 28; 1778: HAY, Aug 3, CG, Oct 2; 1782: CG,
    Dec 31; 1784: KING'S, Feb 26; 1786: CG, Mar 18
--Amitie a l'Epreuve, L' (with Claude Henri de Fusee de Voisenon), 1786: CG,
    Mar 18
--Caprice Amoureux, Le, 1764: DL, Nov 28
--Chercheuse D'esprit, La, 1749: HAY, Nov 17
--Coq du Village, Le, 1749: HAY, Nov 14, 15

293

--Coquette sans la Savoir, La, <u>1749</u>: HAY, Nov 20
--Moissonneurs, Les, <u>1782</u>: CG, Dec 31
Favier (musician), <u>1674</u>: ATCOURT, Feb 0
Favier, Mimi (dancer), <u>1773</u>: KING'S, Oct 23, Nov 30, Dec 7; <u>1774</u>: KING'S, Jan
  29, Feb 17, Mar 8, Apr 14, 19, 28, May 12
Favier, Mimi and Nina (dancers), <u>1773</u>: KING'S, Nov 15, 20
Favier, Nina (dancer), <u>1773</u>: KING'S, Oct 23, Nov 30; <u>1774</u>: KING'S, Jan 29, Feb
  5, 12, 17, Mar 8, 12, 26, Apr 9, 14, 19, 23, 28, May 5, 12, 31, Jun 3
Fawcett, John Jr (actor, singer, author), <u>1791</u>: CG, Sep 21, 28, 30, Oct 13, Nov
  2, 25, Dec 2, 3, 21; <u>1792</u>: CG, Feb 2, 6, 18, Mar 6, 26, 31, Apr 10, 18, 21,
  May 11, 15, 16, 28, 30, Sep 17, 26, Oct 17, 24, 26, 27, Nov 3, 14, Dec 20,
  26; <u>1793</u>: CG, Jan 29, Feb 11, 12, 14, 25, Mar 5, Apr 4, 8, 18, 24, May 3, 15,
  Jun 12, Sep 16, 18, 23, 25, 30, Oct 2, 8, 11, 16, 21, 25, Nov 1, 19, 23, 25,
  Dec 6, 13, 17, 31; <u>1794</u>: CG, Jan 1, 2, 4, 6, 14, 21, Feb 22, 24, Mar 6, 18,
  Apr 7, 10, 12, 23, 25, 29, May 16, 23, 26, Jun 11, 16, HAY, Jul 8, 11, 14,
  22, 26, Aug 4, 9, 11, 12, 18, 23, 28, Sep 1, CG, 15, 17, 22, 26, Oct 1, 8,
  21, 23, 30, Nov 12, 17, 21, 29, Dec 6, 10, 30; <u>1795</u>: CG, Jan 29, 31, Feb 3,
  4, 6, 14, Mar 16, 19, Apr 6, 8, 22, 23, 24, 28, May 1, 8, 13, 14, 25, 29,
  HAY, Jun 9, 11, 13, 15, 20, 22, Jul 1, 16, 20, 22, 31, Aug 3, 14, 18, 21, 29,
  Sep 2, 4, CG, 16, 18, 21, 23, 30, Oct 5, 7, 8, 15, 24, 31, Nov 4, 7, 18, 27,
  30, Dec 5, 7, 9, 21, 26, 29; <u>1796</u>: CG, Jan 13, 23, Feb 2, Mar 14, 19, Apr 5,
  9, 12, 13, 15, 22, 26, 29, May 3, 6, 10, 16, 20, 21, 24, Jun 2, 7, HAY, 11,
  13, 14, 17, 22, 29, Jul 21, 26, 30, Aug 10, 11, 18, 23, 29, 30, Sep 1, 5, CG,
  14, 16, 17, 23, 28, Oct 3, 6, 7, 20, 21, 29, Nov 7, 19, 24, Dec 1, 17, 22;
  <u>1797</u>: CG, Jan 3, 10, Mar 4, 14, Apr 18, 25, 26, May 8, 9, 11, 16, 17, 18, 20,
  23, 31, Jun 2, 5, 8, 10, HAY, 12, 13, 15, 16, 17, 19, 21, 23, 26, 28, Jul 3,
  6, 8, 15, 31, Aug 14, 22, Sep 1, 4, 11, CG, 18, 20, 25, 27, 29, Oct 16, 31,
  Nov 8, 11, 13, 22, Dec 12, 16, 18, 23; <u>1798</u>: CG, Jan 11, Feb 20, Mar 17, 20,
  31, Apr 13, 16, 18, 20, 21, 24, 27, 30, May 9, 11, 25, 28, HAY, Jun 12,
  14, 15, 16, 18, 20, 29, Jul 6, 10, 13, 14, 16, 20, 25, 30, Aug 3, 4, 6, 13,
  14, 28, Sep 7, CG, 26, Oct 5, 8, 11, 25, 31, Nov 7, 20, 21, 23, Dec 8, 11,
  13, 14, 22, 26; <u>1799</u>: CG, Jan 12, 28, Mar 5, 14, Apr 6, 8, 9, 12, 16, 19, 23,
  26, 27, 30, May 3, 13, 15, 24, 25, 28, 31, Jun 1, 3, 5, HAY, 15, 17, 18, 19,
  20, 21, 22, 24, 25, 27, 29, Jul 2, 6, 11, 13, 23, 27, 30, Aug 5, 13, 27, Sep
  2, CG, 16, 25, 27, Oct 2, 7, 17, 18, 21, 24, 25, 31, Nov 8, 11, 14, Dec 16,
  30; <u>1800</u>: CG, Jan 6, 11, 18, Feb 8, Mar 1, 25, 27, Apr 5, 15, 19, 22, 24, 26,
  30, May 6, 7, 12, 15, 17, 27, Jun 2, 12, HAY, 13, 14, 16, 17, 18, 19, 21, 28,
  Jul 1, 2, 5, 15, 26, Aug 7, 8, 14, 19, 20, Sep 1, 3, 10, 13
--Obi; or, Three-Finger'd Jack (pantomime), <u>1800</u>: HAY, Jul 2, 3, 4, 5, 7, 8, 9,
  10, 11, 12, 14, 16, 17, 18, 19, 21, 22, 23, 24, 28, 29, 30, 31, Aug 1, 4, 6,
  8, 9, 11, 12, 13, 22, 25, 28, 30, Sep 3, 10, 11, 12, 13, 15
Fawcett, John Sr (actor, singer), <u>1760</u>: DL, Sep 23, 30, Oct 11, 20, Nov 17, 27;
  <u>1761</u>: DL, Jan 12, 23, May 11, 14, 20, Sep 5, 10, 12, Oct 1, 7, 26, 29, Nov
  24, 27; <u>1762</u>: DL, Apr 22, May 13, 18, Sep 28; <u>1763</u>: CG, Oct 21, Nov 5, 15,
  Dec 29, 30; <u>1764</u>: CG, Jan 14, Feb 22, May 21; <u>1765</u>: KING'S, Feb 15, HAY, Mar
  11; <u>1766</u>: DL, Sep 23, 30, Nov 7, 8, Dec 13; <u>1767</u>: DL, Jan 2, 24, Feb 7, Mar
  28, May 6, 8, 14, 19, Sep 15, 21, 22, Oct 9, Nov 7, 12, 18; <u>1768</u>: DL, Jan 6,
  14, Feb 13, Mar 21, Apr 11, May 6, Sep 17, 24, 28, Oct 3, 7, 13, 21, 28, 31,
  Nov 1, 4, 5, Dec 16, 17; <u>1769</u>: DL, Jan 24, Mar 31, Apr 3, 18, May 1, 6, 15,
  Sep 19, Oct 2, 5, 7, 12, 14, 23, 30, Nov 6, 13, 17, 23, 24, 27, Dec 6, 20;
  <u>1770</u>: DL, Jan 4, 19, Feb 8, 21, Mar 22, 24, May 7, 12, 14, 15, 16, 17, Jun 7,
  Sep 22, 25, 27, Oct 2, 3, 8, 13, 19, 22, 25, 29, Nov 3, 13, 14, 17, 21, 24,
  Dec 6, 13, 20; <u>1771</u>: DL, Jan 2, Mar 7, 23, Apr 1, 2, 30, May 14, 17, Sep 21,
  26, 28, Oct 1, 3, 8, 10, 12, 15, 22, Nov 9, 23, 25, Dec 4, 21, 26; <u>1772</u>: DL,
  Jan 9, Mar 12, 26, 28, Apr 22, 25, May 12, 22, 26, 30, Jun 10, Sep 19, 24,
  29, Oct 1, 13, 20, 21, 24, 30, Nov 12, 16, 17, Dec 2, 18, 30; <u>1773</u>: DL, Jan
  1, 4, 9, 29, Feb 2, Apr 1, 21, 23, May 10, 12, 15, Sep 18, 21, 25, Oct 8, 9,
  11, 25, Nov 2, 9, 13, 25, Dec 3, 10, 21, 27, 31; <u>1774</u>: DL, Jan 19, Feb 8, Mar
  12, 14, 19, 26, Apr 4, 5, 15, 19, May 12, 14, 20, 23, 26, Sep 20, 22, 24, 27,
  Oct 1, 4, 5, 11, 14, 26, Nov 5, 21, Dec 1, 5, 9; <u>1775</u>: DL, Jan 2, Feb 1, 4,
  20, Mar 2, 21, 23, 25, Apr 8, 17, 18, 24, May 1, 2, 3, 13, 16, 18, CG, 27,
  DL, Sep 26, Oct 3, 7, 10, 11, 23, 28, Nov 1, 9, 11, 14, 20, 21, 24, 28, Dec
  7, 11, 15, 29; <u>1776</u>: DL, Feb 15, Mar 14, 18, Apr 9, 20, 22, 25, May 4, 10,
  11, 13, 16, 18, 22, Oct 5, 10, 12, 15, 18, 23, 26, Nov 6, 7, 9, 25, Dec 10,
  28; <u>1777</u>: DL, Jan 1, 4, 8, Mar 1, Apr 22, 25, May 6, Jun 4, Oct 29; <u>1778</u>: DL,
  Mar 2, May 16, Sep 22, 24, Oct 15, 23, Nov 2, 16, Dec 21; <u>1779</u>: DL, Jan 7, 8,
  Feb 8, Mar 13, 16, 22, 23, May 8, 12, 14, 17, 19, Sep 18, 25, Oct 25, 30, Nov
  3, 22, Dec 4, 8, 22, 27; <u>1780</u>: DL, Jan 24, Feb 28, Apr 14, 26, May 5, 10, 12,
  23, Sep 16, 19, 23, 28, Oct 2, 7, 11, 17, 23, 30, Nov 1, 3, 20, 22, 24, 28,
  Dec 1, 4, 6; <u>1781</u>: DL, Jan 9, Apr 21, May 1, 15, Sep 18, 25, Oct 12, 19, Nov
  5, 13, 29, Dec 11; <u>1782</u>: DL, Jan 3, 19, 29, Apr 3, 5, 17, 25, May 3, 9, 16,
  Sep 18, 21, Oct 5, 12, 18, Nov 4, 5, 12, 22, Dec 4, 7, 14, 26; <u>1783</u>: DL, Feb

18, 22, Mar 6, 10, 18, Apr 23, 29, May 12, 20, Sep 23, 30, Oct 2, 11, 13, 17,
20, 22, 24, Nov 3, 13, 14, 18, 20, 26, Dec 2, 5, 10; <u>1784</u>: DL, Jan 3, 8, 13,
16, 17, 31, Mar 6, 29, Apr 14, 28, May 3, 17, 19, Sep 23, 30, Oct 12, 14, 23,
26, Nov 2, 3, 5, 9, 16, 19, 20, 22, 23, 26, Dec 2, 28; <u>1785</u>: DL, Jan 12, 14,
20, 27, Feb 2, 8, 21, Apr 20, 25, 26, May 3, 5, 9, 17, 24, Sep 20, 24, 27,
29, Oct 1, 8, 15, 17, 20, 22, 25, 26, 27, Nov 7, 12, 18, 21, 22, Dec 1, 26,
29, 30; <u>1786</u>: DL, Jan 5, 6, Feb 11, 18, Mar 9, 13, 28, Apr 6, 20, May 23, Sep
23, 26, 30, Oct 3, 5, 7, 9, 10, 24, 25, 30, Nov 15, 25, Dec 5, 19, 26; <u>1787</u>:
DL, Jan 13, 23, 29, Feb 7, Apr 13, May 19, 22, 25, Jun 1, Sep 18, 22, 25, Oct
6, 9, 26, 27, Nov 3, 5, 6, 8, 20, 21, 24, Dec 10, 14, 26; <u>1788</u>: DL, Jan 21,
22, Mar 3, 11, 13, Apr 7, 8, 10, 11, 14, May 14, 22, 23, Jun 2, Oct 2, 4, 7,
13, 16, 20, 22, Nov 6, 10, 17, 25, 28, 29, Dec 4, 6, 17, 22; <u>1789</u>: DL, Jan 6,
8, 10, 17, 31, Feb 7, 16, Mar 21, 24, 28, Apr 21, May 1, 11, 22, Jun 5, 9,
Sep 19, 22, 24, Oct 1, 13, 20, 27, 28, 31, Nov 5, 13, 17, 20, 30, Dec 1, 17,
26; <u>1790</u>: DL, Jan 15, 19, Feb 10, 15, 23, 27, Mar 2, 13, 22, Apr 23, May 7,
14, 15, 28, Sep 30, Oct 7, HAY, 13, DL, 14, 16, 18, 19, 20, 21, 25, 26, 27,
Nov 3, Dec 7, 14, 27; <u>1791</u>: DL, Jan 10, Mar 22, 28, May 19, DLKING'S, Sep 22,
24, 27, Oct 3, 4, 13, 15, 27, 31, Nov 1, 2, 5, 7, 8, 14, 16, 22, 30, Dec 1,
15; <u>1792</u>: DLKING'S, Jan 5, 6, 7, 11, 13, 28, Feb 14, 18, Mar 6, 13, 19, 24,
26, 29, 31, Apr 21, May 23, 31, DL, Sep 18, 25, Oct 4, 9, 11, 13, 18, 27, Nov
10, 21, 26, Dec 4, 10, 15, 17, 26, 27; <u>1793</u>: DL, Jan 16, Feb 9, 16, 23, 26,
Mar 7, 9, Apr 9, 17, 22, 25, 29, May 7, 10, Jun 1, 4
Fawcett, Susan, Mrs John Jr (actor), <u>1791</u>: CG, Oct 3, 17, 21, 27, Nov 2, 4, Dec
3, 21; <u>1792</u>: CG, Apr 21, May 5, 11, 16, 18, Sep 17, 21, 24, 26, Oct 1, 5, Nov
5, 28, Dec 5; <u>1793</u>: CG, Apr 23, May 15, 27, Sep 17, 23, 25, Oct 9, 10, 15,
22, Nov 13, 16, 22, 23, Dec 9, 17, 19, 30; <u>1794</u>: CG, Jan 6, 22, Feb 5, 10,
Mar 6, Apr 12, May 14, 16, Jun 5, HAY, Aug 28, CG, Sep 15, 17, Oct 7, 8, 14,
21, 23, Dec 30; <u>1795</u>: CG, Jan 19, 24, 29, Feb 4, Mar 17, Apr 8, May 1, 8, 14,
27, Sep 21, 23, 28, Dec 5, 15, 22; <u>1796</u>: CG, Apr 15, 29, May 21, Sep 17, Oct
5, 10, 21, 24, Nov 5, 17, 24; <u>1797</u>: CG, Feb 20, May 9, Jun 10, 13, 14, HAY,
19
Fawkener, William (versifier), <u>1789</u>: DL, Mar 21
Fawkes (actor), <u>1743</u>: JS, Mar 16
Fawkes-Pinchbeck Booth, <u>1741</u>: BF, Aug 22, SF, Sep 7; <u>1742</u>: BF, Aug 26; <u>1743</u>:
BFFP, Aug 23
Fawkes-Pinchbeck-Terwin Booth, <u>1740</u>: BFFPT, Aug 23
Fawkes, Mrs (actor), <u>1742</u>: CG, Dec 28; <u>1743</u>: CG, Mar 8, May 4
Fawks's famous boy (entertainer), <u>1722</u>: SOU, Oct 3
Fawns and Nymphs (dance), <u>1741</u>: CG, Jan 28, Feb 6
Fawns' Dance (dance), <u>1726</u>: DL, Nov 18, 23, Dec 12, 29; <u>1727</u>: DL, Feb 8, Apr
20, 24, May 2, Sep 26, Nov 21; <u>1728</u>: DL, May 1, 10, 16, Jun 13; <u>1729</u>: DL, Apr
21, May 1; <u>1730</u>: GF, Mar 10, 12, 14; <u>1735</u>: CG/LIF, Apr 24
Fawns' Dance, Grand (dance), <u>1733</u>: LIF/CG, Apr 23, 25
Fay (dancer), <u>1774</u>: KING'S, Nov 8
Faye, Charles De la (author), <u>1731</u>: LIF, Apr 24
Fayting (Feyting), H (actor), <u>1736</u>: LIF, Sep 30, Oct 14, 21, Dec 7, 16; <u>1737</u>:
LIF, Feb 1
Fear Not Mortal (song), <u>1742</u>: DL, Oct 19
Fearon, James (actor), <u>1771</u>: HAY, May 17, 20, 22, 23, 27, 29, Jun 5, 7, 10, 12,
14, 26, Jul 1, 5, 8, 12, 15, Aug 19, 26, Sep 16, 18, 19, 20; <u>1772</u>: HAY, May
18, 20, 27, Jun 1, 8, 12, 15, 29, Jul 3, 6, 8, 10, 27, Aug 4, 10, 19, Sep 8,
17, 18; <u>1773</u>: HAY, May 17, 19, 24, 26, 28, 31, Jun 4, 7, 14, 18, 28, Jul 2,
21, 28, 30, Aug 4, 11, 23, 27, Sep 3, 16, 17, 18, 20; <u>1774</u>: HAY, Apr 4, 12,
May 16, 30, Jun 1, DL, 2, HAY, 3, 6, 8, 10, 13, 15, 17, 27, Jul 6, 15, Aug
19, 26, Sep 5, 6, 12, 17, CG, 19, 21, 26, Oct 4, 5, 7, 11, 13, 22, 24, 31,
Nov 8, 19, Dec 9, 12, 15, 20, 27; <u>1775</u>: CG, Jan 17, Apr 21, 22, 28, HAY, May
15, CG, 17, 18, 19, 20, HAY, 22, 26, 29, Jun 2, 5, 12, 16, Jul 7, 14, 21, 31,
Aug 2, 9, 16, Sep 4, 11, 13, 16, 18, 19, CG, 25, 29, Oct 6, 11, 13, 18, 21,
23, 25, 28, Nov 4, 13, 28, 30, Dec 1, 9, 26; <u>1776</u>: CG, Jan 1, 5, Feb 5, Apr
26, 27, 30, May 10, HAY, 20, 22, 27, 28, 31, Jun 14, 24, 26, Jul 1, 3, 5, 8,
10, 24, 29, Aug 2, Sep 2, 16, 17, 20, CG, 23, 25, 30, Oct 4, 8, 9, 16, 17,
25, 29, 31, Nov 1, 4, 11, 14, 20, 25, 28, 30, Dec 2, 6, 18, 26, 27;
<u>1777</u>: CG, Jan 8, 17, Feb 22, Apr 7, 14, 16, 28, May 2, 5, HAY, 15, 28, 30,
Jun 6, 9, 11, 19, 26, Jul 7, 15, 18, 24, 30, Aug 7, 9, 12, 14, 18, 19, 25,
29, Sep 3, 18, 19, CG, 22, 24, 26, 29, Oct 8, 10, 15, 16, 23, 27, 30, Nov 1,
6, 7, 13, 18, 21, Dec 5, 26, 29; <u>1778</u>: CG, Jan 15, 19, 20, 21, Feb 6, 24, Mar
2, 9, 14, 23, Apr 7, 11, 21, 22, 25, 27, May 5, 7, 11, 15, Sep 18, 21, Oct 2,
5, 7, 9, 14, 15, 21, 22, 24, 26, Nov 4, Dec 3, 11, 12, 15, 21, 26, 30; <u>1779</u>:
CG, Jan 2, 4, 11, 13, 18, 21, 22, 26, Feb 13, 18, 22, Mar 4, 9, 22, Apr 12,
21, 24, 26, 30, May 6, 10, 12, 13, 18, 20, Sep 20, 24, 27, Oct 1, 11, 13, 20,
23, Nov 1, 4, 8, 9, 10, 11, 16, 22, 23, 25, 27, 30, Dec 3, 11, 29, 31; <u>1780</u>:
CG, Jan 7, 12, 13, 17, 25, Feb 1, 2, 22, Mar 18, Apr 12, 21, 24, 25, May 1,

12, 24, Sep 18, 20, 22, Oct 2, 3, 9, 10, 11, 13, 19, 23, 24, 26, 31, Nov 4,
6, 10, 15, 22, 25, Dec 4, 5, 12; 1781: CG, Jan 1, 4, 12, 25, Feb 14, Mar 3,
Apr 28, 30, DL, May 8, CG, 16, 25, Sep 17, 19, 24, 26, DL, 27, CG, 28, Oct
13, 16, 27, Nov 2, 5, 7, 8, 9, 17, 28, Dec 5, 11, 14, 17, 18, 20, 26, 31;
1782: CG, Jan 3, 4, 5, 7, 9, 11, 16, 22, 25, Feb 4, 5, 14, Mar 16, 19, Apr 1,
4, 10, 12, 17, 20, 23, May 3, 6, 11, 20, 21, Sep 30, Oct 2, 3, 4, 7, 10, 14,
15, 16, 17, 21, 23, 29, Nov 1, 2, 6, 8, 12, 18, 19, 30, Dec 2, 12, 14, 19,
27, 30, 31; 1783: CG, Jan 3, 17, 28, Feb 19, 22, 25, Mar 29, 31, Apr 23, 26,
May 9, 10, 14, 16, 17, 19, 20, 22, 27, 29, DL, Jun 5, CG, Sep 17, 19, 22, 24,
Oct 1, 3, 6, 8, 9, 13, 15, 17, 23, 28, 31, Nov 4, 10, 19, 24, 25, 27, Dec 5,
6, 11, 26, 31; 1784: CG, Jan 7, 9, 14, 16, 22, 26, 29, Feb 5, 13, 20, 21, Mar
4, 6, 20, 22, Apr 13, May 4, 7, 8, 11, 19, 24, 27, Sep 17, 20, 21, 22, 24,
27, 28, 29, Oct 1, 4, 8, 11, 18, 25, 27, 30, Nov 3, 4, 10, 29, 30, Dec 3, 4,
11, 13, 22; 1785: CG, Jan 8, 14, 19, 21, 29, Feb 4, 7, 15, 17, 21, 28, Mar 3,
8, 29, 30, Apr 8, 11, 12, May 4, 6, 7, 12, 13, Sep 21, 23, 26, 28, 30, Oct 3,
5, 10, 27, 28, Nov 1, 2, 9, 14, 18, 19, 23, 24, 26, 29, Dec 1, 2, 7, 8, 14,
21; 1786: CG, Jan 3, 6, 7, 18, 28, Feb 1, 7, 13, 18, 23, 25, Mar 11, 14, Apr
4, 8, 18, 19, 20, 26, May 3, 5, 9, 10, 11, 13, 15, 26, Sep 18, 20, 25, 27,
29, Oct 2, 4, 9, 12, 23, 26, 30, Nov 13, 14, 15, 18, 22, 24, 29, Dec 4, 12,
30; 1787: CG, Jan 2, 4, 6, 8, 11, 26, 27, 31, Feb 6, 9, 10, 13, 20, Mar 12,
26, 27, Apr 11, 16, 17, DL, 18, CG, 25, 26, 27, May 1, 11, 22, Sep 17, 19,
21, 24, 26, 28, Oct 1, 3, 5, 10, 11, 12, 18, 19, 22, 29, 31, Nov 2, 5, 7, 16,
19, 20, 22, 23, Dec 5, 14, 15, 26, 27, 28; 1788: CG, Jan 3, 10, 11, 14, 28,
29, Feb 4, 9, 14, 25, Mar 1, 8, 10, 11, 15, 24, 26, 28, Apr 1, 8, 14, 23, 26,
May 7, 12, 14, 22, Sep 15, 19, 22, 24, Oct 7, 8, 15, 17, 18, 24, 27, 28, 29,
Nov 1, 6, 12, 21, 28, Dec 1, 26, 27, 30, 31; 1789: CG, Jan 2, 20, 21, 28, Feb
6, 11, 14, 19, 21, Mar 3, 28, 31, Apr 14, 15, 20, 21, 28, 29, 30, May 5, 8,
14, 19, 20, 26, 27, Jun 2, 5, 8, 9, 16; 1790: CG, Jun 16
Fearon, Mary, Mrs James (actor), 1771: HAY, Jun 26, Sep 19; 1772: HAY, May 18,
Jun 8, 29, Sep 18; 1773: HAY, May 28, Jul 2, Aug 11, 13, Sep 20; 1774: HAY,
Jun 6, 17, Sep 5; 1775: HAY, Jun 7, 12, Sep 4, CG, Nov 4; 1776: HAY, May 31,
Jul 5; 1777: HAY, Jul 30, CG, Sep 24; 1787: CG, May 11; 1790: CG, Jun 16
Feast of Bacchus, The (dance), 1758: CG, Nov 16, 17, 20, 21, 22, 29, Dec 7, 9,
12, 22, 26, 30; 1759: CG, Jan 2, 12, Mar 20, Apr 20
Feast of Hymen, The. See Porpora, Nicola.
Feast of Thalia, The; or, A Dramatic Olio (play), 1781: HAY, Aug 22; 1785: HAY,
Aug 16
Feast, The. See Manuche, Cosmo.
Feasts of the Piazza y Spagnia (music), 1725: HIC, Mar 19
Feather's Tavern, 1753: DL, Dec 21
Featherstone, Miss (singer), 1751: SF, Sep 9
Federici, Vincenzo (composer), 1789: KING'S, Apr 28; 1790: HAY, Feb 27, Apr 6,
29, May 27, 28; 1791: KING'S, May 14, 19, 24, Jun 4, 21; 1793: KING'S, Feb 5,
Mar 19, Jun 11; 1794: KING'S, Jan 11, Mar 1, Apr 26, May 17, Jun 5; 1795:
KING'S, Feb 20; 1799: KING'S, May 30; 1800: KING'S, Apr 15
--Usurpator Innocente, L' (opera), 1790: HAY, Apr 6, 10, 13, 15, 17, 20, 22,
24, 27, May 21, 25, Jun 1, CG, 26, Jul 3, 17
Federico, Gennaro Antonio (librettist), 1783: CG, Feb 14
Feigned Astrologer, The (play, anon), 1668: NONE, Sep 0
Feigned Courtezans, The. See Behn, Aphra.
Feigned Friendship; or, The Mad Reformer (play, anon), 1699: LIF, May 0
Feild (dancer), 1722: LIF, Mar 13
Feilde, Matthew, 1782: CG, Feb 21
--Vertumnus and Pomona (pastoral), 1782: CG, Feb 21
Feinte Veritable, La; or, The Tender Return (farce), 1735: GF/HAY, Jan 22
Feiston (musician), 1708: SH, Mar 26
Felice Belve (song), 1748: CG, Feb 13, Apr 27
Fell rage (song), 1794: DL, Mar 21
Fell, Mrs William (actor), 1755: BF, Sep 6
Fell's scholars (actors), 1737: LH, Jan 26
Fellowes (actor), 1782: HAY, Sep 21
Fellows, Thomas (mercer), 1767: CG, Apr 9
Felsner (button maker), 1781: DL, May 2
Female Adventure (Pursuit), The; or, Stop Her Who Can (play, anon), 1790: CG,
Apr 29, May 11, Jun 12, Nov 6; 1792: CG, May 16
Female Advocates, The. See Taverner, William.
Female Archer (dance), 1766: CG, Dec 9, 15, 18, 19; 1767: CG, Jan 9, 14, 15,
16, 24, 28, Feb 3, 11, 17, 19, Mar 7, 16, 23, 24, 28, Apr 4, 6, 7, 9, 22, 25,
28, 29, May 2, 4, 6, 13, Oct 29, 31, Nov 9, 11, 27, Dec 11, 16, 28
Female Balloonists (dance), 1785: HAY, Jul 6
Female Captain, The. See Cobb, James, The Contract.
Female Chevalier, The. See Colman the elder, George.

Female Dramatist, The. See Colman the younger, George.
Female Duellist, The. See Fernside.
Female Fop, The. See Sandford.
Female Fortune Teller, The. See Johnson, Charles.
Female Free Mason, The (entertainment), 1737: HAY, Apr 25
Female Friendship (play), 1735: LIF, Sep 2
Female Innocence; or, A School for a Wife (play), 1732: SFLH, Sep 5
Female Inquisition, The (debate), 1755: HAY, Jan 28
Female Minor, The (play, anon), 1760: SF, Sep 18, 19, 20, 22
Female Officer, The. See Kemble, John Philip, The Projects.
Female Orators, The; or, Ladies' Debating Society (prelude, anon), 1780: CG,
    May 12
Female Parson, The. See Coffey, Charles.
Female Prelate, The. See Settle, Elkanah.
Female Rake, The. See Dorman, Joseph.
Female Virtuosos. See Wright, Thomas, No Fool Like Wits.
Female Warriors (dance), 1780: KING'S, Apr 20
Female Wits, The; or, The Triumvirate of Poets at Rehearsal (play, anon), 1693:
    DL, Mar 0; 1696: DL, Sep 0; 1698: DG, Feb 7
Femme Diablesse et les Epouvantes D'Arlequin, La (entertainment), 1725: HAY,
    Feb 15
Femme Jalouse, La. See Jolly, Francois Antoine.
Femme Juge, La (play, anon), 1721: HAY, Dec 19; 1722: HAY, Jan 2
Femme Maitresse (dance), 1764: KING'S, Feb 28, CG, Oct 4, 5, 10, 11, 12, 15,
    16, 23, Nov 1, 10, 14, Dec 6, 8; 1765: CG, Jan 11, May 8
Femme Veange, La; ou, Le Triumphe d'Colombine et d'Arlequin Marquis Ridicule
    (pantomime), 1726: HAY, Mar 28
Femmes Savantes. See Moliere.
Femmes Vengees, Les. See Sedaine, Michel Jean.
Fench, H (actor), 1729: HAY, Feb 25
Fenchurch St, 1745: GF, Mar 12; 1784: HAY, Mar 8
Fencing (entertainment), 1793: DL, May 30
Fenlin, Master (actor), 1740: DL, Oct 14
Fenn (stage doorkeeper), 1739: DL, May 14; 1740: DL, May 21; 1741: DL, May 28;
    1742: DL, May 15; 1743: DL, May 23; 1744: DL, May 21; 1745: DL, May 13
Fenn, Mrs (beneficiary), 1746: DL, May 19
Fennell, James (actor, playwright), 1787: CG, Oct 12; 1789: CG, Oct 16, Nov 2,
    23; 1790: CG, May 15, Oct 27, Nov 8, 22, Dec 6, 10, 11, 20; 1791: HAY, Mar 7;
    see also Cambray
--Advertisement, The; or, A New Way to Get a Husband (farce), 1791: HAY, Mar 7
Fenny (instrumentalist), 1798: HAY, Jan 15
Fenton (actor), 1668: ATCOURT, Feb 4
Fenton, Elijah, 1719: DL, Dec 11; 1720: LIF, Feb 20; 1723: LIF, Feb 22; 1726:
    LIF, Mar 24; 1730: LIF, May 6; 1758: CG, Jan 27; 1770: DL, Mar 20; 1779: CG,
    Nov 10
--Mariamne, 1720: LIF, Feb 20; 1723: LIF, Feb 22, 23, 25, 26, 28, Mar 2, 4, 5,
    7, 9, 12, 14, 16, 18, Apr 1, 15, May 16, Jun 7, Dec 7, 18; 1724: LIF, Jan 29,
    Feb 5, May 12, Nov 12; 1726: LIF, Mar 24, Apr 30; 1727: LIF, Nov 3; 1728:
    LIF, Apr 1; 1730: LIF, May 6; 1733: LIF/CG, Apr 13; 1735: CG/LIF, Mar 13;
    1739: CG, Mar 13, Apr 9, Sep 15; 1745: CG, Mar 11, 12; 1758: CG, Jan 21, 23,
    27, 28, 31, Feb 2, 3, 6, 7, 11, Mar 4, KING'S, 14; 1765: DL, Mar 16; 1770:
    DL, Mar 20; 1774: CG, Mar 14; 1779: CG, Nov 10
Fenton, Lavinia (actor), 1726: HAY, Feb 24, LIF, Jul 15, 22, Aug 19, Oct 3;
    1727: LIF, Feb 13, Apr 26, May 4, Sep 11, Nov 9; 1728: LIF, Jan 29, Mar 9,
    14, 18, 25, 28, Apr 6, 23, 24, 26, 29, May 2, 4, 16, 23
Fenton, Miss (actor), 1786: HAMM, Jul 5, 10, 19, 26
Fenwick (dresser), 1760: CG, Sep 22
Fenwick, John (author), 1798: CG, Feb 13
Fenwick, Lady Mary, 1691: DL, Jan 0
Ferbridge, Jane (actor), 1755: CG, Jan 16
Ferci, Lawrence (equilibrist), 1766: HAY, Oct 27
Ferci, Miss (dancer), 1766: HAY, Oct 27
Ferdinand, Prince, 1759: BFS, Sep 3
Ferdinando. See Porpora, Nicola.
Ferg, Master (actor, dancer), 1737: DL, Nov 7, 11, 12, 19; 1738: DL, Jan 20,
    Feb 28, Mar 3, 13, 20, 21, 25, Apr 12, 13, 14, 21, 22, 24, 26, 27, 29, May 3,
    5, 8, 9, 10, 11, 13, 15, 16, 17, 18, 19, 23, 24, 25, 26, 27, 29, 30, 31, BFH,
    Aug 23, DL, Oct 5, 7, 26, 27, 30, Nov 30, Dec 4, 14, 16, 28; 1739: DL, Jan
    24, Feb 7, Mar 17, 26, 27, Apr 2, 3, 5, 10, 12, 27, 28, 30, May 1, 3, 5, 8,
    11, 14, 16, 18, 19, 22, 23, 26, 30, 31, CG, Aug 2, DL, Oct 10, Nov 13, 20,
    21, Dec 7, 14, 21, 28; 1740: DL, Jan 3, 8, 11, 14, Feb 5, 8, 11, 12, 16, 18,
    19, Mar 4, 6, 8, 10, 18, Apr 7, 11, 14, 19, 21, 22, 26, 30, May 2, 5, 6, 7,

8, 13, 14, 16, 17, 19, 20, 22, 23, 26, 28, BFLP, Aug 23, DL, Oct 14, Dec 26;
1741: CG, Apr 20, May 12, BFLW, Aug 22; 1744: CG, Feb 14
Ferg, Miss (actor, dancer), 1738: BFH, Aug 23; 1739: DL, Oct 10; 1740: DL, Oct
14, Dec 26
Ferguson (actor), 1734: CG/LIF, Dec 30; 1735: CG, Oct 17, Nov 6; 1736: CG, Jan
1, 23, LIF, Mar 31, Apr 16, CG, 30, LIF, May 5, CG, Oct 8, 27; 1737: CG, Jan
10, Feb 3, Mar 15, May 3, 9, 13, 16, 19, 31; 1741: BFH, Aug 22; 1750: SFP,
Sep 7; 1766: CG, Oct 28; 1785: HAY, Jan 31
Ferguson, Miss (actor), 1735: YB, Jul 17; 1736: HAY, Apr 29, LIF, Jun 16, HAY,
29, Jul 14; 1738: CG, Feb 23, Dec 5; 1739: CG, May 17; 1740: CG, Mar 11, Nov
6; 1741: CG, May 8, BFH, Aug 22, CG, Nov 24, Dec 18; 1742: CG, May 6, 12,
BFPY, Aug 25, CG, Dec 7; 1743: SOU, Feb 25, CG, May 4, TCD/BFTD, Aug 23, CG,
Oct 31; 1744: CG, May 2, Nov 27, 29, Dec 21; 1745: CG, May 8, Oct 31, Nov 7;
1746: CG, Feb 10, Apr 5, May 7, Jun 27; 1747: CG, Feb 12, May 15, Oct 31;
1748: CG, Apr 13, 21, 26, 29, BF, Aug 24, SFBCBV, Sep 7, CG, 26; 1749: CG,
Apr 25, Oct 20, Nov 23; 1750: CG, Jan 18, Mar 17, Apr 24, 27, Sep 26, Oct 12,
16, 24, 29, Nov 6; 1751: CG, Apr 12, May 9, Sep 27, 30, Oct 22, Nov 6; 1752:
CG, Apr 4, 28, May 5, Oct 4, 10, 18, Nov 7, 16, Dec 13; 1753: CG, Feb 7, May
9, Sep 10, 12, 17, 24, Oct 8; 1754: CG, Mar 26, Apr 16, Sep 16, 18, 27, Oct
11; 1755: CG, Jan 16, Mar 22, May 9, Oct 1, 3, 17, 21, Nov 3, 8, 12, 19, Dec
4, 5; 1756: CG, Feb 23, Apr 27, May 5, Sep 22, 24, 29, Oct 6, 28, 30, Nov 8,
13, Dec 7, 10; 1757: CG, Feb 9, 14, 16, 18, 19, Apr 15, May 10, 16, Sep 26,
Oct 7, 8, 13, 14, 19, 20, Nov 2, 14, 18, 23, Dec 8, 14; 1758: CG, Apr 28, Sep
27, Oct 2, 9, 24, 25, 30, Nov 13, 16, Dec 18; 1759: CG, Mar 31, Apr 7, 20,
26, 28, May 18, Sep 24; 1760: CG, Jan 14, Apr 28; 1764: CG, Sep 19
Ferguson, Mrs (actor), 1735: YB, Mar 21, SOU, Apr 7, YB, Jul 17; 1736: DL, Feb
28; 1740: CG, May 9; 1745: CG, May 29; 1754: CG, Oct 16; 1759: CG, Oct 1, 3,
5, 10, Nov 24, Dec 5, 8; 1760: CG, Mar 18, May 6, 8, 19, Sep 22, 24, Oct 1,
6, 8, 13, 20, 25, Nov 29; 1761: CG, Mar 25, Apr 20, 27, Sep 9, 11, 18, Oct 2,
5, Nov 2; 1762: CG, Feb 20, May 6, 7, Sep 20, 27, 30, Oct 4, 5, 9, 11, 13,
14, Nov 16; 1763: CG, Mar 5, 26, Sep 19, Oct 5, 7, 8, 12, 26, Dec 26; 1764:
CG, Mar 10, 29, Sep 17, Oct 8, 11, 12, 24, 25, Nov 6; 1765: CG, Sep 16, 18,
30, Oct 5, Nov 13, 28; 1766: CG, Apr 26, May 6, Sep 26, Oct 14, 30, 31, Nov
11, Dec 9; 1767: CG, Jan 1, 23, Sep 23, Nov 10; 1768: CG, Apr 11, May 31, Sep
27, 30; 1769: CG, Mar 27, Dec 27; 1770: CG, May 14, Dec 31; 1771: CG, Sep 28,
Oct 11, 15, Dec 16; 1773: CG, May 20, 22, Oct 4; 1788: CG, Mar 29; 1790: CG,
Dec 11; 1793: KING/HAY, Mar 6, CG, May 10; 1795: DL, May 21; 1797: CG, May 9;
1799: CG, Jun 12
Ferlendis, Alessandro (horn player), 1795: KING'S, Jun 16
Ferlotti, Teresa (dancer), 1794: KING'S, Dec 6; 1795: KING'S, Jan 10
Fermor, Charlotte (correspondent), 1760: DL, Dec 23
Fern (actor), 1749: HAY, Apr 29, May 29; 1750: HAY, Feb 9, 16, 26, Mar 13
Fernside, 1793: DL, May 22
--Female Duellist, The (farce), 1793: DL, May 22
Ferrareni (entertainer), 1754: HAY/SFB, Sep 13
Ferrarese, Sga (singer), 1785: KING'S, Jan 1, 4, 8, Feb 24, 26, Apr 16, 21, May
12, 28, Jun 9; 1786: KING'S, Jan 24, Mar 11, 16, 30, May 20
Ferrari, Giacomo Gotifredo (composer), 1793: DL, May 10, HAY, Nov 30; 1799:
KING'S, May 14; 1800: KING'S, May 13
--Due Svizzeri, I (opera), 1799: KING'S, May 14, 18, 21, 25, 28, Jun 1, 4, 11,
17, 18, 25, 29, Jul 6, 9, 16, 20, Aug 3; 1800: KING'S, May 13, 17, 20, 30,
Jun 17, 19, Jul 1
Ferrars, Earl of, 1763: MARLY, Jun 28
Ferrere (dancer), 1752: DL, Oct 3, 5, 17, 26, Nov 2, 25, 28, Dec 1; 1753: DL,
Jan 1, 5, 15, 22, 23, Feb 5, 19, Mar 20, 26, 31, Apr 24, 25, May 19; 1783:
DL, Sep 18, Oct 13, Nov 8; 1786: DL, May 22; 1787: DL, Jan 29, Feb 15, 24,
May 23, 25, Jun 8, Sep 29, Oct 26, Nov 5, 21, 23
Ferrere, Mme (dancer), 1790: HAY, May 25, 29, Jun 1; 1792: DLKING'S, May 22
Ferrers (actor), 1725: DL, Feb 20, May 11
Ferrers, Captain (spectator), 1660: COCKPIT, Aug 18; 1661: SALSBURY, Mar 25,
VERE, Apr 27, Aug 14, LIF, 17, VERE, Oct 4, LIF, Nov 15, VERE, 27; 1662: LIF,
Oct 18; 1663: BRIDGES, Jun 10, LIF, Dec 26
Ferri, Baldassare. See Eunuch, French.
Perrouh Effendi, Ismail (Turkish ambassador), 1798: CG, May 9; 1800: CG, May
17, DL, Jun 3
Ferry (house servant), 1769: CG, Jan 2
Festin de Pierre, Le. See Moliere.
Festing, John (musician), 1707: YB, Mar 5; 1721: HIC, Mar 15; 1726: HIC, Mar
30; 1729: YB, Feb 28, LIF, Mar 12; 1730: YB, Mar 6; 1731: YB, Mar 26, LIF,
Apr 2; 1732: YB, Mar 29; 1733: YB, Mar 16; 1734: YB, Mar 18, SH, 28, MR, Dec
13; 1735: SH, Mar 28, TB, Apr 24; 1736: MR, Feb 11, YB, Mar 11, HIC, Apr 8,
SH, 16; 1737: YB, Mar 5, DT, Mar 30, DL, May 4, 27; 1740: HIC, Jan 4, Feb 1,

22, Mar 27, 28, Apr 11, 18, 25; 1741: HIC, Jan 16, Feb 19, 27, Mar 5, 6, 13;
    1744: HAY, Apr 4, Nov 5; 1745: HAY, Feb 14; 1762: CG, Dec 8; 1763: CG, Oct 22
Festing, Michael Christian (musician), 1723: HIC, Mar 6; 1724: HIC, Feb 26, Mar
    11; 1726: HIC, Mar 30; 1728: HIC, Mar 15; 1729: YB, Feb 21; 1737: DT, Mar 16
Festival of Anacreon, The (interlude, anon), 1795: DL, May 27
Festival of the Black Prince, The (entertainment), 1773: CG, Apr 24
Festival, The (Impromptu Revel Masque) (masque), 1733: DL/HAY, Nov 9, 15, 26,
    27, 29, Dec 1, 6, 8, 10, 15, 17, 18, 27, 29
Festive Board, The (interlude, anon), 1792: DLKING'S, Apr 19
Fete Anticipated, The (interlude, anon), 1780: CG, Apr 10
Fete Champetre (song), 1774: DL, Nov 26; 1775: DL, Feb 4, 28, Mar 16; 1776: DL,
    Nov 7; 1777: DL, Feb 20; 1780: DL, Feb 28; 1784: DL, May 21
Fete de Campagne, La. See Dorvigny.
Fete de Flora, La (dance), 1775:KING'S, Feb 7, Apr 8
Fete des Matelots et des Provencaux (dance), 1791: KING'S, Apr 14, 16
Fete du Ciel (dance), 1779: KING'S, Mar 25, 27, Apr 10, 17, 24, May 1, 8, 21
Fete du Seigneur (dance), 1791: KING'S, Jun 25, 28, Jul 2, 5
Fete du Village (dance), 1773: KING'S, Apr 1, 24, 27, May 1, 3, 11, 28, Jun 3,
    8; 1776: KING'S, Feb 24, 27, Mar 2, 5, 9, 12, 16, 19, 23, 26, 30, Apr 13, 16,
    18, 23, 25, 27, 30, May 4, 11, 14, 18, Jun 1, 6, 8
Fete Marine (dance), 1786: KING'S, Apr 27, 29, May 23, Jun 13, 24, Jul 4, 8,
    11; 1791: DL, May 20, 25
Fete Pastorale (dance), 1780: KING'S, Apr 22, May 20, 27, Jun 24
Fete Provencale (dance), 1787: KING'S, Mar 8, 10, 29, Apr 28; 1789: KING'S, Jan
    31, Feb 7, 10, 14, CG, Jun 30, Jul 11; 1791: KING'S, May 14, 21, Jun 10, 18,
    21, 25
Fete Villageoise (dance), 1791: PAN, Dec 31; 1792: PAN, Jan 14, HAY, Feb 14,
    Mar 10, 17, May 15
Fete, A (interlude, anon), 1780: CG, Apr 10, May 1, 3, 5; 1781: CG, Apr 3, 7,
    17, 18, 21, 23, 24, 25, DL, 25, 26, CG, 27, DL, 28, CG, 30, DL, May 2, CG, 4,
    5, DL, 7, 10, CG, 11, 12, DL, 15; 1782: CG, May 6, 20; 1783: CG, May 19, HAY,
    Aug 1; 1784: DL, Mar 30, Apr 12, 21
Fetes de Tempe (dance), 1788: KING'S, Feb 28, Mar 1, 4, 13, Apr 5, 22, May 3
Fette Ramsii (dance), 1733: LIF/CG, Mar 15
Fetter Lane, 1737: LIF, Apr 27; 1746: CG, Jan 24
Feudal Times. See Colman the younger, George.
Feversham, Lord. See Dufort, Louis de.
Fevey, Lt, 1759: CG, Oct 22
Feyting. See Fayting.
Fez, Emperor of, 1706: QUEEN'S, May 3, Oct 28
Fialon (dancer), 1791: PAN, Feb 17, 26, Mar 24, May 9, Jun 10; 1792: HAY, Apr
    14; 1794: DL, Oct 31; 1795: DL, Feb 12, May 6, 20, 26; 1796: KING'S, May 12,
    Jun 2, Jul 7, 12, Dec 13; 1797: KING'S, Apr 6, 8, DL, May 22, CG, Oct 21, Nov
    4; 1798: DL, May 16; 1799: KING'S, May 2
Fialon, Mrs (dancer), 1791: PAN, Feb 17; 1795: DL, Feb 12, May 6, 20, 26, Jun
    1, 8
Fichar. See Fisher.
Fickle Fair One, The (play), 1726: LIF, Mar 21, 24
Fickle Shepherdess, The (play, anon), 1703: LIF, Mar 0
Fideli, Sigismondo (singer), 1698: DL, Dec 0, YB, 22; 1699: DL, Feb 28, Apr 15
Fie (actor), 1748: SFP, Sep 7
Fie Ho (song), 1728: LIF, May 8
Fie nay prythee John (song), 1789: HAY, Aug 25
Field (actor), 1794: HAY, May 22
Field (banker), 1750: DL, Apr 3
Field Dance (dance), 1774: KING'S, Jun 3
Field, Ann (actor, singer), 1777: DL, Jan 4, Sep 20, Oct 7, Nov 22, 29, Dec 15;
    1778: DL, Jan 20, May 19, Sep 17, Oct 26, Nov 2, Dec 23; 1779: DL, May 18,
    Sep 18, Oct 21, 30, Nov 3, Dec 14; 1780: DL, Jan 20, Apr 15, May 9, 10, Sep
    23, Oct 5, 10, 26, Nov 23; 1781: DL, Mar 1, 10, Apr 23, May 1, 16, 24, Sep
    15, 25, 27, Oct 12, 19, Nov 13, Dec 28; 1782: DL, Jan 8, 26, Feb 16, Apr 11,
    15, 24, May 25, Sep 18, 19, 24, 28, Oct 3, 10, Nov 7, Dec 26; 1783: DL, Apr
    7, May 5, 12, Sep 16, 18, 30, Oct 7, 8, 13, 16, Dec 2, 10; 1784: DL, Jan 27,
    Feb 3, CG, Mar 23, DL, May 14, 21, Sep 18, 21, 30, Oct 7, 11, 12, 18, 26, Nov
    4, 9, 22, Dec 10; 1785: DL, Jan 12, 22, 27, Feb 2, Apr 6, 14, 22, Sep 17, Oct
    1, 17, 26, Nov 17, 21, 22, Dec 5, 7, 8; 1786: DL, Jan 12, 14, Feb 4, Mar 2,
    4, 7
Field, Benjamin (beneficiary), 1737: HIC, Mar 14
Field, Master John (pianist), 1793: CG, May 21
Field, Mrs (actor), 1748: BFLYY, Aug 24, SFLYYW, Sep 7, BHB, Oct 1, JS, 31
Field, Nathan, 1669: BRIDGES, Jan 12
--Fatal Dowry, The (with Phillip Massinger), 1669: BRIDGES, Jan 12

--Knights of Malta, The. See Fletcher, John.
--Queen of Corinth, The. See Fletcher, John.
--Woman is a Weather Cock, The, <u>1666</u>: NONE, Sep 0
Fieldhouse (actor), <u>1699</u>: LIF, Dec 18; <u>1701</u>: LIF, Dec 0; <u>1702</u>: LIF, Jun 0, Dec
   31; <u>1703</u>: LIF, Feb 0; <u>1704</u>: LIF, Jan 13, Mar 25, Jun 24, Dec 4; <u>1705</u>:
   LIF/QUEN, Feb 22; <u>1706</u>: QUEEN'S, Jun 0; <u>1719</u>: RI, Jul 6; <u>1723</u>: HAY, Apr 22
Fieldhouse, Mrs (actor), <u>1703</u>: LIF, Nov 0; <u>1705</u>: LIF/QUEN, Feb 22
Fielding (actor), <u>1723</u>: LIF, Mar 25
Fielding (actor), <u>1791</u>: HAY, Dec 26
Fielding (beneficiary), <u>1724</u>: DL, May 21; <u>1726</u>: DL, May 17; <u>1727</u>: DL, May 12
Fielding (householder), <u>1757</u>: DL, May 11
Fielding (rioter), <u>1721</u>: LIF, Feb 1
Fielding (wounded in duel), <u>1702</u>: DL, Dec 14
Fielding 's Booth, <u>1729</u>: BFF, Aug 23; <u>1731</u>: SOU, Sep 28
Fielding-Hallam Booth, <u>1738</u>: TC, Aug 7
Fielding-Hippisley Booth, <u>1732</u>: BF, Aug 22; <u>1733</u>: BF, Aug 23, BFFH, Sep 4;
   <u>1736</u>: BFFH, Aug 23
Fielding-Hippisley-Hall Booth, <u>1731</u>: SF/BFFHH, Aug 24, Sep 8
Fielding-Oates Booth, <u>1734</u>: BFFO, Aug 24
Fielding-Reynolds Booth, <u>1728</u>: BFFR, Aug 24, SFFR, Sep 6
Fielding, Allen (actor), <u>1778</u>: DL, Dec 2
Fielding, Henry (author), <u>1728</u>: DL, Feb 16, Apr 22, HAY, Aug 9, DL, Nov 15;
   <u>1729</u>: DL, Apr 30, May 7, Jun 13, 27, Jul 25, HAY, Nov 12, 15, 22, Dec 18;
   <u>1730</u>: HAY, Jan 8, 21, GF, 26, HAY, Feb 6, 12, Mar 30, Apr 24, Jun 23, BFOF,
   Aug 20, SFOF, Sep 9, DL, Oct 24, 28, Nov 25, 30, HAY, 30, DL, Dec 4; <u>1731</u>:
   DL, Feb 8, Mar 20, HAY, 24, LIF, Apr 3, HAY, 22, DL, May 10, Jun 7, 11, Jul
   6, 20, Aug 6, 11, 16, 18, Sep 25, 30, Oct 2, Nov 25, Dec 10; <u>1732</u>: DL, Jan 1,
   10, Feb 14, Mar 23, Apr 26, Jun 1, 23, BF, Aug 16, GF, Oct 11, DL, Nov 6, 7,
   13, 14, Dec 11, 14; <u>1733</u>: DL, Feb 3, 15, 17, 20, Apr 6, 25, 30, May 5, Sep
   26, Oct 10, 15; <u>1734</u>: DL, Jan 15, HAY, Apr 5, BFT, Aug 17, HAY, 21, DL, Oct
   8, LIF, 12, DL, Nov 23, Dec 31; <u>1735</u>: DL, Jan 6, Feb 10, Jul 1; <u>1736</u>: HAY,
   Mar 5, GF, 25, HAY, Apr 29, May 27; <u>1737</u>: DL, Feb 19, HAY, Mar 21, 22, Apr
   13; <u>1738</u>: DL, Aug 19; <u>1742</u>: DL, May 6, 19, BF, Aug 26; <u>1743</u>: DL, Feb 17;
   <u>1745</u>: DL, Oct 17, GF, Dec 2; <u>1748</u>: DL, Jan 22; <u>1749</u>: DL, Feb 27, HAY, Nov 17;
   <u>1752</u>: DL, Apr 6, 13; <u>1755</u>: HAY, Sep 4; <u>1757</u>: CG, Dec 22; <u>1761</u>: DL, Jul 27;
   <u>1769</u>: HAY, Aug 7; <u>1770</u>: DL, Jun 7, CG, Dec 12; <u>1772</u>: HAY, Mar 16; <u>1773</u>: CG,
   Oct 23; <u>1775</u>: HAY, Feb 16, DL, May 13; <u>1776</u>: CHR, Oct 9; <u>1777</u>: CG, Apr 28;
   <u>1778</u>: DL, Nov 30, HAY, Dec 28; <u>1779</u>: DL, Dec 2; <u>1780</u>: CG, Oct 3; <u>1782</u>: HAY,
   Aug 13, Sep 21; <u>1783</u>: DL, Mar 24, HAY, Sep 17; <u>1786</u>: CG, Jan 31, May 9, DL,
   Oct 14; <u>1787</u>: DL, Oct 3; <u>1788</u>: CG, Nov 10; <u>1791</u>: CG, May 2; <u>1793</u>: HAY, Dec
   10; <u>1794</u>: CG, Sep 15; <u>1795</u>: HAY, Aug 11
--Author's Farce, The, <u>1730</u>: HAY, Mar 30, Apr 1, 3, 6, 7, 13, 16, 17, 24, 25,
   May 1, 4, 6, 7, 8, 11, 13, 14, 15, 18, 20, 21, 22, 25, 27, 28, 29, Jun 1, 3,
   4, 5, 8, 10, 11, 12, 16, 17, 19, 20, 22, Jul 3, Oct 21, 23, Nov 18, Dec 23;
   <u>1731</u>: HAY, Jan 4, 7, 8, 13, Feb 3, Mar 19, 31, Apr 5, 7, 9, May 10, Jun 18;
   <u>1732</u>: HAY, May 12; <u>1734</u>: DL, Jan 15, 16, 17, 18, 19, 21, 23; <u>1735</u>: WF, Aug
   23; <u>1748</u>: CG, Mar 28, HAY, May 4
--Coffee House Politician, The; or, The Justice Caught in his Own Trap, <u>1730</u>:
   HAY, Nov 30, LIF, Dec 4, 5, 7, 17; <u>1783</u>: DL, Mar 24
--Covent Garden Tragedy, The (Humours of Covent Garden), <u>1732</u>: DL, Jun 1, 6, 9,
   13, 21; <u>1734</u>: HAY, Apr 17, 18, 19, 29, May 27; <u>1735</u>: YB, Mar 21; <u>1742</u>: BF,
   Aug 26; <u>1778</u>: HAY, Dec 28; <u>1794</u>: CG, Sep 15
--Debauchees, The; or, The Jesuit Caught (The Old Debauchees), <u>1732</u>: DL, Jun 1,
   6, 13, 23, 28, Jul 4, 7; <u>1733</u>: HAY, Mar 27; <u>1745</u>: DL, Oct 17, 19, 22, 24, 26,
   28, 29, 30, 31, Nov 1, 2, 4, 5, 6, 7, 9, 12, 13, 14, 15, 16, 21, GF, Dec 2,
   3, 6, 9, 10, 13, DL, 19, GF, 19, DL, 26; <u>1746</u>: GF, Jan 14, 27, 28, Feb 5, 11,
   Mar 11, DL, Dec 1, 2, 8; <u>1747</u>: DL, Jan 29; <u>1748</u>: DL, Jan 22, 23
--Deborah; or, A Wife For You All, <u>1733</u>: DL, Apr 6
--Don Quixote in England, <u>1734</u>: HAY, Apr 5, 8, 9, 11, 17, 18, 19, 29, Aug 21,
   LIF, Oct 1, SOU, 7; <u>1739</u>: CG, May 17; <u>1744</u>: MFDSB, May 1; <u>1752</u>: DL, Apr 6,
   10, 21, 23, 25, 27, May 1, 2; <u>1759</u>: CG, May 3, 10; <u>1760</u>: SF, Sep 18, 19, 20,
   22; <u>1777</u>: CG, Apr 28, May 7, 15, 21; <u>1782</u>: HAY, Mar 4
--Election, The; or, Bribes on Both Sides, <u>1749</u>: CG, Mar 29
--Eurydice Hissed; or, A Word to the Wise, <u>1737</u>: HAY, Apr 13, 14, 15, 16, 18,
   19, 20, 21, 22, 23, 25, 26, 27, 28, 29, 30, May 2, 6, 11, 12, 23
--Eurydice; or, The Devil Henpecked, <u>1737</u>: DL, Feb 19
--Fathers, The; or, The Good Natured Man, <u>1778</u>: DL, Nov 28, 30, Dec 1, 2, 4, 5,
   7, 8, 9, 12; <u>1779</u>: DL, Jan 16
--Grub Street Opera, The, <u>1731</u>: HAY, Jun 5, 11, 14, Jul 0
--Historical Register, The, <u>1737</u>: HAY, Mar 8, 21, 22, 24, 26, 28, 29, 31, Apr
   2, 11, 12, 13, 14, 15, 16, 18, 19, 20, 21, 22, 23, 25, 26, 27, 28, 29, 30,
   May 2, 3, 5, 6, 11, 12, 17, 18, 19, 23

--Intriguing Chambermaid, The, 1734: DL, Jan 15, 16, 17, 21, 22, 23, 29, 31,
Apr 22, May 13, 16, 21, Nov 11, 13, 16, 19, Dec 4, 7; 1735: DL, Feb 22, Mar
22, Dec 5, 11, 19; 1736: DL, Jan 1, 5, Feb 26, Apr 3, CG, May 17, DL, 22, Oct
2, 21, Nov 8, Dec 9, 17; 1737: DL, Mar 26, CG, Apr 29, DL, May 2, 11, 21, 27,
31; 1738: DL, Mar 2, May 3, 15, Sep 21, Oct 24, Nov 29; 1739: DL, Jan 3, 5,
25, Feb 2, 28; 1740: DL, May 14, Nov 11, 28, Dec 6, 16; 1741: DL, Mar 14, Apr
1, 7, May 13, 21, Sep 15, Oct 8; 1742: DL, May 4, BFPY, Aug 25, DL, Oct 2,
Dec 9; 1743: DL, Apr 13, May 11; 1745: DL, Nov 28, 29, Dec 4, 7, 10; 1746:
DL, Jan 2, GF, Feb 10, DL, 15, 18, GF, 25, DL, Apr 28, Oct 23, 27, 30, Nov 5;
1747: DL, Apr 4, Oct 1, 15, 30, Nov 23, Dec 19; 1748: DL, Jan 5, 21, Mar 14,
19, Apr 2, 13, Oct 4, 13, 14, 22, Nov 2, 8, 18, 21, Dec 3, 10, 23; 1749: DL,
Jan 16, 24, 28, Feb 1, Mar 7, 13, Apr 5, May 16, Sep 28, Oct 13, 18, 23, Nov
4, 8, 24; 1750: DL, Jan 29, Feb 22, Apr 2, 21, 24, Oct 17, 23, 27, Dec 11,
17; 1751: DL, Sep 14, 28, Oct 5, 23, Nov 2, 6; 1752: DL, Feb 8, Mar 3, SFB,
Sep 22, DL, Oct 30, Nov 1, 3, 22, Dec 2, 11, 16; 1753: DL, Apr 2, Oct 3;
1754: DL, Oct 12, 21, Dec 7; 1755: DL, Mar 4, 15, Oct 9, 22; 1756: DL, Apr
23, Oct 7, 21; 1757: DL, Feb 10; 1758: DL, Feb 9, 14, Apr 28, May 11, Oct 12,
19; 1759: DL, Sep 22, Oct 24, Dec 3; 1760: DL, Feb 13, Oct 22, Nov 25; 1761:
DL, Oct 21, Nov 28; 1762: DL, Apr 17, Oct 2, CG, 13, 15; 1763: CG, May 9, DL,
Oct 13; 1764: CG, May 15, 24, Sep 26; 1765: CG, Jan 16, Mar 9, Apr 20, Sep
30, Nov 1, 15; 1766: CG, Jan 31, Apr 3, Oct 29; 1767: CG, Jan 14, Apr 30;
1768: CG, Mar 10, Dec 19; 1769: CG, Feb 1, Oct 11; 1770: CG, Oct 9; 1771: CG,
May 22, Oct 11; 1772: CG, Mar 5, 9, Apr 29, May 23; 1773: DL, Apr 3, 13, CG,
Sep 29; 1785: DL, Apr 1; 1787: CG, Mar 27, Apr 24, 28, May 3, Jun 8, HAY, Aug
14, CG, Oct 18; 1789: CG, May 5, 14; 1790: CG, Feb 23, May 25, DL, Nov 3, 8;
1791: DL, Jan 7, 15, CG, May 3; 1798: CG, Nov 9, 13; 1800: CG, Jan 16
--Letter Writers, The; or, A New Way to Keep a Wife at Home, 1731: HAY, Mar 24,
26, 29, Apr 2; 1783: HAY, Sep 17
--Lottery, The, 1732: DL, Jan 1, 3, 4, 5, 6, 7, 8, D, 12, DL, 20, 21, 22, 25,
27, 28, 29, Feb 1, 10, 11, 12, 26, Mar 4, 7, 14, 18, 28, Apr 21, May 5, 6,
25, Jun 13, Sep 28, Oct 5, 12, 24, Nov 9; 1733: DL, Apr 4, 24; 1734: DL/LIF,
Mar 11, Apr 1, DL/HAY, 27, CG, 30, DL/LIF, May 3, CG, 4, LIF, 16, 29, HAY,
Jun 7, 14, 19, 26, Jul 1, 10, 17, 29, 31, CG/LIF, Sep 20, 30, DL, Oct 29, Nov
21, GF, Dec 2, 3, 4, 5, CG/LIF, 5, GF, 6, DL, 11, CG/LIF, 16; 1735: YB, Mar
12, DL, 17, CG/LIF, Apr 11, GF, 23, DL, May 8, YB, 19, HAY, Jun 12, CG, Sep
29, DL, Nov 12, Dec 3; 1736: DL, Mar 15, 23, GF, Apr 28, DL, Jun 23, Oct 16;
1737: DL, Mar 9, LIF, Apr 27, CG, May 16, DL, Nov 15, 16, 17; 1738: DL, Feb
9; 1739: DL, Jan 18, 24, Apr 12, Oct 23, Nov 7, CG, Dec 6, 12, 21; 1740: DL,
Apr 21; 1742: DL, Mar 30; 1743: CG, Nov 25, Dec 1, 2, 3, 7, 9, 12, 15, 16,
19; 1744: CG, Mar 13, Apr 9, 16, 19, May 2, 4, Oct 8, 10, 15, 18, Nov 2, 9,
27, 28, 29, Dec 22; 1745: CG, Mar 21, Nov 22, Dec 5, 11, DL, 16, 20, 23, 28;
1746: SOU, Oct 27, DL, Dec 20, CG, 20, 23, DL, 26, CG, 30; 1747: CG, May 11,
Nov 24, DL, 27, 28, Dec 1, CG, 4, 5, 7; 1748: DL, Sep 10, 17, 29, CG, Oct 7,
11, DL, 11, CG, 24, DL, Nov 1, Dec 9; 1749: DL, Mar 11, Oct 26, Nov 3, 30;
1750: SFP, Sep 7; 1751: CG, May 2, 6, 11, DL, Oct 11, 19, 24, CG, 26, DL, 30,
Nov 4, CG, 4, 5, 12, DL, 18, CG, 19, Dec 10, DL, 12; 1752: DL, Apr 8; 1753:
DL, Oct 19, CG, 25, DL, 29, CG, 30, Nov 3, 16, 19, 24, 28, 29, Dec 3, DL, 17,
22; 1754: CG, Apr 2, 29, 30, May 14, Oct 11; 1755: CG, Apr 14, DL, Sep 30,
CG, Oct 8, 14, DL, 16, CG, 20, 24; 1756: DL, Nov 13, CG, 29, Dec 3, 7, 11;
1757: CG, Sep 14; 1758: CG, Oct 30, Nov 2, 14, 15, DL, 15, 18, 23, 29, CG,
Dec 1, DL, 6, CG, 13; 1759: DL, Jan 15, CG, Nov 23; 1760: CG, Nov 22, 24, 27;
1767: CG, Feb 19; 1768: DL, Oct 31, Nov 2, 8; 1769: DL, May 11, 16; 1772: DL,
Feb 29, Mar 14, Apr 11, 23; 1773: DL, May 13; 1774: DL, Nov 18, 26, Dec 16;
1775: DL, Jan 20, Nov 25, 29; 1776: DL, Jan 20; 1783: DL, Dec 13
--Love in Several Masques, 1728: DL, Feb 16, 17, 18, 19
--Miser, The, 1733: DL, Feb 17, 19, 20, 24, 27, Mar 1, 3, 6, 13, 17, 27, 30,
Apr 3, 4, 5, 6, 7, 10, 12, 21, 26, May 3, 4, 8, 16, BFCGBH, Aug 23, DL, Oct
24, 26, 27, 29, Nov 16, DL/HAY, 27, 29, Dec 3; 1734: DL, Jan 14, Feb 6, 25,
HAY, Apr 5, 8, LIF, 15, HAY, 17, 29, DL, May 16, JS, 29, 31, RI, Jun 29, HAY,
Aug 14, LIF, Oct 1, DL, 8, Nov 23, Dec 31; 1735: DL, Feb 8, Apr 16, Oct 2,
Nov 13, Dec 15; 1736: DL, Jan 31, Feb 19, GF, Mar 18, 20, 25, Apr 12, 29, DL,
May 6, Oct 25, Nov 30, Dec 18; 1737: DL, Feb 9, May 24, Sep 17; 1738: DL, Feb
11, Apr 11, May 12, Nov 2, 10, Dec 23; 1739: DL, Feb 8, Mar 2, Apr 26, May
25, Sep 15, Nov 2, Dec 7; 1740: DL, Jan 1, Apr 17; 1741: GF, Mar 16, DL, Apr
4, GF, 15, DL, May 2, Sep 17, Nov 9, CG, Dec 12, 15, GF, 26, CG, 31; 1742:
DL, Jan 1, 21, Feb 1, CG, 17, DL, May 1, GF, 18, DL, 19, CG, 25, DL, Sep 25,
JS, Oct 12, CG, Nov 8, DL, 26, Dec 27; 1743: LIF, Apr 4, HAY, 14, CG, May 11,
DL, Oct 4, CG, Nov 17, Dec 7, 30; 1744: DL, Jan 25, CG, Feb 2, Apr 3, 17,
HAY, 20, DL, May 8, HAY, 10, CG, 11, Oct 12, Nov 30, GF, Dec 12, CG, 15;
1745: GF, Jan 3, CG, 25, GF, Mar 7, CG, May 2, Nov 26, DL, Dec 20, GF, 27;
1746: DL, Jan 11, Feb 10, GF, 13, DL, Mar 6, May 16, SOU, Oct 7, CG, 13, GF,
Nov 26, DL, Dec 30; 1747: CG, Jan 22, DL, Mar 17, May 12; 1748: DL, Feb 3;

301

1749: DL, Jan 25, Feb 21, May 12, Oct 24, Dec 5; 1750: DL, Feb 21, CG, Sep
24, Oct 30; 1751: DL, Jan 12, 24, CG, May 13, DL, Sep 12, CG, Oct 8, DL, Dec
27; 1752: CG, Feb 27, Apr 2, 23, Oct 11, Dec 7; 1753: DL, Jan 13, CG, 29, DL,
Feb 20, CG, Mar 27, DL, Sep 11, CG, 17, 19, Oct 15, 16, Nov 23, Dec 21; 1754:
CG, Feb 5, DL, May 17, CG, 17, DL, Sep 14, CG, Oct 11, Dec 2, 20; 1755: CG,
Feb 1, Apr 16, Oct 3, Dec 19; 1756: CG, Jan 21, May 6, DL, 18, CG, Sep 24,
Dec 17; 1757: CG, May 20, Nov 23, Dec 17; 1758: CG, May 8, DL, 17, CG, Sep
27, Nov 22, Dec 19; 1759: CG, Jan 9, DL, 17, CG, Mar 8, Sep 24, Dec 4; 1760:
CG, Feb 23, May 21, DL, Jul 29, CG, Oct 20; 1761: CG, Jan 27, May 14, Sep 11,
Dec 10; 1762: DL, Jan 20, CG, Mar 30, Oct 11, Nov 9; 1763: DL, May 31, CG,
Oct 8, DL, Nov 19, Dec 29; 1764: CG, Jan 20; 1765: DL, Jan 17, 18; 1766: CG,
May 16; 1767: CG, Jan 1, Feb 20, May 9; 1768: CG, Sep 27, Dec 27; 1769: CG,
Jan 5, 24, May 19, Oct 2, Dec 27; 1770: CG, Dec 21; 1771: CG, Jan 17, Oct 30,
DL, Nov 11, CG, 12, Dec 26; 1772: CG, May 6, 29, HAY, Aug 4, CG, Sep 21, Oct
21, Dec 26; 1773: CG, May 17, Dec 2, 3, 31; 1774: CG, Feb 10, Sep 30, Nov 22;
1775: CG, May 30; 1776: HAY, Sep 18; 1777: CG, Oct 1; 1778: CG, Mar 5, CHR,
Jun 24; 1779: DL, Oct 7, 26, Nov 12; 1780: DL, Jan 6, May 26, Oct 3, Nov 20;
1785: HAY, Feb 12; 1786: DL, Oct 30; 1787: CG, Apr 30, May 7; 1788: CG, Jan
21, Feb 18, Apr 5, Nov 10, 11, 13, 18, 24, Dec 20; 1789: CG, Jan 31, Feb 13,
28, Mar 24, HAY, May 25, 29, CG, Nov 7, 17; 1790: CG, Jan 26, Mar 11, May 6;
1791: CG, Dec 2, 7; 1792: CG, Feb 14; 1793: CG, Dec 5; 1795: CG, Apr 8, 23;
1796: HAY, Sep 28; 1797: CG, Nov 21; 1798: CG, Sep 21, 24; 1799: CG, Feb 4,
DL, May 9, CG, Oct 31; 1800: CG, Apr 28, May 1
--Miss Lucy in Town, 1742: DL, May 6, 7, 10, 12, 14, 19, 20, Oct 27, 29, 30,
Nov 1, 2, 3, 6, 12, 15, 19, 30, Dec 1; 1770: DL, Jun 7, CG, Dec 12
--Mock Doctor, The; or, The Dumb Lady Cured, 1732: DL, Jun 23, 28, Jul 4, 7,
28, Aug 1, TC, 4, DL, 11, 15, 19, 21, 22, Sep 8, 12, 14, 16, 19, 21, 30, Oct
3, 7, 10, 17, Nov 16, 30; 1733: DL, Jan 23, GF, Feb 13, HAY, 14, GF, 15, 17,
22, 24, 26, DL, 26, GF, 27, Mar 1, 3, DL, 10, 15, HAY, 20, DL, 26, GF, 28,
30, 31, Apr 2, 4, DL, 9, GF, 10, 11, 12, DL, 13, 16, GF, 17, 18, DL, 18, 23,
HAY, 23, DL, 27, GF, May 4, DL, 9, GF, 10, 11, 14, 15, 16, 23, HAY, 28, Jul
12, CG, Aug 9, RI, Sep 10, GF, 27, DL, Oct 1, GF, 3, 4, DL, 5, DL/HAY, 10,
25, GF, 25, 30, Nov 5, 6, DL/HAY, 14, GF, 20, 21, 27, Dec 13, HAY, 13, DL,
19; 1734: GF, Jan 9, DL/HAY, 11, GF, 19, Feb 5, DL/HAY, Mar 4, GF, 11,
DL/HAY, 25, GF, 28, DL/HAY, Apr 1, HAY, Jun 5, 17, Aug 5, 16, YB, 28, HAY,
Oct 7, DL, 8, 9, HAY, 10, GF, 14, CG/LIF, 18, 23, 24, 26, Nov 1, 7; 1735: GF,
Mar 10, YB, 10, DL, 29, Apr 14, 22, GF, 24, DL, May 9, YB, Jun 3, DL, Jul 1,
LIF, 16, HAY, Aug 4, DL, Sep 27, Nov 27, GF, Dec 3, 4, 5, DL, 17, YEB, 22;
1736: HAY, Feb 11, DL, Mar 20, LIF, 29, DL, Apr 12, GF, 17, LIF, 19, GF, 27,
YB, 27, DL, May 4, 18, HAY, Jun 26, DL, Sep 28, Oct 19, 28; 1737: DL, Mar 19,
29, Apr 20, 23, 27, LIF, May 16, DL, 25, CG, 31, LIF, Jun 22, Aug 5, 9, DL,
Oct 13, 19, Nov 10; 1738: DL, Jan 27, Mar 21, Apr 11, 17, Oct 13, 16, 27;
1739: DL, Jan 4, 6, 10, 15, 31, Mar 26, Apr 25, May 17, CG, 18, DL, 28, CG,
Aug 2, 10, 21, Sep 5, 17, Oct 1, 25, Nov 1, 20, 28, Dec 15, 19; 1740: CG, Jan
25, Mar 11, DL, 22, CG, Apr 14, DL, 14, CG, 18, 25, 29, May 21, DL, 23, 29,
CG, Sep 22, 29, Oct 8, DL, 9, GF, 16, 17, DL, 18, GF, 18, DL, 22, 23, GF, 24,
31, Nov 3, 5, CG, 18, GF, Dec 10, 11; 1741: GF, Jan 20, JS, Feb 20, CG, Mar
2, 30, GF, Apr 6, DL, 20, CG, 23, DL, 27, GF, 29, DL, May 1, 14, 15, 22, 23,
25, 28, NWC, Aug 22, DL, Sep 5, GF, 23, CG, 25, JS, Oct 6, GF, 20, 21, Nov 2;
1742: DL, Mar 20, 22, Apr 1, 5, 6, GF, 20, DL, 27, May 15, Sep 11, SOU, 21,
JS, Oct 12, DL, 25, Nov 4, LIF, 24, 26, 29; 1743: DL, Mar 1, LIF, 8, 15, CG,
Apr 20, LIF, Jun 3, CG, Oct 17, 19, 26, 31, Nov 14, Dec 10; 1744: DL, Mar 12,
HAY, Apr 20, May 10, CG, 11, HAY, 16, Sep 29, CG, Oct 3, HAY, Dec 17; 1745:
DL, Jan 8, 11, JS, 14, DL, 16, GF, 18, 19, 21, 22, 23, 24, 25, 26, DL, Mar
11, GF, 14, 21, CG, Apr 2, 26, Oct 7, DL, 12, GF, 31, Nov 1, 4, CG, 12, 15,
GF, 21, CG, Dec 31; 1746: GF, Jan 15, 22, Feb 3, CG, 13, GF, 17, Mar 10, 18,
CG, May 7, DL, Jun 6, 9, SOU, Sep 17, 25, CG, Oct 1, 4, 17, GF, 30, CG, Nov
4, GF, 6, 7, Dec 15; 1747: GF, Jan 2, CG, Oct 29, Nov 25, Dec 9; 1748: CG,
Jan 1, Apr 14, SOU, Jul 18, CG, Sep 21, 30, BHB, Oct 4, CG, 10, DL, Nov 12,
16, 25, Dec 16; 1749: CG, Jan 3, Mar 14, NWSM, May 16, JS, Jul 3, DL, Sep 16,
CG, Oct 18, Nov 6, 14; 1750: CG, May 3, SFY, Sep 14, CG, Oct 17, Nov 5, DL,
14, 22, 28, Dec 4; 1751: CG, Feb 5, Mar 4, 18, Apr 15, Sep 28, Oct 21, Nov
18; 1752: CG, Jan 27, Feb 1, Apr 22, May 8, Sep 18, SOU, Nov 24; 1753: DL,
Mar 20, Apr 7, CG, May 21, Sep 12, Dec 11; 1754: CG, Feb 12, Sep 16; 1755:
CG, Jan 7, HAY, Aug 21, CG, Oct 3, DL, Nov 6, 11; 1756: DL, Oct 23, Nov 3,
20, 27, Dec 13, ACAD, 15; 1757: DL, Sep 15, Oct 4, 19, Dec 1; 1758: CG, Jan
20, DL, 28, May 5, 8, Sep 26; 1759: DL, Jan 31, Feb 24, CG, May 7, DL, Sep
25, Cct 5, Nov 15, 28, Dec 18; 1760: DL, Jan 16, CG, Apr 15, DL, May 13, Jun
19, CG, Sep 22; 1761: DL, Sep 5, Oct 5, 7; 1762: DL, May 12, CG, 20, Oct 6;
1763: DL, May 31; 1765: CG, Sep 18; 1767: CG, Sep 14, DL, Nov 18, Dec 1;
1769: CG, Oct 12; 1770: CG, Oct 2; 1771: HAY, Jul 5; 1772: HAY, Jul 6, 13,
Aug 7, Sep 9, CG, Nov 21; 1773: HAY, May 31, Jun 23, Jul 21, Sep 20; 1774:

HAY, May 16, Jun 22, Jul 15; <u>1775</u>: HAY, Jul 7; <u>1776</u>: HAY, May 20, Aug 19, CG,
Sep 23; <u>1777</u>: CG, Feb 22, CHR, Jun 25; <u>1778</u>: CHR, Jun 8; <u>1781</u>: CII, Apr 9;
<u>1784</u>: CG, Dec 4, 17; <u>1785</u>: CG, May 17; <u>1787</u>: CG, Feb 13; <u>1788</u>: CG, Mar 11;
<u>1793</u>: HAY, Dec 10, 11, 14, 20, 31; <u>1794</u>: HAY, Jan 14, Feb 6, Apr 1; <u>1795</u>:
HAY, Aug 5, 11, 20; <u>1796</u>: HAY, Jun 14, 28, Jul 13, Aug 4, 15, Sep 16; <u>1797</u>:
HAY, Jun 22, 27, Jul 20, 31, Aug 11; <u>1799</u>: DL, Nov 25, 28, Dec 20, 28
--Modern Husband, The, <u>1732</u>: DL, Feb 14, 15, 16, 17, 18, 19, 21, 22, 24, 26,
28, 29, Mar 2, 18, 30
--Pasquin, <u>1736</u>: HAY, Mar 5, 6, 8, 9, 11, 12, 13, 15, 16, 17, 18, 19, 20, 22,
23, 24, 25, 26, 29, 30, 31, Apr 1, 2, 3, 5, 6, 7, 8, 9, 10, 12, 13, 14, 15,
16, 17, 19, 20, GF, 27, HAY, 27, 29, 30, May 1, 3, 4, 5, 6, 7, 8, 10, 11, 12,
13, 14, 15, 20, 21, 22, 24, 25, 26, Jun 7, 11, 17, 26, Jul 2, BFF, Aug 23,
SOU, Sep 20; <u>1737</u>: LIF, Jan 24, 25, HAY, Feb 9, DL, 19, HAY, 25, Mar 8, 19,
21, Apr 13, 15, May 2, 3, 4, 5, 9; <u>1740</u>: DL, Apr 17, 30, May 16, 22, 28;
<u>1749</u>: CG, Mar 29; <u>1752</u>: CG, Apr 8; <u>1782</u>: HAY, Aug 13
--Pleasures of the Town, The, <u>1730</u>: HAY, Apr 20
--Rape Upon Rape; or, The Justice Caught in His Own Trap, <u>1730</u>: HAY, Jun 23,
24, 26, 30, Jul 1, 2, 3, 10, 21
--Temple Beau, The; or, The Intriguing Sisters, <u>1730</u>: GF, Jan 26, 27, 28, 29,
31, Feb 2, 3, 4, 5, 10, Mar 3, Jun 5, Jul 9; <u>1731</u>: GF, Mar 13, Dec 4; <u>1736</u>:
GF, Mar 25, Apr 27; <u>1782</u>: HAY, Sep 21
--Tom Thumb (Tragedy of Tragedies), <u>1730</u>: HAY, Apr 24, 25, 27, 29, May 1, 4, 6,
7, 8, 11, 13, 14, 15, 18, 20, 21, 22, 25, 27, 28, 29, Jun 1, 3, 4, 5, 8, 10,
11, 12, 16, 17, 19, 20, 22, 23, Jul 1, 2, 3, 17, 18, 22, 23, 24, BFR, Sep 4,
SF, 14, HAY, Oct 23, 26, Nov 11, 30, Dec 4, 7, 14, 23, 30; <u>1731</u>: HAY, Jan 14,
GF, Mar 15, 18, HAY, 19, GF, 20, 22, HAY, 24, 26, GF, 27, HAY, 29, 31, Apr 2,
5, 7, 9, 22, 23, 26, GF, 26, HAY, 28, GF, May 5, HAY, 10, 19, Jun 2, 18;
<u>1732</u>: HAY, Feb 21, Mar 8, Apr 1, LIF, May 2, DL, 3, LIF, 3, DL, 3, LIF, 4,
DL, 12, LIF, 22, DL, 25; <u>1733</u>: DL, May 3; <u>1735</u>: LIF, Aug 6, 8, Sep 2, HAY,
Dec 13; <u>1736</u>: HAY, May 3; <u>1740</u>: DL, Apr 17, CG, 26, DL, 26, 28, 30, CG, May
3, DL, 7, 16, 17, 22, CG, 23, DL, 28; <u>1741</u>: CG, Mar 10, GF, Apr 2, 3, CG, 7,
GF, 16, 21; <u>1742</u>: DL, Mar 29; <u>1743</u>: LIF, Apr 9, HAY, 15; <u>1745</u>: DL, Apr 17,
18, 22, 24, 26, 29, May 7, 10, 13, 23, Oct 8, 10, 15; <u>1746</u>: DL, Jan 29, Feb
5, May 14, 19, Jun 11, 13, Sep 30; <u>1747</u>: GF, Apr 6; <u>1748</u>: DL, Oct 29; <u>1749</u>:
SOU, Oct 16; <u>1751</u>: CG, May 3, 10; <u>1755</u>: DL, Apr 25, 26, May 15, HAY, Sep 4,
6, DL, Oct 27, Nov 1, 28, Dec 15; <u>1756</u>: DL, Apr 5; <u>1759</u>: DL, May 11, 15, 19;
<u>1769</u>: HAY, Aug 7, 9, 14, 29, Sep 6; <u>1770</u>: HAY, Dec 19; <u>1773</u>: CG, Oct 23;
<u>1775</u>: DL, May 13, 15, 16, 19; <u>1776</u>: CHR, Oct 9, 11, 18
--Tumble Down Dick; or, Phaeton in the Suds, <u>1736</u>: HAY, Apr 29, 30, May 1, 4,
5, 6, 7, 8, 10, 11, 13, 14, 15, 20, 21, 22, 24, 25, 27, 28, 29
--Universal Gallant, The; or, The Different Husbands, <u>1735</u>: DL, Feb 10, 11, 12
--Virgin Unmasked, The; or, An Old Man Taught Wisdom, <u>1735</u>: DL, Jan 6, 7, 8, 9,
10, 14, 17, 18, 20, 21, 28, 29, Feb 1, 17, 18, Mar 24, 27, Apr 11, 16, 21,
23, 29, May 17, 22, Jun 3, 9, 11, Sep 6, 9, 11, 30, Nov 22, 24, 28, 29, Dec
18, 22, 30; <u>1736</u>: DL, Jan 3, 6, Apr 1, 10, 15, 16, 29, May 28, Jun 2, Oct 18,
23, Nov 1, 12, 17, YB, Dec 1; <u>1737</u>: DL, Jan 25, Mar 2, 15, Apr 15, 26, May 6,
7, 14, 20, 30, Sep 8, 10, 29, Oct 6, 21, Nov 14; <u>1738</u>: DL, Mar 20, May 22,
31, Sep 7, Dec 6; <u>1739</u>: DL, Jan 1, 23, 26, Mar 3, 8, 22, Apr 27, May 11, 12,
15, 23, Sep 22, 25, Oct 5; <u>1740</u>: DL, Feb 6, Mar 1, 3, 13, 29, Apr 10, May 9,
Sep 27, Oct 7, SOU, 9, DL, Nov 4, 7, 14, GF, 22, 24, 25, 26, DL, 26, GF, 27,
28, Dec 3, 4, 5, DL, 8, GF, 12, DL, 15; <u>1741</u>: GF, Jan 27, 28, Feb 2, 9, 12,
16, 26, 28, Mar 19, DL, 21, GF, Apr 9, 13, DL, 16, GF, 17, DL, May 4, GF, 5,
DL, Jun 4, Sep 8, GF, 14, 18, DL, 22, GF, 25, 30, Oct 19, 22, Nov 27; <u>1742</u>:
GF, Jan 13, 20, JS, 25, GF, Feb 1, 2, 12, 17, 23, DL, Mar 8, 15, GF, 25, DL,
Apr 8, 24, May 6, 18, 22, GF, 27, DL, Sep 16, 21, CG, Oct 4, 6, 9, 11, 13,
14, 18, 21, DL, 26, CG, 27, DL, 27, CG, Nov 6, LIF, Dec 1, 3, 6, 8, 17, 20;
<u>1743</u>: DL, Jan 15, Mar 7, LIF, 14, DL, 14, CG, 22, DL, 24, LIF, Apr 11, DL,
11, CG, 12, HAY, 14, DL, 19, 21, CG, 22, DL, 29, CG, May 3, 6, DL, 9, CG, 11,
Sep 30, Oct 3, DL, 13, CG, Nov 17, 19; <u>1744</u>: CG, Jan 4, 7, DL, 12, Mar 29,
CG, Apr 2, 18, 27, 30, May 7, 9, Sep 24, Nov 14, 17, GF, 26, 29, Dec 4, 10,
15, 29; <u>1745</u>: GF, Jan 31, Feb 1, 5, SMMF, 18, 20, GF, Mar 23, 25, CG, Apr 1,
GF, 4, CG, 23, 27, 30, May 7, 29, BRA, Jun 24, CG, Sep 25, Oct 9, Nov 6, GF,
26, 27, 28, 29, DL, Dec 11, 12, 13; <u>1746</u>: CG, Jan 24, DL, Feb 17, GF, 18, DL,
Mar 17, CG, Apr 19, HAY, 30, DL, Sep 25, Oct 7, SOU, 7, CG, 20, 22, 27, 31,
Nov 6, GF, 10, 11, 26, 27; <u>1747</u>: DL, Jan 17, SOU, 21, GF, Feb 5, DL, Apr 23,
CG, May 7, 13, 22, DL, Oct 23, Nov 6, SOU, 16, DL, Dec 31; <u>1748</u>: DL, Jan 20,
27, Mar 8, Apr 19, CG, 29, May 3, 6, SOU, Aug 1, NTW, Nov 16, DL, 23, 26, Dec
5, 14, 17, NWC, 26, DL, 30; <u>1749</u>: SOU, Jan 2, DL, 20, Feb 3, 20, 27, May 10,
Sep 21, SOU, Oct 2, BHB, 3, DL, 5, 17, 27, Nov 2, 16; <u>1750</u>: SOU, Jan 25, DL,
Sep 8, Nov 1, 17, 26, Dec 1; <u>1751</u>: DL, May 6, 8, 9, 10, Sep 12, 18, JS, Dec
16; <u>1752</u>: NWLS, Nov 20; <u>1754</u>: CG, Oct 29, 30, Nov 1, 8, 20; <u>1755</u>: CG, Jan 28,
Apr 21, May 1, 3, Nov 14, 20, Dec 6; <u>1756</u>: CG, Jan 20, Feb 10, Mar 11, Sep

24, 27, DL, Nov 10, 11, Dec 18; 1757: CG, Jan 11, DL, Oct 13, Nov 12, CG, Dec
5, 23; 1758: DL, Sep 19, CG, Oct 18, DL, 25, Dec 12; 1759: DL, Jan 16, Feb 1,
22, May 30, Oct 6; 1762: CG, Apr 27, DL, May 26; 1765: DL, Dec 7, 9, 20;
1766: DL, Nov 7, 28, Dec 19; 1767: DL, May 12, HAY, Sep 18, DL, Oct 9, 28;
1768: DL, Feb 27, CG, Apr 29, HAY, Jul 6, 20; 1769: DL, May 15, HAY, 15, 17;
1770: HAY, Jun 22; 1771: HAY, May 29, Jun 3, 28; 1772: HAY, May 18, Jun 29;
1773: HAY, May 24, Jun 25, Jul 19, Aug 9; 1775: HAY, May 19, 22; 1786: DL,
Jan 24, 25, 28, CG, 31, Feb 1, DL, 3, 6, CG, 6, DL, 10, 14, 22, 25, 28, Mar
2, 7, 18, 27, Apr 3, 8, 21, 26, May 4, 10, 17, 19, CG, Sep 20, DL, Oct 14,
CG, 20, DL, Dec 1, 15; 1787: DL, Jan 2, Mar 17, RLSN, 30, DL, May 1, HAY, Jun
22, DL, Oct 3, 13, Nov 20; 1788: DL, May 20, HAY, Jul 24, Aug 6, 12, 21;
1789: DL, Mar 23, Apr 30, Oct 1, 3, Dec 2; 1790: HAY, Jun 18, 24, Jul 21, 28,
Aug 18, 26, Sep 2; 1791: DL, Jan 11; 1792: DLKING'S, Jan 11, 17, 21, 25, Feb
1, 6, 18, Apr 23, 30, May 14, 25, HAY, Jun 20, DL, Nov 29, Dec 10, 17; 1793:
DL, Feb 2, Mar 2, Jun 5, HAY, Oct 18; 1794: DL, Apr 21, 22, 23, 24, Sep 20;
1795: DL, Jan 7, May 7, HAY, Aug 29; 1796: DL, May 5, 11, HAY, Sep 3, DL, Oct
3, 31; 1797: DL, Nov 9, Dec 11, 14; 1798: DL, May 19; 1799: DL, Jan 17, May
27, CG, Jun 1, DL, 4, Jul 2, Sep 19, Nov 29, Dec 18; 1800: DL, Feb 12, Mar
15, Apr 26
--Wedding Day, The, 1733: GF, Nov 12; 1743: DL, Feb 17, 19, 21, 22, 24, 26
--Welch Opera, The, 1731: HAY, Apr 22, 23, 26, 28, May 19, 26, 27, Jun 1, 2, 4,
5
Fielding, John (Justice), 1750: JS, Nov 15; 1752: TCJS, Aug 11; 1755: DL, Nov
18, 19; 1757: DL, May 7; 1767: CG, Dec 14; 1773: CG, Jan 22, Apr 19, DL, Sep
18, CG, Oct 27; 1774: CG, Jan 11
Fielding, Miss (actor), 1761: CG, Jan 7, 10, Apr 11; 1762: CG, May 8
Fieri tormenti (song), 1763: KING'S, Apr 25
Fierville (dancer), 1772: KING'S, Nov 14, Dec 1, 8; 1773: KING'S, Jan 2, 5, 12,
19, 26, Feb 2, 20, 23, 25, Mar 9, 16, 18, 23, 30, Apr 1, 3, 13, 17, 19, 20,
24, 27, 29, May 1, 3, 6, 22, 25, 28, Jun 1, 3, 5, 8, 12, 19, Oct 23, Nov 20,
23; 1774: KING'S, Feb 22, Mar 12, 17, 24, Apr 9, 14, 19, May 5, 10, 12, 17,
28, Jun 3; 1775: KING'S, Oct 31, Nov 7; 1776: KING'S, Jan 9, 27, Feb 13, 17,
27, Mar 12, Apr 18, 20, May 30, Jun 8
Fife (actor), 1734: DL, Apr 15; 1736: DL, Jan 12
Fife and Harmony of War (song), 1703: LIF, Jun 14
Fig for the Fellows (entertainment), 1799: CG, Apr 26
Fig-Tree (residence), 1740: CG, Mar 11
Fight off Camperdown (song), 1798: DL, Jun 8; 1800: CG, May 29
Figure Dance (dance), 1737: DL, Mar 19
Figure Dance, Grand (dance), 1782: CG, Apr 2, 27, May 3
Filch, Young (Lilliputian) (dancer), 1729: LIF, May 9, 14, 19
Fildew (actor), 1778: CHR, Jun 1, 3, 8, 15, 18, 22, 24, 26; 1779: HAY, Oct 13;
1781: CII, Mar 15
Filial Pity. See Hill, Aaron.
Filizeau, Miss (actor), 1757: HAY, Aug 22
Filkes (householder), 1742: CG, May 4
Fill round the health good natured and free (song), 1673: DG, May 0
Fill the bowl with rosy wine (song), 1791: DL, May 18
Fille a la Mode, La; ou, Arlequin Badaut de Paris (play), 1720: HAY, Dec 29;
1721: HAY, Mar 9; 1726: HAY, Mar 24
Fille Capitaine, La. See Montfleury, Antoine.
Fille Mal Gardee (dance), 1791: PAN, Apr 30, May 3, 9, 10, 14, 21, 28, Jun 2,
10, 30; 1799: KING'S, Apr 18, DL, May 8, KING'S, 10, Jun 8, Jul 2, 20; 1800:
KING'S, Apr 15, 19
Fille Scavante, La. See Fatouville, Nolant de.
Filles Errantes, Les. See Regnard, Jean Francois.
Filmer, Edward, 1697: LIF, Jun 0
--Unfortunate Couple, The, 1697: LIF, Jun 0; 1704: LIF, Aug 17
--Unnatural Brother, The, 1697: LIF, Jan 0, Jun 0
Filosofo (dance), 1775: KING'S, Nov 16, 18, 28, Dec 5; 1780: KING'S, May 9, 12,
16, Jul 1
Filosofo di Campagna, Il. See Galuppi, Baldassare.
Final, Thomas (musician), 1681: ATCOURT, Nov 15
Finch (bondsman), 1746: CG, Nov 24, Dec 26
Finch (King's servant) 1758: CG, Apr 27
Finch Lane, 1742: GF, Jan 29
Finch, Anne, Countess of Winchelsea (songwriter), 1693: DG, May 0
Finch, Daniel, Earl of Nottingham (spectator), 1689: DLORDG, May 28
Finch, Heneage, Lord Winchelsea (spectator), 1664: BRIDGES, Sep 14; 1694: NONE,
Mar 22
Finch, Mrs (actor), 1695: DL, Sep 0, DG, Nov 0; 1696: DL/DL, Dec 0; 1697: DL,
Feb 0; 1705: DL, Jul 25; 1708: DL/QUEEN, May 19, DL, Jun 26, Jul 27, Aug 4,

Sep 3, 18, 21, 28, Oct 2, 9, 21; 1709: DL, Jan 11, May 2, 24, Nov 26, Dec 7; 1710: DL, Feb 25, Mar 18; 1715: LIF, Jun 14, Oct 11, Dec 12; 1716: LIF, Jun 1, Jul 4; 1717: LIF, May 15, 16, Dec 12, 14; 1718: LIF, Apr 30, Jun 20, Jul 24, RI, Aug 9, 11

Finch, T (costumer), 1787: CG, Nov 1

Find me a lonely cave (song), 1693: NONE, Sep 0; 1698: NONE, Sep 0

Findlay (actor, dancer), 1796: CG, Mar 15, Jun 7; 1797: CG, May 26, Oct 16, Dec 26; 1798: CG, Oct 15; 1799: CG, May 13, 22

Findlay, Master (actor), 1788: HAY, Apr 9

Findon, Daniel (coffee-house proprietor), 1746: GF, Jan 15, 22

Fine Lady's Airs, The. See Baker, Thomas.

Finell (musician), 1675: ATCOURT, Feb 15

Fineschi, Vincenzo (singer), 1787: KING'S, Dec 8; 1788: KING'S, Jan 12, 15, Mar 4, May 15, Jun 26; 1789: KING'S, Jan 10, 24, Feb 28, Mar 21, 24, Apr 4, May 9, 28, Jun 2, CG, Jul 11

Fingalian Dance (dance), 1725: LIF, Apr 22; 1726: LIF, Apr 11, 26, 27, 30, May 3, 14, 24, Aug 5, 9, 16, Sep 14; 1727: LIF, Feb 9, Apr 7, May 4, 22, Oct 26, Nov 1, 16, 23; 1728: LIF, Jan 8, Mar 21, Apr 4, 6, 22, 24, 29, May 16, 20, 22, 29, BFB, Aug 24; 1729: LIF, Jan 13, Mar 10, 17, 27, Apr 10, 11, 24, 26, 28, 30, May 3, 6, 7, 9, 12, 13, 15, 19, 20, 22, 23, BFB, Aug 25; 1730: LIF, Apr 24, 25, 29, May 11, 15, 18, 27, Jul 3, Sep 18, Oct 30, Nov 3, 6, Dec 7; 1731: LIF, Jan 4, May 10, 12, 14, 17, 19, 21, 24, Oct 25, Nov 12, Dec 17; 1732: LIF, Jan 5, Mar 21, 30, Apr 11, 17, May 17, 18, RI, Aug 17, LIF/CG, Sep 25, Oct 2, 9, Nov 7, 16, Dec 4, DL, 18, CG/LIF, 26; 1733: LIF/CG, Jan 12, 15, 18, Feb 2, CG, 8, LIF/CG, Mar 30, Apr 11, 16, 19, 27, May 7, 8, CG, 11, LIF/CG, 15, 19, 24, CG, Oct 26, Nov 1, 23, Dec 4, 11, 28; 1734: DL, Nov 22; 1735: DL, Feb 5, Apr 25; 1737: CG, May 6, 16, 19; 1742: BFHC, Aug 25; 1750: DL, Apr 20; 1755: CG, Nov 26, Dec 1, 3, 5, 11, 16; 1756: CG, Feb 12, Mar 22, 23, 25, 29, 30, Apr 3, 8, 10, 20, 26, 27, 30, May 1, 7, 8, 10, 17; 1757: CG, Apr 27, Oct 13, 21, Nov 1, 3, Dec 12, 15, 19, 20; 1758: CG, Jan 6, 10, 24, Mar 29, Apr 3, 4, 19, HAY, May 18, CG, Nov 11, 27; 1759: CG, Jan 8, 16, 31, Feb 3, 5, 8, Mar 29, Apr 2, 3, 5, 21, 25, 28, May 5, 7, 23, Nov 2, Dec 6, 12, 18; 1760: CG, Mar 17, Apr 8, 9, 10, 12, 18, 22, May 1, 5, 9, 14, 16; 1761: DL, Apr 16, 18, 21, 22, 23; 1763: DL, Oct 25, 27, 29; 1766: CG, May 5; 1767: HAY, Jul 29, Aug 3, 5, 7, 10, 14, 17, Sep 11, 16; 1771: CG, May 15; 1772: CG, Apr 24, May 21, Sep 21, 23, Oct 9, 13, 15; 1773: CG, Feb 19, 27, Sep 29, Oct 1, 5, 14, Dec 6

Fingalian habits, 1724: LIF, Jun 23, Jul 29

Fingalian Revels (dance), 1757: CG, Mar 29, Apr 13, 16, 22, 25, 26, May 24

Fingalian; or, The Female Frolick (dance), 1783: CG, May 28

Finger, Gottfried (composer), 1690: DLORDG, Jan 16; 1691: SH, Nov 23; 1693: SH, Nov 22, YB, 27; 1694: YB, Feb 5, 26; 1695: LIF, Apr 30, YB, Nov 25; 1696: YB, Jan 13, LIF, Mar 0, Apr 0, Nov 14; 1697: YB, Mar 17, Apr 8; 1698: NONE, Sep 0; 1699: YB, Feb 17, DL, Dec 0, DLLIF, 25; 1700: DL, Apr 29, May 16; 1701: DG, Mar 21, 28

Fini (composer), 1750: KING'S, Apr 10

Finley (assistant prompter), 1791: CG, Jun 14; 1792: CG, Jun 1; 1794: CG, Jun 12; 1795: CG, May 30; 1796: CG, May 31; 1797: CG, Jun 6; 1799: CG, May 22

Finley (tumbler), 1702: BFBF, Aug 24; 1704: MF, May 1

Finley-Mrs Barnes Booth, 1704: MF, May 1

Finley, Mrs (dancer), 1702: BFBF, Aug 24

Finley, Mrs (house servant), 1800: CG, Jun 4

Finley's Booth, 1705: MF, May 1

Finney, Mrs (house servant), 1787: DL, Jun 4

Finney, William, 1783: HAY, Aug 27

--Green Room, The; or, Cut and Come Again (prelude), 1783: HAY, Aug 27; 1785: HAY, Jul 26

Finnish tall man (actor), 1741: CG, Nov 26

Finny (ticket deliverer), 1778: DL, May 22; 1779: DL, May 29; 1780: DL, May 23; 1781: DL, May 12; 1782: DL, May 4; 1783: DL, May 31; 1784: DL, May 22; 1785: DL, May 21; 1786: DL, May 29; 1797: CG, Jun 6

Finny, William (sceneman), 1756: CG, May 19; 1757: CG, May 19, Nov 21; 1758: CG, Mar 27, Apr 10, 20, DL, Sep 16

Finta Cameriera, La. See Latille, Gaetano.

Finta Frascatana, La. See Leo, Leonardo.

Finta Principessa, La. See Cherubini, Maria Lorenzo.

Finta Sposa, La (pastiche), 1763: KING'S, Apr 14, 28

Fiorelli, Tiberio (Scaramouch) (actor), 1673: NONE, Apr 21, ATCOURT, Jun 5, Aug 22, NONE, Sep 12; 1675: ATCOURT, Jul 24

Fiorentina, Sga (dancer), 1755: HAY, Sep 1, 11, 15; 1761: SFT, Sep 21; 1762: DL, Oct 9, 14, 27, Nov 23; 1763: DL, Jan 3, Feb 24, Apr 22, May 13

Firbank (dancer), 1704: LIF, Feb 3, 5, 17, Mar 23, Jun 8, 26, Jul 4, DL, 5,

LIF, 27; 1705: LIF, Jan 25, Mar 1, 31, QUEEN'S, Apr 26; 1706: QUEEN'S, Mar
    25, Apr 3, 15, 30, May 15, LIF/QUEN, Jun 12, QUEEN'S, 13, 29
Firbank's scholar (dancer), 1704: LIF, Feb 3, 5, 17, Mar 23, Jun 8, 26, Jul 4,
    27; 1705: LIF, Jan 25
Fire and Water. See Andrews, Miles Peter.
Fire of love in youthful blood, The (song), 1690: DL, Mar 0
Firebrace, Hester, Lady Denbigh, 1700: DLORLIF, Jan 20
Fireworks (entertainment), 1747: KING'S, Feb 24, Mar 24, GF, 30, Apr 4, KING'S,
    May 9, SF, Sep 10; 1749: BFH, Aug 23; 1752: NWLS, Nov 13, 23, 28, 30; 1769:
    MARLY, Aug 10; 1770: RANELAGH, Oct 3; 1780: HAY, Jul 8; 1797: DL, Oct 14, 16
Fireworks, Grand (entertainment), 1768: MARLY, Jul 28
Firske. See Grist, Thomas.
First and Chief (song), 1791: CG, Mar 30; 1793: CG, Mar 20; 1794: CG, Mar 21,
    DL, Apr 9
First Faults. See DeCamp, Maria Theresa.
First Floor, The. See Cobb, James.
First Love. See Cumberland, Richard.
Fischar. See Fisher.
Fischer, Johann Christian (oboist), 1767: KING'S, Jan 23; 1769: KING'S, Feb 3,
    CG, 10, 22, Mar 1, 8, 10, 15, KING'S, Jun 1; 1770: KING'S, Feb 2, DL, Mar 2,
    CG, 7, DL, 23, Apr 6, CG, 21, HAY, May 3; 1771: KING'S, Feb 8, Mar 11; 1772:
    KING'S, Feb 21, HAY, Mar 23, 30, Apr 6, CG, 10, HAY, 27; 1774: KING'S, Feb
    10, DL, 18, Mar 16, HIC, May 9; 1775: KING'S, Jan 26, Mar 8, 10, 22, 24, 29,
    Apr 5, 7; 1776: KING'S, Feb 15, DL, Mar 20; 1780: KING'S, May 31
Fischietti, Domenico (musician), 1761: KING'S, Nov 10; 1767: KING'S, Mar 12;
    1769: KING'S, Jan 28; 1770: KING'S, May 1
--Signor Dottore, Il (opera), 1767: KING'S, Mar 12, Apr 30, May 16, Jun 16;
    1770: KING'S, Jan 9, May 1, 8
--Speziale, Lo (opera), 1769: KING'S, May 6
Fishar (Fischar, Fichar), James (dancer, ballet master), 1761: CG, Dec 10;
    1764: KING'S, Jan 10, Feb 14, 25, Mar 10, 20, 29, Apr 10, May 5, CG, Oct 4,
    15, Dec 12; 1765: CG, Jan 5, 21, 31, Sep 20, Oct 3, 7, 9, 12, 19, 22, Nov 15,
    Dec 6; 1766: CG, Apr 2, 5, 19, Oct 8, 10, 21, 22, 23, Nov 18, 20; 1767: CG,
    Jan 13, 29, Feb 14, 16, 21, Apr 2, 6, 11, 27, May 2, Oct 5, 8, 16, 30, Nov 6,
    Dec 14; 1768: CG, Jan 20, Mar 8, 15, Apr 6, 9, 16, May 12, 13, 25, 28, Sep
    19, 24, 26, Oct 4, 10, 17, 21, 24, 28; 1769: CG, Apr 1, 4, 5, 8, May 9, 12,
    16, 17, 19, Sep 18, 25, 29, Oct 6, Nov 4, 10, Dec 7, 15; 1770: CG, Jan 17,
    Mar 31, Apr 5, 18, 20, 23, May 18, 23, Oct 3, 8, 15, Dec 1, 5, 26; 1771: CG,
    Jan 1, Feb 21, Apr 3, 12, 18, 24, 25, 30, May 8, 25, 28, Sep 27, 28, 30, Oct
    15, 25, Nov 12, Dec 7, 17; 1772: CG, Feb 25, Apr 24, May 8, 15, 21, Sep 30,
    Oct 1, 16, Nov 2, 6, 24, Dec 7, 26; 1773: CG, Feb 6, Mar 20, Apr 16, 17, 24,
    30, May 25, 26, Oct 13, 25, 27, 28, 30, Nov 9; 1774: CG, Jan 3, 7, Mar 19,
    Apr 8, 11, 15; 1775: HAY, Nov 20; 1782: CG, Feb 26
Fishburn, Christopher (author), 1683: MS, Nov 22
Fisher. See Tench, Fisher.
Fisher, J (singer), 1794: DL, Apr 10, May 16, 22, Jun 2, HAY, Jul 9, 24, 25,
    Aug 13, DL, Oct 2, 27, 31, Nov 13, 15, Dec 20, 29; 1795: DL, Jan 19, Feb 17,
    28, Mar 2, Apr 21, Oct 30, Nov 11, 23, 26, Dec 4, 10; 1796: DL, Jan 8, 11,
    18, 23, Feb 27, Mar 3, 12, Apr 30, Jun 1, 11, Sep 29, Oct 19, CG, Nov 5, 9,
    Dec 26; 1797: DL, Jan 7, 14, 17, 20, May 2, 18, Jun 15, Sep 23, Oct 5, 21,
    24, 28, Nov 6, 8, 15, 24, 25, Dec 9, 21; 1798: DL, Jan 16, Feb 1, 24, Mar 24,
    26, May 19, Sep 18, 20, Oct 4, 6, 8, 20, 27, Nov 10, 14, 29, Dec 4, 5, 7, 17,
    29; 1799: DL, Jan 8, 17, 19, 23, Feb 4, 16, Mar 2, 11, Apr 22, 23, May 1, 16,
    20, 24, Jun 13, Jul 2, 4, 5, Sep 19, 21, Oct 19, 26, 31, Nov 6, 14, 16, 29,
    Dec 5, 11, 20; 1800: DL, Jan 1, 3, 6, Feb 12, Mar 11, Apr 5, 29, May 2, 13,
    Jun 12, 18, HAY, Jul 2, 10, 18, Aug 14, Sep 1, 3, 11
Fisher, John Abraham (violinist, composer), 1765: KING'S, Jan 25; 1767: CG, Mar
    2; 1769: HAY, Apr 18, CG, Jul 3; 1770: CG, Jan 5, 27, May 29, MARLY, Sep 11,
    CG, Nov 8, Dec 11; 1771: HAY, Apr 12, DL, Sep 21; 1772: CG, Jan 28; 1774:
    MARLY, Jun 30, CG, Sep 23, Nov 19; 1775: CG, Dec 26; 1776: STRAND, Jan 23,
    CG, Feb 26, Nov 14, 25, Dec 26, 27; 1777: CG, Oct 3, Nov 18, 25; 1778: CG,
    Mar 23, Oct 22; 1779: CG, May 13; 1780: CG, May 6, Sep 25; 1781: CG, Apr 3,
    Oct 20; 1789: CG, Dec 21; 1790: CG, Nov 15; 1791: CG, May 2; 1792: CG, Dec
    20; 1793: CG, Oct 2; 1796: CG, Nov 5; 1799: CG, May 13
--Druids, The (masque), 1774: CG, Nov 19, 21, 22, 23, 25, 28, 30, Dec 5, 6, 8,
    10, 12, 13, 17, 19, 26, 27, 28, 29, 30, 31; 1775: CG, Jan 2, 3, 4, 5, 6, 7,
    9, 10, 11, 12, 13, 14, 16, 18, 19, 20, 25, 27, Feb 6, 10, 14, 18, 20, 22, 24,
    27, 28, Mar 13, 16, 20, 30, Apr 6, 8, 17, 20, 21, 24, 26, May 1, 3, 8, 11;
    1789: CG, Dec 21; 1790: CG, Nov 15; 1793: CG, Oct 2; 1799: CG, May 13
Fisher, Joshua Bridges (actor), 1793: HAY, Aug 20, 27
Fisher, Mrs (actor), 1782: HAY, Sep 21
Fisher, Mrs Alexander (actor), 1752: NWLS, Nov 16, 28, 30; 1776: HAY, Apr 22

Fisher, P (actor), 1776: HAY, Apr 22
Fisheries, Society of Free British, 1757: CG, Dec 15
Fisherman and the River Queen (song), 1800: DL, May 30
Fishermen and Their Wives (dance), 1724: LIF, Jul 31
Fishing Duet (song), 1799: DL, May 21
Fitchett (beneficiary), 1798: DL, Jun 9; 1800: DL, Jun 14
Fitz, Theo (musician), 1675: ATCOURT, Feb 15
Fitz, Thomas (musician), 1675: ATCOURT, Feb 15
Fitz-Crambo, Patrick (author), 1743: DL, Oct 6
Fitzgerald (actor), 1781: HAY, Oct 16; 1782: HAY, Mar 4
Fitzgerald (clothier), 1771: DL, Oct 30, Dec 14; 1773: DL, Oct 7
Fitzgerald (dancer), 1778: DL, Apr 9
Fitzgerald Sr, Mrs (singer), 1729: BFLH, Aug 23, SF, Sep 15
Fitz-Gerald, Katherine (actor), 1675: ATCOURT, Feb 15
Fitzgerald, Mrs (actor), 1771: DL, May 7, 11, 14, 16, 17, Dec 14; 1772: DL, Apr
    2, 4, 25, May 15, Jun 9
Fitzgerald, Mrs (actor, singer), 1714: SH, Apr 6; 1716: LIF, Jan 27, Feb 1, 3,
    6, 16, Mar 3, 10, 15, 17, Apr 23, 25, May 4, Oct 10, 13, 19, Nov 9, DL, Dec
    31; 1717: DL, Jan 2, Feb 4, SH, Mar 13, 27, DL, 30, HIC, May 3, DL, 22, Jun
    6, Oct 9, 25, Nov 6; 1718: TEC, Mar 19, LIF, 22, May 1, 20, Oct 8, 15, 25,
    28; 1720: HIC, Mar 4; 1722: SH, Feb 9; 1723: SH, Mar 6; 1726: HAY, Feb 24;
    1729: BFF, Aug 23; 1730: GF, Oct 23, 26; 1731: GF, Oct 1, 6; 1732: HAY, Mar
    2; 1733: SF/BFLH, Aug 23; 1734: SFG, Sep 7
Fitzgerald, William Thomas (prologuist), 1790: CG, May 5; 1791: CG, Jan 12;
    1792: CG, Dec 1; 1793: CG, Apr 18; 1795: CG, May 1; 1796: CG, Jan 23, Oct 29;
    1797: CG, Jan 10; 1798: CG, Jan 11; 1799: CG, Jan 12, HAY, 24; 1800: CG, Feb
    8
Fitzhenry, Elizabeth (actor), 1765: DL, Oct 15, Nov 15, Dec 6; 1766: DL, Jan
    20, Apr 9; 1767: DL, Oct 27
Fitzherbert, Miss (actor), 1782: HAY, Mar 21, Sep 21, Nov 25
Fitzpatrick (spectator), 1680: DGORDL, Feb 19
Fitzpatrick, Richard (prologuist), 1779: DL, Oct 30; 1781: DL, Nov 27; 1786:
    DL, Jan 14; 1794: DL, Apr 21
Fitzpatrick, Thaddeus, 1752: CG, Nov 2, DL, 13, 16, 18; 1763: DL, Feb 1, CG, 24
Fitzroy Square, 1795: DL, May 18; 1796: DL, May 9
Fitzroy, Anne, Countess of Sussex (actor), 1675: ATCOURT, Feb 15
Five Bells Tavern, 1752: CG, Feb 20, 22; 1754: HAY, Mar 28
Five Thousand a Year. See Dibdin, Thomas John.
Five times by the taper (song), 1796: DL, May 25
Fixed in his everlasting seat (song), 1788: DL, Feb 20; 1789: CG, Mar 27; 1790:
    CG, Mar 3, DL, 10, CG, 24; 1791: CG, Mar 23; 1792: CG, Mar 2; 1793: CG, Mar
    6, 20; 1794: CG, Mar 12, DL, 21, Apr 4, 11; 1795: CG, Mar 4; 1796: CG, Feb
    24; 1797: CG, Mar 10; 1798: CG, Mar 14; 1799: CG, Feb 15, Mar 1; 1800: CG,
    Mar 14
Flack, John Caspar (horn player), 1792: KING'S, Feb 24, Mar 14; 1793: KING/HAY,
    Feb 15, CG, 20; 1794: CG, Mar 7, DL, 12; 1797: CG, Mar 3; 1799: CG, Feb 8;
    1800: CG, Feb 28
Flack, John Caspar and Master (musicians), 1795: CG, Feb 20; 1796: CG, Feb 12;
    1798: HAY, Jan 15, CG, Feb 23
Flack, Master (violinist), 1785: DL, Mar 16; 1792: KING'S, Feb 24
Flag Dance (dance), 1724: LIF, Mar 16, 19, 23, 26, 28, Apr 6, 7, 8, 10, 23, 27,
    28, 29, May 4, Oct 12, Nov 18; 1725: LIF, Mar 18, Apr 5, 14, 19, 23, May 5,
    12; 1726: LIF, Apr 15; 1728: LIF, Mar 25, Apr 30; 1730: LIF, Mar 21, Apr 6,
    10, GF, 16, 20, LIF, May 1, 9, 13, 21, GF, 27, Jun 4, LIF, 4, GF, 9; 1731:
    LIF, Mar 15, 18; 1736: HAY, Feb 20, CG, Mar 20
Flageolet Concerto (music), 1717: LIF, Jul 3
Flaherty, 1771: DL, Nov 14
Flanderkins (dance), 1735: CG/LIF, May 2, CG, 6, 8, CG/LIF, 9, 12, 13, 15, 16,
    20, 22, 26, 27; 1737: DL, Nov 7, 10, 11, 12; 1738: DL, Jan 20, 21, 24, 27,
    28, Feb 3, 6, 28, Mar 13, Apr 24, 29, May 3, 5, 8, 10, 11, 13, 15, 17, 18,
    23, 24, 27, 30, 31, BFH, Aug 23, DL, Oct 5, 7, Nov 30, Dec 16; 1739: DL, May
    14, 31
Flanders, 1679: DG, Sep 0; 1696: LIF, Dec 0; 1702: DL, Dec 8; 1710: QUEEN'S,
    Jul 13; 1746: HAY, Apr 30; 1754: CG, Dec 13
Flavius. See Handel, George Frederic.
Fleaureau (armorer), 1747: DL, Oct 23
Flecknoe, Richard, 1664: LIF, Mar 0; 1671: NONE, Sep 0
--Damoiselles a la Mode, The (Ladies a la Mode, The), 1666: NONE, Sep 0; 1668:
    BRIDGES, Sep 14, 15
--Emilia, 1671: NONE, Sep 0
--Erminia; or, The Fair and Vertuous Lady, 1660: NONE, Sep 0
--Love's Kingdom (Love's Dominion), 1664: LIF, Mar 0; 1673: NONE, Sep 0

Fled is my love (song), 1688: DG, Apr 0
Fleece Coffee House, 1784: HAY, Feb 9
Fleece Tavern, 1660: VERE, Nov 19; 1675: FT, Feb 4; 1700: BF, Aug 0; 1740: GF,
    Nov 3; 1741: GF, Dec 2; 1742: GF, Apr 1; 1746: GF, Jan 20
Fleet Market, 1754: DL, Dec 16
Fleet Prison, 1732: DL, Jan 28; 1742: JS, Nov 9, 25; 1746: DL, Apr 10; 1749:
    HAY, Oct 26
Fleet St, 1697: DG, Jul 1; 1702: LS, Jul 25; 1732: FS, Nov 30; 1733: LIF/CG,
    Apr 21; 1735: CG/LIF, May 27; 1742: CG, Mar 27, GF, Apr 8, JS, 19; 1744: JS,
    Mar 16, DL, Apr 2, May 14; 1746: CG, Jan 24; 1747: DL, Mar 19, HAY, Apr 22;
    1749: DL, Jan 20, BBT, Mar 1; 1750: DL, Feb 21, 26, Mar 6, Oct 1, Nov 28;
    1751: DL, May 14, Dec 17, 18; 1752: DL, Dec 19; 1753: DL, Dec 21; 1754: CG,
    Jan 21, DL, Mar 4, Dec 16; 1756: DL, Mar 9; 1757: DL, Dec 14; 1774: DL, Jan
    19; 1776: KING'S, Nov 2; 1777: CG, May 29; 1780: DL, Apr 28; 1787: CG, May
    23, Jun 15
Fleet, Sir John (Lord Mayor), 1692: CITY, Oct 29
Fleetwood, Charles (actor, proprietor), 1734: DL, Feb 2, Dec 7; 1739: DL, Jan
    31; 1741: DL, Dec 3, 4, 7, 8; 1742: DL, Dec 15; 1743: DL, Apr 5, LIF, Jun 3,
    DL, Sep 13, Oct 6, Nov 26; 1744: DL, Nov 17, 19; 1747: DL, Apr 9, May 18,
    NONE, Jun 6; 1748: DL, Dec 10; 1749: DL, May 16; 1758: DL, Jun 22, Sep 28,
    30, Oct 13, 19, Nov 18; 1759: DL, Jan 3, Feb 1, Apr 17, May 10, Sep 25, Oct
    2, 25, Nov 24, 27, Dec 3, 26; 1760: DL, Jan 24, Feb 8, 13, Mar 24, Apr 7, 9,
    10; 1769: CG, Apr 17
Fleetwood, John Gerrard (actor), 1770: HAY, Aug 8, 13, 22, Sep 1; 1771: HAY,
    Mar 4, Apr 6, 20
Fleming, Robert, 1690: NONE, Sep 0
--Monarchical Image, The, 1690: NONE, Sep 0
Flemish dresses, 1767: CG, Dec 14
Flemish Feast (dance), 1762: DL, Apr 3
Flemish Peasant's Wedding (dance), 1746: CG, Apr 11
Flemming in Wooden Shoes (dance), 1710: GR, Aug 5, 7
Flemming, Count, 1721: KING'S, Apr 15; 1723: KING'S, Jan 15
Flestrin, Quinbus, 1752: DL, Dec 23
Fletcher, John, 1660: NONE, Sep 0; 1662: REDBULL, Jan 22, COCKPIT, Oct 21;
    1666: BRIDGES, Dec 7; 1667: BRIDGES, Sep 25; 1668: LIF, Aug 20; 1669:
    BRIDGES, Jan 12; 1677: DL, Apr 2; 1684: ATCOURT, Feb 11; 1691: NONE, Sep 0;
    1698: DL/ORDG, Nov 0; 1699: DL, Dec 0; 1700: NONE, Apr 11; 1704: LIF, Apr 28;
    1705: QUEEN'S, May 28, DL, Jun 12, Jul 25, 27; 1706: DL, Jan 4, QUEEN'S, Apr
    26; 1707: QUEEN'S, Jan 4, 16, Feb 14, May 26, Oct 30; 1709: DL, Jan 3,
    QUEEN'S, Nov 11; 1710: QUEEN'S, Feb 11, 15, Mar 18, GR, Sep 23; 1711: DL, Jan
    25, DL/QUEEN, Feb 8, DL, May 17, DL/QUEEN, Jun 12, DL, Oct 11, 31; 1712: DL,
    Jan 4, 5, 25, Feb 11, 12, 16, Mar 31, Apr 3, Oct 2, Dec 18, 31; 1713: DL, Feb
    12, Mar 17, May 21, Nov 13, Dec 18; 1714: DL, Jan 12, Feb 22, Apr 8, May 3,
    19, Sep 24, Oct 25, 28, Nov 1, 9, Dec 10, 17; 1715: DL, Jan 28, Feb 10, Aug
    5, 9, 12, Oct 26, Nov 1, 30, Dec 3; 1716: DL, Jan 14, 28, Nov 13, 17; 1717:
    DL, Feb 19, Mar 26, Apr 2, LIF, 11, DL, 13, May 14, Jul 23, 30, Aug 2, Oct
    25, Nov 29, Dec 3; 1718: DL, Jan 23, Feb 15, Jul 18, Aug 5, Oct 24, Dec 31;
    1720: DL, Jan 8, Mar 31, May 7, 25, Jun 21, 30, Jul 21; 1721: DL, Jan 3, 16,
    Mar 18, May 4, Jun 20, Sep 19, Oct 11, 21, 28, Nov 13, 16, 20, 27, 30, Dec
    18; 1722: DL, Jan 4, 5, 17, 19, 24, Apr 7, May 1, 17, 24, Oct 5, LIF, Nov 17,
    19, DL, 29, 30, Dec 5, LIF, 6; 1723: DL, Jan 4, LIF, 23, DL, Feb 4, 8, Apr
    16, LIF, May 29, DL, Oct 18; 1724: DL, Feb 20, Mar 5, LIF, 26, Jun 2; 1725:
    DL, Jan 8, Apr 9, Oct 25, Dec 18; 1726: DL, Mar 24, Oct 22, Dec 8; 1727: DL,
    May 24, Dec 4; 1728: DL, Apr 29; 1729: DL, Jan 21, Jul 15, Nov 18; 1730: DL,
    Jan 3, Feb 24, GF, Apr 7, DL, Oct 8; 1731: DL, Apr 29, Sep 30, Dec 16; 1733:
    DL, Feb 22, Oct 1, DL/HAY, 8, Nov 14, Dec 10, DL, 14, DL/HAY, 17; 1734: DL,
    Jan 3, Oct 23, Dec 17; 1735: DL, Jan 28, 29, Feb 18, Oct 9, CG, Nov 17, DL,
    29, Dec 1, 31; 1736: DL, Mar 2, CG, May 13, 14, Jun 3, Nov 25; 1737: DL, Mar
    17, Sep 3, CG, Oct 26; 1738: CG, Apr 11, DL, Oct 21, Nov 30, Dec 11; 1739:
    CG, Jan 25, Feb 5, Apr 14, DL, May 5, CG, 9, DL, 23, CG, Sep 10, DL, Oct 16,
    CG, Nov 20, 30, Dec 27; 1740: DL, Jan 3, Mar 8; 1741: CG, Oct 7, DL, 10;
    1743: DL, Nov 8, Dec 12; 1744: HAY, Jul 10; 1746: DL, Mar 17, Apr 21; 1747:
    DL, Mar 7; 1749: DL, Oct 5, 7, 9, 19; 1750: CG, Apr 5, DL, Oct 29; 1756: DL,
    Apr 26, CG, Dec 10; 1757: CG, Jan 28, DL, Apr 30, CG, Oct 17; 1758: CG, Feb
    1; 1763: DL, Oct 8; 1767: CG, Dec 14; 1778: CG, Apr 27, HAY, Jul 30; 1779:
    HAY, May 31; 1782: HAY, Nov 25; 1783: CG, Jan 17, Apr 23, May 10, HAY, Aug
    13; 1785: DL, Jan 27, CG, Apr 11; 1787: DL, Oct 26; 1788: CG, Jan 14, Feb 25;
    1791: DL, Mar 22, CG, Jun 1, Nov 5; 1792: DLKING'S, Apr 20; 1795: HAY, Sep
    21; 1796: CG, Nov 24
--Beggar's Bush, The; or, The Royal Merchant (with Phillip Massinger), 1659:
    NONE, Sep 0; 1660: REDBULL, Aug 14, VERE/RED, Nov 7, 20; 1661: VERE, Jan 3,
    Oct 8; 1668: BRIDGES, Apr 24; 1669: BRIDGES, Jan 12; 1674: DL, Mar 26; 1682:

DL, Nov 16; 1686: ATCOURT, Dec 1; 1688: ATCOURT, Feb 13; 1705: DL, Jun 12,
19, 30, Sep 27, Oct 6, Nov 9, Dec 1, 26; 1706: DL, Feb 1, Mar 14, May 25,
QUEEN'S, Oct 22, Nov 8; 1707: QUEEN'S, Feb 14, DL/QUEEN, Nov 14; 1708:
DL/QUEEN, Mar 23; 1710: DL, Apr 15, May 2, GR, Aug 12, DL/QUEEN, Nov 17;
1711: DL/QUEEN, Jun 7; 1712: DL, Jan 25; 1713: DL, Jun 10, Nov 13; 1714: DL,
Dec 17; 1715: DL, Dec 7; 1716: LIF, Jan 4, 9, DL, 24, LIF, Mar 5, Apr 21, Jun
8, Oct 24; 1717: LIF, Jan 15, Nov 22; 1718: LIF, Feb 19, May 15; 1719: LIF,
Feb 21, May 5, Nov 5, Dec 28; 1720: LIF, Feb 22, Apr 30, May 23, Oct 6; 1721:
LIF, Jan 4, Feb 21, Jun 1; 1723: LIF, Jan 11, 21, 28, Mar 11, 23, May 9, 20,
Oct 26, Nov 15, Dec 21; 1724: LIF, Jan 14, Feb 11, Mar 10, May 19, Oct 7, DL,
16, Dec 1; 1725: LIF, Feb 15, Apr 9, May 12, Oct 1, Nov 22; 1726: LIF, Jan 6,
25, Mar 12, May 23, Sep 19, Dec 28; 1727: LIF, Feb 28, Oct 9; 1728: LIF, May
16, Oct 1; 1729: LIF, Jan 20, Nov 18; 1730: LIF, Jan 14, May 20, GF, Oct 21,
LIF, 21, GF, 22, LIF, Dec 1, GF, 9; 1731: GF, Jan 11, LIF, Feb 10, May 25,
Oct 15, Dec 6; 1732: LIF, Jan 20, Mar 13, May 16; 1733: LIF/CG, Apr 2, May
15, CG, Dec 17; 1734: CG, Jan 29; 1735: CG/LIF, Feb 13, GF, Mar 24, CG/LIF,
Apr 15, May 14, CG, Oct 31; 1736: CG, Feb 3, May 14, Dec 20; 1738: CG, Jan 6,
Apr 4, Nov 17, Dec 26; 1739: CG, Feb 12, May 21, Nov 20, 30, Dec 27; 1740:
CG, Feb 18, May 9, Oct 3, DL, 29, 30, 31, CG, Dec 26; 1741: CG, Nov 26, Dec
28; 1742: CG, May 11, Dec 21, 28; 1743: CG, Feb 17, Apr 18, Oct 5, Dec 15;
1744: CG, Feb 14, Apr 30, Oct 15, GF, Dec 22, 29; 1745: GF, Feb 1, CG, Oct
16, Dec 23, GF, 31; 1746: GF, Jan 1, CG, May 3, GF, Nov 14; 1747: CG, Mar 17,
GF, Apr 9; 1748: CG, Jan 27, Feb 25, Nov 16; 1749: CG, Jan 12, Nov 9, Dec 2;
1750: CG, Feb 26; 1751: CG, Nov 14; 1752: CG, Feb 3, 20, May 5, Nov 27; 1753:
CG, Feb 14, Dec 26; 1760: CG, Mar 20, Apr 12, May 14; 1761: CG, Jan 7, 10,
Apr 29, Nov 9, Dec 16; 1767: CG, Dec 14, 15, 16, 17, 19, 21, 23
--Bloody Brother, The; or, Rollo, Duke of Normandy (with Phillip Massinger and
Ben Jonson), 1660: REDBULL, Aug 14, VERE, Dec 6; 1661: VERE, Mar 28; 1667:
BRIDGES, Apr 17; 1668: BRIDGES, Sep 17; 1669: BRIDGES, Jan 12; 1674: DL, Nov
9; 1675: DL, Apr 19; 1682: DL, Feb 4, 6, Nov 16; 1685: DLORDG, Jan 20, Apr
28, NONE, Sep 0; 1687: ATCOURT, Jan 26; 1705: QUEEN'S, Nov 13; 1708: DL, Dec
21
--Bonduca; or, The British Heroine, 1669: BRIDGES, Jan 12; 1695: DL, Sep 0;
1699: DLORDG, Jan 28; 1704: DL, Jan 4; 1706: DL, Feb 12, 18, Jun 6, Dec 19;
1715: DL, Aug 5, 9, 12, 23; 1716: DL, Jun 26, Jul 10; 1718: DL, Jul 25, Aug
22; 1723: HAY, Jan 31; 1729: DL, Jun 13, 18, Jul 15; 1731: DL, Jun 9; 1778:
HAY, Jul 30, 31, Aug 3, 5, 10, 12, 15, 17, 18, 31, Sep 5, 14; 1779: HAY, May
31, Jun 4, 12, 25; 1780: HAY, Jul 10, 22, Aug 2; 1781: HAY, Jun 16; 1793:
KING/HAY, Feb 15; 1795: CG, Apr 24
--Captain, The, 1669: BRIDGES, Jan 12; 1677: DL, Apr 2
--Chances, The, 1660: VERE, Nov 24; 1661: VERE, Apr 27, Oct 9; 1667: BRIDGES,
Feb 5; 1669: BRIDGES, Jan 12; 1682: DL, Dec 30; 1683: MT, Feb 2; 1686:
ATCOURT, Jan 27; 1691: NONE, Sep 0; 1704: DL, Feb 5; 1705: DL, Feb 22; 1708:
DL, Feb 24, Mar 13, Apr 23, Oct 13; 1709: DL, Feb 15, QUEEN'S, Sep 27, Dec 5;
1710: QUEEN'S, Feb 13, May 16, Jun 29, DL/QUEEN, Oct 7; 1711: DL/QUEEN, May
12, DL, Oct 6; 1712: DL, Jan 1, Sep 23; 1713: DL, Oct 21; 1714: DL, Jan 18,
Nov 17; 1715: DL, Jan 17, Feb 25, Mar 17, Oct 27; 1716: IT, Feb 2, DL, Apr 6;
1717: DL, Jan 4, Jun 3, Oct 24; 1718: DL, Apr 1, Oct 27; 1719: DL, Mar 16,
Oct 28; 1720: DL, Jan 4, Apr 5, Oct 12, Dec 28; 1721: DL, Jun 6, Oct 13;
1722: DL, Jan 10, May 7, Dec 3; 1723: DL, May 31, Oct 30; 1724: DL, Feb 24,
May 12, Nov 16; 1725: DL, Dec 9, 15; 1726: DL, Oct 8, Nov 18; 1727: DL, Jan
9; 1728: DL, May 20; 1729: DL, Jan 13, Dec 1; 1730: DL, Dec 2; 1731: DL, Apr
30, Nov 9; 1732: DL, Jan 26; 1738: CG, Apr 12; 1739: DL, Nov 23, 24; 1754:
DL, Nov 4, 7, 8, 12, 14, 16, 19, 21, 26, 28, Dec 4, 6, 14; 1755: DL, Apr 4,
May 16, Nov 28, Dec 15; 1756: DL, Apr 27; 1757: DL, Jan 26, Mar 14; 1758: DL,
Apr 3, 13; 1763: DL, Feb 1; 1772: DL, Apr 22; 1773: DL, Apr 21, 26, May 5,
20, Nov 15, 17; 1774: DL, Feb 1, 28, Mar 1, Apr 13, Dec 7, 15; 1776: DL, Jan
12; 1777: HAY, Aug 19, 23, 28, DL, Dec 4; 1778: DL, Oct 30, 31; 1779: DL, Feb
1, May 26, CG, Dec 11, 15, 20; 1780: CG, Jan 4, 27, Feb 14, Apr 18, Oct 24;
1781: CG, Jan 3, Mar 10, May 5, Oct 3; 1782: CG, Jan 9, Apr 24, DL, May 14,
Nov 26; 1783: DL, May 30, Dec 19; 1784: CG, Jan 7, Apr 15, May 28, Sep 21;
1785: DL, Jan 15, 20, May 21, Nov 3; 1786: DL, May 31, Oct 27, Nov 27; 1787:
DL, Jun 8; 1788: DL, Sep 13, Oct 31; 1791: CG, Jun 1; 1793: DL, Jan 16; 1794:
CG, Apr 12, DL, Jun 14; 1795: DL, Jun 6; 1797: DL, Jan 17, Jun 15
--Coxcomb, The (with Francis Beaumont), 1669: BRIDGES, Jan 12, Mar 17, 23;
1792: DLKING'S, Apr 20
--Cupid's Revenge (Love Despised), 1668: LIF, Aug 17, 20
--Custom of the Country, The (with Phillip Massinger), 1667: BRIDGES, Jan 2,
Aug 1; 1669: BRIDGES, Jan 12
--Double Marriage, The (with Phillip Massinger), 1669: BRIDGES, Jan 12; 1671:
NONE, Sep 0; 1682: DL, Nov 16; 1688: ATCOURT, Feb 6
--Elder Brother, The (with Phillip Massinger), 1660: REDBULL, Aug 14, VERE, Nov

23; <u>1661</u>: VERE, Sep 6; <u>1669</u>: BRIDGES, Jan 12; <u>1677</u>: NONE, Sep 0
--Fair Maid of the Inn, The, <u>1669</u>: BRIDGES, Jan 12
--Faithful Shepherdess, The, <u>1663</u>: SH, Jan 6, BRIDGES, Jun 13; <u>1664</u>: NONE, Sep
0; <u>1668</u>: BRIDGES, Oct 10, 12, 14; <u>1669</u>: BRIDGES, Jan 12, Feb 26; <u>1670</u>:
ATCOURT, Apr 6
--False One, The (with Phillip Massinger), <u>1669</u>: BRIDGES, Jan 12
--Henry VIII. See Shakespeare, William.
--Honest Man's Fortune, The, <u>1668</u>: LIF, Aug 20
--Humourous Lieutenant, The, <u>1660</u>: REDBULL, Aug 14, VERE, Nov 29; <u>1661</u>:
ATCOURT, Apr 20; <u>1662</u>: VERE, Mar 1; <u>1663</u>: BRIDGES, May 7, 8, 9, 11, 12, 13,
14, 15, 16, 18, 19, 20; <u>1666</u>: BRIDGES, Dec 20; <u>1667</u>: BRIDGES, Jan 23; <u>1669</u>:
BRIDGES, Jan 12; <u>1682</u>: DL, Nov 16; <u>1685</u>: DLORDG, Jan 2; <u>1686</u>: ATCOURT, Feb
10, Nov 24; <u>1688</u>: ATCOURT, Feb 27; <u>1697</u>: DL, Jul 0; <u>1704</u>: LIF, Mar 13, Apr 1;
<u>1705</u>: QUEEN'S, Apr 26; <u>1706</u>: QUEEN'S, Feb 2, May 15; <u>1709</u>: DL, Apr 11; <u>1712</u>:
DL, Feb 11, 12, 16, 28, Apr 3, Oct 11; <u>1713</u>: DL, Feb 12, May 21, Nov 14;
<u>1714</u>: DL, Feb 22, May 3; <u>1715</u>: DL, Feb 10, Dec 3; <u>1716</u>: DL, Apr 24, Nov 17;
<u>1717</u>: DL, Apr 2; <u>1718</u>: DL, Jan 13, May 9, Nov 29; <u>1719</u>: DL, Apr 9, Oct 24;
<u>1720</u>: DL, Jan 16, May 12; <u>1721</u>: DL, May 15, Oct 11; <u>1722</u>: DL, May 1; <u>1723</u>:
DL, Feb 4; <u>1724</u>: DL, Jan 29, Apr 18; <u>1726</u>: DL, Oct 22, Dec 8; <u>1728</u>: DL, Apr
29; <u>1729</u>: DL, Jan 21; <u>1730</u>: DL, Jan 3; <u>1744</u>: HAY, Jul 10; <u>1756</u>: CG, Dec 10,
11, 13, 14, 16, 18, 22, 31; <u>1757</u>: CG, Apr 27; <u>1758</u>: CG, Mar 9; <u>1759</u>: CG, Apr
7; <u>1760</u>: CG, Jan 31; <u>1767</u>: CG, Mar 21; <u>1791</u>: DL, Mar 22
--Island Princess, The; or, The Generous Portuguese, <u>1668</u>: BRIDGES, Nov 6;
<u>1669</u>: BRIDGES, Jan 7, 12, Feb 9, Apr 23; <u>1674</u>: DL, Dec 17; <u>1675</u>: ATCOURT, Jun
7; <u>1687</u>: ATCOURT, Apr 25; <u>1698</u>: DL/ORDG, Nov 0, DL, Dec 0; <u>1699</u>: DL/ORDG, Feb
7, DLORLIF, 20, DL/ORDG, Mar 25, Apr 29; <u>1700</u>: DL, Mar 12, Dec 5; <u>1701</u>: DL,
Jan 2; <u>1702</u>: DL, Nov 14; <u>1703</u>: DL, Jan 1, HA, May 18; <u>1704</u>: DL, Jan 18, Mar
23; <u>1706</u>: DL, Jan 8, 9, 10, 11, 15, 17, 18, 31, Feb 7, Mar 7, 16, 25, Apr 18,
Dec 10, 18, 27; <u>1707</u>: DL, Nov 29, Dec 20; <u>1708</u>: DL, Jan 3; <u>1710</u>: GR, Aug 5;
<u>1714</u>: DL, Dec 22, 27, 28, 29; <u>1715</u>: DL, Jan 10, 12, LIF, 25, 26, 27, 28, 29,
Feb 8, DL, 11, LIF, 12, 19, Mar 5, 10, 29, Apr 5, 25, May 12, Oct 6, 13, Nov
26; <u>1716</u>: LIF, Jan 6, Feb 6, Mar 24, Apr 11, May 10, 22, Oct 25, Nov 28, Dec
17, 29; <u>1717</u>: LIF, Jan 31, Feb 26, Apr 13, Jun 3, Nov 15, 21, Dec 13; <u>1718</u>:
LIF, Jan 28, May 13, Dec 2; <u>1719</u>: LIF, Jan 14, May 1, Jun 3, RI, 6; <u>1720</u>:
LIF, Feb 5, 10; <u>1721</u>: LIF, Feb 25, Mar 2, Apr 11, 20, May 12; <u>1722</u>: LIF, Mar
8, 30, Apr 16, May 14, Oct 30; <u>1723</u>: LIF, Jan 7, Mar 25, Apr 29, Jun 6, Nov
2, 7, 8, 9, 20, Dec 11, 26; <u>1724</u>: LIF, Oct 9; <u>1725</u>: LIF, Jan 14, Nov 30;
<u>1726</u>: LIF, Apr 18, May 30, Nov 21; <u>1727</u>: LIF, Oct 26; <u>1728</u>: LIF, Jan 2, Nov
27; <u>1729</u>: LIF, Feb 6, Oct 24; <u>1734</u>: DL, Feb 13, 20, 21, 22, 23, 26, Mar 2,
LIF, May 16; <u>1739</u>: CG, Dec 10, 11
--King and No King (with Francis Beaumont), <u>1660</u>: REDBULL, Aug 14, VERE, Dec 3;
<u>1661</u>: VERE, Mar 14, Sep 26; <u>1662</u>: VERE, Feb 15; <u>1669</u>: BRIDGES, Jan 12, May 6;
<u>1675</u>: DL, Apr 23; <u>1682</u>: NONE, Sep 0; <u>1685</u>: DLORDG, Oct 20; <u>1686</u>: DLORDG, Jan
23, ATCOURT, Dec 9; <u>1687</u>: DLORDG, Jan 6, DL, Feb 22; <u>1692</u>: NONE, Sep 0; <u>1704</u>:
DL, Jun 15; <u>1705</u>: DL, Apr 14, Oct 10; <u>1706</u>: QUEEN'S, Mar 28; <u>1707</u>: QUEEN'S,
Jan 21; <u>1724</u>: LIF, Mar 26; <u>1733</u>: GF, Oct 31, Nov 1; <u>1788</u>: CG, Jan 14
--Knight of the Burning Pestle, The (with Francis Beaumont), <u>1662</u>: VERE, May 5,
7; <u>1666</u>: NONE, Sep 0
--Knights of Malta, The; or, The Humorous Dane (with Phillip Massinger and
Nathan Field), <u>1669</u>: BRIDGES, Jan 12; <u>1690</u>: NONE, Sep 0; <u>1783</u>: CG, Apr 23
--Laws of Candy, The, <u>1669</u>: BRIDGES, Jan 12
--Little French Lawyer, The (with Phillip Massinger), <u>1669</u>: BRIDGES, Jan 12;
<u>1670</u>: IT, Feb 2; <u>1696</u>: NONE, Sep 0; <u>1717</u>: DL, Jul 30, Aug 2, Oct 25; <u>1718</u>:
DL, Jul 18, Aug 5; <u>1720</u>: DL, Jun 30; <u>1721</u>: DL, Jun 16; <u>1749</u>: DL, Oct 7, 9,
10; <u>1778</u>: CG, Apr 27, 30
--Love's Cure; or, The Martial Maid (with Francis Beaumont), <u>1669</u>: BRIDGES, Jan
12; <u>1793</u>: DL, May 22
--Love's Pilgrimage (with Francis Beaumont), <u>1665</u>: MTS, Mar 0; <u>1669</u>: BRIDGES,
Jan 12
--Lover's Progress, The; or, The Wandering Lovers (with Phillip Massinger),
<u>1669</u>: BRIDGES, Jan 12
--Loyal Subject, The, <u>1659</u>: NONE, Sep 0; <u>1660</u>: COCKPIT, Aug 18, SALSBURY, Dec
12; <u>1661</u>: VERE, Feb 5; <u>1669</u>: BRIDGES, Jan 12; <u>1684</u>: NONE, Sep 0; <u>1705</u>: DL,
Jul 25, 27, Sep 25; <u>1706</u>: DL, Jan 4
--Mad Lover, The, <u>1659</u>: NONE, Sep 0; <u>1660</u>: SALSBURY, Dec 12; <u>1661</u>: VERE, Feb 5,
SALSBURY, 9, LIF, Dec 2; <u>1669</u>: LIF, Feb 18; <u>1675</u>: DG, Oct 11; <u>1701</u>: LIF, Jun
24; <u>1703</u>: LIF, Apr 28; <u>1704</u>: LIF, Feb 12, Jul 14, 27, Aug 1; <u>1705</u>: LIF, Jan
25
--Maid in the Mill, The; or, Country Innocence (with William Rowley), <u>1659</u>:
NONE, Sep 0; <u>1660</u>: SALSBURY, Dec 12; <u>1661</u>: SALSBURY, Jan 29, VERE, May 0;
<u>1662</u>: LIF, Jan 29, Apr 1; <u>1668</u>: LIF, Sep 10; <u>1682</u>: NONE, Sep 0; <u>1704</u>: LIF,
Apr 28, Jul 27; <u>1710</u>: DL, Mar 14, 23, Apr 19, GR, Sep 23; <u>1750</u>: CG, Apr 5

--Maid's Tragedy, The (with Francis Beaumont), 1660: REDBULL, Aug 14, VERE, Nov 17; 1661: VERE, May 16; 1662: VERE, Feb 25; 1666: BRIDGES, Dec 7; 1667: BRIDGES, Feb 18, Nov 23; 1668: BRIDGES, Apr 15, May 9; 1669: BRIDGES, Jan 12; 1685: NONE, Sep 0; 1687: DL, Jan 28, DLORDG, Apr 6; 1691: NONE, Sep 0; 1698: LIF, Jul 11; 1704: DL, Feb 3, 4, 15; 1706: QUEEN'S, Nov 2; 1707: QUEEN'S, Nov 6; 1708: DL, Jan 17; 1710: QUEEN'S, Apr 13, DL, Dec 16; 1715: DL, Oct 29, Nov 1, 15, Dec 10; 1716: DL, Apr 16, Dec 29; 1717: DL, Mar 2, Oct 12; 1718: DL, Feb 15, Nov 8; 1719: DL, Oct 31; 1720: DL, Jan 23; 1721: DL, Jan 24, Oct 28; 1723: DL, Mar 21; 1724: DL, Feb 22, May 9; 1725: DL, Dec 18; 1728: DL, Nov 2; 1729: LIF, Nov 8, 10; 1730: LIF, Nov 2; 1732: LIF, Oct 18; 1733: CG, Oct 27; 1735: DL, Nov 29, Dec 1; 1744: CG, Dec 6, 7, 8; 1745: CG, Jan 28, Mar 7; 1785: DL, Jan 27

--Monsieur Thomas; or, Father's Own Son, 1661: VERE, Sep 28, Nov 13; 1662: VERE, Apr 19; 1791: CG, Nov 5

--Nice Valour, The (Passionate Madman, The), 1669: BRIDGES, Jan 12

--Night Walker, The; or, The Little Thief, 1661: SALSBURY, Apr 2; 1662: VERE, Mar 15, 31, May 19; 1664: IT, Nov 1; 1698: DL, Nov 28; 1705: DL, Oct 18, 20

--Noble Gentleman, The (with Rowley, William), 1662: REDBULL, Jan 22; 1669: BRIDGES, Jan 12

--Philaster; or, Love Lies a Bleeding (with Francis Beaumont), 1660: REDBULL, Aug 14, VERE, Nov 13; 1661: VERE, Nov 18; 1662: VERE, Jan 11, Mar 22; 1667: BRIDGES, Nov 16; 1668: BRIDGES, May 30; 1669: BRIDGES, Jan 12; 1671: IT, Nov 1; 1672: LIF, Jun 0, IT, Nov 1; 1674: DL, Oct 24; 1676: DL, May 23; 1683: DLORDG, Feb 0; 1695: DL, Dec 0; 1711: DL, Oct 13, 15, 25, Nov 22, 30; 1712: DL, Jan 26, Mar 31; 1714: DL, Mar 13; 1715: LIF, May 17, DL, Dec 31; 1716: DL, Jan 3, 28; 1722: DL, Nov 29, 30; 1763: DL, Oct 8, 10, 13, 15, 18, 20, 22, 25, 27, 29, Nov 1, 21, Dec 21; 1764: DL, Feb 1, 13, Mar 17, May 2, Oct 19; 1765: DL, Apr 23; 1767: CG, Nov 23, Dec 9; 1768: CG, Jan 2, Feb 11; 1773: DL, May 6; 1774: CG, Oct 20, 26; 1780: CG, Oct 3, 6; 1785: DL, Dec 1; 1796: CG, Nov 24

--Pilgrim, The, 1662: NONE, Sep 0; 1669: BRIDGES, Jan 12; 1671: NONE, Sep 0; 1700: NONE, Apr 11, DL, 29, 30, May 1, Jun 18, Jul 6, Oct 19, Nov 19; 1703: DL, Jul 3, Oct 8, 14, Nov 11, Dec 16; 1704: DL, Jan 14, Mar 23, Nov 3; 1706: DL, Jan 29, Feb 9; 1707: QUEEN'S, Apr 30, May 20, 23, 30, DL/QUEEN, Oct 27, Nov 21; 1708: DL/QUEEN, Jan 5, May 24; 1709: DL, Mar 15, QUEEN'S, Oct 31; 1710: QUEEN'S, Feb 20, Apr 11, May 18, Nov 10; 1711: DL, Nov 5; 1712: DL, Jan 29, Oct 31; 1713: DL, Jan 9, Apr 11, Jun 1, Sep 29; 1714: DL, Jan 15, Sep 24; 1715: DL, Jan 28, LIF, Sep 30, Nov 5; 1716: LIF, Apr 24, DL, Jul 19, Aug 16; 1717: DL, Feb 15, LIF, Nov 4; 1718: LIF, Jan 15, Mar 10, 20; 1719: LIF, Jan 11, DL, Jun 16, Oct 26, LIF, Nov 17; 1720: DL, Jun 11; 1721: LIF, Apr 1, May 19; 1722: LIF, Mar 29, Apr 28; 1723: LIF, Feb 1, 8, May 1, Nov 16, 27, Dec 30; 1724: LIF, Jan 15, 24, Feb 20, Apr 24, Nov 6; 1725: LIF, Jan 15, Apr 12, May 11; 1726: LIF, May 3, Nov 2; 1727: LIF, May 8, Oct 27, Dec 29; 1728: LIF, Mar 14, May 20; 1729: LIF, Apr 8, May 9, Dec 2; 1730: GF, Dec 21, 22, 26, 28, 29; 1731: GF, Jan 8, Feb 9; 1732: GF, Apr 12, LIF, 18; 1733: CG, Dec 3, 19, 28; 1734: CG, May 10; 1738: CG, Apr 25, DL, Nov 30, Dec 2, 4, 5, 16; 1739: DL, May 5; 1740: DL, Jan 3, Mar 8, 10, Dec 18; 1741: DL, Jan 6, Apr 2, CG, Dec 18, 19, 22, 26; 1742: CG, Jan 20, Feb 9, Mar 1, May 10, Dec 7; 1743: CG, May 6; 1744: CG, Dec 21; 1745: CG, Apr 15; 1746: CG, Feb 5, May 7; 1748: CG, Apr 21; 1750: DL, Oct 23, 30, 31, Nov 9; 1751: DL, Jan 1; 1752: CG, May 4, Dec 11; 1762: CG, Feb 15, 17, 18, Mar 8, Apr 27; 1763: CG, May 9; 1780: CG, Apr 21, May 10; 1783: CG, May 9; 1787: DL, Oct 26, 31, Nov 2, 22, 28; 1788: DL, Apr 18

--Prophetess, The; or, Dioclesian (with Phillip Massinger), 1669: BRIDGES, Jan 12; 1690: DG, Jun 0, DL/IT, Oct 21, DG, Nov 17; 1692: DL, Jan 0, DG, May 2; 1693: DG, May 0; 1694: DG, Jan 10; 1697: DG, Mar 9, DLORDG, Dec 4, 18; 1698: DG, Jan 15; 1700: DL, May 16, Jun 1, Nov 21, Dec 4; 1702: DL, Oct 17; 1703: DL, Dec 31; 1704: DL, Jan 4, Feb 7; 1711: SH, Apr 11, May 9; 1712: SH, May 14; 1715: LIF, Dec 3, 5, 6, 7, 8, 9, 10, 19, 20, 26; 1716: LIF, Jan 14, 17, 21, 28, Feb 18, Mar 8, 20, May 3, Nov 2, 15, 24, Dec 14, 27; 1717: LIF, Jan 24, Feb 9, Mar 12, Apr 11, Jun 10, Oct 31, Nov 8, 12, 27, Dec 27; 1718: LIF, Jan 17, May 22, Oct 25, Nov 22; 1724: LIF, Nov 28, 30, Dec 1, 2, 3, 4, 5, 7, 8, 9, 10, 11, 12, 14, 15, 16, 17, 18, 19, 21, 22, 26, 28, 29, 30, 31; 1725: LIF, Jan 2, 8, Apr 1, 8, Nov 20, 26, Dec 11, 29; 1726: LIF, Oct 5, Nov 9, Dec 3; 1727: LIF, Jan 2, Feb 11, Apr 14, Nov 7, 21; 1728: LIF, Oct 9, Nov 5; 1729: LIF, Jan 11, Oct 28, Nov 21; 1730: LIF, Jan 27, Dec 11; 1731: LIF, Jan 18, May 20, Dec 1; 1732: LIF, Mar 6; 1741: SF, Sep 14, 15; 1758: CG, Feb 1, 2, 3, 4, 6, 7, 9, 13, 16, 18, 20, 23, 27, 28, Mar 2, 6, KING'S, 14, CG, 31, Apr 26, Nov 23, 24; 1759: CG, Jan 3, 18, Apr 18, Nov 30, Dec 1; 1760: CG, Apr 15; 1762: CG, May 12; 1784: CG, May 17

--Queen of Corinth, The (with Nathan Field and Phillip Massinger), 1669: BRIDGES, Jan 12

--Rule a Wife and Have a Wife, <u>1659</u>: NONE, Sep 0; <u>1660</u>: SALSBURY, Dec 12; <u>1661</u>: SALSBURY, Apr 1; <u>1662</u>: VERE, Jan 28, Feb 5, 11; <u>1667</u>: ATCOURT, Feb 14; <u>1669</u>: BRIDGES, Jan 12; <u>1682</u>: IT, Nov 1, ATCOURT, 15, DL, 16; <u>1685</u>: ATCOURT, Nov 4; <u>1693</u>: DLORDG, Dec 0; <u>1696</u>: LIF, Oct 0; <u>1700</u>: DL, Dec 6; <u>1701</u>: DL, Mar 24; <u>1702</u>: DL, Oct 16; <u>1703</u>: DL, Nov 29; <u>1704</u>: DL, Feb 19; <u>1705</u>: QUEEN'S, Jun 8, 15, DL, Oct 16, Nov 3; <u>1706</u>: DL, Jan 21, QUEEN'S, Oct 28, Nov 20; <u>1707</u>: QUEEN'S, Feb 12, DL, Dec 15, 17; <u>1708</u>: QUEEN'S, Jan 8, DL, Sep 21; <u>1709</u>: QUEEN'S, Nov 5; <u>1710</u>: QUEEN'S, Feb 25; <u>1711</u>: DL/QUEEN, Feb 1, 8, Jun 12, DL, Oct 31; <u>1712</u>: DL, Jan 5, Apr 26, Oct 2, Dec 31; <u>1713</u>: DL, Mar 17, Oct 28; <u>1714</u>: DL, Jan 12, Apr 8, Oct 25, Dec 10; <u>1715</u>: DL, Feb 24, Mar 12, Apr 28, Oct 26; <u>1716</u>: DL, Jan 14, May 3, Oct 25; <u>1717</u>: DL, Feb 16, May 14, Dec 3; <u>1718</u>: DL, Apr 14, May 30, HC, Oct 23, DL, 24, Dec 31; <u>1719</u>: DL, May 9, Oct 20; <u>1720</u>: DL, Jan 8, Mar 15, May 25; <u>1721</u>: DL, Jan 3, Mar 18, May 4, Sep 19, Nov 27; <u>1722</u>: DL, Jan 19, Apr 4, May 24, Oct 5; <u>1723</u>: DL, Jan 4, Apr 16, Oct 18, Nov 26, Dec 27; <u>1724</u>: DL, Mar 5, Oct 19; <u>1725</u>: DL, Jan 8, Feb 27, Apr 30, Oct 12, Nov 25; <u>1726</u>: DL, Jan 28, Mar 12, Apr 22, Sep 20, Nov 22, Dec 30; <u>1727</u>: DL, May 24, Oct 17, Dec 12; <u>1728</u>: DL, Feb 27, Oct 10, Dec 4; <u>1729</u>: DL, Jan 27, Apr 19, Oct 4, Nov 15; <u>1730</u>: GF, Apr 7, DL, 23, GF, Jul 8, Nov 2; <u>1731</u>: DL, Jan 4, Mar 15, GF, Apr 1, DL, 24, Oct 2, GF, Nov 12, DL, 18, LIF, Dec 15, 16, 18, 21; <u>1732</u>: DL, Jan 14, LIF, Feb 9, Mar 9, DL, 25, LIF, Apr 22, GF, 27, DL, May 1, LIF, 24, LIF/CG, Oct 21, Nov 29, Dec 12, GF, 29; <u>1733</u>: DL, Jan 2, GF, 4, 11, DL, Feb 15, GF, Mar 5, LIF/CG, 29, GF, Apr 10, DL, May 9, LIF/CG, 24, GF, Sep 20, DL, Oct 1, 3, DL/HAY, 8, CG, 31, DL/HAY, Nov 14, CG, 27, GF, 27, DL, Dec 14; <u>1734</u>: DL/HAY, Jan 21, CG, Feb 2, DL, 9, GF, 16, DL, 16, CG, Mar 23, Apr 27, LIF, May 9, GF, 14, Sep 18, DL, Oct 23, CG/LIF, Nov 25, DL, Dec 17; <u>1735</u>: CG/LIF, Jan 2, 14, Feb 6, GF, 11, CG/LIF, Apr 24, LIF, Jun 12, CG, Sep 24, DL, Oct 9, CG, Nov 17, DL, Dec 31; <u>1736</u>: CG, Jan 24, DL, Mar 2, CG, Apr 12, GF, 28, DL, 28, CG, Sep 20, DL, Nov 8; <u>1737</u>: CG, Mar 28, DL, Sep 3; <u>1738</u>: CG, Jan 13, Feb 18, Mar 23, May 6, Sep 18, DL, Oct 21, CG, Nov 25, DL, Dec 11; <u>1739</u>: CG, Feb 5, Apr 14, DL, May 23, CG, Sep 10, DL, Oct 16, CG, Dec 7; <u>1740</u>: DL, Jan 21, CG, Feb 14, DL, Mar 11, CG, Apr 19, Oct 10, GF, Nov 11, CG, Dec 8; <u>1741</u>: CG, Apr 4, GF, 13, CG, May 12, Oct 7, DL, 10, CG, Nov 17, GF, Dec 16; <u>1742</u>: CG, Feb 5, Apr 29, DL, Nov 3; <u>1743</u>: CG, Apr 9, Sep 30; <u>1745</u>: GF, Dec 11; <u>1746</u>: GF, Jan 9, Feb 20, CG, Mar 15; <u>1748</u>: CG, Feb 10, Mar 5; <u>1750</u>: CG, Jan 18, 19, 20, 29, Mar 29, Apr 25, Oct 24; <u>1751</u>: CG, Feb 6, Apr 27, Nov 6; <u>1752</u>: CG, Jan 10, Feb 15, Mar 10, Nov 7; <u>1753</u>: CG, Jan 16; <u>1756</u>: DL, Mar 25, Apr 26, May 12, 21; <u>1757</u>: DL, Mar 22; <u>1758</u>: DL, Nov 23, 29, Dec 21, 30; <u>1759</u>: DL, Feb 24, Apr 2; <u>1760</u>: DL, Jan 19, 22, Apr 25; <u>1761</u>: CG, Mar 25, DL, 31, CG, May 15, Oct 5, DL, Nov 18, 26, Dec 9; <u>1762</u>: DL, May 22, CG, Oct 14, DL, Dec 11, 21; <u>1763</u>: DL, May 10, CG, Oct 26, 28, Nov 2, 8, 11, Dec 2; <u>1764</u>: CG, Jan 12, Mar 6, DL, Apr 24, CG, May 4, DL, 17, CG, Sep 24, Dec 4, 27; <u>1765</u>: DL, May 11, CG, Oct 16, 18, 21, 24, DL, Dec 3; <u>1766</u>: DL, Apr 8, May 14, CG, Nov 27; <u>1767</u>: DL, Mar 7, 16, May 23; <u>1768</u>: HAY, Jul 8; <u>1769</u>: CG, Oct 24, Nov 2, Dec 20; <u>1770</u>: DL, Mar 1, May 18; <u>1771</u>: DL, Jan 4, 8, 15, Jun 1, Nov 13, Dec 16; <u>1772</u>: DL, Feb 1, CG, Oct 23, 27, 28, 31, Nov 3, 5, 19, DL, 30, Dec 11; <u>1773</u>: CG, Jan 2, Oct 6, DL, 22, CG, Dec 2; <u>1774</u>: CG, May 7, DL, Nov 24; <u>1775</u>: DL, Feb 11, Mar 14, May 17, Oct 11, Dec 5, 20; <u>1776</u>: DL, Feb 14, May 2; <u>1777</u>: HAY, Jul 15, 16, Aug 6; <u>1778</u>: DL, Nov 18; <u>1779</u>: DL, Mar 20, Apr 24, Oct 2; <u>1780</u>: CG, Jan 25, DL, May 4, 31, Oct 25, Nov 28; <u>1781</u>: DL, Feb 15, Oct 30; <u>1783</u>: DL, Nov 27; <u>1784</u>: DL, Jan 15, CG, Mar 6, 11, 15, Apr 15, 22, Oct 27, DL, Nov 25; <u>1785</u>: CG, Feb 12, 17, Apr 21, DL, May 5, CG, 11, Oct 27, Dec 13; <u>1786</u>: CG, Feb 2, DL, Oct 28; <u>1787</u>: DL, Jan 10, CG, 31, DL, Feb 2, 19, CG, Nov 20; <u>1788</u>: CG, Feb 12, DL, May 6, CG, Oct 29, DL, Nov 5, 27, Dec 4; <u>1789</u>: CG, Jan 23, Mar 19, Nov 12, 26; <u>1790</u>: CG, Feb 4, Apr 16; <u>1791</u>: CG, Oct 21; <u>1792</u>: CG, Oct 5; <u>1793</u>: CG, Apr 17, Sep 17; <u>1797</u>: DL, Feb 1, 4, Mar 13, Apr 3, CG, Oct 11, DL, 12, CG, 18, 24, DL, Nov 8, 16; <u>1798</u>: DL, Feb 7, CG, Apr 12, May 2, DL, Oct 25; <u>1799</u>: DL, Feb 4, May 14, Sep 28, Oct 14, Nov 13; <u>1800</u>: DL, Jan 3, Feb 6

--Scornful Lady (Bride), The (with Francis Beaumont), <u>1660</u>: VERE, Nov 21, 27; <u>1661</u>: VERE, Jan 4, 25, Feb 12; <u>1662</u>: ATCOURT, Nov 17; <u>1666</u>: ATCOURT, Dec 10, BRIDGES, 27; <u>1667</u>: BRIDGES, Sep 16; <u>1668</u>: BRIDGES, Jun 3, ATCOURT, Nov 21; <u>1669</u>: BRIDGES, Jan 12; <u>1675</u>: IT, Nov 1; <u>1676</u>: NONE, Sep 0; <u>1682</u>: DL, Nov 16; <u>1684</u>: DLORDG, Feb 23; <u>1686</u>: ATCOURT, Feb 3, IT, Nov 1; <u>1690</u>: NONE, Sep 0; <u>1697</u>: DL, Nov 19; <u>1702</u>: LIF, Dec 10; <u>1703</u>: LIF, Feb 11; <u>1704</u>: LIF, Feb 11, Mar 18; <u>1705</u>: QUEEN'S, May 28; <u>1708</u>: DL, Mar 27, Apr 5; <u>1709</u>: DL, Jan 3; <u>1710</u>: QUEEN'S, Feb 11, 15, Mar 18; <u>1711</u>: DL, Jan 25, Mar 22, May 17, Oct 11; <u>1712</u>: DL, Jan 4; <u>1713</u>: DL, Feb 28, Dec 18; <u>1714</u>: DL, May 19, Nov 9; <u>1715</u>: DL, Mar 10, Nov 10, Dec 15; <u>1716</u>: DL, Feb 23, Nov 3; <u>1717</u>: DL, Feb 19, Mar 26; <u>1718</u>: DL, Jan 23, Mar 31; <u>1719</u>: DL, Apr 22, Nov 14; <u>1720</u>: DL, Feb 3, Mar 31, May 7; <u>1721</u>: DL, Jan 16, Apr 28, Oct 21; <u>1722</u>: DL, Jan 24, May 17, Dec 5; <u>1723</u>: DL, Feb 8, Oct 23, Dec 3; <u>1724</u>: DL, Feb 20, May 8, Oct 26; <u>1725</u>: DL, Feb 3, Apr 9, Oct 25; <u>1726</u>: DL, Feb 21, Mar 24, Apr 28, Dec 14; <u>1727</u>: DL, Apr

20, Dec 4; 1728: DL, Dec 2; 1729: DL, Jan 22, Feb 7, Apr 25, Nov 18; 1730:
DL, Feb 24; 1731: DL, Dec 22; 1732: DL, Jan 18; 1733: DL, Feb 22, DL/HAY, Dec
10; 1734: DL/HAY, Feb 7; 1735: DL, Jan 29, Feb 18; 1736: CG, Dec 9, 10; 1737:
DL, Mar 17; 1746: DL, Mar 17, 20, Apr 25; 1747: DL, Oct 17; 1783: CG, Jan 17
--Sea Voyage, The; or, A Commonwealth of Women (Storm, The) (with Phillip
Massinger), 1667: BRIDGES, Sep 25, 26, 27; 1668: BRIDGES, Mar 25, May 16;
1669: BRIDGES, Jan 12; 1702: DL, Jun 9; 1707: DL, Jan 13; 1708: DL, Jun 26,
29, Jul 6; 1710: DL, Apr 12, May 26, GR, Aug 24; 1715: LIF, May 6; 1716: LIF,
Feb 28, Mar 19; 1717: DL, Jul 23, 26; 1720: DL, Jun 21, Jul 21; 1721: DL, Jun
20; 1746: DL, Apr 21
--Spanish Curate (Priest), The (with Phillip Massinger), 1659: NONE, Sep 0;
1660: SALSBURY, Dec 12; 1661: SALSBURY, Mar 16, VERE, Dec 20; 1662: VERE, Jan
1; 1669: BRIDGES, Jan 12, May 17; 1670: NONE, Sep 0; 1676: IT, Feb 2; 1687:
DLORDG, Jan 10, IT, Feb 2, ATCOURT, Apr 11; 1692: NONE, Sep 0; 1722: LIF, Nov
17, 19, 20, Dec 6; 1723: LIF, Jan 23; 1743: DL, Dec 12; 1749: DL, Oct 19;
1783: CG, May 10
--Thierry and Theodorat, 1669: BRIDGES, Jan 12
--Two Noble Kinsmen (with William Shakespeare), 1795: HAY, Sep 21
--Valentinian, 1669: BRIDGES, Jan 12; 1675: NONE, Sep 0; 1684: ATCOURT, Feb 11;
1686: DL, Feb 4; 1687: ATCOURT, May 16; 1688: NONE, Sep 0; 1689: NONE, Sep 0;
1691: NONE, Sep 0; 1693: NONE, Sep 0; 1704: LIF, Feb 3; 1706: DL, Apr 16,
QUEEN'S, Nov 21; 1710: DL, Jan 28, Feb 1; 1711: DL, Apr 21; 1715: LIF, May
24, Jun 14
--Wife for a Month, A, 1659: NONE, Sep 0; 1661: VERE, May 0; 1669: BRIDGES, Jan
12
--Wild Goose Chase, The, 1659: NONE, Sep 0; 1661: VERE, Feb 5; 1668: BRIDGES,
Jan 11; 1669: BRIDGES, Jan 12; 1747: DL, Mar 7, 9
--Wit at Several Weapons (with Francis Beaumont), 1668: LIF, Aug 20
--Wit without Money (with Francis Beaumont), 1660: REDBULL, Aug 14, COCKPIT,
Oct 16, MT, Nov 2, REDBULL, 5; 1663: VERE, Apr 22; 1666: ATCOURT, Oct 11;
1672: LIF, Feb 26; 1707: QUEEN'S, Jan 4, 8, 16, May 26, Oct 30; 1709:
QUEEN'S, Nov 11; 1711: DL, Mar 3; 1712: DL, Dec 18; 1714: DL, Oct 28, Nov 1;
1715: DL, Mar 24, May 10, Nov 30; 1716: DL, Apr 17, Nov 13; 1717: DL, Apr 13,
Nov 29; 1721: DL, Nov 13, 16, 20, 30, Dec 18; 1722: DL, Jan 17, Apr 7, May 2,
Dec 1; 1723: DL, Apr 17, Nov 28; 1724: DL, Jan 31, Apr 15, Oct 21; 1725: DL,
Apr 2, Jun 11, Oct 22; 1726: DL, Feb 8, Nov 15; 1727: DL, Jan 6, Apr 25, Nov
28; 1728: DL, Nov 25; 1729: DL, May 3, Dec 10; 1730: DL, Oct 8, Dec 16; 1731:
DL, Apr 29, Sep 30, Dec 16; 1732: DL, Mar 16; 1733: DL/HAY, Dec 17; 1734:
DL/DL/HA, Jan 31; 1735: DL, Jan 28; 1736: CG, May 13, Jun 3, Nov 25; 1737:
CG, Feb 4, Apr 28, May 10, Oct 26; 1738: CG, Apr 11, Nov 2; 1739: CG, Jan 25,
May 9; 1740: CG, Mar 8, 17, Apr 11, Jun 3, Oct 21, Dec 4; 1748: CG, Apr 11,
May 4; 1753: CG, May 8; 1757: CG, Jan 28, Feb 2, 3, 4, 5, 7, Oct 17, Nov 12;
1758: CG, May 11; 1759: CG, Mar 3; 1760: CG, Jan 9, Feb 4, Apr 28; 1761: CG,
Apr 17, Oct 17; 1764: CG, Feb 11; 1782: HAY, Nov 25
--Woman's Prize, The; or, The Tamer Tamed, 1659: NONE, Sep 0; 1660: REDBULL,
Jun 23, Aug 14, COCKPIT, Oct 30; 1661: VERE, Jul 31, Dec 23; 1668: ATCOURT,
Nov 9; 1669: BRIDGES, Jan 12; 1674: DL, Dec 8; 1757: DL, Apr 30, May 2; 1760:
DL, Apr 30
--Women Pleased, 1668: LIF, Aug 20, ATCOURT, Dec 14, LIF, 26; 1743: DL, Nov 8,
10, 11; 1785: CG, Apr 11
Fletcher, Maria (singer), 1715: LIF, Oct 6, 22, Nov 5; 1716: LIF, Apr 26, May
24, Oct 15, 17, 30; 1717: LIF, Jan 2, Feb 27, Jun 1, 20, Jul 3; 1718: HIC,
Jan 17, YB, Mar 5, LIF, Oct 25, 28, Nov 3, 6, 10, 27, Dec 9; 1719: LIF, Mar
5, Apr 8, 9, 11, 25, May 1, 6, 11, 28, Jun 3; 1720: LIF, Feb 5, 13, HIC, 23,
LIF, Mar 19, 22, 24; 1721: HIC, Mar 3; 1726: LIF, Nov 19, 26; 1727: LIF, Apr
19, Sep 29
Fletcher, Miss (singer), 1796: CG, Mar 16
Fletcher, Miss (singer), 1796: CG, Mar 2, 4, 18
Fletcher, Misses (singers), 1796: CG, Mar 16
Fletcher, Mrs (householder), 1797: DL, Jun 12
Fleureau (householder), 1778: KING'S, Mar 5
Fleuri (dancer), 1705: QUEEN'S, Apr 28
Flexny, William (bookseller), 1761: DL, Mar 14
Flight (dance), 1733: DL, Mar 29, Apr 16, 24, May 18; 1736: DL, Nov 5, 6, 8, 9,
11, 17
Flight (house servant), 1770: CG, May 19, 22; 1771: CG, May 27; 1772: CG, May
25; 1773: CG, May 28; 1774: CG, May 14; 1775: CG, May 27; 1776: CG, May 21
Flingdon, Miss (actor), 1767: CG, Jan 31
Flitch of Bacon, The. See Bate, Henry.
Flocks shall leave the Mountains (song), 1746: CG, Jan 25, Feb 7, 27, Apr 4, 8;
1752: KING'S, Mar 24; 1753: KING'S, Apr 30; 1787: DL, Mar 7; 1790: DL, Feb
24, Mar 12; 1791: DL, Apr 1, CG, 13; 1792: KING'S, Feb 29; 1794: DL, Mar 26;

1795: CG, Mar 13; 1798: CG, Mar 28
Floquet, Etienne Joseph (composer), 1777: KING'S, Nov 4; 1780: KING'S, Apr 22,
May 27; 1783: KING'S, May 8
Flora and Blesa (interlude), 1710: QUEEN'S, Mar 16, Jul 6
Flora. See Hippisley, John.
Flora's Holiday; or, The Shepherds Welcome to the Spring (entertainment), 1736:
CG, May 6, 13
Flora's Vagaries. See Rhodes, Richard.
Florana (dance), 1743: DL, Apr 8, 21, 23, 25, 26, 30, May 2, 3, 4, 5, 7, 12, 19
Flore et Zephire (dance), 1796: KING'S, Jul 7, 9, 12, 16, Nov 26, Dec 6, 13;
1797: KING'S, Jan 7
Florence (play), 1773: KING'S, Nov 15, 20; 1789: KING'S, May 9; 1796: KING'S,
Mar 15; 1799: KING'S, May 30
Florentina, Sga. See Fiorentina, Sga.
Florentine Ladies, The. See Jordan, Thomas.
Florian, Jean Pierre Claris de, 1788: HAY, Aug 22; 1792: DLKING'S, Apr 16
--Bonne Mere, La, 1788: HAY, Aug 22; 1789: CG, Mar 31; 1792: DLKING'S, Apr 16
Floridante. See Handel, George Frederic.
Florio, Charles H (singer, composer), 1792: DLKING'S, May 31; 1794: CG, Mar 7,
21; 1798: DL, Oct 16; 1800: DL, Mar 11, May 29
Florio, Pietro Grassi (flutist), 1762: DL, Feb 26, HAY, Mar 16, DL, 31, HAY,
Apr 22, May 20; 1765: HAY, Mar 11; 1767: DL, Feb 2, May 22; 1768: HAY, Mar 4,
18; 1769: HAY, Feb 15; 1771: CG, Feb 20; 1773: HAY, Mar 17; 1775: KING'S, Jan
26; 1776: KING'S, Feb 15, CG, 23, Mar 22; 1778: CG, Mar 6, 18, Apr 3, KING'S,
4, 9
Florist (dance), 1769: CG, Apr 8
Florizel and Perdita. See Colman the elder, George, The Sheep Shearing.
Florizel and Perdita; or, The Sheep Shearing. See Morgan, MacNamara.
Florizel and Perdita; or, The Winter's Tale. See Garrick, David.
Floro and Blesa. See Bononcini, Giovanni.
Flourishing of the Colors (dance), 1720: KING'S, Apr 29, May 3
Flow thou regal purple stream (song), 1799: CG, Jun 7
Flower (musician), 1675: ATCOURT, Feb 15
Flower Basket Dance (dance), 1774: CG, Apr 15
Flowers of Edinburgh (song), 1772: HAY, Dec 21
Flowing can (song), 1797: HAY, Sep 16
Floyd (actor), 1664: LIF, Aug 13; 1675: NONE, Sep 0
Floyd (actor), 1734: YB, Jul 8
Floyd, Sir Francis, 1660: VERE, Dec 13
Floyd, Miss (actor), 1787: HAY, Jan 8
Fludyer, Thomas (renter), 1758: CG, Mar 4
Flushed with conquest (song), 1800: CG, Mar 19
Flute (music), 1697: LW, Aug 18; 1702: PR, Jun 30, DL, Jul 7, 11, Oct 20; 1703:
DL, May 28, LIF, Jun 11, RIW, Aug 12, YB, Dec 11; 1704: DL, Jan 10, 17, 24;
1705: DL, Dec 19; 1707: YB, Mar 19, DL, 27; 1710: PCGR, Jun 14; 1715: LIF,
Apr 4; 1716: LIF, Apr 9; 1719: HIC, Feb 13; 1720: HIC, Mar 4, LIF, Dec 23;
1722: RI, Jul 23; 1724: HIC, Apr 20; 1729: HIC, Apr 16; 1732: CL, Mar 17;
1735: HIC, Feb 21; 1741: HIC, Jan 16; 1748: DL, Sep 22, Oct 25, 29, Nov 3,
12, 18, 23, 25, 26; 1749: DL, May 8, 11, 12, 16; 1777: KING'S, Mar 20; 1778:
KING'S, Apr 9; 1785: HAY, Feb 28; 1788: CG, Jan 28; 1789: CG, Jan 26; 1794:
DL, Mar 12, Apr 9
Flute a la main Solo (music), 1709: HA, Sep 3; 1711: WCH, Oct 17
Flute a la main Sonata (music), 1707: YB, May 23
Flute and German Flute Concerto (music), 1733: GF, Apr 13
Flute and Hautboy Sonata (music), 1704: YB, Apr 20, Nov 16
Flute and Violin (music), 1703: DL, May 28, Nov 19; 1704: DL, Feb 4, Mar 30;
1706: DL, Jan 4; 1711: GR, Aug 27
Flute and Violin Sonata (music), 1704: YB, Mar 29, DL, Apr 4, YB, May 18; 1708:
SH, Mar 26
Flute and Violin Symphony (music), 1703: RIW, Aug 12
Flute and Violoncello Obligato (music), 1800: CG, Mar 19
Flute Cantata Solo (music), 1718: LR, Dec 3
Flute Chaconne (music), 1719: DL, May 5; 1732: DL, Nov 2, 6, 14
Flute Concerto (music), 1716: LIF, Apr 25, DL, May 31; 1720: LIF, May 5, 12;
1730: DL, May 4, GF, Jun 11; 1731: HAY, May 10; 1732: LIF, Mar 10; 1748: DL,
Sep 17, Oct 18, 19, 22; 1749: DL, Jan 23, Mar 20, Apr 5, May 9; 1770: KING'S,
Feb 2, HAY, Dec 14; 1771: GROTTO, Aug 8; 1774: HAY, Mar 18; 1779: HAY, Mar
17; 1794: DL, Mar 19, 26
Flute Duet (music), 1787: DL, May 4
Flute Obligato (music), 1780: KING'S, Apr 13
Flute Solo (music), 1712: GR, May 19, OS, Nov 28; 1715: LIF, Mar 22, Nov 18;
1716: LIF, Jul 20; 1717: SH, Mar 27, Dec 23; 1718: LIF, May 20, Nov 10, SH,

Dec 23; 1732: CL, Mar 17; 1748: DL, Sep 20
Flute Sonata (music), 1704: YB, Mar 29, Apr 20, May 18, Nov 16
Flute, Oboe, Violin and Violoncello Concertante (music), 1798: CG, Mar 23
Flute, Violin and Hautboy (music), 1703: DL, Apr 19
Fly, fly from my sight (song), 1696: DL, May 0
Fly ye Graces from these Seats (song), 1741: HIC, Apr 24
Fochetti, Vincenzo (singer), 1773: KING'S, Oct 23, Dec 7; 1774: KING'S, Jan 11,
    Feb 10, Mar 17, HIC, May 9, KING'S, Dec 13; 1775: KING'S, Feb 7, Mar 7, 30,
    May 23, Oct 31, Dec 12; 1776: KING'S, Jan 9, Mar 12, 28, Apr 23, Nov 5; 1777:
    KING'S, Feb 4, Apr 1, 17, 29, May 20
Foire de Smirne, La; ou, Les Amans Reunis (dance), 1792: HAY, Apr 14, 17, 19,
    24, 26, 28, May 3, 8, 12, 15, 22, 29, Jun 5, 7, 9
Foire de St Germain, La (farce), 1734: HAY, Nov 13, 21
Foire de St Germain, La. See Regnard, Jean Francois.
Folcad, Miss. See Foulcade, Anne.
Foley (boxkeeper), 1748: DL, May 16; 1749: DL, May 16; 1750: DL, May 10; 1751:
    DL, May 9; 1752: DL, May 2; 1753: DL, May 16; 1754: DL, May 18; 1755: DL, May
    13; 1756: DL, May 14; 1757: DL, May 19; 1758: DL, May 18; 1759: DL, May 30;
    1760: DL, May 16; 1761: DL, May 25; 1762: DL, May 25; 1763: DL, May 17; 1764:
    DL, May 22; 1765: DL, May 21; 1766: DL, May 21; 1767: DL, May 30; 1768: DL,
    May 25; 1769: DL, May 22; 1770: DL, Jun 1
Foley (musician), 1744: JS, Dec 10
Folie (dance), 1717: LIF, Feb 26, Mar 4, 5, 11, Apr 13; 1742: CG, Nov 9
Folie Amoureuse (dance), 1738: DL, Mar 13
Folies Amoureuses, Les. See Regnard, Jean Francois.
Folies d'Espagne (dance), 1718: LIF, May 29; 1789: KING'S, Jun 15, CG, Jul 2;
    1791: KING'S, May 26, Jun 10, 14, 21, Jul 2
Follett, John (actor), 1771: DL, Dec 4, 6, 10; 1772: DL, Jan 1, Mar 28, Apr 22,
    May 25; 1773: HAY, Jul 2, 12, 16, 19, 21, 23, 30, Aug 11, 20, Sep 3, 16, 17,
    18, 20; 1774: HAY, Apr 12, May 30, Jun 8, 13, 17, 27, Jul 6, Aug 19, Sep 2,
    5, 12, 17, 19, 21; 1775: HAY, Sep 21, Oct 30; 1776: DL, Oct 1, 18, Nov 25,
    Dec 10, 28; 1777: DL, Jan 1, 4, Mar 1, Apr 22, May 9, 15, 28; 1778: HAY, Mar
    31; 1785: HAY, Feb 12, Apr 26; 1787: HAY, Jan 8, ROY, Jun 20; 1788: HAY, Apr
    9, 29, Sep 30, Dec 22
Follett Jr, John (actor), 1778: HAY, Mar 31; 1787: HAY, Jan 8; 1788: HAY, Apr
    9, 29, Sep 30, Dec 22; 1789: DL, May 22; 1790: CG, Oct 4, Nov 6, 15, Dec 20;
    1791: CG, May 2, 3, 16, 31, Jun 6, 13, Oct 20, 24, Dec 21, 22; 1792: CG, Mar
    31, Apr 18, May 1, 10, Oct 8, 25, Dec 20, 26; 1793: CG, Mar 11, 16, Apr 8,
    24, May 8, 27, Jun 6, Oct 2, Nov 19, Dec 19; 1794: CG, Feb 6, Mar 25, May 7,
    15, 26, Jun 13, Sep 22, Oct 14, Dec 26; 1795: CG, Mar 14, 19, May 12, Jun 16,
    Sep 25, Oct 5, 12, 23, 24, 29, Nov 9, 12, 16, 27, Dec 21; 1796: CG, Jan 4,
    Mar 15, Apr 9, Jun 1, 4, 7, Sep 17, 26, Oct 7, 24, Nov 19, Dec 19; 1797: CG,
    Mar 16, Apr 8, 19, May 22, Oct 9, 16, Nov 15, 23, 24, Dec 26; 1798: CG, Feb
    12, Mar 19, 29, Apr 9, May 28, Jun 2, Oct 15, 25, Nov 10, 13, Dec 11, 26;
    1799: CG, Jan 15, Jun 1
Follett, John Jr and Mary (actors), 1797: CG, Jun 5; 1798: CG, Jun 6
--Harlequin and Oberon. See Wild, James.
Follett, Mary, Mrs John Jr (actor, singer), 1793: CG, Sep 20, 23, 30, Oct 2, 4,
    7, 9, 19, 24, Nov 12, 28, Dec 7, 9, 14, 19, 27; 1794: HAY, Jan 21, CG, Feb 3;
    1795: CG, Jan 31, Mar 24, Apr 6, 22, May 1, Jun 8, Sep 14, 16, 21, Oct 2, 15,
    19, 24, Nov 4, 16; 1796: CG, Apr 9, 20, Jun 1, 2, Sep 12, 19, 26, Oct 3, 6,
    7; 1797: CG, Feb 18, Mar 16, Apr 8, 25, May 18, 27, Jun 8, 10, Sep 20, 22,
    25, Oct 9, 20, Nov 2, 3, 7, 20, 24, Dec 18, 26; 1798: CG, Feb 12, Mar 19, 31,
    Apr 9, 11, 27, May 7, 23, 25, Jun 6, Sep 17, 28, Oct 5, 8, 11, 15, Dec 15;
    1799: CG, Mar 2, Apr 2, 9, 12, 13, 23, May 21, 28, Jun 7, Sep 18, 30, Oct 4,
    7, Nov 9, 11, Dec 4, 10, 23; 1800: CG, Jan 16, Feb 10, Mar 1, 4, 25, Apr 5,
    29, May 1, 27, Jun 2, 5, 13
Follette (dance), 1725: DL, Sep 23, 28, Oct 2, 18, 25, Nov 16, Dec 7, 20; 1726:
    DL, Jan 5, 27, Feb 8
Follette s'est Ravisee (dance), 1733: LIF/CG, Mar 17, May 14, DL/HAY, Oct 20,
    24, Nov 28, Dec 20, 31; 1734: DL/HAY, Jan 4, Feb 6, Apr 6, DL, 25, DL/HAY,
    27, GF, Sep 11, 13, 16, 18, DL, Oct 3, GF, 14, 16, DL, 26, GF, Dec 3, 4, 5,
    6, 28, 31; 1735: GF, Jan 6, 7, Mar 17, 27, Apr 10, DL, 14, GF, 21, 22, 24,
    28, 30, May 1, 2, 5
Follies of a Day, The. See Holcroft, Thomas.
Follies of the Ages (entertainment), 1764: CG, Mar 26
Folly of Age, The; or, The Accomplished Lady (ballet-pantomime, anon), 1797:
    CG, Jun 9
Fompre, Mrs (actor), 1734: GF/HAY, Nov 20, HAY, Dec 20, 23, GF/HAY, 30; 1735:
    GF/HAY, Jan 9, HAY, 13, GF/HAY, Feb 5, Mar 20, Apr 10, May 2, Jun 2
Fond Echo Forbear (song), 1732: LIF, May 4; 1791: CG, Jun 6
Fond Husband, The. See D'Urfey, Thomas.

Fond Lady, The. See Duffett, Thomas, The Amorous Old Woman.
Fond Shepherd (song), 1698: DL, Mar 0
Fondlewife and Laetitia (entertainment), 1716: GLOBE, Dec 28; 1734: BLO, Jan
    16; 1767: HAY, Aug 14
Fontainbleau. See O'Keeffe, John.
Fontaine (dancer), 1775: DL, Oct 18, Nov 28, Dec 12, 19
Fontaine d'Amour (dance), 1791: PAN, Dec 17, 20, 31; 1792: PAN, Jan 14
Fontainville Forest. See Boaden, James.
Fontenelle, Louisa (actor), 1788: CG, Nov 6, 22, 25; 1789: CG, Feb 3, Mar 3,
    31, Apr 30, May 2; 1790: HAY, Jun 17, 22, 28, 29, Jul 16, 28, Aug 10, 25, Sep
    4, 6; 1791: HAY, Jun 8, 23, Jul 15, 22, 26, 30, Aug 2, 13, 16, 19, 31, Sep 2;
    1792: HAY, Jun 15, 19, 23, Jul 3, 4, 7, 9, 14, Aug 15, 23, Sep 6; 1793: HAY,
    Jun 12, 13, 15, 17, 18, 25, 26, Aug 3, 23, 27
Fonthornoycts, Henricus (musician), 1711: COH, Dec 20
Fonti Amiche (music), 1729: HIC, Apr 16
Fool Made Wise, A. See Johnson, Samuel.
Fool Turned Critic, The. See D'Urfey, Thomas.
Fool, The (play), 1748: JS, May 30
Fool, The. See Topham, Edward.
Fool's Preferment, A. See D'Urfey, Thomas.
Foolish Man and Woman (dance), 1727: KING'S, Mar 16
Fools Have Fortune; or, Luck's All (play, anon), 1679: NONE, Sep 0
Fools' Dance (dance), 1727: LIF, Nov 16, 23
Foord, James (author), 1788: HAY, Aug 18
Foot, Jesse, 1784: DL, Apr 19
--Quacks, The; or, The Credulous Man, 1784: DL, Apr 19
Foote for libelling Peter Paragraph (lecture), 1763: HAY, May 11
Foote, Samuel (actor, dramatist, comedian), 1744: HAY, Feb 6, DL, Mar 10, HAY,
    Apr 6, DL, 13; 1745: DL, Nov 1, 14, 25, Dec 11, 13; 1746: DL, Feb 24, Mar 17,
    Apr 14; 1747: DL, Mar 2, NONE, 27, HAY, Apr 20, 21, 22, 25, 28, CG, May 12,
    HAY, Jun 1, Nov 4, CG, 11, 23, Dec 15; 1748: CG, Jan 14, 27, Feb 2, HAY, 6,
    Apr 18, 21, May 9, Jun 3, Nov 22, Dec 1; 1749: HAY, Jan 16, DL, 18, 19, HAY,
    Feb 11, Mar 10, DL, 18, HAY, Apr 3, DL, 6, HAY, 6; 1750: DL, Jan 22, 26;
    1752: DL, Jan 6, 11, 13, 24, 25, 28; 1753: CG, Mar 24, DL, Oct 20, 24, 27,
    29, 30, Nov 6; 1754: DL, Jan 16, 19, Feb 5, 9, 12, 22, CG, Mar 28, Apr 1, Oct
    14, Nov 12, HAY, Dec 16, DL, 16, HAY, 18; 1755: HAY, Jan 3, 8, CG, 14, Mar
    12, 18, Apr 10, HAY, 12; 1756: CG, Feb 3, 9, 10, 12, 16, 23, Mar 1, 8, 22,
    27, 29, 30, DL, Apr 26, CG, May 7, 10, DL, Oct 14, 29, Nov 1; 1757: DL, Feb
    5, 22, Mar 28, 31, Apr 2, 4, Oct 15, 18, 24; 1758: DL, Jan 26, 30, Feb 1, CG,
    Mar 9, DL, May 4, Oct 17, 27, Nov 1, 14, 17, 24, Dec 18; 1759: DL, May 14,
    HAY, Nov 9; 1760: DL, May 3, HAY, Jun 28, Aug 18, DL, Oct 25, Nov 24, CG, Dec
    18, DL, 19, 22; 1761: CG, Mar 26, DL, Apr 6, CG, 21, DL, 25, May 29, Jun 4,
    15, 18, 26, Jul 2, 21, 27, Aug 8, CG, Nov 10; 1762: CG, Jan 12, 22, HAY, Apr
    28, May 1, DL, 11, HAY, 11, Jun 21, Aug 10, 23, 28, Sep 9, 10; 1763: HAY, May
    9, 11, Jun 9, 20, 27, Jul 6, 18, Aug 5, 29, DL, Nov 30, Dec 5, 9; 1764: HAY,
    Jun 13, 26, Jul 6, 13, 16, 30, Aug 29; 1765: HAY, Jun 10, Jul 8, 15, 31, Aug
    9, 21; 1766: CG, Feb 11, DL, 15, Mar 1, HAY, Jun 18, Jul 1, 12, 15, 23, Aug
    4, 6, KING'S, 20, HAY, 21, KING'S, Sep 9; 1767: HAY, May 29, Jun 4, 5, 8, 22,
    Jul 2, 3, Aug 12, 14, 25, 26, 27, Sep 4, 7, 16; 1768: HAY, May 30, Jun 23,
    Jul 13, 18, Aug 19, 24, DL, Nov 11; 1769: HAY, May 15, 24, 29, Jun 2, 21, Jul
    31, Aug 11, 16, 25, 31; 1770: CG, Feb 15, HAY, Mar 12, DL, Apr 26, HAY, May
    16, 18, 25, 28, 30, Jun 15, 22, Aug 24, 31, Sep 3, CG, 24, HAY, Oct 15, CG,
    23; 1771: HAY, Apr 4, CG, May 1, HAY, 15, 20, 23, 29, Jun 7, 12, 14, 26, 28,
    Aug 19, Sep 2, 18, DL, Dec 19; 1772: DL, Mar 23, HAY, May 18, 20, 22, 27, Jun
    8, 15, 29, Aug 10, Sep 8; 1773: CG, Feb 3, Mar 6, 15, May 8, HAY, 17, 26, 28,
    31, Jun 7, 18, Jul 2, 16, 21, Aug 11, 27, Sep 3; 1774: HAY, May 16, 30, Jun
    3, 6, 8, 10, 17, 27, Jul 15, Aug 19, 26, Sep 5, 12; 1775: HAY, May 15, 17,
    19, 22, 26, 29, Jun 5, 7, 12, Jul 21, 31, Aug 2, 4, 16, 18, 28, Sep 4; 1776:
    HAY, May 20, 22, 27, 28, 31, DL, Jun 1, HAY, 12, 14, 19, 26, Jul 5, 8, 10,
    29, Aug 2, 19, Sep 2, CHR, Oct 7; 1777: HAY, May 30, Jun 6, 9, Jul 7, 16, 30;
    1778: CG, Jan 19, Feb 6; 1779: HAY, Aug 13; 1780: DL, Apr 29; 1781: CG, Apr
    30, HAY, Nov 12; 1782: HAY, Dec 30; 1784: HAY, Sep 17; 1785: HAY, Apr 25, 26,
    CG, May 7; 1787: HAY, Jan 8, CG, Mar 27; 1789: DL, May 5; 1790: DL, May 4,
    12; 1791: DL, Mar 24, HAY, Oct 24; 1792: CG, Apr 10, HAY, Jun 22; 1795: HAY,
    Apr 22; 1799: DL, Apr 24
--Auction of Pictures (entertainment), 1748: HAY, Apr 18, 19, 20, 21, 22, 23,
    25, 26, 27, 28, 29, 30, May 2, 3, 4, 5, 6, 7, 9, 12, 14, 16, 17, 19, 20, 21,
    24, 26, 28, 30, 31, Jun 3, 6, 8, 9, 11, Dec 1, 5, 8, 12, 14, 16, 19, 22, 24,
    28; 1749: HAY, Jan 2, 7, 9, 14, 25, 27, Feb 4, 18, May 1, 6, 10, 15, 19, 26,
    Jun 1
--Author, The, 1757: DL, Feb 2, 5, 7, 9, 12, 15, 17, 19, 22, 26, Mar 1, 5, 10,
    15, 28, Apr 13, 14, 29, May 10, 12, 20, Oct 15, 18, 21, 22, 24, Nov 15, 25,

316

Dec 2, 14, 21; <u>1758</u>: DL, Jan 10, 20, 26, 30, Feb 1, CG, Jul 6, DL, Dec 18;
<u>1760</u>: CG, Dec 18; <u>1769</u>: HAY, Aug 11, 16, 18, 21, 23, Sep 8, 12, 14; <u>1770</u>:
HAY, May 18, 25, 30, Jun 8, Jul 11, 16, 23, Aug 10, Sep 3, 12, CG, Oct 17,
Nov 1, 3, 8, 15, Dec 4, 21; <u>1771</u>: CG, Feb 26, DL, Mar 14, CG, 19, HAY, Apr 4,
CG, 5, DL, 16, 20, HAY, May 23, CG, 23, HAY, Jun 19, Aug 14, 21, Sep 6, 14,
CG, Oct 18, Nov 4, Dec 21; <u>1772</u>: DL, Mar 28, Apr 9, CG, 25, May 12, DL, 18,
HAY, 20, 25, Jun 5, 22, Aug 5, Sep 4, 8, 14, DL, Nov 20, Dec 4; <u>1773</u>: DL, Feb
13, Mar 8, Apr 22, May 17, 25, HAY, Jun 7, 9, Jul 16, Aug 30, Sep 14; <u>1774</u>:
DL, Mar 21, CG, Apr 9, 15, HAY, Jun 3, 10, 17, Jul 1, 13, Aug 24, Sep 14, DL,
Nov 17; <u>1775</u>: DL, Apr 26, May 8, HAY, 15, 17, 29, Jun 14, 28, Jul 12, 21, Aug
14, Sep 1, 20, CG, Nov 28; <u>1776</u>: CG, Jan 4, DL, 26, HAY, May 27, Jun 17, 24,
Jul 31, Sep 11; <u>1777</u>: DL, Feb 20, HAY, Jul 7, 16, 25; <u>1778</u>: CG, Feb 6; <u>1779</u>:
DL, Mar 16, CG, Apr 21; <u>1781</u>: HAY, Jun 1, 6, 12, 26, Jul 10, Aug 4, 25; <u>1782</u>:
HAY, Aug 13, CG, Nov 8, Dec 7; <u>1783</u>: HAY, Jun 4, CG, Oct 28; <u>1784</u>: HAY, Jun
25; <u>1785</u>: DL, Jan 14, 25, HAY, Feb 10, DL, May 26, HAY, Jun 11, Jul 21, Aug
4; <u>1787</u>: HAY, Mar 12; <u>1788</u>: HAY, Jun 23, Sep 13; <u>1790</u>: HAY, Jun 15, 21, Jul
10, 17, Aug 3, CG, Dec 11; <u>1791</u>: CG, Jan 19, HAY, Jul 8, 9, Aug 25; <u>1792</u>:
DLKING'S, Feb 23, Jun 8, HAY, 26, Jul 26, Aug 8; <u>1793</u>: HAY, Jul 20, 25, Oct
21; <u>1794</u>: HAY, Aug 9; <u>1795</u>: HAY, Apr 22; <u>1796</u>: HAY, Jul 11; <u>1797</u>: HAY, Jun
12; <u>1799</u>: DL, Apr 24; <u>1800</u>: HAY, Sep 16
--Bankrupt, The, <u>1773</u>: HAY, Jul 21, 23, 26, 28, 30, Aug 2, 4, 6, 9, 13, 16, 18,
20, 25, 27, Sep 1, 6, 10, 13, 14, 15; <u>1774</u>: HAY, May 16, Jun 1, 15, Jul 1, 8,
Aug 24, Sep 2, 14; <u>1775</u>: HAY, Jun 5, Jul 19, Aug 11; <u>1776</u>: HAY, May 20, 28,
Jul 12, CG, Oct 31, Nov 1, Dec 4
--Capuchin, The, <u>1776</u>: HAY, Aug 19, 21, 23, 26, 28, 30, Sep 4, 9, 13
--Commissary, The, <u>1765</u>: HAY, Jun 10, 11, 14, 17, 19, 21, 24, 26, 28, Jul 1, 3,
5, 8, 10, 12, 17, 22, 26, Aug 5, 12, 15, 19, 23, 26, Sep 2, 4, 10, 12, 13;
<u>1766</u>: HAY, Jul 15, 18, 21, 30, Aug 1; <u>1767</u>: HAY, Jun 4, 10, 19, 25, Jul 20,
Aug 3, Sep 1, 11; <u>1768</u>: HAY, Jul 13, Aug 5, 26, Sep 14; <u>1769</u>: HAY, May 24,
Jun 14, Jul 10, Aug 2, 21, Sep 8, 14; <u>1770</u>: HAY, May 18, 25, Jun 1, 11, Aug
3, 16, Sep 13; <u>1771</u>: CG, May 1, 11, 28, HAY, 29, Jun 17, Aug 16, CG, Sep 23,
30, Oct 9, 16, Nov 1, 9, Dec 11; <u>1772</u>: CG, Jan 15, May 12, HAY, Jun 8, 17,
Aug 5, Sep 14, CG, 25, 30, Oct 13, Nov 9, 23, Dec 22; <u>1773</u>: CG, Feb 6, 23,
May 25, 27, HAY, Jul 2, CG, Oct 22, Nov 5, Dec 11, 18; <u>1774</u>: CG, Feb 4, Apr
22, May 2, 14, 20, 25, HAY, Jun 17; <u>1775</u>: HAY, Jun 7, 30, Aug 9, Sep 13, 20,
CG, Nov 4, 18; <u>1776</u>: HAY, May 31, Jun 12, Aug 9; <u>1777</u>: CG, Sep 24, Oct 17;
<u>1778</u>: CG, May 2, 7, 13, 20, Dec 31; <u>1779</u>: CG, Jan 2, Apr 22, Nov 23; <u>1782</u>:
CG, Oct 2; <u>1784</u>: CG, Aay 11; <u>1785</u>: CG, Nov 29; <u>1787</u>: CG, Oct 1; <u>1788</u>: CG, Apr
1, Oct 17; <u>1789</u>: CG, Oct 21; <u>1791</u>: CG, Nov 25; <u>1793</u>: CG, May 15, HAY, Jun 25,
27, Jul 8, CG, Nov 1
--Cozeners, The, <u>1774</u>: MARLY, Jul 6, HAY, 15, 18, 20, 22, 25, 27, 29, Aug 1, 3,
5, 10, 12, 15, 17, 22, 26, 31, Sep 7, 9, 13, 15; <u>1775</u>: HAY, May 19, 24, Jun
2, 16, 26, Jul 3, 21, Aug 23, Sep 14; <u>1776</u>: HAY, Jun 19, 21, 24, 26, Jul 1,
8, 15, 19, 26, Aug 5, Sep 6, 14; <u>1792</u>: CG, Apr 10
--Devil upon Two Sticks, The, <u>1768</u>: HAY, May 30, Jun 1, 3, 6, 8, 10, 13, 15,
17, 20, 22, 24, 27, 29, Jul 1, 4, 6, 11, 15, 20, 25, 29, Aug 3, 8, 12, 17,
22, 29, Sep 2, 5, 9, 12, 13, 15; <u>1769</u>: HAY, May 15, 17, 19, 22, 26, 31, Jun
7, 12, 19, Jul 5, 24, Aug 4, 28, Sep 4, 13, 15; <u>1770</u>: HAY, May 16, 21, Jun 5,
13, 20, Jul 20, Aug 6, 17, 29, Sep 10, 15; <u>1771</u>: HAY, May 15, Jun 3, 21, Aug
5, 30, Sep 11; <u>1772</u>: HAY, May 27, Jun 1, 10, 24, Jul 27, Sep 9; <u>1773</u>: HAY,
May 31, Jun 25, Jul 12, Aug 23; <u>1774</u>: HAY, Jun 8, 20, 29, Jul 6, Aug 29, Sep
12; <u>1775</u>: HAY, May 15, 17, 29, Jun 19, Jul 5, 24, Aug 18, Sep 8; <u>1776</u>: HAY,
Jun 14, Jul 3, 24, Aug 16, Sep 10; <u>1777</u>: HAY, Jun 6; <u>1778</u>: HAY, Aug 27; <u>1779</u>:
HAY, Aug 13; <u>1780</u>: CII, Apr 19, DL, 29, HAY, Sep 11; <u>1781</u>: HAY, Jun 21, Jul
28; <u>1782</u>: CG, Nov 19, 21, 22, HAY, Dec 30; <u>1783</u>: CG, Jan 11, Feb 15, Mar 22,
May 15, 28, Oct 9, Nov 25, Dec 20; <u>1784</u>: CG, Feb 14, Dec 7, 10, 22; <u>1785</u>: CG,
May 7, HAY, Aug 26, CG, Oct 14, Nov 18; <u>1787</u>: HAY, Jan 8, CG, Feb 20, Mar 17,
Apr 12, Jun 11, HAY, Aug 14, CG, Sep 19, 21; <u>1788</u>: CG, Oct 1, Nov 8; <u>1789</u>:
CG, Oct 31, Dec 4; <u>1790</u>: DL, May 4; <u>1791</u>: HAY, Aug 10
--Diversions of the Morning, The; or, A Dish of Chocolate, <u>1747</u>: HAY, Apr 22,
25, 28, May 2, Jun 1; <u>1753</u>: DL, Nov 19; <u>1758</u>: DL, Oct 17, 27, 30, Nov 1, 6,
9, 14, 17, 28, Dec 18; <u>1759</u>: DL, May 14, 16; <u>1763</u>: HAY, Jul 6, 7; <u>1769</u>: HAY,
Aug 25; <u>1785</u>: HAY, Apr 25
--Englishman in Paris, The, <u>1753</u>: CG, Mar 24, Apr 24, DL, Oct 20, 22, 24, 27,
30, Nov 2, 12, 30, Dec 14, 15, 20; <u>1754</u>: DL, Jan 18, 21, 25, 29, Feb 5, Mar
19, 25, Apr 1, 17, May 4, Sep 28, Oct 5, 8, 17, CG, Nov 12, DL, 25; <u>1755</u>: DL,
Mar 13, 22, Apr 3, 7, Oct 21, 30, Nov 4; <u>1756</u>: DL, Jan 22, CG, Feb 3, DL, Mar
18, CG, 27, DL, Apr 1, CG, May 7, DL, 27, Oct 2, 14, Nov 1, 12, Dec 1; <u>1757</u>:
DL, Mar 21, 31, Sep 22, Oct 12; <u>1758</u>: DL, Feb 6, Mar 18, 31, Apr 17, 24, May
4, Nov 24; <u>1759</u>: DL, Apr 2, 30, May 17, Oct 2; <u>1760</u>: DL, Apr 16, May 1, 12,
14, Dec 19; <u>1761</u>: DL, Apr 16, CG, 21; <u>1762</u>: DL, Feb 19, Apr 23, May 20, 21,
24, 25, Oct 1, CG, 19, 22, 29; <u>1763</u>: CG, Mar 19, DL, Apr 5, May 17, CG, Nov

317

10, Dec 22; 1764: CG, Mar 29, May 5, Oct 3, 17, Nov 27, Dec 27; 1765: CG, Apr 26, Sep 20; 1766: CG, Jan 18, Feb 13, May 1, Oct 22, Nov 11, Dec 20; 1767: CG, Jan 17, Feb 17, Apr 9; 1768: CG, Mar 8, Apr 18, Oct 21, Dec 17; 1769: CG, Jan 18, Apr 11, 19, May 9, Dec 7, 15; 1770: CG, Jan 17, Mar 24, Apr 7, 21; 1771: HAY, May 27, Jun 10, Jul 19, Sep 11, CG, Dec 7; 1772: CG, Apr 28, May 19, 25, Oct 1, 15, 22, Nov 27; 1773: CG, Mar 18, Apr 14, May 11, Oct 27, Nov 13; 1774: CG, Jan 14, Mar 19, Apr 20, Oct 5; 1775: CG, Apr 25, May 12, 17, 24, Oct 18, Nov 9, 25; 1776: CG, Jan 10, Feb 20, Mar 12, Oct 4, Nov 16; 1777: CG, Nov 21; 1778: CG, Apr 28, May 15, HAY, Sep 10, CG, Dec 12; 1779: CG, Mar 25; 1780: CG, Dec 5, 13; 1781: DL, May 8, Dec 27; 1782: DL, May 29, Sep 28, Nov 23, Dec 6, 23; 1783: DL, Jan 14, 20, Feb 1, 24, Oct 4, 8, Nov 29; 1784: DL, Jan 5, Feb 18, Apr 14, May 22; 1785: DL, Jan 11, May 23; 1786: DL, Jan 16, Feb 11, Mar 20, Apr 1, Nov 25; 1787: DL, Oct 6, 25, Dec 12; 1790: CG, Apr 7, May 18; 1792: DLKING'S, Jan 28, 30, Feb 9, May 12, Jun 12, 15, DL, Nov 10; 1794: DL, May 13, 16, Dec 22; 1795: DL, Jan 2, Feb 5

--Knights, The, 1749: HAY, Apr 3, 4, 5, 8, 11, 12, 15, 18, 20, 22, 25, 28, May 1, 6, 10, 15, 19, 26, Jun 1; 1754: DL, Jan 19, Feb 5, 9, 12, 13, 15, 22, CG, Mar 28, Apr 1, Oct 14; 1755: CG, Jan 14; 1756: CG, Mar 22, 25, May 10; 1757: DL, Apr 2, 4, CG, May 4; 1758: CG, Jan 28, 31, Feb 2, DL, 3, CG, Mar 4, 11, 28, Apr 5, 14, 20, May 5, Sep 22, Oct 2, Nov 8, Dec 12; 1759: CG, May 14, Oct 15, 16, 26, Nov 8, 16; 1760: CG, Jan 17, Feb 12, Apr 26, Oct 11, Nov 26, Dec 15, 20; 1761: CG, Jan 21, Sep 26; 1762: CG, Jan 7; 1763: CG, May 16, 25; 1764: CG, Jan 5, May 16, Dec 29; 1765: HAY, Jun 10, 11, 14, 17, 19, 21, Aug 14, CG, Oct 12; 1767: HAY, Aug 10; 1769: CG, Mar 29, Apr 13; 1771: CG, Oct 30; 1772: HAY, Aug 10; 1776: HAY, Jun 26, 28, Jul 5, 17, 22, Aug 7, Sep 9

--Lame Lover, The, 1770: HAY, Jun 22, 25, 27, 29, Jul 2, 4, 6, 11, 16, 23, Aug 1, 10, 20, Sep 5, 12; 1771: HAY, May 23; 1775: HAY, Aug 28, Sep 6; 1789: DL, May 5

--Liar, The, 1761: CG, Sep 25; 1762: CG, Jan 12, 13, 15, 22, HAY, Jun 21, 23, 25, 29, Jul 1, 3, 6, 15, 22, Aug 23, 25, 28, Sep 9; 1763: HAY, Jun 27, 30, Jul 11, 20, 27, Aug 10, 17, 30; 1764: HAY, Jul 30, Aug 1, 3, 8, 17, 27, Sep 5, 11, 14; 1765: HAY, Jul 15, 19, 24, 29, Sep 11; 1767: HAY, Jun 8, Jul 7, 9, 13, 17, 29, Sep 11, 16, DL, Dec 12, 15; 1768: DL, Jan 25, 26, Feb 4, Mar 8, Apr 15, 22, 30, May 9, Nov 17, Dec 9; 1769: DL, Feb 7, 27, May 10, HAY, Aug 16, 23, DL, Dec 13, 22; 1770: DL, Mar 8, May 22, Nov 16, Dec 27; 1771: DL, Jan 12, Mar 5, May 28, HAY, Jun 12, Aug 7; 1772: DL, Jan 3, 20, Mar 23, Sep 19, Nov 27; 1773: DL, Jan 22, Jun 1, Oct 6, Nov 9, Dec 9; 1774: DL, Jan 7, 21, Apr 13, Nov 8, 24, Dec 21; 1775: DL, Jan 19, CG, Apr 22, HAY, Aug 9, 11, 30, Sep 6, 15, 16, DL, 28, Nov 28, CG, 30, Dec 4, DL, 8; 1776: CG, Jan 6, 13, Feb 14, May 21, HAY, 22, 28, Jun 19, Jul 3, Aug 16, 23, CG, Nov 20, Dec 14; 1777: CG, May 24, HAY, Aug 19, 26; 1778: CG, Mar 9, DL, May 5, 25, Oct 3, CG, Dec 15, 29; 1779: DL, Jan 6, May 26; 1780: CG, Apr 24, DL, Nov 11, 18, 27, 29, CG, Dec 4; 1781: DL, Jan 2, 11, May 17, Oct 26, 31, Dec 14; 1782: DL, Apr 13, May 22, Oct 26, Nov 30; 1783: DL, Jan 11, Feb 15, 28, Mar 8, May 15, 28, Jun 2, Sep 18, Oct 17, Dec 22; 1784: DL, Feb 21, May 11, CG, Nov 3; 1785: DL, Mar 17, Apr 14, May 20, Nov 2, 10; 1786: DL, Mar 25, May 31, Nov 29, Dec 8; 1787: DL, May 2, CG, Nov 16; 1788: DL, Apr 25, May 3, 7, 19, 26, 31, Jun 4, Sep 16, 20, 25, Oct 22, Nov 15, 24; 1789: DL, Jan 29, Feb 12, May 9, Jun 12; 1790: DL, May 14, HAY, Aug 7, 9, 13, 18, 24, 30, Sep 4, DL, 14, Oct 5, 9; 1791: DL, Jan 13, Feb 1, May 31, HAY, Aug 15, Sep 7, DLKING'S, Oct 8; 1792: HAY, Jun 22, 28, Jul 19, 28, Aug 25, DL, Sep 25, Nov 6, 20; 1793: DL, Jan 28; 1794: DL, Jun 11, 13, 27, 28, Jul 4, HAY, 12, Aug 8, 19, 29, Sep 15; 1796: DL, Jan 16, HAY, Jun 11, DL, 14, HAY, 18, Jul 18, Aug 4, DL, Sep 24; 1797: HAY, Jun 15, Aug 2; 1798: DL, May 29, Oct 20, Nov 8, 29; 1799: DL, Jul 5; 1800: DL, Jan 14, Mar 11, Apr 5, May 10, HAY, Aug 27

--Maid of Bath, The, 1771: HAY, Jun 26, 28, Jul 1, 3, 5, 8, 10, 12, 15, 17, 19, 22, 26, 29, 31, Aug 2, 9, 14, 21, 23, 28, Sep 4, 10, 12, 14; 1772: HAY, May 18, 20, 25, 29, Jun 5, 12, 22, Jul 22, Aug 21, Sep 4, 10; 1773: HAY, May 28, Jun 7, Jul 7, Sep 8; 1774: HAY, Jun 6; 1775: HAY, Jun 12, 21, Jul 28, Aug 21, 30; 1776: HAY, Jul 5, 22, Aug 7; 1777: HAY, Jul 30; 1787: CG, May 11

--Mayor of Garratt, The, 1763: HAY, Jun 20, 22, 24, 27, 29, 30, Jul 1, 4, 6, 7, 8, 11, 13, 15, 18, 20, 22, 25, 27, 29, Aug 1, 3, 5, 8, 12, 15, 17, 19, 22, 24, 26, 29, 30, 31, Sep 2, 3, DL, Nov 30, Dec 1, 2, 3, 5, 7, 8, 9; 1764: HAY, Jun 26, 28, 29, Jul 3, 5, 6, 10, 16, 20, 25, 30, Aug 1, 6, 10, 17, 20, 27, Sep 5, 11, 14; 1765: HAY, Jul 15, 19, 24, Aug 7, 12, 15, 19, 23, 26, 30, Sep 2, 10, 13; 1766: HAY, Jul 23, 25, 28, 30, Aug 1, 4, 6, KING'S, Sep 9; 1767: HAY, Jun 8, 17, 19, 25, Jul 20, Aug 3, 27, Sep 7, 12; 1768: DL, Apr 9, HAY, Jun 23, Aug 10, Sep 7, 14; 1769: HAY, May 29, Jun 9, 16, Jul 7, 21, Sep 1; 1770: HAY, May 28, Jun 1, 11, Aug 20, Sep 5, 13; 1771: DL, Apr 2, 8, 13, May 3, 14, HAY, 20, Jun 12, Aug 26, Sep 2, 13, DL, 26, Oct 8, Dec 31; 1772: DL, Jan 22, 29, Mar 5, 31, Apr 24, 29, May 2, 11, HAY, 22, 29, Aug 21, Sep 10, DL, Oct 16, 21, Nov 19; 1773: HAY, May 26, Jun 2, 11, 30, Sep 8, DL, Oct 5,

15, Nov 15, Dec 21; 1774: DL, Feb 19, HAY, Jun 6, 24, Sep 2, DL, Nov 4, 12,
23; 1775: DL, Feb 3, Apr 22, HAY, May 26, Jun 9, 21, Jul 19, 26, Aug 16, Sep
14; 1776: HAY, May 31, Jun 21, Jul 29, Aug 9, Sep 13, 23, DL, 28, Oct 3, Nov
8; 1777: DL, May 8, Jun 6, CHR, 20, HAY, Jul 30, Sep 17, 18, 19; 1778: CG,
Jan 15, 16, HAY, Mar 31, CHR, May 27, HAY, Aug 6; 1779: DL, May 18, HAY, Jun
10, 11, Jul 6, 7, 12, 27, Aug 3, 5, 11, 31, DL, Dec 31; 1780: HAY, Jun 23,
29, Jul 3, 27, DL, Sep 28; 1781: HAY, Jun 7, Jul 11; 1784: HAY, Mar 8; 1785:
HAY, Jul 11, 22, Aug 12, 22; 1786: HAY, Mar 6, HAMM, Jun 7; 1788: DL, May 1,
HAY, Jun 11, 26, Jul 1, 5, 25, Aug 9, Sep 3, CG, Oct 24, 28, Nov 15; 1789:
CG, Apr 21, HAY, Jun 29, Jul 8, 9, 25, CG, Dec 4; 1790: HAY, Jun 22, Jul 27;
1791: DL, Apr 5, HAY, Aug 5, 17, 24, Sep 6, 13, CG, 30, Oct 5, 7, 14, Nov 1;
1792: DLKING'S, Feb 27, Mar 5, May 4, DL, Dec 8; 1793: DL, Feb 23, Apr 18,
HAY, Nov 6, 26; 1794: HAY, Aug 11, 21; 1795: DL, Feb 6, HAY, Jun 9, Sep 3;
1796: CG, Dec 1; 1798: DL, Jan 4, 10, Mar 12, HAY, 26, CG, Nov 20
--Minor, The, 1759: HAY, Nov 9; 1760: HAY, Jun 28, Jul 1, 3, 5, 8, 10, 12, 15,
17, 21, 23, 25, 28, 30, Aug 1, 4, 6, 7, 8, 9, 11, 13, 15, 18, 19, 20, 21, 22,
23, 25, 26, 27, 28, 29, 30, Sep 9, DL, Oct 25, Nov 22, CG, 24, DL, 24, CG,
25, DL, 25, 26, CG, 26, 27, DL, 28, CG, 28, 29, DL, Dec 1, 3, CG, 3, DL, 9,
CG, 18, DL, 22; 1761: DL, Jan 9, 19, 24, Apr 22, 25, CG, May 4, 5, DL, 29,
Jun 4, 26, 29, Jul 21, Aug 7, Nov 9, CG, 10; 1762: CG, Jan 22, DL, Mar 30,
Apr 21, CG, 30, DL, May 11, HAY, Jul 8, 10, 13, 20, Sep 2, 8, 11; 1763: HAY,
Jun 20, 22, 24, 29, Jul 1, 8, 15, 25, Aug 3, 12, 15, 26, Sep 2; 1764: HAY,
Jul 16, 18, 27, Aug 13, 24, Sep 3, 12; 1765: HAY, Aug 9, 16, 28, Sep 6; 1766:
HAY, Jun 18, 20, 24, 26, Jul 23, 25, 28, Aug 6, KING'S, 20, HAY, Sep 2; 1767:
HAY, May 29, Jun 2, 15, Aug 19, Sep 4; 1768: HAY, Jul 18, Aug 15, 31; 1769:
HAY, May 29, Jun 9, 16, Jul 7, 21, Aug 11, Sep 12; 1770: DL, Apr 26, 27, 30,
May 12, 17, 21, HAY, Jun 15, Jul 27, Oct 15; 1771: HAY, May 20, Jun 19, Aug
12, Sep 13; 1772: HAY, May 22, Jun 19, Aug 17; 1773: DL, May 1, 11, HAY, 26,
Jun 2, 11, 30, Aug 11, 31; 1774: HAY, Jun 10, 24, Sep 16; 1775: HAY, May 26,
Jun 9, 28, Jul 12, 26, Aug 14, Sep 1, 15; 1776: HAY, May 27, Jun 17, Jul 31,
Aug 14, 27, CHR, Oct 9; 1777: HAY, Jul 7, 16, 25; 1778: CG, Jan 19, 22, 24,
HAY, Aug 20; 1779: CG, Apr 24; 1780: HAY, Sep 8; 1782: CG, Nov 12; 1786: HAY,
Jul 25, Aug 22, 26, Sep 7; 1788: DL, Jan 5, 12, Mar 11, CG, May 14, HAY, Aug
15, Sep 1; 1789: DL, Feb 21, 28, Mar 3, 7, Apr 2, 18, Jun 4, HAY, 23, Jul 9,
Aug 7, Sep 4; 1790: HAY, Jun 14, 19, 29, Jul 15, 31, Aug 5, 17, 26; 1791: CG,
Apr 28, HAY, Jul 1, 5, 21, 29, Aug 12; 1792: DLKING'S, Mar 29; 1797: DL, May
27
--Morning Lectures, 1763: HAY, May 11, 14, 18, 21, 28, Jun 3
--Nabob, The, 1772: HAY, Jun 29, Jul 1, 3, 6, 8, 10, 13, 15, 17, 20, 24, 29,
31, Aug 3, 7, 12, 14, 19, 26, 28, Sep 2, 7, 11, 15; 1773: HAY, May 17, 19,
24, Jun 4, 9, Jul 5, 16, Aug 30, Sep 9; 1774: HAY, May 18, 30, Jun 3, 13, 22,
Jul 4, 13, Aug 8, 19; 1775: HAY, May 22, 31, Jun 14, Jul 17, Aug 4, 25, Sep
11; 1776: HAY, May 22, Jun 28, Jul 17, Aug 12, Sep 11; 1777: HAY, May 30, Jul
11; 1778: HAY, Aug 25; 1781: HAY, Jul 3, 23, 31; 1782: HAY, Jun 4; 1786: DL,
Mar 28
--Orators, The; or, The School of Eloquence Dissected, 1762: HAY, Apr 28, May
1, 4, 6, 8, 11, 18, 20, 22, 25, 26, 29, Jun 1, 3, 5, 8, 10, 12, 16, 21, 23,
25, 29, Jul 1, 3, 6, 8, 10, 13, 15, 20, 22, Aug 30, Sep 6, 9, 10, 14, 16, Oct
25; 1763: HAY, Jul 4, 13, Aug 8, 19, 29, Sep 3; 1764: HAY, Jul 6, 12, 23, Aug
10, 22, 29, Sep 7, 13; 1765: HAY, Jul 31, Aug 7, 14, Sep 3, 9; 1766: HAY, Jul
1, 3, 8, 10, Aug 4; 1767: HAY, Jun 5, 12, Aug 25, 26, Sep 9; 1768: HAY, Aug
24; 1769: HAY, Jun 2, Jul 28; 1771: HAY, Jun 14; 1773: HAY, Sep 3; 1775: HAY,
Aug 16; 1776: HAY, Jul 10; 1780: HAY, Mar 28
--Patron, The, 1764: HAY, Jun 13, 15, 18, 26, 28, 29, Jul 3, 5, 10, 13, 20, 25,
Aug 6, 15, 31, Sep 10; 1765: HAY, Aug 21; 1767: HAY, Aug 12, 27; 1770: HAY,
May 28, Jun 8; 1771: HAY, Jun 7; 1772: HAY, Jun 15; 1774: HAY, Sep 5; 1775:
HAY, Aug 2; 1776: HAY, Jul 29; 1781: HAY, Aug 1; 1792: DL, Dec 28; 1793: DL,
Jan 26
--Rary Shew, 1773: CG, Mar 6
--Sentimental Comedy, A; or, Piety in Pattens (entertainment), 1773: HAY, Aug
23, Sep 3; 1774: HAY, Jun 1, 8, 13, 22, Jul 4, 13, Aug 8, 29, Sep 5, 6, 19;
1775: HAY, Sep 11, 14, 15, 18; 1776: MARLY, May 23, 25, HAY, Jul 10, 15, Aug
7, 9; 1777: HAY, Jun 11, 12, 23, Aug 4, 21, Sep 6; 1778: HAY, May 18, 23, 29,
Sep 18; 1779: HAY, Jun 9, Jul 1, 31; 1780: HAY, Jun 17, 22, Aug 7; 1786: CG,
May 15; 1790: DL, May 12, 19, 27, 31, HAY, Jul 7, 13, 29, Sep 2; 1791: HAY,
Aug 9; 1793: HAY, Jul 5, 9, 10, 16, Aug 7, Sep 10, 21; 1794: HAY, Jul 14, 30,
Aug 21
--Spendthrift, The; or, The Female Conspiracy, 1781: HAY, Nov 12
--Taste; or, Tragedy a la Mode (or, The Diversions of the Morning), 1752: DL,
Jan 6, 11, 13, 21, 22, 23, 24, 28; 1755: CG, Mar 18, Apr 10; 1756: CG, Mar
30, Apr 3, 23, Dec 20, 30; 1758: DL, Oct 17; 1761: DL, Apr 6, May 15; 1762:
DL, May 11, HAY, Sep 10, 11, 14, 16; 1764: HAY, Aug 29, 31, Sep 1, 7, 10, 13;

1770: HAY, Aug 24, Sep 7, 14; 1771: DL, Apr 20, HAY, Jun 7, 17, Aug 16, 23,
Sep 12; 1772: CG, May 11, HAY, Jun 8; 1776: HAY, Jul 10, 12, 15, 19, 26, Aug
5, 12, Sep 6, 14, 23, CHR, Oct 7; 1786: HAMM, Jun 30; 1787: HAY, Apr 30;
1791: HAY, Oct 24
--Tea (entertainment), 1747: HAY, Nov 4, CG, 11, 13, 14, 16, 18, 19, 20, 21,
Dec 15, 22, 23, 30; 1748: CG, Jan 21, 23, 26, 27, 28, Feb 2, 3, HAY, Jun 14,
16; 1749: DL, Apr 6, CG, 7; 1753: DL, Nov 19, 20; 1778: CG, Feb 6
--Trip to Calais, A, 1775: HAY, Aug 4, 16, 18; 1776: HAY, Aug 19
--Writ of Inquiry will be Executed on the Inquisitor General, A, 1754: HAY, Dec
16, 18, 23, 27; 1755: HAY, Jan 1, 3
Foote, Weston, and Shuter in the Shades. See Wilson, Richard, A Peep into
Elysium.
Foote's Vagaries (dance), 1748: CG, Jan 21, Apr 13, May 4, BFH, Aug 24; 1749:
CG, Apr 7; see also Mouse Trap
Footing Dance (dance), 1733: CG, May 1, 2, LIF/CG, 10, BF, Aug 23
Footman Turned Gentleman, The (farce, anon), 1717: LIF, Mar 14; see also
Butcher Turned Gentleman, The
Footman, The (opera, anon), 1732: GF, Mar 7, 9, 11, 14, 18
Fop Song (song), 1706: QUEEN'S, May 2
Fopperwell (actor), 1775: HAY, Oct 30
For all these mercies (song), 1789: CG, Mar 6; 1790: CG, Feb 24, DL, Mar 17;
1791: CG, Mar 11; 1793: CG, Mar 6; 1794: CG, Mar 12, DL, Apr 9; 1795: CG, Mar
13; 1797: CG, Mar 10; 1798: CG, Mar 14, 30; 1799: CG, Feb 15, Mar 13; 1800:
CG, Mar 5
For as in Adam all die (song), 1793: KING/HAY, Feb 20; 1794: DL, Mar 19
For as much as Christ (song), 1794: DL, Apr 10
For behold! darkness shall cover the earth (song), 1790: CG, Mar 26; 1793:
KING/HAY, Feb 20; 1794: DL, Mar 19
For ever! Oh, for ever! (entertainment), 1789: CG, May 15
For Freedom and his Native Land (song), 1782: CG, May 6, 20
For I went with the Multitude (song), 1789: DL, Mar 25
For joys so vast (song), 1790: CG, Feb 26, Mar 19; 1794: CG, Mar 26, Apr 11
For tenderness formed (song), 1786: DL, Jan 14; 1797: CG, May 6
For the horse of Pharaoh (song), 1789: CG, Mar 6; 1791: CG, Mar 11; 1792: CG,
Mar 2; 1797: CG, Mar 10; 1798: CG, Mar 14, 30; 1800: CG, Mar 5
For the Lord is great (song), 1792: CG, Mar 9; 1794: CG, Mar 26
For unto us a Child is born (song), 1789: CG, Apr 3; 1790: DL, Feb 24, Mar 10,
12; 1791: DL, Mar 11, CG, Apr 13; 1792: KING'S, Mar 14, 21, 28; 1793:
KING/HAY, Feb 20; 1794: DL, Mar 12, 14, 19, CG, 26; 1795: KING'S, Feb 27, CG,
Mar 27; 1798: CG, Mar 30; 1799: CG, Mar 15
For us the Zephyr blows (song), 1791: DL, Apr 1; 1792: KING'S, Feb 29; 1794:
DL, Mar 26
Forbes, Margaret (actor), 1768: DL, Nov 1; 1769: MARLY, Aug 10, 17; 1770: HAY,
Dec 14; 1772: MARLY, Aug 20, 25, Sep 1, 7
Forcad, Miss. See Foulcade, Anne.
Force de l'Amour, La (Force of Love) (dance), 1775: DL, Apr 3; 1776: KING'S,
Dec 7, 10, 14, 21; 1777: KING'S, Jan 4, 11, 17, 21, Feb 1, 4, 22, Mar 1, 13,
Jun 3; 1778: DL, Oct 3, 8, 13, 17, 24; 1780: DL, Oct 18, 20, 25; 1781: DL,
May 11
Force of Fashion, The. See Mackenzie, Henry.
Force of Friendship, The. See Johnson, Charles.
Force of Inclination, The (dance), 1734: BFRLCH, Aug 24, Sep 2
Force of Ridicule, The. See Holcroft, Thomas.
Forced Marriage, The. See Moliere.
Forced Marriage, The; or, The Jealous Bridegroom. See Behn, Aphra.
Forcer, Francis (composer), 1676: DG, May 25, Jul 3; 1680: DG, Feb 0
Forcer, Francis (proprietor), 1743: SW, Apr 11
Ford (actor), 1675: ATCOURT, Feb 15
Ford (actor), 1769: HAY, May 29
Ford (actor), 1792: HAY, Nov 26
Ford (treasurer), 1730: LIF, May 4; 1731: LIF, May 26; 1732: LIF, May 8; 1733:
CG, May 4; 1734: CG, May 4; 1735: CG, May 6; 1736: CG, May 4; 1738: CG, May
5; 1740: CG, May 2; 1743: LIF, Apr 6
Ford, Brownlow (actor), 1776: DL, Sep 21
Ford, Harriet Ann (actor, dancer), 1762: DL, Nov 25, 27; 1763: DL, Jan 27, Oct
28, Nov 23, 26, Dec 20; 1764: DL, Jan 13, Feb 24, Sep 22, 25, Dec 26; 1765:
DL, Mar 21, Sep 24, Dec 9, 14; 1766: DL, Mar 22, Apr 18, May 5, Oct 28, 29;
1767: DL, Jan 2, May 21, CG, Sep 14, 23, Oct 19, Nov 14; 1768: CG, Jan 6, 25,
28, Feb 25, Mar 1, 26, Apr 15, Sep 20, 28, Nov 23; 1769: CG, Jan 14, Apr 8,
26
Ford, Henry (numberer), 1731: GF, Apr 6
Ford, Dr James (patentee), 1776: DL, Jan 19, Oct 15; 1780: HAY, Mar 28

Ford, John, 1668: LIF, Aug 20; 1748: DL, Apr 19, 23, 28
--Broken Heart, 1668: LIF, Aug 20
--Lady's Trial, The, 1669: LIF, Mar 3
--Love's Sacrifice, 1663: NONE, Sep 0
--Lover's Melancholy, The, 1668: LIF, Aug 20; 1748: DL, Apr 12, 19, 22, 23, 27,
   28, May 3, 5, 20
--Perkin Warbeck, 1745: DL, Sep 26, GF, Dec 19
--Tis a Pity She's a Whore, 1661: SALSBURY, Sep 9
Ford, Mrs (actor), 1671: LIF, Mar 6
Ford, Richard, 1790: DL, Mar 22; 1791: DL, Mar 22
--Greek Slave, The; or, The School for Cowards, 1791: DL, Mar 22
Ford, Sir Richard, 1662: THAMES, Aug 23
Forde, Miss (actor), 1784: HAY, Feb 23
Forde, Thomas, 1659: NONE, Sep 0
--Love's Labyrinth; or, The Royal Shepherdess, 1659: NONE, Sep 0
Fordyce, Alexander (banker), 1794: CG, May 20
Forecastle Fun; or, Saturday Night at Sea (interlude, anon), 1798: CG, Apr 21,
   May 9
Foreign comedians, 1735: HAY, Mar 13
Foreign Ministers, 1703: DL, Jun 22, Nov 10, Dec 22; 1704: DL, Oct 25, Dec 20;
   1705: DL, Nov 5; 1707: YB, Nov 19; 1710: QUEEN'S, Jul 19; 1718: SH, Dec 23;
   1723: LIF, May 30; 1731: DL, May 18; 1732: LIF, Feb 25, GF, May 4
Foreign Prince, 1731: GF, Jun 1
Foresters' Dance (dance), 1723: DL, May 15; 1724: DL, May 12, 14, 15, 18; 1776:
   CG, Nov 12; 1778: CG, Feb 24; 1779: CG, Sep 24, Dec 17; 1780: CG, Apr 10;
   1781: CG, Apr 3, May 12; 1782: CG, Jan 22, May 6; 1783: CG, May 17, HAY, Jul
   4; 1790: CG, Oct 20; 1791: CG, Oct 6; 1792: CG, Oct 10; 1793: CG, May 30
Forges de Vulcain (dance), 1779: KING'S, Mar 25
Forlivesi, Giuseppe (singer), 1788: KING'S, Apr 5, May 8; 1789: KING'S, Jan 10,
   24, Feb 28, Mar 21, 24, Apr 4, May 9, Jun 2
Formantel, Catherine (singer), 1763: SOHO, Feb 4
Forrest (actor), 1782: HAY, Jan 14, 21
Forrest (attorney), 1746: CG, Nov 24, Dec 27; 1759: CG, Nov 13; 1761: CG, Mar
   7, 10
Forrest, Ebenezer, 1729: LIF, Dec 3
--Momus Turned Fabulist; or, Vulcan's Wedding (musical), 1729: LIF, Dec 3, 4,
   5, 6, 8, 9, 10, 11, 12, 13, 18, 22; 1730: LIF, Feb 3, 4, 5, Mar 3, 31, May 8,
   Jun 12, Dec 15; 1731: LIF, Feb 12, Mar 20, Jun 1, Nov 23; 1733: CG, Jun 26,
   29; 1735: CG, Oct 13; 1737: CG, Apr 28
Forrest, Theodosius, 1775: CG, Oct 17
--Weathercock, The (musical), 1775: CG, Oct 17, 19, 21
Forrest's Coffee House, 1756: DL, Apr 24, CG, Dec 8; 1758: CG, Jul 6
Forrester, Mrs (actor), 1719: LIF, Nov 19; 1720: LIF, May 17; 1721: LIF, Mar 4;
   1729: LIF, Dec 1; 1730: LIF, May 23, HAY, Jun 23, Jul 7, 17, TC, Aug 1, BFR,
   22, Sep 4, LIF, Nov 10; 1731: LIF, Apr 1, 3, May 6, 7, Nov 2; 1732: LIF, Feb
   21, Mar 20, 23, Apr 11, May 26, LIF/CG, Oct 6, 9, 16, Nov 8, CG/LIF, Dec 16,
   LIF/CG, 27; 1733: LIF/CG, Mar 29, 30, Apr 21, CG/LIF, 26, CG, May 1, CG/LIF,
   28, CG, Sep 20, Oct 13, 18, Dec 1, 7; 1734: CG, Feb 26, Mar 5, 28, Apr 1, May
   4, 6, BFHBH, Aug 24, CG/LIF, Sep 27, Nov 7, 11, Dec 5, 30; 1735: CG/LIF, Mar
   11, CG, May 6, Sep 29, Oct 1, Nov 6; 1736: CG, Jan 1, 23, 24, Mar 18, LIF,
   31, CG, Apr 6, LIF, 16, CG, May 17, Oct 8, LIF, 18, CG, Nov 3; 1737: CG, Mar
   15, 28, Apr 11, 26
Forrett (instrumentalist), 1798: HAY, Jan 15
Forster (actor), 1800: HAY, Aug 26, 29
Forster, Ann, Mrs William (actor), 1785: DL, Dec 8; 1786: DL, Jan 12, 14, Feb
   4, 18, 23, Mar 2, 3, 4, 7, 9, 10, Apr 6, May 2, 15, Jun 2, Sep 19, 23, 28,
   Oct 7, 9, 12, Nov 14, Dec 5; 1787: DL, Apr 9, 20, May 4, 8, 16, 29, 30, HAY,
   Jun 18, Jul 2, 16, 21, 23, 27, Aug 3, 4, 10, 14, 21, DL, Sep 18, Oct 4, 11,
   25, Nov 3, 6, 17, 24, Dec 6, 19, 28; 1788: DL, Jan 26, Feb 21, CG, Mar 26,
   DL, Apr 7, May 29, Jun 11, HAY, 12, DL, 13, HAY, Jul 1, 10, 16, 19, Aug 13,
   25, Sep 3, DL, 16, 23, 30, Oct 2, 9, 16, 20, 23, 28, 30; 1789: DL, Jan 17,
   Feb 18, Mar 30, Apr 2
Forster, Mrs (actor), 1796: HAY, Feb 22
Forster, William (flutist, oboist), 1783: HAY, Jun 27; 1784: CG, Jun 10, HAY,
   Jul 28; 1786: HAY, Jul 18; 1787: DL, May 4, HAY, Jul 21; 1788: HAY, Jun 12;
   1789: DL, Sep 26; 1794: CG, Mar 7, HAY, Aug 27; 1795: HAY, Mar 4; 1797: HAY,
   Aug 16; 1798: HAY, Aug 9
Forsyth, Mrs (singer), 1726: HAY, Apr 29, LIF, May 6; 1727: HAY, Mar 17; 1729:
   HIC, Mar 28
Fort St George, 1748: JS, May 30; 1749: HAY, May 16
Forti, Giuseppe (dancer), 1758: KING'S, Nov 11; 1759: KING'S, Jan 16
Forti, Giuseppe and Sga (dancers), 1759: KING'S, May 22

Forti, Sga Giuseppe (dancer), 1758: KING'S, Jan 10, 31, Apr 4, CG, 12
Fortunate Adventurers, The; or, The Successful Lover (farce), 1745: JS, Dec 26
Fortunate Escape (dance), 1780: KING'S, Nov 25, 28, Dec 2, 9, 12, 16, 19; 1781:
    KING'S, Jan 13, Mar 8, Apr 3, 5, 28
Fortunatus. See Woodward, Henry.
Fortune Hunters, The. See Carlisle, James.
Fortune Tellers, The (dance), 1766: DL, Apr 19
Fortune Tellers, The (pantomime, anon), 1740: DL, Jan 15, 16, 17, 18, 19, 21,
    22, 23, Feb 4, 5, 7, 8, 9, 11, 12, 13, 14, 15, 16, 18, 19, 21, Apr 29, May 6,
    Dec 4, 5, 11, 17, 27; 1741: DL, Jan 1, 15, 21, 23, 29, Feb 7, Nov 11, 12, 13,
    14, 16, 27, Dec 31; 1742: DL, Jan 5, 7, Feb 20, 22, 25; 1744: DL, Oct 30, 31,
    Nov 1, 2, 5, 6, 17
Fortune's Favour (dance), 1788: CG, May 28, Oct 10, 17; 1789: CG, Mar 10, 12,
    May 7
Fortune's Fool. See Reynolds, Frederick.
Fortune's Frolic. See Allingham, John Till.
Fortune's Tasks. See Horne, John.
Fortune's Wheel. See Cobb, James.
Forza d'Amore, La (pastiche), 1751: HAY, Jan 19, 26, Feb 2, Mar 5, 19, Apr 20,
    27
Forza de l'Amore, La. See Pescatore, Leonardo.
Fosbrook, Henry (beneficiary), 1798: DL, Jun 9
Fosbrook, Thomas (box-book and housekeeper), 1767: DL, Jan 24; 1775: DL, Jan
    17, Nov 16, 25; 1776: DL, Feb 23, May 14, Sep 21; 1777: DL, Feb 14, May 3,
    Sep 20; 1778: DL, Mar 6, May 12, Sep 17, Dec 7; 1779: DL, Feb 19, May 10, Sep
    18; 1780: DL, May 4; 1781: DL, Mar 2, May 7, Sep 15; 1782: DL, Feb 15, Apr
    29, Sep 17; 1783: DL, Mar 14, May 7, 17, Sep 16; 1784: DL, Feb 27, May 17,
    Aug 20, Sep 16; 1785: DL, Feb 11, May 16, Sep 17; 1786: DL, Mar 3, May 17,
    Sep 16; 1787: DL, Feb 23, May 23, Sep 18; 1788: DL, Feb 8, May 21, Sep 13;
    1789: DL, Feb 27, May 23, Sep 12; 1790: DL, Feb 19, May 21, Sep 11; 1791: DL,
    Mar 11, May 24, DLKING'S, Sep 22; 1792: KING'S, Feb 24, DLKING'S, May 15, DL,
    Sep 15; 1793: DL, Jan 26, May 13; 1794: DL, Mar 12, 14, Apr 21, Jul 2, Sep
    16; 1795: DL, May 26, Jun 5, Sep 17; 1796: DL, May 30, Jun 15, Sep 20; 1797:
    DL, May 31, Jun 13, Sep 19, Oct 27; 1798: DL, May 31, Sep 15, HAY, Dec 17;
    1799: DL, May 24, 30, Jul 3, Sep 17; 1800: DL, May 26
Foster. See Forster.
Foster (beneficiary), 1735: CG/LIF, Jan 14
Foster Lane, 1787: HAY, Mar 12
Foster, Elizabeth, 1750: DL, Mar 28, Apr 2, 4, 5
Foster, Emmanuel (actor), 1769: HAY, Feb 28
Foster, Mrs (clothier), 1772: DL, Oct 30
Foster, Thomas (mercer), 1729: SH, Dec 5
Fotteral, James (actor), 1777: HAY, Aug 29, Sep 19
Foubert (auctioneer), 1737: DL, Mar 17
Foulcade (Folcad, Forcad), Anne (dancer), 1749: DL, Dec 19; 1750: DL, Jan 24,
    Mar 17, Apr 20, 26, 28, May 1
Foulcade, Anne and Miss (dancer), 1750: DL, Feb 14, May 1
Foulis (music copier), 1780: CG, May 29; 1791: DLKING'S, Oct 1
Foulis, John (house servant), 1770: CG, May 29; 1775: CG, May 30
Foulkes (beadle), 1760: DL, May 16
Foullies (dance), 1742: DL, Jan 25, 27, Feb 10
Foundling Hospital, 1749: CHAPEL, May 27; 1750: CHAPEL, Apr 18; 1751: CHAPEL,
    Apr 18, DL, 18, CHAPEL, May 16; 1752: CHAPEL, Apr 9; 1753: CHAPEL, May 1;
    1754: CHAPEL, May 15; 1755: CHAPEL, May 1; 1756: CHAPEL, May 19; 1758:
    CHAPEL, Apr 27; 1774: CHAPEL, Mar 26; 1775: DL, Mar 10, CHAPEL, Nov 23; 1776:
    CHAPEL, Apr 2; 1777: CG, May 20; 1778: CG, May 16, Dec 19; 1779: CG, May 8,
    DL, Dec 18
Foundling, The. See Moore, Edward.
Fount, Sga (spectator), 1710: QUEEN'S, Jul 19, GR, Aug 5
Fountain Court, 1734: YB, Apr 24; 1751: DL, Apr 26
Fountain Tavern, 1744: DL, Nov 24
Fountain, John, 1669: LIF, Feb 25
--Rewards of Virtue, The, 1660: NONE, Sep 0; 1669: LIF, Feb 25
Four Ages of Man (dance), 1784: KING'S, Mar 18, 23, 27, Apr 3
Four and Twenty Fiddlers (song), 1782: CG, Apr 23, May 6, 20, HAY, Aug 28;
    1783: CG, May 7, HAY, Aug 26; 1784: CG, Apr 26, HAY, Aug 24, Sep 17; 1785:
    CG, Apr 11, HAMM, Jul 15, HAY, Aug 23; 1786: CG, Apr 18, HAY, Aug 25, CG, Sep
    22; 1787: HAY, Mar 12, CG, Apr 10, May 21, HAY, Aug 28; 1788: CG, Apr 11;
    1789: CG, Jun 8; 1790: CG, Apr 7; 1795: CG, May 8, 25; 1796: CG, May 26;
    1797: HAY, Aug 8; 1798: CG, May 9; 1799: CG, Apr 6, 8, 16
Four and Twenty Periwigs all on a Row (song), 1788: CG, Mar 26, HAY, Aug 27;
    1789: CG, Apr 20, HAY, Aug 27

Four and Twenty Stock Jobbers (song), 1720: LIF, May 3, 10, 24, BCA, Sep 23;
   1721: LIF, May 4, 29
Four Nations, The (dance), 1783: KING'S, Jun 28
Four Seasons (music), 1704: LIF, Jun 6
Four Seasons (song), 1698: DL/ORDG, Nov 0
Fourberies D'Arlequin, Les; ou, L'Etourdye (pantomime), 1721: HAY, Feb 14
Fourcade, Mimi (actor), 1735: HAY, Apr 16, GF/HAY, Jun 2
Fourner, M (dancer), 1741: GF, Sep 14
Fowler, Miss (actor), 1787: RLSN, Mar 29, 30, 31
Fowler, Mrs Thomas (actor), 1777: HAY, Feb 11; 1778: CHR, Jun 3, 10; 1781: CII,
   Mar 15, 27, 30, Apr 5, 9; 1782: HAY, Jan 14, Mar 4; 1784: HAY, Sep 17; 1787:
   RLSN, Mar 26, 27, 28, 29, 30, 31
Fowlis (house servant), 1746: DL, Apr 24
Fox Chace (entertainment), 1793: CG, Jan 21, Apr 3
Fox, Henry (correspondent), 1734: KING'S, Nov 2; 1736: CG, Nov 13
Fox, Joseph (actor), 1758: CG, Sep 25; 1759: DL, Dec 1, 31; 1760: DL, Feb 13,
   Mar 4, May 3, 8, Oct 20, Nov 22, 29, Dec 12, 17, 26; 1761: DL, Jan 15, Feb
   12, 14, Apr 25, 29, May 30, Sep 14, Oct 31, Nov 6, 9, 10, 12, 21, 28, Dec 11;
   1762: DL, Jan 15, Feb 9, 10, Mar 6, 22, 27, Apr 27, 30, May 25, Sep 25, Oct
   7, 11, 12, 15, 16, Nov 3, 4, 10, 19, 23, 25, 27, Dec 17, 22; 1763: DL, Jan
   17, 19, Feb 3, 24, Apr 13, 23, 29, May 7, Sep 17, 20, 27, Oct 8, 19, 27, Nov
   4, 29, 30, Dec 26; 1764: DL, Jan 7, Mar 20, Apr 2, 12, 14, 26, May 1, 8, 16,
   24, Sep 15, 27, Oct 15, 16, 17, 26, 31, Nov 24, 27; 1765: DL, Jan 1, 15, 22,
   Feb 4, 6, Mar 14, 19, Apr 13, 20, 23, 30, May 21; 1766: DL, Nov 4, 8, Dec 2,
   4, 13; 1767: DL, Jan 2, 24, May 1, 6, 22, Sep 22, 26, Oct 21, 22, Nov 4, 12,
   13, 18, Dec 5, 10, 26; 1768: DL, Jan 6, 9, Feb 13, Apr 8, 9, 27, May 10, 30,
   CG, Sep 26, 30, Oct 5, 17, DL, 21, CG, 22, DL, 28, CG, 29, Nov 22; 1769: CG,
   Feb 7, DL, Apr 4, CG, 24, May 2, 5, 12, 23, Sep 18, 20, Oct 2, 6, 7, 26, Nov
   6, 21, Dec 1, 2, 9, 11; 1770: CG, Jan 1, 3, 5, 10, 20, 25, Feb 7, 9, 24, Mar
   23, 29, Apr 24, May 22, Sep 26, Oct 5, 8, 10, 11, 23, Nov 1, 5, Dec 4, 26;
   1771: CG, Jan 1, 14, 21, 22, Feb 9, Mar 14, Apr 30, May 1, 6, 11, 30, Sep 23,
   25, Oct 2, 7, 9, 11, 14, 15, 18, 25, Nov 4, 5, 11, 12, Dec 11; 1772: CG, Jan
   27, HAY, Mar 16, CG, Apr 11, 22, May 22, 28, Sep 21, 25, Oct 24, Nov 2, 4, 6,
   18, Dec 19, 26; 1773: CG, Jan 28, Mar 22, Apr 3, May 7, 14, 20, 21, 27, Sep
   24, Oct 4, 11, 22, 23, 28, Nov 4, 8, 25, Dec 13, 16, 23; 1774: CG, Jan 3, 5,
   29, Feb 11, Mar 12, Apr 7, 11, 12, May 10, 11, Sep 23, Oct 11, 13, 20, 21,
   Nov 1, 3, 19, Dec 20, 26; 1775: CG, Jan 21, Mar 30, Apr 21, May 2, 4, 19, 20,
   Sep 22, 25, Oct 19, Nov 4, 13, 21, 24, Dec 21; 1776: CG, Apr 16, May 21, Sep
   27, Oct 7, 11, 25, Nov 2, 9, 26, 30, Dec 2; 1777: CG, Jan 3, Mar 31, Apr 28,
   Sep 24, 29, Oct 1, 29, Nov 19; 1778: CG, Jan 20, 29, Feb 7, 11, 28, May 6,
   11; 1779: CG, Mar 27, Apr 19, 23, Oct 23, Nov 8, Dec 17; 1780: CG, May 23
Fox, Lady (spectator), 1669: ATCOURT, Feb 15
Fox, Mrs (actor), 1787: HAY, Jan 8, Mar 12, Apr 30, ROY, Jun 20; 1789: DL, Sep
   24, 26, Oct 13, Nov 13, 17, 20, 23, Dec 7, 26; 1790: DL, Jan 6, 20, 22
Fox, Mrs (spectator), 1686: ATCOURT, Feb 16
Fox, Stag and Hare (song), 1800: CG, Jun 5
Fox, The. See Jonson, Ben, Volpone.
Fox, William (actor), 1781: HAY, Mar 26; 1790: DL, Jun 2, Oct 11, 27, Dec 7,
   14, 15, 22, 23; 1791: DL, Jan 1, Feb 1, Mar 19, May 3, 25
Fox's Coffee House, 1787: HAY, Mar 12
Foxall (house servant), 1735: DL, Jun 3; 1737: DL, May 20
Foxwell (beneficiary), 1745: GF, May 1
Foxwell, Sarah (actor), 1729: LIF, Jan 1
Fra quest Ombra (song), 1755: KING'S, Mar 17
France, King of, 1723: KING'S, Apr 6
France, Queen of, 1785: DL, Feb 18; 1793: CG, Feb 20, KING/HAY, 20, CG, Oct 23
France, 1660: NONE, Sep 0; 1662: LI, Jan 3; 1698: YB, Mar 31; 1699: DL, Apr 15,
   Nov 28; 1700: LIF, Jul 5; 1702: BFBF, Aug 24; 1705: DL, Nov 24; 1713: SH, May
   15, TEC, Nov 26; 1717: SF, Sep 25, LIF, Oct 5; 1718: RI, Aug 30, SF, Sep 6;
   1720: KING'S, Mar 5, DL, Oct 17; 1721: HAY, Feb 9; 1722: SF, Sep 22; 1723:
   RI, Sep 2; 1724: HIC, Dec 21; 1725: DL, Mar 18, HAY, Apr 14, 19, May 7; 1729:
   HAY, May 26; 1730: BFPG/TC, Aug 1; 1732: HAY, Feb 16, DL, Mar 21; 1735: HAY,
   Jun 12; 1741: CG, Apr 20; 1744: CG, Apr 20; 1749: HAY, Nov 17, DL, Dec 28;
   1750: DL, May 21; 1755: DL, Nov 1; 1757: DL, Feb 11, HAY, Dec 26; 1759: CG,
   Sep 24, DL, 25; 1761: BFY, Aug 31; 1763: CG, Oct 15; 1765: DL, Apr 25; 1766:
   DL, Oct 11; 1767: DL, Mar 31; 1768: DL, Oct 14; 1771: KING'S, May 28; 1776:
   DL, Feb 27; 1788: KING'S, Jan 29; 1791: KING'S, May 26; 1793: CG, Jan 23
Frances, Mrs (actor), 1729: BFF, Aug 23
Francesina, Sga (singer), 1737: KING'S, Jan 8, Feb 12, Apr 12, May 24, Oct 29;
   1738: KING'S, Jan 3, 28, Feb 25, Mar 14, Apr 15; 1739: KING'S, Jan 16, Apr 4,
   LIF, Nov 22, Dec 13; 1740: LIF, Feb 27, Mar 26, Nov 22, 29; 1741: LIF, Jan
   10, HAY, Mar 9; 1744: CG, Feb 10, 24, Mar 2, KING'S, Jun 9, Nov 3; 1745:

KING'S, Jan 5, Mar 27, CG, Apr 10, KING'S, May 4; 1746: CG, Feb 14
Franchetti, Elizabeth (author), 1773: DL, Jan 1
Franchi, Angelo (singer), 1783: KING'S, Dec 16; 1784: KING'S, Jan 6, 17, Feb
17, 24, Mar 4, 18, 25, Apr 15, May 8, Jun 12, Dec 18; 1785: KING'S, Jan 4, 8,
25, Feb 26, Mar 17, Apr 2
Francis (actor), 1764: HAY, Sep 1; 1766: HAY, Jun 18, KING'S, Aug 13, 20; 1772:
HAY, Aug 10, Sep 17; 1773: HAY, Jun 18, Jul 19, Aug 6, 11, 13, 27, Sep 3, 14,
15; 1774: HAY, Jun 27, Jul 11, Sep 21; 1775: HAY, May 15, Jul 31, Sep 4;
1776: HAY, Aug 2, Sep 18, 20
Francis (dramatist), 1792: HAY, Jul 25
--Enchanted Wood, The (masque), 1792: HAY, Jul 25, 26, 28, Aug 1, 4, 7
Francis, Captain (spectator), 1700: DLORLIF, Apr 20
Francis, Mary (dancer, singer), 1781: CG, May 1, 18, Oct 16, 24; 1782: CG, Feb
21, Apr 1, 2, 27, May 20, Oct 14; 1783: CG, Oct 13; 1784: CG, Nov 26; 1785:
HAMM, Jun 17, Jul 8, CG, Oct 17, Nov 14; 1788: CG, Jan 14, Oct 13; 1789: CG,
Jun 8, Sep 14, Oct 12; 1790: CG, Sep 13, Oct 6, Nov 26; 1791: CG, Sep 26, Oct
10; 1792: CG, Apr 12, Oct 29, Dec 26
Francis, Messrs (police officers?), 1788: CG, Apr 7
Francis, Miss (dancer), 1719: LIF, Mar 19, Apr 27, May 21, 28, Jun 25, BFBL,
Aug 24, B-L, Sep 5, LIF, Oct 20, 26, 27, Dec 30; 1720: LIF, Mar 8, Apr 29,
30, May 7, 10, 11, 12, 23, 24, 30, Oct 4, Nov 18, Dec 6, 14, 26; 1721: LIF,
Feb 21, 28, Apr 26, 29, May 1, 19, Nov 23; 1722: RI, Aug 20, BFPMB, 25, SF,
Sep 5, 22, LIF, Oct 30, Dec 13
Francis, Dr Philip, 1752: DL, Feb 17, 20; 1754: CG, Jan 26, Feb 23
--Constantine the Great, 1754: CG, Jan 26, Feb 19, 23, 25, 26, 28, Mar 8
--Eugenia, 1752: DL, Feb 17, 18, 20, 22, 24, 25; 1754: CG, Feb 23
Francis, Sarah (actor), 1772: HAY, Jul 10, Sep 17; 1773: CG, May 28, HAY, Aug
2, Sep 3; 1774: HAY, Jun 27; 1775: HAY, Jul 31, Sep 19, 21; 1776: CG, Mar 5,
Apr 27, HAY, Aug 2, Sep 23; 1777: CG, Apr 17, HAY, May 15, Aug 7; 1778: CG,
Mar 30, Apr 7, May 11; 1779: CG, Sep 20; 1780: CG, Apr 7, HAY, Jul 1; 1781:
HAY, Aug 7, 8, 17; 1782: CG, May 10, HAY, Jun 3, Aug 13, 17, 26, 27, Sep 19,
CG, Oct 22; 1783: HAY, Jun 20, 30, Aug 22; 1784: CG, Jan 16, May 15, HAY, Jul
28, Aug 10, 26; 1785: HAY, Jun 2, 16, 29, Aug 31, CG, Sep 23, 30; 1786: CG,
Feb 16, HAY, Jun 9, 12, 29, Jul 19, 29; 1787: HAY, Jun 18, 23, Jul 23, Aug 7,
23, 28; 1788: HAY, Jun 30, Jul 10, Aug 5, 9, 27; 1789: CG, Mar 16, May 28,
HAY, Jun 22, Aug 11, 25, Sep 14, 15, CG, 16, 21; 1790: CG, Oct 4, 29, Nov 1,
6, 11, 12, 18, 19, 20, Dec 15, 20, 22; 1791: CG, Jan 19, 27, Feb 12, Mar 7,
May 2, 3, Jun 6, Sep 16, 17, 20, 21, 28, Oct 3, 28, Nov 2, Dec 21, 22; 1792:
CG, Jan 25, 28, Feb 28, HAY, Apr 16, CG, 17, May 10, Sep 28, Oct 8, 10, 18,
19, 27, Dec 31; 1793: CG, Jan 2, 21, Mar 11, Jun 12
Francis, Sarah, Mrs Francis (actor), 1798: CG, Jun 7
Francis, Thomas Bodley (violinist), 1795: CG, Feb 20, HAY, Mar 4; 1798: CG, Feb
23; 1799: CG, Feb 8; 1800: CG, Feb 28
Francis, William (actor), 1785: HAMM, Jun 17
Francis, William (housekeeper), 1760: CG, Sep 22; 1766: CG, May 15; 1767: CG,
Feb 17, May 18; 1768: CG, May 27, Jun 4; 1769: CG, May 6, 15; 1770: CG, May
18, 24; 1771: CG, May 22; 1772: CG, May 29; 1773: CG, May 28; 1774: CG, May
24; 1775: CG, May 30; 1776: CG, May 21; 1777: CG, May 23, Nov 20; 1778: CG,
May 21; 1779: CG, May 15
Francisco (composer), 1731: LIF, Apr 24
Francisco (dancer), 1728: HAY, Mar 20
Francisco (eunich singer), 1699: DLLIF, Dec 25; 1703: YB, Mar 5, HA, May 18;
1710: PCGR, Jun 14
Francisco (harpsichordist), 1674: SLINGSBY, Dec 2
Francisque, Mme Moylin (actor), 1719: LIF, Jan 13; 1734: GF/HAY, Nov 20, Dec 2,
27, 30; 1735: GF, May 23
Francisque, Moylin (actor), 1719: LIF, Jan 8, 13, 27; 1720: KING'S, May 9, 12,
16, 20, 27, 31; 1721: HAY, Feb 17, Apr 18; 1734: DL/HAY, Jan 12, GF/HAY, Oct
26, HAY, 28, Nov 4, GF/HAY, 6, 20, 22, HAY, Dec 16, GF/HAY, 27, 30; 1735:
HAY, Jan 10, GF/HAY, Feb 6, HAY, 18, GF/HAY, Mar 10, 17, HAY, 19, GF/HAY, Apr
10, HAY, 16, May 9, GF, 23; 1738: HAY, Oct 9, Nov 7
Franck, Johann Wolfgang (musician), 1690: GB, Oct 10; 1691: BG, Apr 2, Sep 17;
1693: YB, Jun 17, BG, Nov 30; 1696: DL, Jan 0
Francklin, Dr Thomas, 1766: DL, Dec 13, 16, 22; 1769: CG, Mar 13; 1775: DL, Jan
21, Feb 3, 7; 1776: HAY, Jun 12
--Contract, The, 1776: HAY, Jun 12, 14; 1779: DL, Apr 5; 1780: HAY, Aug 26
--Earl of Warwick, The, 1766: DL, Dec 13, 15, 16, 18, 20, 22, 23, 29, 30, 31;
1767: DL, Jan 16, 31, Feb 11, 18, Nov 13; 1768: DL, Oct 3, Nov 9; 1769: CG,
Mar 13; 1770: CG, Mar 22, Apr 19, Oct 12; 1773: CG, Apr 19; 1774: DL, Mar 26,
Apr 23; 1775: DL, Apr 24, Nov 14; 1776: DL, Feb 6; 1778: ARME, Jun 22, DL,
Oct 23; 1779: CG, Apr 5, 14; 1780: CG, Nov 14; 1782: CG, Jan 8; 1784: DL, Nov
3, 6, 10; 1785: DL, Sep 29; 1796: CG, May 24; 1797: HAY, Feb 9

--Electra, 1774: DL, Oct 15, 17, 22
--Mary, Queen of Scots, 1773: DL, Apr 19
--Matilda, 1775: DL, Jan 21, 23, 24, 26, 28, 31, Feb 1, 2, 3, 7, 13, Mar 6, Apr
   1, 29, May 27, Dec 2, 13; 1776: DL, Jan 6, Feb 1, Apr 15, Sep 28; 1785: CG,
   Mar 7
Francois (house servant), 1800: DL, Jun 14
Francois a Londres, Le. See Boissy, Louis de.
Francolino, Grimaldo (dancer), 1727: KING'S, Mar 2, Apr 6
Frank (messenger), 1750: DL, Feb 13
Frank, Master (actor), 1770: HAY, Sep 27; 1771: HAY, Apr 4
Franki (instrumentalist), 1794: CG, Mar 7; 1796: CG, Feb 12; 1797: CG, Mar 3
Franklin (actor), 1756: SW, Oct 9
Franklin (actor), 1798: HAY, Apr 23
Franklin, Andrew, 1792: CG, Mar 26; 1797: DL, May 15, Nov 9; 1798: DL, Oct 16;
   1799: HAY, Aug 5, DL, Oct 3; 1800: DL, Mar 11
--Egyptian Festival, The (opera), 1800: DL, Mar 11, 13, 15, 17, 18, 20, 24, 27,
   31, May 29
--Embarkation, The (entertainment), 1799: DL, Oct 3, 5, 7, 8, 10
--Gander Hall (farce), 1799: HAY, Aug 5
--Merode e Selinunte, 1740: HAY, Jan 22, 26, 29, Feb 2, 5, 9, 12, 16, 19, 23,
   26, Mar 1, 4, 8, May 24, 27, 31
--Outlaws, The, 1798: DL, Oct 16, 18, 23, 27, 29, 31, Nov 3
--Trip to the Nore, A (interlude), 1797: DL, Nov 9, 10, 11, 13, 14, 15, 16, 17,
   18, 20, 21, 22, 29, Dec 19, 26, 27
--Wandering Jew, The; or, Love's Masquerade (farce), 1797: DL, May 15, 16, 31,
   Jun 5, 8, Oct 19, 30, Nov 3, Dec 6, 22, 30; 1798: DL, Feb 5, Mar 15, Apr 18
Franklin, R (printer), 1750: DL, Mar 1; 1752: DL, Jan 24, Feb 5; 1753: DL, Feb
   16, 19; 1757: DL, Feb 17; 1758: DL, Jan 26, Mar 3
Franklin, Rev Mr, 1749: DL, May 16
Franklyn (bell ringer), 1757: HAY, Nov 2
Franscisco (actor), 1776: HAY, Sep 16
Fransdorf (house servant), 1768: CG, May 28, 31; 1769: CG, May 20, 22; 1770:
   CG, May 19, 22; 1771: CG, May 25; 1772: CG, May 29; 1773: CG, May 28
Franshaw (dancer), 1675: ATCOURT, Feb 15
Frantzel (Francel) (dancer), 1754: CG, Nov 4, 19; 1755: CG, Jan 4, Apr 16
Fraschetana, La. See Paisiello, Giovanni.
Frasi (singer), 1744: HAY, Apr 4; 1748: KING'S, Apr 5; 1749: HAY, Apr 10; 1753:
   KING'S, Apr 30; 1754: HAY, Feb 11; 1756: KING'S, Apr 5; 1758: CG, Mar 3
Frasi, Giulia (singer), 1742: KING'S, Nov 2, Dec 4; 1743: KING'S, Jan 1, Feb
   22, Mar 30, Apr 5, Nov 15; 1744: KING'S, Jan 3, 31, Mar 28, Apr 3, 24; 1745:
   HAY, Feb 9, Mar 23, CG, Apr 10; 1746: KING'S, Jan 7, 28, HIC, Mar 10, KING'S,
   25, HAY, Apr 23, KING'S, May 13, Nov 4; 1747: KING'S, Apr 14, Nov 14; 1748:
   HAY, Jan 12, CG, Feb 26, KING'S, Mar 1, 5, Apr 5; 1749: CG, Feb 10, KING'S,
   Mar 21, HAY, Apr 6; 1750: CG, Mar 16, KING'S, 31, Apr 3, 10; 1751: HAY, Feb
   5, Mar 19, KING'S, Apr 16, HAY, 27; 1752: CG, Feb 26, KING'S, Mar 24; 1753:
   HAY, Apr 2; 1754: KING'S, Jan 29, Feb 28, Apr 2, 25, CHAPEL, May 15; 1755:
   KING'S, Mar 15, 17; 1756: KING'S, Apr 5, 10, 27, HAB, Dec 9, DL, 20; 1757:
   SOHO, Feb 1, CG, Mar 11, SOHO, 14, DL, 23, CHAPEL, May 5; 1758: KING'S, Jan
   10, 31, CG, Feb 22, Mar 1, KING'S, 6, 14, Apr 6, CHAPEL, 27; 1759: CG, Feb 2,
   SOHO, Mar 1, HAM, Aug 13; 1760: CG, Feb 29, KING'S, Apr 15; 1761: KING'S, Mar
   12; 1762: SOHO, Apr 21; 1767: CG, Mar 6, HAB, Dec 10; 1769: HAY, Apr 18,
   KING'S, Jun 1; 1770: HAY, May 4
Fratelli (musician), 1733: LIF, May 7
Fratesanti (singer), 1743: KING'S, Nov 15; 1744: KING'S, Jan 3, 31, Mar 28, Apr
   3, 24, HIC, May 16
Fratesanti, Sga (singer), 1743: KING'S, Nov 15
Frazier (actor), 1743: BFGA, Aug 23
Frazier, Carey, Countess of Peterborough, 1675: ATCOURT, Feb 15
Frederic (actor, dancer), 1784: KING'S, Dec 18; 1785: KING'S, Jan 1, HAY, Feb
   10, KING'S, 12, Mar 3, 12, 17, Apr 21, May 10, Jun 9, 18
Frederica, Mrs (beneficiary), 1745: HAY, Apr 6
Frederica, Princess, Duchess of York, 1791: CG, Nov 21; 1796: KING'S, Mar 10;
   1800: CG, May 2, Jun 12
Frederick. See Haywood, Eliza.
Frederick, Cassandra (singer), 1749: HAY, Apr 10; 1758: CG, Feb 22, Mar 1, 3,
   CHAPEL, Apr 27; 1759: CG, Feb 2, DL, Mar 23; 1760: SOHO, Jan 18, Feb 14, Mar
   13, HAY, 27, HIC, Apr 29; 1761: SOHO, Jan 21, KING'S, Mar 12; 1768: MARLY,
   Jul 28; 1775: HAY, Oct 30
Frederick, Levy (silk mercer), 1766: DL, Nov 17, Dec 2; 1771: DL, Oct 17; 1772:
   DL, Nov 3, 6, CG, 30; 1773: DL, Apr 12; 1774: DL, Feb 9; 1775: DL, Oct 13,
   31, Nov 30; 1776: DL, Jan 25
Frederick, Miss (actor), 1780: HAY, Nov 13; 1784: HAY, Feb 23

Frederick, Prince, 1728: DL, Dec 19, 26; 1729: LIF, Jan 1, DL, 2, 15
Free Masons, 1728: DL, Dec 30; 1729: DL, Apr 19; 1730: DL, Feb 12, GF, Apr 24,
   DL, 25, May 13, RI, Jun 27; 1731: LIF, Apr 24, DL, 30, GF, Dec 18; 1732: GF,
   Mar 6, LIF, Apr 27, May 13, GF, Nov 29; 1733: HAY, Apr 23, DL, May 1; 1734:
   DL/HAY, May 4, HA, Aug 20; 1735: DL, May 13, TC, 28, HAY, Jun 12, Aug 4, Sep
   29; 1736: LIF, Apr 29, DL, May 4, HAY, Jul 29; 1737: DL, May 7; 1739: DL, May
   15, CG, Aug 10; 1740: CG, Apr 28; 1741: GF, Mar 12, CG, Apr 11, GF, 15, 29,
   JS, May 11, NWGF, Oct 23; 1742: CG, May 4, 14; 1744: JS, Mar 2, DL, May 4;
   1745: CG, May 3; 1747: DL, May 16; 1750: JS, Jul 23; 1751: HAY, Dec 28; 1754:
   HAY/SFB, Sep 26; 1763: MARLY, Jun 28, HAY, Sep 15; 1775: HAY, Sep 21; 1776:
   HAY, Sep 20; 1778: HAY, Mar 31; 1784: HAY, Jan 21; 1785: HAMM, Jul 22
Free Masons' Hall, 1795: CG, Apr 24, May 14; 1796: CG, Apr 26, May 17; 1799:
   CG, Apr 19
Free Masons' Tavern, 1787: CG, Jun 15
Free Thinker; or, The Fox Uncased, The (play), 1737: YB, Apr 14, 28
Freedom and Ease (song), 1747: CG, Apr 24
Freedom and his native Land (song), 1786: HAMM, Jun 5
Freeks, John George (musician), 1758: CHAPEL, Apr 27
Freely I to Heaven Resign (song), 1761: KING'S, Mar 12
Freeman (actor), 1735: YB, Mar 19, TC, May 28, YB, Jul 17, HAY, Dec 13; 1736:
   HAY, Jan 19, LIF, Mar 3, HAY, 5, Apr 26, 29; 1742: LIF, Dec 1, 3, 13, 27;
   1743: LIF, Jan 7, 10, 14, Feb 2, 14, Apr 11, HAY, 14, BFGA, Aug 23; 1745: GF,
   Feb 14, Mar 7; 1746: SFW, Sep 8
Freeman (actor), 1770: HAY, Oct 1; 1778: HAY, Apr 9; 1780: HAY, Nov 13; 1783:
   HAY, Jun 30; 1785: HAY, Jul 13; 1793: HAY, Dec 26
Freeman (disrupter), 1716: DL, Dec 6
Freeman (musician), 1723: BUH, Jan 11
Freeman, John (actor), 1680: DG, Dec 8; 1681: DG, Jan 0, Nov 0; 1683: DL, Dec
   0; 1686: DG, Mar 4; 1688: DL, May 3, NONE, Sep 0; 1689: NONE, Sep 0, DL, Nov
   7, 20; 1690: NONE, Sep 0, DL, Oct 0, Nov 0, Dec 0; 1691: DL, Jan 0, Mar 0,
   NONE, Sep 0; 1692: DL, Feb 0, Mar 0, DG, May 2, DL, Nov 0; 1693: DL, Apr 0;
   1694: DG, Jan 10, DL, Feb 0, Mar 21, DG, May 0; 1695: DG, Apr 0, LIF, 30, DL,
   Sep 0, LIF, 0, Dec 0; 1696: LIF, Mar 0, Apr 0, Jun 0, DG, Oct 0, LIF, 0, Dec
   0; 1697: LIF, Feb 20, Jun 0, Nov 0; 1698: LIF, Jan 0, DL, Mar 0, LIF, Jun 0,
   YB, 7, DL/ORDG, Nov 0; 1699: LIF, Feb 0, Apr 0, DLLIF, 22, DL, Dec 0, LIF,
   18; 1700: LIF, Jan 9, Feb 0, DL, 19, Apr 29, LIF, Dec 0; 1701: LIF, Mar 0,
   Aug 0, Dec 0; 1702: LIF, Dec 31; 1704: LIF, Jan 13, Feb 2, 24, Mar 25, Nov
   13, Dec 4; 1705: LIF/QUEN, Feb 22, LIF, Aug 1, QUEEN'S, Nov 23, Dec 27; 1706:
   QUEEN'S, Jan 3, Jun 0, Oct 30; 1710: DL, Feb 25, Mar 11, 14, GR, Aug 28, 31,
   Sep 1, 28, 30
Freeman, Miss (actor), 1779: HAY, Feb 22
Freeman, Mrs (actor), 1734: HAY, Jun 7, 14, LIF, Aug 20; 1735: LIF, Jul 11, 16,
   23; 1736: HAY, Jun 26; 1741: SF, Sep 14, JS, Nov 9; 1743: LIF, Mar 3, DL, May
   11; 1744: JS, Mar 16, MF, May 3, HAY, Sep 29, Oct 4, 11, GF, Dec 26; 1745:
   GF, Feb 4
Freeman, R (printer), 1749: DL, Nov 2
Freeman, S, Dean of Peterborough, 1697: LIF, Feb 27
Freeman's Court, 1690: HUGHS, Jan 8
Freke (ironmonger), 1771: CG, Nov 5; 1772: CG, Dec 3
Fremble, Master (singer), 1742: SF, Sep 16
French (violinist), 1798: HAY, Jan 15
French Academy, 1737: LH, Jan 26
French Air (song), 1754: DL, Mar 19; 1784: KING'S, Mar 11; 1793: CG, Apr 25
French Ambassador, 1698: ATCOURT, May 13; 1738: HAY, Oct 9
French Andromache Burlesqued (dance), 1716: LIF, Dec 11, 28; 1717: LIF, Feb 1,
   26
French Beau, The. See Pix, Mary.
French children (performers), 1703: DG, Apr 30; 1716: LIF, Dec 18; 1723: LIF,
   May 7; 1728: LIF, Apr 29, May 3, 6; 1739: CG, Dec 22, 26; 1740: CG, Jan 12,
   15, Feb 2, 7, 12, Mar 10, 11, 18, 20, 24, 25, Apr 16, 18, 23, 25, 28, 30, May
   7, 9, 13, 16, 20, 21, Jun 5, Sep 19, 24, Oct 10, 15; 1741: CG, Jan 5, Feb 24,
   Apr 20, May 5, DL, Sep 26, CG, Oct 24; 1745: CG, Jan 1, Nov 23; 1746: CG, Dec
   31; 1753: DL, Nov 1, 8
French Clown (dance), 1706: LIF/QUEN, Jun 12; 1726: LIF, Mar 31; 1731: LIF, May
   13, 28; 1733: LIF/CG, Apr 23; 1735: DL, May 14
French comedians, 1661: COCKPIT, Aug 30, ATCOURT, Dec 2; 1663: NONE, Aug 25;
   1669: ATCOURT, Oct 26; 1672: ATCOURT, Jan 0, Dec 17; 1673: NONE, Sep 12;
   1674: ATCOURT, Feb 0; 1677: ATCOURT, Feb 5, DG, Jun 0, ATCOURT, Nov 0, Dec 4,
   17; 1678: ATCOURT, Apr 12; 1684: ATCOURT, May 26, Oct 29; 1686: DLORDG, Feb
   11; 1688: ATCOURT, Jul 0, Sep 29; 1718: LIF, Nov 7, 26, Dec 10, 19; 1720:
   KING'S, Feb 4, Mar 5, 12, LIF, Apr 4, KING'S, 29, May 6, Jun 13, HAY, Dec 29;
   1721: HAY, Jan 31, Feb 17, Nov 18, Dec 4; 1734: GF/HAY, Oct 26; 1738: HAY,

Oct 4, 7, 9, 12, Nov 7, CG, 10, 13, HAY, 18; 1743: NONE, Jul 13; 1749: DL,
  Nov 14, HAY, 16, 17, 22, Dec 12, 21; 1750: DL, May 22
French Conjuror, The. See Porter, Thomas.
French Country Gentleman (dance), 1761: CG, Dec 10; 1762: CG, Jan 6, 7, 8, 9,
  11, 13, 20, 22, 27, Feb 13, 16, Mar 29
French critics, 1753: DL, Dec 26; 1779: DL, Sep 18
French Cuckold, The. See Moliere.
French Dance (dance), 1718: SF, Sep 6; 1739: SF, Sep 8; 1768: DL, Apr 6
French dancers, 1674: DL, Mar 30; 1755: DL, Nov 6, 8; 1757: DL, Apr 21
French Dancing Master, The. See Cavendish, William.
French Doctor Outwitted, The (droll), 1743: BFHC, Aug 23
French drama, 1661: COCKPIT, Aug 30, ATCOURT, Dec 16; 1677: ATCOURT, May 22;
  1678: ATCOURT, Jan 18, Mar 14; 1697: LIF, Jun 0; 1717: LIF, Oct 5; 1720:
  KING'S, Apr 26, May 31; 1749: HAY, Nov 14; 1766: KING'S, Aug 8; 1774: DL, Oct
  15; 1784: HAY, Aug 21; 1787: HAY, Aug 28; 1788: CG, Apr 29, HAY, Aug 2; 1791:
  DL, May 11
French fashion, 1767: DL, Mar 31; 1775: DL, Oct 7
French Flogged, The. See Stevens, George Alexander.
French Gardener and His Mistress (dance), 1730: DL, Sep 15, 24, Oct 22; 1731:
  DL, Apr 8, 29, May 5, 7, 10, 19; 1733: DL, Apr 4, 30; 1763: CG, Apr 7, 9, May
  11, 17, 20, 25
French Grenadier. See O'Keeffe, John.
French Harp Concerto (music), 1785: DL, Feb 18
French Horn (music), 1724: LIF, Mar 19, Apr 25, 28, DL, May 12, LIF, 27; 1726:
  LIF, Mar 28; 1727: KING'S, Mar 2; 1728: LIF, Mar 18, 21, 27; 1729: LIF, Jan
  16, Mar 5, HAY, 7, HIC, Apr 16, YB, 22; 1732: LIF, Feb 25, HIC, Mar 27, DL,
  May 3; 1733: SH, Mar 19, DL, May 21; 1734: DL/HAY, Feb 4, CG, May 14; 1735:
  HIC, Feb 21, HAY, Mar 26, GF, 29, Apr 22, May 15, LIF, Sep 5, DL, Oct 18, Nov
  17, ST, 26; 1737: SH, Mar 11, LIF, Apr 17, CT, 29; 1741: GF, Mar 12; 1742:
  DL, Feb 17, 19, 20, 23, 26, Mar 2, 11, 15, 18, 29, CG, Apr 22, DL, 28, 30;
  1745: DT, Mar 14; 1746: SPHP, Sep 8; 1747: GF, Mar 24; 1752: CT/HAY, May 5;
  1757: HAY, Oct 3; 1770: KING'S, Mar 22; 1772: CG, Mar 27; 1773: KING'S, Mar
  18; 1795: KING'S, Jun 16
French Horn and Clarinet (music), 1735: ST, Apr 1
French Horn and German Flute (music), 1729: HIC, Mar 12
French Horn and Trumpet (music), 1733: LIF/CG, Apr 25, CG, May 1, LIF/CG, 7;
  1734: YB, Mar 8; 1735: CG, May 8; 1736: LIF, Mar 31, CG, May 11
French Horn and Trumpet Chorus (music), 1738: DL, Mar 3
French Horn and Trumpet Concerto (music), 1733: DL/HAY, Oct 13; 1735: HAY, Mar
  26; 1770: MARLY, Aug 21
French Horn Aubade (music), 1734: HIC, Apr 5
French Horn Concerto (music), 1723: DL, Mar 20; 1724: YB, Mar 27; 1729: HIC,
  Apr 16; 1732: LIF, Mar 10, CL, 17; 1733: DL/HAY, Oct 6; 1734: GF, Sep 9, 11,
  13; 1736: MR, Feb 11, DL, May 22; 1740: DL, May 21; 1743: LIF, Mar 15; 1744:
  HAY, Feb 20, Nov 12; 1752: CT/HAY, Jan 7, 14, 21, 31; 1757: HAY, Sep 2; 1766:
  KING'S, Apr 10; 1770: CG, Mar 2, MARLY, Sep 11; 1772: KING'S, Feb 21, CG, Mar
  6, DL, 11, CG, 13, DL, 18, CG, 20, HAY, 23, DL, 25, HAY, 30, CG, Apr 3, HAY,
  27; 1773: KING'S, Feb 5, CG, 26, Mar 3, 5, 26; 1776: CG, Feb 28, Mar 1, 8;
  1788: DL, Mar 5, 7, KING'S, May 22
French Horn Concerto Obligato (music), 1784: HAY, Apr 27
French Horn Concerto, Grand (music), 1757: HAY, Aug 11, 31, Sep 28
French Horn Duet (music), 1733: DL/HAY, Oct 20
French Horn Solo (music), 1733: DL/HAY, Oct 6; 1734: DL, Apr 29; 1752: CT/HAY,
  Mar 17, 21, Apr 1, 16, 21, May 5; 1759: HAY, Oct 5; 1770: KING'S, Mar 1, 8
French Horn, Hautboy and Harpsichord Trio (music), 1733: DL/HAY, Oct 13
French Lawyer, The. See Fletcher, John, The Little French Lawyer.
French Lute and Arch Lute (music), 1711: COH, Dec 20
French maidens (dancer), 1703: YB, Jul 27, BFG, Aug 23; 1705: LIF/QUEN, Oct 11
French Medley Overture (music), 1784: CG, Nov 16
French music (music), 1660: ATCOURT, Nov 19; 1698: YB, Mar 31; 1701: DG, May
  21; 1719: KING'S, Mar 2; 1726: HAY, May 23; 1789: CG, Sep 21; 1790: CG, Nov 6
French opera, 1674: DL, Mar 27, 30; 1677: ATCOURT, May 29; 1686: DLORDG, Jan
  23, Feb 11; 1784: KING'S, Mar 11, 18
French Peasant (dance), 1706: QUEEN'S, Apr 15, 30, Jun 29; 1707: DL, Feb 20;
  1710: DL, Jan 19, 31, Feb 15, Mar 11, 25, Apr 12; 1714: DL, May 17; 1715: DL,
  Feb 28, LIF, Aug 3, 10, Oct 14; 1716: LIF, May 31, Nov 12; 1717: LIF, May 23,
  DL, Oct 25, LIF, Dec 6, 12; 1718: LIF, Mar 6, May 6, 20, Oct 30, Nov 6, 27;
  1719: LIF, Oct 20, 26; 1720: LIF, May 19; 1722: RI, Aug 20; 1723: LIF, Nov
  28, HAY, Dec 30; 1724: LIF, Apr 7, 10, 24, 28, May 8, 18, 20, 27, Jun 2, RI,
  Jul 11, SOU, Sep 24, LIF, Nov 3; 1725: LIF, Apr 22, 30, May 4, 5, 11, Sep 29,
  Oct 1, 8, Nov 2, 8, 22, Dec 3; 1726: LIF, Jan 3, Apr 13, 14, 29, May 2, 4,
  HAY, 9, DL, 13, LIF, 13, 30, Jul 26, Aug 2, 5, 9, 16, Oct 3, Nov 14, 30;

1727: LIF, Jan 10, Feb 3, 7, 9, Apr 10, 17, 19, 21, 26, DL, May 17, LIF, 18,
22, Sep 13, Oct 26, Nov 1; 1729: DL, Apr 23, LIF, 26, 30, May 6, 9, 13, DL,
14, LIF, 20, HAY, Jun 3, BFF, Aug 23, LIF, Dec 17; 1730: LIF, Mar 21, Apr 10,
24, 25, 30, DL, May 2, LIF, 9, 18, HAY, Jun 27, SFOF, Sep 9; 1731: LIF, Mar
25, May 13, 19, 26, 31; 1732: GF, Jan 27, Apr 20, LIF, 25, GF, 26, 28, LIF,
May 1, 5, DL, Aug 11, GF, Oct 7, 12, 13, 14, 17, 18, 19, 30, LIF/CG, Dec 8,
9, 12, GF, 15, CG/LIF, 16, 19; 1733: CG/LIF, Jan 4, GF, 11, LIF/CG, 11, 31,
GF, Feb 13, LIF/CG, Mar 12, GF, 29, Apr 3, LIF/CG, 11, GF, 25, LIF/CG, May 7,
HAY, 28, CG, Jun 29, Jul 31, Aug 9; 1734: CG, Apr 2, DL/LIF, May 3, CG, 6, 7,
BFRLCH, Aug 24; 1735: DL, Jan 1, Feb 17, Mar 27, May 30, Jun 5, 9, GF/HAY,
Jul 22, DL, Sep 9, GF, 12, 24, Oct 3, HAY, 24, DL, 27, 28, Nov 3, 5, 8, GF,
19, CG, Dec 18, DL, 29; 1736: CG, Jan 1, 2, 7, 9, 12, HAY, 14, CG, 17, 19,
DL, Feb 2, 4, 6, 11, CG, 23, 24, 26, Mar 2, 16, DL, 23, CG, 25, 27, Apr 1, 6,
8, GF, 13, CG, 15, 26, GF, May 5, DL, 5, CG, 6, 8, 11, 13, DL, 31, LIF, Oct
5, CG, Nov 9, 11, Dec 13; 1737: CG, Jan 7, 10, 17, 24, LIF, Mar 26, Apr 2,
18, 21, 28, May 4, CG, 5; 1738: CG, Mar 16, 18, DL, 21, 25, CG, Apr 6, DL,
12, 13, 14, 17, CG, 19, 20, DL, May 5, 19, 22; 1739: CG, Mar 15, Apr 9, DL,
14, May 10, 11, 12, 17, 19, 22, 23, 25, Nov 14, 16, 22, CG, Dec 14, 15, DL,
15, CG, 17, 22, 26; 1740: DL, Feb 9, 14, CG, Mar 10, 18, DL, May 8, 22, Dec
26, 27; 1741: DL, Jan 1, 3, 7, 9, 15, 29, CG, Feb 2, DL, 7, CG, Mar 12, Apr
2, 7, 9, 11, 21, DL, May 25; 1742: DL, Jan 16, 23, Feb 2, Mar 16, GF, May 10;
1743: CG, Mar 24, Apr 9, DL, May 4; 1749: BFCB, Aug 23
French Peasant and His Wife (dance), 1704: DL, Jun 15, 29; 1710: GR, Jul 27,
Aug 5, 7, 12, 17, 24, 26, 28; 1716: LIF, Jul 13
French Peasant, Scaramouch, Harlequin, Cooper and Wife (dance), 1710: GR, Aug
29
French Peasants and their Lasses (dance), 1728: LIF, Apr 29, May 2, 20, Jul 12
French performers, 1703: DG, Apr 30; 1713: TEC, Nov 26; 1718: LIF, Nov 7; 1724:
HIC, Dec 21; 1727: KING'S, Mar 9; 1749: HAY, Nov 7, Dec 2; 1759: DL, Sep 25;
1766: KING'S, Aug 8
French Pieces (entertainment), 1729: HAY, May 26, 29
French playhouse, 1721: LIF, Apr 27; 1734: KING'S, Nov 2; 1741: HAY, Dec 28;
1749: HAY, Nov 22
French Rigadoon (dance), 1741: CG, Apr 20
French royalty, 1670: BRIDGES, May 0
French Sailor and His Lass (dance), 1733: CG, Nov 26, 30, Dec 3, 10, 12, 15,
17, 28, 29, 31; 1734: CG, Jan 3, 4, Feb 14, 18, Mar 11, 18, 19, 25, 28, Apr
22, May 2, 3
French Sailor and His Wife (dance), 1715: LIF, Jan 10; 1716: LIF, Nov 14; 1717:
LIF, Apr 29; 1725: LIF, Oct 25, Nov 2, 8, 11, 17; 1726: LIF, Jan 3, 5, Mar
10, 21, 28, Apr 2, 13, 20, 21, 27, May 10, 12, 13, 19, 25, Sep 19, Oct 3, 19,
Nov 14, 30; 1727: LIF, Jan 31, Feb 7, Mar 11, 13, Apr 3, 5, 10, 17, May 3, 8,
9, 10, 15, 17, 19; 1729: LIF, Apr 8, 17, 29, May 15, Oct 20, Dec 17; 1730:
LIF, Mar 17, Apr 6, May 9, Jun 4, Oct 19, 30, Nov 3, 6; 1731: LIF, Jan 11,
19, Apr 21, Oct 20, 27, Dec 7; 1732: LIF, Jan 5, Feb 7; 1738: CG, Apr 10, 12,
22, 24, May 2, 6, 10
French Sailors' Dance, Grand (dance), 1728: LIF, Apr 22
French Scaramouch (dance), 1700: DL, Dec 13
French Scene (dance), 1717: LIF, May 11
French Shepherd and Shepherdess (dance), 1734: CG, May 1
French singers, 1674: DL, Mar 30
French Song (song), 1693: YB, May 13; 1701: RIW, Aug 11; 1703: DL, Jan 23, Feb
1; 1741: CG, Apr 16; 1746: CG, Mar 17; 1771: DL, Apr 12; 1773: MARLY, Jul 29;
1774: MARLY, Jun 16
French Tambourine (dance), 1731: LIF, Mar 25
French theatre, 1734: GF/HAY, Dec 18; 1759: CG, Sep 24; 1771: DL, Nov 2
French Tumblers, 1700: DL, Dec 13
French Wooden Shoe Dance (dance), 1733: GF, Apr 30
French, Daniel (actor), 1732: TC, Aug 4; 1734: CG, Mar 25; 1735: GF, Mar 27,
CG/LIF, Apr 8; 1736: LIF, Apr 2; 1737: CG, Mar 15, LIF, May 6; 1740: DL, Apr
24; 1741: CG, Apr 1; 1744: HAY, May 10; 1751: HAY, Nov 21
French, James Murphey (author), 1755: DL, Feb 3
French, John (scene painter), 1772: DL, Feb 28, Mar 14, Jun 10, Nov 13, 20, Dec
5, 9, 11; 1773: DL, Jan 1, 8, 22, Feb 19, Mar 6, 20, Apr 3, May 8, Jun 1, 2,
Sep 25, Oct 2, 9, Nov 19, 27, Dec 4, 6, 25; 1774: DL, Jan 1, 3, 21, Feb 22,
Mar 10, 21, 26, Apr 5, 22, May 7, 20, 30, Sep 24, Oct 1, 8, 22, 29, Nov 5,
12, 19, 26, Dec 3, 10, 17, NONE, 24, DL, 31; 1775: DL, Jan 7, 14, 21, 28, Feb
4, 11, 18, 25, Mar 4, 11, 18, 25, Apr 1, 8, 22, 29, May 6, 13, 20, 27
French, Mrs (actor), 1732: TC, Aug 4
French, Samuel (scene painter), 1766: DL, Oct 28, Nov 11, Dec 2, 9, 30; 1767:
DL, Jan 20, Feb 6, Mar 7, Apr 11, 25, May 1, 22; 1771: DL, Sep 21, Oct 15,
19, Nov 2, 8, 30, Dec 7, 12, 14, 21, 28; 1772: DL, Jan 4, 11, 18, Feb 8, 22,

29, Mar 7, 14, 21, 28, Apr 4, 11, 20, 25, May 2, 9, 16, 23, 30, Jun 6, 10,
   Sep 22, 26, Oct 1, 3, 10, 17, 24, 31; 1774: DL, Apr 9, Oct 15, Nov 5; 1775:
   DL, Sep 30, Nov 11; 1776: DL, Jun 8, 10
French, Samuel or Thomas (scene painter), 1777: DL, Jan 1; 1781: DL, Oct 19
French, Thomas (scene painter), 1771: DL, Oct 18, 29, Nov 11, Dec 9, 20, 27;
   1794: DL, Apr 21
Frenchified Lady, The. See Dell, Henry.
Frenchman and Frow (dance), 1737: DL, Mar 2
Frenchman in London, A (play), 1753: CG, Mar 24
Frenchman in the Dairy (dance), 1781: DL, Oct 4, 15, 16, 17, Nov 17, 20, 21
Frenchmen and Frenchwomen (dance), 1702: DL, Aug 22
Frensdorff. See Fransdorf.
Freudenfeld, Auguste (musician), 1726: HIC, Mar 25; 1727: HIC, Mar 15
Friar Bacon and Friar Bungay. See Greene, Robert.
Friar Bacon. See O'Keeffe, John.
Friar Bacon; or, The Country Justice (droll), 1699: BF, Aug 23
Friar Bacon, Friar Bungy and Miles Their Man (droll), 1732: SF, Sep 11
Friar, Mrs (seamstress), 1773: CG, Feb 25
Fribourg (dancer), 1748: SFP, Sep 7
Friend (actor), 1744: MF, Jun 7
Friend in Need is a Friend Indeed!, A. See O'Bryen, Denis.
Friend in Need, A. See Hoare, Prince.
Friend, John (singer), 1799: HAY, Jan 24
Friendly (actor) 1770: HAY, Nov 16, Dec 19
Friendly (actor), 1745: GF, Nov 14
Friendly Impertinent, The (farce, anon), 1734: YB, Mar 27
Friendly Lasses (dance), 1732: GF, Nov 24, 25, 27, 29, 30, Dec 13, 15; 1733:
   GF, Jan 11, 13, Feb 2, 12, Mar 1, Apr 13, 27, May 3, 8, 9, 10, 11, 16, 18,
   22, Sep 25, Oct 9, 15, 16, 26, 29, Nov 9, Dec 14, 20; 1734: GF, Jan 10, 11,
   19, 24, Apr 26, May 7, Oct 16
Friendly, Jack (author), 1748: CG, Nov 7
Friends, The. See Bellamy, Thomas.
Friendship (dance), 1715: LIF, Mar 15
Friendship Betrayed; or, The Injured General (play), 1721: LIF, Jan 27
Friendship Improved. See Hopkins, Charles.
Friendship in Fashion. See Otway, Thomas.
Friendship leads to Love (dance), 1783: KING'S, Dec 6, 27, 30; 1784: KING'S,
   Jan 3, 17, Mar 4, 6, 20
Frightened Song (song), 1784: CG, Apr 13
Frimble, Mrs (actor), 1756: BFSI, Sep 3, SFB, 20
Frimbley (actor), 1789: KHS, Sep 16, WHF, Nov 9, 11; 1799: OCH, May 15
Frimbley, Mrs (actor), 1799: OCH, May 15
Frisby (actor), 1715: DL, Jun 17; 1716: LIF, Mar 19, May 11; 1756: BFSI, Sep 3
Frisk and Fun (dance), 1782: CG, Apr 27, May 9
Frisky Lad, The (dance), 1732: LIF/CG, Nov 16
Frith (dancer), 1757: CG, Oct 22
Frith (householder), 1792: HAY, Nov 26
Frith St, 1707: DS, Jul 22; 1780: HAY, Mar 28; 1782: HAY, Mar 4; 1787: DL, Apr
   25, HAY, Aug 7, 21; 1788: DL, Apr 21, HAY, Aug 15, 20; 1789: DL, Apr 30, HAY,
   Aug 10; 1790: DL, Apr 14, HAY, Aug 13, 31; 1791: DL, Apr 5, HAY, Jul 26, Aug
   31; 1792: DLKING'S, Mar 29, HAY, Aug 20; 1793: DL, Apr 8, CG, May 3, HAY, Aug
   30; 1794: HAY, Jan 27, CG, May 13, HAY, Sep 3; 1795: DL, Apr 16, CG, May 8,
   HAY, Aug 10; 1796: HAY, Sep 7; 1797: DL, Jun 7, HAY, Sep 4; 1798: CG, Apr 24,
   DL, Jun 7, HAY, Sep 7; 1799: DL, Apr 18, CG, 19, HAY, Aug 17
Frodsham (actor), 1777: HAY, Feb 11; 1791: HAY, Dec 26
Frodsham, Sarah (actor), 1783: HAY, Jul 4, 26
Frolic, The (dance), 1734: GF/HAY, Dec 26, 27, 30; 1735: GF/HAY, Jan 2; 1774:
   CG, Apr 16, 19, 20, 25, 26, 27, 28, May 6, 10, 11, Dec 14, 16, 22; 1775: CG,
   Jan 28, 31, Feb 2, 23, Mar 11, 25, 28, Apr 3, 22; 1776: CG, Feb 17, 22, 29,
   Mar 28, Apr 8, 12, May 16, Nov 20, 22; 1777: CG, Apr 19; 1780: CG, Sep 20
Frolicksome Lasses; or, Harlequin Fortune Teller (pantomime), 1747: BFC, Aug 22
Frolics of an Hour, The (interlude), 1795: CG, Jun 2, 16
From Aberdeen to Edinburgh (song), 1696: LIF, Jun 0
From azure plains (song), 1699: DL, May 0
From drinking of sack by the bottle (song), 1686: DL, Jan 0
From England, Sir, I came (song), 1798: HAY, Sep 17
From friends all inspired (song), 1672: DG, Nov 4
From harmony (song), 1784: CG, Apr 27; 1789: CG, Mar 20; 1790: CG, Mar 17;
   1793: CG, Mar 8; 1796: CG, Mar 16; 1797: CG, Mar 22; 1798: CG, Mar 28; 1799:
   CG, Feb 8
From mighty kings (song), 1790: DL, Mar 10; 1791: CG, Mar 23; 1792: CG, Mar 2;
   1793: KING/HAY, Mar 13, CG, 20; 1794: CG, Mar 14, DL, 21, Apr 11; 1795: CG,

Feb 20; 1796: CG, Feb 26; 1797: CG, Mar 31; 1799: CG, Mar 1; 1800: CG, Mar 19
From morn till night I take my glass (song), 1794: CG, May 26; 1800: CG, May 6
From Rosy Bowers (song), 1791: DL, Apr 13; 1793: KING/HAY, Mar 6; see also Rosy
    Bowers
From Shades of Night (song), 1796: DL, Jun 9; 1798: HAY, Sep 17
From the censer curling rise (song), 1789: DL, Mar 20, CG, 20; 1790: CG, Feb
    24, Mar 26; 1791: CG, Mar 11; 1793: CG, Mar 8; 1794: DL, Mar 21, CG, 26, DL,
    Apr 2, 9, 11; 1795: CG, Mar 27; 1796: CG, Mar 16; 1797: CG, Mar 22; 1798: CG,
    Mar 14
From the dread scene (song), 1784: CG, Apr 27
From the mountains lo! he comes (song), 1793: KING/HAY, Feb 27
From tyrant Laws and Customs free (song), 1785: CG, Apr 5
From wave to wave (song), 1789: CG, Mar 20
From where the sun (song), 1800: CG, Jun 16
Froment, Jean Baptiste (dancer), 1739: DL, Mar 10, May 2, 15, 23, 26, Sep 8,
    Oct 6, 19, 26, Nov 1, CG, Dec 4, DL, 6; 1740: CG, Feb 12; 1741: GF, Sep 28,
    Oct 9, 16, 19; 1742: DL, May 3, CG, 21; 1743: DL, Feb 4, 11, May 4, 11, 14;
    1748: CG, Mar 3, Apr 28, Oct 27; 1749: CG, Apr 24, Nov 23; 1750: CG, Apr 28,
    30, Oct 29, Dec 21; 1751: CG, Apr 25, May 4; 1757: HAY, Jun 17, Jul 5, Sep 8,
    14, Oct 3, Dec 26; 1758: HAY, Jan 25, 27; 1761: DL, May 6; 1762: DL, May 12,
    25; 1767: HAY, Jul 17, 20, 29, Aug 31; 1771: HAY, May 2; 1773: DL, Apr 24;
    1774: DL, Apr 20; 1775: DL, Apr 28; 1776: DL, Apr 23; 1777: DL, Apr 19
Froment, Miss (dancer), 1762: DL, May 12, Nov 20, 23, 25; 1767: HAY, Jul 7, 8,
    9, 13, 15, 22, Aug 5, 12, 21, 25, 26, 27, 28, 31, Sep 2, 4, 8, 9, 10, 11, 12,
    14, 16, 18, 21; 1771: HAY, May 2; 1773: DL, Apr 24
Front (actor), 1776: HAY, May 2
Front Long Room, 1729: FLR, Nov 29
Froquett. See Floquet.
Frost (actor), 1784: HAY, Sep 17; 1791: HAY, Mar 7
Frost Music (music), 1704: DL, Jan 4; 1705: DL, Apr 30, Jun 16, 30; 1715: LIF,
    Jan 25, Oct 6, Nov 26; 1716: LIF, Jan 6, Feb 6, May 10, 22, Nov 28
Frost, Mrs (actor), 1733: MEG, Sep 28
Froud, Charles (musician), 1758: SOHO, Apr 1, CHAPEL, 27
Frowde, Philip, 1725: LIF, May 4; 1727: LIF, Jan 16, DL, Dec 13; 1731: LIF, Feb
    3; 1733: CG, Apr 4
--Fall of Saguntum, The, 1727: LIF, Jan 14, 16, 17, 18, 19, 20, 21, 23, 24, 26,
    27, 28, May 18; 1731: LIF, Feb 3
--Philotas, 1731: LIF, Feb 3, 4, 5, 6, 8, 9; 1732: LIF, Apr 29
Frowde, Sir Philip (spectator), 1667: BRIDGES, Aug 12
Fruit Office, 1788: DL, Jun 13
Fryar (hosier), 1745: DL, May 9; 1746: DL, May 7; 1747: DL, May 12; 1749: DL,
    Nov 24; 1750: DL, Jan 3, Feb 13
Frye (hosier), 1751: DL, Dec 17; 1754: DL, May 4
Fryer, Peggy (actor), 1661: LIF/MT, Oct 21; 1720: LIF, Jan 11, Mar 28; 1723:
    HAY, Jan 28
Fugitive, The. See O'Keeffe, John; Richardson, Joseph.
Fulford (actor), 1736: CG, Oct 8, Dec 9, 29; 1737: CG, May 13
Fulford, Mrs (actor), 1737: CG, May 13
Fulham, 1732: FUL, Nov 13; 1789: WHF, Nov 9
Full fathom five (song), 1793: KING/HAY, Feb 15, 27
Fuller (house servant), 1737: DL, May 27; 1738: DL, May 31; 1739: DL, May 26;
    1741: DL, May 28; 1742: DL, May 15; 1743: DL, May 23
Fuller (house servant), 1800: DL, Jun 14
Fuller (spectator), 1760: CG, Mar 12
Fuller, Isaac (scene designer), 1669: BRIDGES, Jun 24
Fuller's Rents (location), 1743: LIF, Mar 3
Fullerton (beneficiary), 1729: HAY, Jul 10
Fullwell (actor), 1745: GF, Feb 14, Apr 15, May 1; 1747: GG, Jan 16, Mar 25
Fullwood (boxkeeper), 1733: HAY, Apr 23; 1736: DL, May 21; 1737: DL, May 25;
    1738: DL, May 31; 1739: DL, May 26; 1740: DL, May 19; 1741: DL, May 28; 1742:
    DL, May 15; 1743: DL, May 23; 1744: DL, May 23
Fun and Frolic; or, Sailors' Revels (interlude), 1799: CG, Apr 6, 8
Funerailles de la Foire & Son Rapel a la Vie, Les (play), 1722: HAY, Jan 8
Funeral Anthems (song), 1759: CG, May 4; 1786: DL, Mar 10; 1789: CG, Mar 6, DL,
    18, 20; 1790: CG, Feb 26, Mar 19; 1791: DL, Mar 23; 1792: KING'S, Feb 24;
    1793: CG, Feb 15, KING/HAY, 22; 1794: CG, Mar 7, DL, Apr 4, 11; 1799: CG, Feb
    8
Funeral, The. See Steele, Sir Richard.
Furbarie per Vendetta, Le; or, Brighella's Revenge Thwarted by Argentina
    (play), 1726: KING'S, Nov 19, Dec 7
Furia di donna irata (song), 1763: KING'S, Apr 25
Furies' Chorus (song), 1789: DL, Oct 13; 1790: DL, Oct 11

Furies' Dance (dance), 1704: DL, Aug 15; 1726: HAY, Apr 27, KING'S, Dec 3;
   1727: LIF, Apr 14; 1739: CG, Jan 20; 1740: DL, Feb 13, Apr 11; 1753: DL, May
   7; 1767: DL, Mar 21, May 13; 1776: DL, Nov 25; 1782: DL, May 10; 1789: DL,
   May 22
Furies' Dance, Grand (dance), 1748: SFP, Sep 7; 1774: KING'S, Nov 8
Furkins (carpenter), 1789: CG, Jun 13; 1790: CG, Jun 8; 1791: CG, Jun 9; 1792:
   CG, May 29; 1795: CG, Jun 13; 1797: CG, May 25; 1798: CG, May 31; 1799: CG,
   May 17; 1800: CG, Jun 4, 7
Furkins, William (housekeeper), 1768: CG, Jun 3, 4; 1769: CG, May 19, 20; 1770:
   CG, May 18, 21; 1771: CG, May 27; 1772: CG, May 23; 1773: CG, May 28; 1774:
   CG, May 14; 1775: CG, May 30; 1776: CG, May 21; 1777: CG, May 23; 1778: CG,
   May 21; 1779: CG, May 15; 1780: CG, May 24; 1781: CG, May 25; 1782: CG, May
   28; 1783: CG, May 31; 1784: CG, May 22; 1786: CG, Jun 1
Furlong (dance), 1732: LIF, May 1
Furnival, Elizabeth, Mrs Thomas (actor), 1731: HAY, Feb 10, 17, 26, Mar 12, 15,
   Apr 22, SFGT, Sep 8; 1737: DL, Mar 17, Apr 12, May 5, Oct 8, 11; 1738: DL,
   Jan 19, Apr 6, May 8, Sep 28, Oct 12, Nov 11, 14, 25; 1739: DL, Mar 8, Apr
   12, May 1, 11; 1745: DL, Nov 6, 14, Dec 11; 1746: DL, Nov 10, Dec 5, 15;
   1747: CG, Jan 12, DL, Feb 2, Mar 3, CG, 23, DL, 24, 28, Apr 9, May 1; 1748:
   DL, Apr 27
Furnival, Thomas (actor), 1730: HAY, Nov 30, Dec 7, 9, 17, 23, 28; 1731: HAY,
   Jan 13, 15, 18, 20, Feb 10, 17, 26, Mar 15, 17, Apr 22, May 12, SFGT, Sep 8;
   1737: DL, Sep 20, 22; 1738: DL, May 17, Sep 14, Oct 26, Nov 4, 9, 30; 1744:
   HAY, Sep 22, 29, Oct 4, 11, 20, GF, Dec 12, 26; 1745: GF, Feb 14, Mar 28, Apr
   22, Oct 28, Nov 4, 11, 12, 13, 14, 19, 22, 26, 27, 28, 29, Dec 2, 4, 6, 9,
   13, 16, 19, 26; 1746: GF, Jan 1, 2, 3, 9, 13, 20, 27, Feb 3, 7, 18, Mar 20,
   SOU, Oct 20, GF, 28, 29, 31, Nov 4, 6, 7, 13, 14, 18, 19, 20, 21, 27, 28, Dec
   1, 9, 10, 11, 12, 17, 18, 22, 31; 1747: GF, Jan 2, 5, 9, 16, 22, 26, 29, Feb
   10, 16, 25, Mar 2, 5, 9, 23; 1748: NWC, Apr 4; 1749: NWLS, Feb 27, HAY, Jun
   1, BFY, Aug 23
Furnival, Thomas and Elizabeth (actors), 1737: DL, May 5
Furnival's Inn, 1745: GF, Mar 18
Furrs (actor), 1707: DL, Dec 26
Fuse, Elena (dancer), 1784: KING'S, Dec 18; 1787: DL, Feb 15, 24
Fustian's Booth, 1736: BFF, Aug 23
Fuzelier, Louis
--Animaux Raisonables, Les (farce), 1734: HAY, Nov 11, 15
--Harlequin and Scaramouch Deserters, 1720: KING'S, Mar 8; 1735: GF/HAY, Jan
   17, Feb 5, HAY, Apr 16, GF/HAY, May 15, HAY, 19
Fye! nay prithee John; or, Handel's Jig (dance), 1735: DL, Sep 25

G, S (poet), 1745: DL, Jan 17
Gabrielle de Vergy. See Belloy, Pierre Laurent Buirette de.
Gabrielli, Caterina (singer), 1775: KING'S, Oct 31, Nov 7
Gabrielli, Francesca (singer), 1775: KING'S, Oct 31, Nov 7, Dec 12; 1776:
   KING'S, Jan 9, Feb 6, 15, 29, Mar 7, Apr 20, May 18, 23
Gadbury (beneficiary), 1728: YB, Mar 13
Gaetani (dancer), 1726: KING'S, Dec 17
Gaetani, Mrs (dancer), 1726: KING'S, Dec 17
Gage, Lord and Lady (spectators), 1738: HAY, Oct 9
Gageure Imprevue, La. See Sedaine, Michel Jean.
Gair (beneficiary), 1743: LIF, Mar 15
Gala (dance), 1782: CG, Apr 2, 9, 17, 27, May 3
Gala, A (celebration), 1789: KING'S, Apr 21
Galatea dry thy tears (song), 1791: DL, Apr 1, CG, 13; 1792: KING'S, Feb 29,
   CG, Mar 9; 1794: DL, Mar 26
Gale (actor), 1735: SOU, Apr 7
Gale (billsticker), 1760: CG, Sep 22
Gale (spectator), 1662: LIF, Apr 2
Gale, Mrs (actor), 1723: HAY, Mar 14
Galeotti. See Gallioti.
Galerati, Caterina (singer), 1714: QUEEN'S, Jan 9, 27, Mar 4, Apr 3, 17, May 1,
   29, Jun 23, KING'S, Oct 23, Nov 16, Dec 30; 1715: KING'S, Feb 26, Apr 23;
   1720: KING'S, Apr 2, 27, Nov 19, Dec 28; 1721: KING'S, Feb 1, Apr 15, May 20
Gallant (pit doorkeeper, boxkeeper), 1717: LIF, Jun 3; 1719: LIF, May 29; 1720:
   LIF, May 30; 1721: LIF, May 26; 1722: LIF, May 22; 1723: LIF, May 21; 1724:
   LIF, May 27; 1725: LIF, May 20; 1726: LIF, May 24; 1729: LIF, May 20; 1730:
   LIF, May 25; 1731: LIF, May 21; 1732: LIF, May 12; 1733: LIF/CG, May 23;
   1734: CG, May 17; 1736: CG, May 25; 1738: CG, May 8; 1739: CG, May 28

Gallant Days of King Arthur (song), 1739: CG, Apr 27
Gallant Peasant (dance), 1767: CG, Jan 13, 17, 31, Feb 2, 3, 4, 5, 6, 7, 9, 18,
   19, HAY, Sep 4, 7
Gallant Shepherd (dance), 1765: CG, Dec 6; 1767: CG, Jan 13, DL, May 18
Gallant Soldier born to Arms (song), 1791: CG, Jun 6, 7, 8, 10, 13; 1797: CG,
   May 31
Gallantry A-la-mode (poem), 1674: DL, Apr 23
Galles, Princesse de, 1749: HAY, Nov 22
Gallet, Sebastian (dancer, ballet master), 1776: DL, Nov 7, Dec 18; 1777: DL,
   Jan 4, 9, Feb 10, Sep 20, Oct 2; 1778: DL, Jan 17; 1796: KING'S, Nov 26, Dec
   27; 1797: KING'S, Jan 17, Feb 7, 25, Mar 11, 28, Apr 25, May 11, Nov 28, Dec
   20; 1798: KING'S, Jan 2, Feb 6, Mar 6, 22, Apr 19, DL, May 9, KING'S, 10, Jun
   14
Galli (singer), 1749: HAY, Apr 10; 1752: KING'S, Mar 24; 1753: KING'S, Apr 30;
   1754: HAY, Feb 13
Galli, Caterina Ruini (singer), 1742: KING'S, Dec 4; 1743: KING'S, Jan 1, Feb
   22, Mar 30, Apr 5; 1744: CG, Mar 2; 1745: HAY, Feb 9, CG, Apr 10; 1747: CG,
   Apr 1, KING'S, Nov 14; 1748: KING'S, Mar 8, CG, 9, 23, KING'S, Apr 5; 1749:
   CG, Feb 10, KING'S, Mar 21, HIC, Apr 21; 1750: CG, Mar 16, DL, 28, KING'S,
   Apr 10; 1751: HAY, Feb 5, Mar 5, KING'S, Apr 16; 1752: CG, Feb 26, KING'S,
   Mar 24; 1753: KING'S, Apr 30; 1754: HAY, Jan 31, Feb 11, 13, CHAPEL, May 15;
   1773: HAY, Feb 26, KING'S, Oct 23, Nov 20, Dec 7; 1774: KING'S, Feb 10, Mar
   8, CHAPEL, 30, KING'S, Apr 19, HIC, May 9, KING'S, 17, Jun 3, Nov 8, Dec 3,
   13; 1775: KING'S, Jan 26, Feb 7, Mar 7, 23, 30, May 6, 23; 1776: KING'S, Feb
   6, 15; 1797: CG, Mar 3, 10, 15, 17, 22, 31; 1799: CG, Mar 15
Gallia, Maria Margarita (singer), 1703: LIF, Jun 1; 1704: YB, Mar 29, Apr 20,
   28, Nov 16; 1706: ATCOURT, Feb 5, QUEEN'S, Mar 7; 1707: DL, Feb 18, Mar 4,
   YB, Apr 4; 1713: QUEEN'S, Jan 10
Galliard (dance), 1723: LIF, Apr 18, May 23, 24, 28
Galliard, John Ernest (composer), 1712: QUEEN'S, May 17; 1717: LIF, Feb 27;
   1718: LIF, Jan 14, 23, Mar 22; 1719: LIF, Apr 11, 13; 1722: DL, Feb 28; 1727:
   LIF, Feb 13; 1734: CG, Mar 16, Apr 2, 25, DL, Dec 12; 1736: CG, Mar 2; 1739:
   KING'S, Apr 14; 1740: HIC, Mar 31; 1741: HAY, Apr 16; 1742: LIF, Jan 29;
   1744: LIF, Dec 11; 1772: CG, Apr 8; 1792: CG, Dec 20; 1793: CG, Dec 19
--Calypso and Telemachus (opera), 1712: QUEEN'S, May 17, 21, 24, Jun 21, 25;
   1717: LIF, Feb 27, Mar 2, 7, 9, 19
--Fair Hypocrite, The; or, The Fond Cuckold, 1745: NWMF, May 13
--Love and Folly, 1739: KING'S, Apr 14; 1740: HIC, Mar 31; 1744: LIF, Dec 11
--Nuptial Masque, The; or, The Triumphs of Cupid and Hymen (masque), 1734: CG,
   Mar 16, 23, 26, Apr 2, 6, 25
Galliardy's School, scholars of (actors), 1732: FUL, Nov 13
Gallic force, in vain (song), 1693: ATCOURT, Nov 4
Gallic Gratitude. See Dodd, James Solas.
Galligantus. See Brooke, Henry.
Gallimaufry, A (interlude, anon), 1795: CG, May 14; 1799: CG, Apr 19
Gallini (payee), 1747: CG, Mar 19
Gallini, Giovanni Andrea (dancer, manager, actor), 1757: CG, Dec 17; 1758: CG,
   Feb 1, Mar 13, Apr 12, 13, 14, KING'S, Nov 11; 1759: KING'S, Jan 16, Mar 20,
   Apr 3, Nov 13; 1760: KING'S, Jan 15, Mar 1, 24, HAY, 27, KING'S, Apr 17, May
   31; 1761: DL, Sep 14, KING'S, Oct 13, Nov 10; 1762: CG, Mar 3, KING'S, Apr
   20; 1763: KING'S, Feb 19, Apr 21, CG, Dec 22; 1764: CG, Jan 20, Mar 20, May
   3; 1765: KING'S, Dec 3; 1787: KING'S, Dec 8; 1789: KING'S, Jan 31, Feb 7, 10,
   CG, Jun 27, Jul 11; 1790: CG, Jul 17
Gallioti, Sga (dancer), 1771: KING'S, Mar 12, May 28
Gallioti, Vincenzo (dancer), 1769: KING'S, Sep 5; 1770: KING'S, Feb 6, 22, May
   19, 24; 1771: KING'S, Feb 9; 1772: KING'S, Jan 14
Gallo-English players, 1749: HAY, Nov 7
Gallot (singer), 1795: DL, Oct 30, Nov 11, Dec 10; 1796: DL, Jan 8, Mar 12, Apr
   30, Sep 29, Oct 19; 1797: DL, Jan 7, May 18, Nov 8; 1798: DL, Jan 16, Feb 20,
   Oct 6, Nov 14, Dec 4, 17, 29, 31; 1799: DL, Jan 19, Nov 14; 1800: DL, Jan 1,
   Mar 11, 13
Galori, Sga (singer), 1758: KING'S, Jan 31
Galuppi, Baldassare (musician), 1741: KING'S, Oct 31, Dec 12; 1742: KING'S, Mar
   2, Apr 20; 1743: KING'S, Jan 1, Apr 5; 1746: KING'S, Jan 28, May 13; 1748:
   KING'S, Jan 16; 1749: KING'S, Mar 21; 1753: KING'S, Apr 30; 1754: KING'S, Feb
   28, CG, Mar 4, Nov 18, KING'S, Dec 17; 1755: KING'S, Feb 18; 1756: KING'S,
   Feb 17; 1757: KING'S, Mar 24, May 31; 1758: KING'S, Apr 6, Nov 11; 1759: CG,
   May 4, MARLY, 10; 1760: MARLY, Jun 18, KING'S, Nov 22; 1761: KING'S, Jan 6,
   HAY, Aug 13, KING'S, Oct 17; 1762: KING'S, Feb 1, CG, Dec 8; 1763: KING'S,
   Feb 3, Apr 25, CG, Oct 22; 1766: KING'S, Mar 13; 1768: KING'S, Apr 21; 1770:
   KING'S, Jan 16; 1771: MARLY, Aug 8; 1772: KING'S, Feb 8, CG, Apr 8; 1773:
   HAY, Mar 17, KING'S, Dec 7; 1775: KING'S, Jan 14; see also Buranello

--Alexander in Persia (opera), 1741: KING'S, Oct 31, Nov 10, 14, 17, 21, 24,
    28, Dec 1, 5; 1742: KING'S, Jan 2, 5, 9, 12, 16, Nov 13, 16, 20, 23, 27;
    1745: CG, Apr 10
--Amanti Ridicoli, Gli (opera), 1768: KING'S, Nov 5, 8, 12, 15
--Arcadia in Brenta, L' (burletta), 1754: CG, Nov 16, 18, 22
--Attalo (opera), 1758: KING'S, Nov 11, 14, 18, 25, 28, Dec 2, 5, 9; 1759:
    KING'S, Jan 13, Mar 12
--Calamita Di Cuori, La (opera), 1763: KING'S, Feb 3, 5, 7, 12, 21, Mar 7, 21,
    Apr 21
--Cameriera Accorta, La (opera), 1754: CG, Mar 4
--Cicisbea alla Moda, La; or, The Modish Coquet (opera), 1759: MARLY, May 10,
    11, 12, 14, 15, 16, 17, 18, 30, Jun 1, 2, 9, 11, 12, 13, 15, 16, 18, 21, 23,
    27, 30, Jul 2, 4, 6, 9, 11, 13, 16, 18, 20, 23, 25; 1760: MARLY, Jul 10, 11,
    12, 14, 15, 16, 17, 18, 21, 22, 23
--Coquette, The (burletta), 1761: HAY, Aug 13, 14, 15; 1771: MARLY, Aug 8, 10,
    20; 1772: MARLY, Aug 31, Sep 2
--Enrico (opera), 1743: KING'S, Jan 1, 4, 8, 11, 15, 18, 22, 25, 29, Feb 1, 5,
    8, 12, 15, 19, Mar 22, 26; 1748: KING'S, Jan 16, 23, Feb 6, 13, 16, Mar 5,
    Apr 5; 1753: KING'S, Nov 27, Dec 1, 4, 8, 11, 15, 18, 22, 29; 1754: KING'S,
    Mar 5, 30
--Eroe Cinese, L' (opera), 1766: KING'S, Apr 12, 26, May 3, 10
--Euristeo (opera), 1757: KING'S, May 31, Jun 4, 7, 11, 14
--Filosofo di Campagna, Il (opera), 1761: KING'S, Jan 3, 6, 13, 20, 27, Feb 3,
    10, 17, 24, Mar 3, 10, 24, 31, Apr 7, 14, 16, 21, Oct 17, 27; 1762: KING'S,
    Feb 15, 22, Mar 8, 15, Apr 29; 1763: DL, Mar 21; 1768: KING'S, Apr 21, 26,
    May 5, 10, Sep 10, 17; 1769: KING'S, Feb 14, 25, May 27, Jun 29; 1770:
    KING'S, Jan 16; 1772: KING'S, Feb 8, 18, 22, 25, 29, Mar 3; 1773: DL, Feb 1
--Mercato di Malmantile, Il (opera), 1761: KING'S, Nov 7, 10, 17, 23, 28, Dec
    2, 7, 14, 21; 1762: KING'S, Jan 4, 25, Apr 14; 1769: KING'S, Jan 28, 31, Feb
    4, 7, 11, 18
--Mondo Nella Luna, Il (opera), 1760: KING'S, Nov 22, 25, 29, Dec 2, 6, 9, 13,
    23, 30; 1761: KING'S, Feb 26
--Nozze di Dorina, Le (opera), 1762: KING'S, Feb 1, 8, Mar 22
--Olimpiade, L' (opera), 1756: KING'S, Feb 10, 17, 21, Mar 6, 9, 13, 20, 23,
    27, Apr 6
--Penelope (opera), 1741: KING'S, Dec 12, 15, 19, 22, 26, 29; 1742: KING'S, Feb
    20, 23, 27; 1754: KING'S, Dec 17, 21, 28; 1755: KING'S, Jan 11, Apr 17
--Puntiglio Amoroso, Il (opera), 1773: KING'S, Dec 7, 14, 18, 21, 23; 1774:
    KING'S, Feb 5
--Ricimero (opera), 1755: KING'S, Feb 18, 22, 25, Mar 1, 4, 8, 15, 18, 22;
    1756: KING'S, Feb 28, Mar 2, 15, 30
--Scipione in Cartagine (opera), 1742: KING'S, Mar 2, 6, 9, 13, 16, 20, 23, 27,
    30, Apr 3, 6, 10, May 29, Jun 1
--Sirbace (opera), 1743: KING'S, Apr 5, 9, 12, 16, 23, 30, May 7, 14, 17
--Trionfo della Continenza, Il (opera), 1746: KING'S, Jan 28, Feb 1, 4, 8, 11,
    15, 18, 22, 25, Mar 1, 25
Gambarini, Elizabetta (singer), 1747: CG, Apr 1; 1761: SOHO, Apr 15
Gambellon (actor), 1728: HAY, Feb 21
Gamble, John (musician), 1662: THAMES, Aug 23; 1675: ATCOURT, Feb 15
Gamerra, Giovanni de (librettist), 1778: KING'S, Feb 7; 1783: KING'S, Nov 29;
    1786: KING'S, May 25
Gamester, The. See Shirley, James; Centlivre, Susannah; Moore, Edward.
Gamesters (dance), 1775: CG, Oct 11, 12, 18, 27, Nov 16, Dec 22; 1776: CG, Mar
    5
Gamesters, The. See Garrick, David.
Gander Hall. See Franklin, Andrew.
Gang (dancer), 1735: CG, Sep 26
Gapatono (actor), 1753: HAY, Mar 13, Apr 10
Gapatono, Sga (actor), 1754: HAY, Apr 1, 22, May 2
Gapper (actor), 1773: DL, Jan 23
Garbutt (beneficiary), 1800: DL, Jun 13
Gard, William (supernumerary), 1767: CG, Oct 8; 1770: CG, Feb 10, 15, 20, 24,
    Mar 20, May 3, 17, 24, 28; 1773: CG, Jan 12, Feb 27, Dec 16; 1779: HAY, Mar 8
Gardel (Guiardele), Favre (dancer), 1779: KING'S, Nov 27, Dec 14; 1780: KING'S,
    Jan 22, Feb 15, Apr 1, 22, May 27; 1782: KING'S, May 9; 1793: KING'S, Jan 26,
    Feb 5, 26, Apr 23, Jun 1, 8, 11, 15; 1794: KING'S, Feb 1, 11, Mar 1, 4, Apr
    1, May 31
Gardel, Mlle Favre (dancer), 1793: KING'S, Jun 1, 8, 11; 1794: KING'S, Mar 1,
    4, 8, 22, Apr 1, 26, May 31; 1798: DL, May 16; 1800: KING'S, Jun 21, 28, Jul
    12, 19
Gardel, Pierre Gabriel (dancer, choreographer), 1780: KING'S, May 9, 25; 1781:
    KING'S, Nov 17, Dec 11; 1782: KING'S, Jan 10, 26, 31, Feb 2, 7, 14, 21, 23,

Mar 19, Apr 11, May 9, Jun 15; <u>1785</u>: KING'S, Mar 3; <u>1786</u>: KING'S, Mar 23;
  <u>1788</u>: KING'S, Feb 21, Apr 3, 26; <u>1789</u>: KING'S, May 14; <u>1796</u>: KING'S, Dec 13
Gardel, Sga (singer), <u>1769</u>: KING'S, Sep 5
Garden (actor), <u>1779</u>: HAY, May 10; <u>1784</u>: HAY, Feb 9
Garden Court, <u>1759</u>: DL, Mar 23
Garden of Love (dance), <u>1777</u>: DL, Apr 22, CG, Nov 11; <u>1778</u>: CG, Jan 28
Gardener and his Wife (dance), <u>1731</u>: DL, Apr 27
Gardener's Wedding, The; or, The Waterman Defeated (farce), <u>1734</u>: MEG, Sep 30,
  Oct 2; <u>1744</u>: HAY, Oct 9, 18, 20
Gardeners' Dance (dance), <u>1726</u>: HAY, Apr 27; <u>1761</u>: HAY, Jun 23, Aug 6; <u>1769</u>:
  CG, Jan 14; <u>1775</u>: CG, Nov 4, 8; <u>1776</u>: DL, Jan 16, 20, May 6, 23; <u>1778</u>: HAY,
  Jun 18, 22, 23, 26, Jul 3, 9, Aug 6, 13
Gardeners' Holiday (dance), <u>1767</u>: DL, Nov 20, 21, 23, 24, 26, Dec 1
Gardeners' Revels (dance), <u>1747</u>: DL, Nov 16, 17, 26
Gardens of Venus, The; or, The Truimphs of Love (entertainment), <u>1733</u>: BFMMO,
  Aug 23
Gardi, Sga (singer), <u>1773</u>: KING'S, Oct 23, Dec 7
Gardin (actor), <u>1784</u>: HAY, Feb 23
Gardiner (boxkeeper), <u>1735</u>: HAY, Dec 17; <u>1743</u>: CG, Apr 29; <u>1744</u>: CG, May 7;
  <u>1745</u>: CG, May 10; <u>1746</u>: CG, May 3; <u>1747</u>: CG, May 16
Gardiner, Luke (prologuist), <u>1781</u>: CG, Nov 17
Gardiner, Matthew, <u>1737</u>: HAY, Feb 28
--Parthian Hero, The; or, Love in Distress, <u>1737</u>: HAY, Feb 28
--Sharpers, The; or, The Female Match-Maker (ballad opera), <u>1737</u>: HAY, Feb 28
Gardiner, Widow (beneficiary), <u>1731</u>: LIF, May 25
Gardner (actor), <u>1779</u>: HAY, Dec 20; <u>1780</u>: CII, Mar 6, 13, 17, 27, Apr 5
Gardner (actor), <u>1792</u>: HAY, Nov 26
Gardner (singer), <u>1799</u>: CG, Sep 30, Oct 7
Gardner, James (actor), <u>1796</u>: HAY, Jun 22; <u>1799</u>: HAY, Jun 29, CG, Sep 18, 30,
  Oct 4, 7, 25, 28, Nov 13, 14, Dec 23; <u>1800</u>: CG, Jan 11, 16, Feb 4, 10, Mar
  17, 25, 27, Apr 5, May 1, 22, Jun 11
Gardner, Miss (actor), <u>1767</u>: HAY, May 29
Gardner, Sarah, Mrs William (actor, playwright), <u>1758</u>: DL, Jun 22; <u>1763</u>: DL,
  Oct 1; <u>1765</u>: CG, Oct 19, Nov 19; <u>1766</u>: CG, Mar 15, Apr 15, 26, Oct 6; <u>1767</u>:
  CG, May 19, HAY, Jun 4, 8, CG, 9, HAY, 12, 15, 17, 22, Jul 2, 6, 15, 22, Aug
  5, 7, 10, Sep 7; <u>1768</u>: CG, Jan 2, May 6, 11, HAY, 30, Jun 8, 22, 23, Jul 8,
  13, Oct 7; <u>1769</u>: CG, Jan 4, Feb 18, Mar 29, May 8, HAY, 15, 24, 29, Jun 7,
  21, Jul 12, 17, Aug 7, 11, 25, CG, Oct 7, 24; <u>1770</u>: CG, Jan 19, 25, Feb 3,
  May 10, HAY, 16, 18, 23, 28, Jun 22, Jul 25, Aug 24, 31, Sep 3, 27, CG, Oct
  17, 19, Nov 2, Dec 5, 22; <u>1771</u>: HAY, Apr 4, CG, 5, 27, May 11, HAY, 15, 17,
  20, 22, 23, 29, 31, Jun 5, 10, 14, Jul 3, 12, 15, 24, Aug 14, 19, 26, 28, Sep
  2, 16, 18, 19, 20, CG, 23, Oct 18, 30, Nov 22, 26, Dec 4, 13, 23; <u>1772</u>: CG,
  Mar 5, DL, 23, CG, 31, Apr 21, 25, May 2, 13, HAY, 25, 27, Jun 8, 15, 24, 29,
  Jul 8, 15, Aug 4, 10, 21, Sep 8, CG, 23, 25, Oct 23, 29; <u>1773</u>: CG, Jan 2, 7,
  Apr 27, HAY, May 17, 19, Jun 4, CG, Sep 24, Oct 6, 15, 21, 22; <u>1774</u>: HAY, Jan
  24, May 30, Jun 1, 3, 6, 8, 13, 15, 17, Jul 15, Aug 19, 26, 29, Sep 19, 21;
  <u>1775</u>: HAY, May 15, 17, 19, 22, 24, 26, 29, Jun 7, Jul 14, 21, Aug 28, Sep 7,
  18, 19, 20, 21; <u>1776</u>: CG, Apr 27, HAY, May 22, 27, 31, Jun 12, 14, 24, Jul 8,
  24, Sep 2, 16, 18, 20, 23; <u>1777</u>: HAY, May 28, 30, Jun 6, 9, 16, Jul 7, 30,
  Aug 7, 9, 23, Oct 9; <u>1781</u>: HAY, Jan 22; <u>1782</u>: HAY, Aug 13, 16; <u>1795</u>: HAY, Apr
  22
--Advertisement, The; or, A Bold Stroke for a Husband (farce), <u>1777</u>: HAY, Aug 9
--Mrs Doggrell in her Altitudes; or, The Effects of a West India Ramble
  (prelude), <u>1795</u>: HAY, Apr 22
Gardner, William (actor, dancer), <u>1750</u>: CG, Oct 30, Dec 21, 26; <u>1751</u>: CG, Apr
  25, May 4, Sep 30, Oct 28, Nov 11, Dec 4; <u>1752</u>: CG, Jan 16, Oct 10, 26, Dec
  7; <u>1753</u>: CG, May 1, 10, 14; <u>1754</u>: CG, Apr 16, 27; <u>1756</u>: DL, Oct 12, 13, 21;
  <u>1761</u>: DL, Jul 2, 27, Aug 7, 8, CG, Dec 11, 30; <u>1762</u>: CG, Jan 5, 12, Apr 17,
  29, May 1, 5, 7, Sep 27, 30, Oct 2, 13, Nov 3, 26; <u>1763</u>: CG, Jan 8, May 14,
  Sep 21, 30, Oct 17, 25, Nov 4, 18, 25, Dec 9; <u>1764</u>: CG, Jan 23, Feb 1, Mar
  29, May 9, 12, 21, Sep 19, 28, Oct 11, 15, 16, 19, 23, Nov 3, 5, Dec 21;
  <u>1765</u>: CG, Jan 8, Apr 16, 19, May 3, 10, 11, 15, HAY, Jun 10, 24, Jul 15, 17,
  31, Aug 8, 9, 21, 30, CG, Sep 18, 27, Oct 4, 14, 15, 17, 23, Nov 11, 18, 23,
  27, Dec 3, 19, 20, 21; <u>1766</u>: CG, Jan 31, Feb 10, Mar 15, 31, Apr 14, 15, 23,
  25, May 6, 13, Sep 22, Oct 6, 16, 17, 18, 20, 31, Nov 4, 7, 21, 28, Dec 4,
  13, 23; <u>1767</u>: CG, Jan 1, 31, Mar 2, 21, 28, Apr 20, 24, 25, 29, May 9, 11,
  13, 27, HAY, 29, Jun 4, 5, 17, 22, 26, 30, Jul 2, 6, 8, 15, 22, 31, Aug 5,
  12, 14, 21, 25, 27, Sep 7, CG, 14, 16, 17, 18, 21, 22, 23, Oct 13, 22, 29,
  Nov 4, 6, 7, 18, 27, Dec 5, 14, 31; <u>1768</u>: CG, Jan 4, 20, Feb 20, 29, Mar 17,
  Apr 13, 20, 22, May 6, 10, 27, 28, HAY, Jun 23, Jul 8, 13, 18, Aug 15, 19,
  24, CG, Sep 20, 21, 22, 23, 26, HAY, Oct 7, CG, 12, 14, 15, 17, 26, Nov 4,
  17, 19, 24, 26, Dec 16, 22; <u>1769</u>: CG, Jan 14, Mar 28, 29, Apr 15, May 8, 10,

25, HAY, Aug 30, Sep 19, CG, 22, 27, Oct 3, 4, 5, 6, Nov 4, Dec 1, 19, 22,
29; 1770: CG, Jan 1, 15, 19, Feb 12, 24, Mar 22, 31, Apr 20, 25, 28, 30, May
1, 8, 10, HAY, 23, Jun 8, 11, 15, 18, Jul 9, 25, Aug 8, 22, Sep 3, 5, CG, 26,
HAY, 27, CG, Oct 5, 8, 11, 12, 17, 25, 27, 29, Nov 1, 5, Dec 12; 1771: CG,
Jan 12, 28, Feb 23, Mar 12, Apr 12, 30, May 6, 13, HAY, 17, CG, 30, HAY, Jun
7, 12, 14, Jul 15, Aug 12, 26, Sep 2, 20, CG, 27, Oct 9, 11, 15, 18, 19, 21,
25, Nov 2, 4, 7, 11, Dec 6, 7, 11, 16, 21, 30; 1772: CG, Jan 9, 21, 27, Feb
1, 24, Mar 10, 24, 30, 31, Apr 25, May 4, 8, 11, 13, HAY, 22, Jun 15, 19, Aug
10, Sep 4, 8, 17, CG, 28, Oct 1, 14, 16, 23, 26, Nov 2, 4, 6, 12, Dec 3;
1773: CG, Jan 6, 25, Feb 23, Mar 15, 22, 30, Apr 3, 16, 19, 23, 28, May 1, 4,
7, 15, 22, Sep 22, Oct 4, 6, 18, 22, 23, 25, 27, Nov 4, 12, 23, 27, Dec 4, 7,
11, 18, 21; 1774: CG, Jan 27, 29, Feb 11, 12, 21, DL, 22, CG, 24, Mar 14, 15,
22, Apr 5, 7, 9, 19, 21, 23, 30, May 11, DL, Jun 2, HAY, Sep 30; 1775: DL,
Feb 23, May 27, Nov 3, 14; 1776: DL, Mar 19, Apr 11, 20, Jun 10, HAY, Jul 29;
1777: DL, Oct 24; 1778: HAY, May 21, 22, Jun 1, 3, 19, Jul 1, 11, 30, Aug 3,
20, 27, Sep 7, 10, 17; 1779: DL, Jun 1, HAY, 4, 10, Jul 5, 6, 31, Aug 13, 17,
24, 31; 1780: DL, Jan 24, 25, May 25, HAY, 30, Jun 2, 5, 6, 9, 10, 13, 14,
26, 29, Jul 1, 8, 29, Aug 14, 17, Sep 8, 11; 1781: DL, May 12, HAY, Jun 7,
15, 21, Jul 2, 9, Aug 7, 17; 1782: DL, Apr 27, HAY, Jun 8, 11, 18, 20, 24,
Jul 4, 16, Aug 9, 17, 30, Sep 16, Dec 30; 1783: DL, May 26, HAY, 31, Jun 6,
13, 20, 25, 30, Jul 4, 5; 1784: HAY, Mar 22, DL, May 22, HAY, 29, Jun 1, 5,
CG, 10, HAY, 12, 14, 22, 25, 28, Jul 6, 28, Aug 2, 5, 9, 16, 20, Sep 6, 13,
17; 1785: DL, May 21, HAY, 28, 30, Jun 2, 3, 7, 15, 21, 24, Jul 11, 13, 19,
21, 26, Aug 6, 23, 26, 31, Sep 2, 9, CG, 21, 23, 26, 28, Oct 13, 28, Nov 10,
14, 28, 30, Dec 14, 30; 1786: CG, Jan 4, Feb 7, 17, Apr 4, 8, 19, 24, May 13,
15, 23, DL, 29, HAY, Jun 9, 14, 16, 20, 28, Jul 7, 8, 13, 14, 18, 21, 25, Aug
12, 29, CG, Sep 18, DL, 19, CG, 20, 27, Oct 4, 6, 23, 30, Nov 14, 25, Dec 4;
1787: CG, Jan 11, 15, Feb 10, 13, Mar 26, Apr 27, May 25, DL, Jun 4, HAY, 13,
14, 18, 20, 21, 23, 27, Jul 2, 19, 25, Aug 4, 17, 29, CG, Sep 24, 28, Oct 17,
18, 22, 29, Nov 9, 14, 19, Dec 10, 20, 27; 1788: CG, Jan 4, 25, 28, Feb 14,
Mar 10, 26, Apr 5, May 12, Jun 3, DL, 6, HAY, 10, 11, 13, 18, 23, Jul 2, 3,
4, Aug 15, 27, Sep 3, 9, CG, 17, 22, 24, Oct 3, 22, 28, Nov 20, Dec 1, 26,
30; 1789: CG, Jan 2, Feb 6, 11, Apr 20, 30, May 5, 7, DL, Jun 10, CG, 16, 17,
HAY, 19, 22, 25, 29, Jul 6, 9, 18, Aug 1, 5, 11, 27, Sep 8, 14, CG, 14, 25,
28, Oct 7, 12, 13, 16, Nov 6, 11, 14, 16, 20, 23, 30, Dec 26; 1790: DL, May
29; 1791: DL, May 31; 1792: DLKING'S, Jun 15
Gardyner's Printing Office, 1749: DL, Apr 10; 1750: DL, Mar 31, Apr 21; 1751:
DL, Apr 26; 1754: DL, May 7; 1755: DL, Apr 24
Garee. See Geree.
Garelli, Giovanni (singer), 1791: PAN, Feb 17, Apr 14, Jun 2; 1792: DLKING'S,
Apr 19; 1793: KING'S, Jan 26, Feb 5, Mar 19, May 14, Jun 1, 11; 1794: KING'S,
Feb 1, Mar 1, 18, Apr 1, 26, 29, May 17, 29, Jun 23
Gargantua, Mynheer, 1734: DL, Feb 23; see also Cajanus, Daniel
Gariboldi, Stefano (double-bass player), 1789: CG, Feb 27
Garland (actor), 1775: DL, Nov 9, 11; 1776: DL, Feb 1, 9, 15, 20, Mar 28, May
4, 11, 15, 22, 24, Jun 10, CHR, Sep 25, Oct 14; 1778: CG, Oct 14, 22; 1779:
CG, Apr 29
Garland (printer), 1772: DL, Oct 1
Garland Dance (dance), 1756: DL, Feb 13, Mar 20, Apr 19, 22; 1763: CG, Mar 15;
1764: DL, Dec 13, 14, 15, 17; 1765: CG, Oct 3, 4, 5, 8, 12, Nov 1, Dec 6, 9,
26; 1766: CG, Jan 20, 22, 27, 29, Oct 23, 29, Nov 1, 6, 11, 12, Dec 3, 5;
1767: CG, Dec 14, 15, 19, 21, 23, 31; 1768: CG, Oct 10, 28, Nov 7, 15, Dec
19; 1769: CG, Jan 7, 12, 20, Mar 13, Apr 8, 17; 1770: CG, Apr 26; 1795: CG,
May 1
Garland Dance, Grand (dance), 1775: DL, Apr 6, 21; 1776: DL, Feb 27, Mar 2, 5,
11, 12, 18, 21, 23, 25, 28, Apr 10, May 2, 9, 30, Jun 10, Oct 9, Nov 26 .
Garlick Hill, 1750: DL, Feb 21
Garman (actor, dancer), 1794: DL, Dec 20; 1795: DL, Jan 19, Oct 30; 1796: DL,
Jan 18, Apr 4, Oct 1, 19, 29, Nov 9, Dec 26; 1797: DL, Jun 10; 1798: DL, Jan
16, Feb 20, May 16, Oct 6, Nov 14, 29, Dec 6; 1799: DL, Jan 19, Feb 5, May
20, Oct 14, 19, Dec 17; 1800: DL, Mar 11
Garman, Miss (actor), 1759: HAY, May 10; 1760: HAY, Jun 2; 1769: CG, May 6, 15,
Nov 4; 1770: CG, May 12
Garnet, Mrs (actor), 1715: LIF, May 24, Jun 23; 1716: LIF, Jan 24, DL, Jul 12;
1717: DL, Feb 25, Oct 21; 1718: DL, Feb 19, May 20, Jun 17, Jul 11, Aug 12,
15, Nov 24, Dec 1, 3, 13; 1719: DL, Jan 16, 24, 26, 31, Feb 3, Jun 9, Oct 14,
15, 17, Nov 3, 7, Dec 11; 1720: DL, Jan 1, May 2, 31, Jun 2, Sep 13, 15, 29,
Oct 4, 20, 29, Nov 18, 21, 22; 1721: DL, Jan 10, Mar 20, Apr 29
Garney (beneficiary), 1746: CG, May 7
Garnier (jeweler), 1743: DL, Mar 10
Garraway's Coffee House, 1753: DL, May 22
Garrelli (actor), 1736: CG, Apr 8

Garrett, Mrs (actor), 1787: HAY, Jun 26
Garrick, David (actor, manager, author), 1740: DL, Apr 15; 1741: GF, Oct 19,
Nov 2, 6, 9, 16, 23, 28, 30, Dec 2, 9, 15; 1742: GF, Jan 5, 14, 23, 27, Feb
3, 18, 22, Mar 6, 9, 11, 13, 15, 18, 22, 27, Apr 1, 6, 19, 22, 26, DL, May 1,
11, GF, 24, DL, 26, 28, 31, Oct 5, 7, 13, 16, 19, 26, 28, Nov 1, 16, Dec 1,
3, 22; 1743: DL, Jan 13, 21, Feb 17, 21, Mar 3, 14, 17, 21, 24, Apr 7, 14,
27, May 2, 6, Sep 13, Oct 6, 15, Dec 2, 6, 7, 9, 10, 13, 14, 15, 17, 20, 22;
1744: DL, Jan 2, 7, Feb 4, 6, 7, 21, Mar 5, 12, 29, Apr 3, 4, 6, 9, 10, 25,
Oct 19, 20, 22, 23, 24, 27, 30, Nov 1, 3, 6, 7, 12, 16, 24, Dec 29; 1745: DL,
Jan 5, 19, 21, Feb 7, 14, 20, Mar 7, 9, 18, Apr 6, 11, 17, 22, Sep 26, Oct
24, Dec 9; 1746: DL, Jan 20, CG, Mar 18, DL, Apr 12, 29, CG, Jun 11, 13, 16,
20, 23, 27, Oct 22, 27, 31, Nov 3, 6, 11, 14, 17, 26, DL, Dec 5, CG, 6, 15,
26; 1747: CG, Jan 2, 12, 17, 20, 31, Feb 4, 12, 19, 26, 27, 28, Mar 5, 6, 12,
14, 19, 24, 30, Apr 6, 7, 9, DL, 9, CG, 20, 27, 28, 30, May 2, 5, 7, NONE,
Jun 6, DL, Sep 15, 17, 19, 22, Oct 3, 8, 15, 17, 20, 21, 23, 24, 28, 30, Nov
6, 10, 16, 18, Dec 4, 5, 14, 16; 1748: DL, Jan 2, 20, 21, Feb 1, 8, 13, 16,
22, 25, Mar 1, 5, 8, 10, 12, 19, 24, May 2, 3, Sep 27, 29, Oct 8, 11, 13, 14,
18, 21, 22, Nov 1, 2, 7, 8, 11, 14, Dec 10, 19, 23; 1749: DL, Jan 2, 18, 20,
Feb 1, 6, Mar 4, 7, 9, 20, Apr 3, 13, 14, 15, May 16, Sep 28, Oct 13, 14, 18,
21, 23, 26, 27, Nov 2, 6, 8, 16, Dec 8, 19, 20, 22; 1750: DL, Jan 6, 22, 25,
29, 31, Feb 10, 16, 19, 23, 24, 28, Mar 13, 15, 19, 26, 27, 31, Apr 4, 5, 9,
20, Sep 8, 11, 21, 25, 27, 28, 29, Oct 1, 2, 16, 19, 20, 22, 23, 24, 29, Nov
1, 6, 7, 8, 13, 14, 28, Dec 3, 15; 1751: DL, Feb 2, 9, 16, 23, Mar 5, 11, 12,
14, 16, Apr 10, 17, 29, May 17, 18, 20, Sep 18, 20, 24, 26, Oct 2, 7, 9, 11,
14, 25, Nov 2, 4, 8, 26, 29, Dec 14, 30; 1752: DL, Jan 11, 25, 28, Feb 3, 6,
8, 13, 17, Mar 7, 9, 12, Apr 14, 17, 20, May 7, Sep 28, Oct 3, 7, 11, 13, 19,
23, 28, 30, CG, Nov 2, DL, 3, 9, 13, 17, 18, 22, 24, 30, Dec 4, 8, 18; 1753:
DL, Feb 7, 26, Mar 3, 10, 12, 15, 19, 20, 22, CG, 24, DL, Apr 2, 3, 7, 26,
28, May 21, 25, Sep 8, 27, 29, Oct 2, 4, 9, 13, 16, 20, 23, 25, 29, CG, 30,
DL, 30, 31, Nov 7, 13, 15, 28, Dec 1, 22; 1754: DL, Jan 5, 23, 24, 26, Feb 1,
18, 25, Mar 18, 19, 23, 25, Apr 16, 20, Oct 3, 11, 16, 21, 24, 30, Nov 2, 6,
7, 16, 22, 30, Dec 7, 17; 1755: DL, Jan 17, 25, Feb 3, 25, Mar 4, CG, 12, DL,
13, 15, 18, 20, Apr 8, 15, May 9, 10, 27, HAY, Sep 15, DL, 25, Oct 2, 4, 8,
10, 17, 23, 27, Nov 1, 6, 7, 13, 15, 17, 18, 21, 24, 28, Dec 4, 6, 11, 19,
23; 1756: DL, Jan 2, 5, 9, 10, 12, 21, 23, Feb 2, 9, 10, 14, 25, 27, Mar 25,
27, 30, Apr 22, 30, May 4, 12, 27, Sep 23, 30, Oct 7, 9, 19, 28, Nov 2, 6,
18, 23, Dec 3, 10, 17; 1757: DL, Jan 18, 19, 24, 26, 27, 29, Mar 7, 8, 21,
22, 24, 28, 29, Apr 2, 14, May 3, 11, 24, Sep 15, 17, 24, 29, Oct 12, 13, 19,
25, 26, 28, Nov 1, 2, 8, 10, Dec 2, 3, 12, 17, 22; 1758: DL, Jan 27, 28, 30,
Feb 11, 21, NONE, Mar 1, DL, 11, 13, 16, 30, Apr 3, 7, 11, 14, 18, Sep 16,
19, 23, 26, Oct 7, 14, 25, Nov 2, 7, 8, 10, 15, 16, 23, Dec 2, 21; 1759: DL,
Jan 3, 12, 13, Feb 3, 14, 15, Mar 3, 20, 24, 27, CG, 28, DL, 31, Apr 5, 7,
17, 21, May 4, Jun 4, Sep 27, 29, Oct 5, 9, 12, 13, 17, 19, 23, 24, 25, 26,
30, Nov 3, 10, 13, 22, 30, Dec 1, 5, 12, 20; 1760: DL, Jan 19, 24, Feb 13,
21, 23, Mar 17, 20, 22, 24, 27, Apr 8, 11, 14, 21, 24, May 10, 22, Sep 30,
Oct 3, 8, 15, 17, 23, 24, Nov 20, 21, 24, Dec 2, 13, 17, 22; 1761: DL, Jan 3,
8, 10, 23, 31, Feb 3, 12, CG, Mar 14, DL, 23, 26, Apr 6, 10, 20, 24, 28, May
28, Jun 3, 4, 15, Jul 27, Sep 12, 14, 18, 19, 23, 29, 30, Oct 1, 7, 13, 16,
20, 21, 24, 31, Nov 7, 18, 23, 28, Dec 11, 14, 17, 23; 1762: DL, Jan 27, 29,
Feb 10, Mar 6, 18, 20, 25, 29, CG, 30, DL, Apr 1, 22, 26, 28, Sep 29, 30, Oct
4, 6, 8, 13, 14, 16, 20, 29, Nov 1, 2, 3, 10, 11, 15, 18, 19, 22, 26, 27, Dec
11, 18; 1763: DL, Jan 17, 19, 26, 27, Feb 1, 3, Mar 1, 15, 19, 21, Apr 4, 29,
May 5, 20, Sep 17, Oct 8, CG, 15, DL, Nov 23, 26, Dec 17; 1765: DL, Jan 1,
Apr 25, Sep 14, Nov 14, 20, 25, Dec 5, 23; 1766: DL, Jan 6, 23, 30, Feb 24,
25, Mar 4, 11, May 22, Oct 10, 11, 18, 23, 25, KING'S, 30, DL, 31, Nov 7, 15,
18, 28, Dec 4, 13; 1767: DL, Jan 2, 24, Feb 3, 12, 17, 23, Mar 7, 23, 30, May
1, 7, 9, 20, 23, 28, Jun 3, HAY, Jul 6, Sep 4, DL, 25, Oct 9, 15, 20, 27, 28,
Nov 7, 11, 18, 23, Dec 1, 3, 5, 14, 16, 19, 23; 1768: DL, Jan 13, 23, Feb 4,
Apr 25, May 26, 31, Aug 18, Sep 8, 22, 29, Oct 5, 6, 11, 14, 15, 17, 20, 25,
28, Nov 9, 15, Dec 9, 14, 23; 1769: DL, Jan 6, 12, 25, 27, Feb 2, 3, 4, 9,
Mar 2, 9, May 11, 18, HAY, Jun 21, DL, Sep 30, CG, Oct 7, DL, 10, 12, 14, 21,
26, Nov 14, 16, 22, 29, CG, Dec 2, DL, 6, 9, 13, 30; 1770: DL, Jan 2, 10, 16,
19, 24, 26, CG, 27, DL, Feb 2, 6, 13, 21, Mar 1, 3, 5, 8, 13, 19, CG, 31, DL,
Apr 30, May 1, CG, 4, DL, 24, Sep 22, 24, Nov 1, 13, 16, 20, 23, 24, 28, Dec
4, 6, 12, 13, 28; 1771: DL, Jan 4, 8, 10, 12, 15, 19, May 24, Jun 1, HAY, 26,
DL, Oct 17, Nov 1, 2, 8, 9, 13, 18, 22, 25, 28, Dec 3, 23, 31; 1772: DL, Jan
11, Feb 28, Mar 2, 3, CG, 5, DL, 10, 13, 23, 26, 31, Apr 23, May 9, 30, Jun
2, Oct 3, 10, 14, 21, GF, 23, DL, 23, 29, Nov 3, 7, 20, 27, 30, Dec 2, 8, 15,
18; 1773: DL, Jan 1, CG, 6, DL, 19, Feb 1, 17, 19, 20, Mar 1, Apr 21, Jun 2,
Sep 18, Oct 1, 2, 8, 14, 19, 20, 22, CG, 23, 27, DL, 28, 30, Nov 6, 12, 15,
CG, 20, DL, 24, Dec 27, 30, 31; 1774: DL, Jan 1, 13, 21, Feb 8, Mar 1, 8, CG,
12, DL, 19, May 5, CG, 12, DL, 13, 17, HG, Aug 19, DL, Sep 17, Oct 8, 13, 15,

336

20, 24, 28, Nov 3, 8, 16, 24, CG, 24, DL, Dec 1, 2, 7, 19; <u>1775</u>: DL, Jan 18,
Feb 16, 17, Mar 4, 18, 27, May 25, 27, Sep 23, 26, Oct 2, 18, 20, 25, 27, 28,
31, Nov 6, 7, 9, 10, 13, 15, 16, 25, 27, 29, Dec 1, 5, 11, 18, 21, 25, 29;
<u>1776</u>: DL, Jan 1, 12, 18, 19, 20, Feb 5, 12, 15, CG, 22, DL, 27, Mar 7, 9, Apr
11, 12, 25, 30, May 2, 7, 9, 13, 16, 21, 23, 24, 27, 30, Jun 1, 3, 5, 8, 10,
Sep 21, Oct 15, 18, 23, 30, Nov 7, 19, Dec 26; <u>1777</u>: CG, Feb 22, DL, 24, CG,
Mar 3, DL, Apr 7, 28, May 8, 9, HAY, 15, Aug 30, DL, Sep 30, CG, Dec 10;
<u>1778</u>: CG, Jan 21, DL, Mar 30, Apr 23, HAY, Jun 11, Jul 11, 30, Aug 27, DL,
Sep 19, Nov 30, Dec 7; <u>1779</u>: DL, Jan 5, 20, Mar 11, CG, Apr 5, 27, HAY, May
31, DL, Sep 18, Nov 20, CG, Dec 11; <u>1780</u>: DL, Feb 28, CG, Mar 14, DL, Apr 21,
HAY, Jun 6, Jul 10, DL, Oct 19, CG, 24; <u>1781</u>: CII, Apr 5; <u>1782</u>: DL, Mar 21,
May 3; <u>1783</u>: CG, May 19, Oct 3, 9; <u>1784</u>: HAY, Mar 22, Sep 17, DL, Nov 22, CG,
30; <u>1785</u>: CG, Jan 8, Mar 29, HAY, Apr 25, CG, May 7, HAMM, Jul 2, HAY, Aug 6,
CG, Sep 30, Oct 5, Nov 8, Dec 5; <u>1786</u>: HAMM, Jun 28, HAY, Aug 29; <u>1787</u>: RLSN,
Mar 29, CG, Apr 11, 16, Oct 1, Nov 14; <u>1788</u>: DL, May 1, HAY, Sep 30; <u>1789</u>:
DL, Feb 16; <u>1790</u>: CG, Jan 22, DL, Feb 27, May 18; <u>1791</u>: CG, Apr 30, May 31,
Jun 1, DLKING'S, Oct 3, Dec 31; <u>1792</u>: HAY, Aug 31, Oct 15; <u>1794</u>: HAMM, Mar
24, CG, Apr 12; <u>1795</u>: DL, Apr 27, CG, Jun 6, WLWS, 19, CG, Dec 22; <u>1796</u>: DL,
May 5; <u>1797</u>: DL, Apr 28, May 24; <u>1798</u>: CG, May 1; <u>1799</u>: HAY, Jun 22
--Bon Ton; or, High Life above Stairs, <u>1775</u>: DL, Mar 18, 27, Apr 4, 8, 29, May
2, 5, 9, 27, Oct 21, 23, 24, 26, 27, Nov 1, 14, 30, Dec 4, 6, 29; <u>1776</u>: DL,
Feb 10, Mar 12, 26, Apr 17, 19, 22, May 6, Jun 5, Oct 9, 31, Nov 11, 15, 30;
<u>1777</u>: DL, Feb 3, 10, 18, Apr 5, 18, 23, 26, May 7, HAY, Aug 18, DL, Oct 30,
31, Nov 5, 17, 27; <u>1778</u>: DL, Jan 20, Feb 11, 14, Apr 11, May 4, 15, 26; <u>1779</u>:
DL, Jan 2, HAY, Jul 20; <u>1780</u>: CII, Feb 29, DL, Apr 19, Oct 20, 26, Nov 2, 16,
20; <u>1781</u>: DL, Jan 15, 18, Mar 26, Apr 25, 30, Oct 6, Dec 15; <u>1782</u>: DL, Apr 8,
Oct 1, 17, Nov 14, 27, Dec 14; <u>1783</u>: DL, Feb 18, Mar 1, Apr 3, 24, 29; <u>1784</u>:
DL, Oct 26, Nov 9, 17, 26; <u>1785</u>: DL, Jan 5, 29, Mar 15, Apr 7, 25, May 10,
HAMM, Jul 6, DL, Oct 6; <u>1786</u>: DL, Mar 16, May 1, 9, 22, HAMM, Jul 21, DL, Oct
12, Nov 13, Dec 9; <u>1787</u>: RLSN, Mar 29, DL, May 7, 18, 24, Nov 6, 26; <u>1788</u>:
DL, Mar 10, 28; <u>1789</u>: HAY, Feb 23, CG, Nov 20, Dec 11; <u>1790</u>: CG, Feb 11, May
1, 8, DL, Nov 2; <u>1791</u>: DL, Jan 28, Feb 22, Mar 15, May 7, HAY, Aug 31,
DLKING'S, Oct 10; <u>1792</u>: DLKING'S, Mar 13, May 10, Jun 7, DL, Oct 15, Nov 28;
<u>1793</u>: DL, Jan 31; <u>1794</u>: DL, May 17, Jun 27; <u>1795</u>: DL, Feb 9, May 29; <u>1796</u>:
HAY, Feb 22, DL, Jun 6, Oct 17, Nov 17; <u>1797</u>: DL, Nov 20, Dec 15; <u>1798</u>: DL,
Sep 25; <u>1799</u>: DL, Mar 30, May 4
--Bundle of Prologues, A (interlude), <u>1777</u>: DL, Apr 28
--Catherine and Petruchio, <u>1754</u>: DL, Mar 18; <u>1756</u>: DL, Jan 21, 23, 24, 26, 27,
28, 29, 31, Feb 2, 3, 4, 23, Mar 13, Apr 6, 28; <u>1757</u>: CG, Mar 26, Apr 15, DL,
18, 21, CG, 21, DL, 30, CG, May 12, 13, 17, Nov 5; <u>1758</u>: CG, Jan 26, Feb 7,
DL, Mar 29, CG, Apr 17, 29, Oct 14, 27, Nov 10, Dec 14; <u>1759</u>: CG, Feb 3, Apr
17, DL, May 10, CG, Oct 13, 19, 27, Nov 6, 15, Dec 3; <u>1760</u>: CG, Jan 8, Feb 1,
DL, Mar 18, CG, 25, 29, DL, 29, CG, Apr 10, May 2, DL, 6, CG, Nov 25, Dec 13;
<u>1761</u>: CG, Jan 9, Mar 7; <u>1762</u>: DL, Jan 27, 28, Feb 4, 6, CG, Mar 22, DL, 29,
CG, Apr 13, DL, May 4; <u>1763</u>: DL, Jan 22, 26, Mar 3, 15, Apr 20, Nov 1; <u>1764</u>:
DL, May 9; <u>1765</u>: CG, Jan 10, 14, 26, Apr 18, May 22, Sep 25; <u>1766</u>: CG, Jan
16, Feb 7, Apr 25, DL, May 2, 3, CG, 6, 16, Nov 1, Dec 12; <u>1767</u>: CG, Jan 24,
May 13; <u>1768</u>: CG, Mar 12, DL, 19, CG, 24, Apr 23, DL, May 13, 23, CG, Nov 3;
<u>1769</u>: CG, Jan 20, Mar 13, DL, Apr 18, CG, 26, May 2, DL, 22; <u>1770</u>: CG, May
22; <u>1771</u>: DL, Jan 2, CG, Apr 12, HAY, May 31, Jun 14, CG, Oct 4, Dec 17;
<u>1772</u>: CG, May 1, 13; <u>1773</u>: DL, Apr 1, Oct 11, CG, Nov 16, 27; <u>1774</u>: DL, Jan
1, 17, HAY, Apr 12, CG, 18, HAY, Jun 13, Jul 4, 22, Aug 5, DL, Nov 30; <u>1775</u>:
DL, Feb 4, 18, May 18, HAY, Jul 14, CG, Dec 20, 21; <u>1776</u>: CG, Jan 3, Feb 13,
17, Mar 14, 23, Apr 19, HAY, 22, CG, May 30, HAY, Jul 24, Aug 21, CG, Oct 11,
Dec 12; <u>1777</u>: HAY, May 1, CG, Nov 19, 24; <u>1778</u>: HAY, Mar 23, CHR, May 29, CG,
Dec 1; <u>1779</u>: CG, Feb 16, Nov 13; <u>1780</u>: CG, Jan 19, DL, Nov 1, 15, CG, Dec 15;
<u>1781</u>: DL, Jan 3, Feb 20, Apr 3, May 19, Oct 24, Dec 11; <u>1782</u>: DL, Apr 23, May
24, Sep 18, Oct 25; <u>1783</u>: DL, Feb 28, Oct 11, Dec 17; <u>1784</u>: CG, Sep 28, DL,
Oct 23; <u>1785</u>: CG, Oct 17; <u>1786</u>: DL, Apr 6, Jun 2, HAMM, 30, DL, Oct 3, Dec 5;
<u>1788</u>: DL, Mar 13, May 5, CG, Nov 22, Dec 15; <u>1789</u>: DL, Jan 10, Mar 30, Apr
28; <u>1790</u>: CG, Mar 13, Apr 6, May 13, HAY, Aug 12, 20, 26, Sep 3, 8; <u>1791</u>: CG,
May 20, HAY, Jun 6, 14, Sep 1, 14, 16, DLKING'S, Nov 30; <u>1792</u>: DLKING'S, Jan
23, 31, Apr 24, May 9, CG, 15, DLKING'S, 28, Jun 9, HAY, Aug 17, Sep 1, 4,
DL, 18, Nov 15, 21, Dec 1; <u>1793</u>: DL, Jan 22, CG, May 10, 23, HAY, Jul 5;
<u>1794</u>: CG, Feb 26, DL, May 30, HAY, Jul 10; <u>1795</u>: CG, Mar 16, Apr 28, Jun 12;
<u>1796</u>: CG, Mar 19, May 3, DL, Jun 13, HAY, 20, 29, Jul 14, 26, CG, Nov 21, Dec
7; <u>1797</u>: DL, Apr 24, May 2, HAY, Jun 13, 20, CG, Nov 9, 15, DL, Dec 21; <u>1798</u>:
HAY, Apr 21, CG, 21, Nov 19, DL, Dec 18, 22; <u>1799</u>: DL, Jan 3, CG, Mar 16, DL,
May 3, CG, 18, DL, 20, Jun 13, 21, 28, CG, Sep 27, DL, Nov 6
--Christmas Tale, A, <u>1773</u>: DL, Dec 27, 28, 29, 30; <u>1774</u>: DL, Jan 1, 4, 6, 8,
11, 14, 17, 19, 21, 26, 28, Feb 4, 7, 10, 17, Mar 7, Apr 5, 11, May 11, Oct
5, 6; <u>1775</u>: DL, Apr 19; <u>1776</u>: DL, Oct 10, 12, 15, 18, 19, 22, 23, 24, 25, 26,

28, 29, 30, Nov 1, 4, 5, 6, 9, 12, 14, 16, 19, 22, 27, 30, Dec 3, 26, 27;
1777: DL, Jan 25, 28, Feb 4, 8, 27, Mar 3, 17, Apr 1, 10, Dec 4, 6, 8, 11,
13; 1778: DL, Apr 23; 1780: DL, Apr 3, 6
--Clandestine Marriage, The (with George Colman the elder), 1766: DL, Feb 7, 8,
15, 20, 22, 24, 25, 27, Mar 1, 3, 4, 6, 8, 10, 11, 13, Apr 3, 10, 24, May 1,
8, 15, Oct 17, 22, Nov 17, 22, 27, Dec 3, 9, 30; 1767: DL, Jan 23, Feb 14,
Mar 23, Apr 7, 20, 30, May 12, 15, Sep 12, 24, Oct 30, Nov 27, Dec 12; 1768:
DL, Jan 5, CG, 9, 11, DL, 11, Feb 6, 12, Apr 7, CG, 22, DL, 28, May 24, Sep
24, Oct 12, Dec 13, 30; 1769: DL, Jan 19, Apr 14, CG, 22, DL, May 15, Sep 16,
Oct 12, Nov 7; 1770: DL, Jan 3, Mar 22, Apr 16, 25, May 17, Oct 2, HAY, 5,
DL, 10, Nov 12, CG, 30, DL, Dec 11, CG, 22; 1771: CG, Jan 2, 18, DL, Mar 19,
Apr 30, CG, May 22, Sep 23, DL, Oct 12, 24, Nov 19, CG, 28; 1772: DL, Jan 9,
Mar 7, May 8, CG, Sep 23, DL, Nov 16, Dec 16, CG, 29; 1773: DL, Jan 14, Feb
6, CG, Sep 24, Dec 18, DL, 21; 1774: CG, Jan 25, DL, Apr 22, Sep 24, Nov 19;
1775: DL, Apr 25, Oct 27, Nov 20, Dec 16; 1776: DL, Jan 5, May 1, Oct 5, 28,
Nov 14, Dec 4; 1777: DL, Apr 10, Sep 25, Dec 8; 1778: DL, Feb 21, HAY, Apr
30, DL, May 1, 13, CHR, Jun 8, DL, Oct 21, Dec 18; 1779: DL, Feb 2, May 7,
Sep 23; 1780: DL, Jan 19, Apr 4, May 5, 22, Oct 10; 1781: DL, Jan 17, Feb 6,
Apr 16, May 11, 21, Sep 20, Nov 3; 1782: DL, Jan 16, Apr 9, May 1, Sep 17,
Nov 20, Dec 21; 1783: DL, Jan 13, Feb 3, Mar 6, 13, Apr 23, May 14; 1784:
HAY, Aug 19, DL, Sep 30, Oct 7, Nov 11; 1785: DL, Jan 24, Mar 3, Apr 1, May
9, HAMM, Jul 8, DL, Oct 25, Nov 25; 1786: DL, Jan 2, May 10, Oct 5, 7, Nov
16; 1787: DL, Oct 9; 1788: DL, Apr 4, May 12; 1789: CG, Nov 27, Dec 2, 15;
1790: CG, Jan 7, Feb 9, May 4, DL, Oct 23, Nov 5, 12; 1791: DLKING'S, Dec 2;
1792: DL, Sep 27, Nov 15; 1793: CG, Oct 11; 1794: DL, Jun 12, 24, Sep 30;
1795: DL, Feb 7, 21, HAY, Apr 22; 1797: DL, Oct 3, 10, Dec 1; 1798: DL, Jan
6, Jun 15, Sep 22, Oct 18; 1799: DL, Jan 16, Apr 30, Sep 21, Oct 24, Dec 19;
1800: DL, Feb 5, 20, Jun 5
--Country Girl, The, 1766: DL, Oct 25, 27, 28, 30, Nov 1, 3, 5, 6, 10, 12, 14,
25, Dec 27; 1767: DL, Jan 1, Apr 29, Nov 16; 1768: DL, Dec 1, 5, 10, 27;
1769: DL, Jan 18, May 10, 23, Sep 30; 1771: DL, Dec 30; 1774: DL, Dec 1, 3,
8, 13, 16; 1775: DL, Mar 7; 1785: DL, Oct 18, 24, 28, Nov 1, Dec 2, 14, 21;
1786: DL, Jan 3, 18, Feb 1, 9, 17, 27, Apr 18, May 3, HAMM, Jun 28, Jul 3,
DL, Sep 21, Nov 29, Dec 20, 29; 1787: DL, Jan 12, 22, 27, Feb 17, 24, Apr 10,
May 4, Sep 22, Oct 3, Nov 8, Dec 3; 1788: DL, Apr 5, Jun 2, Nov 21, Dec 5,
12, 22; 1789: DL, Jan 2, 16, May 23, Jun 1; 1790: DL, Feb 8, Mar 1, 23, May
1, CG, Jun 16, DL, Sep 14, 30, Dec 31; 1791: DL, Jan 24, Mar 29, May 4, 13,
Jun 4, HAY, Aug 2, DLKING'S, Oct 6, 22, Nov 10, 24, Dec 21; 1792: DLKING'S,
Jan 23, Mar 8, 22, Apr 16, May 22, Jun 1, HAY, Oct 15; 1793: DL, Feb 28, Apr
9, 30, May 15; 1794: DL, Jul 2, Oct 21, 22; 1795: DL, Apr 15, 20, 30, May 20,
Jun 3, Nov 3, Dec 3; 1796: DL, Feb 3, Apr 12, 15, May 18, Oct 1, 20, Nov 24,
Dec 22; 1797: DL, May 18, 27, Jun 8, CG, 14, HAY, Sep 18, DL, 26, Nov 22;
1798: DL, Jan 16, Feb 17, May 9, Jun 13, HAY, Sep 17, DL, Dec 21; 1799: DL,
Jan 18, Feb 16; 1800: DL, Mar 10, May 30
--Cymon, 1766: DL, Dec 30; 1767: DL, Jan 2, 3, 5, 6, 7, 8, 9, 10, 12, 13, 14,
15, 17, 19, 20, 21, 22, 26, 27, 28, 29, Feb 2, 3, 6, 10, 13, 16, 20, Mar 10,
Apr 9, May 15, 21, 22, 26, Sep 22, Oct 17, Nov 12; 1768: DL, Feb 13, 15, Mar
22, Apr 15, May 11, Sep 27; 1769: DL, Oct 4; 1770: DL, Jan 23, Feb 5, Mar 24,
29, Apr 23, 30, May 12, 22, Sep 27, Nov 21; 1771: DL, Mar 14, Apr 8, May 11;
1772: DL, Apr 2, 29, May 11, 15, Oct 20, 22, 27, Nov 6, 11, Dec 14; 1773: DL,
Jan 27, Feb 20, Apr 20, May 24; 1778: DL, Jan 17, 20, 22, Feb 6, 14, Apr 7,
May 9, Dec 23; 1779: DL, Mar 23, Oct 21; 1780: DL, Apr 11, May 9, 17, Sep 28,
Oct 24; 1781: DL, May 16; 1782: DL, Apr 18, May 2; 1784: CG, Mar 27, Apr 1,
DL, 14, CG, 21, DL, Nov 26, Dec 1, 6, 20; 1785: DL, Jan 13, Apr 29; 1786: DL,
Jan 6, Mar 20; 1787: CG, May 9, Jun 11, Sep 19, 21; 1788: CG, May 16; 1791:
DLKING'S, Dec 31; 1792: DLKING'S, Jan 2, 3, 4, 5, 6, 7, 9, 10, 11, 12, 13,
14, 16, 17, 19, 20, 26, 27, 30, Feb 1, 3, 6, 9, 10, 13, 16, 17, 25, 28, Mar
5, 15, 22, 27, Apr 30, May 15, 19, DL, Sep 25; 1793: DL, Jan 23, 24, 25, 26,
28, 31, Feb 1, 6, 8
--Enchanter, The; or, Love and Magic, 1760: DL, Dec 13, 15, 16, 18, 29, 30;
1761: DL, Jan 6, 7, 17, 28, 29, Apr 11, 14, 22, May 2, 22, 28; 1762: DL, Feb
3, 11, 12, Mar 2, Apr 20; 1766: DL, Apr 15
--Fairies, The, 1755: DL, Feb 3, 6, 10, 13, 17, 20, 24, Mar 3, 10, 14; 1763:
DL, Nov 23
--Farmer's Return from London, The (entertainment), 1762: DL, Jan 29, Mar 20,
25, 29, 30, Apr 1, 13, 14, 15, 22, 24, 29, May 3, 4, 5, Nov 15, 22, Dec 14;
1766: DL, Apr 19; 1774: DL, Apr 11; 1779: CG, Apr 27, 30, May 1, 12, 18, 20;
1781: CG, May 2, 5, 7, 16, 23
--Florizel and Perdita; or, The Winter's Tale, 1762: DL, Jan 27, 28, Feb 2, 4,
6, Mar 29; 1774: CG, Mar 12
--Gamesters, The, 1757: DL, Dec 5, 22, 23, 26; 1758: DL, Jan 7, 9, 12, 20, Feb
7; 1772: DL, Oct 30, Nov 2, 5, 10, 18, 23, Dec 2, 12; 1773: DL, Jan 1, 2, 20,

Feb 3, 15, Mar 4, 27, Sep 25; <u>1774</u>: DL, Apr 20, May 24, Oct 26; <u>1775</u>: DL, May 19; <u>1776</u>: DL, Nov 6; <u>1779</u>: DL, Mar 13, Apr 26; <u>1782</u>: DL, Oct 5, 16, Dec 27; <u>1783</u>: DL, May 21; <u>1785</u>: DL, May 6; <u>1790</u>: CG, Jan 22
--Guardian, The; or, The Cutter of Colman Street, <u>1759</u>: DL, Feb 3, 6, 7, 8, 9, 10, 13, 14, 15, 17, 19, 21, 23, 27, Mar 10, Apr 18, 24, 26, May 31, Nov 23, 30; <u>1760</u>: DL, Apr 9, 10, Dec 22; <u>1761</u>: DL, Jan 21, Apr 9, Nov 23; <u>1763</u>: DL, May 2; <u>1764</u>: DL, Mar 27; <u>1765</u>: DL, Mar 19, May 6; <u>1767</u>: DL, Mar 21, 24, May 19; <u>1768</u>: DL, Feb 20, Mar 1, Apr 25; <u>1769</u>: CG, Apr 4; <u>1770</u>: CG, Apr 28, Sep 28; <u>1771</u>: DL, Feb 21, Apr 23, CG, May 17, DL, Dec 11; <u>1772</u>: DL, Jan 8; <u>1774</u>: DL, Jan 26, 27, Nov 22; <u>1775</u>: DL, Jan 13, Mar 25, CG, Dec 16, 20; <u>1776</u>: CG, Jan 9, Mar 2; <u>1784</u>: HAY, Jul 12, 14, Aug 2; <u>1785</u>: DL, Feb 2, 7, HAY, Aug 11; <u>1786</u>: HAY, Jul 27; <u>1787</u>: CG, Apr 11, 21, HAY, Aug 4, Sep 14; <u>1788</u>: CG, Apr 24, 29; <u>1796</u>: CG, Nov 25, 29, Dec 3, 14; <u>1797</u>: CG, Apr 26, May 8, HAY, Sep 9, 13, CG, Dec 20; <u>1798</u>: HAY, Aug 22, 27; <u>1799</u>: CG, Feb 4; <u>1800</u>: CG, Feb 3, Jun 10, HAY, Aug 15
--Harlequin's Invasion; or, A Christmas Gambol (pantomime), <u>1759</u>: DL, Dec 31; <u>1760</u>: CG, Jan 1, DL, 1, 2, 3, 4, 7, 8, 9, 11, 12, 14, 15, 21, 22, Feb 8, 18, Mar 3, 4, 15, Apr 7, 8, 19, May 5, 21, 26, Jun 3, Oct 11, 13, 14, 16, 20, 21, 24, Nov 19, Dec 26, 27; <u>1761</u>: DL, Jan 1, 16, Mar 24, 28, May 23, 26, 30, Jun 2, Sep 10, 15, 21, 24, 28, Oct 19, Nov 2, 13, 21, 27, Dec 7, 26; <u>1762</u>: DL, Apr 22; <u>1763</u>: DL, Nov 1; <u>1765</u>: DL, Nov 16, 18, 19, 21, 23, 26, 27, 28, 29, 30, Dec 2, 3, 4, 5, 6, 10, 12, 17, 19, 23, 26, 27, 28; <u>1766</u>: DL, Apr 1; <u>1767</u>: DL, Sep 26, Oct 5, 6, 7, 8, 10, 12, 13, 16, 19, 22, Nov 5, 9, 19, 20, 21, 26, 27, 28, 30, Dec 2, 4; <u>1768</u>: DL, Sep 23, 24, 26, 30, Oct 1, 7, 18, 20, 24; <u>1769</u>: DL, Mar 14, 29, Apr 5, 8, 25, 29, May 12, Sep 21, Oct 2; <u>1770</u>: DL, Feb 12, 14, 16, Apr 16, Sep 29, Oct 29, Nov 2; <u>1771</u>: DL, Mar 21, Apr 17, May 4, 15, Sep 28, Oct 5, 9, 10, 16, 25, 26, Dec 5, 12, 19; <u>1772</u>: DL, Mar 19, Apr 4, 28, May 5, 25, Sep 29, Oct 1, 19, Nov 6, 10, 17, 24, Dec 1, 16; <u>1773</u>: DL, Mar 18, Apr 19, 27, May 3, 7, 12, 19, Oct 25, 26, Nov 10, 16; <u>1774</u>: DL, Feb 5, 12, Apr 8, 14, May 18; <u>1777</u>: DL, Jan 1, 2, 3, 4, 6, 7, 9, 10, 11, 13, 14, 15, 16, 18, 20, 22, 23, 24, 29, 31, Feb 5, 13, 25, Mar 10, 31, Apr 17, 25, 29, Sep 27, Oct 2, 4, Nov 3, 4, 18, 25, Dec 1, 26; <u>1778</u>: DL, Feb 12, May 27, Oct 1, Dec 8, 28; <u>1779</u>: DL, Sep 25, Oct 2, 25; <u>1780</u>: DL, Oct 11, Nov 8, Dec 1, 8, 19; <u>1781</u>: DL, Jan 3, 5, Mar 27; <u>1782</u>: DL, May 3; <u>1786</u>: DL, Dec 26, 27, 28, 30; <u>1787</u>: DL, Jan 1, 5, 9, 11, Feb 7, 10, 12, Apr 11, 16, 24, 30, Jun 5, Sep 25, Oct 2, 15, 22, 29, Nov 5, 9, 14, Dec 3, 7; <u>1789</u>: DL, Sep 19, 24, Oct 8, 19, Dec 14; <u>1790</u>: DL, Apr 19, Oct 19; <u>1792</u>: DL, Dec 27, 31; <u>1793</u>: DL, Jan 2, 7, 8, 14; <u>1796</u>: DL, May 5
--Institution of the Garter, The; or, Arthur's Round Table Restored, <u>1771</u>: DL, Oct 28, 29, 30, 31, Nov 1, 2, 4, 5, 6, 7, 8, 9, 11, 12, 14, 15, 16, 19, 20, 21, 23, 26, 27, CG, 29, DL, 29, 30, CG, Dec 2, DL, 2, 3, 4, 7, 10, 13, 18, 20; <u>1772</u>: DL, Feb 21, 22, 24, Mar 3, 7, 16, 17, May 15, Oct 10, 15; <u>1773</u>: DL, May 29
--Irish Widow, The, <u>1772</u>: DL, Oct 23, 24, 26, 27, 28, 31, Nov 2, 5, 10, 11, 13, 14, 21, 27, Dec 1, 5, 12; <u>1773</u>: DL, Jan 1, 27, Feb 11, 15, 22, Mar 20, 22, Apr 29, May 22, HAY, Sep 18, DL, Nov 1, 6, 9, 12, 17, 22, Dec 6, 23; <u>1774</u>: DL, Jan 8, Mar 12, Apr 16, 27, May 4, 12, 20, 24, Sep 17, Oct 13, Nov 2, 11, 25, Dec 10, 29; <u>1775</u>: DL, Jan 17, 24, Feb 21, Mar 16, 21, Apr 21, Oct 3, 18, 28; <u>1776</u>: DL, Jan 20, CG, Apr 27, DL, May 1, CG, 8, DL, 11, 18, 22, HAY, Sep 17, DL, Dec 14; <u>1777</u>: DL, Apr 19, May 21, 30; <u>1778</u>: HAY, Jan 26, Feb 9, Apr 9, DL, May 2, 9, 12, 14, 18, 20, 22, 28, CHR, Jun 24, DL, Sep 19, Nov 30, Dec 11, 23; <u>1779</u>: DL, Jan 1, 5, Apr 30, May 14, 17, 26, HAY, Sep 8, 13, 15; <u>1780</u>: CII, Apr 5, DL, May 4, 16, 19, HAY, Jul 24, 31, Aug 4; <u>1781</u>: DL, Mar 19; <u>1782</u>: HAY, Jan 14, DL, Apr 6, HAY, 9, DL, 30, May 16, 31, Jun 1, Oct 8, 31, Nov 20, Dec 7, 20; <u>1783</u>: DL, Jan 11, May 6, 26, HAY, Jun 2, DL, Oct 31, Nov 19, HAY, Dec 15; <u>1784</u>: DL, May 27, Sep 21, Oct 5, 30, HAY, Dec 13; <u>1785</u>: DL, Jan 6, HAY, Apr 26, DL, May 12; <u>1786</u>: DL, Apr 28, May 20, HAY, Jul 28; <u>1787</u>: DL, May 9, 25, Jun 7, Sep 29, CG, Oct 19, 25, DL, 27, Nov 16; <u>1788</u>: DL, Mar 6, HAY, Apr 9, CG, 25, DL, May 29; <u>1789</u>: DL, Apr 15; <u>1790</u>: DL, Feb 13, Jun 5; <u>1792</u>: DLKING'S, Jun 4, DL, Oct 2, Nov 3, 14, 24; <u>1793</u>: DL, May 1, 16; <u>1794</u>: DL, May 5, Jul 5; <u>1795</u>: DL, Jan 7, CG, Jun 6; <u>1796</u>: DL, Jun 13; <u>1797</u>: DL, Oct 17, 21, Dec 7, 27; <u>1799</u>: DL, Jun 18, 27, Nov 27
--Isabella; or, The Fatal Marriage, <u>1758</u>: DL, Nov 15, Dec 15; <u>1759</u>: DL, Oct 17, Nov 21; <u>1769</u>: DL, Mar 18; <u>1770</u>: CG, Mar 31, May 4, 5; <u>1772</u>: CG, Mar 30, Apr 2, DL, May 4, CG, 28; <u>1774</u>: DL, Nov 25, 28; <u>1775</u>: DL, Feb 1; <u>1776</u>: DL, Feb 10, HAY, Apr 22; <u>1778</u>: CG, Mar 30, DL, Oct 27; <u>1782</u>: DL, Oct 10, 12, 15, 18, 21, 23, 25, 28, Nov 6, 14, 21, 25, Dec 4, 17; <u>1783</u>: DL, Jan 28, Feb 15, 24, 26, Mar 15, 29, Apr 10, May 6, 19, Jun 5, Oct 8, 31; <u>1784</u>: DL, Feb 2, Mar 2, CG, 20, DL, 25, CG, Apr 15, DL, 20, 30, May 11, HAY, Aug 5, DL, Oct 12, 30, Nov 29, Dec 21; <u>1785</u>: DL, Apr 30; <u>1786</u>: CG, Jan 2, DL, Feb 23, Mar 21, May 11, Oct 12, Dec 13; <u>1787</u>: DL, Mar 27, Apr 21, May 3, 12, Oct 11; <u>1788</u>: DL, Jan 15, Mar 15, CG, Apr 8, 25, DL, Oct 28, Dec 16; <u>1789</u>: DL, Apr 2, CG, May

23; 1790: CG, Apr 29, HAY, Aug 18, DL, Dec 7, 21; 1791: CG, Feb 11, 18; 1792:
DLKING'S, Jan 21, Mar 24, DL, Dec 17; 1793: DL, May 4; 1794: DL, Oct 9, 11;
1795: DL, Jan 3, Apr 14, Sep 19, Nov 2; 1796: DL, Feb 13, Apr 9, 16, Sep 24,
Oct 26, Nov 19, 29; 1797: DL, Jan 16, Apr 4, Oct 30, Dec 4; 1798: DL, Jan 19,
May 28, Dec 3, 18; 1799: HAY, Feb 25, DL, Mar 26, Nov 22; 1800: DL, Feb 10
--Jubilee, The, 1769: DL, Sep 30, Oct 12, 13, 14, 16, 17, 18, 19, 20, 21, 23,
24, 25, 26, 27, 28, 30, 31, Nov 1, 2, 3, 4, 6, 8, 9, 10, 11, 13, 15, 17, 18,
20, 21, 23, 24, 25, 27, 28, 30, Dec 1, 2, 5, 7, 8, 11, 12, 14, 15, 16, 18,
19, 21, 23, 26, 27, 28, 29; 1770: DL, Jan 1, 3, 4, 5, 10, 12, 13, 18, 20, 22,
25, CG, 27, DL, 29, 31, Feb 1, 3, 7, 10, 15, 17, 20, 22, 23, 24, 26, 27, Mar
1, 10, 12, 15, 17, Apr 5, 18, 24, May 1, 26, 29, Jun 5, Oct 3, 4, 5, 6, 8, 9,
10, 11, 12, 22, 26, 30, Nov 3, 7, 9, 12, 15, 19, 22, Dec 5, 8, 11; 1771: DL,
Jan 1, Mar 7, 9, 11, Apr 4; 1772: DL, Mar 2, Jun 10; 1775: CG, Apr 4, DL, Dec
23, 26, 27, 28, 29, 30; 1776: DL, Jan 1, 2, 3, 4, 5, 6, 8, 9, 10, 11, 12, 13,
15, 16, 17, 18, 19, 23, 24, 25, 27, Feb 6, 8, 13, 24, Mar 2, 5, 7, 30, Apr 8,
18, May 24; 1777: DL, Mar 8, 13, 18, Apr 2, 4, 9, 14, 15, 28; 1778: DL, Apr
27, May 6; 1779: DL, Apr 19, 24, 29; 1780: DL, Apr 13, 24, May 8, 22, Dec 12,
22, 26; 1781: DL, Jan 1; 1784: CG, May 7, HAY, Sep 17; 1785: DL, Nov 7, 18,
23, 25, Dec 2, 5, 7, 14, 16, 19, 20, 21, 22; 1786: DL, Dec 21, 22, 23; 1787:
DL, Jan 4, 8, Mar 5; 1789: DL, Sep 22, 29, Oct 5, 6, 12
--Lethe; or, Aesop in the Shades, 1740: DL, Apr 15, May 14; 1741: GF, Apr 7,
15, 20, 24, 27, 30, May 4, Nov 24, 27, 28, Dec 18, 22, 30, 31; 1742: GF, Jan
2, 5, 6, 7, 12, 18, 22, 25, 26, 29, Feb 6, 10, 15, 18, 20, Mar 15, 29, Apr 6,
8, 26, May 21; 1748: DL, Dec 27; 1749: DL, Jan 2, 3, 4, 6, 7, 9, 10, 11, 12,
13, 14, 18, 20, 26, Feb 1, Apr 7, 13, 28, May 11, 16; 1750: DL, Mar 27, 29,
Apr 4, 5, 25, 28, May 2, 11, JS, Jul 23, DL, Sep 18, 22, Oct 16, 22, Nov 13,
15, 20, 24, 30, Dec 5, 7, 12, 19; 1751: DL, Mar 14, Apr 12, 15, 23, 26, 29,
May 1, 7, Sep 24, Oct 2, 7, 15, Nov 8, 16, Dec 5, 9, 17, 23, HAY, 28; 1752:
DL, Jan 31, Feb 15, HAY, Mar 12, DL, 12, Apr 1, 3, 14, 17, 22, HAY, 25, DL,
28, Oct 3, 7, 18, 28, Nov 4, 17, Dec 4, 19; 1753: DL, Mar 15, 17, Apr 9, 26,
May 11, 17, Oct 23, Nov 3, 13, 24, HIC, Dec 31; 1754: HIC, Jan 2, DL, Feb 14,
Mar 16, 30, Apr 2, 24, May 6, 24, Oct 15, Nov 6, 30; 1755: DL, Jan 29, Feb
25, Mar 18, Apr 14, 16, HAY, Sep 11, 15, DL, Oct 24, Nov 5; 1756: DL, Feb 14,
Mar 27, HAY, Apr 19, DL, 22, 30, May 5, 7, 12, 21, 24, 27, 28, Dec 17, 21,
23; 1757: DL, Jan 29, Feb 4, 16, Mar 26, CG, Apr 18, DL, 28, CG, 29, May 16,
18, DL, 24, CG, 25, DL, 31, CG, Oct 21, DL, Nov 2, CG, 7, DL, 16, CG, 16, 22,
Dec 2, DL, 10, CG, 15, 22; 1758: CG, Jan 16, 24, DL, Feb 11, CG, 28, Mar 16,
29, Apr 4, 12, 27, May 3, DL, 23, Jun 1, Sep 19, CG, 29, Oct 11, Nov 1, DL,
8, CG, 20, DL, 21, Dec 13, CG, 18; 1759: DL, Jan 2, CG, 12, Feb 14, 24, DL,
Mar 19, Apr 19, CG, 25, May 5, HAY, 10, CG, 21, Oct 3, DL, 25, CG, Dec 5, 12;
1760: CG, Mar 27, DL, 27, CG, Apr 8, 17, 18, 21, May 8, Oct 1, DL, 8, CG, Nov
19, 21, Dec 16; 1761: CG, Jan 6, DL, 24, CG, Mar 9, DL, Apr 4, CG, 13, 17,
DL, 30, CG, May 14, Oct 3, Nov 11, DL, Dec 14, CG, 16; 1762: CG, Apr 24, Oct
28, Nov 2, DL, 11, CG, 13; 1763: CG, Apr 13, DL, 23, CG, Nov 23; 1764: DL,
Apr 2, CG, Sep 19; 1765: CG, Feb 18, DL, Apr 15, CG, May 16, Sep 23; 1766:
DL, Jan 23, 31, CG, Apr 17, May 2, KING'S, Sep 12, 13, DL, Oct 18; 1767: CG,
Jan 28, DL, May 7, HAY, Jul 6, 10, Aug 21, CG, Oct 16, DL, Nov 23; 1768: DL,
Mar 7, CG, Apr 30; 1769: CG, Apr 12, DL, 24; 1770: CG, Nov 2; 1771: CG, Dec
18; 1772: DL, Jan 11, 14, 16, 18; 1775: DL, Apr 19; 1776: CHR, Oct 9; 1785:
HAY, Apr 25, CG, May 4; 1789: DL, Feb 16
--Lilliput, 1756: DL, Dec 3, 4, 6, 7, 9, 10, 11, 14, 15, 16, 22; 1757: DL, Jan
17, 18, 19, 20, 21, 28, Mar 8; 1777: HAY, May 15, 28, 30, Jun 2, 6, 25, Jul
4, 9, Aug 20, Sep 2
--Linco's Travels (entertainment), 1767: DL, Apr 6, 7, 29, 30, May 4, 15; 1768:
DL, Mar 24, Apr 16, May 2; 1769: DL, Mar 14, Apr 10, May 1; 1770: DL, Mar 22;
1771: GROTTO, Sep 9; 1772: DL, Mar 24, 30, Apr 7, 11, 22, 27, May 19, Jun 2;
1774: DL, Mar 14, Apr 11, 23; 1775: DL, Mar 23; 1781: CII, Apr 9; 1782: DL,
Mar 21, Apr 8, 19, May 8, 9, 14; 1788: CG, May 5, 23, Jun 3; 1791: CG, Jun 3;
1792: CG, May 5; 1797: DL, May 24
--Lying Valet, The (farce), 1741: GF, Nov 30, Dec 1, 2, 3, 4, 5, 7, 8, 9, 10,
12, 19; 1742: GF, Jan 8, 9, 11, 14, 16, 19, 21, 23, Feb 11, 16, 27, Apr 1,
JS, 7, GF, 19, 24, UM, 26, GF, 27, 29, May 1, 5, 6, 10, 14, 17, 18, 19, 24,
JS, Nov 9, 25; 1743: JS, Feb 2, SOU, 18, DL, Mar 3, 8, 15, 17, LIF, 17, DL,
19, LIF, 22, SOU, 30, LIF, Apr 4, DL, 5, 9, 18, HAY, 25, DL, 25, 26, 27, 30,
May 2, 4, 10, 12, 14, 16, 18, 19, 20, Sep 17, 20, 22, 27, 29, Oct 1, CG, 10,
DL, 11, 18, 20, 22, 27, 29, Nov 1, 3, 5, 11, 15, 17, 26, 29, Dec 3, 19; 1744:
DL, Jan 19, Mar 28, CG, 30, DL, Apr 4, 10, 18, HAY, 23, CG, 25, DL, May 9,
11, 23, Sep 20, Oct 11, GF, Nov 30, Dec 11, 12, 17, DL, 18, GF, 21, 28, 31;
1745: GF, Jan 5, 14, 28, 29, Feb 6, SMMF, 11, GF, 11, DL, 12, GF, 25, JS, Mar
8, GF, 19, 26, 28, DL, Apr 6, 20, GF, 29, DL, May 1, 9, GF, Nov 8, 11, 12,
13, 14, DL, 18, 20, GF, 22, 23, Dec 11, HIC, 30, 31; 1746: GF, Jan 9, DL, 11,
GF, 20, Feb 7, DL, 25, GF, Mar 3, HIC, 10, JS, 12, HIC, 14, CG, 18, GF, 20,

340

CG, Apr 21, DL, 30, CG, May 1, Sep 29, Oct 8, DL, 11, 16, 17, SOU, 20, GF,
27, 28, 31, SOU, Nov 6, CG, 11, DL, 12, 25, GF, Dec 9, 10; 1747: GF, Jan 9,
DL, 27, GF, 29, DL, Feb 4, GF, 6, 10, 20, 23, 24, Mar 17, CG, 26, DL, 31, CG,
Apr 7, 22, 29, DL, May 11, 15, CG, 20, SF, Sep 16, DL, 29, Nov 26; 1748: DL,
Jan 2, 26, Feb 2, 8, HAY, 29, DL, Mar 1, 7, 26, 28, Apr 25, May 11, 17, 18,
Sep 13, CG, 23, JS, Oct 31, SOU, 31, DL, Nov 7, 10, HAY, 14, DL, 17, 24, Dec
2, 22, HAY, 27, NWC, 29, DL, 31; 1749: NWMF, Jan 10, DL, 21, Feb 2, 18, Mar
14, JS, 28, CG, Apr 3, DL, 6, HAY, 18, CG, 24, DL, Sep 20, Oct 12, 21, HAY,
26, DL, Nov 6; 1750: DL, Jan 2, BB, 8, DL, 25, Feb 2, 6, 21, 23, SOU, Mar 5,
DL, Apr 30, HAY, Jul 26, DL, Sep 15, Oct 15, Nov 8, 23, Dec 3; 1751: DL, Feb
12, May 2, 9, 14, Sep 7, 13, SF, 18, DL, Nov 9, Dec 16, NWC, 26; 1752: DL,
Jan 29, Feb 6, 29, Mar 16, Apr 30, May 4, Sep 21, Oct 20, Nov 28; 1753: DL,
Sep 8, 18, Oct 4, Nov 5, Dec 21; 1754: DL, Jan 15, Feb 8, CG, Mar 18, 23, 26,
Apr 4, 6, 23, May 20, DL, 21, CG, Sep 23, DL, 26, CG, 27, DL, Oct 14, CG, Nov
2, 13; 1755: SOU, Jan 16, DL, Mar 11, CG, Apr 4, DL, 21, CG, 29, May 19, HAY,
Aug 25, 28, Sep 1, DL, 16, Oct 10, CG, Nov 3, DL, 17, CG, 18, Dec 2, DL, 4,
CG, 15, 22; 1756: CG, Jan 5, DL, Feb 12, CG, 14, Apr 27, DL, May 19, CG, Oct
6; 1757: CG, Jan 5, DL, May 3, 7, 23, Sep 13, CG, Dec 8; 1758: DL, Apr 29,
CG, May 2, Oct 25; 1759: CG, Jan 29, 31, Feb 5, 6, 9, 13, 19, DL, Mar 6, 29,
CG, Apr 2, 5, 18, DL, May 28, Jun 19, CG, Oct 8, 10, 18, DL, 19, CG, Nov 1,
10, 20; 1760: CG, Jan 25, Feb 8, May 12, Oct 21, Nov 17; 1761: CG, Jan 8, Apr
2, 9, 25, May 4, Sep 25; 1762: CG, May 6, DL, Sep 21; 1763: DL, Apr 13; 1764:
DL, Apr 14, May 22, Sep 20, CG, Oct 11, DL, Nov 3; 1765: DL, Jan 15, 29;
1766: HAY, Jul 8, 10, KING'S, Aug 29, Sep 5, 11, 17, 19, DL, Oct 23, 25;
1767: DL, Feb 5, CG, May 19, HAY, Jun 4, 5, 22, Jul 15, Aug 28, Sep 2; 1768:
HAY, Jun 10, 15, Jul 11; 1769: HAY, Jul 17; 1770: DL, Dec 22; 1771: DL, Jan
7, HAY, Jul 3; 1772: DL, Feb 27, Apr 30, HAY, Jun 1, DL, 9, HAY, 24, Jul 17,
DL, Dec 7; 1773: HAY, May 17; 1774: DL, Jan 10, HAY, Jun 1, 8, DL, Dec 2;
1775: DL, May 26, CG, Nov 21; 1776: DL, Mar 25; 1777: CHR, Jun 27; 1778: CHR,
May 25, Jun 10; 1781: CII, Mar 27; 1782: DL, Apr 12, Sep 19, Oct 30; 1784:
HAY, Mar 22, CG, Nov 30, Dec 10; 1785: CG, May 12, HAMM, Jun 17, Jul 1, CG,
Sep 30; 1786: HAMM, Jun 5, HAY, Dec 18; 1787: RLSN, Mar 29, CG, Oct 3, 8;
1788: CG, Jan 12, DL, Oct 2; 1789: DL, Dec 5, 12; 1790: CG, May 26; 1793: CG,
Apr 15, May 29, HAY, Jul 18, 27; 1794: HAY, Mar 13; 1799: HAY, Jun 24, DL,
29, HAY, Sep 5, DL, 21, Dec 11, 21; 1800: DL, Jan 7, Feb 7, Mar 8
--Male Coquette, The; or, 1757, 1757: DL, Mar 24, Dec 3, 5, 6, 7, 9, 12, 15,
17, 20, 29; 1758: DL, Jan 6, 12, 18, Feb 3, Mar 13, Apr 11; 1759: DL, Mar 24,
27, 31, Oct 17, Dec 5; 1760: DL, Apr 24, May 8, 9; 1763: DL, Jan 15, 19;
1765: CG, Jan 21, 24; 1773: DL, Apr 23, 30; 1774: DL, Feb 2, 7, 8; 1775: DL,
Jan 23
--May Day; or, The Little Gipsy, 1775: DL, Oct 28, 30, Nov 4, 6, 7, 8, 9, 10,
18, 21, Dec 9, 14, 18, 29; 1776: DL, Jan 22, 31, Feb 7, 15, Apr 27, Sep 24;
1777: DL, May 16, 23; 1793: CG, May 1; 1798: CG, May 1
--Meeting of the Company, The, 1774: DL, Sep 17, 20, 22, 24, 27, 29, Oct 1, 4,
6, 12, 25; 1775: DL, Sep 23, Dec 25
--Miss in Her Teens; or, The Medley of Lovers, 1746: CG, Dec 27; 1747: CG, Jan
17, 19, 20, 21, 22, 23, 24, 26, 27, 28, 29, 31, Feb 2, 3, 4, 5, 6, 7, 17, GF,
Mar 2, 9, 10, 12, 16, 19, 23, 24, CG, 24, HAY, 24, GF, 26, CG, 30, GF, 30,
CG, 31, GF, 31, Apr 2, CG, 2, 4, GF, 4, CG, 6, GF, 7, CG, 9, 11, GF, 11, CG,
20, HAY, 20, CG, 21, 23, SOU, 27, CG, 27, May 29, BFC, Aug 22, DL, Oct 24,
26, 27, 28, 31, Nov 9, 12, 24, Dec 22, 30; 1748: DL, Jan 1, 12, CG, 14, 15,
SOU, 19, CG, 19, HAY, 25, DL, 28, CG, Feb 8, DL, 9, Mar 10, 15, HAY, 30, CG,
Apr 21, DL, 27, HAY, 30, CG, May 2, HAY, 2, NWSM, 3, DL, 3, CG, 4, NWSM, 4,
CG, 5, NWSM, 5, 6, 9, DL, 13, SOU, Oct 10, DL, 21, 28, NWC, Nov 21, NWSM, 30;
1749: NWMF, Jan 5, DL, 25, HAY, Feb 23, DL, Mar 16, JS, 21, DL, Apr 3, 4, 10,
13, 14, CG, 19, DL, May 1, 12, SFGT, Sep 16, SOUGT, 22, DL, Oct 3, CG, 20,
Nov 9, 13, 30; 1750: DL, Mar 19, 22, CG, 26, DL, 26, CG, Apr 2, DL, 9, 17,
CG, 21, DL, 23, CG, 23, 24, 27, 28, DL, May 3, CG, 7, DL, 8, 10, Oct 23, CG,
24, DL, Nov 6, HAY, 10, DL, 28, Dec 6; 1751: DL, Apr 18, CG, May 9; 1752: DL,
Feb 6, Mar 9, Apr 13, 20; 1753: DL, Apr 5, 12, 28, May 2; 1754: DL, Apr 16,
CG, 17, 19, Oct 23, 25, Nov 27; 1755: DL, Apr 2, 4, CG, 7, 16, DL, 28, 29,
CG, 30, DL, May 2, 3, 6, 8, 12, 13, CG, Dec 11, 19; 1756: DL, Jan 15, 17, 19,
Feb 5, May 10, 18; 1758: HAY, Jan 12, DL, Mar 16, HAY, 16, CG, May 10; 1759:
DL, Apr 5, 20, CG, May 17, DL, 23, CG, 24, DL, 24, Jun 28, CG, Oct 30, 31,
Nov 13, 22; 1760: DL, Mar 6, 8, May 19; 1761: CG, May 8; 1762: DL, Apr 1, 14,
Sep 23, Oct 6, CG, Nov 12, 24, DL, Dec 18; 1763: CG, Jan 24, DL, 29, CG, Mar
21, DL, Apr 11, 26, May 7, Sep 17, Oct 20, CG, Nov 15, 22; 1764: DL, Apr 5,
CG, 24, May 25, Oct 12; 1765: CG, Mar 25, May 7, HAY, Jul 17, 22, 26, Aug 5,
9, 28, Sep 4, 9, 12, CG, Nov 21; 1766: CG, Jan 28, Mar 22, Apr 10, DL, 25,
May 10, 16, 21, HAY, Jun 18, 20, 24, KING'S, Aug 13, 15, Sep 1, HAY, 2,
KING'S, 8, CG, Nov 14; 1767: CG, Jan 21, DL, Apr 27, CG, May 2, DL, 23, HAY,
29, Jun 2, 26, Jul 8, Aug 26, Sep 8, DL, Oct 20; 1768: CG, Feb 5, HAY, Apr

341

28, DL, May 27, HAY, Jun 8, 13, 22, Jul 4; 1769: DL, Feb 13, HAY, 28, CG, May
5, 17, HAY, 24; 1770: DL, Mar 13, CG, May 10, 12, HAY, 16, Aug 30, Oct 5, DL,
Nov 28, Dec 14; 1771: DL, Jan 4, 21, Feb 18, HAY, May 15, DL, 23, Jun 1, HAY,
26, Sep 19, DL, Nov 1, 8; 1772: DL, Jan 25, HAY, May 27, DL, 30, Jun 10, HAY,
Jul 1, Aug 4, DL, Sep 22, Nov 3, 7, Dec 18; 1773: DL, Mar 1, Apr 15, HAY, May
19, DL, 27, HAY, Jul 26, DL, Oct 9, Dec 27, 29; 1774: DL, Jan 15, Feb 1, Apr
22, Sep 22, Nov 3, Dec 17; 1775: DL, May 24, CG, Dec 7, DL, 16; 1776: CG, Feb
9, DL, May 20, Sep 21, CG, 30, Oct 9; 1777: DL, May 13, Jun 5, CHR, 18, HAY,
Aug 7, 12; 1778: HAY, May 22, 27, Jul 11; 1780: CII, Mar 6, 13, HAY, Jun 5,
7, Aug 5; 1782: DL, May 4; 1786: CG, Feb 13, 15; 1787: CG, Apr 26, ROY, Jun
20, CG, Dec 15; 1788: HAY, Apr 29, Sep 30; 1789: DL, Apr 4, 20; 1790: DL, May
27, HAY, Aug 2, 7, 14; 1792: CII, Jan 16, HAY, Feb 6, DL, Nov 27, Dec 12;
1794: HAY, Aug 18; 1795: DL, Jan 21, 22, 28; 1797: HAY, Sep 18
--Neck or Nothing, 1766: DL, Nov 18, 19, 20, 24, 26, 29, Dec 6, 8, 18, 23;
1767: DL, Feb 7, 12; 1774: DL, Jan 19, 20, 24, Feb 3, 17, 28, May 17; 1784:
DL, Feb 10
--Ode upon dedicating a building at Stratford, 1769: DL, Sep 30, Oct 3, 6, 12,
Nov 7, Dec 4; 1770: DL, Jan 16, Mar 19
--Opera of the Fairies, The (musical), 1755: DL, Oct 25, 29, Nov 7
--Peep behind the Curtain, A; or, The New Rehearsal, 1767: DL, Oct 23, 24, 26,
27, 29, 30, 31, Nov 4, 6, 10, 13, 14, 17, 24, Dec 9, 10, 11, 14, 22; 1768:
DL, Jan 7, Feb 3, 5, Mar 5, 17, May 2, Sep 28, Dec 19; 1769: DL, Feb 25, Mar
11, 18, Apr 1, 4, 19; 1770: DL, Mar 22, 26, Apr 28, May 4, 10, 18, 28; 1771:
DL, Mar 23, Apr 26, May 7, 17, Oct 19; 1772: DL, Jan 27, Mar 24, Apr 2; 1773:
DL, Mar 9, 20, 25, May 6, 15; 1774: DL, Mar 17, Apr 23, May 2, 14; 1775: DL,
Feb 24, Mar 2, 20, 30, Apr 24, May 4, 6; 1776: DL, Mar 14, May 3; 1778: DL,
Dec 21; 1779: DL, Mar 23, 25, Apr 7, 16; 1786: HAY, Aug 29; 1790: CG, Mar 27;
1792: CG, Mar 31; 1796: HAY, Sep 5, 6; 1800: CG, Apr 5
--Theatrical Candidates, The, 1775: DL, Sep 23, 26, 28, 30, Oct 3, 5, 7, 10,
11, 12, 13, 20, 21, 23, 24, 27, Nov 7, 28; 1776: DL, Apr 15, 27, 29
Garrick, Epistle to (entertainment), 1760: DL, Dec 6; 1773: DL, Jan 15
Garrick, George (treasurer), 1749: DL, Oct 30, Nov 1, 6; 1750: DL, Jan 1, Apr
9, 28; 1758: NONE, Mar 21; 1759: DL, Dec 12; 1766: DL, Oct 31, Nov 15, 24,
Dec 17; 1767: DL, Jan 23, Mar 7, Apr 11; 1770: DL, Mar 17; 1771: DL, Sep 21,
Oct 23, 29, Dec 13; 1772: DL, Feb 7, Oct 19, 21, Nov 6, Dec 9, 18; 1773: DL,
Jan 8, 29, Feb 2, 3, 4, 6, 16, Mar 9, Apr 1, 3, 17, Nov 6, 8, Dec 17; 1774:
DL, Feb 4, 26, Apr 19, May 7, Nov 25; 1775: DL, Jan 17, Mar 20, May 20, 27;
1776: DL, Jun 10
Garrick, Mrs (actor), 1746: SFW, Sep 8
Garrick, Mrs (payee), 1776: DL, Feb 3
Garrick, Mrs George, 1758: NONE, Mar 21
Garrick, Peter, 1741: GF, Nov 2, Dec 9; 1742: GF, Apr 19
Garrick's Head Coffee House, 1786: DL, May 25
Garter, Knights of the, 1696: LIF, Jul 0
Garth, Sir Samuel, 1704: LIF, Mar 30; 1705: QUEEN'S, Apr 9; 1713: DL, Apr 14;
1734: DL, Jan 3, 4, 8, 9; 1768: CG, Mar 15
--Dispensary, The, 1768: CG, Mar 15; 1773: CG, Jan 6
Garton, Jonathan (treasurer), 1768: CG, May 9; 1769: CG, May 1; 1770: CG, May
7; 1771: CG, Apr 29, Sep 23; 1772: CG, Apr 20; 1773: CG, Jan 6, Apr 12, Dec
31; 1781: CG, May 28; 1783: CG, Jun 6
Garvey, Edmund (scene painter), 1777: CG, Nov 25; 1778: CG, Oct 22; 1779: CG,
Jan 4
Garwood, Mrs (wardrobe keeper), 1773: DL, Apr 12, Jun 2; 1774: DL, Jun 2; 1775:
DL, May 27; 1776: DL, Jun 10
Gasperini, Francesco (musician), 1702: YB, Dec 3, DL, 22; 1703: DL, Jan 23, YB,
28, DL, Feb 1, 11, Mar 13, Apr 19, 23, May 15, 24, 25, 28, Jun 22, RIW, Aug
12, DL, Nov 9, 10, 19, YB, Dec 11, DL, 22; 1704: DL, Jan 1, 12, 25, Feb 4, 9,
15, 21, YB, Mar 24, 29, DL, 30, Apr 4, YB, 28, May 18, DL, Nov 21, 27, Dec
28; 1705: DL, Jan 15, Nov 5, 8, Dec 17, 19; 1706: DL, Jan 3, 4, 29, YB, Mar
6, DL, Apr 3; 1708: SH, Mar 26; 1711: GR, Aug 27, QUEEN'S, Dec 12; 1712:
QUEEN'S, Feb 27, Nov 12, SH, Dec 8; 1723: DL, Mar 20
Gasperini's scholar (musician), 1705: RIW, Jul 14, DL, Oct 12; 1706: DL, Jun 22
Gassmann, Florian Leopold (composer), 1774: KING'S, Jan 11, 15; 1778: KING'S,
Mar 3
--Amore Artigiano, L' (opera), 1778: KING'S, Mar 3, 10, 17, 31, Apr 7, 21
--Contessina, La (opera), 1774: KING'S, Jan 11, 15, 17
Gasthof, Der. See Brandes, Johann Christian.
Gastrill (mercer), 1767: DL, Jan 23, Apr 2
Gastrill and Co (mercers), 1766: DL, Dec 5
Gataker (actor), 1747: RL, Jan 27
Gataker, Thomas, 1730: GF, Dec 16
--Jealous Clown, The; or, The Lucky Mistake, 1730: GF, Dec 16, 17, 18; 1731:

GF, Jan 13, 14
Gates (singer), <u>1708</u>: SH, Feb 4; <u>1717</u>: SH, Mar 27; <u>1723</u>: BUH, Jan 11; <u>1726</u>: IT,
    Feb 2; <u>1731</u>: ACA, Jan 14; <u>1744</u>: KING'S, Jun 9
Gates, Miss (dancer), <u>1738</u>: CG, Apr 27; <u>1740</u>: CG, Mar 27
Gattolini (singer), <u>1787</u>: KING'S, Jan 9, Feb 17, Mar 1
Gaudenzi, Teresa (singer), <u>1783</u>: KING'S, Dec 16
Gaudry (house servant), <u>1792</u>: CG, May 29; <u>1794</u>: CG, Jun 17; <u>1795</u>: CG, Jun 17;
    <u>1799</u>: DL, Jul 3
Gaudry, Ann, Mrs Stephen (actor), <u>1778</u>: DL, Mar 31, May 15, 23, Sep 24, Nov 2;
    <u>1779</u>: DL, Jan 8, Sep 30, Nov 3; <u>1780</u>: DL, Mar 13, Apr 26, Dec 6; <u>1787</u>: HAY,
    May 25, Aug 14; <u>1788</u>: HAY, Jul 10, Aug 5, 9, 11, 13, 18; <u>1789</u>: HAY, Aug 11,
    DL, Nov 13, 14; <u>1790</u>: DL, Jan 13, Oct 11; <u>1791</u>: DL, Mar 22, May 26, HAY, Jul
    30, Aug 31, DLKING'S, Oct 15; <u>1792</u>: DLKING'S, Feb 18, Mar 29, May 23, Jun 13,
    HAY, 15, 23, 25, Jul 25, DL, Oct 11, Nov 21, Dec 26; <u>1793</u>: DL, Mar 7, HAY,
    Aug 3, 12, 16, Sep 2, 11, 19, Oct 10, Nov 16, 19, Dec 26, 27; <u>1794</u>: HAY, Feb
    24, Mar 17, Jul 17, 18, 21, 24, 28, Aug 27; <u>1795</u>: HAY, Jun 13, 20, Jul 22,
    31, Sep 21; <u>1796</u>: HAY, Jul 15, 26, Aug 29; <u>1797</u>: DL, Jan 20, HAY, Jun 23, Jul
    3, Aug 14, 15, 16, 31, DL, Nov 8, Dec 9; <u>1798</u>: DL, Feb 24, HAY, Jun 30, Jul
    21, Aug 3, 11, DL, Nov 14, Dec 4, 15, 29; <u>1799</u>: DL, Jan 19, May 24, HAY, Jun
    25, Jul 9, Aug 21, DL, Oct 14, Nov 14, Dec 11, 28; <u>1800</u>: DL, Jan 1, Mar 11,
    13, Apr 29, May 3, HAY, Jul 2, Aug 14, 29
Gaudry, Anne (actor), <u>1787</u>: DL, Dec 10; <u>1788</u>: DL, Jan 31, Oct 14; <u>1789</u>: HAY,
    Aug 13, DL, Sep 12; <u>1790</u>: DL, Mar 8, May 15, HAY, Jun 15, DL, Oct 14, 21, Dec
    1; <u>1791</u>: HAY, Jun 8, Aug 26, DLKING'S, Dec 31; <u>1792</u>: DLKING'S, May 23, DL,
    Nov 21, Dec 22; <u>1793</u>: DL, Jan 19; <u>1794</u>: DL, Apr 21, 28, May 16, Jun 9, 24,
    Sep 27, Oct 22, 27, 31, Nov 15, Dec 20; <u>1795</u>: DL, Jan 21, May 6, HAY, Sep 21;
    <u>1800</u>: HAY, Jun 13, 16, 17, 27, 28, Jul 2, 5, 7, 30, 31, Aug 8, 19, 20, 27
Gaudry, Joseph (actor, singer), <u>1757</u>: HAY, Sep 12, 14, 28; <u>1759</u>: MARLY, May 10,
    Aug 16, DL, Dec 14; <u>1760</u>: MARLY, Jun 18, Aug 26, HAY, Sep 8; <u>1761</u>: HAY, Jun
    23, Jul 14, 28, Aug 6, 13, 22; <u>1771</u>: CG, Jun 6; <u>1776</u>: DL, Nov 25, Dec 10, 26;
    <u>1777</u>: DL, Jan 1, 4, Apr 22, May 8, Jun 4, Sep 20, Nov 8, Dec 15; <u>1778</u>: DL,
    Jan 5, Feb 6, Mar 16, May 15, 20, 23, Sep 17, 24, Oct 29, Nov 2, Dec 23;
    <u>1779</u>: DL, Jan 27, 29, Mar 11, 13, May 21, Sep 30, Oct 5, 9, 12, 19, 21, 22,
    26, 30, Nov 3, Dec 14, 20, 27; <u>1780</u>: DL, Jan 12, 27, Mar 4, Apr 3, 26, May 2,
    10, Sep 16, 19, 21, 23, 28, Nov 22, 23, Dec 6; <u>1781</u>: DL, Jan 29, Mar 31, Apr
    7, 25, 26, May 1, 10, 15
Gaudry, Joseph and Miss (singers), <u>1757</u>: HAY, Sep 12
Gaudry, Master (actor), <u>1789</u>: HAY, Sep 12
Gaudry, Miss (pianist), <u>1797</u>: HAY, Aug 3
Gaudry, Miss (singer), <u>1757</u>: HAY, Aug 17, 31, Sep 2, 5, 8, 12, 14, 28, Oct 3,
    17; <u>1760</u>: HAY, Feb 14, Jun 2
Gaudry, Richard (actor), <u>1783</u>: HAY, May 31, Jun 3, 12, 20, Jul 26, Aug 1, 13,
    28; <u>1784</u>: HAY, Mar 22, Jun 14, Jul 2, 3, 24, Aug 9, 10, 17, 28, CG, Sep 28,
    Oct 4, 25, Nov 16, Dec 13; <u>1785</u>: HAY, Mar 15, CG, Apr 20, May 7, HAY, Jul 19,
    Aug 2, 4, 6, 19, 25, 31, Sep 16; <u>1786</u>: CG, Jan 18, HAY, Jun 13, 20, Jul 7, 8,
    19, Aug 10, 12, 17, CG, Oct 16, 27, Nov 22, Dec 26; <u>1787</u>: CG, Mar 1, 31, Apr
    10, 13, 20, May 11, Jun 2; <u>1788</u>: HAY, Apr 9, Sep 30
Gaurie, Miss (dancer), <u>1728</u>: HAY, Feb 21
Gauron (Gourion) (dancer, actor), <u>1792</u>: CG, Dec 26; <u>1793</u>: CG, Mar 11; <u>1798</u>: CG,
    Mar 19, DL, Oct 6, Nov 14, Dec 6; <u>1799</u>: DL, Jan 19, Feb 5, Jul 2, Oct 14;
    <u>1800</u>: DL, Mar 11, Jun 13, HAY, Jul 2
Gautherot, Mme (violinist), <u>1789</u>: CG, Feb 27, Mar 6; <u>1790</u>: CG, Feb 19, May 13;
    <u>1793</u>: CG, Feb 15, 20
Gautier (actor), <u>1718</u>: LIF, Jan 3
Gautier, Mlle (dancer), <u>1717</u>: LIF, Oct 25, Nov 1, 8, 15, 22, Dec 6, 11, 13, 27;
    <u>1718</u>: LIF, Jan 1, 3, 15, 24, Feb 19, Apr 16
Gavill. See Cavill, Will.
Gavotte (dance), <u>1773</u>: KING'S, Apr 17, 27, May 22, 25; <u>1778</u>: CG, May 16; <u>1779</u>:
    DL, May 25; <u>1781</u>: KING'S, Apr 26; <u>1782</u>: KING'S, Apr 30; <u>1783</u>: KING'S, May 1;
    <u>1786</u>: KING'S, Jun 1
Gawdrey. See Gaudry.
Gay (tailor), <u>1796</u>: DL, Mar 12, Apr 2, 30, Dec 26; <u>1797</u>: CG, Apr 19; <u>1798</u>: DL,
    Jan 16, Oct 6; <u>1799</u>: DL, Jan 19, May 24, Oct 14, Dec 11; <u>1800</u>: DL, Mar 11,
    Apr 29, HAY, Jul 2
Gay, John (author), <u>1713</u>: DL, May 12; <u>1715</u>: DL, Feb 23; <u>1717</u>: DL, Jan 16; <u>1720</u>:
    DL, Feb 16; <u>1723</u>: KING'S, Feb 2; <u>1724</u>: DL, Jan 15; <u>1728</u>: LIF, Jan 29, Feb 12,
    15, Mar 20; <u>1730</u>: GF, Apr 15, 27; <u>1731</u>: LIF, Mar 26; <u>1732</u>: DL, Dec 16,
    CG/LIF, 26; <u>1733</u>: DL, Feb 3, LIF/CG, 10, 12, 13, HAY, 14, LIF/CG, 15, 17, 19,
    20, CG, 22, LIF/CG, 24, 26, 27, Mar 1, 3, 5, 6, 8, 10, 13, CG/LIF, 26,
    LIF/CG, Apr 25, CG/LIF, 26, May 28, CG, Sep 17, Nov 28, Dec 1; <u>1734</u>: CG, Jan
    8, Mar 5, 9, 16, Apr 29, CG/LIF, Sep 27; <u>1735</u>: CG/LIF, Jan 3, Apr 22, LIF,
    May 21, CG, Oct 1; <u>1736</u>: CG, Feb 14, 20, Mar 4, Apr 1, DL, Sep 21, CG, Oct

27, Nov 3, LIF, 16, 17, 19, 23, CG, Dec 16, 21; 1737: CG, Jan 14, 20, 25, Feb
10, Mar 15, HAY, May 25, LIF, Aug 2, 5, DL, Oct 25, Nov 9; 1738: DL, Jan 25,
Feb 4, Apr 14, CG, 20, DL, 27, May 31, Oct 25, Nov 22, Dec 20; 1739: DL, Jan
10, CG, 19, Mar 13, DL, Apr 5, 23, CG, Aug 10; 1746: DL, Mar 13; 1757: CRT,
Feb 7; 1764: CG, Mar 27; 1771: CG, Apr 27; 1772: DL, Mar 18; 1773: CG, Dec
16; 1776: CG, Feb 3; 1777: HAY, Jun 19; 1782: HAY, Jun 11; 1784: HAY, Aug 10
--Achilles, 1733: LIF/CG, Feb 10, 12, 13, 15, CG, 16, LIF/CG, 17, 19, 20, CG,
22, LIF/CG, 24, 26, 27, Mar 1, 3, 5, 6, 8, 10, 13, Apr 25, CG, May 9, Nov 28;
1734: CG, Feb 28; 1737: CG, Jan 25, 27
--Beggar's Opera, The 1728: LIF, Jan 29, 31, Feb 1, 2, 3, 5, 6, 7, 8, 9, 10,
12, 13, 14, 15, 16, 17, 18, 19, 21, 22, 23, 24, 26, 27, 28, 29, Mar 1, 2, 4,
5, 7, 11, 12, 16, 18, 19, 20, 23, 26, 30, Apr 2, 8, 9, 11, 13, 25, 27, May 1,
4, 7, 9, 10, 16, DL, 17, LIF, 17, 21, 24, 28, 31, Jun 4, 7, 10, 12, 14, 19,
HAY, 24, 26, Jul 3, 8, 10, 15, 22, 24, 29, 31, Aug 5, 7, 14, 16, 20, 22,
BFFR, 24, BFY, 24, SFFR, Sep 6, HAY, 6, SFY, 6, LIF, 13, 20, 23, 25, 27, Oct
4, HAY, 8, 10, LIF, 11, 18, HAY, 24, LIF, 25, 31, Nov 7, HAY, 8, 11, LIF, 14,
15, 21, 28, HAY, 30, LIF, 30, Dec 11, 17, 21, HAY, 23, 30; 1729: LIF, Jan 1,
2, 3, 4, 7, 8, 9, 10, 14, 15, 17, 21, 24, HAY, 25, LIF, 27, Feb 4, 24, 27,
Mar 1, HAY, 5, 8, LIF, 11, HAY, 14, LIF, 20, 24, 25, Apr 7, UM, 7, 15, LIF,
17, 25, HAY, 30, May 1, LIF, 5, 21, HAY, 26, Jul 31, Aug 8, BFRP, 25, LIF,
Oct 1, Nov 6, Dec 3, 17, 31; 1730: LIF, Jan 31, HAY, Mar 18, LIF, 19, 31, GF,
Apr 15, 27, LIF, May 4, RI, Jun 25, LIF, Jul 3, GF, 15, 16, 20, 21, 23, 28,
LIF, Sep 30, GF, Oct 12, 13, LIF, 28, GF, Nov 3, LIF, 20, GF, Dec 2, LIF, 9,
31; 1731: LIF, Jan 22, GF, 27, 28, 29, LIF, Feb 11, GF, 26, Mar 27, LIF, 30,
May 7, Sep 24, Nov 10, GF, 13, 23, LIF, Dec 30; 1732: LIF, Jan 22, HAY, Feb
10, LIF, 21, Mar 7, HAY, 10, 17, GF, May 3, 5, LIF, 23, DL, Jul 11, 14, 18,
21, 25, HAY, 26, DL, 28, Aug 1, 8, 11, 19, 22, RIW/HAY, Sep 4, 6, 8, 12,
LIF/CG, Oct 13, LIF, Nov 15, DL, Dec 16, CG/LIF, 16, 18, DL, 18, CG/LIF, 19,
DL, 19, CG/LIF, 20, 21, 22, 26, 27, 28, 29, 30; 1733: CG/LIF, Jan 1, 2, 3, 4,
5, 6, 8, 9, 10, GF, 24, 25, 26, 29, 31, DL, Feb 10, HAY, 14, Mar 21, 22,
CG/LIF, 26, GF, Apr 3, CG/LIF, 26, May 28, CG, Sep 17, GF, Oct 8, DL, 12, 15,
GF, 17, DL, 22, Nov 6, CG, 15, Dec 1, GF, 26, DL, 26; 1734: CG, Jan 8, DL,
28, GF, Feb 7, LIF, Apr 4, GF, 23, CG, 29, HAY, May 21, LIF, 23, HA, Jun 27,
HAY, Jul 17, Aug 7, 12, CG/LIF, Sep 27; 1735: CG/LIF, Jan 3, GF, 10, Mar 3,
YB, 3, GF, Apr 7, CG/LIF, 8, 22, GF, May 15, YB, 19, LIF, 21, CG/LIF, 30,
HAY, Aug 12, LIF, Sep 2, YB/HAY, 24, CG, Oct 1; 1736: DL, Jan 27, CG, Feb 13,
14, 20, Mar 4, Apr 1, LIF, 20, HAY, Jun 26, Aug 2, DL, Sep 21, CG, Oct 27,
Nov 3, LIF, 16, 17, 19, DL, 19, LIF, 23, CG, Dec 16, 21, DL, 31; 1737: DL,
Jan 1, 4, 5, 7, 8, CG, 14, 20, DL, 20, 22, 28, CG, Feb 10, Mar 15, DL, 19,
CG, Apr 15, DL, May 18, CG, 26, LIF, Jul 29, Aug 2, Sep 7, DL, Oct 25, 26,
28, 29, Nov 9; 1738: DL, Jan 25, Feb 4, Apr 14, CG, 20, DL, 27, May 31, CG,
Sep 1, DL, Oct 25, Nov 22, Dec 20; 1739: DL, Jan 10, CG, 19, Mar 13, DL, Apr
5, 23, CG, 28, DL, May 28, CG, Aug 10, DL, Sep 6, Nov 9; 1740: DL, Jan 29,
Apr 12, CG, 28, DL, May 17, Oct 17, 18, 20, 21, 22, 24, 25, Nov 3, 15, 18,
24, GF, Dec 31; 1741: GF, Jan 1, 2, 3, 5, 6, 7, 8, 9, 10, 12, 13, 14, 27, Feb
3, Apr 8, DL, 22, 29, May 6, GF, 6, DL, 23, Sep 24, 26, 29, Oct 1, 3, JS, 27,
DL, 29, Dec 1, GF, 10, 11, DL, 29; 1742: DL, Jan 12, 23, May 14, GF, 27, DL,
Sep 30, Oct 30, Dec 6; 1743: DL, Jan 14, LIF, Feb 14, 15, DL, 15, LIF, 19,
21, DL, Mar 22, Apr 5, JS, 15, DL, 26, May 10, 19, CG, Nov 7, 9, 11, 12, 23,
Dec 5, 23; 1744: CG, Jan 28, Feb 6, DL, 13, 16, 20, JS, Mar 2, DL, 26, CG,
Apr 25, DL, May 21, NONE, Jun 5, DL, Sep 22, 25, CG, Nov 8, GF, Dec 3, CG, 3,
14, GF, 14, HAY, 26; 1745: GF, Jan 1, CG, 21, HAY, 25, GF, Feb 4, CG, 14,
SMMF, 20, CG, Mar 28, DL, Apr 26, GF, May 1, DL, 8, CG, 29, 31, Sep 30, GF,
Nov 6, 7, 23, CG, 29, DL, 30, Dec 2, 3, CG, 14, 16, 17, DL, 21, CG, 21, DL,
27, NWC, 30; 1746: DL, Jan 13, GF, 15, 22, DL, 27, Feb 3, GF, 5, CG, 10, DL,
11, 25, GF, Mar 4, HIC, 10, CG, 20, 31, Apr 11, DL, 16, CG, 19, DL, May 7,
CG, Jun 9, SOU, Sep 25, DL, 30, Oct 16, 29, GF, Nov 13, DL, 14, GF, Dec 5, 8,
DL, 9, CG, 11, 15, NWC, 22, GF, 29, 30; 1747: GF, Jan 15, DL, 20, GF, 27, CG,
Feb 9, GF, 11, 12, CG, 27, Mar 10, GF, 30, CG, Apr 21, DL, May 13, 25, SF,
Sep 15, DL, 17, CG, Oct 31, Nov 3, 5, 7, 14, SOU, 16, DL, Dec 11, CG, 11, DL,
12, 14, 22, CG, 22; 1748: CG, Jan 1, 26, 27, 28, DL, Mar 28, CG, Apr 14, 23,
DL, May 2, CG, Sep 26, DL, Oct 12, 15, CG, 19, Nov 19, NWC, 21, CG, 29, NWSM,
Dec 29, CG, 29; 1749: SOU, Jan 2, CG, 9, 26, DL, 27, CG, Feb 25, Mar 27, JS,
29, DL, Apr 10, CG, 24, HAY, 29, May 2, 4, 5, 9, 11, CG, 11, HAY, 13, DL, 16,
HAY, 29, 31, Sep 26, BHB, Oct 5, DL, 7, CG, 2 , Nov 14, DL, 29, Dec 27; 1750:
CG, Feb 9, HAY, 9, 16, CG, 17, HAY, 21, CG, 23, HAY, Mar 8, CG, 10, HAY, Apr
17, CG, 20, DL, May 3, 10, Sep 11, CG, Oct 12, DL, 12, 18, Dec 26, CG, 26;
1751: DL, Jan 15, 28, 29, CG, Feb 15, DL, Apr 17, May 13, CG, 14, DL, Sep 7,
SF, 17, CG, 27, 28, 30, Oct 2, 4, 5, 12, 14, 16, 24, 28, 30, Nov 1, 9, 25,
Dec 4, 28; 1752: CG, Jan 16, Feb 5, May 8, Sep 18, DL, Oct 14, CG, 18, Nov 8,
NWLS, 13, DL, 16, CG, 30, DL, Dec 15, CG, 26; 1753: CG, Mar 13, Apr 3, 28,
DL, May 12, Sep 8, CG, 12, Oct 20, Nov 10, DL, Dec 27; 1754: DL, Feb 9, CG,

Mar 21, May 18, DL, 20, CG, Sep 16, DL, Oct 14, 15, 19, CG, Nov 11, 30, DL,
Dec 27; <u>1755</u>: CG, Jan 6, 20, May 17, HAY, Aug 28, Sep 9, DL, 23, CG, Oct 17,
Nov 18; <u>1756</u>: CG, Feb 20, DL, May 8, CG, 21, Sep 22, Nov 3, Dec 29; <u>1757</u>: DL,
Apr 11, CG, 13, DL, May 16, 27, CG, 27, DL, Sep 10, CG, Oct 13, Nov 1, 3, Dec
26; <u>1758</u>: DL, Jan 23, CG, Mar 30, DL, May 11, Jun 22, CG, Oct 9, 11, 19;
<u>1759</u>: CG, Jan 29, 31, Feb 5, 9, Mar 20, DL, May 7, 28, Jun 19, CG, Oct 10,
11, 12, 13, 15, 16, 17, 18, 19, 20, 22, 23, 24, 25, 26, 27, 29, 30, 31, Nov
1, 2, 3, 6, 7, 8, 9, 10, 12, 13, 14, 15, 16, 17, 19, 20, 21, 22, 27, Dec 3;
<u>1760</u>: CG, Jan 5, 8, 12, 17, 25, Feb 1, 8, 12, 21, DL, 21, CG, Mar 24, Apr 10,
May 10, 22, 26, DL, Sep 23, CG, 24, 25, DL, 25, CG, 26, DL, 27, Oct 2, 4, CG,
11, DL, 16, CG, 21, Nov 19, DL, Dec 8, CG, 15; <u>1761</u>: DL, Jan 1, CG, 8, 24,
DL, Mar 14, CG, 27, Apr 8, 9, DL, 20, May 14, CG, 18, DL, Jun 2, Sep 5, CG,
7, 24, Oct 12, 30, DL, Dec 29; <u>1762</u>: CG, Jan 29, Mar 4, DL, Apr 15, CG, 20,
27, May 12, DL, 25, Sep 21, 23, Oct 1, CG, 4, DL, 18, CG, 29, DL, Nov 20, Dec
20; <u>1763</u>: CG, Apr 18, DL, 23, CG, May 4, DL, 23, Sep 17, 29, Oct 4, 11, Nov
5, CG, 22, 29, Dec 9, 28; <u>1764</u>: DL, Feb 16, CG, Mar 22, Apr 24, DL, May 18,
Sep 15, Oct 2, CG, 18, Nov 3; <u>1765</u>: DL, Jan 8, Feb 11, CG, Mar 21, Apr 19,
DL, 24, CG, 27, DL, May 7, CG, 20, DL, Sep 14, CG, Oct 15, Nov 12; <u>1766</u>: DL,
Jan 21, CG, Mar 22, Apr 7, DL, 14, CG, May 5, DL, Sep 25, Oct 2, 13, 20, CG,
Dec 20; <u>1767</u>: CG, Jan 28, DL, Feb 11, CG, Mar 24, DL, Apr 4, CG, 7, 29, May
16, DL, 27, HAY, Aug 5, 7, 10, 17, DL, Sep 16, Oct 12, CG, 13, 15, DL, Dec 4;
<u>1768</u>: CG, Jan 15, Feb 12, DL, Apr 29, CG, 30, May 25, HAY, Jul 27, Aug 1, 10,
Sep 7, DL, 20, CG, Oct 7, DL, Dec 26; <u>1769</u>: CG, Jan 10, May 2, DL, 17, HAY,
Jul 12, 17, Aug 9, 29, DL, Oct 11, CG, Nov 11, 16, 20, Dec 26; <u>1770</u>: DL, Jan
8, 11, CG, Apr 21, DL, 26, CG, May 11, 25, Dec 17, 19; <u>1771</u>: CG, Jan 7, Feb
5, 12, DL, Mar 11, CG, 23, DL, Apr 16, CG, 19, HAY, May 2, DL, Sep 21, CG,
Oct 28, Dec 7, 10, 23, 28; <u>1772</u>: CG, Jan 11, Feb 7, May 20, DL, Sep 22, 24,
29, CG, Oct 13, 15, 29, Nov 17, DL, 21, 24; <u>1773</u>: CG, Jan 21, DL, Feb 9, CG,
22, DL, Mar 18, May 1, Jun 2, Sep 18, CG, Oct 27, Nov 1, 5, Dec 14, 28; <u>1774</u>:
CG, Jan 6, HAY, Apr 4, DL, 14, CG, 22, May 12, 24, DL, 26, CG, 26, HAY, Sep
6, CG, Oct 5, 12, 28, Nov 18; <u>1775</u>: CG, Jan 12, Feb 28, Apr 20, 21, May 16,
HAY, Sep 7, 21, CG, Oct 31; <u>1776</u>: DL, Mar 25, CG, May 4, DL, 6, CG, 18, HAY,
Sep 16, 20, CG, 27, 30, Oct 4, 24, 26, 28; <u>1777</u>: CG, Jan 3, 6, 27, Mar 15,
May 21, HAY, Jun 19, Sep 17, Oct 6, CG, 17, 20, 22, 24, 27, 31, Nov 3, DL, 8,
11, CG, 12, DL, 17, 25, CG, 29, Dec 4, 8, 15, DL, 27, CG, 27; <u>1778</u>: CG, Jan
16, 24, 31, DL, Apr 11, CG, May 1, 2, DL, 11, CG, 14, DL, 25, HAY, Jun 8, 9,
15, 26, Aug 22, CG, Oct 17, Nov 5, Dec 12; <u>1779</u>: DL, Jan 29, Apr 6, CG, 28,
HAY, Aug 27, DL, Oct 5, Nov 2, 13, Dec 18; <u>1780</u>: CG, Feb 8, 12, 19, May 4,
HAY, Jun 5, 8, 9, 10, 12, 17, Aug 30, CG, Sep 21, DL, 21, CG, 22, 25, 29, Oct
16, 25; <u>1781</u>: CG, Jan 9, Feb 27, Apr 24, DL, 26, HAY, Aug 8, 9, 10, 11, 13,
14, 16, 18, 20, 23, 27, 29, 30, Sep 1, 6, 8, 11, 14, DL, Oct 15, CG, 16, DL,
16, 17, CG, 18, DL, Nov 22; <u>1782</u>: DL, Jan 2, Mar 14, CG, Apr 9, DL, 17, 22,
CG, May 4, 6, HAY, Jun 3, 5, 7, 11, 14, 17, 25, Jul 27, Sep 18, CG, Oct 22,
DL, Nov 30; <u>1783</u>: CG, Apr 22, 28, May 3, 13, HAY, Jun 20, CG, Oct 14; <u>1784</u>:
DL, Apr 16, CG, May 1, DL, 15, HAY, 31, Aug 26, 30, DL, Sep 25, Oct 2, 25,
HAY, Dec 13; <u>1785</u>: DL, Jan 5, 21, HAY, 31, DL, Feb 3, HAY, Mar 15, CG, Apr 6,
DL, 15, May 21, HAY, Sep 16, CG, 30, DL, Oct 13, Dec 17; <u>1786</u>: CG, Feb 21,
28, HAY, May 12, DL, 24, HAY, Jul 7, 10, 20, CG, Dec 23, DL, 28; <u>1787</u>: DL,
Feb 22, May 18, Oct 22; <u>1788</u>: DL, Jan 10, 22, CG, Mar 29, HAY, Jun 11; <u>1789</u>:
DL, Jan 8, 15, 29, Feb 12, CG, Mar 3, DL, 5, CG, 7, Apr 29, May 18, HAY, Jun
10, CG, 15, DL, Sep 24, Oct 21, CG, 24, Dec 4; <u>1790</u>: CG, Apr 13, DL, 16, HAY,
Jun 26, Jul 30; <u>1791</u>: CG, Jan 15, 17, 21, 25, Feb 1, Jun 9, HAY, Aug 19, CG,
Sep 20, Nov 12, Dec 8, 31; <u>1792</u>: CG, May 9, Jun 2, HAY, Aug 15, CG, Sep 20;
<u>1793</u>: CG, May 10, Oct 12, 19, Nov 16, Dec 11; <u>1794</u>: CG, Jan 18, May 31, Jun
4; <u>1795</u>: DL, Feb 4, 5, 6, CG, Oct 24, 27, Dec 4; <u>1796</u>: CG, May 3, Dec 27;
<u>1797</u>: CG, Apr 19, May 27, Oct 25, 30, Nov 21; <u>1798</u>: CG, Apr 23, May 21, HAY,
Jun 13, 19, 27, Jul 2, DL, Nov 29, Dec 1, 11, 15; <u>1799</u>: DL, Jul 5, HAY, Aug
10, CG, Sep 18, DL, Oct 19, 26, Nov 12, Dec 17, 27; <u>1800</u>: CG, Jun 10, HAY,
Sep 16
--Captives, The, <u>1724</u>: DL, Jan 10, 15, 16, 17, 18, 20, 21, 22, Feb 4
--Distressed Wife, The, <u>1734</u>: CG, Mar 5, 7, 9, 16; <u>1747</u>: DL, Mar 23; <u>1771</u>: CG,
Apr 27
--Polly (ballad opera), <u>1777</u>: HAY, Jun 19, 20, 23, 25, 30, Jul 2, 4, 9, 22, Aug
15; <u>1782</u>: HAY, Jun 11, 12, 21
--Three Hours after Marriage, <u>1717</u>: DL, Jan 16, 17, 18, 19, 21, 22, 23; <u>1737</u>:
LIF, Aug 5, 9; <u>1746</u>: DL, Mar 13, 15, Apr 10
--What D'ye Call It, The, <u>1715</u>: DL, Feb 23, 24, 25, 26, Mar 1, 5, 7, 14, 19,
21, 26, 28, Apr 2, 4, 5, May 4, 9, Oct 18, 26, Nov 16, 30, Dec 7, 10, 28;
<u>1716</u>: DL, Jan 2, 31, Mar 1, Apr 18, 27, May 21, 23, 30, SF, Sep 25, DL, Oct
17, Nov 1, 13, 27; <u>1717</u>: DL, Feb 5, Apr 4, Oct 24, 29; <u>1718</u>: DL, Mar 11, Apr
1, 14, Jun 4, Oct 21, Nov 10, Dec 30; <u>1719</u>: DL, Apr 14, 17, May 21, Oct 12,
Nov 2; <u>1720</u>: DL, Apr 23, May 26, Oct 14; <u>1722</u>: DL, Apr 7, 13; <u>1723</u>: DL, Jan

8, 19, Apr 17, May 31, Oct 15, 30, Dec 30; 1724: DL, Jan 8, 23, Feb 24, Apr
28, May 21; 1725: DL, Apr 30; 1727: DL, May 2, 19, 26; 1728: DL, May 17;
1729: DL, Jan 22, 27, Feb 5, 17, 20, 24, Mar 3, LIF, 20, 25, DL, Apr 10, 19,
LIF, 21, DL, 22, LIF, 26, DL, May 1, 3, 6, 20, 30, Nov 17, Dec 1; 1730: DL,
Jan 20, LIF, Apr 2, GF, 9, DL, 10, GF, 15, 17, LIF, 24, GF, 27, May 15, 21,
Jun 4, Nov 3; 1731: DL, Mar 15, GF, Apr 1, DL, 1, LIF, 21, DL, 29, May 8,
LIF, 28, DL, Jun 4, Aug 11, 13, 18, Sep 30; 1732: LIF, Feb 7, GF, Apr 14, 17,
24, LIF, May 1, GF, 18, RI, Aug 17, DL, Nov 7; 1733: DL, Feb 3, GF, Apr 24,
May 9; 1735: CG/LIF, Apr 8, GF, 10, 16; 1736: DL, Sep 18, 21; 1737: DL, Mar
4, May 10, 18, 24; 1738: DL, Apr 14; 1739: CG, Jan 16, 19, Mar 13, DL, May 9;
1740: CG, Feb 2, Nov 6; 1741: CG, Dec 16; 1743: DL, Apr 15, CG, Nov 16, 18;
1744: CG, Nov 24; 1745: CG, Apr 3, 4, 22; 1746: CG, Apr 3, May 3, 6, Oct 6,
10, 24, Nov 5, 13; 1748: DL, Feb 3, 4, Mar 21; 1750: CG, Dec 1, 3, 4, 11, 17;
1751: CG, Feb 14, Apr 17, May 8; 1752: CG, Jan 29, Feb 5, Apr 1, 3, May 7,
Oct 2, 9, 24, 31, Dec 8; 1753: CG, Jan 11, Mar 26, 31, Apr 14, 23, Sep 26,
Oct 3, Nov 30; 1754: CG, Mar 30, Sep 30, Oct 17, Dec 13; 1755: CG, Oct 6, 17,
Nov 7, Dec 17, 18, 23; 1756: CG, Sep 29; 1757: CG, Apr 19, Nov 3, 30; 1759:
CG, Apr 23, May 15; 1764: CG, Mar 27, Apr 5; 1769: HAY, May 26, 31, Jun 2;
1772: DL, Apr 20; 1775: CG, Apr 28, May 16; 1782: CG, May 6; 1784: HAY, Aug
10; 1797: CG, Apr 19
--Wife of Bath, The, 1713: DL, May 12, 14, 15; 1730: LIF, Jan 19, 20, 21
Gay, John, sisters of (beneficiaries), 1733: LIF/CG, Feb 13, 19, 24; 1734: CG,
Mar 9
Gay's Head (residence), 1740: DL, May 17
Gayet, Mrs (spectator), 1668: BRIDGES, May 14, 18
Gaylard, Charles James (beneficiary), 1749: JS, Jul 3
Gayward (actor), 1752: SFB, Sep 22
Gazette Extraordinary, A; or, The Illumination. See Pilon, Frederick, The
Illumination.
Gazzaniga, Giuseppe (composer), 1776: KING'S, Mar 28; 1777: KING'S, Apr 17;
1784: HAY, Apr 27; 1786: KING'S, Feb 14; 1787: KING'S, Jan 9; 1789: KING'S,
May 9; 1794: KING'S, Mar 1
--Alcina (L'Isola de Alcina) (opera), 1776: KING'S, Mar 28; 1777: KING'S, Apr
17
--Don Giovanni (opera), 1794: KING'S, Mar 1, 4, 8
--Vendemmia, La, 1789: KING'S, May 9, 12, 14, 16, 23
Gearing, Mrs (toyshop owner), 1742: HAY, Jun 16
Geere, John (author), 1763: DL, Jan 1
Gehot, Joseph (composer, violinist), 1779: CG, Apr 27
Gell (actor), 1795: DL, Nov 20; 1800: HAY, Jul 2
Gelosie Villane, Le. See Sarti, Giuseppe.
Geloso in Cimento, Il. See Anfossi, Pasquale.
Gemelle, Le. See Anfossi, Pasquale.
Geminiani, Francesco (composer), 1718: YB, Dec 10; 1724: HAY, May 8; 1730: DL,
Mar 4; 1732: HIC, Apr 24; 1733: DL/HAY, Oct 13, 20, 27, Dec 1, 20; 1734:
DL/HAY, Jan 4, 10, Feb 4, HIC, Mar 20; 1735: DL, Feb 4, Apr 16, HIC, 17, CG,
May 8, DL, Jun 3, LIF, 19, DL, Dec 6; 1737: DL, May 4, 27; 1742: HAY, Mar 19;
1743: LIF, Mar 15; 1748: HAY, Dec 9; 1750: DL, Mar 16, Apr 11; 1761: SOHO,
Apr 15; 1762: CG, Dec 8; 1763: CG, Oct 22; 1769: CG, Mar 17; 1790: CG, Mar
12; 1791: CG, Apr 15; 1793: CG, Mar 1, 22; 1794: CG, Apr 2; 1795: CG, Mar 6;
1797: CG, Mar 10; 1798: CG, Mar 16
--Inchanted Forest, The (opera), 1761: SOHO, Apr 15
--1st Concerto (1st opera), 1733: DL/HAY, Oct 20
--1st Concerto (2nd opera), 1733: DL/HAY, Oct 13; 1735: DL, Feb 4, Apr 16, Dec
6
--1st Concerto (3rd opera), 1773: DL, Mar 19; 1791: CG, Apr 15; 1794: CG, Apr
2; 1795: CG, Mar 6; 1797: CG, Mar 10; 1798: CG, Mar 16
--3rd Concerto (1st opera), 1734: DL/HAY, Feb 4; 1735: DL, Jun 3
--4th Concerto (2nd opera), 1733: DL/HAY, Oct 27
--6th Concerto (1st opera), 1733: DL/HAY, Dec 1; 1793: CG, Mar 22
Gemmingen, Otto Heinrich Freiherr von, 1794: CG, Feb 5
--Deutsche Hausvater, Der, 1794: CG, Feb 5
Gendon, Mlle (dancer), 1742: DL, Sep 21
General Lying-in Hospital, 1755: KING'S, Apr 17; 1756: KING'S, Apr 29, DL, Dec
18; 1758: KING'S, Apr 26, DL, Dec 20; 1759: CG, Dec 21; 1760: KING'S, May 8;
1761: KING'S, Apr 16, CG, Dec 22; 1762: KING'S, Apr 29, DL, Dec 17; 1763:
KING'S, May 9; 1764: KING'S, May 15; 1765: DL, Dec 18; 1766: CG, Dec 23;
1769: DL, Dec 20; 1771: CG, Dec 20, 30; 1790: DL, May 1; 1797: CG, Jun 21;
1798: CG, Jun 11; 1799: CG, Jun 12; 1800: CG, Jun 13
General Reconcilement (dance), 1741: SF, Sep 14
General View of the Stage, A (book), 1759: CG, Mar 28
General, The. See Boyle, Roger.

Genereux Corsaire (dance), 1741: DL, Oct 21, 22, 23, 26, 27, 28, 30, Nov 2, 6,
    7, 10, 13, 17, 18, 26, Dec 14, 21, 22; 1742: DL, Jan 20, 29, Feb 4, 18, 22,
    Mar 4
Generosita d'Alessandro, La. See Tarchi, Angelo.
Generosite de Scipion (dance), 1776: KING'S, Jan 9, 23, Feb 13, 27, Mar 5
Generous Choice, The. See Manning, Francis.
Generous Conqueror, The. See Higgons, Bevill.
Generous Enemies, The. See Corye, John.
Generous Free-Mason, The. See Chetwood, William Rufus.
Generous Husband, The. See Johnson, Charles.
Generous Impostor, The. See O'Beirne, Thomas Lewis.
Generous Pirate (dance), 1774: CG, Dec 14, 16; 1775: CG, Feb 11
Generous Slave (dance), 1790: HAY, May 13, 27, 28, 29, Jun 1, CG, 15
Generous Sportsman (dance), 1790: HAY, Jun 25, 29, 30, Jul 22, Aug 10, 31
Genii, Ballet of (dance), 1779: KING'S, Feb 23, Mar 2, Apr 15
Genii, The. See Woodward, Henry.
Genius of England (song), 1694: DG, May 0; 1703: DL, Jun 19, Jul 1; 1705: DL,
    Jun 5; 1711: SH, Nov 22; 1715: DL, Aug 19; 1716: DL, Jan 27, Jul 24, Aug 9,
    Oct 30; 1717: LIF, Apr 4, DL, May 30, Jul 4; 1726: LIF, Jun 24, Aug 19, 23;
    1727: LIF, Apr 17, May 3, 19; 1728: LIF, Jul 2; 1739: CG, Nov 7, 9, Dec 12;
    1744: CG, Mar 8; 1745: CG, Oct 18, 21; 1746: CG, Jan 15, Mar 13, 18, Apr 14;
    1748: SOU, Sep 26; 1756: DL, Mar 30; 1798: CG, Feb 28, Mar 9
Genius of Nonsense, The. See Colman the elder, George.
Genlis, Stephanie Felicite Ducrest de Saint Aubin, Comtesse de, 1788: CG, Nov
    28
--Zelie; ou, L'Ingenue, 1788: CG, Nov 28
Genoese Pirate, The. See Cross, John Cartwright.
Genorinij (Genuini), Carlo (machinist), 1761: HAY, Apr 29, RANELAGH, Jun 12
Genteel Dance (dance), 1702: DL, Dec 8; 1706: QUEEN'S, Jun 13
Genteel Round (dance), 1702: DL, Dec 8
Gentili, Giacomo (dancer), 1793: KING'S, Feb 5, 26, Apr 9, 23, Jun 8; 1794:
    KING'S, Jan 11, Mar 1, 4, Apr 1, May 31, DL, Jul 2, KING'S, Dec 6, 20; 1795:
    KING'S, Jan 20, Mar 26, Jun 20; 1796: KING'S, Mar 10, Apr 5, 21, May 12, DL,
    25, KING'S, Jun 2, Jul 7, DL, Oct 1, 29, Nov 8, KING'S, Dec 6, 13, DL, 14,
    26, 27; 1797: DL, Jan 7, KING'S, 10, DL, 12, 31, KING'S, Feb 7, DL, Mar 6,
    KING'S, 11, 28, Apr 6, 25, DL, May 13, 19, 22, KING'S, 25, CG, Jun 14,
    KING'S, 17, Jul 15
Gentle (actor), 1747: RL, Jan 27
Gentle Airs (song), 1789: CG, Mar 20; 1790: DL, Feb 24, CG, 26, DL, Mar 12;
    1791: CG, Mar 23, DL, Apr 13; 1792: CG, Mar 2; 1793: CG, Feb 15, KING/HAY,
    Mar 6, CG, 13, 20; 1794: CG, Mar 7, DL, Apr 4; 1795: CG, Feb 20, Mar 27;
    1796: CG, Feb 26; 1797: CG, Mar 10; 1798: CG, Mar 9, 30; 1799: CG, Feb 20;
    1800: CG, Feb 28
Gentle Jessica (song), 1743: JS, Apr 25
Gentle Parthenissa (song), 1743: DL, Apr 15
Gentle Shepherd, The (song), 1745: DL, Mar 16, Apr 4, 6, 16, 17, 25, 27, May 6,
    13; 1746: DL, Mar 22
Gentle Shepherd, The. See Vanderstop, Cornelius; Tickell, Richard.
Gentle Shepherd, The; or, Patie and Roger. See Ramsay, Allan.
Gentle Sighs (song), 1728: LIF, Jul 2
Gentle Soldier oft you've told me (song), 1793: CG, Mar 23, Apr 3, 9, May 6
Gentleman and Porter Tavern, 1750: DL, Feb 21
Gentleman Cully, The. See Johnson, Charles.
Gentleman Dancing Master, The. See Wycherley, William.
Gentleman Gardiner, The. See Wilder, James.
Gentleman of Venice, The. See Shirley, James.
Gentleman, Francis (actor), 1751: DL, Nov 26; 1752: CG, Mar 6; 1769: DL, Mar
    11, HAY, Sep 19; 1770: HAY, May 16, 18, 30, Jun 18, 22, 25, Jul 25, Aug 8,
    Sep 27, Oct 15, 29; 1771: HAY, May 15, 22, 23, 27, Jun 7, 10, Jul 15, Aug 12,
    19, 26, 28, Sep 2, 16, 20; 1772: DL, Apr 21, HAY, May 22, 27, Jun 8, 29, Jul
    27, Sep 8; 1773: HAY, Sep 3, 18
--Coxcombs, The, 1771: HAY, Sep 16
--Cupid's Revenge, 1772: HAY, Jul 27, 29, 31, Aug 3, 12, 14, 17, 24, 26, 28,
    Sep 2, 7, 11, 15; 1773: HAY, Jun 4, 14, 21
--Modish Wife, The; or, Love in a Puzzle, 1773: HAY, Sep 18; 1780: HAY, Jan 3
--Pantheonites, The, 1773: HAY, Sep 3, 9; 1774: DL, Mar 26, May 5
--Sejanus, 1751: DL, Nov 26
--Tobacconist, The, 1770: HAY, Oct 15; 1771: HAY, Jul 15, 22, Aug 12, Sep 4,
    10, 16, 20; 1772: DL, Apr 21; 1773: DL, Apr 17, HAY, Aug 4, 23, 31; 1775:
    HAY, Sep 19, 21, Oct 30; 1782: HAY, Mar 21; 1784: HAY, Jun 5, 8, 19; 1798:
    CG, Nov 22; 1799: CG, Apr 2; 1800: HAY, Jul 15, 26
Gentleman, The. See Steele, Sir Richard.

Gently Touch the Warbling Lyre (song), 1728: LIF, May 8, 13, 16, 18
Genuini, Charlo. See Genorinij, Carlo.
Geoghegan (printer), 1789: KHS, Sep 16
George (actor), 1745: SMMF, Feb 28; 1748: BFLYY, Aug 24; 1749: SOU, Jan 2, SOU,
    9; 1763: CG, Nov 15; 1764: CG, Jan 14, 16
George (boxkeeper), 1789: DL, Jun 10; 1790: DL, Jun 4; 1791: DL, May 28; 1792:
    DLKING'S, Jun 14; 1793: DL, Jun 5; 1795: DL, May 30; 1796: DL, Jun 14; 1797:
    DL, Jun 14; 1798: DL, Jun 15; 1799: DL, Jul 4, Oct 7; 1800: DL, Jun 17
George and Vulture Tavern, 1732: GV, Feb 10
George Barnwell. See Lillo, George, The London Merchant.
George for England; or, The Triumphs of Roast Beef (droll, anon), 1761: SFW,
    Sep 19, 21
George I, 1753: CG, Nov 12; 1758: CG, Mar 22; see also Highness; King, the;
    Majesty
George II, 1742: DL, Oct 28; 1744: HAY, May 10; 1747: CG, Feb 12; 1759: CG, Dec
    13; 1760: CG, Oct 25, DL, 25, Nov 17; 1761: CG, May 25, Jun 23, Nov 4; 1786:
    NONE, Nov 1; see also Highness; King, the; Majesty
George III and Queen, 1763: DL, Jan 13
George III, 1741: CG, Feb 28, Mar 7, DL, Apr 21, CG, 24, May 15; 1743: CG, Apr
    26; 1744: CG, Feb 1, May 10; 1745: HAY, Mar 5, CG, 11, 28, May 4; 1746: CG,
    Nov 28; 1747: CG, May 14; 1748: CG, Oct 25, Nov 10, Dec 21; 1749: LEI, Jan 7,
    CG, Feb 9, 27, May 4, Dec 16; 1750: CG, Mar 10, 12; 1754: CG, Jan 3; 1760:
    DL, Jan 12, CG, Mar 1, DL, Nov 17; 1761: BFY, Aug 31; 1762: DL, Nov 23; 1763:
    CG, Apr 26; 1767: DL, Dec 14; 1768: CG, Jun 4, Oct 20; 1769: DL, Jan 12;
    1773: DL, Nov 8; 1779: KING'S, Mar 23; 1788: CG, Dec 15; 1790: NONE, Sep 18;
    1794: HAY, Aug 20; 1799: CG, Jun 12; see also Highness; Majesty; King, the;
    Wales, Prince of
George Inn, 1725: BF, Aug 23; 1732: BF, Aug 22; 1733: BF, Aug 23; 1738: BFH,
    Aug 23; 1741: BFH, Aug 22; 1742: BFHC, Aug 25; 1743: BFHC, Aug 23; 1746: BF,
    Aug 23; 1747: BFH, Aug 22; 1748: BF, Aug 24; 1749: BFYT, Aug 23, BFY, 23;
    1753: BFGI, Sep 3, 4, 5; 1754: BFYJN, Sep 3, 4, 5, 6; 1755: BFGT, Sep 3, 5;
    1756: BFGR, Sep 3; 1757: BFG, Sep 5, 6; 1758: BFDVW, Sep 2; 1759: BFS, Sep 3;
    1760: BFS, Sep 3, 4, 5, 6; 1761: BFG, Sep 1, 2, 3, 4, 5, 7
George St, 1736: CG, Apr 27; 1779: CG, Apr 20; 1786: CG, Mar 14; 1787: CG, Apr
    11; 1788: CG, Mar 28; 1797: DL, Jun 6
George Tavern, 1672: WF, Dec 30; 1738: GT, May 1; 1746: GF, Mar 11; 1784: HAY,
    Feb 9; 1789: WHF, Nov 9; 1791: HAY, Oct 24
George, James (actor), 1785: HAY, Apr 25; 1789: WHF, Nov 9
George, John (house servant), 1741: DL, May 23; 1743: DL, May 24; 1745: DL, May
    8; 1746: DL, May 16
George, Master (actor), 1774: CG, Nov 19, Dec 27; 1775: CG, Mar 30
George, Miss (actor, singer), 1783: HAY, Jun 2, 27, Jul 16, 30, Aug 1, 12, 15,
    26, 27, 29, DL, Sep 25, Oct 7, 30, Nov 4, 18, Dec 5; 1784: DL, Jan 3, Feb 27,
    Mar 5, 30, Apr 12, 14, 26, 28, 30, May 3, 5, 7, 12, 17, 18, 20, HAY, Jun 19,
    Jul 7, 24, 28, Aug 2, 3, 5, 10, 24, DL, Oct 7, 14, Nov 12, 19, 22, 26; 1785:
    DL, Feb 2, 8, 11, 19, CG, Mar 12, DL, 28, Apr 6, 14, HAY, May 28, Jun 9, 18,
    Jul 7, 9, 19, 20, Aug 2, 23, Sep 5, DL, Oct 1, 29; 1786: DL, Jan 5, 6, Mar 3,
    4, 10, 22, 24, 29, Apr 4, 25, May 10, 15, HAY, Jun 19, Jul 11, 12, 18, 19,
    20, Aug 3, 12, 15, 29; 1787: DL, Feb 23, Mar 7, HAY, May 16, Jun 20, 21, 26,
    Jul 2, 13, 16, 21, 23, Aug 3, 4, 10, 14, 17, 20, 21; 1788: DL, Feb 8, 20, 22,
    Mar 5; 1789: HAY, May 18, 27, Jun 3, 5, 10, 12, 25, 29, Jul 7, 29, 31, Aug
    11, 12, 27, Sep 12, 15
George, Mrs (actor), 1743: DL, Nov 14; 1744: DL, May 16, HAY, Sep 25, 27, 29,
    Oct 11; 1745: JS, Mar 8; 1749: SOU, Jan 2, 9
George, Sg and Sga (dancers), 1767: DL, Apr 4
George's Coffee House, 1742: GF, Apr 22; 1744: DL, Mar 10; 1747: HAY, Apr 25;
    1752: DL, Nov 15, CG, Dec 12, DL, 19; 1753: DL, May 22; 1758: DL, Mar 10;
    1763: DL, Apr 27; 1784: HAY, Mar 22
Georges Dandin. See Moliere.
Georgia, 1735: HAY, Jun 12
Gerard (dancer), 1753: DL, Mar 26, 31, Sep 13, Oct 12, 13, 24, Nov 26, Dec 19;
    1754: DL, May 2, 15
Gerard, Charles, Earl of Macclesfield, 1663: SH, Jan 6
Gerardy. See Gherardi.
Geree (Garee), John (beneficiary), 1710: CDR, Feb 24; 1711: SH, Jan 11; 1712:
    SH, Feb 7
Gerilda. See Jackson, John, The British Heroine.
German Baron, 1667: BRIDGES, Aug 12; 1776: KING'S, Apr 16
German Camp (dance), 1746: DL, Dec 4, 5, 10, 12, 15, 17, 19, 22; 1747: DL, Jan
    14, 16, 19
German clockworks (entertainment), 1663: BF, Sep 4; 1752: SFB, Sep 22
German Coopers (dance), 1761: HAY, Jun 23, Jul 30, Aug 3

German Flute (music), 1706: YB, Feb 12; 1712: B&S, Nov 24; 1715: GRT, Apr 25;
1717: HIC, May 3; 1718: SH, Dec 23; 1719: HIC, Feb 13, 18; 1720: HIC, Mar 4,
YB, Apr 1, DL, May 24; 1728: LIF, Apr 29, May 6; 1731: GF, Jan 13; 1732: LIF,
Feb 25, HIC, Mar 27; 1733: SH, Mar 19; 1734: SH, Mar 28; 1735: ST, Nov 26;
1741: HIC, Feb 27, Mar 6, 13; 1744: HAY, Oct 4, 18; 1745: CT, Jan 14, DT, Mar
14, SMMF, Jul 11; 1752: CT/HAY, May 5; 1761: HAY, Feb 5; 1762: DL, Mar 31;
1769: HAY, Feb 9; 1772: KING'S, Feb 21; 1774: DL, Oct 6; 1778: KING'S, Apr 4;
1796: CG, Apr 15
German Flute and Violin Sonata (music), 1732: LIF, Mar 10
German Flute Concerto (music), 1720: LIF, Mar 12; 1733: GF, Apr 13; 1735: GF,
Sep 29; 1737: DL, May 4, 27; 1741: HAY, Mar 13, KING'S, 14; 1742: DL, Sep 16,
28; 1743: DL, Jan 4, 6, 7, 15, 17, 19, 22, 25, 27, 29, Feb 1, 5, KING'S, Mar
30, DL, Apr 9, 11, 12, 13, 15, 16, 20, May 23, 24, 26; 1744: SH, Feb 9, HAY,
20, KING'S, Mar 28, CG, Apr 26, HAY, Nov 5; 1748: CG, Apr 26; 1751: DL, Apr
11, 16; 1757: KING'S, Mar 24; 1758: DL, Mar 10; 1759: CG, May 4; 1762: DL,
Feb 26, HAY, Mar 16, Apr 22, May 20; 1765: HAY, Mar 11; 1766: KING'S, Apr 10;
1768: HAY, Mar 4, 18; 1769: HAY, Feb 15; 1770: KING'S, Jun 12; 1771: KING'S,
Feb 8, CG, 20; 1772: KING'S, Feb 21, HAY, Mar 23, Apr 27; 1773: KING'S, Feb
5, HAY, Mar 17; 1774: KING'S, Feb 10; 1775: KING'S, Jan 26; 1776: KING'S, Feb
15, CG, 23, Mar 6, 13, 15, 22; 1778: CG, Mar 6, 25, Apr 3
German Flute Lesson (music), 1709: SH, Aug 25
German Flute Solo (music), 1712: SH, Dec 30; 1715: GRT, Apr 25; 1718: LR, Dec
3; 1722: HAY, May 11; 1729: LIF, Mar 12, 19, DL, 26, LIF, Apr 15, 30, HIC,
30; 1732: GF, Apr 27, May 4, HAY, Jun 1; 1733: HAY, May 26; 1734: HIC, Mar
20, Apr 8; 1735: HAY, Apr 28, GF, Oct 10; 1736: MR, Feb 11, GF, Apr 27; 1737:
DT, Mar 16, CT, Apr 29; 1743: SOU, Mar 30; 1745: HAY, Feb 14; 1748: HAY, Apr
20, Dec 9; 1755: HAY, Feb 13; 1761: HAY, Jan 28; 1772: HAY, Mar 30; 1777: CG,
Feb 28
German Harp (music), 1720: LIF, Feb 27
German Horn Solo (music), 1733: DL, Oct 22
German Hotel, The. See Marshall, James.
German Hunters (dance), 1758: DL, Sep 16, 19, Dec 6, 18; 1759: DL, Jan 13, 19,
May 15
German Hussar (dance), 1742: DL, Apr 8
German Jew; or, The Pedlars (dance), 1749: DL, Dec 9
German Peasant (dance), 1736: DL, May 8
German performers, 1679: SLINGSBY, Nov 20; 1698: SF, Sep 17; 1719: LIF, Jan 22;
1720: LIF, Dec 7; 1726: BFS, Aug 24; 1728: HAY, Apr 3; 1734: DL, Feb 22;
1770: MARLY, Sep 20; 1791: CG, Dec 10; 1798: CG, Dec 11
German Princess, The. See Holden, John.
German Smith (dance), 1765: HAY, Sep 9
German Song (song), 1773: MARLY, Jul 29; 1774: MARLY, Jun 16; 1788: KING'S, Jun
19
German visitors, 1680: EVELYN, Sep 23
Germany, Emperor of, 1728: DL, Sep 28
Germany, 1704: CC, Jun 1; 1724: HIC, Dec 21; 1729: LIF, Feb 7; 1732: HAY, Feb
16, TTT, Mar 10; 1734: GF, May 13; 1754: CG, Nov 4
Germondo. See Traetta, Tommaso.
Gerrard St, 1736: CG, Apr 29; 1754: KING'S, Apr 25; 1778: DL, May 14; 1779: DL,
May 15; 1780: DL, May 10; 1785: DL, Apr 7, May 6; 1790: CG, Feb 11, May 5;
1791: CG, May 14; 1798: KING'S, May 10; 1799: KING'S, Apr 18; 1800: KING'S,
May 8
Gerrard, Miss (actor), 1733: GF, Oct 23, 26, Dec 8, 26; 1734: GF, Jan 2, 7, 8,
12, 18, Apr 26, May 1, BFHBH, Aug 24, GF, Oct 11, 16, 17, 28; 1735: GF, Jan
24, Mar 6, Apr 7, 22, 23, 28, May 5, 8, 15, Sep 26, Nov 17, 26, Dec 8, 17;
1736: GF, Feb 5, 10, 17, 20, Mar 3, 18, HAY, Jun 26, SF, Sep 7, LIF, 28, 30,
Oct 9, 14, 21, Dec 3, 7, 16, 28; 1737: LIF, Feb 1; 1739: BFH, Aug 23; 1740:
GF, Oct 31, Nov 1, 18, 19
Gerum (actor), 1735: LIF, Aug 22
Gervasia (musician), 1768: HAY, Mar 3
Get you hence! (song), 1790: CG, Feb 11
Gething (singer), 1724: DL, Oct 14, 20; 1725: DL, Apr 22, SH, 30
Gevan. See Jevon.
Geves's (householder), 1749: CG, Apr 28
Ghendi (dancer), 1763: HAY, Aug 1
Ghent, 1711: DL, Apr 3
Gherardi (Guerardy) (author), 1725: HAY, Jan 1, 4, 8, 22; 1726: HAY, Apr 14,
May 2
--Retour de la Foire, La (farce), 1718: LIF, Dec 19; 1721: HAY, Jan 12
Gherardi (dancer), 1760: KING'S, Aug 25, Nov 22, Dec 16; 1761: KING'S, Jan 6,
Mar 9, Apr 28, HAY, Jun 23, Aug 6; 1763: HAY, Aug 3, 5; 1764: DL, Jan 13, May
23, HAY, Jun 28, Jul 10, 23, 27, Sep 1, KING'S, Nov 24; 1768: HAY, May 30

Gherardi, Master (dancer), 1764: DL, May 23, HAY, Jun 26, Jul 30, Aug 24
Gherardi, Pietro (singer), 1780: KING'S, Mar 28, Apr 13, May 9, 25, Nov 25, 28,
    Dec 19; 1781: KING'S, Feb 22, Mar 8, Apr 5, Jun 5
Gherardi, Teresa (singer), 1782: KING'S, Nov 2, 14, Dec 19; 1783: KING'S, Jan
    14, 16, Feb 18, 27, Mar 6, 27, Apr 29, May 1, Jun 3, 14
Gherardi's scholars (dancer), 1761: HAY, Jul 16
Gheri (dancer), 1799: DL, Dec 2; 1800: DL, Jun 2
Ghizziello. See Conti, Gioachino.
Ghost, The; or, The Dead Man Alive (farce, anon), 1769: DL, Apr 10, Oct 4;
    1770: DL, Nov 23; 1771: DL, Jan 9, 17, Feb 5, HAY, Apr 20; 1778: CHR, Jun 19,
    26; 1781: HAY, Oct 16; 1783: CG, Apr 23, May 21; 1785: HAMM, Jul 22; 1786:
    HAY, Aug 25; 1787: HAY, Aug 28; 1793: DL, Jan 21, 24, 25; 1795: CG, Oct 19;
    1796: CG, Jan 4, 6; 1797: CG, Feb 18, May 4, Nov 7, Dec 21; 1798: CG, Mar 17,
    HAY, 26, CG, 27, Oct 30, Nov 12; 1799: CG, Nov 9; 1800: CG, Feb 6, May 24
Ghosts of every Occupation (song), 1734: HIC, Jul 10
Ghosts of the Elysian Fields (dance), 1735: HAY, Apr 11
Ghosts, The. See Holden, John.
Giacomazzi (singer), 1768: KING'S, Nov 5, 8
Giacomazzi, Margarita (singer), 1749: CG, Mar 6; 1750: KING'S, Mar 31, Apr 10
Giacomo, Giorgio (singer), 1716: KING'S, Feb 1; see also Berwillibald, Giorgio
    Giacomo
Gianguir (pastiche), 1742: KING'S, Nov 2, 6, 9
Giani (dancer), 1791: DLKING'S, Nov 5, Dec 31; 1796: KING'S, Jul 7, 12
Giani, Sga (actor), 1789: KING'S, Jun 11
Giannina e Bernardone. See Cimarosa, Domenico.
Giant and Dwarf, The; or, Columbine Captive (pantomime, anon), 1798: HAY, Sep
    17
Giant Defeated, The; or, The Reward of Valour (pantomime, anon), 1789: CG, Jun
    12
Giant, Italian (actor), 1760: DL, Apr 14; 1762: CG, Mar 30, Nov 29; 1767: CG,
    May 5, Oct 22, Nov 19; 1768: CG, Sep 24; 1769: CG, Mar 28
Giant, Staffordshire (actor), 1759: HAY, Oct 1
Giardini, Feliae. See DeGiardini, Felice.
Giardinier Italienne, La (dance), 1785: HAY, Jul 1
Giay (musician), 1733: DL/HAY, Oct 6, 20
Gibbin-Mrs Violante Booth, 1726: SF, Sep 7
Gibbon (tumbler), 1713: TEC, Nov 26
Gibbon, Edward (author), 1774: CG, Jan 29
Gibbon, James Deavon (actor), 1797: DL, Nov 7, 23, 25, Dec 8, 9, 14, 18; 1798:
    DL, Feb 13, Mar 3, 22, May 21, 23, 24, Jun 13, 15, 18
Gibbons (actor), 1786: HAMM, Jun 28, Jul 5, 10, 19, 24, 26
Gibbons, Mrs (dancer), 1754: DL, May 2; 1755: DL, May 3, Nov 8; 1756: DL, May
    7; 1757: DL, May 18
Gibbons, Mrs (singer), 1767: MARLY, Sep 18
Gibbons' Tennis Court, 1660: VERE, Nov 8, VERE/RED, 20
Gibbs (actor), 1759: CG, Mar 20, Apr 7, May 3, Nov 5, Dec 10; 1760: CG, Jan 31,
    Feb 14, 18, Mar 6, 17, May 2, 3, 14, Sep 22
Gibbs (pit keeper), 1732: LIF, May 12, GF, 19; 1733: GF, May 21; 1734: GF, May
    20; 1736: GF, May 3
Gibbs (treasurer), 1719: LIF, May 5; 1720: LIF, May 5
Gibbs, Anne (actor), 1661: REDBULL, Mar 23, LIF, Jul 3, 4, 5, 8, Sep 11, Dec
    16; 1662: LIF, Sep 30; 1663: LIF, Jan 6, Feb 23; 1672: ATCOU/DG, Dec 2; 1676:
    DG, Jun 8, Jul 25, Aug 0, Nov 4, Dec 0; 1677: DG, Feb 12, Sep 0; 1678: DG,
    Jan 0, 17, Apr 5, May 28
Gibbs, Henry (policeman), 1750: KING'S, May 16
Gibbs, Maria (actor), 1787: ROY, Jun 20; 1788: DL, Jun 2; 1793: HAY, Jun 15,
    21, Jul 18, 19, Aug 12, Sep 21, 24, Oct 1, 4, 5, 8, 10, 15, 22, 24, 29, Nov
    5, 16, 19, 23; 1794: HAY, Jan 14, Feb 22, Mar 13, Jul 9, 10, 11, 14, 16, Aug
    4, 9, 13, 18, Sep 1, 17, DL, 27; 1795: DL, Jan 22, HAY, Jun 9, 12, 15, 22,
    Jul 1, 8, 16, 22, 30, 31, Aug 3, 7, 21, Sep 2, DL, Oct 8, Dec 2, 9; 1796: DL,
    Jan 23, Mar 12, HAY, Jun 17, 18, 22, 29, Jul 6, 7, 8, 9, 11, 21, 26, 30, Aug
    3, 8, 10, 13, 29, Sep 5, DL, Nov 22, Dec 29; 1797: HAY, Jun 12, 13, 16, 17,
    20, 21, 23, 24, 29, Jul 3, 6, 15, Aug 8, 10, 14, Sep 9, CG, Oct 16, 28, Nov
    8, Dec 12; 1798: CG, Feb 13, Apr 18, 20, 24, May 8, HAY, Jun 12, 14, 15, 16,
    18, 21, Jul 5, 6, 16, 21, 25, 30, Aug 3, 6, 13, 14, 27, 31, Sep 10, CG, 17,
    19, 21, 26, 28, Oct 5, Dec 8; 1799: CG, Jan 25, Mar 5, 14, Apr 6, 23, HAY,
    Jun 17, 19, 20, 21, 24, 25, 29, Jul 6, 11, 20, 27, 30, Aug 5, 13; 1800: CG,
    Apr 26, HAY, Jun 13, 14, 16, 18, 21, 28, Jul 1, 5, 7, Aug 7, 8, 15, 20, 29,
    Sep 1, 3, 10
Gibetti, Sga (singer), 1766: KING'S, Oct 21, Nov 25; 1767: KING'S, Jan 31
Gibraltar. See Dennis, John.
Gibson (actor), 1780: HAY, Mar 28

Gibson (boxkeeper), <u>1780</u>: DL, May 25; <u>1781</u>: DL, May 12; <u>1782</u>: DL, May 4; <u>1783</u>:
DL, May 31; <u>1784</u>: DL, May 24; <u>1785</u>: DL, May 23; <u>1786</u>: DL, May 29; <u>1787</u>: DL,
Jun 4; <u>1788</u>: DL, Jun 12; <u>1789</u>: DL, Jun 12; <u>1790</u>: DL, Jun 5; <u>1791</u>: DL, Jun 1;
<u>1792</u>: DLKING'S, Jun 16; <u>1793</u>: DL, Jun 7; <u>1795</u>: DL, May 30; <u>1796</u>: DL, Jun 14;
<u>1797</u>: DL, Jun 14; <u>1798</u>: DL, Jun 2
Gibson (jeweller), <u>1796</u>: DL, May 27
Gibson Jr, <u>1730</u>: SOU, May 18
--Love at First Sight, <u>1730</u>: SOU, May 18
--Perfidious Brother, The, <u>1730</u>: SOU, May 18
Gibson, William (actor), <u>1739</u>: CG, Sep 17, Oct 1, 4, Nov 6, 20, Dec 10; <u>1740</u>:
CG, Jan 15, Feb 6, Mar 11, 24, Apr 14, 21, 25, 28, May 3, 5, 7, 9, 13, 16,
21, 23, Jun 5, Sep 26, Oct 3, 8, 24, 31, Nov 1, 6, 15, 20, Dec 4, 5; <u>1741</u>:
CG, Jan 2, 7, 15, 19, 22, 23, 27, 28, Feb 2, 7, 16, 26, Mar 5, 9, 12, Apr 1,
11, 17, 30, May 1, 8, 12, Sep 23, 25, Oct 2, 5, 7, 8, 10, 13, 15, 20, 21, Nov
4, 9, 11, 26, Dec 5, 7, 8, 9, 17, 18; <u>1742</u>: CG, Jan 2, Feb 2, 8, 22, 25, Mar
13, 18, Apr 1, 26, May 5, 7, Sep 22, Oct 1, 6, 9, 11, 13, 15, 18, 19, 25, 26,
27, Nov 3, 4, 13, 20, 30, Dec 7, 15, 22; <u>1743</u>: CG, Jan 5, SOU, Feb 18, 25,
CG, Apr 26, May 2, 4, 5, Sep 21, 28, 30, Oct 3, 7, 12, 14, 17, 19, 28, 31,
Nov 2, 4, 16, 19, 21, 28, Dec 3, 8, 12, 17, 19, 27, 31; <u>1744</u>: CG, Jan 7, 11,
24, Feb 3, 28, Mar 8, 13, Apr 19, 23, May 14, Oct 1, 3, 5, 8, 10, 15, 16, 18,
20, 22, 24, 26, 31, Nov 5, 7, 9, 21, 27, Dec 13, 21, 28; <u>1745</u>: CG, Jan 1, 4,
18, Feb 11, 15, Apr 4, 20, 23, 26, Sep 23, 25, 27, Oct 4, 7, 11, 14, 16, 31,
Nov 4, 7, 11, 14, 15, 19, 22, 28, Dec 6, 10, 12, 13; <u>1746</u>: CG, Jan 1, 7, 11,
13, 23, Feb 3, 5, 8, 17, Mar 10, 13, 15, Apr 1, 3, 21, 23, Sep 29, Oct 4, 10,
13, 20, 22, 24, 27, 29, Nov 4, 6, 8, 18, 26, 28, Dec 6, 22, 26, 29; <u>1747</u>: CG,
Jan 20, 26, 31, Feb 3, Mar 7, 17, May 20, Nov 11, 18, 23, Dec 4, 9, 15, 19,
28; <u>1748</u>: CG, Jan 2, 11, 12, 14, 16, 21, 27, 29, Feb 10, 29, Mar 8, 14, 24,
Apr 11, 13, 15, 16, 18, 22, 27, 29, May 3, Sep 21, 28, 30, Oct 3, 10, 14, 17,
22, 25, 27, 29, Nov 4, 9, 15, 16, 24, 26, Dec 20; <u>1749</u>: CG, Feb 4, 23, Mar 2,
6, 13, 14, 29, 31, Apr 5, 6, 11, 17, 21, May 4, Sep 25, 27, Oct 2, 6, 9, 12,
16, 18, 19, 23, 25, 26, 30, Nov 3, 8, 9, 11, 17, 18, 23, Dec 7; <u>1750</u>: CG, Jan
16, 18, 23, Feb 5, 22, Mar 1, Apr 3, 5, 21, 30, Sep 24, 26, 28, Oct 16, 18,
20, 22, 23, 24, 25, 26, 29, Nov 1, 8, 12, 17, 19, 22, 24, 29, Dec 1, 4, 14;
<u>1751</u>: CG, Jan 10, Feb 23, Apr 11, 22, May 1, 16, Oct 7, 8, 11, 17, 19, 25,
29, Nov 4, 6, 14, 16, 18, 21, 22, 26, Dec 5, 10, 14, 16; <u>1752</u>: CG, Jan 6, 18,
Mar 3, 16, DL, 17, CG, 17, 30, Apr 4, 28, May 4, Dec 27; <u>1753</u>: CG, Sep 26,
Oct 5, 10, 22, Nov 5, 9, 12, 14, 28, Dec 26; <u>1754</u>: CG, Apr 6, 17, 24, May 3,
6, 7, 21, Sep 20, 23, 25, 27, Oct 2, 4, 9, 11, 14, 17, 26, Nov 4, 12, 16, 20,
23, 28, Dec 10, 30; <u>1755</u>: CG, Jan 8, 10, 24, 28, Feb 18, Mar 6, 22, Apr 8,
10, 18, May 15, Oct 3, 6, 8, 11, 14, 20, 22, 27, Nov 4, 7, 10, 11, 14, 17,
Dec 3, 5; <u>1756</u>: CG, Jan 6, 15, Feb 9, 19, Mar 23, 25, 27, Apr 3, 20, May 17,
Sep 20, 24, 27, Oct 4, 6, 8, 14, 16, 18, 19, 23, 25, 26, Nov 4, 9, 11, 17,
18, 22; <u>1757</u>: CG, Jan 27, Sep 16, 21, 23, 28, 30, Oct 5, 10, 15, Nov 4, 5, 9,
11, 14, Dec 1, 6, 7, 10, 20; <u>1758</u>: CG, Feb 1, Mar 11, 14, 29, Apr 3, 14, 17,
Sep 25, Oct 2, 4, 20, 26, 27, Nov 1, 2, 4, 7, 9, 14, 18, 21, 23; <u>1759</u>: CG,
Feb 1, 15, Mar 3, 17, May 3, 8, 11, Sep 26, Nov 5, 28, 30, Dec 8, 28, 31;
<u>1760</u>: CG, Jan 9, Feb 7, 28, Mar 20, 25, Apr 8, 17, 18, 22, 24, 29, May 2, 7,
8, 19, Sep 22, Oct 1, 10, 18, Nov 18, 20, 29, Dec 9, 31; <u>1761</u>: CG, Jan 6, 10,
23, Feb 16, Mar 3, 5, 9, 30, Apr 2, 13, 17, 21, 29, May 11, Jun 23, Sep 14,
21, 25, Oct 1, 3, 6, 10, 13, 14, 17, 20, 21, 22, 24, Nov 4, 9, 13, Dec 11,
28, 30; <u>1762</u>: CG, Jan 18, 20, 22, 25, Feb 3, 22, 25, Mar 9, 20, 23, Apr 24,
28, May 4, 6, 11, 14, Sep 24, 27, 30, Oct 2, 9, 12, 16, 19, HAY, 25, CG, Nov
3, 23, 29, Dec 4, 27; <u>1763</u>: CG, Jan 14, May 14, HAY, Aug 5, 22, CG, Sep 26,
Oct 5, 7, 11, 19, Nov 10, 16, 18, 26, Dec 26; <u>1764</u>: CG, Jan 16, 17, Feb 1,
11, 13, 15, Mar 27, Apr 14, May 5, 7, 21, 23, Sep 19, 26, Oct 3, 8, 16, 19,
22, 24, 26, 29, Nov 6, 15, 29, 30, Dec 7; <u>1765</u>: CG, Jan 5, 8, 10, 14, 21, 31,
Feb 18, Mar 26, Apr 11, 16, May 11, 15, 24, Sep 16, 18, 20, 23, 30, Oct 2, 4,
7, 8, 9, 12, 14, 23, 26, 28, Nov 13, 20, 22, 27, Dec 3, 12; <u>1766</u>: CG, Jan 31,
Feb 5, 6, 13, Mar 17, 31, Apr 1, 12, 14, May 6, Sep 22, 26, Oct 6, 10, 21,
22, 23, 25, 30, 31, Nov 19, 25, Dec 4, 9, 10; <u>1767</u>: CG, Jan 23, 29, Feb 21,
28, Mar 2, 21, 23, 28, 31, Apr 24, 25, May 11, Sep 14, 16, 17, 21, 22, 23,
25, Oct 5, 8, 16, 19, 26, Nov 6, 7, 17, 23, Dec 5, 26, 28; <u>1768</u>: CG, Jan 20,
Feb 20, 25, Mar 8, Apr 13, 15, 20, 25, May 13, 24, Sep 19, 20, 21, 22, 26,
28, Oct 6, 10, 14, 17, 21, 22, Nov 4, 9, 17, 24; <u>1769</u>: CG, Jan 2, 14, 28, Mar
16, 28, Apr 7, 11, May 3, Sep 18, 22, 25, 27, 29, 30, Oct 4, 6, 18, 26, 27,
Nov 3, 15, 17, 27, Dec 7, 19, 22, 29; <u>1770</u>: CG, Jan 19, Feb 16, 23, Mar 24,
31, Apr 23, 24, 25, 30, May 1, 8, 9, Sep 26, 28, Oct 1, 2, 8, 10, 16, 18, 23,
25, 27, 29, Nov 8, 17, 23, 29, Dec 3, 13; <u>1771</u>: CG, Jan 25, 28, Apr 5, 10,
12, May 16
Gideon. See Handel, George Frederic.
Giffard, Ann Marcella, Mrs Henry (actor), <u>1729</u>: GF, Nov 4, 7, 8, 10, 17, 21,
24, Dec 1, 3, 8, 20; <u>1730</u>: GF, Jan 9, 13, 26, Feb 9, 10, 24, Mar 17, 30, Apr

1, 2, 6, 7, 9, 15, 16, 17, May 18, 20, 26, 28, Jun 3, 8, Jul 1, 6, 8, 21, Sep
16, 21, 23, 25, 28, 30, Oct 2, 9, 12, 14, 19, 27, 30, 31, Nov 2, 5, 6, 10,
11, 12, 24, 26, 27, 30, Dec 1, 5, 7; 1731: GF, Jan 13, 20, Feb 1, 15, 22, Mar
2, 13, 22, 23, 25, 27, HAY, May 3, 7, GF, Sep 27, Oct 4, 6, 8, 11, 13, 18,
25, 26, Nov 4, 8, 11, 12, 13, 15, 16, 18, 19, 20, 22, 24, 26, Dec 4, 6, 7, 9,
13, 20, 21, 30; 1732: GF, Feb 21, 26, 28, Mar 4, 13, 20, 27, 28, Apr 13, 14,
May 3, 4, 10, Oct 4, 5, 6, 9, 10, 11, 12, 13, 14, 16, 24, 25, 26, Nov 4, 13,
18, 27, 28, 29, Dec 29; 1733: GF, Jan 1, 17, 18, Feb 19, 20, Mar 6, 15, 17,
28, 30, Apr 11, 17, 19, May 9, 29, Sep 12, 17, 19, 20, 21, 27, 28, Oct 3, 4,
5, 9, 15, 18, 19, 24, 25, Nov 5, 8, 10, 14, 29, Dec 13, 18; 1734: GF, Jan 3,
10, 11, 14, 19, Mar 5, Apr 19, May 3, 8, 15, 16, Sep 9, 11, 13, 18, Oct 14,
18, 21, 23, Nov 4, 6, 11, 12, 13, 18, 22, 25, 27, 29, Dec 2, 6, 13, 16, 20;
1735: GF, Jan 1, 2, 3, 4, 6, 11, 13, 20, Feb 5, 6, 8, 22, 24, 25, Mar 10, 17,
20, 29, Apr 9, 14, 16, 22, Sep 10, 12, 15, 17, 22, 24, Oct 3, 6, 8, 15, 27,
Nov 3, 4, 10, 12, 14, 19, 20, 21, 25, 26, Dec 17; 1736: GF, Jan 3, 29, Feb
16, 20, Mar 9, 18, 22, 25, 29, Apr 8, 16, 17, 28, May 5, 13, LIF, Jun 18, Sep
28, Oct 5, 9, 12, 14, 19, 23, 26, 28, Nov 4, 6, 11; 1737: LIF, Feb 12, 21,
Mar 1, 15, 24, Apr 2, 12, 27, May 4, 7; 1738: DL, Feb 2, 10, 28, Mar 2, Apr
29, May 2, Sep 9, 12, 26, Oct 12, 19, 31, Nov 1, 9, Dec 6; 1739: DL, Jan 15,
Feb 13, Mar 22, Apr 7, 10, May 22, 26, Sep 8, 11, 13, 14, 21, Oct 5, Nov 12,
21, 23, Dec 31; 1740: DL, Jan 5, Mar 25, Apr 29, May 2, 6, 9, GF, Oct 18, 20,
21, 23, 24, 27, 28, 29, 31, Nov 3, 4, 12, 13, 17, 19, 20, 24, 25, 26, 27, 28,
Dec 1, 2, 5, 6, 8; 1741: GF, Jan 15, 20, 22, 28, 29, Feb 2, 9, 10, 14, 19,
Mar 7, 10, 19, Apr 7, 9, 15, 27, 28, Sep 14, 16, 21, 23, 25, 28, 30, Oct 5,
7, 13, 16, 19, 23, Nov 4, 6, 9, Dec 2, 16, 26; 1742: GF, Jan 4, 5, 27, Feb 2,
Mar 4, 15, 22, 27, Apr 3, 6, 22, May 17, LIF, Nov 24, 29, Dec 1, 3, 27, 28,
30; 1743: LIF, Jan 10, 21, Feb 2, 9, 11, 17, Mar 22, Apr 4, 5, 9, DL, Oct 6,
8, 11, 13, 15, 20, 25, 27, Nov 4, 8, 17, 18, 24, 26, Dec 1, 12, 19, 20; 1744:
DL, Jan 7, 12, 13, Feb 7, 21, Mar 10, 29, Apr 3, 10, 25, 30, May 1, 11, Sep
15, 18, 27, 29, Oct 4, 6, 11, 13, 17, 24, 30, Nov 3, 5, 16, 24, Dec 11; 1745:
DL, Mar 14, Apr 19, Jun 5, Oct 5, 10, 15, 17, 19, Nov 4, 9, 11, 18, 20, 22,
Dec 12; 1746: DL, Jan 8, Mar 18, Apr 10, Aug 4, 6, 8, Oct 27, Nov 4, 15, Dec
11, 12, 15, 29; 1747: DL, Feb 16, Mar 3, 7, 14, 16, 19, Apr 28, CG, Nov 18,
Dec 4; 1748: CG, Jan 2, 9, 14, 19, 29, Feb 3, 10, 15, Mar 8, Apr 15, 29, Sep
21

Giffard, Edward (actor), 1733: GF, May 16; 1735: GF, May 5; 1736: GF, Apr 26;
   1742: GF, Apr 1, 27, LIF, Dec 6; 1743: LIF, Apr 7; 1745: GF, Mar 19
Giffard, Elizabeth, Mrs William (actor), 1741: GF, Apr 7, Sep 14, 25, 30, Oct
   5, 7, 28, Nov 4; 1742: GF, Feb 2, 11, Mar 2, 23, 25, Apr 21, 27, May 12, 18,
   LIF, Nov 24, 29, Dec 28, 30; 1743: LIF, Jan 10, 21, Feb 11, 28, DL, Oct 4,
   11, Nov 14; 1744: DL, Jan 12
Giffard, Henry (actor), 1729: GF, Oct 31, Nov 3, 4, 5, 6, 7, 8, 10, 11, 17, 20,
   24, Dec 1, 3, 8, 20; 1730: GF, Jan 9, 13, 26, Feb 9, 10, 24, Mar 10, 12, 17,
   Apr 6, 7, 15, 16, 28, May 14, 26, Jun 8, Jul 1, 6, 8, Sep 16, 18, 21, 23, 25,
   28, 30, Oct 2, 9, 19, 21, 24, 27, 30, 31, Nov 2, 5, 6, 12, 24, 26, 27, Dec 1,
   5, 7, 21; 1731: GF, Jan 13, 20, Feb 1, 15, 22, Mar 2, 8, 13, 22, Apr 1, 27,
   HAY, May 3, 7, GF, 17, 20, Sep 27, Oct 6, 8, 11, 13, 18, 25, 26, 27, 30, Nov
   1, 4, 6, 11, 12, 15, 16, 18, 19, 20, 22, 24, Dec 4, 6, 7, 9, 13, 28, 30;
   1732: GF, Feb 2, 4, 5, 21, 26, Mar 6, 20, 27, 28, Apr 12, May 4, 10, Oct 2,
   4, 5, 6, 7, 10, 11, 12, 13, 14, 16, 17, 24, 25, 26, 30, Nov 3, 4, 8, 18, 20,
   27, 28, Dec 1, 18, 29; 1733: GF, Jan 1, 17, 18, 20, Feb 12, 19, 20, Mar 6,
   15, 17, 28, 30, Apr 11, 17, 19, May 9, 29, Sep 10, 12, 17, 19, 20, 21, DL,
   22, GF, 25, 27, 28, DL, 28, Oct 1, GF, 4, 5, 9, 12, 15, DL, 17, GF, 18, 19,
   22, 23, 24, 25, 26, Nov 5, 8, 10, 12, DL, 14, GF, 14, 29, Dec 13, 18, 28;
   1734: GF, Jan 3, 10, 11, 14, 19, 31, Mar 5, 14, 15, 19, Apr 6, 19, 26, May 3,
   6, 8, 14, 15, 16, Sep 9, 11, 13, 16, 18, 20, Oct 14, 16, 18, 21, 23, Nov 4,
   6, 7, 11, 12, 13, 18, 25, 27, 29, Dec 2, 6, 12, 13, 16, 20, 31; 1735: GF, Jan
   3, 4, 6, 11, 13, 20, Feb 5, 6, 8, 24, 25, Mar 10, 17, 20, 29, Apr 9, 16, May
   8, Sep 10, 12, 15, 17, 19, 22, 24, Oct 3, 6, 8, 15, 27, Nov 3, 4, 10, 11, 12,
   14, 19, 20, 21, 24, 25, 26, Dec 17; 1736: GF, Jan 27, 29, Feb 9, 16, Mar 9,
   22, 25, 29, Apr 8, 16, 17, 28, 30, May 5, 13, LIF, Jun 18, Sep 28, Oct 5, 9,
   12, 14, 19, 23, 26, 28, 30, Nov 4, 6, 11, 13, 19, 20, 22, 24, 26, 27, Dec 3,
   10, 20, 22, 31; 1737: LIF, Jan 10, 19, 21, Feb 12, 14, Mar 1, 15, 24, 29, Apr
   2, YB, 14, LIF, 27, 28, May 2, 4, 5, 6; 1738: DL, Mar 2, GF, Jul 11, 26;
   1739: DL, Mar 22, Apr 10, Nov 21, 23; 1740: DL, Mar 25, Apr 15, May 9, GF,
   Oct 18, 20, 21, 22, 27, 31, Nov 4, 13, 14, 15, 17, 18, 19, 20, 24, 25, 26,
   27, 28, 29, Dec 1, 2, 4, 5, 6, 8, 10, 12; 1741: GF, Jan 15, 20, 22, 28, Feb
   2, 9, 10, 19, Mar 7, 16, Apr 7, 9, 17, 23, 27, 28, 30, Sep 14, 16, 18, 21,
   23, 25, 28, 30, Oct 5, 7, 9, 12, 13, 14, 15, 19, 23, 28, Nov 2, 4, 6, 9, 27,
   Dec 2, 9, 16; 1742: GF, Jan 4, 5, 23, 26, 27, Feb 2, 3, Mar 4, 22, 27, 29,
   Apr 1, 22, JS, Nov 9, LIF, 24, 29, Dec 1, 3, 6, 13, 27, 28, 30; 1743: LIF,
   Jan 10, 21, Feb 2, 8, 9, 11, 17, 28, Mar 8, 17, 22, Apr 5, 9, DL, Sep 15, 17,

20, 22, 27, 29, Oct 6, 8, 11, 13, 20, 25, 27, Nov 4, 12, 17, 24, 26, 29, Dec
1, 17, 19; 1744: DL, Jan 7, 12, Mar 10, 29, Apr 10, 25, 30, May 1, 5, 11, 14,
15, 22, 23, Sep 15, 20, 27, 29, Oct 2, 4, 6, 9, 11, 13, 17, 24, 30, Nov 2, 3,
5, 12, 17, 24, Dec 11, 29; 1745: DL, Jan 14, Feb 11, Mar 14, Apr 18, 19, 29,
Oct 10, 15, 17, 22, Nov 14, 18, 20, Dec 10, 11; 1746: DL, Jan 2, 8, 24, 25,
28, Mar 10, 18, Apr 10, May 7, 9, Aug 4, 6, Oct 27, 31, Nov 1, Dec 11, 29;
1747: DL, Jan 2, 15, Mar 3, 14, 16, 19, Apr 20, 23, 29, 30, CG, Nov 18, Dec
9, 19, 28; 1748: CG, Jan 7, 8, 9, 14, 16, 19, 29, Mar 8, Apr 13, 15, 16, 21,
22, Sep 28, Oct 7; 1752: CG, Sep 29, Oct 16, Nov 3, 4, 9, 23; 1759: CG, Dec
15; 1760: CG, Sep 22; 1761: CG, Jan 2; 1772: GF, Oct 23
Giffard, Jane (actor), 1717: LIF, Nov 9, 25, 28; 1718: LIF, Apr 19, SF, Sep 5,
AC, 24, LIF, Oct 15; 1719: LIF, Feb 28, May 7, Oct 5, 31, Nov 3, 13, 16, 18,
19, 21, 23, 26; 1720: LIF, Jan 7, 11, 26, Feb 23, 29, Mar 15, 19, Apr 26, May
5, 11, 17, Jun 7, SFLH, Sep 5, LIF, Oct 1, 8, 11, 15, 18, 20, 22, Nov 1, 2,
3, 15, 26, Dec 17, 21, 22, 27; 1721: LIF, Jan 10, 19, 25, Feb 6, 9, 18, Mar
4, 11, 13, 14, 27, Apr 17, 18, 19, 29, May 5, 10
Giffard, Mrs Joseph (beneficiary), 1735: GF, Apr 24
Giffard, Mrs M (actor), 1733: GF, Apr 6; 1734: GF, Feb 11; 1735: GF, Jan 24,
Feb 4, 25, Mar 10, Apr 9, Sep 24, Nov 11, 20; 1736: GF, Apr 16, LIF, Nov 24,
Dec 7, 17; 1737: LIF, Jan 10, 21, Feb 21, Mar 26, 29, May 17
Giffard, William (actor), 1717: LIF, May 23, Dec 14; 1718: LIF, May 3, SF, Sep
5, AC, 24; 1726: DL, May 7, 19; 1728: LIF, May 16, 22, Jun 25, Jul 2, 5, 19,
HAY, Aug 9, BFHM, 24, LIF, Oct 1, HAY, 15, Nov 14, 19, Dec 7; 1729: HAY, Jan
10, 31, Feb 25, Mar 27, Apr 22, May 2, 7, BF, Aug 26, SF, Sep 8, SOU, 23, GF,
Oct 31, Nov 3, 4, 5, 7, 10, 12, 15, 17, 20, 21, 24, Dec 8, 11, 18; 1730: GF,
Jan 5, 6, 7, 9, 13, 19, 26, Feb 9, 10, 24, Mar 17, 21, 30, Apr 2, 17, 28, May
15, 26, 28, Jun 3, 8, Jul 1, 15, BFPG/TC, Aug 1, BFPG, 20, GF, Sep 16, 18,
25, 28, Oct 2, 9, 14, 20, 21, 24, 26, 27, 30, Nov 10, 11, 12, 20, 24, 27, 30,
Dec 1, 5, 7, 21; 1731: GF, Jan 5, 7, 13, Feb 1, 18, 22, Mar 1, 13, 15, 22,
25, 27, Apr 21, 27, May 5, 7, 17, 20, Jun 1, 2, Oct 6, 8, 11, 18, 25, 26, 27,
29, Nov 1, 6, 11, 15, 18, 20, 22, 26, 27, Dec 4, 13, 20, 21, 28, 30; 1732:
GF, Feb 21, 26, Mar 20, Apr 1, Oct 2, 4, 5, 6, 7, 9, 12, 14, 17, 24, 30, Nov
2, 3, 18, 27, Dec 1; 1733: GF, Jan 8, 18, Feb 12, 20, Mar 6, 15, Apr 6, 11,
DL, Nov 23; 1734: GF, Jan 11, 12, 18, 21, 24, 28, 29, Feb 2, 11, Mar 5, 19,
Apr 18, Sep 11, 18, 20, Oct 16, 23, Nov 11, Dec 6, 16, 20, 31; 1735: GF, Jan
1, 11, 20, Feb 8, 25, Mar 10, 17, Apr 9, 17, May 8, Sep 10, 15, 19, 22, 24,
Oct 3, 6, 8, 27, Nov 10, 11, 12, 19, 20, 21, 24, 25, 26, Dec 8, 17; 1736: GF,
Feb 9, 16, Mar 9, 25, 29, Apr 16, 28, May 5, 13, LIF, Sep 28, Oct 5, 19, 23,
Nov 6, 9, 11, 13, 18, 20, 24, 26, 27, 29, Dec 22; 1737: LIF, Jan 10, 21, Feb
1, 12, 14, 21, Mar 1, 15, 21, Apr 2, 18, 27, May 6; 1740: GF, Oct 28, 29, 30,
Nov 3, 4, 12, 13, 18, 26, 27, 28, 29, Dec 1, 4, 8, 10; 1741: GF, Jan 15, 28,
Feb 2, 10, 14, Mar 16, Apr 7, Sep 14, 18, 21, 23, 25, Oct 2, 5, 7, 19, 23,
Nov 4, 6, 9, 27, Dec 2, 9, 16, 26, 31; 1742: GF, Jan 1, 4, 5, 26, 27, Feb 2,
3, 22, Mar 25, 27, Apr 6, May 6, LIF, Nov 24, 29, Dec 1, 3, 6, 13, 22, 27,
28, 30; 1743: LIF, Jan 10, 14, 21, Feb 2, 9, 11, 17, Mar 17, 22, Apr 4, 5,
DL, Sep 15, 17, 20, 27, 29, Oct 1, 4, 8, 13, 15, 20, 22, 25, 27, Nov 4, 8,
17, 23, 24, 26, 29, Dec 6, 15; 1744: DL, Jan 7, 12, 27, Apr 2, 3, 10, 30;
1752: CG, Sep 18
Giffard, William (Master) (actor), 1731: GF, Nov 24; 1732: GF, Mar 20; 1733:
GF, Apr 6, 11, Sep 10, Dec 28; 1734: GF, Jan 31, Sep 20; 1737: LIF, Mar 1;
1744: DL, Apr 3
Giffard, William and Elizabeth (actors), 1731: HAY, May 7; 1742: GF, Mar 29
Giffard's Nursery, 1747: DL, Mar 19
Gil Blas. See Moore, Edward.
Gilbert (actor), 1729: SOU, Sep 23
Gilbert (beneficiary), 1726: HAY, Apr 12
Gilbert (beneficiary), 1794: CG, Jun 17; 1799: CG, Apr 12
Gilbert-Cooper, John (correspondent), 1748: DL, Dec 23, 26; 1749: DL, Jan 2,
HAY, 7, 16, DL, 17
Gilbert, Miss (actor), 1798: CG, Dec 8; 1799: CG, May 4, 6, Sep 16, 23, Oct 9,
Dec 7; 1800: CG, Jan 16
Gilbert, Mrs (actor), 1749: NWLS, Feb 27
Gilbert, Mrs (actor), 1796: CG, Sep 23, 26, Oct 6, 17, 18, Nov 25, Dec 1, 13,
19; 1797: CG, Jan 10, Feb 18, Apr 8, 19, 25, May 6, 16, 18, Jun 5, 13, Sep
25, Oct 11, 16, 21, Nov 2, 20, Dec 18; 1798: CG, Feb 12, 20, Mar 22, 31, Apr
11, 27, 30, May 15, Sep 17, Oct 1, 5, 8, Nov 9, 12, Dec 11, 15, 26; 1799: CG,
Jan 29, Mar 25, Apr 3, 13, 19, 23, May 3, 7, 28, Sep 18, 30, Oct 7, 11, 21,
24, Nov 11, Dec 23; 1800: CG, Jan 16, 29, Feb 4, 10, Mar 25, Apr 5, 17, May
30, Jun 2
Gilder (composer), 1754: HAY/SFB, Sep 26
Gilding (songwriter), 1766: MARLY, Sep 26
Gildon, Charles, 1659: NONE, Sep 0; 1661: SALSBURY, Jan 29; 1666: NONE, Sep 0;

1667: ATCOURT, May 9; 1679: DL, Mar 0; 1680: DG, Dec 8; 1685: ATCOURT, Dec
14; 1688: DL, Feb 0; 1691: DL, Apr 0; 1692: DL, Jan 0; 1693: DL, Mar 0; 1695:
LIF, Apr 30, NONE, Sep 0, DL, 0, LIF, Dec 0; 1696: DL, Feb 0, May 0, Nov 0,
LIF, 14, DL, 21; 1697: LIF, Feb 20, Jun 0; 1698: LIF, Mar 0; 1701: LIF, Apr
0; 1702: DL, Dec 0
--Love's Victim; or, The Queen of Wales, 1701: LIF, Apr 0
--Patriot, The; or, The Italian Conspiracy, 1680: DG, Dec 8; 1702: DL, Dec 0
--Phaeton; or, The Fatal Divorce, 1698: DL, Mar 0, May 17
--Roman Bride's Revenge, The, 1696: DL, Nov 0
Giles (beneficiary), 1710: DL, Apr 21
Giles (boxkeeper), 1715: LIF, Aug 10; 1717: LIF, Jun 3; 1721: LIF, May 29;
   1722: LIF, Jun 1; 1723: LIF, May 18; 1724: LIF, Jun 1; 1725: LIF, May 21
Giles, Edward (actor), 1730: GF, Jun 19; 1731: GF, May 13; 1732: HAY, Feb 16,
   Mar 2, 17, 23, 31, Apr 4, 27, May 10, Jun 1; 1733: GF, Jan 13, Apr 19, May
   14, HAY, 28, Jul 26, CG, 27, Aug 2, 14, 20; 1734: DL, Jan 15, 19, Feb 4;
   1740: CG, May 29
Giles, Miss (fruit concessionaire), 1781: DL, May 19, Dec 13; 1788: DL, Jun 13
Giles, Mrs (seamstress), 1773: CG, Nov 5
Giles's Coffee House, 1733: GF, May 14
Gill (shoemaker), 1743: LIF, Mar 14
Gill, Mrs (actor), 1728: HAY, Oct 15, 26
Gilles (house servant), 1785: DL, May 21; 1786: DL, May 29; 1787: DL, Jun 4;
   1788: DL, Jun 6; 1789: DL, Jun 10; 1790: DL, May 29; 1791: DL, May 31; 1792:
   DLKING'S, Jun 15; 1793: DL, Jun 6; 1795: DL, Jun 5
Gillet (actor), 1757: HAY, Aug 22
Gillet (house servant), 1795: CG, May 30; 1796: CG, May 31; 1797: CG, May 27
Gillett, 1790: DL, May 29
Gillibrand (house servant), 1734: HAY, Jun 12; 1735: DL, May 23; 1736: DL, May
   21; 1737: DL, May 25, 31; 1739: DL, May 25, 28; 1740: DL, May 19
Gillier (composer), 1703: YB, Apr 28
Gillier (musician), 1758: CHAPEL, Apr 27; 1760: CG, Sep 22
Gillier, Master (dancer), 1740: DL, Apr 24, CG, 25; 1741: DL, Apr 4; 1742: CG,
   Dec 17; 1743: CG, Apr 19
Gillingham (violinist), 1798: HAY, Jan 15
Gillow, Mrs (actor), 1675: DG, Sep 0; 1676: DG, Jun 8, Jul 25; 1677: DG, Mar
   24, Sep 0
Gillow, Thomas (actor), 1671: LIF, Sep 0; 1674: DG, Nov 9; 1675: DG, May 28,
   Sep 0; 1676: DG, Mar 0, Aug 0, Dec 0; 1677: DG, Feb 12, Jun 0, Jul 0, Sep 0;
   1678: DG, Jan 0, May 28, Sep 0, Nov 0; 1679: DG, Mar 0, Apr 0, May 0, Oct 0,
   Dec 0; 1680: DG, Feb 0, Sep 0, Nov 1, Dec 8; 1681: DG, Mar 0; 1682: DG, Jan
   0, Feb 9, Mar 0, DL, Nov 28; 1683: NONE, Sep 0, DL, Nov 12, Dec 0; 1684:
   DLORDG, Aug 0; 1685: DLORDG, Jan 20, DL, May 9, DG, Jul 0, DL, Aug 0; 1686:
   DL, Jan 0, NONE, Sep 0; 1687: ATCOURT, Apr 25; 1729: HAY, Feb 25, Mar 27, 29,
   May 2, 7, 12, 26, 29, Jun 17, Jul 26
Gilmarine, Mrs (actor), 1728: HAY, Feb 21
Gilpin, Miss (actor), 1766: KING'S, Aug 13, 20, 27, HAY, Sep 2
Gilson (singer), 1765: HAY, Mar 11
Gioas Re Di Giuda. See Bach, Johann Christian.
Giocatore, Il. See Orlandini, Giuseppe Maria.
Giordani, Antonia (singer), 1754: CG, Jan 18, Mar 4
Giordani, Francesco (singer), 1754: CG, Jan 18, Feb 11, Mar 4; 1755: HAY, Feb
   3, 17; 1764: KING'S, Nov 27
Giordani, Giuseppe (Giardanello) (singer), 1754: CG, Jan 18, Feb 11, Mar 4;
   1764: KING'S, Nov 27; 1793: KING'S, Jun 11
Giordani, Marina (singer), 1754: CG, Jan 18, Feb 11, Mar 4; 1764: KING'S, Nov
   27
Giordani, Nicolina (singer), 1753: CG, Dec 17; 1754: CG, Jan 18, 19, 28, Feb
   11, Mar 4; 1764: KING'S, Nov 27; see also Spiletta
Giordani, Tommaso (composer), 1764: KING'S, Mar 24, 29, Apr 5; 1766: CHAPEL,
   Apr 30; 1770: KING'S, Feb 6, Dec 18; 1771: KING'S, Feb 8, May 14, 28; 1772:
   KING'S, Feb 21, Apr 21; 1773: KING'S, Feb 5, CG, Mar 19; 1774: KING'S, Mar 8,
   PANT, Apr 4, KING'S, May 17, Jun 3, Nov 8; 1775: KING'S, Mar 7, DL, 20; 1777:
   KING'S, Feb 4, Mar 1, CG, 19, KING'S, Nov 4; 1778: KING'S, Jan 20, Mar 3, May
   30; 1779: HAY, Jul 1; 1781: KING'S, Jun 5, HAY, Jul 18, KING'S, Nov 17; 1782:
   KING'S, Apr 9, May 23, CG, Nov 2; 1783: KING'S, May 1, Nov 29; 1785: CG, Apr
   20; 1787: CG, Oct 31; 1788: CG, Apr 1, Dec 13; 1789: CG, Mar 31, Jun 2, Sep
   23, Nov 24; 1790: DL, Apr 16, CG, Jun 3, DL, Oct 4; 1791: CG, May 18; 1792:
   KING'S, Mar 23, 28, DLKING'S, May 23; 1793: CG, May 3, Oct 24; 1795: HAY, Mar
   4, KING'S, 13
--Antigono (opera), 1774: KING'S, Mar 8, 15, 22, Apr 9, 14, 16, May 5, 10, 14,
   31, Jun 14; 1776: KING'S, May 18, 23, Jun 1, 8, 15, 22, 29; 1777: KING'S, Mar
   1, 8, 20

--Bacio, Il (opera), 1776: KING'S, Jan 9, 16, 23, Feb 3, 13, 20, 27, Mar 5, Apr 25, May 7, 30, Jun 11; 1782: KING'S, Apr 9, Jun 11, 18
Giorgi (dancer), 1757: DL, Oct 4, 20, 29, Dec 23; 1758: DL, Apr 10, Oct 14, 24, 28, Nov 3, Dec 14; 1759: DL, Jan 4, Feb 2, 6, Mar 19, Apr 7, May 17, Sep 25, Oct 6, 16, 17, Nov 17, 24, Dec 31; 1760: DL, Feb 11, Apr 24, 29, May 2, Oct 11, Dec 11, 13; 1761: DL, Mar 7, Apr 20, Sep 8, 10, Oct 26, Nov 3, 28, Dec 28; 1762: DL, Feb 3, Mar 25; 1763: DL, Apr 6; 1764: DL, Sep 22, 25, Oct 20, 29, Nov 2, 10, 13, 28, Dec 13, 14; 1765: DL, Jan 7, 22, Feb 8, 15, Mar 26, 30, Apr 11, 19, May 1, 11, 16, Sep 17, 24, Oct 8, Nov 16, 20; 1766: DL, Jan 6, Feb 3, 7, Mar 17, 22, Apr 14, 15, May 5, Sep 20, 23, 27, 30, Oct 21; 1767: DL, Jan 2, Feb 12, 25, Apr 4, 20, 21, 30, May 8, 15, 22, Sep 19, 21, 22, Oct 22; 1768: DL, Feb 4, 20, Apr 5, 6, 22, 23, May 10, Aug 18, Sep 22, 27, 29, Oct 10, 13, 15, 22; 1769: DL, Mar 13, 16, Apr 26, May 5, Sep 23, Oct 2, 4, 6, 9, Dec 30; 1770: DL, Jan 6, Mar 31, May 2, 15, Sep 22, 25, Nov 29; 1771: DL, Apr 24, May 28, Sep 26, Nov 22, Dec 4, 26; 1772: DL, Apr 24, May 5, 9, Jun 3, Sep 19, Oct 3, 6, Nov 12, Dec 26; 1773: DL, Mar 27, May 8, 12, Sep 21, 25, Oct 9, 13, Nov 25, Dec 27; 1774: DL, Apr 4, 12, 30, May 20, Sep 27, Oct 1, 5, 14, 27, Nov 1, 5, Dec 26; 1775: DL, May 15, Sep 26, 30, Oct 11, 20, Nov 1, 28, Dec 11, 12; 1776: DL, May 18, Oct 9, 24, 26, Nov 6, Dec 10; 1777: DL, Jan 4, Feb 10, HAY, Jun 11; 1782: HAY, Jun 20, Aug 15, 17; 1783: HAY, Jun 13, 30; 1786: KING'S, Mar 23, Dec 23; 1787: KING'S, Jan 20, Mar 13, Jun 14
Giorgi (musician), 1774: HAY, Sep 16
Giorgi, Master (dancer), 1784: HAY, May 28, Aug 28; 1785: HAY, May 28, 31, Jun 1, 23, Aug 31; 1786: HAY, Jun 19, 23, Jul 3, 17; 1787: HAY, May 23, Aug 7, 13
Giorgi, Miss (dancer), 1767: DL, May 8
Giorgi, Rachele Dorta (singer), 1785: KING'S, Jan 25; see also Dorta, Rachele
Giorgi, Sg and Sga (dancers), 1760: DL, Apr 23, May 17, 27, 29; 1761: DL, Apr 3, Sep 19; 1762: DL, Feb 20, Mar 1, Apr 24; 1765: DL, Oct 5; 1767: DL, Jan 24, Sep 12, 17, 23, 26, Oct 10; 1769: DL, Apr 12, May 1; 1770: DL, May 2, Jun 1; 1771: DL, Dec 2
Giorgi, Sga (dancer), 1759: DL, Dec 31; 1760: DL, Feb 11, Apr 24, 29, May 2, Dec 11, 13; 1761: DL, Mar 7, Apr 20, Sep 8, 10, Oct 26, Nov 3, 28, Dec 28; 1762: DL, Feb 3, Mar 25, Sep 21, 28, Oct 15, 21, 22, 27, 29, 30, Nov 5, 23; 1763: DL, Jan 3, 14, Feb 17, 24, Apr 22, 25; 1764: DL, Sep 22, 25, Oct 9, 20, 29, Nov 2, 10, 13, 28, Dec 13, 14; 1765: DL, Jan 18, 22, Feb 8, 15, Apr 13, Sep 17, 24, 26, Oct 8, Nov 16, 20; 1766: DL, Jan 6, Feb 3, 7, Mar 17, 22, Apr 14, 15, May 5, 7, Sep 20, 23, 27, 30, Oct 11, 21, Nov 21, Dec 2; 1767: DL, Jan 2, Apr 9, May 9, 21, Sep 21, 22, Nov 20; 1768: DL, Feb 10, Apr 6, Oct 10; 1769: DL, Mar 13, 16, May 9, 18; 1770: DL, May 15, Sep 22, Oct 30, Nov 3, 12, 19, 29, Dec 1, 11, 12, 13; 1771: DL, Jan 1, May 28, Sep 26, Dec 4, 26; 1772: DL, Sep 19, Oct 3, Nov 12, Dec 2, 26; 1773: DL, Mar 27, May 12, Sep 21, Oct 9, Dec 27
Giorgi's scholars (dancer), 1771: DL, Apr 24, May 23, 25, 30; 1772: HAY, May 18, Jun 15, Aug 4, 10, 17; 1773: DL, May 8, HAY, 17, 19, 26, Jun 14, 30, Jul 7, 12, 21, 30, Aug 4, 11, 23, 27, Sep 3, 9, 14; 1774: HAY, May 16, DL, Jun 2, HAY, 3, Aug 29, Sep 6, DL, Oct 1, 19; 1775: DL, May 15; 1785: HAY, May 31, Jun 17, 25, Jul 5, Aug 31; 1786: HAY, Jun 9, 27, Aug 12; 1787: HAY, Jul 27, Aug 14, 21
Giornovichi (Jarnowick), Giovanni Mane (violinist, composer), 1791: CG, Mar 18; 1793: DL, Mar 7, KING'S, Jun 8; 1794: DL, Mar 12, 14, 19, 21, 26, 28, Apr 2, 4, 9, 11, KING'S, May 15, Jun 3; 1795: DL, May 18; 1796: KING'S, Mar 10, CG, Nov 19
Giovannini, Pietro (librettist), 1786: KING'S, Mar 30
Gipsies, The (dance), 1764: DL, May 23
Gipsies, The. See Dibdin, Charles.
Gipsy Ballad (song), 1794: CG, May 26; see also Wandering Gipsy
Gipsy in a Village (dance), 1764: HAY, Aug 24
Gipsy Tambourine (dance), 1753: DL, Oct 12, 13, 15, 18, Nov 5, Dec 21; 1754: CG, Jan 10, DL, Mar 12, Apr 26
Giraldini (Spanish minister), 1739: DL, Sep 25
Giramondo, Il (opera), 1749: KING'S, Feb 14, 18
Girard, Father, 1732: HAY, Mar 17
Girardeau, Isabella (singer), 1710: QUEEN'S, Jan 10, Mar 23, May 2, Dec 9; 1711: QUEEN'S, Jan 10, Feb 24, Dec 12; 1712: QUEEN'S, Feb 27
Gird on thy sword (song), 1786: DL, Mar 10; 1789: CG, Mar 6, 27; 1790: CG, Feb 24, DL, Mar 17; 1791: CG, Mar 11, DL, Apr 13; 1792: KING'S, Feb 29, CG, Mar 9; 1793: CG, Mar 6; 1794: DL, Mar 12, CG, 12, DL, 14, Apr 2, 10; 1795: KING'S, Mar 13, CG, 13; 1796: CG, Feb 26; 1797: CG, Mar 31; 1799: CG, Feb 20, Mar 13; 1800: CG, Mar 19
Girelli, Maria Antonia (singer), 1772: KING'S, Nov 14; 1773: KING'S, Feb 5, Mar 18
Girl in Style, The. See Scawen, John.

355

Gironimo (musician), 1721: DL, Apr 17
Giroux (ballet master), 1786: KING'S, Jan 24, Mar 11, May 23
Gisbitysky, Mrs (seamstress), 1772: CG, Nov 30
Gismondi, Celeste (singer), 1732: KING'S, Nov 4; 1733: KING'S, Mar 17
Giton (musician), 1675: ATCOURT, Feb 15
Giuliani, Cecilia (singer), 1776: KING'S, Dec 14; 1788: KING'S, Apr 5, May 8;
   1789: KING'S, Jan 24, Feb 28, Mar 7, Apr 2, 4, May 2, Jun 2
Giulio Cesare. See Handel, George Frederic.
Giulio Sabino. See Cherubini, Maria Lorenzo; Sarti, Giuseppe.
Giuochi d'Agrigento, I. See Paisiello, Giovanni.
Giustinelli, Giuseppe (singer), 1763: KING'S, Feb 19, Apr 25, HAY, Jun 9,
   KING'S, Nov 26; 1764: KING'S, Feb 21, Apr 5, DL, Nov 2; 1765: DL, Feb 15;
   1768: KING'S, Feb 5; 1769: HAY, Feb 2
Giustinelli, Sga (singer), 1774: KING'S, Mar 17
Giustino I Imperatore dei Romani (dance), 1794: KING'S, Dec 6
Give glory to his awful name (song), 1789: DL, Mar 20
Give me Wine rosy Wine (song), 1792: CG, May 18
Give round the word (song), 1780: CG, Apr 10, May 3; 1781: CG, Apr 3, May 4;
   1782: CG, May 6, 20; 1783: CG, May 19
Give the vengeance due (song), 1791: CG, Mar 25; 1792: CG, Mar 7; 1794: CG, Mar
   14
Give then royal maid your sorrows over (song), 1693: NONE, Sep 0; 1694: DL, Feb
   0
Gizziello (singer), 1736: CG, May 5, Nov 27; see also Conti, Gioachino
Gladeau, Mrs (singer), 1770: CG, Jan 17
Gladman (trunk maker), 1752: DL, Dec 19
Gladwin (musician), 1741: HIC, Feb 5, HAY, 26; 1744: HAY, Jan 23
Glanville St, 1777: DL, Apr 29; 1778: DL, May 9; 1779: DL, May 8
Glanville, Miss (singer), 1758: MARLY, Sep 11, 18; 1759: MARLY, May 10, Aug 16;
   1760: MARLY, Aug 20; 1761: HAY, Jul 17, Aug 8, 11
Glapthorne, Henry, 1668: LIF, Aug 20
--Argalus and Parthenia, 1661: VERE, Jan 31, Feb 5, Oct 28
--Revenge for Honour, 1668: LIF, Aug 20; 1671: NONE, Sep 0
--Wit in a Constable, 1662: LIF, May 23, CG, 23
Glascot, 1771: DL, Nov 26
Glash (musician), 1714: TEC, May 4
Glass Instrument Concerto (music), 1746: HAY, Apr 23
Glassington, Elizabeth (actor), 1778: CHR, Jun 1, 10
Glassington, Joseph (actor), 1778: CHR, Jun 8, 10; 1785: HAMM, Jul 2
Glassington, Miss (actor), 1782: DL, Apr 11
Glasson, Mlle (dancer), 1741: BFH, Aug 22
Glee (song), 1785: CG, May 26; 1786: CG, Jan 6, HAY, Jul 25; 1787: CG, Apr 27;
   1791: CG, May 2; 1793: CG, Dec 19, 30; 1794: CG, Jan 1, 6, May 7; 1795: CG,
   May 6, Nov 16; 1796: CG, Mar 15, Apr 11, 18, May 9, 20, Oct 24, 31; 1798: CG,
   Apr 21, DL, May 23; 1800: DL, May 10
Glee on the Happy Recovery of His Majesty (song), 1789: DL, May 28
Glen (actor), 1758: HAY, Jan 12, 16
Glen, Mrs (actor), 1755: CG, Feb 24, Apr 19, 29; 1756: DL, Oct 21; 1757: DL,
   Dec 26; 1758: DL, Jan 10, HAY, 12, DL, 1$, HAY, 16, DL, Apr 18, Jun 22, Sep
   21, Oct 30; 1759: DL, Jan 3, Mar 20; 1760: DL, Apr 26
Glindon and Co (publisher), 1795: CG, May 6
Glindon, W (printer), 1795: KING'S, Apr 30, Dec 12; 1796: KING'S, Jan 19, Feb
   16, Apr 16, May 24; 1797: KING'S, Jan 7; 1798: KING'S, Jan 23, Jun 19; 1800:
   KING'S, Jun 17
Globe and Sceptre Tavern, 1742: DL, Apr 21
Globe Tavern, 1749: BBT, Mar 1, HAY, Nov 17; 1781: HAY, Oct 16; 1782: HAY, Mar
   18; 1784: HAY, Jan 21, Feb 9; 1787: CG, Jun 15
Gloria Patri (song), 1786: DL, Mar 10; 1789: CG, Mar 6; 1790: CG, Feb 26, DL,
   Mar 17; 1792: CG, Mar 7; 1793: CG, Feb 22, Mar 20; 1794: CG, Mar 7, DL, Apr
   4, CG, 9; 1795: CG, Feb 20; 1796: CG, Mar 16; 1797: CG, Mar 24; 1799: CG, Feb
   20; 1800: CG, Mar 19
Gloriana. See Lee, Nathaniel.
Glorieux, Le. See Destouches.
Glorious Apollo (song), 1791: DL, May 18
Glorious Day is won (song), 1789: DL, Mar 20
Glorious First of June, The (song), 1795: CG, Jan 19
Glorious First of June, The. See Sheridan, Richard Brinsley.
Glorious Hero may thy Grave (song), 1790: DL, Mar 17
Glorious Ninety-Two (song), 1777: CG, Oct 21
Glorious Queen of Hungary, The; or, The British Troops Triumphant (play), 1743:
   TCD/BFTD, Aug 4, 23
Glory be to the Father (song), 1789: DL, Mar 18, 25; 1790: DL, Feb 26; 1791:

CG, Mar 18, DL, 23; 1792: KING'S, Feb 24, Mar 7; 1793: KING/HAY, Feb 22;
   1794: DL, Apr 10
Glory to God (song), 1789: CG, Mar 6, DL, 20; 1790: DL, Mar 24; 1793: KING/HAY,
   Feb 20; 1794: DL, Mar 19, Apr 4; 1799: CG, Mar 1
Glory's Resurrection. See Settle, Elkanah.
Gloucester Court, 1742: CG, Apr 1; 1784: HAY, Feb 9
Gloucester St, 1782: DL, May 3; 1788: DL, May 14
Gloucester Tavern, 1742: GF, Apr 22
Gloucester, Duke of, 1766: CG, Sep 24; 1767: CG, Jan 1, Apr 23; 1768: CG, Jan
   4, Dec 29; 1770: CG, Jan 5; 1772: CG, Jan 7; 1773: CG, Feb 18, DL, 25; 1774:
   CG, Jan 14; see also Dukes; Princes
Gloucester, Richard Duke of, 1719: BFPM, Aug 24
Gloucester, William Duke of, 1696: LIF, Jul 0; 1697: RICHMOND, Sep 20, 27;
   1700: DLLIF, Aug 6; 1701: YB, Jun 18; see also William, Prince
Gloucestershire, 1720: LIF, Mar 31
Glover (actor, dancer), 1717: KING'S, Mar 16, Apr 11, LIF, 23; 1719: KING'S,
   Feb 12, Mar 2; 1722: HAY, Feb 6; 1723: LIF, Oct 7, 16, 19, Nov 2, 8, 19, 22,
   27, Dec 3, 9, 11, 12, 16, 20; 1724: LIF, Jan 3, 4, Mar 2, 23, 28, Apr 6, 7,
   8, 10, 21, 22, 23, 27, 28, May 2, 4, 12, 13, 15, 19, 20, 22, 25, 26, 27, 28,
   29, Sep 25, 28, 30, Oct 5, 9, 12, 16, 23, 30, Nov 6, 10, 11, 13, 18; 1725:
   LIF, Jan 18, 21, Mar 13, 29, 31, Apr 14, 15, 17, 22, 23; 1726: LIF, Apr 14,
   Oct 3, Nov 2, 14, 21; 1727: LIF, Jan 9, 31, Feb 13, Mar 11, Apr 21, 27, May
   23, Sep 22, 27, Oct 2, 9, 17, 25, 26, 27, Nov 1, 9, 16; 1728: LIF, Jan 8, Mar
   14, Apr 22, May 6, 13, 15, 16, 20, 22, 23, 30; 1730: LIF, Mar 17, Apr 8, 10,
   24, 25, 27, 29, May 1, 4, 11, 15, 23, 27, 28, Sep 23, Oct 1, 7, 19, 30, Nov
   3, 7, Dec 7, 15; 1731: LIF, Jan 4, Apr 3, 8, 22, 28, May 1, 3, 7, 10, 17, 20,
   31, Jun 2, 7, Sep 20, 22, Oct 4, 13, 15, 20, Nov 2, 13, 18, 25, Dec 1, 14,
   17; 1732: LIF, Feb 9, Mar 9, 21, 30, Apr 10, 13, 17, 19, 22, 25, 26, May 1,
   8, 9, 11, 15, 16, LIF/CG, Sep 27, Oct 2, 4, 13, 16, Nov 8, 14, 16, 21, 24,
   Dec 4, 15, 27; 1733: CG/LIF, Jan 9, LIF/CG, 11, 12, 15, 16, 19, 23, Feb 2, 5,
   CG, 8, LIF/CG, Mar 12, CG, 27, LIF/CG, 28, 29, Apr 2, 12, 18, 23, 24, 30, CG,
   May 1, LIF/CG, 3, 7, 8, 10, CG, 16, 17, LIF/CG, 18, 21, CG/LIF, 28, LIF/CG,
   29, Jun 1, CG, Sep 22, Oct 4, 13, 18, Nov 10, 12, 24, Dec 7, 28; 1734: CG,
   Jan 17, 25, Mar 11, 16, Apr 1, 19, 24, 25, 27, 29, 30, May 4, 17, CG/LIF, Sep
   20, Oct 2, 7, 9, 23, 31, Nov 12, 19, 25, Dec 5, 12, 19, 30; 1735: CG/LIF, Jan
   13, 17, Feb 3, 13, 22, Mar 11, 13, 15, Apr 8, 10, 11, 14, 17, 18, 22, 29, May
   2, 5, 16, 19, 20, 27, Jun 2, CG, Sep 29, Oct 3, 13, 17, Nov 6, 11, 19, 28,
   Dec 2, 18; 1736: CG, Jan 1, 9, 10, 17, 23, Feb 23, 24, 26, Mar 2, 11, 20, 23,
   25, 30, Apr 1, 5, 6, 8, 12, 15, 17, 27, 29, 30, May 1, 6, 8, 10, 11, 13, 17,
   20, 24, 27, Jun 4, 14, Sep 22, 29, Oct 4, 6, 8, 27, Nov 3, 11, 23, 26, Dec 6,
   13; 1737: CG, Jan 7, Feb 14, Mar 14, 15, 17, 24, 26, 28, 31, Apr 2, 11, 12,
   14, 15, 19, 21, 22, 25, 29, May 3, 5, 6, 13, 16, 31, Oct 5, 12, 26, 27, Nov
   8, 9, 10, 11, 16; 1738: DL, Jan 3, CG, 3, 25, 31, Feb 2, 3, 13, Mar 2, 7, 13,
   14, 18, 20, 21, 23, Apr 3, 5, 6, 7, 10, 14, 15, 17, 18, 19, 21, 22, 25, 28,
   29, May 1, 2, 10, 11, 15, Oct 13, 18, 23, 26, 28, 30, Nov 2, 13, 18, Dec 5,
   6, 9, 11; 1739: CG, Jan 3, 15, 16, 20, Feb 9, 15, Mar 1, 5, 13, 19, 20, 22,
   26, 27, Apr 3, 7, 9, 14, 23, 24, 25, 26, 27, 30, May 1, 3, 4, 5, 7, 11, 14,
   15, 16, 17, 18, 21, 25, 28, 30, Sep 12, 14, 17, 19, 22, 25, 28, Oct 1, 2, 3,
   23, 27, 31, Nov 1, 3, 6, 7, 8, 10, 12, 13, 14, 15, 21, 23, 24, 26, 28, Dec 1,
   3, 10, 13, 17, 18, 19, 21, 22; 1740: CG, Jan 25, Feb 2, 6, 7, 12, Mar 10, 11,
   18, 24, 25, 27, Apr 9, 14, 16, 18, 23, 25, 28, 29, 30, May 2, 5, 7, 12, 13,
   14, 16, 19, 20, 21, 27, 29, Jun 5, Sep 29, Oct 25, Nov 13, 27, Dec 4, 11;
   1741: CG, Jan 8, 15, Feb 14, Mar 9, Apr 2, 17, 28
Glover, Julia, Mrs Samuel (actor), 1800: CG, Mar 27, Apr 5, 17, 22, 29, May 2,
   10, 15, 20, Jun 2, 7
Glover, Richard, 1753: DL, Dec 1; 1754: DL, Feb 12; 1767: DL, Mar 24; 1769: CG,
   Mar 29; 1771: CG, Mar 12
--Boadicia, 1753: DL, Nov 17, Dec 1, 3, 4, 5, 6, 7, 8, 10, 12, 13; 1754: DL,
   Jan 5, Feb 12
--Medea, 1767: DL, Mar 24; 1768: CG, Mar 17; 1769: CG, Mar 29; 1771: CG, Mar
   12; 1775: DL, Mar 20; 1776: DL, Mar 11, Oct 29; 1779: DL, Mar 25; 1792: CG,
   Mar 26
Glover, Dr William Frederick (actor), 1787: CG, Jun 15
Gluck, Christoph Willibald von (composer), 1742: KING'S, Dec 4; 1746: KING'S,
   Jan 7, Mar 4, 25, HAY, Apr 23; 1753: KING'S, Apr 30; 1770: KING'S, Apr 7;
   1771: KING'S, Apr 30; 1773: KING'S, Mar 9; 1779: KING'S, May 29; 1780:
   KING'S, Mar 9, Apr 20; 1781: HAY, Aug 8; 1782: KING'S, Apr 11, HAY, Jun 3;
   1783: HAY, Jun 5, KING'S, Nov 29; 1785: KING'S, Mar 12, May 12; 1787: DL, May
   11; 1788: KING'S, Mar 4; 1789: CG, May 28, Sep 16; 1790: DL, Mar 24, Apr 16,
   CG, May 6, Oct 19; 1791: CG, Oct 3; 1792: CG, Feb 28, DLKING'S, Mar 19; 1794:
   CG, Nov 17, Dec 26; 1795: KING'S, Apr 30; 1796: KING'S, Apr 7; 1799: KING'S,
   Mar 26, DL, May 24; 1800: CG, Jun 2

--Alceste; ossia, Il Trionfo dell' Amor Conjugale (opera), 1795: KING'S, Apr 30, May 2, 5, 9, 16, 19, 30, Jun 6, 13, 20, 27, Jul 4, 11; 1796: KING'S, Jan 19, 23, 26, 29, Feb 2, 6, Jul 2, 9; 1797: KING'S, Feb 14, 25, Mar 4, May 18, 23; 1800: KING'S, Jun 28, Jul 12, 19, Aug 2
--Artamene (opera), 1746: KING'S, Mar 4, 8, 11, 15, 18, 22, Apr 1, 5, 8, DL, 12, KING'S, 12; 1748: KING'S, Apr 5
--Caduta de Giganti, La; or, The Fall of the Giants (opera), 1746: KING'S, Jan 7, 11, 14, 18, 21, 25, Mar 25
--Ifigenia in Tauride (opera), 1796: KING'S, Apr 7, 9, 12, May 7, 13, 17
--Orfeo ed Eurydice (opera), 1770: KING'S, Apr 7, 17, 21, 28, May 5, 12, 15, 24, 26, Jun 9, 16, 23, 30; 1771: KING'S, Apr 30, May 4, 6, 11, 17, 25; 1773: KING'S, Mar 4, 6, 9, 13, May 25, 28, Jun 8, Dec 7; 1785: KING'S, May 12, 14, 17, 19, 21, 24, Jun 3, 7, 11, 21, 25; 1790: DL, Mar 24; 1792: CG, Feb 28, Mar 6, 13
--Sofonisbe (opera), 1746: KING'S, Mar 4
Gnome, The. See Wewitzer, Ralph.
Go baffled coward (song), 1792: KING'S, Mar 14; 1793: CG, Feb 22; 1794: CG, Mar 26
Go home, unhappy wench (song), 1696: DL, Jan 0
Go injur'd King (song), 1793: CG, Mar 20, 22
Go Jump and Finish Coffee House, 1787: HAY, Mar 12
Go not my Love (song), 1796: DL, May 25
Go patter to lubbers (song), 1790: CG, Dec 1; 1791: CG, Sep 19; 1793: CG, May 21; 1794: CG, Apr 12, Oct 29; 1795: CG, Oct 7; 1797: CG, Oct 2; see also Poor Jack; Life of Poor Jack
Go Perjured Man (song), 1706: DL, Jan 7
Go Rose (song), 1745: CG, Apr 27; 1748: CG, Feb 20, Mar 28, Apr 21, 27, JS, Dec 26; 1750: CG, Apr 19, 24, 25, 27; 1751: CG, Apr 23; 1752: DL, Sep 16
Goadby (actor), 1734: GR, Nov 4
Goblins, The. See Suckling, Sir John.
God preserve His Majesty for Ever and Ever (song), 1792: CG, Dec 26, 29; 1794: CG, May 2, 26; 1800: CG, Jun 2
God preserve the Emperor (song), 1800: CG, Mar 14, 19
God Save the King (dance), 1789: CG, May 10
God Save the King (song), 1736: YB, Mar 4; 1738: DL, Mar 3; 1744: SH, Feb 9; 1745: HAY, Feb 20, DL, Sep 28, CG, Dec 26; 1746: CG, Jan 15; 1757: KING'S, Mar 24; 1758: KING'S, Apr 6; 1760: DL, Nov 21; 1763: KING'S, Apr 25; 1771: CG, Jun 6; 1781: DL, Mar 30; 1786: DL, Mar 10; 1788: CG, Dec 15; 1789: CG, Feb 27, DL, Mar 4, 6, CG, 6, DL, 11, 13, CG, 13, 18, 20, CG, 20, DL, 25, CG, 27, DL, Apr 1, CG, 3, 15, 30, May 5, DL, 11, HAY, Jun 17, Jul 1, KHS, Sep 16, WHF, Nov 11, DL, Dec 16; 1790: DL, Feb 19, CG, 19, DL, 26, CG, Mar 3, 17, DL, Apr 23, May 18; 1791: PAN, Feb 22, CG, Mar 11, DL, 23; 1792: KING'S, Feb 24, CG, Mar 14, Dec 29, 31; 1793: CG, Jan 1, 3, 16, Feb 15, KING/HAY, 15, KING'S, 16, CG, 20, KING/HAY, 22, CG, 22, Mar 1, 6, KING/HAY, 6, CG, 8, 13, KING/HAY, 13, CG, 15, KING/HAY, 20, CG, 20, 22, Apr 24, HAY, Nov 5, CG, 19, 20; 1794: CG, Mar 7, 12, 14, DL, 14, CG, 21, 26, 28, Apr 2, DL, 2, 10, 30, CG, Nov 26; 1797: KING'S, Mar 4, CG, Apr 7, DL, Oct 16; 1798: CG, Jun 4, DL, Oct 2; 1799: CG, Feb 15, 20, Mar 13; 1800: CG, Feb 28, Mar 21, DL, May 15
Goddard (actor), 1716: LIF, Apr 3; 1719: DL, Jun 9
Goddard, Sophia Anne (actor), 1797: DL, Nov 10
Godfrey (spectator), 1676: DG, Jun 2
Godfrey (tailor), 1772: DL, Oct 30
Godwin (actor), 1744: MFHNT, May 1, MF, 3
Godwin (dancer, singer), 1702: DL, Aug 20; 1703: LIF, Jun 11, 14; 1704: LIF, Mar 23, Jul 27; 1706: QUEEN'S, Jan 17, LIF/QUEN, Aug 16
Godwin-Adam Booth, 1743: BFGA, Aug 23
Godwin, Mrs (actor), 1744: MFHNT, May 1, MF, 3
Godwin, Mrs (actor), 1764: CG, Sep 26; 1765: CG, Apr 11, 24, May 9; 1766: CG, Mar 17, Apr 26; 1767: CG, May 11
Godwin's Booth, 1742: BFG, Aug 25; 1743: NONE, Jan 31; 1747: SF, Sep 10
Goethe, Johann Wolfgang von, 1798: CG, Feb 13
--Clavigo, 1798: CG, Feb 13
Goff (proprietor), 1709: HA, Sep 19
Goff (singer), 1730: GF, Nov 28
Going out in the Morning (song), 1781: CG, May 4
Gold (actor), 1744: MFHNT, May 1
Gold, Margaret (actor), 1729: LIF, Jan 1
Golden Anchor Tavern, 1743: LIF, Mar 14
Golden Artichoke Coffee House, 1751: DL, Apr 23
Golden Ball and Dove (residence), 1736: DL, May 8
Golden Ball Tavern, 1739: CG, Mar 13; 1741: DL, May 5; 1742: CG, Apr 30; 1748: KING'S, Mar 1, DL, Apr 14; 1755: DL, Dec 16; 1758: CG, Jan 24

Golden Boar's Head Tavern, 1739: DL, May 11
Golden Bull Tavern, 1738: DL, May 19
Golden Cannister (public house), 1745: CT, Jan 14
Golden Cross Tavern, 1751: DL, May 1; 1777: HAY, Feb 11; 1778: HAY, Mar 31
Golden Days (song), 1799: CG, May 18
Golden Dragon Tavern, 1736: LIF, Apr 19
Golden Fan Tavern, 1742: CG, Apr 20; 1748: DL, Mar 12; 1767: CG, Apr 6
Golden Fleece, Order of the, 1743: LIF, Apr 8
Golden Head Tavern, 1743: CG, Apr 6; 1749: CG, Mar 30
Golden Key Tavern, 1731: DL, Jan 27
Golden Lane, 1749: BF/SFP, Aug 23
Golden Leg Tavern, 1757: DL, Dec 14
Golden Lion Tavern, 1695: SF, Sep 0; 1754: CG, Jan 21
Golden Peruke Tavern, 1740: CR, Feb 29
Golden Pippin, The. See O'Hara, Kane.
Golden Square, 1737: DL, Mar 17; 1745: HAY, Apr 1; 1753: DL, Dec 21; 1764:
   KING'S, Apr 12; 1777: DL, Apr 5; 1778: KING'S, Apr 9, HAY, 29; 1779: HAY, Aug
   10; 1780: KING'S, May 25; 1782: KING'S, Apr 18; 1784: KING'S, Feb 26, HAY,
   Mar 8, KING'S, 18, May 13; 1785: KING'S, Apr 28; 1786: CG, May 24, KING'S,
   25; 1787: KING'S, Mar 15; 1788: KING'S, May 8, 22; 1789: KING'S, Mar 19, Apr
   2, Jun 15, CG, Jul 2; 1790: HAY, May 28; 1792: HAY, Feb 20, Nov 26; 1795:
   KING'S, May 28; 1796: HAY, Mar 28, Aug 30; 1797: HAY, Feb 9, DL, Apr 28,
   KING'S, May 11, CG, 16, HAY, Sep 1; 1798: DL, Apr 27
Golden Star Tavern, 1740: DL, Apr 24; 1741: DL, Apr 4; 1762: HAY, Oct 25
Golden Unicorn Tavern, 1743: HAY, Mar 24
Golden, Mrs (milliner), 1785: HAY, Mar 15
Goldfinch (song), 1759: DL, Mar 29, CG, Apr 30
Goldie, Mrs (actor), 1771: HAY, Jan 28
Goldoni, Carlo, 1749: HAY, Nov 21; 1754: CG, Nov 18, Dec 9; 1760: KING'S, Nov
   22; 1761: KING'S, Jan 6, Apr 28; 1763: KING'S, Feb 3; 1764: DL, Nov 28; 1766:
   KING'S, Nov 25; 1767: KING'S, Feb 24; 1769: KING'S, May 6; 1771: MARLY, Aug
   8; 1773: DL, Feb 1; 1776: DL, Nov 21; 1777: KING'S, Jan 21, Dec 16; 1778:
   KING'S, Mar 26; 1779: DL, Dec 2; 1791: CG, Feb 16; 1798: DL, Jan 25
--Bourru Bienfaisant, Le, 1779: DL, Dec 2
--Padre di Famiglia, Il, 1798: DL, Jan 25
--Serva Amorosa, La, 1798: DL, Jan 25
--Servitore di due Padroni, Il, 1776: DL, Nov 21; 1791: CG, Feb 16
Goldsmith, Oliver, 1758: DL, Nov 2; 1759: DL, Sep 22, CG, 24, DL, 25, Oct 31;
   1760: DL, Mar 17; 1768: CG, Jan 29, Feb 2, 5, 9, 10; 1769: CG, Feb 18; 1771:
   HAY, Jun 26; 1773: CG, Mar 6, 15, Apr 30, May 3, 7, 8, 12; 1774: CG, Apr 28;
   1776: CG, Apr 27; 1784: HAY, Aug 24; 1785: HAY, Aug 23; 1787: HAY, Apr 30,
   CG, May 18; 1788: DL, May 6, HAY, Aug 13; 1789: CG, Apr 20; 1795: HAY, Mar 11
--Good Natured Man, The, 1768: CG, Jan 14, 28, 29, Feb 1, 2, 3, 4, 5, 6, 8, 9,
   10, Mar 21; 1771: CG, Jan 24, 26, Feb 1, May 24; 1773: CG, May 3; 1783: HAY,
   Aug 26, 30; 1784: HAY, Aug 24; 1785: HAY, Aug 23; 1788: HAY, Aug 27; 1789:
   CG, Apr 20; 1800: CG, Apr 22, May 5, 8
--Hermit, The, 1787: HAY, Apr 30; 1788: DL, May 6
--She Stoops to Conquer; or, The Mistakes of a Night, 1773: CG, Mar 6, 13, 15,
   16, 18, 25, 27, 29, Apr 1, 3, 12, 14, 15, 21, 22, 29, 30, May 5, 12, 13, 28,
   31, HAY, Jun 14, 16, 21, 28, Jul 9, CG, Oct 22, 26, Nov 2, 10, 19, Dec 10,
   30; 1774: CG, Jan 19, Feb 8, Apr 28, May 19, Sep 21, Nov 9, Dec 19; 1775: CG,
   Jan 13, Feb 25, Apr 4, May 10, 23, Oct 11, Nov 8; 1776: CG, Feb 7, May 4, Sep
   25, Nov 30; 1777: CG, Jan 22, Apr 25, May 9, HAY, Jun 9, 13, Jul 1, CHR, 2,
   HAY, 14, 29, CG, Dec 5; 1778: CG, Mar 21, May 16, 22, CHR, 29, HAY, Jul 1, 7;
   1779: CG, Jan 21, Nov 27; 1780: CG, Jan 14, May 26; 1781: CG, Jan 12, May 23,
   Nov 2; 1782: CG, May 28; 1785: HAMM, Jul 26, CG, Oct 3, Dec 27; 1786: HAMM,
   Jun 5; 1787: RLSN, Mar 29; 1788: CG, Mar 11, May 24; 1789: CG, Jun 5; 1790:
   CG, May 7, DL, 26, HAY, Sep 29, CG, Oct 1; 1792: CG, May 29; 1793: CG, Jan 2,
   HAY, Oct 15, 18, Nov 8; 1794: CG, Sep 24; 1797: HAY, Jun 20; 1798: CG, Sep
   19; 1799: WRSG, May 17; 1800: DL, May 21
Goldsmiths Jubilee, The. See Jordan, Thomas.
Goldsmiths, Company of, 1674: CITY, Oct 29; 1687: CITY, Oct 29; 1698: CITY, Oct
   29
Goliath. See Atterbury, Luffman.
Gom (Gum), Stephen (carpenter), 1759: CG, Oct 5, 19, 20, Nov 3, 28, Dec 22;
   1760: CG, Dec 23; 1761: CG, Jun 23
Gondeau, Mlle (dancer), 1743: DL, Feb 4, 11, May 4; 1745: CG, May 8, Nov 23,
   29, Dec 27; 1746: CG, Apr 5, 17, May 13, Jun 13, Dec 31; 1747: CG, May 13,
   15; 1748: CG, Mar 3, 14, 28, Apr 12, Oct 27; 1749: CG, Mar 9, Apr 15; 1750:
   CG, May 1, Dec 21, 26; 1751: CG, Apr 25, May 6, Oct 28, Nov 11, Dec 4; 1752:
   CG, Jan 16, Apr 30, Oct 26, Dec 7; 1753: CG, May 3; 1754: CG, May 9; 1755:
   CG, May 13; 1756: CG, May 17; 1757: CG, May 19

Gondolier (dance), 1729: DL, Dec 8; 1731: DL, May 3, 6; 1744: CG, Oct 10, 12,
    15, 16, 18, Nov 27, 29, Dec 3, 11, 14; 1745: CG, Jan 3, Apr 2, 23, 26, May
    14; 1746: CG, Feb 3, Jun 13; 1747: DL, Dec 3; 1748: DL, Feb 3, Apr 19, Oct
    19; 1749: DL, Mar 30, Apr 5; 1751: CG, Jan 17, Apr 12, 26, May 6; 1752: CG,
    Mar 19
Gondolier and Courtezan (dance), 1729: DL, Apr 23, 28, May 7; 1731: DL, May 19
Gondorff, Charles (singer), 1768: HAY, Apr 28
Gooch, Elizabeth Sarah, Mrs William (actor), 1796: HAY, Feb 22
Good (singer), 1703: DL, Dec 27; 1704: DL, Mar 30; 1706: DL, Jan 3
Good Natured Man, The. See Goldsmith, Oliver.
Good neighbor, why do you look away (song), 1694: DL, Sep 0
Good subjects of Old England (song), 1793: CG, Mar 23, Apr 3, May 10; 1794: CG,
    Apr 7; 1795: CG, May 13
Good we wish for (song), 1790: DL, Mar 5
Good, Mrs (beneficiary), 1742: CG, Apr 6
Goodall (actor), 1734: HAY, Jun 7; 1741: CG, Oct 16, Nov 11, Dec 22; 1742: CG,
    Feb 8, May 3, Dec 7; 1743: CG, Apr 28, Oct 31; 1744: CG, Jan 5, 24, Apr 19,
    25, 26, Sep 26, Oct 20; 1746: CG, Apr 22; 1748: HAY, Apr 25; 1750: CG, Apr
    27; 1751: CG, May 4
Goodall, Charlotte, Mrs Thomas (actor), 1788: DL, Oct 2, 22, 23, 25, Nov 8, 28,
    Dec 18; 1789: DL, Jan 7, Feb 20, May 5, 7, 13, 28, Jun 4, 5, 6, 12, HAY, Jul
    30, Aug 11, Sep 7, 15, DL, 15, 17, 19, 22, Oct 8, 13, 24, 31, Nov 5; 1790:
    DL, Jan 15, Feb 11, 15, Apr 30, May 14, 27, Jun 1, 4, HAY, 15, 17, 19, Jul
    16, Aug 10, 12, DL, Sep 11, Nov 4, 12, 17, 24, Dec 1, 3, 6, 8, 10; 1791: DL,
    Jan 14, May 5, 20, 25, 26, 31, HAY, Jun 6, 8, 25, Jul 14, 28, 30, Aug 13, 25,
    29, DLKING'S, Sep 22, 27, Oct 6, Nov 1, 9, 30, Dec 7, 15, 30; 1792: DLKING'S,
    Jan 23, 27, Feb 6, 23, 27, Mar 10, 29, Apr 10, 12, 26, May 19, Jun 4, 5, 15,
    16, HAY, 18, 20, 23, 26, Jul 2, 11, Aug 2, 17, 23, 31, Sep 6, DL, 18, 22, 29,
    Oct 2, 4, 13, 18, 20, Nov 3, Dec 8, 10, 11, 13, 15; 1793: DL, Jan 3, 9, 23,
    Feb 21, 25, Apr 3, 9, May 1, 9, HAY, Jun 28, Jul 3, 5, 13, 25, Aug 1, 3, 27,
    Sep 19, 24, 30, Oct 1, 5, 21, 22, 24, 30, Nov 5, 6, 16, 19, 23, 25, Dec 30;
    1794: HAY, Feb 22, DL, Apr 25, 29, May 5, 9, 30, Jun 16, 19, 23, 26, 27, HAY,
    Jul 9, 10, 18, 21, Aug 9, 13, 22, DL, Sep 16, 18, 20, 27, Oct 20, 31, Nov 7,
    12, 29, Dec 10, 13; 1795: DL, Jan 3, 9, 20, 21, 26, Feb 6, 7, Mar 10, Apr 16,
    May 4, Sep 26, Oct 20, 22, 27, Nov 5, 7, 14, 17, 18, Dec 2, 10, 11, 14, 21,
    30; 1796: DL, Jan 12, 14, Feb 27, 29, Mar 15, May 12, 23, Jun 8, 13, 14, Sep
    20, 27, Oct 1, 8, 15, 27, 28, Nov 10, 22, 26; 1797: DL, Feb 2, Apr 6, 24, May
    1, 24, Jun 13, 14, 15, 16, Sep 19, 26, 28, Oct 26, Nov 11, 18, 28, Dec 2, 9,
    21, 23; 1798: DL, Jan 4, 23, Mar 24, Apr 14, May 7, 8
Goodall, Master (actor), 1761: DL, May 5
Goode (doorkeeper), 1760: CG, Sep 22
Goodenough, Richard Josceline, 1779: CG, Nov 12; 1781: CG, Feb 24, Nov 17
--Cottagers, The, 1779: CG, Nov 12
--William and Nanny (pastoral), 1779: CG, Nov 12, 15, 17, 18, 19, 22, 23, 24,
    25, 26, 27, Dec 22; 1784: CG, Apr 17
Goodfellow (householder), 1745: GF, Mar 12
Goodfellow, J (actor), 1744: HAY, Jun 29, GF, Nov 27, Dec 3, 5, 13, 31; 1745:
    GF, Feb 5, 14, Mar 12, Apr 15, 17, 18, 30, May 1, 2, DL, Oct 8, 12, 17, Nov
    11, 18, 22, 30, Dec 5, 13; 1746: DL, Jan 1, 2, 8, 9, 18, 20, 31, Mar 17, Apr
    10, 15, 21, 22, 23, May 9, Oct 4, 31, Nov 4, 7, GF, Dec 3, 9, 15, 17, 18;
    1747: GF, Jan 5, 16, 26, Feb 12, 16, Mar 2, 5, 9, 19, Apr 2, 7; 1751: NWLS,
    Aug 6, Sep 5; 1752: DL, Jan 11, NWLS, Nov 16, 23, 28, 30, DL, Dec 20
Goodge St, 1782: DL, Mar 19, HAY, Sep 3; 1783: HAY, Aug 29; 1784: DL, Mar 27;
    1785: DL, Mar 17; 1787: HAY, Jul 27; 1792: HAY, Oct 15
Gooding (house servant), 1798: DL, Jun 16; 1799: DL, Jul 3; 1800: DL, Jun 14
Goodman (actor), 1748: Sep 7, SOU, Oct 10; 1758: CHAPEL, Apr 27; 1760: CG, Sep
    22
Goodman (actor), 1782: HAY, Nov 25
Goodman (dancer), 1798: DL, Oct 6, Nov 14, Dec 6; 1799: DL, Jan 19, Feb 5, Oct
    14; 1800: DL, Mar 11
Goodman, Cardell (actor), 1673: LIF, Dec 0; 1674: NONE, Sep 0; 1677: DL, Mar 0,
    17, May 5, Jun 0, Oct 0, Dec 12; 1678: DL, Feb 0, Mar 0; 1680: DL, Feb 0, Mar
    0; 1681: DL, Oct 0; 1682: DL, Feb 4, Mar 11, NONE, Sep 0, DL, Nov 16; 1683:
    NONE, Sep 0, DL, Nov 12; 1684: ATCOURT, Feb 11, NONE, Oct 27; 1685: DL, Dec
    19; 1686: DL, Feb 4, ATCOURT, Oct 27; 1687: NONE, Feb 16
Goodman's Fields Theatre (song), 1733: GF, May 14
Goodshaw, Mrs (actor), 1729: BFF, Aug 23
Goodwin (actor), 1788: HAY, Apr 29
Goodwin (house servant), 1746: DL, May 16; 1747: DL, May 15; 1748: DL, May 9;
    1749: DL, May 5; 1750: DL, May 1; 1751: CG, May 4; 1753: DL, May 15; 1754:
    DL, May 17; 1755: DL, May 15; 1756: DL, May 20; 1757: DL, May 17; 1758: DL,
    May 16; 1759: DL, May 24; 1769: DL, May 19

Goodwin, Eleanor, Mrs Thomas (dancer), 1784: CG, Mar 18, Apr 27, 28, May 21,
     Jun 10, HAY, Jul 13, Aug 26, CG, Sep 20, Oct 6, 8, 22; 1785: CG, Apr 16, 18,
     HAY, Jul 13, 28, Aug 15, 19, 31, CG, Oct 7, 10, Nov 7, 10; 1786: CG, Feb 24,
     Mar 4, HAY, Jun 12, 22, 30, Jul 3, Sep 6, CG, Oct 2, 6, Nov 14, Dec 12; 1787:
     CG, Feb 9, HAY, Aug 6, 14, 21, CG, Sep 28; 1788: CG, Jan 24, 28, Feb 4, May
     28, HAY, Jun 10, 27, Jul 7, Aug 5, 13, 15, Sep 4, CG, 15, Oct 1, 10, 22, 25,
     Nov 7, Dec 26; 1789: CG, Feb 19, Mar 28, May 2, 7, 28, Jun 6, 8, 12, Sep 16,
     30, Oct 2, 21, Nov 19; 1790: CG, Jan 29, Feb 4, Mar 22, 23, Jun 1, HAY, 19,
     25, Jul 1, 13, Aug 11, CG, Oct 4, Nov 23, Dec 20; 1791: CG, May 2, 26, HAY,
     Jun 17, Jul 1
Goodwin, Master (singer), 1796: CG, Dec 19; 1797: CG, Apr 8, Jun 5; 1798: CG,
     Nov 12, Dec 11; 1799: CG, Jan 29, Mar 25, Apr 13, Oct 21; 1800: CG, Jan 16,
     Feb 10
Goodwin, Starling (musician, composer), 1771: GROTTO, Aug 30, Sep 9; 1785: CG,
     Dec 20; 1790: DL, May 20; 1794: CG, Dec 26
Goodwin, Thomas (music copyist), 1784: CG, May 15; 1790: DL, May 20; 1792: CG,
     Jun 1, Dec 20; 1793: CG, Mar 23; 1794: CG, Jun 4; 1795: CG, May 30; 1797: CG,
     May 27; 1798: CG, Feb 12, May 31; 1799: CG, Jun 4; 1800: CG, Jun 10
--Relief of Williamstadt, The; or, The Return from Victory, 1793: CG, Mar 23,
     Apr 1, 2, 3, 9, 10, 12, 13, 15, 16, 29, 30, May 6, 7, 8, 9, 21, 23, Jun 6
Goody Groaner (song), 1791: CG, May 17, 18; see also Stammering Glee
Goodyar (spectator), 1702: DL, Dec 14
Goostree (actor, dancer, machinist), 1795: CG, Apr 6, May 30, Dec 21; 1796: CG,
     May 30; 1797: CG, Mar 16, May 18, Nov 24, Dec 26; 1798: CG, Feb 12, Apr 9,
     May 29, Nov 12; 1799: CG, Jan 29, May 17, Jun 6, Dec 23; 1800: CG, May 23
Goostree, Samuel (dancer, machinist), 1785: HAY, Aug 31; 1786: HAY, Jul 3;
     1795: CG, Oct 23; 1796: CG, Mar 15; 1797: CG, May 26, Nov 24; 1798: CG, Feb
     12, Apr 9; 1799: CG, Apr 13; 1800: CG, Feb 10, HAY, Jul 2
Gopell, Miss (actor), 1793: HAY, Aug 16, 29, Sep 2
Gordian Knot Untied, The. See Walsh, William.
Gordon (musician), 1757: KING'S, Mar 24; 1758: SOHO, Apr 1; 1761: SOHO, Jan 28;
     1762: KING'S, May 11; 1765: KING'S, Nov 23; 1766: KING'S, Oct 21; 1767:
     KING'S, May 9, Oct 27; 1768: KING'S, Feb 20, Nov 3; 1769: KING'S, Jun 29;
     1773: KING'S, Oct 23
Gordon, Alexander (singer, author), 1719: LIF, Dec 7; 1720: LIF, Jan 19, Feb 5,
     10, KING'S, Apr 2, 27, May 30; 1721: YB, Feb 6; 1722: HAY, Jan 26; 1723:
     KING'S, Feb 19, May 14; 1731: HAY, Mar 15; 1739: CG, Dec 17, 20; 1741: CG,
     Apr 4; 1744: DL, Apr 6, HAY, Nov 5; 1745: DL, Apr 3
--Lupone; or, The Inquisitor, 1731: HAY, Mar 15, 16, Apr 9
Gordon, General Patrick (spectator), 1686: DLORDG, May 6
Gordon, Jane Maxwell, Duchess of Gordon, 1800: KING'S, Mar 8, CG, Jun 12
Gordon, Miss (singer), 1770: HAY, Mar 19
Gordon, Mrs (actor), 1784: CG, Oct 4
Gore (singer), 1790: CG, Feb 19, 24, Mar 3, DL, 17
Gore, Mrs (actor), 1786: HAMM, Aug 5; 1795: WLWS, Jun 19
Goreing, Captain (killed), 1685: DG, Jun 10
Gorges, Sir Arthur, 1675: NONE, Sep 0
Gori (actor), 1774: KING'S, Mar 17
Goring, Charles, 1708: DL, Feb 9
--Irene; or, The Fair Greek, 1708: DL, Feb 9, 10, 11
Gorman (house servant), 1798: DL, Jun 16
Gorsuch (actor), 1728: HAY, May 8
Goslin (Gosley) (dancer), 1757: CG, Dec 10; 1758: CG, Feb 1, Apr 28, May 2, Oct
     14, 16, Nov 16, 23; 1759: CG, Dec 10; 1760: CG, Jan 16, 18, Apr 17, Sep 22,
     Oct 20, Dec 11; 1761: CG, Mar 9, Apr 2, Sep 16, 21, 26; 1762: CG, Jan 28
Gosnell, Winifred (actor), 1663: LIF, May 28, 29, Aug 0; 1664: LIF, Sep 10;
     1666: LIF, Dec 26; 1668: LIF, May 31, Jul 28; 1669: LIF, Jan 21
Goss (actor), 1776: HAY, Sep 18
Gottenburgh, 1752: CG, Dec 27
Goudain (actor), 1728: HAY, Feb 21
Gouge (George) (singer), 1698: LIF, Nov 0; 1700: YB, May 8, LIF, Jul 5
Gough (animal trainer), 1791: DLKING'S, Dec 31
Gough, Catherine (actor), 1795: CG, Oct 22, Nov 6, Dec 15
Gould, Grace (wardrobe keeper), 1756: CG, May 21; 1757: CG, May 10; 1758: CG,
     May 8; 1759: CG, May 18; 1760: CG, May 3, Sep 22; 1763: CG, May 14; 1764: CG,
     May 12; 1766: CG, May 15; 1767: CG, Jan 13
Gould, Mrs (house servant), 1738: CG, May 4; 1740: CG, Nov 12, Dec 12
Gould, Robert
--Rival Sisters, The; or, The Violence of Love, 1695: DL, Oct 0
Goulding, George (publisher), 1794: HAY, Jul 26; 1795: HAY, Aug 21
Goupy, Giuseppe (scene painter), 1727: KING'S, Jan 31
Gourion. See Gauron.

Gourlier (dancer), 1798: KING'S, May 10
Gourroin (actor), 1728: HAY, Feb 21
Gout Anglois (dance), 1735: GF/HAY, Jul 22; 1739: DL, Nov 2, 13, 21; 1740: DL,
    Feb 15, 18, May 21
Governante, La. See Bertoni, Fernando Giuseppe.
Governor of Barcelona, The. See Pix, Mary, The Spanish Wives.
Governor of Cyprus, The. See Oldmixon, John.
Governor, The. See Byrn, James.
Gower St, 1785: DL, Apr 30; 1786: DL, Mar 4, May 15; 1787: DL, Jan 29, May 7;
    1788: DL, Jan 21, CG, Apr 23, DL, May 2, 5, Dec 17; 1789: DL, Feb 16, Apr 21,
    CG, 28, DL, May 11, CG, 14; 1790: CG, Apr 27, 30; 1792: CG, May 2; 1793: CG,
    May 8; 1794: CG, May 14; 1795: CG, Apr 22, May 13; 1796: DL, Apr 13, CG, 20,
    HAY, Sep 5; 1797: CG, Apr 26, DL, May 8; 1798: DL, May 7; 1799: DL, Apr 8;
    1800: DL, Apr 28
Gower, Edward (spectator), 1660: VERE, Nov 19, ATCOURT, 19; 1661: ATCOURT, Feb
    26
Goyon (dancer), 1786: KING'S, Dec 23; 1787: KING'S, Jan 6, 16, 20, Feb 13, Mar
    8, 22, May 19, Jun 14
Grabu (Grahme), Louis (composer), 1667: ATCOURT, Oct 1; 1674: DL, Mar 27, 30;
    1678: DG, Jan 0, DL, Feb 0, DG, Jun 0; 1683: DLORDG, Sep 12; 1684: ATCOURT,
    Feb 11; 1685: DLORDG, Jan 1, DG, Jun 3; 1694: SMITHS, Nov 17
Gracchi, the, 1758: CG, Nov 3
Grace (actor), 1788: HAY, Apr 9, Sep 30
Grace (spectator), 1672: BF, Aug 26; 1677: DG, Feb 14
Grace, Anne (actor, dancer), 1721: LIF, Apr 26; 1726: LIF, Jul 5, 22, Aug 2,
    12, 19; 1727: DL, Sep 16; 1728: DL, Jan 10; 1729: DL, Jan 11, 22, 27, Feb 6,
    Mar 4, Apr 12, May 3, 12, 14, Oct 4, Nov 3, 18, Dec 2, 5, 10; 1730: DL, Jan
    9, Feb 10, Apr 20, RI, Jun 24, 27, Jul 16, BFOF, Aug 20, SFOF, Sep 9, DL, Oct
    8, 10, 20, Nov 16, 26, 28, Dec 11; 1731: DL, Jan 8, 20, Feb 8, May 17, RI,
    Jul 1, 8, 15, SF/BFFHH, Aug 24, DL, Sep 30, Oct 2, 9, Nov 1, 24, Dec 10, 17;
    1732: DL, Jan 10, Feb 3, Apr 12, 17, May 12, RI, Aug 17, BF, 22, DL, Sep 23,
    Oct 14, 21, Nov 7, 9, 18, Dec 11, 18; 1733: DL, Jan 9, 17, Feb 12, 15, 17,
    Mar 28, 29, 31, Apr 9, 19, 20, 27, 30, May 1, 7, 14, BFCGBH, Aug 23, DL/HAY,
    Sep 26, Oct 5, 8, 13, 15, 19, 20, 22, 25, 27, Nov 1, 5, 9, 26, 27, 28, Dec 5,
    10, 17, 20; 1734: DL/HAY, Mar 16, 23, 25, 30, LIF, Apr 26, DL, 29, LIF, May
    9, DL, 16, Nov 23; 1735: DL, Jan 28, 29, Feb 4, Mar 1, Apr 14, May 6, Sep 4,
    9, Oct 2, Nov 20, Dec 6; 1736: DL, Jan 28, Feb 21, Apr 15, Oct 23, 25, 29,
    Nov 1, 3, 20, Dec 7, 13, 21, 31; 1737: DL, Mar 15, 17, Oct 21, 25, 27, Nov
    11, 16; 1738: DL, Jan 5, 20, 25, 26, 27, Feb 7, 9, 28, Mar 18, 20, 21, Apr
    27, May 3, 8, 13, 16, Oct 17, 19, 21, 25, Nov 8, 9, 14, Dec 9, 26; 1739: DL,
    Jan 8, 13, 22, 26, Feb 3, 8, Mar 13, 22, Apr 12, 2$, May 19, 28, Oct 4, 6,
    11, 15, 16, 23, 25, 27, 29, Nov 7, 10, 16, 19, 20, 21, 23
Grace, Young (actor), 1733: DL, Mar 31
Gracechurch St, 1742: DL, Apr 21
Graces, The (dance), 1789: HAY, May 22, 25
Gradwell, Thomas (actor), 1668: BRIDGES, Dec 18
Graf von Burgund, Der. See Kotzebue, August Friedrich Ferdinand von.
Grafton St, 1753: DL, Dec 21
Grafton, Duke of (Lord Chamberlain), 1733: DL, May 28, 29; 1746: CG, Nov 4;
    1752: DL, Dec 2; 1754: CG, Jan 18, Feb 11; 1755: HAY, Sep 15
Graham (actor), 1768: HAY, Jun 23, Jul 27, Sep 19; 1771: HAY, Sep 20
Graham (actor), 1777: CHR, Jun 18, 20, 23, 25, 27, 30, Jul 2, 21, 23
Graham (actor, singer), 1798: CG, Apr 28
Graham (bricklayer), 1785: DL, Nov 30
Graham, George (actor), 1777: CHR, Jun 18, 20, 23, 25, 27, 30, Jul 2, 21, 23
Graham, Miss (actor), 1770: HAY, Mar 19
Graham, Mrs (actor), 1748: BFSY, Aug 24; 1754: DL, Feb 25, Apr 29, Dec 9; 1755:
    DL, Jan 22, Apr 16; 1756: DL, Dec 15; 1768: HAY, Jul 13, 22, 25, 27, Aug 15,
    19, Sep 19
Graham, Mrs (actor), 1777: CHR, Jun 20, 23, 27, 30, Jul 21
Graham, Richard, Lord Preston, 1683: DLORDG, Aug 14, Sep 12
Grahme. See Grabu, Louis.
Grainger, Mrs (actor), 1732: HAY, Apr 6; 1735: CG/LIF, Jan 17
Gramachree Molly (song), 1775: DL, May 17; 1778: HAY, Apr 30; 1783: DL, Apr 22,
    May 16; 1784: DL, May 3, 5, 7, 10, 14, 18, 19
Gramont (dancer), 1748: SFP, Sep 7
Gran Brettagna Emula Della Antica Roma, La (cantata), 1760: KING'S, Feb 25
Grand Aga and his Sultana (dance), 1732: LIF, Jan 22, 28
Grand Assembly of Lilliputians, The (play), 1754: SFH, Sep 19
Grand Procession of the Knights (entertainment), 1767: DL, Sep 22
Grand Representation of the Taking of Louisberg (entertainment), 1758: BF, Sep
    2

362

Grand Whisper (song), <u>1733</u>: LIF/CG, Apr 11

Grandchamps (dancer), <u>1749</u>: DL, Oct 24, 28, 31, Nov 1, 9, 27, 30, Dec 2, 6, 23,
28; <u>1750</u>: DL, Jan 4, 18, Mar 10, 13, 15, 17, 22, 27, 29, 31, Apr 2, 9, 17,
21, 23, 27, May 7, 11, Sep 20, 27; <u>1751</u>: CG, Nov 20, Dec 4, 9, 10, 16; <u>1752</u>:
CG, Jan 9, 16, Mar 30, Apr 18, Oct 19, Nov 2, 13, 28, Dec 11, 26; <u>1753</u>: CG,
May 1, Oct 8, 22, 24, 25, 30, Nov 7, 26, Dec 15, 19, 21, 22

Grandis, Sga (singer), <u>1757</u>: KING'S, Mar 24, May 31

Grange Court, <u>1737</u>: LIF, May 5

Granger, Elizabeth (actor, singer), <u>1779</u>: DL, Nov 3, Dec 27; <u>1780</u>: DL, Sep 23;
<u>1781</u>: DL, May 1, Nov 5, 13; <u>1782</u>: DL, Jan 4, Apr 12, 17, 25, Dec 26; <u>1783</u>:
DL, Mar 3, May 2, 12

Granger, Julia (actor, singer), <u>1786</u>: DL, Nov 22; <u>1794</u>: DL, Apr 21, 28, Jun 9,
Sep 27, Oct 14, 31, Nov 15, Dec 20; <u>1795</u>: DL, Jan 19, Feb 12, May 6, HAY, Jun
13, 20, Jul 31, DL, Oct 30, Nov 11, 23, Dec 10; <u>1796</u>: DL, Jan 8, 11, 18, Mar
3, 12, Apr 13, May 23, 25, HAY, Jul 8, 15, 30, Aug 18, 29, DL, Oct 18, 19,
Nov 9; <u>1797</u>: DL, Jan 7, 20, Feb 9, Mar 18, 23, May 13, 24, Jun 10

Granger, Mrs (actor), <u>1764</u>: HAY, Jun 13, Jul 13, Aug 20, Sep 1; <u>1765</u>: HAY, Jun
10, 24, Jul 15, 17, Aug 30; <u>1771</u>: HAY, May 15, 17, 22, 23, 27, 29, 31, Jun 5,
10, 12, 14, Jul 1, 5, 24, Aug 26, Sep 2, 16, 18, 19, 20

Granger, Mrs (actor, dancer), <u>1710</u>: GR, Jun 15, Jul 27, 29; <u>1711</u>: QUEEN'S, May
2, GR, Aug 9

Granger, Samuel (actor), <u>1764</u>: HAY, Jun 13, 26, Jul 6, 13, 23, Aug 20, Sep 1,
DL, 20, 25, Oct 16, 17, 20, 22, Nov 9, 27; <u>1765</u>: DL, Feb 26, Apr 13, May 16

Granier (Greniere) (dancer), <u>1735</u>: GF/HAY, Jan 2, Feb 5; <u>1737</u>: LIF, Jan 19;
<u>1739</u>: BFH, Aug 23; <u>1740</u>: BFH, Aug 23; <u>1741</u>: BFH, Aug 22, GF, Oct 9, 16, Dec
28; <u>1742</u>: GF, Jan 13, 14, Feb 8, LIF, Nov 26, Dec 3, 13, 27; <u>1743</u>: LIF, Jan
7, Feb 17; <u>1745</u>: GF, Feb 14, Apr 15, Dec 4; <u>1746</u>: CG, Dec 27; <u>1747</u>: CG, May
29, Dec 26; <u>1750</u>: HAY, Feb 16, DL, Nov 8; <u>1753</u>: DL, May 12, Nov 14, CG, 20,
DL, 21, CG, Dec 4, 22; <u>1754</u>: DL, Jan 16, Feb 9, CG, 12, DL, Mar 14, 26, CG,
Apr 24, DL, 26, CG, May 1, 4, DL, 4, 10, CG, Nov 23; <u>1755</u>: CG, Jan 4, Apr 1,
2, 11, 14, 18, 23, DL, Oct 8, CG, 22, DL, Nov 8, CG, 14, 15, DL, 15, 22, CG,
26, Dec 3, 9, 17; <u>1756</u>: CG, Jan 21, 26, 31, Feb 21, 24, Mar 15, 20, Apr 20,
28, DL, May 6, Oct 18, CG, 21, Nov 29, Dec 10, 11, 15; <u>1757</u>: CG, Jan 3, 28,
Feb 8, 9, Mar 28, Apr 23, 27, May 2, Oct 12, Nov 2, Dec 14; <u>1758</u>: CG, Feb 1,
Oct 6, Nov 16, 23; <u>1759</u>: CG, Oct 5, Nov 5, 13, Dec 10, 11; <u>1760</u>: CG, Jan 4,
8, 16, 18, Mar 18, 22, Apr 12, 18, 21, 22, May 12, 15, 19, Sep 22, Oct 3, 15,
20, Dec 11, 17; <u>1761</u>: CG, Jan 13, Mar 9, 27, Apr 7, May 5, Sep 16, 21, 26,
Oct 13; <u>1762</u>: CG, Mar 20, Oct 8, Nov 1; <u>1763</u>: CG, Jan 26, Feb 2, 24, Apr 15,
30, May 7, 13, Oct 22, Nov 3, 15; <u>1764</u>: CG, Jan 14; <u>1767</u>: DL, Jan 24, Mar 7;
<u>1774</u>: DL, Oct 1

Granier, J (dancer), <u>1749</u>: CG, Mar 30, Apr 3, 5, 7, 10, 11, 12, 14, 17, 18, 19,
20, 21, 24, 25, May 1, 3

Granier, Jack (dancer), <u>1746</u>: GF, Feb 5, 7, 13; <u>1748</u>: NWC, Apr 4; <u>1749</u>: CG, Mar
29, Apr 28; <u>1756</u>: CG, Mar 1

Granier, Jack and Joseph (dancers), <u>1740</u>: BFH, Aug 23; <u>1741</u>: BFH, Aug 22, GF,
Oct 9; <u>1742</u>: GF, Feb 2, 6, 16, Apr 20, 22, 27, May 18, LIF, Nov 26, 29, Dec
3, 13, 27; <u>1743</u>: LIF, Jan 7, Feb 17, 28, Mar 3, 8; <u>1744</u>: GF, Dec 10; <u>1745</u>:
GF, Feb 4; <u>1746</u>: GF, Jan 31, Feb 17, 24, 25, 27, Mar 10, 11

Granier, Jack and Polly (dancers), <u>1749</u>: CG, Mar 13

Granier, Jack, Joseph and Polly (dancers), <u>1741</u>: GF, Sep 14, 16, Oct 19, 20,
Nov 23, 26, Dec 15, 23; <u>1742</u>: GF, Jan 9, 12, 29, Feb 2, 14, Mar 15, Apr 21;
<u>1743</u>: LIF, Jan 7, Mar 8, 14; <u>1746</u>: GF, Jan 24, Feb 3, 20, Mar 18, 20; <u>1748</u>:
CG, Dec 23, 27

Granier, Joseph (dancer), <u>1746</u>: GF, Feb 5, 7, 13

Granier, Master and Polly (dancers), <u>1742</u>: GF, Jan 4, Feb 6, 16, Apr 20, 22;
<u>1748</u>: CG, Dec 20

Granier, Master Jack or Joseph (dancer), <u>1742</u>: GF, Jan 15, Feb 25, Mar 25, Apr
6, LIF, Nov 29; <u>1748</u>: CG, Mar 14, 24, 31, Apr 18, 29, May 4; <u>1749</u>: CG, Mar 9,
Apr 19; <u>1750</u>: HAY, Mar 8; <u>1752</u>: DL, Dec 15

Granier, Miss (dancer), <u>1787</u>: KING'S, Dec 8

Granier, Mr and Mrs (dancers), <u>1754</u>: CG, Nov 5; <u>1755</u>: CG, Apr 9, 17, 24, 26,
29, May 9; <u>1763</u>: CG, Jan 26

Granier, Mrs (dancer), <u>1747</u>: CG, Jan 29; <u>1755</u>: CG, Apr 1, 2, 11, 14, 23, Oct
23; <u>1756</u>: CG, Mar 20, Apr 28, Oct 21, Nov 29; <u>1757</u>: CG, Feb 8, Oct 12, Nov 2,
Dec 14, 17; <u>1758</u>: CG, Feb 1, Apr 12, 14, May 8, Oct 6, 14, Nov 16, 23; <u>1759</u>:
CG, Nov 5, Dec 10, 13; <u>1760</u>: CG, Jan 16, 18, Apr 12, Sep 22, Oct 3, 15, 20,
Dec 11, 17; <u>1761</u>: CG, Jan 13, Mar 9, 27, Apr 7, May 5, Sep 16, 21, 26, Oct
13; <u>1762</u>: CG, Mar 20; <u>1763</u>: CG, Jan 26

Granier, Polly (dancer), <u>1740</u>: BFH, Aug 23; <u>1741</u>: BFH, Aug 22; <u>1742</u>: GF, Feb
25, Mar 25, Apr 6, May 18, LIF, Nov 26, 29, Dec 3, 13; <u>1745</u>: GF, Feb 4, Oct
28; <u>1746</u>: GF, Jan 31, Feb 5, 7, 13, 17, 24, 25, 27, Mar 10, 11, CG, Dec 5;
<u>1748</u>: CG, Mar 14, 24, 31, NWC, Apr 4, CG, 18, 29, May 4, Oct 27; <u>1749</u>: CG,

Mar 9, 29, 30, Apr 3, 5, 7, 10, 11, 12, 14, 17, 18, 19, 20, 21, 24, 25, 28,
May 1, 3; 1763: CG, Apr 15; 1768: DL, May 4; 1772: KING'S, Nov 14, 21, Dec 5,
8; 1773: KING'S, Jan 2, 5, 12, 15, 26, Feb 2, Mar 9, 16, 18, 23, 30, Apr 1,
17, 24, 27, May 1, 11, Jun 1, 12, 19
Granny's Prediction (pamphlet), 1773: DL, Jan 1
Granom (Granio, Granno, Grannon), John (musician), 1714: SH, Apr 6, QUEEN'S,
May 1; 1715: LIF, Oct 22; 1717: SH, Dec 23; 1718: TEC, Mar 12, SH, Dec 23;
1720: LIF, Mar 12, 24, YB, Apr 1, DL, May 24; 1721: HIC, Mar 1; 1722: DL, Mar
14, HAY, May 11; 1725: SH, May 27; 1729: HIC, Apr 30, SH, Dec 12
Granom, Lewis (musician), 1722: HAY, May 11; 1729: HIC, Jan 4, LIF, Apr 15,
HIC, 30; 1730: LIF, Apr 8
Granom, Lewis or John (musician), 1729: LIF, Apr 15
Grant (actor), 1744: HAY, May 10
Grant (mercer), 1729: LIF, Mar 12
Grant, D (beneficiary), 1754: HAY, Apr 25; 1758: HAY, Mar 13
Granville, Ann (correspondent), 1724: LIF, Dec 12; 1726: LIF, Nov 26; 1729:
KING'S, Dec 20; 1735: KING'S, Mar 15; 1737: CG, Jan 8
Granville, George, Lord Landsdowne, 1685: ATCOURT, Dec 14; 1688: DL, Apr 0;
1695: LIF, Dec 0; 1698: LIF, Jan 0; 1701: LIF, Jan 0, DL, Dec 0; 1703: LIF,
Apr 28; 1706: QUEEN'S, Feb 21; 1721: LIF, Oct 17; 1723: HAY, Dec 19, 20;
1746: DL, Mar 13; 1747: ST, Apr 29; 1755: DL, Feb 3
--British Enchanters, The; or, No Magick Like Love, 1706: QUEEN'S, Feb 21, 23,
25, 26, 28, Mar 2, 5, 9, 12, 26, Apr 2, May 3, Dec 10; 1707: QUEEN'S, Mar 22,
25, Apr 14
--Heroick Love, 1698: LIF, Jan 0; 1713: DL, Mar 19; 1723: HAY, Dec 19, 20;
1725: DL, Oct 21; 1766: DL, Mar 18
--Jew of Venice, The; or, The Female Lawyer, 1701: LIF, Jan 0; 1703: LIF, May
10; 1706: QUEEN'S, Oct 23; 1711: DL, Feb 3, GR, Aug 23, Sep 8; 1715: LIF, Feb
28, Mar 22, Jul 8, Nov 18; 1716: LIF, Jan 20, Jul 20; 1717: LIF, May 16;
1718: LIF, Jan 24, Apr 26; 1719: LIF, Jan 2, BCA, Sep 24; 1720: LIF, Feb 26;
1721: LIF, Mar 28, Oct 17, Nov 10; 1722: LIF, Jan 5, Nov 16; 1723: LIF, Jan
25; 1724: BPT, Mar 18; 1727: LIF, Apr 17, Nov 13, 30; 1728: LIF, May 23;
1729: LIF, Jan 23, May 2, Dec 16; 1730: LIF, Oct 7, Nov 21; 1731: LIF, Feb
22, Oct 20; 1732: LIF, Jan 25; 1734: CG, Feb 8; 1735: CG/LIF, Feb 11; 1736:
CG, Feb 12; 1739: CG, Jan 23; 1747: ST, Apr 29; 1748: SOU, Oct 31
--Peleus and Thetis, 1747: ST, Apr 29
--She Gallant, The; or, Once a Lover and always a Lover, 1695: LIF, Dec 0;
1717: LIF, Jan 17, 18, May 20; 1746: DL, Mar 13, Apr 5
Granville, Miss (singer), 1758: MARLY, Aug 21
Grasetti, Maria (singer), 1717: KING'S, Feb 2, Mar 2
Grassi (singer), 1766: KING'S, Oct 21, Dec 27; 1770: KING'S, Feb 2
Grassi, Cecilia (singer), 1769: KING'S, Sep 5; 1770: KING'S, Mar 1, 22, May 10;
1771: KING'S, Jan 10, Feb 8, 9, 28, May 6; 1772: DL, Mar 6, HAY, 23, 30, Apr
6, KING'S, 21, HAY, 27, KING'S, May 28; 1773: HAY, Apr 19
Grateful Acknowledgment, The (musical address), 1775: HAY, Feb 2
Grateful Hearts enjoy the Blessing (song), 1789: CG, Apr 3; 1794: CG, Mar 26,
Apr 11; 1798: CG, Mar 28, 30; 1800: CG, Mar 5
Grateful Servant, The. See Shirley, James.
Grattan, Henry (correspondent), 1767: DL, Oct 27
Gratulatory Epilogue (song), 1747: CG, Apr 24
Graun (composer), 1755: HAY, Apr 18; 1757: KING'S, Mar 24; 1770: CG, Mar 16
Graves, James (beneficiary), 1710: CDR, Feb 24; 1711: PH, Mar 1
Graves, Richard (author), 1796: DL, May 2
Gray (actor), 1728: DL, Nov 15; 1729: DL, Jun 13; 1730: DL, Apr 23, Dec 4;
1731: DL, Jul 23, Aug 6, 11, Oct016, Nov 25; 1732: DL, Mar 21, May 6, 12, Aug
1, BF, 22, DL, Nov 17, Dec 26; 1733: DL, Feb 17, Mar 31, BFCGBH, Aug 23,
DL/HAY, Oct 12; 1734: DL/HAY, Feb 7, 22, DL, Apr 15, LIF, May 23, HAY, Jun 7,
Jul 19, BFFO, Aug 24, DL, Oct 21, Nov 1; 1735: DL, Jan 22, May 14, Jul 1,
GF/HAY, 22, HAY, Aug 4, GF/HAY, 8, HAY, 12, GF/HAY, 21, DL, Sep 15, Oct 31;
1736: DL, Jan 12, Feb 28, BFFH, Aug 23, DL, Oct 12, Dec 4, 31; 1737: DL, May
21; 1738: DL, Jan 24, Feb 23, May 30, Oct 3, 30; 1739: DL, Jan 13, Mar 29,
Apr 5, May 28, Oct 1, 10, 15, Nov 15, 22, Dec 11, 31; 1740: DL, Jan 5, 15,
Apr 8, May 19, BFHC, Aug 23, DL, Dec 4, 18; 1741: DL, May 12, 28, BFH, Aug
22, DL, Oct 31, Nov 11, Dec 4, 7, 19; 1742: DL, Mar 29, Apr 20, May 13, BFHC,
Aug 25, DL, Sep 25, Oct 2, 7, 13; 1743: DL, May 10, Oct 25, Dec 6, 9; 1744:
DL, Jan 17, Mar 12, Apr 9, May 8, Cct 11, Nov 2; 1745: DL, Jan 8, 16, GF, May
1, DL, 7, Jun 5, Nov 18, Dec 11, 27; 1746: DL, Jun 11, Sep 30, Oct 23; 1747:
DL, Jan 17, May 4, Oct 17; 1748: DL, May 9, Nov 29; 1749: DL, May 9; 1750:
DL, Jan 4, May 3; 1751: DL, May 8; 1752: DL, May 4, Dec 8; 1753: DL, May 14,
21; 1754: DL, May 20; 1755: DL, May 12, Oct 17, Nov 8, 15; 1756: DL, Apr 29,
May 13, Nov 18; 1757: DL, Sep 29; 1758: DL, May 9, Nov 16; 1759: DL, May 28,
Oct 30; 1760: DL, Oct 3

Gray (actor), 1785: HAY, Jan 31; 1791: HAY, Dec 12
Gray (boxkeeper), 1795: DL, Jun 5; 1796: DL, Jun 15; 1797: DL, Jun 16
Gray (house servant), 1769: CG, Jan 6
Gray (house servant), 1786: CG, May 18; 1787: CG, May 19; 1788: CG, May 27;
    1789: CG, Jun 16
Gray, James (constable), 1746: DL, May 3
Gray, Master (singer), 1800: CG, May 15, 28
Gray, Miss (dancer), 1773: DL, May 10
Gray, Mrs Thomas Brabazon (actor, singer), 1785: CG, Sep 23, Oct 17, Nov 14;
    1787: CG, Jan 27, Dec 3, 17; 1788: CG, Jan 7, Sep 22, Dec 29; 1789: CG, Sep
    14, Oct 12, Dec 21; 1790: CG, Jan 23, Mar 1, May 24, 27, Sep 13, Oct 6, Nov
    26; 1791: CG, May 26, Sep 26, Oct 3, 10, Dec 22; 1792: CG, Feb 28, Apr 12,
    May 10, Oct 8, 19, 29; 1793: CG, Apr 8
Gray, Sarah Jane (actor, singer), 1796: CG, Oct 17, Dec 19; 1797: CG, Apr 25,
    May 18, Sep 25, Oct 16, Nov 2, Dec 18; 1798: CG, Mar 19, Apr 9, Sep 17, Oct
    8, 15, Nov 12, Dec 11, 15, 26; 1799: CG, Jan 29, Mar 2, 4, 26, Apr 22, May 4,
    10, 14
Gray, Thomas (author), 1769: HAY, Feb 2; 1795: HAY, Mar 11; 1799: HAY, Sep 16;
    1800: CG, Jun 16
Gray, Thomas (spectator), 1736: GF, Jan 3, CG, Jun 9, Oct 1; 1742: KING'S, Apr
    20; 1746: DL, Oct 4; 1751: DL, Feb 12; 1755: KING'S, Dec 9
Gray, Thomas Brabazon (actor), 1791: CG, Apr 30, Oct 20, Nov 19, Dec 10, 21,
    22; 1792: CG, Jan 23, Feb 28, Mar 1, 22, 31, Apr 12, May 19, 28, 29, Oct 8,
    19, 25, 29, Nov 5, HAY, 26, CG, Dec 20, 22, 26, 29, 31; 1793: CG, Jan 9, Feb
    25, Mar 23, Apr 4, 30, May 3, 10, 24, Jun 8, 12, Sep 20, 23, 30, Oct 2, 7, 9,
    12, Nov 5, 18, 19, Dec 9, 16, 27; 1794: CG, Feb 4, Apr 30, Oct 7, 20, 30, Nov
    15, Dec 26; 1795: CG, Jan 31, Feb 20, Mar 11, 16, Apr 29, Oct 24, Nov 4, Dec
    21, 28; 1796: CG, Jan 4, Feb 2, Apr 26, 30, May 31, Sep 16, 26, Oct 6, 14,
    24, Nov 19, Dec 12, 19; 1797: CG, Feb 18, Mar 16, Apr 8, 25, 27, May 6, 18,
    19, 20, 22, 23, Jun 14, Sep 25, Oct 2, 16, 18, 20, 31, Nov 2, 24, Dec 16, 18,
    26; 1798: CG, Feb 9, 12, Mar 15, 17, 19, 31, Apr 9, 16, 21, 28, May 8, 12,
    14, 28, Jun 4, 11, Sep 17, HAY, 17, CG, Oct 8, 11, 25, 31, Nov 12, Dec 11,
    15, 26; 1799: CG, Jan 29, Mar 2, 4, 16, 25, 26, Apr 3, 22, May 10, 14
Gray's Bard (entertainment), 1798: HAY, Sep 17
Gray's Inn Coffee House, 1737: LIF, Mar 9
Gray's Inn Gate, 1737: LIF, Mar 9; 1756: DL, Mar 9
Gray's Inn Passage, 1744: HAY, Apr 23; 1745: GF, Feb 26
Gray's Inn, 1736: LIF, Apr 29, CG, May 24; 1742: JS, Oct 12; 1751: DL, Dec 17;
    1761: DL, Mar 14; 1779: HAY, May 10; 1782: CG, Apr 26; 1790: DL, Apr 6
Graydon (actor), 1668: NONE, Sep 0, BRIDGES, Nov 6
Graziani, Clementina (actor), 1789: KING'S, Jan 10, May 2
Greak (householder), 1794: CG, May 23
Great Almonry, 1744: CG, Jan 19
Great Augustus like the glorious sun (song), 1682: DG, Jan 23
Great Britain still her Charter boasts (song), 1793: CG, Mar 23; 1798: CG, Feb
    9, May 8, 28, Jun 4; 1799: CG, May 28; 1800: CG, Apr 15, 19
Great Brookfield, 1745: MF, May 2
Great Buckingham St, 1780: CG, Mar 14
Great Chelsea, 1733: CHE, May 9
Great Concert Hall, 1757: BF, Sep 3; 1759: BFY, Sep 3
Great Favourite, The. See Howard, Sir Robert.
Great Fire, 1668: NONE, Oct 29
Great Fives Court, 1746: SFY, Sep 8
Great George St, 1784: HAY, Jul 24
Great Hart St, 1777: CG, May 13
Great Jehovah's awful Word (song), 1789: CG, Apr 3; 1790: CG, Feb 26; 1791: CG,
    Mar 23; 1792: CG, Mar 2; 1797: CG, Mar 10, 15, Apr 7; 1798: CG, Mar 30
Great Jove once made love like a bull (song), 1692: DL, Jan 0
Great Maddox St, 1777: CG, Apr 25, May 20; 1778: CG, May 16
Great Marlborough St, 1779: DL, May 7; 1781: DL, May 16; 1782: KING'S, Apr 11,
    May 16, Jun 5; 1788: KING'S, Apr 17; 1789: KING'S, May 21; 1792: DLKING'S,
    Mar 26; 1793: DL, Mar 18; 1795: DL, Apr 27, CG, Jun 2; 1796: DL, May 2; 1797:
    DL, May 1; 1798: DL, Apr 23; 1799: DL, May 29
Great Mary-le-Bone St, 1770: MARLY, Aug 21; 1782: KING'S, Mar 7; 1783: KING'S,
    Mar 6; 1784: KING'S, Mar 4
Great Mogul, 1737: HAY, Mar 8; see also Fielding, Henry
Great Newport St, 1736: DL, May 8; 1743: CG, Apr 6; 1786: CG, May 2; 1787: CG,
    Mar 13
Great Ormond St, 1743: CG, Mar 24; 1744: CG, Apr 4
Great Piazza Coffee Room, 1756: LRRH/PCR, Feb 18, PCR, 21, LRRH/PCR, 25, Mar 4,
    10, 17, PCR, 24, 31
Great Piazza, 1740: CG, Mar 10; 1743: DL, Jan 13; 1744: DL, Feb 25, Mar 5, 13;

365

1752: DL, Jan 6; 1753: DL, Mar 20; 1771: CG, May 10; 1773: DL, May 12, CG,
    20; 1777: CG, May 7; 1778: CG, May 5; 1779: DL, Apr 14, CG, 30; 1790: DL, May
    11; 1791: DL, May 11
Great Portland St, 1788: CG, Feb 5; 1794: HAY, May 22
Great Pulteney St, 1778: HAY, Apr 29; 1784: KING'S, Feb 26, Mar 18, May 13;
    1785: KING'S, Apr 28; 1786: KING'S, May 25; 1788: CG, Apr 11; 1796: HAY, Aug
    30; 1797: HAY, Feb 9, DL, Apr 28, KING'S, May 11; 1798: DL, Apr 27
Great Queen of Hymen's hallowed fires (song), 1696: DG, Oct 0
Great Queen St, 1736: DL, Mar 23, CG, Apr 6, DL, 13, LIF, 19; 1737: HIC, Apr 1,
    CG, 11; 1740: CG, Mar 18, DL, 25, CG, Apr 9, DL, 15, 25; 1741: DL, Mar 14,
    CG, Apr 7, DL, 13, Dec 21; 1742: CG, Mar 6, 15, DL, Apr 30; 1743: DL, Mar 8,
    15, Apr 7; 1744: CG, Mar 13; 1745: DL, Mar 20, Apr 16; 1746: CG, Mar 10, DL,
    10, Apr 12, 29; 1747: DL, Mar 7; 1748: DL, Mar 21; 1749: DL, Mar 13, Apr 14;
    1750: DL, Mar 13; 1751: DL, Mar 11, Apr 23, 30; 1752: DL, Mar 7, Apr 17;
    1753: DL, Mar 19, Apr 30; 1757: DL, Mar 22, Apr 18, 30; 1759: DL, Apr 18;
    1762: CG, Apr 23; 1764: DL, May 15; 1765: DL, Mar 18; 1777: CG, Apr 5, 19;
    1778: CG, Mar 31, DL, Apr 7; 1779: CG, Apr 10; 1780: CG, Apr 1, DL, 5, 22;
    1782: DL, Apr 1, CG, 9; 1783: DL, Apr 3, 24; 1784: DL, Mar 30, Apr 26, CG,
    27, May 18; 1785: CG, Mar 30, DL, Apr 4, CG, 13, 18; 1786: DL, Apr 19, CG,
    21, May 3, 26; 1787: CG, Apr 25, May 3, 23, Jun 15; 1788: DL, Apr 2, May 14;
    1790: DL, Apr 7; 1791: DL, Apr 27, CG, Jun 1; 1792: DLKING'S, Apr 10, CG, May
    18; 1794: DL, Mar 12, HAY, Aug 30; 1795: DL, Apr 24; 1796: DL, May 5; 1797:
    DL, May 12, 19; 1798: DL, May 11, CG, 16; 1799: CG, Mar 5, DL, Apr 17, CG,
    23; 1800: CG, Apr 5, DL, May 16
Great Room, 1701: RIW, Aug 11; 1709: HA, Jul 30; 1721: RI, Oct 23; 1731: STA,
    Aug 9; 1732: TTT, Mar 3, 10, RIW/HAY, Sep 12; 1734: GR, Nov 4; 1735: YB/HAY,
    Oct 1; 1751: CT, Dec 3; 1754: HIC, Jan 2, SOHO, Mar 26, 28, KING'S, Apr 2,
    DL, Nov 22, HAY, Dec 16, 18; 1755: SOHO, Mar 11; 1756: SOHO, Feb 2, Mar 16,
    BFGR, Sep 3; 1757: SOHO, Feb 1, CRT, 7, SOHO, Mar 14; 1758: SOHO, Mar 31;
    1759: SOHO, Mar 1, MARLY, Apr 16; 1760: SOHO, Jan 18, Feb 14; 1761: SOHO, Jan
    21, 28, Apr 15; 1762: SOHO, Feb 9, Apr 21; 1763: SOHO, Feb 4; 1764: CG, Jun
    5; 1765: MARLY, Oct 5; 1773: CR, Apr 21, 30; 1774: GRP, Jul 23; 1776: DL, Jun
    1
Great Russel St, 1741: CG, Mar 17; 1742: LIF, Jan 29, DL, Mar 12, CG, 30; 1757:
    CG, Apr 13; 1777: CG, Apr 8; 1778: DL, May 27; 1780: CG, Apr 12, 27; 1781:
    CG, Apr 23, 24, May 4; 1782: HAY, Jan 14, CG, Apr 16, 29; 1783: CG, Apr 5,
    DL, 25; 1784: CG, Mar 27, DL, Apr 28, HAY, Jul 30, Aug 20; 1786: CG, May 6,
    20; 1790: CG, Apr 21; 1791: CG, May 5; 1792: CG, Apr 18, DLKING'S, 26; 1793:
    CG, Apr 24, HAY, Aug 1; 1794: CG, May 7, HAY, Aug 13; 1795: CG, Apr 29; 1796:
    CG, Apr 8, May 17; 1797: CG, May 6, DL, Jun 2; 1798: CG, May 1; 1800: HAY,
    Aug 12
Great Shier Lane, 1748: DL, Apr 19
Great Square, 1782: CG, Apr 26
Great Storm of 1703, 1703: DL, Nov 27
Great Suffolk St, 1732: LIF, Apr 13; 1739: DL, Apr 7; 1763: HAY, Sep 5; 1767:
    CG, Mar 31; 1777: KING'S, Mar 13, Apr 17; 1779: KING'S, Apr 29; 1780: KING'S,
    Apr 27; 1781: KING'S, Mar 15; 1782: DL, Apr 17; 1786: KING'S, Mar 23; 1787:
    HAY, Aug 14; 1788: KING'S, Apr 3; 1789: CG, Apr 21; 1790: HAY, Mar 25; 1800:
    DL, Jun 2
Great Tichfield St, 1787: CG, Apr 20
Great Wild St, 1738: CG, May 1; 1748: HAY, Nov 14; 1772: CG, May 6; 1777: DL,
    Apr 19; 1799: CG, Jun 5
Greatest Glory of a Prince is the Conquest of His Own Passions, The (play),
    1726: KING'S, Nov 1
Greatheed, Bertie, 1788: DL, Mar 29; 1789: DL, Mar 17; 1796: DL, May 23
--Regent, The, 1788: DL, Mar 29, Apr 1, 3, 26, May 3, 13, 17, 20, 24, 27; 1789:
    DL, Mar 17; 1792: DLKING'S, Mar 17; 1793: DL, Jan 7; 1796: DL, Feb 20
Greatorex, Thomas (organist), 1789: CG, Mar 20, Apr 30; 1790: CG, Feb 19, Mar
    17; 1791: CG, Mar 16, Apr 6, 13; 1792: CG, Feb 29, Mar 28, 30; 1794: KING'S,
    May 15
Greber, Giacomo (composer), 1703: LIF, Jun 8, 11; 1704: DL, Jan 29, Feb 12, 19,
    26, Apr 22, 29, May 31, CC, Jun 7, DL, Jul 5
Grecian Coffee House, 1697: LIF, Feb 19; 1752: DL, Mar 17; 1753: DL, Apr 3;
    1754: CG, Jan 29
Grecian Daughter, The. See Murphy, Arthur.
Grecian Sailors (dance), 1735: CG/LIF, Apr 17, 21, May 19; 1737: CG, Mar 26,
    31, Apr 2, 12, 19, 21, 22, 25, 29, May 3, 5, 6, 13, 16, 31, Oct 5, 12; 1738:
    CG, Mar 20, 21, Apr 14, 18, 19, 21, 22, 25, 28, 29, May 1, 2, 10, 11, 15, Oct
    20; 1739: CG, Jan 15, Apr 9, 23, 24, 25, May 1, 4, 7, 11, 14, 15, 16, 17, 18,
    21, 25, 28, 30, Sep 12, 14, 17, 19, Oct 2, Nov 10, 12, Dec 1, 3, 18; 1740:
    CG, Feb 6, Mar 10, 11, May 2, 7, 12, 19, 20, Jun 5; 1741: CG, Jan 8; 1753:
    CG, Apr 9

Gree (beneficiary), 1741: DL, May 15
Greek dresses, 1767: DL, Nov 5
Greek Slave, The. See Ford, Richard.
Greek St, 1740: DL, Apr 24; 1741: DL, Apr 4; 1743: DL, May 18; 1758: KING'S, Apr 6
Greek tragedy, 1772: CG, Nov 21; 1774: CG, Oct 3
Green (actor), 1729: FLR, Nov 29, Dec 1; 1731: HAY, Jun 2; 1735: HAY, Aug 12; 1736: LIF, Apr 29; 1737: HAY, Jan 26
Green (actor), 1785: HAY, Apr 25
Green (banker), 1798: DL, Oct 27
Green (beneficiary), 1741: GF, Jan 22
Green (prompter), 1736: DL, Nov 19, 23; 1737: DL, Apr 12, Oct 1; 1738: DL, Jan 19, 26, Apr 6, 13, May 17, Sep 30; 1739: DL, Jan 16, Apr 5, 25, May 12, 15, 30, Oct 17, 27, Nov 15, 20; 1740: DL, Jan 15, Feb 6, Mar 11, Apr 17, May 2, 9, 19, 20, Sep 16, Oct 15, 27, Nov 19, Dec 4; 1741: DL, Jan 15, Feb 6, May 15, Sep 15, Oct 6, 8, 9, 15, Nov 2, 4, 11, 18, 21, Dec 4; 1742: DL, Mar 8, 29, Apr 20, May 8, Sep 11, 14, 16, 25, Oct 2, 7, 13, Nov 4, 8, 16; 1743: DL, Jan 27, Feb 10, Apr 15, May 10, Nov 1, 4, 8, 14, 15, 17, 18, 29, Dec 1, 9, 12, 15, 16, 17; 1744: DL, Jan 7, Feb 21, Mar 12, 29, Apr 2, 26, May 5, 9, 15, 16, 22, Sep 18, 27, Oct 6, 19, 22, 30, Nov 1, 2, 3, 5, 6, 24, Dec 19; 1745: DL, Jan 8, 22, Feb 20, Mar 7, 16, Apr 30, May 1, 8, Jun 5; 1747: DL, Apr 9, May 18
Green (singer), 1749: NWSM, May 10, 15, BF/SFP, Aug 23; 1755: DL, May 2
Green Canister Coffee House, 1748: DL, Apr 19
Green Door (householder), 1740: DL, Apr 25; 1741: DL, Apr 13; 1742: DL, Feb 1, 24; 1743: DL, Apr 7
Green Gates Theatre, 1721: GG, Mar 22
Green Goose Fair, 1682: DG, Jun 10; 1748: HAY, Apr 18
Green Lamp (householder), 1747: CG, Apr 29
Green Man Coffee House, 1792: HAY, Oct 15
Green Park, 1749: DL, Apr 27; 1781: DL, Apr 30
Green Room, The. See Finney, William.
Green Room, 1737: DL, Oct 6; 1743: DL, Jan 17; 1763: DL, Nov 19; 1768: DL, Oct 21
Green Sleeves (dance), 1718: DL, Jul 11; 1720: DL, Jul 7
Green St, 1796: DL, Nov 29
Green Willow (song), 1791: CG, Jun 3
Green, Dr (composer), 1753: KING'S, Apr 30; 1755: SOHO, Jan 16
Green, Henry (songwriter), 1780: CG, Apr 11
Green, Jane, Mrs Henry (actor), 1747: DL, Sep 19, 24, 29, Oct 1, 3, 15, 24, Nov 10, 16, 17, 18, 25, Dec 4, 5, 12, 16, 26; 1748: DL, Jan 20, Feb 1, Apr 14, 19, 28, May 2, Sep 10, 13, 15, 17, 27, Oct 1, 8, 11, 13, 15, 18, 19, 21, 22, 29, Nov 1, 9, 11, Dec 22, 26, 28; 1749: DL, Jan 2, 13, 18, Apr 4, 5, 15, May 8, 16, Sep 16, 20, 21, 22, 26, Oct 3, 10, 18, 19, 21, 23, 26, 28, 30, Nov 9, 17, 21, Dec 8, 9, 12, 18; 1750: DL, Jan 1, 19, 29, 31, Feb 7, Mar 27, May 7, 22, Sep 8, 11, 13, 15, 18, 21, Oct 16, 20, 22, 23, 29, Nov 1, 2, 3, 8, 12, 14, 15, 28, Dec 14, 26; 1751: DL, Jan 5, 7, 26, Mar 12, Apr 9, 16, 18, 27, May 6, 7, 10, Sep 7, 12, 13, 17, 21, 24, 26; 1753: DL, Oct 30; 1754: CG, Oct 11, 23, 28, 29, Nov 6, Dec 5; 1755: CG, Jan 7, 9, 18, Feb 8, Mar 12, Apr 2, 4, 21; 1756: CG, Sep 24, 27, 29, Oct 1, 18, 21, Nov 8, 13; 1757: CG, Jan 14, 17, 20, 21, Mar 21, Apr 18, May 12, 16, 20, 25, Sep 14, 26, Oct 7, 12, 21, Nov 2, 18, 23, Dec 5; 1758: CG, Jan 26, Mar 11, 29, Apr 3, 21, 25, May 10, Sep 18, 27, 29, Oct 9, 13, 14, 18, 24, 25, Nov 18; 1759: CG, Jan 17, Mar 20, Apr 20, 21, May 2, 17, 24, Sep 24, 28, Oct 1, 3, 8, 10, 13, 30, Dec 18; 1760: CG, Mar 6, 24, Apr 25, May 2, 6, 12, Sep 22, 24, Oct 1, 6, 8, 14, 20, Nov 25; 1761: CG, Jan 2, 8, 17, 28, Feb 17, Apr 1, 17, 20, 29, May 8, Oct 26, Nov 11, Dec 10, 11; 1762: CG, Feb 15, 22, Mar 13, 22, Apr 27, May 3, 6, 8, 20, Oct 11, 23, 28, 29; 1763: CG, Feb 14, Apr 12, 16, 27, 30, May 9, Oct 8, 12, 14, 15, 20, Nov 22, 23; 1764: CG, Jan 4, 9, Apr 27, May 3, 14, Sep 17, 19, 24, Oct 11, 12, 18, 20, 30; 1765: CG, Jan 10, Mar 21, Apr 23, 29, Sep 16, 18, 23, 25, Oct 5, 10, 15, Nov 28; 1766: CG, Mar 15, Apr 2, 7, 18, 21, 26, May 16, Oct 14, 15, Nov 1, Dec 16, 20, 30; 1767: CG, Jan 1, 28, 31, Feb 21, May 2, 19, 22, Sep 14, 15, 17, 26, Oct 13, 16, 26, 31, Nov 23, 27, 28; 1768: CG, Jan 9, 29, Feb 5, 25, Mar 10, 12, 24, Apr 23, Sep 27, Oct 7, 11, 12, 15, Nov 3, 8, 9, 16, Dec 19; 1769: CG, Jan 14, Mar 4, 16, Apr 1, 4, 12, 22, 26, 27, 28, May 5, 6, 10, 18, Sep 25, 30, Oct 2, 6, 7, 11, 12, 27, Nov 11, 23, Dec 2; 1770: CG, Jan 3, 6, 17, Feb 3, Mar 13, Apr 20, 26, 28, May 1, 2, 10, 22, Sep 24, 28, Oct 1, 2, 9, 19, 23, Nov 8, 14, 16, 30, Dec 17, 21; 1771: CG, Jan 9, 26, 28, Feb 9, Apr 10, 12, 25, 30, Sep 23, 25, 27, 30, Oct 4, 11, 14, 19, 28, 30, Nov 5, 8, 19, Dec 18, 21, 23; 1772: CG, Jan 15, 29, Mar 5, DL, 23, CG, 23, Apr 4, 22, 25, May 4, 5, 12, 29, Sep 21, 23, Oct 7, 9, 13, 29, Nov 21, Dec 5, 11; 1773: CG, Jan 14, 28, Mar 15, Apr 16, 23, May 3, Sep 20, 24, 27,

29, Oct 1, 8, 9, 15, 21, 22, 27, Nov 6, 16, 20, 27, Dec 2, 3, 23; 1774: CG, Jan 29, Mar 22, Apr 23, 25, Sep 21, 26, Nov 4, 22, 25, 29, Dec 2; 1775: CG, Jan 12, 17, Mar 20, Apr 1, 19, 21, DL, May 11, CG, Sep 20, 22, Oct 9, 11, 13, 20, 23, 24, 31, Nov 1, 13, 16, 21, Dec 2, 21; 1776: CG, Jan 9, 24, Feb 9, Mar 5, 30, Apr 11, 12, May 13, Sep 25, 27, Oct 11, 24, 25, Nov 2, 9, 14, Dec 5, 12; 1777: CG, Jan 2, 25, 31, Feb 5, Mar 15, Apr 29, Sep 22, 26, Oct 1, 3, 17, 20, 29, Nov 12, 17, 19, Dec 5, 19, 20, 26; 1778: CG, Jan 15, Feb 6, Apr 23, Sep 23, Oct 2, 9, 17, 23, 29, Nov 4, 12, 14, Dec 1, 2; 1779: CG, Jan 4, 21, 26, May 15, Sep 20, 22, Nov 6, 13, 22, 23, 27, Dec 1, 11, 18; 1780: CG, Jan 7, Apr 11, May 23, 26

Green, Jonathan (boxkeeper), 1749: CG, Apr 29; 1750: CG, May 3; 1751: CG, May 11; 1752: CG, May 8; 1753: CG, May 17; 1754: CG, May 20; 1755: CG, May 16; 1756: CG, May 18; 1757: CG, May 17; 1758: CG, May 9; 1759: CG, May 24; 1760: CG, May 16, Sep 22; 1761: CG, May 14; 1763: CG, May 24; 1764: CG, May 24; 1765: CG, May 24; 1766: CG, May 16; 1767: CG, May 22; 1768: CG, Jun 2, 3; 1769: CG, May 18; 1770: CG, May 26, 28? 1771: CG, May 24; 1772: CG, May 27; 1773: CG, May 27; 1774: CG, May 19; 1775: CG, May 24; 1776: CG, May 18; 1777: CG, May 22; 1778: CG, May 20; 1779: CG, May 18; 1780: CG, May 19; 1781: CG, May 22; 1782: CG, May 22; 1783: CG, May 30; 1784: CG, May 27; 1786: CG, May 30; 1787: CG, May 31; 1788: CG, May 17; 1789: CG, Jun 16; 1790: CG, Jun 12; 1791: CG, Jun 14; 1792: CG, May 25

Green, Master (musician), 1770: MARLY, Aug 21; 1771: CG, May 15, GROTTO, Aug 30, Sep 3, 9; 1772: CG, Apr 9; 1773: MARLY, Sep 3; 1774: HAY, Mar 25

Green, Master W (actor), 1734: JS, May 24, DL, Dec 6; 1735: DL, May 22, 29, GF/HAY, Jul 15, 18, Aug 1, HAY, 12, DL, Oct 25, Nov 21; 1736: DL, May 20, HAY, Jun 29, DL, Dec 20; 1737: DL, Jan 6, May 13; 1738: DL, May 3; 1739: DL, Oct 13

Green, Miss (actor), 1777: CG, Jan 8, 11, May 15, Sep 29, Oct 6; 1778: CG, Jan 15, 20, 21, May 6, 14, Sep 28; 1779: CG, Jan 19, Feb 2, Apr 12, 29, May 3, 10, Nov 8, 19, 30; 1780: CG, Feb 1, 2, Apr 12, 21, May 12, 17; 1781: HAY, Jan 22; 1782: HAY, Jan 21

Green, Mrs (actor), 1732: TC, Aug 4; 1735: SOU, Apr 7

Green, Mrs (house servant), 1782: CG, May 15; 1784: HAY, Mar 8; 1786: CG, Jun 1

Green, Mrs P (actor), 1773: CG, Nov 12, Dec 9, 16, 21; 1774: CG, Mar 12, Apr 12, May 11, 20

Green, Mrs William (actor), 1780: CG, Oct 31, Nov 24; 1781: CG, Jan 1, 18, Feb 14

Green, Samuel (organ builder), 1794: KING'S, May 15

Greene, Alexander
--Politician Cheated, The, 1662: NONE, Sep 0

Greene, Robert
--Friar Bacon and Friar Bungay, 1662: COCKPIT, Oct 21

Greenleaf, Miss (actor), 1785: HAY, Jan 31

Greenvil. See Granville.

Greenwich Hospital, 1778: DL, Jan 2, Oct 8; 1779: DL, Oct 5; 1797: DL, Nov 9

Greenwich Park. See Mountfort, William.

Greenwich Pensioner (song), 1790: DL, May 4, 19, 27, 28, CG, Nov 23, 26, Dec 1; 1791: CG, Sep 19; 1793: CG, May 21; 1794: CG, Apr 12, May 10, Oct 29; 1795: CG, Oct 7; see also Twas in the good ship Rover

Greenwich, 1709: GR, Jun 6; 1710: QUEEN'S, May 24, GR, Aug 26, Sep 1, 28; 1711: GR, May 21; 1721: GR, Dec 15; 1731: LIF, Jan 11; 1767: DL, Nov 2; 1797: DL, Nov 9; 1798: WRSG, Jun 8

Greenwich, 1767: DL, Nov 2

Greenwood, Mrs (actor), 1749: BFCB, Aug 23

Greenwood, Thomas (scene painter), 1771: DL, Nov 26; 1772: DL, Feb 24; 1774: DL, Nov 5; 1775: DL, Nov 11; 1777: DL, Jan 1, CG, Nov 25; 1778: CG, Oct 22; 1782: DL, Dec 26; 1784: DL, Jan 7, Sep 23; 1785: DL, Dec 8, 26; 1786: DL, Jan 14, Oct 24; 1787: DL, Nov 8, 21, Dec 26; 1788: DL, Sep 23, Nov 10; 1789: DL, Nov 13, 24, Dec 26; 1790: DL, Oct 26, Nov 17, Dec 27; 1791: DL, Jan 1, DLKING'S, Sep 29, Dec 31; 1792: DLKING'S, May 23, DL, Oct 18, Nov 21; 1794: DL, Apr 21, Jun 9, Oct 28, 31, Dec 20; 1795: DL, May 6; 1796: DL, Jan 18, Mar 12, Apr 2, Sep 29, Nov 9, KING'S, Dec 13, DL, 26; 1797: KING'S, Jan 10, Feb 7, Apr 6, DL, Dec 14

Greenwood, Thomas Jr (scene painter), 1798: DL, Jan 16, Oct 6; 1799: DL, Jan 19, May 24, Oct 14, Dec 11; 1800: DL, Mar 11, Apr 29

Greetinge (musician), 1675: ATCOURT, Feb 15

Gregg's Coffee House, 1743: DL, Apr 18

Gregorian Song (song), 1741: CG, Apr 30; 1742: CG, Apr 26, May 3

Gregorians, Society of, 1735: HAY, Jul 10; 1736: GF, Apr 12, May 6; 1740: DL, May 13; 1741: CG, Apr 30; 1742: CG, Apr 26

Gregory, Elizabeth, Mrs John (actor), 1754: CG, Jan 10, Mar 14, 23; 1755: CG, Mar 12; 1757: CG, Jan 5, 14, Feb 21, Mar 26; 1765: DL, Oct 15

Gregson (actor), 1788: DL, Mar 29; 1789: DL, Mar 17, Oct 1, Dec 26; 1790: DL, Mar 8, May 15, 29, Oct 7, 14; 1791: DLKING'S, Oct 31, Dec 31; 1792: DLKING'S, Feb 18, Mar 17, Apr 16, Jun 4, 13, HAY, Jul 25, DL, Sep 25, Oct 2; 1793: DL, Mar 11, 19; 1794: DL, Apr 21, 29, May 5, 13, 19, Jun 9, Sep 27, Oct 7, Nov 15; 1795: DL, Jan 31, Feb 4, Jun 5, Sep 29, Oct 1, 30, Nov 11, 23, Dec 2, 4, 10; 1796: DL, Jan 18, Feb 27, Mar 12, Apr 2, 4, 30, May 4, Jun 4, Oct 10, 19, Nov 9, Dec 26; 1796: DL, Jun 11; 1797: DL, Jan 7, 20, Feb 9, 16, Sep 23, Nov 7, 8, 25, Dec 21; 1798: DL, Jan 16, Feb 20, 27

Gregson (house servant), 1791: DL, May 31; 1793: DL, May 31; 1797: DL, Jun 10; 1798: DL, Jun 2; 1799: DL, Jul 2; 1800: DL, Jun 13

Greniere. See Granier.

Grenoust (musician), 1715: LIF, May 13

Gresham (shoemaker), 1742: DL, Apr 29

Gresham's Warehouse, 1757: CG, Mar 31

Greshamers, 1667: LIF, Oct 5

Gresnick, Antoine Frederic (composer)
--Alceste (opera), 1786: KING'S, Dec 23, 30; 1787: KING'S, Jan 2, 6, 20, Feb 6, 10, 13, 24, Mar 8

Gresset, Jean Baptiste Louis
--Mechant, Le, 1792: HAY, Jun 30

Gretna Green. See Stuart, Charles.

Gretry, Andre Ernest Modeste (composer), 1776: DL, Dec 5; 1779: KING'S, Feb 23; 1781: KING'S, Mar 8, Nov 17; 1783: KING'S, Feb 27; 1786: KING'S, Apr 27, CG, Oct 16, DL, 24; 1787: CG, Mar 12, DL, Nov 8; 1788: DL, Sep 23, CG, Nov 6, Dec 13; 1789: CG, Sep 28, Nov 24; 1790: DL, Apr 16; 1793: CG, Feb 25; 1794: CG, Nov 17, Dec 26; 1796: CG, Nov 19
--Epreuve Villageoise, L' (opera), 1786: KING'S, Apr 27
--Evenements Imprevus, 1794: CG, Dec 26
--Panurge (opera), 1786: KING'S, Apr 27
--Zemira e Azor (opera), 1776: DL, Dec 5; 1779: KING'S, Feb 23, Mar 2, 6, 9, 16, 20, Apr 6, 13, 15, 20, 27; 1781: KING'S, Mar 8, 15; 1783: KING'S, Feb 23, Mar 2, 6, 9, 16, 20, Apr 6, 13, 15, 20, 27; 1796: KING'S, Jul 23, 30, Nov 26, 29, Dec 3; 1797: KING'S, Feb 14

Gretton, John, 1795: CG, Jun 6; 1800: CG, Jun 16
--Masque in Honor of the Nuptials of His Royal Highness, 1795: CG, Jun 6

Greville (actor), 1785: HAY, Jan 31

Greville, Susan (actor), 1770: CG, Jan 17; 1772: HAY, Sep 18; 1773: HAY, Sep 18, DL, Nov 1, 9, 12, 20, Dec 11; 1774: DL, Feb 2, 9, 17, Mar 10, 22, 26, Apr 16, 19, May 4, Sep 17, 20, 24, 29, Oct 6, 12, 29, Nov 16, Dec 1; 1775: DL, Jan 23, Feb 23, Mar 28, Apr 8, 21, May 12, Sep 26, Oct 3, 5, 7, 31, Nov 20, 23, Dec 11, 12; 1776: DL, Jan 3, 20, Mar 21, Apr 17, 22, May 8, HAY, Sep 16, 17, DL, 26, Oct 12, Nov 9, 25, Dec 10, 14, 17, 31; 1777: DL, Mar 31, Apr 22, 29, Jun 6; 1778: HAY, May 18, Jul 30, Sep 2; 1782: HAY, Jan 14; 1785: HAY, Mar 15, Apr 26; 1788: HAY, Apr 9; 1795: CG, Jun 6

Grey. See Gray.

Grey (actor), 1770: HAY, Dec 19

Grey, Charles (patron), 1797: KING'S, May 18, CG, Jun 14

Greyhound Inn, 1682: BF, Aug 24; 1719: BFBL, Aug 24; 1722: BFB, Aug 25; 1741: BFTY, Aug 22; 1743: BFYWR, Aug 23; 1747: BFC, Aug 22; 1757: BF, Sep 3; 1759: BFY, Sep 3, BF, 4; 1760: BFG, Sep 3, 4, 5, 6; 1761: BFY, Aug 31, Sep 3, 4, 5, 7; 1762: BFY, Sep 3

Gricourt (dancer), 1786: KING'S, Dec 23; 1787: KING'S, Jan 16, 20, Feb 13, Mar 13, 22, Jun 14

Grieston (parson), 1755: DL, Sep 27

Griffin (actor, singer), 1778: HAY, Jul 1, 9, 30, Aug 3, 21, 22

Griffin (bookseller), 1769: CG, Feb 25; 1771: CG, Oct 15; 1772: CG, Dec 3

Griffin, Benjamin (actor, author), 1715: LIF, Feb 16, Jun 2, 14, 23, Aug 17, Sep 29, Oct 5, 11, 12, 24, Dec 12; 1716: LIF, Jan 4, 24, Apr 3, Jul 4, Aug 3, Oct 20, Nov 9; 1717: LIF, Feb 2, 25, Apr 29, May 16, Oct 17, 25, 26, 29, Nov 1, 9, 11, Dec 7, 12; 1718: LIF, Feb 3, Apr 19, 28, Jul 9, Oct 6, 15, 31, Nov 3, 24; 1719: LIF, Jan 2, Feb 7, 21, Mar 30, Apr 28, BFBL, Aug 24, LIF, Oct 2, 5, 7, 10, 13, 17, Nov 3, 5, 12, 13, 17, 23; 1720: LIF, Jan 11, 26, Feb 8, 26, Mar 15, Oct 1, 11, 13, 22, Nov 2, 18, 19, 26, 29, Dec 17, 26; 1721: LIF, Jan 4, 10, 25, Apr 1, 10, 17, Sep 27, DL, 30, Oct 9, 25; 1722: DL, Feb 2, 15, Apr 10, Sep 15, 27, Oct 2, 26, 30, Nov 7, Dec 11; 1723: DL, Apr 2, May 15, Sep 14, 28, Oct 3, 10, 28; 1724: DL, Apr 16, 28, May 6, 7, Sep 12, 29, Oct 27, Nov 19, Dec 18; 1725: DL, Jan 4, Feb 18, 20, Apr 29, Sep 11, 14, 28, Oct 5, 14, 27, Nov 29, Dec 18; 1726: DL, Jan 3, 12, Apr 19, May 23, Sep 15, 29, Oct 20, Nov 9, 12, 16, Dec 12; 1727: DL, Jan 20, Feb 11, 21, Apr 18, 19, 29, Sep 9, 21, 23, 30, Oct 12, Nov 9, Dec 13; 1728: DL, Feb 16, Mar 9, May 1, 8, 17, Sep 21, Oct 3, Nov 2, 8; 1729: DL, Jan 7, 20, Feb 3, 6, Apr 22, 23, May 3, 6, 7, 12, 14, Jun 13, 20, 27, Jul 25, Sep 23, Oct 16, 22, Nov 8, 21, 27, 28,

FLR, 29, Dec 1, DL, 3, 8; 1730: DL, Jan 9, 24, Feb 10, Apr 24, May 2, 11, Sep
19, 29, Oct 6, 8, 20, Nov 16, 18, 24, 25; 1731: DL, Feb 8, Mar 15, 16, Apr 8,
21, 26, May 3, 10, 12, 17, 19, Sep 18, 21, 28, 30, Oct 2, 5, 7, 14, 21, 30,
Nov 6, 10, 13, Dec 1, 7; 1732: DL, Feb 10, Mar 23, 30, Apr 14, 25, 27, 28,
May 1, 4, 5, 9, 12, Sep 19, 21, 23, 26, 28, 30, Oct 10, 12, 19, 28, 31, Nov
7, 9, 11, 13, 21, 24, Dec 14, 18; 1733: DL, Jan 2, 16, 19, 22, 26, 29, Feb
17, Mar 28, Apr 4, 6, 9, 19, 24, May 7, 14, 24, 29, Jun 4, 9, BFCGBH, Aug 23,
Sep 4, DL/HAY, 26, Oct 3, 5, 6, 8, 12, 13, 15, 17, 19, 25, Nov 9, 27, Dec 10,
12, HAY, 13, DL/HAY, 19, 20; 1734: DL/HAY, Jan 2, 21, HAY, Feb 12, DL/HAY,
Mar 12, 23, Apr 1, LIF, 15, DL/HAY, 18, 20, DL, 22, DL/HAY, 26, May 1, DL,
16, Sep 7, 19, 26, 30, Oct 3, 8, 9, 14, 17, 19, 21, 23, 25, Nov 2, 8, 20, Dec
6; 1735: DL, Jan 11, 23, 29, Feb 4, 10, Mar 6, 10, 13, Apr 11, 16, May 2, Sep
1, 4, 9, 13, 15, 18, 25, 30, Oct 2, 4, 9, 11, 21, 23, 24, 28, Nov 1, 17, 19,
21, 29, Dec 6; 1736: DL, Feb 9, 20, Mar 11, 25, Apr 8, 12, 15, Aug 26, Sep 4,
7, 9, 14, 16, 18, 21, 23, Oct 9, 13, 21, 22, 25, 30, Nov 2, 3, 6, 8, 12, 19,
23, Dec 7, 17, 21; 1737: DL, Feb 5, Mar 17, 22, Apr 15, May 5, Aug 30, Sep
10, 15, 17, 20, 24, 27, 29, Oct 8, 20, 24, 27, 31, Nov 12, 14, 15; 1738: DL,
Jan 5, 14, 19, 26, 31, Feb 2, 16, Mar 2, 20, Apr 11, 14, 26, 28, May 13, Sep
7, 9, 16, 19, 21, 23, Oct 3, 17, 20, 21, 26, 27, Nov 2, 3, 8, 11, 14, 20, 25,
27, 29; 1739: DL, Jan 1, 3, 13, Feb 1, 7, Mar 10, 20, 27, 29, 31, Apr 25, 28,
May 1, 19, Sep 1, 4, 15, 18, Oct 3, 4, 6, 8, 9, 10, 15, 16, 18, 19, 20, 22,
24, 25, 27, Nov 7, 10, 16, 20, Dec 8, 14; 1740: DL, Jan 16, Feb 7, 18; 1741:
GF, Apr 15; 1745: GF, Nov 18; 1748: HAY, Apr 25
--Humours of Purgatory, The, 1716: LIF, Apr 3, 4, 6; 1745: GF, Nov 18, 19, 20,
25; 1748: HAY, Apr 25
--Injured Virtue; or, The Virgin Martyr, 1714: SOU, Nov 1
--Love in a Sack, 1715: LIF, Jun 14, Jul 5, 7, 21, Aug 23, 31; 1716: LIF, Jan
16
--Masquerade, The; or, An Evening's Intrigue, 1717: LIF, May 16
--Whig and Tory; or, The Double Deceit, 1720: LIF, Jan 26, 27, 28, 29, Feb 1,
2, 4, 16, 25, Dec 17, 19; 1729: DL, Jul 25, 29, Aug 1; 1730: DL, Apr 24;
1731: DL, Jan 6
Griffin, Edward (actor), 1668: ATCOURT, Feb 4; 1679: DL, Feb 0
Griffin, Mrs (actor), 1729: FLR, Nov 29, Dec 1
Griffin, Phillip (Captain) (actor), 1673: LIF, Mar 0, Dec 0; 1674: DL, May 16;
1675: DL, Jan 25, May 10; 1676: DL, Jan 29, Dec 11; 1677: DL, Mar 0, 17, May
5, Oct 0, Dec 12; 1678: DL, Feb 0, Mar 0; 1681: DL, May 0, Oct 0; 1682: DL,
Feb 4, Mar 11, NONE, Sep 0, DL, Nov 16; 1683: NONE, Sep 0, DL, Nov 12, Dec 0;
1684: ATCOURT, Feb 11, DL, Mar 0; 1685: DLORDG, Jan 20, DL, May 9, Aug 0;
1686: DL, Jan 0, DG, Mar 4; 1687: ATCOURT, Apr 25; 1688: DL, Feb 0, May 3,
NONE, Sep 0; 1689: NONE, Sep 0; 1691: NONE, Sep 0; 1698: DL, Jun 2; 1700: DL,
Nov 8; 1701: DL, Feb 4, May 12, 31, Dec 0; 1702: DL, Feb 0, Dec 0; 1703: DL,
Apr 23, Jun 9, Nov 12, 18, Dec 2; 1704: DL, Jan 26, May 0, Jun 13, 15; 1705:
DL, Jun 5, Jul 25; 1706: DL, Apr 0; 1707: DL, Oct 18, 25, 29
Griffin, Robert (renter), 1758: CG, Jan 6, Feb 23
Griffith (actor), 1702: LIF, Dec 31; 1705: DL, Feb 6; 1712: DL, Apr 12, May 3;
1714: DL, Nov 30, Dec 6
Griffith (actor), 1750: DL, Sep 18, Oct 13, Dec 21; 1755: CG, Oct 24
Griffith (actor), 1786: HAMM, Jun 5
Griffith (actor, prologuist), 1779: HAY, Dec 20
Griffith (dancer), 1725: LIF, May 5
Griffith, Elizabeth, 1769: DL, Feb 4; 1772: CG, Mar 5; 1779: DL, Dec 2
--Double Mistake, The, 1766: CG, Jan 9, 10, 11, 13, 14, 15, 16, 17, 18, 21, 23,
25, 28, Feb 17, Apr 16
--Platonic Wife, The, 1765: DL, Jan 22, 23, 24, 25, 26, 28, 29, 31
--School for Rakes, The, 1769: DL, Feb 4, 6, 7, 11, 13, 14, 15, 16, 18, 20, 21,
Mar 30, Apr 6, 20, May 4, 23, Sep 26, Oct 13, 14, Nov 3; 1770: DL, Jan 13,
May 5, Oct 5; 1771: DL, Apr 10, Oct 28; 1776: DL, Apr 26
--Times, The, 1779: DL, Dec 2, 4, 6, 7, 8, 9; 1780: DL, Feb 1, 17, 21
--Wife in the Right, A, 1772: CG, Mar 5, 9
Griffith, Mrs (actor), 1751: CG, May 14; 1752: CG, May 2, Nov 30; 1753: CG, Mar
26, May 5, Sep 12; 1754: CG, Jan 22, Apr 27, Sep 16, Dec 30; 1755: CG, Mar
22, May 9, 13; 1758: CG, Feb 11; 1763: CG, May 14; 1765: DL, Jan 24; 1766:
CG, Jan 9, May 15; 1767: CG, May 18; 1768: CG, Jun 3, 4; 1769: CG, May 19,
22; 1770: CG, May 19, 22; 1771: CG, May 22
Griffith, R (printer), 1750: DL, Apr 28, Oct 13; 1753: DL, Oct 30; 1755: CG,
Mar 12, DL, Nov 14, 24; 1760: CG, Mar 12
Griffith, Richard (actor), 1764: DL, Sep 18, 29, Oct 13; 1765: DL, Jan 5, 24,
Feb 13, Apr 15, May 6; 1770: HAY, May 18, Aug 1, Oct 1, 5; 1771: HAY, Jun 7,
DL, Oct 12, Nov 11, Dec 2, 4, 10, 26; 1772: DL, Jan 20, Feb 26, Apr 21, 22,
29, May 12, 25, HAY, Jun 8, Aug 10, DL, Sep 29, Oct 16, 21, 23, 30, Dec 7, 8,
18, 26; 1773: DL, Jan 1, Apr 1, 3, 17, 21, 23, May 8, 12, 17, 24, 26, 28, 31,

Jun 2, Sep 25, Oct 11, 25, Nov 9, 26, Dec 11, 15, 27; <u>1774</u>: DL, Jan 14, 15,
Feb 8, 17, Mar 3, 19, 22, 26, Apr 4, 5, 15, 19, 25, May 7, HAY, 30, Aug 19,
Sep 19, DL, 20, 29, Dec 16; <u>1775</u>: DL, Feb 3, HAY, May 19, 22, Jun 5, 7, 12,
Jul 19, 26, Aug 2, 16, Sep 4, 7, 16, 19, 20, 21, DL, 26, Oct 3, 7, Nov 9, 11,
Dec 1; <u>1776</u>: DL, Jan 20, 26, Mar 18, May 4, 11, HAY, 28, 31, DL, Jun 1, HAY,
14, 19, 26, Jul 5, 8, 10, 29, Aug 2, Sep 6, 20
Griffith, Richard (author)
--Variety, <u>1782</u>: DL, Feb 23, 25, 26, 28, Mar 2, 4, 5, 7, 9, 11, Apr 12
Griffith, S (house servant), <u>1760</u>: CG, May 19; <u>1761</u>: CG, May 15
Griffith, Sarah (florist), <u>1768</u>: CG, Jan 6
Griffith, Thomas (actor), <u>1730</u>: DL, Apr 2, 30, May 12; <u>1744</u>: CG, Jan 24
Griffiths (actor), <u>1792</u>: CG, Dec 26
Griffiths (boxkeeper), <u>1795</u>: DL, Jun 6; <u>1796</u>: DL, Jun 13
Griffiths (dancer), <u>1799</u>: CG, Dec 23; <u>1800</u>: CG, Jan 10
Griffiths (house servant), <u>1750</u>: CG, May 7
Griffiths (singer), <u>1789</u>: CG, Feb 27, Mar 27; <u>1790</u>: CG, Feb 19, 24, Mar 3, 26;
<u>1791</u>: CG, Mar 11, 18, 23, 25, 30, Apr 13
Griffiths, John (actor), <u>1770</u>: HAY, May 16, 23, 28, 30, Jun 18, 22, 25, 27, Jul
9, 20, Aug 8, 31, Sep 3, 13, Oct 1; <u>1771</u>: HAY, Jun 24, Jul 3, Aug 5, Sep 16,
18, 19, 20; <u>1772</u>: DL, Jan 1, HAY, Jun 1, 24, Sep 17, 18, DL, Oct 16, 28, CG,
Nov 4, DL, 10; <u>1773</u>: DL, Sep 23, 25; <u>1774</u>: DL, Feb 15, May 19, HAY, Sep 19,
DL, 29, Oct 4, 5, 18, 24, 26, 27, 28, 29, Nov 1, 21, 26, Dec 2, 3, 9, 26, 27;
<u>1775</u>: DL, Jan 2, 18, 21, 23, Feb 4, 17, 20, 23, Mar 2, 21, 23, 25, Apr 17,
18, 24, 29, May 2, 6, 12, HAY, 15, 17, DL, 19, HAY, 29, DL, Sep 23, 28, Oct
11, 12, 17, 23, Nov 1, 3, 6, 23, 25, Dec 7, 11; <u>1776</u>: DL, Jan 27, Feb 12, 24,
Mar 14, 18, 25, 28, Apr 10, 22, May 8, 11, HAY, 31, Aug 9, Sep 16, 17, DL,
21, HAY, 23, DL, 26, Oct 1, 8, 10, 12, 15, 23, 29, Nov 6, 9, 16, 21, 25, 29,
Dec 28, 31; <u>1777</u>: DL, Jan 1, 28, Mar 13, Apr 7, 18, 21, May 9, 15, HAY, 30,
DL, Jun 6, HAY, 6, 9, 16, 19, 26, Jul 18, 30, Aug 7, 19, 25, Sep 10, 17, 18,
DL, 27, 30, Oct 7, 17, 18, Nov 10, 14, 18, Dec 13; <u>1778</u>: DL, Jan 1, Feb 2,
10, Mar 16, May 15, Sep 19, 24, Oct 1, 8, 15, Nov 4, 10; <u>1779</u>: DL, Jan 8, Apr
12, 13, 16, 22, May 11, 18, 21; <u>1780</u>: DL, Feb 22, Sep 23, 30, Oct 11, 17, 30,
Nov 1, 4, Dec 4, 27; <u>1781</u>: DL, Jan 9, 16, Feb 17, Mar 19, 31, May 22, Sep 18,
25, Oct 12, 16, 19, Nov 10, Dec 11; <u>1782</u>: DL, Jan 22, Mar 21, Apr 12, May 13,
18; <u>1785</u>: HAY, Jan 31; <u>1786</u>: HAY, Mar 6, Dec 18; <u>1787</u>: HAY, Jan 8, Mar 12;
<u>1788</u>: HAY, Apr 29, Sep 30
Griffiths, Master (actor), <u>1797</u>: CG, Apr 8
Griffiths, Miss (actor), <u>1798</u>: HAY, Jun 13, 19, 21, 27, Jul 5, 11, 13, Aug 4,
6, 11, 21, 23, 29, Sep 7, 14; <u>1799</u>: HAY, Jun 18, 28, DL, Jul 4, HAY, 5, 13,
16, 19, Aug 10, 21, 28
Griffiths, Miss (author), <u>1792</u>: HAY, Aug 23
Griffiths, Mrs (beneficiary), <u>1747</u>: CG, May 22
Grig St, <u>1753</u>: DL, Mar 26
Grigg (beneficiary), <u>1729</u>: HAY, Jul 16
Grignions (time keeper), <u>1754</u>: DL, Nov 18
Grignon (watchmaker), <u>1744</u>: DL, Dec 13
Grigsby's Coffee House, <u>1748</u>: CG, Nov 7; <u>1750</u>: DL, Jan 11; <u>1751</u>: DL, May 14;
<u>1752</u>: DL, Nov 15, CG, Dec 12; <u>1753</u>: DL, May 7; <u>1755</u>: DL, Apr 28; <u>1757</u>: DL,
May 6
Grim the Collier of Croyden; or, The Devil and his Dame (play, anon), <u>1661</u>:
NONE, Sep 0
Grimaesse (actor), <u>1729</u>: LIF, Apr 8
Grimaldi (dancer), <u>1740</u>: CG, Feb 12, Oct 10; <u>1741</u>: CG, Jan 5, Feb 24, Oct 24;
<u>1742</u>: CG, Nov 1, 2, 9, 20
Grimaldi, Catherine (dancer), <u>1778</u>: DL, Sep 26; <u>1779</u>: DL, May 5
Grimaldi, Catherine, Joseph and William (dancers), <u>1789</u>: DL, Dec 26
Grimaldi, Cavaliero Nicolini (singer), <u>1708</u>: QUEEN'S, Dec 14; <u>1709</u>: QUEEN'S,
Jan 19, Mar 2, May 28, Oct 20, Nov 17; <u>1710</u>: QUEEN'S, Jan 10, Mar 23, Apr 25;
<u>1711</u>: QUEEN'S, Jan 10, Feb 24, Apr 4, Dec 12; <u>1712</u>: QUEEN'S, Feb 27, Mar 22,
Jun 4, 11, 14; <u>1715</u>: KING'S, May 7, 25, Jun 25; <u>1716</u>: KING'S, Feb 1, Mar 10,
Apr 18, May 2; <u>1717</u>: KING'S, Jan 5, Feb 2, 16, HIC, Mar 20, KING'S, 21, Apr
11; <u>1722</u>: LIF, May 4
Grimaldi, Giuseppe (dancer, actor), <u>1758</u>: KING'S, Jan 10, 31, DL, Oct 12, Nov
2, Dec 2, 14, 26; <u>1759</u>: DL, Jan 4, Feb 21, Oct 6, 16, Nov 8, Dec 1, 31; <u>1760</u>:
DL, Feb 11, Apr 17, May 10, Oct 2, 7, 8, 11, Nov 17, Dec 3, 13; <u>1761</u>: DL, Feb
12, Mar 26, Apr 18, Sep 10, Oct 10, 14, 26, Nov 3, 28, 30, Dec 12, 15, 28;
<u>1762</u>: DL, Jan 27, Feb 3, Mar 22, Apr 24, Oct 15, Nov 5, 23, 27; <u>1763</u>: DL, Jan
3, Mar 15, Apr 6, 13, 25, May 31, Oct 4, 28, Nov 10, 12, 15, 19, Dec 1, 17,
26; <u>1764</u>: DL, Jan 23, Feb 24, Mar 8, 10, 15, 19, 26, May 4, Sep 25, Oct 9,
Nov 13, 14, 28, Dec 13, 26; <u>1765</u>: DL, Jan 18, 22, Feb 15, Apr 9, 13, 19, 20,
May 1, 10, Sep 24, Oct 28, Nov 16; <u>1766</u>: DL, Jan 6, Apr 28, Sep 27, Oct 21,
23, 29, Dec 2; <u>1767</u>: DL, Jan 2, Mar 17, May 6, 8, SW, 13, Jun 13, DL, Sep 15,

22, 23, Oct 10, 28, Nov 16, Dec 26; 1768: DL, Feb 4, Apr 26, Sep 8, 20, 22,
    27, Oct 10, 11, 20, Dec 30; 1769: DL, Apr 12, 26, Sep 26, Oct 4, Nov 14;
    1770: DL, May 2, HAY, 16, DL, Oct 13, Dec 1; 1771: DL, Apr 24, Oct 21, Dec
    26; 1772: DL, May 5, Oct 3, Nov 18, Dec 26; 1773: DL, Mar 27, May 4, Sep 21,
    25, Oct 9, 20, Nov 25, Dec 27; 1774: DL, Jan 29, Apr 28, CG, Sep 19, DL, 29,
    Oct 5, 14; 1775: DL, Jan 2, Feb 10, Mar 23, May 6, Oct 11, 17, 20, Nov 2, 11,
    Dec 11; 1776: DL, Apr 23, Jun 10, Oct 1, 24, Nov 26; 1777: DL, Jan 4, Apr 26;
    1778: CG, Apr 29, DL, Oct 8; 1779: DL, Jan 8, May 5, 11, Sep 21, 30, Oct 5,
    30; 1780: DL, Jan 3, 12, May 5, 9; 1781: DL, Jan 29, May 14, Sep 20; 1782:
    DL, Jan 3, 17, May 6, Sep 20, Nov 4, Dec 9, 26; 1783: DL, Jan 10, Sep 23, Oct
    13, Nov 8; 1784: DL, Jan 7, 13, Feb 3, May 7, CG, 8, DL, Sep 23, Dec 20;
    1785: DL, Jan 20, Sep 27, Dec 26, 29; 1786: DL, Jan 3, HAY, Jul 3, Sep 4
Grimaldi, Giuseppe and Sga (dancers), 1767: DL, Jan 24
Grimaldi, Joseph (dancer), 1784: CG, May 8; 1788: DL, Nov 10; 1789: DL, Feb 7;
    1790: DL, Mar 8, May 15, Oct 14, Dec 27; 1795: DL, Feb 4; 1796: DL, Oct 19,
    25, Nov 9, 11, 12, 16, 18, 24, 26, Dec 14, 15, 26; 1797: DL, Jan 20, Feb 1,
    16, Mar 6, Sep 23, Oct 12, Nov 4, 8, 9, 11, 15, Dec 21; 1798: DL, Jan 4, 16,
    Feb 17, 20, May 11, Oct 4, 6, Dec 6, 21; 1799: DL, Jan 19, Feb 4, 5, May 1,
    20, Jun 13, Sep 28, Oct 8, 26, 31, Nov 6, Dec 2; 1800: DL, Jan 1, 4, 18, Mar
    10, 11, May 29, Jun 2
Grimaldi, Maria, Sga Joseph (dancer), 1800: DL, Jun 2
Grimaldi, Sg and Sga (dancers), 1742: CG, Nov 20
Grimaldi, Sga (dancer), 1742: CG, Nov 20
Grimaldi, Sga (singer), 1726: LIF, May 6
Grimaldi, Sga Giuseppe (dancer), 1752: SFB, Sep 22; 1765: DL, Sep 24; 1768: DL,
    Apr 6
Grimaldi's scholars (dancers), 1768: DL, Apr 26; 1774: DL, Apr 28
Grimberg. See DeGrimbergue.
Grimwood (actor), 1750: SFYW, Sep 7
Grimwood, Mrs (actor), 1750: SFYW, Sep 7
Griselda. See Bononcini, Giovanni.
Grist, Harriet (actor), 1792: CG, Oct 11; 1793: CG, Jan 29, Mar 23, Apr 24, Jun
    1, Oct 1, 3, 9, 22, 30, Nov 9, 12, Dec 18
Grist, Thomas (actor), 1775: DL, Oct 2, 17, 19, Nov 21, 22, 24; 1776: DL, Jan
    1, Apr 12, Nov 4, 25, Dec 10, 14, 17; 1777: DL, May 15, 30
Groans of Ghosts, The (song), 1673: DG, Jul 3
Groath, Mrs (tenant), 1771: DL, Sep 26; 1772: DL, Sep 19; 1773: DL, Sep 18;
    1776: DL, Jan 25, Mar 23, Jun 10
Groce, Miss (actor), 1768: CG, Apr 30, May 25, HAY, Jul 8
Grocers Hall, 1683: CITY, Oct 29
Grocers, Company of, 1659: CITY, Oct 29; 1661: CITY, Oct 29; 1672: CITY, Oct
    29; 1673: CITY, Oct 29; 1678: CITY, Oct 29; 1681: CITY, Oct 29; 1692: CITY,
    Oct 29; 1695: CITY, Oct 29
Grognet, Mlle (dancer), 1733: DL, Oct 12, 15, 24, 31, Nov 21, Dec 1, 5, 7, 13;
    1734: DL, Jan 15, 21, Feb 4, Mar 7, DL/LIF, 11, DL/HAY, 18, DL/LIF, Apr 1,
    LIF, 15, 18, DL/HAY, 26, JS, May 31; 1735: CG/LIF, Feb 13, Apr 24, GF/HAY,
    May 5, CG/LIF, 9, 20
Grondeur. See Palaprat, Jean.
Groom (banker), 1772: DL, Dec 15
Groom and the Cook, The; or, Daniel and Dishclout's Law Suit (monologue), 1799:
    CG, May 14
Grosman, John Joseph (musician), 1758: CHAPEL, Apr 27
Gross, Mrs (actor), 1751: DL, Sep 7; 1762: DL, May 24
Grossi (Ciface, Cifeccio, Siface), Giovanni Francesco (singer), 1687: ATCOURT,
    Jan 30, NONE, Apr 19
Grossman (musician), 1743: LIF, Mar 15
Grosvenor Place, 1777: CG, Apr 10
Grosvenor Square, 1733: LIF/CG, Apr 24; 1738: GF, Sep 16; 1739: DL, May 4;
    1743: NONE, Jan 31, DL, Apr 15; 1747: DL, Apr 28; 1755: KING'S, Apr 17; 1756:
    KING'S, Apr 29, DL, Dec 18; 1757: CG, Mar 17, Dec 2; 1769: DL, Mar 9; 1776:
    HAY, Oct 7; 1786: HAY, Aug 10; 1787: KING'S, Apr 26, HAY, Aug 3; 1792: HAY,
    Nov 26; 1795: CG, May 16; 1796: CG, Apr 29, DL, Nov 29; 1797: CG, May 20;
    1799: CG, May 31; 1800: DL, Jun 7
Grosvenor St, 1728: DL, Nov 19; 1730: DL, Oct 23; 1753: DL, May 22; 1756: DL,
    Nov 12; 1758: DL, Mar 7, 10; 1759: CG, May 8; 1763: DL, Apr 27
Grotesque Ballet, Grand (dance), 1737: DL, Oct 18
Grotesque Dance (dance), 1704: DL, Feb 17; 1706: DL, Jan 3, Jun 25, 28; 1707:
    YB, Nov 19; 1717: DL, Jan 3, Apr 2; 1726: KING'S, Dec 21; 1727: KING'S, Jan
    12, 25, Mar 16, 23, Apr 8; 1786: HAMM, Jul 26
Grotesque Lilliputians, Grand (dance), 1756: BFSI, Sep 3
Grotesque Minuet (dance), 1758: CG, Apr 20
Grotesque Pantomime Dance (dance), 1736: CG, Mar 20

Grotta di Trofonio, La. See Casti, Giovanni Battista.
Grotto Gardens, 1771: GROTTO, Jun 22; 1772: GROTTO, Aug 17
Grotto Tavern, 1787: HAY, Mar 12
Group of Lovers, The; or, Beauty at her levee (song), 1791: CG, May 19, Jun 1;
   1792: CG, May 30; 1796: CG, Apr 29, May 27; 1797: CG, May 11, 20, HAY, Aug 8;
   1798: HAY, Aug 28; 1799: CG, Apr 26, May 28
Grove, The. See Oldmixon, John.
Grove, W (actor), 1733: HAY, May 26
Grover (actor), 1771: HAY, May 20, 22, Jul 1, Aug 28, Sep 18; 1772: HAY, Jun
   29, Aug 10
Groves (singer), 1781: DL, May 23; 1782: HAY, Jan 14
Grub St, 1698: LIF, Nov 0; 1736: LIF, Dec 11
Grub Street Opera, The. See Fielding, Henry.
Grubb, John (author, proprietor), 1796: DL, May 17
--Alive and Merry (farce), 1796: DL, May 17, 18, 19, 28, Jun 4, 10
Grullo and Moschetta. See Orlandini, Giuseppe Maria.
Grumbler, The. See Sedley, Sir Charles.
Gruttschreiber, J A, 1798: CG, Apr 17
--Siri Brahe; oder, Die Neugierigen, 1798: CG, Apr 17
Gryffin. See Griffin.
Guaccini, Pietro (singer), 1713: QUEEN'S, Mar 28; 1719: YB, Dec 19
Guadagni (Guadini), Gaetano (singer), 1748: KING'S, Nov 8; 1749: KING'S, Mar
   21; 1750: CG, Mar 16, KING'S, 31, Apr 10; 1751: KING'S, Apr 16, HAY, 27;
   1753: KING'S, Apr 30; 1754: CG, Nov 18; 1755: DL, Feb 3, KING'S, Mar 17;
   1768: KING'S, Nov 8; 1769: KING'S, Mar 16, Sep 5; 1770: KING'S, Jan 27, Feb
   2, 22, Mar 1, 8, DL, 14, 16, KING'S, 22, HAY, May 4, KING'S, Jun 12; 1771:
   CG, Mar 13, HAY, Apr 17, CHAPEL, 27, KING'S, 30
Guadagni, Sga (singer), 1767: KING'S, Oct 27, Nov 7, Dec 1, 8, 12, 15, 19, 22;
   1769: KING'S, May 16, Sep 5, Nov 7; 1770: KING'S, Apr 24, May 22, Jun 19, 26;
   1771: CG, Mar 1, KING'S, 21
Guadeloupe, 1795: CG, May 6
Guard, William (master carpenter), 1777: CG, Oct 20; 1778: CG, May 6; 1779: CG,
   May 12; 1780: CG, May 17, Sep 25; 1781: CG, May 8; 1782: CG, May 21, Oct 4;
   1783: CG, May 27; 1784: CG, May 26; 1785: CG, Oct 3; 1786: CG, May 23, Sep
   25; 1787: CG, Jun 5, Sep 24
Guarda nel mio taddio (song), 1793: KING/HAY, Feb 15, 27, Mar 8
Guardian Angels (song), 1774: CG, Dec 23
Guardian Outwitted (dance), 1790: CG, Apr 8, 17; see also Tuteur Trompe, Le
Guardian Outwitted, The (musical), 1764: CG, Dec 12, 13, 14, 15, 17, 18
Guardian, The. See Cowley, Abraham.
Guardian, The; or, The Cutter of Coleman Street. See Garrick, David.
Guarducci, Tommaso (singer), 1766: KING'S, Oct 21, Dec 27; 1767: KING'S, Mar 5,
   May 2, Oct 27; 1768: CG, Feb 24, KING'S, Mar 10
Guarini, Giovanni Battista (composer), 1668: LIF, Aug 20
Guastatore, Il (dance), 1753: CG, Apr 30
Guaxandi, Antonio (singer), 1731: KING'S, Dec 7
Guerin (dancer), 1755: CG, Nov 1, Dec 17; 1756: CG, Jan 2, 21, 22, Feb 14, Mar
   1, 2, 30, Apr 22; 1757: CG, Sep 21, Nov 5, 7, 29, Dec 7; 1758: CG, Apr 8, 28,
   May 2
Guerin, Mrs (actor, dancer), 1758: CG, Feb 1, Apr 28, May 2
Guering (musician), 1730: HIC, Apr 15
Guerini (actor, author), 1763: DL, Jan 3
--Magician of the Mountain, The (pantomime), 1763: DL, Jan 3, 4, 5
Guerre Ouverte. See Dumaniant.
Guest, George (singer), 1784: DL, Mar 19; 1785: DL, Mar 11
Guglielmi, Pietro (composer), 1767: KING'S, Oct 27; 1768: KING'S, Jan 16, Mar
   10, 26, May 24, Nov 19; 1769: KING'S, Sep 5, Dec 12; 1770: KING'S, Jan 13,
   Mar 8, 31, Apr 7, May 19; 1771: KING'S, Feb 8, 23, 28, Apr 30, Nov 2, 23;
   1772: KING'S, Jan 14, Feb 21, Mar 24, 26, May 30; 1775: KING'S, Nov 16; 1779:
   HAY, Aug 14; 1781: KING'S, Nov 17; 1790: CG, Mar 8; 1791: PAN, Mar 1, KING'S,
   May 12, HAY, Jun 25, PAN, Dec 17, 31; 1792: HAY, Apr 12, CG, May 22, DL, Nov
   21; 1794: KING'S, Mar 1, 18, Apr 26, DL, May 16, Oct 27; 1795: KING'S, Feb
   20, 27; 1796: KING'S, Dec 6; 1798: KING'S, Jan 9; 1799: CG, Apr 19, KING'S,
   May 30
--Amor fra le Vendemmie, L' (opera), 1796: KING'S, Dec 6, 10, 13, 17, 20, 23,
   27, 31; 1797: KING'S, Jan 3
--Assembla, L' (opera), 1772: KING'S, Mar 17, 24, 28, 31, Apr 7
--Bella Pescatrice, La (opera), 1791: PAN, Mar 1, 3, 5, 8, 10, 12, 15, 19, 22,
   24, 26, 29, Apr 2, 5, 12, 28, May 3, 9, 24, Jun 3, 23, Jul 19; 1792: HAY, Apr
   12, 19, 26, May 1, 10, 15, 22, 29, Jun 5, 9, DL, Nov 21; 1794: KING'S, Mar
   18, 22, 25, 29
--Carnovale Di Venezia (opera), 1772: KING'S, Jan 14, 17, 20, 25, 28, Feb 4,

Mar 10, 17
--Costanza Di Rosinella, La (opera), 1770: KING'S, Mar 31
--Debora and Sisara (oratorio), 1795: KING'S, Feb 20
--Demetrio (opera), 1772: KING'S, May 30, Jun 3, 5
--Disertore, Il, (opera), 1770: KING'S, May 19; 1771: KING'S, Nov 23, 29, Dec
  14, 21; 1772: KING'S, Jan 4, 11
--Ifigenia in Aulide (opera), 1768: KING'S, Jan 16, 23, Feb 6, 20, 23
--Pastorella Nobile, La (opera), 1791: PAN, Dec 17, 20, 31; 1792: PAN, Jan 7,
  14
--Pazzie D'Orlando, Le (opera), 1771: KING'S, Feb 23, 26, Mar 2, 5, 9, 16, Apr
  1, 6, 20, 21, Jun 1, 15; 1772: KING'S, Feb 21, Mar 26, Apr 9, 11, 21, May 14
--Ratto de la Sposa, Il (opera), 1768: KING'S, Mar 26, Apr 5, 19
--Viaggiatori Ridicoli, I (opera), 1768: KING'S, May 24, 28, 31, HAY, Jun 4,
  KING'S, 7, 11, 18, 21, 25, 28, 30, Nov 15, 19, 22, 26, 29, Dec 3, 6, 10;
  1769: KING'S, Jan 14, 17, Feb 21, May 20, Jun 24, Dec 12, 19; 1770: KING'S,
  Jan 9, May 22, 29; 1771: KING'S, May 21, Jun 22, Nov 2, 9, 12, 16, Dec 7, 10,
  17, 28; 1772: KING'S, Jan 7, Feb 1, Mar 7; 1775: KING'S, Mar 30, Apr 25, May
  2
Guglielmi, Pietro and Sga, 1771: KING'S, Mar 21; 1772: KING'S, Mar 26
Guglielmi, Sga Pietro (singer), 1770: KING'S, Jan 13, Feb 1, 2, 3, 10, Mar 1,
  22, 29, May 19, Jun 12; 1771: KING'S, Jan 10, 12, Feb 8, 28, Mar 21, Nov 2;
  1772: KING'S, Feb 21, Mar 26, Apr 7, 9, May 19, 28
Guiardele. See Gardel.
Guichard, Jean Francois, 1778: DL, Mar 16
--Bucheron, Le; ou, Les Trois Souhaits, 1778: DL, Mar 16
Guidetti, Giovanni (dancer), 1766: DL, Oct 11; 1767: DL, Jan 2, 24, Feb 25, Mar
  23, May 21, Jun 1
Guidi, Antonia (dancer), 1769: KING'S, Sep 5; 1770: KING'S, Feb 6, 22, May 19,
  24; 1771: KING'S, Mar 12, Apr 1, May 23, 28, Jun 15; 1772: KING'S, Jan 14,
  Apr 25, 28, May 5, 9, 12, 14, 16, 23, 28, Jun 3, 9, 11
Guildford, Earl of. See North, George Augustus.
Guildhall, 1660: CITY, Jul 5; 1673: CITY, Oct 29; 1681: CITY, Oct 29; 1687:
  CITY, Oct 29; 1732: DL, Feb 1, Sep 28; 1734: DL, Oct 29; 1745: DL, Dec 5, 9,
  CG, 9, DL, 14, CG, 14, 16, 17, 21; 1746: CG, Dec 20, DL, 20; 1748: CG, Oct 7;
  1751: DL, Dec 17; 1772: DL, Feb 29
Guilford (actor), 1792: HAY, Nov 26
Guimard, Marie Madeleine (dancer), 1789: KING'S, Apr 28, May 2, 7, 14, 23, Jun
  9, 15
Guinquette, La; or, Harlequin Turned Tapster (farce), 1716: DL, Apr 11, 13, 20,
  23, 30
Guirlande Enchantee, La (pantomime), 1725: HAY, Jan 20
Guise (boxkeeper), 1735: CG/LIF, May 20; 1736: CG, May 18; 1737: CG, May 12;
  1738: CG, May 11; 1739: CG, May 15; 1740: CG, May 16
Guishard (actor), 1789: HAY, Aug 11; 1790: HAY, Jul 16; 1791: DLKING'S, Oct 15
Guitar (music), 1764: DL, Mar 24; 1773: CG, Apr 27; 1778: KING'S, Feb 24; 1779:
  KING'S, May 15; 1780: KING'S, Apr 22, May 9, 20; 1781: DL, May 19
Guittard (song), 1757: HAY, Oct 21
Gulgulachem-Chemaunim (Chinese mandarin), 1735: LIF, Jun 19
Gulick, Mrs (actor), 1718: LIF, Oct 15; 1719: LIF, May 25, Nov 7, 13, 26; 1720:
  LIF, Jan 7, 26, Feb 17, 23, 29, Mar 17, Apr 19, May 14, Jun 7, BFBL, Aug 23,
  LIF, Dec 8; 1721: LIF, Mar 14, Apr 13, May 19, 29, SF, Sep 8, LIF, Nov 13,
  Dec 11; 1722: LIF, Mar 15, 28, May 16; 1724: RI, Jun 27, 29, Jul 11, 18
Gull (actor), 1791: HAY, Mar 7; 1792: HAY, Feb 20
Gum. See Gom, Stephen.
Gunning, Elizabeth (novelist), 1791: HAY, Aug 13
Gunning, General John, 1791: HAY, Aug 13
Gunning, Susannah (novelist), 1791: HAY, Aug 13
--Siri Brahe, 1798: CG, Apr 17
Gustave Vasa; or, Gustavus the Great, King of Sweden. See Piron, Alexis.
Gustavus III, King of Sweden, 1798: CG, Apr 17
Gustavus Vasa. See Brooke, Henry.
Guy (householder), 1778: HAY, Aug 25; 1779: HAY, Aug 25
Guy (plumber), 1767: DL, Jan 23
Guy Fawkes!; or, The Fifth of November (interlude, anon), 1793: HAY, Nov 5
Guy, Earl of Warwick (droll), 1730: SFLH, Sep 8; 1731: BFLH, Aug 24
Guzman. See Boyle, Roger.
Guzman, Elhadge (Moroccan messenger), 1710: QUEEN'S, May 4
Gwatkin, Mrs, 1776: DL, May 13
Gwilliam (violinist), 1792: CG, Feb 24; 1793: CG, Feb 15; 1794: CG, Mar 7;
  1795: CG, Feb 20; 1796: CG, Feb 12; 1797: CG, Mar 3; 1798: CG, Feb 23; 1799:
  CG, Feb 8; 1800: CG, Feb 28
Gwinn (actor), 1716: LIF, Jul 18

Gwinn (doorkeeper), 1719: LIF, May 13; 1720: LIF, May 11; 1721: LIF, May 10;
   1722: LIF, May 23; 1723: LIF, May 15; 1724: LIF, May 20; 1725: LIF, May 12;
   1726: LIF, May 25; 1727: LIF, May 17; 1728: LIF, May 23; 1729: LIF, May 14;
   1730: LIF, May 21; 1731: LIF, May 26; 1732: LIF, May 18; 1733: CG, May 16;
   1734: CG, May 15; 1735: CG/LIF, May 20; 1736: CG, May 18; 1737: CG, May 12;
   1740: CG, May 21; 1741: CG, May 6; 1742: CG, May 17; 1743: CG, May 9; 1744:
   CG, May 9; 1745: CG, May 13; 1746: CG, May 5; 1747: CG, May 19; 1748: CG, May
   6
Gwinn (musician), 1751: DL, May 4; 1753: CG, Apr 28
Gwinn, Lucy (house servant), 1754: CG, May 4; 1756: CG, May 21; 1757: CG, May
   19; 1758: CG, Apr 22; 1759: CG, Dec 8; 1760: CG, May 3, Sep 22; 1762: CG, May
   13; 1763: CG, May 14
Gwinn, Widow (beneficiary), 1738: CG, May 15; 1739: CG, May 23; 1742: CG, Mar
   1; 1745: CG, Apr 23
Gwinn, Widow (householder), 1744: CG, Apr 16
Gwyn, Mrs (silk dyer), 1746: DL, Apr 22
Gwyn, Nell (actor), 1663: BRIDGES, Nov 3; 1664: NONE, Sep 0, BRIDGES, Nov 0;
   1665: BRIDGES, Apr 0, LIF, 3; 1666: NONE, Sep 0, BRIDGES, Dec 8; 1667:
   BRIDGES, Jan 23, BRI/COUR, Feb 0, Mar 2, LIF, 7, BRI/COUR, 25, BRIDGES, Apr
   8, May 1, BRI/COUR, 24, NONE, Jul 13, BRIDGES, Aug 22, 26, Sep 20, Oct 5, 19,
   NONE, 26, BRIDGES, Nov 11, 16, Dec 26, 28; 1668: BRIDGES, Jan 11, Feb 20, 27,
   May 7, Jun 12, NONE, Sep 0, BRIDGES, 14, Dec 18; 1669: BRIDGES, Jan 7, 16,
   NONE, Feb 10, BRIDGES, May 6, Jun 24; 1670: BRI/COUR, Dec 0; 1674: DG, Sep 0,
   Oct 0, Nov 2, 11, 26, Dec 2, 9; 1675: DG, Jan 21, Feb 27, Mar 3, 19, 24, Jun
   12, 15, 22, 23, 24, 29, Sep 24, 25, Oct 8, 11, DL, 27, DG, Nov 0, Dec 0;
   1676: DG, Jan 0, 10, Feb 0, Mar 11, May 9, 25, Jun 8, 9, Jul 3, 25, Sep 12,
   21, 23, 25, Oct 2, 5, 11, 12, 16, 18, 26, 27, Nov 1, 4; 1677: DG, Sep 0;
   1678: DG, Apr 5; 1680: DG, Feb 26; 1682: DL, Feb 4
Gyles, Daniel, 1768: CG, Apr 30
Gyrowetz, Adalbert (author), 1790: CG, Oct 4; 1791: HAY, Jun 25; 1792: CG, Feb
   28

H, E, 1772: DL, Sep 29
H, T, 1762: DL, Nov 2
Haberdashers Hall, 1682: DG, Apr 0; 1756: HAB, Dec 9; 1767: HAB, Dec 10
Haberdashers, Company of, 1664: CITY, Oct 29; 1699: CITY, Oct 30
Habgood, Thomas (musician), 1758: HAY, Mar 13
Habington, William, 1668: LIF, Aug 20
--Queen of Arragon, The, 1668: LIF, Aug 20, ATCOURT, Oct 14, LIF, 19
Habito, Mrs (actor), 1742: BFPY, Aug 25
Hackett (actor), 1743: SF, Sep 8; 1744: HAY, Sep 27, 29, Oct 4, 11, 13
Hackett, John (actor), 1748: CG, Mar 28; 1749: CG, Oct 6, Nov 1, 8; 1750: CG,
   Apr 26, Nov 19, 22; 1755: HAY, Sep 1, 6; 1756: CG, May 5; 1757: CG, May 20;
   1758: CG, May 12
Hackett, Sir James (wounded), 1684: DLORDG, Oct 29
Hacketts (beneficiary), 1799: CG, May 29; 1800: CG, Jun 11
Hackney, 1722: CLA, May 4
Had I a Heart for Falsehood framed (song), 1791: CG, Jun 4
Haddington Masque, The. See Jonson, Ben.
Haddington, Thomas Earl of (spectator), 1741: KING'S, Dec 19
Haddock (house servant), 1736: CG, May 10
Hadfield, James (attempted assassin of George III), 1800: DL, May 15
Hadley (actor), 1734: BFHBH, Aug 24
Hadley (machinist), 1775: DL, May 27
Hadley and Co (smiths), 1776: DL, Jun 10
Hagen, V (musician), 1735: HIC, Feb 21, May 5
Hagley, Miss (actor, singer), 1789: DL, Feb 27, Mar 18, 20, 25, May 11, 28, Sep
   15, 22, 26, Oct 10, 17, 26, 27, 28, Nov 4, 13, Dec 7, 9, 12, 15, 23, 26;
   1790: DL, Feb 19, 24, 26, Mar 5, 10, 11, 12, 13, 19, 24, Apr 16, 24, May 25,
   31, Oct 4, 7, 11, 16, 21, 26, 27, Nov 19, Dec 7, 8; 1791: DL, Jan 1, Feb 10,
   Mar 11, 23, Apr 1, 8, 13, 28, May 19, DLKING'S, Sep 27, 29, Oct 3, 4, 29, Nov
   2, 5, 9, 26, 29, Dec 1, 31; 1792: DLKING'S, Jan 21, Feb 8, 11, 18, KING'S,
   24, 29, DLKING'S, Mar 10, KING'S, 14, 23, DLKING'S, 27, KING'S, 28, DLKING'S,
   29, KING'S, 30, DLKING'S, May 14, 21, 31
Hague (actor), 1748: HAY, Dec 9; 1776: HAY, May 2
Hague, The, 1659: NONE, Sep 0
Haigh, Thomas (violinist), 1795: HAY, Mar 4
Hail Fellows Well Met (farce, anon), 1792: CG, May 8, HAY, Aug 9
Hail, immortal Bacchus (song), 1761: KING'S, Mar 12

Hail, mighty Joshua (song), 1791: CG, Mar 23; 1792: CG, Mar 9
Hail to the Brave (song), 1795: CG, May 6
Hail to the myrtle shade (song), 1680: DG, Sep 0
Hail, Windsor (song), 1742: NWC, Dec 27; 1743: JS, Apr 25
Haines. See Haynes.
Haines, John (waiter), 1749: ∂AY, Nov 17
Hale (beneficiary), 1711: SOU, Feb 6
Hale (paper hanger), 1795: CG, Oct 24
Hale, Ann, Mrs Sacheverel (actor), 1739: CG, Oct 3, 29, Nov 3, Dec 15; 1740:
   CG, Jan 12, Mar 10, May 12, Sep 22, 24, Oct 6, 29, Nov 7, 18, Dec 10; 1741:
   CG, Jan 12, 22, Mar 2, 9, 16, Apr 1, 11, 30, May 12, 15, Oct 29, 31, Nov 9,
   11, 30, Dec 1, 4, 7, 9; 1742: CG, Feb 2, 3, 22, Mar 8, Apr 1, 10, 23, 24, May
   4, 6, 7, 10, 14, 25, Sep 29, Oct 4, 6, 9, 11, 16, 21, 25, 29, Nov 3, 8, 13,
   25, 29, Dec 22; 1743: CG, Jan 18, Apr 26, May 2, 4, 5, LIF, Jun 3, CG, Sep
   28, Oct 7, 12, 24, 26, 29, Nov 2, 16, 17, 18, 19, 21, 30, Dec 9, 12; 1744:
   CG, Jan 14, Feb 7, 23, 28, Mar 30, Apr 19, May 14, Sep 21, 28, Oct 3, 8, 10,
   22, 24, 26, 29, Nov 1, 7, 21, 22, 27, 28, 30, Dec 10, 11, 12, 17; 1745: CG,
   Jan 4, 7, 11, Feb 12, Apr 17, May 8, 10, Sep 27, Oct 2, 4, 7, 9, 11, 16, 29,
   31, Nov 4, 7, 8, 11, 12, 13, 14, 15, 16, 18, 22, 23, 25, 26, 30, Dec 2, 10,
   12; 1746: CG, Jan 2, 7, 11, 23, Feb 3, 6, 17, Mar 13, Apr 23, Oct 1, 8, 10,
   13, 15, 29, Nov 3, 8, 11, 14, 17, 18, 26, Dec 10, 17, 26, 27; 1747: CG, Jan
   31, Feb 2, 3, 12, Mar 7, 17, Apr 4, May 5, Nov 11, 16, 18, Dec 15, 17, 28;
   1748: CG, Jan 2, 7, 8, 12, 14, 15, 21, 27, 29, Feb 10, 15, Mar 8, 24, Apr 11,
   13, 15, 18, 21, 22, 26, 29, Oct 7, 10, 14, 24, 27, 29, Nov 3, 9, 16, 21, 26,
   28, Dec 21, 26; 1749: CG, Jan 2, 11, 25, 28, Feb 6, 18, Mar 31, Apr 5, HAY,
   6, CG, 7, 11, 17, 21, Sep 29
Hale, Mary Ann (actor, singer), 1777: HAY, May 30, Jun 19, Jul 15, 18, Aug 9,
   12, 19, 25, Sep 17, 18, Oct 13; 1778: HAY, Mar 31, Jun 19, Jul 2, 11, Aug 3,
   Sep 7; 1779: HAY, Jun 10, 18, Jul 1, Aug 6, 31; 1780: HAY, May 30, Jun 13,
   15, 23, DL, Oct 26; 1781: DL, Jan 22, Apr 18, 24, HAY, Jun 1, 8, 12, Jul 6,
   Aug 8, 22, Sep 13, DL, Oct 13, 18; 1782: DL, Jan 26, Apr 13, HAY, Jun 3, 6,
   11, Jul 30, Aug 17, 27, DL, Sep 18, Oct 26, 29, 30, Nov 16, Dec 26; 1783: DL,
   Jan 15, Apr 21, May 2, 12, HAY, 31, Jun 10, 30, Jul 26, Aug 20, 22, DL, Sep
   18, Nov 12, Dec 2, 29; 1784: DL, Feb 3, Mar 29, Apr 16, May 24, HAY, Jun 1,
   4, 14, Jul 28, DL, Sep 16, 18, 25; 1785: DL, Jan 12, 20, 24, Mar 17, Apr 27,
   May 3, 11, 23, HAY, 31, Jun 2, 21, 29, Jul 19, Aug 31, DL, Sep 27, Oct 13,
   Nov 2, 9, 26, Dec 7; 1786: DL, Jan 4, May 26, Jun 1; 1787: DL, May 21, ROY,
   Jun 20; 1788: HAY, Jun 16; 1789: HAY, May 29, Jun 8, 19, 26; 1790: HAY, Jun
   19, 29, Aug 7, 20; 1791: HAY, Jun 6, 16, 17, 23, Jul 15, 30, Aug 15, 16, 31;
   1792: HAY, Jun 15, 18, 20, 22, 23, 25, 27, Jul 25; 1793: HAY, Jun 12, 29, Jul
   10, 15, Aug 12, 16, Sep 2, 11, 21, Oct 1, 5, 29, Nov 19, Dec 26; 1794: HAY,
   Jan 4, 27, Feb 1, 20, 24, Jul 8, 9, 12, 14, 17, 18, 21, 24, 28, Aug 4, 27,
   Sep 17; 1795: HAY, Jun 16, 20, Jul 1, 13, 20, 31, Aug 21, Sep 21; 1796: HAY,
   Jun 11, Jul 9, Aug 10, 13, 17, 29, Sep 17; 1797: DL, Apr 28, May 24, Jun 15,
   HAY, 15, 16, 23, 24, Jul 4, Aug 14, 15, 31; 1798: HAY, Jun 13, 27, 30, Jul 6,
   21, Aug 3, 11, 25, Sep 5; 1799: HAY, Jun 15, 25, 29, Jul 6, 9, 17, Aug 21,
   26; 1800: HAY, Jun 14, Jul 2, Aug 8, 14, 20, 27, 29
Hale, Mr and Mrs (actors), 1745: CG, Apr 20
Hale, Sacheverel (actor), 1732: LIF, May 2, BFB, Aug 23, LIF/CG, Dec 26; 1733:
   LIF/CG, Apr 12, CG, May 1, LIF/CG, 19, CG, Jun 26, Jul 6, 27, Aug 2, 20, Sep
   22, 27, Oct 2, 11, 13, 25, 26, 27, 29, 31, Nov 1, 3, 5, 9, 10, 21, 26, 30,
   Dec 3, 4, 20; 1734: CG, Jan 4, 5, 18, 23, Mar 28, Apr 16, May 3, 16, 17,
   BFHBH, Aug 24, CG/LIF, Sep 18, 20, 23, 25, RI, 26, CG/LIF, Oct 9, 11, 14, 18,
   19, 29, Nov 1, 4, 11, 14, 25, 28, Dec 26; 1735: CG/LIF, Jan 9, 21, 23, 25,
   Feb 3, 11, 13, 15, Mar 11, 13, 20, 22, 29, Apr 9, 10, May 5, 9, 16, 27, CG,
   Sep 12, 16, 19, 24, 29, Oct 3; 1737: CG, Oct 7, Nov 2, 4, 9, 18; 1738: CG,
   Jan 3, 6, 9, 13, 18, 25, Feb 6, 13, 16, 23, Mar 13, 25, Apr 7, 10, 12, 17,
   24, 28, May 10, 18, Sep 18, 20, 22, 25, 29, Oct 2, 4, 6, 9, 13, 14, 16, 18,
   20, 21, 23, 31, Nov 4, 7, 9, 15, 17, 20, 28, Dec 2, 4, 5, 7; 1739: CG, Jan 4,
   17, Feb 9, 10, 14, 23, 26, Mar 3, 13, 27, Apr 3, 12, 24, May 1, 2, 7, 17, 25,
   Aug 21, BFHCL, 23, CG, Sep 5, 7, 10, 12, 14, 15, 17, 22, 27, 28, Oct 2, 3, 4,
   5, 6, 8, 9, 10, 22, 24, 25, 26, 29, 30, Nov 6, 17, 20, 22, Dec 1, 4, 6, 10,
   15, 19, 29; 1740: CG, Jan 12, 15, 25, Mar 11, 18, 20, Apr 14, May 2, 5, 9,
   12, 23, Jun 5, Sep 19, 24, 26, 29, Oct 1, 3, 6, 8, 22, 24, 29, 31, Nov 1, 4,
   6, 7, 15, 20, Dec 5, 6, 10, 13, 19, 29; 1741: CG, Jan 2, 6, 7, 12, 21, 22,
   27, 28, 29, Feb 7, 12, 14, 17, 24, 26, Mar 5, 7, 9, 12, 16, Apr 1, 3, 9, 11,
   15, 17, 22, May 1, 11, 12, Sep 21, 23, 25, 30, Oct 2, 5, 8, 13, 15, 20, 21,
   24, 26, 29, 30, 31, Nov 2, 4, 7, 9, 11, 23, 26, 27, Dec 1, 7, 9, 11, 12, 17,
   18; 1742: CG, Jan 2, 19, 23, Feb 3, 4, 10, 15, 22, 25, 27, Mar 13, 18, 27,
   Apr 1, 26, May 1, 4, 7, Sep 22, Oct 1, 4, 6, 9, 11, 13, 16, 18, 19, 21, 25,
   26, 29, Nov 3, 4, 8, 11, 13, 15, 20, 22, 29, 30, Dec 7, 15, 21, 22; 1743: CG,
   Jan 5, 18, Mar 15, Apr 9, 26, May 2, 4, 5, Sep 28, Oct 3, 5, 7, 10, 12, 14,

17, 19, 21, 24, 26, 28, 29, 31, Nov 2, 4, 16, 17, 18, 19, 21, 28, 30, Dec 3,
8, 9, 12, 14, 16, 27, 31; 1744: CG, Jan 4, 5, 7, 11, 24, Feb 3, 7, 23, 28,
Mar 3, 8, 13, Apr 19, May 14, Sep 24, 26, 28, Oct 1, 3, 5, 8, 10, 15, 16, 18,
20, 24, 26, 29, 31, Nov 5, 7, 9, 12, 21, 22, 27, 29, 30, Dec 5, 6, 10, 11,
12, 13, 17, 21, 26, 28; 1745: CG, Jan 1, 2, 4, 7, 14, 18, 23, Feb 9, 15, Mar
11, 14, Apr 17, 20, 23, 25, 26, May 3, 13, Sep 23, 25, 27, Oct 2, 4, 7, 9,
11, 14, 16, 18, 29, 31, Nov 2, 4, 7, 9, 11, 12, 13, 14, 15, 16, 18, 19, 22,
23, 25, 26, 28, 30, Dec 2, 5, 6, 10, 12, 13; 1746: CG, Jan 2, 7, 11, 13, 23,
25, Feb 5, 6, 8, 17, Mar 10, 13, 15, Apr 1, 3, 7, 22, 23, 28
Hales, Mrs (house servant), 1747: CG, May 22; 1750: CG, May 7; 1760: CG, Sep 22
Half an Hour after Supper (interlude, anon), 1789: HAY, May 25, 27, 29, Jun 12,
15, 19, 24, 26, Jul 21, Aug 1, 13, 21; 1790: HAY, Jun 14, 23, Jul 6, 14, 16,
22, Aug 7; 1791: HAY, Jun 16, 20, 24, Jul 4, 9, 16, 18, 23, 29, 30, Aug 4,
29; 1792: HAY, Jun 29, Jul 6, 19, 25, Aug 6; 1793: HAY, Jun 17, 21, Jul 1,
13, Aug 3, 10, Sep 12, Nov 25; 1794: HAY, Jan 15, 29, Feb 20, Mar 8, Jul 12,
21, Aug 22; 1795: HAY, Jun 16, Jul 1, Aug 19, Sep 5; 1796: HAY, Jul 2, Aug
10, 17; 1797: HAY, Jun 28, Jul 4, 6, Aug 9; 1798: HAY, Jun 27, Jul 3
Half and Half (song), 1800: HAY, Sep 10
Half Pay Officers, The. See Molloy, Charles.
Halfmoon Inn, 1721: BF/SF, Sep 2; 1729: SOU, Sep 23; 1731: SFGT, Sep 8; 1736:
NONE, Sep 7
Halfmoon St, 1756: DL, Nov 12; 1781: CG, Mar 27; 1782: CG, Mar 18; 1786: CG,
May 5; 1787: CG, Mar 26, Apr 27; 1788: CG, Mar 10, Apr 18; 1789: CG, Mar 28,
May 12; 1790: CG, Mar 22; 1791: CG, Apr 11; 1792: CG, Mar 26; 1793: CG, Mar
18, May 2; 1794: CG, Apr 7, May 10; 1795: CG, Mar 16, May 7; 1796: CG, Mar
14, Apr 19; 1798: CG, Apr 18; 1799: CG, Apr 12, May 15; 1800: CG, Apr 19, May
13
Halfmoon Tavern, 1749: DL, Feb 9, CG, Apr 28; 1784: HAY, Jan 21
Halford (leather gilder), 1774: CG, Mar 3
Halford, Mrs (singer), 1766: CG, Oct 21, Nov 21; 1767: CG, May 20
Haliburton (house servant), 1777: CG, May 24; 1778: CG, May 22; 1779: CG, May
15; 1782: CG, May 29; 1783: CG, Jun 4
Halifax, Lord (spectator), 1761: DL, Jul 27
Halifax, Lord. See Saville, George.
Hall (actor), 1770: HAY, Dec 14
Hall (actor), 1782: HAY, May 6; 1784: HAY, Nov 16; 1785: HAY, Apr 25
Hall (musician), 1675: ATCOURT, Feb 15
Hall (wardrobe keeper), 1703: DL, Apr 23, Jun 16, Oct 15; 1704: DL, Apr 6, Jun
21; 1705: DL, Jun 19; 1707: DL, Apr 14; 1708: DL, Oct 7; 1710: DL, Mar 9,
QUEEN'S, Apr 27
Hall-Leigh Booth, 1721: SFHL, Sep 2
Hall-Miller Booth, 1728: BFHM, Aug 24
Hall-Oates Booth, 1729: BF, Aug 26
Hall, Elizabeth (actor), 1664: NONE, Sep 0, BRIDGES, Nov 0; 1667: BRIDGES, Jan
23, LIF, Mar 30; 1668: BRIDGES, Dec 19
Hall, Jacob (acrobat), 1668: BF, Aug 29, SF, Sep 21; 1671: CITY, Oct 30; 1679:
BF, Sep 3
Hall, John (actor), 1715: LIF, Jan 4, 7, Feb 3, Apr 4, May 26, Jun 2, 7, 23,
Aug 3, 11, Oct 5, 10, Dec 12; 1716: LIF, Jan 4, 24, Apr 20, 27, Jul 4, Aug 3,
Oct 10, Nov 5, 10; 1717: LIF, Jan 22, Feb 11, May 10, Jun 3, Jul 10, Oct 15,
Nov 6, 20; 1718: LIF, Jan 2, Feb 3, Apr 28, Jun 30, Jul 24, SF, Sep 5, AC,
24; 1719: LIF, Mar 30, Apr 30; 1720: SFLH, Sep 5, SOU, Oct 10, LIF, Dec 8;
1721: LIF, Jan 19, Feb 6, Apr 1, 10, May 12, 23, SFHL, Sep 2, LIF, Oct 12,
25, 26, 31, Nov 13, 27, Dec 1, 11, 27; 1722: LIF, Jan 9, 13, Mar 29, 31, Apr
13, 24, May 21, 25, SOU, Sep 26, LIF, Oct 2, 6, 11, 12, 16, 18, 20, 22, 26,
29, Nov 7, 13, 14, 17, 30, Dec 8, 15, 21; 1723: LIF, Jan 3, 11, Apr 6, May 7,
18, 21, 23, Sep 28, 30, Oct 4, 9, 19, 22, 24, 25, 29, 31, Nov 1, 12, 16, 18,
19; 1724: LIF, Mar 23, May 6, 19, 27, Jun 23, Jul 14, 31, Sep 23, 25, 28, Oct
7, 12, 23, 27, 30, Nov 3, 6, 13, 17; 1725: LIF, Jan 4, 11, 19, Feb 27, Mar
11, 29, Apr 7, 17, 28, May 21, Oct 1, 4, 11, 16, 27, Nov 6, 8, 12, 24, 29,
Dec 2, 15; 1726: LIF, Feb 19, Apr 11, 18, May 3, 4, 12, Sep 14, 21, 26, 28,
Oct 3, 19, 24, Nov 2, 11, 21, 30, Dec 14; 1727: LIF, May 4, BF, Aug 21, LIF,
Sep 11, 18, 20, 27, Oct 2, 9, 31, Nov 1, 17, Dec 11; 1728: LIF, Jan 8, 29,
Apr 6, 23, 24, 26, 30, May 11, BFHM, Aug 24, LIF, Sep 30, Oct 1, Nov 11, 19,
20, Dec 31; 1729: LIF, Jan 16, Mar 3, 17, Apr 8, 15, 16, 17, 19, 23, 24, 30,
May 6, 12, 15, BF, Aug 26, LIF, Sep 19, 24, 29, Oct 3, 8, 29, 30, Nov 13, 14,
Dec 3; 1730: LIF, Jan 2, 19, 26, Apr 2, 23, 27, 30, May 11, 15, 18, 23, 25,
Jul 3, RI, 16, LIF, Sep 18, 21, Oct 5, 7, 23, 26, 31, Nov 10, Dec 4, 15;
1731: LIF, Jan 20, 21, Apr 3, 23, 24, 26, May 1, 5, 10, 21, Jun 2, RI, Jul 1,
8, SF/BFFHH, Aug 24, LIF, Sep 27, Oct 13, 18, 25, 27, 30, Nov 2, 12, 18, Dec
9; 1732: LIF, Jan 7, Feb 14, 15, 21, Mar 20, Apr 18, 27, May 2, 9, 22, RI,
Aug 17, LIF/CG, Sep 25, Oct 6, 9, 16, 21, 28, 30, Nov 8, 9, 17, 22, 24, Dec

15, CG/LIF, 16; 1733: LIF/CG, Jan 18, 31, Feb 3, 10, Mar 26, 29, 30, Apr 3,
CG, 4, LIF/CG, 10, 11, 13, 19, 21, 27, CG, May 1, LIF/CG, 7, 19, 24, CG/LIF,
28, BFCGBH, Sep 4, CG, 17, 20, 27, 29, Oct 4, 9, 11, 16, 18, 26, 29, 31, Nov
28, 30, Dec 3, 4, 15, 17, 20, 31; 1734: CG, Jan 23, Mar 5, 18, 28, Apr 30,
May 2, 3, RI, Jun 27, BFRLCH, Aug 24, Sep 2, CG, 2, CG/LIF, 20, RI, 26,
CG/LIF, 27, Oct 9, LIF, 12, CG/LIF, 14, 16, 29; 1738: CG, Jan 25; 1742: CG,
Oct 28; 1743: CG, Sep 26; 1749: BF/SFP, Aug 23
Hall, John (carpenter) and Hall (boxkeeper), 1784: CG, May 22, 29; 1786: CG,
May 31, Jun 1; 1787: CG, May 30, Jun 2; 1788: CG, May 27, 30; 1789: CG, Jun
5, 13; 1790: CG, May 29, Jun 12; 1791: CG, Jun 2, 14; 1792: CG, May 12, 25;
1794: CG, Jun 4, 12; 1795: CG, Jun 4; 1796: CG, Jun 3, 4; 1797: CG, May 25;
1798: CG, May 31; 1799: CG, May 21, 22; 1800: CG, Jun 3, 4
Hall, John (real estate), 1708: DL, Sep 7
Hall, Mrs (beneficiary), 1707: YB, Apr 2
Hall, Mrs (boxkeeper), 1797: CG, Jun 8
Hall, William (musician), 1699: YB, Mar 8; 1701: YB, Mar 3; 1707: YB, Apr 2
Hall's Booth, 1720: SOU, Nov 28
Hallam (actor), 1725: DL, Feb 18, Apr 30, May 19, Oct 5; 1726: DL, May 7, Oct
1, Nov 16; 1727: DL, May 22, Sep 30, Oct 6; 1728: DL, Mar 19, May 17, Oct 08,
30; 1729: GF, Nov 3, 5, 6, 8, 11, 14, 20, 24, Dec 3, DL, 26; 1730: GF, Jan 5,
9, 23, HAY, Feb 18, 23, Mar 12, 20, 30, Apr 20, 24, May 1, DL, 2, 18, Oct 1,
HAY, Nov 16, 20, DL, 24, 30, HAY, Dec 9, DL, 11, HAY, 28; 1731: HAY, Jan 15,
18, 20, DL, 27, Feb 8, HAY, 10, DL, 22, HAY, 26, Mar 15, 17, 24, Apr 22, DL,
May 12, HAY, 12, 13, DL, Oct 5, 21, Nov 25, Dec 1, LIF, 3, DL, 21; 1732: DL,
Mar 21, LIF, May 2, DL, 5, Dec 11; 1733: HAY, Mar 20, 26, CG, May 1, DL, Jun
4, DL/HAY, Oct 12, DL, 24, CG, Nov 26, DL, Dec 19, 21; 1734: DL, Jan 3, 15,
19, HAY, Feb 12, Apr 5, DL/HAY, 26, May 1, HAY, 27, JS, 29, HAY, Jun 5, 17,
19, 21, Jul 19, 26, 31, Aug 14, 16, HA, 20, DL, Sep 26, HAY, Oct 7, CG/LIF,
18, DL, 21, Nov 22, Dec 6; 1735: DL, Jan 22, 29, Feb 25, YB, Mar 21, DL, Apr
28, May 2, 10, CG, Nov 22, DL, Dec 12; 1736: CG, Sep 29; 1737: YB, Apr 14,
CG, Sep 30, Nov 2, 9, 15, 17; 1738: CG, Jan 16, 17, 20, 25, Feb 6, 13, 16,
23, Mar 13, 20, 25, Apr 12, 22, 24, 25, Jun 30, Jul 7, 11, 21, Aug 1, 22, Sep
20, 22, 25, 29, Oct 6, 11, 14, 20, 24, 28, 30, Nov 4, 17, 18, 23, 29, Dec 2,
4, 5, 7; 1739: CG, Jan 22, Feb 3, 9, 10, 14, 16, Mar 13, Apr 23, 25, May 25,
Aug 2, Sep 5, 15, 19, 22, 25, 27, 29, Oct 4, 6, 9, 10, 22, 25, 26, 29, 30,
Nov 2, 5, 6, 9, 10, 17, 20, Dec 6, 10, 21; 1740: CG, Jan 15, 17, Mar 11, 27,
Apr 9, 21, 25, 28, May 3, 5, 7, 9, 12, 23, 27, Jun 5, Sep 19, 24, 26, Oct 1,
3, 23, 24, 25, 27, 29, 31, Nov 4, 15, 20, Dec 6, 10; 1741: CG, Jan 2, 7, 15,
22, 23, 27, 28, Feb 12, 26, Mar 7, 10, 16, 30, Apr 1, 7, 9, May 4, BFH, Aug
22; 1742: DL, Oct 16, 21, Nov 1, 16, Dec 9; 1743: DL, Jan 27; 1745: GF, Dec
4; 1746: GF, Jan 1, 2, 13, Mar 22, Oct 28, 31, Nov 4, 6, 14, 18, 19, 21, 26,
27, Dec 3, 5, 9, 17, 29; 1747: GF, Jan 2, 5, 9, 16, 21, 22, 26, 29, Feb 3,
13, 20, Mar 2, 30, HAY, Apr 22, CG, Dec 1; 1752: NWLS, Nov 13, 16, 20, 23,
28, 30; 1756: BFSI, Sep 3, 4, 6; 1764: CG, Feb 10, May 15; 1765: CG, Apr 12,
13, May 10; 1766: CG, Jan 31, May 5, Sep 22, Oct 1, Nov 26; 1767: CG, Jan 12,
Mar 21, May 14; 1768: CG, Feb 20, Mar 10, Nov 17
Hallam (actor), 1798: WRSG, Jun 8; 1799: WRSG, May 17
Hallam-Chapman Booth, 1736: BFHC, Aug 23
Hallam, Adam (actor), 1728: DL, Mar 19, Oct 18; 1730: DL, May 18, 27, Nov 25,
30; 1731: DL, Jan 20, Apr 19, 24, May 4, 7, 12, 17, SF/BFMMO, Aug 26, DL, Sep
18, Oct 16, 30, Nov 22, 25, Dec 10; 1732: DL, Feb 14, Mar 14, Apr 14, 17, May
1, 2, 3, 5, 10, 12, BF, Aug 22, DL, Sep 21, 28, Oct 5, 10, 17, 24, Nov 4,
LIF/CG, 7, DL, 11, 16, 21, 24, Dec 14, 20, 22; 1733: DL, Jan 11, Feb 22, Apr
9, 13, 19, 30, May 1, 5, 14, 24, 29, CG, Aug 9, BFCGBH, 23, DL/HAY, Oct 5, 6,
10, 12, 17, 19, 22, 25, Nov 5, 9, 23, 26, 28, Dec 5, 10, 17, 19, 22; 1734:
DL/HAY, Jan 12, 17, Mar 25, CG, 28, DL/HAY, 30, Apr 2, 18, DL, 22, 23,
DL/HAY, 26, CG, May 3, DL, 13, 15, BFHBH, Aug 24, CG, Sep 2, CG/LIF, 18, 20,
30, Oct 11, 18, Nov 1, 4, 7, 11, 14, 21, 25, 28, Dec 5, 26; 1735: CG/LIF, Jan
6, 25, Feb 3, 13, Mar 18, 20, 24, 25, Apr 8, 10, 11, 17, 18, LIF, 19, CG/LIF,
21, CG, 25, CG/LIF, May 9, 16, CG, Sep 12, 19, 24, 26, 29, Oct 20, 22, 25,
29, 31, Nov 4, 10, 15, 22, Dec 8, 31; 1736: CG, Jan 9, 10, Feb 10, 26, Mar
15, 18, 22, 29, Apr 6, 8, 29, LIF, May 5, CG, 17, Sep 22, 24, 29, Oct 4, 6,
LIF, 18, CG, 20, 23, 25, 29, Nov 1, 4, Dec 2, 9, 20, 29; 1737: CG, Feb 15,
24, 26, Mar 24, 31, Apr 11, 14, 26, May 31, Sep 16, 19, 26, 30, Oct 5, 14,
19, 22, 28, 29, Nov 1, 4; 1738: CG, Jan 3, 25, Jun 27, Nov 27; 1739: CG, Aug
31; 1741: CG, Apr 11
Hallam, G (actor), 1745: GF, Dec 2; 1746: GF, Oct 29, Nov 18, 19, 21, 26
Hallam, Isabella (actor), 1752: CG, Sep 22, Oct 2, 27; 1753: CG, May 18, Sep
21, 26, Nov 22; 1754: CG, Sep 20, 30; 1755: CG, Oct 6, Dec 12, 13; 1756: CG,
Sep 29, Oct 13; 1757: CG, Jan 27, Feb 19, Oct 19, Nov 7, 11, 26; 1758: CG,
Jan 7; 1761: CG, Apr 10; 1762: CG, Apr 12, 22, Sep 20, Oct 1, 5, 6, 16, 26,
Nov 1, 5, 29, Dec 8; 1763: CG, Jan 8, 24, 28, Feb 14, Mar 21, Apr 15, 22, 25,

May 20, 23, Sep 19, 21, 30, Oct 7, 12, 14, 15, 18, 20, 21, 22, Nov 3, 4, 18;
1764: CG, Jan 9, 19, 20, 28, Feb 1, 8, 11, 15, 22, Mar 20, Apr 25, May 11,
21, Oct 25, 27, 29, 30, 31, Nov 5, 6, 14, 16, 29, Dec 11, 12, 19; 1765: CG,
Jan 3, 8, 15, 17, 18, 31, Feb 19, Mar 11, 16, 18, 28, Apr 8
Hallam, Lewis (actor), 1745: GF, Jan 31, Feb 9, 14, Mar 7, Apr 1, 22, Oct 28,
Nov 4, 11, 13, 14, 18, 19, 22, 27, 28, 29, Dec 2, 4, 11, 27, 30; 1746: GF,
Jan 1, 6, 13, 17, 20, 27, 31, Feb 3, 7, Oct 28, 29, 31, Nov 4, 6, 7, 13, 14,
18, 19, 20, 21, 26, 28, Dec 3, 9, 10, 11, 12, 15, 17, 18, 22, 29; 1747: GF,
Jan 2, 5, 9, 16, 22, 26, Feb 5, 16, 24, Mar 2, 9, Apr 2; 1748: NWC, Apr 4;
1749: NWLS, Feb 27; 1750: HAY, Jul 26; 1751: NWLS, Aug 6, Sep 5; 1775: CG,
Jan 3
Hallam, Lewis and Mrs (actors), 1746: GF, Mar 17; 1747: GF, Mar 9
Hallam, Mrs (actor), 1731: LIF, Sep 27, Oct 11, 18, 20, 25, 27, Nov 4, 8, 17,
Dec 1, 3, 9, 14; 1732: LIF, Jan 19, Feb 14, 15, 28, Mar 25, Apr 10, 11, 26,
29, CG/LIF, Sep 22, LIF/CG, 27, 29, Oct 2, 6, 11, LIF, 18, LIF/CG, 20, 25,
28, 30, Nov 4, 7, 13, Dec 4, 7, 15; 1733: LIF/CG, Jan 1, CG, Feb 8, Apr 4,
LIF/CG, 12, 13, CG, May 1, 2, LIF/CG, 3, 7, CG, 17, Oct 6, 11, 13, 20, 23,
25, 26, 27, Nov 5, 16, 19, 26, Dec 8, 15; 1734: CG, Jan 9, Feb 14, Mar 18,
28, Apr 18, May 9, 17, CG/LIF, Sep 18, 20, 25, 30, Oct 7, 9, 14, 25, Nov 4,
Dec 26; 1735: CG/LIF, Jan 6, 9, 25, 31, Feb 11, 22, Mar 25, Apr 9, May 2, 27,
YB, Jul 17, CG, Sep 12, 29, Oct 8, 10, 20, 25, Nov 4, 6, 10, 13, 15, 22;
1736: CG, Feb 21, Mar 9, 16, 20, 29, Apr 13, 29, Oct 1, 4, 6, 11, 13, 15, 20,
23, 30, Nov 1, 4, 22, 26, Dec 4, 29; 1737: CG, Jan 21, Feb 15, 26, Mar 24,
31, May 3, Sep 16, 21, 23, Oct 7, 14, 17, 19, 21, 22, 27, 31, Nov 1, 4, 19;
1738: CG, Jan 3, 17, Feb 6, Mar 13, 20, 25, Apr 7, 14, 17, Jul 21, Sep 15,
25, 29, Oct 4, 6, 9, 14, 16, 18, 24, 28, 31, Nov 4, 11, 22, 23, 29; 1739: CG,
Jan 4, 15, 17, 23, Feb 10, 26, Apr 3, 25, Aug 31, Oct 8, 9, 22, 25, Nov 2, 9,
17, 22, 24, 27, 28; 1740: CG, Jan 15, Apr 21, Jun 5; 1745: GF, Feb 9, 14, Mar
7, Oct 28, Nov 11, 12, 13, 14, 18, 19, 25, 28, Dec 2, 4, 6, 11, 13, 16, 19;
1746: GF, Jan 1, 3, 6, 10, 13, 17, 20, 27, Feb 3, 7, 13, Mar 15, Oct 27, 28,
29, 31, Nov 4, 6, 7, 13, 14, 18, 19, 20, 21, 26, 27, 28, Dec 1, 2, 9, 10, 11,
12, 15, 17, 18, 22, 27, 31; 1747: GF, Jan 2, 9, 16, Feb 2, 5, 16, 20, Mar 9,
19, 26, Apr 2, HAY, 22; 1748: NWC, Apr 4; 1749: NWLS, Feb 27; 1751: NWLS, Sep
5
Hallam, Thomas (actor), 1734: LIF, May 9, JS, 29
Hallam, William (actor), 1730: HAY, Mar 30, Apr 8; 1733: BFCGBH, Aug 23, Sep 4;
1736: CG, Mar 27, LIF, Apr 16; 1737: CG, Nov 9; 1738: CG, Feb 13, 16, 23, Mar
25, Apr 25, Jun 27, 30, Jul 7, 11, Aug 1, 29, Dec 2, 4, 5; 1739: CG, Feb 10,
16; 1745: GF, Dec 16, 23, 26; 1746: GF, Jan 2, 27, Feb 24, Mar 17, Nov 28,
Dec 12; 1747: GF, Jan 9, Feb 3, 25, Mar 2, 9, 16; 1756: NWGF, Mar 18, SW, Oct
9
Hallam's Booth, 1737: BF, Aug 23; 1738: BFH, Aug 23, SFH, Sep 5; 1739: BFH, Aug
23; 1740: BFH, Aug 23; 1741: BF, Aug 22
Hallam's New Theatre, 1744: MFHNT, May 1, MF, 3, DL, 11
Hallandall (musician), 1754: HAY, Feb 13
Hallelujah Chorus (song), 1789: DL, Mar 25, CG, Apr 3; 1790: DL, Feb 24, CG,
Mar 26; 1791: DL, Mar 11, CG, Apr 6, 15; 1792: KING'S, Mar 14, 28; 1793:
KING/HAY, Feb 20, Mar 20, CG, 22; 1794: DL, Mar 12, 14, 19, Apr 2; 1795: CG,
Feb 27, Mar 27; 1798: CG, Mar 30; 1799: CG, Mar 15
Hallet, Benjamin (musician), 1751: HAY, Dec 27; 1752: CT/HAY, Jan 7, 14, 31,
Feb 6, 13, Mar 17, 21, Apr 14, 16, May 5; 1753: HAY, Apr 10; see also Cupid
Halley (house servant), 1786: CG, Jun 2; 1789: CG, Jun 5
Halling (actor), 1779: HAY, Dec 27
Halpin, John Edmund (actor), 1796: DL, Nov 2
Halsted (boxkeeper), 1710: DL, Apr 18
Ham (actor), 1757: DL, Oct 11
Hambleton, the Misses (singers), 1731: GF, Jun 1, 3
Hamersley (haberdasher), 1747: CG, Feb 24
Hamilton (actor), 1732: GF, Oct 10, Nov 8; 1733: GF, Sep 20, Oct 9, 15, 18, 23,
Nov 29, Dec 8, 12; 1734: GF, Jan 10, May 3, 10, Sep 11, 16, Oct 16, 18, Nov
27, 29; 1735: GF, Jan 1, 3, 6, 8, 11, 13, 17, 24, Feb 4, 11, 24, Mar 6, 10,
Sep 15, 17, 19, 22, 24, Oct 15, Nov 4, 11, 14, 17, 20, 21, 25, 26, Dec 6, 8,
17; 1736: GF, Feb 9, Mar 9, 29, Apr 8, 28, May 3, 5, 13, LIF, Sep 28, Oct 9,
12, 23, Nov 9, 11, 13, 18, 27, Dec 3, 22; 1737: KING'S, Jan 8, LIF, 19, 21,
Mar 1, 29, Apr 12, 25, 27, May 6, 10
Hamilton (actor), 1774: HAY, Sep 21; 1775: HAY, Feb 20, Nov 20; 1776: HAY, Oct
7; 1779: HAY, Jan 11, Mar 8; 1780: HAY, Jan 17
Hamilton (actor), 1792: HAY, Oct 22
Hamilton (beneficiary), 1720: LIF, Feb 5, 10
Hamilton, Captain Edward (naval officer), 1800: CG, Apr 5
Hamilton, Duke of, 1730: HIC, Apr 15
Hamilton, Esther, Mrs John (actor), 1754: CG, Oct 2, 4, 7, 15, 16, 18, 29, Nov

1, 4, 14, 25, 28; <u>1755</u>: CG, Jan 7, 18, 22, 24, 28, Feb 8, 24, Apr 1, 8, Oct
6, 10, 11, 16, 27, 31, Dec 4; <u>1756</u>: CG, Jan 2, 6, Feb 26, Mar 18, 22, Apr 6,
20, May 26, Sep 27, Oct 11, 15, 19, 21, 22, 23, 27, 28, Nov 4, 11, Dec 1;
<u>1757</u>: CG, Jan 28, Feb 19, Apr 15, 22, May 6, 11, 16, Sep 14, 16, 21, 23, 26,
28, 30, Oct 3, 7, 10, 12, 14, 15, 17, 19, 20, 22, 27, 28, 31, Nov 4, 5, 7,
11, 14, 16, 18, 23, Dec 1, 2, 9, 15, 20; <u>1758</u>: CG, Feb 1, Mar 11, 14, Apr 3,
Sep 18, 20, 22, 25, 27, 29, Oct 13, 20, 23, 24, 25, 26, Nov 2, 3, 4, 7, 13,
14, 16, 18, 21, 23, 29, Dec 12; <u>1759</u>: CG, Jan 18, Feb 14, Mar 1, 3, 5, 8, 17,
19, 24, 27, Apr 23, May 3, 7, 8, 11, 17, Sep 24, 26, 28, Oct 1, 5, Nov 5, 26,
30, Dec 6, 10, 11, 14, 17, 18, 19, 20, 21, 22, 31; <u>1760</u>: CG, Jan 4, 9, 14,
Feb 28, Mar 17, 25, Apr 17, 18, 24, 29, May 2, 7, 8, 12, Sep 22, Oct 6, 8,
14, 15, 17, 18, 20, Dec 29; <u>1761</u>: CG, Jan 6, 23, Mar 3, 5, 25, 26, 30, Apr 2,
6, 17, 27, May 4, 11, Oct 3, 13, 14, 15, 17, 20, 22, 23, 26, 27, 31, Nov 4,
6, Dec 10, 28; <u>1762</u>: CG, Feb 22, Mar 23, May 11
Hamilton, James (actor), <u>1668</u>: ATCOURT, Feb 4
Hamilton, Master J (actor, singer), <u>1736</u>: GF, Mar 9, LIF, Sep 28, Oct 9, Dec 7;
<u>1737</u>: LIF, Feb 1, Apr 2, DL, Nov 19; <u>1738</u>: DL, May 16, BFH, Aug 23, DL, Oct
30, Dec 4; <u>1739</u>: DL, Feb 7
Hamilton, Master W (actor, singer), <u>1736</u>: LIF, Oct 9; <u>1737</u>: LIF, Mar 1, Apr 2,
May 10, DL, Nov 19; <u>1738</u>: DL, May 16, BFH, Aug 23, DL, Oct 30, Dec 4; <u>1739</u>:
DL, Feb 7
Hamilton, Masters W and J (actors, singers), <u>1735</u>: GF, Jan 25, Feb 17, Mar 6,
Apr 9, May 2; <u>1736</u>: GF, Mar 3, Apr 8, LIF, Dec 31; <u>1737</u>: LIF, Apr 2, 12, 14,
May 4, 10, 17, Jul 26; <u>1738</u>: DL, May 16, TC, Aug 7
Hamilton, Miss (actor), <u>1769</u>: CG, May 12, HAY, Aug 30; <u>1770</u>: HAY, Aug 22, Sep
1; <u>1771</u>: HAY, Apr 6, CG, May 6
Hamilton, Miss (actor), <u>1777</u>: DL, May 13; <u>1779</u>: HAY, Jan 11; <u>1780</u>: HAY, Jan 17
Hamilton, Miss (actor), <u>1792</u>: CII, Jan 16
Hamilton, Mr and Mrs (actors), <u>1733</u>: GF, Apr 11
Hamilton, Mrs (actor), <u>1719</u>: LIF, May 6; <u>1732</u>: GF, Oct 4, 6, 7, 17, 25, 26, 30,
Nov 3, 18, 27, 28, Dec 18; <u>1733</u>: GF, Feb 26, Mar 5, 6, 15, 30, Apr 11, 13,
19, 25, May 8, 9, 10, 11, 18, Sep 12, 17, 21, 24, 25, 27, Oct 1, 9, 12, 18,
22, 24, 26, Nov 8, 14, 29, Dec 12, 13; <u>1734</u>: GF, Jan 10, 11, 19, 31, Mar 5,
BFHBH, Aug 24, GF, Sep 9, 11, 13, 16, 25, Oct 11, 14, 16, 17, 21, 23, Nov 7,
12, 13, 18, 27, Dec 9, 13, 20, 31; <u>1735</u>: GF, Jan 3, 6, 8, 10, 11, 13, 20, 24,
Feb 5, 6, 17, 24, 25, Mar 6, 20, 24, 29, Apr 9, 14, 17, 18, May 3, 8, Sep 12,
15, 17, 19, 22, Oct 6, 15, Nov 3, 6, 10, 12, 20, 21, 24, Dec 8, 17; <u>1736</u>: GF,
Jan 29, Feb 9, Mar 9, Apr 8, LIF, Sep 28, Oct 5, 9, 12, 21, 23, 26, Nov 9,
13, 18, 24, 26, 27, 29, Dec 3, 7, 16, 20, 22, 27, 31; <u>1737</u>: LIF, Jan 20, 21,
Feb 1, 12, 14, 21, Mar 15, 21, Apr 2, 25, 27, May 2, 4, 6, 7, Jun 15, Jul 26,
Aug 5; <u>1738</u>: DL, Jan 14, Feb 6, May 16, CG, Jun 27, 30, Aug 1; <u>1739</u>: DL, Jan
20, Feb 3, 5, Mar 10, 31, Apr 10, 25, May 25, 28
Hamilton, Mrs (beneficiary), <u>1781</u>: CG, May 19; <u>1782</u>: CG, May 10; <u>1783</u>: CG, May
29; <u>1784</u>: CG, May 11, 24
Hamilton, Newburgh, <u>1712</u>: DL, Jun 5; <u>1715</u>: LIF, Jun 23
--Doating Lovers, The; or, The Libertine Tamed, <u>1715</u>: LIF, Jun 23, 27, 28
--Petticoat Plotter, The, <u>1712</u>: DL, Jun 5, Jul 4, 18, 29, Aug 12; <u>1715</u>: LIF,
Nov 17, 18; <u>1718</u>: LIF, Apr 18; <u>1728</u>: HAY, Aug 19
Hamilton, William (actor), <u>1766</u>: KING'S, Aug 8, 18, 25, Sep 13; <u>1767</u>: HAY, Sep
18, 21; <u>1768</u>: HAY, Jul 6, Aug 8, 19, Sep 19, CG, Nov 4, 26; <u>1769</u>: CG, Jan 7,
May 12, HAY, 15, 26, Jun 2, 5, 7, Jul 17, Aug 7, 11, 25, 30, Sep 11, CG, Oct
7, Nov 3, 17, 29, Dec 29; <u>1770</u>: CG, Jan 27, Apr 25, May 2, HAY, 16, 18, CG,
22, HAY, 23, 28, Jun 18, 22, Jul 9, 20, Aug 1, 8, 24, Sep 20, CG, Oct 1, 13,
17, Dec 26; <u>1771</u>: CG, Jan 1, Feb 21, Apr 2, 12, 27, HAY, May 15, 17, CG, 21,
HAY, 22, 29, 31, Jun 14, 21, Jul 12, 24, Sep 14, CG, Oct 4, 15, Dec 19; <u>1772</u>:
CG, Jan 4, Feb 25, HAY, Mar 16, CG, May 25, Nov 14, Dec 7; <u>1773</u>: CG, Jan 19,
Apr 23, 27, May 4, HAY, 17, 19, CG, 24, HAY, 28, 31, Jun 7, 18, 28, Jul 19,
21, 28, Aug 11, 27, Sep 3, 17, CG, 20, Oct 28, Nov 16, Dec 1; <u>1774</u>: CG, Jan
29, Apr 4, HAY, 4, CG, 9, 11, 23, May 16
Hamilton, William (scene painter), <u>1790</u>: CG, Dec 20; <u>1795</u>: KING'S, Mar 21
Hamlen (actor), <u>1784</u>: HAY, Apr 30
Hamlet. See Shakespeare, William.
Hamlet, Miscellaneous Observations on (pamphlet), <u>1752</u>: DL, Jan 22
Hammersley and Co (bankers), <u>1795</u>: DL, Oct 8; <u>1798</u>: DL, Nov 10
Hammersmith, <u>1786</u>: HAMM, Jul 10; <u>1793</u>: KING'S, Feb 19; <u>1794</u>: HAMM, Mar 24;
<u>1798</u>: CG, Apr 24; <u>1799</u>: CG, Apr 19
Hammond, Anthony (poet), <u>1755</u>: DL, Feb 3
Hammond, Henry (spectator), <u>1700</u>: LIF, Mar 11
Hammond, J (publisher), <u>1790</u>: HAY, Apr 6, 29, May 29; <u>1793</u>: KING'S, Feb 5, 26,
Mar 19, Apr 23, May 14; <u>1800</u>: KING'S, Jan 11
Hammond, William (spectator), <u>1664</u>: LIF, Jan 0
Hamoche, Mrs (beneficiary), <u>1722</u>: HAY, Feb 26

Hamoir, John (dancer), 1766: KING'S, Nov 25; 1768: DL, Nov 5, Dec 1; 1770: CG,
   Oct 10, 16, 17, Dec 26; 1771: CG, Jan 1, Feb 21, Apr 3, 22, Oct 15; 1772: CG,
   Feb 25, Mar 26, Apr 22, May 7, 9, 14; 1784: DL, Jan 13, Feb 3, May 19, Nov
   26; 1785: DL, Jan 11, May 5, Oct 17, 18, 24, Dec 26; 1786: DL, Jan 6, 16, Apr
   24, Jun 6, Nov 25, Dec 5; 1787: DL, Feb 15, May 30, Jun 8, Oct 6, 26, Nov 1,
   5, 23, Dec 26; 1788: DL, Apr 16, May 6, 30, Jun 2, 3, Sep 18, Nov 10, 19, Dec
   22; 1789: DL, Apr 15, May 22, 27, Jun 9, 10; 1790: DL, Jan 26, 27, Feb 18,
   May 15, Sep 30, Oct 26, Dec 18, 27; 1791: DLKING'S, Oct 3, Nov 5, Dec 2, 10;
   1792: DLKING'S, Jan 28, Mar 19, Jun 7, DL, Nov 10, 21; 1793: DL, May 13;
   1794: DL, May 16, Jun 2, 9, 12, 16, 23, 25, Jul 4, 5; 1796: KING'S, Jul 7, 12
Hamoir, John and Miss (dancers), 1768: DL, Nov 5; 1770: CG, Nov 29; 1771: CG,
   Oct 4, 31; 1783: DL, Dec 4; 1784: DL, Mar 8, Apr 26, May 17, 21, Sep 16, Oct
   28, Nov 9, Dec 3; 1785: DL, Jan 20, May 21
Hamoir (Armoy), Miss (dancer), 1766: KING'S, Nov 25; 1767: SW, May 13; 1768:
   DL, Nov 5, Dec 1; 1770: CG, Oct 10, 16, 17, Dec 26; 1771: CG, Jan 1, Feb 21,
   Apr 3, Oct 15, Nov 4; 1772: CG, Feb 25, Apr 22, May 7, 14; 1784: DL, Mar 8,
   Nov 9
Hamon, William (spectator), 1664: LIF, Jan 0; 1665: LIF, Jan 6
Hamond (actor), 1749: HAY, Nov 14; 1750: DL, May 22
Hampstead Fair, 1748: HAY, Apr 18
Hampstead Heath. See Baker, Thomas.
Hampstead Road, 1735: TC, Aug 4; 1736: TCP, Aug 4
Hampstead Song (music), 1734: HA, Sep 11
Hampstead Wells, 1709: HA, Jul 30; 1723: HA, Jul 8; 1724: HA, May 4
Hampstead, 1707: HA, Aug 1; 1709: HA, Sep 19; 1732: HA, Jun 6; 1734: CG, Mar
   25, HA, Jun 27, Sep 2; 1735: GF, Mar 27; 1736: LIF, Apr 2; 1759: HAM, Aug 13;
   1768: CG, Oct 24; 1775: DL, Dec 25
Hampton Court, 1662: THAMES, Aug 23; 1718: NONE, Aug 29, RI, 30, SF, Sep 6, DL,
   24, Oct 7, 10, 14, 17, 24, Nov 15; 1731: LIF, May 25, DL, Jun 14, 17, Jul 2,
   Oct 19; 1732: DL, Jul 14
Hampton Gardens, 1774: HG, Aug 19
Hampton Green, 1731: DL, Jul 9
Hampton, 1767: CG, May 23; 1770: DL, Sep 22, 24; 1775: DL, May 27
Hancks (coal merchant), 1747: CG, Jan 13
Hancock, Thomas (actor), 1660: REDBULL, Nov 5; 1661: NONE, Sep 0
Handel Commemoration (music), 1784: CG, Apr 27, May 17, 26; 1785: DL, Feb 11,
   25; 1789: CG, Mar 6
Handel (Hendel), George Frederic (composer), 1710: QUEEN'S, Dec 6; 1711:
   QUEEN'S, Feb 24; 1712: QUEEN'S, Nov 22, 26; 1713: QUEEN'S, Jan 10, 21, 24,
   Feb 4, 21, Mar 17, May 16; 1714: SH, Feb 22; 1715: KING'S, May 25; 1717:
   KING'S, Mar 21; 1718: DL, May 16; 1719: HIC, Feb 18; 1720: KING'S, Apr 27;
   1721: KING'S, Apr 15, Jul 5, Dec 9; 1722: SH, Feb 9, LIF, Apr 4; 1723:
   KING'S, Jan 12, DL, Mar 20, KING'S, May 14; 1724: KING'S, Feb 20, LIF, Mar
   19, YB, 27, LIF, Apr 25, KING'S, Oct 17, 31; 1725: KING'S, Feb 13; 1726:
   KING'S, Feb 8, Mar 12, May 5, LIF, 11; 1727: KING'S, Jan 31, Nov 11; 1728:
   KING'S, Feb 17, Apr 30; 1729: DL, Feb 26, SH, Mar 14, HIC, Apr 16, KING'S,
   Dec 2; 1730: KING'S, Feb 24, DL, May 13, LIF, 14, GF, 22; 1731: KING'S, Jan
   12, ACA, 14, KING'S, Feb 2, HIC, 4, LIF, Mar 26, May 24, GF, Jun 3, LIF, 7;
   1732: KING'S, Jan 15, Feb 15, DL, Mar 7, CL, 17, GF, 30, LIF, Apr 13, YB, 20,
   GF, 27, KING'S, May 2, DL, 3, LIF, 9, GF, 11, HAY, 17, LIF, 18, KING'S, 23,
   DL, Jul 7, HAY, 26, KING'S, Nov 4, Dec 5; 1733: KING'S, Jan 27, HAY, Feb 28,
   KING'S, Mar 17, LIF/CG, 30, KING'S, Apr 7, 14, GF, 23, HAY, 23, LIF/CG, 25,
   CG, May 1, LIF/CG, 7, 18, 24, KING'S, Jun 22, CG, Aug 9, DL/HAY, Oct 20, 27,
   HAY, Nov 19, DL/HAY, Dec 1, KING'S, 4, DL/HAY, 20, LIF, 29; 1734: DL/HAY, Jan
   4, KING'S, 5, 26, DL/HAY, 26, Feb 4, DL/LIF, Mar 11, KING'S, 11, 13, HIC, 20,
   KING'S, 23, Apr 2, 6, 9, HH, 26, LIF, 26, KING'S, 30, DL/HAY, May 1, CG, 14,
   15, KING'S, 18, Oct 23, CG/LIF, Nov 4, CG, 8, CG/LIF, 9, MR, Dec 13; 1735:
   CG, Jan 8, HIC, Feb 21, YB, 28, CG, Mar 12, CG/LIF, 15, CG, 19, SH, 28, CG,
   28, Apr 16, DL, 22, CG/LIF, May 2, CG, 6, 8, CG/LIF, 9, LIF, 21, CG/LIF, 27,
   DL, Jun 3, GF/HAY, Jul 15, HAY, Dec 13; 1736: HAY, Jan 14, MR, Feb 11, CG,
   19, Mar 3, 27, LIF, 31, CG, Apr 12, SH, 16, CG, 29, May 4, 11, 12, 17, DL,
   22, CG, Jun 4, Nov 23, 27, YB, Dec 1; 1737: CG, Jan 8, 12, Feb 7, 16, Mar 16,
   23, HIC, Apr 7, CG, 13, CT, May 2, DL, 4, LIF, 4, CG, 16, 18; 1738: KING'S,
   Jan 3, CG, 18, KING'S, Feb 25, DL, Mar 3, 21, KING'S, 28, CG, Apr 8, KING'S,
   15, CG, May 3, DL, 17, KING'S, Dec 29; 1739: KING'S, Jan 16, CRT, 18, KING'S,
   Mar 20, Apr 4, 13, 19, DL, 24, 30, KING'S, May 1, CG, 15, 25, Nov 7; 1740:
   LIF, Feb 27, DL, Mar 17, 20, LIF, 28, HIC, Apr 2, DL, 14, HIC, 18, DL, 22,
   May 17, 21, 26, LIF, Nov 22; 1741: LIF, Jan 10, HAY, Feb 3, LIF, 7, HAY, 26,
   HIC, 27, Mar 5, CG, 10, GF, 12, HIC, 13, DL, 14, KING'S, 14, LIF, Apr 4, DL,
   8, 20, HIC, 24, CG, May 14, KING'S, Nov 21, CG, 30; 1742: DL, Mar 12, Apr 1,
   6, CG, 22, GF, 22, CG, 23, GF, 29, HAY, Jun 16; 1743: CG, Feb 18, 23, LIF,
   Mar 15, CG, 16, KING'S, Nov 15, 19; 1744: SH, Feb 9, CG, 10, HAY, 15, CG, 24,

381

Mar 2, 28, Apr 17, KING'S, Jun 9, 22, Oct 22, Nov 3, 5, Dec 1; 1745: CG, Jan
5, KING'S, 5, 17, DL, Mar 20, KING'S, 27, CG, Apr 10, KING'S, May 4, DL, 13,
Nov 14, 15, 16; 1746: CG, Jan 25, Feb 14, KING'S, Mar 25, CG, Apr 29, DL, May
8; 1747: KING'S, Feb 24, CG, Mar 6, 20, Apr 1, 15, KING'S, Nov 12, Dec 5;
1748: HAY, Jan 12, KING'S, Feb 20, Mar 8, 14, Apr 5, CG, 13, 15, HAY, Dec 9;
1749: CG, Feb 28, Mar 3, KING'S, 21, CG, 31, VAUX, Apr 21, HIC, 21, CG, May
1; 1750: CG, Mar 1, DL, Apr 2, KING'S, 10, DL, 11, CHAPEL, May 1; 1751:
KING'S, Apr 16, DL, 18, Nov 12, HAY, Dec 27, 30; 1752: HAY, Jan 2, CG, Mar
18, KING'S, 24, DL, Apr 3, CG, 15, Nov 4; 1753: CG, Mar 12, HAY, Apr 2,
KING'S, 30, CG, May 10; 1754: DL, Jan 23, HAY, Feb 13, KING'S, 28, Mar 12,
Apr 6, CG, 22, KING'S, 25; 1755: SOHO, Mar 11, KING'S, 17; 1756: SOHO, Feb 2,
DL, 9, CG, Mar 5, SOHO, 16; 1757: CRT, Feb 7, CG, 25, Mar 11, SOHO, 14,
KING'S, 24, CG, Apr 22, HAY, May 2, Aug 31, Sep 2, 8, 14, 28, Oct 17; 1758:
KING'S, Jan 31, CG, Mar 3, KING'S, 6, CG, 18, KING'S, Apr 6; 1759: SOHO, Mar
1, CG, 23, May 4, RANELAGH, Jun 13; 1760: SOHO, Jan 18, RANELAGH, Jun 11;
1761: CG, Feb 25, KING'S, Mar 12, DL, Apr 14, Oct 26; 1762: DL, Feb 26, CG,
Mar 3, 19, 24, Apr 23, KING'S, May 11, DL, Oct 25, CG, Dec 8; 1763: CG, Feb
18, 23, Mar 4, DL, Apr 27, MARLY, Jun 28, CG, Oct 22, Nov 3; 1764: DL, Mar
16, KING'S, Apr 12; 1765: KING'S, Jan 25, CG, Mar 1; 1766: CG, Mar 5; 1767:
CG, Mar 6, 27, Apr 8, May 23; 1768: HAY, Mar 2, CG, 11; 1769: CG, Feb 10, 22,
Mar 1, 3; 1770: DL, Mar 16, CG, Apr 21; 1771: GROTTO, Aug 30; 1772: CG, Mar
6, DL, 6, 11, 18, CG, 27, DL, 27, CG, Apr 10; 1773: DL, Feb 26, Mar 5, 12,
HAY, 26; 1774: HAY, Feb 18, 23, 25; 1775: KING'S, Jan 26, Mar 8, DL, 15,
KING'S, 24; 1776: DL, Feb 23, CG, 28; 1777: DL, Dec 15; 1778: DL, Mar 27, CG,
Apr 8; 1779: KING'S, Mar 11, DL, 12, KING'S, Nov 27; 1780: HAY, Jul 8; 1781:
DL, Mar 30; 1782: DL, Feb 15, Mar 15, CG, Nov 2, 25; 1783: CG, Jan 18,
KING'S, Mar 6, CG, May 6; 1784: KING'S, Mar 4, 18, DL, 24, CG, Apr 27; 1785:
KING'S, Feb 24, Apr 21, May 12; 1786: DL, Mar 10; 1787: DL, Feb 23, KING'S,
Mar 1, HAY, Aug 6, DL, Sep 18; 1788: CG, Jan 28, DL, Feb 8, 22, CG, Apr 1,
Nov 6; 1789: CG, Jan 26, KING'S, Feb 7, DL, 27, Mar 6, CG, 6, DL, 11, 20, CG,
20, 31, May 20, Sep 23, 28, Nov 24; 1790: DL, Feb 24, 26, Mar 3, CG, 8, DL,
10, 12, 17, 19, 24, CG, May 6, 24, Jun 2, Oct 19; 1791: CG, Mar 18, DL, 23;
1792: KING'S, Feb 24, CG, 24, 28, KING'S, 29, CG, Mar 2, 7, 9, KING'S, 14,
CG, 14, 16, 21, KING'S, 21, 23, 28, 30; 1793: CG, Feb 20, KING/HAY, 22, CG,
22, Apr 25, May 11; 1794: CG, Mar 7, 14, 21, KING'S, May 15, HAY, Aug 18;
1795: CG, Feb 20, 27, KING'S, 27, CG, Mar 6, KING'S, 13, CG, 27, May 16;
1796: CG, Feb 12, 17, 19; 1797: CG, Mar 3, 15, 24, Sep 29; 1798: CG, Feb 23,
28, Mar 9, 14, 23; 1799: CG, Feb 8, 15, 20, 22, Mar 1, 6, 13, 15, Sep 16;
1800: CG, Feb 28, Mar 5, 19, 28, Apr 4
--Acis and Galatea (serenata), 1731: LIF, Mar 26; 1732: HAY, May 17, 19,
KING'S, Jun 10, 13, 17, 20, Dec 5, 9, 12, 16; 1734: KING'S, May 7; 1736: CG,
Mar 24, 31; 1739: LIF, Dec 13, 20; 1740: LIF, Feb 6, 14, 21, Mar 28; 1741:
LIF, Feb 28, Mar 11; 1742: CG, Apr 23; 1744: SH, Feb 9; 1745: CG, Apr 10;
1746: CG, Jan 25; 1748: KING'S, Apr 5, HAY, 20; 1749: HIC, Apr 21, DL, Nov
27, 28, 29; 1750: DL, Feb 12, Apr 27; 1753: HAY, Apr 2; 1754: HAY, Feb 13;
1755: DL, Dec 15, HAY, 15; 1756: SOHO, Feb 2; 1752: CRT, Feb 7, HAY, May 2,
RANELAGH, Jun 9; 1758: HAY, Feb 2, SOHO, Mar 31, Apr 1, RANELAGH, Jun 14;
1759: HAM, Aug 13; 1762: SOHO, Feb 9, HIC, 12; 1763: SOHO, Feb 4, CG, Mar 16;
1764: HAY, Nov 13; 1766: CG, Feb 21, 26, RANELAGH, Jun 20, MARLY, Sep 26;
1767: CG, Mar 27, Apr 3; 1768: CG, Mar 11; 1769: CG, Feb 17; 1770: DL, Mar
16; 1771: DL, Mar 13; 1772: DL, Mar 18, Apr 3; 1773: DL, Mar 5, 24, MARLY,
May 27, 29, Jun 3, 4, 10, 17, 24, 26; 1774: DL, Mar 11; 1775: DL, Mar 15, Apr
5; 1776: DL, Feb 23, Mar 8; 1777: DL, Feb 28, Mar 14, CG, 19, 21; 1778: DL,
Mar 6, CG, 6, 11, 25, DL, 27, CG, Apr 3; 1779: DL, Feb 26, Mar 3, HAY, 19;
1780: DL, Feb 18, Mar 3; 1781: DL, Mar 14, 16, 30; 1782: DL, Feb 22, Mar 8;
1783: DL, Mar 14, CG, Apr 28, May 6; 1784: DL, Mar 5, 24, CG, Apr 27; 1785:
DL, Feb 18; 1786: KING'S, Feb 18, 21; 1787: DL, Mar 7, 9; 1788: DL, Feb 22,
Mar 5; 1789: DL, Mar 6, 27, CG, Apr 3; 1790: DL, Feb 24, CG, Mar 3, DL, 5,
10, CG, 17, DL, 19, CG, 26; 1791: CG, Mar 23, DL, Apr 1, CG, 13; 1792:
KING'S, Feb 29, Mar 7, CG, 9, 14, 21, 23, KING'S, 28, 30; 1793: KING/HAY, Mar
6, 8, CG, 8, 20, 22; 1794: CG, Mar 12, DL, 14, 26, Apr 2; 1795: CG, Mar 13,
18; 1796: CG, Mar 16; 1797: CG, Mar 24; 1798: CG, Mar 2, 28; 1799: CG, Feb
22; 1800: CG, Mar 21
--Admeto (oratorio), 1754: KING'S, Mar 12, 16, 19, 23, Apr 6
--Admetus (opera), 1727: KING'S, Jan 25, 31, Feb 4, 7, 11, 14, 18, 21, 25, 28,
Mar 4, 7, 11, 14, 18, 21, 25, Apr 4, 15, 18, Sep 30, Oct 3, 7, 14, 17, Nov 4;
1728: LIF, Mar 18, 21, KING'S, May 25, 28, Jun 1, 11; 1731: KING'S, Dec 7,
11, 14, 18; 1732: KING'S, Jan 4, 8, 11; 1733: DL/HAY, Dec 1; 1734: DL/HAY,
Jan 4, 10; 1735: GF/HAY, Aug 21; 1792: CG, Mar 9
--Aetius (opera), 1732: KING'S, Jan 14, 15, 18, 22, 25, 29
--Agrippina (opera), 1720: KING'S, Apr 27
--Alcina (opera), 1735: CG, Apr 16, 19, 23, 26, 30, May 3, 7, 10, 14, 17, 21,

28, Jun 4, 12, 18, 25, 28, Jul 2, 5, DL, Dec 6; 1736: CG, Nov 6, 10, 13, 27,
DL, Dec 15; 1737: CG, Jun 10, 21; 1761: KING'S, Mar 12; 1786: DL, Mar 10;
1787: DL, Feb 23, KING'S, Mar 1; 1788: DL, Feb 8; 1789: DL, Mar 18; 1790: DL,
Feb 24, 26; 1791: DL, Mar 23; 1792: KING'S, Feb 24; 1793: KING/HAY, Feb 22;
1797: CG, Mar 17; 1799: CG, Mar 6
--Alexander (opera), 1726: KING'S, May 5, 7, 10, 12, 14, 17, 19, 21, 24, 2$,
31, Jun 4, 7, 11; 1727: KING'S, Dec 26, 30; 1728: KING'S, Jan 2, 6; 1729:
HIC, Apr 16; 1731: LIF, Apr 29; 1732: KING'S, Nov 22, 25, 28, Dec 2, 19, 26,
30; 1733: DL/HAY, Oct 20, HAY, Nov 19; 1734: DL/HAY, Jan 26; 1744: DL, Feb
16; 1751: HAY, Dec 27; 1752: HAY, Jan 2
--Alexander Balus (opera), 1748: CG, Mar 23, 25, 30, DL, Apr 15; 1754: CG, Mar
1, 6; 1768: CG, Mar 16; 1773: DL, Mar 17; 1786: DL, Mar 10; 1789: DL, Mar 18,
CG, Apr 3; 1790: DL, Feb 26; 1791: DL, Mar 11, 23, Apr 1; 1792: KING'S, Feb
24; 1793: KING/HAY, Feb 22, CG, Mar 8; 1798: CG, Mar 14; 1800: CG, Mar 19
--Allegro ed Il Penseroso, L' (music), 1741: DL, Mar 14, LIF, Apr 8; 1743: CG,
Mar 18; 1744: CG, Apr 17; 1754: CG, May 23; 1755: CG, Feb 21; 1757: SOHO, Feb
1; 1759: RANELAGH, Jun 13; 1760: RANELAGH, Jun 11; 1764: CG, Mar 9, 30; 1772:
DL, Mar 11; 1773: DL, Mar 12; 1775: DL, Mar 22; 1776: DL, Mar 13; 1777: DL,
Mar 12; 1778: DL, Mar 13; 1780: DL, Mar 10; 1782: DL, Feb 15; 1783: DL, Mar
7, 21; 1784: DL, Feb 27, CG, Apr 27; 1785: DL, Feb 23; 1788: CG, Jan 28, Feb
5; 1789: CG, Jan 26, DL, Mar 6, CG, 20, DL, 25; 1790: CG, Feb 26, Mar 3, DL,
10, CG, 17, Jun 2; 1791: CG, Mar 18, DL, 25, CG, 30, Apr 6, DL, 13, CG, 15;
1792: CG, Feb 24, Mar 14, KING'S, 14, CG, 14, 21, KING'S, 28, 30, CG, 30;
1793: CG, Feb 22, KING/HAY, Mar 6, 8, CG, 20; 1794: DL, Mar 12, 14, CG, 21,
DL, Apr 2, CG, 2, DL, 2, 9, CG, 11; 1795: CG, Mar 4, 25; 1796: CG, Feb 17,
26; 1797: CG, Mar 17; 1798: CG, Feb 28, Mar 28; 1799: CG, Mar 1, 15; 1800:
CG, Feb 28
--Allegro, Il Penseroso, ed Il Moderato, L' (music), 1740: LIF, Feb 27, Mar 6,
10, 14, Apr 23; 1741: LIF, Jan 31, Feb 7, 21, Mar 24; 1754: KING'S, Apr 25;
1759: SOHO, Mar 1; 1780: DL, Feb 25; 1781: DL, Mar 21, 23
--Amadis; or, The Loves of Harlequin and Colombine (opera), 1715: KING'S, May
25, Jun 11, 15, 18, 28, Jul 2, 7, 9, Aug 27; 1716: KING'S, Feb 16, 21, Mar 3,
6, Jun 20, Jul 12; 1717: KING'S, Feb 16, 23, Mar 21, Apr 11, May 30; 1718:
LIF, Jan 24, 29, 31, Feb 7, 14, 19, Mar 3, 13, 29, Apr 3, 15, 16, May 1;
1719: LIF, Jan 9, 11, Feb 4, Mar 10, 21, Apr 1; 1720: LIF, Mar 19, Apr 22;
1721: LIF, Jan 7, 14, 19, 26, Feb 14, Mar 9, 23, 28; 1722: LIF, Mar 3, 12,
17, Apr 2, 10, 16, May 4, 14, Dec 27, 29; 1723: LIF, Feb 11, Mar 11, 19, 21,
May 2, 31; 1724: LIF, Jan 4, Oct 5, 27
--Arbaces (opera), 1734: KING'S, Jan 5, 8, 12, 15, 19, 22, Mar 26, 28, 30
--Ariadne in Crete (opera), 1734: KING'S, Jan 26, 29, Feb 2, 5, 9, 12, 16, 19,
23, 26, Mar 2, 5, 9, 12, Apr 16, 20; 1735: CG/LIF, May 2, CG, 6, 8, CG/LIF,
20, DL, Jun 3, LIF, 19; 1736: HAY, Jan 14, CG, May 11; 1751: HAY, Dec 27;
1752: HAY, Jan 2; 1789: CG, Mar 20; 1790: CG, Mar 3; 1791: DL, Mar 11, CG,
18; 1792: CG, Feb 24, Mar 21; 1793: CG, Feb 20, KING/HAY, Mar 13, CG, 22;
1794: CG, Mar 7, DL, Apr 4; 1795: CG, Feb 27, Mar 27; 1797: CG, Mar 17; 1798:
CG, Mar 2; 1799: CG, Feb 20, Mar 15; 1800: CG, Mar 5
--Ariodante (opera), 1734: CG/LIF, Nov 4; 1735: CG, Jan 8, 11, 15, 18, 22, 29,
Feb 5, 12, 20, 24, Mar 3; 1736: CG, May 5, 7
--Atalanta (opera), 1736: CG, May 12, 15, 19, 22, 26, 29, Jun 2, 9, Nov 20, 27;
1738: DL, Mar 3; 1790: DL, Mar 17; 1794: DL, Apr 9
--Athalia (oratorio), 1735: CG, Apr 1, 2, 3, 9, 12, HAY, 16; 1756: CG, Mar 5,
10, 12; 1786: DL, Mar 10; 1789: DL, Mar 18, 20, CG, 20, Apr 3; 1790: DL, Feb
24, CG, 24, 26, DL, 26, CG, Mar 3, 5, DL, 10, 17; 1791: CG, Mar 11, 23, DL,
23, CG, 25, DL, Apr 1, 13; 1792: CG, Feb 24, Mar 2, 7, KING'S, 23, 28, 30;
1793: CG, Feb 15, KING/HAY, 22, CG, 22, Mar 6, KING/HAY, 6, CG, 8, 20; 1794:
CG, Mar 7, 12, DL, 26; 1795: CG, Feb 20, Mar 4, 18, 25; 1796: CG, Feb 24, 26,
Mar 16; 1797: CG, Mar 10; 1798: CG, Mar 9, 14, 30; 1799: CG, Feb 20; 1800:
CG, Feb 28, Mar 5
--Belshazzar (oratorio), 1745: KING'S, Mar 27, 29, Apr 23; 1751: CG, Feb 22,
27; 1754: CG, Apr 22; 1758: CG, Feb 22, KING'S, Apr 6
--Berenice (opera), 1737: CG, May 18, 21, 25, Jun 15; 1789: CG, Apr 3; 1791:
CG, Mar 23; 1792: CG, Mar 7; 1793: CG, Mar 20; 1794: CG, Mar 26; 1797: CG,
Mar 22; 1799: CG, Mar 1
--Caius Fabricius (opera), 1733: KING'S, Dec 4, 8, 15, 22
--Choice of Hercules (oratorio), 1753: CG, Mar 9, 14; 1755: CG, Feb 14, 19;
1761: KING'S, Mar 12; 1782: DL, Feb 15
--Deborah (oratorio), 1733: KING'S, Mar 17, 27, 31, Apr 3, 7, 10; 1734: KING'S,
Apr 2, 6, 9; 1735: CG, Mar 26, 28, 31, Apr 1; 1744: KING'S, Nov 3, 24; 1754:
CG, Mar 8, 13; 1756: CG, Mar 19; 1764: CG, Mar 14, Apr 6; 1766: CG, Feb 14;
1767: CG, Mar 11; 1771: DL, Mar 8; 1781: DL, Mar 9; 1789: CG, Apr 3; 1790:
CG, Feb 26, Mar 17; 1791: DL, Mar 11, CG, 23; 1792: CG, Mar 2, 9; 1793: CG,
Feb 15, 22, Mar 20; 1794: CG, Mar 7, DL, 12, 14, CG, 26, DL, Apr 9, 11,

KING'S, 26; 1795: CG, Feb 20, Mar 25; 1796: CG, Feb 26, Mar 16; 1797: CG, Mar
   31; 1798: CG, Mar 9; 1799: CG, Feb 8, Mar 15; 1800: CG, Feb 28, Mar 21
--Deidamia (opera), 1741: LIF, Jan 10, 17, 24, HAY, Feb 10; 1786: DL, Mar 10;
   1789: DL, Mar 18; 1790: DL, Feb 26; 1791: DL, Mar 23; 1792: KING'S, Feb 24;
   1793: KING/HAY, Feb 22
--Dettingen Te Deum (song), 1793: CG, Feb 15, Mar 13; 1794: CG, Mar 7; 1795:
   CG, Feb 20; 1796: CG, Feb 24; 1797: CG, Mar 22; 1798: CG, Mar 9; 1799: CG,
   Feb 8; 1800: CG, Mar 19
--Dido (opera), 1737: CG, Apr 13, 20, 27, Jun 1
--Esther (oratorio), 1732: CR, Feb 23, Mar 1, 3, YB, Apr 20, KING'S, May 2, 6,
   9, 13, 16, 20; 1733: KING'S, Apr 14, 17; 1735: DL, Feb 4, CG, Mar 5, 7, 12,
   14, 19, 21, Apr 1, DL, 16; 1736: CG, Apr 7, 14; 1737: CG, Apr 6, 7; 1740:
   LIF, Mar 26; 1743: CR, Feb 24; 1751: CG, Mar 15; 1755: SOHO, Mar 11; 1757:
   CG, Feb 25, Mar 2; 1767: CG, Mar 6; 1768: CG, Feb 26; 1779: DL, Feb 24; 1786:
   DL, Mar 10; 1789: CG, Mar 6, DL, 18, CG, 20; 1790: CG, Feb 24, DL, 26, CG,
   26, Mar 3, DL, 10, 17; 1791: DL, Mar 11, CG, 11, 18, DL, 23, Apr 1, CG, 6,
   13, 15; 1792: KING'S, Feb 24, CG, 24, Mar 9, KING'S, 14, CG, 21, KING'S, 23,
   30; 1793: CG, Feb 15, 20, KING/HAY, 22, Mar 6, CG, 13, KING/HAY, 13, CG, 20,
   22; 1794: CG, Mar 7, DL, 21, CG, 26, Apr 9, DL, 11; 1795: CG, Feb 20, Mar 4;
   1796: CG, Feb 24; 1797: CG, Mar 22, 31; 1798: CG, Mar 9; 1799: CG, Feb 8;
   1800: CG, Feb 28, Mar 19
--Ezio (opera), 1786: DL, Mar 10; 1789: DL, Mar 18; 1790: DL, Feb 24, 26, CG,
   Mar 17; 1791: DL, Mar 23; 1792: KING'S, Feb 24, CG, Mar 2; 1793: CG, Feb 20,
   KING/HAY, 22; 1798: CG, Mar 14, 30; 1799: CG, Feb 8, Mar 6
--Flavius (opera), 1723: KING'S, May 14, 18, 21, 25, 27, 30, Jun 11, 15; 1732:
   KING'S, Apr 17, 18, 22, 25, 29; 1739: DL, Apr 24, Nov 7; 1740: DL, Mar 22
--Floridante (opera), 1721: KING'S, Dec 9, 13, 16, 20, 23, 27, 30; 1722:
   KING'S, Jan 3, 5, Feb 13, 20, Apr 25, 28, May 23, 26, Dec 4, 8, 11, 15, 18,
   22, 26; 1727: KING'S, Apr 29, May 2; 1733: KING'S, Mar 3, 6, 10, 13, May 8,
   15, 19
--Gideon (oratorio), 1769: CG, Feb 10, 15; 1770: DL, Mar 9; 1790: CG, Mar 17;
   1794: DL, Apr 11; 1800: CG, Mar 5
--Giulio Cesare (opera), 1787: KING'S, Mar 1, 3, 6, 17, 20, 24, 27, 31, Apr 14,
   Jun 2, 16
--Hercules (oratorio), 1745: KING'S, Jan 5, 9, 12; 1749: CG, Feb 24, 28, Mar 1;
   1752: CG, Feb 21; 1790: CG, Feb 26, Mar 3; 1791: CG, Mar 23, 25, Apr 6, 13;
   1792: CG, Mar 9
--Hester (oratorio), 1767: CG, May 23
--Hymen (operetta), 1740: LIF, Nov 22, 29, Dec 13
--Israel in Babylon (opera), 1764: KING'S, Apr 12; 1765: KING'S, Jan 25, CG,
   Mar 1; 1768: HAY, Mar 2; 1770: CG, Mar 28; 1791: DL, Mar 11, CG, 23
--Israel in Egypt (oratorio), 1739: KING'S, Apr 4, 11, 13, 17; 1740: LIF, Apr
   1; 1756: CG, Mar 17, 24; 1757: CG, Mar 4; 1708: CG, Feb 24; 1765: CG, Mar 13;
   1766: CG, Mar 5; 1767: CG, Mar 13; 1769: CG, Mar 3; 1771: DL, Feb 22; 1777:
   DL, Feb 26, Mar 7; 1786: DL, Mar 10; 1789: CG, Mar 6, DL, 18, CG, 20, 27, Apr
   3; 1790: CG, Feb 24, DL, 24, 26, CG, 26, Mar 3, 17; 1791: CG, Mar 11, DL, 11,
   CG, 23, DL, 23, CG, 25, DL, Apr 13; 1792: KING'S, Feb 24, CG, Mar 2, KING'S,
   21; 1793: CG, Feb 15, KING/HAY, 15, 22, CG, Mar 6, 8, 13; 1794: CG, Mar 7,
   DL, 12, 14, CG, 14, 21, DL, 26, CG, 26, DL, Apr 2, CG, 9, DL, 9, CG, 11, DL,
   11; 1795: CG, Feb 20, 27, Mar 13, 25; 1796: CG, Feb 24, Mar 2; 1797: CG, Mar
   10, 15, 24, 31; 1798: CG, Mar 9, 14, 28, 30; 1799: CG, Feb 8, 15, 20, Mar 13;
   1800: CG, Mar 5
--Jephtha (oratorio), 1752: CG, Feb 26, 28, Mar 4, Apr 15; 1753: CG, Mar 16,
   21, Apr 12, May 9; 1756: CG, Apr 2; 1758: CG, Mar 1, KING'S, Apr 6; 1761:
   KING'S, Mar 12; 1763: CG, Mar 9; 1776: DL, Mar 6; 1777: CG, Mar 7; 1784: DL,
   Mar 17, CG, Apr 27; 1786: DL, Mar 10; 1789: DL, Mar 18, CG, 20, DL, 25, CG,
   27, Apr 3; 1790: CG, Feb 24, DL, 26, CG, 26, Mar 3, DL, 10, CG, 17; 1791: CG,
   Mar 11, 18, 23, DL, 23, 25; 1792: KING'S, Feb 24, CG, Mar 2, KING'S, 7, CG,
   9, KING'S, 23, 28, 30; 1793: CG, Feb 15, KING/HAY, 22, CG, Mar 6, 8,
   KING/HAY, 13, CG, 20; 1794: CG, Mar 7, DL, 12, CG, 12, DL, 14, 21, CG, 26,
   DL, Apr 2, 4, 9; 1795: CG, Feb 20, Mar 13, 25; 1796: CG, Feb 24, 26, Mar 16;
   1797: CG, Mar 10, 17, 22, 31, Apr 7; 1798: CG, Mar 2, 9, 28, 30; 1799: CG,
   Feb 8, 15, 20; 1800: CG, Feb 28, Mar 5, 19
--Joseph (oratorio), 1768: CG, Mar 2; 1780: DL, Mar 1; 1786: DL, Mar 10; 1789:
   DL, Mar 18, CG, 20, DL, 20; 1790: DL, Feb 24, CG, 26, DL, Mar 5; 1791: DL,
   Mar 11, CG, 23, DL, 23, Apr 1; 1792: KING'S, Feb 24, Mar 23, 30; 1793:
   KING/HAY, Feb 22, CG, Mar 6, 8, KING/HAY, 13; 1794: CG, Mar 12; 1795: CG, Feb
   20, Mar 13; 1796: CG, Mar 16; 1797: CG, Mar 22; 1798: CG, Mar 14, 28; 1799:
   CG, Feb 8
--Joseph and His Brethren (oratorio), 1744: CG, Mar 2, 7, 9, 14; 1745: KING'S,
   Mar 15, 22; 1747: CG, Mar 18, 20, 25; 1755: CG, Feb 28; 1757: CG, Mar 9;
   1772: DL, Mar 27

--Joshua (oratorio), <u>1748</u>: CG, Mar 9, 11, 16, 18; <u>1749</u>: CG, Mar 13; <u>1752</u>: CG,
Feb 14, 19; <u>1754</u>: CG, Mar 22; <u>1769</u>: CG, Feb 24; <u>1778</u>: DL, Apr 1; <u>1786</u>: DL,
Mar 10; <u>1787</u>: DL, Feb 23; <u>1788</u>: DL, Feb 8; <u>1789</u>: CG, Mar 6, DL, 20; <u>1790</u>: DL,
Feb 24, CG, 24, DL, 26, Mar 17, CG, 17, DL, 24; <u>1791</u>: CG, Mar 11, DL, 11, CG,
23, DL, 23; <u>1792</u>: KING'S, Feb 24, 29, Mar 7, CG, 7, 9, KING'S, 28; <u>1793</u>:
KING/HAY, Feb 15, 22, CG, Mar 6; <u>1794</u>: CG, Mar 12, DL, 12, 14, 21, CG, 26,
DL, Apr 2, 9; <u>1795</u>: CG, Feb 27, Mar 13; <u>1796</u>: CG, Feb 26, Mar 16; <u>1797</u>: CG,
Mar 10; <u>1798</u>: CG, Feb 28, Mar 14, 28, 30; <u>1799</u>: CG, Feb 15, Mar 1, 13; <u>1800</u>:
CG, Feb 28, Mar 5
--Jubilate (anthem), <u>1731</u>: ACA, Jan 14; <u>1789</u>: CG, Mar 6, DL, 18; <u>1790</u>: CG, Feb
26, DL, 26, Mar 17; <u>1791</u>: CG, Mar 18, DL, 23; <u>1792</u>: KING'S, Feb 24, Mar 7;
<u>1793</u>: CG, Feb 22, KING/HAY, 22; <u>1794</u>: CG, Mar 7, DL, Apr 4; <u>1795</u>: CG, Feb 20;
<u>1796</u>: CG, Mar 16; <u>1797</u>: CG, Mar 24; <u>1799</u>: CG, Feb 20; <u>1800</u>: CG, Mar 19
--Judas Maccabaeus (oratorio), <u>1747</u>: CG, Apr 1, 3, 8, 10, 13, 15, May 4; <u>1748</u>:
CG, Feb 26, Mar 2, 4, 31, Apr 1, 4, KING'S, 5, CG, 7; <u>1750</u>: CG, Mar 9, 14,
28, 29, 30, HAY, Oct 18; <u>1751</u>: CG, Mar 20, HAY, Dec 27; <u>1752</u>: CT/HAY, Jan 7,
14, 31, CG, Mar 18, 20; <u>1753</u>: CG, Mar 23, 28, 30, KING'S, May 7; <u>1754</u>: CG,
Mar 27, Apr 3; <u>1755</u>: CG, Mar 12, 14; <u>1756</u>: CG, Mar 26, 31; <u>1757</u>: CG, Mar 25;
<u>1758</u>: CG, Mar 3, 8; <u>1759</u>: CG, Mar 23, 28; <u>1760</u>: SOHO, Jan 18, CG, Mar 19, 21,
DL, May 14; <u>1761</u>: CG, Feb 6, 11; <u>1762</u>: CG, Mar 5, 10, 17, SOHO, Apr 21; <u>1763</u>:
CG, Mar 2; <u>1764</u>: CG, Mar 23, Apr 4; <u>1765</u>: CG, Feb 22, Mar 8, 22; <u>1766</u>: CG,
Feb 28, Mar 14; <u>1767</u>: CG, Mar 20, Apr 1; <u>1768</u>: CG, Mar 4, 18; <u>1769</u>: HAY, Feb
10, CG, 22, HAY, Mar 3, CG, 10, HAY, Apr 18; <u>1770</u>: DL, Mar 7, CG, 7, DL, 21,
HAY, May 4; <u>1771</u>: CG, Feb 15, DL, 20, Mar 6, CG, 20, HAY, Apr 12; <u>1772</u>: CG,
Mar 11, DL, 13, Apr 1; <u>1773</u>: DL, Feb 26, Mar 3, CG, 12, DL, 19; <u>1774</u>: DL, Feb
18, Mar 9; <u>1775</u>: DL, Mar 3, 10, KING'S, 29, Apr 5; <u>1776</u>: CG, Feb 23, DL, 28;
<u>1777</u>: CG, Feb 14, DL, 21, CG, Mar 14; <u>1778</u>: DL, Mar 11, 20, CG, 27; <u>1779</u>: DL,
Feb 19, Mar 10, 17; <u>1780</u>: DL, Feb 16, Mar 8; <u>1781</u>: DL, Mar 7; <u>1782</u>: DL, Feb
20; <u>1783</u>: DL, Mar 19; <u>1784</u>: DL, Mar 19, CG, Apr 27; <u>1785</u>: HAY, Feb 23, DL,
Mar 4; <u>1786</u>: DL, Mar 22; <u>1787</u>: DL, Feb 23, Mar 28; <u>1788</u>: DL, Feb 8, 27, Mar
12; <u>1789</u>: DL, Mar 6, 13, 18, CG, 20, 27, Apr 3; <u>1790</u>: CG, Feb 26, DL, 26, CG,
Mar 5, DL, 10, 12, CG, 19, 26; <u>1791</u>: DL, Mar 11, 18, CG, 23, DL, 23, CG, 25,
DL, 25, CG, 30, Apr 6, 15; <u>1792</u>: CG, Feb 24, KING'S, 24, 29, CG, Mar 2,
KING'S, 9, CG, 9, 16; <u>1793</u>: KING/HAY, Feb 15, CG, 15, 20, KING/HAY, 22, CG,
Mar 6, KING/HAY, 13, CG, 13, 20, KING/HAY, 22, CG, 22; <u>1794</u>: CG, Mar 7, 12,
DL, 12, CG, 14, 21, DL, 21, 26, CG, 26, DL, Apr 2, 4, 9, 11; <u>1795</u>: CG, Feb
20, Mar 4, 13, 25; <u>1796</u>: CG, Feb 24, 26, Mar 16; <u>1797</u>: CG, Mar 10, 17, 31;
<u>1798</u>: CG, Mar 16, 28, 30; <u>1799</u>: CG, Feb 15, 20, Mar 1, 13, 15; <u>1800</u>: CG, Feb
28, Mar 5, 19
--Jupiter in Argos (musical), <u>1739</u>: KING'S, May 1, 5
--Justin (opera), <u>1737</u>: CG, Feb 7, 16, 19, 22, 25, Mar 2, 4, May 4, 11, Jun 8
--Lotharius (opera), <u>1729</u>: KING'S, Dec 2, 6, 9, 13, 16, 20, 30; <u>1730</u>: KING'S,
Jan 3, 10, 13
--Messiah, The (oratorio), <u>1743</u>: CG, Mar 23, 25, 29; <u>1745</u>: KING'S, Apr 9, 11;
<u>1749</u>: CG, Mar 23; <u>1750</u>: CG, Apr 12, CHAPEL, 18, May 1, 15; <u>1751</u>: CHAPEL, Apr
18, May 16; <u>1752</u>: CG, Mar 25, 26, CHAPEL, Apr 9; <u>1753</u>: CG, Apr 13, CHAPEL,
May 1; <u>1754</u>: NONE, Apr 5, CHAPEL, May 15; <u>1755</u>: CG, Mar 19, 21, CHAPEL, May
1; <u>1756</u>: CG, Apr 7, 9, CHAPEL, May 19; <u>1757</u>: CG, Mar 30, Apr 1, CHAPEL, May
5; <u>1758</u>: CG, Mar 10, 15, 17, KING'S, Apr 6, CHAPEL, 27; <u>1759</u>: CG, Mar 30, Apr
4, 6; <u>1760</u>: CG, Mar 26, 28, KING'S, Apr 15, 24; <u>1761</u>: CG, Mar 11, 13; <u>1762</u>:
DL, Mar 24, 26, CG, 31, DL, 31, CG, Apr 2, RANELAGH, Jun 16; <u>1763</u>: CG, Mar
23, 25; <u>1764</u>: CG, Apr 11, 13; <u>1765</u>: CG, Mar 27, 29; <u>1766</u>: CG, Mar 19, 21;
<u>1767</u>: CG, Apr 8, 10, HAB, Dec 10; <u>1768</u>: HAY, Mar 9, 11, CG, 23, HAY, 23, CG,
25, HAY, 25; <u>1769</u>: KING'S, Feb 3, HAY, 17, Mar 1, 10, CG, 15, HAY, 17, CG,
17; <u>1770</u>: CG, Mar 2, 21, DL, 23, Apr 4, 6; <u>1771</u>: CG, Feb 20, 22, Mar 8, 13,
DL, 20, 22; <u>1772</u>: CG, Mar 6, 18, Apr 1, 3, DL, 8, 10; <u>1773</u>: HAY, Feb 26, CG,
Mar 3, 5, DL, 26, HAY, 26, DL, 31, CG, 31, Apr 2, DL, 2; <u>1774</u>: HAY, Feb 18,
DL, Mar 16, HAY, 18, DL, 18, CHAPEL, 26; <u>1775</u>: KING'S, Mar 10, 17, DL, 24,
31, Apr 7, KING'S, 7, CHAPEL, Nov 23; <u>1776</u>: CG, Mar 1, 13, 22, DL, 27, 29,
CHAPEL, Apr 2; <u>1777</u>: CG, Feb 19, DL, 19, Mar 19, 21; <u>1778</u>: CG, Mar 13, 20,
DL, Apr 8, 10; <u>1779</u>: HAY, Mar 3, 10, DL, 24, HAY, 26, DL, 26; <u>1780</u>: DL, Mar
15, 17; <u>1781</u>: DL, Apr 4, 6; <u>1782</u>: DL, Mar 20, 22; <u>1783</u>: DL, Apr 2, 9, 11;
<u>1784</u>: DL, Mar 3, Apr 2; <u>1785</u>: DL, Feb 16, Mar 16, 18; <u>1786</u>: DL, Mar 3, 24;
<u>1787</u>: DL, Mar 14, 16; <u>1788</u>: DL, Feb 13, Mar 14; <u>1789</u>: CG, Feb 27, Mar 13, DL,
25, Apr 1, CG, 3; <u>1790</u>: CG, Feb 19, DL, 19, 24, Mar 5, 10, CG, 12, DL, 17,
24, CG, 26; <u>1791</u>: DL, Mar 11, 16, CG, 16, DL, Apr 1, 6, CG, 8, 13, 15; <u>1792</u>:
CG, Feb 29, KING'S, Mar 2, 14, 23, 28, CG, 28, KING'S, 30; <u>1793</u>: KING/HAY,
Feb 20, CG, Mar 1, 8, 13, 15, KING/HAY, 15, 20, 22, CG, 22; <u>1794</u>: DL, Mar 12,
14, 19, CG, 26, DL, 28, CG, 28, DL, Apr 2, 4, 12; <u>1795</u>: CG, Feb 27, Mar 11,
20, 27; <u>1796</u>: CG, Feb 19, Mar 11, 18; <u>1797</u>: CG, Mar 3, 15, 29, Apr 5; <u>1798</u>:
HAY, Jan 15, CG, Feb 23, Mar 21, 30; <u>1799</u>: HAY, Jan 24, CG, Feb 13, Mar 8,
15, HAY, 29; <u>1800</u>: CG, Mar 7, 26

--Nabal (oratorio), 1764: DL, Mar 16, CG, 21; 1789: CG, Apr 3; 1790: CG, Mar 17; 1794: CG, Mar 26; 1798: CG, Mar 28, 30; 1800: CG, Mar 5
--Occasional Oratorio, The (pastiche), 1738: KING'S, Mar 28; 1746: CG, Feb 14, 19, 26; 1747: CG, Mar 6, 11, 13; 1763: CG, Feb 18, 25; 1786: DL, Mar 10; 1788: DL, Feb 8; 1789: CG, Mar 6, DL, 18, 20; 1790: CG, Feb 24, DL, 26; 1791: DL, Mar 23, CG, Apr 13; 1792: KING'S, Feb 24, CG, Mar 2, KING'S, 28; 1793: KING/HAY, Feb 22, CG, Mar 6; 1794: CG, Mar 12, DL, 21, 26, Apr 9, 10, 11; 1795: CG, Mar 4; 1796: CG, Feb 26; 1797: CG, Mar 10; 1798: CG, Mar 28; 1799: CG, Feb 15, Mar 13
--Omnipotence (oratorio), 1774: HAY, Feb 25, Mar 2, 4, 9, 11, 16, 23, 25; 1776: CG, Feb 28; 1777: CG, Feb 26; 1778: CG, Apr 8; 1779: HAY, Mar 24
--Orestes (opera), 1734: CG, Dec 18, 21, 28; 1735: CG/LIF, Apr 17, CG, Nov 19, 28, Dec 2; 1736: CG, Mar 2, 15, 27, Apr 8, 12, 17, 27, 29, 30, May 1, 10
--Orlando (opera), 1733: KING'S, Jan 27, Feb 3, 6, 10, 17, 20, Mar 3, Apr 21, 24, May 1, 5, 8
--Otho (opera), 1723: KING'S, Jan 12, 15, 19, 22, 26, 29, Feb 2, 5, 9, 12, 16, Mar 26, Jun 4, 8, Dec 11, 14, 18, 21, 28; 1724: KING'S, Jan 1; 1726: KING'S, Feb 5, 8, 12, 15, 19, 22, 26, 28, Mar 5, 8; 1727: KING'S, Apr 11, 13; 1733: KING'S, Nov 13, 17, 20, 24; 1734: KING'S, Dec 5, 10, 14, 17, 21, 23; 1745: CG, Apr 10; 1748: HAY, Dec 9; 1752: CT/HAY, Jan 14, 31; 1770: DL, Mar 14; 1771: GROTTO, Aug 30, Sep 3; 1789: DL, Mar 20; 1790: DL, Mar 17; 1791: DL, Apr 1
--Parnasso in Festa (serenata), 1734: KING'S, Mar 11, 13, 16, 19, 23; 1737: CG, Mar 9, 11; 1740: LIF, Nov 8; 1741: KING'S, Mar 14
--Parthenope (opera), 1730: KING'S, Feb 24, 28, Mar 3, 7, 10, 14, 17, Dec 12, 15, 19, 29; 1731: KING'S, Jan 2, 5, 9; 1737: CG, Jan 29, Feb 2, 5, 9
--Pastor Fido, Il (opera), 1712: QUEEN'S, Nov 22, 26, 29, Dec 3, 6, 10, 27; 1713: QUEEN'S, Feb 21; 1734: KING'S, May 18, 21, 24, 28, Jun 4, 8, 11, 18, 22, 25, 29, Jul 3, 6, CG, Nov 8, CG/LIF, 9, 13, 16, 20, 23; 1735: CG/LIF, Apr 17; 1739: CG, Mar 22
--Porus (opera), 1731: KING'S, Feb 2, 6, 9, 13, 16, 20, 23, 27, Mar 2, 6, 9, 13, 16, 20, 23, LIF, 26, KING'S, 27, DL, Apr 26, 27, 29, May 6, LIF, 17, DL, Jul 27, SF/BFFHH, Aug 24, Sep 8, KING'S, Nov 23, 27, 30, Dec 4; 1732: LIF, Mar 10; 1733: DL/HAY, Dec 1, 3; 1734: DL/HAY, Jan 10; 1735: GF, Apr 22; 1736: CG, Dec 1, 8, 11, 15, 22; 1737: CG, Jan 5
--Ptolomy (opera), 1728: KING'S, Apr 30, May 4, 7, 11, 14, 18, 21; 1729: LIF, Mar 5, HIC, Apr 16, 30; 1730: KING'S, May 19, 23, 26, 30, Jun 2, 6, 13; 1732: CL, Mar 17, LIF, Apr 19; 1733: KING'S, Jan 2, 9, 13, 16; 1734: DL/HAY, Feb 4; 1786: DL, Mar 10; 1787: DL, Feb 23; 1789: DL, Mar 18; 1790: DL, Feb 26; 1791: DL, Mar 23; 1792: KING'S, Feb 24; 1793: KING/HAY, Feb 22; 1797: CG, Mar 31
--Radamistus (opera), 1720: KING'S, Apr 27, 30, May 4, 7, 11, 14, 18, 21, Jun 8, 22, Dec 28, 31; 1721: KING'S, Jan 4, 21, 25, Mar 21, 25, Nov 25, 29, Dec 2, 6; 1724: YB, Mar 27; 1729: HIC, Apr 16; 1789: DL, Mar 20
--Redemption (music), 1785: DL, Feb 11; 1786: DL, Mar 10, 15, 17, 22, 29, 31, Apr 5, 7; 1787: DL, Feb 23, 28, Mar 2, 23, 30; 1788: DL, Feb 8, 15, 29; 1789: DL, Mar 11, 18, Apr 3; 1790: DL, Feb 26, Mar 26; 1791: CG, Mar 11, DL, 23, CG, 23, DL, 23, 30, Apr 8, 15; 1792: KING'S, Feb 24, Mar 16; 1793: KING/HAY, Feb 22, Mar 1; 1794: CG, Mar 14, DL, 21, Apr 2, 10; 1795: CG, Feb 20, 27, Mar 13, 25; 1796: CG, Feb 24, 26; 1797: CG, Mar 10; 1799: CG, Feb 15; 1800: CG, Feb 28
--Richard I, King of England (opera), 1727: KING'S, Nov 8, 11, 14, 18, 21, 25, 28, Dec 2, 5, 9, 12, 16
--Rinaldo (opera), 1711: QUEEN'S, Feb 24, 27, Mar 3, 6, 10, 13, 17, 20, 24, Apr 11, 25, May 5, 9, 26, Jun 2; 1712: QUEEN'S, Jan 23, 26, 29, Feb 7, 9, 13, 23, Mar 6, Apr 1; 1713: QUEEN'S, Mar 24, May 6, 9; 1714: KING'S, Dec 30; 1715: KING'S, Jan 4, 8, 15, 22, 27, 29, Feb 5, 12, 19, Jun 25; 1717: KING'S, Jan 5, 12, 19, 23, 26, Feb 9, Mar 9, May 2, 18, Jun 5; 1731: KING'S, Apr 6, 10, 20, 24, 27, May 1
--Rodelinda (opera), 1725: KING'S, Feb 13, 16, 20, 25, 27, Mar 2, 6, 9, 13, 16, 20, 30, Apr 3, 6, Dec 18, 21, 23, 28; 1726: KING'S, Jan 1, 4, 8, 11, DL, Apr 28; 1729: HIC, Apr 16; 1731: KING'S, May 4, 8, 11, 15, 18, 22, 25, 29; 1748: DL, Sep 22; 1770: DL, Mar 14, 16; 1782: DL, Feb 15; 1786: DL, Mar 10; 1787: DL, Feb 23, KING'S, Mar 1; 1789: DL, Mar 18; 1790: DL, Feb 26, Mar 5; 1791: DL, Mar 23; 1792: KING'S, Feb 24, CG, Mar 9; 1793: CG, Feb 15, KING/HAY, 22
--Roxana; or, Alexander in India (opera), 1743: KING'S, Nov 15, 19, 26, 29, Dec 3, 6, 10, 13, 17, 20, 27, 31; 1744: KING'S, Mar 6, 10, 13, 17; 1746: KING'S, Apr 15, 19, 22, 26, 29, May 3, 6, 10; 1747: KING'S, Feb 24, 28, Mar 3, 7, 10, 14, 17, 21; 1748: KING'S, Feb 20, 27, Mar 8, 12
--Ruth (oratorio), 1768: CHAPEL, May 25; 1769: KING'S, Apr 5; 1771: CHAPEL, Apr 27; 1774: CHAPEL, Mar 30; 1776: CHAPEL, Apr 3
--Samson (oratorio), 1734: GF/HAY, Dec 2, 9; 1735: GF/HAY, Feb 12; 1743: CG, Feb 18, 23, 25, Mar 2, 9, 11, 16, 31; 1744: CG, Feb 24, 29, Mar 13, Apr 2,

28; <u>1745</u>: KING'S, Mar 1, 8, CG, Apr 10; <u>1746</u>: DL, Jan 4; <u>1747</u>: ST, Apr 29;
<u>1749</u>: CG, Mar 3, 8, 10, 15; <u>1750</u>: CG, Apr 4, 6, DL, 26; <u>1751</u>: CT, Mar 16;
<u>1752</u>: HAY, Jan 2, CG, Feb 26, Mar 6, 11, 13; <u>1753</u>: CG, Apr 4, 6, 11; <u>1754</u>:
CG, Mar 29, KING'S, Apr 2, 25, CG, May 3; <u>1755</u>: CG, Feb 26, Mar 7; <u>1756</u>: HAB,
Dec 9; <u>1757</u>: SOHO, Mar 14; <u>1758</u>: KING'S, Mar 6, Apr 6; <u>1759</u>: CG, Mar 14, 16,
21; <u>1760</u>: CG, Feb 22, 27; <u>1761</u>: CG, Feb 27, Mar 6; <u>1762</u>: CG, Feb 26, DL, Mar
10, 19, CG, 26; <u>1763</u>: CG, Mar 18; <u>1764</u>: CG, Mar 28, RANELAGH, Jun 13; <u>1765</u>:
CG, Mar 6, 20; <u>1766</u>: CG, Feb 21, Mar 12; <u>1767</u>: CG, Mar 18; <u>1768</u>: CG, Feb 19,
Mar 9; <u>1769</u>: HAY, Feb 22, CG, Mar 1, HAY, 8, CG, 8; <u>1770</u>: DL, Mar 2, CG, 14,
DL, 30; <u>1771</u>: DL, Feb 15, CG, Mar 1, DL, 1; <u>1772</u>: CG, Mar 13, DL, 20; <u>1773</u>:
CG, Mar 10, 17, DL, 26; <u>1774</u>: DL, Feb 23, HAY, 23, DL, Mar 4; <u>1775</u>: DL, Mar
8, KING'S, 8, 22; <u>1776</u>: CG, Mar 8, DL, 22; <u>1777</u>: CG, Feb 21, DL, Mar 5; <u>1778</u>:
DL, Mar 25; <u>1779</u>: DL, Mar 5; <u>1780</u>: DL, Feb 23; <u>1782</u>: DL, Mar 6; <u>1783</u>: DL, Mar
26; <u>1784</u>: DL, Mar 10, HAY, 10, CG, Apr 27; <u>1785</u>: DL, Mar 11; <u>1786</u>: DL, Mar
10; <u>1788</u>: DL, Feb 20, 22; <u>1789</u>: CG, Mar 6, DL, 18, 25, CG, 27, Apr 3; <u>1790</u>:
DL, Feb 24, CG, 26, DL, 26, CG, Mar 3, DL, 5, 10, 17, CG, 17, 19; <u>1791</u>: CG,
Mar 11, DL, 11, CG, 23, DL, 23, CG, Apr 13; <u>1792</u>: CG, Feb 24, KING'S, 24, 29,
CG, Mar 2, KING'S, 7, CG, 9, KING'S, 14, CG, 21, KING'S, 23, 30; <u>1793</u>: CG,
Feb 15, KING/HAY, 15, 22, CG, 22, Mar 6, 8, 20, KING/HAY, 22, CG, 22; <u>1794</u>:
CG, Mar 7, DL, 12, CG, 12, DL, 14, 21, 26, CG, 26, DL, Apr 2, 9, 11; <u>1795</u>:
CG, Feb 20, 27, KING'S, 27, CG, Mar 4, 13, KING'S, 13, CG, 25; <u>1796</u>: CG, Feb
24, 26, Mar 16, DL, May 11; <u>1797</u>: CG, Mar 10, 15, 22, 24, Apr 7; <u>1798</u>: CG,
Mar 2, 9, 14, 28, 30; <u>1799</u>: CG, Feb 15, 20, Mar 1, 13, 15; <u>1800</u>: CG, Feb 28,
Mar 5, 14, 19, 21
--Saul (oratorio), <u>1739</u>: KING'S, Jan 8, 16, 23, Feb 3, 10, Mar 27, Apr 19, DL,
30; <u>1740</u>: LIF, Mar 21; <u>1741</u>: HIC, Feb 5, LIF, Mar 18; <u>1744</u>: CG, Mar 16, 21;
<u>1745</u>: KING'S, Mar 13; <u>1750</u>: CG, Mar 2, 7; <u>1754</u>: CG, Mar 15, 20; <u>1759</u>: CG, May
4; <u>1769</u>: CG, Oct 7; <u>1786</u>: DL, Mar 10; <u>1787</u>: DL, Feb 23; <u>1789</u>: CG, Mar 6, DL,
18, CG, 27, Apr 3; <u>1790</u>: DL, Feb 24, CG, 24, DL, 26, CG, 26, DL, Mar 17, CG,
19; <u>1791</u>: CG, Mar 11, DL, 23, CG, 25, DL, Apr 1, 13; <u>1792</u>: KING'S, Feb 24,
29, CG, Mar 2, 9, KING'S, 30; <u>1793</u>: CG, Feb 15, KING/HAY, 22, CG, Mar 6;
<u>1794</u>: CG, Mar 7, DL, 12, CG, 12, DL, 14, CG, 21, DL, 21, Apr 2, 4, 10, 11,
CG, 11; <u>1795</u>: CG, Feb 20, Mar 13, 25; <u>1796</u>: CG, Feb 24, 26, Mar 16; <u>1797</u>: CG,
Mar 10, 31; <u>1798</u>: CG, Mar 9, 28; <u>1799</u>: CG, Feb 8, 15, 20, Mar 13, 15; <u>1800</u>:
CG, Feb 28, Mar 14, 19, 21
--Scipio (opera), <u>1726</u>: KING'S, Mar 12, 15, 19, 22, 26, 29, Apr 2, 12, 16, 19,
23, 26, DL, 28, KING'S, 30; <u>1729</u>: DL, Mar 26; <u>1730</u>: KING'S, Oct 31, Nov 3, 7,
10, 14, 17, 21; <u>1748</u>: KING'S, Apr 5; <u>1789</u>: CG, Mar 20; <u>1790</u>: CG, Mar 17;
<u>1792</u>: CG, Mar 14; <u>1793</u>: CG, Feb 22, Mar 20; <u>1794</u>: CG, Mar 14; <u>1795</u>: CG, Mar
4; <u>1797</u>: CG, Mar 15; <u>1798</u>: CG, Mar 30; <u>1799</u>: CG, Feb 20, Mar 15; <u>1800</u>: CG,
Mar 19
--Semele (oratorio), <u>1744</u>: CG, Feb 10, 15, 17, 22, KING'S, Dec 1, 8; <u>1745</u>: CG,
Apr 10; <u>1746</u>: DL, Apr 15; <u>1762</u>: CG, Mar 19; <u>1786</u>: DL, Mar 10; <u>1788</u>: DL, Feb
8; <u>1789</u>: CG, Mar 6, DL, 18, CG, Apr 3; <u>1790</u>: DL, Feb 24, CG, 24, DL, 26;
<u>1791</u>: DL, Mar 23, CG, 23; <u>1792</u>: KING'S, Feb 24; <u>1793</u>: KING/HAY, Feb 22, CG,
Mar 6; <u>1794</u>: CG, Mar 12; <u>1796</u>: CG, Feb 26; <u>1797</u>: CG, Mar 10; <u>1798</u>: CG, Mar 2;
<u>1799</u>: CG, Feb 8, 15, Mar 6; <u>1800</u>: CG, Feb 28
--Siroe (opera), <u>1728</u>: KING'S, Feb 14, 17, 19, 24, 27, Mar 2, 9, 12, 16, 19,
23, 26, 30, Apr 2, 6, 9, 13, 23, 27; <u>1729</u>: HIC, Apr 16; <u>1732</u>: LIF, Mar 10,
CL, 17
--Solomon (oratorio), <u>1749</u>: CG, Mar 17, 20, 22, May 1; <u>1750</u>: DL, Mar 28; <u>1754</u>:
SOHO, Mar 26; <u>1759</u>: CG, Mar 2, 7; <u>1765</u>: CG, Mar 15, MARLY, Aug 6; <u>1767</u>:
MARLY, Sep 18; <u>1782</u>: DL, Feb 27; <u>1789</u>: DL, Mar 20, CG, 20; <u>1790</u>: CG, Feb 24,
26, DL, Mar 5, 10, CG, 17; <u>1791</u>: CG, Mar 11, 18, DL, 25, Apr 1; <u>1792</u>: CG, Feb
24, KING'S, 29, Mar 7, 14, CG, 14, KING'S, 23, 28; <u>1793</u>: CG, Feb 15, Mar 8,
KING/HAY, 15; <u>1794</u>: CG, Mar 7, DL, 12, 14, CG, 21, DL, 21, CG, 26, DL, Apr 2,
9, 11; <u>1795</u>: CG, Feb 20, Mar 13; <u>1796</u>: CG, Feb 24, Mar 16; <u>1797</u>: CG, Mar 22,
31; <u>1798</u>: CG, Mar 14, 23; <u>1799</u>: CG, Feb 8, 20, Mar 1, 13; <u>1800</u>: CG, Mar 5, 21
--Sosarmes (opera), <u>1732</u>: KING'S, Feb 14, 15, 19, 22, 26, 29, Mar 4, 7, 11, 14,
18, 21, LIF, Apr 19; <u>1734</u>: HH, Apr 26, KING'S, 27, 30, May 4; <u>1786</u>: DL, Mar
10; <u>1787</u>: KING'S, Mar 1; <u>1789</u>: DL, Mar 18; <u>1790</u>: CG, Feb 24, DL, 26, Mar 12;
<u>1791</u>: CG, Mar 11, DL, 23, CG, Apr 13; <u>1792</u>: CG, Feb 24, KING'S, 24, CG, Mar
23, KING'S, 30; <u>1793</u>: KING/HAY, Feb 22, CG, Mar 6; <u>1794</u>: CG, Mar 12; <u>1797</u>:
CG, Mar 22; <u>1799</u>: CG, Feb 15, Mar 15
--Susanna (oratorio), <u>1749</u>: CG, Feb 2, 10, 15, 17, 22, Mar 31, May 1; <u>1759</u>: CG,
Mar 9; <u>1786</u>: DL, Mar 10; <u>1789</u>: DL, Mar 18, KING'S, May 9; <u>1790</u>: CG, Feb 26,
DL, 26, Mar 10, CG, 17; <u>1791</u>: DL, Mar 23; <u>1792</u>: KING'S, Feb 24, Mar 7; <u>1793</u>:
KING/HAY, Feb 22; <u>1794</u>: DL, Apr 2
--Te Deum (anthem), <u>1731</u>: ACA, Jan 14; <u>1772</u>: DL, Mar 11; <u>1773</u>: DL, Mar 12;
<u>1789</u>: DL, Mar 18; <u>1790</u>: DL, Feb 26; <u>1791</u>: CG, Mar 11, DL, 23; <u>1792</u>: KING'S,
Feb 24, Mar 23, 30; <u>1793</u>: KING/HAY, Feb 22; <u>1794</u>: DL, Apr 11, KING'S, May 15
--Terpsicore (musical), <u>1734</u>: CG/LIF, Nov 9, 13, 16, 20, 23

--Theodora (oratorio), 1750: CG, Mar 16, 21, 23; 1755: CG, Mar 5; 1761: CG, Feb 25; 1767: CG, Mar 25; 1786: DL, Mar 10; 1787: DL, Feb 23; 1788: DL, Feb 8; 1789: CG, Mar 6, DL, 18, CG, May 20; 1790: CG, Feb 24, DL, 26, Mar 10, CG, 26; 1791: CG, Mar 11, DL, 23; 1792: KING'S, Feb 24, CG, Mar 2, KING'S, 7; 1793: KING/HAY, Feb 15, 22, CG, Mar 6; 1794: DL, Mar 12, CG, 12, DL, 14, 21, Apr 2, CG, 11; 1795: CG, Feb 27, Mar 25; 1796: CG, Feb 24, 26; 1797: CG, Mar 10; 1798: CG, Mar 14, 30; 1799: CG, Feb 8
--Theseus (opera), 1713: QUEEN'S, Jan 10, 14, 17, 21, 24, 28, Feb 4, 11, 14, 17, Mar 17, Apr 15, 18, May 16
--Triumph of Time and Truth (Trionfo del Tempo e Della Verita, Il) (oratorio), 1737: CG, Mar 23, 25, Apr 1, 4; 1739: KING'S, Mar 3; 1757: CG, Mar 11, 16, 18, 23; 1758: CG, Feb 10, 15; 1760: CG, Mar 7; 1789: CG, Mar 20, Apr 3; 1790: DL, Feb 24, CG, 26, Mar 3, 17; 1791: CG, Mar 23, DL, Apr 13; 1792: CG, Mar 2; 1793: CG, Mar 6, KING/HAY, 13; 1794: DL, Mar 14, Apr 2, 11; 1795: CG, Mar 13; 1796: CG, Feb 24; 1797: CG, Mar 15; 1800: CG, Mar 14
--Wenceslaus (opera), 1731: KING'S, Jan 12, 16, 19, 23
--Xerxes (opera), 1738: KING'S, Apr 15, 18, 22, 25, May 2
--Grand Concerto, 1743: LIF, Mar 15; 1746: KING'S, Mar 25; 1748: KING'S, Apr 5; 1749: KING'S, Mar 21; 1750: KING'S, Apr 10; 1751: KING'S, Apr 16; 1752: KING'S, Mar 24; 1753: KING'S, Apr 30; 1755: KING'S, Mar 17; 1790: DL, Mar 17
--1st Grand Concerto, 1790: CG, Mar 26; 1791: CG, Mar 18; 1793: CG, Mar 20
--5th Grand Concerto, 1789: CG, Mar 20; 1790: CG, Feb 24; 1791: CG, Mar 11, DL, 11; 1792: CG, Mar 2; 1793: CG, Mar 6; 1794: CG, Mar 21, 26; 1796: CG, Mar 16; 1798: CG, Mar 9; 1799: CG, Feb 15; 1800: CG, Mar 19
--11th Grand Concerto, 1790: CG, Mar 3; 1791: CG, Mar 23; 1794: CG, Mar 12, Apr 3
Handelian Society, 1791: DL, Apr 13
Hanes. See Haynes.
Hang this whining way (song), 1691: DL, Dec 0
Hanging and Marriage. See Carey, Henry.
Hanmeuze, Mrs (beneficiary), 1751: CG, May 14
Hanmore (house servant), 1750: CG, May 7
Hanmore, Mrs (house servant), 1747: CG, May 22; 1749: CG, May 3; 1760: CG, Sep 22
Hannah Hewit. See Dibdin, Charles.
Hannah. See Worgan, James.
Hannah, Mrs, 1761: DL, Jul 27
Hannibal. See Dekker, Thomas.
Hanover Square Rooms, 1789: DL, Mar 6; 1791: KING'S, Mar 26
Hanover Square, 1743: CG, Feb 18; 1744: CG, Feb 10, KING'S, Nov 3; 1745: KING'S, Jan 17, MF, May 2; 1777: CG, Apr 25, May 20; 1778: CG, May 16; 1793: CG, Apr 25; 1796: CG, Apr 15; 1798: CG, Apr 17; 1799: CG, Apr 9, May 24; 1800: CG, Apr 17, May 17
Hanover St, 1739: CG, Dec 15; 1742: CG, Apr 20; 1743: HAY, Mar 24, CG, Apr 15; 1744: CG, Apr 3, 17; 1746: CG, Apr 16; 1747: CG, Apr 27; 1789: CG, Jun 8
Hanover, Court of, 1703: YB, Jul 27; 1710: QUEEN'S, Nov 25; 1731: LIF, May 6
Hanover, Sophia, Princess of, 1710: QUEEN'S, Nov 25
Hanoverian succession, 1724: RI, Aug 3
Hanson (beneficiary), 1722: LIF, May 29; 1723: LIF, Jun 3
Hanson (poulterer), 1754: DL, Dec 16
Hanson, Mrs (dresser), 1719: LIF, May 28; 1724: LIF, Jun 3; 1725: LIF, May 24
Hanson, Sir Robert (Lord Mayor), 1672: CITY, Oct 29
Hants, 1788: DL, Apr 14
Hanyours, Master (actor), 1756: DL, May 5
Happy Bride (song), 1750: NWSM, Aug 20; 1764: CG, May 8
Happy Captive, The. See Theobald, Lewis.
Happy Constancy, The. See Jacob, Hilderbrand.
Happy Day (song), 1761: KING'S, Mar 12
Happy Discovery, The (play), 1769: CG, Apr 5
Happy Gallant, The; or, The Modern Wife (play, anon), 1755: BF, Sep 6
Happy Hero, The (play), 1746: BFWF, Aug 25
Happy if still they reign in pleasure (song), 1789: CG, Mar 20; 1790: CG, Mar 17
Happy Iphis (song), 1790: CG, Mar 3; 1791: CG, Mar 11; 1794: CG, Mar 7, Apr 9; 1795: CG, Feb 20, Mar 25; 1796: CG, Mar 16; 1797: CG, Apr 7; 1799: CG, Feb 20
Happy Lovers (dance), 1742: CG, Oct 6, 11, 13, 14, 21, Dec 7, 11, 14, 17, 22; 1743: CG, May 4, 6, 9
Happy Lovers, The. See Ward, Henry.
Happy Nuptials, The. See Carey, Henry.
Happy Pair (song), 1739: DL, Apr 3, 10, 24, 25, 26, 30, May 16; 1741: DL, May 9, Oct 15, 20, 31, Nov 13, 14, 17, 24, 27, Dec 5, 7, 8, 11, 17, 19, 26, 31; 1742: DL, Jan 16, 19, 20, 26, 28, Feb 2, 12, 18, 27, Mar 6, 9, 16, May 4, 17,

Sep 23, Oct 29; <u>1789</u>: CG, Apr 3; <u>1790</u>: CG, Mar 26; <u>1791</u>: CG, Mar 25; <u>1792</u>:
 CG, Mar 7; <u>1794</u>: CG, Mar 14, DL, Apr 9; <u>1795</u>: DL, Feb 12
Happy Shepherd and Shepherdess (dance), <u>1735</u>: DL, May 17
Happy Shepherd, The (music), <u>1720</u>: LIF, Mar 22
Happy Sisters (dance), <u>1789</u>: HAY, Jul 8
Happy Stratagem, The (dance), <u>1799</u>: DL, Jul 1
Happy they (song), <u>1790</u>: CG, Mar 19; <u>1794</u>: CG, Mar 26, Apr 11
Happy Villagers (dance), <u>1766</u>: CG, Dec 15, 18; <u>1767</u>: CG, Jan 9, 14, 16
Happy we (song), <u>1787</u>: DL, Mar 7; <u>1791</u>: DL, Apr 1; <u>1792</u>: KING'S, Feb 29; <u>1794</u>:
 DL, Mar 26
Happy we who free from love (song), <u>1697</u>: DL, Sep 0
Happy were the Days (song), <u>1800</u>: CG, May 17
Harangue in a Tub (entertainment), <u>1776</u>: CHR, Oct 9
Harbin (actor), <u>1733</u>: GF, Sep 25, Oct 24, Nov 29, Dec 12, 31; <u>1734</u>: GF, Jan 14,
 19, 21, 31, Feb 11, Mar 5, May 7, Sep 16, 20, 25, Oct 16, Nov 18, 25, Dec 6,
 16; <u>1735</u>: GF, Jan 1, 6, Feb 5, 11, Apr 22, May 3
Harbin, Tom (beneficiary), <u>1748</u>: CG, Nov 7, 15, Dec 14, 15
Harcourt, Elizabeth, Lady (spectator), <u>1780</u>: DL, May 24
Harcourt, Mrs (actor), <u>1705</u>: QUEEN'S, Dec 27; <u>1706</u>: QUEEN'S, Jan 8, Feb 11
Harcourt, <u>1700</u>: DLORLIF, Jan 23
Harden, <u>1718</u>: DL, Jul 25
Harder (actor), <u>1744</u>: HAY, May 10
Hardwicke, Lord. See Yorke, Philip.
Hardwicke, Thomas (architect), <u>1793</u>: KING'S, Feb 19
Hardy (beneficiary), <u>1726</u>: LIF, May 19
Hardy, Lord (actor), <u>1701</u>: DL, Dec 0
Harem of Ispahan (dance), <u>1774</u>: KING'S, Jan 29, Feb 5, 17, 22, Mar 12, Apr 28
Hargrave (actor), <u>1796</u>: CG, Oct 6, 13, 26, Dec 19; see also Snow, Robert
Hargraves, H S (boxholder), <u>1796</u>: DL, May 23
Hargreaves (smith), <u>1757</u>: CG, Dec 19; <u>1760</u>: CG, Jan 19
Harington, Dr Henry (composer), <u>1790</u>: DL, Apr 16; <u>1791</u>: CG, May 17; <u>1793</u>: CG,
 Dec 19
Hark, hark, the horrid sound (song), <u>1792</u>: CG, Mar 7; <u>1794</u>: CG, Mar 14
Hark, hark, to the Woodlands (song), <u>1791</u>: HAY, Dec 12
Hark, how the songsters (song), <u>1693</u>: NONE, Sep 0
Hark, my Damilcar (song), <u>1694</u>: NONE, Sep 0
Hark, the Drum beats to Arms! (song), <u>1794</u>: CG, May 7
Hark, the hollow woods (song), <u>1789</u>: HAY, Aug 25
Hark, the Lark at Heaven's Gate sings (song), <u>1784</u>: CG, Apr 24; <u>1787</u>: DL, Feb
 1, Nov 5; <u>1788</u>: HAY, Aug 22; <u>1790</u>: CG, May 13; <u>1791</u>: CG, Jun 6; <u>1792</u>: CG, May
 19; <u>1793</u>: CG, Nov 18, 22; <u>1794</u>: CG, Oct 7; <u>1797</u>: DL, Mar 6; <u>1800</u>: CG, May 13
Hark, the litdle warbling Choir (song), <u>1742</u>: DL, Oct 8
Hark, the storm grows (song), <u>1667</u>: BRIDGES, Sep 25
Hark, the trumpet sounds (song), <u>1793</u>: KING/HAY, Mar 15
Hark, the watch dogs bark (song), <u>1793</u>: KING/HAY, Feb 15, 27
Hark, 'tis the Linnet (song), <u>1790</u>: CG, Mar 17; <u>1704</u>: DL, Apr 4; <u>1798</u>: CG, Mar
 14
Hark, ye Madam (song), <u>1696</u>: LIF, Jun 0; <u>1704</u>: LIF, Jul 27
Harland (actor), <u>1695</u>: DG, Apr 0, DL, Sep 0, Nov 0; <u>1696</u>: DL, Feb 0, May 0, DG,
 Jun 0, DL, Jul 0, DL/DL, Dec 0; <u>1697</u>: DL, Jan 0, Feb 0, May 8, 31, Jul 0, Sep
 0, NONE, 0; <u>1698</u>: DL, Feb 0
Harlequin (Arlequin). See also Arlequin.
Harlequin a Blunderer (pantomime), <u>1720</u>: KING'S, Mar 19
Harlequin a Man of Good Fortune. See Regnard, Jean Francois.
Harlequin a Merry Spirit (pantomime), <u>1720</u>: KING'S, Mar 29, LIF, Apr 5
Harlequin a Savage (farce), <u>1735</u>: GF/HAY, Jun 2, 4
Harlequin a Sham Astrologer (pantomime), <u>1720</u>: KING'S, Mar 24, 26, LIF, Apr 5
Harlequin always Harlequin. See Biancolelli, Pierre Francoise Dominique.
Harlequin and a Countryman (dance), <u>1715</u>: LIF, May 13; <u>1722</u>: LIF, Jan 1; <u>1732</u>:
 WINH, May 27, SOU, Oct 12
Harlequin and Clown (dance), <u>1746</u>: GF, Feb 10
Harlequin and Dame Ragonde (dance), <u>1716</u>: LIF, Oct 18
Harlequin and Faustus. See Wild, James.
Harlequin and Harlequinette (dance), <u>1734</u>: GF, Apr 27; <u>1735</u>: DL, May 30, Jun 2,
 9, LIF, 12; <u>1736</u>: DL, Apr 1
Harlequin and Oberon. See Wild, James.
Harlequin and Pirotte (dance), <u>1725</u>: DL, Apr 20
Harlequin and Punch (dance), <u>1715</u>: LIF, Apr 18, May 2, 5, Jun 7, DL, Oct 24;
 <u>1720</u>: LIF, Nov 28; <u>1721</u>: LIF, Jan 2, 23; <u>1722</u>: LIF, Apr 26; <u>1723</u>: DL, Nov 21;
 <u>1724</u>: DL, Apr 29
Harlequin and Quixotte. See Cross, John Cartwright.
Harlequin and Scaramouch Deserters. See Fuzelier, Louis.

Harlequin Anna Bullen (burlesque), 1727: LIF, Dec 11, 12, 13, 14, 15, 16, 19
Harlequin Barber; or, Mezzetin in the Suds (pantomime), 1741: CG, Apr 20; 1754:
    SFY, Sep 18, 19, 20, 21, 23, 24
Harlequin Buffoon at Court, a Dumb Spy, and Condemned to the Stirpado (play),
    1726: KING'S, Nov 1
Harlequin Captain of the Bandittos, Thief, Spy, Head Serjeant, Judge, and
    Hangman (pantomime), 1727: KING'S, Jan 16
Harlequin Captive. See Theobald, Lewis.
Harlequin Captive; or, the Sallee Rover (pantomime), 1748: BFP, Aug 24
Harlequin Captive; or, The Magic Fire. See Linley, William.
Harlequin Conjuror; or, Pantaloon Dissected (pantomime), 1754: SFH, Sep 19
Harlequin Conqueror (entertainment), 1728: HAY, May 27
Harlequin Dance (dance), 1705: DL, Jan 1; 1706: DL, Mar 28; 1710: DL, Feb 4,
    Jun 6, GR, Aug 7; 1714: DL, Apr 30, May 17, 31, Dec 1; 1715: DL, Feb 28, LIF,
    Oct 7, 14; 1716: DL, May 25, 30, LIF, Oct 18, 19, 25, 26, 29, 30; 1717: LIF,
    Mar 25, 30, Nov 1, Dec 6; 1718: DL, May 8, 27, LIF, Nov 27; 1719: DL, May 2,
    5, LIF, 26, Jun 3; 1720: DL, May 17, 20, Jun 14; 1722: DL, Mar 15, Apr 9, May
    21, Jun 26, Jul 6; 1723: DL, May 15; 1725: DL, Mar 18, Oct 14; 1726: DL, Feb
    18, HAY, Apr 13, DL, 21, May 4, 9, 17; 1727: KING'S, Mar 16, DL, 20, Apr 10,
    LIF, 14, 26, May 9; 1728: DL, Apr 8, 11, May 7, 8, 17, 22, Oct 21, Nov 7;
    1729: LIF, Mar 27, Apr 12, DL, 28, May 1, 2, HAY, 12, DL, Jun 20, 24, BFF,
    Aug 23, DL, Sep 30, GF, Dec 19, 20; 1730: GF, Mar 2, DL, May 4, GF, Sep 18;
    1731: GF, Jan 21, DL, Mar 22, 29, Apr 27, May 5, 6, 7, 10; 1732: DL, May 3,
    25, 29, Jun 6, 23, 28, Jul 4, 7, RIW/HAY, Sep 4, 12, GF, Oct 10; 1733: DL,
    May 18, DL/HAY, Dec 12, HAY, 13; 1734: CG, Apr 17, May 1, HAY, Jun 5, 24, 28,
    Aug 7, 22, GF/HAY, Nov 20; 1735: GF/HAY, Mar 21, Apr 25, CG/LIF, 29, CG, May
    6; 1736: CG, Jan 9, 12, HAY, Feb 20, CG, 23, Mar 2, 22, 29, LIF, 31, CG, Apr
    5, 10, May 1, LIF, 5, CG, 6, 10, DL, 15, CG, 17, LIF, Nov 22, 23, 26; 1737:
    DL, Feb 22, HAY, Mar 3, DL, 5, 14, 19, 21, 22, Apr 2, May 4, 5, 9, 14, 18,
    24, 26, 27, 30, 31, Jun 11; 1739: DL, Apr 14, CG, May 21; 1740: CG, Dec 16,
    20; 1741: CG, Jan 10, Feb 6; 1742: CG, Oct 11, DL, Nov 17, 19; 1743: CG, Apr
    22; 1747: SOU, Jan 21; 1749: DL, Mar 14; 1751: DL, Apr 26; 1757: CG, Apr 27
Harlequin Dead and Revived (pantomime, anon), 1720: KING'S, Mar 5
Harlequin Dissected; or, The Biter Bit (farce), 1743: TCD/BFTD, Aug 23
Harlequin Doctor Faustus. See Thurmond, John.
Harlequin Englishman; or, The Frenchman Bit (or, The Spaniard Outwitted)
    (pantomime), 1742: GF, Mar 1, 2, 4, 6, 8, 9, 11, 13, 16, 20, 23, NWC, Dec 27
Harlequin Every-where. See Dibdin, Charles, The Mirror.
Harlequin Executed; or, The Farmer Disappointed (pantomime), 1716: LIF, Dec 26,
    29; 1717: LIF, Jan 1, 29, Feb 6, 28, Apr 27, May 10, 20, 30; 1718: LIF, Jan
    8, 10, 15, Apr 23; 1720: LIF, Jan 15, 20, May 25; 1722: LIF, Feb 2, 3, 5
Harlequin Fortune Teller (pantomime), 1748: NWSM, May 3, 4, 5, 6, 9; 1750:
    NWSM, May 10
Harlequin Freemason. See Dibdin, Charles.
Harlequin Grand Volgi. See Roger.
Harlequin Happy and Poor Pierrot Married. See Roger.
Harlequin Happy at Last (pantomime), 1742: UM, Oct 4
Harlequin Happy; or, Jack Spaniard Bit (pantomime), 1740: TCLP, Aug 4
Harlequin Happy; or, The Frenchman Bit (pantomime, anon), 1747: SMMF, Jul 20
Harlequin Happy; or, The Miller Bit (pantomime, anon), 1745: SMMF, Jul 11
Harlequin Hermit (pantomime, anon), 1744: MF, Jun 11
Harlequin Hulla (farce), 1734: GF/HAY, Oct 26; 1735: HAY, Apr 25, May 2, GF,
    May 23
Harlequin Hussar (pantomime), 1743: TCD/BFTD, Aug 4; 1760: HAY, Jun 2
Harlequin Hydaspes. See Aubert, Isabella.
Harlequin Imprisoned; or, The Country Wake (pantomime), 1748: SFP, Sep 7, 12
Harlequin in Constantinople (pantomime), 1720: KING'S, Mar 12
Harlequin in the City (pantomime), 1734: GF, Oct 17, 18, 21, 23
Harlequin Incendiary; or, Colombine Cameron (pantomime, anon), 1746: DL, Mar 3,
    4, 6, 8, 11, 20, 31, Apr 1, 2, 5, BFWF, Aug 25
Harlequin Inchanted (pantomime), 1753: DL, Apr 25
Harlequin Invader (pantomime), 1746: BFLY, Aug 25
Harlequin Invisible in the Emperor of China's Court (play), 1724: LIF, Apr 8
Harlequin Junior; or, The Magic Cestus (pantomime, anon), 1784: DL, Jan 7, 8,
    9, 10, 12, 13, 14, 15, 16, 17, 19, 20, 21, 22, 23, 24, 26, 27, 28, Feb 3, 5,
    7, 9, 11, 12, 16, 19, 20, 23, 26, Mar 1, 4, 18, 22, Apr 23, May 12, 19, Sep
    23, 25, 28, Oct 2, 11, 25, Nov 2, 8, 12, 18, Dec 1, 6, 20, 27, 30; 1785: DL,
    Jan 1, 10; 1787: DL, Dec 26, 27, 28, 29, 31; 1788: DL, Jan 2, 3, 4, 7, 8, 9,
    10, 11, 14, 15, 16, 18, 19, 22, 25, 26, Feb 11, 18, 21, Mar 3, 24, 25, 26,
    Apr 3, 17, Nov 10, 13; 1790: DL, May 15
Harlequin Magician; or, Mezzetin Deceived (pantomime), 1754: BFYJN, Sep 3, 4,
    5, 6

Harlequin Man and Woman (dance), 1703: DL, Dec 22; 1704: DL, Aug 16; 1710: DL,
    Mar 11; 1722: DL, Feb 5; 1726: LIF, Oct 12; 1735: GF/HAY, Apr 7, HAY, May 26
Harlequin Mezzetin and Colombine (dance), 1716: DL, May 10, 15
Harlequin Mountebank; or, The Squire Electrified (pantomime), 1750: NWC, Apr
    16; 1756: DL, May 11, 15
Harlequin Orpheus; or, The Magical Pipe (pantomime, anon), 1735: DL, Mar 3, 4,
    6, 8, 11, 15, 18, 25, Apr 7, 8, 9, 10, 12, 17, 24, 26, 30, May 3, 12, 15, 16,
    19, 21, 26, 27, 28, Jun 2, 5
Harlequin Peasant; or, A Pantomime Rehearsal (pantomime, anon), 1793: HAY, Dec
    26, 27, 28, 30, 31; 1794: HAY, Jan 3, 4, 6, 7, 8, 9, 13, 16, 18, 21, 23, 28,
    31, Feb 7, 10, 17
Harlequin Prince by Magic Art (pantomime), 1770: GRP, Dec 10
Harlequin Punch and Colombine (dance), 1736: CG, Jun 4
Harlequin Punchanello and Dame Ragonde (dance), 1716: LIF, Jan 11
Harlequin Rambler. See O'Keeffe, John.
Harlequin Ranger. See Woodward, Henry.
Harlequin Restored; or, Taste a la Mode (pantomime, anon), 1736: DL, Jan 12,
    13, 14, 15, 16, 17, 19, 20, 21, 22, 23, 24, 26, 27, 28, 29, 31, Feb 2, 3, 4,
    5, 7, 9, 10, 11, 12, 13, 14, 16, 17, 18, 19, 21, 23, 24, Apr 13, 30, May 11,
    12, 13, 31, Oct 5, 7, 9, 13, 14, 15, 26, 27, 29, Nov 5, 6, 9, Dec 20, 21, 22,
    23, 27, 28, 29; 1737: DL, Jan 3, 14, 15, 17, Apr 11, 14, May 4; 1738: DL, May
    10, 13, Oct 10, 12, 14, Nov 27; 1740: BFLP, Aug 23; 1755: SOU, Jan 20, 27
Harlequin Restored; or, The Country Revels (pantomime), 1732: DL, Dec 14, 15,
    16, 18, 19; 1733: DL, May 24, Dec 5, 6; 1735: DL, Oct 7, 9, 11, 14, 16, 18,
    20, 21, 22, 23, 24, 25, 28, 29, 30, 31, Nov 1, 3, 7, 8, 11, 14, 17, 18, 20,
    25, 26, Dec 1, 2, 4, 8, 12, 13
Harlequin Sailor (Mariner); or, The Wapping Landlady (farce, anon), 1746: MF,
    May 5, SFY, Sep 8
Harlequin Scapin; or, The Old One Caught in a Sack (play), 1740: BFHC, Aug 23
Harlequin, Scaramouch, and a Countryman (dance), 1721: LIF, Apr 25
Harlequin, Scaramouch, Cooper and his Wife (dance), 1710: GR, Aug 17, 26
Harlequin Sclavonian; or, Monsieur in the Suds (farce, anon), 1744: MFHNT, May
    1, MF, 3
Harlequin Shepard. See Thurmond, John.
Harlequin Shipwrecked (pantomime), 1736: GF, Feb 20, 21, 23, 24, 25, 26, 27,
    28, Mar 1, 2, 3, LIF, Oct 21, 23, 26, 28, 30, Nov 2, 4, 5, 6, 9, 11, 13, 16,
    17, 18, 19, 20, 22, 23, 24, 26, 27, 29, 30, Dec 1, 2; 1737: LIF, Jan 15, 17,
    19, 20, 21; 1739: DL, Feb 10, Mar 10, 15, 19, 24, 29, 31, Apr 2, 14, 23, May
    1, 8, 10, 19, Sep 8, 11, 13, 15, 18, 20, 21, 24, Oct 6, 8, 24, 25, Nov 9, Dec
    6, 7, 8, 10; 1740: DL, Jan 5, 7, 29, 31, Feb 1, Apr 8, 12, May 1, 8, 26, Nov
    17, 18, 20, 21, 24, 25, 27; 1741: DL, Dec 4, 5, 7, 8, 9, 10, 11, 12, 16, 19,
    23, 26, 29; 1742: DL, Jan 5, 8, 12, 16, 19, 26, Feb 2, 11, 13, 15, 17, 23,
    Mar 18, 23; 1744: DL, Nov 10, 12, 13, 14, Dec 7, 8, 10, 21, 22, 28; 1745: DL,
    Jan 3, 5, 10
Harlequin Skeleton. See Phillips, Edward, The Royal Chace.
Harlequin Sorcerer. See Theobald, Lewis.
Harlequin Statue. See Yarrow, Joseph.
Harlequin Student; or, The Fall of Pantomime (pantomime, anon), 1741: GF, Feb
    25, Mar 3, 5, 9, 10, 14, 17, 21, 30, 31, Apr 1, May 6
Harlequin Teague. See O'Keeffe, John.
Harlequin the Man in the Moon (pantomime), 1741: SF, Sep 14, 15
Harlequin Tiresias (farce), 1734: HAY, Dec 4
Harlequin Triumphant (farce, anon), 1743: SF, Sep 8; 1752: SFB, Sep 22
Harlequin Turned Cook (farce), 1746: NWC, Sep 25
Harlequin Turned Dancing-Master; or, The Highlander Bit (farce), 1730: GF, Apr
    1, 16, 28, Jun 3, 25
Harlequin Turned Fortuneteller (farce), 1747: JS, Feb 3
Harlequin Turned House Breaker (pantomime), 1720: LIF, Feb 13
Harlequin Turned Into a Dog (dance), 1732: WINH, May 27
Harlequin Turned Judge (pantomime), 1717: DL, Dec 5, LIF, 11, DL, 30; 1718: DL,
    Jan 22, Mar 1, 3, 22, 24, Apr 18, Oct 4, Nov 4, 5, Dec 20; 1719: DL, Jan 1,
    24, Apr 7; 1720: DL, Jun 6; 1721: DL, Mar 28; 1723: DL, May 7, 30
Harlequin Turned Philosopher; or, The Country Squire Outwitted (farce), 1739:
    BFH, Aug 23
Harlequin Woman (dance), 1739: CG, May 21, 23
Harlequin's Chaplet. See Wild, James.
Harlequin's Contrivance; or, The Jealous Yeoman Defeated (farce), 1732: GF, Apr
    21, 25, May 10
Harlequin's Contrivance; or, The Plague of a Wanton Wife (farce), 1730: BFR,
    Aug 22, Sep 4, SFP, 9, SF, 14
Harlequin's Distress; or, The Happiness of Colombine (droll, anon), 1739: TC,
    Aug 8

Harlequin's Frolic; or, A Voyage to Prussia (pantomime), 1757: HAY, Jun 17, 20,
   23, 28, Jul 1, 5, 8, 27, 29, Aug 3, 5, 11, 13, 17, 19, 24, 26, 27, 29, 31,
   Sep 2, 5, 8, 12, 14, 16, 23, 28, Oct 3, 5, 12, 17, 21, Dec 26, 27, 28; 1758:
   HAY, Jan 6, May 18
Harlequin's Frolics (pantomime, anon), 1776: CG, Dec 26, 27, 30, 31; 1777: CG,
   Jan 1, 2, 4, 6, 7, 9, 10, 11, 14, 16, 21, 23, 24, 27, Apr 1, 3, 15, May 10,
   20
Harlequin's Frolics; or, The Power of Witchcraft (pantomime, anon), 1789: DL,
   Dec 26, 28, 29, 30, 31; 1790: DL, Jan 2, 4, 5, 7, 9, 11, 12, 14, 16, 21, 26,
   27, 29, Feb 2, 4, 8, Mar 1
Harlequin's Frolics; or, The Rambles of Covent Garden (pantomime), 1748: BFH,
   Aug 24
Harlequin's Gambols. See Sylphs, The.
Harlequin's Invasion. See Garrick, David.
Harlequin's Jacket; or, The New Year's Gift (pantomime, anon), 1775: DL, Jan 2,
   3, 4, 7, 9, 11, 12, 14, 16, 26, 27, 28, 31, Feb 7, 11, 23, Mar 6, 11, Apr 1,
   6, 28, May 10, 27, Oct 11, CG, 13, DL, 13, 14; 1782: DL, Jan 3
Harlequin's Jubilee. See Woodward, Henry.
Harlequin's Maggot (pantomime), 1757: HAY, Aug 22
Harlequin's Medley (pantomime, anon), 1797: CG, Jun 9
Harlequin's Museum; or, Mother Shipton Triumphant (pantomime, anon), 1792: CG,
   Dec 20, 21, 22, 26, 27, 28, 29, 31; 1793: CG, Jan 1, 2, 3, 4, 5, 7, 8, 9, 10,
   11, 12, 14, 15, 17, 18, 19, 21, 22, 23, 24, 25, 26, 28, Feb 2, 4, 5, 6, 8, 9,
   11, 12, 14, 16, 18, 19, 21, 23, Apr 1, 2, 3, Nov 19, 20, 27, Dec 2; 1798: CG,
   Jun 2; 1799: CG, May 13
Harlequin's Return. See Cross, John Cartwright.
Harlequin's Treasure; or, Jewels New Set (pantomime, anon), 1796: CG, Mar 15,
   17, 19, 28, 29, 31, Apr 2, 4, 6, 7, 11, 18, May 2, 9, 19, 23, Jun 7, Oct 24,
   27, 31, Nov 1
Harlequin's Triumph. See Thurmond, John.
Harlequin's Vagaries (pantomime), 1757: SF, Sep 17, 19, 20, 21, 22
Harlequin's Whim; or, A True Touch of the Times (farce), 1745: MF, May 7
Harlequiness (dance), 1716: LIF, Oct 19
Harley (actor), 1796: HAY, Feb 22; 1797: HAY, May 10; 1798: HAY, Mar 26
Harley, Abigail, 1718: DL, Apr 22
Harley Jr, Edward (correspondent), 1718: DL, Apr 22
Harley, Sir Edward, 1677: DG, Nov 17
Harley, George Davies (actor, author), 1789: CG, Sep 25, Oct 16, Nov 6, 10, 20,
   23, Dec 5, 14; 1790: CG, Jan 4, 29, Mar 22, Apr 14, May 3, 5, 24, Oct 11, 18,
   Nov 1, 4, 8, 23, Dec 20, 31; 1791: CG, Jan 12, 27, Feb 11, Apr 5, 16, May 10,
   Jun 1, 6, Sep 19, 23, Oct 3, 17, 24, 28, Nov 4, Dec 3; 1792: CG, Jan 6, Feb
   18, Mar 26, Apr 10, 21, 28, May 11, 18, 19, Sep 17, 24, Oct 1, Nov 5, 21, 24,
   Dec 1, 20, 26, 27; 1793: CG, Jan 21, Mar 4, Apr 4, 8, DL, 23, CG, May 23, 24,
   27, 30, Sep 23, 25, Oct 3, 4, 5, 9, 10, 14, Nov 13, 18, Dec 19, 30; 1794: CG,
   Jan 6, 13, Feb 1, Mar 6, May 6, 14, 19, 21, 26, 30, Jun 5, Sep 15, 17, 29,
   Oct 7, 15, 21, 30, Nov 22; 1795: CG, Jan 6, 8, 19, 24, 31, Feb 4, 21, Mar 16,
   28, Apr 24, May 2, 7, 13, 14, 18, 27, 29, Jun 3, 10, Sep 14, 23, 25, 28, Oct
   2, 8, 14, 16, 19, 22, 23, Nov 4, 7, 27, Dec 7, 9, 21, 22, 23, 26; 1796: CG,
   Jan 6, 8, 13, Mar 19, May 12, 27
Harley, Lady, 1673: NONE, Apr 21
Harley, Mrs (actor), 1781: HAY, Jan 22, Mar 26
Harlot's Progress, The. See Cibber, Theophilus.
Harlot's Progress, The; With the Comical Humours of the Yorkshire Waggoner
   (play), 1733: BFYY, Aug 23, SFYY, Sep 10
Harlowe, Master (actor), 1792: DLKING'S, Jan 21, DL, Dec 17; 1794: DL, Apr 21
Harlowe, Sarah (actor), 1786: HAMM, Jul 19, 24, 26, HAY, Dec 18; 1787: HAY, Jan
   8; 1790: CG, Nov 4, 23, 26, 30, Dec 2, 17, 20; 1791: CG, Feb 16, Mar 12, 14,
   May 10, 11, 24, Sep 14, 17, 26, Oct 10, 20, Dec 8; 1792: CG, Jan 6, Feb 6, 8,
   9, 11, 13, 18, Mar 6, 26, 31, Apr 10, 12, May 11, 15, 19, 23, 28, 30, Sep 17,
   19, 20, 21, 24, 26, Oct 3, 8, 10, 12, 17, 19, 26, 29, Nov 3, Dec 31; 1793:
   CG, Jan 23, Feb 25, Mar 18, Apr 4, 8, May 1, 8, 21, 23, Jun 10; 1794: HAY,
   Jan 14, Feb 11, 22, 24, Jul 14, 17, 18, 21, 23, 24, Aug 1, 4, 9, 11, 13, 18,
   27, 29, 30, Sep 3, 5, 6, 10, 17; 1795: HAY, Jun 9, 13, 20, 22, 25, 27, Jul 6,
   22, 25, 31, Aug 11, 18, 21, 25, Sep 21; 1796: HAY, Jun 11, 13, 14, 17, 22,
   25, 30, Jul 2, 5, 11, 15, 23, 26, 28, 30, Aug 11, 30, Sep 2, 12, 16; 1797:
   HAY, Jun 12, 13, 15, 16, 19, 21, 22, 23, Jul 3, 4, 10, 13, 15, Aug 8, 9, 14,
   15, 22, 28, Sep 4, 8, 16, 18; 1798: HAY, Jun 12, 14, 15, 16, 18, 20, 23, 27,
   30, Jul 14, 16, 17, 20, 25, 30, Aug 11, 29, Sep 3, 14, 17; 1799: HAY, Jun 15,
   17, 18, 19, 22, 27, 28, Jul 2, 6, 9, 17, 23, 26, 27, Aug 27; see also
   Waldron, Mrs
Harman (actor), 1756: BFSI, Sep 3
Harman (house servant), 1800: DL, Jun 14

Harman (prologuist), 1698: LIF, May 0
Harman, Mrs (actor), 1756: BFSI, Sep 3, SFB, 20
Harmonic Festival, An (interlude, anon), 1790: CG, May 24; 1797: CG, May 24
Harmonic Jubilee, An (interlude, anon), 1786: CG, May 22; 1798: HAY, Aug 14
Harmonic Pasticcio, An (interlude, anon), 1796: HAY, Aug 23
Harmonical Meeting, 1771: HAY, Apr 17, May 2
Harmony Harmony (song), 1796: DL, May 25
Harold, Mrs (actor), 1725: LIF, Dec 15
Haron (musician), 1758: CHAPEL, Apr 27
Harp (music), 1712: MA, May 21; 1714: SH, May 27; 1718: YB, Mar 5, TGB, 7;
    1724: LIF, Mar 16; 1725: HIC, May 31; 1741: HIC, Feb 19, Mar 13; 1751: DL,
    May 4; 1753: DL, Mar 27, 29, CG, Apr 28; 1755: DL, Apr 2, May 8; 1758: DL,
    Mar 29; 1759: HAY, Oct 1; 1760: DL, Apr 22, CG, May 6, 7, DL, 14; 1763: CG,
    Apr 11, 13, May 2; 1774: KING'S, Feb 24; 1782: CG, Apr 27; 1785: KING'S, Mar
    12; 1789: DL, Mar 6, KING'S, Apr 2, Jun 15; 1791: CG, Mar 18, 30, KING'S, Jun
    6, DLKING'S, Nov 19, 22, CG, Dec 2; 1792: KING'S, Mar 23; 1793: DL, May 23,
    CG, Jun 6; 1794: CG, Feb 6, DL, Apr 9, CG, May 2, Nov 3; 1795: CG, Mar 5, DL,
    May 4, CG, Oct 12, Dec 30; 1796: CG, Mar 14, May 18, DL, Jun 9, CG, Oct 31;
    1797: CG, May 24; 1798: CG, Feb 14, May 25, 28; 1800: CG, Mar 4, 31, May 17
Harp and Lute Imitation (music), 1714: QUEEN'S, May 1
Harp and Piano Forte Duet (music), 1800: CG, Mar 7, KING'S, May 29
Harp Concerto (music), 1739: CG, Apr 26; 1741: HIC, Feb 27, Mar 5; 1796: CG,
    Feb 12, 17, 24, Mar 2, 11, 16
Harp Concerto, Grand (music), 1789: DL, Mar 11
Harp Lesson (music), 1760: CG, May 1
Harp Organisee Lesson (entertainment), 1719: LIF, Jan 22
Harp Serenata (music), 1789: DL, Mar 6, 11
Harp Solo (music), 1718: LR, Dec 3; 1740: CG, Apr 9
Harp Sonata (music), 1734: HAY, Apr 3
Harp Voluntary (music), 1737: CT, Apr 29
Harpe (dancer), 1675: ATCOURT, Feb 15
Harper (actor), 1755: BF, Sep 6
Harper (actor), 1787: RLSN, Mar 28; 1790: HAY, Sep 29
Harper (taverner), 1759: CG, May 8
Harper, Elizabeth (actor), 1778: HAY, May 22, Jun 8, 10, 24, Jul 9, 21, Aug 3,
    17, 25, Sep 10; 1779: HAY, Jun 7, 12, 18, Jul 1, 30, Aug 14, 17, 25, 27, Sep
    15; 1780: HAY, Jun 3, 5, 13, 15, 24, 28, Jul 8, Aug 17, 21, 29, 31, Sep 5;
    1781: HAY, Jun 1, 9, 12, 16, 26, Jul 9, 18, Aug 7, 15, 17, 22, 28, Sep 3, 4,
    5, CG, 21, 24, 26, Oct 13, 16, 23, 27, Nov 7, 12, 24, 28, Dec 5, 22; 1782:
    CG, Feb 2, 21, Mar 23, Apr 9, HAY, Jun 4, 10, 13, 17, 20, 22, Jul 13, 30, Aug
    9, 15, 23, 24, 27, 30, Sep 20, CG, 25, 30, Oct 7, 9, 22, 23, Nov 2, Dec 14,
    27; 1783: CG, Jan 23, 29, Feb 11, 18, 25, DL, Mar 14, CG, Apr 28, May 12, 24
Harper, John (actor, singer), 1719: B-L, Sep 5, BCA, 24, LIF, Oct 13, 15, Nov
    5, 7, 17, 18, 19, 23, 26, Dec 28; 1720: LIF, Jan 11, 26, Feb 23, Mar 15, May
    3, 5, 10, 11, 12, 23, 24, BCA, Sep 23, SOU, Oct 10, LIF, 11, 18, 22, Nov 10,
    18, 26; 1721: LIF, Feb 16, 21, Apr 1, 29, May 4, 18, 29, 30, HAY, Jul 14, DL,
    28, Aug 18, BFLGB, 24, SF, Sep 8, DL, Oct 25; 1722: DL, Jan 16, Apr 14, 16,
    May 3, Jul 6, RI, 23, Aug 20, BFLSH, 25, DL, Oct 2, 19, 20, 22, Dec 4; 1723:
    DL, Jan 7, Apr 19, May 11, 20, 30, HA, Jul 22, DL, 23, 26, 30, Aug 6, 9, 12,
    16, Sep 24, Oct 1, 8, 10, 18, 24, Nov 12, Dec 30; 1724: DL, Apr 28, May 16,
    22, RI, Jun 22, 27, 29, Jul 4, 11, 13, 18, Aug 3, BFL, 22, DL, Sep 17, 19,
    Oct 19, 24, Nov 2, 6, 7, 21; 1725: DL, Jan 20, 27, Feb 20, 22, Apr 21, May
    11, 19, 21, Sep 7, 18, 21, 25, Oct 12, 14, 15, 23, 25, 28, Nov 2, 3, 27, 29,
    Dec 9, 13; 1726: DL, Jan 12, 26, Feb 11, Mar 17, Apr 22, May 11, 23, Jun 3,
    Sep 10, 15, 17, 20, 22, Oct 1, 13, 18, 20, 22, 27, Dec 12, 14, 17, 30; 1727:
    DL, Jan 20, 27, Feb 8, 21, 27, Apr 19, 24, May 1, 5, 15, 22, BF, Aug 22, DL,
    Sep 9, 19, 28, Oct 3, 6, 7, 17, 19, 20, Nov 1, 9, 18, 21, Dec 4, 13; 1728:
    DL, Jan 2, Feb 16, Mar 9, 30, Apr 29, May 1, 10, 14, 17, 20, 22, 29, Sep 10,
    26, 28, Oct 10, 23, 24, 28, 30, 31, Nov 7, 8, 12, 14; 1729: DL, Jan 2, 7, 13,
    21, 22, Feb 3, 6, 15, 24, 25, Apr 11, 16, 23, May 3, 7, 12, 14, 28, BFLH, Aug
    23, SF, Sep 15, DL, 23, 25, 30, Oct 9, 14, 16, 21, 23, 30, Nov 3, 6, 7, 14,
    18, 22, 24, 27, 28, Dec 1, 3, 5, 8, 10, 13, 26; 1730: DL, Jan 3, 9, Feb 10,
    Mar 30, Apr 22, 24, May 11, 13, BFLH, Aug 24, 31, SFLH, Sep 8, SFG, 8, DL,
    17, 19, 22, 29, Oct 1, 6, 8, 10, 20, Nov 18, 25, 26, 30, Dec 2, 4; 1731: DL,
    Jan 20, Feb 8, Mar 8, 15, 16, 20, 29, Apr 1, 8, 21, 26, May 3, 12, 19, 31,
    Jun 7, 11, Jul 20, 23, Aug 6, 16, BFLH, 24, SFLH, Sep 8, DL, 25, 30, Oct 2,
    7, 14, 16, 19, 21, 30, Nov 6, 8, 10, 24, Dec 2, 3, 17, 22, 29; 1732: DL, Jan
    1, 10, 14, Feb 1, 11, 14, Mar 11, 23, Apr 1, 12, 17, 25, 27, 28, May 1, 3, 4,
    12, Sep 26, 28, Oct 3, 10, 12, 14, 17, 19, 21, Nov 9, 13, 14, 18, 21, Dec 6,
    9, 11, 22; 1733: DL, Jan 2, 16, 19, 26, 29, Mar 28, May 3, 14, 21, 29, Jun 4,
    TC, Jul 30, SF/BFLH, Aug 23, DL/HAY, Sep 26, Oct 8, 10, 12, 15, 22, 25, Nov
    1, 9, 12, 16, HAY, 19, 20, DL/HAY, 21, 28, Dec 5, 12, 17, 20, HAY, 26; 1734:

DL/HAY, Jan 10, 21, HAY, Feb 12, DL/HAY, Mar 12, 16, 25, 26, Apr 17, 18, 20,
DL, May 15, LIF, 29, RI, Sep 2, DL, 7, 12, 14, 19, 28, Oct 14, 19, 22, 23,
26, 29, Nov 1, 2, 8, 16, 18, 22, Dec 6, 14; 1735: DL, Jan 3, 6, 20, 22, 23,
28, Feb 10, 14, 25, Mar 3, 6, 20, Apr 7, 11, 21, 23, May 6, 14, 29, Jun 9,
Sep 1, 4, 6, 9, 15, 18, Oct 4, 9, 21, 23, 25, 30, 31, Nov 3, 10, 12, 21, 22;
1736: DL, Jan 3, Feb 5, Apr 6, 12, LIF, 14, DL, Sep 9, 16, 21, 23, Oct 16,
18, 20, 22, 29, Nov 1, 8, 12, 15, 19, 20, 23, Dec 7, 31; 1737: DL, Jan 6, Feb
5, 10, 28, Mar 1, 10, Apr 11, 12, 13, 15, 27, Aug 30, Sep 1, 3, 8, 27, 29,
Oct 1, 8, 11, 21, 24, 25, 27, Nov 1, 11, 15, 16; 1738: DL, Jan 5, 14, 19, 24,
25, 26, 31, Mar 2, 20, 21, Apr 14, 17, 26, 27, 28, May 3, 8, 13, 17, Sep 7,
9, 14, 16, 21, 28, 30, Oct 18, 20, 21; 1739: DL, Apr 5; 1740: DL, Apr 28;
1741: DL, Apr 24; 1742: DL, May 1
Harper, Master (actor), 1737: DL, Nov 19; 1738: DL, Dec 4
Harper, Miss (singer), 1771: MARLY, Jun 4, 6, 11, 13, 18, 20, 25, 27, Jul 2, 4,
9, 11, 13, 16, 18, 20, 23, 30, Aug 13, 15, 17, 22, 24, Sep 3, 5, 17; 1773:
HAY, Feb 26
Harper, Mrs (actor), 1755: BF, Sep 6
Harper, Mrs John (beneficiary), 1742: DL, May 1, 11
Harpsichord (music), 1701: RIW, Aug 11; 1710: YB, May 1; 1713: HIC, Mar 25,
QUEEN'S, May 16; 1717: SH, Mar 27; 1718: LIF, May 1, LR, Dec 3; 1719: HIC,
Feb 18, LIF, Apr 3; 1720: SH, Mar 9; 1721: GG, Mar 22, LIF, 29; 1722: HIC,
Mar 16; 1723: SH, Mar 6; 1724: LIF, Mar 19, Apr 25; 1728: YB, Mar 13, HAY,
Apr 3; 1729: HAY, Jan 28, DL, Jul 29, Aug 9; 1730: GF, Jun 30; 1731: LIF, May
24; 1732: LIF, Feb 25; 1733: HAY, Mar 29; 1737: HIC, Apr 7; 1738: HAY, Mar 3;
1749: HAY, Apr 10; 1758: DL, Mar 18, SOHO, Apr 1; 1768: DL, Apr 27; 1791:
KING'S, Apr 9
Harpsichord and Hautboy Concerto (music), 1760: HAY, Feb 15
Harpsichord and Organ (music), 1764: CG, Jun 5
Harpsichord and Violin Sonata (music), 1731: LIF, May 24; 1733: HAY, May 26
Harpsichord and Violoncello Concerto (music), 1736: HIC, Jan 21
Harpsichord Concerto (music), 1739: DL, Jan 17; 1741: HAY, Feb 26, GF, Apr 29;
1752: CG, Apr 17; 1755: SOHO, Mar 11; 1757: DL, Jan 21; 1759: HAM, Aug 13;
1765: HAY, Mar 11; 1766: DL, Dec 3, 4; 1767: DL, Jan 1, Apr 25, May 23, Jun
3; 1768: DL, Apr 9; 1769: DL, Apr 1; 1770: HAY, Sep 20; 1771: CG, May 1, 23;
1772: HAY, Apr 27; 1773: CG, May 25
Harpsichord Lesson (music), 1716: LIF, Apr 26; 1717: LIF, May 7; 1720: LIF, Mar
12; 1721: LIF, Mar 18, May 2; 1724: LIF, Apr 28, 30; 1726: LIF, May 11; 1730:
GF, May 12, 13, 22; 1731: LIF, Apr 2, HIC, 9, DT, 23, LIF, May 24; 1732: GF,
Apr 27, HAY, Jun 1; 1733: LIF/CG, May 18; 1734: HIC, Apr 8, CG, May 14; 1737:
HIC, Mar 24; 1741: HIC, Feb 5; 1768: HAY, Mar 3
Harpsichord Solo (music), 1711: HDS, Apr 24; 1714: HIC, Apr 28, 29; 1717: SH,
May 10; 1729: HIC, Apr 16; 1734: HIC, Mar 20
Harpsichord Sonata (music), 1784: KING'S, Mar 4
Harpsichord Voluntary (music), 1729: DL, Jul 29
Harpsichord, Bass Viol and Violin (music), 1722: LIF, Feb 27
Harrache (jeweller), 1755: DL, Dec 16; 1759: DL, Apr 30
Harrache (toy maker), 1744: DL, Mar 5
Harricks, William, 1778: HAY, Jan 26; 1779: HAY, Mar 15; 1783: HAY, Dec 15
--Mirror for the Ladies, A (interlude), 1779: HAY, Mar 15
Harriett, Captain (actor), 1784: DL, Aug 20
Harrington (actor), 1733: CG, May 1, 16, DL/HAY, Oct 8, 10, Dec 17, 19, 20;
1734: DL/HAY, Jan 12, Mar 16, CG, 28, May 3, 13; 1736: LIF, Oct 9; 1739: CG,
Oct 22; 1740: CG, Jan 15, Feb 2, Mar 11, Apr 25, May 2, 3, 21, Sep 22, Oct
24, Nov 6; 1741: CG, Jan 2, Mar 2, 19, Apr 17, May 11, 15, BFTY, Aug 22, CG,
Sep 23, 25, Oct 13, 20, 21, Nov 11, 30, Dec 9; 1742: CG, Jan 2, 14, 23, Feb
9, 25, Mar 13, 27, Apr 10, May 5, 7, 10, 14, Oct 1, 9, 13, 25, 26, 27, Nov 4,
13, Dec 7; 1743: CG, Apr 19, May 4, Sep 21
Harrington (actor), 1780: HAY, Jan 3
Harrington (boxkeeper), 1744: CG, Apr 28; 1745: CG, May 6; 1747: CG, May 12
Harrington, Hurlo (prompter), 1749: DL, Sep 23
Harrington, J (actor), 1734: GR, Nov 4
Harrington, John (musician), 1795: KING'S, May 14; 1798: HAY, Jan 15
Harrington, John (prompter), 1748: CG, Apr 26; 1749: DL, Sep 23
Harrington, Miss (actor), 1733: LIF/CG, Apr 18
Harrington, R (actor), 1734: GR, Nov 4
Harriott, Sir (spectator), 1760: CG, Feb 16
Harris (actor), 1715: DL, Aug 9
Harris (actor), 1729: HAY, Dec 18; 1730: HAY, Mar 30, Apr 6, 20; 1735: TC, May
28; 1746: SFW, Sep 8; 1749: BFHG, Aug 23
Harris (actor), 1773: CG, Oct 16, 28; 1774: CG, Jan 3, Mar 15, Apr 13, Sep 23,
Oct 19, 20, Nov 19; 1775: CG, Jun 1, Oct 17; 1776: CG, Apr 13
Harris (actor), 1784: HAY, Mar 8; 1789: WHF, Nov 9; 1790: DL, Dec 27; 1791: DL,

Feb 7, CG, Mar 11
Harris (hosier), 1753: DL, Mar 26
Harris (house servant), 1790: DL, Jun 2; 1791: CG, Jun 14
Harris Jr (actor), 1730: HAY, Mar 30
Harris-Godwin Booth, 1749: BFHG, Aug 23
Harris, Henry (actor), 1661: LIF, Jun 28, Aug 15, 24, Sep 11, LIF/MT, Oct 21,
    LIF, Dec 16; 1662: LIF, Mar 1, Sep 30, Oct 18, ATCOURT, 27; 1663: LIF, Jan 6,
    8, Feb 23, Jul 22, Oct 24, Dec 10, 22; 1664: LIF, Mar 0, NONE, Apr 27, LIF,
    Jul 20, Aug 13, Sep 10, Nov 5, Dec 2; 1665: LIF, Apr 3; 1667: BRIDGES, Jan
    24, LIF, Feb 0, 27, Mar 7, Aug 15, Sep 4, Nov 7, BRIDGES, Dec 11; 1668: LIF,
    Jan 6, Feb 6, Mar 26, Apr 29, May 2, 11, ATCOURT, 29, LIF, Jul 6, Aug 29,
    BRIDGES, Nov 6; 1669: LIF, Feb 25, Apr 16, May 12, BRIDGES, Jun 24; 1670:
    LIF, Apr 0, NONE, Sep 0, LIF, Nov 0, BRI/COUR, Dec 0; 1671: LIF, Jan 10, Mar
    6, Jun 0, DG, Nov 0, 9; 1672: DG, Jan 31, Jul 4, Aug 3, Nov 4, ATCOU/DG, Dec
    2; 1673: DG, Feb 18, LIF, Mar 0, DG, May 0, Jul 3, Aug 9, 20; 1675: ATCOURT,
    Feb 15, DL, Apr 30, DG, May 28, Sep 0; 1676: DG, Jan 10, Mar 0, 11, Jun 8,
    Jul 3, 25, Aug 0; 1677: DG, Feb 12, May 12, 31, Sep 0; 1678: DG, Jan 0, Apr
    5, May 28, Sep 0, Nov 0; 1679: DG, Apr 0, Sep 0, Dec 0; 1681: DG, Apr 0
Harris, James (author)
--Spring, The, 1762: DL, Oct 20, 22, 23, 25, 26, 29, Nov 19, 22
Harris, James, 1749: CG, Feb 10
Harris, Joseph (actor, author), 1670: BRIDGES, Aug 0; 1673: LIF, Dec 0; 1674:
    DL, May 16; 1675: DL, Jan 25, May 10, Aug 0; 1676: DL, Jan 29; 1685: DLORDG,
    Jan 20, DL, Aug 0; 1686: DL, Jan 0, Apr 0; 1687: ATCOURT, Apr 25; 1689: DL,
    Nov 7, 20; 1691: DL, Mar 0, DG, May 0, DL, Dec 0; 1692: DL, Feb 0, Mar 0;
    1694: DL, Feb 0, DG, May 0; 1696: LIF, Jun 0, Dec 0; 1697: LIF, Jun 0; 1699:
    LIF, May 0; 1700: LIF, Jan 9; 1701: LIF, Jan 0, Mar 0; 1705: DL, Jun 12;
    1709: QUEEN'S, Dec 12
--City Bride, The; or, The Merry Cuckold, 1696: LIF, Mar 0
--Love's a Lottery, and a Woman the Prize, 1699: LIF, Mar 0
Harris, Miss (actor), 1779: HAY, Mar 15, May 10; 1781: HAY, Mar 26
Harris, Mrs (actor), 1696: DL, Feb 0; 1697: NONE, Sep 0
Harris, Mrs (actor), 1736: HAY, Feb 19
Harris, Mrs (actor), 1775: HAY, Feb 2
Harris, Mrs (actor), 1794: DL, May 16, 30, Dec 20, 23; 1795: DL, Feb 12
Harris, Mrs (dancer), 1790: DL, Oct 26; 1791: DLKING'S, Nov 5; 1792: DLKING'S,
    Mar 19, DL, Nov 21, Dec 27
Harris, Mrs (house servant), 1786: CG, Jun 2; 1788: CG, May 24; 1790: CG, Jun
    12; 1792: CG, May 12
Harris, Peter (dancer, choreographer), 1767: CG, May 1, 6, 13; 1768: CG, Mar
    17, Apr 11, Jun 3, Sep 22, Oct 4, Dec 22; 1769: CG, Apr 22, 26, May 25, Oct
    4; 1770: CG, May 17, Sep 26, Nov 23; 1771: CG, May 11, 28, Oct 15, 30; 1772:
    CG, May 1, 22, Sep 28, Oct 17, Nov 4, 17, Dec 15; 1773: CG, Apr 26, 27, Dec
    8; 1774: CG, Feb 17, Apr 16, May 13; 1775: CG, May 3, Sep 27, Nov 18, Dec 7;
    1776: CG, May 3, 15, Oct 9, 31, Nov 12; 1777: CG, Jan 21, Feb 15, May 20, Sep
    24, Oct 1, 3, Nov 3, 4; 1778: CG, Apr 20, May 16, HAY, Sep 10, CG, 21, Oct
    23, Nov 10, 25; 1779: CG, May 3, 8, Oct 8, 13, 22, Nov 9; 1780: CG, Apr 17,
    May 8, 16, Sep 25, Oct 3, Nov 6, Dec 5; 1781: CG, Feb 13, May 18, Sep 26, Oct
    20, Nov 1, Dec 19; 1782: CG, Apr 1, 2, 17, May 3, 25, Sep 25, Oct 7, 8, Nov
    29, Dec 6, 11, 20, 31; 1783: CG, Feb 21, Apr 25, 28, May 17, 24, 26, Sep 17,
    22, Oct 1, Nov 19; 1784: CG, Feb 13, Mar 6, Apr 27, 28, May 21, Jun 10, Sep
    17, 22, Oct 6, 8, 27, Dec 1; 1785: CG, Jan 14, Apr 9, 18, May 18; 1787: CG,
    May 31; 1789: CG, Jun 4
Harris, T (actor), 1696: LIF, Nov 14
Harris, Thomas (proprietor), 1767: CG, Jun 9; 1768: CG, Mar 1, Oct 24; 1773:
    CG, Mar 6; 1774: CG, Apr 9; 1777: CG, Jan 10; 1780: CG, May 29; 1781: CG, May
    28; 1782: HAY, Aug 22, CG, Oct 3; 1783: CG, Jun 6; 1784: CG, Jun 2; 1788: CG,
    Jan 14; 1791: CG, Feb 4, DL, Jun 4; 1794: HAY, Aug 23, 28; 1795: CG, Dec 21;
    1796: CG, Jan 23; 1797: CG, Jan 10, HAY, Sep 1; 1798: CG, Feb 14; 1799: CG,
    Jun 10
Harris, William (actor), 1668: NONE, Sep 0
Harrison (actor), 1785: HAMM, Jul 15, 22, 26
Harrison (actor, dancer), 1724: SF, Sep 2; 1725: LIF, Jan 21, Nov 13; 1726:
    LIF, Jul 5, 29, Sep 23; 1727: LIF, Sep 29; 1728: LIF, Oct 14; 1729: LIF, Oct
    3, Nov 1, 11; 1730: LIF, Jan 2, Oct 9, Dec 15; 1733: HAY, Apr 18
Harrison (beneficiary), 1726: DL, May 10
Harrison (beneficiary), 1776: CHR, Oct 4
Harrison (composer), 1711: YB, May 24, Jul 16
Harrison (pit office keeper), 1721: LIF, May 23; 1722: LIF, May 10; 1723: LIF,
    May 27; 1725: LIF, May 10; 1726: LIF, May 23
Harrison (tenant), 1772: DL, Jun 10; 1773: DL, Jun 2; 1774: DL, Jun 2; 1775:
    DL, May 27; 1776: DL, Jun 10

Harrison and Co (printers), 1784: HAY, Mar 17, Jun 19; 1785: DL, Dec 8; 1787: HAY, May 16; 1788: HAY, Aug 18, 22
Harrison, Elizabeth (author), 1724: DL, Jan 21
Harrison, J (dancer), 1748: DL, Feb 9, CG, Apr 18, BFLYY, AUG 24, BFH, 24, SFLYYW, Sep 7, BHB, Oct 1, DL, 27; 1749: DL, Feb 21, CG, Apr 24, DL, May 9, Oct 24, Nov 9, Dec 2, 28; 1750: DL, May 2, Nov 13; 1751: DL, May 6, Dec 26; 1752: DL, Jan 28, Apr 25, 27; 1753: DL, May 11; 1754: DL, Apr 26, May 16; 1755: DL, Apr 25, May 6, Oct 8, Nov 8; 1756: DL, Apr 29, May 10, 18, SFB, Sep 20; 1757: DL, May 2; 1758: DL, May 8; 1759: DL, May 21; 1760: DL, May 8
Harrison, J, scholars of (dancers), 1759: DL, May 21; 1760: DL, May 8
Harrison, Miss (actor), 1746: GF, Feb 24
Harrison, Miss (actor), 1763: HAY, Jul 6; 1767: CG, Jan 31; 1776: HAY, Sep 20; 1781: HAY, Jan 22
Harrison, Mrs (beneficiary), 1733: CG, May 16
Harrison, Mrs Samuel (singer), 1793: KING/HAY, Feb 15, 20, 22, 27, Mar 6, 13, 15, 20
Harrison, Samuel (singer, composer), 1776: CG, May 11; 1777: HAY, May 15, Jul 18; 1778: CG, Apr 1; 1789: CG, Feb 27, Mar 6, 20, 27, Apr 3; 1790: CG, Feb 19, 24, 26, Mar 3, 10, 17, 19, 26; 1791: CG, Mar 11, 18, 23, 25, 30, Apr 6, 13, 15; 1792: CG, Feb 24, Mar 2, 7, 9, 14, 16, 21, 23; 1793: KING/HAY, Feb 15, 20, 22, 27, Mar 6, 13, 15, 20, 22; 1794: DL, Mar 12, 19, 21, Apr 2, 4, 9, 11, KING'S, May 15, CG, 23, 26; 1795: KING'S, Feb 20, 27, Mar 13; 1796: DL, Apr 30
Harrison, Samuel and Mrs (singers), 1793: KING/HAY, Mar 6
Harrogate Theatre, 1789: CG, Jan 10
Harrolt (actor), 1740: BFLP, Aug 23
Harrop, Sarah (singer), 1777: CG, Feb 14, Mar 19
Harry the Smuggler, 1749: HAY, Apr 8
Hart (actor), 1744: HAY, Apr 6; 1747: GF, Jan 5
Hart (haberdasher), 1772: DL, Jan 7
Hart (numberer), 1775: DL, Mar 20
Hart (singer), 1674: DG, Apr 30, May 16; 1675: ATCOURT: Feb 15
Hart (singer), 1792: CG, Feb 28
Hart and Feather Tavern, 1746: CG, Feb 18
Hart St, 1705: TGB, Mar 2; 1721: GB, Mar 15; 1732: GF, Oct 11; 1743: JS, Mar 31; 1754: DL, Nov 22, HAY, Dec 16; 1760: CG, Sep 22; 1768: CG, Jun 4; 1782: CG, Sep 23; 1787: DL, May 4; 1789: CG, Jun 27; 1792: CG, Mar 5, Sep 17; 1793: CG, Feb 15, Sep 16; 1794: CG, Mar 7, Sep 15; 1795: CG, Feb 20, Sep 14; 1796: CG, Feb 12, Sep 12; 1797: CG, Mar 3, DL, May 17, Jun 12, HAY, Aug 10, CG, Sep 18, Dec 6; 1798: CG, Feb 9, 23, Sep 17; 1799: CG, Sep 16
Hart, Charles (actor), 1659: NONE, Sep 0; 1660: NONE, Sep 0, COCKPIT, Oct 8, REDBULL, Nov 5, VERE, 17, Dec 3, 6; 1661: NONE, Sep 0; 1662: VERE, Jan 28, Jul 23; 1663: VERE, Mar 0, BRIDGES, May 7, NONE, Sep 0; 1664: NONE, Sep 0; 1665: BRIDGES, Jan 14, Apr 0; 1666: NONE, Sep 0, BRIDGES, Dec 7, ATCOURT, 10, BRIDGES, 27; 1667: BRI/COUR, Feb 0, BRIDGES, 5, Apr 17, May 1, Aug 26, Sep 20, Oct 19, Nov 2, 16, Dec 7, 28; 1668: BRIDGES, Apr 7, Jun 12, Sep 14, Nov 6, Dec 18; 1669: BRIDGES, Feb 6, May 6, Jun 24; 1670: BRI/COUR, Dec 0; 1671: BRIDGES, Mar 0; 1672: BRIDGES, Jan 0, LIF, Mar 0, Apr 0, DG, Jul 4, NONE, Sep 0, LIF, Nov 0; 1673: LIF, May 0, NONE, Jul 0; 1674: DL, May 16, OXFORD, Jul 0; 1675: DL, Jan 12, 25, Apr 23, 30, NONE, Sep 0, DL, Nov 17; 1676: DL, Jan 29, ATCOURT, May 29, DL, Sep 9, Dec 11; 1677: DL, Jan 12, Mar 17, Dec 12; 1678: DL, Feb 0, Mar 0; 1680: DL, Sep 0; 1682: NONE, Sep 0, DL, Nov 16; 1685: DL, May 9, Dec 19; 1698: DL, Feb 0
Hart, James (composer), 1671: DG, Nov 0; 1674: DG, Apr 30; 1675: NONE, Sep 0; 1677: NONE, Sep 0
Hart, Miss (actor), 1760: DL, Oct 22; 1761: DL, May 11
Hart, Mrs (actor), 1744: HAY, Apr 6; 1746: GF, Dec 29
Hart, Philip (composer), 1703: SH, Mar 3
Hart, Richard (actor), 1671: BRIDGES, Jun 0
Hartford Bridge. See Pearce, William.
Hartle, Mrs (dancer), 1769: CG, May 19, 25; 1770: CG, May 18; 1771: CG, May 22; 1772: CG, May 1, 29; 1773: CG, May 26, 28; 1774: CG, May 18, 20, DL, Oct 29; 1775: DL, May 8, 25
Hartley, Elizabeth (actor), 1772: CG, Oct 5, Nov 6, 21, Dec 3; 1773: CG, Feb 23, Mar 1, 6, 20, 22, 30, Apr 3, 15, 28, May 1, 4, 7, 17, Sep 22, Oct 11, 21, 23, 25, Dec 4, 11, 14, 21; 1774: CG, Feb 9, 11, Mar 12, 14, 15, 22, Apr 13, 19, May 11, Oct 3, 4, 15, Nov 5, Dec 9, 17, 26; 1775: CG, Jan 7, DL, Feb 10, CG, Mar 2, 13, DL, 30, CG, May 17, Oct 17, 21, 30, Nov 13; 1776: CG, May 6, 10, Oct 2, Nov 4, 14, 25, Dec 2, 6, 18, 26; 1777: CG, Feb 1, 13, 22, Mar 17, Apr 12, 28, May 5, 13, 14, Sep 24, Oct 6, 8, 10, 30, Nov 1, 7, Dec 3; 1778: CG, Jan 3, 19, Feb 2, Apr 6, Dec 8, 26; 1779: CG, Jan 18, 22, Feb 2, 23, Mar 11, Apr 24, May 6, 10, 20, Sep 27, Oct 11, 18, 23, 29, DL, Nov 20, CG, 30,

Dec 6, 9, 16, 27; 1780: CG, Jan 3, 17, Feb 1, 22, Mar 4, Apr 7, 10, 12, May 29
Hartry, John (actor), 1760: HAY, Sep 9, 11; 1761: CG, May 5, Jun 23; 1766: DL, Oct 31, Nov 18; 1767: DL, Jan 24, Apr 21, May 1, 19, Sep 26, Oct 20, 22, 23, Nov 7, 18, Dec 16, 26; 1768: DL, Jan 9, Feb 29, Mar 19, Apr 9, 14, May 6, CG, 13, DL, 27, Sep 17, 20, 26, 28, Oct 10, 13, 20, 28, 31, Nov 8, Dec 16; 1769: DL, Jan 20, 25, Mar 28, Apr 3, 10, 18, CG, 28, DL, May 3, Sep 19, 21, Oct 4, 7, 13, 14, 21, Nov 14, 22, Dec 6, 16, 23; 1770: DL, Jan 3, 16, 19, Feb 2, Mar 22, 31, Apr 3, May 11, 14, 15, 16, 17, 19, Jun 7, Sep 29, Oct 3, 9, 13, 31, Nov 3, 13, 15, 16, 17, 23, Dec 6, 22, 31; 1771: DL, Jan 2, Mar 7, 23, Apr 2, 5, 17, 19, 23, 30, May 14, 27, 29, Sep 26, 28, Oct 1, 8, 17, 22, Nov 8, 9, 14, 18, 23, 25, Dec 3, 26; 1772: DL, Jan 15, Feb 17, 27, 29, Apr 4, 20, 25, May 4, 12, 22, Sep 29, Nov 3, 17, 20, Dec 7; 1773: DL, Jan 1, Feb 17, 18, Apr 1, May 13, 15, Sep 28, Oct 2, 11, 14, Dec 16; 1774: DL, Jan 10, 19, 26, Feb 5, Mar 17, Apr 8, 18, 19, May 12, Oct 1; 1775: HAY, Feb 20
Hartry, Mrs (actor), 1775: HAY, Feb 20
Harts-Horn Inn Yard, 1722: BFLSH, Aug 25
Hartson, Hall, 1767: HAY, Sep 8; 1768: DL, Jan 6
--Countess of Salisbury, The, 1767: HAY, Aug 21, 24, 26, 28, 31, Sep 2, 8, 10, 12, 14; 1768: DL, Jan 6, 8, 12, 20, Apr 13, Oct 7, 13, 21, CG, 26, DL, 26, CG, 29, Nov 2, 14; 1769: DL, Apr 4, CG, 26, DL, Nov 24; 1773: DL, Apr 23; 1775: CG, Apr 3; 1777: CG, Apr 7, 17; 1778: CG, Apr 7; 1779: DL, Mar 16; 1780: CG, Jan 12, HAY, Aug 14, 16; 1781: DL, Jan 9; 1784: DL, Mar 6, 9, Apr 13; 1794: CG, Jun 5; 1797: DL, Dec 8, 30
Harvard. See Havard.
Harvay (Harve), Mlle (dancer), 1725: DL, Mar 18, Apr 20, LIF, May 19
Harvelt (actor), 1740: SF, Sep 9
Harvest Home (song), 1717: DL, Aug 6
Harvest Home. See Dibdin, Charles.
Harvey (actor), 1733: CG, Aug 20
Harvey (dancer), 1748: DL, Oct 27; 1749: DL, Jan 27, Feb 21, Apr 10; 1750: DL, Nov 27, Dec 31; 1751: DL, Jan 2, Mar 12, 19, May 3, Sep 21, Nov 5, 15, 19, 23, Dec 20, 26; 1752: DL, Jan 20, 28, Feb 5, Mar 7, Apr 2, 20, 23, 27, Sep 19, Oct 10; 1753: DL, May 1, 18
Harvey (musician), 1795: CG, Feb 20; 1796: CG, Feb 12
Harvey, Lady Elizabeth, 1668: BRIDGES, Dec 18; 1669: BRIDGES, Jan 13
Harvey, Miss (dancer), 1785: KING'S, Jun 18, 25; 1786: KING'S, Feb 18, Apr 6, May 23, Jun 6, Jul 1; 1788: KING'S, Feb 21, Apr 3, May 15, 31
Harvey, Mrs (actor), 1758: HAY, Jan 16, 25
Harvey, Mrs (actor), 1794: HAY, Jul 17, 18, 21, 24, Aug 27, 29; 1798: HAY, Apr 23
Harwood, Miss (dancer), 1738: DL, Jan 6, May 5, 29, 30, Dec 4
Harwood, Ralph (actor), 1775: DL, Mar 28
Harwood, Robert (prompter), 1774: Dl, May 19; 1775: DL, May 8; 1776: DL, May 3, Jun 10; 1777: DL, Apr 22; 1778: DL, May 18; 1779: DL, May 7; 1780: DL, May 9; 1781: DL, May 17, Oct 12; 1782: DL, May 8; 1783: DL, May 15; 1784: DL, May 18; 1785: DL, May 12; 1786: DL, May 22, Oct 16; 1787: HAY, Jan 8
Haseler (Hasely) (beneficiary), 1794: CG, Jun 14; 1795: CG, Jun 10; 1796: CG, May 21; 1797: CG, Jun 2; 1798: CG, May 31; 1799: CG, May 17; 1800: CG, Jun 4
Haskey (beneficiary), 1787: CG, Jun 5
Haskey, Miss (dancer), 1792: HAY, Jul 25, DL, Dec 27
Haskey, Mrs (actor, dancer), 1785: DL, May 20, Dec 26; 1786: DL, May 29; 1787: DL, Jun 1; 1788: DL, Jun 5; 1790: DL, Oct 26; 1791: DLKING'S, Nov 5; 1792: DLKING'S, Mar 19, HAY, Jul 25, DL, Nov 21, Dec 27; 1793: HAY, Jun 21, Oct 10, Dec 26; 1794: HAY, Jan 4, DL, May 16, 30, Dec 20, 23; 1795: DL, Feb 12, HAY, Sep 21, DL, Oct 30; 1796: DL, Jan 18, Mar 1, HAY, Jul 15, DL, Oct 1, 29, Dec 26; 1797: DL, Jun 10, HAY, Jul 13; 1798: DL, Jan 16, Feb 20, May 16, HAY, Jun 13, Jul 17, Aug 3, Sep 5; 1799: HAY, Jun 25, Aug 10, 17, 26
Haslang, Count, 1761: CG, Oct 9
Hasse, Johann Adolph (musician, composer), 1734: KING'S, Oct 29; 1736: KING'S, Nov 23, 27, 30, Dec 4, 14, 18, 21; 1737: KING'S, Jan 1; 1739: HAY, Dec 15; 1740: HAY, Mar 15; 1741: HIC, Mar 26, Apr 24, KING'S, Oct 31; 1742: KING'S, Nov 2; 1743: LIF, Mar 15; 1748: KING'S, Mar 14, 26, Apr 5, May 7; 1752: CT/HAY, May 5; 1754: KING'S, Jan 29, Feb 28, Nov 9; 1755: KING'S, Mar 17, Apr 12, Nov 29; 1756: DL, Apr 2; 1757: KING'S, Jan 18, Mar 24, DL, 25, KING'S, Apr 26; 1758: DL, Mar 10, KING'S, Apr 18; 1759: CG, May 4, DL, Dec 14; 1761: HAY, Jun 23, Jul 28; 1762: KING'S, May 11; 1764: KING'S, Mar 29; 1766: KING'S, Feb 20; 1771: HAY, Apr 17; 1777: KING'S, Mar 1
--Artaserse; or, Le Pazzie D'Orlando (opera), 1754: KING'S, Jan 29, Feb 2, 9, 16, 23, Mar 2, 9, 26, Apr 20; 1766: KING'S, Feb 20, 22, 25, Mar 1; 1772: KING'S, Apr 21, 25, 28, May 2, 5, 9, 12, 16, 23, 26, 30, Jun 9, 11, 20, Dec 1, 5, 15, 19, 22, 26; 1773: KING'S, Jan 2, 5, 12, 15, Feb 5, Mar 23, Apr 20,

29, Jun 12; 1774: KING'S, May 17, 20
--Artaxerxes (opera), 1734: KING'S, Oct 29, Nov 2, 5, 9, 12, 16, 19, 23, 26,
    30, Dec 3, 7, 28, 31; 1735: KING'S, Jan 4, 7, 11, 14, 18, 21, 25, 28, Mar 15,
    18, CG, 19, KING'S, 22, Apr 22, 26, 29, May 17, 23, 27, 31, Jun 3; 1736:
    KING'S, Jan 3, 10, 13, 17, Mar 27, 30, Jun 1, 5; 1738: DL, Apr 12; 1741: DL,
    Oct 24; 1742: DL, Feb 3
--Dido (opera), 1748: KING'S, Mar 14, 26, Apr 2, 16, 23, 26, 30
--Ezio (opera), 1755: KING'S, Apr 12, 19, 26, 29, May 3, 6, 10, 13, 16, 20, 24,
    27, Jun 7, Nov 29, Dec 2, 6; 1764: KING'S, Nov 24, 27, Dec 1, 4, 8, 11, 15,
    18, 22; 1765: KING'S, Jan 15, 22, Feb 12, 19, 26, Mar 21, 26, Apr 20, 24, May
    4; 1766: KING'S, Dec 20, 27; 1767: KING'S, Jan 10, 17; 1770: KING'S, Jan 13,
    20, 23, 27, Feb 3, 10, 24, Mar 10; 1771: KING'S, Feb 8
--Ipermestra, L' (opera), 1746: KING'S, Mar 4; 1754: KING'S, Nov 9, 12, 16, 19,
    23, 26, 29, Dec 3, 7, 10, 14, 31; 1755: KING'S, Jan 4, 7, Apr 10, 22; 1756:
    KING'S, May 25, 29, Jun 3, 12, 19
--Olimpia in Ebuda (opera), 1740: HAY, Mar 15, 18, 22, 25, 29, Apr 8, 12, 15,
    19, 22, 26, 29, May 3, 6, 15
--Pellegrini, I (oratorio), 1757: DL, Mar 25; 1764: KING'S, Apr 5
--Re Pastore, Il (opera), 1757: KING'S, Jan 18, 22, 25, 29, Feb 1, 5, 8, 12,
    15, 19, 22, 26, Apr 26, May 10; 1765: KING'S, Mar 7; 1778: KING'S, May 30,
    Jun 5
--Ridiculous Guardian, The (opera), 1761: HAY, Jul 28, 30, 31, Aug 3, 7
--Semiramide Reconosciuta, La (opera), 1748: NWSM, May 3, KING'S, 7, 14
--Siroe (opera), 1736: KING'S, Nov 23, 27, 30, Dec 4, 11, 14, 18, 21; 1737:
    KING'S, Jan 1, 4, Feb 1, 5, 8
--Tutor, The (burletta), 1759: DL, Dec 14, 15; 1765: DL, Feb 4, 5
Hassell, Robert (renter), 1758: CG, Mar 16
Haste, Lorenzo, haste away (song), 1779: CG, Nov 11; 1781: CG, Nov 8
Haste, my Nannet (song), 1779: DL, Mar 12
Haste, thee nymph (song), 1790: CG, Mar 17; 1791: CG, Mar 18, DL, 25; 1793: CG,
    Mar 20, Apr 11; 1794: CG, Mar 21, DL, Apr 9; 1799: CG, Mar 15
Hastings (house servant), 1717: LIF, May 28; 1719: LIF, May 13; 1722: LIF, May
    19
Hastings (spectator), 1760: CG, Mar 12
Hastings, Theophilus, Earl of Huntington, 1667: BRIDGES, Apr 15, LIF, May 6;
    1698: DLORLIF, Jul 13
Haswell (actor), 1744: HAY, Dec 26
Hat, The (entertainment), 1721: HAY, Jan 2, Feb 2, 20
Hatchet (house servant), 1749: CG, Apr 22
Hatchett, William, 1730: HAY, Apr 8; 1733: HAY, May 31; 1737: HAY, Apr 25
--Rival Father, The; or, The Death of Achilles, 1730: HAY, Apr 8, 9, 22
Hathorne (treasurer), 1745: CG, May 1
Hatley (house servant), 1788: CG, May 24
Hatsell (mercer), 1771: DL, Dec 12; 1772: DL, Jan 6, Mar 26, Jun 10, Dec 8;
    1773: DL, Mar 1, Jun 2, Nov 19; 1774: DL, Jan 21, Feb 22, Jun 2, Oct 20, Nov
    11; 1775: DL, Jan 10, Feb 23, Oct 27, Nov 3, Dec 8; 1776: DL, Jan 26, Jun 10;
    1777: DL, Feb 25
Hatten (actor), 1734: YB, Jul 8
Hatton (sword cutler), 1799: DL, Oct 14
Hatton Buildings, 1667: BRIDGES, Apr 15
Hatton Garden, 1673: HG, Sep 23; 1720: CGR, Jun 22; 1721: GG, Mar 22; 1743: CG,
    Nov 17; 1762: HAY, Oct 25; 1794: CG, May 24; 1795: CG, May 29
Hatton, Alice (spectator), 1700: DLORLIF, Jan 20
Hatton, Ann, Mrs William T P (actor, singer), 1793: HAY, Jun 14, 17, 21, Jul
    10, 18, 19, 30, Aug 3, 6, 12, 16, Sep 2, 10
Hatton, Lady. See Yelverton, Frances.
Hatton, Mrs (actor), 1725: DL, Feb 20, 22
Hatton, William T P (actor), 1789: WHF, Nov 9
Haughton (actor), 1757: CG, May 16
Haughton (Houghton) (actor, dancer), 1724: RI, Jun 27, 29, Jul 4, SOU, Sep 24;
    1725: BF, Aug 23, DL, Nov 19, Dec 6; 1726: DL, Feb 11, Apr 23, 26, 27, 30,
    May 2, 4, 13, LIF, 17, DL, Jun 3, LIF, Jul 15, 22, Aug 12, 19, DL, Oct 1, 27,
    Nov 2, 15, 23, 30, Dec 7, 14, 30; 1727: DL, Feb 27, Mar 23, Apr 12, 20, 21,
    28, 29, May 2, 5, LIF, 8, 15, DL, 22, 26, Oct 6, 30, Nov 1, 14; 1728: LIF,
    Jan 29, DL, Mar 30, LIF, Apr 24, DL, 24, 25, May 6, 9, LIF, 20, Jun 25, Jul
    5, 19, DL, Sep 19, Oct 10, 30, Nov 15; 1729: LIF, Jan 16, May 12, DL, 14, 26,
    28, BFB, Aug 25, DL, Dec 12, 26; 1730: DL, Apr 11, 14, 23, 24, 27, 29, 30,
    May 1, 4, 11, LIF, 14, DL, 15, 19, RI, Jun 24, 27, Jul 16, DL, Oct 1, LIF, 7,
    DL, 10, LIF, 12, DL, 22, 28, Nov 23, 30, Dec 4, LIF, 4; 1731: LIF, Jan 8, 13,
    DL, 27, LIF, Feb 3, 27, DL, Apr 1, LIF, 3, GF, 23, DL, May 3, 7, LIF, 20, RI,
    Jul 1, 15, 22, DL, Oct 16, LIF, 20, DL, 26, Nov 22, 25, Dec 2, LIF, 8, 9, DL,
    15, 28; 1732: LIF, Feb 1, DL, 2, 22, Mar 4, LIF, 20, DL, 21, Apr 17, 21, 22,

26, 28, 29, May 1, LIF, 1, 2, DL, 2, 3, 6, 12, RI, Aug 17, BFB, 23, DL, Sep
23, 28, LIF/CG, Oct 6, DL, 14, 17, 19, 21, 26, Nov 7, 8, 10, 14, 17, 20;
1733: DL, Jan 11, 23, 25, 31, Feb 2, CG, 8, DL, Mar 5, 8, 15, 26, 28, 29, 31,
Apr 4, LIF/CG, 10, 12, DL, 16, 20, 24, 25, 30, May 1, CG, 1, DL, 2, 5, 7,
LIF/CG, 7, DL, 9, 14, CG, 16, DL, 18, 21, BF, Aug 23, CG, Sep 20, 29, Oct 2,
DL/HAY, 25, CG, Nov 16, HAY, 19, DL/HAY, 24, CG, 26, 30, Dec 3, 4, 20, 28;
1734: DL/HAY, Jan 7, 23, CG, Feb 26, Mar 16, 21, 28, Apr 1, 19, 27, May 10,
13, RI, Jun 27, BFFO, Aug 24, CG/LIF, Sep 20, GF, Oct 7, 9, 28, Nov 18, Dec
2, 12; 1735: GF, Jan 13, CG/LIF, 20, GF, 24, CG/LIF, Feb 11, GF, Mar 6,
CG/LIF, 11, GF, 13, 20, 29, Apr 23, CG/LIF, 23, GF, 30, May 3, CG/LIF, 16,
LIF, Aug 29, GF, Sep 24, Oct 15, Nov 6, CG, 10, GF, 17, 19, CG, 22, GF, 25,
Dec 4, 5, 6, 10, 11, 15, 17; 1736: GF, Feb 6, 10, 17, 20, Mar 3, 22, 25, CG,
27, GF, 29, Apr 1, LIF, 2, GF, 6, 8, 12, LIF, 16, GF, 28, 29, CG, 30, GF, May
4, 5, CG, 14, LIF, Jun 16, CG, Sep 20, LIF, 28, 30, Oct 5, 9, CG, 11, LIF,
21, CG, Nov 1, LIF, Dec 7, 16; 1737: LIF, Feb 1, CG, Mar 15, LIF, 21, 24, 26,
31, Apr 2, 19, 27, CG, May 16, DL, Oct 22, Nov 10; 1738: CG, Jan 5, DL, 11,
13, 14, 28, Feb 3, CG, 6, DL, 20, 21, 23, CG, 23, DL, 28, Mar 9, 13, 16, 23,
Apr 11, 21, 22, 24, 26, 29, May 1, 2, 3, 5, CG, 5, DL, 6, 8, 9, 12, 16, CG,
Oct 4, 30, Nov 18, Dec 9; 1739: CG, Jan 20, 22, Feb 10, May 3, Dec 20; 1740:
CG, Oct 13, 22, Dec 12, 17, 19, 20, 22, 29, 30; 1741: CG, Jan 2, 7, 8, 10,
21, 27, 28, 29, 31, Feb 3, 6, 7, 17, 23, 24, 28, Mar 5, 16, 17, 19, 31, Apr
21
Haughton (pit doorkeeper), 1710: DL, May 10
Haughton, Hannah (actor), 1734: GF, Dec 6; 1742: LIF, Nov 26; 1743: LIF, Feb
14, Apr 4; 1744: HAY, Oct 20, GF, Dec 4, 10, 12, 15, 18, 19, 21, 26, 31;
1745: GF, Mar 7, 25, Apr 15, DL, Jun 5; 1746: GF, Feb 13, 17, 24, Mar 6, CG,
Jun 11, 27, Oct 3; 1747: CG, Feb 12; 1748: CG, Jan 19, Mar 21, 28, Apr 13,
15, 29, May 4, Sep 26, 28, Oct 3, 14, 27, 29, Nov 3, 16, 26, Dec 22, 26;
1749: CG, Jan 2, 3, 28, Mar 14, 29, Apr 15, 19, 24, Sep 27, 29, Oct 18, 20,
24, 25, 30, Nov 3, 9, 16, 23, Dec 8, 26; 1750: CG, Jan 17, 18, Feb 7, Apr 7,
30, HAY, Jul 26, CG, Sep 24, 26, Oct 12, 22, 23, 24, 29, Nov 6, 22, 29, Dec
4, 18, 21, 26; 1751: CG, Apr 16, 22, 25, 26, May 1, 4, 9, 16, Sep 25, 27, 30,
Oct 8, 17, 22, 28, 29, Nov 6, 14, 18, 26, 28, Dec 4; 1752: CG, Jan 18, Mar
30, Apr 15, 28, Sep 25, 29, Oct 4, 10, 11, 14, 16, 18, 23, 26, 27, 31, Nov 2,
7, 9, 16, DL, Dec 18; 1753: DL, Jan 9, 22, 23, 24, Feb 7, Apr 12, 26, Sep 18,
Oct 10, 24, Nov 7, 26, Dec 26; 1754: DL, Jan 16, 19, Feb 20, 21, 22, 23, Mar
19, Apr 18, 20, Sep 19, Oct 8, Nov 30, Dec 4, 9, 12; 1755: DL, Jan 15, 17,
21, 22, Feb 25, Mar 4, 18, 20, Apr 12, 15, May 6, Oct 3, 7, 27, 31, Nov 22,
26, 28, Dec 1, 5; 1756: DL, Jan 10, 20, Apr 6, 10, 27, May 14, 24, Sep 28,
Oct 14, 18, 21, 27, Nov 2, 12, Dec 27; 1757: DL, Jan 26, Apr 27, 30, May 17,
23, Oct 7, 12, Nov 10, Dec 27; 1758: DL, Jan 19, Apr 3, 7, 18, May 15, Oct
14, 25, 27, Dec 29; 1759: DL, Jan 6, Feb 15, Mar 3, 20, 31, Apr 7, 19, 30,
May 16, Jun 28, Nov 10, 13, 16, 30, Dec 5, 18, 31; 1760: DL, Mar 20, 24, Apr
18, 19, 22, 24, May 16, Jun 19, Oct 17, 22, 24; 1761: DL, Jan 31, Apr 3, 17,
24, May 25, 28, Jun 15, Jul 2, 27, Sep 23, 24, Oct 14, 20, 29, Nov 2, 6, 10,
14, Dec 23; 1762: DL, Jan 7, 11, Apr 16, May 7, 10, 12, 17, Sep 18, 29, Oct
4, 11, 12, 25, 28, Nov 12, 19, Dec 27; 1763: DL, Jan 18, Apr 6, May 17, Sep
27, 29, Oct 1, 19, 21, Dec 5, 26, 28; 1764: DL, Jan 4
Haughton, Mrs (actor, dancer), 1724: RI, Jun 27, 29, Jul 4, 11, 13, 18, SOU,
Sep 24; 1725: BF, Aug 23; 1726: HAY, Feb 24, SFSE, Sep 8; 1727: DL, Oct 6, 9,
Nov 1; 1728: DL, Mar 30, Nov 18; 1729: DL, May 14, GF, Oct 31, Nov 3, 5, 6,
7, 8, 10, 12, 14, 20, 24, 25, Dec 8, 20; 1730: GF, Jan 5, 7, 9, 16, 19, 26,
Feb 9, 10, Mar 5, 12, 17, 21, Apr 7, 10, 14, 15, 24, 28, May 15, 19, 29, Jun
1, 3, 8, 12, 30, Jul 1, 6, 8, BFPG/TC, Aug 1, BFPG, 31, GF, Sep 16, 18, 23,
25, 28, 30, Oct 2, 5, 14, 19, 20, 21, 24, 27, 30, 31, Nov 2, 5, 10, 12, 26,
27, 28, Dec 1, 5, 7, 21; 1731: GF, Jan 13, 14, 15, 16, 20, Feb 1, 13, 15, 18,
27, Mar 1, 2, 4, 6, 11, 13, 16, 22, Apr 1, 6, 23, 26, 27, May 5, 7, 14, 17,
Jun 1, 8, Oct 6, 13, 25, 26, 27, 29, Nov 8, 11, 12, 16, 19, 20, 26, Dec 1, 4,
6, 13, 18, 20, 21, 28, 30; 1732: GF, Jan 13, Feb 21, 26, Mar 7, 20, Apr 17,
May 4, Oct 5, 7, 10, 11, 13, 24, 25, 26, Nov 2, 3, 8, 10, 28, Dec 20, 29;
1733: GF, Jan 17, 18, 24, Feb 1, 5, 15, Mar 5, 8, 12, 17, 28, Apr 11, 13, 20,
23, May 9, 23, HAY, 28, BF, Aug 23, GF, Sep 10, 12, 14, 17, 19, 20, 24, 27,
28, Oct 5, 8, 12, 22, 23, 26, Nov 10, 12, 13, 29, Dec 31; 1734: GF, Jan 10,
11, Feb 7, 11, Apr 19, 26, May 17, 20, Sep 13, 16, 20, Oct 18, Nov 22, 29,
Dec 6, 12, 20, 31; 1735: GF, Jan 1, 3, 4, 9, 10, 11, 13, 20, Feb 8, 24, 25,
Mar 24, Apr 10, 16, 22, 23, 24, May 1, Sep 10, 12, 17, 19, Nov 3, 10, 11, 12,
19, 21, 24, 25; 1736: GF, Feb 9, Mar 9, 25, Apr 8, 16, 28, LIF, Oct 12, 23,
Nov 6, 29, Dec 3, 7, 16, 31; 1737: LIF, Mar 29, May 4; 1740: BFHC, Aug 23;
1743: LIF, Apr 11
Haughty Strephon (song), 1752: DL, Jan 24, Feb 10
Haunted Tower, The. See Cobb, James.
Hautboy (music), 1702: PR, Jun 30; 1703: LIF, Jun 11; 1709: SH, Nov 30; 1712:

B&S, Nov 24, SH, Dec 30; 1713: SH, Feb 23; 1719: HIC, Feb 13; 1720: HIC, Mar
   4, YB, Apr 1, LIF, Dec 23; 1723: HIC, Mar 6; 1729: HIC, Apr 16, May 21; 1732:
   LIF, Feb 25; 1735: HAY, Jan 31; 1746: SFHP, Sep 8; 1761: HAY, Feb 5; 1770:
   CG, Feb 24; 1771: HAY, Apr 12; 1776: STRAND, Jan 23; 1778: KING'S, Feb 7, Mar
   19, Apr 4; 1780: KING'S, Jan 22; 1781: KING'S, Mar 15; 1787: CG, Mar 31;
   1788: CG, Feb 5, Mar 10; 1789: DL, Mar 20, CG, May 20; 1791: CG, May 27, Sep
   23; 1793: CG, Apr 11, Oct 29; 1795: CG, Jun 10; 1796: CG, May 25; 1798: HAY,
   Aug 9; 1800: HAY, Aug 26
Hautboy and Flute (music), 1725: DL, May 10
Hautboy and Flute Concerto (music), 1722: DL, Mar 14
Hautboy and French Horn Duet (music), 1772: CG, Apr 10
Hautboy and Violin (music), 1703: YB, Dec 11; 1733: HIC, Apr 27
Hautboy Concerto (music), 1714: TEC, May 4; 1716: LIF, May 10, Jun 4; 1722:
   HAY, May 11; 1726: HIC, Mar 16; 1729: HIC, Apr 16; 1732: CL, Mar 17; 1733:
   HIC, Mar 16, DL/HAY, Dec 1, 3; 1735: DL, Feb 4, Apr 16, CG, May 8, DL, Jun 3,
   Jul 1, GF/HAY, 15, DL, Dec 6; 1737: HIC, Apr 1, DL, May 4, 27; 1741: KING'S,
   Mar 14; 1743: LIF, Mar 15, KING'S, 30; 1744: KING'S, Mar 28, HAY, Apr 4;
   1745: HAY, Mar 23; 1752: CG, Feb 26; 1755: HAY, Feb 13; 1757: KING'S, Mar 24,
   DL, 25; 1758: DL, Mar 10, SOHO, Apr 1, KING'S, 6; 1759: CG, Feb 2, DL, Mar
   23, 30, CG, May 4, Nov 30; 1761: KING'S, Mar 12; 1762: DL, Mar 5, 26, HAY,
   May 20; 1763: KING'S, Apr 25, CG, Oct 13, 25, Dec 8; 1764: CG, Jan 19,
   CHAPEL, Feb 29, HAY, Nov 13; 1765: CG, Jan 28; 1767: KING'S, Jan 23; 1768:
   KING'S, Feb 5, HAY, 19, 24, Mar 9, 16; 1769: KING'S, Feb 3, HAY, 10, CG, 10,
   22, Mar 1, 8, 10, HAY, 10, CG, 15, KING'S, Jun 1, MARLY, Aug 17, 24, CG, Oct
   10; 1770: KING'S, Feb 2, DL, Mar 2, CG, 7, DL, 23, Apr 6, HAY, May 3; 1771:
   KING'S, Feb 8, Mar 21; 1772: KING'S, Feb 21, HAY, Mar 30, Apr 27; 1773:
   KING'S, Feb 5; 1774: KING'S, Feb 10, DL, 18, Mar 16; 1775: KING'S, Jan 26,
   DL, Mar 3, 8, 10, 17, 22, 24, KING'S, 29; 1776: KING'S, Feb 15; 1778: CG, Mar
   6, DL, 11, CG, 18; 1779: DL, Feb 24, Mar 5, HAY, 17, 24; 1780: DL, Feb 16,
   25; 1781: DL, Mar 7, CG, 23, DL, Apr 6, KING'S, Jun 14, 16; 1782: DL, Feb 15,
   27, Mar 20; 1783: DL, Mar 19; 1785: DL, Mar 4; 1786: DL, Mar 8, 22, 31; 1787:
   DL, Mar 9; 1788: DL, Feb 8, 20, Mar 5; 1789: DL, Mar 6, CG, 6, DL, 25, CG,
   27, Apr 3; 1790: DL, Feb 24, CG, 26, DL, Mar 10; 1791: DL, Mar 23, CG, Apr 6;
   1792: KING'S, Feb 29, CG, Mar 9, KING'S, 28; 1793: KING/HAY, Mar 13, 22;
   1794: DL, Mar 12; 1795: KING'S, May 14
Hautboy Duet (music), 1754: DL, Mar 27
Hautboy Solo (music), 1714: TEC, May 4; 1717: SH, Mar 27; 1718: LR, Dec 3;
   1719: YB, Dec 19; 1721: LIF, Apr 17, May 9; 1722: HAY, May 11; 1723: DL, Mar
   20; 1724: HIC, Feb 26; 1729: HIC, Apr 16; 1730: LIF, May 13; 1731: LIF, Apr
   2; 1732: LIF, Mar 10, CL, 17; 1733: HIC, Apr 20; 1740: HIC, Mar 31; 1761:
   HAY, Jan 28; 1774: HIC, May 9
Hautboy Sonata (music), 1712: OS, Nov 28
Hautboy, Flute and Hunting Horn (music), 1704: CC, Jun 1
Hautboy, Flute and Violin Concerto (music), 1723: DL, May 15
Hautboy, Trumpet and Kettle Drum (music), 1731: SF/BFFHH, Aug 24
Hauteroche, Noel le Breton, Sieur de
--Cocher Suppose, Le, 1722: HAY, Jan 5, Feb 26, Apr 10
--Dame Invisible, La, 1721: HAY, Apr 24
--Deuil, Le (farce), 1721: HAY, Jan 17, Dec 21
Havard (actor), 1791: HAY, Sep 26
Havard, Elizabeth, Mrs William (actor), 1745: CG, Oct 2, 29, 31, Nov 14, 19,
   23; 1746: CG, Jan 1, 7, 10, Feb 6, Mar 20, Apr 14, 15, Oct 1, Dec 11, 19, 31;
   1747: CG, Jan 28, Feb 11; 1748: DL, Mar 31, Oct 15, 29, Nov 14; 1749: DL, May
   16, Sep 26, 28, Oct 30; 1750: DL, Mar 29, Sep 11, Oct 29, Nov 7; 1751: DL,
   Sep 7, Oct 11; 1752: DL, Jan 8, Sep 16, Oct 14, 19; 1753: DL, Sep 8, 27;
   1754: DL, Oct 14, Nov 22; 1755: DL, Jan 22, Sep 23, Oct 31, Nov 1; 1757: DL,
   Apr 11, Sep 10; 1758: DL, Jun 22; 1759: DL, Mar 27, May 28, Jun 19; 1760: DL,
   May 23, Sep 23, 30; 1761: DL, Sep 5, Oct 1; 1762: DL, Jan 5; 1764: DL, Apr
   14, 27
Havard, William (actor, author), 1730: BFPG, Aug 20, HAY, Oct 21, Nov 9, 13,
   30, GF, Dec 10, 12, 17, 21, 30; 1731: GF, Jan 5, 22, 25, Feb 8, 12, 18, 22,
   Mar 1, 16, 20, Apr 6, 8, 20, May 7, 14, Jun 1, 2, 3, Sep 27, Oct 8, 11, 18,
   25, 26, 29, Nov 1, 4, 8, 12, 15, 18, 20, 24, 26, Dec 4, 6, 9, 13, 21, 28, 30;
   1732: GF, Mar 20, Apr 14, May 4, 15, Oct 2, 4, 5, 6, 7, 12, 13, 14, 17, 18,
   26, 30, Nov 4, 27, 28, Dec 18, 29; 1733: GF, Mar 15, 17, Apr 11, 17, 19, May
   3, 9, HAY, 28, GF, Sep 10, 12, 14, 17, 19, 20, 25, Oct 1, 5, 9, 12, 15, 18,
   24, 25, Nov 5, 8, 10, 12, 13, 29, Dec 12, 18, 31; 1734: GF, Jan 3, 14, 31,
   May 6, Sep 11, 13, 16, 20, Oct 14, 16, 23, Nov 7, 22, 25, 27, 29, Dec 6, 16,
   31; 1735: GF, Jan 6, 8, 11, 24, Feb 4, 5, 22, 25, Mar 17, 24, Apr 14, 30, Sep
   10, 12, 15, 17, 19, Oct 3, 6, 10, 15, 27, Nov 4, 11, 21, 24, 26, Dec 6, 8,
   17; 1736: GF, Jan 29, Feb 9, 16, Mar 9, 18, 23, 25, 29, Apr 6, 8, 16, 28, May
   5, 13, LIF, Jun 8, 18, Sep 28, Oct 5, 9, 12, 14, 19, 28, Nov 4, 6, 9, 11, 13,

18, 20, 24, 26, 27, 29, Dec 20, 22; 1737: LIF, Feb 12, 14, Mar 1, Apr 18, 27,
May 2, 4, Jun 15, DL, Sep 3, 6, 8, 10, 15, 17, 22, 24, 29, Oct 1, 20, 21, Nov
1, 15, 16, 19; 1738: DL, Jan 19, 26, 31, Feb 10, Mar 20, 25, Apr 6, 17, 22,
May 2, 6, Sep 7, 12, 14, 16, 30, Oct 12, 17, 18, 20, 21, 27, 30, Nov 1, 2,
11, 18, 20, 23, 29, 30, Dec 6, 18; 1739: DL, Jan 2, 13, 16, 22, 26, Feb 13,
Mar 8, 10, 20, 22, Apr 10, 14, 30, May 18, 19, 25, Sep 1, 13, 14, 15, 18, 20,
22, 24, Oct 9, 10, 15, 16, 17, 18, 20, 22, 23, 24, 25, 29, Nov 7, 8, 19, 20,
21, 23, Dec 10, 14, 22, 31; 1740: DL, Jan 3, 8, 19, Feb 16, Mar 11, 13, Apr
17, May 2, 9, 20, Sep 6, 16, 23, 25, Oct 2, 4, 9, 10, 11, 13, 14, 16, 27, 29,
Nov 7, 10, 11, 13, 19; 1741: DL, Feb 5, 14, 24, Mar 21, 30, Apr 2, 4, 28, May
7, 12, 14, 21, Sep 8, 10, 12, 17, 19, Oct 6, 8, 9, 10, 12, 15, Nov 11, 16,
20, 21, Dec 7, 8, 11, 12, 14, 16, 19; 1742: DL, Jan 4, 6, 8, 22, Feb 11, 12,
13, 15, Mar 6, 8, 27, 29, Apr 19, 24, 28, May 3, 25, 28, Sep 11, 14, 18, 25,
28, Oct 2, 5, 7, 9, 12, 13, 16, 18, 26, Nov 1, 3, 4, 12, 16, 19; 1743: DL,
Jan 11, 27, 28, Feb 4, 10, 11, Mar 14, SOU, 30, DL, Apr 8, 18, 29, LIF, Jun
3, DL, Sep 13, Dec 1, 6, 10, 15, 16, 17, 19, 21; 1744: DL, Jan 7, 12, 13, 27,
Feb 21, 25, Mar 1, Apr 2, 3, 10, 18, 23, 25, 30, May 1, 4, 22, 23, Sep 15,
18, 20, 27, 29, Oct 4, 6, 9, 11, 13, 17, 19, 20, 22, 24, 27, 30, Nov 5, 6,
15, 16, Dec 5, 19; 1745: DL, Jan 4, 12, 14, Feb 11, 13, 20, Mar 7, 18, Apr
19, 24, Sep 24, 26, 28, Oct 1, 3, 12, 15, 17, 19, 22, Nov 1, 4, 9, 11, 18,
20, 22, 23, 26, 28, Dec 5, 11, 12, 13, 17, 20, 30; 1746: DL, Jan 8, 14, 18,
Mar 13, 17, 18, Apr 4, 11, 15, 23, May 9, Aug 6, CG, Sep 29, Oct 6, 8, 10,
13, 20, 24, 27, Nov 4, 6, 8, 11, 13, 24, 28, Dec 2, 8, 19, 22, 26, 27, 29;
1747: CG, Jan 17, 20, 26, Feb 2, 6, 11, 12, Mar 7, 17, DL, 19, CG, 23, 26,
28, 30, Apr 4, 20, DL, Sep 15, 22, Oct 1, 3, 17, 20, 24, 30, Nov 2, 4, 6, 10,
13, 16, 17, 26, Dec 4, 5, 16; 1748: DL, Jan 6, 12, 18, Feb 1, 3, 9, 13, Mar
10, 19, 31, Apr 21, 28, May 16, Sep 10, 13, 15, 17, 20, 24, 27, 29, Oct 1, 8,
11, 13, 18, 19, 22, 28, Nov 1, 3, 4, 8, 9, 11, 14, 23, 28, 29, Dec 21, 28;
1749: DL, Jan 9, 20, 25, Feb 6, 21, Mar 7, 16, 31, Apr 5, 10, 15, May 8, Sep
16, 19, 20, 21, 28, Oct 3, 10, 11, 13, 17, 18, 21, 23, 24, 26, 28, Nov 4, 9,
16, 27, Dec 7, 8, 9, 12, 18, 20; 1750: DL, Jan 6, 22, 31, Feb 7, Mar 13, 19,
26, 29, May 10, Sep 8, 13, 15, 21, 22, 25, 27, 28, Oct 13, 15, 16, 19, 20,
23, 24, 26, 30, Nov 1, 2, 3, 5, 7, 8, 12, 13, 15, 28, Dec 3, 14; 1751: DL,
Jan 15, Feb 18, Mar 12, Apr 17, 19, Sep 10, 12, 13, 14, 17, 18, 19, 20, 21,
24, 26, Oct 2, 7, 10, 11, Nov 2, 4, 7, Dec 10; 1752: DL, Jan 6, 28, Feb 3, 6,
13, 17, Mar 7, Apr 1, 3, 10, 11, 14, 20, 21, 27, May 12, Sep 16, 19, 21, 23,
26, 28, 30, Oct 3, 7, 10, 13, 16, 19, 21, 23, 26, 28, Nov 3, 4; 1753: DL, Feb
7, 8, 22, 28, Mar 19, 22, 26, 29, Apr 7, 9, 12, CG, 23, DL, 25, 28, May 1, 4,
7, 17, 18, 21, 22, Sep 11, 13, 15, 18, 20, 22, 25, 27, Oct 2, 3, 4, 6, 9, 16,
18, 20, 23, 24, 25, 30, Nov 1, 5, 7, 8, 14, 15, 26, Dec 1; 1754: DL, Jan 7,
16, 23, Feb 20, Mar 25, Apr 1, 16, Jul 2, Sep 14, 21, 24, 26, Oct 1, 8, 10,
11, 16, 18, 21, 22, 23, 25, 29, Nov 4, 11, 22, Dec 13, 17; 1755: DL, Jan 6,
15, 17, 22, 25, Feb 18, 22, Mar 4, CG, 12, DL, 15, 18, Apr 3, May 27, Sep 13,
16, 18, 20, Oct 3, 4, 7, 8, 10, 23, 24, 27, 28, 31, Nov 1, 4, 6, 17, 22, 26,
Dec 1, 4, 18, 23; 1756: DL, Jan 10, 21, Feb 11, 27, Mar 25, Apr 1, 6, May 5,
10, 14, 18, 24, Sep 21, 25, 28, 30, Oct 2, 5, 9, 13, 14, 16, 19, 21, 23, 27,
28, 29, Nov 2, 4, 17, 19, Dec 11, 15, 27; 1757: DL, Jan 18, 22, 24, Mar 22,
24, Apr 12, 20, 26, Sep 13, 17, 20, 22, 24, 27, Oct 4, 7, 8, 11, 12, 15, 18,
29, Nov 4, 8, 10, 15, 19, Dec 2, 3, 27; 1758: DL, Jan 24, Feb 4, 21, Mar 11,
13, 16, 31, Apr 7, 18, 25, May 2, 17, Jun 1, Sep 16, 19, 21, 23, 26, 28, Oct
10, 12, 14, 18, 25, 27, 30, Nov 1, 4, 13, 15, 17, 18, 23, Dec 13, 18; 1759:
DL, Jan 3, 13, 17, Feb 1, Mar 3, 20, 24, 31, Apr 5, 19, 21, 26, May 9, 11,
14, 16, Jun 28, Jul 12, Sep 22, 25, 29, Oct 2, 4, 11, 12, 16, 17, 19, 22, 23,
26, Nov 1, 2, 5, 10, 13, 17, 30, Dec 5, 12, 20; 1760: DL, Jan 1, 11, 16, 19,
Feb 13, Mar 17, 27, Apr 11, 22, 24, 28, May 7, 8, 16, Jun 19, Sep 20, 30, Oct
7, 9, 10, 11, 14, 18, 22, 24, Nov 20, 27, Dec 2, 11, 17, 30; 1761: DL, Jan 8,
23, 28, 31, Mar 26, 28, 30, Apr 18, 23, 29, May 1, 18, 28, Sep 8, 10, 15, 17,
18, 21, 23, 24, 25, 26, 28, 30, Oct 1, 14, 17, 20, 26, 27, 31, Nov 4, 18, 21,
28, Dec 11, 23; 1762: DL, Jan 7, 20, 27, 29, Feb 20, 22, Mar 1, 25, 29, May
17, Sep 18, 25, 28, 29, Oct 4, 5, 6, 9, 12, 15, 16, 20, 23, 29, 30, Nov 1, 2,
3, 4, 12, 19, 26, Dec 6, 11, 22; 1763: DL, Jan 14, 17, Mar 1, 14, Apr 6, May
14, 31, Sep 20, 24, 27, Oct 1, 24, 31, Nov 4, 7, 9, 14, 15, 19, 22, 29, Dec
1, 10, 14; 1764: DL, Jan 4, 9, 13, 18, 23, 27, Feb 23, Mar 3, 20, 31, Apr 2,
7, 24, 25, 27, May 11, 24, Sep 20, 22, 25, 29, Oct 4, 9, 16, 17, 20, 23, 26,
31, Nov 5, 9, 17, 24, 27, Dec 18; 1765: DL, Jan 2, 15, 18, 23, 24, Feb 4, Mar
16, 23, 26, Apr 12, May 1, 4, 11, 18, Sep 17, 26, Oct 2, 9, 14, 15, 22, 23,
25, 28, Nov 11, 14, 20, Dec 3, 5, 6; 1766: DL, Jan 6, 9, 13, 24, Feb 3, 11,
20, Mar 18, 20, Apr 7, 9, 11, 25, May 2, 5, 10, 22, Sep 30, Oct 8, 16, 21,
23, 24, 29, Nov 4, 8, 20, 21, 24; 1767: DL, Jan 24, Feb 7, 21, Mar 7, 21, 24,
28, 30, Apr 4, 11, 24, May 8, 16, Jun 1, Sep 17, 21, 23, 26, Oct 9, 10, 22,
23, 28, Nov 4, 5, 19, 20, 24, 26, Dec 15; 1768: DL, Jan 9, 14, Feb 27, Mar
15, Apr 8, HAY, Aug 8, DL, Sep 23, 26, 29, Oct 20; 1769: DL, May 8; 1772: DL,

401

Jun 4; 1774: HAY, Sep 21
--Elopement, The (farce), 1763: DL, Apr 6
--King Charles I, 1737: LIF, Feb 8, Mar 1, 3, 4, 5, 7, 8, 10, 12, 14, 17, 19,
    22, 28, Apr 11, 13, 15, 19, 25, May 10, 18; 1740: DL, May 9; 1744: DL, Jan
    12, Mar 1; 1748: DL, Apr 23; 1781: CG, Apr 2; 1785: HAY, Jan 31
--Regulus, 1744: DL, Jan 12, Feb 21, 23, 25, 27, 28, Mar 1, Apr 18
--Scanderbeg, 1733: GF, Mar 15, 26; 1744: DL, Mar 1
Havard, William and Mrs (actor), 1747: CG, Apr 27
Have at All; or, The Midnight Adventure. See Williams, Joseph.
Have mercy upon me (song), 1793: CG, Mar 20
Havers (renter), 1750: DL, Jan 31
Hawker (beneficiary), 1729: LIF, May 6
Hawker, Essex (actor, author), 1723: HAY, Dec 12; 1724: HAY, Feb 27; 1729: LIF,
    Apr 10, 19; 1730: LIF, Apr 20
--Country Wedding and Skimmington, The (farce), 1729: DL, Jul 18, 22, 25, Aug
    1, 7; 1730: DL, May 11, 14, Oct 20; 1731: GF, Feb 5, 17; 1732: DL, May 8
--Wedding, The, 1729: LIF, May 6, 27; 1730: LIF, Apr 20, 27, 29, May 6, 15, 20;
    1731: GF, Jan 23, 25, 26, 27, 28, 29, Feb 5, 6, 17, 18; 1733: LIF/CG, Apr 3,
    May 3
Hawkes (coal merchant), 1781: CG, May 28; 1789: CG, Oct 9
Hawkes (tallow chandler), 1786: CG, Mar 6
Hawkesworth, John, 1756: DL, Dec 15, 23; 1759: DL, Dec 1; 1761: DL, Jan 31;
    1769: CG, Apr 17; 1773: DL, Nov 18; 1774: DL, Mar 23; 1792: HAY, Aug 31
--Edgar and Emmeline (entertainment), 1761: DL, Jan 31, Feb 2, 3, 5, 7, 9, 10,
    24, Mar 5, 9, Apr 2, Sep 25, Dec 5, 11; 1762: DL, Mar 23, 25; 1763: DL, Jan
    27, 28, Feb 22, Apr 28, Dec 20; 1764: DL, Mar 29; 1767: DL, Apr 29; 1768: CG,
    Mar 26, Apr 8; 1770: CG, Mar 22; 1774: DL, Apr 19; 1795: DL, Apr 27
--Fall of Egypt, The, 1774: DL, Mar 23, 25; 1775: DL, Mar 29
Hawkesworth, Walter, 1664: BRIDGES, May 2
--Labyrinthus, 1664: BRIDGES, May 2
Hawkin (house servant), 1796: CG, May 21; 1799: CG, May 29
Hawkins (actor), 1741: JS, Nov 9
Hawkins (actor), 1793: HAY, Dec 26; 1794: DL, Oct 31; 1796: DL, Jan 11; 1800:
    HAY, Jul 2
Hawkins, James (composer), 1691: NONE, Sep 0
Hawkins, William (author), 1759: CG, Feb 15; 1773: CG, May 1
Hawksby (Hawksly) (actor), 1757: DL, May 13; 1758: DL, May 9; 1765: DL, May 22;
    1768: DL, Jan 14, Feb 6, 11
Hawley, Rouse (musician), 1719: HIC, Mar 6
Hawling, Francis, 1723: DL, Aug 16
--Impertinent Lovers, The; or, A Coquet at Her Wits End, 1723: DL, Aug 16
Hawtin (actor, dancer), 1792: CG, Dec 20, 26; 1793: CG, Apr 8, Oct 2, 12, Dec
    19; 1794: CG, May 31, Sep 22, Dec 26; 1795: CG, May 12, Jun 4; 1796: CG, Jan
    23, 25, Feb 1, 18, 27, Mar 15, Jun 4, 7, Oct 24, Dec 19; 1797: CG, Feb 18,
    Mar 4, 7, 16, Apr 8, 27, May 3, 8, 9, 15, 18, Jun 7, 9, Sep 29, Oct 16, Nov
    4, Dec 26; 1798: CG, Mar 31, Apr 9, May 18, 28, Jun 2, Oct 15; 1799: CG, Jan
    29, Mar 25, Apr 13, 19, 23, May 13, 28, Oct 7, 21, 25, Dec 23; 1800: CG, Feb
    10, Apr 5, 29, Jun 2, 10, HAY, Jul 3, 18
Hay (house servant), 1794: CG, Jun 17; 1795: CG, Jun 10; 1796: CG, Jun 3; 1797:
    CG, Jun 7; 1798: CG, May 18; 1799: CG, May 22; 1800: CG, Jun 3
Hay (musician), 1758: DL, Mar 3; 1759: HAM, Aug 13, CG, Nov 30; 1760: KING'S,
    Apr 24; 1763: CG, Feb 18; 1764: HAY, Nov 13; 1766: CG, Feb 21, RANELAGH, Jun
    20; 1767: HAB, Dec 10; 1773: KING'S, Feb 5; 1775: CHAPEL, Nov 23
Hay, Harriett Sylvester, 1796: CG, May 27; 1797: CG, May 17
Hay, Master (actor), 1728: HAY, Feb 16
Hayden (composer), 1730: GF, Dec 19; 1732: GF, May 4, 15, 17, 23
Hayden Cantata (song), 1731: GF, May 13
Haydn, Franz Joseph (composer, conductor), 1783: HAY, Aug 1; 1785: CG, May 12;
    1787: CG, Mar 12; 1788: CG, Dec 13; 1789: DL, Feb 27, Mar 20; 1790: CG, Oct
    4; 1791: KING'S, Mar 31, Apr 9, 26, May 12, 19, Jun 2, CG, Dec 10, PAN, 31;
    1792: CG, Nov 3; 1793: CG, Mar 11, Sep 16; 1794: HAY, Jul 28, CG, Nov 17, Dec
    26; 1795: KING'S, Feb 20, 27, HAY, Mar 4, KING'S, 28, CG, Apr 6, 9; 1796: DL,
    Apr 30; 1799: KING'S, Mar 26, CG, May 15, OCH, 15, HAY, Aug 13, Sep 16; 1800:
    CG, Mar 14, 19, 28, Apr 2
--Creation, The (oratorio), 1800: CG, Mar 28, Apr 2, 4
Haydock (beneficiary), 1734: LIF, May 16; 1735: DL, May 22
Haydon Square, 1733: GF, Feb 12, Mar 30
Hayes (actor), 1736: LIF, Oct 21; 1737: CG, Oct 17, 19; 1738: BFP, Aug 23, CG,
    Oct 4; 1739: CG, Apr 29, May 8, 21, BFH, Aug 23; 1740: BFH, Aug 23
Hayes (actor), 1762: CG, Oct 18, 25; 1763: CG, Feb 3, Apr 25, May 9, HAY, Jun
    9, 20, Aug 1, CG, Sep 23, Oct 10, 15, 25, 26, Dec 9; 1764: CG, Jan 21, May
    16, HAY, Jun 13, 26, Jul 6, 13, 23, CG, Sep 24, Oct 5, 11, Nov 1, 16; 1765:

CG, Apr 9, May 24
Hayes (pit office keeper), 1753: DL, May 5; 1757: DL, May 2; 1758: DL, Apr 27;
1759: DL, May 15; 1760: DL, Apr 21; 1762: DL, Apr 21
Hayes, Charlotte (spectator), 1760: CG, Oct 16; 1774: CG, Feb 26
Hayes, F (actor), 1775: HAY, Feb 2; 1780: HAY, Mar 28; 1781: HAY, Mar 26
Hayes, Miss (actor), 1739: BFH, Aug 23; 1740: BFH, Aug 23
Hayes, Mr and Charlotte (spectators), 1760: DL, Feb 21
Hayes, Philip (composer), 1760: DL, Apr 16, May 8; 1786: CG, Apr 28, Oct 16;
1790: CG, Jun 1
Hayles, Henry (scene keeper, boxkeeper), 1677: DL, Dec 12, 26
Hayley, William, 1784: HAY, Aug 18, Sep 2; 1789: DL, Nov 7, CG, 10; 1790: CG,
Jan 29; 1792: CG, Apr 17
--Eudora, 1790: CG, Jan 29
--Lord Russel, 1784: HAY, Aug 18, 21, 23, 27, Sep 6; 1785: HAY, Jun 1, 2, 27,
Aug 1, 31; 1786: HAY, Jun 22
--Marcella, 1789: DL, Nov 7, CG, 10, 13
--Two Connoisseurs, The, 1784: HAY, Sep 2, 4, 7, 10, 14; 1785: HAY, Jun 4, 10,
30, Jul 7, Aug 31; 1786: HAY, Jun 23; 1787: HAY, Jun 23
--Zelma; or, The Will o' th' Wisp, 1792: CG, Apr 17, 19, 26, May 3
Haym, Nicolino Francesco (composer), 1705: QUEEN'S, Nov 17; 1706: DL, Jan 29,
Mar 30, Apr 3; 1708: QUEEN'S, Dec 14; 1711: QUEEN'S, Dec 26; 1712: DL, Jan
18, QUEEN'S, Dec 10; 1713: QUEEN'S, Jan 10, HIC, Apr 17, 24; 1714: QUEEN'S,
Jan 27; 1715: KING'S, Feb 26; 1720: KING'S, Apr 27; 1723: KING'S, Jan 12, Feb
19, May 14; 1724: KING'S, Jan 14, Feb 20, Apr 18, Oct 31; 1725: KING'S, Feb
13; 1726: KING'S, Jan 15; 1727: KING'S, Jan 31, May 6; 1728: KING'S, Feb 17,
Apr 30; 1735: GF/HAY, Mar 21
--Camilla (opera), 1706: DL, Mar 30, Apr 6, 11, 23, 30, May 16, 23, Jun 4, Jul
5, DG, Aug 1, Nov 26, DL, Dec 12, 14, QUEEN'S, 16, DL, 17, 21, 28; 1707: DL,
Jan 4, 11, 18, 25, 29, Feb 1, ATCOURT, 6, DL, 8, 12, 15, 27, Mar 8, 13, 29,
Apr 24, May 15, 24, Nov 15, DL/QUEEN, Dec 6, QUEEN'S, 9, DL/QUEEN, 9, 13;
1708: DL/QUEEN, Jan 27, 31, Feb 3, SH, 4, DL/QUEEN, 7, 10, 21, Mar 13, SH,
26, DL/QUEEN, 27, Apr 6, 24; 1709: QUEEN'S, Jan 25, 27, 29, Feb 2, 5, 12, 16,
19, Mar 17, Apr 5, 27, May 7, 21, Oct 20, Nov 7, 14, Dec 2, 13; 1717: LIF,
Jan 2, 5, 9, 12, 16, 19, 23, 26, Feb 13, 16, 20, Apr 2, 9, Jun 20, Jul 3;
1719: LIF, Feb 24, Mar 9, 14, Apr 16; 1726: LIF, Nov 19, 22, 24, 25, 26, 29,
Dec 1, 6, 8, 10, 13, 17, 20, 31; 1727: LIF, Jan 3, 5, 12, 25, Feb 1, 8, Mar
16, Apr 6, 12, 24, 27, May 12, Nov 2, 8, Dec 7; 1728: LIF, Nov 16, Dec 14;
1730: LIF, Apr 25, 30; 1733: LIF/CG, Apr 11
--Croesus (opera), 1714: QUEEN'S, Jan 27, 29, Feb 3, 9, 13, 16, 20, 23, 27, Mar
31, May 8, 22
--Dorinda (opera), 1712: QUEEN'S, Dec 10, 13, 17, 20, 31; 1713: QUEEN'S, Jan 3,
31, Feb 7, Mar 21, Apr 25; 1714: QUEEN'S, Jan 9, 16, 23
--Elisa (opera), 1726: KING'S, Jan 15, 18, 22, 25, 29, Feb 1
--Pyrrhus and Demetrius (opera), 1708: QUEEN'S, Dec 11, 14, 18, 21, 23, 28, 30;
1709: QUEEN'S, Jan 1, 5, 8, 12, 15, 19, 22, Feb 9, 12, 16, 23, 26, Mar 8, 22,
29, Apr 2, 9, 12, 16, 30, May 4, 14, 28, Jun 4, Oct 27, Nov 3, 10, 29, Dec 9,
16, 30; 1710: QUEEN'S, Jan 6, Feb 3, Mar 21, Dec 6, 9, 13, 16, 30; 1711:
QUEEN'S, Jan 3, 6, Feb 3, 13, May 12; 1716: KING'S, Mar 10, 13, 17, HIC, 21,
KING'S, 24, Apr 4, 11, May 2, 15, 26, 31, Jun 2; 1717: KING'S, Feb 2, Mar 2
Haym's scholar (musician), 1713: HIC, Apr 24
Haymakers' Dance (dance), 1757: CG, Apr 23, 29; 1772: HAY, Aug 17; 1773: HAY,
May 26, Jun 2, 11, Jul 28, 30; 1774: DL, Jun 2, HAY, Aug 3; 1775: HAY, Jun 5,
21, 26, Jul 28, Aug 4, 14, Sep 13; 1776: HAY, May 27, 28, Jul 8, 10, Aug 9;
1777: HAY, Jun 18
Hayman (actor), 1736: DL, Feb 28; 1743: LIF, Feb 14, Mar 21, Apr 5, 8, CG, Oct
5, 17, Dec 12, 14; 1744: CG, Jan 11, Mar 12, Apr 30, May 2, Sep 19, Oct 3, 8,
Nov 2, 5, 9, 27, Dec 6, 21; 1745: CG, Mar 11, Apr 4, 20, 23, 26, May 6, 8,
Sep 23, 25, Oct 7, Nov 7, 26; 1746: CG, Jan 11, Feb 5, GF, 5, CG, 24, Mar 10,
13, 18, Apr 1, 7, May 1, Sep 29, Oct 1, Dec 6, 19
Hayman, Mrs (beneficiary), 1747: CG, May 22
Haymer (merchant), 1749: DL, Apr 5
Haymes, Thomas (actor, singer), 1789: DL, Sep 19, 24, Oct 1, 10, 20, Nov 5, 21,
Dec 10, 14, 17, 22, 26; 1790: DL, Jan 15, 19, Feb 3, 13, Mar 22, Apr 23, 30,
May 14, 15, 20, 25, 28, Oct 7, HAY, 13, DL, 14, 16, 21, 26, Nov 3, 4, 5, Dec
8, 14, 27; 1791: DL, Jan 10, 27, Feb 1, 10, Mar 19, 22, Apr 28, May 10, 14,
19; 1795: CG, Jan 2, 14, Feb 21, Mar 16, Apr 8, 28, May 14, Jun 16, Sep 14,
21, 23, 28, Oct 14, 16, 19, 22, Nov 4, 6, 25, 27, Dec 7, 9, 21, 23; 1796: CG,
Mar 15, 17, 30, Apr 1, 19, 23, 29, May 18, 28, Jun 3, 7, Sep 12, 14, 17, 19,
23, 26, 30, Oct 5, 6, 7, 17, 18, 20, 21, 24, Nov 3, 5, Dec 1, 15, 27; 1797:
CG, Jan 3, 7, 10, Feb 18, Mar 13, Apr 19, 26, May 6, 16, 17, 18, 19, Jun 8,
13, 21
Haynes, John (prologuist), 1690: DL, Dec 0; 1749: HAY, Nov 17

403

Haynes (Haines, Hanes), Joseph (actor, author), 1668: BRIDGES, Mar 7, May 7, NONE, Sep 0, BRIDGES, Dec 18; 1669: BRIDGES, Mar 17, LIF, Dec 14; 1671: BRIDGES, Dec 7; 1672: DG, Jul 4, LIF, Nov 0; 1674: DL, May 16, Nov 19; 1675: DL, Jan 12, 25, Apr 23, May 10, Jul 0, Aug 0; 1676: DL, Jan 29, Dec 11; 1677: DL, Mar 0, May 5, Jun 0; 1678: DL, Mar 0; 1679: DL, Mar 0; 1682: NONE, Sep 0; 1684: DL, Mar 0, DG, Jun 0, DLORDG, Aug 0; 1685: DG, Jul 0, DL, Aug 0, BF, 0; 1689: DLORDG, Apr 0; 1691: NONE, Sep 0; 1692: DL, Mar 0; 1693: DL, Mar 0, Apr 0, DG, May 0; 1694: DG, May 0; 1696: DL, Feb 0, Mar 0, DG, Jun 0, DL, Jul 0, DG, Oct 0, DL, Nov 21, DL/DL, Dec 0; 1697: DL, May 8, 31, NONE, Sep 0, LIF, Nov 0; 1698: DL, Dec 0; 1699: DL, Apr 0, Nov 28; 1700: DL, Mar 0, YB, 20, DL, Apr 29, Oct 0; 1735: DL, Jun 3; 1736: DL, May 25; 1752: DL, Apr 3; 1764: CG, Apr 28; 1779: HAY, Oct 18; 1791: CG, May 18
--Epilogue Riding on an Ass (entertainment), 1752: DL, Apr 21; 1754: CG, May 17; 1765: CG, May 15; 1766: CG, Apr 15, 19, HAY, Aug 21; 1770: CG, Mar 26; 1771: CG, Mar 18; 1776: CG, May 10, HAY, Sep 18; 1782: HAY, Aug 27, Sep 16; 1783: CG, May 9, HAY, Aug 13, 27; 1784: HAY, Aug 10; 1785: HAY, Feb 12, CG, May 7, HAY, Aug 16
--Fatal Mistake, A; or, The Plot Spoiled, 1689: DLORDG, Apr 0; 1691: NONE, Sep 0; 1695: NONE, Sep 0
Haynes, Mrs (singer), 1700: LIF, Jul 5; 1701: YB, May 5
Haynes's Recantation Prologue (entertainment), 1689: DLORDG, Apr 0, NONE, Sep 0
Haynes's Reformation Prologue (entertainment), 1692: DLORDG, Jan 2
Hayns, Mrs (actor), 1730: HAY, Mar 11
Hays (dresser), 1760: CG, Sep 22
Hays, Mrs (actor), 1717: LIF, Dec 7
Hayward, Miss (actor), 1767: DL, Jan 24; 1770: HAY, Jul 9, Aug 22, 27, Sep 1, 3, DL, Oct 27, Dec 13; 1771: DL, Mar 21, Apr 23, May 27, Oct 19, 28, Nov 4; 1772: DL, Feb 28, Mar 23, 28
Haywood (Hayward), Eliza (actor, author), 1717: LIF, Apr 23; 1721: LIF, Mar 4; 1723: DL, Aug 12; 1729: LIF, Mar 4; 1730: HAY, Apr 8; 1732: HAY, Mar 2; 1733: HAY, May 31; 1736: HAY, Jan 21; 1737: HAY, Mar 14, 21, Apr 13, 25, May 23; 1743: DL, Dec 10; 1781: HAY, Jan 22; 1792: HAY, Dec 26
--Arden of Feversham, 1736: HAY, Jan 21
--Fair Captive, The, 1715: LIF, May 21; 1721: LIF, Mar 4, 6, 7, Nov 16
--Frederick, Duke of Brunswick Lunenberg, 1729: LIF, Mar 4, 6, 8
--Love in Excess, 1737: HAY, May 23
--Opera of Operas, The; or, Tom Thumb the Great, 1733: HAY, May 31, Jun 4, 6, 8, 11, 13, 15, 18, 20, 22, 25, 27, DL/HAY, Oct 29, 31, Nov 1, 3, 5, 6, DL, 7, DL/HAY, 7, 8, DL, 9, DL/HAY, 9, 10, 12, DL, 13, DL/HAY, 13, 15, 16, 17, DL, Dec 13, DL/HAY, 28; 1734: DL/HAY, Jan 21, 28; 1740: CG, Apr 30
--Wife to be Let, The, 1723: DL, Aug 12, 13, 14; 1781: HAY, Jan 22; 1792: HAY, Dec 26
Haywood, Mrs (beneficiary), 1770: DL, May 28
Hazard (actor), 1748: BF, Aug 24, SFBCBV, Sep 7
He bids the circling season (song), 1789: DL, Mar 20
He chose a mournful muse (song), 1790: DL, Feb 24; 1791: CG, Mar 25, Apr 13; 1792: CG, Mar 7; 1794: CG, Mar 14
He comes (song), 1789: DL, Mar 18; 1790: DL, Feb 26, CG, Mar 3; 1791: DL, Mar 11, 23, CG, Apr 6, 13; 1792: CG, Mar 21; 1793: CG, Feb 20, KING/HAY, 22, CG, Mar 20; 1795: CG, Mar 4; 1800: CG, Feb 28
He delivered the poor (song), 1794: DL, Apr 11
He gave them hailstones (song), 1786: DL, Mar 10; 1789: CG, Mar 6, DL, 18; 1790: CG, Feb 24, DL, 24, 26; 1791: CG, Mar 11, DL, 23; 1792: KING'S, Feb 24, CG, Mar 2, KING'S, 21; 1793: CG, Feb 15, KING/HAY, 22; 1794: CG, Mar 7, DL, 12, 14, Apr 2, 10; 1795: CG, Feb 20, KING'S, 27, CG, Mar 25; 1796: CG, Feb 24; 1797: CG, Mar 10; 1798: CG, Mar 9, 30; 1799: CG, Feb 15, Mar 13; 1800: CG, Mar 5
He has left me-the Youth, the dear youth I adore (song), 1800: CG, May 17
He layeth the beams (song), 1790: DL, Feb 26, CG, Mar 17; 1791: DL, Mar 23, CG, 23; 1792: KING'S, Feb 24, CG, Mar 2; 1793: CG, Feb 20, KING/HAY, 22, Mar 1; 1794: DL, Mar 12, CG, 14, DL, 14, Apr 2, 10; 1795: CG, Feb 27; 1798: CG, Mar 14, 30; 1799: CG, Feb 8, Mar 6
He led her by the milk-white hand (song), 1699: DL, May 0
He led them through the deep (song), 1790: CG, Mar 19; 1794: CG, Mar 26, Apr 11
He measureth the waters (song), 1791: CG, Feb 26, Mar 23; 1794: CG, Mar 14, DL, Apr 10; 1795: CG, Feb 27; 1799: CG, Mar 6
He rebuked the Red Sea (song), 1789: CG, Apr 3; 1790: CG, Feb 26; 1791: CG, Mar 23; 1794: CG, Apr 11; 1795: CG, Mar 25; 1798: CG, Mar 14
He shall feed his flock (song), 1758: KING'S, Apr 6; 1790: DL, Mar 17; 1793: KING/HAY, Feb 20; 1794: DL, Mar 19
He sitteth at the right hand of God (song), 1786: DL, Mar 10; 1789: DL, Mar 18; 1790: DL, Feb 26; 1791: DL, Mar 23; 1792: KING'S, Feb 24; 1793: KING/HAY, Feb

22; <u>1794</u>: DL, Apr 10
He smote all the first born (song), <u>1789</u>: CG, Apr 3; <u>1790</u>: CG, Mar 17; <u>1791</u>:
DL, Mar 11, CG, 23; <u>1793</u>: CG, Mar 8; <u>1794</u>: CG, Mar 7, DL, 26, Apr 11; <u>1795</u>:
CG, Feb 20; <u>1798</u>: CG, Mar 14
He sung Darius great and good (song), <u>1790</u>: DL, Feb 24; <u>1791</u>: CG, Mar 25; <u>1792</u>:
CG, Mar 7; <u>1794</u>: CG, Mar 14
He that dwelleth (song), <u>1793</u>: KING/HAY, Feb 20; <u>1794</u>: DL, Mar 19
He trusted in God (song), <u>1793</u>: KING/HAY, Feb 20; <u>1794</u>: DL, Mar 19
He was brought as a lamb (song), <u>1786</u>: DL, Mar 29; <u>1789</u>: DL, Mar 18; <u>1790</u>: DL,
Feb 26; <u>1791</u>: DL, Mar 23; <u>1792</u>: KING'S, Feb 24; <u>1793</u>: KING/HAY, Feb 22, Mar
1; <u>1794</u>: DL, Apr 10
He was cut off (song), <u>1790</u>: CG, Mar 26; <u>1793</u>: KING/HAY, Feb 20; <u>1794</u>: DL, Mar
19
He was despised and rejected (song), <u>1758</u>: KING'S, Apr 6; <u>1786</u>: DL, Mar 3;
<u>1793</u>: KING/HAY, Feb 20, CG, Mar 13, 22; <u>1794</u>: DL, Mar 19; <u>1795</u>: CG, Mar 20,
27; <u>1797</u>: CG, Mar 3, 15; <u>1799</u>: CG, Feb 13, Mar 15
He was eyes unto the blind (song), <u>1786</u>: DL, Mar 10; <u>1787</u>: DL, Feb 23; <u>1789</u>:
CG, Mar 6, DL, 18, CG, 27; <u>1790</u>: DL, Feb 26, CG, 26; <u>1791</u>: DL, Mar 23, Apr 8;
<u>1792</u>: KING'S, Feb 24, CG, Mar 9; <u>1793</u>: KING/HAY, Feb 22, Mar 22; <u>1794</u>: CG,
Mar 26, DL, Apr 10, CG, 11; <u>1795</u>: CG, Feb 20; <u>1796</u>: CG, Feb 24; <u>1797</u>: CG, Mar
22; <u>1798</u>: CG, Mar 14; <u>1799</u>: CG, Feb 15, Mar 13; <u>1800</u>: CG, Feb 28
He Would be a Soldier. See Pilon, Frederick.
He Would if He Could. See Bickerstaff, Isaac.
He's aye kissing me (song), <u>1778</u>: DL, Apr 28, May 14, 15; <u>1779</u>: HAY, May 10;
<u>1780</u>: DL, Apr 7
He's Much to Blame. See Holcroft, Thomas.
Head (actor), <u>1744</u>: HAY, Apr 6
Head, Richard
--Hic and Ubique; or, The Humours of Dublin, <u>1662</u>: NONE, Sep 0
Heafford (plasterer), <u>1760</u>: CG, Feb 2; <u>1772</u>: CG, Jan 17; <u>1773</u>: CG, Jan 18
Heaphy, Mrs Tottenham, Alice (actor), <u>1794</u>: HAY, Jun 2
Hear a Nation's deep Distress (song), <u>1789</u>: DL, Mar 20
Hear, Jacob's God (song), <u>1790</u>: CG, Mar 17; <u>1791</u>: CG, Mar 11; <u>1793</u>: CG, Feb 15;
<u>1794</u>: CG, Mar 7; <u>1795</u>: CG, Feb 20; <u>1798</u>: CG, Mar 28; <u>1799</u>: CG, Mar 13; <u>1800</u>:
CG, Mar 5
Hear us, O God (song), <u>1793</u>: CG, Mar 8; <u>1797</u>: CG, Mar 24
Hear us, O Lord (song), <u>1791</u>: DL, Mar 11; <u>1797</u>: CG, Mar 17
Hear, Ye Gods of Britain (song), <u>1716</u>: DL, Jun 26
Heard, Ann, Mrs William (actor), <u>1772</u>: CG, May 23; <u>1776</u>: CG, May 11; <u>1777</u>: CG,
May 9; <u>1778</u>: CHR, May 25, 29, Jun 1, 3, 18, 24; <u>1783</u>: DL, May 23, Nov 22;
<u>1784</u>: DL, May 15; <u>1785</u>: DL, Jan 20, May 20, Sep 27, Dec 26; <u>1786</u>: DL, Feb 10,
May 26, Nov 25, Dec 14, 16; <u>1787</u>: DL, May 30, Jun 1, Sep 20, Oct 2, Dec 6, 7;
<u>1788</u>: DL, Jun 5, 6, Sep 16, 25, Nov 1, 10, 15; <u>1789</u>: DL, Jan 5, Apr 21, May
22, Jun 9, Sep 15, 17, 19, 24, 29, Oct 8, 10, Dec 5, 8; <u>1790</u>: DL, Mar 8, May
15, Jun 2, Oct 4, 14, 27, Nov 5, 10, Dec 1; <u>1791</u>: DL, Apr 2, 4, DLKING'S, Oct
3, 4, 11, Nov 22, Dec 1, 2; <u>1792</u>: DLKING'S, Feb 4, 8, Jun 13, DL, Sep 15, 20;
<u>1793</u>: DL, Jan 29, Mar 12, Jun 5, HAY, 21, Aug 12, Sep 21, Nov 5, Dec 26;
<u>1794</u>: HAY, Jan 2, 4, Feb 20, Mar 13, 17, DL, May 20, 22, HAY, Jul 8, 12, Aug
20, DL, Oct 13, 21, Nov 12, 19, Dec 12; <u>1795</u>: DL, Jan 23, May 12, 29, HAY,
Jun 16, Jul 4, Aug 17, DL, Sep 17, 24, 26, Dec 2; <u>1796</u>: DL, Jan 2, 11, 18,
Mar 15, Apr 13, May 12, HAY, Jun 17, Aug 17, Sep 5, DL, Oct 4, 6, Nov 9, 22
Heard, Elizabeth (actor), <u>1782</u>: DL, Dec 26; <u>1783</u>: DL, Mar 10, CG, 29, DL, Apr
10, Sep 23; <u>1784</u>: CG, Jan 16, Feb 10, DL, Mar 6, May 10, 15, Sep 16, Nov 5;
<u>1785</u>: DL, Nov 7; <u>1786</u>: DL, Feb 1; <u>1787</u>: DL, Jun 1, Dec 10; <u>1788</u>: DL, Jun 6,
Oct 14, 20; <u>1789</u>: HAY, May 25, 29, Jun 3, 8, DL, 9, HAY, 17, Jul 9, 11; <u>1790</u>:
DL, Mar 18, 22, Apr 30, May 11, 12, HAY, Jun 14, 17, 25, Jul 5, 28, Aug 6, 7,
10, 11, DL, Sep 16, Oct 2, 26, 27; <u>1791</u>: DL, Mar 2, 4, 5, May 10, 20, HAY,
Jun 16, 17, 18, 28, Jul 1, 9, 15, 26, Aug 13, 15, 16, 18, Sep 2, DLKING'S,
27, Oct 1, 3, 4, Nov 5, 11, 15, 22, Dec 1, 2; <u>1792</u>: DLKING'S, Jan 7, Feb 23,
May 22, 23, Jun 13, 15, HAY, 18, 22, 26, 29, 30, Jul 7, 16, 28, Aug 9, 15,
23, 28, Sep 5, 6, DL, 27, Nov 2, Dec 21, 22, 28; <u>1793</u>: DL, Jan 5, 16, 21, 28,
Feb 4, 21, 25, Mar 5, 7, Apr 3, 5, 22, 23, 29, May 1, 3, 7, 10, Jun 1, 3, 10,
HAY, 12, 14, 15, 17, 21, 22, 25, 26, 29, Jul 18, 25, Aug 7, 12, Sep 19, 21,
26, 28, Oct 1, 5, 8, 21, 22, 24, 30, Nov 4, 5, 25, 27, 29, 30, Dec 5, 19;
<u>1794</u>: HAY, Jan 2, 9, 10, 13, 14, Feb 20, Mar 13, 17, DL, May 3, 13, 23, Jun
12, 14, 20, Jul 2, HAY, 8, 9, 11, 12, 17, 22, Aug 4, 9, 13, 20, Sep 10, DL,
27, 30, Oct 22, 31, Nov 1, 5, 15, 29, Dec 12, 20; <u>1795</u>: DL, Jan 13, 24, 26,
Feb 12, Mar 3, Apr 24, May 4, 9, 20, 26, 27, Jun 1, 3, 6, HAY, 11, 16, 18,
22, 24, 27, Jul 22, 25, Aug 7, 29, DL, Oct 6, 22, Nov 3, 6, 26, Dec 12, 14,
15, 17, 19; <u>1796</u>: DL, Jan 5, 16, 18, Feb 20, 22, 27, Apr 2, 13, 18, 20, 26,
May 6, 23, Jun 3, 4, 7, 8, 11, HAY, 11, 14, 17, 20, 29, 30, Jul 6, 11, 12,
15, 21, 26, Aug 3, 8, 13, 17, 23, Sep 17, DL, 20, 24, Oct 1, 3, 13, 24, 25,

27, Nov 1, 2, 8, 9, 10, 22, 23, Dec 7, 20, 26; 1797: DL, Jan 12, 17, 20, 27,
Feb 2, Mar 4, Apr 27, 28, May 1, 12, 15, 19, 24, 27, Jun 7, 12, HAY, 15, 17,
21, 22, 23, 29, Jul 3, 4, 6, 8, 10, 13, Aug 5, 9, 10, 14, 15, 21, 30, Sep 8,
11, DL, 26, 28, Oct 5, 7, 12, 14, 19, 28, Nov 10, 11, 14, 18, 20, 21, 24, Dec
9; 1798: DL, Jan 9, Feb 27, Apr 9, 14, May 7, 9, 11, 24, 29, Jun 1, 12, HAY,
12, 13, 14, 15, 16, 19, 20, 21, 23, 27, 28, 29, 30, Jul 17, 20, 30, Aug 3,
11, 21, 30, Sep 12, DL, 20, Oct 8, 11, 20, Nov 10, 28, Dec 4, 7, 8, 10, 12,
HAY, 17, DL, 19, 21, 27, 29; 1799: DL, Jan 11, Feb 4, 14, 19, Apr 19, 22, 23,
24, May 2, 8, 9, 16, Jun 10, HAY, 17, 18, DL, 19, HAY, 21, 22, 24, 25, DL,
29, Jul 1, 3, 4, 5, HAY, 8, 12, 16, 17, 26, Aug 13, 17, 26, 27, DL, Sep 21,
28, Oct 1, 5, 29, 30, 31, Nov 12, 14, 25, Dec 26, 30; 1800: DL, Jan 4, 11,
14, 18, 25, Feb 1, 4, 7, 12, Mar 10, 24, 27, Apr 21, 28, 29, May 1, 10, 19,
30, Jun 5, 7, 9, 10, 11, 17
Heard, William, 1776: DL, Jun 5
--Snuff Box, The; or, A Trip to Bath, 1775: HAY, Mar 23
--Valentine's Day, 1776: DL, Mar 23
Heart in Love's Empire, A (song), 1672: DG, Jul 4
Heart of Oak (song), 1761: CG, Apr 23, May 1
Heart of Steel (song), 1796: CG, May 16
Heart the seat of soft delight (song), 1748: KING'S, Apr 5; 1784: DL, Mar 5;
    1789: CG, Apr 3; 1791: DL, Apr 1, CG, 13; 1792: KING'S, Feb 29, CG, Mar 9;
    1794: DL, Mar 14, 26
Heartfree (author), 1766: DL, Jan 23
Heartless, Mrs (actor), 1746: SFW, Sep 8
Hearts of Oak (entertainment), 1762: DL, Jan 15, 16, 18, 20, 22, 23, 27, 28,
    29, Feb 22, 27, Mar 2, 9, 15, 18, 23, 27, Apr 3, 21, May 7, 8, 17, 18, 19,
    21, 24, Sep 25, Oct 4, 22, Nov 4, 10, 13, 16; 1763: DL, May 6; 1765: DL, Apr
    20, May 1, 9, 14, Dec 16; 1766: DL, Feb 7, 18, Apr 4, 12, 29, May 14; 1767:
    DL, Feb 12, 23, Apr 21, 22, 23, 25, 28, 29, May 6, 8, Oct 22, 27, Nov 6, 23,
    Dec 2, 19; 1768: DL, Apr 7, 9, Oct 13, 27; 1769: DL, Apr 1, 6, 14, 21, 26;
    1770: DL, Mar 31, Apr 3
Hearts of Oak (song), 1796: CG, May 12; 1797: CG, May 2, Oct 18, 20; 1798: CG,
    Apr 24, May 9
Heartwell, Henry, 1798: CG, May 23; 1799: HAY, Jul 13
--Castle of Sorrento, The (opera), 1799: HAY, Jul 13, 15, 16, 17, 18, 19, 20,
    22, 23, 24, 25, 29, Aug 2, 7, 8, 12, 14, 16, Sep 2, 9, 10, 12, 14; 1800: CG,
    Apr 26, May 6, HAY, Jun 14, Jul 25, Aug 2, 5, 21, Sep 8
--Reformed in Time (opera), 1798: CG, May 23, 25, 29, 31, Oct 5
Heath (beneficiary), 1738: CG, Aug 29
Heath, Francis (house servant), 1739: DL, May 31; 1744: DL, May 21; 1747: DL,
    May 15; 1750: DL, Mar 8; 1753: DL, May 19; 1767: DL, Jan 24, Feb 9; 1771: DL,
    Nov 14; 1772: DL, Apr 9; 1774: DL, May 19; 1775: DL, May 27, Dec 9; 1776: DL,
    Jun 10, Oct 15
Heath, Miss (actor), 1755: DL, Nov 8; 1762: DL, Mar 29; 1763: DL, Mar 21; 1765:
    DL, Mar 18
Heath, Mr and Mrs (house servants), 1767: DL, Jan 24; 1775: DL, Sep 30
Heath, Mrs, 1773: DL, Mar 29
Heathcot (beneficiary), 1790: CG, May 29; 1791: CG, Jun 2; 1792: CG, May 25;
    1794: CG, Jun 4; 1795: CG, Jun 4
Heather, Master (actor), 1798: DL, Oct 15, Nov 3; 1799: DL, Apr 5, May 4, Jul
    1, Sep 28, Nov 7; 1800: DL, Jan 1, Jun 5
Heatly (actor), 1770: HAY, Dec 19
Heatly, Mrs (actor), 1770: HAY, Dec 19
Heaving of the Lead (song), 1797: CG, Jun 10
Hebden (bassoonist), 1745: DT, Mar 14; 1758: CHAPEL, Apr 27
Hecate's Prophecy (entertainment), 1758: DL, Apr 14
Hecuba. See West, Richard; Delap, John.
Hedge Lane, 1763: HAY, Sep 5
Hedges (actor), 1780: HAY, Nov 13; 1782: HAY, Jan 21
Hedges, Mrs (actor), 1780: HAY, Jun 9, DL, Dec 8; 1782: DL, May 8, 11, 31, Sep
    19; 1783: DL, Feb 7, Mar 10, May 9, Sep 23, 30, Oct 7, Dec 10; 1784: DL, Apr
    26, May 3, 20, Sep 21, Nov 4, 5; 1785: DL, May 11, Nov 7, 17, 22; 1786: DL,
    May 24; 1789: DL, Jun 5; 1790: DL, Mar 8, 22, May 15, 28, CG, Jun 16, DL, Oct
    14; 1791: DL, May 10; 1795: DL, Feb 6, 12, May 6; 1796: DL, Jan 18
Heele (surveyor), 1776: DL, Jun 10; 1778: DL, Dec 18
Heemskirk. See Hemskirk.
Heffinal, Dr. See Hiffernan, Paul.
Heidegger, John James (proprietor, author), 1713: QUEEN'S, Feb 26, Apr 11;
    1714: QUEEN'S, Mar 4; 1715: KING'S, May 25; 1717: LIF, Oct 5; 1733: KING'S,
    Jun 22; 1734: KING'S, Nov 2; 1737: KING'S, Apr 25; 1738: KING'S, May 23, Jul
    26; 1741: KING'S, Dec 1; 1745: DL, Oct 24
--Ernelinda (opera), 1713: QUEEN'S, Feb 26, 28, Mar 3, 7, 10, 14, 28, Apr 11,

May 2, 30; 1714: QUEEN'S, Apr 3, 7, 17, 24, May 12, Jun 5, 23, KING'S, Nov
  16, 20, Dec 4, 18; 1715: KING'S, Apr 2, 9
Heigho for a Husband. See Waldron, Francis Godolphin.
Heinel, Mlle (dancer), 1770: KING'S, May 19; 1771: KING'S, Dec 17, 21, 28;
  1772: KING'S, Jan 4, 7, 11, 14, Feb 1, 4, 8, 18, 22, 25, 29, Mar 3, 7, 10,
  12, 17, 24, 31, Apr 4, 7, 9, 21, 25, 28, May 9, 12, 14, 23, 30, Jun 3, 5;
  1773: KING'S, Jan 5, 12, 19, 26, Feb 2, 20, 23, 25, Mar 9, 16, 18, 30, Apr 1,
  3, 13, 17, 19, 20, 24, 27, 29, May 1, 3, 6, 11, 22, 25, 28, Jun 1, 3, 5, 8;
  1774: KING'S, Mar 24; 1776: KING'S, May 30
Heir at Law, The. See Colman the younger, George.
Heir of Lynne (ballad), 1793: CG, Apr 25
Heir of Morocco, The. See Settle, Elkanah.
Heiress, The. See Cavendish, William; Burgoyne, Lieutenant-General John.
Heiress, The; or, The Antigallican. See Mozeen, Thomas.
Heiress, The; or, The Salamanca Doctor Out Plotted. See Centlivre, Susannah.
Hele. See Heele.
Helena, Miss (spectator), 1679: BF, Sep 3
Helm (dancer, actor), 1773: CG, Dec 31; 1774: CG, Oct 7, 15, Nov 19, Dec 1, 14,
  16, 27; 1775: CG, Jan 24, Mar 30, May 12, KING'S, Oct 31, Nov 7, 28; 1776:
  KING'S, Jan 9, 20, Feb 3, 13, 24, Mar 12, 19, 28, Apr 18, 25, May 30, Jun 8,
  DL, Oct 24, Nov 1, 6, 7, Dec 18; 1777: DL, Feb 10, Apr 22; 1779: HAY, Feb 22,
  Mar 15; 1780: DL, Nov 4, Dec 4, 27; 1781: DL, Jan 16, May 15, 18, Sep 18, Nov
  5, 10; 1782: DL, Apr 12, 25, May 7, 16, 18, CG, Oct 22, Nov 1, 18, 28, 29,
  Dec 3, 14, 31; 1783: CG, Jan 1, 17, 28, Apr 23, May 16, 17, 29, 31, Oct 6,
  13, 14, Dec 6; 1784: CG, Jan 16, 26, 29, Feb 12, Mar 1, 23, Apr 13, May 6,
  11, 18, 20, 24, 26, Jun 10, Sep 20, 28, Oct 11, Nov 16, 30, Dec 3, 4; 1785:
  CG, Jan 8, Feb 28, Mar 7, 29, Apr 1, 6, 22, May 7, Sep 21, 23, 30, Oct 12,
  17, Nov 10, Dec 14; 1786: CG, Jan 4, 31, Feb 7, 11, Mar 13, Apr 4, 8, 18, 24,
  May 3, 15, 18, 24, Sep 20, Oct 4, 6, 9, Nov 18, Dec 15, 30; 1787: CG, Feb 6,
  10, 13, Mar 31, Apr 16, 30, May 11, Jun 2, Sep 17, 21, 28, Oct 3, 22, Nov 9,
  Dec 5, 15; 1788: CG, Jan 18, 21, Mar 1, 11, 24, Apr 1, May 12, Jun 4, Oct 22,
  Nov 12, 22, 26, Dec 1; 1789: CG, Feb 17, 21, Apr 30, Jun 16; 1798: CG, Feb 12
Helm, Miss (actor), 1753: CG, Oct 8, Nov 7, 9, 10, Dec 11; 1754: CG, Apr 18,
  Sep 16, 18, 27, Dec 10; 1755: CG, Oct 17, Nov 10, Dec 4; 1756: CG, Apr 29,
  May 5, Sep 22, Oct 28, Nov 9, 11, Dec 23; 1757: CG, Feb 18, Apr 30, May 27,
  Oct 13, 20, Nov 9, 15, 18; 1758: CG, Jan 11, Mar 13, Apr 22, Sep 18, 20, Oct
  9, Nov 9; 1759: CG, May 3, 18, Oct 1, 10; 1760: CG, Jan 16, Feb 21, Apr 12,
  May 8, DL, Jul 29, CG, Sep 22, 24, Oct 20; 1761: CG, Apr 17, May 11, Sep 16,
  Oct 5, 14; 1762: CG, Mar 29, Apr 17, Oct 4, 13, 14, Dec 27; 1763: CG, Mar 26,
  May 7, 18, Sep 30, Oct 12, 26; 1764: CG, Mar 27, May 5, Sep 24, Oct 5, 12;
  1765: CG, May 3, Oct 16, Nov 15, 28; 1766: CG, Apr 25, Oct 14, Nov 18, 27;
  1767: CG, May 9, Sep 14, Oct 5, 9, Nov 28; 1768: CG, Feb 25, Oct 22, Dec 26;
  1769: CG, Jan 23, Apr 24, Oct 12, 20, 24, Dec 20; 1770: CG, Jan 27, Apr 30,
  May 2, Oct 2, Dec 26; 1771: CG, Jan 1, 15, Apr 23, 29, Sep 23, Oct 2, 11;
  1772: CG, Mar 23, Apr 27, May 29, Sep 25, Oct 23, Dec 11; 1773: CG, Apr 21,
  May 8, 25, Oct 15, 22, Dec 23; 1774: CG, Jan 3, 29, Apr 11, 12
Help, Galatea (song), 1791: DL, Apr 1; 1792: KING'S, Feb 29; 1794: DL, Mar 26
Hemans, William (actor), 1747: RL, Jan 27
Hemet, Miss (singer, actor), 1780: HAY, Jun 24, Nov 13; 1781: HAY, Jan 22;
  1782: HAY, Mar 18, Apr 9, May 6, Nov 25; 1783: HAY, Sep 17; 1784: HAY, Feb
  23; 1785: HAY, Jan 31
Heminge (Hemmings), William (actor, author), 1687: DLORDG, Mar 26
--Eunuch, The, 1676: NONE, Sep 0; 1687: ATCOURT, Jan 30, DLORDG, Mar 26, DL,
  May 12
--Fatal Contract, The, 1663: NONE, Sep 0
Hemley, Mrs (actor), 1788: HAY, Dec 22; 1789: HAY, Feb 23
Hemlock Court, 1737: LIF, Apr 2
Hemming's Row, 1788: DL, May 6
Hemmings (actor), 1740: GF, Dec 15; 1741: GF, Feb 19
Hemmings, Elizabeth (singer), 1710: YB, May 1
Hemmings, Robert (actor), 1747: RL, Jan 27
Hempson, Celestina (singer), 1733: LIF, Dec 29; 1734: LIF, Feb 26, Apr 10, May
  11; see also Celeste, Sga
Hemskirk (actor), 1745: NWC, Dec 30
Hemskirk (singer), 1751: DL, Apr 22
Hemskirk, J (actor), 1736: HAY, Feb 16, LIF, Mar 31; 1739: BF, Aug 27, SF, Sep
  8; 1740: SOU, Oct 9, GF, Nov 22, Dec 6, 15; 1741: GF, Jan 27, Feb 16, 19, Mar
  12, Apr 15, 17, 29, Sep 16, Oct 9, 16, Nov 4, Dec 10; 1742: GF, Feb 3, 18,
  LIF, Dec 1, 6, 13; 1743: LIF, Jan 7, 14, Feb 14, 17, HAY, Apr 14; 1745: NWC,
  Dec 30
Hemsted (actor), 1784: HAY, Aug 13
Hence loathed melancholy (song), 1790: DL, Mar 10, CG, 17; 1791: CG, Mar 18,

407

30; 1794: CG, Mar 21, DL, Apr 9
Hence vain deluding joys (song), 1791: CG, Mar 18, 30; 1792: CG, Feb 24; 1794:
   CG, Mar 21, DL, Apr 9
Hendel. See Handel.
Henderson (actor), 1779: HAY, Jan 11; 1780: HAY, Jan 17
Henderson (singer), 1794: DL, Oct 31; 1796: DL, Jan 11
Henderson (ticket deliverer), 1790: DL, May 29; 1791: DL, May 31; 1792:
   DLKING'S, Jun 15; 1793: DL, Jun 6; 1795: DL, Jun 5; 1796: DL, Jun 10; 1797:
   DL, Jun 15; 1798: DL, Jun 16; 1799: DL, Jul 3; 1800: DL, Jun 13
Henderson, John (actor), 1768: CG, Oct 24; 1777: HAY, Jun 11, 26, Jul 15, 24,
   Aug 7, 19, 25, Sep 3, DL, 30, Oct 7, 14, 17, 28, Nov 24, 29, Dec 4, 13, 18;
   1778: DL, Jan 2, 24, Feb 10, 24, Mar 5, 31, Sep 17, 19, 22, 29, Oct 1, CG, 5,
   DL, 13, 17, 28, 31, Nov 4, 7, Dec 19, 22; 1779: CG, Jan 1, DL, 5, Feb 8, Mar
   22, Apr 10, CG, 24, 26, DL, Jun 1, CG, Oct 18, 23, 30, Nov 1, 10, 13, 19, 22,
   Dec 11, 17, 31; 1780: CG, Jan 12, 25, Mar 14, DL, Apr 7, CG, 27, May 1, 12,
   Oct 2, 9, 11, 19, 23, 24, 26, 30, Nov 1, 4, 10, Dec 12, 27; 1781: CG, Jan 4,
   29, 31, Feb 10, Mar 23, 31, Apr 18, 20, HAY, Aug 24, CG, Sep 17, Oct 3, 13,
   22, 23, 26, 31, Nov 3, 6, 17, Dec 5, 8, 11, 17, 18, 31; 1782: CG, Jan 3, 5,
   7, 10, 22, Feb 9, Mar 19, Apr 17, 20, DL, May 15, CG, Oct 3, 4, 8, 10, 14,
   17, 21, Nov 1, 18, 29, 30, Dec 12, 14, 20, 30; 1783: CG, Jan 1, 28, Feb 19,
   Mar 29, 31, Apr 1, May 7, 17, 19, Sep 24, 26, Oct 3, 6, 9, 11, 13, 15, 17,
   20, Nov 4, 10, 13, 24, 27, Dec 1, 31; 1784: CG, Jan 3, 7, 9, 16, 23, 26, DL,
   Feb 10, CG, 10, 11, Mar 4, 6, 16, 20, 23, 30, Sep 17, 20, 21, 27, 28, 29, Oct
   4, DL, 9, CG, 11, 18, 27, 30, Nov 4, 13, 29; 1785: CG, Jan 19, 21, Feb 8, 28,
   Mar 3, 7, 8, 15, Apr 2, 8, 12, 23, May 7, 13, 18, Sep 21, 26, 28, Oct 12, 17,
   27, 31, Nov 1, 2, 4, 8; 1786: CG, Feb 25
Hendon, 1783: CG, Jan 29
Henery (dancer), 1774: KING'S, Dec 13; 1775: KING'S, Apr 18, Jun 6, 17, 24, Oct
   31
Henley (actor), 1785: HAY, Feb 10
Henley, Anthony (poet), 1693: DL, Feb 0, DLORDG, Dec 0
Henley, Rev John (orator), 1729: YB, Apr 15; 1747: HAY, Apr 21; 1752: CT/HAY,
   Mar 21, HAY, 28, CT/HAY, May 5
Henley, Mrs (actor), 1784: HAY, Dec 13; 1785: HAY, Jan 31, Feb 10, Mar 15;
   1793: CG, Dec 7, 11, 18, 19, 30, 31; 1794: CG, Jan 3, Feb 10, 22, Apr 25, 29,
   May 26, Jun 11, Sep 22, 26, 29, Oct 3, 7, 10, 22, 30, Nov 7; 1795: CG, Jan
   12, 31, Feb 5, 14, Mar 9, 17; 1796: CG, Sep 19, 26, 28, Oct 6, 7, 24, Dec 19;
   1797: CG, Jan 10, Feb 18, Mar 16, Apr 8, 19, 25, May 18, 22, Jun 5, 8, 9, Sep
   25, Oct 16, Nov 2, Dec 16, 18, 26; 1798: CG, Feb 12, Mar 19, 31, Apr 9, 20,
   May 12, Jun 2
Henley, Sir Robert (author), 1731: DL, Aug 18
Henniker, John (antiquary prologuist), 1791: CG, May 10
Henning (pit office keeper), 1760: CG, Sep 22
Henny, Madam de (dancer), 1753: CG, May 14
Henpecked Captain, The. See Cross, Richard.
Henrie, Mrs (actor), 1752: CG, Oct 26
Henrietta St, 1731: DL, Jan 27; 1738: DL, May 19; 1739: DL, May 11; 1743: CG,
   Mar 14; 1751: DL, Mar 12, Dec 17; 1753: DL, Mar 22; 1754: DL, Mar 23; 1755:
   DL, Mar 17; 1757: DL, Mar 28; 1758: DL, Mar 16; 1778: CG, Mar 23; 1779: DL,
   Apr 16, CG, 27; 1784: DL, Apr 13; 1785: CG, Apr 23; 1786: KING'S, Apr 6, DL,
   28; 1791: PAN, Feb 17, CG, May 28; 1792: CG, May 15; 1793: CG, May 21, DL,
   24; 1794: HAY, Jun 2; 1795: DL, May 2; 1796: DL, May 12; 1797: DL, May 25
Henrietta-Maria, Queen Dowager, 1669: NONE, Sep 3
Henriette-Anne, Princess, 1669: BRIDGES, Jun 24
Henry (actor), 1769: HAY, Feb 28
Henry (actor), 1777: CHR, Jun 18, 20, 23, 25, 27, 30, Jul 2, 21; 1782: HAY, Mar
   4
Henry and Emma. See Bate, Henry.
Henry and Emma; or, The Nut Brown Maid. See Arne, Dr Thomas A.
Henry Frederick, Prince, 1753: CG, Mar 24; 1755: CG, Dec 18; 1757: CG, Nov 5;
   1758: CG, Feb 4; 1760: CG, Dec 19; 1761: CG, Sep 24, Oct 8; 1768: CG, Jan 14,
   May 5; 1769: CG, Feb 13
Henry II. See Bancroft, John.
Henry II; or, The Fall of Rosamond. See Hull, Thomas.
Henry III of France Stabbed by a Fryer. See Shipman, Thomas.
Henry IV. See Shakespeare, William.
Henry V. See Shakespeare, William.
Henry VI. See Shakespeare, William.
Henry VII. See Macklin, Charles.
Henry VII's Chapel, 1753: KING'S, Apr 30; 1758: KING'S, Apr 6; 1759: CG, Feb 2
Henry VIII. See Shakespeare, William.
Henry, John (actor), 1779: DL, Oct 16, Nov 15; 1780: DL, Jan 8, 24, 28, Feb 2,

Apr 18, 21
Henry, Luigi (dancer), <u>1775</u>: KING'S, Jan 17; <u>1776</u>: DL, Oct 26; <u>1777</u>: DL, Oct 2,
    31, Nov 11, 25; <u>1778</u>: DL, Jan 17, 28, Feb 19, Mar 24, Oct 3, Nov 2, Dec 11;
    <u>1779</u>: KING'S, Feb 23, Mar 2, DL, May 5, 8, 17, 25, Sep 28, Nov 3, 20, KING'S,
    27, Dec 14; <u>1780</u>: KING'S, Feb 19, DL, 24, 28, KING'S, Apr 22, DL, May 2, 5,
    KING'S, 9, DL, Sep 23, 30, Oct 2, 18, 19, Nov 11, KING'S, 28, Dec 2, 16;
    <u>1781</u>: DL, Jan 2, KING'S, 13, DL, 18, KING'S, 23, DL, 31, KING'S, Feb 22, DL,
    Mar 12, KING'S, 29, DL, Apr 25, 30, May 1, 8, KING'S, Jun 5, DL, Sep 20, Oct
    4, 19, Nov 13, KING'S, 17, 28, Dec 11; <u>1782</u>: KING'S, Feb 2, DL, 12, KING'S,
    21, Mar 19, May 25, Nov 2, Dec 12, 17; <u>1783</u>: KING'S, Jan 11, Feb 15, Mar 13,
    Apr 10, May 1, 31, Nov 29, Dec 6; <u>1784</u>: KING'S, Jan 17, Feb 14, Mar 11, 18,
    May 11, 13, 20, 29, Jun 26, Dec 18; <u>1785</u>: KING'S, Jan 1, 11, Feb 5, Mar 3,
    May 12; <u>1786</u>: KINCS, Feb 18, 25, Mar 11, 21, 23, Apr 1, May 23, Jun 6, Dec
    23; <u>1787</u>: KING'S, Jan 6, 20, Mar 8, May 19, Dec 8; <u>1788</u>: KING'S, Jan 15, 29,
    Feb 21, 28, Mar 1, 13, Apr 3, May 15, 31, Jun 14
Henry, Mrs (actor), <u>1788</u>: CG, Jan 25, HAY, Jul 24; <u>1789</u>: DL, Nov 21; <u>1790</u>: DL,
    May 26
Henry, Prince, <u>1749</u>: CG, Dec 16; <u>1750</u>: CG, Mar 12; <u>1752</u>: CG, Dec 30; <u>1755</u>: CG,
    Dec 18; <u>1761</u>: CG, Sep 24, Oct 8; <u>1766</u>: CG, Sep 24; see also Highness; Princes
Henry's Cottage Maid (song), <u>1791</u>: DL, May 19
Heraclius. See Carlell, Lodowick.
Herbert, Lady Henrietta, <u>1767</u>: CG, May 23
Herbert, Lady Katherine, <u>1675</u>: ATCOURT, Feb 15
Herbert, Lord Edward, <u>1767</u>: CG, May 23
Herbert, Lord, <u>1721</u>: KING'S, Apr 15
Herbert, Miss (actor), <u>1794</u>: HAY, May 22; <u>1797</u>: HAY, Dec 4; <u>1798</u>: HAY, Mar 26
Herbert, Philip, Earl of Pembroke, <u>1675</u>: DLORDG, Dec 2
Herbert, Sir Henry (master of the revels), <u>1660</u>: NONE, Aug 7, REDBULL, 14, Nov
    5, 6, VERE/RED, 7, VERE, 8, 9, 10, 12, 13, 15, 16, 17, 19, VERE/RED, 20,
    VERE, 21, 22, 23, 24, 26, 29, Dec 1, 3, 6, 8; <u>1661</u>: VERE, Jan 9, 31, Feb 5,
    May 0, Oct 26, Nov 29, Dec 10, 11, 13, 16, 18, 20, 23, 28, 30; <u>1662</u>: VERE,
    Jan 6, 10, 11, 21, 28, Feb 15, 25, 27, Mar 1, 3, 11, 15, LIF, Apr 1, VERE, 4,
    19, 23, May 5, 12, 17, Jun 2, 6, Jul 7, 23; <u>1663</u>: LIF, Jun 0, BRIDGES, Nov 0,
    3, LIF, Dec 22; <u>1664</u>: LIF, Aug 13, BRIDGES, Sep 14, NONE, Nov 0, LIF, 5;
    <u>1671</u>: LIF, Mar 9; <u>1672</u>: DG, Mar 9; <u>1680</u>: DG, Feb 26; <u>1769</u>: CG, Sep 30, Oct 2,
    7, 12, 17, Nov 21; <u>1777</u>: CHR, Jun 27; <u>1796</u>: HAY, Feb 22
Herbert, Thomas, Lord Pembroke, <u>1680</u>: DG, Feb 26; <u>1697</u>: LIF, Feb 27
Hercules and Omphale (music), <u>1746</u>: NWC, Sep 15
Hercules and Omphale. See Byrn, James.
Hercules. See Motteux, Peter Anthony; Rossi, Giacomo; Handel, George Frederic.
Here a sheer hulk (song), <u>1790</u>: CG, Nov 23; <u>1791</u>: CG, Sep 19; <u>1793</u>: CG, May 21;
    <u>1794</u>: CG, Apr 12; <u>1799</u>: CG, Apr 19; see also Tom Bowling
Here amid these shady woods (song), <u>1786</u>: DL, Mar 10; <u>1789</u>: CG, Apr 3; <u>1793</u>:
    CG, Mar 8; <u>1798</u>: CG, Mar 14
Here and There and Every Where. See Delpini, Carlo Antonio.
Here we laugh and work together (song), <u>1796</u>: CG, Apr 12, May 12, 28
Here's a health to all good lasses (song), <u>1790</u>: CG, Apr 21, DL, May 20; <u>1791</u>:
    DL, May 18
Here's to the maiden of bashful fifteen (song), <u>1781</u>: DL, Sep 27
Hereford Society, <u>1778</u>: HAY, Mar 31
Herle, Mrs (actor), <u>1733</u>: DL, May 5, Oct 10, 24, Dec 14; <u>1734</u>: DL, Jan 3, 8,
    Feb 4, DL/LIF, Mar 11, LIF, Apr 15, DL/LIF, May 3, JS, 31, BFHBH, Aug 24,
    HAY, Oct 7, GR, Nov 4; <u>1736</u>: LIF, Mar 31, BFHC, Aug 23; <u>1738</u>: BFP, Aug 23
Herman von Unna. See Skjoldebrand, Anders Fredrik Count.
Hermione, The. See Dibdin, Thomas John.
Hermit, The (song), <u>1787</u>: HAY, Apr 30
Hermit, The. See Goldsmith, Oliver.
Hermit, The; or, Harlequin at Rhodes. See Dance, James.
Hermitage Bridge, <u>1763</u>: HAY, Sep 15; <u>1782</u>: HAY, Mar 18; <u>1784</u>: HAY, Feb 9
Hero and Leander (droll), <u>1728</u>: BFLHS, Aug 24
Herod and Antipater. See Markham, Gervase.
Herod and Mariamne. See Pordage, Samuel; Fenton, Elijah, Mariamne.
Herod the Great. See Boyle, Roger.
Heroic Ballet (dance), <u>1785</u>: KING'S, Mar 17
Heroic Comic Dance, Grand (dance), <u>1732</u>: DL, May 3
Heroic Footman, The (farce, anon), <u>1736</u>: HAY, Feb 16
Heroic General, The; or, Briton's Darling (farce, anon), <u>1746</u>: SFY, Sep 8
Heroic Historic Ballet (dance), <u>1775</u>: KING'S, Feb 7, 14, Mar 23, Apr 4, 8
Heroic Love. See Granville, George.
Heroic Lover, The. See Cartwright, George.
Heroic Taylors, The (play), <u>1760</u>: BFG, Sep 4, 5, 6
Heroine (dance), <u>1705</u>: DL, Feb 24, Mar 1

Heroine of the Cave, The. See Hiffernan, Dr Paul.
Herold, Mrs (actor), 1723: HAY, Dec 12; 1724: HAY, Feb 5, Mar 9; 1726: LIF, Jun
     24, Jul 15
Heron (musician), 1760: CG, Sep 22; 1767: CG, Dec 28; 1774: CG, Jan 14
Heron, Mary (actor), 1721: DL, Apr 25, May 16, 26, Jul 28, Sep 9, Nov 25, Dec
     19; 1722: DL, Feb 10, May 24, Oct 13, 17, 24; 1723: DL, Feb 6, May 16, 22,
     Oct 16, 21, 23, Nov 6, 16, 19; 1724: DL, Feb 6, Apr 22, May 1, 8, 13, 22, Sep
     17, Oct 24, 28, Nov 6, 10, 13, 21, 27, Dec 21; 1725: DL, Jan 5, 20, 25, Feb
     3, 20, Apr 21, 23, 30, Jun 14, Sep 4, 7, 21, Oct 2, 12, 15, 18, 20, 23, 25,
     Nov 2, 3, 8, 22; 1726: DL, Jan 3, Mar 28, 31, Apr 21, Oct 13, Dec 6, 7, 14,
     17, 20; 1727: DL, Feb 11, Apr 8, 10, 14, May 8, 15, Nov 18, Dec 4; 1728: DL,
     Jan 3, Apr 2, May 15, Sep 12, 17, Oct 8; 1729: DL, Jan 24, 29, Feb 15, Jun
     13, 27, Jul 18, 25, Sep 13, Nov 8, Dec 10, 13; 1730: DL, Jan 20, Mar 30, Apr
     15, May 11, 13, Oct 8, 22, 28, Nov 18, 26, Dec 4; 1731: DL, Jan 11, 20, Feb
     8, Mar 15, 29, Apr 19, 21, 28, May 3, 13, Sep 23, 25, 28, 30, Oct 2, Nov 1,
     6, 23, 24, Dec 16, 22; 1732: DL, Jan 10, Feb 2, 11, 14, Mar 27, 30, Apr 14,
     22, 27, 29, May 4, Oct 10, 12, 28, Nov 10, 18, 21, 24, Dec 6, 8; 1733: DL,
     Jan 2, 22, 26, Feb 6, 22, Mar 5, 8, 12, 29, Apr 16, 23, 24, May 1, 14, 29,
     Jun 4, DL/HAY, Sep 26, Oct 3, 6, 8, 13, 15, 20, 22, 25, 27, Nov 5, 9, 27, Dec
     5, 8, 10, 17; 1734: DL/HAY, Jan 12, HAY, Feb 12, DL/HAY, Mar 4, 12, 18, 23,
     30, Apr 1, 2, 20, DL, 22, DL/HAY, 26, DL, 29, DL/HAY, May 1, DL, 16, Oct 17,
     21, 23, 25, 26, Nov 2, 6, 16, 22, 25, Dec 6, 19; 1735: DL, Jan 20, 28, 29,
     Feb 10, 24, Mar 22, Apr 21, 23, 25, May 14, 29; 1736: DL, Mar 5, Apr 16;
     1749: DL, Nov 29; 1750: DL, Jan 8
Herpst (house servant), 1768: CG, Jan 2
Herqui, Bay of, 1796: CG, Apr 15
Herriette (dancer), 1675: ATCOURT, Feb 15
Herriman, Master (actor), 1767: SW, May 13, Jun 13; 1769: MARLY, Aug 17; 1775:
     HAY, Mar 23
Herring and Chas (merchants), 1772: DL, Dec 9
Herringman, Henry (printer), 1668: BRIDGES, Jun 22
Herrington (actor), 1787: ROY, Jun 20, HAY, Aug 29
Herron, Master (actor), 1796: DL, Nov 9
Herschel, Friedrich Wilhelm (composer), 1783: HAY, Aug 1
Herschell (musician), 1760: HAY, Feb 15
Hertford (actor), 1778: HAY, Apr 30
Hertford, Lady (correspondent), 1743: DL, Jan 17, Feb 17, CG, 25, KING'S, Nov
     15
Hervey, John (spectator), 1711: QUEEN'S, Apr 25; 1712: QUEEN'S, Apr 5; 1730:
     DL, Dec 11; 1732: DL, Jan 4; 1734: KING'S, Nov 2; 1735: CG/LIF, May 1; 1736:
     CG, Nov 13
Hervey, Lady, 1711: QUEEN'S, Apr 25; 1712: QUEEN'S, Apr 5; 1761: DL, Jun 18
Hervey, Miss. See Harvey, Miss.
Hervey, Mrs (actor), 1736: HAY, Jan 14
Hervigni, Mlle. See D'Hervigni, Mlle.
Hesse, Frederick (renter), 1758: CG, Mar 2
Hesse, Prince and Princess Landgrave of, 1703: DL, Nov 19
Hesse, Prince of, 1746: DL, Jun 3
Hesse, Princess of, 1746: CG, Oct 31, Nov 7, 10, 12
Hester. See Handel, George Frederic.
Hetheril (beneficiary), 1748: DL, May 20
Heureuse Erreur, L'. See Patrat, Joseph.
Heureux Evenement, L' (dance), 1787: KING'S, Jan 20, Mar 13, Jun 14
Heureux Naufrage, L' (dance), 1796: KING'S, Jul 7, 9, 12, 16
Heureux Naufrage, L'. See Rotrou, Jean de.
Heureux Retour, L'; ou, Le Vainqueur Genereux (dance), 1797: KING'S, Mar 28,
     Apr 1, 6
Heutte (Huette), Mlle (dancer), 1751: CG, Apr 12, 17, 26, 30, May 4, 11, 14,
     17; 1754: CG, Apr 27, May 4
Hewardine, William (actor), 1787: CG, May 14; 1792: HAY, Apr 16
Hewer, Mrs (spectator), 1667: LIF, Mar 7
Hewer, W (spectator), 1667: BRIDGES, Apr 9, LIF, Oct 14, Nov 7; 1668: LIF, Jun
     24, Aug 31, BRIDGES, Oct 12; 1669: LIF, Apr 16
Hewetson and Lonsdale (lace mercers), 1772: CG, Mar 19, Nov 27; 1773: DL, Mar
     1; 1774: CG, Mar 21, DL, Jun 2, Nov 25; 1775: DL, May 27; 1777: DL, Feb 7
Hewetson, Messrs (lacemen), 1759: CG, Oct 25; 1760: CG, Mar 8, Nov 27; 1761:
     CG, Mar 3; 1767: DL, Jan 23; 1772: DL, Jun 10; 1776: DL, Jun 10; 1794: CG,
     Nov 29
Hewetson's Great Room, 1729: BOS, Jan 21
Hewitt (householder), 1782: HAY, Jan 14
Hewitt, Sir George (spectator), 1673: LIF, Jun 30
Hewitt, John (actor, author), 1733: SF/BFLH, Aug 23, DL, Sep 28, Oct 1, 31, Nov

13, 14, 26, Dec 5, 11, 17; <u>1734</u>: DL, Jan 22, Feb 11, Mar 7, DL/HAY, Apr 20,
  DL, 23, LIF, 26, May 9, DL, 13, 15, HAY, 27, Jun 12, DL, Sep 14, 24, Oct 5,
  8, 9, 14, 19, 22, 23, 26, Nov 8, 25; <u>1735</u>: DL, Jan 13, May 22, Jun 3; <u>1736</u>:
  DL, Jun 2, LIF, Sep 28, Oct 5, 9, 28, Nov 4, 16, 20, 26, 29, Dec 7, 16, 20,
  31; <u>1737</u>: LIF, Jan 10, 19, Feb 21, DL, May 27
--Fatal Falshood, <u>1734</u>: DL, Feb 11, 12, 14, 15
--Tutor for the Beaus, The; or, Love in a Labyrinth, <u>1737</u>: LIF, Feb 21, 22, 24
Hewlett (actor), <u>1721</u>: SFHL, Sep 2, LIF, Oct 26; <u>1722</u>: LIF, Jan 22
Hews (actor), <u>1661</u>: NONE, Sep 0
Hewson (actor), <u>1730</u>: HAY, Sep 18; <u>1731</u>: GF, Mar 15, 18, HAY, May 4; <u>1733</u>: BF,
  Aug 23, DL, Oct 1, 10, 24, Nov 13, 23, 26, Dec 5, 7; <u>1734</u>: DL, Jan 15, 19,
  31, Feb 4, 16, HAY, Apr 5, 17, LIF, May 17, HAY, 27
Hewson (musician), <u>1675</u>: ATCOURT, Feb 15
Hewson, <u>1774</u>: CG, May 25
Hey Ho Who's Above? (song), <u>1728</u>: LIF, Apr 23
Heyborn, Miss (actor), <u>1782</u>: HAY, Mar 4
Heyborn, Mrs (actor), <u>1782</u>: HAY, Jan 21
Heydegger. See Heidegger.
Heyden (composer), <u>1718</u>: SF, Sep 3
Heyward (dancer), <u>1767</u>: DL, Jan 24
Heywood, Thomas, <u>1791</u>: HAY, Aug 16
--Fair Maid of the West, The, <u>1662</u>: REDBULL, Mar 25; <u>1791</u>: HAY, Aug 16
--Love's Mistress; or, The Queen's Mask (Psyche), <u>1661</u>: SALSBURY, Mar 2, VERE,
  11, SALSBURY, 25, VERE, Oct 26; <u>1665</u>: BRIDGES, May 15; <u>1668</u>: BRIDGES, Aug 15;
  <u>1669</u>: BRIDGES, May 24; <u>1675</u>: DG, Feb 27, Mar 1, 2, 3, 4, 5, 6, 9, Jun 24, DL,
  Aug 0, 27, DG, Sep 25, Oct 8; <u>1676</u>: DG, Jan 0; <u>1682</u>: DG, Jan 19; <u>1689</u>: NONE,
  Sep 0; <u>1697</u>: DG, Apr 8; <u>1704</u>: DL, Jun 9, 21
--Queen Elizabeth's Troubles and the History of Eighty Eight, <u>1667</u>: BRIDGES,
  Aug 17
--Rape of Lucrece, The, <u>1661</u>: LIF, Jul 8
--Royal King, and The Loyal Subject, The, <u>1661</u>: NONE, Sep 0
--Wise Woman of Hogsdon, The, <u>1671</u>: NONE, Sep 0
Hibernia Freed. See Phillips, William.
Hibernian Dotage; or, The Lover's Last Blunder (dance), <u>1786</u>: CG, Nov 14; see
  also Dotage
Hic and Ubique. See Head, Richard.
Hickey, <u>1753</u>: CG, May 21
Hickford, <u>1749</u>: HIC, Apr 21
Hickford's Room, <u>1697</u>: HIC, Dec 9; <u>1707</u>: HIC, Apr 2; <u>1733</u>: HIC, Jun 15; <u>1737</u>:
  DL, Mar 17; <u>1744</u>: HIC, May 16; <u>1746</u>: HIC, Feb 3, Mar 10; <u>1749</u>: HIC, Apr 21;
  <u>1750</u>: HIC, May 18; <u>1751</u>: HIC, May 23; <u>1753</u>: HIC, Dec 31; <u>1758</u>: SOHO, Apr 1;
  <u>1760</u>: HIC, Apr 29; <u>1762</u>: HIC, Feb 12; <u>1773</u>: HIC, May 18
Hickman, Jack (doorkeeper), <u>1749</u>: DL, Nov 4; <u>1751</u>: DL, Dec 28
Hicks (actor), <u>1729</u>: HAY, Jan 31, Mar 29, May 7, Jun 14, Nov 12, Dec 18; <u>1730</u>:
  HAY, Jan 21, Mar 11, 20, 30, Apr 20, Jun 17, 23, Jul 17, BFR, Aug 22, Sep 4,
  SF, 14, HAY, Oct 21, 23, Nov 16, Dec 28; <u>1731</u>: HAY, Jan 18, Feb 3, Mar 5, 24,
  May 12, SFGT, Sep 8; <u>1732</u>: HAY, Mar 8, May 8, 15, TC, Aug 4, HAY, Nov 29;
  <u>1733</u>: HAY, Feb 14, Mar 14, 16, 19, 20, 22, 26, Apr 18, Jul 26, SF/BFLH, Aug
  23; <u>1734</u>: DL, Jan 19, Feb 4, HAY, Apr 5, SFL, Sep 7
Hicks (boxkeeper), <u>1780</u>: DL, May 20; <u>1781</u>: DL, May 24; <u>1782</u>: DL, May 29; <u>1783</u>:
  DL, May 28; <u>1784</u>: DL, May 25; <u>1785</u>: DL, May 25; <u>1786</u>: DL, May 31; <u>1787</u>: DL,
  Jun 6; <u>1788</u>: DL, Jun 10; <u>1789</u>: DL, Jun 6; <u>1790</u>: DL, Jun 3; <u>1791</u>: DL, Jun 1;
  <u>1792</u>: DLKING'S, Jun 16; <u>1793</u>: DL, Jun 10; <u>1795</u>: DL, May 30; <u>1796</u>: DL, Jun 14
Hicks (songwriter), <u>1704</u>: LIF, Jun 24
Hickson, Mrs (actor), <u>1740</u>: BF/WF/SF, Aug 23; <u>1748</u>: BFLYY, Aug 24, HAY, Sep 5,
  SFLYYW, 7, BHB, Oct 1, JS, 31
Hide and Seek. See Walter, William.
Hide me from day's garish eye (song), <u>1782</u>: DL, Feb 15; <u>1791</u>: CG, Mar 18; <u>1792</u>:
  CG, Feb 24; <u>1794</u>: CG, Mar 21
Hide, Mrs (actor), <u>1734</u>: HAY, Apr 5
Hidou, Mme (dancer), <u>1774</u>: DL, Oct 4, Nov 5, Dec 7, 8; <u>1775</u>: DL, Jan 24, Mar
  13, Apr 1, 3, 6, May 25, 27, Oct 7
Hiens (tailor), <u>1750</u>: DL, Jan 15
Hiffernan (Heffinal), Dr Paul, <u>1753</u>: CG, Dec 17; <u>1754</u>: DL, Jan 5, CG, 22, Feb
  23; <u>1759</u>: CG, Apr 20; <u>1761</u>: DL, Apr 1; <u>1768</u>: DL, Apr 6; <u>1770</u>: DL, May 1;
  <u>1774</u>: DL, Mar 19; <u>1775</u>: DL, Mar 25
--Heroine of the Cave, The, <u>1774</u>: DL, Mar 19, Apr 5; <u>1775</u>: DL, Mar 25; <u>1784</u>:
  CG, Mar 22
--Lady's Choice, The, <u>1759</u>: CG, Apr 20
--Maiden Whim, The; or, The Critical Minute, <u>1756</u>: DL, Apr 24; <u>1759</u>: CG, Apr 20
--National Prejudice, The, <u>1768</u>: DL, Apr 6
--New Hippocrates, The; or, A Lesson for Quacks, <u>1761</u>: DL, Apr 1, 13

Higden, Henry, 1693: DL, Mar 0
--Wary Widow, The; or, Sir Noisy Parrot, 1693: DL, Mar 0
Higgins (actor), 1782: HAY, Jan 21
Higgins (entertainer), 1709: QUEEN'S, Dec 7, 8, 10, 12, 17, 19, 26, 27, 28, 29
Higginson (actor), 1715: DL, Dec 6; 1717: DL, Aug 6; 1718: DL, May 28
Higginson, Mrs (actor), 1799: CG, Nov 11, 18; 1800: CG, May 20
Higgons, Bevill (prologuist), 1698: LIF, Jan 0; 1701: LIF, Jan 0, DL, Dec 0
--Generous Conqueror, The; or, The Timely Discovery, 1701: DL, Dec 0
High Holborn, 1749: DL, May 16; 1758: CG, Mar 22; 1779: HAY, Aug 20; 1783: CG,
    Apr 23; 1784: CG, Apr 13, DL, May 3; 1785: CG, Mar 29; 1786: CG, Apr 24;
    1787: CG, Apr 16; 1792: CG, Apr 10; 1793: CG, Apr 8; 1794: CG, Apr 23, HAY,
    Jun 2, CG, 5; 1795: CG, Apr 8; 1796: CG, Mar 30, DL, Jun 2; 1798: CG, May 30
High Life below Stairs. See Townley, James.
High mettled racer (song), 1794: CG, May 26; 1798: CG, May 28; see also See the
    course throng'd with gazers
High minded soldier (song), 1788: HAY, Aug 28
High rolling seas that bear afar (song), 1796: CG, May 25
High Rope Vaulting (entertainment), 1702: BFGB, Aug 24; 1703: BFG, Aug 23
High Rope Walking (entertainment), 1724: BFP, Aug 22
High St, 1796: CG, Apr 12, 20, May 12, 28
Highat, 1735: LIF, Sep 2
Highland Competition Prize (music), 1791: CG, May 18
Highland Dance (dance), 1703: DL, Jun 18; 1722: LIF, May 2, 23; 1723: LIF, May
    15; 1725: LIF, May 18; 1729: LIF, May 3; 1730: GF, Oct 21, 23; 1732: DL, Apr
    21, Jul 7, Aug 11, 17, 19, YB, Nov 30; 1733: HAY, Mar 19; 1743: BFHC, Aug 23;
    1746: JS, Dec 10
Highland Fair, The. See Mitchell, Joseph.
Highland Festivity (dance), 1795: CG, Nov 25, 26; 1796: CG, Apr 26, May 28
Highland Fling (dance), 1791: CG, May 18
Highland Lad (song), 1750: DL, Apr 28, 30
Highland Laddie (song), 1784: DL, May 7; 1786: CG, Apr 28; 1790: CG, Jun 1;
    1798: CG, Apr 28
Highland Lass (dance), 1732: DL, Apr 17
Highland Lassie (song), 1784: DL, May 12
Highland Lilt (dance), 1702: DL, Dec 8; 1703: DL, Feb 12; 1704: DL, Oct 20;
    1723: DL, Nov 20; 1724: RI, Jul 4, 11
Highland Lovers (dance), 1799: CG, Apr 23, May 14, 25
Highland Reel (dance), 1749: CG, Apr 24; 1750: CG, Apr 28, 30; 1768: CG, Mar 7,
    14, 17, 19, 22, Apr 9, 13, 22, 28, 29, May 2, 30, 31, Jun 4; 1773: CG, May
    19, Nov 12, 15, 18, 23, 27, Dec 15, 23; 1774: CG, Jan 12, Feb 2, Mar 19, Apr
    9, 23; 1781: DL, Oct 29; 1782: DL, Oct 16; 1783: DL, Mar 6, 29, Apr 7; 1784:
    DL, Oct 18; 1786: DL, Feb 23, May 19, 26, Sep 28; 1787: DL, May 23, 31; 1789:
    DL, May 27, Jun 5, 9, 10; 1790: DL, Jun 1; 1794: CG, May 23, HAY, Aug 5;
    1798: CG, Apr 28, May 5, 22
Highland Reel, The. See O'Keeffe, John.
Highland, Richard (cook), 1766: CG, Oct 6
Highlander (dance), 1730: LIF, Mar 21; 1732: BFMMO, Aug 23
Highlander and His Mistress (dance), 1729: LIF, Apr 8, 17, 21, 26, 29, May 1,
    7, 8, 12, 14, 19, Oct 6; 1730: LIF, Mar 17, Apr 8, 10, May 21, Oct 7, Dec 7;
    1731: LIF, Apr 1, 8, 21, 28, May 1, 12, 14, 21, 26, 28, Jun 7; 1732: LIF, Mar
    9, Apr 10, 11, 12, 13; 1737: CG, Apr 2; 1740: DL, Apr 18
Highlander and His Wife (dance), 1731: LIF, Mar 18, 22, Apr 29, May 7, 13
Highley (building account), 1766: DL, Oct 10, Nov 22, Dec 26; 1773: DL, Dec 9;
    1774: DL, Mar 3, Nov 18; 1776: DL, Jun 10
Highmore, John (proprietor), 1730: DL, Feb 19, GF, Jun 3; 1732: DL, Jul 14;
    1733: DL, Mar 24, Jun 4, 9, Jul 5; 1743: LIF, Mar 8; 1744: CG, Mar 29; 1747:
NONE, Jun 6
Highness, Her, 1680: DG, Sep 0; 1697: YB, Feb 24; 1698: YB, May 4, 25; 1699:
DL/ORDG, Apr 29; 1716: KING'S, May 9; 1718: RI, Jul 28; 1720: DL, Dec 10;
    1723: DL, Apr 29; 1726: HAY, Mar 11; 1735: HAY, Jan 13, DL, Dec 10; 1736: CG,
Jan 14, 29, DL, May 8, LIF, Jul 7, RI, Aug 28, LIF, Nov 19
Highness, His, 1669: LIF, Apr 20, BRIDGES, 24, LIF, May 10, BRIDGES, 24; 1670:
BRIDGES, May 0; 1674: ATCOURT, Dec 15; 1675: ATCOURT, Feb 15; 1694: DG, Jan
10; 1697: NONE, Sep 0; 1714: DL, Dec 16, 21, 31; 1715: KING'S, Jan 4, DL, 8,
13, KING'S, 15, DL, 18, 21, KING'S, 22, DL, 25, 27, 29, Feb 1, 3, KING'S, 5,
DL, 8, 10, KING'S, 12, DL, 15, 17, KING'S, 19, DL, 22, 24, KING'S, 26, DL,
28, Mar 3, KING'S, 5, DL, 8, 10, KING'S, 12, DL, 15, KING'S, 19, May 14, 21,
DL, Jun 3, KING'S, Jul 2, 9; 1716: DL, Jan 19, KING'S, May 15, DL, 18, Nov
22, 28, 30, Dec 3, 6, 10, 13; 1717: DL, Jan 8, 11, 14, 25, Feb 7, 11, Mar 4,
May 3, LIF, Oct 7, DL, 18, 23, Nov 22, LIF, 25, DL, 29; 1718: LIF, Apr 3, DL,
18, 22, Jun 6, RI, Jul 26, Aug 23, DL, Nov 6, 14, 20, 25, Dec 2, LIF, 12, DL,
15, LIF, 19; 1719: DL, Jan 5, 9, LIF, Feb 5, DL, 6, KING'S, 26, DL, Mar 3, 5,

31, Apr 14, LIF, 24, RI, Jun 6, BFSL, Aug 24, DL, Oct 23, 26, 29, LIF, Nov 2,
DL, 20; 1720: LIF, Jan 8, DL, 18, 22, Feb 16, LIF, Mar 7, KING'S, 22, LIF,
May 4, Oct 24, DL, Nov 2; 1721: DL, Mar 6, Oct 25, Dec 11, LIF, 14; 1722: DL,
Dec 21; 1723: DL, Mar 11, LIF, Apr 22; 1725: DL, Dec 2; 1727: DL, Apr 21, WS,
Dec 14; 1728: LIF, Dec 28; 1729: DL, Jan 4, LIF, 7, 11, DL, 16, LIF, Feb 6,
DL, Mar 11, HIC, 12, DL, 18, 29, LIF, Apr 8, 22, HAY, 28, LIF, 29, May 3, DL,
6, LIF, 21, BFR, Aug 25, 26, DL, Nov 1, 6, 8, LIF, 11, DL, 15, LIF, 22, 27,
DL, 29, LIF, Dec 3, 8, 18, DL, 27; 1730: LIF, Jan 5, DL, 8, 19, LIF, Feb 12,
DL, Mar 5, 9, LIF, 12, 17, Apr 2, 30, HAY, May 14, KG, Oct 22, RI, 27, LIF,
Nov 11, DL, 19, 26, Dec 10, LIF, 16; 1731: LIF, Jan 14, 27, Mar 11, Apr 27,
DL, May 1, LIF, 6, Oct 29, DL, Nov 29, Dec 8, 16, LIF, 21, DL, 22, 30; 1732:
LIF, Jan 7, D, 12, DL, 19, 26, Feb 2, LIF, Mar 9, DL, 13, 16, 27, Apr 13, Dec
14; 1733: GF, Jan 20, LIF/CG, Mar 12, DL, 26, 29, Apr 19, CG, Dec 1; 1734:
CG, Mar 11, DL/HAY, 18, CG, Apr 1, 6, 17, DL/HAY, 18, 24, DL, Sep 30, Oct 10,
17, 24, Nov 4, HAY, 8, DL, 11, 18, GF/HAY, 18, DL, Dec 2, GF/HAY, 6, DL, 12,
HAY, 16, GF/HAY, 30; 1735: GF/HAY, Jan 17, HAY, 27, GF/HAY, Feb 14, DL, Mar
17, HAY, 24, GF/HAY, Apr 10, DL, May 5, Jun 9, Sep 1, Nov 19, KING'S, 25, CG,
27, DL, Dec 3, 10, 17, 31, CG, 31; 1736: DL, Jan 8, CG, Feb 4, DL, Mar 8, 15,
HAY, 29, DL, Apr 3, CG, 29; 1743: NONE, Jul 13; 1748: DL, Jan 14
Highnesses, Their, 1661: ATCOURT, Feb 25; 1675: ATCOURT, Feb 15; 1680: DLORDG,
May 6; 1683: DG, May 31; 1699: DG, Dec 7; 1715: DL, Mar 17; 1717: DL, Mar 7,
11, KING'S, 14, DL, 18, 28; 1719: RI, Jul 6; 1720: KING'S, May 31, Jun 9;
1721: DL, Jan 23, Feb 3, Mar 13, Oct 19, Nov 13, HAY, Dec 15; 1722: HAY, Jan
8, Feb 2, DL, Mar 5, 12, RI, Aug 20, DL, Oct 10, 19, Nov 2; 1723: DL, Apr 26,
RI, Sep 2, DL, Nov 13, 20, Dec 13; 1724: DL, Jan 17, LIF, 24, 31, Feb 10, DL,
Mar 16, Apr 17, RI, Aug 3, DL, Oct 23; 1725: LIF, Feb 5, DL, Mar 4, 11, Oct
27, Nov 2, 10, 17, 24, Dec 15; 1726: DL, Mar 3, 7, Apr 20, KING'S, May 5,
LIF, Nov 25, DL, Dec 16; 1727: DL, Mar 9, 16; 1728: LIF, Nov 16; 1729: BFR,
Aug 25; 1734: GF/HAY, Nov 6, HAY, 14, CG/LIF, 25, GF/HAY, Dec 5; 1735: DL,
Dec 31; 1736: DL, Feb 11, CG, 26, KING'S, May 4, DL, 5, CG, 12, DL, 19,
KING'S, Jun 15, DL, 23, LIF, Jul 1; 1737: CG, Mar 30, Apr 6, 20
Hildersley (wig maker), 1759: CG, Oct 15
Hill (actor), 1695: DL, Sep 0, Dec 0; 1696: DL, Feb 0, Jul 0
Hill (actor), 1728: HAY, Oct 15, 26, Nov 19, Dec 7; 1729: HAY, Jan 27, 31, Mar
27, LIF, Apr 12, HAY, 22, May 7; 1732: KING'S, Dec 5, NONE, 25, DL, 28; 1733:
DL, Apr 5, Jul 5, CG, Aug 20; 1736: BFFH, Aug 23, DL, Nov 13, 23, Dec 30;
1737: DL, Jan 29, Apr 12, May 20, 26, Sep 8, 22, Oct 1, 21, 25; 1738: DL, Jan
11, 19, Feb 23, 28, Mar 4, 25, Apr 6, 10, May 1, 3, 6, 17, 26, Sep 14, 21,
30, CG, Oct 21, Nov 6, 9, 13, 29, Dec 2, 4, 5; 1739: CG, Jan 4, 17, Feb 10,
DL, 13, CG, 16, 22, 24, Mar 3, 13, 27, Apr 15; 1740: TC, Aug 4; 1742: DL, Mar
13, 25, May 8, 12; 1744: HAY, Feb 6, Sep 29; 1752: DL, Dec 9, 22, 23; 1753:
DL, Jan 1, 13; 1754: SFH, Sep 19; 1758: DL, Dec 21
Hill (actor), 1786: CG, May 30, HAMM, Jun 5, 7, 28, 30, Jul 5, 7, 12, 19, 26,
Aug 5; 1790: CG, May 29; 1791: CG, Jun 2; 1792: CG, May 25; 1793: CG, Mar 11
Hill (singer), 1794: CG, Mar 7, 21, Jun 10; 1796: CG, May 31; 1797: CG, Jun 8;
1798: CG, May 31
Hill, Aaron, 1709: DL, Nov 23; 1710: DL, Jan 3, 9, Apr 27, QUEEN'S, Nov 22;
1716: LIF, Feb 7; 1721: LIF, Mar 4, Apr 21, HAY, Nov 18; 1722: HAY, Jan 20;
1723: HAY, Jul 24, DL, 30, Aug 2, Dec 5; 1731: DL, Feb 23, Dec 10; 1733: CG,
Aug 21; 1734: CG, Jan 9, DL, Feb 11, CG/LIF, Oct 23; 1735: CG, Apr 25, YB,
May 29, GF, Nov 26, 27, 28, 29, Dec 1, 2, 3; 1736: DL, Jan 12, LIF, Jun 18;
1746: DL, Dec 1; 1749: DL, Apr 15; 1750: DL, Feb 3, 9; 1758: HAY, Mar 6, 16;
1769: CG, Mar 28; 1786: HAY, Jul 25; 1793: HAY, Dec 2
--Alzira; or, The Americans (Spanish Insult Repented), 1736: LIF, Jun 18, 22,
25, Jul 1, 2, 7, 14, 16, 21, Oct 14; 1737: LIF, Apr 21, May 16; 1744: DL, Apr
30; 1755: CG, Mar 18, 20; 1756: CG, Apr 29; 1758: CG, Jan 11, 13, Apr 19
--Athelwold, 1731: DL, Dec 10, 11, 13; 1771: HAY, Mar 11, Apr 1, 24
--Elfrid; or, The Fair Inconstant, 1710: DL, Jan 3, 4, 5, 9, Feb 21; 1723: HAY,
Jul 24
--Fatal Extravagance, The, 1730: LIF, Feb 21, 24, 26, 28, Mar 5, 10, Apr 21,
May 12; 1733: CG, Jun 26, 29, Jul 27, 31; 1734: JS, Apr 29, CG/LIF, Nov 25;
1735: YB, Mar 12, Jul 17; 1736: HAY, Feb 2, Jul 30; 1793: HAY, Dec 2; 1794:
CG, May 14
--Fatal Vision, The; or, The Fall of Siam, 1716: LIF, Feb 7, 8, 9, 11, 13, 14,
Mar 6
--Filial Pity, 1733: DL, Jul 5
--Insolvent, The; or, Filial Piety, 1758: HAY, Mar 6, 11, 16
--Merope, 1730: LIF, Apr 16; 1731: LIF, Feb 27, Mar 1, 2; 1737: KING'S, Jan 8,
15, 18, 22, 25, 29; 1749: DL, Apr 4, 15, 17, 18, 19, 20, 21, 22, 24, 25, May
6, 12, 13; 1750: DL, Jan 31, Feb 1, 2, 3, 5, 9, 12, 20, Mar 31, Apr 25; 1753:
DL, Mar 19, Apr 10, May 19, Oct 23, Nov 24; 1754: DL, Apr 17; 1755: DL, Oct
25, 28, 30, Nov 3, 10, 19, Dec 3; 1756: DL, Jan 22, Feb 2, Apr 20, May 6, Oct

2, Dec 3, 31; 1757: DL, Jan 22, Feb 15, CG, Mar 12, DL, May 13, Oct 15; 1758:
DL, Jan 13, Apr 12, Dec 13; 1759: DL, Feb 3, Nov 1; 1760: DL, Jan 7, Oct 11,
Dec 1, 5; 1766: DL, Jan 6, 13, 17; 1767: DL, Sep 26; 1770: DL, Apr 19; 1773:
DL, Jan 13, 15, 18, Apr 3, 24, Nov 25; 1777: CG, Jan 17, 18, 20, DL, 22, 25;
1778: DL, Dec 19; 1779: DL, Jan 5, 8, 25; 1787: CG, Jan 15; 1797: CG, Nov 29
--Squire Brainless; or, Trick Upon Trick, 1710: DL, Apr 27, 28, 29
--Walking Statue, The; or, The Devil in the Wine Cellar, 1710: DL, Jan 9, 10,
12, 13, 16, 17, 21, 28, 31, Feb 3, 7, 8, 15, 18, 21, Mar 25, Apr 10, 12, 15,
27, May 11, 17, GR, Jun 19, Jul 29, Aug 7, 14, 21; 1711: DL/QUEEN, Apr 30,
DL, May 8, 31, DL/QUEEN, Jun 5, 12, Jul 13; 1712: DL, Feb 6, SPS, 12, DL, May
15, 19, 20, Jun 10, 19; 1713: DL, Jun 10; 1714: DL, Apr 19, Jun 14, Jul 13;
1715: LIF, Jan 21, 22, Feb 24, Mar 19, 22, Sep 28; 1716: LIF, Jan 2, Apr 24,
Jul 25, Aug 17, Nov 30; 1717: LIF, May 28, Jun 28; 1718: LIF, Jun 4; 1719:
LIF, May 5; 1720: LIF, Mar 31, May 4, 10; 1721: LIF, Feb 6, 13; 1722: LIF,
May 2, 8, 21, 22; 1723: DL, Jul 26, 30, Aug 2; 1726: LIF, Apr 11; 1729: DL,
Jun 20, 24, 30; 1731: LIF, Apr 1; 1737: CG, Mar 15; 1746: GF, Mar 17; 1749:
JS, Dec 27; 1769: CG, Mar 28; 1786: HAY, Jul 25
--Zara, 1735: YB, May 28, 29, 30, 31, Jun 2, YB/HAY, 6, YB, 13, YB/HAY, 18, Jul
9; 1736: DL, Jan 12, 13, 14, 15, 16, 17, 19, 20, 21, 22, 23, 24, 26, 27, 28;
1737: HIC, Apr 1, DL, May 4; 1741: DL, May 28; 1742: JS, Apr 7; 1751: CG, Mar
16, 19, May 3, Oct 21, Nov 8; 1752: CG, Jan 2, 27, Mar 14, Apr 13, May 15,
Dec 12; 1753: CG, Jan 20; 1754: DL, Mar 25, Apr 24; 1755: DL, Apr 8, CG, 29,
DL, 30, May 9, CG, Oct 30, Nov 1, 3, 17, 26, Dec 9, 10, 15, 18, 19; 1756: DL,
Feb 10; 1757: DL, Jan 27, Feb 1, 9, 16, Mar 26, May 31, Oct 25, Nov 2; 1758:
DL, Jan 10, 11, 16, Feb 11, Apr 22, Nov 8, Dec 20; 1759: CG, Jan 11, 19, DL,
Feb 13, Mar 19, May 2, 31, Nov 3, Dec 5, CG, 12, DL, 14; 1760: DL, Mar 27,
Oct 8; 1761: DL, Feb 5, Mar 5, Apr 8, 27, Sep 29, CG, Oct 19, DL, Nov 17;
1762: DL, Nov 27, Dec 17; 1763: DL, Apr 30; 1764: DL, Jan 7, 16, 26, Feb 2;
1765: DL, Feb 6, Apr 29, Oct 12; 1766: DL, Jan 23, 31, Apr 19, Oct 18; 1767:
DL, Nov 11, 14; 1768: CG, May 10, DL, Oct 11, CG, Nov 19; 1769: CG, Feb 21,
May 3, DL, 8; 1770: DL, Jan 2, Nov 28; 1771: DL, Nov 18; 1772: DL, Jan 16,
Nov 7; 1773: DL, May 22, Oct 8, Dec 13; 1774: DL, May 13, Oct 13, CG, Dec 3,
8, DL, 31; 1775: CG, Feb 3, DL, Mar 7, CG, Oct 12, DL, 25, Dec 14; 1776: CG,
Jan 31, DL, Feb 3, Mar 7, CG, Dec 3; 1779: CG, Feb 9, 12; 1780: DL, Dec 15;
1781: DL, Jan 2, Feb 1, 3, Oct 11; 1782: CG, Jan 9, 10, 17, Mar 21, Oct 10,
Nov 25; 1784: CG, Mar 4, Sep 28, DL, Nov 13, 16, 17, 24; 1785: DL, Dec 26;
1791: CG, Oct 7; 1796: CG, Dec 19
Hill, Abraham (spectator), 1663: VERE, Mar 0; 1676: DG, May 25
Hill, Colonel, 1684: DLORDG, Oct 29
Hill, G B, 1775: DL, Mar 27
Hill, James (actor), 1798: CG, Oct 8, 15, Nov 7, 12, 17, Dec 15, 26; 1799: CG,
Jan 5, 29, Mar 2, 5, 25, Apr 9, 30, May 7, 10, 22, 24, Jun 7, Sep 16, 30, Oct
4, 7, 21, 24, Nov 5, 9, 11, 12, 13, 14, Dec 16; 1800: CG, Jan 16, 25, 27, 28,
29, Mar 4, Apr 5, 15, 26, 30, May 1, 13, 17, 22, Jun 11, 13, HAY, 14
Hill, Dr John (author, critic), 1740: CG, Feb 6, 12; 1751: DL, Mar 7; 1752: DL,
Nov 11, 27, Dec 2, HAY, 14; 1753: DL, Mar 20; 1756: DL, Apr 26; 1759: DL, May
1; 1761: BFG, Sep 1
--Rout, The, 1758: DL, Dec 20, 21, 23, 27, 28; 1759: DL, May 1
Hill, Messrs (wax chandlers), 1791: CG, Jun 14; 1795: CG, Sep 28
Hill, Miss (actor), 1794: CG, Sep 24; 1795: CG, Mar 28, Apr 6, May 30
Hill, Mrs (actor, dancer), 1723: LIF, May 3, 10, HAY, Dec 12, 16; 1724: HAY,
Jan 3, 16, May 6, DL, 22; 1725: SH, Apr 30; 1728: HAY, Aug 9; 1729: HAY, Jan
27, Feb 11, 25, Mar 29, May 12, 26, LIF, Oct 15, 22, 24, Nov 1, Dec 16, HAY,
27; 1730: LIF, Jan 2, HAY, Feb 23, LIF, Apr 10, May 20, SOU, Sep 24, LIF, 25;
1731: GF, May 13; 1732: GF, May 19; 1734: GF, Apr 18, May 8, 22, YB, Aug 28;
1737: DL, May 20, Oct 25; 1740: BF/WF/SF, Aug 23, BFH, 23; 1741: BFH, Aug 22;
1743: TCD/BFTD, Aug 23; 1744: HAY, Sep 29, Oct 4, 11, 18, 20, Nov 1, 5, GF,
Dec 3, JS, 10
Hill, Captain Richard (spectator), 1692: DL, Dec 9; 1697: DLORLIF, Sep 15
Hill, Tom (spectator), 1668: BRIDGES, Oct 12
Hill, Will (beneficiary), 1749: CG, Apr 28
Hill's Booth, 1754: SFH, Sep 19
Hiller (actor), 1734: YB, Jul 8
Hilliad (book), 1753: DL, Jan 13, Mar 20
Hilliard, Miss (actor, dancer), 1734: CG, Mar 16, CG/LIF, Dec 30; 1735: CG/LIF,
Mar 29, CG, Nov 6, 15, Dec 11; 1736: CG, Jan 1, 21, 23, Mar 6, 18, May 6, 11,
13, Sep 22, Oct 8, 20, Nov 3, 26; 1737: CG, Feb 14, Apr 26, Oct 7, Nov 9;
1738: CG, Jan 3, Feb 13, Mar 14, Apr 11, 14, May 10, Jun 27, Jul 11; 1741:
CG, Sep 28, Oct 7, 15, 17, 31; 1742: CG, Jan 2, Feb 25, Mar 6, Apr 22, 27,
May 5, 7, Oct 6, 9, 16, 26, Nov 15, 25, Dec 21; 1743: CG, Jan 8, 18, Feb 4,
Mar 8, Apr 21, 29, Sep 23, 30, Oct 19, Nov 7, 19, 21, Dec 3, 16, 20, 29;
1744: CG, Jan 11, 14, Apr 6, May 2; 1746: DL, Feb 6, Apr 24, 25; 1748: CG,

Apr 20; 1750: CG, Jan 31, Feb 7, Mar 19, 29, 31, Apr 5, 17, 18, 20, 21, 23,
24, Sep 26; 1751: CG, Jan 17, Apr 12, 17, 18, Sep 25, Oct 9, 21, Nov 11;
1752: CG, Jan 23, Mar 17, 19, Apr 13, 15, Dec 7, 16, 18; 1753: CG, Feb 6, Mar
29, Apr 9, 30, May 9, Oct 18, 20, 25, Nov 3; 1754: CG, Jan 5, Apr 4, 25, May
6; 1755: CG, Nov 14, 15, 26, Dec 3, 9; 1756: CG, Jan 21, 26, 31, Feb 12, 21,
24, Mar 15, 30, Apr 19, 20, May 26, Dec 10, 11, 15, 16, 17; 1757: CG, Jan 3,
28, Mar 26, 28, 29, Apr 15, 23, 26, Oct 13, Nov 11, Dec 7, 17; 1758: CG, Feb
1, Apr 12, 14, 20, 22, Oct 4, Nov 1, 11, 23; 1759: CG, Apr 21, Nov 2, 13, 30,
Dec 6, 12; 1760: CG, Jan 4, 8, 16, Mar 18, 22, Apr 8, 10, 12, 18, 21, 22, May
1, 12, 15, 19; 1763: DL, Oct 4, 25, Dec 26, 28; 1766: CG, May 5, Nov 18;
1767: CG, Apr 27
Hillier, Miss (singer), 1741: CG, May 15
Hilligsberg, Janet (dancer), 1788: KING'S: Feb 12; 1793: KING'S, Jun 1; 1795:
DL, Feb 12, KING'S, Mar 26, May 16; 1797: KING'S, Nov 28; 1798: KING'S, Apr
19, DL, May 9, KING'S, 10, Dec 8; 1799: KING'S, Mar 26, May 2, DL, 8; 1800:
KING'S, Jan 11, 28, Feb 18, Mar 1, 4, DL, May 14, KING'S, Jul 19
Hilligsberg, Mlle (dancer), 1787: KING'S, Dec 8; 1788: KING'S, Jan 12, 15, 29,
Feb 21, 28, Mar 13, Apr 3, 19, May 29, 31; 1790: HAY, Jan 7, Feb 13, Mar 25,
Apr 6, 15, 22, May 4, 13, 27, 28, CG, Jul 6, 10; 1791: KING'S, Mar 10, 26,
Apr 12, 14, May 5, 19, 26, Jun 4, 10, 14, 25, 28, PAN, Dec 17, 31; 1792: HAY,
Feb 14, Mar 10, Apr 14; 1793: KING'S, Jan 26, Feb 5, 26, Apr 6, 23, Jun 1, 8,
11; 1794: KING'S, Jan 11, Mar 1, 4, 22, Apr 1, May 31, DL, Jul 2, KING'S, Dec
6, 20; 1795: KING'S, Jan 20, Mar 26, 28, Apr 7, Jun 20; 1796: KING'S, Jan 2,
9, Feb 20, Mar 1, 5, 8, 10, Apr 2, 21, May 12, DL, 25, KING'S, Jun 2, Jul 2,
7, 16, 23, Nov 26, Dec 6, 13; 1797: KING'S, Jan 7, 10, 17, Feb 7, Mar 11, 28,
Apr 6, 25, May 11, 13, DL, 22, KING'S, 25, CG, Jun 14, KING'S, 17, CG, Oct
21, 28, 31, Nov 4, KING'S, 28, Dec 20; 1798: KING'S, Feb 6, Mar 22, Apr 19,
26, DL, May 9, KING'S, 10, CG, Jun 11, KING'S, 14, Dec 8; 1799: KING'S, Jan
29, Mar 26, Apr 18, May 2, DL, 8; 1800: KING'S, Jan 11, 28, Mar 1, 4, Apr 15,
May 8, DL, 14, KING'S, 29, Jun 24, 28
Hilligsberg, Mlle E (dancer), 1794: DL, Jul 2
Hilligsberg, Mme M L (dancer), 1794: KING'S, Jan 11, Feb 1; 1795: KING'S, Mar
26
Hillingdon Churchyard, 1761: CG, Nov 26
Hillingsworth, Miss. See Illingham, Miss.
Hillman, Mrs (seamstress), 1766: DL, Oct 9, Dec 30
Hills (singer), 1741: JS, Oct 27
Hilton, John (composer), 1792: CG, May 11
Hilton, Mrs (actor), 1792: CII, Jan 16
Hilton, 1718: DL, May 28; 1719: DL, May 19
Hinchcliff (mercer), 1773: DL, Jun 2
Hinchinbroke, Lord. See Montagu, Edward.
Hind (actor), 1730: SOU, Sep 24; 1732: BFMMO, Aug 23, GF, Oct 5; 1733: HAY, Mar
19; 1734: SFL, Sep 7, GF, 25, Oct 17, 28, Dec 9; 1735: GF, Jan 13, 24, Mar 6,
CG, Nov 22; 1741: GF, Dec 10; 1745: HAY, Apr 1; 1746: SOU, Oct 16; 1778: DL,
May 25; 1779: DL, May 28
Hind, Mrs (actor), 1732: HAY, Jun 1, BFMMO, Aug 23; 1733: HAY, Mar 19; 1748:
BFP, Aug 24
Hindle, John (singer), 1792: CG, Mar 16, 21, 23
Hindmarsh, John (violinist), 1790: HAY, Sep 29
Hindmarsh, Mrs John (singer), 1795: CG, Mar 11, 13, 18, 20, 25, 27; 1798: HAY,
Aug 23
Hindy-Gylesangbier (Chinese mandarin), 1735: LIF, Jun 19
Hint to the Theatres, A (pantomime), 1736: HAY, Dec 3, 8; 1737: NWLS, May 30
Hint, William (correspondent), 1744: CG, Oct 10, DL, 13, 20, 23, Nov 3, 10
Hiorne, Miss (actor), 1778: HAY, Dec 28
Hippisley-Bullock-Hallam Booth, 1734: BFHBH, Aug 24
Hippisley-Chapman Booth, 1740: BFHC, Aug 23; 1741: BFH, Aug 22; 1742: BFHC, Aug
25; 1743: BFHC, Aug 23
Hippisley-Chapman-Legar Booth, 1739: BFHCL, Aug 23
Hippisley, Elizabeth (actor), 1736: CG, Mar 22; 1740: GF, Oct 22, 28, 31, Nov
15, 22, 26, 29, Dec 1, 4, 5, 8, 15; 1741: GF, Jan 15, 20, 27, Feb 2, 5, 14,
19, Mar 3, 7, 16, 19, Apr 7, 13, 15, 20, 24, 30, Sep 14, 16, 21, 25, 28, 30,
Oct 2, 5, 7, 19, 23, 28, Nov 6, 9, 27, 30, Dec 2, 9, 26; 1742: GF, Jan 1, 5,
18, 22, 25, 26, 27, Feb 3, Mar 1, 27, Apr 1, 6, 19, 22, May 1, 6, 10, 21, 24,
CG, Oct 4, 13, Nov 8, 22, Dec 7; 1743: LIF, Feb 14, SOU, 18, LIF, Mar 8, Apr
4, 11, CG, Sep 28, 30, Oct 7, 10, 29, Nov 18, 19, 30; 1744: CG, Jan 5, Feb
28, Mar 30, May 1, 7, Sep 24, 26, Oct 10, 24, 26, 29, Nov 8, Dec 10, 11;
1745: CG, Jan 7, Mar 14, 28, Apr 1, 17, 19, 20, 23, May 1, 7, 15, 29, Sep 25,
27, 30, Oct 2, 9, 29, Nov 6, 7, 8, 9, 12, 13, 16, 20, 22, 23, 25, 26, 28, 30,
Dec 5, 10, 12, 13, GF, 23; 1746: GF, Jan 2, CG, 7, Feb 6, 8, 17, 24, Mar 10,
13, 18, Apr 1, 8, 15, 24, Sep 29, Oct 6, 8, 20, 29, Nov 3, 6, 8, 26, Dec 10,

11, 19, 26; 1747: CG, Jan 17, 26, 31, Feb 4, 7, 12, Mar 7, May 7, 19, 20, 22,
DL, Sep 19, Oct 1, CG, 31, Nov 23, Dec 15; 1748: CG, Jan 2, 8, Feb 13, Apr
12, 22, BFSY, Aug 24, CG, Sep 26, Oct 7, 17, 29, Nov 9; 1749: CG, Mar 2, 31,
BFY, Aug 23, CG, Oct 20, 25, 26, 30, Nov 8, 23, 24; 1750: CG, Jan 18, HAY,
Jul 26, CG, Oct 12, 24, 29, Nov 12, 22, Dec 4; 1751: CG, Jan 18; 1752: DL,
Dec 19, 20; 1753: DL, Feb 3, Mar 3, 22, Apr 30, May 11, Sep 15, 25, Oct 20,
31; 1754: DL, Apr 30, Nov 7; 1755: DL, Mar 20, Apr 25, 29, May 6, Sep 18, Oct
7, 17, Nov 8, 15, 28; 1756: DL, Apr 29, May 14, Oct 13, 21, Nov 18; 1757: DL,
Jan 26, May 9, Sep 29, Oct 15, Nov 19; 1758: DL, Apr 3, 18, May 9, Sep 16,
28, Oct 3, 19, 25, Nov 16, Dec 13, 18; 1759: DL, Jan 3, 4, Feb 1, 26, Mar 20,
24, May 7, 21, Sep 22, Oct 6, 17, 25, 30, Nov 1, 6, 9, 10, 17, 19, 24, Dec
12; 1760: DL, Mar 11, 20, Apr 11, 21, 22, 29, May 7, 16, Sep 20, 30, Oct 3,
11, 22, Nov 20, Dec 30; 1761: DL, Jan 10, Apr 17, 24, May 14, Sep 8, 10, 14,
Oct 24, 29, Nov 10, 14, 21, 28, Dec 11, 17, 23; 1762: DL, Feb 20, Mar 22, May
6, 8, 17, Oct 9, 11, 15, Nov 10, 19, Dec 6, 27; 1763: DL, Jan 15, Mar 1, 15,
Apr 11, Sep 22, Oct 8, Nov 14, Dec 15, 28; 1764: DL, Jan 3, 4, 27, Mar 20,
24, May 3, 11, 19, 21, Oct 19, 20, 25, Nov 8, 17, 22, Dec 8; 1765: DL, Jan 2,
3, 24, Feb 4, 16, Mar 23, Apr 13, 26, May 18, Sep 24, Oct 5, 15, 22, Nov 15,
Dec 7; 1766: DL, Jan 24, Feb 1, Mar 15, 22, Apr 16, 25, Oct 16, Dec 4; 1767:
DL, May 2, 4, 20, 22, Sep 17, 19, 26, Oct 6, 21, Nov 18, Dec 7; 1768: DL, Jan
9, 19, Feb 27, Mar 21, Apr 27, 28, Sep 17, Oct 20, Nov 21, Dec 3, 6, 12
Hippisley, Jenny (actor), 1735: CG/LIF, Mar 18; 1740: DL, Jan 11
Hippisley, John (actor, dancer, author), 1722: LIF, Nov 7, 13, 17, 23, 30, Dec
5, 8, 10, 14, 15, 21, 31; 1723: LIF, Jan 3, 10, 11, 12, 29, Feb 1, 12, 13,
Mar 25, Apr 4, 6, 16, 18, May 3, 18, Sep 28, 30, Oct 7, 14, 18, 22, 31, Nov
1, 2, 12, 14, 16, 19, 21, 28, Dec 2, 6, 11, 12, 16, 27; 1724: LIF, Mar 16,
23, Apr 6, 24, 28, May 19, 21, 27, Jun 3, 4, Sep 23, 28, Oct 7, 9, 14, 23,
27, 30, Nov 3, 6, 11, 13, 18, 20, 25, 26; 1725: LIF, Jan 4, 11, 16, Feb 27,
Mar 11, 13, 29, 31, Apr 5, 7, 19, 26, May 12, 19, 20, 21, Sep 29, Oct 1, 4,
11, 13, 19, 21, 23, 26, 28, Nov 2, 8, 12, 18, 23, 24, 30, Dec 2, 3, 7, 8, 15,
16; 1726: LIF, Jan 7, Feb 19, Mar 21, Apr 11, 18, 25, May 3, 4, 11, 12, Sep
12, 14, 19, 26, 28, Oct 3, 12, 19, 24, Nov 2, 11, 21, 30, Dec 14; 1727: LIF,
Jan 4, 9, Mar 20, Apr 5, 19, 26, May 9, 19, 22, Sep 11, 13, 15, 27, Oct 2, 9,
17, 21, 26, 31, Nov 16, 17, Dec 11, 14; 1728: LIF, Jan 29, Mar 9, 14, 21, 25,
28, Apr 4, 6, 23, 24, 26, 30, May 11, 15, Sep 18, 30, Oct 1, 21, Nov 1, 11,
20, Dec 28, 31; 1729: LIF, Feb 6, 7, 22, Mar 3, 10, 15, 17, Apr 8, 9, 10, 11,
15, 17, 24, 26, 29, 30, May 3, 7, 15, Sep 19, 22, 24, 26, Oct 3, 8, 15, 20,
22, 24, 30, 31, Nov 1, 4, 7, 8, 13, 14, Dec 3; 1730: LIF, Jan 2, 19, 26, Feb
3, Apr 2, 13, 30, May 7, 11, 14, 15, 18, 20, 23, 25, Jun 1, BFR, Aug 22, LIF,
Sep 18, 21, 23, 25, Oct 5, 7, 9, 12, 19, 23, 26, 30, 31, Nov 2, 3, 6, 7, 10,
13, 23, Dec 3, 4, 15; 1731: LIF, Jan 4, 8, 9, 20, Mar 22, 25, Apr 1, 3, 23,
26, May 1, 5, 13, 20, 21, 25, Jun 2, 8, RI, Jul 1, 8, 15, 22, SF/BFFHH, Aug
24, LIF, Sep 20, 22, 27, 29, Oct 1, 4, 11, 13, 20, 25, 27, 30, Nov 2, 6, 8,
12, 13, 17, 18, 25, Dec 1, 3, 6, 8, 9, 11, 15, 29; 1732: LIF, Jan 7, 10, 18,
19, 28, Feb 3, 14, 15, 21, Mar 20, 23, 30, Apr 10, 14, 18, 27, May 1, 5, 9,
BF, Aug 22, CG/LIF, Sep 22, LIF/CG, 25, 27, 29, Oct 2, 4, 6, 9, 16, LIF, 18,
LIF/CG, 20, 21, 23, 25, 28, 30, Nov 1, 3, 7, 8, 9, 11, 14, 17, 18, 22, 24,
Dec 4, 7, CG/LIF, 16, LIF/CG, 27; 1733: LIF/CG, Jan 15, 18, Feb 5, CG, 8, Mar
27, LIF/CG, 29, 30, 31, Apr 2, 10, 11, 12, 17, 27, CG, May 1, 2, LIF/CG, 7,
10, 19, 24, CG/LIF, 28, LIF/CG, Jun 1, BF, Aug 23, BFFH, Sep 4, CG, 17, 20,
22, 25, 27, 29, Oct 2, 4, 6, 9, 11, 13, 16, 18, 19, 25, 27, 29, 31, Nov 1, 3,
8, 9, 16, 19, 21, 26, 30, Dec 3, 4, 7, 8, 17, 20, 31; 1734: CG, Jan 23, 25,
Feb 11, 26, Mar 18, 25, 28, Apr 1, 6, 16, 19, BFHBH, Aug 24, CG, Sep 2, HA,
2, RI, 9, CG/LIF, 18, 20, 23, 25, RI, 26, CG/LIF, 27, Oct 2, 7, LIF, 12,
CG/LIF, 14, 16, 18, 23, 25, 29, Nov 11, 14, 19, 21, 25, Dec 5, 19, 30; 1735:
CG/LIF, Jan 6, 17, 21, 23, Feb 3, 4, 8, LIF, 12, CG/LIF, 13, 22, LIF, Mar 3,
CG/LIF, 11, 18, 20, 29, Apr 9, 17, 18, LIF, 19, CG/LIF, 21, 22, CG, 25,
CG/LIF, May 1, 2, 5, CG, 6, CG/LIF, 9, 15, 16, LIF, 21, CG/LIF, 27, Jun 2,
CG, Sep 12, 16, 17, 24, 26, 29, Oct 1, 8, 13, 15, 17, 20, 22, 24, 29, 31, Nov
6, 7, 10, 15, 22, 29, Dec 8, 15, 30, 31; 1736: CG, Feb 10, 26, Mar 6, 18, 20,
22, 27, 29, LIF, Apr 2, CG, 8, 13, LIF, 16, CG, 29, May 1, 3, LIF, 5, CG, 13,
20, BFFH, Aug 23, CG, Sep 17, 20, 22, 24, 29, Oct 1, 4, 8, 11, 13, LIF, 18,
CG, 20, 22, 23, 25, 27, 29, Nov 1, 3, 11, 15, 25, 26, 29, Dec 2, 9, 20, 29;
1737: CG, Jan 7, 10, 17, 21, 28, Feb 3, Mar 12, 15, 24, 28, Apr 2, 12, 14,
15, 26, 28, May 3, 6, 31, Oct 3, 5, 7, 10, 12, 17, 21, 24, 26, 28, 29, Nov 1,
2, 12, 14, 17, 18; 1738: CG, Jan 3, 5, 6, 9, 13, 17, 18, 25, 31, Feb 13, 16,
23, Mar 13, 14, 18, 25, Apr 4, 7, 10, 12, 17, 20, 22, 24, 25, May 18, Sep 25,
27, Oct 2, 4, 6, 9, 11, 13, 14, 16, 18, 20, 23, 26, 30, Nov 2, 7, 11, 13, 15,
17, 18, 20, 23, 24, 25, 28, Dec 2, 4, 5, 12; 1739: CG, Jan 8, 16, 20, 22, 24,
Feb 9, 10, 16, 26, Mar 15, 19, 27, Apr 3, 5, 12, 24, 25, May 2, 7, 8, 11, 17,
18, 23, 25, 28, BFHCL, Aug 23, CG, Sep 12, 14, 17, 19, 22, 25, 27, 28, Oct 1,
3, 4, 5, 8, 10, 20, 25, 26, 29, Nov 1, 2, 6, 9, 10, 13, 17, 20, Dec 1, 4, 6,

7, 10, 13, 15, 17, 21, 29; <u>1740</u>: CG, Jan 12, 15, 17, Feb 2, 12, Mar 11, 18,
24, 25, 27, Apr 9, 23, 28, May 2, 5, 7, 9, 21, 27, Jun 5, BFHC, Aug 23, CG,
Sep 19, 22, 24, 26, 29, Oct 1, 3, 6, 10, 22, 23, 24, 25, 27, 29, Nov 1, 6,
DL, 6, CG, 10, 15, Dec 4, 5, 6, 10, 13, 29; <u>1741</u>: CG, Jan 2, 5, 6, 15, 19,
21, 22, 23, 27, 29, Feb 7, 14, 24, 28, Mar 2, 7, 10, 30, Apr 1, 3, 10, 11,
15, 22, 24, 25, May 1, 4, 7, 11, 12, BFH, Aug 22, CG, Sep 21, 23, 25, 28, 30,
Oct 2, 5, 7, 10, 20, 21, 24, 26, 29, 30, 31, Nov 2, 7, 9, 11, 23, 26, 27, Dec
1, 11, 12, 18; <u>1742</u>: CG, Jan 2, 5, 19, 23, Feb 3, 10, 22, 25, 27, Mar 6, 13,
22, 27, Apr 1, 19, 24, May 4, 5, 7, BFHC, Aug 25, CG, Sep 29, Oct 1, 6, 9,
11, 15, 16, 19, 25, 26, 27, 28, 29, Nov 8, 11, 13, 15, 19, 20, 22, 25, 30,
Dec 7, 21; <u>1743</u>: CG, Jan 8, 18, Feb 9, Mar 8, 15, 17, 22, Apr 26, May 4, 5,
BFHC, Aug 23, CG, Sep 21, 23, 26, 30, Oct 5, 10, 12, 14, 17, 19, 21, 24, 29,
31, Nov 7, 16, 17, 18, 19, 21, Dec 3, 8, 9, 12, 16, 17, 19, 26; <u>1744</u>: CG, Jan
4, 7, 11, 14, 24, Feb 14, 28, Mar 12, 30, Apr 19, May 1, 14, Sep 19, 21, Oct
1, 3, 5, 8, 10, 15, 20, 22, 29, 31, Nov 1, 7, 8, 9, 21, 24, 27, 28, 29, 30,
Dec 5, 6, 8, 10, 11, 12, 17, 21; <u>1745</u>: CG, Jan 1, 2, 4, 7, 18, 23, Feb 11,
Apr 1, 20, 25, 26, May 1, 13, Sep 23, 30, Oct 2, 4, 7, 9, 11, 16, 29, Nov 2,
7, 8, 9, 11, 13, 14, 18, 19, 20, 22, 23, 25, 26, 30, Dec 2, 5, 6, 10, 12, 13,
21; <u>1746</u>: CG, Jan 2, 7, 11, 13, 23, 25, Feb 3, 5, 6, 17, Mar 13, 15, 18, Apr
3, 21, 22, 28, Sep 29, Oct 6, 8, 10, 13, 15, 17, 29, Nov 1, 3, 6, 17, 18, 24,
26, Dec 3, 6, 8, 10, 11, 17, 22, 26, 27, 29, 31; <u>1747</u>: CG, Jan 17, 26, 31,
Feb 2, 3, 5, 6, 7, 11, Mar 7, DL, 19, CG, Apr 2, 20, Dec 1; <u>1760</u>: CG, Apr 9;
<u>1762</u>: CG, Apr 16, 28, 30, May 11, DL, 17, HAY, Oct 25; <u>1763</u>: HAY, Sep 7;
<u>1790</u>: HAY, Sep 29
--Flora; or, Hob in the Well (Hob's Opera), <u>1729</u>: LIF, Apr 17, 18, 19, 21, 23,
28, 29, 30, May 1, 2, 3, 7, 8, 12, 14, 15, 19, 23, HAY, Jul 26, Aug 2, 19,
BFB, 25, LIF, Sep 19, SOU, 23, LIF, 24, BLA, 30, LIF, Oct 6, 8, 29, Nov 7,
11, HAY, 26, 29, LIF, Dec 1, 15, 18, 29; <u>1730</u>: LIF, Jan 23, Feb 2, HAY, Mar
12, LIF, 14, Apr 3, 17, 25, May 9, 13, 23, 25, GF, 27, Jun 9, 15, 16, 19, 22,
29, Jul 1, 3, 8, 14, 22, BFPG, Sep 1, LIF, Oct 7, GF, 7, LIF, 12, GF, 20,
LIF, 23, GF, 24, 27, 29, LIF, 30, Nov 6, GF, 7, 10, 20, 24, Dec 1, LIF, 5, 7,
GF, 11; <u>1731</u>: LIF, Jan 11, GF, 15, LIF, 19, GF, 19, Mar 1, HAY, 10, GF, Apr
22, LIF, 26, May 19, 21, 25, 31, Jun 7, BFB, Aug 26, LIF, Oct 13, GF, 25, 26,
LIF, 27, GF, 29, Nov 4, LIF, 29, GF, Dec 3, 4, LIF, 7; <u>1732</u>: LIF, Jan 5, GF,
25, 26, LIF, Feb 4, GF, 19, 26, 29, Mar 6, 13, 20, 23, 28, Apr 12, 18, LIF,
19, 22, 25, 26, GF, May 23, LIF/CG, Sep 25, Oct 9, 25, Nov 7, 16; <u>1733</u>:
LIF/CG, Jan 18, 20, GF, Apr 6, LIF/CG, 10, 12, 18, GF, 23, 27, CG, May 4,
LIF/CG, 10, 15, 21, HAY, 26, CG, Sep 27, GF, Oct 9, 10, 12, 23, CG, 31, Nov
20, Dec 4, GF, 8, 18, HAY, 26; <u>1734</u>: DL/HAY, Jan 2, CG, 3, DL/HAY, 4, GF, 8,
DL/HAY, 9, 10, GF, 12, DL/HAY, 16, GF, 18, CG, 22, DL/HAY, 23, GF, 26, CG,
Mar 25, 28, GF, May 22, CG, Sep 2, RI, 26, DL, 28, Oct 1, 4, GF, 16, CG/LIF,
Nov 19; <u>1735</u>: YB, Mar 3, CG/LIF, 22, GF, 27, SOU, Apr 7, LIF, 16, GF, 17, 28,
May 5, DL, 7; <u>1736</u>: CG, Mar 22, LIF, Apr 2, CG, 27, 29, May 18, Jun 4, RI,
Aug 28, CG, Sep 17, Dec 6; <u>1737</u>: CG, Jan 10, Feb 3, LIF, 25, CG, Mar 19, Apr
21, LIF, May 6, CG, Sep 26, 28, Oct 3; <u>1738</u>: CG, Mar 13, 21, Apr 21, May 6,
Oct 18; <u>1739</u>: CG, Jan 15, May 1, DL, 14, CG, Nov 7, Dec 17; <u>1741</u>: GF, Feb 6,
10, Apr 23, NWC, Aug 22; <u>1743</u>: SOU, Feb 25; <u>1744</u>: CG, May 1, DL, 16; <u>1745</u>:
GF, Mar 18, Apr 30, CG, May 1, 6, 10, 13, GF, Dec 26, 27, 30, 31; <u>1746</u>: GF,
Jan 1, 2, 7, 17, Feb 20, Mar 6, NWSM, Jul 28, SOU, Nov 3, GF, Dec 16, 17, 22,
26, 27; <u>1747</u>: GF, Jan 26, 27, Feb 4, DL, 10, GF, 11, DL, 12, 14, 17, GF, 19,
DL, 21, GF, 24, DL, 26, Mar 5, Apr 7, May 1, 5, 12; <u>1748</u>: DL, Jan 9, 11, Feb
11, CG, Dec 21, 22; <u>1749</u>: NWLS, Feb 27, CG, Apr 10, Oct 16, 19, 23, 28, Nov
2; <u>1750</u>: CG, Apr 30, May 1, Oct 13, 15, 18, 23, Nov 14, Dec 13, 18; <u>1751</u>: CG,
Jan 29, Apr 10, 26, NWLS, Aug 6, 7, CG, Oct 18, HAY, Nov 21; <u>1752</u>: CG, Jan
25, Feb 4, Apr 30, Oct 4, 6, Dec 12; <u>1753</u>: CG, Jan 9, Apr 2, 12, Dec 5; <u>1754</u>:
CG, Apr 30, Sep 25; <u>1755</u>: CG, Nov 15; <u>1757</u>: CG, May 6, 11, 19; <u>1758</u>: CG, Nov
27; <u>1760</u>: CG, Apr 9, 24, 30, May 7, 15, Sep 29, Nov 20; <u>1761</u>: CG, Apr 28, May
5, 13; <u>1767</u>: DL, Apr 11, 20, 23, May 11, 15, 16, Dec 7, 16; <u>1768</u>: DL, Jan 23,
28, HAY, Aug 8, 12, Sep 13, DL, 17; <u>1769</u>: DL, Dec 6; <u>1770</u>: DL, Mar 3, CG, Apr
25, HAY, Jun 25; <u>1771</u>: DL, Nov 25; <u>1774</u>: DL, Nov 29, Dec 19; <u>1784</u>: CG, May
26; <u>1786</u>: CG, Dec 12, 13, 14, 18, 20; <u>1787</u>: CG, Jan 26, May 16, Nov 22; <u>1788</u>:
CG, Apr 8, Nov 19; <u>1789</u>: CG, Dec 10; <u>1791</u>: CG, Jan 12, Jun 8, 15, Dec 3;
<u>1795</u>: DL, Jun 3, HAY, Jul 6, 9
--Journey to Bristol, A; or, The Honest Welshman, <u>1731</u>: LIF, Apr 23, May 13;
<u>1733</u>: LIF/CG, Apr 2, 21
--Sequel to the Opera of Flora, The; or, Hob's Wedding, <u>1732</u>: LIF, Mar 20, Apr
10, 21, May 5
Hippisley Jr, John (author), <u>1750</u>: DL, Jan 1
Hippisley, Master (actor), <u>1740</u>: CG, Apr 26; <u>1741</u>: CG, Mar 10
Hippomene et Atalante (dance), <u>1779</u>: KING'S, Mar 25, May 21, Jun 5, 26; <u>1800</u>:
KING'S, Mar 4, 8, 22, Apr 22, 29, Jul 19
His body is buried (song), <u>1793</u>: CG, Feb 15

417

His hideous love (song), 1791: CG, Mar 23, DL, Apr 1; 1792: KING'S, Feb 29;
    1794: DL, Mar 26
His mighty arm (song), 1792: KING'S, Mar 28; 1793: CG, Mar 20; 1797: CG, Mar 31
His yoke is easy (song), 1793: KING/HAY, Feb 20; 1794: DL, Mar 19
Historical and Succinct Account of the late Riots at the Theatres, An
    (pamphlet), 1763: DL, Mar 1
Historical Register, The. See Fielding, Henry.
Historical Tragedy of the Civil War, An. See Cibber, Theophilus.
History and Fall of Domitian, The. See Massinger, Phillip.
History of Charles VIII of France, The. See Crowne, John.
History of Hengist, the Saxon King of Kent, The (play, anon), 1700: DL, Jun 3
History of John Gilpin the Linen Draper (entertainment), 1785: DL, Apr 11
History of King Henry the VIIIth and Anna Bullen, The (droll), 1732: BFMMO, Aug
    23
History of Mr Shuter and the Sow (entertainment), 1759: CG, Mar 22
History of Pope Joan, The; or, A Discovery of the Debaucheries and Villanies of
    the Popish Faction (play, anon), 1679: CS, Dec 17
History of the Famous Friar Bacon, The (droll), 1720: SFLH, Sep 5
History of Tom Jones the Foundling, in his Married State, The (book), 1749: DL,
    Dec 4
Hitchcock (actor), 1760: CG, Apr 12; 1761: CG, Apr 11
Hitchcock, Mary Anne (actor), 1770: HAY, Oct 29; 1777: HAY, May 15; 1778: HAY,
    Jun 1; 1779: HAY, Jun 2; 1781: HAY, Jul 18, Aug 22, Sep 5, 7
Hitchcock, Robert (actor, playwright), 1773: HAY, Sep 16; 1777: HAY, May 15,
    Jun 6, Jul 7, Aug 25, Sep 3, Oct 9; 1779: HAY, Jun 2, Jul 17, Aug 10, 13;
    1780: HAY, May 30, Jun 6, 23, Sep 11; 1798: CG, Nov 12
--Coquette, The; or, The Mistakes of the Heart, 1777: HAY, Oct 9
--Macaroni, The, 1773: HAY, Sep 16
Hitchcock, Sarah, Mrs Robert (actor), 1747: CG, May 12; 1748: CG, Apr 29; 1750:
    CG, Apr 27; 1758: CG, Apr 22; 1759: CG, Apr 28; 1760: CG, May 3; 1761: CG,
    Apr 11; 1767: CG, May 9; 1768: CG, May 27; 1769: CG, May 6; 1770: CG, May 18;
    1771: CG, May 22; 1772: CG, May 23; 1773: CG, May 22; 1774: CG, May 7; 1775:
    CG, May 30; 1776: CG, May 22; 1777: HAY, Jun 9, 11, 16, 19, 26, 27, Jul 3,
    18, 24, Aug 18, 22, Sep 10; 1778: HAY, May 22, Jun 1, 3, 8, 10, 12, Jul 2, 9,
    22, Aug 3, 7, 21, Sep 2, 7, 17, 18; 1779: HAY, Jun 2, 7, 17, Jul 2, 5, 16,
    20, Aug 6, 17, 18, 27, 31; 1780: HAY, May 30, Jun 2, 3, 5, 9, 13, 14, 24, Jul
    15, Aug 10, 12, 17, 24; 1781: HAY, Jun 5, 6, Jul 18, 21, Aug 15, 24, Sep 12
Hither haste the young and gay (song), 1798: CG, Apr 9
Ho un non so che nelcor (song), 1714: QUEEN'S, May 1, 29, Jun 23
Hoadley, John (author, songwriter), 1731: LIF, Apr 30; 1755: SOHO, Jan 16;
    1777: DL, Mar 12
--Contrast, The, 1731: LIF, Apr 30, May 4, 8
Hoadly, Benjamin
--Suspicious Husband, The, 1747: CG, Feb 12, 13, 14, 16, 17, 18, 19, 20, 21,
    23, 24, 25, 26, 27, 28, DL, Mar 2, CG, 7, 19, 21, 24, NONE, 27, CG, Apr 28,
    30, May 2, 8, Nov 18, 19, 20, 21, 25, DL, Dec 4, 5, 7, 8, 9, 10, 21, CG, 29;
    1748: DL, Jan 16, HAY, 25, CG, Feb 3, DL, 5, CG, 8, Mar 3, DL, 12, Apr 19,
    May 3, 17, Sep 27, Oct 25, Nov 26, Dec 29; 1749: DL, Jan 31, HAY, Feb 23, DL,
    Mar 13, Apr 26, CG, Oct 23, 24, DL, 26, CG, Nov 7, DL, 18, CG, 30; 1750: CG,
    Jan 13, Feb 6, DL, 10, Mar 24, CG, Apr 24, DL, May 17, 21, 22, Oct 16, Nov 8,
    10; 1751: DL, Apr 12, 22, May 11, CG, 16, DL, Oct 9, Nov 14, CG, 26, Dec 13;
    1752: DL, Jan 24, Feb 10, Mar 16, Apr 15, May 12, CG, Sep 25, 27, Oct 20, Nov
    14, DL, 22, CG, Dec 2, DL, 5, CG, 12, 22; 1753: CG, Jan 12, DL, 19, CG, Feb
    1, DL, Mar 27, CG, May 5, DL, 25, CG, Sep 14, DL, Oct 13, Nov 17, CG, Dec 10;
    1754: DL, Jan 2, Feb 23, CG, Mar 7, DL, 21, Apr 18, May 28, CG, Oct 4, Nov
    21, DL, Dec 7; 1755: CG, Jan 8, DL, 14, CG, Feb 5, DL, Apr 11, CG, May 19,
    DL, Sep 25, Oct 22, Nov 24; 1756: DL, Feb 16, Mar 29, CG, Apr 20, DL, Sep 23,
    CG, Nov 11; 1757: CG, Jan 4, DL, Feb 3, 10, Apr 13, May 11, Sep 15, Nov 3,
    CG, 18, Dec 21; 1758: DL, Feb 14, Mar 29, CG, Sep 20, DL, Oct 21, 31; 1759:
    DL, Mar 22, Apr 20, CG, May 21, DL, Oct 5, Nov 20; 1760: DL, Jan 10, Mar 11,
    Apr 19, Jun 3, Oct 17, Nov 18; 1761: DL, Feb 12, CG, Apr 6, DL, 7, Sep 12,
    CG, 30, DL, Nov 20; 1762: DL, Jan 14, Mar 13, Apr 16, Sep 30, Oct 26, Dec 13;
    1763: DL, Apr 19, May 6; 1764: DL, Jan 25, 31, Feb 15, 29, Oct 25, Nov 26,
    Dec 28; 1765: DL, Feb 13, Apr 18, May 9, Oct 24; 1766: DL, May 12, Nov 28,
    Dec 19; 1767: DL, Mar 19, CG, Apr 11, May 1, DL, 29, Jun 3, Oct 15, Dec 23;
    1768: DL, May 4, 26, Aug 18, Oct 6, Dec 23; 1769: DL, May 11, 20, Dec 6;
    1770: DL, Nov 23; 1771: DL, Jan 10, Nov 25, Dec 6; 1772: DL, Mar 10, CG, 23,
    26, Apr 24, May 15, DL, Nov 27, CG, Dec 11; 1773: CG, Jan 12, DL, 22, CG, May
    26, DL, Oct 20; 1774: DL, Jan 18; 1775: CG, Mar 20, DL, 28, CG, May 5, DL,
    13, CG, Sep 20; 1776: CG, Mar 30, DL, May 23, Jun 1, CG, Dec 5; 1777: CG, Apr
    26, CHR, Jun 23; 1778: CG, Sep 23, Nov 6, Dec 19; 1779: CG, Jan 8, Mar 11,
    DL, May 10, CG, Nov 6; 1780: DL, Apr 1, 6, CG, 17, CII, 19, CG, May 18, Oct

6, Dec 28, 29; <u>1781</u>: CG, May 19, Oct 23; <u>1782</u>: DL, May 7, CG, 22, Nov 27;
<u>1783</u>: DL, Jan 3, 17, Oct 18, Nov 4; <u>1784</u>: DL, Jan 8, May 20; <u>1785</u>: HAY, Apr
26, CG, Nov 7, 26; <u>1787</u>: CG, May 23; <u>1788</u>: CG, Jan 2, Oct 10, DL, Dec 18;
<u>1789</u>: CG, Dec 31; <u>1790</u>: CG, Jan 9, 27, Feb 5, Apr 28, DL, May 14, CG, Jun 8,
Sep 17, Dec 15, 22; <u>1791</u>: DL, May 20, CG, Jun 8, Sep 16; <u>1792</u>: CG, Jun 1, Sep
19, 28; <u>1793</u>: CG, May 23, Sep 20, Dec 23; <u>1794</u>: CG, May 20, Jun 17, Sep 15;
<u>1795</u>: CG, Jan 9, May 7, Jun 17, Oct 2; <u>1796</u>: CG, Dec 21; <u>1797</u>: DL, Feb 7, CG,
Apr 29, DL, Jun 14, CG, Sep 22, Dec 30; <u>1798</u>: CG, May 3; <u>1799</u>: CG, Sep 20,
Dec 27; <u>1800</u>: CG, Jan 8
--Tatlers, The, <u>1797</u>: CG, Apr 29
Hoadly, Dr Benjamin, <u>1747</u>: CG, Feb 12, Mar 7; <u>1797</u>: CG, Apr 29
Hoadly, Rev John (clergyman), <u>1747</u>: CG, Feb 12; <u>1777</u>: DL, Mar 12
Hoare, Katherine (actor), <u>1779</u>: HAY, Feb 22
Hoare, Messrs (bankers), <u>1776</u>: KING'S, Nov 2
Hoare, Prince, <u>1790</u>: DL, Apr 16; <u>1791</u>: DL, May 3, DLKING'S, Oct 15; <u>1792</u>:
DLKING'S, May 23, DL, Oct 11; <u>1793</u>: DL, Mar 11, HAY, Dec 16; <u>1795</u>: HAY, Sep
2; <u>1796</u>: CG, Feb 2, DL, Apr 30, May 10; <u>1797</u>: DL, Feb 9, CG, Apr 25; <u>1798</u>:
DL, Nov 14; <u>1799</u>: HAY, Jul 30; <u>1800</u>: DL, Apr 28, May 10
--Captive of Spilburg, The, <u>1798</u>: DL, Nov 14, 15, 16, 17, 19, 20, 21, 22, 23,
24, Dec 5, 7, CG, 11, DL, 12, 14, 19, 20, 28
--Cave of Trophonius, The (opera), <u>1791</u>: DL, May 3, 21, DLKING'S, Oct 15, 17,
22, 26, 29; <u>1792</u>: DL, Oct 11, 16
--Children, The; or, Give Them their Way, <u>1800</u>: DL, Apr 28
--Friend in Need, A (opera), <u>1797</u>: DL, Feb 7, 9, 10, 11, 13, 14, 15, 17, 20,
22, 24
--Indiscretion, <u>1800</u>: DL, May 8, 10, 13, 22, 24, 28, Jun 9
--Italian Villagers, The (opera), <u>1797</u>: CG, Apr 25, 27, 28, May 1, 3, 5, Dec
16; <u>1798</u>: CG, Apr 21; <u>1799</u>: CG, Apr 6; <u>1800</u>: CG, May 22
--Julia; or, Such Things Were, <u>1796</u>: DL, May 2
--Lock and Key (farce), <u>1796</u>: CG, Feb 2, 3, 4, 5, 6, 9, 11, 13, 15, 16, 18, 20,
22, 23, 25, 27, 29, Mar 1, 3, 5, 7, 8, 10, 12, Apr 2, 7, 14, 26, 28, May 5,
13, Sep 16, Oct 19, Nov 2, 30, Dec 8; <u>1797</u>: CG, Feb 1, May 6, Jun 1, HAY, Jul
1, 3, 8, 13, 22, Aug 12, CG, Sep 25; <u>1798</u>: CG, Feb 22, Apr 17, May 22, HAY,
Jul 10, Aug 2, 20, Sep 10; <u>1799</u>: CG, Apr 9, 26, May 31, Oct 2, Dec 12; <u>1800</u>:
CG, Apr 19, 24
--Mahmoud; or, The Prince of Persia, <u>1796</u>: DL, Apr 30, May 4, 7, 9, 10, 17, 19,
25, 28, Jun 1, 4, 6, 9, 10, 11, 15; <u>1797</u>: CG, Mar 31; <u>1798</u>: HAY, Sep 17
--My Grandmother (farce), <u>1793</u>: HAY, Dec 16, 17, 18, 23, 31; <u>1794</u>: HAY, Jan 4,
8, 10, 16, 23, 31, Feb 3, 10, 11, 14, 18, 25, Mar 3, 10, 18, 22, 29, Apr 3,
7, 8, DL, May 9, 12, 15, 22, 29, Jun 3, 5, 27, 28, HAY, Aug 29, Sep 1, 2, 8,
9, 12, 15, DL, 16, 20, Oct 7, 29, Nov 12, 28; <u>1795</u>: DL, Jan 13, 26, 29, Feb
7, Apr 17, May 14, 21, 26, Jun 4, 8, HAY, 11, Jul 10, 18, 27, Aug 8, 15, 27,
Sep 12, DL, 22, Oct 20, Nov 23, Dec 30; <u>1796</u>: DL, Jan 12, Mar 10, Apr 2, 7,
19, May 9, 24, 31, Jun 14, HAY, 25, Aug 2, DL, Oct 1, Nov 12; <u>1797</u>: DL, Jan
27, Feb 22, Mar 14, Apr 8, May 3, Jun 15, HAY, 17, Jul 24, Aug 7, DL, Oct 16,
Nov 10, Dec 26; <u>1798</u>: DL, Mar 5, HAY, Jun 21, 25, 30, Jul 7, 17, 24, Aug 3,
16, DL, Sep 18, Dec 8; <u>1799</u>: DL, Jan 15, Mar 7, Apr 6, May 24, Jun 11, 26,
HAY, Jul 5, 11, Aug 1, 19, Sep 6, DL, Nov 13, 19, Dec 16; <u>1800</u>: DL, Feb 11,
May 8, HAY, Jun 27
--No Song No Supper (farce), <u>1790</u>: DL, Apr 16, 26, May 3, 10, 17, 24, Oct 4,
12, 21, 28, Nov 4, 11, 15, 18, 22, 29, Dec 2, 6, 9, 10, 13, 15, 17, 20; <u>1791</u>:
DL, Feb 5, 14, 24, 28, Mar 10, 29, Apr 12, May 3, 12, 16, 24, Jun 4,
DLKING'S, Sep 24, 27, Oct 6, 11, 15; <u>1792</u>: DLKING'S, Mar 27, May 21, Jun 1,
5, DL, Sep 20, 22, Oct 4, 6, 11, 30, Nov 13; <u>1793</u>: DL, Jan 10, 18, Feb 5, 9,
12, 19, May 9, 21, HAY, Aug 6, Oct 22, 26, 31, Nov 8, 13, 21, Dec 2, 5, 9,
11; <u>1794</u>: HAY, Jan 10, 17, 29, Feb 3, 20, DL, Apr 25, 26, May 2, 9, 21, 28,
Jun 6, 10, 25, 30, Jul 2, Sep 23, 25, Oct 11, 21, 31, Nov 19, Dec 3, 10;
<u>1795</u>: DL, Jan 27, Feb 10, Apr 18, 28, May 13, 22, Jun 2, 6, Sep 17, 29, Oct
17, 26, Nov 3, 27, Dec 11, 26; <u>1796</u>: DL, Jan 14, Feb 11, Mar 7, 14, 30, Apr
8, May 13, 23, Jun 3, HAY, Jul 8, Aug 3, DL, Sep 27, Oct 22, Nov 16, Dec 2;
<u>1797</u>: DL, Jan 19, 25, Feb 4, 23, Apr 19, CG, 26, DL, May 4, Jun 10, CG, 14,
HAY, Sep 4, DL, 23, 26, Oct 24, Dec 5, 29; <u>1798</u>: DL, Jan 2, Feb 2, May 10,
HAY, Jul 13, 28, Aug 10, 25, DL, Oct 2, Nov 10, Dec 28; <u>1799</u>: DL, Jan 10, Feb
25, Apr 3, May 17, CG, 24, DL, Jun 25, Jul 4, Oct 12, 24, Dec 4; <u>1800</u>: DL,
Jan 28, Apr 25, May 9, 27, Jun 2
--Prize, The; or, 2.3.5.8, <u>1793</u>: DL, Mar 11, 19, 21, 23, Apr 2, 4, 6, 11, 12,
16, 20, 26, 27, 30, May 2, 3, 4, 6, 11, HAY, Aug 30, Sep 30, Oct 3, 9, 14,
17, 24, 28, Nov 2, 7, 11, 12, 13, 18, 22, 28, Dec 3, 6, 11, 13; <u>1794</u>: HAY,
Jan 9, 10, 18, 22, 27, Feb 1, 3, 7, 11, 13, 21, Mar 4, 13, 20, 25, Apr 5, DL,
May 12, 13, 19, 26, Jun 4, HAY, Sep 6, DL, 18, Oct 4, 28, Nov 21, Dec 5, 17;
<u>1795</u>: DL, Jan 20, 31, Feb 2, 14, Apr 20, 30, May 18, 19, Jun 1, HAY, Aug 10,
25, DL, Sep 19, Oct 21, 31, Nov 25, Dec 31; <u>1796</u>: DL, Jan 9, Mar 10, Apr 6,

14, 28, May 26, Jun 13, HAY, Jul 11, 18, 30, Aug 24, Sep 1, 10, DL, 20, Oct
18, Nov 24; 1797: DL, Jan 18, Feb 3, Mar 6, Apr 6, May 10, 11, Jun 13, Sep
21, Oct 3, 27, Nov 18, Dec 12; 1798: DL, Jan 2, Feb 26, Mar 24, Jun 2, 16,
Sep 22, Nov 6, 30; 1799: DL, Jan 1, 18, Apr 10, May 15, Jun 8, Jul 1, HAY,
Aug 17, DL, Sep 17, 28, Oct 31, Dec 7; 1800: DL, Jan 22, Mar 31, Jun 5
--Sighs; or, The Daughter, 1799: HAY, Jul 30, 31, Aug 1, 2, 3, 6, 7, 8, 9, 14,
15, 16, 24, Sep 2, 9, 12; 1800: HAY, Jun 18, 23, 25, Jul 4, 11, 21, Aug 1,
Sep 2
--Three and the Deuce!, The (farce), 1795: HAY, Aug 31, Sep 2, 3, 4, 5, 8, 9,
10, 11, 12, 14, 15, DL, Oct 8; 1796: DL, May 25
Hob (actor), 1751: HAY, Nov 21
Hob. See Doggett, Thomas.
Hob's Opera. See Hippisley, John, Flora.
Hob's Wedding. See Leigh, John.
Hobart, Lord (spectator), 1748: DL, Feb 25
Hobbe, Mrs (householder), 1778: HAY, Apr 29
Hobby Horse, The. See Thompson, Edward.
Hobler (actor), 1788: HAY, Aug 5, 8; 1789: HAY, Aug 11, 13, Sep 12; 1791:
DLKING'S, Oct 15; 1792: DLKING'S, May 23, 25; 1793: HAY, Aug 3, 15, Oct 10;
1794: DL, Jun 9, 12, 23, 25
Hobson (stage doorkeeper), 1735: LIF, May 21; 1737: DL, May 25; 1738: DL, May
18; 1739: DL, May 25; 1740: DL, May 22; 1741: DL, May 22; 1742: DL, May 22,
Sep 11, 21, Dec 15; 1743: DL, Mar 8, 10, 14, 15, 17, 1(, 22, Apr 5, 7, 18,
29, May 4, 6, 11; 1744: DL, Feb 25, Mar 5, 12, Apr 4, 10, 21, 27, May 4, 5,
11, 14, 22, Sep 15; 1745: DL, Mar 11, 14, 20, Apr 1, 16, 17, 20, May 10, Sep
19; 1746: DL, Mar 10, 13, 18, Apr 3, 8, 10, 12, 29, May 12, Sep 23; 1747: DL,
Feb 11, 23, Mar 7, 14, 16, 23, 24, Apr 4, May 13, Sep 15; 1748: DL, Mar 7,
10, 12, 14, 15, 21, 22, 26, 31, Apr 2, 12, 13, 18, 19, 27, 28, 29, May 18,
Sep 10; 1749: DL, Feb 9, Mar 7, 13, 14, 29, 31, Apr 1, 3, 5, 7, 10, 13, 14,
26, 28, May 1, 8, 9, 12, Sep 16; 1750: DL, Jan 9, Feb 21, 22, Mar 10, 13, 17,
19, 20, 22, 24, 31, Apr 2, 4, 21, May 4, 7, 17, Sep 8; 1751: DL, Mar 11, 14,
16, 19, Apr 11, 12, 17, 19, 20, 22, 24, 30, May 2, 10, 22
Hobson, Mrs, 1749: DL, Nov 18, Dec 23, 30; 1750: DL, Jan 20, Mar 3, 12, Apr 17,
28
Hobson's Choice; or, Thespis in Distress (burletta), 1787: ROY, Jul 3
Hobster (wine merchant), 1769: CG, Apr 3
Hochbrucher, Johann Baptist (harpist), 1779: KING'S, Feb 23
Hockbrucker (musician), 1743: LIF, Mar 15
Hockley, 1699: DLLIF, Sep 12
Hodge Podge (song), 1735: CG/LIF, May 5
Hodge Podge, The; or, A Receipt to Make a Benefit (interlude, anon), 1781: HAY,
Aug 28, 31; 1796: HAY, Aug 30
Hodges (office keeper), 1762: DL, May 25; 1765: DL, May 18; 1766: DL, May 20;
1768: DL, May 27; 1769: DL, May 20; 1771: DL, May 29; 1772: DL, Jun 10; 1773:
DL, Jun 1; 1774: DL, May 27; 1775: DL, May 18; 1776: DL, May 20; 1777: DL,
Jun 4; 1778: DL, May 26; 1779: DL, Jun 1
Hodges, Thomas, 1749: BF/SFP, Aug 23
Hodges, William (scene painter), 1788: DL, Feb 25
Hodgins, Henry (scene painter), 1779: CG, Jan 4, Nov 30; 1780: CG, Dec 29;
1781: CG, May 28, Oct 1, Dec 26; 1782: CG, Oct 10, Nov 25; 1783: CG, Jan 18,
Sep 22, Dec 23; 1784: CG, Jan 29, Sep 20, Dec 27; 1785: CG, Oct 13, Dec 20;
1786: CG, Dec 26; 1787: CG, Nov 5, Dec 26; 1788: CG, Sep 22, Dec 26; 1789:
CG, Sep 28, Dec 21; 1790: CG, Sep 29, Nov 15, Dec 20; 1791: CG, Sep 17, Oct
20, Dec 21; 1792: CG, Dec 1, 20; 1793: CG, Mar 11, Oct 2, 12, Dec 19; 1794:
CG, Feb 22, Sep 22, Nov 17, Dec 26; 1795: CG, Apr 6, Dec 21; 1796: CG, Mar
15, Apr 9, Oct 24; 1798: CG, May 28; 1799: CG, May 13, Sep 23; 1800: CG, May
1
Hodgins, Master (actor), 1792: CG, Dec 26
Hodgson (coal merchant), 1771: CG, Nov 18; 1772: CG, Nov 16
Hodgson (Hudson, Hodson), John (actor), 1690: DL, Jan 0, NONE, Sep 0, DL, 0,
NONE, 0, DL, Oct 0, Nov 0, Dec 0; 1691: DL, Jan 0, Mar 0, Apr 0, DG, May 0,
NONE, Sep 0; 1692: DL, Jan 0, Feb 0, Mar 0, Apr 0, Nov 0, 8; 1692: DL, Apr 0,
DG, May 0; 1695: LIF, Sep 0, Dec 0; 1696: LIF, Jun 0, Nov 14, Dec 0; 1697:
LIF, Apr 0, May 0, Jun 0, Nov 0, ATCOURT, 4; 1698: LIF, Apr 0, YB, 25; 1699:
LIF, Feb 0, May 0; 1700: LIF, Jan 9, Apr 0, Sep 25; 1701: LIF, Mar 0, Apr 0;
1721: DL, Jun 2
Hodgson, Mrs (actor), 1693: DL, Feb 0, NONE, Sep 0, DLORDG, Dec 0; 1694: DL,
Jan 10, DLORDG, Feb 0, DL, 0, Mar 21, DG, May 0, NONE, Sep 0; 1695: LIF, Aug
0, Sep 0, NONE, 0, LIF, Dec 0; 1696: DL, Apr 0, LIF, 0, Jun 0, Nov 14; 1697:
LIF, Jun 0, ATCOURT, Nov 4
Hodgson, Mrs (singer), 1700: YB, Mar 20; 1701: DG, Mar 21, YB, 24; 1702: LIF,
Jun 22, YB, Jul 2, LIF, Dec 29; 1703: YB, Mar 19, LIF, Apr 28, Oct 25, YB,

Dec 11; <u>1704</u>: LIF, Mar 23, YB, 29, LIF, Apr 29, Jun 1, 8, Jul 4, 10, Aug 9;
<u>1705</u>: LIF, Mar 1, YB, 7, LIF, Aug 7, LIF/QUEN, Oct 11, 17; <u>1706</u>: QUEEN'S, Jan
2, LIF/QUEN, 25, ATCOURT, Feb 5, QUEEN'S, Apr 15; <u>1710</u>: DL, Apr 22; <u>1718</u>:
LIF, May 20; <u>1719</u>: LIF, May 18
Hodson, William, <u>1779</u>: DL, Dec 13; <u>1781</u>: DL, May 1; <u>1783</u>: DL, Mar 24
--Adventures of a Night, The (farce), <u>1783</u>: DL, Mar 24, 27, 31, Apr 1, 5, May
1, 3, 10, 13, 22, 27
--Zoraida, <u>1779</u>: DL, Dec 13, 14, 15, 23; <u>1780</u>: DL, Jan 4, 13, 17, 25, Feb 2, 8,
Mar 11; <u>1781</u>: DL, May 1
Hoffman (instrumentalist), <u>1798</u>: HAY, Jan 15
Hoffman, Sophia (pianist), <u>1797</u>: DL, May 18
Hogarth, William (painter), <u>1742</u>: CG, Mar 22; <u>1783</u>: CG, Apr 26; <u>1786</u>: CG, Apr
18; <u>1789</u>: HAY, May 18
Hogg, Alex (printer), <u>1792</u>: DLKING'S, May 29
Hoggins, Philip (actor), <u>1772</u>: CG, Oct 27
Hogia, Jusep (Tunisian ambassador), <u>1733</u>: DL, Oct 22
Hojah, Cossam (Tripoline ambassador), <u>1728</u>: HAY, Oct 24
Holbein, Hans (painter), <u>1757</u>: DL, Jan 1
Holborn Bars, <u>1724</u>: BPT, Feb 21; <u>1749</u>: DL, Feb 9
Holborn, <u>1723</u>: BHT, Dec 23; <u>1736</u>: HAY, Apr 6, CG, May 6; <u>1737</u>: LIF, Mar 9, CG,
Apr 25, HAY, May 2; <u>1739</u>: CG, Nov 7; <u>1744</u>: CG, Apr 20, DL, May 14, 17; <u>1745</u>:
GF, Mar 18; <u>1748</u>: HAY, Apr 18; <u>1749</u>: CG, Apr 28; <u>1750</u>: BB, Jan 8, DL, Nov 28;
<u>1751</u>: DL, Dec 17; <u>1752</u>: DL, Nov 15; <u>1756</u>: DL, Mar 9; <u>1757</u>: DL, Dec 21; <u>1760</u>:
HAY, Aug 15; <u>1761</u>: DL, Mar 14; <u>1779</u>: DL, May 5, HAY, 10; <u>1783</u>: DL, Apr 26;
<u>1787</u>: HAY, Mar 12; <u>1789</u>: CG, May 2; <u>1790</u>: CG, May 3; <u>1792</u>: HAY, Oct 15
Holcomb, Henry (actor, singer), <u>1706</u>: DL, Mar 30, May 25, Jun 1, 18, 20, DG,
Nov 1, DL, Dec 3; <u>1707</u>: DL, Mar 4; <u>1710</u>: YB, Mar 31, Apr 17, QUEEN'S, Jun 29;
<u>1729</u>: DL, Feb 26
Holcroft (actor), <u>1770</u>: HAY, May 28, Jun 27, Jul 25, Aug 1, 24, 31
Holcroft, Thomas (actor, playwright), <u>1777</u>: DL, Jan 4, 10, Mar 1, Apr 21, 23,
30, May 28, 31, Jun 2, Sep 20, Oct 2, 17, Nov 12; <u>1778</u>: DL, Jan 1, 5, Feb 2,
10, 24, May 1, 19, 23, Sep 17, 24, Oct 1, 8, 15, Nov 2, 4, Dec 21; <u>1779</u>: DL,
Jan 8, Mar 13, May 7, 18, 19, Sep 25, Oct 5, 7, 30, Nov 3, 11, Dec 2, 4, 27;
<u>1780</u>: DL, Jan 12, 24, Apr 5, 14, 26, 29, May 10, 20, 31, Sep 19, 21, 23, 30,
Oct 3, 11, 17, Nov 8, 9, Dec 1, 4, 6, 27; <u>1781</u>: DL, Jan 9, 16, 26, Apr 25,
May 1(10, 15, Sep 18, 20, 25, Oct 4, CG, 13, DL, 26, CG, Nov 1, DL, 5, CG,
6, DL, 13; <u>1782</u>: DL, Feb 2, Apr 6; <u>1784</u>: HAY, Aug 2, CG, Dec 14, 15, 16;
<u>1785</u>: CG, Apr 1, HAMM, Jul 25, CG, Nov 10; <u>1786</u>: HAY, Jun 20; <u>1787</u>: DL, Mar
12; <u>1790</u>: CG, Nov 11; <u>1791</u>: CG, Feb 4; <u>1792</u>: CG, Feb 18; <u>1793</u>: CG, Oct 8;
<u>1794</u>: CG, Feb 5, Sep 15; <u>1795</u>: CG, May 2; <u>1796</u>: DL, Jan 23, CG, May 6, DL,
Dec 6; <u>1798</u>: DL, Jan 25, CG, Feb 13, HAY, Jun 23; <u>1799</u>: CG, Apr 2
--Choleric Fathers, The (opera), <u>1785</u>: CG, Nov 10, 11, 12, 15, 16, 18, 24
--Crisis, The; or, Love and Fear (opera), <u>1778</u>: DL, May 1
--Deserted Daughter, The, <u>1795</u>: CG, May 2, 4, 5, 9, 11, 12, 15, 18, 20, 26, 28,
Jun 1, 15, Oct 14, 21, 28, Dec 2; <u>1796</u>: CG, May 16; <u>1798</u>: CG, May 16; <u>1800</u>:
CG, May 2
--Duplicity, <u>1781</u>: CG, Oct 13, 17, 19, 23, 26, 30, Nov 1, 6, Dec 28; <u>1796</u>: CG,
May 6
--Follies of a Day, The; or, The Marriage of Figaro, <u>1784</u>: CG, Dec 14, 15, 16,
17, 18, 20, 22, 31; <u>1785</u>: CG, Jan 1, 3, 4, 5, 11, 13, 15, 18, 20, 22, 25, 29,
Feb 1, 3, 5, 12, 22, Mar 1, 19, Apr 19, May 10, 27, HAMM, Jul 25, CG, Oct 26,
Dec 28; <u>1786</u>: CG, Jan 11, Feb 1, Apr 1, May 10; <u>1787</u>: HAY, Aug 21, CG, Nov 8;
<u>1788</u>: CG, Jun 3; <u>1789</u>: DL, May 27, Nov 7, 11, 19, CG, 21, 24, 28, Dec 7, 10,
17; <u>1790</u>: CG, Jan 6, Mar 25, Apr 12, 24, DL, 30, May 11, 12, CG, 14, Jun 3,
HAY, 17, 23, Jul 2, 12, Aug 11, DL, Oct 9, CG, 29; <u>1791</u>: CG, Feb 28, Mar 10,
DL, May 10, CG, 17, DL, 23, CG, Sep 20, Nov 9, DLKING'S, 11, CG, 15,
DLKING'S, 19; <u>1792</u>: CG, Feb 4, Apr 25, DLKING'S, 26, CG, Oct 27, Nov 13;
<u>1793</u>: CG, Apr 5, May 24, Oct 19, Dec 17; <u>1794</u>: CG, Feb 25, May 2, 9, Jun 5,
Oct 3; <u>1795</u>: CG, Apr 22, Jun 6, Dec 4; <u>1796</u>: CG, Apr 12, 19, DL, May 12, 20,
30, Jun 2, HAY, Aug 8, 24, Sep 17, CG, Oct 17, Nov 23, Dec 5; <u>1797</u>: DL, Feb
2, 8, Mar 4, 27, Apr 4, HAY, Aug 10, DL, Dec 23; <u>1798</u>: DL, Jan 3, Feb 19, Apr
9, CG, May 16, DL, 30, Jun 1, CG, Oct 1, Nov 16; <u>1799</u>: CG, Apr 23, HAY, Aug
13, 23; <u>1800</u>: DL, Jan 11, 31, CG, May 15, DL, 24, Jun 17
--Force of Ridicule, The, <u>1796</u>: DL, Nov 29, Dec 6
--He's Much to Blame, <u>1798</u>: CG, Feb 13, 14, 15, 16, 17, 19, 20, 22, 24, 26, 27,
Mar 1, 3, 5, 6, 10, 13, 17, 24, 27, Jun 5, 7
--Inquisitor, The, <u>1798</u>: HAY, Jun 23, 25, 26
--Knave or Not, <u>1798</u>: DL, Jan 18, 23, 25, 26, 27, 31, Feb 1, 6, 7
--Love's Frailities; or, Precept against Practice, <u>1794</u>: CG, Feb 5, 6, 7, 8,
11, 12
--Man of Ten Thousand, The, <u>1796</u>: DL, Jan 23, 26, 27, Feb 2, 4, 6, 9
--Masked Friend, The, <u>1781</u>: CG, Oct 13; <u>1796</u>: CG, May 6; <u>1797</u>: CG, Jun 1, 9

--Noble Peasant, The (opera), 1784: HAY, Aug 2, 4, 7, 9, 11, 12, 14, 16, 23,
   25, 31, Sep 3, 15
--Old Cloathsman, The (opera), 1799: CG, Apr 2, 3, 8
--Rival Queens, The; or, Drury-Lane and Covent-Garden (prelude), 1794: CG, Sep
   15
--Road to Ruin, The, 1792: CG, Feb 18, 20, 21, 23, 25, 27, Mar 1, 3, 5, 8, 10,
   12, 13, 15, 17, 19, 20, 22, 24, 27, 29, Apr 9, 11, 13, 16, 17, 19, 20, 23,
   24, 26, 30, May 3, 7, 14, 21, 31, Sep 17, Oct 11, 18, 25, Nov 1, 8, 15, 22,
   29, Dec 6, 13; 1793: CG, Jan 4, 11, 18, Mar 23, Apr 10, May 3, 21, Jun 12,
   Oct 3, 8, Nov 19, Dec 26; 1794: CG, Feb 13, HAMM, Mar 25, CG, May 7, Jun 3;
   1795: CG, Jan 8, Mar 5, Oct 8; 1796: CG, May 20, Oct 14; 1797: CG, Jun 5;
   1798: CG, Apr 19, HAY, Aug 14, 25, Sep 7, 12, CG, Oct 3, 10; 1799: CG, May 7,
   HAY, Jun 29, Jul 3, CG, Oct 2; 1800: CG, Jan 3, Jun 11
--School for Arrogance, The, 1791: CG, Feb 4, 5, 8, 10, 12, 14, 17, 19, 22, 24;
   1793: CG, Oct 5, 8, Nov 13, 20; 1794: CG, Feb 15, May 15; 1795: CG, Feb 6,
   Jun 12; 1796: CG, Jun 2; 1797: CG, Jun 9; 1799: CG, Jun 5
--Seduction, 1787: DL, Mar 10, 12, 13, 17, 19, 22, 24, 26, Apr 12, May 1, 5, 17
Hold John (song), 1731: LIF, May 28
Hold, John, E're You Leave Me (song), 1710: QUEEN'S, Jul 6, 26
Holden, John, 1665: LIF, Apr 17
--German Princess, The, 1664: LIF, Apr 15
--Ghosts, The, 1665: LIF, Apr 17
Holden, Mrs (actor), 1662: LIF, Mar 1
Holderness, Lord, 1761: CG, Apr 3
Holford (coal merchant), 1799: CG, Nov 4
Holiday (actor), 1791: HAY, Oct 24
Holinshead's Chronicles, 1759: DL, Jul 12
Holland (beneficiary), 1740: CG, May 29
Holland, C (actor), 1782: HAY, Mar 4, 18; 1785: HAY, Feb 10
Holland, Charles (actor), 1755: DL, Oct 13, 25, 28, 30; 1756: DL, Jan 1, 21,
   Feb 27, Apr 20, 29, Oct 2, 27, Nov 12, 24, Dec 11; 1757: DL, Jan 18, Mar 8,
   24, Apr 26, 28, May 3, 23, Oct 15, 20, Nov 4, Dec 8; 1758: DL, Jan 24, 28,
   Feb 1, 21, Mar 11, Apr 22, 25, May 15, Jun 1, Oct 12, 17, 19, 24, Nov 1, 3,
   4, 14, Dec 13, 16, 28; 1759: DL, Jan 3, 6, 12, 18, Feb 1, Mar 3, 26, 31, Apr
   19, 21, 23, May 11, 14, 18, Jun 4, Oct 4, 11, 19, 25, Nov 1, 3, 5, 9, 13, 17,
   24, 30, Dec 1, 31; 1760: DL, Jan 1, 11, 24, Feb 13, 21, Mar 17, 24, Apr 8,
   11, 14, 15, 28, May 1, 8, Sep 20, Oct 8, 11, 18, 24, 25, Nov 20, Dec 11, 30;
   1761: DL, Jan 3, 10, 23, 28, 31, Apr 6, 9, 18, 23, 24, May 11, 18, 25, 29,
   Sep 8, 10, 15, 21, 24, 26, 28, 29, 30, Oct 20, 26, Nov 4, 6, 9, 21, 28, Dec
   11, 26, 30; 1762: DL, Jan 2, 19, 27, Feb 20, 22, Mar 1, 15, 25, 30, Apr 1,
   30, May 7, 10, Sep 25, 28, Oct 4, 5, 7, 9, 12, 15, 20, 25, 28, 29, Nov 1, 3,
   4, 17, 27, Dec 6, 22; 1763: DL, Jan 19, 26, Feb 3, Mar 15, 17, 26, Apr 4, 20,
   Sep 20, 27, Oct 12, 14, 17, 24, 31, Nov 4, 7, 9, 14, 22, 29, Dec 1, 5, 14,
   26; 1764: DL, Jan 3, 7, 14, 18, Feb 14, 18, 21, 25, Mar 27, Apr 2, 12, May
   24, Sep 20, 22, 27, Oct 4, 9, 13, 16, 17, 18, 23, 24, 26, 31, Nov 5, 8, 9,
   17, 24, 27, Dec 8, 13; 1765: DL, Jan 1, 3, 24, Feb 4, 6, Mar 18, 19, 26, Apr
   20, Sep 17, 19, 21, 24, Oct 9, 11, 12, 14, 15, 23, 25, 28, 30, 31, Nov 11,
   15, 20, Dec 6, 7, 23; 1766: DL, Jan 6, 9, 13, 22, Feb 13, 20, 25, Mar 11, 18,
   20, 22, Apr 7, May 5, Sep 27, Oct 7, 8, 9, 16, 17, 18, 21, 24, 25, Nov 4, 17,
   20, 24, Dec 6, 13; 1767: DL, Jan 24, 31, Feb 7, 19, Mar 21, 24, 28, 30, 31,
   Apr 11, 20, 22, 28, 29, May 1, 4, 9, HAY, 29, DL, Sep 12, 15, 17, 19, 23, Oct
   8, 10, 14, 26, 29, 31, Nov 4, 5, 11, 13, 16, 19, 20, 21, 24, 28, Dec 5, 15,
   CG, 31; 1768: DL, Jan 23, Feb 27, Mar 15, 21, 24, Apr 4, 6, Sep 17, 26, Oct
   1, 3, 5, 8, 10, 11, 14, 17, 18, 19, 31, Dec 1, 3, 17; 1769: DL, Jan 9, Feb 4,
   Mar 13, 16, 18, 30, Apr 10, 21, 25, 28, May 16, Sep 19, 23, 26, 28, 30, Oct
   9, 14, 17, 18, 23, 30, 31, Nov 1, 13, 15, 18, 27, Dec 7
Holland, Charles (actor), 1796: DL, Oct 31, Nov 7, 9, 28, Dec 9; 1797: DL, Jan
   2, 20, Feb 3, Mar 6, 11, 14, May 9, 12, 17, Jun 12, Oct 5, 7, 12, 14, 16, 17,
   19, 26, Nov 4, 7, 9, 13, 21, 23, 24, 25, 27, Dec 2, 8; 1798: DL, Feb 13, 26,
   Mar 17, May 7, 11, 24, Jun 6, Sep 15, 18, 20, 25, 29, Oct 4, 11, 16, Nov 13,
   16, 26, Dec 27; 1799: DL, Feb 4, 14, 23, Apr 23, May 9, 20, 24, Jun 18, 29,
   Jul 1, Sep 17, 19, 21, 28, Oct 1, 3, 7, 12, 21, 29, 31, Nov 8, 14, 25, 27,
   Dec 11, 26, 30; 1800: DL, Jan 18, Mar 11, Apr 19, 28, 29, May 1, 10, 21, 23,
   Jun 18
Holland, John (dancer), 1772: DL, Nov 21; 1773: DL, Mar 25, Apr 1, CG, Oct 23;
   1774: DL, Jan 1, KING'S, Apr 28, May 12, CG, Sep 28, Nov 19, Dec 26; 1775:
   CG, May 26, Nov 18, Dec 7; 1776: CG, May 3; 1777: DL, Apr 3, CG, Oct 1, Nov
   3, DL, 7, CG, 11, DL, 11; 1778: CG, Apr 20, May 22, Oct 23, Nov 25; 1779: CG,
   May 3, DL, 14, CG, 21, Sep 22, 24, Oct 22, Nov 9, 23; 1780: CG, Jan 8, May 8,
   18; 1781: CG, May 18
Holland, John Joseph (scene painter), 1794: CG, Dec 26
Holland, Lord, 1745: DL, Apr 27

Holland, Miss (actor), 1777: CHR, Jun 23
Holland, Miss (singer), 1800: CG, Jun 16
Holland, Mrs (actor), 1728: HAY, May 8
Holland, W A (actor, dancer), 1792: CG, Oct 15, 18, Nov 16, 24, Dec 26; 1793:
    CG, Mar 11, 23, May 4, 10, 27, Sep 16, Oct 2, 18, Nov 12, 19, Dec 19, HAY,
    23, CG, 31; 1794: CG, Jan 21, Feb 6, 12, Apr 7, May 9, 26, Jun 6, Sep 22, Oct
    1, 14, 20; 1795: CG, Feb 19, 26, Apr 6, 28, May 12, 13, 29, Jun 6, Sep 14,
    21, Oct 2, 8, 23, Nov 13, 25, 27, Dec 9, 21; 1796: CG, Jan 4, 23, 25, Feb 1,
    Mar 15, 30, Apr 8, 9, 12, 15, 19, 20, 26, May 10, 16, 28, Jun 2
Holland, 1683: DLORDG, Feb 0; 1709: QUEEN'S, Dec 7; 1732: HAY, Feb 16; 1746:
    SFLY, Sep 8; 1799: DL, Oct 3
Hollar (clothing designer), 1757: DL, Jan 1
Hollendulla (musician), 1760: HAY, Feb 15
Holliday, Elizabeth (actor), 1723: LIF, Jun 3; 1725: LIF, May 14; 1728: LIF,
    Jan 29, Apr 24, May 8, Nov 23, Dec 28; 1729: LIF, Jan 16, 18, Apr 19, 23, 26,
    May 3, 7, 22, Oct 29, 30, Nov 4; 1730: LIF, Jan 22, Mar 17, 21, Apr 2, 30,
    May 7, 11, 15, 23, 25, Sep 18, Oct 7, 19, 23, Nov 7, 23, 30, Dec 2; 1731:
    LIF, Jan 8, 9, 20, Apr 3, 21, May 6, 20, Jun 2, Sep 20, Oct 20, 27, Nov 12,
    Dec 1, 3, 8; 1732: LIF, Jan 5, 7, Feb 14, Apr 26, 27, May 1, 9, 11, LIF/CG,
    Oct 6, 11, 25, 28, Nov 7, 8, 18, 22, Dec 28; 1733: LIF/CG, Jan 15, 23, 31,
    DL, Feb 8, 22, Mar 15, LIF/CG, 26, DL, Apr 4, 9, 19, May 1, 14, 21, 24, Sep
    24, Oct 17, 24, 31, Nov 5, 13, 14, 21, 26, Dec 7, 11, 21; 1734: DL, Feb 11,
    Mar 7, DL/LIF, 11, DL/HAY, 25, 28, LIF, Apr 15, 18, DL, 23, DL/HAY, 26, May
    8, DL, 15, DL/HAY, 23, DL, Sep 7, 24, Oct 3, 8, 14, 22, 25, Nov 2, 4, 16, 20,
    22, Dec 6, 14; 1735: DL, Jan 7, 11, 28, 29, Feb 10, Mar 6, Apr 28, May 14,
    Jul 1, LIF, Aug 1, DL, Sep 4, 9, 11, 13, 20, 25, 27, Oct 2, 11, 21, 25, 27,
    28, 30, 31, Nov 3, 4, 6, 19, 21, 24, 29, Dec 26; 1736: DL, Jan 3, Feb 5, 9,
    20, Mar 13, Apr 12, 15, 29, May 4, 26, Aug 26, Sep 9, 11, 14, 16, 18, 23, Oct
    7, 19, 25, 27, 30, Nov 1, 3, 4, 6, 13, 15, 20, 22, Dec 7, 17, 21; 1737: DL,
    Jan 6, 10, Feb 10, Mar 10, 15, 17, 22, Apr 12, 15, 27, May 5, 7, Aug 30, Sep
    1, 6, 8, 10, 15, 17
Hollingsworth (actor), 1767: CG, Jan 31; 1771: CG, Sep 28; 1773: CG, May 22,
    Sep 24; 1774: CG, Jan 3, Apr 11, Sep 23, Oct 7, 11, 21, Nov 19, Dec 27; 1775:
    CG, Jan 3, Mar 30, May 4, 30
Hollingsworth (dresser), 1760: CG, Sep 22
Hollingsworth, Mrs (charwoman), 1760: CG, Sep 22
Hollingsworth, Thomas (actor), 1787: DL, Dec 12, 26; 1788: DL, Jan 5, 14, 23,
    Apr 4, 14, 18, 28, May 1, 8, 21, Sep 13, 18, 27, 30, Oct 2, Nov 8, 10, 17,
    27, Dec 4, 6, 11, 12, 22; 1789: DL, Jan 3, Apr 14, May 27, Jun 11, Sep 12,
    17, Oct 1, 8, 22, 24, 31, Nov 13, Dec 3, 5, 17, 22, 26; 1790: DL, Mar 22, Apr
    23, 27, May 14, 15, Oct 7, 11, HAY, 13, DL, 16, 21, Nov 1, Dec 10, 11, 22,
    27; 1791: DL, Jan 1, 10, Feb 10, Mar 4, Apr 2, 16, May 10, 11, 18, DLKING'S,
    Sep 22, 29, Oct 1, 3, 31, Nov 4, 8, 14, Dec 7; 1792: DLKING'S, Jan 6, 9, 13,
    28, Feb 7, 13, 27, Mar 6, 10, 12, 29, Apr 10, 24, May 17, Jun 9, 11, 13, DL,
    Sep 18, 19, 22, 25, 29, Oct 4, 9, Nov 5, 10, 16, 23, 26, Dec 10, 27, 28;
    1793: DL, Jan 5, 16, Feb 16, 21, Mar 12, 14, 21, Apr 9, 17, May 7, 10, 22,
    Jun 1, HAY, Sep 24; 1794: DL, May 3, Jul 2, Sep 23, 27, Oct 18, 20, Nov 3,
    Dec 5, 9, 12, 13, 20, 23; 1795: DL, Jan 3, 5, 6, 23, 31, Feb 2, 6, Apr 17,
    May 9, 12, 22, 29, Jun 3, Sep 17, 22, Oct 6, 27, 30, Nov 6, 7, 10, 26, Dec 2,
    7, 10, 12, 18, 19, 21; 1796: DL, Jan 18, Feb 27, Mar 12, 19, 28, Apr 25, 29,
    May 13, 17, 24, 28, Jun 4, 8, 11, 13, Sep 20, 29, Oct 1, 3, 4, 8, 10, 15, 19,
    24, 25, 28, Nov 8, 9, 10, 18, 22, Dec 5, 7, 16, 26; 1797: DL, Jan 12, 17, Feb
    7, 9, 17, Mar 23, Apr 24, 27, May 12, 15, 22, 24, Jun 7, 12, HAY, 13, DL, Sep
    23, 26, 28, 30, Oct 5, 7, 17, 19, 23, 28, Nov 4, 9, 10, 11, 14, 15, 17, 23,
    24, 25, 27, 28, Dec 2, 5, 12, 19, 20, 21, 23; 1798: DL, Jan 4, 9, 16, 25, Feb
    12, 13, 22, 27, Mar 8, Apr 14, 25, May 21, 24, Jun 6, 7, 12, Sep 20, 25, 27,
    Oct 4, 6, 8, 9, 11, 16, 27, Nov 10, 13, 14, 19, 22, 26, 28, 29, Dec 4, 5,
    HAY, 17, DL, 19, 28; 1799: DL, Jan 11, 19, Feb 14, 19, 23, Mar 2, 4, Apr 8,
    13, 17, 22, May 1, 3, 8, 9, Jun 10, 18, Oct 1, 5, 7, 8, 10, 12, 14, 19, 22,
    26, 29, 31, Nov 8, 12, 14, 16, 25, 27, 29, 30, Dec 7, 14, 17; 1800: DL, Jan
    3, 4, 7, 18, Feb 1, Mar 8, 17, 27, Apr 15, 28, May 19, 23, Jun 7
Holliss, 1767: CG, Mar 24
Hollogan (scene painter), 1794: CG, Nov 17, Dec 26; 1795: CG, Apr 6, Dec 21;
    1796: CG, Mar 15, Apr 9, Oct 24, Nov 5, Dec 19; 1797: CG, Mar 16, Oct 2, Nov
    24, Dec 26; 1798: CG, Feb 12, Apr 9, Oct 15, Nov 12, Dec 11; 1799: CG, Jan
    29, Apr 19, Sep 23, Dec 23; 1800: CG, Jan 16, May 1
Holloway (dancer), 1772: CG, May 1; 1773: CG, Apr 24, May 21; 1774: CG, Sep 26;
    1775: CG, May 8; 1776: CG, May 4, 15; 1777: CG, May 20; 1778: CG, May 16;
    1779: CG, May 8; 1780: CG, May 8, 16, 18; 1781: CG, May 18; 1782: HAY, Mar
    18, CG, Apr 1, 27, May 11, 25
Holloway, Mr and Mrs (dancers), 1773: CG, May 21; 1774: CG, May 11; 1776: CG,
    May 15; 1777: CG, May 20

Holloway, Mrs (dancer), 1773: CG, Apr 24
Holman (financier), 1772: DL, Feb 8
Holman, Joseph George (actor, playwright), 1768: CG, Oct 24; 1784: CG, Oct 25,
    Nov 5, 12, Dec 3, 13, 30; 1785: CG, Jan 12, Feb 4, 15, Mar 3, 7, 15, Apr 12,
    18, 22, Sep 23, 26, Oct 17, Nov 14, 28, Dec 1, 5, 10, 13, 14; 1786: CG, Jan
    4, 6, 18, 24, 31, Feb 2, Mar 6, 11, 14, Apr 4, 8, 19, May 9, 11, 13, Sep 20,
    27, Oct 2, 4, 6, 23, 26, 30, Nov 15, 22, 27, Dec 4, 6, 20; 1787: CG, Jan 11,
    15, 31, Feb 10, Mar 27, Apr 11, 14, 27, May 1, 4, 15, 21; 1789: CG, Sep 14,
    18, 25, Oct 7, 12, Nov 10, 12, 16, 20, 23, 27, 30, Dec 14, 21, 26, 31; 1790:
    CG, Jan 13, 29, Feb 11, 22, Mar 18, 22, 27, Apr 14, 29, May 5, 11, 18, 20,
    24, Sep 13, 17, Oct 6, 11, 15, 18, 20, 23, 27, Nov 1, 3, 6, 11, 23, 27, 30,
    Dec 2, 6, 10, 17, 20, 31; 1791: CG, Jan 3, 12, Feb 11, 12, Apr 5, 16, 30, May
    10, Jun 6, Sep 12, 16, 17, 23, 26, Oct 3, 6, 10, 12, 17, 20, 21, 24, 27, 28,
    Nov 4, 24, 29, Dec 3, 21, 26; 1792: CG, Jan 6, Feb 18, Mar 26, Apr 10, 12,
    May 2, 5, 11, 19, 30, Jun 2, Sep 17, 24, 28, Oct 5, 8, 10, 12, 15, 29, 31,
    Nov 3, 5, 6, 7, 10, 12, 14, 24, Dec 1, 5, 20; 1793: CG, Jan 14, 21, Apr 11,
    15, 24, May 8, 24, Sep 16, 17, 20, 30, Oct 3, 4, 5, 8, 9, 11, 14, 23, 28, Nov
    13, 18, 23, Dec 19, 20, 30; 1794: CG, Jan 6, 14, Feb 1, 5, 18, Mar 17, Apr 7,
    May 6, 16, 19, 26, 30, Jun 5, Sep 15, 22, 29, Oct 1, 7, 8, 15, 20, 23, Nov 8,
    19, 20, 21, 22, Dec 6; 1795: CG, Jan 6, 8, 19, 29, Feb 6, 21, Mar 16, Apr 22,
    24, May 1, 8, 14, 27, Jun 3, 17, Sep 14, 18, 25, 28, 30, Oct 2, 7, 8, 12, 16,
    22, 23, 30, Nov 6, Dec 7, 9, 15, 22, 23, 26, 31; 1796: CG, Jan 6, Apr 1, 19,
    22, 26, May 6, 17, 21, 24, DL, 27, CG, 28, Jun 2, 6, Sep 12, 19, 21, 26, Oct
    5, 10, 14, 20, Nov 5, 19, Dec 10, 17, 21, 26; 1797: CG, Jan 4, 7, 10, Feb 27,
    Mar 14, 16, 23, 30, Apr 8, 29, May 6, 16, 31, Jun 1, 13, Sep 18, 22, 25, Oct
    2, 4, 11, 12, 13, 28, Nov 3, 4, 11, 18, 20, 23, Dec 27; 1798: CG, Jan 5, 11,
    Feb 6, 9, Mar 20, 31, Apr 10, 17, 19, 30, May 4, 12, 15, 23, 28, 30, 31, Sep
    17, 26, Oct 1, 3, 5, 8, Nov 7, Dec 8; 1799: CG, Jan 12, Apr 9, 16, 27, May
    15, 22, Jun 5, 7, HAY, 29, Aug 21, CG, Sep 16, 20, 23, 30, Oct 2, 7, 9, 14,
    29, Nov 7, 8, 14, Dec 10, 23, 30; 1800: CG, Jan 16, DL, Feb 6, CG, Mar 22,
    Apr 17, 24, 30, May 10, 13, 20, 27, 29, Jun 2, 7, HAY, Aug 14
--Abroad and at Home (opera), 1796: CG, Nov 19, 21, 22, 23, 25, 28, DL, 29, CG,
    29, 30, Dec 1, 3, 5, 7, 9, 13, 15, 17, 23, 29, 30; 1797: CG, Jan 3, 6, 9, 13,
    16, 19, Feb 17, 21, May 2, 11, 15, 30, Oct 31; 1799: CG, Apr 6, May 3, Jun 6;
    1800: CG, Jan 11, May 22
--Red Cross Knights, The, 1799: HAY, Aug 21, 23, 26, 28, 30, 31, Sep 6, 14
--Votary of Wealth, The, 1799: CG, Jan 12, 14, 16, 17, 18, 19, 22, 23, 25, 28,
    31, Feb 5, 9, 12, 16, 21, 26, Mar 4, 12, May 21, Jun 8, Sep 25; 1800: CG, Apr
    17
--What a Blunder (opera), 1800: HAY, Aug 13, 14, 15, 16, 18, 19, 20, 22, 25, 27
Holman, Master (actor), 1737: DL, Nov 19; 1738: DL, Oct 30, Dec 4; 1739: DL,
    Feb 7
Holmden (tailor), 1774: CG, Apr 8
Holme and Cooper (timber merchants), 1773: CG, Jan 29; 1774: CG, Apr 20
Holmes (actor), 1747: GF, Jan 5
Holmes (actor), 1779: HAY, Mar 15, May 10, Oct 18; 1781: HAY, Jan 22
Holmes (actor), 1795: HAY, Sep 21; 1797: HAY, Jan 23, 26, May 10
Holmes (musician), 1708: SH, Feb 4, Mar 26
Holmes, James (bassoonist), 1790: CG, Feb 19; 1793: KING/HAY, Mar 13, 15; 1795:
    KING'S, Feb 27, Jun 16; 1798: HAY, Jan 15
Holmes, Sir John (duellist), 1669: BRIDGES, Mar 4; 1679: DG, Jun 21
Holofernes (puppetry), 1663: NONE, Aug 6
Holt (actor, dancer), 1729: HAY, Mar 29, Dec 18; 1732: WINH, May 27, DL, 29,
    Jun 6, 23, Aug 15, 17, GF, Dec 20; 1733: GF, Jan 10, Apr 20, May 4, DL/HAY,
    Oct 6, 25, 27, Nov 8, HAY, 19, DL/HAY, 24, 26, Dec 1, 28; 1734: DL/HAY, Jan
    7, 12, 23, 29, Feb 7, 20, Mar 12, 18, 19, Apr 1, DL, 15, 23, DL/HAY, 26, DL,
    29, May 15; 1744: HAY, Jun 29
Holt (house servant), 1769: CG, Jan 6
Holt, Mrs (actor), 1721: BF/SF, Sep 2; 1728: HAY, Nov 19; 1729: HAY, Feb 25
Holt, Mrs (householder), 1737: DL, Apr 23; 1739: DL, Mar 26, May 2
Holtham (Holtman), Edward (actor), 1744: HAY, Sep 27, 29, Oct 11, Dec 26; 1748:
    CG, Oct 17, 24, 28, Nov 10, 15, 16, 24, Dec 26; 1749: CG, Apr 21, 24, May 4,
    BFCB, Aug 23, CG, Oct 2, 19, 20, Nov 9, 17, 23; 1750: CG, Jan 24, Mar 17, Apr
    26, May 1, 10, Oct 12, 22, 26, 29, Nov 6; 1751: CG, Jan 18, Mar 7, Apr 16,
    Sep 23, 27, 30, Oct 11; 1752: CG, Mar 16, Apr 28, May 2, 4, Oct 9, 10, 18,
    24, Nov 28, Dec 11, 13; 1753: CG, Feb 7, Mar 24, May 1, 7, Sep 12, Oct 5, 30;
    1754: CG, Jan 22, Mar 9, Apr 22, 25, May 2, 4, 7, Sep 16, 20, 25, Oct 2, 15,
    24, Nov 12, Dec 10; 1755: CG, Jan 16, Mar 18, Apr 28, 30, May 15, Oct 10, 17,
    22, 27, Nov 8, 10, 12, 13, 21, Dec 3, 4; 1756: CG, Mar 27, 30, May 5, 17, Sep
    20, 22, 24, Oct 28, Nov 8, 9, 22, 24, Dec 6, 7, 10, 20; 1757: CG, Jan 27, Feb
    9, 16, 21, Apr 30, May 4, 16, 20, 25, Sep 23, Oct 5, 8, 10, 13, 14, 20, 22,
    Nov 2, 5, 7, 9, 11, 18; 1758: CG, Apr 3, 12, 22, Sep 25, Oct 4, 9, 30, Nov 9,

13, 21; 1759: CG, Jan 4, 6, Feb 1, 26, Mar 3, 17, 20, Apr 7, 25, 28, May 7,
11, 18, Sep 26, Oct 5, 10, Nov 28, Dec 10, 12, 31; 1760: CG, Jan 9, 11, Feb
14, Mar 18, 24, Apr 8, 29, May 12, 14, Sep 22, 24, Oct 1, 8, 10, 17, 25, Nov
18; 1761: CG, Mar 25, Apr 2, 10, 17, 20, 27, 29, May 5, 11, Sep 7, 14, 23,
Oct 3, 5, 13, 17, 31, Nov 6, Dec 11, 28, 29; 1762: CG, Jan 12, Feb 15, Mar
20, Apr 16, 21, 24, 28, May 7, 12, Sep 27, Oct 2, 4, 8, 13, 14, 16, 19, 20,
28, Nov 8, 12, Dec 8; 1763: CG, Jan 8, Apr 25, May 2, 9, 16, Sep 30, Oct 22,
26, Nov 3, 10, 15, 22, 23, 26; 1764: CG, Jan 9, 14, Feb 11, 17, Mar 27, Apr
2, May 11, 15, 21, Sep 19, 28, Oct 8, 17, 18, 23, 26, Nov 15, 16; 1765: CG,
Apr 19, May 11, 20, Sep 20, 23, 27, Oct 4, 9, 15, 30, Nov 22; 1766: CG, Jan
9, 31, Mar 22, Apr 8, May 3, 5, 6, Sep 22, Oct 6, 18, 21, 22, 31, Nov 7, 8,
14, Dec 2, 20; 1767: CG, Jan 28, 29, 31, Feb 28, Apr 25, May 13, Sep 14, 18,
19, Oct 5, 9, 13, Nov 10, Dec 22; 1768: CG, Jan 8, 16, 29, Feb 1, 5, 20, 25,
Mar 8, Apr 29, 30, May 25, 28, Sep 30, Oct 7, 21, 27, Nov 4, 8, 17, Dec 16;
1769: CG, Jan 19, Feb 6, Mar 29, Apr 12, May 5, 12, 15, Oct 2, Nov 4, 11, 17,
23, Dec 1, 2, 6, 7; 1770: CG, Jan 27, 29, Apr 25, May 12, Sep 24, Oct 1, 11,
Nov 2, Dec 17, 26, 28; 1771: CG, Jan 1, 26, Feb 21, Apr 22, 30, May 21, Sep
30, Oct 15, 16, 28, Nov 19, Dec 19; 1772: CG, Feb 25, May 25, Oct 13; 1773:
CG, Mar 15, May 24, HAY, Jul 21, CG, Oct 27, 28, Nov 25, Dec 23; 1774: CG,
Feb 9, Apr 11, May 16; 1778: HAY, Apr 30
Holton, Miss (actor), 1782: HAY, Jan 21
Holy Lord God Almighty (song), 1786: DL, Mar 29; 1787: DL, Feb 23; 1789: DL,
Mar 18; 1790: DL, Feb 26; 1791: CG, Mar 11, DL, 23; 1792: KING'S, Feb 24, CG,
Mar 9; 1793: CG, Feb 15, KING/HAY, 22; 1794: CG, Mar 7, DL, 21, Apr 2, CG, 4,
DL, 10; 1795: CG, Feb 20; 1796: CG, Feb 24; 1797: CG, Mar 10, 22; 1798: CG,
Mar 9; 1799: CG, Feb 8
Home, John, 1757: CG, Mar 12; 1758: DL, Feb 21; 1760: DL, Feb 21; 1769: DL, Feb
23; 1773: DL, Feb 27, Mar 2, 8; 1776: CG, Mar 18; 1778: CG, Jan 21; 1797:
HAY, Dec 4; 1799: OCH, May 15
--Agis, 1758: DL, Feb 18, 20, 21, 23, 25, 27, 28, Mar 2, 4, 6, 7, 9, 14; 1761:
DL, Jan 23, Feb 3; 1797: HAY, Dec 4
--Alfred, 1778: CG, Jan 21, 22, 23, DL, Mar 30
--Alonzo, 1773: DL, Feb 1, 22, 25, 27, Mar 1, 2, 4, CG, 6, DL, 6, 8, 9, 11, 13,
16, 18, 22; 1798: CG, May 1
--Douglas, 1757: CG, Mar 12, 14, 15, 17, 18, 19, DL, 29, CG, Apr 2, 12, 14, 20,
28; 1758: DL, Feb 21, Mar 2, CG, 16; 1759: CG, Mar 24, Apr 21, Nov 23; 1760:
DL, Jan 11, 14, 23, CG, Nov 22; 1761: DL, Apr 18, Oct 26; 1762: DL, May 11;
1768: DL, Nov 10, 12, 15, 29; 1769: DL, Feb 2, Apr 17, Dec 1; 1770: DL, Mar
10, HAY, 19, Nov 21; 1771: DL, Mar 9, May 6, Oct 30; 1775: CG, Apr 8; 1776:
CG, Jan 15, 17, 19, 22, Feb 2, 16, 22, 27, Mar 16, 18, Apr 15, Oct 15, 31;
1777: CG, Mar 3, Nov 27; 1778: CG, Apr 4, CHR, May 27; 1779: CG, Jan 14, 23,
Apr 30, HAY, May 10; 1780: HAY, Jun 2, 7, 22, Jul 14, Aug 16, DL, Dec 4, 11,
21; 1781: DL, Jan 23, 25, May 19; 1783: CG, Nov 13, 15, 20, 22, 29, DL, Dec
22, 31; 1784: CG, Jan 1, DL, 2, Feb 10, 28, CG, Mar 8, DL, Apr 1, May 4, 8,
HAY, Aug 13, DL, Oct 9, Nov 13, CG, Dec 30; 1785: CG, Mar 15, Apr 1, DL, 9,
HAMM, Jun 27, Jul 2, DL, Sep 22, Nov 15, CG, Dec 29; 1786: HAMM, Jun 7, 28,
HAY, Dec 18, DL, 19; 1787: DL, Mar 31, Apr 28, CG, Dec 28; 1788: DL, Jan 8,
HAY, Jul 2, DL, Dec 9; 1790: CG, Apr 29, Oct 4, Dec 20; 1791: HAY, Dec 12;
1792: DLKING'S, Feb 23, Apr 24, CG, Dec 20, HAY, 26; 1793: DL, Jan 4, Mar 16;
1794: CG, Jan 13, 29, DL, Jun 6, Oct 2, 4; 1795: DL, Jan 29, Apr 29, May 2,
HAY, Aug 29, DL, Nov 16; 1796: DL, Jan 18, CG, Oct 26, DL, Nov 2; 1797: DL,
Jan 6, CG, Oct 23, 26; 1798: CG, Apr 16, HAY, 23, WRSG, Jun 8, DL, Dec 27;
1799: DL, Jan 10, Mar 16, Apr 13, OCH, May 15, DL, Dec 30; 1800: CG, Apr 29
--Fatal Discovery, The, 1769: DL, Feb 23, 25, 27, 28, Mar 2, 4, 6, 7, 9, Apr
13; 1776: CG, Mar 18
--Siege of Aquileia, The, 1760: DL, Feb 21, 23, 25, 26, 28, Mar 1, 4, 6, 8, 10
Homer's Head (print shop), 1750: CG, Nov 5
Homme a Bonne Fortune, L'. See Baron, Michel.
Honest Friends and Jovial Souls (song), 1782: CG, May 6
Honest Man's Fortune, The. See Fletcher, John.
Honest Thieves, The. See Knight, Thomas.
Honest Yorkshireman, The. See Carey, Henry.
Honesty in Tatters (song), 1797: CG, May 17
Honey Moon, The. See Linley, William.
Honeycott, John (schoolmaster), 1711: CLK, Feb 6; 1712: CLKCS, Feb 6
Honi Soit qui mal y Pense (dance), 1799: KING'S, Apr 18, DL, May 8
Honiton, 1749: DL, Mar 20; 1765: MARLY, Oct 5
Honorata Poverta di Rinaldo, L' (pantomime, anon), 1727: KING'S, Jan 4
Honorius. See Ciampi, Lorenzo.
Honour and Arms (song), 1743: CG, Apr 16; 1747: ST, Apr 29; 1750: DL, Apr 26;
1752: KING'S, Mar 24, CG, Apr 25; 1754: CG, May 3; 1757: CG, May 13; 1789:
DL, Mar 25, CG, 27; 1791: DL, Mar 11, CG, 11; 1792: CG, Mar 9, KING'S, 14;

425

1793: CG, Mar 6; 1794: CG, Mar 12, DL, 21, Apr 2; 1795: CG, Mar 25; 1796: CG,
   Mar 16; 1798: CG, Mar 9; 1799: CG, Mar 13
Honywood, Colonel Philip (renter), 1758: CG, Feb 27
Hood (publisher), 1794: DL, Oct 28
Hood (waterer), 1767: CG, Feb 4
Hood, Captain Alexander, 1798: CG, May 9
Hook (carpenter), 1736: DL, May 14
Hook, Harriet Horncastle
--Double Disguise, The (farce), 1784: DL, Mar 8, 9, 11, 13, 15, 16, 20, 23, Apr
   3, 12, 26, May 13, 20, Nov 1, 3; 1785: DL, Apr 8, 19; 1786: DL, Apr 18; 1787:
   DL, Apr 18, 28, May 4, 28, Jun 6; 1788: DL, May 30
Hook, James (composer), 1760: CG, Oct 16; 1767: DL, Apr 22; 1769: MARLY, Aug
   10, 17; 1770: DL, Mar 31, MARLY, Jul 17, Sep 4, 11, HAY, 20; 1771: HAY, Apr
   12, CG, May 1, MARLY, May 23, Jun 27, Jul 13, HAY, 24, MARLY, Aug 22, GROTTO,
   24, MARLY, Sep 5, 10, 12, 17; 1772: HAY, Jul 27, Aug 17, MARLY, 28; 1773: CG,
   May 6, MARLY, Aug 3, 27; 1775: HAY, Mar 23, Aug 21; 1776: CG, Mar 20; 1777:
   DL, Mar 11, HAY, Jul 18; 1778: CG, Mar 6, 18, Nov 23; 1779: CG, Oct 8; 1780:
   CG, Apr 19; 1782: CG, May 6, DL, Nov 5, Dec 11; 1783: DL, Apr 7; 1785: DL,
   Apr 15, CG, 25, DL, May 3; 1786: CG, Mar 18, DL, May 3, 22, CG, 22; 1787: CG,
   Mar 12, DL, May 18; 1788: CG, Jan 28, DL, May 6; 1789: CG, May 5; 1790: DL,
   May 19; 1791: CG, May 18, 27, 31, Jun 6; 1793: CG, Mar 18, Dec 19; 1794: CG,
   May 23; 1795: DL, May 6, Jun 2; 1796: DL, May 11, Jun 3; 1797: DL, May 20,
   CG, 23, DL, Jun 8, CG, Oct 4; 1798: DL, May 23, Jun 8; 1799: DL, May 9, 17
--Ascension, The (oratorio), 1776: CG, Mar 20; 1778: CG, Mar 18
--Dido (opera), 1771: HAY, Jul 24, 26, 29, 31, Aug 2, 7
--Dilettante, Il (burletta), 1772: MARLY, Aug 28, Sep 1; 1773: MARLY, Jul 29,
   Aug 3, 10, 24, Sep 8, 11; 1774: MARLY, Jun 16, Aug 4, 6
--Divorce, The (musical), 1773: MARLY, Aug 27
--Love and Innocence (pastoral serenata), 1769: MARLY, Aug 10, 17, 24
Hook Jr, James
--Diamond Cut Diamond; or, The Venetian Revels (opera), 1797: CG, May 23, 25,
   Oct 4, 6
--Jack of Newbury (opera), 1795: DL, Mar 14, 17, 23, May 6, 7, 8, 11, 15
Hook, Mrs (actor), 1702: DL, Nov 13, 26, Dec 14
Hooke (actor), 1786: CG, Nov 14; 1787: HAY, Jan 8
Hooke, Miss (actor), 1782: HAY, Jun 11, 18, 20, 21, 29, Jul 2, 5, Aug 23; 1783:
   HAY, Jun 7, 13, 14, 27, 30, Jul 4; 1784: HAY, May 29, Jun 14, 17, Jul 15, 19,
   28, Sep 14; 1785: HAY, Jun 7; 1787: HAY, Jan 8
Hooke, Robert (spectator), 1673: DG, Jul 29, Aug 21; 1675: DL, Aug 0
Hooker, Sir William (Lord Mayor), 1673: CITY, Oct 29
Hookham and Carpenter (printers), 1794: CG, Mar 25, HAY, Aug 18
Hookham, T (printer), 1788: CG, Apr 8
Hoole, John, 1768: CG, Dec 3, 21; 1770: CG, Feb 24, Mar 1, 10, 15; 1775: CG,
   Mar 2; 1794: CG, May 30
--Cleonice, Princess of Bithynia, 1775: CG, Mar 2, 4, 6, 7, 9, 11, 13, 14, 16,
   23
--Cyrus, 1768: CG, Dec 3, 5, 6, 8, 10, 13, 15, 17, 19, 21; 1769: CG, Jan 3, 13,
   31, Feb 7, 11, 23, Mar 2, 9, 30, Apr 6, 20, May 22, 25, Oct 28, Nov 1, 18;
   1770: CG, Jan 10, 26, Feb 13, Apr 2, Dec 4, 6, 12, 20; 1771: CG, Feb 14, Mar
   19, Apr 15, May 2, Oct 18, Nov 23; 1772: CG, Jan 29, Mar 14, May 18; 1774:
   CG, Apr 11; 1775: CG, Apr 18; 1776: DL, Mar 11, 14; 1794: CG, May 30
--Timanthes, 1770: CG, Feb 23, 24, 26, 27, Mar 1, 3, 5, 6, 8, 10, 12, 13, 15,
   17, 19, 22, May 28, Oct 5, 20, Nov 27; 1771: CG, Mar 14, Apr 8, May 30, Nov
   11, Dec 17; 1772: CG, Apr 9, May 7; 1773: CG, Apr 3; 1774: CG, Feb 11; 1775:
   DL, Mar 21
Hooly and Fairly (song), 1754: DL, May 10; 1755: DL, Apr 2, 16, 25, 28, 29;
   1756: DL, May 5; 1757: HAY, Aug 31, Sep 2, 28; 1780: HAY, Jan 17; 1782: HAY,
   Mar 18
Hooly and Fairly; or, The Highland Lad and Lowland Lass (pastoral, anon), 1798:
   CG, Apr 28, May 5, 22
Hooper (beneficiary), 1730: GF, Jun 17; 1731: GF, May 12
Hooper, Rachel (actor), 1742: LIF, Dec 13; 1743: LIF, Feb 14, 28, Mar 21; 1746:
   GF, Feb 5, Mar 17; 1747: GF, Mar 5; 1748: HAY, Mar 31; 1749: HAY, Nov 9, 11;
   1750: HAY, Apr 9; 1751: DL, Apr 22; 1757: HAY, Oct 21
Hooper, S (printer), 1767: CG, Mar 13
Hooper's Square, 1741: GF, Apr 22; 1745: GF, Mar 18
Hop-Pickers, The (dance), 1775: CG, May 12
Hop, The (prelude), 1791: DL, May 12
Hope thou cheerful ray of light (song), 1796: CG, Oct 17
Hope told a flattering tale (song), 1794: DL, Apr 9; 1797: CG, May 9; 1799: CG,
   Jun 12
Hoper, Mrs

--Battle of Poictiers, The; or, The English Prince, 1747: GF, Mar 5, 14
--Cyclopedia, The, 1748: HAY, Mar 31, Apr 13
--Queen Tragedy Restored, 1749: HAY, Nov 9, 11
Hophye, Mme (actor), 1753: HAY, Mar 13
Hopkins and Co (ironmongers), 1773: DL, Jun 2; 1774: DL, Jan 21, Jun 2, Oct 20;
    1775: DL, May 27
Hopkins, Charles, 1693: DLORDG, Nov 0; 1695: LIF, Aug 0; 1697: LIF, Nov 0;
    1699: LIF, Nov 7
--Boadicea, Queen of Britain, 1697: LIF, Nov 0; 1699: LIF, Nov 7
--Friendship Improved; or, The Female Warriour, 1699: LIF, Nov 7; 1702: LIF,
    Dec 7
--Pyrrhus, King of Epirus, 1693: DLORDG, Nov 0; 1695: LIF, Aug 0
Hopkins, Elizabeth (actor), 1776: DL, Oct 19, 25, Nov 4, 9, 16, Dec 16, 18, 28;
    1777: DL, Jan 9, 22, Feb 17, Apr 7, 17, May 1, 3, Jun 6, Sep 20, 23, Oct 28,
    Nov 4, 13, 29, Dec 3, 4, 11; 1778: DL, Jan 23, Feb 10, Mar 30, Apr 27, May 1,
    12, 21
Hopkins, Elizabeth, Mrs William (actor), 1761: DL, Nov 14, 21; 1762: DL, Jan
    22, 26, Feb 9, Mar 30, May 7, 10, Oct 28, Nov 3, 26, Dec 6, 14; 1763: DL, Jan
    8, 15, Mar 17, Apr 6, 20, 26, Sep 20, Oct 17, Nov 4, 14, 23, Dec 14; 1764:
    DL, Jan 9, Feb 15, 18, 21, 25, Mar 3, 31, Apr 26, May 24, Oct 11, 16, 22, 24,
    25, Nov 8, 17, Dec 18; 1765: DL, Jan 1, 2, 14, 18, 24, Feb 6, Mar 16, 18, 19,
    Apr 20, 26, 27, 30, May 11, 17, Sep 19, 26, Oct 9, 11, 12, 22, 24, CG, Nov
    13; 1766: DL, Mar 18, 20, 22, Apr 1, 5, 8, 12, 15, 22, 25, 28, May 3, 9, 10,
    13, 22, Oct 21; 1767: DL, Feb 9, 18, 21, Mar 7, 24, Apr 21, 22, May 2, 4, 9,
    Jun 1, Sep 18, 23, Oct 13, 14, 21, 23, 26, 29, Nov 4, 13, 19; 1768: DL, Jan
    9, Mar 15, 17, 21, Apr 4, 18, 26, May 25, 31, Aug 18, Sep 17, 23, 26, 28, 29,
    Oct 3, 4, 10, 19, 31, Nov 21, Dec 28; 1769: DL, Jan 25, Apr 28, May 4, 15,
    Sep 16, 19, 23, 26, Oct 3, 17, 21, 30, Nov 1, 2, 9, 13, 15, 18, 21, 22; 1770:
    DL, Feb 27, Mar 17, 20, 22, Apr 3, May 17, 19, 28, Oct 2, 3, 5, 8, 16, 18,
    23, 24, 26, Nov 6, 9, 10, Dec 6; 1771: DL, Jan 19, Mar 18, 23, Apr 2, 8, 9,
    17, May 4, 7, 17, Sep 24, 28, Oct 12, 19, 25, 28, 31, Nov 6, 9, Dec 3; 1772:
    DL, Jan 17, 20, Feb 3, Mar 7, 17, 24, 30, Apr 20, 27, May 13, 19, 30, Jun 3,
    Sep 19, 26, Oct 15, 24, 28, 31, Nov 9, 16, 20, 28, Dec 8, 18, 29; 1773: DL,
    Feb 4, Mar 9, 23, 30, Apr 19, 21, 27, 30, Sep 21, 23, Oct 14, Nov 4, 15, 20,
    26, Dec 10, 11, 16, 21; 1774: DL, Jan 20, 22, 24, Feb 8, 15, Mar 15, 17, 22,
    26, Apr 11, May 4, 10, 17, 18, 28, Sep 17, 22, 24, Oct 4, 12, 14, 15, 24, Nov
    11, Dec 7, 19; 1775: DL, Jan 11, Feb 23, Mar 2, 20, Apr 24, May 6, CG, Jun 1,
    DL, Sep 23, Oct 3, 7, 17, 23, 24, 26, 30, Nov 4, 20, 25, Dec 11; 1776: DL,
    Jan 13, 20, 27, Feb 13, 15, Mar 7, 11, 14, 21, Apr 8, 10, 17, 26, May 13, Sep
    21, Oct 1, 5, 12, 23, 29, 30, Nov 5, 28, Dec 31; 1777: DL, Jan 16, 28, Mar
    13, Apr 7, 11, Sep 20, 23, 25, 30, Oct 7, Dec 4; 1778: DL, Jan 8, 10, 23, Mar
    12, Apr 9, 20, 21, 27, Sep 19, Oct 3, 8, 19, 21, 26, 31, Nov 14, 20, 30, Dec
    21; 1779: DL, Jan 23, Feb 3, CG, Mar 4, DL, 25, Apr 28, May 15, 25, Sep 18,
    23, 25, 30, Oct 5, 9, 16, 19, 30, Nov 5, 9, 17, 19, 20, Dec 29; 1780: DL, Jan
    11, 26, Feb 22, Apr 13, 14, 21, Sep 16, 21, 23, Oct 5, 7, 10, 12, 19, 23, 26,
    28, 31, Nov 2, 8, 29; 1781: DL, Feb 12, Apr 21, May 5, 17, Sep 18, 20, 22,
    25, 29, Oct 2, 12, 13, 15, 16, 27, 29, Nov 10, 20; 1782: DL, Jan 26, Feb 25,
    Mar 21, Apr 15, 19, 23, 30, May 7, 14, 18, Sep 17, 18, 24, Oct 1, 3, 10, 12,
    26, Nov 2, 5, 7, 26, CG, 29, DL, 30; 1783: DL, Jan 3, 15, 29, Feb 7, 12, 18,
    Mar 10, 17, 24, Apr 28, 29, May 12, Sep 18, 20, 23, 25, 30, Oct 14, 18, 30,
    Nov 12, Dec 5, 10, 12, 19; 1784: DL, Jan 1, 3, 10, 28, Feb 3, 10, 14, Mar 8,
    Apr 19, May 5, 15, 17, 21, Sep 16, 18, 21, 25, 28, 30, Oct 11, Nov 1, 5, 12,
    13, 19, Dec 10; 1785: DL, Jan 13, 20, Feb 21, Mar 8, 30, Apr 8, 18, 20, 27,
    May 26, Sep 17, 20, 22, 24, 27, Oct 11, 13, 25, Nov 3, 7, 17, 18, 21, 22, Dec
    5, 7; 1786: DL, Jan 4, Mar 28, Apr 1, 18, 26, May 25, Sep 16, 19, 23, 30, Oct
    7, 24, 27, Nov 14, 18, Dec 26, 28; 1787: DL, Jan 13, 23, 26, 29, Apr 10, 18,
    20, May 3, 23, 30, 31, Jun 1, Sep 18, 20, 25, Oct 9, 27, 30, Nov 10, 27, Dec
    6, 7, 8, 19; 1788: DL, Jan 26, Feb 7, Mar 29, Apr 10, 28, May 1, 6, 14, 21,
    22, Jun 6, Sep 13, 16, 25, 27, 30, Oct 7, 14, 20, 25, Nov 12, 17, 19; 1789:
    DL, Jan 8, Feb 18, 28, Apr 14, 21, May 27, Jun 4, Sep 12, 15, 19, 24, 29, Oct
    22, 31, Nov 7, 18, 24, Dec 2, 10, 22; 1790: DL, Feb 15, 27, Mar 2, 18, 22,
    Apr 14, May 26, 29, Jun 1, Sep 16, Oct 2, 18, 19, 20, 21, 23, 25, 27, Nov 1,
    3, Dec 3; 1791: DL, Mar 4, Apr 30, May 26, 31, DLKING'S, Sep 29, Oct 1, 3,
    10, 20, Nov 4, 7, 11, 14, 30, Dec 1, 2, 14; 1792: DLKING'S, Jan 7, 9, Mar 1,
    Apr 20, 28, DL, Sep 15, 19, 22, 27, Oct 13, 18, 20, Nov 12, Dec 27; 1793: DL,
    Jan 16, Mar 5, 12, 14, Apr 5, 17, May 7, Jun 3, 5, 6, 7, HAY, Sep 21, 24, 26,
    30, Oct 1, 8, 15, 22, 29, Nov 5, 23, Dec 19, 23, 30; 1794: HAY, Jan 14, 21,
    Feb 22, DL, Apr 28, May 2, 3, 8, Jun 12, 14, 16, 23, Jul 7, HAY, 9, 14, 22,
    Aug 4, 9, 18, 27, Sep 1, 3, DL, 16, HAY, 17, DL, 27, 30, Oct 13, Nov 1, 5,
    Dec 5, 10, 12; 1795: DL, Feb 6, Mar 14, Apr 24, May 18, Jun 6, HAY, 9, 12,
    15, 16, 18, 19, Jul 1, 8, 20, 25, 30, Aug 21, DL, Oct 3, 6, 15, 22, Nov 10,
    14, 23, Dec 1, 2, 12, 18, 19, 30; 1796: DL, Jan 13, 25, Feb 1, 27, Apr 25,

May 5, Jun 1, 8, HAY, 11, 13, 18, 30, Jul 6, 7, 8, 9, 23, 30, Aug 10, 18, Sep 5, 7, 17

Hopkins, Miss (actor, singer), 1793: CG, Sep 20, 25, Oct 8, 9, 16, 22, 25, 28, Nov 1, 11, Dec 27, 30; 1794: CG, Jan 13, 27, Feb 13, 18, 22, Mar 4, Apr 10, 12, 29, 30, May 20, 23, 30, Jun 5, 14, 16, Sep 17, 22, 26, 29, Oct 14, 20, 21, 30, Nov 8, Dec 6, 10, 18; 1795: CG, Feb 3, 6, Apr 6, 8, 23, 24, May 1, 6, Jun 5

Hopkins, Priscilla (actor), 1764: DL, May 24; 1765: DL, Apr 30; 1771: DL, Oct 28, Nov 22, Dec 20; 1772: DL, Apr 27, May 30, Jun 10, Oct 6, 30, Dec 2; 1773: DL, Jan 1, Mar 2, Apr 19, May 6, Jun 2, Sep 23, 25, Oct 18, 28, Nov 9, 25, Dec 21; 1774: DL, Jan 19, Feb 2, Mar 3, Apr 9, 26, 29, May 10, 28, Sep 29, Oct 8, Nov 4, 10, Dec 2; 1775: DL, Jan 2, 23, Mar 18, May 19, 25, Sep 23, Oct 24, Nov 2, 6, 9, 14, 18, 20, 23, 28, Dec 19, 26; 1776: DL, Jan 20, 27, Feb 12, 15, 22, Mar 7, 12, 14, 25, 28, Apr 8, 17, 20, 22, 26, May 3, 8, 16, 22, 27, HAY, Sep 17, DL, Oct 1, 12, 24, Nov 7, 20, 21, Dec 4, 14; 1777: DL, Jan 28, Apr 7, 21, May 8, Sep 25, 30, Oct 9, 18, 22; 1778: DL, Jan 2, 10, Apr 21, 27, May 21

Hopkins, Priscilla and Elizabeth (actors), 1778: DL, May 1
Hopkins, William (prompter), 1763: DL, Nov 23; 1778: DL, Apr 27; 1779: DL, Jan 5, Apr 19; 1780: DL, Apr 13
Hopkins, William and Elizabeth (actors), 1762: DL, Apr 13; 1764: DL, May 3; 1767: DL, Jan 24; 1769: DL, Apr 8; 1770: DL, Apr 16; 1772: DL, Apr 27
Hopton (actor), 1791: HAY, Dec 26
Horace. See Philips, Katherine.
Horace, 1754: CG, Jan 26; 1773: DL, Mar 22
Horaces, Les. See Corneille, Pierre.
Horden, Hildebrand (actor), 1695: DL, Sep 0, Oct 0, DG, Nov 0, DL, 0, Dec 0; 1696: DL, Jan 0, Feb 0, Mar 0, Apr 0, May 18; 1697: DL, Sep 0; 1701: DL, Dec 0

Horn and Morn (song), 1782: DL, Feb 15
Horn Tavern, 1746: CG, Jan 24; 1788: HAY, Sep 30
Horn, Carl Friedrich (composer), 1800: DL, Jun 7
Hornbolt (singer), 1705: DL, Jul 18
Hornbolt, Mrs (singer), 1705: DL, Oct 2
Horne (instrument maker), 1767: CG, Dec 14
Horne and Co (coal merchants), 1783: DL, Dec 18
Horne, John (actor), 1784: DL, Aug 20, 25; 1786: HAY, Jun 20
Horne, John (author)
--Fortune's Tasks; or, The Fickle Fair One, 1683: NONE, Sep 0
Horne, John (treasurer, Middlesex Hospital), 1757: DL, Dec 21
Hornpipe (dance), 1713: DL, Jun 10; 1722: LIF, Mar 31, Apr 5, 20, May 2, 4, 7, 10, 14, 18, 23, Jun 1, HAY, 28, SFW, Sep 5, SOU, Oct 3, LIF, 22; 1727: KING'S, Mar 16; 1730: LIF, Apr 6, 27, May 21, Oct 31; 1732: LIF, Jan 7, 18, 19, Feb 21, Mar 7, HAY, 8, 17, LIF, 21, 30, Apr 11, 17, 18, 19, 22, 24, 25, 26, 27, 28, May 1, 2, 3, 4, 5, 8, 10, 11, 15, 16, 17, 18, RI, Aug 17, BFB, 23, GF, Nov 25, 27, 29, 30, DL, Dec 18; 1733: GF, Jan 26, 29, HAY, Feb 14, Mar 14, 20, 22, 26, Apr 18, 23, LIF/CG, 30, CG, May 16, 17, GF, 21, BFMMO, Aug 23, DL, Oct 12, 15, 22, Dec 26; 1734: DL, Jan 28, GF, May 13, SFG, Sep 7, GF, Oct 16, Dec 20; 1735: BF, Aug 23, LIF, Sep 2, 5; 1736: HAY, Jan 19, Feb 16, LIF, Mar 31, Apr 16, CG, 30, LIF, May 5, CG, Oct 27; 1737: CG, Jan 10, Feb 3, Mar 15, May 3, 9, DL, 13, CG, 13, 16, 19, 31; 1738: DL, Apr 27, May 10, 31, Oct 25, CG, Dec 8; 1739: CG, May 8, 10, 11, 14, 15, DL, 28, CG, 28, 29, Aug 10, 21, Dec 8; 1740: DL, Apr 12, May 17, 19, 20, 22, BFLP, Aug 23, DL, Oct 20, 21, 22, 24, 25, GF, 28, DL, Nov 3, 7, 15, 18, 24; 1741: GF, Jan 20, Feb 2, 5, 9, Mar 16, 19, Apr 2, 6, 7, 8, 13, 14, 15, DL, 22, GF, 30, CG, Dec 9, 11; 1742: DL, Jan 12, GF, 12, DL, 23, GF, Feb 2, DL, 5, CG, Mar 27, JS, Apr 7, DL, 30, May 4, 8, 13, 17, 24, Sep 30; 1743: LIF, Feb 17; 1744: DL, Sep 22; 1745: GF, Apr 15, 26, SMMF, Jul 11; 1746: GF, Jan 14, 24, 31, Feb 17, 27, Mar 4, 10, 11, 18, May 1, BFYB, Aug 25, GF, Dec 5; 1747: GF, Jan 29, Feb 25, Mar 31, Apr 6, CG, May 7, BFC, Aug 22; 1748: NWC, Apr 4, DL, 14, CG, 18, DL, 25, NWSM, May 4, DL, 16, SFLYYW, Sep 7, SFBCBV, 7, SOU, Oct 24, JS, Dec 26; 1749: DL, Apr 7, 12, 14, 28, May 2, 5, 8, 9, 11, 12, SOU, Sep 18, DL, Oct 30, Nov 23; 1750: BB, Jan 8, DL, 11, HAY, Feb 16, Mar 8, DL, Apr 16, 18, 20, May 2, 4, 8, Sep 21, 27, Oct 15, 17, 22, 29; 1751: DL, Jan 1, 2, 3, 10, Apr 16, 26, May 4, CG, 6, DL, 6, 8, 9, 10, 13, Oct 18, 29, Dec 17; 1752: DL, Mar 16, 30, Apr 2, 8, 16, 17, 21, 23, 25, 27, 30, CG, 30, DL, May 1, 2, 4, 5, 12, Sep 28, Nov 16, Dec 15, HAY, 18; 1753: DL, Feb 6, HAY, Mar 13, DL, 31, Apr 7, HAY, 10, DL, 12, 24, May 4, 11, 12, 14, 15, 17, 18, BFSY, Sep 3, DL, 11, 13, 15, Dec 11; 1754: DL, Jan 16, 18, Feb 1, 4, 5, Mar 14, 26, Apr 26, May 7, 13, 15, 16, 17, 18, 21, 22, Sep 21, HAY, Dec 9, DL, 16; 1755: CG, Feb 8, Mar 17, DL, Apr 2, 3, 7, 10, CG, 15, DL, 21, CG, 24, DL, 24, 25, 29, May 3, 5, 6, 8, 12, 13, HAY, Aug 28, Sep 1, BF, 3, HAY, 4, 9, 11, 15, DL, Nov 21,

22; <u>1756</u>: DL, Apr 21, CG, 22, DL, 23, 30, May 7, 8, 10, CG, 10, 11, DL, 13,
14, 17, 18, 20, Aug 12; <u>1757</u>: CG, Apr 16, 18, 23, 25, 26, DL, 27, May 2, CG,
4, DL, 5, 7, 12, 14, 17, CG, 17, DL, 18, 19, 20, 23, HAY, Sep 2, 8, Oct 3;
<u>1758</u>: CG, Apr 21, 22, DL, May 8, 9, 12, 16, 17, 18, CG, Oct 9; <u>1759</u>: CG, Jan
29, 31, Mar 20, DL, May 2, 11, CG, 16, DL, 17, CG, 17, DL, 19, 21, 29, 30,
Jun 19, 28, MARLY, Aug 9, 16, HAY, Sep 21, 25, CG, Oct 10, 12, 23, Nov 2, 13;
<u>1760</u>: CG, Jan 8, Mar 24, Apr 10, DL, 17, 22, HAY, 30, CG, 30, DL, May 8, 9,
13, 15, 16, 19, SF, Sep 18, CG, 24; <u>1761</u>: CG, Mar 24, 26, Apr 11, DL, 16, CG,
24, 27, May 1, 7, 8, 11, 18, DL, 25, 27, Jun 19, CG, 23, DL, Aug 8, HAY, 22,
DL, Dec 17, 19, 22; <u>1762</u>: DL, Mar 30, CG, Apr 17, DL, 26, 30, May 1, 3, 7,
CG, 7, DL, 10, 11, 14, CG, 17, DL, 18, 20, 26, Sep 18, CG, Dec 30; <u>1763</u>: DL,
Apr 5, CG, 8, 18, DL, 25, 26, CG, 29, DL, 30, CG, May 13, 16, 18, 20, 26,
HAY, Jul 20, 27, Sep 7, CG, Dec 8; <u>1764</u>: CG, Mar 26, 27, DL, Apr 3, CG, 5, 9,
10, 12, DL, 12, CG, 14, 27, 28, DL, May 4, CG, 5, 7, 9, 11, 12, 14, 16, DL,
17, CG, 18, 23, 24, 25, HAY, Sep 1, 3; <u>1765</u>: CG, Mar 14, 26, Apr 9, 10, 12,
DL, 16, CG, 17, 18, DL, 27, CG, 29, 30, May 3, 7, 8, 9, 10, 11, 15, DL, 22,
CG, 22, 23, 24, HAY, Jun 10, Aug 7, 9, 28, Sep 2, 9; <u>1766</u>: CG, Mar 18, Apr 8,
9, 12, 25, 29, DL, 30, CG, May 3, 6, 7, DL, 13, CG, 14, 16, Dec 23; <u>1767</u>: CG,
Feb 5, DL, Apr 27, CG, May 1, 6, 9, 13, HAY, Jul 20, 22, 24, 27, Aug 5, 7,
10, 17, Sep 11, 12, 16, DL, 16, HAY, 18; <u>1768</u>: CG, Jan 25, 28, Feb 25, Apr
15, KING'S, May 5, CG, 12, 13, 24, 26, Jun 3, DL, Sep 20, CG, 24; <u>1769</u>: DL,
Apr 14, CG, 22, DL, May 10, 12, CG, 19, KING'S, Nov 28; <u>1770</u>: CG, Apr 20, 21,
May 18, DL, 21, CG, 23, DL, 23, Jun 4, MARLY, Aug 28, HAY, Oct 5, Dec 19;
<u>1771</u>: DL, May 21, 22, 29, HAY, Jun 14, Jul 3, GROTTO, Aug 30, HAY, Sep 16;
<u>1772</u>: DL, Apr 20, CG, May 1, DL, 6, 13, CG, 23, DL, 27, CG, 29, DL, Jun 1,
10, HAY, Dec 21; <u>1773</u>: DL, Apr 3, CG, 24, 30, DL, May 14, CG, 21, 22, 24, 25,
DL, 25, CG, 28, DL, 28; <u>1774</u>: CG, Apr 16, DL, 28, 30, CG, May 7, 14, DL, 16,
18, CG, 20, DL, 23, Jun 2; <u>1775</u>: HAY, Feb 2, 20, CG, Apr 18, 19, May 4, DL,
8, HAY, Sep 20, Nov 20; <u>1776</u>: CG, Mar 19, May 11, DL, 15, 24, CHR, Sep 25,
CG, 27, CHR, Oct 18; <u>1777</u>: DL, Apr 30, May 15, 28, HAY, Sep 17, Oct 9, CG,
17, 20, 22, 24, 27, 31, Nov 3, DL, 8, CG, 12, 29, Dec 4, 27; <u>1778</u>: CG, Jan
16, 24, HAY, Apr 29, CG, May 1, DL, 2, CG, 2, 14, DL, 18, 21, CHR, 25, 27,
Jun 1, HAY, 8, CG, Oct 17, Dec 12; <u>1779</u>: HAY, Jan 11, DL, 29, Apr 6, CG, 23,
28, May 4, HAY, 10, DL, 11, 21, 26, HAY, Aug 27, DL, Oct 5, HAY, 18; <u>1780</u>:
CG, Feb 8, CII, Apr 5, 19, DL, May 5, HAY, Jun 5, CG, Sep 21, DL, 21; <u>1781</u>:
DL, Apr 18, 26, May 4, CG, 19, DL, 23, 25, 26, HAY, Aug 8, 10, DL, Oct 15,
16, CG, 16, DL, 17; <u>1782</u>: DL, Jan 2, HAY, 21, DL, Mar 14, HAY, 18, DL, Apr
17, 22, 27, HAY, May 6, DL, 9, 14, 15, 16, 31, HAY, Jun 3, Sep 18, 21, CG,
Oct 22, HAY, Nov 25, DL, 30; <u>1783</u>: CG, Apr 22, DL, 26, CG, May 3, 13, DL, 20,
21, 23, CG, 29, DL, 31, HAY, Jun 20, CG, Oct 14; <u>1784</u>: HAY, Feb 9, Mar 8, DL,
Apr 16, HAY, 30, May 10, DL, 15, 17, 19, 21, 27, HAY, Aug 26, DL, Sep 25,
HAY, Dec 13; <u>1785</u>: HAY, Jan 31, Feb 14, Mar 15, CG, Apr 6, DL, 8, May 19, 20,
23, CG, 24, HAMM, Jul 1, 2, 8, CG, Sep 30, DL, Oct 13; <u>1786</u>: DL, Jun 6, HAMM,
Jul 26, CG, Dec 23, DL, 28; <u>1787</u>: DL, Feb 22, May 18, 31, Jun 7; <u>1788</u>: DL,
Jan 22, KING'S, Feb 21, 26, Mar 8, 15, CG, 29, HAY, Apr 9, Jun 11; <u>1789</u>: DL,
Jan 8, CG, Mar 3, HAY, Jun 10, DL, Sep 24, CG, Oct 24; <u>1790</u>: DL, Apr 16, Jun
2, HAY, 26; <u>1791</u>: CG, Jan 15, DL, May 26, CG, Jun 3, 9, Sep 20, Nov 12; <u>1792</u>:
CG, May 9, Sep 20, Dec 26; <u>1793</u>: CG, Apr 11, 17, May 10, 31, DL, Jun 5, CG,
Oct 12, Nov 16, 19, Dec 11; <u>1794</u>: CG, Apr 23, May 31, Jun 4; <u>1795</u>: DL, Feb 6,
CG, Apr 28, KING'S, May 16, DL, Jun 6, CG, Oct 2, 24, Nov 13, 26; <u>1796</u>:
KING'S, Feb 6, CG, May 3, DL, Oct 29, CG, Dec 27; <u>1797</u>: DL, Jun 10, HAY, Aug
3, DL, Nov 9; <u>1798</u>: CG, May 8, DL, 31, CG, Jun 5, DL, Nov 14, 15, 21, 23, 24,
29, Dec 5, 6; <u>1799</u>: CG, May 14, HAY, Aug 10, DL, Oct 19, Dec 2, 17; <u>1800</u>: CG,
May 23, Jun 11, 13, HAY, Sep 16

Hornpipe in Fetters (dance), <u>1796</u>: CG, Mar 15, Oct 24; <u>1797</u>: CG, Oct 25; <u>1798</u>:
CG, Apr 23, May 21; <u>1799</u>: CG, May 17, Sep 18; <u>1800</u>: CG, Jun 10
Hornpipe on Skates (dance), <u>1771</u>: KING'S, Mar 12, Apr 2, 13, May 28
Hornpipical Ballet, Grand (entertainment), <u>1762</u>: BFY, Sep 3
Horns Inn, <u>1719</u>: BFPM, Aug 24; <u>1720</u>: BFPMJ, Aug 23; <u>1723</u>: BFPJ, Aug 22; <u>1724</u>:
BFP, Aug 22; <u>1733</u>: BFAP, Aug 23
Horriban, Miss (actor), <u>1732</u>: HAY, Nov 29
Horse and away to Newmarket (song), <u>1741</u>: DL, May 23
Horse and Four (dance), <u>1754</u>: HAY, Mar 4
Horse and his rider (song), <u>1786</u>: DL, Mar 10; <u>1789</u>: CG, Mar 6, DL, 18, CG, 27;
<u>1790</u>: CG, Feb 24, DL, 26, CG, Mar 26; <u>1791</u>: CG, Mar 11, DL, 23; <u>1792</u>: CG, Mar
2, KING'S, 21; <u>1793</u>: CG, Feb 15, KING/HAY, 22, CG, Mar 13; <u>1794</u>: DL, Mar 12,
CG, 14, DL, 14, Apr 2, CG, 9; <u>1795</u>: KING'S, Feb 27, CG, 27, Mar 25; <u>1796</u>: CG,
Feb 26; <u>1797</u>: CG, Mar 10; <u>1798</u>: CG, Mar 14, 30; <u>1799</u>: CG, Feb 8
Horse and the Widow, The. See Dibdin, Thomas John.
Horse Guards, <u>1778</u>: CG, May 8
Horses When with Glory Burning (song), <u>1749</u>: KING'S, Mar 21
Horsfall (actor), <u>1789</u>: DL, Nov 13, 14; <u>1790</u>: DL, Jan 8; <u>1791</u>: DLKING'S, Oct

15; 1792: DLKING'S, May 23, 25; 1793: HAY, Aug 3, 15, Oct 10; 1794: DL, May
16, 22, Jun 2, 12, 21, 23; 1795: DL, Feb 24
Horsfield, Mrs (spectator), 1668: BRIDGES, May 18
Horshoe Tavern, 1724: HT, Mar 13
Horsington, Margaretta (actor), 1732: LIF, Feb 29, May 2, LIF/CG, Oct 9; 1733:
LIF/CG, Jan 18, Mar 12, Apr 18, CG, May 2, Jul 6, Aug 14, Oct 18; 1734: CG,
Feb 26, May 3, 7, CG/LIF, Nov 11, Dec 5, 30; 1735: CG/LIF, Jan 17, LIF, Feb
12, CG/LIF, Mar 29, Apr 9, May 5, 12, 16, CG, Sep 16, 29, Oct 17, 20, Nov 6,
21, Dec 1; 1736: CG, Jan 1, 24, Feb 9, Mar 20, LIF, Apr 2, May 5, CG, Jun 3,
Oct 1, 8, 13, LIF, 18, CG, Nov 3, 23, 29; 1737: CG, Mar 28, May 3, 9, LIF,
Jul 26, Aug 2, CG, Sep 26, Oct 5, 21, Nov 17, 18; 1738: CG, Jan 13, Apr 17,
27, Jul 11, Aug 29, Sep 18, Oct 16, Nov 7, 11, 13, 18, 21; 1739: CG, Jan 17,
Feb 9, Sep 10, 21, 22, Oct 2, 3, 8, Dec 15; 1740: CG, Mar 25, Apr 14, 28, Oct
6, 8, 22; 1741: CG, Jan 2, 21, Feb 24, 28, Apr 2, May 6, 12, DL, Oct 10;
1742: DL, Sep 14, 28, Oct 9, Nov 3, 8, 19; 1743: DL, Apr 27, LIF, Jun 3, DL,
Sep 20, 24, Oct 11, 25, Nov 8, 26; 1744: DL, Mar 12, May 14, Sep 20, 29, Oct
6, Nov 1, 2, 16, Dec 11; 1745: DL, Jan 10, Feb 13, Mar 12, Jun 5, Sep 21, 28,
Oct 17, Nov 26, Dec 16; 1746: DL, Feb 3, Sep 25, 30; 1747: DL, Jan 3, Sep 24,
Oct 21, Nov 2
Horsley (beneficiary), 1730: GF, Jun 17
Hortolana, The (play), 1727: KING'S, Feb 16
Horton (actor), 1727: LIF, May 2
Horton, Captain (actor), 1738: CG, Sep 1
Horton, Christiana (actor), 1715: DL, Jun 6, Jul 1, Dec 6; 1716: DL, Mar 6, Jul
12, 19, Aug 9, Sep 29, Oct 4, 9, 13, 24, 29, Nov 14; 1717: DL, May 11, 14,
30, Oct 1, 10, Nov 6, 8, 18, 25, Dec 3, 30, 31; 1718: DL, Feb 14, Mar 17, Nov
13, 19, 27, 28, Dec 19, 22, 31; 1719: DL, Jan 2, 16, 29, Apr 30, Sep 19, 22,
Oct 16, 27, Nov 23; 1720: DL, May 3, 10, 30, Jun 11, Jul 7, Sep 20, 29, Oct
4, 5, 7, 15, 20, 29, Nov 2, 7, 29, Dec 1, 8; 1721: DL, Feb 23, Mar 2, 18, Apr
13, 14, 18, 26, May 29, Jul 28, Aug 1, 8, 18, Sep 9, 12, 19, Oct 3, 9, 10,
18, 24, Nov 1, 3, 11, 17, Dec 16, 28; 1722: DL, Jan 5, 6, Apr 12, 16, Sep 8,
18, 27, Oct 2, 5, 9, 17, 19, 22, 26, Dec 4, 22, 26; 1723: DL, Jan 2, Mar 16,
25, 28, Apr 1, 19, May 10, 20, 24, Jun 4, Sep 17, 24, Oct 1, 3, 18, 21, 28,
29, Nov 1, 2, 7, 8, 14, 15, 22, Dec 20, 30; 1724: DL, Apr 8, 11, May 14, 16,
Sep 15, 17, 19, 29, Oct 10, 14, 19, 29, Nov 6, 7, 13, Dec 3, 18; 1725: DL,
Jan 4, 9, 20, 27, Apr 5, 15, 21, 24, May 11, 21, Sep 7, 9, 14, 28, 30, Oct 5,
7, 12, 15, 20, 27, Nov 1, 3, 6, 12, 17, 27, Dec 13; 1726: DL, Jan 3, 5, Apr
28, May 4, 12, 23, Sep 6, 8, 10, 20, 22, 27, 29, Oct 6, 11, 15, Nov 9, 16;
1727: DL, Jan 20, 25, 27, Feb 8, 11, Apr 8, 17, 20, 24, May 8, 10, Sep 19,
21, 26, 30, Oct 7, 9, 12, 14, 17, 18, 20, 23, 30, Nov 22, Dec 9; 1728: DL,
Jan 2, 5, Mar 25, May 15, 23, Sep 26, Oct 3, 10, 22, 23, 25, 28, Nov 8, 12;
1729: DL, Jan 1, 15, 20, 31, Feb 1, 22, 25, Mar 8, 10, 25, Apr 11, 12, 23,
May 6, 14, 20, Sep 25, Oct 2, 4, 7, 9, 14, 16, 21, 22, 28, Nov 1, 3, 6, 12,
17, 21, 22, 24, 27, Dec 2, 19, 20; 1730: DL, Mar 19, Apr 10, 14, 27, Sep 15,
17, 22, 24, Oct 1, 10, 24, Nov 20, 24, 25, Dec 11; 1731: DL, Jan 11, 27, Mar
15, 29, Apr 3, 8, 21, May 1, 3, Sep 21, 23, 25, 28, Oct 2, 5, 19, Nov 6, 13,
23, Dec 1, 17, 21; 1732: DL, Jan 3, 26, Feb 2, 3, 11, 14, Mar 14, 20, 23, 30,
Apr 1, 24, 27, 29, May 5, 10, Sep 19, 28, Oct 3, 5, 12, 21, 28, Nov 4, 7, 13,
14, 16, 21, 24, Dec 6, 14, 20; 1733: DL, Jan 2, 13, 16, 20, 23, 25, 26, Feb
17, Mar 5, 12, 28, Apr 11, 16, 18, 19, May 1, 5, 10, 15, 29, Sep 24, 28, Oct
1, 5, 17, 24, 31, Nov 5, 13, 14, 23, Dec 5, 11, 17, 21; 1734: DL, Feb 11, Mar
4, 7, DL/LIF, 11, DL/HAY, 25, DL/LIF, Apr 1, LIF, 15, 18, DL/HAY, 20, DL, 23,
DL/HAY, 24, LIF, 26, DL/HAY, May 4, LIF, 9, CG/LIF, Sep 30, Oct 7, 9, 11, 16,
18, Nov 1, 12, 21, 25, 28; 1735: CG/LIF, Jan 9, 10, 16, 21, 25, 31, Feb 22,
Mar 13, Apr 10, 21, CG, 25, CG/LIF, May 1, 2, CG, 6, Sep 16, 17, 19, 24, 26,
Oct 8, 10, 17, 25, Nov 1, 7, 8, 13, 29, Dec 8, 31; 1736: CG, Jan 8, 10, Feb
10, 21, 26, Mar 9, 11, 18, 29, Apr 6, 8, 29, May 3, 13, 17, 24, Sep 15, 17,
20, 22, 27, 29, Oct 1, 4, 6, 8, 15, 25, 30, Nov 8, 11, 15, 22, 26, Dec 2, 9;
1737: CG, Jan 8, 10, Feb 3, 7, 14, 24, 26, Mar 7, 14, 17, 24, 31, Apr 11, 26,
May 31, Sep 16, 19, 21, 26, 28, 30, Oct 3, 7, 10, 14, 19, 21, 22, 24, 26, 27,
28, 31, Nov 1, 15, 17, 18, 19; 1738: CG, Jan 9, 13, 18, 25, 26, 31, Feb 6,
Mar 16, Apr 7, 10, 12, 24, May 18, Sep 15, 18, 20, 27, 29, Oct 9, 11, 13, 18,
20, 21, 23, 24, 28, 31, Nov 2, 7, 9, 11, 15, 18, 20, 22, 23, 27, 28, 30, Dec
7; 1739: CG, Jan 4, 17, 22, Feb 16, 24, 26, Mar 3, 13, 15, Apr 5, 25, May 1,
2, Aug 2, 21, 31, Sep 5, 10, 12, 14, 15, 17, 21, 22, 25, 28, 29, Oct 2, 3, 4,
5, 6, 9, 23, Nov 5, 6, 9, 10, 22, 28, Dec 4, 10, 15, 19, 21; 1740: CG, Jan
12, 17, Mar 18, 20, 25, 27, Apr 14, 28, May 7, 12, Sep 15, 22, 24, 26, 29,
Oct 1, 6, 8, 23, 27, 31, Nov 1, 4, 7, 20, Dec 4, 5, 6, 13, 19, 29; 1741: CG,
Jan 6, 21, 22, 23, 28, Feb 7, 12, 17, 24, 26, Mar 7, 12, 16, 30, Apr 1, 11,
17, 27, May 4, 12, Sep 21, 23, 25, 28, Oct 2, 5, 7, 8, 10, 13, 24, Nov 4, 9,
11, 23, 27, Dec 7, 11, 12, 17; 1742: CG, Jan 2, 19, Feb 4, 10, 15, 22, 27,
Mar 18, 20, 27, Apr 1, 24, May 1, 4, 5, Oct 6, 9, 11, 13, 15, 16, 18, 19, 27,

28, Nov 4, 8, 20, 22, 29, 30, Dec 22; 1743: CG, Jan 18, Feb 9, 14, Mar 15,
21, Apr 9, May 5, Sep 23, 26, 28, 30, Oct 3, 7, 10, 12, 14, 17, 19, 24, 26,
28, 31, Nov 2, 4, 17, 18, 21, 28, 30, Dec 3, 8, 9, 17, 19; 1744: CG, Feb 23,
Mar 29, DL, Nov 19, CG, Dec 10, 11, 12, 17, 26, 29; 1745: CG, Jan 1, 2, 4, 5,
23, Feb 9, Mar 14, 21, Apr 22, 29, May 4, 13, Oct 2, 4, 7, 9, 11, 18, Nov 9,
11, 12, 16, 19, 26, 28, 30, Dec 5, 6, 10, 12; 1746: CG, Jan 25, Feb 17, Mar
15, Apr 1, 5, 21, Jun 13, 16, 23, 27, Oct 3, 6, 20, Nov 24, 26, Dec 2, 10,
22, 29; 1747: CG, Jan 26, 31, Feb 2, 3, Mar 7, Apr 6, May 20, Nov 16, Dec 9,
28; 1748: CG, Jan 2, 7, 8, 12, 14, 15, 16, 19, 21, 29, Feb 1, 15, Mar 14, 24,
Apr 11, 16, 18, 26, 29, Sep 23, 28, 30, Nov 9, 24, Dec 9, 20, 22; 1749: CG,
Mar 29, 30, Apr 10, 11, May 1, Sep 27, Oct 2, 6, 9, 19, Nov 1, 16, 17, 18,
Dec 8, 16, 28; 1750: CG, Jan 4, 16, Feb 2, 22, Mar 1, 17, Apr 3, 5; 1752: DL,
Apr 20; 1753: DL, May 25; 1754: DL, May 30; 1756: DL, May 24, Dec 4
Horton, Mrs (ticket deliverer), 1798: DL, Jun 11
Horwell (actor), 1779: HAY, Oct 18; 1781: HAY, Nov 12; 1782: HAY, Nov 25; 1792:
HAY, Apr 16
Horwood, Jesse (ticket holder), 1764: KING'S, Apr 12
Hosannah to the Son of David (song), 1786: DL, Mar 10; 1789: DL, Mar 18; 1790:
DL, Feb 26; 1791: DL, Mar 23; 1792: KING'S, Feb 24; 1793: KING/HAY, Feb 22;
1794: DL, Apr 10
Hosier Lane, 1698: BF, Aug 23; 1699: BF, Aug 23; 1703: BFPD, Aug 23; 1727: BF,
Aug 21; 1733: BFCGBH, Aug 23; 1742: BF, Aug 26; 1743: TCD/BFTD, Aug 23; 1754:
BFSIY, Sep 3; 1755: BF, Sep 6
Hoskins, Sir John (spectator), 1674: DG, Jun 20; 1675: DG, Jun 25; 1676: DG,
May 25
Hospital for Fools, An. See Miller, James.
Hospital Gate, 1697: BF, Aug 24; 1699: BF, Aug 23; 1700: BF, Aug 0; 1701: BF,
Aug 25; 1702: BFBF, Aug 24, BFGB, 24; 1703: BFPBS, Aug 23, BFG, 23; 1721:
BFLGB, Aug 24; 1723: BFL, Aug 22; 1724: BFL, Aug 22; 1727: BF, Aug 22; 1733:
BFMMO, Aug 23, SF/BFLH, 23; 1735: BF, Aug 23; 1738: BFP, Aug 23; 1741: BFH,
Aug 22, BFLW, 22; 1742: BFPY, Aug 25; 1743: BFFP, Aug 23, BFGA, 23; 1746:
BFLY, Aug 25, BFYB, 25, BFWF, 25; 1748: BFH, Aug 24, BFSY, 24; 1749: BF/SF,
Aug 23, BFCB, 23
Hospital of Incurables, Venice, 1772: CG, Apr 8
Hospitality (song), 1797: CG, May 9
Hote du Village, L' (dance), 1754: CG, Nov 19
Hotel, The. See Vaughan, Thomas.
Hotham. See Holtham.
Hotspur (author), 1774: DL, Jan 13
Houblon, Sir John (Lord Mayor), 1695: CITY, Oct 29
Houblon, Winn (spectator), 1680: DL, Jan 27
Hough (actor), 1735: DL, Oct 7, Nov 15, 20; 1736: DL, Jan 12, May 13, 24, Oct
5, Dec 4, 20; 1737: DL, May 4, 23, Oct 27; 1738: DL, Sep 23, Oct 3, 10, Dec
15; 1739: DL, Mar 10, May 26, Sep 8, 26, Nov 22, Dec 6, 11, 21; 1740: DL, Jan
4, 5, Apr 8, Oct 27, Nov 19, Dec 4, 19; 1741: DL, Feb 24, May 28, Oct 31, Nov
11, Dec 4; 1742: DL, Apr 20, 26
Hough (beneficiary), 1759: CG, May 12
Hough (boxkeeper), 1795: DL, Jun 5; 1796: DL, Jun 15; 1797: DL, Jun 16; 1798:
DL, Jun 14; 1800: DL, Jun 14
Hough (house servant), 1772: CG, Jan 6
Hough, J
--Second Thought is Best, 1778: DL, Mar 30
Hough, Mrs (actor), 1741: DL, Nov 12
Houghton. See Haughton.
Houghton, Widow (beneficiary), 1739: CG, May 16
Houlton, Robert (journalist), 1795: CG, Feb 14, Apr 29, May 1
Hounslow Heath, 1772: CG, Jan 31
Hounslow, 1720: HOUN, Jun 13
Hour Before Marriage, An (play, anon), 1772: CG, Jan 22, 25
House of Commons, 1666: NONE, Nov 29; 1702: SH, Jan 31, CC, May 21; 1737: CG,
Jun 1; 1751: DL, Oct 30; 1769: DL, Feb 4
House of Lords, 1691: DL, Dec 16, NONE, 17; 1737: NONE, Jun 4, 6; 1776: DL, Mar
14
Hovel, The (opera, anon), 1797: DL, May 23
How beautiful are the feet (song), 1786: DL, Mar 3; 1793: KING/HAY, Feb 20;
1794: DL, Mar 19; 1798: CG, Mar 30
How blest the maid (song), 1790: CG, Feb 26; 1791: CG, Apr 6, 13; 1792: CG, Mar
9
How calm Eliza are these groves (song), 1697: DL, Sep 0
How comes it now good Mrs Spratt (song), 1699: DL, May 0
How excellent thy name (song), 1786: DL, Mar 10; 1789: DL, Mar 18, CG, Apr 3;
1790: DL, Feb 24, 26, CG, 26; 1791: DL, Mar 23; 1792: KING'S, Feb 24; 1793:

KING/HAY, Feb 22; 1794: DL, Mar 21, Apr 2, 10; 1795: KING'S, Mar 13
How frail is old age to believe (song), 1678: DG, Jun 0
How great are the blessings of government made (song), 1685: DG, Jul 0
How happy I am the fair sex can defy (song), 1696: DG, Oct 0
How happy is she (song), 1695: DL, Oct 0
How happy's the husband (song), 1694: DL, Jan 0
How long must women wish in vain (song), 1692: DL, Feb 0
How merrily we live (song), 1781: DL, Apr 25, May 7, 10; 1787: HAY, Aug 21;
    1791: CG, May 3, 16; 1792: CG, Apr 18; 1793: CG, Apr 24; 1794: CG, May 7;
    1800: CG, Apr 23
How much I love thee (song), 1790: CG, Nov 23; 1791: CG, Sep 19; 1792: CG, May
    19; 1793: CG, May 21; 1794: CG, Apr 12, Oct 29; 1795: CG, Oct 7; 1796: CG,
    Apr 8
How pleasant is mutual love (song), 1672: ATCOU/DG, Dec 2
How retched is the slave to love (song), 1676: DG, May 25
How shall we mortals spend our hours (song), 1789: CG, May 5; 1790: CG, Apr 21;
    1795: CG, May 16
How stands the glass around (song), 1790: CG, Apr 21, May 24; 1791: CG, May 3;
    1792: CG, Apr 18; 1793: CG, Mar 23, Apr 3, 24; 1794: CG, May 7; 1800: CG, Apr
    23
How sweet in the woodlands (song), 1782: HAY, Jan 14, DL, Apr 20; 1786: CG, May
    22; 1787: HAY, Aug 14
How sweet's the love that meets return (song), 1785: HAY, Feb 10, Jul 28, Aug
    15; 1786: CG, Apr 21, HAY, Jun 22, Sep 12
How to be Happy. See Brewer, George.
How to Grow Rich. See Reynolds, Frederick.
How unhappy a lover am I (song), 1670: BRI/COUR, Dec 0
How vain is man (song), 1789: CG, Mar 27; 1790: DL, Mar 17; 1791: DL, Mar 25;
    1794: DL, Apr 9
How willing my paternal love (song), 1792: KING'S, Mar 23, 30; 1793: CG, Mar 8;
    1794: CG, Mar 26; 1796: CG, Feb 24, Mar 16; 1798: CG, Mar 2; 1799: CG, Feb
    15, Mar 15
How, Mr (spectator), 1700: DL, Mar 13
How, Sir Scroope (spectator), 1680: DG, Feb 2
Howard (actor), 1733: CG, May 2; 1735: CG/LIF, Feb 13; 1736: CG, May 31; 1745:
    GF, Feb 28, Dec 2; 1751: CG, Sep 30, Oct 28, Nov 11, Dec 4, 9; 1752: CG, Feb
    11, Mar 17, Apr 13, 18, Oct 10, 18, 21, 26, 30, Dec 7; 1753: CG, Jan 6, Apr
    28, May 2, Oct 10, Dec 15; 1754: CG, Jan 12, Apr 26, May 1, 2, Nov 5, 16, 20,
    Dec 30; 1755: CG, Apr 2, 9, 24, 28, Oct 20, 22, Nov 17; 1756: CG, Apr 24, May
    6, Oct 4, 6, 21; 1757: CG, Apr 27, May 3, Oct 12, Dec 7, 10; 1758: CG, Feb 1,
    Apr 13, Oct 6, Nov 1, 30; 1762: CG, Dec 8; 1763: CG, Oct 22; 1773: HAY, May
    17, Jun 7, 18, 30, Jul 21, 28, Aug 11, 23, Sep 8; 1779: HAY, Oct 13
Howard St, 1748: SFLYYW, Sep 12
Howard, Barbara, Countess of Suffolk, 1674: ATCOURT, Dec 22; 1675: ATCOURT, Feb
    15
Howard, Charles, Earl of Berkshire, 1668: ATCOURT, Jan 13
Howard, Edward, 1667: BRIDGES, Apr 15, 20, 22
--Change of Crowns, The, 1667: BRIDGES, Apr 15, 22
--Man of Newmarket, The, 1678: DL, Mar 0
--Six Days' Adventure, The; or, The New Utopia, 1671: LIF, Mar 6
--Usurper, The, 1664: BRIDGES, Jan 2; 1668: BRI/COUR, Dec 2, 3, 7
--Women's Conquest, The, 1670: LIF, Nov 0
Howard, H (actor), 1760: DL, Apr 22
Howard, Henry (author)
--United Kingdoms, The, 1662: NONE, Sep 0
Howard, Henry, 11th Duke of Norfolk (spectator), 1680: DL, Jun 1
Howard, Henry, 12th Duke of Norfolk (rioter), 1691: NONE, Dec 17
Howard, James, 1662: LIF, Mar 1
--All Mistaken; or, The Mad Couple, 1667: BRIDGES, Sep 20, Dec 28; 1668:
    BRIDGES, Jul 29; 1677: DG, Feb 0
--English Monsieur, The, 1663: BRIDGES, Jul 30; 1666: BRIDGES, Dec 8; 1667:
    BRIDGES, Oct 29; 1668: BRIDGES, Apr 7; 1673: NONE, Sep 0
Howard, Lady Elizabeth (spectator), 1671: NONE, Mar 4; 1673: DG, Jul 3
Howard, Mrs (actor), 1696: LIF, Jun 0, Dec 0; 1697: LIF, Feb 27, Jun 0; 1699:
    LIF, May 0
Howard, Mrs (beneficiary), 1747: GF, Feb 6
Howard, Sir Philip, 1668: BRIDGES, Dec 19
Howard, Sir Robert, 1662: ATCOURT, Nov 27; 1665: BRIDGES, Feb 0; 1666: ATCOURT,
    Oct 18; 1668: BRIDGES, Feb 20, LIF, May 5, 8; 1669: BRIDGES, Feb 27, Mar 4;
    1697: NONE, Sep 3; 1715: DL, Jul 19, 22, 29, Aug 19; 1718: LIF, Jun 30, DL,
    Jul 1, RI, Aug 2, DL, 12, Dec 1; 1719: DL, Jan 29, Oct 19; 1720: DL, Jan 15,
    Feb 15; 1721: DL, Nov 29; 1797: CG, May 9, HAY, Jun 29; 1798: HAY, Jun 21

--Blind Lady, The, 1659: NONE, Sep 0
--Committee, The; or, The Faithful Irishman, 1662: ATCOURT, Nov 27; 1663:
  BRIDGES, Jun 12; 1667: BRIDGES, May 13, Aug 13, Oct 28; 1668: BRIDGES, May
  15; 1669: ATCOURT, Feb 8; 1671: IT, Feb 2; 1675: DL, Nov 11; 1685: DLORDG,
  Dec 30; 1686: IT, Feb 2, DLORDG, Apr 8, OXFORD, Jul 0, ATCOURT, Nov 17; 1687:
  DLORDG, Feb 1; 1689: DLORDG, Nov 28; 1697: LIF, Oct 27; 1699: DL, Oct 24;
  1701: LIF, Mar 6; 1702: DL, Jan 24; 1704: DL, Apr 26, 29, May 20, Oct 28, 31,
  IT, Nov 1, DL, 2, 7, 23, Dec 28; 1705: DL, Jan 29, Apr 11, Jun 30, Sep 29,
  LIF/QUEN, Oct 17, DL, Nov 10, QUEEN'S, Dec 5; 1706: QUEEN'S, Jan 7, LIF/QUEN,
  25, DL, Mar 28, LIF/QUEN, Jul 6, Aug 21, QUEEN'S, Oct 17, Dec 2; 1707: DL,
  Mar 20, 25, Jun 2, QUEEN'S, Oct 21, DL, 21, Nov 13; 1708: DL, Jan 29, Oct 15;
  1709: DL, Feb 3, May 26, Nov 28, Dec 9; 1710: QUEEN'S, Apr 10, Jul 19,
  DL/QUEEN, Nov 8; 1711: DL/QUEEN, Apr 30, May 7, DL, Dec 10; 1712: DL, Apr 12,
  Oct 13; 1713: DL, Jan 23, Oct 30; 1714: DL, Jan 29, Dec 6; 1715: DL, Jan 6,
  LIF, Jul 12, 20; 1718: LIF, Jun 30, DL, Jul 1, LIF, 2, 4, DL, 4, RI, Aug 2,
  DL, 12, RI, 23, LIF, Oct 31, Nov 17, DL, Dec 1, LIF, 22; 1719: DL, Jan 6, 29,
  LIF, Apr 8, 28, DL, May 2, LIF, 28, DL, Jun 5, Oct 19, LIF, Nov 23; 1720: DL,
  Jan 15, Feb 15, Apr 21, LIF, May 3, DL, 17, LIF, 27, Oct 11, DL, 29; 1721:
  DL, Jan 11, LIF, 31, DL, Apr 11, LIF, May 1, 17, DL, Jul 18, Aug 1, Oct 9,
  Nov 29; 1722: DL, Feb 6, LIF, Mar 5, 6, 28, DL, May 8, LIF, 22, DL, Sep 27,
  Dec 11; 1723: DL, Feb 7, Mar 28, LIF, Apr 16, DL, May 13, Oct 3, Dec 2, DT,
  6; 1724: DL, Jan 28, LIF, Feb 4, DL, Apr 7, May 4, LIF, 6, DL, Sep 29, Oct 8,
  Nov 23; 1725: LIF, Feb 1, Apr 26, DL, May 3, LIF, 26, DL, Sep 14, LIF, Dec 4,
  DL, 10; 1726: DL, Mar 21, LIF, Apr 26, DL, May 6, Sep 29, Nov 11, Dec 19;
  1727: DL, Mar 21, Apr 18, Oct 12, Dec 27; 1728: DL, Mar 5, May 16, Oct 3, Dec
  9; 1729: DL, Feb 18, Apr 10, May 12, Oct 22, GF, Dec 1, 2, 13; 1730: GF, Jan
  17, Mar 9, DL, Apr 22, GF, May 15, Nov 26; 1731: GF, Mar 18, Nov 16; 1732:
  GF, Jan 3, 4, 5, 6, 7, 8, 10, 11, 12, 14, 15, 17, 18, 26, LIF, 28, GF, Feb 7,
  28, Mar 2, LIF, 21, DL, 30, GF, Apr 11, DL, 15, GF, 21, May 2, DL, 9, LIF,
  18, DL, Sep 19, GF, Nov 8, DL, 10, 22, 23, Dec 27; 1733: DL, Jan 22, GF, Mar
  10, DL, Apr 23, LIF/CG, May 10, DL, 17, DL/HAY, Oct 3, GF, 23, DL/HAY, 31,
  Nov 15, HAY, Dec 13, DL, 21, GF, 27; 1734: BLO, Jan 16, DL, 25, DL/HAY, Feb
  6, May 1, LIF, 29, DL, Sep 26, GF, Oct 18, DL, Nov 6, GF, Dec 21, DL, 28;
  1735: DL, Feb 20, GF, Mar 6, Apr 28, DL, May 2, 29, Sep 13, Nov 14, GF, 25;
  1736: DL, Jan 1, GF, Mar 4, DL, 9, LIF, 31, DL, Apr 10, CG, May 3, DL, Sep
  14, Nov 17, Dec 2, LIF, 18; 1737: LIF, Jan 7, CG, Feb 3, DL, May 3, LIF, 6,
  CG, 23, DL, Sep 10; 1738: DL, May 19, Oct 27, Dec 7; 1739: DL, Feb 9, Mar 5,
  CG, Apr 5, DL, May 14, CG, 16, DL, Dec 14, 28; 1740: DL, Feb 12, CG, Mar 18,
  Apr 23, DL, May 19, CG, Sep 24, DL, Oct 2, Nov 22, GF, 25, DL, Dec 2, GF, 11;
  1741: GF, Apr 27, DL, May 21, GF, Oct 13, Dec 29; 1742: DL, Jan 6, 9, 28, Apr
  20, GF, May 3, DL, Oct 9, Nov 15, LIF, Dec 1; 1743: DL, Jan 4, 20, Feb 9,
  LIF, Apr 6, JS, 7, DL, Sep 22; 1744: DL, Oct 2, Dec 26; 1745: GF, Jan 4, 5,
  DL, 22, GF, Feb 4, DL, 19, SMMF, 28, DL, Apr 15; 1746: DL, Jan 2, 3, 4, 6, 7,
  17, GF, Feb 7, DL, 7, May 2, CG, Oct 15, 17, SOU, 27, DL, 31, GF, Nov 21, 24,
  25, DL, Dec 2; 1747: DL, Jan 14, GF, 21, DL, Feb 7, GF, 13, Mar 17, CG, May
  12, DL, 15, Oct 29, CG, Dec 17; 1748: CG, Feb 11, Mar 17, Apr 28; 1749: CG,
  Jan 25, SOU, 26, NWLS, Feb 27, CG, May 1, Oct 11, 13, Nov 27; 1750: CG, Oct
  15, Nov 21, Dec 28; 1751: CG, Nov 7; 1752: CG, Jan 1, Feb 6, Apr 9, May 7,
  Sep 20, Oct 26, Dec 20, 29; 1753: CG, Feb 20, Oct 3, 29, Dec 6, 28; 1754: CG,
  Oct 9, Nov 5; 1755: CG, Feb 6, May 20, Oct 18; 1756: CG, May 14, Oct 20, Nov
  23, Dec 27; 1757: CG, Jan 24, Apr 18, Sep 21, Nov 21; 1758: CG, Jan 25, May
  12, Sep 22, Nov 10, Dec 28; 1759: CG, Feb 14, Dec 6, 26; 1760: DL, Dec 29;
  1765: DL, May 6; 1766: DL, May 3; 1768: DL, May 13; 1769: DL, May 17; 1770:
  DL, May 3; 1771: DL, Apr 17, May 17, Dec 26; 1772: DL, Apr 27, Jun 3; 1773:
  DL, Jan 1, May 8; 1774: DL, Apr 19, May 16; 1775: DL, Apr 17, May 24; 1776:
  DL, May 4, Oct 12, 15; 1777: DL, Apr 21, May 15; 1778: DL, Apr 21; 1779: DL,
  May 25, Dec 29; 1780: DL, Mar 27, May 6, Nov 8; 1783: DL, Feb 12; 1785: DL,
  May 26; 1787: DL, Dec 27; 1788: DL, Feb 7, Jun 10; 1797: CG, May 9, HAY, Jun
  29; 1798: HAY, Jun 21
--Country Gentleman, The, 1669: BRIDGES, Feb 27
--Duke of Lerma, The, 1668: BRIDGES, Apr 18
--Great Favourite, The; or, The Duke of Lerma, 1668: BRIDGES, Jan 11, Feb 20,
  Apr 18; 1669: BRIDGES, Jan 12
--Indian Queen, The. See, Dryden, John.
--Surprisal, The, 1662: VERE, Apr 23; 1667: BRIDGES, Apr 8, Aug 26, Dec 26;
  1668: BRIDGES, Apr 17, May 1; 1689: NONE, Sep 0; 1715: DL, Aug 19
--Vestal Virgin, The; or, The Roman Ladies, 1664: BRIDGES, Dec 0; 1665:
  BRIDGES, Feb 0
Howard, Samuel (singer, composer), 1732: CR, Feb 23; 1794: CG, Apr 10, Sep 17,
  Dec 26; 1795: CG, Jan 12
Howard, Thomas (actor), 1668: ATCOURT, Feb 4
Howard, Thomas, 10th Duke of Norfolk (spectator), 1669: BRIDGES, May 24

433

Howard, William (violinist), 1792: CG, Feb 24
Howard, William, Lord Stafford, 1669: BRIDGES, May 24
Howe, John (spectator), 1700: DL, Mar 13
Howe, Lady Anne (correspondent), 1681: DLORDG, Dec 18; 1682: DG, Jan 25
Howe, W (spectator), 1668: BRIDGES, Sep 28
Howell (actor), 1799: CG, Apr 13, 25, Oct 21, Dec 23; 1800: CG, Feb 10, 12, May
    7, 27, HAY, Jul 2
Howell (beneficiary), 1723: BELH, May 20
Howell (singer), 1693: ATCOURT, Apr 30; 1699: YB, Jan 4
Howey, Mrs (actor), 1723: HAY, Dec 12; 1724: HAY, Feb 5
Howland St, 1787: KING'S, May 24; 1788: KING'S, Mar 6; 1789: KING'S, Jun 11;
    1790: DL, Feb 1; 1791: DL, Feb 5; 1792: DLKING'S, May 30; 1793: DL, Mar 11,
    HAY, Dec 16; 1794: CG, May 16, HAY, Aug 23; 1795: DL, May 18; 1796: CG, Apr
    26, DL, May 9
Hoy, Robert (actor), 1791: CG, Jun 6
Hubbard, Lord, 1748: DL, Feb 22
Hubert (actor), 1777: CHR, Jun 20
Huddart, Thomas (actor), 1798: CG, Oct 15
Huddersfield, 1799: CG, Apr 16
Huddy (rope maker), 1773: CG, Jan 18; 1774: CG, May 9
Huddy, Master (actor), 1732: GF, Mar 20, Dec 1
Huddy, Mrs (ticket holder), 1746: GF, Jan 20
Huddy, Philip (actor), 1723: LIF, May 10, BFPJ, Aug 22, SF, Sep 5, SOU, 25;
    1724: LIF, May 13, Jul 3, 21, 31, Aug 11, BFP, 22, SF, Sep 5; 1725: LIF, May
    1, 21, BF, Aug 23; 1726: HAY, Feb 24; 1727: LIF, May 19; 1729: GF, Dec 8, 19;
    1730: GF, Jan 9, 13, 19, Feb 12, 24, Mar 17, 30, Apr 2, 6, 7, 15, 27, 28, May
    26, Jun 17, Jul 6, 7, 8, BFPG/TC, Aug 1, BFPG, 20, SFP, Sep 9, GF, 23, 25,
    Oct 5, 22, 27, 30, Nov 2, 5, 6, 10, 12, 20, 30, Dec 1, 4, 8, 21, 31; 1731:
    GF, Jan 5, 20, 26, Feb 15, 18, 22, 27, Mar 2, Apr 1, 27, May 7, 14, TC, Aug
    4, 12, SF/BFFHH, 24, GF, Sep 27, SOU, 28, GF, Oct 8, 13, 26, 29, Nov 1, 4, 5,
    6, 8, 9, 12, 13, 15, 16, 24, Dec 1, 6, 7, 20, 30; 1732: GF, Feb 2, 26, Mar
    20, 28, 30, Apr 12, May 3, BF, Aug 22, GF, Oct 2, 5, 11, 12, 16, 30, Nov 2,
    4, 8, 18, 29, Dec 1; 1733: GF, Jan 8, 17, 24, Feb 5, 19, 20, Mar 15, 17, 28,
    Apr 3, 9, 11, 17, BF, Aug 23, GF, Sep 10, 19, 24, 25, 27, Oct 1, 8, 9, 12,
    15, 18, 19, 23, 26, Nov 5, 8, 10, 29, Dec 18, 26, 31; 1734: GF, Jan 3, 19,
    28, 31, Feb 7, 11, Apr 18, 26, RI, Jun 27, BFFO, Aug 24, GF, Sep 11, 20, Oct
    16, 18, 21, Nov 7, 18, 25, 27, 29, Dec 6, 12, 16; 1735: GF, Jan 8, 10, 11,
    13, Feb 8, 22, 24, Mar 24, 27, May 3
Hudibras; or, Trulla's Triumph (opera, anon), 1730: LIF, Mar 9
Hudson (actor), 1787: ROY, Jun 20
Hudson (painter), 1750: DL, Jan 22
Hudson (singer), 1760: SOHO, Jan 18; 1762: HIC, Feb 12, RANELAGH, Jun 11; 1771:
    HAY, Apr 15, May 2
Hudson, Mrs (actor), 1771: HAY, Apr 15
Hudson, Mrs (actor), 1785: HAY, Jan 31
Hue and Cry, The. See Inchbald, Elizabeth.
Huffer, The (poem), 1676: NONE, Sep 0
Hugdson. See Hudson.
Huggins (artificial flower maker), 1795: CG, Jun 12
Huggins, William (librettist), 1733: LIF, Feb 16
Hugh Morgan's Lamentation (song), 1759: BFY, Sep 3
Hughes (actor), 1755: BF, Sep 6
Hughes (actor), 1795: CG, Apr 8; 1796: DL, May 2
Hughes (actor, singer), 1700: DL, Feb 19; 1702: HAW, Jun 1, DL, 9, PR, 30, HAW,
    Jul 27, DL, Dec 8; 1703: DL, Jan 23, Feb 1, 11, SH, Mar 3, HA, May 18; 1704:
    DL, Jan 4, YB, Mar 29; 1705: DL, Jan 16, Feb 14, 26, Apr 10, Jun 26, Oct 16,
    20, Nov 5, 7, 9, Dec 7, 26, 31; 1706: DL, Jan 16, 25, 28, Mar 2, 5, 30, Apr
    2, 16, Jun 11, 18, 20; 1707: DL, Feb 18, Mar 4, 17, 27, Apr 1, YB, 18, DL,
    Nov 11, 22, 25, 28, 29, Dec 10, 17, 27, 30; 1708: DL, Jan 3; 1710: QUEEN'S,
    Feb 16; 1717: LIF, Feb 27, SH, Mar 13, 27, Dec 23; 1718: YB, Dec 5; 1726: IT,
    Feb 2
Hughes (boxkeeper), 1731: LIF, Jun 2; 1732: LIF, May 16; 1733: CG, May 17
Hughes (executor), 1750: CG, Feb 2
Hughes (linen draper), 1761: CG, Mar 26; 1772: CG, Jan 3, Feb 3, 29, Mar 3, Nov
    23, Dec 14; 1774: CG, Mar 21
Hughes (porter), 1781: DL, Sep 29
Hughes (tailor), 1750: DL, Jan 31
Hughes and Bates (linen drapers), 1760: CG, Feb 9; 1774: CG, Mar 21
Hughes, Charles (circus manager), 1791: DLKING'S, Dec 31; 1792: DLKING'S, Apr
    30; 1798: CG, May 28
Hughes, John, 1712: QUEEN'S, May 17; 1716: DL, Jan 12; 1720: DL, Feb 16, 17;
    1722: CLA, May 4, DL, Dec 6; 1733: LIF/CG, Mar 15, 17, Apr 24; 1735: DL, Mar

22; <u>1737</u>: DL, Jan 14, 15, 18, 29, Apr 26; <u>1738</u>: DL, Jan 28; <u>1739</u>: DL, Jan 23;
    <u>1758</u>: CG, Mar 29; <u>1773</u>: MARLY, Aug 27; <u>1779</u>: CG, Mar 20
--Apollo and Daphne (masque), <u>1716</u>: DL, Jan 12, 14, 16, 21, 24; <u>1773</u>: MARLY,
    Aug 27
--Siege of Damascus, The, <u>1720</u>: DL, Feb 17, 18, 19, 20, 22, 23, 24, 25, 26, Apr
    29; <u>1722</u>: CLA, May 4, DL, Dec 6; <u>1733</u>: LIF/CG, Mar 15, 17, Apr 24; <u>1735</u>: DL,
    Mar 22; <u>1737</u>: DL, Jan 11, 12, 14, 15, 18, 29, Apr 26, Oct 19; <u>1738</u>: DL, Jan
    28, Mar 25, Dec 6; <u>1739</u>: DL, Jan 23, Apr 14, Dec 31; <u>1743</u>: CG, Jan 5, 6, 7,
    8, 10, 11, 12, 13, 14, 15, 29, Mar 3, 10, Apr 5, 19, May 23; <u>1744</u>: CG, Feb 3,
    27, JS, Mar 20, CG, Oct 5, Nov 26; <u>1745</u>: CG, Jan 3, GF, Mar 12; <u>1747</u>: CG, Jan
    20, Feb 10; <u>1748</u>: HAY, Dec 27; <u>1749</u>: CG, Feb 23; <u>1750</u>: CG, Feb 5; <u>1751</u>: CG,
    Nov 11, Dec 2, 5, 6, 7, 9, 11, 12, 23; <u>1752</u>: CG, Jan 11, 25, Feb 4, Mar 9,
    Apr 15, HAY, 25, CG, May 1, Dec 9, 15, 30; <u>1753</u>: CG, Apr 7, May 11, Nov 28,
    Dec 28; <u>1754</u>: CG, Jan 3, Apr 4; <u>1756</u>: CG, Apr 3; <u>1758</u>: CG, Mar 29, May 4, Oct
    27, DL, Nov 18, 21, 25, 28, Dec 5; <u>1759</u>: CG, Jan 13, Feb 13, May 12; <u>1760</u>:
    CG, Feb 7, Dec 31; <u>1765</u>: HAY, Jan 28, CG, May 15; <u>1766</u>: DL, Nov 8, 11, 18;
    <u>1770</u>: DL, Jan 27, 29, 31, Feb 3, 10, 17; <u>1772</u>: CG, Mar 24, Apr 27; <u>1776</u>: DL,
    Mar 14, 28; <u>1780</u>: CG, Jan 13, 17, 24; <u>1785</u>: CG, Feb 17, 21, 28
Hughes, Margaret (actor), <u>1661</u>: NONE, Sep 0; <u>1663</u>: VERE, Mar 0; <u>1668</u>: BRIDGES,
    May 7, Jun 12, NONE, Sep 0, BRIDGES, Nov 6; <u>1669</u>: BRIDGES, Feb 6, Jun 24;
    <u>1676</u>: DG, Mar 0, Jul 25, Aug 0, Dec 0; <u>1677</u>: DG, Feb 12, Mar 24, May 31, Jun
    0
Hughes, Miss (actor), <u>1732</u>: GF, Apr 10; <u>1733</u>: DL, Oct 17; <u>1734</u>: JS, May 23, 24,
    HAY, 27, JS, 29, 31; <u>1735</u>: GF, Jan 6, 15, 24, Feb 4, Apr 18, Sep 24, Oct 15,
    Nov 14, 17; <u>1736</u>: GF, Feb 20, Mar 3, 25, Apr 6, 16, 17, May 3, LIF, Oct 5,
    21, 26, Dec 7, 17; <u>1737</u>: LIF, Jan 21, Feb 12, 14, 21
Hughes, Miss H (actor), <u>1734</u>: JS, May 31
Hughes, Miss J (actor), <u>1733</u>: HAY, May 28
Hughes, Miss M (actor), <u>1733</u>: HAY, May 28; <u>1735</u>: GF, Mar 25
Hughes, Mrs (singer), <u>1703</u>: DL, Feb 12
Hughs (public house), <u>1690</u>: HUGHS, Jan 8
Hulet (beneficiary), <u>1778</u>: DL, May 19
Hulet (housekeeper), <u>1767</u>: DL, Jan 24
Hulett, Charles (actor), <u>1720</u>: LIF, May 21; <u>1721</u>: LIF, May 9, Nov 28; <u>1722</u>:
    LIF, Feb 13, May 7, 15, Jun 13, Aug 1, BFLSH, 25, LIF, Oct 27; <u>1723</u>: LIF, Jan
    10, HAY, Mar 14, LIF, May 3, 17, Oct 4; <u>1724</u>: LIF, Feb 24, Apr 21, 27, May
    15, Jul 3, 21, 31, Aug 11, Sep 28; <u>1725</u>: LIF, Jan 11, Mar 29, Apr 7, 14, May
    1, 21; <u>1726</u>: LIF, May 18, Oct 24; <u>1727</u>: LIF, Jan 16, Apr 7, May 2, 8, 15, 19,
    BF, Aug 22; <u>1729</u>: HAY, Feb 25, Mar 5, 27, 29, May 2, 7, Jun 17, Jul 26, 31,
    DL, Aug 16, HAY, 19, BFF, 23, BFR, 25, LIF, Sep 12, SF, 15, LIF, 17, Oct 3,
    10, 13, Nov 4, 8, 25, Dec 3, 15; <u>1730</u>: LIF, Jan 19, 26, Apr 20, May 18, Jul
    3, BFLH, Aug 31, SFG, Sep 8, SFLH, 8, LIF, 16, 21, Oct 5, 12, 14, 27, Nov 2,
    6, 10, 23, Dec 4, 30; <u>1731</u>: LIF, Jan 5, 13, Feb 3, 27, Apr 1, 3, 23, May 6,
    17, 20, TC, Aug 4, 12, BFLH, 24, SF, Sep 8, SFLH, 8, LIF, 17, 20, 22, 27, 29,
    Oct 6, 11, 13, 25, Nov 4, 17, Dec 1, 3, 9, 15; <u>1732</u>: LIF, Jan 10, 26, Feb 5,
    22, Mar 23, 25, Apr 10, 11, 18, 24, 29, May 2, 3, 22, GF, Oct 2, 4, 7, 11,
    13, 18, 24, Nov 4, 18, Dec 2, 29; <u>1733</u>: GF, Jan 8, 24, Feb 5, 12, 19, 20, Mar
    5, 8, 15, 17, 30, Apr 3, 6, 16, 19, May 4, 5, 18, HAY, 28, CG, Jun 26, Jul 6,
    SF/BFLH, Aug 23, GF, Sep 10, 14, 20, 24, 25, 28, Oct 5, 8, 11, 12, 15, 18,
    22, 26, Nov 5, 7, 8, 10, 13, 29, Dec 13, 18, 26, 28; <u>1734</u>: GF, Jan 3, 14, 31,
    Feb 7, 11, Mar 5, 18, 19, Apr 1, 26, 27, May 15, 16, 23, BFHBH, Aug 24, SFL,
    Sep 7, GF, 16, 20, 25, Oct 16, 21, 23, 28, Nov 4, 7, 11, 18, 22, 25, 27, 29,
    Dec 2, 13, 16, 31; <u>1735</u>: GF, Jan 4, 10, 13, Feb 5, 25, Mar 17, 20, 24, 29,
    Apr 9, 14, 15, 22, May 3, 15, Sep 10, 15, 19, Oct 3, 8, Nov 19
Hulett, Mrs (actor), <u>1731</u>: TC, Aug 12, SF, Sep 8
Hull (musician), <u>1732</u>: HIC, Apr 24
Hull, Mrs (actor), <u>1770</u>: CG, Apr 26; <u>1771</u>: CG, Apr 24, Oct 7; <u>1772</u>: CG, Apr 22,
    May 4; <u>1773</u>: CG, May 1, Dec 11; <u>1774</u>: CG, Mar 7, Sep 19, Oct 4, 7, 13, 14,
    22, Dec 9; <u>1775</u>: CG, Jan 3, May 20
Hull, Thomas (actor, author), <u>1759</u>: CG, Oct 5, 18, 20, Nov 26; <u>1760</u>: CG, Jan
    18, Apr 25, May 1, Sep 22, Dec 9; <u>1761</u>: CG, Mar 9, 24, 25, 28, Apr 1, 2, 17,
    23, 24, 28, May 1, 8, 11, 12, 14, Sep 7, 9, 11, 14, 23, 25, Oct 5, 10, 13,
    17, 20, 22, 23, Nov 4, 13, 24, Dec 30; <u>1762</u>: CG, Jan 14, 18, Mar 9, 13, 20,
    Apr 3, 12, 13, 16, 21, 24, 29, 30, May 6, 14, Sep 22, 24, 27, Oct 2, 4, 9,
    11, 12, 14, 20, 21, Dec 4; <u>1763</u>: CG, Apr 15, 26, Sep 21, 23, 26, Oct 8, 17,
    26, Nov 10, 18, Dec 26; <u>1764</u>: CG, Jan 17, Feb 11, Mar 29, Apr 28, May 21, 24,
    Sep 19, 21, 24, 26, Oct 5, 8, 17, Nov 19, Dec 21, 22; <u>1765</u>: CG, Jan 8, 14,
    DL, Feb 15, CG, 18, May 2, 11, Sep 30, Oct 2, 7, 14, 16, 22, 23, 28, 30, Nov
    11, 19, 20, 27, 28, 30, Dec 4, 12, 26; <u>1766</u>: CG, Jan 9, 31, Feb 5, Apr 2, 14,
    15, 19, 25, 26, May 6, 12, 13, 16, Sep 22, 24, 26, Oct 6, 21, 23, 28, 30, 31,
    Nov 8, 11, 17, 25, 27, 28, Dec 8; <u>1767</u>: CG, Jan 1, 31, Feb 6, 9, 27, Mar 2,
    10, 23, 31, Apr 24, 25, May 6, 7, 8, 9, 19, 21, Jun 9, Sep 16, 21, 22, 23,

25, Oct 26, 30, Nov 4, 6, 7, 17, Dec 8, 14, 17, 21, 28; 1768: CG, Jan 13, 20, 22, Feb 20, Mar 8, Apr 20, 25, 26, 29, May 4, Jun 3, Sep 20, 22, 26, 27, 29, Oct 4, 6, 10, 17, 21, 24, 25, Nov 4, 9, 17, 19, Dec 3; 1769: CG, Jan 2, 28, Mar 28, Apr 1, 5, 7, 17, 25, May 3, 16, 23, 24, Sep 20, 22, 25, 30, Oct 2, 4, 6, 7, 18, 24, Nov 1, 3, 4, 15, 17, 27, Dec 1, 2, 7, 19, 29; 1770: CG, Jan 2, 3, 4, 6, 11, 19, 31, Feb 2, 3, 12, Mar 20, 24, Apr 26, May 7, 9, 19, Sep 26, Oct 1, 8, 11, 16, 18, 19, 25, 29, Nov 1, 5, 23, Dec 3, 4, 7, 13, 21; 1771: CG, Jan 4, 5, 8, 12, Mar 12, Apr 5, 9, 11, 16, 23, 24, 27, 30, May 3, 6, 13, Sep 25, 30, Oct 2, 7, 9, 11, 15, 18, 19, 25, 30, Nov 4, 5, 7, 8, 16, 21, 26, Dec 7, 9, 11, 21, 30; 1772: CG, Jan 1, 4, 14, 27, Feb 1, Mar 21, 24, 31, Apr 7, 22, May 4, 8, 11, Sep 21, 28, Oct 1, 5, 14, 17, 23, 24, 26, 30, Nov 2, 6, 14, 21, Dec 3, 14, 28; 1773: CG, Jan 6, 7, 16, 25, Feb 23, Mar 22, 30, Apr 13, 16, 23, 27, May 1, 4, 6, 7, 10, 14, 28, Sep 22, 27, Oct 4, 6, 9, 11, 15, 16, 18, 21, 23, 25, 27, Nov 8, 12, 23, Dec 3, 7, 11, 17, 21, 23; 1774: CG, Jan 3, 4, 10, 12, 24, Feb 7, Mar 12, 14, 15, 22, Apr 5, 9, 11, 12, 13, 19, 20, 23, May 2, 7, 11, Sep 19, 23, 26, Oct 3, 4, 5, 13, 14, 15, 19, 20, 22, 24, 26, 29, 31, Nov 8, 24, Dec 3, 9, 15, 17, 20, 26; 1775: CG, Jan 3, Mar 2, 4, 18, Apr 22, 26, May 5, 6, 9, 17, Sep 20, 22, 25, 27, 29, Oct 12, 18, 19, 21, 23, 25, 28, 30, Nov 9, 13, 14, Dec 1, 29; 1776: CG, Jan 1, Feb 5, 22, Mar 18, DL, Apr 9, CG, 22, 27, May 1, 8, 10, 13, Sep 23, 25, Oct 4, 7, 8, 17, Nov 11, 12, 14, 15, 19, 21, 25, 28, 29, Dec 2, 4, 6, 18, 26, 27; 1777: CG, Jan 8, 17, Feb 1, 5, Apr 14, 16, 29, May 13, 29, HAY, Jun 16, CG, Sep 22, 24, 29, Oct 3, 6, 15, 17, 21, 23, Nov 1, 4, 6, 7, 13, 18, 21, Dec 3, 10, 19, 26; 1778: CG, Jan 3, 20, 21, Feb 10, 24, 26, Mar 7, 14, 23, Apr 11, 27, May 5, 6, 9, 11, 15, Sep 21, 28, Oct 5, 12, 15, 16, 22, 24, 26, 27, 28, 30, 31, Dec 3, 8, 12, 17, 30; 1779: CG, Jan 4, 13, 18, 22, Feb 2, 12, 23, Mar 4, 20, 22, Apr 5, 24, 27, May 3, 6, 15, 20, Sep 20, 24, 27, Oct 1, 13, 16, 18, 23, 29, Nov 1, 8, 10, 13, 19, 22, Dec 1, 9, 16, 22, 23, 31; 1780: CG, Jan 17, Apr 27, May 3, 29, Jun 1, Oct 3, 4, 9, 19, 23, 26, 30, Nov 1, 10, 14, 24, 27, Dec 5, 12, 27; 1781: CG, Jan 2, 4, 8, 13, 15, 17, 18, Feb 15, Apr 2, 21, May 14, 28, Sep 21, 24, Oct 31, Nov 5, 9, Dec 5, 8, 10, 17, 18, 20, 31; 1782: CG, Jan 1, 3, 5, 7, 8, 10, 22, Feb 5, Mar 19, Apr 17, 23, May 1, 2, 6, 20, HAY, Jun 19, CG, Oct 4, 7, 10, 14, 17, 21, 31, Nov 1, DL, 16, CG, 18, Dec 2, 9, 14, 19, 30, 31; 1783: CG, Jan 1, DL, 11, CG, 27, Feb 19, Mar 29, Apr 5, 7, 23, 26, May 5, 17, 19, Sep 17, 19, 22, 24, Oct 2, 6, 9, 11, 13, 15, 20, Nov 8, 10, 27, Dec 11, 26, 31; 1784: CG, Jan 9, 12, 22, 31, Feb 5, 18, Mar 1, 4, 22, Apr 13, May 17, 26, Jun 2, Sep 17, 20, 24, 27, 28, Oct 4, 6, 8, 11, 18, 25, 30, Nov 13, 29, Dec 13, 27; 1785: CG, Jan 8, 19, 21, DL, Feb 2, CG, 14, 28, Mar 8, DL, Apr 7, CG, 8, 22, May 7, Sep 21, 28, Oct 5, 28, 29, Nov 1, 2, 9, 14, Dec 10, 14, 26, 30; 1786: CG, Jan 2, 6, 7, 18, Feb 7, 11, 25, Mar 6, Apr 4, 19, 24, 26, May 3, 5, 13, Sep 18, 20, 25, 27, Oct 6, 23, 30, Nov 22, 29, Dec 4, 15, 19; 1787: CG, Jan 6, 8, DL, 23, CG, Mar 26, Apr 11, 17, 24, 25, 27, May 4, 21, Sep 17, 24, Oct 1, 10, 12, 17, 29, 31, Nov 7, 9, 14, 19, 22, Dec 27; 1788: CG, Jan 4, 14, 18, 29, Mar 10, 24, Apr 11, May 2, Sep 17, 19, 22, Oct 15, DL, Nov 6, CG, 12, 26, Dec 26; 1789: CG, Jan 2, 8, 10, 20, 21, Feb 11, Apr 20, 30, May 22, 26, Jun 16, Sep 14, 18, Oct 6, 9, 12, 16, Nov 5, 19, 20, 23, 30, Dec 26; 1790: CG, Jan 23, 29, Feb 11, 25, Apr 7, 30, May 13, 18, 20, 24, 31, Jun 2, Sep 13, 15, 29, Oct 6, 8, 11, 13, 18, 20, 23, Nov 1, 4, 8, 23, 27, Dec 2, 6, 14; 1791: CG, Jan 7, Feb 11, Apr 16, 30, May 2, 31, Sep 12, 26, Oct 6, 7, 10, 12, 17, 20, 24, Nov 4, Dec 21, 26; 1792: CG, Mar 26, HAY, Apr 16, CG, 17, 18, May 11, 17, 18, 19, 22, Sep 21, Oct 1, 8, 10, 12, 15, 29, 31, Nov 5, 12, 14; 1793: CG, Apr 15, May 24, Sep 16, 18, 23, HAY, 24, CG, 27, 30, Oct 5, 7, 8, 14, 25, Nov 1, 23, 28; 1794: CG, Jan 3, 6, Feb 1, Mar 17, 25, Apr 12, 29, May 14, 16, 30, Sep 17, 22, Oct 1, 6, 8, 15, 17, 20, Nov 12, Dec 6; 1795: CG, Jan 19, Feb 21, Mar 17, Apr 29, May 1, 22, 25, Jun 3, 5, Sep 14, 18, 21, 25, 28, 30, Oct 16, 23, Dec 9, 31; 1796: CG, Jan 8, 13, Apr 5, May 21, 24, Jun 7, Sep 19, 21, 26, Oct 10, DL, 18, CG, 20, 24, Nov 5, 24, Dec 19; 1797: CG, Jan 7, 10, Feb 18, Apr 25, May 4, 10, 16, 31, Sep 18, 22, Oct 2, 6, 13, 16, 21, Nov 2, 18, 20, Dec 16; 1798: CG, Jan 5, Feb 9, Apr 10, 17, May 4, 12, 30, Jun 11, Sep 21, Oct 8, 15; 1799: CG, Mar 5, Apr 12, May 6, 20, Jun 5, Sep 23, 30, Oct 4, 7, 17, 29, Dec 30; 1800: CG, Jan 29, DL, Apr 14, CG, May 21, 22

--All in the Right, 1766: CG, Apr 26
--Disinterested Love, 1798: CG, May 30
--Fairy Favour, The, 1766: CG, Dec 2; 1767: CG, Jan 31, Feb 2, 3, 4, 5, 6, 9, 17, 19, Mar 10, 26
--Fatal Interview, The, 1782: DL, Nov 16, 18, 19
--Henry II; or, The Fall of Rosamond, 1773: CG, May 1, Dec 11, 14, 31; 1774: CG, Jan 12, 14, 17, 20, 22, 24, 27, 28, Feb 24, Mar 3, 7, 8, 17, Apr 4, 20, May 5, 23, Oct 17, 24, Nov 5, 28, Dec 13; 1775: CG, Jan 21, Apr 1, May 22, Oct 30, Dec 26; 1776: CG, Dec 26; 1782: CG, Dec 31; 1787: HAY, Jul 25, DL, Dec 26; 1791: HAY, Dec 26; 1796: DL, Apr 2

--Iphigenia; or, The Victim, 1778: CG, Mar 23
--Love Finds the Way (opera), 1777: CG, Nov 18, 19, 20, 21, 22, 24, 26, 28, Dec
  2, 6; 1778: CG, Apr 25, May 8, 20; 1779: CG, Apr 7
--Perplexities, The, 1767: CG, Jan 31, Feb 2, 3, 4, 5, 6, 7, 9, 10, 19, Mar 4
--Spanish Lady, The, 1765: CG, May 2; 1769: CG, Dec 11, 12, 13, 14, 16, 23;
  1770: CG, Jan 23, 25, Feb 27, Mar 5, 17, Apr 26, May 26; 1772: CG, Apr 11,
  May 2; 1776: DL, Apr 9
Hull, 1777: HAY, Oct 9; 1785: DL, Mar 31
Hulmandel (musician), 1772: HAY, Apr 27
Hulme (actor), 1779: HAY, Dec 27
Hulstone (actor), 1735: YB, Jul 17, HAY, Dec 13
Humane Society, 1784: CG, Dec 21; 1800: CG, Jun 16
Hume, David (correspondent), 1757: CG, Mar 12
Hummel, Johann Nepomuk (pianist), 1791: KING'S, May 19
Hummell, J Lewis (singer), 1793: KING/HAY, Feb 15; 1794: CG, Mar 7
Humour Out of Breath. See Day, John.
Humourist, The. See Cobb, James.
Humourists, The. See Shadwell, Thomas; Cibber, Theophilus.
Humourous Election, The (opera, anon), 1734: HAY, Jul 26, 29, 31, Aug 5
Humourous Lieutenant, The. See Fletcher, John.
Humourous Lovers, The. See Cavendish, William.
Humourous Medley (dance), 1734: HA, Sep 2
Humourous Physician, The; or, A Cure for All Ills (play), 1757: BFG, Sep 5, 6
Humours of a Country Fair (dance), 1796: CG, May 10
Humours of an Election, The. See Pilon, Frederick.
Humours of Bartholomew Fair (song), 1759: BFS, Sep 3
Humours of Bedlam (dance), 1723: LIF, Nov 16, 27; 1724: LIF, Apr 24, Nov 6;
  1725: LIF, Jan 15; 1726: LIF, May 3, Nov 2; 1727: LIF, May 8; 1728: LIF, Mar
  14, May 20; 1729: LIF, May 9; 1732: GF, Apr 12
Humours of Bedlam. See Fletcher, John, The Pilgrim.
Humours of Billingsgate (play, anon), 1731: DL, Nov 12
Humours of Blackwall, The; or, The Indiaman Returned (dance), 1775: CG, Apr 29,
  May 9, 11, 19, 22, 30
Humours of Cloth Fair (dance), 1754: SFP, Sep 18
Humours of Covent Garden. See Fielding, Henry, The Covent Garden Tragedy.
Humours of Epsom Downs (song), 1743: JS, Mar 23
Humours of Harlequin, The (play), 1729: HAY, Feb 25, 27, Mar 1, 3, 5, 6, 8, 12,
  14, 19, 28, Apr 8, May 1, 26, Jun 13, 14, 21, 24, 25, 26, 27, 28, Jul 1, 5,
  9, 10, 12, 16, 19, 23, 26, 28, Aug 2, 13, BFR, 25, SF, Sep 8, HAY, Nov 26,
  29, Dec 5; 1730: HAY, Jan 16, Feb 4, 6, 12
Humours of Harlequin, The; or, The Life and Death of Dr Faustus (farce, anon),
  1732: TC, Aug 17
Humours of Leixlip (dance), 1777: CG, Apr 25, 30, May 2, 7, 12, 26, Oct 8, 10,
  Nov 19, Dec 22; 1779: CG, Feb 25; 1780: CG, Sep 27, Oct 2, 3, 6, 18, 19, Nov
  2; 1781: CG, Apr 20, 26
Humours of Marriage (dance), 1727: LIF, Apr 7
Humours of Mayfair (dance), 1743: MF, May 9
Humours of Newmarket (dance), 1776: CG, May 3, 6, 8, 13, 14, 15, 17, 18, 23,
  27, 30, Jun 1; 1777: CG, Apr 28, May 5, Oct 1; 1778: CG, Apr 20; 1779: CG,
  May 3, 8, DL, 14; 1780: CG, May 8, 10, 12, 16, 18, 19, 24; 1781: CG, May 18;
  1782: CG, Apr 1, May 11; 1783: CG, May 26
Humours of Oxford, The. See Miller, James.
Humours of Purgatory, The. See Griffin, Benjamin.
Humours of Sir John Brute, The (play, anon), 1791: HAY, Dec 26
Humours of Sir John Falstaff, Justice Shallow, and Ancient Pistol, The
  (medley), 1734: HAY, Jun 3, 4, 5
Humours of the Age (entertainment), 1761: CG, Mar 30; 1762: CG, Mar 22; 1763:
  CG, Mar 17
Humours of the Age, The. See Baker, Thomas.
Humours of the Army, The. See Shadwell, Charles.
Humours of the Turf, The. See Downing, George.
Humours Reconciled, The. See Jonson, Ben.
Humphrey (actor), 1798: WRSG, Jun 8; 1799: WRSG, May 17
Humphrey, Duke of Gloucester. See Philips, Ambrose.
Humphrey, Pelham (composer), 1667: BRIDGES, Sep 25, ATCOURT, Nov 16; 1671:
  BRIDGES, Mar 0, DG, Nov 0
Humphreys (beneficiary), 1792: DLKING'S, Jun 15; 1793: DL, Jun 6; 1795: DL, Jun
  4; 1796: DL, Jun 15; 1797: DL, Jun 15; 1798: DL, Jun 16; 1799: DL, Jul 3;
  1800: DL, Jun 14
Humphreys (house servant), 1757: DL, May 20; 1758: DL, May 17; 1760: DL, May
  15; 1764: DL, May 18; 1766: DL, May 16; 1767: DL, May 30; 1768: DL, May 30;
  1769: DL, May 19; 1770: HAY, Sep 20; 1771: DL, May 28; 1772: DL, Jun 5; 1773:

DL, May 31; 1774: DL, May 26; 1775: DL, May 24; 1776: DL, May 17
Humphreys, Miss (actor), 1769: DL, May 19
Humphreys, Mr and Mrs (actors), 1799: WRSG, May 17
Humphreys, Mrs (actor), 1798: WRSG, Jun 8; 1799: WRSG, May 17
Humphreys, Mrs (haberdasher), 1766: DL, Dec 30
Humphreys, Richard (pugilist), 1788: CG, Dec 30
Humphreys, Samuel (author), 1731: KING'S, Jan 12, HAY, 20, KING'S, Feb 2, Apr
   6; 1732: KING'S, Jan 15, Feb 15, Nov 4; 1733: KING'S, Jan 27, Mar 17, Apr 14,
   LIF, 16
Humphries (linen draper), 1772: CG, Jan 23
Humphries, Eliza (actor), 1797: DL, Oct 14, Nov 20, 28; 1800: DL, Jun 18
Humphry (house servant), 1750: CG, Jan 3
Hungarian acrobats, 1743: LIF, May 6
Hungarian and Two Tyroleans (dance), 1740: CG, Nov 28
Hungarian comedians, 1744: HAY, Dec 26
Hungarian Dance (dance), 1739: DL, Apr 24, 25, May 15; 1740: DL, Mar 22, Apr
   10, 18; 1753: CG, Mar 31
Hungarian Gambols (dance), 1761: CG, Mar 9, Apr 4, 25, Sep 21
Hungarian Peasants (dance), 1752: DL, Nov 25, 27, Dec 5, 21; 1767: HAY, Aug 5
Hungarian Volunteers (spectators), 1749: JS, Mar 27
Hungersford Market, 1758: HAY, Jan 27
Hungry Fox one day did spy (song), 1799: CG, Oct 7
Huniades. See Brand, Hannah.
Hunt (actor), 1782: HAY, Nov 25
Hunt (fireworks maker), 1796: DL, Dec 26
Hunt the Slipper. See Knapp, Henry.
Hunt, Henrietta, Mrs William (actor), 1777: CG, Apr 22; 1778: CG, Apr 28
Hunt, Mrs (actor), 1675: ATCOURT, Feb 15; 1699: LIF, Dec 18
Hunt, Mrs (actor), 1704: LIF, Feb 2; 1705: LIF/QUEN, Feb 22; 1710: DL, Feb 25,
   May 23, Jun 6; 1715: LIF, Jan 4, 7, 8, Mar 26, May 10, Jun 2, 14, 23, Aug 11,
   Oct 5, 11, 24, Nov 29, 30, Dec 12; 1716: LIF, Mar 10, Apr 14, 27, DL, Jul 12,
   Oct 29, Dec 5; 1717: DL, Jan 16, Aug 6, 22, Nov 6, 13; 1718: DL, Apr 29, Jul
   11, Aug 15; 1719: DL, Jan 10, 29, Jun 9, Oct 22, 28, Nov 14
Hunt, Mrs (actor), 1771: DL, Oct 1, 8, 22, Nov 13, Dec 14; 1772: DL, May 27,
   Sep 26, 29, Oct 1, Nov 9, 12, 18; 1773: DL, Apr 19, May 3, 10, HAY, Sep 20,
   DL, 21, Oct 9, 25, Nov 2, 25, Dec 27; 1774: DL, Jan 19, Mar 17, 19, Apr 15,
   May 10, 14; 1775: CG, Apr 28
Hunt, Mrs (spectator), 1668: LIF, Oct 19
Hunt's Court, 1745: CG, Apr 26; 1747: CG, May 11; 1748: CG, Apr 13
Hunter (actor), 1783: HAY, Dec 15; 1784: HAY, Feb 23, Mar 22, Apr 30; 1791:
   HAY, Dec 12; 1792: HAY, Feb 6
Hunter (house servant), 1755: DL, May 15
Hunter, Maria (actor), 1773: DL, Jan 12; 1774: CG, Oct 1, 21, 24; 1775: CG, Oct
   2, 13, Nov 13, Dec 8, 29; 1776: CG, Jan 1, Feb 9, 22, May 8; 1777: HAY, May
   15, 30, Jun 11, 26, Jul 15, Aug 7, 19, Sep 10; 1782: CG, Apr 17, DL, 30, CG,
   Oct 14, Nov 1, Dec 4, 27, 31; 1783: CG, May 19, 20; 1785: HAY, Apr 26; 1788:
   HAY, Apr 9, 29; 1791: HAY, Dec 26; 1792: HAY, Apr 16; 1799: CG, Jun 12, HAY,
   Oct 21
Hunter, Widow, 1767: DL, Feb 4; 1772: DL, Jan 18; 1774: DL, Jan 11; 1775: DL,
   Jan 6; 1776: DL, Jan 13
Hunters, The (dance), 1764: DL, Feb 24, 27; 1768: DL, Dec 1
Hunting Cantata (song), 1785: DL, Apr 1
Hunting Dance (dance), 1777: CG, Feb 18, Apr 16
Hunting Duet (song), 1785: DL, May 19; 1786: DL, May 25
Hunting Music (music), 1735: GF, May 15
Hunting Song (song), 1726: DL, May 17; 1744: HAY, Jan 23; 1761: DL, Oct 26;
   1762: CG, Apr 20; 1766: CG, Apr 18; 1770: DL, May 18; 1771: GROTTO, Sep 3, 9;
   1774: HAY, Sep 5; 1776: HAY, Feb 22, Sep 2, CG, Oct 23; 1778: CG, Mar 25,
   HAY, 31, Aug 21; 1779: HAY, Mar 15, May 10; 1784: DL, May 12; 1786: DL, May
   22, 24; 1787: HAY, Aug 21; 1788: CG, May 16, DL, 26; 1789: CG, May 6, Jun 8;
   1791: KING'S, May 19; 1793: CG, Nov 18; 1797: CG, Jun 13; 1799: CG, Jun 7;
   1800: CG, May 20
Hunting Symphony (music), 1791: KING'S, May 19
Huntington Divertisement (interlude), 1678: MTH, Jun 20
Huntington, Earl of. See Hastings, Theophilus.
Huntington, Lord, 1763: DL, Oct 20
Huntley, Miss (actor), 1790: CG, Dec 20
Huntsman, Horn and Pack of Dogs (entertainment), 1702: DL, Aug 22; 1703: DL,
   Jun 18; 1704: DL, Jun 5; 1710: DL, May 26
Huntsman's sweet Hallo (song), 1781: CG, Feb 26, May 4, 7; 1782: CG, Feb 26,
   Mar 5, HAY, 18, CG, Apr 26, May 4; 1783: CG, May 16, 21; 1784: CG, May 18
Hurd, 1776: DL, Jun 3

Hurdy Gurdy (music), 1754: HAY, Jul 4, Sep 10
Hurlothrumbo. See Johnson, Samuel.
Hurlstone, Thomas, 1792: HAY, Apr 16, CG, May 10, Oct 27; 1793: CG, May 3;
    1794: HAY, Aug 23; 1795: CG, Feb 14
--Crotchet Lodge (farce), 1795: CG, Feb 14, 17, 19, 21, 24, 26, 28, Mar 3, 7,
    10, 14, 17, Apr 27, 29, May 14, HAY, Aug 21, CG, Oct 24, 27, Dec 18; 1796:
    CG, Apr 9; 1797: CG, Jun 2, Nov 21; 1798: CG, Nov 21
--Just in Time (opera), 1792: CG, May 10, Oct 27, 30, Nov 2, 10, 13, 17, 20,
    23; 1794: CG, Jan 21
--To Arms; or, The British Recruit (Who's Afraid?) (interlude), 1793: CG, May
    3, 15; 1795: CG, Mar 16, 28, Apr 22, 29, May 21
Hurly-Burly; or, The Fairy of the Well (or, Chiswick Fair) (pantomime), 1785:
    DL, Dec 26, 27, 28, 29, 30, 31; 1786: DL, Jan 2, 3, 9, 10, 11, 12, 13, 19,
    20, 23, 26, 27, 31, Feb 1, 2, 9, 17, HAMM, Jul 26; 1787: DL, Nov 21, 23, 24
Hurrel (actor), 1741: TC, Aug 4
Hursfall (barber), 1761: CG, Apr 25
Hurst (actor), 1754: CG, Nov 20, Dec 10; 1755: CG, May 9; 1757: HAY, Oct 31
Hurst (actor), 1782: HAY, Nov 25
Hurst (beneficiary), 1724: LIF, Apr 25
Hurst, Master (actor), 1756: DL, Dec 3; 1759: DL, Apr 5; 1765: DL, Feb 4
Hurst, Miss (actor), 1781: HAY, Mar 26, Oct 16
Hurst, Richard (actor), 1765: DL, Oct 22, 28, Dec 6, 18; 1766: DL, Jan 17, 24,
    29, Feb 5, 11, 13, Mar 15, Apr 9, CG, May 3, DL, 3, HAY, Jun 26, Jul 1, 15,
    31, KING'S, Aug 8, 13, 18, HAY, 21, KING'S, 25, 27, Sep 5, 9, 13, 15, 19, DL,
    Oct 17, 18, 23, 29, Nov 4, 8, 17, 20, Dec 2, 4, 6; 1767: DL, Jan 24, Feb 7,
    Apr 24, May 11, 13, Sep 12, HAY, 16, DL, 21, HAY, Oct 10, 21, 22, 26,
    28, 29, Nov 4, 11, 24, Dec 26, 28; 1768: DL, Jan 14, Feb 27, Mar 8, 15, 21,
    Apr 12, 21, 27, May 4, Sep 8, 20, 24, 26, 28, Oct 10, 11, 13, 14, 20, 21, 31,
    Nov 1, 4, 5, 24, Dec 3, 16, 17, 21, 28; 1769: DL, Jan 21, 27, Mar 16, Apr 7,
    13, May 1, 3, 5, 22, Sep 16, 23, 28, Oct 7, 9, 13, 14, 23, 30, Nov 4, 9, 14,
    18, 21, 23, 24, 27, 28, 29, Dec 13; 1770: DL, Jan 13, 19, 27, Mar 1, 20, 22,
    26, 31, May 5, 15, 16, 17, 30, Sep 22, Oct 2, 3, 5, 8, 9, 24, 25, 31, Nov 3,
    5, 9, 10, 13, 16, 17, 19, 28, Dec 17; 1771: DL, Jan 4, Mar 7, Apr 5, 6, 9,
    24, May 3, 10, Sep 26, 28, Oct 1, 12, 17, 28, Nov 4, 8, 13, 18, 21, 23, Dec
    2, 4; 1772: DL, Feb 26, Mar 12, 26, 28, May 14, 16, 30, Sep 19, Oct 10, 13,
    16, 17, 21, 24, 29, 31, Nov 3, 4, 7, 9, 16, 17, 30, Dec 30; 1773: DL, Jan 13,
    19, Feb 2, 18, Mar 30, Apr 23, 27, 30, May 4, 10, 12, 19, Sep 21, Oct 2, 5,
    8, 19, 22, 28, Nov 2, 4, 6, 13, 20, 24, 25, Dec 3, 20, 21, 27; 1774: DL, Jan
    19, Feb 2, Mar 12, 14, 15, 19, Apr 12, 28, May 4, 18, 28, Sep 17, 22, 27, Oct
    1, 4, 13, 20, 21, 27, 28, Nov 1, 3, 4, 19, 24, 29; 1775: DL, Feb 17, Mar 20,
    21, 23, 25, Apr 17, May 1, 6, 24, Sep 26, Oct 3, 5, 10, 11, 12, 20, 25, Nov
    3, 4, 6, 9, 20, 21, 27, Dec 7, 26; 1776: DL, Feb 2, 12, Mar 28, Apr 18, 26,
    29, May 11, 13, 18, 22, Sep 24, Oct 5, 9, 10, 12, 18, 22, 23, 26, Nov 4, 25,
    Dec 14, 28; 1777: DL, Jan 4, 22, Feb 17, Mar 13, Apr 24, 26, 29, May 15, Jun
    6, Sep 25, 27, 30, Oct 7, 17, 31, Nov 4, 18, 24, 29, Dec 3, 13, 18; 1778: DL,
    Jan 2, 5, 24, Feb 10, 19, Mar 30, May 5, 21, Sep 24, 26, 29, Oct 15, 16, 21,
    26, 28, 30, Nov 4, 9, 11, 16, 18, Dec 11, 19, 21, 22; 1779: DL, Feb 8, Mar
    22, 25, Apr 19, CG, May 4, DL, 4, 21, Oct 30, Nov 1, 8, 11, 20, 22, 24, Dec
    10, 20, 28, 30; 1780: DL, Jan 19, 28, Apr 10, 17, 18, 21, 26, 28
Hurst, Robert, 1724: LIF, Aug 11
--Roman Maid, The, 1724: LIF, Aug 11, 14, 18; 1725: LIF, Jan 20
Hurst, T (actor), 1768: DL, Oct 10
Hus, Jean Baptiste (dancer), 1787: KING'S, Jan 20, Feb 13, Mar 8, 22, May 17
Hus, Mlle (dancer), 1787: KING'S, Feb 13
Husband His Own Cuckold, The. See Dryden Jr, John.
Husband, Benjamin (actor), 1696: LIF, Oct 0; 1701: LIF, Mar 0, Dec 0; 1702: DL,
    Nov 0, 26, Dec 0, 14; 1704: DL, May 0; 1705: QUEEN'S, Nov 23, Dec 27; 1706:
    QUEEN'S, Feb 11, 21, LIF/QUEN, Apr 11, QUEEN'S, Jun 0, Oct 26, Dec 27, 30;
    1707: QUEEN'S, Jan 14, 20, Feb 12, 14, 15, 18, Mar 27, Jul 4, 10, Aug 1, 12,
    DL/QUEEN, Oct 20, 22, 25, QUEEN'S/DL, Nov 8, DL/QUEEN, 10, 14, 19, 25, Dec 27;
    1708: DL/QUEEN, Jan 1, DL, 31, Feb 9, 14, Apr 10, 15, 22, DL/QUEEN, May 20,
    DL, 31, Jun 10, 15, 17, 19, Jul 20, Aug 28, 31, Sep 9, 11, 18, 21, 23, 25,
    28, 30, Oct 9, 19, Dec 21, 31; 1709: DL, Jan 1, Feb 5, 11, 25, Mar 5, Apr 27,
    May 10, Jun 2, QUEEN'S, Sep 24, Oct 1, 4, 8, 22, 28, 29, 31, Nov 4, 8, Dec
    12; 1710: QUEEN'S, Apr 19, 20, May 11, Jun 1, 5, GR, 19, 21, 24, Jul 1, 3, 6,
    8, 10, 12, 15, 27, Aug 12, QUEEN'S, 16, GR, 19, 26, 28, 31, Sep 9, DL/QUEEN,
    Oct 5, Nov 13, 17, 18, DL, 20, 21, Dec 9; 1711: DL/QUEEN, Feb 8, DL, Mar 8,
    May 18, Jun 29, Jul 6, 10, GR, Aug 2, DL, Oct 31, Nov 3; 1712: DL, May 27,
    Jul 4, Aug 8, Oct 22, Nov 7; 1714: DL, Feb 2, May 17; 1715: LIF, Jan 3, 4, 7,
    Feb 2, 3, 5, Apr 18, May 24, Oct 7, 12, 24, Nov 30, Dec 12; 1716: LIF, Jan 3,
    4, Apr 13, Oct 10, Nov 5; 1717: LIF, Jan 8, 10, 22, Apr 11, Oct 15, 26, Nov
    6, 14, 20, 26, Dec 9; 1718: LIF, Jan 7, Apr 16

Husbands (actor), 1741: JS, Nov 9
Hush ye pretty warbling Choir (song), 1733: DL/HAY, Oct 27, Dec 31; 1734:
    DL/HAY, Feb 4, Mar 4, Apr 6; 1787: DL, Mar 7; 1790: CG, Mar 17, 26; 1791: DL,
    Apr 1, CG, 13; 1792: KING'S, Feb 29; 1794: DL, Mar 26; 1796: CG, Mar 16
Hussar (dance), 1720: DL, Feb 10, Mar 31, Apr 26, Sep 13; 1721: DL, Apr 11;
    1722: DL, Jan 8, Mar 15, May 19, Oct 25; 1723: DL, Mar 28, May 10, 21, Oct 3,
    Nov 20; 1724: DL, Apr 7, 8; 1725: DL, Mar 15, 18, Oct 2, 23; 1726: DL, Jan
    24, Mar 24, 28; 1728: DL, Mar 7, 16, May 2, 9; 1732: DL, May 10; 1734:
    DL/HAY, Feb 20, Mar 5, 9; 1742: CG, Apr 5; 1743: DL, Apr 25, May 16, 23
Hussar and Wife (dance), 1721: DL, Mar 16, 25
Hussey (actor, dancer), 1732: LIF, Nov 20; 1735: CG, Mar 28; 1736: LIF, Mar 31,
    Sep 28, Oct 21; 1739: KING'S, Jan 16; 1743: LIF, Jun 3; 1744: DL, May 21;
    1746: DL, Apr 22, NWSM, Jul 28; 1747: GF, Mar 3; 1752: SFB, Sep 22; 1755:
    HAY, Sep 3; 1757: HAY, Oct 31, Dec 26; 1760: HAY, Jun 2, CG, Dec 11; 1761:
    CG, Mar 9, May 8, 25, Sep 21, 26, 29; 1762: CG, Apr 17, May 11, 13; 1763: CG,
    Jan 26, May 13; 1764: CG, Jan 14, May 22; 1765: CG, May 22, Oct 28; 1766: CG,
    May 6, Oct 25, Nov 18; 1767: CG, Apr 27, Oct 17; 1768: CG, May 27; 1769: CG,
    May 6, Nov 4; 1770: CG, May 18, 23; 1771: CG, Jan 11, 29, Apr 12, May 17, 22,
    Sep 30, Oct 11; 1772: CG, May 1, 16, Sep 30; 1773: CG, Apr 24; 1774: CG, May
    20; 1775: CG, May 26
Hussey-Phillips Booth, 1746: SFHP, Sep 8
Hussey, J (dancer), 1758: HAY, Jan 6
Hussey, John (actor), 1778: HAY, Sep 8; 1780: HAY, Sep 2
Hussey, Master (actor), 1757: HAY, Jun 17, Jul 5, Aug 22
Hussey, Mrs (beneficiary), 1746: NWSM, Jul 28
Hussey, T (dancer), 1757: HAY, Dec 26
Hussey's Booth, 1745: MF, May 6, 10; 1746: BF, Aug 23; 1747: BFH, Aug 22; 1748:
    BFH, Aug 24; 1749: BFH, Aug 23
Hussy, Lady Sarah (spectator), 1697: LIF, Feb 27; 1700: LIF, Jan 29
Hust (actor), 1755: DL, Nov 8
Hust, Master (actor), 1755: DL, Nov 8
Hutchinson (attorney), 1772: CG, Dec 14
Hutchinson (haberdasher), 1773: DL, Nov 10
Huttley (actor), 1793: HAY, Aug 6
Hutton (actor), 1773: HAY, Jun 2, 28, Jul 2, 19, Aug 11, 13, 16, 23, 27, Sep 3,
    17, 18; 1775: HAY, Sep 7, Oct 30; 1776: HAY, Aug 27; 1777: HAY, Sep 17
Hutton, Miss (actor, dancer), 1720: LIF, Dec 6, 14, 26; 1721: LIF, Feb 21, 28,
    Apr 29, Oct 17, Dec 14; 1722: LIF, Jan 13, Mar 13, 29, 31, Apr 20, 24, May 2,
    7, 8, 10, 18
Hutton, Mrs (actor), 1749: HAY, Oct 17
Huygens, van Constantijn (Dutch spectator), 1689: BF, Aug 26, ATCOURT, Nov 15,
    DL, Dec 4; 1693: DL, Jan 16; 1695: DLORLIF, Dec 9
Hyam, Mrs (actor), 1781: HAY, Nov 12; 1783: HAY, Sep 17
Hyanson (actor), 1784: DL, Aug 20, 27
Hydaspes. See Mancini, Francesco.
Hyde (actor), 1733: GF, Apr 17, Sep 17, DL, Oct 19; 1734: DL/HAY, May 2; 1735:
    DL, Feb 5; 1736: CG, Feb 24; 1737: DL, Mar 4; 1738: DL, May 11; 1739: CG, Sep
    25, Dec 6
Hyde (actor), 1760: HAY, Jun 28
Hyde (engraver), 1757: DL, Apr 19
Hyde Park Hospital, 1750: DL, Apr 9
Hyde Park. See Shirley, James.
Hyde Park, 1669: BRIDGES, Apr 24; 1686: DLORDG, May 6; 1695: DLORLIF, Jun 22;
    1696: MF, May 0; 1697: LIF, Mar 9; 1701: MF, May 1; 1704: MFFB, May 1; 1736:
    CG, Oct 4; 1748: NWSM, May 3; 1762: CHAPEL, May 18; 1764: CHAPEL, Feb 29;
    1766: CHAPEL, Apr 30; 1774: CHAPEL, Mar 30; 1776: KING'S, Apr 16; 1777: CG,
    Apr 10; 1791: PAN, Feb 17, Dec 17
Hyde, Edward, Earl of Clarendon, 1669: BRIDGES, Feb 27; 1675: ATCOURT, Apr 22;
    1684: CITY, Oct 29
Hyde, J (trumpeter), 1792: KING'S, Feb 24; 1794: DL, Mar 14, 19; 1798: HAY, Jan
    15
Hyde, Mrs (beneficiary), 1751: HAY, Nov 21
Hydropique Amoureux, L' (dance), 1741: DL, Feb 9, 10, 17
Hylas et Temire (dance), 1799: KING'S, Apr 18, May 2, Jun 8, 15, Jul 13, 16;
    1800: KING'S, Jan 28, Feb 1, 4, 8, 18, 22, Mar 1
Hymen. See Handel, George Frederic; Allen.
Hymen's Temple; or, The Shepherd's Wedding (dance), 1748: DL, Feb 9, 12, Mar 24
Hymen's Triumph (dance), 1764: CG, Mar 20
Hymen's Triumph; or, Trick upon Trick (pantomime, anon), 1737: LIF, Feb 1, 2,
    3, 4, 5, 7, 8, 9, 10, 11, 12, 14, 15, 16, 17, 19, 21, 22, 24, Mar 10, 14, 15,
    17, 19, 22, 28, 29, Apr 19, 20
Hymn to the Sun (song), 1694: ATCOURT, Jan 1

Hymn, Solemn (music), 1774: DL, Mar 19
Hypochondriac, The (farce, anon), 1718: LIF, Apr 28; 1719: LIF, Apr 28; 1720: LIF, Jan 9, 21, Feb 8, 19
Hypocrite, The. See Shadwell, Thomas; Bickerstaff, Isaac.

I am a jolly gay Pedlar (song), 1796: CG, May 16, Jun 1; 1797: CG, May 22; 1798: CG, Mar 19; 1799: CG, Mar 2; 1800: CG, Mar 4, 8, Jun 5
I attempt from Love's sickness to fly (song), 1695: DG, Apr 0
I blush in the Dark (song), 1785: CG, Apr 20
I burn, I burn (song), 1694: DG, May 0; 1717: LIF, Nov 9; 1718: LIF, Apr 24; 1720: LIF, Oct 4; 1722: LIF, Mar 31; 1723: LIF, Jan 2, Oct 4; 1728: LIF, Apr 24; 1733: GF, Dec 31
I can dance and sing (song), 1795: CG, Mar 19
I come not (song), 1792: KING'S, Mar 14
I come to sing (song), 1695: DG, Apr 0
I courted and writ (song), 1696: DG, Oct 0
I feel the deity within (song), 1790: CG, Mar 19; 1791: CG, Apr 15; 1792: CG, Mar 9; 1793: CG, Mar 13; 1794: CG, Mar 7, DL, 26; 1795: CG, Feb 20; 1798: CG, Mar 28; 1799: CG, Feb 20; 1800: CG, Mar 19
I have a silent sorrow here (song), 1798: DL, Mar 24, HAY, Aug 23, DL, Sep 15; 1799: DL, Apr 6, Nov 27; 1800: DL, Mar 4
I have lost my Anna (song), 1777: CG, Oct 8
I know that my redeemer liveth (song), 1786: DL, Mar 3, 24; 1787: DL, Mar 30; 1790: CG, Mar 26; 1792: KING'S, Mar 28; 1793: KING/HAY, Feb 20, CG, Mar 8; 1794: DL, Mar 19, 28; 1795: CG, Mar 20, 27; 1797: CG, Mar 3; 1798: CG, Mar 30; 1799: CG, Feb 13
I looked, I looked, and saw within the Book of Fate (song), 1691: DLORDG, Dec 0
I Must have a Comforter (opera), 1736: TC, Aug 4
I never loved any dear Mary but you (song), 1795: DL, Jun 2; 1798: DL, Jun 8
I never saw a face till now (song), 1684: DL, Apr 0
I once had virtue, wealth, and fame (song), 1690: DLORDG, Mar 0
I rage, I melt, I burn (cong), 1790: DL, Mar 10; 1791: DL, Apr 1, CG, 13; 1792: KING'S, Feb 29, CG, Mar 14, 21; 1794: DL, Mar 26; 1798: CG, Mar 28
I rise with the morn (song), 1800: DL, May 10
I scorn you (song), 1715: LIF, Aug 23
I see she flies me (song), 1693: NONE, Sep 0
I sigh and lament (song), 1795: KING'S, Mar 13
I sighed and owned my love (song), 1694: DL, Feb 0
I sighed and pined (song), 1688: DG, Apr 0
I sing the produce of the vine (song), 1791: DL, Apr 1
I sit on my sunkie (song), 1791: CG, May 18
I sup with Gobble (song), 1795: CG, Nov 16
I tell thee, Charmion (song), 1695: LIF, Apr 30
I that once was a Ploughman a Sailor am now (song), 1795: DL, Jun 2
I was called knowing Joey (song), 1795: CG, May 25; 1796: CG, Apr 5; 1797: CG, May 9; 1799: CG, Apr 26
I went to Sea (song), 1799: CG, Mar 16, Dec 9
I whistle and drive my team (song), 1792: CG, May 28
I will give thanks unto thee (song), 1798: CG, Feb 28
Ibbeston (ticket holder), 1748: DL, Sep 27
Ibbings, Mrs. See Evans, Susannah.
Ibbott, Miss (actor), 1760: CG, Oct 22, 25
Ibrahim, The Illustrious Bassa. See Settle, Elkanah.
Ibrahim, the Thirteenth Emperour of the Turks. See Pix, Mary.
Idalide. See Sarti, Giuseppe.
Idle Nymph (song), 1780: CG, Apr 10
If all that I love is her Face (song), 1741: DL, Nov 24
If Celia you had youth and all (song), 1696: DL, Nov 0
If e'er the Cruel Tyrant Love (song), 1762: CG, Apr 3, DL, May 13, 18; 1782: CG, Feb 26
If God be for us (song), 1793: KING/HAY, Feb 20; 1794: DL, Mar 19
If God could lengthen life forever (song), 1750: DL, Apr 26
If I give thee honour due (song), 1793: CG, Mar 20; 1794: CG, Mar 21, DL, Apr 9
If Love be a Fault (song), 1741: DL, May 27, Jun 4
If Love's a Sweet Passion (song), 1751: CG, Apr 24; 1752: CG, Apr 25, May 4, 6; 1754: CG, May 13, 20; 1766: KING'S, Sep 13
If mortals laugh and sing (song), 1696: DG, Oct 0
If thou wilt give me back my love (song), 1688: DG, Apr 0
If Tis Joy to Wound a Lover (song), 1733: DL/HAY, Oct 13

If Wine and Music have the Power (song), 1711: YB, Jul 16
If you travel the wide world all over (song), 1792: CG, Apr 21
If you will love me (song), 1694: DG, May 0
Ifigenia in Aulide. See Guglielmi, Pietro; Bertoni, Fernando Giuseppe;
    Cherubini, Maria Lorenzo.
Ifigenia in Tauride. See Gluck, Christoph Willibald von.
Ignoramus, The. See Ruggle, George.
Iliff (Ilett), Edward Henry (actor, playwright), 1788: HAY, Jul 2, Aug 5, 15,
    18, 25, Sep 6, 15; 1789: HAY, May 18, 20, 25, 29, Jun 1, 3, 15, 17, 22, 26,
    30, Jul 9, 11, 30, 31, Aug 11, 25, Sep 2, 9, 12, 14, 15; 1790: HAY, Jun 14,
    15, 17, 22, Jul 5, 7, 28, Aug 4, 11, 13, 16; 1791: HAY, Jun 8, 13, 16, 18,
    20, Jul 1, 7, 8, 15, 30, Aug 18, 31; 1798: DL, Jun 6
--Ugly Club, The (burlesque), 1798: DL, Jun 6
Iliff, Edward Henry and Maria (actor), 1789: HAY, Jul 31; 1790: HAY, Aug 4;
    1791: HAY, Aug 12
Iliff, Maria, Mrs Edward Henry (actor, singer), 1789: HAY, May 18, Jun 5, 10,
    12, Jul 31, Aug 11; 1790: HAY, Jun 15, 29, Jul 16, Aug 4, 20; 1791: HAY, Jun
    8, 23, Jul 30, Aug 12; 1794: DL, Dec 20; 1795: DL, Jan 19, Feb 6; 1798: CG,
    Feb 12, Mar 31, Apr 9, 14, 18, 19, Sep 17, 26, Oct 8, Nov 6, 12, Dec 11, 15,
    26; 1799: CG, Mar 2, 5, 9, Apr 2, 9, 13, 23, May 28, Sep 30, Oct 7, 21, 24,
    Nov 15, 18, Dec 23; 1800: CG, Jan 16, Feb 7, 10, Mar 25, May 1, 17, Jun 2
I'll bless my King and cheerly sing (song), 1794: CG, May 9
I'll hurry, hurry, hurry, hurry thee (song), 1698: NONE, Sep 0
I'll mount to yon blue coelum (song), 1688: DG, Apr 0
I'll never love thee more (song), 1660: DH, Mar 28
I'll proclaim the wondrous story (song), 1790: DL, Mar 17; 1791: DL, Apr 1;
    1792: KING'S, Mar 14; 1794: DL, Mar 21
I'll sail upon the Dog-star (song), 1688: DG, Apr 0
I'll Tell You What. See Inchbald, Elizabeth.
I'll to the well trod stage anon (song), 1791: CG, Mar 18; 1792: CG, Feb 24,
    Mar 21
Illingham (Hillingsworth), Miss (dancer), 1797: DL, Nov 8; 1798: DL, Jan 16,
    Feb 20, May 16; 1799: DL, Jan 19, Mar 2
Illingworth, Mrs (singer), 1799: DL, May 24, 29
Illumination; or, The Glaziers Conspiracy. See Pilon, Frederick.
I'm jolly Dick the Lamplighter (song), 1790: CG, Nov 23; 1791: CG, Sep 19;
    1793: CG, May 21; 1794: CG, Apr 12, Oct 29; 1795: CG, Oct 7, Nov 4; 1797: CG,
    Oct 2; 1799: CG, Mar 16, 25; see also Lamplighter, The
Imaginary Cuckolds, The. See Moliere.
Imer, Sga (singer), 1746: KING'S, Jan 7, 28, Mar 25, May 13
Imitation of a Country Farmer's Daughter (dance), 1705: LIF/QUEN, Sep 28
Imitation of Birds and Beasts (song), 1724: RI, Jul 11
Imitation of Mademoiselle and her Dancing Dog (dance), 1707: DL, Oct 31
Imitation of the Tattoo (music), 1720: DL, May 20
Imitation; or, The Female Fortune-Hunters. See Waldron, Francis Godolphin.
Imitations (entertainment), 1703: DL, Jun 18, 19; 1710: DL, May 26; 1718: LIF,
    Dec 26; 1768: HAY, Oct 7; 1770: HAY, Sep 27; 1771: DL, May 4; 1772: DL, May
    2, CG, 15, HAY, Aug 10, 24, Sep 17, 18; 1773: MARLY, Jul 29, HAY, Aug 11, Sep
    3, 17, 18; 1774: HAY, Jan 24, CG, Mar 26, DL, Apr 27, May 5, 9, 10, 19, HAY,
    Jun 10, Aug 29, Sep 6, 19, 30, CG, Dec 1; 1775: DL, Apr 22, HAY, Aug 28, Sep
    4, 7, 16, 18, 19, 21, Oct 30; 1776: DL, Apr 12, HAY, Aug 27, Sep 18, 23, CHR,
    23, 30, Oct 2, 4, 14, 16, 18; 1777: HAY, Feb 11, CG, Apr 14, HAY, Sep 17, Oct
    9; 1778: HAY, Jan 26, CG, May 22, HAY, Dec 28; 1779: CG, Apr 24, DL, May 7,
    HAY, Dec 20; 1780: HAY, Jan 3, Mar 28, DL, Apr 21, HAY, Aug 2, 17, 31; 1781:
    HAY, Aug 21, 29; 1782: HAY, Jan 14, DL, Apr 17, CG, 17, HAY, Aug 9, 27, CG,
    Nov 6; 1783: DL, Apr 25, HAY, Aug 20, 27, CG, Dec 6; 1784: HAY, Mar 22, DL,
    Apr 28, HAY, Jul 30, Aug 20, 26, Sep 17, Dec 13; 1785: HAY, Jan 24, 31, Feb
    7, 12, 14, 21, 24, 28, Mar 7, 10, CG, 12, HAY, 14, CG, 19, HAY, Apr 11, 15,
    18, DL, 18, HAY, 26, 29, CG, May 7, HAMM, Jul 2, 4, 22, 25, HAY, 26; 1786:
    HAY, Mar 6, CG, May 24, HAY, Jul 25, Aug 22; 1787: HAY, Jan 8, Mar 12, 26,
    DL, Apr 9, 25, HAY, Aug 21; 1788: CG, Apr 25, HAY, 29, CG, May 14; 1789: CG,
    May 15, 21, 23, HAY, 29, Jul 31, Aug 12, 25; 1790: CG, Apr 29, HAY, Aug 4,
    18; 1791: CG, Apr 28, May 10, Jun 15, HAY, Aug 27; 1792: CG, Apr 28, Jun 2;
    1794: HAY, Jan 14; 1795: CG, May 6, DL, Jun 3, HAY, 9, CG, 16; 1796: DL, Apr
    13, CG, May 20, DL, 21, 27, CG, Jun 2, HAY, Jul 7, Aug 23, 30, Sep 17; 1797:
    CG, May 22, 30, DL, Jun 9, 12, HAY, Aug 3, 8, 14, 22; 1798: CG, Apr 9, May
    25, DL, Jun 12, HAY, Aug 14, Dec 17; 1799: HAY, Feb 25, Apr 17, CG, Jun 1, 7,
    12, HAY, Sep 16; 1800: CG, May 15, DL, 30, CG, Jun 5, 12, 13, DL, 18, HAY,
    Sep 16
Imitative Song (song), 1785: DL, Apr 18, May 5, 6, 16, HAY, Aug 19; 1786: DL,
    Apr 4
Immortal Lord of Earth and Skies (song), 1789: CG, Apr 3; 1790: CG, Feb 26;

1800: CG, Feb 28
Immyns (singer), 1740: LIF, Mar 26
Impartial (author), 1768: KING'S, Nov 8
Impartial Examen of the Present Contests, An (pamphlet), 1744: DL, Nov 19
Imperial Captives, The. See Mottley, John.
Imperial Tragedy, The. See Killigrew, William.
Impertinent Lovers, The. See Hawling, Francis.
Imposters, The; or, A Cure for Credulity. See Reed, Joseph.
Impostor, The. See Shirley, James.
Impostor, The; or, The Biter Bit; With the Comical Humours of Vizard The Biter
    (farce, anon), 1734: BFHBH, Aug 24
Impostors, The. See Cumberland, Richard.
Imposture Defeated. See Powell, George.
Impresario, The. See Sani, Domenico.
Imprisonment of Harlequin, The (pantomime, anon), 1740: GF, Dec 15, 16, 17, 18,
    19, 20, 22, 26, 27, 29, 30, 31; 1741: GF, Jan 1, 2, 3, 5, 6, 7, 8, 9, 10, 12,
    13, 14, 17, 19, 21, 23, 24, 26, 31, Feb 3, 7, 24, Oct 9, 12, 13, 14, 15, 16,
    23, 24, 26, 27, 29, 30, 31, Nov 5, Dec 11, 16, 17, 26; 1742: GF, Mar 27, 30,
    Apr 3, 5, 10, 21, 28, May 7, LIF, Dec 27, 28, 30; 1743: LIF, Jan 3, 5, Feb
    10, 14, 15, 19, 21; 1746: SFW, Sep 8; 1750: SFP, Sep 7, 8, 10/12, 13; 1752:
    SFP, Sep 21, 22
Impromptu Faragolio, An (entertainment), 1757: HAY, Sep 13, 14, 16, 23, 28, Oct
    3, 5, 12
Impromptu Revel Masque. See The Festival.
In all our Cynthia's shining sphere (song), 1697: DG, Jun 0
In and Out Loobies round about (song), 1745: GF, Feb 4
In Gieste (song), 1795: KING'S, Feb 27
In infancy our hopes and fears (song), 1762: CG, Apr 3
In love should there meet a fond pair (song), 1771: MARLY, Aug 15; 1778: HAY,
    Aug 25
In Merry Sherwood (song), 1795: CG, Dec 21
In my Father's Mud Cabin (song), 1796: HAY, Sep 1; 1797: CG, May 20; 1799: CG,
    Apr 30
In Phyllis all vile jests are met (song), 1682: DG, Apr 0
In praise of a Country Life (song), 1722: SF, Sep 5
In Praise of Ancient Britons (song), 1724: BPT, Feb 21
In praise of Barreled October (song), 1754: HAY/SFB, Oct 1
In praise of English Plumb Pudding (song), 1735: LIF, Sep 2; 1736: HAY, Feb 16
In praise of Fishing (song), 1724: LIF, Jul 31; 1725: LIF, Mar 29, May 21
In praise of Love and Wine (song), 1723: LIF, Nov 2; 1724: LIF, Jan 3, Apr 23,
    30, May 4, 19, Oct 9; 1725: LIF, Mar 11, Apr 19, 23, Oct 13; 1726: LIF, Apr
    13; 1727: LIF, Oct 26
In praise of Tea and Bread and Butter (song), 1733: BFAP, Aug 23
In praise of the Duke of Cumberland (song), 1745: SMMF, Jul 11; 1746: DL, Mar
    22, BFWF, Aug 25, SFW, Sep 8, SFY, 8
In praise of the Tars who have leathered (song), 1799: CG, Oct 7
In praise of their Wives (song), 1746: SOU, Oct 27
In search of a Pirate (song), 1798: CG, Oct 15
In storms when clouds (song), 1793: CG, May 10
In sweetest harmony (song), 1786: DL, Mar 10, 29; 1787: DL, Feb 23; 1789: DL,
    Mar 18; 1790: CG, Feb 24, DL, 26, Mar 26; 1791: DL, Mar 23, CG, 23; 1792:
    KING'S, Feb 24, CG, Mar 2; 1793: KING/HAY, Feb 22; 1794: CG, Mar 21, DL, Apr
    10, CG, 11; 1795: CG, Mar 25; 1797: CG, Mar 10; 1798: CG, Mar 9; 1799: CG,
    Feb 15, Mar 15; 1800: CG, Feb 28
In the day of Thy Power (song), 1789: DL, Mar 25
In the days of Herod (song), 1794: DL, Apr 10
In the dead of the night (song), 1794: DL, Nov 1; 1795: DL, May 4; 1797: DL,
    May 29; 1799: DL, Apr 24, CG, May 3
In the downhill of life (song), 1792: CG, May 15
In the golden barge we ride (song), 1780: HAY, Jun 15
In the Pleasant Month of May (song), 1728: LIF, Apr 23, 24, May 8, 29, Jun 25
In the Shady Blest Retreat (song), 1770: CG, May 1
In the spring when the meadows (song), 1798: CG, Apr 9
In these delightful groves (song), 1691: NONE, Sep 0
In vain against Love I strove (song), 1692: DL, Nov 8
In vain do idle vi'lets blow (song), 1787: HAY, Aug 10
In vows of everlasting truth (song), 1797: DL, Feb 11
Inauguration Speech (entertainment), 1751: HAY, Dec 27; 1752: CT/HAY, Jan 7
Incantation (song), 1698: DL/ORDG, Nov 0; 1752: DL, Mar 21, Apr 11
Ince (beneficiary), 1797: CG, Jun 6; 1798: CG, May 19; 1799: CG, May 29
Inchanted Forest, The. See Geminiani, Francesco.
Inchanted Island, The; or, Harlequin Fortune-Teller (pantomime), 1755: BF, Sep

443

3, 4, 5, 6

Inchbald, Elizabeth, Mrs Joseph (actor, playwright), 1780: CG, Oct 3, 6, 9, 11,
13, 18, 24, 30, Nov 4, 8, 13, 14, Dec 12; 1781: CG, Jan 4, 18, Feb 24, Apr 2,
18, 28, Sep 19, Oct 3, 13, 16, 23, Nov 5, 9, 28, Dec 11, 18, 31; 1782: CG,
Jan 3, 5, 7, 8, Mar 19, Apr 17, 23, HAY, Jun 3, 20, Jul 16, Aug 26; 1783:
HAY, Jun 13, 20, Jul 5, Aug 19, 26, Sep 12, CG, Oct 3, 9, 14, 15, Nov 10,
19; 1784: CG, Jan 3, 7, 12, 16, Feb 18, Mar 6, May 8, 17, DL, 26, HAY, 29,
31, Jul 6, Aug 24, 26, CG, Sep 17, 21, 22, 24, 28, 29, Oct 27, Nov 4, 10, 11,
13, 30, Dec 1; 1785: CG, Jan 8, 21, Feb 4, 7, 15, DL, 21, CG, Mar 5, 7, Apr
8, 11, 12, May 7, 18, HAY, 28, Jun 2, 4, 7, 16, Jul 23, 26, Aug 4, 13, 23,
Sep 2, 7, CG, 28, 30, Oct 12, 19, 22, 27, Nov 2, 7, 9, 23, Dec 7, 8, 10, DL,
19, CG, 26, 30; 1786: CG, Jan 7, Feb 7, Mar 6, 11, Apr 18, 27, May 3, 5, 13,
20, 26, HAY, Jun 16, 20, 22, 23, Jul 8, 24, DL, Sep 16, CG, Oct 9, 12; 1787:
CG, Jan 8, 31, Feb 9, 10, Mar 15, 26, Apr 11, 17, May 22, 23, Jun 2, HAY, 20,
22, Jul 27, CG, Oct 3, 17, 22, 31, Nov 5, 7, 19, Dec 15; 1788: CG, Jan 4, 10,
29, Feb 9, Mar 31, Apr 5, 29, HAY, Jun 19, Jul 2, 3, Aug 25, 27, CG, Oct 8,
10, 18, Nov 28; 1789: CG, Jan 2, 8, 15, 20, Feb 11, 19, 21, 23, Mar 3, Apr
20, 28, May 14, HAY, Jul 6, 15, Sep 8; 1791: DL, May 11, HAY, Jul 9; 1792:
CG, Apr 10, HAY, Jun 30, Aug 23; 1793: CG, Jan 29, Mar 7; 1794: DL, Nov 1;
1797: CG, Mar 4, Nov 13; 1798: CG, Oct 11, 17; 1799: CG, Nov 30; 1800: CG,
Apr 23
--All on a Summer's Day, 1787: CG, Dec 15
--Animal Magnetism, 1788: CG, Apr 24, 29, May 1, 6, 9, 13, 20, 22, 26, Jun 5,
6, 9, Sep 15, 26, Oct 16, 22, 25, 31, Nov 5, 17, 24, 27, Dec 5; 1789: CG, Jan
17, Feb 7, Mar 3, Jun 17, Sep 16, 23, Oct 20, Nov 14; 1790: CG, Mar 6, Jun
11, Oct 19; 1791: CG, Dec 13; 1792: CG, Nov 24; 1794: CG, Mar 18, Jun 14;
1797: CG, May 31
--Appearance is against Them (farce), 1785: CG, Oct 22, 24, 26, 27, 28, 29, Nov
10, 12, 15, 16, 18, Dec 8, 10
--Child of Nature, The, 1788: CG, Nov 28, 29, Dec 2, 4, 6, 8, 10, 11, 12, 16,
17, 18, 23; 1789: CG, Jan 3, 14, 22, 27, Feb 2, 9, 18, 26, Mar 9, 17, Apr 23,
May 13, Jun 3, 12, Oct 6; 1790: CG, Jan 28, Apr 27, May 17, HAY, Aug 11, CG,
Dec 18; 1791: CG, Jan 7; 1792: CG, Apr 18; 1794: CG, Oct 30; 1795: CG, Mar
14, DL, Apr 16, May 4, 19, 21, 27, Jun 2, WLWS, 19, DL, Nov 17, Dec 1, 8, 15,
22, 29; 1796: DL, Feb 11, 20, 25, Mar 10, 14, Sep 20, Dec 1; 1797: DL, May
15, Jun 6; 1798: DL, Jun 8, CG, 11; 1799: DL, Jan 31, Feb 19, May 2; 1800:
DL, Apr 1, CG, 23, May 13, 23, Jun 12, DL, 12, 18
--Cross Partners, 1792: HAY, Aug 21, 23, 24, 25, 27, 29, Sep 1, 4, 6, 7, 8
--Every One has His Fault, 1793: CG, Jan 29, 31, Feb 1, 2, 5, 6, 7, 8, 9, 12,
14, 16, 19, 21, 23, 25, 26, 28, Mar 2, 5, 7, 9, 11, 14, 16, 19, 21, Apr 3, 9,
13, 16, May 27, Jun 11, Oct 1, Nov 7; 1794: CG, Apr 25; 1795: CG, May 13;
1796: CG, Apr 20, May 27; 1797: CG, May 17; 1798: CG, May 1, 22; 1799: CG,
May 24, Oct 16, HAY, 21; 1800: CG, Jan 10, Jun 3
--Hue and Cry, The (farce), 1791: DL, May 11; 1797: CG, Nov 13
--I'll Tell You What, 1785: HAY, Jul 30, Aug 4, 6, 8, 10, 12, 13, 15, 17, 18,
20, 22, 24, 29, 30, Sep 3, 6, 7, 8, 10, 13, 15; 1786: CG, May 20, HAY, Jun
13, 17, 24, 27, Jul 1, 11, 25, Aug 2, 11, Sep 4; 1787: HAY, Jun 11, 19, Aug
16; 1788: HAY, Jun 17, 24, Jul 29, 31, Sep 6; 1790: HAY, Aug 16, Sep 11;
1791: DL, May 11, HAY, Jun 13; 1792: HAY, Jul 4, 9, 14; 1794: HAY, Jul 10,
Aug 5
--Lover's Vows, 1798: CG, Oct 11, 12, 17, 18, 19, 22, 24, 25, 26, 29, 30, 31,
Nov 1, 2, 5, 6, 8, 9, 10, 17, 20, 22, 24, 27, 29, Dec 1, 5, 7, 18, 22; 1799:
CG, Jan 2, 8, 11, 24, 29, Feb 7, 14, 18, Mar 2, 9, 30, Apr 12, May 30, Jun
12, Oct 10, 26, Dec 19, 27; 1800: CG, Apr 19, Jun 5
--Married Man, The, 1789: HAY, Jul 15, 17, 18, 21, 24, 28, Aug 1, Sep 4; 1790:
HAY, Jun 14
--Midnight Hour, The, 1787: CG, May 22, 24, 29, Jun 1, 6, 8, 9, 12, 13, 15, Oct
11, 20, 24, 27, 30, Nov 1, 3, 6, 10, 13, 17, 21, 24, 27, 28, Dec 1, 4, 6, 8,
11, 13, 19, 22; 1788: CG, Jan 8, 19, 23, 26, Feb 2, 26, Mar 4, 15, Apr 2, 17,
22, Jun 6, 9, Oct 7, 21, Nov 17, 25, Dec 11; 1789: CG, Jan 13, Feb 23, Mar
26, May 27, Jun 3, 11, 17, Oct 24, Dec 19; 1790: CG, Jan 12, Mar 2, 20, Apr
17, May 19, Dec 14, 18; 1791: CG, Mar 2, May 31, Nov 12, 19, Dec 20; 1792:
CG, Feb 7, May 23, Oct 19, Dec 5; 1793: CG, Oct 22, 26, Nov 2, Dec 11; 1794:
CG, Mar 3, May 31; 1795: CG, Feb 4, 7, Oct 5; 1796: CG, Sep 14, Dec 13; 1797:
CG, Mar 9, May 30; 1799: CG, May 31
--Mogul Tale, A; or, The Descent of the Balloon (farce), 1784: HAY, Jul 6, 7,
9, 13, 16, 20, 21, 23, Aug 4, 14, 16; 1785: HAY, May 28, 31, Jun 6, Jul 2,
16, Sep 7, 10, 13; 1786: HAY, Jul 8, 14, 15, 20, Aug 15; 1787: HAY, Jun 20,
Jul 5, 27, Aug 8, 27, Sep 3; 1788: HAY, Jul 3, Aug 1, Sep 1, 8, 12, 15; 1789:
HAY, Jun 8, Jul 6, Sep 8; 1790: HAY, Jun 25, Jul 3, 19; 1791: HAY, Jun 14,
17, Jul 12; 1792: HAY, Sep 5, 8, 15; 1793: HAY, Jun 22, Jul 8, 17, 26, Aug
29, Sep 7; 1794: HAY, Jul 11, 18, 19, Aug 2; 1796: HAY, Aug 23, 26, Sep 1, 8,

14; <u>1797</u>: HAY, Jun 12, 16, Aug 30; <u>1798</u>: HAY, Jun 18, Jul 30, Aug 15; <u>1799</u>:
  HAY, Jun 17, Jul 10, Sep 11; <u>1800</u>: HAY, Sep 10, 13
--Next Door Neighbors, <u>1791</u>: HAY, Jul 9, 11, 12, 14, 18, 20, 23, 27, 28, 29,
  Aug 13, 30; <u>1792</u>: HAY, Jul 16, Aug 18
--Simple Story, A, <u>1791</u>: DL, May 11
--Such Things Are, <u>1786</u>: CG, Dec 20; <u>1787</u>: CG, Feb 10, 13, 14, 15, 16, 19, 22,
  24, 27, Mar 1, 3, 5, 8, 10, 12, 19, 22, 29, Apr 9, 19, May 2, 8, Jun 7, Oct
  5, Nov 15, 23; <u>1788</u>: CG, Jan 3, May 7; <u>1789</u>: CG, May 26; <u>1790</u>: CG, May 18;
  <u>1791</u>: DL, May 11; <u>1792</u>: CG, Apr 10; <u>1793</u>: CG, Apr 24; <u>1796</u>: CG, May 28; <u>1798</u>:
  CG, May 28
--Wedding Day, The (farce), <u>1794</u>: DL, Oct 16, 18, 21, 23, 25, 27, 29, 31, Nov
  1, 3, 4, 5, 7, 8, 11, 14, 15, 17, 18, 22, 25, 26, Dec 2, 15, 20; <u>1795</u>: DL,
  Jan 9, Apr 14, 25, May 4, 15, Sep 19, Nov 10, Dec 10; <u>1796</u>: DL, Feb 20, Apr
  13, 26, 29, May 10, 16, Oct 29, Nov 2, Dec 9; <u>1797</u>: DL, May 1, 9, 29, Nov 17;
  <u>1798</u>: DL, Apr 30, Jun 12; <u>1799</u>: DL, Jan 31, Apr 24, Jun 5; <u>1800</u>: DL, Mar 13,
  20, Apr 24, May 6
--Widow's Vow, The (farce), <u>1786</u>: HAY, Jun 20, 21, 22, 23, 26, 27, 30, Jul 7,
  12, 15, Aug 8, 19, Sep 1; <u>1787</u>: HAY, Jul 3, 6, Aug 2, 15, 18, 24, Sep 1, 11
--Wise Man of the East, The, <u>1799</u>: CG, Nov 30, Dec 2, 3, 4, 5, 6, 7, 10, 12,
  14, 18, 28; <u>1800</u>: CG, Jan 2, 15
--Wives as they Were, and Maids as they Are, <u>1797</u>: CG, Mar 4, 6, 7, 9, 11, 13,
  14, 16, 18, 21, 23, 25, 28, 30, Apr 1, 4, 6, 18, 20, 22, May 8, 12, 18, 25,
  Nov 4, 16; <u>1798</u>: CG, Apr 11; <u>1800</u>: CG, May 28
--Young Men and Old Women, <u>1792</u>: HAY, Jun 30, Jul 2, 4, 10, 12, 17
Inchbald, George (actor), <u>1786</u>: CG, Sep 25, Oct 4, 16, 18
Inchbald, Joseph (actor), <u>1770</u>: DL, Oct 8, 11, 20; <u>1771</u>: DL, Jan 12, 17, Feb
  21, Apr 9, May 10, Oct 10, 12, 28, CG, Nov 4, DL, 15, Dec 4; <u>1772</u>: DL, Feb
  26, 28, Mar 28, Apr 4, 22, May 5, 20, Oct 1
Incledon, Charles Benjamin (actor, singer), <u>1790</u>: CG, Sep 17, Oct 1, 5, 6, 12,
  15, 19, 23, Nov 23, 26, Dec 1, 20; <u>1791</u>: CG, Jan 12, Feb 12, Mar 11, 18, 23,
  25, 30, Apr 6, 13, 15, 28, 30, May 2, 3, 5, 6, 10, 16, 17, 18, 19, 20, 24,
  27, 28, 31, Jun 1, 3, 4, 6, 8, 10, 13, Sep 19, 20, 21, 23, 26, 30, Oct 3, 10,
  19, 20, Nov 1, 15, 19, 21, 25, Dec 3, 10, 15; <u>1792</u>: CG, Feb 2, KING'S, 24,
  CG, 25, 28, KING'S, 29, Mar 14, 23, 28, 30, CG, Apr 12, 17, 18, 25, May 5, 9,
  10, 11, 15, 18, 19, 24, 28, Sep 19, 24, Oct 3, 8, 12, HAY, 15, CG, 19, 27,
  29, Nov 3, Dec 20, 26; <u>1793</u>: CG, Jan 9, 25, Feb 15, 20, 22, 25, Mar 1, 6, 8,
  13, 15, 20, 22, 23, Apr 3, 4, 8, 9, 10, 11, 24, 25, May 1, 3, 10, 11, 15, 16,
  21, 23, 27, Jun 6, 10, 12, Sep 16, 18, 23, 25, 30, Oct 1, 2, 7, 10, 12, 15,
  24, 29, Nov 1, 2, 5, 7, 18, 22, 28, 30, Dec 4, 6, 7, 9; <u>1794</u>: CG, Jan 21, 24,
  Feb 10, 22, Mar 7, 14, 21, Apr 7, 10, 12, 23, 25, 29, May 2, 6, 7, 9, 10, 13,
  14, 21, 22, 23, 24, 26, 28, Jun 2, 3, 5, 9, 11, Sep 15, 17, 19, 22, 24, 26,
  Oct 1, 3, 20, 21, 23, 29, 30, Nov 7, 11, 15, 17; <u>1795</u>: CG, Jan 29, 31, Mar
  16, Apr 6, 8, 24, 28, May 1, 6, 7, 8, 13, 14, 16, 19, 21, 25, 27, 29, Jun 1,
  2, 5, 6, 8, 10, 12, 16, Sep 14, 16, 18, 21, 23, 28, Oct 2, 5, 7, 8, 14, 15,
  22, 24, Nov 4, 6, 14, 27, Dec 9, 21, 28; <u>1796</u>: CG, Jan 13, Feb 2, Mar 14, Apr
  1, 5, 9, 12, 15, 19, 26, 29, DL, 30, CG, 30, May 3, 6, 10, 12, 16, 17, 20,
  23, 24, 26, 27, 28, Jun 1, 2, Sep 14, 16, 17, 19, 21, 23, 26, 30, Oct 5, 6,
  7, 17, 20, 21, Nov 5, 10, 12, 19, 24, Dec 15, 19, 22, 27, 28, 29; <u>1797</u>: CG,
  Jan 3, 10, 25, Feb 18, Apr 25, 29, May 2, 9, 11, 16, 17, 18, 19, 20, 22, 23,
  24, 30, 31, Jun 1, 5, DL, 6, CG, 8, 10, 13, Sep 20, 25, 27, 29, Oct 2, 4, 11,
  16, 18, 20, 25, 30, 31, Nov 1, 2, 10, 13, 15, 21, Dec 16, 18, 19; <u>1798</u>: CG,
  Jan 1, Feb 9, 12, 14, 23, Mar 2, 9, 14, 15, 28, 30, 31, Apr 14, 16, 17, 21,
  24, 27, 28, May 1, 5, 7, 8, 9, 10, 12, 14, 15, 16, 22, 23, 24, 25, 28, Jun 1,
  2, 4, 6, 7, Oct 5, 8, 11, 25, 31, Nov 1, 7, 12, 17, Dec 11, 15, 21, 26; <u>1799</u>:
  CG, Jan 5, 14, 17, 22, 26, Feb 8, 13, 15, 20, Mar 1, 5, 6, 13, 15, 16, Apr 2,
  6, 9, 12, 16, 18, 19, 23, 26, 30, May 3, 4, 7, 13, 14, 15, 18, 24, 25, 28,
  31, Jun 1, 3, 5, 6, 7, Sep 16, 18, 20, 25, 27, 30, Oct 2, 7, 16, 21, 24, 28,
  Nov 7, 14, Dec 2, 4, 7, 9, 10; <u>1800</u>: CG, Jan 11, 16, 25, 27, 28, Feb 4, 19,
  28, Mar 1, 5, 14, 17, 19, 21, 25, Apr 5, 15, 19, 22, 23, 26, 29, May 1,
  2, 6, 7, 10, 13, 15, 17, 20, 22, 24, 27, 29, 30, Jun 2, 5, 6, 12
Inconstant, The. See Farquhar, George.
Incostanza Deluza, L' (song), <u>1745</u>: HAY, Feb 9, 16, 23, Mar 2, 9, 16, 23, 30,
  Apr 1, 6, 20; <u>1746</u>: DL, Apr 12
Independent Patriot, The. See Lynch, Francis.
India, <u>1782</u>: DL, May 16; <u>1784</u>: HAY, Sep 17; <u>1790</u>: CG, Apr 7
Indian (spectator), <u>1742</u>: DL, Jan 30
Indian Ballet (dance), <u>1779</u>: KING'S, Nov 27
Indian children, <u>1695</u>: DG, Apr 0
Indian Dance (dance), <u>1717</u>: LIF, Dec 28; <u>1718</u>: LIF, Jan 1, 2, 13, Mar 18; <u>1729</u>:
  GF, Dec 12; <u>1734</u>: GF, May 20; <u>1735</u>: GF, Mar 20; <u>1741</u>: DL, Apr 9, May 5; <u>1777</u>:
  HAY, Jun 19; <u>1782</u>: HAY, Jun 11
Indian Dance, Grand (dance), <u>1718</u>: LIF, Jan 10, Feb 1, May 3

Indian Emperor, The. See Dryden, John.
Indian Empress, The; or, The Conquest of Peru (play, anon), 1731: HAY, Feb 13,
    17, 18
Indian King, American, 1710: QUEEN'S, Apr 24, 25, DL, 25, QUEEN'S, 27, 28, DL,
    28, YB, May 1; 1720: YB, Apr 1; 1730: LIF, Sep 28, Oct 1; 1734: LIF, Aug 20,
    CG/LIF, Sep 20; 1766: HAY, Sep 2; see also American Princes
Indian Merchant, The; or, The Happy Pair (play, anon), 1742: BFPY, Aug 25, SF,
    Sep 8
Indian Peasants (dance), 1756: DL, May 15, 19, 21, 24; 1757: DL, Jan 27, Feb
    10, 21
Indian Queen (public house), 1747: CG, May 11
Indian Queen, The. See Dryden, John.
Indian Song (song), 1790: CG, Nov 23; 1791: CG, Sep 19; 1794: CG, Apr 12; see
    also Dear Yanco say, and true he say
Indian Tambour (dance), 1704: DL, Mar 30
Indian Trumpet Song (song), 1704: LIF, Jun 8
Indian War Dance, Grand (dance), 1790: HAY, Jul 16, 23
Indian War Song (song), 1791: CG, Jun 6, 7, 8
Indian's Ransom (dance), 1787: CG, Feb 17, Apr 11, May 12
Indianer in England, Die. See Kotzebue, August Friedrich Ferdinand von.
Indians, American, 1734: CG/LIF, Sep 23, DL, Oct 4, HAY, 7, LIF, 12; 1742: DL,
    May 6; 1791: DLKING'S, Dec 31
Indiscreet Lover, The. See Portal, Abraham.
Indiscretion. See Hoare, Prince.
Industrious Farmer (dance), 1763: KING'S, Apr 14, 28
Industrious Lovers, The; or, The Yorkshireman Bit (play), 1749: BF/SFP, Sep 7,
    8, 9, 11, 12
Ines de Castro. See Bianchi Jr, Francesco.
Ines de Castro; or, Royal Justice. See LaMotte, Houdart de.
Infelice van mi lagno (song), 1750: KING'S, Apr 10; 1751: KING'S, Apr 16
Infernal Spirits' Dance, Grand (dance), 1729: DL, May 28, Oct 30
Infernals, The (dance), 1741: BFH, Aug 22
Inflexible Captive. See More, Hannah.
Ingall (actor), 1784: HAY, Dec 13; 1792: HAY, Oct 15
Ingall, Mrs (actor), 1748: BFLYY, Aug 24, SFLYYW, Sep 7, BHB, Oct 1
Inganno Fortunato, L'; or, The Happy Delusion (pantomime, anon), 1727: KING'S,
    Jan 25
Inglese in Italia, L'. See Anfossi, Pasquale.
Ingrat, L'. See Destouches.
Ingrateful Lover (song), 1691: DL, Dec 0
Ingratitude of a Common-Wealth, The. See Tate, Nahum.
Ingratitudine Punita, La (pastoral opera), 1748: HAY, Jan 12, 26, Feb 2,
    KING'S, Mar 1, Apr 5
Inimitable Dexterity of Hand (entertainment), 1733: MEG, Sep 28
Injured Innocence. See Bellers, Pettiplace.
Injured Love; or, The Lady's Satisfaction (play, anon), 1711: DL, Apr 7, 9, 10,
    13, 14, 16; 1721: LIF, Dec 18, 19, 20, 21, 30; 1722: LIF, Apr 26, Dec 14;
    1723: LIF, Jan 8, May 24
Injured Lovers, The. See Mountfort, William.
Injured Merchant, The; or, The Extravagant Son (play), 1755: SF, Sep 18
Injured Princess, The. See D'Urfey, Thomas.
Injured Virtue. See Griffin, Benjamin.
Injurious charmer of my vanquished heart (song), 1684: ATCOURT, Feb 11
Inkle and Yarico. See Colman the younger, George.
Innamorate Del Cicisbeo, L' (opera), 1767: KING'S, Apr 2
Inner Temple Hall, 1682: IT, Nov 1
Inner Temple, Society of the, 1734: IT, Feb 2
Inner Temple, 1662: MT, Nov 1; 1668: NONE, Feb 0; 1673: IT, Nov 1; 1699: LIF,
    Dec 18; 1734: DL, Sep 21; 1744: IT, Feb 23
Innocent Mistress, The. See Pix, Mary.
Innocent Theft, The. See Kelly, John, Timon in Love.
Innocent Usurper, The. See Banks, John.
Innocent Wife, The. See Ravenscroft, Edward.
Innocente e quell'affetto (song), 1757: KING'S, Mar 24
Inquisitor, The. See Holcroft, Thomas.
Insolvent, The. See Hill, Aaron.
Inspector. See Hill, Dr John.
Institution of the Garter, The. See Garrick, David.
Intennerir mi sento (song), 1754: KING'S, Feb 28
Interlude (entertainment), 1749: KING'S, Feb 28; 1762: DL, Feb 20; 1770: HAY,
    Mar 12; 1772: CG, May 11; 1773: CG, May 8; 1798: CG, Feb 9
Interlude between Plutus and Wit (entertainment), 1777: CG, Apr 28; 1780: CG,

Apr 12, 24; 1784: DL, May 17

Interlude from the Register Office (entertainment), 1776: CG, Apr 27, HAY, Sep 23

Interlude of City Customs, An (interlude), 1703: DL, Jun 30

Intrigants, Les. See Dumaniant.

Intrigues at Versailles, The. See D'Urfey, Thomas.

Intrigues D'Arlequin, Les (pantomime), 1725: HAY, Feb 23; 1726: HAY, Apr 18; 1735: HAY, Mar 13, 14, GF/HAY, Apr 7, HAY, May 28

Intrigues of a Morning, The; or, An Hour in Paris (farce), 1792: CG, Apr 18, May 17

Intriguing Captains, The; or, The Lover's Contrivance (play, anon), 1756: SFB, Sep 20, SF, 22, 23

Intriguing Chambermaid, The. See Fielding, Henry.

Intriguing Footman, The (play, anon), 1792: CG, Apr 21

Intriguing Footman, The; or, Jack Spaniard Bit (play), 1749: BFHG, Aug 23

Intriguing Footman, The; or, The Spaniard Outwitted (farce, anon), 1742: BFG, Aug 25

Intriguing Harlequin, The; or, Any Wife Better Than None (farce, anon), 1734: SFG, Sep 7

Intriguing Lover, The; or, A Tit-Bit for a Nice Palate (play, anon), 1757: SF, Sep 17, 19, 20, 21, 22

Invader of his Country. See Shakespeare, William, Coriolanus.

Invasion, The. See Pilon, Frederick.

Invill, Kiza (dancer, actor), 1772: CG, May 1; 1773: CG, Apr 24, May 26; 1774: CG, May 18, 20; 1775: CG, Mar 20; 1781: CG, Oct 16; 1782: CG, Apr 27; 1784: HAY, Aug 26; 1785: HAY, Aug 31; 1786: CG, Nov 14; 1787: CG, Sep 28; 1788: CG, Jan 21, HAY, Aug 5, 11; 1791: G, Jun 6

Invill, 1788: HAY, Aug 5

--Gnome, The. See Wewitzer, Ralph.

Invisible Mistress, The (farce, anon), 1788: DL, Apr 21

Invocation to Diana, The (song), 1699: DL, Dec 0

Ion (beneficiary), 1720: LIF, May 23

Ipermestra, L'. See Hasse, Johann Adolph; Sarti, Giuseppe.

Iphigenia in Aulide; or, The Sacrifice of Iphigenia (dance), 1793: KING'S, Apr 23, 27, 30, May 4, 7, 11, 14, 17, 21, 25, 28, Jun 11, 15, 18, 22, 25, 29

Iphigenia. See Dennis, John; Porpora, Nicola.

Iphigenia; or, The Victim. See Hull, Thomas.

Iphigenie (play), 1722: HAY, Jan 23

Iphigenie en Aulide. See Racine, Jean.

Iredale (beneficiary), 1789: CG, Jun 16; 1790: CG, Jun 12; 1791: CG, Jun 14; 1792: CG, Jun 1

Ireland (actor), 1741: GF, Apr 22; 1747: GF, Mar 31

Ireland (upholsterer), 1772: DL, Mar 26; 1773: DL, Jun 22; 1774: DL, Jun 2, Oct 20; 1775: DL, Feb 23; 1776: DL, Jun 10

Ireland, John (critic), 1779: CG, May 5

Ireland, Master (actor), 1759: HAY, Apr 18

Ireland, Samuel (engraver), 1796: DL, Apr 2

Ireland, William Henry, 1796: DL, Apr 2

--Vortigern, 1796: DL, Apr 2

Ireland, 1662: LI, Jan 3; 1664: BRIDGES, Sep 14; 1668: LIF, May 11; 1689: DLORDG, Nov 28; 1690: DG, Jun 0; 1698: DL, Jun 2; 1699: DLLIF, Dec 25; 1705: LIF/QUEEN, Oct 17, LIF, 20; 1708: DL/QUEEN, Jun 4; 1712: DL, Apr 12; 1714: DL, Nov 30; 1715: DL, Jan 22, 24, LIF, May 16, 24; 1716: LIF, Oct 6; 1717: LIF, Feb 4, Apr 23; 1718: LIF, Sep 26; 1723: HAY, May 24; 1724: YB, Mar 27, HAY, May 8; 1726: DL, May 7; 1728: DL, Sep 10; 1729: HAY, May 2, Aug 6; 1732: CL, Mar 17, GF, Oct 26; 1741: CG, May 1, DL, Oct 28, KING'S, Nov 21; 1743: DL, Oct 8; 1746: GF, Mar 18; 1747: JS, Feb 3; 1749: HAY, Mar 10, DL, May 16; 1750: DL, Jan 20, Sep 8, 18; 1751: DL, Sep 26, Oct 3, 22; 1752: DL, Sep 23, CG, 25, 29; 1753: CG, Feb 21, DL, Mar 13, Oct 9; 1754: CG, Nov 5; 1756: CG, Mar 23; 1758: DL, Sep 16, 19, Oct 27; 1759: DL, Sep 22, HAY, Oct 3, DL, Nov 5; 1761: BFY, Aug 31, BFG, Sep 1, CG, Oct 3; 1762: CG, Oct 5; 1763: DL, Sep 27; 1765: DL, Jan 1, Oct 15; 1768: DL, May 12, CG, Oct 24; 1770: CG, Sep 24; 1771: DL, Jan 1, Sep 26, CG, Oct 31; 1775: DL, Feb 17, CG, Oct 13; 1780: CG, Feb 22, Mar 14; 1786: CG, Apr 2, HAY, Aug 29; 1792: CG, Apr 21, HAY, Aug 15; 1793: CG, Mar 18; 1794: CG, May 23, HAY, Aug 28; 1796: CG, May 16; 1797: CG, May 20; 1799: HAY, Aug 27

Irena (play, anon), 1663: NONE, Sep 0

Irene. See Johnson, Samuel, Mahomet and Irene.

Irene; or, The Fair Greek. See Goring, Charles.

Irish (boxkeeper), 1792: DLKING'S, Jun 15; 1793: DL, Jun 6; 1795: DL, Jun 6; 1796: DL, Jun 13; 1797: DL, Jun 16; 1798: DL, Jun 14; 1799: CG, Mar 2

Irish Air (song), 1783: CG, Apr 7; 1793: CG, Apr 25; 1797: CG, Nov 24; 1799:

CG, Jun 6
Irish and Scotch Medley Overture (music), 1772: HAY, Mar 16
Irish Ballad (song), 1729: HAY, May 29; 1742: DL, Mar 8, 22; 1784: HAY, Aug 3
Irish Bird Catchers (dance), 1789: DL, May 19, 23, Jun 6, 12; 1790: DL, Jan 23,
    Feb 3, 10, 13, Jun 5
Irish Comic Song (song), 1798: CG, May 9; 1800: CG, May 7
Irish Dance (dance), 1700: LIF, Jul 5; 1703: DL, Feb 3; 1704: LIF, Jun 26;
    1724: LIF, Jun 23, Jul 29; 1725: LIF, Mar 13, Apr 10, 28, May 1, 3, 4, 5, 6,
    10, 12, 17, 19, 21, 24; 1752: SFB, Sep 22; 1777: CG, Apr 25; 1796: CG, Apr 13
Irish Drinking Song (song), 1790: CG, Nov 23; 1791: CG, May 3, 16, Sep 19;
    1792: CG, Apr 18; 1793: CG, Apr 24; 1794: CG, Apr 12; see also Of the
    ancients it's speaking
Irish Evidence, The; or, The Mercenary Whore (play, anon), 1682: BF, Aug 24
Irish Fair (dance), 1772: DL, Oct 23, 24, 26, 27, 28, 31, Nov 2, 5, 14, 21, Dec
    5, 12; 1773: DL, Jan 27, Feb 11, 15, 22, Apr 29, May 22, 26, 27, Sep 18, 21,
    Oct 27, Nov 1, 6, 12, 17, 22, Dec 1, 6, 15, 23; 1774: DL, Jan 8, Feb 3, 26,
    Mar 12, 17, Apr 11, 13, 16, 19, 20, 21, 25, 27, May 4, 12, Sep 17, Oct 13,
    24, Nov 2, 3, 11, 25, 29, Dec 3, 10, 29; 1775: DL, Jan 17, Feb 3, 21, Mar 16,
    21, 28, Apr 21, 26, May 4, Oct 3, 13, 18, Dec 1, 23; 1776: DL, Feb 9, Mar 14,
    Apr 11, 25, May 7, 11, 18, 22, Oct 31, Nov 28, Dec 14, 19; 1777: DL, Mar 10,
    11, Apr 19, 26, May 30; 1778: DL, May 8, 9, Sep 29; 1780: DL, May 4, Sep 30,
    Oct 30, Nov 2, Dec 8; 1781: DL, Mar 19, Apr 16, 27, May 9, 16; 1782: DL, Apr
    6, 20, 24, May 16, 30, 31, Jun 1, Oct 5, 31, Nov 5; 1783: DL, Feb 22; 1784:
    DL, Sep 21; 1786: DL, Apr 28; 1787: DL, May 9, 25, Jun 7, Sep 29, Oct 27;
    1788: DL, Mar 6, May 30, Jun 3; 1789: DL, Apr 15
Irish Fine Lady, The. See Macklin, Charles.
Irish Harp (music), 1712: SH, May 14; 1717: CORH, Apr 26
Irish Haymakers (dance), 1767: DL, Sep 19, Oct 14, 21, Nov 10, Dec 3; 1768: DL,
    Mar 17, Apr 6, Oct 15, 22, 29; 1769: DL, Feb 14, Sep 23; 1799: CG, Jun 1, 6
Irish Hospitality. See Shadwell, Charles.
Irish Humour (dance), 1703: DL, Jun 16
Irish Jig (dance), 1717: LIF, Mar 18; 1777: CG, Apr 25
Irish Landlord and Landlady (dance), 1757: HAY, Oct 3
Irish Legacy, The. See Arnold, Samuel James.
Irish Lilt (dance), 1762: DL, Oct 23, 25, 26, Dec 27; 1763: DL, Jan 13, 18, 27,
    Feb 2, 14, 22, Mar 7, 19, Apr 8, 20, May 7, 9, 11, 14, 16, 28, Sep 22, 27,
    Oct 21, Nov 28, Dec 10, 12, 13, 15; 1764: DL, Jan 12, Mar 26, 27, 29, 31, Apr
    3, 7, 10, 12, 24, 25, 26, May 3, 5, 7, 8, 16, Oct 6, 11, 18, Nov 8, Dec 22,
    26, 29; 1765: DL, Jan 10, Feb 14, Mar 16, 18, 23, Apr 10, 11, 15, May 7, 13,
    17, 20, Oct 1, 4, 7; 1766: DL, Mar 17, Apr 4, 5, 7, 9, 11, 15, 21, 23, 26,
    28, May 3, 6, 9, 12; 1767: DL, Apr 30, May 2, 4, 9, 11, CG, Sep 21, Oct 5, 6,
    13, 15, 28, Nov 12, Dec 3, 15, 28; 1768: CG, Jan 28, Feb 4, 11, Mar 7, 8, 21,
    24, 26, Apr 6, 8, 12, 20, 30, Sep 30, Oct 1, 5, 13; 1769: CG, Jan 19, 25, Feb
    1, Mar 11, 28, Apr 1, 3, 5, 7, 14; 1770: CG, Apr 2, 19, 25, May 11, 23; 1772:
    CG, Oct 28; 1773: CG, Apr 14, 19, 23, May 1, 4, 10, 14, 27, Oct 5, 13, Nov
    10, 17; 1774: CG, Mar 21, Apr 7, Dec 2; 1775: CG, May 6, Jun 1; 1776: CG, May
    20, Nov 9; 1778: CG, Apr 24, 25; 1785: CG, May 24; 1786: CG, May 27; 1787:
    CG, Feb 8; 1788: CG, Mar 15, 28; 1790: CG, Oct 20, Dec 11; 1791: CG, Oct 6,
    Nov 9; 1792: CG, Oct 10; 1793: CG, Sep 27; 1795: CG, May 30
Irish Milkmaids (dance), 1765: DL, Mar 21, 25, May 10; 1766: DL, May 5
Irish Mimic, The. See O'Keeffe, John.
Irish Newsman (song), 1798: CG, Jun 5; 1799: HAY, Sep 16
Irish performers, 1774: CG, Apr 12
Irish Pipes (music), 1794: CG, Feb 6
Irish Rorotorio (song), 1747: DL, Apr 25
Irish Song (song), 1713: SH, Mar 23; 1728: LIF, Apr 26; 1730: LIF, May 23;
    1743: IT, Dec 26; 1746: DL, Jan 2; 1785: HAY, Feb 10; 1793: CG, May 24, Dec
    19; 1794: CG, Jan 1, Apr 7; 1795: CG, May 13, Nov 16; 1796: CG, Apr 15; 1797:
    CG, May 16; 1800: CG, Apr 23, May 10
Irish Tar, The. See Oulton, Walley Chamberlain.
Irish Trot (dance), 1702: DL, Aug 20; 1704: LIF, Jul 24, Aug 9; 1705: LIF, Jan
    25, Oct 12; 1710: GR, Aug 7; 1719: RI, Jun 6; 1720: LIF, Jan 11, DL, Apr 5,
    26, May 17; 1721: LIF, Apr 29; 1723: HAY, Jan 28; 1733: HAY, Mar 19, DL, May
    14, CG, Aug 14, 16, 21; 1734: DL/HAY, Feb 20, Mar 5, DL, Apr 25, DL/HAY, May
    4, LIF, 23, DL, Oct 9; 1735: HAY, Oct 24; 1736: HAY, Jan 19, Feb 2, LIF, Jun
    16; 1737: LIF, Jun 15; 1740: GF, Dec 12; 1746: SOU, Oct 27
Irish tunes, 1745: DL, Jan 17
Irish Turf Cutters (dance), 1759: CG, Oct 15
Irish way of settling a Quarrel (entertainment), 1795: CG, May 6
Irish Wedding (dance), 1775: CG, Dec 12, 13, 14
Irish Whim (song), 1704: LIF, Jun 8
Irish Widow, The. See Garrick, David.

Irishman in London, The. See Sheridan, Thomas.
Irishman in London, The; or, The Happy African. See Macready, William.
Irishman in Spain, The. See Stuart, Charles.
Irishman's Peep at the Continent (song), 1795: CG, May 1, 6, 19, 21, Jun 2, 5
Irishman's Tour through London (entertainment), 1794: CG, Apr 29; 1795: CG, Jun 8
Irishmen, 1767: HAY, Aug 21, CG, Nov 10, 12
Iron Chest, The. See Colman the younger, George.
Iron Mongers, Company of, 1685: CITY, Oct 29
Ironmonger (residence), 1746: DL, Apr 8
Ironmonger Lane, 1751: DL, Mar 7
Ironside and Belchior (bankers), 1748: CG, Mar 31, Apr 11
Irresolu, L'. See Destouches.
Irwich (composer), 1788: CG, Dec 13
Irwin (actor), 1790: HAY, Sep 29
Irwin, Lady A (spectator), 1733: KING'S, Mar 17, 27
Irwin, Mrs (singer), 1700: DL, Feb 19
Is not the King most mighty (song), 1791: DL, Mar 11; 1792: KING'S, Mar 14, 30
Isaac (dancer), 1675: ATCOURT, Feb 15; 1705: YB, Jan 4; 1712: QUEEN'S, Mar 22; 1715: LIF, Mar 15; 1716: LIF, Jan 10
Isaac. See Jomelli, Niccolo.
Isaac's scholar (dancer, singer), 1702: DL, May 2, Dec 29
Isabella. See Garrick, David.
Isabella, Miss. See Young, Isabella.
Island of Slaves, The. See Clive, Catherine.
Island of St Marguerite, The. See St John, John.
Island Princess, The. See Fletcher, John.
Island Queens, The. See Banks, John.
Islanders, The. See Dibdin, Charles.
Isle des Amazones, L' (opera), 1724: HAY, Dec 17
Isle des Esclaves, L'; or, Harlequin in the Island of Slaves (pantomime), 1735: HAY, Feb 21
Isle Desert, L' (dance), 1773: KING'S, Feb 2, 9
Isle Sauvage, L'. See Saint-Foix, Germain Francois Poulain de.
Isleworth, 1774: DL, Jan 21
Islington, Strong Man from (entertainer), 1734: DL/HAY, Mar 2
Islington, 1734: LIF, Sep 6; 1735: CG/LIF, Jan 14, CG, Jun 24; 1743: SW, Apr 11; 1744: DL, May 11
Ismael, Emperour Muley (Moroccan emperor), 1710: QUEEN'S, May 4
Isola D'Amore, L'. See Sacchini, Antonio Maria Gasparo.
Isola del Piacere, L'. See Martin y Soler, Vicente.
Isola Disabitata, L'. See Jomelli, Niccolo.
Israel in Babylon. See Handel, George Frederic.
Israel in Egypt. See Handel, George Frederic.
Israelites, The. See Smollett, Dr Tobias.
Issipile. See Sandoni, Pietro; Cocchi, Gioacchino; Anfossi, Pasquale.
Istowlawleys, King of the (Indian visitor), 1719: LIF, Dec 21; see also American Princes; Indian Kings, American
Isum (beneficiary), 1707: YB, Jan 27
It must be so (song), 1793: CG, Mar 6; 1794: CG, Mar 12; 1795: CG, Mar 13; 1796: CG, Feb 26; 1799: CG, Feb 15
It Should Have Come Sooner (farce, anon), 1723: DL, Jul 30, Aug 2, 9
Italian Air (song), 1757: HAY, Aug 11, 31, Sep 2; 1784: DL, May 20, 21; 1787: DL, Mar 28; 1791: DL, May 26; 1793: KING/HAY, Mar 13, CG, Apr 25; 1794: CG, May 2; 1796: CG, May 10
Italian Air, Mock (song), 1735: DL, Apr 29, May 7, 9, 14, 20; 1760: HAY, Sep 8
Italian Bagpiper (dance), 1754: CG, Nov 26
Italian Bakers (dance), 1766: DL, Oct 11, 13, 15, 21, Nov 3, 6, 10, 14, 25, 27, Dec 23
Italian Burletta Song, Mock (song), 1761: CG, May 4
Italian Cabaret (dance), 1748: DL, Nov 9, 12, 18, 24, Dec 29; 1749: DL, Jan 10
Italian Cantata (song), 1720: LIF, Feb 5, 10
Italian Cantata, Mock (song), 1757: CG, May 6
Italian Cantata, 1711: QUEEN'S, May 12
Italian Canzonetta (song), 1780: KING'S, Apr 13, 18
Italian Catch (song), 1727: KING'S, Apr 6, 14; 1791: KING'S, Jun 2
Italian Chaconne (dance), 1752: DL, Mar 16
Italian children (performers), 1705: QUEEN'S, Apr 14, 24
Italian comedians, 1667: ATCOURT, Nov 15; 1673: NONE, Apr 21; 1675: NONE, Jun 20; 1683: NONE, Apr 0, WINDSOR, Aug 0; 1724: HAY, Dec 17; 1726: HAY, Mar 24, KING'S, Sep 21, 28, Nov 23, 26; 1749: HAY, Nov 7
Italian comedy, 1673: ATCOURT, May 29; 1724: HAY, Dec 17; 1725: HAY, Jan 11,

22; <u>1749</u>: HAY, Nov 14, 20; <u>1753</u>: DL, Oct 9; <u>1761</u>: DL, Jun 18; <u>1782</u>: CG, Oct
3; <u>1785</u>: DL, Dec 26
Italian Comic Song (song), <u>1762</u>: HAY, Apr 22
Italian Concerto (music), <u>1722</u>: DL, Mar 14
Italian Consort (music), <u>1702</u>: YB, Nov 19, Dec 3
Italian Dance (dance), <u>1715</u>: DL, Nov 14; <u>1743</u>: CG, Apr 22
Italian Dialogue (song), <u>1715</u>: LIF, Apr 26; <u>1716</u>: LIF, May 4
Italian Duet (song), <u>1733</u>: DT, May 30; <u>1779</u>: HAY, Mar 3; <u>1784</u>: HAY, Apr 27
Italian Fireworks (entertainment), <u>1747</u>: BFC, Aug 22; <u>1748</u>: NWSM, May 3, 4,
BFH, Aug 24; <u>1754</u>: SFH, Sep 19
Italian Fishermen (dance), <u>1754</u>: DL, Oct 22, Nov 5; <u>1755</u>: DL, Apr 1
Italian Gamesters (dance), <u>1776</u>: CG, Mar 5, 23, May 10
Italian Gardener (dance), <u>1742</u>: DL, Dec 31; <u>1743</u>: DL, Jan 11, 12, 14, 18, 20,
28, Feb 3, 15, Mar 10, 19, 21, 26, Apr 28; <u>1752</u>: DL, Dec 21, 22; <u>1759</u>: DL,
Oct 6, 25, Nov 7; <u>1760</u>: DL, Dec 3, 9, 12; <u>1761</u>: DL, Jan 19, Feb 23, Mar 27,
Apr 20, May 6, Oct 10; <u>1762</u>: DL, May 3; <u>1763</u>: DL, Apr 25, Nov 19, 26, Dec 2,
5, 29; <u>1772</u>: CG, Apr 24; <u>1774</u>: CG, Sep 19; <u>1775</u>: CG, Oct 11, Nov 10; <u>1776</u>:
CG, Jan 10, 11, 17, Feb 20, 24, Mar 2, 4, May 17, 21
Italian Giant. See Giant, Italian.
Italian habits, <u>1754</u>: BFSIY, Sep 3, DL, Nov 4, 7
Italian Harp (music), <u>1717</u>: CORH, Apr 26
Italian Husband, The. See Ravenscroft, Edward.
Italian Interludes (entertainment), <u>1703</u>: YB, Jul 27, 30
Italian Jealousy; or, French Gallantry (entertainment), <u>1729</u>: LIF, Apr 8
Italian lady (beneficiary), <u>1729</u>: YB, Apr 18
Italian Laughing Song (song), <u>1773</u>: MARLY, Aug 10; <u>1781</u>: DL, Apr 25, May 7,
HAY, Aug 31
Italian manner, <u>1754</u>: DL, Nov 4, 7
Italian Masquerade (dance), <u>1743</u>: DL, Nov 10, 12, 15, 19, 22, 26, Dec 1, 7, 12,
16, 28; <u>1744</u>: DL, Jan 2, 9, 19
Italian Mimic Night Scene (dance), <u>1702</u>: DL, Oct 20; <u>1716</u>: DL, Mar 8, 20, Oct
22, 24, 26, 29, 31, Nov 12, 14, LIF, Dec 26; <u>1717</u>: DL, Jan 2, 9, Feb 5, 14
Italian Monk, The. See Boaden, James.
Italian Music (music), <u>1667</u>: NONE, Feb 12, 16; <u>1680</u>: EVELYN, Sep 23; <u>1687</u>:
ATCOURT, Jan 5; <u>1699</u>: YB, Feb 17; <u>1701</u>: DG, May 21; <u>1707</u>: YB, Mar 19; <u>1712</u>:
OSG, Apr 9; <u>1713</u>: SH, Dec 30; <u>1720</u>: LIF, Feb 5
Italian Night Scene (dance), <u>1702</u>: DL, Aug 22; <u>1705</u>: LIF, Oct 8; <u>1709</u>: DL, Dec
27; <u>1710</u>: DL, Jan 12, Mar 7, 25, Apr 12, 25, May 23, 30, Jun 6, GR, Jul 6, 8,
Aug 21; <u>1715</u>: LIF, Mar 31, Oct 24, 25, 26, Nov 10, 12, Dec 21, 22, 27; <u>1716</u>:
DL, Apr 20, LIF, 21, DL, May 7, LIF, Dec 29; <u>1717</u>: DL, Feb 18, LIF, Apr 22;
<u>1718</u>: DL, Mar 31, RI, Jul 26, AC, Sep 24; <u>1736</u>: HAY, Feb 20
Italian opera, <u>1674</u>: NONE, Jan 5; <u>1710</u>: GR, Jun 21; <u>1712</u>: QUEEN'S, Dec 10;
<u>1723</u>: KING'S, Apr 2; <u>1727</u>: LIF, Feb 13; <u>1729</u>: LIF, Mar 19; <u>1732</u>: HAY, Apr 20;
<u>1734</u>: KING'S, Nov 2; <u>1736</u>: CG, Nov 27; <u>1739</u>: HAY, Dec 26; <u>1743</u>: CG, Mar 2;
<u>1746</u>: DL, Jan 4; <u>1760</u>: KING'S, Aug 25; <u>1761</u>: KING'S, Jun 3; <u>1790</u>: CG, Jul 24;
<u>1792</u>: HAY, Jan 30; <u>1793</u>: DL, Jan 26; <u>1794</u>: DL, Apr 29, May 24; <u>1797</u>: KING'S,
Jul 18
Italian Peasant and the Happy Slave (dance), <u>1758</u>: HAY, May 18
Italian Peasants (dance), <u>1740</u>: CG, Nov 3, 21, 28, Dec 2, 5, 9, 11, 13, 30;
<u>1741</u>: CG, Jan 3, 8, 28, Feb 12, Mar 5, 7, 9, 10, 30, Apr 14, 29, Oct 24, 28,
30, DL, Dec 5, 7, 10, 16, 23; <u>1742</u>: DL, Jan 5, 8, 12, 22, 26, 28, Feb 5, 15,
16, 17, 19, 20, 23, Mar 2, 4, 8, 15, 20, 22, 29, Apr 6, 21, CG, May 21, DL,
22, CG, Dec 10, 13; <u>1746</u>: DL, Feb 6, 7, 10, 20, 24, 27, CG, Mar 6, 8, DL, 10,
17, CG, 22, 31, DL, Apr 4, 7, 9, CG, 9, DL, 10, 11, 14, 17, 18, 21, 24, 28,
Jun 6, 9, 11, 13; <u>1753</u>: CG, Nov 20, 22, 30, Dec 1, 4, 5, 6, 7, 11, 19; <u>1754</u>:
CG, Apr 4, 6, 17, 18, 19, 22, 23, 26, 30, May 3, 4, 6, 7, 8, 9, 14, 18, 21;
<u>1755</u>: CG, Apr 14, 22, May 6, 7, 9, 13, 16, 20, Nov 26; <u>1756</u>: CG, Apr 24, 27,
May 17; <u>1757</u>: HAY, Aug 11, Sep 2, DL, Oct 4, 6, 11, 12, 19, 28, Nov 1, 3, 5,
17, 19, 25, Dec 12, 15, 20; <u>1758</u>: DL, Jan 6, 9, 18, 26, Feb 3, Apr 7, 14, 17,
22, 25, May 1, 6, 23; <u>1759</u>: DL, Feb 6, 7, 24; <u>1767</u>: HAY, Jul 29, 31, Aug 3,
5, 14; <u>1773</u>: HAY, Jun 14, 18, Jul 23; <u>1780</u>: HAY, May 30, Aug 24; <u>1781</u>: HAY,
Aug 15
Italian performers, <u>1660</u>: SF, Sep 13; <u>1693</u>: YB, Jan 10; <u>1701</u>: BF, Aug 25; <u>1702</u>:
YB, Nov 3; <u>1711</u>: FE, Nov 7; <u>1715</u>: SH, May 2, 5; <u>1727</u>: KING'S, Mar 9; <u>1749</u>:
KING'S, Feb 18; <u>1752</u>: HAY, Mar 12, CG, Dec 30; <u>1756</u>: BFGR, Sep 3; <u>1758</u>: HAY,
Jan 25; <u>1766</u>: KING'S, Aug 8; <u>1767</u>: SW, Jun 13; <u>1771</u>: GROTTO, Aug 27, 29, 30,
31, Sep 9; <u>1797</u>: KING'S, Jul 18
Italian Postures (entertainment), <u>1719</u>: KING'S, Mar 5, 19
Italian puppet play, <u>1662</u>: CG, May 9; <u>1667</u>: CC, Aug 21
Italian Robbers (dance), <u>1762</u>: DL, Oct 9, 11, 12
Italian Rondeau (song), <u>1779</u>: HAY, Mar 17
Italian Scaramouch (dance), <u>1701</u>: BF, Aug 25; <u>1702</u>: BFGB, Aug 24; <u>1704</u>: LIF,

Jul 10, Aug 17; <u>1706</u>: QUEEN'S, Jan 8, 14, 17, 22, 23, Apr 30; <u>1710</u>: DL, Mar
  11, GR, Jul 3, Aug 12
Italian Scena (entertainment), <u>1793</u>: KING/HAY, Mar 6; <u>1796</u>: CG, May 10
Italian Scene Painters, <u>1709</u>: QUEEN'S, Apr 2
Italian Serio-Comic Song (song), <u>1785</u>: HAY, Feb 14
Italian Shadows (dance), <u>1720</u>: LIF, Apr 9, 18, 19, 22, 26, May 3, 11, 25, SFLH,
  Sep 5, SOU, Oct 10, Nov 28; <u>1737</u>: BF, Aug 23, SF, Sep 7
Italian Sonata (music), <u>1703</u>: YB, Jan 28, Feb 24, DL, Apr 23, May 24, 25, LIF,
  Jun 14, RIW, Aug 12, DL, Nov 9, Dec 22; <u>1704</u>: DL, Jan 25, Feb 21, Mar 30, Nov
  18, 27, Dec 28; <u>1705</u>: HDR, Jan 2, DL, 15, Nov 5, Dec 17; <u>1706</u>: DL, Feb 16;
  <u>1708</u>: SH, Mar 26
Italian Song (song), <u>1667</u>: BRIDGES, Aug 12, NONE, Sep 9; <u>1692</u>: DLORDG, Aug 24;
  <u>1699</u>: YB, Feb 17; <u>1701</u>: YB, Mar 26, RIW, Aug 11; <u>1703</u>: DL, Jan 23, YB, 28,
  DL, Feb 1, 11, LIF, Jun 1, DL, Nov 30, Dec 14, LIF, 21; <u>1704</u>: DL, Jan 4, 18,
  29, LIF, Feb 1, DL, 12, 22, LIF, Mar 7, DL, 14, YB, Apr 20, DL, 22, 29, YB,
  May 18, DL, 31, CC, Jun 7, DL, 21, Jul 5, YB, Nov 16, Dec 30; <u>1705</u>: DL, Jan
  4, 16, LIF, Feb 9, DL, Apr 13, 18, Jun 16, 23, 26, Oct 24, Nov 6, QUEEN'S,
  Nov 17, DL, Dec 1, 15, QUEEN'S, 31; <u>1706</u>: DL, Jan 12, 29, Feb 23, YB, Mar 13,
  DL, Apr 13, DL/DG, Nov 21, DL, Dec 5; <u>1707</u>: DL, Feb 4, 20, YB, Mar 5, Apr 4,
  DL, Nov 15; <u>1710</u>: YB, Apr 17, QUEEN'S, Jun 29, Aug 16; <u>1712</u>: GR, May 19, SML,
  21; <u>1715</u>: LIF, Feb 26, 28, SH, May 2, LIF, 5, DL, Jul 1; <u>1716</u>: HIC, Mar 21,
  DL, May 25; <u>1717</u>: LIF, Nov 26; <u>1718</u>: YB, Mar 5, LIF, Oct 11; <u>1720</u>: LIF, May
  23; <u>1721</u>: DL, Aug 9, LIF, Dec 7, 18, 19, 20; <u>1722</u>: DL, Apr 21; <u>1723</u>: DL, Apr
  1, LIF, May 3, DL, 23, Jun 6, Oct 9, LIF, 10, HAY, Dec 12; <u>1724</u>: DL, Jan 29,
  Feb 1, BPT, 21, LIF, Mar 16, 26, DL, May 22, LIF, Jun 4, DL, Oct 8, 14, 20,
  LIF, 22, Nov 3, 12; <u>1725</u>: LIF, Mar 13, Apr 12, DL, 22, SH, 30, DL, May 8, Dec
  8; <u>1726</u>: DL, Jan 1, 8, 18, HAY, Feb 24, LIF, Mar 28, 31, Apr 22, 29, DL, 29,
  LIF, May 6, DL, Oct 1; <u>1727</u>: LIF, Jan 9, Apr 19, 24, 27, May 17; <u>1728</u>: LIF,
  Mar 9, HAY, Apr 3; <u>1729</u>: LIF, Mar 5, HAY, 7, HIC, Apr 30, SF, Sep 15; <u>1730</u>:
  GF, Apr 14, LIF, May 14, GF, Jun 16; <u>1731</u>: CRT, Mar 10, DL, Apr 22, GF, Jun
  3, Sep 29, Oct 1, 6, DL, Nov 19; <u>1732</u>: HIC, Mar 27, DL, Apr 25, 28, May 4, 6,
  HIC, 10, GF, 19, HAY, Jun 1, DL, Nov 14; <u>1733</u>: HAY, Mar 14, DL, May 9, CG,
  16, DT, 30; <u>1734</u>: DL/HAY, Feb 22, Mar 5, DL, May 13, JS, 31, GF, Sep 9, 16,
  18, 20, Oct 16; <u>1735</u>: GF, Mar 17, HAY, 22, GF, 29, Apr 9, 16, 21, 24, 29, May
  6, Oct 13, Nov 3, 19; <u>1736</u>: GF, Feb 4, 6, 17, Mar 22, Apr 6, 13, May 4, DL,
  Dec 15; <u>1737</u>: LIF, Mar 21, 31, HIC, Apr 1, LIF, 2, 12, 14, 18, 21, 27, 28,
  May 5, Sep 7; <u>1738</u>: DL, Mar 3; <u>1739</u>: DL, May 3; <u>1742</u>: DL, Feb 25, Mar 8, Apr
  5; <u>1743</u>: DL, Apr 22; <u>1744</u>: SH, Feb 9; <u>1747</u>: DL, Apr 2; <u>1748</u>: CG, Feb 13, Mar
  14; <u>1751</u>: CG, Apr 23; <u>1752</u>: CT/HAY, Jan 31; <u>1753</u>: HAY, May 3; <u>1754</u>: HAY, Feb
  13; <u>1756</u>: DL, Mar 27; <u>1766</u>: DL, Apr 4, 29; <u>1767</u>: CG, Apr 29; <u>1770</u>: HAY, Aug
  31; <u>1771</u>: CG, Mar 1; <u>1773</u>: HAY, May 5, MARLY, Jul 29; <u>1774</u>: HAY, Feb 25;
  <u>1775</u>: KING'S, Mar 24; <u>1776</u>: HAY, Apr 18; <u>1780</u>: HAY, Mar 28; <u>1782</u>: DL, Apr 24,
  Oct 5; <u>1783</u>: CG, Oct 11; <u>1784</u>: DL, Apr 12; <u>1788</u>: DL, Jun 7; <u>1791</u>: KING'S, May
  19
Italian Song, Mock (song), <u>1735</u>: LIF, Jun 12; <u>1736</u>: CG, Mar 27, LIF, Apr 2, 16,
  CG, May 1, 13, 17, 24, Jun 4; <u>1746</u>: DL, Nov 1; <u>1763</u>: DL, Mar 21; <u>1764</u>: DL,
  Nov 28; <u>1766</u>: HAY, Jul 31; <u>1774</u>: MARLY, Jun 16; <u>1795</u>: HAY, Aug 21; <u>1798</u>: HAY,
  Aug 28, Sep 7; <u>1799</u>: HAY, Aug 27
Italian Spiletta (entertainment), <u>1759</u>: HAY, Sep 21, 25
Italian Theatre, Paris, <u>1726</u>: HAY, Mar 31
Italian Theatre, <u>1726</u>: HAY, Mar 31
Italian vaulting (entertainment), <u>1701</u>: LIF, Oct 21
Italian Villagers, The. See Hoare, Prince.
Italy, <u>1664</u>: BRIDGES, Aug 2; <u>1668</u>: BRIDGES, Oct 12; <u>1674</u>: SLINGSBY, Dec 2;
  <u>1675</u>: ATCOURT, Sep 29; <u>1687</u>: ATCOURT, Jan 30; <u>1698</u>: PEPYS'S, May 30; <u>1699</u>:
  DL, Apr 15; <u>1701</u>: YB, Mar 26; <u>1703</u>: LIF, Jun 1, Nov 29; <u>1704</u>: YB, Mar 24;
  <u>1705</u>: QUEEN'S, Apr 9; <u>1706</u>: BF, Aug 27; <u>1708</u>: DL/QUEEN, Feb 7; <u>1713</u>: QUEEN'S,
  Mar 28; <u>1714</u>: QUEEN'S, Jan 9, 23, KING'S, Dec 30; <u>1715</u>: HIC, Apr 6, SH, Jun
  30, GRT, Jul 23; <u>1716</u>: LIF, Apr 11, Oct 25; <u>1718</u>: AC, Sep 24; <u>1719</u>: LIF, Apr
  16, Dec 7; <u>1720</u>: LIF, Jan 19, KING'S, Feb 18, LIF, Jun 6; <u>1722</u>: HAY, Jan 26;
  <u>1723</u>: KING'S, Jan 12; <u>1724</u>: HAY, Mar 18, KING'S, Oct 17, HIC, Dec 21; <u>1726</u>:
  HAY, Mar 4; <u>1727</u>: KING'S, Mar 23; <u>1728</u>: HIC, Mar 20; <u>1730</u>: LIF, May 13; <u>1732</u>:
  HAY, Feb 16, Apr 19, KING'S, Nov 4; <u>1733</u>: HAY, Aug 20; <u>1734</u>: YB, Mar 8, Apr
  5, LIF, 20; <u>1736</u>: DL, Apr 22; <u>1737</u>: KING'S, Apr 25, BF, Aug 23, SF, Sep 7;
  <u>1739</u>: HAY, Dec 15; <u>1740</u>: HIC, Mar 3; <u>1741</u>: TC, Aug 4; <u>1743</u>: KING'S, Nov 15;
  <u>1744</u>: HIC, May 16; <u>1748</u>: KING'S, Nov 8; <u>1749</u>: KING'S, Feb 28, CG, Mar 6, HAY,
  Apr 3; <u>1752</u>: CT/HAY, May 9, HAY, Dec 11; <u>1753</u>: HAY, Mar 13; <u>1760</u>: SOHO, Mar
  13, KING'S, Aug 25; <u>1761</u>: KING'S, Jan 13; <u>1762</u>: KING'S, Apr 14, RANELAGH, Jun
  16; <u>1763</u>: DL, Sep 17; <u>1764</u>: KING'S, Jan 10; <u>1765</u>: DL, Apr 25; <u>1766</u>: KING'S,
  Oct 21; <u>1773</u>: HAY, Feb 26, KING'S, Oct 23; <u>1776</u>: DL, Mar 20; <u>1779</u>: HAY, Mar
  17; <u>1788</u>: KING'S, Mar 4; <u>1790</u>: CG, Mar 17, DL, 22; <u>1791</u>: DLKING'S, Nov 21;
  <u>1794</u>: KING'S, Dec 6; <u>1799</u>: DL, Jul 1

Iver's Wine Vaults, 1778: HAY, Apr 29
Ives (actor), 1750: HAY, Feb 26, Mar 13
Ives (actor), 1798: WRSG, Jun 8
Ives, Miss (actor, singer), 1795: CG, Sep 14, 21, Oct 19, 24, Nov 9, 16; 1796:
     CG, Apr 9, 26
Ives, Thomas (trustee), 1717: SH, Feb 27
Ivory, Abraham (actor), 1671: BRIDGES, Dec 7
Ivy Lane, 1751: DL, Apr 23; 1755: DL, Nov 18

Jack (blacksmith), 1771: CG, Nov 5; 1773: CG, Jan 20; 1774: CG, May 4
Jack (singer), 1675: ATCOURT, Feb 15
Jack and his Charming Fanny (song), 1799: HAY, Aug 22
Jack at the Windlass (song), 1794: CG, Apr 7; 1795: CG, May 13; 1797: CG, May
     11, 20; 1798: CG, May 28, 30; 1800: CG, Apr 15
Jack of Newbury. See Hook Jr, James.
Jack of the Green (dance), 1735: DL, Sep 30
Jack Rattling (song), 1795: WLWS, Jun 19
Jack Tar's Delight (dance), 1788: DL, Jun 5
Jack the Giant Killer (droll), 1730: HAY, Jul 7, 10
Jack the Giant Queller. See Brooke, Henry.
Jack thou art a toper (song), 1785: DL, May 11; 1789: CG, May 5, 29; 1791: CG,
     May 17
Jackman, Isaac, 1777: DL, Mar 20, Apr 7; 1781: DL, Nov 10; 1785: HAY, Mar 15;
     1789: CG, Mar 31
--All the World's a Stage (farce), 1777: DL, Apr 7, 16, 24, May 1, 2, 3, 5, 10,
     12, 20, 26, CHR, Jul 21, 23, DL, Sep 20, 30, Nov 8, 15; 1778: DL, Apr 7, HAY,
     29; 1780: DL, Sep 23; 1781: DL, Jan 8, 13, Feb 22, Mar 15, 31, Apr 23, May
     11, 26, Oct 16, Nov 22; 1782: DL, Jan 2, CG, May 17, DL, 30, Oct 3, 15, CG,
     Nov 4; 1783: DL, Jan 4, Feb 8, 19, Mar 4, 18, May 2, 16, Oct 14, 27, Dec 30;
     1784: DL, May 6, CG, 19, DL, 24, Sep 18, Oct 9, Dec 14; 1785: DL, Feb 4, 15,
     Mar 12, HAY, 15, DL, 31, Sep 24, Oct 17, Nov 16, Dec 8; 1786: DL, Jan 17, Apr
     20, HAMM, Jul 19, DL, Sep 16; 1787: DL, Mar 8, Jun 6, Sep 20, Oct 26, Nov 13;
     1788: DL, Feb 25, Jun 5; 1789: DL, Feb 28, Sep 17, Nov 18; 1791: DL, Apr 30,
     May 14, 28, DLKING'S, Sep 29, Oct 17, Nov 17, Dec 31; 1792: DLKING'S, Apr 18,
     20, DL, Sep 15, Oct 8, Nov 22; 1793: HAY, Sep 24, Oct 3, 9, 17, Nov 9, 28;
     1794: DL, Jun 5, Jul 5, 7, HAY, 9, 18, 29; 1795: DL, Jan 21, HAY, Jul 8, 23;
     1796: DL, Apr 30, HAY, Jul 8; 1797: DL, Nov 15
--Divorce, The (farce), 1781: DL, Nov 10, 12, 13, 15, 17, 19, 20, 22, Dec 17,
     18, 19, 20, 21, 22, 29; 1782: DL, Jan 31, Mar 2, 19, Apr 2, 16, May 2, 9, 21,
     Sep 24, Oct 15, 23, Nov 13; 1783: DL, Jan 16, 28, Feb 27, Mar 25, Apr 30, May
     14; 1788: HAY, Aug 29; 1789: DL, Apr 14, May 28, Jun 11, Sep 17; 1793: DL,
     Jan 5, 9, 15, 29, Feb 23, HAY, Dec 19; 1794: HAY, Jan 3
--Man of Parts, The, 1789: CG, Mar 31
--Milesian, The (opera), 1777: DL, Mar 20, 22, Apr 3, 8, 11, 12; 1778: DL, May
     14
Jackson (actor), 1744: HAY, Sep 27; 1745: GF, Feb 14, Apr 15, May 1, Dec 4;
     1748: BF, Aug 24, SFBCBV, Sep 7; 1750: HAY, Feb 9, 16, 26, Mar 13
Jackson (actor), 1759: CG, Dec 12
Jackson (dancer), 1777: CG, Apr 25; 1779: CG, Apr 28, Nov 9, Dec 4; 1780: CG,
     May 23, Oct 11, 18; 1781: CG, May 1, 19, Oct 24, Dec 13; 1782: CG, May 10;
     1783: CG, May 23, 29; 1784: CG, May 11, HAY, Sep 17; 1785: HAY, Feb 10, CG,
     May 24; 1786: CG, May 30, Nov 14; 1787: CG, May 19; 1788: CG, May 12, 15,
     HAY, Dec 22; 1789: CG, Jun 1, 6, 8, Sep 16, Dec 21; 1790: CG, Mar 1, May 27,
     Oct 4; 1791: CG, May 2, 26, Jun 13, Dec 22; 1792: CG, May 12, Oct 8, Dec 26;
     1793: CG, Mar 11, May 27, Dec 19; 1794: CG, May 23, 26, 31; 1795: CG, Feb 19,
     May 30, Oct 23, Nov 16; 1796: CG, Apr 8, Jun 3; 1797: CG, May 29; 1798: CG,
     Jun 5, Oct 15; 1799: CG, Mar 2, 5, Apr 13, Jun 4; 1800: CG, Jun 11
Jackson (lyricist), 1754: HAY/SFB, Sep 26
Jackson (receiver), 1748: DL, May 3
Jackson (violinist), 1758: CHAPEL, Apr 27; 1761: HAY, Jan 28, Feb 5
Jackson (violinist), 1797: CG, Mar 3; 1798: HAY, Jan 15, CG, Feb 23; 1799: CG,
     Feb 8; 1800: CG, Feb 28
Jackson, E (publisher), 1797: KING'S, Nov 28; 1798: KING'S, Jan 23, Feb 20, Mar
     10, Apr 21, 26, Dec 29; 1800: KING'S, Jun 21
Jackson, Hester, Mrs John (actor), 1775: HAY, Jul 7, CG, Sep 25, Oct 2, 16, 21,
     Nov 4, 9, 13; 1776: CG, Jan 5, Mar 5, May 1, 18, Oct 7, 17, 31, Nov 11, 21,
     Dec 17; 1777: CG, Jan 8, 17, Feb 1, 22, 25, May 2, 7, 13, Sep 24, 29, Oct 10,
     21, 30, Nov 7, Dec 10, 26, 29; 1778: CG, Jan 21, Feb 5, 13, 25, Mar 14, 23,
     Apr 22, May 5, 6, 9, 15, Sep 25, Oct 5, 12, 14, 21, 24, 26, Nov 4, 6, 9, 10,

452

21, Dec 17, 26; 1779: CG, Jan 4, 13, 18, 22, Feb 23, Mar 22, Apr 30, DL, May
    10, CG, 20, Oct 13, 29, Nov 1, 6, 8, 16, 22, 25, 29, Dec 6, 27; 1780: CG, Jan
    25, Feb 17, 21, Apr 7, May 1; 1796: DL, Nov 9
Jackson, J, 1766: CG, Nov 28, Dec 5
Jackson, Jane (singer), 1795: DL, Nov 11, 23, Dec 10; 1796: DL, Jan 8, 11, 18,
    Mar 3, 12, Apr 30, Oct 19; 1797: DL, Jan 7, Feb 9, 16, Jun 10, Oct 31, Nov 8,
    Dec 9, 11; 1798: DL, Jan 16, Feb 20, 24, Jun 16, Oct 6, Nov 14, 26, Dec 4,
    29; 1799: DL, Jan 19, Mar 2, HAY, 29, DL, Apr 6, May 4, 8, 24, Oct 14, Nov
    14; 1800: CG, Jun 16
Jackson, John (actor, author), 1762: DL, Oct 7, 15, Nov 4; 1763: DL, Apr 20,
    May 12, HAY, Jun 20, Jul 6, Aug 1, 5, Sep 7, DL, Oct 17, 31, Nov 4, 9, 29,
    Dec 1; 1764: DL, Jan 4, 18, Feb 14, 15, 28, Mar 20, Apr 2, May 5, Sep 22, Oct
    9, 17, 23, 24, Nov 5, 24, 27; 1765: DL, Jan 2, 15, Mar 25, Apr 22, May 4;
    1768: CG, May 30; 1775: HAY, Jul 7, 14; 1776: CG, May 1; 1777: CG, May 7;
    1778: CG, May 5
--British Heroine, The (Gerilda; or, The Siege of Harlech), 1778: CG, May 5
--Eldred; or, The British Freeholder, 1775: HAY, Jul 7, 10, 14; 1776: CG, May 1
Jackson, John and Hester (actor), 1776: CG, May 1
Jackson, Master (dancer), 1775: CG, Apr 29, Dec 12; 1776: CG, Jan 2, Oct 15;
    1777: CG, Jan 22, Apr 25, Oct 8, 21; 1778: CG, Jan 21, 28, Mar 9, May 2, Nov
    27; 1779: CG, Feb 16, 25, May 21
Jackson, Miss (actor), 1743: CG, Mar 8; 1744: CG, Jan 14, Dec 8; 1745: CG, May
    7; 1747: GF, Mar 26
Jackson, Miss (actor), 1768: HAY, Jun 23
Jackson, Miss (actor), 1780: HAY, Apr 5, Nov 13; 1781: HAY, Mar 26
Jackson, Mrs (actor), 1740: DL, Oct 17, Dec 4; 1741: DL, Oct 31, Nov 11, Dec 4;
    1742: CG, Apr 27, Sep 29, NWC, Dec 27, CG, 29; 1749: HAY, Apr 29; 1768: HAY,
    Jun 23, Jul 8, 27
Jackson, Mrs (actor), 1782: HAY, Mar 4; 1791: HAY, Dec 26
Jackson, Mrs (clothier), 1773: DL, Feb 15
Jackson, Thomas (actor), 1768: HAY, Jun 8, 23, Jul 6, 27, Aug 8, 19, 24, Dec
    19; 1770: HAY, Oct 29; 1775: HAY, Sep 19, Nov 20; 1776: HAY, May 22, 27, Jun
    19, 26, Jul 8, 10, Sep 16, 18, 23, Oct 7; 1777: HAY, May 15, 28, 30, Jun 6,
    9, Jul 7, 18, 24, 30, Aug 9, 19, 25, 29, 30, Sep 3, 10, 17, 19, Oct 9, 13;
    1778: HAY, May 21, 27, Jun 11, CHR, 24, HAY, Jul 1, 9, Aug 20, 27, Sep 2, 8;
    1779: HAY, Jun 2, 4, 7, 10, 18, Jul 1, 15, 17, Aug 13, 14, 18, 31, Sep 8, 17,
    Dec 27; 1780: HAY, Apr 5; 1782: HAY, Mar 21, May 6, Nov 25; 1787: HAY, Mar 12
Jackson, William (singer, musician, composer), 1741: CT, Mar 13; 1742: JS, Apr
    7; 1766: CG, Apr 18; 1767: CG, Nov 4; 1772: DL, Apr 20; 1780: DL, Dec 27;
    1783: DL, Dec 5; 1789: DL, Apr 14; 1795: HAY, Mar 4; 1796: CG, Nov 19
--Lycidas (musical), 1767: CG, Nov 4
--Metamorphosis, The (opera), 1783: DL, Dec 5, 8, 9
Jackson's Brother (musician), 1741: CT, Mar 13
Jackson's Habit Warehouse, 1751: DL, Apr 17
Jacky and the Cow (song), 1796: DL, Apr 13, HAY, Sep 1; 1800: CG, May 7
Jacob Gawkey's Rambles through Bath (entertainment), 1794: HAY, Jun 2
Jacob, Benjamin (organist), 1799: HAY, Jan 24
Jacob, Elizabeth Brydges (spectator), 1699: DLLIF, Apr 22
Jacob, Hildebrand, 1738: CG, Jan 25
--Fatal Constancy, The, 1723: DL, Apr 22, 23, 26, 29; 1724: DL, Feb 12, 13
--Happy Constancy, The, 1738: CG, Jan 25
--Nest of Plays, The, 1738: CG, Jan 25, DL, 28
--Prodigal Reformed, The, 1738: CG, Jan 25
--Trial of Conjugal Love, 1738: CG, Jan 25
Jacobs (actor), 1768: HAY, Jun 23, Jul 18, 27, Aug 8, 24, Oct 7; 1769: HAY, May
    15, 22, 26, 29, Jun 2, 5, 7, 9, Jul 12, Aug 7, 11, 14, 25, Sep 1, 11; 1770:
    DL, Jan 16, Apr 16, HAY, May 16, 18, DL, 18, 21, HAY, 23, 28, Jun 15, 25, Aug
    24, DL, Oct 13, Nov 17, Dec 5; 1771: DL, Mar 7, Apr 17, May 27, Nov 11, Dec
    4, 26, 30; 1772: DL, Mar 26, Apr 20, 22, 29, May 12, HAY, 18, 20, 22, DL, 25,
    HAY, 27, Jun 5, 12, 29, Jul 3, 6, 8, 10, Aug 5, 10, 19, 28, Sep 8, DL, Oct 3,
    21, Nov 20, Dec 26; 1773: DL, Apr 19, 23, 29, HAY, May 17, DL, 22, 24, HAY,
    26, 28, 31, Jun 4, 7, 18, 28, Jul 2, 21, 30, Aug 11, 25, 27, Sep 3, 16, DL,
    25, Oct 14, 25, Nov 9, 25, Dec 30; 1774: DL, Feb 2, 5, 9, Mar 14, Apr 19,
    HAY, May 16, DL, 18, HAY, 30, Jun 1, 3, 6, 8, 10, 17, 24, 27, Aug 19, Sep 5,
    12, 17, 21; 1775: HAY, Mar 23, May 15, 17, 19, 22, 26, 29, Jun 5, 7, 12, Jul
    7, 14, 31, Aug 2, Sep 4, 18, 20, 21, Oct 30
Jacobs (actor), 1783: HAY, Sep 17
Jacobs, Miss E (actor, singer), 1798: DL, Nov 14, Dec 4, 29; 1799: DL, Jan 19,
    Mar 2, May 24, Oct 14, Nov 14, Dec 11, 28; 1800: DL, Jan 1, Mar 11, 13, Apr
    29, Jun 6
Jacobs, Miss R (actor), 1799: DL, Jan 19, Mar 2
Jacobs, Mlle (dancer, actor), 1791: PAN, Feb 17, Mar 22, DLKING'S, Nov 5; 1792:

DLKING'S, Mar 19, May 23, Jun 13, HAY, 27, Jul 25

Jacobs, Mrs (dancer), 1725: HAY, May 7

Jacobs, Richard (carpenter), 1794: DL, Mar 19; 1795: DL, Feb 12, May 6; 1796:
DL, Jan 18, Nov 9, Dec 26; 1797: DL, Jun 10; 1798: DL, Jun 16; 1799: DL, Jul
3

Jacolet (dancer), 1788: KING'S, Jan 29, Mar 13, May 15

J'aime la Liberte (song), 1738: DL, Apr 17

Jalousie of Three Pierrots (dance), 1727: LIF, Apr 21

Jalousie sans Raison (dance), 1790: HAY, Mar 25, Apr 15, 17, 22, 29, May 4, 11,
15, 18, 20

Jalousies de Serail (dance), 1789: KING'S, Mar 17, 19, 21, Apr 2, 4, May 2, 5,
21

Jaloux de Sabuse. See Campistron, Jean Galbert de.

Jaloux Puni (dance), 1793: KING'S, Jun 1, 4, 8, 11, 15, 22

Jaloux sans un Rival, Le (dance), 1772: KING'S, May 14

Jalouzie (dance), 1740: DL, Apr 10, 22

Jamaica Coffee House, 1777: HAY, Oct 13; 1782: HAY, Mar 18

Jamaica, 1692: SF, Sep 13

James (actor), 1671: NONE, Sep 0

James (actor), 1781: HAY, Jan 22, Mar 26; 1782: HAY, Jan 21, Nov 25

James (boxkeeper), 1677: DL, Dec 12, 26

James (composer), 1741: GF, Apr 29

James (dancer), 1723: HAY, Feb 13, Apr 22, Dec 30; 1724: LIF, Jul 14, 29, SOU,
Sep 24

James (rioter), 1773: CG, Nov 18; 1775: CG, Feb 24

James (spectator), 1677: DL, Dec 12, 26

James I, 1700: DLANDLIF, Jun 14; 1704: LIF, Jul 10; 1714: DL, Jun 25; 1720: DL,
Jul 19; 1735: LIF, Jun 19; 1741: GF, Feb 17; 1755: HAY, Sep 4; 1799: DL, Oct
7; see also Highness; King, the; Majesty

James II (Duke of York), 1661: NONE, May 5, LIF, Jun 28, VERE, Sep 7, LIF/MT,
Oct 21; 1663: LIF, Oct 24; 1664: LIF, Aug 13; 1667: BRI/COUR, Mar 2, BRIDGES,
Apr 15, Aug 17, LIF, Oct 15, BRIDGES, 19; 1668: LIF, May 2, 8, ATCOURT, Oct
14, Nov 30, LIF, Dec 21; 1670: ATCOURT, Apr 6; 1673: YH, May 5; 1679: DG, Sep
0; 1680: DG, Feb 0, 2; 1682: DG, Apr 21, May 31, DLORDG, Oct 24; 1683:
DLORDG, Sep 12, CITY, Oct 29; 1685: DL, May 9, BF, Aug 0, ATCOURT, Dec 14;
1689: DLORDG, Nov 28; 1745: MF, May 2; see also Duke; Highness; King, the;
Majesty

James Square, 1751: DL, Mar 18

James St, 1697: HIC, Dec 9; 1707: HIC, Apr 2; 1734: JS, Apr 22; 1735: CG/LIF,
Mar 25; 1736: CG, Mar 16; 1740: CG, May 12; 1741: JS, Feb 20, May 19, Sep 29,
Oct 6; 1742: JS, Oct 12; 1744: DL, Feb 25, Mar 5, 29; 1747: DL, Mar 17, HAY,
Apr 20; 1748: DL, Mar 26; 1749: BBT, Mar 1, DL, 18, 30, Apr 5; 1750: JS, Jan
25, DL, Mar 19, CG, 31; 1751: DL, Apr 15, Dec 17; 1752: DL, Mar 17, TCJS, Aug
11; 1753: DL, Apr 3; 1754: CG, Jan 19, DL, May 4; 1756: JS, Mar 18, DL, May
1; 1757: DL, Feb 22, May 3; 1758: DL, Apr 10; 1766: JS, Jan 6; 1775: CG, Jun
1; 1777: CG, Mar 22, May 14; 1790: DL, Apr 16; 1794: CG, Apr 30; 1798: CG,
May 30

James, Dr (physician), 1751: DL, Feb 27

James, Harris (actor), 1732: GF, Oct 14, 16, Dec 1, 18, 20; 1733: GF, Jan 13,
20, 23, Feb 5, 13, Mar 10, 27, Apr 11, 13, 19, 27, May 8, DL, 9, GF, Sep 10,
24, 27, Oct 1, 19, 23, 25, Nov 10, 14; 1734: CG, Jan 23, Apr 16, May 7, 9,
HAY, Jun 3, 7, 12, 14, 24, 28, Jul 5, 19, 31, CG/LIF, Sep 20, DL, 24, RI, 26,
CG/LIF, Oct 9, LIF, 12, CG/LIF, 16, 18, 29, Nov 1, 21, Dec 5; 1735: CG/LIF,
Jan 21, 23, Feb 3, 13, Mar 20, 29, SOU, Apr 7, CG/LIF, May 16, 27, CG, Sep
26, 29, Oct 1, 8, 13, 29, Nov 10, 29, Dec 27; 1736: CG, Jan 9, Mar 6, 18, 20,
23, 25, 27, 29, Apr 6, LIF, 16, CG, 29, 30, May 1, 3, 10, 13, 17, 20, Jun 14,
Sep 17, 20, 24, 29, Oct 1, 4, 13, 20, 22, 25, 29, Nov 1, 11, 25, 26, 29, Dec
20; 1737: CG, Feb 3, 15, Mar 15, Apr 14, 26, 29, May 9, 31, LIF, Jul 26, Aug
2, 5, CG, Sep 21, 30, Oct 24, 26, DL, 27, CG, 28, 29, Nov 1, 2, 9, 14, 17;
1738: CG, Jan 3, 6, 9, 19, 24, 25, Feb 13, 16, 23, Mar 4, 20, 25, Apr 22, 25,
May 8, 10, Sep 27, Oct 2, 6, 11, 13, 20, 30, Nov 2, 11, 13, 15, 17, 20, 23,
Dec 2, 4, 5, 11, 12; 1739: CG, Jan 16, 20, 22, Feb 10, 16, Mar 27, Apr 3, 5,
12, 25, May 2, 14, 17, 23, 25, 30, Aug 31, Sep 5, 7, 14, 17, 19, 22, 25, 27,
28, Oct 3, 5, 8, 10, 25, 29, 30, Nov 6, 9, 30, Dec 4, 6, 10, 13, 29; 1740:
CG, Jan 12, 15, 17, Feb 2, Mar 18, 24, 27, Apr 14, May 3, 5, 7, 9, 12, 27,
29, Jun 5, TC, Aug 4, CG, Sep 19, 22, 24, 26, Oct 1, 3, 6, 8, 22, 23, 24, 25,
27, 29, Nov 1, 4, 6, 15, Dec 4, 10, 13, 29; 1741: CG, Jan 2, 6, 23, 27, Feb
7, 14, 19, 24, 28, Mar 7, 16, Apr 3, May 2, 4, 11, 12, 14, BFH, Aug 22, CG,
Sep 21, 28, 30, Oct 2, 10, 15, 20, 21, 24, 26, 29, Nov 7, 26, 27, 30, Dec 1,
7, 11, 18; 1742: CG, Jan 2, 19, Feb 22, 25, Mar 9, 27, Apr 1, JS, 7, CG, May
3, 4, 5, 7, 11, Oct 9, 15, 27, 29, Nov 20, Dec 7, 22; 1743: CG, Jan 8, Feb 9,
JS, Mar 16, CG, Apr 20, May 4, 5, TCD/BFTD, Aug 4, CG, Sep 21, 23, Oct 14,

19, 21, Nov 2, 7, 16, 19, 25, Dec 3, 8, 9, 17, 19; 1744: CG, Jan 5, 18, Feb
28, Mar 13, Apr 6, 7, 27, May 9, Sep 21, 26, Oct 1, 10, 15, 22, 29, 31, Nov
8, 24, 28, 29, Dec 12, 17, 21; 1745: CG, Jan 4, 23, Feb 11, Apr 17, 20, 26,
29, May 13, Sep 23, 25, 30, Oct 11, 16, 29, Nov 8, 13, 15, 22, 23, 25, Dec 5,
10, 13, 20; 1746: CG, Jan 7, 9, Feb 3, 5, 6, 17, Mar 13, Apr 3, 21, 22, 23,
26, 28, Sep 29, Oct 1, 3, 6, 8, 15, 29, Nov 6, 8, 17, 18, Dec 11, 19, 26, 27;
1747: CG, Feb 2, 3, 6, 12, Mar 17, 30, Apr 6, May 15, 20, Oct 31, Nov 11, 13,
16, 18, 23, Dec 9, 15, 17, 19; 1748: CG, Jan 2, 7, 12, 14, 15, 21, 27, 29,
Feb 8, 15, Mar 14, 24, 28, Apr 11, 13, 15, 18, 21, 22, 26, 27, 28, 29, DL,
Sep 10, 13, 22, 24, 27, Oct 13, 29, Nov 11, 12, 14, 29, Dec 21, 26, NWC, 26,
DL, 28; 1749: DL, Jan 17, Feb 4, Mar 16, 29, 30, Apr 10, 12, Sep 16, 19, 28,
Oct 3, 26, 30, Nov 15, 27, Dec 18, 20, 28; 1750: DL, Jan 1, Feb 21, 23, Mar
17, 26, Apr 17, 19, 20, Sep 13, 15, 18, 21, 22, 25, 28, Oct 29, 30, Nov 2, 7,
14, Dec 14, 31; 1751: DL, Jan 5, 12, Mar 16, Apr 9, 18, 29, May 17, Oct 12
James, Harris and Mrs (actors), 1739: CG, May 14
James, little (spectator), 1668: LIF, Jan 6
James, Mrs (actor), 1669: BRIDGES, Jun 24; 1670: BRI/COUR, Dec 0; 1671:
BRIDGES, Mar 0, Jun 0; 1672: LIF, Apr 0, Nov 0; 1673: LIF, May 0; 1674: LIF,
Mar 0; 1675: DL, Jan 12, 25, May 10; 1676: DL, Jan 29
James, Mrs Harris (actor), 1733: HAY, Feb 14; 1736: CG, May 10, Nov 26, Dec 16,
29; 1737: CG, Jan 25, Feb 1, LIF, 1, CG, 26, Apr 29, LIF, Aug 2, CG, Sep 16,
19, 26, Oct 24, Nov 9, 17; 1738: CG, Jan 3, 19, Feb 6, 16, 23, Mar 13, Apr
12, Sep 20, 22, Oct 6, 11, 24, Nov 11, 20, 27, 29, Dec 4, 5, 16; 1739: CG,
Jan 3, 17, 20, 22, Feb 14, 26, Mar 20, May 1, Sep 5, 12, 14, 25, 28, 29, Oct
4, 22, 25, 26, 30, Nov 10, 13, Dec 1, 4, 6, 15; 1740: CG, Jan 17, Feb 2, Mar
11, Apr 28, May 5, Sep 26, 29, Oct 23, 27, 29, 31, Nov 1, 6, 10, GF, Dec 5,
CG, 29; 1741: CG, Jan 2, 21, 22, 29, Feb 7, 28, Mar 7, 16, Apr 3, 24, May 1,
BFH, Aug 22, CG, Sep 25, Oct 29, 30, Nov 7, 9, 23, 26, 27, Dec 7, 11, 12;
1742: CG, Jan 23, Feb 22, 25, 27, Apr 1, May 3, 5, 7, Sep 29, Oct 9, 19, 25,
26, 27, 28, 29, Nov 30; 1743: CG, Mar 1, Oct 29, Nov 28, 30, Dec 10, 14, 27;
1744: CG, Jan 3, 18, Apr 10, 19, 27, May 14, Sep 21, Oct 16, 24, 31, Nov 12,
28, Dec 13, 26, 28; 1745: CG, Mar 11, Apr 1, 15, 16, 17, 25, 26, May 4, 21,
Sep 23, 25, Oct 2, 4, 31, Nov 8, 18, 19, 23, 25, 28, 30, Dec 2, 6; 1746: CG,
Jan 7, 9, 10, 11, 13, 25, Feb 3, 6, 17, Mar 4, Apr 1, 3, 7, 18, 23, 28, Sep
29, Oct 3, 20, 27, Nov 1, 13, 17, 18, 24, 28, Dec 6, 10, 22, 27, 29; 1747:
CG, Jan 26, Feb 12, Apr 20, Nov 16, Dec 28; 1748: CG, Jan 9, 12, 16, 29, Mar
28, Apr 22, 26, DL, Sep 15, 29, Oct 6, 8, 27, 29, Nov 29, Dec 26; 1749: DL,
Jan 14, Apr 3, 12, May 1, 12, Oct 3, 30, Nov 9, 21, Dec 28; 1750: DL, Apr 19,
May 1, Sep 28, Oct 15, 22, 29, Nov 12, 15, Dec 31; 1751: DL, May 1, Sep 14,
17, 20, 21, Oct 22, Nov 7; 1752: DL, Jan 1, Mar 9, Apr 13, 21, Oct 5, 10, 13,
Nov 25, 27, Dec 5, 7, 19; 1753: DL, Jan 3, 22, 24, Apr 14, 23, 27, May 15,
18, Sep 13, Oct 4, 10, 13, 18, 20, Nov 8, 26; 1754: DL, Jan 16, Feb 20, Apr
18, Sep 19, Oct 10, 11, 18, 23, Nov 22
Jameson (actor), 1782: HAY, Mar 21
Jameson, Mary (singer), 1773: CG, Sep 29, Oct 13; 1774: CG, Feb 4, 7, Mar 19,
Apr 7, 9, 15; 1775: HAY, Feb 16, May 1
Jameson, Miss (actor), 1782: HAY, Nov 25
Jamie's Return (dance), 1786: HAY, Jul 6, Sep 2, 15; 1787: HAY, Jun 29, Jul 3,
28; 1788: DL, Nov 13; 1789: DL, Jan 7, 17, Feb 20
Jane (spectator), 1667: BRIDGES, Sep 20
Jane Shore. See Rowe, Nicholas.
Janeway's Coffee House, 1750: DL, Nov 28; 1751: DL, May 14; 1752: DL, Dec 19
Janiewicz, Felix (violinist), 1793: KING/HAY, Feb 15, 20, Mar 6
Janno (Janny) (actor, dancer), 1733: BFMMO, Aug 23, BFCGBH, Sep 4, DL/HAY, 26,
Oct 3, 12, 19, 24, 25, Nov 14, 23, 24, 26, Dec 3, 12, HAY, 13, DL/HAY, 19,
22; 1734: DL/HAY, Jan 12, 29, Feb 7, 20, 22, Mar 12, BFHBH, Aug 24, DL, Sep
19, Oct 3, 21, Nov 22; 1735: DL, Feb 5, 14, Apr 25, Oct 1, 7, 31, Nov 15, 20,
Dec 6; 1736: DL, Jan 3, May 24, BFHC, Aug 23, DL, Sep 7, Oct 5, 12, Nov 2,
11, Dec 4; 1737: DL, Apr 19, May 23, BF, Aug 23, SF, Sep 7; 1740: BFH, Aug
23; 1741: CG, Jan 21, Feb 17; 1747: GF, Jan 16
Jansolin (Jansolet), Mme (dancer), 1756: CG, May 19; 1757: CG, Apr 30; 1758:
CG, Feb 1, Apr 8, 28, May 2, Oct 14, Nov 16, 23; 1759: CG, May 16, Dec 10;
1760: CG, Jan 16, 18, Apr 11, May 8, Sep 22, Oct 20, Dec 11; 1761: CG, Mar 9,
May 8, 25, Sep 16, 21, 26, Nov 25; 1762: CG, Jan 28, May 7
Janson (musician), 1772: DL, Mar 6, 11, 13, 18, 20, 25, 27, Apr 3
Janson (singer), 1787: CG, Nov 16, Dec 3, 17; 1788: CG, Jan 7, 14, Mar 1, Sep
22, Dec 15, 29
January and May (dance), 1788: HAY, Jun 27, Aug 5
Jaquis, Gervase (spectator), 1667: BRIDGES, Apr 15, LIF, May 6
Jar Tavern, 1744: CG, Apr 20
Jardin (dancer), 1750: CG, Feb 7, Mar 1, 19, Apr 3, 17, 19, 21, 24, 28, Dec 21,
22, 26; 1751: CG, Jan 3, 17, Apr 12, 25

Jardiniere (dance), 1787: KING'S, Mar 22, Apr 17, Jun 5
Jardiniers (dance), 1754: CG, Mar 7, 25
Jardiniers Suedois (dance), 1740: DL, Nov 29, Dec 1, 2, 3, 19, 22, 29, 30;
    1741: DL, Jan 2, 3, 6, 10, 12, 13, 14, 24, 28, Feb 3, 6, Mar 2, 5, 19, Apr
    15, 21, May 18, 20, BFLW, Aug 22, DL, Nov 28, 30, Dec 2, 15, 17, 22, 28;
    1742: DL, Jan 4, 13, 21, Feb 8, 24, Apr 8, CG, Nov 20, 22, 23, 27, 29, 30,
    Dec 3, 4; 1744: CG, Apr 16, 23
Jarnowick. See Giornovichi, Giovanni Mane.
Jarratt, Miss (singer), 1772: DL, Nov 3, 6, Dec 8; 1773: DL, Jan 4, Mar 30, Apr
    16, Sep 28, Nov 2, Dec 11, 27; 1774: DL, Jan 26, Feb 2, 15, Apr 29, May 14,
    16, 18, Sep 20, 22, 29, Oct 5, 12, 14, Nov 22; 1775: DL, Mar 21, 23, Apr 17,
    21, 22, May 13, Sep 26, 30, Oct 17, 20, 28, Dec 1, 16, 29; 1776: DL, Apr 24,
    May 4, 20, 22, 23, Sep 21, 26, Oct 1, 5, 15, 18, Nov 4, 16, 21, 25, Dec 5,
    10; 1777: DL, Jan 4, Apr 22, May 6, HAY, Oct 6
Jarvis (actor), 1734: CG, May 15; 1735: CG/LIF, May 15; 1736: CG, May 17; 1737:
    CG, May 3; 1738: CG, May 10; 1739: CG, May 18; 1740: CG, May 23; 1744: HAY,
    May 16, Jun 29
Jarvis (beneficiary), 1755: CG, Apr 30; 1756: CG, May 5; 1760: CG, Apr 12;
    1761: CG, Apr 11; 1762: CG, May 8
Jarvis (stationer), 1758: CG, Apr 19
Jarvis, J (publisher), 1785: KING'S, Feb 26, May 12, 28; 1786: KING'S, Mar 16;
    1789: DL, Nov 24; 1790: DL, Sep 11; 1791: DL, Jan 1
Jarvis, Miss (actor), 1744: HAY, May 10
Jarvis, Mrs (ticket deliverer), 1758: CG, May 8
Jatter (actor), 1661: NONE, Sep 0
Jay (beneficiary), 1748: SOU, Jul 18
Jay, Sir James (physician), 1763: DL, Apr 27
Je Ne Sca Quoi, La. See Smart, Christopher.
Je Ne Scai Quoi (dance), 1732: DL, Aug 17, 19, 22, LIF/CG, Nov 16; 1733: CG,
    Mar 27, LIF/CG, Apr 11; 1737: LIF, Jul 26, Aug 2, 9, CG, Sep 26, Oct 3; 1738:
    CG, Jan 21, 25, Mar 16, 21, Apr 5, 11, 12, 17, 24, 25, 26, 27, May 1, 2, 3,
    5, 10, 11, 15, 16, 18; 1739: CG, Apr 23, 25, 26, 27, May 1, 2, 4, 7, 9, 10,
    14, 15, 16, 23, 24, 25, 29, 30, Nov 23, 26, Dec 1, 3, 17; 1740: CG, Jan 8,
    Mar 24, Apr 9, 23, 29, May 2, 5, 12, 13, 19, 20, 27, Oct 8, 23; 1742: CG, Oct
    15, 18, 19; 1752: CG, Apr 15; 1757: HAY, Nov 2
Je suis Lindor (song), 1788: KING'S, May 29
Jeaffreson, Christopher (correspondent), 1684: DLORDG, Oct 29
Jealous (ticket deliverer), 1789: CG, Jun 13; 1790: CG, Jun 8; 1791: CG, Jun 9;
    1792: CG, Jun 1; 1794: CG, Jun 17
Jealous Clown, The. See Gataker, Thomas.
Jealous Doctor, The; or, The Intriguing Dame (pantomime), 1717: LIF, Apr 29,
    May 1, 3, 4, 7, 21, Oct 25, 29, 30, Nov 1, 2, 4, 9, 16, 21, 25, 30, Dec 12,
    20, 31; 1718: LIF, Jan 21, Feb 22, 24, Mar 31, May 13, 15, 20; 1719: LIF, Apr
    4; 1720: LIF, Feb 26, Mar 14, Apr 20, 27, May 5, 7, 12, Dec 15, 28, 29; 1721:
    LIF, Jan 31, Feb 8, Mar 21, May 5, 11, Nov 20, 21, Dec 28; 1722: LIF, Jan 11,
    Apr 4, Nov 21, Dec 22; 1723: LIF, Jan 7, Apr 16; 1724: LIF, Apr 10, 22, May
    12, 13, 22, 25, Jul 10; 1726: LIF, Jul 19, 26, Aug 19, 23
Jealous Farmer Deceived. See Yarrow, Joseph, Harlequin Statue.
Jealous Harlequin (dance), 1776: DL, Jan 17, 18, Feb 29, Apr 24, May 4
Jealous Husband Outwitted, The (play), 1732: RIW/HAY, Sep 11, 15, 18, 20; 1746:
    CG, Apr 14
Jealous Husband, The (farce, anon), 1777: CG, Apr 7
Jealous Husband, The; or, Modern Gallantry (play, anon), 1732: GF, Feb 21, 22,
    24
Jealous Lovers, The. See Randolph, Thomas.
Jealous Peasant (dance), 1766: DL, Nov 11, 13, Dec 4, 12; 1767: DL, Mar 23, May
    13
Jealous Savoyard (dance), 1741: BFH, Aug 22
Jealous Taylor, The; or, The Intriguing Valet (farce, anon), 1731: HAY, Jan 13,
    14, 15, 18, 25, 27, Feb 3, 4, 10, 26, Mar 5, 12, 17, 19, May 28, Jun 5, 7, 14
Jealous Wife, The. See Colman the elder, George.
Jealous Woodcutter (dance), 1762: CG, Oct 23, 25, 26, 28, 29, Nov 2, 4, 10, 12,
    13, 19, 20, Dec 7, 8, 14, 16, 17, 22, 27, 28; 1763: CG, Jan 20, Feb 8, 19,
    22, Mar 3, 15, 17, 19, 21, May 9, 14; 1764: CG, Nov 1, 2, 16, 21, 24, Dec 6,
    11; 1765: CG, Jan 19, 25, Mar 30, Apr 26, May 2, 10, 23; 1771: CG, Oct 4, 18,
    23, 26, Nov 2
Jealousy between Three Lilliputians (dance), 1735: GF/HAY, Mar 21
Jealousy Deceived; or, The Amours of Harlequin (pantomime), 1730: GF, Jan 7, 8,
    9, 12, 15, 16, Feb 16, 19, Mar 31, May 18, 22, 29
Jefferies, Master (actor), 1740: BF/WF/SF, Aug 23
Jefferson (actor), 1777: CHR, Jun 20; 1788: HAY, Dec 22
Jefferson, Elizabeth, Mrs Thomas (the first) (actor), 1753: DL, Oct 6, Dec 26;

1754: DL, Jan 7, Oct 10, 18; 1755: DL, Feb 3, Apr 29, May 9, Oct 3, Dec 18;
  1756: DL, May 3, Sep 25, 28, Oct 27; 1757: DL, May 3, Sep 13, 27, Oct 29, Dec
  17; 1758: DL, May 2, 3, 4
Jefferson, Rebecca, Mrs Thomas (the second) (actor), 1772: DL, Mar 23; 1773:
  DL, Oct 6, 19, 20, 22; 1774: DL, Jan 13, Mar 12, 15, 21, Apr 19, Nov 8, 17,
  24; 1775: DL, Jan 18
Jefferson, Thomas (actor), 1753: DL, Oct 24, 31, Nov 15, 26, Dec 1, 18; 1754:
  DL, Jan 23, Apr 30, May 4, Nov 6, 11; 1755: DL, Feb 18, Mar 4, Apr 29, Sep
  18, Oct 7, 14, 23, Nov 6, 8, 15, Dec 4, 6, 19; 1756: DL, Jan 2, 10, 12, 21,
  Feb 27, Apr 10, 24, 29, May 3, Sep 18, 25, 30, Oct 9, 14, 15, 23, 28, Nov 18,
  23, Dec 10, 15; 1757: DL, Jan 7, 22, Feb 22, Mar 21, 24, Apr 18, May 3,
  7, Sep 13, 17, 20, 24, Oct 15, 19, 28, Nov 1, 2, 4, 19, Dec 2, 3, 10, 22;
  1758: DL, Feb 1, Mar 4, Apr 7, 27, May 2, 17, 23; 1767: DL, Sep 17, 18; 1768:
  DL, Sep 28, 29, Oct 1, 18, 25, 28, Nov 7, 10, 17, Dec 3, 17; 1769: DL, Feb
  23, Mar 11, 31, Apr 15, 21, Sep 19, 21, Oct 20, 26, 31, Nov 1, 8, 13, 16, 17,
  23, 27, 28, Dec 1, 4; 1770: DL, Jan 16, 19, 25, Feb 27, Mar 24, 26, Apr 7,
  17, May 3, Sep 25, Oct 3, 4, 6, 12, 15, 24, Nov 17, Dec 4, 13; 1771: DL, Feb
  21, Mar 9, 18, 23, Apr 2, 3, 5, 6, 17, 20, May 1, Oct 22, 23, 26, 29, 30, Nov
  9, 26, 27, Dec 4, 10, 26, 31; 1772: DL, Jan 1, Mar 17, 26, Apr 4, 6, May 4,
  12, 29, 30, Oct 16, 21, 29, Nov 3, 6, 12, Dec 15, 18, 31; 1773: DL, Jan 1,
  21, 26, Feb 1, 8, 11, 18, 23, 25, 27, Mar 27, Apr 16, 21, May 13, 19, 20, Sep
  28, 30, Oct 2, 9, 20, 23, Nov 6, 9, 15, Dec 10; 1774: DL, Jan 13, Feb 8, 9,
  Mar 14, 15, 19, 22, Apr 8, 25, May 16, Sep 20, 22, 29, Oct 1, 4, 6, 8, 20,
  27, 28, Nov 1, 16, 25, Dec 7, 9; 1775: DL, Jan 18, Feb 23, Mar 21, 25, 28,
  Apr 1, 4, 17, 21, May 10, Sep 23, 26, 28, Oct 3, 5, 7, 12, 21, 23, 27, Nov 6;
  1776: DL, Jan 3, Feb 10, 12, Apr 10, 24, May 4, 10, 23, Sep 21, 24, 26, Oct
  8, 9, 12, 15, 18, 23, 25, Nov 9, 16; 1777: DL, May 1, 28
Jefferson, Thomas and Mrs (actors), 1758: DL, Sep 16
Jeffrey, H (printer), 1752: DL, Dec 22
Jeffreys, George Chancellor (spectator), 1688: DL, May 3
Jeffreys, George, 1724: LIF, Feb 24; 1726: LIF, Feb 19; 1731: LIF, Feb 27
--Edwin, 1724: LIF, Jan 24, Feb 24, 25, 27, 29, Mar 3, 5
Jeffreys, Sir Robert (Lord Mayor), 1685: CITY, Oct 29
Jeffries (actor), 1767: HAY, Jul 6
Jeffries, Mrs (actor), 1764: HAY, Aug 20, Sep 1; 1767: HAY, Jun 8, 15, 17, Jul
  2, 6, 22, 31, Aug 10, 12, 25, 27, Sep 2, 7, 21, DL, 25, Oct 15, 23, 30, Nov
  7, 28, Dec 12, 19; 1768: DL, Jan 23, Mar 21, 24, Apr 13, 14, 28, May 24, 25,
  Aug 18, Sep 8, 23, 24, 27, 30, Oct 5, 6, HAY, 7, DL, 8, 15, Nov 17, Dec 1,
  14; 1769: DL, Jan 27, Apr 18, 28, HAY, Jun 5, 21, Jul 12, 21, Aug 11, 14, 16,
  25, 30, DL, Sep 16, 30, Oct 4, 5, 10, 17, 18, Nov 9, 29, Dec 6, 11, 13, 14,
  21, 23; 1770: DL, Jan 16, Mar 3, 27, 31, Apr 26, 28, May 17, HAY, 18, 23, Jun
  15, 18, Jul 9, 25, Aug 24, Sep 3, DL, 27, Oct 2, 18, 22, Nov 9, 15, 16, 20,
  23, 24, Dec 5, 29; 1771: DL, Apr 12, 26, May 11, 27
Jehovah crowned (song), 1786: DL, Mar 10; 1789: CG, Mar 6, DL, 18, CG, 27;
  1790: DL, Feb 26, CG, Mar 3; 1791: DL, Mar 11, 23, CG, Apr 6, 13; 1792:
  KING'S, Feb 24, CG, Mar 21; 1793: CG, Feb 20, KING/HAY, 22, Mar 1, CG, 20;
  1794: DL, Apr 10; 1795: CG, Mar 4; 1800: CG, Feb 28
Jehovah is my shield (song), 1786: DL, Mar 10; 1789: DL, Mar 18; 1790: DL, Feb
  26; 1791: DL, Mar 23; 1792: KING'S, Feb 24; 1793: KING/HAY, Feb 22; 1794: DL,
  Apr 10
Jehu (farce, anon), 1779: DL, Feb 20
Jekyll, Joseph (versifier), 1780: DL, May 24; 1788: CG, Apr 8
Jell, Mrs (actor), 1728: HAY, Aug 9
Jellico (actor), 1782: HAY, Jan 21
Jemimah, Lady (spectator), 1661: BF, Aug 31; 1663: BRIDGES, May 7; 1664: NONE,
  Oct 17
Jemmat, Catherine (author), 1771: DL, Jan 1
Jemmy Jumps in the Dumps (entertainment), 1792: CG, May 10
Jenerosita per Forza di Pantalone Economo in Campagna (entertainment), 1726:
  KING'S, Dec 17
Jenkins (actor), 1731: TC, Aug 12, SFGT, Sep 8, SOU, 28, GF, Oct 29, Nov 4, 5,
  8, 13, Dec 8, 30; 1732: GF, Feb 2, Mar 7, 20, 28, Apr 27, 28, May 9, 10, Oct
  5, 14, 18, Nov 4, Dec 1, 20, 29; 1733: GF, Jan 20, 24, Feb 5, Mar 8, Apr 3,
  11, 13, 19, May 8, HAY, 28, BF, Aug 23, GF, Sep 10, 14, 19, 20, Oct 8, 9, 11,
  19, 25, Nov 5, 13, 29, Dec 8, 12, 15, 26; 1734: GF, Jan 19, 31, Feb 7, 11,
  May 1, 10, 20, Sep 11, 16, 20, 25, Oct 14, 16, Nov 7, 18, 22, 25, Dec 6;
  1735: GF, Jan 8, 10, 24, Feb 7, 11, Mar 29, Apr 9, 23, 28, May 3, 5
Jenkins (actor), 1749: BFC, Aug 23
Jenkins (trumpeter), 1773: DL, Jun 2, Dec 28
Jenkins, George (drummer), 1798: HAY, Jan 15
Jenkinson, William (drummer), 1794: CG, Mar 7; 1796: CG, Feb 12; 1797: CG, Mar
  3; 1798: CG, Feb 23; 1799: CG, Feb 8; 1800: CG, Feb 28

457

Jennens (librettist), 1744: KING'S, Jun 9; 1745: KING'S, Mar 27
Jennens, Robert (spectator), 1696: LIF, Nov 14, 19, DL, 21
Jenner, Charles (author), 1773: CG, Feb 6
Jennings (actor), 1779: DL, Oct 12
Jennings (glover), 1767: DL, Apr 4; 1772: DL, Jun 10; 1773: DL, Jun 2; 1775:
    DL, May 27; 1776: DL, Mar 16, Jun 10
Jennings (householder), 1746: GF, Mar 11
Jennings (ticket deliverer), 1782: CG, May 29; 1783: CG, Jun 4
Jennings, Mrs (actor), 1662: ATCOURT, Nov 1; 1668: LIF, Feb 6; 1669: LIF, Dec
    14; 1670: LIF, Sep 20; 1671: LIF, Jan 10; 1675: ATCOURT, Feb 15
Jennings, Robert (renter), 1758: CG, Mar 6
Jenny (actor), 1759: DL, Apr 27
Jenny bright as the day (song), 1754: CG, May 8
Jenny come tie me (dance), 1735: DL, Jul 1
Jenny gin you can love (song), 1688: DG, Apr 0
Jenny's Whim. See O'Keeffe, John.
Jephson, Robert, 1775: DL, Feb 17; 1779: DL, Feb 8; 1781: CG, Nov 17; 1785: CG,
    May 12; 1787: CG, Mar 12, DL, Apr 14; 1789: DL, Feb 16; 1791: CG, Feb 16;
    1796: DL, Nov 12, 15
--Braganza, 1775: DL, Feb 17, 18, 20, 21, 22, 24, 25, 27, Mar 2, 4, 6, 9, 11,
    13, Apr 6, May 9, Nov 3, 30, Dec 21; 1776: DL, Jan 4, Feb 13, Mar 19, Oct 10;
    1777: DL, Apr 16, Nov 18; 1778: DL, Oct 15; 1779: DL, Feb 8; 1782: DL, Mar
    16; 1785: DL, May 24, Oct 20, Nov 5
--Campaign, The; or, Love in the East Indies (opera), 1785: CG, May 12, 14, 19;
    1787: CG, Mar 12
--Conspiracy, The, 1796: DL, Nov 12, 15, 17, 19
--Count of Narbonne, The, 1781: CG, Nov 17, 19, 20, 21, 22, 23, 24, 26, 27, 29,
    30, Dec 1, 3, 15, 27; 1782: CG, Jan 2, 12, 19, 26, May 6, 13, Oct 3, 24, Nov
    28; 1783: CG, Jan 13, May 23; 1784: CG, Jan 26, Jun 14; 1787: DL, Feb 10, Mar
    8, 15, 31; 1790: CG, Mar 22, Apr 26; 1791: CG, Sep 19; 1793: DL, Mar 2; 1795:
    CG, Mar 16, Apr 30; 1798: DL, Apr 30
--Julia; or, The Italian Lover, 1787: DL, Apr 14, 16, 26, Nov 27, Dec 11, 13,
    15, 18, 20, 22, 29; 1788: DL, Jan 1
--Law of Lombardy, The, 1779: DL, Feb 8, 9, 12, 13, 15, 16, 20, 22, 23, Apr 21;
    1789: DL, Feb 16
--Two Strings to Your Bow (farce), 1791: CG, Feb 16, 18, 21, 23, 26, Mar 8, Apr
    5, Jun 13, Dec 8; 1792: CG, Oct 12, Nov 7, Dec 19; 1793: CG, May 3, Jun 8,
    Nov 11, 23, Dec 4; 1794: CG, Oct 30; 1795: CG, Jan 31, Jun 13; 1796: CG, Dec
    9; 1797: CG, Feb 25, Jun 8, HAY, 21, 24, Jul 25; 1798: HAY, Jun 16, Jul 16,
    31, Aug 11, 30, Sep 14, CG, Nov 17; 1799: CG, Jan 16, HAY, Feb 25; 1800: CG,
    Mar 27
Jephson, W (spectator), 1689: DG, Jun 13
Jephtha. See Handel, George Frederic.
Jeptha's Rash Vow; or, The Virgin Sacrifice (droll), 1698: BF, Aug 23, 25;
    1703: BFPBS, Aug 23; 1718: SF, Sep 6; 1733: SF/BFLH, Aug 23, Sep 10; 1750:
    SFYW, Sep 7, 8, 10, 11, 12, 13
Jermaine (actor), 1681: DL, Oct 0
Jermoli, Guglielmo (singer), 1777: KING'S, Nov 4, Dec 16; 1778: KING'S, Jan 20,
    Mar 3, 26, Apr 2, 9, May 5, Nov 24, Dec 22; 1779: KING'S, Apr 29, May 15
Jermoli, Sga (singer), 1777: KING'S, Nov 4; 1778: KING'S, Jan 20, Mar 3, 10,
    26, Apr 2, May 5, Nov 24, Dec 22; 1779: KING'S, Feb 23, Apr 29
Jermyn St, 1753: KING'S, May 12; 1780: CG, Mar 29; 1781: CG, Feb 26; 1795:
    KING'S, Mar 26
Jerningham, Edward, 1777: DL, Mar 11; 1793: CG, Mar 18, Nov 13; 1794: CG, May
    10; 1795: DL, Apr 17; 1797: CG, Apr 29
--Margaret of Anjou (interlude), 1777: DL, Mar 11; 1793: CG, Mar 18, May 2;
    1794: CG, May 10
--Siege of Berwick, The, 1793: CG, Nov 13, 14, 19, 21, Dec 5, 12; 1794: CG, Jan
    24
--Welch Heiress, The, 1795: DL, Mar 23, Apr 17, 20
Jeronimo is Mad Again. See Kyd, Thomas.
Jerrold, Miss (actor), 1780: CII, Apr 19
Jerrold, Mrs Samuel (actor), 1780: CII, Feb 29, Mar 6, 13, 17, 27, Apr 5, 19;
    1799: WRSG, May 17
Jerrold, Robert (actor), 1780: CII, Feb 29, Mar 6, 13
Jerrold, Samuel (actor), 1780: CII, Feb 29, Mar 6, 13, 17, 27, Apr 19
Jerrold, Samuel and Mrs (actors), 1780: CII, Apr 19
Jerry Sneak in his Glory (song), 1799: DL, May 4
Jersey, Lord, 1750: DL, Feb 24
Jerusalem Chamber, 1730: DL, Oct 27
Jerusalem Coffee House, 1749: CG, Apr 28; 1756: DL, Nov 12
Jerusalem Lodge, 1778: HAY, Jan 26

Jervais (ticket deliverer), 1754: CG, May 4
Jervis, Admiral Sir John, 1st Earl of St Vincent, 1797: DL, Mar 6, HAY, May 10,
    KING'S, 18, CG, Dec 19
Jesuit, The. See Marriott, Reverend George.
Jesuits, 1684: MS, Nov 22; 1692: DL, Mar 0
Jeu D'Amour et du Hazard, Le. See Marivaux, Pierre Carlet de Chamblain de.
Jeu D'Esprit (entertainment), 1792: CG, May 16, 19, 28, 30; 1794: CG, May 16
Jeunesse (dance), 1727: DL, Apr 14, 22, 25, May 4, 8, 15; 1728: DL, May 9
Jeux d'Egle (dance), 1800: KING'S, Jan 11, Feb 11, 18, 22, 25
Jevon (actor), 1731: DL, Aug 6; 1733: HAY, Mar 20, 26
Jevon (Gevan, Jeuan, Jevarns, Jevorne), Thomas (actor, author), 1675: DG, May
    28, NONE, Sep 0; 1676: DG, Mar 11, May 25, Nov 4; 1677: DG, Feb 12, Mar 24,
    May 31, Jun 0, Jul 0, Sep 0; 1678: DG, Jan 0, Apr 5; 1679: DG, Sep 0, Oct 0,
    Dec 0; 1680: DG, Jun 0, Dec 8; 1681: DG, Mar 0; 1682: DG, Jan 0, 23, Mar 0,
    Apr 0, NONE, Sep 0, DL, Nov 28; 1683: DG, May 31, NONE, Sep 0, DL, Dec 0;
    1684: DL, Mar 0, DLORDG, Aug 0; 1685: DG, Jul 0, DL, Aug 0, NONE, Sep 0;
    1686: DL, Jan 0, DG, Mar 4, 6, DL, Apr 0, NONE, Sep 0; 1687: DG, Mar 0; 1688:
    DL, Feb 0, DG, Apr 0, DL, May 3
--Devil of a Wife, The; or, The Comical Transformation, 1686: DG, Mar 4, 6;
    1692: NONE, Sep 0; 1694: NONE, Sep 0; 1704: LIF, Jun 30, Aug 17; 1715: LIF,
    Jul 5, 7, 21, Aug 31, Oct 3, Nov 17; 1716: LIF, Jan 10, Apr 2, Jul 13, Oct
    29; 1717: LIF, Jul 5, Nov 5; 1718: LIF, Jan 6, Jun 27, Oct 9, Dec 1; 1719:
    LIF, Jun 17, Oct 20, Dec 3; 1720: LIF, Jan 22, Feb 12, 27, Oct 31; 1722: LIF,
    Aug 3; 1724: LIF, Apr 6, May 8, Nov 11; 1725: LIF, Feb 4, 5; 1730: GF, Oct 5,
    6, 7, 15, 29, Dec 30; 1731: GF, Jan 6, 26, May 12, DL, Aug 6
Jevon, Mrs (actor), 1720: LIF, Mar 14
Jew and the Doctor, The. See Dibdin, Thomas John.
Jew in Distress, The; or, Harlequin turned Sharper (pantomime), 1755: SF, Sep
    18
Jew of Venice, The. See Granville, George.
Jew, The. See Cumberland, Richard.
Jew, 1775: DL, Oct 28; 1776: DL, Jan 25, Feb 10, Mar 30
Jew's Harp (music), 1751: HAY, Dec 27; 1752: CT/HAY, Jan 7, 14, 31, Feb 11, CT,
    Mar 7, CT/HAY, 17, 21, Apr 1, May 5, HAY, Dec 7, 18; 1753: HAY, Mar 29; 1754:
    HAY, Jul 4, Sep 10
Jewell, Anne, Mrs William (actor), 1769: HAY, Feb 2, 22, 23, Jun 12, 21, Jul
    12, 28, Aug 7, 25, 28, 30; 1770: HAY, May 16, 21, 23, Jun 5, 22, Jul 20, Aug
    1, 31, Sep 3; 1771: HAY, May 23, Jun 3, 5, 10, 26, Jul 24, Aug 12, 19; 1772:
    HAY, Mar 16, DL, 23, HAY, May 18, 27, Jun 10, Jul 27, Aug 3; 1773: HAY, May
    28, 31, Jun 4, Jul 2, 5, 21, Aug 23, 27, Sep 3, 17; 1774: HAY, May 16, 30,
    Jun 1, 6, 8, 10, Jul 11, 15, Aug 8, 26, Sep 5, 6, 12, 16, 19, 30; 1775: DL,
    Sep 30, CG, Oct 2, DL, 21, Nov 28; 1776: DL, Feb 8, Mar 26, Apr 12, HAY, May
    20, 28, Jun 14, 19, Jul 5, 8, 10, Aug 19, 26, Sep 2, 16; 1777: HAY, May 28,
    Jun 6, 11, Jul 7, 15, 30, Aug 30, Sep 3, 17; 1778: HAY, May 18, 21, 22, Jun
    1, 11, Aug 20, 27, Sep 7, 18; 1779: HAY, Jun 2, 4, 9, Aug 13, Sep 15, 17;
    1780: HAY, May 30, Jun 17, Jul 29, Sep 8, 11; 1781: HAY, Jun 21, Aug 22
Jewell, William (treasurer), 1765: HAY, Aug 8; 1766: HAY, Jun 18, Sep 2; 1767:
    HAY, May 29, Aug 14; 1768: HAY, May 30, Aug 19; 1769: HAY, May 15, Aug 25;
    1770: HAY, May 16, Aug 31; 1771: HAY, May 15, Aug 19; 1772: HAY, May 18, Aug
    24; 1774: HAY, Sep 5; 1775: HAY, May 15, Sep 4; 1776: HAY, Sep 2; 1777: HAY,
    Sep 3, 17; 1778: HAY, Sep 2, 18; 1779: HAY, Aug 13; 1780: HAY, Aug 22; 1781:
    HAY, Aug 21, KING'S, Nov 17; 1782: HAY, Aug 16; 1783: HAY, Aug 22; 1784: HAY,
    Aug 13; 1785: HAY, Aug 11; 1786: HAY, Aug 4; 1787: HAY, Aug 14; 1788: HAY,
    Aug 13; 1789: HAY, Aug 31; 1790: HAY, Jan 7, Apr 15, Sep 6; 1791: HAY, Sep 5;
    1792: HAY, Sep 10; 1793: KING'S, Jan 26, HAY, Sep 9; 1794: HAY, Sep 8; 1795:
    HAY, Sep 7; 1796: HAY, Sep 9; 1797: HAY, Sep 11; 1798: HAY, Aug 18, Sep 10;
    1799: HAY, Sep 9; 1800: HAY, Sep 8
Jewish Courtship (interlude, anon), 1787: DL, Apr 23
Jewish Education. See Baddeley, Robert.
Jig (dance), 1700: LIF, Jul 5; 1714: DL, May 3, 14; 1717: DL, Oct 30; 1741: DL,
    Apr 4
Jinghall, Mrs (actor), 1740: BF/WF/SF, Aug 23
Jo Son quell Pellegrino (song), 1750: KING'S, Apr 10
Joan of Arc. See Cross, John Cartwright.
Joan said to John (song), 1789: HAY, Aug 25
Joanna. See Cumberland, Richard.
Joanni, Signior. See Draghi, Giovanni Baptista.
Job, D (printer), 1750: DL, Dec 10
Jockey Dance (dance), 1743: BFGA, Aug 23; 1744: MF, May 3, Jun 7; 1746: HAY,
    Apr 30, BFYB, Aug 25; 1748: HAY, Apr 30, BHB, Oct 4, NWSM, Dec 29; 1749:
    NWMF, Jan 5, 10; 1790: CG, May 27; 1791: CG, Feb 5, May 2, 7, 14, 24; 1792:
    CG, May 12

Jodrell, Richard Paul, 1779: HAY, Jul 17; 1783: HAY, Aug 22
--Seeing is Believing (farce), 1783: HAY, Aug 22, 23, 25, Sep 1, 3, 5, 8, 10;
  1784: HAY, Jun 10, 17, 21, 23; 1785: HAY, Jun 13, Jul 12, Aug 5; 1786: HAY,
  Aug 10, 14, 22, Sep 7, 11; 1787: HAY, Aug 1, 6, 30; 1788: DL, May 7, HAY, Jun
  18, 20, Jul 7, 11, 23, Aug 6, Sep 1; 1789: HAY, Jun 17, Jul 18; 1790: HAY,
  Jun 17, 24, Jul 20, 24, Aug 18, 26, Sep 11; 1791: HAY, Jun 18, 24, 25, Jul 4,
  11, 12, 20, 28, Aug 1, 6, 27, Sep 14; 1792: HAY, Jun 18, 21, 23, Aug 18;
  1793: HAY, Jun 14, 18, 19, Jul 6; 1794: HAY, Sep 10; 1795: HAY, Jun 27, Jul
  2; 1799: HAY, Jul 26, 30, Aug 21, Sep 3
--Widow and no Widow, A, 1779: HAY, Jul 17, 19, 21, 22, 26, 27, 29, Aug 4, 7,
  12, 28; 1780: HAY, Jul 15, 19, 28, Sep 2
Joe Haynes meets 'em (song), 1697: DG, Jun 0
Joe's Coffee House, 1753: DL, Dec 21
Johanna von Montfaucon. See Kotzebue, August Friedrich Ferdinand von.
Johannot, Richard (singer), 1792: HAY, Oct 15
John Bull Half Seas Over (entertainment), 1782: HAY, Nov 25
John E're You Leave Me. See Hold, John E're You Leave Me.
John Gilpin's Ride (entertainment), 1786: DL, Apr 26; 1787: RLSN, Mar 29
John St Theatre, New York, 1799: CG, May 18
John St, 1786: CG, May 24; 1788: CG, Feb 5; 1792: CG, Apr 12; 1793: CG, Apr 11;
  1794: CG, May 6; 1795: CG, Apr 24; 1796: CG, Apr 1; 1797: CG, Apr 29
John's Coffee House, 1741: GF, Apr 23
Johnes, Thomas (member of Parliament for Cardigan), 1778: DL, Nov 30
Johnny and Kate (song), 1759: DL, Apr 24
Johns (actor), 1770: HAY, Dec 19
Johnson (actor), 1742: BFHC, Aug 25, BFPY, 25, DL, Dec 15; 1743: JS, Jan 5,
  BFYWR, Aug 23; 1744: CG, Apr 20, DL, 30, MFHNT, May 1, HAY, Sep 27, 29, Oct
  4, GF, Dec 26; 1745: DT, Mar 14, SMMF, Jul 11, CG, Sep 23, Oct 18, Nov 22,
  Dec 11, 13; 1746: CG, Feb 8, Mar 13, Apr 7, 21, 23, SOU, Oct 16; 1747: DL,
  Sep 22; 1748: DL, Sep 17, JS, Oct 31, NWC, Dec 26
Johnson (actor), 1752: DL, Jan 3; 1753: DL, May 18, Oct 9; 1754: DL, Mar 14,
  Jul 2, Oct 18; 1755: DL, Oct 3, 25, 31; 1756: DL, Mar 16, May 11, Sep 28, Oct
  5; 1757: DL, Jan 22, Oct 29; 1758: DL, Nov 16
Johnson (actor), 1763: HAY, Jun 20, Jul 6, 18, Aug 1, 29, Sep 5, 7; 1764: DL,
  Dec 13; 1765: HAY, Jun 10, Jul 15, Aug 9, 21, 30; 1766: DL, Apr 16, KING'S,
  Aug 15, 25; 1770: DL, Dec 4; 1771: HAY, Apr 15, DL, Dec 31; 1772: DL, Mar 26;
  1774: HAY, May 16, 30, Jun 8, 17, 27, Aug 24, 29; 1775: HAY, Mar 23; 1776:
  HAY, Sep 17
Johnson (actor), 1791: HAY, Sep 26, Oct 24, Dec 12; 1792: CII, Jan 16, HAY, Oct
  22; 1794: HAMM, Mar 24
Johnson (gallery keeper), 1677: DL, Dec 12, 26; 1700: DL, Jun 3
Johnson (housekeeper, doorkeeper), 1759: DL, Jan 8; 1761: DL, Sep 5; 1765: DL,
  May 11, Sep 14; 1766: DL, May 10; 1767: DL, Jan 24; 1772: DL, Apr 23, Sep 19
Johnson (musician), 1724: YB, Mar 27
Johnson (property man), 1752: DL, Dec 14; 1753: DL, May 10
Johnson (singer), 1749: HAY, Apr 29, BFC, Aug 23; 1750: HAY, Feb 9, 16, 26, CG,
  Oct 8
Johnson, Benjamin (actor), 1695: DL, Sep 0, Oct 0, Nov 0; 1696: DL, Jan 0, Feb
  0, Mar 0, DG, Jun 0, DL, Sep 0, Nov 21; 1697: DL, May 31, DG, Jun 0, NONE,
  Sep 0; 1698: DL, Feb 0, Jun 0, DL/ORDG, Nov 0, DL, Dec 0; 1699: DL, Apr 0,
  Nov 28; 1700: DL, Mar 0, Apr 29, Jun 3, Jul 9; 1701: DL, Mar 1, Apr 0, May
  31, Dec 0; 1702: DL, Nov 0, Dec 14; 1703: DL, Jan 27, Mar 11, Apr 10, May 21,
  Jun 4, 23; 1704: DL, Jan 26, ATCOURT, Feb 28, LIF, Mar 30, DL, May 25, Dec
  26; 1705: DL, Apr 11, Jul 25, Oct 30, Nov 20; 1706: DL, Apr 1, QUEEN'S, Nov
  28, Dec 2, 3, 27; 1707: QUEEN'S, Jan 11, 13, 14, 17, Feb 18, 21, Mar 27, Apr
  30, Jun 18, 20, 27, Jul 1, 4, 8, 22, 26, 30, Aug 12, DL/QUEEN, Oct 18, 20,
  22, 23, 27, 28, 29, Nov 1, QUEEN'S, 22, DL/QUEEN, Dec 27; 1708: DL/QUEEN, Jan
  1, DL, 15, Feb 6, 7, 26, Mar 8, 9, 18, Apr 10, 17, 19, 27, May 21, Jun 5, 15,
  19, 24, 26, Jul 1, 3, 29, Aug 28, 31, Sep 3, 4, 9, 14, 16, 18, 28, Oct 2, 5,
  7, 14, 15, 18, 22, Dec 14, 18, 22, 28, 30, 31; 1709: DL, Jan 1, 3, 4, 17, 18,
  26, Feb 2, 16, 19, 26, Mar 14, 15, 17, 21, 31, Apr 9, 25, 30, May 3, QUEEN'S,
  Sep 22, 24, Oct 6, 17, 21, 22, 25, 28, 31, Nov 4, 9, 18, 19, Dec 12; 1710:
  QUEEN'S, Jan 7, 11, 14, 18, 21, Feb 20, May 6, 15, 19, 29, Jun 1, 5,
  DL/QUEEN, Oct 5, Nov 8, QUEEN'S, 10, DL/QUEEN, 11, 13, 15, 16, 18, DL, 21,
  25, 27, 28, Dec 1, 2, 4, 7, 9, 14, 15, 18, 22; 1711: DL, Jan 9, 15, 19, 20,
  26, 29, Feb 10, DL/QUEEN, 17, DL, Mar 8, Apr 7, 26, May 21, 31, DL/QUEEN, Jun
  22, DL, 26, Jul 3, 10, Aug 3, 17, 31, Sep 22, 27, 29, Oct 12, 16, 20, 26, 27,
  29, 30, Nov 1, 2, 5, 6, 8, 20, 26, Dec 8, 10, 31; 1712: DL, Apr 29, May 13,
  Jul 4, 22, Aug 8, 26, Sep 25, Oct 4, 7, 10, 13, 15, 17, 22, 29, 31, Nov 26,
  Dec 12, 27; 1713: DL, Jan 14, 29, Feb 9, 13, Mar 3, 16, Apr 20, May 11, 18,
  Jun 5, 12, 19, Sep 29, Oct 23, Nov 9, Dec 2, 18; 1714: DL, Mar 31, Apr 12,
  May 5, 17, 21, 26, 28, Jun 2, 4, 18, 25, 29, Jul 2, 13, Oct 22, Nov 9, 26,

Dec 6, 8, 20; 1715: DL, Jan 22, Feb 4, 12, 15, 22, 23, Mar 8, 19, Apr 2, 30,
Jun 6, 24, 28, Jul 1, 6, Nov 12, Dec 9, 12, 30; 1716: DL, Jan 17, 25, 26, Feb
1, 9, 18, 23, Mar 3, 10, Apr 2, 9, May 9, Jun 15, Jul 12, 19, Oct 2, 6, 9,
12, 16, 19, 22, 24, 27, 29, Nov 2, 3, 12, 14, Dec 4, 14; 1717: DL, Jan 9, 16,
31, Feb 15, Mar 1, Apr 8, Jun 10, 24, Jul 2, 16, Aug 6, 9, Sep 28, Oct 1, 3,
15, 16, 21, Nov 6, 8, 20, 25, 27, Dec 4, 31; 1718: DL, Jan 20, 23, 27, Feb
19, Mar 24, Apr 3, 5, 19, May 28, Jun 11, 27, Jul 1, 11, NONE, 30, DL, Aug 1,
20, Sep 20, 27, Oct 2, 7, 10, 11, 15, 17, Nov 12, 18, 19, 24, 26, 27, 28, Dec
1, 10, 11; 1719: DL, Jan 6, 28, Apr 22, Sep 12, 15, 17, 19, 24, Oct 7, 8, 14,
16, 22, 23, Nov 2, 3, 6, 11, 14, 23, Dec 2; 1720: DL, Jan 1, 12, 13, Feb 15,
Mar 19, 31, May 20, Jun 7, 11, Jul 7, Sep 15, 17, 29, Oct 4, 6, 7, 13, 15,
29, Nov 2, 10, 12, 18, 21, Dec 5, 8; 1721: DL, Jan 13, 16, 25, Mar 7, 23, Apr
13, 26, May 5, 29, Aug 9, Sep 9, 12, 14, 16, 26, 28, 30, Oct 3, 4, 9, 10, 12,
16, 18, 21, 23, 25, 31, Nov 7, 8, 17, 28, Dec 22; 1722: DL, Jan 9, 15, 16,
Apr 5, May 22, Jul 10, Sep 11, 15, 18, 20, 25, 27, Oct 10, 12, 15, 16, 17,
19, 20, 22, 24, 31, Dec 5, 26; 1723: DL, Jan 17, 28, Feb 5, Mar 25, May 11,
20, Jun 3, 4, Sep 17, 19, 21, 24, 28, Oct 1, 3, 8, 10, 21, 22, 23, 29, Nov 1,
6, 14, 19, 21, 22, Dec 30; 1724: DL, Feb 17, Apr 8, 28, May 1, 22, Sep 12,
15, 17, 19, 29, Oct 14, 22, 24, 27, 28, 29, Nov 6, 10, 13, 26, 27, Dec 7;
1725: DL, Feb 3, 18, Mar 31, Apr 15, 21, 22, 30, May 11, Sep 7, 9, 11, 14,
16, 18, 21, 25, Oct 5, 7, 9, 15, 20, 23, 25, Nov 8, 22, 29; 1726: DL, Jan 5,
26, Mar 24, May 23, Sep 6, 10, 13, 17, 22, 24, 29, Oct 6, 11, 15, 20, 27, Nov
12, 16, 26, Dec 12, 14; 1727: DL, Jan 20, Apr 6, May 2, 15, 19, 22, Sep 14,
19, 23, 26, 30, Oct 3, 5, 9, 12, 20, 23, 26, 30, Nov 1, 21, Dec 4; 1728: DL,
Jan 3, 5, Mar 9, 28, Apr 2, May 17, Sep 10, 12, 17, 19, 21, 26, 28, Oct 3,
17, 21, 23, 25; 1729: DL, Jan 1, 3, 22, 29, 31, Feb 3, 6, Mar 27, HAY, 29,
DL, Apr 16, 22, 23, HAY, May 2, 3, DL, 3, 6, HAY, 19, DL, Sep 13, 25, 30, Oct
2, 9, 14, 22, 23, 30, Nov 17, 18, 27, Dec 2, 3, 4, HAY, 18; 1730: DL, Jan 24,
HAY, Feb 23, Mar 13, DL, Apr 13, 14, May 2, Sep 12, 15, 17, 22, 24, Oct 10,
22, Nov 24, 25, 30; 1731: DL, Feb 8, Mar 15, 20, Apr 1, 8, May 1, 3, 7, 10,
19, Sep 18, 25, 28, Oct 5, 7, 9, 21, 30, Nov 8, 22, 23, Dec 1, 2, 17, 22, 29;
1732: DL, Feb 10, HAY, Mar 2, 8, DL, 20, 23, 30, Apr 17, HAY, 20, DL, 25,
HAY, 26, DL, 29, HAY, May 1, DL, 4, 5, Sep 19, 28, 30, Oct 3, 10, 17, 21, 28,
Nov 9, 11, 13, 14, 24, Dec 9, 26; 1733: DL, Jan 19, 22, Feb 3, 22, Mar 15,
28, Apr 6, 11, 23, 24, May 1, 14, 29, Jun 4, DL/HAY, Sep 26, Oct 3, 6, 10,
12, 17, 22, 25, 27, Nov 9, 16, 23, Dec 10, 19, 20, 22; 1734: HAY, Feb 12,
DL/HAY, Mar 12, 25, Apr 17, 18, 20, DL, 22, DL/HAY, May 1, DL, 15, Sep 7, 19,
24, 26, Oct 3, 5, 14, 17, 19, 22, Nov 8, 16, 22, Dec 6; 1735: DL, Jan 29, Mar
10, 13, 27, Apr 11, 14, LIF, 18, DL, May 1, 2, Sep 1, 4, 11, 13, 15, 18, 25,
Oct 21, 23, 24, GF, 27, DL, 27, 31, Nov 1, 3, GF, 4, DL, 7, 10, GF, 15, DL,
17, GF, 19, DL, 20, 21, GF, 26, Dec 17; 1736: DL, Jan 3, GF, 3, 29, Feb 16,
Mar 9, DL, 11, 13, 20, GF, 22, DL, 29, LIF, 31, GF, Apr 8, 16, 17, LIF, Jun
18, DL, Sep 4, 7, 9, 11, 14, 18, 21, LIF, 28, DL, Oct 7, 9, 12, LIF, 14, DL,
19, LIF, 19, DL, 21, 22, 23, LIF, 28, DL, 29, 30, Nov 1, 3, LIF, 4, DL, 12,
15, 19, LIF, 20, 26, 27, DL, Dec 7, LIF, 20; 1737: DL, Jan 6, LIF, 10, DL,
Feb 10, LIF, 12, 14, 21, Mar 1, HAY, 3, DL, 17, LIF, 21, DL, 26, LIF, Apr 21,
May 2, DL, Aug 30, Sep 6, 10, 15, 22, 24, Oct 20, 24, CG, Nov 2, DL, 11, 14,
15, 16; 1738: DL, Jan 19, 23, 31, CG, Feb 6, 13, 23, DL, 28, Mar 2, CG, 13,
DL, 18, 20, Apr 14, 17, 28, May 1, 3, 6, Sep 7, 9, 14, 16, 21, Oct 3, 17, 18,
20, 23, 27, Nov 3, CG, 4, DL, 9, 17, 20, 29, CG, 30, DL, 30, CG, Dec 2, 4, 5;
1739: CG, Jan 4, DL, 8, 22, 26, CG, Feb 22, DL, Mar 20, 22, 29, Apr 28, May
9, 16, 18, 19, CG, 25, DL, Sep 1, 4, 8, CG, 15, DL, 18, 20, 22, CG, 27, 29,
DL, Oct 10, 11, 13, 20, 22, CG, 23, DL, 23, 24, 25, CG, Nov 5, DL, 7, 19, 20,
21, CG, Dec 6, 10, DL, 14, 26; 1740: DL, Jan 3, 16, Feb 7, CG, Mar 11, DL,
13, 20, 29, Apr 22, 29, May 30, Sep 6, 9, 11, 25, 30, Oct 2, 4, 9, 10, 11,
13, 14, 15, Nov 10, 13, 27, 28, 29, Dec 18, 19; 1741: DL, Jan 6, Feb 14, 24,
Mar 21, Apr 3, May 13, 14, 21, 25, Sep 5, 12, 19, Oct 6, 8, 9, 21, Nov 2, 16,
21, Dec 7; 1742: DL, Jan 4, 6, Feb 11, 12, 13, Mar 27, JS, Apr 7, DL, 24, May
12
Johnson, Captain (rioter), 1749: DL, Dec 2
Johnson, Charles (author), 1701: LIF, Aug 0; 1704: LIF, Oct 2; 1705: LIF/QUEN,
Feb 22; 1710: QUEEN'S, May 1; 1711: DL, Jan 20, Nov 12; 1712: DL, Nov 7;
1714: DL, Jan 5; 1715: DL, Feb 4; 1716: DL, Feb 3; 1717: DL, Feb 25; 1719:
DL, Jan 16; 1723: DL, Jan 9; 1726: LIF, Jan 7; 1729: DL, Feb 6; 1730: DL, Dec
11; 1732: DL, Apr 17, Dec 11; 1762: CG, Dec 8; 1778: CG, Nov 23, Dec 21;
1782: CG, Apr 10; 1789: DL, May 1
--Caelia; or, The Perjured Lover, 1732: DL, Dec 11, 12
--Country Lasses, The; or, The Custom of the Manor (Country), 1715: DL, Feb 4,
5, 7, 9, May 5, 17, Jun 2, Jul 6; 1716: DL, May 14; 1724: RI, Jul 13; 1729:
DL, Jun 27, Jul 4, 8, Aug 9; 1730: DL, May 11, Nov 18; 1734: GF, Dec 2, 3, 4,
5, 14; 1735: GF, Jan 17, Mar 4; 1736: GF, Mar 29, LIF, Dec 14, 15, 22; 1739:
CG, Mar 27, 31, Apr 2, May 15; 1740: CG, May 15, 17, 28, Nov 15, Dec 16;

461

1741: CG, May 5; 1744: JS, Mar 16; 1745: GF, Apr 2, May 3; 1746: CG, Apr 22,
     25; 1747: CG, Feb 6, Dec 19, 26; 1749: SOU, Feb 13; 1751: CG, Dec 14, 17, 19,
     27; 1752: CG, Jan 22, Feb 22, Apr 14, Nov 1; 1753: CG, Jan 17, Oct 24, Nov
     29; 1756: CG, Jan 6, 7, 8, 9, 10, 13, 14, 23, Feb 11, 17, Apr 19, May 18, 19,
     Oct 19, Dec 6, 15, 21; 1757: CG, Jan 18, May 12, Sep 16, Nov 30; 1758: CG,
     May 5; 1759: CG, Mar 17, May 29, Dec 31; 1760: CG, Jan 10, May 3; 1761: CG,
     Jan 23, May 12, Oct 22, Nov 12; 1763: CG, Nov 26, 30, Dec 3; 1764: CG, Feb 4,
     Nov 15; 1765: CG, Jan 17, Nov 22, Dec 5; 1767: CG, Feb 28, May 12; 1769: CG,
     Nov 17; 1778: HAY, Apr 29, CG, Nov 23, Dec 21; 1789: DL, May 1
--Ephesian Matron, The, 1732: DL, Apr 17, 29
--Female Fortune Teller, The, 1726: LIF, Jan 7, 8, 10, 11, 12, 13, 21
--Force of Friendship, The, 1710: QUEEN'S, Apr 17, 20, May 1
--Generous Husband, The; or, The Coffee House Politician, 1711: DL, Jan 20, 22,
     23
--Gentleman Cully, The, 1701: LIF, Aug 0, DL, 13
--Love in a Chest, 1710: QUEEN'S, May 1
--Love in a Forest, 1723: DL, Jan 9, 10, 11, 12, 14, 15
--Masquerade, The, 1719: DL, Jan 16, 17, 19, 20, 21, 22, 27, NONE, Mar 26, DL,
     Apr 3
--Medea, 1730: DL, Dec 11, 12, 14
--Successful Pirate, The, 1712: DL, Nov 7, 8, 10, 11, Dec 16
--Sultaness, The, 1717: DL, Feb 25, 26, 27, 28
--Victim, The, 1714: DL, Jan 5, 6, 7, 8, 9, 11
--Village Opera, The, 1729: DL, Feb 6, 7, 8, 10, 11, 27, Apr 8; 1730: HAY, Jan
     8, 9, 16; 1756: DL, Mar 23; 1762: CG, Dec 8
--Villagers, The, 1756: DL, Mar 23
--Wife's Relief, The; or, The Husband's Cure, 1711: DL, Nov 12, 13, 15, 16, 17,
     19, 20, Dec 1, 14, 29; 1712: DL, Feb 4; 1713: DL, Nov 3, 11; 1715: LIF, Oct
     7, 8, 19, Nov 25; 1717: LIF, Jan 11, Nov 26; 1718: LIF, Jan 27, Apr 5; 1722:
     HAY, Dec 17; 1723: DT, Nov 26; 1728: LIF, Jul 19, 23; 1736: LIF, Oct 5, 7,
     DL, 13, 14, 15, LIF, 16, DL, 16, 18, 20, Nov 10; 1737: DL, Jan 25, LIF, Feb
     11, May 17; 1741: GF, Feb 2, 6; 1742: GF, Jan 4; 1750: HAY, Jul 26; 1761: CG,
     Mar 26, Apr 16, May 7, Oct 31; 1782: CG, Apr 10, 19, May 24
Johnson, E (publisher), 1779: CG, Apr 30
Johnson, Elizabeth, Mrs John (actor), 1798: CG, Sep 28, Oct 5, 11, Dec 11;
     1799: CG, Jan 14, 23, May 18, Oct 10, Nov 30; 1800: CG, May 28
Johnson, Henry (box-bookkeeper), 1776: KING'S, Nov 2; 1778: KING'S, Nov 24;
     1779: KING'S, Nov 27; 1781: KING'S, Nov 17; 1788: KING'S, Feb 21
Johnson, John (actor), 1783: HAY, Sep 17; 1784: HAY, Jan 21; 1787: HAY, May 16,
     18, 23, 25, Jun 18, 20, 22, 26, 27, Jul 3, 7, 19, 23, 25, 27, Aug 1, 3, 4, 7,
     14, 17, 21, 22, 29, Sep 5, 8; 1788: HAY, Jun 10, 12, 18, 23, 30, Jul 2, 3,
     10, 24, Aug 5, 9, 27, 28, Sep 3, 9; 1789: HAY, May 20, 25, Jun 1, 3, 5, 8,
     12, 17, 19, 22, 25, 30, Jul 4, 6, 30, Aug 5, 11, Sep 8; 1790: DL, Oct 23;
     1791: HAY, Jul 30; 1792: HAY, Feb 6, Jun 18, 20, 22, 23, 26, Jul 3, 16, 25,
     31, Aug 2, 6, 9, 15, 17, 23, 31; 1796: HAY, Jun 22; 1799: CG, May 18
Johnson, John (architect), 1793: KING'S, Feb 19
Johnson, Master (actor), 1762: DL, Feb 26, Mar 3, 5, RANELAGH, Jun 11
Johnson, Miss (actor), 1723: DL, Apr 6; 1724: DL, Jan 27, Oct 28, Nov 10; 1725:
     DL, Feb 13, Apr 7, 22, May 17; 1726: DL, May 17
Johnson, Miss (actor), 1767: RANELAGH, Jun 1
Johnson, Mrs (actor), 1670: LIF, Jan 0, Apr 0, Nov 0, Dec 10; 1672: DG, Nov 4,
     ATCOU/DG, Dec 2; 1673: DG, May 0, Jul 3
Johnson, Mrs (actor), 1725: DL, Jan 9
Johnson, Mrs (actor), 1748: NWC, Dec 26, 29; 1749: SOU, Jan 2; 1761: DL, Mar
     26, May 21, 28; 1763: HAY, Sep 5, 7; 1767: HAY, Aug 5, 7, DL, Sep 15, Oct 10;
     1769: DL, May 6, Sep 19; 1770: DL, Oct 8; 1771: DL, Nov 12; 1772: DL, May 30;
     1774: DL, Feb 11; 1775: DL, Mar 6, 18, Oct 23, 30
Johnson, Mrs (actor), 1781: DL, Feb 17, HAY, Oct 16; 1784: HAY, Jan 21, Mar 8;
     1792: CII, Jan 16; 1794: HAMM, Mar 24
Johnson, Nathaniel
--Pyrander, 1662: NONE, Sep 0
Johnson, Rev Dr Samuel (governor of the College of New York), 1763: DL, Apr 27
Johnson, Samuel (actor), 1776: CHR, Sep 23, 25, 27, 30, Oct 2, 4, 7, 9, 11, 14,
     16, 18; 1777: HAY, Feb 11; 1778: HAY, Mar 23; 1779: HAY, Mar 15; 1781: HAY,
     Jan 22; 1782: HAY, Mar 4, 21, Apr 9, May 6
Johnson, Samuel (actor, author), 1737: LIF, Jan 10; 1741: HAY, Apr 11, May 15
--All Alive and Merry; or, Men in Pursuit of Money, 1737: LIF, Jan 10, 11, 12,
     13, 14, 15, 17, May 10, BF, Aug 23, SF, Sep 7; 1746: BFWF, Aug 25
--Blazing Comet, The, 1732: HAY, Mar 2, 3, 6, 8, 27, Apr 19, 20, 26
--Cheshire Comicks, The; or, The Amours of Lord Flame, 1730: HAY, Feb 23, 25,
     27, Apr 15
--Fool Made Wise, A, 1741: HAY, Apr 11, 13, 18

--Hurlothrumbo; or, News from Terra Australis Incognita, 1729: HAY, Mar 29, Apr
   7, 9, 10, 11, 12, 14, 15, 16, 17, 18, 19, 21, 22, 23, 25, 26, 30, May 2, 3,
   5, 8, 9, 10, 12, 13, 14, 17, 19, Dec 18, 27, 29, 31; 1730: HAY, Jan 29, Feb
   18, 23, Mar 13, Apr 20; 1731: HAY, Aug 20; 1732: HAY, Mar 2, May 1; 1734:
   HAY, May 21; 1735: LIF, Apr 18; 1737: LIF, Jan 10; 1741: HAY, May 15
--Sir John Falstaff in Masquerade, 1741: HAY, Apr 11, 13, 18
Johnson, Dr Samuel (lexicographer), 1747: DL, Sep 15; 1749: DL, Feb 6, 9, 15,
   20; 1750: DL, Apr 5; 1771: HAY, Jun 26; 1775: DL, Mar 27; 1777: CG, May 29;
   1791: DL, Jun 4
--Mahomet and Irene, 1748: DL, Nov 29; 1749: DL, Jan 15, Feb 6, 7, 9, 11, 13,
   14, 15, 16, 18, 20; 1750: DL, Apr 4
Johnson, Widow (beneficiary), 1747: CG, Apr 25; 1748: CG, Mar 29
Johnson's Music Shop, 1746: HIC, Mar 10
Johnston (actor), 1756: DL, Apr 29, Nov 6; 1757: DL, Jan 22, Oct 13; 1758: DL,
   Oct 7; 1759: DL, Jan 4, Feb 26, Apr 7, Jul 12, Oct 4, 30, Nov 19, 22; 1760:
   DL, Mar 25, Jul 29, Oct 2, 3, Dec 17; 1761: DL, Mar 23, Sep 14, 17, Oct 7;
   1762: DL, Mar 27, Oct 5, 15, Nov 2, 10, Dec 11; 1763: DL, May 19, Sep 22, Oct
   28, 31, Nov 2; 1764: DL, Sep 25, Oct 20, Dec 27; 1765: DL, Apr 13, Sep 24,
   Oct 5, Nov 16; 1766: DL, Jan 6, Apr 22, KING'S, Sep 13, DL, 27, Oct 29, Dec
   4, 10; 1767: DL, Sep 15, 17, 23, Oct 23, CG, Nov 4; 1768: DL, Sep 26, 28, Oct
   11, 25, Dec 7, 30; 1769: DL, Apr 12, Sep 26, Nov 16; 1770: DL, Mar 22, May 5;
   1771: DL, Mar 23, Apr 6, 26, Oct 19, Dec 26; 1772: DL, Oct 3, 21, Dec 15;
   1773: DL, Mar 9; 1774: DL, Jan 13, Feb 18, Mar 14, 15, 17, May 9; 1775: DL,
   Jan 10, 18, 24, Feb 2, Mar 2, 3, May 27; 1777: HAY, Oct 9; 1778: DL, Jan 1
Johnston (actor), 1784: HAY, Jan 21; 1786: HAMM, Jun 5, 7, 28, 30, Jul 5, 10,
   26, Aug 5
Johnston (actor), 1797: HAY, Sep 18
Johnston (stage doorkeeper), 1762: DL, Apr 2, May 26, Sep 18; 1763: DL, May 14,
   Sep 17; 1764: DL, May 12, Sep 15; 1765: DL, Mar 18; 1766: DL, Sep 20, Nov 21;
   1767: DL, Jan 12, 24, Feb 28, Mar 21, 30, May 16, Jun 3, Sep 26, Dec 19;
   1768: DL, May 7, Jun 21, Sep 17; 1769: DL, May 15; 1770: DL, Mar 2, May 19;
   1771: DL, Feb 15, May 23, Oct 23, 30, Dec 3; 1772: DL, Feb 18, Mar 6, May 29,
   Jun 10; 1773: DL, Feb 26, May 12, 27, Sep 18, Nov 6; 1775: DL, Oct 21; 1776:
   DL, Jan 8, Feb 1
Johnston, A (dancer), 1787: DL, May 18, Jun 7; 1798: DL, Dec 5, 6; 1799: DL,
   Feb 5
Johnston, A (featherman), 1772: DL, Jun 10; 1773: DL, Jun 2; 1774: DL, May 20,
   Jun 2; 1775: DL, May 20
Johnston, Alexander (machinist), 1789: DL, Jun 9; 1790: DL, Jun 1; 1791: DL,
   May 25, DLKING'S, Oct 1; 1792: CG, Apr 12; 1793: KING'S, Apr 23; 1794: DL,
   Apr 21, Dec 20; 1795: DL, Feb 12, May 6, Oct 21, Nov 23; 1796: DL, Jan 18,
   Mar 12, Apr 2, 30, Jun 7, Nov 9, Dec 26; 1797: DL, Jun 9; 1798: HAY, Jul 21,
   DL, Oct 6; 1799: DL, Jan 19, KING'S, Mar 26, DL, May 24, Jun 21, Oct 14, Dec
   11; 1800: DL, Mar 11, Apr 29
Johnston, Captain (spectator), 1760: DL, Mar 10
Johnston, Helen, Mrs Roger (actor), 1767: DL, Sep 16, 17, 18, 21, 26, Oct 10,
   20, Nov 20, 21, 24, Dec 3; 1768: DL, Mar 15, 21, Apr 4, 14, 15, 23, Sep 17,
   26, 28, 29, Oct 5, Nov 21, Dec 16, HAY, 19; 1769: DL, Jan 6, 9, 20, 25, Mar
   18, Apr 10, May 1, 22, Sep 19, Oct 2, 17, 30, Nov 2, 8, 11, 13, 22, Dec 13;
   1770: DL, Feb 13, May 12, 30, Sep 22, Oct 3, 12, 16, 17, 18, 20, 29, Dec 6,
   19, 31; 1771: DL, Apr 2, 26, May 11, Sep 21, 28, Oct 10, 15, 19, 25, 28, 29,
   Nov 9, Dec 3, 4; 1772: DL, Mar 12, May 4, 19, Jun 2, Oct 1, 14, 16, 24, Nov
   12, 20, 28, Dec 17, 18, 22; 1773: DL, Jan 29, Feb 10, 11, Mar 26, Apr 23, May
   13, 31, Oct 2, 14, Nov 13, 24, Dec 16, 27, 31; 1774: DL, Jan 4, 14, Feb 2, 7,
   8, Apr 28, May 4, 9, 28, HAY, Sep 6, DL, 22, Oct 4, 5, 8, 20, 24, Nov 8, 9,
   11, 25; 1775: DL, Jan 4, 23, Feb 17, May 1, 10, 12, 13, 20, HAY, Sep 21, DL,
   Oct 3, 14, 21, 26, Nov 9, 18, 21, 25, 30, Dec 5, 11; 1776: DL, Feb 10, Mar
   18, 23, 25, 28, May 6, 22, Jun 10, Oct 10, 12, 18, 19, 23, 25, Nov 5, 7, 9,
   Dec 10, 28; 1777: DL, Feb 17, Apr 21, 24, May 19, Sep 25, 27, 30, Oct 7, Nov
   8, 13, 14, 18, 29; 1778: DL, Mar 30, Apr 23, May 5, 14, 23, Sep 19, Oct 3,
   15, 20, 23, 26, 27, Nov 16, Dec 11; 1779: DL, Jan 7, Mar 11, Apr 9, 12, 16,
   May 15, Oct 30; 1780: DL, Oct 3, 11, 12, 23, Nov 1, 27, Dec 8; 1781: DL, Jan
   6, Feb 17, Mar 27, May 1
Johnston, Henry Erskine (actor), 1797: CG, Oct 23, Nov 2, 29; 1798: CG, Jan 4,
   DL, 16, CG, Apr 17, 28, May 30, DL, Jun 12, HAY, 23, 28, Jul 16, 21, Sep 3,
   CG, Oct 11, 25, Nov 12, Dec 11, 21, 22; 1799: CG, Jan 12, Mar 2, 5, 16, Apr
   8, 19, 23, 27, 30, May 15, 18, Jun 1, 12, HAY, 15, 18, 24, CG, Sep 25, Oct 9,
   10, 18, 21, Nov 14, 30; 1800: CG, Jan 16, Feb 8, Apr 1, 22, 26, 29, May 10,
   12, 13, Jun 2, 6, HAY, 13
Johnston, Henry Erskine and Nannette (actors), 1800: CG, Apr 29
Johnston, J (abused spectator), 1744: DL, Nov 24
Johnston, J (music keeper), 1771: DL, Oct 26; 1772: DL, Jun 10; 1773: DL, Jun

2, Nov 25, 29; 1774: DL, Jan 21, Jun 2, Nov 18, 25; 1775: DL, Jan 10, Feb 7,
    Apr 1, May 27, Oct 19, Dec 1; 1776: DL, Mar 23, Apr 12
Johnston, J (wardrobe keeper), 1767: DL, Jan 24, Apr 29, May 4
Johnston, Master (actor), 1759: HAY, May 10
Johnston, Mr and Mrs (actors), 1786: HAMM, Aug 5
Johnston, Mr and Mrs (beneficiaries), 1769: DL, May 6
Johnston, Mrs (actor), 1760: DL, Jul 29, Dec 17; 1761: DL, Feb 12, 14, Jun 15;
    1766: KING'S, Aug 27, 29, Sep 9, 17, 19; 1767: HAY, Jul 31, Aug 14
Johnston, Mrs (actor), 1786: HAMM, Jun 5, 7, 28, 30, Jul 5, 7, 10, 19, 24, 26,
    Aug 5
Johnston, Mrs J (beneficiary), 1770: DL, May 12
Johnston, Nannette, Mrs Henry Erskine (actor), 1798: HAY, Sep 3, 12, CG, 17,
    Oct 11; 1799: CG, Jan 12, Mar 2, 5, 14, 16, 25, Apr 19, 23, May 13, Jun 12,
    Sep 25, Oct 10, 11, Nov 30; 1800: CG, Jan 16, Feb 8, 19, Apr 29, May 1, Jun 2
Johnston, R (gilder), 1771: DL, Nov 25; 1772: DL, Jan 6, Feb 24, Mar 16; 1773:
    DL, Mar 1; 1776: DL, Jun 10
Johnston, Roger (actor), 1779: DL, Apr 22, Oct 23; 1780: DL, Sep 30
Johnston, Roger (author), 1790: DL, Dec 27
--Fairy Favour, The; or, Harlequin Animated (pantomime), 1790: DL, Dec 27, 28,
    29, 30, 31; 1791: DL, Jan 3, 4, 6, 17, 19, 20, 22, 24, 26, 27, 31, Feb 7, 11,
    21, 23, Mar 1, 14, 21, 28, Apr 11
Johnstone (actor), 1780: HAY, Nov 13; 1785: HAY, Mar 15
Johnstone (author), 1778: CG, Dec 8
--Buthred, 1778: CG, Dec 8, 10, 12, 14; 1779: CG, Jan 12
Johnstone, Ann (actor), 1798: CG, Jan 4; 1799: CG, Jun 12
Johnstone, James, 1786: HAY, Jul 24
--Disbanded Officer, The; or, The Baroness of Bruchsal, 1786: HAY, Jul 24, 26,
    27, 29, 31, Aug 1, 5, 7, 8, 28, Sep 8; 1787: HAY, Jun 22; 1788: HAY, Jun 19,
    Jul 29
Johnstone, John Henry (actor, singer), 1783: CG, Oct 2, 14, 24, 27, Nov 4, 8,
    Dec 18; 1784: CG, Jan 21, 27, 29, Feb 23, Mar 27, Apr 17, 26, 27, 28, May 7,
    25, 29, Sep 17, 21, 22, Oct 4, 12, 18, 25, 28, Nov 10, 16, Dec 27; 1785: CG,
    Mar 19, 30, Apr 5, 6, 11, 12, 18, May 4, 12, 17, Sep 19, 21, 23, Oct 5, 7,
    14, 17, 20, 21, Nov 3, 4, 5, 10, 14, 19, Dec 5, 8; 1786: CG, Jan 18, Feb 7,
    13, 17, 18, 21, 23, 28, Mar 7, 14, 16, 18, 25, Apr 1, 20, 28, May 22, HAMM,
    Jul 10, CG, Sep 18, Oct 4, 9, 12, 16, 21, 23, 31, Nov 15, 22, 24, 25, Dec 1,
    5, 6, 8, 16, 23; 1787: CG, Jan 4, 17, Mar 1, 12, 31, Apr 10, 28, May 9, 15,
    21, Sep 17, 19, 21, 24, 26, 28, Oct 1, 3, 17, 18, 19, 22, 31, Nov 14, Dec 3,
    21, 22; 1788: CG, Jan 10, 14, 28, Mar 28, Apr 1, 2, 8, 14, 16, May 12, 22,
    Sep 15, 17, 19, 22, 24, 26, 29, Oct 1, 8, 17, 18, 21, 22, 25, Nov 1, 6, Dec
    13, 15, 29; 1789: CG, Jan 27, Feb 6, 11, 14, 20, 24, Mar 31, Apr 14, 15, 21,
    May 2, 5, 20, 29, Jun 2, DL, 13, CG, Sep 14, 16, 18, 23, 25, 28, Oct 2, 7,
    12, 13, 20, 21, 23, 28, 31, Nov 6, 10, 11, 14, 20, 21, 24, 28, Dec 4, 12;
    1790: CG, Mar 8, 18, Apr 13, 16, 21, May 5, 6, 13, 24, Sep 13, 15, 17, Oct 6,
    12, 13, 15, 19, 20, 30, Nov 4, 9, 11, 23, 26, Dec 2, 11, 20, 28; 1791: CG,
    Jan 15, Feb 4, 12, Apr 28, May 3, 5, 6, 14, 17, 18, 20, 31, Jun 6, 7, HAY,
    25, Jul 19, 20, 30, Aug 19, 26, CG, Sep 12, 14, 17, 19, 26, 28, 30, Oct 3, 6,
    10, 19, Nov 1, 2, 5, 7, 12, 15, 25, 26, Dec 10, 15; 1792: CG, Feb 25, 28,
    DLKING'S, Mar 29, CG, Apr 12, 18, 21, May 2, 15, 22, DLKING'S, Jun 7, HAY,
    18, 23, Jul 3, Aug 2, 15, 22, CG, Sep 17, 19, 20, 21, 24, 26, 28, Oct 3, 5,
    8, 10, 19, 26, 27, 29, Nov 7, Dec 13; 1793: CG, Jan 9, 25, Mar 18, Apr 4, 24,
    25, May 3, 10, 11, 15, 21, 24, DL, Jun 3, CG, 12, HAY, 13, 17, 29, Jul 9, 19,
    Aug 3, 8, 12, 27, 28, CG, Sep 18, HAY, 19, CG, 20, HAY, 21, CG, 25, 27, 30,
    Oct 1, 4, HAY, 7, CG, 7, 8, 15, 18, 24, 29, Nov 1, 2, 5, 7, 18, 23, Dec 7,
    10; 1794: CG, Jan 3, 21, Feb 22, Apr 7, 10, 12, 29, May 2, 6, 7, 9, 13, 16,
    23, 26, 31, Jun 6, HAY, Jul 8, 11, 16, 17, 21, Aug 9, 18, 19, 23, 25, 28, Sep
    3, CG, 15, 17, 19, 22, 24, 26, Oct 3, 7, 8, 17, 20, 21, 29, 30, Nov 12, 15,
    Dec 30, 31; 1795: CG, Jan 2, 29, Feb 6, HAY, Mar 4, CG, 19, Apr 22, 23, 28,
    May 1, 6, 13, 14, 16, 19, 21, 25, DL, Jun 1, CG, 2, 5, 8, HAY, 11, 15, 19,
    20, Jul 16, 31, Aug 14, 25, Sep 2, 4, CG, 14, 16, 18, 21, 23, 25, 28, Oct 5,
    7, 14, 30, Nov 6, 9, 16, 18, 25, 27, DL, Dec 10, CG, 21, 23, 29; 1796: CG,
    Jan 2, 23, 25, 28, Feb 1, Apr 5, 9, 12, 15, 19, 26, 29, May 12, 18, 20, 24,
    26, Jun 2, HAY, 11, 17, 22, 25, Jul 15, Sep 1, CG, 19, 21, 26, 30, Oct 3, 5,
    6, 7, 17, 18, 20, 21, 29, Nov 4, 19; 1797: CG, Feb 18, 27, May 2, 9, 11, 16,
    17, 20, Jun 8, HAY, 15, 16, 17, 21, 23, 26, 29, Jul 8, 15, Aug 4, 7, 11, 24,
    Sep 1, CG, 20, 22, 27, 29, Oct 2, 11, 20, 21, 31, Nov 11, 15, 22, Dec 12, 19,
    28; 1798: CG, Jan 1, Feb 9, Mar 15, 17, 31, Apr 11, 17, 21, 24, May 8, 9, 12,
    14, 24, 28, 31, Jun 1, HAY, 14, 15, 16, 20, 21, 29, Jul 14, 20, 21, Aug 6,
    11, 14, 28, Sep 7, 10, CG, 17, 19, 26, Oct 8, Nov 7, 12, Dec 15, 26; 1799:
    CG, Jan 22, 25, 28, Mar 5, 14, 16, 27, Apr 6, 9, 12, 16, 26, 30, May 3, 4,
    13, 28, Jun 1, 3, 5, 6, HAY, 20, 21, 22, 24, 25, Jul 2, 12, 13, 16, 20, Aug
    13, 27, Sep 2, CG, 23, 27, 30, Oct 7, 11, 17, 18, 24, 25, Dec 16; 1800: CG,

Jan 11, 29, Feb 19, Mar 1, Apr 15, 19, 22, 23, 26, 30, May 6, 7, 20, 22, 30,
HAY, Jun 13, 14, 16, 17, 19, Jul 7, Aug 14, 19, 23, 29, Sep 1
Johnstone, Maria Ann, Mrs John Henry (actor, singer), 1783: CG, Sep 17, 19, 22,
Oct 6, 16, Nov 8, Dec 12, 15, 20; 1784: CG, Jan 2, 19, Feb 9
Join with thee calm peace and quiet (song), 1791: CG, Mar 18; 1794: CG, Mar 21,
DL, Apr 9
Jolly (dancer), 1756: CG, May 11, 18; 1757: HAY, Jul 1, 5, Aug 22, 27, 31, Sep
2, 14, 28, Oct 3, 12, 17, 21, Dec 26; 1758: HAY, Mar 13, May 18
Jolly breeze that comes whistling (song), 1698: LIF, Nov 0
Jolly Crew, The; or, Tars at Anchor (interlude, anon), 1799: CG, Apr 16
Jolly God (song), 1761: KING'S, Mar 12
Jolly, Francois Antoine
--Femme Jalouse, La; or, The Jealous Wife, 1735: HAY, Jan 27, 29
Jolly, George (manager), 1661: REDBULL, Mar 23, May 28, COCKPIT, Nov 13,
SALSBURY, 26; 1662: REDBULL, Jan 22, Mar 25, May 26, COCKPIT, Oct 21
Jomelli, Niccolo (composer), 1749: KING'S, Mar 21; 1752: KING'S, Mar 24; 1754:
KING'S, Apr 23; 1755: KING'S, Nov 11, Dec 9; 1757: KING'S, Mar 24; 1759:
KING'S, Nov 13; 1760: SOHO, Mar 13, HAY, 27; 1761: SOHO, Jan 21; 1762:
KING'S, May 15; 1763: KING'S, Apr 25; 1767: KING'S, Apr 9; 1770: KING'S, Feb
22, Mar 1, CG, 16; 1771: KING'S, Feb 28; 1772: CG, Apr 8; 1774: KING'S, Apr
19, May 10, 17; 1780: KING'S, Apr 1, May 9; 1789: DL, Feb 27, Mar 20; 1797:
DL, Dec 14
--Andromaca (opera), (play), 1755: KING'S, Nov 11, 15, 22
--Attilio Regolo (opera), 1754: KING'S, Apr 23, 27, 30, May 4, 7, 11, 14, 18,
21, 25; 1762: KING'S, May 15, 22, 26, Jun 3
--Demofoonte (opera), 1755: KING'S, Dec 9, 13, 16, 20, 27, 30; 1756: KING'S,
Jan 3, 10, 13, 17, 20, 24, 27, 31, Feb 3, 7, Mar 15, Apr 3, 27, 29, May 1;
1757: KING'S, Mar 24
--Don Trustullo (intermezzo), 1767: KING'S, Apr 9, May 16, Jun 16
--Isaac (oratorio), 1761: SOHO, Jan 21; 1792: KING'S, Mar 28
--Isola Disabitata, L'; or, The Deserted Island (opera), 1760: SOHO, Mar 13,
HAY, 27, HIC, Apr 29
--Passione, La (Passion, The) (opera), 1770: KING'S, Mar 1, 8, 15, CG, 16,
KING'S, Jun 12; 1771: KING'S, Feb 28, Mar 7
--Uccellatrice, L' (intermezzo), 1770: KING'S, Feb 22
Jona (house servant), 1755: CG, Apr 30; 1756: CG, May 5
Jona, Widow (beneficiary), 1756: CG, Dec 8; 1758: CG, Dec 13, 21
Jonathan (actor), 1759: CG, Dec 10; 1761: CG, Oct 13
Jones (actor), 1717: DL, May 30; 1723: HAY, Apr 15; 1729: HAY, Jan 10, Feb 1,
Dec 18; 1730: HAY, Jan 21, 29, Feb 6, 23, Mar 11, 12, 30, Apr 6, 8, 20, 24,
May 1, Jun 17, 23, 27, Jul 17, TC, Aug 1, BFR, 22, Sep 4, SFP, 9, SF, 14,
HAY, 18, Oct 21, 23, Nov 9, 13, 16, 30, Dec 9, 17, 28; 1731: HAY, Jan 13, 14,
15, 18, 20, Feb 3, 10, 17, 26, Mar 15, 17, 19, 24, Apr 22, May 12, 13, 17,
19, TCY, Aug 9, BFLH, 24, SFLH, Sep 8, SOU, 28, SUN, Nov 30; 1732: HAY, Feb
16, Mar 2, 8, 17, 23, 31, Apr 4, 27, May 8, 10, 15, DL, 29, HAY, Jun 1, DL,
1, 23, Aug 1, 4, 11, 15, 17, BFMMO, 23, DL, Sep 19, 28, Oct 17, Nov 14, 17,
21, GF, 30, DL, Dec 6, 11, 14, 18, 26; 1733: HAY, Mar 20, 26, DL, 28, 31, Apr
9, 19, 24, May 3, 5, 7, CG, Jul 6, HAY, 26, CG, 27, Aug 2, BFCGBH, 23, BFMMO,
23, BFCGBH, Sep 4, DL, 26, Oct 10, 24, 31, Nov 13, 21, 23, 26, Dec 5, 21, 31;
1734: DL, Jan 3, 15, 19, DL/HAY, 28, Mar 16, 30, HAY, Apr 5, DL/HAY, 26, 27,
DL/LIF, May 3, DL, 15, LIF, 23, JS, 23, HAY, Jun 3, 7, 19, 21, 24, Jul 19,
26, 31, Aug 7, 16, LIF, 20, DL, Sep 19, HAY, Oct 7, DL, 21, 22, Nov 1, 20,
Dec 6; 1735: DL, Jan 22, YB, Mar 21, DL, Apr 19, May 14, TC, 28, LIF, Jun 12,
DL, Jul 1, GF/HAY, 15, 18, 22, Aug 1, HAY, 4, GF/HAY, 21, LIF, 25, HAY, 26,
LIF, 29, Sep 2, 5, DL, Oct 31, Nov 19, HAY, Dec 13, 17; 1736: HAY, Jan 19,
Feb 19, Mar 5, CG, 27, HAY, Apr 7, 29, Jun 26, Jul 30, TC, Aug 4, BFFH, 23,
SOU, Sep 20; 1737: LIF, Jan 22, Feb 1, HAY, Mar 14, 21, Apr 13; 1740: BFLP,
Aug 23, SF, Sep 9, CG, 24, DL, Dec 4; 1741: CG, Jan 12, GF, Apr 15, TC, Aug
4, BFH, 22; 1743: JS, Mar 16; 1744: MFHNT, May 1, HAY, 16, MF, Jun 7, JS, Dec
10; 1745: GF, Apr 15; 1746: GF, Nov 25; 1747: ST, Apr 29; 1748: HAY, May 2,
BFP, Aug 24, BF, 24, SFBCBV, Sep 7, HAY, Dec 9; 1749: SOU, Jan 2; 1750: SFYW,
Sep 7
Jones (actor), 1756: BFSI, Sep 3
Jones (actor), 1762: CG, Sep 22; 1765: HAY, Aug 30; 1767: CG, Jan 29; 1770:
HAY, Dec 14; 1771: HAY, Mar 4, Sep 19; 1772: HAY, Aug 4
Jones (actor), 1772: DL, Dec 26; 1773: DL, Sep 25, Oct 28, Nov 25; 1774: DL,
Feb 9, Apr 15, 19, HAY, May 16, 30, Jun 3, 8, 13, 15, 17, 27, Aug 19, Sep 5,
12; 1775: HAY, May 15, 17, 24, 29, Jul 7, 14, 17, 21, 31, Aug 2, 16, CG, Oct
13, Nov 21, 28, Dec 21, 26, 29; 1776: CG, Jan 2, 5, 12, Feb 17, Mar 9, Apr
30, May 13, HAY, 20, 22, 27, Jun 14, Jul 24, 29, Aug 2, CG, Sep 23, 27, Oct
7, 11, 17, 25, Nov 13; 1777: CG, Jan 8, Apr 28, May 9, Sep 22, 29, Oct 1, 20,
23, Nov 19; 1778: CG, Jan 19, 20, Feb 2, 23, Mar 14, May 11, 14, Oct 2, 12,

14, 15, 21, 26, Dec 1, 21; 1779: CG, Jan 13, 22, Feb 8, 22, Apr 22, 23, 24,
26, 27, 29, 30, May 19, Sep 22, Oct 1, 6, 20, Nov 4, 8, 13, 16, 22, 23, Dec
21; 1780: CG, Jan 18, Feb 3, 22, Mar 6, 13, DL, 14, CG, 14, 18, Apr 25, May
17, 18, 19, Sep 18, Oct 2, 10, 11, 13, 19, 21, 26, 30, 31, Nov 4, 15, Dec 15;
1781: CG, Jan 25, DL, Feb 12, CG, 15, Apr 26, 28, May 3, Sep 17, 24, 26, 28,
Oct 1, 29, Nov 2, 21, Dec 11, 12, 26, 31; 1782: CG, Jan 5, 11, Feb 9, Mar 16,
Apr 10, May 3, 6, 7, 8, 11, 14, 17, Sep 23, 25, Oct 7, 8, 16, 22, Nov 1, 2,
8, 12, 30, Dec 3, 12, 30; 1783: CG, Apr 1, 22, May 20, 23, 28, Jun 6, Sep 19,
22, 26, Oct 1, 2, 3, 10, 14, 17, 28, Nov 8, 10, Dec 6; 1784: CG, Jan 6, 29,
Feb 9, Mar 9, 16, May 8, 15, 18, Sep 17, 20, 28, 29, Oct 1, 11, 25, 28, Nov
16, 25, Dec 3, 14; 1785: CG, Mar 29, May 7, 11, 18, DL, Oct 18, Dec 1, CG, 7,
DL, 8, 26, 28; 1786: DL, May 26, Sep 19, 21, 23, Oct 3, Nov 25, Dec 7; 1787:
DL, Jan 13, Feb 16, May 3, Jun 1, 8, Sep 18, 22, Oct 24, 26, Nov 21, 24, 27,
Dec 8, 26; 1788: DL, Feb 7, Mar 3, Apr 14, 15, Jun 5, Sep 13, 30, Oct 4, 25,
Nov 10, 21, 28, 29, Dec 6, 22; 1789: DL, Jan 1, 17, Feb 7, Mar 9, 21, 24, May
22, 27, Jun 9, 13, Sep 12, Oct 1, 3, 31, Nov 13, Dec 26; 1790: DL, Feb 8, 10,
Mar 22, Apr 19, May 15, Jun 2, 3, Sep 14, Oct 7, 14, 21, 26, Nov 19, Dec 27;
1791: DL, May 10, 19, DLKING'S, Oct 6, 31, Nov 5, 10, 14, 22, 29; 1792:
DLKING'S, Jan 7, 18, Feb 18, Mar 6, 10, 26, 29, 31, Apr 10, 25, May 17, Jun
13, DL, Sep 25, Oct 4, 9, 31, Nov 5, Dec 3, 10, 26, 27; 1793: DL, Feb 16, 28,
Mar 9, May 14, 21, 22, 31, Jun 5; 1794: DL, Apr 21, May 1, 2, 3, 5, 19, Jun
14, 17, Sep 18, 23, Oct 31, Nov 11, Dec 5, 6, 9; 1795: DL, Jan 3, 5, 8, 12,
24, Feb 6, May 26, Jun 4, Sep 22, Oct 27, Nov 3, 6, 7, 20, Dec 19, 23; 1796:
DL, Jan 2, 18, Feb 27, Apr 11, 18, 25
Jones (actor), 1776: CHR, Oct 2, 7; 1777: HAY, Oct 9; 1779: HAY, Mar 8, Dec 27;
1780: CII, Feb 29, Mar 17, 27, Apr 5, 19; 1781: HAY, Mar 26, CII, 30, Apr 5,
HAY, Oct 16; 1782: HAY, Jan 21, Nov 25; 1784: HAY, Jan 21, Nov 16; 1785: HAY,
Mar 15; 1787: HAY, Jan 8, RLSN, Mar 30; 1789: WHF, Nov 9, 11; 1793: HAY, Sep
24, 30, Oct 3, 4, 7, 8, 15, 24, 29, Nov 16, Dec 26, 30; 1794: HAY, Mar 27,
May 22, Sep 17; 1796: HAY, Sep 16; 1797: HAY, Jan 23, May 10
Jones (bookseller), 1750: DL, Nov 28
Jones (box-office keeper), 1748: DL, May 9; 1749: DL, May 2; 1750: DL, May 8;
1773: DL, May 21; 1774: DL, May 16; 1776: CG, Apr 29
Jones (composer), 1723: DL, Aug 12
Jones (dancer), 1720: SOU, Oct 3; 1722: LIF, Mar 31, Apr 5, 20, May 2, 4, 7,
10, 14, 18, 23, Jun 1, HAY, 28, SFW, Sep 5, SOU, 25, Oct 3, LIF, 22; 1730:
LIF, Oct 31; 1732: LIF, Jan 7, 18, 19, Feb 21, Mar 7, 21, 27, 30, Apr 11, 17,
18, 19, 22, 24, 25, 26, 27, 28, May 1, 2, 3, 4, 5, 8, 9, 10, 11, 16, 17, 18,
TC, Aug 4, BFB, 23, GF, Oct 5, 11, 13, 14, 16, 17, 23, 24, 25, 27, 28, 30,
Nov 2, 4, 8, 13, 15, 17, 23, 24, 25, Dec 15, 18, 29; 1733: GF, Jan 11, 12,
13, 23, 26, 29, Feb 2, HAY, Mar 16, 20, 22, 26, Apr 18, 23, LIF/CG, 30, CG,
May 1, 2, 4, LIF/CG, 10, CG, 16, 17, HAY, 26, Jun 4, 11, 13, 15, 18, BFMMO,
Aug 23; 1742: GF, Jan 12, DL, May 15
Jones (gallery doorkeeper), 1721: LIF, Jun 6; 1722: LIF, May 28; 1723: LIF, Jun
6; 1724: LIF, May 26; 1725: LIF, May 25; 1729: LIF, May 20
Jones (house servant), 1735: CG/LIF, May 26; 1736: CG, May 31; 1737: CG, May
19; 1738: CG, May 16
Jones (laceman), 1772: DL, Jan 6; 1773: DL, Jun 2, Dec 2; 1774: DL, Feb 22;
1776: DL, Jan 26
Jones (musician), 1728: YB, Mar 13; 1729: DL, Mar 26; 1730: GF, Jun 30; 1737:
LIF, May 4
Jones (musician), 1750: DL, Mar 28; 1752: DL, Apr 29; 1760: CG, Sep 22
Jones (numberer), 1718: DL, May 29; 1719: DL, May 27; 1720: DL, May 19; 1725:
DL, May 12; 1726: DL, May 12; 1727: DL, May 19; 1728: DL, May 22; 1729: DL,
May 9; 1730: DL, May 7; 1731: DL, May 17; 1732: DL, May 9; 1734: DL/HAY, May
8; 1735: DL, May 20
Jones (singer), 1715: LIF, Jan 25, Feb 9, 28, Mar 3, 21, Apr 4, 19; 1717: LIF,
Jan 2, Oct 31, Nov 12, Dec 27; 1718: TEC, Mar 19
Jones (singer), 1798: CG, May 9, Dec 11; 1799: CG, May 4, 13; 1800: CG, Jan 16
Jones (trumpeter), 1770: MARLY, Aug 21; 1771: CG, May 15, GROTTO, Aug 30, Sep
3, 9; 1774: HAY, Mar 25
Jones, C (harpist), 1798: HAY, Jul 21
Jones, Charles (actor), 1734: DL, Jan 15; 1740: CG, Jan 17; 1743: LIF, Jan 21,
DL, Sep 27, Oct 18; 1745: CG, May 8
Jones, Edward (harpist), 1776: CG, Mar 15, 20, 27; 1777: CG, May 3; 1795: CG,
Apr 6; 1798: CG, Feb 23
Jones, Elizabeth (actor), 1793: CG, Nov 18
Jones, George (dancer), 1793: CG, Mar 11
Jones, Griffith (pianist), 1799: CG, Feb 8; 1800: CG, Feb 28
Jones, Henry, 1753: CG, Feb 21; 1755: DL, Oct 24; 1758: DL, Jun 1; 1760: DL,
Jan 1; 1774: DL, Mar 19, CG, Dec 26; 1775: DL, Mar 25
--Earl of Essex, The, 1751: CG, Feb 27; 1753: CG, Feb 17, 20, 21, 22, 23, 24,

26, 27, 28, Mar 1, 2, 3, 5, 8, 12, 13, 15, May 16, 23, Dec 11, 12, 13, 14;
1754: CG, Jan 1, Mar 25, Apr 26, May 10; 1755: CG, Feb 24, 27, Apr 1, 19, Oct
11, DL, 24, CG, 25, DL, 25, Nov 18, Dec 16, CG, 20; 1756: CG, Jan 3, DL, 8,
Apr 22, CG, Oct 27; 1757: DL, Jan 24, 29, Feb 12, May 14, CG, 17, Oct 3, Nov
22; 1758: CG, Jan 16, May 3, DL, Jun 1, CG, Sep 29, Nov 11, Dec 12, 21; 1759:
CG, Jan 1, Mar 1, Apr 20, Dec 21; 1760: DL, Jan 1, CG, 1, DL, Apr 12, CG, 19,
Oct 15, 22, 25, Dec 29; 1761: CG, Oct 27; 1762: CG, Nov 30; 1763: CG, Dec 27;
1764: CG, Jan 14; 1765: CG, Dec 10; 1766: CG, Nov 18; 1770: CG, Apr 24, Oct
10, Nov 12, Dec 28; 1771: CG, Oct 7, 17, Nov 13; 1773: CG, Nov 8, Dec 16;
1774: CG, Dec 26; 1775: DL, Mar 25; 1778: HAY, Apr 29, CHR, Jun 19; 1781: DL,
Feb 12; 1782: CG, Apr 17; 1784: HAY, Aug 18; 1785: DL, Apr 27; 1790: CG, Dec
31; 1791: CG, Jan 6, 13, 20, 24, 31, Feb 25, Apr 11, May 14, Oct 3, 31, Dec
27; 1792: CG, May 24, Sep 24, Dec 31; 1793: CG, Dec 26, 30; 1794: CG, Dec 26;
1795: CG, Jan 12, May 27; 1796: HAY, Apr 27; 1799: CG, Dec 23
Jones, Jenny (actor), 1732: HAY, Mar 8, 23, May 8, RIW/HAY, Sep 4; 1734: LIF,
   Oct 1; 1735: GF/HAY, Aug 8, HAY, Dec 13, 17; 1736: HAY, Feb 19, Mar 5
Jones, Jere (tavern keeper), 1745: CG, May 8
Jones, John (musician), 1726: LIF, Apr 30
Jones, Martha Elizabeth, Mrs James (actor), 1791: DL, May 26; 1793: DL, May 14,
   HAY, Jun 21, Jul 5, 13, Oct 30, Dec 26; 1794: HAY, Jan 4, DL, May 3, HAY, 22,
   Jul 10, DL, Nov 19; 1795: DL, Feb 6, 12, HAY, Aug 3, Sep 21, DL, Oct 21, Dec
   2; 1796: DL, Jan 18, Jun 7, HAY, 11, 13, 14, 29, Jul 6; 1797: DL, May 19,
   HAY, Jun 13, 16, 22, Jul 10, 13, DL, Oct 12, Nov 24, 28, Dec 21; 1798: DL,
   Mar 24, May 11, HAY, Jun 13, Jul 17, Aug 3, DL, Nov 10, 22, 29, Dec 21; 1799:
   DL, Apr 8, 22, May 3, HAY, Jun 22, 25, Aug 10, DL, Oct 5, 19, Nov 25, Dec 7,
   12
Jones, Master (actor), 1772: CG, Feb 3, May 29, Sep 28; 1773: CG, May 22, Oct
   4; 1774: CG, Oct 22; 1775: CG, Oct 13; 1776: CG, Jan 1, Nov 1, 11; 1777: CG,
   Nov 7
Jones, Miss (actor), 1780: HAY, Sep 25; 1781: CII, Mar 15
Jones, Miss (actor, dancer, singer), 1729: HAY, May 29; 1730: HAY, Mar 12, Apr
   6, 24, May 1, BFR, Sep 4, SF, 14, HAY, Oct 23; 1731: HAY, Jan 14, Mar 19, May
   4; 1732: HAY, Feb 16, Mar 8, 17, 23, Apr 27, May 8, 10, 15, LIF, Nov 20, HAY,
   29; 1733: LIF, Mar 7, HAY, 27, BFCGBH, Aug 23, DL/HAY, Oct 29, Nov 24, 26,
   Dec 27; 1734: DL/HAY, Jan 5, 12, Mar 21, HAY, Apr 5, DL, 15, 29, May 13, HAY,
   27, Jun 3, 5, 19, 28, Jul 5, 10, 26, 31, Aug 7, 14, 16, LIF, 20, HAY, 21, 22,
   GF, Sep 9, 11, 13, 25, LIF, Oct 1, GF, 28, Nov 7, 8, 18, Dec 2, 16; 1735: GF,
   Jan 24, YB, Mar 3, GF, 6, 17, 20, 27, Apr 7, 9, 21, 22, 23, 24, May 1, 3, 15,
   GF/HAY, Jul 18, 22, HAY, Aug 4, GF/HAY, 8, HAY, 12, GF/HAY, 21, HAY, 26,
   YB/HAY, Sep 17, GF, Oct 13, 15, Nov 6, 12, 15, 17, 19, HAY, Dec 13, GF, 17,
   HAY, 17; 1736: HAY, Jan 19, GF, Feb 4, 5, 10, 17, HAY, 19, GF, 20, Mar 3, Apr
   17, DL, 22, HAY, 26, GF, 28, HAY, 29, GF, May 3, HAY, 13, 27, Jun 26, LIF,
   Jul 1, HAY, 30, SOU, Sep 20, LIF, Oct 5, 21, Nov 16, Dec 3, 7, 16; 1737: LIF,
   Feb 21, Mar 21, HAY, 21, LIF, Apr 12, 14, 18, 25, 27, 29, 30, May 2, 4, HAY,
   5, LIF, 6, 7, 17, 18; 1738: DL, Oct 30; 1739: DL, Dec 26; 1740: DL, Jan 15,
   Feb 13, 14, Mar 29, Apr 11, 29, May 13, 14, GF, Oct 24, 28, Dec 6; 1741: GF,
   Mar 3, 12; 1742: JS, May 31; 1743: SOU, Feb 18; 1746: GF, Mar 22; 1748:
   BFLYY, Aug 24, BFSY, 24, SFLYYW, Sep 7, BHB, Oct 1; 1750: HAY, Jul 26; 1756:
   BFSI, Sep 3, SFB, 20
Jones, Miss (singer), 1797: HAY, Jan 23, May 10
Jones, Miss and Jenny (actors), 1734: HA, Sep 2
Jones, Mrs (actor), 1779: HAY, May 10; 1784: HAY, Dec 13
Jones, Mrs (actor), 1799: WRSG, May 17
Jones, Mrs (actor, singer), 1728: HAY, Dec 10; 1729: HAY, May 7, 26, Jun 14,
   BFR, Aug 25, SF, Sep 8; 1730: HAY, Apr 8, 24, May 4, SF, Sep 14; 1731: HAY,
   Mar 24, Apr 22; 1733: HAY, Jun 4; 1734: HAY, Jun 5; 1735: GF, Mar 29; 1736:
   BFFH, Aug 23, LIF, Sep 28; 1740: DL, Mar 8, GF, Oct 31, Nov 25, Dec 12, 15;
   1741: GF, Jan 15, 20, 27, 28, Feb 5, 6, 14, 19, Mar 12, 16, 19, DL, 24, GF,
   Apr 2, 14, 15, 16, 22, Sep 14; 1757: BFG, Sep 5
Jones, Mrs (seamstress), 1753: DL, Mar 26
Jones, Mrs (singer), 1762: CG, Oct 8, Nov 1, 15; 1763: CG, Jan 24, May 2, 17,
   Sep 21, Oct 3, 14, Nov 15, 29; 1764: CG, Jan 3, May 4, 21, Sep 21, Oct 1, Nov
   5, 7; 1765: CG, May 6, 11, Oct 3, 7, 14, 22, Dec 6, 9, 23; 1766: CG, Apr 30,
   May 19, Oct 21, Nov 21; 1767: CG, Feb 14, May 11, Sep 25, Oct 30, Nov 4, Dec
   2; 1768: CG, Jan 20, Feb 13, May 7, Sep 26, Oct 5, 17; 1769: CG, May 9, 25,
   Oct 6; 1770: CG, Jan 3, Mar 29, May 16, 26, Oct 8; 1771: CG, Apr 30, May 15,
   Oct 25, Dec 11; 1772: CG, Jan 27, Apr 9, May 21, Nov 2, Dec 26; 1773: CG, Mar
   22, Apr 3, May 19, 22, Oct 23, Dec 13; 1774: CG, Feb 11, May 13, Oct 13;
   1775: CG, May 4, DL, 27, CG, Sep 25, Oct 19; 1776: CG, May 4
Jones, R (dancer), 1733: HAY, Feb 14, Mar 14, 16, 20, 22, 26, Apr 18, 23, May
   26, BFMMO, Aug 23; 1734: DL, Feb 4
Jones, Shatford (prologuist), 1779: HAY, Oct 18

467

Jones, William (coal merchant), 1759: CG, Nov 10; 1766: CG, Oct 21
Jones, William (publisher), 1788: DL, Nov 5
Jones's scholar (dancer), 1732: HAY, Mar 17
Jonno, Master (dancer), 1749: DL, Nov 9, 10
Jonson, Ben, 1660: NONE, Sep 0; 1662: NONE, Sep 0; 1663: NONE, Mar 0; 1668:
LIF, Feb 22, Aug 20; 1670: LIF, Nov 0; 1677: DL, Dec 12, 26; 1685: BF, Aug
26; 1695: DL, Nov 0; 1697: DL, Sep 0; 1699: DLLIF, Sep 12; 1700: DLLIF, Feb
0, LIF, 0; 1702: DL, Jun 3, Aug 18, LIF, Oct 9; 1703: DL, May 21, Jun 12, Oct
11, Nov 3, 24, Dec 13; 1704: DL, Feb 14, 23, Mar 25, Apr 8, Sep 28, Oct 23,
Nov 29; 1705: DL, Jan 8, Mar 22, Jun 5, Nov 8; 1706: QUEEN'S, Dec 3; 1707:
QUEEN'S, Jan 1, 2, 7, Feb 21, DL/QUEEN, Oct 28, Nov 13; 1708: DL/QUEEN, Jan
7, Apr 21, DL, 27, DL/QUEEN, Jul 15; 1709: DL, Jan 4, Feb 19, 21, 22, 26, 28,
Mar 1, May 11, 27; 1710: QUEEN'S, Jan 9, 11, 14, 23, Feb 9, Jun 1, 9; 1711:
DL, Feb 10, Aug 24, Nov 1, Dec 8; 1712: DL, Feb 19, Apr 1, 29, Aug 26, Nov
17; 1713: DL, Jan 14, Nov 2, 24, Dec 1, 14, 21, 22; 1714: DL, May 12, Oct 27;
1715: DL, Mar 3, Jun 28, Nov 3; 1716: DL, Jan 25, 26, Dec 10; 1717: DL, Jan
31, LIF, Apr 11, DL, May 15, 25, Jul 16; 1718: DL, Jan 20, Jun 27, Oct 17,
Nov 18, 26; 1719: DL, Apr 28, Aug 4, Nov 3; 1720: DL, Mar 19, 22, Jun 10, Aug
22, Sep 15, Nov 12, 16; 1721: DL, Jan 31, Feb 28, Oct 25, 26, Nov 22, Dec 22;
1722: DL, Jan 9, May 23, Oct 10, 24; 1723: DL, Feb 14, Mar 23, Oct 10, Nov 6,
21; 1724: DL, Feb 10, May 15, Oct 28, Dec 31; 1725: LIF, Jan 11, DL, Apr 6,
15, Nov 8; 1726: DL, Jan 5, Oct 15, 20, 25, Nov 17; 1727: DL, Jan 10; 1728:
DL, Mar 9, Apr 2, Oct 26; 1729: DL, Jan 29, 31, Feb 3, LIF, Mar 27, DL, Dec
3; 1730: LIF, Jun 1, DL, Sep 24; 1731: LIF, Jan 4, DL, 8, Oct 7, 9, 30, LIF,
Dec 11; 1732: DL, Mar 9, Nov 9; 1733: DL/HAY, Dec 12, 19, 20, 22, 27, 28, 29,
31; 1734: DL/HAY, Jan 1, 2, 4, 5, 25, Mar 16, 21, Apr 6, DL, 15, DL/HAY, 27,
DL, Sep 19, Dec 3; 1735: DL, Feb 1, Mar 13, Apr 14, 26, May 22, LIF, Aug 25,
DL, Sep 15, Nov 18, 20; 1736: DL, Mar 29, May 28, Oct 21, 22, 23; 1737: DL,
Nov 14, 15, 16; 1738: DL, Feb 18, 20, May 27; 1739: DL, Jan 26, Mar 20, 26,
Oct 23, 24; 1740: DL, Oct 9, 10, 11, CG, Dec 10, 31; 1741: DL, May 12; 1742:
DL, Feb 11, 12, May 31, Dec 15; 1744: DL, Apr 3; 1745: CG, Apr 17, Dec 3, 28;
1746: CG, Apr 21; 1747: DL, Oct 21; 1748: CG, Mar 5, DL, Apr 23, Nov 7; 1749:
DL, Oct 14; 1750: DL, Nov 14, Dec 17; 1751: DL, Oct 22, Nov 23, 29, Dec 4;
1752: DL, Feb 3, Oct 26; 1755: DL, Dec 11; 1757: DL, Mar 7; 1758: DL, Jan 27;
1771: HAY, Sep 16, CG, Nov 12, 26; 1772: DL, Apr 21; 1774: CG, Nov 19; 1776:
DL, Dec 28; 1783: HAY, Sep 12, CG, Oct 3; 1784: CG, Apr 26, HAY, May 31, Jun
5; 1785: DL, Feb 21; 1791: DLKING'S, Oct 3, Dec 27; 1795: HAY, Sep 21; 1796:
CG, May 16, 19
--Alchemist, The, 1660: VERE, Dec 0; 1661: VERE, Jun 14, 22, Aug 14, Dec 16;
1662: VERE, Feb 13, NONE, Sep 0; 1664: BRIDGES, Aug 3; 1668: LIF, Feb 22;
1669: BRIDGES, Jan 12, Apr 17; 1674: DL, Nov 12; 1675: DL, Oct 26; 1700:
DLLIF, Feb 0; 1701: DL, Mar 27, Apr 1; 1702: LIF, Oct 9; 1709: DL, Feb 19,
21, 22, 28, Mar 26, Apr 4, May 11; 1710: QUEEN'S, Jan 14, 23; 1711: DL, Feb
10, Apr 6, Dec 8; 1712: DL, Feb 19; 1713: DL, Dec 21, 22; 1721: DL, Oct 25,
26, 27, Nov 22; 1723: DL, Oct 10, Dec 4, 13; 1726: DL, Oct 20, Nov 17; 1727:
DL, Jan 10; 1728: DL, Mar 9, Oct 26; 1729: DL, Feb 3, Dec 3; 1731: DL, Jan 8,
Oct 7; 1732: DL, Mar 7, Nov 9; 1733: DL, Jan 19, DL/HAY, Dec 12, 20, 28, 31;
1734: DL/HAY, Jan 4, 25, Mar 16, Apr 6, 27, DL, Sep 19, Dec 3; 1735: DL, Feb
1, Apr 26, Sep 15, 16, Nov 18, Dec 19; 1736: DL, Apr 13, Oct 22; 1737: DL,
Nov 15; 1738: DL, Feb 21, May 27; 1739: DL, Mar 20, 26, Oct 24; 1740: DL, Oct
10, CG, Dec 10, 31; 1742: DL, Feb 12, 16, 17; 1743: DL, Mar 21, Apr 8, 19,
21, May 7, Dec 16; 1744: DL, Jan 2, 28, Feb 4, Apr 9, Nov 6, 19, Dec 22;
1745: DL, Jan 10, Feb 8, Apr 17, Sep 28, Nov 21; 1746: DL, Feb 22, Mar 31,
Aug 11, Sep 25, Nov 25; 1747: DL, Sep 22, Oct 21, Nov 12, 25; 1748: DL, Mar
24, Apr 29, Nov 7; 1749: DL, Apr 12, May 1, Oct 14, Nov 14, Dec 2; 1750: DL,
Apr 18, Nov 14, 30, Dec 13; 1751: DL, Jan 9, 25, May 2; 1753: DL, Mar 20, Apr
14, 30; 1755: DL, Dec 11, 12, 20, 30; 1756: DL, Jan 17, Feb 5, 19, Apr 21;
1757: DL, Mar 7, Apr 19; 1758: DL, Jan 27, Feb 18, Nov 7, 22; 1759: DL, Jan
2, Mar 15, Oct 9, Nov 6; 1760: DL, Jan 21, Apr 17, Oct 15, Dec 18; 1761: DL,
Apr 14, Oct 16, Nov 27; 1762: DL, Jan 23, Mar 9, Apr 20, Nov 18, Dec 2, 15,
16; 1763: DL, Apr 9, Dec 17; 1764: DL, Jan 2; 1766: DL, Oct 31, Nov 13; 1767:
DL, May 19, Oct 20; 1768: DL, Feb 25, Mar 7; 1769: DL, Jan 25, Apr 29, Nov
22; 1770: DL, Feb 6, HAY, Oct 15, DL, Dec 6; 1771: DL, Dec 3; 1772: DL, Apr
21, Nov 20; 1773: DL, Feb 13, Oct 14; 1774: DL, Mar 24, Oct 24, Dec 6; 1775:
DL, Nov 25; 1776: DL, Jan 18, Apr 11; 1782: DL, Mar 21, Apr 5, 10, 19, 26,
May 31, Oct 12, 21, Nov 2, 28, Dec 3, 18, 21; 1783: DL, Sep 25, Oct 21; 1784:
HAY, Jun 5; 1785: DL, Jan 13, 18, Feb 26; 1787: DL, Apr 10
--Bartholomew Fair, 1661: VERE, Jun 8, 27, Sep 7, Nov 12, Dec 18; 1664:
BRIDGES, Aug 2; 1667: BRIDGES, Apr 2; 1668: BRIDGES, Sep 4; 1669: BRIDGES,
Jan 12, ATCOURT, Feb 22; 1682: DL, Nov 16; 1702: DL, Jun 3, Aug 18; 1704: DL,
Mar 25, Apr 8, Sep 28; 1705: DL, Jan 8; 1707: QUEEN'S, Aug 12, 14, 22,
DL/QUEEN, Oct 22; 1708: DL/QUEEN, Jul 15, DL, Aug 26, 31; 1710: QUEEN'S, Jun

1; <u>1711</u>: DL, Mar 8, Aug 24; <u>1712</u>: DL, Aug 26; <u>1713</u>: DL, Jan 14, Dec 1; <u>1715</u>: DL, Jun 28; <u>1716</u>: DL, Dec 10; <u>1717</u>: DL, Jul 16; <u>1718</u>: DL, Mar 24, Jun 27, Nov 26; <u>1719</u>: DL, Apr 28, Aug 4; <u>1720</u>: DL, Jan 13, Jun 10, Aug 22, Oct 31; <u>1722</u>: DL, Jul 10, Dec 21; <u>1731</u>: DL, Oct 30; <u>1735</u>: LIF, Aug 25

--Cataline's Conspiracy, <u>1667</u>: BRIDGES, Dec 7, 11; <u>1668</u>: BRIDGES, Jan 11, Dec 18, 19; <u>1669</u>: BRIDGES, Jan 2, 12, 13, NONE, Feb 10; <u>1673</u>: NONE, Sep 0; <u>1675</u>: DL, Mar 8

--Cynthia's Revels, <u>1669</u>: BRIDGES, Jan 12

--Devil is an Ass, The, <u>1663</u>: NONE, Mar 0; 1669; BRIDGES, Jan 12

--Eastward Ho. See Chapman, George.

--Every Man in His Humour, <u>1669</u>: BRIDGES, Jan 12; <u>1670</u>: BRIDGES, Mar 0; <u>1725</u>: LIF, Jan 11, 12, 13; <u>1750</u>: DL, Dec 17; <u>1751</u>: DL, Nov 23, 29, Dec 2, 4, 6, 9, 11, 13, 19, 21; <u>1752</u>: DL, Jan 10, 16, 25, 31, Feb 3, 7, Mar 10, Apr 4, May 8, Nov 30, Dec 1, 23; <u>1753</u>: DL, Jan 15, 29, Mar 1, 31, Apr 27, May 3; <u>1754</u>: DL, Mar 19, Apr 4, May 24, Oct 30, Dec 3, 12; <u>1755</u>: DL, Jan 31, Mar 17, Apr 3, May 7, Dec 6, 17; <u>1756</u>: DL, Feb 17, Apr 5, Dec 10; <u>1757</u>: DL, Jan 12, Feb 21, Mar 31, Apr 27, Oct 19; <u>1758</u>: DL, Feb 9, Apr 11, May 31; <u>1759</u>: DL, Mar 31, May 4, Nov 13, Dec 22; <u>1760</u>: DL, Jan 12, Mar 4, Oct 24, Dec 31; <u>1761</u>: DL, Apr 1, 15, Oct 20, 22, Dec 18; <u>1762</u>: DL, Oct 4, CG, 25, 26, 28, Nov 2, DL, 3, CG, 4, 10, 13, 19, 27, Dec 3; <u>1763</u>: DL, Jan 5, CG, 12, 26, Feb 11, Mar 15, Apr 13, May 6, Oct 10, Nov 23, Dec 22; <u>1764</u>: CG, Jan 5, Feb 16, Mar 26, Apr 14, May 22, HAY, Sep 1, CG, Oct 16, Nov 1, 21; <u>1765</u>: CG, Jan 5, 24, Mar 12, Apr 12, May 6, Oct 8, Nov 16, Dec 18; <u>1766</u>: CG, Feb 4, Mar 18, Apr 9, 30, DL, May 22, CG, Oct 22, Nov 15, Dec 8; <u>1767</u>: CG, Jan 5, Feb 12, Mar 10, Apr 22, May 5, 14, Sep 17, DL, Oct 9, Nov 7, CG, 24; <u>1768</u>: DL, Jan 7, CG, 26, Feb 18, Apr 16, DL, 21, CG, May 12, Sep 21, Nov 1, Dec 9; <u>1769</u>: DL, Jan 27, Feb 9, CG, 25, Apr 29, May 10, 24, Sep 27, Nov 22, DL, 29; <u>1770</u>: CG, Jan 20, DL, May 24, Nov 16; <u>1771</u>: HAY, May 17, DL, Nov 1, CG, 7, DL, 8, CG, 14, Dec 18; <u>1772</u>: CG, Jan 8, Feb 20, Mar 19, May 25, Oct 14, DL, 29, CG, Dec 15; <u>1773</u>: CG, Jan 22, Feb 13, May 18, DL, Oct 2, 6, CG, Nov 23; <u>1774</u>: CG, Jan 21, Apr 16, DL, Oct 20, Dec 29; <u>1775</u>: DL, Oct 5, Dec 18; <u>1776</u>: DL, Feb 9, Apr 25; <u>1777</u>: CG, Apr 10; <u>1778</u>: DL, Jan 2, Feb 7, Oct 28; <u>1779</u>: DL, Apr 23, May 14, 17, CG, Oct 1, DL, Nov 24; <u>1780</u>: DL, Jan 12, Apr 28, May 25, Nov 3; <u>1781</u>: DL, May 23, Sep 29, Nov 20; <u>1782</u>: DL, Apr 10, Nov 22; <u>1784</u>: DL, Jan 16, Mar 9, Nov 23; <u>1785</u>: DL, Dec 30; <u>1786</u>: DL, May 29, Oct 30, Nov 15, Dec 30; <u>1787</u>: DL, Jun 7; <u>1788</u>: DL, May 23; <u>1791</u>: DLKING'S, Oct 3; <u>1798</u>: CG, May 15, 25

--Every Man out of His Humour, <u>1669</u>: BRIDGES, Jan 12; <u>1675</u>: DL, Jul 0

--Haddington Masque, The, <u>1774</u>: CG, Nov 19

--Humours Reconciled, The, <u>1669</u>: BRIDGES, Jan 12

--Magnetic Lady, The, <u>1669</u>: BRIDGES, Jan 12

--Masque of Oberon, <u>1771</u>: CG, Nov 12

--New Inn, The; or, The Light of Heart, <u>1669</u>: BRIDGES, Jan 12; <u>1748</u>: DL, Apr 23

--Poetaster, The, <u>1668</u>: LIF, Aug 20

--Rollo, Duke of Normandy. See Fletcher, John.

--Sad Shepherd, <u>1783</u>: CG, Oct 3; <u>1795</u>: HAY, Sep 21

--Sejanus, <u>1669</u>: BRIDGES, Jan 12

--Silent Woman, The (Madame Epicene), <u>1660</u>: REDBULL, Jun 0, Aug 14, VERE, Nov 10, ATCOURT, 19, VERE, Dec 4; <u>1661</u>: VERE, Jan 7, May 25; <u>1663</u>: NONE, Mar 0; <u>1664</u>: IT, Feb 2, BRIDGES, Jun 1; <u>1666</u>: ATCOURT, Dec 10; <u>1667</u>: BRIDGES, Apr 16; <u>1668</u>: BRIDGES, Sep 18, 19; <u>1669</u>: BRIDGES, Jan 12; <u>1673</u>: NONE, Jul 0; <u>1685</u>: DLORDG, Jan 15; <u>1700</u>: DLLIF, Feb 0, DL, Dec 21; <u>1701</u>: DL, Jun 5; <u>1703</u>: DL, May 7, Oct 11, Dec 13; <u>1704</u>: DL, Feb 14, Oct 23; <u>1706</u>: DL, Feb 2; <u>1707</u>: QUEEN'S, Jan 1, 2, 7, Feb 21, DL/QUEEN, Oct 28, Nov 13; <u>1708</u>: DL/QUEEN, Jan 7, Apr 21; <u>1709</u>: DL, Jan 4, Mar 1, May 31; <u>1710</u>: QUEEN'S, Jan 11, Feb 9, Jun 9, DL, Nov 28; <u>1711</u>: DL, Mar 5, Nov 1; <u>1712</u>: DL, Apr 1; <u>1713</u>: DL, Mar 3, Nov 2, Dec 14; <u>1714</u>: DL, Oct 27; <u>1715</u>: DL, Mar 3, Nov 3; <u>1716</u>: DL, Jan 25, Dec 4; <u>1717</u>: DL, May 25; <u>1718</u>: DL, Jan 20, Nov 18; <u>1719</u>: DL, Nov 3; <u>1720</u>: DL, Sep 15, Nov 16; <u>1721</u>: DL, Feb 28; <u>1722</u>: DL, Jan 9, May 23, Oct 24; <u>1723</u>: DL, Feb 14, Nov 6; <u>1724</u>: DL, Feb 10, Oct 28, Dec 31; <u>1725</u>: DL, Apr 6, Nov 8; <u>1726</u>: DL, Oct 25; <u>1728</u>: DL, Apr 2; <u>1729</u>: DL, Jan 29; <u>1730</u>: DL, Dec 21; <u>1731</u>: DL, Oct 9; <u>1732</u>: DL, Mar 9; <u>1733</u>: DL/HAY, Dec 12, 22, 29; <u>1734</u>: DL/HAY, Jan 1, 5, Mar 21, DL, Apr 15; <u>1735</u>: DL, Apr 14, May 22, Nov 20, Dec 20; <u>1736</u>: DL, Mar 29, May 28, Oct 23; <u>1737</u>: DL, Nov 16; <u>1738</u>: DL, Feb 18; <u>1739</u>: DL, Jan 26, Oct 23; <u>1740</u>: DL, Oct 11; <u>1741</u>: DL, May 12; <u>1742</u>: DL, Feb 13; <u>1745</u>: CG, Apr 17, Nov 23, Dec 3, 28; <u>1746</u>: CG, Feb 18, Mar 8; <u>1748</u>: CG, Mar 28; <u>1749</u>: DL, May 1; <u>1752</u>: DL, Oct 21, 24, 26, 27, 31, Nov 1, 11; <u>1776</u>: DL, Jan 13, 15, 17, 23; <u>1784</u>: CG, Apr 26

--Staple of News, <u>1669</u>: BRIDGES, Jan 12

--Tale of a Tubb, <u>1669</u>: BRIDGES, Jan 12

--Volpone; or, The Fox, <u>1662</u>: ATCOURT, Oct 16; <u>1665</u>: BRIDGES, Jan 14; <u>1667</u>: ATCOURT, Aug 28; <u>1669</u>: BRIDGES, Jan 12; <u>1676</u>: DL, Jan 17; <u>1700</u>: DLLIF, Feb 0, DL, May 2, Dec 27; <u>1701</u>: DL, Mar 18, Jun 19; <u>1703</u>: DL, May 21, 24, 25, Jun

12, Nov 3, 24; 1704: DL, Feb 23, Jun 17, Nov 29; 1705: DL, Jun 5, Nov 8;
1706: QUEEN'S, Dec 3; 1708: DL, Apr 27; 1709: DL, Feb 26, May 27; 1710:
QUEEN'S, Jan 9, DL, Nov 25; 1712: DL, Apr 29, Nov 17; 1713: DL, Nov 24; 1714:
DL, May 12; 1715: DL, Mar 19; 1716: DL, Jan 26; 1717: DL, Jan 31, May 15;
1718: HC, Oct 16, DL, 17; 1720: DL, Mar 19, 22, Nov 12; 1721: DL, Jan 31, Dec
22; 1722: DL, Oct 10; 1723: DL, Mar 23, Nov 21; 1724: DL, May 15; 1725: DL,
Apr 15; 1726: DL, Jan 5, Oct 15; 1727: DL, Jan 12, LIF, Nov 15, 16, 23; 1728:
LIF, Mar 11, May 29, Oct 21; 1729: DL, Jan 31, LIF, Mar 27, Oct 17; 1730:
LIF, Jun 1, DL, Sep 24; 1731: LIF, Jan 4, DL, Oct 5, LIF, Dec 11; 1732: LIF,
Feb 5, LIF/CG, Nov 11; 1733: LIF/CG, Jan 11, Feb 3, Apr 19, CG, Nov 3, 24,
DL/HAY, Dec 12, 19, 27; 1734: CG, Jan 2, DL/HAY, 2, CG, Feb 26, Apr 24; 1735:
DL, Mar 13, May 7, Nov 17, Dec 18; 1736: DL, May 8, Oct 21, CG, Nov 15, 17,
Dec 30; 1737: CG, Mar 19, Apr 19, Oct 10, DL, Nov 14; 1738: DL, Feb 20, May
24, CG, Oct 23, Nov 16; 1739: DL, Oct 22, CG, Dec 21; 1740: DL, Oct 9; 1741:
DL, Apr 13; 1742: DL, Feb 11, CG, Oct 15, Nov 24; 1743: CG, Feb 4, Dec 17;
1744: CG, Jan 17; 1745: CG, Feb 11; 1746: CG, Apr 21; 1748: CG, Apr 18, Dec
20, 23; 1749: DL, May 1, CG, Nov 18; 1750: CG, Jan 8; 1753: CG, Nov 12, Dec
15; 1754: CG, Oct 17; 1771: CG, Nov 26, 27, 29, Dec 2, 31; 1772: CG, Jan 6,
28, Feb 18; 1773: CG, Jan 7, 20; 1783: HAY, Sep 12, 13; 1784: HAY, May 31,
Jun 7, Jul 2, 29, Sep 9; 1785: DL, Feb 21, Mar 7, Apr 13; 1788: DL, May 19
Jordan, Dorothy (actor), 1785: DL, Oct 18, Nov 11, 18, 21, Dec 1, 3, 8, 17;
1786: DL, Jan 9, 10, 24, Mar 21, 27, Apr 28, Sep 21, 23, 26, 30, Oct 10, 14,
21, 24, Nov 21, Dec 11, 14; 1787: DL, Feb 15, Apr 13, 17, May 2, Sep 22, Oct
3, 15, 22, 26, Nov 1, 2, 8; 1788: DL, Apr 8, 11, 16, May 2, Sep 18, 23, 25,
Oct 4, 11, 13, 22, Nov 19, 21, 28, Dec 12, 17; 1789: DL, Jan 26, 28, Mar 5,
9, 23, Apr 15, 21, May 1, CG, 2, DL, Jun 13; 1790: DL, Feb 8, 10, 12, 15, 18,
23, 27, Mar 2, 8, 13, 22, Apr 14, 26, CG, 29, DL, May 8, CG, Jun 16, HAY, Aug
18, DL, Sep 14, 16, 30, Oct 4, 7, 12, 14, 18, 20, 25, 27, Nov 1, 3, 17, Dec
3, 8; 1791: DL, Jan 11, Mar 7, 22, Apr 5, 7, 27, May 10, CG, 10, DL, 18, 19,
28, HAY, Jul 26, Aug 2, DLKING'S, Sep 22, 24, Oct 1, 3, 4, 6, 10, 20, 25, Nov
1, 4, 8, 14, 16, 18, 26, Dec 10, 31; 1792: DLKING'S, Mar 17, Apr 16, 20, May
1, 8, 17, DL, Dec 10; 1793: DL, Feb 25, 28, Mar 4, 7, 14, 21, Apr 1, 5, 9,
17, 22, 25, 29, May 13, 22, 24, Jun 1; 1794: DL, Jul 2, Oct 22, 27, 29, 30,
Nov 1, 5, 7, 14, 15, 29, Dec 5, 10, 12; 1795: DL, Jan 3, 15, Apr 16, 17, 24,
29, May 4, 9, 12, 26, 29, Sep 17, Nov 3, 5, 7, 10, 12, 14, 17, 19, 24, 26,
Dec 1, 7, 10, 14, 21; 1796: DL, Jan 12, Feb 1, 27, Mar 14, Apr 2, 25, 28, 29,
May 5, 13, Jun 9, Oct 1, 4, 8, 24, 25, 28, Nov 2, 10, 14, Dec 1; 1797: DL,
Apr 19, 28, May 8, 12, 17, 24, 29, Jun 5, 7, 9, CG, 10, 13, DL, 14, CG, 14,
HAY, Sep 18, DL, 19, 21, 26, 28, Oct 5, 7, 12, 21, Nov 11, 17, 21, 23, 24,
28, 30, Dec 11, 14; 1798: DL, Jan 23, 25, Feb 13, 17, 22, Mar 8, Apr 14, 30,
May 7, 11, 19, 21, 24, 30, Jun 1, 5, 8, CG, 11, HAY, Aug 21, DL, Sep 15, 29,
Oct 4, 11; 1799: DL, Jan 31, Feb 4, 7, 9, 14, 16, 19, 23, HAY, 25, DL, Mar 2,
Apr 8, 10, 17, 19, 22, 24, 27, May 3, 4, 24, 27, CG, Jun 1; 1800: DL, Mar 10,
13, 15, 17, 22, 24, 27, Apr 1, 16, 18, 23, 25, 26, 28, May 10, 12, 16, 21,
26, 29, Jun 2, 5, 12, CG, 12, DL, 13, CG, 13, DL, 16, Jul 1
Jordan, Mrs (actor), 1688: DG, Apr 0; 1689: DL, Nov 7, 20; 1690: DL, Jan 0, Mar
0, DLORDG, 0
Jordan, Thomas, 1659: NONE, Dec 18; 1660: REDBULL, May 0, Jun 23, ATCOURT, Aug
16, VERE, Dec 8; 1661: REDBULL, May 28; 1667: NONE, Sep 0; 1675: CITY, Oct
29; 1676: CITY, Oct 30; 1677: CITY, Oct 29; 1678: CITY, Oct 29; 1679: CITY,
Oct 29; 1680: CITY, Oct 29; 1681: CITY, Oct 29; 1682: CITY, Oct 30; 1683:
CITY, Oct 29; 1684: CITY, Oct 29
--Bacchus Festival; or, A New Medley, 1660: VH, Apr 12
--Florentine Ladies, The, 1659: NONE, Sep 0
--Goldsmiths Jubilee, The; or, London's Triumph, 1674: CITY, Oct 29
--London in its Splendor, 1673: CITY, Oct 29
--London in Luster, 1679: CITY, Oct 29
--London Triumphant; or, The City in Jollity and Splendour (pageant), 1672:
CITY, Oct 29
--London's Glory; or, The Lord Mayor's Show (pageant), 1680: CITY, Oct 29
--London's Joy; or, The Lord Mayor's Show (pageant), 1681: CITY, Oct 29
--London's Resurrection to Joy and Triumph, 1671: CITY, Oct 30
--London's Royal Triumph for the City's Loyal Magistrate, 1684: CITY, Oct 29
--Love Hath Found Out His Eyes; or, Distractions, 1660: REDBULL, May 0
--Triumphs of London, The, 1675: CITY, Oct 29; 1678: CITY, Oct 29; 1683: CITY,
Oct 29; 1691: CITY, Oct 29; 1692: CITY, Oct 29; 1693: CITY, Oct 30; 1694:
CITY, Oct 29; 1695: CITY, Oct 29; 1699: CITY, Oct 30
--Wealth Outwitted; or, Money is an Ass, 1667: NONE, Sep 0
Joseph and His Brethren. See Handel, George Frederic.
Joseph Andrews. See Pratt, Samuel Jackson.
Joseph. See DeFesch, William; Handel, George Frederic.
Joshua. See Handel, George Frederic.

Jossett (dancer), 1750: CG, Feb 7, Mar 1, 19, Apr 3
Joueur, Le. See Regnard, Jean Francois.
Joules (actor), 1781: CG, Mar 3, Oct 13, Dec 6, 8; 1782: CG, May 20, Oct 17;
    1783: CG, Apr 12; 1784: CG, May 18
Journey to Bristol, A. See Hippisley, John.
Journey to Paris. See Observations on His Journey to Paris.
Jovial Coopers (dance), 1757: CG, Nov 7, 10, 14, 16, 18, 19, 21, 22, 23, 25,
    28, 30, Dec 2, 5, 6, 8, 9; 1758: CG, Feb 14, 18, 25, Apr 10
Jovial Crew, The (dance), 1746: GF, May 1
Jovial Crew, The. See Brome, Sir Richard.
Jovial Gardeners (dance), 1763: CG, Mar 12, 26; 1771: CG, Nov 4, 6
Jovial Jack Tars; or, All Well Matched (entertainment), 1749: BFCB, Aug 23, 24,
    25, 26, 28
Jovial Sailors (dance), 1784: DL, Mar 20, 22, Apr 12, May 5, 10; see also Merry
    Sailors
Joy to the Happy Pair (song), 1742: GF, Feb 2
Joy, William and Richard (weight lifters), 1699: ATCOURT, Nov 15, DG, 29, Dec
    7; 1700: DG, Jan 3
Joyce (actor), 1777: HAY, Oct 13
Joyce, Anthony (spectator at puppetry), 1663: NONE, Aug 6
Joyce, Kate (spectator at puppetry), 1662: NONE, Aug 6
Joyce, Mary (spectator at puppetry), 1663: NONE, Aug 6
Joyner, William
--Roman Empress, The, 1670: BRIDGES, Aug 0
Joyous Return of the Brave British Tars from the Conquest of Cape Breton, The
    (entertainment), 1758: BFDVW, Sep 2
Joys Immortal (song), 1717: LIF, Dec 2, 7
Joys in gentle strains (song), 1789: CG, Apr 3; 1796: CG, Mar 16
Jozzi (singer), 1746: KING'S, Jan 7, 28, Mar 25, May 13
Jubal's Lyre (song), 1760: DL, May 14; see also O had I Jubal's Lyre
Juber (dancer), 1791: KING'S, May 26
Jubilate. See Handel, George Frederic.
Jubilee Ball (dance), 1749: BFCB, Aug 23, 24, 25, 26, 28
Jubilee Concert (music), 1753: BFSY, Sep 3
Jubilee Dicky (actor), 1703: DL, Jun 19, Oct 28; 1710: GR, Jun 15, 21, Aug 12,
    24, Sep 11; 1716: DL, Apr 14, SF, Sep 25; 1717: TC, Aug 5; 1720: BFPMJ, Aug
    23; 1723: DL, Apr 16; 1724: SF, Sep 2, HAY, Oct 13; 1731: DL, Feb 10, GF, Nov
    15; 1732: DL, Apr 21; 1733: DL, May 5; see also Norris, Henry
Jubilee Dicky's son (dancer), 1713: DL, Jun 10
Jubilee, The. See Garrick, David.
Jubilitat Deo (anthem), 1702: CC, May 21
Judas Maccabaeus. See Handel, George Frederic.
Judd Place West, 1796: DL, May 20; 1798: DL, May 23; 1799: DL, Apr 18, HAY, Aug
    20; 1800: DL, May 21
Judge Tycho's Sentence (entertainment), 1774: DL, May 5, 9, 12
Judgment of Paris; or, The Truimphs of Beauty (ballad opera), 1731: LIF, May 6;
    1733: DL, Jan 31, Feb 6, 8, 10, 12, 13, 15
Judgment of Paris, The (dance), 1733: LIF/CG, Mar 28; 1757: CG, Dec 17, 23;
    1758: CG, Jan 9, 13, 20, 26, 28, 31, Feb 2, 7, 11, Mar 4, 9, 11, 13, 14, 18,
    Apr 5, 7, 10, 12, 13, 14, 17, 22; 1760: KING'S, Mar 24; 1764: CG, May 3, 4, 8
Judgment of Paris, The. See Congreve, William.
Judicious Choice (song), 1767: DL, May 26
Judith. See DeFesch, William; Arne, Dr Thomas A.
Jugement de Paris (dance), 1785: KING'S, Feb 12, 15, 26
Juggling (entertainment), 1746: HIC, Feb 3, Mar 10
Julia; or, Such Things Were. See Hoare, Prince.
Julia; or, The Italian Lover. See Jephson, Robert.
Julian (actor), 1733: MEG, Sep 28; 1734: MEG, Sep 30; 1740: DL, May 28, BFHC,
    Aug 23, GF, Oct 21, 24, 25, 27, 30, 31, Nov 6, 13, 15, 18, 21, 22, 25, 28,
    29, Dec 1, 4, 5, 6, 8, 10, 12, 15; 1741: GF, Jan 15, 20, 27, 28, 29, Feb 2,
    12, 14, 16, Mar 3, 19, Apr 2, 17, 27, BFTY, Aug 22, GF, Sep 14, 16, 18, 21,
    25, 30, Oct 2, 5, 9, 16, 28, Nov 6, 9, 27, Dec 9, 10, 29; 1742: GF, Jan 1, 4,
    18, Feb 3, Mar 1, 25, 27, 29, May 3, 18, JS, Oct 12, LIF, Nov 29, Dec 1, 3,
    6, 13, 22, 27, 28, 30; 1743: LIF, Jan 7, 14, Feb 2, 14, 17, 28, Apr 4, 5,
    HAY, 14; 1745: GF, Oct 28, Nov 4, 11, 12, 14, 18, 22, 26, 27, Dec 2, 4, 6, 9,
    11; 1746: GF, Jan 1, 2, 3, 6, 13, Feb 3, 7, 18, 24, 27
Juliana. See Crowne, John.
Juliano, Master (musician), 1796: KING'S, Mar 10
Julien, Mme (dancer), 1784: KING'S, Dec 18
Julietta (singer), 1743: KING'S, Nov 15
Juliot, Solomon Paul (renter), 1758: CG, Mar 9
Julius Caesar. See Shakespeare, William.

Jump through a Tub of Fire (entertainment), 1780: DL, May 9, 12; 1797: CG, Jun 9

Junes, Nassar (Syrian prince), 1722: LIF, May 18
Juniper, Jack (author), 1736: HAY, Aug 2
Junius Brutus. See Duncombe, William; Bertoni, Fernando Giuseppe.
Juno in her Cups (entertainment), 1784: HAY, Sep 17
Jupiter and Alcmena (pantomime), 1746: NWC, Sep 25
Jupiter and Alcmena. See Dibdin, Charles.
Jupiter and Europa; or, The Intrigues of Harlequin (pantomime), 1723: LIF, Mar 23, 25, 26, Apr 2, 17, 20, 22, May 1, 16, 25, 30, Jun 7, Oct 19, 26, Nov 15, Dec 6, 10, 14, 19, 27, 28; 1724: LIF, Jan 1, Mar 10, 12, Jun 4, Sep 25, Oct 20, 29, Nov 5, 14, 27; 1725: LIF, Jan 5, Oct 21, 27, 29, Nov 4, 5, 27, Dec 7; 1726: LIF, Jan 4, Oct 17, 29; 1727: LIF, Jan 13, Apr 28, Oct 27, Nov 3
Jupiter and Io (entertainment), 1735: GF, Jan 23, 24, 25, 27, 28, 29, 31, Feb 1, 3, 4, 5, 6, 7, 8, 10, 11, 12, 13, 14, 15, 17, 18, 20, 22, 24, 25, 27, Mar 1, 3, 4, 6, 8, 11, 15, 18, 22, 25, Apr 7, 8, 12, 14, 15, 25, 26; 1736: GF, Mar 3, 4, 5, 6, 8, 9, 11, 13, 23, Apr 5
Jupiter and Juno (play, anon), 1740: TCLP, Aug 4
Jupiter in Argos. See Handel, George Frederic.
Jupp (house servant), 1767: CG, Dec 28; 1769: CG, Jan 2; 1774: CG, Jan 14
Just in Time. See Hurlstone, Thomas.
Justice Busy. See Crowne, John.
Justin. See Handel, George Frederic.
Justly these evils (song), 1790: CG, Feb 26, Mar 19; 1791: CG, Mar 11; 1792: KING'S, Mar 30; 1799: CG, Mar 15

K Tow oh Koam, King of the River Nation (spectator), 1710: QUEEN'S, Apr 28
K, J (letter writer), 1731: GF, Nov 16
Kanari (dance), 1734: GF, May 20
Karba (musician), 1726: HAY, Mar 11, DL, Apr 28
Karmazin (musician), 1752: DL, Oct 16
Karney (actor), 1734: JS, May 24; 1736: DL, May 22; 1737: DL, May 14
Karver (Kawer), Miss (actor), 1736: HAY, May 27; 1737: HAY, Mar 21; 1739: DL, Dec 26; 1740: DL, Feb 13, May 28, Oct 22, Nov 24, Dec 4; 1741: DL, May 23; 1748: HAY, Nov 22; 1760: HAY, Feb 14
Katchpole, Sir John (spectator), 1687: DL, Jan 28
Kate of Aberdeen (song), 1775: CG, May 10, 23; 1776: CG, May 7; 1780: HAY, Jul 27; 1781: DL, May 9; 1782: DL, May 1; 1783: CG, May 26
Katharine and Petruchio. See Garrick, David, Catherine and Petruchio.
Katharine Oggy (song), 1798: CG, Apr 28
Katharine, Mme (singer), 1754: HAY, Nov 28, Dec 9
Katt, Lady, 1711: QUEEN'S, Apr 25
Kauntze, George (flutist), 1798: HAY, Jan 15
Kay, Arthur (spectator), 1700: DL, Mar 12, LIF, 12
Kaye (French horn player), 1790: CG, Feb 19; 1791: CG, Mar 11; 1792: CG, Feb 24; 1793: CG, Feb 15
Kaygill (Cagle, Keygille) (pit doorkeeper), 1760: DL, May 6; 1763: DL, May 17; 1764: DL, May 21, 22; 1765: DL, May 21; 1766: DL, May 21; 1767: DL, Jun 1; 1768: DL, May 30; 1769: DL, May 19; 1770: DL, May 30; 1771: DL, May 28; 1772: DL, Jun 5; 1773: DL, Jun 2; 1774: DL, May 28; 1775: DL, May 26; 1776: DL, May 22; 1777: DL, Jun 2; 1778: DL, May 23; 1779: DL, May 28; 1781: DL, May 18
Keale (actor), 1749: HAY, May 16
Keally, 1701: DG, Mar 21
Kean, Edmund (actor), 1791: DLKING'S, Dec 31; 1796: DL, Jun 8
Kean, Moses (actor), 1784: HAY, Mar 22, Aug 26; 1785: HAY, Jan 24, 31, Feb 7, 24, CG, May 7; 1787: HAY, Jan 8, Jun 23; 1789: DL, Jun 4, HAY, Aug 25; 1790: HAY, Jul 5; 1791: HAY, Aug 18, Sep 16
Kear, James Thomas (actor, singer), 1757: HAY, Oct 17, 21, Dec 26; 1758: HAY, Jan 6, 12, 25, Feb 2, MARLY, Aug 21, Sep 5, 11, 18; 1760: DL, Oct 20; 1761: DL, May 11; 1765: DL, May 1, 7, Sep 14; 1766: DL, Jan 6, Feb 3, 7, May 13, Sep 25, 27, Dec 4; 1767: DL, Jan 24, Apr 4, May 26, Sep 16, 23; 1768: DL, Jan 14, Apr 22, 25, 27, May 11, Sep 20, 22, 28; 1769: DL, Mar 16, Apr 12, May 9, Oct 9, 11, 14; 1770: DL, Jan 4, Mar 22, May 7, 18, Oct 3, 13, 23, 25, Nov 1, 3, 14, 19, Dec 13; 1771: DL, Mar 7, 11, 23, Apr 1, 6, 24, May 25, 27, Sep 21, Oct 10, Nov 28, Dec 2, 26; 1772: DL, Mar 26, Apr 25, Jun 1, Sep 22, 29, Oct 1, 21, Nov 12, Dec 2, 21, 26, 30; 1773: DL, May 10, 19, Sep 25, Oct 9, 25, Nov 2, 9, 25, Dec 3, 27; 1774: DL, Jan 18, 19, Mar 14, 19, Apr 8, 15, May 18, Oct 5, 8, 11, 14, Nov 5, 21, Dec 9, 26; 1775: DL, Jan 2, Feb 1, Mar 21, 23, May 1, 3, 19, Oct 7, 10, 11, 28, Nov 9, 11, 28, Dec 7, 11; 1776: DL, Feb 1,

9, 15, 20, Mar 14, 18, 25, May 10, 22, Oct 10, 15, 18, Nov 25, Dec 10; 1777:
    DL, Jan 1, 4, Mar 1, Apr 22, May 6, 9, 28, Oct 29, Nov 14; 1778: DL, Mar 2;
    1784: HAY, Sep 17
Kearby, J (publisher), 1779: CG, Nov 12
Kearny (actor), 1769: HAY, May 24, 26, 29, Jun 2, 5, 7, 9, Jul 12, 17, 21, Aug
    7, 9, 14, 25, 29, 30, Sep 11
Kearsley, C and G (publishers), 1791: CG, Feb 16; 1792: HAY, Aug 23
Kearsley, George (printer, publisher), 1767: CG, Mar 4; 1772: DL, Feb 18; 1778:
    CG, Feb 4, DL, 19, HAY, Aug 7, CG, Sep 18, 28, Oct 2, Nov 4; 1779: CG, Jan 4,
    Apr 27, May 6, Oct 6, 20, Nov 30, DL, Dec 13; 1780: CG, Jan 18, Feb 1, Apr
    25, Jun 26, Oct 19, Nov 15, 25, Dec 29; 1781: CG, Oct 1, DL, Nov 10; 1782:
    CG, Feb 9; 1784: CG, Oct 29; 1785: DL, Feb 8
Keasberry, William (actor, manager of Bath Theatre), 1768: HAY, Sep 19; 1770:
    HAY, Sep 20; 1789: CG, May 22
Keate, George (author, painter), 1767: DL, Jan 2; 1781: HAY, Aug 8
Keating (actor), 1789: DL, Oct 31
Keating (beneficiary), 1715: LIF, Oct 31
Keating (house servant), 1753: DL, May 15
Keeffe, Mrs. See O'Keeffe, Mary.
Keel (stationer), 1766: DL, Nov 3
Keely (actor), 1733: DL/HAY, Nov 24
Keen (actor), 1736: LIF, Mar 31
Keen (dancer), 1789: DL, Jan 8, May 27, Jun 9, 10, Sep 24, Dec 26
Keen, Miss (dancer), 1785: HAY, Dec 26
Keen, William (actor), 1764: DL, May 11, Dec 26; 1765: DL, Jan 22, May 16, HAY,
    Jun 10, Jul 31, Aug 21, DL, Oct 2, 25, Nov 21, 25, Dec 6, 7; 1766: DL, Jan 6,
    Mar 22, Apr 7, 18, 25, May 13, HAY, Jun 26, Jul 1, 15, KING'S, Aug 8, 13, 18,
    HAY, 21, KING'S, 25, 27, Sep 13, 19, DL, 27, Oct 8, 24, HAY, 27, DL, 29, Nov
    4, 8, 24, Dec 4, 20; 1767: DL, Jan 24, Feb 7, 10, Mar 7, 30, May 13, 26, HAY,
    Jun 4, 5, 22, 26, 30, Jul 2, 8, 15, 29, 31, Aug 12, 21, 25, 27, Sep 1, DL,
    15, HAY, 18, 21, DL, Oct 14, Nov 4, 19, 24, Dec 15, 26; 1768: DL, Jan 6, 14,
    Mar 15, 26, Apr 27, May 11, HAY, Jul 13, 27, Aug 8, 24, DL, Sep 8, 17, 20,
    26, 28, Oct 10, 11, 13, 21, Nov 4, 10, Dec 16, 17, 30; 1769: DL, Feb 23, Apr
    18, May 9, Sep 16, 26, Oct 2, 7, 9, 13, 14, 21, 30, 31, Nov 8, 17, 24, 27,
    Dec 1, 6, 12, 23; 1770: DL, Jan 4, 16, 27, Apr 7, 20, May 14, 16, Jun 1, Sep
    22, Oct 3, 8, 9, 12, 13, 25, 29, 31, Nov 3, 14, 15, 17, 19, 24, Dec 5, 13;
    1771: DL, Jan 1, 2, Mar 7, 9, 14, Apr 1, 6, 13, 17, May 1, 15, Sep 26, 28,
    Oct 1, 10, 21, 29, 30, Nov 9, 14, 19, 25, Dec 2, 4; 1772: DL, Jan 8, 11, Mar
    12, 26, 28, Apr 21, 22, 25, May 12, 26, Sep 19, Oct 1, 6, 16, 21, 24, 30, Nov
    12, 17, 18, 20, Dec 17, 18, 26, 30; 1773: DL, Jan 21, Feb 11, 17, Apr 13, 17,
    23, May 10, 12, 13, 18, Sep 21, 25, 28, 30, Oct 13, 14, 19, 23, Nov 2, 13,
    Dec 21; 1774: DL, Feb 2, 7, 8, 19, Mar 14, 19, 21, Apr 4, 19, 28, May 4, 14,
    Sep 24, 29, Oct 1, 4, 8, 21, 24, 26, 27, Nov 1, 17, 29, Dec 9, 26; 1775: DL,
    Jan 3, 23, Feb 17, Mar 18, 23, 25, Apr 17, 29, May 1, 10, 12, 13, 15; 1778:
    HAY, Dec 28; 1781: HAY, Aug 10
Keene, Edward (musician), 1699: YB, May 12; 1700: YB, Mar 19; 1703: YB, Mar 12;
    1729: YB, Apr 2
Keene, Mrs (house servant), 1730: LIF, May 25; 1747: CG, May 22
Keene, Theophilus (actor), 1704: DL, Mar 6; 1705: DL, Mar 29, Jun 12, Jul 25,
    Dec 3; 1706: DL, Apr 0, 8, QUEEN'S, Oct 26, Nov 13, 14, 29, Dec 3, 10, 14,
    16; 1707: QUEEN'S, Jan 4, 14, 25, Feb 14, 15, 18, Mar 1, 8, YB, 26, QUEEN'S,
    Apr 1, 21, 30, May 2, 26, Jun 13, 18, 25, Jul 4, 22, 30, Aug 1, 12, Oct 21,
    DL/QUEEN, 22, 23, 25, 27, QUEEN'S, Nov 6, QUEEN/DL, 8, DL/QUEEN, 10, 14, 15,
    19, QUEEN'S, 22, DL/QUEEN, 25, QUEEN'S, Dec 13, YB, 17, DL/QUEEN, 27, 31;
    1708: DL/QUEEN, Jan 1, DL, 15, 31, Feb 9, 14, 23, Mar 13, 18, DL/QUEEN, 23,
    DL, 25, Apr 15, 19, 26, 27, May 21, 31, Jun 15, 19, Jul 1, 3, 27, Aug 4, 28,
    31, Sep 4, 7, 9, 11, 14, 18, 25, 28, 30, Oct 2, 5, 9, 14, 23, 25, Dec 21;
    1709: DL, Jan 1, 11, 15, 26, Feb 5, 25, 26, Mar 3, 15, 19, 21, 24, 31, Apr 2,
    5, 9, 11, 27, May 2, 18, Jun 2, Sep 6, Nov 23, 25, 30, Dec 3, 10, 31; 1710:
    DL, Jan 3, 14, 18, 21, 26, 28, Feb 11, 16, Apr 15, 21, 22, May 23, DL/QUEEN,
    Nov 11, 16, 17, DL, 20, 25, 27, 30, Dec 2, 14, 16, DL/QUEEN, 29; 1711:
    DL/QUEEN, Jan 8, DL, 18, 20, 27, DL/QUEEN, Feb 17, DL, 24, 27, Mar 20, Apr
    21, DL/QUEEN, May 1, 3, DL, 18, 21, 22, Jul 10, Sep 25, Oct 2, 10, 13, 18,
    20, 24, 27, 29, 30, Nov 3, 5, 6, 8, 10, 23, 24, 26, 27, Dec 3; 1712: DL, May
    8, 22, Jun 2, Jul 1, 4, 29, Aug 1, Sep 30, Oct 4, 10, 11, 14, 16, 20, 21, 23,
    28, 29, Nov 1, 7, Dec 12; 1713: DL, Jan 5, 10, 15, 29, Mar 9, 14, 16, 28, Apr
    14, May 4, 11, 18, Jun 5, 12, 19, Oct 13, 23, Nov 16, 23, 25, 27; 1714: DL,
    Jan 5, Mar 31, Apr 26, May 7, 21, 28, Jun 2, 4, 18, 25, Oct 26, Dec 18; 1715:
    LIF, Jan 3, 4, 11, Feb 3, 5, Mar 12, 26, May 24, Jun 23, Aug 11, Oct 5, 10,
    22, 24, 25, 26, 27, Nov 7, 29; 1716: LIF, Jan 3, 4, Feb 4, 21, Mar 3, Apr 17,
    Jul 11, Oct 18, 20, 23, 26, 27, Nov 9, 10, 17, 22, Dec 1, 13; 1717: LIF, Jan
    8, 29, Feb 11, 28, Mar 11, 16, 19, 28, Apr 13, May 18, DL, Sep 28, LIF, Oct

473

5, 9, 12, 15, 24, 26, Nov 6, 14, 16, 19, Dec 3, 9, 10, 21; 1718: LIF, Jan 7, 22, 23, Feb 1, 15, 27, Mar 1, 3, Apr 15, 23, May 15, DL, Jul 25, NONE, 30

Keene, Widow (beneficiary), 1718: LIF, Dec 4; 1719: LIF, May 1; 1720: LIF, Mar 14; 1721: LIF, Mar 25; 1724: LIF, May 28; 1725: LIF, May 24; 1729: LIF, May 19

Keeting (ticket deliverer), 1800: CG, Jun 10

Keisher (Kisheir) (house servant), 1743: DL, May 24; 1744: DL, May 21

Keitch (musician), 1719: CGR, Mar 18, MTH, Apr 29, HIC, May 7; 1720: LIF, Dec 23; 1721: LIF, May 9; 1726: HIC, Mar 16

Keith (actor), 1723: DL, Jun 12

Keller (composer), 1703: DL, Apr 27, YB, Dec 11; 1704: YB, Apr 28

Kelley (victim), 1718: LIF, Jun 20, NONE, Jul 12

Kellnar (actor), 1735: GF, Dec 17; 1736: LIF, Sep 28

Kellom (choreographer), 1717: LIF, Feb 21

Kellom's scholar (dancer), 1716: LIF, Apr 30, May 10, 18, Nov 15, 28, 29; 1717: LIF, Jan 4, 7, 11, 14, 15, 31, Mar 2, Apr 8, May 16, Jun 1, 7, 12; 1718: DL, Nov 17, 28

Kelly (actor), 1732: HAY, Mar 13; 1733: HAY, Mar 14, LIF, Apr 16, CG, May 16, 17, DL/HAY, Oct 29, Nov 26; 1734: DL/HAY, Jan 12, 28, Mar 21, DL, Apr 15, 29, HIC, May 2; 1735: GF, Feb 14, Mar 6, 20, Apr 23, May 6, Sep 10, 15, 26, Oct 15, Nov 26, Dec 17; 1736: GF, Feb 4, 10, 17, 20, Mar 3, DL, Apr 22, GF, 29, May 4, LIF, Sep 28, Oct 5, 21, Dec 3, 7, 17, 31; 1737: LIF, Feb 1, Apr 25, 29, 30, May 6; 1739: KING'S, Jan 16

Kelly (actor), 1749: HAY, Nov 14; 1750: DL, May 22

Kelly (actor, mimic), 1787: HAY, Mar 26

Kelly, Earl of. See Erskine, Thomas Alexander.

Kelly, Hugh, 1770: DL, Mar 3, 5, 6; 1771: CG, Feb 23; 1773: DL, Dec 11; 1774: CG, Dec 6; 1776: CG, Feb 9, CHR, Sep 23; 1777: CG, May 13, 29; 1800: CG, May 24

--Clementina, 1771: CG, Feb 23, 25, 26, 28, Mar 2, 4, 5, 7, 9

--False Delicacy, The, 1768: DL, Jan 23, 25, 26, 27, 28, Feb 1, 2, 3, 5, 6, 9, 10, 11, 16, 20, 23, Mar 12, Apr 20, May 12, Oct 8, Dec 15; 1769: DL, Mar 14, Apr 26, Oct 18; 1770: DL, Jan 10, Mar 6; 1773: DL, Apr 16; 1782: DL, Oct 14; 1783: DL, May 20

--Man of Reason, The, 1776: CG, Feb 9

--Romance of an Hour, The, 1774: CG, Dec 2, 3, 7, 9, 14, 16, 22; 1775: CG, Feb 11, Apr 1, 19, Dec 2, 13; 1784: HAY, Nov 16; 1788: CG, Apr 26; 1797: HAY, May 10

--School for Wives, The, 1773: DL, Dec 10, 11, 13, 17, 20, 22, 23, 30, 31; 1774: DL, Jan 3, 5, 7, 10, 12, 13, 15, 18, 20, 24, 27, Feb 3, 5, 12, 15, Mar 10, Apr 7, 9, May 25, Oct 12; 1775: DL, Jan 3, Feb 9, Apr 3, May 11; 1776: DL, Apr 17, CHR, Sep 23; 1777: CG, May 2; 1782: CG, May 11, 21; 1784: HAY, Nov 16; 1787: CG, Apr 16, May 16; 1788: CG, Mar 15, DL, Apr 28; 1789: CG, Mar 28; 1790: CG, Apr 20; 1791: CG, May 18; 1793: CG, Jun 8; 1794: CG, Jan 22, May 13, Jun 13; 1796: CG, Oct 5, Dec 16; 1797: CG, May 22; 1800: CG, May 10, Jun 4

--Word to the Wise, A, 1770: DL, Mar 3, 5; 1777: HAY, May 1, CG, 13, 29; 1784: HAY, Jan 21

Kelly, John, 1732: LIF, Mar 25; 1733: DL, Dec 5; 1735: DL, Jan 22

--Married Philosopher, The, 1732: LIF, Mar 25, 28, Apr 1, 15, 20; 1733: CG/LIF, Mar 26, CG, 27

--Plot, The, 1735: DL, Jan 22, 24, 25

--Timon in Love; or, The Innocent Theft, 1733: DL, Dec 5, 6, 8; 1736: CG, Mar 23

Kelly, Mark (actor), 1795: DL, Feb 12, 17, Jun 4

Kelly, Michael (actor, singer, composer), 1787: DL, Apr 20, 30, May 11, Sep 27, Oct 4, 25, Nov 8, Dec 17, 19; 1788: DL, Jan 26, 28, Feb 25, Apr 7, May 1, 6, 8, Sep 23, Oct 9, 14, 23, 25, Nov 1, Dec 17; 1789: DL, Jan 8, Feb 16, 18, 27, Mar 6, 9, 18, 20, 25, Apr 14, 17, 20, KING'S, 21, CG, May 15, DL, 19, 23, 27, 28, KING'S, Jun 11, DL, Sep 22, 24, 26, Oct 10, 13, 15, 22, 26, 28, Nov 4, 13, 24, 30, Dec 3, 7; 1790: DL, Feb 19, 24, 26, Mar 5, 12, Apr 16, 30, May 4, 31, Jun 1, HAY, 3, DL, Sep 11, Oct 4, 11, Nov 30, Dec 8; 1791: DL, Jan 1, Feb 10, Mar 25, Apr 1, 28, May 3, 19, Jun 4, DLKING'S, Sep 22, 27, 29, Oct 15, 25, 29, Nov 2, 9, 12, 16, 17, 30, Dec 7, 31; 1792: KING'S, Feb 24, DLKING'S, Mar 10, KING'S, 14, DLKING'S, 17, KING'S, 23, 28, 30, DLKING'S, May 23, DL, Sep 18, 20, 27, Oct 9, 11, 13, 18, Nov 10, 21, Dec 13, 14; 1793: DL, Jan 23, KING'S, 26, Feb 5, CG, 15, 20, 22, KING'S, 26, CG, Mar 6, 8, 13, KING'S, 19, CG, 20, 22, DL, May 7, KING'S, 14, Jun 11, 25; 1794: DL, Mar 12, 19, 26, Apr 2, 4, 9, 10, 11, 21, 25, 26, May 3, 9, 16, 17, 19, Jun 9, Jul 2, Sep 27, Oct 6, 7, 11, 20, 27, Nov 3, Dec 20; 1795: DL, Jan 3, Feb 6, KING'S, 7, CG, 20, 27, Mar 11, 13, 18, 20, 25, 27, KING'S, Apr 14, 30, DL, May 6, 18, KING'S, 26, DL, 27, KING'S, Jun 23, DL, Sep 17, 29, Oct 1, 6, 30, Nov 11, KING'S, Dec

12, DL, 18; <u>1796</u>: KING'S, Jan 2, 19, CG, Feb 12, 26, DL, Mar 12, CG, 16,
KING'S, Apr 7, DL, 30, May 11, 25, Sep 22, 27, 29, Oct 10, 19, Nov 10, Dec 5;
<u>1797</u>: DL, Jan 7, Feb 9, 16, Mar 6, May 8, 22, Sep 23, 26, Oct 7, 19, 23, Nov
7, 8, 20, 24, Dec 14; <u>1798</u>: DL, Jan 16, 20, Feb 2, Mar 6, Apr 24, May 9, 23,
31, HAY, Jun 13, 27, Jul 5, 11, DL, Sep 27, 29, Oct 2, 6, 16, 18, Nov 14, 29,
Dec 13, 29; <u>1799</u>: DL, Jan 19, Mar 2, Apr 2, 20, 25, CG, 30, DL, May 7, 8, 24,
Jun 28, Sep 17, 24, Oct 14, 19, 24, Nov 16, Dec 11, 17; <u>1800</u>: DL, Jan 1, 21,
28, Feb 1, 6, Mar 6, 11, 13, Apr 28, 29, May 14, 16, Jun 6
Kelly, Mrs (actor), <u>1743</u>: TCD/BFTD, Aug 4
Kelly, Mrs, Coffee House, <u>1753</u>: DL, Dec 11
Kellyad, The (criticism), <u>1767</u>: DL, Jan 16
Kelm (house servant), <u>1792</u>: CG, Jun 1
Kemble, Charles (actor, author), <u>1794</u>: DL, Apr 21, 25, May 1, 3, 19, Jun 9, 21,
23, 24, 25, 28, Jul 2, HAY, 12, 21, 22, 26, Aug 4, 9, 18, 20, 23, Sep 3, DL,
23, 27, Oct 7, 14, 18, 22, 28, 29, Nov 1, 14, Dec 6, 12, 20; <u>1795</u>: DL, Jan
21, 23, 26, Feb 17, 21, 28, Mar 12, 14, 21, May 26, Jun 6, HAY, 13, 15, 20,
Jul 25, 31, Aug 3, 13, 18, 21, 24, 25, 31, DL, Sep 19, 22, 24, 26, 29, Oct 1,
12, 27, 30, Nov 3, 6, 7, 10, 12, 19, 20, 23, Dec 9, 18; <u>1796</u>: DL, Feb 20, Mar
15, Apr 2, 20, 25, 29, May 2, 4, 7, 13, 23, 24, 28, Jun 1, 4, HAY, 13, 16,
17, 22, 25, 30, Jul 5, 6, 15, 23, 26, 30, Aug 2, 8, 10, 11, 18, 23, 29, 30,
Sep 1, 5, 7, 16, DL, 20, 24, 29, Oct 1, 10, 13, 19, Nov 2, 3, 9, 15, 18, 26,
28, Dec 6, 14, 23, 29, 30; <u>1797</u>: DL, Jan 17, Feb 1, 8, 22, Mar 6, 7, 11, 20,
21, Apr 28, May 1, 8, 19, 24, 27, 29, Jun 9, HAY, 12, 13, DL, 15, HAY, 17,
19, 20, 23, 29, Jul 3, 8, 10, 15, 20, Aug 5, 8, 9, 14, 15, 19, 28, Sep 4, 8,
DL, 19, 23, 26, 28, 30, Oct 3, 5, 12, 14, 16, 21, 26, 30, Nov 1, 4, 7, 9, 10,
14, 15, 17, 21, 23, 25, Dec 8, 9; <u>1798</u>: DL, Mar 5, 8, 22, Apr 14, 30, May 11,
30, Jun 2, 7, HAY, 12, 14, 18, 20, 21, 23, 30, Jul 14, 16, 21, Aug 11, 21,
29, 30, Sep 3, 10, DL, 18, 20, 22, 25, 29, Oct 2, 4, 9, 16, 27, 30, Nov 6,
16, 22, 26, Dec 3, 21, 27, 29; <u>1799</u>: DL, Jan 8, 9, 11, Feb 28, Mar 2, Apr 17,
19, 22, 23, May 1, 3, 4, 24, 30, HAY, Jul 1, 2, 5, 6, 9, 12, 16, 20, 27, 30,
Aug 13, 15, 21, 26, DL, Sep 17, 19, 21, 24, Oct 1, 3, 7, 21, 29, Nov 2, 16,
22, 29, Dec 7, 9, 11, 26, 30; <u>1800</u>: DL, Jan 1, 2, 11, 25, Feb 15, Mar 10, 11,
Apr 15, 18, Jun 11, HAY, 13, 14, 17, 18, 19, Jul 2, 15, Aug 7, 8, 12, 13, 21
--Point of Honour, The, <u>1792</u>: CG, May 8; <u>1800</u>: HAY, Jul 15, 16, 17, 18, 19, 22,
23, 25, 26, 29, 30, Aug 4, 6, 9, 11, 21, 28, Sep 1, 5, 15
Kemble, Elizabeth (actor), <u>1783</u>: DL, Feb 22, Oct 16, 20, Nov 14; <u>1784</u>: DL, Jan
3, 22, 23, May 10, Oct 26, Nov 2, 15, Dec 3; <u>1785</u>: DL, Apr 20, 27, May 30
Kemble, Elizabeth and Frances (actors), <u>1785</u>: DL, Apr 23
Kemble, Elizabeth, Mrs Stephen George (actor), <u>1783</u>: CG, Nov 24, Dec 6, 23, 27,
29, 31; <u>1784</u>: CG, Jan 5, 9, 14, 19, 26, 29, Feb 10, 13, 18, Mar 16, Apr 13,
17, May 10, 17, 18, 26, 27; <u>1787</u>: HAY, May 18, 23, Jun 13, 18, 21, Jul 23,
Aug 4, Sep 5; <u>1788</u>: HAY, Jun 10, 13, 23, 24, 30, Jul 2, 4, 7, 10, 12, 24, Aug
9, 22, 26, 28, Sep 3; <u>1789</u>: HAY, May 18, Jun 1, 17, 19, 22, 25, 30, Jul 15,
Aug 5, 11, 21, 27, Sep 15; <u>1790</u>: HAY, Jun 14, 15, 18, 28, Jul 7, Aug 2, 11,
14, 16; <u>1791</u>: HAY, Jun 8, 10, 13, 18, 20, 23, 25, Jul 9, 28, 30, Aug 10, 16,
24, 27; <u>1792</u>: HAY, Jul 3, 4, 6, 9, 10, 16, 25, Aug 2, 9, 20, 22, Sep 1, 5;
<u>1793</u>: HAY, Jun 12, 13, 14, 17, 18, 22, 29, Aug 3, 6, 12, 27; <u>1794</u>: HAY, Jul
8, 10, 11, 14, 18, 21, 22, 24, Aug 9, 12, 20, 22, 23, 27, 28, Sep 1, 3; <u>1795</u>:
HAY, Jun 9, 10, 11, 12, 13, 15, 16, 20, Jul 25, 31, Aug 3, 7, 18, 21, 29;
<u>1796</u>: HAY, Jun 11, 13, 14, 16, 17, 22, 25, 30, Jul 7, 14, 15, 21, 23, 30, Aug
3, 8, 10, 11, 23, 29, 30, Sep 1, 3, 7, 16
Kemble, Frances (actor), <u>1783</u>: DL, Jan 6, Mar 3, 17, 18, May 3, Oct 11, 24;
<u>1784</u>: DL, Jan 1, Mar 6, Apr 24, 26, HAY, Jul 12, Aug 18, Sep 2, DL, Oct 9,
18, 23, 27, Nov 3, 16, Dec 10; <u>1785</u>: DL, Jan 14, Feb 2, Sep 22, 24, 29, Oct
6, Nov 8, 18, Dec 2, 5, 26; <u>1786</u>: DL, Jan 5, Feb 15, 18, Mar 4, 9, 25
Kemble, Frances Crawford (actor), <u>1791</u>: HAY, Aug 16
Kemble, Henry Stephen (actor), <u>1796</u>: HAY, Jul 5, 29
Kemble, John Philip (actor, author, manager), <u>1758</u>: DL, Sep 16, 19; <u>1759</u>: DL,
Jan 12; <u>1760</u>: DL, Nov 17; <u>1764</u>: DL, Apr 12, 14; <u>1767</u>: DL, Nov 6; <u>1769</u>: CG,
Oct 18, Nov 11; <u>1770</u>: CG, Jan 19; <u>1772</u>: DL, Sep 22, 26, Oct 1, 16, 20, 23,
Nov 3, CG, 4, DL, 12, Dec 2, 8, 18; <u>1773</u>: DL, Mar 9, CG, Apr 24, May 8, Sep
29, DL, Oct 6, 9, CG, 9, DL, 19, 22, CG, 27, DL, Nov 2, 6, CG, 27, DL, Dec
11, 13, 27; <u>1774</u>: DL, Sep 17, 22, Oct 4, Nov 5, Dec 1, 19; <u>1775</u>: DL, Jan 21,
Feb 17, Mar 6, 30, Apr 1, May 3, 12, Sep 23, Oct 5, 11, 18, 24, 31, Nov 6, 9,
24, 29, Dec 1, 12, 18; <u>1776</u>: DL, Jan 13, 18, 20, Feb 1, 2, 5, 15, 24, Mar 14,
Apr 11, 19, May 9, 13, 27, 30, Jun 3, 5, 8, Sep 28, CG, Nov 14, DL, 25, 29,
Dec 10, 23; <u>1778</u>: DL, Sep 17; <u>1780</u>: CG, Mar 18; <u>1783</u>: DL, Sep 30, Oct 4, 20,
Nov 6, 14, 22, Dec 6, 10, 15; <u>1784</u>: DL, Apr 13, 24, 28, May 8, 10, 17, Sep
21, Oct 5, 27, Nov 2, 15, 22, Dec 2; <u>1785</u>: DL, Jan 27, Mar 8, 31, Apr 4, 25,
Sep 17, Oct 1, 6, 8, 15, 20, 26, 27, Nov 12, 17, 18, 21, 22, Dec 26; <u>1786</u>:
DL, Jan 5, Feb 11, 18, Mar 4, 9, 13, 25, Apr 6, May 15, Sep 19, Oct 3, 5, 7,
9, 16, 19, 23, 24, Nov 22, 25, Dec 6, 11, 21; <u>1787</u>: DL, Jan 13, 23, 29, Feb

7, 20, Mar 8, 12, 29, Apr 13, 14, 16, 26, May 1, 7, Sep 18, 29, Oct 6, 15,
20, 26, 27, 30, Nov 3, 5, 6, 20, 24, 29, Dec 3, 8, 11, 14, 26; 1788: DL, Jan
3, 21, 25, 31, Feb 1, Mar 13, 29, Apr 28, 30, May 1, 5, Sep 16, 30, Oct 2, 9,
11, 14, 16, 20, 28, Nov 1, 5, 6, 11, 12, 17, 25, 28, Dec 9; 1789: DL, Jan 1,
6, 10, 13, 17, 19, Feb 3, 7, 16, 24, Mar 17, 19, 21, 30, Apr 2, 16, 20, May
1, 8, 11, 13, 15, Sep 12, 15, 17, Oct 1, 3, 13, 24, 28, Nov 2, 6, 7, CG, 10,
DL, 27, 30, Dec 7, 14, 22; 1790: DL, Jan 1, Feb 3, Mar 8, 22, Apr 7, 14, May
18, 26, Oct 7, 11, 12, 14, 21, 27, Nov 1, 10, 17, Dec 7, 9, 30; 1791: DL, Jan
31, Mar 21, 28, Apr 4, 28, 29, May 14, DLKING'S, Sep 27, Oct 1, 3, 17, 25,
31, Nov 7, 9, 14, 29, Dec 1, 6, 12; 1792: DLKING'S, Jan 4, 18, 21, 24, 28,
Feb 2, 4, 14, 18, 23, Mar 1, 6, 10, 13, 17, 26, 31, Apr 14, 27, 28, May 28,
DL, Sep 15, 22, 25, Oct 4, 31, Nov 2, 5, Dec 13, 17, 21, 26, 28; 1793: DL,
Jan 4, 7, 23, 24, 29, Feb 5, 9, 12, 16, 23, 26, Mar 2, 5, 9, 12, 18, Apr 22,
23, May 9, HAY, Aug 3, 6, Sep 19, 24, 30, Oct 15, 21, 24, 28, Nov 4, 19;
1794: DL, Mar 12, Apr 21, 25, 26, 29, May 1, 3, 9, Jun 6, 9, 17, Jul 2, Sep
18, 23, 27, Oct 4, 7, 9, 11, 14, 18, 21, 25, 28, 31, Nov 5, 6, 7, 15, 18, 29,
Dec 6, 12, 30; 1795: DL, Jan 26, Feb 28, Mar 3, 10, 14, 21, Apr 27, HAY, Aug
29, DL, Sep 19, 22, 24, 29, Oct 5, 12, 20, 21, 22, 27, Nov 5, 16, 20, 23, Dec
2, 11, 18, 23; 1796: DL, Jan 23, Feb 15, 27, Mar 12, Apr 2, 18, 20, 30, May
2, 4, 23, Jun 1, 8, Sep 29, Oct 3, 6, 10, 13, 15, 22, 24, 26, Nov 5, 8, 9,
15, 19, 22, 23, Dec 9, 16, 20; 1797: DL, Jan 2, 6, 10, 12, 20, Feb 1, 3, Mar
6, 20, May 1, Sep 26, 28, 30, Oct 5, 12, CG, 23, DL, 30, Nov 2, 4, 7, 15, 17,
21, 23, 24, 25, 28, Dec 2, 8, 14; 1798: DL, Feb 26, Mar 5, 17, 24, Apr 30,
May 24, Jun 6, Sep 15, 18, 20, 25, Oct 2, 4, 9, 11, 27, Nov 6, 10, 13, 16,
Dec 3, 29; 1799: DL, Jan 9, 12, 25, Feb 4, 11, 14, Apr 8, 22, 23, 24, 30, May
1, 6, 7, 20, 24, Sep 19, 24, 28, Oct 1, 3, 5, 7, 12, 17, 21, 22, Nov 8, 22,
25, 27, 29, CG, 30, DL, Dec 7, 9, 11, 28; 1800: DL, Jan 25, Feb 3, Apr 29
--Coriolanus; or, The Roman Matron, 1789: DL, Jan 20, Feb 7, 10, 14, 21, 24,
Mar 3, 7, 14; 1792: DLKING'S, Mar 31, Apr 21; 1793: DL, Feb 23, May 21; 1796:
DL, Apr 18, Oct 3; 1797: DL, Feb 27
--Farm House, The, 1789: DL, May 1, 2, 6, 12, Jun 1; 1790: DL, Feb 23, Apr 12,
23, HAY, Jul 28, Aug 5; 1791: HAY, Jul 15; 1792: DL, Dec 15; 1793: DL, Feb 1;
1795: CG, Oct 9, 16; 1796: CG, Jun 3, Oct 25; 1797: CG, Apr 25, Sep 18; 1799:
CG, Sep 18
--Lodoiska, 1794: DL, May 7, 9, 12, 15, 17, 22, 23, 26, 27, 28, 29, 30, Jun 2,
4, 6, 9, 11, 12, 13, 14, 16, 17, 18, 19, 20, 21, 23, 24, 25, 26, 27, 28, 30,
Jul 3, 4, 5, 7, Sep 20, 25, 27, 30, Oct 2, 6, 9, 13, 16, 22, 23, 25, Nov 6,
10, 13, 20, 24, 27, Dec 4, 8, 11, 16, 18, 30, 31; 1795: DL, Jan 1, 8, 10, 12,
15, 17, 21, 24, 26, 31, Feb 3, 4, Oct 1, 3, 5, 8, 12, 19, 22, 27, Nov 2, 9,
12, 17, 21, 24, 28, Dec 3, 5, 9; 1797: DL, Feb 16, 18, 21, 23, 25, 28, Mar 2,
7, 9, 13, 18, 21, 25, Apr 18, 29, May 13, 25, Jun 2, 8; 1800: DL, Jan 1, 2,
3, 6, 8, 9, 13, 15, 16, 18, 23, 27, 29, Feb 6, 7, Apr 14, 15, 16, 17, 18, May
13, 16, 22, 28
--Love in Many Masks, 1790: DL, Mar 8, 9, 13, 20, 27, Apr 10, 17, May 15, Oct
14
--Pannel, The, 1788: DL, Nov 28, Dec 1, 3, 5, 9, 12, 20; 1789: DL, Jan 9, 14,
22, Feb 6, 13, 23, Mar 12, 31, Apr 29, May 4, 14, 16, Jun 1; 1790: DL, Feb
10, 15, Mar 20, Apr 7, 14, 23, Oct 14, Nov 12, 23; 1791: DL, Jan 14, Feb 25,
Mar 22, Apr 9, May 4, 18, Jun 2, DLKING'S, Sep 22, Oct 27, Nov 2, Dec 15;
1792: DLKING'S, Jan 13, Feb 2, 13, 20, Mar 3, 31; 1793: DL, Apr 9, 15, 24,
May 23; 1794: DL, Dec 29; 1795: DL, Jan 1, 3, 9, 14, Apr 22, May 2, 8, Dec
21; 1796: DL, Feb 25, Apr 19, Nov 10, Dec 3; 1797: DL, May 6; 1798: DL, Apr
14, May 8; 1800: DL, Mar 27, May 12, Jun 6
--Projects, The (farce), 1786: DL, Feb 18
--School for Scandal Scandalized, The (interlude), 1780: CG, Mar 18
--Trick upon Trick (farce), 1789: DL, Dec 19, 22
Kemble, Priscilla, Mrs John Phillip (actor), 1787: DL, Dec 8, 10, 11, 14, 27,
28; 1788: DL, Jan 2, 4, 9, 11, Feb 7, 25, Mar 15, 31, Apr 8, 25, 29, 30, May
23, 26, Jun 11, Sep 16, 18, 20, 23, 25, Oct 4, 25, Nov 1, 8, 28, Dec 1, 18;
1789: DL, Jan 7, Mar 5, Apr 20, 21, May 1, Jun 4, Sep 19, 29, Oct 8, 10, 17,
Nov 21, 27, Dec 2; 1790: DL, Jan 15, Feb 10, 15, 23, Mar 8, 22, May 14, Jun
1, Sep 14, Oct 4, 9, 14, 18, 23, 27, Nov 5, 10, Dec 1, 3; 1791: DL, Jan 27,
Apr 4, May 20, 26, 31, DLKING'S, Sep 22, 27, Oct 3, 4, 8, 10, 24, Nov 4, Dec
2; 1792: DLKING'S, Feb 4, 8, Apr 10, 20, May 17, DL, Sep 15, 20, 25, 27, Oct
4, 13, 18, Nov 2, Dec 10, 15; 1793: DL, Jan 1, 9, 29, Feb 25, Mar 4, 12, Apr
9, 17, 29, May 24, Jun 5; 1794: DL, Apr 25, May 22, Jun 12, 16, 19, 20, 28,
Jul 2, Sep 30, Oct 21, 22, 29, Nov 12, 14, Dec 5; 1795: DL, Jan 3, Sep 24,
26, Nov 3, 10, 12, 19, Dec 9, 21; 1796: DL, Jan 12, Feb 1, May 13, 23
Kemble, Roger (actor), 1788: HAY, Aug 26
Kemble, Stephen George (actor, author), 1783: CG, Sep 24, Oct 8, Nov 4, Dec 29;
1784: CG, Jan 16, DL, 22, CG, Feb 10, Mar 22, May 4, 17; 1787: HAY, May 16,
18, 25, Jul 7, 20, 25, Aug 28, Sep 5, 14; 1788: HAY, Jun 18, 23, Jul 24, Aug

2, 9, 26, 28, Sep 3; 1789: HAY, May 18, 20, 25, Jun 1, 15, 17, 22, 24, 25,
   30, Jul 15, Aug 5, 27, Sep 12; 1790: HAY, Jun 14, 18, 28, Jul 7, Aug 11;
   1791: HAY, Jun 10, 16, 18, 29, Jul 9, Aug 16, 27, 29, 31, Sep 2, 5, 7
--Northern Inn, The; or, The Days of Good Queen Bess (farce), 1791: HAY, Aug 16
Kemp (actor), 1723: HAY, Mar 14, Apr 15, 22; 1744: HAY, May 10; 1759: CG, Nov
   10, Dec 15, 29, 31; 1760: CG, Jan 8, 12, 19, 26, Feb 2, 9, 16, 23, Mar 1, 8,
   15, 22, 29, Apr 19, May 10, 16, 28
Kempton, Matthew (actor), 1673: LIF, Dec 0
Kempton, Mrs (gallery keeper), 1677: DL, Dec 26
Kenaston. See Kynaston.
Kendrick. See Kenrick.
Kennedy (actor), 1745: GF, Feb 14, 20, Mar 7, May 2, 3, Nov 11, 12, 13, 14, 18,
   19, 22, 26, 27, 28, 29, Dec 2, 4, 10, 11, 27; 1746: GF, Jan 1, 2, 3, 6, 13,
   17, 27, Feb 3, 7, 10, Mar 4, 6, CG, Jun 16, 23, 27, Oct 22; 1747: CG, Mar 28,
   Dec 9, 28; 1748: CG, Jan 12, 27
Kennedy (actor), 1760: DL, Dec 29; 1761: DL, Apr 13, May 1, Sep 21, 26, 30, Oct
   13, Nov 4, 14, 18, 28; 1762: DL, Mar 25, Apr 26, 30, May 7, 13, 20; 1763:
   HAY, May 9, Jun 20, 24, Jul 6, Aug 1, Sep 5, 7; 1774: HAY, Apr 4, DL, May 6,
   CG, 12, DL, 25, 30, HAY, 30, Jun 15, Aug 19, Sep 5, 17, 21; 1778: HAY, Dec
   28; 1779: HAY, Mar 15
Kennedy Jr (actor), 1774: HAY, May 16
Kennedy, Agnes, Mrs Thomas (actor), 1779: HAY, Jul 16; 1784: CG, Nov 16, 20,
   25, 26, Dec 3, 27, 28; 1785: CG, Jan 6, Mar 3, 29, Apr 1, 2, 11, May 6, 28,
   Oct 3, 7, Nov 22, 26, 30, Dec 1, 9, 10, 20, 22, 26, 30; 1786: CG, Jan 3, 7,
   20, 28, Feb 11, 16, Sep 18, Oct 2, 19, Nov 27, Dec 13, 15, 30; 1787: CG, Jan
   6, 12, 31, Apr 17, 25, 27, DL, May 9, CG, 14, 16, 21, DL, 22, CG, 23
Kennedy, Margaret, Mrs Morgan Hugh (actor, singer), 1779: CG, Jan 26, 27, Feb
   13, DL, 19, CG, 23, DL, 26, Mar 3, 12, 19, CG, 20, 22, DL, 26, Apr 6, CG, 7,
   10, 19, 21, May 6, 13, HAY, Jul 16, 17, 20, CG, Sep 22, 27, Oct 6, 8, 20. 29,
   Nov 30, Dec 18; 1780: CG, Feb 1, 8, 17, Mar 14, Apr 1, May 12, Sep 20, 21,
   Oct 3, 30, Nov 15, 25, Dec 8; 1781: CG, Jan 18, Apr 3, 17, 25, May 1, 2, 12,
   HAY, Aug 22, CG, Sep 17, 24, 26, Oct 11, 16, 24, 30, Nov 2, 12, 28, Dec 26;
   1782: CG, Feb 21, Mar 16, HAY, 21, CG, Apr 9, May 6, 11, 20, Sep 25, 27, Oct
   7, 22, 30, Nov 2, Dec 14, 27, 30, 31; 1783: CG, Jan 23, Apr 5, 7, 22, 26, May
   3, 6, 7, 20, 24, Sep 22, 26, Oct 6, 8, 14, 16, 24, 28, 29, Nov 4, 8, 10;
   1784: CG, Jan 19, DL, Feb 27, Mar 5, CG, 20, Apr 17, 24, 27, May 1, Sep 21,
   Oct 4, 12, 15, 25, 28, Nov 6, 16; 1785: HAY, Feb 23, CG, Mar 19, 30, Apr 6,
   8, 12, 18, May 4, 12, 18, Sep 21, 23, 30, Oct 7, 14, 17, 20, 21, Nov 3, 10,
   14, 21, Dec 26, 30; 1786: CG, Jan 2, 6, 18, Feb 21, 23, Mar 11, 18, Apr 20,
   21, May 6, 22, HAMM, Jul 24, CG, Oct 9, 16, 21, 23, 26, 31, Nov 15, 23, 24,
   Dec 1; 1787: CG, Jan 13, Mar 12, 26, 31, Apr 27, May 3, Sep 17, 24, Oct 1,
   18, 22, Nov 19, Dec 3, 21, 22; 1788: CG, Jan 4, 14, Feb 4, 5, Mar 24, 29, Apr
   1, 2, 30, May 12, 22, Jun 6, Sep 19, 22, 26, 29, Oct 1, 3, 13, 16, 17, 21,
   Nov 1, 3, Dec 29; 1789: CG, Jan 2, Feb 6, 14, Mar 31, Apr 2; 1790: HAY, Aug
   18; 1796: DL, Apr 30
Kennedy, Master (actor), 1760: DL, Oct 3, Dec 17; 1761: DL, Jan 31, Sep 25, Oct
   23, Dec 11, 28; 1762: DL, May 7
Kennedy, Miss (actor), 1753: CG, Dec 10; 1754: CG, Jan 22, Apr 19
Kennedy, Mr and Mrs (actors), 1761: DL, Apr 13; 1762: DL, Apr 26
Kennedy, Mrs (actor), 1745: GF, Feb 14, Mar 7, Nov 13, 14, Dec 4, 26; 1746: GF,
   Jan 6, 13, 17, 20, 27, Feb 7, Nov 18, 19, 20
Kennedy, Mrs (actor), 1792: HAY, Nov 26
Kennedy, Mrs (actor, singer), 1760: DL, Oct 10, 14, 17, 22, Dec 5, 8, 29; 1761:
   DL, Jan 3, Apr 1, 7, 13, 18, May 7, 11, 18, Sep 19, 25, Oct 17, 27, Nov 14,
   Dec 30; 1765: HAY, Jun 24, Jul 31, Aug 8, 12
Kennedy, Polly (actor), 1773: CG, Nov 5; 1774: DL, May 6
Kennedy, Thomas (actor), 1784: CG, Oct 4, 21, 29, 30, Nov 4, 16, Dec 27; 1785:
   CG, Jan 27, Feb 2, 21, Mar 7, 29, Apr 1, 8, 22, May 6, 7, 24, Sep 23, 26, DL,
   27, CG, 28, Oct 3, 12, 17, 19, 22, Nov 1, Dec 14, 26; 1786: CG, Jan 3, Feb
   16, Mar 4, Apr 18, May 13, 26, 29, Oct 9, 25, Nov 29, Dec 11, 21; 1787: CG,
   Jan 2, 6, Feb 6, Mar 15, 27, Apr 11, 12, 25, 30, May 4, 23
Kennedy, Thomas and Agnes (actors), 1786: CG, May 26; 1787: CG, May 23
Kennington Green, 1793: DL, May 10
Kennington Lane, 1782: DL, Apr 16; 1783: DL, Apr 7; 1784: DL, Apr 12; 1785: DL,
   Apr 1; 1786: DL, Kensington Division, 1748: HAY, Apr 18
Kennington, 1792: DLKING'S, May 22, HAY, Jul 31
Kenniston. See Kynaston.
Kenny (actor), 1776: CHR, Sep 23, 25, 27, 30, Oct 2, 4, 14, 16, 18; 1777: HAY,
   Feb 11, Jun 6, 19, Jul 15, 18, 24, Aug 7, 12, 14, Sep 3, 15; 1778: HAY, Jan
   26, Mar 23, 24, 31, Apr 29, 30, May 18, Jun 1, Jul 2, 30, Aug 6, 27, Sep 4,
   8, DL, 24, Oct 15, Nov 2, Dec 21; 1779: DL, Jan 8, May 5, HAY, Jun 4, 18, 22,
   Jul 1, 16, 17, 31, Aug 13, 14, 24, 28, 31, Sep 17, DL, Oct 30, Nov 3; 1780:

DL, Apr 26, 29, May 5, 17, HAY, 30, Jun 9, 13, 14, 23, 26, Jul 8, 10, 15, 29,
    Aug 14, 26, 31, Sep 5, 11, 25; 1781: HAY, Jun 9, 16, 21, Jul 18, Aug 1, 8,
    22, 24, 25, 29, Sep 4, Oct 16; 1782: HAY, Jun 3, 4, 10, 11, 12, Jul 5, Aug 5,
    8, 13, 17, Sep 16, 18, DL, Dec 30; 1783: DL, Jan 9, 29, Feb 8, Mar 6, May 12,
    23, HAY, Jun 3, 5, 12, 20, 30, Jul 8, Aug 1, 22, 23, 28, DL, Oct 13, 14, Nov
    8, 20, 22, 24, Dec 2, 5; 1784: DL, Jan 7, 9, Mar 6, May 3, 15
Kenny (musician), 1713: SH, Feb 23; 1714: SH, Feb 22; 1715: SH, May 2; 1717:
    SH, May 10; 1718: TEC, Mar 12; 1724: LIF, Mar 19, Apr 25
Kenny, Mrs (actor), 1776: CHR, Oct 16
Kenrick (Kendrick) (actor, singer), 1783: HAY, Sep 17, Dec 15; 1787: CG, Mar
    31; 1791: HAY, Jul 30, CG, Oct 20; 1792: CG, Feb 28, HAY, Jun 23, CG, Dec 31;
    1793: HAY, Jun 17, Aug 3, 12, 16, Sep 2, 19, CG, Oct 2, 24, Nov 19, 28; 1794:
    HAY, Jul 17, 18, 21, 24, Aug 27; 1795: CG, Apr 24, HAY, Jun 13, 20, Jul 31;
    1796: HAY, Jul 15, CG, Oct 6; 1797: CG, Feb 18, HAY, Jun 23, Aug 15, 16;
    1798: HAY, Jun 30, Jul 21, Aug 11, CG, Nov 12, Dec 11, 26; 1799: CG, Jan 21,
    Apr 2, May 4, HAY, Jul 9, 13, Aug 21, Sep 2, 9, CG, Dec 23; 1800: CG, Jan 16,
    HAY, Jun 14, Jul 2, Aug 14, 29, Sep 1, 11
Kenrick, Dr William, 1748: DL, Mar 10; 1766: DL, Apr 12; 1767: DL, Dec 5; 1772:
    MARLY, Jul 2; 1773: CG, Nov 20; 1774: DL, Jan 19, Mar 9, 23, MARLY, Jul 6;
    1778: CG, Nov 23, Dec 21; 1779: HAY, Dec 27
--Duellist, The, 1773: CG, Nov 16, 19, 20, 22, 27; 1774: HAY, Sep 21
--Falstaff's Wedding, 1766: DL, Apr 12, 14; 1774: DL, Mar 9, DT, 16, DL, 23,
    MARLY, Jul 6; 1779: HAY, Dec 27
--Lady of the Manor, The, 1778: CG, Nov 21, 23, 25, 26, 30, Dec 1, 2, 4, 9, 16,
    18, 22, 31; 1779: CG, Jan 25, Oct 8, Nov 5; 1788: CG, Jan 28, 31, Feb 7, 23,
    Mar 4, Apr 19; 1789: CG, May 5, Nov 14
--Spendthrift, The; or, A Christmas Gambol (farce), 1778: CG, Dec 21, 23
--Widowed Wife, The, 1767: DL, Dec 4, 5, 7, 8, 9, 10, 11, 12, 17, 18, 21; 1768:
    DL, Jan 1, 15, 21, Feb 22, Mar 14; 1769: DL, Apr 28
Kensington Gardens. See Cobb, James.
Kensington Gravel Pits, 1769: CG, May 1
Kensington Stage (entertainment), 1788: CG, Mar 26
Kent (actor), 1786: HAY, Mar 6; 1794: HAMM, Mar 24; 1795: WLWS, Jun 19; 1799:
    DL, Jul 2; 1800: DL, Jun 13
Kent (attorney), 1750: CG, Feb 2
Kent St, 1789: KHS, Sep 16
Kent, Mary Anne (actor), 1794: HAMM, Mar 24, HAY, May 22; 1795: WLWS, Jun 19
Kent, Master (actor), 1795: WLWS, Jun 19
Kent, Miss C (entertainer), 1794: HAMM, Mar 24; 1795: WLWS, Jun 19
Kent, Mrs (actor), 1692: DL, Nov 8; 1693: DL, Feb 0; 1694: DL, Jan 0, DG, May
    0, DL, Sep 0; 1695: DL, Dec 0; 1696: DL, Jan 0, Mar 0, Sep 0, Nov 21, DL/DL,
    Dec 0; 1697: DL, Jan 0, May 8; 1698: DL, Mar 0, Jun 0, DL/ORDG, Nov 0; 1699:
    DL, Apr 0; 1700: DL, Jul 9, Oct 0; 1701: DL, May 31, Dec 0; 1702: DL, Feb 0,
    Aug 20, Nov 0, Dec 0; 1703: DL, Jun 23, Jul 6; 1704: DL, May 0; 1705: DL, Apr
    23; 1707: DL, Oct 23, Dec 26; 1708: DL, Apr 27, Jun 15, 26, Jul 3, 10, Oct
    21, 26; 1709: DL, May 24, Nov 25, 28, Dec 6, 7; 1710: DL, Mar 27, Apr 12, GR,
    Jun 15, 21, 24, 28, Jul 3, 6, 8, 10, 12, 20, 22, 29, Aug 7, 19, 24, 26, Sep
    9, 11, 23, 28, 30; 1712: SML, Jul 9; 1715: LIF, Jan 4, 11, 13, Feb 3, May 12,
    Jun 23, Oct 11, 12, 22, 24, Dec 12; 1716: LIF, Apr 27, May 8, Oct 10, 18;
    1717: LIF, Jan 28, Feb 11, May 20, Oct 24, 26, Nov 20, Dec 7, 14; 1718: LIF,
    Jan 2, Feb 3, 18, Jun 30, Sep 26, Oct 11, 15
Kent, Sophia (actor), 1795: WLWS, Jun 19
Kent, Thomas (actor), 1690: DL, Sep 0; 1691: NONE, Sep 0; 1692: DL, Mar 0;
    1694: DL, Sep 0; 1695: DL, Oct 0; 1696: DL, Feb 0; 1699: DL, Apr 0, Dec 0;
    1701: DL, Feb 4; 1702: DL, Dec 0; 1704: EL, Jan 26; 1705: DL, Jan 18, Jun 12;
    1706: DL, Apr 8, QUEEN'S, Oct 30, Dec 28; 1707: QUEEN'S, Jan 4, Feb 14
Kent, Thomas (pit keeper), 1677: DL, Dec 12, 26
Kent, W (actor), 1795: WLWS, Jun 19
Kent, 1762: DL, Sep 21
Kentish Barons, The. See North, Francis.
Kentish Strong Man, 1699: DLLIF, Sep 12, DG, Nov 25, Dec 7; 1700: DG, Jan 3
Kentish Town, 1787: DL, Mar 27; 1796: CG, Apr 22
Keppel, Admiral Augustus, 1779: HAY, Mar 17, CG, Apr 12
Kerneguy, Lady (spectator), 1668: LIF, Dec 3
Keroualle, Louise de, Duchess of Portsmouth, 1668: BRIDGES, Dec 18; 1674: NONE,
    Sep 0; 1678: ATCOURT, Jan 18; 1680: DG, Feb 2, DL, Jun 2; 1685: DLORDG, Jan
    1; 1686: ATCOURT, Feb 16
Kerridge (actor), 1785: HAMM, Jun 27, Jul 1, 4, 6, 8, 15, 22, 25, 26, 27
Ketch. See Kytch.
Kettle Drum (music), 1697: LW, Jul 21; 1703: LIF, Jun 11; 1712: B&S, Nov 24;
    1727: LIF, Mar 20, Apr 21; 1728: LIF, Apr 22, May 6, 13, 20; 1731: GF, Mar
    23, LIF, Apr 22, Jun 7; 1732: LIF, Apr 13, May 9; 1733: LIF/CG, Mar 30, CG,

478

May 1, 2, DL, 21; <u>1734</u>: DL/LIF, Mar 11, DL/HAY, May 1; <u>1735</u>: LIF, Sep 5;
<u>1736</u>: DL, Mar 27, CG, May 11, 17; <u>1737</u>: HIC, Apr 7; <u>1738</u>: CG, Apr 8; <u>1740</u>:
DL, Apr 26; <u>1741</u>: GF, Mar 12; <u>1744</u>: HAY, Feb 15; <u>1746</u>: SFHP, Sep 8; <u>1748</u>:
HAY, Dec 9; <u>1753</u>: HAY, Mar 29, BFSY, Sep 3; <u>1755</u>: BFGT, Sep 3, SFG, 18; <u>1762</u>:
CG, Apr 23; <u>1786</u>: DL, Jan 20
Kettle Drum and Trumpet (music), <u>1727</u>: KING'S, Mar 2; <u>1729</u>: HAY, Jan 31; <u>1732</u>:
DL, May 3; <u>1733</u>: HAY, Apr 23; <u>1751</u>: HAY, Dec 27; <u>1752</u>: CT/HAY, Jan 7
Kettle Drum Preamble (music), <u>1727</u>: LIF, May 10; <u>1729</u>: LIF, May 6; <u>1730</u>: LIF,
Mar 17, Apr 2, 22, May 9, DL, 13, LIF, 14; <u>1731</u>: LIF, May 3, 24, GF, Jun 3;
<u>1732</u>: DL, May 3, LIF, 9, GF, 11, LIF, 18, DL, Jul 7, HAY, 26; <u>1733</u>: HAY, Feb
28, LIF/CG, Mar 28, Apr 25, May 7, 24, CG, Aug 9; <u>1734</u>: DL, Feb 25, LIF, Apr
26, CG, May 14, HAY, Nov 14; <u>1735</u>: CG/LIF, Mar 15, Apr 9, May 12, LIF, 21,
CG/LIF, 27, DL, 30, Jun 2, LIF, 12, HAY, Dec 13; <u>1736</u>: MR, Feb 11, LIF, Mar
31, DL, Apr 1, 13, CG, Jun 4, HAY, Jul 29, YB, Dec 1; <u>1737</u>: DL, Apr 2, CG,
26, HAY, May 3, DL, 4, CG, 10, 16; <u>1738</u>: DL, Feb 28, Mar 3, 21, CG, Apr 8,
DL, 29, CG, May 3, DL, 5, 10, 17, 29, CG, Dec 11, DL, 14; <u>1739</u>: DL, Apr 7,
CG, May 15, DL, 22, CG, 25, Nov 7, Dec 15; <u>1740</u>: DL, Apr 14, 22, May 14, 17,
21, 26; <u>1741</u>: CG, Mar 10, DL, Apr 20, CG, May 12, 14, DL, 28, CG, Nov 30;
<u>1742</u>: CG, Apr 22, GF, 22, 29, HAY, Jun 16; <u>1743</u>: JS, Jan 5, LIF, Mar 15, JS,
23; <u>1744</u>: JS, Mar 2; <u>1745</u>: GF, Mar 23, DL, May 13; <u>1746</u>: DL, May 8, SOU, Sep
25; <u>1748</u>: HAY, Dec 9; <u>1752</u>: CT/HAY, Jan 7; <u>1756</u>: DL, Aug 12; <u>1757</u>: HAY, Aug
3, 5, 31, Sep 2, 8
Kettle, Tilly (portrait painter), <u>1781</u>: CG, Dec 26
Kew. See Cue.
Key and Garter Tavern, <u>1741</u>: DL, Mar 24
Key Tavern, <u>1660</u>: CITY, Oct 29
Key to the Lock, A. See O'Keeffe, John.
Keygille. See Kaygill.
Keynlas (actor), <u>1784</u>: HAY, Mar 8
Keys (actor, dancer), <u>1791</u>: DLKING'S, Nov 5; <u>1792</u>: DLKING'S, Mar 19, HAY, Jul
25, DL, Nov 21, Dec 27; <u>1793</u>: DL, Jun 5, HAY, Dec 26; <u>1794</u>: DL, Jun 9, Sep
27, Oct 27, Nov 10, Dec 20; <u>1795</u>: DL, Jan 19, Oct 30; <u>1796</u>: DL, Jan 18, Mar
12, 19, 28, Apr 4
Keys (box-office keeper), <u>1791</u>: CG, Jun 2; <u>1792</u>: CG, May 25
Keys, Mrs (haberdasher), <u>1772</u>: CG, Feb 1
Keyton (house servant), <u>1753</u>: DL, May 15
Kickaraboo (song), <u>1798</u>: DL, May 7
Kickill (actor), <u>1762</u>: HAY, May 1
Kicking up a Row (song), <u>1799</u>: CG, Apr 16
Kidwell (musician), <u>1675</u>: ATCOURT, Feb 15
Kilburn, Master (actor), <u>1733</u>: DL, Nov 7; <u>1734</u>: DL, Feb 4
Kilburne (beneficiary), <u>1738</u>: CG, Aug 29
Kilby, Elizabeth (actor), <u>1728</u>: HAY, Jul 1, Aug 5, 9, Sep 6, LIF, Nov 23; <u>1729</u>:
LIF, Apr 17, 23, May 7, 15, BFR, Aug 25, LIF, Sep 19, Oct 15, Dec 29; <u>1730</u>:
HAY, Mar 5, LIF, May 18, 25, BFOF, Aug 20, SFOF, Sep 9, LIF, 25, Oct 7, Nov
6, 7, 10, Dec 4; <u>1731</u>: LIF, Jan 20, May 17, 21, Oct 4, 11, 13, Nov 6, 12;
<u>1732</u>: LIF, Feb 21, Mar 20, Apr 17, 18, 21, LIF/CG, Sep 25, Oct 4, Nov 8,
CG/LIF, Dec 16, LIF/CG, 27; <u>1733</u>: LIF/CG, Jan 18, Apr 3, CG, 4, LIF/CG, 19,
25, CG, May 1, LIF/CG, 8, 14, CG/LIF, 28, CG, Sep 27, 29, Oct 13, 19, 25, 26,
29, Nov 28, 29, Dec 1, 7; <u>1734</u>: CG, Jan 25, Feb 26, Mar 16, 28, Apr 1, 6, Sep
2, CG/LIF, 23, 25, RI, 26, CG/LIF, 27, Oct 29, Nov 11, 19, 21, Dec 5; <u>1735</u>:
CG/LIF, Feb 4, 13, Mar 11, 22, Apr 9, 11, 22, CG. 25, CG/LIF, May 16, CG, Sep
12, 26, 29, Ocv 1, 20, 24, 29, Nov 29, Dec 30; <u>1736</u>: CG, Jan 1, 23, Feb 26,
Mar 18, LIF, Apr 2, CG, 6, 26, May 3, LIF, 5, CG, 6, 11, Jun 3, 8, LIF, 16,
HAY, 29, CG, Sep 15, 17, Oct 8, 13, LIF, 18, CG, 20, 25, 29, Nov 3, 11, 26,
Dec 6; <u>1737</u>: CG, Jan 17, 21, 25, Feb 15, Mar 15, 28, Apr 11, 15, Sep 26, Oct
5, 12, 17, 28, 29, Nov 16; <u>1738</u>: CG, Jan 3, 9, 31, Feb 13, Mar 20, Apr 17,
18, 20, 22, 24, 26, Sep 25, 27, Oct 2, 4, 6, 13, 20, 26, 28, 30, Nov 11, 15,
18, 27; <u>1739</u>: CG, Jan 20, Feb 9, 24, DL, Mar 10, CG, Apr 23, DL, 28, May 2,
CG, 7, DL, 16, CG, 17, DL, 19, CG, Jun 1, DL, Sep 6, CG, 22, 25, 28, Oct 3,
5, 8, 26, 29, Nov 3, 9, Dec 4, 13; <u>1740</u>: CG, Jan 12, Feb 12, Apr 28, 29, May
2, 12, Sep 22, Oct 10, 22, 27, 29, Nov 1, 6; <u>1741</u>: CG, Jan 2, 5, 6, 21, 27,
Feb 14, 17, 24, 28, Mar 16, Apr 3, 6, 17, 22, 24, 28, May 11, 19, Sep 21, 28,
Oct 5, 17, 24, 29, 31, Nov 7, 26, 27, Dec 1, 7; <u>1742</u>: CG, Jan 5, 23, Feb 3,
25, May 1, 7, Oct 16, 28, 29, Nov 15, Dec 21, 22; <u>1743</u>: CG, Jan 8, Feb 4, 9,
Mar 8, Apr 13, 18, May 20, Sep 23, 26, Oct 7, 14, Nov 16, 19, Dec 26, 27;
<u>1744</u>: CG, Jan 4, 14, Feb 13, 14, Mar 27, Dec 8, 18; <u>1745</u>: CG, Jan 1, Mar 28,
Apr 19
Kilkenny (dance), <u>1734</u>: CG, Apr 19, 24, 27, 29, May 4; <u>1737</u>: CG, Mar 24; <u>1739</u>:
CG, Nov 8, 10, 13, 14, 15, 21, 23, 24, Dec 19, 21; <u>1740</u>: CG, Jan 25, Apr 23,
May 20, Dec 11; <u>1741</u>: CG, Mar 9
Killigrew (renter), <u>1750</u>: DL, Apr 3

Killigrew, Charles (master of the revels), 1679: DL, Feb 0
Killigrew, Henry (proprietor), 1662: LIF, Oct 18; 1666: MOORFLDS, Sep 1; 1667:
    LIF, Jul 20
Killigrew, Thomas (author, patentee), 1660: COCKPIT, Oct 8, REDBULL, Nov 5,
    VERE, 8; 1661: VERE, Nov 29; 1663: VERE, Mar 0, BRIDGES, May 7; 1664:
    BRIDGES, Jan 25, Aug 2, Nov 0; 1767: NONE, Feb 12, BRIDGES, 14, NONE, Sep 9;
    1668: NURSERY, Sep 0; 1669: BRIDGES, Mar 6; 1682: DL, Nov 16; 1719: DL, Feb
    14; 1750: DL, Apr 3
--Bellamira, Her Dream; or, The Love of Shadows, 1662: NONE, Sep 0
--Chit Chat, 1719: DL, Feb 14, 16, 17, 19, 21, 23, 24, 26, 28, Mar 2, 19, Apr
    3, RI, Jun 6, DL, Nov 20
--Cicilia and Clarinda; or, Love in Arms (opera), 1662: NONE, Sep 0; 1667:
    BRIDGES, Feb 14
--Claracilla, 1660: REDBULL, Aug 14, VERE, Dec 1; 1661: VERE, Jul 4; 1663:
    ATCOURT, Jan 5; 1669: BRIDGES, Mar 9
--Parson's Wedding, The, 1664: BRIDGES, Oct 5, 11, NONE, Nov 0; 1672: LIF, Jun
    0
--Princess, The; or, Love at First Sight, 1661: VERE, Nov 29
--Thomaso; or, The Wanderer, 1662: NONE, Sep 0; 1664: BRIDGES, Nov 0
Killigrew, William
--Imperial Tragedy, The, 1668: NURSERY, Sep 0
--Ormasdes, 1663: NONE, Sep 0
--Pandora, 1664: LIF, Apr 0
--Siege of Urbin, The, 1664: NONE, Sep 0
--Zelindra, 1662: VERE, Mar 3
Kilmarnock, Lord (rebel), 1746: DL, Aug 4
Kilvington (householder), 1797: CG, May 30; 1798: CG, May 25
Kinaston. See Kynaston.
Kind Appointment (song), 1764: CG, May 8
Kind der Liebe, Das. See Kotzebue, August Friedrich Ferdinand von.
Kind Keeper, The. See Dryden, John.
Kindersley (spectator), 1759: CG, Oct 22
Kindness hath resistless charms (song), 1684: ATCOURT, Feb 11
King (actor), 1778: CHR, May 25; 1779: HAY, Mar 15; 1792: HAY, Feb 6
King (boxkeeper) 1703: DL, Jun 14; 1707: DL, Apr 16; 1708: DL/QUEEN, Jun 4;
    1714: DL, Jun 16; 1715: DL, Jun 10; 1716: DL, Jun 9; 1717: DL, Jun 7; 1718:
    DL, May 23; 1719: DL, May 21; 1720: DL, May 30; 1721: DL, Jun 1; 1722: DL,
    May 19; 1723: DL, May 27; 1724: DL, May 16
King (dancer), 1767: CG, Apr 27, DL, May 4, 15; 1770: CG, May 3; 1771: CG, Apr
    26; 1772: CG, May 1; 1774: CG, May 18, 20; 1775: CG, May 15, 26
King (singer), 1726: IT, Feb 2
King and Co (haberdashers), 1775: DL, May 27
King and No King. See Fletcher, John.
King and the Miller of Mansfield, The. See Dodsley, Robert.
King and Titi, The; or, The Medlars (farce, anon), 1737: HAY, May 25
King Arthur. See Dryden, John.
King Charles I. See Havard, William.
King Edgar and Alfreda. See Ravenscroft, Edward.
King Edward III with the Fall of Mortimer (play), 1710: QUEEN'S, Mar 11
King Edward IV; or, The Lives of Robin Hood and Little John (droll), 1751: SF,
    Sep 7, 9, 10, 11
King Egbert, King of Kent and Monarch of England; or, The Union Of The Seven
    Kingdoms (play), 1719: BFSL, Aug 24
King Harry's Head Tavern, 1745: GF, Feb 26, Mar 18; 1746: GF, Mar 4
King Henry and Rosamond (play, anon), 1692: DL, Nov 9
King Henry the Fourth of France. See Beckingham, Charles.
King John. See Shakespeare, William.
King Lear. See Shakespeare, William.
King of Morocco's Diversions (dance), 1727: KING'S, Mar 2
King Pepin's Campaign. See Shirley, William.
King shall rejoice (song), 1761: KING'S, Mar 12; 1789: CG, Mar 20
King Square Court, 1774: DL, Feb 24
King St Coffee House, 1751: DL, Dec 17
King St, 1661: VERE, Feb 5; 1736: CG, Mar 18; 1737: DL, Mar 10; 1738: CG, Mar
    16; 1741: DL, Mar 31; 1742: DL, Mar 15, 30; 1743: DL, Mar 14; 1744: DL, Mar
    13; 1745: CG, Apr 18; 1746: DL, Apr 3; 1747: DL, Mar 31, CG, Apr 20; 1750:
    DL, Dec 10; 1751: DL, Mar 18; 1752: DL, Feb 22; 1760: CG, Jan 4, DL, 16;
    1762: DL, Apr 20; 1764: KING'S, Apr 12; 1765: KING'S, Apr 24; 1774: CG, May
    12, DL, 25, 30, HAY, Jun 7; 1777: DL, Mar 11, Apr 29; 1778: DL, Mar 30; 1779:
    DL, Mar 16; 1780: CG, Apr 11; 1783: DL, Apr 26; 1784: DL, Apr 14; 1785: HAY,
    Apr 26, Aug 2; 1786: DL, Apr 25, HAY, Aug 3; 1787: DL, May 9, HAY, Jul 19,
    Aug 10; 1789: DL, Apr 17, CG, 30, May 6; 1790: DL, May 4; 1791: CG, May 3,

DL, 6; 1792: DLKING'S, May 1, HAY, Nov 26; 1793: DL, Apr 25; 1795: CG, Jun 6;
1796: KING'S, Mar 10, CG, May 18; 1797: CG, May 24; 1798: CG, Apr 28, HAY,
Aug 23; 1799: CG, May 7, HAY, Aug 22; 1800: CG, Apr 30, DL, May 20
King William's Happy Deliverance and Glorious Triumph over His Enemies (droll),
1696: MF, May 0
King, George, 1786: CG, Nov 14, 24, Dec 11; 1787: CG, Jan 13, Mar 27, 31, Apr
11, 27, May 23
King, John (dancer), 1788: CG, Apr 1, May 12, Dec 26; 1789: CG, Jun 16; 1790:
CG, Oct 4; 1791: CG, May 3, Sep 12, Oct 20, Nov 2, Dec 22; 1792: CG, Jan 25,
28, 31, Jun 2, Nov 6, Dec 26; 1793: CG, Mar 11, Sep 17, Dec 19; 1794: CG, Feb
26; 1795: CG, Jun 10, 17, Oct 26, Nov 16; 1796: CG, Mar 15, Jun 6; 1799: CG,
Apr 23, May 13, Oct 7; 1800: CG, Mar 25
King, Mary, Mrs Henry (actor), 1775: DL, Oct 2, 13, 18, 21, 24, Nov 4, 23, Dec
12, 26; 1776: DL, Jan 19, 20, 31, Feb 6, 10, 22, Mar 7, Apr 22, May 4, 8;
1800: HAY, Jun 27
King, Mary, Mrs Thomas (dancer), 1766: DL, Sep 25, 27, 30, Oct 11, 29, Nov 11;
1767: DL, Jan 2, Feb 12, 25, Mar 2, 3, 17, 24, Apr 4, 21, 24, 27, 30, May 6,
8, 18, 21, Sep 12, 15, 16, 17, 19, 22, 23, Oct 22, Nov 16, Dec 26; 1768: DL,
Jan 11, 16, Feb 12, 20, Apr 6, 16, 22, May 4, 5, Aug 18, Sep 8, 20, 22, 29,
Oct 10, 11, 13, 15, 22, Nov 1, 2, 3, Dec 5, 7, 30; 1769: DL, Mar 13, Apr 12,
May 18, Sep 23, 26, Oct 4, 6, 11, 14, Dec 6, 30; 1770: DL, Jan 6, Mar 31, Apr
20, May 2, 5, 17, Oct 3, 13, Nov 3, 17, 29, Dec 7, 13, 21; 1771: DL, Jan 15,
Mar 7, 11, Apr 6, Oct 21, Nov 22, Dec 26; 1772: DL, Mar 26, May 9; 1775: DL,
May 8
King, Master (actor), 1750: DL, May 3; 1765: CG, Apr 29; 1766: CG, Apr 21
King, Matthew Peter (pianist, composer), 1787: HAY, Aug 10; 1791: CG, May 24;
1793: CG, May 16
--Primrose Green; or, Love in the Country, 1791: CG, May 24
King, Miss (actor), 1782: HAY, Dec 30
King, Mrs (actor), 1736: LIF, Apr 29; 1740: JS, Oct 6; 1742: DL, May 13, 14,
Sep 21, 25; 1743: DL, Jan 20, Feb 4, May 10, Sep 17, Oct 20, Dec 1; 1744: DL,
May 1, 14, Sep 20, Nov 7, 27; 1745: DL, Feb 11, Apr 19, 30, May 8, Jun 5, Sep
24, Nov 18, 28, 30; 1746: DL, Mar 13, Apr 14, May 1
King, Mrs (dancer), 1749: NWLS, Feb 27; 1759: DL, Oct 27
King, Robert (composer), 1684: DL, Apr 0, DLORDG, Aug 0; 1685: DL, May 9; 1690:
DL, Mar 0, DLORDG, 0; 1691: BG, Sep 17; 1692: DL, Feb 0; 1698: YB, Jan 17;
1702: SHG, May 12
King, the, 1660: NONE, Aug 7, ATCOURT, Nov 19, VERE/RED, 20, VERE, Dec 13;
1661: ATCOURT, Feb 25, Apr 20, LIF, Jun 28, Aug 15, VERE, 27, NONE, Sep 0,
VERE, 7, LIF, 11, VERE, Oct 10, LIF/MT, 21; 1662: LI, Jan 3, ATCOURT, Feb 11,
Oct 2, 8, 27, Nov 10, 17, Dec 1, 8; 1663: ATCOURT, Jan 5, SH, 6, ATCOURT, Feb
23, BRIDGES, May 8, LIF, Jul 22, ATCOURT, Dec 10, LIF, 22; 1665: LIF, Apr 3;
1666: NONE, Jul 17, ATCOURT, Oct 11, 29, BRIDGES, Dec 20, ATCOURT, 28; 1667:
NONE, Feb 12, BRI/COUR, Mar 2, 5, BRIDGES, Apr 15, 16, 20, LIF, May 6,
BRIDGES, 18, LIF, Aug 15, BRIDGES, 17, Sep 25, 27, ATCOURT, Oct 1, BRIDGES,
7, LIF, 15, BRIDGES, 19, 29, LIF, Nov 7, ATCOURT, 16, BRIDGES, 16, 21, 23,
Dec 11; 1668: BRIDGES, Jan 4, 11, ATCOURT, 13, BRIDGES, 20, LIF, Feb 6,
BRIDGES, 20, LIF, 22, BRIDGES, Mar 2, LIF, 26, BRIDGES, Apr 7, LIF, May 2,
BRIDGES, 18, ATCOURT, 29, BRIDGES, Jul 14, 31, Sep 28, Nov 6, BRI/COUR, Dec
3, BRIDGES, 18, LIF, 21, 29; 1669: BRIDGES, Jan 2, 7, 13, 16, 21, 29, Feb 2,
ATCOURT, 22, LIF, 25, BRIDGES, 27, Mar 23, ATCOURT, Oct 26; 1670: ATCOURT,
Apr 6, DOVER, May 11, NONE, Jun 22; 1671: ATCOURT, Nov 14, DG, 15; 1672:
NONE, Jan 9, LIF, Feb 26, DG, Jul 4; 1673: YH, May 5; 1674: DG, May 16, NONE,
Sep 0, CITY, Oct 29, DG, Dec 2; 1675: DG, Jan 8, 22, DL, 25, DG, Feb 27, DL,
Mar 8, ATCOURT, Apr 22, DL, 23, May 4, 7, DG, Sep 0, ATCOURT, 29; 1676: CITY,
Oct 30; 1677: ATCOURT, May 29, DL, Jul 0, DG, Nov 5, 17, DL, Dec 12, 26;
1678: ATCOURT, Jan 18, Mar 14; 1679: DL, Feb 0, DG, Jun 21, NONE, Sep 0;
1681: DL, Oct 0, DLORDG, Nov 12, ATCOURT, 15; 1682: DG, Jan 25, DL, Feb 4,
Nov 16; 1683: DL, Jan 19, WINDSOR, Aug 0; 1684: DLORDG, May 24; 1685: DLORDG,
Jan 15, 22, 27, Apr 28, DL, May 11, DG, Jun 3, ATCOURT, Oct 10, Nov 30, Dec
14, DL, 19, DLORDG, 30; 1686: DLORDG, Jan 23, DL, Feb 4, DLORDG, 8, 11,
ATCOURT, 16, DLORDG, Apr 8, May 6, 10, Oct 6, 13; 1687: DLORDG, Jan 20, Apr
6, DL, May 12; 1688: ATCOURT, Feb 6, DL, Apr 0, May 15, CITY, Oct 28; 1689:
YB, Nov 11, ATCOURT, 15; 1690: ATCOURT, Jan 1; 1692: CITY, Oct 29; 1693:
ATCOURT, Nov 4; 1696: LIF, Dec 0; 1697: ATCOURT, Feb 6, RICHMOND, Sep 27;
1698: YB, Jan 10; 1699: LIF, Mar 4, ATCOURT, Nov 15; 1714: KING'S, Oct 26;
1715: DL, Jan 5, KING'S, 15, Apr 9, Jul 23, Aug 27; 1716: KING'S, Feb 1, Mar
3, 10, DL, Apr 7, KING'S, Jun 30; 1717: KING'S, May 13, NONE, Sep 13, DL, Dec
19; 1718: DL, Apr 22, RI, Aug 30, DL, Nov 15; 1719: KING'S, Feb 12, 21, DL,
Mar 30, Apr 6, 22, LIF, 25; 1720: KING'S, Mar 8, Apr 27; 1721: KING'S, Mar 7,
Apr 15, May 3, DL, 18, Nov 21; 1722: KING'S, Apr 25, May 9, Oct 27; 1723:
KING'S, Jan 22, LIF, Apr 20, KING'S, May 18; 1724: KING'S, Jan 11, DL, Mar 5;

1726: KING'S, Jan 11, 15, Feb 8, Mar 8, 15, May 31, Oct 5, 21, 28, Nov 5, 7, 12, 16, 19, 30; 1727: DL, Sep 28, Nov 7, KING'S, Dec 5; 1728: DL, Jan 27, KING'S, Feb 17, LIF, 22, KING'S, Mar 9, 12, DL, 14, KING'S, 19, 30, Apr 2, May 7, DL, Nov 13, 20, 30, Dec 11; 1729: LIF, Jan 16, DL, 28, Feb 5, Mar 6, 13, Oct 28, Nov 12, 19, 26, KING'S, Dec 13; 1730: KING'S, Feb 14, LIF, 19, 26, KING'S, 28, Mar 17, DL, 19, Apr 2, GF, 28, DL, Oct 28, Dec 10, 17; 1731: KING'S, Mar 9, 16, DL, 18, KING'S, 20, LIF, 25, KING'S, 27, Apr 6, 10, 20, May 1, 18, DL, Nov 12, LIF, 18, KING'S, Dec 4; 1732: SJP, Apr 27, KING'S, May 9, 16, DL, Nov 24, KING'S, Dec 9; 1733: KING'S, Mar 31, May 29, Jun 5, DL, 9, KING'S, 26, Nov 6, Dec 22; 1734: KING'S, Feb 2, 5, LIF, Sep 6, KING'S, Oct 23, Nov 5, GF/HAY, 6, CG/LIF, 9; 1735: CG, Jan 8, LIF, Feb 27, KING'S, Dec 16; 1736: KING'S, Jun 22; 1737: KING'S, May 17; 1739: CG, Jan 11, KING'S, 16; 1740: CG, Oct 25, Nov 27; 1744: DL, May 11; 1746: CG, Nov 25, 28, Dec 9, 17; 1747: CG, Jan 2, 14, 27, Feb 17, May 20, DL, Oct 28, KING'S, Dec 26; 1748: DL, Jan 8; 1754: DL, Nov 19; 1756: DL, Nov 8; 1757: DL, Nov 23, 29; 1762: DL, Nov 12, Dec 16; 1764: DL, Feb 11; 1769: DL, Jan 12, Feb 9, Oct 12, 25, Nov 16; 1770: DL, Mar 8, Sep 27, Oct 10, 24, Dec 12; 1771: DL, Jan 9; 1787: KING'S, Mar 1, CG, Dec 12; 1789: KING'S, Apr 21, DL, Dec 16; 1791: KING'S, Mar 26

King, Thomas (actor, manager, author), 1748: DL, Oct 19, Nov 3, Dec 26, 28; 1749: DL, Jan 2, 18, 25, Feb 6, 21, Apr 28, 29, May 12, Sep 21, 22, Oct 5, 11, 17, 19, 24, 25, Nov 1, 4, Dec 18, 26; 1750: DL, Jan 1, 2, 4, 6, 22, CG, Feb 14, DL, 24, Mar 13, 17, 29, Apr 2, 9, 17, 25, 28, Sep 8; 1751: DL, Oct 28, Nov 2, 16, Dec 2; 1752: DL, Mar 3; 1753: DL, Jan 9, 24, Nov 8, CG, 12, Dec 31; 1754: CG, Jan 26; 1755: DL, Nov 8, 12, 27; 1758: CG, Jan 6; 1759: DL, Sep 22, Oct 2, 11, 27, 31, Nov 9, 17, 24, Dec 12, 18, 31; 1760: DL, Jan 10, 24, Mar 6, 20, 29, CG, 29, DL, Apr 9, 17, May 8, CG, Sep 25, DL, 30, Oct 3, 11, Nov 17, 21, Dec 5, 11, 29; 1761: DL, Jan 10, 31, Feb 5, 12, Mar 26, Apr 1, 6, 17, 24, 25, 28, May 18, 28, Jun 18, Jul 27, Sep 8, 10, 15, 19, 25, Oct 10, 24, 27, 29, Nov 9, 14, 28, Dec 11, 17; 1762: DL, Jan 7, 27, 29, Feb 20, Mar 1, 6, 20, 22, 25, 27, 29, 30, Apr 1, 21, 22, 30, May 4, 6, 7, 10, 11, 14, 17, Sep 23, 25, 30, Oct 8, 9, 12, 14, 21, 23, 25, 29, 30, Nov 3, 4, 10, 11, 12, Dec 1, 15, 22, 27; 1763: DL, Jan 5, 7, 22, 27, Mar 14, 19, 21, 24, Apr 5, May 13, 14, 18, 26, Sep 17, 20, 27, Oct 1, 8, 12, 14, 17, 20, 29, Nov 1, 4, 8, 10, 15, Dec 1, 10, 14, 17, 20, 28; 1764: DL, Jan 3, 14, 18, 23, Feb 2, 6, Mar 10, 24, 31, Apr 2, 3, 7, 10, 12, 14, 28, May 9, 24, Sep 15, 18, 25, Oct 2, 4, 6, 9, 13, 18, 22, 25, 26, Nov 8, 9, 17, Dec 18; 1765: DL, Jan 23, Feb 4, 7, Mar 18, 19, 26, 30, Apr 16, 20, 26, May 1, 17, 18, 22, Sep 14, 17, 19, 21, Oct 1, 18, 23, 24, 31, Nov 16, 20, Dec 7; 1766: DL, Jan 23, 29, Feb 3, 8, 13, 20, Mar 15, 20, Apr 1, 12, 16, 19, 22, 25, May 3, 5, 10, 17, CG, Oct 25, DL, Nov 17, CG, 18, DL, 18, Dec 10, 12; 1767: CG, Jan 1, DL, 2, 24, Feb 5, 9, 21, 23, CG, Mar 6, DL, 28, Apr 4, 6, 7, 29, 30, May 6, 7, 8, 23, 26, Sep 12, 22, 23, 26, Oct 9, 10, 14, CG, 17, DL, 22, 23, 27, Nov 12, 20, 26, 28, Dec 2, 5, 19, CG, 28, 31; 1768: DL, Jan 19, 23, Mar 15, 17, 19, 21, 24, Apr 6, 9, 12, 14, 16, 18, 22, May 2, 4, 6, HAY, Jun 23, DL, Sep 23, 24, 26, 27, 28, 30, Oct 4, 5, 8, 13, 15, 18, 19, CG, 24, DL, 25, 31, Nov 5, 17, Dec 16; 1769: CG, Jan 2, DL, 20, 27, Feb 3, 4, Mar 14, 16, Apr 3, 7, 10, CG, 11, DL, 12, CG, 12, DL, 15, 18, 24, 28, May 1, 16, 20, Sep 16, 19, 21, 26, Oct 3, 4, 5, 6, 9, 10, 13, 14, 17, 18, Nov 8, 15, 16, 23, 29, Dec 8, 26; 1770: CG, Jan 3, DL, 16, CG, 27, DL, Feb 3, Mar 1, 3, 5, 22, 27, Apr 3, 20, May 3, 14, 16, 17, Sep 27, CG, Oct 1, DL, 2, 3, 4, 5, 9, 12, 15, 18, 22, 23, 26, Nov 3, 16, 24, 26, Dec 4, 5, 20, CG, 26, DL, 29, 31; 1771: CG, Jan 1, DL, 2, 4, 19, CG, Feb 21, DL, Mar 7, 14, 18, 21, 23, Apr 5, 6, 9, 20, 26, May 8, 14, Sep 24, Oct 1, 3, 8, 9, 12, 15, CG, 15, DL, 19, 24, 26, 28, 29, 31, Nov 2, 8, 11, 13, 26, 27, 29, Dec 10, 11, 30, 31; 1772: DL, Jan 1, 4, CG, 6, DL, 20, Feb 17, CG, 25, DL, 29, Mar 12, 21, 23, 24, 28, 30, Apr 2, 4, 7, 21, 29, May 9, 12, 13, 18, Sep 26, Oct 8, 10, 15, 20, 28, 29, 30, Nov 2, 11, 12, 16, 17, 20, 30, Dec 2, 8, 15; 1773: DL, Jan 4, CG, 5, DL, Feb 1, 3, 4, 11, 18, 25, Mar 1, 4, 9, 23, 25, 29, 30, Apr 3, 13, 16, 17, CG, 24, DL, 30, May 1, CG, 8, 11, DL, 13, 17, Jun 2, Sep 23, 25, Oct 2, 11, 18, 19, 22, 30, Nov 1, 2, 6, 13, 20, 27, Dec 4, 10, 11, 13, 17, 18, 21, 25, 30; 1774: DL, Jan 1, CG, 3, DL, 8, 13, CG, 14, DL, 15, 19, 21, 22, 29, Feb 5, 12, 15, 26, Mar 5, 12, 14, 15, 17, 19, 21, 26, Apr 4, 9, 12, 15, 16, 19, 23, 29, 30, May 2, 7, 10, 14, 20, 21, 30, Jun 2, Sep 17, CG, 23, DL, 24, Oct 1, 8, 12, 14, 15, 20, 24, 26, Nov 5, 7, 10, 17, 18, 24, 30, Dec 1, 19; 1775: DL, Jan 11, 18, HAY, Feb 2, DL, Mar 2, 10, 18, 23, Apr 8, 19, 21, 22, May 5, 6, 10, 13, 27, Sep 26, 30, Oct 5, 7, 11, 20, 21, 24, Nov 6, 9, 18, 20, 22, 23, 25, 28, Dec 11, 29; 1776: DL, Jan 13, 26, Feb 1, 3, 5, 10, 22, 24, Mar 2, 7, 12, 14, 26, Apr 8, 9, 15, 17, 24, 26, May 8, 9, 11, 16, Jun 5, 10, HAY, 12, DL, Sep 21, 26, Oct 5, 9, 12, 19, 25, 30, Nov 6, 11, 19, 21, 29, Dec 18, 31; 1777: DL, Jan 16, Feb 24, Mar 1, 4, 13, 31, Apr 2, 7, 8, 29, May 8, Sep 25, Oct 9, 22, 31, Nov 13, Dec 3, 11; 1778: DL, Jan 23, Mar 5, 12, Apr 9, 27, Sep 26, Oct 6, 8, 13, 19, 20, 21, Nov

18, 20, 28, 30, Dec 21; 1779: DL, Jan 2, 25, Feb 3, 20, Mar 13, Apr 10, 19,
May 10, 15, Sep 21, 23, 30, Oct 2, 9, 12, 19, 30, Nov 9, 15, 18, Dec 2, 3,
11; 1780: DL, Jan 3, 18, 28, Feb 19, 22, Mar 4, Apr 1, 10, 19, May 24, Oct 5,
10, 12, 14, 20, 25, 28, 31, Nov 2, 10, Dec 4, 7, 19; 1781: DL, Jan 6, Mar 10,
Apr 18, 24, HAY, Aug 10, DL, Sep 20, 27, 29, Oct 2, 6, 12, 13, 18, 30, Nov 6,
7, 15; 1782: DL, Jan 22, Feb 7, 23, 25, Apr 11, May 7, 8, 10, Sep 17, 19, 26,
28, Oct 1, 5, 14, 29, Nov 12, Dec 26; 1783: DL, Jan 3, 10, 14, 24, 29, Feb 3,
7, 22, Mar 3, 20, Apr 29, May 5, 12, 15; 1784: DL, Sep 30, Oct 18, 26, Nov 4,
22, 25, Dec 3, 10, 22; 1785: DL, Feb 21, Apr 11, 20, 25, May 6, 11, HAY, Sep
2, DL, 20, Oct 4, 6, 18, 25, 26, 31, Nov 5, 18, 26, Dec 5, 8, 26; 1786: DL,
Jan 3, 14, Feb 18, Mar 27, Apr 6, 26, May 17, 25, HAY, Aug 17, DL, Sep 16,
21, 23, 28, Oct 7, 10, 12, 26, 28, Nov 14, 25, Dec 11, 21, 26; 1787: DL, Jan
24, Mar 12, 29, Apr 13, KING'S, 24, May 21, DL, 21, KING'S, 23, HAY, Aug 17,
DL, Sep 18, 22, Oct 2, 6, 9, 13, 15, 20, 24, 26, Nov 6, 10, 24, 29; 1788: DL,
Jan 2, 5, 25, Feb 25, Apr 10, 11, 28, May 6, 14, 22, HAY, Aug 25, DL, Sep 13;
1789: CG, Apr 15, CG, Nov 20, 27, Dec 11, 18; 1790: CG, Jan 13, 22, Feb 11,
May 1, 12, DL, Oct 23, 25, 27, Nov 1, 2, 10, 16, Dec 1, 31; 1791: DL, Jan 24,
Mar 2, 31, HAY, Aug 31, DLKING'S, Sep 27, Oct 1, 3, 6, 10, 20, Nov 1, 29, Dec
2; 1792: DLKING'S, Apr 20, 26, 27, HAY, Aug 6, 23, 31, Sep 5, DL, 15, 22, 27,
Oct 4, 13, 15, 31, Dec 18; 1793: DL, Feb 14, 28, Mar 4, 7, 14, Apr 3, 22;
1794: DL, Apr 25, May 17, 20, 23, Jun 2, 10, 12, 17, Jul 2, Sep 30, Oct 22,
29, Nov 1, 5, 12, Dec 10, 12; 1795: DL, Jan 24, Feb 9, 12, 28, Mar 16, Apr
16, May 4, 12, 26, 29, Sep 17, 22, 26, Oct 20, 22, Nov 3, 7, 10, 12, 14, 17;
1796: DL, Feb 1, Apr 2, 13, 20, 29, Jun 6, HAY, Jul 7, DL, Sep 27, 29, Oct 1,
4, 8, 15, 17, 24, Nov 1, 2, 8, 21, Dec 20; 1797: DL, Jan 27, Mar 30, Apr 19,
24, May 15, CG, 18, DL, 24, 29, Jun 12, Sep 19, 21, 26, 28, 30, Oct 3, 5, 7,
14, 26, Nov 17, 18, 20, 24, 28, Dec 5; 1798: HAY, Jan 15, DL, May 18, 24, Jun
2, 8, 16, Sep 22, 25, Oct 4, 9, 20; 1799: DL, Jan 8, 9, Feb 1, 14, 16, 19,
Apr 8, 19, 24, May 24, Sep 19, 21, 24, Oct 15, 17, 22; 1800: DL, Feb 8, 12,
15, Mar 6, 10, 13, May 10, 15, Jun 12, HAY, Aug 12
--Love at First Sight, 1763: DL, Oct 17, 18, 19, 21, 25, 26, Nov 22
--Lovers' Quarrels, 1790: CG, Feb 11, 12, May 8, 12, Oct 15, Nov 2; 1791: CG,
Mar 4, May 27, Nov 29; 1792: CG, Feb 3, May 1, Nov 10; 1793: CG, Apr 4, Oct
23, Nov 6; 1794: CG, Feb 27, May 23; 1795: CG, Jan 29, May 7; 1796: CG, Apr
22, Dec 15, 17; 1797: CG, May 6, 24; 1798: CG, Mar 31, Sep 26, Nov 15; 1799:
CG, May 10, Nov 8; 1800: CG, Apr 29
--Triumph of Mirth, The; or, Harlequin's Wedding (pantomime), 1782: DL, Dec 26,
27, 28, 30, 31; 1783: DL, Jan 1, 3, 7, 8, 10, 13, 15, 17, 18, 21, 22, 24, 27,
31, Feb 3, 5, 6, 7, 11, 12, 14, 20, 22, 25, Mar 3, 10, 17, Oct 13, 16, Nov 5
--Wit's Last Stake, 1768: DL, Apr 14; 1769: DL, Jan 20, 21, 24, 25, 27, Feb 1,
3, 6, 11, Sep 19; 1770: DL, Dec 31; 1771: DL, Jan 18; 1772: DL, Feb 17, Mar
2, Nov 12; 1779: HAY, Mar 8, May 10; 1780: HAY, Jan 3; 1784: HAY, Feb 9;
1792: HAY, Oct 22; 1799: DL, Apr 24, 25
King, Thomas and Mrs (actors), 1767: DL, Jan 24
King, William (actor), 1799: CG, Mar 25, Apr 2, 5, 11, 13, 22, Jun 6, Sep 30,
Oct 21, Dec 23; 1800: CG, Jan 16, Feb 10, Mar 4, Apr 15, 23, May 7, Jun 2, 6
King's Arms Tavern, 1714: SOU, Nov 1; 1723: KAT, Dec 4; 1736: CG, Apr 27; 1738:
CG, May 1; 1741: DL, Sep 5; 1742: DL, Feb 1, Mar 12, Apr 1; 1743: DL, Apr 18;
1748: DL, Apr 13; 1749: HAY, Nov 17; 1750: DL, Oct 1; 1753: CG, Feb 23; 1787:
HAY, Mar 12; 1789: CG, Apr 15, WHF, Nov 9
King's Bench, 1669: NONE, Jan 5; 1680: DG, Feb 9; 1717: SFBL, Sep 9; 1722: SFM,
Sep 5; 1733: DL/HAY, Nov 16, HAY, 20; 1738: CG, Feb 13; 1741: CG, Jan 12, GF,
Apr 23; 1746: GF, Feb 10; 1750: DL, May 14; 1753: DL, Feb 6; 1755: DL, Sep
27; 1761: SOHO, Jan 28; 1762: DL, Jan 29; 1763: HAY, Jun 9; 1772: DL, Oct 3;
1775: CG, Feb 24
King's Chapel, 1767: CG, May 23
King's Choir (singers), 1729: CRT, Dec 5
King's Gate St, 1744: DL, May 14
King's Head Tavern, 1731: TCY, Aug 9; 1741: BFTY, Aug 22; 1749: CG, Apr 28,
BFC, Aug 23; 1751: DL, May 2; 1776: HAY, Oct 7; 1780: CII, Mar 17; 1784: HAY,
Mar 8; 1789: KHS, Sep 16
King's Passage, 1749: DL, May 16
King's Row, 1799: DL, Apr 25
King's scholars, the (actors), 1717: WS, Apr 23; 1718: WS, Jan 24; 1721: WS,
Nov 21; 1722: WS, Jan 23, 26; 1724: WS, Nov 13; 1727: WS, Dec 14; 1728: WS,
Jan 15; 1735: WS, Dec 5; 1745: WS, Jan 11
King's Yard, 1753: KING'S, Mar 2
Kingham, Mrs (actor), 1780: CII, Feb 29, Mar 6, 13, 17, 27, Apr 5, 19; 1781:
HAY, Mar 26
Kingiston. See Kynaston.
Kings (four Indian visitors), 1710: QUEEN'S, Apr 27
Kings shall be thy nursing fathers (song), 1790: CG, Mar 17, 26; 1791: CG, Mar

23; 1792: CG, Mar 9; 1793: CG, Mar 8; 1794: CG, Mar 21; 1795: CG, Mar 18;
  1796: CG, Mar 16
Kingston, Duchess of, 1775: HAY, Aug 4, 16, 18
Kingston, 1737: DL, Sep 13
Kingswood (featherman), 1771: CG, Dec 2; 1772: CG, Apr 21; 1774: CG, Apr 8
Kingswood (maker of artificial flowers), 1784: DL, Jan 3
Kinnaird, George, 7th Baron (patron), 1797: KING'S, May 18, CG, Jun 14
Kinski, Count (German ambassador), 1728: DL, Sep 28; 1731: KING'S, Nov 13, 16,
  DL, 17, 29
Kippling, John (actor), 1784: HAY, Jun 5, Aug 24, Sep 17; 1787: ROY, Jun 20
Kirby (actor), 1748: CG, Dec 6
Kirby St, 1794: CG, May 24; 1795: CG, May 29
Kirby, Miss (actor, singer), 1778: DL, May 23, Sep 24, 26, Oct 15, 31, Nov 2,
  Dec 22; 1779: DL, Jan 8, Mar 22, May 10, 18, 19, 21, Sep 21, 28, 30, Oct 26,
  30, Nov 3, 6, Dec 2, 27, 31; 1780: DL, Jan 3, 20, 28, Feb 28, Apr 1, 3, 5,
  15, 26, May 2, 6, 9, Sep 16, 19, 21, 23, 28, Oct 3, 5, 17, 19, 20, 30, Nov 1,
  10, 13, 18, Dec 4, 6, 8, 16, 19; 1781: DL, Jan 16, Feb 8, 15, 17, Mar 6, 10,
  12, May 1, 10, 17, 23, 24, Dec 14; 1782: HAY, Jul 27, Aug 5, 6, 15
Kirby, Mrs (actor), 1739: CG, Oct 2
Kirby, Mrs (actor), 1767: HAY, Jun 4, 10, Jul 2, 8, 22, Aug 5, Sep 7, 16
Kirk (coppersmith), 1771: CG, Oct 2
Kirk (dancer), 1788: DL, Jun 6; 1789: DL, Dec 26; 1790: DL, Oct 26, Dec 27
Kirk (house servant), 1776: DL, Jun 10, Nov 1; 1777: DL, Apr 30; 1778: DL, May
  18; 1779: DL, May 21; 1780: DL, May 16; 1781: DL, May 23; 1788: DL, Jun 6;
  1790: DL, May 29; 1791: DL, May 26
Kirk, Mrs (actor), 1729: GF, Dec 1; 1730: GF, Jan 13, 19, Feb 6, 7, 9, HAY, Mar
  11, GF, 12, 17, 30, Apr 6, May 18
Kirkham (actor), 1690: DL, Sep 0, Dec 0; 1691: DL, Jan 0, Mar 0
Kirkman (harpsichord maker), 1769: CG, May 10, Jun 6; 1770: CG, May 29; 1772:
  DL, Jun 10; 1773: DL, Jun 2; 1776: DL, Jun 10
Kirkman (house servant), 1749: CG, Oct 19, Dec 5; 1750: CG, Mar 26
Kirkman, Francis (author), 1659: NONE, Sep 0
Kirkman, James T (author), 1761: CG, Jan 28; 1767: CG, Nov 28
Kirkpatrick (actor), 1777: CG, Nov 7
Kirton, Miss (actor, singer), 1791: DLKING'S, Oct 15; 1792: DLKING'S, Feb 18,
  Mar 29, May 23, DL, Oct 11, Nov 21, Dec 22, 26; 1793: DL, Jan 19, CG, Oct 12,
  21, 24, 28, 29, Nov 11, 28, Dec 7, 19; 1794: CG, Apr 30, Oct 22; 1795: CG,
  Jan 12, 31, Mar 9, 14, 16, Jun 6, 10, Sep 14, 21, Oct 12, 24, Nov 4, 9, 16,
  27, Dec 7; 1796: CG, Feb 2, Apr 2, 14, 16, May 17, 25, 31
Kisheir. See Keisher.
Kiss Accepted and Returned, The. See Lampe, John Frederick.
Kiss, The (dance), 1791: HAY, Jul 1
Kit Katters, 1700: LIF, Jan 9
Kitty and Jemmy (dance), 1798: DL, May 16
Kitty Conolly and Jack the Painter (entertainment), 1797: DL, May 24
Kitty Grogan. See Tho I'm no Dancing Master.
Kitty; or, The Female Phaeton (song), 1757: HAY, Sep 8, 12, 28, Oct 3
Klanert, Charles Moritz (actor), 1798: CG, Oct 8, Nov 7, 12, Dec 26; 1799: CG,
  Jan 29, Mar 25, Apr 9, May 6, 13, Jun 7, 8, Sep 18, 20, 23, 25, 30, Oct 7,
  14, 21, 24, 29, 31, Nov 11, 12, 14, 30, Dec 2, 5, 10, 23; 1800: CG, Jan 16,
  Feb 4, 8, Mar 4, 25, 27, Apr 5, 24, 25, 28, 30, May 1, 5, 7, 13, 17, 23, 27,
  Jun 2, HAY, 13, 14, 16, 17, 19, 21, Jul 1, 2, 5, 15, Aug 7, 8, 14, 20, 23, 29
Klein (dancer), 1706: DL, Jun 28, Jul 5, DG, 9
Knapp (actor), 1697: LIF, Jun 0, Nov 0; 1701: LIF, Mar 0, Dec 0; 1702: LIF, Dec
  31; 1703: LIF, Nov 0; 1704: LIF, Mar 25, Dec 4; 1705: LIF/QUEN, Feb 22, LIF,
  Aug 1, QUEEN'S, Nov 23; 1706: QUEEN'S, Jan 3, Apr 30; 1707: QUEEN'S, Jan 4,
  May 9; 1710: DL, Mar 21; 1715: LIF, Jan 7, Feb 3, Mar 26, Apr 30, May 24, Jun
  2, 23, Aug 17, Sep 29, Oct 5, 7, 10, 11, 24, 28, Nov 29, 30, Dec 12; 1716:
  LIF, Jan 4, Apr 3, 11, 25, Jul 4, Oct 10, 20, Nov 6; 1717: LIF, Jan 22, Feb
  11, 25, May 20, Nov 6, 26, 28, Dec 14; 1718: LIF, Feb 3, May 13, Jun 30, Jul
  24, Oct 3, 31; 1719: LIF, Feb 7, 21, Apr 28, Jun 17; 1720: SFLH, Sep 5
Knapp (actor), 1782: HAY, Mar 4; 1784: HAY, Aug 21
Knapp, Henry, 1780: CG, Nov 4
--Excise-Man, The (farce), 1780: CG, Nov 4
--Hunt the Slipper (farce), 1784: HAY, Aug 21, 23, 25, 28, 31, Sep 3; 1785:
  HAY, Jun 3, 9, Jul 6, 16, Aug 13, 20; 1786: HAY, Jun 9, 19
Knapp, Mrs (actor), 1719: LIF, Nov 13; 1720: LIF, May 14, BFPMJ, Aug 23, LIF,
  Nov 22, Dec 17, 21; 1721: LIF, May 15, 29, BF/SF, Aug 24
Knapton, J and P (printers), 1750: DL, Oct 9
Knave or Not. See Holcroft, Thomas.
Knavery in All Trades; or, The Coffee-House (play, anon), 1663: NONE, Dec 26
Knee Dance (dance), 1727: KING'S, Mar 2

Knellar (actor), 1736: GF, Feb 20
Knepp (Kneap, Knipp, Nep), Elizabeth (actor), 1663: BRIDGES, Nov 3; 1664:
  BRIDGES, Nov 0; 1666: MOORFLDS, Aug 22, NONE, Oct 25, ATCOURT, 29, NONE, Nov
  14, ATCOURT, Dec 10, BRIDGES, 27; 1667: BRIDGES, Jan 2, 15, 23, 24, BRI/COUR,
  Feb 0, BRIDGES, 5, NONE, 12, LIF, 27, Mar 30, BRIDGES, Apr 16, May 1, 22, Aug
  12, 17, 22, 24, NONE, Sep 9, BRIDGES, 14, Oct 5, 19, Dec 30; 1668: LIF, Jan
  6, BRIDGES, 11, Feb 20, Mar 25, Apr 7, 17, LIF, May 2, BRIDGES, 7, 9, 15, 16,
  18, Jun 3, 12, NONE, Sep 0, BRIDGES, 4, 18, 19, 28, BRI/COUR, Dec 2; 1669:
  BRIDGES, Jan 1, Feb 2, Jun 24; 1670: BRIDGES, Aug 0; 1671: BRIDGES, Mar 0;
  1672: LIF, Nov 0; 1673: LIF, Mar 0; 1675: DL, Jan 12, Aug 0, NONE, Sep 0;
  1676: DL, Dec 11; 1677: DL, Mar 0; 1678: DL, Mar 0; 1710: DL, Feb 25
Knerber (musician), 1744: HAY, Sep 5
Knife Grinder's Song (song), 1790: CG, Apr 22
Knife Grinders (dance), 1760: CG, Apr 17, 21, May 2, 3, 12, 16; 1763: CG, Oct
  12, 15, 20, 26, 27, 28, Nov 8, 10, 16, 17, 18, 19, 24; 1764: CG, Jan 3, 6,
  12, Feb 18, 24, 25, 29, Mar 1, 19, Apr 7, 10, 27, May 10, 16
Knight (actor), 1797: HAY, Sep 18
Knight (banker), 1748: DL, May 3
Knight (tinman), 1749: DL, Nov 8, Dec 11; 1750: DL, Jan 9, Feb 8, Mar 8, Apr 17
Knight of the Burning Pestle, The. See Fletcher, John.
Knight, Frances Maria (actor), 1676: DL, Dec 11; 1677: DL, Oct 0; 1684: DL, Apr
  0; 1685: DL, Aug 0; 1688: DL, May 3, NONE, Sep 0; 1689: DL, Mar 0, Nov 7, 20;
  1690: DL, Jan 0, Sep 0, Oct 0, Dec 0; 1691: DL, Jan 0, Apr 0, BG, 2, NONE,
  Sep 0; 1692: DL, Nov 0; 1693: DL, Apr 0, DG, May 0, NONE, Sep 0; 1694: DL,
  Feb 0, Mar 21, DG, May 0, DL, Sep 0; 1695: DG, Apr 0, DL, Sep 0, Oct 0, Nov
  0, Dec 0; 1696: DL, Feb 0, Mar 0, Apr 0, May 0, Sep 0; 1697: DL, Jan 0,
  DLLIF, Feb 15, DL, May 31; 1698: DL, Feb 0, Mar 0, Jun 0; 1699: DL, Dec 0;
  1700: DL, Mar 0, Nov 23, Dec 9; 1701: DL, May 31; 1702: DL, Nov 26; 1703: DL,
  Mar 11, Apr 10, Jun 23; 1704: DL, Jan 26, Mar 6, May 0, 31, Dec 7; 1706: DL,
  Mar 27; 1707: DL, Oct 18, 23, 25, Dec 4, 26; 1708: DL, Jan 15, Mar 8, 9, Apr
  17, 19, DL/QUEEN, 21, DL, 26, DL/QUEEN, May 25, DL, Jun 5, Sep 14, 16, 21,
  23, 25, 30, Oct 2, 18, 19, 22, 23, 26, Dec 18, 21, 30; 1709: DL, Jan 3, 4, 8,
  17, 22, 26, Feb 5, 16, Mar 5, 8, 21, 22, Apr 9, 30, May 2, 18, 24, Nov 23,
  24, 25, Dec 3, 7, 10, 17; 1710: DL, Jan 3, 14, 18, 31, Feb 11, 16, Mar 11,
  27, Apr 21, 22, May 23, DL/QUEEN, Nov 15, 18, DL, 20, 21, 23, 25, 27, 28, Dec
  1, 9, 11, 15, 16, 21; 1711: DL, Jan 27, DL/QUEEN, Feb 8, 17, DL, 19, 24,
  DL/QUEEN, 26, DL, Mar 10, DL/QUEEN, 24, DL, Apr 7, May 10, 18, 21, 22, Jun
  26, Jul 3, Aug 17, Oct 2, 8, 9, 18, 20, 23, 27, 29, 30, 31, Nov 3, 7, 9, 23,
  24, Dec 31; 1712: DL, Mar 17, May 19, 20, Jun 2, Sep 20, Oct 2, 4, 7, 10, 15,
  20, 21, 28, 30, Nov 1; 1713: DL, Jan 5, 10, 29, Feb 9, 11, 19, Mar 3, 14, May
  27, Jun 3, 5, Oct 13, Nov 16, 19, 27, 28, Dec 2; 1714: DL, Jan 5, Mar 29, May
  5, 12, Jun 18, Oct 26, Nov 27, Dec 6, 8; 1715: LIF, Jan 8, 11, Feb 2, 3, 5,
  16, Mar 26, 31, Apr 30, Sep 29, Oct 4, 22, 28, Nov 30; 1716: LIF, Jan 3, Apr
  5, 27, Oct 18, 23, Nov 10, 13, 26, Dec 13; 1717: LIF, Jan 8, 10, Feb 11, Mar
  11, 16, 30, Apr 1, May 18, Oct 24, Nov 11, 14, 20, Dec 9, 14; 1718: LIF, Jan
  2, Mar 1, 31, Apr 23, Oct 1, 4, 6, 18, 31, Nov 13, 24, 25, Dec 6; 1719: LIF,
  Jan 3, Feb 28, Mar 30, Apr 2; 1723: LIF, Sep 28, 30, Oct 10, 31, Nov 14, 21,
  26; 1724: LIF, Mar 26, Apr 7, 21, 22, 25, May 26, Jun 3
Knight, Margaret, Mrs Thomas (actor), 1795: CG, Apr 23, Sep 25, 30, Oct 9, 15,
  Nov 18; 1796: CG, Mar 30, May 6, 20, 21, Oct 25, Nov 19; 1797: CG, Jan 3, Feb
  20, 27, Mar 13, Apr 8, May 9, 17, Jun 1, Sep 18, 29, Oct 31, Nov 3, 22, 23;
  1798: CG, Feb 6, Mar 20, Apr 26, May 15
Knight, Mary (singer), 1674: SLINGSBY, Dec 2; 1675: ATCOURT, Feb 15
Knight, Mrs (actor), 1749: HAY, Apr 29, May 2, 29; 1750: HAY, Feb 9, 16, 26
Knight, Thomas (actor), 1795: CG, Sep 25, 30, Oct 5, 9, 15, 19, 30, Nov 9, Dec
  7, 9, 21, 29; 1796: CG, Jan 4, 8, Feb 2, Mar 14, 19, 30, Apr 23, May 6, 12,
  21, Sep 12, 16, 17, 21, 30, Oct 6, 7, 20, 24, 25, Nov 7, 19, 24, 25; 1797:
  CG, Jan 3, 17, 18, Feb 18, 20, 23, 27, Mar 13, Apr 19, 25, May 8, 9, 12, 16,
  23, 30, Jun 1, 14, Sep 18, 22, 25, 27, 29, Oct 11, 20, 28, 31, Nov 3, 7, 15,
  Dec 12, 16, 19, 20; 1798: CG, Jan 11, Feb 7, 10, Mar 17, 20, 31, Apr 13, 24,
  27, 30, May 1, 8, 15, 17, 24, 31, HAY, Aug 11, CG, Sep 17, 19, 28, Oct 3, 5,
  11, 15, 30, 31, Nov 6, 7, 9, 23; 1799: CG, Jan 25, Feb 4, 7, Mar 14, Apr 2,
  6, 9, 16, 30, May 7, 15, 25, 31, Jun 7, Sep 18, 20, Oct 2, 4, 10, 16, 24, 25,
  Nov 9, 11, 14, 30, Dec 30; 1800: CG, Jan 6, 11, 16, Feb 3, 8, Apr 22, 24, 26,
  30, May 20, 27, 29, Jun 12
--Honest Thieves, The; or, The Faithful Irishman (farce), 1797: CG, May 9, 10,
  12, 13, 19, Jun 7, 10, HAY, 29, Jul 1, 7, 18, Aug 3, CG, Sep 27, 29, Oct 25,
  Nov 17; 1798: CG, Mar 13, 15, Apr 18, May 9, 23, HAY, Jun 21, Jul 5, Aug 14,
  CG, Sep 19; 1799: CG, Jan 25, Jun 3, Oct 25; 1800: CG, May 10
--Turnpike Gate, The (opera), 1799: CG, Oct 28, Nov 7, 14, 15, 16, 18, 19, 20,
  21, 22, 23, 25, 26, 27, 28, 29, Dec 3, 5, 6, 11, 13, 14, 17, 19; 1800: CG,
  Feb 5, 11, Mar 18, May 22, Jun 11

Knight, Thomas and Margaret (actors), 1796: CG, May 6; 1797: CG, May 19; 1798:
    CG, May 15
Knight, Ursula (actor), 1676: DL, Dec 11
Knights (actor), 1784: HAY, Mar 8, Apr 30; 1793: HAY, Dec 26; 1794: DL, Oct 31;
    1796: DL, Jan 11; 1800: HAY, Jul 2
Knights of Malta, The. See Fletcher, John.
Knights of St Patrick (song), 1783: DL, May 12
Knights, The. See Foote, Samuel.
Knightsbridge, 1743: LIF, Mar 21; 1800: DL, May 21, HAY, Aug 5
Knipe, Captain Charles, 1715: LIF, Jun 2; 1716: LIF, Jun 4
--City Ramble, The; or, The Humours of the Counter, 1715: LIF, Jun 2, 6, 7, Jul
    8, Oct 17, Nov 4, 28, Dec 31; 1717: LIF, Nov 13, 18; 1718: LIF, Jan 27; 1736:
    CG, Mar 27
Knipp, Mrs. See Knepp, Elizabeth.
Kniveton, Margaretta Priscilla, Mrs Thomas (actor), 1771: CG, Oct 4, 9, 14, 19,
    Nov 9, 18, 28, Dec 9, 18, 23, 27; 1772: CG, May 11, Nov 14, Dec 5, 19; 1773:
    CG, Jan 22, Mar 15, 23, May 6, 28, Sep 24, 27, Oct 8, 21, 22, Nov 20, Dec 1,
    7
Kniveton, Mr and Mrs (actors), 1772: CG, May 11; 1773: CG, May 11; 1774: CG,
    May 3
Kniveton, Thomas (actor), 1770: CG, Apr 24, May 1, 22, Nov 30; 1771: CG, Jan 4,
    26, Apr 10, 12, 24, 27, May 9, Sep 23, Oct 4, 15, 25, 30, Nov 26; 1772: CG,
    Mar 5, Apr 21, 22, 25, May 4, 11, Sep 21, 23, 28, Oct 16, 22, 27, Nov 2, 6,
    Dec 29; 1773: CG, Jan 6, 7, Sep 22, 24, Oct 4, 9, 25, Nov 20, 23, Dec 17;
    1774: CG, Jan 5, 29, Mar 12, Apr 12, 23, May 3
Knott (actor), 1729: SF, Sep 8, HAY, Nov 29; 1730: HAY, Feb 12, Mar 30, Apr 20,
    TC, Aug 11, BFR, 22, Sep 4
Know Your Own Mind. See Murphy, Arthur.
Knowles (actor), 1770: HAY, Jun 18, 22, Aug 8, Oct 15; 1771: HAY, May 15, 17,
    20, 23, 29, Jun 14, Sep 18
Knowles, Widow (beneficiary), 1751: HAY, Nov 21
Knox, Mrs (actor), 1785: HAY, Apr 25
Knyvett, Charles (organist, pianist), 1775: DL, May 27; 1789: CG, Feb 27; 1790:
    CG, Feb 19, Jun 2; 1791: CG, Mar 11; 1792: CG, Feb 24; 1794: CG, May 23, 26
Koerbitz, Christiano Tedeschini (actor), 1754: CG, Nov 18
Kolowiky (musician), 1761: HAY, Jan 28, Feb 5
Kontzen (musician), 1729: HAY, Jan 28, LIF, Feb 7
Kontzen's father (musician), 1729: HAY, Jan 28
Kotzebue, August Friedrich Ferdinand von, 1798: DL, Mar 24, CG, Oct 11; 1799:
    CG, Apr 8, 9, 12, 13, DL, 22, May 24, HAY, Jun 15, Jul 30, CG, Nov 30; 1800:
    CG, Jan 16, DL, Feb 1
--Armuth und Edelsinn, 1799: HAY, Jul 30
--Graf von Burgund, Der, 1799: CG, Apr 12
--Indianer in England, Die, 1799: DL, Apr 22
--Johanna von Montfaucon, 1800: CG, Jan 16
--Kind der Liebe, Das, 1798: CG, Oct 11
--Menschenhass und Reue, 1798: DL, Mar 24
--Opfertod, Der, 1799: HAY, Jun 15
--Reconciliation, 1799: CG, Apr 13
--Schreibepult, Das; oder, Die Gefahren der Jugend, 1799: CG, Nov 30
--Spanier in Peru, Die, 1799: DL, May 24
--Versohnung, Die, 1799: CG, Apr 8
--Wildfang, Der, 1800: DL, Feb 1
--Witwe und das Reitpferd, Die, 1799: CG, May 4
Kraus, Widow (beneficiary), 1756: DL, Nov 12
Kreutzer, Rudolph (composer), 1794: DL, Jun 9, Sep 27; 1795: DL, Oct 1; 1797:
    DL, Feb 16; 1800: DL, Jan 1
Krumpholtz, Johann Baptist (composer), 1794: CG, Apr 25
Krumpholtz, Mme Johann Baptist (harpist), 1789: DL, Mar 6, 11, KING'S, Apr 2
Kurz, 1758: CHAPEL, Apr 27
Kyd, Thomas
--Jeronimo is Mad Again, 1668: NURSERY, Feb 24
Kynaston (musician), 1718: YB, Dec 5
Kynaston (Kenniston, Kingiston) (renter), 1750: DL, Feb 7
Kynaston, Edward (actor), 1659: NONE, Sep 0; 1660: COCKPIT, Aug 18, Oct 8,
    REDBULL, Nov 5, VERE, 19, Dec 6; 1661: VERE, Jan 7, Dec 28; 1663: NONE, Sep
    0; 1665: BRIDGES, Jan 14, Apr 0; 1666: NONE, Sep 0, ATCOURT, Dec 10, BRIDGES,
    27; 1667: BRIDGES, Apr 16, 17, Oct 19; 1668: BRIDGES, Sep 14, Nov 6, Dec 18;
    1669: BRIDGES, Feb 1, 2, 9, Jun 24; 1670: BRIDGES, Aug 0, BRI/COUR, Dec 0;
    1671: BRIDGES, Mar 0, Jun 0; 1672: BRIDGES, Jan 0, LIF, Apr 0, Nov 0; 1673:
    LIF, May 0; 1675: DL, Jan 12, 25, Apr 23, 30, May 10, Nov 17; 1676: DL, Jan
    29, ATCOURT, May 29, DL, Sep 9, Dec 11; 1677: DL, Jan 12, Mar 17; 1682: NONE,

Sep 0, DL, Nov 16, 28; 1683: DG, May 31, NONE, Sep 0; 1684: ATCOURT, Feb 11,
DL, Mar 0; 1685: DLORDG, Jan 20, DL, May 9; 1686: DL, Jan 0, Apr 0; 1687:
ATCOURT, Apr 25; 1688: DG, Apr 0; 1689: DL, Mar 0, Nov 7, Dec 4; 1690:
DLORDG, Mar 0, NONE, Sep 0, DL, Oct 0, Nov 0, Dec 0; 1691: DL, Mar 0, DG, May
0, NONE, Sep 0, DL, Dec 0; 1692: DL, Mar 0, Apr 0, Jun 0, Nov 8; 1693: NONE,
Sep 0, DL, Oct 0; 1694: DL, Jan 0, 13, Feb 0, NONE, Jul 0; 1695: LIF, Dec 0;
1696: LIF, Apr 0, Oct 0; 1697: LIF, Nov 0; 1698: LIF, Jan 0, Mar 0, Apr 0,
May 0, Jun 0
Kynaston, Thomas (trustee), 1733: DL, Jun 4
Kytch (Ketch, Kitch) (musician), 1709: H&P, Jun 18; 1716: LIF, May 10, 18, Jun
4; 1717: SH, Mar 27; 1719: HIC, Feb 13, 18, YB, Dec 19; 1720: HIC, Feb 23,
Mar 4, YB, Apr 1; 1721: HIC, Mar 15, LIF, Apr 17, HAY, Aug 2; 1722: HIC, Feb
16, HAY, May 11; 1723: HIC, Mar 6, HAY, 6, DL, 20, HAY, Apr 5, May 24; 1724:
HIC, Feb 26, Mar 18, YB, 27, HIC, Apr 17, HAY, May 8; 1729: HIC, Apr 16;
1731: LIF, Apr 2, HAY, May 10; 1734: MR, Dec 13; 1735: HAY, Jan 31

L, E (author), 1747: DL, Oct 20
L, H (tax proposer), 1746: DL, Jan 10
LaBack (dancer), 1736: LIF, Mar 31
LaBane (singer), 1714: LIF, Dec 22
L'Abbe (LAbbree, LaBee) (dancer), 1698: ATCOURT, May 13; 1701: LIF, Jun 24;
1702: LIF, Dec 11, DL, 29; 1703: LIF, Feb 11, Jun 1, 11, DL, Nov 30, Dec 14,
LIF, 21; 1704: DL, Jan 4, 18, LIF, Feb 1, DL, 22, Mar 14, LIF, 30, Dec 12;
1705: DL, Jan 16, QUEEN'S, Nov 17, 20, LIF/QUEN, Dec 4, QUEEN'S, 8, 12,
LIF/QUEN, 26; 1706: ATCOURT, Feb 5; 1710: QUEEN'S, Aug 16; 1713: DL, Jun 12
L'Abbe Jr (dancer), 1706: QUEEN'S, May 29, Jun 29, LIF/QUEN, Jul 6; 1712: DL,
May 30
L'Abbe Sr or Jr (choreographer), 1731: DL, Mar 22; 1735: CG/LIF, May 9; 1737:
CG, Apr 25, May 13
L'Abbe's brother (dancer), 1705: LIF, Feb 20
L'Abbe's scholars (dancer), 1705: LIF, Feb 20, Mar 10; 1706: QUEEN'S, Apr 25
LaBee. See L'Abbe.
Labisle (dancer), 1730: BFPG/TC, Aug 1
Laborie (dancer), 1782: KING'S, Dec 10; 1786: KING'S, Dec 23; 1787: KING'S, Jan
6, 20, Feb 13, Mar 8, 22, May 19, Jun 14; 1790: HAY, Jan 7, Feb 13, Mar 25,
Apr 6, 15, 22, May 4, 13, 27, CG, Jul 6, 10; 1791: PAN, Dec 17; 1792: HAY,
Feb 14, Mar 10, 17, Apr 14; 1797: KING'S, Nov 28; 1798: KING'S, Feb 6, Mar
22, Apr 19, 26, DL, May 9, KING'S, 10, CG, Jun 11, KING'S, 14, Dec 8; 1799:
KING'S, Apr 18, May 2, DL, 8; 1800: KING'S, Jan 11, 28, Mar 1, 4, DL, May 14,
KING'S, 29, Jun 24, 28
Laborie, Master (dancer), 1798: KING'S, May 10
Laborie, Mme Lombard (dancer), 1797: KING'S, Nov 28, Dec 20; 1798: KING'S, Feb
6, Apr 19, 26, DL, May 9, KING'S, 10, CG, Jun 11, KING'S, 14, Dec 8; 1799:
KING'S, Jan 29, Feb 12, Mar 26, May 2, DL, 8; 1800: KING'S, Jan 11, 28, Mar
1, 4, Apr 15, DL, May 14, KING'S, 29, Jun 24, 28
Labours of Hercules (dance), 1726: KING'S, Oct 21
Labyrinth, The (play, anon), 1664: BRIDGES, May 2
Labyrinth, The; or, The Country Madcap (dance), 1797: DL, Mar 6, 9, 13
Labyrinthus. See Hawkesworth, Walter.
Lacam (renter), 1758: CG, Mar 27
Lacam, Mrs (renter), 1758: CG, Mar 27
Lace Lappet, 1755: DL, Dec 16
Lacey, Mrs (actor), 1737: HAY, Mar 21; 1740: SF, Sep 9
Lackington, Allen and Co (publishers), 1797: CG, Nov 24; 1798: CG, Oct 15;
1800: CG, Jan 16
Lackit (actor), 1746: SFW, Sep 8
LaCourt (scene painter), 1750: CG, Mar 10
LaCroix (dancer), 1741: DL, Oct 21, Nov 28, Dec 14, 18; 1742: DL, Jan 6, Feb
24, Mar 13
Lacy, F (actor), 1730: HAY, Jun 23
Lacy, James (actor, proprietor), 1727: LIF, May 2, 19; 1728: LIF, Jan 29, May
20, 22, Jul 5, 19, HAY, Nov 14, 19, Dec 7; 1729: HAY, Jan 10, 31, DL, Jun 13,
GF, Nov 3, 10, HAY, 12, GF, 14, HAY, 15, GF, 21, 24, Dec 1, 3, 8, 16, 17,
HAY, 18; 1730: HAY, Jan 8, GF, 12, HAY, 21, Feb 6, Mar 11, 12, GF, 17, HAY,
20, GF, 30, HAY, 30, Apr 2, 7, May 13, 28, Jun 3, 9, HAY, 27, Jul 7,
BFLH, Aug 31, SFLH, Sep 8, SFG, 8, HAY, 18, Nov 9, 18, 20, 30, Dec 7, 17, 28;
1731: HAY, Jan 13, 15, 18, 20, Feb 17, 26, Mar 15, 24, May 12, LIF, Oct 11,
Dec 9; 1732: LIF, Apr 24, May 2, Oct 18, LIF/CG, 20, 25, 27, 30, Nov 4, Dec
4, 14; 1733: LIF/CG, Jan 1, Feb 5, Apr 10, CG, Oct 2, 31, Nov 9, 10, 14, 19,

30, Dec 1, 3, 17, 20; 1734: CG, Jan 1, 5, 18, Apr 29, May 3, 4, 7, 17, BFFO,
Aug 24, LIF, Oct 1, HAY, 7; 1735: LIF, Jul 11, 16, 23, 30, Aug 1, 6, 22, 25,
29, Sep 2, 5, YB/HAY, 17; 1736: HAY, Mar 5, Apr 29, TC, Aug 4, SOU, Sep 20;
1737: HAY, Mar 5, 14, 21, Apr 13, May 4; 1738: CG, Feb 13, Mar 2, YB, 26, 28,
Apr 9; 1741: BFH, Aug 22; 1742: DL, May 12; 1743: CG, Apr 20; 1744: HAY, Nov
1; 1745: DL, Sep 28; 1746: DL, Jan 20, Apr 12, Nov 4, 7, 15; 1747: DL, Jan
24, Apr 9, 11; 1748: CG, Oct 25; 1749: DL, May 16, Nov 2, CG, 11, DL, 27, Dec
5, 22, 26, CG, 26; 1750: CG, Jan 4, DL, 6, 13, CG, 16, DL, 22, 29, Feb 8, 10,
CG, 20, Mar 1, DL, 26, Apr 7, 9, CG, 21, 26, Sep 28, Oct 26, Nov 29, Dec 1;
1751: CG, Jan 1, 25, Feb 23, Mar 16, Apr 16, 23; 1752: DL, Jan 11, Sep 26,
Oct 20, Nov 4, 13, 25, 28, Dec 4, 8; 1753: DL, May 1, 2, 21, Sep 8, Oct 3, 4,
6, 22, Nov 5, 8, 15; 1754: DL, Jan 23, May 6; 1755: DL, Nov 13, 15; 1759: DL,
Dec 12; 1761: DL, Jun 4; 1766: DL, Jan 23, Oct 11; 1767: DL, Jan 24, Dec 19;
1772: DL, Dec 17; 1774: DL, Jan 21
--Fame; or, Queen Elizabeth's Trumpets (farce), 1737: HAY, May 4
Lacy, John (actor, author), 1660: NONE, Sep 0, COCKPIT, Oct 8, REDBULL, Nov 5,
VERE, Dec 0; 1661: NONE, Sep 0; 1662: VERE, Mar 11, Apr 23, May 17, 21, 22,
ATCOURT, Nov 27; 1663: VERE, Mar 0, BRIDGES, May 8, Jun 10, 12, 13, NONE, Sep
0; 1664: BRIDGES, Dec 0; 1665: BRIDGES, Jan 14; 1666: BRIDGES, Mar 19, NONE,
Sep 0, ATCOURT, Dec 10, BRIDGES, 27; 1667: BRIDGES, Apr 9, 15, 16, 20, 22,
May 1, 13, NONE, Jul 13, BRIDGES, Aug 13; 1668: BRIDGES, Apr 28, Jul 31, Sep
14; 1669: BRIDGES, Jan 11, 16, 19, NONE, Feb 10, BRIDGES, Apr 17; 1671:
BRIDGES, Mar 0, Dec 7; 1675: DL, Apr 23, May 10; 1679: DL, Feb 0; 1701: LIF,
Mar 6
--Dumb Lady, The; or, The Farriar the Physician, 1669: NONE, Sep 0
--Old Troop, The; or, Monsieur Ragout, 1664: BRIDGES, Dec 0; 1668: BRIDGES, Jul
31, Aug 1; 1680: NONE, Sep 0; 1705: LIF, Oct 20; 1707: QUEEN'S, Jul 30; 1714:
DL, Jul 27, 30; 1717: DL, Aug 6
--Sauny the Scot. See Shakespeare, William, The Taming of the Shrew.
--Sir Hercules Buffoon; or, The Poetical Squire, 1684: DG, Jun 0
Lacy, Mrs (actor), 1696: LIF, Mar 0
Lacy, Mrs (actor), 1728: LIF, Jan 29, May 2, 30, Jul 2; 1730: HAY, Jun 23, SFG,
Sep 8, SFLH, 8, HAY, Nov 9, 13, 20, 30, Dec 7, 23, 28; 1731: HAY, Jan 13, 14,
15, 18, 20, Feb 10, 26, Mar 24, Apr 22, SF/BFMMO, Aug 26; 1733: CG/LIF, Mar
26; 1734: CG, Jan 15, 23, Mar 5, BFFO, Aug 24, SFL, Sep 7, HAY, Oct 7; 1736:
BFFH, Aug 23
Lacy, Theodore (actor), 1730: GF, May 26
Lacy, Thomas (actor), 1746: DL, Apr 29
Lacy, Thomas Hailes (spectator), 1698: LIF, Jul 11
Lacy, Willoughby (actor, manager), 1774: DL, Mar 22, May 5, Oct 8, 11, 27;
1775: DL, Oct 20; 1776: DL, Mar 14, Jun 3, Sep 21, Oct 9, 10, 15, Nov 5;
1777: DL, Feb 3, 17, Mar 13, 20, Apr 11, 24; 1778: DL, Apr 23; 1784: HAY, Sep
13; 1785: HAY, Jun 24, Sep 9; 1786: HAY, Jul 14; 1798: HAY, Dec 17; 1800: DL,
Jun 18
Lacy Jr, Willoughby (actor), 1795: HAY, Sep 21
Lad of the Hills, The. See O'Keeffe, John.
Ladbrook, Sir Robert, 1763: DL, Oct 8
Ladbrooke, Widow (beneficiary), 1756: CG, Nov 25
Ladd (actor), 1739: CG, Dec 10; 1740: CG, Feb 12, Mar 18; 1741: CG, Feb 24
Ladd (actor), 1773: MARLY, Sep 3
Ladd (singer), 1758: CHAPEL, Apr 27
Ladder Dance (dance), 1702: MF, May 5; 1706: LIF/QUEN, Jan 25, HAW, Aug 10, 17;
1710: GR, Aug 5, 7, 12, 17, 19, 24, 26, Sep 1; 1718: AC, Sep 24; 1723: RI,
Sep 2
Ladies a la Mode, The. See Flecknoe, Richard, The Damoiselles a la Mode.
Ladies of Honour (play), 1669: ATCOURT, Feb 22
Ladies Preservative in the Three Chief Characteristicks of Beauty, The (book),
1729: DL, Mar 6
Ladies Visiting Day, The. See Burnaby, William.
Ladies' Frolick, The. See Dance, James.
Lads and Lasses (dance), 1716: DL, May 16, Oct 18; 1717: DL, Feb 13; 1720: DL,
Jan 14, May 20, Sep 20; 1722: LIF, May 18; 1723: DL, Nov 22, Dec 31; 1724:
DL, Feb 11, Apr 15; 1725: DL, May 21; 1728: LIF, Apr 22; 1729: LIF, Apr 22;
1730: DL, Apr 15, GF, Jun 1, 12
Lads and Lasses Dance, Grand (dance), 1728: LIF, May 15
Lads and lasses, blithe and gay (song), 1694: DG, May 0
Lady Errant, The (play), 1671: LIF, Mar 9; 1672: DG, Mar 9
Lady Fair, 1690: NONE, Sep 8; 1693: SF, Sep 7; 1753: SFP, Sep 18
Lady Jane Gray. See Banks, John, The Innocent Usurper; Rowe, Nicholas.
Lady Moore. See Carey, Henry.
Lady of the Manor, The. See Kenrick, Dr William.
Lady Pentweazle in Town (interlude, anon), 1787: CG, Mar 27

Lady Pentweazle Scene (entertainment), 1760: CG, Dec 18; 1761: CG, Apr 13, May
    5; 1762: DL, May 11; 1776: HAY, Sep 23, CHR, Oct 7
Lady Pentweazle's Vagaries (dance), 1753: BFSY, Sep 3
Lady's Choice, The. See Hiffernan, Dr Paul.
Lady's Lamentation (song), 1737: DL, Mar 12, CG, 26, Apr 14, 18, 25, 29, May 2,
    DL, 3, CG, 6, HAY, 6, CG, 9, 13, 16, 19, DL, 19, CG, 31, LIF, Jul 26, Aug 2,
    CG, Sep 26; 1738: DL, Apr 22
Lady's Lamentation for their Adonis, The (poem), 1692: DL, Dec 9
Lady's Last Stake, The. See Cibber, Colley.
Lady's Lesson (song), 1755: CG, Apr 2
Lady's Opera, The. See Gay, John, The Beggar's Opera.
Lady's Oratory (entertainment), 1729: YB, Apr 15, 22, 29
Lady's Revenge, The. See Popple, William.
Lady's Trial, The. See Ford, John.
Lady's Triumph, The. See Theobald, Lewis.
Laferry (dancer), 1702: DL, Oct 23; 1703: DL, Feb 12, May 28, Oct 16, Nov 1,
    17, Dec 22, 27; 1704: DL, Apr 18, 27, Aug 15, Nov 13, Dec 1; 1705: DL, Jan
    12, Mar 19
LaFevre (actor), 1728: HAY, Mar 20
Lafevre, Master (dancer), 1732: RIW/HAY, Sep 4, 12
LaFond, Mlle (dancer), 1772: KING'S, Dec 1, 5; 1773: KING'S, Jan 2, 5, 12, 15,
    Feb 16, 20, Mar 9, 16, 18, 23, 30, Apr 1, 17, 24, May 22, 25, 28, Jun 1, 19
LaFont, Joseph de, 1779: CG, Apr 30
--Naufrage, Le, 1779: CG, Apr 30
--Trois Freres Riveaux, Les, 1722: HAY, Jan 6, Feb 8, Mar 8
LaFont (LeFont), Mrs (dancer), 1741: CG, Nov 26; 1742: CG, Jan 8, Feb 22, Oct
    25, Nov 2, Dec 21; 1743: CG, Mar 8, Apr 23, Oct 3, Dec 20, 21; 1744: CG, Jan
    14, Feb 14, Mar 3, May 4; 1746: CG, Dec 6, 31; 1747: CG, Feb 28, May 15;
    1748: CG, Mar 3, 14, Apr 29, DL, Oct 27; 1749: DL, Feb 21, May 11, Oct 11,
    18, 24, Nov 9, 27, 29, Dec 2, 28; 1750: DL, Jan 1, Apr 5, May 1
LaFontaine (beneficiary), 1735: HAY, Mar 29
LaFontaine, Jean de (author), 1758: CG, Nov 9
Laforest (dancer), 1704: DL, Jun 9, Aug 16; 1705: DL, Jan 1, Jul 3, 5, 18, Oct
    2, 16, Nov 12, Dec 17; 1706: DL, Jan 14; 1727: DL, May 31
Laforest (Lafory), Mrs (dancer), 1727: DL, May 31
LaFoy (actor), 1729: LIF, Oct 15
LaFoy, Mrs (actor), 1732: LIF/CG, Nov 8, 9
Lagarde. See Legar.
Lagarroune, Mrs (beneficiary), 1725: HAY, Apr 7
Laggat (actor), 1799: WRSG, May 17
L'Agile (actor), 1740: GF, Nov 6, Dec 15; 1750: NWC, Apr 16
LaGrange's Medicinal Warehouse, 1765: DL, Apr 26
Laguerre, John (actor, dancer, singer), 1725: LIF, Apr 23; 1726: LIF, Oct 24;
    1727: LIF, Oct 26; 1728: LIF, Apr 26, May 18, Nov 23; 1729: LIF, Apr 17, Oct
    6, 15, 22; 1730: LIF, Jan 2, Apr 6, 10, 17, 24, 29, Sep 25, Oct 27, Nov 10,
    Dec 15; 1731: LIF, Mar 15, Apr 3, 24, 26, 28, May 6, 19, 20, Oct 11, 13, Nov
    2, 6, 18, Dec 1; 1732: LIF, Feb 4, Mar 20, 23, Apr 18, 21, 22, 25, 27, 28,
    LIF/CG, Sep 25, Oct 4, Nov 13, 24, Dec 27, 28; 1733: LIF/CG, Jan 18, Feb 10,
    Mar 29, Apr 11, 18, May 3, CG, 4, LIF/CG, 14, 19, 21, CG, Sep 27, Oct 11, 13,
    20, Nov 28, Dec 7, 18; 1734: CG, Jan 1, 25, Feb 13, Mar 16, Apr 1, 16, 18,
    24, 27, May 1, 3, 4, 6, 13, BFRLCH, Aug 24, Sep 2, CG, 2, RI, 26, DL, 28, 30,
    Dec 12; 1735: DL, Jan 6, Mar 3, Apr 7, 21, Jun 9, Sep 6; 1736: CG, Mar 6, 18,
    Apr 12, 27, May 4, 6, 13, 18, Sep 17, Oct 8, 20, Nov 3, 22, 23, 26; 1737: CG,
    Jan 4, 10, 25, Feb 14, Mar 17, Apr 18, 21, May 31, Sep 21, 26, Oct 7, 26, Nov
    8; 1738: CG, Jan 3, 23, Feb 13, Mar 7, 14, Apr 11, 19, 21, May 5, 6, 15, Sep
    15, Oct 4, 6, 18, 28, Nov 18, Dec 9; 1739: CG, Mar 5, May 24, Aug 29, 31, Sep
    7, 21, 22, Oct 3, 25, 26, Nov 1, 7, Dec 1, 4, 14, 17, 18; 1740: CG, Jan 5,
    10, 15, Feb 12, Mar 18, Apr 16; 1741: GF, Feb 6, Apr 16, 23; 1742: CG, May
    12; 1743: SOU, Feb 18; 1745: CG, Jan 25, Apr 4, May 1, 6, Sep 27; 1746: CG,
    Apr 18, 29; 1747: CG, Dec 28; see also Legar
Laguerre, John (painter), 1748: CG, Mar 29, DL, 29
Laguerre, Mary, Mrs John (the first) (dancer), 1725: LIF, Apr 14, 20, 23, 28,
    May 4, 5, 11, 20, 22, Oct 1; 1726: LIF, Mar 10, 26, May 3, 12, Oct 3, 24, Nov
    14; 1727: LIF, Jan 7, 9, Feb 9, May 12, Sep 22, 27, 29, Oct 2, 12, 26, Nov 9;
    1728: LIF, Mar 9, Apr 29, May 13, 15, 20, 30, Sep 18; 1729: LIF, Jan 16, Feb
    6, Mar 20, Apr 17, 26, May 1, 3, Sep 24, Oct 15, 20, 22, Nov 1, Dec 17; 1730:
    LIF, Jan 2, 26, Mar 16, 17, Apr 8, 10, 17, 24, May 9, 11, 20, 25, Jun 4, Sep
    25, Oct 7, 9, 12, 19, 27, 30, Nov 3, 6, Dec 7, 15; 1731: LIF, Jan 11, 19, Mar
    15, 18, 22, Apr 1, 3, 21, 26, 28, 29, May 1, 5, 6, 7, 12, 13, 14, 19, 21, 24,
    26, 28, Jun 7, Sep 22, Oct 1, 4, 11, 13, 20, 27, Nov 6, 13, 18, 25, Dec 6, 7,
    14; 1732: LIF, Jan 5, 7, 22, 26, 28, Feb 7, Mar 9, 20, 30, Apr 10, 11, 12,
    13, 14, 17, 21, 24, 25, May 10, 13, 17, 24, 29, LIF/CG, Sep 25, 27, Oct 2, 4,

Nov 1, 8, 9, 13, 16, 24, Dec 8, CG/LIF, 19, LIF/CG, 28; 1733: LIF/CG, Jan 16,
23, Feb 2, CG, 8, LIF/CG, Mar 12, 15, 17, CG, 27, LIF/CG, 28, 29, 30, Apr 2,
11, 12, 16, 18, 23, CG, May 1, LIF/CG, 7, 8, 10, 14, CG, 16, 17, LIF/CG, 18,
21, 24, CG/LIF, 28, LIF/CG, 29, 31, Jun 1, CG, Sep 22, 25, Oct 4, 9, 13, 16,
18, 20, Nov 1, 16, Dec 7, 17; 1734: CG, Jan 25, Feb 26, Apr 1, 16, 19, 24,
27, 29, May 4, 6, DL, Oct 10, Dec 12; 1736: CG, Apr 27, Oct 8, 27, Nov 3, 9,
11, 23, Dec 13, 28; 1737: CG, Jan 7, Feb 14, Mar 7, 15, 17, 24, 26, 28, Apr
2, 12, 14, 15, 25, 26, 28, 29, May 9; 1739: CG, Mar 27
Laguerre, Mr and Mrs (actors), 1733: LIF/CG, Apr 18; 1734: CG, Apr 19
Laguerre, Mrs (actor), 1731: LIF, May 13
Laguerre, Mrs John (the second), 1749: BF/SFP, Aug 23; 1750: SOU, Mar 5
Lahante (dancer), 1794: KING'S, Mar 1, 4, 8, Apr 1, Dec 20; 1795: KING'S, Jan
20, Mar 26, Jun 20; 1796: KING'S, May 12, Jul 7, 12
LaHarpe, Jean Francois de, 1766: DL, Dec 13
--Conte de Warwick, Le, 1766: DL, Dec 13
Lahaussage (musician), 1770: KING'S, Mar 8, 22, 29
Lair (actor), 1744: DL, Feb 1
Laird and Highland Attendance Dance, Grand (dance), 1704: LIF, Apr 28
Laithfield (dancer), 1704: LIF, Jul 27
Lake, Warwick (spectator), 1697: DLDGLIF, Jan 22; 1698: DLORLIF, Feb 15
L'Alamaine (embroiderer), 1772: CG, Feb 21
LaLauze Jr (dancer), 1726: HAY, Apr 18, 25, 27, May 6, 9
LaLauze, Charles (dancer, ballet master, pantomime writer), 1726: HAY, Apr 14,
27, May 9; 1728: HAY, Feb 21, Mar 27; 1732: RIW/HAY, Sep 4, 8, 11, 12; 1734:
DL, Oct 23, Nov 1, 7, Dec 4, 9, 11, 12, 19; 1735: DL, Jan 17, 18, 21, 28, 29,
Feb 4, 5, 13, 14, 17, 22, 27, Mar 3, 10, 27, Apr 7, 11, 14, 15, 22, 25, May
2, 7, 14, Jun 9, CG, Oct 3, 6, 13, 15, 28, 31, Nov 11, 13, 19, 28, Dec 2, 12,
30, 31; 1736: CG, Jan 1, 2, 7, 9, 10, 14, 23, Feb 23, 26, Mar 6, 15, 16, 20,
22, 23, 25, 27, 29, 30, Apr 1, 5, 6, 8, 10, 12, 15, 17, 26, 27, 29, May 1, 3,
6, 8, 10, 11, 13, 17, 20, 25, Jun 4, Nov 9, 11, 26, Dec 6, 13, 28, 30; 1737:
CG, Jan 7, 24, 28, Feb 1, 14, Mar 7, 10, 14, 15, 17, 19, 24, 26, 28, 31, Apr
2, 11, 12, 14, 15, 19, 22, 25, 26, 28, 29, May 2, 3, 5, 6, 9, 12, 16, 31;
1738: CG, Feb 13, 20, Mar 13, 14, 16, 20, 21, 23, Apr 4, 5, 6, 7, 10, 11, 12,
15, 18, 19, 20, 21, 22, 24, May 2, 5, 6, 10, 15, Oct 28, Nov 18, Dec 9, 13;
1739: CG, Jan 20, Feb 9, 24, Mar 15, 20, 22, 26, 27, Apr 3, 9, 24, 25, 27,
30, May 1, 2, 3, 4, 9, 14, 17, 18, 21, 23, 24, 25, 28, 29, 30, DL, Nov 14,
16, 22, Dec 8, 10, 12, 14, 15, 19, 22; 1740: DL, Jan 15, Feb 9, 14, 16, 18,
Apr 10, 17, 18, 22, 26, 28, 29, May 2, 5, 7, 9, 12, 14, 15, 16, 17, 19, 20,
21, 22, 26, 28, 29; 1741: CG, Jan 21, Feb 17, 28, Apr 6, 24, Oct 15, 24, 27,
Nov 26, Dec 7, 8, 10, 12, 14, 21, 22; 1742: CG, Jan 5, 11, Mar 1; 1743: CG,
Feb 4, Apr 13, May 20, TCD/BFTD, Aug 4, CG, Dec 20; 1744: CG, Apr 6, 16, Oct
22, Nov 17, Dec 8; 1745: CG, Jan 14, 25, Mar 18, 28, Apr 2, 23, 24, May 4, 6,
7, 10, Oct 29, Dec 20; 1746: CG, Jan 1, Apr 14, Dec 19; 1747: CG, Mar 9, Apr
22, 23, 24, Dec 26; 1748: CG, Mar 3, Apr 20, Oct 27, Nov 16, Dec 26; 1749:
CG, Apr 12, Oct 24, Nov 23; 1750: CG, Jan 8, Feb 7, Apr 18, 25, Oct 29, Dec
21, 26; 1751: CG, May 1, Sep 30, Oct 28, Nov 11, 13; 1752: CG, Mar 30, Apr
15, Oct 10, 18, Nov 2, 28, Dec 7; 1753: CG, Apr 25, Dec 15; 1754: CG, May 1,
Nov 5; 1755: CG, Apr 23, Oct 22; 1756: CG, Apr 28, Oct 21; 1757: CG, Apr 27,
May 3, Oct 12; 1758: CG, Apr 19, Oct 6; 1759: CG, Apr 25, Nov 5, Dec 10;
1760: CG, Jan 16, Apr 23, Sep 22, Oct 15, 20; 1761: CG, Apr 22, May 25, Sep
25, Oct 10, 13; 1762: CG, Jan 28, Apr 28, Nov 1; 1763: CG, Apr 29; 1768: CG,
Dec 26; 1769: CG, Feb 13, Mar 7, Apr 29; 1770: HAY, Feb 14, CG, 15; 1771:
HAY, Mar 11, Apr 1, 24; 1776: CG, May 4; 1792: CG, Dec 20
LaLauze, Miss (dancer), 1759: CG, Apr 25; 1760: CG, Apr 23; 1761: CG, Apr 22;
1762: CG, Apr 28; 1763: CG, Apr 29; 1764: KING'S, Mar 29; 1769: CG, Apr 29;
1770: HAY, Feb 14; 1771: HAY, Mar 11, Apr 1; 1776: CG, May 4
LaLauze's scholar (dancer), 1742: CG, Apr 29; 1744: CG, Apr 7, 16; 1747: CG,
Apr 23; 1748: CG, Apr 20; 1749: CG, Apr 12; 1754: CG, May 1; 1763: CG, Apr 29
Lally, Edward (actor, dancer), 1719: DL, Nov 10; 1720: DL, Feb 1, 12, 29, Mar
15, Apr 5, 9, 19, 25, 26, May 9, 11, 12, 16, 17, 18, 21, 26, 27, 31, Jun 1,
2, Sep 13, 20, 27, Oct 6, 22, 25, 31, Nov 8, 23, Dec 7, 9; 1721: DL, Feb 7,
Mar 13, Apr 11, 12, 25, 29, May 1, 16, 22, 31, LIF, Oct 3, 17, Dec 14; 1722:
LIF, Mar 13, 29, 31, Apr 6, 10, 20, 24, 26, May 2, 7, 8, 10, 16 18, 25, Jun
1, Oct 16, 30, Nov 7, Dec 13; 1723: LIF, Feb 13, 19, Mar 25, Apr 29, May 18,
23, 24, 28; 1724: LIF, Oct 16, 23, 30, Nov 3, 10, 11, 13, 18; 1725: LIF, Jan
4, 18, 21, Mar 13, 18, 29, 31, Apr 7, 17, 20, 22, 26, 28, May 1, 7, 10, 12,
14, 17, 18, 19, 20, 21, 22, 24, Sep 29, Oct 1, 4, 13, 19, 21, 22, Nov 3, 8,
9, 11, 12, 13, 18, 22, 24, 29, 30, Dec 2, 8; 1726: LIF, Jan 3, 14, Mar 21,
Apr 18, 19, 21, 22, May 3, 16, 17, 19, 26, 30, Sep 14, 16, 23, 26, 30, Oct 5,
12, 24, 29, Nov 9, 21; 1727: LIF, Jan 9, 31, Jun 7
Lally, Michael (dancer), 1721: LIF, Oct 17; 1722: LIF, May 7, Oct 30, Nov 7,
Dec 13; 1723: LIF, Feb 13, 19, Mar 25, May 15, 18, 23; 1724: DL, Jan 27;

1725: DL, Feb 20, Sep 28, Oct 7, 25, Nov 16, 19, Dec 6, 16; 1726: DL, Jan 25,
Mar 21, 31, Apr 15, 23, 26, 27, 30, May 2, 3, 4, 13, 16, 18, 19, 23, 25, Oct
25, Nov 2, 15, 23, 30, Dec 7, 12, 14, 17, 30; 1727: DL, Feb 8, 10, 18, 27,
Mar 20, 23, Apr 12, 15, 17, 18, 19, 20, 25, 26, 27, 28, 29, May 2, 3, 4, 8,
10, 15, 17, 22, 24, 26, Sep 26, Oct 5, 6, 7, 12, 19, Nov 1, 9, 14, 18, 21;
1728: DL, Feb 21, 29, Mar 19, 28, Apr 4, 8, 11, 24, 25, May 1, 6, 7, 9, 10,
15, 16, 17, 23, Jun 13, Sep 12, 17, 19, 26, Oct 10, 18, 21, 24, 30, 31, Nov
15; 1729: DL, Jan 14, 27, Mar 22, 24, Apr 10, 22, 28, 30, May 1, 26, 28, Oct
9, Nov 3, Dec 8, 12, 26; 1730: DL, Jan 1, Apr 10, 11, 13, 14, 15, 16, 18, 22,
23, 24, 27, 29, 30, May 1, 4, 15, 19, Oct 1, 8, 10, 22, 28, Nov 19, 30, Dec
3, 4; 1731: DL, Jan 27, Apr 1, May 6, 7, Oct 16, 26, Nov 22, 25, Dec 15, 28;
1732: DL, Feb 2, 22, Mar 4, 21, Apr 18, 21, 22, 24, 26, 27, 29, May 10, 12,
25, Nov 8, 17, 20, Dec 22, 26; 1733: DL, Jan 23, Feb 12, Mar 26, 31, Apr 16,
20, 23, May 7, Oct 10, 12, 24, Nov 13, 21, 26, Dec 1, 5; 1734: DL, Feb 4, 13,
Mar 7, DL/LIF, 11, DL/HAY, 19, 23, 26, 30, DL/LIF, Apr 1, LIF, 15, DL, 15,
DL/HAY, 26, 27, DL, May 15, CG/LIF, Oct 2, Nov 18, 21, 29, Dec 14, 19, 30;
1735: CG/LIF, Jan 17, Feb 13, Mar 13, 15, 20, 22, 24, 25, Apr 8, 9, 10, 11,
14, 15, 24, 29, Jun 2, CG, Sep 26, Nov 6, 15; 1736: CG, Jan 21, 23, Apr 5,
26; 1737: CG, Mar 28; 1738: CG, Mar 21; 1739: CG, Mar 26; 1740: CG, Mar 24;
1741: CG, Mar 17; 1742: CG, Mar 30; 1743: CG, Apr 14
Lally, Samuel (dancer), 1728: DL, Mar 19, Apr 11, 24, May 3, 7, 8, 10, 22, Oct
18, 21, Nov 7, 8, 12; 1729: DL, Jan 14, 31, Mar 10, 25, 27, Apr 9, 10, 23,
28, 30, May 1, 2, 7, Jun 20, 24, Aug 7, Oct 9, Nov 3, Dec 12; 1730: DL, May
4, 15, Oct 28, Dec 4; 1731: DL, Apr 27, May 3, 5, 7, 10, 19, Oct 16, 26, Nov
22, 25, Dec 15; 1732: DL, Feb 22, Mar 21, Apr 18, 27, 28, May 2, 3, 12, 29,
Jun 6, 23, 28, Jul 4, 7, Oct 19, Nov 8, 17, Dec 14, 26; 1733: DL, Jan 23, Feb
12, Mar 26, 31, Apr 16, 20, 30, May 5, 7, Sep 26, Oct 10, 12, 17, 19, 24, Nov
2, 13, 23, 26, Dec 5; 1734: DL, Jan 22, Feb 4, Mar 7, DL/LIF, 11, DL/HAY, 12,
16, 18, 28, DL/LIF, Apr 1, DL/HAY, 1, LIF, 15, DL, 15, 22, 25, DL/HAY, 26,
27, DL, 29, DL/HAY, May 1, DL/LIF, 3, DL/HAY, 8, DL, 13, 15, DL/HAY, 22, 23,
LIF, 29, CG/LIF, Nov 29, Dec 14, 30; 1735: CG/LIF, Jan 13, 14, 17, Feb 3, 13,
Mar 15, 20, 24, 25, Apr 11, 14, 17, CG, Jun 24
Lally's brother (dancer), 1720: DL, May 21, 23; 1721: DL, May 23; 1722: LIF,
May 2
Lally's scholar (dancer), 1720: DL, Apr 5, 26, May 5, 26
LaLoge (dancer), 1728: LIF, Apr 30
Lalonese (tailor), 1775: DL, Dec 7
Lamash (LeMarsh), Philip (actor), 1773: HAY, May 19, Jul 21, 28, Aug 11, 27,
Sep 3; 1774: DL, Sep 29, Oct 5, 8, 24, Nov 5, 30; 1775: DL, Jan 2, 10, 18,
23, Mar 2, 18, Apr 19, May 1, 11, 12, 19, 27, Sep 30, Oct 11, 21, 28, Nov 6,
25, Dec 11; 1776: DL, Jan 23, Feb 10, 12, 26, Mar 7, 14, 18, 25, Apr 15, 17,
22, May 3, 11, 22, Sep 21, 26, Oct 9, 18, Nov 6, 9; 1777: DL, Feb 24, Apr 3,
7, 18, 22, May 8, 14, Sep 30, Oct 2, 14, 17, 18, 22, 31, Nov 4, 14, 19, 24,
29, Dec 3, 15; 1778: DL, Jan 17, 22, Feb 2, 10, Apr 7, 9, 20, May 8, HAY, 18,
22, Jun 1, 19, Jul 2, 11, 30, Aug 21, Sep 2, DL, 17, 19, 22, 26, 29, Oct 6,
15, 22, Nov 4, 6, 10, 14, Dec 21; 1779: DL, Jan 2, 5, 7, 26, Feb 20, Mar 13,
Apr 19, May 5, 6, 10, HAY, 31, DL, Jun 1, HAY, 2, 7, 9, 10, 18, Jul 1, 20,
Aug 6, 14, 24, DL, Oct 30, Nov 1, 17, 25, Dec 2, 4, 8, 9, 21, 30; 1780: DL,
Jan 11, 26, Apr 3, 4, 7, 14, 19, 21, 29, May 2, HAY, 30, Jun 3, 5, 13, 15,
17, 24, Jul 10, 24, Aug 4, 5, 24, Sep 2, DL, 16, 23, 26, Oct 5, 14, 20, Nov
15, 29; 1781: DL, Mar 10, 31, May 5, 8, 10, 24, HAY, 30, Jun 1, 7, 9, 12, 16,
Jul 6, 23, Aug 7, 21, DL, Sep 15, 25, 27, 29, Oct 6, 12, 16, 24, 27, Nov 13,
15, Dec 6; 1782: DL, Jan 3, 31, Apr 17, 27, May 11, Sep 17, 18, 20, 21, 24,
26, 28, Oct 1, 3, 5, 10, 14, 24; 1787: DL, Oct 2, 3, 6, 13, 26, Nov 6, 10,
22, 27, Dec 1, 7, 26; 1788: DL, Jan 2, 21, Apr 8, 14, 18, 21, 28, May 14, Oct
2, 4, 7, 23, Nov 5, 10, 14, 25, Dec 5; 1789: DL, Jan 26, Feb 16, Apr 21, May
7, Jun 2, 4, Sep 22, 26, Oct 1, 10, Dec 5, 10, 26; 1790: DL, Jan 19
Lamb (actor), 1774: HAY, Jan 24
Lamb (publishing house), 1747: NONE, Mar 27
Lamb, Charles (critic), 1782: HAY, Dec 30
Lamb, Margaret (bond holder), 1749: CG, Dec 20; 1759: CG, Oct 8; 1760: CG, Mar
15, Sep 22; 1761: CG, Apr 3, 28
Lamb, William (epiloguist), 1799: DL, May 24
Lamb's Conduit Fields, 1778: CG, May 16
Lamb's Conduit, 1742: DL, Apr 1
Lamball, Mrs (actor), 1739: DL, May 3; 1740: GF, Oct 31, Nov 18, Dec 1, 2, 10,
12; 1741: GF, Jan 20, 27, 29, Mar 3, Apr 9, 14; 1742: CG, May 7, JS, Oct 12;
1743: LIF, Apr 4, 8, BFHC, Aug 23
Lambe (decedant), 1764: HAY, Nov 13
Lambe, Widow (beneficiary), 1764: HAY, Nov 13
Lambert, George (scene painter), 1752: CG, Feb 1, 11; 1753: CG, Jan 13; 1757:
CG, Sep 14, Dec 5; 1758: CG, Mar 4; 1759: CG, Sep 24; 1760: CG, Feb 19, May

23, Sep 22; 1769: CG, Nov 4, 6; 1773: MARLY, Sep 3; 1789: CG, Dec 21; 1790:
CG, Nov 15; 1796: CG, Mar 15, Oct 24; 1799: CG, May 13
Lambeth St, 1746: GF, Mar 4, 10; 1747: GF, Mar 16
Lambeth Wells, 1698: LW, Jun 8, 29
Lambeth, 1788: DL, May 7; 1789: DL, May 22; 1790: DL, May 14; 1791: DL, May 12,
HAY, Aug 2, 26, Sep 16
Lame Lover, The. See Foote, Samuel.
Lamentation of Mary Queen of Scots (song), 1782: CG, Apr 9
Laments (music), 1791: CG, May 18
Lamercier, 1772: DL, Oct 10
Lamote (householder), 1733: LIF/CG, Mar 28
Lamotte, Franz (violinist), 1776: KING'S, Feb 15, CG, 23, 28, Mar 1, 6, 8, 20,
22, 27; 1777: CG, Feb 14, 19, Mar 19
LaMotte, Houdart de, 1734: GF/HAY, Dec 30; 1763: DL, Jan 19
--Ines de Castro; or, Royal Justice, 1734: GF/HAY, Dec 30; 1735: GF/HAY, Apr 10
Lamound (dancer), 1743: CG, Dec 20
Lamour (musician), 1707: YB, Apr 18
Lamp (ticket deliverer), 1789: CG, Jun 13; 1791: CG, Jun 9; 1792: CG, Jun 1
Lampe (beneficiary), 1729: HAY, Mar 7
Lampe, Isabella, Mrs John Frederick (singer), 1738: CG, Oct 9, Dec 9; 1739: CG,
Feb 9, Mar 20, Apr 28, May 8, Aug 29, 31, Sep 7, 21, Oct 10, 20, 31, Dec 1,
10, 14, 15, 17, 18; 1740: CG, Jan 1, 5, 15, Feb 12, Mar 18, Apr 30, Jun 5,
Sep 19, 26, Oct 1, 10, 22, Dec 16, 29; 1741: CG, Jan 5, Feb 16, 24, Mar 30,
Apr 10, 11, 18, Sep 28, 30, Oct 21, 24, Nov 26; 1742: CG, Jan 8, Apr 22, 30,
May 5; 1743: DL, Feb 2, 11, HAY, Mar 24, DL, Apr 14; 1744: CG, Jan 14, HAY,
19, CG, Feb 9, Mar 3, HAY, Apr 16, 19, CG, 21, Oct 1, 31, Dec 8, 29; 1745:
CG, Jan 1, 14, 25, HAY, Feb 14, CG, Apr 4, 25, Sep 27, Nov 14, 15, 23, Dec
13; 1746: CG, Jan 8, 25, Apr 18, Jun 27, Nov 4, 6, Dec 29, 31; 1747: DL, Mar
16, CG, 26, Nov 23; 1748: CG, Mar 14, 21, Apr 13; 1751: CG, Nov 11, Dec 9;
1752: CG, Jan 2, 7, 8, Feb 11, Mar 17, Apr 13, 18, Oct 10, 21, 26, 30, Dec 7,
8; 1753: CG, Jan 6, May 2, Oct 10; 1754: CG, Mar 25, Apr 17, 26, May 2, Nov
16, 20, Dec 30; 1755: CG, Apr 2, 9, 24, 28, Oct 20, Nov 17; 1756: CG, Apr 24,
May 6, Oct 4, 6, Dec 10; 1757: CG, Apr 22, 27, Dec 7, 10; 1758: CG, Feb 1,
Mar 13, Apr 13, 24, Nov 1, 23; 1759: CG, Apr 3, 7, 23, Nov 30; 1760: CG, Jan
16, 18, 31, Feb 11, Mar 27, Apr 8, 14, 17, 18, Sep 22, 29, Oct 3, 20, Dec 11;
1761: CG, Apr 2, 10, Sep 16, 25, 26; 1762: CG, May 4, 11, Sep 22, Oct 8, Nov
1, 15; 1763: CG, Jan 24, May 2, 17, Sep 21, Oct 3, 14, 21, Nov 15; 1764: CG,
Jan 3, 16, May 4, 21, Sep 21, Oct 1, 18, Nov 5, 7; 1765: CG, May 6, 11, Oct
3, 7, 9, 14, 22, Dec 6, 9, 23; 1766: CG, Apr 30, May 13, 19, Oct 21, HAY, 27,
CG, Nov 18, 21; 1767: CG, Jan 29, Feb 14, May 11, SW, 13, Jun 13, CG, Sep 19,
25, Oct 5, 9, 30, Nov 4, Dec 2; 1768: CG, Jan 20, Feb 13, May 7, Sep 26, Oct
5, 10, 17; 1769: CG, May 9, 25, Oct 6, Nov 7; 1770: CG, Jan 3, Mar 29, May
16, 26, Oct 8; 1771: CG, Mar 14, Apr 30, May 15, 30, Oct 25, Dec 11; 1772:
CG, Jan 27, Apr 9, May 21, Nov 2, Dec 26; 1773: CG, Mar 22, Apr 3, May 19,
Oct 23, Dec 13; 1774: CG, Feb 11, May 13, Oct 13; 1775: CG, May 4, Sep 25,
Oct 19; 1776: CG, May 4; 1781: CG, May 19; 1782: CG, May 10; 1783: CG, May
29; 1784: CG, May 11; 1786: CG, Jun 1; 1787: CG, Jun 2; 1788: CG, May 31;
1790: CG, Jun 8; 1794: CG, Jun 14
Lampe, John Frederick (singer, composer), 1732: HAY, Mar 13, Nov 14, 16, Dec
18; 1733: HAY, Feb 23, Mar 16, DL, Sep 26, Nov 7, 9, Dec 7, 13; 1734: DL, Jan
3, HIC, Apr 5, LIF, May 9, DL, 16, LIF, 16; 1736: DL, Sep 7; 1737: DL, Apr
29; 1739: CG, Mar 20; 1740: CG, Feb 12, Apr 30, BFLP, Aug 23; 1741: CG, Apr
18; 1743: HAY, Mar 24; 1744: HAY, Jan 19, 23, Apr 16; 1745: CG, Jan 25, Apr
3, 4, Sep 27, Oct 11, 14; 1746: CG, Jan 8; 1748: CG, Mar 14, Apr 13, HAY, Dec
9; 1749: CG, Oct 19, Dec 5; 1750: CG, Mar 26; 1751: CG, Dec 2, 9; 1752: CG,
Apr 20; 1754: CG, May 2; 1755: CG, Apr 28; 1756: CG, Apr 24; 1758: CG, Apr
13; 1760: CG, Sep 22; 1762: CG, Mar 30
--Britannia (opera), 1732: HAY, Nov 14, 16, 20, 23, 27; 1733: DL, Oct 3; 1734:
GF, Feb 12, 13, 14, 15, 16, 18, 19, 20, 21, 22, 23, 25, 26, 28, Mar 2, 4, 7,
9, 12, 14, 16, 21, 23, 26, 30, Apr 1, 2, 4, 6, 15, 16, 17, 22, 23, 25, 29,
May 2, 9, 23, Sep 26, 27, 30, Oct 1, 2, 3, 4, 5, 7, 9, 11, 17, Nov 19, 20,
21, 22, 25, 26, 27, 28, 29, Dec 11; 1735: GF, Apr 9, May 2, 3, 8, 9, Nov 7,
10, 11; 1736: GF, Apr 8, LIF, Dec 8, 9, 10, 11, 13, 14, 15, 16, 17, 18, 20,
21, 22, 27, 28, 29, 30
--Dione (opera), 1733: HAY, Feb 21, 23, 27, Mar 16
--Kiss Accepted and Returned (operetta), 1744: HAY, Apr 16, 19
--Orpheus and Eurydice (musical), 1740: CG, Feb 12, 13, 14, 15, 16, 18, 19, 21,
23, 25, 26, 28, Mar 1, 3, 4, 6, 8, 13, 15, 17, 22, 29, Apr 7, 8, 10, 11, 12,
15, 17, 19, 22, 24, 26, 29, May 1, 6, 8, 10, 15, 17, 22, 26, 28, 30, Jun 3,
10, 13, BF/WF/SF, Aug 23, 29, Sep 8, CG, Oct 10, 11, 13, 15, 16, 17, 18, 20,
21, 30, Nov 12, 14, 17, Dec 3, 6, 8, 18, 26, 27; 1741: CG, Jan 5, 6, 9, 16,
19, Feb 10, 16, 21, 24, Mar 14, 21, 31, Apr 4, 14, 15, 29, May 19, Oct 24,

26, 28, Nov 7, 9, 14, 16, 17, 19, 20, 21, Dec 19, 28, 29, 30; 1742: CG, Jan
2, 13, 20, 26, 29, Feb 5, 9, 11, 17, 19, 25, Mar 8, 16, 20, 23, 29, Apr 3, 8,
10, 19, 24, 27, 29, May 13; 1744: CG, Feb 14, 16, 18, 20, 21, 23, 25, 27, Mar
1, 10, 17, 27, May 21, 23; 1745: CG, Jan 1, 2, 4, 5, 7, 11, 18, 19, 23, Feb
9, 12, 13, 28, Mar 4, 9, 16, 23, 26, Apr 6, 19, 20, May 21, Nov 23, 25, 26,
27, 30, Dec 2, 6, 7, 10, 13, 19, 21, 23, 26, 28; 1746: CG, Jan 4, 7, 8, 16,
22, 29, 31, Feb 1, 11, 17, 22, Mar 8, 20, 22, 31, Apr 5, 25, 30, May 13, Dec
31; 1747: CG, Jan 1, 15, Feb 10, 26, 28, Mar 5, 9, 16, 17, 28, Apr 20, 25,
May 1, Dec 1; 1755: CG, Jan 29, 31, Feb 1, 3, 4, 5, 6, 7, 8, 10, 11, 13, 15,
17, 18, 20, 22, 24, 25, 27, Mar 1, 3, 4, 13, 20, 31, Apr 5, 12, 19, May 14,
22; 1756: CG, Jan 6, 7, 8, 9, 10, 13, 14, 23, 27, Feb 4, 17, 19, Mar 6, 9,
13, 18, Apr 19, 21, May 5, 12, 26, Oct 13, 14, 18, 20, 22, 26, 29, Nov 1, 5,
11, 16, 22, 23, 25, 27, 30, Dec 2, 4, 6, 9, 14, 16, 21, 27, 29; 1757: CG, Jan
4, 6, Oct 19, 20, 22, 24, 27, Nov 4, 8, 16, 17, 24, Dec 13, 28; 1758: CG, Jan
12; 1768: CG, Jan 6, 7, 8, 9, 11, 12, 13, 14, 15, 16, 18, 21, 23, 26, Feb 12,
23, Apr 14, 22, May 7, 26, 27, 30, Jun 3, Sep 20, 23, 29, Oct 6, 10, 14, 18,
20; 1775: CG, Oct 13, 16, 20, 23, 24, 25, 30, 31, Nov 1, 2, 6, 7, 24, Dec 1,
8, 15, 19; 1787: CG, Oct 15, 22
--Pyramus and Thisbe (mock opera), 1745: CG, Jan 23, 25, 26, 28, 29, 31, Feb 1,
2, 4, 5, 6, 7, 8, 11, Mar 2, 5, 12, 25, 30, Apr 16, 25, Sep 27, Oct 4, 11,
16, 28, 31, Nov 8, 19, 28, Dec 20; 1746: CG, Jan 14, 18, Feb 7, 18; 1748: CG,
Apr 13; 1751: CG, Dec 2, 9; 1752: CG, Apr 3; 1754: CG, May 2
--Queen of Spain, The; or, Fairinelli at Madrid (musical), 1744: HAY, Jan 19,
23, Apr 16, 19; 1745: HAY, Feb 14
--Sham Conjurer, The (masque), 1741: CG, Apr 18, 21, 22
Lampe, John Frederick and Isabella, 1748: CG, Sep 22
Lamplighter (dance), 1757: CG, Apr 29, May 4, 6, 12, 13, 16; 1760: CG, Mar 18,
22, 25, Apr 8, 9, 24, 25, 30, May 1, 2, 3, 5, 6, 7, 8, 15; 1764: DL, Oct 29,
31, Nov 5, 7, 14, Dec 12; 1765: DL, Feb 19; 1768: CG, Nov 1, 2, 8, 16, 17,
18, 21, 24, Dec 9; 1769: CG, Feb 2, 13, Apr 22, May 2, Oct 5, 20, 26, Dec 22;
1770: CG, Jan 18, 22, 24, Mar 26, Oct 9, 12, Nov 14; 1771: CG, Oct 16, 22,
29; 1772: CG, Feb 21; 1773: CG, Dec 7, 8, 29; 1774: CG, Feb 22, Nov 9, 10;
1796: CG, Jun 3
Lamplighter, The (song), 1790: CG, Apr 30, Nov 23; 1791: CG, Sep 19; 1794: CG,
Apr 12; see also I'm jolly Dick the Lamplighter
Lampoe (music), 1729: DL, Mar 26
Lampugnani, Giovanni Battista (composer), 1741: KING'S, Oct 31; 1742: KING'S,
Apr 20, Nov 2; 1743: KING'S, Nov 15; 1744: KING'S, Apr 24; 1745: CG, Apr 10;
1746: KING'S, Apr 15; 1747: KING'S, Feb 24; 1748: KING'S, Mar 8; 1749:
KING'S, Mar 21; 1754: KING'S, Nov 9; 1755: KING'S, Jan 14
--Alceste (opera), 1744: KING'S, Apr 24, 28, May 1, 5, 8, 11, 15, 19, 26, Jun
2, 5, 9, 16
--Alphonso (opera), 1744: KING'S, Jan 3, 7, 10, 14, 17, 21, 24, 28
--Demetrio (opera), 1744: KING'S, Apr 24
--Siroe (opera), 1755: KING'S, Jan 14, 18, 25, 28, Feb 1, 4, 8, 11, 15, Apr 5,
8, 15; 1756: KING'S, May 4, 8, 11, 15, 18, 22; 1763: KING'S, Dec 13, 17, 20,
22, 31; 1764: KING'S, Jan 3, 7, 21, 24, Feb 18, Apr 10; 1786: DL, Mar 10;
1787: DL, Feb 23; 1789: CG, Mar 6, DL, 18; 1790: DL, Feb 26; 1791: DL, Mar
23; 1792: KING'S, Feb 24; 1793: KING/HAY, Feb 22, Mar 22; 1794: CG, Mar 26;
1797: CG, Mar 22; 1798: CG, Mar 14; 1799: CG, Mar 13
Lancashire Hornpipe (dance), 1717: SF, Sep 25
Lancashire Witch (public house), 1742: JS, Apr 19
Lancashire Witches, The. See Shadwell, Thomas.
Lancashire, 1737: LIF, Mar 9
Lancetti (musician), 1733: LIF, May 7
Land of Enchantment, The (interlude, anon), 1785: CG, Apr 18, May 4
Land of Potatoes (song), 1793: CG, Apr 25, HAY, Aug 27; 1795: CG, Apr 28, May
7, 14; 1796: CG, Apr 5, 29; 1797: CG, May 9; 1799: CG, Apr 26
Landall (undertaker), 1772: DL, Jun 10; 1773: DL, Oct 29; 1774: DL, Jun 2;
1776: DL, Feb 13
Lane (actor), 1775: HAY, May 24, Jul 7, 14, 31, Aug 9, 28, Sep 18, 19, 20
Lane (dancer), 1675: ATCOURT, Feb 15
Lane (tailor), 1749: DL, Dec 8; 1750: DL, Jan 3, 19
Lane, Charlotte (dressmaker), 1755: CG, Sep 29, Oct 17, 24, Nov 1, 8, 15, 22,
29, Dec 5, 13
Lane, Mrs, 1747: CG, Mar 26
Lane, Sir Thomas (Lord Mayor), 1694: CITY, Oct 29
Lane, William (actor), 1791: HAY, Sep 26; 1792: HAY, Apr 16
Lane, William (publisher), 1790: CG, May 5; 1791: CG, Jan 12, Sep 23; 1792: CG,
Apr 18; 1793: HAY, Aug 12; 1794: HAY, Feb 8
Langbourn-Ward Coffee House, 1743: CG, Nov 17
Langford (tailor), 1771: DL, Nov 13

Langford, Abraham (composer), 1736: GF, Feb 10; 1753: CG, Apr 5; 1758: CG, Mar 7

--Lover His Own Rival, The, 1736: GF, Feb 10, 11, 12, 13, 16, 17, Mar 18, 25, 29, Apr 1, 6, 8, 13, 16, LIF, Jun 8, Dec 3; 1737: HAY, Mar 7, LIF, 24; 1743: MF, May 9, 10; 1753: CG, Apr 5, 28, 30, May 1, 7, 14, 15, 17, 18, Sep 10, 21, Oct 1, Nov 22, Dec 7, 19; 1754: CG, Oct 4, 28, Dec 5, 17; 1755: CG, Apr 1, Oct 21; 1756: CG, Jan 24, Apr 20, May 24, Oct 1; 1757: CG, Jan 7, Sep 28, Dec 12; 1758: CG, Feb 25

Langford, Robert (auctioneer), 1767: HAY, May 29; 1776: DL, Oct 9, 10, 15
Langlois (house servant), 1771: DL, May 21; 1776: DL, May 24, Jun 10
Langrish, Master (actor), 1781: CG, Jan 31, DL, Sep 18; 1782: CG, Jan 7, May 6
Langrish, Miss (actor), 1779: CG, Oct 11, Nov 1, Dec 7; 1780: CG, Jan 12, DL, Apr 10, CG, May 3, HAY, Aug 14, CG, Oct 9, DL, Oct 23, CG, Nov 15; 1781: DL, Jan 9, CG, 24, Mar 24, Apr 3, Nov 2; 1782: CG, Jan 7, Mar 19, Apr 27, May 6, 11, 21; 1783: HAY, Aug 19; 1785: HAY, Jun 3, 9, 13, 28, Aug 6, 16, 19, 26, Sep 16
Langrish, Timothy (dancer), 1767: CG, Jan 31; 1773: CG, Apr 26, 30, May 3; 1774: CG, Apr 16; 1775: CG, Apr 29, May 5, 6, 13, 29; 1776: CG, Jan 2, Oct 15; 1777: CG, Jan 22, Apr 25, May 13, Oct 21, Dec 29; 1778: CG, Jan 21, 28, Feb 23, May 2, Oct 22, Nov 27; 1779: CG, Apr 28, May 21, Sep 22, Oct 22, Nov 15, Dec 29; 1780: CG, Apr 1, May 6, Sep 18, 25, 27, Oct 11, 18; 1781: CG, Feb 13, May 1, Oct 20, 24, Dec 13; 1782: CG, Feb 21, Apr 1, 2, 27, May 17, 28
Laniere (beneficiary), 1725: HAY, Apr 7
Lanoe, Charles (renter), 1758: CG, Mar 4
Lansdowne, Lord. See Granville, George.
Lany (dancer), 1774: KING'S, Nov 8, 19, Dec 13; 1775: KING'S, Jan 17, Feb 7, Mar 23, Apr 4, 8, 18, 22, 25, 27, Jun 6, 17, 24
Lanyon (Lanyam) (actor, dancer), 1723: LIF, Mar 25, May 22, Oct 19, Nov 2, 27, Dec 9, 11, 12, 20; 1724: LIF, Jan 4, Mar 2, 14, Apr 6, 7, 10, 27, May 2, 4, 8, 12, 13, 15, 16, 18, 22, 26, 27, 28, Jun 2, 3, Sep 25, 28, 30, Oct 5, 9, Nov 6; 1725: LIF, Jan 21, Mar 13, 31, Apr 17, May 6, Oct 21, 27, Nov 3, 13, 30, Dec 2; 1726: LIF, Jan 14, Apr 21, 30, May 3, 10, Sep 16, 23, 26, 30, Oct 3, 5, 24, 29, Nov 2, 9, 14, 21, Dec 3; 1727: LIF, Jan 31, Feb 13, 27, Sep 20, 22, 29, Oct 12, 27, Nov 7, 9, 17, Dec 19; 1728: LIF, Mar 14, Apr 22, May 6, 11, 15, 20, 22, 23, Sep 30, Oct 9, 14, 26, Nov 23; 1729: LIF, Jan 16, 18, 31, Feb 6, Apr 22, Oct 3, 10, 15, 24, 28, Nov 1, 4; 1730: LIF, Jan 2, Apr 10, 25, May 9, 14, Sep 21; 1741: GF, Apr 9
Laoeudaimonos; or, A People Made Happy (masque, anon), 1789: DL, May 19
LaPierre (dancer), 1740: DL, Oct 27, 31, Nov 17, Dec 4, 10; 1741: DL, Mar 17, Apr 9; 1742: DL, Sep 21, LIF, Dec 3, 6, 13, 27; 1743: LIF, Jan 7, BFFP, Aug 23
Lapper (actor, dancer), 1770: HAY, Oct 5; 1779: HAY, May 10
LaPrue (dancer), 1729: HAY, Jun 11
Lapthorne, Richard (spectator), 1691: BF, Aug 8
Larbor, 1767: DL, Jun 1
Larevier. See LaRiviere.
Larfay (beneficiary), 1725: LIF, May 22
Large Room, 1753: BFSY, Sep 3, 5, 6
Largeau, Master (actor), 1756: DL, Dec 3
LaRiviere (dancer), 1765: KING'S, Jan 5, CG, May 9; 1766: CG, Dec 9, 15; 1767: CG, Feb 21, Oct 5, 24, 29; 1774: DL, Nov 5; 1775: DL, Apr 3, 28, Dec 4, 19; 1776: DL, Apr 15, Jun 10
LaRiviere, Mme (dancer), 1767: CG, Mar 16
Lark Concerto (song), 1757: HAY, Sep 12
Lark, The (song), 1785: DL, Apr 8
Lark's Shrill Note (song), 1762: DL, May 11; 1766: DL, Apr 21, 26
Larken, Edmund (beneficiary), 1744: SH, Feb 9
Larkin (actor), 1756: DL, Aug 12; 1771: DL, Apr 17; 1772: CG, May 12
Larkman (boxkeeper), 1794: CG, Jun 12; 1795: CG, Jun 4; 1796: CG, Jun 3; 1797: CG, May 27; 1798: CG, May 29; 1799: CG, May 21; 1800: CG, Jun 4
Larks awake the drowsy morn, The (song), 1682: DL, Mar 0
L'Armand, (dancer), 1749: BFY, Aug 23
L'Armand, Mme (dancer), 1749: BFY, Aug 23
LaRoche, James (singer), 1695: LIF, Dec 0; 1696: LIF, Mar 0, Nov 14; 1697: LIF, Jun 0, ATCOURT, Nov 4
LaRoche, Mme (musician), 1677: ATCOURT, May 22
LaRoche, Mrs (actor), 1767: CG, Nov 4, Dec 12, 22
Laroon, F (actor, singer), 1702: DL, Dec 8; 1703: DL, Jan 23, Feb 1, 12; 1704: YB, Mar 29; 1706: QUEEN'S, Mar 7
Larpenini (singer), 1767: KING'S, Mar 21
Larpent, John (?) Francis, 1760: DL, Oct 13
Larry Grogon (dance), 1739: DL, Dec 7; 1740: DL, May 21
Lascelles, Colonel, 1770: CG, Nov 8

Lascelles, Miss (actor), 1800: CG, Jun 3
Lascells (Lassels) (actor), 1736: LIF, Mar 29, GF, May 5; 1741: CG, Jan 27, Apr
    1, Sep 25, Nov 11, 23, 30, Dec 9, 18
Lascells, Thomas (beneficiary), 1735: CG/LIF, May 14
Laschi, Anna (actor), 1748: KING'S, Nov 8; 1749: KING'S, Apr 22
Laschi, Filippo (singer), 1748: KING'S, Nov 8; 1749: KING'S, Feb 28, Mar 21;
    1750: KING'S, Mar 20, 27, 31, Apr 10; 1757: HAY, Jun 17, Jul 5
Lascia cadermi in Volto (song), 1741: DL, Oct 24; 1742: DL, Feb 3
Lascia giacer sul prato (song), 1757: KING'S, Mar 24
Lasciar t'amato bene (song), 1754: KING'S, Feb 28
Lass of Patie's Mill (song), 1727: LIF, Mar 13, Apr 7, May 3; 1728: LIF, Mar 28
Lass of Richmond Hill (song), 1790: DL, May 19, 25
Lass of the Mill (song), 1753: DL, Mar 27, 29, May 18
Lass that was Laden with Care (song), 1760: CG, May 6
Lass there lives upon the green, A (song), 1695: DL, Nov 0
Lassells, Mrs (actor), 1691: DL, Mar 0, Apr 0; 1692: DL, Jan 0, Mar 0; 1693:
    DL, Mar 0, Apr 0; 1697: LIF, Jun 0
Lassy (dancer), 1760: CG, Sep 22
Last of the Family, The. See Cumberland, Richard.
Last Shilling (song), 1800: CG, May 7
Last Time I Cam o'er the Moor (song), 1762: HAY, Apr 28
Last Whitsunday they brought me (song), 1796: DL, Apr 2
Late Revolution, The; or, The Happy Change (play, anon), 1689: NONE, Sep 0
Late Theatre, 1740: GF, Oct 15
Late Wells, 1745: GF, Mar 11, 12, 14, Apr 19, 23, May 2, Oct 28; 1746: GF, Oct
    27, 28
Lathbury (house servant), 1743: DL, May 24; 1745: DL, May 9; 1746: DL, May 16;
    1747: DL, May 14
Latille, Gaetano (composer), 1748: KING'S, Nov 29; 1749: KING'S, Jan 21; 1755:
    KING'S, Mar 17
--Finta Cameriera, La (opera), 1749: KING'S, Jan 21
--Madame Ciana (opera), 1750: KING'S, Jan 13, 16, Feb 3, HAY, Apr 18, 19, 21
--Orazio (opera), 1748: KING'S, Nov 29, Dec 3, 6, 10, 13, 17; 1749: KING'S, Jan
    14, 17, Feb 21, Mar 7, Jun 10
Latimer, Lord. See Osborne, Edward.
Latin Prologue (entertainment), 1749: HAY, May 27, Jun 24
Latin school, 1679: CS, Dec 17
Latin Song (song), 1688: DL, May 12; 1701: RIW, Aug 11; 1715: SH, Jun 30
LaTour (musician), 1703: DL, Apr 19; 1704: YB, Apr 28; 1706: YB, Feb 12; 1707:
    YB, Apr 18; 1800: KING'S, May 29
LaTour, Miss (dancer, actor), 1725: LIF, Oct 26, Nov 2, 8, 11, 18, 24, Dec 3;
    1726: LIF, Jan 5, Mar 31, Apr 21, 29, May 3, 11, 12, 16, 17, 19, 24, 25, 26,
    30, Oct 19; 1727: LIF, Feb 13, Apr 21, 27, May 9, Jun 7, Nov 9; 1728: LIF,
    Apr 22, 30, May 6, 11, 15, 22, 23, 30, Jun 25, Oct 14, 26, Nov 8, 23; 1729:
    LIF, Jan 16, 18, Feb 6, Mar 20, 27, Apr 8, 12, 19, 22, 26, May 8, Oct 15, 22,
    24, Nov 1, 4; 1730: LIF, Jan 2, Mar 17, Apr 8, 10, 25, 27, 29, 30, May 1, 4,
    11, 15, 23, 27, 28, Sep 23, 25, Oct 1, 7, 9, 19, 27, 30, Nov 3, 7, Dec 7, 12,
    15; 1731: LIF, Jan 4, Apr 3, 8, 22, 28, May 1, 3, 6, 7, 10, 17, 31, Jun 2, 7,
    Sep 20, 22, Oct 4, 11, 13, 15, 20, Nov 2, 6, 8, 12, 13, 18, 25, Dec 7, 14,
    17; 1732: LIF, Feb 9, Apr 10, 22, 25, 26, May 1, 5, 16, 26, LIF/CG, Sep 27,
    Oct 2, 4, 13, 16, LIF, 18, LIF/CG, 25, Nov 8, 16, 25, Dec 4, 8, 12, 15,
    CG/LIF, 16, 19, LIF/CG, 27; 1733: CG/LIF, Jan 4, LIF/CG, 11, 12, 15, 18, 19,
    23, 27, 31, Feb 2, 5, 6, CG, 8, LIF/CG, Mar 12, CG, 27, LIF/CG, 28, Apr 11,
    12, 16, 18, 23, 30, CG, May 1, LIF/CG, 3, 7, 8, CG, 11, LIF/CG, 14, CG, 16,
    Oct 16, 27, DL/HAY, 27, Nov 12, 17, HAY, 19, DL/HAY, 23, 24, 26, 28, Dec 1,
    3, HAY, 13, DL/HAY, 20, 31; 1734: DL/HAY, Jan 1, 2, 10, 16, Feb 4, 6, 20, Mar
    9, 12, 16, 19, Apr 2, DL, 4, 22, DL/HAY, 26, 27, DL, 29, DL/HAY, May 1, 22,
    23, LIF, 29
Latourdy (dancer), 1705: DL, Nov 7
Latter, Mrs, 1761: CG, Mar 10
Lauchery (dancer), 1755: DL, Nov 3, 4, 8; 1761: DL, Nov 19, 28; 1762: DL, Jan
    27, Feb 3, Mar 25, Oct 7, 15, 22, 29, Nov 23; 1763: DL, Jan 3, Feb 24, Apr 6,
    May 31, Oct 4, 28, Dec 1, 17, 26; 1764: DL, Jan 23, Feb 24, Mar 19, Apr 5,
    25, Oct 9, 29, Nov 2, 10, Dec 14; 1765: DL, Jan 7, 18, Feb 8, Mar 30, May 14;
    1773: DL, Dec 9; 1774: DL, Sep 27, Nov 18, Dec 16, 19; 1775: DL, Feb 2, Sep
    30, Oct 7, Nov 1; 1776: DL, Jun 10
Lauda, The (song), 1759: CG, May 4
Lauder (singer), 1752: HAY, Mar 7, Apr 15; 1753: HAY, Apr 14; 1754: HAY, Feb 2,
    5, Mar 28, Aug 27, Sep 10, HAY/SFB, 26, Oct 1, HAY, Nov 28; 1755: HAY, Jun
    30; 1756: HAY, Apr 8, 19, Jun 3; 1757: HAY, Apr 22, Aug 22, 31, Sep 2, 5, 8,
    14, 23, 28, Oct 3; 1758: HAY, Jan 25, 27, Mar 13, Apr 28, May 18; 1759: HAY,
    Jun 8; 1760: HAY, Feb 21, Sep 1, 8, Dec 19; 1761: HAY, Mar 9, May 11, Dec 16;

1762: HAY, Feb 19, Apr 28, Jul 28, Sep 17, Dec 8; 1763: HAY, Mar 8, May 3,
      Sep 15; 1764: HAY, Apr 9, Sep 17, Dec 12; 1765: HAY, May 16; 1766: HAY, May
      19; 1768: HAY, Feb 22; 1769: HAY, Feb 27, Dec 18
Lauder, Widow (beneficiary), 1772: HAY, Sep 21, Dec 21
Lauderdale, Lord. See Maitland.
Laudermey, Miss (actor), 1792: HAY, Nov 26
Laugh and a Cry (song), 1790: CG, Apr 6
Laugh When You Can. See Reynolds, Frederick.
Laughing Bacchanalian (dance), 1771: HAY, Aug 12
Laughing Song (song), 1788: CG, Feb 5; 1791: DL, Mar 25; 1800: CG, May 28, Jun
      13
Laundress's Visiting Day (dance), 1746: DL, Dec 27, 29, 31; 1747: DL, Jan 2, 5,
      8, 12, 14
Laura et Lenza (dance), 1800: KING'S, May 8, 13, 24, Jun 19, 24, 28, Jul 1, 8,
      15, 26, Aug 2
Laurence, French (lawyer, versifier), 1787: DL, Apr 20
Laurent (dancer), 1799: CG, May 28
Laurenti, Marianna (singer), 1790: HAY, Jan 7, Feb 2
Lauretta (dance), 1790: HAY, Apr 22
Lavenu, Lewis (violinist), 1791: CG, Mar 30; 1792: CG, Feb 24; 1793: CG, Feb
      15; 1794: CG, Mar 7; 1795: CG, Feb 20, 27; 1796: CG, Feb 17; 1797: CG, Mar 3;
      1798: CG, Feb 23; 1799: CG, Feb 8
Laver, Mrs (singer), 1797: HAY, Jan 23
Laving (dancer), 1705: DL, Dec 17
Law (confectioner), 1750: DL, Nov 28
Law against Lovers, The. See Davenant, Sir William.
Law of Lombardy, The. See Jephson, Robert.
Law, William (divine), 1773: DL, Jan 1
Lawder (actor), 1734: GR, Nov 4
Lawley (beneficiary), 1743: DL, May 24
Lawr, Mrs (actor), 1775: CG, May 11, Oct 13; 1776: CG, May 11
Lawrence (actor), 1743: TCD/BFTD: Aug 4
Lawrence (actor), 1785: DL, Dec 1; 1787: DL, Jan 13, HAY, Jun 23, Jul 19, 21,
      23, 27, Aug 7, 28, Sep 8
Lawrence (actor, singer), 1706: QUEEN'S, Mar 7, Jun 29, LIF/QUEN, Jul 6, Aug
      21; 1707: DL, Feb 24, Mar 4, Apr 1, Oct 21, 29, Nov 25, 28, 29, Dec 4, 10,
      17, 18, 27, 30; 1708: DL, Jan 3; 1709: QUEEN'S, Mar 2, SH, Aug 25, HA, Sep 3;
      1710: QUEEN'S, Jan 10, SH, Mar 22, QUEEN'S, 23, YB, Apr 17; 1711: QUEEN'S,
      Jan 10, Feb 24, RIW, Jul 21, QUEEN'S, Dec 12; 1712: SH, Mar 6, Apr 4; 1713:
      SH, Mar 23; 1714: QUEEN'S, Jan 27, Mar 4; 1715: KING'S, Feb 26, LIF, Apr 30;
      1716: KING'S, Apr 18, LIF, Oct 29; 1717: LIF, Oct 31, Nov 12, Dec 27
Lawrence (boxkeeper), 1719: LIF, May 13; 1721: LIF, May 25; 1722: LIF, May 21;
      1723: LIF, May 20; 1724: LIF, May 16; 1725: LIF, May 19; 1726: LIF, May 14;
      1728: LIF, May 30; 1729: LIF, May 22; 1730: LIF, Jun 1; 1731: LIF, Jun 2;
      1732: LIF, May 15; 1735: CG/LIF, May 22; 1737: CG, May 9; 1738: CG, May 12;
      1739: CG, May 25; 1740: CG, May 21; 1741: CG, May 5; 1742: CG, May 7; 1743:
      CG, May 3; 1744: CG, May 11; 1745: CG, May 13; 1746: CG, May 3; 1747: CG, May
      16, 20; 1748: CG, May 4; 1749: CG, Apr 29; 1750: CG, May 3; 1751: CG, May 13;
      1752: CG, May 6; 1753: CG, May 18; 1754: CG, May 21; 1755: CG, May 19; 1756:
      CG, May 18; 1757: CG, May 10
Lawrence (glockenspiel player), 1796: CG, Jun 2; 1797: CG, May 18
Lawrence (paper hanger), 1766: DL, Nov 3; 1771: DL, Dec 12; 1773: DL, Mar 1,
      Dec 2; 1774: DL, Nov 18; 1776: DL, Apr 11
Lawrence, Sir John (Lord Mayor), 1664: CITY, Oct 29
Lawrence, Miss (dancer), 1770: CG, Mar 22; 1772: CG, May 1
Lawrence, Thomas (actor), 1784: DL, Aug 20
Laws (actor), 1741: GF, Oct 9; 1746: GF, Mar 22; 1747: GF, Mar 26
Laws of Candy, The. See Fletcher, John.
Lawson (actor), 1693: DL, Apr 0
Lawson (musician), 1744: CG, Apr 26, HAY, Nov 5; 1748: CG, Apr 26
Lawson, Abigail (actor), 1692: DL, Jan 0; 1694: DL, Sep 0; 1695: LIF, Apr 30,
      Sep 0, Dec 0; 1696: LIF, Mar 0, Oct 0, Nov 14, Dec 0; 1697: LIF, May 0, Jun
      0, ATCOURT, Nov 4; 1698: LIF, Mar 0; 1699: LIF, May 0; 1701: LIF, Jan 0;
      1702: LIF, Dec 31; 1703: LIF, Feb 0, Mar 0; 1704: LIF, Dec 4
Lawson, Mrs (actor), 1755: DL, Nov 8, 15
Lawson, Mrs (actor), 1794: HAY, May 22
Lawton, Mrs (actor), 1703: LIF, Nov 0
Lawyer Nonsuited, The (farce, anon), 1782: HAY, May 6
Lawyer, The. See Williamson, James Brown.
Lawyer's Feast, The. See Ralph, James.
Lawyer's Panic, The. See Dent, John.
Lax (dancer), 1715: LIF, Mar 1; 1719: LIF, Oct 5, 27

Lax, Mrs (dancer), 1738: SFH, Sep 5; 1740: BFLP, Aug 23
Laye (musician), 1726: IT, Feb 2
Layfield (actor), 1750: DL, Nov 3, 13, 15, 30, Dec 6, 26; 1751: DL, Apr 27, May
   2, 6
Layfield, Lewis (actor, dancer), 1704: LIF, Jul 10, Aug 17; 1706: QUEEN'S, Jan
   8, 14, 17, 22, 23, LIF/QUEN, 25, QUEEN'S, Feb 2, 4, 9, Mar 25, Apr 20, 30,
   Jun 29, LIF/QUEN, Aug 10, HAW, 17; 1709: DL, Dec 15, 30; 1710: DL, Jan 12,
   14, 31, Feb 4, 11, Mar 11, 14, 25, Apr 12, May 23, 26, GR, Aug 12; 1711: PH,
   Mar 1; 1728: HAY, Oct 26, Nov 19
Layfield, Mrs (actor), 1728: HAY, Dec 7, 10
Layley (house servant), 1775: CG, May 30
Lazzarini, Gustavo (singer), 1791: PAN, Feb 17, Mar 1, Apr 14, May 14, Jun 2,
   16, Dec 17, 31; 1792: HAY, Feb 14, 28, Mar 31, Apr 12
L'Cler (musician), 1751: DL, Apr 11, 16
L'Clert (dancer), 1755: DL, Nov 8
L'Contri, Mlle. See DeLaCointrie, Mme.
Lea Church, 1762: DL, Sep 21
Leach (actor, singer), 1779: HAY, Oct 18; 1780: CII, Feb 29, Mar 6, 13, 17, 27,
   Apr 5, 19
Leach (beneficiary), 1746: DL, Apr 23
Leach, Mrs M (actor), 1800: HAY, Aug 15
Leacy, Mrs (actor), 1727: LIF, Dec 11
Lead House, 1745: GF, Feb 26
Leadbetter (beneficiary), 1726: LIF, May 16
Leadenhall St, 1663: BF, Aug 25; 1787: HAY, Mar 12
Leak, Elizabeth (actor, singer), 1793: KING/HAY, Feb 15, 20, 22, 27, Mar 6, 13,
   20; 1794: HAY, Jan 21, Feb 11, 24, DL, Mar 12, 19, 26, Apr 2, 4, 9, 10, 11,
   21, 25, 28, May 2, 8, 16, 19, Jun 9, Jul 2, HAY, 8, 14, 17, 18, 21, 22, 24,
   26, Aug 1, 4, 12, 18, 23, 27, 29, Sep 3, DL, 16, HAY, 17, DL, 23, 27, Oct 7,
   14, 27, 31, Nov 15, Dec 12, 20, 30; 1795: DL, Jan 21, 27, KING'S, Feb 20, DL,
   24, KING'S, 27, Mar 13, DL, 14, Apr 16, May 1, 2, 4, 6, 21, 27, 29, 30, Jun
   3, HAY, 9, 10, 11, 13, 15, 20, Jul 6, 16, 20, 30, 31, Aug 14, 21, 25, 29, Sep
   1, 2, DL, 19, 24, 26, 29, Oct 1, 8, 30, Nov 2, 11, 23, Dec 2, 10; 1796: DL,
   Jan 11, 18, Feb 1, CG, 12, 17, 19, 26, DL, Mar 3, 7, CG, 16, DL, 19, 28, Apr
   2, 13, 25, 30, May 11, 13, 25, 27, 30, 31, Jun 1, 8, 9, HAY, 11, 13, 14, 15,
   22, 25, Jul 1, 2, 5, 8, 14, 15, Aug 23, 30, Sep 1, DL, 24, 27, 29, Oct 1, 6,
   10, Nov 5, 28, Dec 6, 10; 1797: DL, Jan 7, 20, Feb 7, 17, 21, 22, 24, 27, Mar
   6, 23, May 1, 12, 13, 17, 20, 23, 31, Jun 6, 14, Sep 26, Oct 7, 16, 30, 31,
   Nov 7, 8, 21, 24, Dec 9, 11, 20; 1798: HAY, Jan 15, DL, Feb 13, 16, 20, Mar
   22, 24, Apr 28, May 7, 23, 24, 31, Jun 5, Sep 15, 18, 27, Oct 2, 6, 11, 15,
   16, 31, Nov 1, 3, 22, Dec 3, 21; 1799: DL, Jan 8, HAY, 24, DL, Mar 26, Apr 4,
   5, 16, May 7, 9, 13, 24, Jun 28, Nov 6, 7, 13, 14, 20, 22, 27, Dec 11; 1800:
   DL, Mar 4, 6, 10, Apr 1, 16, 29, May 29, Jun 3
Leander (musician), 1770: MARLY, Aug 21
Leander, Lewis Henry (French horn player), 1792: CG, Feb 24; 1793: CG, Feb 15,
   Mar 20; 1798: CG, Feb 28
Leander, Lewis Henry and Vincent Thomas (French horn players), 1784: HAY, Apr
   27; 1790: CG, Feb 19; 1791: CG, Mar 11; 1795: KING'S, Jun 16
Leanerd, John
--Counterfeits, The, 1678: DG, May 28
--Country Innocence, The; or, The Chamber-Maid Turn'd Quaker, 1677: DL, Mar 0
--Rambling Justice, The; or, The Jealous Husbands, 1678: DL, Feb 0; 1693: NONE,
   Sep 0
Leap over Fourteen Men (entertainment), 1719: KING'S, Mar 7
Leap over Man upon a large Coach Horse (entertainment), 1719: LIF, Feb 5,
   KING'S, Mar 5
Leap over 12 Hoops (entertainment), 1719: KING'S, Mar 2
Leap over 16 Naked Swords (entertainment), 1719: KING'S, Mar 12
Leap through a Cask on Fire (entertainment), 1780: CG, May 6; 1783: CG, May 23
Leap through a Cask stopped at both Ends (entertainment), 1719: KING'S, Mar 19
Leap through a Hogshead of Real Water (entertainment), 1794: CG, Jun 13
Leap through a Tub of Fire (entertainment), 1784: DL, May 7
Leap through a Wheel of Fireworks (entertainment), 1797: CG, Jun 5
Leap Year (dance), 1784: CG, Oct 22, Nov 10, 24; 1785: CG, Apr 16, May 16, Oct
   10, 19, Dec 8; 1786: CG, Feb 18, 27, May 11, 13, Oct 6; 1787: CG, Apr 25, 27,
   Sep 26; 1788: CG, Jan 28; 1789: CG, Mar 5
Lear (actor), 1778: CHR, Jun 22, 24, 26
Leary (householder), 1777: KING'S, May 1; 1778: KING'S, May 28
Leave, leave these useless arts (song), 1692: NONE, Sep 0
Lebeck's Head Coffee House, 1746: CG, Jan 24
LeBlanc (dancer), 1733: BFCGBH, Sep 4; 1734: GF, Apr 27
LeBlanc, Mlle (spectator), 1661: LIF, Nov 15

LeBlanc, Mrs (actor), 1777: DL, May 28
Leblond (dancer), 1735: YB/HAY, Sep 17
LeBoeuf (dancer), 1783: CG, Oct 9; 1784: CG, Apr 17, May 8
LeBreton (choreographer), 1774: KING'S, May 5
LeBrun (actor, dancer), 1717: KING'S, Mar 30, DL, Oct 12; 1726: HAY, May 9;
    1732: DL, Nov 17, Dec 18, 22; 1733: DL, Mar 10, 31, Apr 4, 24, May 1, 2, 5,
    9, 18, 21, 24, BF, Aug 23, BFFH, Sep 4, DL, 26, Oct 10, 12, 15, 17, 19, 22,
    24, 27, 31, Nov 2, 13, 21, 23, 26, Dec 5, 7, 13, 26, 31; 1734: DL, Jan 28,
    31, Feb 4, Mar 7, DL/LIF, 11, DL/HAY, 12, 18, 25, 28, 30, Apr 1, 6, DL, 15,
    22, DL/HAY, 26, DL, 29, DL/HAY, May 1, 3, DL, 15, DL/HAY, 22, 23, LIF, 29,
    DL, Sep 10, 12, 19, 26, Oct 5, 8, 9, 10, 21, 22, 26, Nov 1, 7, 16, 19, 22,
    Dec 4, 9, 11, 12; 1735: DL, Jan 16, 17, 20, 21, 22, 28, 29, Feb 4, 5, 13, 14,
    15, Mar 3, 29, Apr 7, 11, 14, 15, 16, 18, 21, 22, 25, May 1, 2, 5, 6, 7, 8,
    9, 14, 20, 22, 23, 29, Jun 3, 11, Jul 1, Sep 1, 15, 25, 30, Oct 4, 7, 31, Nov
    3, 6, 12, 13, 15, 19, 20, Dec 17, 18, 22, 26, 27; 1736: DL, Jan 3, 5, 6, 9,
    12, Feb 28, Mar 3, 20, 23, 27, 29, Apr 5, 6, May 3, Sep 7; 1738: TC, Aug 7,
    BFP, 23, SFH, Sep 5; 1756: DL, May 20; 1757: DL, May 18
LeBrun, Francesca, Mrs Ludwig August (singer), 1778: KING'S, Jun 13, 20; 1779:
    KING'S, Nov 27, Dec 14; 1780: KING'S, Jan 22, Mar 9, Apr 22, 27, May 31, Dec
    23; 1781: KING'S, Jan 23, Mar 8, 15, 29, Apr 3
LeBrun, Ludwig August (oboist), 1778: KING'S, Feb 7, Mar 6, 19, Apr 4; 1780:
    KING'S, Jan 22; 1781: KING'S, Mar 15, 25; 1782: KING'S, Jan 26, Feb 23, Apr
    11, Jun 14, 16
LeBrun, Mrs (dancer), 1726: HAY, Apr 20, May 9; 1736: CG, Oct 8, Nov 3, 9, 11,
    26, Dec 13; 1737: CG, Jan 7, Feb 14, Mar 7, 15, 17, 19, 26, 28, Apr 12, 15,
    25, 26, 28, 29, May 5, 9, 12; 1738: CG, Feb 13, Mar 16, 20, Apr 10, 12, 20,
    27, 28, 29, May 2, 3, 6, 8, 11, 12, 15, 16, TC, Aug 7, BFP, 23, SFH, Sep 5,
    CG, Oct 26, 28, 30, Nov 18, Dec 9; 1739: CG, Jan 3, 6, 18, 20, Feb 15, Mar 5,
    Apr 9, May 5, 8, 21, 23, Sep 22, Oct 3, 15, Dec 4, 10; 1740: CG, Feb 12, Mar
    25, May 7, 9, 14, 29, Oct 10, 29, Dec 29; 1741: CG, Jan 5, Feb 24, Oct 24,
    30, Nov 7, 26, Dec 15, 28, 30; 1742: CG, Jan 2, 8, 21, 25, Feb 22, Mar 23,
    Apr 30, May 5, 10, Oct 1, 25, Nov 2, Dec 21; 1743: CG, Mar 8, May 4, Oct 3,
    Dec 20; 1744: CG, Jan 14, Feb 14, Mar 3, Apr 6, 28, Oct 10, 22, Dec 8; 1745:
    CG, Jan 1, 14, May 2, 7, Nov 14, 23; 1746: CG, Apr 30, May 13, Jun 13, Dec
    31; 1747: CG, May 15
LeCharmante, Mme (actor), 1736: HAY, Apr 29; see also Beaumaunt, Mlle
LeCointe (Cointe) (dancer), 1756: CG, Apr 22, May 10, 11, 18; 1757: HAY, Sep 14
LeCoudriere (actor), 1727: BF, Aug 21
LeCouteux (musician), 1773: MARLY, Jun 15
Lecture on Conjurors (entertainment), 1765: DL, Mar 30
Lecture on Heads, A.   See Stevens, George Alexander.
Lecture on Hearts and Dissertation on Noses (entertainment), 1776: CHR, Sep 23
Lecture on King Henry IV, Part I (entertainment), 1774: MARLY, Jul 6
Lecture on Life (entertainment), 1763: DL, Apr 5
Lecture on Macbeth, and Measure for Measure (entertainment), 1774: DT, Mar 16
Lecture on Mimicry (entertainment), 1774: GRP, Jul 23; 1776: DL, Jun 1
Lecture on Oratory (entertainment), 1791: DL, Mar 24
Lecture upon Lectures (entertainment), 1776: DL, Jun 1
Lectures on English Oratory (entertainment), 1763: HAY, May 9, 11, 14
Lecuss, Mrs (renter), 1758: CG, Mar 18
LeDet (dancer), 1778: KING'S, Nov 24, Dec 22, 29; 1779: KING'S, Jan 23, Feb 23,
    Mar 2, 25, May 15, 29, Jun 19
Ledger, John (actor), 1776: CG, Jan 5, 12, Apr 30, May 4; 1777: CG, May 9;
    1778: CG, Feb 23, May 12, Oct 14; 1779: CG, Apr 23, 29, May 3, Oct 6; 1780:
    CG, Feb 2, Apr 25, May 17, Nov 15; 1781: CG, Jan 25, May 3, 16, HAY, Jun 16,
    Aug 7, 15, 17, 29, CG, Sep 17, Nov 2; 1782: CG, May 8, 11, HAY, Jun 12, Jul
    5, Aug 5, 9, 13, 19, CG, Oct 22, Nov 2, 20, 30, Dec 3; 1783: CG, May 15, HAY,
    31, Jun 3, 12, 30, Jul 7, 26, Aug 1, 28, CG, Oct 14, 17; 1784: CG, Jan 29,
    Feb 12, May 12, 26, HAY, Jun 1, 2, 14, 19, Jul 27, Aug 10, CG, Sep 20, 28,
    29, Oct 28; 1785: CG, Feb 28, Apr 6, May 7, HAY, 30, Jul 19, 20, Aug 2, 3, 4,
    6, 31, CG, Sep 26, 30, Oct 3, 17, 22, Nov 10, 29, Dec 26; 1786: CG, Feb 11,
    May 18, HAY, Jun 13, 14, 20, 26, Jul 11, 12, CG, Sep 25, Oct 18, Nov 22, Dec
    15, 23; 1787: CG, Feb 10, May 28, HAY, Jul 7, 13, 19, Aug 4, 29, CG, Oct 31,
    Nov 5; 1788: CG, Jan 18, Mar 11, 29, Apr 23, May 12, 30, HAY, Jun 10, 19, 23,
    Aug 5, 13, 27, Sep 3, 9, CG, Oct 8, 22, Nov 26, Dec 15, 20; 1789: CG, Jan 31,
    Feb 6, Apr 14, 30, May 20, Jun 5, HAY, 23, 25, Jul 3, 7, Aug 5, 11, CG, Oct
    13, Nov 7, 11, Dec 26; 1790: CG, Jan 22, 23, Mar 18, 27, May 27, HAY, Jun 15,
    26, 28, 29, Jul 5, 16, 28, Aug 12, Sep 4, CG, Oct 4, 8, Nov 1, 15; 1791: CG,
    Apr 16, 28, May 14, 26, HAY, Jun 10, CG, 13, HAY, 18, 20, 23, 30, Jul 9, 15,
    20, 22, Aug 5, 24, CG, Oct 12, Nov 9, Dec 2; 1792: CG, Feb 18, Mar 6, May 29,
    HAY, Jun 15, 20, 22, Jul 3, 14, 16, 23, Aug 2, 6, 22, Sep 4, CG, 26, 28, Oct
    12, 26; 1793: CG, Jan 7, Apr 18, HAY, Jun 11, 12, 13, 18, 25, 29, Jul 5, 9,

15, Aug 3, 5, 14, 27, CG, Oct 12, 16, Nov 11, 25, 30, Dec 5, 17; <u>1794</u>: CG,
   Jun 6, HAY, Jul 8, 9, 10, 11, 12, 17, 21, 22, 29, Aug 4, 11, 12, 13, 20, 23,
   CG, Sep 15, 24, Oct 3, 23, 30; <u>1795</u>: CG, Mar 19, Apr 7, May 1, Jun 4, HAY, 9,
   10, 11, 15, 16, 20, Jul 1, 3, 4, 8, 16, 20, 22, 25, 30, 31, Aug 3, 14, 27,
   Sep 2, CG, 14, 23, Oct 2, 7, 8, 16, 19, 22, 24, Nov 9, Dec 5, 9; <u>1796</u>: CG,
   Jan 23, Apr 1, 29, May 23, Jun 7, HAY, 11, 13, 14, 16, 18, 22, 25, 29, 30,
   Jul 4, 5, 6, 8, 9, 14, 15, 21, 23, 26, Aug 8, 10, 13, 15, 18, Sep 7, CG, 16,
   17, 21, 26, 30, Oct 21, Dec 9; <u>1797</u>: CG, Jan 4, Mar 4, May 9, 16, 18, HAY,
   Jun 13, 15, 16, 17, 20, 21, 22, 23, 24, 28, Jul 3, Aug 4, 5, 9, 15, 28, 30,
   31, CG, Sep 22, 29, Oct 4, 25, Nov 3, 4, 8, 21, Dec 23, 27; <u>1798</u>: CG, May 31,
   HAY, Jun 12, 13, 14, 15, 16, 18, 19, 20, 21, 23, 30, Jul 14, Aug 3, 4, 11,
   21, 25, 29, Sep 3, 5, 10; <u>1799</u>: CG, May 21, HAY, Jun 18, 19, 20, 21, 22, 24,
   25, 29, Jul 2, 9, 10, 12, 23, Aug 10, 26; <u>1800</u>: CG, May 23, HAY, Jun 13, 16,
   19, 20, Jul 5, 7, Aug 20, 23, 27
Ledger, Richard (ticket deliverer), <u>1778</u>: CG, May 22; <u>1779</u>: CG, May 15; <u>1780</u>:
   CG, May 24; <u>1781</u>: CG, May 25; <u>1782</u>: CG, May 28; <u>1783</u>: CG, May 29; <u>1784</u>: CG,
   May 11; <u>1786</u>: CG, May 30; <u>1787</u>: CG, Jun 5
Lediard, Thomas, <u>1732</u>: HAY, Nov 16
Lediger (musician), <u>1675</u>: ATCOURT, Feb 15
Ledley (wax chandler), <u>1759</u>: CG, Dec 12; <u>1760</u>: CG, Jan 10, Feb 1, 28, May 2,
   Nov 25, Dec 9; <u>1761</u>: CG, Jan 14, Feb 7, Mar 5
LeDuke (dancer), <u>1675</u>: ATCOURT, Feb 15
Ledwith (actor), <u>1770</u>: HAY, Oct 5
Lee (actor), <u>1779</u>: HAY, Dec 27
Lee (beneficiary), <u>1734</u>: DL, May 21
Lee (boxkeeper), <u>1729</u>: HAY, May 14; <u>1730</u>: HAY, Apr 20; <u>1731</u>: HAY, Apr 9; <u>1732</u>:
   HAY, Feb 21; <u>1733</u>: HAY, Apr 23
Lee, Mrs, Booth of, <u>1725</u>: SF, Sep 8; <u>1730</u>: SOU, Oct 8; <u>1733</u>: SF, Sep 10, SOU,
   Oct 18; <u>1748</u>: BFLYY, Aug 24
Lee's Booth, <u>1721</u>: BFLGB, Aug 24, SF, Sep 8; <u>1723</u>: BFL, Aug 22; <u>1724</u>: WINH, Apr
   13, BFL, Aug 22, SF, Sep 7; <u>1729</u>: SF, Sep 15, SOU, Oct 14; <u>1730</u>: SOU, May 18;
   <u>1731</u>: SOU, Jun 11; <u>1732</u>: SOU, Oct 12; <u>1733</u>: TC, Jul 30; <u>1734</u>: SFL, Sep 7,
   SOU, Oct 7; <u>1735</u>: TC, May 28; <u>1738</u>: SFL, Sep 5
Lee's Old Theatre, <u>1735</u>: SFLT, Sep 4
Lee's Playhouse, <u>1735</u>: SFLP, Sep 4; <u>1736</u>: SFL, Sep 7
Lee-Hallam Booth, <u>1737</u>: SF, Sep 7
Lee-Harper Booth, <u>1724</u>: SF, Sep 7; <u>1726</u>: SFLH, Sep 8; <u>1727</u>: BF, Aug 22; <u>1728</u>:
   SFLH, Sep 6; <u>1729</u>: BFLH, Aug 23, SF, Sep 15; <u>1730</u>: BFLH, Aug 24, 31, SFLH,
   Sep 8, SOU, 24; <u>1731</u>: BFLH, Aug 24, SF, Sep 8, SFLH, 8; <u>1732</u>: SFLH, Sep 5,
   SFLHO, 5; <u>1733</u>: SF/BFLH, Aug 23, Sep 10, SF, 10
Lee-Harper-Spiller Booth, <u>1722</u>: BFLSH, Aug 25; <u>1726</u>: BFLHS, Aug 24; <u>1728</u>:
   BFLHS, Aug 24, SFLHS, Sep 6
Lee-Phillips Booth, <u>1739</u>: BF, Aug 27; <u>1740</u>: TCLP, Aug 4, BFLP, 23, SF, Sep 9;
   <u>1742</u>: SOU, Sep 21
Lee-Walker Booth, <u>1720</u>: SFLW, Sep 5
Lee-Woodward Booth, <u>1741</u>: TC, Aug 4, BFLW, 22, SF, Sep 14
Lee-Yates Booth, <u>1746</u>: SFLY, Sep 8; <u>1747</u>: SF, Sep 9; <u>1748</u>: BFLYY, Aug 24, BHB,
   Oct 1
Lee-Yates Jr Booth, <u>1746</u>: BFLY, Aug 25
Lee-Yates-Warner Booth, <u>1747</u>: BFLYW, Aug 22; <u>1748</u>: SFLYYW, Sep 7, 8, 9, 10, 12,
   13; <u>1749</u>: BF/SF, Aug 23, 24, 25, 26, 28, SF/SF, Sep 7, BF/SF, 8, 9, 11, 12
Lee, G (printer), <u>1733</u>: SF/BFLH, Aug 23
Lee, Harriet, <u>1787</u>: DL, Nov 10; <u>1796</u>: DL, Apr 20
--New Peerage, The; or, Our Eyes may Deceive Us, <u>1787</u>: DL, Nov 10, 12, 13, 15,
   17, 19, 21, 23, 26
Lee, Henry (actor, author), <u>1796</u>: CG, Oct 6, 13, 14, 29, Nov 19, 21, Dec 1, 7,
   19; <u>1797</u>: CG, Jan 24, 25, Feb 18, 23, Mar 4, 6, 7, Apr 25, Sep 25, Nov 4, 21,
   24, Dec 28; <u>1798</u>: CG, Feb 12, Mar 19, Apr 11, 21, May 7, HAY, Jul 6
--Throw Physick to the Dogs! (Caleb Quotem and His Wife!) (farce), <u>1798</u>: HAY,
   Jul 6, 7
Lee, James Nathaniel (actor, singer), <u>1788</u>: CG, Apr 23, Sep 22, Dec 15, 20;
   <u>1789</u>: CG, Feb 11, Apr 30, May 27, 28, Sep 21, Oct 7, 12, Nov 7, Dec 21; <u>1790</u>:
   CG, Jan 23, Mar 1, 27, Apr 14, May 27, Sep 13, Oct 4, 6, Nov 11, 15, 26;
   <u>1791</u>: CG, Feb 4, PAN, 17, CG, May 3, 16, 31, Jun 13, Sep 26, Oct 10; <u>1792</u>:
   CG, Jan 16, 23, Oct 8, 10, 27, 29, Nov 23; <u>1793</u>: CG, Mar 11; <u>1795</u>: CG, Sep
   14, 21; <u>1796</u>: CG, Mar 15, Apr 26, Sep 16, 19, 26, Nov 14; <u>1797</u>: CG, May 18,
   Nov 2; <u>1798</u>: CG, Feb 9, Sep 17, 21, Oct 3, 8, 11, Nov 1, 10, Dec 11, 15;
   <u>1799</u>: CG, Jan 12, 14, 17, 29, Mar 2, 4, Apr 3, 9, 13, 23, 24, 25, May 4, 6,
   13, 15, 21, 28, Sep 30, Oct 2, 7, 21, 31, Nov 11, 12, Dec 4, 27; <u>1800</u>: CG,
   Jan 16, Feb 10, Mar 4, 25, Apr 5, 23, 26, 29, May 1, 7, 23, 27, Jun 2
Lee, John (actor), <u>1671</u>: LIF, Sep 0; <u>1674</u>: DG, Nov 9; <u>1675</u>: NONE, Sep 0; <u>1676</u>:
   DG, Jul 3, Aug 0, Dec 0; <u>1677</u>: DG, Mar 24, Jun 0, Sep 0

Lee, John (actor, author), 1745: GF, Oct 28, Nov 11, 13, 18, 19, 22, 26, 27,
    Dec 2, 4, 6, 9, 13, 16; 1746: GF, Jan 9, Mar 3, Oct 27, 29, Nov 4, 11, 13,
    14, 19, 20, 28, Dec 3, 9, 10, 11, 16, 27, 29, 31; 1747: GF, Jan 2, 5, 9, 16,
    22, 26, 29, Feb 2, 5, 10, 16, Mar 2, 5, 9, 12, HAY, Apr 22, DL, Nov 14, Dec
    3, 16, 26; 1748: DL, Jan 2, Mar 19, Apr 14, Sep 13, Oct 6, 8, 13, 28, Nov 2,
    4, 14, 29; 1749: DL, Jan 9, Feb 21, Apr 15, May 1, Sep 19, 28, Oct 5, CG, 23,
    Nov 4, Dec 28; 1750: CG, Jan 4, 16, Feb 22, Mar 1, 12, 20, Apr 2, 7, 28, Oct
    13, 23, 31, Nov 5, DL, 13, Dec 27; 1751: DL, Jan 4, 26, Feb 23, Mar 11, 14,
    Apr 23, 29, Sep 26, Oct 22, 31, Nov 2, 4, 28, Dec 31; 1752: DL, Jan 28, Apr
    6, 10; 1757: CG, Nov 11, 12, 18, Dec 5; 1758: CG, Jan 24, Apr 10, DL, Sep 19;
    1762: DL, Feb 22, May 11, Sep 28, Oct 2, 5, 6, 28, Nov 1, 3, 4, 17, Dec 31;
    1763: DL, Jan 17, Apr 6, May 2, 10, 18, Sep 20, Oct 8, 17, 24, 31, Nov 4, 7,
    9, 29, Dec 5; 1764: DL, Jan 2, 13, 16, 18, Feb 18, 21, Mar 20, Apr 10, 12,
    24, 25, 27, May 9, 19, Sep 20, 22, 27, Oct 15, 17, 19, 26, Nov 5, 9, 27;
    1765: DL, Jan 2, 14, 15, 23, 24, Feb 4, 6, Mar 2, 16, 26, Apr 11, 13, 26, May
    6, 11, 18, Sep 21, Oct 12, 14, 22, 28, Nov 11, 22, 25, Dec 6, 7, 9; 1766: DL,
    Jan 6, 9, 13, Feb 20, Mar 15, 20, 22, Apr 9, 18, May 2, 5, 21, 22, KING'S,
    Aug 8, 13, 25, Sep 5, 9, 13, 15; 1767: DL, Jan 24; 1768: CG, Apr 13, HAY, Jun
    23, Jul 8, Aug 19, Sep 19; 1770: CG, Jan 5, DL, 10; 1772: CG, May 29; 1773:
    CG, Apr 27; 1774: CG, Oct 1, 11, 22, Nov 8, Dec 2, 3, 20; 1775: CG, Jan 17,
    18, 28, Feb 21, 24, Mar 2, Apr 4, 19, Sep 29, Nov 9; 1776: CG, Feb 5, Mar 23,
    Nov 12, 25, Dec 16; 1777: CG, Jan 8, Apr 4, Sep 29; 1779: CG, Sep 0
--Man of Quality, The (Miss Hoyden), 1773: CG, Apr 27; 1774: DL, Mar 15; 1776:
    DL, Mar 28, Apr 10, 24, CG, 30, May 4, DL, 7, CHR, Sep 25; 1784: HAY, Aug 6;
    1790: CG, May 5
Lee, Mary (actor), 1670: LIF, Jan 0, Sep 20, Nov 0; 1671: NONE, Mar 4, LIF, 6,
    15, Sep 0; 1673: DG, May 0, Jul 3; 1674: DG, Nov 9; 1675: DG, May 28, Sep 0;
    1676: DG, Jan 10, Mar 0, 11, Jun 8, Jul 3, Nov 4, Dec 0; 1677: DG, Feb 12,
    Jul 0, Sep 0; 1678: DG, May 28, Sep 0, Nov 0; 1679: DG, Mar 0, Apr 0, May 0,
    Dec 0; 1680: DG, Jan 0, Feb 0, Sep 0; 1682: DG, Apr 0; 1683: DG, May 31; see
    also Slingsby, Lady
Lee, Miss (actor), 1742: DL, Apr 3, May 25, Nov 8; 1743: DL, May 2
Lee, Miss (actor), 1761: CG, Apr 11, May 8
Lee, Mrs (actor), 1735: DL, Apr 16
Lee, Mrs (actor), 1759: CG, Dec 20, 29; 1760: CG, Mar 20, Apr 19, May 14, Oct
    6; 1761: CG, Mar 25, 26, 30, Apr 29, May 11
Lee, Mrs (actor), 1762: DL, Sep 21, Oct 14, 26, Nov 3; 1763: DL, Jan 15, Mar
    26, Apr 26, Oct 8, 17, 19, Nov 30, Dec 10, 17; 1764: DL, Jan 14, 18, Feb 21,
    Mar 3, 26, May 3, 8, 22, Sep 20, Oct 6, 18, 19, 22, Nov 9; 1765: DL, Jan 2,
    24, 26, Mar 23, May 8, Oct 18, 31, Nov 23, Dec 3, 26; 1766: DL, Feb 13, Apr
    18, 29, May 5, Oct 9, 29, Dec 6; 1767: DL, Jan 31, Feb 7, 9, Mar 7, 28, Apr
    11, 27, 30, May 4, 8, Sep 12, 18, 25
Lee, Mrs (actor), 1778: HAY, Mar 23, 31
Lee, Mrs (director of booth), 1748: BFLYY, Aug 24; 1749: NWSM, May 3, BF/SF,
    Aug 23; 1750: SFYW, Sep 7; 1755: SFG, Sep 18
Lee, Nathaniel, 1672: DG, Aug 3; 1673: DG, Feb 18; 1678: DG, Sep 0; 1680: DG,
    Dec 8; 1682: DL, May 29, DLORDG, Jul 18; 1707: DL, Oct 18; 1709: GR, Jun 20;
    1710: QUEEN'S, Jun 29; 1716: DL, Aug 9, 14, Oct 30; 1718: DL, Feb 22; 1721:
    DL, Nov 2, 3, Dec 2; 1722: DL, Jan 23, LIF, Nov 8, 24; 1723: LIF, Jan 1, 26,
    May 10, Sep 28, Dec 17; 1724: LIF, Jul 3, 7, Sep 23, Nov 19; 1725: LIF, Oct
    11; 1726: LIF, Apr 14, Sep 28, Dec 30; 1727: LIF, Oct 31; 1728: LIF, Jan 1,
    Nov 11; 1729: LIF, Oct 13; 1730: LIF, Oct 5; 1731: LIF, Apr 24; 1735: CG, Nov
    10, 11, Dec 12; 1736: CG, Dec 27; 1737: CG, Feb 18; 1739: CG, Oct 1; 1755:
    CG, Jan 10; 1776: CHR, Oct 7
--Caesar Borgia, Son of Pope Alexander the Sixth, 1679: DG, May 0; 1695: NONE,
    Sep 0; 1704: LIF, Jun 8; 1706: QUEEN'S, Jan 11; 1707: QUEEN'S, Aug 19; 1719:
    DL, Jan 3, 5, NONE, Mar 26
--Constantine the Great, 1683: DL, Nov 12
--Duke of Guise. See Dryden, John
--Gloriana; or, The Court of Augustus Caesar, 1676: DL, Jan 29; 1698: NONE, Sep
    0
--Lucius Junius Brutus, 1680: DG, Dec 8
--Mithridates, 1678: DL, Feb 0; 1681: BF, Sep 9, DL, Oct 0; 1684: NONE, Sep 0;
    1686: DL, Feb 4; 1692: NONE, Sep 0; 1695: NONE, Sep 0; 1704: DL, Oct 14, Nov
    30; 1708: DL, Feb 14, Mar 22; 1709: GR, Jun 20; 1711: DL, Dec 13, 15, 20;
    1715: DL, Mar 21; 1716: DL, Feb 25; 1717: DL, Mar 9, Dec 28; 1721: DL, Mar 2;
    1723: DL, Mar 4; 1724: DL, Feb 15; 1726: DL, Nov 29; 1727: DL, Mar 18; 1728:
    DL, Apr 13; 1729: DL, Jan 25; 1734: DL, Apr 22; 1736: LIF, Oct 19, 21; 1737:
    LIF, Mar 31; 1738: CG, Nov 9, 10, Dec 19; 1794: DL, Nov 12
--Oedipus. See Dryden, John.
--Princess of Cleve, The, 1680: DG, Sep 0; 1696: NONE, Sep 0
--Rival Queens, The; or, Alexander the Great (Alexander), 1677: DL, Mar 17, Dec

26; <u>1681</u>: ATCOURT, Nov 15; <u>1683</u>: NONE, Sep 0; <u>1685</u>: DL, Dec 19; <u>1686</u>: ATCOURT, Oct 27; <u>1687</u>: NONE, Feb 16; <u>1690</u>: DLORDG, Jan 16; <u>1691</u>: NONE, Sep 0; <u>1692</u>: DL, Dec 2; <u>1693</u>: NONE, Sep 0; <u>1698</u>: DLORLIF, Feb 24, DL, Nov 19; <u>1699</u>: LIF, Jan 5, 6; <u>1701</u>: DL, Feb 20, 22, Apr 5; <u>1703</u>: LIF, Jun 1; <u>1704</u>: DL, Jun 13; <u>1705</u>: QUEEN'S, Dec 19; <u>1706</u>: QUEEN'S, May 2, Nov 4, Dec 30; <u>1707</u>: QUEEN'S, Jan 22; <u>1708</u>: DL, Jan 31, Apr 13, Sep 25; <u>1709</u>: DL, Feb 11, Apr 5, GR, Jun 20; <u>1710</u>: DL, Jan 23, QUEEN'S, Jun 29, GR, Jul 6; <u>1712</u>: DL, May 1, Nov 13; <u>1715</u>: LIF, Apr 26, Jul 27; <u>1717</u>: LIF, Mar 16, Apr 27; <u>1718</u>: LIF, Oct 4; <u>1722</u>: LIF, Dec 1, 3, 4, 28; <u>1723</u>: LIF, Jan 24, Mar 30, Nov 26, Dec 28; <u>1724</u>: LIF, Mar 14; <u>1725</u>: LIF, Jan 7, Feb 23, Oct 15; <u>1726</u>: LIF, Apr 16, Nov 8; <u>1727</u>: LIF, Nov 14; <u>1729</u>: LIF, Nov 20, Dec 15; <u>1732</u>: LIF, Apr 10; <u>1733</u>: GF, Nov 29, 30, Dec 1, 3, 4, 5, 6, 7, 21; <u>1734</u>: GF, Jan 23, Mar 11, Nov 25, 26; <u>1735</u>: GF, Jan 9, CG, Oct 25, 27, 28, Nov 11, Dec 1, 26; <u>1736</u>: CG, Jan 19, Mar 16, Oct 6, Nov 18, DL, 22, 23, 24, 26, CG, Dec 27; <u>1737</u>: DL, Jan 26, CG, Feb 18, Oct 22; <u>1738</u>: CG, Jan 10, Oct 24; <u>1739</u>: CG, Jan 2, Feb 22, Sep 29, Oct 1, Dec 26; <u>1740</u>: CG, Oct 31; <u>1741</u>: CG, Mar 19, TC, Aug 4; <u>1743</u>: DL, Jan 27, Feb 2, Nov 17, Dec 26; <u>1749</u>: CG, Mar 14; <u>1755</u>: CG, Nov 17; <u>1756</u>: CG, Jan 15, 17, 19, 20, 22, 24, 26, 28, 31, Feb 7, 10, 12, 17, 21, Mar 11, 16, Apr 10, Oct 25, Nov 2, 6, Dec 1; <u>1757</u>: CG, Jan 3, Feb 14, Mar 28, Apr 29, Dec 20, 22, 29, 31; <u>1758</u>: CG, Jan 6, Feb 25, Mar 28, Nov 14, 15, Dec 29; <u>1759</u>: CG, Jan 8, Mar 19, Apr 23; <u>1760</u>: CG, Mar 25, Apr 23; <u>1761</u>: CG, Jan 15, Mar 3, 31, Apr 18; <u>1762</u>: CG, Mar 23, Apr 13, 26, Oct 6; <u>1764</u>: DL, Mar 20, 22, Apr 9, 23, CG, May 9, DL, 23; <u>1765</u>: DL, Jan 15, 16, 19, 21, Feb 23, Mar 2, 9, 21, CG, 26, DL, Apr 8, 30; <u>1766</u>: DL, Apr 9, 18; <u>1767</u>: CG, Mar 23, DL, 30, CG, Apr 21, DL, 21, 23, 24, May 2, CG, 25, HAY, Jul 31; <u>1768</u>: DL, Mar 15, Sep 28, Oct 7; <u>1769</u>: DL, Mar 11, CG, Dec 15; <u>1770</u>: CG, Jan 5, Mar 24, Apr 17; <u>1771</u>: CG, Apr 9, 22, May 11, 21; <u>1772</u>: CG, Apr 7, 30, May 19, DL, Oct 16, 19, 26, Dec 3; <u>1773</u>: CG, Mar 30, Apr 21, May 11, 15, Dec 21; <u>1774</u>: CG, Mar 26, DL, Apr 8, CG, 18, May 2, DL, 4, 12, CG, Oct 4, DL, 8, CG, 10, DL, 11, CG, 17, DL, 21, Nov 2, CG, Dec 27; <u>1775</u>: CG, Jan 23, May 2, Nov 13; <u>1776</u>: DL, Mar 28, CG, Apr 10, CHR, Oct 7, DL, Nov 5; <u>1777</u>: DL, Feb 17, CG, May 5, 6; <u>1778</u>: DL, Mar 30, CG, Apr 22, DL, May 4, CG, 13, 23, Dec 26; <u>1779</u>: DL, Apr 12, CG, May 1; <u>1780</u>: CG, Apr 10, DL, 17, May 10, Nov 27; <u>1781</u>: DL, Apr 17; <u>1782</u>: CG, Apr 12, Dec 27; <u>1783</u>: DL, Apr 21, CG, 28, May 24; <u>1784</u>: DL, Apr 26; <u>1785</u>: CG, May 4; <u>1786</u>: CG, May 15; <u>1787</u>: CG, Oct 22, 26, Dec 17; <u>1788</u>: CG, May 19; <u>1789</u>: CG, Apr 28, May 12; <u>1792</u>: CG, Apr 12; <u>1794</u>: CG, May 6, 28, DL, Nov 19; <u>1795</u>: CG, Mar 28, DL, Nov 23, 25, 27, 30, Dec 4, 7, 14, 21, 28; <u>1796</u>: DL, Jan 1, 13, 25, Apr 12; <u>1799</u>: CG, Apr 9, 15, Oct 14
--Sophonisba; or, Hannibal's Overthrow, <u>1675</u>: DL, Apr 30, May 4, 7, 10, Nov 6, Dec 29; <u>1676</u>: DL, Nov 27; <u>1680</u>: NONE, Sep 0; <u>1684</u>: NONE, Sep 0; <u>1692</u>: NONE, Sep 0; <u>1696</u>: NONE, Sep 0; <u>1700</u>: DL, Jul 8; <u>1704</u>: LIF, Oct 16, Nov 3; <u>1706</u>: QUEEN'S, Jan 18, Jun 26; <u>1707</u>: QUEEN'S, Aug 1; <u>1708</u>: DL, Jun 17, Sep 11; <u>1709</u>: DL, Dec 31; <u>1711</u>: DL, Jul 17; <u>1712</u>: DL, Jul 18; <u>1715</u>: LIF, Apr 18, Nov 15; <u>1717</u>: LIF, Feb 7, Mar 5, Nov 19; <u>1724</u>: LIF, Jul 3, 7, 10; <u>1725</u>: DL, Feb 1, 2; <u>1726</u>: LIF, Apr 11, May 18; <u>1728</u>: LIF, Jul 5
--Theodosius; or, The Force of Love, <u>1680</u>: DG, Sep 0; <u>1683</u>: NONE, Sep 0; <u>1691</u>: NONE, Sep 0; <u>1694</u>: DG, Jun 12; <u>1696</u>: NONE, Sep 0; <u>1703</u>: LIF, Jun 5; <u>1704</u>: LIF, Feb 5; <u>1707</u>: QUEEN'S, Apr 3; <u>1711</u>: GR, Sep 20; <u>1715</u>: LIF, Mar 31, Apr 29; <u>1717</u>: LIF, Mar 11; <u>1719</u>: LIF, Dec 26; <u>1721</u>: DL, Nov 2, 3, Dec 2; <u>1722</u>: DL, Jan 23, Mar 12, Apr 23, Dec 22; <u>1723</u>: DL, May 8, Nov 7, Dec 19; <u>1724</u>: DL, Oct 13, Nov 30; <u>1725</u>: DL, Apr 24, Jun 7, Nov 1; <u>1726</u>: DL, Jan 21, Mar 26, May 20; <u>1727</u>: DL, Apr 17, Oct 13; <u>1728</u>: DL, Oct 1, Nov 21; <u>1729</u>: DL, Jan 15, Mar 3; <u>1730</u>: DL, Apr 27, Oct 24; <u>1731</u>: DL, Jan 5; <u>1733</u>: DL, May 5, Dec 17; <u>1734</u>: GF, Jan 3, 4, 5, DL, 26, GF, Feb 6, 12, Mar 9, Nov 18; <u>1735</u>: GF, May 9, HAY, Jun 12, CG, Nov 1, 3, Dec 4; <u>1736</u>: CG, Feb 23, Apr 3, Sep 15, Nov 23; <u>1737</u>: CG, Feb 14, Nov 19; <u>1738</u>: CG, Mar 16, May 10, Sep 15, Nov 14; <u>1739</u>: CG, Feb 8, Sep 21; <u>1743</u>: CG, Apr 9; <u>1746</u>: DL, Dec 12, 15, 16, 17, 18; <u>1747</u>: DL, Apr 9; <u>1748</u>: CG, Dec 9; <u>1749</u>: CG, Jan 4; <u>1750</u>: CG, Feb 2, 13; <u>1751</u>: CG, Apr 10; <u>1752</u>: CG, Mar 7, 23; <u>1753</u>: CG, Jan 8, 9, 10, 11, Feb 8, 19, Mar 31, May 2, Nov 19, 20; <u>1754</u>: CG, Feb 21, Apr 22, May 14; <u>1755</u>: CG, Nov 19, Dec 22; <u>1756</u>: CG, Mar 27, Apr 30, Oct 30, Nov 15; <u>1757</u>: CG, Apr 16, Dec 14; <u>1758</u>: CG, Mar 18, May 10, Nov 25, Dec 18, 20; <u>1759</u>: CG, Feb 7, May 5, Dec 5; <u>1760</u>: CG, Jan 2; <u>1761</u>: CG, Feb 16, Apr 25, Oct 1; <u>1763</u>: CG, Nov 16; <u>1764</u>: CG, Jan 23, Oct 19; <u>1765</u>: CG, Jan 28; <u>1766</u>: CG, Mar 31, KING'S, Sep 19, CG, Dec 4; <u>1767</u>: CG, Jan 22, May 5, HAY, Jul 8, 10; <u>1768</u>: DL, Apr 27; <u>1769</u>: DL, Apr 12; <u>1770</u>: CG, May 8, DL, Oct 5, 25; <u>1771</u>: CG, Apr 20, DL, 23; <u>1772</u>: DL, Dec 30; <u>1773</u>: DL, Dec 3; <u>1774</u>: DL, Apr 29; <u>1775</u>: CG, Apr 22, May 15; <u>1780</u>: CG, Nov 24; <u>1786</u>: CG, Feb 23, 27; <u>1789</u>: HAY, Feb 23; <u>1797</u>: DL, Jan 20, 21, 23, 26, 28
--Tragedy of Nero, The, <u>1674</u>: DL, May 16; <u>1675</u>: DL, Aug 0; <u>1695</u>: NONE, Sep 0
Lee, Rachel (actor), <u>1693</u>: DL, Feb 0
Lee, Sarah Jane, Mrs Henry (actor), <u>1795</u>: CG, Mar 19, 21, Apr 23, 27, May 1, 13, 19, 25, Jun 8; <u>1796</u>: CG, Oct 14, 21, 29, Nov 10, 11

Lee, Sophia, 1780: HAY, Aug 5; 1796: DL, Apr 20
--Almeyda, Queen of Granada, 1796: DL, Apr 14, 16, 20, 21, 22, 23, May 16
--Chapter of Accidents, The, 1780: HAY, Aug 5, 7, 9, 12, 15, 18, 19, 21, 23,
    25, 28, Sep 9, 13, 14, 15; 1781: DL, May 8, HAY, Jun 7, 9, 13, 20, 23, 27,
    30, Jul 4, 7, 13, 17, 19, 25, Aug 2, 6, 31, Sep 7; 1782: CG, Apr 23, 29, DL,
    May 11, CG, 17, 23, HAY, Jun 10, 19, Jul 11, 15, 22, Aug 3, 12, 23, Sep 11;
    1783: CG, Apr 7, May 2, 27, HAY, Jun 16, Aug 15; 1784: CG, Feb 18, DL, Apr
    21, HAY, Jul 20; 1785: HAY, Jun 6, Jul 29; 1786: CG, May 3, 22, HAY, Jun 15,
    Jul 4, Aug 4, 24; 1787: CG, Apr 17, May 18, HAY, Jul 4, 13, Aug 9, Sep 13;
    1788: HAY, Jun 12, 21, 28, Jul 30, Aug 21; 1789: HAY, Jun 24, Jul 4, 23, Aug
    18; 1790: CG, May 31, HAY, Jun 17; 1791: CG, Apr 30, Jun 2; 1793: DL, Feb 14,
    Apr 26, HAY, Jun 15, 21, 27, Jul 12, Sep 3, Oct 1, Dec 9, 11, 13; 1794: HAY,
    Jun 2; 1795: HAY, Aug 7, CG, Sep 25; 1796: CG, May 6, HAY, Aug 3; 1797: DL,
    Jan 14, HAY, Jul 6, 12; 1799: HAY, Feb 25; 1800: CG, May 29
Lee, W and A (publishers), 1789: HAY, Aug 25
Lee, William (author), 1775: KING'S, Nov 7
Leeds, Duke of (patron), 1735: KING'S, Mar 15
Leeds, Duke of. See Osborne.
Leeds, 1770: DL, Oct 8; 1785: DL, Nov 21
Leek, The (dance), 1741: GF, Dec 23; 1742: GF, Feb 8, 11, 17, 24, Mar 15, 18,
    25, Apr 1, 21, 26
Leeson (haberdasher), 1753: DL, Dec 11
Leeson, Henrietta Amelia (actor), 1775: CG, Nov 3, 8, 11, Dec 7; 1776: CG, Feb
    7, Sep 30, Nov 1, Dec 5, 17; 1777: CG, Jan 8, 17, Feb 1, 6, 27, May 2, 24,
    Sep 24, Oct 23; 1778: CG, Jan 19, Feb 3, 6, Mar 2, 23, Apr 25, May 16, Sep
    18, 25, Oct 14; 1779: CG, Mar 9, Apr 5, 21, 24, 30
Leete (singer), 1793: KING/HAY, Feb 27, Mar 1, 8, 13, 15; 1798: HAY, Jan 15;
    1799: HAY, Jan 24, Mar 29
Lefevre (actor), 1738: HAY, Oct 9
LeFevre (dancer), 1753: DL, Nov 1, 8, 10, 17, 21, Dec 19
Lefevre, Joseph (lute player), 1788: KING'S, May 22
LeFevre, Mlle (actor), 1738: HAY, Oct 9
LeFevre, Mlle (dancer), 1711: QUEEN'S, Mar 20
Lefevre, Mrs (actor, singer), 1778: HAY, Feb 9, Mar 24, Apr 29, CHR, May 25,
    29, Jun 3, HAY, Sep 17, Dec 28; 1779: HAY, Mar 8, 15, Jul 31, Aug 14, 31, Oct
    13, Dec 20; 1780: HAY, Jan 3, Mar 28, May 30, Jun 13, Sep 5, 25; 1781: HAY,
    Jun 9, Jul 21, 27, Aug 8, 22, Oct 16; 1782: HAY, Mar 4, Jun 3, 10, 11, 22,
    Aug 13, 17, 27, Sep 16, 18; 1783: HAY, Jun 5, 13, 20, Jul 2, Aug 12, 13, 22,
    Dec 15; 1784: HAY, Jan 21, Feb 9, Mar 22, May 29, Jun 28, Jul 28, Aug 26, Sep
    17; 1785: HAY, Jun 2, 7, Jul 1, Aug 31; 1786: HAY, Dec 18; 1787: HAY, May 23,
    Jun 13, 18, 25; 1788: HAY, Jun 20, 26, Jul 14, Aug 5, 9; 1789: HAY, May 20,
    29, Jun 1, 10, 12, Jul 21, Aug 29, CG, Sep 21, Oct 12, Nov 16, Dec 21; 1790:
    CG, Jan 23, Apr 24, May 27, Oct 6, Nov 26, Dec 6; 1791: CG, Mar 5, May 26;
    1792: CG, May 12
Leffler, James Henry (bassoonist), 1794: CG, Dec 26; 1795: HAY, Mar 4; 1796:
    CG, Feb 12; 1797: CG, Mar 3; 1798: CG, Feb 23; 1799: CG, Feb 8; 1800: CG, Feb
    28
Leffler, T (musician), 1795: HAY, Mar 4
Lefond, Mlle. See LaFond, Mlle.
LeFont, Mrs. See LaFont, Mrs.
Lefrond (actor), 1733: HAY, Mar 16, 26
Leg Tavern, 1740: LG, Apr 7
Legar (Leguerre, Lagarde) (actor, dancer, singer), 1719: LIF, Apr 30; 1720:
    KING'S, Apr 27, Dec 28; 1721: LIF, Apr 20, May 10; 1722: LIF, Apr 5, 24, HAY,
    May 11; 1723: LIF, Jan 9, Mar 25, Apr 22, Oct 14, 19, Nov 2, 22, Dec 20;
    1724: LIF, Jan 3, KING'S, Feb 20, LIF, Apr 9, 23, 30, May 4, 6, 19, 30, Jun
    4, Sep 25, 30, Oct 9, Nov 4; 1725: LIF, Jan 21, Mar 11, 29, Apr 7, 15, 16,
    Oct 13, 21, Nov 3, 13, 22, Dec 2, 8; 1726: LIF, Jan 14, Mar 19, 21, Apr 2,
    11, 13, 14, 15, 19, 20, 25, 27, May 20, Sep 16, 23, 26, 30, Oct 5, 29, Nov
    19; 1727: LIF, Feb 13, Apr 28, Sep 22, 29, Oct 12, 27, Nov 7, 9; 1728: HAY,
    Mar 27, LIF, 27, May 2, 15, Sep 30, Oct 9, 14, 23, 26; 1729: LIF, Jan 18, Mar
    17, Apr 8, 19, Sep 19, Oct 3, 6, 10, 28, Nov 1, 4; 1730: LIF, Feb 2, May 14,
    23, Sep 21, Oct 1, 7, 9, Nov 7, Dec 11, 30; 1731: LIF, Mar 26, GF, Apr 1,
    LIF, 8, Sep, 27, Oct 4, 15, Nov 13; 1732: LIF, Feb 28, May 5, LIF/CG, Oct 13,
    30, Nov 8; 1739: BFHCL, Aug 23, CG, Oct 10, 30, 31, Dec 10; 1743: SOU, Feb
    25, LIF, Apr 6; see also Laguerre
Legar, Mr and Mrs (actors), 1725: LIF, Apr 16; see also Laguerre
Legar, Mrs (dancer), 1724: LIF, Sep 25, 30, Oct 5, 7, 9, 12, 16, 23, 27, 30,
    Nov 6, 11, 13, 17, 18; 1725: LIF, Jan 4, 16, 18, 21, Feb 27, Mar 13, 29, 31,
    Apr 5, 15, 17, 22, 30, Sep 29, Oct 4, 8, 13, 19, 26, Nov 2, 6, 12, 22, 29;
    1726: LIF, Mar 19, 21, Apr 2, 11, 13, 14, 16, 20, 22, 29, 30, May 4, 13, 30,
    Sep 12, 14, 16, 19, 30, Oct 7, 29, Nov 2, 21, 30, Dec 5, 9, 14; 1727: LIF,

Jan 31, Feb 13, Apr 17, Sep 15, 20, 25, Oct 9, 27, Nov 1, Dec 9; 1728: LIF,
Jan 8, Mar 14, 21, 25, Apr 4, May 6, 11, 15, 16, 18, Dec 31; 1729: LIF, Jan
18, Mar 10, Apr 8, 15, 17, 19, 21, 24, 29, 30, May 7, 8, 12, 14, 15, 19, Sep
26, Oct 8, 10, 24, Nov 4; 1730: LIF, May 21, Sep 23, Oct 1, 31, Nov 7, 26;
1731: LIF, Jan 19, Mar 22, 25, Apr 8, May 25, Oct 15; 1732: LIF, Jan 19, Feb
28, Mar 23, Apr 10, LIF/CG, Oct 13; 1733: LIF/CG, Feb 5; see also Laguerre,
Mrs
Legatoire Universel, Le. See Regnard, Jean Francois.
Lege (actor), 1728: HAY, Feb 21
Leger (dancer), 1782: KING'S, Feb 23, Mar 9, 19
Legg, Jonathan (singer, actor), 1751: CG, Nov 11, Dec 4; 1752: CG, Feb 11, Mar
17, Apr 25, Oct 21, 26, 30, Dec 7; 1753: CG, May 2, 10, Oct 10, Dec 27; 1754:
CG, May 3, 8, CHAPEL, 15, CG, Nov 16, 20; 1755: CG, Apr 9, May 8, Oct 29, Nov
17; 1756: CG, May 14, Oct 4, 6; 1757: CG, May 13, Dec 7, 10; 1758: CG, Feb 1,
May 3, Nov 1, 23; 1759: CG, Feb 23, May 15, Nov 5, 30, Dec 10; 1760: CG, Jan
16, 18, Apr 8, 17, May 7, Sep 22, 29, Oct 15, 20, Dec 11; 1761: CG, Apr 2,
May 1, Sep 16, 25, 26, Oct 13; 1762: CG, Jan 28, May 6, 11, Sep 22, Oct 8,
Nov 1, 15; 1763: CG, Jan 24, 26, May 11, 17, MARLY, Jun 28, CG, Sep 21, Oct
3, 14, Nov 15, Dec 2, 13, 17; 1764: CG, Jan 3, 14, Feb 22, May 11, 21, Sep
21, Oct 1, 18, Nov 5, 7; 1765: CG, May 8, 11, MARLY, Aug 6, CG, Oct 3, 7, 9,
14, 22, 28; 1766: CG, Feb 5, May 7, Oct 14, 21, Nov 4, 18, 21; 1767: CG, Jan
29, Feb 14, May 11, Sep 14, 19, 25, Oct 5, 9, 17, 27, 30, Nov 4; 1768: CG,
Jan 20, Mar 15, May 7, Sep 24, 26, Oct 5, 15, 17, 24, Dec 26; 1769: CG, Jan
19, Apr 29, May 9, 25, Oct 6, 30, Dec 9; 1770: CG, Jan 3, Mar 29, May 16, Sep
26, Oct 8, Nov 12; 1771: CG, Mar 14, Apr 22, 30, May 15, 30, Sep 25, Oct 25;
1772: CG, Jan 27, 31, May 21, Nov 2, Dec 26; 1773: CG, Jan 23; 1774: DL, Oct
5, 14, 17, Nov 5, 21, Dec 9; 1775: DL, Jan 2, Mar 2, 21, 23, Apr 17, May 1,
3, 15, Oct 7, 11, 28, Nov 9, 11, 28, Dec 7, 11; 1776: DL, Feb 1, Mar 14, May
10, 11, 22, Jun 10, Oct 18, Nov 25, Dec 10; 1777: DL, Jan 1, 4, Mar 1, Apr
22, May 6, 9, 28, Sep 20, Dec 4, 13; 1778: DL, Jan 5, 17, May 8, 23, HAY, Jun
12, Sep 7, DL, 24, Nov 2, Dec 29; 1779: DL, Apr 7, May 8
Legg, Mrs Jonathan (beneficiary), 1779: DL, May 19
Legh, Richard (spectator), 1666: LIF, Dec 0; 1667: BRIDGES, Jan 2
Legrand, Louis, 1723: LIF, Feb 18
--Cartouche; or, The French Robbers (farce), 1723: LIF, Feb 18, 19, 20, 21, Mar
19, May 2, Jun 3, Dec 3; 1727: LIF, Mar 18, KING'S, Apr 6, 14; 1730: LIF, Mar
2
Legrand, Marc-Antoine
--Animaux Raisonables, Les; ou, Ulysses & Circe (opera), 1721: HAY, Mar 23;
1725: HAY, Jan 29, Feb 22
--Belphegor; or, Arlequin Aux Enfers (farce), 1735: HAY, Jan 3, Apr 11
LeGrande, Mrs (actor), 1677: DG, Sep 0; 1678: DG, Jan 0
LeGrange (dancer), 1736: HAY, Feb 20
Leguard. See Delaguarde.
Leguerre. See Legar.
Legyt (spectator), 1760: CG, Feb 16
Leicester (beneficiary), 1735: HAY, Jul 10
Leicester Court, 1783: CG, May 10; 1784: CG, May 7; 1785: DL, Mar 31
Leicester Fields, 1733: HIF/CG, Mar 28; 1735: DL, Apr 21; 1736: DL, Apr 15;
1737: DL, Apr 16; 1739: DL, Apr 12; 1740: DL, Apr 16; 1742: CG, Apr 21; 1746:
DL, Apr 8; 1747: CG, Apr 29, May 11; 1748: DL, Apr 12, CG, 13, 14; 1749: DL,
Mar 14, Apr 7; 1750: DL, Jan 9, Mar 17; 1751: DL, Apr 20; 1752: DL, Mar 16,
Apr 1; 1754: DL, Mar 26; 1762: HAY, Sep 7; 1767: CG, Apr 6; 1778: KING'S, Apr
30; 1779: KING'S, May 13, HAY, Aug 17, Oct 13; 1781: KING'S, Feb 22, Mar 29;
1783: CG, May 10; 1784: DL, Apr 24, May 7, CG, 7, 10, DL, 20; 1785: DL, Mar
31; 1787: DL, Apr 18; 1790: CG, Jun 16; 1791: KING'S, May 26; 1795: DL, May
21; 1796: DL, Apr 12; 1797: DL, May 23; 1798: DL, May 9, 24
Leicester House, 1749: DL, Jan 2, 20
Leicester Place, 1799: CG, May 18
Leicester Square, 1751: DL, Apr 11; 1794: HAY, Jun 2; 1795: DL, Apr 14; 1796:
DL, May 13; 1797: HAY, Jan 23, DL, May 22; 1798: HAY, Mar 26; 1799: DL, Apr
15, May 8, 9, HAY, Aug 15, Oct 21; 1800: DL, May 14, Jun 6
Leicester St, 1742: HAY, Jun 16; 1781: KING'S, Feb 22, Mar 29; 1787: DL, Apr
18; 1799: HAY, Oct 21
Leicester, Eliza, Mrs Thomas (actor), 1778: HAY, Mar 24; 1793: CG, Oct 7, 9,
18, 19, 25, Nov 7, 15, 16, 21, Dec 6, 11, 18; 1794: CG, Apr 12
Leicestershire, 1734: DL, Dec 26
Leigh (dancer), 1710: DL, Mar 25, Apr 12, May 23; 1712: DL, Jun 12; 1715: DL,
Nov 2
Leigh (rioter), 1773: CG, Nov 18
Leigh (ticket deliverer), 1737: LIF, Jun 15
Leigh St, 1788: DL, May 8; 1790: DL, May 19

Leigh-Hall Booth, <u>1720</u>: SFLH, Sep 5, SOU, Oct 10
Leigh, Anthony (actor), <u>1670</u>: LIF, Jan 0; <u>1671</u>: LIF, Sep 0; <u>1673</u>: DG, May 0;
<u>1676</u>: DG, Jan 10, Mar 11, May 25, Jul 25, Nov 4, Dec 0; <u>1677</u>: DG, May 31, Jun
0, Sep 0; <u>1678</u>: DG, Jan 0, 17, Apr 5, May 28, Jun 0; <u>1679</u>: DG, Mar 0, Apr 0,
May 0, Sep 0, NONE, 0; <u>1680</u>: DG, Jan 0, Jun 0, Sep 0, Nov 1; <u>1681</u>: DG, Sep 0,
Nov 0, DG/IT, 22; <u>1682</u>: DG, Jan 0, 23, Feb 9, Apr 0, NONE, Sep 0; <u>1683</u>: DL,
Jan 19, DG, May 31, Jul 0, NONE, Sep 0, DL, Dec 0; <u>1684</u>: DL, Mar 0, Apr 0,
DLORDG, Aug 0; <u>1685</u>: DL, May 9, Jul 0, Aug 0, NONE, Sep 0; <u>1686</u>: DL, Jan 0,
Apr 0, OXFORD, Jul 0, NONE, Sep 0; <u>1687</u>: DG, Mar 0; <u>1688</u>: DL, Feb 0, DG, Apr
0, DL, May 3, NONE, Sep 0; <u>1689</u>: DL, Mar 0, Apr 0, NONE, Sep 0, DL, Dec 4;
<u>1690</u>: DL, Jan 0, Mar 0, DLORDG, 0, DG, Jun 0, NONE, Sep 0, DL, 0, DL/IT, Oct
21, DL, Nov 0, Dec 0; <u>1691</u>: DL, Jan 0, Apr 0, NONE, Sep 0; <u>1692</u>: DL, Jan 0,
Apr 0, Jun 0, Nov 0, 8, NONE, Dec 21; <u>1693</u>: NONE, Jan 0
Leigh, Elinor, Mrs Anthony (actor), <u>1670</u>: LIF, Jan 0, Nov 0; <u>1671</u>: LIF, Jan 10,
Mar 6, 15, DG, Nov 0; <u>1672</u>: DG, Jul 4; <u>1673</u>: DG, Mar 12; <u>1676</u>: DG, Jan 10;
<u>1677</u>: DG, Mar 24, Jun 0; <u>1680</u>: DG, Jun 0, Sep 0; <u>1681</u>: DG, Nov 22; <u>1684</u>: DL,
Apr 0; <u>1686</u>: NONE, Sep 0; <u>1688</u>: NONE, Sep 0; <u>1689</u>: DL, Mar 0, NONE, Sep 0,
DL, Dec 4; <u>1690</u>: DLORDG, Mar 0, NONE, Sep 0, DL, Dec 0; <u>1691</u>: DL, Jan 0;
<u>1692</u>: DL, Feb 0, Nov 0; <u>1693</u>: DL, Feb 0, Mar 0, Apr 0, DG, May 0, DL, Oct 0;
<u>1694</u>: DL, Feb 0, Mar 21, DG, May 0; <u>1695</u>: LIF, Apr 30, Sep 0, Dec 0; <u>1696</u>:
LIF, Apr 0, Oct 0, Nov 14, Dec 0; <u>1697</u>: LIF, May 0, Jun 0, Nov 0; <u>1698</u>: LIF,
Mar 0, Nov 0
Leigh, Elizabeth (actor), <u>1681</u>: NONE, Sep 0; <u>1699</u>: LIF, Dec 18; <u>1700</u>: LIF, Jan
9, Mar 5; <u>1701</u>: LIF, Jan 0, Mar 0, Aug 0; <u>1702</u>: LIF, Jun 0; <u>1703</u>: LIF, Feb 0,
Mar 0, Apr 28, May 21, Jun 1, Nov 0; <u>1704</u>: LIF, Jan 13, Jun 6, Dec 4; <u>1706</u>:
QUEEN'S, May 2, Nov 22, 25, Dec 2, 3, 5, 7, 13, 27; <u>1707</u>: QUEEN'S, Jan 20,
May 23, Jun 10, 25
Leigh Jr, Francis (actor, dancer), <u>1728</u>: DL, Nov 14; <u>1730</u>: DL, Oct 28; <u>1731</u>:
DL, Nov 25; <u>1732</u>: DL, Mar 21, May 6, Aug 1, 17, BF, 22, DL, Nov 16, Dec 18;
<u>1733</u>: DL, Jan 23, Mar 31, May 3, 9, BFCGBH, Aug 23, Sep 4, DL, Oct 10, 24,
31; <u>1734</u>: DL, Feb 4, DL/HAY, Mar 16, DL, Apr 15, DL/HAY, 26, May 24, DL, Sep
19, Oct 9, 21, Nov 1, 8, Dec 6; <u>1735</u>: DL, Jan 22, Feb 14, YB, Mar 21, DL, Apr
25, May 14, 22, 23, LIF, Jun 12, DL, Jul 1, GF/HAY, 22, Aug 21, DL, Sep 11,
13, 15, Oct 2, Nov 15, 21; <u>1736</u>: DL, Feb 9, 28, May 18, 21, Aug 26, Sep 7,
SFL, 7, DL, 14, 28, Oct 12, 22, 25, Nov 22, 24, 26, Dec 7, 31; <u>1737</u>: DL, Jan
26, 29, May 17, 20, 25, Sep 10, 17, Oct 13, 25, 27, Nov 12, 15; <u>1738</u>: DL, Jan
12, 19, 24, 26, Feb 23, Apr 13, May 3, Sep 23, Oct 3, 16, 30, Nov 2, Dec 15;
<u>1739</u>: DL, Jan 16, Feb 1, 9, Mar 20, Apr 5, May 2, 19, 28, Sep 6, 22, 26, Oct
10, 13, Nov 7, 19, 22, Dec 11, 14, 31; <u>1740</u>: DL, Jan 15, Mar 25, Apr 17, 29,
May 9, BFH, Aug 23, DL, Sep 20, Oct 10, 14, 15, 17, 27, Nov 17, 24, Dec 2, 4,
26; <u>1741</u>: DL, May 21, Sep 17, Oct 6, 9, 20, Nov 11, 21; <u>1742</u>: DL, Jan 4, 6,
Feb 12, Mar 27, 29, Apr 5, 20, 26, Oct 2, 7, 9, 12, 16, Nov 1, Dec 17; <u>1743</u>:
DL, Feb 10, Mar 21, Apr 18, 21, Sep 13; <u>1744</u>: DL, May 23, Sep 18, 20, Oct 2,
19, SOU, 20; <u>1745</u>: DL, Jan 11, 16, Apr 19, 30, May 7, Sep 28, Oct 8, Nov 1,
19, 20, 30, Dec 16, 20, 30; <u>1746</u>: DL, Jan 2, Apr 7, 10, 15, 23, 26, May 9,
16, Jun 11, 13, Aug 6, Sep 25, 27, 30, Oct 11, 23, 31, Dec 12, 30; <u>1747</u>: DL,
Jan 15, Feb 7, 24, Mar 28, 30, Apr 11, May 1, 5, SF, Sep 14, BHB, 26, DL, Oct
21, 24, 29; <u>1748</u>: DL, Jan 6, Feb 3, Apr 19, May 4
Leigh Sr, Francis (actor), <u>1707</u>: DL, Apr 3, Oct 18, 25, Dec 26; <u>1708</u>: DL, Mar
18, SH, 26, DL, May 29, Aug 31, Sep 4, 14, 16, 18, 21, 28, Oct 2, 5, 25, Dec
21; <u>1709</u>: DL, Jan 18, Feb 15, 16, 24, Mar 17, Apr 12, May 17, 31, Jun 1, Sep
6, Nov 26, Dec 3, 6, 7, 9, 10, 17; <u>1710</u>: DL, Jan 14, Feb 1, 6, 7, 9, 25, Mar
11, May 3, Jun 2, GR, 21, 24, 28, Jul 1, 8, 10, 12, 20, 22, 27, 29, Aug 3, 5,
7, 10, 12, 14, 19, 24, 28, Sep 9, 11, DL, Dec 7; <u>1711</u>: DL/QUEEN, Feb 17, DL,
Mar 17, Apr 21, May 18, 21, DL/QUEEN, 29, DL, 31, DL/QUEEN, Jun 5, 22, GR,
Jul 26, DL, Oct 13, 16, 30, Nov 23, Dec 6; <u>1712</u>: DL, Jan 19, May 19, Jun 2,
5, 9, Jul 18, Nov 7, 26, Dec 30; <u>1713</u>: DL, Jan 5, 19, 29, Feb 9, 13, Mar 16,
May 12, 18, Jun 17, 19, Nov 9, 25, 27, Dec 2; <u>1714</u>: DL, May 17, 21, 28, Jun
2, 4, 18, 25; <u>1715</u>: LIF, Jan 8, Mar 26, Apr 19, Jun 7, 23, Aug 3, 10, Oct 10,
12, DL, Nov 9, Dec 12, 31; <u>1716</u>: DL, Jan 11, Feb 3, May 8, 9, Jul 12, 19, Oct
9, 11, 16, 29, Dec 5; <u>1717</u>: DL, Jan 2, 12, 16, May 4, 14, Jun 6, 10, Oct 9,
14, Nov 6, 13, 18, 20, 25, Dec 31; <u>1718</u>: DL, Feb 14, 19, Mar 24, Apr 1, 14,
17, 25, Jun 11, Jul 11, Aug 1, RI, 2, DL, 20, Oct 2, 8, 15, 20, 24, Nov 27,
Dec 11, 19; <u>1719</u>: DL, Apr 23, May 23
Leigh, John (actor, author), <u>1715</u>: LIF, Jan 3, 4, 7, 8, 11, Feb 2, 3, 5, 16,
Mar 19, 26, Apr 30, Jun 2, 23, Aug 11, Sep 28, 29, Oct 4, 5, 7, 10, 12, 28,
Nov 29, 30; <u>1716</u>: LIF, Jan 3, 4, Feb 21, Mar 24, Apr 27, Jul 4, 11, Aug 3,
Oct 10, 18, 20, 23, Nov 5, 9, 10, 13, Dec 1, 4; <u>1717</u>: LIF, Jan 10, 28, Mar
11, 16, 18, May 18, Jun 25, Jul 10, TC, Aug 5, NONE, Sep 12, SF, 25, LIF, Oct
15, 17, 26, Nov 6, 11, 14, 16, 19, 20, 26, 28, Dec 3, 7, 9, 10, 14; <u>1718</u>:
LIF, Jan 2, 7, 11, Feb 1, 18, Mar 1, 3, Apr 19, 23, Jun 20, 30, Jul 9, RI,
19, LIF, 24, RI, Aug 2, LIF, 6, RI, 9, 11, 16, 23, SF, Sep 3, 5, LIF, 26, 29,

30, Oct 1, 4, 6, 8, 11, 15, 16, 18, 31, Nov 11, 13, 24, 25, Dec 6; <u>1719</u>: LIF,
Jan 3, 16, Feb 7, 21, 28, Mar 19, 30, Apr 2, Oct 2, 5, 7, 10, 13, 15, 17, 31,
Nov 3, 5, 7, 13, 18, 19, 21, 23, 24, 26, Dec 10; <u>1720</u>: LIF, Jan 7, 11, 26,
Feb 11, 23, 26, Mar 17, 19, Apr 9, 18, 26, 30, May 11, 17, 25, SFLH, Sep 5,
LIF, Oct 6, 8, SOU, 10, LIF, 11, 13, 15, 18, 20, 27, Nov 1, 2, 3, 10, 15, 19,
22, 29, Dec 1, 17, 21, 22, 27, 31; <u>1721</u>: LIF, Jan 17, 28, Feb 25, Mar 4, 11,
23, Apr 17, 19, 25, May 5, 10, 15, 29, SFHL, Sep 2, LIF, 27, Oct 12, 19, 24,
26; <u>1722</u>: LIF, May 4, Jun 13, Aug 1, Sep 29, Oct 1, 2, 9, 13, 18, 20, 26, Nov
7, 8, 12, 17, 22, Dec 1, 15, 20, 21, 31; <u>1723</u>: LIF, Jan 3, 7, 11, Feb 22, Apr
18, May 9, Oct 24, 31, Nov 1, 2, 14, 18, 21, Dec 7; <u>1724</u>: LIF, Mar 19, 23,
26, Apr 22, May 19, Jul 3, 14, 21, 31, Aug 11, Oct 7, 9, Nov 17, 19; <u>1725</u>:
LIF, Jan 4, Oct 11
--Hob's Wedding, <u>1720</u>: LIF, Jan 11, 12, 13, 14, 15, 16, 18, 22, 29, Feb 6, 12,
27; <u>1723</u>: HAY, Jan 28
--Pretenders, The; or, Kensington Gardens, <u>1719</u>: LIF, Nov 21, 26, 27, 28, 30,
Dec 1, 2, 16
Leigh (Lee), Michael (actor), <u>1690</u>: DL, Mar 0, Sep 0; <u>1691</u>: NONE, Sep 0, DL,
Dec 0; <u>1692</u>: DL, Feb 0, Mar 0, Nov 8; <u>1693</u>: DL, Apr 0; <u>1694</u>: DL, Feb 0, May
0, Sep 0, NONE, 0; <u>1695</u>: DL, Sep 0, Nov 0, DG, 0, DL, Dec 0; <u>1696</u>: DG, Jun 0,
LIF, 0, Nov 14; <u>1697</u>: DL, Feb 0, May 8, ATCOURT, Nov 4; <u>1701</u>: LIF, Jan 0;
<u>1702</u>: LIF, Dec 31; <u>1703</u>: LIF, Nov 0; <u>1704</u>: LIF, Mar 25, Jun 8, DL, Oct 18,
LIF, Dec 4; <u>1705</u>: LIF/QUEN, Feb 22, Oct 30
Leigh, Mrs (actor), <u>1718</u>: RI, Aug 23; <u>1724</u>: SF, Aug 28
Leigh, Widow (beneficiary), <u>1720</u>: DL, Jun 1; <u>1721</u>: DL, May 30; <u>1722</u>: DL, May
28; <u>1723</u>: DL, Jun 4; <u>1724</u>: DL, May 25; <u>1725</u>: DL, May 24; <u>1726</u>: DL, May 17
Leinster, Captain (spectator), <u>1691</u>: DLORDG, Mar 17
Leinster, Duchess of. See St George, Emilia Olivia.
Leinster, Duke of. See Schomberg, Meinhardt.
Leire (beneficiary), <u>1744</u>: TB, Apr 17
Leith, <u>1752</u>: CG, Dec 27
Leitherfull (actor), <u>1680</u>: DG, Sep 0
Leke, Robert, Lord Deincourt, Earl of Scarsdale, <u>1675</u>: ATCOURT, Feb 15; <u>1699</u>:
DLORLIF, Feb 20
Lelauze. See LaLauze.
LeMarch (actor), <u>1773</u>: HAY, Sep 16
LeMarsh. See Lamash.
LeMash. See Lamash.
Lemercier (dancer), <u>1781</u>: DL, May 17; <u>1782</u>: DL, Jan 11, 21, Feb 19, 23, Mar 7,
Apr 5, 25, May 10, 17
LeMesurier, Paul (Lord Mayor), <u>1794</u>: DL, Jul 2
LeMierre, Antoine Marin, <u>1790</u>: CG, May 5
--Veuve du Malabar, La, <u>1790</u>: CG, May 5
Lemon St, <u>1740</u>: CG, Apr 21; <u>1741</u>: NWGF, Oct 23; <u>1743</u>: LIF, Mar 14, Apr 7; <u>1745</u>:
GF, Feb 4, Mar 21, Oct 28; <u>1746</u>: GF, Mar 3, Oct 27, Nov 13; <u>1749</u>: NWLS, Feb
27; <u>1751</u>: NWLS, Aug 6, 7, Sep 5; <u>1752</u>: NWLS, Nov 13, 16, 20, 23, 30; <u>1754</u>:
NWLS, Mar 1
LeMont (dancer), <u>1748</u>: SFP, Sep 7
Lendrick (actor), <u>1780</u>: HAY, Apr 5
Leneker (beneficiary), <u>1717</u>: HIC, May 3; <u>1719</u>: HIC, Feb 18
L'Englois. See Langlois.
Lennard (beneficiary), <u>1722</u>: LIF, May 23
Lennard, Thomas, Lord Sussex, <u>1686</u>: DLORDG, Dec 22
Lennet (actor), <u>1791</u>: HAY, Oct 24
Lennox, Charles, Duke of Richmond, <u>1693</u>: DL, Apr 0; <u>1694</u>: DGORDL, Jun 28
Lennox, Charlotte, <u>1750</u>: HAY, Feb 22; <u>1769</u>: CG, Feb 18; <u>1775</u>: DL, Nov 9; <u>1776</u>:
DL, Dec 28
--Old City Manners, <u>1775</u>: DL, Nov 9, 11, 13, 15, 17, 20, 27, Dec 14; <u>1776</u>: DL,
Jan 1, 8, Nov 9, Dec 28
--Sister, The, <u>1769</u>: CG, Feb 18
Lenten Prologue Refused by the Players, A (broadside), <u>1683</u>: NONE, Apr 11
Leo, F (composer), <u>1742</u>: KING'S, Apr 20
Leo, Leonardo (composer), <u>1732</u>: KING'S, Nov 4; <u>1741</u>: KING'S, Oct 31; <u>1742</u>:
KING'S, Apr 20; <u>1748</u>: KING'S, Dec 31; <u>1754</u>: CG, Feb 11; <u>1770</u>: CG, Mar 16
--Amor Costante, L' (opera), <u>1754</u>: CG, Feb 11, 13, 15, 18, 20
--Amor Vuol Sofferenza (opera), <u>1748</u>: KING'S, Dec 31
--Finta Frascatana, La (opera), <u>1748</u>: KING'S, Dec 31
Leonard (beneficiary), <u>1720</u>: LIF, Jun 2; <u>1725</u>: LIF, May 7
Leonard (dancer), <u>1675</u>: ATCOURT, Feb 15; <u>1694</u>: DGORDL, Jun 28
Leonard (duellist), <u>1694</u>: DGORDL, Jun 28
Leonard, Mrs (actor), <u>1733</u>: HAY, May 28
Leonardi (dancer), <u>1744</u>: DL, Dec 14, 15, 17, 19, 21, 26, 28; <u>1745</u>: DL, Jan 10
Leonardi, Pietro (singer), <u>1761</u>: KING'S, Nov 10

Leoni (Lyon, Master), Michael (singer, actor), 1760: DL, Dec 13; 1761: DL, Apr
    11, May 22, Sep 10, CG, 21; 1762: DL, May 8; 1770: CG, Jan 27, 31, May 1,
    HAY, Oct 1; 1771: GROTTO, Aug 24, Sep 3; 1774: CG, Oct 13, Nov 1; 1775: CG,
    Apr 25, May 8, Oct 2, 14, 18, Nov 21; 1776: STRAND, Jan 23, CG, Feb 3, 23,
    Apr 20, Oct 7, Nov 4, 9, 14, 25, 28, 30, Dec 6; 1777: CG, Jan 25, Apr 5, Oct
    8, 29, 30, Dec 3, 26; 1778: CG, Jan 8, Feb 4, Mar 31, DL, Sep 17, CG, 28, Oct
    22, 23, Nov 3, 5, Dec 11; 1779: CG, Jan 4, Mar 20, 22, DL, Apr 6, CG, 10, 17,
    Dec 18, 29; 1780: CG, Jan 7, 29, Mar 27, Apr 3, 18, May 1, Nov 13, 15, 18,
    25; 1781: CG, Mar 3, 31, Apr 25, May 2, Oct 10, 13, 24, Nov 7, 9, 10, 12, 28;
    1782: CG, Feb 2; 1784: CG, May 1; 1785: CG, Apr 5, 20; 1787: CG, Jan 13, Mar
    31, Apr 21; 1788: CG, Apr 30, Jun 2; 1791: CG, Jun 4
Lepicq, Charles (dancer), 1782: KING'S, May 2, 25, Jun 5, Nov 2, 9, 30, Dec 12;
    1783: KING'S, Jan 11, 16, Feb 13, 15, Mar 13, Apr 10, May 1, 8, 31, Jun 28,
    Nov 29, Dec 6, 16, 27, 30; 1784: KING'S, Mar 4, 6, 18, 20, 25, Apr 24, May
    13, 20, Dec 18; 1785: KING'S, Jan 1, 11, 22, Feb 5, 12, Mar 3, 12, 17, Apr 7,
    14, 21, May 12, 24, Jun 18, 21, 25, 28; 1786: KING'S, Mar 23; 1789: KING'S,
    Jun 15
Leporello (composer), 1794: KING'S, Mar 1
LePost, Mimi (dancer), 1727: KING'S, Mar 23
Leppie (Lepye) (dancer), 1755: CG, Jan 4, Apr 15, 18, May 6; 1756: CG, Nov 29,
    Dec 10; 1757: CG, Feb 8, 9, 16, Apr 26, 27, May 2, Nov 2, Dec 10, 17; 1758:
    CG, Feb 1, Apr 14, 20, Oct 14, Nov 1, 16, 23; 1759: CG, Oct 5, Dec 10, 11;
    1760: CG, Jan 16, 18, Apr 8, 12, 17, 18, 22, 25, Oct 11, 20, Dec 11, 17;
    1761: CG, Mar 9, Apr 2, 21, May 25, Sep 16, 21, 26, Oct 13; 1762: CG, Apr 30,
    May 11, DL, Oct 7, 22, 29; 1763: DL, Jan 3; 1764: CG, Oct 23, Nov 1, Dec 12;
    1765: CG, Mar 26, Apr 18, 30, Oct 28, Nov 15; 1769: DL, Oct 4; 1770: KING'S,
    May 19, HAY, Dec 10; 1771: HAY, Sep 16, KING'S, Nov 2, Dec 10; 1772: KING'S,
    Jan 11, Nov 14, 21, Dec 8; 1773: KING'S, Jan 2, 5, 15, 26, Mar 9, 16, 18, 23,
    30, Apr 1, 17, 24
Leppie Jr (dancer), 1770: KING'S, May 19
Leppie, Mrs (dancer), 1758: CG, Feb 1, Apr 22, Oct 14, Nov 16, 23; 1759: CG,
    Apr 28, Dec 10; 1760: CG, Jan 16, 18, Apr 12, Oct 11, 20; 1761: CG, Mar 9,
    May 7, Sep 16, 21; 1762: CG, Jan 28, DL, Nov 23
Leppie's scholar (dancer), 1761: CG, May 7
Leprue (actor), 1729: HAY, Feb 25
Lepulley (dancer), 1782: HAY, Jan 21
LeRiche (musician), 1697: HIC, Dec 9, YB, 16; 1698: ROBERTS, Mar 23; 1700: LIF,
    Sep 25
LeRoy (dancer), 1675: ATCOURT, Feb 15
Leroy (scene painter), 1777: DL, Jan 1
LeRoy, Mlle (dancer), 1737: BF, Aug 23, SF, Sep 7
LeSac (choreographer), 1700: LIF, Jul 5
LeSac (dancer), 1710: GR, Jul 27, 29, Aug 3, 5
LeSac (dancer), 1725: LIF, Nov 2, 8, Dec 3; 1726: LIF, May 3, 11, 12, 16, 24,
    25; 1727: LIF, May 9; 1729: HAY, Jun 24; 1732: LIF, Oct 18, LIF/CG, 25, 30,
    Nov 8, 9, 16, Dec 8, CG/LIF, 19; 1733: LIF/CG, Jan 12, 18, 19, 23, 27, Feb 2,
    CG, 8, LIF/CG, Mar 12, CG, 27, LIF/CG, 28, Apr 12, 16, 18, 30, May 3, 7, 8,
    10, 14, CG, 16, 17, LIF/CG, 18, 21, 24, Jun 1, CG, Sep 22, Oct 4, 11, 18, 27,
    Nov 10, 12, 24, Dec 7, 28; 1734: CG, Jan 1, 14, 17, 25, Feb 26, Mar 11, 16,
    Apr 1, 27, May 1, 7, 15, RI, Sep 12, CG/LIF, 20, 25, Oct 2, 7, 14, 23, 26,
    31, Nov 1, 19, 25, 29, Dec 5, 12, 19, 30; 1735: CG/LIF, Jan 13, 14, 17, Feb
    3, 13, 22, Mar 11, 15, YB, 21, CG/LIF, 25, Apr 9, 14, 15, 17, 18, May 2, CG,
    6, 8, CG/LIF, 9, 12, 13, 15, 16, 19, 20, 22, 27, Jun 2, GF, Oct 15, Nov 3, 6,
    12, 14, 15, 17, 19, 28, Dec 4, 6, 8, 10, 12, 15, 17; 1736: GF, Feb 4, 5, 16,
    HAY, 20, GF, 20, Mar 3, 25, Apr 1, 6, 12, 27, 28, May 6, 10, LIF, Jul 1, Sep
    30, Oct 5, 9, 21, Dec 7, 15, 16; 1737: LIF, Jan 5, Feb 1, DL, 10
LeSac, Master (actor), 1732: GF, Dec 18
LeSac, Master (dancer), 1725: LIF, Oct 26, Nov 11, 18, 24; 1726: LIF, Jan 5,
    Mar 31, Apr 21, 29, May 17, 19, 26, 30, Oct 19
LeSage Jr (actor, dancer), 1734: GF/HAY, Nov 20, Dec 2, 9, HAY, 13, 20, 23,
    GF/HAY, 30; 1735: GF/HAY, Jan 8, 9, HAY, 13, GF/HAY, 16, Feb 5, 13, HAY, Mar
    19
LeSage Sr (actor), 1734: GF/HAY, Nov 20, Dec 2, 9, HAY, 13, 20, 23, GF/HAY, 27,
    30; 1735: GF/HAY, Jan 8, 9, HAY, 13, GF/HAY, 16, Feb 5, 13
LeSage, Alain Rene, 1726: HAY, May 9
--Arlequin Hulla (farce), 1722: HAY, Mar 5, 8, 12, 27, 30; 1734: GF/HAY, Nov 6,
    18, Dec 6; 1735: GF/HAY, Jan 17, Feb 28, HAY, Mar 24; 1749: HAY, Nov 22, 24
--Arlequin Invisible, a la Cour du Roy de la Chine (farce), 1721: HAY, Dec 4,
    15
--School of Lovers, The (farce), 1720: LIF, Apr 4
LeSage, J B (witness), 1738: HAY, Nov 7
LeSage, Mrs (actor), 1734: HAY, Dec 13

LeSage, Mrs Jr (dancer), 1734: HAY, Dec 20, 23, GF/HAY, 27; 1735: HAY, Jan 13,
    GF/HAY, Feb 5
Lescot (dancer), 1758: KING'S, Jan 10, 31
Lescot, Mme (dancer), 1758: KING'S, Jan 10, 31
Leserve, Anna Maria (actor, singer), 1787: HAY, Apr 30; 1791: CG, Jun 13, Sep
    26, Oct 3, 10, 20, Nov 4, Dec 21, 22; 1792: CG, Feb 28, Mar 10, Apr 12, 17,
    May 10, 15, Oct 8, 12, 19, 24, 29, 30, Dec 26; 1793: CG, Apr 8, May 10, 31,
    Sep 23, 30, Oct 2, 7, 9, 24, 25, Nov 11, 22, 28, Dec 7, 19, 27; 1794: CG, Jan
    6, 9, Feb 5, 26, Mar 6, May 6, Sep 22, 29, Oct 7, 20, 30, Dec 6; 1795: CG,
    Jan 31, Mar 16, 19, Apr 7, 8, 24, May 12, 29, Jun 6, Sep 14, 21, 28, 30, Oct
    8, 14, 15, 19, 24, 30, Nov 4, 9, 27; 1796: CG, Jan 23, Feb 1, 4, 16, Mar 30,
    Apr 23, 26, May 3, 16, 23, Jun 3, 7, Sep 12, 16, 19, 26, Oct 6, 7, 14, 29,
    Nov 21, Dec 9, 19; 1797: CG, Jan 10, Feb 18, 27, Mar 13, 16, Apr 8, 25, May
    18, 26, Jun 13, HAY, 20, 21, 23, Aug 14, 15, 24, CG, Sep 25, Oct 6, 13, 16,
    21, Nov 2, 11, 15, 20, Dec 8, 18, 23, 26; 1798: CG, Jan 31, Feb 12, Mar 31,
    Apr 9, 10, 19, May 18, 28, 30, 31, HAY, Jun 16, 30, Jul 6, 21, Aug 11, 21,
    Sep 10, CG, 17, 19, Oct 1, 3, 8, 11, Nov 6, 12, 17, 23, Dec 11, 15, 26; 1799:
    CG, Jan 29, Mar 2, 16, 25, Apr 2, 9, 13, 19, 23, 26, May 10, 14, 23, 28, Jun
    7, 12, HAY, 15, 22, 24, Jul 9, Aug 17, 21, CG, Sep 18, 27, 30, Oct 2, 7, 9,
    10, 16, 21, 24, 25, 29, 31, Nov 11, Dec 10, 23; 1800: CG, Jan 18, 29, Feb 10,
    Mar 17, 25, 27, Apr 5, 29, 30, May 1, 2, 20, 23, 29, Jun 2, HAY, Jul 1, 2,
    Aug 14, 29, Sep 1
Leslie (Lislie) (ticket delivere), 1779: DL, May 28; 1780: DL, May 25; 1781:
    DL, May 18; 1782: DL, May 4; 1783: DL, May 26; 1784: DL, May 15; 1785: DL,
    May 21
Lesly, George
--Divine Dialogues (entertainment), 1683: NONE, Sep 0
Lessing, Gotthold Ephraim, 1786: HAY, Jul 24; 1794: DL, Oct 28
--Minna von Barnhelm, 1786: HAY, Jul 24
Lessingham, Jane (actor), 1756: CG, Nov 18; 1762: CG, Feb 3, Mar 9, 20, Apr 19,
    24, Oct 21, Nov 8; 1763: CG, Apr 23, May 6, Sep 23; 1764: DL, Oct 29; 1765:
    DL, Jan 23, May 17, 18, 27, Oct 18; 1767: DL, Apr 29, May 6, 25, 26, 29, Jun
    3, CG, Sep 26, Oct 6, 22, Nov 7, 17; 1768: CG, Jan 9, Feb 29, Apr 20, May 27,
    31, Sep 22, 23, Oct 12, 14, Nov 16, Dec 3, 16, 22, 29; 1769: CG, Apr 1, 19,
    20, 22, Oct 3, 4, 5, Nov 17, Dec 12, 22; 1770: CG, Jan 6, 12, Apr 5, 28, Oct
    26, 27, Nov 16, 30; 1771: CG, Apr 3, 20, 27, May 17, Sep 23, Oct 22, Nov 2,
    25, Dec 6, 9; 1772: CG, Jan 20, Feb 3, 22, Mar 23, Apr 21, 22, Sep 21, 23,
    28, Oct 16, 19, 30, Nov 12, Dec 11, 22; 1773: CG, Apr 17, 27, Nov 12, 18, Dec
    7, 8, 9, 18; 1774: CG, Jan 15, 25, DL, Apr 5, CG, 7, Sep 21, 28, Oct 26, 27,
    Nov 3, 8, 12; 1775: CG, Jan 17, Feb 11, Mar 20, Apr 19, May 4, 18, 20, Sep
    20, 27, 29, Oct 4, 6, 11, 24, Nov 24, 28, Dec 16, 28; 1776: CG, Jan 9, 24,
    Mar 2, Apr 27, Sep 23, 25, Oct 29, Nov 7, 26; 1777: CG, Jan 2, 25, Apr 16,
    May 29, Sep 22, 26, Oct 15, 16, 23, Dec 5; 1778: CG, Jan 29, Feb 6, 13, 28,
    Mar 14, Apr 24, 27, Sep 18, 23, 25, 30, Oct 2, 9, 15; 1779: CG, Jan 11, 13,
    22, 26, Apr 27, DL, May 5, CG, Oct 29, Nov 4, 6, 30, Dec 31; 1780: CG, Jan 7,
    Sep 18, Oct 6, 19, 21, Nov 2; 1781: CG, Jan 18, Feb 15, Apr 21, May 28, Nov
    8, Dec 5; 1782: CG, Jan 4, 18, Mar 16, Oct 29, Nov 14, 27
Lesson for Lawyers, A. See Baddeley, Robert.
Lester (ticket deliverer), 1798: CG, Jun 5
L'Estoile, Claude de
--Belle Esclave, La, 1725: HAY, Jan 15
L'Estrade (actor), 1739: CG, Oct 3
Lestrade (dancer), 1740: CG, May 13, Oct 29, Dec 29; 1741: CG, Feb 10; 1742:
    CG, Jan 8
L'Estrange Jr, J (beneficiary), 1732: TTT, Mar 3
L'Estrange, Joseph (actor), 1774: CG, Oct 20, 31, Dec 3, 9, 15, 17, 26; 1775:
    CG, Jan 7, Feb 21, Mar 2, 18, 28, Apr 22, May 20, HAY, 22, Jun 7, 28, Jul 12,
    14, 19, 21, 31, Sep 4, 16, 21, CG, 25, Oct 12, 17, 19, 21, 25, 28, 30, Nov 4,
    14, Dec 1, 9; 1776: CG, Jan 1, Feb 22, 26, Mar 16, 18, Apr 26, May 7, HAY,
    22, 27, 28, 31, Jun 14, Jul 10, Aug 2, 19, Sep 2, 17, 20, CG, Oct 2, 7, 8,
    16, 17, 31, Nov 1, 11, 12, 13, 14, 21, 28, Dec 2, 6, 18, 27; 1777: CG, Jan 8,
    17, Feb 25, Apr 7, 14, 16, May 7, 14, CHR, Jun 18, 20, 25, 27, CG, Sep 29,
    Oct 6, 15, 16, 21, 30, Nov 1, 6, 7, 13; 1778: CG, Jan 3, 15, 19, 20, 21, Feb
    10, 16, 24, Mar 2, 7, 23, 30, Apr 7, 11, 21, 27, May 5, 6, 9, 11, 15, Sep 21,
    28, Oct 5, 9, 21, 22, 24, 26, 28, 31, Nov 4, 19, Dec 3, 8, 26; 1779: CG, Jan
    18, 19, 22, Feb 12, Mar 4, 9, 22, Apr 6, 8, 23, 24, 26, 27, 29, 30, May 6,
    13, 18, 20, Sep 20, 24, Oct 1, 4, 6, 11, 13, 18, 20, 23, 29, Nov 1, 8, 10,
    11, 16, 19, 22, 30, Dec 3, 16, 31; 1780: CG, Jan 12, 17, 25, Feb 17, 22, Apr
    21, 25, 27, May 10, Jun 1, Oct 2, 3, 4, 9, 11, 18, 19, 23, 26, Nov 4, 6, 10,
    13, 15, 24, Dec 27; 1781: CG, Jan 16, 18, 31, Feb 24, Apr 2, May 7, 10, 16,
    Sep 24, Oct 5, 23, 31, Nov 2, 5, 8, 28, Dec 5, 10, 11, 17, 20, 31; 1782: CG,
    Jan 1, 5, 7, 10, Feb 5, Mar 14, 19, Apr 17, May 11, 20, 21, Oct 3; 1783: CG,

May 27; 1784: DL, Jan 9, HAY, 21, CG, Jun 10; 1785: HAY, Feb 12, Mar 15, Apr
   26; 1787: ROY, Jun 20; 1788: HAY, Apr 9, 29, Dec 22
L'Estrange, Sir Roger (author), 1717: DL, Jul 9, 11
Let all the Angels (song), 1793: KING/HAY, Feb 20; 1794: DL, Mar 19
Let bards elate (song), 1793: CG, May 21; see also Peggy Perkins
Let Caesar and Urania live (song), 1737: CG, Mar 14; 1745: CG, Mar 14
Let every shepherd bring his lass (song), 1698: DL, Mar 0
Let fame sound the Trumpet (song), 1786: HAMM, Jul 10
Let Festal Joy Triumphant Reign (song), 1754: CG, Apr 22
Let Masonry be now my Theme (song), 1735: DL, May 13, HAY, Aug 4; 1737: DL, May
   7; 1738: CG, May 1
Let Matrimony be now my Theme (song), 1734: DL/HAY, May 4
Let me wander not unseen (song), 1742: DL, Apr 6, 21, 22, 23, 27, May 8, 17,
   18, Sep 25, 28, Oct 2; 1743: LIF, Mar 21; 1789: CG, Mar 20, DL, 25; 1790: CG,
   Mar 3, DL, 10; 1791: CG, Mar 30, DL, Apr 13; 1792: KING'S, Mar 14, 30; 1793:
   CG, Mar 20; 1794: DL, Mar 12, 14, CG, 21, DL, Apr 2, 9; 1796: CG, Feb 17;
   1799: CG, Mar 15
Let monarchs fight (song), 1694: DG, Jan 10
Let no rage thy bosom fire (song), 1762: CG, Apr 3, 24
Let not Age (song), 1784: CG, May 15
Let old Timotheus yield the prize (song), 1791: CG, Mar 25; 1792: CG, Mar 7;
   1794: CG, Mar 14
Let other Men sing of their Goddess's bright (song), 1791: CG, May 5
Let the bells now ring (song), 1670: NONE, Sep 0
Let the bright seraphim (song), 1790: CG, Mar 17, 26; 1791: DL, Mar 11; 1792:
   CG, Feb 24, KING'S, 29, Mar 7, CG, 9; 1793: KING/HAY, Feb 15, CG, Mar 8;
   1794: DL, Mar 12, 14, CG, 26, DL, Apr 9, CG, 11; 1795: CG, Mar 13; 1796: CG,
   Feb 24, Mar 2, 16; 1797: CG, Mar 15; 1798: CG, Mar 14; 1799: CG, Mar 1; 1800:
   CG, Mar 5
Let the dreadful engines (song), 1694: DG, May 0; 1702: DL, Nov 19, Dec 8;
   1704: DL, Jun 7
Let the merry bells (song), 1793: CG, Mar 20
Let the soldiers (song), 1694: DG, Jan 10
Let the whole earth stand in awe (song), 1790: CG, Mar 3; 1792: CG, Mar 9
Let their celestial concerts all unite (song), 1790: CG, Mar 17, 26; 1791: CG,
   Apr 13; 1792: CG, Feb 24, Mar 21; 1793: CG, Mar 8; 1794: DL, Apr 9, 11; 1795:
   CG, Mar 13; 1797: CG, Mar 15; 1799: CG, Mar 1; 1800: CG, Mar 5
Let them come if they dare (song), 1798: CG, Mar 9, 14
Let those Youths who freedom prize (song), 1697: DG, Jun 0
Let us break (song), 1793: KING/HAY, Feb 20; 1794: DL, Mar 19
Let us love and let us drink (song), 1795: CG, May 1, 8; 1797: CG, May 2
Let us revel and roar (song), 1695: LIF, Dec 0
Let ye Soldiers (song), 1694: DG, Jan 10
Let's drink dear friends (song), 1672: DG, Jul 4
Let's imitate her notes above (song), 1784: CG, Apr 27, May 17; 1791: CG, Mar
   25; 1792: CG, Mar 7, KING'S, 28; 1794: CG, Mar 14
Let's sing old Rose and burn the Bellows (song), 1783: HAY, May 31; 1788: HAY,
   Aug 22, Sep 2; 1789: CG, May 5; 1790: DL, May 20; 1791: CG, May 17; 1800: CG,
   Apr 26
Letang (dancer), 1675: ATCOURT, Feb 15
Letelier (singer), 1675: ATCOURT, Feb 15
LeTemps (dancer), 1674: DL, Mar 30
LeTexier, Anthony, 1770: DL, Apr 27; 1788: HAY, Aug 22; 1789: CG, Mar 31; 1791:
   KING'S, May 19; 1799: KING'S, Jan 29, May 30
Lethe Rehearsed (pamphlet), 1749: DL, Feb 1
Lethe.   See Garrick, David.
Letsam (boxkeeper), 1757: CG, May 18; 1758: CG, May 8; 1759: CG, May 18; 1760:
   CG, May 15, Sep 22; 1761: CG, May 13
Letteney (actor, singer), 1788: CG, Dec 26; 1789: CG, Sep 14, Oct 12, Dec 21,
   29; 1790: CG, Jan 23, Mar 1, Apr 14, May 27, Jun 16, Sep 13, Oct 4, 6, Nov 6,
   15, 26; 1791: CG, Feb 4, May 3, 16, 26, 31, Jun 13, Sep 26, Oct 10, Dec 21;
   1792: CG, Jan 5, Feb 28, Mar 31, Apr 12, 18, May 10, 12, Oct 8, 29; 1798: CG,
   Feb 12; 1799: CG, Jan 29, Mar 25, Apr 13, 25, Dec 23; 1800: CG, Jan 10, Feb
   10
Letter of Complaint, A (criticism), 1747: DL, Mar 19
Letter Writers, The. See Fielding, Henry.
Leucippo. See Vento, Mathias.
Levace (dancer), 1742: NWC, Dec 27
Leveridge, Richard (actor, singer, composer), 1695: DG, Apr 0, DL, Oct 0, Nov
   0; 1696: LIF, Apr 0, DG, Aug 0, Oct 0, DL, Nov 0; 1697: DL, Jan 0, DG, Jun 0;
   1698: DL, Mar 0, YB, May 28, Jun 7, DL/ORDG, Nov 0; 1699: DL, May 0, DLLIF,
   Dec 25; 1702: DL, Nov 14, 19, 21, Dec 8, 22; 1703: DL, Jan 23, Feb 1, 3, 11,

Mar 13, Apr 19, 23, May 13, 28, Jun 12, 16, 17, 19, 22, Jul 1, Oct 19, Nov 2, 8, 10, 27, 29, Dec 14; 1704: DL, Jan 1, 4, 18, 25, Feb 4, 24, 29, LIF, Mar 7, DL, 20, 23, May 25, Jun 7, 9, 13, 19, 29, Jul 1, Nov 23, Dec 2, 6, 16, 20; 1705: DL, Jan 2, 11, 15, 16, Feb 5, 8, 14, 26, 27, Apr 10, May 16, 22, Jun 5, 9, 16, 26, Oct 13, Nov 5, Dec 29, 31; 1706: DL, Jan 1, 7, 10, 16, 21, 25, 28, Feb 1, ATCOURT, 5, DL, 19, 26, Mar 2, 5, 26, 27, 30, Apr 2, DG, Nov 1, DL/DG, 2, DL, Dec 3, 10; 1707: DL, Jan 2, 7, 13, 21, 23, Feb 20, 24, Mar 1, 3, 4, 17, 27, Apr 1, 3, YB, May 23, DL, Oct 28, 29, Nov 11, 22, 25, 28, 29, DL/QUEEN, Dec 6, DL, 10, 17, 18, 27, 30; 1708: DL, Jan 3, QUEEN'S, 20, Feb 26; 1710: QUEEN'S, Jul 6, 13, 21, 26; 1711: RIW, Jul 21, SH, Nov 22; 1712: SH, Apr 4, QUEEN'S, May 17, GR, Jul 19, QUEEN'S, Nov 22, Dec 10; 1713: QUEEN'S, Jan 10, CA, Mar 20, QUEEN'S, May 6, DL, Jun 5; 1714: DL, Jun 18, Oct 21, LIF, Dec 28, 29; 1715: LIF, Jan 17, 25, Feb 9, Mar 3, 14, 21, 22, 24, 31, Apr 4, 9, 18, 19, 23, 26, 28, May 2, 3, 6, 10, 18, 24, Jun 1, Oct 6, 15, 18, Nov 1, 11, Dec 28; 1716: LIF, Feb 1, 10, 16, Mar 3, 6, 10, 15, Apr 11, 25, May 2, 4, Oct 15, 29, 30, Nov 9, 28; 1717: LIF, Jan 2, Feb 4, 27, Mar 19, 23, Apr 4, 13, May 13, 15, Jun 1, Oct 31, Nov 12, 15, Dec 9, 13, 31; 1718: LIF, Jan 14, 17, 20, Mar 4, 11, 22, Apr 5, 24, May 1, 6, 20, Oct 8, 15, 21, 25, 27, 28, Nov 10, 18, Dec 9, 11; 1719: LIF, Jan 31, Apr 8, 11, 20, May 1, 11, 12, Jun 3; 1720: LIF, Feb 5, Mar 19, 22, 24, Apr 9, 28; 1722: LIF, Mar 12; 1723: LIF, Nov 2, 22, Dec 20; 1724: LIF, Jan 3, Mar 3, 23, 26, 28, Apr 6, 7, 9, 13, 23, 30, May 4, 6, 19, 30, Sep 30, Oct 9; 1725: LIF, Jan 21, Mar 11, 15, 18, 29, 31, Apr 2, 5, 7, 10, 15, 16, 20, 23, 30, Oct 13, Nov 3, 13, 22, 30, Dec 2, 8; 1726: LIF, Jan 14, Mar 19, 21, Apr 2, 11, 13, 14, 15, 18, 19, 20, 25, 26, 27, May 4, 13, 20, 30, Sep 16, 23, 26, 30, Oct 5, 24, Nov 19, 21, 26; 1727: LIF, Feb 13, Mar 13, 20, 23, Apr 12, Sep 22, 29, Oct 12, 26, Nov 7, 9, 17; 1728: LIF, Mar 9, YB, 13, LIF, 25, 28, Apr 1, 6, 23, 24, 29, 30, May 2, 3, 13, 15, 16, 18, 23, 29, Sep 30, Oct 9, 14, 23, 26, Nov 23; 1729: LIF, Jan 31, Apr 11, Sep 26, Oct 3, 6, 15, 24, 28, Nov 1, 4; 1730: LIF, Jan 2, Mar 16, 17, Apr 10, 15, 22, 23, 24, 29, May 1, 14, 27, Sep 21, SOU, 24, LIF, 25, Oct 1, 9, Nov 7, Dec 11, 15, 30; 1731: LIF, Mar 15, 22, 26, GF, Apr 1, LIF, 3, 8, 24, 28, 29, May 3, 12, 14, 19, 20, Sep 27, Oct 4, 15, Nov 6, 13, 18, Dec 1; 1732: LIF, Feb 28, Mar 30, Apr 19, 28, May 5, 8, LIF/CG, Oct 4, 13, 30, Nov 8, 13, 24, Dec 27; 1733: LIF/CG, Feb 10, LIF, Mar 7, LIF/CG, 15, 29, 30, Apr 11, 18, 20, CG, May 1, 2, LIF/CG, 3, CG, 4, LIF/CG, 14, 24, 29, CG, Oct 6, 11, 13, 20, Nov 28, Dec 7, 18; 1734: CG, Jan 1, 25, Feb 13, 26, Mar 16, 18, 28, Apr 1, 16, 18, 24, 27, May 1, 3, 4, 6, 9, 13, 14, 15, CG/LIF, Oct 2, Nov 25, Dec 19, 30; 1735: CG/LIF, Feb 13, Mar 15, 18, 20, 25, Apr 15, 21, 22, May 2, 5, GF, 5, DL, 20, CG/LIF, Jun 2, CG, Sep 26, Oct 17, Nov 6, 15, Dec 11; 1736: CG, Jan 1, 21, 23, Mar 6, 18, LIF, Apr 2, CG, 12, 17, 27, 30, May 4, 6, 13, 18, 24, Jun 4, Sep 22, Oct 8, 20, Nov 3, 22, 23, 26; 1737: CG, Jan 4, 25, Feb 14, Mar 17, Apr 12, 18, 19, 21, 22, May 5, 12, 31, Oct 7, Nov 8; 1738: CG, Jan 3, 23, Feb 13, Mar 7, 14, Apr 11, 12, 18, 19, May 2, 5, 6, 10, 12, 15, Oct 4, 6, 28, Nov 18, Dec 6; 1739: CG, Jan 6, 15, 20, Feb 24, Mar 2, 5, Apr 27, May 8, 17, 18, 23, 24, 25, Sep 22, Oct 3, 10, 20, 25, 26, 30, 31, Nov 1, 10, 16, Dec 4, 10; 1740: CG, Jan 22, Feb 12, Mar 18, Apr 16, 30, Jun 5, Sep 19, 26, Oct 1, 22, Dec 16, 29; 1741: CG, Jan 5, 21, Feb 16, 17, 24, 28, Mar 30, Apr 10, 13, 17, 18, 24, 25, 30, May 6, Sep 28, Oct 8, 17, 21, 24, 27, Nov 2, 26; 1742: CG, Jan 5, Mar 15, Apr 19, 22, May 5, 17, 21, Oct 9, 16; 1743: CG, Jan 8, Feb 4, Apr 15, Oct 7, Nov 25, Dec 3, 20, 26; 1744: CG, Jan 14, Feb 14, Mar 3, 14, 15, 28, 29, 30, Apr 2, 3, 6, 12, 16, 17, 19, 30, Oct 1, 22, 31, Dec 8, 29; 1745: CG, Jan 1, 14, Apr 24, May 3, Oct 29, Nov 14, 15, Dec 13; 1746: CG, Jan 1, 8, Apr 16, Jun 27, Nov 6, 8, Dec 26, 29; 1747: CG, Mar 19, 26, Apr 24, Nov 23, Dec 26; 1748: CG, Mar 3, 18, 24, 31, Oct 27, Nov 16, Dec 10; 1749: CG, Apr 14, May 4, Oct 12, 24, Nov 23; 1750: CG, Mar 27, 29, Nov 8, Dec 21, 26; 1751: CG, Apr 16, 19, 24; 1755: DL, Feb 21; 1758: CG, Mar 22; 1790: CG, May 6
--Pyramus and Thisbe, 1716: LIF, Apr 11, Oct 25, 26, 29, Nov 21, 22, Dec 29; 1717: LIF, Jan 25, 31, Mar 23; 1723: RI, Sep 2
Leveridge's Coffee House, 1718: LIF, Mar 4, 17
Leverton (bricklayer), 1761: CG, Feb 23
Leverton and Co (bricklayers), 1772: CG, Jan 17; 1773: CG, Jan 29
Leverton, Mrs (mantua maker), 1772: CG, Jan 16; 1773: CG, Jan 15, Apr 14
Leveson, Sir Richard, 1660: NONE, Sep 13, VERE, Nov 19, ATCOURT, 19, VERE, Dec 6, 8; 1661: ATCOURT, Feb 26, NONE, May 5
Leveson, Sir William, 1688: DL, Apr 0
Levett, Sir Richard (Lord Mayor), 1699: CITY, Oct 30
Levi (doorkeeper), 1741: GF, May 6; 1742: GF, May 10, 18; 1743: LIF, Apr 6; 1778: HAY, Dec 28
Leviez (Livier), Charles (dancer), 1734: DL, Oct 28, Nov 1, Dec 12, 21; 1735: DL, Jan 18, 21, 28, Feb 5, 18, Mar 3, 15, Apr 7, CG, Sep 26, Oct 3, 17, Nov 6, 15, 28, Dec 2; 1736: CG, Jan 1, 9, 10, 21, 23, Feb 23, Mar 2, 6, 11, Apr

29, May 6, 8, 11, 17, BFHC, Aug 23, DL, Sep 9, Oct 2, 12, Nov 2; 1737: DL,
Feb 10, Mar 10, 14, Apr 2, 11, 13, May 4, 5, 6, 7, 9, 11, 13, 14, 16, 18, 19,
20, 24, 25, 26, 27, 30, 31, Jun 11, Oct 25; 1738: DL, Jan 19, 20, 24, 28, Feb
1, 6, Mar 3, 13, Apr 12, 21, 22, 24, 26, May 1, 2, 10, 11, 18, 19, 22, 24,
25, 30, 31, Sep 23, Oct 3, 10, 30, Dec 15; 1739: DL, Feb 5, Mar 10, May 1, 2,
5, 9, 11, 14, 15, 16, 19, 23, 26, 28, 31, Sep 8, 13, 26, Oct 9, 16, 18, 19,
22, 26, 27, 31, Nov 1, 22, 28, Dec 6, 11, 19; 1740: DL, Jan 5, 7, 15, Feb 13,
Apr 10, 11, 17, 28, 29, May 2, 5, 7, 8, 9, 12, 14, 15, 16, 17, 19, 20, 21,
22, 26, 28, 29, Oct 13, 14, 15, 16, 27, 31, Nov 17, Dec 4, 10, 19, 26; 1741:
DL, Jan 20, 26, Mar 17, Apr 27, May 7, 12, 28, Oct 12, 27, Nov 4, 11, Dec 4;
1742: DL, Jan 6, Mar 8, Apr 30; 1743: DL, Feb 4, 11, Apr 25, Oct 13, 15, Nov
19, 23, 26; 1744: DL, Jan 5, 17, 19, Feb 1, 3, 6, 16, Apr 6, 20, May 24, Oct
2, 17, 19, 24, 30, Nov 7; 1745: DL, Apr 27, Dec 17; 1746: DL, Mar 3, Apr 24,
25, Jun 6; 1747: DL, Jan 24, Apr 23, May 16, Nov 2, 13, 16; 1748: DL, Apr 15,
Oct 27; 1749: DL, Apr 14, Dec 11; 1750: DL, Jan 13, Mar 26, Apr 27, Dec 26;
1751: DL, Apr 24, Oct 16; 1752: DL, Apr 16, Oct 12; 1753: DL, Jan 1, 15, 17,
Feb 19, Apr 25, Oct 17, Nov 14; 1754: DL, Apr 26, Oct 31, Dec 5; 1755: DL,
Apr 1, 22, Nov 22; 1756: DL, Mar 29, Apr 22, May 11, Oct 18; 1757: DL, Apr
29; 1758: DL, Jan 13, Apr 24; 1759: DL, Apr 30, May 4, 9, Dec 7; 1760: DL,
Apr 23, Oct 7; 1761: DL, Apr 18, HAY, Jun 23, DL, Oct 23, Dec 12; 1762: DL,
May 3
Leviez's scholars (dancer), 1738: DL, May 19
Lewendahl, Marshall, 1755: DL, Nov 14
Lewes (spectator), 1661: SALSBURY, Mar 26
Lewes, Catharine Maria, Mrs Charles Lee (actor), 1790: CG, Jul 16; 1791: HAY,
Mar 7
Lewes, Charles Lee (actor), 1766: CG, Nov 25; 1767: CG, Mar 21, Apr 11, May 15,
26, Sep 23, Nov 6; 1768: CG, Feb 20, May 3, Jun 4, Sep 22, Oct 4, 6, Nov 4,
17, 19, Dec 26; 1769: CG, Feb 4, 20, 28, Apr 29, May 1, 3, Sep 27, 30, Oct 4,
7, Nov 4, Dec 11, 29; 1770: CG, Jan 15, 25, Mar 22, May 8, 10, 14, 28, Sep
26, Oct 1, 15, 17, 19, 25, Nov 2, 5, 12, 15, 17, 23, Dec 12, 21, 26; 1771:
CG, Jan 1, 28, Feb 6, 21, Apr 3, 6, 16, 18, 20, 22, May 1, 3, Sep 23, Nov 22,
25, Dec 18, 19, 21, 23, 26; 1772: CG, Jan 21, 31, Feb 24, Mar 16, 17, 19, 23,
26, 31, Apr 11, 22, 27, May 8, Sep 21, 28, Oct 14, 16, Nov 6, 30, Dec 3, 5,
11, 15, 26; 1773: CG, Jan 6, 16, 21, 28, Feb 1, 10, 17, Mar 15, 29, Apr 16,
17, 27, May 3, 7, 12, 17, 19, Sep 22, 27, Oct 6, 8, 9, 22, 28, Nov 12, 23,
25, 27, Dec 7, 8, 9; 1774: CG, Jan 3, 5, 26, 29, Mar 12, 15, 26, Apr 9, 11,
12, 23, 28, May 3, 6, Sep 19, 28, 30, Oct 7, 11, 13, 26, Nov 4, 12, 19, Dec
1, 2, 27; 1775: CG, Jan 3, 17, Feb 9, Mar 20, 30, Apr 19, 22, May 2, 6, 9,
17, 18, Jun 1, HAY, Sep 19, CG, 20, 25, 27, Oct 6, 9, 11, 13, 24, Nov 1, 3,
21, 30, Dec 2, 7, 8, 16, 19, 23, 26, 29; 1776: CG, Jan 13, 24, Feb 3, 9, 12,
26, Mar 2, 5, 25, 30, Apr 26, 27, 30, May 6, 10, 13, Sep 25, 27, 30, Oct 16,
17, 29, Nov 2, 7, 15, 19, 20, 25, 30, Dec 17, 19, 21, 26; 1777: CG, Jan 2,
Feb 22, Mar 17, Apr 7, 14, 16, 23, 26, 28, 29, May 2, 12, 13, 24, 29, Sep 22,
Oct 1, 10, 16, 20, 30, Nov 1, 3, 17, 20, 21, 25, Dec 5, 10, 20, 29; 1778: CG,
Jan 15, Feb 6, 23, Mar 9, 12, Apr 21, 22, 25, 27, 29, May 5, 7, Sep 18, 23,
30, Oct 2, 5, 7, 9, 12, 14, 15, 16, 21, 24, Nov 4, 5, Dec 2, 11, 12, 15, 19,
21; 1779: CG, Jan 4, 21, 26, Feb 15, 22, 23, Mar 4, 20, Apr 12, 21, May 3, 6,
18, Sep 20, 22, 27, Oct 1, 6, Nov 10, 11, 16, 22, 23, 27, Dec 3, 9, 18, 23;
1780: CG, Jan 7, Feb 1, 2, 22, Apr 3, 7, 17, 19, 21, 24, Jun 26, Sep 18, 21,
Oct 11, 31, Nov 2, 4, 8, 10, 15, 22, Dec 4, 5, 28; 1781: CG, Jan 12, 25, Feb
14, 24, Mar 8, HAY, 14, CG, 24, Apr 20, 21, 28, Sep 19, 26, Oct 5, 13, 30,
Nov 2, 8, Dec 5; 1782: CG, Jan 5, 11, 18, Feb 9, 11, Mar 16, 19, Apr 1, 3, 8,
10, 17, 20, 23, 24, May 3, 6, 7, 11, 28, Sep 23, Oct 3, 4, 8, 15, 16, 18, 19,
23, 29, Nov 2, 6, 14, 16, Dec 6, 12; 1783: CG, Jan 3, 17, 28, Apr 25, DL, Sep
16, Oct 16, Nov 3, 18, 27, 28; 1784: DL, Jan 10, 28, CG, 29, DL, Feb 14, Apr
19, Oct 11; 1785: DL, May 9; 1790: CG, Apr 7, Jul 16; 1791: HAY, Mar 7; 1792:
HAY, Feb 20
Lewis (actor), 1730: HAY, Jul 17, Nov 16; 1732: LIF, Jan 12
Lewis (attorney), 1749: DL, Jan 19
Lewis (payee), 1750: DL, Feb 23
Lewis (ticket deliverer), 1751: DL, May 13; 1752: DL, May 2
Lewis, C (actor), 1764: HAY, Sep 1
Lewis, C (publisher), 1788: CG, Apr 29
Lewis, David, 1727: LIF, May 2
--Philip of Macedon, 1727: LIF, Apr 29, May 2, 11
Lewis, Father (executed), 1679: DG, May 0
Lewis, Henrietta Amelia, Mrs William Thomas (actor), 1779: CG, Oct 11, Nov 1,
13, 23, 27; 1780: CG, Jan 12, Mar 14, 18, Apr 3, May 24, Oct 2, 9, Dec 29;
1781: CG, Jan 12, 24, 25, Feb 14, Mar 8, Apr 2, 18, 28, May 19, Oct 16, Nov
2; 1782: CG, Apr 1, 27, May 1, DL, 16, CG, 21, 25, 29, Sep 23, Oct 14, 22,
23, Nov 2, 12, 14, 27, 30, Dec 12, DL, 19; 1783: CG, Jan 17, DL, May 26, CG,

Sep 19, Oct 1, 8, 10, 14, 17, Dec 26; 1784: CG, Feb 13, May 13, DL, 24, CG,
29, Oct 29, Nov 3, 13, Dec 3, 28; 1785: DL, May 23, CG, 26, Sep 26, Oct 3,
Nov 1, 9, Dec 7, 22; 1786: CG, Jan 14, Feb 4, DL, May 29, CG, Sep 18, 20, 22,
29, Nov 29, Dec 30; 1787: CG, Jan 23, 26, DL, Jun 4, CG, Nov 16, 28, Dec 15;
1788: CG, Jan 11, Feb 14, 25, Mar 11, 24, May 14, DL, Jun 6, CG, Oct 17, Nov
12, Dec 30, 31; 1789: CG, Jun 5, DL, 9, CG, Oct 9, 31; 1790: CG, Jan 23, Mar
27, May 7, Sep 15, Oct 1, 5, 13, 27, Dec 17; 1791: CG, May 24
Lewis, J (portrait painter), 1754: CG, Sep 20
Lewis, Matthew Gregory, 1797: CG, Mar 16, DL, Dec 14; 1798: DL, Jan 25, Mar 24,
May 19, 21; 1799: DL, Apr 8, 22, CG, 30, DL, Dec 7; 1800: DL, May 30
--Castle-Spectre, The, 1797: DL, Dec 11, 14, 15, 16, 18, 20, 21, 22, 26, 27,
28, 29; 1798: DL, Jan 1, 2, 3, 4, 5, 8, 9, 10, 11, 15, 22, 29, Feb 2, 5, 12,
19, 26, Mar 5, 12, 15, 19, 22, Apr 9, 13, 18, 21, 25, May 2, 10, 21, 23, 29,
31, Jun 6, 11, 18, Sep 29, Oct 8, 15, 23, Nov 1, 7, 17, 24, Dec 22, 28; 1799:
DL, Jan 5, 12, Feb 5, 12, Apr 8, 22, CG, 30, DL, May 7, 16, 21, Jul 3, Sep
17, 26, Oct 23, 30, Nov 15, Dec 4, 7; 1800: DL, Jan 16, Feb 1, 17, 22, Apr
25, May 26, Jun 2
--East Indian, The, 1799: DL, Apr 22, May 1, Dec 7, 10, 12, 14, 17
--Twins, The; or, Is It He or his Brother? (farce), 1799: DL, Apr 8
Lewis, Miss (actor), 1735: LIF, Jun 19
Lewis, Mrs (actor), 1757: CG, Dec 19; 1762: CG, Sep 27, Oct 20; 1763: CG, Apr
15, May 7
Lewis, Mrs (beneficiary), 1711: GR, Sep 13
Lewis, P (comedian), 1774: DL, Jan 1
Lewis, Philip (actor), 1752: DL, Dec 8; 1753: DL, Jan 1, May 16, Oct 20; 1755:
DL, Oct 17, Nov 12, 15; 1756: DL, Jan 21, Apr 29, May 20, Nov 18; 1761: CG,
Sep 23, Dec 11; 1762: CG, Jan 22, Feb 15, May 13, Sep 24, Oct 2; 1763: CG,
Jan 8, Feb 1, 3, Apr 25, HAY, May 9, CG, 9, 14, HAY, Jun 27, Jul 6, Aug 1, 5,
22, 29, Sep 5, 7, CG, 26, 28, 30, Oct 15, Nov 10, 23; 1764: CG, Feb 9, Mar 8,
27, Apr 2, 5, 28, May 12, 15, HAY, Jun 13, 26, Jul 6, 18, 23, Aug 20, 29, Sep
1, CG, 26, 28, Oct 3, 16, 17, 20, Nov 1; 1765: CG, Jan 28, Feb 18, Apr 19,
May 9, 11, Sep 27, 30, Oct 2, 4, 8, 10, 11, 14, 17, 19, 30, Nov 19, Dec 6,
20; 1766: CG, Jan 6, 31, Feb 6, Mar 11, Apr 26, May 12, KING'S, Aug 13, 18,
HAY, 21, KING'S, 25, 27, Sep 12, CG, 22, Oct 6, 8, 16, 22, 29, 30, Nov 8, Dec
11; 1767: CG, May 26; 1768: CG, Sep 24, 27, Oct 4, HAY, 7, CG, 10, 17, 24,
26, Nov 1, 4, 21, 26, Dec 9, 16, 19, 22; 1769: CG, Jan 23, 25, Feb 2, 4, 25,
Mar 29, Apr 7, 11, 17, 28; 1770: CG, Mar 3, Oct 29; 1773: HAY, May 26, 31;
1774: HAY, Sep 30; 1775: HAY, Feb 2, Mar 23, Sep 4, 20, 21; 1776: HAY, May 2,
CHR, Sep 23, 25, 27, 30, Oct 4, 7, 9, 11, 16, 18; 1777: HAY, Apr 22; 1779:
HAY, May 10; 1782: HAY, Mar 21
Lewis, Robert, 1758: CG, Mar 14
Lewis, William Thomas (actor, manager), 1773: CG, Oct 15, Nov 12, 20, 24; 1774:
CG, Jan 5, 29, Feb 9, 15, 26, Mar 12, 15, 22, Apr 5, 7, 12, 18, 19, 21, 23,
Sep 21, 23, Oct 3, 7, 11, 13, 21, 26, 27, Nov 8, 19, 24, 25, Dec 9, 15, 20;
1775: CG, Jan 17, Feb 11, 21, Mar 2, 18, 20, Apr 8, 22, May 4, 9, 17, 20, Sep
20, 22, 25, 29, Oct 4, 13, 20, 21, 24, 25, Nov 1, 3, 10, 14, 24, Dec 1, 8;
1776: CG, Jan 5, 6, 24, Feb 5, 9, Mar 5, 19, 23, 30, Apr 26, 27, May 1, 6, 8,
10, 13, Sep 23, Oct 15, 16, 17, 25, 31, Nov 1, 2, 4, 7, 12, 14, 15, 21, 26,
Dec 5, 6, 12, 17, 18; 1777: CG, Jan 2, Feb 1, 5, 22, Mar 17, Apr 7, 14, 16,
28, May 2, 7, 13, Sep 22, 24, 29, Oct 6, 8, 10, 15, 21, 30, Nov 6, 12, 13,
19, 27, Dec 3, 10, 19; 1778: CG, Jan 3, 21, 29, 31, Feb 2, 10, 13, 16, 24,
25, 28, Mar 2, 7, 14, 23, 30, Apr 11, 21, Sep 23, 28, Oct 2, 9, 14, 15, 21,
22, 23, 24, 26, 28, 29, 31, Nov 10, 21, Dec 1, 3, 11, 17; 1779: DL, Jan 5,
CG, 11, 13, 22, 26, Feb 23, Mar 9, Apr 5, 6, 27, 30, May 6, 10, 15, 18, DL,
Jun 1, CG, Sep 24, 27, Oct 4, 11, 13, 23, 29, Nov 4, 6, 8, 9, 13, 16, 19, 22,
23, 25, 30, Dec 1, 3, 9; 1780: CG, Jan 7, 25, Feb 1, 22, Mar 18, Apr 3, 7,
12, 21, May 3, 24, Jun 1, Sep 18, 20, 22, Oct 2, 3, 4, 6, 10, 18, 21, 31, Nov
8, 14, 24, 27, Dec 12, 15, 27; 1781: CG, Jan 10, 18, 25, Feb 10, 14, 15, 24,
Mar 24, Apr 2, 21, 28, May 10, 14, Sep 17, 19, 21, 24, 28, Oct 5, 13, 16, 23,
31, Nov 17, Dec 10, 11, 18, 20; 1782: CG, Jan 1, 4, 8, 11, 18, 22, Feb 9, Mar
19, Apr 10, 23, May 3, 11, Sep 23, 27, Oct 3, 7, 8, 9, 18, 19, 23, Nov 27,
29, 30, Dec 2, 6, 14, 19; 1783: CG, Jan 1, 3, 17, 27, 28, Feb 25, Apr 1, 5,
7, 23, 30, May 9, 19, 20, DL, Jun 2, CG, 6, Sep 19, 22, 26, Oct 1, 8, 9, 15,
17, 20, 31, Nov 13, 24, Dec 5, 6; 1784: CG, Jan 3, 14, 22, 23, 26, 29, 31,
Feb 5, 13, 18, 20, Mar 1, 6, 16, Apr 3, May 8, 12, 17, 26, 29, Jun 2, Sep 17,
24, 28, 29, Oct 1, 6, 25, 27, 28, Nov 10, 11, 16, Dec 14, 28; 1785: CG, Jan
14, Feb 8, Mar 5, 8, 15, 19, 29, Apr 2, 18, May 4, 7, 13, 26, Sep 26, 28, Oct
5, 7, 10, 17, 19, 26, 27, 29, Nov 3, 7, 14, 19, Dec 7, 10, 14, 22, 28, 29,
30; 1786: CG, Jan 3, 7, 14, 20, 28, Feb 1, 7, 11, 13, 16, 18, Mar 4, 11, Apr
8, 18, May 9, 22, 26, HAY, Jul 25, CG, Sep 18, 29, Oct 4, 12, 19, 23, Nov 13,
15, 18, 22, Dec 1, 7, 13, 15, 30; 1787: CG, Jan 4, 6, 11, 31, Feb 10, Mar 15,
31, Apr 16, 17, 27, 30, May 22, 23, Sep 24, 26, 28, Oct 5, DL, 6, CG, 11, 17,

Nov 2, 5, 7, 8, 14, 20, 22, 28, Dec 5, 15; 1788: CG, Jan 2, 3, 4, 9, 10, 15,
  17, 18, 21, 29, Feb 4, 14, 25, Mar 15, 28, Apr 2, 8, 14, 23, Jun 9, Sep 17,
  19, 22, 24, 26, Oct 7, 8, 10, 15, 17, 18, 29, Nov 1, 6, 7, 21, 22, 26, 28,
  Dec 19, HAY, 22, CG, 27, 30, 31; 1789: CG, Jan 2, 8, 15, 20, 28, Feb 3, 11,
  Mar 5, 28, Apr 4, 14, 15, 20, 30, May 8, 15, 19, 26, Sep 14, 16, 18, Oct 2,
  6, 7, 24, Nov 2, 5, 12, 19, 21, Dec 5, 31; 1790: CG, Jan 13, 23, Feb 25, Mar
  13, 18, 27, Apr 20, 21, May 18, 31, Sep 13, 15, 17, 29, Oct 8, 15, 23, 29,
  Nov 3, 30, Dec 2, 10, 14, 15, 28; 1791: CG, Jan 3, 7, Feb 4, Mar 12, Apr 11,
  16, May 5, 10, 11, 18, 19, 20, 24, Sep 12, 14, 16, 17, 20, 21, 26, Oct 12,
  13, 20, 21, Nov 5, 24, 26; 1792: CG, Feb 6, 8, 18, Mar 31, Apr 10, 18, May 5,
  15, Jun 1, Sep 17, 28, Oct 3, 5, 8, 12, 17, 24, 26, 27, 31, Nov 6, 14, 28,
  Dec 1, 5, 8; 1793: CG, Jan 29, Mar 23, Apr 8, 18, 24, May 8, 10, Sep 16, 17,
  18, 20, 27, Oct 1, 2, 3, 4, 5, 7, 9, 10, 15, 18, 19, 25, 29, Nov 1, 19, 23,
  Dec 18; 1794: CG, Jan 3, 22, Feb 5, 24, 26, Apr 7, 12, 25, May 14, 26, Sep
  15, 19, Oct 3, 20, 23, 30, Nov 12, 20, 21, 22, 25, Dec 6, 10, 31; 1795: CG,
  Jan 6, 8, 10, 23, 24, 29, 31, Mar 16, 19, 28, Apr 22, May 1, 2, 8, 13, 25,
  29, Sep 16, 21, 30, Oct 2, 7, 8, 14, Nov 4, 7, 27, Dec 4, 9, 15; 1796: CG,
  Jan 2, 23, Mar 14, 19, Apr 5, 20, May 21, 28, Jun 1, 6, 7, DL, 9, CG, Sep 16,
  19, 23, Oct 14, 17, 20, 29, Nov 5, 21, Dec 21, 22, 31; 1797: CG, Jan 4, 10,
  17, Mar 4, 16, Apr 8, May 8, 12, Sep 18, 20, 22, Oct 4, 6, 11, 16, 28, Nov 2,
  4, 15, 18, 22, Dec 18, 23, 28; 1798: CG, Jan 11, Feb 6, 13, Mar 20, 31, Apr
  13, 19, 27, 30, May 15, 16, 22, 24, 28, Sep 21, Oct 1, 3, 5, 8, Nov 5, 7, Dec
  8; 1799: CG, Jan 12, Mar 16, Apr 16, 26, 27, May 15, 22, 24, 28, 31, Sep 16,
  20, 25, 27, Oct 2, 7, 11, 16, 17, 18, 25, 31, Nov 11, 30, Dec 30; 1800: CG,
  Jan 7, 29, Mar 27, Apr 5, 22, 24, May 2, 12, 15, 17, 27, 28, Jun 2, 7, 12
Lewiss (dancer, singer), 1796: CG, Dec 19; 1797: CG, May 26; 1798: CG, Oct 25,
  Dec 11; 1799: CG, Jan 14, 29, Mar 4, 25, Oct 26, Dec 23; 1800: CG, Jan 16,
  Feb 10, Mar 4, 25, Apr 5, 23, 29, May 1, 27, Jun 2
L'Herondell's School, 1736: CHE, May 24, 26, 28; 1739: CHE, May 8
L'Homme, Miss (actor), 1732: BFMMO, Aug 23
Liar, The. See Corneille, Pierre, The Mistaken Beauty; Foote, Samuel.
Liberal Opinions. See Dibdin, Thomas John.
Libertine, The. See Shadwell, Thomas, Don John.
Liberty Alone (song), 1747: CG, May 4
Liberty Asserted. See Dennis, John.
Liberty Hall. See Dibdin, Charles.
Liberty; or, Two Sides of the Water (entertainment), 1790: HAY, Aug 13, 16, 17,
  Oct 13
Liberty; or, We Slaves Rejoice (dance), 1789: HAY, Aug 5
Licensing Act, 1737: LIF, Mar 19, DL, May 24, NONE, 28, Jun 4, CG, 8, 10, DL,
  11, LIF, 15, NONE, 18, CG, 25, NONE, Jul 0; 1738: CG, Jan 25; 1744: DL, Nov
  19; 1745: GF, Apr 16; 1753: SFP, Sep 18
Lick at the Town, A. See Woodward, Henry.
Liddel (actor), 1784: HAY, Feb 23
Liddel, Mrs (actor), 1782: HAY, Mar 4
Liddell, 1773: DL, May 12
Lidl (musician), 1776: KING'S, Feb 15
Lie of the Day, The. See O'Keeffe, John.
Liege, John (boxkeeper), 1735: HAY, Mar 19, Apr 18
Lieutenant, The. See Fletcher, John, The Humourous Lieutenant.
Life and Death of Common Sense, The. See Wilson, Richard.
Life and Death of Doctor Faustus, The. See Mountfort, William.
Life and Death of Harlequin, The (pantomime, anon), 1776: CHR, Oct 14
Life and Death of Sir Walter Raleigh, The. See Sewell, George, Sir Walter
  Raleigh.
Life is but a little span (song), 1698: DL, Mar 0
Life of a Beau (song), 1738: DL, May 13, 29; 1739: DL, May 19, Sep 15; 1740:
  DL, Apr 15, 17; 1741: JS, Oct 27, Nov 9; 1743: CG, Nov 17; 1745: DL, Dec 20;
  1749: DL, Jan 25, Mar 13, Oct 24; 1751: DL, Jan 12, Sep 12; 1753: DL, Jan 13;
  1754: DL, Sep 14, CG, Oct 11; 1756: DL, May 18; 1758: DL, May 17; 1759: DL,
  Jan 17; 1762: DL, Jan 20; 1763: DL, Nov 19; 1765: DL, Jan 18
Life of a Belle (song), 1740: DL, May 14, 29; 1744: CG, Dec 10; 1746: DL, Feb
  24, Dec 30; 1757: CG, May 25
Life of Mother Shipton, The. See Thomson, Thomas.
Life of Poor Jack (song), 1797: CG, May 17; see also Poor Jack; Go patter to
  lubbers
Life's Vagaries. See O'Keeffe, John.
Lift up your heads O ye gates (song), 1789: CG, Apr 3; 1790: CG, Mar 26; 1793:
  KING/HAY, Feb 20; 1794: DL, Mar 19
Light (music seller), 1774: HAY, Jun 7
Lightfoot, William (painter), 1659: CITY, Oct 29; 1660: CITY, Oct 29
Ligonier, Miss, 1759: CG, Oct 22

Like a bright cherub (song), <u>1790</u>: CG, Mar 17; <u>1794</u>: DL, Apr 11; <u>1800</u>: CG, Mar 5
Like Father, Like Son. See Behn, Aphra.
Like Master, Like Man (play, anon), <u>1705</u>: LIF, Jan 25
Like Master, Like Man. See Ryder, Thomas.
Like the raging Ocean (song), <u>1789</u>: DL, Mar 20
Like to Like; or, A Match Well Made (play, anon), <u>1701</u>: DL, Mar 15; <u>1723</u>: LIF, Nov 28, 29
Lilborne, Mrs (actor), <u>1670</u>: LIF, Nov 0
Lilleston, Thomas (actor), <u>1660</u>: COCKPIT, Feb 4, REDBULL, Nov 5; <u>1661</u>: LIF, Jun 28, Aug 24, LIF/MT, Oct 21; <u>1662</u>: LIF, Oct 18, ATCOURT, 27, Nov 1; <u>1663</u>: LIF, Dec 22; <u>1664</u>: LIF, Aug 13
Lillier, Charles (ticket seller), <u>1711</u>: YB, May 24
Lilliput. See Garrick, David.
Lilliputian Camp (dance), <u>1767</u>: DL, Feb 27, 28, Mar 2, 3, 5, 12, 14, 16, 17, 26, Apr 2, May 6, 7, 14, Dec 2, 4, 14, 21; <u>1768</u>: DL, Apr 26, Sep 22, Oct 26; <u>1769</u>: DL, Mar 28; <u>1775</u>: DL, May 6
Lilliputian Fisherman (dance), <u>1762</u>: DL, Nov 20, 22
Lilliputian Performance (music), <u>1797</u>: DL, May 18, 20
Lilliputian Punch (dance), <u>1738</u>: DL, Apr 12, 13
Lilliputian Sailors (dance), <u>1755</u>: DL, Oct 30, 31, Nov 1, 3, 4, 6, 7, 10, 17
Lilliputian Scotch Dance (dance), <u>1735</u>: GF/HAY, Mar 3, 10, Apr 7
Lilliputians (performers), <u>1727</u>: DL, May 1, 8; <u>1729</u>: LIF, Jan 1, BOS, 21, LIF, 24; <u>1731</u>: YB, Apr 7; <u>1732</u>: DL, Aug 11, 19; <u>1734</u>: JS, Apr 22; <u>1735</u>: GF/HAY, Feb 6, YB, Mar 12, HAY, 29, GF/HAY, Apr 7, HAY, 18, GF/HAY, 25, May 1, 2, HAY, 26, GF/HAY, Jun 2, HAY, 29, Jul 7; <u>1737</u>: LIF, Apr 2, May 7, DL, Oct 18, 25, Nov 2, 7, 19; <u>1738</u>: DL, May 10, 16, 18, 19, 29, BFH, Aug 23, DL, Dec 4; <u>1739</u>: DL, May 22; <u>1744</u>: DL, Feb 3, 6; <u>1754</u>: HAY, Jul 4, 18, Aug 1, BFSIY, Sep 3, HAY/SFB, 19; <u>1757</u>: DL, Jan 18, HAY, Jun 17, Sep 2, 14; <u>1777</u>: HAY, Jul 18
Lillo, George, <u>1730</u>: LIF, Nov 10; <u>1731</u>: DL, Jun 22; <u>1735</u>: DL, Jan 13, Jul 1, LIF, Aug 1; <u>1736</u>: HAY, May 27; <u>1738</u>: CG, Aug 1; <u>1740</u>: DL, Feb 23, 26, 28, Mar 3; <u>1741</u>: GF, Feb 14; <u>1755</u>: HAY, Sep 4; <u>1759</u>: DL, Jul 12; <u>1782</u>: HAY, Jun 29; <u>1783</u>: HAY, Jun 30; <u>1784</u>: CG, Feb 10, HAY, Jun 17; <u>1790</u>: CG, Apr 14
--Arden of Feversham, <u>1759</u>: DL, Jul 12; <u>1790</u>: CG, Apr 14
--Christian Hero, The, <u>1735</u>: DL, Jan 13, 14, 15, 16
--Elmerick, <u>1740</u>: DL, Feb 23, 25, 26, 28, Mar 1, 3
--Fatal Curiosity, The; or, Guilt it Own Punishment, <u>1736</u>: HAY, May 27, 28, 29, 31, Jun 1, 2, 21; <u>1737</u>: HAY, Mar 21, 22, 24, 26, 28, 29, 31, Apr 2, 11, 12, May 2; <u>1741</u>: GF, Feb 14, 17, Mar 3; <u>1742</u>: JS, Nov 22; <u>1755</u>: HAY, Sep 4; <u>1782</u>: HAY, Jun 29, Jul 1, 3, 5, 8, 10, 12, 18, 31, Aug 8, 19; <u>1783</u>: HAY, Jun 28, 30, Jul 22; <u>1784</u>: CG, Feb 10, HAY, Jun 17, Jul 6; <u>1786</u>: HAY, Jun 29; <u>1797</u>: DL, May 1, 6
--London Merchant, The; or, George Barnwell, <u>1731</u>: DL, Jun 22, 25, 30, Jul 2, 6, 9, 13, 16, 20, 23, 27, 30, Aug 3, 11, 13, 16, 20, BFB, 26, SFGT, Sep 8, GF, 27, 29, Oct 1, 4, 15, DL, 16, 23, 28, 29, GF, Nov 10, DL, 11, GF, 29, DL, Dec 9, GF, 10, 27, DL, 27; <u>1732</u>: GF, Jan 13, DL, 20, GF, Feb 15, DL, Apr 10, GF, 13, DL, May 17, LIF, 22, DL, 29, HAY, Jun 1, DL, Aug 21, GF, Oct 16, DL, 26, GF, Dec 28; <u>1733</u>: GF, Jan 6, HAY, Mar 26, CG, Aug 7, 10, 17, DL, Oct 10, GF, 19, HAY, Dec 26; <u>1734</u>: JS, Apr 22, May 24, HAY, Jun 17, Aug 22; <u>1735</u>: GF, Feb 22, YB, Jun 3, DL, Jul 1, 4, LIF, 11, GF/HAY, 15, LIF, Aug 1, YB/HAY, Oct 1, GF, 8, DL, Dec 26; <u>1736</u>: GF, Mar 1, LIF, Apr 9, HAY, 26, YB, 26, HAY, May 27, Jun 21, LIF, Nov 9; <u>1737</u>: LIF, Feb 8, HAY, Mar 21, 28, YB, Apr 14, HAY, May 2, LIF, Jun 22; <u>1738</u>: CG, Aug 1, 4; <u>1740</u>: DL, Feb 23, 26, 28, Mar 3, CG, May 23, GF, Oct 29, Nov 7; <u>1741</u>: GF, Feb 14, 28, Mar 31, DL, Jun 4, GF, Oct 2, JS, Nov 9, GF, Dec 8; <u>1742</u>: GF, Mar 23, SOU, Sep 27, JS, Nov 8; <u>1743</u>: HAY, Mar 23, DL, Oct 1, Dec 27; <u>1744</u>: DL, May 16, MF, Jun 6, GF, Dec 11; <u>1745</u>: GF, Jan 17, Nov 25, Dec 10; <u>1746</u>: GF, Feb 11, SOU, Nov 6, GF, 13; <u>1747</u>: GF, Feb 2, 19, SMMF, Aug 28; <u>1748</u>: DL, Apr 27, JS, Jun 14, Oct 31, NWC, Dec 29; <u>1749</u>: DL, May 8, SFP, Sep 15, DL, 22, 23, 30, Oct 31, Dec 26, CG, 26; <u>1750</u>: BB, Jan 8, DL, Feb 15, May 8, Sep 18, 20, Dec 27; <u>1751</u>: DL, May 14, Dec 26; <u>1752</u>: NWLS, Nov 20; <u>1753</u>: DL, Dec 26; <u>1756</u>: DL, Jan 1, 20, May 13; <u>1757</u>: DL, May 23; <u>1758</u>: DL, May 15; <u>1759</u>: DL, Jan 6, May 17, Jul 12, Dec 31; <u>1760</u>: DL, May 13; <u>1761</u>: DL, May 25, Nov 6, Dec 28; <u>1763</u>: DL, May 17, Dec 26; <u>1764</u>: DL, Apr 12; <u>1765</u>: DL, Jan 1, Apr 8, May 9, Sep 26, 28, Oct 1, 7, 21, Nov 18, Dec 26; <u>1766</u>: DL, May 13; <u>1767</u>: DL, Jun 1, Oct 23, CG, 26, Nov 2, 9, DL, Dec 26; <u>1768</u>: CG, Jan 18, May 2, 23, DL, Sep 23, CG, Nov 9; <u>1769</u>: CG, Jan 9, Apr 10, May 17, DL, 22, CG, Sep 25, Nov 9, DL, 9, Dec 26; <u>1770</u>: CG, Jan 29, May 10, DL, 28, Jun 4, CG, Oct 1, 22, DL, Nov 9, CG, 9, Dec 26; <u>1771</u>: CG, Apr 18, DL, May 20, CG, 27, Sep 30, Nov 9; <u>1772</u>: CG, Jan 3, Apr 20, DL, Nov 9, Dec 26; <u>1773</u>: CG, May 28, Sep 27, Dec 27; <u>1774</u>: DL, May 28, CG, Sep 26; <u>1775</u>: CG, Jan 2, Oct 23, DL, Dec 23, 26; <u>1776</u>: DL, May 17, CHR, Oct 11; <u>1777</u>: DL, Jun 6, CHR, 30, CG, Dec 26; <u>1778</u>: CG, Jan 5, DL, May 21, CHR, Jun 9, DL, Nov 9;

1779: CG, Jan 4, DL, Dec 28; 1780: CII, Mar 27, DL, Nov 9; 1781: CII, Apr 9,
DL, May 12, CG, Nov 9, Dec 26; 1782: DL, May 29, HAY, Jun 29; 1783: DL, Apr
21, HAY, Jun 30, CG, Dec 26, DL, 29; 1784: DL, May 19, HAY, Jun 17, CG, Dec
27; 1785: DL, Nov 9, CG, Dec 26; 1786: DL, Dec 26; 1787: DL, Feb 12, Apr 30,
Sep 25, Nov 9, Dec 27; 1788: DL, Mar 24, Sep 20; 1789: DL, Jun 10, Dec 7;
1796: DL, Nov 28, 30, Dec 2, 7, 12, 19, 26, CG, 26; 1797: DL, Jan 9, 31, Feb
17, Apr 17, Nov 9; 1798: DL, Nov 9, 26, Dec 17; 1799: DL, Jan 14, Dec 26;
1800: DL, Apr 14
--Marina, 1738: CG, Aug 1, 4, 8
--Sylvia; or, The Country Burial (opera), 1730: LIF, Nov 10, 11, 12; 1736: CG,
Mar 18
Lilly, William (astrologer), 1681: DL, May 0
Lilt (dance), 1770: CG, Nov 16; 1771: CG, Feb 26; 1772: CG, Mar 26, 30, Apr 11,
May 20, 26
Linco's Travels. See Garrick, David.
Lincoln (organ builder), 1799: HAY, Jan 24
Lincoln, Miss (actor), 1745: GF, Feb 4, 14, Mar 5, 12, Apr 6, NWC, Dec 30;
1746: HIC, Feb 3, Mar 10, NWC, Sep 15; 1747: SF, Sep 14
L'Inconnue, Mlle (dancer), 1723: LIF, Nov 2, 7, Dec 11; 1724: LIF, Oct 9; 1726:
HAY, May 9
L'Inconu, de (dancer), 1730: HAY, Jun 27
Lindar, Miss (actor, singer), 1715: DL, Dec 6; 1717: DL, May 14, 22, Jul 23,
26, Oct 26, 30, Nov 7, 22, 27, Dec 3; 1718: DL, Jan 7, 21, 23, 27, 28, 31,
Feb 6, Mar 4, 18, Apr 25, 29, May 7, 8, 14, 19, 21, 27, 29, Jun 6, 11, 13,
17, 27, Jul 11, 18, 22, Aug 1, Oct 2, 8, 10, 14, 15, 20, 22, 24, 27, 29, Nov
6, 7, 14, 19, 24, 28, Dec 2, 10, 11, 15; 1719: DL, Jan 7, 8, Feb 3, 7, Mar
16, 19, Apr 11, 16, 20, 21, 23, 30, May 2, 4, 5, 7, 9, 11, 12, 13, 14, 21,
30, Jun 16, Jul 31, Sep 15, 29, Oct 12, 16, 19, 26, 30, Nov 9, 16, 21, 23,
25, 27; 1720: DL, Jan 13, Mar 29, Apr 5, 9, 19, 25, 26, May 5, 16, 20, 21,
23, 25, 26, Jun 7, 14, 21, Jul 7, Nov 23, Dec 17; 1721: DL, Jan 17, May 23,
29, Jun 20, Jul 4, Aug 1, 9, 15, 18, Oct 14; 1722: DL, May 17, 21, Jun 26,
Jul 3, 6, 10; 1723: DL, Jan 7, 9, 22, 24, May 13, 23, Jun 6, Jul 12, Aug 2,
9, 12, 16, Sep 17, Oct 1, 9, Nov 8, 22, 23; 1724: DL, Jan 27, Apr 15, 29, May
2, 14, 18, Sep 15, 17; 1725: DL, Feb 20, Mar 1, Apr 2, 21, May 8, 17, Sep 7,
Oct 19, Nov 19, Dec 6; 1726: DL, Feb 11, May 11, Sep 10, Nov 2, 11, 15, 26,
Dec 7; 1727: DL, Feb 21, May 3, 4, 8, 22, 26, Sep 9, 19, Oct 7, Nov 1, 14;
1728: DL, Mar 16, 19, 30, Apr 30, May 3, 6, 17, Sep 26, Oct 10, 18, 30, Nov
15; 1729: DL, Jan 7
Lindebleim, Joanna Maria ("the Baroness") (singer), 1703: DL, Jan 23; 1707:
DL/QUEEN, Dec 6; 1708: QUEEN'S, Feb 26, Apr 10, Dec 14; 1709: QUEEN'S, Mar
29; 1711: QUEEN'S, May 12; 1713: HIC, Apr 24, May 27; 1714: HIC, Mar 17;
1715: HIC, Apr 6; 1716: HIC, Mar 21; 1717: HIC, Apr 12; see also Maria,
Joanna
Lindley, Master (actor), 1767: CG, Jan 31, Mar 26
Lindley, Robert (violoncellist), 1792: KING'S, Mar 7, 9; 1794: KING'S, May 15;
1795: KING'S, Mar 13, Jun 16; 1798: HAY, Jan 15
Lindores, Lady (spectator), 1760: DL, Feb 21
Lindsey (Lynsey), Mrs (singer), 1697: DG, Jun 0, DL, Sep 0; 1698: DL, Mar 0,
Jun 0, DL/ORDG, Nov 0; 1699: YB, Apr 28; 1700: DL, Feb 19; 1702: YB, Jul 2,
DL, 11, Dec 8, 22; 1703: DL, Feb 1; 1704: DL, Jan 4, Mar 23, YB, 29; 1705:
DL, Jan 16, Apr 10, May 16, 22, Jun 5, 9, 26, Oct 13, Nov 5, 9, Dec 7, 26,
31; 1706: DL, Jan 1, 21, 25, 28, ATCOURT, Feb 5, DL, 26, Mar 2, 5, 27, 30,
Apr 2, DG, Nov 1, DL, Dec 3, 10; 1707: DL, Jan 13, 21, Feb 20, Mar 4, 17, 20,
27, Apr 1, 3, YB, May 23, DL/QUEEN, Dec 6, DL, 17, 18; 1708: DL, Jan 3,
QUEEN'S, Feb 17, 26; 1709: QUEEN'S, Mar 2, Apr 5; 1710: QUEEN'S, Jan 10, Mar
16, Jul 6; 1711: YB, Mar 23; 1712: GR, Jul 19; 1730: HAY, Jan 8, 16, 21, Feb
2
Line (house servant), 1738: CG, Apr 21; 1749: CG, Apr 25
Lingo's Opinions on Men and Manners (entertainment), 1787: CG, Apr 10, 17, HAY,
Aug 28; 1788: HAY, Aug 27; 1790: CG, Apr 7
Lings (house servant), 1800: DL, Jun 14
Lings, John (actor), 1764: DL, May 22; 1765: DL, May 17; 1766: DL, May 21;
1767: DL, May 27, HAY, Jun 26, Aug 5; 1768: DL, May 13, 23, HAY, Jul 25, Aug
8, Oct 7; 1769: HAY, May 15, DL, 17, HAY, 26, Jun 5, Jul 12, 17, Aug 18, 30,
Sep 1, 11, 19; 1770: DL, May 7, HAY, 16, 23, 28, DL, 28, HAY, 30, Jun 18, 25,
27, Jul 25, Aug 1, 31; 1771: HAY, May 15, 20, 22, DL, 25, HAY, 31, Jun 5, 14,
Jul 1, Aug 28, DL, Dec 26; 1772: DL, Apr 22, HAY, May 27, DL, Jun 3, HAY, 29,
Jul 3, 10, Aug 10, Sep 17, DL, Oct 3, Dec 26; 1773: DL, Feb 13, HAY, May 17,
DL, 28, HAY, 31, Jun 18, Jul 28, Aug 11, 27, DL, Sep 25; 1774: DL, May 16, 24
Lings, Miss (dancer), 1772: DL, May 5, Jun 3, HAY, Aug 10, Sep 17, DL, Dec 26;
1773: DL, May 28, HAY, Jun 16, 18, Jul 28, DL, Sep 25; 1774: DL, Apr 19, May
24; 1778: CG, May 2, Oct 22; 1779: CG, Apr 28, Nov 9; 1780: CG, Apr 17, May

16, 23

Lini, Francesco (singer), <u>1754</u>: CG, Jan 18, Feb 11, Mar 4

Linike (beneficiary), <u>1724</u>: HAY, Mar 27

Linike, Widow (beneficiary), <u>1726</u>: HIC, Mar 16

Link Boy (song), <u>1792</u>: CG, May 28

Linkmen's Dance (dance), <u>1712</u>: DL, Jun 12; <u>1713</u>: DL, May 27; <u>1714</u>: DL, May 31;
   <u>1716</u>: DL, Apr 9

Linley, Elizabeth Ann (singer), <u>1769</u>: KING'S, Apr 5; <u>1773</u>: DL, Feb 26, Mar 10,
   KING'S, Apr 12

Linley, Maria (singer), <u>1776</u>: DL, Feb 23, Mar 1, 20, CHAPEL, Apr 2, 3; <u>1777</u>:
   DL, Feb 14; <u>1778</u>: DL, Mar 6, 27; <u>1779</u>: DL, Mar 12, 19; <u>1781</u>: DL, Mar 2, 30;
   <u>1782</u>: DL, Feb 15; <u>1783</u>: DL, Mar 7, 12, 14, 19

Linley, Mary (singer), <u>1769</u>: CG, Oct 7, Dec 11; <u>1773</u>: DL, Feb 26, KING'S, Apr
   12; <u>1776</u>: DL, Mar 1, 20, CHAPEL, Apr 2, 3; <u>1777</u>: DL, Feb 14; <u>1778</u>: DL, Mar 6,
   27; <u>1779</u>: DL, Feb 19; <u>1780</u>: DL, Feb 11

Linley, Mary and Miss (musicians), <u>1776</u>: DL, Mar 20

Linley, Mrs (wardrobe keeper), <u>1781</u>: DL, Jan 16

Linley Jr, Thomas (violinist, composer), <u>1772</u>: HAY, Mar 30; <u>1773</u>: KING'S, Apr
   12; <u>1776</u>: DL, Mar 6, 20, 27, CHAPEL, Apr 2, DL, Dec 5; <u>1777</u>: DL, Jan 4, Feb
   14, Mar 12; <u>1778</u>: DL, Feb 19, Mar 6, 18; <u>1784</u>: DL, Nov 9; <u>1785</u>: DL, Oct 17;
   <u>1786</u>: DL, Dec 5; <u>1789</u>: DL, Oct 13; <u>1790</u>: DL, Oct 11; <u>1791</u>: DLKING'S, Nov 9;
   <u>1792</u>: DL, Dec 13; <u>1793</u>: HAY, Nov 19; <u>1797</u>: DL, Feb 22, Dec 9; <u>1799</u>: DL, May
   4, Nov 14

--Lyric Ode, A, <u>1776</u>: DL, Mar 20

Linley Sr, Thomas (composer, conductor, proprietor), <u>1767</u>: CG, Feb 19, Dec 14,
   19; <u>1773</u>: DL, Feb 26, Mar 5, 19, 26; <u>1776</u>: DL, Jan 19, Feb 28, Mar 1, Sep 21,
   Oct 15, Nov 25, Dec 5; <u>1777</u>: DL, Jan 4, Nov 8; <u>1778</u>: DL, Oct 15; <u>1779</u>: DL,
   Jan 29, Mar 11, Oct 5, Dec 14; <u>1780</u>: DL, Jan 3, Sep 21, Nov 23; <u>1781</u>: DL, Jan
   29, Mar 10, 28, Oct 15, 29, Nov 3, 29, Dec 13; <u>1782</u>: DL, Mar 16, Nov 30, Dec
   26; <u>1784</u>: DL, Apr 16, Sep 25, Nov 4, 22; <u>1785</u>: DL, Mar 18, Apr 8, Oct 13, Dec
   8, 26; <u>1786</u>: DL, Jan 14, Apr 24, May 5, Sep 23, Oct 24, Dec 28; <u>1787</u>: DL, May
   18, Nov 12, 21; <u>1788</u>: DL, Jan 22, Feb 25, Nov 17, 25; <u>1789</u>: DL, Jan 8, Feb
   27, Mar 9, May 28, Sep 15, 24, Nov 24; <u>1790</u>: DL, Mar 5, May 31; <u>1791</u>: DL, Mar
   11; <u>1792</u>: KING'S, Feb 24, Mar 14, 28, 30; <u>1793</u>: KING/HAY, Feb 15, Mar 6, DL,
   May 10, 24, HAY, Nov 30; <u>1794</u>: DL, Mar 12, Apr 21, Jul 2, Oct 7; <u>1795</u>: DL,
   Sep 29; <u>1796</u>: DL, Apr 25, Oct 10, Dec 26; <u>1797</u>: DL, Nov 7; <u>1798</u>: DL, Sep 18;
   <u>1800</u>: CG, Jun 2

--Song of Moses, The (ode), <u>1777</u>: DL, Mar 12; <u>1778</u>: DL, Mar 18

Linley, William (composer), <u>1796</u>: DL, Jan 18, Apr 2, Nov 9; <u>1797</u>: DL, Jan 7,
   Nov 9; <u>1798</u>: DL, Mar 24; <u>1799</u>: DL, Nov 16; <u>1800</u>: DL, Jan 21

--Harlequin Captive; or, The Magic Fire (pantomime), <u>1796</u>: DL, Jan 18, 19, 20,
   21, 22, 23, 25, 26, 27, 28, 29, Feb 1, 2, 3, 4, 5, 6, 8, 9, 11, 13, 15, 16,
   18, 22, 23, 25, 27, 29, Mar 1, 12, 17, 19, 28, CG, 29, DL, Apr 4, 11, Nov 9,
   11, 15, 19

--Honey Moon, The (opera), <u>1797</u>: DL, Jan 7

--Pavilion, The (Ring, The; or, Love Me for Myself) (entertainment), <u>1799</u>: DL,
   Nov 16, 18; <u>1800</u>: DL, Jan 21

Linnet (actor), <u>1734</u>: BFFO, Aug 24; <u>1740</u>: GF, Oct 20, 22, 23, 24, 28, 30, 31,
   Nov 13, 18, 19, 24, 25

Linnet, Mrs (actor), <u>1740</u>: GF, Oct 30, Nov 1, 22

Linton (actor, singer), <u>1789</u>: HAY, Aug 11; <u>1790</u>: CG, Jun 8, HAY, Jul 16, CG,
   Nov 15; <u>1791</u>: CG, Jun 9, HAY, Jul 30, Aug 31, CG, Oct 20, Dec 13; <u>1792</u>: CG,
   Feb 28, Mar 31, Apr 18, May 10, 19, 29, HAY, Jun 23, CG, Oct 19, Dec 20, 22,
   26, 29, 31; <u>1793</u>: CG, Feb 25, Mar 23, Apr 4, 24, 25, May 10, HAY, Jun 17, Aug
   3, 12, 16, Sep 2, CG, 23, 30, Oct 2, 7, 9, 24, Nov 18, 19, 28, Dec 7, 19;
   <u>1794</u>: CG, Feb 6, 22, Mar 7, 10, 21, 31, Apr 7, May 2, 7, 23, 24, 26, Jun 14,
   HAY, Jul 17, 18, 21, 24, Aug 27, CG, Sep 22, 26, 29, Oct 7, 14, 20, 30, Nov
   7, Dec 26; <u>1795</u>: CG, Jan 31, Feb 20, Mar 4, Apr 6, 24, 28, May 6, 13, 14, 16,
   Jun 6, 10, HAY, 13, 20, Jul 31, CG, Sep 14, 21, Oct 12, 15, 19, 24, Nov 4,
   14, Dec 21; <u>1796</u>: CG, Feb 2, Mar 14, 15, Apr 5, 9, 15, 19, 26, 29, May 16,
   20, 25, HAY, Jul 15, Aug 29, CG, Sep 12, 19, 26, Oct 6, 7, 17, 24, Nov 19,
   Dec 19; <u>1797</u>: CG, Jan 10, Feb 18, Mar 16, Apr 8, 25, May 6, 11, 18, 19, 20,
   23, HAY, Jun 23, Jul 3, Aug 14, 15, CG, Sep 25, Oct 16, 18, 25, 31, Nov 2,
   13, 24, Dec 18, 26; <u>1798</u>: CG, Jan 1, Feb 9, 12, Mar 17, 19, 31, Apr 9, 21,
   May 8, 28, Jun 4, HAY, 30, Jul 21, Aug 11, 21, 28, CG, Sep 17, 26, Oct 8, 11,
   15, 25, 31, Nov 12, Dec 11, 15, 26; <u>1799</u>: CG, Jan 21, 29, Mar 2, 25, Apr 2,
   6, 9, 13, 16, 23, 25, 26, May 4, 13, 24, 28, Jun 1, 3, 6, 7, 8, HAY, 20, Jul
   9, 13, Aug 21, Sep 2, CG, 18, 30, Oct 2, 7, 24, Nov 9, 11, 14, Dec 5, 10, 16,
   23; <u>1800</u>: CG, Jan 16, Feb 10, Mar 25, Apr 5, 15, 19, 23, 26, May 1, 2, 6, 13,
   17, 22, Jun 2, 5, 6, HAY, 14, 16, Jul 2, 21, 28, 30, Aug 1, 2, 22

Linton, Charles (musician), <u>1784</u>: CG, Sep 28

Linton, J (singer, actor), <u>1796</u>: CG, Oct 6, Dec 19; <u>1797</u>: CG, Jan 24, 25, Feb

18, Mar 6, Apr 25, May 18, Oct 16, Dec 26; 1798: CG, Dec 11; 1799: CG, Jan
14, 29, Feb 11, Apr 13, 23, 24, May 4, Dec 23; 1800: CG, Jan 16, Feb 10
Linton, Master (singer), 1798: CG, Nov 12; 1800: CG, Jan 16
Linton, Mrs (ticket deliverer), 1786: CG, Jun 2; 1787: CG, Jun 2; 1788: CG, May
31; 1789: CG, Jun 13; 1796: CG, Jun 4; 1797: CG, Jun 8; 1798: CG, Jun 5;
1800: CG, Jun 11
Lintott (printer), 1716: DL, Mar 5
Linus (author), 1746: DL, Jan 4
Lion calls not (song), 1791: DL, Apr 1
Lionel and Clarissa. See Bickerstaff, Isaac.
Liparotti (scene painter), 1796: KING'S, Jul 7; 1797: KING'S, Jan 7
Lipmann (beneficiary), 1762: DL, May 8
Lipparini, Agostino (singer), 1791: PAN, Mar 1, May 14, Jun 16, Dec 17; 1792:
HAY, Feb 14, 28, Mar 31, Apr 12
Lipparini, Giuseppe (singer), 1791: PAN, Mar 1, May 14, Dec 17; 1792: HAY, Mar
31, Apr 12
Liquor Pond St, 1720: LIF, Mar 31
Lisbon Opera, 1782: KING'S, Mar 2
Lisbon, 1750: DL, Jan 6; 1762: DL, Nov 2
Lisburne, Lady (spectator), 1699: LIF, Jan 5
Lisle (actor), 1684: DL, Mar 0
Lisle de la Drevetiere, L F
--Arlequin Conjurer, Statue Enfant, Moor and Skeleton (farce), 1735: HAY, Jan
31
--Arlequin Sauvage (farce), 1734: HAY, Oct 28, Dec 12, 19; 1735: HAY, Jan 20,
GF/HAY, Feb 6, HAY, 10, GF/HAY, 20, HAY, 26, Mar 5, GF/HAY, 21, HAY, 26, Apr
18
--Faucon, Le; ou, Les Oyes de Boccace; or, Harlequin an Anchoret, 1735: HAY,
Feb 21, Mar 7, 29, May 28
--Faulcon Court, 1747: SOU, Jan 21
--Timon le Misantrope, 1726: HAY, May 11; 1734: HAY, Oct 30, GF/HAY, Nov 6;
1735: GF/HAY, Jan 22, Apr 14, HAY, May 21; 1736: CG, Mar 23
Lisle St, 1789: CG, Mar 31; 1791: KING'S, May 19; 1797: HAY, Jan 23, DL, May
22; 1798: HAY, Mar 26; 1799: DL, Apr 15
Lisley, Jane (actor), 1777: HAY, Aug 28, Sep 3, 10, 19
Listen listen (song), 1796: DL, May 25
Listen to the voice of love (song), 1796: DL, May 11, 30; 1797: DL, May 18;
1799: DL, May 9
Listening crowd (song), 1790: DL, Mar 17; 1791: CG, Mar 25; 1792: CG, Mar 7;
1794: CG, Mar 14
Liston, John (actor), 1799: HAY, Aug 15
Litchfield St, 1795: DL, May 20
Litchfield, Harriett Sylvester, Mrs John (actor), 1796: CG, May 27; 1797: HAY,
Feb 9, CG, May 17, Jun 12, Sep 20, 29, Oct 2, 11, 31, Nov 8, 20, 29, Dec 21;
1798: CG, Jan 4, May 7, 30, Jun 11, Sep 19, 21, 28, Oct 5, 15, 30, Nov 5, 20,
22, 23, Dec 17, 26; 1799: CG, Jan 17, Mar 28, Apr 6, 9, 23, 27, May 6, 18,
22, 25, 31, Jun 12, Sep 16, 23, 27, Oct 4, 7, 14, 18, 24, 25, 28, 29, Nov 9,
Dec 4, 23; 1800: CG, Jan 11, 18, Apr 24, Jun 7, 12
Litchfield, John (actor, prologuist), 1793: HAY, Dec 23; 1795: CG, Jun 3; 1797:
HAY, Feb 9
Litchfield, John and Harriett Sylvester (actors), 1797: HAY, Feb 9
Litchfield, Lord, daughter of, 1699: LIF, Jan 5
Literary Fund, The, 1792: HAY, Apr 16
Little (actor, singer), 1791: CG, Jun 9, HAY, Jul 30, Aug 31, CG, Oct 20; 1792:
CG, May 12, HAY, Jun 23, CG, Dec 31; 1793: HAY, Jun 17, Aug 3, 12, 15, CG,
Oct 2, 24, Nov 19, 28; 1794: CG, May 31, HAY, Jul 17, 18, 21, 24, Aug 27, CG,
Oct 22; 1795: CG, Jan 31, Apr 24, Jun 10, HAY, 13, 20, Jul 31, CG, Sep 21,
Nov 4, 30; 1796: CG, Jan 1, Apr 26, May 21, 31, HAY, Jul 15, Aug 29, CG, Sep
19, 26, Oct 6; 1797: CG, Feb 18, May 18, Jun 2, HAY, 23, Aug 14, 15, CG, Nov
2, Dec 18, 26; 1798: CG, May 19, HAY, Jun 30, Jul 21, Aug 11, CG, Oct 8, Nov
12, Dec 11, 15, 26; 1799: CG, Jan 14, 29, Feb 11, Mar 2, Apr 9, 13, May 4,
Jun 8, HAY, Jul 9, 13, Aug 21, Sep 2, 9, CG, 30, Oct 7, Nov 11; 1800: CG, Jan
16, Feb 10, Mar 4, May 1, Jun 11, HAY, 14, Jul 2, Aug 14, 29, Sep 1, 11
Little (gallery boxkeeper), 1731: DL, May 17; 1732: DL, May 9; 1734: DL, May
21; 1736: HAY, Jul 29; 1737: DL, May 27; 1741: GF, Nov 2, 16, Dec 9; 1742:
GF, Apr 19
Little Bess the Ballad Singer (song), 1798: DL, May 24
Little Bridges St, 1735: HAY, Mar 22; 1748: DL, Apr 19; 1778: DL, May 9; 1779:
DL, May 8; 1780: DL, May 6; 1787: DL, Feb 2
Little Britain, 1742: DL, Apr 21, 30; 1744: DL, Mar 1; 1758: CG, Jul 6
Little Brookfield, 1743: MF, May 9; 1745: MF, May 2
Little Chapel St, 1751: DL, May 22

516

Little Charles St, <u>1793</u>: DL, Jun 1
Little Dutchwoman (dance), <u>1730</u>: DL, May 2, 27, Sep 15
Little Farthing Rushlight (song), <u>1792</u>: HAY, Aug 22; <u>1793</u>: DL, Apr 8, May 7;
   <u>1794</u>: HAY, Jan 27, Jul 22; <u>1795</u>: DL, Apr 16, HAY, Jun 16, DL, Oct 15; <u>1796</u>:
   CG, May 18, Jun 4, HAY, 11; <u>1797</u>: CG, Apr 19, May 16, Jun 8, HAY, 12; <u>1798</u>:
   CG, Feb 20, Apr 28, HAY, Jun 15; <u>1799</u>: CG, May 3, 7, HAY, Jun 15, Aug 20;
   <u>1800</u>: CG, Jan 29, Apr 17, Jun 11, HAY, Jul 1
Little Flute (music), <u>1728</u>: YB, Mar 13; <u>1729</u>: HIC, Apr 16; <u>1732</u>: TTT, Mar 3;
   <u>1735</u>: GF/HAY, Jul 15
Little Flute Concerto (music), <u>1716</u>: DL, Jun 6; <u>1718</u>: DL, May 16, LR, Dec 3;
   <u>1721</u>: LIF, May 9; <u>1722</u>: DL, Mar 14, HAY, May 11, DL, 11; <u>1723</u>: DL, May 2, 28,
   Jun 25, RI, Sep 2; <u>1724</u>: DL, May 12; <u>1725</u>: DL, Mar 31, May 19; <u>1726</u>: LIF, Apr
   30, DL, May 23, 25; <u>1727</u>: DL, May 15; <u>1729</u>: HIC, Apr 16; <u>1730</u>: DL, Apr 29,
   May 2; <u>1733</u>: DL, May 9; <u>1734</u>: GF, May 8
Little Flute Solo (music), <u>1730</u>: DL, Apr 16
Little French Lawyer, The. See Fletcher, John.
Little Harlequin (dance), <u>1728</u>: DL, May 3
Little Hunchback, The. See O'Keeffe, John.
Little Ormond St, <u>1739</u>: CG, Nov 7
Little Peggy's Love (dance), <u>1796</u>: KING'S, Apr 21, 23, May 3, 13, DL, 25,
   KING'S, 28, Jun 4, Jul 16, 23
Little Piazza, <u>1751</u>: DL, Apr 16; <u>1762</u>: CG, Mar 20; <u>1777</u>: DL, Apr 26
Little Pig lays without any Straw (song), <u>1792</u>: CG, May 16, 19, 28, 30; <u>1794</u>:
   CG, May 16
Little Pipe Solo (music), <u>1723</u>: DL, Jun 6
Little Queen St, <u>1777</u>: CG, Apr 22; <u>1778</u>: CG, Apr 28; <u>1794</u>: HAY, Jun 2; <u>1797</u>:
   CG, Apr 19; <u>1798</u>: CG, Apr 11
Little Russel St, <u>1708</u>: DL, Sep 7; <u>1737</u>: LIF, Mar 24; <u>1750</u>: DL, Apr 21; <u>1751</u>:
   DL, Apr 26; <u>1752</u>: DL, Apr 6, 10, 15; <u>1753</u>: DL, Apr 27; <u>1777</u>: DL, Mar 31, Apr
   7; <u>1778</u>: DL, Apr 9, 27, May 1, 11, 14; <u>1779</u>: DL, Apr 5, 19, May 1; <u>1780</u>: DL,
   Mar 28, Apr 13, 17, 26; <u>1781</u>: DL, Apr 28; <u>1782</u>: DL, Apr 18, May 9, 10; <u>1783</u>:
   DL, Apr 29; <u>1784</u>: DL, Apr 19; <u>1785</u>: DL, Apr 11; <u>1786</u>: DL, Apr 26, May 22, 24,
   25, Jun 6; <u>1787</u>: HAY, Jan 8, DL, Apr 23, May 22; <u>1789</u>: DL, May 19; <u>1790</u>: DL,
   May 27; <u>1791</u>: DL, May 10, 20; <u>1792</u>: DLKING'S, May 8, Jun 7; <u>1794</u>: DL, Mar 12,
   Apr 21, Jul 2; <u>1796</u>: DL, Sep 20; <u>1797</u>: DL, Oct 27; <u>1798</u>: DL, Sep 15; <u>1799</u>:
   DL, May 18, Sep 17
Little Sailor Boy (song), <u>1795</u>: CG, Apr 28, May 7
Little Taffline; or, The Silken Sash (song), <u>1796</u>: DL, May 25, HAY, Aug 23, Sep
   17; <u>1797</u>: DL, May 31, HAY, Aug 10; <u>1798</u>: DL, May 24, HAY, Aug 23, Dec 17;
   <u>1799</u>: HAY, Aug 24; <u>1800</u>: DL, Jun 3, HAY, Aug 23
Little these evils (song), <u>1792</u>: KING'S, Mar 23
Little Waist (song), <u>1796</u>: DL, Jun 3
Little Warwick St, <u>1756</u>: CG, Dec 8
Little Wild St, <u>1742</u>: DL, Apr 26; <u>1743</u>: CG, Apr 27; <u>1744</u>: CG, Apr 25; <u>1746</u>: CG,
   Apr 26; <u>1747</u>: DL, Feb 18, 23; <u>1750</u>: DL, Mar 20; <u>1751</u>: DL, Jan 24, Mar 19, Apr
   29; <u>1752</u>: DL, Mar 19, Apr 13; <u>1753</u>: DL, Apr 14; <u>1754</u>: DL, Apr 18; <u>1778</u>: HAY,
   Mar 31; <u>1785</u>: DL, May 3; <u>1786</u>: DL, May 5
Little Windmill St, <u>1784</u>: HAY, Feb 9
Little, Master (singer), <u>1798</u>: CG, Nov 12; <u>1799</u>: CG, Apr 13; <u>1800</u>: CG, Jan 16,
   Feb 10
Littlegood, Master (actor), <u>1735</u>: YB, May 19
Littlejohn, Mrs (actor), <u>1739</u>: DL, Feb 1, May 4
Littleton (actor), <u>1735</u>: LIF, Jul 23, Aug 6, 8, 25, Sep 5; <u>1736</u>: CG, Mar 27,
   BFHC, Aug 23; <u>1739</u>: CG, Aug 2, 21, BFH, 23, CG, Sep 5, 27; <u>1740</u>: BFH, Aug 23;
   <u>1742</u>: GF, Apr 19; <u>1743</u>: TCD/BFTD, Aug 4
Littleton, Master (actor), <u>1735</u>: LIF, Aug 22, 29; <u>1736</u>: LIF, Mar 31; <u>1738</u>: BFH,
   Aug 23
Littleton, William Henry, 3rd Baron, <u>1771</u>: HAY, Jun 26; <u>1784</u>: DL, Apr 12
Littlewood, John (actor), <u>1668</u>: NONE, Sep 0; <u>1669</u>: BRIDGES, Jun 24; <u>1670</u>:
   BRIDGES, Aug 0, BRI/COUR, Dec 0; <u>1671</u>: BRIDGES, Dec 7
Live and love (song), <u>1785</u>: CG, Apr 5
Live Lumber; or, Unburied Dead (prelude, anon), <u>1796</u>: CG, Mar 30
Lively Lad and Lass (dance), <u>1735</u>: DL, Jan 21, 28
Liveridge. See Leveridge.
Liverpool Prize, The. See Pilon, Frederick.
Liverpool Theatre, <u>1787</u>: DL, Dec 12; <u>1790</u>: DL, Feb 10; <u>1792</u>: CG, Nov 9; <u>1794</u>:
   CG, Feb 1; <u>1798</u>: DL, Jun 18
Liverpool, <u>1760</u>: CG, Oct 10; <u>1763</u>: CG, May 18; <u>1774</u>: DL, Jan 13; <u>1783</u>: DL, Mar
   18; <u>1792</u>: DLKING'S, Feb 7; <u>1794</u>: DL, Mar 12; <u>1795</u>: DL, Jan 20; <u>1796</u>: DL, Apr
   29, HAY, Jun 16, DL, Nov 28
Livery Rake, The. See Phillips, Edward.
Livier. See Leviez.

517

Liviez. See Leviez.
Livigni, Filippo (librettist), 1782: KING'S, Nov 2; 1785: KING'S, Apr 2
Llewellin, Miss (actor), 1785: HAY, Apr 8
Lloyd (actor), 1703: LIF, Nov 0
Lloyd (actor), 1768: HAY, Jul 13, 25, 27, Aug 8; 1770: HAY, Oct 1, 5, 15, 29,
    Nov 16, 21, Dec 19; 1771: HAY, Jan 28, Mar 4, Sep 19, 20; 1772: HAY, May 18,
    27, Jun 29, Jul 3, Aug 4, 10, Sep 17, 18; 1773: HAY, May 17, 24, 26, 28, 31,
    Jun 4, 7, 11, 14, 16, 18, 28, Jul 2, 21, 30, Aug 4, 11, 27, Sep 3, 16, 18;
    1774: HAY, May 16, 30, Jun 1, 3, 6, 8, 10, 13, 17, 27, Jul 6, Aug 19, Sep 5,
    6, 12, 17, 21, 30; 1775: HAY, Feb 2, May 15, 17, 19, 22, 26, 29, Jun 5, 7,
    12, 16, Jul 7, 14, 21, 31, Aug 2, 16, 28, Sep 4, 19, 20, 21, Oct 30; 1776:
    HAY, May 20, 27, 28, 31, Jun 14, Jul 1, 5, 10, 24, 29, Aug 2, Sep 16, 17, 18,
    23, CHR, 30, HAY, Oct 7, CHR, 9, 14; 1781: HAY, Nov 12; 1782: HAY, Jan 14;
    1784: HAY, Mar 8, Apr 30, CG, Oct 4, Nov 12, HAY, 16; 1787: HAY, Mar 12
Lloyd (actor), 1789: HAY, Jun 1
Lloyd (house servant), 1782: CG, May 8; 1783: CG, May 29; 1795: CG, Jun 10;
    1798: CG, May 19; 1799: CG, Jun 4
Lloyd (instrumentalist), 1797: CG, Mar 3
Lloyd (printer), 1773: DL, Jan 15
Lloyd (ticket deliverer), 1789: CG, Jun 13
Lloyd (valet), 1746: DL, May 19; 1747: DL, May 11; 1751: DL, May 13, Sep 21;
    1752: DL, May 2; 1754: DL, May 8; 1768: DL, Sep 29
Lloyd, Elizabeth (actor), 1779: HAY, Jul 15, Aug 18, 21, 31, Sep 8; 1780: HAY,
    Jun 13, 23, Sep 5; 1781: HAY, Jun 8, 15, Aug 1, 21; 1782: HAY, Jun 20, Aug 5;
    1783: HAY, Jun 13, 24, Jul 26, Aug 19, 22, 27; 1784: HAY, Mar 22, May 27, 29,
    Jun 5, 10, 14, 26, Jul 12, Aug 21, 26; 1785: HAY, Feb 12, Jun 3, 7, 11, 13,
    Jul 19, 29, Aug 11, 16
Lloyd, Mrs (actor, singer), 1788: CG, Dec 26; 1790: CG, Sep 13, Oct 4, Nov 27,
    Dec 20, 22; 1791: CG, Mar 7, 31, May 26, Sep 26, Oct 3, Dec 13, 22; 1792: CG,
    Feb 28, Apr 12, May 10, Dec 26; 1793: CG, Apr 8, Sep 23, 30, Oct 2, 7, 9, 24,
    Nov 28, Dec 7, 19, 27; 1794: CG, May 6, Sep 15, 22, 29, Oct 20; 1795: CG, Jan
    31, Apr 24, May 18, Sep 14, 21, Oct 15, 19, Nov 4, 9, Dec 11; 1796: CG, Apr
    9, May 10, 16, Jun 6, Sep 12, 17, 19, 26, Oct 6, 7, Dec 19; 1797: CG, Feb 18,
    Apr 25, May 18, Jun 5, 9, Sep 25, Oct 16, Nov 2, 15, Dec 18, 26; 1798: CG,
    Feb 12, Mar 31, Apr 9, Jun 2, Sep 17, Oct 8, Nov 12, Dec 11, 15, 26; 1799:
    CG, Jan 29, Mar 25, Apr 3, 13, 19, May 28, Sep 30, Oct 7, 21, 24; 1800: CG,
    Jan 16, Feb 10, Mar 25, May 1, 23, Jun 2, HAY, Jul 2, Aug 14
Lloyd, Robert, 1760: DL, Nov 17, Dec 6; 1761: DL, Feb 12; 1764: DL, Nov 28, 29;
    1795: HAY, Mar 11
--Arcadia; or, The Shepherd's Wedding, 1761: DL, Oct 26, 27, 28, 30, 31, Nov 6,
    7, 10, 24, 26
--Capricious Lovers, The (opera), 1764: DL, Nov 28, 29, 30, Dec 1, 3, 4, 5, 6,
    7; 1765: DL, Mar 2, 5, 7, 9, 11, 14, 25, Apr 30; 1766: DL, Mar 17, Apr 11,
    May 9; 1767: DL, May 4, 8; 1782: DL, Apr 24, Oct 5
Lloyd, T A, 1781: HAY, Nov 12
--Romp, The (farce), 1778: CG, Mar 28; 1781: HAY, Nov 12; 1785: DL, Nov 21, 24,
    28, 30, Dec 1, 3, 6, 9, 13, 17, 23; 1786: DL, Jan 3, 4, 6, 18, 21, Feb 4, 7,
    13, 16, 21, 24, Mar 6, 11, 14, 21, 30, Apr 4, 17, 20, 25, 27, May 5, 12, 16,
    18, 24, HAMM, Jul 28, HAY, Aug 3, 7, HAMM, 8, HAY, 16, CG, Sep 25, 27, DL,
    30, CG, Oct 2, DL, 10, CG, 16, DL, 17, 21, Nov 23, Dec 16; 1787: DL, Jan 29,
    Feb 8, Mar 20, 29, Apr 17, 21, CG, May 18, HAY, Jun 26, 29, Jul 10, Aug 30,
    Sep 15, CG, Oct 12; 1788: DL, Apr 8, 11, May 16, 24, Sep 25, Oct 13, 24;
    1789: DL, Mar 23, Apr 16, 25, CG, May 2, DL, 20, HAY, 22, Jun 3, 12, 19, Jul
    15; 1790: DL, Feb 18, Mar 13, 23, Apr 6, 12, 20, 28, May 5, 13, HAY, Sep 29,
    DL, Oct 7, 23, Dec 16, 22; 1791: DL, Feb 9, 17, Mar 7, DLKING'S, Oct 4; 1792:
    CG, Mar 10; 1793: DL, Apr 5, 29; 1795: DL, May 5, 9, CG, Sep 30, DL, Dec 7;
    1796: DL, May 6; 1797: CG, Mar 13; 1798: CG, Nov 6, 8; 1799: DL, Apr 22
Lloyd's Coffee House, 1748: CG, Nov 15; 1794: DL, Jul 2; 1797: CG, Jun 14, DL,
    Oct 27; 1798: CG, Feb 9, DL, Sep 15
Lo a stranger now before you (song), 1777: DL, Feb 10
Lo behold a sea of tears (song), 1671: LIF, Jun 0
Lo he is our God (song), 1794: DL, Mar 26; 1795: KING'S, Feb 27
Lo here my love (song), 1791: DL, Apr 1, CG, 13; 1792: KING'S, Feb 29; 1794:
    DL, Mar 26
Lo we all attend (song), 1790: CG, Mar 3
Loach (actor), 1779: HAY, Jan 11
Loader (actor), 1774: CG, Nov 19, Dec 27; 1775: CG, Mar 30; 1785: HAY, Jan 31
Loathsome urns (song), 1792: CG, Mar 2
Locanda, La. See Paisiello, Giovanni.
Locandiera, La. See Cimarosa, Domenico.
Locatelli, Pietro Antonio (composer), 1733: HIC, Apr 27
Lochaber (song), 1774: HAY, Feb 25

Lochaber no more (song), 1784: HAY, Feb 9
Lochery. See Laughery.
Lock and Key Tavern, 1751: DL, Apr 29; 1754: DL, May 2; 1756: DL, Apr 29
Lock and Key. See Hoare, Prince.
Lock Hospital, 1747: CG, Feb 25, DL, Apr 10; 1749: HAY, Jan 2; 1750: DL, Apr 9;
    1751: CHAPEL, Apr 18; 1753: DL, May 22; 1754: CG, May 23; 1755: DL, Apr 15;
    1756: DL, Apr 2; 1758: DL, Dec 13; 1762: CHAPEL, May 18, DL, Dec 15; 1764:
    CHAPEL, Feb 29; 1766: CHAPEL, Apr 30; 1767: CHAPEL, May 13, CG, Dec 22, 23;
    1768: HAY, Feb 15, CHAPEL, May 25; 1771: CHAPEL, Apr 27; 1774: CHAPEL, Mar
    30; 1776: CHAPEL, Apr 3
Locke (hatter), 1767: DL, Mar 23
Locke, Matthew (composer), 1661: NONE, Apr 22; 1663: LIF, Oct 0, ATCOURT, Dec
    10; 1673: DG, Jul 3; 1674: DG, Apr 30; 1675: DG, Feb 27; 1676: DG, Nov 4, DL,
    18; 1677: ATCOURT, May 22; 1704: DL, Jun 9; 1776: DL, Nov 25; 1777: DL, Apr
    22; 1778: DL, Jan 5, HAY, Sep 7, DL, 24; 1781: DL, Nov 5; 1785: DL, Feb 2,
    KING'S, Mar 17, DL, Oct 1; 1786: DL, Oct 9; 1787: DL, Nov 3; 1788: DL, Oct
    16; 1792: DLKING'S, Feb 18, DL, Dec 26; 1794: DL, Apr 21, Oct 7; 1795: DL,
    Sep 29; 1796: DL, Oct 10; 1797: DL, Nov 7; 1798: DL, Sep 18
Lockhart (actor), 1771: HAY, Apr 15
Lockhart, Miss (singer), 1789: DL, Feb 27, Mar 18, 20, 25
Lockits, 1700: DL, Mar 13
Lockman, John (librettist), 1736: DT, Apr 16; 1740: HIC, Jan 4; 1743: CG, Nov
    17; 1744: DL, Apr 2; 1745: DL, Nov 14; 1756: CG, Dec 17; 1757: CG, Dec 15;
    1764: CG, Dec 11; 1765: DL, Apr 22
Loder, Mrs (beneficiary), 1741: GF, Dec 21
Lodgings to Let for Single Gentlemen (song), 1797: DL, Apr 28; 1799: DL, Apr 19
Lodi, Sga (singer), 1711: HDS, Apr 24; 1713: HIC, Mar 25; 1714: HIC, Apr 28;
    1715: GRT, Apr 26
Lodi, Stella (singer), 1773: KING'S, Oct 23, Nov 20, Dec 7; 1774: KING'S, Jan
    11
Lodoiska. See Kemble, John Philip.
Loeli, D (author), 1736: KING'S, Apr 13
Loft, Mrs (actor), 1782: HAY, Jan 21
Logan, Maria (actor), 1783: HAY, Jun 18; 1784: CG, May 7, HAY, Jun 28; 1785:
    HAY, Jun 11, Aug 25; 1793: HAY, Jun 15; 1795: HAY, Aug 3, 21, CG, Oct 15, Nov
    16, 20, 25, 26, 27, 30, Dec 4, 7, 15, 18, 23; 1796: CG, Mar 14, 30, Apr 26,
    May 25, Jun 3, HAY, 16, Aug 8, 10, 18, 23, 30, CG, Sep 19, 26, 28, Oct 6, 7,
    17, 18, 29, Nov 24, Dec 9, 10, 15; 1797: CG, Feb 18, 20, Mar 13, Apr 8, May 6
Lokes and Co (wax chandlers), 1788: DL, Oct 28; 1789: DL, Dec 15
Lolli, Antonio (violinist), 1785: DL, Feb 23
Lombard St, 1735: LIF, Jun 19; 1748: DL, May 2; 1749: CG, Apr 28; 1753: DL, Dec
    21
Lomphergall (dance), 1734: GF, May 17
Londinium Triumphans. See Tatham, John.
London Assurance Office, 1782: CG, Nov 26
London Cuckolds, The. See Ravenscroft, Edward.
London Hermit, The. See O'Keeffe, John.
London Hospital, 1787: ROY, Jun 20
London in its Splendor. See Jordan, Thomas.
London in Luster. See Jordan, Thomas.
London is a Fine Town (song), 1717: LIF, Nov 5; 1718: LIF, Jan 6, Aug 6, RI, 16
London Lying-in Hospital, 1756: HAB, Dec 9; 1757: CG, Dec 15; 1759: CG, Jan 9;
    1761: DL, Dec 15; 1762: CG, Dec 22; 1764: DL, Dec 19; 1765: CG, Dec 21; 1767:
    HAB, Dec 10; 1768: DL, Dec 20; 1769: CG, Dec 20; 1771: DL, Dec 17; 1773: CG,
    Dec 18, 31; 1775: CG, Dec 22; 1776: DL, Dec 17; 1778: DL, Dec 18; 1782: DL,
    Dec 19
London Merchant, The. See Lillo, George.
London Prentice, The. See DeFesch, William.
London Road, 1789: DL, Apr 2; 1790: HAY, Oct 13; 1791: DL, Mar 24, HAY, Aug 26;
    1792: DLKING'S, Mar 19
London Spa Fields, 1735: WF, Aug 23
London Spa, 1741: NWC, Aug 22; 1746: NWC, Sep 15; 1748: NWC, Nov 21, Dec 26,
    29; 1749: NWC, Nov 27; 1750: NWC, Apr 16
London Triumphant. See Jordan, Thomas.
London's Anniversary Festival. See Taubman, Matthew.
London's Annual Triumph. See Taubman, Matthew.
London's Glory Represented by Time, Truth, and Fame. See Taubman, Matthew.
London's Glory. See Jordan, Thomas.
London's Great Jubilee. See Taubman, Matthew.
London's Joy. See Jordan, Thomas.
London's Resurrection to Joy and Triumph. See Jordan, Thomas.
London's Royal Triumph for the City's Loyal Magistrate. See Jordan, Thomas.

London's Triumph. See Tatham, John.
London's Triumph; or, The Goldsmith's Jubilee. See Taubman, Matthew.
London's Yearly Jubilee. See Taubman, Matthew.
Long (actor), 1780: HAY, Mar 28
Long (householder), 1746: DL, Apr 28
Long (supplier), 1760: CG, Mar 17
Long (ticket deliverer), 1792: DLKING'S, Jun 15; 1793: DL, Jun 6
Long Acre, 1718: LIF, Jun 20, NONE, Jul 12; 1735: CG/LIF, Mar 25; 1736: CG, Mar
   16, May 4; 1739: CG, Dec 15; 1742: CG, Apr 20; 1743: HAY, Mar 24, CG, Apr 6,
   15; 1744: CG, Jan 19, DL, Mar 5, CG, Apr 3, 17; 1746: CG, Apr 16; 1747: CG,
   Apr 27, May 7; 1748: CG, Apr 13; 1749: CG, Mar 30; 1750: KING'S, Mar 13;
   1751: DL, Apr 29, Dec 17; 1752: DL, Apr 2, 14; 1754: DL, May 2, 4; 1755: CG,
   Jan 8, Dec 16; 1756: DL, Jan 22, Apr 29, CG, Dec 15; 1764: DL, Dec 12; 1765:
   CG, Dec 17; 1768: DL, Dec 16; 1771: DL, Dec 21; 1772: DL, Sep 29; 1776: DL,
   Dec 19; 1777: DL, Apr 21, CG, 28, May 6, 14; 1778: DL, Apr 30, CG, May 19;
   1779: CG, May 13, DL, 19; 1780: CG, Apr 22, DL, May 6, CG, 12; 1781: DL, May
   16; 1784: CG, May 8; 1785: CG, Apr 15, HAY, Jul 19; 1786: CG, May 2, DL, 2,
   CG, 10, 15; 1787: CG, Mar 13; 1789: CG, Jun 8; 1790: CG, May 24; 1791: CG,
   Jun 6; 1792: DLKING'S, May 10, CG, 16, HAY, Oct 15; 1794: DL, Mar 12, HAY,
   Jun 2; 1796: CG, Apr 22; 1798: CG, May 12; 1799: CG, May 10; 1800: CG, Apr 23
Long Ave, 1746: DL, Apr 25
Long betwixt Love and fear Phillis tormented (song), 1672: LIF, Nov 0
Long by adverse motion (song), 1789: DL, Mar 20
Long Live the King (song), 1742: GF, Apr 22; 1745: GF, Oct 28
Long Minuet (dance), 1787: CG, Dec 26; 1789: CG, Jun 8; 1795: CG, Nov 9, 16
Long Room, 1718: LR, Dec 3; 1724: HA, May 4; 1734: HA, Sep 2; 1759: HAM, Aug
   13; 1768: CG, Oct 24
Long Whitson Holiday (dance), 1733: DL, May 14
Long, Jane (actor), 1661: LIF, Dec 16; 1663: LIF, Jan 8, Feb 23, Oct 0,
   ATCOURT, Dec 10; 1664: LIF, Mar 0, NONE, Apr 27, LIF, Aug 13, Sep 10; 1665:
   LIF, Apr 3; 1666: NONE, Sep 0; 1667: LIF, Nov 7; 1668: NONE, Sep 0; 1669:
   LIF, Dec 14; 1670: LIF, Feb 19, Nov 0; 1671: LIF, Jan 10, Mar 6, 15, Jun 0;
   1672: DG, Nov 4; 1673: DG, Feb 18
Long, Lady (spectator), 1700: DLORLIF, Jan 20
Long, Miss (dancer), 1774: HAY, Apr 4
Long's Coffee House, 1758: CG, Jul 6
Longbottom (actor), 1728: HAY, May 8; 1729: HAY, Jul 16, DL, Aug 16
Longdale (actor), 1795: HAY, Sep 21
Longley, E (boxkeeper), 1771: CG, May 27; 1772: CG, May 29; 1773: CG, May 28;
   1774: CG, May 14; 1776: CG, May 22; 1777: CG, May 23; 1778: CG, May 22; 1779:
   CG, May 19; 1780: CG, May 26; 1781: CG, May 26; 1782: CG, May 29; 1783: CG,
   Jun 4; 1784: CG, May 29; 1786: CG, May 27; 1787: CG, Jun 5; 1788: CG, May 17;
   1789: CG, Jun 6; 1790: CG, Jun 8; 1791: CG, Jun 9; 1792: CG, Jun 1; 1797: DL,
   Nov 25; 1798: DL, Jun 7
Longman, James, and Broderip, Francis (music publishers), 1784: HAY, Mar 3, CG,
   Dec 27; 1786: CG, Oct 16, Dec 26; 1787: CG, Apr 24; 1788: CG, Dec 13; 1790:
   CG, May 6; 1793: CG, May 21; 1794: HAY, Jun 2; 1797: CG, Jun 21; 1798: CG,
   Jun 11
Longman, Thomas Norton (publisher), 1782: CG, Mar 16; 1788: CG, May 22; 1789:
   CG, May 15, HAY, Aug 11, CG, Oct 7; 1791: HAY, Jul 30, CG, Nov 5; 1792: CG,
   Apr 21, Sep 17; 1793: CG, Feb 25, Apr 18, May 11; 1794: CG, Apr 10, Oct 23,
   30, Dec 6; 1795: CG, Jan 31, Feb 14, 21, Mar 19, Apr 6, 23, May 1, Jun 3,
   HAY, 20, CG, Oct 23, Nov 7; 1796: CG, Jan 23, Feb 2, Mar 19, Apr 9, HAY, Jun
   11, CG, Oct 29, Nov 5, 19, Dec 19; 1797: CG, Jan 10, Mar 16, DL, Apr 28, HAY,
   Jul 15, CG, Dec 26; 1798: CG, Jan 11, DL, Mar 24, CG, Nov 12, 23, Dec 8;
   1799: CG, Jan 12, Apr 8, 27, Jun 12, Oct 31; 1800: CG, Feb 8, Mar 25
Longman, Thomas Norton, and Rees, Owen (publishers), 1800: CG, May 12
Longueville, Lady. See Yelverton, Barbara.
Longueville, Viscount. See Yelverton, Henry.
Longville (beneficiary), 1718: LIF, Jan 15; 1721: LIF, Mar 28; 1723: LIF, Dec
   12
Lonsdale (dancer), 1779: HAY, Oct 18, Dec 27
Lonsdale, Mark, 1784: DL, Nov 4; 1791: CG, Jun 6; 1794: CG, Dec 26; 1795: CG,
   Dec 21
--Mago and Dago; or, Harlequin the Hero (pantomime), 1794: CG, Dec 26, 27, 29,
   30, 31; 1795: CG, Jan 1, 2, 3, 5, 6, 7, 12, 13, 14, 15, 19, 20, 21, 22, 23,
   26, 27, 28, Feb 9, 12, 16, 23, Mar 2
--Spanish Rivals, The (farce), 1784: DL, Nov 4, 5, 6, 10, 15, 19, 20, 27, Dec
   2; 1785: DL, Apr 8
--Tipoo Saib; or, British Valour in India (pantomime), 1791: CG, Jun 6, 7, 8,
   10, 13
Lonzetti (musician), 1754: HAY, Feb 13

Look before You Leap. See Robson, Horatio Edgar.
Look down (song), <u>1698</u>: DL, Mar 0
Look down fair nymph and see (song), <u>1686</u>: DL, Jan 0
Look round and here behold (song), <u>1697</u>: DG, Jun 0
Looking Glass for the Times (entertainment), <u>1784</u>: HAY, Aug 19, 20
Lops, Rosa (singer), <u>1791</u>: KING'S, Mar 31, Apr 16, May 14
Lord Bacon's Head Tavern, <u>1756</u>: DL, Mar 9
Lord Chamberlain, <u>1666</u>: ATCOURT, Oct 18; <u>1668</u>: BRIDGES, Dec 18; <u>1669</u>: BRIDGES,
   Jan 13, Mar 4, 6, ATCOURT, Oct 26; <u>1671</u>: NONE, Apr 1; <u>1676</u>: DL, Sep 9; <u>1682</u>:
   DG, Aug 10; <u>1683</u>: DL, Jan 19; <u>1691</u>: NONE, Dec 17; <u>1692</u>: NONE, Apr 9; <u>1696</u>:
   NONE, Oct 26; <u>1697</u>: ATCOURT, Feb 6, NONE, Jun 4, DG, Jul 1; <u>1700</u>: DLLIF, Aug
   6; <u>1706</u>: YB, Mar 18; <u>1707</u>: DL/QUEEN, Dec 31; <u>1709</u>: DL, Jun 7; <u>1718</u>: HC, Sep
   23; <u>1719</u>: DL, May 9, KING'S, Nov 27, 30, Dec 2, DL, 19; <u>1720</u>: DL, Jan 23, Feb
   2, 16, Mar 3; <u>1733</u>: DL, May 28; <u>1737</u>: NONE, Jun 4; <u>1739</u>: CG, Mar 27; <u>1740</u>:
   DL, Jan 4; <u>1742</u>: DL, May 6; <u>1743</u>: DL, Oct 8; <u>1744</u>: HAY, Oct 22, Nov 10; <u>1745</u>:
   CG, Dec 21; <u>1746</u>: CG, Nov 4; <u>1751</u>: DL, Mar 20, Nov 29; <u>1752</u>: HAY, Mar 31, DL,
   Nov 18, Dec 2; <u>1753</u>: DL, Mar 20, CG, Apr 11; <u>1754</u>: HAY, May 29; <u>1757</u>: KING'S,
   May 31, Sep 20, DL, Dec 29; <u>1758</u>: DL, Dec 18; <u>1759</u>: HAY, Jan 12, DL, 22;
   <u>1763</u>: KING'S, Mar 5, HAY, May 21, Aug 29; <u>1764</u>: CG, Jun 5; <u>1767</u>: DL, Sep 28;
   <u>1768</u>: KING'S, May 12, HAY, Sep 19, Oct 7; <u>1770</u>: HAY, May 4, Oct 1; <u>1771</u>: HAY,
   May 2, Sep 18, 20; <u>1772</u>: DL, Feb 8; <u>1773</u>: HAY, Sep 17; <u>1774</u>: HAY, Jan 24, Sep
   16, 19, 30; <u>1775</u>: HAY, Feb 2, 20, Aug 4, Nov 20; <u>1776</u>: HAY, Apr 22, Oct 7;
   <u>1777</u>: HAY, Feb 11, Apr 22, May 1, Sep 16, 17, 18, 19, Oct 6, 9, 13; <u>1778</u>:
   HAY, Jan 26, Feb 9, Mar 23, 24, 31, Apr 9, 29, 30, Sep 16, 17, 18, Dec 28;
   <u>1779</u>: HAY, Jan 11, May 10, Sep 16, 17, Oct 13, 18, Dec 20, 27; <u>1780</u>: HAY, Jan
   3, 17, Mar 28, Apr 5, Sep 25, Oct 30, Nov 13; <u>1781</u>: HAY, Jan 22, Mar 26, Nov
   12; <u>1782</u>: HAY, Jan 14, 21, Mar 18, 21, May 6, Sep 16, 18, 19, 20, 21, CG, Oct
   31, HAY, Nov 25, Dec 30; <u>1783</u>: HAY, Sep 17, Dec 15; <u>1784</u>: HAY, Jan 21, Feb 9,
   23, Mar 3, 8, 10, 22, Apr 30, DL, Aug 20, 25, 27, 28, HAY, Sep 17, Nov 16,
   Dec 13; <u>1785</u>: HAY, Jan 24, 31, Feb 7, 10, 12, 14, 21, 23, 24, 28, Mar 7, 10,
   14, 15, Apr 8, 11, 15, 18, 25, 26, 29, Sep 16, Dec 26; <u>1786</u>: CG, Feb 13, HAY,
   Mar 6, NONE, Nov 1, HAY, Dec 18; <u>1787</u>: HAY, Jan 8, Mar 12, 26, Apr 30; <u>1788</u>:
   HAY, Apr 9, 29, Sep 30, Dec 22; <u>1789</u>: HAY, Feb 23; <u>1790</u>: NONE, Sep 18, HAY,
   29, Oct 13; <u>1791</u>: KING'S, Feb 23, HAY, Mar 7, Aug 13, Sep 16, Oct 24, Dec 12,
   26; <u>1792</u>: DLKING'S, Jan 30, HAY, Feb 6, 20, Apr 16, Oct 15, 22, Nov 26, Dec
   26; <u>1793</u>: CG, Nov 20; <u>1794</u>: HAY, May 22, Jun 2, Sep 1, 17; <u>1795</u>: HAY, Mar 4,
   Apr 22, Sep 21; <u>1796</u>: HAY, Feb 22, Mar 28, Apr 27, Sep 16, 17, 28, DL, Nov
   12; <u>1797</u>: HAY, Jan 23, 26, Feb 9, May 10, Sep 16, 18, Dec 4; <u>1798</u>: HAY, Jan
   15, Mar 26, Apr 21, 23, Sep 17, Dec 17; <u>1799</u>: HAY, Jan 24, 28, Feb 25, Apr
   17, Sep 16, Oct 21; <u>1800</u>: HAY, Feb 3, Sep 16
Lord Chancellor, <u>1660</u>: MT, Nov 2; <u>1682</u>: DL, Mar 21; <u>1697</u>: IT, Nov 1
Lord gave (song), <u>1793</u>: KING/HAY, Feb 20; <u>1794</u>: DL, Mar 19
Lord in thee (song), <u>1792</u>: KING'S, Mar 23, 30; <u>1794</u>: DL, Apr 11; see also O
   Lord in thee have I trusted
Lord is a Man of War (song), <u>1786</u>: DL, Mar 10; <u>1789</u>: DL, Mar 18; <u>1790</u>: DL, Feb
   26, CG, Mar 3; <u>1791</u>: DL, Mar 23; <u>1792</u>: KING'S, Feb 24; <u>1793</u>: KING/HAY, Feb
   22; <u>1794</u>: DL, Apr 10; <u>1799</u>: CG, Feb 20
Lord Mayor, <u>1659</u>: CITY, Oct 29, NONE, Dec 18; <u>1660</u>: CITY, Oct 29; <u>1661</u>: CITY,
   Oct 29; <u>1662</u>: THAMES, Aug 23; <u>1663</u>: BF, Aug 25, CITY, Oct 29; <u>1664</u>: CITY, Oct
   29; <u>1666</u>: CITY, Oct 29; <u>1667</u>: CITY, Oct 29; <u>1668</u>: NONE, Oct 29; <u>1669</u>: CITY,
   Oct 29; <u>1670</u>: CITY, Oct 29; <u>1671</u>: CITY, Oct 30; <u>1672</u>: CITY, Oct 29; <u>1673</u>:
   CITY, Oct 29; <u>1674</u>: CITY, Oct 29; <u>1675</u>: CITY, Oct 29; <u>1676</u>: CITY, Oct 30;
   <u>1677</u>: CITY, Oct 29; <u>1678</u>: CITY, Oct 29; <u>1679</u>: CITY, Oct 29; <u>1680</u>: CITY, Oct
   29; <u>1681</u>: CITY, Oct 29; <u>1682</u>: BF, Aug 23, CITY, Oct 30; <u>1683</u>: DL, Jan 19,
   CITY, Oct 29; <u>1684</u>: CITY, Oct 29; <u>1685</u>: CITY, Oct 29; <u>1686</u>: CITY, Oct 29;
   <u>1687</u>: CITY, Oct 29; <u>1688</u>: CITY, Oct 28; <u>1689</u>: CITY, Oct 29; <u>1690</u>: NONE, Sep
   8; <u>1691</u>: BF, Aug 3, 8, CITY, Oct 29; <u>1692</u>: CITY, Oct 29; <u>1693</u>: CITY, Oct 30;
   <u>1694</u>: BF, Sep 1; <u>1697</u>: BF, Aug 24; <u>1698</u>: CITY, Oct 29; <u>1699</u>: BFPD, Aug 23,
   CITY, Oct 30; <u>1700</u>: BF, Jun 25; <u>1717</u>: NONE, Sep 12; <u>1729</u>: SF, Sep 8; <u>1730</u>:
   GF, Apr 28, BFPG, Aug 20; <u>1749</u>: DL, Apr 27; <u>1752</u>: DL, Nov 9; <u>1762</u>: BFY, Sep
   3, HAY, 7; <u>1794</u>: DL, Jul 2; <u>1797</u>: DL, Oct 27
Lord Mayor's Day; or, A Flight from Lapland. See O'Keeffe, John.
Lord Mayor's Pageant, <u>1659</u>: CITY, Oct 29; <u>1661</u>: CITY, Oct 29; <u>1662</u>: CITY, Oct
   29; <u>1663</u>: CITY, Oct 29; <u>1664</u>: CITY, Oct 29; <u>1666</u>: CITY, Oct 29; <u>1671</u>: CITY,
   Oct 30; <u>1672</u>: CITY, Oct 29; <u>1673</u>: CITY, Oct 29; <u>1674</u>: CITY, Oct 29; <u>1675</u>:
   CITY, Oct 29; <u>1676</u>: CITY, Oct 30; <u>1677</u>: CITY, Oct 29; <u>1678</u>: CITY, Oct 29;
   <u>1679</u>: CITY, Oct 29; <u>1680</u>: CITY, Oct 29; <u>1681</u>: CITY, Oct 29; <u>1682</u>: CITY, Oct
   30; <u>1683</u>: CITY, Oct 29; <u>1684</u>: CITY, Oct 29; <u>1685</u>: CITY, Oct 29; <u>1686</u>: CITY,
   Oct 29; <u>1687</u>: CITY, Oct 29; <u>1688</u>: CITY, Oct 28; <u>1689</u>: CITY, Oct 29; <u>1693</u>:
   CITY, Oct 30; <u>1694</u>: CITY, Oct 29; <u>1695</u>: CITY, Oct 29; <u>1698</u>: CITY, Oct 29;
   <u>1699</u>: CITY, Oct 30
Lord Mayor's Show, The; or, Four and Twenty Alderman (song), <u>1800</u>: DL, Apr 28

Lord of Eternity (song), 1790: CG, Mar 17; 1792: CG, Mar 2; 1793: CG, Feb 15;
    1794: CG, Mar 7; 1795: CG, Feb 20; 1796: CG, Mar 16; 1797: CG, Mar 31; 1799:
    CG, Mar 15
Lord of the Manor, The. See Burgoyne, Lieutenant-General John.
Lord remember David (song), 1789: DL, Mar 18; 1790: DL, Feb 26; 1791: DL, Mar
    23; 1792: KING'S, Feb 24, Mar 30; 1793: KING/HAY, Feb 22, CG, Mar 6; 1794:
    DL, Mar 12, CG, 12, DL, 14, Apr 2, 10; 1795: CG, Mar 13, 25; 1796: CG, Feb
    26; 1797: CG, Mar 22; 1798: CG, Mar 14; 1799: CG, Feb 15, Mar 15; 1800: CG,
    Feb 28
Lord Russel. See Hayley, William; Stratford, Thomas.
Lord said unto the Lord (song), 1789: DL, Mar 25
Lord shall reign (song), 1789: CG, Mar 6, 27; 1791: CG, Mar 11; 1792: CG, Mar
    2; 1793: CG, Feb 15, Mar 13; 1794: CG, Mar 14, Apr 9; 1795: CG, Feb 27, Mar
    25; 1797: CG, Mar 10; 1798: CG, Mar 14, 30; 1800: CG, Mar 5
Lord shall send (song), 1789: DL, Mar 25
Lord swear and will not repent (song), 1789: DL, Mar 25
Lord to thee (song), 1794: DL, Mar 21; 1795: CG, Mar 25; 1796: CG, Feb 24, Mar
    2
Lord Treasurer, 1677: DL, Jul 0
Lord upon Thy Right Hand (song), 1789: DL, Mar 25
Lord what is man (song), 1786: DL, Mar 10; 1788: DL, Feb 8; 1790: DL, Feb 24;
    1792: KING'S, Feb 24; 1793: CG, Mar 6; 1794: CG, Mar 12, DL, Apr 4, 10; 1796:
    CG, Feb 26; 1797: CG, Mar 10; 1798: CG, Mar 2; 1799: CG, Feb 8, Mar 6
Lord worketh wonders (song), 1794: CG, Mar 21; 1799: CG, Mar 1
Lord, John? (horn player), 1794: CG, Mar 7
Lordly Husband, The (play, anon), 1737: HAY, May 16
Lorenzi, Giovanni Battista (librettist), 1792: HAY, Mar 31
Lorenzini, Caterina (singer), 1780: KING'S, Dec 23; 1781: KING'S, Mar 8, Apr 5,
    Jun 5, 23, Nov 17, Dec 11; 1782: KING'S, Jan 10, 12, Mar 2, 7, 16, Apr 9, May
    25
Lorenzo. See Merry, Robert.
Lorenzo, Vicenzo (dancer), 1773: KING'S, Oct 23
Loriners Hall, 1737: LH, Jan 26
Lorrain (dance), 1731: DL, Oct 26, Nov 11; 1732: DL, Apr 19
Lorrain, Duke of (spectator), 1731: HC, Oct 18, LIF, 29, KING'S, Nov 1, 13, 16,
    DL, 17, KING'S, 23, DL, 29, KING'S, 30, LIF, Dec 2
Lort (equilibrist), 1749: SFP, Sep 15, SOU, 18
Lort, John (manager), 1662: LI, Jan 3
Lost Lady, The. See Berkeley, William.
Lost Lover, The. See Manley, Mary.
Lost Picture (dance), 1765: CG, May 9
Lothario (opera), 1741: CG, Mar 7
Lothario (song), 1749: CG, Apr 5, 14
Lotharius. See Handel, George Frederic.
Lottery Office, 1792: CG, Feb 8
Lottery, The (play, anon), 1728: HAY, Nov 14, 19, 20, 21, 23, Dec 10; 1729:
    HAY, Jan 2
Lottery, The. See Sewell, George; Fielding, Henry.
Lotti, Antonio (composer), 1731: ACA, Jan 14
Lottini, Antonio (singer), 1737: KING'S, Jan 1, 25, Feb 19, Mar 26; 1738:
    KING'S, Jan 3, 28, Apr 15
Louch, Mrs (beneficiary), 1742: CG, Mar 11; 1743: CG, Apr 16
Loud as the thunder (song), 1794: DL, Mar 26
Louille, Mlle Sophie (dancer), 1774: KING'S, Nov 19
Louis XVI, 1793: CG, Jan 23, DL, 24
Louisa Anne, Princess, 1735: GF/HAY, Jan 9; 1760: CG, Apr 26, Dec 19; 1766: CG,
    Oct 23, Nov 20, Dec 18; 1767: CG, Jan 15, 29, Feb 19, Apr 23, DL, May 7, CG,
    15; 1768: CG, Jan 14, Feb 4, 22, DL, May 13; see also Princesses
Lourdet de Santerre, Jean Baptiste (author), 1778: CG, Oct 2
Loutherbourgh (actor), 1776: CHR, Oct 14
Louvicini, Sga (singer), 1705: QUEEN'S, Dec 15, 19, 31; 1706: DL, Jan 29
Louvre (dance), 1724: LIF, May 5, 16, 20, 25, 26, 27, 28, 29, Jun 1; 1725: LIF,
    May 21; 1726: LIF, Apr 14, 20, May 14; 1727: LIF, Mar 11, Oct 26; 1731: LIF,
    May 3; 1732: LIF, May 1, 24, RIW/HAY, Sep 4, 12; 1733: LIF/CG, Apr 23; 1734:
    GF, Apr 27, CG, May 8; 1735: GF/HAY, Jul 15; 1736: CG, Apr 26; 1737: CG, Mar
    24, DL, May 11; 1739: CG, Mar 22; 1740: DL, Mar 22, Apr 25, May 15, CG, Dec
    20; 1741: CG, Jan 7, 10, Feb 14, Mar 7, 12, 17, Apr 2, 24, 29, DL, May 13,
    14; 1742: CG, Jan 11, 16, Mar 30, Apr 1, 5, 20, 29, May 21; 1743: LIF, Mar 3,
    22, CG, 24, Apr 14, 18, 22; 1744: CG, Apr 4, 16, 24; 1745: CG, Apr 2, 18, 19,
    23; 1746: CG, Apr 2, DL, 3, CG, 15, DL, 16, 24; 1747: DL, Apr 2; 1748: DL,
    Mar 24, 26, Apr 15, CG, 19, HAY, May 2; 1750: DL, Mar 17, CG, 31, Apr 18, 23,
    28; 1751: DL, Apr 11, 16, May 8; 1752: DL, Mar 16, CG, Apr 13, 15, 18, 22,

DL, 27; <u>1753</u>: DL, Mar 31, CG, Apr 9, DL, 24, CG, 30, May 1; <u>1754</u>: DL, Mar 26,
CG, Apr 16, May 4; <u>1755</u>: CG, Apr 23, DL, 24, 29; <u>1757</u>: DL, May 18, HAY, Sep
8, 14; <u>1758</u>: CG, Apr 19, DL, May 2, 10; <u>1759</u>: DL, May 15, 23; <u>1760</u>: DL, May
7; <u>1762</u>: CG, Apr 28; <u>1763</u>: CG, Apr 29; <u>1766</u>: KING'S, Mar 13; <u>1767</u>: DL, May
12, 15; <u>1769</u>: CG, Apr 29; <u>1770</u>: HAY, Feb 14; <u>1771</u>: HAY, Mar 11, Apr 1, May 2,
DL, 8; <u>1772</u>: DL, May 8; <u>1773</u>: DL, Apr 22, KING'S, Jun 12, 19; <u>1774</u>: DL, Apr
20; <u>1775</u>: KING'S, Apr 22, 25, DL, 28, KING'S, May 6, 11, 16, 27, 30; <u>1776</u>:
DL, Apr 23
Louvre and Bretagne (dance), <u>1731</u>: LIF, Apr 5
Louvre and Minuet (dance), <u>1735</u>: GF/HAY, Jul 18; <u>1741</u>: CG, Apr 15; <u>1747</u>: GF,
Apr 4; <u>1749</u>: DL, Mar 14, 30, CG, Apr 21; <u>1750</u>: DL, May 1; <u>1751</u>: CG, Apr 12,
18, 26, May 4; <u>1753</u>: DL, Mar 26; <u>1754</u>: CG, Apr 4, DL, 6, CG, 25, 27; <u>1755</u>:
CG, Apr 22; <u>1756</u>: CG, Apr 27, 28, DL, May 5; <u>1757</u>: CG, Apr 26, DL, May 6;
<u>1760</u>: CG, Apr 23, DL, 29; <u>1761</u>: CG, Apr 22, DL, 28, May 5, 6; <u>1762</u>: DL, Apr
21, May 12; <u>1763</u>: DL, Apr 30; <u>1767</u>: DL, May 22; <u>1768</u>: DL, May 10; <u>1773</u>: DL,
Apr 24, CG, May 21
Louvre and Tambourine (dance), <u>1736</u>: CG, Apr 8
Louvre Minuet (dance), <u>1777</u>: DL, Apr 23
Lovat, Lord (on trial), <u>1747</u>: CG, Mar 18
Lovattini (singer), <u>1766</u>: KING'S, Oct 21, Nov 25; <u>1767</u>: KING'S, Jan 31, Feb 24,
Mar 12, Apr 9, Oct 27, Nov 7; <u>1768</u>: KING'S, Apr 21, Nov 8; <u>1769</u>: KING'S, Mar
2, May 23, Sep 5, Nov 7; <u>1770</u>: KING'S, Feb 22, May 19, Nov 6, Dec 4, 8; <u>1771</u>:
KING'S, Mar 14, Apr 25; <u>1772</u>: HAY, Apr 6, KING'S, 9; <u>1774</u>: KING'S, Dec 13;
<u>1775</u>: KING'S, Mar 7, 30, May 23
Love (singer), <u>1743</u>: DL, May 26
Love (song), <u>1748</u>: HAY, Apr 20
Love a la Mode. See Macklin, Charles.
Love alone can here alarm me (song), <u>1696</u>: LIF, Nov 14
Love and a Bottle. See Farquhar, George.
Love and a Bumper (play, anon), <u>1718</u>: LIF, Mar 4
Love and Danger. See Davenant, Sir William.
Love and Duty. See Slade, John.
Love and Duty; or, The Distressed Bride. See Sturmy, John.
Love and Empire; or, Virtue Triumphant (farce), <u>1750</u>: NWSM, May 1, SFB, Sep 8,
10, SF, 11, SFB, 12
Love and Folly. See Galliard, John Ernest.
Love and Friendship. See DeFesch, William.
Love and Glory. See Phillips, Thomas.
Love and Honour. See Davenant, Sir William.
Love and Honour; or, Britannia in Full Glory at Spithead (interlude, anon),
<u>1794</u>: CG, May 9
Love and Innocence. See Hook, James.
Love and Jealousie (dance), <u>1729</u>: DL, Oct 18, 22
Love and Jealousy; or, The Downfall of Alexander the Great (entertainment),
<u>1733</u>: BF, Aug 23
Love and Madness! See Waldron, Francis Godolphin.
Love and Money. See Benson, Robert.
Love and Resolution. See Arne, Dr Thomas A.
Love and Revenge. See Settle, Elkanah.
Love and Revenge; or, The Vintner Outwitted (opera, anon), <u>1729</u>: HAY, Nov 12,
13, 14, 15, 18, 20, Dec 5, 22; <u>1730</u>: HAY, Feb 12, Mar 20
Love and War. See O'Keeffe, John.
Love and Wine (song), <u>1725</u>: LIF, Apr 7; <u>1726</u>: LIF, Apr 14, 27; <u>1728</u>: LIF, May
15; <u>1733</u>: GF, Mar 17, May 22
Love at a Loss. See Trotter, Catherine.
Love at a Venture. See Centlivre, Susannah.
Love at First Sight. See Crauford, David; Gibson Jr; King, Thomas.
Love Betrayed. See Burnaby, William.
Love Despised. See Fletcher, John, Cupid's Revenge.
Love Finds the Way. See Hull, Thomas.
Love for Love (dance), <u>1787</u>: HAY, Jun 25, 27, Jul 20, 23, 27, 30
Love for Love. See Congreve, William.
Love for Money. See D'Urfey, Thomas.
Love Hath Found Out His Eyes. See Jordan, Thomas.
Love in a Camp. See O'Keeffe, John.
Love in a Chest. See Johnson, Charles.
Love in a Forest. See Johnson, Charles.
Love in a Labyrinth; or, School for a Wife (play, anon), <u>1746</u>: BFLY, Aug 25
Love in a Mist. See Cunningham, John.
Love in a Riddle. See Cibber, Colley.
Love in a Sack. See Griffin, Benjamin.
Love in a Tubb. See Etherege, Sir George.

Love in a Veil. See Savage, Richard.
Love in a Village. See Bickerstaff, Isaac.
Love in a Wood. See Wycherley, William.
Love in Excess. See Haywood, Eliza.
Love in her eyes (song), 1752: KING'S, Mar 24; 1784: DL, Mar 5; 1787: DL, Mar
    7; 1791: DL, Apr 1, CG, 13; 1792: KING'S, Feb 29, CG, Mar 23; 1794: DL, Mar
    26
Love in Low Life; or, A Press Gang at Billingsgate. See Carey, Henry, Nancy.
Love in Many Masks. See Kemble, John Philip.
Love in Several Masques. See Fielding, Henry.
Love in the City. See Bickerstaff, Isaac.
Love in the Dark. See Fane, Sir Francis.
Love in the East. See Cobb, James.
Love in the Suds (play), 1772: MARLY, Jul 2
Love is the Doctor. See Moliere.
Love Lies a Bleeding. See Fletcher, John, Philaster.
Love Lost in the Dark; or, The Drunken Couple (play, anon), 1679: NONE, Sep 0
Love Makes a Man. See Cibber, Colley.
Love Match, The (play, anon), 1762: CG, Mar 13, 15
Love Runs All Dangers (pantomime, anon), 1733: HAY, Mar 16, 20, 21, 22, 26, Apr
    23
Love sounds the alarm (song), 1735: DL, Apr 29; 1787: DL, Mar 7; 1791: CG, Mar
    23, DL, Apr 1; 1792: KING'S, Feb 29; 1794: DL, Mar 26
Love the Leveller; or, The Pretty Purchase (play, anon), 1704: DL, Jan 22, 26,
    27
Love thou art best of human joys (song), 1693: DG, May 0
Love thou maddening power (song), 1787: DL, May 11; 1800: CG, May 24
Love Tricks. See Shirley, James.
Love Triumphant (dance), 1764: CG, May 3
Love Triumphant; or, Nature Will Prevail. See Dryden, John.
Love Triumphant; or, The Rival Goddesses. See Bellamy, Daniel.
Love Will Find Out The Way (play, anon), 1660: NONE, Sep 0
Love Without Interest; or, The Man Too Hard for the Master (play, anon), 1699:
    DL, Apr 0
Love would Invade me (song), 1713: QUEEN'S, Apr 25; 1735: HAY, Jan 31
Love, James (actor), 1762: DL, Sep 21, 25, 30, Oct 4, 12, 13, 16, 29, Nov 1, 3,
    17, 18, 23, Dec 6, 11, 14, 20; 1763: DL, Jan 18, 19, Feb 24, Mar 21, 26, Apr
    15, 26, May 2, 9, 14, 17, 31, Sep 22, 27, 29, Oct 15, 19, Nov 7, 8, 9, 14,
    15, 23, 26, 29, Dec 1, 5, 14, 17, 24, 26; 1764: DL, Jan 4, 16, 18, 23, 25,
    Feb 11, 14, Mar 20, 24, Apr 2, 12, 24, May 11, Sep 18, 27, Oct 4, 9, 16, 17,
    23, 25, 26, Nov 7, 9, 27; 1765: DL, Jan 1, 15, Feb 4, Mar 18, 19, Apr 13, 15,
    19, 22, May 1, 11, 17, 22, Sep 21, Oct 9, 18, 23, 24, 28, 31, Nov 20, 22, Dec
    3, 6, 7, 20, 23; 1766: DL, Jan 6, 9, 13, 24, Feb 3, 20, Mar 15, 18, Apr 7, 9,
    12, 16, 22, May 3, 5, 20, 21, Sep 20, 23, 27, Oct 9, 17, 21, 24, 31, Nov 7,
    17, 20, 28; 1767: DL, Mar 7, 21, Apr 4, 21, 24, 25, May 6, 8, 23, Sep 12, 15,
    18, 19, 25, Oct 9, 14, 15, 20, 22, 23, 30, Nov 6, 12, 18, 20, 21, 23, 24, 28,
    Dec 1, 2, 5; 1768: DL, Jan 9, 14, Mar 17, Apr 9, 11, May 26, Aug 18, Sep 17,
    22, 24, 28, Oct 5, 6, 13, 15, 18, Nov 21, 24; 1769: DL, Jan 6, 25, Mar 16,
    29, Apr 1, 10, 24, 28, May 1, 15, Sep 16, Oct 2, 6, 9, 10, 13, 14, 17, 21,
    23, Nov 2, 8, 20, 22, Dec 4, 6, 8, 13, 16; 1770: DL, Jan 19, Feb 7, 13, Mar
    1, 13, 22, Apr 2, May 2, 3, 17, 30, Sep 22, Oct 2, 9, 12, 13, 16, 17, 18, 25,
    29, Nov 3, 6, 15, HAY, 16, DL, 19, 20, 23, Dec 6, 20; 1771: DL, Jan 4, 31,
    Mar 18, 23, Apr 1, 2, 26, May 8, 14, 17, 27, Sep 26, Oct 1, 10, 12, 15, 19,
    25, 29, Nov 6, 13, 14, 21, 25, 28, Dec 2, 3, 10, 21, 26; 1772: DL, Jan 1, 15,
    Feb 4, 21, Mar 23, Apr 7, May 11, 29, Jun 3, 5, 10, Oct 8, 13, 14, Nov 16,
    17, 20, 27, 28, 30, Dec 22, 29; 1773: DL, Jan 1, 19, Feb 11, Apr 13, Oct 8,
    14, 22, Nov 2, 24, Dec 10; 1774: DL, Jan 29; see also Dance, James
Love, Master (musician), 1763: DL, Dec 28; 1767: DL, Apr 25; 1768: DL, Apr 9,
    27; 1769: DL, Apr 1
Love, Mrs (dancer), 1741: BFH, Aug 22
Love, Mrs James (actor), 1763: DL, Apr 9, May 28, 31, Sep 17, Dec 26; 1764: DL,
    Mar 31, Apr 12, May 1, 9, Sep 15, Oct 6; 1765: DL, Jan 22, Sep 14, Oct 18,
    Nov 27, Dec 16; 1766: DL, Mar 18, Apr 22, 25, Sep 25; 1767: DL, May 6, Oct
    12, 15, 20, 23, Nov 12, 26; 1768: DL, Feb 20, Mar 10, Apr 14, Aug 18, Sep 20,
    24, 28, Oct 6, 18; 1769: DL, Feb 13, Apr 3, 10, May 1, Oct 4, 10, 11, 14, Nov
    7, Dec 6, 18, 19; 1770: DL, Jan 6, Mar 1, 22, 24, 27, Apr 3, May 17, Sep 25,
    Oct 2, 3, 25, Nov 3, 21, 22, 23, 24, 28, Dec 5, 20, 22; 1771: DL, Jan 4, 19,
    22, Mar 7, 11, 12, 21, 23, Apr 5, 9, 15, 26, May 10, 14, Sep 21, 24, Oct 8,
    12, 15, 17, 19, Nov 1, 2, 8, 11, 13, 25, Dec 6, 21; 1772: DL, Jan 4, 20, Feb
    21, 27, Mar 21, 30, Apr 6, 20, May 13, Sep 22, 26, Oct 6, 13, 28, Nov 16, 27,
    30, Dec 2, 7; 1773: DL, Feb 27, Mar 9, 27, Apr 21, May 13, Sep 18, 23, Oct 8,
    13, 16, 20, 22, Nov 2, 15, 26, Dec 21, 27; 1774: DL, Jan 5, 10, Mar 17, Apr

15, May 3, 9, HAY, 16, 30, DL, Jun 2, HAY, 13, Jul 6, 11, 18, Aug 1, 26, Sep
6, 19, DL, 22, 24, 27, Oct 11, 14, 19, Nov 1, 7, 24, Dec 7, 9; 1775: DL, Mar
2, 23, 28, Apr 8, 22, May 1, 3, 6, 11, 17, HAY, 19, 31, Jul 7, 31, Aug 21,
28, Sep 7, 21, DL, 30, Oct 5, 7, 11, Nov 20, Dec 7, 16; 1776: DL, Mar 7, 14,
25, Apr 8, 9, May 8, HAY, 20, DL, 22, 24, Jun 3, HAY, 19, Jul 1, 8, 24, Sep
16, 17, 18, 20, DL, 21, HAY, 23, DL, 26, Oct 5, 18, 30, Nov 25, Dec 10; 1777:
DL, Jan 1, 4, 8, Mar 1, 13, Apr 1, 21, 22, May 9, 14, CG, 21, HAY, 28, Jun 9,
11, 16, 19, Jul 3, 24, Aug 9, 12, 19, 25, 28, 30, Sep 3, 17, 19, DL, 20, 23,
25, Oct 2, HAY, 6, DL, 7, Nov 8, 12, Dec 4; 1778: DL, Jan 5, 13, 22, Feb 21,
May 14, HAY, 18, 21, 22, Jun 1, 3, 8, 12, Aug 21, Sep 7, 10, DL, 24, 29, Oct
6, 8, 10, 15, 21, 31, Nov 2, 18, Dec 21; 1779: DL, Jan 8, 29, Mar 18, Apr 16,
May 15, Jun 1, HAY, 2, 7, 9, 17, Jul 5, 17, Aug 27, DL, Sep 23, 30, Oct 2, 7,
12, 19, 25, Nov 3, Dec 22, 27; 1780: DL, Apr 26, May 10, HAY, 30, Jun 3, 5,
14, 17, Jul 15, Aug 5, 10, 17, Sep 5, DL, 16, 19, 21, 23, 26, 28, Oct 2, 10,
11, 12, 25, 26, Nov 1, 3, 9, 10, 17, 28, Dec 1, 6, 7; 1781: DL, Jan 6, 26,
Mar 10, Apr 26, May 1, 8, 24, HAY, Jun 1, 7, Aug 7, 15, 21, 22, DL, Sep 15,
20, 29, Oct 2, 4, 12, 15, 29, 30, Nov 5, 6, 13, 15, 21, 29, Dec 11; 1782: DL,
Jan 3, 19, 26, Feb 14, Mar 9, Apr 3, 15, 17, 18, 25, May 3, 4, 7, 8, 11, 14,
29, HAY, Jun 10, 11, Aug 13, 17, 23, 24, 27, 30, DL, Sep 17, 18, HAY, 18, DL,
19, 28, Oct 3, 8, 10, 16, Nov 7, 22, 26, 30, Dec 5, 7, 26; 1783: DL, Jan 25,
Mar 3, 20, 24, May 5, 12, 20, HAY, Jun 2, 16, 18, 30, Jul 5, 8, 26, Aug 13,
15, 22, 26, 29, DL, Sep 16, 20, 25, Oct 4, 7, 8, 11, Nov 13, 14, 21, 27, Dec
2, 19; 1784: DL, Jan 16, 31, Feb 3, 24, Mar 20, 29, Apr 14, 16, 19, 21, May
3, 15, HAY, Jun 14, 28, Jul 7, 20, 24, 28, Aug 5, 6, 10, 17, 24, Sep 2, DL,
16, 18, 23, 25, 30, Oct 12, 14, 18, 19, 23, Nov 2, 4, 9, 16, 22, 23, 25, 26,
Dec 10, 28; 1785: DL, Jan 11, 12, 20, 22, Feb 2, Mar 28, Apr 1, 14, May 3,
HAY, Jun 2, 4, 6, 9, 11, 16, Jul 19, Aug 2, 8, 16, 23, 31, Sep 16, DL, 17,
27, Oct 13, 15, 17, 26, Nov 3, Dec 5, 7, 26; 1786: DL, Jan 5, 6, 9, 14, 16,
Feb 23, Mar 9, Apr 6, May 2, 29, HAY, Jun 12, 15, 17, 19, 23, 29, Jul 7, 10,
13, 18, 21, Aug 10, DL, Sep 26, 28, Oct 3, 7, 12, 24, 25, 27, Nov 25, Dec 5;
1787: DL, Jan 10, 13, 18, Apr 9, 27, May 11, 18, 22, 28, 30, Jun 7, HAY, 13,
21, 23, Jul 4, 23, Aug 10, DL, Sep 20, 27, Oct 6, 11, Nov 8, 21, Dec 6, 14,
17, 26, 28; 1788: DL, Jan 22, Feb 21, Mar 3, 13, 24, 31, May 14, 22, 23, Jun
2, HAY, 12, 30, Jul 4, 10, Aug 5, 15, 26, 27, DL, Sep 13, 18, 23, Oct 20, 28,
Nov 1, 17, 19, 25, 28, Dec 4; 1789: DL, Jan 8, 10, Apr 21, May 23, 27, Jun
13; 1790: DL, Jun 1
Love's a Jest. See Motteux, Peter Anthony.
Love's a Lottery. See Harris, Joseph.
Love's a sweet passion (song), 1753: DL, May 15
Love's Contrivance. See Centlivre, Susannah.
Love's Cruelty. See Shirley, James.
Love's Cure. See Fletcher, John.
Love's Frailties. See Holcroft, Thomas
Love's goddess sure (song), 1692: ATCOURT, Apr 30
Love's Kingdom. See Flecknoe, Richard
Love's Jealousy. See Payne, Nevil.
Love's Labour Lost. See Shakespeare, William.
Love's Labyrinth. See Forde, Thomas.
Love's Last Shift. See Cibber, Colley.
Love's Martyr. See Wharton, Anne.
Love's Metamorphoses. See Vaughan, Thomas.
Love's Mistress. See Heywood, Thomas.
Love's Mystery (play, anon), 1660: VERE, Nov 12
Love's Pilgrimage. See Fletcher, John.
Love's Quarrel (play, anon), 1661: SALSBURY, Apr 6
Love's Reward; or, The Unnatural Mother (play, anon), 1697: LIF, Sep 0
Love's Sacrifice. See Ford, John.
Love's the Cause and Cure of Grief. See Cooke, Thomas.
Love's Triumph. See Motteux, Peter Anthony.
Love's Triumph; or, The Happy Fair One (play, anon), 1718: SF, Sep 3; 1720:
BFBL, Aug 23
Love's Triumph; or, The Royal Union. See Cooke, Edward.
Love's Victim. See Gildon, Charles.
Loveday, Thomas (actor), 1660: COCKPIT, Oct 8; 1663: VERE, Mar 0, NONE, Sep 0;
1667: BRIDGES, Oct 5
Lovelace (boxkeeper), 1703: DL, Jun 14; 1707: DL, Apr 16; 1708: DL/QUEEN, Jun
4; 1710: DL, Apr 15; 1711: SH, May 9; 1715: LIF, Jun 1; 1716: LIF, Jun 5;
1717: LIF, May 30; 1719: LIF, May 26; 1720: LIF, May 10; 1721: LIF, May 22;
1722: LIF, May 24; 1723: LIF, May 23; 1724: LIF, May 19; 1725: LIF, May 18;
1726: LIF, May 23
Lovell, Mrs (actor), 1686: NONE, Sep 0
Lovell, Thomas (actor), 1660: REDBULL, Nov 5; 1661: LIF, Aug 24, Sep 11, Dec

16; <u>1663</u>: LIF, Jan 6, Oct 0, ATCOURT, Dec 10
Lovely Nan (song), <u>1796</u>: HAY, Sep 1; <u>1799</u>: CG, May 3
Lovely Nancy (song), <u>1779</u>: HAY, Mar 17
Lovely Selina, innocent and free (song), <u>1680</u>: DG, Sep 0
Loveman (actor), <u>1767</u>: HAY, Jun 4, 5, 15, 26, Jul 2, 10, Aug 5, 21, 25, Sep 18,
   21; <u>1768</u>: HAY, Jun 17, Jul 13, 25, 27, Aug 15, 24, Sep 19
Lovemore (actor), <u>1751</u>: SF, Sep 9
Lover His Own Rival, The. See Langford, Abraham.
Lover in Disguise (dance), <u>1785</u>: HAY, Jun 27
Lover, The. See Cibber, Theophilus.
Lover's Lesson (song), <u>1751</u>: CG, Apr 24
Lover's Luck, The. See Dilke, Thomas.
Lover's Melancholy, The. See Ford, John.
Lover's Metamorphosis, The; or, More Ways Than One to Win Her (play, anon),
   <u>1756</u>: SFW, Sep 18, 20, SF, 21
Lover's Opera, The. See Chetwood, William Rufus.
Lover's Progress, The. See Fletcher, John.
Lover's Rapture (song), <u>1755</u>: HAY, Aug 21
Lover's Vows. See Inchbald, Elizabeth.
Lovers of Their Country, The; or, Themistocles and Aristides. See Madden,
   Samuel, Themistocles.
Lovers' Quarrels. See King, Thomas.
Loves of Baldo and Media, The (play, anon), <u>1712</u>: GR, Jul 19
Loves of Damon and Clemene, The; or, The Metamorphosis of Leander (en
   tertainment), <u>1727</u>: LIF, Mar 20
Loves of Ergasto, The (opera), <u>1705</u>: QUEEN'S, Apr 9, 10, 11, 12, 13, 24, 25
Loves of Harlequin and Colombine (dance), <u>1717</u>: LIF, Apr 23; <u>1724</u>: BFL, Aug 22
Loves of John and Jane (song), <u>1783</u>: HAY, Aug 1
Loves of Mars and Venus (play, anon), <u>1717</u>: DL, Mar 2, 5, 9, 12, 16, 21, 23,
   Oct 12, 19, 26, Nov 2, 4, 5, 9, 16, 23, 30, Dec 26; <u>1718</u>: DL, Jan 1, 18, Feb
   15, 22, Mar 15, 29, Apr 5, Oct 11, Nov 8, Dec 2, 26; <u>1719</u>: DL, Jan 10, 31,
   Feb 5, Dec 29; <u>1720</u>: DL, Jan 8, 21, Feb 8, 15, Mar 7, 26, May 3; <u>1724</u>: DL,
   Jan 27, 28, 29, Feb 7, 12; <u>1725</u>: LIF, Apr 5; <u>1739</u>: DL, May 2, 3, 4, 5; <u>1746</u>:
   CG, Apr 17
Loves of Mars and Venus, The. See Motteux, Peter Anthony.
Lovesick King, The. See Brewer, Anthony.
Loving and beloved again (song), <u>1699</u>: LIF, Mar 0
Loving Enemies, The. See Maidwell, Lewis.
Low Layton, <u>1743</u>: DL, May 16
Lowder (actor), <u>1735</u>: LIF, Jul 23, 30, Aug 22, 29, Sep 5, YB/HAY, 17, GF, Nov
   11; <u>1736</u>: HAY, Mar 5, Apr 26, 29, Jun 26; <u>1737</u>: LIF, Jun 15; <u>1740</u>: GF, Oct
   21, 22; <u>1741</u>: BFTY, Aug 22; <u>1748</u>: BFSY, Aug 24
Lowe (actor), <u>1683</u>: DL, Dec 0; <u>1684</u>: DL, Mar 0; <u>1685</u>: DLORDG, Jan 20, DL, Aug
   0; <u>1686</u>: DL, Jan 0, DG, Mar 4
Lowe and Co, Mrs (glaziers), <u>1772</u>: DL, Jun 10; <u>1773</u>: DL, Mar 1, Jun 2; <u>1774</u>:
   DL, Jan 21, Jun 2; <u>1775</u>: DL, Feb 23, May 27
Lowe and Lewis (woolen drapers), <u>1771</u>: CG, Nov 27; <u>1772</u>: CG, Dec 1; <u>1774</u>: CG,
   Jan 6, Apr 19
Lowe and Lucas (linen drapers), <u>1772</u>: CG, Apr 22
Lowe, James (beneficiary), <u>1752</u>: CT/HAY, Mar 12
Lowe, Joseph (citizen), <u>1752</u>: CG, Dec 28; <u>1753</u>: CG, Jan 6
Lowe, Margaret (actor), <u>1729</u>: LIF, Jan 1
Lowe, Mrs (actor), <u>1737</u>: LIF, Mar 9; <u>1743</u>: JS, Apr 25; <u>1749</u>: DL, Nov 18; <u>1771</u>:
   DL, Nov 22
Lowe, Thomas (singer, actor), <u>1732</u>: HIC, Mar 27, KING'S, May 2; <u>1740</u>: DL, Apr
   23, Sep 11, 20, 27, Oct 2, 9, 17, 23, 27, Nov 1, 11, 19, 24, 26, 28, 29, Dec
   10, 20; <u>1741</u>: DL, Jan 15, 24, CT, Mar 13, DL, 17, 24, 30, Apr 3, 7, 8, 16,
   18, 20, 22, 24, 27, 28, 29, May 1, 2, 4, 5, 7, 9, 12, 13, 14, 15, 22, 25, 26,
   27, 28, Jun 4, Sep 5, 8, 10, 15, 17, 29, Oct 3, 8, 15, 24, 31, Nov 2, 6, 9,
   11, 13, 14, 21, 24, 27, 30, Dec 1, 3, 5, 7, 8, 9, 10, 11, 12, 14, 15, 16, 17,
   18, 19, 26, 28, 31; <u>1742</u>: DL, Jan 1, 5, 8, 13, 14, 18, 19, 20, 22, 26, 27,
   29, Feb 2, 3, 4, 10, 11, 15, 16, 17, 26, 27, Mar 1, 11, 12, 13, 15, 16, 20,
   22, 23, 25, 27, 29, 30, Apr 5, 6, 17, 20, 21, 22, 24, 26, 27, 28, 29, Sep 11,
   14, 16, 21, 23, 25, 28, 30, Oct 2, 7, 12, 19, 21, 26, 27, Nov 1, 11, 15, 17,
   23, 25, 26, 27, 29, Dec 3, 4, 6, 9, 13, 15, 22; <u>1743</u>: DL, Jan 1, 3, 7, 10,
   11, 15, 18, 19, 20, Feb 4, 14, 15, CG, 18, 23, DL, Mar 12, 14, 15, Apr 13,
   14, 15, 20, 27, 29, May 4, 5, 6, 7, 10, 11, 12, 14, 16, 18, 20, 23, 24, LIF,
   Jun 3, DL, Oct 8, NWLS, Nov 1; <u>1744</u>: DL, Sep 22, 27, 29, Oct 2, 6, 9, Nov 8,
   16, 22, 24, 26, 27, 28, 29, 30, Dec 1, 3, 4, 5, 6, 8, 11, HAY, 11, DL, 12,
   13, 14, 17, 19, 22, 26, 27, 29, 31; <u>1745</u>: DL, Jan 3, 4, 7, 8, 10, 14, 17, 31,
   Feb 5, 11, 12, 15, Mar 9, 11, 14, DT, 14, DL, Apr 3, 4, 15, 17, 18, 22, 24,
   25, 29, 30, May 1, 6, 7, 8, 9, 10, 13, Jun 5, Sep 19, 21, 24, 26, 28, Oct 1,

526

12, 17, 19, 29, 30, 31, Nov 1, 2, 4, 5, 6, 7, 9, 11, 12, 13, 15, 16, 18, 19,
20, 21, 23, 25, 26, 27, 28, 30, Dec 4, 5, 6, 7, 9, 10, 11, 12, 13, 16, 17,
20, 28, 30, 31; 1746: DL, Jan 2, 3, 4, 10, 11, 14, 16, 17, 22, 23, 24, 25,
28, 29, 31, Feb 6, 7, 8, 10, 13, 15, 20, 22, 24, 27, Mar 1, 3, 10, 13, 15,
17, 18, 22, Apr 3, 4, 7, 8, 9, 10, 11, 14, 15, 17, 18, 19, 21, 22, 23, May 3,
8, 9, 12, 16, 19, Jun 6, Sep 23, 25, 27, 30, Oct 4, 14, 23, 25, 27, 30, 31,
Nov 1, 5, 7, 22, 25, 28, Dec 15, 20, 26, 30; 1747: DL, Jan 10, 22, 24, Feb 9,
10, 28, Mar 7, 12, 21, 23, 30, Apr 4, 10, 21, 29, 30, May 5, 7, 16, Sep 15,
17, 19, 24, Oct 29, Nov 2, 7, 10, 13, 27, Dec 3; 1748: DL, Jan 6, 9, CG, Mar
9, DL, 21, CG, 23, DL, 28, Apr 12, 13, 20, 25, May 2, 4, CG, Sep 26, 28, Oct
7, 11, 14, Nov 11, 16, 28, Dec 10, 21, 26; 1749: CG, Feb 10, Mar 9, 31, Apr
4, 17, HAY, 19, CG, May 4, Sep 25, 27, 29, Oct 6, 12, 16, 19, 20, 24, 27, Nov
4, 17, 23; 1750: CG, Mar 16, 27, 29, Apr 5, 19, 28, 30, MARLY, Aug 16, CG,
Sep 24, 26, Oct 12, 13, 16, 18, 19, 23, 27, 29, Nov 5, 8, 17, Dec 21, 22;
1751: HAY, Feb 5, CG, Mar 1, 14, Apr 16, 18, 20, 24, May 2, 4, 14, Sep 23,
25, 27, 30, Oct 17, 18, 19, 26, 28, Nov 4, 16, Dec 9; 1752: CG, Jan 18, Feb
6, Mar 9, 17, Apr 3, 13, 18, 25, 27, Sep 18, 20, 29, Oct 4, 6, 10, 18, 21,
30, 31, Nov 3, 4, Dec 4, 8; 1753: CG, Jan 6, Apr 5, 28, May 2, 11, Sep 10,
12, 14, 17, 24, Oct 5, 10, 22, 25, Nov 5, Dec 5, 15; 1754: CG, Mar 25, 26,
Apr 6, 22, 25, 26, May 2, 13, 15, 20, Sep 16, 18, 20, 23, 25, 27, Oct 2, 4,
7, 9, 11, 29, Nov 4, 5, 12, 16, 20; 1755: CG, Mar 22, Apr 2, 9, 15, 22, 24,
28, May 12, Sep 29, Oct 1, 8, 10, 16, 17, 20, 21, 22, Nov 4, 11, 14, 15, 17,
Dec 5; 1756: CG, Jan 6, Apr 19, 20, 24, May 6, 17, 20, Sep 20, 22, 24, 27,
Oct 1, 4, 6, 19, 21, 25, 26, Nov 4, 8, 22, 29, Dec 21; 1757: CG, Jan 8, Apr
19, May 3, 6, Sep 14, 16, 23, 26, 28, 30, Oct 10, 12, 13, 31, Nov 4, 14, 18,
Dec 5, 6, 7, 10, 26; 1758: CG, Feb 1, Mar 30, Apr 13, Sep 18, 25, 27, Oct 2,
4, 6, 9, 18, 30, Nov 1, 3, 4, 21, 23, 27; 1759: CG, Feb 15, Mar 17, 22, DL,
23, CG, Apr 3, 23, 30, May 3, 25, Sep 24, 26, Oct 5, Nov 5, 23, 30, Dec 8,
11, 31; 1760: CG, Jan 16, 18, 19, Feb 14, Mar 17, 18, 27, Apr 8, 9, 10, 17,
24, May 7, 9, 15, DL, Sep 23, Oct 7, 20, Nov 17, 22, Dec 2, 11, 13, 30; 1761:
DL, Jan 12, 23, Mar 30, Apr 3, 13, 29, Sep 5, 8, 18, 23, 28, Oct 7, 12, 16,
26, 29, 31, Nov 4; 1762: DL, Jan 5, 15, 27, Feb 3, 17, 20, Mar 1, 27, Apr 15,
May 13, 19, HAY, Sep 1, DL, Oct 5, 30, Nov 23; 1763: DL, Jan 17, Apr 13,
MARLY, Jun 28; 1765: DL, Apr 24, MARLY, Aug 6; 1766: DL, Jan 6, MARLY, Sep
26; 1767: DL, Jan 27, MARLY, Sep 18; 1771: DL, Nov 5
Lowe's scholars (actor), 1714: MEG, Apr 1
Lowen, John (actor), 1663: LIF, Dec 22
Lower Brook St, 1795: CG, May 16; 1796: CG, Apr 29; 1797: CG, May 20
Lower Charlotte St, 1791: CG, May 11
Lower Cross St, 1762: HAY, Oct 25
Lower Eaton St, 1797: DL, Jun 2
Lower Gower St, 1800: CG, May 20
Lower, William
--Amourous Fantasme, The, 1659: NONE, Sep 0
Lowland Festivity (dance), 1799: CG, May 22
Lowndes, C (publisher), 1790: DL, Oct 26, Dec 27; 1791: DLKING'S, Nov 5; 1792:
DL, Oct 18; 1793: DL, Mar 7, May 10, HAY, Nov 30; 1794: DL, Jul 2, Sep 16,
Oct 7; 1795: DL, Feb 12, May 6, Sep 17, Nov 23; 1796: DL, Jan 18, Feb 27, Sep
20; 1797: DL, Jan 7, Mar 6, Sep 19, Oct 7; 1798: DL, Sep 15, Nov 10; 1799:
DL, Sep 17
Lowndes, Thomas and William (publishers), 1750: DL, Jan 1; 1751: DL, Jan 1;
1764: CG, Oct 16; 1776: CG, Nov 7; 1778: DL, Oct 15; 1779: HAY, Oct 13; 1780:
DL, Sep 16; 1783: HAY, Aug 22, CG, Oct 10; 1784: DL, Feb 14; 1785: DL, Nov
21; 1786: HAY, Aug 10; 1788: DL, Feb 25, HAY, Aug 2; 1789: HAY, Jun 3; 1792:
CG, Oct 24, DL, Dec 8
Lowther (actor), 1737: HAY, Mar 21, Apr 13
Lowther, Anthony (spectator), 1667: BRI/COUR, Mar 25; 1668: BRIDGES, Feb 7
Loyal and Generous Free Mason (dance), 1731: LIF, Apr 5
Loyal Brother, The. See Southerne, Thomas.
Loyal Effusion, A. See Dibdin, Charles.
Loyal General, The. See Tate, Nahum.
Loyal Protestant, The (song), 1679: DG, Sep 0
Loyal Song (song), 1793: CG, May 10; 1796: CG, Apr 15; 1798: DL, May 23, CG,
Nov 7
Loyal Subject, The. See Fletcher, John.
Loyd. See Lloyd.
Loyde. See Lloyd.
Lucas (beneficiary), 1731: GF, Mar 16; 1746: DL, Mar 1
Lucas (dancer), 1755: CG, Apr 15, 18, May 6; 1756: KING'S, Mar 30, CG, Apr 22,
Dec 10, 11, 16, 17; 1757: CG, Jan 28, Mar 26, 28, 29, Apr 15, 27, May 2, 3,
10, Oct 13, Nov 11, Dec 10; 1758: CG, Feb 1, Apr 17, 28, May 8, Oct 4, 14,
Nov 11, 16, 23; 1759: CG, May 21

Lucas (tinman), 1794: DL, Jul 7
Lucas, Dr, 1784: DL, Aug 20
Lucas, Henry (actor), 1775: HAY, Mar 23; 1778: HAY, Mar 24; 1779: HAY, Oct 13;
    1784: DL, Aug 20
Lucas, Mrs (actor), 1779: HAY, Oct 13
Lucas, Mrs (actor, dancer), 1693: NONE, Sep 0; 1695: DL, Nov 0; 1696: DL, Jan
    0, Apr 0, DG, Jun 0, DL, Sep 0; 1697: DG, Jun 0; 1700: DL, Oct 0; 1701: DL,
    Apr 0, Dec 0; 1702: DL, Aug 18, 20, Nov 0; 1703: DL, Jan 27, Feb 12, Apr 10,
    May 28, Jun 23, Jul 3, Oct 26, Nov 1, 5, 17, Dec 2; 1704: DL, Apr 27, Aug 15,
    Nov 13, 27, Dec 7; 1705: DL, Jan 12, 18, Oct 30, Nov 20, Dec 17; 1707: DL,
    Oct 23, Dec 26
Lucca Opera, 1785: KING'S, Jan 8
Lucchesina, Sga (singer), 1737: KING'S, May 24, Oct 29; 1738: KING'S, Jan 3,
    28, Feb 25, Mar 14, Apr 15; 1739: KING'S, Jan 16, CG, Mar 10
Lucchi (dancer), 1757: DL, Dec 23
Lucchi, Sga (dancer), 1757: DL, Oct 4, 20, Nov 26; 1758: DL, Apr 10, 15, 19,
    Oct 14, 24, 28, Nov 3, Dec 14; 1759: DL, Jan 4, Feb 2, 6, Mar 19, Apr 7, May
    17; 1760: DL, Dec 13; 1761: DL, Apr 11; 1767: DL, Jan 24; 1768: DL, Apr 30
Luchino (musician), 1753: KING'S, Nov 20
Luciani (singer), 1768: KING'S, Nov 5, 8
Luciet, Miss (dancer), 1798: DL, Oct 6, Nov 14, Dec 6; 1799: DL, Jan 19, Feb 5,
    Oct 14; 1800: DL, Mar 11
Lucinda, close or veil those eyes (song), 1688: DL, Feb 0
Lucinda is bewitching fair (song), 1695: DL, Apr 1
Lucio Vero. See Sacchini, Antonio Maria Gasparo.
Lucius Junius Brutus. See Lee, Nathaniel.
Lucius Papirius. See Caldara, Antonio.
Lucius, the First Christian King of Britain. See Manley, Mary.
Lucius Verus (opera, anon), 1715: KING'S, Feb 26, Mar 5, 12, 19, Apr 2, 23, 30;
    1716: KING'S, Feb 1, 4, 11
Lucius Verus (pastiche), 1747: KING'S, Nov 12, 14, 21, 28, Dec 5, 12, 19, 26;
    1748: KING'S, Jan 2, 9, HAY, 12, KING'S, Mar 14, 19
Lucius Verus. See Ariosti, Attilio.
Lucky Chance, The. See Behn, Aphra.
Lucky Discovery, The. See Arthur, John.
Lucky Escape (dance), 1792: CG, May 19, 28, Nov 16; 1793: CG, Jan 16, May 4,
    DL, 24, CG, Jun 3, 10, Sep 16; 1794: CG, May 9, 21, HAY, Sep 17, CG, Oct 1;
    1795: CG, Oct 8; 1796: CG, Mar 30; 1800: DL, Jun 2
Lucky Escape, The. See Robinson, Mary.
Lucky Prodigal, The; or, Wit at a Pinch (play, anon), 1715: LIF, Oct 24, 25,
    26, 27
Lucky Return (dance), 1786: DL, Jan 5, Feb 18, Mar 18, Apr 6, 17, 20, 28, 29,
    May 3, 17, 22, Jun 7, Dec 28; 1787: DL, May 30, Jun 8; 1788: DL, Jan 5, Feb
    1, Mar 10
Lucretia (play), 1726: KING'S, Dec 31
Lucrezia Romana Violata, da Sesto Tarquinio (musical), 1726: KING'S, Dec 31
Lucuss (renter), 1758: CG, Feb 23
Ludgate Hill, 1740: APH, Mar 28; 1748: DL, Sep 27; 1749: HAY, Feb 10; 1751: DL,
    Nov 26, Dec 18; 1753: DL, Dec 11
Ludgate St, 1723: DT, Nov 12; 1724: DT, Dec 2; 1729: SH, Dec 5; 1744: SH, Feb
    9; 1751: CG, Nov 19
Ludgate, 1661: BF, Aug 31
Ludger, Conrad (translator), 1799: CG, Apr 13
Ludlow Castle, 1738: DL, Mar 4; 1739: DL, Nov 28; 1740: DL, Dec 10; 1744: CG,
    Mar 3
Luellin (spectator), 1661: BF, Aug 31; 1664: BRIDGES, Oct 11
Luffingham's Great Room, 1723: HA, Jul 8
Lullaby (song), 1794: DL, Mar 28, Apr 12, CG, May 9; 1795: DL, May 18; 1796:
    DL, May 25; 1799: CG, May 24
Lully (dancer), 1717: LIF, Nov 15
Lully (musician), 1705: DL, Apr 10; 1707: YB, May 23
Lully, John Baptist (composer), 1686: DLORDG, Feb 11; 1706: QUEEN'S, Apr 8;
    1719: KING'S, Mar 2
Lumber Troopers, Company of (spectators), 1731: LIF, Apr 26; 1733: DT, Apr 5;
    1734: YB, Nov 25
Lumley, Lady Ann (spectator), 1731: LIF, Mar 11
Lun (actor), 1717: LIF, Apr 22, 29, May 30, Oct 25, Nov 1, 22, Dec 11, 27;
    1718: LIF, Jan 10, 24, May 1; 1719: LIF, Jan 9; 1720: LIF, Jan 23, May 5, Dec
    15, 22, 28; 1721: LIF, Jan 7, Apr 25, Oct 10; 1722: LIF, Jan 1, 15; 1723:
    LIF, Mar 25, Apr 27, May 2, Oct 14, 19, Dec 20; 1724: LIF, Jan 4, Sep 25, 30,
    Oct 5, Nov 4; 1725: LIF, Jan 21, Apr 17, Oct 21, Nov 3, 13; 1726: LIF, Jan 4,
    14, Sep 16, 23, 30, Oct 17; 1727: LIF, Jan 13, Feb 13, Mar 20, Apr 28, Sep

22, 29, Oct 12, 27, Nov 9; 1728: LIF, Oct 14, 26, Nov 23; 1729: LIF, Jan 18,
Apr 8, 22, Oct 15, Nov 1, 4; 1730: LIF, Jan 2, Sep 25, Oct 1, 9, Nov 7, Dec
15; 1731: LIF, Oct 4, 15, Nov 6, 13, 18; 1732: LIF, Feb 1, 5, 14, LIF/CG, Oct
4, 13, Nov 8, 24, Dec 27; 1733: LIF/CG, Jan 23, CG, Oct 13, Dec 7; 1734: CG,
Jan 25, Feb 26, Apr 1, CG/LIF, Oct 2, Dec 19, 30; 1735: CG/LIF, Feb 13, Jun
2, CG, Sep 26, Oct 17, Nov 6; 1736: CG, Jan 1, 23, Mar 6, Sep 22, Oct 4, 8,
Nov 3, 26; 1737: CG, Feb 14, Oct 7; 1738: CG, Feb 13, Oct 28, Nov 18; 1739:
CG, Jan 20, Feb 24, DL, Mar 1, CG, Sep 22, Oct 20, 26, Nov 12, Dec 4; 1740:
CG, Feb 12, Oct 10, 22, Dec 29; 1741: CG, Jan 5, 21, Feb 17, 24, 28, Apr 24,
Oct 24, Nov 4, 26; 1742: CG, Jan 5, Feb 1; 1746: CG, Nov 24; 1747: CG, Dec
26; 1750: CG, Feb 7; 1751: CG, Nov 11; 1752: CG, Nov 2, 9; 1770: CG, Jan 27;
1792: CG, Dec 20; see also Rich, John
Lun Jr (actor), 1734: GF, Sep 25, Oct 17, 28, Nov 18, Dec 9; 1735: GF, Jan 13,
24, Feb 17, Mar 6, May 3, Sep 17, Nov 6, 17; 1736: GF, Feb 20, Mar 3, LIF,
Oct 9, 21, Dec 7, 16, 31; 1737: LIF, Feb 1, DL, Oct 22, 27; 1738: DL, Jan 24,
May 8, Sep 23, Oct 30, Dec 7, 15; 1739: DL, Feb 7, Mar 10, May 18; 1741: CG,
Apr 6, 28; 1770: HAY, Feb 14; 1771: HAY, Mar 11
Lun's Ghost; or, The New Year's Gift (pantomime, anon), 1782: DL, Jan 3, 4, 5,
7, 8, 9, 10, 11, 12, 14, 15, 16, 17, 18, 19, 22, 29, Mar 14
Lunati, C A (composer), 1724: HIC, Apr 20
Lunatic, The (play, anon), 1729: HAY, Feb 27, Mar 1, 3, 6
Lunatics (dance), 1740: DL, Dec 13, 15, 18; 1741: DL, Jan 6
Lunenburg, Duke of, 1719: YB, Dec 19
Lungi del caro bene (song), 1789: DL, Mar 6
Lupi, Edwardo (composer), 1732: HIC, Mar 31
Lupino, Miss (dancer), 1799: CG, Jan 29; 1800: DL, May 14, Jun 2
Lupino, Thomas (tailor, costume designer), 1758: CG, Feb 13; 1760: CG, Feb 9,
26, Oct 25; 1761: CG, Mar 23, Oct 10; 1766: CG, Dec 27; 1768: CG, Jan 21;
1774: DL, Nov 25; 1775: DL, Feb 3, KING'S, Nov 7; 1776: DL, Nov 7; 1782:
KING'S, Nov 2; 1784: KING'S, Mar 18; 1788: KING'S, Jan 29; 1791: PAN, Feb 17,
May 9, Jun 16; 1794: CG, Nov 17
Lupino, Thomas Frederick (scene designer), 1792: CG, Dec 20; 1793: CG, Dec 19;
1794: DL, Jun 9, CG, Nov 17, Dec 26; 1795: CG, Apr 6, Dec 21; 1797: CG, Oct
2, Nov 24, Dec 26; 1798: CG, Feb 12, Mar 31, Apr 9, May 28, Oct 15, Nov 12,
Dec 11; 1799: CG, Jan 29, Apr 19, Sep 23, Dec 23; 1800: CG, Jan 16, May 1
Lupone. See Gordon, Alexander.
Lushington, William (steward), 1797: KING'S, May 18, CG, Jun 14
Lusinghe piu Care (song), 1729: HIC, Apr 16; 1734: DL/HAY, Jan 26, Feb 4; 1748:
CG, Feb 15; 1750: CG, Apr 19
Lusinghe vezzose (song), 1714: QUEEN'S, May 1, Jun 23
Lusini, Caterina (singer), 1783: KING'S, Nov 29; 1784: KING'S, Jan 17, Feb 17,
Mar 4, May 8, Jun 17
Lussant, Mlle (dancer), 1753: DL, Sep 13, Oct 9, 17, 24, Nov 21, 23, Dec 19,
26; 1754: DL, Jan 7, 28, Mar 14, Jul 2
Lute (music), 1708: SH, Feb 4, Mar 26; 1723: HIC, Mar 6; 1800: DL, May 12, 23,
30
Lute Concerto (music), 1733: HIC, Apr 20
Lute Solo (music), 1728: HIC, May 15; 1736: HIC, Jan 21, LIF, Mar 8
Lute, Mandolin, Bass Viol and Hautboy (music), 1718: WEYS', Feb 12
Lutte Marine (dance), 1773: DL, Apr 22
Luxborough, Lady, 1749: DL, Feb 20
Luxmore (ticket deliverer), 1786: CG, Jun 1; 1787: CG, Jun 5; 1788: CG, May 27;
1789: CG, Jun 5; 1790: CG, May 29; 1791: CG, Jun 2
Lyar, The. See Foote, Samuel, The Liar; Corneille, Pierre, The Mistaken
Beauty.
Lyceum Theatre, 1790: CG, Nov 23
Lycidas. See Jackson, William.
Lydall, Edward (actor), 1661: NONE, Sep 0; 1668: BRIDGES, Jun 12, NONE, Sep 0,
BRIDGES, Nov 6; 1669: BRIDGES, Jun 24; 1670: BRIDGES, Aug 0, BRI/COUR, Dec 0;
1671: BRIDGES, Jun 0; 1672: LIF, Apr 0; 1673: LIF, Mar 0, May 0, Dec 0; 1674:
LIF, Mar 0, DL, May 16; 1675: DL, Jan 12, 25, Apr 23, May 10, Aug 0, NONE,
Sep 0; 1676: DL, Jan 29; 1677: DL, Mar 0, 17, Jun 0
Lydell, Cleomire (actor), 1711: PU, May 14
Lydell, Dorindall (actor), 1711: PU, May 14
Lydell, Miss (actor), 1712: SML, Jun 4, 11, 18, Jul 9
Lying Lover, The. See Steele, Sir Richard.
Lying Valet, The. See Garrick, David.
Lying-in Hospital, 1750: KING'S, Mar 13; 1755: CG, Jan 8, Dec 16; 1757: CG, Dec
2, 15; 1766: CG, Dec 17; 1772: DL, Dec 19, 22
Lylett (beneficiary), 1720: LIF, Jun 2
Lylinston. See Lilleston.
Lylly (musician), 1675: ATCOURT, Feb 15

Lynam (beneficiary), <u>1732</u>: LIF, May 11; <u>1738</u>: CG, May 6
Lynch (actor), <u>1782</u>: HAY, Jan 21
Lynch, Francis, <u>1737</u>: LIF, Feb 12
--Independent Patriot, The; or, Musical Folly, <u>1737</u>: LIF, Feb 12, 14, 15
Lyne, John (beneficiary), <u>1741</u>: HIC, Feb 5
Lyngs. See Lings.
Lynham (actor), <u>1746</u>: SOU, Oct 16, GF, 29
Lynn, Mrs (haberdasher), <u>1773</u>: CG, Jan 7, Feb 1
Lynsey, Mrs. See Lindsey, Mrs.
Lyon (ticket deliverer), <u>1781</u>: DL, May 12; <u>1782</u>: DL, Apr 27; <u>1783</u>: DL, May 31;
    <u>1784</u>: DL, May 22; <u>1785</u>: DL, May 21; <u>1786</u>: DL, May 29; <u>1787</u>: DL, Jun 4; <u>1788</u>:
    DL, Jun 6
Lyon, B (wardrobe keeper), <u>1772</u>: DL, Jun 10
Lyon, Master. See Leoni, Michael.
Lyon, Miss (actor, singer), <u>1781</u>: HAY, May 30, Jun 5, 11, 15, 22, Aug 8, Oct
    16; <u>1784</u>: CG, Oct 4
Lyon, Samuel Thomas (violinist), <u>1798</u>: HAY, Jan 15
Lyon, Thomas (bassoonist), <u>1790</u>: CG, Feb 19; <u>1791</u>: CG, Mar 11; <u>1792</u>: CG, Feb
    24; <u>1798</u>: HAY, Jan 12
Lyon, William (actor), <u>1732</u>: GF, Nov 25, 28, Dec 4; <u>1733</u>: GF, Jan 18, 20, 24,
    Feb 5, 19, Mar 5, Apr 19, CG, Aug 2, 14, 20, GF, Sep 10, 19, 24, Oct 1, 3, 5,
    9, 17, 19, 24, Nov 10, 14, 28, 29, Dec 8, 13, 18, 26, 27, 28; <u>1734</u>: GF, Jan
    3, 10, 19, 21, 24, 31, Feb 2, 11, Apr 1, May 15, 17, 20, 22, Sep 9, 13, 16,
    20, Oct 16, 18, 23, Nov 7, 13, 27, Dec 2, 13, 16, 20, 31; <u>1735</u>: GF, Jan 3, 4,
    6, 8, 13, 24, Feb 5, 6, 24, Mar 10, 17, 25, 29, May 15, Sep 10, 12, 15, 17,
    19, 24, Oct 3, 6, 15, 27, Nov 4, 6, 10, 11, 14, 17, 20, 21, 24, 25, 26, Dec
    8, 17; <u>1736</u>: GF, Jan 29, Feb 5, 9, Mar 3, 9, 18, 29, Apr 8, 16, 17, 28, May
    3, 5, 13, LIF, Sep 28, Oct 5, 9, 12, 23, 26, Nov 4, 6, 11, 13, 16, 18, 20,
    24, 26, 27, 29, Dec 3, 7, 11, 16, 22, 31; <u>1737</u>: LIF, Jan 10, 15, 21, Feb 12,
    14, 21, Mar 29, Apr 18, 25, 27, 30, May 2, 4, 6, Jun 15, Jul 26, Aug 5, CG,
    Sep 30, Nov 9; <u>1738</u>: CG, Feb 6, 23, Mar 4, 13
Lyon, William (author)
--Wrangling Lovers, The; or, Like Master Like Man (farce), <u>1770</u>: HAY, Jul 9,
    Aug 22, 27; <u>1771</u>: HAY, May 17; <u>1779</u>: HAY, Mar 15, Dec 20; <u>1786</u>: HAMM, Aug 5
Lyons (singer), <u>1784</u>: HAY, Sep 17
Lyons, John (actor), <u>1781</u>: HAY, Jan 22, Mar 26; <u>1782</u>: HAY, May 6, Nov 25; <u>1783</u>:
    HAY, Aug 23; <u>1784</u>: HAY, Jun 17, Aug 10, 31, Sep 11; <u>1785</u>: HAY, Jun 16, 21,
    Jul 11, 13, 19, 20, 23, Aug 2, 3, 4, 31, DL, Dec 1; <u>1786</u>: HAY, Jun 12, 13,
    20, 28, Jul 12, 18, 19, 24, Aug 12, 17, 29; <u>1787</u>: HAY, May 23, 25, Jun 21,
    22, 27, Jul 2, 7, 20, 21, 23, 28, Aug 4, 17, Sep 8, DL, 22, Nov 10; <u>1788</u>: DL,
    Apr 14, May 7, Jun 5, HAY, 10, 12, 13, 18, 19, 30, Jul 4, 10, Aug 5, 9, 16,
    29, Sep 9, DL, Oct 4, Nov 17, 28, 29, Dec 6, 22; <u>1789</u>: DL, Feb 16, 19, Mar
    21, 24, May 22, 27, Jun 2, 13, HAY, 19, 22, Jul 1, Aug 11, Sep 12, 14, 15,
    DL, 17, 24, Oct 13, 28, Nov 5, 13, 17, 20, 24, Dec 2, 22, 26, 28; <u>1790</u>: DL,
    Feb 10, 11, Mar 8, 22, Apr 19, 23, May 4, 11, 14, 15, 28, Jun 3, HAY, 15, 16,
    17, 19, 22, 26, Jul 5, 16, Aug 10, 12, 23, 31, Sep 4, DL, 11, HAY, 13, DL,
    Oct 11, 14, 25, 26, Nov 3, 17, Dec 27, 29; <u>1791</u>: DL, Jan 10, Apr 30, May 10,
    11, 19, HAY, Jun 6, 18, 23, Jul 7, 30, Aug 5, 10, 24, 31, Sep 2, DLKING'S,
    22, 29, Oct 15, Nov 4, 5, 7, 12, 16, 22, 30, Dec 1; <u>1792</u>: DLKING'S, Jan 7,
    18, 31, Feb 4, 7, 18, Mar 1, 13, 26, 29, Apr 12, 14, 28, May 17, 23, Jun 13,
    HAY, 15, 20, 23, 30, Jul 11, 14, 18, 25, Aug 2, 9, 17, 23, 31, DL, Sep 15,
    29, Oct 4, 9, 11, 13, HAY, 15, DL, 18, Nov 21, Dec 10, 14, 26, 27, 28; <u>1793</u>:
    DL, Feb 12, 25, Mar 9, 11, 12, Apr 5, 16, 22, 23, May 7, 29, Jun 5, HAY, 17,
    21, 25, 26, 29, Jul 5, 18, 23, Aug 3, 5, 6, 12, 15, Sep 19, 21, 24, 28, 30,
    Oct 1, 4, 5, 8, 10, 15, 21, 24, 29, 30, Nov 5, 6, 16, 19, 22, Dec 16, 26, 30;
    <u>1794</u>: HAY, Jan 16, 27, Feb 8, 22, 24, Mar 13, DL, Apr 21, 25, 28, May 1, 3,
    6, 12, 16, 30, Jun 9, 10, 12, 28, Jul 4, HAY, 8, 9, 10, 11, 12, 17, 19, 21,
    22, 24, Aug 11, 13, 20, 27, DL, Sep 16, HAY, 17, DL, 27, Oct 14, 27, 31, Nov
    15, 18, 24, Dec 9, 20; <u>1795</u>: DL, Feb 6, 12, 28, Mar 2, 3, May 6, HAY, Jun 9,
    10, 11, 13, 15, 20, Jul 1, 8, 18, 25, 31, Aug 3, 27, 29, Sep 2; <u>1796</u>: HAY,
    Jun 11, 13, 14, 16, 22, 25, 29, 30, Jul 4, 5, 8, 9, 12, 15, 21, 23, 26, Aug
    8, 10, 11, 13, 18, 27, 29, Sep 7; <u>1797</u>: HAY, Jun 13, 15, 16, 17, 19, 20, 21,
    22, 24, 28, Jul 3, 18, 21, Aug 1, 9, 15, 23, 28, 31, Sep 8, 18; <u>1798</u>: HAY,
    Jun 12, 13, 15, 16, 18, 19, 21, 30, Jul 14, 21, Aug 3, 4, 11, 15, 23, 28, 29,
    31, Sep 3; <u>1799</u>: HAY, Jun 15, 17, 18, 20, 22, 24, 25, 26, Jul 2, 5, 6, 9, 13,
    23, Aug 10, 13, 17, 21
Lyric Ode, A. See Linley Jr, Thomas.
Lysaght, Edward (songwriter), <u>1784</u>: CG, Apr 17
Lysaght, N (spectator), <u>1689</u>: DG, Jun 13
Lyttleton, Lord, <u>1749</u>: CG, Jan 13
Lyttleton, Sir Charles (spectator), <u>1677</u>: ATCOURT, Nov 10

M Thurot's Trip to Carrickfergus (entertainment), 1761: CG, Apr 16
M, A (blind beneficiary), 1748: SOU, Oct 12
M, I (author), 1748: CG, Mar 5
Ma chere Amie (song), 1787: RLSN, Mar 27, 28, CG, Apr 21; 1788: DL, May 23, Jun
   3, 11; 1797: CG, May 23
Macaroni Adventurer, The; or, Woman's a Riddle (play, anon), 1778: HAY, Dec 28
Macaroni, The. See Hitchcock, Robert.
MacArthur (instrumentalist), 1800: CG, Feb 28
MacArthur, Miss (pianist), 1796: CG, Mar 4, 16; 1797: CG, Mar 17, Apr 5, 7
Macartney, Alexander (actor), 1799: CG, Oct 14, 17, 29, Nv 9, Dec 23; 1800: CG,
   May 17
Macartney, Charles Justin (actor), 1799: CG, Dec 9
Macarty, Colonel (spectator), 1679: DLORDG, Jan 6
Macbeth. See Shakespeare, William.
Macchierini, Giuseppa (singer), 1782: KING'S, Jan 12
Macclean (dancer), 1749: DL, Oct 11
Macdonogh, Dr, 1771: CG, Dec 30
Macdougall (house servant), 1800: DL, Jun 14
MacEvoy (householder), 1746: CG, Feb 18
MacGeorge (actor), 1762: HAY, May 1, Sep 16
MacGeorge, Miss (actor), 1789: CG, Sep 21
MacGuire (actor), 1733: MEG, Sep 28
Macheath in the Shades; or, Bayes at Parnassus (ballad opera, anon), 1735:
   CG/LIF, Mar 11
Macheath turned Pirate; or, Polly in India (opera, anon), 1737: HAY, May 25
Machen (actor), 1729: HAY, Feb 11, Mar 29, May 2, 7, Jul 16, Aug 19, BFR, 25,
   GF, Nov 8, Dec 3, 4, 11, 12; 1730: GF, Mar 7, 17, 30, Apr 6, LIF, May 7, GF,
   22, 26, Jun 3, 4, 17, 19, Jul 1, 22, BFPG/TC, Aug 1, BFPG, 20, GF, Oct 2, 5,
   9, 14, 19, 31, Nov 5, 10, 11, 12; 1731: GF, Jun 2, SOU, Sep 28; 1732: HAY,
   May 15, Nov 29; 1733: HAY, Feb 20, Mar 14, 19, 20, 26, 27, Apr 18; 1734: DL,
   Jan 19, HAY, Apr 5, May 27, Aug 16, 22; 1735: YB, Mar 19, 21, LIF, Jul 16,
   23, HAY, Aug 4, LIF, 6, 8, 22, 25, 29, YB/HAY, Sep 17, 24, Oct 1, HAY, Dec
   13, 17; 1736: HAY, Feb 16, 19, Mar 5, Apr 29, May 3, Jun 26, Aug 2; 1737:
   HAY, Mar 21, Apr 13; 1742: JS, Apr 7, May 31; 1743: JS, Jan 5; 1748: SFP, Sep
   7; 1749: BF/SFP, Aug 23
Machin (singer), 1774: DL, Nov 28; 1775: DL, Oct 26, Nov 24, Dec 7; 1776: DL,
   Jan 19, Feb 13, Mar 26, Jun 10
Machin, OBrien (actor), 1778: HAY, Feb 9, CHR, Jul 30
Mackarel, Elizabeth (actor), 1674: DL, Nov 19
Mackarnea (actor), 1748: BFLYY, Aug 24
Mackdonald (merchant), 1770: CG, Mar 1
Mackennea (actor), 1748: JS, Oct 31
MacKenzie (actor), 1734: SFL, Sep 7; 1736: SF, Sep 7; 1741: BFTY, Aug 22
Mackenzie (beneficiary), 1723: LIF, May 14; 1724: LIF, May 25
Mackenzie, Henry, 1784: CG, Feb 10; 1787: HAY, Sep 5; 1789: CG, Dec 5
--Force of Fashion, The (False Shame), 1789: CG, Dec 5, 8
--Shipwreck, The, 1784: CG, Feb 10
Mackintosh (ticket deliverer), 1784: HAY, Feb 9
Mackintosh, John (bassoonist), 1798: CG, Feb 23; 1799: CG, Feb 8; 1800: CG, Feb
   28
Mackintosh, W (publisher), 1779: KING'S, Nov 27; 1780: KING'S, Jan 22, Feb 8,
   Dec 19
Macklew, E (publisher), 1782: CG, Feb 9
Macklin, Anne, Mrs Charles (actor), 1739: DL, Dec 8, 10, 14, 22; 1740: DL, Jan
   7, 12, 15, 21, 29, Feb 1, 2, 8, 18, Mar 17, 22, Apr 9, 12, 16, 22, 25, Sep
   11, 23, Oct 2, 11, 13, 14, 15, 18, 23, 28, Nov 1, 6, 7, 11, 17, 24, Dec 15;
   1741: DL, Jan 15, Feb 2, Apr 24, 29, May 21, 27, Sep 5, 8, 12, 15, 24, Oct 9,
   23, Nov 11, 20, Dec 7; 1742: DL, Jan 4, 6, Feb 12, 13, Mar 8, 22, 29, Apr 20,
   May 6, 10, 12, Sep 21, 30; 1743: DL, Jan 14, Feb 17, Mar 21, Apr 13, May 11,
   LIF, Jun 3; 1744: HAY, Apr 6, 20, May 10, 16, Jun 29; 1745: DL, Mar 7, 16,
   Apr 20, 26, CG, May 29, DL, Sep 21, 24, 28, Oct 1, 3, 8, 10, 12, 15, 22, Nov
   1, 25, 26, 30, Dec 10; 1746: DL, Jan 2, Feb 24, Mar 13, 17, Apr 4, 10, 15,
   23, Jun 6, 11, Sep 25, 30, Oct 2, 4, 27, 31, Nov 7, 22, 28; 1747: DL, Jan 3,
   14, 21, Feb 10, 18, 26, Mar 3, 23, 24, Apr 24, May 5, 13, 14, Sep 17, 19, 24,
   26, Oct 1, 17, 21, 29, Nov 25, Dec 17, 30; 1748: DL, Jan 6, 9, 12, 25, 28,
   Feb 3, Mar 22, 24, Apr 12, 14, 22, 27, 28; 1750: CG, Sep 24, 26, 28, Oct 15,
   16, 20, 22, 27, 31, Nov 12, 22, 28, 29, Dec 3, 10, 21; 1751: CG, Apr 22, 24,
   May 9, Oct 7, 8, 9, 19, 22, Nov 7, 11, 13, 18, 21, Dec 10; 1752: CG, Jan 3,
   6, Mar 3, 16, 30, Apr 4, Sep 20, Oct 4, 10, 11, 14, 19, 21, 24, Nov 3, 16,

531

Dec 8, 19; <u>1753</u>: CG, Mar 19, 20, 24, DL, Dec 20; <u>1754</u>: DL, Nov 7, Dec 13;
<u>1755</u>: DL, Jan 23, Feb 7, May 6, Oct 8, 13, Nov 6, 28; <u>1756</u>: DL, May 10, 14,
Oct 9, 13, 21, 23, Nov 3, 12, Dec 15; <u>1757</u>: DL, Jan 26, May 2, Oct 1; <u>1758</u>:
DL, Mar 13, Apr 3, 18, May 2, Sep 28, Oct 18, Dec 28, 30
Macklin, Charles (actor, playwright), <u>1730</u>: SOU, Sep 24; <u>1731</u>: GF, Apr 5, 19,
28; <u>1733</u>: DL, Oct 31, Nov 21, Dec 11, 21; <u>1734</u>: DL, Jan 3, 15, 19, DL/LIF,
Mar 11, DL/HAY, 30, HAY, Apr 5, DL, 22, 23, LIF, 26, DL/LIF, May 3, HAY, 27,
DL, Sep 24, 26, HAY, Oct 7, DL, 8, 22, Nov 8, 16, 20, 22, Dec 12, 14; <u>1735</u>:
DL, Jan 6, 11, 20, 22, Feb 25, Mar 22, Apr 21, 24, May 6, 10, 16, 20, Dec 12;
<u>1736</u>: DL, Jan 31, Feb 5, 7, 18, 20, 21, 26, Mar 13, 25, LIF, Apr 14, DL, 17,
May 6, Sep 4, 7, 11, 18, 23, 28, Oct 2, 12, 13, 20, 25, Nov 1, 2, 9, 13, 15,
20, 23, 27, Dec 4, 7, 17, 20, 21, 27, 31; <u>1737</u>: DL, Jan 6, 27, Feb 10, 19,
28, Mar 1, 12, Apr 12, 27, May 5, 17, Jun 11, Aug 30, Sep 6, 8, 10, 13, 15,
17, 20, 22, 24, 27, 29, Oct 8, 11, 13, 20, 21, 22, 24, 25, 27, 31, Nov 11,
15, 16, 17; <u>1738</u>: DL, Jan 5, 14, 24, 25, 26, Feb 2, Mar 2, 20, 21, Apr 14,
17, 27, 28, May 2, 3, 5, 8, 9, 13, 17, 25, 26, Sep 7, 9, 14, 19, 21, 23, 28,
Oct 3, 16, 17, 18, 20, 24, 25, 27, 30, Nov 2, 3, 8, 11, 14, 25, 29, 30, Dec
7, 9, 15, 26, 28; <u>1739</u>: DL, Jan 1, 8, 13, 22, 26, Feb 7, Mar 10, 20, 22, 27,
29, 31, Apr 9, 10, 25, 28, May 2, 9, 15, 28, Sep 1, 4, 6, 11, 15, 18, 20, 22,
26, Oct 4, 10, 13, 15, 18, 19, 23, 24, 25, 27, Nov 7, 8, 10, 15, 16, 19, 21,
Dec 8, 10, 11, 14, 22, 26, 31; <u>1740</u>: DL, Jan 5, 16, Feb 13, Mar 13, 17, 18,
22, 29, Apr 12, 15, 17, 19, 22, 23, 28, 29, May 6, 8, 9, 13, 14, 23, Sep 6,
9, 13, 20, 23, 25, 27, 30, Oct 2, 4, 9, 10, 11, 13, 14, 15, 17, 23, 27, 28,
29, Nov 1, 7, 8, 11, 13, 17, 24, 27, 28, Dec 6, 13, 15, 18, 19, 26; <u>1741</u>: DL,
Jan 6, 15, Feb 2, 14, 24, Mar 14, Apr 3, 4, 7, 27, 29, May 1, 12, 14, 21, 25,
Sep 5, 8, 12, 15, 17, 19, 22, 24, Oct 8, 9, 10, 15, 20, 21, 23, 31, Nov 2,
11, 16, 20, 21, Dec 16; <u>1742</u>: DL, Jan 6, 7, 8, 22, Feb 11, 12, 13, Mar 22,
27, 29, Apr 20, 22, 26, 27, May 6, 22, Sep 11, 14, 16, 18, 21, 25, 28, 30,
Oct 2, 7, 9, 12, 16, 18, 27, Nov 1, 8, 12, 16, 19, 22, Dec 22; <u>1743</u>: DL, Jan
11, 28, Feb 17, Mar 3, 21, Apr 7, May 9, LIF, Jun 3, DL, Sep 13, Oct 6, 15,
Dec 6, 12, 14, 19; <u>1744</u>: HAY, Jan 21, Feb 6, 13, 23, Apr 6, 20, May 10, 16,
Jun 29, Jul 6, 10, DL, Nov 10, Dec 19, 22, 26, 28; <u>1745</u>: DL, Jan 4, 5, 7, 8,
19, 21, 25, 26, 31, Feb 13, 14, 20, Mar 7, 30, Apr 19, 20, 26, CG, May 29,
DL, Sep 19, 21, 24, 26, 28, Oct 1, 3, 5, 8, 10, 12, Nov 20, 23, 26, 28, 30,
Dec 5, 10, 16, 20; <u>1746</u>: DL, Jan 18, 20, 31, Feb 24, Mar 13, 17, Apr 4, 11,
15, 21, 23, Sep 23, 25, 30, Oct 4, 23, 27, Nov 7, 21, 22, 28, Dec 20, 26, 30;
<u>1747</u>: DL, Jan 3, Mar 12, 16, 24, 30, Apr 4, 20, 28, 30, May 5, Sep 15, 17,
19, 22, 24, 26, Oct 1, 3, 15, 17, 21, 24, Nov 2, 7, 16, 17, 27, Dec 4, 5, 16,
26; <u>1748</u>: DL, Jan 6, 12, 18, Feb 3, 13, 22, Mar 22, 24, Apr 19, 23, 28, May
3, 4; <u>1749</u>: BBT, Mar 1; <u>1750</u>: CG, Sep 24, 26, 28, Oct 16, 18, 20, 24, 25, 27,
30, 31, Nov 28, 29, Dec 3, 10, 21; <u>1751</u>: DL, Mar 7, 16, CG, Apr 10, 19, May
9, Oct 7, 8, 9, 11, 19, 22, 25, Nov 11, 13, 16, 21, 28, Dec 10, DL, 30; <u>1752</u>:
CG, Jan 3, 6, 28, Mar 3, 30, Apr 4, 8, May 4, Sep 18, Oct 4, 6, 10, 11, 14,
19, 21, 24, Nov 3, 16, 28, Dec 8, 11, 19, 21; <u>1753</u>: CG, Feb 6, Mar 20, 24,
DL, Oct 30, Dec 15, 20; <u>1754</u>: DL, Jan 5, Mar 25, Nov 22, HAY, Dec 16, DL, 16,
HAY, 18, 23; <u>1756</u>: DL, Mar 29; <u>1759</u>: DL, Dec 12, 19; <u>1760</u>: DL, Jan 17, CG,
Dec 19, 23, 31; <u>1761</u>: CG, Jan 2, 10, 14, 17, 20, 28, 29, 31, Feb 2, 3, 7, 9,
19, 21, 26, 28, Mar 12, Apr 1, 4, DL, 24; <u>1763</u>: CG, Apr 12; <u>1764</u>: CG, Apr 10;
<u>1765</u>: CG, Apr 9; <u>1766</u>: CG, Apr 2; <u>1767</u>: DL, Apr 6, CG, 6, Sep 21, Oct 6, 10,
Nov 28, Dec 5; <u>1768</u>: CG, Feb 29; <u>1769</u>: CG, Apr 1; <u>1770</u>: CG, Apr 5; <u>1771</u>: CG,
Apr 3, Oct 22, 31, Nov 2; <u>1773</u>: CG, Mar 6, Apr 16, 17, Oct 5, 22, 23, 30, Nov
18, 20, 27; <u>1775</u>: CG, Feb 24, May 18, 25, Jun 1, Oct 6, 19, 24; <u>1776</u>: DL, Jun
1, CG, Oct 29, Nov 7, 11, 15, Dec 2, 17; <u>1777</u>: CG, Jan 2, Mar 22, Apr 16, Oct
1, HAY, 9, CG, 16, 23, Nov 1; <u>1778</u>: CG, Mar 24; <u>1779</u>: CG, Feb 25, Nov 11, 27;
<u>1780</u>: CG, Apr 5, Nov 2, Dec 14; <u>1781</u>: CG, May 10, 28, Oct 5, Nov 8; <u>1782</u>: CG,
Jan 18, Mar 5, Oct 19, 29; <u>1783</u>: CG, Apr 30, Dec 5; <u>1784</u>: CG, Jan 29, Feb 12,
May 20, Oct 28, Nov 10; <u>1786</u>: CG, Feb 11, 18, Mar 2, 30, HAY, Jul 25, CG, Oct
12, Dec 15; <u>1787</u>: CG, May 5, Dec 20; <u>1788</u>: CG, Jan 10, 18, Apr 28, Oct 18,
Nov 19, 26; <u>1789</u>: CG, Feb 18, May 7; <u>1791</u>: CG, May 5, Nov 26; <u>1794</u>: CG, May
20; <u>1796</u>: HAY, Jun 16
--Club of Fortune Hunters, The; or, The Widow Bewitched, <u>1748</u>: DL, Apr 12, 22,
27, 28
--Covent Garden Theatre; or, Pasquin turned Drawcansir, Censor of Great
Britain, <u>1752</u>: CG, Apr 8; <u>1753</u>: DL, Dec 20
--Henry VII; or, The Popish Impostor, <u>1746</u>: DL, Jan 14, 18, 20, 21; <u>1753</u>: DL,
Dec 20
--Irish Fine Lady, The (True-Born Irishman, The), <u>1767</u>: CG, Nov 23, 28; <u>1779</u>:
HAY, Oct 9
--Love a la Mode, <u>1759</u>: DL, Dec 12, 13, 15, 19, 21, 22, 27; <u>1760</u>: DL, Jan 17,
18, 23, Feb 6, 7, 12, 14, 19, Mar 25, Apr 12, 18, May 17, 20, 23, 27, 29, CG,
Dec 19, 23, 31; <u>1761</u>: CG, Jan 2, 10, 14, 17, 20, Feb 2, 3, 5, 7, 9, 10, 19,
21, 26, 28, Mar 12, 14, Apr 1, 3, 15, DL, 24, May 4, 18; <u>1762</u>: DL, May 6;

1763: CG, Apr 12, 20, DL, May 3; 1764: CG, Apr 10, 12; 1765: CG, Apr 9, DL,
May 6; 1766: CG, Apr 2; 1767: CG, Apr 6, Jun 9, Sep 21, 26, Oct 6, 10, 14,
21, 28, Nov 21, Dec 10; 1768: CG, Jan 1, 22, 25, Feb 29, Apr 6, 20, DL, 26;
1769: CG, Apr 1; 1770: CG, Apr 5, DL, May 3; 1771: HAY, Jan 28, CG, Apr 3,
27, May 6, Oct 22, 24, 26, 29, 31; 1772: CG, Apr 22; 1773: DL, Apr 15, CG,
16, 17, Oct 5, 14, Nov 18; 1774: DL, Apr 6, 11; 1775: CG, May 18, 29, Oct 6,
27; 1776: DL, Apr 8, CG, 13, Oct 29, Nov 4, 11, 22, Dec 19; 1777: CG, Jan 15,
Feb 15, Mar 22, Apr 19, Oct 16, 28, Nov 4, 13, Dec 22; 1778: CG, Mar 24, Apr
24; 1779: CG, Feb 25, Nov 11, 20, 27; 1780: CG, Jan 8, 28, Apr 5, 29, Nov 2,
6, 9, 16, 23, 30, Dec 7, 14; 1781: CG, Feb 13, 20, Nov 8, 15, Dec 4; 1782:
CG, Apr 8, Oct 29, Dec 3; 1783: CG, Feb 13, Apr 30, Dec 5, 16; 1784: CG, Mar
18, Nov 3, 10; 1785: CG, Feb 14; 1786: CG, Feb 18, Oct 12, Dec 19; 1787: CG,
Feb 8, May 5, Jun 15, Dec 20; 1788: CG, Jan 10, 24, Feb 14, 16, Apr 3, 17,
28, Oct 18; 1790: CG, Nov 27; 1791: CG, May 5, Nov 26, Dec 17; 1792: CG, Jan
24; 1794: DL, May 13, 15, 17, 19, 20, 23
--Man of the World, The, 1781: CG, May 10, 15, 17, 21, 28, Oct 5, 11, 24, 25,
Dec 12; 1782: CG, Jan 24, 31, Feb 6, Mar 5, 16, Apr 5, 11, 18, May 14, Oct
19, Nov 20; 1783: CG, Jan 9, Mar 25, Jun 6; 1784: CG, Jan 29, Feb 12, 28, Mar
9, May 20, Oct 28, Dec 9; 1785: CG, Feb 24; 1786: CG, Feb 11, Mar 2, 9, 30,
Dec 15; 1787: CG, Feb 2, Mar 8, 20, May 5, Jun 13; 1788: CG, Jan 18, Feb 1,
Mar 3, Apr 7, 28, Nov 19, 26; 1790: CG, Sep 29, Oct 22, 30; 1797: CG, May 16,
26
--Married Libertine, The, 1761: CG, Jan 28, 29, 31, Feb 2, 3, 5, 7, 9, 10
--Suspicious Husband Criticized; or, The Plague of Envy, 1747: DL, Mar 16, 24,
26, Apr 30
--True-Born Scotsman, The, 1781: CG, May 10
--Will and No Will, A; or, A Bone for Lawyers (or, A New Case for the Lawyers),
1746: DL, Apr 23; 1748: DL, Mar 22, 29, 31, Apr 11, 21, 22; 1756: DL, Mar 29
Macklin, Charles and Anne (actors), 1750: DL, Sep 8
Macklin, Maria (actor, dancer), 1742: DL, Mar 8, Dec 20; 1745: DL, Feb 2, 20,
Oct 8, 19; 1746: DL, Jan 8, Apr 17, Sep 30, Nov 15; 1747: DL, Mar 16, Apr 29;
1751: CG, Apr 10, 24, Oct 23, 25, 26; 1752: CG, Apr 8; 1753: CG, Mar 24, Apr
24, DL, Oct 20, 27, Dec 20; 1754: DL, Jan 16, 19, Feb 5, Apr 8, 20, Sep 26,
28, Oct 14, Nov 7, Dec 7, 17; 1755: DL, Jan 15, 25, Feb 8, 18, 25, Mar 22,
Apr 22, May 5, Sep 13, 18, 20, 23, 25, Oct 7, 21, Nov 26, 28, Dec 1, 2, 23;
1756: DL, Feb 24, Mar 27, 29, Apr 20, 22, 28, 29, May 3, 24, Sep 18, 23, 28,
30, Oct 2, 13, Nov 6, 17, 23, Dec 27; 1757: DL, Jan 11, 22, 26, Feb 22, Mar
24, 28, Apr 2, 11, 12, 15, 30, May 2, 7, Sep 10, 15, 20, 22, Oct 8, 13, 29,
Nov 19, 22, 29, Dec 3, 22, 27; 1758: DL, Jan 19, 24, Feb 1, Mar 13, 18, Apr
3, 18, 24, Jun 22, Sep 16, 19, 26, Oct 3, 7, 18, 21, Nov 10, 24, Dec 2; 1759:
DL, Feb 1, 2, 15, Mar 24, 27, Apr 2, 30, May 7, 9, 16, 23, Jun 19, Sep 22,
29, Oct 2, 4, 5, 11, 17, Nov 22, Dec 12, 19; 1760: DL, Jan 24, Feb 8, Mar 20,
24, 25, Apr 21, 24, May 1, 7, 8, 16, CG, Sep 22, 29, Oct 1, 13, 23, 25, Dec
19; 1761: CG, Jan 2, 10, 17, 28, Feb 17, Apr 1, 6, 21, 22, May 25; 1762: CG,
Sep 22, 27, 30, Oct 1, 5, 12, 19, 21, Nov 1, 3, 15, 16, 29, 30, Dec 27; 1763:
CG, Feb 15, Mar 19, 21, Apr 5, 12, May 11, 14, 26, Oct 3, 5, 7, 14, 17, 19,
21, 24, 29, Nov 7, 10, 16, 26, Dec 16, 27, 29; 1764: CG, Jan 16, 28, Feb 1,
9, 13, Mar 27, 29, Apr 10, May 12, Sep 17, 19, 21, Oct 1, 3, 5, 10, 15, 16,
19, 20, 22, 24, Nov 6, 15, 29, 30; 1765: CG, Jan 21, Feb 18, Apr 9, May 9,
Sep 18, 20, Oct 2, 3, 5, 9, 10, 11, 17, 23, 26, Nov 19, 22, Dec 3, 10; 1766:
CG, Jan 9, Feb 6, 13, Apr 1, 2, 15, 25, May 13, Oct 16, 21, 22, 25, 28, 30,
Nov 18, 21, 25, 28, Dec 6, 10, 16, 23; 1767: CG, Jan 23, 31, Feb 28, Mar 2,
Apr 6, 11, 24, 28, May 19, Sep 19, 21, Oct 6, Nov 6, 27, 28, Dec 26; 1768:
CG, Jan 22, Feb 23, 25, Mar 8, 24, Apr 6, 20, 25, Sep 23, 29, 30, Oct 6, 10,
15, 21, Nov 8, Dec 22; 1769: CG, Jan 2, Mar 16, 28, Apr 1, DL, May 3, CG, 9,
Sep 20, 30, Oct 3, 5, 27, Nov 3, 17, 23, 27, Dec 7; 1770: CG, Jan 6, 17, Apr
5, 20, 25, Sep 24, Nov 23, Dec 3; 1771: CG, Jan 4, Apr 3, May 3, Oct 22, Nov
16, 19, 21, Dec 6, 7; 1772: CG, Jan 4, Feb 22, DL, Mar 23, CG, Apr 22, 25,
May 8, Sep 25, Oct 1, Nov 12, Dec 3, 22, 28; 1773: DL, Feb 1, CG, 3, Mar 6,
Apr 16, 17, 23, May 6, 11, 26, Sep 20, Oct 5, 18, 27, Nov 11, Dec 17, 18;
1774: CG, Jan 15, Apr 5, Sep 19, Oct 5, 22, 27, Nov 3, Dec 6, 12; 1775: CG,
Apr 25, May 9, 17, 18, 25, 26, Oct 4, 6, 18, 24; 1776: CG, Jan 1, Feb 20, Mar
12, Apr 13, 19, 27, May 13, Oct 4, 15, 29, Nov 7, 11, 15, Dec 17; 1777: CG,
Jan 2, Apr 19
Macklin's Coffee House, 1755: DL, Jan 17, Apr 14; 1756: LRRH/PCR, Feb 18
Mackmillan, Mrs. See McMillen, Mrs.
Maclean (actor), 1730: LIF, Dec 4
Macleish (printer), 1788: CG, Dec 6; 1791: CG, May 31; 1792: CG, Apr 30; 1793:
CG, Oct 17; 1796: CG, Apr 16
Macleish, E (printer), 1797: CG, Mar 3; 1798: CG, Feb 23; 1799: CG, Feb 8, Sep
16
Macleish, H (printer), 1791: CG, Mar 11; 1792: CG, Feb 24; 1793: CG, Feb 15;

1794: CG, Mar 7, Nov 17; 1796: CG, Feb 12, May 10
Maclelan (actor), 1742: DL, Sep 28, Dec 14; 1743: DL, May 16
Macloughlin. See Macklin.
MacMahon, P (bookkeeper), 1785: KING'S, Jun 18
Macnally, Leonard, 1782: CG, May 7, Sep 23; 1783: CG, Apr 23, 26, May 19; 1784:
   CG, Apr 17; 1785: CG, Apr 2; 1786: CG, Apr 1, Oct 16; 1787: CG, May 21; 1789:
   CG, Nov 28
--April Fool, The; or, The Follies of a Night (farce), 1786: CG, Apr 1, 28, May
   5
--Cantabs, The (farce), 1787: CG, May 21
--Coalition (farce), 1783: CG, May 19
--Fashionable Levities, 1785: CG, Apr 2, 4, 9, 16, 26, 29, May 9, 20; 1792: CG,
   Mar 31, May 8, 16; 1793: CG, Apr 8, May 1, Jun 6; 1797: CG, May 6; 1800: CG,
   Jun 2
--New Occasional Prelude, A (prelude), 1782: CG, Sep 23
--Retaliation; or, The Citizen a Soldier (farce), 1782: CG, May 7, 8, 9, 10,
   14, 23, 28, Sep 25, Oct 7, 22, Nov 7, Dec 18; 1783: CG, Apr 26, Oct 2; 1784:
   CG, Feb 7, Apr 20, May 22, Nov 25, Dec 7, 20; 1785: CG, May 12, Nov 22; 1798:
   CG, Apr 20
--Richard Coeur de Lion, 1786: CG, Oct 16, 18, 19, 20, 21, 23, 25, 26, 28, 30,
   Nov 18, 20, Dec 18
--Robin Hood; or, Sherwood Forest (opera), 1779: CG, Nov 12; 1784: CG, Apr 17,
   19, 20, 30, May 3, 5, 11, 12, 13, 14, 19, 24, 31, Oct 12, 15, 22, Nov 2, 9,
   Dec 10; 1785: CG, Mar 12, Apr 15, Oct 21, Nov 29, Dec 2; 1786: CG, Jan 17,
   Apr 28, May 31, HAMM, Jun 28; 1787: CG, Oct 18, 20, 24, 25, 27, 30, Nov 1, 3,
   6, 10, 13, 17, 21, 24, 27, Dec 1, 4, 6, 8, 11, 13, 19; 1788: CG, Jan 8, 19,
   26, Feb 2, 26, Apr 15, 25, May 13, Oct 21, Nov 27; 1789: CG, Jan 7, 24, Apr
   21, Jun 2, Oct 28, Nov 28, Dec 15; 1790: CG, Mar 23, Oct 13, Nov 12, 18, Dec
   15; 1791: CG, Feb 12, Apr 7, May 7, 11, Jun 2, Sep 28, Oct 12, 29; 1792: CG,
   Mar 31, Apr 11, 28; 1793: CG, Jun 12, Sep 20, Nov 14; 1794: CG, May 2, 5, 8,
   Oct 7; 1795: CG, Jun 8; 1796: CG, Oct 3, Dec 12; 1797: DL, Jun 6; 1798: CG,
   Apr 16, Oct 8; 1799: CG, Jan 24, DL, May 4, CG, Sep 25, Nov 12; 1800: DL, Jun
   3
--Tristram Shandy, 1783: CG, Apr 26, May 1, 3, 7, 9, 12, 13, Sep 17, Oct 21,
   24; 1784: CG, Jan 21, Feb 14, Oct 8, 15, Nov 27; 1794: CG, Apr 12
Macquire (actor), 1740: BF/WF/SF, Aug 23
Macquire, Mrs (actor), 1740: BF/WF/SF, Aug 23
Macready, William (actor, playwright), 1786: CG, Sep 18, 20, 27, 29, Oct 12,
   18, 19, 21, 23, 30, Nov 13, 22, 29, Dec 13, 20, 21, 30; 1787: CG, Jan 6, 15,
   26, 31, Feb 6, 10, 13, Mar 26, 27, 31, Apr 11, 14, 16, 25, 26, 27, 30, May 1,
   HAY, Aug 28, CG, Sep 17, 24, 28, Oct 1, 5, 10, 11, 12, 17, 18, 19, 22, 29,
   Nov 5, 7, 19, 20, Dec 10, 15, 27; 1788: CG, Jan 3, 5, 15, 21, Feb 5, 9, 23,
   Mar 1, 10, 11, 24, Apr 14, 23, 26, May 2, 12, 14, 23, Sep 22, Oct 3, 8, 29,
   Nov 6, 7, 12, 28, Dec 1, 26, 27, 31; 1789: CG, Jan 8, 10, 20, 21, Feb 11, 21,
   Mar 5, 31, Apr 14, 20, 28, 30, May 5, 14, 15, 26, Jun 16, 17, Sep 14, 25, 30,
   Oct 2, 6, 7, 9, 12, 16, 30, Nov 2, 5, 12, 13, 16, 20, 23, 27, Dec 5, 11, 26;
   1790: CG, Jan 4, 22, 29, Feb 5, 23, 27, Mar 27, Apr 7, 14, 29, May 5, 11, 18,
   Jun 10, Sep 13, 29, Oct 4, 5, 6, 11, 13, 18, 20, 25, Nov 3, 4, 6, 8, 11, 22,
   23, Dec 2, 6, 10, 31; 1791: CG, Jan 3, 14, 26, Feb 2, 16, Mar 12, Apr 11, 16,
   28, May 2, 3, 6, 10, 11, 18, 31, Jun 1, 3, 10, Sep 12, 17, 21, 23, 26, Oct 3,
   6, 7, 10, 12, 17, 21, 24, Nov 4, 24, Dec 1, 3, 13, 15, 21, 26; 1792: CG, Feb
   2, 6, 8, 18, 23, Mar 6, 22, 26, 31, Apr 10, 12, 18, 21, May 5, 30, Sep 17,
   24, 26, Oct 1, 5, 8, 10, 12, 15, 17, 18, 26, 29, 31, Nov 3, 5, 6, 7, 12, 24,
   Dec 1, 5, 20, 27; 1793: CG, Jan 2, 14, Feb 14, Mar 4, 5, Apr 8, 11, 24, 25,
   May 8, 24, 27, Jun 8, Sep 16, 17, 18, 23, 25, 30, Oct 1, 4, 7, 9, 10, 14, 16,
   17, 18, 21, 29, 30, 31, Nov 1, 11, 13, 18, 23, Dec 6, 19, 20, 30; 1794: CG,
   Jan 6, 14, 22, Feb 1, 13, 22, Mar 6, 17, Apr 12, 23, May 19, 22, Jun 4, 5,
   Sep 17, 22, 29, Oct 1, 7, 8, 15, 20, 21, 30, Nov 12, 20; 1795: CG, Jan 6, 19,
   24, 31, Feb 3, 14, 21, Mar 5, 28, Apr 6, 23, 24, 27, 29, May 1, 8, 13, 14,
   22, 25, 27, Jun 3, 5, 6, 8, 10, 17, Sep 14, 16, 18, 21, 23, 25, 28, 30, Oct
   2, 5, 8, 15, 16, 19, 22, 23, 24, 30, Nov 4, 18, 25, 27, Dec 4, 7, 9, 15, 21,
   30; 1796: CG, Jan 2, 6, 8, 13, 23, 25, 28, Feb 1, Mar 14, Apr 1, 5, 19, 20,
   23, 29, May 6, 12, 20, 21, 24, 28, Jun 6, Sep 12, 14, 16, 17, 19, 23, 26, 30,
   Oct 5, 6, 10, 13, 14, 17, 18, 20, 21, 24, 29, Nov 5, 7, 19, Dec 9, 10, 15,
   19, 21, 22; 1797: CG, Jan 4, 10, Feb 20, 23, 27, Apr 8, May 6, 9, 16, 17, 31,
   Jun 1, 2, 10, 13; 1798: HAY, Dec 17
--Bank Note, The; or, Lessons for Ladies, 1795: CG, May 1, 6, 19, 21, Jun 2, 5,
   Sep 18
--Irishman in London, The; or, The Happy African (farce), 1792: CG, Apr 21, May
   2, 11, 16, 28, 30, HAY, Aug 15, CG, Sep 17, Oct 1, 11, Dec 18; 1793: CG, Mar
   18, Apr 6, 12, 15, 29, May 9, Jun 4, Sep 25, Oct 15, Nov 5, Dec 14; 1794: CG,
   Mar 1, 22, Apr 5, May 5, 23, Jun 17, HAY, Aug 28, CG, Oct 21; 1795: CG, Feb

2, May 16, Sep 23, Dec 11; 1796: CG, Apr 5, May 30, Oct 21, Nov 28; 1797: CG,
    May 11, 20, HAY, Jun 15, 19, 30, Jul 11, 28, CG, Oct 31; 1798: HAY, Apr 23,
    Jul 20, Aug 28; 1799: HAY, Apr 17, Aug 27, CG, Oct 18; 1800: HAY, Aug 19
MacSwiney, Owen (proprietor), 1705: DL, Mar 29; 1706: DL, Mar 30; 1736: CG, Apr
    1; 1737: CG, Mar 21; 1745: DL, Mar 30; see also Swiny, Owen
Maculla (boxkeeper), 1746: DL, May 14; 1747: DL, May 14
Mad Bess (song), 1737: CG, Mar 10; 1745: CG, Apr 15; 1749: DL, Apr 5; 1772: DL,
    May 6; 1781: HAY, Aug 28; 1786: DL, Apr 25; 1787: HAY, Aug 10; 1790: DL, Mar
    17, CG, Jun 2, 7; 1791: DL, Apr 1, 26; 1792: CG, Mar 7, KING'S, 30; 1793: CG,
    Feb 20, KING/HAY, 27, CG, Mar 6, KING/HAY, 13, CG, 20, 22; 1794: CG, Mar 12,
    DL, 14, CG, 26, Apr 25, May 20; 1795: CG, Mar 4, 18; 1796: CG, Feb 26, Mar
    16, May 18, 24, 25, HAY, Aug 30; 1797: CG, Mar 24, 31; 1798: CG, Mar 9, 30;
    1799: CG, Feb 20, Mar 13; 1800: CG, Mar 14
Mad Captain, The. See Drury, Robert.
Mad Catherina (dance), 1763: CG, Apr 15
Mad Couple. See Howard, James.
Mad Dance (dance), 1718: LIF, Apr 24; 1730: BFPG/TC, Aug 1, 24
Mad Dialogue (song), 1703: DL, Jun 22; 1705: DL, May 22, Jul 3; 1706: DL, Jan
    21; 1707: DL, Jan 13, Apr 3; 1711: GR, Sep 8; 1716: DL, May 30, Jun 6; 1717:
    DL, May 22; 1718: LIF, Apr 5, 24, May 6, DL, 21; 1731: GF, Jan 13
Mad Doctor (dance), 1760: DL, Oct 14, 15, 17, 23, Nov 22, 24, 25, 27, Dec 1,
    12; 1761: DL, Jan 9
Mad House, The. See Baker, Richard.
Mad Lover, The. See Fletcher, John.
Mad Lovers, The; or, Sport Upon Sport: With the Comical Humours of Squire
    Graygoose (play), 1738: TC, Aug 7
Mad Man and Mad Lady (song), 1710: QUEEN'S, Jul 6
Mad Men and Women (dance), 1720: KING'S, May 3
Mad Robin (song), 1731: LIF, Apr 8
Mad Song (song), 1703: LIF, Jun 14; 1704: LIF, Apr 29; 1716: DL, May 30; 1722:
    LIF, Apr 28; 1784: HAY, Sep 17
Mad Tom (song), 1730: GF, Jun 29, Jul 14; 1731: GF, May 14, 17, SFLH, Sep 8;
    1732: GF, Apr 24, May 19; 1741: DL, May 26, Dec 10; 1748: SOU, Sep 26, Oct
    10; 1749: JS, Mar 15; 1754: HAY, Sep 10; 1774: CG, Apr 8, 29; 1780: CG, Apr
    10, 18; 1781: CG, Apr 3, 18, 25; 1782: CG, May 6, 20; 1784: CG, Apr 24; 1790:
    CG, Jun 3; 1799: CG, Apr 6, May 18, HAY, Sep 16
Mad Tom of Bedlam. See Doggett, Thomas.
Mad World, My Masters, A. See Middleton, Thomas.
Madam Epicene. See Jonson, Ben, The Silent Woman.
Madam Fickle. See D'Urfey, Thomas.
Madame Ciana. See Latille, Gaetano.
Madan (spectator), 1760: CG, Mar 29
Madden (clothier), 1750: DL, Jan 1
Madden, Master (actor), 1749: LEI, Jan 7
Madden, Miss (dancer), 1766: KING'S, Aug 25, 27, Sep 9, 13; 1767: DL, May 18;
    1768: CG, May 27, 28; 1769: CG, May 6, 11, 17, Nov 4; 1770: CG, May 18; 1771:
    CG, May 22
Madden, Samuel, 1729: LIF, Feb 10
--Themistocles, the Lover of His Country, 1729: LIF, Feb 10, 11, 12, 13, 14,
    15, 17, 18, 20; 1770: HAY, Feb 14
Maddin (actor), 1781: HAY, Mar 26
Maddin, Miss (actor), 1781: HAY, Mar 26
Maddison, Robert (author), 1763: CG, Feb 18
Maddocks (Maddox) (actor), 1715: DL, Apr 20, SF, Sep 5; 1716: DL, Jun 8
Maddocks, Anthony (acrobat), 1752: CG, Nov 2, DL, 6, CG, Dec 4; 1757: HAY, Oct
    3; 1758: DL, Oct 27; 1770: HAY, Dec 10
Maddocks, Miss (actor), 1746: GF, Oct 27, 28, 31, Nov 6, 13
Maddocks, Mrs Walter (actor, singer), 1794: DL, Oct 13, 27, Nov 15, Dec 20, 23;
    1795: DL, Jan 6, 10, Feb 6, 26, 28, Mar 7, Jun 3, 6, Sep 22, Oct 20, 30, Nov
    11, 20, 23, 26, Dec 10; 1796: DL, Jan 2, 8, 11, 13, 16, 18, Feb 1, Mar 3, 12,
    Apr 9, 12, 13, 26, 30, May 11, Sep 29, Oct 11, 19, Nov 2, 9; 1797: DL, Jan 7,
    17, 20, Feb 1, 9, 16, May 5, 24, Sep 21, 23, 30, Oct 3, 12, 14, 19, Nov 8,
    17, Dec 20, 21; 1798: DL, Jan 16, Feb 20, Jun 7, Sep 20, 22, Oct 6, 9, 27,
    Nov 14, 26, 28, 29, Dec 4, 29; 1799: DL, Jan 19, Mar 2, 4, 11, May 3, Sep 21,
    24, Oct 1, 14, 19, Nov 6, 14, 29, Dec 2; 1800: DL, Jan 1, Feb 6, Apr 29, CG,
    May 23
Maddocks, Walter (actor), 1787: DL, Oct 18; 1789: DL, Sep 17, 19, 22, 24, Oct
    1, 13, 27, 31, Nov 5, 13, 17, 20, Dec 2, 3, 26; 1790: DL, Jan 15, 19, Feb 10,
    15, 18, Mar 8, 18, 22, Apr 20, 23, May 4, 8, 14, 15, 25, 28, Jun 2, 4, Oct 2,
    7, 14, 18, 19, 25, 26, 27, Nov 4, 17, Dec 7, 14, 27, 29; 1791: DL, Jan 10,
    Mar 21, Apr 28, 30, May 10, 11, 26, DLKING'S, Sep 22, 29, Oct 4, 10, 15, 27,
    31, Nov 1, 2, 4, 5, 7, 8, 9, 10, 11, 16, 22, Dec 1, 15; 1792: DLKING'S, Jan

5, 6, 13, 18, 21, 24, 28, Feb 8, 18, 23, Mar 6, 10, 13, 17, 19, 29, 31, Apr
10, 12, 16, 20, 24, 25, 28, May 1, 5, 17, 23, Jun 13, 15, DL, Sep 15, 25, 26,
29, Oct 4, 9, 11, 13, 18, 31, Nov 10, 21, 26, Dec 3, 4, 13, 17, 21, 27, 28;
1793: DL, Jan 4, 7, 16, Feb 9, 16, 23, 26, Mar 5, 7, 9, 12, 21, Apr 3, 6, 9,
16, 17, 18, 22, 23, 25, 27, 29, May 1, 7, 10, 15, 27, 28, 31, Jun 1, 3, 10,
HAY, Oct 1, 3, 4, 7, 8, 10, 11, 15, 18, 21, 22, 24, 30, Nov 4, 5, 6, 13, 16,
19, 23, 29, Dec 14, 23, 26, 28, 30; 1794: HAY, Jan 3, 4, 13, 24, 27, Feb 12,
22, 24, Mar 10, 27, 29, 31, DL, Apr 21, 25, 28, 29, May 1, 5, 6, 8, 12, 16,
30, Jun 6, 9, 27, Jul 2, Sep 16, 23, 27, Oct 4, 14, 27, 28, 31, Nov 15, 18,
29, Dec 5, 6, 9, 12, 20, 30; 1795: DL, Jan 8, 13, 15, 20, 23, 24, 27, Feb 3,
10, 12, 17, 21, 28, Mar 3, 5, 21, Apr 14, 16, May 6, 26, Jun 4, Sep 19, 22,
24, Oct 1, 3, 5, 6, 8, 20, 21, 30, Nov 2, 6, 7, 10, 11, 16, 17, 19, 20, 23,
26, Dec 2, 10, 11, 14, 19, 30, 31; 1796: DL, Jan 18, 23, Feb 1, 13, 15, 27,
29, Mar 12, 17, 19, 28, Apr 2, 9, 15, 18, 25, 29, 30, May 9, 13, 17, 18, 23,
26, Jun 4, 10, 11, 13, Sep 20, 22, 24, 29, Oct 1, 3, 6, 8, 10, 11, 13, 15,
19, 22, 24, 26, 27, 28, 29, Nov 2, 5, 9, 10, 18, 22, 23, 26, 28, Dec 2, 9,
12, 16, 20, 26; 1797: DL, Jan 7, 10, 12, 17, 20, 21, 24, 27, Feb 1, 2, 3, 7,
9, 16, 18, 22, Mar 6, 20, Apr 6, 28, May 1, 2, 4, 12, 16, 23, 24, Jun 7, 13,
16, Sep 21, 23, 26, 28, 30, Oct 5, 7, 12, 14, 16, 17, 21, 24, 28, 30, Nov 2,
4, 7, 8, 9, 11, 15, 17, 18, 21, 23, 24, 25, 28, Dec 2, 8, 9, 11, 20, 21, 23,
27; 1798: DL, Jan 4, 6, 16, 23, Feb 3, 13, 16, 20, Mar 17, Apr 30, May 9, 14,
19, 21, 24, 30, Jun 6, 7, 15, 16, Sep 15, 18, 20, 22, 25, 27, 29, Oct 2, 4,
6, 9, 11, 13, 15, 16, 20, 27, 30, Nov 10, 13, 14, 16, 22, 26, 29, Dec 3, 4,
21, 27, 29; 1799: DL, Jan 2, 8, 11, 18, 19, Feb 4, 14, 19, 26, Mar 2, Apr 5,
8, 18, 19, 24, 27, May 3, 4, 20, 24, Jun 5, 18, 21, 26, 29, Jul 5, Sep 17,
19, 21, 24, 26, Oct 1, 3, 5, 7, 8, 12, 14, 17, 19, 21, 26, 29, Nov 2, 6, 8,
13, 14, 16, 22, 25, 27, 29, Dec 2, 7, 11, 14, 30; 1800: DL, Jan 1, 4, 11, 18,
21, 25, Feb 19, Mar 10, 11, 13, Apr 28, 29, May 19, Jun 11, 12, 18
Madhouse, The. See Baker, Richard.
Madman, The (burletta), 1770: MARLY, Aug 28, 30, Sep 8
Madman's Dance (dance), 1702: LIF, Dec 29
Madre non mi conosci (song), 1763: KING'S, Apr 25
Madrid Opera, 1800: KING'S, Jan 11
Madrid, 1723: RI, Sep 2
Madrigal (song), 1731: ACA, Jan 14; 1797: CG, May 23
Madrigal and Truletta. See Reed, Joseph.
Maestra, La. See Cocchi, Gioacchino.
Maestri d'Balli (dance), 1758: KING'S, Jan 10
Maestro di Cappella, Il; or, The Music Master (dance), 1754: DL, Oct 22
Maffei (author), 1757: CG, Mar 12
Maffei, Sga (singer), 1791: KING'S, Apr 16, Jun 2
Maffet (actor), 1796: HAY, Apr 27
Magalli, Sga (singer), 1760: SOHO, Feb 14, KING'S, 25, May 31
Maggot (dance), 1718: DL, Jun 13, Jul 18, Nov 7; 1733: DL, Oct 17, 19, Nov 2;
    1734: DL/HAY, Mar 30; 1738: DL, Apr 21, 22, 26, May 6, 9; 1740: DL, May 7, 15
Maggot, The. See Egleton, Mrs.
Magic Banner, The. See O'Keeffe, John.
Magic Cavern, The. See Wewitzer, Ralph.
Magic Girdle, The. See Barthelemon, Francois Hippolyte.
Magic Lanthorn (entertainment), 1775: NONE, Apr 10, MARLY, May 30, DL, Dec 25
Magic Oak, The. See Dibdin, Thomas John.
Magic Picture, The. See Bate, Henry.
Magic Scene (entertainment), 1758: DL, Apr 28, May 4, 11, 17
Magician no Conjurer, The. See Merry, Robert.
Magician of the Mountain, The. See Guerini.
Magician, The; or, Harlequin a Director (pantomime, anon), 1721: LIF, Mar 16,
    30, Apr 11, 12, 20, 22, 28, May 3, 10, Jun 8, Nov 4, 11, 18, 22, Dec 7, 21,
    26, 29; 1722: LIF, Jan 4, 5, 13, 15, 18, 19, 20, Feb 1, 10, 12, 24, 26, Mar
    1, 5, 26, 27, Apr 5, 11, 13, 19, May 1, Oct 19, 25, 29, Nov 14, Dec 8, 28;
    1723: LIF, Jan 9, 21, 25, Feb 14, Mar 28, Apr 19, Oct 14, 29, Nov 4, 5; 1724:
    LIF, Apr 30, Nov 4; 1725: LIF, Jan 16; 1780: CG, Dec 29
Magnes (musician), 1729: DL, Jul 29, Aug 9
Magnet, The (musical, anon), 1771: MARLY, Jun 27, Jul 2, 4, 6, 9, 11, 13, 16,
    20, 27, Aug 13, 15, 17, 22, 24, 27, 29, 31, Sep 5, 7, 10, 12, 17; 1772:
    MARLY, Sep 7, 10, 15; 1773: MARLY, Jul 8, Aug 5; 1774: MARLY, Jun 18
Magnetic Lady, The. See Jonson, Ben.
Magnificat (music), 1750: DL, Apr 11
Magnifique, Le (dance), 1784: KING'S, Mar 11
Magnus (actor), 1693: NONE, Sep 0; 1698: DL, Mar 0
Magnus's son, 1697: DL, Feb 0; 1698: DL/ORDG, Nov 0
Mago and Dago. See Lonsdale, Mark.
Magpie Tavern, 1744: HAY, Apr 23

Maguire (actor), 1761: CG, Sep 30, Oct 3, Nov 2, Dec 11; 1762: CG, Feb 15, May 1

Maguire, Mrs (actor), 1761: DL, Jul 2, CG, Oct 3; 1762: CG, May 1, HAY, Aug 30

Mahmoud. See Hoare, Prince.

Mahomet and Irene. See Johnson, Dr Samuel.

Mahomet the Impostor. See Miller, James.

Mahomet. See Voltaire.

Mahomet, Ach (Algerian ambassador), 1732: TC, Aug 17

Mahon (householder), 1778: DL, Apr 2; 1779: DL, Mar 23

Mahon, Gertrude (actor), 1780: CG, Dec 12; 1781: CG, Feb 14, Apr 21

Mahon, John (clarinetist), 1773: HAY, Feb 26, Mar 3, 5, 17, 24, 26; 1774: PANT, Apr 4; 1770: HAY, Feb 16, Mar 9; 1783: DL, Mar 21; 1784: DL, Mar 19, Apr 12, HAY, Aug 3, 5; 1790: CG, Feb 19; 1792: CG, Feb 24, Mar 14; 1793: CG, Feb 15; 1794: CG, Mar 7; 1795: CG, Feb 20, 27; 1796: CG, Oct 17, Nov 19; 1797: CG, Mar 3, 17; 1800: CG, Apr 2

Mahon, Mrs (actor), 1766: CG, Oct 18, Nov 18; 1767: CG, Jan 10, 21, 29, Feb 19, May 26, HAY, Aug 5, 10, 14, Sep 4, 18, 21

Mahon, Robert (actor, singer), 1767: CG, Oct 13, 20, 23, 26, 30, Nov 7, Dec 2, 14; 1768: CG, Jan 20, Feb 25, Apr 19, 30, May 13, 24, HAY, Jun 27, 29, Jul 6, 8, Aug 1, 8, 19, 24, Sep 7, CG, 24, 26, 28, Oct 5, HAY, 7, CG, 7, 10, 17, Nov 25, 26, Dec 12; 1769: CG, Feb 21, Mar 4, 16, Apr 17, 22, 25, May 1, 3, 6, 23; 1775: CG, Oct 2, 6, 17, 24, 28, Nov 13, 21, 24, Dec 1, 26; 1776: CG, Jan 12, Feb 12, 26, Mar 25, Apr 16, 27, May 6, Sep 25, Oct 7, 8, 9, 15, 25, 29, Nov 9, Dec 4, 26; 1777: CG, Jan 1, 2, 13, 25, Feb 13, 25, Mar 8, 31, Apr 23, 28, 29, May 2, 5, Sep 22, 26, Oct 1, 16, 21, 23, 29, Nov 3, 25; 1778: CG, Jan 8, 29, Feb 4, 5, 12, 26, Mar 19, 30, Apr 11, May 6, 11, 12, 15, 22, Oct 14, 23, 27, Nov 4, Dec 19; 1779: CG, Jan 1, 4, 25, Feb 3, 13, Mar 22, 27, Apr 5, 10, 12, 21, May 6, 13, 20; 1782: CG, Sep 23, 27, Oct 3, 7, 8, 9, 14, 15, 22, 28, 29, Nov 1, 2, 18, 30, Dec 14, 27, 31; 1783: CG, Jan 4, 17, Feb 19, Mar 29, May 9, 14, 19, 20, 23, Sep 22, 24, 26, Oct 3, 6, 8, 13, 14, 17, 21, Nov 6, 8, 19, Dec 5, 11; 1784: CG, Jan 7, 9, 16, 21, 24, 29, Feb 4, 9, 13, 14, 23

Mahon, Sarah (singer), 1789: CG, Mar 6, 20, 27, Apr 3; 1790: CG, Feb 19, 24, 26, Mar 3, 17, 26; 1796: CG, Oct 17

Mahon, W (musician), 1791: CG, Mar 11

Mai l'Amorio verace (song), 1746: KING'S, Mar 25

Maid in the Mill, The. See Fletcher, John.

Maid of Bath, The. See Foote, Samuel.

Maid of Honour, The. See Massinger, Phillip.

Maid of Kent, The. See Waldron, Francis Godolphin.

Maid of the Mill, The. See Bickerstaff, Isaac.

Maid of the Moor (song), 1797: DL, Apr 28

Maid of the Oaks, The. See Burgoyne, Lieutenant-General John.

Maid of the Rock (song), 1793: KING/HAY, Mar 6, 13

Maid the Mistress. See Dibdin, Charles.

Maid's Last Prayer, The. See Southerne, Thomas.

Maid's the Mistress, The. See Taverner, William; O'Keeffe, John.

Maid's Tragedy Altered, The. See Waller, Edmund.

Maid's Tragedy, The. See Fletcher, John.

Maid's Wish (song), 1740: BFLP, Aug 23, SF, Sep 9

Maiden Captain, The (play, anon), 1720: KING'S, Mar 17

Maiden fresh as a rose (song), 1693: DL, Apr 0

Maiden Lane, 1738: DL, May 17; 1750: CG, Apr 2; 1756: HAB, Dec 9; 1767: HAB, Dec 10; 1777: HAY, Aug 25; 1778: DL, Mar 31; 1795: DL, May 27; 1797: CG, May 23, Jun 9; 1798: CG, May 23

Maiden Queen. See Dryden, John, Secret Love.

Maiden Queen, The; or, The Rival Generals (play, anon), 1745: NWMF, May 13

Maiden Whim, The. See Hiffernan, Dr Paul.

Maiden's Case (song), 1729: BFRP, Aug 25

Maidens listen (song), 1794: CG, May 9

Maids have a Care (song), 1746: SFHP, Sep 8

Maidstone, 1798: CG, Nov 23

Maidwell, Lewis
--Loving Enemies, The, 1680: DG, Jan 0

Maidwell's scholar (lyricist), 1689: NONE, Aug 5

Maidwell's School, 1689: NONE, Aug 5

Maigre, Mons De la Soup (actor), 1736: HAY, Apr 29; see also Lauder

Maillard (dancer), 1726: HAY, May 3, 9

Maine, John (gallery doorkeeper), 1721: LIF, Jun 6; 1722: LIF, May 28; 1723: LIF, May 21; 1724: LIF, Jun 2; 1725: LIF, May 7; 1726: LIF, May 30; 1729: LIF, May 19; 1730: LIF, Jun 1

Mainwaring (author), 1706: DL, Mar 30

Maisonneurs Distresse (dance), 1776: KING'S, Apr 25

Maitland (beneficiary), 1720: LIF, Jun 2
Maitland, James, 8th Earl of Lauderdale (patron), 1794: DL, Jul 2
Maitland, John, Lord Lauderdale, 1660: VERE, Dec 13; 1667: BRIDGES, May 1
Maitre Etourdi, Le.   See Quinault, J B.
Majesties, Their, 1662: THAMES, Aug 23, ATCOURT, Oct 16, CITY, 29; 1664:
   BRIDGES, Jan 25; 1666: ATCOURT, Oct 18; 1667: ATCOURT, Oct 25, Nov 15; 1668:
   ATCOURT, Feb 4; 1670: ATCOURT, Apr 6; 1672: ATCOU/DG, Dec 27; 1674: ATCOURT,
   Sep 10, NONE, Dec 14; 1675: ATCOURT, Feb 2, 15, 22; 1680: DL, May 31; 1683:
   CITY, Oct 29; 1689: CITY, Oct 29; 1690: ATCOURT, Nov 4; 1691: BG, Apr 23;
   1692: CITY, Oct 29; 1693: ATCOURT, Jan 1, 2, Nov 4; 1694: ATCOURT, Jan 1, DG,
   Jun 12; 1727: DL, Nov 7, KING'S, Dec 26; 1728: DL, Mar 7, 14, KING'S, 16, DL,
   Oct 26, Dec 11; 1729: DL, Mar 6, 13, SH, 14; 1730: DL, Apr 2, Oct 28, Nov 12,
   KING'S, 17, 24, 28, Dec 1, LIF, 3, KING'S, 15, 19; 1731: KING'S, Jan 16, 23,
   Feb 13, 16, 20, 23, 27, DL, Mar 4, 18, KING'S, May 4, 8, 11, HC, Oct 18, DL,
   28, GF, 30, DL, Nov 12, KING'S, 13, 16, 23, 27, 30, Dec 7, 11, 14, 18; 1732:
   KING'S, Jan 8, 18, 22, 25, 29, Feb 15, 19, 22, 26, DL, Mar 2, KING'S, 11, 21,
   25, Apr 1, 22, 25, May 2, GF, Oct 11, LIF/CG, 28, KING'S, Nov 4, 7, 25, DL,
   30, KING'S, Dec 2, 16, 19, 26, 30; 1733: CG/LIF, Jan 4, KING'S, 13, LIF/CG,
   23, CG, 24, DL, 25, KING'S, 27, Feb 6, 20, DL, 22, KING'S, Mar 3, 17, 27, Apr
   24, May 1, 22, DL, Oct 27, KING'S, 30, Nov 13, 20, CG, 29; 1734: KING'S, Jan
   5, 12, 29, Feb 12, DL, 13, KING'S, 19, Mar 5, DL, 7, KING'S, 12, 13, GF, 15,
   CG, 21, KING'S, May 24, LIF, Jun 15, KING'S, Jul 3, 6, DL, Sep 19, CG/LIF,
   Nov 4, KING'S, Dec 10, CG, 18; 1735: DL, Jan 23, CG, 29, KING'S, Feb 1, 8,
   CG, 12, LIF, 27, CG, Mar 12, DL, May 10, CG, 14, KING'S, Oct 28, DL, Nov 5,
   8, 15, CG, 19, KING'S, 25; 1736: KING'S, Jan 24, CG, Feb 5, 23, 25, DL, Mar
   3, KING'S, May 8, CG, 12; 1737: CG, May 18, KING'S, 31, Oct 29; 1761: DL, Sep
   14, CG, 24, DL, 30, Oct 1, CG, 8, DL, 15, 22, 26, CG, 29, DL, Nov 5, KING'S,
   10, DL, 12, CG, 19, DL, 26, Dec 3, KING'S, 5, CG, 10, DL, 31; 1762: CG, Jan
   7, KING'S, 11, DL, 21, Feb 4, CG, 11, KING'S, 15, CG, 26, Mar 3, 10, 17, 24,
   31, Apr 15, DL, 29, CG, Oct 7, Nov 4, DL, 11, KING'S, 13, CG, 25, Dec 30;
   1763: KING'S, Jan 8, CG, 27, KING'S, Feb 3, DL, 7, CG, 18, KING'S, 19, CG,
   23, KING'S, 26, CG, Mar 2, 9, 16, 23, Apr 14, KING'S, May 14, CG, Oct 13, Nov
   3, 17, Dec 8, DL, 15, 29; 1764: CG, Jan 5, DL, 12, CG, 19, KING'S, 21, CG,
   Feb 23, Mar 9, 14, 21, 28, 30, Apr 4, 11, Oct 4, DL, 11, CG, 18, Nov 1, DL,
   8, KING'S, 24, Dec 1, CG, 6, KING'S, 8, DL, 13, CG, 27; 1765: KING'S, Jan 5,
   DL, 10, CG, 24, KING'S, 26, DL, Feb 14, KING'S, 16, CG, 18, 22, DL, Nov 14,
   CG, 21, KING'S, 23, DL, Dec 5, KING'S, 14, CG, 26; 1766: DL, Jan 23, KING'S,
   25, CG, Feb 14, 17, 19, KING'S, 22, CG, 26, Mar 5, DL, 6, CG, 12, 14, 19, DL,
   Apr 17, Nov 13, KING'S, 15, 18, CG, 20, KING'S, 22, DL, 27, KING'S, 29, Dec
   2, DL, 4, CG, 18, KING'S, 20; 1767: DL, Jan 1, KING'S, 6, DL, 8, CG, 15, 29,
   KING'S, 31, Feb 3, DL, 5, 12, KING'S, 14, 17, CG, 19, KING'S, 21, DL, 26, Mar
   2, CG, 6, KING'S, 7, 10, CG, 11, 13, DL, 16, CG, 18, 20, 25, 27, KING'S, 28,
   CG, Apr 1, 3, 8, 10, 23, DL, May 7, KING'S, Oct 27, DL, Dec 14; 1768: KING'S,
   Jan 9, DL, 11, CG, 14, DL, 21, CG, 25, DL, 28, KING'S, 29, CG, Feb 4, KING'S,
   6, DL, 8, CG, 11, KING'S, 13, DL, 15, CG, 19, 22, 24, 26, DL, 29, CG, Mar 2,
   4, KING'S, 5, DL, 7, CG, 9, 11, 14, 16, 18, 23, 25, KING'S, Apr 26, CG, May
   5, DL, Oct 6, CG, 13, DL, 20, KING'S, 22, Nov 5; 1769: CG, Jan 5, KING'S, 7,
   DL, 12, KING'S, 14, CG, 19, KING'S, 28, DL, Feb 9, CG, 10, 13, 15, 17, 22,
   24, Mar 1, 3, 8, 10, KING'S, 11, CG, 15, 17, Oct 19, Nov 2, KING'S, 7, CG,
   23, Dec 14; 1770: KING'S, Jan 13, DL, Mar 1, 2, 7, 9, 14, 16, 21, 23, 28, 30,
   Apr 4, 6, KING'S, 7, DL, Sep 27, CG, Oct 3, DL, 10, CG, 17, DL, 24, KING'S,
   Nov 6, 27, CG, Dec 5; 1771: KING'S, Jan 29, Feb 9, DL, 15, 20, 22, 27, Mar 1,
   6, 8, 13, 15, 20, HAY, Apr 4, DL, Oct 9, CG, 16, DL, 24, CG, 30, KING'S, Nov
   2, DL, 20, KING'S, Dec 17; 1772: KING'S, Feb 29, DL, Mar 6, KING'S, 7, DL,
   11, 13, KING'S, 14, 17, DL, 18, 20, 25, 27, Apr 1, 3, 8, 10, KING'S, May 2,
   9, 23, Jun 3, DL, Oct 21, CG, 28, KING'S, Nov 14, CG, 18, Dec 2; 1773:
   KING'S, Jan 5, 12, DL, Mar 10, 12, 17, 19, 24, 26, 31, Apr 2, KING'S, 3, DL,
   21, CG, May 5, KING'S, 11, DL, Jun 2, CG, Oct 13, 20, DL, Nov 3, CG, 10, 24,
   KING'S, Dec 4, CG, 8; 1774: CG, Jan 5, DL, Apr 13, CG, 27, DL, Jun 2, Nov 2,
   KING'S, 8, CG, 9, DL, 23, CG, 30, DL, Dec 7, KING'S, 10, CG, 14; 1775: DL,
   Jan 11, 25, KING'S, 31, CG, Feb 1, KING'S, 4, 14, DL, 15, KING'S, 18, 21, Mar
   8, DL, 10, 13, KING'S, 17, 22, 24, 29, 31, Apr 5, 7, DL, May 5, HAY, 17, DL,
   27, HAY, Jun 14, Jul 19, Aug 2, 30, Sep 13, DL, Oct 5, CG, 11, Nov 29, DL,
   Dec 6, KING'S, 12, CG, 13; 1776: DL, Jan 10, Feb 7, KING'S, 17, DL, 23, Mar
   1, CG, 4, DL, 8, 15, 22, 29, Jun 5, 10, HAY, 12, 26, Jul 10, 24, Sep 4, DL,
   Oct 9, CG, 16, DL, Nov 1, KING'S, 2, CG, 6, DL, 13, CG, 20, KING'S, 26, DL,
   Dec 4, CG, 11, DL, 18; 1777: CG, Jan 22, DL, 29, CG, Feb 5, DL, 14, 28, Mar
   7, 14, 21, Apr 9, CG, 30, DL, May 7, CG, 12, DL, 21, CG, 26, KING'S, 31, HAY,
   Oct 9, KING'S, Nov 4; 1778: KING'S, Jan 3, DL, 7, CG, 14, DL, 21, CG, 28, DL,
   Feb 11, CG, 18, DL, 25, Mar 6, CG, 9, DL, 13, 20, 27, Apr 3, 10, KING'S, 11,
   DL, May 13, CG, 25, HAY, Jun 10, 24, Sep 11, DL, Nov 18, KING'S, 24, CG, 27,
   KING'S, Dec 12; 1779: DL, Jan 11, CG, Apr 9, KING'S, 20, DL, 23, 30, CG, May

7, DL, 14, KING'S, Nov 27, DL, Dec 3, CG, 10, DL, 17; 1780: CG, Jan 14, DL,
Feb 7, 11, CG, 14, DL, 18, 25, CG, 28, DL, Mar 10, 13, 17, CG, Apr 17, 24,
May 29, Nov 6, 13, DL, 20, KING'S, 25, CG, 27, Dec 4, 28; 1781: KING'S, Jan
2, CG, 11, DL, 17, CG, 26, DL, Feb 1, CG, 8, 15, DL, Mar 2, 9, 15, 16,
KING'S, 17, DL, 23, 30, KING'S, 31, Apr 21, CG, 26, KING'S, May 5, CG, 28,
KING'S, 29, HAY, 31, Jun 14, 21, Jul 19, Aug 30, DL, Nov 8, KING'S, 17; 1782:
KING'S, Jan 1, CG, 9, KING'S, Feb 9, DL, 15, 22, KING'S, Apr 13, May 11, 17,
HAY, Jul 24, Aug 7, CG, Oct 2, DL, 24, KING'S, Nov 2, CG, 7, DL, 20, CG, 27,
KING'S, Dec 10; 1783: DL, Jan 2, 9, CG, 16, DL, 20, 23, 28, CG, Feb 3, DL,
Mar 14, 21, 28, Apr 4, 11, 12, Jun 5, HAY, Jul 2, DL, Oct 8, CG, 22, DL, Nov
5, CG, 12, DL, 19, CG, 26, KING'S, 29, DL, Dec 10; 1784: DL, Feb 27, Mar 5,
CG, 11, DL, 12, 19, KING'S, 20, DL, 26, Apr 2, CG, May 14, DL, 27, CG, Jun 2,
HAY, 9, CG, Oct 21, Nov 3, DL, 17, CG, Dec 1, DL, 15, KING'S, 18, CG, 31;
1785: CG, Jan 27, Feb 3, DL, 7, 11, CG, 17, DL, 18, 24, 25, Mar 4, 11, 12,
CG, 17, DL, 18, Apr 14, KING'S, May 17, DL, 18, HAY, Jun 1, KING'S, Jul 2,
HAY, Aug 17, DL, Sep 22, 24, CG, Oct 5, DL, Nov 2, CG, 16; 1786: DL, Jan 18,
KING'S, 24, CG, 25, DL, Feb 2, 6, CG, 13, DL, 20, CG, 27, May 19, KING'S, 23,
DL, 30, HAY, Jun 14, CG, Sep 22, DL, Oct 5, 7, CG, 19, Nov 16, DL, 30, CG,
Dec 14, KING'S, 23; 1787: DL, Feb 5, CG, 12, 19, Mar 8, KING'S, 17, DL, 22,
KING'S, May 8, 22, DL, Jun 9, CG, 15, Oct 25, DL, Nov 14, CG, 28, Dec 12;
1788: DL, Jan 2, CG, 16, 23, DL, Feb 1, KING'S, 5, CG, 14, KING'S, Apr 8, 29,
CG, Jun 9; 1789: CG, Nov 18, Dec 2, DL, 16; 1790: CG, Jan 13, Nov 17, DL, 25,
CG, Dec 1, DL, 15, CG, 29; 1791: CG, Jan 20, DL, 26, CG, Feb 7, DL, 14, CG,
21, PAN, 22, DL, 28, CG, Mar 7, PAN, 19, CG, May 13, PAN, 21, DL, Jun 4, CG,
13, HAY, 22, CG, Dec 7, 28; 1792: DLKING'S, Jan 4, CG, Feb 6, 13, DLKING'S,
20, CG, Mar 15, Jun 2, Oct 24, Nov 7, 21, Dec 5, DL, 14, CG, 19; 1793: CG,
Jan 2, 16, 23, Feb 4, Apr 15, May 29, Jun 5, HAY, 19, CG, Oct 23, Nov 6, 20,
Dec 4, 18; 1794: CG, Jan 1, 16, 22, 27, HAY, Feb 3, CG, 10, HAY, 17, CG, 24,
HAY, Mar 3, KING'S, Apr 12, CG, May 5, KING'S, Jun 3, CG, Nov 26, Dec 10, DL,
31; 1795: CG, Jan 14, Feb 16, Apr 20, 27, Oct 30; 1796: CG, Jan 21, DL, Feb
1, KING'S, Apr 26, CG, Nov 2, 16, 30, Dec 14; 1797: CG, Jan 12, 19, 25, Feb
1, 6, 13, 20, 27, May 8, Nov 3, 8, 22, Dec 6, 19, 20; 1798: CG, Jan 15, 25,
31, Feb 8, 15, 22, Mar 1, 8, 15, 29, Apr 26, Oct 24, Nov 7, 21, 28, Dec 5,
19; 1799: CG, Jan 16, 21, 28, Feb 4, Mar 7, 14, Apr 4, 11, 18, May 9, DL, Jun
5, CG, Nov 6, 20, Dec 18; 1800: CG, Jan 15, DL, 22, CG, 29, DL, Feb 6, CG,
13, DL, 20, CG, 27, DL, Mar 6, CG, 13, DL, 20, CG, 27, DL, Apr 3, CG, 24, DL,
May 1, CG, 8, DL, 15

Majesty, Her, 1663: NONE, Sep 0; 1664: NONE, Sep 0; 1675: ATCOURT, Feb 15;
1681: ATCOURT, Nov 15; 1689: DLORDG, May 28; 1692: ATCOURT, Apr 30; 1702: SH,
Jan 31, May 7; 1703: LIF, Feb 11, DL, Apr 19, HA, May 18; 1704: DL, Feb 8,
LIF, 19, DL, 29, LIF, Mar 21, DL, Apr 25, LIF, May 23, Jun 6; 1705: DL, Feb
7, LIF/QUEN, Sep 28; 1706: ATCOURT, Feb 5, YB, Dec 20; 1707: ATCOURT, Feb 6,
DL, 20, QUEEN'S, Mar 22, DL, Apr 3; 1708: DL, Jan 15, DL/QUEEN, Feb 21, SH,
Mar 26, DL, Aug 28; 1709: DL, Nov 23; 1710: DL, Feb 28, QUEEN'S, Jul 13;
1711: QUEEN'S, Feb 13, GR, Sep 8; 1712: DL, Jan 7, QUEEN'S, Mar 22; 1713: DL,
Sep 24; 1729: RI, Aug 6; 1731: DL, Mar 22, LIF, May 6; 1732: DL, Sep 8; 1733:
GF, Mar 1; 1734: CG, Jan 11; 1735: DL, Sep 15, Oct 1; 1736: GF, Jan 27, DL,
Nov 4; 1761: CG, Sep 24; 1772: KING'S, Jan 17; 1780: KING'S, Jan 18; 1789:
CG, Apr 15, KING'S, May 12; 1797: CG, Jun 21; 1798: CG, Jun 11; 1799: CG, Jun
12; 1800: CG, Jun 13

Majesty, His, 1660: CITY, Jul 5, Oct 29, ATCOURT, Nov 19; 1661: NONE, Apr 22,
VERE, Nov 26; 1662: ATCOURT, Jan 16; 1665: ATCOURT, Feb 2; 1666: ATCOURT, Nov
26; 1667: BRIDGES, Apr 22; 1668: BRIDGES, Jun 12; 1671: ORMONDS, Feb 27,
ATCOURT, Sep 19, LIF, Nov 18; 1672: CC, Nov 11; 1673: LIF, Jun 7, ATCOURT,
Aug 22, NONE, Sep 0, CITY, Oct 29; 1674: DG, Mar 17, May 16; 1675: ATCOURT,
Jul 24; 1676: ATCOURT, Jan 18, DL, Feb 14, DG, Nov 4; 1677: ATCOURT, May 22,
29; 1680: DG, Feb 2, 9; 1681: DG, Jan 29; 1682: DLORDG, Jan 10, DL, Feb 22,
Mar 2, 21, DLORDG, Jul 18; 1683: DLORDG, Sep 12; 1684: ATCOURT, Oct 29,
DLORDG, 29, MS, Nov 22; 1685: DLORDG, Jan 1; 1687: CITY, Oct 29; 1688: DL,
Apr 0; 1689: ATCOURT, Nov 4; 1691: DL, Dec 16; 1695: CITY, Oct 29; 1697: YB,
Mar 24; 1698: ATCOURT, May 13; 1699: DG, Dec 7; 1701: YB, Jun 18; 1714: DL,
Dec 13, KING'S, 30; 1715: LIF, Mar 10, 15, KING'S, Apr 2, DL, 7, KING'S, 23,
DL, Jun 3; 1717: KING'S, Feb 16, 23, Mar 16, DL, 25, KING'S, 30, DL, Apr 1,
KING'S, 4, DL, May 6, LIF, 11, NONE, Sep 13; 1718: NONE, Aug 29, HC, Sep 23,
DL, 24, HC, Oct 1, DL, 7, 14, 17, 24, Nov 22, LIF, 26; 1719: DL, Mar 30, Apr
6, 20, 22, LIF, 25, DL, Dec 14; 1720: DL, Jan 23, Mar 3, 17, Apr 4, KING'S,
5, LIF, 9, KING'S, May 11, Dec 28; 1721: LIF, Mar 4, May 8, DL, 18, Nov 21;
1722: HAY, Apr 10; 1723: KING'S, Jan 12, Feb 9, 23, DL, Mar 18, LIF, Apr 20,
KING'S, May 27; 1724: KING'S, Feb 20; 1726: LIF, Mar 17, KING'S, May 5, Sep
28, Oct 5, 21, 28, Nov 1, 5, 7, 12, 16, 19, 23, 26, 30, Dec 3, 7, 10, 14, 17,
21, 28, 31; 1727: KING'S, Jan 4, 12, 16, 25, Feb 9, 16, Mar 2, 9, 16, 23, Apr
6, 8, 25, LIF, May 10, DL, Sep 28; 1728: DL, Nov 13, 20, 30, Dec 11; 1729:

DL, Jan 28, Feb 5, Oct 28, Nov 12, 19, 26; 1730: KING'S, Mar 21; 1731: DL,
Jan 13, LIF, Mar 25, GF, Apr 23, 26, LIF, May 25, HAY, Aug 20, GF, Oct 11,
DL, 30; 1732: DL, Sep 27, GF, Oct 2, 11, LIF/CG, 28, GF, 30, DL, Nov 24;
1733: KING'S, Mar 17, DL, May 28, DL/HAY, Sep 26; 1734: DL, Sep 19, CG/LIF,
Nov 4, DL, 15; 1735: DL, Sep 1; 1737: CG, May 18; 1738: HAY, Oct 9; 1739: CG,
Jan 20, DL, Feb 10, CG, 14, Oct 27; 1740: HAY, Feb 9, CG, 12, HAY, Mar 15,
CG, Apr 12, HAY, 15, May 10, CG, Oct 25; 1741: CG, Feb 14, DL, Mar 5, KING'S,
Oct 31, DL, Dec 3; 1742: CG, Mar 4, KING'S, Nov 2, DL, 13; 1744: DL, Sep 15,
HAY, Nov 8; 1745: DL, Apr 22, 27, Sep 28, LIF, Oct 7; 1746: KING'S, Jan 7,
DL, Jun 3, KING'S, Nov 4, DL, Dec 3; 1747: CG, Jan 13, DL, Feb 11, CG, 17,
DL, Oct 28, KING'S, Nov 14, DL, Dec 9; 1748: DL, Jan 8, Nov 30, KING'S, Dec
17, DL, 21, KING'S, 31; 1749: DL, Jan 5, Mar 1, Oct 28, Nov 1, HAY, 22, Dec
21, DL, 22; 1750: CG, Feb 14, DL, Mar 10, 17; 1751: DL, Jan 17, Oct 28, Nov
29, Dec 18, CG, 20; 1752: CG, Jan 14, Feb 22, SF, Sep 16, DL, Dec 2, CG, 2;
1753: CG, Jan 17, Feb 6, DL, Nov 8, KING'S, 13; 1754: CG, Mar 2, SFH, Sep 19,
KING'S, Nov 9, CG, 9; 1755: CG, Jan 4, KING'S, 25; 1756: DL, Nov 8, KING'S,
Dec 11; 1757: DL, May 7, CG, Nov 29; 1758: KING'S, Nov 11; 1760: CG, Dec 2,
19, DL, 23; 1761: DL, Jan 16, 20, 23, CG, Feb 11, DL, 19, CG, Mar 3, DL, Apr
15, May 12, 28, KING'S, Jun 3, CG, Sep 24; 1762: KING'S, Jun 5; 1763: KING'S,
Nov 26; 1766: DL, Jan 23, KING'S, Oct 21; 1767: DL, Mar 26, Sep 28, CG, 28;
1768: CG, May 13, DL, 13; 1769: CG, Jun 6; 1771: CG, Jun 6; 1773: DL, Feb 26;
1774: KING'S, Jan 17; 1776: DL, Jun 5, HAY, 12; 1786: CG, Jun 5; 1788: DL,
Jun 13; 1789: DL, Feb 27, May 19; 1790: CG, Feb 19, DL, Apr 23; 1791: PAN,
Feb 17, KING'S, Mar 26, PAN, Jun 3; 1792: DLKING'S, Jan 30; 1793: KING/HAY,
Feb 15, KING'S, Jun 4; 1794: KING'S, May 15, CG, Jun 4, 17, KING'S, 23; 1796:
CG, Feb 12, DL, May 16, HAY, Sep 16, 17; 1797: KING'S, Mar 11, DL, May 23,
CG, Jun 13; 1798: CG, Feb 28, Oct 15; 1799: HAY, Sep 16; 1800: CG, Mar 29,
Jun 6
Major, J (printer), 1755: DL, Nov 18
Major, Miss (actor), 1745: GF, Nov 4; 1747: GF, Feb 10, 20
Majorano, Gaetano (singer), 1737: KING'S, Oct 29; 1738: KING'S, Jan 3, 28, Mar
14
Make haste, my shepherd, come away (song), 1676: DG, Jul 3
Malade Imaginaire, Le. See Moliere.
Malbrough (dance), 1784: CG, May 8, Jun 2
Male Coquette, The. See Garrick, David.
Male, George (actor, dancer), 1796: DL, Dec 26; 1797: DL, Feb 16, Dec 21; 1798:
DL, Jan 16, Feb 20, May 16, 21, Oct 6, Nov 14, Dec 5
Male, Miss (dancer), 1735: YB/HAY, Sep 17, Oct 1; 1736: CG, Jan 23, LIF, Apr
16, CG, May 17, Nov 23; 1737: CG, May 3
Malin (water bailiff), 1662: THAMES, Aug 23
Mall, The. See Dover, John.
Mallet, David, 1731: DL, Feb 22, 23; 1739: DL, Feb 13; 1745: DL, Mar 20; 1751:
DL, Feb 23, Mar 8; 1755: DL, May 9; 1759: DL, Mar 3; 1762: DL, Nov 26; 1763:
DL, Jan 19; 1767: DL, Apr 9
--Alfred the Great, 1745: DL, Mar 20, Apr 3, 25; 1746: DL, May 12; 1751: DL,
Feb 21, 23, 25, 26, 28, Mar 2, 4, 5, 6, 7, 8, 9, 12, Apr 17, 19; 1753:
KING'S, May 12; 1754: DL, Mar 27, CG, Apr 26, May 3; 1755: DL, Mar 19; 1759:
CG, Feb 2, DL, Mar 23, 30, CG, May 12; 1760: CG, Mar 27; 1761: KING'S, Mar
12; 1762: DL, Mar 17, CG, 23; 1773: DL, Oct 6, 9, 11, 12, 13, 15, 16, 18, 21,
25, Nov 1, 6, 9, 25, Dec 28
--Britannia (masque), 1755: DL, May 9, 10, 14, 16, 21, 27; 1756: DL, Feb 10,
19, Mar 30; 1757: DL, May 11; 1758: DL, May 2, 8
--Elvira, 1762: DL, Nov 26; 1763: DL, Jan 19, 20, 21, 22, 24, 25, 26, 27, 28,
29, Feb 1, 17, 24, Mar 8
--Eurydice, 1731: DL, Feb 22, 23, 24, 25, 26, 27, Mar 1, 2, 4, 6, 9, 11, 13,
Apr 26; 1759: DL, Mar 3, 6, 10, 13, 17
--Mustapha, 1739: DL, Feb 13, 14, 15, 16, 17, 19, 20, 21, 22, 24, 27, 28, Mar
1, 3
Mallet, Elizabeth (spectator), 1667: LIF, Feb 4; see also Wilmot, Elizabeth
Mallet
Mallicoe (singer), 1772: KING'S, Apr 25
Mallin (actor), 1744: HAY, Jun 29
Malloin, Miss (actor), 1728: HAY, Feb 21
Malme (house servant), 1768: CG, Dec 29; 1774: CG, Jan 14
Malone (actor), 1732: TC, Aug 4; 1741: TC, Aug 4; 1743: TCD/BFTD, Aug 4, SF,
Sep 8; 1745: NWC, Dec 30; 1746: HIC, Mar 10, 14, SFW, Sep 8; 1748: DL, Apr
23, NWC, Dec 26, 29; 1749: SOU, Jan 9, NWLS, Feb 27, BFC, Aug 23; 1750: SFYW,
Sep 7
Malone, Edmond (author), 1747: CG, Feb 12
Malone, Mrs (actor), 1743: TCD/BFTD, Aug 4
Malpas, Lord (spectator), 1731: DL, Dec 8

Malta, 1727: KING'S, Mar 2, Apr 6
Malter (dancer), 1733: CG, Nov 8, 13, 26, 28, 29, 30, Dec 1, 3, 8, 10, 12, 15,
    17, 20, 22, 28, 29, 31; 1734: CG, Jan 2, 3, 4, 7, 9, 10, 11, 12, 14, Feb 14,
    18, 22, 26, Mar 5, 7, 11, 12, 16, 18, 19, 21, 25, 28, Apr 1, 2, 16, 17, 18,
    19, 22, 26, 27, 30, May 1, 2, 3, 4, 6, 7, 14, GF/HAY, Nov 20, HAY, Dec 13,
    23, GF/HAY, 27, 30; 1735: GF/HAY, Mar 3, HAY, 19, May 9, GF, 23; 1740: DL,
    Nov 4, 6, 10, 11, 12, 17, 18, Dec 4, 10, 26, 27; 1741: DL, Jan 1, 6, 7, 9,
    15, 21, 23, 24, 29, Feb 3, 7, 19, Mar 7, 14, 17, 21, 30, 31, Apr 2, 6, 7, 8,
    9, 17, 18, 20, 21, 24, 27, 28, 30, May 1, 2, 4, 5, 9, 14, 15, 21, 22, 23, 25,
    26, 27, 28
Malter (Maltair), Master (dancer), 1749: DL, Dec 19, 20; 1750: DL, Jan 6, 24,
    Feb 14, Mar 17, Apr 26, 28, May 1
Malter, Mlle (dancer), 1734: GF/HAY, Dec 2, HAY, 13, 23, GF/HAY, 27, 30; 1735:
    GF/HAY, Jan 16, HAY, Apr 16, May 9, GF, 23; 1740: DL, Nov 4, 6, 10, 11, 12,
    17, 18, Dec 4, 10, 26, 27; 1741: DL, Jan 1, 6, 7, 9, 15, 21, 23, 24, 29, Feb
    3, 7, 19, Mar 7, 14, 17, 21, 30, 31, Apr 2, 6, 7, 8, 9, 14, 17, 18, 20, 21,
    24, 27, 28, 30, May 1, 2, 4, 9, 14, 15, 21, 22, 23, 25, 26, 27, 28
Malter, Mr and Mlle (actors), 1735: GF/HAY, Jan 8; 1740: DL, Nov 3
Malthus, Daniel (landlord), 1767: DL, Jan 9; 1772: DL, Feb 4; 1773: DL, Jan 22;
    1774: DL, Jan 14; 1775: DL, Feb 24; 1776: DL, Feb 9
Malton, Thomas (scene painter), 1790: CG, Dec 20; 1793: CG, Dec 19; 1794: DL,
    Apr 21, Jun 9, CG, Sep 22
Mamamouchi. See Ravenscroft, Edward.
Man and Wife. See Colman the elder, George.
Man is for the woman made (song), 1695: DL, Sep 0
Man Milliner, The. See O'Keeffe, John.
Man of Business, The. See Colman the elder, George.
Man of Mode, The. See Etherege, Sir George.
Man of Newmarket, The. See Howard, Edward.
Man of Parts, The. See Jackman, Isaac.
Man of Quality, The. See Lee, John.
Man of Reason, The. See Kelly, Hugh.
Man of Taste, The. See Miller, James.
Man of Ten Thousand, The. See Holcroft, Thomas.
Man of the World, The. See Macklin, Charles.
Man of War and Sea Fight (entertainment), 1761: DL, Apr 24; 1762: DL, May 19;
    1771: DL, Apr 5, 17; 1772: DL, Apr 27, Jun 3; 1779: DL, May 25
Man, Boy and Ass (entertainment), 1790: CG, Apr 16; 1799: DL, Apr 24
Man, Henry, 1780: CG, Apr 21
--Elders, The (farce), 1780: CG, Apr 21, May 1, 3, 5
Man's Bewitched, The. See Centlivre, Susannah.
Man's the Master, The. See Davenant, Sir William.
Managed Horse (entertainment), 1703: YB, Jul 27
Management. See Reynolds, Frederick.
Manager an Actor in Spite of Himself, The. See Bonnor, Charles, Tran
    sformation.
Manager in Distress, The. See Colman the elder, George.
Manasseh. See Worgan, James.
Manby, R (printer), 1751: DL, Nov 26
Manchester Square, 1791: PAN, Jun 2
Manchester Theatre, 1777: DL, Apr 26, HAY, Jun 9; 1780: DL, Oct 17; 1783: HAY,
    Jul 4; 1788: DL, Nov 10; 1792: CG, Mar 10; 1798: HAY, Aug 14, DL, Nov 17
Manchester, Duke of (spectator), 1729: DL, Nov 1
Manchester, Earl of. See Montagu, Edward.
Manchester, 1737: LIF, Mar 9; 1783: DL, Dec 22; 1784: DL, Jan 10, Apr 24; 1785:
    DL, Mar 8; 1786: DL, Feb 18; 1787: DL, Mar 29; 1792: DLKING'S, Apr 28, CG,
    Nov 2; 1795: DL, Apr 27; 1796: HAY, Sep 28; 1799: CG, Apr 16
Mancini, Francesco (composer), 1701: DL, Jan 31; 1710: QUEEN'S, Mar 23; 1720:
    LIF, Feb 5
--Hydaspes (opera), 1710: QUEEN'S, Mar 2, 6, 16, 23, 25, 30, Apr 1, 12, 15, 18,
    21, 28, May 2, 5, 12, 23, 30, Nov 22, 25, 29, Dec 2, 20, 22, 27; 1711:
    QUEEN'S, Feb 7, 10, 17, 20, Apr 4, 7, 28, May 30, Jun 2, Nov 21, 24, Dec 5,
    8, 26; 1712: QUEEN'S, Jan 12, 17, Feb 20, Mar 27, 29, Apr 26, SML, May 21,
    QUEEN'S, 31; 1715: KING'S, May 7, 11, 14, 21, Jun 2, Jul 23, Aug 27; 1716:
    KING'S, May 9
Mancini, Rosa (singer), 1743: KING'S, Nov 15; 1744: KING'S, Jan 3, 31, Mar 28,
    Apr 3, 24
Mandajors de Ours, Jean Pierre
--Arlequin Vale de Deux Maitres, 1791: CG, Feb 16
Mandane. See Brevio.
Mandelitta (music), 1707: HIC, Apr 2
Mandolin Concerto (music), 1728: HIC, May 15; 1768: HAY, Mar 3

Manesiere, Louisa (dancer), <u>1761</u>: CG, Oct 31, Dec 10; <u>1762</u>: CG, Jan 28, Feb 12,
    Mar 22, 27, Apr 19, Oct 8, 23, Nov 24, 25; <u>1763</u>: CG, Jan 26, Feb 24, Mar 8,
    Apr 8, May 16, 20, Oct 5, 14, Nov 1, 15, Dec 22; <u>1764</u>: CG, Jan 20, Mar 20,
    May 3, Oct 1, 4, Nov 1, 7, Dec 12; <u>1765</u>: CG, Jan 31, Mar 7, 11, Apr 18, Oct
    12, 19, 22, Nov 15, 26, Dec 6; <u>1766</u>: CG, Mar 11, Oct 8, 10, Nov 18, 20, 21,
    Dec 15; <u>1767</u>: CG, Jan 13, Feb 14, 21, Apr 11, 27, May 2, Sep 21, Oct 5, 8,
    12, 16, 21, 30, Nov 6, 16, 19, 23, Dec 9; <u>1768</u>: CG, Mar 7, 8, Apr 16, May 13,
    24, Sep 19, 26, 30, Oct 4, 10, 28, Nov 1, Dec 12; <u>1769</u>: CG, Mar 14, Apr 8,
    27, Sep 18, 25, 29, Oct 5, 6, Nov 4, 10, 23, Dec 7, 15; <u>1770</u>: CG, Jan 27, Mar
    29, 31, Apr 2, 20, May 1, Oct 1, 3, 9, 15, 24, Nov 3, 16, Dec 1, 5, 26; <u>1771</u>:
    CG, Jan 1, Feb 21, Apr 12, 23, 24, May 28, Sep 27, Oct 9, 15, 16, 25, 30, Nov
    4, 12, Dec 17, 21; <u>1772</u>: CG, Feb 25, Mar 12, 23, 26, 28, Apr 6, 24, May 1,
    Oct 16, Nov 2, 6, 17, 24, Dec 7, 26; <u>1773</u>: CG, Feb 6, Mar 20, Apr 24, 26, May
    19, 26; <u>1774</u>: CG, Apr 15
Manessier (oboist), <u>1798</u>: HAY, Jan 15
Mangora, King of the Timbusians. See Moore, Thomas.
Manina, Sga (singer), <u>1712</u>: QUEEN'S, May 17; <u>1713</u>: QUEEN'S, Jan 10, Apr 25, May
    6; <u>1714</u>: QUEEN'S, May 1, Jun 23; <u>1720</u>: LIF, Dec 23
Manley, Mary, <u>1696</u>: LIF, Apr 0, DL, Sep 0; <u>1706</u>: QUEEN'S, Dec 16; <u>1717</u>: DL, May
    11; <u>1720</u>: DL, Feb 20, Apr 27
--Almyna; or, The Arabian Vow, <u>1706</u>: QUEEN'S, Dec 16, 17, 18
--Double Mistress, The; or, 'Tis Well 'Tis No Worse, <u>1720</u>: DL, Feb 20
--Lost Lover, The; or, The Jealous Husband, <u>1696</u>: DL, Mar 0
--Lucius, the First Christian King of Britain, <u>1717</u>: DL, May 11, 13, 18; <u>1720</u>:
    DL, Apr 27
--Royal Mischief, The, <u>1696</u>: LIF, Apr 0, DL, Sep 0
Manly (actor), <u>1742</u>: JS, May 31; <u>1743</u>: JS, Jan 5
Mann, Horace (correspondent), <u>1741</u>: KING'S, Oct 31, Nov 10, Dec 22; <u>1742</u>: DL,
    May 6, KING'S, 25; <u>1743</u>: CG, Feb 23, KING'S, Apr 19, Aug 14; <u>1745</u>: DL, Mar
    28; <u>1746</u>: DL, Dec 5; <u>1748</u>: DL, Feb 16, 25; <u>1773</u>: CG, Mar 19
Mann, James (renter), <u>1758</u>: CG, Mar 2
Mann, Mary (actor), <u>1728</u>: HAY, Aug 9, BFHM, 24, HAY, Oct 15, 26, Nov 14, 19;
    <u>1729</u>: HAY, Feb 25, Mar 27, 29, Apr 8, May 26, 29, Jun 14, Jul 23, BFR, Aug
    25, SF, Sep 8, SOU, 23, HAY, Nov 29; <u>1732</u>: HAY, Mar 8, Jun 1, DL, Nov 17, Dec
    6, 11, 14, 18, 26; <u>1733</u>: DL, Jan 23, 29, Feb 12, Mar 26, 28, 31, Apr 6, 16,
    20, May 7, HAY, Jul 26, BFCGBH, Aug 23, Sep 4, DL/HAY, 26, Oct 3, 5, 6, 8,
    10, 12, 15, 19, 20, 22, 24, 25, 27, Nov 1, 8, 9, 14, 15, HAY, 19, DL/HAY, 23,
    24, 26, 27, 28, Dec 1, 5, 10, HAY, 13, DL/HAY, 19, 20, 22, HAY, 26, DL/HAY,
    28, 31; <u>1734</u>: DL/HAY, Jan 2, 4, 7, 12, 16, 23, 28, 29, Feb 4, 6, 20, Mar 4,
    9, 12, 16, 19, 25, Apr 1, 2, DL, 4, DL/HAY, 6, DL, 15, DL/HAY, 17, 18, DL,
    25, DL/HAY, 26, 27, DL, 29, DL/HAY, May 1, LIF, 9, DL, 13, 16, LIF, 23, HAY,
    27, LIF, 29, JS, 31, BFRLCH, Aug 24, Sep 2, DL, 7, 10, 12, 19, 24, 26, Oct 3,
    5, 8, 21, 23, 25, 26, 28, Nov 1, 16, 20, 22, Dec 9, 11, 14, 17, 21, 26, 28,
    31; <u>1735</u>: DL, Jan 1, 11, 17, 18, 20, 21, Feb 4, 13, 14, 17, 18, 22, 27, Mar
    3, 6, 10, 27, Apr 7, 11, 14, 25, 28, May 8, 14, 29, Jun 3, 11, LIF, Jul 16,
    Aug 6, 25, DL, Sep 9, 15, 30, Oct 1, 2, 7, 22, 30, Nov 3, 6, 7, 13, 15, 17,
    19, 20, 25, Dec 6, 18, 27; <u>1736</u>: DL, Jan 3, 12, Feb 5, 12, 13, 14, 28, Mar 3,
    11, 22, 23, 25, 27, Apr 8, 10, 12, LIF, 14, DL, 15, 16, 29, 30, May 4, 11,
    14, 20, 21, Sep 7, 25, 30, Oct 2, 5, 9, 12, 22, 29, Nov 2, 13, 17, 23, Dec 4,
    9, 10, 17, 20, 31; <u>1737</u>: DL, Jan 27, Feb 14, Mar 4, Apr 27, 28, 29, May 4,
    20; <u>1738</u>: DL, Sep 16, 23, Oct 3, 10, 16, 21, 26, 27, 30, Dec 7, 15; <u>1739</u>: DL,
    Jan 26, Feb 5, 7, Mar 10, Apr 14, May 28; <u>1740</u>: BFLP, Aug 23, DL, Oct 14, 27,
    Nov 17, Dec 26; <u>1741</u>: DL, Nov 11, Dec 4; <u>1744</u>: DL, Jan 5, 17, Feb 1, Mar 15,
    Apr 19, Oct 17, 24, 30, Nov 7, 10; <u>1746</u>: DL, Apr 25
Mann, Mrs, <u>1772</u>: DL, Jun 10
Manners, John, Earl of Rutland (Lord Roos), <u>1675</u>: BF, Sep 3; <u>1676</u>: CITY, Oct
    30; <u>1677</u>: DL, Jan 19
Manners, Katherine, Countess of Rutland (Lady Roos), <u>1676</u>: NONE, Sep 0; <u>1681</u>:
    DLORDG, Dec 18; <u>1682</u>: DG, Jan 25, Aug 4; <u>1685</u>: DLORDG, Jan 1, DL, Dec 26,
    DLORDG, 30, OLDFIELD, 30; <u>1686</u>: NONE, Jan 7, DLORDG, 23, ATCOURT, 27, DL, Feb
    4, DLORDG, 6, 11, ATCOURT, 16, DG, Mar 6; <u>1688</u>: DL, May 12
Manning (justice), <u>1738</u>: HAY, Oct 9
Manning (merchant), <u>1772</u>: DL, Dec 14
Manning, Francis, <u>1696</u>: LIF, Jul 0; <u>1702</u>: DL, Nov 0
--All for the Better; or, The Infallible Cure, <u>1702</u>: DL, Nov 0
--Generous Choice, The, <u>1700</u>: LIF, Feb 0
Manning, William (steward), <u>1797</u>: KING'S, May 18, CG, Jun 14
Mannington (beneficiary), <u>1710</u>: DL, Apr 20
Mansel St, <u>1733</u>: GF, Apr 2
Mansel, Elizabeth (actor), <u>1795</u>: CG, Oct 8, Nov 7, 27; <u>1796</u>: CG, Mar 14, 30,
    31, Apr 8, 19, 23, 28, May 21, 24, Sep 12, 17, 30, Oct 5, 6, 21, 25, 26, Nov
    7, Dec 9, 21, 22, 26, 29, 30, 31; <u>1797</u>: CG, Jan 27, 28, Feb 18, 20, 23, Apr

8, 29, May 9, 16, 17, 31, Jun 1, Sep 18, 22, 27, 29, Oct 12, 13, 16, 23, 31, Nov 3, 18, 20, Dec 12, 18, 28; 1798: CG, Feb 6, Mar 31, Apr 13, 17, 19, May 15, 23, 24, Jun 5, Sep 19, 21, Oct 1, 31, Nov 7, 9, 17, 22, 23, Dec 8; 1799: CG, Jan 25, Mar 14, 28, Apr 10

Mansel, Robert (actor), 1798: CG, Sep 19, Nov 9, 17, 23; 1799: CG, Feb 7, DL, 26, CG, Mar 14, Apr 6, 9, 23, May 6, 14, Sep 23, 25, 30, Oct 7, 14, 18, 24, 25, Nov 7, Dec 30; 1800: CG, Jan 18, 29, Mar 27, Apr 5, May 12, 13

Mansell, Mary (actor), 1772: DL, Sep 26, Oct 1, 10, 16, 23, 31, Nov 3, 4, 9, 16, 21, Dec 26; 1773: DL, Jan 13, 16, 23, Feb 27, Apr 16, May 14, 19

Mansfield St, 1733: GF, Mar 28; 1741: GF, Dec 2; 1742: GF, Mar 18

Mansfield, Lord, 1773: CG, Nov 18

Manship (musician), 1701: YB, Mar 26; 1709: HA, Jul 30, Sep 3, GO, Nov 21, SH, 30; 1710: SH, Mar 22, YB, Apr 17

Mansill (actor), 1792: HAY, Feb 6

Mansion of Peace (song), 1785: DL, May 3; 1790: CG, Mar 3, 10; 1791: CG, Mar 18, Apr 15; 1792: CG, Mar 7, 14, 21, 23; 1793: KING/HAY, Feb 15, Mar 20; 1794: DL, Apr 4, 11

Manstead (actor), 1778: HAY, Apr 29

Mantagnana, Antonio (singer), 1732: KING'S, Mar 25; 1737: KING'S, Feb 12

Mantelli (musician), 1719: YB, Dec 19

Manual Exercise (entertainment), 1782: HAY, Mar 4; 1783: HAY, Aug 15; 1784: DL, Apr 12; 1795: DL, May 20, 22

Manuche, Cosmo
--Feast, The, 1664: NONE, Sep 0

Manuel, Mrs (actor), 1667: BRIDGES, Aug 12

Manwayring, Arthur (author), 1693: DL, Mar 0

Many rend the skies (song), 1789: CG, Mar 20; 1790: DL, Feb 24, CG, Mar 3; 1791: DL, Mar 11, CG, 25; 1792: KING'S, Feb 29, CG, Mar 7, KING'S, 7; 1793: CG, Mar 20; 1794: CG, Mar 14, DL, 26, Apr 4, 11; 1795: KING'S, Mar 13; 1798: CG, Mar 28; 1799: CG, Mar 1

Manziotti, Antonio (singer), 1763: KING'S, Nov 26

Manzoletto (singer), 1775: KING'S, Oct 31; 1779: KING'S, Jan 23, Feb 23, Jul 3, Nov 27, Dec 14; 1780: KING'S, Jan 22, Mar 9, Apr 13, May 9, 25, Nov 25, 28, Dec 23; 1781: KING'S, Jan 23, Mar 29, Apr 5, May 1, Nov 17, Dec 11; 1782: KING'S, Jan 10, 12, Mar 7, 16, May 25

Manzoli, Giovanni (singer), 1764: KING'S, Nov 24; 1765: KING'S, Jan 26, Mar 2, 7, 21, 28

Mapp, Mrs (bone-setter), 1736: LIF, Oct 16

Mapples, Mrs John (singer), 1778: HAY, Feb 9, Sep 7

Maquignons (dance), 1742: CG, Mar 9, 13, 15, 18, 22

Mara, Gertrude Elizabeth, Mme Giovanni Battista (actor, singer), 1786: KING'S, Feb 14, Mar 7, 21, Apr 6, May 4, 25, Jun 13, Dec 23; 1787: KING'S, Jan 20, DL, Feb 23, KING'S, Mar 1, DL, 7, 9, KING'S, 15, 22, DL, 28, KING'S, 29, DL, 30, KING'S, Apr 17, May 1, Jun 5; 1788: DL, Feb 8, 20, 22, Mar 5, 12, 14, Apr 7, May 28; 1790: HAY, Apr 6, 29, May 28, 29; 1791: PAN, Feb 17, Apr 14, Jun 2, DLKING'S, Nov 17, 19, 21; 1792: DLKING'S, May 23, Jun 11, DL, Nov 10; 1793: KING'S, Feb 5, CG, 15, 20, 22, Mar 1, 6, 8, 13, KING'S, 19, CG, 22, DL, May 23, KING'S, Jun 11; 1794: CG, Mar 7, 12, 14, 21, 26; 1796: CG, Feb 24, 26, Mar 2, 11, 16, Apr 30, May 25, DL, Jun 9; 1797: CG, Mar 3, 10, 15, 17, 22, 24, 31, Oct 25, Nov 9, 15, 21, Dec 5; 1798: KING'S, Jan 31, CG, Feb 23, 28, Mar 2, 9, 14, 28, 30, Apr 21, 23, 25, May 10, 14, 17; 1799: CG, Feb 8, 13, 15, 20, Mar 1, 13, 15; 1800: DL, Mar 11, CG, Apr 2, Jun 16

Mara, Giovanni Battista (violoncellist), 1787: KING'S, Mar 1, DL, 21; 1788: DL, Feb 22; 1792: DLKING'S, May 23, DL, Nov 12; 1796: CG, Feb 12

Maranesi, Casimo (dancer), 1752: CG, Oct 10, 28, Dec 2, 4, 19; 1753: CG, Feb 6, 14, Mar 31, Apr 30, Oct 20, Dec 10; 1754: CG, Mar 2, 7, 14, 19, 25, 26, 30, Apr 29, May 22, KING'S, Nov 9; 1755: KING'S, Mar 18; 1756: KING'S, Apr 6; 1758: KING'S, Apr 4; 1759: KING'S, Nov 13; 1760: KING'S, Jan 15, Mar 1, Apr 17, May 31, CG, Sep 22, Oct 10, 25, Nov 19, 28, Dec 15, 18; 1761: CG, Jan 2, 3, 10, 24, Mar 9, Apr 16, 21, 23, 29, May 1, 4, 8, 13, 14, 25, Sep 14, 21, 25, Oct 1, 12, Dec 10; 1762: CG, Jan 7, Feb 2, Apr 19, 21, 22, 23, Sep 22, Oct 1, Nov 1, Dec 8; 1765: KING'S, Dec 3

Maranesi, Sg and Sga (dancers), 1760: CG, Oct 11, 13, 14, 25; 1761: CG, Sep 18; 1762: CG, Apr 21, 27, Oct 19; 1763: CG, Jan 26

Maranesi, Sga Casimo (dancer), 1760: CG, Sep 22, Oct 10, 20, Nov 19; 1761: CG, May 25, Sep 25, Oct 1, 8, 13; 1762: CG, Jan 28, Apr 27, Oct 8, Nov 1, 5; 1763: CG, Apr 22

Marcadet (dancer), 1797: KING'S, Jan 17, Feb 7

Marcelia. See Boothby, Frances.

Marcella. See Hayley, William.

Marcelle (dancer), 1732: LIF, Apr 13

Marcello, Benedetto (composer), 1763: CG, Mar 4; 1792: KING'S, Mar 14

March (music), 1736: DL, May 7, 25, 28, Oct 23; 1737: DL, May 27; 1751: HAY,
    Dec 27; 1752: CT/HAY, Jan 7, 14, 31; 1786: DL, Mar 22, CG, Apr 18; 1789: DL,
    Mar 18, CG, 20; 1790: DL, Feb 26, Mar 17, CG, 17; 1791: DL, Mar 23; 1792:
    KING'S, Feb 24, CG, Mar 14; 1793: CG, Feb 22, KING/HAY, 22, CG, Mar 20; 1794:
    CG, Mar 14; 1795: CG, Mar 4; 1796: CG, Mar 16; 1797: CG, Mar 15, 31; 1798:
    CG, Mar 30; 1799: CG, Feb 8, 20, Mar 15; 1800: CG, Mar 19
March, Grand (music), 1758: HAY, Mar 13; 1794: CG, May 2; 1799: CG, Mar 1
Marchand de Smyrne, Le (dance), 1798: KING'S, Dec 26; 1799: KING'S, Jan 1, Feb
    2, 12
Marchesa Giardiniera, La. See Anfossi, Pasquale.
Marchese Tulipano, Il. See Paisiello, Giovanni.
Marchesi, Luigi (singer), 1788: KING'S, Apr 5, May 8, 29; 1789: KING'S, Jan 24,
    Feb 7, 28, Apr 2, 4, 30, Jun 2; 1790: HAY, Apr 6, 29, May 28, 29
Marchesini, Maria Antonia (Antonia, Marie) (singer), 1737: KING'S, Apr 25, 26,
    May 24, Oct 29; 1738: KING'S, Jan 3, 28, Mar 14; 1739: CG, Mar 10
Marchetti (singer), 1773: KING'S, Oct 23, Dec 7; 1774: KING'S, Jan 11, Mar 8,
    Apr 19, HIC, May 9, KING'S, 17, Jun 3
Marchi, Antonio (librettist), 1735: CG, Apr 16
Marcucci, Sga (dancer), 1764: KING'S, Jan 10, Feb 21
Mardette, Mrs (dancer), 1740: DL, Dec 4
Mareis, Pasqualino de (musician), 1736: CG, Feb 19
Marella (musician), 1755: HAY, Jan 29, Feb 13; 1756: HAY, Mar 25
Mareschi, Sga (singer), 1757: KING'S, Mar 24, May 31
Marforio (farce, anon), 1736: CG, Apr 10
Margaret of Anjou. See Jerningham, Edward.
Margaret St, 1746: HIC, Mar 10; 1782: KING'S, May 9, 23; 1783: CG, Feb 14;
    1795: DL, May 1; 1796: DL, May 11; 1797: DL, May 18
Margaret's Ghost Appearing to William (song), 1728: LIF, May 3
Margarita, Sga (singer), 1707: DL, Apr 1, HIC, 2, DL, May 13, DL/QUEEN, Dec 6,
    DL, 18; 1708: QUEEN'S, Dec 14; 1710: QUEEN'S, Mar 18; 1712: QUEEN'S, May 17,
    Dec 10; 1713: QUEEN'S, Apr 25, May 6; 1714: QUEEN'S, Jan 27, Mar 4, May 1,
    29, Jun 23; 1715: DL, Oct 20, Nov 1, 15, 18; 1716: DL, Jan 12; 1717: LIF, Jan
    2; 1718: YB, Mar 5; 1719: LIF, Mar 5, CGR, 18, LIF, Apr 9, 11, 16, 25, May
    12, 28; 1722: HIC, Mar 8; 1723: HAY, Mar 13
Margate Theatre, 1788: CG, Oct 22; 1789: CG, Nov 13; 1795: DL, Jan 22; 1796:
    DL, Oct 27; 1797: DL, Nov 10, HAY, Dec 4
Margate, 1788: CG, Oct 22; 1789: DL, Sep 19, Dec 10
Margery. See Carey, Henry.
Margherita, Sga (singer), 1733: DL, May 21
Maria; or, The Beggar Girl (song), 1799: CG, Jun 7
Maria, Joanna (singer), 1703: DL, Jan 23, Feb 1; 1705: QUEEN'S, Nov 17; 1706:
    DL, Mar 30; see also Lindebleim, Joanna Maria
Maria, Princess (actor), 1735: GF/HAY, Jan 9; see also Princesses
Maria, The (dance), 1740: CG, Mar 25
Mariage d'Orphee et d'Eurydice, Le. See Chapotan.
Mariage de Figaro, Le. See Beaumarchais, Pierre Augustin Caron de.
Mariage de Pesant, Le (play, anon), 1744: MFMCB, May 1
Mariage du Village (dance), 1764: KING'S, Feb 21, Mar 20, 29, Apr 14, May 5, 8
Mariage Force, Le. See Moliere.
Mariage Mexicain (dance), 1800: KING'S, Feb 25, Mar 1, 4, 22, Apr 29, Jun 10,
    17, 21, Jul 15, 26
Mariages Flamands (dance), 1790: HAY, Feb 13, 20, 27, Apr 6, 13, 17, May 20,
    25, Jun 12, CG, 15
Mariamne. See Pordage, Samuel, Herod and Mariamne; Fenton, Elijah.
Marian. See Brooke, Frances.
Mariane, Mlle (dancer), 1760: CG, Sep 22, Dec 11, 17; 1761: CG, Mar 9, May 8,
    25, Sep 16, 21, 26; 1762: CG, Jan 28
Marie (Maria, Marriee) (dance), 1718: LIF, May 15; 1720: DL, Apr 5; 1725: LIF,
    Dec 16; 1727: LIF, Mar 23; 1732: LIF, Apr 25; 1733: LIF/CG, Apr 30; 1734: CG,
    Apr 24, May 6, 17; 1738: CG, Mar 23; 1740: CG, Mar 25; 1742: CG, Apr 20;
    1759: CG, Apr 25
Marie, Mrs (beneficiary), 1726: DL, May 20
Mariet, Mlle (dancer), 1743: BFFP, Aug 23; 1749: DL, Oct 24, Nov 9, 27, Dec 2,
    28; 1750: DL, Jan 1, Feb 19, Nov 27, Dec 26; 1751: DL, Jan 18, Feb 18, Apr
    24, 27, Oct 16, Dec 26; 1752: DL, Oct 12; 1753: DL, Jan 1, 15, 17, Feb 19,
    Apr 25, Oct 9, 17, Nov 14, 21, Dec 26; 1754: DL, Jan 7, Oct 18, 31, Nov 5,
    Dec 5, 9, 12; 1757: DL, Oct 29; 1758: DL, Jan 13, Oct 5, 20, Nov 27; 1759:
    DL, May 15, Oct 4; 1760: DL, Apr 22, Oct 2, 7; 1761: DL, Mar 14
Marigi. See Morigi.
Marina. See Lillo, George.
Marinari, Gaetano (scene designer, machinist), 1786: KING'S, Mar 23; 1788:
    KING'S, Jan 29; 1790: HAY, May 13; 1793: KING'S, Feb 26, Apr 23; 1794:

KING'S, Apr 26, DL, Oct 31; <u>1795</u>: DL, Feb 12, May 6, HAY, Jun 20, DL, Oct 21,
   Nov 23; <u>1796</u>: DL, Feb 27, KING'S, Apr 7, DL, 30, HAY, Sep 1, DL, Nov 15, Dec
   26; <u>1797</u>: HAY, Jul 8, Aug 15, KING'S, Nov 28; <u>1798</u>: KING'S, Jan 9, HAY, Jun
   23, 29, 30, Jul 21, DL, Nov 14; <u>1799</u>: KING'S, Jan 22, Mar 26, DL, May 24,
   HAY, Jul 9, 20, Aug 13, DL, Dec 11; <u>1800</u>: KING'S, Apr 15, HAY, Jun 17
--Triumph of Hymen, The, <u>1795</u>: DL, May 6, 7, 8, 11, 15
Marine Boys Marching to Portsmouth (dance), <u>1757</u>: HAY, Jun 17, Aug 11, 31, Sep
   2, 8, 28, Oct 17
Marine Society, <u>1757</u>: DL, May 11, KING'S, Jun 18; <u>1758</u>: KING'S, May 4,
   RANELAGH, Jun 14; <u>1759</u>: DL, Mar 30, Dec 5
Marinelli (dancer), <u>1796</u>: CG, Dec 19
Mariners, The. See Birch, Samuel.
Mariners' Song (song), <u>1794</u>: CG, May 26; <u>1798</u>: CG, May 8; <u>1799</u>: CG, Apr 6;
   <u>1800</u>: CG, May 22
Mariniere (dance), <u>1744</u>: DL, Jan 28
Mariottini (dancer), <u>1773</u>: KING'S, Oct 23, Nov 20, 23, 30, Dec 7; <u>1774</u>: KING'S,
   Jan 11, 29, Feb 5, 12, 17, Mar 8, 12, 26, Apr 9, 14, 19, 23, 28, May 5, 12,
   28, 31, Jun 3
Marivaux, Pierre Carlet de Chamblain de, <u>1779</u>: DL, Apr 5; <u>1786</u>: HAY, Aug 29
--Arlequin Poli par l'Amour (farce), <u>1734</u>: HAY, Oct 31, GF/HAY, Nov 18, 20,
   HAY, Dec 23; <u>1735</u>: HAY, Jan 15, 31, GF/HAY, May 5; <u>1738</u>: HAY, Oct 9
--Double Inconstance, La; ou, Arlequin a la Cour Malgre Luy, <u>1734</u>: HAY, Nov 11;
   <u>1735</u>: HAY, Jan 23, Feb 3, 10, 26, Mar 5, Apr 23
--Fausse Suivante, La; ou, Le Fourbe Puni, <u>1779</u>: DL, Apr 5
--Jeu D'Amour et du Hazard, Le; ou, Arlequin Maitre et Valet, <u>1734</u>: HAY, Oct
   31, Nov 29; <u>1735</u>: GF/HAY, Mar 3, HAY, May 8; <u>1749</u>: HAY, Nov 20; <u>1786</u>: HAY,
   Aug 29
--Surprise de l'Amour, La; or, Harlequin in Love Against his Will (farce),
   <u>1735</u>: HAY, Feb 1
Mark when beneath the western main (song), <u>1800</u>: CG, May 17
Marked you her eye of heavenly blue? (play), <u>1787</u>: CG, Dec 22
Market Day, The (dance), <u>1785</u>: DL, Oct 24, 25, 26, 28, Nov 3, 15, 21
Market House, <u>1744</u>: MFHNT, May 1
Market Lane, <u>1720</u>: KING'S, May 14; <u>1769</u>: KING'S, Feb 24; <u>1774</u>: KING'S, Nov 8;
   <u>1776</u>: KING'S, Mar 26, Nov 2; <u>1777</u>: KING'S, Nov 4; <u>1778</u>: KING'S, Nov 24; <u>1779</u>:
   KING'S, Nov 27; <u>1780</u>: KING'S, Feb 26, Nov 25; <u>1782</u>: KING'S, Nov 2; <u>1783</u>:
   KING'S, Nov 29; <u>1784</u>: KING'S, Jun 3, Dec 21; <u>1786</u>: KING'S, Jan 24, Dec 23;
   <u>1791</u>: DLKING'S, Sep 22; <u>1793</u>: KING'S, Jan 26; <u>1794</u>: KING'S, Dec 6; <u>1796</u>:
   KING'S, Nov 26; <u>1797</u>: KING'S, Jan 7
Market St, <u>1757</u>: DL, Dec 21; <u>1777</u>: DL, May 6
Market, The (dance), <u>1757</u>: DL, Nov 26, 29, 30, Dec 1, 8, 10, 14, 19, 22, 27;
   <u>1758</u>: DL, Feb 9, Apr 19
Markham, Gervase
--Herod and Antipater, <u>1668</u>: LIF, Aug 20
Markham, Mrs (actor), <u>1721</u>: DL, May 23, Aug 4, Oct 27, Dec 12; <u>1722</u>: DL, Jan
   26, May 23
Marklew, Mrs (dancer), <u>1774</u>: DL, May 18; <u>1776</u>: CHR, Sep 25; <u>1777</u>: DL, Oct 31
Markordt, J (composer), <u>1780</u>: CG, Oct 3
Marks (actor), <u>1782</u>: HAY, Nov 25
Marks (house servant), <u>1776</u>: CG, May 21; <u>1778</u>: CG, May 21; <u>1779</u>: CG, May 15;
   <u>1780</u>: CG, May 24; <u>1781</u>: CG, May 25; <u>1782</u>: CG, May 28; <u>1783</u>: CG, May 31; <u>1784</u>:
   CG, May 22; <u>1786</u>: CG, May 27; <u>1787</u>: CG, May 30; <u>1788</u>: CG, May 30; <u>1798</u>: DL,
   Jun 16; <u>1799</u>: DL, Jul 3; <u>1800</u>: DL, Jun 14
Marlborough (actor), <u>1781</u>: CII, Mar 15
Marlborough (song), <u>1784</u>: CG, Mar 11, 13
Marlborough Place, <u>1792</u>: DLKING'S, May 22, HAY, Jul 31
Marlborough St, <u>1791</u>: DL, Apr 4
Marlborough, Duchess of (spectator), <u>1699</u>: DL, Dec 0; <u>1727</u>: MH, Jun 7; <u>1737</u>:
   HAY, May 23
Marlborough, Duke of, <u>1704</u>: DL, Aug 11; <u>1706</u>: YB, Dec 20; <u>1709</u>: QUEEN'S, Mar
   17; <u>1710</u>: QUEEN'S, Jul 13
Marlbro' Dance (dance), <u>1784</u>: KING'S, Mar 2
Marley, Robert (coach maker), <u>1761</u>: CG, Jan 23
Marlow (actor), <u>1747</u>: RL, Jan 27
Marlow, Mrs (actor), <u>1723</u>: HAY, Dec 12
Marlowe, Christopher
--Doctor Faustus, <u>1662</u>: REDBULL, May 26, NONE, Sep 0; <u>1675</u>: DG, Sep 24, 28
Marlton (actor), <u>1779</u>: HAY, Oct 13
Marmion, Shackerley
--Rampant Alderman, The; or, News from the Exchange (Fine Companion), <u>1684</u>:
   NONE, Sep 0
Marmontel, Jean Francois (librettist), <u>1776</u>: DL, Dec 5; <u>1780</u>: DL, Dec 27; <u>1782</u>:

CG, Dec 20; 1784: CG, Oct 27; 1785: CG, Nov 23; 1787: CG, Feb 9; 1789: CG,
  Nov 19; 1792: CG, Oct 3; 1796: KING'S, Apr 2, Jul 23
--Silvain, 1780: DL, Dec 27
Marow, Lady. See Cayley, Mary.
Marplot in Lisbon. See Centlivre, Susannah.
Marplot. See Centlivre, Susannah.
Marplot's Address (entertainment), 1778: HAY, Mar 23
Marquis Buildings, 1766: DL, Sep 23
Marr, Harry (actor), 1740: BFHC, Aug 23, GF, Nov 24, 25, 28, 29, Dec 1, 8, 12,
  15; 1741: GF, Jan 15, 20, 27, 29, Feb 2, 10, 19, Mar 3, 16, 19, Apr 15, 24,
  BFTY, Aug 22, GF, Sep 30, Oct 9, 16, 19, 23, Dec 29, 30; 1742: GF, Jan 1, 4,
  25, Feb 1, Mar 27, Apr 6, 24, May 6, 18, DL, Oct 13, Nov 24, Dec 14; 1743:
  DL, Jan 27, Feb 10, 14, SOU, Mar 30, DL, Apr 27, May 23, 24; 1744: HAY, Jun
  29; 1745: DL, Mar 30, Oct 8, Nov 18, 22; 1746: DL, Jan 2, 8, 24, Apr 10, 14,
  16, 23, 26, May 9, 19, CG, Jun 20, 27, DL, Oct 27, 31, Nov 12; 1747: DL, Feb
  7, Mar 7, 16, 28, May 11, Sep 22, Oct 29, 30, Dec 16, 17; 1748: DL, Mar 22,
  Oct 8, 15, 29, Nov 14, 29; 1749: HAY, Jan 7, DL, 25, Feb 21, Apr 29, May 9,
  12, BFY, Aug 23, DL, Oct 3, 13, 26, Dec 20; 1750: DL, Jan 6, 22, Feb 10, May
  3, Sep 18, 25, 28, Oct 16, 30, Nov 1, 8; 1751: DL, Jan 12, Apr 27, May 6, Sep
  12, 18, 24, 26, Oct 9, Nov 2; 1752: DL, Mar 30, Apr 1, Sep 30, Oct 3, 16, 23,
  Nov 3, 22, Dec 8; 1753: DL, May 17, 18, 21, Sep 11, 25, Oct 13, 23; 1754: DL,
  Feb 20, Apr 30, May 2, Sep 14, Oct 1, 10, 24; 1755: DL, May 3, Oct 4, 17, Nov
  8, 15; 1756: DL, Jan 21, Mar 27, May 18, Sep 25, 30, Nov 4, 18; 1757: CG, May
  27, DL, Sep 24, 29, Nov 4; 1758: DL, May 9, 17, Sep 26, Nov 16; 1759: DL, Sep
  29, Oct 30; 1760: DL, Apr 28, May 12, Oct 3, Nov 27, Dec 29; 1761: DL, Jun
  15, Jul 2, 27, Aug 8, Sep 14, 15; 1762: DL, May 17, Sep 21, Oct 6, Nov 3, 5,
  10, 23, 30, Dec 22; 1763: DL, May 31, Sep 20, 27, Oct 8, 10, 19, 27, 31, Nov
  19, 30; 1764: DL, Jan 4, Sep 27, Oct 15, 16; 1765: DL, Apr 13, May 6, Oct 9,
  Nov 16; 1766: DL, Jan 13, 24, Apr 12, May 3, Sep 23, Dec 2, 4; 1767: DL, Jan
  24, May 1, Sep 15, Oct 14; 1768: DL, Apr 9, Sep 17; 1769: DL, Sep 19, Oct 31;
  1770: DL, Oct 3; 1776: DL, May 7; 1777: DL, Jan 1
Marr, Miss (house servant), 1756: DL, May 7
Marriage a la Mode. See Dryden, John; Boadens, Charles, Modish Couple.
Marriage a la Mode; or, Conjugal Douceurs. See Murphy, Arthur.
Marriage Act, The. See Dibdin, Charles.
Marriage Broker, The. See W, M.
Marriage Feast (dance), 1773: DL, May 4
Marriage Hater Matched, The. See D'Urfey, Thomas.
Marriage Night, The. See Cary, Henry.
Marriage, The (dance), 1726: LIF, Apr 29
Married Beau, The. See Crowne, John.
Married Libertine, The. See Macklin, Charles.
Married Man, The. See Inchbald, Elizabeth.
Married Philosopher, The. See Kelly, John.
Married Un-Married, The; or, The Widow'd Wife (farce, anon), 1796: HAY, Sep 1
Marriot, F (actor, author), 1784: HAY, Mar 22; 1787: RLSN, Mar 26, 27, 28, 29,
  30, 31, ROY, Jun 20
Marriot, F and Mrs (actors), 1787: RLSN, Mar 29
Marriot, Mrs F (actor), 1787: RLSN, Mar 26, 27, 28, 29, 30, 31
Marriott, Rev George
--Jesuit, The, 1773: CR, Apr 14, 21, 30, HIC, May 18
Marriott's Great Room, 1722: RI, Jul 23
Marry or Do Worse. See Walker, William.
Mars and Venus (dance), 1740: CG, Nov 21, Dec 5, 11, 13; 1741: CG, Jan 17, 29;
  1742: CG, Feb 22
Mars and Venus (musical, anon), 1704: LIF, Jan 29, Feb 17, Jun 30
Mars and Venus; or, The Mouse Trap (entertainment), 1717: LIF, Nov 22, 29, Dec
  6, 13; 1718: LIF, Jan 1; 1723: LIF, Apr 27; 1725: LIF, Apr 17, 21; 1739: DL,
  May 2, 3, 4
Marseilles (dancer), 1786: KING'S, Mar 11, 23
Marseilles Sailor (dance), 1732: DL, Mar 30
Marsh Jr, Alphonso (composer), 1675: ATCOURT, Feb 15
Marsh Sr, Alphonso (composer), 1668: BRIDGES, Jun 12; 1670: BRI/COUR, Dec 0;
  1673: LIF, Mar 0; 1675: ATCOURT, Feb 15
Marsh, C (printer), 1756: DL, Jan 23
Marsh, Charles, 1738: CG, Aug 22, 30
--Amasis, King of Egypt, 1738: CG, Aug 22, 30
Marsh, Mrs (actor), 1788: HAY, Apr 9
Marsh's Coffee House, 1751: DL, May 14
Marshall (actor), 1724: SF, Sep 2
Marshall (actor), 1730: HAY, Jan 29, Feb 23, Mar 12, 20, 30, Apr 20, 24, May 1,
  DL, Dec 9, 22, 29; 1731: DL, Jan 19, Feb 17, 22, Apr 3, May 7, 19, 31, Jun

11, Nov 22; 1732: DL, Feb 3, Mar 14, Apr 24, May 2; 1733: DL, Sep 28, Oct 1,
8, 17, 31, Nov 5, 13, 14, 21, 23, 26, Dec 17; 1734: DL, Jan 3, Feb 11, Mar 7,
LIF, May 9, CG/LIF, Sep 18, Nov 4, 14, Dec 26; 1735: CG/LIF, Feb 15, May 1,
16, Jun 17, CG, Sep 24, Oct 20, 25, 31, Nov 1, 4, 7, 10, 13, 15, 22, 29, Dec
11; 1736: CG, Mar 16, 20, Apr 6, May 1, 17, Jun 14, Sep 15, 20, Oct 6, 11,
13, 15, LIF, 18, CG, 20, 23, Nov 1, 11, Dec 20, DL, 31; 1737: CG, Jan 10, DL,
29, Oct 25; 1738: DL, Jan 12, Feb 23, Apr 13, May 17, 30, Sep 23, Nov 30, Dec
15; 1739: DL, Jan 16, CG, 18, DL, May 26, 28, Sep 6, 26, Nov 15, 20; 1740:
DL, Jan 3, GF, Nov 4, 12, 13, 17, 20, Dec 2, 4, 5, 10; 1741: GF, Jan 15, Feb
2, 5, 19, Mar 19, TC, Aug 4, GF, Sep 14, 18, 28, Oct 12, 19, 23, 28, Nov 4,
Dec 9, 16; 1742: GF, Jan 4, 5, Feb 3, Mar 4, 25, 27, Apr 10; 1745: DL, Oct
12, Nov 4, 22, Dec 5, 10; 1746: DL, Jan 18, 31, Apr 23; 1758: DL, Jun 22;
1773: DL, Oct 29
Marshall (actor), 1755: HAY, Sep 1, 9; 1758: HAY, Jan 18; 1765: HAY, Jul 15,
31, Aug 7
Marshall (commentator on murder), 1697: DLORLIF, Sep 15
Marshall (householder), 1755: DL, Apr 11; 1778: HAY, Apr 9
Marshall (plumber), 1776: DL, Jun 10
Marshall (timber merchant), 1747: CG, Apr 22
Marshall and Co (plumbers), 1772: DL, Mar 26; 1773: DL, Jun 2; 1774: DL, Jun 2;
1775: DL, Feb 23; 1776: DL, Jan 26
Marshall St, 1756: HAY, Mar 25
Marshall, Anne, (Mrs Quinn, Wyn, Gwinn) (actor), 1660: NONE, Sep 0; 1662: VERE,
Jan 28; 1663: VERE, Mar 0, BRIDGES, May 7, NONE, Sep 0; 1664: BRIDGES, Jan
25, Feb 1, NONE, Sep 0, BRIDGES, Nov 0; 1665: BRIDGES, Jan 14, Apr 0; 1667:
BRI/COUR, Feb 0, Sep 0; 1668: BRIDGES, Jun 12, 27; 1677: DG, Mar 24, Jul 0;
Sep 0; 1678: DG, Jan 17, Apr 5, Nov 0; 1681: DL, May 0; 1682: DL, Feb 4
Marshall, James, 1790: CG, Nov 11; 1791: CG, Feb 4
--German Hotel, The, 1790: CG, Nov 11, 12, 13, 16, 18, 20, 25, Dec 1, 14, 15,
21; 1791: CG, Jan 1, 4
Marshall, Miss (actor), 1772: GROTTO, Aug 17
Marshall, Miss (actor), 1784: HAY, Nov 16
Marshall, Mr and Mrs (actors), 1737: DL, May 4
Marshall, Mrs (actor), 1736: LIF, Oct 19, Nov 20, Dec 7, DL, 15, LIF, 17, DL,
31, LIF, 31; 1737: LIF, Feb 14, 21, Mar 21, DL, May 13, LIF, 17, DL, 19, Sep
10, 15, Oct 11, 25, Nov 1, 12; 1738: DL, Jan 25, Feb 2, Mar 20, Apr 13, 17,
CG, 20, DL, 27, CG, Jun 30, Jul 7, 11, Aug 1, 29, DL, Oct 10, 25, 27, Nov 3,
11, CG, 18; 1739: DL, Feb 1, Mar 12, CG, 20, DL, 27, May 14, CG, 17, DL, 18,
19, CG, 28, DL, 28, Sep 4, 6, 8, 11, 15, 22, Oct 8, Nov 7, 15, 21, 23, Dec 8;
1740: DL, Jan 16, Feb 13, Mar 11, 25, Apr 12, 21, May 6, 19, 28; 1742: DL,
Jan 22, May 25; 1743: HAY, Apr 14
Marshall, Rebecca (actor), 1663: NONE, Sep 0; 1665: LIF, Apr 3; 1666: BRIDGES,
Dec 7, ATCOURT, 10, BRIDGES, 27; 1667: BRI/COUR, Feb 0, BRIDGES, 5, Apr 17,
BRI/COUR, May 24, BRIDGES, Aug 24, LIF, Sep 11, BRIDGES, Oct 19, NONE, 26;
1668: BRIDGES, Jan 24, ATCOURT, 27, BRIDGES, Feb 27, Apr 7, May 7, Jul 11,
Nov 6; 1669: BRIDGES, Jun 24; 1670: BRIDGES, Aug 0, BRI/COUR, Dec 0; 1671:
BRIDGES, Jun 0; 1672: BRIDGES, Jan 0, LIF, Apr 0, Jun 0, Nov 0; 1673: LIF,
May 0; 1674: DL, May 16, OXFORD, Jul 0; 1675: DL, Apr 23, NONE, Sep 0, DL,
Nov 17; 1676: DL, Jan 29, ATCOURT, May 29, DL, Dec 11; 1677: DL, Jan 12, 18,
Mar 0, 17, DG, May 31
Marshall, Rebecca and Anne (actors), 1661: NONE, Sep 0; 1666: NONE, Sep 0;
1667: NONE, Oct 26; 1668: BRIDGES, Sep 14
Marshall, Samuel (beneficiary), 1711: CLH, Apr 25
Marshall, Stephen (divine), 1667: NONE, Oct 26
Marshall, Thomas (actor, singer), 1781: HAY, Jun 1, 26, Jul 18, 28, Aug 15;
1790: CG, Sep 17, Oct 6, 13, 15, Nov 4, 11, 26, Dec 20, 27; 1791: CG, Jan 3,
14, Feb 4, Mar 5, May 2, 6, 19, Jun 1, 4, Sep 14, 16, 21, 23, Oct 10, 17, 19,
20, 27, Nov 1, 19, 24, Dec 21, 22; 1792: CG, Feb 28, Mar 6, 10, 26, Apr 10,
12, May 10, 11, 19, 22, Jun 2, Sep 19, 21, 24, 26, 28, Oct 1, 3, 8, 19, 24,
26, 29, Nov 5, Dec 13, 31; 1793: CG, Apr 3, 9, 24, May 24, Jun 10
Marshall, William (actor), 1724: RI, Aug 3
Marshalsea Prison, 1715: SF, Sep 5; 1720: SOU, Oct 3; 1721: SF, Sep 8; 1724:
SF, Sep 7; 1726: SOU, Sep 27; 1731: SF, Sep 8; 1735: SFLT, Sep 4; 1737: SF,
Sep 7; 1750: DL, May 7
Marsollier des Vivetieres, Benoit Joseph (librettist), 1787: CG, Apr 24; 1798:
DL, Nov 14, CG, Dec 11
--Camille; ou, Le Souterrain, 1798: DL, Nov 14, CG, Dec 11
--Nina; ou, La Folle par Amour, 1787: CG, Apr 24
Marson (actor), 1776: CHR, Oct 9
Marston, John, 1751: DL, Oct 22; 1776: DL, Dec 28
--Eastward Ho. See Chapman, George.
Marten, John (actor), 1738: DL, May 26, CG, Oct 2; 1739: CG, Apr 3, 12, May 17,

18, 23, Aug 2, 21, 31, DL, Sep 22, Oct 11, Nov 23, Dec 31; 1740: DL, Feb 7,
   Mar 20, Apr 15, 17, 22, 25, May 9, 12, Oct 27, Nov 6, 10, 19, 29, Dec 15, 19;
   1741: DL, Jan 15, Feb 24, Apr 3, May 12, 13, 14, Jun 4, BFTY, Aug 22, CG, Sep
   25, 30, Oct 13, 15, 21, 28, 31, Nov 11, 26, Dec 16, 18; 1742: CG, Jan 2, 19,
   Feb 3, 5, 11, 23, 25, 27, Mar 6, 13, 27, Apr 1, 6, 20, 24, 26, May 4, 5, 7,
   11, Sep 29, Oct 9, 14, 16, 25, 26, 29, Nov 3, 15, 20, 22, 30, Dec 7, 28;
   1743: SOU, Feb 18, CG, 22, Apr 9, May 2, 4, 11, Sep 28, 30, Oct 5, 7, 14, 21,
   29, 31, Nov 16, 19, Dec 3, 8, 9, 12, 16, 19; 1744: CG, Jan 5, 11, Feb 14, 28,
   Mar 13, 28, Apr 25, 30, May 1, 9, Sep 24, 26, Oct 1, 3, 8, 10, 15, 22, 24,
   29, 31, Nov 9, 27, 28, 29, 30, Dec 5, 12, 17, 21, 29, 31; 1745: CG, Jan 1, 2,
   23, Apr 4, 17, 20, 23, 30, May 13, 29, Sep 25, 27, Oct 9, 16, 29, Nov 7, 9,
   13, 14, 15, 19, 22, 23, 25, 28, Dec 2, 5, 10, 13; 1746: CG, Jan 2, 7, 11, 13,
   Feb 3, 5, 8, 10, 24, Mar 8, 10, 13, 15, Apr 1, 3, 4, 22, 28, Jun 9, 23, 27,
   Sep 29, Oct 1, 6, 8, 10, 13, 20, 29, Nov 3, 8, 17, 18, 24, Dec 6, 19, 26, 27,
   29, 31; 1747: CG, Jan 29, Feb 2, 6, 7, 11, Mar 7, 17, May 6, 15, 22; 1748:
   CG, Apr 18, 21, 22, 27, 29, May 2, 3, Sep 30, Oct 7, 11, 14, 17, 27, 29, Nov
   16, 26, 28, Dec 9, 20; 1749: CG, Jan 2, 25, Mar 2, 4, 9, Apr 4, 11, 17, 20,
   May 4, Sep 25, 29, Oct 2, 6, 11, 12, 18, 25, 26, 27, 30, Nov 1, 8, 9, 17, 18,
   21, 24, Dec 7, 27; 1750: CG, Jan 18, 24, Feb 2, 22, Mar 17, Apr 30, Sep 24,
   26, Oct 15, 16, 22, 24, 26, Nov 6, 8, 12, 17, 19, 22, 28, 29, Dec 4, 10;
   1751: CG, Apr 16, 19, May 4, 8, Sep 23, 25, Oct 8, 9, 17, 29, Nov 6, 11, 14,
   22, Dec 10, 14; 1752: CG, Jan 3, 29, Mar 3, 16, 17, 30, Apr 4, 21, 28, 29,
   30, May 4, Sep 22, Oct 2, 4, 9, 11, 19, 23, 24, 30, Nov 1, 7, 9, 27, Dec 11,
   13, 14; 1753: CG, Feb 7, 12, Mar 19, 20, May 10, 18, Nov 9, 13, 15, 23, 29,
   30, Dec 26; 1754: CG, Mar 9, Apr 1, 18, 20, 30, May 4, 7, 9, 14, 15, Sep 20,
   27, 30, Oct 7, 9, 11, 14, 18, 29, Nov 1, 6, 16, 23; 1755: CG, Jan 28, Apr 2,
   18, May 6, Oct 3, 6, 16, 24, Nov 10, 11, 14, 17, 19, 22, Dec 3, 4; 1756: CG,
   Jan 6, Feb 19, Mar 18, May 11, Sep 20, 22, 24, 27, 29, Oct 6, 11, 19, 28, 30,
   Nov 9, 17, 29, Dec 10; 1757: CG, Jan 27, 28, Feb 9, May 9, Sep 16, 23, 28,
   Oct 14, 17, 20, Nov 5, 9, 11, 16, 23, Dec 6, 10, 14; 1758: CG, Mar 9, Apr 3,
   14, 17, May 2, Sep 25, 27, Oct 20, 23, 25, Nov 9, 13, 18, Dec 18; 1759: CG,
   Feb 1, Mar 3, 17, 22, 27, Apr 7, May 11, Sep 24, 26, 28, Oct 1, 3, 5, Dec 5,
   31; 1760: CG, Jan 9, 31, Feb 14, Mar 18, 20, 24, Apr 9, 29, May 2, 5, 6, 19,
   Sep 22, Oct 6, 8, 13, 17, 18, 20, Nov 18; 1761: CG, Jan 6, 7, Feb 16, Mar 9,
   25, Apr 2, 17, 20, 29, May 5, Sep 9, 11, 18, Oct 1, 2, 5, 13, 14, 17, Nov 9,
   17, Dec 28; 1762: CG, Jan 28, Feb 15, Apr 3, 21, 27, May 5, Sep 20, Oct 5, 9,
   11, 14, 16, 20, 25, Nov 16, Dec 4, 27; 1763: CG, Apr 20, 25, May 9, Sep 19,
   Oct 8, 10, 15, 18, 19, 21, 26, Nov 8, 10, 16, 18, Dec 22; 1764: CG, Feb 11,
   15, 18, Mar 6, 8, 27, May 14, 18
Marten, Miss (actor), 1761: DL, Jan 31
Marten, Mrs (actor), 1732: HAY, Mar 10; 1742: CG, Apr 24; 1744: CG, May 14;
   1745: CG, Nov 25; 1746: CG, Dec 26; 1747: CG, Jan 17; 1752: CG, Dec 8
Marten, Widow (beneficiary), 1765: CG, May 7
Marteneni (artificial flower seller), 1795: CG, Jan 28
Martha, Mrs (spectator), 1661: VERE, Oct 8
MArthur. See MacArthur.
Martial (actor), 1769: HAY, Feb 28
Martial Music (music), 1735: HA, Oct 1; 1791: HAY, Oct 24
Martial Nymph, The; or, The Conquered Scythian (dance), 1792: DLKING'S, Jun 7
Martial Overture (music), 1795: HAY, Jul 16
Martial Queen, The. See Carleton, R.
Martial Song (song), 1788: HAY, Sep 30
Martin (actor), 1729: HAY, Aug 6, DL, 16; 1734: GF, Nov 13, Dec 2, 13; 1735:
   GF, Jan 13, 24, Mar 6, 10, Apr 9, May 3, HIC, 15; 1736: SH, Apr 16; 1737:
   LIF, Apr 30, CG, Sep 30; 1738: DL, May 26, CG, Dec 20; 1739: DL, Oct 29;
   1740: DL, Oct 4
Martin (actor), 1742: CG, Feb 19; 1743: CG, Oct 24; 1748: CG, Apr 11; 1750: CG,
   May 7; 1752: CG, Apr 29; 1754: CG, Feb 12; 1756: DL, May 5, CG, 19, Oct 22,
   DL, Dec 3; 1757: CG, May 19; 1758: CG, May 8; 1759: CG, May 18; 1760: CG, Feb
   2, Apr 10, May 28; 1763: CG, Jan 26; 1764: CG, Feb 1; 1767: CG, Apr 27
Martin (actor), 1791: HAY, Oct 24; 1796: HAY, Feb 22, Apr 27
Martin (boxkeeper), 1710: DL, May 16; 1715: LIF, Aug 10
Martin (wardrobe keeper), 1760: CG, Jan 14; 1767: CG, May 27
Martin y Soler (Martini), Vicente (composer), 1750: HIC, May 18; 1754: DL, Jan
   23; 1757: KING'S, Mar 24; 1783: KING'S, Nov 29; 1789: KING'S, Jan 10, DL, Nov
   24; 1790: HAY, Feb 27, CG, May 6, Oct 19; 1791: DL, Jan 1, Apr 13, DLKING'S,
   Sep 29, CG, Oct 3; 1792: DLKING'S, Mar 19; 1793: KING'S, Feb 26, DL, May 10,
   HAY, Nov 30; 1794: KING'S, May 17, CG, Nov 17, KING'S, Dec 6; 1795: KING'S,
   Jan 27, HAY, Mar 4, KING'S, May 26, 28; 1797: KING'S, Apr 18; 1799: CG, Mar
   15
--Albero di Diana, L' (opera) 1797: KING'S, Apr 18, 22, 25, 29, May 9, 27, Jun
   6

--Burbero di.Buon Cuore, Il (opera), 1794: KING'S, May 17, 20, 27, 31
--Cosa Rara, La (opera), 1789: KING'S, Jan 10, 13, 17, 20, Feb 3, 10, 17, 24,
    Mar 7, May 2; 1791: DL, Jan 1
--Isola del Piacere (opera), 1795: KING'S, May 26, 28, Jun 2, 9
--Nozze dei Contadini Spagnuoli, Le (intermezzo), 1795: KING'S, May 28
--Scola dei Maritati, La (opera), 1795: KING'S, Jan 27, 31, Feb 3, 21, 24, Mar
    3, 17, Apr 7, 25, 28, May 14, Jun 30, Jul 7; 1798: KING'S, Jan 23, 27, 31,
    Feb 10, 13, 17, Mar 6
--5th Concerto, 1799: CG, Mar 15
Martin, Jonathan (musician), 1763: CG, May 13
Martin, Mary (correspondent), 1772: DL, Apr 23
Martin, Mrs (actor), 1695: LIF, Sep 0; 1697: LIF, Nov 0; 1698: LIF, May 0, Jun
    0; 1699: LIF, Apr 0, May 0, Dec 0; 1700: LIF, Dec 0; 1701: LIF, Jan 0, Mar 0,
    Aug 0, Nov 0; 1703: LIF, Mar 0
Martin, Mrs (actor), 1725: LIF, Oct 25; 1726: LIF, Feb 19, Jul 5, 15, 22, 29,
    Aug 2, 19, Nov 30; 1727: LIF, Apr 5, 10, May 17, Dec 11; 1728: LIF, Jan 29,
    Jun 25, Aug 2; 1729: LIF, May 15, BFB, Aug 25, LIF, Dec 18; 1730: HAY, Jan 8,
    16, 21, Feb 4, 6, 12, 18, 23, Mar 5, 11, 30, Apr 20, May 1, LIF, 18, RI, Jun
    24, Jul 16, LIF, Oct 12, Nov 10; 1731: LIF, Apr 1, 23, 29, May 6, RI, Jul 1,
    8, 15, 22, BFB, Aug 26, LIF, Oct 20; 1732: LIF, Jan 26, 28, Feb 14, 21, HAY,
    Mar 23, 31, Apr 1, LIF, 18, HAY, 27, LIF, May 2, 31, RI, Aug 17, BFB, 23,
    LIF/CG, Sep 27, Oct 2, 28, Nov 8, Dec 14, CG/LIF, 16; 1733: LIF/CG, Jan 20,
    HAY, Feb 21, Mar 19, LIF/CG, Apr 30, CG/LIF, May 28, BF, Aug 23, CG, Sep 17,
    20, 25, 27, 29, Oct 16, Nov 1, 30; 1734: CG, Feb 18, Mar 28, HAY, Apr 5, CG,
    16, HAY, 17, RI, Jun 27, BFFO, Aug 24, CG, Sep 2, CG/LIF, 23, RI, 26, CG/LIF,
    27, MEG, 30, CG/LIF, Oct 14, 16, Nov 7, 14, 19, Dec 5, 30; 1735: CG/LIF, Jan
    17, 21, Mar 11, 20, 25, 29, Apr 17, CG, 25, CG/LIF, May 5, 9, 15, 27, CG, Sep
    16, 26, 29, Oct 1, 20, Nov 29; 1736: CG, Feb 26, Mar 18, Apr 8, May 3, Jun 4,
    LIF, 16, CG, Sep 17, Oct 8, 25, Nov 11; 1737: CG, Feb 3, Mar 10, 15, Sep 16,
    Oct 3, 28, Nov 18; 1738: CG, Jan 9, 25, Feb 13, Sep 27, Oct 13, 20, Nov 7,
    Dec 2; 1739: CG, Feb 16, Apr 5, May 2, 7, 17, 28, Aug 2, Sep 10, 14, 27, Oct
    26, Nov 6; 1740: CG, Jan 12, Feb 12, Mar 18, 25, May 5, 12, Sep 22, 24, Oct
    10, Nov 1; 1741: CG, Jan 5, 15, 23, 27, Feb 7, Mar 7, 9, Apr 30, Sep 28, Oct
    24, Dec 9; 1742: CG, Jan 2, Feb 22, Mar 13, 27, Apr 1, 6, May 4, Nov 25, 30;
    1743: CG, Feb 9, May 4, 11, Sep 23, Oct 19, 21, 29, 31, Nov 7, 19, Dec 9;
    1744: CG, Jan 14, Feb 14, 28, May 1, Sep 21, Oct 10, 29, Nov 1, 27, 30, Dec
    12; 1745: CG, Jan 1, May 1, 14, Sep 30, Oct 29, Nov 7, 8, 23; 1746: CG, Oct
    1, 13, 29, Dec 17, 31
Martin, Mrs (actor), 1758: HAY, Jan 12, 16
Martin, Mrs (house servant), 1760: CG, Sep 22
Martin, Robert (machinist), 1759: CG, Oct 8
Martinelli (machinist), 1795: CG, Apr 6; 1796: CG, Mar 15, Oct 24; 1797: CG,
    Oct 30
Martini (dancer), 1776: DL, Jan 16, 17, 26, Jun 1, 5
Martlet Court, 1741: DL, Jan 16; 1751: DL, Apr 24; 1754: DL, May 4; 1755: DL,
    Apr 25; 1767: CG, Mar 24; 1777: CG, May 5; 1780: DL, May 6, 10; 1783: DL, May
    12; 1786: DL, May 3; 1787: CG, May 9; 1790: CG, Apr 22, DL, May 27; 1791: CG,
    May 6, 20, Jun 4; 1792: CG, Apr 25, DLKING'S, Jun 7; 1793: CG, May 1, 16;
    1794: CG, May 9, Jun 11; 1795: CG, May 6, Jun 12; 1796: CG, Apr 15, DL, May
    17; 1797: CG, May 11; 1798: CG, May 9, DL, Jun 6; 1799: DL, Apr 19, CG, May
    3, DL, 7; 1800: CG, May 7
Martyn, Benjamin, 1730: DL, Jan 26
--Timoleon; or, Liberty Restored, 1730: DL, Jan 26, 27, 28, 29, 31, Feb 2, 3,
    4, 5, 6, 7, 9, 16, 17, May 13, Nov 17; 1733: GF, Feb 20, 22, 24, 27; 1750:
    JS, Nov 15; 1772: DL, Mar 28
Martyr, Margaret (actor, singer), 1780: CG, Nov 13, 15, 25, Dec 9, 12, 16;
    1781: CG, Mar 31, Apr 24, May 2, 7, Sep 17, 24, Oct 16, 23, 24, 25, 31, Nov
    7, Dec 26; 1782: CG, Feb 21, Mar 16, 18, Apr 30, May 1, HAY, Sep 18, CG, 25,
    27, Oct 7, 9, 16, Nov 8, 9, 25, Dec 6, 14, 20, 27, 31; 1783: CG, Feb 5, Mar
    3, Apr 5, 7, 23, May 6, 9, 16, 19, 24, Sep 22, 26, Oct 2, 3, 6, 8, 9, 10, 21,
    24, Nov 4, 8, 19; 1784: CG, Jan 13, 29, Feb 21, 23, Mar 6, 20, 23, 27, Apr
    17, 27, May 7, 10, 17, 18, 25, 26, Jun 14, Sep 21, 22, Oct 4, 8, 12, 18, 25,
    27, 28, Nov 6, 16, Dec 6, 14; 1785: CG, Mar 7, 12, 30, Apr 2, 5, 8, 11, 12,
    15, 18, 22, 25, May 4, 6, 7, 12, Sep 19, 21, 23, 30, Oct 7, 14, 17, 20, 21,
    26, Nov 3, 4, 10, 14, 19, 21, 23, Dec 5, 8, 14, 26, 28; 1786: CG, Jan 2, 6,
    14, 18, Feb 1, 17, 23, 25, Mar 14, 18, Apr 1, 4, 24, May 6, 9, 10, 15, 22,
    26, 27, Sep 18, Oct 9, 16, 21, 23, 26, 31, Nov 15, 22, 23, 25, 30, Dec 1, 5,
    6, 12, 23, 26; 1787: CG, Jan 4, Feb 9, Mar 12, 31, Apr 10, 16, 24, 25, 27,
    May 9, 11, 15, 21, Sep 17, 19, 21, 24, 26, Oct 1, 5, 17, 18, 19, 22, 31, Nov
    8, Dec 3, 21, 22; 1788: CG, Jan 14, 28, Feb 5, 9, Mar 11, 24, 26, 29, Apr 1,
    2, 8, 11, 25, May 12, 22, Sep 17, 19, 22, 24, 26, 29, Oct 1, 3, 8, 13, 17,
    21, 22, Nov 1, Dec 13, 26, 29; 1789: CG, Jan 3, Feb 6, 14, 19, 21, Mar 3, 31,

Apr 30, May 5, 6, 15, 22, 28, Jun 2, 8, Sep 14, 16, 18, 23, 25, 28, Oct 2, 7,
12, 13, 16, 21, 23, 24, 28, 30, 31, Nov 10, 11, 14, 19, 21, 24, 28, Dec 3,
10, 12, 21; <u>1790</u>: CG, Jan 23, Mar 8, 18, 22, 27, Apr 12, 20, 21, 22, 29, May
5, 6, 7, 11, 13, Jun 1, 4, 16, HAY, Aug 18, CG, Sep 13, 15, 17, Oct 1, 5, 6,
12, 13, 15, 19, 23, 29, 30, Nov 3, 6, 11, 15, 16, 23, 25, 26, Dec 2, 8, 20,
28; <u>1791</u>: CG, Jan 12, 15, 26, Feb 11, Apr 28, 30, May 2, 5, 6, 18, 19, 27,
31, Jun 7, Sep 12, 14, 16, 17, 19, 20, 21, 23, 26, 28, 30, Oct 5, 10, 19, 20,
Nov 1, 2, 7, 25, Dec 3, 8, 10, 15; <u>1792</u>: CG, Feb 2, 23, 25, 28, Mar 31, Apr
10, 12, 17, 18, 21, 25, May 10, 11, 19, 22, Sep 26, Oct 19, 22, 25, 27, 29,
31, Nov 24, Dec 1, 3, 4, 13, 20, 22; <u>1793</u>: CG, Feb 25, Apr 4, 11, 24, 25, May
1, 3, 10, 11, 15, 21, 24, Jun 1, 4, 5, 12, Sep 16, 17, 18, 20, 23, 25, 27,
30, Oct 1, 2, 4, 5, 7, 9, 10, 11, 12, 18, 19, 24, 29, Nov 1, 2, 5, 7, 13, 15,
18, 22, Dec 6, 7, 9, 17; <u>1794</u>: CG, Jan 14, 21, Feb 6, 22, Apr 7, 10, 12, May
2, 6, 9, 13, 22, 23, 28, Jun 11, Sep 15, 17, 19, 22, 24, 26, 29, Oct 1, 3, 7,
10, 14, 17, 20, 21, 23, 29, Nov 7, 11, 15, 17, 21, Dec 6, 26, 30; <u>1795</u>: CG,
Jan 2, 6, Feb 14, Mar 14, 16, Apr 6, 28, May 1, 6, 8, 13, 14, 29, Jun 9, 10,
Sep 14, 16, 18, 21, 23, 25, 28, Oct 2, 5, 7, 8, 12, 14, 15, 19, 22, 24, 31,
Nov 6, 9, 14, 16, 25, 27, Dec 4, 5, 7, 21; <u>1796</u>: CG, Jan 4, Feb 2, Mar 15,
30, Apr 5, 9, 12, 15, 26, 29, May 3, 10, 16, 18, 20, 23, Sep 12, 14, 16, 17,
19, 21, 23, 26, 30, Oct 3, 5, 6, 17, 18, 20, 21, 24, Nov 12, 19, 24, Dec 15,
27, 31; <u>1797</u>: CG, Jan 3, 10, Apr 8, 19, 25, 26, May 2, 9, 11, 16, 17, 18, 22,
23, 24, Jun 8, 21, Sep 20, 22, 25, 27, 29, Oct 2, 4, 25, 31, Nov 1, 2, 8, 10,
11, 15, Dec 16, 28; <u>1798</u>: CG, Jan 1, Feb 9, 20, Mar 19, 31, Apr 9, 11, 16,
18, 21, 24, May 1, 7, 9, 10, 14, 16, 23, 24, 28, Jun 2, 4, 7, Sep 17, 19, 26,
Oct 1, 5, 8, 11, Nov 10, Dec 15; <u>1799</u>: CG, Jan 5, 17, 22, HAY, Feb 25, CG,
Mar 16, Apr 6, 9, 12, 16, 30, May 3, 13, 14, 15, 22, 24, 25, 28, Jun 6, 7,
Sep 16, 18, 20, 23, 25, 27, 30, Oct 2, 7, 11, Dec 2, 4, 7, 9, 10, 16; <u>1800</u>:
CG, Jan 11, 29, Mar 1, Apr 5, 15, 17, May 7, 30, Jun 13
Maruso, Don Bartholomeo Bernalte (Spanish dignitary), <u>1702</u>: LIF, Dec 11; <u>1703</u>:
DL, Jan 1
Marvell, Andrew (author), <u>1675</u>: ATCOURT, Jul 24; <u>1677</u>: DG, Nov 17
Marvelous, The (entertainment), <u>1798</u>: CG, Apr 24
Mary Gray (song), <u>1781</u>: DL, May 9
Mary Retrouve, Le. See D'Ancourt, Florent Carton.
Mary Scot (song), <u>1730</u>: DL, Apr 28; <u>1739</u>: DL, Mar 26, Apr 24, 30; <u>1740</u>: DL, Apr
30, May 12; <u>1741</u>: DL, Apr 6; <u>1744</u>: CG, Jan 19; <u>1754</u>: DL, May 10
Mary St, <u>1793</u>: CG, May 24
Mary-le-Bone Church, <u>1774</u>: DL, Mar 22
Mary-le-Bone Gardens, <u>1754</u>: SFH, Sep 19; <u>1758</u>: MARLY, Jun 8, 27; <u>1759</u>: MARLY,
Apr 16, KING'S, 21, MARLY, May 30; <u>1760</u>: MARLY, Jun 3, HAY, Sep 8; <u>1762</u>: DL,
Nov 23; <u>1763</u>: MARLY, Jun 28; <u>1767</u>: MARLY, Jun 8; <u>1771</u>: MARLY, May 23, HAY,
Sep 18; <u>1772</u>: MARLY, Jul 2; <u>1773</u>: MARLY, May 27; <u>1774</u>: DL, Mar 22; <u>1775</u>:
MARLY, May 30; <u>1776</u>: CG, Apr 16, MARLY, May 27; <u>1777</u>: CG, May 5; <u>1793</u>:
KING'S, Feb 19
Mary-le-Bone St, <u>1735</u>: HAY, Mar 29; <u>1776</u>: HAY, Oct 7; <u>1796</u>: HAY, Mar 28
Mary, Lady (actor), <u>1670</u>: ATCOURT, Apr 6; <u>1675</u>: ATCOURT, Feb 15
Mary, Lady (equilibrist), <u>1702</u>: BFBF, Aug 24; <u>1703</u>: MF, May 0; <u>1704</u>: MF, May 1
Mary, Princess (actor), <u>1730</u>: DL, Oct 28; <u>1732</u>: DL, Mar 16
Mary, Queen of Scots. See Francklin, Dr Thomas; St John, John.
Mary, Queen, Birthday Song for (song), <u>1697</u>: LW, Aug 18
Mary, Queen, <u>1667</u>: BRIDGES, Aug 17, 22, Nov 2, Dec 30; <u>1689</u>: NONE, Apr 11;
<u>1690</u>: ATCOURT, Nov 4; <u>1691</u>: ATCOURT, Jan 1; <u>1694</u>: DL, Jan 13, NONE, Dec 28;
<u>1696</u>: DL, Dec 0; see also Highness; Majesty; Queen, the
Mary's dream (The moon had climbed the highest hill) (song), <u>1792</u>: KING'S, Mar
28; <u>1794</u>: CG, May 26
Mascarade, La (dance), <u>1742</u>: DL, Oct 9, 12, 14, 16, 18, 21, 22, Nov 5, 12, 15
Mascarille, Madame la Marquise de, <u>1736</u>: HAY, Jun 7
Mascherata, La (dance), <u>1775</u>: KING'S, Mar 23, Apr 4, 6, May 11
Masefield (paper hanger), <u>1772</u>: CG, Oct 24
Masked Friend, The. See Holcroft, Thomas.
Mason (actor), <u>1732</u>: HAY, Mar 2, May 17; <u>1734</u>: GR, Nov 4
Mason (actor), <u>1748</u>: SFLYYW, Sep 7, BHB, Oct 1
Mason (actor), <u>1780</u>: HAY, Nov 13
Mason (beneficiary), <u>1746</u>: DL, May 19; <u>1747</u>: DL, May 11
Mason (boxkeeper), <u>1743</u>: CG, May 9; <u>1744</u>: CG, May 11; <u>1745</u>: CG, May 14; <u>1746</u>:
CG, May 6; <u>1750</u>: CG, May 7
Mason (house servant), <u>1786</u>: CG, Jun 2
Mason (singer), <u>1703</u>: DL, Nov 25, 29, Dec 27
Mason, John, <u>1668</u>: LIF, Aug 20
--Muliasses the Turk, <u>1668</u>: LIF, Aug 20
Mason, M (witness), <u>1735</u>: GF/HAY, Mar 18
Mason, Miss (singer), <u>1794</u>: DL, Apr 9

Mason, Mrs (actor), 1748: NWC, Dec 29
Mason, Robert (violoncellist), 1786: DL, Mar 29; 1789: DL, Mar 25; 1790: DL,
    Feb 24, Mar 5, 17; 1791: DL, Mar 11, Apr 13; 1792: KING'S, Feb 24, 29, Mar
    21; 1793: KING/HAY, Feb 15, Mar 6; 1794: DL, Mar 12
Mason, Susannah (actor, singer), 1732: HAY, Mar 13, Nov 16; 1733: HAY, Jun 4,
    DL, Nov 7; 1734: DL, Jan 3, Feb 4, DL/HAY, Mar 21, DL, Apr 15, 29, JS, May 31
Mason, William, 1755: KING'S, Dec 9; 1772: CG, Nov 21; 1773: CG, Feb 2; 1776:
    CG, Dec 6; 1779: CG, Feb 23; 1781: CG, Mar 23
--Caractacus (reading), 1773: CG, Nov 5; 1776: CG, Dec 6, 9, 10, 11, 12, 16,
    31; 1777: CG, Jan 7, 10, 16, 23, 29, Feb 7, Apr 5, 23, May 10, Dec 3; 1778:
    CG, Jan 9, Oct 22, Nov 3, 17; 1785: CG, Oct 17
--Elfrida (oratorio), 1772: CG, Nov 21, 23, 24, 25, 26, 27, 28, 30, Dec 1, 2,
    3, 5, 7, 9, 10, 12, 16, 18, 23; 1773: CG, Jan 11, 13, 15, 19, 20, 26, 27, Feb
    2, 3, 4, 16, 25, Oct 21, Nov 16, Dec 8; 1774: CG, Oct 3, Nov 11; 1775: CG,
    Jan 27; 1777: CG, May 14; 1779: CG, Feb 23, 27, Mar 6, 11, 16, 18, Apr 12;
    1781: CG, Mar 23; 1783: CG, Apr 5; 1785: DL, Apr 14, 16; 1792: CG, Nov 24
Mason, 1775: DL, Feb 17
Masonic Address (entertainment), 1784: HAY, Jan 21
Masonic Melange, A. See Whitfield, John.
Masonry Ode (song), 1754: HAY/SFB, Sep 26; 1766: MARLY, Sep 26; 1774: DL, Apr
    27, May 9, 10
Masons at Work (dance), 1764: KING'S, Nov 24
Masons et Sabotiers (dance), 1741: DL, Jan 20, 22, 26, 28, 31, Mar 3, 19, Apr
    11, 15, 25, 30, Oct 27, 28, Nov 3, 6, 7, 9, 20, 23, Dec 18, 30; 1742: DL, Jan
    1, 9, 29, BFPY, Aug 25, SF, Sep 8, SOU, 27
Masons' benefit, 1741: JS, May 11
Masons' Dance (dance), 1736: DL, May 4
Masons' Prologue (entertainment), 1757: HAY, Sep 23
Masons' Song (song), 1731: LIF, Apr 5; 1732: HAY, Apr 19; 1735: DL, May 13,
    HAY, Jun 12; 1736: LIF, Apr 29; 1738: CG, Aug 29; 1739: CG, Aug 10, DL, Sep
    14; 1740: CG, Apr 28; 1741: GF, Mar 12, CG, Apr 11, GF, 15; 1742: CG, May 4;
    1744: DL, May 4; 1745: CG, May 3; 1747: DL, May 16; 1753: HAY, Apr 14; 1754:
    HAY, Feb 2, HAY/SFB, Sep 26; 1757: HAY, Sep 23; 1761: HAY, Mar 9; 1790: DL,
    Apr 20
Masque (entertainment), 1663: ATCOURT, Jul 2; 1665: ATCOURT, Feb 2; 1691: NONE,
    Sep 0; 1697: LW, Jul 3; 1698: DL/ORDG, Nov 0; 1701: DL, Aug 23; 1703: DL, May
    24, Dec 11; 1704: DL, Feb 3, 4, Mar 23, 28, May 27, Dec 6; 1705: DL, Jan 26;
    1706: DL, Jan 1, Mar 5, Jun 22, DG, Nov 23; 1707: DL, Dec 10; 1715: LIF, Mar
    24, Nov 11; 1716: LIF, May 2; 1729: DL, Apr 23; 1730: DL, Oct 1, KG, 22;
    1733: CG, May 1, LIF/CG, 1, CG, 2, LIF/CG, 29; 1734: LIF, May 16; 1776: CG,
    May 6; 1779: CG, May 10; 1780: CG, Apr 12; 1793: HAY, Dec 5
Masque Ball Scene (entertainment), 1787: CG, May 21
Masque in Honor of the Nuptials of His Royal Highness. See Gretton, John.
Masque of Hercules. See Motteux, Peter Anthony.
Masque of Oberon. See Jonson, Ben.
Masque, Grand (entertainment), 1724: DL, Oct 1, 3; 1746: DL, Jan 31
Masquerade Anticipated, A (interlude, anon), 1792: CG, May 28
Masquerade Ballet (dance), 1778: KING'S, May 28
Masquerade Dance (dance), 1732: GF, Dec 27; 1733: GF, Jan 6, 10, Feb 15, May 3,
    4, 14, 15, 16, 22, Sep 21, Nov 7; 1749: DL, Apr 1; 1751: DL, Oct 19; 1753:
    DL, Mar 26; 1754: DL, Mar 30, Apr 30; 1755: CG, Apr 15; 1756: DL, Nov 8;
    1758: DL, Jan 25, Sep 30; 1760: CG, Sep 29; 1762: DL, Apr 27; 1766: DL, Oct
    23; 1767: DL, Apr 6, May 18; 1771: CG, Apr 6; 1777: KING'S, Feb 4, Mar 4, CG,
    Oct 15; 1778: KING'S, Mar 3, 10, 17, 31, Apr 28, 30, May 5, 12, 30, Jun 5;
    1779: KING'S, Dec 14, 21; 1780: KING'S, Feb 8, 19, Apr 4, 11, CG, Oct 19, Dec
    30; 1782: DL, Apr 25, May 10; 1785: CG, Jan 21, Nov 2; 1786: CG, Jan 24, May
    13; 1787: CG, Apr 11, HAY, Aug 17, CG, Nov 7; 1788: CG, Apr 14; 1789: CG, Jan
    20; 1794: CG, Nov 12; 1797: CG, Oct 6
Masquerade Dance, Grand (dance), 1733: GF, Apr 10, 17, 23; 1748: CG, Dec 26,
    27; 1757: DL, Mar 22
Masquerade de Florana, La (dance), 1743: DL, Mar 19, 26, Apr 8
Masquerade Polish Dance (dance), 1758: DL, Apr 27
Masquerade Scene (entertainment), 1752: CG, Dec 18; 1757: DL, Jan 6; 1765: DL,
    Mar 30; 1768: DL, Nov 29, Dec 7; 1769: CG, Jan 6, DL, Feb 2, CG, Mar 28, Oct
    7, DL, 7; 1776: CG, Oct 7, DL, Dec 10; 1777: CG, Sep 29; 1778: CG, Jan 12,
    DL, Feb 10, 19, May 23, CG, Oct 26; 1779: DL, Dec 27, CG, 31; 1781: DL, May
    1, CG, Sep 24; 1782: CG, Oct 7, DL, Nov 16; 1783: DL, Feb 18, Mar 3, CG, Sep
    22; 1785: HAY, Dec 26; 1786: DL, Apr 26, CG, Oct 23; 1787: DL, Jan 29, HAY,
    May 25, DL, Nov 5, CG, 12; 1788: DL, Apr 30, CG, Sep 22; 1789: CG, Sep 14,
    DL, Nov 27; 1790: CG, Oct 25; 1791: CG, Sep 26; 1792: DLKING'S, May 17, CG,
    19, Oct 8, DL, Nov 2, CG, 26; 1794: CG, Feb 10; 1795: CG, Jan 5; 1796: DL,
    Oct 25; 1797: DL, Jan 12, Mar 6, 23, May 19, Nov 10; 1798: DL, May 24, Oct

551

11; <u>1799</u>: DL, May 9, Jul 4, Oct 12, 29, Nov 20
Masquerade Warehouse, <u>1792</u>: HAY, Feb 6
Masquerade, Grand (entertainment), <u>1768</u>: DL, Nov 9; <u>1795</u>: CG, Sep 21; <u>1796</u>: CG,
    May 17, Sep 19, Oct 27; <u>1797</u>: CG, Nov 2; <u>1799</u>:, CG, Dec 9; <u>1800</u>: CG, Mar 27
Masquerade, La (dance), <u>1764</u>: KING'S, Mar 31, Apr 10, 14, May 5, 8, 15
Masquerade, The. See Johnson, Charles.
Masquerade, The; or, An Evening's Intrigue. See Griffin, Benjamin.
Masqueraders, The (dance), <u>1731</u>: LIF, Nov 2, 3; <u>1732</u>: DL, May 3, 9; <u>1733</u>: GF,
    Mar 1, 26, 29, May 5, 10, 18; <u>1734</u>: DL, Nov 22; <u>1735</u>: DL, Feb 5, Apr 25
Masques, The (dance), <u>1731</u>: DL, Nov 3, Dec 15, 16; <u>1732</u>: DL, Apr 17, 18, 21,
    26, 28, May 1, 2, 4, 6
Massaniello. See D'Urfey, Thomas.
Massey (actor), <u>1748</u>: NWC, Apr 4, NWSM, May 4, CG, 6, BFP, Aug 24; <u>1749</u>:
    BF/SFP, Aug 23, Sep 7; <u>1758</u>: HAY, Dec 28; <u>1760</u>: HAY, Apr 30; <u>1767</u>: CG, Sep
    14, 17, Oct 8; <u>1775</u>: HAY, Feb 2, CG, May 9
Massey (actor), <u>1776</u>: CHR, Sep 23, 25, 30, Oct 2, 4, 9; <u>1777</u>: HAY, May 15, 30,
    Jun 6, 9, 11, 19, 26, Jul 2, 15, 18, 24, 30, Aug 7, 14, 18, 19, Sep 3, 10,
    16, 17, 18, 19, Oct 13; <u>1778</u>: HAY, Feb 9, Mar 24, 31, Apr 9, 29, 30, May 18,
    21, 22, CHR, 27, 29, HAY, Jun 1, CHR, 1, 3, HAY, 8, CHR, 9, 10, HAY, 11, 12,
    CHR, 15, 18, 19, HAY, 19, CHR, 22, 24, HAY, 25, CHR, 26, HAY, Jul 1, 2, 11,
    30, Aug 6, 17, 22, 26, 27, Sep 2, 7, 10, 18; <u>1779</u>: HAY, May 31, Jun 7, 10,
    12, 17, Jul 15, Aug 6, 17, 18, 24, 27, Oct 13; <u>1780</u>: HAY, Mar 28, May 30, Jun
    3, 5, 15, 28, 29, Jul 1, 8, 10, 29, Aug 5, 17, Sep 2; <u>1781</u>: HAY, May 30, Jun
    1, 7, 8, 11, 12, 14, 16, Jul 23, Aug 1, 7, 8, 15, 17, 24, 25, 31; <u>1782</u>: HAY,
    Jun 3, 4, 6, 11, 12, 13, 18, Jul 17, 25, Aug 8, 13, 16, 17, 24, 30, Sep 10,
    18; <u>1783</u>: HAY, May 31, Jun 2, 6, 7, 12, 18, 20, 30, Jul 4, 5, 28, Aug 1, 13,
    20, 23, 26; <u>1792</u>: HAY, Nov 26
Massey, Mr and Mrs (actors), <u>1778</u>: HAY, Feb 9
Massey, Mrs E (actor), <u>1776</u>: CHR, Sep 23, 27, Oct 4; <u>1777</u>: HAY, Aug 7, 14, 29;
    <u>1778</u>: HAY, Feb 9, Apr 9, Jun 10, 19, Jul 30, Sep 7, 17; <u>1779</u>: HAY, May 31,
    Jul 2, 31, Aug 24, Oct 13; <u>1780</u>: HAY, Jul 1, 10; <u>1781</u>: HAY, Jun 16, Aug 7
Massimino (actor, singer), <u>1777</u>: KING'S, May 15
Massinger, Phillip, <u>1669</u>: BRIDGES, Jan 12; <u>1719</u>: DL, Jun 9, Oct 29; <u>1720</u>: DL,
    Jun 6; <u>1722</u>: LIF, Jun 13; <u>1748</u>: DL, Oct 19; <u>1778</u>: CG, Apr 27; <u>1779</u>: CG, Oct
    13, Nov 10; <u>1781</u>: CG, Sep 17; <u>1783</u>: CG, Apr 23, DL, 29, CG, May 10, Nov 8;
    <u>1785</u>: DL, Jan 27; <u>1793</u>: DL, May 22; <u>1796</u>: CG, Apr 19, DL, May 23; <u>1798</u>: CG,
    May 30
--Bashful Lover, The, <u>1669</u>: BRIDGES, Jan 12; <u>1798</u>: CG, May 30
--Beggar's Bush, The. See Fletcher, John.
--Bloody Brother, The. See Fletcher, John.
--Bnndman, The; or, Love and Liberty, <u>1659</u>: NONE, Sep 0; <u>1661</u>: SALSBURY, Mar 1,
    19, 26, VERE, May 0, LIF, Nov 4, 25; <u>1662</u>: LIF, Apr 2; <u>1664</u>: LIF, Jul 28;
    <u>1719</u>: DL, Jun 9, 12, Oct 29; <u>1720</u>: DL, Jun 6; <u>1779</u>: CG, Oct 13, 15, 20, 27,
    Nov 3, 18, Dec 30
--City Madam, The, <u>1783</u>: DL, Apr 29
--Custom of the Country, The. See Fletcher, John.
--Double Marriage, The. See Fletcher, John.
--Duke of Milan, <u>1669</u>: BRIDGES, Jan 12
--Elder Brother, The. See Fletcher, John.
--Emperor of the East, The, <u>1669</u>: BRIDGES, Jan 12
--False One, The. See Fletcher, John.
--Fatal Dowry, The. See Field, Nathan.
--History and Fall of Domitian, The; or, The Roman Actor, <u>1669</u>: BRIDGES, Jan
    12; <u>1691</u>: NONE, Sep 0; <u>1722</u>: LIF, Jun 13, 15, 20, Jul 25, Nov 22; <u>1794</u>: DL,
    Oct 2, 18; <u>1796</u>: DL, May 23
--Knights of Malta, The. See Fletcher, John.
--Little French Lawyer, The. See Fletcher, John.
--Lover's Progress, The. See Fletcher, John.
--Maid of Honour, The, <u>1785</u>: DL, Jan 27, 29, Feb 10
--New Way to Pay Old Debts, A, <u>1662</u>: REDBULL, Jan 25; <u>1708</u>: DL, Aug 4; <u>1748</u>:
    DL, Oct 19, 20, 21; <u>1749</u>: DL, Jan 23, May 11; <u>1759</u>: DL, May 11; <u>1760</u>: DL, May
    8; <u>1769</u>: DL, Oct 21, 24, 27; <u>1781</u>: CG, Apr 18, 26, May 8, 16, 24, Sep 17, Dec
    14; <u>1782</u>: CG, Jan 16, Feb 1, Apr 2; <u>1783</u>: CG, Apr 1, May 16, Sep 26, DL, Nov
    14, 17, Dec 4; <u>1784</u>: DL, Jan 26, Feb 9, Mar 18, May 26, CG, 27, DL, Nov 2;
    <u>1785</u>: DL, May 17, CG, 18, Oct 12; <u>1786</u>: DL, Jan 5; <u>1787</u>: DL, Jan 13, Dec 14;
    <u>1788</u>: DL, Mar 25, Jun 12; <u>1796</u>: CG, Apr 19
--Picture, The, <u>1783</u>: CG, Nov 8
--Prophetess, The. See Fletcher, John.
--Queen of Corinth, The. See Fletcher, John.
--Renegado, The, <u>1662</u>: VERE, Jun 6
--Rollo, Duke of Normandy. See Fletcher, John, The Bloody Brother.
--Royal Merchant, The. See Fletcher, John, The Beggar's Bush.

552

--Sea Voyage, The. See Fletcher, John.
--Spanish Curate, The. See Fletcher, John.
--Storm, The. See Fletcher, John, The Sea Voyage.
--Unnatural Combat, The, 1669: BRIDGES, Jan 12
--Very Woman, A, 1661: LIF, Jul 11
--Virgin Martyr, The. See Dekker, Thomas.
Massingham (boxkeeper), 1792: DLKING'S, Jun 15; 1793: DL, Jun 6; 1795: DL, Jun
    5; 1796: DL, Jun 15; 1797: DL, Jun 13, 14; 1798: DL, Jun 15; 1799: DL, Jul 4;
    1800: DL, Jun 17
Massingham Jr (ticket deliverer), 1795: DL, Jun 5; 1796: DL, Jun 15; 1798: DL,
    Jun 16
Massink. See Messink.
Master I have (song), 1783: HAY, Sep 9; 1784: HAY, Aug 17
Master of the King's Music, 1674: DL, Mar 30; 1685: DG, Jun 3; 1724: DL, May 6
Master of the Mint, 1674: SLINGSBY, Dec 2
Master of the Revels, 1679: DL, Feb 0; 1681: DG, Sep 0; 1697: DG, Jul 1; 1699:
    DL, Dec 0
Master Teddy O'Shaughnessey's History of Himself (song), 1795: CG, May 1, 8;
    1796: CG, Apr 26, May 24, 26; 1797: CG, May 2; 1798: CG, Apr 24
Masters (ticket deliverer), 1789: CG, Jun 6; 1794: CG, Jun 4; 1798: CG, May 18;
    1799: CG, May 17
Masters, Mrs (actor, singer), 1788: CG, May 31; 1789: CG, Sep 14, Oct 12, Dec
    21; 1790: CG, Jan 23, Mar 1, May 24, 27, Sep 13, Oct 6, Nov 26; 1791: CG, May
    26, Sep 26, Oct 6, 10, Dec 21, 22; 1792: CG, Feb 28, Apr 12, 17, May 10, 12,
    HAY, Jun 18, 23, Jul 25, Aug 9, CG, Oct 8, 19, 29, Dec 26; 1793: CG, Apr 8,
    HAY, Jun 12, 17, 21, Aug 3, 12, 16, Sep 2, CG, 23, 30, Oct 2, 7, 9, 12, 21,
    28, Nov 11, Dec 27; 1794: CG, Apr 30, HAY, Jul 17, 18, 21, 24, 28, Aug 27,
    CG, Sep 22, Oct 20; 1795: CG, Feb 3, May 18, 30, Jun 6, Sep 14, 21, Oct 15,
    19, Nov 4, 9, 16; 1796: CG, Jan 1, Apr 9, 26, May 16, 31, HAY, Jul 15, Aug
    29, CG, Sep 12, 19, 26, Oct 6, 7, Dec 19; 1797: CG, Feb 18, Apr 25, May 18,
    27, HAY, Jun 23, Aug 14, 15, 24, CG, Sep 25, Oct 16, Nov 2, Dec 18, 26; 1798:
    CG, Feb 12, Apr 27, HAY, Jun 30, Jul 21, Aug 11, CG, Sep 17, Oct 8, 25, 29,
    Nov 12, Dec 11, 15, 26; 1799: CG, Jan 29, Mar 25, Apr 2, 13, 19, May 28, HAY,
    Jul 9, Aug 21, CG, Sep 30, Oct 7, 21, 24, Nov 11, Dec 23; 1800: CG, Jan 16,
    Feb 10, Mar 25, May 1, 23, HAY, Jul 2, Aug 14, 29
Masters, Mrs (dancer), 1775: CG, Oct 13, 17, 21, Nov 21, Dec 26; 1776: CG, Jan
    15, Feb 16, Mar 23, May 4
Masters, Mrs (singer), 1675: ATCOURT, Feb 15
Masterson, Mrs (actor), 1775: CG, Sep 25, Oct 2
Match in Newgate, A. See Bullock, Christopher.
Matelot (dance), 1727: DL, May 17; 1730: DL, May 18, Sep 17, Oct 22; 1733:
    LIF/CG, Apr 30; 1740: DL, Jan 31, Feb 1, 2, 4, 7, 9, 16, 18, 19, Mar 22, 24,
    25, Apr 9, 14, 15, 16, 21, 26; 1741: DL, Jan 12, 13, 16, 22, 24, 27, 31, Feb
    6, CG, 7, DL, 10, 12, 19, CG, Mar 2, DL, 2, 5, CG, 7, DL, 12, 16, CG, 17, Apr
    3, 9, 16, DL, 17, 23, May 9, CG, 11, DL, 11, CG, 12, DL, 18, 21, 22, 27, Nov
    10, 13, 17, 18, 28, 30, CG, 30, DL, Dec 2, 8, CG, 9, 11, DL, 14, CG, 16, DL,
    18, 23, 28; 1742: DL, Jan 6, 7, 11, 14, 16, 18, Feb 1, 5, 6, 11, 12, 27, Mar
    11, CG, Apr 21, DL, 23, Oct 9, 12, 14, 16, 18, 21, 22, 25, 28, Nov 1, 3, 27;
    1743: CG, Mar 24, Apr 9; 1754: CG, Mar.30, Apr 29; 1757: HAY, Oct 21; 1776:
    KING'S, May 16
Matelot Basque (dance), 1752: DL, Oct 5, 7, 10, 12, 14, 17, 18, Nov 6, 23, Dec
    11, 14, 22; 1753: DL, Mar 26, 31, Apr 3, 9, 14, 30
Matelot Provencal (dance), 1764: KING'S, Jan 10, 14, 24, Feb 14, 25, 28, Mar
    29, 31, Apr 10, 14, May 15, CG, Oct 4, 5, 10
Matelot Tambourine (dance), 1741: DL, May 28
Matelote Polonnes (dance), 1741: DL, Dec 31
Matheis (singer), 1734: CR, Nov 27
Mather, Mrs (actor), 1800: HAY, Sep 16
Mather, Mrs (beneficiary), 1744: CG, Apr 7
Mathews, Catherine Mary (dancer), 1772: CG, May 1, 22; 1773: CG, Apr 24, 26,
    May 26; 1774: CG, Apr 15, 16, May 18, 20; 1775: CG, Apr 29, May 3, 11, 26,
    Sep 27, Oct 13, 31, Nov 18; 1776: CG, Jan 23, 24, Apr 13, May 15, Oct 9, Nov
    25; 1777: CG, Jan 21, Feb 15, Sep 24, Oct 1, 3, Nov 25; 1778: CG, May 12, 16,
    Sep 21, Oct 14, 17, 22, Nov 25; 1779: CG, Sep 22, Oct 8, 13, 22, Nov 9, Dec
    29; 1780: CG, Apr 17, May 6, 8, 10, 16, Sep 25, 27, Oct 3, Nov 6, 28; 1781:
    CG, May 7, 18, Sep 26, Oct 20, Nov 1, Dec 19, 26; 1782: CG, Apr 1, 2, 9, 17,
    27, May 17, Sep 25, Oct 7, 8, 22, Nov 29; 1783: CG, Apr 22, 25, 28, May 23,
    24, 26, Sep 17, 22, Nov 19; 1784: CG, Feb 13, Apr 28, May 21, Sep 17, 22, Oct
    6, Dec 1; 1785: CG, Jan 14, Apr 16, 18
Mathews, James (actor), 1786: HAY, Jun 9, 17, 19; 1787: HAY, May 16, Jul 16,
    21, 23, Aug 10, 14, 21; 1788: HAY, Jun 12, Jul 2, Aug 5, 11, 22, 27, 28, Sep
    2; 1789: HAY, May 18, 25, Jun 5, 10, 12, 17, 23, Jul 29, Aug 5, 10, 11, 28

Mathews' Academy, 1760: HAY, Aug 15
Mathias (King's messenger), 1769: CG, Jun 6
Matilda. See Francklin, Dr Thomas.
Matin, Midi, et le Soir, Le (interlude), 1788: DL, May 6, 8
Mativeoff, Andreas Artemonides (Russian ambassador), 1708: DL, Jun 3
Matlose (dance), 1727: DL, May 8, 15
Matrimonial Squabble, The; or, A Cure for Jealousy (interlude), 1741: BFH, Aug
    22
Matrimonio Segreto, Il. See Cimarosa, Domenico.
Matrimony. See Abington, Frances.
Matriomonio Disturbato, Il; or, Pantalon's Marriage Disturbed (play, anon),
    1726: KING'S, Nov 26
Matrone D'Ephese, La; ou, Arlequin Diane (play, anon), 1725: HAY, Apr 16
Mattei, Sga Colomba (singer), 1754: KING'S, Nov 9; 1755: KING'S, Mar 17, Apr
    15; 1756: SOHO, Feb 2, Mar 16, KING'S, Apr 5, 10; 1757: KING'S, Sep 20; 1758:
    KING'S, Jan 10, 31, Apr 6, 18, 26, Nov 11; 1759: KING'S, Jan 16, Mar 5, Nov
    13; 1760: KING'S, Jan 15, Feb 25, Mar 1, Apr 17, May 3, 31, Aug 25, Nov 22,
    Dec 16; 1761: KING'S, Feb 7, Jun 3, Sep 19, Oct 13, 27; 1762: KING'S, Mar 1,
    May 11, 15, Jun 5, Nov 13; 1763: KING'S, May 31; 1765: KING'S, Dec 3
--Promesse del Ciels, Le (serenata), 1761: KING'S, Sep 19
Matteis, Nicholao (musician), 1674: SLINGSBY, Dec 2; 1675: SLINGSBY, Jan 19;
    1679: SLINGSBY, Nov 20; 1698: YB, May 30
Matthews (dancer, singer), 1735: HAY, Dec 13; 1739: CG, May 21, DL, Oct 10, 16,
    18, 22, 24, 25, 26, 27, 29, 31, Nov 1, 2, 10, 13, 20, 21, Dec 7, 12, 14, 28,
    29; 1740: DL, Jan 5, 7, 8, 11, 14, Feb 2, 5, 7, 11, 15, 16, 18, 19, 21, May
    21, GF, Oct 29, Nov 10, 13, 17, 18, 20, 22, 24, 27, Dec 1, 2, 3, 4, 5, 15;
    1741: GF, Jan 20, Feb 2, 9, CG, Nov 30, Dec 9; 1742: DL, May 25; 1743: HAY,
    Mar 23, DL, May 26; 1744: JS, Dec 10; 1746: CG, Mar 22, Apr 5, 7, DL, May 2,
    NWC, Oct 20, SOU, Nov 6, CG, Dec 16, 27; 1747: CG, Apr 23, May 4, 7, DL, Nov
    2, 13, 16, 17, Dec 12, 14, 15, 26; 1748: DL, Jan 8, 14, 18, Feb 9, Mar 14,
    24, Apr 14, 23, 25, May 6, HAY, Sep 5, DL, 20, Oct 15, 27, 29, Nov 7, 9, 12,
    16, 25, 30, Dec 21, JS, 26, DL, 26, 27; 1749: DL, Jan 7, 9, Feb 2, 4, 21, Mar
    13, 14, Apr 12, 14, May 16, BFCB, Aug 23, DL, Sep 26, 28, Oct 11, 18, 23, 28,
    30, 31, Nov 1, 7, 9, 23, 27, Dec 2, 7, 13, 23, 26, 27; 1750: DL, Jan 4, 11,
    18, 19, Feb 21, Mar 10, 13, 17, 27, 31, Apr 5, 16, NWC, 16, DL, 18, 20, 27,
    28, May 4, 7, Sep 11, 20, 21, 27, Oct 13, 15, 17, 20, 22, 29, Nov 7, 13, 17,
    Dec 12; 1751: DL, Jan 22, Feb 16, 23, Apr 8, 9, 10, 12, 16, 20, 22, 24, 26,
    May 1, 3, 6, 11, Sep 7, 10, Oct 1, 9, 15, 17, 18, 19, 28, 29, Nov 5, 18, Dec
    7, 13, 14, 16, 17, 26; 1752: DL, Jan 18, 27, Feb 5, Apr 2, Oct 14, 19, Nov
    16; 1753: DL, Mar 31, Apr 7, 12, 24, Sep 8, 11, 13, 15, Oct 9; 1754: DL, Sep
    21, Oct 3, 11, 14, Dec 16; 1755: DL, Apr 2, 3, 7, 10, 21, Sep 23, Oct 8, Nov
    8, 21, 22; 1756: DL, Apr 21, 23, 30, May 1, 8, 14, Oct 18; 1757: DL, Apr 11,
    27, Sep 10; 1759: DL, May 7, Jun 28, Dec 1; 1760: HAY, Aug 15; 1761: CG, Oct
    13; 1762: DL, May 11, Nov 23; 1763: DL, Jan 3; 1766: KING'S, Aug 25, Sep 5,
    DL, Nov 22
Matthews, Brander (author), 1773: DL, Feb 1
Matthews, Miss (actor), 1756: DL, Dec 3; 1757: HAY, Jun 17; 1758: DL, May 12,
    Dec 7; 1759: DL, Apr 5; 1765: DL, Nov 16; 1766: KING'S, Sep 1; 1767: DL, Jan
    24, May 15, 19, Sep 26, Dec 12; 1768: DL, Jan 28, Aug 18, Sep 23, 26
Matthews, Mrs (actor), 1749: DL, Feb 23; 1750: DL, Oct 1; 1753: DL, Jan 1;
    1755: DL, Nov 8, 15; 1756: DL, Apr 29; 1760: DL, Jul 29, Oct 20; 1761: DL,
    Dec 28
Matthews' scholar (dancer), 1748: DL, Dec 26; 1749: DL, Apr 7, 12
Mattley, Mary (haberdasher), 1759: CG, Nov 1
Mattocks, George (actor, singer), 1749: DL, Oct 20; 1750: DL, Jan 18, 20, Nov
    13, Dec 13; 1751: DL, Apr 25, May 4, Sep 14, 17, 19, 20, 21, Oct 3, 4, 16,
    25, 29, Nov 20, Dec 26; 1752: DL, Jan 1, 9, 28, Mar 2, 9, 17, Apr 23, 25, 28,
    May 2, 5; 1757: CG, Nov 1, Dec 16; 1758: CG, Feb 1, Apr 24, Nov 1, 23; 1759:
    DL, Mar 23, CG, 26, Apr 3, May 1, 3, Nov 30, Dec 10; 1760: CG, Jan 18, Feb
    14, Apr 8, 17, 25, May 21, Sep 22, 29, Oct 3, 6, 15, 20, Nov 22, 28, 29, Dec
    11, 22; 1761: CG, Jan 10, Mar 25, Apr 2, 20, 23, Sep 9, 14, 16, 18, 21, 25,
    26, Oct 9, 13, 24, Nov 4; 1762: CG, Jan 12, 13, 28, Feb 2, Mar 13, 20, Apr
    20, 21, 26, 27, May 11, Sep 22, 24, 29, Oct 1, 8, 25, 26, Nov 1, 3, 15, Dec
    8; 1763: CG, Jan 24, 26, Feb 24, Apr 26, May 14, Sep 19, 21, 28, Oct 3, 8,
    10, 11, 14, 22, Nov 3, 15, Dec 2, 12, 20, 29, 30; 1764: CG, Jan 3, 4, 13, 14,
    16, Feb 22, Mar 24, 27, Apr 7, 10, 28, May 1, 18, 21, 26, Sep 17, 21, 28, Oct
    1, 18, 23, 24, 26, 27, Nov 1, 5, 7, 16, 23, Dec 12; 1765: CG, Jan 31, Apr 9,
    12, 22, May 2, 11, Sep 16, 27, Oct 3, 4, 7, 8, 9, 12, 14, 22, 28, Nov 20, Dec
    6, 7; 1766: CG, Feb 5, 6, Mar 20, Apr 4, 19, May 12, Oct 10, 14, 18, 21, 22,
    Nov 15, 21, Dec 3, 8; 1767: CG, Jan 5, 21, 29, 31, Feb 14, 19, 21, Apr 6, 7,
    11, 21, 27, May 14, 21, 22, Sep 15, 16, 17, 18, 19, 25, Oct 6, 8, Dec 2, 4,
    5, 14, 30; 1768: CG, Jan 1, 6, 15, 20, 26, Feb 1, 25, 27, Apr 5, 8, 12, May

5, 13, 24, 25, Jun 3, Sep 19, 21, 24, 26, 30, Oct 5, 17, 22, 24; 1769: CG,
Jan 14, Feb 18, HAY, 22, CG, Mar 16, Apr 3, 8, 11, 15, 25, May 9, Sep 18, 20,
27, 29, 30, Oct 6, 14, 17, 20, 27, Nov 11, 24, Dec 5, 11, 15; 1770: CG, Jan
3, 25, Feb 23, 27, Mar 8, 10, 27, 31, Apr 3, 7, 23, 25, May 1, HAY, 3, CG, 9,
19, Sep 24, 26, 28, Oct 2, 5, 8, Nov 8, 12, 14, 30, Dec 12, 13, 17; 1771: CG,
Feb 8, Mar 12, 14, Apr 3, 4, 5, 6, 8, 12, 30, May 3, 17, 28, Sep 23, 25, 27,
Oct 22, 28, Nov 1, 7, 8, 9, 12; 1772: CG, Jan 2, Feb 20, 24, Mar 2, DL, 23,
CG, 30, 31, Apr 7, 11, 23, May 2, 20, Jun 1, Sep 23, 25, 30, Oct 13, 14, 17,
Nov 2, 4, Dec 26; 1773: CG, Feb 6, Mar 20, 22, 27, Apr 13, 14, 17, 20, 23,
May 11, Sep 20, 24, 29, Oct 5, 6, 16, 23, 27, Nov 26, 30, Dec 13, 16; 1774:
CG, Jan 29, Feb 7, Mar 14, 19, 26, May 14, Sep 19, 23, 28, Oct 11, 13, 15,
19, 20, Nov 1, 19, 29, Dec 1, 20, 27; 1775: CG, Jan 12, 21, Mar 30, Apr 1, 4,
24, May 15, 18, Sep 20, 22, 25, 27, Oct 6, 16, 17, 18, 19, 31, Nov 13, 21,
Dec 5; 1776: CG, Feb 5, 26, Apr 9, 15, May 13, 18, 20, Sep 27, Oct 7, DL, 9,
CG, 9, 15, 25, 29, Nov 9, 12, 13, 14, 18, Dec 2, 4, 23, 27; 1777: CG, Jan 3,
Feb 25, Mar 31, Apr 14, 22, 29, May 5, Sep 26, 29, Oct 3, 15, 16, 23, 29, 30,
Nov 18; 1778: CG, Jan 29, Feb 4, 24, 26, Apr 11, DL, May 2, CG, 6, HAY, 22,
CG, Sep 18, 25, 28, Oct 23, 26, 27, Nov 23; 1779: DL, Jan 5, CG, Mar 22, 27,
Apr 19, May 6, 13, Sep 22, 24, Oct 8, 16, 20, Nov 8, 11, DL, 27; 1780: CG,
Feb 1, 5, 17, Mar 11, 14, 29, Apr 3, 7, 17, 24, 25, 27, Sep 20, Oct 19, Nov
2, 13, 25, Dec 9, 12, 16; 1781: CG, Jan 13, 16, Mar 31, Apr 2, DL, 21, CG,
24, Sep 17, 21, 24, 26, Oct 19, 23, 25, 27, 31, Nov 8, 12, 28, Dec 5; 1782:
CG, Jan 22, Feb 2, 14, Apr 17, Sep 25, Oct 7, 9, 29, Nov 2, 6, 8, Dec 6, 27;
1783: CG, Feb 19, Mar 3, May 3, 16, 17, 24, Sep 22, Oct 6, 21, 28, Nov 8, Dec
5, 6; 1784: CG, Jan 9, Apr 23, 27, May 7
Mattocks, George and Isabella (actors), 1797: CG, Oct 11
Mattocks, Isabella, Mrs George (actor), 1765: CG, Apr 8, 12, 13, 16, 18, 23,
24, 30, May 2, 7, 8, 23, Sep 16, 20, 27, Oct 4, 5, 8, 10, 12, 25, Nov 12, 28,
Dec 3, 6, 20; 1766: CG, Jan 9, Feb 5, 8, Apr 11, 14, 16, 18, CHAPEL, 30, CG,
May 8, 9, Sep 22, Oct 8, 10, 14, 16, 18, Nov 4, 11, 12, Dec 1, 3, 16, 31;
1767: CG, Jan 21, 23, Feb 5, 11, 17, 21, Mar 23, 28, Apr 4, 7, 11, 24, 27,
May 7, 11, 12, CHAPEL, 13, CG, Sep 16, 18, 19, 22, Oct 5, 8, 27, 28, Nov 4,
7, 10, 17, 18, 23, 27, Dec 5, 8, 14; 1768: CG, Jan 9, 16, 18, 23, 29, Feb 25,
HAY, Mar 4, CG, Apr 5, 12, 16, 19, May 5, 11, 24, CHAPEL, 25, CG, 26, Jun 2,
Sep 19, 21, 23, 24, 28, 30, Oct 5, 7, 10, 14, 15, 22, Nov 1, 4, 9, 18, Dec 3,
12, 21; 1769: CG, Jan 14, 26, 28, Feb 20, Mar 14, 16, 31, Apr 5, 10, May 15,
16, 17, 23, 24, Sep 18, 20, 22, 25, 29, Oct 3, 7, 18, 20, 25, 27, 30, Nov 1,
4, 15, 24, Dec 1, 2, 11, 15, 20, 22, 30; 1770: CG, Jan 3, 5, 23, 24, 25, Feb
3, 9, 23, 27, Mar 8, 20, 22, 29, Apr 2, 7, 20, 26, 30, May 1, HAY, 3, CG, 11,
25, Sep 24, 26, 28, Oct 1, 2, 5, 11, 12, 19, 25, 27, Nov 5, 8, 12, 30, Dec 4,
12; 1771: CG, Jan 4, 25, Feb 9, Mar 23, Apr 4, 6, 12, 18, 19, 20, 22, 23, 24,
25, 27, CHAPEL, 27, CG, May 1, 25, Sep 23, 25, 27, 30, Oct 2, 16, 18, 19, 23,
28, Nov 1, 2, 4, 5, 8, 9, 21, Dec 14, 17; 1772: CG, Jan 15, 18, 21, 25, Feb
20, 22, Mar 5, 21, 23, DL, 23, CG, 24, 28, 30, 31, Apr 4, 7, 11, 20, 21, 23,
25, May 2, 4, 5, 8, 14, 16, 19, 22, 26, Sep 21, 23, 30, Oct 12, 13, 14, 16,
17, 21, 26, 29, Nov 4, 21, Dec 3, 11, 22; 1773: CG, Jan 6, 14, 28, Feb 6, 19,
22, 26, Mar 3, 19, 20, 27, 29, Apr 13, 19, 20, 23, May 3, 11, 27, 28, Sep 24,
27, 29, Dec 8, 16, 21, 23; 1774: CG, Jan 7, 15, 25, 29, Mar 12, 17, 19, 22,
26, Apr 5, 7, 8, 11, 19, 20, 26, May 2, 3, 5, 9, 10, 11, 12, 18, 25, Sep 19,
21, 23, 26, 28, Oct 3, 5, 7, 11, 14, 15, 19, 20, 21, 27, Nov 2, 3, 12, 29,
Dec 1, 3, 15, 20; 1775: CG, Jan 3, 21, Feb 7, 11, 21, DL, Mar 10, CG, 18, 20,
25, Apr 4, 19, 25, 28, May 3, 4, 9, 15, 16, DL, 19, CG, 22, 23, 24, 25, 30,
Sep 20, 22, 27, Oct 12, 13, 16, 17, 18, 20, 23, 30, 31, Nov 1, 3, 11, 13, 14,
21, Dec 29; 1776: CG, Jan 5, STRAND, 23, CG, Feb 5, 9, 26, Mar 5, 16, 25, 30,
Apr 16, 26, 27, May 6, 13, Sep 27, Oct 9, 15, 16, 17, 25, Nov 2, 4, 7, 8, 9,
12, 15, Dec 2, 4, 5, 17; 1777: CG, Feb 5, 22, DL, Mar 22, CG, 31, Apr 7, 14,
16, 28, 29, DL, May 5, CG, 29, Sep 26, Oct 3, 8, 10, 17, 23, 29, 30, Nov 1,
12, 20, 21, Dec 19; 1778: CG, Jan 15, 29, Feb 13, 24, 26, Mar 5, 14, 23, 28,
Apr 21, 25, May 11, 22, Sep 18, 21, 23, 25, Oct 2, 5, 7, 9, 12, 14, 23, 27,
29, DL, Nov 12, CG, 23, Dec 11, 12; 1779: CG, Jan 13, Feb 23, Mar 27, Apr 6,
27, May 10, 15, 18, Sep 22, 24, 27, Oct 8, Nov 4, 22, Dec 1, 3; 1780: DL, Jan
5, CG, 18, Feb 22, Mar 14, 18, 27, Apr 3, 7, 12, May 3, Sep 20, 22, Oct 3, 6,
10, Nov 8, 27, Dec 4, 5, 15; 1781: CG, Jan 1, 10, 12, Feb 10, 15, 24, Mar 22,
24, Apr 2, 7, 18, 28, 30, Sep 19, 21, 26, 28, Oct 19, 23, 26, 27, 30, Nov 2,
28, Dec 8, 18; 1782: CG, Jan 4, 18, 25, Feb 2, 9, Mar 11, 19, Apr 4, 10, 17,
May 7, 11, 28, Sep 23, 25, 30, Oct 3, 8, 9, 17, 18, Nov 6, 14, 27, 29, Dec 6;
1783: CG, Jan 3, Feb 25, Apr 5, 12, May 7, Oct 2, 8, 11, 15, 16, 17, Dec 6;
1784: CG, Jan 14, 23, Feb 20, Mar 16, Apr 13, 14, May 8, 12, 13, DL, 20, CG,
26, 29; 1786: CG, Sep 18, 29, Oct 4, 19, 25, Nov 13, 15, 24, Dec 13, 20, 30;
1787: CG, Jan 2, 6, 26, 27, Feb 10, Mar 27, 31, Apr 16, 17, 30, Sep 19, 28,
Oct 3, 5, 11, 18, 31, Nov 2, 8, 22, 23, 28, 30, Dec 5, 15; 1788: CG, Jan 3,
9, 11, 21, Feb 23, Mar 11, 15, Apr 2, 8, 29, May 12, Sep 15, 24, 26, Oct 7,

15, 17, 24, Nov 1, 7, 10, 21, 22, 27, 28, Dec 19, 31; <u>1789</u>: CG, Jan 28, Feb
24, Mar 28, Apr 30, May 5, 8, 14, 26, Jun 5, Sep 14, 18, Oct 2, 6, 20, 24,
Nov 7, 19, 20, 27, Dec 2; <u>1790</u>: CG, Jan 13, 23, Feb 11, 23, Mar 8, 13, 27,
Apr 7, 20, 27, 29, May 5, 7, 18, Sep 15, Oct 1, 15, 19, 23, Nov 11, 25, Dec
2, 14, 17; <u>1791</u>: CG, Jan 7, 12, Feb 2, 4, Mar 12, 14, Apr 5, May 3, 10, 11,
18, 20, 24, Jun 6, Sep 12, 14, 30, Oct 13, 20, 27, Nov 19, 29, Dec 2, 3, 13;
<u>1792</u>: CG, Feb 6, 8, 18, Apr 10, 18, 21, Sep 17, 19, 20, 21, Oct 1, 3, 12, 17,
19, 24, Nov 10, 24, 28; <u>1793</u>: CG, Jan 2, 29, Apr 15, 24, May 1, 2, 8, 10, 15,
23, 24, 31, Jun 6, Sep 20, 27, Oct 1, 3, 5, 8, 9, 10, 11, 15, 17, 23, 25, Nov
1, 2, 9, 16, 23, Dec 5, 18; <u>1794</u>: CG, Jan 14, 22, Feb 5, 22, 24, 26, Mar 18,
Apr 7, 12, 23, May 7, 16, 26, Jun 5, Sep 15, 26, Oct 8, 17, 23, 30, Nov 19,
20, 22, Dec 6, 8, 10; <u>1795</u>: CG, Jan 8, 24, 29, 31, Feb 6, Apr 8, 22, 28, 29,
May 1, 2, 13, 21, Jun 2, 5, 12, Sep 14, 18, Oct 2, 5, 7, 8, 14, Nov 4, Dec
15, 31; <u>1796</u>: CG, Jan 8, 23, DL, 25, CG, Mar 14, 19, Apr 5, 8, 12, 13, 20,
22, 23, May 28, Jun 2, 6, 7, Sep 12, 14, 16, 21, 26, 28, Oct 5, 14, 29, Nov
7, 17, Dec 14, 17, 21, 22; <u>1797</u>: CG, Jan 4, 7, 10, Feb 23, 25, Mar 4, 16, Apr
8, 29, May 6, 16, 17, 31, Jun 8, 10, 13, Sep 22, 27, Oct 4, 16, 28, Nov 4,
11, 15, 20, 21, Dec 8, 18, 20, 23; <u>1798</u>: CG, Jan 11, Feb 6, 13, Mar 31, Apr
10, 19, 20, 30, May 1, 16, 22, 24, 28, Jun 5, Sep 26, Oct 3, Nov 5, 7, 9, 23,
Dec 8, 26, 29; <u>1799</u>: CG, Feb 4, Mar 16, Apr 2, 19, 26, May 22, 24, 31, Jun 5,
HAY, 22, 29, CG, Sep 16, 20, 27, Oct 2, 16, 17, 25, Nov 8, 11, 30; <u>1800</u>: CG,
Jan 16, Feb 3, 4, Mar 27, Apr 22, 23, 24, 30, May 2, 7, 29, Jun 2, 7
Mattocks, Master (actor, dancer), <u>1746</u>: SFHP, Feb 21, Sep 8; <u>1748</u>: BFH, Aug 24;
<u>1749</u>: DL, Sep 21, 22, 23, 30, Oct 11, 17, 18, 20, 23, 24, 30, Nov 7, 9, 10,
14, 15, 17, 18, 21, 23, 25, 28, Dec 2, 22, 28, 29; <u>1750</u>: DL, Jan 4, 11, 18,
Feb 9, 15, Apr 25, 26, 28, 30, May 4, Sep 18, 20, 27, Oct 1, 13, 30; <u>1751</u>:
DL, Apr 25, May 1, 6, 8, 9, 10, Sep 13, Oct 1, 2
Mattocks, Miss (actor), <u>1746</u>: SOU, Oct 7, 16; <u>1748</u>: CG, Jan 14, May 2, 5; see
also Maddocks, Miss
Mattocks, Miss (actor), <u>1774</u>: CG, May 12; <u>1775</u>: CG, Apr 20
Maudet, Mlle (dancer), <u>1741</u>: BFH, Aug 22; <u>1742</u>: CG, Jan 8, 21, 25, Feb 22, May
8, Oct 1, Dec 21; <u>1743</u>: CG, Mar 8
Maudlin, the Merchant's Daughter of Bristol (play, anon), <u>1720</u>: BFPMJ, Aug 23;
<u>1729</u>: BF, Aug 26; <u>1734</u>: SFG, Sep 7; <u>1746</u>: SFLY, Sep 8
Mauly (actor), <u>1749</u>: HAY, Nov 14; <u>1750</u>: DL, May 22
Mawby (violoncellist), <u>1798</u>: HAY, Jan 15
Mawley (actor), <u>1733</u>: DL/HAY, Oct 12
Mawson (mercer), <u>1776</u>: DL, Jan 15
Maxfield (actor), <u>1744</u>: GF, Dec 26; <u>1745</u>: GF, Feb 14, Mar 7, Apr 2
Maxfield, George (actor), <u>1675</u>: ATCOURT, Feb 15
Maxwell, Mrs (beneficiary), <u>1798</u>: DL, Jun 11
May (beneficiary), <u>1721</u>: DL, May 30; <u>1722</u>: DL, May 29; <u>1724</u>: DL, May 18; <u>1725</u>:
DL, May 14; <u>1726</u>: DL, May 12; <u>1727</u>: DL, May 19
May balmy peace (song), <u>1794</u>: DL, Apr 11
May Day Dance (dance), <u>1728</u>: LIF, May 2
May Day Frolic, The (dance), <u>1762</u>: DL, May 1
May Day Garland (dance), <u>1770</u>: DL, May 17, 18
May Day Morning, The (dance), <u>1761</u>: DL, Apr 16, 21
May Day; or, The Little Gipsy. See Garrick, David.
May Day; or, The Merry Milkmaids of Islington (play, anon), <u>1746</u>: DL, May 2
May every Hero fall like thee (song), <u>1790</u>: DL, Mar 17
May Game (dance), <u>1748</u>: DL, Feb 9
May Morning's Adventure (song), <u>1734</u>: GF, May 1
May no rash intruder (song), <u>1789</u>: CG, Mar 20; <u>1790</u>: CG, Feb 26; <u>1792</u>: KING'S,
Mar 7; <u>1794</u>: CG, Mar 21; <u>1795</u>: KING'S, Feb 27, CG, Mar 13; <u>1799</u>: CG, Mar 1;
<u>1800</u>: CG, Mar 5
May our Navy Old England for ever protect (song), <u>1794</u>: CG, May 2; see also Our
Laws, Constitution and King; Though Hurricanes rattle
May the Prince and his Bride (song), <u>1795</u>: CG, Apr 9
May, Benjamin (manager), <u>1747</u>: DL, May 14; <u>1755</u>: HAY, Sep 9, 11, 15; <u>1759</u>: DL,
Jan 10
May's Buildings, <u>1741</u>: DL, May 5
Mayer (mercer), <u>1772</u>: CG, Mar 7
Mayers, Mrs (dancer), <u>1704</u>: DL, Jan 12, 18, 24, Feb 1, LIF, 1, DL, 4, 8, 15,
22, 26, 29, Mar 14, 20, 23, LIF, 30, DL, Apr 3
Mayfair, <u>1696</u>: MF, May 0; <u>1699</u>: DL, May 0; <u>1701</u>: DL, May 31; <u>1702</u>: BFGB, Aug
24; <u>1703</u>: BFG, Aug 23; <u>1705</u>: DL, Apr 30, MF, May 1, QUEEN'S, 3; <u>1708</u>:
DL/QUEEN, May 1; <u>1709</u>: DL, Apr 29; <u>1714</u>: SF, Aug 31; <u>1744</u>: MF, Jan 25, MFDSB,
May 1, DL, 11; <u>1745</u>: DL, Apr 22, MF, May 2; <u>1746</u>: NWMF, Oct 6; <u>1748</u>: HAY, Apr
18, NWSM, Nov 30, Dec 26, 29; <u>1749</u>: NWMF, Jan 5, 10, NWSM, May 3, 10, 15, 16;
<u>1752</u>: HAY, Mar 31
Mayle (beneficiary), <u>1741</u>: DL, May 14; <u>1742</u>: DL, May 13; <u>1743</u>: DL, May 12;

1744: DL, May 15
Maynard (actor), 1733: HAY, Mar 27
Mayne (house servant), 1768: CG, Jan 2; 1772: CG, Jan 7
Mayne, Jasper
--City Match, The, 1668: BRIDGES, Sep 28
--Schemers, The; or, The City Match, 1755: DL, Apr 15, 17
Mayo, Mrs (actor), 1756: CG, May 8; 1757: CG, Oct 21
Mayor of Garratt, The. See Foote, Samuel.
Mayor of Quinborough, The. See Middleton, Thomas.
Mazarin, Mme (spectator), 1678: ATCOURT, Jan 18
Mazzinghi, Joseph (composer), 1786: KING'S, Mar 11; 1787: KING'S, Jan 9, Dec 8;
    1788: KING'S, Jan 15, 29, Apr 5, May 8, 15; 1789: KING'S, Jan 10, 24, Mar 24,
    31, May 9, 28; 1791: PAN, Feb 17, Mar 1, 19, Apr 14, May 14, Jun 16, CG, Dec
    3, PAN, 17, 31; 1792: CG, Feb 2, HAY, 14, 28, CG, 28, HAY, Mar 10, 31, Apr
    12, 14; 1794: CG, Nov 17; 1795: KING'S, Mar 26, Jun 20; 1796: KING'S, Feb 20,
    Mar 1, 10, Jun 14, Dec 13; 1797: KING'S, Jan 17, Feb 7, Apr 6; 1798: KING'S,
    May 10, CG, Oct 25, Nov 12; 1799: CG, Mar 16, Oct 24, Nov 14; 1800: CG, Apr
    29, May 1, 17
--Tesoro, Il (opera), 1796: KING'S, Jun 14, 18, Jul 5
Mazzioti, Antonio (singer), 1764: KING'S, Feb 21, Apr 5
Mazzoni (singer, composer), 1754: KING'S, Feb 28; 1786: KING'S, Mar 11
Mazzoni, Sga (dancer), 1773: KING'S, Oct 23, Nov 20, 30, Dec 7; 1774: KING'S,
    Jan 11, 29, Feb 5, 12, Mar 17, 24, Apr 9, 19, 28, May 5, 12, 28, Jun 3
McClean (dancer), 1765: HAY, May 16
McDonald (actor), 1790: CG, Jun 12, 16
McDonald (M'Donald) (beneficiary), 1778: DL, May 25; 1779: DL, May 28; 1780:
    DL, May 20
McDonald (singer, actor), 1772: HAY, Sep 21; 1775: HAY, Feb 20, Nov 20; 1776:
    HAY, Oct 7; 1777: HAY, Apr 22; 1779: HAY, Jan 11, Mar 8; 1780: HAY, Jan 17;
    1782: HAY, Mar 18; 1784: HAY, Feb 9; 1785: HAY, Jan 24
McDonald, Andrew, 1787: HAY, Sep 5
--Vimonda, 1787: HAY, Sep 5, 6, 7, 10; 1788: HAY, Aug 28; 1789: HAY, Jun 17
McGeorge, Horatio Thomas (actor), 1766: HAY, Jun 18, 26, Jul 1, 15, 18, 23, 31,
    KING'S, Aug 8, 13, 18, 20, 25, 27, HAY, Sep 2, KING'S, 9, 12, 13, 15; 1770:
    HAY, May 16, 28, 30, Jun 18
McGeorge, Miss (actor), 1789: CG, Sep 30, Oct 12, Nov 11; 1790: CG, Mar 1, May
    27
McGeorge, Mrs (actor), 1766: HAY, Jun 18, Jul 3, 8, 15, 18, 31, KING'S, Aug 13,
    HAY, 21, KING'S, 25, 27, 29, HAY, Sep 2, KING'S, 5, 9, 13, 15; 1770: HAY, May
    30, Jul 25, Aug 1, 24, 30, 31; 1786: DL, Dec 6; 1792: HAY, Apr 16
McGregor (bagpiper), 1791: CG, May 18
McGuire, Mrs (actor), 1762: HAY, Aug 10
McIntosh (ticket deliverer), 1776: HAY, Oct 7
McLane (bagpiper), 1791: CG, May 18
MClean (actor), 1772: HAY, Dec 21
McLean (beneficiary), 1758: HAY, Mar 13
McMahon (actor), 1766: KING'S, Sep 12, 13
McMillan (stationer), 1783: DL, Jan 14
McMillen (shoemaker), 1771: DL, Nov 19, CG, Dec 10; 1772: CG, Dec 1; 1774: CG,
    Jan 18, May 14
McMillen, Mrs (merchant), 1773: CG, Feb 8
McNally, Mrs, 1784: DL, Aug 20
McNeil (dancer), 1749: DL, Oct 18, 23, 24, Nov 9, 27, Dec 2, 28; 1750: DL, Jan
    1, 18, Feb 19, 21, Apr 5, NWC, 16, DL, 20, Oct 20, Nov 15, 27, Dec 6; 1751:
    DL, Jan 2, May 1
McPherson (actor), 1770: HAY, Mar 19; 1771: HAY, Jun 26
M'Cready (ticket deliverer), 1779: HAY, Dec 27
McTavish (bagpiper), 1791: CG, May 18
M'Donald. See McDonald.
Me when the sun (song), 1791: CG, Mar 30; 1792: CG, Feb 24; 1794: CG, Mar 21
Mea vita mio bene (song), 1758: KING'S, Apr 6
Meachen (actor), 1732: HAY, May 10
Mead (singer), 1799: DL, Feb 4, 9, Mar 2, Apr 16, 23, 29, May 24, Oct 14, Nov
    14, Dec 11, 28; 1800: DL, Jan 1, Mar 11, 13, Apr 29, May 3
Meadows (actor), 1785: HAMM, Jul 1, 4, 8, 11, 15, 25, 26, 27; 1786: HAMM, Jun
    5, 7, 28, 30, Jul 5, 10; 1792: CII, Jan 16
Meadows, William (actor), 1785: HAY, Feb 12, Jun 9, 28, Aug 2, 8, 19, 23, 26,
    31, Sep 16, CG, 19, 23, Oct 17, Nov 4, 14, Dec 5, 26; 1786: CG, Feb 4, Mar
    18, May 24, HAY, Jun 9, 13, 19, Jul 3, 7, 25, Aug 3, 10, 12, Sep 4; 1787:
    HAY, May 16, 18, 23, 25, Jun 26, Jul 2, 16, 19, 21, 23, Aug 4, 10, 14, 21;
    1790: CG, Jun 16
Meads, Mrs (actor), 1740: BFH, Aug 23

Meanwell, T (author), 1748: CG, Nov 15
Meard's Court, 1746: DT, Mar 14
Meares (tailor), 1757: CG, Nov 12; 1759: CG, Nov 10, 17, 24, Dec 1, 8; 1760:
    CG, Jan 5, 12, 19, 26, Feb 2, 9, 16, Mar 1, 8, 22, 29, Apr 14, 28, Sep 22
Mears, Miss (actor, dancer), 1730: DL, May 15, Oct 28, Dec 4; 1731: DL, Feb 8,
    Jun 11, Jul 23, Oct 16, Nov 25, Dec 28; 1732: DL, Feb 22, Mar 21, Apr 28, May
    2, 3, 6, 10, 12, 25, 29, Jun 1, 23, Aug 1, 17, BF, 22, DL, Sep 19, 23, Oct
    19, Nov 8, 17, 20, Dec 6, 11, 14, 18, 26; 1733: DL, Jan 23, Feb 12, Mar 26,
    31, Apr 16, 30, May 5, 7, 9, Oct 10, 12, 24, 31, Nov 13, 21, 23
Mears, William (printer), 1711: SOU, Feb 6; 1716: LIF, Apr 11
Measure for Measure. See Shakespeare, William.
Mechant, Le. See Gresset, Jean Baptiste Louis.
Mechel (Michel) (dancer), 1740: CG, Sep 19, 29, Oct 1, 3, 6, 8, 23, 27, 31, Nov
    3, 7, 13, 15, 18, 19, 20, 25, :7; Dec 2, 4, 5, 9, 11, 12, 13, 16, 19, 20, 30;
    1741: CG, Jan 2, 3, 7, 10, 12, 15, 17, 27, 28, 29, Feb 2, 6, 7, 23, Mar 2, 5,
    7, 9, 10, 12, 16, 17, 30, Apr 1, 2, 3, 6, 7, 8, 9, 10, 11, 13, 16, 17, 18,
    20, 21, 28, May 11, 12, 14, 15, DL, Sep 26, 29, Oct 12, 15, 21, 31, Nov 4,
    14, Dec 19, 30, 31; 1742: DL, Jan 15, Mar 29, Apr 8; 1745: DL, Nov 2, 9, 14,
    20, 21, 23, 25, 29, Dec 2, 3, 5, 7, 9, 10, 11, 13, 17, 26, 28, 31; 1746: DL,
    Jan 1, 4, 6, 7, 8, 23, Apr 16, May 2, 7, 8, 9, 19, Jun 9, 11, Dec 3, 4, 8,
    16, 17, 27, 29; 1747: DL, Apr 25, 28, 30, May 4
Mechel Jr (dancer), 1741: CG, Apr 20; 1742: DL, Apr 8; 1746: DL, Apr 16
Mechel, Mlle (dancer), 1740: CG, Sep 19, 29, Oct 1, 3, 6, 8, 23, 27, 31, Nov 3,
    7, 13, 15, 25, 27, Dec 2, 4, 5, 9, 11, 12, 13, 16, 19, 20, 30; 1741: CG, Jan
    2, 3, 10, 12, 15, 17, 27, 28, 29, Feb 2, 6, 7, 23, Mar 2, 5, 7, 17, 30, Apr
    1, 2, 3, 6, 7, 8, 9, 10, 11, 13, 16, 18, 20, 21, 22, 25, 28, May 2, 11, 12,
    14, 15, DL, Sep 26, 29, Oct 12, 15, 21, 31, Nov 4, 14, Dec 8, 9, 16, 19, 30;
    1742: DL, Jan 5, 15, Mar 29, Apr 8; 1745: DL, Nov 2, 11, 14, 15, 18, 27, 29,
    Dec 2, 3, 5, 9, 10, 11, 13, 17, 20, 31; 1746: DL, Jan 1, 7, 8, 10, 13, 17,
    24, Apr 3, 16, May 2, 7, 8, 9, 19, Jun 9, 11, Dec 3, 4, 8; 1747: DL, Apr 2,
    6, 25, 28, 30, May 4
Mechel, Mons and Mlle (dancers), 1745: DL, Sep 26, Oct 12, 28, 29; 1746: DL,
    Apr 16
Mechels, the (dancers), 1741: DL, Dec 5, 8; 1742: DL, Jan 16, 19, Feb 17, Mar
    18, 22, 25, Apr 8, May 26, 28, 31; 1745: DL, Oct 1, Nov 5, 7, Dec 20, 23;
    1746: DL, Jan 22, Feb 3, 6, 13, Mar 3, 13, Apr 16, 30, May 1, 16, Jun 6, 13;
    1747: DL, Mar 7, 9, 10, 12, 14, 17, 21, 23, 28, 30, 31, Apr 2, 9, 10, 21, 22,
    23
Mechin (actor), 1729: HAY, Mar 27
Mechlin. See Macklin.
Mecklenberg, Charlotte, Princess of, 1761: BFY, Aug 31, SFT, Sep 21
Medbourne, Matthew (actor), 1662: NONE, Sep 0, LIF, 30, ATCOURT, Nov 1; 1663:
    LIF, Feb 23, Oct 0, ATCOURT, Dec 10, LIF, 22; 1664: LIF, Aug 13, Nov 5; 1665:
    LIF, Apr 3; 1666: BRIDGES, Mar 19; 1670: BRIDGES, May 0; 1671: LIF, Jan 10,
    Mar 6, 15, Jun 0, Sep 0, DG, Nov 0; 1672: DG, Jan 31, Aug 3, Nov 4; 1673: DG,
    Feb 18, May 0, Jul 3; 1674: DG, Nov 9; 1675: DG, May 28, NONE, Sep 0, DG, 0;
    1676: DG, Jan 10, Mar 0, Jun 8, Jul 3, 25, Aug 0, Nov 4, Dec 0; 1677: DG, Feb
    12, Mar 24, Jul 0, Sep 0; 1678: DG, Jan 0, May 28, Nov 0
Medea and Jason (ballet), 1781: HAY, Aug 8, 9, 10, 11, 13, 14, 16, 18, 20, 23,
    27, 29, 30, Sep 1, 6, 8, 11, 14, 15; 1782: HAY, Jun 3, 5, 7, 14, 17, 21, 25,
    28, Jul 4, 6, 11, 15, 18, 23, 25, 27, Aug 1, 12; 1783: HAY, Jun 5, 6, 9, 20,
    28, Jul 11, 18, 25, 26, Aug 2, 6; 1784: HAY, Aug 26; 1785: HAY, Mar 10
Medea. See Johnson, Charles; Glover, Richard.
Medecin Malgre Lui, Le. See Centlivre, Susannah, Love's Contrivance; Moliere.
Medee et Jason (dance), 1781: KING'S, Mar 29, 31, Apr 3, 17, 21, 24, 26, May 1,
    10, 12, 22, 31, Jun 9, 12, 19, 21, 26, 30, Jul 3; 1782: KING'S, Apr 11, 25,
    May 16, 21, Jun 3, 25
Medhurst (pastry cook), 1799: HAY, Apr 17
Medina, Miss (singer, actor), 1740: GF, Dec 31; 1741: GF, Feb 3, 59, Dec 10;
    1742: GF, Jan 18, 21, 27, Apr 19, 22, 29, May 27; 1746: GF, Feb 18, 27; 1749:
    DL, Feb 21, 23
Meditation (music), 1715: DL, Apr 20
Medlam, 1767: DL, Jan 14, Apr 24
Medley (actor), 1796: DL, May 11
Medley Cantata (song), 1771: MARLY, Aug 3, 20; 1772: HAY, Aug 10
Medley Concert, A; or, An Impromptu of Whim, Novelty and Amusement (e
    ntertainment), 1757: HAY, Jun 15, 17, 20, 23, 28, Jul 1, 5, 8, 27, 29, Aug 3,
    5, 11, 13, 17, 19, 22, 24, 26, 27, 29, 31, Sep 2, 5, 8, 12, Oct 12, 17, 21,
    Dec 26, 27, 28; 1758: HAY, Jan 6
Medley Dance (dance), 1703: LIF, Jun 11
Medley Epilogue (entertainment), 1761: CG, Mar 14; 1762: CG, Mar 30
Medley Hodge-Podge (entertainment), 1731: LIF, May 28

558

Medley Hornpipe (dance), 1765: CG, Apr 30, May 13; 1766: CG, Apr 30; 1794: CG, May 2
Medley of Jokes (dance), 1730: GF, Jul 17; 1731: GF, Oct 20; 1736: GF, May 6; 1742: DL, May 25; 1743: HAY, Mar 23; 1749: BFCB, Aug 23
Medley of Lovers (song), 1798: CG, May 30
Medley Overture (music), 1735: DL, May 17, GF/HAY, Aug 21, LIF, Sep 5, GF, Oct 15, DL, 18, 21, Nov 17; 1736: HAY, Jan 14; 1760: RANELAGH, Jun 11; 1773: DL, Nov 9; 1776: DL, Apr 22
Medley Prologue (entertainment), 1799: DL, Apr 8
Medley, The (dance), 1734: CG/LIF, Dec 14; 1735: CG/LIF, Jan 13, 14, Feb 3; 1764: DL, Nov 20, 26, 27, Dec 10, 27, 28, 31; 1765: DL, Jan 1, 3, 8, 10, 14, 17, 18, 29, Feb 2, 5, 7, 14, Mar 21, 23, 25, 26, 30, Apr 10, 11, 12, 13, 15, 17, 20, 22, 24, 25, 29, 30, May 2, 4, 8; 1768: DL, Apr 16, 18, 23, 27, 28, May 2, 4, 5, 6, 7, 9, 23, 31; 1771: DL, Apr 24, May 23, 25, 30; 1772: HAY, May 18, 20; 1773: DL, May 8, HAY, 17, 19, Jun 11, Jul 5; 1775: HAY, Jun 12, 14, 16, Jul 5, 7, 19, 31, Aug 11, 18, 25, Sep 1, 8, 14; 1776: HAY, Jul 17, 19, Aug 5, 14; 1784: HAY, May 28, Jun 7, Jul 27
Medley, The (entertainment), 1732: LIF, May 4, 8, 10; 1733: LIF/CG, Apr 2, 17; 1735: LIF, Apr 19; see also Drunken Man
Medley, The; or, Harlequin At-All. See Messink, James.
Medonte. See Sarti, Giuseppe.
Meeting of the Company, The. See Garrick, David.
Megalli, Domenico (singer), 1760: KING'S, Apr 17
Meggs, Mary (orange woman), 1666: BRIDGES, Aug 29; 1667: BRIDGES, Aug 22, 26
Mehun. See Mohun.
Melcomb, Lord, 1761: DL, Jun 18, Jul 27
Mellini (singer), 1750: KING'S, Feb 3, Apr 10
Mellini, Eugenia (singer), 1749: KING'S, Mar 21, Apr 15; 1750: KING'S, Mar 31, Apr 10, HAY, 28; 1754: CG, Nov 18; 1755: HAY, Jan 29
Mellish (actor), 1736: YB, Apr 26
Mellish (composer), 1790: DL, May 20
Mellon, Harriot (actor), 1795: DL, Jan 31, Sep 24, Oct 1, 15, 30, Nov 11, 14, 23, 26, Dec 1, 3, 7, 10, 14, 18, 30; 1796: DL, Jan 8, 11, 12, 16, 18, 29, Feb 20, 27, Mar 3, 5, 12, 14, Apr 13, 30, May 6, 23, Jun 8, Sep 20, 24, Oct 6, 13, 15, 19, Nov 8, 9, 18, Dec 6, 20, 21; 1797: DL, Jan 10, 12, 27, Feb 7, Apr 18, 19, May 12, 17, 23, 26, Jun 7, Sep 21, 23, 30, Oct 3, 7, 28, Nov 2, 4, 15, 18, 30, Dec 9, 11, 23; 1798: DL, Jan 23, Feb 13, May 9, 19, 29, Jun 1, 6, 12, 13, Sep 22, 25, 27, Oct 4, 6, 9, 11, 13, 15, 20, Nov 22, Dec 14, 21; 1799: DL, Jan 5, 9, 17, Feb 1, 14, 23, Mar 9, Apr 5, 8, 17, May 3, 18, 28, Jun 29, Jul 1, 2, Sep 21, 24, 28, Oct 1, 5, 8, 12, 22, 26, Nov 14, 25; 1800: DL, Jan 11, 14, 18, 25, Feb 8, Mar 10, 27, May 1, 24
Melmoth, Charlotte, Mrs Courtney (actor), 1774: CG, Feb 26, Apr 11, 25, Oct 4, 20, 22, 24, Nov 19, Dec 26; 1775: CG, Feb 20; 1776: DL, Nov 25; 1777: DL, Feb 17
Melmoth, Courtney (actor), 1774: CG, Oct 1, 20, Nov 19; 1775: CG, Feb 20
Melmoth, Mr and Mrs (actors), 1775: CG, Apr 18
Melocosmiotes, A (interlude, anon), 1796: CG, May 16
Melvin, John (dancer), 1792: DL, Dec 27
Memi, Mlle (dancer), 1749: DL, Nov 9, 27; 1750: DL, Feb 19, Nov 27
Memorable 13th of September (or, The Siege of Gibraltar) (song), 1790: CG, May 18, 24; see also September the Thirteenth proud Bourbon may mourn
Men Tedela (song), 1746: KING'S, Mar 25
Menage (dancer), 1779: DL, Dec 10, 17; 1780: DL, Apr 18; 1782: DL, May 10, 15, Sep 28; 1784: DL, May 22; 1785: HAY, Apr 15; 1786: DL, Apr 24; 1787: DL, Jan 29; 1789: HAY, May 22, Jun 10, Jul 8; 1702: DL, Dec 27
Menage, Arabella (actor, dancer), 1792: DL, Dec 27; 1798: DL, Oct 6, Nov 14, Dec 4, 17, 29; 1799: DL, Jan 1, 7, 19, 23, Feb 4, May 17, 24, Oct 24, 29, Nov 14, Dec 2, 11; 1800: DL, Jan 1, Feb 17, Mar 10, 11, Apr 29, May 23, 29
Menage, Frederick (dancer, actor), 1792: HAY, Jul 25; 1793: CG, Mar 11, KING'S, Jun 4, 11, HAY, Oct 1, Dec 26; 1794: HAY, Jan 4, DL, Apr 25, May 14, KING'S, 31; 1795: DL, Feb 12, Apr 16, HAY, Jun 10, Aug 27, DL, Sep 26; 1796: KING'S, Jul 7, 12, HAY, 29, Aug 10, DL, Oct 1, 10, 29; 1797: DL, Feb 16, Mar 6, KING'S, Apr 6, DL, May 13, HAY, Jun 26, Jul 7, Aug 19, DL, Sep 19, Nov 7, KING'S, 28; 1798: DL, Mar 22, May 9, 16; 1799: KING'S, Mar 26, DL, May 8; 1800: HAY, Jul 2
Menage, Frederick and Mary (dancers), 1793: DL, May 31; 1794: HAY, Jul 19; 1795: DL, Jun 1; 1796: HAY, Sep 7, DL, Oct 19
Menage, Mary (actor, dancer, singer), 1791: PAN, Feb 17, Mar 19, 22, 24, Dec 17; 1792: HAY, Mar 10, Apr 14, Jun 19, Jul 25, Aug 9, DL, Oct 4, 11, 13, 18, Nov 5, 21, Dec 26, 27; 1793: DL, Mar 7, KING'S, Apr 23, DL, May 10, 31, KING'S, Jun 1, HAY, 12, Aug 3, 6, 12, 23, Sep 19, 30, Oct 1, Nov 19, 30, Dec 26; 1794: HAY, Jan 4, Feb 8, 24, DL, Apr 21, 25, 29, May 16, 19, 24, Jun 9,

Jul 2, HAY, 17, 18, 21, 24, 28, Aug 22, 27, DL, Sep 27, Oct 7, 22, 27, 31,
Nov 15, Dec 20; 1795: DL, Jan 19, Feb 12, Apr 16, 27, May 6, 20, 26, HAY, Jun
9, 10, 13, 20, Jul 31, Aug 18, DL, Sep 26, 29, Oct 30, Nov 11, 23, Dec 10,
30; 1796: DL, Jan 8, 11, 18, Mar 3, 12, Apr 25, 30, May 4, Jun 4, HAY, 13,
15, 25, Jul 9, 15, Aug 29, DL, Sep 29, Oct 10, 19, Nov 9; 1797: DL, Jan 7,
20, Feb 9, 16, Mar 6, KING'S, Apr 6, HAY, Jun 19, 23, 24, Aug 9, 14, 15, 24,
Sep 4, DL, Nov 7, 8, Dec 9; 1798: DL, Jan 16, Feb 20, 24, Mar 6, May 16, Jun
4, HAY, 12, 20, 30, Jul 13, 21, Aug 2, 11, 20, DL, Oct 6, Nov 14, 26, Dec 4,
29; 1799: DL, Jan 19, Mar 2, 4, 11, 26, May 4, 24, HAY, Jul 9, 10, 23, Aug 5,
13, 21, DL, Oct 12, 14, Nov 14, Dec 11; 1800: DL, Jan 1, Mar 11, Apr 29, HAY,
Jun 16, 21, Jul 2, 26, 28, Aug 14, 20
Menage, Miss E (dancer), 1792: HAY, Jul 25
Menasier, Sga. See Manesiere, Sga.
Mendenia, Sga (singer), 1754: HAY, Apr 22
Mendez (actor), 1767: HAY, Jun 22, Aug 12
Mendez (actor), 1781: HAY, Nov 12
Mendez (treasurer), 1763: HAY, Aug 11
Mendez, Moses (author, renter), 1746: DL, Mar 18; 1749: DL, Dec 2; 1750: DL,
Dec 13; 1751: DL, Nov 19
--Chaplet, The (musical), 1749: DL, Dec 2, 4, 5, 6, 7, 8, 9, 11, 12, 13, 14,
15, 16, 18, 19, 21, 23, 28, 30; 1750: DL, Jan 4, 11, 18, 23, Feb 8, 10, 13,
20, Mar 13, 20, 24, 31, Sep 20, 21, 27, Oct 19, 26, Nov 7; 1751: DL, Feb 16,
Mar 11, 18, Apr 19, 30, May 4, 17, Oct 1, 3, 9, 12, 17, Nov 15, 19, Dec 4,
13, 19; 1752: DL, Jan 28, Feb 3, Apr 24, May 12, Sep 23, 28, Oct 10, 19;
1753: DL, Mar 1, 19, 20, 29, Apr 24, May 18, 25, Sep 13, 20, Oct 2, 11, Nov
1, 6, 15; 1754: DL, Jan 16, Feb 6, Apr 26, May 9, Oct 3, 30, Nov 22, Dec 3;
1755: DL, Jan 25, Apr 8, Sep 27, Oct 18, Nov 27, Dec 11, 12, 17; 1756: DL,
Jan 10, Feb 16, Apr 8, May 3, Oct 19, 30, Dec 8; 1757: DL, Feb 18, Apr 15,
19, 26, Sep 29, Oct 6, Nov 18, Dec 13; 1758: DL, Jan 25, CG, Apr 24, DL, 27,
Sep 30, Oct 7, 21, Dec 4, 9; 1759: DL, Mar 17, Nov 22; 1760: CG, Oct 3; 1761:
DL, Jan 12, 13, 15, CG, Apr 6, DL, 8, CG, 11, DL, 18, CG, May 6, DL, 11, CG,
12, Sep 18, Oct 1, DL, 7, CG, 10, DL, 24; 1762: DL, Feb 10, CG, Apr 22, Oct
26; 1763: CG, Apr 5; 1764: DL, Apr 26, CG, Nov 16, Dec 1; 1765: CG, Jan 25,
Oct 8, Nov 30, Dec 21; 1766: CG, Feb 3; 1767: CG, Apr 27, May 14, Sep 16;
1768: CG, Jan 29, DL, Apr 11; 1769: CG, Oct 20, 26, Dec 4; 1770: CG, May 18,
Sep 24; 1771: DL, Feb 9, 14, Apr 11, Sep 24; 1772: DL, Mar 26; 1773: DL, Mar
29; 1774: CG, Jan 29, May 19, Oct 11; 1775: CG, Jan 17; 1782: DL, Apr 20;
1784: DL, Dec 18, 21; 1785: DL, Jan 4; 1794: DL, Oct 16, 18
--Double Disappointment, The, 1746: DL, Mar 18, 22, Apr 3, 7, 11, 14, 17, 22,
May 3, 7, Nov 1, 4, 7, 8, 10, 11, 15, 17, 18, 20, 22, 24, 26, Dec 6, 9, 27;
1747: DL, Jan 20, 24, Feb 5, Mar 2, 23, Apr 10, 21, 25, 28, May 6, 8, 14, 16,
Sep 19, 22, Oct 17, 20, 21, Nov 4, 10, Dec 15, 29; 1748: DL, Jan 13, Mar 3,
Apr 12, 18, 23, May 9, 25; 1752: DL, Oct 11, 16, 17, 23, Nov 30, Dec 1, 5, 7,
13, 20, 21, 23; 1753: DL, Feb 6, 23, Mar 27, 31, Apr 10, May 9, 14, 15, 16;
1754: CG, Apr 25, May 3, 4, 7, 13, 15, 18, 21, Oct 2, 26, 31, Dec 3; 1755:
CG, Apr 25, May 15, Oct 10, Dec 9, 12, 31; 1756: CG, Jan 31, Sep 24; 1757:
CG, Jan 3, Apr 22, May 10, 20, Sep 23; 1758: CG, Oct 4, 23, Nov 9, 22; 1759:
CG, Mar 22; 1760: DL, Apr 29, May 3, Sep 20, CG, Oct 8, DL, Nov 27, 28; 1761:
CG, Apr 22, DL, May 20, Sep 12, Nov 30; 1762: DL, May 15, Sep 28, CG, Oct 8;
1767: DL, Nov 7; 1771: DL, Apr 30; 1773: HAY, Jun 16
--Robin Hood (musical), 1750: DL, Dec 11, 13, 14, 15, 17, 22
--Shepherd's Lottery, The (musical), 1751: DL, Nov 11, 19, 20, 21, 22, 23, 25,
26, 30, Dec 2, 3, 7, 10, 20, 21; 1752: DL, Jan 17, 25, Mar 7, Apr 2, 4, 9;
1753: DL, Apr 27, May 25, Sep 22, Oct 5, Nov 26; 1754: DL, Apr 4, 18
Mendez, Tabitha (renter), 1758: CG, Apr 29
Mendoza, Daniel (pugilist), 1789: CG, Jan 5
Menechmes, Les. See Regnard, Jean Francois.
Mengozzi, Bernardo (singer), 1786: KING'S, Dec 23; 1787: KING'S, Feb 17, 27,
Mar 1, 15, Apr 17, 24, May 1, 29, Jun 16
Menschenhass und Reue. See Kotzebue, August Friedrich Ferdinand von.
Menteur, Le. See Corneille, Pierre.
Mentoreni, Sga (dancer), 1754: HAY, Mar 11, 30, Apr 1
Mentz, Elector of, 1772: CG, Mar 6, DL, 11
Meraspe o L'Olimpiade. See Rolli, Paolo Antonio.
Mercante Prodigo, Il; or, Harlequin a Prodigal Merchant (farce), 1726: KING'S,
Nov 16
Mercato di Malmantile, Il. See Galuppi, Baldassare.
Mercer (spectator), 1664: LIF, Sep 10, Dec 2; 1665: LIF, Apr 3; 1666: MOORFLDS,
Aug 22, Sep 1; 1667: BRIDGES, Apr 8, Sep 16, Oct 28; 1668: NURSERY, Jan 7,
LIF, May 7, 11, BRIDGES, 14, 18, LIF, Jun 24, BF, Aug 29, BRIDGES, Oct 12
Mercer, Mary (spectator), 1668: LIF, Aug 31
Mercers, Company of, 1686: CITY, Oct 29

Merchant of Venice, The. See Shakespeare, William.
Merchant Taylors' School, scholars of, 1665: MTS, Mar 0
Merchant Taylors, Company of, 1660: CITY, Oct 29; 1666: CITY, Oct 29; 1680:
    CITY, Oct 29; 1682: CITY, Oct 30; 1693: CITY, Oct 30
Merchant Taylors' Hall, 1678: MTH, Jun 20; 1690: MTH, Mar 27; 1753: KING'S, Mar
    2
Merchant, Mrs (actor), 1678: DL, Feb 0, Mar 0
Mercier, Louis Sebastien (author), 1791: HAY, Jul 9; 1800: HAY, Jul 15
Mercurians, Society of, 1741: JS, Nov 9
Mercury Harlequin. See Woodward, Henry.
Mercy (musician), 1716: LIF, Apr 9; 1719: HIC, Feb 13; 1735: YB, Apr 1
Meredith (actor), 1789: CG, Apr 28; 1792: HAY, Apr 16; 1797: HAY, Jan 23, 26,
    May 10; 1798: HAY, Mar 26
Meredith (house servant), 1745: HAY, Mar 4; 1751: HAY, Dec 20; 1754: HAY, Apr
    22
Meredith (singer), 1773: HAY, Feb 26, Apr 23; 1778: CG, Mar 6
Meredith (singer), 1794: DL, Mar 12, 19, 26, Apr 2, 4, 9, 10, 11; 1798: CG, Jun
    11
Meredith, Amos (author), 1729: HAY, Mar 29
Meredith, Miss, 1760: CG, Mar 29
Merighi Song (song), 1731: DL, May 6
Merighi, Antonia (singer), 1729: KING'S, Dec 2; 1730: KING'S, Feb 24, Apr 4,
    May 19, Nov 3; 1731: KING'S, Feb 2, Apr 6, DL, Jul 27; 1736: KING'S, Nov 23,
    CG, 27; 1737: KING'S, Jan 8, Feb 12, Apr 12, May 24, Oct 29; 1738: KING'S,
    Jan 3, 28, Feb 25, Mar 14, Apr 15
Merit, Miss (actor), 1753: HAY, Mar 13
Merit, Mrs (chimney sweeper), 1772: DL, Apr 24
Merlin. See Phillips, Edward, The Royal Chace.
Merlin the British Enchanter; or, St George for England, (play, anon), 1738:
    SFL, Sep 5
Merlin the British Enchanter; or, The Child has Found his Father (droll), 1724:
    SF, Sep 2
Merlin; or, The British Enchanters (play), 1731: SFGT, Sep 8
Merlin; or, The Devil of Stonehenge. See Theobald, Lewis.
Merlin; or, The Enchanter of Stonehenge (pantomime), 1767: SW, May 13, Jun 13
Merlin, Joseph (instrument maker), 1777: DL, Jan 4
Mermaid Court, 1726: SOU, Sep 27; 1735: SFLT, Sep 4; 1736: SF, Sep 7; 1738:
    SFH, Sep 5
Mermaid, The (farce), 1792: CG, Mar 26
Merode e Selinunte. See Franklin, Andrew.
Merope. See Hill, Aaron; Bianchi Jr, Francesco.
Merrifield (dancer), 1763: CG, May 13; 1764: CG, May 22; 1765: CG, May 20;
    1769: CG, Nov 4; 1770: CG, May 12; 1771: CG, May 17; 1772: CG, Apr 20, May 1,
    16; 1773: CG, Apr 15, 24, May 26; 1774: CG, May 18; 1775: HAY, Feb 2, CG, May
    26, HAY, Oct 30; 1776: CG, May 15
Merrivale (actor), 1724: LIF, May 20, SOU, Sep 24
Merry Andrew (droll), 1668: BF, Aug 29
Merry Beggars (song), 1731: DL, Apr 5
Merry Beggars, The (play, anon), 1756: BFGR, Sep 3
Merry Cobler (song), 1746: GF, Feb 17
Merry Cobler of Castlebury, The. See Stuart, Charles, The Cobler of
    Castlebury.
Merry Cobler of Preston, The. See Bullock, Christopher, The Cobler of Preston.
Merry Cobler, The. See Coffey, Charles.
Merry Conceited Humours of Bottom the Weaver, The (droll, anon), 1661: ATCOURT,
    Apr 20
Merry Counterfeit, The. See Behn, Aphra.
Merry Couple, The (dance), 1732: LIF/CG, Nov 16
Merry Devil of Edmonton, The (play, anon), 1661: VERE, Aug 10; 1662: VERE, Jan
    6; 1669: BRIDGES, Jan 12; 1690: NONE, Sep 0
Merry Gardeners (dance), 1786: HAY, Jun 23, 27
Merry Lass (dance), 1732: GF, Mar 6, 16, Apr 18, May 2, 10, 15, 17, 18, 23, Oct
    26, 27, Nov 14, 15; 1733: GF, Jan 12; 1774: HAY, Jun 13; 1775: HAY, May 31,
    Jun 2, 7, 9, 19, 28, 30, Jul 3, 17, 21, 24, Aug 2, 9, 21, 28, Sep 6, 11, 15;
    1776: HAY, May 20, 22, 31, Jun 17, 19, 21, Jul 5, 12, 15, 26, 31, Aug 7, 16;
    1777: HAY, Jun 11, Jul 7, 28; 1778: HAY, May 18, 22, 29, Jun 1, 5, 11, 12,
    15, 16, 22; 1785: HAY, Jun 23, 25, Jul 5, 30
Merry Masqueraders, The. See Aubin, Mrs.
Merry Milkmaids of Islington, The; or, The Rambling Gallants Defeated (play,
    anon), 1661: LIF, Jul 5, 9; 1679: NONE, Sep 0
Merry Month of May (song), 1728: LIF, Apr 30, May 2, 3, 11, 16, 30; 1730: LIF,
    May 1

Merry Peasants (dance), 1775: DL, Oct 18, 19, 24, 26, 27, Nov 9, 10, 16, 21, 23, 27, Dec 9, 29; 1776: DL, Jan 2, 10
Merry Roundelay (song), 1782: HAY, Apr 9, May 6; 1783: CG, May 17; 1784: DL, May 5, 24
Merry Sailor and the Lively Lass, The (dance), 1735: DL, Dec 27
Merry Sailors (dance), 1767: CG, Oct 9, 10, 14, 16, 27, 31, Nov 10, 27, Dec 9, 11, 16, 22, 30; 1768: CG, Jan 2, 22, 25, Feb 4, 10, 22, 27, Mar 5, Apr 5, 11, 18, 22, May 4, Jun 1, 2, Sep 20, 27, Oct 13, 21, 26, Nov 19, 25; 1769: CG, Jan 17, Mar 16, Apr 4, 15, 25, 26, May 5, 8, 9, 10, 15, 18, 25, Oct 18, Nov 1, 2, Dec 8, 16, 29; 1770: CG, Feb 6, 8, 12, May 15, 16, 22, Oct 15, 17, 26; 1771: CG, Jan 29, Feb 4, 8, 16, 28, Apr 1, Oct 26; 1772: CG, Jan 17, Apr 25, Oct 12, Nov 4, 12, 23, 28, Dec 10, 19, 31; 1773: CG, Feb 8, Apr 21, May 18, Oct 7, Nov 18, 24, Dec 4; 1774: CG, Feb 12, Apr 18, 29, Oct 26, 27, Nov 4, 7; 1775: CG, Apr 1, 8, 25; 1776: CG, Mar 14, 30, Apr 11, 27, May 14, Nov 6, 7; 1777: CG, Jan 10; 1778: CG, Sep 25; 1781: CG, Feb 13, Sep 21; 1782: CG, Apr 8, May 28; 1783: CG, Feb 21, DL, May 2, HAY, Sep 17; 1784: DL, Apr 12; 1785: CG, Sep 19, Dec 7; 1788: CG, May 15; 1793: CG, Apr 25; see also Jovial Sailors
Merry Sherwood. See Pearce, William.
Merry Sketch of Folly and Fashion, A (interlude, anon), 1790: CG, Jul 16
Merry Throwster, The (opera, anon), 1731: GF, Mar 8
Merry Wife Constant, The (dance), 1733: LIF/CG, May 14
Merry Wives of Broad Street, The. See Shadwell, Charles.
Merry Wives of Windsor, The. See Shakespeare, William.
Merry Woodcutters (dance), 1784: DL, Dec 3
Merry, Anne, Mrs Robert (actor), 1791: CG, Sep 12, 16, 19, 23, 26, Oct 24, Nov 4, Dec 15, 21, 26; 1792: CG, Feb 18, Apr 12, 18, May 2, 5
Merry, Robert, 1789: DL, May 11, CG, 15, Oct 7; 1790: CG, Apr 6, 14, 29, May 18, Dec 20; 1791: CG, Apr 5, May 14, Nov 5; 1792: CG, Feb 2; 1796: DL, Apr 2
--Lorenzo, 1791: CG, Apr 5, 7, 9, 14, 27, May 7
--Magician no Conjurer, The (opera), 1792: CG, Feb 2, 3, 4, 7
Messiah, The. See Handel, George Frederic.
Messin, Count (died), 1754: DL, Feb 7
Messink (actor), 1734: HIC, Apr 5; 1741: DT, Feb 19; 1742: CG, Mar 27; 1743: DL, Feb 2, HAY, Mar 24; 1744: HAY, Jan 19, CG, Mar 3, HAY, Nov 5; 1745: CG, Jan 14; 1746: CG, Apr 29; 1748: CG, Apr 26; 1750: DL, Dec 13
Messink Jr (actor), 1745: HAY, Feb 14; 1748: HAY, Dec 9
Messink, James (actor, pantomime writer), 1767: DL, Sep 26, Oct 8, 22, Nov 26, Dec 26; 1768: DL, Feb 29, Apr 9, 23, Sep 8, 20, 26, 28, Oct 10, 13, 31, Nov 5; 1769: DL, Apr 3, 10, 26, Sep 21, Oct 4, 5, 14; 1770: DL, Mar 22, May 2, 7, 14, 29, Jun 7, Sep 29, Oct 3, 13, 25, Nov 3, 17; 1771: DL, Feb 5, Mar 7, 23, Apr 1, 2, 24, Sep 26, 28, Oct 1, 3, 21, Nov 11, Dec 26; 1772: DL, Jan 28, Apr 20, May 5, Sep 29, Oct 3, 16, Nov 17, 18, Dec 26; 1773: DL, Feb 5, May 8, Sep 21, 25, Oct 25, Nov 2, 25; 1774: DL, Apr 15, 19, 21, 30, May 14, Sep 20, 29, Oct 1, 14, Nov 5, 7; 1775: DL, Jan 2, 19, Mar 23, May 10, Sep 26, Oct 11, 17, Nov 17, 22, 23, 24, Dec 2, 11, 29; 1776: DL, Apr 12, 23, May 11, Sep 26, Oct 1, 9; 1777: DL, Jan 1, May 15, CG, Nov 25; 1778: CG, Feb 23, Apr 30, Oct 14, 22; 1779: CG, Apr 24, May 12, Oct 20, 23; 1780: CG, May 6, 17, Sep 25, Oct 2, Dec 29; 1781: CG, May 3, Oct 1, 20, Dec 26; 1782: CG, May 8; 1792: CG, Dec 20; 1796: CG, Mar 15, Oct 24
--Choice of Harlequin, The; or, The Indian Chief (pantomime), 1781: CG, Dec 26, 27, 28, 29, 31; 1782: CG, Jan 1, 2, 3, 4, 5, 7, 8, 9, 10, 11, 12, 14, 15, 16, 17, 18, 19, 21, 22, 23, 24, 25, 26, 28, 29, 31, Feb 1, 2, 4, 5, 6, 7, 28, Mar 2, 4, 7, 9, 11, 12, Apr 3, 11, 15, 22, May 16, 20, 27, Oct 10, 14, 17, 21, 24, 28, Nov 1, 9, 11; 1783: CG, Sep 22, 29, Oct 6, 20, 22, 29, Nov 3; 1789: CG, Dec 21; 1790: CG, Nov 15; 1793: CG, Oct 2; 1796: CG, Mar 15, Oct 24; 1799: CG, May 13
--Elopement, The (pantomime), 1767: DL, Dec 26, 28, 29, 30, 31; 1768: DL, Jan 1, 2, 4, 5, 6, 8, 9, 11, 12, 14, 15, 18, 19, 20, 21, 22, 29, Feb 6, 11, 16, 22, 23, 25, Mar 14, Apr 16, 19, 20, 21, May 12, 26, Sep 8, 20, Oct 10, 19, 21, 22; 1770: DL, Oct 13, 15, 16, 18, 19, 23, 24, 31, Nov 1, 5, 6, 8, 10, 14, 17, 30, Dec 1; 1771: DL, Jan 5, Feb 1, 8, Mar 4, Apr 6, 24, May 2, 9, Oct 21, 22, 23; 1772: DL, May 16, 19, Nov 18, 23, 25, 28, Dec 17; 1773: DL, Apr 24, May 4, 8, 21, Sep 21, 23, 28, Oct 7, 14, 20, 29, Nov 18; 1774: DL, Apr 4, 30, Sep 29, Oct 4, 6, 12, 26, 27, 29, 31, Nov 9, 19, 28, Dec 26, 27; 1775: DL, Apr 27, Oct 17, 19, 30, Nov 2, 3; 1776: DL, Apr 23, Oct 1, 8, 12, Nov 18, 20, 29; 1777: DL, Nov 10, 11, 13, Dec 27; 1779: DL, May 11, Sep 21, 28, Oct 16, Nov 19, Dec 29; 1780: DL, Oct 23, 24, 30, Dec 5, 27; 1781: DL, Jan 10, 17; 1784: DL, May 7; 1786: HAMM, Aug 8; 1789: DL, Dec 26
--Medley, The; or, Harlequin At-All (pantomime), 1778: CG, Oct 14, 15, 16, 17, 19, 26, Nov 2, 14, 18, 30, Dec 7, 9, 14, 28, 30, 31; 1779: CG, Mar 13, Apr 23
--Norwood Gypsies, The (pantomime), 1777: CG, Nov 25, 26, 27, 28, 29, Dec 1, 2,

3, 4, 5, 6, 8, 9, 15, 26, 27, 29, 30, 31; <u>1778</u>: CG, Jan 1, 2, 3, 5, 6, 7, 8, 9, 10, 12, 13, 14, 17, 20, 26, 27, 31, Feb 3, 9, 14, Mar 16, 19, Apr 9, 23, 30, May 4, 14, 25, Oct 22, 27, Nov 3; <u>1779</u>: CG, May 12; <u>1780</u>: CG, May 6, 8, 10, 16, 17, 20, Sep 25, 27, Oct 2, 9, 16, Nov 28, Dec 2, 11, 18, 20; <u>1781</u>: CG, Oct 20, 22, 27, 29; <u>1789</u>: CG, Dec 21; <u>1790</u>: CG, Nov 15; <u>1793</u>: CG, Oct 2; <u>1799</u>: CG, May 28, 30
--Pigmy Revels, The; or, Harlequin Foundling (pantomime), <u>1772</u>: DL, Dec 14, 26, 28, 29, 30, 31; <u>1773</u>: DL, Jan 1, 2, 4, 5, CG, 6, DL, 6, 7, 8, 9, 11, 12, 13, 14, 15, 16, 18, 20, 21, 23, 25, 26, 28, Feb 6, 9, 12, 16, 18, 20, 25, Mar 15, 16, May 20, Sep 25, Oct 21, 23, 27, Nov 3, 20; <u>1774</u>: DL, Apr 20, 28
Messis, Mrs (actor), <u>1733</u>: GF, May 7
Metamorphoses D'Arlequin, Les (pantomime, anon), <u>1724</u>: HAY, Dec 17, 18; <u>1725</u>: HAY, Mar 4, May 5; <u>1726</u>: HAY, Apr 13
Metamorphoses of Cartouche, The (pantomime, anon), <u>1727</u>: LIF, Apr 24
Metamorphoses of Harlequin, The (pantomime, anon), <u>1732</u>: TC, Aug 4; <u>1741</u>: CG, Nov 7; <u>1745</u>: CG, Jan 1; <u>1756</u>: CG, Jan 6, Oct 13
Metamorphoses of the Windmills (dance), <u>1741</u>: CG, Apr 20
Metamorphoses, The. See Dibdin, Charles.
Metamorphosis of the Beggar's Opera, The (ballad opera), <u>1730</u>: HAY, Mar 11
Metamorphosis, The. See Jackson, William.
Metamorphosis, The; or, The Old Lover Outwitted. See Corey, John.
Metamorphosis, The; or, Wizard of the Village (dance), <u>1765</u>: DL, Apr 27
Metastasio, Pietro Bonaventura, <u>1731</u>: KING'S, Feb 2; <u>1732</u>: KING'S, Nov 4; <u>1734</u>: KING'S, Oct 29; <u>1735</u>: KING'S, Nov 25; <u>1736</u>: KING'S, Nov 23; <u>1742</u>: KING'S, Apr 20, Dec 4; <u>1744</u>: KING'S, Apr 24; <u>1748</u>: KING'S, Mar 14, 26, May 7; <u>1754</u>: KING'S, Apr 23, Nov 9; <u>1755</u>: KING'S, Apr 12, Dec 9; <u>1756</u>: KING'S, Feb 17; <u>1760</u>: SOHO, Mar 13; <u>1761</u>: SOHO, Jan 21; <u>1768</u>: HAY, Feb 24; <u>1770</u>: CG, Mar 16, Apr 4; <u>1771</u>: CG, Mar 6; <u>1772</u>: HAY, Apr 6; <u>1773</u>: CG, Mar 19; <u>1774</u>: KING'S, Dec 3; <u>1778</u>: KING'S, May 30, Nov 28; <u>1779</u>: KING'S, Jan 23, Nov 27; <u>1784</u>: KING'S, May 8; <u>1785</u>: KING'S, Jan 8, Apr 16; <u>1786</u>: KING'S, Feb 14, Dec 23; <u>1789</u>: KING'S, Jun 2; <u>1790</u>: HAY, Apr 6; <u>1792</u>: DLKING'S, May 23; <u>1796</u>: DL, Nov 15; <u>1800</u>: KING'S, May 22
--Alessandro Nell Indie (opera), <u>1756</u>: KING'S, Dec 11, 14, 18, 21; <u>1757</u>: KING'S, Jan 4, 8, 11, 15, Mar 1, 5; <u>1761</u>: KING'S, Oct 13, 24, Nov 7, 14, 21, 28, Dec 5, 12, 19; <u>1764</u>: KING'S, Mar 13, 17, 20, 24, 31, Apr 7, 14, 28, May 15; <u>1774</u>: KING'S, Dec 3, 10, 17, 31; <u>1789</u>: KING'S, Jun 2
Metburn. See Medbourne.
Mettalcourt, C (dancer), <u>1780</u>: CG, Dec 5
Metteer (actor), <u>1755</u>: HAY, Sep 1, 3, 9, 11, 15
Meuniers Amoureux de la Coquette (dance), <u>1741</u>: GF, Sep 14
Meure, Hutchinson (financier), <u>1747</u>: DL, Apr 9
Mew (actor), <u>1723</u>: HAY, Mar 14, Apr 15, 22
Mew's Coffee House, <u>1746</u>: DT, Mar 14; <u>1756</u>: DL, Apr 24
Mexicains (dance), <u>1775</u>: KING'S, Feb 7
Meyer, Charles (harpist), <u>1791</u>: CG, Oct 24, Dec 2; <u>1792</u>: KING'S, Mar 23, HAY, Apr 17
Meyer, Jeremiah (author), <u>1792</u>: CG, Apr 17
Meyer, Philipp Jacob (harpist), <u>1789</u>: KING'S, Jun 15; <u>1791</u>: CG, Mar 18, KING'S, May 23, Jun 6, DLKING'S, Nov 19, 22; <u>1792</u>: HAY, Apr 14; <u>1793</u>: DL, May 23; <u>1794</u>: DL, Apr 9; <u>1795</u>: DL, May 4, 21; <u>1799</u>: KING'S, May 30
Meyers (singer), <u>1796</u>: DL, Sep 29, Oct 19, Nov 9; <u>1797</u>: DL, Jan 7, Feb 9, May 18, Nov 8; <u>1798</u>: DL, Jan 16, Feb 1; <u>1799</u>: DL, Jan 19, 28
Meyler, William (prologue and epilogue writer), <u>1786</u>: CG, Mar 14
Mezierres (dancer), <u>1787</u>: KING'S, Dec 8
Mezzetin a Clown and two Chairmen (dance), <u>1703</u>: LIF, Jun 8
MGeorge. See McGeorge.
Mi Credi In Fedele (song), <u>1729</u>: LIF, Mar 5
Mi Dona mi Vende (song), <u>1762</u>: KING'S, May 11
Mi Volgo (song), <u>1729</u>: DL, Mar 26; <u>1733</u>: DL/HAY, Oct 13
Mia speranza, La (song), <u>1729</u>: HIC, Apr 30
Micco, Tuskeestannagee Whosly Powov (American Indian), <u>1719</u>: LIF, Dec 21; see also American Princes; Indian Kings, American
Michael (actor), <u>1744</u>: HAY, Sep 29
Michan (singer), <u>1776</u>: DL, Nov 25
Michel, Master (dancer), <u>1785</u>: HAY, Jul 1
Michel, Miss (dancer), <u>1785</u>: HAY, Jul 1
Michel, Pierre (dancer), <u>1786</u>: KING'S, Apr 1
Micheli, Sga (singer), <u>1774</u>: KING'S, Jan 11, Apr 19
Michell, Betty (spectator), <u>1667</u>: BRIDGES, Feb 5
Michell, Mary (renter), <u>1758</u>: CG, Feb 23
Michell, Mr and Master (dancers), <u>1800</u>: CG, Apr 29
Michelli, Leopoldo (singer), <u>1762</u>: HAY, Apr 22; <u>1765</u>: KING'S, Jan 26, Mar 28;

1766: KING'S, Nov 25; 1767: KING'S, Oct 27; 1773: KING'S, Nov 20, Dec 7;
1774: KING'S, Mar 8, 17, Jun 3; 1776: KING'S, Nov 2, 5; 1777: KING'S, Jan 21,
Feb 4, Mar 1, 13, 15, Apr 1, 29, May 15, 20, 24, Nov 4, 8, Dec 16; 1778:
KING'S, Jan 20, Mar 3, 26, Apr 2, May 5, Nov 28, Dec 22; 1779: KING'S, Apr
29, May 29, Nov 27; 1780: KING'S, Jan 22, Feb 8, Mar 9, Apr 13, 22, May 9,
25, Nov 25, 28, Dec 19, 23; 1781: KING'S, Jan 23, Apr 5, Jun 5, 23, Nov 17,
Dec 11; 1782: KING'S, Jan 10, 12, Mar 7, Apr 9, May 25; 1783: KING'S, Jun 3
Micho (spectator), 1734: LIF, Aug 20, CG/LIF, Sep 23
Mid Watch (song), 1793: CG, Apr 11, 24, May 10, 23; 1794: CG, Apr 7, 23, Jun 9,
11; 1795: CG, Mar 16, May 1, 13, 21, DL, Jun 6, CG, 12; 1796: CG, Apr 15;
1797: CG, Jun 1; 1798: CG, May 8, 25; 1799: CG, Mar 16, Apr 12, 18, Jun 3;
1800: CG, Jun 2
Midas. See O'Hara, Kane.
Midburn. See Medbourne.
Middle Temple Lane, 1786: DL, Jun 6
Middle Temple, 1659: MT, Nov 0; 1660: MT, Nov 2; 1662: MT, Nov 1; 1723: DL, Feb
15; 1761: CG, Feb 2
Middlebrook (feather man), 1749: DL, Nov 7
Middlehurst, Mrs (beneficiary), 1743: CG, Apr 16
Middlemist (actor), 1761: HAY, May 11, Dec 16; 1762: HAY, Feb 19, Apr 28, Jul
28, Sep 17, Dec 8; 1763: HAY, Mar 8, May 3; 1764: HAY, Dec 12; 1769: HAY, Feb
27, Dec 18; 1772: HAY, Sep 21; 1775: HAY, Feb 20, Nov 20; 1776: HAY, Oct 7;
1779: HAY, Jan 11, Mar 8; 1780: HAY, Sep 25; 1782: HAY, Mar 18; 1784: HAY,
Feb 9; 1785: HAY, Jan 24
Middlesex Hospital for Sick and Lame, and Lying-In Married Women, 1755: CG, Dec
5; 1757: DL, Dec 21; 1759: CG, Jan 16, DL, Dec 18; 1761: CG, Dec 16; 1763:
DL, Dec 20; 1764: CG, Dec 11; 1765: KING'S, Apr 24; 1766: DL, Dec 17; 1767:
CG, Dec 18, 23; 1770: DL, Dec 18, CG, 21; 1772: CG, Dec 22, 31; 1775: DL, Dec
16; 1776: CG, Dec 20; 1779: DL, Dec 21; 1781: CG, Dec 21; 1782: DL, Dec 21;
1792: HAY, Oct 15
Middlesex Sessions, 1660: COCKPIT, Feb 4
Middlesex, Lord (actor, opera patron), 1728: HAY, Feb 16; 1739: HAY, Dec 1;
1746: DL, Dec 5
Middlesex, 1660: NONE, Aug 20; 1692: CITY, Oct 29; 1698: DLLIF, May 10, 12;
1709: HA, Sep 19; 1731: HAY, Aug 20; 1742: JS, Oct 12; 1744: HAY, May 10, DL,
11, MEG, Sep 18; 1745: CG, Feb 20; 1746: NONE, May 30; 1748: HAY, Apr 18;
1768: CG, Jun 4; 1772: GF, Oct 23; 1776: DL, Jan 1
Middleton (actor), 1734: HAY, Apr 17; 1740: BFLP, Aug 23; 1741: TC, Aug 4;
1749: BFC, Aug 23; 1750: SFP, Sep 7
Middleton (color man), 1774: DL, Oct 20
Middleton's Booth, 1741: TC, Aug 4; 1745: MF, May 7
Middleton-Cushing Booth, 1744: MFMCB, May 1
Middleton, Charles, Earl of (correspondent), 1685: ATCOURT, Nov 30; 1687: DL,
May 12
Middleton, James (actor), 1788: CG, Sep 22, Oct 27; 1789: CG, Feb 3, Apr 28,
May 15, 22; 1793: CG, Sep 23, Oct 7, 9, 18, Nov 2, 13, 18, 23; 1794: CG, Jan
3, 6, 22, Feb 18, Mar 6, 25, Apr 12, May 5, 16, 19, 26, 28, Sep 29, Oct 6, 7,
8, 23, Nov 8; 1795: CG, Jan 19, 23, Feb 4, 21, Mar 7, 9, 10, 19, Apr 24, May
1, 2, 29, Jun 2, 3, Sep 14, 16, 18, 28, Oct 5, 7, 9, 14, 19, 23, Nov 6, 7,
Dec 9; 1796: CG, Jan 2, 8, 13, Mar 19, Apr 19, 20, 23, 26, May 17, 27, Sep
12, 14, 21, 23, 26, Oct 5, 6, 10, 20, 25, 26, 29, Nov 24, Dec 19, 29; 1797:
CG, Jan 25, Mar 20, Apr 29, May 4, 9, 31, Jun 10; 1798: DL, Oct 13, Dec 4,
19; 1799: DL, Jan 19, Mar 2
Middleton, Mrs (actor), 1722: BFPMB, Aug 25, SF, Sep 5; 1723: BFPJ, Aug 22, SF,
Sep 5, SOU, 25; 1740: BFLP, Aug 23, GF, Oct 21, 22, 23, 25, 29, 30, Nov 15,
18; 1741: TC, Aug 4
Middleton, Mrs (spectator), 1667: BRIDGES, Feb 5
Middleton, Robert (dancer), 1778: CHR, Jun 22, HAY, Dec 28; 1779: HAY, Mar 15,
Oct 13; 1782: HAY, Mar 21, May 6, Sep 21, Nov 25; 1783: HAY, Sep 17; 1784:
HAY, Feb 9; 1785: HAY, Jan 31
Middleton, Thomas, 1665: NONE, May 4; 1676: NONE, Sep 0; 1677: DG, Sep 0; 1786:
CG, Apr 1; 1789: DL, Nov 7
--Changeling, The (with William Rowley), 1659: NONE, Sep 0; 1661: SALSBURY, Feb
23; 1668: ATCOURT, Nov 30; 1789: DL, Nov 7
--Counterfeit Bridegroom, The; or, The Defeated Widow, 1676: NONE, Sep 0; 1677:
DG, Sep 0
--Mad World, My Masters, A, 1661: LIF, Jul 5; 1715: LIF, Feb 3; 1786: CG, Apr 1
--Mayor of Quinborough, The (with William Rowley), 1660: NONE, Sep 0; 1669:
BRIDGES, Jan 12; 1710: QUEEN'S, Apr 29
--More Dissemblers than Women, 1669: BRIDGES, Jan 12
--No Wit, No Help, Like a Woman's, 1676: NONE, Sep 0; 1677: DG, Sep 0
--Puritan, The; or, Widow of Watling Street, 1663: NONE, Sep 0; 1714: DL, Jun

--Spanish Gypsies, The (with William Rowley), 1668: BRIDGES, Mar 7
--Widow, The, 1660: REDBULL, Aug 14, VERE, Nov 16; 1661: VERE, Jan 8; 1662:
    ATCOURT, Jan 16; 1665: NONE, May 4; 1669: BRIDGES, Jan 12; 1672: NONE, Sep 0
Midnight Hour, The. See Inchbald, Elizabeth.
Midnight Thoughts (prose), 1748: HAY, Sep 5
Midnight Wanderers, The. See Pearce, William.
Midnight, Dorothy (actor), 1752: CT/HAY, Mar 17, 21, Apr 1, 21, May 5; 1753:
    HAY, Mar 13, 27, 31, Apr 10, May 3; 1754: HAY, Apr 1, 22, HAY/SFB, Sep 26;
    1757: HAY, Aug 11, 17, 22, 31, Sep 2, 8, 14, 16, 28, Oct 3, Nov 2; 1758: HAY,
    Jun 1; 1759: HAY, Sep 28; 1760: HAY, Feb 14
Midnight, Mary (actor), 1750: DL, Oct 29; 1751: CT, Dec 3, HAY, 27; 1752: HAY,
    Jan 2, CT/HAY, 7, 21, 31, HAY, Mar 28, CT/HAY, Apr 1, May 5, HAY, Dec 26;
    1753: HAY, Mar 1, 13, 27, BFSY, Sep 3; 1754: HAY, Apr 22, 25, Sep 10,
    HAY/SFB, 19, HAY, Nov 8; 1755: HAY, Sep 1, BF, 6, HAY, 9, 11, 15; 1757: HAY,
    Aug 5, 11, 31, Sep 2, 28; 1758: HAY, May 18; 1760: HAY, Feb 14, Sep 8
Midnight's Intrigues, The. See Behn, Aphra, The Feigned Courtezans.
Midshipman, The (song), 1795: WLWS, Jun 19
Midst of the Sea (song), 1799: HAY, Sep 2
Midsummer Night's Dream, A. See Shakespeare, William.
Midsummer Whim (dance), 1732: DL, May 29, Jun 6, 23, 28, Jul 7
Midwood (cheesemonger), 1745: GF, Mar 21
Miell, William (actor), 1768: HAY, Jul 25, 27
Mighty master (song), 1792: CG, Mar 7; 1794: CG, Mar 14
Mighty power (song), 1789: CG, Apr 3; 1790: CG, Feb 24; 1791: CG, Mar 11; 1792:
    CG, Mar 7; 1795: CG, Mar 25; 1796: CG, Feb 26; 1797: CG, Mar 10; 1799: CG,
    Mar 1
Migliavacca, G A (librettist), 1758: KING'S, Jan 31
Milan Opera, 1793: KING'S, Feb 5
Milan, 1729: HIC, May 21; 1750: HIC, May 18; 1757: KING'S, Mar 24; 1772: CG,
    Mar 27; 1773: KING'S, Oct 23; 1780: KING'S, Apr 22; 1782: KING'S, Feb 23, Apr
    11, Nfv 2; 1791: PAN, Jun 2; 1800: KING'S, Jan 11
Milbourn (grocer), 1754: CG, Jan 19
Milburne (Milbank), Charles (actor), 1785: HAY, Jul 13, Aug 19, 31; 1786: HAY,
    Jul 3, Sep 4; 1787: HAY, Sep 6; 1788: HAY, Aug 5, 13, CG, Dec 13, 15; 1789:
    CG, Mar 5, Apr 14, May 5, HAY, Jul 7, Aug 11, Sep 14, 15, CG, Oct 2, 9, Nov
    16, Dec 3; 1790: CG, Oct 4, 13, Dec 6, 20; 1791: CG, Jan 14, Apr 16, 25, May
    2, Oct 12, 17, Dec 21; 1792: CG, Mar 31, May 10
Mildmay (spectator), 1697: DLLIF, Feb 15
Mile End Fair, 1733: MEG, Sep 28; 1742: UM, Oct 4; 1748: HAY, Apr 18
Mile End Old Town, 1744: MEG, Sep 18
Miles Gloriosus (play), 1718: WS, Jan 24
Miles, Francis (dancer, actor), 1740: BFH, Aug 23; 1741: BFH, Aug 22; 1744: DL,
    Oct 2, 19; 1745: DL, Jan 14; 1746: DL, Mar 3, Apr 2, GF, Oct 27, 29, Nov 13,
    14, 19, 24, Dec 5, 15; 1747: GF, Jan 5, 9, 16, 26, Feb 13, 16, Mar 2, 10;
    1748: NWC, Apr 4; 1750: CG, Oct 29, Dec 21; 1751: CG, May 1, 6, 7, Sep 30,
    Oct 28; 1752: CG, Mar 30, Apr 30, Oct 10, 18, Nov 9, 28, Dec 7; 1753: CG, Apr
    25, May 3, 5, 9, 15, 21, Dec 15; 1754: CG, Apr 30, Sep 16, Nov 5; 1755: CG,
    Apr 23, May 2, Oct 22; 1756: CG, Apr 28, May 1, 13, Sep 22, Oct 21; 1757: CG,
    May 2, 3, Oct 12, 13; 1758: CG, Feb 1, Apr 19, 21, May 2, Oct 6, 9, 19; 1759:
    CG, Apr 30, Oct 10, Nov 5, Dec 10; 1760: CG, Jan 16, 19, Apr 22, 23, 28, May
    5, 7, 8, 14, Sep 22, Oct 15, 20; 1761: CG, Mar 9, Apr 27, Sep 16, 21, Oct 13;
    1762: CG, Jan 28, Apr 27, 28, May 11, Nov 1; 1763: CG, Jan 14, 17, 20, 26,
    Apr 27, Oct 8, 14, 15, Dec 20; 1764: CG, Mar 13, Apr 27, Oct 18, 24, Nov 5;
    1765: CG, Apr 29, May 10, Oct 9, 28, Nov 1; 1766: CG, Apr 21, Oct 18, 25;
    1767: CG, Jan 29, Apr 27, May 1, Sep 18, 19, Oct 9, 17, 26, Dec 4, 7; 1768:
    CG, Jan 6, Mar 15, Apr 16, 22, May 2, 12, Sep 20, 24, Oct 24, Dec 26; 1769:
    CG, Jan 19, Feb 4, 13, 20, 28, Mar 7, Apr 21, May 19, Oct 2, 23, Nov 4; 1770:
    CG, Jan 27, Mar 31, Apr 20, May 3, Oct 1, Dec 26; 1771: CG, Jan 8, Apr 11,
    12, 26, May 2
Miles, John (treasurer), 1698: IT, Feb 2
Miles, Mary, Mrs Francis (actor, dancer), 1744: DL, Oct 2, 17; 1745: DL, Jan
    14; 1746: GF, Oct 27, Nov 13, 18, 24, Dec 15, 29; 1747: GF, Feb 13, 16, Apr 4
Miles, Mrs (actor), 1748: NWC, Apr 4
Miles, Mrs (dancer), 1690: DL, Jan 0; 1691: NONE, Sep 0
Miles, Widow (beneficiary), 1780: CG, May 23
Miles, William (rioter), 1773: CG, Nov 18; 1775: CG, Feb 24
Miles, William Augustus, 1773: DL, Sep 18; 1779: HAY, Jul 1; 1780: DL, Apr 14
--Artifice, The (opera), 1780: DL, Apr 14, 15, 20, 25, 27, May 3
--Summer Amusement. See Andrews, Miles Peter.
Milesian, The. See Jackman, Isaac.
Military Dance (dance), 1788: KING'S, Jan 12, 15, Feb 12, Apr 5, 10

Military Exercise (entertainment), 1781: HAY, Aug 28
Military Manoeuvres (entertainment), 1799: DL, Apr 25, Sep 24
Military Overture (music), 1793: CG, May 1
Milk Pail Dance (dance), 1734: GF, Jan 7, 8, 12, 18, 28, Apr 24, 26, May 1, 3,
    6, 7, 8, 20
Milk Pail Song (song), 1734: GF, Jan 2, 7, 8, 12, 18
Milkmaid (entertainment), 1776: MARLY, May 27, 30, Jun 1, 8
Milkmaids' Dance (dance), 1713: DL, Jun 17; 1716: DL, Jul 24; 1728: LIF, May 3,
    8, 11, 13, 29, 30; 1739: BFH, Aug 23; 1765: DL, Dec 9; 1766: DL, Mar 22, Apr
    16, 18
Milkmaids' Holiday (dance), 1759: CG, Apr 21, 23, 30, May 1, 7, 8, 11, 12;
    1760: CG, Apr 22; 1763: CG, Mar 15
Milkmaids' Song (song), 1716: DL, Jul 24; 1728: LIF, May 8, 29
Mill Bank, 1739: DL, May 8; 1744: DL, May 4
Mill Yard, 1746: GF, Mar 3
Millan (ticket deliverer), 1756: DL, Jan 22
Miller (actor), 1745: GF, Mar 21; 1748: BFSY, Aug 24
Miller (actor), 1761: DL, Jun 15, 18, Jul 2, 27, Aug 8
Miller (actor), 1771: HAY, May 15, 17, 20, 31, Jun 14, Jul 5, 10, Aug 5
Miller (bassoonist), 1741: HAY, Feb 3, HIC, Mar 5, 6, KING'S, 14, HIC, Apr 10;
    1743: KING'S, Mar 30, JS, Apr 7; 1744: KING'S, Mar 28, HAY, Apr 4; 1745: HAY,
    Feb 14, CG, Apr 10; 1746: KING'S, Mar 25; 1748: KING'S, Apr 5, HAY, Dec 9;
    1749: KING'S, Mar 21; 1750: KING'S, Apr 10; 1751: KING'S, Apr 16; 1752:
    KING'S, Mar 24; 1753: KING'S, Apr 30; 1754: KING'S, Feb 28; 1755: KING'S, Mar
    17; 1756: KING'S, Apr 5; 1757: KING'S, Mar 24; 1758: KING'S, Apr 6, CHAPEL,
    27; 1760: CG, Sep 22; 1763: KING'S, Apr 25
Miller (beneficiary), 1770: CG, May 19, 22; 1771: CG, May 25; 1772: CG, May 29
Miller (householder), 1749: DL, Feb 9; 1750: DL, Feb 9; 1753: DL, Mar 6; 1756:
    DL, Jan 22; 1758: DL, Mar 2, 7
Miller (shoemaker), 1750: DL, Jan 4
Miller (ticket deliverer), 1777: CG, May 24; 1778: CG, May 22; 1779: DL, May 5;
    1781: DL, May 4; 1782: DL, May 9; 1784: DL, May 17; 1785: DL, May 17
Miller's Booth, 1696: MF, May 0; 1699: BF, Aug 23; 1702: MF, May 5
Miller and His Wife (dance), 1710: DL, Apr 12; 1711: GR, Aug 30; 1712: GR, Jul
    19; 1736: DL, May 12, Sep 7; 1739: DL, May 10; 1740: CG, Jan 12, 15, 17, 19,
    22, 24, 25, Mar 10, 11, 18, 20, Apr 16, 18, Sep 19, 24, Oct 1, 6, 23, 31, Nov
    13, 15, Dec 2, 12, 19; 1741: CG, Jan 27, BFH, Aug 22, DL, Oct 15, Nov 24
Miller Outwitted, The; or, Harlequin Statue (pantomime), 1752: CG, Mar 30
Miller-Hall-Milward Booth, 1727: BF, Aug 21
Miller-Mills-Oates Booth, 1731: SF/BFMMO, Aug 26, Sep 8; 1732: BFMMO, Aug 23;
    1733: BFMMO, Aug 23
Miller, A (printer), 1745: DL, Apr 1; 1749: CG, Jan 17, DL, Apr 19; 1750: DL,
    Feb 12; 1751: DL, Feb 21, 28, Mar 6, 8; 1754: CG, Feb 26, DL, Mar 27; 1755:
    CG, Jan 15, Mar 13; 1757: CG, Mar 17, 18; 1758: DL, Mar 2
Miller, Anne (actor, singer), 1794: DL, Jun 9, Oct 28, Dec 12, 19; 1795: DL,
    Oct 1, 27, Nov 23; 1796: DL, Feb 15, Apr 2, 30, May 23, 30, Sep 27, Oct 25,
    Nov 9, 26, 28, Dec 29, 30; 1797: DL, Jan 2, Feb 28, Sep 19, Oct 3, Nov 9, 10,
    Dec 9; 1798: DL, May 11, Jun 7, Sep 22, 25, Nov 26, Dec 19; 1799: DL, Jan 8,
    11
Miller, D, 1744: DL, Nov 24
Miller, his Wife, and a Town Miss (dance), 1710: GR, Aug 7, 12
Miller, J A (insurance man), 1749: DL, Dec 22
Miller, James (author), 1730: DL, Jan 9; 1734: HAY, Feb 12; 1735: DL, Mar 6;
    1737: DL, Feb 28; 1738: DL, Jan 26, Feb 16; 1739: DL, Nov 15; 1743: LIF, Apr
    11; 1744: CG, Mar 2, DL, Apr 25, Nov 24; 1745: DL, Feb 11; 1749: DL, Feb 9
--Art and Nature, 1738: DL, Feb 16, 21
--Coffee House, The, 1738: DL, Jan 26, 28; 1739: DL, Sep 15
--Hospital for Fools, An, 1739: DL, Nov 15, 16, 17
--Humours of Oxford, The, 1730: DL, Jan 9, 10, 12, 13, 14, 15, 16; 1744: DL,
    Apr 28; 1779: HAY, Mar 15; 1780: HAY, Mar 28
--Mahomet the Imposter (Mahomet and Palmira), 1744: DL, Apr 25, 26, 27, 28, Nov
    24; 1749: DL, Feb 9; 1765: DL, Nov 25, 26, 28, Dec 2, 4, 10, 12; 1766: DL,
    Jan 6, 7, 15, 25, Feb 15, May 7, Nov 26; 1767: CG, Dec 8; 1768: CG, May 4,
    Oct 24, 31; 1771: HAY, Apr 6, CG, May 6; 1772: CG, Feb 1, 8, 17; 1776: DL,
    Apr 19; 1778: DL, Nov 11, 13, 17, Dec 14; 1779: DL, Jan 18, May 28, Nov 2, 8,
    16; 1785: HAY, Feb 24; 1786: CG, Apr 4, Dec 4; 1795: DL, Apr 27; 1796: CG,
    Oct 13, 18
--Man of Taste, The; or, The Guardians, 1735: DL, Mar 6, 8, 11, 15, 18, 25, 29,
    Apr 7, 8, 9, 10, 12, 15, 17, 24, 30, May 3, 12, 15, 16, 19, 21, 26, 27, 28,
    30, Jun 2, Sep 9, Nov 22, Dec 4, 22; 1736: DL, Feb 26, Apr 30, May 22; 1737:
    DL, Mar 3, 7, 14, 21, Apr 15, May 20; 1738: DL, May 13; 1739: DL, Apr 25;
    1743: LIF, Feb 28, Apr 11; 1752: DL, Mar 10

--Mother-in-Law, The; or, The Doctor's the Disease, <u>1734</u>: HAY, Feb 9, 12,
DL/HAY, 13, 14, HAY, 15, DL/HAY, 16, 18, 19, 20, 21, 22, 23, 25, 26, 28, Mar
2, 5, 7, 9, 12, Apr 1, May 3, DL, Oct 19, Nov 1, 18; <u>1735</u>: DL, Jan 4, Mar 17,
Oct 23; <u>1736</u>: DL, Feb 23, Jun 2, Nov 12, Dec 29; <u>1737</u>: DL, May 25, Oct 24;
<u>1739</u>: DL, Apr 28; <u>1740</u>: DL, Feb 7
--Picture, The; or, Cuckold in Conceit, <u>1745</u>: DL, Feb 11
--Universal Passion, The, <u>1736</u>: HAY, Jan 19, 20; <u>1737</u>: DL, Feb 28, Mar 1, 3, 7,
8, 14, 21, 24, 28, 31; <u>1741</u>: DL, Mar 14, Apr 17
Miller, James William (dancer, actor), <u>1773</u>: CG, Apr 24, 30, May 25, 28; <u>1774</u>:
CG, Jan 15, 29, Feb 19, Apr 15, May 24; <u>1775</u>: CG, May 27; <u>1776</u>: HAY, Apr 22,
CG, May 21, 22; <u>1777</u>: HAY, Oct 9; <u>1780</u>: HAY, Jan 3; <u>1784</u>: HAY, Feb 23; <u>1787</u>:
CG, Jun 5; <u>1788</u>: CG, May 30; <u>1790</u>: CG, May 27; <u>1792</u>: HAY, Feb 6; <u>1796</u>: HAY,
Feb 22
Miller, Joseph (actor), <u>1704</u>: LIF, Mar 25; <u>1705</u>: LIF, Aug 1; <u>1709</u>: DL, Dec 3,
10, 17; <u>1710</u>: DL, Jan 31, Mar 14, 21, 27, Jun 6; <u>1715</u>: DL, Feb 4, 22, 23, Apr
30, May 7, Jun 6, 24, 28, Jul 1, 6, Aug 9, Dec 6, 31; <u>1716</u>: DL, Jan 17, 25,
Feb 9, Mar 3, 10, Apr 2, Jun 15, Jul 12, 19, Oct 2, 19, 22, 23, 27, 29, Nov
2, 12, 13, 27, Dec 4; <u>1717</u>: DL, Jan 16, Feb 15, Mar 1, Apr 25, May 10, Jun 3,
6, 24, Jul 2, 16, Aug 6, 22, Oct 3, 15, 16, 21, 25, 30, Nov 6, 8, 18, 19, 27,
Dec 4; <u>1718</u>: DL, Jan 7, 20, Feb 11, 19, Mar 24, Apr 3, 19, 23, 29, May 3, 13,
Jun 11, 17, 27, Jul 1, 11, 18, RI, 19, 28, DL, Aug 1, RI, 2, DL, 15, Sep 27,
Oct 7, 10, 15, 20, 28, 29, 30, Nov 12, 18, 19, 24, 26, Dec 1, 10, 11, 16;
<u>1719</u>: DL, Jan 6, 16, 28, Feb 14, Apr 11, 13, May 6, 8, Jun 9, BFPM, Aug 24,
RI, Sep 5, DL, 15, 22, 24, Oct 9, 10, 14, 15, 16, 19, 22, 23, Nov 2, 3, 6, 7,
11, 16, 20, 30, Dec 2; <u>1720</u>: DL, Jan 2, 5, 12, 13, 15, Apr 21, May 10, 20,
Jun 2, 11, 30, Jul 7, BFPMJ, Aug 23, DL, Sep 13, 15, 17, 20, 24, Oct 4, 7,
13, 15, 17, 20, 29, Nov 7, 18, 22, Dec 5, 6, 8, 17; <u>1721</u>: DL, Jan 13, 25, 27,
Mar 23, Apr 13, 14, 15, May 5, 26, 29, Jun 20, 27, Jul 18, 28, Aug 4, 15, 18,
BF/SF, 24, DL, Sep 12, 26, 28, 30, Oct 2, 3, 4, 5, 9, 10, 12, 16, 17, 18, 23,
24, 25, Nov 7, 8, 13, 17, 18, 28, 30, Dec 1; <u>1722</u>: DL, Jan 5, 9, Mar 29, Apr
14, May 2, 22, 25, RI, Jul 23, Aug 20, BFPMB, 25, SFM, Sep 5, DL, 18, 20, 22,
25, 27, Oct 2, 8, 12, 15, 16, 19, 20, 22, 24, 25, 31, Dec 4, HAY, 17; <u>1723</u>:
DL, Jan 7, 9, 17, 23, HAY, 31, DL, Feb 5, 6, HAY, 13, Mar 14, DL, 28, May 11,
15, 20, 23, Jun 4, Sep 17, 19, 24, Oct 1, 3, 8, 9, 10, 16, 19, 22, 24, 28,
Nov 1, 6, 8, 12, 14, 18, 19, 22, Dec 30; <u>1724</u>: DL, Feb 6, 17, Apr 15, 29, May
1, 16, 20, RI, Aug 3, DL, Sep 15, 17, 19, SOU, 24, DL, 26, 29, Oct 8, 14, 21,
24, 28, 29, Nov 2, 6, 10, 21, 26, 27, Dec 7, 18; <u>1725</u>: DL, Jan 4, 20, 25, Feb
20, Apr 7, 21, 28, 30, May 11, 19, 21, Sep 4, 7, 9, 14, 18, 21, 25, 28, Oct
7, 9, 15, 18, 22, 23, 26, 27, 28, Nov 2, 3, 8, 22, 29, Dec 9, 13; <u>1726</u>: DL,
Jan 11, 26, Feb 11, Mar 17, 21, May 7, 11, Jun 3, Sep 3, 10, 15, 17, 22, 24,
29, Oct 1, 6, 11, 18, 20, 22, 27, Nov 9, 15, Dec 7, 12; <u>1727</u>: DL, Jan 20, 27,
Feb 8, 21, Apr 8, 12, 19, 24, 25, 29, May 2, 3, 4, 5, 15, 19, 22, BF, Aug 21,
DL, Sep 7, 9, 14, 19, 26, 28, Oct 3, 5, 6, 9, 12, 19, 20, 30, Nov 1, 9, 18,
21, 28, Dec 5; <u>1728</u>: DL, Jan 2, 3, 5, 10, Feb 14, 16, Mar 9, Apr 2, 4, 22,
29, May 10, 17, 20, 29, BFHM, Aug 24, DL, Sep 10, 12, 17, 26, Oct 3, 12, 17,
21, 23, 24, 25, 30, 31, Nov 7, 8, 12; <u>1729</u>: DL, Jan 2, 7, 13, 20, 21, 29, Feb
3, 6, 15, 18, 24, Apr 10, 11, 14, 16, 22, May 3, 7, 9, 14, 30, WINH, Jul 19,
DL, Sep 13, 20, 23, 30, Oct 2, 9, 14, 16, 21, 22, 23, 30, 31, Nov 7, 14, 17,
21, 24, Dec 1, 2, 3, 4, 8, 10, 13, 26; <u>1730</u>: DL, Jan 3, 8, Feb 10, Mar 30,
Apr 17, May 13; <u>1731</u>: SF/BFMMO, Aug 26; <u>1732</u>: GF, Jan 3, 20, 22, 27, 29, Feb
2, 5, 7, 8, 9, 10, 12, 17, 19, 26, Mar 7, 23, 27, Apr 1, 10, 12, 14, 18, 19,
26, 27, 28, May 1, 2, 3, 4, 10, 11, 15, BFMMO, Aug 23, DL, Nov 22, 23, 25,
28, Dec 8, 9, 14, 26; <u>1733</u>: DL, Jan 12, 13, 16, 19, 22, 26, Feb 3, 6, Mar 10,
15, 28, Apr 6, 9, 23, 24, 26, May 1, 7, 14, 18, 24, 29, Jun 4, BFMMO, Aug 23,
RI, Sep 10, DL/HAY, 26, Oct 3, 5, 6, 10, 12, 15, 19, 22, 25, 27, Nov 1, 9,
26, 27, Dec 17, 20, 22; <u>1734</u>: DL/HAY, Jan 2, HAY, Feb 12, DL/HAY, Mar 12, 23,
25, 30, Apr 17, 18, 20, DL, 22, DL/HAY, May 1, DL, 15, RI, Sep 2, DL, 7, 10,
19, 24, 26, Oct 3, 14, 17, 19, 21, 22, Nov 2, 8, 16, 20, 22, Dec 6, 14; <u>1735</u>:
DL, Jan 23, 28, Mar 6, Apr 11, 14, May 2, 14, Sep 1, 4, 6, 9, 11, 13, 15, 18,
25, Oct 21, 23, 24, 27, 30, 31, Nov 3, 19, 20, 21; <u>1736</u>: DL, Jan 3, Mar 11,
13, Apr 5, 12, LIF, 14, DL, 15, Aug 26, Sep 7, 9, 11, 14, 16, 18, 21, 23, Oct
5, 7, 9, 19, 22, 23, 30, Nov 1, 3, 12, 15, 19, 20, Dec 7, 17; <u>1737</u>: DL, Jan
6, 29, Feb 5, 10, 19, Mar 10, 22, 29, Apr 12, 15, May 5, 18, Aug 30, Sep 6,
10, 15, 22, Oct 6, 11, 20, 21, 24, Nov 1, 11, 15, 16; <u>1738</u>: DL, Jan 5, 14,
19, 31, Feb 2, 16, 23, Mar 2, 20, 21, Apr 13, 14, 17, 28, 29, May 1, 3, 6,
13, 27, Aug 16, Dec 14
Miller, Krazinsky (composer), <u>1795</u>: DL, Feb 12, 13
Miller, Miss (actor), <u>1779</u>: HAY, Mar 15
Miller, Miss E (actor), <u>1761</u>: CG, Oct 9, 10, 23; <u>1762</u>: CG, Jan 13, 28, Mar 13,
Apr 26, May 12, Sep 24, 29, 30, Oct 8, 20, 25, Nov 1, 15, Dec 8; <u>1763</u>: CG,
Jan 24, 26, Apr 27, Sep 21, 28, Oct 3, 5, 10, 11, 14, 22, 26, Nov 3, 10, 15,
18, Dec 7, 12; <u>1764</u>: CG, Jan 14, Feb 22, Apr 10, 12, 28, May 21, Sep 17, 21,

24, 28, Oct 1, 11, 18, 23, 24, 26, Nov 1, 5, 7, 23, Dec 12; 1765: CG, Jan 4,
21, 26; 1769: CG, Oct 18, Nov 13; 1770: CG, Feb 16, Apr 30, May 7, 8, Oct 10,
18, 29, Nov 1, 5, 29, Dec 28; 1771: CG, Jan 28, Apr 9, 23, 29, 30, Sep 25,
Oct 2, 7, 11, 15, 25, Nov 4, 5, 26, Dec 21, 30; 1772: CG, Jan 15, Feb 18, Mar
5, DL, 18, CG, Apr 30, May 11, Sep 28, Oct 5, 26, Nov 2, 4, Dec 3, HAY, 21;
1773: CG, Jan 7, 14, 25, Feb 23, 25, Mar 6, 30, Apr 16, 28, May 24, Sep 24,
Oct 4, 11, 16, 18, 21, Nov 4, 8, 20, 27, Dec 4, 6, 13, 21, 31; 1774: CG, Jan
12, Mar 17, Apr 18, 20, 21, May 5
Miller, Mrs (actor), 1723: HAY, Mar 14
Miller, Mrs (actor), 1730: SOU, Sep 24; 1732: HAY, Mar 8; 1735: TC, May 28,
GF/HAY, Jul 18, HAY, Aug 4; 1740: DL, Apr 19; 1749: BF/SFP, Aug 23; 1758: DL,
Apr 29
Miller, Rev (author), 1744: DL, Apr 28
Miller, William (actor), 1779: HAY, Oct 18
Miller, William (publisher), 1792: CG, Dec 1; 1800: HAY, Aug 14
Miller, William Edward (singer), 1794: KING'S, Jan 11, Mar 1, DL, 12, 19, 21,
KING'S, Apr 1, DL, 2
Miller's Holiday, The; or, Love in a Furz-Bush (farce, anon), 1730: TC, Aug 11
Miller's Jealousy (dance), 1738: CG, Mar 20
Miller's Wife (dance), 1710: GR, Aug 19, 28
Millerd (composer), 1793: KING'S, Apr 23
Millerd, Marie Elizabeth Anne (dancer), 1793: KING'S, Jan 26, Feb 5, 26, Apr 6,
23, Jun 1, 8, 11
Millers and Colliers (dance), 1767: DL, Mar 17
Millers and Courtezan (dance), 1742: GF, Feb 2, 6, 13, Mar 15, Apr 22, 29;
1743: LIF, Jan 7
Millers' Dance (dance), 1704: DL, Jun 5, Aug 10; 1707: DL, Dec 26; 1710: DL,
Mar 25, Apr 25, May 23, GR, Aug 24; 1712: DL, Jun 12; 1715: LIF, Aug 10, 23,
Oct 12; 1726: LIF, Jun 17; 1740: DL, May 8, SOU, Oct 9; 1742: DL, Feb 25;
1756: DL, May 12; 1757: DL, Jan 29, Feb 12, 26, Mar 1; 1758: DL, Oct 12, 13,
18, 23; 1760: DL, May 10, Oct 7; 1765: DL, Jan 18, 26, Feb 9
Millico (singer), 1772: KING'S, Apr 21, Nov 14; 1773: KING'S, Feb 5, 25, Mar 4,
6, Oct 23, Nov 20, 27; 1774: KING'S, Jan 29, Feb 10, 24, Mar 8, Apr 19, HIC,
May 9, KING'S, 17, Jun 3
Millidge, Elizabeth, Mrs Josiah (actor), 1768: DL, Sep 26, Oct 4, 6, 8, 10, 31,
Nov 17, Dec 16; 1769: DL, Mar 29, May 12, Sep 16, 21, Oct 3, 18, Dec 4, 6;
1770: DL, Mar 6, 8, May 19, 22, Oct 13, 23, Nov 6, 13, 16, 17; 1771: DL, May
17, Oct 17, Nov 25, 28; 1772: DL, Jan 3, Feb 29, May 25, Sep 19, Nov 3, Dec
21, 26; 1773: DL, Feb 4, Mar 30, Apr 16, May 13, Sep 25, Oct 6, 28, Nov 10,
Dec 11, 27; 1774: DL, Jan 18, Feb 15, Apr 16, May 9, 10, 18, Sep 29, Oct 8,
12, 28, Dec 16, 21; 1775: DL, Jan 2, Feb 23, Apr 1, May 17, 19, Sep 23, 28,
Oct 11, Nov 6, 9, 25; 1776: DL, Jan 13, 27, Feb 12, Apr 17, 22, May 24
Millidge, Josiah (printer), 1774: DL, May 30; 1775: DL, Mar 7
Millon (actor), 1728: HAY, Feb 21
Mills (actor), 1774: HAY, Jan 24; 1778: HAY, Mar 24; 1779: HAY, Mar 15, Oct 18;
1784: HAY, Feb 23, Mar 8
Mills (dancer), 1783: DL, May 31, Sep 27, Nov 4; 1784: DL, Mar 20, Apr 16, Sep
25; 1785: DL, Jan 6, 20, Mar 7, Apr 8, May 19, 20, 23, Sep 22, 27, Oct 13;
1786: DL, Apr 20, 24, 28, May 19, 26, Sep 28, Dec 28; 1787: DL, Feb 22, May
23, Jun 1; 1788: DL, Jan 5, 22, Feb 1, Mar 6, 10
Mills Jr (actor), 1721: DL, Nov 30; 1723: DL, Feb 15, Dec 5; 1724: DL, Dec 9,
22; 1725: DL, Nov 29; 1730: DL, Dec 11; 1731: DL, Mar 20; 1732: DL, Feb 14;
1733: DL, Feb 17, Jun 4; 1735: DL, Jan 28, Mar 6
Mills, Elizabeth (actor), 1750: DL, Apr 21
Mills, Elizabeth, Mrs William (the second) (actor), 1737: DL, Sep 22, 27, 29,
Oct 1, 4, 11, 21, 22, 31, Nov 1, 2, 4, 11, 12, 17, 19; 1738: DL, Jan 5, 14,
31, Feb 2, 11, 16, Mar 20, 21, Apr 17, 22, 24, May 6, 13, Sep 12, 14, 19, 23,
28, 30, Oct 18, 19, 20, 24, 27, 30, Nov 2, 3, 4, 8, 14, 20, 30, Dec 1, 9, 26;
1739: DL, Jan 8, 22, 31, Feb 1, 3, Mar 8, 10, 22, 27, 31, Apr 9, 25, 26, 28,
30, May 12, 18, 19, Sep 15, 18, 20, 22, 24, Oct 3, 4, 5, 11, 17, 18, 19, 20,
25, 26, 27, Nov 5, 7, 8, 10, 12, 13, 15, 16, 19, 28, Dec 10, 22, 26, 28;
1740: DL, Jan 3, 16, Feb 14, 16, 23, Mar 25, Apr 16, 17, 22, May 6, 13, 20,
26, 29, 30, Sep 9, 13, 16, 18, 20, 23, 25, Oct 2, 13, 16, 27, 28, Nov 4, 6,
8, 11, 13, 19, 28, Dec 6, 10, 15, 18; 1741: DL, Jan 6, Feb 2, Mar 17, 30, Apr
4, 16, 24, May 14, 21, 25, Jun 4, Sep 5, 10, 12, 17, 22, Oct 8, 9, 12, 20,
21, 23, Nov 4, 11, 20, Dec 7, 8, 12, 19; 1742: DL, Jan 4, 6, Feb 16, Mar 8,
27, 29, Apr 5, 22, 28, Sep 18, 21, 25, 28, Oct 9, 12, 13, 16, Nov 1, 4, 8,
12, 22, Dec 14, 22; 1743: DL, Jan 18, 27, 28, Feb 4, 10, 11, Mar 24, Apr 20,
Sep 13, Dec 17, 20, 21, 22, 29; 1744: DL, Jan 7, 13, 25, Mar 12, 30, Apr 2,
23, HAY, Sep 25, 27, Oct 11, DL, Nov 19, Dec 29; 1745: DL, Jan 4, 24, 25, 26,
Feb 1, 5, 11, 13, 14, Mar 16, Apr 20, Sep 19, 21, 24, Oct 3, 8, 15, Nov 1,
25, 28, Dec 10, 17; 1746: DL, Jan 14, Feb 10, 13, 17, 24, Mar 8, 10, Apr 10,

568

23, 28, May 9, Oct 2, 23, 25, Nov 1, 5, 7, GF, 13, DL, Dec 11, 20, 26, 29;
1747: DL, Jan 2, Feb 23, Mar 7, 23, 30, Apr 30, May 16, Oct 1, 15, 24, Nov
16, Dec 3; 1748: DL, Jan 18, Mar 19, Apr 25, 27, Sep 10, 15, 17, 22, 29, Oct
8, 13, 28, 29, Nov 1, 28, Dec 28; 1749: DL, Jan 25, Feb 21, Sep 16, Oct 17,
24, 30, Nov 9, 15, 16, Dec 7, 9, 18; 1750: DL, Mar 13, Apr 18, 21, Sep 13,
15, 21, 22, 27, Oct 26, 29, Nov 2, 3, 8, 12, 13, 24, Dec 27; 1751: DL, Jan 4,
5, 12, 26, Feb 18, 21, Apr 26, 29, Sep 12, 13, 14, 17, Oct 2, 3, 10, Nov 16;
1752: DL, Jan 28, Feb 6, Apr 3, 9, 10, 27, Sep 16, 21, 26, 28, Oct 7, 10, 16,
Nov 8, Dec 18, 19, 29; 1753: DL, Jan 2, 3, 13, 22, Feb 22, Apr 28, May 4, 18,
Sep 11, 18, 22, 29, Oct 3, 9, 12, 18, 20; 1754: DL, Jan 23, Feb 20, 22, Mar
23, May 7, 27, Sep 14, 24, Oct 8, 12, 23, Dec 13; 1755: DL, Apr 15, 24, Sep
13

Mills, Henry (actor), 1799: CG, Sep 18, 30, Oct 21, 29, Dec 23; 1800: CG, Jan
10

Mills, John (actor), 1695: DG, Apr 0, DL, Sep 0, Nov 0, Dec 0; 1696: DL, Jan 0,
Feb 0, May 0, DG, Jun 0, DL, Jul 0, Sep 0, Nov 21; 1697: DL, Feb 0, DG, Jun
0, DL, Jul 0, NONE, Sep 0, DL, 0; 1698: DL, Mar 0, Jun 0, DL/ORDG, Nov 0, DL,
Dec 0; 1699: DL, Apr 0, Nov 28, Dec 0; 1700: DL, Feb 19, Mar 0, Jul 9, Oct 0,
Nov 23, Dec 9; 1701: DL, Feb 4, Mar 1, Apr 0, May 12, 31, Dec 0; 1702: DL,
Feb 0, Oct 17, Nov 0, 26, Dec 0, 14; 1703: DL, Jan 27, Mar 11, Apr 10, Jun 4,
Oct 27, Dec 2; 1704: DL, Jan 26, Mar 6, May 0, Jun 9; 1705: DL, Jan 18, Mar
29, Apr 23, 30, Jun 12, 16, Jul 25, Oct 30, Nov 20, Dec 3; 1706: DL, Apr 0,
2, BF, Aug 27, QUEEN'S, Oct 26, 30, Nov 2, 7, 13, 14, 20, 22, 29, Dec 2, 3,
5, 7, 13; 1707: QUEEN'S, Jan 1, 4, 13, 14, 18, 25, Feb 3, 14, 15, Mar 8, 27,
Apr 30, May 2, 26, Jun 2, 10, 18, 20, 25, 27, Jul 4, 10, 22, 26, Aug 12,
DL/QUEEN, Oct 18, 20, QUEEN'S, 21, DL/QUEEN, 22, 23, 25, 27, 28, 31, QUEEN'S,
Nov 6, DL/QUEEN, 10, 11, 14, 15, 18, 19, QUEEN'S, 22, DL/QUEEN, 25, QUEEN/DL,
Dec 6, DL/QUEEN, 27, 31; 1708: DL/QUEEN, Jan 1, DL, 15, 31, Feb 3, 4, 6, 9,
14, 23, 24, 26, QUEEN/DL, Mar 4, DL, 8, 15, 16, 18, 27, Apr 10, 17, 26, 27,
29, May 31, Jun 5, 15, 19, DL/QUEEN, 22, DL, 24, 26, Jul 1, 3, 10, 20, 29,
Aug 4, Oct 12, 13, 14, 15, 16, 18, 21, 22, 23, 25, 26, Dec 14, 18, 22, 28,
30, 31; 1709: DL, Jan 3, 4, 5, 7, 8, 10, 15, 18, 21, 22, 25, 26, 27, 29, Feb
4, 11, 16, 19, 26, Mar 3, 5, 14, 15, 19, 31, Apr 9, 14, 26, 30, May 3, 12,
18, 20, Jun 2, QUEEN'S, Sep 22, 27, 29, Oct 1, 4, 6, 8, 11, 17, 22, 25, 28,
31, Nov 4, 8, 9, 11, 12, 15, 18, 19, Dec 12; 1710: QUEEN'S, Jan 5, 18, 19,
21, Feb 4, 11, 13, 16, Mar 4, 11, Apr 20, May 6, 15, 16, 25, 29, Jun 1, 5, 9,
16, Jul 26, DL/QUEEN, Oct 4, 7, Nov 4, 6, 7, 8, QUEEN'S, 10, DL/QUEEN, 11,
13, 14, 15, 16, 17, 18, DL, 20, 25, 27, 28, 30, Dec 1, 4, 11, 12, 14, 15, 16,
18, 21, 22, 30; 1711: DL, Jan 9, 11, 15, 16, 19, 20, 25, 26, 27, Feb 3, 10,
15, 19, 22, Mar 3, 8, 10, DL/QUEEN, Apr 5, DL, 7, May 8, DL/QUEEN, 11, DL,
15, 18, 21, 22, DL/QUEEN, 29, Jun 22, DL, 26, 29, Jul 3, 27, Aug 3, 17, 31,
Sep 22, 25, Oct 2, 6, 9, 10, 11, 12, 13, 18, 19, 20, 22, 23, 24, 26, 27, 29,
Nov 1, 2, 3, 5, 6, 8, 9, 10, 23, 26, 29, Dec 3, 8, 10, 13, 18, 21, 31; 1712:
DL, Jan 19, Mar 17, 31, Jun 2, Jul 1, 4, 22, Aug 8, 26, Sep 20, 23, 25, 30,
Oct 4, 8, 10, 13, 15, 16, 17, 20, 22, 23, 29, 30, 31, Nov 1, 3, 7, 25, 28,
Dec 12; 1713: DL, Jan 6, 14, 15, 19, 29, Feb 9, 19, 28, Mar 3, 9, 14, 16, Apr
14, May 11, 13, 18, Jun 5, Sep 29, Oct 13, Nov 16, 19, 23, 25, 28, Dec 2, 18;
1714: DL, Jan 5, 28, Feb 2, Mar 8, 29, 31, Apr 26, 27, May 5, 28, Jun 2, 18,
25, 29, Jul 2, 20, Oct 26, Nov 3, 9, 15, 25, 26, 27, Dec 6, 8, 9, 16, 20;
1715: DL, Jan 24, Feb 4, 12, 15, 21, 22, 25, 28, Mar 14, 26, 28, Apr 2, 19,
20, 30, May 17, 18, 20, 24, Jun 6, 24, 28, Jul 1, 6, Oct 13, 22, Nov 9, 12,
19, 29, Dec 6, 9, 12, 17, 30, 31; 1716: DL, Jan 5, 7, 10, 11, 13, 17, 21, 24,
25, 26, Feb 1, 9, 18, 21, 23, 25, Mar 3, 10, 19, Apr 2, 16, Jun 15, 26, Jul
12, 19, Aug 9, Sep 29, Oct 2, 6, 11, 12, 13, 15, 16, 17, 19, 22, 23, 24, 25,
27, 29, Nov 1, 2, 3, 5, 6, 13, 14, 27, Dec 4, 5, 15, 17, 27, 29; 1717: DL,
Jan 2, 4, 5, 9, 24, 26, 31, Feb 2, 15, 25, Mar 1, 7, Apr 11, May 8, 10, 11,
22, Jun 10, 18, 24, Jul 2, 16, Aug 9, 13, Oct 1, 3, 10, 11, 15, 16, 21, 24,
25, 26, 28, Nov 6, 8, 13, 18, 19, 20, 23, Dec 3, 4, 6, 31; 1718: DL, Jan 7,
13, 20, 23, 27, 29, Feb 1, 18, Mar 1, 4, 6, 8, 17, 22, 24, Apr 5, 19, May 13,
20, 28, Jun 11, 17, 27, Jul 8, 11, 25, NONE, 30, DL, Aug 1, 15, 20, Sep 20,
25, 27, Oct 2, 4, 7, 10, 11, 17, 20, 21, 22, 24, 25, 27, 28, 30, 31, Nov 8,
12, 13, 18, 19, 24, 26, 27, 28, 29, Dec 1, 3, 10, 11, 13, 16; 1719: DL, Jan
24, Feb 14, Mar 5, 7, May 4, 8, 11, Jun 9, 12, 26, Jul 28, Sep 12, 15, 19,
22, 24, 29, Oct 3, 7, 8, 9, 13, 14, 15, 16, 17, 20, 22, 24, 28, 30, 31, Nov
2, 3, 6, 7, 11, 14, 16, 17, 18, 19, 20, 21, 23, 24, 26, Dec 5, 8, 11; 1720:
DL, Jan 1, 5, 8, 12, 13, Feb 15, 17, Mar 14, 19, Apr 2, 21, May 30, Jun 2, 7,
11, Jul 7, Sep 10, 13, 15, 17, 20, 22, 29, Oct 1, 6, 7, 12, 13, 15, 17, 20,
29, Nov 2, 4, 7, 10, 11, 12, 18, 19, 21, 22, 26, 28, 29, Dec 1, 5, 6, 8, 17;
1721: DL, Jan 3, 10, 16, 17, 19, 23, 24, 25, 27, Feb 3, 10, Mar 2, 9, 23, Apr
13, 18, 26, May 15, 29, Jun 20, 27, Jul 28, Aug 1, 4, 8, Sep 9, 14, 16, 19,
23, 26, 28, 30, Oct 2, 3, 4, 5, 6, 7, 9, 10, 11, 12, 13, 14, 16, 17, 18, 19,
20, 23, 24, 25, 28, 31, Nov 3, 4, 7, 8, 11, 13, 14, 15, 16, 17, 25, Dec 1,

12, 22, 28; 1722: DL, Jan 6, 9, 26, Feb 19, Mar 8, Apr 13, 14, 17, May 2, 5,
22, Sep 8, 11, 15, 20, 25, 27, 29, Oct 2, 5, 6, 8, 10, 11, 12, 13, 15, 17,
18, 19, 20, 22, 23, 24, 25, 27, 31, Nov 1, 5, 7, Dec 3, 7, 22, 26; 1723: DL,
Jan 7, 8, 9, 17, 28, Feb 4, 5, 6, 15, Mar 2, 11, 14, 21, Apr 22, May 10, 20,
23, Jun 3, Sep 14, 19, 21, 24, 28, Oct 1, 3, 5, 9, 10, 12, 15, 18, 21, 22,
26, 29, 30, 31, Nov 1, 2, 4, 6, 7, 9, 12, 16, 18, 19, 21, 22, Dec 5, 30;
1724: DL, Jan 15, 27, Feb 6, 12, 15, 17, 22, Mar 9, Apr 8, 15, 18, 25, 28,
May 1, 14, 22, Sep 12, 17, 19, 24, 29, Oct 10, 17, 19, 20, 21, 22, 27, 28,
31, Nov 2, 4, 6, 10, 13, 14, 16, 19, 21, 26, 27, Dec 3, 7, 9; 1725: DL, Jan
25, Feb 1, 9, Mar 8, Apr 15, 20, 21, 22, 24, May 8, 11, Sep 7, 11, 14, 16,
25, 30, Oct 2, 5, 9, 12, 13, 14, 15, 16, 18, 20, 21, 22, 23, 26, 28, Nov 1,
2, 4, 6, 8, 10, 12, 20, 22, Dec 9, 18, 22; 1726: DL, Jan 3, 5, 22, Feb 2, Mar
10, May 11, 12, 18, 23, Sep 6, 8, 10, 13, 17, 20, 22, 24, 27, 29, Oct 13, 15,
18, 20, 22, 27, Nov 4, 12, 15, 16, 19, 29, Dec 3, 7, 15, 20, 21; 1727: DL,
Jan 16, 20, 21, 25, 27, Feb 4, 11, 23, Mar 13, Apr 17, 29, May 8, 15, 22, Sep
14, 16, 19, 21, 23, 28, 30, Oct 3, 5, 9, 12, 14, 17, 19, 20, 21, 23, 26, Nov
4, 18, 28, 30, Dec 5, 9, 13, 30; 1728: DL, Jan 2, 3, 10, Feb 16, Mar 9, 11,
21, Apr 1, 2, 13, 29, May 1, 20, 23, 31, Sep 7, 10, 17, 19, 21, 26, 28, Oct
1, 3, 5, 10, 17, 21, 22, 23, 24, 31, Nov 9, 12, Dec 6; 1729: DL, Jan 1, 2, 7,
11, 13, 15, 21, 25, 29, 31, Feb 1, 3, 15, 22, 24, Mar 11, Apr 8, 16, 17, 23,
May 7, 14, Sep 11, 18, 20, 23, 25, 27, 30, Oct 4, 7, 9, 14, 21, 22, 25, 28,
30, 31, Nov 1, 3, 4, 7, 8, 12, 17, 19, 24, 25, 27, 28, 29, Dec 1, 3, 4, 5,
13, 20; 1730: DL, Jan 3, 9, 21, 24, 26, Feb 28, Mar 16, 19, Apr 14, 27, Sep
12, 15, 17, 19, 22, 24, 26, 29, Oct 1, 3, 6, 17, 22, 24, Nov 16, 20, 24, 25,
26, 28, 30, Dec 1, 2, 11; 1731: DL, Jan 8, 20, 27, Feb 8, 17, 22, Mar 8, 15,
16, Apr 3, 10, 19, 21, May 1, 10, 13, Sep 18, 21, 25, Oct 2, 5, 7, 9, 14, 19,
21, Nov 1, 5, 6, 9, 10, 15, 23, 24, Dec 1, 2, 7, 10, 18, 21, 29; 1732: DL,
Jan 3, 10, 15, Feb 2, 3, 10, Mar 6, 14, 20, 23, 30, Apr 1, 17, 24, 27, 28,
29, May 4, 5, Sep 19, 21, 23, 26, 28, 30, Oct 3, 5, 12, 17, 19, Nov 4, 7, 9,
11, 13, 14, 18, 21, Dec 11; 1733: DL, Jan 2, 15, 16, 19, 20, 25, Mar 5, 8,
28, 29, Apr 4, 18, 23, 27, 30, May 2, 5, 10, 29, Jun 4, DL/HAY, Sep 26, Oct
3, 6, 8, 10, 12, 13, 15, 17, 20, 27, Nov 1, 5, 10, 23, 26, 28, Dec 12, 19,
20, 22; 1734: DL/HAY, Jan 12, HAY, Feb 12, DL/HAY, Mar 4, 12, 23, 25, 30, Apr
2, 17, 18, 20, DL, 22, DL/HAY, 26, DL, 29, DL/HAY, May 1, DL, 15, RI, Sep 2,
DL, 12, 14, 19, 24, 26, 28, Oct 9, 14, 17, 21, 22, 23, 24, 25, 26, Nov 2, 4,
8, 22, 25, Dec 19; 1735: DL, Jan 13, 23, Feb 4, 24, Mar 6, 10, 13, 22, Apr
11, 14, 21, 23, 25, 28, May 2, Sep 1, 9, 11, 13, 15, 20, 23, 27, 30, Oct 4,
9, 21, 24, 25, 27, 31, Nov 1, 4, 6, 12, 17, 20, 24, Dec 6; 1736: DL, Jan 3,
Feb 9, Mar 11, 15, Apr 12, 15, 29, May 4, 26, Aug 26, Sep 4, 7, 9, 14, 16,
18, 21, Oct 7, 9, 19, 21, 22, 23, 27, Nov 2, 4, 8, 15, 22, 23, Dec 17; 1737:
DL, Jan 14, Feb 5, 28, Mar 1, 10, 12, 15, 17
Mills, John (actor), 1782: CG, Apr 30, Sep 23, Nov 25; 1783: CG, Jan 3, Feb 19,
May 15
Mills, Louisa Henrietta Hannah, Mrs Henry (actor), 1798: CG, Oct 3, Nov 6, 12,
Dec 26; 1799: CG, Jan 28, Mar 16, Apr 13, May 7, 28, Oct 2, 7, 16, 17, 24,
28, Dec 9; 1800: CG, Jan 8, Feb 10, Mar 27, Apr 5, 22, 29, May 1, 12, 15, 23,
Jun 2
Mills, Master (dancer), 1775: HAY, Nov 20; 1778: DL, Sep 26; 1779: DL, May 5
Mills, Miss (actor), 1739: DL, Nov 21; 1748: JS, Oct 31
Mills, Miss (actor), 1752: DL, Dec 8; 1753: DL, May 21, Oct 9; 1754: DL, Feb 9;
1755: DL, Oct 17, Nov 8, 15; 1756: DL, Apr 29, Nov 18; 1757: DL, May 9, Sep
29; 1758: DL, Nov 16; 1759: DL, Jan 3, Feb 26, Oct 30; 1760: DL, Jan 24, Oct
3; 1761: DL, Sep 14, Nov 10; 1762: DL, Oct 11, 28, Nov 10; 1763: DL, May 31,
Oct 8; 1764: DL, Apr 12, Oct 19; 1765: DL, Apr 13; 1766: DL, Feb 20, Dec 4;
1767: DL, Jan 24, May 6, CG, Sep 14, Nov 7, 10, 23, Dec 31; 1768: CG, Jan 16,
Feb 13, Mar 24, Apr 13, Sep 30, Nov 8, Dec 16; 1769: CG, May 12, Oct 17, 24;
1770: CG, Feb 12, Sep 24, HAY, Oct 29, Dec 14; 1771: CG, Jan 12
Mills, Miss (actor), 1800: CG, Jan 7, Apr 29, May 10, 12, 13, 17, 23, 30, Jun 2
Mills, Mr and Mrs William, 1733: DL, Apr 9; 1749: DL, Apr 10; 1750: DL, Mar 31
Mills, Mrs (actor), 1696: DL, Feb 0, Mar 0, May 0, DG, Jun 0; 1698: DL, Dec 0;
1703: DL, Apr 10; 1704: DL, Jul 11; 1706: QUEEN'S, Nov 25; 1707: QUEEN'S, Jan
4, Mar 8, Jun 20, 25, 27, Jul 4; 1708: DL, Jun 15, 19, DL/QUEEN, 22, DL, 26,
Jul 1, DL/QUEEN, 15; 1709: DL, Jan 4, Mar 17, May 12, 18; 1710: QUEEN'S, Apr
10; 1711: DL/QUEEN, May 29, DL, Aug 3, Oct 12; 1713: DL, Jun 23; 1714: DL,
Jun 18; 1715: DL, May 27, Jul 19, Aug 5; 1716: DL, May 31, Jul 31; 1717: DL,
May 25, Nov 27
Mills, Mrs (actor), 1736: HAY, Apr 26
Mills, Mrs (actor), 1782: HAY, Dec 30
Mills, Mrs (actor, singer), 1795: DL, Oct 30; 1796: DL, Jan 18, Nov 9; 1798:
DL, Nov 29, HAY, Dec 17; 1799: HAY, Aug 10, DL, Oct 19
Mills, Mrs (beneficiary), 1788: DL, Jun 5
Mills, Peter (architect), 1661: NONE, Apr 22; 1662: THAMES, Aug 23

Mills, Susan, Mrs John (actor), 1783: DL, Feb 18
Mills, Theodosia, Mrs William (the first) (actor), 1727: DL, Sep 28, Oct 5, 6,
7, 12, 14, 19, 23, 30, Nov 1, 18, Dec 6; 1728: DL, Jan 2, 3, 5, 10, Feb 16,
Mar 2, 16, 19, 25, 28, 30, Apr 8, 25, May 2, 10, 16, 17, 20, 23, Sep 7, 12,
17, 19, 26, Oct 10, 17, 18, 21, 24, 25, 28, 30, 31, Nov 7, 8, 12, 15, 18;
1729: DL, Jan 1, 27, 31, Feb 1, 6, 15, Mar 13, 18, 25, Apr 9, 19, 22, May 8,
14, 16, 26, 28, Sep 11, 30, Oct 2, 9, 21, 30, Nov 1, 6, 7, 14, 17, 24, 28,
Dec 4, 5, 13; 1730: DL, Mar 16, Apr 13, 14, 21, 25, May 4, 11, Sep 15, 17,
Oct 3, 6, 10, 22, Nov 16, 26, 30; 1731: DL, Mar 15, 29, Apr 21, 30, May 1, 3,
7, 10, Jun 11, Jul 6, Aug 6, 16, Sep 25, 28, Nov 6, 9, 10, 22, 23, 24, Dec 3,
18; 1732: DL, Feb 10, 11, Mar 23, Apr 18, 22, 27, 28, May 4, 8, 12, Sep 23,
26, 30, Oct 3, 10, 12, Nov 14, 18, 24, Dec 6; 1733: DL, May 19
Mills, William (actor), 1712: SML, May 21, Jun 18; 1715: DL, Jun 17; 1718: DL,
May 27, Jun 17; 1719: DL, Jan 28, Mar 7, May 2, Jun 9, Dec 11; 1720: DL, Feb
17, May 9, Dec 17; 1721: DL, May 8; 1722: DL, Jan 26, Feb 19, May 7, Dec 3;
1723: DL, Jan 9, May 9, Oct 30, Nov 12; 1724: DL, Feb 17, May 4, Sep 29, Nov
16; 1725: DL, Jan 9, Feb 1, 4, Apr 9, 19, 20, 22, 26, May 7, Sep 14, 16, 21,
Oct 5, 9, 21, 25, Nov 20, Dec 9; 1726: DL, Feb 2, May 2, 18, Sep 13, 24, 29,
Oct 11, 20, Nov 1, 19, 26, Dec 12, 14, 17, 20, 28; 1727: DL, Feb 4, 21, Mar
13, 16, Apr 24, 26, 29, May 10, 22, Sep 7, 9, 14, 23, 30, Oct 12, 17, 21, 23,
30, Nov 1, 6, 22, 27, 30, Dec 4, 7, 8, 9; 1728: DL, Jan 4, Feb 26, Mar 9, 25,
Apr 13, 25, May 20, Sep 12, 19, 21, Oct 3, 8, 10, 12, 17, 28, Nov 2, 8, 9;
1729: DL, Jan 1, 2, 11, 13, 20, 22, 25, 28, Feb 3, 25, Apr 11, 19, 23, May 3,
6, 7, 9, 28, Sep 13, 18, 20, 23, 27, Oct 4, 7, 11, 16, 22, 23, 30, Nov 6, 12,
18, 19, 21, 22, 25, 27, Dec 1, 2, 3, 4, 27; 1730: DL, Jan 9, 21, 24, 26, Apr
14, 25, Sep 12, 15, 19, 24, 29, Oct 8, 20, Nov 18, 20, 25, 28, 30, Dec 1, 2;
1731: DL, Jan 11, 20, 27, Feb 8, 22, Mar 15, 16, 22, 29, Apr 1, 3, 8, 30, May
7, 18, 19, 31, Jun 11, 22, Jul 20, Aug 18, SF/BFMMO, 26, DL, Sep 18, 21, 23,
25, Oct 2, 7, 14, 16, 21, 30, Nov 8, 9, 15, 22, 23, Dec 2, 3, 21, 22; 1732:
DL, Feb 3, 11, Mar 14, 20, Apr 1, 17, 22, 25, May 3, 8, Jun 1, 9, Aug 1, 4,
15, 21, BFMMO, 23, DL, Sep 19, 21, 23, 26, Oct 3, 5, 17, 19, 26, 28, Nov 7,
9, 11, 13, 14, 18, 21, Dec 6, 9, 11, 14, 20; 1733: DL, Jan 2, 25, 26, Feb 22,
Mar 5, 8, 12, 28, 29, Apr 4, 9, 13, 16, 19, 24, 30, May 3, 10, 24, BFMMO, Aug
23, RI, Sep 10, DL/HAY, 26, Oct 3, 6, 8, 10, 12, 13, 15, 19, 20, 25, 27, Nov
1, 10, 23, 26, 27, 28, Dec 5, 10, 12, 17, 20, 22, HAY, 26; 1734: DL/HAY, Jan
12, 17, HAY, Feb 12, DL/HAY, 22, Mar 12, 23, 25, Apr 2, 6, 17, 18, DL, 22,
DL/HAY, 26, DL, 29, DL/HAY, May 1, DL, 15, 16, RI, Sep 2, DL, 7, 10, 12, 14,
19, 24, 26, Oct 3, 5, 8, 9, 12, 14, 19, 21, 22, 23, 25, Nov 2, 8, 16, 25, Dec
14, 19, 31; 1735: DL, Jan 11, 13, 20, 23, 29, Feb 4, 10, 24, Mar 10, 13, 22,
Apr 11, 14, 18, 21, 23, 25, 28, May 2, 14, Jun 9, Jul 1, LIF, Aug 1, DL, Sep
1, 4, 6, 9, 11, 13, 15, 18, 20, 23, 25, 27, 30, Oct 2, 4, 7, 9, 11, 21, 23,
27, 28, 30, 31, Nov 1, 3, 6, 7, 10, 17, 20, 24, 29, Dec 6, 26; 1736: DL, Jan
3, 19, Feb 5, 9, 20, Mar 11, 13, 23, Apr 12, LIF, 14, DL, 15, 29, May 4, Aug
26, Sep 4, 9, 11, 14, 16, 21, Oct 5, 7, 9, 12, 13, 19, 21, 22, 23, 25, 27,
29, 30, Nov 1, 2, 3, 6, 8, 11, 12, 13, 15, 19, 20, 22, 23, Dec 1, 7, 14, 21;
1737: DL, Jan 10, 24, 27, Mar 22, Apr 12, 15, 19, 26, 27, May 2, 5, 7, 24,
Aug 30, Sep 1, 3, 6, 8, 10, 15, 17, 20, 22, 24, 27, 29, Oct 1, 6, 11, 19, 20,
24, 27, 31, Nov 1, 4, 11, 12, 14, 15, 16, 17, 19; 1738: DL, Jan 5, 14, 19,
31, Feb 2, 10, 16, 28, Mar 2, 4, 16, 20, 21, Apr 17, 22, 29, May 2, 6, 8, 13,
Sep 7, 9, 12, 14, 16, 19, 21, 23, 26, 28, 30, Oct 3, 13, 17, 18, 19, 20, 21,
24, 26, 27, 30, 31, Nov 1, 2, 3, 4, 8, 9, 14, 20, 25, Dec 6, 9, 26; 1739: DL,
Jan 3, 8, 15, 22, 26, 31, Feb 1, 3, 13, Mar 8, 13, 17, 20, 27, 31, Apr 9, 25,
26, 28, 30, May 1, 19, Sep 1, 4, 8, 11, 13, 15, 18, 20, 21, 22, 24, Oct 3, 4,
5, 6, 8, 9, 10, 11, 16, 17, 19, 20, 22, 23, 24, 25, 27, Nov 3, 5, 7, 8, 10,
12, 16, 19, 20, 28, Dec 14, 22, 31; 1740: DL, Jan 5, 16, 19, Feb 7, 13, 16,
23, Mar 11, 13, 17, 20, 25, 27, Apr 14, 16, 17, 22, 29, 30, May 6, 16, 26,
29, 30, Sep 6, 9, 11, 13, 16, 18, 20, 23, 25, 27, 30, Oct 2, 4, 7, 9, 10, 11,
13, 14, 16, 27, 28, 29, Nov 1, 4, 6, 8, 10, 11, 13, 19, 27, Dec 10, 15, 20;
1741: DL, Jan 15, Feb 2, 14, Mar 14, 17, 31, Apr 4, 6, 16, 24, May 14, 21,
25, Jun 4, Sep 5, 8, 10, 12, 15, 17, 19, 22, Oct 6, 8, 9, 10, 12, 15, 21, 23,
Nov 2, 4, 11, 16, 20, 21, Dec 7, 8, 12, 16, 19; 1742: DL, Jan 6, 22, Feb 11,
12, 13, Mar 8, 9, 20, 27, 29, Apr 5, 22, 24, 28, May 28, Sep 11, 14, 16, 18,
21, 25, 28, Oct 2, 5, 7, 9, 13, 26, 28, Nov 1, 2, 3, 4, 8, 12, 16, 19, 22,
Dec 9, 11, 14, 17; 1743: DL, Jan 11, 27, 28, Feb 4, 10, 11, Mar 3, 14, 21,
24, Apr 7, 11, 12, LIF, Jun 3, DL, Sep 13, Dec 6, 12, 13, 15, 16, 17, 20;
1744: DL, Jan 7, 13, 25, 27, Feb 3, 21, Apr 2, 3, 9, 17, 23, May 1, 4, 14,
HAY, Sep 25, 27, Oct 4, 11, 20, Dec 11, DL, 18, 19, 22, 27, 28; 1745: DL, Jan
4, 14, 26, Feb 11, 13, 14, 20, Apr 6, 20, 24, Sep 19, 21, 24, 26, 28, Oct 3,
5, 8, 10, 15, Nov 9, 11, 22, 23, 25, 28, Dec 5, 11, 13; 1746: DL, Feb 8, 10,
12, Mar 1, 10, 13, 17, Apr 4, 11, 14, 15, 23, 28, Jun 13, Sep 23, 25, 27, Oct
4, 23, 25, 27, Nov 1, 4, 7, 21, 28, Dec 20, 26, 29, 30; 1747: DL, Jan 2, 24,
RL, 27, DL, Feb 2, Mar 3, 7, 12, 16, 23, 24, 28, 30, Apr 21, 23, 28, May 5,

16, Sep 15, 19, 26, Oct 17, 21, 29, 30, Nov 2, 7, Dec 16; <u>1748</u>: DL, Jan 6,
12, Feb 3, Mar 24, Apr 25, May 16, Sep 10, 13, 20, Oct 4, 13, 18, 28, Nov 7,
9, Dec 21; <u>1749</u>: DL, Apr 3, 10, Sep 19, 20, Oct 11, 14, 17, 23, 28, Nov 27,
Dec 9; <u>1750</u>: DL, Feb 17, 22, Mar 22, Apr 16, 18, 20
Milman St, <u>1732</u>: LIF, May 9; <u>1733</u>: LIF/CG, May 8; <u>1736</u>: CG, May 6; <u>1737</u>: CG,
Apr 25
Milsintown, Viscount, <u>1749</u>: LEI, Jan 7
Milton, John, <u>1738</u>: DL, Mar 4; <u>1739</u>: DL, Nov 28; <u>1740</u>: DL, Dec 10; <u>1742</u>: DL,
Mar 8, 20, 30, Apr 1, 6, 21; <u>1744</u>: CG, Feb 24, Mar 3, DL, Apr 2; <u>1745</u>: CG,
Jan 14; <u>1746</u>: CG, Feb 14; <u>1747</u>: CG, Mar 26; <u>1748</u>: CG, Dec 10; <u>1749</u>: CG, Mar
3; <u>1750</u>: DL, Feb 28, Mar 28, Apr 2, 4, 5; <u>1752</u>: DL, Mar 31, Apr 21; <u>1755</u>: DL,
Feb 3; <u>1756</u>: HAY, Mar 25; <u>1759</u>: RANELAGH, Jun 13; <u>1760</u>: CG, Feb 29, RANELAGH,
Jun 11; <u>1761</u>: CG, Mar 6; <u>1764</u>: CG, Mar 30; <u>1766</u>: KING'S, Sep 13; <u>1767</u>: CG,
Nov 4; <u>1769</u>: HAY, Feb 2; <u>1772</u>: DL, Mar 11, CG, Apr 8, 10, Oct 17; <u>1773</u>: HAY,
Mar 17, CG, May 6; <u>1774</u>: DL, Mar 2; <u>1792</u>: CG, Feb 24; <u>1793</u>: CG, Feb 22; <u>1794</u>:
CG, Mar 21; <u>1795</u>: HAY, Mar 11; <u>1796</u>: CG, Feb 17; <u>1798</u>: CG, Feb 28; <u>1799</u>: HAY,
Sep 16
--Comus, <u>1738</u>: DL, Mar 4, 6, 7, 9, 11, 14, 23, Apr 3, 4, 5, May 4, 15; <u>1739</u>:
DL, Apr 3, 7, 27, Nov 28, 29, 30, Dec 1, 3, 4, 5, 6; <u>1740</u>: DL, Jan 10, Mar
17, 25, 29, Apr 8, 14, 16, 19, 25, May 1, 7, 9, Dec 10, 11, 13, 17; <u>1741</u>: DL,
Jan 31, Feb 10, Mar 17, Apr 16, May 22, Oct 12, 13, 14, 30, Nov 19, Dec 30;
<u>1742</u>: DL, Jan 2, 15, Feb 9, Apr 1, May 15; <u>1743</u>: DL, Jan 18, Feb 11, 12, LIF,
28, DL, Mar 8, 14, Apr 14, May 16; <u>1744</u>: CG, Mar 3, 5, 6, HAY, Oct 20; <u>1745</u>:
CG, Jan 14, DL, 14, 15, CG, 16, 17, DL, 24, CG, 26, Feb 6, Mar 25, GF, Apr
17, DL, Dec 17, 19; <u>1746</u>: DL, Jan 15, Feb 17; <u>1747</u>: DL, Jan 24, CG, Mar 26,
Apr 29, DL, Nov 13; <u>1748</u>: DL, Dec 10, CG, 10, 12, 13, 15, 16; <u>1749</u>: DL, May
16, Oct 11, 12, 19; <u>1750</u>: DL, Jan 24, Feb 28, CG, Mar 27, DL, Apr 2, 4, 5,
May 10, Oct 13; <u>1751</u>: DL, May 3; <u>1752</u>: DL, Nov 28, 29; <u>1753</u>: DL, May 5; <u>1755</u>:
CG, Apr 9; <u>1756</u>: DL, Nov 24, 26, Dec 1, 7, 9; <u>1758</u>: DL, Nov 3, 6; <u>1759</u>: DL,
Apr 18, Nov 23, 24, 26; <u>1760</u>: CG, Jan 18, 19, 21, 22, 23, 26, 29, Feb 2, 5,
11, Mar 27, Apr 14, Dec 11, 13, 30; <u>1761</u>: CG, Jan 9, 21, Mar 7, Apr 3, Sep
26, Oct 8, Nov 11; <u>1762</u>: CG, Mar 22, 27, Apr 29, Oct 8, 27; <u>1763</u>: CG, Apr 22,
Nov 15; <u>1764</u>: CG, Jan 4, Mar 24, Apr 28, May 26, Nov 7; <u>1765</u>: CG, Mar 14, Apr
24, Oct 22; <u>1766</u>: CG, Mar 20, May 2; <u>1767</u>: CG, Feb 14, Mar 30, Oct 30; <u>1771</u>:
MARLY, Aug 15, 20, 27; <u>1772</u>: CG, Feb 26, May 26, Oct 17, 19, 20, 24, 27, 28,
30, 31, Nov 3, 14, 19, Dec 3, 15, 17; <u>1773</u>: CG, Jan 1, 11, 14, 18, 29, Feb
10, Mar 4, 27, Apr 15, Oct 16, 19, 20, 26, Nov 4, 11, 17; <u>1774</u>: CG, May 12,
Oct 19, 21, 25, Nov 5, 12, 17, Dec 21; <u>1775</u>: CG, Feb 8, 17, 25, Mar 14, 21,
25, DL, May 1; <u>1776</u>: CG, Mar 16, 18, Oct 7, 8, 14, 23, 28, 30; <u>1777</u>: CG, Jan
7, 8, 17, 20, 22, Feb 3, 5, 6, 20, 25, Mar 4, 8, 15, Oct 30, Nov 1, 7, 10,
Dec 12, 13, DL, 15, 16, CG, 16, 17, DL, 17, CG, 18, DL, 19, 22, 23, CG, 23,
DL, 29, 31; <u>1778</u>: DL, Jan 7, 23, 26, 31, Feb 5, 17, 24, Mar 9, CG, May 1, 19,
23, DL, Sep 17, 22, 24, 26, Dec 5, 15; <u>1779</u>: CG, Mar 22, DL, Apr 6, 13, CG,
13, DL, May 1, 5, 8, CG, 20, DL, Sep 18, 23, Oct 22, Dec 20; <u>1780</u>: CG, Feb
17, 21, Mar 11, 16, 29, Apr 15, 27, May 25, Jun 1, HAY, 24, 26, 27, Jul 1, 6,
Aug 1, 3, 19, 29, 30, DL, Oct 10, 21, 28, Nov 7, CG, 13, 14, DL, 23, 30, Dec
20; <u>1781</u>: DL, Jan 19, 22, 25, Feb 19, Mar 10, May 9, Sep 27, Oct 4, 13, CG,
23, 26, DL, Dec 7; <u>1782</u>: DL, Jan 24, CG, Feb 18, 23, 26, DL, 28, Mar 16, CG,
Apr 26, May 13, 22, 24; <u>1783</u>: DL, Apr 7, CG, May 16, 20, HAY, Jun 27, 28, Jul
1, 7, 10, 30, Aug 7, DL, Oct 7, Nov 15, 27, Dec 16; <u>1784</u>: DL, Feb 2, 28, CG,
Mar 23, Apr 3, DL, 27, CG, Jun 10, HAY, Jul 28, DL, Oct 7, Nov 11; <u>1785</u>: CG,
Mar 7, Apr 5, 15, 22, DL, 23, May 6, 24, CG, Sep 23, Nov 2; <u>1786</u>: CG, Apr 1,
DL, May 15, HAY, Jul 18, 29, Aug 1; <u>1787</u>: CG, Mar 31, Apr 14, HAY, Jul 21,
Sep 7, DL, Oct 4, 9, 11, 16, 20, 24, 31, Nov 2, 13, Dec 1, 4, 6, 10, 14;
<u>1788</u>: DL, Jan 23, Feb 2, CG, 5, DL, 9, CG, Mar 10, DL, Apr 2, CG, 24, DL, 28,
May 12, 23, HAY, Jun 12, 14, 21, DL, Oct 23, Nov 8, Dec 15, 30; <u>1789</u>: DL, Jan
7, 13, Feb 11, HAY, 23, DL, May 9, Sep 26, Oct 21; <u>1790</u>: DL, May 20, Nov 30,
Dec 8; <u>1791</u>: CG, May 27, Sep 23, DLKING'S, Oct 29, 31, Nov 28; <u>1792</u>:
DLKING'S, Mar 12, Apr 17, CG, May 18, DL, Sep 27; <u>1793</u>: CG, Apr 11, HAY, Aug
28, 29, Sep 2, CG, Oct 29; <u>1794</u>: CG, Mar 27, DL, Jun 12, HAY, Aug 27; <u>1795</u>:
DL, May 27, CG, Jun 10, Nov 27; <u>1796</u>: CG, May 25; <u>1797</u>: CG, Jan 10, Mar 7,
DL, Nov 24, 30, Dec 4, 8, 18; <u>1798</u>: DL, Feb 5, Apr 25, Jun 18; <u>1799</u>: CG, Jun
7, Dec 10; <u>1800</u>: CG, Mar 22
--Paradise Lost (epic poem), <u>1799</u>: HAY, Sep 16
--Samson Agonistes, <u>1749</u>: CG, Mar 3; <u>1752</u>: DL, Feb 20; <u>1761</u>: CG, Mar 6
Milward, Mary, Mrs William (beneficiary), <u>1742</u>: DL, Mar 9, CG, 25
Milward, William (actor), <u>1723</u>: HAY, Dec 12; <u>1724</u>: HAY, Feb 5, 13, Mar 9; <u>1726</u>:
LIF, Feb 19, May 13, 24, Jun 17, 24, Jul 5, 15, 22, Aug 2, 12, 19, Sep 28,
Oct 3, 12, Nov 8, 10, 14, 18, 30; <u>1727</u>: LIF, Jan 16, 31, Apr 7, 26, May 2, 4,
15, 19, BF, Aug 21, LIF, Sep 11, 15, 20, 25, Oct 2, 9, 17, 19, 21, 26, 31,
Nov 16, 17, Dec 11, 15, 16; <u>1728</u>: LIF, Jan 8, 17, 29, Mar 21, 28, Apr 1, 4,
23, 24, 26, May 11, 15, 23, 30, Jun 25, Jul 2, 5, 19, Aug 2, Sep 16, 18, 30,

Oct 1, 7, 21, Nov 1, 11, 20, Dec 7, 31; <u>1729</u>: LIF, Jan 13, 31, Feb 3, 6, 7,
10, 22, Mar 3, 4, Apr 8, 10, 16, 17, 19, 23, 30, May 7, 15, Sep 12, 17, 19,
22, 24, 26, 29, Oct 3, 13, 20, 24, 30, Nov 4, 8, 13, 25, Dec 3, 15, 27; <u>1730</u>:
LIF, Jan 19, 26, Mar 17, 21, Apr 2, 20, 24, May 6, 7, 11, 13, 18, 20, 23, 25,
Jun 1, RI, 24, 27, Jul 16, Aug 6, LIF, Sep 16, 18, 21, 23, Oct 5, 7, 12, 14,
23, Nov 2, 3, 6, 13, 23, Dec 3, 4, 30; <u>1731</u>: LIF, Jan 4, 9, 11, 13, 20, 21,
Feb 3, 27, Mar 8, 22, Apr 1, 3, 23, 24, May 5, 10, 17, 20, 25, Jun 2, RI, Jul
1, 8, 15, 22, LIF, Sep 17, 20, 22, 27, 29, Oct 1, 6, 11, 13, 18, 20, 25, 27,
30, Nov 4, 8, 12, 17, Dec 1, 3, 6, 9, 11, 15; <u>1732</u>: LIF, Jan 7, 10, 18, 26,
Feb 14, 15, 21, Mar 2, 23, 25, Apr 10, 11, 18, 24, 26, 27, 29, May 9, 22,
CG/LIF, Sep 22, LIF/CG, 27, 29, Oct 4, 9, 11, LIF, 18, LIF/CG, 21, 25, 27,
28, 30, Nov 1, 3, 4, 7, 8, 9, 11, 17, 18, 22, Dec 4, 14, 15, CG/LIF, 16,
LIF/CG, 28; <u>1733</u>: LIF/CG, Jan 15, 20, Feb 5, CG, 8, LIF/CG, Mar 15, 26, CG,
27, LIF/CG, Apr 2, CG, 4, LIF/CG, 10, 12, 13, 17, CG, May 1, 2, LIF/CG, 7,
24, DL/HAY, Oct 10, 12, 17, 22, 25, Nov 1, 5, 9, 14, 23, 26, 27, 28, Dec 10,
19, HAY, 26; <u>1734</u>: HAY, Feb 1, DL/HAY, 6, Mar 12, 25, 30, Apr 1, 2, 17, 18,
20, 26, RI, Jun 27, Sep 2, DL, 7, 10, 14, 24, 28, Oct 3, 5, 8, 9, 12, 14, 17,
24, 25, 26, Nov 4, 8, 16, 20, 25, Dec 6, 14, 19, 31; <u>1735</u>: DL, Jan 13, 20,
29, Feb 24, Mar 6, 10, 13, 22, Apr 11, 14, 21, May 14, Jul 1, LIF, Aug 1, DL,
Sep 1, 4, 6, 9, 11, 18, 20, 23, 25, 27, 30, Oct 2, 7, 11, 21, 24, 25, 27, 28,
30, Nov 1, 3, 4, 7, 12, 17, 19, 20, 21, 24, 29, Dec 26; <u>1736</u>: DL, Jan 12, Feb
5, 9, Mar 11, 13, 20, LIF, Apr 14, DL, May 26, Aug 26, Sep 4, 7, 9, 11, 18,
21, 23, Oct 5, 7, 9, 12, 19, 21, 23, 27, 30, Nov 1, 2, 3, 4, 6, 11, 13, 17,
19, 20, 22, Dec 14, 17, 21, 30; <u>1737</u>: DL, Jan 6, 10, 14, 21, 24, Feb 28, Mar
1, 10, 12, 15, 17, 22, Apr 15, 27, May 2, 7, 14, 27, Aug 30, Sep 1, 3, 6, 8,
10, 20, 22, 24, 29, Oct 1, 6, 11, 19, 20, 21, 31, Nov 1, 4, 12, 14, 17, 19;
<u>1738</u>: DL, Jan 11, 14, 19, 31, Feb 2, 10, 28, Mar 2, 4, 16, 21, 25, Apr 6, 17,
22, 29, May 3, 6, 8, 13, Sep 7, 9, 12, 14, 16, 19, 21, 26, 28, 30, Oct 12,
13, 18, 19, 20, 21, 24, 26, 27, 30, 31, Nov 1, 3, 4, 9, 20, 30, Dec 6, 9, 26;
<u>1739</u>: DL, Jan 3, 13, 22, 31, Feb 1, 3, 13, Mar 8, 10, 13, 17, 27, 31, Apr 25,
30, May 15, 18, Sep 1, 4, 8, 11, 13, 14, 18, 20, 21, 22, 24, Oct 5, 8, 9, 10,
13, 15, 16, 17, 18, 19, 20, 22, Nov 3, 5, 8, 12, 19, 20, 28, Dec 10, 31;
<u>1740</u>: DL, Jan 3, 16, 19, Feb 16, 23, Mar 11, 13, 17, 20, 25, 27, Apr 16, 22,
29, May 2, 6, 20, 30, Sep 6, 9, 11, 13, 16, 20, 27, 30, Oct 4, 7, 9, 13, 14,
15, 16, 27, 29, Nov 4, 7, 10, 11, 13, 19, 27, 29, Dec 6, 8, 10, 18, 20; <u>1741</u>:
DL, Jan 6, 15, Feb 2, 14, Mar 14, 17, 31, Apr 16, 24, May 13, 14, 25, Sep 5,
12, 15, 19, 22, Oct 6, 8, 9, 10, 12, 15, 20, 21, Nov 2, 4, 11, 16, 20, Dec 8,
14, 16, 19; <u>1742</u>: DL, Jan 22, 26, 27, Feb 1, 6, 10, Mar 9; <u>1743</u>: LIF, Apr 11
Mimic Comic Opera Song (song), <u>1761</u>: DL, Apr 1, 2, 13, 15, 21, May 8; <u>1763</u>: DL,
May 9
Mimic Ladder Entertainment (entertainment), <u>1704</u>: DL, Jun 5
Mimic Night Scene (dance), <u>1717</u>: DL, May 16, 31
Mimic Song (song), <u>1732</u>: GF, Oct 26, Nov 8, 24; <u>1734</u>: GF, Apr 27
Mimic Song of the Country Life (song), <u>1715</u>: DL, May 24, Jun 2, 6, 28, Jul 26;
<u>1716</u>: DL, May 3, 25, 30, Jun 19; <u>1717</u>: DL, Jun 27, Aug 9; <u>1718</u>: DL, May 30,
Jun 27, Nov 26; <u>1719</u>: LIF, May 29; <u>1722</u>: RI, Aug 20, BFPMB, 25; <u>1724</u>: RI, Jun
29
Mimicotti, Sga (singer), <u>1757</u>: HAY, Jun 28, Aug 11, 31, Sep 2, 8, 14, 28, Oct
3; <u>1760</u>: HAY, Sep 8
Mimie, Mrs (actor), <u>1734</u>: GF/HAY, Dec 9, HAY, 13, GF/HAY, 27; <u>1735</u>: GF/HAY, Jan
8, 9, HAY, 13
Mimus (eulogy), <u>1749</u>: HAY, Jun 24
Mine Hand be Strenghtened (anthem), <u>1775</u>: DL, Mar 22
Mines (boxkeeper), <u>1717</u>: LIF, Jun 3; <u>1721</u>: LIF, May 23; <u>1722</u>: LIF, May 22;
<u>1724</u>: LIF, May 22; <u>1726</u>: LIF, May 12; <u>1729</u>: LIF, May 19; <u>1731</u>: LIF, May 25;
<u>1732</u>: LIF, May 15; <u>1733</u>: LIF/CG, May 23; <u>1734</u>: CG, May 17; <u>1735</u>: CG/LIF, May
13; <u>1736</u>: CG, May 25; <u>1738</u>: CG, May 8; <u>1739</u>: CG, May 28; <u>1740</u>: CG, May 19;
<u>1741</u>: CG, May 12; <u>1742</u>: CG, May 14; <u>1743</u>: CG, May 9; <u>1744</u>: CG, May 11
Minet (actor), <u>1733</u>: HAY, Jun 4
Mingotti (musician), <u>1755</u>: KING'S, Mar 17; <u>1756</u>: DL, Apr 2, KING'S, 5; <u>1757</u>:
KING'S, May 31
Mingotti, Regina (singer), <u>1754</u>: KING'S, Nov 9; <u>1755</u>: KING'S, Mar 15, 17, Apr
12, Jun 7, Nov 29; <u>1756</u>: KING'S, Mar 15, DL, Apr 2, KING'S, 3, 5, 6, 10, Dec
11; <u>1757</u>: KING'S, Jan 18, Mar 24, DL, 25, KING'S, Apr 30, May 10, 31, Jun 18;
<u>1758</u>: DL, Mar 10; <u>1759</u>: CG, May 4, KING'S, 14; <u>1763</u>: KING'S, Nov 26, Dec 13;
<u>1764</u>: KING'S, Feb 21, Mar 29, Apr 5
Miniature Picture, The. See Craven, Elizabeth Baroness.
Ministers, Foreign, <u>1733</u>: DL, Oct 17, Nov 24; <u>1734</u>: DL/HAY, Mar 16, DL, May 21;
<u>1739</u>: CG, Jan 20
Minna von Barnhelm. See Lessing, Gotthold Ephraim.
Minnes, J (spectator), <u>1668</u>: BF, Sep 7
Minns (Mynns) (actor), <u>1696</u>: LIF, Jun 0; <u>1705</u>: LIF, Aug 1, LIF/QUEN, Oct 30,

QUEEN'S, Nov 23; <u>1706</u>: QUEEN'S, Jan 3, Feb 11, Apr 30, Oct 30; <u>1707</u>: QUEEN'S, Jan 4, May 9; <u>1723</u>: HAY, Jan 31, Feb 13, Mar 14; <u>1729</u>: GF, Nov 7, 10, 11, 12, 14, 17, 21, Dec 3; <u>1730</u>: GF, Mar 30, Apr 28, Jun 3, 9, Jul 10, Nov 10; <u>1731</u>: SOU, Sep 28; <u>1732</u>: HAY, Feb 16, Mar 2, 23, Apr 27, May 8, 10; <u>1733</u>: HAY, Mar 19, Apr 18, CG, Jul 6

Minns, Mrs (actor), <u>1715</u>: SF, Sep 5; <u>1717</u>: LIF, Dec 30; <u>1718</u>: RI, Aug 23; <u>1724</u>: SF, Aug 28

--Siege of Troy, The, <u>1715</u>: SF, Sep 5

Minor, The. See Foote, Samuel.

Minories, <u>1742</u>: GF, Mar 25; <u>1744</u>: HAY, Apr 23; <u>1746</u>: GF, Mar 11

Minors, Sybilla (actor), <u>1741</u>: DL, Nov 11, 12; <u>1742</u>: DL, Apr 20, May 8, 26, Oct 7, Nov 1, Dec 22; <u>1743</u>: DL, May 10; <u>1744</u>: HAY, Apr 6, 20, May 10, 16, DL, Dec 27; <u>1745</u>: DL, Jan 29, Feb 2, 4, 7, 9, 20, May 7, Oct 19, Nov 30, Dec 12, 13, 30; <u>1746</u>: DL, Jan 10, 17, 18, 28, Mar 4, 10, 13, Apr 4, 7, 21, 23, Jun 11, 13, Sep 30, Oct 25, Nov 1, 7, Dec 26; <u>1747</u>: DL, Feb 2, 11, Mar 7, 16, 23, Apr 22, 28, 29, Dec 5, 12; <u>1748</u>: DL, Mar 1, 10, 19, May 2, 6, SFP, Sep 7; <u>1749</u>: CG, Sep 29, Oct 23, Nov 9, Dec 26; <u>1750</u>: CG, Jan 11, Mar 17, Apr 27, DL, Sep 8, 22, Oct 16, Nov 7, 14, 15, 24, 28, Dec 14; <u>1751</u>: DL, Feb 2, 14, 16, 23, Mar 12, 14, 16, May 1, 18, Sep 7, 10, 14, 17, 21, 26, Oct 2, 4, 7, 9, 11, 22, 28, 29, Nov 7, 8, 9, 16, 28, 29, Dec 10, 26; <u>1752</u>: DL, Jan 6, Feb 13, Mar 9, 10, Apr 3, 4, 6, 13, 27, Sep 19, 21, 28, 30, Oct 3, 5, 10, 11, 19, 30, Nov 22, 30, Dec 8, 18, 19, 29; <u>1753</u>: DL, Jan 1, 3, 8, 15, 17, Feb 19, Mar 19, 22, Apr 5, 25, 28, 30, May 4, 11, 17, 18, 21, 25, Sep 8, 25, 27, 29, Oct 2, 9, 10, 13, 18, 20, 23, 31, Nov 1, 14, 26, Dec 20, 26; <u>1754</u>: DL, Jan 7, 23, Feb 9, 12, 20, Apr 16, 30, May 2, 13, 14, 24, Sep 14, 19, 26, Oct 1, 3, 5, 15, 18, 21, 23, 29, 30, Nov 6, 22, Dec 5, 7, 9, 13, 17; <u>1755</u>: DL, Jan 6, 22, Apr 2, 19, 21, May 6, Sep 13, 16, 18, 25, 27, Oct 2, 3, 7, 13, 17, 24, 25, 28, 31, Nov 1, 17, 22, 26, Dec 4, 6, 23; <u>1756</u>: DL, Jan 1, 2, 12, 21, Mar 23, 27, 29, Apr 3, 24, 30, May 10, 12, 14, Sep 18, 23, 28, Oct 2, 7, 13, 15, 18, 21, 23, 28, Nov 6, 11, 12, 18, 23, Dec 10, 15, 27; <u>1757</u>: DL, Jan 18, Mar 24, Apr 20, May 2, 3, 9, 23, Sep 13, 15, 17, 20, 29, Oct 6, 8, 19, 26, 27, 29, Nov 10, 15, 16, 18, Dec 3, 8, 10, 27; <u>1758</u>: DL, Jan 13, 24, Mar 13, 16, Apr 18, 29, May 1, 2, 15, Sep 16

Minstrel's Song (song), <u>1796</u>: CG, Mar 14, May 18; <u>1797</u>: CG, May 24; see also Where is that towering spirit fled

Minton (actor), <u>1797</u>: HAY, Dec 4

M'Intosh. See Mackintosh.

Minuet (dance), <u>1717</u>: DL, Oct 30; <u>1726</u>: LIF, Apr 14, DL, May 6; <u>1731</u>: DL, Mar 25, LIF, May 3; <u>1732</u>: DL, Mar 13, 16, 23, LIF, Apr 25, May 1, 24, DL, 25, LIF, Oct 18, DL, Nov 6, 14; <u>1733</u>: CG, Mar 27, LIF/CG, Apr 23, DL, 30, LIF/CG, 30, GF, 30, DL, May 5, HAY, 28; <u>1734</u>: DL/HAY, Mar 18, DL/LIF, Apr 1, LIF, 15, 18, GF, 19, CG, 24, May 8, 17, JS, 31, HAY, Jun 19, Aug 14, LIF, 20, HAY, 22; <u>1735</u>: DL, Mar 13, 17, 22, CG/LIF, Apr 14, 24, GF/HAY, May 5, DL, 17, CG/LIF, 20, YB, Jun 3, LIF, 19, Jul 11, GF/HAY, 15, DL, Nov 5; <u>1736</u>: DL, Apr 3, GF, May 6, DL, 7, 14, 19, 20, 25, 27, 28; <u>1737</u>: DL, Mar 5, CG, 19, 24, Apr 2, LIF, 18, CG, 25, DL, 30, May 4, LIF, 4, DL, 5, CG, 5, DL, 9, 11, CG, 12, 13, DL, 30, Nov 2, 7; <u>1738</u>: DL, Feb 25, Mar 3, 13, CG, 21, 23, DL, May 5, 12, 19, 22, 25, 29, 30; <u>1739</u>: CG, Mar 22, 26, DL, Apr 9, 12, 14, 24, 25, 26, May 9, 16, CG, Dec 15; <u>1740</u>: DL, Mar 22, CG, 24, 25, DL, Apr 24, 25, CG, 25, 29, May 5, DL, 7, CG, 12, 13, DL, 15, CG, Dec 9; <u>1741</u>: CG, Jan 10, Feb 14, Mar 7, 17, Apr 2, DL, 4, CG, 20, 2 , DL, 27, CG, 28, 29, DL, May 1, 12, 13, 14, 28, JS, Oct 27; <u>1742</u>: CG, Jan 11, Mar 30, Apr 1, 5, DL, 19, CG, 20, DL, 23, CG, 23, 29, May 1, DL, 7, CG, 11, 21; <u>1743</u>: LIF, Mar 3, 22, CG, 24, Apr 6, LIF, 7, CG, 14, 16, 18, 22, 23, 28, DL, May 11; <u>1744</u>: CG, Apr 4, 7, 16, 24, DL, May 1; <u>1745</u>: CG, Apr 2, 16, 18, 19, 23, May 6, DL, 8, 9, CG, 29; <u>1746</u>: CG, Mar 17, Apr 2, DL, 3, CG, 8, 14, 15, DL, 16, 24; <u>1747</u>: DL, Apr 2, 21, CG, May 13, DL, Sep 29; <u>1748</u>: DL, Mar 24, 26, HAY, Apr 14, DL, 15, CG, 19, 21, HAY, May 2; <u>1749</u>: CG, Apr 12, 24; <u>1750</u>: DL, Mar 17, CG, 31, Apr 18, DL, 20, CG, 23, 28, DL, 28, May 3; <u>1751</u>: DL, Apr 11, 16, CG, May 1, DL, 4, 8; <u>1752</u>: DL, Mar 16, CG, 19, Apr 13, 15, 18, 22, DL, 27; <u>1753</u>: DL, Mar 31, CG, Apr 9, DL, 24, CG, 30, May 1, DL, 1, 2, 8, 12, CG, 14, DL, 14, 17, CG, Oct 25; <u>1754</u>: DL, Mar 26, CG, 30, Apr 16, 23, DL, May 2, CG, 4; <u>1755</u>: CG, Mar 17, KING'S, 18, CG, Apr 15, DL, 22, CG, 23, DL, 24, 28, 29, May 5; <u>1756</u>: DL, Mar 29, KING'S, 30, Apr 6, CG, 22, DL, 22, May 13, 20, Nov 8; <u>1757</u>: CG, Jan 10, Mar 12, DL, 22, CG, 29, DL, Apr 2, 12, CG, 16, DL, 25, CG, 27, DL, 29, CG, May 25, HAY, Aug 31, Sep 8, 14, 28, DL, Nov 8; <u>1758</u>: DL, Mar 18, CG, Apr 11, 12, DL, 14, 18, CG, 19, DL, 24, 27, May 2, 10; <u>1759</u>: KING'S, Mar 20, HAY, Apr 18, CG, 25, 27, DL, May 9, 15, CG, 16, DL, 21, 23, Dec 19; <u>1760</u>: KING'S, Mar 24, DL, Apr 9, CG, 11, DL, 16, CG, 17, 22, 25, DL, May 1, 7, 8, HAY, Jun 5; <u>1761</u>: CG, Jan 2, Apr 1, DL, 8, 10, 18, 29, 30, CG, May 8, HAY, Aug 6, 22; <u>1762</u>: DL, Mar 20, CG, Apr 17, 21, 23, 27, 28, DL, 28; <u>1763</u>: CG, Mar 26, Apr 12, KING'S, 21, CG, 29, May 13; <u>1764</u>: CG, Apr 10, May 3, 22, DL, 23, CG, Oct 17; <u>1765</u>: CG, Apr 9,

DL, 11, 16, CG, 18, DL, 19, CG, 23, 26, May 9, 20, 22; 1766: KING'S, Mar 13,
CG, Apr 2, 5, 19, 25, DL, May 5, CG, 6, DL, 7, CG, 9; 1767: DL, Mar 31, CG,
Apr 6, 11, DL, 20, CG, 27, DL, May 8, CG, 9, DL, 12, 13, 15, 16, 18, 26;
1768: DL, Apr 5, CG, 6, 9, DL, May 4, 7, CG, 27, 31; 1769: CG, Apr 1, 4, 5,
8, 27, 29, May 6, 12, 17; 1770: HAY, Feb 14, CG, Apr 5, 17, 18, 20, DL, 27,
28, CG, May 1, DL, 2, CG, 3, 18, 23, 25, DL, 30, Jun 4, HAY, Dec 19; 1771:
HAY, Mar 11, DL, 18, HAY, Apr 1, CG, 3, 6, DL, 22, CG, 26, HAY, May 2, DL, 8,
CG, 17, 22, 25, DL, Sep 21; 1772: CG, Apr 22, May 1, 5, DL, 8, CG, 8, DL, 9,
CG, 15, 16, 21, 23, DL, Nov 21; 1773: KING'S, Apr 1, CG, 16, 17, DL, 22,
KING'S, 24, CG, 24, KING'S, 27, CG, May 3, 12, 18, 26; 1774: CG, Apr 12, 15,
DL, 20, KING'S, 28, DL, 30, CG, May 7, KING'S, 12, CG, 14, 16, 18, 20, HAY,
Jun 10, 24; 1775: CG, Apr 22, DL, 28, CG, May 12, 15, 16, 18, KING'S, 25, CG,
26, Oct 24; 1776: CG, Apr 13, DL, 23, CG, May 3, 4, 11, Oct 4, 7, Nov 16, 30;
1777: CG, Jan 2, KING'S, Feb 4, CG, Apr 19, 26, 29, May 20, Sep 29, Nov 21;
1778: CG, Jan 12, KING'S, Mar 10, CG, Apr 28, May 16, 22, KING'S, 26, 28,
HAY, Sep 10, CG, Oct 26, Dec 12; 1779: CG, Mar 25, KING'S, Apr 15, CG, 19,
28, May 8, DL, 17, CG, Nov 8, KING'S, Dec 14, 21; 1780: KING'S, Feb 8, 19,
Apr 4, DL, 18, KING'S, 20, DL, May 2, CG, 16, 18, Dec 5, 13; 1781: KING'S,
Apr 26, CG, May 18, Sep 24, DL, Dec 27; 1782: KING'S, Mar 19, DL, Apr 25, CG,
27, DL, May 10, 16, KING'S, Jun 5, HAY, 20, 22, Aug 21, 29, Sep 4, 6, 13, DL,
28, CG, Oct 7, DL, Nov 23, Dec 6; 1783: KING'S, Mar 13, May 1, HAY, Jun 13,
KING'S, 19, CG, Sep 22, DL, Oct 4, Nov 29; 1784: DL, Apr 12, May 22; 1785:
KING'S, Apr 14; 1786: DL, Sep 26; 1787: CG, Apr 27; 1788: DL, Apr 14; 1789:
CG, Sep 30, DL, Dec 1, 15; 1792: DLKING'S, Jan 28, DL, Nov 10; 1793: DL, May
13; 1794: DL, May 16, CG, 24; 1797: DL, Nov 10, 14; 1798: CG, May 16; 1800:
CG, Mar 27

Minuet and Allemande (dance), 1780: CG, May 16; 1781: DL, May 11; 1782: CG, Apr
 2
Minuet and Cotillion (dance), 1776: CG, May 15; 1787: DL, Jun 4
Minuet and Gavotte (dance), 1779: CG, May 21; 1782: DL, May 8, KING'S, 9, DL,
 17; 1783: KING'S, May 8; 1785: KING'S, Apr 7; 1789: DL, Dec 9
Minuet and Louvre (dance), 1735: GF, Apr 17; 1736: CG, Mar 25, GF, Apr 13;
 1748: CG, Apr 28; 1769: DL, May 2; 1770: DL, May 10
Minuet and Quadrille (dance), 1786: DL, Jun 6
Minuet and Waltz (dance), 1800: CG, May 2
Minuet Dauphin (dance), 1778: KING'S, May 28
Minuet de la Cour (dance), 1776: KING'S, Apr 25, 30, May 4, 7, 11, 18, Jun 6,
 8; 1777: CG, Apr 4, DL, 19, CG, 26, KING'S, May 8, CG, 20, KING'S, Jul 5, DL,
 Nov 7, 11, CG, 18; 1778: KING'S, Apr 28, DL, May 2, 8, 11, 12, 13, 15, CG,
 16, DL, 18, 25, 26, 27, Sep 19, Dec 23; 1779: DL, Jan 29, Mar 16, CG, May 8,
 DL, 25; 1780: DL, Jan 7, Sep 19, 26, Oct 18, Nov 17, Dec 23; 1781: DL, Jan
 24, HAY, Mar 26, DL, Apr 27, May 5, 8, HAY, Jul 23; 1782: DL, Jan 4, 19, 21,
 Mar 18, Apr 8, 12, 29, May 15, 29, HAY, Aug 15, DL, Sep 17, Oct 7, Nov 5, Dec
 9, CG, 11; 1783: DL, Jan 31, Apr 7, KING'S, May 1; 1784: DL, May 14, 18, CG,
 21; 1785: DL, Jan 11, CG, May 18, DL, 20, 23, HAY, Dec 26; 1786: DL, Jan 16,
 Mar 20, Apr 6, 20, Jun 1, KING'S, 1, DL, Nov 25; 1787: DL, Apr 13, May 31,
 Oct 6, Dec 12; 1788: HAY, Sep 4, 11; 1789: KING'S, Jun 15, CG, Jul 2; 1790:
 DL, Jun 2; 1791: CG, Feb 15, KING'S, May 26, Jun 6; 1797: KING'S, Apr 6, Jun
 15; 1798: KING'S, Apr 19; 1799: DL, May 3; 1800: CG, May 23, KING'S, Jun 19
Minuet de la Cour and Allemande (dance), 1777: CG, May 9; 1781: DL, Apr 3;
 1784: DL, Apr 21, May 17; 1786: DL, May 2, 26; 1788: DL, Jun 6; 1795: CG, Sep
 21; 1796: CG, May 17
Minuet de la Cour and Gavotte (dance), 1778: KING'S, Mar 3, 10, 17, 31, Apr 30,
 May 12, 30, Jun 5; 1780: CG, May 16; 1784: KING'S, Mar 11; 1785: DL, May 17,
 CG, 28; 1789: DL, Jan 17, HAY, Jul 16, DL, Nov 21; 1790: HAY, Jun 19, CG, Jul
 10; 1791: DL, May 24; 1793: DL, Jun 4; 1797: DL, Jun 10; 1799: CG, Jun 8
Minuet de la Cour en Quatre (dance), 1781: CG, May 18
Minuet de la Ville (dance), 1782: KING'S, Apr 30
Minuet de Volage (dance), 1792: HAY, Mar 10
Minuet et Marie (dance), 1733: GF, Apr 20
Minuet of Iphigenia (dance), 1789: KING'S, Apr 28, May 28, Jun 6, 16, CG, Jul 2
Mirror for the Ladies, A. See Harricks, William.
Mirror, The (play, anon), 1737: HAY, Jan 26
Mirror, The; or, Harlequin Every-where. See Dibdin, Charles.
Mirsa (dance), 1782: KING'S, May 9, 16, 25
Mirth admit me of thy crew (song), 1764: CG, May 11; 1784: CG, Apr 27; 1791:
 CG, Mar 18, 30; 1793: CG, Mar 20; 1794: CG, Mar 21, DL, Apr 9; 1798: CG, Feb
 28; 1799: CG, Mar 15
Mirth and Jollity (dance), 1776: CG, Jan 2, 3, 4, 6, 8, 9, 13, 15, Feb 5, 9,
 Mar 19, Apr 17, 18, 26, 30, May 1, 9, Oct 15, 29; 1777: CG, Jan 1, 15, Mar
 22, Oct 21
Mirth by Moonshine (dance), 1787: CG, Sep 28, Oct 19, 29; 1788: CG, Jan 21, Sep

15; 1789: CG, Jan 13, May 6, 12
Mirth gives courage (song), 1746: CG, Apr 16; 1747: CG, Apr 24; 1748: CG, Mar
   31; 1749: CG, Apr 14; 1750: CG, Mar 09
Misanthrope, Le. See Moliere.
Misaubain, Mrs (householder), 1744: CR, Mar 21
Miscellanies in Prose and Verse (book), 1771: DL, Jan 1
Misdale (actor), 1760: HAY, Jun 28
Miser Bit, The; or, Harlequin Reveller (farce, anon), 1742: BFPY, Aug 25, SF,
   Sep 8, SOU, 27
Miser Outwitted, The; or, Phelim in the Suds (farce, anon), 1754: SFG, Sep 21,
   23, 24
Miser, The. See Moliere, L'Avare; Shadwell, Thomas; Fielding, Henry.
Miser, The; or, Wagner and Abericock. See Thurmond, John.
Miser's Passport (song), 1743: CG, Apr 15; 1744: CG, Apr 17; 1745: CG, Apr 24
Miserere Mei Deus (music), 1743: KING'S, Apr 19, 26; 1772: CG, Mar 27, Apr 8;
   1773: HAY, Mar 3, 17; 1790: CG, Mar 17, 19
Miseries of Love, The (play, anon), 1732: HAY, Nov 29
Misero Pergoletto (song), 1763: KING'S, Apr 25
Misery of Civil War, The. See Crowne, John.
Mislebrook (beneficiary), 1757: CG, May 20; 1758: CG, May 12; 1759: CG, May 25;
   1760: CG, May 19, Sep 22; 1762: CG, May 21; 1763: CG, May 26
Miss in Her Teens. See Garrick, David.
Miss Lucy in Town. See Fielding, Henry.
Miss Midnight's Medley Concert (entertainment), 1757: HAY, Nov 2, 4, 7, 9
Misses' Lamentation (song), 1704: LIF, Jun 1
Mississippi (play, anon), 1720: LIF, May 4
Mississippi River, 1719: LIF, Dec 21
Mist (iron monger), 1796: CG, Feb 15
Mist (journalist), 1722: DL, Jan 8
Mist and Co (braziers), 1776: DL, Mar 16, Apr 11
Mist and Sons (ironmongers), 1779: DL, Nov 8
Mistake of a Minute, The (farce, anon), 1787: DL, Apr 23
Mistake, The. See Vanbrugh, Sir John.
Mistake, The; or, All is Right at Last (dance), 1742: BFHC, Aug 25
Mistaken Beauty. See Corneille, Pierre.
Mistaken Husband, The. See Dryden, John.
Mistakes, The (play, anon), 1690: DL, Dec 0
Mistress Mine (song), 1790: HAY, Aug 20
Mitchel, Mons and Mlle (dancers), 1745: DL, Sep 26
Mitchell, Colin (actor), 1778: HAY, Sep 17; 1779: HAY, Feb 22, Mar 8, May 10;
   1785: HAY, Feb 10
Mitchell, John (renter), 1758: CG, Feb 23
Mitchell, Joseph (author), 1721: LIF, Apr 21; 1731: DL, Mar 20; 1793: HAY, Dec
   2
--Fatal Extravagance, The, 1721: LIF, Apr 21, 22, Nov 22; 1722: LIF, Jan 11,
   May 7; 1724: LIF, May 2
--Highland Fair, The; or, Union of the Clans, 1731: DL, Mar 20, 23, 27, Apr 20
Mitchell, Miss (actor), 1779: HAY, Oct 18
Mitchell, Miss (actor), 1798: CG, Sep 26, 28, Oct 8, Nov 12, Dec 15, 26; 1799:
   CG, Mar 2, 4, Apr 9, May 13, 27, 31
Mitchell, Mrs (actor), 1660: NONE, Sep 0
Mitchell, Richard (beneficiary), 1741: CG, Dec 11
Mitermayer (scene painter), 1757: KING'S, Mar 8
Mithridate. See Racine, Jean.
Mithridates. See Lee, Nathaniel; Porpora, Nicola.
Mitre Court, 1753: DL, Dec 21
Mitre Tavern, 1735: CG/LIF, Jan 14; 1740: CG, May 12; 1750: DL, Feb 21
Mitridate a Sinope. See Sarti, Giuseppe.
Mitridate. See Terradellas, Domenico; Sacchini, Antonio Maria Gasparo.
Mitteer, Mrs (actor), 1774: HAY, Sep 17, 30
M'Kenna (beneficiary), 1749: JS, Mar 27
M'Knowl (householder), 1799: CG, Jun 5
M'Lane, Miss (singer), 1768: HAY, Dec 19
M'Mahon (actor), 1766: KING'S, Aug 13; 1767: HAY, Sep 9
M'Millin (actor), 1780: HAY, Apr 5
M'Nab (actor), 1785: HAY, Jan 24
M'neale. See McNeil.
Mob in Despair, The (farce, anon), 1737: HAY, Jan 26
Mock (merchant), 1760: CG, Jan 26
Mock Astrologer. See Dryden, John, Evening's Love.
Mock Countess, The (ballad opera, anon), 1733: DL, Apr 30, May 14; 1734:
   CG/LIF, Nov 11, 12; 1735: CG/LIF, May 15, 22; 1737: CG, Mar 7; 1738: CG, Aug

1, 4, 8

Mock Doctor, The. See Fielding, Henry.
Mock Duellist, The. See Belon, Peter.
Mock Italian-English Ballad (song), 1735: DL, May 6, 22, 23, 29, Jun 3
Mock Lawyer, The. See Phillips, Edward.
Mock Marriage, The. See Scott, Thomas.
Mock Mason, The. See Chetwood, William Rufus.
Mock Minuet (dance), 1733: LIF/CG, Apr 12, 18, 19, May 7, CG, 11, LIF/CG, 15,
   19, 24, DL/HAY, Oct 27, 29, 31, Nov 22, Dec 1, 5, 19, 20; 1746: GF, Jan 14;
   1753: CG, Mar 31, Apr 30; 1754: CG, Apr 29; 1771: DL, Apr 19, May 15; 1772:
   DL, Jan 21; 1777: DL, Nov 14; 1779: DL, Jan 7, Dec 8; 1780: DL, May 25, Sep
   16; 1783: DL, Oct 2; 1784: DL, Oct 14; 1785: DL, Sep 29, Nov 15; 1787: DL,
   Sep 22; 1788: DL, Oct 4; 1791: CG, Apr 11, DL, May 19, HAY, Oct 24, DLKING'S,
   Nov 22; 1792: DL, Oct 9; 1794: DL, Jun 25; 1795: DL, Jan 23; 1796: CG, Mar
   14, DL, Jun 4, Sep 20; 1797: DL, Jun 16, HAY, Aug 5, DL, Nov 14; 1798: CG,
   Apr 27, May 15, HAY, Aug 30, DL, Sep 20, HAY, Dec 17; 1799: DL, Mar 9, HAY,
   Aug 26, DL, Oct 1, Dec 17
Mock Officer, The; or, The Captain's Lady (play, anon), 1733: DL, Mar 28
Mock Orators, The; or, The Kept Mistress (play, anon), 1756: DL, Apr 10, Oct 23
Mock Pompey (farce), 1706: QUEEN'S, Jul 31
Mock Tempest, The. See Duffett, Thomas.
Modena, Duke of, 1676: DG, Apr 30; 1678: ATCOURT, Nov 0
Modena, Mary, Duchess of (died), 1687: NONE, Jul 24
Modena, Prince of (spectator), 1735: DL, Oct 21, CG, 24, DL, 27, KING'S, 28,
   GF, Nov 5, CG, 6, DL, 11, 13
Moderation and Alteration (song), 1776: CHR, Sep 23; 1780: CG, Apr 22; 1781:
   HAY, Aug 17, 24, 31; 1785: CG, May 4, 16; 1788: HAY, Aug 22
Modern Antiques. See O'Keeffe, John.
Modern Breakfast. See Siddons, Henry.
Modern Fine Gentleman, The. See Garrick, David, The Male Coquette.
Modern Husband, The. See Fielding, Henry.
Modern Madness; or, A Touch of the Times (play, anon), 1749: BFCB, Aug 23, 24,
   25, 26, 28
Modern Midnight Conversation, A (entertainment), 1742: CG, Mar 22
Modern Pimp, The; or, The Doctor Deceived (entertainment), 1736: BFHC, Aug 23;
   1741: BFH, Aug 22
Modern Prophets, The. See D'Urfey, Thomas.
Modern Traveller (entertainment), 1767: DL, Mar 31
Modern Wife, The (play, anon), 1771: CG, Apr 27
Modern Wife, The. See Stevens, John.
Modett, Mlle (dancer), 1742: BFHC, Aug 25
Modish Couple, The. See Boadens, Charles.
Modish Husband, The. See Burnaby, William.
Modish Wife, The. See Gentleman, Francis.
Modista Raggiratrice, La. See Paisiello, Giovanni.
Moegan, Francis (spectator), 1674: WF, Oct 31
Moench (Munich), Simon Frederic (scene painter), 1773: KING'S, May 6; 1791:
   PAN, May 9, 21, Jun 10, 16
Moffett, Mrs (actor), 1724: LIF, Jun 23, Jul 3, 21, 31, Aug 11, Oct 14, Nov 18;
   1725: LIF, Jan 11, Mar 29, Apr 10, 23, May 17, 21, Oct 15, Nov 24, Dec 8, 16,
   31; 1726: LIF, Jan 7, Feb 19, Mar 24, Apr 11, May 4, 11, 13; 1727: LIF, Sep
   25, Oct 25
Moffett, Mrs (actor), 1743: BFYWR, Aug 23
Moffett, Mrs (dresser), 1775: DL, May 27
Moggy and Jemmy; or, The Union Feast (dance), 1799: DL, Jan 14, 18, Feb 5
Moggy Lauder (music), 1791: CG, May 20
Moglie Fedele, La. See Alessandri, Felice.
Mogul Tale, A. See Inchbald, Elizabeth.
Mohammed, Sidi (Tunisian ambassador), 1733: DL, Oct 22, DL/HAY, Nov 1
Mohammedanism, 1775: CG, Mar 18
Mohocks (Indians), 1710: YB, May 1
Mohun, Charles, 4th Baron (murderer), 1692: DL, Dec 2, 9; 1697: DLORLIF, Sep 15
Mohun, Michael (actor), 1660: NONE, Sep 0, COCKPIT, Oct 8, REDBULL, Nov 5,
   VERE, 15, 17, VERE/RED, 20, VERE, 22, Dec 0, 3, 6; 1661: NONE, Sep 0; 1662:
   VERE, Jan 28; 1663: VERE, Mar 0, BRIDGES, May 7, NONE, Sep 0; 1664: NONE, Sep
   0; 1665: BRIDGES, Jan 14, Apr 0; 1666: NONE, Sep 0, BRIDGES, Dec 7, ATCOURT,
   10; 1667: BRI/COUR, Feb 0, BRIDGES, Apr 16, 17, Oct 5, 19, Dec 7, 26; 1668:
   BRIDGES, Jun 12, Sep 14, Nov 6, Dec 18; 1669: BRIDGES, Feb 6, Apr 17, May 6,
   Jun 24; 1670: BRIDGES, Aug 0, BRI/COUR, Dec 0; 1671: BRIDGES, Mar 0, Jun 0;
   1672: BRIDGES, Jan 0, LIF, Feb 26, Apr 0, Nov 0; 1673: LIF, May 0; 1674: LIF,
   Mar 0, DL, 26, May 16; 1675: DL, Jan 12, 25, Apr 23, 30, May 10, NONE, Sep 0,
   DL, Nov 17; 1676: DL, Jan 29, ATCOURT, May 29, DL, Sep 9; 1677: DL, Jan 12,

Mar 17, Oct 0, Dec 12, 26; <u>1678</u>: DL, Feb 0, Mar 0; <u>1681</u>: DL, May 0; <u>1682</u>: DL, Feb 4, NONE, Sep 0, DL, Nov 16; <u>1698</u>: DL, Feb 0
Moissonneurs de la Styrie (dance), <u>1742</u>: DL, Nov 22, 24, 25, 26, 30, Dec 1, 3, 6, 8, 11, 14, 16, 17, 18, 21, 23, 27; <u>1743</u>: DL, Jan 28, Feb 3, 26, 28, May 7
Moissonneurs, Les (dance), <u>1778</u>: KING'S, Dec 22, 29; <u>1779</u>: KING'S, Jan 5, 23, 29, Feb 2, 9, 27, Mar 11, May 25, 29, Jun 15, 19, 26, 29
Moissonneurs, Les. See Favart, Charles Simon.
Molbery (actor), <u>1782</u>: HAY, Mar 4
Moleck, Bell Ara (Mason), <u>1744</u>: JS, Mar 2
Moliere (Jean Baptiste Poquelin), <u>1667</u>: LIF, Aug 15; <u>1669</u>: LIF, Jun 14; <u>1670</u>: BRIDGES, May 0; <u>1687</u>: NONE, Sep 0; <u>1693</u>: DG, May 0; <u>1704</u>: LIF, Aug 9; <u>1706</u>: QUEEN'S, Jul 31; <u>1718</u>: LIF, Jun 20, 25; <u>1719</u>: LIF, Jan 13, 27, KING'S, Mar 14, LIF, Jun 24; <u>1720</u>: KING'S, Apr 29, Jun 13, 17; <u>1721</u>: HAY, Jan 19, Feb 3, 10, 14, 27, Mar 2, 13, Apr 24, Dec 4, 11, 14, 29; <u>1722</u>: HAY, Jan 1, 4, Feb 6, Mar 15, 26, Apr 2; <u>1724</u>: LIF, Jul 14, 17, HAY, Dec 30; <u>1725</u>: HAY, Jan 18, 22, Feb 11, May 7; <u>1726</u>: HAY, Apr 15, LIF, Jun 17, CLAR, Nov 14; <u>1727</u>: WS, Dec 14; <u>1732</u>: DL, May 12, Jun 23, Jul 28, Aug 1, 22, BF, 22, DL, Sep 8, 19, Nov 16, 30; <u>1733</u>: DL, Feb 20, Mar 10, HAY, 20, DL, Apr 19, May 9, 14, 18, BF, Aug 23, DL/HAY, Oct 10, 25, Nov 9, 14, Dec 12, HAY, 13; <u>1734</u>: DL, Jan 3, 4, DL/HAY, 9, 11, DL, 23, DL/HAY, Feb 16, 20, 21, 22, 23, Mar 5, 9, 12, 25, LIF, Apr 4, DL/HAY, May 3, DL, Oct 8, 9, 19, HAY, Nov 1, DL, 18, GF/HAY, 20, DL, 23, GF/HAY, 28, Dec 11, 18, HAY, 20, 23, DL, 31; <u>1735</u>: HAY, Jan 13, 15, GF/HAY, Feb 6, HAY, 7, 18, DL, Mar 17, HAY, 19, CG/LIF, 20, DL, 29, Apr 14, 16, 22, GF/HAY, May 2, HAY, 8, 9, 19, DL, Jul 1, LIF, 30, Aug 1, DL, Sep 27, Oct 2, 23, Dec 15; <u>1736</u>: DL, Jan 31, Feb 19, 23, Mar 20, Apr 12, May 6, Jun 2, Sep 28, Oct 19, 25, 28, Nov 12, 30, Dec 7, 8, 18; <u>1737</u>: DL, Mar 29, May 24, 25, 30, Sep 17, Oct 13, 19, 24, Nov 10; <u>1738</u>: DL, Jan 27, Feb 11, Mar 20, 21, Apr 11, 17, May 12, 30, Oct 16, 27, Nov 2, 10, Dec 23; <u>1739</u>: DL, Jan 4, 15, CG, Aug 2, 10, 21, Sep 5, Oct 25, Nov 20; <u>1743</u>: LIF, Feb 28; <u>1747</u>: DL, Nov 25; <u>1749</u>: HAY, Nov 15, 22; <u>1750</u>: HAY, Mar 7; <u>1767</u>: CG, Jan 10; <u>1768</u>: DL, Nov 17; <u>1769</u>: DL, Mar 28; <u>1772</u>: CG, Jan 25; <u>1780</u>: HAY, Apr 5; <u>1781</u>: CG, Apr 18; <u>1782</u>: CG, Apr 4; <u>1784</u>: CG, Oct 6; <u>1785</u>: CG, Oct 29; <u>1789</u>: CG, Nov 5; <u>1792</u>: CG, Apr 18, HAY, Aug 31; <u>1793</u>: HAY, Dec 10; <u>1795</u>: HAY, Aug 11; <u>1797</u>: CG, Apr 29
--Amour Medicin, L' (Love is the Doctor), <u>1734</u>: LIF, Apr 4
--Amphitrion, <u>1721</u>: HAY, Dec 11, 22; <u>1722</u>: HAY, Mar 15; <u>1734</u>: HAY, Dec 20; <u>1735</u>: HAY, Jan 1
--Avare, L' (Miser, The), <u>1721</u>: HAY, Feb 3; <u>1722</u>: HAY, Jan 1, Feb 6; <u>1732</u>: SS, Nov 1; <u>1734</u>: HAY, Nov 1; <u>1735</u>: HAY, Mar 12; <u>1750</u>: HAY, Feb 26, Mar 1, 7, 13
--Bourgeois Gentilhomme, Le, <u>1720</u>: KING'S, Apr 29, May 10; <u>1721</u>: HAY, Feb 27, Mar 4; <u>1722</u>: HAY, Mar 26; <u>1735</u>: HAY, Jan 13, 15; <u>1737</u>: KING'S, May 21
--Cocu Imaginaire, Le, <u>1721</u>: HAY, Mar 2, Dec 22; <u>1722</u>: HAY, Jan 4, Apr 2; <u>1735</u>: HAY, May 8, 9
--Ecole des Femmes, L', <u>1721</u>: HAY, Mar 13, Apr 28; <u>1735</u>: GF/HAY, Mar 20, May 2; <u>1749</u>: HAY, Nov 15; <u>1797</u>: CG, Apr 29
--Ecole des Maris, L', <u>1721</u>: HAY, Dec 14; <u>1722</u>: HAY, Jan 16; <u>1734</u>: GF/HAY, Dec 18; <u>1735</u>: HAY, Mar 7
--Etourdi, L' (farce), <u>1710</u>: QUEEN'S, Jun 16; <u>1720</u>: KING'S, May 9, Jun 9; <u>1734</u>: HAY, Dec 12, 19; <u>1735</u>: GF/HAY, Jan 21, HAY, Mar 26
--Facheaux, Les, <u>1725</u>: HAY, Jan 18
--Femmes Savantes, <u>1693</u>: DG, May 0
--Festin de Pierre, Le (farce), <u>1721</u>: HAY, Mar 6; <u>1722</u>: HAY, Jan 11; <u>1725</u>: HAY, Apr 7; <u>1735</u>: GF/HAY, Jan 8, Mar 17
--French Cuckold, The (farce), <u>1735</u>: GF/HAY, Feb 6, 14, Mar 3, Apr 7, May 5, Jun 2, 4
--Georges Dandin, <u>1719</u>: LIF, Jan 27; <u>1721</u>: HAY, Jan 9, Feb 14, Dec 14; <u>1722</u>: HAY, Mar 27; <u>1725</u>: HAY, Jan 18; <u>1735</u>: HAY, May 9; <u>1747</u>: DL, Nov 25; <u>1769</u>: DL, Mar 28; <u>1781</u>: CG, Apr 18
--Imaginary Cuckolds, The, <u>1733</u>: DL, Apr 11, 19, 25, May 18
--Malade Imaginaire, Le; or, The Mother-In-Law, <u>1720</u>: KING'S, Jun 13, 17; <u>1734</u>: HAY, Dec 23; <u>1735</u>: HAY, Feb 7
--Mariage Force, Le (Forced Marriage, The), <u>1721</u>: HAY, Jan 5, Feb 17, Mar 16, Dec 11; <u>1722</u>: HAY, Jan 2; <u>1724</u>: HAY, Dec 30; <u>1725</u>: HAY, Jan 25; <u>1726</u>: HAY, Apr 15, 18; <u>1735</u>: HAY, Feb 7, 18, Mar 19; <u>1736</u>: CG, Apr 8, CHE, May 24, 26, 28
--Medecin Malgre Lui, Le (Doctor against His Will, The), <u>1721</u>: HAY, Jan 19, Feb 10; <u>1725</u>: HAY, Jan 7, 22, May 7; <u>1734</u>: GF/HAY, Nov 28, Dec 11
--Misanthrope, Le, <u>1721</u>: HAY, Dec 29
--Monsieur de Pourceaugnac, <u>1792</u>: CG, Apr 18
--Precieuses Ridicules, Les, <u>1722</u>: HAY, Feb 1, 12; <u>1735</u>: GF/HAY, Mar 10; <u>1737</u>: LH, Jan 26; <u>1750</u>: HAY, Mar 7, 8
--Tartuffe, Le; or, The Hypocrite, <u>1669</u>: LIF, Jun 14; <u>1670</u>: BRIDGES, May 0;

1671: BRIDGES, Jan 25; 1687: NONE, Sep 0; 1718: LIF, Jun 20, 25, Jul 3; 1719:
    LIF, Jan 13, Jun 24; 1721: HAY, Jan 24, 31, Dec 4; 1725: HAY, Feb 11, Apr 30;
    1726: CLAR, Nov 14; 1734: GF/HAY, Nov 18, 20, HAY, 27; 1735: HAY, Jan 10,
    GF/HAY, Mar 10, Apr 21, HAY, May 19; 1749: HAY, Nov 22, 24; 1784: CG, Oct 6;
    1785: CG, Oct 29; 1789: CG, Nov 5
Molinarella, La. See Paisiello, Giovanni, L'Amore Contrastato.
Molini, Miss (actor), 1798: DL, Feb 17, Nov 28, Dec 21
Molipitano, Claudio (actor), 1751: CT, Dec 3
Molloy (wine merchant), 1743: LIF, Mar 14
Molloy, Charles, 1715: LIF, Feb 16; 1716: LIF, Feb 21; 1718: LIF, Apr 19; 1720:
    LIF, Jan 11; 1724: LIF, Feb 24; 1726: LIF, Dec 14; 1793: HAY, Nov 23
--Coquet, The, 1718: LIF, Apr 19, 21, 22; 1793: HAY, Nov 23
--Half Pay Officers, The, 1720: LIF, Jan 11, 12, 13, 14, 15, 16, 18; 1723: HAY,
    Jan 28; 1730: HAY, Mar 12
--Perplexed Couple; or, Mistake upon Mistake, 1715: LIF, Feb 16, 17, 18
Moment Aurora (song), 1799: CG, Mar 16, Dec 9
Momus Turned Fabulist. See Forrest, Ebenezer.
Momus, Grand Dance in (dance), 1729: LIF, Dec 17; 1730: RI, Jun 24, LIF, Dec 3,
    15; 1731: LIF, Mar 15, Apr 28, Nov 18; 1732: LIF, Jan 7, Apr 12, 21; 1733:
    CG, Mar 27, LIF/CG, Apr 18, DL/HAY, Nov 24, Dec 31; 1734: DL/HAY, Jan 3, 4,
    5, 9, 21, 26, Mar 16, 23, 28, 30, Apr 2, 6, 26, DL, 29, DL/HAY, May 4, CG, 6,
    9; 1739: CG, Dec 4, 5, 7, 20; 1740: CG, Jan 10, 12, 19, 22, 24, 26, 29, 31,
    Feb 2, 4, 9; 1741: CG, Feb 28; 1746: CG, Apr 9
Monarchical Image, The. See Fleming, Robert.
Monari, Sga Fabris (dancer), 1766: KING'S, Jan 25
Monck (house servant), 1760: CG, Jan 5, 12, 19
Monck, Elizabeth Cavendish, Duchess of Albemarle (actor), 1676: DG, Mar 0
Monck, George, 1st Duke of Albemarle, 1660: FH, Apr 12, NONE, 23, ATCOURT, Nov
    19; 1679: DLORDG, May 15
Monckton (Monck), Miss (musician), 1791: HAY, Jun 25
Moncrieff, John, 1755: CG, Mar 6
--Appius, 1755: CG, Feb 27, Mar 1, 6, 8, 10, 11, 13, 15
Monday (house servant), 1799: DL, Jul 2; 1800: DL, Jun 14
Monday Society, 1732: CRT, Nov 20
Mondini (singer), 1755: KING'S, Mar 17; 1756: DL, Apr 2
Mondini, Sga (singer), 1754: KING'S, Nov 9; 1756: DL, Apr 2, KING'S, 5, 10
Mondo Nella Luna, Il. See Galuppi, Baldassare.
Mondozie, Miss (dancer), 1748: HAY, May 2
Monet, Jean, 1750: DL, May 14, 17, 21, 22; 1751: CG, Jan 15; 1766: DL, Oct 11;
    1767: DL, Mar 23
Monetti (dancer), 1783: KING'S, Dec 6; 1784: KING'S, Jan 17
Money (actor), 1782: HAY, Mar 21
Money at a Pinch. See Robson, Horatio Edgar.
Money the Mistress. See Southerne, Thomas.
Monford. See Mountfort.
Monk (actor), 1749: SOU, Jan 9
Monk (machinist), 1770: CG, Apr 5
Monk and Hird (button makers), 1771: CG, Nov 28
Monk, Mrs (actor), 1785: HAMM, Jun 17, 27, Jul 1, 4, 6, 8, 15, 22, 25, 26, 27
Monk, The (novel), 1797: CG, Mar 16
Monlass (actor), 1733: GF, Dec 10, 13, 26, 27, 31; 1734: GF, Jan 08, 21, 25,
    31, Feb 11, May 7, 17, HAY, Jun 5, 17, 21, GF, Sep 13, 20, 25, Oct 16, 17,
    18, Nov 18, Dec 11, 13, 16, 31; 1735: GF, Jan 6, 10, 18, Apr 23, 25, May 3, 5
Monlass, Mrs (actor), 1733: GF, Dec 11, 12, 13, 26, 31; 1734: GF, Jan 8, Feb 2,
    Apr 18, May 3, 7, 10, 14, 17, 22, HAY, Jun 3, 5, 7, 14, 24, GF, Nov 27, 29,
    Dec 11, 13, 31; 1735: GF, Jan 10, 13, 24, Feb 4, 11, 12, Apr 7
Monlass, Young (actor), 1735: GF, Feb 27
Monmouth Court, 1763: HAY, Sep 5
Monmouth, Duchess of. See Scott, Anne.
Monmouth, Duke of. See Scott, James.
Monmouth, Lord. See Mordaunt, Charles.
Monmouth, 1759: HAY, Sep 21
Monmouth's Glory (song), 1746: SOU, Nov 6
Monody on the Death of Garrick, The (entertainment), 1779: DL, Mar 11, 13, 18,
    20, 25, Apr 10, 17, 21, 26, May 24, Jun 3; 1781: DL, Mar 28; 1782: DL, Mar
    16; 1789: DL, Mar 27, Apr 3; 1792: HAY, Nov 26
Monody on the Death of General Wolfe (entertainment), 1760: SF, Sep 18
Monody on the late John Henderson (entertainment), 1787: HAY, Mar 26; 1789:
    HAY, Feb 23; 1791: HAY, Dec 26
Monody to the Memory of John Howard (entertainment), 1790: CG, May 18
Mons, Sga (singer), 1717: HIC, Apr 10, Dec 18; 1718: YB, Mar 27; 1719: KING'S,
    Apr 25

Monsieur de Pourceaugnac. See Moliere.
Monsieur Defeated (song), 1746: GF, Feb 17
Monsieur Grimaudin (farce), 1721: HAY, Mar 9
Monsieur Ragou. See Lacy, John.
Monsieur Thomas; or, Father's Own Son. See Fletcher, John.
Monsieur Tonson (entertainment), 1795: CG, May 14, DL, Jun 3, CG, 5, HAY, Aug
    21, 29; 1796: CG, Apr 26, May 17, DL, Jun 13
Monsigny, Pierre Alexandre (composer), 1773: DL, Nov 2; 1777: HAY, Aug 30
--Bella Arsene, La (opera), 1795: KING'S, Dec 12, 15, 19, 22, 26, 29; 1796:
    KING'S, Mar 10, 12
Monster Discovered (entertainment), 1790: DL, May 11
Monstrum Horrendum; or, The Practice of a Modern Comic Entertainment
    (pantomime), 1732: HAY, May 12
Montagnana, Antonio (singer), 1731: KING'S, Dec 7; 1732: KING'S, Jan 15, Feb
    15, May 2, 23, Jun 10, Nov 4; 1733: KING'S, Jan 27, Mar 17, LIF, Dec 29;
    1734: LIF, Feb 26, May 11, KING'S, Oct 29; 1735: KING'S, Feb 1, Apr 8, May 3,
    Nov 25; 1736: KING'S, Jan 24, Apr 13, Nov 23, CG, 27; 1737: KING'S, Jan 8,
    Apr 12, Oct 29; 1738: KING'S, Jan 3, 28, Feb 25, Mar 14, Apr 15
Montagu, Constantia (actor), 1779: HAY, Jun 18, Jul 17, 31
Montagu, Duchess of (spectator), 1710: QUEEN'S, Jul 13
Montagu, Duke of (spectator), 1715: SF, Sep 15; 1722: HAY, Jan 20; 1729: GF,
    Dec 10; see also Dukes
Montagu, Edward, Earl of Manchester (Lord Chamberlain), 1699: DLLIF, Dec 25
Montagu, Edward, Lord Hinchinbroke, 1661: VERE, Jan 8; 1667: BRIDGES, Oct 23
Montagu, Edward, Lord Sandwich, 1662: ATCOURT, Oct 2; 1668: LIF, Dec 8
Montagu, George (correspondent), 1746: CG, Nov 4; 1752: CT/HAY, May 5; 1760:
    DL, Nov 21, 24; 1761: DL, Jun 18, Jul 27
Montagu, Master (actor), 1749: LEI, Jan 7
Montagu, Mrs (subscriber), 1772: CG, Mar 5
Montague House, 1741: CG, Mar 17; 1742: CG, Mar 30
Montague, Anne (spectator), 1680: DG, Nov 1
Monteux. See Motteux.
Montevolli (singer), 1741: KING'S, Nov 10
Montfleury, Antoine
--Ecole de Jaloux, L'; or, The Fausse Turquise, 1721: HAY, Jan 12, Feb 13
--Fille Capitaine, La; ou, Colombine Fille Scavante, 1718: LIF, Dec 17; 1720:
    KING'S, Apr 26; 1721: HAY, Jan 10; 1725: HAY, Apr 19; 1726: HAY, Apr 14;
    1734: HAY, Nov 4, Dec 20, GF/HAY, 30; 1735: GF/HAY, Feb 6, 20, Apr 25
Montgomery (actor), 1752: DL, Mar 12
Montgomery (singer), 1735: HAY, Aug 4; 1738: CG, Aug 29; 1739: DL, May 28;
    1741: GF, Apr 29
Monticelli, Angelo Maria (singer), 1741: KING'S, Oct 31, Dec 12, 19; 1742:
    KING'S, Jan 19, Mar 2, Apr 13, 20, Nov 2, Dec 4; 1743: KING'S, Jan 1, Feb 22,
    Mar 30, Apr 5, Nov 15; 1744: KING'S, Jan 3, 31, Mar 6, 28, Apr 3, 24, Jun 22;
    1746: KING'S, Jan 7, 28, Mar 25, May 13
Montier. See Mountier.
Montier, Mrs (actor), 1744: JS, Dec 10
Montigny (beneficiary), 1727: LIF, May 15
Montijo, Count de (spectator), 1732: DL, Nov 21; 1733: HAY, Jun 11
Montreal, 1765: MARLY, Oct 5
Monument Booth, 1700: BF, Aug 0; 1701: MF, May 1
Monza, Carlo (composer), 1778: KING'S, Nov 28
Monza, Maria (actor), 1741: LIF, Jan 10, HIC, Apr 28
Monzani, Tebaldo (flutist), 1785: HAY, Feb 28; 1798: CG, Mar 23, Apr 23
Moody, John (actor), 1759: DL, Jan 12, May 22, Sep 22, 27, Oct 12, 22, 30, 31,
    Dec 1, 12, 20, 31; 1760: DL, Feb 8, Mar 6, 20, Apr 25, 29, May 16, Sep 20,
    Oct 3, 11, Dec 4, 12, 17, 29; 1761: DL, Feb 12, Apr 3, 4, 17, 24, 25, 29, May
    14, Sep 10, 12, 19, Oct 24, 29, 31, Dec 11; 1762: DL, Jan 29, Mar 15, Apr 1,
    29, 30, May 6, 13, 18, 19, 26, Sep 21, 23, 25, 28, Oct 7, 8, 13, Nov 3, 6,
    10, Dec 18, 22, 27, 28; 1763: DL, Jan 5, 8, 15, 17, 27, Feb 5, 15, 24, Mar
    21, Apr 11, 21, May 3, 7, 14, 19, 28, Sep 17, 22, Oct 12, 19, 24, 31, Nov 9,
    29, 30, Dec 27, 28; 1764: DL, Jan 13, 18, 23, Feb 13, 18, Apr 12, 27, May 11,
    Sep 18, 20, 22, 25, Oct 4, 13, 15, 17, 20, Nov 9, 27, Dec 10, 12, 27; 1765:
    DL, Jan 22, 23, 24, Apr 13, 15, 26, May 6, 18, Sep 19, Oct 5, 14, Nov 16, Dec
    7, 14, 20; 1766: DL, Jan 6, 9, 23, Feb 5, Mar 15, 20, Apr 12, 16, 22, 25, May
    3, CG, 3, DL, 19, 20, 22, Oct 7, 9, 18, 23, 28, 29, Dec 2, 4; 1767: DL, Jan
    24, Feb 7, Mar 21, Apr 11, 27, May 1, 6, 8, HAY, 29, DL, Sep 15, 16, 17, 19,
    26, Oct 9, 20, 22, 23, Nov 7, 12, 18, 23, 26, 28, 30, Dec 1, 7, 16, 26; 1768:
    DL, Mar 26, Apr 9, 14, 26, Sep 8, 17, 20, 23, 26, 28, 29, Oct 3, 5, 10, 11,
    13, 15, 28, 31, Dec 7, 20, 21, 30; 1769: DL, Jan 16, 24, 27, Feb 13, Mar 28,
    29, 31, Apr 7, 10, 24, 29, May 1, Sep 21, 26, Oct 4, 6, 10, 11, 13, 14, 16,
    17, 21, 23, Nov 4, 29, Dec 4, 6, 23; 1770: DL, Jan 4, Feb 21, Mar 13, 22, 31,

Apr 3, 17, May 3, 5, 7, 24, Sep 29, Oct 3, 9, 13, 18, 29, Nov 3, 6, 14, 15,
16, 17, 23, 24, 26, 28, Dec 5, 20; 1771: DL, Jan 19, Mar 7, 11, 14, 21, 23,
Apr 1, 2, 5, 6, 9, 15, 17, 26, 30, May 11, 17, Sep 21, 24, 28, Oct 1, CG, 4,
DL, 15, 19, 21, Nov 1, 2, 6, 8, 14, 25, 27, 28, Dec 21, 26; 1772: DL, Jan 4,
20, Mar 21, 23, 26, Apr 20, 25, 27, May 13, Jun 1, 3, 10, Sep 22, 26, 29, Oct
13, 21, 23, 28, 29, Nov 17, 18, 20, 28, Dec 8, 21, 29; 1773: DL, Jan 1, 19,
26, Feb 22, Mar 9, 30, Apr 15, May 7, 10, HAY, 17, DL, 17, 27, HAY, 28, 31,
Jun 7, 14, 16, 18, Jul 2, 5, 21, 28, Aug 27, DL, Sep 18, CG, 22, DL, 23, Oct
2, 8, 25, Nov 1, 2, 9, 24, 26, Dec 7, 11, 16, 27; 1774: DL, Jan 18, Feb 9,
15, Mar 14, 17, 21, 22, Apr 6, 11, 12, 19, May 7, 9, 18, Jun 2, Sep 17, 20,
22, 29, Oct 1, 6, 8, 12, 14, CG, 15, DL, 20, Nov 3, 5, 7, 11, 17, 24, 29, Dec
19, 26; 1775: DL, Feb 23, Mar 2, 23, Apr 8, 17, 21, May 6, 12, Sep 23, 26,
Oct 3, 5, 11, 20, 26, Nov 28, Dec 5, 7, 11, 16; 1776: DL, Jan 3, 26, 27, Feb
17, Mar 7, 12, 14, 25, Apr 8, 17, 22, 24, May 4, 11, 16, 18, Sep 21, 26, Oct
9, 15, 18, 30, Nov 5, 7, 9, 19, 25, 28, 29, Dec 14, 18, 26, 27; 1777: DL, Jan
1, 4, 16, 28, Feb 20, 24, Mar 13, 20, Apr 3, 22, 28, 29, May 19, Sep 20, 23,
25, 27, HAY, Oct 6, DL, 9, 17, CG, 24, DL, Nov 8, Dec 3, 11, 13; 1778: DL,
Jan 2, 5, 10, 22, Feb 2, 24, Mar 5, 12, 16, 30, Apr 9, 21, May 2, Sep 17, 19,
22, 24, 26, Oct 1, 8, 13, 15, 28, Nov 2, 14, 18, 20, 28, Dec 11, 19, 21;
1779: DL, Jan 5, 23, 29, Mar 13, 16, Apr 9, May 15, 21, 25, Jun 1, Sep 25,
28, 30, Oct 2, 5, 9, 12, 30, Nov 3, 5, 6, CG, 11, DL, 11, CG, 12, DL, 17, 18,
CG, 22, DL, 22, Dec 20, 29; 1780: DL, Feb 22, 28, Mar 4, Apr 4, 7, 26, May 2,
4, 10, Sep 19, 21, 23, 26, Oct 2, 5, 11, 12, 17, 25, 26, Nov 2, CG, 2, DL, 8,
10, 17, Dec 1, 6, 7, 8, 19; 1781: DL, Jan 26, Mar 19, Apr 18, 28, May 5, 7,
10, Sep 15, 25, Oct 2, 4, 15, 25, 27, 29, 30, Nov 5, 6, 7, 10, 13, 21; 1782:
DL, Jan 19, 26, Apr 6, 11, 30, May 3, 10, Sep 18, 24, 28, Oct 3, 8, 16, Nov
2, 7, 30, Dec 5, 7; 1783: DL, Jan 10, 15, Feb 12, Mar 6, May 2, 5, 12, Sep
20, 25, 27, Oct 16, 31, Nov 12, 13, 20, 21, 27, 28, Dec 2, 12; 1784: DL, Jan
10, 28, Feb 3, 14, Apr 16, CG, May 1, DL, 5, Sep 16, 18, 21, 23, 25, 28, Oct
11, 14, 18, 26, Nov 9, 22, 25, Dec 10, 22, 28; 1785: DL, Jan 6, 14, 22, Feb
2, Apr 1, 5, 11, May 3, 26, Sep 27, Oct 1, 4, 13, 17, 31, Nov 18, Dec 5, 7,
26, 29; 1786: DL, Jan 4, 9, Feb 18, 23, Apr 28, May 25, Jun 1, Sep 26, 28,
30, Oct 9, 25, 26, 28, Nov 14, Dec 5, 11, 21, 26, 28; 1787: DL, Jan 18, 24,
Apr 13, May 9, 11, 16, 23, 30, 31, Jun 1, Sep 20, 25, 27, 29, Oct 15, 24, Nov
3, 6, Dec 6, 7, 8, 28; 1788: DL, Jan 22, Feb 7, Apr 8, 14, 21, 28, May 6, 14,
21, 22, Jun 6, HAY, Aug 29, DL, Sep 23, 25, 27, Oct 2, 11, 16, 20, 25, Nov 5,
12, 19, 29, Dec 17; 1789: DL, Jan 1, 7, 8, Feb 16, Mar 19, Apr 14, 15, May
27, Jun 3, 4, 13, Sep 15, 17, 19, 22, 24, 29, Oct 3, 13, Nov 21, 24, 27, Dec
2; 1790: DL, Feb 10, 13, 15, Mar 2, Apr 14, 20, Jun 1, Sep 11, Oct 11, 12,
18, 19, 20, 27, Nov 1, Dec 3; 1791: DL, Jan 25, Apr 27, 28, May 31, DLKING'S,
Sep 22, 24, Oct 1, 3, 10, 20, 25, Nov 7, 8, 9, 29, Dec 1; 1792: DLKING'S, Jan
7, Feb 8, 18, Jun 4, 15, DL, Sep 18, 22, Oct 2, 18, 31, Nov 2, Dec 13, 26,
27; 1793: DL, Jan 5, Mar 4, 12, 14, Apr 17, 22, 25, May 24, Jun 1, 5; 1794:
DL, Apr 21, 25, May 3, 5, 17, 19, Jun 10, 16, 17, 23, Sep 18, 27, Oct 7, 20,
29, 31, Nov 5, 7, 14, 15, Dec 5, 10, 13; 1795: DL, Jan 26, Feb 6, 12, May 4,
Sep 29, Oct 8, 22, 27, Nov 5, 10, 12, 14, 26, Dec 2, 14; 1796: DL, Feb 27,
Jun 8, 13
Moon St, 1797: CG, May 4
Moone (mercer), 1730: LIF, May 27
Moor (householder), 1742: DL, Mar 22, Apr 29
Moor (spectator), 1700: DLORLIF, Jan 23
Moor of Venice, The. See Shakespeare, William, Othello.
Moor, Henrietta (actor), 1698: LIF, Mar 0, Apr 0, DL, Dec 0; 1699: LIF, Nov 7,
DL, 28; 1700: DL, Mar 0, Apr 29, Jul 9, Oct 0, Dec 9; 1701: DL, Mar 1, May
31; 1702: DL, Jul 11, Nov 0, 26, Dec 14; 1703: DL, Jan 27, Mar 11; 1704: DL,
Jan 26, Jun 7, Dec 7; 1705: DL, Mar 29; 1707: DL, Mar 3, 17, Oct 18, 25;
1708: DL/QUEEN, Feb 21, DL, Mar 8, 16, 27, Apr 10, 17, 22, DL/QUEEN, May 24,
25, DL, Jun 15, Jul 3, DL/QUEEN, 15, DL, 29, Aug 4, 31, Sep 3, 7, 18, 21, 28,
Oct 18, 19, 25, Dec 20, 31; 1709: DL, Jan 3, 10, Mar 4, 15, 22, Apr 12, 30,
May 7, 17, 24, Sep 6, Nov 24, 26, 28, Dec 3, 17; 1710: DL, Jan 9, 31, Feb 11,
16, 25, Mar 14, Jun 6
Moor's St, 1740: DL, May 5
Moore (house servant), 1737: DL, May 30; 1738: DL, May 29; 1741: DL, May 22;
1743: DL, May 14
Moore (householder), 1747: DL, Mar 23, Apr 28
Moore (lyricist), 1745: DL, Sep 21
Moore (tailor), 1750: DL, Apr 9
Moore, Charles (prologuist), 1799: CG, Nov 30
Moore, Counsellor, 1798: CG, Dec 8
Moore, Edward, 1748: DL, Feb 13; 1751: DL, Feb 2; 1753: DL, Feb 7; 1771: DL,
Mar 16; 1790: CG, Apr 29, Nov 6
--Foundling, The, 1748: DL, Feb 13, 15, 16, 18, 19, 20, 22, 23, 25, 27, 29, Mar

1, 3, 5, 7, 8, 15, 17, Apr 16, May 11; <u>1749</u>: DL, Jan 20, 21, Mar 11; <u>1750</u>: DL, Mar 26; <u>1751</u>: DL, Feb 2; <u>1764</u>: DL, Apr 10; <u>1765</u>: DL, Oct 3, 5, 17, Dec 18; <u>1767</u>: DL, Nov 6, Dec 29; <u>1770</u>: DL, Feb 7, Oct 13; <u>1779</u>: HAY, Feb 22; <u>1782</u>: DL, Mar 21, Apr 4, Sep 20, Dec 31; <u>1783</u>: DL, May 28; <u>1786</u>: CG, Apr 8, 25, Oct 4, 11, 31; <u>1787</u>: DL, Jun 6, CG, Sep 28; <u>1788</u>: CG, May 15; <u>1789</u>: WHF, Nov 11; <u>1793</u>: DL, Jan 9, Jun 10; <u>1794</u>: DL, Jun 18, 19; <u>1795</u>: DL, Feb 13
--Gamester, The, <u>1753</u>: DL, Feb 7, 8, 9, 10, 12, 13, 14, 15, 16, 17, 19, 24, Mar 10, Apr 5; <u>1771</u>: DL, Mar 16, Apr 3, May 3, GROTTO, Jun 22, 25, 29, Aug 8, 22, 24, 27, 29, 30, 31, Sep 3, 9, DL, Oct 5, 18, Nov 7; <u>1772</u>: DL, Jan 14, May 6, Oct 23, Dec 28; <u>1774</u>: DL, Apr 26, May 27; <u>1775</u>: DL, Jan 2, Dec 19, 27; <u>1777</u>: DL, Apr 17; <u>1779</u>: DL, Apr 10, 17, 20, 27, Nov 13, 15; <u>1780</u>: DL, Jan 3, CG, May 10; <u>1781</u>: CG, Jan 4, 29, Apr 5; <u>1782</u>: CG, Jan 3; <u>1783</u>: DL, Nov 22, 24, 26, 29, Dec 6, 18, CG, 31; <u>1784</u>: DL, Jan 29, Feb 13, Apr 3, Oct 5, 16; <u>1785</u>: DL, Jan 25, Apr 12, Nov 12; <u>1786</u>: DL, May 27, CG, Sep 25, DL, Oct 16, Dec 15; <u>1787</u>: DL, Oct 30; <u>1788</u>: DL, Apr 29, Nov 1; <u>1789</u>: DL, Mar 10, CG, Apr 4; <u>1790</u>: CG, Apr 21; <u>1791</u>: DL, Apr 4; <u>1792</u>: DLKING'S, Feb 4, 21; <u>1793</u>: DL, Jan 29, Feb 19, Apr 29, May 25; <u>1794</u>: DL, May 20, 22, 29, Jun 4, HAY, Aug 20, DL, Oct 20, 21, Nov 8; <u>1795</u>: DL, Mar 24, Sep 24, Nov 13; <u>1796</u>: DL, Feb 5, Apr 27, Oct 6, 17, Dec 23; <u>1797</u>: DL, Apr 1, CG, May 4, DL, Nov 15; <u>1798</u>: DL, Jan 17, Mar 10, Apr 27, Nov 6, 30; <u>1799</u>: DL, Dec 3, 9; <u>1800</u>: DL, Mar 25
--Gil Blas, <u>1751</u>: DL, Jan 25, Feb 2, 4, 5, 6, 7, 8, 9, 11, 12; <u>1764</u>: DL, Mar 26; <u>1776</u>: CG, Mar 19; <u>1790</u>: CG, Apr 29, Nov 6
Moore, Henry (spectator), <u>1660</u>: COCKPIT, Oct 16; <u>1661</u>: VERE, Jan 4, Nov 27; <u>1665</u>: LIF, Jan 4; <u>1693</u>: NONE, Sep 0; <u>1695</u>: DG, Apr 0
Moore, Sir John (actor), <u>1732</u>: CR, Feb 23; <u>1733</u>: GF, Sep 25, Nov 29, Dec 12; <u>1734</u>: GF, Jan 14, 21, Feb 11, May 7, Sep 16, 20, Oct 16, Nov 18, Dec 6; <u>1735</u>: GF, Jan 24, Feb 4, May 2, 3; <u>1736</u>: LIF, Apr 20
Moore, John (Lord Mayor), <u>1681</u>: CITY, Oct 29
Moore, Master (actor), <u>1754</u>: DL, Oct 31, Nov 5; <u>1755</u>: DL, Feb 3, Apr 28, May 3, BF, Sep 6; <u>1756</u>: DL, Apr 29, May 10; <u>1757</u>: HAY, Jun 17, Oct 31; <u>1764</u>: HAY, Aug 20, Sep 1; <u>1770</u>: HAY, Oct 29; <u>1772</u>: HAY, Aug 10
Moore, Mrs (actor), <u>1715</u>: LIF, Jan 7, 8, Feb 2, Mar 26, May 5, Aug 11, Oct 4, 5, 11, 12, 28, Nov 30, Dec 12; <u>1716</u>: LIF, Apr 3, May 7, Oct 10; <u>1717</u>: DL, May 10, Jun 24; <u>1718</u>: DL, May 8, 28, Jul 11, Aug 15, Oct 15; <u>1719</u>: DL, May 9, Jun 9; <u>1720</u>: DL, Jan 13, May 7; <u>1721</u>: DL, May 13, Aug 4, Oct 17, 20, Dec 15; <u>1722</u>: DL, Jan 9, Feb 15, May 10, Oct 12, 24, 25, Nov 7, Dec 7; <u>1723</u>: DL, Jan 22, May 10, 15, Sep 14, Oct 28, Nov 6, 18; <u>1724</u>: DL, Apr 29, May 9, Oct 28, Nov 2, 10, 19; <u>1725</u>: DL, May 7, Oct 2, 28, Nov 8; <u>1726</u>: DL, Jan 3, May 16, Oct 18; <u>1727</u>: DL, Jan 20, Feb 11, Apr 8, May 10, Sep 14, 21, 28, Oct 19; <u>1728</u>: DL, Jan 10, Feb 16, Apr 2, May 8, 20, Oct 17, 24, 31; <u>1729</u>: DL, Jan 29, Apr 16, May 16, Oct 21, Nov 8
Moore, Mrs (actor), <u>1733</u>: HAY, Mar 14; <u>1735</u>: SOU, Apr 7
Moore, Mrs (actor), <u>1775</u>: HAY, Mar 23
Moore, Mrs (beneficiary), <u>1711</u>: TGB, Apr 2
Moore, Mrs (house servant), <u>1735</u>: DL, Jul 1; <u>1740</u>: DL, May 28; <u>1742</u>: DL, Feb 24, Mar 20
Moore, Mrs Mark (actor), <u>1784</u>: HAY, Jan 21
Moore, Susan (actor), <u>1778</u>: CG, May 23
Moore, Thomas, <u>1717</u>: LIF, Dec 14
--Mangora, King of the Timbusians, <u>1717</u>: LIF, Dec 14, 16, 17, 18, 28; <u>1718</u>: LIF, Jan 2
Moorehead, John (violinist, composer), <u>1799</u>: CG, Feb 8, May 4, Oct 7, Dec 23; <u>1800</u>: CG, Feb 8, 28, May 28, DL, Jun 5
Moorgate Coffee House, <u>1750</u>: DL, Nov 28
Moorish Ambassador, <u>1682</u>: DL, Feb 4, 6, DG, Jun 17
Moorish Dance (dance), <u>1726</u>: HAY, May 9; <u>1727</u>: LIF, Jan 9, 10, 31, Apr 27; <u>1729</u>: DL, May 2, GF, Dec 15, 16; <u>1730</u>: GF, Jan 17, 19, 22, 23, Mar 21; <u>1732</u>: GF, Feb 15, LIF, Apr 22; <u>1733</u>: CG, Aug 2; <u>1735</u>: GF, Mar 29, HAY, Dec 29; <u>1738</u>: DL, Nov 23, 24, 29, Dec 2, 14, 16, 28, 30; <u>1739</u>: DL, Jan 2, 3, 4, 6, 13, Apr 12, 14, 28, May 3, 5; <u>1743</u>: DL, May 26
Moorish Dance, Grand (dance), <u>1728</u>: LIF, Apr 22, May 6, 13, 20, 22, 23; <u>1729</u>: DL, Apr 23, May 26; <u>1730</u>: DL, May 13; <u>1731</u>: DL, May 7; <u>1732</u>: DL, Nov 8; <u>1733</u>: DL, Jan 23; <u>1736</u>: HAY, Feb 20; <u>1739</u>: DL, Jan 17, 19, May 9
Moorish War Dance, Grand (dance), <u>1730</u>: LIF, Apr 10
Moorland (actor), <u>1780</u>: HAY, Apr 5
Moran, C, <u>1765</u>: DL, Sep 14
Mordaunt (actor), <u>1732</u>: HAY, Mar 31
Mordaunt, Charles, Lord Monmouth, <u>1698</u>: DL, May 5
Mordaunt, Lady Mary (actor), <u>1663</u>: SH, Jan 6; <u>1669</u>: LIF, Feb 1; <u>1670</u>: ATCOURT, Apr 6; <u>1675</u>: ATCOURT, Feb 15
Mordecai's Beard. See Baddeley, Robert.
More (pastry maker), <u>1780</u>: DL, Apr 28

More Dissemblers than Women. See Middleton, Thomas.
More Frightened than Hurt! (farce, anon), 1785: HAY, Aug 16
More Gentle than the Southern Gale (song), 1775: CG, Apr 4
More Ways than One to Win Her. See Cowley, Hannah.
More, Hannah, 1776: DL, May 13; 1777: CG, Dec 10; 1779: CG, May 6, Dec 9
--Fatal Falsehood; 1779: CG, May 6, 11, 14, 17, Dec 9, 13; 1780: CG, Feb 5, Apr
  25
--Inflexible Captive, The, 1775: DL, May 2
--Percy, 1777: CG, Dec 9, 10, 11, 12, 13, 15, 16, 17, 18, 20, 22, 30; 1778: CG,
  Jan 1, 7, 10, 17, 26, 31, Feb 4, 7, 21, Mar 28, Dec 17; 1779: CG, Jan 7, May
  6, Dec 9; 1780: HAY, Jul 6, 12; 1782: CG, Dec 5, 19; 1785: CG, Dec 10, 12,
  21; 1786: DL, Mar 25, Apr 1, May 6, 20, Oct 19; 1787: DL, Sep 29, Oct 4, Nov
  27; 1788: DL, Jan 3; 1797: CG, Oct 12
Moreau (composer), 1799: KING'S, Mar 26
Moreau, Anthony (dancer), 1714: LIF, Dec 28; 1715: LIF, Jan 10, 14, 25, Feb 1,
  3, 9, 26, Mar 1, 3, Apr 4, 19, 22, 25, 29, 30, May 2, 9, 10, 12, 24, Jun 7,
  Oct 13, 14, 24, 26, 28, 29, 31, Nov 1, 4, 17, 19, 21, 22, 23, Dec 13, 17, 28,
  30; 1716: LIF, Jan 11, 18, 19, Feb 16, Mar 22, Apr 5, 6, 9, 30, May 10, 18,
  24, Jun 1, 4, 12, Oct 10, 12, 19, 23, 25, 29, 30, 31, Nov 9, 12, 14, 15, 22,
  24, 28, 29, Dec 12, 17, 21, 29, 31; 1717: LIF, Jan 4, 7, 10, 11, 14, 15, 17,
  22, 25, 31, Feb 2, 6, 26, Mar 2, 4, 18, 30, Apr 4, 13, 23, 27, May 7, 10, 11,
  16, 23, 27, 28, Jun 1, 7, Oct 14, 15, 21, 22, 24, 29, Nov 9, 15, Dec 6, 9,
  11, 12, 13, 28; 1718: LIF, Jan 1, 2, 7, 10, 13, 15, 21, Feb 1, 20, Mar 1, 6,
  8, 10, 18, Apr 15, 16, May 3, 6, 15, 20, Jun 4, RI, Jul 26, 28, Aug 2, LIF,
  6, Sep 26, 29, Oct 1, 3, 4, 6, 9, 11, 21, 31, Nov 3, 10, 13, 17, 18, 24, 29,
  Dec 1, 4, 9, 22, 26; 1719: LIF, Jan 3, 9, 13, 14, Feb 9, 16, 24, Mar 19, Apr
  3, 4, 8, 9, 28, 29, 30, May 7, 13, 19, 25, RI, Aug 31, Sep 5; 1728: LIF, Oct
  1, 9, 14, 21, Nov 23, Dec 31; 1729: LIF, Jan 13, 16, 18, Feb 6, Mar 20, 27,
  Apr 8, 11, 12, 15, 16, 19, 22, 26, 30, May 1, 6, 9, 13, 14, 19, 20
Moreau, Mrs (dancer), 1718: LIF, Mar 13, Apr 15, 16, May 1, Jun 30, RI, Jul 26,
  28, Aug 2, LIF, 6, RI, 9, LIF, Sep 26, 29, Oct 3, 4, 6, 9, 11, 15, 21, 31,
  Nov 3, 10, 11, 13, 17, 18, 24, 29, Dec 1, 4, 9; 1719: LIF, Jan 3, 9, 13, 14,
  Feb 9, 16, 24, 28, Mar 19, Apr 3, 4, 10, RI, Aug 31, Sep 5; 1728: LIF, Oct 1,
  21, 23, 26, Nov 23, Dec 31; 1729: LIF, Jan 13, 16, 18, Feb 6, Apr 11, 12, 16,
  19, Oct 6; 1736: CG, Sep 22, Oct 4, 8, Nov 3, 9, 22, 26; 1737: CG, Jan 28,
  Feb 14, Mar 7, 24, May 12, Sep 21, 30, Oct 7; 1738: CG, Feb 2, 3, 13, Mar 2,
  7, 13, 16, 18; 1746: GF, Nov 21, 26, 27, 28, Dec 3, 5, 10, 11, 12, 22; 1747:
  GF, Jan 5, 9, 16, Feb 2, 6, 20, 24, Mar 10, 24, 26, HAY, Apr 22, BFC, Aug 22
Morell (actor), 1729: HAY, May 26, 29
Morella. See Marella.
Morelli, Giovanni (singer), 1787: KING'S, Apr 24, Jun 7, CG, Oct 31, KING'S,
  Dec 8; 1788: KING'S, Jan 12, 15, Feb 5, 7, Mar 4, May 15, Jun 19; 1791: PAN,
  May 14, Jun 16; 1792: KING'S, Feb 24, 29, Mar 14, 21, 23, 28, 30, DLKING'S,
  Apr 19; 1793: KING'S, Jan 26, KING/HAY, Feb 15, 20, KING'S, 26, KING/HAY, 27,
  Mar 8, 13, 15, KING'S, May 14, Jun 25; 1794: KING'S, Jan 11, Feb 1, Mar 1,
  18, Apr 1, May 17, 29, Jun 5; 1795: KING'S, Jan 10, 27, Apr 14, May 26, 28,
  Jun 23, 30, Dec 12; 1796: KING'S, Feb 16, Mar 15, 29, Apr 16, May 5, Jun 14,
  Jul 23, Nov 26, Dec 6, 20; 1797: KING'S, Jan 7, Feb 14, Mar 14, Apr 18, Jun
  8, Jul 18; 1798: KING'S, Jan 23, Feb 10, Mar 10, 22, Apr 10, 21, Jun 5, Dec
  26; 1799: KING'S, Mar 26, Apr 13, May 14, Jun 25; 1800: KING'S, Jan 11, Feb
  18, May 13, Jun 17
Moretti, Sga (singer), 1750: KING'S, Mar 31
Morey, Master (dancer), 1779: DL, May 18
Morgan (actor), 1776: HAY, May 2, CHR, Oct 4; 1784: HAY, Feb 23
Morgan (composer), 1697: DL, Sep 0
Morgan (singer), 1746: DL, Nov 7
Morgan (ticket deliverer), 1757: CG, May 27; 1758: CG, May 12; 1759: CG, May 25
Morgan Jr (actor), 1742: DL, Sep 18, 21, 25, 28, Oct 2, 7, 9, 12, 18, Dec 14,
  22; 1743: DL, Jan 28, Feb 10, 17, Mar 21, Apr 15, May 9, 26, BFHC, Aug 23,
  DL, Oct 20, 22, Nov 12, 15, 18, 23, 26, 29, Dec 1, 9, 16; 1744: DL, Jan 12,
  Feb 1, Apr 2, 3, 9, 17, May 1, 22, 23, HAY, Oct 11, DL, 17; 1745: DL, Apr 17,
  29, May 8, Jun 5, GF, Nov 4, 11, 12, 13, 18, 19, 21, 23, 26, 27, 28, Dec 2,
  4, 11; 1746: GF, Jan 1, 2, 6, 10, 13, 15, 17, 20, 27, 31, Feb 3, 7, 13, 18,
  24, Mar 4, CG, Jun 13, 23, 27, Sep 29, Oct 1, 6, Nov 6, Dec 26; 1747: CG, Mar
  28, May 12, 16, Nov 16, Dec 9, 17; 1748: CG, Jan 12, 14, 15, 21, 27, Mar 14,
  28, Apr 13, 15, 21, 22, 26, 27, 28, May 2, BFP, Aug 24, SFP, Sep 7, SOU, 26,
  Oct 10, 24, NWC, Dec 26, 29; 1749: SOU, Jan 2, 26, Feb 20, HAY, Apr 29, May
  26, BF/SFP, Aug 23, Sep 7, SOU, Oct 16; 1750: HAY, Feb 16, 1756: DL, May 24;
  1757: DL, May 27; 1758: DL, Jun 22
Morgan, Henrietta Maria, Mrs Robert (actor), 1721: SF, Sep 8; 1722: RI, Jul 23,
  LIF, Aug 1, BFLSH, 25, LIF, Dec 15; 1723: LIF, Nov 28, Dec 7; 1724: LIF, Jun
  23, Jul 3, 14, BFP, Aug 22, SF, Sep 5, LIF, Oct 23, Nov 25; 1725: LIF, Feb

27, Oct 4, 26, Dec 3; <u>1726</u>: LIF, Jan 7, Jun 17, 24, Jul 5, 15, 22, Aug 2, 12,
SFSE, Sep 8, LIF, Oct 3, Nov 8, 30; <u>1727</u>: LIF, Apr 28, May 4, 8, 17, 18, BF,
Aug 22, LIF, Sep 11, Oct 2; <u>1728</u>: LIF, Jan 29, Mar 21, Apr 6, 24, Jul 2, 5,
Aug 2, BFHM, 24; <u>1729</u>: LIF, Mar 4, Apr 30, May 13, 15, 23, BFB, Aug 25; <u>1730</u>:
LIF, Apr 8, 27, May 7, 25, RI, Jun 24, Jul 16, BFLH, Aug 31, SFG, Sep 8,
SFLH, 8, HAY, Nov 9, 13, 16, 20, Dec 9, GF, 14, 15, 16, 21; <u>1731</u>: GF, Jan 2,
13, 20, 27, Feb 1, 11, 18, Mar 2, 13, 18, 20, 22, Apr 1, 6, 27, 28, May 7,
11, 14, 17, 21, 22, Jun 1, 2, 3, RI, Jul 1, 8, 15, 22, BFLH, Aug 24, SFLH,
Sep 8, GF, Oct 25, 27, 29, Nov 8, 12, 13, 16, 17, 20, Dec 4, 6, 7; <u>1732</u>: GF,
Feb 21, Mar 16, 23, 27, Apr 12, 19, May 3, 4, RI, Aug 17, BFB, 23, GF, Oct 2,
4, 6, 11, 16, 25, 26, 30, Nov 2, 8, 18, 28, Dec 29; <u>1733</u>: GF, Jan 1, 18, 24,
Feb 5, Mar 17, Apr 25, May 9, 29, SF/BFLH, Aug 23, GF, Sep 12, 17, 20, 21,
25, Oct 1, 4, 12, 15, 17, 18, 19, 23, 24, 26, Nov 8, 10, 14, CG, Dec 3; <u>1734</u>:
SFL, Sep 7; <u>1735</u>: LIF, Aug 29
Morgan, James (actor), <u>1765</u>: CG, Oct 26, 30, Nov 13, 27; <u>1766</u>: CG, Apr 25, 26,
29, Oct 25, Nov 1, 8, 25, Dec 9; <u>1767</u>: CG, Jan 10, 24, Apr 11, 25, Sep 14,
26, Dec 7, 17, 21, 26; <u>1768</u>: CG, Jan 4, 6, 7, 8, 20, 29, Feb 1, Mar 8, 24,
Apr 25, May 7, 26, 28, HAY, Jul 13, 18, Aug 26, CG, Sep 20, 26, 30, Oct 4, 6,
17, 21, 24, 28, Nov 4, 16, 21, Dec 30; <u>1769</u>: CG, Jan 19, Feb 27, Apr 7, DL,
7, CG, 20, May 19, HAY, 29
Morgan, MacNamara, <u>1753</u>: CG, Nov 3; <u>1754</u>: CG, Jan 22, Mar 25; <u>1758</u>: CG, Mar 13;
<u>1768</u>: DL, Mar 15; <u>1774</u>: DL, Apr 12; <u>1790</u>: CG, Feb 11
--Florizel and Perdita; or, The Sheep Shearing, <u>1754</u>: CG, Mar 25, Apr 17, 24;
<u>1758</u>: CG, Mar 13, 14; <u>1759</u>: CG, Mar 24, 27, Apr 7, 24, May 2; <u>1760</u>: CG, Dec
22; <u>1761</u>: CG, Jan 13, Mar 24, Apr 16; <u>1762</u>: CG, Mar 20, 23, May 3; <u>1768</u>: DL,
Mar 15; <u>1769</u>: DL, Apr 7; <u>1771</u>: DL, Apr 9; <u>1774</u>: DL, Apr 12, May 7; <u>1790</u>: CG,
Feb 11, May 28, Nov 27; <u>1798</u>: CG, May 12
--Philoclea, <u>1754</u>: CG, Jan 19, 22, 23, 24, 25, 28, 29, 31, Feb 2, 4
Morgan, Master (actor), <u>1762</u>: CG, Oct 20, Dec 27; <u>1763</u>: CG, Feb 1, Sep 28,Oct
19, Nov 10; <u>1764</u>: CG, Jan 26, Mar 8, 20, May 7, 21, Oct 11, 16, 17, Nov 3,
30; <u>1765</u>: CG, Apr 19, May 24, Oct 15
Morgan, Master (dancer), <u>1746</u>: GF, Oct 27, Nov 13, 24, Dec 15, 17; <u>1747</u>: GF,
Jan 5, 9, Feb 10, 13, 16, 20; <u>1750</u>: HAY, Feb 16
Morgan, Mr and Mrs (actors), <u>1733</u>: GF, Apr 16
Morgan, Mrs (actor), <u>1748</u>: BFP, Aug 24, SFP, Sep 7, SOU, 26, Oct 24, NWC, Dec
26, 29; <u>1749</u>: SOU, Jan 2, 9, 26, BF/SFP, Aug 23, Sep 7, SOU, 18
Morgan, Mrs (actor), <u>1768</u>: HAY, Aug 5
Morgan, Robert (actor), <u>1716</u>: LIF, Apr 27, Aug 3; <u>1719</u>: LIF, Nov 13, 17; <u>1720</u>:
LIF, Jun 7, Nov 19, Dec 8; <u>1721</u>: LIF, Apr 1, May 16, 19, 23, BFLGB, Aug 24,
SF, Sep 8, LIF, Oct 26; <u>1722</u>: LIF, Mar 5, 15, 29, 31, Apr 26, Jun 1, Aug 1,
BFLSH, 25, LIF, Oct 18, 20, 22, 29, 30, 31, Nov 3, 7, 17, 21, 29, 30, Dec 14,
21; <u>1723</u>: LIF, Jan 11, Feb 1, 4, 15, Apr 4, 16, May 8, Sep 30, Oct 31, Nov
12; <u>1724</u>: LIF, Jan 3, Mar 16, May 8, 19, Jun 23, Jul 3, 14, 21, 31, Sep 28,
Oct 7, 30, Nov 25; <u>1725</u>: LIF, Mar 11, 31, Apr 7, 26, May 17, 21, Sep 29, Oct
1, Nov 12, Dec 2, 3, 15; <u>1726</u>: LIF, May 10, 12, 13, 18, 24, Jun 17, 24, Jul
5, 15, 22, Aug 2, 12, 19, SFSE, Sep 8, LIF, 12, 19, 26, Nov 11; <u>1727</u>: LIF,
Apr 5, 19, May 2, 19, BF, Aug 22, LIF, Sep 13, 15, Oct 9, 17, Nov 17, Dec 11;
<u>1728</u>: LIF, Jan 29, Mar 25, Apr 6, 23, 24, May 16, Aug 2, Nov 20; <u>1729</u>: HAY,
Jan 25, BFLH, Aug 23, LIF, Sep 12, SF, 15, LIF, 26, Oct 3, 24, 29, Nov 13,
Dec 3; <u>1730</u>: LIF, Jan 1, May 7, 11, 18, 25, RI, Jun 24, 27, Jul 16, BFLH, Aug
31, SFLH, Sep 8, LIF, 16, 21, 23, Nov 6, HAY, 9, 13, 16, 20, 30, Dec 4, 9,
GF, 14, 15, 16, 18, 21, 30, LIF, 30; <u>1731</u>: GF, Jan 2, 19, 20, 23, 26, Feb 8,
18, 20, 22, 26, 27, Mar 1, 2, 13, 18, 22, 23, 30, Apr 1, 5, 20, 27, 28, May
4, 7, 15, 17, 20, 21, Jun 1, 2, RI, Jul 1, 15, 22, BFLH, Aug 24, SFLH, Sep 8,
GF, Oct 18, 25, 27, 29, Nov 1, 5, 6, 8, 9, 11, 12, 17, 20, 22, Dec 1, 4, 6,
13, 21, 28; <u>1732</u>: GF, Jan 3, 21, 29, Feb 2, 26, Mar 20, 27, Apr 12, 27, May
3, 11, RI, Aug 17, BFB, 23, GF, Oct 2, 4, 6, 14, 17, 24, 25, 26, 30, 31, Nov
3, 8, 27, 28, Dec 1, 22; <u>1733</u>: GF, Jan 1, 20, 24, Feb 13, 19, Mar 5, 28, 30,
Apr 13, 16, May 22, HAY, 28, GF, 29, RI, Aug 20, SF/BFLH, 23, GF, Sep 10, 17,
21, 25, 27, 28, Oct 1, 4, 9, 12, 15, 17, 18, 19, 22, 23, 24, 25, 26, Nov 14,
CG, 26, Dec 3, 7, 8, 17, 20, 22; <u>1734</u>: CG, Jan 1, 16, 23, Feb 21, Mar 5, Apr
15, 20, May 3, 7, RI, Jun 27, YB, Jul 8, CG, Sep 2, SFL, 7, CG/LIF, 18, 23,
25, LIF, Oct 1, CG/LIF, 7, 18, 25, Nov 1, 11, 14, 21, Dec 5, 12; <u>1735</u>:
CG/LIF, Jan 17, 23, Feb 3, LIF, 12, CG/LIF, 13, LIF, Mar 3, CG/LIF, 11, 29,
Apr 9, 11, 17, 18, May 2, 5, 16, LIF, 21, Aug 29
Morgan, Young (actor), <u>1732</u>: BFB, Aug 23
Morgan, <u>1753</u>: CG, Nov 1
Morgann, Maurice (versifier), <u>1786</u>: CG, Feb 10
Morichelli-Bosello, Anna (singer), <u>1794</u>: KING'S, May 17, Jun 5, Dec 6; <u>1795</u>:
KING'S, Jan 10, 27, Feb 3, Apr 14, May 14, 26, 28, Jun 23, 30
Morigi, Andrea (singer), <u>1766</u>: KING'S, Oct 21, Nov 25; <u>1767</u>: KING'S, Jan 31,
Feb 24, Apr 9, Oct 27; <u>1768</u>: KING'S, Mar 10, May 5, Nov 8; <u>1769</u>: KING'S, Sep

584

5, Nov 7; 1770: KING'S, Mar 22, May 19; 1771: KING'S, Jan 10, Feb 9, 28, Mar
  14, Jun 29; 1772: KING'S, Feb 21; 1781: KING'S, Dec 11; 1782: KING'S, Jan 10,
  Mar 2, Apr 9, Nov 2, Dec 19; 1783: KING'S, Mar 27, Jun 3, 14; 1785: KING'S,
  May 24, 28; 1786: KING'S, Jan 24, Mar 11, 16, May 20; 1787: KING'S, Jan 9,
  Feb 17, 20, 27, Apr 24, Dec 8; 1788: KING'S, Feb 5, Mar 4, May 15; 1793:
  KING'S, Jan 29, May 14, Jun 1
Morigi, Margherita (singer), 1782: KING'S, Nov 12, 14; 1783: KING'S, Feb 18,
  Mar 6; 1786: KING'S, May 20; 1788: KING'S, May 15
Morlaco, Il (dance), 1752: CG, Dec 19; 1753: CG, Feb 6
Morland (actor), 1743: DL, Dec 12, 14, 15, 20, 21, 22, 23, 28, 30; 1744: DL,
  Jan 4, 12, Feb 1, Mar 12, 29, Apr 9, 17, May 1, 5, 11, 14, 16, 17, 22, 23
Morland (actor), 1771: DL, Nov 8
Morland, Mrs (actor), 1770: DL, Oct 29, Nov 1, 13, 27, Dec 5; 1771: DL, Apr 3,
  May 10, Oct 5, 12, 17, 28, Nov 9, 15, 25; 1772: DL, Apr 25
Morland, Susannah (spectator), 1667: LIF, Sep 16
Morland's School, 1722: CLA, May 4
Morley (actor), 1785: HAY, Apr 25
Morley, Lady Penelope (spectator), 1696: DL, Nov 6, 21, 23, 25, Dec 29; 1697:
  DL, Jan 2, DL/DL, 22, DG, Mar 9, 13, DL, 27, Apr 5, DG, 8, DL, 23, May 8,
  DL/DL, 24, DG, 25, DL, 26, 27, 31, Jun 5, 12, 18, Nov 19, 26, DLORDG, Dec 4,
  DL, 9; 1698: DL, Jan 5, 18, DG, Feb 7, 25, Mar 19, DL, Nov 19, 26, 28; 1699:
  DLORDG, Jan 28, DL, Feb 2, 3, DL/ORDG, 7, Mar 25, DL, Jun 29, Oct 24, 28, Nov
  11, 21, 28, Dec 14, 16; 1700: DL, Feb 3, 10, 13, 19, May 2, Jun 15, 18
Morley, Thomas (composer), 1790: DL, May 20; 1791: DL, May 18
Morley, William (treasurer), 1681: DL, May 11
Morn, who night adorning (song), 1787: CG, Oct 18
Morning Hymn (song), 1772: CG, Apr 8, 10; 1773: HAY, Mar 17
Morning Lark (song), 1789: CG, Apr 3; 1799: CG, Feb 15
Morning Lectures. See Foote, Samuel.
Morning Ramble, The. See Payne, Henry Nevil.
Morning's Frolick, A; or, A Ramble Through Covent Garden (play, anon), 1755:
  BFGT, Sep 3, 5, 6
Mornington, Lord. See Wellesley, Garret.
Moroccan Ambassador, 1682: DL, Jan 14, DG, 19, Feb 1, 16, DL, 28, DG, Mar 0,
  May 17, DLORDG, Jul 6; 1691: DLORDG, Nov 24, BG, Dec 5; 1698: DL, Jul 9;
  1700: DL, Jun 1, 3; 1706: QUEEN'S, May 3, Oct 28; 1707: YB, Mar 5, QUEEN'S,
  Jul 3; 1714: SH, Apr 6; 1725: DL, Oct 14; 1726: HIC, Apr 1; 1737: LIF, Sep 7;
  1756: DL, May 4
Moroccan performers, 1698: SF, Sep 17
Moroccan Woman (rope dancer), 1698: BF, Aug 25
Morocco, Emperor of, 1700: YB, Jun 21; 1708: DL, Oct 9; 1709: DL, Jun 1; 1724:
  HAY, Jan 16, DL, 31, Feb 7, May 22; 1726: DL, Mar 8, LIF, 31, HAY, Apr 25,
  LIF, Aug 9, 19, 23, Sep 30, Oct 29; 1738: CG, Apr 8; 1739: DL, Sep 14; 1794:
  HAY, Sep 1
Morosini, Chevalier (Venetian ambassador), 1763: DL, May 2
Morphew (actor), 1794: HAMM, Mar 24
Morphy (musician), 1712: SH, May 14, MA, 21; 1717: CORH, Apr 26; 1718: TGB, Mar
  7; 1725: HIC, May 31
Morrel (singer), 1750: SFYW, Sep 7, 10
Morrell, Rev Dr Thomas (librettist), 1737: CG, Mar 23; 1746: CG, Feb 14; 1747:
  CG, Apr 1; 1757: CG, Mar 11; 1764: DL, Mar 16; 1769: CG, Feb 10
Morrice, Miss (actor), 1740: CG, Nov 7
Morrill (actor), 1747: SF, Sep 24
Morris (actor), 1746: CG, Oct 15, Nov 3; 1747: CG, Jan 29, Dec 17; 1748: CG,
  Jan 7, 8, 12, 19, 29, Mar 17, 28, Apr 21
Morris (actor), 1765: CG, Oct 2, 28, Dec 6; 1766: CG, Jan 31, Mar 22, Apr 23,
  Sep 22, Oct 6, 25, Nov 18; 1767: CG, Apr 21, May 8, 21, Sep 16, 17, 18, 22,
  23, Oct 5, 6, 8, 9, 17, Nov 4, 23, 27, 28, Dec 5, 17, 26, 28; 1768: CG, Jan
  4, 6, 7, 8, 29, Feb 1, Mar 8, May 3, 5, 28, Sep 20, 21, 24, 26, Oct 4, 6, 15,
  21, 26, 27, Nov 4, 24, Dec 7, 9, 16, 26; 1769: CG, Jan 7, 10, 12, 14, 19, Apr
  8, 15, 21, 29, May 3, 8, 9, 10, Sep 18, 22, 27, 30, Oct 2, 6, 7, 23, Nov 3,
  4, 17, 21, Dec 1, 7, 20, 22, 29; 1770: CG, Jan 13, 18, 19, 24, 27, Mar 23,
  27, 31, Apr 20, 30, May 1, 9, 14, Oct 1, 5, 11, 15, 23, 25, 27, Nov 2, 5, 12,
  22, 23, 30, Dec 26; 1771: CG, Jan 1, 4, 28, Feb 21, Apr 3, 12, 16, 22, 27,
  30, May 1, 4, 30, Sep 23, 27, Oct 15, 22, Nov 4, 7, 11, 21, 29, Dec 7, 9, 19,
  21, 23; 1772: CG, Jan 1, 4, 31, Feb 17, 24, 25, Mar 5, 23, Apr 25, May 9, 11,
  Sep 28, Oct 1, 13, 14, 15, 16, 20, 23, 30, Nov 2, 4, 6, 30, Dec 26; 1773: CG,
  Jan 6, 16, Apr 3, May 3, 14, 24; 1774: HAY, Jan 24, Apr 4, 12, CG, May 14,
  20; 1775: HAY, Sep 20, Oct 30; 1777: CG, May 24, HAY, Oct 9; 1782: HAY, Mar
  21, May 6
Morris (dancer), 1752: DL, Sep 19; 1753: DL, May 4, 14, 17, Nov 26; 1754: DL,
  Feb 7, 16, Apr 26, May 7; 1755: DL, Apr 24, 29, May 5, 15, Nov 8; 1756: DL,

May 13, 20; 1757: DL, May 18, 23, HAY, Aug 22, Sep 2, 8, 14, 28, Oct 3, DL,
   Nov 30, Dec 27; 1758: DL, May 9, 11, 16, Jun 22; 1759: DL, May 28, Jun 19
Morris (doorkeeper), 1733: GF, May 16; 1734: GF, May 13; 1742: GF, May 10, 18
Morris (Morrice) (actor), 1732: HAY, Mar 2, GF, May 10, TC, Aug 4, RIW/HAY, Sep
   4, 11; 1733: GF, Feb 3, HAY, Jul 26, CG, Aug 2, GF, Sep 19, 24, Oct 17, Dec
   14, 26; 1734: GF, Feb 11, Apr 19, Sep 25, Nov 18; 1735: GF, Jan 24, Feb 4, 6
Morris (ticket deliverer), 1779: DL, May 28; 1780: DL, May 25; 1781: DL, May
   26; 1782: DL, May 31; 1784: DL, May 26
Morris (woolen draper), 1759: CG, Dec 11
Morris Dance (dance), 1704: LIF, Aug 17; 1712: DL, Aug 5, 8, 15, 22, 26; 1714:
   DL, Jul 13; 1716: LIF, Jan 10; 1796: CG, Jan 4
Morris, A (actor), 1792: HAY, Apr 16
Morris, Catherine (actor, singer), 1777: HAY, May 15, Jul 15, 18, CG, Nov 7,
   Dec 20; 1778: CG, Jan 20, Feb 2, Mar 2, May 5, 12, HAY, Sep 7, CG, Oct 5;
   1779: CG, Mar 9, Oct 6, Nov 1, 30; 1780: CG, Feb 22, 24, 26, Apr 7, 10, 11,
   12, 19, 22, Oct 9, Nov 1, 13, 24, 25, Dec 28; 1781: CG, Jan 15, Mar 3, Sep
   24, Oct 16, 23, 25, Nov 2, 12, 19, Dec 8, 17; 1782: CG, Jan 16, Feb 21, Apr
   10, May 11, 27, HAY, Jun 3, 7, 12, 18, 22, Jul 13, 16, 17, 25, Aug 6, 9, 13,
   15, 16, 17, 23, 24, Sep 18, 19, 20, CG, 30, Oct 3, 7, 17, 22, Nov 18, 19, 21,
   25, 29, Dec 6, 27; 1783: CG, Feb 25, Apr 5, 7, 22, 23, 25, May 12, 16, 19,
   24, HAY, Jun 2, 7, 18, 20, 24, 27, 30, Jul 4, 5, 8, 16, 26, Aug 1, 13, 15,
   20, 22, 27, 28, 29, Sep 10; 1784: HAY, Jun 5, CG, 10, HAY, 10, 14, 26, Jul 6,
   7, 12, 19, 24, 28, Aug 2, 10, 17, 19, 21, 26
Morris, Charles (prologuist), 1793: DL, Apr 3; 1799: DL, Mar 2
Morris, Edward, 1790: DL, Mar 18; 1793: DL, Apr 3; 1799: DL, Mar 2
--Adventurers, The (farce), 1790: DL, Mar 18, 20, 25, Apr 8, 13, 21, May 31,
   Oct 2; 1791: DL, Feb 19
--False Colours, 1793: DL, Apr 3, 4, 5, 11, 12, 15, 24, May 1, 2
--Secret, The, 1799: DL, Mar 2, 4, 5, 7, 9, 11, 12, 14, 25, 27, 28, 29, Apr 1,
   3, 5, 12, May 30, Nov 16, 19, 26; 1800: DL, Jan 1, 8, Feb 13
Morris, Master (actor), 1784: HAY, Aug 10
Morris, Master (dancer), 1741: DL, May 25; 1742: GF, May 10, DL, 24; 1743: SF,
   Sep 8
Morris, Miss (actor), 1768: CG, Nov 26; 1769: CG, Jan 11, 28, Feb 18, Apr 15,
   May 1, 16; 1770: CG, Jan 1, Mar 24
Morris, Miss (actor), 1779: HAY, Dec 27
Morris, Miss (actor), 1792: CG, Nov 14, Dec 20; 1794: CG, Mar 25, May 19, 28,
   Oct 6, 20, Dec 29; 1795: CG, Jan 19, Mar 28, Apr 8, May 27, Jun 3, Sep 21,
   28, Oct 23; 1796: CG, Jan 8, 13, 14, Apr 22, DL, May 12, CG, Sep 19, 21, Oct
   10, 29, Nov 24, Dec 26; 1797: CG, Jan 7, DL, May 25, CG, 31, Jun 2
Morris, Mrs (actor), 1782: HAY, Sep 18; 1784: HAY, Aug 10; 1785: HAY, Aug 31
Morris, Mrs (singer, dancer), 1740: BFH, Aug 23; 1742: NWC, Dec 27; 1743: SF,
   Sep 8
Morris, Mrs (ticket deliverer), 1775: CG, May 4; 1776: CG, May 11; 1777: CG,
   May 9
Morris, Mrs (ticket deliverer), 1800: CG, Jun 10
Morris, Robert (scene painter), 1796: CG, Jun 6; 1797: CG, Jun 8; 1799: CG, Jun
   8
Morris, Robert (spectator), 1735: NONE, Sep 11
Morris, Thomas (actor, songwriter), 1785: CG, Apr 2; 1788: CG, Apr 8; 1792:
   HAY, Apr 16; 1796: DL, Jun 3; 1797: DL, Jun 8; 1798: DL, May 23, Jun 8
Morris, Widow (ticket deliverer), 1798: CG, Jun 5
Morris, 1747: CG, Feb 25
Morris, 1760: CG, Feb 4
Morrison (actor), 1777: HAY, Oct 13
Morrison (householder), 1744: CG, Jan 19
Morrison, Ana Maria (actor, dancer), 1737: DL, Nov 19; 1738: DL, May 19, 25,
   26, 31, BFH, Aug 23, DL, Oct 30, Dec 4; 1739: DL, Feb 7, Apr 28, May 1, 2,
   11, 30, Oct 10; 1740: DL, Apr 24, CG, 25, May 7, DL, 8, CG, 23; 1741: CG, May
   12, Oct 13; 1742: CG, Oct 4, 13, 27; 1743: CG, Apr 29, Sep 28, Oct 26, Dec
   19; 1744: CG, May 2, Oct 24, Nov 22; 1745: CG, May 8, Nov 15, 28; 1746: CG,
   Feb 8, 24, 25, Mar 13, 18, Apr 1, 22, May 2, Jun 27, Oct 20, Nov 6; 1747: CG,
   Jan 26, May 15, Nov 23, Dec 28; 1748: CG, Jan 29, Feb 15, Mar 24, Apr 14, 26,
   Sep 21, 26; 1749: CG, Mar 29, Apr 20, 22, Sep 25, Oct 2, 12, 20, Nov 23;
   1750: CG, Feb 22, Apr 27, May 10, Oct 12, 26, 29, Nov 8, 19, 29; 1751: CG,
   Jan 1, Feb 23, Apr 24, May 9, Sep 27, 30, Oct 29, Nov 13, 22; 1752: CG, Mar
   17, 30, Apr 28, May 2, Sep 22, Oct 10, 18, 30, Nov 9, Dec 13, 26; 1753: CG,
   Jan 19, Apr 25, May 1, 18, Sep 10, 12, 21, 24, 26, Oct 5
Morrison, Ann Maria (actor), 1772: HAY, Sep 17
Morrison, Master (dancer), 1749: DL, May 2
Morrison, Miss (Mrs) (actor), 1760: CG, Sep 22, 24, Oct 23; 1764: CG, Apr 28
Morrison, Mrs (actor, singer), 1741: JS, Nov 9; 1742: JS, May 31

Morse, Mrs (Miss) (actor), 1731: GF, Oct 13, 27, Nov 8; 1732: HAY, Mar 2, 17,
   May 10, 15, TC, Aug 4, BF, 22; 1733: HAY, Mar 20, 26, BFCGBH, Aug 23, DL, Oct
   8, Nov 23
Mort d'Hercule, La (dance), 1791: KING'S, Apr 11, 12, May 3, 5, Jun 2
Mort de Cesar, La. See Voltaire.
Mort de Lucresse, La (play, anon), 1726: HAY, Apr 22
Mort du Capitaine Cook, La. See Arnould.
Mortellari, Michele (composer), 1786: KING'S, Feb 14, May 25; 1788: KING'S, May
   29
--Armida (opera), 1786: KING'S, May 25, Jun 1, 10, 17, 24, Jul 1, 11; 1791:
   PAN, Feb 17, 19, 22, 26, Mar 12, CG, Apr 6, PAN, 7, 9
Mortimer (box-office keeper), 1757: DL, May 19; 1758: DL, May 16; 1759: DL, May
   28; 1760: DL, May 12; 1761: DL, May 20; 1762: DL, May 18; 1763: DL, Jan 3,
   May 13; 1764: DL, May 17; 1765: DL, May 17; 1766: DL, May 14; 1767: DL, Jan
   24, May 27; 1768: DL, May 13, 23; 1769: DL, May 17; 1770: DL, May 28; 1771:
   DL, May 25, Dec 26; 1772: DL, Jun 3; 1773: DL, May 28; 1774: DL, May 24, Sep
   17; 1775: DL, May 23, 27, Sep 26; 1776: DL, May 18; 1777: DL, May 30; 1778:
   DL, May 22; 1779: DL, May 29; 1780: DL, May 23; 1781: DL, May 25
Morton (actor), 1736: YB, Apr 26
Morton (actor), 1792: HAY, Oct 15; 1793: HAY, Oct 1
Morton, Mary (actor), 1778: CG, Apr 4, 6, 7, 9, 21, 22, 24, 29, May 1, 6, 12,
   14, 19, Sep 18, 28, Oct 9, 14, 15, 16, DL, 17, CG, 22, 23, 24, 26, 27, 29,
   Nov 4, 5, 19, Dec 21, 26; 1779: CG, Jan 14, Feb 13, 15, 22, 23, Mar 22, 27,
   Apr 5, 6, 10, 26, 27, 28, 30, May 4, 13, 18, 24, Sep 20, 24, 27, Oct 1, 4,
   16, 18, Nov 9, 11, 22, Dec 3, 17, 18; 1780: CG, Jan 26, Feb 2, 5, 17, 22, Mar
   14, 27, 29, Apr 3, 7, 19, 21, 25, 27, May 1, 3, 5, 6, 23, 25, Sep 18, 20, 22,
   25, Oct 2, 10, 18, 19, 23, 31, Nov 2, 4, 8, 13, 15, 22, 24, 27, Dec 9, 22;
   1781: CG, Jan 13, Feb 14, 24, Mar 24, 31, Apr 2, 3, May 2, 7, 28, Sep 19, 21,
   24, 26, 28, Oct 16, 19, 20, 23, 24, 25, 27, Nov 5, 7, 8, 12, 17, Dec 17, 26;
   1782: CG, Jan 1, 16, Feb 9, Mar 14, Apr 10, 12, May 3, 6, 27, Oct 8, 9, 15,
   18, 22, 24, 29, 31, Nov 18, Dec 6, 27, 31; 1783: CG, Jan 3, 17, 23, Feb 17,
   Mar 3, Apr 5, 7, 22, 25, May 10, 19, 20, 21, Sep 17, 22, Oct 6, 9, 14, 16,
   31, Nov 6, 8, 13, 25, Dec 5; 1784: CG, Jan 3, 14, 21, 22, 26, 29, Feb 10, 13,
   19, 20, Mar 27, Apr 3, 24, 26, May 7, 8, Jun 14, Oct 1, 4, 8, 12, 18, 25, 27,
   28, 29, Nov 3, 10, 11, 25, Dec 3, 6, 21, 22; 1785: CG, Jan 14, Feb 8, 21, Mar
   5, 7, 15, Apr 1, 5, 6, 12, 22, May 6, 7, 13, 25, 26, Sep 19, 23, 28, 30, Oct
   7, 10, 14, 17, 19, 21, 22, 27, Nov 3, 10, 14, Dec 8, 10, 29; 1786: CG, Jan 3,
   18, 20, 28, 31, Feb 13, 16, 17, 18, 21, Mar 16, 18, 20, 30, Apr 4, Oct 12,
   19, 21, 23, Nov 13, 14, 24, 27, 30, Dec 1, 13, 15, 23, 30; 1787: CG, Jan 6,
   11, 13, 15, 31, Feb 20, Mar 1, 31, Apr 11, 14, 16, 18, 27, May 5, 16, 21, Jun
   11, Sep 21, 24, Oct 1, 3, 5, 12, 22, Nov 2, 20, 22, 23, 28, 30, Dec 3, 17,
   28; 1788: CG, Jan 9, 10, 14, 15, 18, Feb 4, 5, 9, 25, Mar 1, 15, 26, 29, Apr
   1, 2, 8, 11, 14, 30; 1799: CG, Apr 23
Morton, Mrs (actor), 1736: YB, Apr 26, CG, Nov 25
Morton, Thomas, 1792: CG, Dec 1; 1795: HAY, Jun 20; 1796: CG, Jan 23, Apr 26;
   1797: CG, Jan 10, HAY, 23; 1798: CG, Jan 11; 1800: CG, Feb 8
--Children in the Wood, The (opera), 1793: HAY, Oct 1, 2, 3, 4, 5, 8, 9, 11,
   19, 23, 25, 26, 29, Nov 1, 4, 11, 16, 20, 22, 25, 27, 29, Dec 2, 4, 6, 10,
   12, 14, 19, 21; 1794: HAY, Jan 1, 2, 4, 8, 11, 15, 16, 20, 23, 25, 27, 31,
   Feb 5, 7, 10, 15, 18, 21, 27, Mar 4, 10, 13, 18, 22, 25, 27, 29, Apr 5, 8,
   DL, 24, 25, 29, May 1, 7, 13, 14, 24, 31, Jun 11, 27, 30, HAY, Jul 18, 19,
   Aug 25, 30, Sep 5, 9; 1795: DL, Apr 16, HAY, Jun 10, 19, Jul 3, 10, 15, 30,
   Aug 5, 24, DL, Sep 26, Oct 13, Nov 5, 26; 1796: DL, Jan 2, HAY, Jul 5, 12,
   21, 29, Aug 6, 18, 24, Sep 7; 1797: DL, Feb 16, 21, May 8, 10, HAY, Aug 19,
   21, 25, 26, Sep 2, 7, DL, 19, 30, Oct 14, Nov 1, Dec 2; 1798: DL, Jan 6, Mar
   22, Apr 28, May 21, HAY, Jun 28, Jul 4, 10, 18, Aug 9, 18, Sep 1, 14, DL, 29,
   Nov 1, 13, Dec 15, 29; 1799: DL, Jan 9, HAY, Jun 18, Jul 4, Aug 24, DL, Sep
   26, Oct 30, Nov 15, Dec 10, 30; 1800: DL, Feb 10
--Columbus; or, A World Discovered, 1792: CG, Dec 1, 3, 4, 7, 8, 10, 11, 12,
   14, 15, 17, 18, 19; 1793: CG, Jan 1, 3, 5, 8, 10, 12, 15, 17, 19, 22, 24, 26,
   28, Feb 11, 12, 18, Mar 12, Apr 1, 2, Jun 10, Oct 4, Nov 8; 1794: CG, Jun 11;
   1795: CG, Jan 6
--Cure for the Heart Ache, A, 1797: CG, Jan 10, 11, 12, 14, 17, 18, 20, 21, 23,
   24, 26, 27, 28, 31, Feb 2, 3, 4, 6, 7, 8, 9, 10, 11, 14, 15, 16, 17, 18, 20,
   22, 23, 24, 25, 28, Mar 2, 20, 27, Apr 3, 17, 21, 24, May 10, 13, 29, Jun 7,
   Oct 16, Nov 8, Dec 22, 29; 1798: CG, Mar 26, Jun 6, Sep 21; 1799: CG, Apr 19,
   Jun 3, Oct 17; 1800: CG, Jan 13, Apr 1
--Secrets Worth Knowing, 1798: CG, Jan 9, 11, 12, 13, 15, 16, 17, 18, 19, 20,
   23, 24, 26, 27, 31, Feb 1, 3, 10, Mar 8, Apr 14, Nov 7; 1799: CG, May 25;
   1800: CG, Apr 24
--Speed the Plough, 1800: CG, Feb 8, 10, 11, 12, 13, 14, 15, 17, 18, 19, 20,
   21, 22, 24, 25, 27, Mar 1, 3, 4, 6, 8, 11, 15, 18, 20, 22, 24, 25, 29, Apr 1,

3, 14, 16, 18, 21, 25, 28, May 3, 9, 19, 26, Jun 9
--Way to Get Married, The, 1796: CG, Jan 23, 25, 26, 27, 28, 29, Feb 1, 3, 4,
    5, 8, 9, 11, 13, 15, 16, 18, 20, 22, 23, 25, 27, 29, Mar 1, 3, 5, 7, 8, 10,
    12, 17, 31, Apr 6, 14, 21, 26, 28, May 5, 19, Jun 7, Sep 16, Oct 19, Nov 2,
    Dec 8, 30; 1797: CG, Feb 1, Apr 19, Dec 23; 1799: CG, Apr 26, Jun 1, Oct 25
--Zorinski, 1795: HAY, Jun 20, 22, 23, 24, 25, 26, 27, 29, 30, Jul 2, 6, 9, 11,
    14, 21, 27, Aug 4, 17, 31, Sep 7; 1796: CG, Apr 26, May 7, HAY, Sep 1; 1797:
    HAY, Jul 8; 1798: HAY, Jun 29; 1799: HAY, Aug 13, 27; 1800: HAY, Jun 17, 24
Moseley, John (renter), 1660: REDBULL, Nov 5; 1692: DL, Nov 8
Moser (actor), 1768: KING'S, Mar 10
Moses (actor), 1729: HAY, Feb 1
Moses (pit doorkeeper), 1730: GF, Jun 25; 1731: GF, May 17; 1732: GF, May 22
Moses and the children of Israel (song), 1789: DL, Mar 18; 1790: DL, Feb 26;
    1791: DL, Mar 23; 1792: KING'S, Feb 24; 1793: KING/HAY, Feb 22; 1794: DL, Apr
    10
Moss (actor), 1769: HAY, Feb 28; 1772: HAY, Jun 12; 1773: HAY, May 17, 24, 28,
    31, Jun 4, 11, 14, 16, 18, 28, Jul 2, 12, 16, 19
Moss (actor), 1776: CG, May 8
Moss (actor), 1781: HAY, Nov 12
Moss, Mary (actor), 1776: HAY, Oct 7; 1777: HAY, Apr 22
Moss, Miss (actor), 1731: GF, Oct 11; 1734: DL, Jan 8
Moss, Mrs (dancer), 1704: DL, Oct 20, 27, Nov 13, 18, 24, Dec 6; 1705: DL, Jan
    1, 8, 15, 16, 26, Feb 12, Mar 3, Jun 9, 26, 28, Jul 3, 5, Oct 16, Nov 5, 7,
    12, Dec 12, 19, 27, 31; 1706: DL, Jan 5, 14, 21, 24, 25, Apr 1, 3, 13
Moss, William Henry (actor), 1786: DL, Oct 30; 1787: HAY, May 16, 18, 23, 25,
    Jun 16, 20, 22, Jul 2, 4, 5, 13, 16, 25, Aug 4, 7, 10, 14, 21, 28, Sep 8;
    1788: HAY, Jun 10, 11, 12, 16, 19, 20, Jul 2, 10, 24, Aug 5, 9, 11, 13, 20,
    22, 25, 27, DL, Oct 2; 1789: HAY, May 20, 25, 27, Jun 1, 3, 5, 8, 10, 19, 22,
    24, 26, 27, 29, Jul 3, 7, 30, 31, Aug 1, 5, 11, 25, Sep 8; 1790: HAY, Jun 15,
    16, 17, 18, 22, 25, 26, 29, 30, Jul 5, Aug 2, 4, 11, 16, 20
Mossop, Henry (actor), 1751: DL, Sep 13, 26, 27, Oct 5, 7, 10, 16, CG, 16, DL,
    Nov 4, 8, 28, Dec 10; 1752: DL, Jan 11, 15, 28, Feb 6, 11, Mar 12, 30, Apr 1,
    10, Sep 21, 26, 30, Oct 11, 16, 28, Nov 4, 18, 28, Dec 7, 15; 1753: DL, Jan
    6, 18, Feb 7, 22, 26, Mar 3, Apr 2, May 7, 9, Sep 18, 25, Oct 3, 6, 25, 29,
    31, Nov 5, Dec 1, 22; 1754: DL, Jan 9, 14, 23, Feb 25, Mar 25, Apr 20, Sep
    24, Oct 1, 8, 10, 29, Nov 4, 6, 11, 30, Dec 9, 17, 28; 1755: DL, Feb 22, 25,
    Mar 14, 15, Apr 30, May 1, Sep 13, Oct 10; 1756: DL, Sep 18, 21, 25, Oct 16,
    27, 29, Nov 1, 4, 17, 19, 23, 24, Dec 11, 27; 1757: DL, Jan 27, Mar 21, 26,
    Apr 26, 30, Sep 13, 20, 22, 27, Oct 4, 6, 7, 11, 18, 20, 25, Nov 1, 4, 15,
    26, Dec 8; 1758: DL, Jan 19, 28, Feb 21, Mar 25, 30, Apr 8, 25, May 2, 3, Sep
    19, 21, Oct 10, 12, 18, 24, 30, Nov 2, 3, 4, 8, 17, 18, Dec 28; 1759: DL, Jan
    20, Feb 1, 7, 15, Mar 24, Apr 21, May 23, 29, Sep 22; 1768: DL, Nov 11; 1770:
    CG, Nov 8; 1772: DL, Mar 18; 1773: CG, Oct 23; 1785: HAY, Apr 26; 1799: DL,
    Sep 26
Most Knowing Least Understanding, The; or, Harlequin's Metamorphosis
    (pantomime, anon), 1726: KING'S, Oct 28
Mosticelli (singer), 1746: KING'S, Mar 25
Motezuma. See Sacchini, Antonio Maria Gasparo.
Mother Shipton. See Colman the elder, George.
Mother Shipton's Review of the Audience (entertainment), 1785: CG, Mar 29;
    1787: CG, Apr 16; 1789: CG, Apr 14
Mother Shipton's Wish; or, Harlequin's Origin (entertainment), 1735: GF, Jan 24
Mother-in-Law, The. See Miller, James.
Motley (beneficiary), 1721: LIF, Nov 7
Motley (dancer), 1675: ATCOURT, Feb 15
Mott (ticket deliverer), 1788: CG, May 24; 1790: CG, Jun 12; 1791: CG, Jun 14
Mott, Mrs (haberdasher), 1771: DL, Oct 15
Mottett, Mrs (actor), 1727: BF, Aug 21
Motteux, Mrs (actor), 1743: SF, Sep 8; 1744: TB, Mar 22
Motteux, Peter Anthony, 1693: YB, Jun 17; 1695: LIF, Sep 0, DL, 0; 1696: LIF,
    Jun 0, Nov 14, 19; 1697: LIF, Jun 0, Nov 0; 1698: DL/ORDG, Nov 0; 1699: LIF,
    Apr 0, DL, Dec 0; 1700: ATCOURT, Nov 4; 1702: DL, Dec 14; 1704: DL, Feb 22;
    1705: DL, Jan 18, QUEEN'S, Dec 27; 1706: QUEEN'S, Mar 7; 1707: DL, Apr 1;
    1708: QUEEN'S, Feb 26, DL, Dec 14; 1723: DL, Jul 30, Aug 6, 16; 1778: CG, Feb
    4
--Acis and Galatea; or, The Country Wedding, 1702: LIF, Dec 11; 1703: LIF, Feb
    11, Apr 28; 1704: LIF, Feb 12, 15, Jul 14; 1705: LIF, Mar 31; 1706: QUEEN'S,
    Mar 28, LIF/QUEN, Apr 1, QUEEN'S, 26; 1709: QUEEN'S, Nov 12, 19, 22, Dec 22,
    31; 1710: QUEEN'S, Jan 21, Mar 7; 1714: DL, Jul 27, 30; 1715: LIF, Nov 22,
    24, 28, Dec 16, 31; 1716: LIF, Jan 13, Apr 14; 1719: LIF, Oct 29; 1723: DL,
    Jul 16, 19, 23, 26, 30, Aug 6, 9, 16; 1724: DL, May 5, 6, 7, 9, 15, 18, 25,
    Oct 30; 1725: DL, May 17, 24; 1728: DL, Mar 30, Apr 2, 23; 1729: BF, Aug 26;

1739: CG, Mar 20
--All Without Money, 1697: LIF, Jun 0
--Beauty in Distress, 1698: LIF, Apr 0
--Britain's Happiness, 1704: DL, Feb 22, LIF, Mar 7
--Farewell Folly; or, The Younger the Wiser, 1705: DL, Jan 18, 19, 20, 22, 23,
   Feb 7
--Hercules (masque), 1697: LIF, Jun 0
--Love's a Jest, 1696: LIF, Jun 0; 1704: LIF, Jul 27; 1711: DL, Aug 31
--Love's Triumph (opera), 1708: QUEEN'S, Feb 26, 28, Mar 2, 6, 9, 20, 23, Apr
   17
--Loves of Mars and Venus, The (pantomime), 1696: LIF, Nov 14, 16, 17, 18, 19,
   20; 1797: LIF, Jun 0; 1778: CG, Feb 4
--Natural Magick, 1697: LIF, Jun 0
--Temple of Love, The, 1706: QUEEN'S, Mar 7, 16
Mottley, John, 1720: LIF, Feb 29; 1721: LIF, Apr 13, May 3; 1728: HAY, May 8,
   Oct 15; 1730: GF, Jun 8; 1731: GF, Feb 15, DL, Aug 6
--Craftsman, The; or, The Weekly Journalist (play), 1728: HAY, Oct 15, 17, 19,
   26, 31, Nov 1; 1731: GF, Feb 15, 16
--Imperial Captives, The, 1720: LIF, Feb 20, 29, Mar 1, 3, 5, 21
--Penelope, 1728: HAY, May 8, 9, 17
--Widow Bewitched, The, 1730: GF, Jun 8, 10, 11, 15, 22, 23, Jul 2; 1786: DL,
   Apr 26
Moudet, Mlle (dancer), 1740: DL, Dec 10; 1741: DL, Mar 17, CG, Nov 26, Dec 15,
   28, 30; 1742: CG, Jan 8, Sep 29
Moult, George (spectator), 1699: BF, Aug 30, DLLIF, Sep 12
Moultrie, George, 1798: CG, Mar 17, HAY, Aug 11
--Devil of a Lover, A (farce), 1798: CG, Mar 13, 17, 24
--False and True, 1798: HAY, Aug 11, 13, 15, 17, 20, 22, 27, 30, Sep 4, 14;
   1799: CG, Apr 30, HAY, Jul 16, 24, Sep 4; 1800: HAY, Jun 25
Mount Lebanon, 1730: HAY, Apr 22
Mount St, 1786: KING'S, Mar 16, HAY, Aug 10; 1787: KING'S, Apr 26, HAY, Aug 3;
   1788: KING'S, Feb 21; 1789: KING'S, May 28; 1790: HAY, May 27; 1791: KING'S,
   May 23
Mount-Edgcumbe, Richard, Earl of (composer), 1800: KING'S, May 22
--Zenobia of Armenia (opera), 1800: KING'S, May 22
Mount, Mrs (actor), 1744: HAY, Dec 26
Mount's Coffee House, 1753: DL, May 22; 1756: DL, Nov 12; 1758: DL, Mar 10;
   1759: CG, May 8; 1763: DL, Apr 27; 1776: HAY, Oct 7
Mountain Grecian (dance), 1739: SF, Sep 8
Mountain, John (violinist), 1790: CG, Feb 19, May 13; 1791: CG, Mar 11; 1792:
   CG, Feb 24; 1793: CG, Feb 15; 1795: HAY, Mar 4, CG, May 19; 1797: CG, Jun 21;
   1798: CG, Jun 11; 1799: CG, Jan 29, Apr 6
Mountain, Rosemond, Mrs John (actor, singer), 1787: CG, Sep 17, 19, 21, 24, 28,
   Oct 1, 5, 11, 19, 22, 31, Nov 7, Dec 3; 1788: CG, Jan 3, 4, 14, 21, Feb 4, 5,
   14, Mar 11, Apr 15, 16, 26, May 3, 8, 12, 21, Jun 6, Sep 15, 17, 19, 22, 24,
   26, 29, Oct 8, 16, 17, 18, 21, 22, Nov 3, 10, 21, Dec 29; 1789: CG, Jan 2, 3,
   10, Feb 6, Mar 5, 28, 31, Apr 4, 20, 30, May 6, 19, 26, 28, Jun 2, 8, 11, Sep
   14, 16, 18, 23, 25, 28, Oct 2, 12, 13, 16, 20, 21, 23, 28, 30, 31, Nov 6, 7,
   11, 19, 21, 28, 30, Dec 12, 21; 1790: CG, Jan 23, Feb 4, Mar 8, 22, Apr 7,
   12, 20, 21, 22, May 5, 7, 11, 13, 18, 24, Jun 4, Sep 13, 15, 17, 29, Oct 1,
   5, 6, 12, 15, 20, 23, Nov 10, 15, 16, 19, 23, 25, 26, Dec 2, 8, 11, 20, 28;
   1791: CG, Jan 12, 29, Feb 11, Mar 31, Apr 28, 30, May 5, 6, 18, 27, 31, Jun
   6, 7, 10, 13, Sep 12, 14, 16, 17, 19, 21, 23, 26, 28, 30, Oct 3, 5, 6, 10,
   19, 20, Nov 7, 9, 15, 19, 21, 25, Dec 2, 15, 23; 1792: CG, Feb 2, 25, 28, Mar
   22, 26, Apr 10, 12, 17, 18, May 10, 11, 18, 19, 22, 28, Sep 26; 1793: CG, Sep
   17, 20, 25, 27, 30, Oct 1, 2, 5, 7, 9, 10, 15, 18, 21, 29, Nov 1, 2, 12, 13,
   15, 18, 22, 23, 28, 30, Dec 5, 7, 9, 14, 17, 19, 26; 1794: CG, Jan 3, 21, Feb
   1, 4, 5, 6, 13, 14, Mar 6, 11, 15, Apr 7, 10, 12, 23, 25, 29, May 2, 6, 14,
   16, 17, 23, 28, Jun 11, 16, Sep 17, 19, 22, 29, Oct 3, 7, 8, 14, 17, 20, 23,
   29, 30, Nov 7, 11, 15, 17, 19, 20, 22, Dec 29, 30, 31; 1795: CG, Jan 2, 8,
   31, HAY, Mar 4, CG, 14, 17, Apr 6, 8, May 19, 21, 25, 27, Jun 8, 10, 16, Sep
   14, 16, 18, 21, 23, 25, Oct 5, 7, 12, 19, 22, 31, Nov 4, 6, 9, 14, 16, 27,
   Dec 5, 7, 9, 21, 22, 29, 31; 1796: CG, Jan 2, 4, 13, Mar 15, Apr 1, 5, 9, 12,
   15, 20, 26, 29, 30, May 10, 12, 16, 20, 27, 28, Jun 6, Sep 12, 16, 17, 19,
   21, 23, 26, 30, Oct 3, 6, 7, 24, Nov 5, 24, Dec 22; 1797: CG, Jan 3, 4, 7,
   10, Feb 18, 24, 25, Mar 16, Apr 8, 25, May 6, 9, 16, 18, 20, 22, 23, 27, 31,
   Jun 1, 5, 6, 7, 8, Sep 20, 22, 25, 27, 29, Oct 2, 4, 6, 9, 11, 20, 21, Nov 1,
   2, 3, 11, 13, 15, 21, Dec 16, 18; 1798: CG, Jan 1, 11, Feb 12, 20, Mar 17,
   19, Apr 10, 19, 28, May 7, 9, 10, 12, 14, 15, 23, 24, 28, Jun 1, 4; 1800:
   HAY, Jun 16, 20, 25, 26, 28, Jul 1, 2, 25, 30, 31, Aug 2, 7, 12, 14, 23, 26,
   Sep 1, 3, 11, 16
Mountaineers, The (dance), 1773: DL, Sep 30, Oct 2, 6, 7, Nov 2, 15, 24; 1774:

DL, Mar 12, 15, Apr 5, 26, 29, May 3, 16

Mountaineers, The. See Colman the younger, George.

Mountaineers, The; or, The Woodland Sports (dance), 1784: CG, Dec 1; 1785: CG, Apr 6

Mountebank, The; or, The Country Lass (masque), 1715: LIF, Dec 21, 22, 27, 28; 1716: LIF, Jan 10, 19, Feb 20, Mar 5, May 28

Mountford (master carpenter), 1776: CG, Oct 26; 1777: CG, May 9

Mountfort (actor), 1729: BFF, Aug 23

Mountfort (singer), 1728: YB, Apr 12

Mountfort, Mrs (actor), 1728: HAY, Nov 14, 19, Dec 7; 1729: HAY, Jan 25, 31, Feb 11, 25, Mar 27, 29, May 26, 29, Jun 14, 17, Jul 31, Aug 2, DL, 16, HAY, 19, BFF, 23, BFR, 25, SF, Sep 8, GF, Oct 31, Nov 4, 5, 6, 11, 13, 17, 20, 25, 28, Dec 6, 8, 10, 17, 18, 30; 1730: GF, Jan 1, Feb 9, Mar 12, 17, 30, Apr 2, 6, 8, 10, 16, 24, 28, May 27, 28, Jun 3, 8, 12, 23, 25, 30, Jul 1, 6, 10, 13, 17, 21, BFPG/TC, Aug 1, BFPG, 31, GF, Sep 18, 21, 23, 28, Oct 5, 12, 14, 21, 24, 27, 30, Nov 2, 10, 11, 27, Dec 1, 12, 28; 1731: GF, Jan 23, HAY, Feb 10

Mountfort, Susannah, Mrs William (actor), 1680: DG, Feb 0; 1682: DL, Nov 16; 1686: DL, Apr 0, NONE, Sep 0; 1687: DLORDG, Jan 3, DG, Mar 0, ATCOURT, Apr 25; 1688: DL, May 3, NONE, Sep 0; 1689: DL, Mar 0, Apr 0, NONE, Sep 0, DL, Dec 4; 1690: DL, Jan 0, Sep 0, DL/IT, Oct 21; 1691: DL, Apr 0, NONE, Sep 0, DL, Dec 0; 1692: DL, Nov 0; 1693: DL, Feb 0, Mar 0, Apr 0, DG, May 0, DL, Oct 0; 1694: DL, Jan 0; 1695: DL, May 0; 1704: ATCOURT, Feb 28, LIF, Mar 21, Jun 26, Oct 16, Dec 4; 1705: DL, Jun 14, 16, Oct 16, 18, 30, Nov 6, 20; 1706: DL, Mar 28, Apr 8; 1707: DL, Jan 1, Mar 11, 25, 27, Oct 21, 28, Nov 20, Dec 2, 17; 1708: DL, Jan 15; 1712: DL, Oct 4, 13, 20, 30, Nov 26, Dec 17, 27; 1713: DL, Jan 6, 29, May 12, 29, Jun 19, Nov 9, 11, 16, 25; 1714: DL, Apr 23, May 28, Jun 4, Oct 22, Nov 27, Dec 4, 6; 1715: DL, Jan 5, 25, Feb 4, 22, Mar 26, Apr 19, May 20, 24, Oct 22, Nov 19, Dec 17, 20, 30; 1716: DL, Jan 17, 23, Feb 9, 21, Apr 16, Oct 4, 12, 15, 24, Nov 12, 26, Dec 15, 29; 1717: DL, Jan 26, Apr 8, 11, Oct 1, 14, 16, 21, 28, Nov 27, Dec 30; 1718: DL, Jan 25, 27, Feb 19, Mar 20, LIF, Oct 21

Mountfort, William (actor, author), 1662: NONE, Sep 0; 1678: DG, May 28; 1680: DG, Jun 0; 1682: NONE, Sep 0, DL, Nov 28; 1683: DG, May 31, NONE, Sep 0, DL, Dec 0; 1684: DL, Mar 0; 1685: DLORDG, Jan 15, DL, May 9, NONE, Sep 0, DL, Dec 19; 1686: NONE, Jan 18, DL, Apr 0; 1687: DG, Mar 0, ATCOURT, Apr 25; 1688: DL, Feb 0, DG, Apr 0, DL, May 3, NONE, Sep 0; 1689: DL, Mar 0, Apr 0, DLORDG, Oct 0, DL, Nov 7, Dec 4; 1690: DL, Jan 0, DLORDG, 16, DL, Sep 0, NONE, 0, DL, Oct 0, Nov 0, ATCOURT, 4, DL, Dec 0; 1691: DL, Jan 0, Mar 0, Apr 0, NONE, Sep 0, DLORDG, Oct 10, DL, Dec 0; 1692: DL, Jan 0, Apr 0, Jun 0, Nov 8, Dec 2, 9; 1693: NONE, Jan 0, Sep 0; 1697: LIF, Mar 13; 1704: LIF, Nov 13; 1708: DL, Apr 20; 1710: DL, Jan 31; 1718: DL, Jul 25; 1723: HAY, Dec 26, 30; 1724: HAY, Jan 31; 1731: HAY, May 12

--Edward III (with John Bancroft), 1690: DL, Nov 0, DLORDG, 0; 1691: DL, Feb 4, DLORDG, Oct 10; 1692: DL, Nov 8; 1731: HAY, May 12

--Fall of Mortimer, The, 1731: HAY, May 12, 13, 14, 17, 21, 24, 26, 27, 28, Jun 1, 2, 4, 5, 7, 14, 30, Jul 21; 1732: FS, Nov 30

--Greenwich Park; or, The Merry Citizens (Humourous Old Rake), 1691: DL, Apr 0; 1697: DL, Oct 16; 1704: DL, Apr 22, 26; 1705: DL, Mar 1, Dec 21; 1708: DL, Apr 17, 20, Oct 18, Dec 29; 1715: DL, Jun 21, 24, Jul 1, 15; 1716: DL, Jan 4, Feb 8, May 2, Nov 14; 1717: DL, Feb 11, Apr 4, May 27; 1718: DL, Feb 6, May 28, Nov 28; 1719: DL, Nov 23; 1723: HAY, Dec 26, 30; 1730: DL, Oct 10, 13, 15, Dec 3, 28; 1731: DL, Apr 23, Nov 12, Dec 17; 1732: DL, May 6, Oct 21; 1735: DL, Nov 10, 11, Dec 27; 1736: DL, Feb 27, Oct 29; 1741: CG, Jan 29, 31, Feb 2, 3, 6

--Injured Lovers, The; or, The Ambitious Father, 1688: DL, Feb 0

--Life and Death of Doctor Faustus, The, 1685: NONE, Sep 0; 1697: LIF, Mar 13; 1724: HAY, Jan 31, Feb 1, 4, 18

--Successful Strangers, The, 1690: DL, Jan 0; 1692: NONE, Sep 0; 1695: NONE, Sep 0; 1708: DL, Jul 20, 22; 1710: DL, Jan 31; 1711: DL, Jun 29; 1728: LIF, Jun 25, 28

--Zelmane; or, The Corinthian Queen, 1704: LIF, Nov 13, 18

Mountier, Thomas (actor), 1731: HAY, May 6; 1732: LIF, Mar 10, 22, HIC, 27, Apr 5, DL, 25, HAY, May 17, Nov 16; 1733: HAY, Jun 4, DL, Nov 7, 16, 26; 1734: DL, Feb 4, DL/HAY, Mar 21, DL, Apr 15, 29; 1740: HIC, Mar 19

Mountstevens, 1680: ATCOURT, Feb 20

Mourn all ye Muses (song), 1791: DL, Apr 1; 1792: KING'S, Feb 29; 1794: DL, Mar 26

Mourning Bride, The. See Congreve, William.

Mouse Trap, The; or, Foote's Vagaries (dance), 1748: CG, Mar 28; see also Foote's Vagaries

Mouth of the Nile, The. See Dibdin, Thomas John.

Mowatt, Miss (actor), 1760: CG, Jan 24, 28, Feb 13, Mar 6, Apr 30; 1761: DL,

HAY, 26, CG, 27, Aug 14, 20, BF, 23, DL, Sep 26, Oct 10, 17, 24, 31, Nov 13,
14, 23, 26, 27, Dec 7, 11, 21, 26; 1734: DL, Jan 3, 8, 15, 19, 28, Feb 4,
DL/LIF, Mar 11, DL/HAY, 25, 30, HAY, Apr 5, DL, 15, LIF, 15, DL/HAY, 20, 26,
LIF, May 9, DL, 15, 16, LIF, 23, HAY, Aug 16, 21, BFRLCH, 24, Sep 2, CG/LIF,
18, 23, 25, 27, LIF, Oct 1, CG/LIF, 9, 18, 29, Nov 7, 11, 14, 19, 21, 25, Dec
5, 12, 26, 30, 31; 1735: CG/LIF, Jan 3, 6, 23, 28, LIF, Mar 3, CG/LIF, 11,
20, 29, Apr 8, 9, 17, 18, 22, May 1, 15, 16, LIF, 21, CG/LIF, 26, LIF, Jul
11, 16, 23, 30, Aug 1, 6, 25, 29, Sep 2, 5, CG, 12, 16, 17, 24, 26, 29, Oct
1, 13, 17, 20, 29, 31, Nov 6, 7, 10, 22, Dec 8, 27; 1736: CG, Jan 9, Mar 15,
18, 20, 22, 27, LIF, Apr 2, CG, 6, 8, LIF, 16, CG, 29, 30, May 3, LIF, 5, CG,
13, 17, 20, BFHC, Aug 23, CG, Sep 15, 17, 20, 24, 29, Oct 4, 13, LIF, 18, CG,
20, 23, 25, 27, 29, Nov 1, 25, 29, Dec 2, 9, 20, 29; 1737: CG, Jan 10, 21,
25, Feb 3, Mar 15, 24, 28, Apr 14, 15, 26, 28, May 9, LIF, Jun 15, Jul 26,
Aug 2, 5, CG, Sep 16, 21, 30, Oct 3, 5, 12, 17, 26, 28, 29, Nov 1, 2, 9, 14,
18; 1738: CG, Jan 3, 6, 9, 13, 17, Feb 6, 13, 16, 23, Mar 14, 25, Apr 7, 12,
20, 22, 25, May 3, 10, 18, Aug 30, Sep 18, 27, Oct 2, 4, 6, 9, 11, 14, 20,
26, 30, Nov 2, 7, 17, 23, 28, 29, Dec 2, 4, 5, 12; 1739: CG, Jan 8, Feb 10,
16, Mar 20, 27, Apr 3, 23, 24, 25, May 1, 7, 15, 17, 23, 25, Aug 31, Sep 5,
7, 10, 14, 17, 19, 21, 22, 27, 28, Oct 1, 2, 3, 5, 8, 10, 22, 25, 29, Nov 6,
9, 13, 20, Dec 1, 10, 15; 1740: CG, Jan 15, 17, Feb 2, Mar 11, 24, 27, Apr
14, 18, 28, May 3, 5, 9, 21, 23, 27, Jun 5, Sep 19, 22, 26, Oct 1, 3, 6, 8,
22, 23, 25, 29, Nov 1, 15, GF, 18, CG, Dec 4, 10, 29, 30; 1741: CG, Jan 2, 6,
12, 15, 21, 23, 27, 29, Feb 14, 19, Mar 2, 9, 10, 30, Apr 3, 7, 10, 11, 17,
18, 21, 22, 25, May 1, 4, 11, 12, BFH, Aug 22, CG, Sep 21, 25, Oct 2, 7, 10,
20, 21, 24, 26, 29, Nov 9, 23, 26, 27, 30, Dec 1, 7, 9, 11, 18; 1742: CG, Jan
19, May 7, 18, BFHC, Aug 25; 1743: CG, Jan 27; 1749: CG, Apr 15
Mullart, William and Mrs (actors), 1736: CG, May 3; 1737: CG, Apr 28
Mullet (actor), 1731: HAY, Jul 21
Mulliner (actor), 1754: HAY, Nov 28, Dec 9
Mullins (shoemaker), 1785: CG, Nov 4
Mumford, Miss (actor), 1734: JS, May 29
Munck (singer), 1758: CHAPEL, Apr 27
Munden, Joseph Shepherd (actor, singer), 1779: HAY, Jan 11, Oct 13, 18, Dec 27;
1780: HAY, Jan 3, 17; 1790: CG, Dec 2, 10, 17; 1791: CG, Jan 26, Feb 2, 4,
16, Mar 14, Apr 11, 16, May 2, 5, 6, 14, 18, 19, 24, Jun 1, 3, 6, Sep 12, 14,
17, Oct 3, 10, 12, 19, 20, Nov 4, 5, 19, 24, 29, Dec 3, 21, 22; 1792: CG, Feb
2, 18, 23, Mar 26, 31, Apr 10, 17, 18, May 2, 10, 11, 15, 18, 28, 30, Sep 17,
19, 21, 24, 28, Oct 8, 10, 12, 19, 25, 26, 27, 29, 31, Nov 3, 5, 6, 7, 10,
14, 17, Dec 1, 3, 8, 20, 21, 22, 26, 27; 1793: CG, Jan 2, 9, 29, Feb 25, Mar
18, Apr 4, 8, 15, 18, 25, May 1, 3, 10, 11, 24, 27, Sep 16, 18, 23, 25, 27,
30, Oct 1, 2, 3, 4, 8, 9, 10, 12, 15, 16, 18, 22, 23, 24, 25, 29, Nov 2, 5,
9, 11, 12, 23, 30, Dec 6, 9; 1794: CG, Jan 14, 21, 22, Feb 5, 6, 22, Apr 7,
10, 12, 23, 29, May 2, 13, 16, 22, 28, 29, Jun 11, Sep 15, 17, 19, 22, 24,
26, 29, Oct 1, 3, 8, 10, 14, 17, 21, 23, 30, Nov 7, 11, 12, 17, 19, 21, 22,
Dec 6, 10, 31; 1795: CG, Jan 2, 6, 8, 23, 29, 31, Feb 3, 6, Mar 14, 16, 19,
28, Apr 22, 23, May 1, 2, 6, 8, 13, 14, 16, 20, 21, 25, 27, 29, Jun 2, 4, 6,
8, 12, 16, Sep 14, 16, 18, 21, 23, 25, 30, Oct 2, 5, 7, 8, 14, 15, 19, 22,
24, 30, 31, Nov 4, 7, 14, 18, 25, 27, Dec 9, 14, 15, 21, 22, 23, 29, 31;
1796: CG, Jan 2, 8, 23, Feb 2, Mar 14, 30, Apr 5, 12, 13, 15, 20, 22, 23, 26,
29, May 6, 10, 16, 18, 20, 21, 23, 26, 27, Jun 2, 7, Sep 12, 14, 16, 17, 19,
21, 23, 26, 28, 30, Oct 5, 6, 14, 17, 18, 20, 21, 29, Nov 5, 19, 21, 24, 25,
Dec 9, 15, 17, 22, 27; 1797: CG, Jan 3, 7, 10, Feb 20, 23, 27, Mar 4, 16, Apr
19, 25, 29, May 2, 6, 9, 11, 16, 17, 18, 20, 22, 23, 31, Jun 1, 5, 8, 13,
HAY, 15, 16, 20, 21, 23, 29, Jul 3, 6, 8, 10, 13, 15, Aug 4, 8, 10, 17, 21,
CG, Sep 18, 20, 22, 25, 27, 29, Oct 4, 6, 11, 16, 20, 25, 28, 31, Nov 1, 4,
10, 11, 13, 18, 22, 23, Dec 12, 16, 18, 19, 20, 23; 1798: CG, Jan 11, Feb 9,
Mar 17, 20, 31, Apr 10, 11, 17, 19, 20, 21, 24, 27, 28, 30, May 1, 5, 7, 9,
10, 12, 15, 16, 17, 18, 22, 23, 24, 28, 30, 31, Jun 2, 6, HAY, 12, 14, 16,
21, 23, 29, Jul 5, 10, 17, 20, 21, 25, Aug 6, 11, 14, 16, 21, 23, 28, Sep 3,
7, 10, CG, 17, 19, 21, 26, 28, Oct 1, 3, 5, 8, 11, 31, Nov 1, 5, 7, 10, 12,
17, 24, Dec 8, 26; 1799: CG, Jan 12, 17, 22, 25, 26, 28, Feb 4, Mar 5, 14,
16, Apr 2, 6, 8, 9, 12, 16, 18, 19, 26, 27, 30, May 3, 7, 13, 15, 18, 22, 24,
28, 31, Jun 1, 3, 5, 7, Sep 16, 20, 23, 25, 27, 30, Oct 2, 4, 7, 10, 11, 16,
17, 18, 21, 24, 25, 28, 31, Nov 8, 11, 13, 14, 30, Dec 2, 4, 7, 16; 1800: CG,
Jan 11, 16, 18, Feb 3, 8, Mar 1, 17, 25, 27, Apr 5, 15, 17, 19, 22, 23, 24,
26, 30, May 1, 2, 6, 7, 10, 12, 13, 15, 20, 27, 28, 29, 30, Jun 2, 5, 7
Mungo Dance (dance), 1773: DL, Apr 22
Munich. See Moench.
Munich, 1782: KING'S, Mar 16
Munier, Mrs (actor), 1759: DL, Nov 19
Munro (musician), 1722: HIC, Mar 16; 1728: YB, Mar 13
Munro (ticket deliverer), 1734: DL, May 21

593

Munro, Henry (oboist), <u>1792</u>: CG, Feb 24; <u>1793</u>: CG, Feb 15; <u>1794</u>: CG, Mar 7;
   <u>1795</u>: CG, Feb 20; <u>1796</u>: CG, Feb 12; <u>1797</u>: CG, Mar 3; <u>1798</u>: CG, Feb 23; <u>1799</u>:
   CG, Feb 8; <u>1800</u>: CG, Feb 28
Munro, Samuel (violinist), <u>1796</u>: CG, Feb 12; <u>1797</u>: CG, Mar 3; <u>1798</u>: CG, Feb 23;
   <u>1799</u>: CG, Feb 8; <u>1800</u>: CG, Feb 28
Muntford. See Mountfort.
Muraile (dancer), <u>1675</u>: ATCOURT, Feb 15
Murden (actor), <u>1763</u>: HAY, Jun 20, Aug 5, Sep 5, 7; <u>1765</u>: CG, Jan 17, 21, May
   2, 9, 11, Sep 20, Oct 5, 14, 15, Dec 6, 21; <u>1766</u>: CG, Jan 9, 31, Apr 2, 25,
   29, HAY, Jun 26, Jul 1, 3, 8, 18, 23, 31, KING'S, Aug 8, 13, 18, 25, 27, 29,
   Sep 9, CG, Oct 1, 6, 15, 22, Dec 23; <u>1767</u>: CG, Jan 31, Mar 21, Apr 25, May
   12, 15, 26
Mure, Hutchison (renter), <u>1758</u>: CG, Feb 25, Apr 18
Mure, Mary (renter), <u>1758</u>: CG, Apr 18
Murgatroyd, Miss (actor), <u>1748</u>: DL, Dec 26; <u>1749</u>: DL, Sep 26, Dec 18, 20, 26;
   <u>1750</u>: DL, Jan 6, 27, Feb 14
Murphin (actor), <u>1772</u>: GROTTO, Aug 17
Murphy (actor), <u>1792</u>: CII, Jan 16
Murphy (bagpiper), <u>1798</u>: CG, May 5, 28, HAY, Jul 21; <u>1799</u>: CG, Jan 29, 31, Mar
   2
Murphy, Arthur (actor, author), <u>1753</u>: CG, Nov 1, 3, 10, 14, DL, Dec 1, CG, 11,
   17, DL, 26; <u>1754</u>: CG, Jan 10, DL, 16, CG, Oct 18, Nov 15, 23; <u>1755</u>: CG, Mar
   18, 22, Apr 2, 4, 17, 18, May 5, DL, Sep 20, Oct 24, Nov 4, Dec 8, 23; <u>1756</u>:
   DL, Jan 2, 8, 12, Feb 27, Apr 3, 26, May 7; <u>1757</u>: DL, Dec 3; <u>1758</u>: DL, Mar
   30; <u>1759</u>: DL, Apr 21; <u>1760</u>: DL, Jan 24, 26, Nov 17; <u>1761</u>: DL, Jan 3, 10, 15,
   Jun 15; <u>1764</u>: CG, Jan 9; <u>1765</u>: DL, Mar 23; <u>1767</u>: CG, Jan 10, DL, Apr 22;
   <u>1768</u>: DL, Feb 27; <u>1772</u>: DL, Feb 26, 29, Mar 9, 16; <u>1773</u>: CG, Feb 23, Mar 30;
   <u>1774</u>: CG, Oct 31; <u>1775</u>: DL, Nov 27; <u>1776</u>: CG, Mar 30, Apr 26, Sep 23; <u>1777</u>:
   CG, Feb 22, Apr 1, Nov 6, 18; <u>1781</u>: CG, Jan 31, DL, Feb 17; <u>1785</u>: CG, Oct 17;
   <u>1786</u>: CG, Feb 25; <u>1787</u>: CG, May 14, ROY, Jun 20; <u>1788</u>: HAY, Sep 30; <u>1789</u>: CG,
   Nov 28; <u>1791</u>: CG, Feb 2; <u>1793</u>: DL, Mar 18; <u>1795</u>: HAY, Mar 4
--All in the Wrong, <u>1761</u>: DL, Jun 15, 16, 18, 19, 22, 24, 26, 29, Jul 16, 23,
   Aug 8, Nov 10, 11, 16, 19, 25, Dec 4, 19, 31; <u>1762</u>: DL, Jan 16, Feb 9, Apr
   13, May 14, Oct 11, Nov 13, Dec 9; <u>1763</u>: DL, Jan 8, 13, Mar 7, May 4, Oct 21,
   Dec 7, 15; <u>1765</u>: DL, Jan 3, 10, Apr 16, Sep 24, Nov 12; <u>1766</u>: DL, Jan 14;
   <u>1768</u>: DL, Jan 19, May 25, Oct 4; <u>1769</u>: DL, Oct 3, 19, 25, Dec 14; <u>1770</u>: DL,
   May 19, Oct 23; <u>1771</u>: DL, May 15; <u>1773</u>: DL, Feb 4; <u>1774</u>: DL, May 10; <u>1776</u>:
   CG, Apr 26, Oct 16, Dec 20; <u>1777</u>: CG, Apr 22, May 20; <u>1778</u>: CG, Apr 21, Oct
   9; <u>1779</u>: CG, Jan 20, May 18, Dec 3; <u>1780</u>: CG, Jan 29, May 17; <u>1783</u>: CG, Jan
   3, 8, 16, May 22; <u>1784</u>: CG, Feb 20, 24, Mar 29, Apr 16, May 6; <u>1785</u>: CG, Jan
   14, Feb 2, 3, May 5, Oct 10, DL, 26, CG, Nov 23; <u>1786</u>: CG, Jan 21, Nov 13,
   16; <u>1787</u>: CG, Feb 9, DL, Mar 29, CG, Nov 2, Dec 21; <u>1788</u>: CG, Apr 21, Nov 21;
   <u>1789</u>: DL, Jan 13, 27, Feb 17, CG, Nov 19, Dec 30; <u>1790</u>: DL, May 18; <u>1793</u>: DL,
   Apr 22, May 3, 9, 30; <u>1796</u>: DL, Jun 8; <u>1797</u>: DL, Jan 27, Nov 18
--Alzuma, <u>1773</u>: CG, Feb 19, 23, 25, Mar 1, 2, 4, 6, 8, 9, 11, 13, 30, Apr 12
--Apprentice, The (farce), <u>1756</u>: DL, Jan 2, 3, 5, 6, 7, 8, 9, 10, 12, 14, 16,
   20, Feb 2, Mar 15, 22, 25, Apr 26, Sep 18, Oct 15, Nov 4; <u>1757</u>: DL, Mar 14,
   22, Apr 12, Sep 20, Oct 27; <u>1758</u>: DL, Feb 2, Mar 14, Apr 3, 7, 14; <u>1759</u>: DL,
   Apr 27, May 7, 29, Nov 24; <u>1760</u>: DL, Mar 11, Apr 17, May 15; <u>1762</u>: DL, May 7,
   8, Nov 3; <u>1763</u>: CG, Feb 14, 19, Mar 3, 15, Apr 6, 11, 22, May 18, Dec 9;
   <u>1764</u>: CG, Mar 22, May 9, DL, 21, CG, 23, HAY, Jul 23, Aug 8, 15, 22, Sep 12,
   CG, Nov 3; <u>1765</u>: CG, May 11, 24, Oct 15, Dec 19; <u>1766</u>: CG, Jan 25, Feb 18,
   Mar 11, Apr 8, 29, May 8, HAY, Jun 26, Jul 1, CG, Oct 18, Nov 6; <u>1767</u>: CG,
   Jan 16, Feb 14, Apr 25, Oct 8, Dec 17, 22; <u>1768</u>: CG, Feb 8, Mar 3, 22, Apr
   19, Oct 4, 17, 28, Dec 15, HAY, 19; <u>1769</u>: CG, Feb 27, Mar 14, Apr 28, May 25,
   HAY, Sep 19; <u>1770</u>: CG, Jan 18, Mar 19, 29, Apr 27, HAY, Oct 1; <u>1771</u>: HAY, Jun
   21, Aug 9, CG, Nov 11, Dec 14; <u>1772</u>: CG, Jan 29, Mar 10, Apr 7, 23, May 20,
   30, HAY, Jul 3, Sep 18, CG, 28, Oct 5, Nov 26, HAY, Dec 21; <u>1773</u>: CG, Feb 8,
   Mar 8, Apr 12, May 15, HAY, Jun 28, Jul 23, Sep 16, CG, Nov 9; <u>1774</u>: CG, Mar
   21, Apr 12, 19, HAY, Sep 21; <u>1775</u>: CG, Feb 23, Apr 8, May 4, Nov 8, 21, 22,
   Dec 14, 18; <u>1776</u>: CG, Feb 29, Mar 28, Nov 9; <u>1777</u>: CG, Sep 29, Oct 13, 24,
   29, Nov 15; <u>1778</u>: CG, Mar 30, HAY, Aug 27, Sep 2, CG, Oct 23, Nov 23; <u>1779</u>:
   CG, Feb 18, Apr 15, Nov 9; <u>1780</u>: CG, Jan 20, HAY, Jun 6, 9, 10, 15, 20, Aug
   9, CG, Sep 20, Nov 25; <u>1781</u>: DL, Jan 16, 20, 27, Apr 26, May 5, HAY, Jul 9,
   DL, Sep 18, CG, Oct 16, DL, 22, Nov 27, CG, 28, DL, Dec 13; <u>1782</u>: DL, Apr 22,
   May 18, Nov 1, Dec 4; <u>1783</u>: DL, Jan 6, 9, Feb 19, Apr 25, Jun 5, Oct 20, Nov
   3, Dec 5; <u>1784</u>: DL, Apr 15, HAY, Sep 17, DL, Oct 12; <u>1785</u>: DL, Feb 22, HAY,
   24, Apr 8, HAMM, Jul 2, HAY, Aug 6, Sep 8; <u>1786</u>: HAY, Jun 9; <u>1788</u>: CG, Mar
   26, DL, Dec 6; <u>1789</u>: DL, Dec 17; <u>1790</u>: DL, Jun 4; <u>1791</u>: DL, Jan 10; <u>1792</u>:
   DLKING'S, Jan 6, 23, Feb 3, May 16, 30, DL, Nov 26, HAY, 26; <u>1793</u>: DL, Feb 6,
   Mar 16, May 29, Jun 4; <u>1796</u>: DL, Nov 18, 25, Dec 1, 15; <u>1797</u>: DL, Mar 11, Apr
   26, Nov 4; <u>1798</u>: DL, Jan 5, 22, Oct 4, Dec 4; <u>1799</u>: DL, Jan 12, Feb 5, May

28, Jun 6, 19, Oct 26, Nov 22, Dec 13, 31; 1800: DL, Jan 20, Feb 8, Mar 18,
Apr 22, May 17
--Choice, The, 1765: DL, Mar 23, 26; 1766: DL, Mar 18; 1772: CG, Mar 30
--Citizen, The, 1761: DL, Jul 2, 4, 7, 9, 13, 16, Aug 5, 8; 1762: HAY, Aug 10,
13, 19, 23, 25, 27, 28, Sep 3, 7, CG, Nov 15, 17, 20, 25, Dec 1, 7; 1763: CG,
Jan 19, Feb 26, Mar 5, 17, Apr 16, 18, 30, May 17, HAY, Jul 18, 22, 29, Aug
10, 11, 24, 31, Sep 7, CG, 23, 26, Oct 3, 5, DL, 8, CG, 10, 11, 13, 25, Nov
29, Dec 8, 21, 31; 1764: CG, Jan 11, Feb 18, Mar 26, Apr 2, 9, 30, May 7, 26,
HAY, Jul 12, 13, 18, 27, Aug 3, 13, 24, Sep 3, CG, Oct 1, 4, 15, Nov 7, 21,
Dec 7; 1765: CG, Mar 12, 19, Apr 10, 16, 30, May 15, HAY, Jul 8, 10, 12, Aug
8, 21, Sep 11, CG, Nov 12, Dec 2; 1766: CG, Jan 21, Mar 3, DL, 20, CG, Apr 5,
11, 23, May 3, 9, HAY, Jul 31, CG, Oct 8, 10, 23, Nov 12, Dec 1, 16, 23, 31;
1767: CG, Mar 7, 16, 23, 30, Apr 7, May 12, HAY, Jun 12, Jul 3, Sep 4, 9, CG,
18, Dec 18; 1768: CG, Jan 5, Feb 6, Mar 5, Apr 5, 9, May 24, Oct 7, Nov 17,
29, Dec 10; 1769: CG, Mar 16, DL, Apr 3, CG, 10, May 16, Sep 29, Oct 16, 19;
1770: CG, Feb 26, Apr 2, 17, May 25, HAY, Aug 31, Nov 16; 1771: HAY, Jan 7,
CG, Apr 6, HAY, May 31, CG, Dec 17; 1772: CG, Mar 24, Apr 9, DL, 29, CG, May
22, DL, 22, CG, Oct 12, Nov 28, Dec 21; 1773: CG, Jan 29, Mar 2, May 1, 20,
DL, 24, 28, Dec 30; 1774: DL, Jan 14, HAY, 24, DL, Mar 3, CG, 12, Apr 6, 22,
23, 27, May 11, Nov 2, 15; 1775: CG, Mar 6, 27, Apr 18, May 22, Dec 5, 6;
1776: CG, Mar 21, HAY, May 2, CHR, Oct 14, CG, Nov 8, 29; 1777: CG, Apr 29,
May 12, HAY, Jun 30, Jul 2, 11, Aug 9, 14, 22, CG, Nov 20; 1778: CG, Mar 31,
CHR, Jun 1; 1779: HAY, Jul 15, 16, 22, 23, 26, Aug 12, 18, 21; 1780: DL, Apr
5, Sep 21, Nov 11, Dec 6; 1781: DL, Jan 15, Oct 26; 1782: DL, Feb 12, 16, CG,
May 29, HAY, Sep 21, DL, Oct 18; 1783: DL, Mar 29, Apr 25, Oct 22, 28, Dec 9;
1784: HAY, Jul 8, CG, Nov 16, Dec 14; 1785: DL, Apr 26; 1787: RLSN, Mar 26,
CG, May 14; 1788: CG, Jan 5, Feb 23, 28, HAY, Sep 30; 1789: HAY, Sep 7, DL,
Oct 20, Nov 3, 10, CG, 13, DL, 26, CG, Dec 5, DL, 11, 19; 1790: DL, Feb 1, 9,
16, 25, Mar 11, Apr 15, HAY, Jun 17, 23, 30, Jul 7, Aug 5, 16, 28, DL, Oct
16; 1791: DL, Jan 5, 18, 28, Feb 22, Apr 29, May 13, 17, HAY, Jul 14,
DLKING'S, Oct 13, Nov 1, 21; 1792: DLKING'S, Jan 12, 24, Feb 14, HAY, Apr 16,
DLKING'S, May 17, Jun 11, HAY, Jul 11, DL, Oct 27, Nov 23; 1793: DL, May 30,
HAY, Jul 13, Aug 1, Oct 30, Nov 15; 1794: HAY, Jan 9, 24, Feb 17, Mar 11, Apr
1, DL, May 6, 20, 27, Dec 31; 1795: DL, Jan 16, Feb 9, HAY, Aug 3, DL, Oct
30; 1796: DL, Apr 18, HAY, 27, DL, May 4, HAY, Jul 6, 18, Aug 9, DL, Oct 10,
Nov 17, Dec 16; 1797: DL, Apr 1, CG, Nov 3, DL, 21, 23, HAY, Dec 4, DL, 13;
1798: DL, Jan 11, Apr 13, May 12, Jun 14, Sep 15; 1799: DL, Apr 13; 1800: DL,
Mar 17, May 2, Jun 11, 14
--Desert Island, The, 1760: DL, Jan 24, 25, 26, 28, 29, 31, Feb 1, 2, 4, 5, 9
--Englishman Returned from Paris, The, 1756: CG, Feb 3, 5, 9, 11, 12, 13, 16,
18, 20, 23, 25, 27, Mar 1, 4, 8, 15, 29, Apr 1, DL, 3, CG, Oct 11, 12, 15,
19, 28, DL, 29, CG, Nov 2, Dec 1, 15; 1757: CG, Mar 1, 29, Apr 13, Dec 14,
17, 19; 1758: CG, Jan 13, 21, Feb 11, Mar 9, Apr 7, 10, 28, May 12, Oct 16,
21, Dec 19; 1759: CG, Jan 15, 16, Feb 8, 27, Apr 30, Oct 11, 20, 24, Nov 3,
12, 19, 27, Dec 21; 1760: CG, Jan 5, Feb 21, Mar 22, Oct 13, 14; 1761: CG,
May 1, Oct 12; 1763: HAY, Aug 5, 22; 1766: CG, Apr 7, HAY, 30; 1770: CG, Nov
17
--Grecian Daughter, The, 1772: DL, Feb 25, 26, 27, 29, Mar 2, 5, 7, 9, 12, 14,
16, Apr 30, May 14, 28, Oct 13; 1774: DL, Mar 12; 1775: CG, Mar 27, 30, Apr
24, DL, May 16, Oct 10, CG, 25, Nov 20; 1776: CG, Jan 5, 12, Feb 7, 12, Apr
9, 22, May 20, Nov 28; 1777: CG, Mar 31, May 6, Nov 13, Dec 1; 1778: CG, Feb
12, Apr 20, 30, Dec 3; 1779: CG, Apr 13; 1780: HAY, Jun 14, 19, DL, Oct 11,
Nov 15; 1781: DL, Jan 4; 1782: CG, Oct 21, 28, DL, 30, Nov 1, 4, 13, 27, Dec
9, 12; 1783: DL, Jan 2, CG, Feb 10, DL, 19, Mar 4, 27, Apr 12, May 17, Oct
14, Nov 19, CG, 27, Dec 1, 4; 1784: CG, Jan 8, 27, Feb 31, CG, Feb 9, 26, Apr
12, DL, 22, Oct 19, Nov 27, CG, 29; 1785: DL, Mar 17, May 4, Oct 15, CG, 28,
31, Nov 4; 1786: CG, Jan 5, 16, Feb 14, Apr 26, DL, May 30, CG, Sep 27, DL,
Oct 23, CG, Dec 27; 1787: DL, Jan 2, Apr 26, CG, May 28, Oct 15, DL, 18, CG,
Dec 27; 1788: CG, May 17, DL, Nov 4; 1789: DL, Feb 28, CG, Dec 26; 1790: DL,
Dec 14; 1791: CG, Dec 27; 1792: DLKING'S, Feb 11, 27, CG, Nov 12, DL, Dec 31;
1793: DL, Feb 2, Apr 27; 1794: CG, Mar 17, 24, HAY, 31, CG, May 30, Oct 1,
DL, Dec 15, 16, CG, 27; 1795: DL, Oct 19; 1796: DL, Jan 4, 6, Feb 1, May 6,
Oct 13, 29, Nov 12; 1797: DL, Mar 11, May 9, Nov 21; 1798: CG, Jan 5, DL, Mar
13, Nov 16, Dec 20; 1799: DL, Jan 28, Apr 11, Oct 21
--Know Your Own Mind, 1777: CG, Feb 22, 24, 25, Mar 1, 4, 6, 8, 11, 13, 18, 20,
Apr 1, 3, 10, 12, 24, 30, May 8, Oct 10, 30, Dec 23; 1778: CG, Jan 2, Feb 3,
Mar 10, Apr 29, Oct 14; 1779: CG, Jan 15, Mar 16; 1780: CG, Apr 7, May 19;
1781: CG, Feb 14; 1786: CG, Dec 13; 1789: DL, Apr 21, Oct 8, 10, 15, 22, 29,
Nov 14, 19; 1790: DL, Jan 22, May 7, 19, Nov 5, Dec 9; 1791: DL, May 3,
DLKING'S, Oct 4, Dec 9, 23; 1792: DLKING'S, Jun 14, DL, Sep 20, Nov 7, Dec 4;
1793: DL, Jan 11; 1795: DL, Jan 17, Dec 9; 1796: DL, Jan 19, Dec 29; 1797:
DL, Feb 15, Mar 16; 1798: DL, May 11

--Marriage a la Mode; or, Conjugal Douceurs, 1760: DL, Mar 24; 1767: DL, Apr 22
--News from Parnassus (prelude), 1776: CG, Sep 23, 25, 27, 30
--No One's Enemy but His Own, 1763: CG, Dec 31; 1764: CG, Jan 9, 10, 11, 19;
    1774: CG, Oct 26, 28, Nov 1, 7, 9, 11
--Old Maid, The, 1756: CG, Feb 26, DL, Mar 27, May 4; 1761: DL, Jul 2, 4, 7, 9,
    13, 16, 21, Aug 5, 7, Nov 14, 17, 18, 20, Dec 2, 3, 9, 15, 17, 18; 1762: DL,
    Feb 2, 8, 15, 18, Mar 20, Apr 26, 28, CG, May 1, HAY, Aug 10, 13, 19, 27, Sep
    3, 7, DL, 18, CG, 20, 29, 30, Oct 4, 7; 1763: DL, Jan 7, 17, 21, Mar 24, CG,
    26, Apr 29, May 4, 13, Sep 21; 1764: CG, Feb 21, May 12, DL, Oct 2, CG, 16,
    DL, 31; 1765: DL, Feb 1, HAY, Jun 24, 26, 28, Jul 1, 3, 5, 29, Sep 3, 6, CG,
    Dec 20; 1766: CG, Jan 7, Feb 8, Mar 15, Apr 1, HAY, Jul 3, 15, DL, Nov 8, 15,
    Dec 17, 30, 31; 1767: HAY, Jun 15, Jul 2, DL, Nov 11, Dec 5; 1768: DL, Feb 1,
    CG, 27, DL, May 25, HAY, Jun 17, 20, 24, CG, Sep 19, DL, Nov 1; 1769: DL, Apr
    22; 1770: DL, Feb 8, CG, Nov 14, DL, Dec 17; 1772: DL, May 14, 28, Oct 17,
    Dec 8, 23; 1773: DL, Jan 19, Dec 20; 1777: CG, Jan 25, 31, Feb 11, Apr 30,
    Sep 26; 1778: HAY, Apr 30, CHR, Jun 9, Jul 30, CG, Oct 9; 1781: CII, Mar 15;
    1795: DL, May 4; 1796: CG, May 27; 1797: DL, Oct 26
--Orphan of China, The, 1755: DL, Dec 19; 1756: DL, Jan 5; 1759: DL, Apr 21,
    23, 25, 28, May 1, 3, 5, 8, 12; 1760: DL, Feb 13, 16; 1764: DL, Apr 2, 26,
    May 5, Nov 24; 1765: DL, Mar 5, Apr 15, Oct 25, 29; 1766: DL, Feb 17, Nov 24;
    1767: DL, Feb 4, Nov 19; 1768: DL, Dec 17; 1777: CG, Nov 6, 8, 17; 1787: HAY,
    Mar 26
--Rival Sisters, 1793: DL, Mar 18, 19, 23, Apr 2, 6, 10, 13
--School for Guardians, The, 1766: CG, Dec 31; 1767: CG, Jan 10, 12, 13, 15,
    17, 20, Feb 18; 1777: CG, Nov 18
--Spouter, The; or, The Triple Revenge, 1756: DL, Apr 26
--Three Weeks after Marriage, 1776: CG, Mar 30, Apr 8, 11, 12, 17, 18, 25, May
    2, 9, 16, 20, 23, 27, Jun 1, Oct 2, CHR, 7, CG, 25, Nov 6; 1777: CG, Feb 18,
    Apr 5, 11, 18, May 13, 19, Nov 12, 14, 22; 1778: CG, Feb 20, Mar 28, Apr 4,
    Oct 29; 1779: CG, Feb 12, Mar 13, Apr 10, 28, May 5, Nov 22; 1780: CG, Sep
    22, Dec 8; 1781: CG, Feb 8, May 2, Sep 21, Nov 10; 1782: CG, May 25, Oct 9,
    Nov 5; 1783: CG, Apr 12, May 26, Oct 14; 1784: CG, May 12; 1785: CG, Mar 5,
    10, 14, 17, 31, Apr 7, 21, May 11, 26, Oct 19, Nov 19, 30, Dec 13, 17; 1786:
    CG, Feb 10, 25, May 4, Oct 19; 1787: CG, Jan 31, Apr 17, Nov 26; 1788: CG,
    Jan 15, Feb 12, May 29, Nov 7; 1789: CG, Mar 19, Apr 17, Jun 15, Nov 12, 26;
    1790: CG, Mar 8; 1791: CG, Mar 12; 1792: CG, Feb 8, May 18; 1793: CG, Oct 9,
    Nov 19, 21; 1794: CG, Mar 15, HAY, May 22; 1795: CG, May 1, Jun 2, Dec 15;
    1796: CG, Apr 15; 1797: CG, Oct 11, 18, 24; 1798: CG, Jan 31, Nov 5, 7; 1799:
    CG, Apr 12; 1800: DL, Jun 5, CG, 12
--Upholsterer, The, 1758: DL, Mar 30, Apr 1, 4, 6, 8, 12, 13, 18, 19, 26, May
    6, 10, 31; 1759: DL, Mar 26; 1760: DL, Apr 11, 21; 1761: CG, Jun 23; 1763:
    CG, Oct 26, 28, Nov 2, 8, 11, 17, 18, Dec 1, 14, 29; 1764: CG, Jan 4, 10, Feb
    20, Mar 24, Apr 3, 14, 27, May 1, 3, 11, Sep 24, Oct 8, Nov 2, 26, Dec 6, 11;
    1765: CG, Jan 2, Feb 25, Mar 14, 21, Apr 17, 23, 27, May 14, 23, Oct 5, Nov
    20, 29, Dec 17; 1766: CG, Jan 17, 29, Feb 25, Mar 20, Apr 14, 21, May 5, Oct
    15, 21, Nov 13; 1767: CG, Jan 9, Feb 11, 18, Mar 24, 31, Apr 22, 29, May 16,
    Sep 17, Nov 20, Dec 21; 1768: CG, Feb 3, 4, 16, Mar 1, 19, May 10, 25, Oct
    12, Nov 1, 19, Dec 6, 23; 1769: CG, Feb 2, Mar 6, 18, Apr 3, 7, 15, 22, May
    8, 18, Oct 6, 21, Dec 8; 1770: CG, Jan 19, Mar 13, 27, Apr 23, May 4; 1771:
    CG, Apr 10, HAY, May 22, Aug 28, CG, Nov 8, Dec 10, 13; 1772: CG, Jan 24, DL,
    Mar 21, CG, May 4, 26, Oct 9, Nov 24; 1773: CG, Mar 13, Apr 14, May 4, Oct 1,
    30; 1774: CG, Feb 2, Mar 22, Apr 25, May 17, Nov 29; 1775: CG, Feb 21, Apr
    25, May 20, Nov 16, 27; 1776: CG, Jan 11, Mar 7, 26, Oct 24, Nov 9; 1777: CG,
    Nov 17, 18, Dec 19; 1778: CG, May 9, Dec 2, 10; 1779: CG, Apr 9, May 13, Dec
    18; 1780: CG, Jan 18, Feb 1, 28, Sep 21, Nov 24, Dec 23; 1781: CG, Mar 24,
    May 10; 1782: CG, Apr 24, Sep 23; 1784: CG, Dec 1; 1791: CG, Feb 2; 1794: CG,
    Apr 23
--Way to Keep Him, The, 1760: DL, Jan 24, 25, 26, 28, 29, 31, Feb 1, 2, 4, 5,
    9, Mar 18, Apr 26, May 29; 1761: DL, Jan 10, 12, 13, 15, 16, 20, 22, 27, Feb
    10, Mar 27, Dec 17, 21; 1762: DL, Jan 21, Mar 27; 1763: DL, Mar 19, Apr 11,
    May 28; 1764: DL, Jan 3, 10, 12, Mar 29, Nov 8, Dec 31; 1765: DL, Feb 7, Apr
    11, May 14, Oct 11, Nov 27, 29; 1766: DL, Jan 28; 1767: DL, Apr 22; 1768: CG,
    Mar 24, DL, Apr 6, 18, May 9, Oct 19, CG, Nov 8, 16, Dec 30; 1769: DL, Apr
    18, May 20, Nov 15, CG, 23, DL, Dec 19; 1770: DL, Jan 1, CG, May 21, DL, 22,
    CG, Sep 24, Oct 3, DL, 26, CG, Nov 7, Dec 29; 1771: CG, Jan 24, DL, Apr 20,
    May 23, Oct 31, CG, Nov 19; 1772: CG, Jan 7, DL, Feb 25, May 25, Oct 15;
    1773: DL, Jan 15, Apr 22; 1774: DL, Jan 22, May 12; 1776: CG, Jan 24, Mar 4,
    DL, 21, CG, May 15; 1777: DL, Mar 31, Apr 16; 1779: DL, Mar 15; 1780: CG, Jan
    7, 15; 1781: DL, Apr 24, Oct 16, 18, 23, 31, Nov 9, 19; 1782: DL, Mar 18, Apr
    19, Oct 29, Dec 3; 1783: DL, Jan 8; 1785: CG, Mar 5, 10, 14, 17, 31, Apr 7,
    DL, May 11, CG, Oct 19, DL, Nov 5, 26, 29, 30; 1786: DL, Feb 6, May 18, HAMM,
    Aug 8; 1787: CG, Mar 15, Apr 23, DL, May 21, Sep 25, Oct 2, 16; 1788: DL, Jan

9, Mar 27, CG, Apr 25, DL, May 19; 1789: CG, Jan 15, Dec 11; 1790: CG, Jan 15, Feb 12, Apr 29, DL, Dec 1; 1791: DLKING'S, Dec 19; 1793: CG, Oct 15, 17; 1794: CG, Jan 25; 1797: CG, Dec 8; 1798: CG, Jan 3
--What We Must All Come To, 1763: CG, Dec 31; 1764: CG, Jan 9; 1767: DL, Apr 22; 1776: CG, Mar 30
--Zenobia, 1768: DL, Feb 27, Mar 1, 3, 5, 8, 10, 19, May 11, 12, Dec 3, 6, 12; 1769: DL, Mar 13; 1770: DL, Feb 3, Mar 26, Apr 5, May 1, Nov 17, Dec 18; 1771: DL, May 10; 1773: DL, May 19; 1775: DL, Mar 21; 1776: CG, Nov 21, 23, Dec 23; 1777: CG, Oct 21; 1784: CG, Jan 22; 1786: CG, May 5; 1787: CG, Jan 8, Oct 31
Murray (actor), 1772: HAY, Dec 21
Murray and Greenlaw (publishers), 1778: DL, Mar 30
Murray, Andrew (actor), 1781: CII, Apr 5; 1784: HAY, Feb 9; 1785: HAY, Jan 24, HAMM, Jun 17; 1791: HAY, Dec 12; 1792: HAY, Dec 26; 1797: HAY, Dec 4
Murray, Ann, Mrs Charles (actor), 1799: CG, May 10
Murray, Charles (actor), 1796: CG, Sep 30, Oct 13, 20, 24, 26, Nov 5, 19, 21, 24, 25, Dec 19, 21, 26, 28; 1797: CG, Jan 10, Feb 13, 18, 20, Apr 25, 29, May 4, 6, 16, 17, DL, 29, CG, 31, Jun 10, 13, 14, Sep 18, 22, 25, 27, Oct 2, 6, 12, 13, 16, 20, 21, 23, 28, Nov 3, 11, 18, 20, 23, 29, Dec 8, 12, 16, 20, 26, 27; 1798: CG, Jan 4, Feb 13, Mar 20, 31, Apr 17, 28, 30, May 4, 9, 10, 12, 15, 22, 23, 24, 28, 30, Jun 1, Sep 17, 21, 28, Oct 1, 5, 11, 15, 19, Nov 23; 1799: CG, Jan 12, Feb 4, Mar 14, 16, Apr 8, 9, 12, 16, 23, 30, May 4, 6, 10, 15, 18, 24, Sep 20, 23, 25, 30, Oct 4, 9, 10, 14, 16, 17, 18, 21, 24, Nov 7, 30, Dec 23, 30; 1800: CG, Jan 16, 29, Feb 3, 8, 15, 19, Mar 27, Apr 22, 23, 26, 29, 30, May 2, 12, 13, 23, 27, 29, Jun 2
Murray, Harriet (actor), 1798: CG, May 12; 1799: CG, Mar 16, 25, May 10, Jun 10, Oct 17, Nov 30; 1800: CG, Jan 29, Feb 8, Mar 27, Apr 5, 22, 23, 26, 30, May 12, 13, 23, 29, Jun 2
Murray, John (publisher), 1781: CG, Apr 20; 1787: HAY, Sep 5
Murray, Mrs (actor), 1791: HAY, Dec 12; 1792: HAY, Feb 6, Dec 26
Murray, Sir Robert (spectator), 1667: NONE, Feb 12
Murry (actor), 1749: SOU, Jan 9
Musardo (actor), 1754: HAY, Sep 10
Muscovita, Sga. See Panichi, Lucia.
Muscovy, Czar of, 1697: DLORDG, Dec 18; 1698: DG, Jan 15, YB, Feb 10, DL, 12, DLORLIF, 24; 1708: DL, Jun 3
Muse of Newmarket, The; or, Mirth and Drollery (entertainment), 1679: NONE, Sep 0; 1746: DL, May 2
Muses on Mount Parnassus (dance), 1787: KING'S, Mar 1
Muses' Looking Glass, The. See Randolph, Thomas.
Music a la Mode; or, Bayes in Chromatics (burletta), 1764: DL, Apr 12, 14
Music in Four Acts (entertainment), 1762: RANELAGH, Jun 16
Music School, 1672: WF, Dec 30; 1673: WF, Sep 4, 27, Nov 20, Dec 22; 1674: WF, Jan 12, Apr 20, Sep 29, Oct 31; 1675: BANNSTER, Nov 25; 1678: EB, Nov 22, 25; 1679: EB, Jan 9
Music spread thy voice (song), 1789: CG, Mar 20; 1794: CG, Mar 26
Music; or, A Parley of Instruments. See Banister, John.
Musical Address (song), 1799: DL, May 9; 1800: DL, Jun 7
Musical Courtship (song), 1791: CG, May 6, 27
Musical Dialogue (song), 1706: QUEEN'S, Mar 4
Musical Dramatick Poem, A (entertainment), 1741: HIC, Feb 6, 13, 20
Musical Elegy on the late Mr Palmer (song), 1798: HAY, Aug 23
Musical Epilogue (song), 1741: CG, Apr 10; 1743: CG, Apr 15; 1787: HAY, Aug 14, 21
Musical Imitations (entertainment), 1771: MARLY, May 23, Jun 4, Jul 18, 27, Aug 3, 8, 20, 22, 27, 29, Sep 3, 5, 10, 17; 1772: MARLY, Aug 20, 25
Musical Lady, The. See Colman the elder, George.
Musical Prologue (song), 1760: KING'S, Dec 16
Musical Society, 1728: CRT, Dec 18
Musicians' Fund, 1772: KING'S, Feb 21
Musidorus (author), 1766: KING'S, Jan 25
Mussini, Nicolo (singer), 1790: HAY, Feb 27, Mar 25, Apr 6, Jun 8, CG, Jul 10
Mussolini (musician), 1773: CG, Apr 27
Mussot, Jean Francois. See Arnould.
Mussulmo, Mahomet Acmed Vizaro (entertainer), 1747: BFH, Aug 22
Must I my Acis still bemoan? (song), 1776: DL, Feb 23; 1787: DL, Mar 7; 1791: DL, Apr 1; 1792: KING'S, Feb 29; 1794: DL, Mar 26
Mustapha. See Boyle, Roger; Mallet, David.
Mutes (actor), 1760: CG, Apr 14
Mutineers, The; or, Love in Excess (farce, anon), 1744: JS, Dec 10
Mutius Scaevola. See Rolli, Paolo Antonio.
Mutual Deception, The. See Atkinson, Joseph.

Muzette (dance), <u>1725</u>: DL, Feb 9, Mar 31; <u>1726</u>: DL, Feb 8, Mar 31, Apr 21, 27,
29, May 3, 4, 5, 13, 17, 25; <u>1727</u>: DL, Apr 20, May 2, 10, 19, 22; <u>1728</u>: DL,
May 7, 15; <u>1729</u>: DL, May 2, Oct 9; <u>1732</u>: DL, Apr 18, LIF/CG, Oct 25; <u>1733</u>:
LIF/CG, Apr 30, May 14, 18, 21, Jun 1; <u>1739</u>: CG, Dec 22, 26; <u>1741</u>: CG, Mar
30, Apr 8, May 12, 15, DL, Nov 14, Dec 3; <u>1742</u>: CG, Apr 5, 20, Dec 1, 2, 9,
10, 13; <u>1743</u>: CG, Apr 8
Muzioli (dancer), <u>1763</u>: CG, Mar 8
My arms against this Gorgias (song), <u>1790</u>: DL, Mar 10, 12, CG, 19; <u>1791</u>: CG,
Apr 15; <u>1794</u>: CG, Mar 7; <u>1795</u>: CG, Feb 20; <u>1798</u>: CG, Mar 28, 30
My bliss too long (song), <u>1781</u>: CG, Nov 8
My cup is full (song), <u>1799</u>: CG, Mar 13
My dear Molly-oh! what Folly (song), <u>1797</u>: CG, Jun 9
My dearest, my fairest (song), <u>1696</u>: DL, Apr 0
My Dolly was the fairest Thing (song), <u>1800</u>: CG, Apr 26, May 2
My Faith and Truth (song), <u>1744</u>: CG, Mar 13, Apr 2, 28; <u>1746</u>: DL, Jan 4, 16,
Mar 1, Apr 10; <u>1790</u>: DL, Mar 17, 24; <u>1793</u>: KING/HAY, Feb 15; <u>1794</u>: DL, Apr 4,
11; <u>1796</u>: CG, Feb 24, DL, May 11; <u>1797</u>: CG, Mar 10; <u>1798</u>: CG, Mar 9; <u>1799</u>:
CG, Mar 15; <u>1800</u>: CG, Mar 14, 21
My Fond Shepherd (song), <u>1757</u>: CG, May 2; <u>1760</u>: DL, Apr 16
My Friend is the Man I'd copy through Life (song), <u>1799</u>: DL, May 17
My God my soul is vexed (song), <u>1789</u>: DL, Mar 25
My Grandmother. See Hoare, Prince.
My Heart is inditing (song), <u>1761</u>: KING'S, Mar 12; <u>1775</u>: DL, Mar 17; <u>1777</u>: CG,
Mar 19, 21; <u>1781</u>: DL, Mar 30; <u>1787</u>: DL, Mar 7; <u>1788</u>: DL, Mar 5
My Joe Jannet (song), <u>1791</u>: CG, May 18
My Lucy, alas, is no more (song), <u>1784</u>: DL, Apr 12; <u>1787</u>: HAY, Aug 14
My mother bids me bind my hair (song), <u>1799</u>: HAY, Aug 13, Sep 16
My mother had a maid called Barbara (song), <u>1795</u>: CG, Apr 24; <u>1796</u>: CG, Mar 14,
Apr 1, May 17
My name's O'Flanagan (song), <u>1795</u>: CG, Nov 16
My name's Ted Blarney (song), <u>1792</u>: CG, May 28
My name's Tippy Bob (song), <u>1795</u>: CG, May 16
My Nightgown and Slippers. See Colman the younger, George.
My Poll and my Partner Joe (song), <u>1791</u>: DL, May 17, 18; <u>1792</u>: DLKING'S, Apr 10
My Song shall be Alway (song), <u>1740</u>: HIC, Apr 2
My sweet, pretty Mogg (song), <u>1779</u>: HAY(Oct 18
My sweetest Honoria (song), <u>1793</u>: CG, Apr 25
My wife has a tongue as good as e'er twanged (song), <u>1683</u>: NONE, Sep 0
My Willy was a Sailor bold (song), <u>1798</u>: CG, Oct 15
Mylius, Christlob (visitor), <u>1753</u>: CG, Nov 12
Mynit, William (actor), <u>1732</u>: HAY, Nov 16; <u>1733</u>: HAY, Mar 14, 16, 20, 21
Mynns. See Mines; Minns.
Mynns, Mrs. See Minns, Mrs.
Myra's Choice (song), <u>1730</u>: GF, Jun 2
Myres (musician), <u>1675</u>: ATCOURT, Feb 15
Myrtillo (dance), <u>1716</u>: DL, May 31, Dec 13; <u>1717</u>: DL, Jan 29, Feb 6, Mar 14;
<u>1718</u>: DL, Mar 13, Oct 18; <u>1719</u>: DL, Mar 5, Apr 18, Oct 7, Nov 10; <u>1720</u>: DL,
Feb 29, Apr 18, 26, Oct 18; <u>1721</u>: DL, Feb 25, Apr 14, LIF, Oct 17, DL, 19,
LIF, 21, DL, 23; <u>1722</u>: DL, Mar 10, LIF, May 2, 10, 23, DL, 25, 29, Oct 15,
LIF, Dec 13, 22; <u>1723</u>: LIF, Feb 13, DL, Apr 29, May 9, LIF, 15, 18, Oct 7;
<u>1724</u>: DL, Feb 1, LIF, Apr 8, DL, 13, LIF, 21, 24, 27, 28, May 2, 7, 12, 16,
22, Nov 3, 10, 13, 18; <u>1725</u>: DL, Feb 4, Mar 31, Apr 2, LIF, 14, DL, 16, LIF,
20, DL, 24, LIF, 26, 30, DL, 30, May 13, LIF, 18, 22, DL, Sep 25, LIF, Oct 4,
DL, 7, LIF, 8, DL, Nov 27, Dec 16; <u>1726</u>: DL, Jan 25, Mar 21, LIF, Apr 22, DL,
Dec 17; <u>1727</u>: DL, Feb 10, 18, Mar 13, May 24, Oct 5; <u>1728</u>: DL, Mar 28, Apr 8,
May 23, Sep 12, Oct 21; <u>1729</u>: LIF, Apr 22, 26, May 8, 22; <u>1730</u>: DL, Apr 13,
May 4; <u>1732</u>: DL, Apr 18, 26, 27, May 4, Sep 8; <u>1735</u>: DL, May 7
Myrtillo. See Cibber, Colley.
Myself I shall adore (song), <u>1745</u>: CG, Apr 10; <u>1748</u>: CG, Apr 13; <u>1757</u>: CG, Apr
22
Myslivecek, Josef (composer), <u>1778</u>: KING'S, Nov 28; <u>1779</u>: KING'S, Nov 27
Mysteries of the Castle, The. See Andrews, Miles Peter.
Mysterious Husband, The. See Cumberland, Richard.
Mytton (tavern keeper), <u>1746</u>: CG, Apr 24

N, Lord, <u>1691</u>: DLORDG, Oct 1
N, N (author)
--Rome's Follies; or, The Amorous Fryars, <u>1681</u>: NONE, Sep 0
N, N (dancer), <u>1776</u>: KING'S, Jan 9, Feb 13, Mar 7

N, N (singer), 1760: KING'S, Aug 25
Nabal. See Handel, George Frederic.
Nabbes, Thomas (author), 1746: DL, May 2
Nabob, The. See Foote, Samuel.
Nag's Head Tavern, 1787: HAY, Mar 12
Naiads' Dance (dance), 1799: CG, Dec 10
Nailer (beneficiary), 1723: DL, May 28
Naked Boy Coffee House, 1751: DL, Mar 12
Nancy of the Dale (song), 1786: DL, May 5
Nancy. See Carey, Henry.
Nando's Coffee House, 1745: DL, Apr 16; 1750: DL, Nov 28; 1751: DL, May 14
Nanetta E Lubino. See Pugnani, Gaetano.
Nanfan, Master (dancer), 1741: GF, Feb 19, Mar 3, Apr 28, BFTY, Aug 22
Nanine. See Voltaire.
Nanny O (song), 1745: DL, Apr 17, 22, 29; 1752: DL, Apr 24
Nansan, Master (beneficiary), 1737: LIF, May 7, 10
Napier, Mrs (actor), 1676: DG, Aug 0, Nov 4, Dec 0; 1677: DG, May 31
Napier, William (viola player), 1795: CG, Feb 20, 27
Naples Bay. See Cross, John Cartwright.
Naples Opera, 1782: KING'S, May 2, Nov 30
Naples Theatre, 1759: HAY, Jan 12, MARLY, Apr 16; 1784: KING'S, Dec 18
Naples, King of, 1794: KING'S, May 15
Naples, 1728: HAY, Apr 3; 1736: TC, Aug 4; 1749: KING'S, Feb 28; 1763: KING'S,
    Mar 24; 1789: KING'S, Mar 24; 1792: HAY, Mar 31; 1793: KING'S, May 14; 1794:
    KING'S, Mar 18, May 15, Jun 23; 1795: KING'S, Feb 20; 1796: KING'S, Feb 16,
    Apr 16, Dec 6; 1797: KING'S, Apr 27; 1798: KING'S, Apr 21, 26; 1799: KING'S,
    Jan 22
Narcissus. See Scarlatti, Dominico.
Narcotic, The. See Powell, James.
Nardini (composer), 1773: HAY, Feb 26, DL, Mar 5
Nares, Rev Robert (prologuist), 1793: CG, Jan 29
Nares' scholars (singer), 1771: DL, Nov 12, Dec 4; 1772: DL, Mar 3, May 23, Dec
    11
Narr (actor), 1776: DL, Mar 28; see also Marr
Narrative of the Rise and Progress of the Disputes (pamphlet), 1768: CG, Mar 1
Nasaquitine, Don John de, 1749: DL, Jan 27
Nasce al Bosco (song), 1764: KING'S, Mar 29; 1786: DL, Mar 10; 1789: DL, Mar
    18; 1790: DL, Feb 24
Nash, Joseph (actor), 1776: DL, Dec 31; 1777: DL, Jan 1, Feb 24, Oct 17; 1778:
    DL, Jan 3, Feb 24, May 19, Nov 10, Dec 21; 1779: DL, Jan 8, Mar 13, Apr 28,
    Oct 5; 1780: DL, Jan 26, May 5, 17, Sep 30, Oct 17, Nov 4, Dec 27; 1781: DL,
    May 18, Sep 25; 1782: DL, Jan 3, May 16; 1786: HAY, Mar 6, HAMM, Aug 5
Nash, Miss (actor), 1782: HAY, Nov 25
Naso, Miss (dancer), 1735: HAY, Jun 12
Nasolini, Sebastiano
--Andromaca (opera), 1790: HAY, May 28, 29, Jun 8, CG, 15, 19, Jul 6
Nassau (dance), 1733: CG, Nov 12, 13, 14, 15, 16, 20, 23, 28, 30, Dec 6, 11,
    17, 28; 1734: CG, Jan 17, 21, Mar 11, 12, 19, Apr 16, 18, 22, 26, 27, May 1,
    CG/LIF, Oct 26, 31
Nassau St, 1736: CG, Apr 29; 1742: DL, Apr 5, 22; 1743: DL, Apr 20; 1744: DL,
    Apr 9, 23, HAY, Dec 11; 1791: CG, Feb 15; 1792: CG, Apr 14; 1793: CG, Apr 17
Natalia, The (music), 1734: DL/HAY, Jan 26
Nathan, Mrs (singer), 1789: HAY, Feb 23
National Prejudice, The. See Simon; Hiffernan, Dr Paul.
Natural Magick. See Motteux, Peter Anthony.
Natural Son, The. See Cumberland, Richard.
Naturalizing Bill, 1753: DL, Sep 8
Nature Framed thee sure for loving (song), 1746: DL, Apr 12
Nature Will Prevail. See Walpole, Horace.
Naufrage, Le. See LaFont, Joseph de.
Naumann, Johann Gottlieb (composer), 1790: CG, Dec 20; 1794: KING'S, Dec 20
Naval History (song), 1800: CG, Apr 26, May 2
Naval Interlude, A (interlude, anon), 1798: HAY, Mar 26
Naval Pillar, The. See Dibdin, Thomas John.
Naval Review, Grand (entertainment), 1776: DL, Nov 9; 1781: DL, May 10; 1783:
    DL, Sep 27; 1785: DL, Jan 6; 1794: CG, May 9
Naval Volunteers, The; or, Britain's Bulwark (interlude, anon), 1795: CG, Apr
    28, May 7
Navy and Army of Britain forever (song), 1799: CG, Oct 7
Nawcheys, Emperor of the (American Indian), 1719: LIF, Dec 21; see also
    American Princes; Indian Kings, American
Nayler (actor), 1741: TC, Aug 4

Naylor (Nailor) (actor), 1740: GF, Nov 3, 4, 15, Dec 15; 1741: GF, Jan 15, Feb
    9, 10, 19, Mar 3, Sep 16, 23, Oct 9, 16, 19, Nov 4, 9, Dec 9, 16, 23; 1742:
    GF, Apr 21, May 18, LIF, Dec 27; 1743: LIF, Jan 7, Feb 14, HAY, Apr 14; 1744:
    MF, Jun 7, HAY, Sep 27, 29, Oct 4, 11, 18; 1745: GF, Apr 15
Naylor (gallery doorkeeper), 1726: LIF, May 30; 1731: LIF, May 21; 1732: LIF,
    May 15; 1734: CG, May 17; 1738: CG, May 8; 1739: CG, May 28; 1740: CG, May
    19; 1741: CG, May 7; 1742: CG, May 11
Naylor, Miss (actor, dancer), 1740: GF, Oct 24, 29, Nov 10, Dec 15; 1741: GF,
    Jan 15, Feb 10, Apr 2, 16, Oct 9, 19; 1742: GF, Jan 19, Feb 3, 19, Mar 29,
    Apr 24, LIF, Dec 27; 1743: LIF, Apr 4
Naylor, Mrs (actor), 1765: CG, May 16; 1766: CG, May 9; 1767: CG, May 20; 1768:
    CG, May 25; 1769: CG, May 17, 18; 1770: CG, May 25; 1771: CG, May 28
Neale (actor), 1784: HAY, Sep 17
Neale (grocer), 1762: HAY, Sep 7
Neale (hat maker), 1775: DL, Oct 24
Neale, Charles (musician, actor), 1720: HIC, Mar 4, LIF, Dec 23; 1722: SH, Feb
    9; 1727: LIF, May 10; 1729: LIF, May 6; 1731: LIF, May 24; 1732: LIF/CG, Oct
    6, 16, Nov 8, 22, Dec 7, 14, 27, 28; 1733: LIF/CG, Jan 15, CG/LIF, 25,
    LIF/CG, 27, CG, Feb 8, LIF/CG, Mar 29, 30, Apr 24, 30, CG, May 1, LIF/CG, 8,
    10, Jun 1, CG, Sep 15, 20, 25, 27, 29, Oct 4, 6, 9, 11, 19, 29, Nov 1, 3, 14,
    16, 17, 21, Dec 20, 31; 1734: CG, Jan 1, 16, Mar 5, 28, Apr 16, May 2, 7,
    CG/LIF, Oct 7, LIF, 12, CG/LIF, 18, 29, Nov 1, 7, 21, Dec 5, 31; 1735:
    CG/LIF, Jan 6, 17, 21, Feb 3, 4, Mar 20, 29, Apr 9, 10, CG, 25, CG/LIF, May
    1, 2, 12, 13, 14, DL, Jul 1, GF/HAY, 15, CG, Sep 16, 17, 26, Oct 8, 13, 24,
    29, Nov 7, 10, 22, 29, Dec 8, 27; 1736: CG, Jan 8, 9, Feb 26, May 13, 20, 24,
    31, Sep 17, 24, 29, Oct 1, 20, 25, 29, Nov 1, 8, 11, 15, 25, Dec 6; 1737: CG,
    Jan 10, Feb 15, Apr 26, May 10, Sep 30, Oct 3, 5, 10, 21, 26, 28, 29, Nov 2,
    10; 1738: CG, Jan 9, 18, 25, Feb 16, 23, Mar 14, 20, 25, Apr 28, May 5, Sep
    22, 27, Oct 6, 13, 20, 23, 30, Nov 2, 8, 11, 15, 28, Dec 4, 5, 11; 1739: CG,
    Jan 8, 20, Feb 10, 16, 26, Mar 27, Apr 3, 5, 25, May 5, 7, 11, 17, 21, 23,
    25, Sep 12, 14, 17, 22, 25, 28, Oct 5, 10, 25, 26, 29, Nov 6, 9, 10, 13, 17,
    20, Dec 6, 10, 15, 19, 21; 1740: CG, Jan 12, 15, Mar 11, 18, 24, 27, May 2,
    9, Jun 5, Sep 19, 22, 24, 26, 29, Oct 1, 3, 8, 24, 27, 29, Nov 1, 6, 10, 15,
    Dec 4, 10, 13, 19, 20, 22, 29; 1741: CG, Jan 2, 6, 7, 9, 12, 15, 21, 23, Feb
    7, 14, Mar 30, Apr 3, 7, 11, 17, 27, 30, DL, Sep 5, 8, 10, 12, 15, 22, Oct 6,
    21, Nov 2, 9, 11, 16, 20, 21, CG, 30, DL, Dec 7, 12; 1742: DL, Jan 4, 6, 8,
    Feb 11, 12, 13, Mar 29, Apr 24, 29, May 6, 10, 12, 18, 27, 28, Sep 11, 18,
    25, 28, Oct 2, 7, 9, 12, 18, 26, 27, Nov 1, 8, 12, 16, 19, Dec 14, CG, 22,
    DL, 22; 1743: DL, Jan 28, Feb 17, Mar 21, SOU, 30, DL, Apr 7, 15, 27, Sep 15,
    17, 20, 22, 24, 29, Oct 4, 11, 13, 22, 25, Nov 8, 12, 23, 26, 29, Dec 1, 9,
    15, 16; 1744: DL, Jan 7, 13, 27, Mar 10, 12, Apr 2, 3, 17, 23, May 1, CG, 2,
    DL, 4, 14, Sep 15, 18, 20, 29, Oct 2, 6, 9, 19, 22, 24, 30, Nov 1, 2, 6, 16,
    Dec 11, 19; 1745: DL, Jan 4, 10, Feb 11, Apr 17, 19, May 1, Sep 19, 21, 24,
    26, 28, Oct 3, 10, 12, 15, 17, Nov 1, 14, 18, 22, 23, 25, 26, Dec 11, 13, 20,
    30; 1746: DL, Jan 2, 14, Mar 13, 18, Apr 4, 15, 18, 21, 23, May 14, Sep 23,
    25, Oct 2, 23, 27, 31, Nov 1, 5, 7, 21, Dec 1, 26, 29, 30; 1747: DL, Jan 2,
    3, Mar 3, 7, 23, 24, 28, Apr 11, 28, Sep 15, 22, 24, Oct 3, 15, 21, 24, 29,
    30, Nov 16, 17, Dec 16; 1748: DL, Jan 6, 12, 18, 22, Feb 3, Mar 19, Apr 13,
    28, May 6, Sep 17, 20, Oct 8, 13, 19, 28, 29, Nov 1, 3, 7, 9, 11, 14, Dec 21,
    26, 28; 1749: DL, Jan 13, Apr 7, May 16, Sep 20, 21, 28, Oct 13, 14, 17, 18,
    28, 30, Nov 21, Dec 30; 1750: DL, Jan 10, 13, 23
Nealson (actor), 1744: HAY, Apr 6
Neapolitan Dance (dance), 1710: GR, Jul 22
Neate, Charles (pianist), 1800: CG, Feb 28, Apr 4
Neck or Nothing. See Garrick, David.
Necromancer, The; or, Harlequin Doctor Faustus (pantomime), 1723: LIF, Dec 20,
    21; 1724: LIF, Jan 7, 8, 9, 10, 11, 13, 14, 15, 16, 17, 18, 20, 21, 22, 23,
    24, 25, 27, 28, 29, 31, Feb 1, 3, 4, 5, 6, 7, 8, 10, 11, 12, 13, 14, 15, 17,
    18, 20, 22, Mar 3, 7, 14, 17, 21, 24, Apr 11, 18, May 1, 21, 30, Jun 5, Sep
    30, Oct 2, 17, 24, 31, Nov 7, 21, 23; 1725: LIF, Jan 1, 7, 9, Mar 20, 30, Apr
    9, 24, May 27, Nov 3, 10, 19, 25, Dec 1, 13, 22, 27, 28; 1726: LIF, Jan 6,
    11, Apr 12, Sep 16, Oct 10, 21, Nov 7, Dec 5; 1727: LIF, Jan 11, May 30, Sep
    22, Oct 6, 23, 25, Nov 6, Dec 9, 18, 28, 29, 30; 1728: LIF, Jan 22, 26, Oct
    26, 29, Nov 2, 29, Dec 30; 1729: LIF, Jan 28, Feb 1, 3, 11, 22, Mar 3, 13,
    May 2, Sep 26, 29, Oct 10, 30, Nov 29, Dec 2, 13, 22, 27; 1730: LIF, Jan 22,
    29, Oct 1, 2, 21, 26, Nov 4, Dec 29; 1731: LIF, Jan 27, 29, Mar 9, Oct 15,
    22, Nov 4, 5, 27, 30, Dec 6, 8, 22, 29; 1732: LIF, Jan 12, 17, 18, 20, Feb 1,
    5, 8, 22, 29, May 29, 31, LIF/CG, Oct 13, 21, 23, 28, Nov 3, Dec 26; 1734:
    CG, Feb 26, 28, Mar 2, 4, 14, 30, Apr 4, 15, 20, 23, May 24, CG/LIF, Oct 2,
    4, 16, 19, 21, 25, GF, 28, 29, CG/LIF, 29, GF, 30, 31, Nov 1, 4, CG/LIF, 4,
    GF, 5, CG/LIF, 5, GF, 6, CG/LIF, 6, GF, 7, 11, 12, 13, CG/LIF, 14, GF, 14,
    15, 16, CG/LIF, Dec 6, 19, 26, 27; 1735: CG/LIF, Jun 2, CG, Sep 24, 26, Oct

1, 6, 8, 10, Nov 1, 3, GF, 17, 18, 20, 21, 22, 24, CG, Dec 10, 11, 17, 20,
22, 29, 31; 1736: CG, Sep 22, 24, 27, Oct 1, Dec 28; 1737: CG, Jan 13, 14,
18, Oct 7, 14, 17, 19, 21, 22, 24; 1738: CG, Apr 3, Oct 4, 9, 11, 14, 16, 21,
Nov 9, Dec 8; 1739: CG, Jan 2, Feb 14, May 8, 10, 12, 21, Oct 20, 22, 24, 30,
Nov 30; 1740: CG, Jan 1, Oct 22, 29, Nov 4, 5, Dec 29; 1741: CG, Jan 1, Sep
28, Oct 2, 5, 7, 10, 13, 14, 21, 30, Nov 4, 23, Dec 21; 1742: CG, Jan 1, Oct
16, 29; 1743: CG, Jan 27, Feb 3, Apr 29, Dec 26; 1744: CG, Jan 10, 31, Feb 9,
Mar 31, Apr 21, Oct 31, Nov 1, 3, 8, 12, Dec 31; 1745: GF, May 6, 9; 1751:
CG, Nov 11, 13, 14, 16, 20, 21, 22, 23, 25, 26, 27, 28, 29, 30, Dec 2, 3, 20,
27, 30; 1752: CG, Jan 2, 4, 10, 14, 18, 22, 24, Dec 7, 11, 13, 14, 15, 16,
19, 20, 27, 29; 1753: CG, Jan 5; 1766: CG, Nov 8, Dec 8; 1767: CG, Oct 12,
Nov 6; 1793: CG, Dec 19
Nee Galon, Le (dance), 1754: HAY, Jul 9
Needham, Dr Jaspar (spectator), 1697: LIF, Feb 22
Neglected Virtue; or, The Unhappy Conquerors (play, anon), 1696: DL, Feb 0
Negligente, Il. See Ciampi, Lorenzo.
Negri, Maria Catterina (singer), 1733: KING'S, Oct 30, Nov 13, Dec 4; 1734:
KING'S, Jan 26, Mar 13, Apr 2, 27, May 18, CG/LIF, Nov 9; 1735: CG, Jan 8,
Mar 5, Apr 16; 1736: CG, May 12, Dec 8; 1737: CG, Jan 12, Feb 16, Mar 9, 23,
May 18
Negri, Maria Rosa (singer), 1733: KING'S, Oct 30, Dec 4; 1734: KING'S, Mar 13,
Apr 2, 27, CG/LIF, Nov 9
Negri, Teresa (singer), 1794: KING'S, Mar 1, 18
Negro boy (musician), 1737: SH, Mar 11; 1738: DL, Mar 3
Negro Boy (song), 1799: CG, Jun 7
Negro Dance (dance), 1788: CG, Oct 22, 25; 1789: CG, Jan 1, Mar 10, May 6, Jun
18, Oct 13, Dec 22; 1791: CG, Apr 28, Nov 2, 9; 1792: CG, Apr 25, May 30, Sep
26; 1794: CG, Jun 14; 1796: CG, Apr 15; 1798: CG, Oct 15; 1799: CG, Mar 5,
May 13, Jun 5, Dec 16; 1800: CG, Apr 23
Negro Song (song), 1743: IT, Dec 26; 1790: CG, Apr 22; 1795: CG, May 6; 1797:
CG, May 11
Negus (singer), 1786: DL, Mar 8, 10
Nel pensare al gran cimento (song), 1758: KING'S, Apr 6; 1762: KING'S, May 11
Nel pugnar (song), 1740: DL, Mar 25
Nel riposo (song), 1786: DL, Mar 10, 29
Nelson (actor), 1766: HAY, Jun 26, Jul 1, 15, KING'S, Aug 13, 18, Sep 5
Nelson (actor), 1778: HAY, Apr 9
Nelson (actor, musician), 1736: LIF, Nov 20; 1740: GF, Oct 20, 23, Nov 4, 22,
24, 28, Dec 11, 15; 1741: GF, Jan 15, 29, Feb 10, Mar 3, 7, 12, Apr 24; 1744:
HAY, May 10, Jun 29
Nelson, Admiral Lord, 1798: DL, Oct 2
Nelson, Master (actor), 1778: CHR, May 29, Jun 1, 3, 8, 10, 18, 26
Nelson, Mrs (actor), 1733: GF, Apr 30
Neopolitan band, 1736: BFF, Aug 23, NONE, Sep 7
Neopolitan Punch (dance), 1742: DL, Dec 31; 1743: DL, Jan 11, 12, 14, 18, 20,
Feb 15, Mar 24, Apr 6, 11, 23, 26
Neopolitans, The (dance), 1753: DL, Nov 1, 3, 5, 7, 13
Nep, Mrs. See Knepp, Elizabeth.
Nepolitano, Egidio Duni (composer), 1737: KING'S, May 24
Neptune (song), 1793: HAY, Nov 19, Dec 26
Neptune and Amphitrite (masque), 1727: DL, May 22; 1729: DL, May 28, Oct 30;
1745: GF, Feb 14, Dec 4; 1746: DL, Jan 31, Feb 1, 4, 5, 18, May 19; 1747: DL,
Dec 26; 1750: DL, Jan 1, 19; 1789: DL, Oct 13; 1790: DL, Jan 25, Oct 11;
1791: DLKING'S, Nov 9, 25, Dec 14, 27; 1792: DLKING'S, Apr 12, May 8, DL, Dec
13; 1793: DL, Jan 2, May 7, HAY, Nov 19; 1797: DL, Feb 22, 28, Mar 18, Dec 9,
23; 1798: DL, Feb 24, Jun 5; 1799: DL, May 4, Nov 14
Neptune's Address to His Most Sacred Majesty Charles the Second. See Tatham,
John.
Neptune's Palace (masque), 1740: BFH, Aug 23
Neptune's Prophecy (entertainment), 1792: DLKING'S, May 23, 25, 28, Jun 2, 11
Nerborn (musician), 1798: HAY, Jan 15
Neri, G B (author), 1709: QUEEN'S, Mar 2
Neri, Gaetano (actor), 1790: HAY, Jan 7, Feb 2, 27, Jun 3
Neri, Michaelangelo (actor), 1794: KING'S, Dec 20
Nericault, Philippe (author), 1777: CG, Feb 22; 1780: DL, Nov 22; 1781: HAY,
Nov 12; 1789: HAY, Jul 15; 1790: DL, Nov 17; 1791: CG, Feb 4, HAY, Jul 9;
1792: HAY, Aug 23; see also Destouches
Nerina (opera), 1751: HAY, Feb 16, 23, Mar 2
Nerone (pastiche), 1753: KING'S, Nov 13, 17, 20, 24; 1754: KING'S, Feb 12, 28
Nesbit, J, 1794: DL, Jul 2
Nest of Fools. See Brome, Sir Richard, The Northern Lass.
Nest of Plays, The. See Jacob, Hildebrand.

Nestor's Advice to his Master when in Council (song), 1739: CG, Apr 27
Netley Abbey. See Pearce, William.
Neuman, Henry, 1799: HAY, Jun 15
--Family Distress, 1799: HAY, Jun 15, 17, 18, 19, 20
Nevelong. See Nivelon.
Nevil, George, Lord Abergavenny (spectator), 1697: LIF, Mar 4
Nevill, Mrs (actor), 1782: DL, Mar 14, May 4
Neville, Edward, 1779: CG, Oct 20
--Plymouth In An Uproar (farce), 1779: CG, Oct 20, 22, 25, 27, 29, 30, Nov 1,
   3, 8
Neville, Sylas (diarist), 1767: DL, Mar 31, Apr 21, CG, 24, DL, 25, CG, May 5,
   DL, 18, HAY, Jun 25, 26, 30, CG, Oct 6, DL, 9, CG, Dec 9, DL, 15, 23, CG, 26,
   31
New Anthem. See Shaw Jr, Thomas.
New Athenian Comedy, The. See Settle, Elkanah.
New Bagnio, 1739: DL, Apr 7
New Blown Rose (song), 1785: CG, Apr 25
New Bond St, 1757: DL, Dec 14; 1761: DL, Apr 30; 1782: HAY, Jan 14; 1786: DL,
   May 24; 1792: HAY, Feb 6
New Broad Court, 1748: CG, Apr 15
New Brooms! See Colman the elder, George.
New Buildings, 1758: CG, Mar 13, Apr 20; 1788: DL, May 6
New Church, 1752: CG, Feb 20; 1753: DL, Dec 11; 1780: DL, Apr 28
New Crown Court, 1757: DL, Apr 25, 26; 1759: DL, Apr 20; 1779: CG, May 4
New Divertisement, The. See Cross, John Cartwright.
New Eclogue, A. See Veracini, Francis.
New Exchange Row, 1745: DL, Mar 11; 1747: DL, Mar 16
New General Lying-in Hospital, 1769: CG, Dec 22; 1770: CG, May 22, Dec 22;
   1778: CG, May 23; 1780: HAY, Aug 2, CG, Dec 22
New Hall, 1676: DG, Mar 0
New Hay at the Old Market. See Colman the younger, George.
New Hippocrates, The. See Hiffernan, Dr Paul.
New Impromptu, A (entertainment), 1757: HAY, Oct 31
New Inn Coffee House, 1778: DL, Apr 21
New Inn, The. See Jonson, Ben.
New Inn, 1736: HAY, Feb 16
New Invention (entertainment), 1710: GR, Jul 22
New Lisle St, 1795: DL, Apr 14; 1796: DL, Apr 12; 1798: DL, May 9; 1799: DL,
   May 8; 1800: DL, May 14, Jun 6
New Long Room, 1735: HA, Oct 1
New Made Nobleman, The (play, anon), 1662: REDBULL, Jan 22
New Mariners (song), 1794: CG, May 23; 1798: CG, May 9
New Nelson St, 1779: DL, May 7
New North St, 1739: DL, Apr 3; 1740: DL, Apr 9; 1750: DL, Mar 24; 1791: DL, May
   17; 1793: DL, May 24; 1795: DL, Jun 2; 1796: DL, Jun 3; 1797: DL, Jun 8;
   1798: DL, Jun 8; 1799: DL, May 17; 1800: DL, Jun 4
New Occasional Prelude, A. See Macnally, Leonard; Cumberland, Richard.
New Ormond St, 1777: DL, Mar 17; 1778: DL, Apr 6, CG, 22; 1779: DL, Mar 27;
   1780: DL, Apr 3
New Palace Yard, 1777: CG, Mar 17
New Peerage, The. See Lee, Harriet.
New Proteus, The (play, anon), 1727: KING'S, Mar 16
New Pye St, 1777: DL, Apr 23
New Readings by Johnny Bulcalf; with his Journey to London (interlude), 1785:
   DL, May 12
New Road, 1796: DL, May 20
New Round Court, 1776: HAY, Oct 7; 1777: HAY, Oct 13
New Sketch of his own picture (entertainment), 1762: DL, May 18
New Spain. See Scawen, John.
New St Square, 1731: LIF, Apr 26
New St, 1742: DL, Apr 26; 1743: DL, May 4; 1749: DL, Mar 7; 1765: DL, Apr 26;
   1780: HAY, Aug 17; 1798: CG, Apr 17; 1799: CG, Apr 9; 1800: CG, Apr 17
New Trade for a Jew (song), 1794: CG, Dec 26; 1795: CG, Jan 12
New Way of Wooing, The (dance), 1735: DL, Jul 1
New Way to Pay Old Debts, A. See Massinger, Phillip.
New Year's Day Song and Music (music), 1703: LIF, Feb 11
New York Coffee House, 1763: DL, Apr 27
New York, College of, 1763: DL, Apr 27
Newberry (actor), 1706: DL, Apr 16, 17; 1707: YB, Apr 18; 1715: LIF, Jun 3;
   1717: LIF, Oct 31, Nov 12, Dec 27; 1718: TEC, Mar 19, LIF, Apr 15
Newberry (printer), 1751: DL, Mar 7
Newberry, John (printer), 1752: CT/HAY, Mar 21, DL, Apr 17, CT/HAY, May 5;

1756: DL, Jan 22
Newbold (actor, singer), 1783: DL, Nov 8; 1784: DL, Nov 9, 22; 1785: DL, May
    20, HAMM, Jun 17, 27, Jul 1, 2, 6, DL, Oct 17, 26; 1786: DL, Mar 9, May 26,
    Sep 30, Oct 7, Dec 5; 1787: DL, May 3, 16, Jun 1; 1788: DL, Apr 8, Oct 13
Newbough, Prince of (spectator), 1675: ATCOURT, Jun 7
Newbury Town Hall, 1780: DL, May 24
Newby, Mrs (actor), 1776: CHR, Oct 16; 1778: CHR, Jun 8, 10, 18, 22, 26
Newcastle Theatre, 1784: CG, Nov 16; 1792: HAY, Jun 18, CG, Oct 11; 1799: DL,
    Sep 10, 21
Newcastle, Duchess of. See Cavendish, Margaret.
Newcastle, Duke of. See Cavendish, William.
Newcomb (confectioner), 1799: HAY, Apr 17
Newcombe's School, 1722: CLA, May 4
Newest Humours of Harlequin (dance), 1703: DG, Apr 30
Newgate and Tyburn (entertainment), 1733: BFAP, Aug 23
Newgate Market, 1755: DL, Nov 18
Newgate St, 1736: CG, Apr 28; 1751: DL, Apr 23
Newgate, 1678: DG, Nov 0; 1685: ATCOURT, Dec 14; 1692: DL, Mar 0; 1695: DG, Jun
    25; 1722: LIF, Nov 26; 1737: DL, Mar 5; 1755: DL, Sep 27; 1760: HAY, Aug 15
Newhouse (dancer), 1707: HA, Aug 1
Newhouse (dancer), 1715: LIF, Feb 8, Mar 3, 26, Apr 22, DL, Jun 2, LIF, Nov 22,
    25, 28, Dec 21, 28; 1716: LIF, Jan 11, 19, May 18, 31, Jul 13, 18, 25, Oct
    19, Nov 15, 28, 29; 1717: LIF, Jan 1, Apr 8, May 16, 23, Jun 7, Nov 8, 15,
    22, Dec 6; 1718: LIF, Jan 1, 2, 3, 4, 15, 24, Mar 8, Apr 16, May 15, Jun 27,
    Jul 18, Aug 6, Nov 13; 1719: LIF, Jan 9, May 7, 13, 21, 25, 28, 29, Jun 3,
    25, BFBL, Aug 24, B-L, Sep 5, LIF, Oct 5, 20, 27, Dec 30; 1720: LIF, Feb 27,
    Mar 26, Apr 30, May 11, 12, 23, 25, 30, Jun 6, Oct 4, Nov 18, 19, Dec 6, 14,
    22, 26; 1721: LIF, Feb 1, 21, 28, Apr 26, 29, May 1, 9, Dec 14; 1722: LIF,
    Apr 20, 24, May 8, 10, 16, 18, 25, RI, Aug 20, BFPMB, 25, SF, Sep 5, LIF, Oct
    16, 30, Nov 7, Dec 13; 1723: LIF, Feb 13, 19, Mar 25, Apr 27, May 6, 15, 23,
    28, Oct 7, 16, 19; 1724: LIF, Mar 2, 14, 23, Apr 6, 7, 10, 21, 23, 27, May 2,
    4, 5, 12, 13, 15, 16, 18, 19, 20, 22, 25, 27, 28, 29, Jun 1, 3, 23, Jul 14,
    29, Sep 28, Nov 6, 10, 18, 27; 1725: LIF, Jan 21, Mar 13, 29, 31, Apr 7, 10,
    17, 22, 28, May 1, 3, 4, 5, 6, 7, 10, 12, 14, 17, 18, 19, 20, 21, 22, 24, 25,
    27, Oct 4, 21, Nov 13, 30, Dec 2; 1726: LIF, Jan 14, Apr 11, 20, 21, 26, 27,
    30, May 3, 14, 24, 26, Jun 17, 21, 24, Jul 1, 5, 15, 19, 22, 26, 29, Aug 2,
    5, 9, 16, Sep 14, 23, 26, 30, Oct 5, 24, 29, Nov 2, 9, 21, Dec 3; 1727: LIF,
    Jan 9, 31, Feb 9, 13, Mar 20, Apr 7, 10, 21, 27, May 4, 8, 22, Sep 20, 29,
    Oct 12, 26, 27, Nov 1, 7, 9, 16, 17, 23, Dec 19; 1728: LIF, Jan 8, Mar 14,
    21, Apr 4, 6, 22, 24, 29, May 2, 6, 8, 11, 13, 15, 16, 18, 22, 23, 29, Sep
    30, Oct 9, 14, Nov 23; 1729: LIF, Jan 13, 16, 18, 31, Feb 6, Mar 10, 17, 20,
    27, Apr 8, 10, 11, 19, 22, 24, 26, 28, 30, May 3, 6, 7, 8, 9, 12, 13, 15, 19,
    20, 21, 22, 23, Oct 3, 15, 22, 24, 28, Nov 1, 4, 11; 1730: LIF, Jan 2, 26,
    Apr 10, 24, 25, 27, 29, May 7, 9, 11, 14, 15, 18, 27, Jul 3, Sep 18, 21, 25,
    Oct 1, 9, 27, 30, Nov 3, 6, 7, Dec 7, 11, 15, 30; 1731: LIF, Jan 4, Apr 3, 5,
    28, May 3, 6, 10, 12, 14, 17, 19, 20, 21, 25, 31, Jun 2, Sep 22, 27, Oct 4,
    11, 15, 25, 27, Nov 2, 6, 12, 13, 18, 25, Dec 1, 14, 17; 1732: LIF, Jan 5,
    GF, Mar 6, LIF, 21, 30, Apr 11, 17, 22, 25, 26, May 17, 18, 22, LIF/CG, Sep
    25, 27, Oct 2, 4, 9, 13, 16, LIF, 18, LIF/CG, 30, Nov 7, 8, 16, 21, 24, Dec
    4, 8, 15, CG/LIF, 19, 26, LIF/CG, 27, CG/LIF, 28; 1733: LIF/CG, Jan 12, 15,
    18, 23, Feb 2, CG, 8, LIF/CG, Mar 12, CG, 27, LIF/CG, 28, 30, Apr 11, 12, 16,
    18, 19, 20, 21, 23, 27, CG, May 1, LIF/CG, 7, 8, CG, 11, LIF/CG, 14, 15, CG,
    16, LIF/CG, 19, 24, CG, Oct 11, 13, 26, Nov 1, 23, Dec 4, 7, 11, 28; 1734:
    CG, Jan 1, 14, 25, Feb 26, Apr 1, 27, May 1, 7; 1741: GF, Feb 16
Newington Butts, 1779: CG, May 8
Newington Green, 1732: LIF, Jun 9
Newington, 1787: RLSN, Mar 28
Newman (actor), 1744: HAY, May 10
Newman (actor), 1781: CII, Mar 15
Newman (prompter), 1703: DL, Jul 5; 1705: DL, Jun 30; 1707: QUEEN'S, May 9;
    1708: DL, Jun 10; 1709: DL, May 19; 1710: QUEEN'S, May 3; 1711: DL/QUEEN, May
    25; 1712: DL, Jun 19; 1713: DL, Jun 19; 1714: DL, Jun 4
Newman (proprietor), 1794: HAMM, Mar 24
Newman, Mrs (actor), 1695: DL, Sep 0, Oct 0
Newman, Mrs (actor), 1729: HAY, Dec 5, 18; 1730: HAY, Jan 21, Feb 12, Mar 20
Newmarket, 1675: ATCOURT, Feb 22; 1679: NONE, Sep 0; 1681: DL, Oct 0; 1746: DL,
    May 2
Newmarket's Delight (dance), 1735: DL, Oct 1
Newport (actor), 1776: CHR, Oct 2
Newport Market, 1757: DL, Dec 21
Newport St, 1741: CG, Apr 20; 1756: DL, Jan 22
Newport, Andrew (spectator), 1660: NONE, Sep 13, VERE, Dec 6, 8

Newport, Francis (spectator), 1661: NONE, May 5
News from Parnassus. See Murphy, Arthur.
Newspapers, The (entertainment), 1786: HAY, Aug 3
Newstead, Mrs (actor), 1730: SFP, Sep 9, SF, 14
Newth (actor), 1695: DG, Nov 0; 1696: DL, Jul 0; 1699: DL, Apr 0
Newton (actor), 1767: HAY, Jun 4, 5, 10, 17, 22, 26, Jul 2, 6, Aug 5, 25, Sep
    4, 7, 9, 18
Newton (actor), 1776: CHR, Sep 23, 27, 30, Oct 14, 18; 1777: CHR, Jun 23, 25,
    27, 30, Jul 2, 21, 23; 1778: HAY, Mar 24, CHR, May 25, 27, 29, Jun 1, 3, 8,
    9, 10, 15, 18, 19, 22, 24, 26; 1779: DL, May 28; 1780: HAY, Mar 28, Apr 5,
    DL, May 17, CG, Oct 13, Nov 15, Dec 15; 1781: CG, May 3, DL, 5, CG, 16, Sep
    17, Oct 13, Nov 2; 1782: CG, Apr 1, DL, 27, CG, May 7, 8, HAY, Nov 25; 1783:
    DL, May 26; 1784: DL, May 15, CG, Oct 29, Dec 14; 1785: CG, Mar 29, May 7,
    11, DL, 27, CG, Sep 26, 30, Oct 17, Nov 10; 1786: CG, Feb 17, May 18, DL, Jun
    2
Newton, Isaac, 1756: DL, Feb 9
Newton, Miss (dancer), 1769: DL, Apr 14
Newton, Miss C (actor), 1776: CHR, Oct 14
Newton, Mrs (beneficiary), 1776: HAY, May 2
Newton, Mrs (boxkeeper), 1776: CHR, Oct 14
Newton, Rev Thomas (correspondent), 1741: GF, Dec 15; 1742: GF, Jan 14
Newton's Warehouse, 1735: DL, Mar 29; 1753: DL, Apr 2; 1754: DL, Mar 25; 1755:
    DL, Mar 15; 1757: DL, Mar 26
Newtone (dancer), 1743: CG, Dec 21, 26
Next Door Neighbors. See Inchbald, Elizabeth.
Niais and Niaise (dance), 1727: KING'S, Mar 16
Niaise, Les (dance), 1741: CG, May 15
Niblett, Mrs (charwoman), 1760: CG, Sep 22
Nice Valour, The. See Fletcher, John.
Nichelman (composer), 1755: HAY, Apr 18
Nichol (baker), 1751: DL, May 1; 1777: DL, Apr 22; 1778: DL, May 4; 1779: DL,
    May 15; 1780: DL, May 10
Nichol (wire monger), 1767: DL, Jan 28, Feb 20
Nichola (musician), 1697: YB, Jan 7; 1698: YB, May 30
Nicholas (composer), 1710: SH, Mar 22
Nicholas Lane, 1747: CG, Apr 20
Nicholas, Mrs (singer), 1737: LIF, Sep 7
Nicholes (actor), 1784: HAY, Nov 16
Nicholini (dancer), 1748: HAY, Apr 14
Nicholl (baker), 1752: DL, Apr 13
Nicholls (actor), 1750: NWC, Apr 16
Nicholls (actor), 1791: HAY, Dec 26
Nicholls (dresser), 1760: CG, Sep 22; 1771: CG, Dec 2
Nicholls, Mrs (actor), 1729: HAY, Jan 25
Nicholls, William, 1749: DL, Jan 20
Nichols (actor, singer), 1728: HAY, Oct 15; 1729: HAY, Jan 10, Feb 1, 11; 1733:
    SF/BFLH, Aug 23, DL, Oct 10, Nov 7, 26, Dec 5; 1734: DL, Jan 3, 8, Feb 4, GF,
    Apr 1, 2, 24, May 3, 16, Nov 4, 8, 12, Dec 16; 1735: GF, Jan 24, Apr 23, May
    5, Nov 17, Dec 17; 1736: GF, Feb 20, Mar 3, LIF, Sep 28, Oct 9, 21, Dec 7,
    17; 1737: LIF, Jan 24, Feb 1; 1739: BFH, Aug 23; 1746: CG, Apr 19
Nichols (gilder), 1774: CG, May 14
Nichols, Deputy (register for the Literary Fund), 1792: HAY, Apr 16
Nichols, R H (author), 1750: CHAPEL, May 1
Nicholson (dancer), 1745: CG, Jan 3; 1746: CG, May 2; 1747: HAY, May 28; 1748:
    HAY, May 2
Nicholson (spectator), 1664: BRIDGES, Jan 2
Nicholson (violinist), 1758: CHAPEL, Apr 27
Nicholson, Margaret (attempted assassin of the King), 1786: DL, Sep 16
Nicholson, William (author), 1781: CG, Oct 13
Nick-all, J (author), 1749: HAY, Feb 10
Nicketerotion at the Meeting of Antony and Cleopatra (song), 1790: CG, May 24
Nicknackatory, A (interlude, anon), 1796: CG, Apr 26
Nicks (violinist), 1795: HAY, Mar 4; 1796: CG, Feb 12; 1797: CG, Mar 3; 1798:
    CG, Feb 23; 1799: CG, Feb 8; 1800: CG, Feb 28
Nicol, G and W (publishers), 1784: DL, Dec 2; 1794: CG, May 19; 1797: DL, May 8
Nicolai, Johann Gottlieb (author), 1792: DLKING'S, Apr 16
Nicolina, Sga (actor), 1756: CG, Jan 12
Nicolini (actor, singer, dancer), 1781: HAY, Aug 8; 1782: HAY, Jun 3; 1783:
    HAY, Jun 5; 1785: HAY, Jul 13, Aug 31; 1790: DL, Oct 26; 1791: DLKING'S, Nov
    5; 1792: DLKING'S, Mar 19, DL, Nov 21; 1794: DL, May 16, Jun 9, Sep 27, Oct
    27, Nov 10, Dec 20; 1795: DL, Jan 19, Feb 3, Oct 30; 1796: DL, Jan 18, Apr 4,
    Oct 1, 29, Nov 9, Dec 26; 1798: DL, Jan 16, 24, 26

Nicolini (singer), 1709: QUEEN'S, Jan 19, 25, Jun 4; 1710: QUEEN'S, Mar 9, 18,
    21; 1712: SML, Jun 4; 1715: KING'S, Jun 25; 1716: KING'S, Feb 11, May 2;
    1720: KING'S, Dec 28; 1729: HIC, Apr 16
Nicolini, C (publisher), 1800: KING'S, Apr 15
Nicoll (Nicolls, Nichols, Nicols), George (rope maker), 1766: DL, Nov 26; 1771:
    DL, Oct 24; 1772: DL, Nov 27; 1773: DL, Oct 6; 1774: DL, Oct 14; 1775: DL,
    Jan 20, Nov 3; 1785: DL, Dec 20; 1790: DL, Nov 20
Nicols, Miss (dancer), 1777: CG, Apr 25; 1778: CG, Jan 28
Niddity Nod (song), 1786: DL, May 24
Nie Jaloux (dance), 1754: HAY, Jul 11, 16, Aug 6
Nield, Jonathan (singer), 1795: CG, Feb 20, 27, Mar 11, 13, 20, 25, 27; 17962
    CG, Feb 12, 17, 24, 26; 1799: HAY, Mar 29
Nieri, Isaia (dancer), 1754: KING'S, Nov 9
Nigh (actor), 1794: DL, Oct 31; 1796: DL, Jan 11; 1800: HAY, Jul 2
Night (song), 1767: DL, Mar 28
Night Scene (dance), 1703: DL, Oct 7, Dec 15; 1704: DL, Jan 11; 1709: DL, Dec
    30; 1710: DL, Jan 19, GR, Aug 5, 7; 1711: GR, Sep 3; 1716: LIF, May 18, Nov
    5; 1724: HAY, Jan 13
Night Thoughts (poem), 1794: HAY, Jun 2
Night Walker, The. See Fletcher, John.
Night's Adventure of a Buck, The (entertainment), 1758: DL, May 4
Nightingale Chorus (song), 1789: CG, Mar 20; 1791: CG, Mar 18; 1792: CG, Feb
    24, Mar 14
Nightingale, The (song), 1703: LIF, Jun 8; 1797: HAY, Sep 1, 16
Nigri (composer), 1772: CG, Mar 27, Apr 10; 1773: HAY, Mar 17, CG, 19
Nile, 1798: DL, Oct 2
Nimmo, Widow, 1767: DL, Apr 25
Nina. See Wolcot, John; Paisiello, Giovanni.
Nina; ou, La Folle par Amour. See Marsollier des Vivetiers, Benoit Joseph.
Ninetta. See Cimarosa, Domenico.
Ninette a la Cour (dance), 1781: KING'S, Feb 22, 24, 27, Mar 1, 6, 10, 13, 17,
    20, 24, 27, Apr 28, May 5, 15, 19, 26, 29, Jun 23, Jul 3; 1786: KING'S, Jun
    1, 6, 13, 20, 27, Jul 1, 4, 11; 1789: KING'S, May 14, 21; 1791: KING'S, Jun 6
Nipclose, Sir Nicholas, 1771: CG, Nov 4, DL, Dec 11, 17; 1772: DL, Jan 1
Nitteti. See Sacchini, Antonio Maria Gasparo; Anfossi, Pasquale.
Nivelon (dancer), 1740: DL, Oct 13, 14, 16, 24, 27, 31, Nov 14, 15, 17, 18, 22,
    25, Dec 4, 10, 13, 26; 1741: DL, Jan 1, 7, 9, 15, 29, Feb 7, Mar 17
Nivelon, C (dancer), 1781: KING'S, Nov 17, Dec 11; 1782: KING'S, Jan 10, 29,
    Feb 2, 7, 14, 21, 23, Mar 19, Apr 11, May 2, 7, 9, 16, 25; 1784: KING'S, Dec
    18; 1785: KING'S, Jan 1, 11, 22, Feb 5, 12, 26, Mar 3, 12, 17, Apr 21, May
    12, Jun 9, 18, 28; 1789: KING'S, Mar 17, 31, Apr 28, May 7; 1793: KING'S, Jan
    26, Feb 5, 26, Apr 6, 23, Jun 4, 11
Nivelon, Francis (dancer), 1699: DLORLIF, Nov 9; 1702: DL, Aug 20; 1723: LIF,
    Oct 29, Nov 2, 8, 16, 22, 27, 28, Dec 3, 9, 11, 12, 14, 16, 20; 1724: LIF,
    Jan 3, 4, Feb 3, Mar 2, 16, 19, 23, 24, 26, 28, Apr 6, 7, 8, 10, 23, 24, 27,
    28, 29, 30, May 4, 8, 18, 20, 22, Jun 4, Sep 25, 28, 30, Oct 5, 9, 12, 14,
    16, 23, 30, Nov 3, 6, 11, 13, 18; 1725: LIF, Jan 4, 18, 21, Mar 11, 16, 18,
    29, 31, Apr 5, 10, 14, 15, 19, 22, 23, 26, 28, 30, May 3, 4, 5, 6, 11, 12,
    26, Sep 29, Oct 1, 4, 8, 13, 19, 21, 22, 25, Nov 2, DL, 3, LIF, 3, 8, 9, 12,
    13, 18, 22, 23, Dec 2, 3; 1726: LIF, Jan 3, 5, 14, Mar 10, 19, 21, 28, 31,
    Apr 2, 11, 13, 14, 15, 18, 19, 20, 22, 25, 26, 27, 29, May 2, 3, 4, 13, 16,
    17, 20, 23, 25, 30, Sep 16, 23, 26, 30, Oct 3, 5, 12, 24, Nov 2, 9, 14, 21,
    30, Dec 3; 1727: LIF, Feb 3, 7, 8, 9, 13, Mar 11, 13, 16, 20, 23, Apr 3, 5,
    6, 7, 10, 12, 17, 19, 24, 26, 27, May 3, 4, 8, 9, 10, 12, 15, 17, 18, 19, 22,
    Sep 13, 15, 20, 22, 29, Oct 2, 9, 12, 17, 26, Nov 1, 7, 9, 16, 17, 23; 1728:
    LIF, Jan 8, Mar 9, 18, 21, 25, 28, Apr 1, 4, 6, 23, 24, 29, 30, May 2, 8, 23,
    29; 1729: LIF, Oct 10, 15, 20, 22, 24, 28, Nov 1, 4; 1730: LIF, Jan 2, Feb 3,
    Mar 17, 21, Apr 6, 8, 10, 13, 15, 24, 25, 30, May 1, 4, 9, 13, 21, Jun 4, RI,
    24, LIF, Sep 18, 23, 25, Oct 1, 7, 9, 19, 27, 30, Nov 3, 6, 7, Dec 11, 15;
    1731: LIF, Jan 4, 11, 19, Mar 15, 18, 22, 25, Apr 1, 3, 5, 22, 23, 24, 26,
    28, 29, May 1, 5, 6, 12, 13, 14, 21, 28, 31, Jun 2, 7, Oct 4, 11, 13, 15, 20,
    Nov 6, 8, 12, 13, 18, Dec 7, 14; 1732: LIF, Jan 5, 19, Feb 9, Mar 9, 20, 23,
    Apr 10, 12, 14, LIF/CG, Sep 25, 27, Oct 2, 4, 9, 13, 16, LIF, 18, LIF/CG, 25,
    30, Nov 8, 14, 16, 21, 24, Dec 4, 8, 15, CG/LIF, 19, LIF/CG, 27; 1733:
    LIF/CG, Jan 23, 27, Feb 2, 3, CG, 8, LIF/CG, Mar 12, 15, 17, CG/LIF, 26, CG,
    27, LIF/CG, 28, 29, 30, Apr 2, 3, 12, 16, 18, 23, 30, CG, May 1, LIF/CG, 3,
    CG, 4, LIF/CG, 7, 8, 10, 14, CG, 16, 17, LIF/CG, 21, 23, 24, 31, DL/HAY, Oct
    13, 15, 20, 24, 27, Nov 24, 26, 28, Dec 12, HAY, 13, DL/HAY, 19, 20, 22, 31;
    1734: DL/HAY, Jan 1, 4, 10, GF, 12, DL/HAY, 12, 16, 28, Feb 4, 6, 20, Mar 4,
    5, 9, 12, 16, 18, 19, 23, 25, 26, 28, 30, Apr 2, DL, 4, DL/HAY, 6, DL, 15,
    25, DL/HAY, 26, 27, DL, 29, DL/HAY, May 1, DL, 13, Sep 7, 12, 19, 24, Oct 3,
    8, 10, 23, 26, Nov 7, Dec 4, 9, 11, 12, 26, 28, 31; 1735: DL, Jan 1, 11, 17,

18, 21, 28, 29, Feb 4, 13, 14, 15, Mar 3, 27, Apr 7, 11, 14, 18, 19, 21, 22, 23, 25, 28, May 1, 5, 6, 7, 8, 14, 22, 23, 29, Jun 3, 9, 11, CG, Sep 24, Oct 3, 6, 13, 15, 17, 28, Nov 6, 11, 13, 15, 19, 22, 24, 28, Dec 2, 12, 18, 27; 1736: CG, Jan 1, 2, 9, 19, 21, 23, Mar 6, 15, 16, 20, 22, 23, 25, 27, 30, Apr 1, 5, 6, 8, 12, 15, 17, 27, 29, May 1, 3, 6, 8, 10, 11, 17, 18, 20, 25, Jun 4, Sep 17, 22, 29, Oct 4, 6, 8, 20, 27, Nov 3, 9, 11, 23, 26, Dec 6, 13, 30; 1737: CG, Jan 7, 17, 24, 28, Feb 1, 14, Mar 7, 10, 14, 15, 17, 19, 24, 26, 28, Apr 11, 12, 14, 15, 19, 22, 25, 26, 28, 29, May 2, 3, 5, 6, 9, 12, 16, 31, Oct 7; 1738: CG, Feb 8, 9, 10, 13, Mar 13, 14, 16, 20, 21, 23, Apr 4, 5, 6, 7, 10, 11, 12, 15, 18, 20, 21, 22, 27, 28, 29, May 2, 3, 5, 6, 8, 11, 12, 15, 16

Nivelon, Francis and Louis (dancers), 1723: LIF, Oct 18, 24, 29, Nov 19, 28; 1724: LIF, Mar 23, 26, 28, Apr 6, 7, 8, 9, 10, May 4

Nivelon, Louis (dancer), 1723: LIF, Nov 2, 8, 27, Dec 3, 9, 11, 12, 14, 16, 20; 1724: LIF, Jan 4, Mar 2, 23, 24, Apr 7, 10, 28

Nivelon, Mlle (actor), 1741: BFH, Aug 22

Nivelon's scholar (dancer), 1736: CG, Mar 20, Apr 8, 12, May 8, 14, 17, 18

Nix (Nicks), Samuel (boxkeeper), 1780: DL, May 17; 1781: DL, May 16; 1782: DL, May 13; 1783: DL, May 16; 1784: DL, May 14; 1785: DL, May 13; 1786: DL, May 24; 1787: DL, May 28; 1788: DL, May 26; 1789: DL, Jun 8; 1790: DL, May 31; 1791: DL, May 23; 1792: DLKING'S, Jun 7; 1793: DL, Jun 3; 1795: DL, Jun 6; 1796: DL, Jun 13; 1797: DL, Jun 16; 1798: DL, Jun 14

Nix, William (boxkeeper), 1798: DL, Jun 14

Nix, 1773: CG, Dec 31

No cruel father (song), 1790: CG, Feb 24; 1793: CG, Mar 6; 1794: CG, Mar 12, DL, Apr 4; 1798: CG, Mar 28

No Fool Like the Old Fool (play, anon), 1676: DL, Jun 13

No Fool Like the Old One; or, The Lucky Discovery (droll, anon), 1751: SF, Sep 9

No Fools Like Wits. See Wright, Thomas.

No good without an exception (song), 1794: CG, May 2

No Joke Like a True Joke (farce, anon), 1732: HAY, May 24

No kissing at all (song), 1715: DL, May 24, Jul 26; 1728: LIF, Mar 9, 25, Apr 24, May 13, 16; 1731: LIF, Mar 22; 1732: LIF, Mar 30, May 8; 1733: LIF/CG, Apr 11

No longer heave the heartfelt sigh (song), 1798: CG, Oct 15

No Matter What (play, anon), 1758: DL, Apr 25

No more shall Edom (song), 1789: DL, Mar 20; 1791: DL, Mar 11, CG, 23

No more to Ammon's God (song), 1789: CG, Apr 3; 1790: CG, Mar 17, 26; 1791: CG, Mar 18, 30; 1792: CG, Mar 2; 1793: CG, Mar 6; 1794: CG, Mar 12; 1795: CG, Mar 13; 1796: CG, Feb 24, 26, Mar 2; 1797: CG, Mar 22; 1798: CG, Mar 28; 1799: CG, Feb 15; 1800: CG, Feb 28

No more, ye infidels (song), 1790: CG, Mar 17

No never (song), 1754: CG, May 8, 13, 15, 20

No, no, every morning my beauties renew (song), 1698: NONE, Sep 0

No, no, my Heart (song), 1729: HIC, Apr 30

No, no, no, no, resistance is but vain (song), 1693: DL, Feb 0

No, no, poor suffering heart no change endeavour (song), 1692: DL, Apr 0

No non sai (song), 1753: KING'S, Apr 30

No non Temer (song), 1729: DL, Mar 26

No oh Dio (song), 1729: HIC, Apr 16

No One's Enemy but His Own. See Murphy, Arthur.

No Song No Supper. See Hoare, Prince.

No sport to the chace can compare (song), 1783: HAY, Aug 1

No Wit like a Woman's (farce, anon), 1769: DL, Mar 28, 31; 1780: HAY, Apr 5; 1781: CG, Apr 18

No Wit, No Help, Like a Woman's. See Middleton, Thomas.

Noah's Flood. See Ecclestone, Edward.

Noake. See Nokes.

Noaseman (dancer), 1723: HAY, Dec 26, 30

Noble (actor), 1734: YB, Jul 8; 1736: YB, Dec 1; 1737: HAY, Mar 7

Noble (actor), 1779: HAY, Oct 18

Noble (dancer, actor), 1790: CG, Jun 4, 12; 1791: CG, Jun 9; 1792: CG, Mar 31; 1794: CG, Jun 14; 1795: CG, Jun 10, Nov 16; 1796: CG, May 21; 1797: CG, Jun 2; 1798: CG, Mar 31, Apr 9, May 19; 1799: CG, Jun 8, Oct 21; 1800: CG, Apr 5, Jun 4, 11

Noble (upholsterer), 1772: CG, Feb 26; 1773: CG, Jan 20, Oct 19; 1774: CG, Mar 3

Noble Englishman, The; or, The History of Darius King of Persia and the Destruction of Babylon (entertainment), 1721: SF, Sep 8

Noble Gentleman, The. See Fletcher, John.

Noble Peasant, The. See Holcroft, Thomas.

Noble Pedlar, The. See Carey, George Saville.
Noble Soldier, The; or, Love in Distress (musical, anon), 1717: SFBL, Sep 9;
    1719: B-L, Sep 5
Noble Stroller, The; or, The Humours of Avignon and Cripplegate (interlude,
    anon), 1723: SOU, Sep 24
Noble, Eustace le, 1718: LIF, Dec 10, 12
--Deux Arlequins, Les, 1718: LIF, Dec 10, 12; 1720: KING'S, May 31; 1721: HAY,
    Feb 2; 1725: HAY, May 7; 1734: GF/HAY, Nov 28, Dec 11; 1735: GF/HAY, Mar 3,
    21, Apr 25
Nobleman, The; or, Family Quarrel. See Cooper, Elizabeth.
Nobleman, The; or, The Great Man. See Tourneur, Cyril.
Nobody (song), 1786: HAMM, Jun 5
Nobody. See Robinson, Mary.
Nocchiero s'abbandona (song), 1757: KING'S, Mar 24
Noche Hollandaise (dance), 1778: KING'S, Nov 24, 28, Dec 22, 29; 1779: KING'S,
    Jan 5, Feb 2
Nodder (actor), 1743: DL, May 2
Noel (musician), 1752: CG, Jan 6, CT/HAY, Apr 1, 21, May 5; 1757: HAY, Sep 5,
    8, 14
Noel, Bridget (spectator), 1676: NONE, Sep 0; 1685: DLORDG, Dec 30, OLDFIELD,
    30
Noel, Katherine (spectator), 1671: BRIDGES, Jan 2, NONE, Feb 4, ATCOURT, 6, 20,
    NONE, Mar 4, 16
Noel, Miss (actor), 1785: HAY, Apr 25
Noferi, Giovanni Battista (dancer), 1778: KING'S, Feb 24; 1779: KING'S, May 15;
    1780: KING'S, Apr 13, 20, 22, May 9, 20; 1782: KING'S, Apr 11
Nofferi (musician), 1770: KING'S, Feb 2
Noisy, Mlle (dancer), 1705: QUEEN'S, Nov 15, 17, 20, LIF/QUEN, Dec 4, QUEEN'S,
    8, 12; 1706: QUEEN'S, Jan 2
Nokes (actor), 1792: DL, Nov 21, Dec 27
Nokes, James (actor), 1659: NONE, Sep 0; 1660: REDBULL, Nov 5; 1661: SALSBURY,
    Jan 29, LIF, Dec 16; 1662: LIF, Mar 1, NONE, Sep 0; 1663: LIF, Feb 23, Dec
    22; 1664: LIF, Mar 0, Aug 13; 1665: LIF, Apr 3; 1667: LIF, Aug 15; 1668: LIF,
    Feb 6, May 2, NONE, Sep 0, LIF, Dec 8, ATCOURT, 28; 1669: LIF, Dec 14; 1670:
    LIF, Nov 0, BRI/COUR, Dec 0; 1671: LIF, Mar 6; 1672: DG, Feb 6, Jul 4, Aug 3,
    ATCOU/DG, Dec 2; 1675: NONE, Sep 0; 1676: DG, Jan 10, Nov 4, Dec 0; 1677: DG,
    May 31; 1678: DG, Jan 17, Jun 0; 1679: DG, Mar 0, NONE, Sep 0, DG, 0, Oct 0;
    1680: DG, Jun 0, Sep 0, Nov 1, Dec 8; 1681: DG, Jan 0, Nov 0, DG/IT, 22;
    1682: DG, Jan 0, Apr 0, NONE, Sep 0; 1685: DG, Jul 0; 1686: DL, Jan 0, Apr 0,
    NONE, Sep 0; 1688: DG, Apr 0, NONE, Sep 0; 1689: DL, Mar 0, Apr 0, NONE, Sep
    0; 1690: DL, Jan 0, Mar 0, NONE, Sep 0, DL/IT, Oct 21, DL, Nov 0; 1691: DL,
    Apr 0, NONE, Sep 0; 1696: NONE, Sep 8
Nokes, Mrs (actor), 1728: HAY, Nov 19; 1729: HAY, Jan 31, Feb 25, May 7, 12,
    26, 29, Jun 14, 17, Jul 5, 26, Aug 8, BFR, 25, SF, Sep 8, SOU, 23, HAY, Nov
    15, 22, Dec 18; 1730: HAY, Jan 8, 21, Feb 6, 23, Mar 11, 20, Jun 17, Jul 17,
    TC, Aug 1, BFR, 22, Sep 4, SFP, 9, SF, 14, HAY, Oct 21, 26, Nov 13, 16, 30,
    Dec 9, 14, 23, 28; 1731: HAY, Jan 15, 18, 20, Feb 3, 10, 26, Mar 10, 17, Apr
    22, May 19
Nokes, Robert (actor), 1660: REDBULL, Nov 5; 1662: ATCOURT, Nov 1; 1663: LIF,
    Feb 23, Oct 0; 1676: DG, Jan 10
Noland (actor), 1736: LIF, Mar 31
Non andrai farfalone amoroso (song), 1792: DLKING'S, Apr 19
Non ch'amarmi (song), 1741: DL, Oct 15, 16, 20, Dec 3
Non era ancora sorta l'Aurora (song), 1792: KING'S, Mar 21
Non fau in che parlo (song), 1764: KING'S, Mar 29
Non lo diro col Labro (song), 1729: HIC, Apr 30; 1732: LIF, Apr 19
Non pavento il pastorello (song), 1751: KING'S, Apr 16
Non pensi (song), 1755: KING'S, Mar 17
Non piu andrai (song), 1792: KING'S, Mar 28; 1793: KING/HAY, Feb 15, 27, Mar 8
Non vi piacque ingiusti Dei (song), 1754: KING'S, Feb 28; 1755: KING'S, Mar 17
Non-Common Pleas, Court of, 1733: HAY, May 26
None are so Blind as Those Who Won't See. See Dibdin, Charles.
Nonini (singer), 1782: KING'S, Mar 2, Apr 9, Jun 15
Nonjuror, The. See Cibber, Colley.
Noontide Air (song), 1739: DL, Apr 3, 7, 9, 12, 25, 27, 28, May 3, CG, Nov 9;
    1740: DL, Mar 17, 25, 29, Apr 14, 16, 19, May 9, 12, 22; 1741: DL, May 9, 12,
    22, 27, 28, Dec 10, 11; 1742: DL, Apr 27, May 1; 1743: DL, Mar 14, LIF, 21,
    DL, May 23; 1744: HAY, Oct 20; 1746: GF, Mar 17; 1780: CG, Apr 15; 1789: HAY,
    Feb 23
Nootka Sound. See Byrn, James.
Nor on beds of fading flowers (song), 1777: CG, Jan 7; 1791: CG, May 27; 1792:
    CG, May 18; 1793: CG, Apr 11

Nora, Miss (actor), 1734: CG/LIF, Oct 29
Norbury (house servant), 1769: CG, May 20, 22; 1770: CG, May 19, 22; 1771: CG,
  May 25; 1772: CG, May 29; 1773: CG, May 28; 1774: CG, May 24
Norfolk (glazier), 1776: DL, Jan 5, Mar 25, Jun 10
Norfolk St, 1692: DL, Dec 9; 1699: YB, Mar 8; 1701: YB, Mar 3; 1707: YB, Apr 2;
  1778: KING'S, Nov 24; 1779: DL, May 4; 1787: CG, Nov 16; 1794: CG, May 20;
  1795: CG, May 21; 1800: DL, Jun 5
Norfolk, Duke of. See Howard, Henry (11th Duke); Howard, Henry (12th Duke);
  Howard, Thomas.
Norman, Miss (actor, dancer), 1733: GF, Dec 21, 26; 1734: GF, Feb 11, Apr 26,
  HAY, Jun 7, 28, BFRLCH, Aug 24, GF, Dec 12; 1735: GF, Jan 9, 10, 24, Feb 4,
  Mar 6, 25, 29, Apr 30, CG, Oct 3, 17, Nov 6; 1736: CG, Jan 1, 9, 10, 23, Feb
  23, Mar 6, 11, May 6, 11, Oct 8, Nov 3, 9, Dec 4; 1737: CG, Jan 28, Feb 14,
  Mar 7, 24, Apr 25, May 12, 13, Oct 7; 1738: CG, Feb 3, 13, Mar 2, 7, 16, 18,
  Apr 24, 25, Oct 4, Nov 18, Dec 9, 11; 1739: CG, Jan 18, 20, Feb 15, Mar 5,
  Apr 28, Sep 21, Oct 10; 1743: CG, Oct 17; 1744: CG, Jan 14, Oct 10, Nov 27;
  1746: GF, Feb 10
Norman, Mrs (beneficiary), 1718: YB, Dec 10
Norman, Samuel (woodcarver), 1766: CG, Nov 13
Normanby, Lord. See Sheffield, John.
Normand, Mlle (dancer), 1789: KING'S, Jan 10, 31, Feb 10, 14, Mar 10, CG, Jun
  27, 30
Norolk, Mrs (glazier), 1778: DL, May 14
Norris (dresser), 1760: CG, Sep 22
Norris St, 1777: CG, May 22; 1778: CG, May 20; 1779: CG, May 18; 1780: CG, May
  19
Norris-Chetwood-Orfeur-Oates Booth, 1724: SF, Sep 2
Norris, Henry (actor), 1662: LIF, Sep 30, ATCOURT, Nov 1; 1664: LIF, Mar 0, Aug
  13, Nov 5; 1670: LIF, Sep 20, Nov 0; 1671: BRIDGES, Jan 2, LIF, 10, Mar 15,
  Jun 0, Sep 0, DG, Nov 0; 1672: DG, Jan 31, Aug 3, Nov 4; 1673: DG, Feb 18,
  Mar 12; 1674: DG, Nov 9; 1675: DG, May 28, NONE, Sep 0; 1676: DG, Jun 8, Jul
  3, Aug 0, Nov 4, Dec 0; 1677: DG, Feb 12, Jun 0, Sep 0; 1678: DG, Jan 0, Sep
  0, Nov 0; 1679: DG, Mar 0, Apr 0, Dec 0; 1680: DG, Feb 0, Dec 8; 1681: DG,
  Jan 0, Mar 0; 1682: DG, Jan 0; 1683: NONE, Sep 0, DL, Dec 0; 1685: DL, Aug 0;
  1686: DG, Mar 4; 1687: ATCOURT, Apr 25
Norris (Norreys, Norice), Henry (actor, booth proprietor), 1699: DL, Nov 28,
  Dec 0; 1700: DL, Apr 29, Jul 9, Oct 0, Dec 9; 1701: DL, Apr 0, May 31, Dec 0;
  1702: DL, Feb 0, Nov 0; 1703: DL, Apr 10, Jun 4, 19, 23, 30, Oct 28; 1704:
  DL, Jan 7, 26, Jun 23, Dec 26; 1705: DL, Jan 18, Feb 20, Mar 29, Apr 23, Jun
  12; 1706: DL, Apr 0, 1, 8, BF, Aug 27, QUEEN'S, Nov 13, 14, 22, 25, Dec 3, 5,
  7, 11, 13, 14; 1707: QUEEN'S, Jan 1, 4, 13, 14, 18, Feb 14, 18, Mar 8, 27,
  Apr 30, May 26, Jun 2, 10, 13, 18, 20, 25, 27, Jul 1, 4, 30, Aug 12,
  DL/QUEEN, Oct 18, 20, QUEEN'S, 21, DL/QUEEN, 22, 27, 28, 29, 31, Nov 1,
  QUEEN'S, 6, DL/QUEEN, 10, 11, 14, 18, Dec 27, 31; 1708: DL/QUEEN, Jan 1, DL,
  Feb 3, 4, 6, 7, 23, 24, 26, Mar 13, 16, 18, Apr 10, 22, 26, 27, 29, DL/QUEEN,
  May 20, DL, 21, Jun 5, 11, 15, 19, 26, Jul 1, 20, 29, Aug 4, 28, 31, Sep 4,
  Oct 7, 12, 13, 14, 15, 16, 19, 22, Dec 14, 21, 28, 31; 1709: DL, Jan 1, 4,
  10, 18, 21, 27, 29, Feb 1, 2, 19, 23, 24, 26, Mar 3, 14, 15, 17, 22, 28, 31,
  Apr 4, 11, 12, 30, May 3, 17, 18, Sep 6, Nov 24, 26, 28, Dec 3, 6, 7, 9, 10,
  17; 1710: DL, Jan 9, 14, 25, 31, Feb 1, 9, 11, 18, Mar 11, 14, 21, 27, Apr
  15, 21, May 23, GR, Jun 19, 28, Jul 1, 8, 10, 12, 20, 27, 29, Aug 3, 5, 7,
  10, 12, 14, 19, 24, 28, Sep 9, 11, 20, 23, 30, DL/QUEEN, Nov 4, 6, 7, 8, 9,
  QUEEN'S, 10, DL/QUEEN, 15, 17, DL, 21, 25, 28, Dec 2, 5, 7, 11, 14, 15, 18,
  DL/QUEEN, 29, DL, 30; 1711: DL, Jan 11, 19, 20, 25, 26, DL/QUEEN, Feb 8, DL,
  10, DL/QUEEN, 17, DL, Mar 3, 8, 17, Apr 7, 21, DL/QUEEN, May 11, 12, DL, 15,
  18, 21, 22, 31, DL/QUEEN, Jun 5, 22, DL, 26, 29, Jul 3, 10, DL/QUEEN, 13, DL,
  27, Aug 3, 17, 31, Sep 25, 27, 29, Oct 4, 6, 9, 10, 11, 12, 13, 16, 22, 24,
  26, 30, 31, Nov 1, 2, 5, 6, 8, 12, Dec 8, 10, 18, 31; 1712: DL, Jan 19, May
  15, Jun 2, 5, Jul 4, 22, Aug 1, 26, Sep 23, 30, Oct 2, 6, 8, 10, 13, 16, 20,
  22, 31, Nov 3, 7, 26, Dec 27; 1713: DL, Jan 5, 6, 12, 14, 19, 29, Feb 9, 13,
  Mar 3, 16, May 11, 12, 25, Jun 5, 12, 17, 18, 19, Sep 29, Nov 9, 11, 16, 23,
  25, 27, Dec 2, 18; 1714: DL, Jan 28, Mar 31, Apr 27, May 5, 17, 21, 26, 28,
  Jun 2, 4, 18, 25, Jul 13, 20, SF, Aug 31, DL, Oct 22, Nov 9, 15, 24, 27, Dec
  6, 8, 16; 1715: DL, Feb 4, 12, 21, 22, 23, 25, 28, Mar 5, 8, Apr 2, 19, 30,
  May 18, 20, 31, Jun 6, 28, Aug 9, SF, Sep 15, DL, Oct 13, Dec 9, 20, 30, 31;
  1716: DL, Jan 13, 17, 25, 26, Feb 9, 13, 18, 21, 23, Mar 3, 10, Apr 2, 14,
  May 8, 9, Jun 15, 19, Jul 12, 19, SF, Sep 25, DL, 29, Oct 2, 4, 9, 11, 12,
  15, 16, 19, 22, 29, Nov 3, 13, 27, Dec 4, 5, 14; 1717: DL, Jan 4, 12, 16, 31,
  Feb 14, 15, Mar 26, May 10, 14, Jun 10, 14, 24, 27, Jul 16, 30, TC, Aug 5,
  SF, Sep 9, DL, Oct 1, 9, 10, 14, 15, 16, 24, 25, 28, Nov 6, 8, 13, 18, 19,
  20, 25, Dec 3, 4, 31; 1718: DL, Jan 7, 20, 23, 27, Feb 19, Mar 24, Apr 21,
  Jun 11, 17, 27, Jul 1, 11, 18, RI, 19, DL, 22, Aug 1, RI, 2, DL, 15, SF, Sep

6, DL, 27, Oct 2, 8, 10, 15, 17, 20, 22, 24, 27, 28, 30, Nov 12, 18, 19, 26,
27, Dec 1, 11, 16; 1719: DL, Jan 16, 28, Apr 14, May 8, 19, RI, Jun 6, DL, 9,
RI, Jul 6, BFBL, Aug 24, DL, Sep 17, 19, 22, 24, 29, Oct 7, 9, 15, 16, 21,
22, 27, 28, 30, Nov 3, 6, 7, 11, 16, 18; 1720: DL, Jan 1, 5, 12, 13, Feb 5,
Mar 19, Apr 19, 21, May 20, Jun 2, 11, 30, Jul 7, 19, BFPMJ, Aug 23, DL, Sep
10, 13, 15, 17, 20, 22, 29, Oct 3, 4, 5, 7, 12, 15, 17, 20, 29, Nov 1, 2, 7,
11, 12, 21, 22, Dec 5, 6, 8, 17; 1721: DL, Jan 25, 27, Mar 23, 28, Apr 10,
13, 25, 26, May 5, 29, Jun 16, 20, Jul 28, Aug 1, 4, 18, BF/SF, 24, DL, Sep
9, 12, 16, 19, 21, 26, 28, Oct 2, 3, 4, 5, 6, 10, 12, 13, 16, 17, 18, 20, 21,
24, 25, Nov 1, 13, 17, 25, 30, Dec 1, 22; 1722: DL, Jan 9, Apr 7, 10, 14, May
2, 8, 22, Sep 11, 13, 18, 20, 27, Oct 8, 9, 10, 12, 17, 19, 22, 24, 25, 26,
30, Dec 3, 4, 5, 7, 26; 1723: DL, Jan 7, 9, 17, 23, Feb 5, 6, Apr 16, May 11,
20, 22, 23, Jun 4, BFPJ, Aug 22, RI, Sep 2, DL, 17, 19, 24, 26, Oct 1, 3, 8,
9, 18, 21, 23, 29, 30, Nov 1, 6, 8, 12, 15, 18, 21, 22, Dec 30; 1724: DL, Feb
6, 17, Apr 7, 15, 18, 28, May 1, 6, 16, 22, LIF, Jun 23, RI, 27, 29, Jul 4,
11, 13, 18, LIF, 31, SF, Sep 2, DL, 15, 17, 19, 22, 29, Oct 8, HAY, 13, DL,
19, 21, 27, 28, 29, Nov 2, 6, 10, 13, 16, LIF, 25, DL, 26, Dec 7, 18; 1725:
DL, Jan 20, 25, Feb 18, 20, Apr 2, 9, 15, 21, 30, May 8, 11, LIF, 21, DL, 21,
BF, Aug 23, DL, Sep 9, 14, 18, 25, 28, Oct 2, 5, 9, 12, 15, 18, 20, 22, 25,
28, Nov 3, 8, LIF, Dec 3, DL, 7, 9, 13; 1726: DL, Jan 5, 24, 26, Mar 17, 28,
May 11, LIF, 17, DL, 23, LIF, 26, DL, Jun 3, LIF, 24, Aug 2, 19, DL, Sep 6,
17, 20, 22, 24, 29, Oct 1, 11, 15, 18, 22, 27, Nov 9, 15, 16, 26, Dec 7, 14,
21; 1727: DL, Jan 27, Feb 8, Apr 8, 14, 25, 29, May 2, 5, LIF, 8, DL, 8, 22,
Sep 9, 12, 14, 26, 28, 30, Oct 3, 5, 6, 9, 12, 17, 19, 20, 23, 30, Nov 28,
Dec 4, 5, 13; 1728: DL, Jan 2, Apr 2, 8, 29, May 1, 8, 10, 17, 20, Sep 10,
12, Oct 3, 10, 17, 21, 23, 24, 30, 31, Nov 7, 12, 14; 1729: DL, Jan 1, 2, 13,
20, 21, 22, 29, 31, Feb 24, Apr 9, 16, 22, 23, May 3, 6, 14, Jun 27, Sep 13,
30, Oct 4, 14, 16, 21, 22, 27, 30, 31, Nov 3, 7, 14, 18, 21, 24, 25, 27, FLR,
Dec 1, DL, 1, 4, 5, 26; 1730: DL, Jan 3, 9, GF, 22, DL, Feb 12, Apr 14, 18,
May 2, 13, 18, Sep 15, 24, Oct 1, 3, 8, 20, 28, Nov 24; 1731: DL, Feb 10, GF,
Nov 15, 16, 17, 19, 20, 22, 27, Dec 1, 4, 21, 28; 1732: GF, Jan 20, 29, Feb
5, 8, 26, Mar 4, 7, 27, 28, Apr 10, 12, DL, 21, GF, 27, May 4, 11, 23, TC,
Aug 4, GF, Oct 2, 4, 6, 7, 10, 11, 12, 14, 17, 26, 30, Nov 2, 3, 8, 22, Dec
1, 18, 29; 1733: GF, Jan 1, 18, 20, 24, Feb 5, 13, 19, Mar 30, Apr 17, 18,
24, 30, DL, May 5, GF, 8, 9, HAY, 28, DL, Jun 9, BFMMO, Aug 23, GF, Sep 10,
12, 17, DL, 28, Oct 1, 10, GF, 10, DL, 24, 31, Nov 14, 21, 23, 26, Dec 5, 7,
11, 21; 1734: DL, Jan 3, 15, 19, DL/LIF, Mar 11, JS, May 31, BFFO, Aug 24,
GF, Sep 9, 20, 25, Oct 17, Nov 8, 13, Dec 2, 16, 20, 21; 1735: GF, Jan 24,
Feb 12, 17, Mar 6, 24, Apr 9, 10, 23, Sep 12, 17, 22, 26, Oct 6, 15, Nov 3,
6, 10, 11, 14, 17, 24, 25, Dec 8; 1736: GF, Feb 20, Mar 9, 25, 29, Apr 16,
17, 29, May 6, 13, LIF, Oct 5, 9, 12, 23, Nov 6, 11, 13, 18, 29, Dec 22;
1737: LIF, Jan 10, Feb 1, Mar 15, 21, 29, Apr 12, 14, 18, 25, 27, 30, May 6;
see also Jubilee Dicky
Norris Jr, Henry (actor), 1712: SML, May 21, Jun 11, 18; 1715: DL, Feb 23, Aug
9, Dec 6; 1718: SF, Sep 6; 1719: DL, Jan 28; 1721: DL, May 31; 1724: RI, Jun
27, 29, Jul 11, 13, 18, SF, Sep 2, HAY, Oct 13; 1726: LIF, Jul 19
Norris, Miss (actor), 1730: HAY, Dec 21; 1732: GF, Apr 10, DL, 21; 1733: GF,
May 5, DL, 5, Oct 17, Nov 26; 1734: DL, Feb 4, GF, May 8, JS, 24, GF, Dec 6;
1735: GF, Mar 20, Apr 29; 1736: LIF, Oct 19, Dec 27; 1737: LIF, Mar 1, Apr 2,
May 10
Norris, Miss (dancer, actor), 1707: DL, Nov 4, 6, 28, 29, DL/QUEEN, Dec 9, DL,
17; 1708: DL, Jan 3, Jun 15, 26, Jul 3, 20, 29, Aug 28, Sep 11, 14, 25, 28
Norris, Miss (singer), 1748: CG, Dec 10, 26, 27; 1749: CG, Mar 9, 14, 31, Apr
5, May 4, DL, Oct 11, 17, Dec 2; 1750: DL, Jan 1, 4, 29, Feb 15, 24, Mar 15,
Apr 2, 3, 23, Sep 20, Oct 1, 13, 30, Nov 13, Dec 13, 18; 1751: DL, Jan 28,
Feb 23, Mar 12, Apr 17, Sep 7, Oct 1, Nov 19; 1752: DL, Apr 10, 18, 25, Sep
23, 26, Oct 11, 14
Norris, Mrs (actor), 1662: LIF, Sep 30, ATCOURT, Nov 1; 1664: LIF, Aug 13;
1665: LIF, Apr 3; 1667: LIF, Aug 15; 1669: LIF, Dec 14; 1671: LIF, Mar 15;
1672: DG, Jan 31, Aug 3; 1673: DG, Mar 12, May 0; 1676: DG, Jan 10, Aug 0;
1677: DG, Mar 24, May 31, Jun 0, Jul 0, Sep 0; 1678: DG, Jun 0; 1679: DG, Mar
0, Sep 0; 1680: DG, Jan 0, Jun 0; 1681: DG, Jan 0, DG/IT, Nov 22; 1682: DG,
Jan 0, Apr 0; 1683: DG, Jul 0, DL, Dec 0; 1684: DLORDG, Dec 0
Norris, Mrs (actor), 1703: DL, Jun 4; 1705: DL, Jul 25; 1708: DL, Jan 31,
DL/QUEEN, Feb 21, DL, May 21, Jun 24, Jul 27, Sep 3, Oct 25
Norris, Mrs (actor), 1731: GF, Dec 1, 17, 28, 29; 1732: GF, Jan 21, Apr 10, 28,
May 4, Oct 25, Nov 3, 8; 1733: HAY, May 28
Norris, Thomas (singer), 1762: DL, Oct 9, 11, 22, 25; 1763: DL, Apr 27; 1764:
DL, Feb 27; 1772: DL, Mar 6, GROTTO, Aug 17; 1773: DL, Feb 26, Nov 9, 25;
1774: DL, Mar 12, CHAPEL, 26, DL, May 3, Sep 29, Oct 4, 14, 27, Dec 26; 1775:
DL, Jan 3, Feb 17, Mar 10, May 6, 12, Oct 11, 23, 25, Nov 1, 3, 4, 9, 11, 14,
21, CHAPEL, 23, DL, Dec 11; 1776: DL, Mar 1, 14, 18, 28, CHAPEL, Apr 2, DL,

10, 19, 20, 22, May 11, 13, 18, 22; <u>1777</u>: DL, Feb 14; <u>1778</u>: Mar 6, 27; <u>1779</u>:
DL, Feb 19, Mar 12, 26; <u>1780</u>: DL, Feb 11; <u>1781</u>: DL, Mar 2, 30; <u>1782</u>: DL, Feb
15; <u>1783</u>: DL, Mar 14; <u>1784</u>: DL, Feb 27; <u>1785</u>: DL, Feb 11
Norris, William (actor), <u>1776</u>: DL, Sep 21, Oct 23, Nov 4, 9, 16, Dec 10, 28;
<u>1777</u>: DL, Jan 1, 4, 28, Feb 17, 24, Mar 13, Apr 2, 17, 18, 24, May 6, 8, Sep
25, 30, Oct 18, Nov 4, 29; <u>1778</u>: DL, Jan 5, 22, 24, Mar 30, Apr 23, May 15,
23, Sep 19, 24, Oct 1, 21, Nov 10, 16, Dec 21, 22; <u>1779</u>: DL, Mar 16, 18, 22,
27, Apr 10, 12, 19, May 25, Jun 1, Sep 18, CG, 20, DL, 23, Oct 2, 7, 16, Nov
15, Dec 13, HAY, 20, DL, 27; <u>1780</u>: DL, Jan 3, 24, Apr 29, May 2, 10, CG, 18,
DL, Sep 16, 19, 23, Oct 3, 10, 17, 25, Nov 1, 4, 11, 13, 22, 24, 27, 29, Dec
4, 15; <u>1781</u>: DL, Jan 9, 20, Mar 31, May 1, 17, 22, 24, Sep 18, 20, 25, Oct
16, 22, 29, 30, Nov 13, Dec 11; <u>1782</u>: DL, Jan 3, Apr 15, 23, 24, 25, 27, May
15, CG, 20, DL, Sep 17, HAY, 21, DL, 24, Oct 1, 3, 5, 10, Nov 1, 12, Dec 26;
<u>1783</u>: DL, Feb 22, Mar 6, 17, 18, Apr 24, May 2, Oct 31; <u>1784</u>: DL, Mar 5
Norsa, Hannah (actor), <u>1732</u>: CG/LIF, Dec 16; <u>1733</u>: LIF/CG, Feb 10, Mar 29, Apr
12, 18, CG/LIF, 26, LIF/CG, 27, May 7, 15, 19, 21, CG/LIF, 28, CG, Jun 26,
Jul 6, 27, Aug 2, 3, 9, 14, 20, Sep 17, 27, 29, Oct 11, 13, 18, 29, Nov 26,
28, Dec 7, 28; <u>1734</u>: CG, Jan 1, 9, 17, 23, 25, Feb 13, 26, Mar 5, 11, 16, 18,
28, Apr 1, 30, May 3, 7, Sep 2, CG/LIF, 20, 23, 27, 30, Oct 2, 9, 11, 18, 31,
Nov 1, 11, 12, 19, 21, Dec 5, 19; <u>1735</u>: CG/LIF, Jan 17, 23, 31, Feb 3, LIF,
12, CG/LIF, 13, Mar 11, 20, Apr 11, 14, 15, 21, 22, 29, May 1, 15, 16, YB,
19, LIF, 21, CG/LIF, 26, Jun 2, YB, 3, HAY, 12, CG/LIF, 17, CG, Sep 12, 16,
19, 26, 29, Oct 1, 10, 13, 17, 22, 24, 25, 29, Nov 7, 15, Dec 27; <u>1736</u>: CG,
Feb 10, 28, Mar 6, 15, 18, 20, LIF, Apr 2, CG, 6, 12, 13, 29, 30, May 1, 3,
4, HAY, Jun 29, Jul 7
Norsa, Master (actor), <u>1734</u>: JS, May 24; <u>1735</u>: YB, Mar 10, 21, May 19, Jun 3;
<u>1736</u>: HAY, Jun 29
Norsa, Master and Miss (beneficiaries), <u>1735</u>: YB, May 19
Norsa Jr, Miss (dancer), <u>1735</u>: YB, Mar 10, CG/LIF, Apr 29, CG, May 6
North Audley St, <u>1792</u>: HAY, Nov 26
North Country Maggot (dance), <u>1733</u>: GF, May 4
North Hall, <u>1706</u>: NH, Jul 29
North St, <u>1751</u>: DL, Apr 10, May 14; <u>1777</u>: CG, May 10; <u>1778</u>: CG, May 9; <u>1779</u>:
CG, May 1; <u>1780</u>: CG, Apr 28; <u>1792</u>: DLKING'S, May 29
North, Francis, <u>1788</u>: HAY, Jul 10; <u>1791</u>: HAY, Jun 25; <u>1794</u>: HAY, Feb 22; <u>1797</u>:
HAY, Jul 15; <u>1800</u>: DL, Apr 29
--Kentish Barons, The, <u>1791</u>: HAY, Jun 25, 27, 28, 30, Jul 2, 5, 7, 13, 16, 25
North, George Augustus, 3rd Earl of Guildford, <u>1797</u>: DL, Oct 27
North, Lord (chancellor), <u>1777</u>: CG, Feb 28
North, Lord, son of, <u>1749</u>: LEI, Jan 7
North, Roger (spectator), <u>1673</u>: DG, Jul 3; <u>1685</u>: DG, Jun 3; <u>1691</u>: DG, May 0
North, Sir Christopher (spectator), <u>1667</u>: BRIDGES, Dec 30
Northampton, Countess of (spectator), <u>1734</u>: DL, Nov 27
Northamptonshire, <u>1677</u>: DL, Jul 0
Northern Castle, The (play, anon), <u>1667</u>: BRIDGES, Sep 14
Northern Heiress, The. See Davys, Mary.
Northern Heroes, The (play, anon), <u>1748</u>: BF, Aug 24, SFBCBV, Sep 7, 8, 9, 10,
12, 13
Northern Inn, The. See Kemble, Stephen George.
Northern Lass, The. See Brome, Richard.
Norton (author), <u>1744</u>: DL, Apr 28
Norton (beneficiary), <u>1797</u>: CG, May 25; <u>1798</u>: CG, May 19; <u>1799</u>: CG, Jun 4
Norton (chorus), <u>1749</u>: DL, Nov 24, Dec 6, 7, 8, 9, 11, 13, 15, 16, 18, 19, 21,
23, 30; <u>1750</u>: DL, Jan 1, 5, 12, 19, 24, 31, Feb 1, 3, 5, 9, 12, 13, 20, 26,
27, Mar 1, 3, 5, 6, 8, 12, 13, 20, 24, 31, Apr 5, 7, 23, 24, 27
Norton St, <u>1789</u>: CG, May 5
Norton, Captain (beneficiary), <u>1743</u>: CG, Oct 28
Norton, Martha (actor, singer), <u>1794</u>: HAY, Jul 17, 18, 21, 24, 28, Aug 27, CG,
Oct 22; <u>1795</u>: CG, Jan 31, May 1, 6, 19, 30, Jun 2, 6, HAY, 13, 20, Jul 31,
CG, Sep 14, 21, Oct 19, Nov 4, 16, 30, Dec 7, 18; <u>1796</u>: CG, Jan 1, Feb 2, Mar
14, 30, Apr 2, 9, 13, May 16, 31, HAY, Jul 15, Aug 29, CG, Sep 12, 16, 19,
23, 26, 28, Oct 6, 7, 14, 29, Dec 19; <u>1797</u>: CG, Feb 18, 27, Mar 4, 6, Apr 8,
19, 25, May 16, 18, Jun 2, 5, 13, HAY, 23, Jul 3, Aug 14, 15, 24, CG, Sep 25,
Oct 16, Nov 2, 10, 23, 24, Dec 18, 26; <u>1798</u>: CG, Feb 12, 13, 16, Mar 29, Apr
9, 19, 20, 27, May 31, HAY, Jun 30, Jul 6, 10, 21, Aug 11, 25, CG, Sep 17,
Oct 3, 8, Nov 12, 21, Dec 15, 26; <u>1799</u>: CG, Jan 29, Mar 25, Apr 3, 9, 13, 19,
May 14, 28, Jun 4, 7, HAY, 29, Jul 9, Aug 21, CG, Sep 18, 30, Oct 2, 7, 21,
24, Nov 11, Dec 10, 23; <u>1800</u>: CG, Jan 16, Feb 10, Mar 17, 25, Apr 5, 29, May
20, Jun 2, HAY, Jul 2, Aug 14, 29
Norton, Mary (actor), <u>1662</u>: ATCOURT, Dec 1, LIF, 27
Norton, Miss (dancer), <u>1798</u>: CG, Dec 11; <u>1800</u>: CG, May 1
Norton, Mrs (actor), <u>1742</u>: CG, Jan 23

Norton, Richard
--Pausanius, the Betrayer (Lover) of his Country, 1696: DL, Apr 0
Norwich Company, 1770: DL, Sep 25; 1798: CG, Dec 15
Norwich Stuff Warehouse, 1762: DL, Apr 20
Norwich Theatre, 1770: DL, Oct 29; 1772: HAY, Sep 18; 1777: HAY, Aug 7, Oct 9;
    1780: HAY, Aug 29, Nov 13; 1781: HAY, Jan 22; 1785: CG, Sep 19; 1786: CG, Jan
    28, 31, HAY, Mar 6, CG, Nov 13; 1789: CG, Jan 29, Sep 25; 1790: CG, May 5;
    1793: CG, Nov 14; 1794: HAY, Jun 2, CG, Sep 15; 1795: CG, May 8; 1796: CG,
    Oct 5; 1798: DL, Oct 20; 1799: DL, Feb 26
Norwich, 1662: REDBULL, Jan 25, Mar 25; 1671: NONE, Sep 0; 1699: LIF, Dec 18;
    1770: HAY, Sep 27; 1774: DL, Oct 8; 1792: DLKING'S, Jan 18
Norwood Gypsies, The. See Messink, James.
Nosegay (dance), 1767: DL, Apr 27; 1770: HAY, Jun 11, 13, 15, 29, Jul 2, 4, 9,
    11, 13, Aug 8, Sep 3, 5, 7, 10, 11; 1771: HAY, May 31, Jun 3, Jul 1, Aug 7,
    9, Sep 11, 12; 1773: DL, May 5; 1775: CG, May 26; 1783: HAY, Jun 11; 1786:
    HAY, Jun 14
Nosegay Lovers (dance), 1783: HAY, Jun 4
Nosegay of Weeds, A. See O'Keeffe, John.
Nosom (house servant), 1737: LIF, Jun 15
Nossiter, Maria Isabella (actor), 1753: CG, Oct 10, 23, 30, Nov 1, 14, Dec 11;
    1754: CG, Jan 21, 22, Mar 18, 25; 1755: CG, Mar 12, Dec 6, 12; 1756: CG, Feb
    26, Mar 1, 18, 22, 29, Apr 1, 3, Oct 4, 11, 13, 15, 18, 25, 27, 30; 1757: CG,
    Jan 11, 27, Mar 28; 1758: CG, Oct 25, 26, Nov 23, Dec 29; 1759: CG, Jan 3,
    12, Mar 22, 24, Apr 5, 7
Nost, Mrs (actor), 1774: HAY, Apr 12, Sep 17, 21; 1775: HAY, Feb 2, Oct 30;
    1777: HAY, May 1; 1778: CHR, Jul 30
Not unto us (song), 1792: CG, Mar 14
Note of Hand, The. See Cumberland, Richard.
Nothing but a Place (song), 1795: HAY, Mar 4
Notoriety. See Reynolds, Frederick.
Nott (dancer), 1729: HAY, May 26, Jun 14, Jul 23, Dec 27; 1732: TC, Aug 4
Nottingham St, 1733: LIF/CG, May 8; 1735: CG/LIF, May 12
Nottingham, Earl of. See Finch, Daniel.
Nottingham, Mrs (actor), 1728: HAY, Dec 23; 1730: HAY, Mar 18
Nourse, J (publisher), 1747: NONE, Mar 27
Nous Faut Partir, Il (play), 1749: HAY, Dec 2
Nouveau Ballet Comique & Autres Danses (dance), 1725: HAY, Mar 8
Novella, The. See Brome, Richard.
Novelty, The (entertainment), 1768: SW, Apr 4
Noverre (dancer), 1755: DL, Nov 8
Noverre, Jean Georges (dancer, ballet master), 1755: DL, Nov 8, 15; 1757: DL,
    Nov 8, 18; 1758: DL, Mar 18, Apr 14, 18, 27, May 1, 2, Sep 23, 30, Oct 7, Nov
    3, Dec 8; 1759: DL, Jan 4, Mar 20, 27, Apr 18, 27, Sep 25, Oct 16, 23, Nov
    22, Dec 1, 19; 1760: DL, Apr 9, 29, May 7, HAY, Jun 5, DL, Sep 20, Dec 19;
    1761: DL, Apr 28, 29, Nov 3, Dec 26; 1762: DL, Feb 19, Mar 20, Apr 3, 27, 28,
    May 13, Oct 1; 1763: DL, Mar 1, Apr 30; 1764: DL, May 23; 1765: DL, Apr 16;
    1766: DL, May 5, 7; 1767: DL, May 12; 1769: DL, May 2; 1770: DL, May 10;
    1771: DL, May 8; 1772: DL, May 8; 1781: KING'S, Nov 17, Dec 11; 1782: KING'S,
    Jan 10, 26, 29, Feb 2, 23, Mar 19, Apr 11, May 2, Jun 5; 1783: KING'S, May 1;
    1787: KING'S, Dec 8; 1788: KING'S, Jan 15, 29, Feb 12, 28, Mar 13, Apr 3, 17;
    1789: KING'S, Jan 31, Mar 3, 17, 31, Apr 28, May 7, 21; 1793: KING'S, Jan 26,
    Feb 26, Apr 6, 23; 1794: KING'S, Jan 11, Mar 1, 11, Apr 1, Jun 23; 1795: CG,
    Apr 6, KING'S, May 14; 1796: KING'S, Dec 13; 1797: CG, Nov 4
Noverre, Miss (dancer), 1755: DL, Nov 1, 4, 8
Noverre, Mrs (dancer), 1755: DL, Nov 8
Novestris, 1781: HAY, Aug 8; 1782: HAY, Jun 3; 1783: HAY, Jun 5; 1784: HAY, Aug
    26; see also Colman Sr, George
Novosielski, Michael (scene painter), 1781: KING'S, Feb 22, Mar 29, Jun 5, Nov
    17; 1782: KING'S, May 2, Nov 2; 1783: KING'S, Nov 29; 1784: KING'S, Mar 18,
    Apr 15, May 8, Dec 18; 1785: KING'S, May 12; 1791: DLKING'S, Oct 20
Now a different Measure try (song), 1790: CG, Feb 26
Now after the death (song), 1794: DL, Apr 10
Now Deborah (song), 1794: DL, Apr 10
Now heaven in all her glory shone (song), 1790: DL, Feb 24; 1794: DL, Apr 10;
    1796: CG, Feb 26
Now is the Month of Maying (song), 1790: DL, May 20; 1791: DL, May 18
Now landed from the ocean (song), 1795: CG, May 1, 8
Now strike the golden lyre (song), 1791: CG, Mar 25; 1792: CG, Mar 7; 1794: CG,
    Mar 14
Now the elders (song), 1794: DL, Apr 10
Now the Men and the Maids are Making of Hay (song), 1730: LIF, May 1
Now the Tones all must droop (song), 1682: DG, Jan 23

Now when I think thee upon (song), 1789: DL, Mar 25
Now when Joseph was sold (song), 1794: DL, Apr 10
Now when the fullness of time (song), 1794: DL, Apr 10
Now's Your Time, Taylors! Sound Men and True! (entertainment), 1794: CG, Apr 23
Nowland (actor), 1732: HAY, Nov 29
Nozze dei Contadini Spagnuoli, Le. See Martin y Soler, Vicente.
Nozze del Tamigi e Bellona, Le. See Bianchi Jr, Francesco.
Nozze di Dorina, Le. See Galuppi, Baldassare; Sarti, Giuseppe.
Nozze di Figaro, Le. See Mozart, Wolfgang Amadeus.
Nugent (actor), 1784: HAY, Nov 16
Nugent, General, 1736: HAY, May 25; 1737: DL, May 26
Nugent, Master (actor), 1749: LEI, Jan 7
Nuit aux Aventures, La. See Dumaniant.
Nume Alata (song), 1713: QUEEN'S, Apr 25
Numi se giusti siete (song), 1757: KING'S, Mar 24
Numidian Dance (dance), 1730: LIF, Mar 17, Apr 8, 25, 27, 29, May 1, 4, 11, 15,
   23, 27, 28, Sep 23, Oct 7, 19, 30, Nov 3, Dec 7; 1731: LIF, Jan 4, Apr 8, May
   1, Jun 7, Oct 20; 1732: LIF, Apr 10, May 16, LIF/CG, Dec 4, 15
Numitor. See Porta, Giovanni.
Numps's Courtship. See Piece, Dr.
Nunnery, The. See Pearce, William.
Nunns, John (actor), 1785: HAY, Jul 29
Nunns, Mrs John (actor), 1785: HAY, Jun 11, 29
Nuptial Masque, The. See Galliard, John Ernest.
Nut Brown Maid, The (poem), 1774: CG, Apr 13; 1775: DL, Apr 20; 1779: HAY, Oct
   18; 1781: DL, Apr 23; 1782: DL, Apr 24
Nuttall (merchant), 1760: CG, Feb 9
Nuttall, Mrs (merchant), 1768: CG, Mar 18
Nuvoletta (song), 1737: DL, Jan 15, 18
Nymph and a Swain, A (song), 1695: LIF, Apr 30
Nymph's Refusal (song), 1787: CG, Apr 24
Nymphe et Chasseur (dance), 1789: KING'S, Mar 3, 10, 19, May 23, 26, Jun 6, 11,
   13, 16, CG, Jul 2
Nymphes de Diane (dance), 1778: KING'S, Nov 24, Dec 22, 29; 1779: KING'S, Jan
   5, 23, 29, Feb 2, 6; 1781: KING'S, Jan 23, 29, Feb 10, Mar 17
Nymphs and Shepherds (song), 1759: CG, May 12; 1760: CG, Mar 27; 1762: CG, Mar
   23; 1763: CG, Apr 23, 26; 1774: HAY, Jun 7
Nymphs of the Plain (song), 1697: DG, Jun 0

O Baal (song), 1790: CG, Mar 17; 1791: CG, Mar 23; 1792: CG, Mar 2; 1793: CG,
   Feb 15; 1794: CG, Mar 7, DL, Apr 4, 9; 1795: CG, Feb 20; 1796: CG, Mar 16;
   1797: CG, Mar 31; 1798: CG, Mar 9; 1799: CG, Mar 15; 1800: CG, Mar 21
O be kind, my dear, be kind (song), 1685: DL, May 9
O Beauteous Queen, Enclose those Eyes (song), 1748: CG, Mar 8; 1794: CG, Mar
   26, Apr 11; 1800: CG, Mar 14
O Bless the Genial Bed with chast delights (song), 1695: DG, Apr 0
O bring me wine (song), 1795: CG, May 6, 13, 16; 1796: CG, Apr 29; 1797: CG,
   May 20, DL, Jun 6; 1798: DL, May 23; 1800: DL, May 29
O Care Parollette (song), 1733: DL/HAY, Nov 22
O Change beyond Report (song), 1798: CG, Mar 30
O che Salvo (song), 1764: KING'S, Mar 29
O come let us worship (song), 1789: CG, Mar 6, 27; 1790: CG, Mar 3; 1791: CG,
   Mar 11, DL, 11; 1792: KING'S, Mar 14; 1793: KING/HAY, Feb 15, CG, 22; 1794:
   DL, Mar 12; 1797: CG, Mar 24; 1798: CG, Mar 28
O da Pastor (song), 1746: KING'S, Mar 25
O Death, where is thy sting? (song), 1793: KING/HAY, Feb 20; 1794: DL, Mar 19
O didst thou know the pains (song), 1790: DL, Mar 10; 1791: DL, Apr 1; 1792:
   KING'S, Feb 29; 1794: DL, Mar 26
O ever in my bosom live (song), 1796: CG, May 16, Jun 1; 1797: CG, May 22;
   1798: CG, Mar 19; 1799: CG, Mar 2, 5, 9; 1800: CG, Mar 4, 8, Jun 5
O Fairest of Ten Thousand Fair (song), 1750: KING'S, Apr 10
O fatal day (song), 1790: CG, Feb 24; 1792: CG, Mar 2; 1794: CG, Mar 21, Apr
   11; 1795: CG, Mar 25; 1797: CG, Mar 10; 1798: CG, Mar 9; 1799: CG, Feb 15,
   Mar 15; 1800: CG, Feb 28
O Father, whose Almighty power (song), 1791: CG, Mar 23; 1795: KING'S, Feb 27
O filial piety (song), 1790: CG, Feb 24; 1793: CG, Mar 6; 1794: CG, Mar 12, DL,
   Apr 4; 1798: CG, Mar 28
O first created beam (song), 1786: DL, Mar 10; 1789: CG, Mar 6, DL, 18; 1790:
   CG, Feb 24, DL, 26; 1791: CG, Mar 11, DL, 11, 23; 1792: KING'S, Feb 24, CG,

Mar 2, KING'S, 14; <u>1793</u>: KING/HAY, Feb 15, 22, CG, Mar 6; <u>1794</u>: CG, Mar 12, DL, 21, Apr 10; <u>1795</u>: CG, Feb 27, KING'S, Mar 13, CG, 25; <u>1796</u>: CG, Feb 24; <u>1797</u>: CG, Mar 10, 22, Apr 7; <u>1798</u>: CG, Mar 14; <u>1799</u>: CG, Mar 13; <u>1800</u>: CG, Feb 28
O gentle maid (song), <u>1795</u>: CG, Mar 18
O God, Tis Thou (song), <u>1789</u>: DL, Mar 20
O God, who in thy heavenly hand (song), <u>1789</u>: CG, Mar 20; <u>1790</u>: CG, Feb 26; <u>1791</u>: CG, Mar 23; <u>1793</u>: CG, Mar 6; <u>1794</u>: CG, Mar 12; <u>1795</u>: CG, Mar 13; <u>1796</u>: CG, Mar 16; <u>1799</u>: CG, Feb 8, Mar 6
O Godlike Youth (song), <u>1790</u>: CG, Feb 24; <u>1793</u>: CG, Feb 15, Mar 13
O had I Jubal's Lyre (song), <u>1786</u>: DL, Mar 10; <u>1787</u>: DL, Feb 23; <u>1788</u>: DL, Feb 8; <u>1789</u>: CG, Mar 6, DL, 18, CG, 27; <u>1790</u>: DL, Feb 24, CG, 24, DL, 26, Mar 12; <u>1791</u>: DL, Mar 11, CG, 11, DL, 23; <u>1792</u>: KING'S, Feb 24, CG, Mar 21, KING'S, 28; <u>1793</u>: KING/HAY, Feb 22; <u>1794</u>: CG, Mar 12, DL, 14, Apr 2, 10; <u>1795</u>: CG, Feb 27, Mar 27; <u>1798</u>: CG, Feb 28, Mar 28; <u>1799</u>: CG, Mar 1; see also Jubal's Lyre
O how you protest (song), <u>1695</u>: DL, Sep 0
O inespettata Sorte (song), <u>1748</u>: KING'S, Apr 5
O Judah boast (song), <u>1789</u>: DL, Mar 20; <u>1792</u>: CG, Feb 24; <u>1793</u>: CG, Mar 8; <u>1798</u>: CG, Mar 14
O lead me to some peaceful gloom (song), <u>1695</u>: DL, Sep 0; <u>1704</u>: DL, Jun 21
O let eternal honors (song), <u>1791</u>: CG, Mar 23; <u>1794</u>: CG, Mar 14; <u>1796</u>: CG, Feb 26
O let the merry peal go on (song), <u>1792</u>: CG, May 11
O Liberty (song), <u>1790</u>: DL, Mar 17; <u>1791</u>: DL, Mar 11; <u>1792</u>: KING'S, Feb 29; <u>1793</u>: CG, Mar 13; <u>1794</u>: CG, Mar 26, Apr 11; <u>1795</u>: CG, Mar 13, 25; <u>1796</u>: CG, Mar 16; <u>1797</u>: CG, Mar 31; <u>1799</u>: CG, Feb 15
O Lord, in thee have I trusted (song), <u>1791</u>: CG, Mar 11; see also Lord in thee
O love, if e'er thou'lt ease a heart (song), <u>1671</u>: DG, Nov 0
O love, that stronger art than wine (song), <u>1686</u>: DL, Apr 0
O Lovely Peace (song), <u>1749</u>: KING'S, Mar 21; <u>1750</u>: CG, Mar 29; <u>1793</u>: KING/HAY, Feb 15
O Lovely, Fair and Faithful Youth (song), <u>1753</u>: KING'S, Apr 30
O magnify the Lord (song), <u>1789</u>: CG, Mar 20; <u>1790</u>: CG, Mar 17; <u>1791</u>: DL, Mar 11, CG, 23; <u>1792</u>: KING'S, Mar 14, 30; <u>1793</u>: CG, Feb 15, KING/HAY, 27; <u>1794</u>: CG, Mar 7, DL, 12, 14, Apr 2; <u>1795</u>: CG, Feb 20, KING'S, 27; <u>1797</u>: CG, Mar 10; <u>1798</u>: CG, Mar 9; <u>1799</u>: CG, Feb 8, Mar 6
O mirror of our fickle state (song), <u>1798</u>: CG, Mar 28, 30
O Nanny, wilt thou go with me (song), <u>1787</u>: DL, May 28
O Peace, thou fairest child of Heaven (song), <u>1745</u>: DL, Apr 25; <u>1746</u>: DL, May 12; <u>1748</u>: CG, Mar 31; <u>1751</u>: DL, Feb 26
O Phoebus (song), <u>1793</u>: KING/HAY, Mar 20
O ruddier than the Cherry (song), <u>1741</u>: HIC, Apr 24; <u>1742</u>: CG, Apr 23; <u>1745</u>: CG, Apr 10; <u>1764</u>: CG, May 11; <u>1784</u>: DL, Mar 5; <u>1787</u>: DL, Mar 7; <u>1790</u>: DL, Mar 10; <u>1791</u>: DL, Apr 1, CG, 13; <u>1792</u>: KING'S, Feb 29, CG, Mar 14, 21; <u>1794</u>: DL, Mar 26; <u>1798</u>: CG, Mar 28
O sad virgin (song), <u>1791</u>: CG, Mar 18, 30; <u>1792</u>: CG, Feb 24; <u>1794</u>: CG, Mar 21; <u>1796</u>: CG, Feb 17; <u>1798</u>: CG, Feb 28
O say, Bonny Lass will you carry a Wallet? (song), <u>1788</u>: CG, May 12, DL, Jun 10; see also Say Bonny Lass
O sing praises unto the Lord (song), <u>1792</u>: CG, Mar 9
O sing unto the Lord (anthem), <u>1740</u>: HIC, Apr 2, 11, 18
O Sleep, Why dost thou leave me? (song), <u>1745</u>: CG, Apr 10; <u>1746</u>: DL, Apr 15; <u>1748</u>: CG, Feb 13; <u>1749</u>: KING'S, Mar 21; <u>1750</u>: CG, Apr 19; <u>1794</u>: CG, Mar 12, Apr 4
O take him gently from the pile (song), <u>1695</u>: LIF, Dec 0
O the pleasures of the plains (song), <u>1789</u>: CG, Apr 3; <u>1791</u>: DL, Apr 1, CG, 13; <u>1792</u>: KING'S, Feb 29; <u>1793</u>: CG, Mar 8; <u>1794</u>: DL, Mar 26; <u>1798</u>: CG, Mar 28
O the Sweets in Friendship Found (song), <u>1741</u>: HIC, Apr 24
O thou almighty power (song), <u>1789</u>: DL, Mar 20
O thou that tellest good tidings (song), <u>1790</u>: CG, Mar 26; <u>1793</u>: KING/HAY, Feb 20; <u>1794</u>: DL, Mar 19
O thou wert born to please me (song), <u>1791</u>: CG, May 27
O What a Charming Thing's a Battle (song), <u>1771</u>: MARLY, Jul 18, GROTTO, Sep 3, 9, MARLY, 17; <u>1772</u>: DL, May 18; <u>1773</u>: DL, May 13, HAY, Aug 23, 31, Sep 3, 16, DL, Dec 21; <u>1774</u>: DL, Apr 8, HAY, Jun 7; <u>1775</u>: DL, Apr 26; <u>1777</u>: DL, Apr 21, Dec 30; <u>1781</u>: CG, May 7; <u>1789</u>: DL, Jun 3, 12; <u>1793</u>: CG, Mar 23, Apr 3, 9, 10, DL, Jun 1
O why did e'er my thoughts aspire (song), <u>1684</u>: DL, Apr 0
O worse than death (song), <u>1790</u>: CG, Feb 24; <u>1791</u>: CG, Mar 11; <u>1792</u>: CG, Mar 2; <u>1793</u>: CG, Mar 6; <u>1794</u>: CG, Mar 12, Apr 4, 11; <u>1795</u>: CG, Mar 25; <u>1796</u>: CG, Feb 26; <u>1797</u>: CG, Mar 10; <u>1798</u>: CG, Mar 14, 30

O worship the Lord (song), 1790: CG, Mar 3; 1792: CG, Mar 9
Oakes, Miss (actor), 1772: GROTTO, Aug 17
Oakly (actor), 1735: YB, Mar 19
Oakman, J, 1767: DL, Apr 20
--Athiest, The (fable), 1767: DL, Apr 20
Oates (singer, musician), 1737: DL, May 7; 1738: CG, May 1
Oates Jr (dancer), 1734: DL, Apr 25, DL/HAY, May 4, DL, 16, LIF, 23, BFFO, Aug
   24, DL, Oct 9; 1735: DL, May 13, LIF, Jun 12, HAY, Oct 24; 1736: LIF, Apr 16,
   DL, May 7, LIF, Jun 16; 1737: LIF, Apr 2, 21, 28; 1738: CG, May 1; 1739: CG,
   May 2, Aug 2; 1740: CG, May 12, BFHC, Aug 23, CG, Sep 26, Oct 10; 1741: CG,
   Jan 5, Apr 2; 1750: CG, Apr 26
Oates-Fielding Booth, 1730: BFOF, Aug 20, SFOF, Sep 9
Oates, Ann (actor), 1732: BFMMO, Aug 23
Oates, Dr, 1683: DL, Jan 19
Oates, James (actor, singer), 1715: DL, Dec 6; 1718: DL, Feb 19, May 1, RI, Aug
   9; 1719: DL, Jan 28, May 7, Jun 9, BFPM, Aug 24, DL, Dec 11; 1720: DL, May
   20, SFLH, Sep 5, DL, Dec 17; 1721: DL, May 19, Jun 20, Aug 1, 4, 18, BF/SF,
   24, SFHL, Sep 2, DL, 12, Nov 30; 1722: DL, Jan 5, 26, May 9, RI, Jul 23,
   BFPMB, Aug 25, SF, Sep 5, DL, 18, Oct 8; 1723: DL, May 17, Jun 4, Jul 5, 16,
   Aug 12, BFPJ, 22, SF, Sep 5, DL, 17, Dec 5; 1724: DL, May 5, SF, Sep 2, DL,
   15, Oct 29; 1725: DL, Apr 21, 30, May 4, 17, Sep 7, 9, Dec 4; 1726: DL, May
   3, 11, Sep 10, 24, Oct 1, 11; 1727: DL, Feb 21, Mar 16, Apr 19, May 2, BF,
   Aug 21, DL, Sep 9, 14, 19, 26, 28, Oct 6, 9, Dec 13; 1728: DL, Mar 30, May
   16, 17, 29, BFHM, Aug 24, DL, Sep 12, 26, Oct 17, 30, Nov 15; 1729: DL, Jan
   2, 7, Feb 6, May 1, 3, 7, 12, 14, BF, Aug 26, DL, Sep 13, 23, Oct 9, Nov 7,
   Dec 2, 4, 10, 26, 29; 1730: DL, Jan 9, Feb 10, Mar 30, Apr 29, May 1, 13, 19,
   BFOF, Aug 20, SFOF, Sep 9, DL, 17, 29, Oct 1, 3, 6, 8, 20, Nov 23, 30, Dec 4;
   1731: DL, Feb 8, Apr 3, 8, 21, 26, May 3, 7, 10, 12, 17, 19, Jun 7, 11, Jul
   20, 23, Aug 6, 11, 16, SF/BFMMO, 26, DL, Sep 25, 30, Oct 2, 9, 16, 30, Nov 6,
   10, 22, 23, Dec 2, 18; 1732: DL, Feb 10, Mar 30, Apr 17, 25, May 1, 12, HAY,
   15, BFMMO, Aug 23, DL, Sep 19, 30, Oct 3, 10, 12, 17, 28, Nov 6, 7, 9, Dec
   11, 14, 22; 1733: DL, Jan 8, 29, Feb 15, 17, Mar 28, 31, Apr 24, 30, May 1,
   3, 14, BFMMO, Aug 23, DL/HAY, Sep 26, Oct 3, 5, 6, 8, 10, 12, 17, 22, 25, 27,
   Nov 1, 9, 23, Dec 17, 19, 20, 22; 1734: DL/HAY, Jan 17, HAY, Feb 6, DL/HAY,
   22, Mar 12, 25, Apr 18, 20, DL, 22, 25, DL/HAY, May 1, 3, DL, 15, BFFO, Aug
   24, DL, Sep 7, 19, Oct 3, 5, 8, 14, 17, 19, 22, 26, Nov 1, 6, 8, Dec 14;
   1735: DL, Jan 22, 23, 28, Feb 14, Mar 22, Apr 11, 14, 16, 28, May 2, 13, 14,
   LIF, Jun 12, DL, Sep 4, 13, 15, 18, 25, Oct 2, 9, 23, 24, 25, 31, Nov 3, 6,
   13, 19, 20, 29; 1736: DL, Jan 3, Feb 7, 18, Mar 11, May 7, LIF, Jun 16, DL,
   Aug 26, Sep 14, 18, 23, Oct 9, 22, 23, 25, 30, Nov 1, 3, 8, 12, 15, 19, 20,
   22, Dec 17, 31; 1737: DL, Mar 17, May 11, 27, Jun 11, Aug 30; 1738: CG, May
   1; 1739: CG, May 2; 1740: CG, Jan 22, Feb 2, Mar 11, 25, May 12, Nov 6, Dec
   13, 20, 22; 1741: CG, Jan 9, Feb 19, 24, 28, Mar 7, 16, 30, Apr 11, 16, 23,
   May 1; 1743: DL, Nov 14; 1745: GF, Nov 5, Dec 11; 1746: DL, May 8, CG, Jun
   11, 16, 27, DL, Aug 4, 6, 11; 1747: DL, May 6; 1748: CG, Jan 29, Mar 3, 14,
   28, Apr 13, 14, 28, Sep 26, Oct 17, Nov 4, 16, 24, Dec 22, 23; 1749: CG, Feb
   23, Mar 2, 14, 29, Apr 11, 21, May 4, BFY, Aug 23, CG, Sep 27, Oct 2, 19, 20,
   24, 26, Nov 1, 8, 9, 17, 23; 1750: CG, Feb 5, Apr 20, May 2; 1751: CG, May 9
Oates, Master and Miss (dancers), 1736: LIF, Jun 16; 1737: DL, May 11, LIF, Jun
   15, CG, Sep 21; 1738: CG, May 1, 18, Jun 27; 1739: CG, May 2
Oates, Miss (dancer, actor), 1730: BFOF, Aug 20, SFOF, Sep 9; 1731: DL, May 31,
   Jun 11, Jul 23, Aug 6, 16, 18, 20, SF/BFMMO, 26, DL, Oct 2, Nov 25; 1732: DL,
   Jan 1, Mar 21, May 1, 17, BFMMO, Aug 23, LIF/CG, Nov 16; 1733: LIF/CG, Jan
   18, Feb 10, Apr 13, May 10, BFMMO, Aug 23, DL/HAY, Oct 15, 25, 29, Nov 9, 24,
   26, Dec 6, 15, HAY, 26, DL/HAY, 27; 1734: DL/HAY, Jan 12, Feb 22, Mar 21, 30,
   DL, Apr 25, 29, DL/HAY, May 4, DL, 16, LIF, 23, DL/HAY, 24, BFFO, Aug 24, DL,
   Sep 19, HAY, Oct 7, DL, 9, Nov 1; 1735: DL, May 6, 13, 14, LIF, Jun 12, Jul
   11, HAY, Oct 24; 1736: DL, May 7, LIF, Jun 16, Sep 30, Oct 5, 9, 21, Nov 16,
   Dec 7, 16; 1737: LIF, Jan 19, Feb 1, Apr 2, 18, 21, 28, May 4, 7, DL, 11,
   LIF, Jun 15, Jul 26, Aug 2, 5, 9, CG, Sep 26, Oct 3, 7, 12, Nov 16; 1738: CG,
   Jan 3, 20, 21, 25, 28, 31, Feb 2, Mar 16, 21, Apr 4, 5, 11, 12, 17, 24, 25,
   26, 28, 29, May 1, 2, 3, 5, 6, 8, 10, 11, 12, 15, 16, 18, Sep 22, 27, Oct 4,
   20, 23, 26, 28, Nov 8, 13, 18, 20, Dec 5, 6, 9, 11; 1739: CG, Jan 3, 6, 8,
   15, 16, 18, 20, Feb 9, 15, Mar 5, 13, 15, 19, 22, 26, 27, Apr 2, 3, 7, 9, 23,
   24, 25, 26, 27, 30, May 1, 2, 4, 5, 7, 8, 9, 10, 11, 14, 16, 17, 18, 23, 24,
   28, 29, Aug 2, 21, 29, Sep 5, 7, 10, 12, 15, 17, 19, 22, 28, Oct 2, 3, 15,
   20, 30, Nov 1, 3, 6, 7, 8, 9, 10, 13, 14, 15, 16, 20, 21, 23, 24, 26, 28, Dec
   1, 3, 4, 6, 8, 10, 12, 13, 14, 17, 18, 19, 21, 29; 1740: CG, Jan 3, 4, 5, 8,
   15, 17, Feb 2, 6, 7, 12, Mar 10, 20, 24, 25, 27, Apr 9, 14, 16, 18, 23, 28,
   29, May 2, 5, 7, 9, 12, 13, 14, 19, 20, 21, 23, 27, 29, Jun 5, Sep 19, 29,
   Oct 3, 6, 8, 10, 22, 23, 29, 31, Nov 3, 7, 13, 15, 18, 19, 20, Dec 12, 19,
   22, 29; 1741: CG, Jan 5, 7, Feb 24, 28, Mar 2, 12, 16, 31, Apr 3

O'Beirne, Thomas Lewis, 1780: DL, Nov 22
--Generous Impostor, The, 1780: DL, Nov 22, 23, 24, 25, Dec 2, 5, 13
Obeldiston. See Olbeldiston.
Obert, Mrs. See Aubert, Isabella.
Obi. See Fawcett Jr, John.
Oboe (music), 1781: KING'S, Mar 15; 1790: CG, Mar 3
Oboe and Piano Forte (music), 1792: DLKING'S, May 1
Oboe Concerto (music), 1753: KING'S, Apr 30; 1754: KING'S, Feb 28; 1755:
  KING'S, Mar 17; 1762: KING'S, May 11; 1766: KING'S, Apr 10; 1772: HAY, Mar
  23; 1776: DL, Mar 20; 1784: DL, Mar 10; 1790: CG, Mar 17; 1792: KING'S, Mar
  14, 21; 1793: CG, Feb 15, KING/HAY, 27, CG, Mar 13, 22; 1794: CG, Mar 7, 21,
  DL, 28; 1795: CG, Feb 20; 1796: CG, Feb 24, 26; 1797: CG, Mar 22; 1798: CG,
  Feb 28, Mar 14, 30; 1799: CG, Feb 8; 1800: CG, Feb 28, Mar 5, 21
Oboe Obligato (music), 1786: CG, May 2
O'Brien, Martha Maria (actor), 1780: HAY, Jan 3
O'Brien, William (actor, author), 1758: DL, Jun 22, Oct 3, 10, 19, 21, Nov 8,
  13, 17, Dec 20, 28; 1759: DL, Jan 20, Feb 3, Mar 24, 31, Apr 17, 26, May 16,
  Jun 28, Sep 22, Oct 5, 16, 17, 25, 31, Nov 2, 8, 13, 30, Dec 19; 1760: DL,
  Jan 10, Feb 8, Mar 6, 24, Apr 11, 21, 22, 24, 29, May 8, 16, Sep 30, Oct 8,
  10, 14, 17, 24, Dec 22, 30; 1761: DL, Jan 31, Feb 5, 12, Apr 10, Jun 15, Jul
  2, 27, Aug 8, Sep 8, 10, 12, 17, 19, 25, Oct 14, 20, 24, Nov 10, 14, 23, 28,
  Dec 11, 14; 1762: DL, Jan 11, 13, 15, Feb 10, Mar 15, 25, Apr 1, May 7, 17,
  19, 26, Sep 18, 23, 30, Oct 4, 8, 9, 11, 25, 28, 29, Nov 10, 22, 26, Dec 6,
  10, 22; 1763: DL, Jan 15, 18, 27, Feb 3, Mar 15, 21, 26, Apr 12, 23, May 2,
  Sep 17, 22, 24, 29, Oct 1, 12, 14, 19, 21, 28, 29, Nov 2, 4, 9, Dec 20; 1764:
  DL, Jan 4, 9, 13, 25, 27, Feb 18, 21, Mar 24, 27, 29, Apr 2, 3, 7, 9; 1770:
  HAY, Mar 19; 1772: CG, Dec 5, DL, 8, CG, 15
--Cross Purposes, 1772: CG, Dec 5, 7, 8, 9, 10, 11, 12, 14, 16, 18, 23; 1773:
  CG, Jan 1, 13, 15, Feb 2, 25, Mar 6, 23, Oct 8, 13, Nov 23; 1774: CG, Mar 14,
  Apr 13, 26, May 10, 13, HAY, Jun 15, 20, 29, Jul 18, 27, Aug 3, CG, Nov 4,
  14, 18, Dec 23; 1775: CG, Apr 3, 29, May 12, HAY, 24, CG, 27, HAY, Aug 2, 7,
  Sep 13, CG, Oct 9, 26, Nov 10, 29; 1776: CG, Mar 9, May 15, 18, Sep 27, Oct
  16, Dec 9; 1777: CG, Feb 5, May 9, 22, CHR, Jun 30, CG, Oct 20, Nov 6; 1778:
  CHR, Jun 22, CG, Oct 2, Dec 8; 1779: CG, Mar 20, May 7, Sep 22; 1780: CG, Feb
  22; 1782: CG, Nov 2; 1783: CG, Jan 28, Oct 10; 1784: CG, Jan 23, Sep 17;
  1787: HAY, Sep 8; 1789: DL, Dec 10; 1790: CG, Oct 5; 1792: DLKING'S, Jan 9,
  DL, Sep 19; 1796: CG, Jan 8, 20; 1797: CG, Feb 22, 23, Apr 29, May 23, HAY,
  Jul 13, 17, 21, 29, Aug 9; 1798: CG, May 24, HAY, Jul 17, Aug 8, Sep 3, CG,
  Oct 31; 1799: CG, Nov 11
--Duel, The, 1772: DL, Dec 8
O'Bryan, Captain Charles (actor), 1668: ATCOURT, Jan 13, Feb 4
O'Bryen, Denis, 1783: HAY, Jul 5
--Friend in Need is a Friend Indeed!, A, 1783: HAY, Jul 5, 7, 8, 10, 14, 15,
  18, 25, Aug 2
Observations on his Journey to Paris (entertainment), 1764: CG, Apr 14, May 18;
  1765: CG, Apr 11, 24, HAY, Aug 8; 1766: HAY, Sep 2; 1767: CG, Mar 24, HAY,
  Aug 14; 1768: CG, Mar 21; 1769: CG, May 1; 1775: CG, Mar 28; 1780: HAY, Nov
  13; 1781: HAY, Nov 12; 1784: HAY, Mar 22; 1785: HAY, Mar 15; 1788: CG, Apr
  26, May 19; 1789: CG, May 22
Observations on the Importance of Theatres (pamphlet), 1769: DL, Jan 2
Occasional Oratorio, The. See Handel, George Friedric
Occhiette Furbetti (song), 1790: HAY, Jun 10
Ocean (cantata), 1799: HAY, Mar 29
Ockman (beneficiary), 1747: DL, May 18
Octave (acrobat), 1719: KING'S, Mar 2, 19
Octave Dragon (farce, anon), 1726: HAY, May 3
Octave Etourdi (farce, anon), 1726: HAY, Apr 15
Octave Flute (music), 1712: B&S, Nov 24; 1775: HAY, Feb 16
Octavius, Prince, 1779: KING'S, Mar 23
Oddities, The. See Dibdin, Charles.
Oddwell (actor, singer), 1796: CG, Oct 6; 1797: CG, Feb 18, Apr 25, May 18, Dec
  26; 1798: CG, Nov 12, Dec 11, 26; 1799: CG, Jan 14, 21, 29, Feb 11, Apr 2, 3,
  13, 23, May 4, Jun 7, Oct 24, Dec 10, 23; 1800: CG, Jan 16, Feb 10, May 1
Ode (song), 1772: MARLY, Aug 25, 28; 1786: DL, Mar 9; 1795: CG, Jun 6
Ode for the Prince's Birthday (song), 1716: HIC, Dec 13; 1772: MARLY, Sep 1, 7
Ode in Honour of Great Britain (song), 1745: DL, Mar 20
Ode in Praise of Music (music), 1703: SH, Mar 3
Ode of Horace (song), 1715: YB, May 28
Ode of Odes (music), 1776: HAY, Apr 18
Ode on Charity (song), 1779: DL, Mar 19
Ode on St Cecilia's Day. See Dryden, John.
Ode on the Glorious Beginning of Her Majesty's Reign (music), 1704: DL, Jan 4

Ode on the King (music), 1716: HIC, Dec 13
Ode on the King's Birthday (entertainment), 1692: COURT, Nov 5; 1693: ATCOURT,
    Nov 4
Ode on the Passions (entertainment), 1774: CG, Apr 18, May 25; 1781: CG, Mar
    23, 31; 1784: CG, Apr 27, May 17; 1785: HAY, Apr 26; 1788: DL, Apr 30, May
    19; 1790: HAY, Sep 29; 1791: CG, Feb 15; 1792: DLKING'S, Mar 26, CG, Apr 14,
    28; 1793: CG, Apr 17; 1794: HAY, Aug 30; 1795: DL, Apr 14, CG, 24, DL, May
    30, WLWS, Jun 19; 1796: CG, Mar 14, HAY, 28, DL, Apr 12, HAY, 27, Sep 16;
    1797: HAY, Aug 22, Sep 18; 1798: CG, Apr 18, May 15, DL, Jun 15; 1799: DL,
    May 16, CG, Jun 12; 1800: CG, Apr 19
Ode on the Power of Music (entertainment), 1763: DL, Mar 12
Ode on the Recovery of His Majesty (entertainment), 1789: DL, May 11
Ode to Echo (song), 1760: DL, Apr 16, May 8
Ode upon dedicating a building at Stratford. See Garrick, David.
Ode upon the Happy Accession of Her Majesty to the Throne (music), 1704: DL,
    Jan 4
Ode Upon the Happy Return of King Charles II to his Languishing Nations
    (entertainment), 1660: NONE, May 29
Odell, George C D (author), 1773: CG, Oct 23
Odell, Miss (beneficiary), 1731: GF, Oct 27
Odell, Mrs (beneficiary), 1735: TC, Aug 18; 1751: DL, Feb 21
Odell, Thomas (proprietor, author), 1721: LIF, Jan 19; 1729: HAY, May 7, GF,
    Dec 30; 1730: GF, Apr 28, Jun 27; 1731: GF, May 21, Jun 2, 4; 1735: DL, Jun
    11, GF, Nov 3, HAY, Dec 29; 1736: LIF, Jun 8, HAY, Jul 30; 1744: HAY, Oct 11,
    16
--Chimera, The; or, An Hue and Cry to Change Alley, 1721: LIF, Jan 19, 20, 21,
    25
--Patron, The; or, Statesman's Opera (opera), 1729: HAY, May 7
--Prodigal, The; or, Recruits for the Queen of Hungary, 1744: HAY, Aug 28, Oct
    11, 13, 16
--Smuglers, The, 1729: HAY, May 7
Odenato and Zenobia. See Sarti, Giuseppe.
Oder (beneficiary), 1717: LIF, Jun 3
Odi grand Ombra (song), 1793: KING/HAY, Mar 15
Odiham, 1788: DL, Apr 14
Odingsells, Gabriel, 1725: LIF, Feb 27, Dec 8; 1730: DL, Mar 30
--Bath Unmasked, The, 1725: LIF, Feb 27, Mar 1, 2, 4, 6, 8, 9, 16, Apr 17, 30,
    May 27, Oct 26; 1728: LIF, Mar 21
--Bayes Opera, 1730: DL, Mar 30, 31, Apr 1; 1731: DL, Jul 23, 27
--Capricious Lovers, The (opera), 1725: LIF, Dec 8, 9, 10
Odio vinto dall' Eroismo, L' (dance), 1795: KING'S, Jun 13, 16, 20
Odo il suo no de quendiaccenti (song), 1762: KING'S, May 11
Oedipe. See Voltaire.
Oedipus Tyrannus. See Sophocles.
Oedipus, King of Thebes. See Dryden, John.
Of Age To-morrow. See Dibdin, Thomas John.
Of all sensations Pity brings. See Soldier's Grave.
Of all the world's enjoyments (song), 1699: DL, May 0
Of English Brown Beer (song), 1742: CG, Mar 15; see also Praise of Good English
    Beer
Of plighted Faith (song), 1796: DL, May 25
Of the ancients it's speaking (song), 1790: CG, Nov 23; 1791: CG, May 3, Sep
    19; 1792: CG, Apr 18; 1793: CG, Apr 24, May 21; 1794: CG, Apr 12, Oct 29;
    1795: CG, Oct 7; 1797: CG, Oct 2; 1799: CG, Mar 16, 27, Apr 18, Dec 9; see
    also Irish Drinking Song
Officier en Recrue, L'. See Farquhar, George, The Recruiting Officer.
Offild. See Oldfield.
Offrande a Terpsichore, L' (dance), 1797: KING'S, Nov 28, Dec 2, 20, 30; 1798:
    KING'S, Feb 6
Offrandes a l'Amour, Les (dance), 1787: KING'S, Dec 8; 1788: KING'S, Jan 3, 12,
    15, Feb 5, 23, 26, Mar 1, Apr 17, 19, 22, May 8
Oft have our footsteps (song), 1798: CG, Apr 9
Oft on a plat of rising ground (song), 1782: DL, Feb 15; 1789: CG, Mar 20;
    1790: CG, Mar 3, DL, 10; 1791: CG, Mar 18; 1793: CG, Mar 20; 1794: CG, Mar
    21, DL, Apr 9; 1795: KING'S, Feb 27; 1799: CG, Mar 15
Ogden (actor), 1773: MARLY, Sep 3
Ogden, Henrietta Maria, Mrs John (dancer), 1724: LIF, Mar 14, 23, 28, Apr 6, 7,
    8, 10, 21, 22, 23, 27, 28, May 2, 4, 5, 8, 12, 13, 15, 16, 18, 20, 22, 26,
    27, 28, Jun 1, 2, 3, 23, Jul 29, SOU, Sep 24, LIF, 30, Oct 9, Nov 10, 13, 18;
    1725: LIF, Jan 21, Mar 11, 13, 29, 31, Apr 7, 10, 14, 15, 17, 20, 22, 23, 28,
    May 1, 3, 4, 5, 6, 7, 10, 12, 14, 17, 18, 19, 20, 21, 22, 24, 25, Oct 4;
    1726: LIF, Jan 11, 14, Mar 26, Apr 11, 16, 20, 21, 26, 27, 30, May 3, 14, 24,

26, Jun 17, 21, 24, Jul 1, 5, 15, 19, 22, 29, Aug 2, 5, 9, 16, 19, 23, Sep
14, 16, 30, Oct 3, 7, 24, Nov 9, 14, 21, Dec 3, 9; 1727: LIF, Jan 9, 31, Feb
9, 13, Mar 20, Apr 7, 10, 21, 27, May 4, 8, 22, Oct 12, 26, Nov 1, 7, 9, 16,
23, Dec 9, 22; 1728: LIF, Jan 8, Mar 21, Apr 4, 6, 22, 24, 29, May 6, 8, 11,
15, 16, 18, 22, 23, 29, Jun 25, Jul 2, Aug 2, BFB, 24, LIF, Oct 9, 14, 26,
Nov 8; 1729: LIF, Jan 13, 16, 18, Feb 6, Mar 10, 17, 20, 27, Apr 8, 10, 11,
19, 22, 24, 26, 28, 30, May 3, 6, 7, 8, 9, 12, 13, 15, 19, 20, 22, 23, BFB,
Aug 25, LIF, Oct 10, 15, 22, 24, Nov 1, 4; 1730: LIF, Jan 2, Apr 10, 24, 25,
29, 30, May 1, 6, 11, 15, 18, 20, 23, 27, Jun 1, Jul 3, RI, 16, LIF, Sep 18,
25, Oct 1, 9, 27, 30, Nov 3, 6, 7, Dec 7, 15; 1731: LIF, Jan 4, Apr 3, 28,
May 3, 6, 10, 14, 17, 19, 20, 21, RI, Jul 1, BFB, Aug 26, LIF, Sep 22, Oct 4,
11, 15, 25, 27, Nov 2, 6, 8, 12, 13, 18, 25, Dec 1, 7, 14, 17; 1732: LIF, Jan
5, 19, Mar 21, 27, 30, Apr 11, 17, 18, 19, 22, 25, 26, 27, 28, May 1, 2, 3,
4, 5, 8, 9, 10, 11, 16, 17, 18, RI, Aug 17, BFB, 23, LIF/CG, Sep 25, 27, Oct
2, 4, 9, 13, 16, LIF, 18, LIF/CG, Nov 7, 8, 16, 21, 24, Dec 4, 8, 15, CG/LIF,
19, 26, LIF/CG, 27, CG/LIF, 28; 1733: LIF/CG, Jan 12, 15, 16, 18, 23, Feb 2,
CG, 8, LIF/CG, Mar 12, CG, 27, LIF/CG, 28, 29, 30, Apr 2, 11, 12, 16, 18, 19,
20, 21, 23, 24, 27, 30, CG, May 1, 2, LIF/CG, 3, CG, 4, LIF/CG, 7, 8, 10, CG,
11, LIF/CG, 15, CG, 16, 17, LIF/CG, 18, 19, 21, 24, CG/LIF, 28, LIF/CG, 29,
Jun 1, CG, 26, 29, Aug 14, 17, 21, BF, 23, CG, Sep 22, 25, 27, Oct 4, 6, 13,
16, 26, 27, Nov 1, 12, 23, Dec 4, 7, 11, 28; 1734: CG, Jan 17, 25, Feb 26,
Mar 11, 16, Apr 1, May 9, 10, 14, 15, 16, 17, CG/LIF, Sep 20, Oct 2, 31, Dec
5, 12, 19, 30; 1735: CG/LIF, Jan 13, Feb 13, 22, Apr 17, May 2, CG, 6, 8,
CG/LIF, 9, 12, 13, 15, 16, 20, 22, 26, 27, Jun 2, CG, Sep 26, Oct 3, 13, 17,
Nov 6, 11, Dec 18; 1736: CG, Jan 1, 9, 10, 23, Feb 23, 26, Mar 6, 11, May 6,
11, Sep 22, 29, Oct 4, 6, 8, 27, Nov 3, 9, 23, 26; 1737: CG, Jan 28, Feb 14,
Mar 7, 24, 28, Apr 15, May 6, 12, 16, 19; 1748: BFLYY, Aug 24
Ogden, John (actor), 1715: LIF, Feb 7, Oct 11, 24, Dec 12; 1716: LIF, Jan 24,
Mar 19, Apr 3, May 8, Jul 4, Oct 18, Dec 4; 1717: LIF, May 15, 16, Nov 16,
19, 20, 26, 28, Dec 14; 1718: LIF, Jan 7, Feb 3, 18, Apr 23, Jun 20, 30, Jul
9, 24, RI, Aug 2, 9, 11, LIF, Sep 26, 30, Oct 1, 3, 4, 11, 16, 31, Nov 11,
25, Dec 6; 1719: LIF, Jan 16, Feb 7, 21, Apr 29, BFBL, Aug 24, LIF, Oct 2, 5,
7, 10, 13, Nov 5, 7, 12, 13, 18, 19, 21, 23, Dec 10; 1720: LIF, Jan 7, Feb
11, 23, Mar 28, Apr 26, May 5, 14, 30, BFBL, Aug 23, LIF, Oct 1, 11, 15, 22,
Nov 1, Dec 27, 31; 1721: LIF, Apr 17, 19, 21, Oct 21, 24, Nov 4, 9; 1722:
LIF, May 15, Jun 13, Aug 1, Oct 18, Nov 8, 22, 26; 1723: LIF, Dec 17; 1724:
LIF, Mar 19, 28, Apr 6, 29, May 8, 18, 20, 27, Jun 23, Jul 3, 14, 21, 31, Aug
11, Sep 23, SOU, 24, LIF, 28, Oct 27, Nov 11, 12; 1725: LIF, Apr 7, 14, 23,
May 6, 21, Sep 24, Oct 11, Nov 11, 29; 1726: LIF, Mar 24, May 10, 18, Jun 17,
24, Jul 5, 22, Aug 2, 19, Sep 19, 28, Nov 10, 18; 1727: LIF, Jan 16, Apr 10,
19, May 2, 8, 19, 22, Sep 20, 25, Oct 19, 31, Dec 11; 1728: LIF, Jan 8, 17,
Apr 23, 29, May 15, 16, 23, Jun 25, Jul 2, 5, 19, Aug 2, Sep 16, Nov 11, Dec
28; 1729: LIF, Jan 13, Feb 10, Apr 16, 17, 26, BFB, Aug 25, LIF, Sep 29, Oct
13, Nov 14, 25; 1730: LIF, Jan 19, Apr 20, May 6, 11, 13, 14, 15, 18, RI, Jun
27, LIF, Oct 5, 7, 12, 26, Nov 3, Dec 30; 1731: LIF, Jan 8, 13, 19, 21, Feb
3, 27, May 6, 12, 17, 20, 25, RI, Jul 1, 8, 15, 22, BFB, Aug 26, LIF, Sep 17,
27, 29, Oct 6, 13, 18, 20, Dec 1, 6, 8, 9; 1732: LIF, Feb 5, 15, Apr 24, May
1, 31, Jul 3; 1733: LIF/CG, Feb 5; 1737: CG, May 6
Ogilby, John (composer), 1664: ATCOURT, Jan 0
Ogilvie, Ann (actor), 1767: HAY, May 29, Jun 22, 25, 26, Jul 15, Aug 14, Sep 7,
CG, Nov 7; 1768: CG, Feb 13, May 4, HAY, Aug 15, 24, CG, Sep 30, Oct 4, 7;
1769: CG, Apr 28, May 5, 23, HAY, 24, 26, 29, Jun 5, 21, Jul 12, 17, Aug 31,
Sep 19, CG, 20, Nov 9; 1770: CG, Jan 3, 18, Feb 12, Mar 24, Apr 21, 24, May
12, HAY, Sep 27, Oct 5, 15; 1771: CG, Jan 12, Nov 11, Dec 6, 11; 1772: CG,
Apr 9, May 30, Sep 28, Nov 6, 12; 1773: CG, Feb 10, May 20, Dec 18, 22; 1774:
CG, Mar 21, May 4, Oct 15, Nov 19; 1775: CG, Feb 23, Apr 22
Oglethorpe, Theophilus (spectator), 1700: DL, Mar 13
Ogn' Amante (song), 1757: KING'S, Mar 24
Oh all ye gods of Holy Truth (song), 1695: NONE, Sep 0
Oh dear, sweet sir you look so gay (song), 1697: DG, Jun 0
Oh dio mancar mi Sento (song), 1750: KING'S, Apr 10
Oh Joshua! (song), 1794: DL, Apr 10
Oh tis Elysium All (song), 1754: KING'S, Feb 28
Oh welcome home, my dearest Jack (song), 1795: CG, Nov 16
Oh why to be happy (song), 1795: CG, Apr 28; 1796: CG, Mar 14, Apr 12, May 12,
28; 1797: CG, May 11, 20
O'Hara, Kane, 1764: CG, Feb 22; 1773: CG, Feb 6, 9, Mar 11; 1775: CG, Jan 21;
1777: HAY, Aug 22; 1778: HAY, Aug 7; 1780: CG, Oct 3; 1796: CG, Nov 5
--April-Day (burletta), 1777: HAY, Aug 22, 26; 1778: HAY, Aug 7, 11
--Golden Pippin, The, 1772: CG, Dec 7; 1773: CG, Feb 6, 8, 9, 12, 13, 17, 20,
27, Mar 9, 11, Apr 21, 22, Oct 20, Nov 26, 30, Dec 2, 3, 4, 7, 9, 11, 13, 31;
1774: CG, Jan 1, Oct 15, 27, 29, Nov 3, 8, 16, 24, Dec 15, 20; 1775: CG, Jan

21, Feb 9, 15, 23, Mar 7, 21, 23; 1776: CG, Oct 15, 17, 21, 23, 26, 30; 1777:
CG, Jan 13, 18, 27, 29, Feb 7, 24, Mar 1, 6, 11; 1780: CG, Feb 5, Mar 4, 7,
9, 31, Dec 9, 19; 1781: CG, Feb 7, Oct 24, 25, 26, Nov 23, Dec 17; 1782: CG,
Feb 9, Dec 4, 6; 1783: CG, May 24, Jun 3; 1787: HAY, Jul 16, 17, 20, 24, Aug
1, 25, 29, Sep 5; 1792: CG, May 11; 1796: CG, Oct 7, Nov 5
--Midas (burletta), 1764: CG, Feb 22, 23, 24, 25, 27, 28, 29, Mar 1, 2, 3, DL,
16; 1766: CG, Feb 5, 6, 10, 11, 15, 17, 20, 22, 24, 27, Mar 1, 4, 6, 8, 10,
13, 18, 31, Apr 4, 9, 15, 16, 28, 30, May 7, 15, Oct 14, 16, Nov 7, 13; 1767:
CG, Feb 10, 12, 28, Mar 5, 12, 19, Apr 4, 24, 28, May 4, 6, 11, Oct 27, 31,
Nov 5, 6, 24, 27, Dec 5, 9, 11; 1768: CG, Jan 2, 19, 28, Feb 9, 18, Mar 21,
Apr 7, Jun 4, Sep 30, Oct 15, 29, Nov 5, 12, 16, 24, Dec 1, 9, 16; 1769: CG,
Feb 7, 11, 16, 23, Mar 2, 9, 30, May 23, Sep 20, Oct 3, 17, 24, Dec 9, 19;
1770: CG, Jan 3, 20, Mar 10, 12, HAY, Aug 1, 3, 6, 16, CG, Sep 26, Oct 10,
11, 13, 30, Nov 13, Dec 7, 15; 1771: CG, Mar 7, May 9, 16, Sep 25, Oct 2, 7,
14, 23, 25, Dec 19; 1772: CG, Mar 28; 1773: CG, Feb 6, Sep 24, 27, Oct 4, 9,
12, 15, 18, 25, Nov 8, 15, 19, 22, Dec 21; 1774: CG, Jan 24, Feb 3, 21, 26,
Mar 10, 15, 24, May 5, 26; 1775: CG, Jan 21, Nov 13, 14, 15, 17, 20; 1776:
CG, May 6, 7, HAY, Sep 18, CHR, 23; 1777: CG, Mar 31, Apr 2, 8, 10, 12, 21,
May 2, HAY, Jun 9, 13, 18, Jul 1, 14, 16, Aug 22, 23, Sep 4, 8, 10, 11; 1778:
CG, Jan 29, Apr 25, May 5, HAY, Jun 12, 16, 17, 23, Jul 17, 20, 25, Aug 7,
24; 1779: CG, Mar 27, Apr 6, 16, 20, May 1, 18, HAY, Jun 17, 19, 24, 26, Jul
17, 19, 30, Aug 12, CG, Sep 24, Oct 4, 13, 23; 1780: HAY, May 30, Aug 2, CG,
Oct 3; 1781: CG, Apr 2, 23, May 24, HAY, Aug 15, CG, Oct 19; 1782: CG, Feb
18, 19; 1783: HAY, Aug 26; 1784: CG, Apr 26, 28, May 18, HAY, Jul 24, 26, Aug
3, CG, Oct 18, Dec 13, 15; 1785: CG, Mar 12, 19, May 16, HAMM, Jul 15, CG,
Nov 2, 4, 28; 1786: CG, Apr 21, Dec 5; 1787: CG, May 30, HAY, Aug 10, CG, Sep
24; 1788: CG, May 15, 27, Sep 17; 1789: CG, Feb 16, Apr 28, May 11, Jun 16,
HAY, Jul 29, CG, Oct 23; 1791: CG, May 6; 1794: CG, Nov 7, 10; 1795: CG, Feb
13, Nov 14
--Tom Thumb (burlesque), 1780: CG, Oct 3, 4, 6, 10, 11, 13, 18, 26, 27, 31, Nov
1, 8, 10, 11, 17, 21, 27, Dec 23; 1781: CG, Feb 10, 14, 22, 23, 26, 27, Apr
3, 7, 17, 21, 24, May 4, 11, HAY, Aug 22, 24, CG, Oct 10, 30, Nov 1, 3, 14,
Dec 7, 13, 19, 22; 1782: CG, Feb 11, 16, 26, Mar 5, 14, Apr 2, 20, 27, May 4, Sep
27, Oct 4, 8, 11, 19, Nov 29; 1783: CG, Feb 28, Apr 1, May 2, 20, 27, Jun 4,
Sep 26, Oct 15, Dec 11; 1784: CG, Jan 22, Apr 13, 15, DL, 28, CG, Nov 6, 29;
1785: CG, Mar 1, Apr 8, Nov 21, Dec 9; 1786: CG, May 13, 20, Nov 23; 1788:
CG, Mar 29, Apr 11, May 5, 28, Jun 3, Oct 3; 1789: CG, Feb 13, 20, May 19,
29, Oct 16, Nov 23; 1790: CG, Feb 10, Apr 7, 28, Dec 8; 1791: CG, Feb 8, Sep
16; 1792: CG, May 12; 1793: CG, Jan 23, Jun 5, Sep 17; 1794: CG, Oct 10, 15,
24; 1795: CG, May 6, 21; 1796: CG, May 18; 1797: CG, Apr 19; 1799: CG, May 3;
1800: CG, Apr 17
--Two Misers, The (musical), 1775: CG, Jan 21, 23, 24, 26, 31, Feb 1, 2, 3, 4,
7, 16, Mar 4, 9, 11, 28, Apr 27, May 5, 10, 19, 26, Sep 20, 22, Oct 4, 12,
Nov 3; 1776: CG, Apr 9, May 1, 10, Dec 2, 3, 5; 1777: CG, Mar 17, 18, Oct 15,
Nov 14, Dec 11; 1778: CG, Jan 28; 1779: CG, Dec 17; 1786: CG, Apr 4, 19, Nov
30; 1787: CG, Feb 1, 22, Oct 5; 1788: CG, May 24; 1790: CG, Apr 12, May 5;
1794: CG, Apr 25
Oiseleurs, Les (dance), 1779: KING'S, Jan 23, 29, Feb 6, 9, 27, Mar 11, Apr 29,
May 13
Oithona (dramatic poem), 1768: HAY, Mar 3
O'Keeffe (Keeffe), Mary, Mrs John (actor), 1778: CG, Jan 12, DL, Nov 25, Dec
11; 1779: CG, Feb 20
O'Keeffe, John (actor, author), 1778: CG, Jan 12, HAY, Jul 2, Aug 14, DL, Nov
25; 1779: CG, Feb 20, HAY, Aug 14, Oct 13; 1781: HAY, Jun 16, Sep 4, CG, Nov
24, 28; 1782: CG, Feb 9, Mar 16, Apr 1, HAY, Jun 4, Jul 5, Aug 17, CG, Sep
25, Nov 2, 25; 1783: CG, Feb 14, 25, Apr 7, HAY, May 31, Jul 26, Aug 12, 28,
CG, Nov 4, 8, Dec 23; 1784: CG, Jan 29, HAY, Aug 20, Sep 6, CG, Nov 16; 1785:
CG, Feb 7, May 12, HAY, 30, Jun 16, HAMM, Jul 25, HAY, Aug 24, CG, Oct 7, Nov
3, Dec 20; 1786: CG, Feb 17, HAMM, Jul 5, 7, 10, HAY, Aug 12, CG, Dec 1;
1787: CG, Jan 27, Mar 12, Oct 31; 1788: CG, Mar 1, Apr 1, HAY, Jul 2, Aug 18,
CG, Nov 6, Dec 26; 1789: CG, Feb 3, Apr 4, 14, Nov 28; 1790: CG, Mar 8, HAY,
Sep 4, CG, Nov 4; 1791: CG, Mar 14, Apr 16; 1793: CG, May 11, HAY, Jun 29,
CG, Nov 23; 1794: CG, May 16, HAY, Sep 1; 1795: CG, Mar 19, Apr 23, Dec 21;
1796: CG, Mar 19, Apr 9, 23, HAY, Jun 22, CG, Oct 7, Nov 5; 1797: CG, May 17,
Dec 19; 1798: DL, May 19, Jun 5, 6; 1800: CG, Jun 12
--Agreeable Surprise, The, 1781: HAY, Sep 1, 3, 4, 5, 7, 10, 12, 13, 15, CG,
Nov 24, 26, 27, 29, 30, Dec 1, 18, 20; 1782: CG, Apr 1, HAY, Jun 4, 6, 8, 15,
22, 28, 29, Jul 6, 8, 10, 12, 22, 26, 31, Aug 3, 7, Sep 7, 9, 12, 14, 20;
1783: CG, Apr 7, HAY, May 31, Jun 3, 5, 9, 12, 17, 23, 28, Jul 2, 11, 17, 22,
25, Aug 2, 6, 9, 25, Sep 1, 5, 10; 1784: CG, Jan 13, 15, 17, HAY, May 28, Jun
1, 8, 9, 15, 18, 29, Jul 2, 3, 5, 31, Aug 18, 20, 27, Sep 4, 6, 15; 1785:
HAY, May 30, Jun 1, 4, 14, 30, Jul 4, 7, 9, 18, 30, Aug 24, 27; 1786: HAY,

Jun 14, 16, 28, HAMM, 30, Jul 5, HAY, 6, HAMM, 12, HAY, Aug 5, 24, 31, Sep
15; 1787: HAY, May 23, Jun 14, 18, 23, 27, Jul 5, 14, 20, 26, 30, Aug 20, 23,
Sep 15; 1788: HAY, Jun 10, 13, 18, 20, 28, Jul 11, 31, Aug 19, Sep 2, 6, 13;
1789: HAY, Jun 19, 23, 30, Jul 8, 20, 24, 27, Aug 3, 6, 8, 29, Sep 1, 10, 15;
1790: HAY, Jun 18, 23, Jul 5, 22, Aug 5; 1791: HAY, Jun 13, 18, 22, Aug 10;
1792: HAY, Jul 9, 11, 16, 18, 21, 23, 30, Aug 4, 13, 20, 27, Sep 5, 11, 15;
1793: DL, Apr 8, HAY, Aug 27, Sep 11; 1794: HAY, Aug 12, 15, 19, 23, Sep 9;
1795: DL, Apr 16, HAY, Jun 10, 12, Jul 1, 7, 28, Aug 4, 18, Sep 4, 8, CG, Dec
5, 10; 1796: HAY, Jun 14, 21, Jul 16, Aug 16; 1797: HAY, Jun 13, 22, 27, Jul
1, 12, Aug 18, 24, 31, Sep 8, CG, Nov 8, Dec 23; 1798: CG, Feb 10, DL, Jun 6,
HAY, 18, 26, Jul 9, 26, Aug 13, Sep 6, 13, DL, 27; 1799: DL, May 2, WRSG, 17,
HAY, Jun 17, Jul 3, Aug 8, 9; 1800: CG, Jun 12, HAY, 21, 28, Jul 1, 10, 31,
Aug 29
--Aladin; or, The Wonderful Lamp, 1788: CG, Dec 26, 27, 29, 30, 31; 1789: CG,
Jan 1, 2, 3, 5, 6, 7, 8, 9, 10, 12, 14, 16, 19, 22, 24, 27, 28, 29, Feb 3,
23, Apr 13, 15; 1797: CG, Jun 9; 1798: CG, Jun 2
--Alfred; or, The Magic Banner, 1796: HAY, Jun 22
--Banditti, The; or, Love's Labyrinth (opera), 1781: CG, Nov 28; 1782: CG, Nov
2
--Basket Maker, The (opera), 1790: HAY, Sep 4, 7, 9, 10, 13; 1800: CG, Jun 12
--Beggar on Horseback, A (farce), 1785: HAY, Jun 16, 17, 18, 20, 22, 23, 25,
28, 29, Jul 14; 1786: HAY, Jun 10, 12, Jul 14, Aug 4, 17, 23; 1787: HAY, Jun
20, Jul 23, Aug 3; 1788: HAY, Jun 30, Jul 23, 25; 1797: HAY, Aug 8; 1800: CG,
Jun 12
--Birth Day, The; or, The Prince of Arragon, 1783: HAY, Aug 12, 14, 16, 21, 23,
25
--Blacksmith of Antwerp, The (farce), 1785: CG, Feb 7, 8; 1800: CG, Jun 12
--Britain's Brave Tars!!; or, All for St. Paul's, 1797: CG, Dec 19, 21
--Castle of Andalusia, The, 1781: CG, Nov 28; 1782: CG, Nov 2, 4, 5, 6, 7, 8,
9, 11, 12, 13, 14, 15, 16, 19, 21, 22, 23, Dec 7, 11, 13, 18, 21, 28; 1783:
CG, Jan 2, 7, 11, 14, 16, 21, 25, Feb 11, 15, 20, Mar 15, 22, Apr 7, 21, May
1, 12, HAY, Sep 9, CG, Oct 28, Nov 6, 11, 19, 25, Dec 3, 20; 1784: CG, Jan
24, Feb 7, 17, Mar 13, 30, Apr 23, 24, HAY, Aug 17; 1785: CG, Mar 30, Apr 25,
May 21, Oct 14, Nov 29; 1786: CG, Apr 20, 29, May 19, Nov 24; 1787: CG, May
10; 1788: CG, Apr 1, 9, May 14, 21; 1789: CG, Mar 31, Sep 23, Oct 17, Dec 18;
1790: CG, Feb 3, Mar 20, Apr 24; 1791: CG, May 5, 26, Sep 30, Oct 14; 1792:
CG, May 23; 1793: CG, Jan 9, Jun 4, Sep 25, Oct 22, Nov 12, Dec 17, 21; 1794:
CG, Jan 11, Feb 15, Jun 12, Oct 3; 1795: CG, Jan 7, Jun 4, Sep 23; 1796: CG,
May 10, Oct 21; 1797: CG, Jun 6, Sep 27, 29, Dec 5; 1798: CG, Apr 25; 1799:
DL, May 4, CG, Sep 27; 1800: CG, Jun 12
--Czar, The, 1790: CG, Mar 8, 11, 13, 16, Nov 4; 1800: CG, Jun 12
--Dead Alive, The (opera), 1781: HAY, Jun 16, 18, 19, 21, 23, 27, 30, Jul 3, 7,
13, 16, 26, 31, Aug 3; 1782: HAY, Jul 5, 10, 11, 15, 18, Aug 23; 1783: HAY,
Aug 1, 8, 13, 19; 1784: HAY, Aug 20; 1785: HAY, Aug 16, 24; 1786: HAY, Sep 9;
1787: HAY, Jul 25; 1788: HAY, Aug 25; 1792: HAY, Aug 2; 1794: HAY, Jul 22,
24, Aug 1, 7, 13, 29; 1795: HAY, Jun 15, 17, Jul 3, 16, 20, Aug 6, 22, Sep 1,
5; 1796: HAY, Jun 13, 23, Jul 28, Aug 13, 25; 1797: HAY, Jun 28, Jul 27;
1798: DL, Jun 6, HAY, Aug 4, 8; 1799: HAY, Jun 18; 1800: CG, Jun 12
--Doldrum, The; or, 1803 (farce), 1796: CG, Apr 23, 25, 27, 30, May 2, 4, 7,
11, 25, Sep 12; 1797: CG, Feb 27; 1800: CG, Jun 12
--Eleventh of June, The; or, The Daggerwoods at Dunstable (interlude), 1798:
DL, Jun 5, 7, 13
--Farmer, The (farce), 1787: CG, Oct 26, 31, Nov 2, 7, 8, 14, 15, 20, 22, 26,
29, 30, Dec 5, 7, 10, 12, 14, 17, 20; 1788: CG, Jan 21, 25, 29, Feb 1, 7, 18,
19, 21, 25, 28, Mar 3, 6, 13, Apr 5, 10, 17, 24, May 1, 6, 20, 29, Jun 5, 9,
Sep 24, Oct 6, 20, 27, Nov 12, 26, Dec 9, 11, 19; 1789: CG, Jan 14, 22, Feb
2, 9, 18, 23, Mar 9, 26, Apr 23, May 4, 23, Jun 16, Sep 14, 30, Oct 17, 19,
Nov 4, 25, Dec 16; 1790: CG, Jan 6, 27, Feb 2, 20, Mar 15, Apr 12, 23, 28,
May 4, Jun 11, Dec 2, 4, 7, 16, 18; 1791: CG, Jan 18, Feb 5, 7, 15, 22, Apr
14, May 4, 21, Jun 14, Sep 12, Oct 13, Nov 21, Dec 6; 1792: CG, Jan 6, Feb
27, Apr 20, May 16, 24, Sep 21, Oct 31, Dec 17; 1793: CG, Jan 29, May 8, 31,
Sep 27, Oct 17, Dec 16; 1794: CG, Feb 19, Jun 5, 16, HAY, Aug 23, CG, Oct 17,
Nov 13; 1795: CG, Feb 11, Mar 26, May 30, Sep 14, Dec 1; 1796: CG, May 6, 31,
Sep 21, Nov 4, Dec 16; 1797: CG, Feb 15, Sep 22, Nov 11, 23; 1798: CG, Feb 6,
May 3, 18, DL, Jun 6, CG, 11, HAY, Aug 6, CG, Sep 19; 1799: CG, Jan 12, May
20, Sep 23, Nov 2; 1800: CG, Feb 7, Jun 3, 12
--Fontainbleau; or, Our Way in France (opera), 1784: CG, Nov 16, 17, 18, 20,
23, 25, 27, 30, Dec 1, 2, 4, 7, 8, 10; 1785: CG, Jan 6, Feb 19, Apr 27, May
25, HAY, Aug 9, CG, Oct 7, Nov 3, 22; 1786: CG, Jan 10, Apr 21, May 19, 23,
HAMM, Jul 10, CG, Dec 1, 18; 1787: CG, Apr 24, May 17; 1788: CG, Mar 15, Apr
2, 26, May 8, 28, Sep 26, Dec 23; 1789: CG, May 20, 25, Sep 16, Oct 2, Dec
29; 1790: CG, Feb 18, Apr 22, Oct 15, Nov 2; 1791: CG, May 3, Jun 4, Sep 14;

1792: CG, Oct 3; 1793: CG, Jun 7, Oct 5, 15; 1794: CG, Jan 4; 1795: CG, Jan 29, KING'S, Dec 12; 1796: CG, Apr 5, May 26; 1798: CG, May 24, DL, Jun 6; 1800: CG, Jun 12

--French Grenadier, 1800: CG, Jun 12

--Friar Bacon; or, Harlequin's Adventures in Lilliput, Brobdignag (pantomime), 1783: CG, Dec 23, 26, 27, 29, 30, 31; 1784: CG, Jan 1, 2, 3, 5, 6, 7, 8, 9, 10, 12, 29; 1789: CG, Dec 21; 1790: CG, Nov 15; 1793: CG, Oct 2; 1799: CG, May 13

--Fugitive, The (opera), 1790: CG, Mar 8, Nov 4, 5, 6, 8

--Harlequin Rambler; or, The Convent in an Uproar (pantomime), 1783: CG, Dec 23; 1784: CG, Jan 29, 31, Feb 2, 3, 4, 5, 6, 9, 11, 17, 23, Mar 2, 8, Apr 12, 17, 19, May 3, 14, 20, 31, Sep 20, 27, Oct 4, 11, Nov 4; 1789: CG, Dec 21; 1790: CG, Nov 15; 1793: CG, Oct 2; 1799: CG, May 13

--Harlequin Teague; or, The Giant's Causeway (pantomime), 1782: HAY, Aug 17, 19, 20, 21, 22, 24, 26, 29, 31, Sep 2, 4, 5, 6, 7, 9, 10, 11, 12, 13, 14, 18, 19, 20; 1783: HAY, Jun 28, 30, Jul 1, 4, 9, 12, 14, 15, 21, 23, Aug 4, 5, 18, Sep 1, 3; 1785: HAY, Jul 13, 18, 20, 25, 27, 28, Aug 1, 25, 30; 1786: HAY, Sep 4, 6, 11, 13

--Highland Reel, The (opera), 1788: CG, Nov 6, 7, 8, 10, 11, 13, 15, 18, 20, 22, 25, Dec 1, 3, 8, 12, 17; 1789: CG, Jan 6, 19, 29, Feb 13, Apr 4, 27, May 2, 8, 15, 27, Jun 9, Sep 28, Oct 6, 14, 27, Nov 9, 18, 23, Dec 7, 14; 1790: CG, Jan 12, 26, Feb 6, 16, Apr 5, 24, May 20, 29, Jun 12, Oct 5, Nov 9, 17; 1791: CG, Feb 17, Apr 16, Nov 7; 1792: CG, Feb 20, Apr 14, Oct 5, Dec 3; 1793: CG, May 6, Oct 10, Dec 12; 1794: CG, Mar 25, Apr 1, May 24, Jun 4, Nov 11; 1795: CG, Feb 13, Mar 21, Oct 22; 1796: CG, Sep 19; 1797: CG, Nov 1; 1798: CG, May 30, Nov 1; 1799: CG, May 22, Sep 20; 1800: CG, Jun 12

--Irish Mimic, The; or, Blunders at Brighton (farce), 1795: CG, Apr 23, 25, 30, May 2, 9, 20, Jun 1, 3, HAY, Aug 21, CG, Nov 18, 21, 24, 28, Dec 3, 8; 1796: CG, Mar 19, Apr 22, May 12, Jun 6, Oct 29; 1797: CG, Feb 20, May 4, Oct 11, Nov 22; 1798: CG, Feb 3; 1799: CG, Jan 28, May 29, Oct 17; 1800: CG, Feb 27, Jun 7, 12

--Jenny's Whim; or, The Roasted Emperor (farce), 1794: HAY, Sep 1

--Key to the Lock, The (farce), 1788: HAY, Aug 18

--Lad of the Hills, The; or, The Wicklow Gold Mine (Wicklow Mountains, The) (opera), 1796: CG, Apr 9, 11, 13, 23, May 16, Oct 7, 10, 12, 13, 14, 26, Dec 10; 1797: CG, Mar 4, Sep 25; 1800: CG, Jun 12

--Lie of the Day, The; or, A Party at Hampton Court, 1789: CG, Feb 3; 1796: CG, Mar 19, 30, Apr 2, 7, May 24; 1798: CG, Apr 13, 26; 1799: CG, May 31; 1800: CG, Jun 12

--Life's Vagaries, 1795: CG, Mar 19, 21, 23, 24, 26, Apr 7, 9, 10, 11, 13, 14, 15, 16, 18, 20, 21, Nov 27; 1796: CG, Jun 4; 1799: CG, May 28; 1800: CG, Jun 12

--Little Hunchback, The; or, A Frolick in Bagdad (farce), 1789: CG, Apr 14, 18, 22, May 4, Jun 13, Oct 2, 6, 13, 28; 1790: CG, Mar 4, 9, Apr 8, 24; 1791: CG, Jan 14, Mar 1, Sep 23; 1792: CG, Feb 13, Sep 26; 1793: CG, Oct 30; 1800: CG, Jun 12

--London Hermit, The; or, Rambles in Dorsetshire, 1793: HAY, Jun 29, Jul 1, 2, 4, 5, 6, 9, 10, 11, 13, 16, 18, 23, 24, 31, Aug 2, 12, Sep 10, 12, 21, 28; 1794: CG, Apr 29, HAY, Jul 8, 12, Aug 1, 12, 16, Sep 11; 1795: HAY, Jun 11, 18, Jul 15, 23, Aug 11, 25, 28, CG, Dec 29; 1796: CG, Jan 7, 22, HAY, Jun 17, Jul 4; 1797: HAY, Jun 17, 27, Jul 13, Sep 7; 1798: DL, Jun 6, HAY, 15, Jul 7; 1799: HAY, Jun 21, 28, Aug 17; 1800: CG, Jun 12, HAY, Jul 3, 7, 14, 28, Aug 13, 30

--Lord Mayor's Day; or, A Flight from Lapland (pantomime), 1782: CG, Nov 25, 26, 27, 28, 30, Dec 2, 4, 5, 9, 10, 12, 16, 19, 21, 23, 26, 27, 28, 30; 1783: CG, Jan 1, 2, 7, 18, 20, 21, 22, 23, 24, 25, 27, Feb 5, 7, 24, Mar 10, Apr 21, May 28, Nov 10, 11, 17, 24; 1784: CG, Nov 9, 18; 1789: CG, Dec 21; 1790: CG, Nov 15; 1793: CG, Oct 2; 1795: CG, Nov 9, 10, 12, 16, 23; 1798: CG, Jun 2

--Love and War (opera), 1785: CG, May 12; 1787: CG, Mar 12, 15, 19, 20, 22, 29, Apr 13, 18, 23, May 9, 25, Jun 2, Oct 1; 1788: CG, Apr 19, May 2, 30, HAY, Aug 13, CG, Oct 17; 1789: CG, Feb 2, 9, Oct 21, Dec 5, 18; 1790: CG, Apr 26, Jun 8; 1791: CG, Nov 25, Dec 16; 1793: CG, May 15, Nov 1

--Love in a Camp; or, Patrick in Prussia (farce), 1786: CG, Feb 17, 20, 22, 23, 27, Mar 2, 4, 6, 9, 25, Apr 22, 27, May 18, 26, Jun 1, Sep 18, 22, 29, Nov 25, Dec 9; 1787: CG, Feb 3, 15, 19, 22, Mar 22, HAY, Apr 30, CG, May 7, 16, 19, Jun 5, Oct 10, 17, 26; 1788: CG, Apr 4, 16, 23, May 3, 8, 23, Sep 22, Oct 15; 1789: CG, Jan 23, Feb 11, May 12, 26, Jun 4, Oct 7, Nov 5, Dec 8; 1790: CG, Feb 6, 10, 27, Apr 21, May 27, Nov 11; 1791: CG, Feb 24, May 19, Jun 1, Sep 17, Nov 5; 1792: CG, May 9, Oct 10, Dec 1; 1793: CG, May 30, Jun 6, Oct 4; 1794: CG, Apr 30, May 31; 1795: CG, Nov 25; 1796: CG, Oct 18; 1798: CG, Apr 11; 1800: CG, May 30, Jun 12

--Magic Banner, The; or, Two Wives in a House, 1796: HAY, Jun 22, 23, 24; 1800:

CG, Jun 12
--Maid's the Mistress, The (burletta), 1783: CG, Feb 14, 17
--Man Milliner, The (farce), 1787: CG, Jan 27; 1800: CG, Jun 12
--Modern Antiques; or, The Merry Mourners (farce), 1791: CG, Mar 14, 15, 17,
19, 21, 22, 24, 26, 28, 29, 31, Apr 2, 4, 12, 26, May 13, 23, Jun 9, Sep 14,
Nov 12, Dec 10; 1792: CG, Jan 6, Feb 10, Apr 12, May 4, 8, Sep 19, Dec 18;
1793: CG, Nov 9, 20, Dec 7; 1794: CG, Mar 4, May 20, Sep 26; 1795: CG, Feb 5;
1796: CG, Apr 13, Sep 28; 1797: CG, May 27; 1800: CG, Jun 12
--Nosegay of Weeds, The; or, Old Servants in New Places (farce), 1798: DL, Jun
6
--Olympus in an Uproar; or, The Descent of the Deities (burletta), 1796: CG,
Nov 5, 7, 8, 9, 10, 11, 12, 14, 15, 17, 18, 26, Dec 2, 6
--Omai; or, A Trip round the World (pantomime), 1785: CG, Dec 20, 21, 22, 23,
26, 27, 28, 29, 30, 31; 1786: CG, Jan 2, 3, 4, 5, 6, 7, 9, 10, 11, 12, 13,
14, 16, 17, 18, 19, 20, 21, 23, 24, 25, 26, 27, 28, Feb 4, 13, 14, 21, 24,
Mar 13, Apr 3, 6, 17, 20, 25, May 1, 8, 16, 19, Jun 5, Oct 9, 27, Nov 27, Dec
2, 4; 1788: CG, Mar 24, 25, 27, 31, Apr 7, 9, 15, 29, Jun 5; 1789: CG, Dec
21; 1790: CG, Nov 15; 1793: CG, Oct 2; 1799: CG, May 13
--Peeping Tom (opera), 1784: HAY, Sep 6, 7, 8, 9, 10, 11, 13, 15; 1785: HAY,
May 30, Jun 1, 7, 10, 11, 21, 24, 27, Jul 8, 15, Sep 3; 1786: HAY, Jun 14,
15, 24, HAMM, 28, Jul 3, HAY, 4, 8, HAMM, 10, HAY, 13, Aug 9, 21, 30, Sep 5,
12; 1787: HAY, Jun 21, 25, 30, Jul 11, 18, 24, 28, Aug 16, 23, 29, Sep 15;
1788: HAY, Jun 13, 17, 27, Jul 7, 14, 17, 26, Aug 2, 16, Sep 1, 5, 11; 1789:
CG, Apr 20, HAY, Jun 22, 27, Jul 1, 8, 16, 20, 27, Aug 6, 8, 20, 29, 31, Sep
5, 11, 12; 1790: HAY, Jun 16, Jul 15, 31; 1791: HAY, Aug 10; 1792: HAY, Aug
22, 24, 30, Sep 5, 10, 12, 15; 1793: HAY, Jun 14, 19, 26, Jul 1, 2, 10, 19,
23, 31, Aug 23, 30, Sep 3, 9, 12; 1794: HAY, Jan 27, Jul 22, 29, Aug 25, Sep
11, 15; 1795: HAY, Jun 16, 26, Jul 4, 14, 22, Aug 7, 12, 24, Sep 1, DL, Oct
15, 17, 24, 29, Nov 6, 13, 30, Dec 17; 1796: HAY, Jun 11, 15, 24, 30, Jul 4,
20, 27, Aug 19, Sep 13; 1797: CG, May 16, 18, HAY, Jun 12, 22, Jul 1, 10, 26,
Aug 22, 28, Sep 6, 16; 1798: CG, Feb 20, Mar 8, HAY, Jun 15, 18, 22, Jul 12,
27, Aug 17, Sep 1, 8; 1799: HAY, Jun 15, 26, Aug 20, Sep 16; 1800: CG, Jan
29, Jun 12, HAY, 23, Jul 1, 12, 29
--Pharo Table, The, 1789: CG, Apr 4, 13; 1790: CG, Apr 21
--Poor Soldier, The (opera), 1783: CG, Apr 7, Oct 29, Nov 4, 5, 7, 8, 12, 13,
14, 15, 18, 20, 21, 22, 27, 28, 29, Dec 2, 4, 8, 9, 10, 11, 12, 13, 17, 18,
19, 22; 1784: CG, Jan 26, 28, Feb 10, 19, 26, Mar 1, 9, 16, 20, 25, Apr 1,
12, 29, Jun 2, Sep 21, Oct 13, 20, 26, Nov 8, 13, 19, 24, Dec 3, 11, 18, 23;
1785: CG, Feb 3, 12, 19, 22, 26, Mar 3, 15, Apr 4, 9, 23, 30, May 10, 20, 27,
HAMM, Jul 25, CG, Oct 20, Nov 1, 9, 25, Dec 3, 12, HAY, Dec 26; 1786: CG, Feb 16,
Apr 8, May 25, 29, Jun 2, HAMM, Jul 5, 7, CG, Oct 31, Nov 21, Dec 11, 13, 15;
1787: CG, Feb 2, 7, 14, 24, Mar 3, Apr 25, May 4, 23, 31, Jun 8, Sep 17, Oct
11, Dec 18; 1788: CG, Mar 28, Apr 11, 18, May 3, 19, 21, 31, Sep 19, Oct 10,
29, Nov 21, Dec 2; 1789: CG, Jan 21, Mar 16, Sep 25, Oct 9, Nov 6, 16, 27,
Dec 9; 1790: CG, Jan 28, Feb 5, Apr 20, 30, May 15, 26, Sep 17, 29, Nov 13,
Dec 17; 1791: CG, Feb 19, Apr 9, 29, May 10, Jun 4, Oct 19, Nov 11, 23; 1792:
CG, Jan 26, Feb 21, Mar 17, Apr 27, May 29, Sep 20, 24, Oct 17, Dec 4; 1793:
CG, Apr 18, May 16, Oct 1, 18, 31; 1794: CG, Feb 21, Mar 25, HAMM, 25, CG,
May 6, Sep 19; 1795: CG, Feb 7, DL, May 4, CG, Jun 6, Sep 18; 1796: CG, Jan
23, Sep 30; 1797: DL, Jun 7, HAY, Sep 1, CG, 20, 27, Nov 16; 1798: CG, Feb 1,
Apr 14, May 19, HAY, Aug 21; 1799: CG, Jan 22, May 1, OCH, 15, HAY, Aug 28,
31, CG, Sep 30, Nov 5, Dec 20; 1800: CG, Feb 7, May 24, Jun 12, HAY, Aug 26
--Positive Man, The (farce), 1779: HAY, Oct 13; 1782: CG, Mar 14, 16, 21, 23,
Apr 5, 6, 13, 18, Oct 16, 26, Nov 18, Dec 11; 1783: CG, Feb 20, Nov 19; 1784:
CG, Jan 19, 23, Apr 30, May 24, Sep 22, Oct 12, 13, 21, Nov 15, Dec 6; 1788:
CG, Feb 7, 9, Mar 13, Apr 24; 1789: CG, Feb 21, Mar 14, Oct 30; 1790: CG, Apr
10, May 4; 1792: CG, Feb 16, 23, May 9; 1793: CG, Dec 6, 10; 1796: CG, May
20; 1797: CG, May 17, 25; 1800: CG, Jun 12
--Prisoner at Large, The (farce), 1788: HAY, Jul 2, 4, 8, 12, 16, 18, 28, Aug
28, Sep 10; 1789: HAY, Aug 5, 26; 1792: CG, Mar 6, Oct 26, 30, Nov 2, 17, 23;
1793: CG, Jun 7, Oct 9, 16, Nov 21, Dec 14; 1794: CG, May 9, Jun 12, HAY, Aug
4, 7, 16, 23; 1795: CG, Feb 3, Jun 4, HAY, 19, 22, Jul 4, 13, 31, Aug 17, 31,
Sep 9; 1796: CG, Apr 29, May 26, HAY, Jun 17, Jul 13, 29, Aug 22, CG, Sep 17,
Nov 22; 1797: CG, Feb 28, May 2, Jun 6, HAY, 15, 16, 23; 1798: HAY, Jun 14,
Jul 25, Aug 7, Sep 4, CG, Nov 14; 1799: CG, Apr 6, HAY, Jun 19, Jul 8; 1800:
CG, Jan 18, Jun 12, HAY, Aug 20
--Rival Soldiers, The (farce), 1793: CG, May 11; 1797: CG, May 17, HAY, Jun 28,
Jul 6, CG, Oct 11; 1798: CG, Apr 18, Nov 8; 1799: CG, Apr 20
--Shamrock, The; or, The Anniversary of St. Patrick (opera), 1783: CG, Apr 7,
8, Nov 4
--She Gallant, The; or, Square-Toes Outwitted (farce), 1779: HAY, Oct 13; 1782:
CG, Mar 16

--She's Eloped!, <u>1798</u>: DL, May 17, 19
--Siege of Curzola, The (opera), <u>1786</u>: HAY, Aug 12, 14, 16, 19, 21, 23, 30;
    <u>1787</u>: HAY, Jul 2, 4, 9, Aug 9
--Son-in-Law, The (farce), <u>1779</u>: HAY, Aug 14, 16, 18, 23, 26, 27, 28, 30, Sep
    1, 2, 3, 6, 9, 10, 14, 15, Oct 13; <u>1780</u>: HAY, Jun 13, 16, 19, 21, 23, 30, Jul
    4, 7, 13, 18, 20, 26, 31, Aug 8, 22, 24, 25, 31, Sep 5; <u>1781</u>: CG, Apr 30,
    HAY, Jun 9, 13, 15, 16, 20, 28, Jul 4, 12, 17, 19, Aug 2, 6, 21, 22, Sep 4,
    CG, Dec 5, 6, 8, 11, 12, 14; <u>1782</u>: CG, Apr 1, 19, 26, HAY, Jun 4, 10, 13, 17,
    20, 26, Jul 1, 5, 13, 20, Aug 2, 27, 28, Sep 3; <u>1783</u>: CG, Apr 7, HAY, May 31,
    Jun 5, 9, 13, 19, 26, Jul 2, 11, 18, 24, 31, Aug 6, 11, Sep 3, 12; <u>1784</u>: CG,
    Jan 14, 16, 20, HAY, May 29, Jun 14, 24, Jul 1, 15, 17, 22, 29, Aug 14, 20,
    Sep 1, 6, 14; <u>1785</u>: HAY, May 30, Jun 1, 2, 8, Jul 1, 5, Aug 17, 24, 27, Sep
    6; <u>1786</u>: HAY, Jun 29, Jul 6, 8, Aug 11, 18, Sep 2, 8, 14; <u>1787</u>: HAY, Jun 25,
    28, Jul 12, 14, 28, Aug 2, 22, Sep 13; <u>1788</u>: HAY, Jun 13, 20, 24, 27, Jul 17,
    19, 29, Sep 5, 9, 13; <u>1789</u>: HAY, Jun 27, Jul 2, 10, 13, 21, 30, Aug 10, 12,
    19, 25, Sep 3, 11; <u>1790</u>: HAY, Jun 23, Jul 5, 9, Aug 11, Sep 3, 14, Oct 13;
    <u>1791</u>: HAY, Jun 30, Jul 2, 13, 18, 26, 28, Sep 8; <u>1792</u>: HAY, Jun 15, Jul 3,
    11, 18, Aug 1, 7, 16, 21, 29, Sep 3; <u>1793</u>: HAY, Jun 11, 18, 28, Jul 4, 6, 11,
    22, Aug 2, 23, Sep 5, 10, 13; <u>1794</u>: CG, Apr 29, HAY, Jul 18, 29, Aug 26, Sep
    5, 13; <u>1795</u>: HAY, Jun 16, 23, 30, Jul 7, 23, 29, Aug 13, 28, DL, Dec 2, 4;
    <u>1796</u>: DL, Jan 1, HAY, Jul 5, 8, 12, 26, 29, Aug 1, 5, 11, 25, 30, Sep 12;
    <u>1798</u>: DL, May 7, 18, Jun 6, Dec 21; <u>1799</u>: CG, Apr 30; <u>1800</u>: CG, Jun 12
--Sprigs of Laurel (opera), <u>1793</u>: CG, May 11, 13, 14, 17, 20, 22, 25, 28, Sep
    17, 18, 30, Oct 7, 14, Nov 8, 25; <u>1794</u>: CG, Feb 14, Mar 11, May 7, 14, 30,
    Sep 15, Oct 27; <u>1795</u>: CG, May 19, Oct 14, Nov 19, Dec 17; <u>1796</u>: CG, May 24,
    Oct 20; <u>1797</u>: CG, May 17; <u>1798</u>: DL, Jun 6; <u>1800</u>: CG, Jun 12
--Tantara Rara Rogues All!; or, Honesty the best Policy (farce), <u>1788</u>: CG, Mar
    1, 8; <u>1800</u>: CG, Jun 12
--Tony Lumpkin in Town; or, The Dilettante (farce), <u>1778</u>: HAY, Jul 2, 3, 7, 8,
    21, 28, Aug 6, 14, 28; <u>1779</u>: HAY, Jun 7, Aug 6, 7, 9, 10, 14, 19; <u>1782</u>: CG,
    Apr 1; <u>1800</u>: CG, Jun 12
--Toy, The; or, Hampton Court Frolics, <u>1789</u>: CG, Jan 31, Feb 3, 4, 5, 6, 10,
    12, 14, 16, 19, Mar 2; <u>1790</u>: CG, Mar 18, Nov 30; <u>1792</u>: CG, May 15; <u>1796</u>: CG,
    Mar 19; <u>1800</u>: CG, Jun 12
--Wild Oats; or, The Strolling Gentlemen, <u>1791</u>: CG, Apr 16, 25, 29, May 4, 9,
    12, 13, 16, 21, 25, 30, Jun 7, 15, Oct 12, 19, 26, Nov 3, 10, 17, 22, Dec 1,
    12, 15, 19; <u>1792</u>: CG, Jan 9, 18, 26, Feb 9, 15, Apr 27, Oct 31, Nov 19, 30,
    Dec 28; <u>1793</u>: CG, Mar 18, Apr 12, May 15, Sep 16, Oct 31, Dec 10; <u>1794</u>: CG,
    Feb 19, Nov 21; <u>1195</u>: CG, May 22, Sep 30, Nov 25; <u>1798</u>: CG, Mar 20, Jun 4,
    DL, 6; <u>1799</u>: CG, Apr 16, May 29; <u>1800</u>: CG, May 27, Jun 12
--World in a Village, The, <u>1793</u>: CG, Nov 23, 25, 26, 27, 28, 29, 30, Dec 2, 3,
    4, 6, 10, 13; <u>1794</u>: CG, Jan 2, 10, 17, 23, Feb 14, May 16, 31, Jun 4, 16, Oct
    8, Nov 4; <u>1795</u>: CG, May 30; <u>1800</u>: CG, Jun 12
--Young Quaker, The, <u>1783</u>: HAY, Jul 26, 28, 29, 31, Aug 4, 5, 7, 9, 11, 14, 16,
    21, 29, Sep 2, 4, 6, 9, 11, 15; <u>1784</u>: HAY, Jun 14, 18, 24, 29, Jul 3, 16, 27,
    Aug 3, 20, Sep 1, 11; <u>1785</u>: HAY, Jul 19; <u>1786</u>: HAY, Jul 18, Aug 25; <u>1787</u>:
    HAY, Jun 21, 26, Jul 11, 18, 26, 31, Aug 10, 20; <u>1788</u>: HAY, Jun 20, Jul 4,
    18, Aug 11; <u>1789</u>: HAY, Aug 12; <u>1791</u>: HAY, Jun 23, Aug 12; <u>1792</u>: HAY, Jun 15,
    Jul 10; <u>1793</u>: HAY, Jun 18; <u>1795</u>: HAY, Aug 21, 27; <u>1796</u>: HAY, Aug 10, 23;
    <u>1797</u>: HAY, Aug 8; <u>1798</u>: DL, Jun 6, Nov 22, 27; <u>1800</u>: CG, Jun 12, HAY, Aug 8
Olbeldiston (actor, dancer), <u>1733</u>: BFMMO, Aug 23, DL, Oct 10, 15, 24, Nov 13,
    Dec 5; <u>1734</u>: DL, Feb 4, Mar 7, DL/LIF, Apr 1, DL, 23, HAY, Jun 24, 28, Jul
    10, LIF, Aug 20; <u>1739</u>: BFH, Aug 23; <u>1740</u>: BFH, Aug 23; <u>1741</u>: GF, Jan 20, Feb
    19, Mar 3, BFH, Aug 22, GF, Oct 2, 12, 16, Dec 28; <u>1742</u>: GF, Jan 13, 14, Feb
    8
Old Anacreon (song), <u>1735</u>: GF, May 5
Old Bailey, <u>1718</u>: NONE, Jul 10; <u>1735</u>: DL, May 16; <u>1736</u>: HAY, Apr 26; <u>1784</u>: HAY,
    Jan 21
Old Batchelor, The. See Congreve, William.
Old Bethlem, <u>1798</u>: HAY, Jan 15
Old Bond St, <u>1782</u>: HAY, Jan 14; <u>1784</u>: DL, May 20
Old Boswell Court, <u>1722</u>: MBS, Mar 26
Old Broad St, <u>1737</u>: LH, Jan 26
Old Castle Tavern, <u>1779</u>: HAY, May 10
Old Chiron (song), <u>1752</u>: CG, Apr 25; <u>1753</u>: CG, Apr 28
Old City Manners. See Lennox, Charlotte.
Old Cloathsman, The. See Holcroft, Thomas.
Old Crown Inn, <u>1799</u>: OCH, May 15
Old Debauchees, The. See Fielding, Henry, The Debauchees.
Old England forever (song), <u>1742</u>: CG, Apr 19, May 21; <u>1745</u>: CG, Apr 24; <u>1792</u>:
    CG, Dec 26; <u>1793</u>: CG, Jan 3, Nov 19
Old England will be England still (song), <u>1794</u>: CG, Apr 25; <u>1797</u>: CG, May 31

Old England's tree of Liberty (song), 1798: CG, Apr 20
Old Fool (dance), 1763: DL, Apr 30
Old Friend Pickle Herring (entertainment), 1705: BF, Aug 27
Old Gravel Lane, 1735: YEB, Dec 22; 1748: NTW, Nov 16
Old Ground Young (dance), 1770: CG, May 1, 4, 5, 8, 9, Nov 23, 24, Dec 5, 10,
    18; 1771: CG, Mar 14, 18, 19, Apr 2, 9, 23, Oct 30, Nov 1; 1772: CG, Mar 31,
    Apr 4, 6, 23, 28, 29, 30, May 8, 25, 27, Sep 28, Oct 1, 5, 14, Dec 9, 11, 22;
    1773: CG, May 12, 15, Dec 8, 18; 1774: CG, Feb 5, 19, Mar 14, 22, Apr 5, 13,
    May 2
Old Hob and his Wife (entertainment), 1722: SFM, Sep 5
Old Jewry, 1742: DL, Apr 21
Old Maid, The. See Murphy, Arthur.
Old Man Bit, The; or, Harlequin Skeleton (farce), 1742: JS, Oct 12
Old Man Metamorphosed (dance), 1770: CG, Apr 20, Dec 1, 11
Old Mode and the New, The. See D'Urfey, Thomas.
Old Round Court, 1746: CG, Jan 24
Old St, 1771: DL, Dec 17; 1773: CG, Dec 18; 1775: CG, Dec 22; 1776: DL, Dec 17;
    1778: DL, Dec 18; 1782: DL, Dec 19
Old Straw (interlude, anon), 1796: DL, Jun 7
Old Towler (song), 1794: CG, Jan 24, Feb 10, May 14, 24, Jun 3, 9, Nov 15;
    1795: CG, Apr 8, 24, 28, May 1, 19, Jun 5, 6, 8, 16, Sep 28, Nov 6; 1796: CG,
    Apr 5, 12, 19, 20, 29, May 3, 12, 17; 1797: CG, May 2, 9, 20, Oct 30, Nov 21;
    1798: CG, Apr 21, 28, May 5, 8, 9, 15, 23, Jun 1, 2, 6; 1799: CG, Jan 5, May
    7, 13, 24, 31, Jun 5, Sep 16; 1800: CG, Mar 17, Apr 15, May 2, 7, 17, 24, 27,
    29
Old Troop, The. See Lacy, John.
Old Widow Bewitched, The; or, The Devil to do about Her (play, anon), 1758:
    BFDVW, Sep 2, 4, 5, 6, SFW, 18, 19, 20, 21
Old Witch of Endor, The; or, Harlequin Turned Beau (pantomime), 1753: SFP, Sep
    27
Old Woman nursing her Grandchild (entertainment), 1704: DL, Jun 5
Old Woman of Eighty (song), 1787: RLSN, Mar 27; 1797: HAY, Aug 10
Old Woman's Oratory, The. See Smart, Christopher.
Old Woman's Song (song), 1704: LIF, Jun 8, Jul 10; 1719: RI, Jun 6
Old Woman's Whim (dance), 1754: HAY, Jul 18
Old Women Weatherwise (entertainment), 1770: HAY, Mar 17, DL, May 11, 31, HAY,
    Oct 1
Oldfield (householder), 1778: CHR, May 25
Oldfield (Offied) (singer), 1773: MARLY, Sep 3; 1778: HAY, Sep 7; 1783: HAY,
    Jun 30; 1785: HAY, Jul 13
Oldfield (Offild), Anne (actor), 1699: NONE, Sep 0; 1700: DL, Feb 19, Apr 29,
    Jul 6, Oct 0, Nov 23; 1701: DL, Feb 4, Mar 1, May 12, Dec 0; 1702: DL, Jan 0,
    Feb 0; 1703: DL, Feb 18, Mar 11, Apr 10, Jun 4, Dec 2; 1704: DL, Mar 6, 28,
    Dec 7; 1705: DL, Jan 18, Feb 22, Apr 23, Oct 30, Nov 20, Dec 3; 1706: DL, Feb
    26, Mar 30, Apr 0, 8, 16, QUEEN'S, Nov 7, 13, 14, 22, 25, Dec 3, 7, 14; 1707:
    QUEEN'S, Jan 1, 4, Feb 4, 25, Mar 1, 8, 24, 27, Apr 21, 30, May 26, Jun 10,
    DL/QUEEN, Oct 18, 20, 23, 27, 28, 31, Nov 1, 10, 11, 20, 25, QUEEN/DL, Dec 6,
    QUEEN'S, 13, DL/QUEEN, 26, 31; 1708: QUEEN'S, Jan 8, DL, Feb 4, 7, 14, 23,
    24, Mar 16, 18, Apr 17, 22, 26, Oct 2, 5, 7, 12, 13, 18, 19, 25, Dec 14, 18,
    22; 1709: DL, Jan 5, 8, 11, 27, 29, Feb 12, Mar 3, 14, 15, 31, QUEEN'S, Sep
    22, 24, 27, 29, Oct 1, 4, 6, 17, 21, 22, 25, 28, 29, 31, Nov 5, 8, 11, 12,
    19, Dec 5, 12; 1710: QUEEN'S, Jan 5, 7, 11, 12, 19, 21, 26, Feb 2, 11, 13,
    18, Mar 4, Jun 29, Jul 6, 13, 19, 21, DL/QUEEN, Oct 4, 5, 7, Nov 4; 1711: DL,
    Jan 9, 11, 15, 25, 26, DL/QUEEN, Feb 8, DL, 9, DL/QUEEN, 12, DL, 15, 19, 22,
    DL/QUEEN, 26, DL, Mar 3, 5, 6, 10, 22, Apr 7, DL/QUEEN, 30, DL, May 5, 15,
    22, DL/QUEEN, 26, DL, Sep 22, 25, 27, Oct 6, 9, 10, 11, 17, 18, 23, 24, 31,
    Nov 1, 2, 8, 12, 23, 26, 29, Dec 3, 10, 13, 18; 1712: DL, Jan 19, Feb 28, Mar
    17, Apr 3, May 6, Sep 20, 23, 25, Oct 2, 8, 11, 16, 22, Nov 3, 25, 27, 28,
    Dec 6, 12, 17, 27; 1713: DL, Jan 15, 29, Feb 19, 28, Mar 2, 9, 14, Apr 14,
    May 7, Oct 15, 22, Nov 9, 23, 28, Dec 18; 1714: DL, Jan 5, 26, 28, Feb 2, Mar
    1, 29, Apr 27, May 3, 26, 28, Sep 23, 27, Oct 11, 22, 25, Nov 9, 15, 26, 27,
    Dec 2, 16, 21; 1715: DL, Feb 10, 19, 25, 28, Mar 8, 10, 21, 28, Apr 2, 19,
    20, May 17, 24, Oct 22, Nov 9, 16, 19, Dec 9, 12, 16; 1716: DL, Jan 5, 25,
    Feb 21, 23, 25, Mar 5, 8, 10, 12, 13, Apr 26, May 9, Jun 15, Oct 9, 11, 12,
    15, 16, 17, 19, 23, 25, 27, Nov 1, 2, 3, 12, 13, 27, Dec 4, 14, 15, 17, 27;
    1717: DL, Jan 4, 9, 16, 24, 26, Feb 25, Mar 11, May 11, Jun 14, Nov 15, 20,
    23, 25, 26, 27, 28, 30, Dec 3, 4, 6; 1718: DL, Jan 7, 13, 20, 22, 23, 29, Feb
    14, 22, Mar 8, 13, 17, Apr 1, 15, 19, May 14, 20, Jun 4, Oct 2, 8, 10, 11,
    15, 21, 24, 25, 27, 28, 30, 31, Nov 4, 18, 24, 29, Dec 3, 10, 13, 16, 19, 29;
    1719: DL, Jan 7, 16, 24, Feb 4, 14, Mar 3, 7, Apr 11, 14, 16, 17, 25, 29, Sep
    24, Oct 1, 3, 7, 8, 9, 13, 14, 15, 17, 20, 21, 23, 24, 28, Nov 10, 11, 14,
    17, 20, Dec 2, 5, 11; 1720: DL, Jan 8, 12, Feb 2, Mar 3, Apr 2, 21, 23, May

10, 23; 1721: DL, Jan 2, 3, 6, 10, 13, 16, 19, 20, 25, 27, Feb 3, 14, 28, Mar
2, 6, 7, Apr 11, 14, 15, May 2, 15, Sep 19, 21, 28, Oct 2, 4, 9, 11, 12, 17,
19, 21, 23, Nov 4, 8, 11, 13, 14, 16, 24, 25, 28, Dec 12; 1722: DL, Jan 6, 9,
26, Mar 5, 31, Apr 13, May 2, Sep 8, 13, 20, 27, Oct 2, 5, 8, 11, 12, 13, 15,
16, 18, 25, 27, Nov 7, Dec 5; 1723: DL, Jan 8, 17, 23, Feb 4, 15, Mar 2, 4,
11, Apr 1, Sep 14, 19, Oct 1, 3, 9, 18, 23, 25, 26, 31, Nov 2, 14, 16, 18,
Dec 5, 20; 1724: DL, Jan 15, 27, Feb 15, Mar 5, Apr 15, 18, Sep 17, 29, Oct
8, 10, 14, 19, 20, 21, Nov 2, 7, 10, 14, 19, 21, 26, Dec 7, 9, 22; 1725: DL,
Jan 9, 27, Feb 3, 9, Mar 4, May 27, 31, Jun 11, Sep 7, 14, 25, Oct 7, 9, 12,
13, 18, 22, 23, 25, 26, 28, Nov 2, 6, 12, 20, 27, 29, Dec 10; 1726: DL, Jan
3, 11, 28, Mar 3, Sep 8, 10, 15, 17, 20, 24, 27, 29, Oct 6, 13, 18, 22, 27,
Nov 15, 19, 26, 29, Dec 7, 9, 12, 14, 15, 17; 1727: DL, Jan 3, 5, 7, 14, 16,
27, Feb 7, 9, 11, 23, Mar 9, 13, Apr 11, 12, 24, Sep 14, 19, 21, 28, Oct 5,
7, 12, 14, 17, 19, 21, Nov 9, 18, 22, 27, 28, 30, Dec 4, 9, 13; 1728: DL, Jan
5, 10, Feb 16, Mar 7, 11, Apr 13, 29, Sep 7, 26, Oct 3, 8, 10, 17, 21, 22,
24, 25, 28, 31, Nov 8, 9, 19, 25, 27, Dec 2, 4, 9, 12, 16, 17, 26; 1729: DL,
Jan 21, 25, Feb 1, 15, 18, 25, Mar 6, Apr 16, 17, Sep 11, 18, 30, Oct 2, 4,
9, 11, 16, 21, 22, Nov 1, 6, 7, 8, 18, 19, 22, Dec 4, 10, 13, 20, 27; 1730:
DL, Jan 3, 9, 21, 26, Feb 28, Mar 19, Apr 2, 18, 20, 23, Sep 19, Oct 23, 27,
Nov 3, Dec 17; 1731: LIF, May 14; 1747: CG, Feb 28
Oldfield, 1685: OLDFIELD, Dec 30
Oldham, John (songwriter), 1684: MS, Nov 22
Oldman (actor), 1738: SFL, Sep 5
Oldmeadow (actor), 1785: HAMM, Jun 17, Jul 2
Oldmixon, George (translator), 1734: KING'S, Mar 13
Oldmixon, John, 1697: LIF, Jun 0, IT, Nov 1; 1698: LIF, Nov 0; 1700: LIF, Feb
0; 1703: LIF, Jan 0
--Amintas, 1697: NONE, Sep 0
--Governor of Cyprus, The, 1703: LIF, Jan 0
--Grove, The; or, Love's Paradise, 1700: DLORLIF, Jan 20, DL, Feb 19
--Thyrsis; or, The Lost Shepherdess, 1697: LIF, Jun 0; 1711: PU, Apr 3
Oldmixon, Miss (actor), 1749: HIC, Apr 21
Olimpia in Ebuda. See Hasse, Johann Adolph.
Olimpiade, L' (pastiche), 1769: KING'S, Nov 11, 18, 25, Dec 2, 9, 16, 19, 23;
1770: KING'S, Jan 6, Feb 1, 17, Mar 3, 17, 24, 27, May 10, 31; 1771: KING'S,
Feb 8; 1774: KING'S, Jun 3, 7, 11, 18, 25
Olimpiade, L'. See Pergolesi, Giovanbattista; Galuppi, Baldassare; Arne, Dr
Thomas A; Bertoni, Fernando Giuseppe; Cimarosa, Domenico.
Oliphant's Coffee House, 1748: DL, Apr 14
Olive (house servant), 1768: CG, Jan 2
Olive, Mrs (actor), 1743: CG, Dec 17
Oliver (actor), 1757: DL, Mar 24
Oliver (beneficiary), 1761: CG, May 12
Oliver, James (musician), 1798: HAY, Jan 15
Oliver, John (spectator), 1676: DG, Jun 2; 1677: BF, Aug 27
Olivier (dancer), 1782: KING'S, Mar 19
Olla Podrida, An (interlude, anon), 1798: HAY, Sep 7
Olympus in an Uproar. See O'Keeffe, John.
Olzi (Olsii), Gioseppe (musician), 1703: LIF, Nov 29; 1704: YB, May 18
Omaggio, L'. See Bianchi, Giovanni Battista.
Omai. See O'Keeffe, John.
Ombra cara (song), 1726: LIF, Mar 28; 1729: HIC, Apr 16; 1789: DL, Mar 20
Ombre D'Arlequin, L' (play, anon), 1725: HAY, Mar 29; 1726: HAY, Mar 24
Ombre piante (song), 1729: HIC, Apr 30
Ombres des Amants Fideles (dance), 1734: DL/HAY, Jan 12, 29, Feb 4
Omer, Mme (dancer), 1791: PAN, Feb 17
Omnipotence. See Handel, George Frederic.
On Nee Yeath Tow no Riow, King of Granahjoh-Hore (spectator), 1710: QUEEN'S,
Apr 28
On, on, my dear Brethren (song), 1734: DL/HAY, May 4; 1735: DL, May 13, HAY,
Aug 4; 1736: DL, May 4; 1737: DL, May 7; 1738: CG, May 1; 1739: DL, May 15,
28; 1741: GF, Apr 29; 1747: DL, May 16
On our paternal (song), 1789: DL, Mar 20
On the charmer fondly gazing (song), 1789: DL, Mar 20, 25; 1791: DL, Mar 11;
1792: KING'S, Mar 14, 30
On the lake of Killarney (song), 1791: CG, May 18
On the pleasant banks of Tweed (song), 1793: KING/HAY, Mar 15
On the Stage (poem), 1736: DL, Apr 1
On the Unhappy Conflagration of the Theatre Royal, January 25th, 1672 (poem),
1672: BRIDGES, Jan 25
One and All (music), 1798: CG, Oct 24
One night while all the village slept (song), 1678: DL, Feb 0

One Thousand Fairy Scenes (song), 1733: DL/HAY, Dec 3
One Tun Coffee House, 1749: CG, Apr 28; 1751: DL, May 2; 1787: HAY, Mar 12
Onofreo (singer), 1775: KING'S, Oct 31, Nov 7; 1776: KING'S, Jan 27
Onorati, Giacomo (dancer), 1794: KING'S, Dec 6, 20; 1795: KING'S, Jan 20, Feb
    28, Mar 26, Jun 13, Dec 12; 1796: KING'S, Feb 2, 20, Mar 1, 10, Apr 2, 21,
    May 12
Openshaw, 1737: LIF, Mar 9
Opera de Compagne Precede du Grondeur, L'. See Dubresney, Charles Riviere.
Opera du Gueux, L'. See Gay, John, The Beggar's Opera.
Opera of Operas, The. See Haywood, Eliza.
Opera of the Fairies, The. See Garrick, David.
Opera Song (song), 1707: DL, Oct 29; 1709: SH, Aug 25; 1711: GR, Sep 8, WCH,
    Oct 17; 1712: OS, Nov 28; 1713: HIC, Apr 9, QUEEN'S, 25, Jun 9, 20; 1721:
    KING'S, Jun 14; 1722: KING'S, Feb 15, Mar 6; 1726: HAY, Mar 4, Apr 29; 1727:
    HAY, Mar 17; 1731: DT, Jul 7; 1737: HAY, May 3
Opera, An (first in England), 1674: NONE, Jan 5
Opfertod, Der. See Kotzebue, August Friedrich Ferdinand von.
Opinion of the Ancients (song), 1736: CG, Apr 12, 17, May 11; 1739: CG, Apr 27
Opportunity, The. See Shirley, James.
Opposition. See Ryder, Thomas.
Opprimete i contumaci (song), 1762: KING'S, Mar 1
Or let the merry bells (song), 1790: CG, Mar 3, DL, 10; 1791: CG, Mar 18, 30,
    DL, Apr 13; 1792: KING'S, Mar 14, 30; 1794: CG, Mar 21; 1799: CG, Mar 15
Oracle, The. See Cibber, Susannah.
Oram, John (scene painter), 1749: DL, Nov 2, 27; 1750: DL, Feb 10, Apr 7; 1755:
    DL, Jan 4; 1758: DL, Dec 29; 1759: DL, Jan 1
Orange Inn, 1743: LIF, Mar 22
Orange Moll. See Meggs, Mary.
Orange St, 1786: DL, May 1
Orange Warehouse, 1777: DL, Apr 29
Orange Women, 1735: DL, Jul 1
Orange, Prince and Princess of, 1734: GF, Mar 15, KING'S, 16, DL/HAY, 18,
    KING'S, 19
Orange, Prince of, 1670: ATCOURT, Nov 4, LIF, 5; 1684: ATCOURT, May 26, Jun 10;
    1733: DL, Nov 7, GF, 7, KING'S, 10, 13; 1734: GF, Feb 11, KING'S, Mar 5, 9,
    12, 13, CG, 21, Apr 1, DL, 4, CG, 6, DL/HAY, 18, HA, Sep 11; 1740: CG, Nov
    20; see also William III
Orange, Princess of, 1677: ATCOURT, Nov 10; 1734: KING'S, Apr 2, Jul 6, LIF,
    Oct 1, GF/HAY, 26, HAY, 28, Nov 1; 1736: CG, Dec 11, KING'S, 11; 1741:
    KING'S, Mar 14; 1759: CG, Oct 15, Nov 23; see also Mary, Queen
Oration (entertainment), 1702: SH, Jan 31, May 7, CC, 21; 1716: DL, May 29;
    1738: YB, Mar 26, 28; 1752: CT/HAY, Apr 1, May 5; 1757: HAY, Sep 8, Oct 3;
    1760: HAY, Feb 14
Oration in Favour of Matrimony (entertainment), 1751: CT, Dec 3
Oratorio on the Divine Veracity. See Barbandt, Charles.
Orators, The. See Foote, Samuel.
Oratory (entertainment), 1740: CAC, Mar 12, 14, APH, 28, LG, Apr 7
Oratory a la mode de Theatre (medley), 1757: HAY, Aug 22, Sep 2
Orazio. See Latille, Gaetano.
Orbin, Miss (actor), 1733: HAY, Mar 26
Order of British Bucks (entertainment), 1761: CG, Apr 16
Ordinary, The. See Cartwright, Sir William.
Oreste et Electre (dance), 1775: KING'S, May 25
Orestes. See Theobald, Lewis; Handel, George Frederic; Voltaire.
Orfeo e Eurydice (dance), 1773: KING'S, Nov 30; 1774: KING'S, Jan 11, 15, 17,
    Mar 8, Apr 14
Orfeo ed Eurydice. See Gluck, Christoph Willibald von.
Orfeo. See Bertoni, Fernando Giuseppe.
Orfeur (actor), 1720: LIF, Dec 8; 1721: LIF, Nov 13; 1722: LIF, Jan 22, May 15,
    Aug 1, BFLSH, 25, HAY, Dec 17; 1723: HAY, Jan 31, Feb 13, Mar 14, Apr 15,
    BFPJ, Aug 22, SF, Sep 5, SOU, 25; 1724: LIF, May 28, RI, Jun 27, Jul 4, 11,
    13, 18, SF, Sep 2
Orfeur, Mrs (actor), 1722: HAY, Dec 17; 1723: HAY, Jan 31, Mar 14, Apr 15, 22,
    BFPJ, Aug 22, SF, Sep 5, SOU, 25, LIF, Oct 18; 1724: LIF, May 28, RI, Jun 27,
    29, Jul 4, SF, Sep 2
Organ (music), 1736: SH, Apr 16, DL, 22; 1738: KING'S, Mar 28; 1753: HAY, Apr
    2; 1761: HAY, Feb 5; 1762: DL, Mar 31; 1763: DL, Dec 28; 1774: CHAPEL, Mar
    26; 1775: CHAPEL, Nov 23; 1789: CG, Apr 30; 1790: CG, Feb 19; 1791: CG, Mar
    11, 16, Apr 6, 13; 1792: CG, Feb 24, 29, Mar 28, 30; 1793: CG, Feb 15; 1794:
    CG, Mar 7, Apr 4; 1799: HAY, Jan 24
Organ Concerto (music), 1735: CG, Apr 1; 1737: CG, Mar 16, 23; 1739: KING'S,
    Feb 17, Mar 3, 20, LIF, Nov 22, 27, Dec 13, 20; 1740: LIF, Feb 21, 27, Mar 6,

21, 26, 28, Apr 1, 23, Nov 8; 1741: LIF, Jan 31, Feb 28, Mar 11, Apr 8; 1743:
CG, Mar 18, 23, 25, 29, 31; 1744: CG, Feb 29, Mar 2, 7, 9, 14, 16, 21,
KING'S, Nov 24; 1745: DL, Apr 3; 1746: CG, Feb 14; 1750: CG, Mar 16, 21, 23;
1751: HAY, Feb 5, CG, 22, 27, Mar 1, 6, 8, 13, 15, 20; 1754: KING'S, Apr 25;
1755: DL, Mar 14, 19; 1756: DL, Apr 2; 1758: DL, Mar 10, MARLY, Aug 21; 1759:
SOHO, Mar 1, DL, 23, 30, CG, May 4, RANELAGH, Jun 13, MARLY, Aug 9; 1761: CG,
Feb 6, DL, 27; 1762: CG, Feb 26, DL, Mar 26, SOHO, Apr 21, CHAPEL, May 18;
1763: CG, Feb 18; 1764: CG, Mar 9; 1765: CG, Feb 22; 1766: CG, Feb 26; 1767:
CG, Mar 6; 1768: CG, Feb 19; 1769: MARLY, Aug 17; 1770: DL, Mar 7, MARLY, Jul
17, RANELAGH, 27, MARLY, Aug 21, Sep 4, 11; 1771: DL, Feb 15, MARLY, May 23,
Jun 27, Jul 13, Aug 3, 22, Sep 5, 10, 12, 17; 1773: CG, Mar 3, DL, 3, 10, 17,
CG, 19, DL, 24; 1774: HAY, Feb 18, DL, 23; 1775: DL, Mar 3, 8, KING'S, 8, DL,
15, 17, 24; 1776: DL, Feb 23, Mar 1, 6, 15, 22, 29; 1777: DL, Feb 14; 1778:
DL, Mar 6; 1779: DL, Feb 19, 24, Mar 3, 12, 19; 1780: DL, Feb 11, 16, Mar 3,
15; 1781: DL, Mar 2, 7, Apr 4; 1782: DL, Feb 20, 27, Mar 22; 1783: DL, Mar
14, 26; 1784: HAY, Mar 3, DL, 12; 1785: HAY, Feb 23; 1789: CG, Mar 20; 1793:
CG, Mar 8; 1794: CG, Mar 19, 26, Apr 11; 1797: CG, Mar 24; 1799: CG, Feb 22
Organ Voluntary (music), 1755: HAY, Feb 13
Organ with three Voices (entertainment), 1702: DL, Aug 22; 1703: DL, Jun 18;
    1704: DL, Jun 5
Orione. See Bach, Johann Christian.
Orlandini, Giuseppe Maria (composer), 1721: KING'S, Feb 1; 1737: KING'S, Jan 1,
    25, Feb 19
--Giocatore, Il; or, The Gamester (interlude), 1737: KING'S, Jan 1, 4, 15, 18,
    22, Feb 12, 15
--Grullo and Moschetta (interlude), 1737: KING'S, Feb 19, 22, 26, Mar 5, 8, 19,
    22, Apr 19, 23, May 14, 17
--Pourceaugnac and Grilletta (musical), 1737: KING'S, Jan 25, 29, Feb 1, 5, 8,
    Mar 12, 15
Orlando (actor), 1744: GF, Dec 15
Orlando. See Handel, George Frederic.
Orleans, Henriette Anne, Duchess of, 1670: NONE, Jun 22
Ormasdes. See Killigrew, William.
Orme (ticket deliverer), 1786: CG, May 31; 1787: CG, May 19
Orme, Miss (actor), 1785: CG, Feb 5, Mar 7, Sep 23, Oct 17, 26, Nov 14; 1786:
    CG, Apr 28, Oct 28
Orme, Mrs (beneficiary), 1714: SH, May 27
Ormick (dancer), 1742: LIF, Nov 26
Ormisda. See Cordans, Bartholomeo.
Ormiston (actor), 1792: HAY, Oct 22
Ormond, Duchess of. See Butler, Elizabeth Preston.
Ormond, Duke of. See Butler, James.
Ormophan, Tichucbactey (Chinese mandarin), 1735: LIF, Jun 19
Oroonoko. See Southerne, Thomas.
Orpen, Miss (married), 1774: DL, Mar 22
Orphan Bess the Beggar Girl (song), 1799: DL, May 9
Orphan of China, The. See Murphy, Arthur.
Orphan, The. See Otway, Thomas.
Orpheo (dance), 1784: KING'S, Mar 6, 9, 13, HAY, Apr 30, May 10
Orpheus (opera, anon), 1736: KING'S, Mar 2, 6, 9, 13, 16, 20, Apr 6, 10, 17,
    29, May 1, Jun 8, 15, 22
Orpheus and Eurydice (dance), 1791: KING'S, Mar 10, 26, 31, Apr 14, 16, May 12,
    14, 17, 19, 23, Jun 29
Orpheus and Eurydice (masque, anon), 1673: DG, Jul 3
Orpheus and Eurydice. See Weaver, John; Lampe, John Frederick.
Orpheus Seeking After Eurydice (concert), 1744: HIC, May 16
Orpin (actor), 1746: GF, Oct 28, 29
Orrery, brother and sister, 1668: LIF, Dec 8
Orrery, Earl of. See Boyle.
Orrery, John, Earl of, 1751: DL, Nov 26
Orsato (musician), 1799: CG, May 18
Orton, Jacob (author), 1776: DL, Jan 1
Osbaldiston. See Olbeldiston.
Osborn, Margaret (actor), 1671: LIF, Sep 0; 1672: DG, Jan 31, Aug 3, Nov 4;
    1673: DG, Mar 12, May 0; 1674: DG, Nov 9; 1676: DG, Jul 3, Aug 0; 1677: DG,
    Sep 0; 1680: DG, Feb 0; 1681: DG, Nov 0, DG/IT, 22; 1682: DG, Jan 0; 1683:
    DG, May 31, Jul 0; 1685: DL, Aug 0; 1690: DL, Mar 0, Dec 0; 1691: DL, Jan 0,
    Apr 0, NONE, Sep 0
Osborne (actor), 1785: HAY, Feb 10
Osborne (treasurer), 1770: CG, May 22; 1773: HAY, Jul 5, 21, 28, Aug 4, 11, 27,
    Sep 3
Osborne, Dorothy, Lady Temple, 1664: ATCOURT, Jan 0

Osborne, Edward, Lord Latimer, 1677: DL, Jul 0
Osborne, Francis, 5th Duke of Leeds (author), 1790: DL, Nov 17; 1794: DL, Jul
    2; 1797: KING'S, May 18, CG, Jun 14, DL, Oct 27
Osborne, Henrietta (actor), 1759: DL, Oct 8; 1761: CG, Jun 23; 1763: HAY, Jun
    20, 27, Aug 1, 11, Sep 5, 7; 1775: HAY, Oct 30
Osborne, Master (singer), 1733: GF, Nov 12; 1735: GF/HAY, Aug 21; 1736: LIF,
    Dec 7, 17
Osborne, Peregrine, Viscount Dunblaine, 1675: ATCOURT, Feb 15
Osborne, Thomas, Earl of Darby, Marquis of Carmarthen, 3rd Duke of Leeds, 1683:
    DL, Jan 19; 1697: DLORDG, Dec 18; 1698: DL, Feb 12
Oscar and Malvina. See Byrn, James.
Osmond the Great Turk. See Carlell, Lodowick.
Ossian (poet), 1768: HAY, Mar 3
Ossian, 1791: CG, Oct 20; 1794: CG, Oct 14; 1798: CG, Mar 19; 1800: CG, Mar 4
Ossory, Earl of. See Butler, Thomas.
Oswald (house servant), 1751: DL, Feb 1; 1752: DL, Apr 9
Oswald (musician), 1743: DL, Dec 1, 3; 1759: HAY, Jan 12, Mar 29
Oswald, J (printer), 1751: DL, Feb 27
Oswald's Music Shop, 1759: MARLY, Jul 26
Othello. See Shakespeare, William.
Otho. See Handel, George Frederic.
Ottey, Sarah (musician), 1720: SH, Mar 9; 1721: LIF, Mar 29; 1722: LIF, Feb 27
Otway, Thomas, 1670: LIF, Sep 20; 1673: DG, Feb 18; 1676: DG, Dec 0; 1677: DG,
    May 31; 1679: DG, Jun 21; 1682: DG, Feb 9, Apr 21, May 31; 1686: DL, Nov 29;
    1697: LIF, Feb 20; 1703: LIF, Sep 27; 1704: LIF, Aug 9; 1705: DL, May 28, 29;
    1711: DL, Jul 3; 1712: DL, May 9, 12; 1713: DL, May 13, Oct 31; 1714: DL, May
    7, Oct 30; 1715: DL, Mar 14, Jun 17, Dec 13; 1716: DL, Jan 20, May 7, Dec 3;
    1717: DL, Jan 11, Nov 21; 1718: DL, Mar 22; 1719: DL, Mar 5, Nov 26; 1720:
    DL, Jan 5, Mar 12, Nov 19, Dec 6, 15; 1721: DL, Jan 28, May 6, Sep 23, Dec 1,
    LIF, 2, 4; 1722: LIF, Jan 9, DL, 20, LIF, Feb 24, Apr 5, DL, May 26, Oct 6,
    Nov 1, LIF, 30, Dec 13; 1723: DL, Feb 2, LIF, 5, DL, Apr 6, LIF, May 23, DL,
    29, Oct 12, Nov 12, LIF, 19; 1724: LIF, Jan 3, DL, Feb 8, LIF, May 16, 21,
    DL, 21, Oct 31, LIF, Nov 3; 1725: DL, Jan 16, LIF, Nov 8; 1726: HAY, Feb 24,
    DL, May 16; 1727: LIF, Apr 7, WS, Dec 14, LIF, 16; 1729: LIF, Feb 7, HAY, 11;
    1731: LIF, Oct 25; 1732: LIF, Feb 1, DL, Dec 20; 1733: LIF/CG, Apr 12, CG,
    Oct 2, DL/HAY, Nov 10; 1734: DL, Nov 21; 1735: DL, Jan 6, Mar 3, May 17, Jun
    9, HAY, Jul 10, DL, Sep 23; 1736: DL, Mar 8, LIF, Apr 29, HAY, Dec 3, DL, 14,
    CG, 18; 1737: CG, Jan 7, DL, 19, Sep 1, Oct 22; 1738: DL, Jan 11, Feb 3, 7,
    23; 1739: DL, Mar 15; 1740: GF, Nov 17, DL, Dec 5; 1748: CG, Mar 8; 1750: DL,
    Jan 20, 22; 1753: DL, Apr 30, CG, Oct 30; 1757: CG, Mar 12; 1771: DL, Nov 2;
    1779: HAY, Oct 18; 1792: DLKING'S, Apr 14
--Alcibiades, 1675: DG, Sep 0; 1686: NONE, Sep 0
--Athiest, The; or, The Second Part of the Souldiers Fortune, 1683: DG, Jul 0
--Caius Marius, 1679: DG, Oct 0; 1682: DL, Jan 14; 1692: DLORDG, Mar 16; 1693:
    ATCOURT, Jun 10; 1695: NONE, Sep 0; 1699: DL, Nov 11; 1701: DL, Apr 12; 1703:
    DL, Dec 18; 1704: DL, Feb 10, 24; 1705: DL, Dec 22; 1706: QUEEN'S, Apr 6;
    1707: QUEEN'S, Feb 18, 19; 1710: DL, Feb 18, May 17, GR, Aug 28; 1711: DL,
    Mar 17; 1712: DL, May 12, SML, Jul 9, DL, Nov 20; 1713: DL, Jun 18, Oct 31;
    1714: DL, Oct 30; 1715: DL, Feb 21; 1716: DL, Jan 13; 1717: DL, May 10, Nov
    19; 1720: DL, Jan 5, Dec 6, 15; 1721: DL, May 6, Dec 1; 1723: DL, Nov 12;
    1724: DL, Feb 8, Nov 24; 1727: DL, Apr 29; 1735: LIF, Aug 15, 22, Sep 2
--Cheats of Scapin, The; or, The Miser Outwitted, 1676: DG, Dec 0; 1684:
    DLORDG, Dec 0; 1687: IT, Nov 1; 1703: DG, Apr 30; 1704: LIF, Aug 9; 1705:
    QUEEN'S, Dec 3; 1710: DL, Jan 16, 17, QUEEN'S, Jul 19; 1715: LIF, Jan 18, 20,
    Aug 4; 1716: DL, Aug 16, Nov 16; 1717: DL, Jul 4; 1724: LIF, May 21, Jun 4,
    Nov 13; 1725: LIF, Jan 22, Feb 20, Nov 24; 1726: LIF, Jan 27, Oct 19; 1727:
    LIF, Feb 13, 14, Nov 28, Dec 5, WS, 14; 1729: LIF, May 2; 1730: LIF, Jan 7,
    Feb 16, Apr 4, HAY, 6, LIF, 13, Dec 21; 1731: LIF, Mar 25; 1732: HAY, Feb 16;
    1733: BF, Aug 23; 1734: CG, Feb 11; 1735: CG/LIF, Feb 8; 1736: CG, Mar 29,
    30, Apr 15, 28, May 10, 14, 24, 27, Jun 1, BFFH, Aug 23; 1737: CG, Jan 28,
    Feb 1, 8, Mar 17, 24, 31, Apr 2; 1738: CG, Apr 10, Nov 13, 14, Dec 11; 1739:
    CG, Jan 3, Mar 15, Apr 7; 1740: CG, Feb 16, Mar 27, Sep 24, Oct 3, Nov 3;
    1741: CG, May 7; 1742: SF, Sep 16; 1744: CG, May 14; 1745: CG, Nov 20; 1747:
    SF, Sep 10; 1753: DL, Apr 30, May 1, 22, Sep 25, 29, Oct 6; 1755: CG, Jan 8,
    10, 11, 15, 16, 21, 23, 25, Mar 17, Apr 9, 22, 26, May 6, 12, 13, 16, Oct 11,
    Nov 1, 5, 19, Dec 5, 8, 20; 1756: CG, Jan 29, Feb 21, Apr 22, Oct 16, Nov 18,
    Dec 23; 1757: CG, Feb 21, Mar 7, Sep 21, Nov 1, 21, 28, Dec 10, 29; 1758: CG,
    Jan 6, Mar 7, Sep 20, Nov 13; 1759: CG, Feb 21, Mar 29, May 12, 18, Oct 12,
    23, Nov 7, 21; 1760: CG, Mar 3, Apr 14; 1761: CG, Mar 26; 1762: CG, Sep 27;
    1763: CG, May 11, 26, Oct 7; 1764: CG, Sep 21, Dec 8; 1765: CG, Mar 23, Oct
    3; 1766: HAY, Jul 18, 21, KING'S, Aug 27, Sep 3, 10, 15; 1767: HAY, Jun 10,
    30; 1770: CG, Apr 24, May 1; 1772: CG, May 11; 1776: CG, Jan 15; 1786: CG,

Nov 13, 16, Dec 1, 8, 16; <u>1787</u>: CG, May 3, Jun 8; <u>1788</u>: CG, Jan 5, Nov 6;
<u>1789</u>: CG, May 16, 18, 29; <u>1792</u>: DL, Dec 21, 22, 29; <u>1793</u>: DL, Jan 4, 11, 19,
26, Feb 11, 16, 26, Apr 23, 30, Jun 7; <u>1794</u>: DL, Apr 24
--Don Carlos, <u>1676</u>: DG, Jun 8, 9, 10, 12, 13, 14, 15, 16, 17, 19, Oct 12; <u>1678</u>:
NONE, Sep 0; <u>1685</u>: NONE, Sep 0; <u>1694</u>: NONE, Sep 0; <u>1703</u>: LIF, Sep 27; <u>1704</u>:
LIF, Feb 18; <u>1708</u>: DL, Jul 27; <u>1712</u>: DL, Aug 12; <u>1715</u>: DL, Jun 17; <u>1728</u>: HAY,
Dec 7; <u>1734</u>: BFT, Aug 17, BFFO, 24; <u>1736</u>: BFFH, Aug 23
--Friendship in Fashion, <u>1678</u>: DG, Apr 5; <u>1750</u>: DL, Jan 20, 22
--Orphan, The; or, The Unhappy Marriage, <u>1680</u>: DG, Feb 0, Mar 6; <u>1682</u>: DG, Feb
9; <u>1684</u>: NONE, Sep 0; <u>1687</u>: ATCOURT, Jan 10; <u>1690</u>: NONE, Sep 0; <u>1692</u>: DL, Feb
9, Mar 3; <u>1695</u>: NONE, Sep 0; <u>1699</u>: DL, Nov 21; <u>1704</u>: DL, Jul 7; <u>1705</u>:
QUEEN'S, Dec 11; <u>1706</u>: QUEEN'S, Jun 29, LIF/QUEN, Aug 10; <u>1707</u>: QUEEN'S, Mar
1; <u>1709</u>: DL, Nov 30; <u>1710</u>: GR, Aug 14; <u>1711</u>: DL, Feb 27; <u>1712</u>: DL, Mar 13,
Jul 29; <u>1713</u>: DL, Mar 28, Nov 10; <u>1714</u>: DL, May 7; <u>1715</u>: LIF, Jan 3, 22, DL,
Mar 14, LIF, Nov 23; <u>1716</u>: DL, Jan 21; <u>1717</u>: DL, Feb 2, Mar 7, 23, 28, May
23, Oct 26; <u>1718</u>: DL, Feb 4, Nov 22, Dec 2; <u>1719</u>: BR, Apr 2, DL, 18, Nov 21,
Dec 31; <u>1720</u>: HIC, Feb 2, DL, Mar 5; <u>1721</u>: DL, Jan 17, Mar 13, GB, 15, GG,
22, LIF, Oct 5, DL, 14, LIF, Nov 23; <u>1722</u>: DL, Feb 3, HAY, May 25, Jun 8, 21,
LIF, Oct 6, 23, DL, Nov 1; <u>1723</u>: LIF, Jan 31, DL, Feb 9, Apr 6, LIF, Dec 10,
DL, 17; <u>1724</u>: LIF, Mar 12, DL, 28, Oct 17; <u>1725</u>: DL, Feb 13, May 20, Oct 16;
<u>1726</u>: HAY, Feb 24, DL, Mar 19, May 9, LIF, Nov 14; <u>1727</u>: DL, Jan 21, Mar 6,
Apr 22; <u>1728</u>: DL, Apr 1, HAY, May 27, DL, Oct 15, HAY, Nov 14; <u>1729</u>: DL, Jan
9, HAY, 27, Feb 27, DL, Apr 8, Oct 25, GF, Nov 4, 19; <u>1730</u>: DL, Mar 21, Apr
16, GF, May 21, DL, Sep 26, GF, Nov 24, LIF, Dec 14; <u>1731</u>: DL, Jan 2, GF, 7,
DL, Feb 17, Mar 30, HAY, Apr 20, GF, 21, HAY, May 4, GF, 5, Jun 3, Nov 24;
<u>1732</u>: LIF, Jan 12, GF, Feb 19, LIF, 26, GF, Apr 18, DL, 24, HAY, May 8,
LIF/CG, Oct 11, GF, Nov 18, LIF/CG, Dec 11, DL, 20; <u>1733</u>: GF, Apr 24, DL, May
15, CG, Oct 13, GF, Nov 8, CG, Dec 5; <u>1734</u>: GF, Feb 21, Mar 4, YB, 27, LIF,
Apr 18, YB, Aug 28, CG/LIF, Oct 11, GF, 21; <u>1735</u>: CG/LIF, Jan 4, HAY, Aug 4,
CG, Sep 19, Nov 8; <u>1736</u>: GF, Mar 6, YB, Apr 27, CG, 30, Sep 27, Dec 18; <u>1737</u>:
CG, Jan 7, HAY, Feb 12, DL, Mar 15, Apr 20, May 21, Sep 1, Oct 22; <u>1738</u>: CG,
Jan 26, DL, Feb 7, Oct 19; <u>1739</u>: CG, Feb 24, DL, Mar 15, Oct 5; <u>1740</u>: DL, Jan
15, Oct 7, CG, Nov 7, GF, 17, DL, Dec 5; <u>1741</u>: JS, Feb 20, GF, Nov 6, 7, 30,
Dec 5, 9, 17, 19; <u>1742</u>: GF, Jan 19, Feb 19, Mar 2, 8, 29, Apr 24, DL, 28, May
11, CG, Oct 4, DL, 5, 22, CG, Nov 9, DL, Dec 11; <u>1743</u>: CG, Feb 19, SOU, 25,
CG, Mar 19, DL, Apr 20, CG, 29, DL, Oct 6, CG, 26, DL, Dec 10, 29; <u>1744</u>: DL,
Feb 7, Mar 13, Apr 18, Oct 27, Nov 13, CG, 22, 23, JS, Dec 3, DL, 3; <u>1745</u>:
DL, Feb 2, Apr 24, May 23, BRA, Jun 24, DL, Oct 19, Dec 9; <u>1746</u>: GF, Jan 3,
29, DL, Apr 12, 17, NWMF, Oct 6, CG, Nov 11, DL, 15, 17, 18, 19, 20, Dec 10,
GF, 15, CG, 23; <u>1747</u>: SOU, Jan 21, DL, 27, Feb 28, Mar 2, 26, HAY, Apr 20,
DL, 23, Nov 18, 19, 20, 21, 30, Dec 19; <u>1748</u>: DL, Jan 20, HAY, Feb 29, DL,
Mar 31, Oct 11, CG, 24, DL, Nov 10, CG, 22, NWSM, Dec 26; <u>1749</u>: DL, Jan 28,
Mar 20, JS, 28, DL, May 16, SOU, Oct 2, DL, Dec 8, 11; <u>1750</u>: DL, Jan 20, CG,
Feb 20, DL, Mar 20, Apr 9, HAY, Oct 18, CG, 19; <u>1751</u>: CG, Jan 14, DL, Mar 14,
CG, Apr 12, DL, Oct 7, 8, 11, CG, 17, 18, Nov 18, DL, 21; <u>1752</u>: DL, Jan 2,
CG, 21, DL, Mar 17, CG, Apr 1, DL, 13, CG, 22, DL, Oct 3, CG, 27, Nov 20;
<u>1753</u>: DL, Jan 23, CG, Feb 13, 17, Mar 29, DL, Apr 9, CG, 24, DL, Oct 2, 15,
CG, Nov 22; <u>1754</u>: CG, Feb 14, DL, Apr 1, CG, May 1, DL, Oct 21; <u>1755</u>: DL, Jan
16, Apr 7, Nov 17, CG, Dec 6, 12, 13; <u>1756</u>: DL, Apr 29, CG, May 20, Oct 13;
<u>1757</u>: DL, Jan 18, Mar 8, Apr 18, CG, 25, Nov 26; <u>1758</u>: CG, Jan 23, Oct 6, DL,
19, 23, 26, Nov 11, 30, CG, Dec 11, DL, 19; <u>1759</u>: DL, Feb 7, 23, May 19, Oct
25, CG, Dec 7; <u>1760</u>: DL, Jan 4, Mar 17, Apr 10, 14, CG, Oct 23, Dec 16; <u>1761</u>:
CG, Sep 28; <u>1762</u>: CG, Nov 1; <u>1764</u>: CG, Jan 28, DL, Feb 8, 14, 17, 20, 22, Apr
7, 30, May 12, CG, 25, DL, Oct 23, Nov 7; <u>1765</u>: DL, Mar 23, May 4, Sep 21,
Oct 26; <u>1766</u>: DL, Feb 4, 8, KING'S, Sep 5, 8, DL, 27, Nov 21; <u>1767</u>: DL, May
22, HAY, Sep 16, CG, Oct 19, DL, Nov 21, CG, Dec 12; <u>1768</u>: DL, Jan 4, HAY,
Apr 28, DL, May 2; <u>1769</u>: DL, Apr 10, May 5, CG, Oct 18, 20, 23, Nov 8, 13;
<u>1770</u>: CG, Jan 5, 9, Feb 1, May 15, DL, 30, HAY, Aug 22, 27, DL, Oct 17, CG,
18, Nov 22; <u>1771</u>: DL, Mar 7, HAY, Apr 20, DL, Oct 15, Nov 2; <u>1772</u>: DL, Feb
21, CG, May 16, DL, Dec 22; <u>1774</u>: DL, May 27; <u>1776</u>: DL, Mar 23, CG, Nov 1;
<u>1777</u>: DL, Jan 1; <u>1778</u>: CG, Mar 2, 16, HAY, Apr 9, CG, 20, 30; <u>1779</u>: CG, Mar
9, Oct 11, Nov 1, 30, Dec 2; <u>1781</u>: CII, Apr 5; <u>1782</u>: DL, Dec 26; <u>1783</u>: CG,
Mar 31; <u>1785</u>: CG, Feb 4, 7, 10, 21, Dec 1, 6, 15; <u>1786</u>: CG, Jan 13, 19, 26,
Feb 9, Mar 2, Apr 27, Oct 2; <u>1787</u>: CG, Jan 27, DL, Feb 7, RLSN, Mar 27, CG,
May 22; <u>1788</u>: CG, Oct 27; <u>1790</u>: CG, Oct 27, Nov 5, Dec 9; <u>1791</u>: CG, Oct 28;
<u>1793</u>: CG, Jan 21; <u>1797</u>: CG, Oct 9, 11, 13, 20, Nov 10, Dec 26; <u>1798</u>: CG, Apr
9, May 29, Oct 1; <u>1799</u>: CG, Oct 9
--Soldier's Fortune, The, <u>1677</u>: DG, May 31; <u>1680</u>: DG, Jun 0, Nov 1; <u>1681</u>: DG,
Mar 1, 8, Apr 18; <u>1682</u>: DG, Nov 9; <u>1685</u>: IT, Nov 2; <u>1694</u>: NONE, Sep 0; <u>1699</u>:
NONE, Sep 0; <u>1705</u>: DL, May 28, 29, Oct 23; <u>1708</u>: DL, Mar 9; <u>1709</u>: DL, Jan 17;
<u>1711</u>: DL, Jul 3; <u>1716</u>: DL, Jan 17, 20, May 29; <u>1717</u>: DL, Jan 11; <u>1722</u>: LIF,
Jan 9, Feb 24, 26, Mar 1, Apr 5, May 2, Nov 30, Dec 13; <u>1723</u>: LIF, Feb 5, May

    23, Nov 19; 1724: LIF, Jan 3, 23, May 16, Nov 3; 1725: LIF, Feb 16, Apr 6,
    27, Nov 8; 1726: LIF, Feb 24, Dec 22; 1736: LIF, Apr 29, HAY, Dec 3, 8; 1748:
    CG, Mar 8; 1779: HAY, Oct 18
--Titus and Berenice, 1676: DG, Dec 0
--Venice Preserved; or, A Plot Discovered, 1680: DG, Feb 0; 1682: DG, Feb 9,
    11, Apr 21, May 31; 1695: NONE, Sep 0; 1700: DL, Feb 3; 1701: DL, Jan 18;
    1703: DL, Nov 20; 1704: DL, Jan 15, 29, Nov 11; 1705: QUEEN'S, Apr 28, DL,
    Dec 13; 1707: QUEEN'S, Feb 22, DL, Apr 22, QUEEN'S, May 9, DL/QUEEN, Nov 15;
    1708: DL/QUEEN, Jun 4; 1709: DL, Mar 19; 1710: QUEEN'S, Feb 25, Apr 26, GR,
    Jun 24; 1711: DL, Jan 16, GR, Aug 20, Sep 17; 1712: DL, May 9; 1713: DL, May
    13, Oct 8; 1714: DL, Mar 6, Nov 3; 1715: DL, Dec 13; 1716: DL, May 7, Dec 3;
    1717: DL, Nov 21; 1718: DL, Mar 22, Oct 4; 1719: DL, Mar 5, Nov 26; 1720: DL,
    Jan 11, Mar 12, May 27, Nov 19; 1721: DL, Jan 28, May 8, Sep 23, LIF, Dec 2,
    4; 1722: DL, Jan 20, May 26, Oct 6, LIF, Nov 29; 1723: DL, Feb 2, HAY, 13,
    DL, May 29, Oct 12, Dec 14; 1724: HAY, Mar 9, DL, 19, May 21, Oct 31; 1725:
    DL, Jan 16, 28, May 14, Nov 10; 1726: DL, Feb 17, May 16; 1727: LIF, Apr 7,
    Dec 16; 1729: HAY, Jan 10, 22, Feb 1, LIF, 7, HAY, 11, LIF, Nov 1, GF, 21,
    DL, 29, GF, Dec 4; 1730: GF, May 12, DL, Oct 17, GF, Nov 30; 1731: DL, Jan 7,
    GF, 25, LIF, Oct 25; 1732: LIF, Feb 1, LIF/CG, Sep 29, Dec 27, DL, 30; 1733:
    DL, Jan 27, LIF/CG, Apr 12, DL, May 10, CG, Oct 2, DL/HAY, Nov 10; 1734: CG,
    Feb 9, DL, Oct 24, Nov 21; 1735: DL, Jan 6, Mar 3, GF, 17, DL, May 17, Jun 9,
    HAY, Jul 10, DL, Sep 23, GF, Oct 3, CG, Nov 19, 26, 27; 1736: DL, Mar 8, GF,
    22, CG, Oct 11, DL, Dec 14, CG, 14; 1737: DL, Jan 19, CG, Sep 23; 1738: CG,
    Jan 5, DL, 11, Feb 3, 23, CG, Sep 25, DL, Oct 31, CG, Dec 15; 1739: CG, Feb
    3, DL, Sep 14, CG, Nov 2, DL, 17; 1740: GF, Oct 18, DL, Dec 8; 1742: GF, Apr
    1, 3, 5, May 17, CG, Oct 1, Nov 1, Dec 23; 1743: CG, Feb 2, DL, Mar 14, CG,
    17, DL, 19, CG, 26, DL, Apr 6, CG, 27, DL, May 13, Nov 18, CG, Dec 31; 1744:
    CG, Jan 31, DL, Mar 29, CG, Apr 16, DL, 28, CG, Sep 24, DL, Oct 23, Nov 15;
    1745: GF, Feb 5, CG, 5, GF, 11, DL, Apr 16, CG, Oct 14, GF, Nov 8, CG, Dec
    31; 1746: CG, Jan 24, Oct 4; 1747: GF, Jan 26, Feb 4, DL, 16, 17, CG, Mar 5,
    24, 30, Apr 9, 11, DL, Oct 20, 31, Nov 27, CG, Dec 1, 4, 5, 7; 1748: DL, Feb
    8, Mar 5, 7, May 25, CG, Oct 22, Nov 7, DL, 8, HAY, 14; 1750: CG, Jan 23, Mar
    15, JS, 28, DL, Oct 24, 25, 27; 1751: DL, Mar 18, CG, Dec 16, 18; 1752: CG,
    Jan 17, Mar 6, 19, May 9, TCJS, Aug 11, DL, Oct 28, Nov 14, NWLS, 28, CG, Dec
    21, 23; 1753: CG, Jan 3, 5, Mar 17, DL, 24, CG, Apr 14, DL, Oct 25, 29, Nov
    10, CG, 14, 15, 16, 17, Dec 5, 17, 22, 27; 1754: DL, Feb 14, CG, Mar 2, 30,
    May 6, Nov 23, 25, 26; 1755: CG, Jan 23, SOU, 27, DL, Mar 14, 15, CG, Apr 5,
    29, Nov 14; 1757: DL, Apr 26, Oct 7, 11, 14; 1758: HAY, Jan 18, 23; 1759: DL,
    Mar 20, DL, 24; 1760: DL, Mar 17, Apr 15; 1761: CG, Mar 9, DL, Apr 23; 1762:
    DL, Feb 22, CG, Apr 26, May 14, DL, Oct 20, Nov 16, CG, Dec 4; 1763: DL, Mar
    26, Nov 18, 22, 24, Dec 16, 22; 1764: CG, Jan 17, DL, 28, Feb 8, Mar 13, May
    4, Oct 31, Nov 3, 21; 1765: DL, Feb 12, Mar 14, Apr 12, Oct 2, 4, 8, Nov 1,
    13; 1766: DL, Jan 6, 22, Apr 16, KING'S, Aug 13, 15, Sep 10, DL, Oct 8, 11,
    14, Nov 19; 1767: HAY, Jun 26, CG, Sep 16, Nov 14, DL, Dec 15; 1768: CG, Nov
    24, Dec 31; 1770: DL, Apr 7, CG, May 10, HAY, 30, Sep 1, CG, Oct 23, HAY, 29,
    CG, 30; 1771: CG, Jan 5, DL, Apr 13; 1772: DL, Apr 9; 1773: DL, Jan 21, 25,
    Mar 25, Sep 28, Oct 23; 1774: DL, Dec 9; 1775: DL, May 3, Sep 28, CG, Oct 28;
    1776: DL, Jan 12, CG, Oct 8, DL, 8; 1777: CHR, Jul 3; 1778: DL, Mar 16, CG,
    Apr 11, May 23, CHR, Jun 15; 1779: CG, Mar 22, Apr 16; 1781: DL, Mar 19;
    1782: CG, Feb 5, DL, Dec 14, 20; 1783: DL, Jan 9, 16, 25, Feb 4, 17, 24, Mar
    11, 25, Apr 8, May 10, 27, Oct 17, 27, CG, Dec 11, 18, DL, 20; 1784: CG, Jan
    13, DL, Feb 18, Mar 27, Apr 15, May 13, Nov 20; 1785: DL, Jan 4, 17, CG, 19,
    24, 28, DL, Apr 2, CG, 13, DL, Oct 8; 1786: DL, Feb 11, CG, 25, DL, Mar 28,
    HAMM, Jul 5, DL, Oct 3, Nov 13, Dec 9; 1787: CG, Jan 1, DL, Apr 17, Jun 9,
    HAY, Jul 19, DL, Oct 6, 23, CG, 29; 1788: DL, Jan 17, Mar 4, Nov 6, Dec 30;
    1789: CG, Jan 21; 1790: CG, Apr 29, Nov 23, 29; 1791: HAY, Oct 24; 1792:
    DLKING'S, Jan 28, Apr 14; 1793: DL, Feb 26; 1794: CG, Feb 1, 4; 1795: DL, Oct
    21, 26, 29
Oulton, Walley Chamberlain, 1779: CG, Apr 30; 1783: HAY, Sep 17; 1785: CG, Nov
    8; 1787: DL, Sep 18; 1789: CG, Jun 2, HAY, 3, 17; 1791: DLKING'S, Nov 26, Dec
    31; 1792: HAY, Jul 7; 1794: CG, Feb 5; 1795: CG, May 12; 1797: HAY, Aug 24;
    1798: CG, May 8
--All in Good Humour (interlude), 1792: HAY, Jul 7, 11, 13, 16, 18, 27, Aug 3,
    7, 13, 16, 23; 1793: HAY, Jun 26, 29, Jul 5, 11, 30, Aug 9, Nov 29; 1794:
    HAY, Jan 20, 29, Feb 1, Mar 1, 31, Jul 8, 15, 23, Sep 2, 8; 1795: HAY, Jun
    24, 29, Jul 6, 11, 17, Aug 1, 17, 26, Sep 10; 1796: HAY, Jun 20, 27, 30, Jul
    19; 1798: HAY, Jul 14, Sep 4; 1799: HAY, Jul 16, 17, 22, 25, Sep 7
--As It Should Be, 1789: HAY, Jun 3, 5, 8, 10, 17, 25, Aug 14
--Botheration; or, A Ten Years Blunder, 1798: CG, May 8, 10, 11, 17, 21, Jun 5,
    Sep 17
--Irish Tar, The; or, Which is the Girl (interlude), 1797: HAY, Aug 24
--Perseverance; or, The Third Time the Best (interlude), 1789: CG, Jun 2

Our Laws, Constitution and King (song), 1795: CG, Apr 28; 1797: CG, May 20; 1800: CG, Apr 15, 19; see also May our Navy Old England for ever Protect; Though Hurricanes rattle
Our Navy see, spread o'er the Seas (song), 1756: DL, Apr 10
Our simple tale thus ended (song), 1795: CG, May 25; 1796: CG, Apr 19
Our Tars so Fam'd in Story (song), 1798: DL, May 23
Ousley (lyricist), 1686: DL, Apr 0
Outlaws, The. See Franklin, Andrew.
Outom (musician), 1675: ATCOURT, Feb 15
Outropers-Office, 1690: GB, Oct 10
Outsim, Che-sazan (Chinese mandarin), 1735: LIF, Jun 19
Over hill and valley (song), 1793: KING/HAY, Mar 13, 15, 20
Over Mountains and Moorlands (song), 1771: GROTTO, Aug 24
Over the Hills and Far away (song), 1746: CG, Feb 7
Ovid's Metamorphosis, 1661: COCKPIT, Aug 30; 1734: GF, Apr 19
Owen (house servant), 1742: DL, May 25; 1743: DL, May 2; 1745: GF, May 1; 1746: GF, Feb 25; 1747: GF, Mar 24
Owen (musician), 1758: CHAPEL, Apr 27
Owen, J (publisher), 1793: DL, May 22
Owen, Miss (actor), 1796: CG, Sep 26, Oct 6, 7, Dec 19; 1797: CG, Feb 18, Apr 25, May 18, Jun 6
Owen, W (printer), 1749: DL, Mar 1; 1750: CG, Nov 5; 1751: DL, Feb 4; 1752: DL, Dec 23; 1756: NONE, Dec 25
Owen, William (actor), 1785: HAY, Mar 15
Owen's Coffee House, 1750: DL, Feb 22; 1760: HAY, Aug 15
Owenson, Robert (actor), 1771: CG, Nov 4, 6, Dec 11, 17, 21, 30; 1772: CG, Feb 21, May 8, 13, 19, Sep 28, 30, Nov 6, Dec 3, 26; 1773: CG, Jan 23, 25, Mar 22, Apr 16, 26, May 7, 8, 10, 14, 17, 21, 24, Sep 22, Oct 8, 25, 28, Nov 4, 27, Dec 13, 16, 21; 1774: CG, Jan 1, 3, 27, 29, Feb 24, 26, Mar 15, 22, Apr 7, 13, 15, 26, 30, May 3, 10, 11, HAY, 30, DL, Jun 2, HAY, 8, 13, 15, 17, 27, Aug 19, Sep 5, 12, 17, 19, 21
Owl (song), 1754: HAY, Jul 23, Aug 8
Oxendon St, 1733: LIF/CG, Mar 28; 1785: KING'S, Jun 9; 1787: KING'S, Jun 7
Oxford gentleman (actor), 1743: JS, Apr 25; 1755: BFGT, Sep 3, 5
Oxford Road, 1745: BRA, Jun 24; 1766: CG, Dec 23; 1771: CG, Dec 20, 30; 1772: DL, Dec 22; 1791: PAN, May 9; 1792: CG, May 22; 1794: HAY, Jun 2; 1796: CG, May 3
Oxford St, 1778: HAY, Apr 29; 1779: DL, May 17; 1786: CG, May 11; 1789: DL, Apr 14; 1791: PAN, Feb 17, HAY, Oct 24; 1795: CG, Feb 20, Jun 2
Oxford, Earl of. See DeVere, Aubrey.
Oxford, Earl of, 1728: LIF, Feb 12
Oxford, University of, 1703: DL, Jul 16
Oxford, 1661: REDBULL, Mar 23, LIF, Jul 3, 4, 5, 6, 8, 9, 10, 11, NONE, 13, Sep 0; 1663: VERE, Mar 0, BRIDGES, Nov 3; 1669: NONE, Jul 0; 1670: NONE, Jun 22; 1671: LIF, Jun 0, OXFORD, Jul 0, NONE, Oct 26; 1673: NONE, Jul 0; 1675: ATCOURT, Jul 24; 1680: DL, Jul 0, NONE, Sep 0; 1681: DL, Mar 0; 1682: OXFORD, Jul 10, 18; 1686: OXFORD, Jul 0; 1690: ATCOURT, Nov 4; 1691: OXFORD, Jun 30; 1692: NONE, Sep 0; 1693: ATCOURT, Jan 2, OXFORD, Jul 7; 1694: ATCOURT, Jan 1; 1698: NONE, Sep 0, LIF, Nov 0; 1703: DL, Jul 16; 1704: DL, Jul 7, LIF, Dec 2; 1713: DL, Jun 23; 1730: GF, May 12, SOU, Oct 8; 1731: SOU, Sep 28; 1732: GF, May 19, SOU, Oct 12; 1733: SOU, Oct 18; 1743: KING'S, Apr 19; 1748: HAY, Dec 5, 12; 1750: DL, Jan 1; 1754: DL, Dec 4; 1772: DL, Dec 2; 1776: DL, Mar 20; 1777: CG, Feb 28; 1783: HAY, Jun 2
Oxfordshire, 1745: GF, Dec 19
Oxonian in Town, The. See Colman the elder, George.
Ozanne, Mrs (dancer), 1739: CG, Jan 20, May 8, 30, Sep 22, Oct 3, 15, Dec 4, 10; 1740: CG, Feb 12, Mar 25, May 3, 5, 13, Oct 10, 11; 1741: CG, Jan 5, Feb 24, Apr 22, 23, 25, 27, 30, May 1, 2, 4, 5, 7; 1744: CG, Dec 8; 1745: CG, Jan 1, 14, Nov 14, 29
Ozell, John, 1716: LIF, May 14
--Cato of Utica, 1716: LIF, May 14, 15, 16, Dec 21
Ozmyn and Daraxa. See Boaden, James.

P, D M (author), 1719: KING'S, Feb 19
Pacchierotti, Gasparo (singer), 1778: KING'S, Nov 28; 1779: KING'S, Jan 23, Mar 6, 11, 25, May 29, Nov 27, Dec 14; 1780: KING'S, Jan 22, Mar 9, Apr 22, May 31; 1781: KING'S, Mar 15, Nov 17, Dec 18; 1782: KING'S, Jan 8, 12, Mar 7, 16, May 25, Nov 14; 1783: KING'S, Jan 7, Feb 18, Mar 6, Apr 29, Nov 29; 1784: KING'S, Jan 17, Feb 17, Mar 4, May 8; 1791: PAN, Feb 17, 26, Apr 14, Jun 2

Paccini, Gertrude (dancer), 1775: DL, Sep 26, Oct 2, 20, Nov 28; 1776: DL, Jan 16, 17, 26, Feb 27, Mar 2, 11, 30, Apr 10, KING'S, 20, DL, 22, Jun 1

Pacini, Andrea (actor), 1724: KING'S, Oct 31, Dec 1; 1725: KING'S, Feb 13, Apr 10, May 11

Pack (actor), 1756: BFSI, Sep 3

Pack of Dogs (entertainment), 1704: DL, Jun 5; 1710: DL, May 26

Pack-Spiller-Hall Booth, 1718: SF, Sep 5

Pack, Captain (composer), 1680: DG, Nov 1; 1681: DG, Jan 0; 1682: DL, Nov 28; 1683: DG, Jul 0; 1684: DL, Apr 0

Pack, George (actor), 1676: CITY, Oct 30; 1682: DL, Mar 0; 1693: DL, Apr 0; 1694: DG, May 0; 1700: LIF, Jan 9, Feb 0, Dec 0; 1701: LIF, Jan 0, Mar 0, Apr 0, Nov 0, Dec 0; 1702: LIF, Jun 0, Oct 21, Dec 31; 1703: LIF, Feb 0, Apr 28, May 21, Nov 0; 1704: LIF, Feb 2, Mar 25, 30, Aug 1, Dec 4; 1705: LIF, Jan 25, LIF/QUEN, Feb 22, LIF, Mar 1, LIF/QUEN, Sep 28, Oct 17, 30, QUEEN'S, Dec 27; 1706: QUEEN'S, Jan 17, Mar 7, Apr 20, 30, May 2, Jun 0, 29, Nov 14, 25, Dec 7, 11; 1707: QUEEN'S, Feb 10, 15, Apr 30, May 9, 26, Jun 2, 10, Jul 1, 4, 10, 22, 30, Aug 12, DL/QUEEN, Oct 27, 29, 31, Nov 1, 11, 18; 1708: DL, Feb 3, 6, 7, Mar 8, Apr 17, 22, DL/QUEEN, May 24, DL, Jun 19, 26, DL/QUEEN, Jul 15, DL, 20, Aug 4, Oct 7, Dec 14, 18, 20, 21, 28, 29; 1709: DL, Jan 11, 29, Feb 19, Mar 2, 15, 17, 28, 29, Apr 11, 25, 30, May 3, 12, 17, Sep 6, Nov 24, 26, 28, Dec 3, 6, 7, 8, 10, 17, 26; 1710: DL, Jan 9, 12, 14, 31, Feb 1, 11, 25, Mar 11, 14, 23, 27, Apr 15, May 3, 10, 16, 18, 23, 30, Nov 23, Dec 1, 5, 7, 12, 30; 1711: DL, Jan 9, Feb 10, 27, May 4, 15, 18, 21, DL/QUEEN, 29, DL, Jun 26, 29, Jul 6, 27, Aug 3, 17, 24, 31, Sep 22, 29, Oct 6, 9, 12, 13, 16, 19, 22, Nov 5, 7, 12, Dec 8, 18; 1712: DL, Jan 19, May 13, 22, 30, Jun 2, 5, Jul 11, 22, Aug 1, 5, 12, 26, Sep 23, 25, 30, Oct 11, 14, 15, 31, Nov 3, 7, 26, Dec 27; 1713: DL, Jan 5, 6, 14, 26, 29, Mar 3, 28, May 12, 21, Jun 12, 17, 18, Sep 29, Nov 11, 25, 27; 1714: DL, Jan 28, Mar 31, Apr 27, May 5, 7, 17, Jun 11, 25, Jul 20, 27, Oct 22, Dec 16; 1715: LIF, Jan 3, 5, 6, 7, 8, 14, 25, Feb 2, 3, 9, 16, 21, Mar 14, 21, 22, 24, 31, Apr 4, 18, 19, DL, 20, LIF, 23, 28, May 24, Jun 1, 2, 7, 23, Aug 11, 23, Sep 28, Oct 6, 7, 11, 15, 24, Nov 29, Dec 12, 28; 1716: LIF, Jan 3, 4, Feb 10, Mar 15, 19, Apr 11, 27, Jun 12, Oct 15, 19, 29, Nov 5, 9, 28, Dec 13; 1717: LIF, Jan 2, 10, 28, Feb 6, 11, Mar 23, 25, 30, Apr 13, Jun 1, SF, Sep 9, 25, LIF, Oct 17, 24, 26, Nov 5, 6, 15, 20, 23, 26, 28, Dec 7, 9, 13, 28, 31; 1718: LIF, Jan 2, 6, 14, 18, Feb 3, Mar 6, 22, Apr 19, May 1, RI, Aug 16, SF, Sep 5, AC, 24, LIF, Oct 3, 15, 18, 24, Nov 8, 24, Dec 1, 9; 1719: LIF, Jan 3, Feb 21, 28, Mar 16, Apr 2, 9, 11, May 1, Jun 3, Oct 5, 10, 15, 29, Nov 5, 12, 13, 17, 26, Dec 30; 1720: LIF, Mar 8, 19, Apr 30, May 11, 24, Jun 9, Nov 22, 26, Dec 6, 7, 15, 20, 26; 1721: LIF, Jan 3, 4, 10, 13, 19, 25, Feb 16, Apr 1, 10, 17, 20, May 5, 10, 15, Jun 6; 1722: LIF, Mar 10; 1724: LIF, Apr 21, May 7

Pack, Major Richardson (prologuist and epiloguist), 1719: LIF, Jan 16, DL, Dec 11

Pack, Mrs (beneficiary), 1719: LIF, May 28

Pack's Invitation to the Town (song), 1724: LIF, May 7

Packer (actor), 1713: DL, Nov 9; 1716: LIF, Apr 14

Packer, John Hayman (actor), 1758: DL, Jun 22, Sep 19, 26, 28, Oct 12, 17, 19, 21, 25, 27, Nov 2, 3, 14, 15, 16, 18, 23, Dec 20; 1759: DL, Jan 3, Mar 3, 31, Apr 7, 21, May 19, 21, Jun 19, 28, Jul 12, Sep 25, 27, 29, Oct 4, 5, 9, 17, 19, 25, 30, 31, Nov 1, 5, 10, 13, 22, 24, Dec 1, 20, 31; 1760: DL, Jan 10, 19, Feb 8, 13, 21, Mar 4, 20, 24, 25, Apr 11, 22, 28, 30, May 3, 5, 7, 16, Sep 30, Oct 3, 7, 11, 15, 17, 18, 23, Nov 27, Dec 17, 29; 1761: DL, Jan 3, 8, 23, Mar 23, 26, Apr 1, 6, 17, 25, May 11, 28, Sep 5, 8, 10, 12, 14, 15, 18, 19, 28, Oct 7, 14, 20, 27, 29, 31, Nov 6, 10, 18, 20, 28, Dec 17, 23, 30; 1762: DL, Jan 11, 20, 23, 29, Mar 6, 25, 27, 30, Apr 1, 26, 28, 29, 30, May 4, 6, 15, 17, Sep 18, 23, 25, 30, Oct 4, 6, 7, 11, 13, 16, 20, 25, 29, Nov 2, 3, 4, 10, 16, 17, 18, 19, 27, Dec 10, 11, 18, 22, 27; 1763: DL, Jan 14, 17, 18, 19, Mar 1, 14, 15, 26, Apr 6, 20, May 10, 14, 17, 31, Sep 17, 20, 22, 27, 29, Oct 8, 14, 17, 19, 21, 24, 29, 31, Nov 2, 4, 7, 9, 19, 22, 29, Dec 1, 5, 10, 14, 17, 26, 28; 1764: DL, Jan 4, 7, 23, 25, 27, Feb 11, 18, Mar 13, 20, 24, 26, 27, 31, Apr 10, 12, 24, 25, 26, May 1, 2, 11, Sep 18, 20, 25, 27, Oct 2, 4, 6, 9, 15, 22, 24, 25, 26, 31, Nov 5, 9, 17, 24, 27, 28, Dec 8, 13; 1765: DL, Jan 1, 2, 3, 15, 18, Feb 4, 6, Mar 2, 14, 16, 18, 19, 23, Apr 13, 20, 26, May 2, 11, 22, Sep 17, 19, 21, 24, Oct 2, 3, 12, 14, 15, 18, 21, 22, 23, 24, 25, 28, 30, Nov 14, 15, 20, Dec 3, 6; 1766: DL, Jan 6, 9, 14, Mar 15, 18, 20, Apr 1, 7, 9, 12, 16, 18, 22, 25, 26, 28, May 5, 19, 20, 21, 22, Sep 20, 23, 30, Oct 8, 9, 16, 18, 21, 23, 24, 29, 31, Nov 4, 8, 18, 20, 24, 26, 28, Dec 4, 6, 10, 13, 15, 29; 1767: DL, Jan 24, Feb 7, 9, 19, Mar 7, 21, 24, 28, 30, 31, Apr 11, 27, May 4, 6, 8, 16, 28, Jun 1, Sep 15, 17, 21, 26, Oct 6, 8, 9, 10, 14, 15, 20, 21, 22, 23, 28, 29, Nov 4, 6, 11, 12, 13, 19, 20, 21, 24, 26, 28, Dec 14, 15, 16, 19, 28; 1768: DL, Jan 9, 14, 19, Feb 27, Mar 15, 21, Apr 19, 22, 23, 25, May 3, 6, Sep 17, 22, 23, 27, 28, 29, Oct 1, 3,

4, 5, 6, 10, 11, 13, 15, 20, 21, 25, 31, Nov 1, 4, 10, 17, 21, 24, Dec 3, 17, 28; 1769: DL, Jan 20, 25, 27, Feb 13, Mar 18, Apr 10, CG, 26, DL, May 1, Sep 16, 19, 21, 23, Oct 2, 3, 4, 6, 7, 10, 13, 17, 23, 30, Nov 1, 2, 4, 9, 11, 14, 15, 16, 18, 21, 22, 27, 29, Dec 1, 6, 13, 16, 27; 1770: DL, Jan 2, 4, 16, 19, 27, Feb 7, 8, Mar 1, 8, 13, 20, 22, 26, 27, Apr 7, 19, 20, May 7, 15, 30, Sep 22, Oct 3, 8, 9, 13, 15, 16, 17, 18, 20, 23, 24, 29, 31, Nov 3, 5, 10, 13, 14, 16, 17, 19, 23, 28, Dec 4, 6, 13, 17, 20, 29; 1771: DL, Jan 4, 19, Feb 18, Mar 9, 12, 14, 16, 23, Apr 2, 5, 13, 26, May 4, 27, Sep 24, 26, 28, Oct 1, 5, 10, 15, 17, 19, 24, 25, 30, Nov 2, 4, 6, 8, 9, 13, 18, 21, 23, 25, 27, 28, Dec 2, 3, 4, 21, 31; 1772: DL, Jan 4, 7, 15, Feb 21, 26, Mar 3, 21, 28, Apr 4, 6, 22, 25, May 4, 13, 14, 30, Sep 19, 26, Oct 1, 13, 16, 17, 23, 24, 29, 31, Nov 3, 4, 7, 12, 17, 19, 20, 27, 28, 30, Dec 15, 18, 22, 29; 1773: DL, Jan 13, 19, 21, 26, Feb 2, 4, 18, Mar 9, 20, 23, Apr 21, 27, 30, May 10, 12, 17, 19, Sep 21, 23, Oct 5, 8, 14, 18, 19, 20, 22, 23, 28, Nov 2, 6, 13, 15, 20, 24, 25, Dec 16, 20; 1774: DL, Jan 13, Feb 2, 8, 19, Mar 12, 17, 19, 21, 22, 26, Apr 26, May 4, 7, 9, 10, 27, Sep 17, 22, 27, Oct 1, 4, 6, 14, 15, 21, 24, 28, Nov 1, 3, 7, 10, 11, 17, 24, Dec 7, 9, 19, 26; 1775: DL, Jan 2, 4, 18, Feb 17, 23, Mar 2, 23, 25, 28, Apr 8, 24, May 1, 16, Oct 10, 11, 14, 17, 20, 23, 26, Nov 1, 3, 4, 6, 14, 21, 25, Dec 7, 11, 19; 1776: DL, Jan 3, 12, 26, Feb 10, 12, 22, Mar 11, 14, 23, Apr 8, 12, 15, 19, May 3, 8, 13, 16, 18, 22, 23, 27, Oct 8, 9, 10, 12, 18, 22, 23, 26, 29, 30, Nov 5, 21, 25, 28, Dec 10, 18; 1777: DL, Jan 22, Feb 20, Mar 13, 31, Apr 11, 17, 22, 29, May 8, Sep 20, 27, 30, Oct 7, 14, 17, 22, 31, Nov 4, 18, 24, 29, Dec 3, 4, 11, 18; 1778: DL, Jan 5, 22, Feb 2, 10, 24, Mar 16, May 23, Sep 17, 19, 22, 24, 26, 29, Oct 6, 8, 15, 17, 23, 26, 27, 31, Nov 2, 4, 11, 16, 18, Dec 19, 21, 22; 1779: DL, Feb 8, Mar 16, 22, 25, Apr 10, 16, May 10, 15, Jun 1, Sep 18, 21, 25, 30, Oct 2, 9, 16, 21, 30, Nov 5, 8, 11, 15, 20, Dec 13, 20, 27; 1780: DL, Jan 11, 12, 24, 28, 29, Apr 1, 18, 26, Sep 16, Oct 2, 5, 11, 12, 14, 17, 19, 23, 25, Nov 1, 4, 9, 10, 29, Dec 6; 1781: DL, Jan 6, 26, Feb 3, 12, 17, Mar 19, 29, Apr 18, 23, May 1, 8, CG, 14, DL, 15, 24, Sep 18, 25, 27, 29, Oct 2, 4, 12, 19, 30, Nov 5, 7, 27, Dec 27; 1782: DL, Mar 16, 21, 23, Apr 11, 23, 24, 25, May 7, 8, 10, 14, 29, Sep 19, 24, 26, 28, Oct 1, 10, 30, Nov 8, 26, Dec 14, 26; 1783: DL, Jan 10, 15, Feb 18, 22, Mar 3, 10, 18, Apr 21, 24, 28, May 31, Sep 20, 23, 30, Oct 4, 7, 8, 11, 14, 16, 17, 20, 24, Nov 12, 20, 27, 29, Dec 5, 10, 12, 19, 29; 1784: DL, Jan 3, 10, 22, 23, Feb 14, Mar 6, Apr 28, May 10, 21, Sep 16, 21, Oct 11, 12, 18, 19, 23, 26, Nov 3, 4, 5, 15, 17, 19, 20, 22, 25, Dec 2, 3, 11; 1785: DL, Jan 11, 14, 20, 27, Feb 2, 21, Mar 8, Apr 7, 14, 18, 27, May 3, 24, 27, Sep 17, 20, 24, 29, Oct 1, 8, 15, 20, 26, 27, 31, Nov 3, 7, 9, 17, 18, 21, 22, Dec 1, 26; 1786: DL, Jan 4, 16, 24, Feb 8, 18, 23, Mar 4, 25, 28, Apr 6, CG, 26, DL, Jun 1, Sep 16, Oct 3, 5, 7, 9, 12, 14, 19, 23, 24, 26, 27, 28, Nov 25, Dec 6, 19, 26; 1787: DL, Jan 11, 23, 29, Feb 7, Mar 8, 29, Apr 13, 14, May 3, 7, 19, 31, Jun 1, Sep 18, 25, 29, Oct 3, 6, 9, 11, 13, 18, 24, 26, 27, 30, Nov 3, 5, 6, 10, 16, 20, 24, 27, 29, Dec 8, 10, 11, 26; 1788: DL, Jan 2, 21, Mar 13, 29, Apr 30, May 1, 5, 6, 7, 21, Jun 6, Sep 13, 16, 20, 27, 30, Oct 2, 7, 9, 14, 16, 25, 28, Nov 1, 4, 5, 6, 17, 25, 28; 1789: DL, Jan 1, 6, 10, 17, 19, 27, 31, Feb 16, 21, Mar 17, 21, 23, Apr 21, Jun 4, Sep 12, 19, 22, Oct 1, 10, 13, 24, 28, Nov 27, 30, Dec 2, 14; 1790: DL, Feb 13, Apr 20, 30, May 8, 18, 26, Oct 7, 11, 21, 23, 27, Nov 3, 5, 10, Dec 3, 7, 14; 1791: DL, Jan 11, Mar 21, 28, Apr 4, 27, 28, May 14, 31, DLKING'S, Sep 27, Oct 3, 4, 31, Nov 7, 8, 9, 14, 29, 30, Dec 2, 7, 12; 1792: DLKING'S, Jan 18, 21, 28, Feb 4, 11, 14, 18, 23, Mar 1, 6, 10, 13, 17, 26, Apr 12, Jun 4, DL, Sep 15, 18, 20, 25, 27, Oct 2, 4, 13, 31, Nov 2, 5, 10, 29, Dec 13, 17, 21, 26, 28, 31; 1793: DL, Jan 3, 7, 9, 29, Feb 5, 9, 12, 16, 26, Mar 2, 4, 5, 9, 18, Apr 22, 27, Jun 1, 5; 1794: DL, Apr 21, 25, 26, 29, May 1, 2, 15, 16, 19, 22, 23, 30, Jun 4, 12, 17, 19, 23, Jul 5, Sep 18, 23, 30, Oct 7, 11, 20, 21, 25, 29, 31, Nov 1, 11, 12, 18, 29, Dec 6, 9, 12, 13, 16, 20, 30; 1795: DL, Jan 7, 26, Feb 5, Mar 10, 14, 21, Apr 27, Sep 19, 24, 26, 29, Oct 8, 12, 19, 21, 27, Nov 6, 10, 12, 20, 23, 26, Dec 9, 10, 11, 18, 23, 28, 30; 1796: DL, Jan 13, 25, 29, Feb 15, Apr 2, 11, 25, 29, 30, May 5, 11, 23, Jun 8, 13, 14, Sep 24, 27, Oct 3, 6, 10, 13, 17, 24, Nov 2, 5, 9, 26, 28, Dec 9, 16, 20, 21, 29, 30; 1797: DL, Jan 2, 12, 20, 27, Feb 1, 8, 16, 20, 22, Mar 6, 7, 20, Apr 19, 24, 28, May 4, 8, 12, 16, 23, 27, Jun 7, Sep 19, Oct 5, 7, 12, 30, Nov 4, 7, 9, 15, 17, 18, 21, 23, 25, Dec 1, 2, 8, 9, 11, 14, 21; 1798: DL, Apr 30, May 11, 23, 24, Jun 7, Sep 18, 22, 25, 29, Oct 2, 4, 11, 15, 27, Nov 6, 13, 16, 26, Dec 3, 4, 19; 1799: DL, Jan 15, 17, 31, Feb 4, 14, Apr 17, 23, May 3, 4, 20, 31, Jun 12, Sep 19, 26, 28, Oct 1, 3, 7, 12, 21, 30, 31, Nov 6, 8, 14, 22, 29, Dec 9, 19, 23, 26; 1800: DL, Feb 5, 12, 18, 20, Mar 20, 25, 29, Apr 29, May 21, Jun 11, 18

Packer, Mrs (actor), 1723: LIF, Oct 4; 1759: DL, May 14
Packet of News (entertainment), 1764: DL, Apr 3, May 9
Packet-Boat, The. See Birch, Samuel
Packington, Miss (beneficiary), 1734: DL, May 13

632

Packwood, Miss (dancer), 1800: CG, May 2

Pacsible. See Paisible.

Pacuvius (play), 1699: LIF, Dec 0

Pad, The. See Woodbridge, Robert.

Padbury (coal merchant), 1794: HAY, Jun 2

Paddick (actor), 1735: SOU, Apr 7; 1744: HAY, Sep 27, 29, Oct 4, 6, 11, 13, 18;
1745: CG, Sep 23, Oct 31, Nov 22; 1746: CG, Apr 29, Jun 11, 16, 23, Sep 29;
1747: CG, Dec 9, 19; 1748: CG, Jan 12, 21, 27, Feb 29, Mar 24, 28, Apr 14,
27, 28, 29, BF, Aug 24, SFBCBV, Sep 7, CG, 26, Oct 3, Nov 16, 24; 1749: CG,
Apr 11, DL, Oct 28, Nov 4, Dec 19; 1750: DL, Jan 17, Apr 30, May 2, Sep 28,
Oct 22, 30; 1751: DL, Jan 7, May 4, CG, Dec 14; 1752: CG, Jan 6, Feb 6, Mar
17, 30, Apr 28, May 4, 5, Oct 2, 24, 25, 30, Nov 1; 1753: CG, Jan 22, 31, May
1, Sep 26, Oct 17, 24; 1754: CG, Feb 12, May 14, Oct 2, 14, Nov 6; 1755: CG,
May 9

Paddick (ticket deliverer), 1786: CG, Jun 1

Paddick, Mrs (wardrobe keeper), 1748: BF, Aug 24, SFBCBV, Sep 7; 1757: CG, May
19; 1758: CG, Feb 7, Apr 8; 1760: CG, Apr 12, Sep 22; 1763: CG, May 14; 1766:
CG, May 15; 1767: CG, May 18; 1768: CG, Jan 6, Mar 10, May 27; 1769: CG, May
6, 10; 1770: CG, May 18, 26; 1771: CG, May 27; 1772: CG, May 23; 1773: CG,
May 22; 1774: CG, May 14, 25; 1775: CG, May 27

Paddington Green, 1786: CG, Apr 26

Paddy O'Blarney (song), 1796: HAY, Sep 1

Paddy's Description of Pizarro (song), 1800: HAY, Aug 29, Sep 10

Paddy's Ramble from Dublin to London (song), 1789: CG, Mar 31

Padington (actor), 1743: BFYWR, Aug 23

Padlock, The. See Bickerstaff, Isaac.

Padouana (dancer), 1746: DL, Dec 27, 29; 1747: DL, Jan 31, Feb 4, 7

Padouana, Sga (dancer), 1746: DL, Nov 21, Dec 8, 16, 29; 1747: DL, Jan 5, 21,
22, 24, Feb 16, 23, 27, Mar 3, 5, 12, 14, 17, 19, 23, 26, 30, 31, Apr 6, 7,
10, 11, 20, 21, 22, 23, 25, 27, 29

Padre Amanta (song), 1729: DL, Mar 26

Padre conquesto Amplesso (song), 1762: KING'S, May 11

Padre di Famiglia, Il. See Goldoni, Carlo.

Padre e Il Figlio Rivali, Il. See DeGiardini, Felice.

Padrone Servo, ed il Servo Padrone pes Impegno D'Honore (pantomime, anon),
1726: KING'S, Dec 28

Padua, 1752: CT/HAY, Mar 21; 1753: HAY, Mar 13

Paer (composer), 1792: DLKING'S, May 23

Paganini, Angiola (singer), 1760: KING'S, Aug 25, Nov 22; 1761: KING'S, Jan 6,
Mar 9, Apr 28, Nov 10, Dec 2; 1762: KING'S, Mar 8; 1769: CG, Feb 10

Paganini, Carlo (singer), 1760: KING'S, Aug 25, Nov 22; 1761: KING'S, Jan 6,
Mar 9, Apr 28, Nov 10; 1762: KING'S, Mar 29; 1769: CG, Feb 17, 24, Mar 3, 17

Paganini, Carlo and Angiola (singers), 1761: KING'S, Jan 6, Mar 9; 1762:
KING'S, Apr 14

Page (actor), 1742: JS, Apr 19, BF, Aug 26; 1748: JS, Oct 31

Page (house servant), 1758: DL, May 17; 1759: DL, May 28; 1760: DL, May 12;
1769: DL, May 17; 1770: DL, May 28; 1771: DL, May 25; 1772: DL, Jun 3, 10;
1773: DL, May 28, Jun 2; 1774: DL, May 24, Jun 2; 1775: DL, May 23, 27; 1776:
DL, May 18, Jun 10; 1777: DL, May 30; 1778: DL, May 22; 1779: DL, May 29;
1780: DL, May 23

Page (housekeeper, stage doorkeeper), 1741: CG, May 14, Nov 11; 1742: CG, Feb
15, Mar 1, 6, 18, 27, Apr 1, 20, 21, May 21; 1743: CG, Apr 15, 27, May 6;
1744: CG, Jan 7, 19, Mar 13, Apr 3, 17, May 1, 4, Sep 19; 1745: CG, Mar 6,
11, 28, Apr 2, May 14, Sep 23; 1746: CG, Apr 16, May 6, Sep 29; 1747: CG, Mar
31, Apr 20, May 19, Oct 29; 1748: CG, Feb 8, Mar 21, 28, Apr 11, 14, May 5,
Sep 21; 1749: CG, Apr 22, Sep 25; 1750: CG, Mar 27, Apr 2, DL, 23, CG, May 4,
Sep 24; 1751: CG, Apr 19, May 4, Sep 23; 1752: CG, Mar 30, May 2

Page, John (singer), 1792: CG, Feb 24, Mar 9, 21; 1795: CG, Jun 17; 1797: CG,
Apr 7; 1798: HAY, Jan 15; 1799: HAY, Jan 24, CG, Feb 13, 15, Mar 1, 6, 13,
15; 1800: CG, Apr 2, Jun 16

Page, John (spectator), 1659: MT, Nov 0

Page, Mrs (actor), 1742: JS, Nov 8

Page, Nicolino (beneficiary), 1712: SML, Jun 4

Paget, Colonel (patron), 1735: KING'S, Mar 15

Paget, William (actor), 1730: HAY, Jun 23, 27, Jul 7, BFOF, Aug 20, SFOF, Sep
9; 1731: DL, Feb 8, 15, 17, Mar 20, Apr 5, 19, May 10, 12, 19, Oct 16; 1732:
DL, Feb 14, Mar 23, Apr 17, May 5, Jun 1, 23, Aug 1, 15, 17, Sep 21, LIF/CG,
Oct 6, LIF, 18, LIF/CG, 23, 25, 30, Nov 4, 7, 17, 18, Dec 4, 15, CG/LIF, 26;
1733: LIF/CG, Feb 5, Apr 2, CG, 4, LIF/CG, 10, 12, 21, 23, CG, May 1, LIF/CG,
7, CG, 16, CG/LIF, 28, DL, Sep 26, Oct 1, Nov 2, 5, 14, 23, 26, Dec 7, 11,
26; 1734: DL, Jan 28, Feb 11, DL/HAY, Mar 30, Apr 16, LIF, May 9, DL/HAY, 17,
HAY, 27; 1735: CG/LIF, Feb 15, Mar 11, May 27, HAY, Aug 26, CG, Sep 29, Oct

13, 20, 22, Nov 8, 10, 22, Dec 6, 27; 1736: CG, Jan 8, 9, Feb 13, Mar 20, 27, 29, LIF, Apr 2, CG, 13, LIF, 16, CG, May 17, 20, Jun 14, LIF, 16, CG, Sep 15, 27, 29, Oct 11, 20, 22, 23, Nov 1, 8; 1737: CG, Feb 26, Mar 14, 15, 28, 31, Apr 11, 14, 25, May 3, 16; 1740: DL, May 28, BFHC, Aug 23, GF, Oct 20, 21, 22, 23, 24, 25, 27, 31, Nov 3, 4, 12, 15, 17, 18, 20, 24, 28, 29, Dec 2, 4, 10, 12; 1741: GF, Jan 15, 20, 27, 29, Feb 9, 10, 12, 14, 19, 28, Mar 7, 19, Apr 2, 15, 17, Sep 23, 28, 30, Oct 2, 5, 15, 16, 19, 23, Nov 4, 6, 9, 27, 30, Dec 2, 9, 10, 16; 1742: GF, Jan 1, 5, 18, Feb 3, Mar 27, 29, Apr 1, 8, BFHC, Aug 25, JS, Nov 9, 25; 1744: HAY, Sep 22, 27, 29, Oct 4, 11, GF, Dec 3, 4, 15, 22, 26; 1745: GF, Feb 14, Mar 7, Apr 17, Oct 28, Nov 4, 5, 8, 11, 12, 13, 14, 18, 19, 22, 23, 25, 26, 27, 28, 29, Dec 2, 4, 6, 9, 11, 13, 16, 19, 28; 1746: GF, Jan 1, 2, 3, 10, 13, 17, 20, 27, Feb 3, 7, Mar 3, 4, CG, May 2, Jun 13, 16, 20, 27, NWMF, Oct 6, SOU, 20, 21, GF, 27, 28, 29, 31, Nov 6, 7, 13, 14, 18, 19, 20, 21, Dec 1, 3, 5, 9, 10, 11, 12, 15, 17, 18, 22, 31; 1747: GF, Jan 5, 9, 16, 21, 22, 26, Feb 5, 23, 25, Mar 2, 5, Apr 6, CG, Nov 23, Dec 4, 9; 1748: CG, Feb 25, 29, Apr 13, 14, 25, 27, 29, May 2, 4, BF, Aug 24, SFP, Sep 7, SFBCBV, 7, CG, 26, 28, Oct 14, 17, 24, Nov 4, 12, 16, 24; 1749: CG, Mar 2, 14, Apr 5; 1755: HAY, Sep 11, 15
Paget's sons (actor), 1747: GF, Apr 6
Pagitt (musician), 1675: ATCOURT, Feb 15
Pagod (dancer), 1728: LIF, Apr 22
Pain (actor), 1736: YB, Apr 26
Pain (actor), 1762: DL, Nov 23
Pain, Nevil. See Payne, Henry Nevil.
Paine, James (architect), 1793: KING'S, Feb 19
Painter in Love with his Picture (dance), 1761: CG, May 8
Painter, Elizabeth (actor), 1769: HAY, Sep 19; 1781: HAY, Oct 16
Painter, Joshua (actor), 1776: HAY, May 2; 1778: HAY, Mar 24, Jul 1, 2, 30, Aug 21, 22, 27, CG, Oct 14; 1779: CG, Apr 23, May 19, HAY, Jun 18, Jul 1, 17, 31, Aug 13, 24, 28, CG, Sep 27; 1780: CG, Jan 7, Feb 2, May 23, HAY, Jun 9, 14, 26, Jul 15, Aug 17, 26, Sep 11; 1781: CG, Mar 3, Apr 28, May 3, HAY, Jun 16, 21, Aug 7, 8, 22, 25, 29, Sep 4, CG, 17, Oct 13, Nov 17, 24; 1782: CG, Apr 1, May 8, 17, HAY, Jun 3, 4, 12, Jul 5, Aug 13, 16, 17, Sep 16, 18, CG, Oct 23, Dec 3, 14; 1783: CG, May 28, HAY, 31, Jun 2, 5, 20, 30, Jul 8, Aug 1, 13, 23, 26, CG, Oct 1, 14; 1784: CG, Jan 29, Mar 6, May 15, 26, HAY, Jun 1, 9, 17, Aug 10, 24, 26, 28, CG, Sep 20; 1785: CG, Apr 6, May 7, 11, HAY, 30, Jun 11, 16, Jul 13, 20, 26, Aug 2, 23, 25, 31, CG, Sep 26, 30, Oct 3, 27; 1786: CG, Apr 24, May 18, 24, HAY, Jun 12, 14, 16, 26, Aug 10, 12, 17; 1787: CG, Jan 31, Mar 1, May 19, HAY, Jun 16, Jul 23, Aug 4, 29, CG, Nov 20; 1788: CG, Mar 1, 11, May 12, 15, HAY, Jun 10, 16, 23, 30, Jul 2, 10, Aug 5, 9, 15, 16, 22, 26, 27, Sep 3, 9, CG, Oct 29; 1789: CG, Feb 6, Apr 14, 20, 30, May 20, Jun 5, 6, HAY, 23, 25, 26, Aug 5, 11, CG, Nov 11, 12; 1790: CG, Mar 1, 18, May 27, HAY, Jun 15, 19, 28, 29, Jul 5, Aug 24, 31
Painter, Sarah Lenox (actor), 1780: CII, Mar 6; 1781: HAY, Aug 7, 8, CG, Oct 16; 1782: HAY, Jun 3, CG, Oct 14, HAY, Dec 30; 1783: HAY, Jun 5, 30, Jul 26, Aug 1, 13, CG, Oct 13; 1784: HAY, Aug 10, Sep 17; 1785: HAY, Jul 19, Aug 31; 1786: HAY, Jul 3, Sep 4
Painter's Art (entertainment), 1776: CHR, Oct 7
Pair-Royal of Coxcombs, The. See Philips, Joan.
Paisible, James (musician), 1675: ATCOURT, Feb 15; 1677: ATCOURT, May 22; 1698: YB, Mar 16; 1702: DL, Oct 20; 1703: YB, Mar 19, DL, Apr 19, May 15, 28, RIW, Aug 12, DL, Nov 19, YB, Dec 11; 1704: DL, Jan 17, Feb 4, YB, Mar 29, DL, 30, Apr 4, YB, 20, 28, May 18, DL, Dec 15, 28; 1705: DL, Apr 10, Nov 8, Dec 17; 1706: DL, Jan 4; 1707: YB, May 23; 1708: SH, Mar 26; 1710: PCGR, Jun 14; 1712: SH, Dec 8; 1713: HIC, Mar 25; 1715: DL, Apr 28, Jun 2, Nov 2; 1716: DL, Apr 16, May 31, Jun 6, Nov 29; 1717: DL, Mar 1, SH, 27, Dec 23; 1718: TEC, Mar 12, DL, May 16, SH, Dec 23; 1719: DL, May 9
Paisiello, Giovanni (composer), 1776: KING'S, Nov 5; 1777: KING'S, Nov 4; 1778: KING'S, Mar 26, Dec 22; 1779: KING'S, May 29; 1780: KING'S, Mar 9; 1781: KING'S, Apr 5; 1785: CG, May 12; 1786: DL, Jan 14, KING'S, 24, Mar 11; 1787: KING'S, Feb 17, CG, Mar 12, KING'S, Apr 24, HAY, Aug 4, CG, Oct 31, KING'S, Dec 8; 1788: KING'S, Feb 5, 21, May 15; 1789: KING'S, Jun 11, DL, Nov 24; 1790: HAY, Feb 27, May 27, Jun 3; 1791: DL, Jan 1, KING'S, Mar 26, 31, Apr 2, 26, DL, May 3, KING'S, 12, PAN, 14, Jun 16, HAY, 25, DLKING'S, Sep 29; 1792: HAY, Feb 28, KING'S, 29, Mar 14, 21, 23, 28, HAY, 31; 1793: KING'S, Jan 26, Feb 5, KING/HAY, 15, CG, 25, KING/HAY, Mar 15, KING'S, May 14, CG, 16; 1794: KING'S, Feb 1, Apr 1, DL, 9, CG, 10, May 2, KING'S, 15, 29, Jun 5, 23, CG, Sep 17, KING'S, Dec 6; 1795: KING'S, Jan 10, Mar 13, Apr 14; 1796: CG, Feb 2, KING'S, Apr 16, DL, 30; 1797: KING'S, Jan 7, Apr 27, Nov 28; 1798: DL, Jan 16, KING'S, Apr 26, Dec 26, 29; 1799: CG, Apr 19, KING'S, May 30, Jun 25; 1800: KING'S, Jan 11, DL, Feb 1, KING'S, Apr 24, Jun 21
--Amore Contrastato, L'; or, La Molinarella (opera), 1791: PAN, May 14, 17, 21,

26, 31, Jun 7, 14, 30, Jul 5, 12; 1794: KING'S, Dec 6, 9, 13, 16
--Barbiere di Siviglia, Il; or, The Spanish Barber (opera), 1786: DL, Jan 14;
   1789: KING'S, Jun 11, 15, CG, Jul 4, 11; 1790: HAY, Jun 3, 5, 10; 1792:
   KING'S, Mar 14, 23; 1793: KING'S, Jan 26, 29, Feb 2, 23; 1798: KING'S, Jun 5,
   9, 12, 26, 30
--Conte Ridicolo, Il (opera), 1787: KING'S, Dec 8; 1795: KING'S, Apr 14, 18,
   May 12
--Didone (opera), 1799: KING'S, May 30, Jun 8, 11, 15, 22, Jul 27
--Discordia Conjugale, La; ou, Le Vane Gelosie (opera), 1792: PAN, Jan 10, 14,
   HAY, Mar 27, 31, Apr 10, 14, 28, May 12
--Due Contesse, Le (opera), 1777: KING'S, Nov 4, 11, 18, 25, Dec 2, 9; 1778:
   KING'S, Jan 13
--Elfrida (opera), 1798: KING'S, Apr 26, 28, May 5, 8, 10, 12, 19, 25, 29, Jun
   14, 16, Jul 3, 7, 14, 21, 28, Aug 4, Dec 29; 1799: KING'S, Jan 5, 19, Feb 26,
   Mar 12, May 2, 4, 7, 10, 14, 25, 28, Jun 1, 17, 18, Jul 13; 1800: KING'S, Jun
   21, Jul 5, 26
--Fraschetana, La (opera), 1776: KING'S, Nov 5, 12, 19, 26, 30, Dec 2, 7, 10,
   17, 21; 1777: KING'S, Jan 4, 11, 17, 28, Feb 22, 25, Mar 18, Apr 8, May 1, 6,
   15, Jun 17; 1778: KING'S, Dec 22, 29; 1779: KING'S, Jan 5, 12, 19, Feb 2;
   1781: KING'S, Apr 5, 24, May 1, 5, 12, 17, 19, 22, 29, 31, Jun 9, 12, 19;
   1788: KING'S, May 15, 22, 27, Jun 3, 10, 19; 1794: KING'S, Jun 5, 10, 17, 21,
   28; 1799: KING'S, Mar 26, 30, Apr 2, 6, 16
--Giuochi d'Agrigento, I (opera), 1793: KING'S, Feb 5, 9, 12, 16, 19, May 4
--Locanda, La (opera), 1791: PAN, Jun 16, 18, 21, 28, Jul 2, 5, 9, 14, 18;
   1792: HAY, Feb 28, Mar 1, 3, 6, 8, 10, 13, 15, 17, 20, 22, 24, 27, 29, Apr
   17, 24, May 3, 8, 19, 24, Jun 2, 7
--Marchese Tulipano, Il; ou, Le Finte Contesse (Marchese Villano, Il) (opera),
   1778: KING'S, Mar 26; 1786: KING'S, Jan 24, 28, 31, Feb 4, 7, 11, Apr 18, 20,
   Jun 20, Jul 4
--Modista Raggiratrice, La (opera), 1796: KING'S, Apr 16, 19, 21, 23, 26, 30,
   May 3, 12, 21, Jun 2, 28; 1797: KING'S, Jan 7, Feb 7, 11, 21, Mar 7
--Nina (opera), 1797: KING'S, Apr 27, 29, May 2, 6, 11, 13, 16, 20, 25, Jul 4,
   8, 22, Dec 9, 26; 1798: KING'S, Jan 2, 16, 31; 1800: KING'S, Apr 24, 29, May
   3
--Pirro (opera), 1791: KING'S, Feb 23, Mar 10, 22
--Prova Dell' Opera, La (interlude), 1794: KING'S, Apr 1, 29
--Re Teodoro in Venezia, Il; or, Theodore at Venice (opera), 1787: KING'S, Dec
   8, 11, 15, 18, 22; 1788: KING'S, Jan 3, 5, 8, 12, Feb 2, 16, 26, May 6; 1795:
   KING'S, Apr 14
--Schiavi per Amore, Gli (opera), 1787: KING'S, Apr 24, 26, 28, May 5, 8, 12,
   15, 17, 22, 24, 29, Jun 7, 12, 14, 19, 23, 26, 30, Jul 5; 1788: KING'S, Feb
   5, 7, 9, 21, 23, 28, Mar 1, 11, 13, Apr 3, 8, DL, Jun 5, KING'S, 19, 26;
   1790: HAY, May 27; 1797: KING'S, Mar 14, 18, 21, 25, 28, Apr 6, May 25, Jun
   2; 1798: KING'S, Dec 26; 1799: KING'S, Jan 1, 8, 15, Feb 12, 19
--Serva Padrona, La (opera), 1794: KING'S, May 29, Jun 3, 23, 24, Jul 1, 3, 5;
   1799: KING'S, Jun 25, 29, Jul 6, 9, 16, 20, Aug 3
--Te Deum, Grand (anthem), 1794: KING'S, May 15
--Tutor Burlato, Il (opera), 1787: KING'S, Feb 17, 20, Mar 10
--Zingari in Fiera, I (opera), 1793: KING'S, May 14, 17, 21, 25, 28, Jun 1, 8,
   18, 22, 25, 29; 1795: KING'S, Jan 10, 13, 17, 20, 24, Feb 17; 1800: KING'S,
   Jan 11, 14, 18, 21, 25, 28, Feb 1, 4, Mar 4, 22, 29, May 8, Jun 24, Jul 15,
   29
Palace Yard, 1724: PY, Apr 20; 1793: DL, May 27
Paladini, Luigi (dancer), 1775: KING'S, Oct 31, Nov 7, 16, 28; 1776: CG, Oct 23
Palatine, Elector of, 1712: QUEEN'S, Mar 27, OSG, Apr 9; 1719: DL, Mar 11;
   1721: YB, Jan 9; 1722: HAY, Mar 16
Palemon and Lavinia (dance), 1782: CG, Feb 21
Palin, Miss (actor), 1728: LIF, Jan 17, 29, Apr 24, May 23, Jun 25, Jul 5, 19;
   1729: LIF, May 12; 1733: CG, Jul 6
Pall Mall, 1702: WH, Jan 14; 1709: H&P, Jun 18; 1733: GF, May 14, PM, Dec 24;
   1734: PM, Nov 29; 1739: DL, Apr 24; 1741: DL, Mar 24; 1742: GF, Apr 22; 1744:
   CG, Apr 18, DL, Dec 13; 1745: DL, Apr 1; 1749: CG, Jan 17, DL, Feb 9, 15;
   1750: DL, Feb 27, Mar 5, 28, Apr 4, Nov 28; 1751: DL, Feb 5; 1752: CG, Mar
   18, DL, Dec 22; 1753: DL, Feb 9, CG, 23, DL, Mar 6, Dec 21; 1754: CG, Jan 24,
   29; 1755: DL, Dec 16; 1756: DL, Jan 22; 1757: CG, Mar 17, DL, Apr 23; 1758:
   DL, Jan 26, Mar 2, 7, 10; 1759: DL, Apr 30, CG, May 8; 1763: DL, Apr 27;
   1765: DL, Dec 18; 1769: KING'S, Feb 24; 1774: KING'S, Nov 8; 1776: KING'S,
   Nov 2; 1777: KING'S, Mar 20, Nov 4; 1778: KING'S, Nov 24; 1779: KING'S, Nov
   27; 1780: KING'S, Nov 25; 1781: HAY, Jun 20, Oct 16, KING'S, Nov 17; 1782:
   HAY, Mar 18, KING'S, Nov 2; 1783: KING'S, May 1, HAY, Jun 20, KING'S, Nov 29;
   1784: HAY, Jan 21, Feb 9, KING'S, Mar 11, 25, CG, Apr 28, KING'S, May 20, Jun
   3, Dec 18, 21; 1785: KING'S, Mar 17, Apr 7, 14; 1786: KING'S, Jan 24, CG, Apr

28, KING'S, Dec 23; <u>1787</u>: KING'S, Mar 22, HAY, Jul 21, KING'S, Dec 8; <u>1788</u>:
DL, May 28, HAY, Jul 23; <u>1789</u>: KING'S, Jan 10, May 7; <u>1790</u>: HAY, Jan 7; <u>1791</u>:
KING'S, May 12, PAN, Dec 17; <u>1792</u>: DLKING'S, Mar 27, May 8; <u>1793</u>: KING'S, Jan
26, DL, May 9; <u>1794</u>: KING'S, Jun 5, Dec 6; <u>1795</u>: KING'S, Apr 30, May 14;
<u>1796</u>: KING'S, Jul 23, Nov 26; <u>1798</u>: CG, Apr 23, HAY, Aug 18; <u>1799</u>: KING'S,
May 30
Pallavicino, V (composer), <u>1769</u>: KING'S, May 6
Palli, Sga (singer, actor), <u>1748</u>: HAY, Jan 12
Palm, Miss (actor), <u>1734</u>: JS, May 29
Palma (singer), <u>1744</u>: HAY, Apr 4, HIC, May 16; <u>1745</u>: HAY, Apr 1
Palma, Bernardo (singer), <u>1736</u>: KING'S, Jan 24, ST, Feb 11
Palma, Phillippo (singer), <u>1736</u>: DL, Apr 22
Palma, Sga (singer), <u>1746</u>: HIC, Mar 10
Palmer (actor), <u>1723</u>: HAY, Apr 22
Palmer (house servant), <u>1743</u>: CG, May 9; <u>1744</u>: CG, May 11; <u>1745</u>: CG, May 14;
<u>1746</u>: CG, May 6; <u>1747</u>: CG, May 19; <u>1748</u>: CG, May 5
Palmer (musician), <u>1770</u>: HAY, Dec 14; <u>1771</u>: GROTTO, Aug 8
Palmer (wax chandler), <u>1766</u>: DL, Nov 4; <u>1767</u>: DL, May 9; <u>1771</u>: CG, Dec 11;
<u>1772</u>: DL, Jan 6, CG, Feb 17, Apr 11, Nov 12, Dec 30; <u>1773</u>: CG, Oct 29, Dec
18; <u>1774</u>: DL, Jan 7, CG, 19, DL, Jun 2; <u>1775</u>: DL, May 27; <u>1776</u>: DL, Jan 19,
Apr 11, Jun 10
Palmer Family, <u>1766</u>: DL, Jan 6
Palmer, Barbara Villiers, Countess of Castlemaine (spectator), <u>1661</u>: ATCOURT,
Apr 20, VERE, Jul 23, Aug 27, Sep 7; <u>1662</u>: VERE, May 21, ATCOURT, Nov 17;
<u>1664</u>: LIF, Mar 7; <u>1665</u>: ATCOURT, Feb 2, LIF, Apr 3; <u>1666</u>: ATCOURT, Oct 29;
<u>1667</u>: LIF, Feb 4, BRIDGES, 5, LIF, May 21, BRIDGES, Aug 26, BF, 30; <u>1668</u>:
ATCOURT, Jan 13, Feb 4, BRIDGES, Apr 7, LIF, May 5, BRIDGES, Dec 18, LIF, 21;
<u>1669</u>: BRIDGES, Jan 13
Palmer, H (actor), <u>1760</u>: DL, Jun 19
Palmer, Hannah Mary, Mrs John (actor), <u>1761</u>: DL, Apr 27, 29, May 2, 5, 6, 13,
18, Sep 17, 19, 24, Oct 1, 24, 27, Nov 10, 23, Dec 26; <u>1762</u>: DL, Jan 15, Feb
10, Mar 1, 15, 20, 22, 27, Apr 14, 24, 30, May 13, 14, 19, Sep 18, 25, Oct 7,
8, 11, 23, 30, Nov 22, Dec 10; <u>1763</u>: DL, Feb 3, Mar 1, 7, 14, Apr 16, May 2,
Sep 22, 24, 27, Oct 12, 21, 31, Nov 9, 15, Dec 10; <u>1764</u>: DL, Mar 20, 24, 27,
Apr 9, 10, 12, 27, 30, May 1, 8, 9, 19, Sep 18, 20, 22, 29, Oct 4, 6, 9, 13,
15, 16, 17, 20; <u>1765</u>: DL, Jan 3, 7, 15, Feb 5, Mar 16, 18, 19, Apr 10, 19,
22, 23, May 1, 4, 16, 20, 22, Sep 17, 19, 24, 26, Oct 3, 9, 14, 30, 31, Nov
11, 23, 25, Dec 5, 23, 27; <u>1766</u>: DL, Jan 9, Feb 3, 20, Mar 15, Apr 7, 9, 15,
25, May 16, 20, 21, Sep 20, 27, Oct 7, 10, 17, 25, Nov 4, 17, 26, 28, Dec 2,
13; <u>1767</u>: DL, Jan 31, Feb 19, 21, Mar 21, 30, Apr 4, 11, 20, 29, May 16, 20,
Jun 1, HAY, 10, 12, Jul 2, Aug 5, DL, Sep 12, 17, 19, 21, 23, Oct 8, 15, 23,
26, Nov 6, 13, 16, 25, Dec 5; <u>1768</u>: DL, Jan 19, Feb 20, Apr 5, 6, 14, 22;
<u>1773</u>: HAY, Jul 5, 30, Aug 11, 23, 27; <u>1774</u>: HAY, May 16, 30, Jun 1, Jul 6,
11, Aug 19; <u>1775</u>: HAY, May 22, Jul 7, Aug 9, Sep 4, 11, 16, 18, 20; <u>1776</u>:
HAY, May 20, 22, Sep 23
Palmer, Hannah, Mrs William (actor), <u>1768</u>: DL, Oct 13; <u>1769</u>: DL, Oct 13; <u>1771</u>:
DL, May 27; <u>1773</u>: DL, Apr 30; <u>1774</u>: DL, Mar 14; <u>1776</u>: DL, May 11, HAY, 22,
Jul 3, 10, 24, Sep 16, DL, Dec 31; <u>1777</u>: HAY, May 30, Jun 2, 30, Jul 15, Aug
4, 19, Sep 17, 19; <u>1778</u>: HAY, May 21, Aug 21, Sep 18; <u>1779</u>: HAY, Jun 4, 10,
Jul 14, 17; <u>1780</u>: DL, May 5, HAY, 30, Jun 29, Jul 29, Sep 2; <u>1781</u>: HAY, May
30, Jun 7, Jul 23, Aug 8, 29; <u>1782</u>: HAY, Jun 3, 4, 18, Aug 13, 27; <u>1783</u>: HAY,
Jun 7, 20, Aug 22
Palmer, Jemima Sarah (actor), <u>1794</u>: HAY, Jul 25, Aug 27; <u>1798</u>: HAY, Jun 18;
<u>1799</u>: HAY, Feb 25, Aug 21
Palmer the elder, John (actor), <u>1748</u>: HAY, May 2, BFP, Aug 24, SFP, Sep 7, DL,
29, Oct 28, 29, Nov 3, 4, 28, Dec 26; <u>1749</u>: DL, Feb 21, Mar 9, Apr 28, 29,
May 8, Sep 16, 21, 22, Oct 13, 17, 24, 30, Nov 2, 4, 28, Dec 7, 18, 20, 26,
28; <u>1750</u>: DL, Jan 6, 18, 22, Mar 13, 19, 22, Apr 3, 19, May 1, 4, Oct 15, 20,
23, 26, 29, Nov 1, 2, 3, 5, 7, 13, 15, 24, Dec 3, 14, 19, 31; <u>1751</u>: DL, Jan
1, 7, 12, 16, 18, Feb 2, 16, 23, Mar 12, 16, Apr 12, 22, 23, 24, 29, May 1,
SF, Sep 9, DL, 10, 12, 13, 14, 17, 19, 21, 24, Oct 3, 9, 11, 17, 22, 29, Nov
16, 29, Dec 14; <u>1752</u>: DL, Jan 1, 11, Feb 3, 8, Mar 7, 9, 10, 12, Apr 8, 10,
21, Sep 19, 23, 26, 30, Oct 5, 7, 10, 12, 19, 21, 26, Nov 3, 22, 23, 25, 27,
30, Dec 7, 8, 18, 20, 29; <u>1753</u>: DL, Jan 2, 3, 8, 13, 18, 22, Feb 6, Mar 22,
Apr 2, 5, 7, 24, May 2, 4, 21, 25, Sep 11, 13, 15, 20, 22, 25, 29, Oct 6, 9,
10, 12, 13, 18, 24, Nov 6, 7, 8, 14, 15, 26, Dec 20; <u>1754</u>: DL, Jan 7, 16, 23,
Feb 1, Mar 19, 23, Apr 16, May 15, Sep 14, 17, 19, 21, 26, Oct 1, 3, 5, 10,
18, 22, 23, 30, Nov 4, 7, 22, Dec 7; <u>1755</u>: DL, Jan 6, 15, 17, 22, 25, Feb 18,
Mar 4, CG, 12, DL, 13, 20, Apr 4, 5, 15, May 1, 5, Sep 13, 16, 18, 20, 25,
27, CG, 29, DL, Oct 2, 7, 13, 17, 27, 31, Nov 1, 4, 12, 22, 26, 28, Dec 1, 4,
6, 11, 18; <u>1756</u>: DL, Jan 9, Feb 24, Mar 23, 27, 29, 30, Apr 3, 5, 10, 20, May
5, 12, 17, 18, 24, 27, Sep 18, 23, 25, 28, 30, Oct 5, 7, 13, 14, 19, 23, 28,

29, Nov 2, 4, 6, 11, 12, 18, Dec 10, 15, 27; 1757: DL, Jan 3, 22, 26, Feb 22,
Mar 7, 24, KING'S, 26, DL, Apr 15, 20, 30, May 2, 11, 23, Sep 15, 24, 27, 29,
Oct 4, 6, 7, 8, 12, 13, 18, 19, 26, 29, Nov 4, 8, 10, 19, 22, Dec 3, 22, 27;
1758: DL, Jan 24, 27, Feb 1, 20, Mar 13, 16, 30, Apr 3, 25, May 4, 17, Sep
16, 21, 23, 26, 28, Oct 3, 7, 14, 18, 21, 25, 27, 30, Nov 1, 7, 10, 13, 14,
15, 16, 17, 23, 24, Dec 18, 20, 28; 1759: DL, Jan 17, 20, Feb 27, Mar 24, 26,
31, Apr 2, 7, 26, 27, May 11, 14, 16, 21, Sep 22, 25, 27, 29, Oct 2, 5, 9,
12, 16, 17, 19, 22, 23, 26, 27, 30, 31, Nov 2, 9, 10, 13, 17, 22, Dec 1, 12,
19; 1760: DL, Jan 10, 19, 24, Mar 20, 22, 24, Apr 9, 11, 21, 24, 28, 29, 30,
May 7, 8, 12, 15, 16, Jul 29, Sep 20, 30, Oct 3, 7, 9, 10, 14, 15, 17, 23,
24, Nov 17, 27, Dec 2, 29, 30; 1761: DL, Jan 10, Feb 12, Mar 23, 26, 28, 31,
Apr 16, 20, 24, 28, 29, May 1, 5, 11, 28, 29, Sep 8, 10, 14, 17, 19, 23, 25,
26, 30, Oct 1, 7, 10, 13, 14, 16, 17, 20, 24, 31, Nov 18, 20, 28, Dec 23;
1762: DL, Jan 7, 11, 15, 20, 21, Feb 10, 19, 20, Mar 20, 25, 27, Apr 22, 30,
HAY, May 1, DL, 10, 15, 19, 20, 21, Sep 18, 25, 28, 29, 30, Oct 1, 4, 5, 6,
7, 8, 9, 13, 14, 23, 29, Nov 2, 10, 12, 17, 18, 19, 26, Dec 1, 10, 11; 1763:
DL, Jan 14, 15, 17, 18, Mar 1, 19, 21, Apr 4, May 10, Sep 20, 22, 24, 29, Oct
1, 12, 19, 24, 29, 31, Nov 2, 8, 15, 19, 29, Dec 1, 5, 14, 17; 1764: DL, Jan
3, 9, 13, 14, 25, 27, Mar 24, 26, 31, Apr 24, 25, HAY, Jun 26, Jul 6, 13, 23,
Aug 20, DL, Sep 18, 20, 22, 27, 29, Oct 4, 9, 13, 15, 17, 18, 20, 22, 25, 26,
Nov 8, 12, 17, Dec 13, 18; 1765: DL, Jan 18, Feb 2, Mar 18, 19, Apr 13, May
11, 18, 22, Sep 17, 19, 21, Oct 3, 11, 14, 23, 24, 28, 30, 31, Nov 14, 20,
Dec 3, 5, 7, 23; 1766: DL, Jan 9, Feb 13, 20, Mar 15, Apr 2, 16, 25, May 3,
10, 14, 19, 20, 21, 22, HAY, Jun 18, 26, Jul 1, 3, 15, 23, 31, KING'S, Aug 8,
13, 18, 20, HAY, 21, KING'S, 25, 27, HAY, Sep 2, KING'S, 9, 12, 13, 15, DL,
20, 30, Oct 9, 10, 17, 21, 23, 25, 31, Nov 17, 18, 20, 28, Dec 2, 4, 6, 9,
10, 15; 1767: DL, Jan 9, 24, 31, Feb 19, Mar 7, 21, Apr 11, 22, 29, 30, May
12, 19, HAY, 29, Jun 4, 5, 8, 10, 12, 15, 17, 22, 26, 30, Jul 2, 3, 6, 15,
22, 31, Aug 5, 7, 14, 25, 27, DL, Sep 12, 17, HAY, 18, DL, 21, HAY, 21, DL,
25, Oct 7, 8, 9, 14, 15, 20, 22, 28, 29, Nov 6, 16, 20, 26, 28, Dec 1, 16;
1768: DL, Jan 13, 14, 16, Feb 9, Mar 17, 21, 24, Apr 4, 6, 29, May 30, 31
Palmer the younger, John (actor), 1762: DL, May 20, 21, 24, 25; 1763: DL, May
17, Nov 9, Dec 26; 1764: DL, Feb 18, Mar 13, 20, Apr 7, 12, May 21, HAY, Jun
13, DL, Oct 2; 1765: DL, Apr 10; 1766: DL, Oct 7, 13, Dec 2; 1767: DL, Jan
24, Apr 11, 22, 27, 30, May 6, 8, 20, 25, 26, HAY, 29, Jun 1, 4, 5, 8, 17,
19, 22, 25, Aug 12, 21, DL, Sep 19, 26, Oct 10, 20, 21, 23, Nov 5, 12, Dec 2,
5, 7, 12, 19, 21; 1768: DL, Jan 6, 23, Mar 21, Apr 6, 19, 21, 27, 30, May 3,
4, 5, 6, 9, 30, Sep 24, 26, 27, 28, Oct 5, 8, 10, 15, 21, 28, 31, Nov 10, 17,
Dec 1, 16, 17; 1769: DL, Jan 25, 27, Feb 4, 13, 23, HAY, 28, DL, Mar 11, 28,
29, 31, Apr 19, 28, May 1, Sep 16, 23, 26, 30, Oct 7, 10, 17, 18, 23, 28, 30,
Nov 2, 18, 22, 24, 27, 28, 29, Dec 1, 4, 8, 12, 13, 23; 1770: DL, Jan 6, Feb
21, Mar 3, 13, 20, 22, 24, 26, 31, Apr 19, 26, 27, May 9, 15, 17, 30, Sep 22,
25, Oct 2, 5, 8, 18, 25, 29, 31, CG, Nov 2, DL, 6, 10, 15, 16, 17, 21, 24,
28, Dec 6, CG, 12, DL, 13, 29; 1771: DL, Jan 10, 12, Mar 5, 9, 16, 23, Apr 6,
13, 20, 26, May 11, Sep 21, 26, 28, Oct 5, 12, 15, 19, 24, 28, 30, Nov 1, 8,
11, 14, 15, 22, 23, 28, Dec 3, 4, 21, 30; 1772: DL, Jan 3, 7, Feb 26, Mar 12,
26, 28, Apr 6, 21, May 4, 12, Jun 10, Sep 19, 22, 24, Oct 13, 16, 21, 23, 31,
Nov 4, 12, 16, 20, Dec 4, 17, 21; 1773: DL, Jan 13, Feb 2, 27, Mar 9, 23, 30,
Apr 1, 16, 17, 23, 27, 29, 30, May 1, 6, 12, HAY, 17, DL, 17, HAY, 19, DL,
19, 27, 31, HAY, 31, Jun 14, 16, 18, Sep 16, DL, 18, 21, Oct 5, 6, 8, 9, 14,
18, 19, Nov 20, 25, 26, Dec 10, 11, 21, 27; 1774: DL, Jan 1, 18, 19, Feb 2,
5, 9, 15, Mar 12, 14, 15, 17, 19, 22, Apr 4, 6, 12, 21, 25, 26, 28, May 4,
18, 26, HAY, Jun 8, 15, 27, Jul 4, 13, 15, 22, DL, Sep 20, 22, 24, Oct 5, 8,
12, 15, 21, 24, 27, Nov 4, 7, 8, 10, 25, Dec 1, 13, 16, 17, 29; 1775: DL, Jan
2, 4, 11, 21, 27, Feb 17, Mar 18, 20, 21, 25, 28, Apr 19, 20, 21, 24, May 12,
25, 27, Sep 23, 26, 28, Oct 3, 10, 14, 17, 24, Nov 3, 4, 9, 14, 17, 18, 20,
25, Dec 2, 11, 12, 16, 19; 1776: DL, Jan 9, 13, 27, Feb 15, 22, Mar 7, 11,
14, 18, 28, Apr 10, 17, 18, 24, 25, 26, May 8, 13, HAY, 20, 22, DL, 23, HAY,
27, 28, DL, Jun 5, HAY, Jul 3, Aug 19, Sep 2, 16, 17, 20, 20, DL, 21, HAY, 23,
DL, 26, 28, Oct 1, 5, 10, 12, 19, 22, 29, Nov 4, 9; 1777: DL, Jan 16, 20, 22,
25, 27, Mar 4, 13, 20, Apr 7, 11, 17, 22, May 6, 8, HAY, 15, 28, 30, Jun 2,
6, 9, 11, 26, 27, 30, Jul 15, 24, Aug 7, 14, 19, 25, 28, 29, 30, Sep 3, DL,
27, 30, Oct 4, 7, 14, 17, 18, 22, Nov 4, 13, 14, 18, 24, 29, Dec 3, 8, 13,
18; 1778: DL, Jan 10, 22, 24, Feb 2, 18, Mar 12, 30, Apr 9, 20, 23, May 5,
16, HAY, 18, 21, 22, Jun 1, 10, 11, 19, Jul 1, 2, 11, 30, Aug 21, Sep 7, 10,
DL, 19, 22, 26, 29, Oct 1, 3, 6, 15, 17, 20, 21, 23, 26, 27, Nov 7, 10, 11,
20, Dec 19, 21, 22; 1779: DL, Jan 7, 23, Mar 13, 16, 22, 25, Apr 5, 10, 12,
16, 19, 28, May 10, 15, 21, HAY, 31, DL, Jun 1, HAY, 2, 4, 10, 18, Jul 1, 15,
16, 17, 20, 31, Aug 17, 24, 28, 31, Sep 7, DL, 18, 21, 23, Oct 7, 9, 16, 21,
23, 30, Nov 8, 11, 15, 18, 22, 24, Dec 2, 8, 9, 13, 20; 1780: DL, Jan 1, 11,
18, 24, 26, 28, Feb 22, Mar 16, 30, Apr 10, May 12, 24, HAY, 30, Jun 2, 5, 9,
13, 14, 15, 24, Jul 1, 6, 10, 13, 24, 29, Aug 5, 14, 16, 22, 24, 26, Sep 5,

637

DL, 16, 19, 26, Oct 2, 3, 5, 10, 11, 14, 23, Nov 1, 2, 3, 4, 13, 17, 18, 22,
29, Dec 4, 27; 1781: DL, Jan 6, 9, 26, Feb 17, Mar 10, 27, Apr 2, 18, 23, 28,
May 8, 17, HAY, 30, Jun 4, 5, 6, 7, 8, 9, 12, 13, 15, Jul 9, 18, 23, Aug 7,
21, 22, 24, 28, 31, DL, Sep 15, 18, 20, 25, 27, 29, Oct 4, 6, 12, 24, 25, 29,
Nov 10, 15, 27, Dec 13, 14, 27; 1782: DL, Jan 19, Feb 25, Mar 16, 19, 21, Apr
11, 23, 24, 30, May 4, 7, 8, 11, 14, 18, 31, HAY, Jun 4, 6, 10, 11, 12, 13,
15, 20, 24, 29, Jul 16, 30, Aug 5, 6, 9, 15, 26, 27, Sep 3, DL, 17, 18, 19,
20, 21, 24, 26, 28, Oct 1, 5, 8, 10, 12, 14, 26, 30, Nov 5, 7, 22, 26, 29,
Dec 7, 11; 1783: DL, Jan 3, 24, 29, Feb 7, 22, Mar 10, 17, 20, 24, 29, Apr 7,
29, May 2, 9, 12, HAY, 31, Jun 2, 3, 4, 5, 6, 7, 10, 13, 16, 18, 24, 27, 30,
Jul 2, 5, 26, Aug 12, 19, 22, 26, 27, 29, Sep 12, DL, 16, 18, 23, 25, Oct 2,
4, 7, 8, 11, 14, 16, 18, 20, 21, 24, 29, Nov 3, 13, 14, 18, 20, 21, 22, Dec
6, 12, 19, 22; 1784: DL, Jan 1, 3, 16, 17, 22, Feb 10, Mar 6, 27, Apr 19, 21,
26, 28, May 3, 5, 17, 21, HAY, 28, 29, 31, Jun 1, 2, 4, 14, 17, 19, 22, 26,
Jul 8, 20, 28, Aug 2, 3, 5, 6, 18, 19, 24, Sep 2, DL, 28, 30, Oct 5, 7, 9,
12, 14, 18, 19, 21, 23, 26, 28, Nov 2, CG, 3, DL, 3, 4, 5, 13, 15, 16, 23,
Dec 2, 3, 10, 11, 22, 28; 1785: DL, Jan 11, 13, 20, 22, 27, Feb 21, Mar 17,
30, Apr 11, 15, 18, 20, May 3, 6, 24, HAY, 28, 31, Jun 2, 3, 4, 6, 7, 11, 15,
17, 21, Jul 19, 23, 26, 29, Aug 4, 23, 30, Sep 2, DL, 20, 22, 27, 29, Oct 4,
13, 15, 18, 20, 22, 25, 26, 27, Nov 2, 3, 7, 11, 12, 18, Dec 5, 30; 1786: DL,
Jan 5, 9, 14, 16, Feb 15, 18, 20, 23, Mar 4, 25, 28, Apr 4, 26, May 15, Jun
1, 2, 6, HAY, 12, 13, 15, 16, 21, 22, 23, 26, 28, 29, Jul 12, 13, 18, 19, 21,
24, Aug 12, 17, 29, DL, Sep 16, 21, 23, 26, 28, 30, Oct 3, 7, 12, 16, 19, 21,
23, 25, 26, 27, 30, Nov 14, 15, 18, 25, 29, Dec 6, 19, 21; 1787: DL, Jan 13,
24, Feb 12, Mar 12, 27, Apr 10, 13, 14, 23, May 3, Jun 1, 6, ROY, 20, Jul 3,
DL, Sep 18, Dec 11; 1788: DL, Apr 25, May 5, 6, 7, 14, 19, 21, 22, 23, Jun 2,
9, HAY, 10, 12, 17, 19, 26, Jul 10, 24, Aug 9, 22, 25, 29, Sep 9, DL, 13, 16,
23, 27, Oct 2, 4, 7, 9, 14, 23, 28, Nov 1, 4, 5, 8, 11, 19, 25, Dec 5, 9, 18;
1789: DL, Jan 1, 7, 13, 20, 26, Feb 17, Apr 2, May 19, 22, 23, Jun 13, HAY,
Jul 15; 1790: DL, May 14, HAY, Aug 7, 10, 12, 13, 16, 19, 20, 23, 25, 31, Sep
1, DL, 14, 16, HAY, Oct 13, DL, 18, 20, 21, 23, 26, 27, Nov 1, 3, 10, 17, Dec
7, 8, 14, 29; 1791: DL, Jan 1, Feb 10, Mar 22, 24, Apr 2, 4, 5, 27, May 20,
Jun 4, HAY, 6, 8, 10, 13, 17, 18, 20, Jul 9, 14, 30, Aug 15, 24, 26, 31,
DLKING'S, Sep 27, 29, Oct 1, 3, 6, 8, 10, 20, 29, 31, Nov 4, 5, 7, 8, 14, 30,
Dec 2; 1792: DLKING'S, Jan 18, 21, 28, 31, Feb 4, 7, 11, 23, Mar 1, 19, 26,
29, Apr 10, 12, 19, 20, 28, May 22, 28, Jun 15, HAY, 18, 20, 22, 23, 27, Jul
4, 23, 25, Aug 2, 9, 17, 23, 28, Sep 1, DL, 15, 18, 22, 25, 27, Oct 9, 13,
16, 18, 20, Nov 5, 10, 15, 17, Dec 8, 17, 28, 31; 1793: DL, Jan 4, 9, 16, 29,
Feb 12, 14, 21, 25, 28, Mar 4, 9, 12, 14, 18, Apr 1, 23, 26, HAY, Oct 8;
1794: DL, Apr 21, 25, 26, May 1, 3, 5, 8, 15, 16, 19, 22, 23, 30, Jun 2, 6,
9, 10, 12, 14, 16, 19, 25, 26, 28, Jul 2, HAY, 9, 10, 12, 18, 21, 25, Aug 9,
18, 20, 27, 30, Sep 3, DL, 16, 20, 27, 30, Oct 4, 7, 11, 14, 18, 21, 22,
25, 28, 29, Nov 3, 5, 8, Dec 3, 5, 6, 10, 12, 16, 19, 30; 1795: DL, Jan 2, 5,
20, 22, Feb 12, 28, Mar 3, HAY, 4, 11, DL, 14, 21, Apr 14, 17, 22, 27, May 6,
12, 30, Jun 3, 6, Sep 17, 19, 22, 24, 26, 29, Oct 1, 3, 6, 19, 22, 26, Nov 3,
6, 10, 12, 14, 16, 19, 23, 26, Dec 10, 11, 18, 23, 30; 1796: DL, Jan 5, 16,
23, 29, Feb 1, 27, Mar 15, Apr 12, 13, 14, 16, 20, 26, May 12, 23, 25, 30,
Jun 2, 4, 7, 8, HAY, 11, 13, DL, 13, HAY, 14, 16, 20, 22, 29, Jul 15, 16, 21,
23, 26, 30, Aug 3, 8, 13, 29, 30, Sep 1, 16, 17, DL, 20, 22, 24, 27, HAY, 28,
DL, 29, Oct 1, 4, 6, 8, 10, 11, 13, 22, 25, 27, 28, Nov 1, 2, 5, 8, 9, 10,
15, 23, 26, 29, Dec 6, 21, 26, 30; 1797: DL, Jan 7, 14, 17, 27, Feb 1, 2, 3,
7, 16, 20, 22, Mar 6, 20, Apr 6, 24, 28, May 1, 12, 17, 19, Jun 7, 12, HAY,
13, 15, 19, 20, 22, 23, 24, 26, Jul 3, 6, 8, 10, 15, Aug 5, 8, 10, 14, 15,
22, Sep 4, 9, DL, 19, 26, 30, Oct 3, 7, 12, 14, 21, 30, Nov 4, 7, 10, 11, 14,
15, 17, 18, 20, 21, 23, 24, Dec 9, 14, 21, 23; 1798: DL, Jan 16, 23, 25, Feb
3, 9, 12, 20, Mar 8, 24, Apr 27, May 11, 19, 21, 24, 29, 30, Jun 4, 6, 12,
15, 18, HAY, Aug 18, DL, Sep 15
Palmer, John and Mrs (actors), 1767: DL, Jan 24
Palmer, John and Robert (actors), 1775: DL, Nov 24
Palmer Jr, John (actor), 1791: HAY, Jun 20, Jul 9, 30; 1792: DLKING'S, Feb 18,
Mar 19, HAY, Jun 18, 23, 29, Jul 16, Aug 9, Sep 1; 1793: HAY, Jun 12, 14, 17,
21, 29, Jul 4, 18, 23, Aug 3, 6, 12, Sep 2, 3, 7, 19, 21, 24, 28, 30, Oct 4,
8, 10, 11, 15, 17, 21, 29, Nov 5, 14, 15, Dec 9; 1794: HAY, Jul 8, 9, 10, 12,
16, 17, 18, 21, 22, 29, Aug 9, 20, 22, 27, 30, Sep 6, 10; 1795: HAY, Jun 9,
10, 11, 13, 16, 27, Jul 1, 16, 25, 31, Aug 7, 10, 29, 31, Sep 21; 1796: HAY,
Jun 11, 14, 15, 17, 20, 22, 25, 29, 30, Jul 5, 6, 8, 9, 11, 12, 14, 15, 23,
30, Aug 3, 8, 11, 12, 17, 18, 30, Sep 5, 7, 17; 1797: HAY, Jun 12, 13, 15,
17, 19, 20, 21, 22, 23, 24, 26, 29, Jul 4, 6, 10, Aug 2, 9, 14, Sep 4, 8, 12,
14, 18; 1798: HAY, Apr 23, DL, May 19, Jun 7, HAY, 12, DL, 13, HAY, 14, 15,
16, 18, 19, 20, 21, 27, 28, 29, Jul 6, 14, 20, 21, 23, Aug 30, 31, Sep 3, 7;
1799: HAY, Feb 25, Jun 15, 17, 18, 19, 20, 21, 24, 25, 26, 27, 29, Jul 16,
17, 26, Aug 5, 17, 26, 27; 1800: HAY, Jun 13, 16, 17, 19, 28, Jul 1, 2, 3, 7,

15, 21, Aug 8, 12, 14, 19, 20, 21, 22, 26, 29, Sep 3, 6
Palmer, K (actor), 1776: HAY, Aug 2
Palmer, Martha Elizabeth (actor), 1782: DL, Jan 3; 1783: DL, Nov 20, Dec 10;
  1784: DL, Nov 16; 1785: DL, Jan 14, 20, May 9, Sep 27, Nov 22, Dec 1, 26;
  1786: DL, Feb 15, Mar 28, May 17, HAY, Jun 29; 1787: DL, Jan 5, HAY, Jun 23,
  Aug 28; 1788: DL, May 5, Jun 5, HAY, Aug 5, 9, 18, 26, 27, DL, Nov 11; 1789:
  HAY, Jun 22, DL, Nov 13, 14; 1790: DL, Jan 22, Feb 5, Apr 16, HAY, Jun 17,
  Jul 5, 16, 19, Aug 4, 6, 12, DL, Oct 11, 26, Nov 19; 1791: DL, Mar 22, May
  10, HAY, Jun 6, 30, Jul 7, 14, Aug 18, DLKING'S, Nov 5, 30; 1792: DLKING, Jan
  7, 31, HAY, Jun 15, Jul 11, Aug 9, 17, 31, DL, Sep 18
Palmer, Martha Elizabeth and Jemima Sarah (beneficiaries), 1798: HAY, Aug 18
Palmer, Master (actor), 1766: KING'S, Sep 5; 1767: HAY, Jun 22; 1769: HAY, May
  26, Jun 5; 1770: DL, May 30, Jun 4; 1771: DL, May 28; 1772: DL, Jun 5; 1773:
  DL, May 31; 1798: DL, Mar 6, 20, Jun 4
Palmer, Miss (actor), 1767: HAY, Aug 21, Sep 16; 1768: DL, Jan 4, 6; 1769: DL,
  Apr 10; 1772: DL, Dec 22
Palmer, Mrs (actor), 1729: HAY, Jan 2, May 7, 26, 29, Jun 14, 17, BFR, Aug 25,
  SF, Sep 8, BLA, 30, GF, Nov 3, 5, 6, 14, 20, Dec 1, 17; 1730: GF, Feb 12, 16,
  Mar 30, Apr 2, 6, 16, 28, May 21, 27, 28, Jun 8, 9, 12, 18, 23, 25, 26, 29,
  Jul 6, 8, 17, BFPG/TC, Aug 1, BFPG, 31, GF, Sep 18, 21, 23, 28, 30, Oct 5, 9,
  12, 14, 20, 24, 27, 30, Nov 6, 10, 11, 26, Dec 16; 1731: GF, Jan 23, Feb 18,
  Mar 1, 2, 8, 15, 22, Apr 5, 8, 20, 21, 27, May 4, 11, 14, 15, 17, Jun 1, 2,
  Sep 27, Oct 6, 8, 11, 13, 18, 27, 29, Nov 1, 5, 6, 11, 12, 13, 16, 20, 22,
  24, Dec 6, 8, 20, 21; 1732: GF, Feb 2, Mar 7, 27, Apr 10, 27, 28, May 1, 3,
  4, 12, 17, 22, BF, Aug 22, HAY, Nov 29; 1733: HAY, Feb 14
Palmer, Mrs (actor), 1780: CII, Mar 17; 1781: CII, Mar 15, 27, 30, Apr 5, 9
Palmer, Mrs (actor), 1793: HAY, Dec 27; 1794: HAY, Jan 4
Palmer, Mrs A (actor), 1786: DL, Oct 3, Dec 2; 1787: DL, Jan 18, Apr 10; 1788:
  DL, Jan 9, Apr 15, May 26
Palmer, Robert (actor), 1775: DL, May 27; 1776: HAY, May 20, 22, 28, 31, Jun
  12, Jul 3, 24, Aug 19, Sep 16, 17, 20, DL, 21, HAY, 23, DL, Oct 9, 10, 18,
  Nov 25, Dec 14, 28; 1777: DL, Jan 1, Feb 17, Mar 20, Apr 2, 30, May 1, 6, 8,
  HAY, 28, 30, DL, Jun 4, HAY, 6, 16, 26, 30, Jul 7, 15, 24, Aug 7, 9, 18, 19,
  25, 29, 30, Sep 3, 9, 10, 19, DL, Oct 7, 17, Nov 18, 24, 29, Dec 3, 11, 18;
  1778: DL, Jan 1, 2, 5, 22, Feb 2, Mar 30, HAY, May 18, DL, 18, HAY, 21, DL,
  23, HAY, Jun 1, 3, 11, 19, Jul 2, 11, 30, Aug 20, 21, 22, 27, Sep 2, 7, DL,
  22, 24, 26, 29, Oct 1, 8, 15, 16, 26, 28, Dec 8, 10, 11, 21; 1779: DL, Jan 8,
  Feb 1, 9, 20, Mar 13, 22, May 11, 17, 21, HAY, 31, DL, Jun 1, HAY, 2, 4, 10,
  Jul 5, 15, 17, 20, 31, Aug 6, 13, 17, 18, 24, Sep 8, DL, 18, 21, 25, 28, 30,
  Oct 5, 23, Nov 24, Dec 20, 27; 1780: DL, Jan 24, Feb 3, Apr 7, 12, 18, 20,
  21, May 2, 9, HAY, 30, Jun 9, 14, 23, 24, Jul 1, 6, 10, 13, 15, 20, 24, 29,
  Aug 14, 17, 26, Sep 5, 8, 11, DL, 16, 30, Oct 2, 5, 10, 11, 17, 19, 23, 25,
  30, Nov 1, 3, 4, 10, 14, 18, 22, 24, 27, Dec 1, 6, 8, 27; 1781: DL, Jan 16,
  Feb 12, 17, Mar 10, 19, May 1, 10, 16, 17, 24, HAY, 30, Jun 1, 8, 16, 21, Jul
  9, Aug 1, 7, 8, 17, 22, 24, 28, DL, Sep 18, 20, 25, 27, 29, Oct 6, 19, 29,
  30, Nov 5, 7, 15, 21, 27, Dec 14; 1782: DL, Jan 1, 3, 12, 22, Feb 25, Mar 16,
  CG, Apr 3, DL, 12, 17, 25, 27, 30, May 2, 3, 4, 24, 25, HAY, Jun 3, 4, 6, 13,
  29, Jul 16, 30, Aug 9, 13, 15, 16, 17, 27, DL, Sep 19, 20, 24, 28, Oct 8, 10,
  22, 25, 26, 30, Nov 1, 2, 4, 8, 12, 22, Dec 5, 7, 11, 14, 26, 27; 1783: DL,
  Jan 4, 29, Feb 18, Mar 6, 10, 17, 18, 20, Apr 7, CG, 8, DL, 24, 29, May 2,
  10, 14, HAY, 31, Jun 3, 4, 6, 10, 16, 18, 20, 27, 30, Jul 4, Aug 13, 19, 22,
  29, Sep 12, DL, 18, 23, 27, 30, Oct 7, 8, 11, 13, 14, 17, 20, 24, 29, 31, Nov
  14, 15, 18, 22, 27, Dec 2, 5; 1784: DL, Jan 1, 3, 7, 13, 16, 17, Feb 3, 10,
  Mar 29, Apr 19, 21, 24, 26, May 3, 7, 21, HAY, 28, 29, 31, Jun 1, 2, 4, 5,
  10, 14, 17, 25, 26, 28, Jul 6, 8, 12, 13, 15, 30, Aug 18, 21, 26, Sep 13, DL,
  18, 21, 23, Oct 5, 7, 12, 18, 19, 21, 23, 26, 27, Nov 2, 4, 5, 19, 20, 22,
  23, 25; 1785: DL, Jan 6, 14, 20, 24, 27, Feb 2, 8, 21, Mar 8, 17, 31, Apr 4,
  11, 18, 20, 25, 27, May 24, HAY, 28, 31, Jun 2, 3, 6, 13, 16, 21, 24, 29, Jul
  13, 20, 21, 26, Aug 1, 4, 11, 16, 26, 31, Sep 2, 9, DL, 17, 20, 24, 29, Oct
  1, 6, 8, 15, 20, 26, Nov 2, 7, 8, 11, 12, 17, 18, 21, Dec 30; 1786: DL, Jan
  5, 14, Feb 11, 18, 20, 23, Mar 28, Apr 4, 6, 28, May 1, 15, 17, HAY, Jun 10,
  12, 13, 15, 19, 20, 26, 28, 29, Jul 3, 11, 14, 18, 19, 21, 25, 27, 28, 29,
  Aug 4, 10, 12, 17, 29, Sep 4, DL, 16, 19, 21, 23, 28, Oct 3, 5, 9, 12, 16,
  21, 23, 25, 28, Nov 15, 25, 29, Dec 19, 26; 1787: DL, Jan 13, 18, 23, 29, May
  7, 9, 16, 19, HAY, Jun 11, 13, 16, 18, 20, 21, 23, 25, 27, 28, Jul 4, 7, 13,
  19, 20, 21, Aug 4, 7, 21, 28, Sep 8, DL, 18, 20, 22, 25, 29, Oct 6, 9, 11,
  13, 18, 20, 26, 27, Nov 3, 5, 6, 24, Dec 5, 6, 7, 14; 1788: DL, Jan 2, 5, 12,
  Mar 13, 29, Apr 8, 10, 14, 17, 21, 25, 29, May 6, 7, 14, Jun 6, HAY, 10, 12,
  16, 17, 18, 20, 23, 26, 28, Jul 2, 4, 7, 10, 24, Aug 2, 9, 13, 15, 18, 26,
  27, DL, Sep 16, 18, 25, 30, Oct 4, 7, 9, 21, 28, Nov 5, 6, 8, 12, 25, 28, 29,
  Dec 8, 18; 1789: DL, Jan 7, 10, 17, Feb 3, 16, 21, 28, Apr 4, 14, 15, 20, 21,
  May 11, 22, Jun 3, 13, HAY, 15, 17, 19, 22, 24, 26, 27, 29, 30, Jul 7, 9, 11,

15, 30, 31, Aug 1, 5, 11, 25, 27, Sep 7, 9, DL, 12, 17, 19, 26, 29, Oct 1, 10, 17, 20, 24, 31, Nov 5, 7, 24, Dec 1, 10; 1790: DL, Jan 19, Feb 10, 27, Mar 8, 18, 22, Apr 14, 30, May 7, 14, 20, 27, Jun 1, HAY, 14, 15, 17, 18, 19, 22, 26, 29, 30, Jul 5, 7, 16, 20, 28, Aug 2, 4, 6, 7, 11, 12, 16, 20, 25, Sep 4, DL, 14, 16, Oct 2, 7, HAY, 13, DL, 14, 16, 19, 25, 27, Nov 1, 2, 3, 4, 5, 10, 17, 20, Dec 1, 7, 14; 1791: DL, Jan 1, Feb 15, Mar 22, 31, Apr 30, May 10, 12, 19, 31, HAY, Jun 6, 8, 13, 16, 17, 18, 20, 23, 30, Jul 1, 8, 9, 14, 15, 22, Aug 9, 13, 15, 16, 18, 31, Sep 16, DLKING'S, 22, 27, 29, Oct 1, 3, 4, 8, 10, 13, 24, 31, Nov 4, 5, 7, 10, 11, 22, 30; 1792: DLKING'S, Jan 5, 7, 9, 18, 21, 24, 28, Feb 2, 8, 23, Mar 6, 10, 26, 29, May 9, 17, 22, HAY, Jun 15, 18, 20, 22, 26, 27, 29, 30, Jul 4, 7, 11, 14, 16, 23, 25, 31, Aug 2, 6, 9, 15, 17, 20, 28, 31, Sep 6, DL, 15, 18, 19, 20, 22, 25, 27, 29, Oct 9, 15, 16, 27, Nov 7, 27, Dec 3, 4, 10, 17, 21, 27, 28; 1793: DL, Jan 1, 3, 5, 21, Feb 14, 16, 26, Mar 4, 9, 12, Apr 3, 5, 9, 11, May 23, 24; 1794: HAY, Sep 1, 2, 5, 8, 10, 15, DL, 20, 23, Oct 9, 11, 20, 29, 31, Nov 5, 10, 12, Dec 3, 5, 8, 12, 13, 30; 1795: DL, Jan 8, 12, 19, 20, 22, 23, 26, Feb 9, 28, Apr 17, 22, 23, 24, May 6, 12, 18, 26, 29, Jun 1, Sep 17, 19, 22, 26, Nov 24, Dec 1, 2, 9, 11, 17, 19, 21, 26, 30; 1796: DL, Jan 5, 7, 12, 16, 23, Feb 20, 22, 27, 29, Mar 12, 19, 28, Apr 18, 26, May 12, 13, 28, Jun 2, 6, 8, HAY, 11, DL, 11, 13, HAY, 13, DL, 14, HAY, 16, 17, 18, 20, 22, 25, 29, 30, Jul 5, 6, 7, 8, 9, 11, 12, 14, 23, Aug 3, 8, 10, 11, 17, 18, 26, 29, 30, Sep 5, 17, DL, 24, 27, 29, Oct 3, 4, 10, 13, 15, 17, 19, 24, 25, 27, 28, Nov 1, 5, 8, 10, 22, 28, Dec 6, 16, 29; 1797: DL, Jan 14, Feb 2, 7, 16, Mar 6, Apr 6, 19, 24, 27, 28, May 8, 12, 15, 17, 18, 24, Jun 2, HAY, 12, 13, 15, 17, 19, 23, 26, Jul 3, 4, 6, 10, 13, 19, Aug 5, 7, 8, 9, 10, 11, 14, 15, 21, 28, Sep 4, 9, 14, DL, 19, 21, 23, Oct 5, 7, 14, Dec 6, 7, 9, 11, 13, 21, 23; 1798: DL, Jan 9, 23, Feb 13, 19, 22, Mar 3, 8, 24, Apr 13, 14, May 7, 11, 16, 19, 24, 29, 30, Jun 6, HAY, 12, 13, 15, 20, 21, 23, 27, 28, 30, Jul 5, 10, 16, 17, 20, 21, 25, Aug 3, 7, 23, 27, 29, 30, 31, Sep 3, 10, DL, 15, 18, 20, 22, 25, 29, Oct 4, 6, 9, 13, 20, 27, Nov 10, 13, 22, 26, 28, Dec 5, HAY, 17, DL, 19, 21; 1799: DL, Jan 8, 11, Feb 23, 26, Mar 2, Apr 8, 22, 25, 27, May 1, 3, 24, Jun 10, 15, 18, 19, 20, 21, 22, 25, 27, DL, Jul 1, HAY, 2, 4, 9, 10, 11, 12, 17, 19, 20, 23, 26, 27, 30, Aug 5, 10, 13, 17, 21, 24, 26, 27, Sep 13, 14, DL, 17, 19, 21, 24, 26, Oct 1, 3, 5, 8, 22, 29, 31, Nov 8, 12, 16, 27, 29, Dec 2, 7, 11; 1800: DL, Jan 4, 11, 14, 18, Feb 12, Mar 10, 17, 27, Apr 28, May 1, 10, 30, Jun 12, HAY, 14, 18, 21, Jul 5, 7, 15, Aug 7, 8, 12, 14, 15, 19, 20, 23, 27, 29, Sep 11

Palmer Sr, Robert (pit doorkeeper), 1754: DL, May 21; 1755: DL, May 6; 1756: DL, May 10; 1759: DL, May 29; 1760: DL, May 15; 1763: DL, May 17; 1764: DL, May 21; 1767: DL, May 28; 1772: DL, Jun 5; 1775: DL, May 24; 1776: DL, May 17; 1777: DL, Apr 30; 1778: DL, May 18; 1779: DL, May 21; 1780: DL, May 9; 1781: DL, May 24; 1782: DL, May 29; 1783: DL, May 28; 1784: DL, May 26; 1785: DL, May 25; 1786: DL, May 31; 1787: DL, Jun 6

Palmer, Thomas (epiloguist), 1798: CG, Oct 11; 1800: CG, Jun 5

Palmer, William (actor), 1775: DL, Nov 24; 1785: CG, Sep 19, 23, 26, 28, Oct 19, 22, Nov 2, 9, 14, Dec 5, 10, 13, 14, 26, 30; 1786: CG, Jan 5, 31, Feb 4, 7, 8, 13, 17, 18, 25, Mar 6, 7, 18, Apr 1, 18, 19, 24, 26, May 3, 9, 11, 13, 15; 1787: ROY, Jun 20

Palmer, Wingfield (actor), 1763: DL, Nov 15, 23; 1768: DL, Apr 29, Sep 30, Oct 5, Nov 21; 1769: DL, Jan 25, 27, Apr 5, 11, May 12, 19, Sep 21, 26, Oct 2, 5, 17, 21, 27, Nov 2, 3, 22, 29, Dec 16; 1770: DL, May 14, 18, 24, Oct 3, 16, 18, 22, Nov 3, 15, 16, 24, Dec 5, 6; 1771: DL, Jan 16, Mar 7, 12, Apr 5, 6, 15, May 17, 20, Sep 21, Oct 3, 17, 25, Nov 8, 11, 22, Dec 3, 5, 26; 1772: DL, Jan 15, Feb 18, Mar 26, Apr 22, May 12, Jun 3, Sep 29, Oct 6, 19, 21, 29, Nov 20, Dec 8, 26; 1773: DL, Jan 4, Feb 27, Apr 15, 21, 23, 30, Sep 25, Oct 2, 13, 14, Nov 9, 15, Dec 11, 27; 1774: DL, Jan 5, 19, Feb 2, 9, 15, Mar 14, 15, Apr 16, May 11, 14, 25; 1775: DL, Oct 24

Palmerini (singer), 1727: KING'S, Jan 31, Oct 21, Nov 11; 1728: KING'S, Feb 17

Palms, Miss (actor), 1729: BLA, Sep 30; 1730: HAY, Jan 8, Feb 6, 18, 23, Mar 11, 20, 30, Apr 20, 30, Jul 17, BFR, Aug 22, Sep 4, SFP, 9, HAY, Dec 28; 1731: HAY, Mar 17; 1732: HAY, Mar 2, Apr 4, May 15, Jun 1; 1733: HAY, Mar 14, 16, 20, 26, Apr 18, Jun 4, DL, Nov 7, 13, Dec 5; 1734: DL, Feb 4, DL/LIF, Apr 1, DL, 15

Paluprat, Jean
--Grondeur, 1722: HAY, Jan 19, 25, Mar 30

Pamela. See Dance, James.

Pan and Syrinx (masque), 1740: CG, Dec 16, 17

Pan and Syrinx. See Theobald, Lewis.

Panchaud (boxkeeper), 1792: DLKING'S, Jun 15; 1793: DL, Jun 6; 1795: DL, Jun 6; 1796: DL, Jun 13; 1797: DL, Jun 16; 1798: DL, Jun 14

Pandora. See Killigrew, William.

Pandours (dance), 1754: DL, Nov 4, 5, 8

Panichi, Lucia (La Moscovita) (singer), 1739: CG, Mar 10; 1740: HAY, Jan 22, Mar 15, May 10; 1741: KING'S, Oct 31, Nov 10, Dec 12, 19; 1742: KING'S, Jan 19, Mar 2, Apr 13, 20
Pannel, The. See Kemble, John Philip.
Pantalon (dancer), 1727: KING'S, Mar 2, LIF, Apr 24, KING'S, 25; 1728: HAY, Apr 3
Pantalon a Broker, Broken Merchant and Desperately in Love, Harlequin His Shopkeeper (pantomime), 1726: KING'S, Nov 7
Pantalon Baron di Sloffenburgo (pantomime), 1726: KING'S, Dec 10
Pantaloon and Enamorata (dance), 1742: CG, Apr 20, 23, 26, 30, May 3, 4, 5, 10, 12, 14, 18, Dec 15; 1743: CG, Feb 4
Pantaloon and his Wife (dance), 1720: KING'S, Mar 12
Pantaloon's Death (entertainment), 1797: CG, Jun 9
Pantheon (show room), 1774: PANT, Mar 30
Pantheonites, The. See Gentleman, Francis.
Pantomime (entertainment), 1720: KING'S, Mar 29; 1747: SF, Sep 15, SOU, Oct 5, 22; 1748: SOU, Sep 26; 1752: HAY, Dec 11
Pantomime Ballet (dance), 1767: CG, Apr 27, May 15, 18, 21, 22
Pantomime Dance (dance), 1738: CG, Apr 20, 28, May 3, 8, 11, 12, 15, 16; 1747: SOU, Jan 21; 1755: KING'S, Mar 18, DL, Dec 3, 5, 8, 10, 15, 16, 18, 22, 27, 29, 30, 31; 1756: DL, Jan 6, 14, 16, 20, CG, May 11, 14, 17; 1759: MARLY, Sep 7; 1761: DL, Mar 7, Jun 16; 1767: DL, Feb 25, 26, 27, 28, CG, Sep 26, Oct 6, 8, 16, 20, 23, Nov 6, 13, 20; 1768: CG, Jan 5, DL, Nov 16, 23, Dec 7; 1769: CG, May 16, 17, DL, Nov 16, 17; 1770: CG, Nov 29, 30, Dec 8, 12, 22; 1771: HAY, Jul 3, 5, 10, 12, 15, Sep 4; 1773: DL, Apr 22
Pantomime de Suisse et d'Allemande (dance), 1740: CG, May 13
Pantomime du Charpentier (dance), 1754: HAY, Aug 6, 29, Sep 10, HAY/SFB, 13, 17, 26, Oct 1, 10; 1755: HAY, Feb 10
Pantomimical Interlude (entertainment), 1779: HAY, Mar 15; 1785: HAY, Dec 26; 1788: HAY, Sep 30; 1796: CG, Jun 4
Panton St, 1697: HIC, Dec 9; 1733: HIC, Jun 15; 1746: HIC, Feb 3, Mar 10, 14; 1748: KING'S, Mar 1, HAY, Apr 21; 1749: DL, Mar 14; 1750: DL, Mar 17; 1751: DL, Apr 11; 1762: HAY, Sep 7; 1770: GRP, Dec 10; 1774: GRP, Jul 23; 1775: NONE, Apr 10; 1776: DL, Jun 1; 1789: HAY, Aug 12; 1792: HAY, Feb 6; 1793: DL, Jun 1, HAY, Aug 6; 1797: KING'S, Jun 8; 1800: KING'S, Jun 19
Panurge. See Gretry, Andre Ernest Modeste.
Papal Tyranny in the Reign of King John. See Cibber, Colley.
Papendick, George (manuscript seller), 1799: CG, Apr 9
Papillon (actor, singer, musician), 1728: LIF, May 20, Oct 14, Nov 23; 1729: LIF, Jan 18, Apr 19, Nov 11; 1730: LIF, Jan 2, May 7, 14, Sep 21, Dec 15; 1731: LIF, Apr 24, May 17, 20, SFLH, Sep 8, LIF, 27, ST, Oct 21, LIF, Nov 13, 18, Dec 1; 1732: LIF, May 17, LIF/CG, Oct 30, Nov 24
Paquorel (dancer), 1738: HAY, Oct 9
Paradies, Domenico (composer), 1747: KING'S, Jan 17; 1748: KING'S, Apr 5; 1749: KING'S, Mar 21, HAY, Apr 10; 1751: KING'S, Apr 16; 1760: SOHO, Mar 13; 1762: CG, Dec 8; 1763: CG, Oct 22
--Phaeton (opera), 1747: KING'S, Jan 17, 24, 27, 31, Feb 3, 7, 10, 14, 17, 21; 1750: CG, Mar 29
Paradise Lost. See Smith, John Christopher; Milton, John.
Paradise Regained. See Barbandt, Charles.
Paradise St, 1776: CHR, Sep 23; 1777: CG, May 5
Paradise Transplanted and Restored (puppetry), 1660: NONE, Sep 0; 1671: NONE, Mar 31; 1673: HG, Sep 23
Paradox, The; or, Maid, Wife and Widow (interlude, anon), 1799: CG, Apr 30, May 10
Parant (actor), 1749: HAY, Nov 14; 1750: DL, May 22
Pardini (musician), 1714: HIC, May 20; 1724: HIC, Apr 17; 1727: SG, Mar 8; 1728: HIC, Mar 27
Parents and Children (entertainment), 1786: HAMM, Jun 28, 30, Jul 10
Paretti (actor), 1762: HAY, Mar 16
Parfett, Miss, 1768: CG, Apr 30
Pariati, Pietro (author), 1724: KING'S, Dec 1
Paris Opera, 1703: DL, Jan 2, Feb 18; 1709: QUEEN'S, Feb 5; 1710: QUEEN'S, Aug 16; 1716: DL, Apr 11, LIF, Oct 18, 23; 1717: LIF, Apr 23, Oct 25; 1723: LIF, Oct 18; 1730: LIF, Nov 23; 1732: LIF, Apr 13, DL, Sep 23; 1739: BF, Aug 27, SF, Sep 8; 1740: TCLP, Aug 4; 1742: CG, Oct 23; 1750: DL, Oct 31; 1752: HAY, May 21, CG, Oct 10; 1774: KING'S, May 5; 1775: DL, Oct 18; 1784: KING'S, Dec 18; 1786: KING'S, Dec 23; 1789: KING'S, Mar 17; 1791: CG, Oct 20; 1793: KING'S, Jan 26, Apr 23
Paris Theatre, 1718: LIF, Nov 7; 1721: HAY, Jan 16; 1732: GF, Oct 4; 1784: CG, Apr 17, HAY, May 10
Paris, 1668: ATCOURT, Jan 13, LIF, Feb 11; 1682: DL, Nov 28; 1683: DLORDG, Aug

14, Sep 12; <u>1686</u>: DLORDG, Feb 11; <u>1699</u>: LIF, Apr 10, DLLIF, Sep 12, DLORLIF,
Nov 9, LIF, Dec 0; <u>1705</u>: LIF/QUEN, Nov 6; <u>1716</u>: DL, Apr 4; <u>1717</u>: KING'S, Mar
16; <u>1719</u>: LIF, Jan 29, KING'S, Feb 12; <u>1720</u>: KING'S, Feb 4, Mar 29, LIF, Apr
5, Jun 6; <u>1721</u>: HAY, Jan 31; <u>1723</u>: LIF, May 7, RI, Sep 2; <u>1724</u>: HIC, Apr 20;
<u>1725</u>: LIF, Oct 23; <u>1726</u>: HAY, Mar 31, Apr 11; <u>1727</u>: DL, May 17, BF, Aug 21;
<u>1728</u>: LIF, Apr 29, Oct 1; <u>1729</u>: DL, May 14, HAY, Jun 3, BFF, Aug 23; <u>1731</u>:
LIF, Mar 15; <u>1732</u>: HAY, Mar 17, DL, Jul 28, TC, Aug 4, BF, 22; <u>1733</u>: DL/HAY,
Oct 6, DL, 12; <u>1734</u>: DL, Oct 28; <u>1735</u>: GF/HAY, Feb 24, YB, May 29, DL, Nov
18, CG, Dec 31; <u>1736</u>: HAY, Feb 20, Apr 29, DL, Nov 18; <u>1738</u>: HAY, Oct 4;
<u>1739</u>: SF, Sep 8, CG, 17, 19; <u>1740</u>: DL, Oct 13, Nov 3; <u>1741</u>: BFH, Aug 22, DL,
Oct 21, CG, Nov 11, Dec 15; <u>1743</u>: TCD/BFTD, Aug 23; <u>1745</u>: DL, Sep 26; <u>1749</u>:
DL, Feb 2, BFY, Aug 23; <u>1751</u>: DL, May 18, 20; <u>1752</u>: DL, Oct 3, Nov 25; <u>1753</u>:
CG, Mar 10, DL, 26, 31, CG, Dec 10, 17; <u>1754</u>: CG, Nov 26; <u>1755</u>: DL, Nov 14,
Dec 19; <u>1756</u>: DL, Jan 5; <u>1766</u>: DL, Oct 11, Dec 13; <u>1772</u>: DL, Mar 6; <u>1773</u>: CG,
Apr 24, KING'S, Oct 23; <u>1777</u>: KING'S, Jul 5; <u>1782</u>: KING'S, May 9; <u>1783</u>: CG,
Oct 9; <u>1784</u>: KING'S, Feb 26, CG, Jun 14, Dec 14; <u>1785</u>: CG, May 6, HAMM, Jul
25; <u>1786</u>: KING'S, Mar 23, Apr 27, HAY, Sep 6, KING'S, Dec 23; <u>1787</u>: CG, Apr
24; <u>1789</u>: KING'S, Feb 10, CG, 27, Mar 16, KING'S, Apr 28, May 7, 14, CG, Sep
21; <u>1790</u>: CG, Feb 19, Dec 20; <u>1791</u>: CG, Oct 20; <u>1793</u>: DL, Jan 24; <u>1795</u>:
KING'S, Apr 30; <u>1796</u>: KING'S, Feb 9, Apr 7, CG, Nov 10, KING'S, Dec 13; <u>1797</u>:
KING'S, Jan 10; <u>1799</u>: KING'S, May 2
Parish, Miss (dancer), <u>1774</u>: CG, Apr 15; <u>1777</u>: CG, Apr 25; <u>1778</u>: CG, May 2;
<u>1779</u>: CG, Apr 28; <u>1784</u>: HAY, Apr 30
Parisien Dupe dans Londres, Le; ou, La Fille A La Mode (play, anon), <u>1719</u>: LIF,
Jan 1
Parisienne, La Petite (actor), <u>1748</u>: CG, Mar 28
Parisot, Mlle (dancer), <u>1796</u>: KING'S, Feb 9, Mar 1, 8, 10, Apr 2, 21, May 12,
DL, 25, KING'S, Jun 2, Jul 2, 7, 23, DL, Oct 1, 29, Nov 8, KING'S, 26, Dec 6,
13, 23; <u>1797</u>: KING'S, Jan 10, 17, Feb 7, Mar 11, 28, Apr 6, 8, 25, DL, May
22, KING'S, 25, CG, Jun 14, KING'S, 17; <u>1798</u>: DL, Jan 16, Feb 20, May 16, 24,
31, Jun 18, Oct 6, Nov 26, Dec 6; <u>1799</u>: DL, Jan 19, Mar 2, May 2, 3, Jul 1;
<u>1800</u>: KING'S, Jan 11, 28, Mar 1, 4, DL, 6, KING'S, Apr 15, DL, May 14,
KING'S, 29, Jun 24, 28
Park Lane, <u>1791</u>: HAY, Aug 10; <u>1792</u>: CG, May 8, HAY, Aug 9
Park Place, <u>1718</u>: WEYS', Feb 12; <u>1737</u>: DL, Mar 5
Park Row, <u>1800</u>: DL, May 21, HAY, Aug 5
Park St, <u>1799</u>: CG, May 31; <u>1800</u>: DL, Jun 7
Park Theatre, New York, <u>1799</u>: CG, May 18
Parke, John (oboist), <u>1769</u>: MARLY, Aug 10, 17, 24; <u>1771</u>: HAY, Apr 12; <u>1774</u>: DL,
Nov 7; <u>1776</u>: DL, Jan 16, 24, Mar 7, Jun 10; <u>1778</u>: DL, Mar 11; <u>1779</u>: DL, Feb
24, Mar 26, Apr 13, Sep 23; <u>1780</u>: DL, Feb 16, Oct 10; <u>1781</u>: DL, Mar 7; <u>1782</u>:
DL, Feb 15, 27, Mar 20; <u>1783</u>: DL, Mar 19, Oct 7; <u>1784</u>: DL, Mar 10, Oct 7;
<u>1785</u>: DL, Mar 4; <u>1787</u>: DL, Oct 16; <u>1788</u>: DL, Feb 8, 20, Mar 5; <u>1789</u>: DL, Oct
21; <u>1790</u>: DL, Dec 8; <u>1792</u>: KING'S, Feb 29, DL, Sep 27; <u>1795</u>: DL, May 27;
<u>1797</u>: DL, Nov 24
Parke, Mary Hester (singer, pianist), <u>1785</u>: DL, Mar 11; <u>1794</u>: CG, Mar 7, 14;
<u>1795</u>: CG, Feb 20, 27, Mar 4, 11, 13, 18, 20, 25, 27; <u>1796</u>: CG, Feb 12, 17,
24, 26, Mar 16
Parke, William Thomas (oboist), <u>1784</u>: CG, Mar 23; <u>1785</u>: CG, Mar 7, Apr 15, 22,
Sep 23; <u>1786</u>: DL, Mar 8, CG, May 2; <u>1787</u>: DL, Mar 9, CG, 31, Apr 24; <u>1788</u>:
CG, Jan 28, Feb 5, Mar 10; <u>1789</u>: CG, Jan 26, DL, Mar 6, 20, 25, CG, May 20;
<u>1790</u>: DL, Feb 24; <u>1791</u>: DL, Mar 23, CG, May 27, Sep 23; <u>1792</u>: KING'S, Feb 24,
Mar 14; <u>1793</u>: KING/HAY, Feb 27, Mar 22, CG, Apr 11, Oct 29; <u>1794</u>: DL, Mar 12,
28, CG, Apr 10, May 9, Sep 17; <u>1795</u>: CG, May 12, 19, Jun 10, Nov 27; <u>1796</u>:
CG, Feb 2, May 25; <u>1797</u>: CG, Jan 10, Mar 3, 22, Jun 21; <u>1798</u>: CG, Feb 23, Mar
23, 30, Jun 11; <u>1799</u>: CG, Jan 8, Feb 8, 15, Apr 2, Jun 7, Dec 10; <u>1800</u>: CG,
Feb 28, Mar 14, 21
Parker (actor), <u>1740</u>: TC, Aug 4
Parker (actor), <u>1755</u>: HAY, Sep 1, 9, 11, 15; <u>1758</u>: HAY, Feb 2; <u>1770</u>: HAY, Oct 1
Parker (actor), <u>1779</u>: HAY, Dec 27; <u>1780</u>: HAY, Apr 5, Nov 13; <u>1784</u>: HAY, Feb 23
Parker (payee), <u>1776</u>: DL, May 23
Parker-Dogget Booth, <u>1699</u>: BF, Aug 23; <u>1703</u>: BFPD, Aug 23
Parker, Edmond (pianist), <u>1799</u>: CG, May 15, Jun 12
Parker, Miss (actor), <u>1797</u>: HAY, Dec 4
Parker, Mrs (actor), <u>1720</u>: LIF, Oct 15, 18; <u>1723</u>: LIF, Oct 4, 22, Nov 2, 4, 26,
Dec 2, 7, 12; <u>1724</u>: LIF, Feb 24, Mar 16, 26, Apr 7, 9, 14, 27, 28, 29, Jun 1,
Aug 11, Sep 23, Oct 22, Nov 4, 12, 17, 18, 20, 24, 26; <u>1725</u>: LIF, Jan 4, 16,
Feb 27, Mar 13, Apr 5, 14, Sep 24, Oct 4, 11, 15, 23, 26, 28, Nov 2, 4, 9,
11, 17, 18, 23, Dec 2, 7, 8, 16; <u>1726</u>: LIF, Jan 7, Mar 19, 21, Apr 22, 30,
Sep 26
Parker, Mrs (actor), <u>1775</u>: HAY, Oct 30
Parker, Sophia, Mrs William (dancer), <u>1797</u>: CG, Nov 24, Dec 26; <u>1798</u>: CG, Feb

12, Mar 19; 1799: CG, Oct 7, 21, 24, Dec 23; 1800: CG, Feb 10, Mar 4
Parker's Booth, 1703: BFP, Aug 23
Parkinson, C (instrumentalist), 1792: KING'S, Feb 24, Mar 14
Parkinson, Jeremiah (bassoonist), 1786: DL, Apr 5; 1788: DL, Feb 20; 1789: DL,
    Mar 6, 25; 1790: DL, Feb 24, Mar 24; 1791: DL, Mar 30; 1792: KING'S, Feb 24,
    Mar 14, 23; 1793: CG, Feb 20; 1794: DL, Mar 12; 1795: CG, Feb 20; 1796: CG,
    Feb 12, 26; 1797: CG, Mar 3, 17; 1798: CG, Feb 23, Mar 9; 1799: CG, Feb 8,
    20; 1800: CG, Feb 28, Mar 19
Parks, 1776: DL, Feb 12
Parliament St Coffee House, 1758: CG, Jul 6
Parliament St, 1793: DL, May 27; 1799: HAY, Apr 17
Parliament, 1667: BRIDGES, Nov 2; 1680: DG, Jan 0; 1681: DG, Jan 0, DL, May 0;
    1683: DL, Jan 19; 1689: CITY, Oct 29; 1700: DLANDLIF, Jun 14; 1734: DL, Dec
    2; 1735: DL, Mar 6; 1737: HAY, Feb 19, DL, May 24; 1738: DL, Jan 28, CG, Feb
    13; 1744: HAY, Aug 28; 1749: HAY, Nov 22, 29, 30; 1756: HAY, Jan 14; 1780:
    KING'S, Dec 16; 1790: CG, May 20; 1796: CG, Jun 7; 1798: CG, May 5
Parlour (actor), 1722: HAY, Jun 28, BFPMB, Aug 25, SF, Sep 5; 1723: DL, Jul 5,
    HA, 22, DL, Aug 12
Parlour, Mrs (actor), 1721: LIF, Oct 17, Nov 29; 1722: LIF, Jan 12, Apr 26, May
    3, 18, 25, Jun 1, 13, HAY, 28, BFPMB, Aug 25, LIF, Nov 14; 1723: LIF, Feb 13
Parma, Duke of, 1788: KING'S, May 22
Parma, Prince of (spectator), 1698: DL, Jul 5
Parma, 1800: KING'S, Apr 15
Parnasso in Festa. See Handel, George Frederic.
Parodia del Pastor Fido, La (play, anon), 1727: KING'S, Apr 25, 26, 27, May 10
Parosasi. See Pergolesi.
Parr (beneficiary), 1753: DL, May 15; 1754: DL, May 17; 1755: DL, May 6
Parracide, The. See Sterling, James.
Parracide, The; or, Innocence in Distress. See Shirley, William.
Parrot Coffee House, 1760: DL, Mar 24
Parrott (coal merchant), 1787: DL, Jan 9
Parry (actor), 1739: CG, Apr 26; 1740: CG, Apr 9, 30, TCLP, Aug 4, BFLP, 23,
    SF, Sep 9; 1741: HIC, Feb 19, 27, Mar 5, 13
Parry (musician), 1753: DL, Mar 27, 29, CG, Apr 14; 1755: SOHO, Mar 11, DL, Apr
    2, May 8; 1757: DL, Mar 31, May 14; 1760: CG, Apr 19; 1763: CG, May 2
Parry (singer), 1772: DL, Mar 6; 1773: DL, Feb 26; 1775: DL, Mar 10
Parry, Thomas (wine merchant), 1739: CG, Jan 8
Parsley (actor), 1780: HAY, Apr 5
Parsloe (actor), 1780: CII, Apr 5; 1797: CG, Dec 26; 1798: CG, Feb 12, Mar 19,
    Apr 9
Parsloe's Grand Medley (entertainment), 1752: SFB, Sep 22
Parson's Dream, The. See Killigrew, Thomas, The Parson's Wedding.
Parson's Green, 1789: WHF, Nov 9
Parson's Wedding, The. See Killigrew, Thomas.
Parsonage (tenant), 1774: DL, Jun 2; 1775: DL, May 27; 1776: DL, Jun 10
Parsons (actor), 1792: CII, Jan 16; 1794: HAMM, Mar 24
Parsons, Alderman, 1732: GF, Feb 7
Parsons, Eliza (author), 1792: CG, Apr 18
Parsons, J (publisher), 1793: CG, May 27
Parsons, Mrs (actor), 1703: LIF, Mar 0, Nov 0; 1705: LIF/QUEN, Feb 22
Parsons, Mrs (actor), 1762: HAY, Aug 23, Sep 16, DL, 21, Dec 14; 1763: DL, Jan
    15, 29, Feb 1, Mar 12, 26, May 23; 1764: HAY, Jul 30, Aug 20, Sep 1; 1765:
    HAY, Jul 15, 31, Aug 30; 1772: HAY, May 18, 22, 27, Jul 15, 27, Aug 4, Sep
    17, 18; 1776: HAY, Jul 29
Parsons, Mrs (actor), 1792: CII, Jan 16; 1794: HAMM, Mar 24
Parsons, Theo (songwriter), 1693: SH, Nov 22
Parsons, William (actor), 1762: DL, Sep 21, 25, Oct 6, 7, 19, 28, 29, Nov 3, 5,
    10, 12, Dec 27; 1763: DL, Jan 7, 15, 17, 29, Feb 24, Mar 1, 14, 26, Apr 5,
    29, May 4, 6, 7, 16, 18, 26, 31, Sep 17, Oct 4, 8, 14, 19, 21, 28, Nov 9, 23,
    26, 29, Dec 1, 26, 28; 1764: DL, Jan 13, 18, 20, 27, Feb 11, 21, Mar 20, 31,
    Apr 2, 27, May 11, HAY, Jun 13, 26, Jul 6, 13, 16, 23, Aug 20, Sep 1, DL, 15,
    22, 25, Oct 15, 17, 19, 23, 26, Nov 9, 13, 27; 1765: DL, Jan 3, 18, 22, 24,
    Feb 1, 4, 23, Mar 19, Apr 9, 13, 17, 22, 26, HAY, Jun 10, Jul 15, 31, Aug 8,
    9, 21, 30, DL, Sep 14, 21, 24, 26, Oct 28, Nov 16, Dec 7, 12, 14, 21, 23;
    1766: DL, Jan 6, 9, 22, 23, 24, 29, Feb 11, 13, Apr 12, 16, 22, May 9, 19,
    Sep 25, 27, Oct 9, 18, 28, 31, Nov 7, 18, Dec 2, 4; 1767: DL, Jan 2, 24, Apr
    11, 22, CG, May 18, DL, 27, Sep 15, 16, 22, 26, Oct 9, 20, 23, 28, CG, Nov 4,
    DL, 23, 26, 28, Dec 7, 16; 1768: DL, Jan 9, 19, 28, Mar 24, Apr 14, CG, May
    27, 28, DL, Sep 17, 20, 23, 26, 27, 28, Oct 4, 5, 20, 31, Nov 5, Dec 9; 1769:
    DL, Jan 20, 25, Mar 31, Apr 3, HAY, 18, DL, 21, 24, 25, 27, May 15, Sep 19,
    21, Oct 2, 3, 4, 5, 11, 14, 17, 23, Nov 14, 17, 22, 23, Dec 6, 8, 13, 16, 23;
    1770: DL, Jan 6, 16, 19, Feb 8, 9, 22, Mar 22, 27, 31, Apr 2, 23, May 2, 3,

7, 14, 15, 21, 23, 26, Sep 22, 25, 27, 29, Oct 3, 5, 18, 19, 22, 23, 25, Nov
3, 13, 14, 15, 16, 24, Dec 5, 6, 19, 31; 1771: DL, Jan 19, Feb 21, Mar 7, 11,
12, 14, 18, Apr 1, 5, 6, 15, 17, 23, May 1, 10, 14, 27, 30, Sep 21, 24, 28,
Oct 3, 8, 17, 19, 26, 28, Nov 2, 6, 9, 14, 16, 22, 25, Dec 3, 11, 12, 14, 26;
1772: DL, Jan 4, 11, 15, Feb 17, 29, Mar 18, 21, 23, 26, Apr 2, 4, 6, 7, 20,
22, 25, 27, 28, HAY, May 18, Jun 1, 8, 10, 15, 29, Jul 6, 8, 15, 27, Aug 10,
26, Sep 17, 18, DL, 19, 22, 26, 29, Oct 6, 10, 19, 20, 21, 23, 30, Nov 3, 6,
12, 20, 26, Dec 15, 29; 1773: DL, Jan 4, 9, Feb 10, 18, 25, 27, Mar 23, Apr
16, 21, 23, 30, May 1, 6, 8, 10, 13, 17, 25, Jun 2, Sep 18, HAY, 20, DL, 23,
25, Oct 2, 6, 13, 14, 19, 25, 28, Nov 1, 2, 15, 17, 19, 27, Dec 27; 1774: DL,
Jan 4, 5, 6, 8, 13, 19, Feb 7, 8, 12, 14, Mar 1, 14, 15, 26, Apr 11, 13, 15,
16, 19, 29, May 3, 7, 9, 14, 17, 20, 25, Sep 17, 20, 24, 27, Oct 4, 5, 11,
14, 20, 24, 26, 28, Nov 1, 7, 8, 11, 22, 26, 29, Dec 1, 7, 9; 1775: DL, Jan
18, 23, Feb 1, Mar 18, 23, Apr 17, 19, 21, 22, 25, 27, May 19, Sep 28, 30,
Oct 3, 5, 7, 10, 21, 23, 28, 30, Nov 1, 6, 9, 14, 18, 20, 21, 23, 25, 28, Dec
4, 5, 7, 11, 29; 1776: DL, Jan 3, 13, Feb 1, 3, 10, 12, 15, Mar 7, 9, 25, 28,
Apr 8, 12, 13, 17, 20, 24, May 4, 6, 8, 11, 16, HAY, 22, 31, DL, Jun 3, HAY,
12, 14, 19, 26, Jul 3, 5, 8, 10, Aug 2, 19, Sep 2, 16, 17, 20, DL, 21, HAY,
23, DL, 24, 26, Oct 1, 5, 9, 10, 15, 18, 19, 30, Nov 6, 7, 9, 21, 25, 28, 29,
30, Dec 14, 17, 18, 28, 31; 1777: DL, Jan 1, 16, Feb 24, Mar 1, Apr 7, 22,
28, 29, May 8, 9, HAY, 28, 30, Jun 6, 16, 19, 26, 27, 30, Jul 15, 18, 30, Aug
9, 18, 19, 25, 29, 30, Sep 3, 17, 19, DL, 20, 23, 25, 27, Oct 2, 4, HAY, 6,
DL, 7, 14, 17, 22, 29, 31, Nov 8, 13, 24, Dec 4, 11, 13; 1778: DL, Jan 2, 5,
8, 10, 17, 22, 23, Feb 10, 24, Mar 5, 12, 16, Apr 9, 20, 21, May 2, HAY, 18,
21, 22, Jun 1, 3, 8, 11, 19, Jul 2, 30, Aug 6, 17, 21, 27, Sep 7, DL, 17, 19,
22, 24, 29, Oct 1, 3, 6, 8, 10, 13, 15, 17, 19, 20, 21, 28, 31, Nov 4, 14,
20, 30, Dec 19, 21, 23; 1779: DL, Jan 2, 5, 29, Mar 11, 13, 18, Apr 5, 10,
16, 19, 28, May 15, 19, 21, 25, HAY, 31, DL, Jun 1, HAY, 2, 4, 7, 9, 12, 19,
Jul 1, 5, 15, 20, Aug 6, 11, 12, 13, 14, 20, 24, 27, 31, Sep 8, DL, 21, 23,
25, 30, Oct 5, 9, 19, 21, 25, 30, Nov 6, 17, 18, 19, 22, 24, 27, Dec 4, 9,
20, 22, 29; 1780: DL, Jan 5, 11, 26, Feb 22, 28, Mar 14, Apr 3, 4, 14, 19,
21, 26, May 4, 10, 23, 24, Sep 19, 21, 23, 26, 28, Oct 2, 5, 7, 10, 12, 14,
17, 18, 20, 31, Nov 2, 3, 8, 10, 17, 22, 28, Dec 1, 4, 6, 7, 27; 1781: DL,
Jan 6, Mar 10, Apr 18, 21, 28, May 5, 15, Sep 15, 20, 22, 25, 27, 29, Oct 2,
6, 12, 13, 15, 16, 25, 27, Nov 5, 6, 7, 10, 15, 20, Dec 13; 1782: DL, Jan 19,
21, Feb 19, 25, Mar 7, 21, Apr 6, 15, May 2, 3, 7, 8, 14, 18, HAY, Jun 4, 10,
11, 12, 13, 20, Jul 2, 17, Aug 5, 6, 15, 27, DL, Sep 17, 18, 19, 20, 21, 24,
26, Oct 1, 3, 5, 8, 10, 26, Nov 5, 7, 12, 22, 26, 27, 29, Dec 11; 1783: DL,
Jan 10, 15, 24, 27, 29, Feb 7, 12, 22, Mar 3, 6, 20, 24, Apr 28, 29, May 2,
5, 12, 20, HAY, Jun 2, 3, 4, 5, 6, 13, 18, 24, Jul 5, 26, Aug 13, 22, 26, 29,
Sep 12, DL, 16, 18, 20, 25, 27, 30, Oct 28, 29, 30, 31, Nov 3, 12, 13, Dec
19, 30; 1784: DL, Jan 3, 7, 10, 16, 17, 22, 26, 28, 31, Feb 3, 10, 11, 14,
Mar 8, 20, 29, Apr 1, 14, 19, 30, May 3, 7, 10, 15, 17, HAY, 18, 29, 31, Jun
2, 10, 14, 26, Jul 6, 8, 12, 27, 30, Aug 2, 10, 19, 25, Sep 2, 13, DL, 16,
18, 21, 30, Oct 11, 14, 18, 21, 26, 28, Nov 1, 2, 4, 12, 13, 16, 22, 23, 26,
Dec 10, 22, 28; 1785: DL, Jan 11, Feb 2, 21, Mar 30, Apr 1, 2, 8, 15, 20, 25,
27, May 3, 6, 26, HAY, 28, Jun 2, 3, 4, 7, 11, 13, 16, 18, 24, Jul 9, 18, 21,
30, Aug 4, 11, 17, 23, Sep 2, DL, 17, 20, 22, 24, Oct 1, 4, 6, 11, 13, 15,
20, 22, 25, 31, Nov 1, 3, 11, 17, 18, Dec 5, 7, 30; 1786: DL, Jan 14, Feb 18,
20, Mar 20, 27, 28, Apr 4, 6, 18, 28, May 25, Jun 1, HAY, 10, 12, 13, 16, 20,
23, 29, Jul 8, 13, 17, 18, 19, 21, 24, 25, 27, 28, Aug 10, 15, 17, DL, Sep
16, 19, 21, 23, 28, Oct 7, 9, 10, 12, 17, Nov 14, 15, 18, 25, 27, Dec 2, 4,
11, 21, 22; 1787: DL, Apr 9, 18, 19, 20, May 9, 11, 17, 22, 23, 25, 30, 31,
Jun 8, HAY, 11, 13, 18, 20, 21, 22, 23, 25, Jul 3, 19, 23, Aug 1, 3, 4, 14,
17, 21, 28, Sep 14, DL, Oct 9, 13, 15, 20, Dec 5, 6, 8, 12; 1788: DL, Mar 10,
25, 31, Apr 2, 10, 21, 28, 30, May 7, 12, HAY, Jun 16, 17, 18, 19, 26, 30,
Jul 3, 4, Aug 4, 25, 29, DL, Sep 18, 27, 30, Oct 7, 9, 11, 20, 21, 22, 25,
Nov 8, 19; 1789: DL, Feb 16, Apr 14, 20, May 27, Oct 3, 6, 17, Dec 2; 1790:
HAY, Aug 13, 25, Sep 11, Oct 13, DL, 20, 23, 25, 27, Nov 10, 11; 1791: DL,
Jan 28, Feb 15, Apr 12, 27, HAY, Jun 6, 8, 10, 13, 17, 23, Jul 26, 30, Aug 2,
10, 19, 31, DLKING'S, Sep 27, 29, Oct 3, 10, 20, 24, 25, 31, Nov 29, Dec 1,
16, 31; 1792: DLKING'S, Mar 29, Apr 10, 20, May 29, HAY, Jun 15, 19, 22, 23,
29, Jul 4, Aug 6, 15, Sep 5, DL, 15; 1793: DL, Jan 1, Mar 14, HAY, Jun 11,
13, 15, 17, 18, 22, 29, Aug 3, 12, Sep 19, 21, 24, Oct 5, 15, 22, 24, 29, Nov
5, 16, 23, Dec 7, 17; 1794: HAY, Jan 7, 11, Feb 5, DL, May 16, 17, HAY, Jul
8, 9, 10, 11, 14, 17, 21, 22, 25, Aug 9, 13, 14, Sep 17, DL, Oct 27, 31, Nov
7, 12, Dec 10, 12, 30; 1795: DL, Jan 2, 19
Parsons, Sir William (composer), 1793: KING/HAY, Mar 6; 1797: DL, May 8; 1798:
DL, May 23
Parsons, William (poet), 1788: DL, Jan 31
Partenio. See Veracini, Francis.
Parthenope. See Handel, George Frederic.

Parthian Hero, The. See Gardiner, Matthew.
Parti de Chasse d' Henry IV, Le (dance), 1784: KING'S, Dec 18
Parting Lovers (dance), 1740: BFLP, Aug 23; 1741: GF, Apr 16, 30
Parting Lovers, The. See Carey, Henry, Nancy.
Parto da te ben mio (song), 1758: KING'S, Apr 6
Parto non ho Costanza (song), 1749: KING'S, Mar 21
Parton (musician), 1765: KING'S, Jan 25
Partridge (hosier), 1772: CG, Nov 23; 1773: CG, Jan 14; 1774: CG, Jan 6, May 17
Partridge (ticket deliverer), 1784: CG, May 29
Partridge and Franks (hosiers), 1771: CG, Nov 27
Partridge, James (renter), 1758: CG, Mar 7
Partridge, Simon (cobler), 1752: DL, Dec 22
Parvisol (householder), 1778: DL, Apr 30
Parys (actor), 1791: CG, Apr 28
Pas de Basque (dance), 1783: KING'S, Jan 11, 16, 25, 28, Jun 21; 1784: KING'S,
    Jun 8
Pas de Bernois (dance), 1788: KING'S, Feb 21, 23, 26, Mar 4, 15
Pas de Cinq (dance), 1773: KING'S, Mar 18, 23, Jun 19; 1788: KING'S, Feb 21,
    23, 26, Mar 4, 15
Pas de Deux (dance), 1743: CG, Apr 6, 22; 1771: KING'S, Jun 1; 1773: KING'S,
    Jan 12, 15, 19, Feb 9, 20, 23, 27, Mar 16; 1774: KING'S, Nov 19, Dec 3, 13;
    1775: KING'S, Jan 17, Apr 18, 22, 25, May 16, 27, 30, Jun 6, 17, 24; 1776:
    KING'S, Apr 18; 1777: KING'S, Feb 25, May 15; 1780: KING'S, Apr 20, May 9;
    1781: KING'S, Mar 15, Apr 5; 1782: KING'S, Nov 30, Dec 10, 19; 1783: KING'S,
    Feb 13, 18, Apr 10, May 1, 8, CG, 9, KING'S, Jun 3, 21, Dec 16; 1784: KING'S,
    Jan 17, Mar 20, Apr 15, CG, May 21; 1785: KING'S, Jan 15, Apr 7, Jun 28;
    1786: KING'S, Jun 1; 1787: KING'S, Mar 8; 1788: KING'S, Jan 15, Feb 21, 26,
    Mar 15, May 15; 1791: KING'S, May 19, 26; 1794: CG, Oct 20; 1796: KING'S, Feb
    20, Mar 5, 8
Pas de Deux Anacreontique (dance), 1778: KING'S, Dec 22; 1789: KING'S, Apr 28,
    May 28, Jun 6, CG, Jul 2
Pas de Deux du Masque (dance), 1778: KING'S, Feb 24; 1779: KING'S, May 15, 25,
    Jun 29
Pas de Deux Provencal (dance), 1787: HAY, Aug 7
Pas de Deux Russe (dance), 1787: KING'S, Mar 8, 13, Jun 16, 19; 1789: KING'S,
    May 2, 7, Jun 6
Pas de Huit (dance), 1784: KING'S, Mar 18
Pas de Lapons; or, Laplanders' Dance (dance), 1783: KING'S, Feb 13
Pas de Quatre (dance), 1755: CG, Jan 4, 23; 1777: KING'S, Nov 4; 1785: KING'S,
    Apr 21; 1786: KING'S, Apr 27; 1800: DL, May 14
Pas de Quatre de Panurge (dance), 1788: KING'S, Apr 3; 1798: KING'S, Mar 22,
    24, Apr 21, CG, Jun 11; 1800: KING'S, Apr 29
Pas de Sept (dance), 1788: KING'S, Feb 21, 23, 26, Mar 4, 15
Pas de Six de la Rosieu (dance), 1789: KING'S, May 21, CG, Jul 2
Pas de Trois (dance), 1734: CG, Mar 21; 1756: CG, Apr 22; 1772: KING'S, Jun 11,
    20; 1773: DL, Apr 22, KING'S, Nov 20; 1783: KING'S, Nov 29; 1784: KING'S, Jan
    17; 1785: KING'S, Mar 12, Apr 7; 1786: KING'S, Apr 27; 1787: KING'S, Mar 22;
    1788: KING'S, Feb 21, 23, 26, Mar 4, 15; 1791: KING'S, May 26, Jun 2, 6;
    1793: KING'S, Jun 4; 1796: KING'S, Mar 5, Jul 16, 23; 1798: KING'S, Apr 26;
    1799: CG, May 25
Pas de Trois en Berger Gallante (dance), 1772: KING'S, May 28
Pas de Trois et de Quatre (dance), 1793: KING'S, Feb 16
Pas Russe (dance), 1788: KING'S, Feb 21, 23, 26, Mar 4, 15; 1790: HAY, Apr 22,
    May 13, 15, CG, Jul 10; 1791: KING'S, May 19, 23, CG, Nov 21; 1793: DL, May
    31, Jun 7; 1795: KING'S, Mar 26, May 16; 1796: HAY, Sep 7, 16; 1797: CG, Jun
    9; 1798: KING'S, May 10
Pas Seul (dance), 1780: KING'S, Apr 22, May 20; 1781: KING'S, Mar 15, Apr 5,
    Nov 20, 28, Dec 11; 1782: KING'S, Feb 2, 28, Apr 30, Nov 19; 1783: KING'S,
    Feb 13, Apr 10, May 1, 8, 31, Jun 28, Nov 29; 1784: KING'S, Jan 3, Mar 11,
    May 13; 1786: KING'S, Apr 27; 1788: KING'S, Feb 21, 23, 26, Mar 4, 15; 1791:
    KING'S, May 26; 1792: HAY, Feb 6, Nov 26; 1793: KING'S, Jun 11; 1796: KING'S,
    May 12; 1798: DL, May 11, 16, 31; 1799: DL, May 2, CG, 25; 1800: DL, May 29,
    Jun 2
Pas, Grand (dance), 1796: CG, Nov 21
Paschal (dance), 1731: LIF, May 19
Paskin (ticket deliverer), 1792: CG, May 29; 1794: CG, Jun 17; 1795: CG, Jun
    17; 1796: CG, Jun 3; 1797: CG, May 25; 1798: CG, May 31; 1799: CG, May 21;
    1800: CG, Jun 4
Pasmore (beneficiary), 1760: CG, Nov 21
Pasquale (musician), 1732: HIC, Apr 24, May 5; 1745: HAY, Apr 1; 1750: DL, Sep
    25; 1751: KING'S, Apr 16; 1752: CG, Apr 18; 1754: KING'S, Feb 28
--Triumphs of Hibernia, The (masque), 1752: CG, Apr 18

Pasquale Jr (musician), 1745: HAY, Apr 1
Pasqualigo, Benedetto (librettist), 1783: KING'S, Jan 7
Pasqualino (musician), 1733: HIC, Apr 20, 27, May 25; 1748: KING'S, Apr 5;
    1749: KING'S, Mar 21; 1750: KING'S, Apr 10; 1752: KING'S, Mar 24; 1753:
    KING'S, Apr 30; 1754: HAY, Feb 11; 1755: KING'S, Mar 17; 1756: KING'S, Apr 5;
    1758: KING'S, Apr 6; 1759: CG, Feb 2; 1762: RANELAGH, Jun 16
Pasquarielle (actor), 1736: CG, Apr 8
Pasquin. See Fielding, Henry.
Pasquin et Marforio (pantomime, anon), 1718: LIF, Nov 26; 1721: HAY, Jan 6;
    1725: HAY, Mar 11
Pasquin's Budget. See Dibdin, Charles.
Pasquinades Italiennes, Les; ou, Arlequin Medecin de Moeurs (pantomime), 1719:
    LIF, Jan 6
Pass (ticket seller), 1794: HAY, Jun 2
Passacaille (dance), 1706: QUEEN'S, Jun 13; 1716: LIF, May 7; 1719: LIF, Mar
    19, Apr 27; 1720: DL, Apr 5; 1721: DL, May 10; 1723: DL, May 16, Jul 23, 26,
    Aug 6, 9; 1724: DL, Feb 10, Mar 26, May 12, LIF, Oct 14, 16, Nov 11, 13;
    1725: DL, May 10, 12, Oct 2, LIF, 13, DL, 18, LIF, Nov 9, DL, Dec 21; 1726:
    DL, Mar 31, Apr 15, LIF, May 2, DL, 9; 1732: GF, May 10; 1735: GF, Sep 12,
    Oct 3, 13; 1773: KING'S, Mar 23, Apr 24, May 3, 22, Jun 19; 1776: KING'S, Nov
    30, Dec 17; 1777: KING'S, Jan 11; 1782: KING'S, Nov 9, 14, Dec 28; 1783:
    KING'S, Nov 29
Passacaille de Zaid (dance), 1754: DL, Mar 26
Passagier che su la Sponda (song), 1748: KING'S, Apr 5
Passaglia, Salvadore (singer), 1756: SOHO, Feb 2, Mar 16, KING'S, Apr 5, 10;
    1757: KING'S, Mar 24, DL, 25, KING'S, May 31; 1758: KING'S, Jan 10, 31, Apr 6
Passe Pied (dance), 1776: DL, Mar 19
Passerini (musician), 1754: KING'S, Jan 29, Feb 28; 1760: SOHO, Jan 18, Feb 14
Passerini, Christina (singer), 1754: KING'S, Apr 2, CHAPEL, May 15; 1755: DL,
    Feb 3, HAY, Apr 18; 1756: SOHO, Feb 2, Mar 16; 1757: KING'S, Mar 24, DL, 25,
    KING'S, Apr 30, May 31; 1758: CG, Feb 10; 1760: SOHO, Jan 18, Feb 14; 1761:
    SOHO, Jan 21
Passini (singer), 1774: KING'S, Nov 8, Dec 3; 1775: KING'S, Jan 14, 26, Feb 7,
    Mar 23, May 6
Passion of Love I never felt (song), 1791: CG, May 18
Passion of Sappho, The (music), 1711: YB, May 24, Jul 16; 1718: LIF, Nov 15
Passion, The. See Jomelli, Niccolo, La Passione.
Passionate Madman, The. See Fletcher, John, The Nice Valour.
Passionate Pilgrim (poem), 1793: CG, Oct 9
Passione, La. See Jomelli, Niccolo.
Passive Husband, The. See Cumberland, Richard, A Word for Nature.
Pasteurs Joyeux (dance), 1743: CG, Jan 19, 21, 24, 25
Pastimes of Terpsichore (dance), 1783: KING'S, Dec 6, 16, 27, 30; 1784: KING'S,
    Jan 3, Feb 3
Paston (violinist), 1764: KING'S, Apr 12
Pastor Fido (dance), 1740: CG, Mar 25; 1742: DL, Apr 23
Pastor Fido; or, The Faithful Shepherd. See Settle, Elkanah.
Pastor Fido, Il. See Handel, George Frederic.
Pastor, Il (song), 1753: KING'S, Apr 30
Pastoral Ballet (dance), 1774: KING'S, Jan 29, Feb 5, 12, Mar 8, Apr 28, Nov
    19, Dec 3, 13; 1775: KING'S, Jan 17, May 25; 1776: KING'S, Jan 20, 23, 27,
    Feb 3, 6, 13, 17, 29, Mar 7, 14, 28, Apr 9, 20, May 16; 1779: KING'S, Nov 27;
    1780: KING'S, Jan 22, Feb 15, 19, Mar 18, Apr 8, 13, 18, 25, May 2, 25; 1783:
    KING'S, Feb 13
Pastoral Cantata (song), 1724: HIC, Mar 20
Pastoral Dance (dance), 1674: ATCOURT, Dec 22; 1716: DL, Dec 13; 1718: LIF, Jun
    4; 1719: LIF, Jan 5; 1724: LIF, May 19, 29, Oct 12, 14, 16, 23, Nov 11; 1725:
    LIF, May 7, 14, 17, 20, Sep 29; 1726: LIF, Jan 5, Apr 19, May 3, DL, 3, 4, 6,
    LIF, 9, DL, 13, 23, 25, LIF, Jun 24, Jul 29, Aug 19, 23, Sep 14, Oct 3, Nov
    14; 1727: LIF, Feb 3, Apr 6, 27, DL, May 1, 3, 5, LIF, Oct 2, 9, 17, 26, Nov
    1, 16; 1728: LIF, Jan 8, DL, May 3, 7, 10, LIF, 13, 16, 30, Oct 23; 1731:
    LIF, Mar 22, 29, Apr 22, 24; 1732: LIF, Feb 28, 29, Apr 12, 13, GF, 21, LIF,
    May 5, 15, DL, Aug 15; 1733: HAY, May 28; 1734: GF, Sep 20, Oct 14, Dec 6;
    1735: GF, Jan 17, Mar 27, CG/LIF, Apr 15, GF, 17, May 5, CG/LIF, 9, GF, Oct
    6, 10; 1736: HAY, Feb 20; 1738: DL, May 2; 1748: DL, Mar 26, Apr 12, 25, 28,
    29, May 3, 5, 9, 18, 20; 1749: DL, Mar 30; 1755: CG, Apr 23; 1756: CG, Apr
    28; 1757: DL, Oct 20; 1758: DL, Oct 24; 1759: CG, Mar 24; 1760: DL, Dec 11;
    1762: DL, Mar 1, Oct 30; 1763: DL, Nov 15; 1765: CG, Apr 18, DL, May 1; 1768:
    KING'S, May 5; 1769: CG, Dec 15, 21; 1770: CG, Dec 5, 19; 1772: KING'S, Mar
    17, 21, Apr 7, CG, 24, KING'S, May 16, 19, 23, Jun 9; 1773: KING'S, Jan 12,
    15, 26, Feb 2, 20, 23, 27, Mar 23, Apr 17, 27, May 1, 11, Jun 1, 12, HAY, 16,
    KING'S, Nov 20, 23, Dec 7; 1774: KING'S, May 31; 1775: DL, Apr 28; 1776: CG,

Nov 23, Dec 19; 1777: CG, Jan 15, Mar 22, Apr 26, HAY, Jul 18, Aug 22, Nov 23; 1780: DL, Feb 28, Nov 23; 1781: CG, May 18, KING'S, Nov 17, 20, 24, 28, Dec 20; 1782: KING'S, Jan 10, 26, 29, Feb 2, 7, 14, 16, 23, 28, Mar 7, Apr 20, May 4; 1787: HAY, Aug 6; 1792: CG, May 24
Pastoral Dance, Grand (dance), 1735: CG/LIF, Apr 14; 1774: DL, Apr 20
Pastoral Dialogue (song), 1700: LIF, Jul 5; 1705: DL, Jan 2; 1716: DL, Jun 19, Jul 24; 1731: DL, Aug 20; 1732: LIF, Mar 30; 1752: CG, Dec 8; 1754: DL, Mar 28; 1764: CG, Jan 19, 20
Pastoral Entertainment, A. See Bononcini, Giovanni.
Pastoral Entree (dance), 1775: KING'S, Oct 31
Pastoral Lovers (dance), 1783: DL, Sep 18, 25, Oct 9, Nov 29
Pastoral Mask (music), 1710: YB, May 3
Pastoral Minuet (dance), 1784: KING'S, Feb 26
Pastoral Pantomime (dance), 1755: CG, Apr 16
Pastoral Pas de Deux (dance), 1784: HAY, May 10
Pastoral Song (song), 1715: LIF, May 3; 1780: DL, Nov 23; 1786: HAMM, Jun 28
Pastoral Sports (dance), 1782: CG, Oct 8, 9, 29; 1784: CG, Sep 22, Oct 1, 18; 1785: CG, Feb 14, May 5
Pastore, Il (dance), 1752: CG, Dec 19; 1753: CG, Jan 5, 8, 27, 29, Feb 2, 6, 10, 14, 20, Mar 5, 8, 10, 12, 15, 17, 20, 27, 31, Apr 10, 23
Pastorella io giurerei (song), 1751: KING'S, Apr 16
Pastorella Nobile, La. See Guglielmi, Pietro.
Pastorelli, Giovanna (singer), 1794: KING'S, Jan 11, Feb 1, Mar 1, Jun 5, Dec 6; 1795: KING'S, Jan 10, 17, 24, 27, Apr 14, 30, May 14, 26, 28, Jun 2, 23, Dec 12; 1796: KING'S, Jan 19, Feb 16, Mar 10, Apr 7, 16, Jun 14, Dec 6, 20; 1797: KING'S, Jan 7, Feb 25, Apr 18, Jun 8, 10, Nov 28, Dec 2, 20; 1798: KING'S, Jan 23, Feb 20, Mar 22, Apr 10, 21, 26, Dec 8, 29; 1799: KING'S, Jan 22; 1800: KING'S, Mar 18
Pastres (dance), 1741: DL, Apr 4
Pate, William (singer), 1692: DG, May 2; 1695: LIF, Apr 30; 1696: DL, Sep 0; 1698: DL, Mar 0, YB, May 28, PEPYSS, 30, YB, Jun 7, DL/ORDG, Nov 0; 1699: DL, May 0, Dec 0, YB, 13; 1700: DL, Feb 19, Apr 29; 1703: DL, Feb 11, HA, May 18
Patence (dancer), 1770: HAY, Dec 19
Patentee, The; or Some Reflections in Verse (pamphlet), 1700: DLLIF, May 13
Patents all the Rage (song), 1798: CG, Apr 20, May 28, HAY, Aug 28
Paternoster Lane, 1749: DL, Feb 14
Paternoster Row, 1736: CG, Mar 30; 1737: CT, Feb 18, CG, Apr 14; 1739: CG, Apr 25; 1740: CG, Apr 18; 1744: DL, Apr 2, CG, 20; 1745: CT, Jan 14, HAY, Apr 1; 1747: CG, Mar 19; 1749: DL, Feb 15; 1750: DL, Jan 4, Mar 5, Apr 4; 1751: CT, Mar 16; 1752: CT/HAY, Jan 7, 14, 21, 31, Feb 4, 11, 18, CT, Mar 7, DL, Nov 27; 1756: DL, Jan 5, 22, Dec 21; 1757: DL, Jan 29; 1787: CG, Jun 15; 1788: HAY, Sep 30
Paterson (actor), 1733: MEG, Sep 28
Patie and Peggy. See Cibber, Theophilus.
Patient Grisell (puppetry), 1667: BF, Aug 30; 1717: BF, Aug 26
Patler (actor), 1721: LIF, Nov 13
Patrat, Joseph, 1786: HAY, Jun 20; 1798: CG, Apr 24, HAY, Jun 12
--Anglais, L'; ou, Le Fou Raisonnable, 1798: CG, Apr 24
--Heureuse Erreur, L', 1786: HAY, Jun 20
Patria, Gregorio (oboist), 1789: CG, Feb 27; 1790: CG, Feb 19, Mar 3; 1791: CG, Mar 11; 1792: CG, Feb 24; 1793: CG, Feb 15
Patrick (tin man), 1772: CG, Feb 24, Dec 14; 1773: CG, Feb 2; 1774: CG, Mar 3
Patrick in Prussia. See O'Keeffe, John, Love in a Camp.
Patrick, Richard (doorkeeper), 1723: HAY, Apr 15; 1729: HAY, Jan 31
Patriot Merchant, The; or, The Cheats of the Times (droll, anon), 1733: BFAP, Aug 23
Patriot, The (play, anon), 1784: HAY, Feb 23
Patriot, The; or, The Italian Conspiracy. See Gildon, Charles.
Patron, The. See Foote, Samuel.
Patron, The; or, Statesman's Opera. See Odell, Thomas.
Pattenden (actor), 1741: TC, Aug 4, GF, Sep 28, Oct 19, Nov 4, Dec 15, 29; 1742: GF, Jan 1, 5, Apr 24, May 18, LIF, Dec 1, 13, 27; 1743: LIF, Feb 14, Mar 24, TCD/BFTD, Aug 23
Patterson (beneficiary), 1772: CG, May 29
Patterson (chandler), 1759: CG, Nov 9; 1771: CG, Oct 7
Patterson, Miss (actor), 1782: HAY, Sep 21
Patterson, William
--Arminius, 1731: GF, Jan 13; 1737: CG, Jan 8, 12, 15, 19, 22, 26, Feb 12; 1740: DL, Jan 4
Pattinson (tallow chandler), 1759: CG, Nov 24; 1760: CG, Jan 17, Feb 16, Apr 11, May 16, 28, Dec 20; 1761: CG, Jan 10, 27, 31, Feb 7; 1771: CG, Nov 6, Dec 30; 1772: CG, Feb 19, Mar 28, Apr 11, Nov 12, Dec 9; 1773: CG, Jan 14, Feb 4,

Apr 1, Nov 10, Dec 17; 1774: CG, Jan 12, Feb 8, Mar 10, Apr 14; 1776: CG, Dec
16; 1780: CG, May 29
Pattison, Miss (actor), 1736: HAY, Jan 14; 1737: HAY, Mar 7
Pattocks, Miss (beneficiary), 1746: SOU, Oct 7
Paul (actor), 1715: LIF, Oct 20; 1716: LIF, May 31; 1722: HAY, Dec 17; 1723:
HAY, Jan 31; 1734: DL, Feb 28, JS, May 23, GR, Nov 4
Paul (singer), 1742: JS, May 31
Paul and Virginia. See Cobb, James.
Paul Baker's Court, 1780: DL, Mar 31
Paul et Virginie (dance), 1795: KING'S, Mar 26, Apr 7, 11, 30, May 12, 26, 28;
1796: KING'S, Jan 2, 9, 16, 19, Feb 9, 16
Paul Prigg's Description of his Journey (entertainment), 1787: RLSN, Mar 29
Paul, Master (singer), 1796: CG, Dec 19; 1797: HAY, May 10, CG, Jun 5
Paul's Alley, 1698: CLARK'S, Apr 1
Paul's Head Coffee House, 1750: DL, Nov 28
Paulet (dancer), 1733: HAY, May 28
Paulet, Master (dancer), 1733: BFCGBH, Aug 23
Paulet, Mrs (actor), 1726: DL, Nov 2; 1727: DL, Nov 14
Paulet's son (dancer), 1725: LIF, Apr 19
Paulina, Mrs (singer), 1713: HIC, May 27
Pausanius, the Betrayer of his Country. See Norton, Richard.
Pavilion, The. See Linley, William.
Pawlet, Kitty (beneficiary), 1720: CGR, Jun 22
Pawlet's Great Dancing Room, 1702: PR, Jun 30
Paxton, William (violoncellist), 1761: HAY, Jan 28, Feb 5; 1764: KING'S, Apr
12; 1775: DL, Mar 22, Apr 7; 1782: CG, Dec 31
Paye, Miss (singer), 1787: CG, Dec 3, 17; 1788: CG, Jan 14, May 22, Sep 22, Dec
29; 1792: CG, Dec 26; 1793: CG, Sep 30, Oct 2, 7, 9, 24, Dec 27; 1794: CG,
Jan 9
Payler (actor), 1778: HAY, Dec 28
Payne (actor), 1736: LIF, Mar 31
Payne (actor), 1785: HAMM, Jun 17, 27, Jul 1, 2, 4, 6, 8, 15, 22, 25, 26, 27
Payne (actor), 1786: HAY, Dec 18
Payne (bookseller), 1756: DL, Jan 22; 1760: CG, Dec 30
Payne (house servant), 1745: DL, May 13
Payne (publisher), 1792: DLKING'S, Jan 18
Payne and Boquet (booksellers), 1750: DL, Apr 4
Payne, Henry Nevil, 1672: DG, Aug 3, Nov 4
--Fatal Jealousy, 1672: DG, Aug 3
--Love's Jealousy, 1672: DG, Aug 3, Nov 4
--Morning Ramble, The; or, Town Humours, 1672: DG, Aug 3, Nov 4
--Siege of Constantinople, The, 1674: DG, Nov 2
Payne, J (printer), 1756: DL, Dec 21
Payne, Jonathan (actor), 1772: HAY, Sep 18
Payne, Master (actor), 1785: HAMM, Jun 17, Jul 2, 4, 25, 27
Payne, Mrs (innkeeper), 1749: DL, Feb 14
Payne, Mrs Jonathan (actor), 1772: HAY, Sep 18
Paysan (dance), 1741: DL, Apr 9; 1757: HAY, Jun 17
Paysan Mantaignez (dance), 1733: GF, Apr 20
Paysanne (dance), 1751: CG, Apr 26, 29, May 4, 7, 11
Paysanne Distraite (dance), 1777: KING'S, May 20, 24, 27, Jun 10, 17, 21, 24,
28
Paysans Allemands (dance), 1742: DL, Apr 3, 10, 19, May 7; 1756: CG, Apr 22
Paysans de Bordeaux (dance), 1741: CG, Apr 22
Paysans Gallants (dance), 1755: CG, Dec 3, 11, 16; 1756: CG, Apr 1, 29, May 3,
4, 6, 10, 20, 24
Paysans Iroquois (dance), 1756: CG, Apr 22
Paysans Legers (dance), 1743: BFFP, Aug 23
Paysans Moisonneurs (dance), 1743: CG, Oct 26, Nov 30, Dec 7, 8, 13, 16
Paysans Voles (dance), 1779: KING'S, May 15, 25, 29, Jun 5, 15, 19
Pazzie D'Orlando, Le. See Guglielmi, Pietro.
Pea-Hen Tavern, 1792: HAY, Nov 26
Peace in Europe (serenata, anon), 1749: KING'S, Apr 29
Peace to the soul (song), 1800: CG, Jun 16
Peacock Coffee House, 1743: HAY, Mar 23; 1749: DL, Jan 20; 1750: DL, Mar 6
Peacop (housekeeper), 1744: DL, May 15; 1745: DL, May 1; 1746: DL, May 7; 1747:
DL, May 8; 1757: DL, May 13; 1758: DL, May 2; 1759: DL, May 11; 1760: DL, Apr
28
Peake, Richard (treasurer), 1799: DL, Jun 5, Nov 2
Peale, Sir John (Lord Mayor), 1686: CITY, Oct 29
Pearce (actor), 1728: HAY, Aug 9, Oct 15; 1729: HAY, Jan 2, 31, Mar 29, May 7,
29, Jun 17, Jul 10, 26, BFR, Aug 25, SF, Sep 8, GF, Nov 11, 17, Dec 3, 5;

16, 22, Dec 8; <u>1779</u>: CG, Jan 1, May 1, Oct 23, Nov 10, Dec 11; <u>1780</u>: CG, Jan
17, Feb 17, Apr 28, Oct 19, 23, 24, 30; <u>1781</u>: CG, Feb 24, Apr 2, 18, 28, May
9
Peirce, Mrs (singer), <u>1675</u>: ATCOURT, Feb 15
Peircival. See Percival.
Peire. See Peer.
Peirson. See Pierson.
Peite (house servant), <u>1744</u>: DL, May 22
Pelerins Voyageur (dance), <u>1742</u>: DL, Feb 17, 19
Peleus and Thetis. See Granville, George.
Pelham (dancer), <u>1717</u>: LIF, Nov 8, Dec 9; <u>1718</u>: RI, Jul 28
Pelham (spectator), <u>1698</u>: DLLIF, Feb 26
Pellegrini, Cavaliero Valeriano (singer), <u>1712</u>: OSG, Apr 9; <u>1713</u>: QUEEN'S, Feb
26, May 2; see also Valeriano, Cavaliero
Pellegrini, I. See Hasse, Johann Adolph.
Pelling (dancer, actor), <u>1717</u>: LIF, Nov 22, Dec 6; <u>1718</u>: LIF, Jan 1, 2, 3, 4,
15, 24, 27, Feb 4, Mar 8, 10, Apr 15, 16, RI, Jul 26, LIF, Aug 6; <u>1719</u>: LIF,
Jan 9, Apr 29, May 7, 13, 21, 25, 28, 29, Jun 25, BFBL, Aug 24, B-L, Sep 5,
LIF, Oct 5, 27, Dec 30; <u>1720</u>: LIF, Jan 23, Mar 26, Apr 30, May 11, 12, 19,
23, 24, 25, 30, Jun 6, 7, Oct 4, Dec 28; <u>1721</u>: LIF, May 15, Oct 10, 17, Dec
14; <u>1722</u>: LIF, Jan 1, Mar 13, 29, 31, Apr 6, 20, 24, 27, May 2, 7, 8, 10, 16,
18, 25, Jul 27, Oct 16, 30, Nov 7, Dec 13; <u>1723</u>: LIF, Feb 13, 19, Mar 25, May
18, 23, 24, 28, Oct 7, 16, 19, Nov 2, 8, 19, 27, Dec 11; <u>1724</u>: LIF, Jan 3, 4,
Mar 14, Apr 6, 7, 21, May 4, 12, 13, 30, Jun 23, Jul 14, 29, Sep 25, 28, 30,
Oct 5, 9, 17, Nov 3, 6, 10, 13; <u>1725</u>: LIF, Jan 21, Mar 11, 13, 29, 31, Apr
14, 17, 20, 22, May 22, Oct 4, 21, Nov 3, 13, 30, Dec 2; <u>1726</u>: LIF, Jan 14,
Apr 18, 21, 22, 30, May 3, Jun 17, 21, 24, Jul 15, 19, 22, 26, Sep 16, 23,
26, 30, Oct 5, 24, 29, Nov 2, 9, 21, Dec 3; <u>1727</u>: LIF, Jan 9, Feb 13, Mar 20,
Apr 21, 27, May 8, Sep 20, 22, 29, Oct 12, 27, Nov 7, 9, 17, Dec 19; <u>1728</u>:
LIF, Mar 14, Apr 22, May 3, 6, 11, 15, 18, 22, 23, Sep 30, Oct 9, 14, 21, 23,
26, Nov 23, Dec 12, 31; <u>1729</u>: LIF, Jan 16, 18, 31, Feb 6, Mar 10, 20, 27, Apr
8, 10, 11, 15, 19, 22, 24, May 20, 21, 22, Oct 3, 15, 22, 24, 28, Nov 1, 4,
Dec 16; <u>1730</u>: LIF, Jan 2, Apr 10, 22, 25, 27, 29, 30, May 14, Sep 21, 25, Oct
9, 27, Nov 7, Dec 11, 15, 30; <u>1731</u>: LIF, Apr 3, 5, 28, May 3, 5, 6, 20, Sep
27, Oct 4, 11, Nov 2, 6, 8, 12, 13, 18, 25, Dec 1, 7, 14; <u>1732</u>: LIF, Apr 13,
17, 18, 22, 24, 25, 26, 27, 28, May 2, 5, 8, 9, 17, LIF/CG, Oct 4, 30, Nov 8,
24, Dec 8, CG/LIF, 19, LIF/CG, 27; <u>1733</u>: LIF/CG, Jan 1, 15, 23, Mar 12, CG,
27, LIF/CG, 28, Apr 2, 12, 16, 18, 23, 24, CG, May 1, LIF/CG, 3, 7, 8, CG,
16, LIF/CG, 24, CG, Jun 26, Sep 20, 25, 29, Oct 4, 11, 13, 31, Nov 1, 10, 12,
Dec 7, 28; <u>1734</u>: CG, Jan 1, 14, 17, 25, Feb 26, Mar 11, 16, Apr 27, May 1, 6,
7, 15, DL, Sep 7, 10, 19, 24, 26, Oct 3, 5, 8, 10, 17, 21, 22, 25, 28, Nov 1,
16, 22, Dec 9, 11, 12, 17; <u>1735</u>: DL, Jan 17, 18, 21, 28, Feb 5, 13, 14, Mar
3, 25, Apr 7, 11, 25, May 7, 14, 17, Jun 5, Sep 15, Oct 1, 7, 22, Nov 17, 20;
<u>1736</u>: DL, Jan 3, Feb 28, Mar 27, Apr 6, 30, May 14, 15, 21, Aug 26, Oct 2, 5,
12, Nov 3, 11, 13, Dec 4; <u>1737</u>: DL, Jan 26, Feb 10, Apr 11, May 3, 13, 19,
20, Oct 22; <u>1738</u>: DL, Jan 19, 20, 24, 28, Feb 1, 6, Mar 13, Apr 12, May 12,
13, 17, 22, 23, Sep 23, Oct 3, 30, Dec 7, 15; <u>1739</u>: DL, Feb 5, 7, May 1, 2,
5, 9, 11, 14, 16, 19, 23, 28, 31, Sep 13, 26, Oct 9, 10, 16, 18, 22, 26, 27,
31, Nov 20, 22, Dec 8, 10, 11, 12, 14, 19; <u>1740</u>: DL, Jan 7, 15, Feb 16, 18,
BFH, Aug 23; <u>1741</u>: BFH, Aug 22; <u>1742</u>: LIF, Dec 3, 13, 27; <u>1743</u>: LIF, Jan 7,
Feb 17; <u>1745</u>: DL, Jan 14, Dec 17; <u>1747</u>: DL, Nov 2, 13, 16; <u>1748</u>: DL, Oct 27;
<u>1749</u>: DL, Feb 21, Oct 11, 18, 24, Nov 9, 27, Dec 2, 28; <u>1750</u>: DL, Jan 1, Feb
19, Apr 5, Nov 13, 27; <u>1751</u>: DL, Dec 26; <u>1752</u>: DL, Jan 28
Pelling, Mrs (dancer), <u>1726</u>: LIF, Sep 14, 16, 19, 23, 30, Oct 12, 24, Nov 9,
21, Dec 3, 5; <u>1727</u>: LIF, Jan 9, 31, Feb 13, Mar 20, Sep 15, 22, 27, 29, Oct
2, 9, 12, 17, 25, 26, Nov 1, 7, 9, 16, Dec 22; <u>1728</u>: LIF, Jan 8, Apr 30, Oct
9, 14, 26, Nov 23, Dec 12; <u>1729</u>: LIF, Jan 13, 16, 18, Feb 6, Mar 10, 17, 20,
Apr 19, 22, 26, May 8, Oct 22, 24, 28, Nov 4; <u>1730</u>: LIF, Jan 2, Apr 25, 27,
30, Oct 9, 27, Nov 7, Dec 11, 14, 15; <u>1731</u>: LIF, Apr 3, 28, May 3, 5, 6, 20,
Oct 4, Nov 6, 8, 12, 13, 18, Dec 1, 7; <u>1732</u>: LIF, Mar 9, 21, 30, Apr 13, 17,
19, 22, 24, 25, 26, May 5, 8, 9, 11, 15, LIF/CG, Oct 13, Nov 8, 14, 16, 17,
21, 24, Dec 8, CG/LIF, 19, LIF/CG, 27; <u>1733</u>: CG/LIF, Jan 9, LIF/CG, 11, 12,
16, 19, 23, Feb 2, 5, CG, 8, LIF/CG, Mar 12, CG, 27, LIF/CG, 28, 29, Apr 2,
12, 16, 18, 23, 30, CG, May 1, LIF/CG, 3, 7, 8, 10, CG, 16, 17, LIF/CG, 21,
24, CG/LIF, 28, LIF/CG, 29, CG, Jun 26, Oct 13, 16, 18, 27, Nov 12, Dec 7;
<u>1734</u>: CG, Apr 1, May 6, DL, Sep 7, 10, 19, 24, 26, Oct 3, 5, 8, 10, 17, 21,
25, 28, Nov 1, 16, 22, Dec 9, 11, 12, 17, 21; <u>1735</u>: DL, Jan 17, 18, 21, 28,
Feb 5, 13, 14, Mar 3, 15, 25, Apr 7, 25, 26, May 7, 14, Jun 5, Oct 7, 22, Nov
15, 17, 20, Dec 6; <u>1736</u>: DL, Jan 12, Feb 28, Mar 27, Apr 6, 10, May 14, 20,
21, Sep 7, Oct 2, 12, Nov 2, Dec 4; <u>1737</u>: DL, Feb 14, May 3, 13, Nov 10;
<u>1738</u>: DL, Jan 24, 28
Pelopida. See Barthelemon, Francois Hippolyte.

651

Pelotti, Sga (singer), 1713: QUEEN'S, Mar 28, May 6
Pemberton (singer), 1780: DL, May 17; 1781: DL, May 5; 1782: DL, Apr 27, Nov 6;
    1783: DL, May 26; 1784: DL, May 15, CG, Oct 25, Nov 12; 1785: DL, May 20, CG,
    Nov 14; 1786: CG, Jan 18, DL, May 26, CG, Jun 2, Oct 23; 1787: CG, Jan 29
Pembroke Hall, 1751: DL, Mar 7
Pembroke, Countess of. See Queroulle, Henrietta.
Pembroke, Earl of. See Herbert.
Pendarves, Mrs (correspondent), 1724: LIF, Dec 12; 1726: LIF, Nov 26; 1729: DL,
    Feb 26, LIF, Mar 12, KING'S, Dec 20; 1734: KING'S, Apr 2, HH, 26, KING'S, 30;
    1735: KING'S, Mar 15; 1736: CG, Nov 27; 1737: CG, Jan 8; 1739: HAY, Dec 1
Pender L'Amico (song), 1748: KING'S, Apr 5
Pendrell (beneficiary), 1720: LIF, May 27
Pendry (actor), 1710: GR, Sep 28, 30; 1715: DL, Feb 23, Aug 9
Penelope. See Mottley, John; Galuppi, Baldassare.
Penelope; or The Fair Disconsolate (mock opera, anon), 1734: HAY, Jul 5, 8, 19
Penkethman-Boheme Booth, 1722: SF, Sep 5
Penkethman-Bullock Booth, 1722: SF, Sep 22
Penkethman-Bullock-Simpson Booth, 1703: BFPBS, Aug 23
Penkethman-Giffard Booth, 1730: BFPG, Aug 20, BFPG/TC, 24, BFPG, 31, Sep 1
Penkethman-Miller Booth, 1719: BFPM, Aug 24
Penkethman-Miller-Boheme Booth, 1722: BFPMB, Aug 25
Penkethman-Miller-Norris Booth, 1720: BFPMJ, Aug 23; 1721: BF/SF, Aug 24, Sep 2
Penkethman-Norris Booth, 1718: SF, Sep 6; 1723: BFPJ, Aug 22, SOU, Sep 24
Penkethman-Pack Booth, 1717: SF, Sep 9
Penkethman, Mrs (actor), 1737: LIF, Mar 29; 1738: TC, Aug 7, BFP, 23; 1740: DL,
    Oct 14, 17, 27, Nov 17, 24, 29, Dec 4, 26; 1741: DL, May 15
Penkethman, Widow (beneficiary), 1726: DL, May 19; 1727: Dl, May 15; 1728: DL,
    May 29
Penkethman (Penkeman, Pinkiman, Pinkyman), William (actor), 1692: DL, Nov 0;
    1693: DL, Feb 0; 1694: DL, Sep 0; 1695: DG, Nov 0; 1696: DL, Jan 0, Feb 0,
    Mar 0, Apr 0, DG, Jun 0, Aug 0, DL, Sep 0, DL/DL, Dec 0; 1697: DL, Jan 0, Feb
    0, May 8, 31, DG, Jun 0, DL, Jul 0, Sep 0, NONE, 0; 1698: DL, Jun 0, DL/ORDG,
    Nov 0, DL, Dec 0; 1699: DL, Apr 0, May 0, Nov 28; 1700: DL, Apr 29, Jul 9,
    Nov 23, Dec 9; 1701: DL, Mar 1, Apr 0, May 31, Jun 7, 13, Dec 0; 1702: DL,
    Jan 0, Feb 0, Jul 7, 11, Aug 20, 22, Sep 18, Oct 26, Nov 26, Dec 0, 14; 1703:
    DL, Jan 27, Feb 12, Mar 11, Apr 10, 27, DG, 30, DL, May 28, YB, Jul 27, 30,
    BFPBS, Aug 23, DL, Oct 21, Dec 2; 1704: DL, Jan 26, Feb 1, ATCOURT, 28, LIF,
    Mar 30, ATCOURT, Apr 24, MFFB, May 1, DL, Jun 5, Jul 1, 11, Aug 10; 1705: DL,
    Jan 18, Mar 29, Apr 23, Jun 12, 23, LIF/QUEN, Oct 11, DL, 24, 25, 30, Nov 20,
    Dec 17; 1706: DL, Feb 4, Mar 4, Apr 0, 1, BF, Aug 27, DL/DG, Nov 21, DG, 28,
    DL, Dec 3, 19; 1707: DL, Jan 27, Feb 24, Mar 6, 11, 17, 25, Apr 3, Oct 23,
    25, 28, Nov 4, 6, 11, 13, Dec 2, 10, 26; 1708: DL/QUEEN, Feb 2, DL, 4,
    DL/QUEEN, 5, DL, 24, Mar 8, 16, 18, DL/QUEEN, Apr 7, 8, DL, 17, 19, 26, May
    21, DL/QUEEN, 24, 25, Jun 4, DL, Oct 12, 13, 14, 15, 16, 18, 21, 25, 26, Dec
    14, 18, 22; 1709: DL, Jan 10, 11, 12, 13, 14, 18, 25, 27, Feb 4, 16, 19, Mar
    4, 8, 14, 15, 19, 21, 31, Apr 4, 25, 30, May 25, 31, QUEEN'S, Sep 27, Oct 1,
    6, 17, 22, 28, 31, Nov 8, 11, 18, 19, Dec 12; 1710: QUEEN'S, Jan 5, 7, 12,
    14, 18, 19, 21, 23, Feb 13, Mar 4, Apr 13, May 1, 6, 16, 24, 29, GR, Jun 15,
    24, 26, 28, Jul 3, 8, 10, 15, 20, Aug 5, 7, 10, 17, 26, Sep 1, 7, 9, 23,
    DL/QUEEN, Oct 7, Nov 6, 8, QUEEN'S, 10, DL/QUEEN, 16, 18, DL, 30, Dec 1, 4,
    5, 7, 9, 14, 15, 16, 18, 22; 1711: DL, Jan 9, 11, 15, 16, 19, 26, Feb 10,
    DL/QUEEN, 17, DL, 22, Mar 17, Apr 7, 23, May 22, 31, Sep 22, Oct 4, 6, 8, 16,
    20, 26, 30, Nov 2, 5, 8, 10, 23, 26, 29, Dec 8, 10, 18, 21; 1712: DL, May 5,
    Jun 2, Jul 11, 22, Sep 23, 25, Oct 6, 7, 11, 13, 15, 17, 20, 22, 23, 31, Nov
    3, 7, 26, Dec 12; 1713: DL, Jan 5, 29, Mar 16, Apr 6, May 11, 12, Jun 5, 18,
    19, Sep 29, Oct 23, Nov 16, 18, 27; 1714: DL, Jan 28, Apr 19, 26, SF, Aug 31,
    DL, Nov 23, 24, 26, 29; 1715: DL, Jan 12, 13, 14, 25, Feb 10, 12, 15, 21, 22,
    23, 25, 26, 28, Apr 2, 4, SF, Sep 15, DL, Nov 19, Dec 9, 12, 20; 1716: DL,
    Jan 13, 23, Feb 1, 3, 9, 18, Mar 10, Apr 2, 5, 16, May 14, 30, Jun 15, 21,
    26, SF, Sep 25, DL, Oct 4, 16, 19, 22, 27, Nov 2, 14, 26, 27, Dec 29; 1717:
    DL, Jan 4, 5, 9, 16, 26, Feb 15, Mar 1, Apr 4, May 10, 14, 22, 25, 30, SF,
    Sep 9, NONE, 13, SF, 25, DL, Oct 3, 9, 16, 21, 24, Nov 18, 19, 20, Dec 4, 31;
    1718: DL, Jan 7, 13, Feb 14, 19, Mar 1, 22, Apr 1, 5, 19, 21, May 14, 27, 28,
    NONE, 31, DL, Jun 6, RI, Jul 19, 26, 28, Aug 2, 16, 23, 30, SF, Sep 6, DL,
    25, Oct 2, 4, 7, 10, 11, 20, 27, 30, Nov 8, 24, 27, 28, 29, Dec 10, 13, 19;
    1719: DL, Apr 9, May 5, RI, Jun 6, Jul 6, BFPM, Aug 24, DL, Sep 15, 19, 22,
    24, Oct 3, 7, 8, 14, 15, 24, 27, 28, 31, Nov 10, 11, 19, 23, 26; 1720: DL,
    Jan 5, 12, Feb 5, Apr 7, 21, May 5, 20, BFPMJ, Aug 23, SFLH, Sep 5, DL, 20,
    Oct 1, 3, 5, 6, 12, 13, 15, 20, 29, Nov 2, 18, 19, Dec 5, 6, 8, 17; 1721: DL,
    Jan 23, 24, 25, 27, Feb 14, Mar 27, May 3, 5, 15, 26, BF/SF, Aug 24, DL, Sep
    14, 16, 23, 28, Oct 7, 9, 10, 11, 13, 16, 17, 18, 23, 25, 28, Nov 1, 7, 8,
    25, Dec 1, 15; 1722: DL, Jan 4, 5, 8, 15, Apr 10, 12, May 3, 18, 22, RI, Jul

23, Aug 20, BFPMB, 25, SF, Sep 5, SFM, 5, SF, 22, DL, 27, 29, Oct 6, 9, 12, 13, 15, 20, 22, 25, 26, 30, 31, Dec 3, 4, 26; 1723: DL, Jan 9, 16, 17, 23, 28, Feb 4, 5, Mar 21, 28, Apr 1, May 6, 20, RI, Sep 2, DL, 19, 21, Oct 5, 10, 12, 16, 28, 29, 30, Nov 1, 8, 12, 15, 16, 18, 19, Dec 20, 30; 1724: DL, Feb 17, 22, Apr 7, 18, 28, May 1, 6, 7, 16, 22, RI, Jun 22, Aug 3, SF, Sep 2, SOU, 24, HAY, Oct 13, DL, 27; 1725: DL, May 13, BF, Aug 23, DL, Sep 20, Oct 2; 1729: LIF, Apr 19, 23, 30, BF, Aug 26, SF, Sep 8, LIF, 22, SOU, 23, GF, Nov 17, 18, 20, 24, Dec 1, 3, 15, 18, 19, 20; 1730: GF, Jan 5, 6, 7, 9, 13, 19, 26, Feb 7, 9, 10, 16, Mar 17, 30, 31, Apr 2, 6, 7, 9

Penkethman Jr, William (actor), 1729: LIF, Mar 25, Nov 17; 1730: GF, Apr 9, 15, 17, 20, 28, May 26, 28, Jun 2, 3, HAY, 4, GF, 8, 12, 16, 17, 19, Jul 6, 8, 10, BFPG/TC, Aug 1, BFPG, 20, 31, SFP, Sep 9, GF, 16, 18, 23, 25, 28, 30, Oct 5, 9, 12, 19, 20, 21, 24, Nov 2, 3, 6, 10, 11, 26, Dec 1, LIF, 8, 30; 1731: GF, Jan 6, LIF, Mar 22, Apr 3, GF, 29, LIF, May 10, TC, Aug 4, 12, SF/BFFHH, 24, LIF, Sep 27, SOU, 28, LIF, Oct 1, 6, 25, 30, Nov 8, 12, 25, Dec 3, 9, 29; 1732: LIF, Jan 7, 28, Feb 3, 14, Mar 23, 30, Apr 18, 24, May 3, BF, Aug 22, CG/LIF, Sep 22, LIF/CG, 27, Oct 2, 20, 23, 27, 28, 30, Nov 1, 7, 8, 11, Dec 7, GF, 18; 1733: GF, Jan 1, 13, 23, Feb 5, 19, Mar 5, 17, 27, 28, 30, Apr 4, 11, 16, 18, May 8, 9, 22, 29, BF, Aug 23, GF, Sep 10, 12, 20, 25, 27, Oct 1, 4, 9, 12, 15, 18, 22, 23, 25, Nov 10, 14, 28, Dec 8, 12, 13, 18, 31; 1734: GF, Jan 10, 19, 21, 24, 28, 31, Apr 6, 19, 27, May 1, 3, 6, 15, BFRLCH, Aug 24, Sep 2, GF, 9, 11, 13, 16, 20, 25, Oct 14, 16, 17, 18, 23, 28, Nov 6, 7, 13, 18, 27, 29, Dec 2, 6, 9, 13, 16, 20, 23, 31; 1735: GF, Jan 3, 8, 11, 13, 24, Feb 6, 11, 17, 24, 25, Mar 6, 10, 17, 24, 29, Apr 9, 10, 16, 22, 23, 30, May 2, 3, 8, 15, Sep 15, 17, 19, 22, 24, Oct 3, 6, 15, 27, Nov 3, 6, 10, 14, 17, 20, 24, 25, Dec 8; 1736: GF, Feb 5, 9, 10, 11, 17, 20, Mar 3, 9, 18, 25, 29, Apr 16, 17, 28, May 13, LIF, Jun 8, Oct 5, 9, 12, 21, 23, 26, Nov 6, 11, 13, 18, 20, 24, 26, 27, 29, Dec 3, 7, 16, 22, 31; 1737: LIF, Jan 10, 21, Feb 1, 21, DL, Mar 4, LIF, 15, 21, 24, 29, Apr 22, 27, 28, May 2, 6, 17, Jul 26, Aug 5, CG, Sep 19, 23, 28, Oct 17, Nov 9, 17; 1738: CG, Jan 3, 25, Feb 16, Mar 25, Apr 7, 12, 24, 25, Jun 27, 30, Jul 7, 11, Aug 1, TC, 7, BFP, 23, CG, Sep 18, 20, Oct 4, 6, 9, 21, 28, Dec 4; 1739: CG, Jan 16, 20, 22, Feb 10, 14, 24, Mar 3, 27, Apr 5, May 7, 17, 18, DL, Sep 8, 11, 20, 27, Oct 10, 13, 24, 26, 29, Nov 7, 15, 20, 23, Dec 6; 1740: DL, May 16; 1745: MF, May 7

Penkethman's Booth, 1704: MFFB, May 1; 1705: MF, May 1; 1706: MF, May 1, BF, Aug 27; 1707: MF, May 13; 1716: SF, Sep 25; 1717: SF, Sep 20, 25; 1718: SF, Sep 3; 1722: SF, Sep 24; 1723: SF, Sep 5, SOU, 25; 1724: BFP, Aug 22, SF, Sep 5; 1730: SFP, Sep 9; 1738: BFP, Aug 23

Penkethman's Dancing Dogs (entertainment), 1707: BF, Aug 30

Penkethman's Theatre, 1709: GR, Jun 6; 1711: GR, May 21; 1719: RI, Jun 6; 1720: RI, Aug 29; 1722: RI, Jul 23; 1723: RI, Sep 2

Penn, John, 1796: HAY, Mar 28

--Battle of Eddington, The; or, British Liberty, 1796: HAY, Mar 28; 1797: HAY, Jan 23, 26, May 10

Penn, Sir William (spectator), 1661: VERE, Sep 28, Oct 26, Nov 25, 29, Dec 30; 1662: VERE, Jan 1, Feb 5, Mar 31, May 19; 1664: BRIDGES, Aug 4, Sep 28; 1665: BRIDGES, Jan 13; 1666: BRIDGES, Aug 29, MOORFLDS, Sep 1; 1667: BRI/COUR, Mar 25, BRIDGES, May 1, BRI/COUR, 24, BRIDGES, Aug 13, LIF, 15, BRIDGES, 17, 26, LIF, Sep 5, BRIDGES, 20, LIF, Nov 7; 1668: BRIDGES, Feb 7, 18, May 9, BF, Sep 7, BRIDGES, 19

Pennington (actor), 1744: HAY, Apr 6, May 10, 16, Jun 29

Pennington, Miss (actor), 1790: HAY, Sep 29

Pennington's (watchmaker), 1779: CG, May 3

Pennsylvania Coffee House, 1763: DL, Apr 27

Penny Lottery (entertainment), 1698: DG, Oct 18

Penny, Catherine (counterfeiter), 1743: DL, Mar 7

Peno si per un Ingrata (song), 1749: KING'S, Mar 21

Penray. See Pendry.

Penryn, 1755: HAY, Sep 4

Pensa che amante (song), 1755: KING'S, Mar 17

Pensa che il Cielo trema (song), 1746: KING'S, Mar 25

Penseroso, Il (song), 1742: GF, Feb 2

Pentland (actor), 1780: HAY, Jan 17

People of Jerusalem (song), 1794: DL, Apr 10

People that walked (song), 1790: CG, Mar 26; 1793: KING/HAY, Feb 20; 1794: DL, Mar 19

Peplow (actor), 1723: DL, Aug 12; 1726: DL, May 10, Oct 1; 1727: DL, May 22, Oct 6; 1730: DL, Oct 6, 28; 1731: DL, Aug 11; 1732: DL, May 6, Aug 1, TC, 4; 1733: DL, Mar 31, DL/HAY, Oct 12; 1734: DL/LIF, May 3, DL, 21, Oct 21; 1735: DL, Jul 1, HAY, Aug 4, 12; 1736: DL, Sep 25; 1737: DL, May 20, Oct 25, 27; 1738: DL, May 30, Sep 23, Dec 15; 1739: DL, May 28, Sep 26, Dec 11; 1740: DL, Jan 16, May 21

Peplow, Mrs (actor), 1739: DL, May 28
Pepo. See Pieppo.
Pepoli, Count Alexander (librettist), 1795: KING'S, May 14
Peppet, Mrs (boxkeeper), 1723: HAY, Apr 22
Pepusch, Godfrede (musician), 1704: LIF, Apr 4
Pepusch, John Christopher (musician, composer), 1704: LIF, Apr 4; 1707: DL, Apr
    1, YB, 18; 1710: YB, Mar 31, PCGR, Jdn 14; 1714: SH, Jan 28; 1715: DL, Mar
    12, Apr 20, Nov 23; 1716: DL, Jan 23, Apr 12, 17; 1717: LIF, Jul 3; 1718:
    LIF, Nov 18; 1719: LIF, Apr 25; 1724: LIF, Dec 12; 1725: LIF, Apr 15; 1726:
    LIF, Mar 31, May 4, 6; 1727: HAY, Mar 17, YB, Apr 26; 1729: HIC, Apr 16, LIF,
    May 6; 1730: LIF, May 21, 25; 1731: LIF, Apr 29; 1732: HIC, Mar 31, LIF, May
    9; 1733: CG, May 1, LIF/CG, 8, 24, DL/HAY, Dec 1; 1735: DL, Jun 3; 1737: CR,
    Apr 29; 1781: HAY, Aug 8; 1782: HAY, Jun 3; 1784: HAY, Aug 26; 1789: CG, Dec
    21; 1790: CG, Nov 15; 1792: CG, Dec 20; 1793: CG, Oct 2, Dec 19
--Dido and Aeneas (masque), 1716: DL, Apr 17, 24, 25, 30, May 15
--Thomyris, Queen of Scythia; or, The Royal Amazon, 1707: DL, Apr 1, 5, 15, 19,
    26, May 3, 6, 13, 20, QUEEN'S, Dec 9, DL, 18; 1708: QUEEN'S, Jan 13, 17, 20,
    24, SH, Feb 4, DL/QUEEN, 14, QUEEN'S, 17, SH, Mar 26, DL/QUEEN, Apr 6,
    QUEEN'S, 10, 13, 20, May 1, 20; 1709: QUEEN'S, Nov 17, 21, 24, Dec 6, 20;
    1710: QUEEN'S, Jan 3, Feb 7, 23, Mar 9; 1712: QUEEN'S, Mar 22, Apr 5; 1716:
    KING'S, May 2; 1717: LIF, May 9, Jun 1; 1718: LIF, Dec 9, 11, 18, 20; 1719:
    LIF, Jan 7, 10, Feb 12, 14, 19, Apr 23; 1728: LIF, Jan 12, 15, 24, Nov 9, 12
Pepys (actor), 1777: HAY, May 1
Pepys, Barbara (spectator), 1669: LIF, Feb 18, BRIDGES, Mar 9
Pepys, Elizabeth (spectator), 1661: LIF, Aug 23, NONE, Dec 4; 1662: VERE, May
    21, LIF, Sep 30; 1663: BF, Sep 4; 1664: BRIDGES, Jun 1, BF, Sep 2, NONE, 30;
    1666: ATCOURT, Dec 17; 1667: BRIDGES, Feb 5, NONE, Mar 1, BRIDGES, Apr 8,
    NONE, Oct 31, BRIDGES, Nov 1; 1668: NURSERY, Feb 24, BRIDGES, Jun 20,
    BRI/COUR, Dec 2; 1669: BRIDGES, Jan 7, Mar 9
Pepys, Samuel (spectator), 1685: ATCOURT, Oct 10; 1698: PEPYSS, May 30
Per le porte del tormente (song), 1733: DL/HAY, Oct 20, 25, HAY, Nov 19; 1734:
    DL/HAY, Jan 4, 5, Mar 4, Apr 2
Per lei fra l'armi (song), 1755: KING'S, Mar 17
Per Pieta nell' Incostanza Delusa (song), 1745: CG, Apr 10; 1746: KING'S, Mar
    25, DL, Apr 12
Peralta, Sga (singer), 1756: SOHO, Feb 2; 1757: HAY, Jun 17, Jul 5
Perceval, Sir John, 1707: DL, Feb 1; 1709: QUEEN'S, Jan 19, Sep 15; 1713: DL,
    Apr 14, May 7
Perceval, Philip, 1707: DL, Feb 1
Percey (boxkeeper), 1772: DL, Jun 9; 1774: DL, May 27; 1775: DL, Jan 20, May
    18; 1776: DL, Jan 19, Jun 10; 1777: DL, Jun 4; 1778: DL, May 26; 1779: DL,
    Jun 1; 1780: DL, May 25; 1781: DL, May 26; 1782: DL, May 31; 1784: DL, May
    27; 1785: DL, May 26; 1786: DL, Jun 1; 1787: DL, Jun 7; 1788: DL, Jun 11;
    1789: DL, Jun 11; 1790: DL, Jun 4; 1791: DL, May 28; 1792: DLKING'S, Jun 14;
    1793: DL, Jun 5; 1795: DL, May 30; 1796: DL, Jun 14; 1797: DL, Jun 14; 1798:
    DL, Jun 15; 1799: DL, Jul 4; 1800: DL, Jun 17
Percey, Miss (actor), 1778: HAY, Dec 28
Percival, Helena (spectator), 1679: BF, Sep 3
Percival, Susannah (actor), 1681: DL, Oct 0; 1682: DL, Mar 0; 1683: DG, May 31,
    Jul 0, DL, Dec 0; 1684: DL, Mar 0, Apr 0, NONE, Aug 0, DLORDG, 0; 1685:
    DLORDG, Jan 20, DG, Jul 0, DL, Aug 0; 1686: DL, Jan 0, DG, Mar 4, DL, Apr 0
Percival, Thomas (actor), 1672: DG, Jan 31; 1674: DG, Nov 9; 1675: NONE, Sep 0;
    1676: DG, May 25, Jul 3, 25, Aug 0, Dec 0; 1677: DG, Feb 12, Mar 24, May 31,
    Jun 0, Jul 0, Sep 0; 1678: DG, Jan 0, May 28; 1679: DG, Apr 0, May 0, Oct 0;
    1680: DG, Feb 0, Dec 8; 1682: DG, Jan 0, 23, Feb 9, DL, Nov 28; 1683: NONE,
    Sep 0, DL, Dec 0; 1684: DLORDG, Aug 0; 1685: DLORDG, Jan 20, DG, Jul 0, DL,
    Aug 0; 1686: DL, Jan 0, DG, Mar 4; 1693: BF, Aug 31
Percy St, 1777: CG, Apr 16; 1778: CG, Apr 24
Percy. See More, Hannah.
Percy, Jeremiah (real estate), 1766: DL, Oct 17
Percy, John (composer), 1785: CG, Apr 6; 1791: CG, Jun 3; 1793: KING/HAY, Feb
    20, DL, May 27
Perdona Amato Bene (song), 1749: KING'S, Mar 21
Pere de Famille, Le. See Diderot, Denis.
Peretti, Niccolo (singer), 1762: CG, Feb 2, HAY, Apr 22, CG, Nov 15; 1763: CG,
    Jan 24, Feb 24, May 10, Oct 3, KING'S, Nov 26, CG, Dec 12, 29; 1764: KING'S,
    Feb 21, Apr 5, CG, May 10; 1776: KING'S, Feb 29
Perez (Peris), Admiral (spectator), 1738: CG, Apr 8; 1739: DL, Sep 14
Perez, Davide (composer), 1754: KING'S, Feb 28; 1755: KING'S, Mar 17, Apr 12,
    26, May 20, Nov 29; 1758: KING'S, Jan 31, Apr 6, 18; 1759: KING'S, Apr 21,
    Dec 15; 1760: KING'S, Mar 1; 1761: KING'S, Mar 14; 1764: KING'S, Feb 21, Mar
    29

--Arminio (opera), 1760: KING'S, Mar 1, 8, 10, 15, 22, 29, Apr 12, 19
--Didone Abbandonata, La (opera), 1761: KING'S, Mar 14, 28, Apr 4, 11, 18, 25,
  May 2, 16, 23, 30
--Farnace (opera), 1759: KING'S, Apr 21, 24, 28, May 1, 5, 8, 12, 15, 19, 26,
  29, 31, Jun 4, 9, 16, 22, MARLY, Aug 16, KING'S, Dec 15, 22, 29; 1760:
  KING'S, Jan 5, Mar 3, 10, 24
--Senocrita (opera), 1764: KING'S, Feb 21, 25, 28, Mar 3, 10, 27
Perez, Hag Abdelcader (Moroccan ambassador), 1724: HAY, Jan 16, DL, 31, Feb 7,
  May 22
Perez, Sga (dancer), 1788: KING'S, May 22
Perfect History of the Creation of the World, The (puppetry), 1726: BFY, Aug 26
Perfidious Brother, The. See Theobald, Lewis; Gibson Jr.
Pergolesi, Giovanbattista (composer), 1742: KING'S, Apr 20; 1744: HIC, May 16;
  1750: KING'S, Mar 27; 1753: KING'S, Apr 30; 1754: CG, Jan 18; 1755: HAY, Jan
  29, KING'S, Mar 17; 1758: DL, Mar 10, MARLY, Jun 8; 1759: HAY, Jan 12, CG,
  May 4, MARLY, Jul 26; 1760: MARLY, Jun 3; 1761: HAY, Jul 14; 1763: KING'S,
  Mar 24; 1770: KING'S, Mar 8, MARLY, Jun 16, Aug 7; 1771: KING'S, Feb 28, DL,
  Apr 12; 1772: CG, Mar 27, Apr 8; 1773: HAY, Mar 17; 1776: CG, Mar 6; 1789:
  DL, Mar 25; 1783: CG, Feb 14, 17; 1793: CG, Mar 20; 1796: CG, Nov 5
--Olimpiade, L' (opera), 1742: KING'S, Apr 20
--Serva Padrona, La; or, The Servant Mistress (opera), 1750: KING'S, Mar 27;
  1755: HAY, Jan 29, Feb 7; 1758: MARLY, Jun 8, 10, 13, 14, 15, 17, 20, 21, 22,
  23, 24, 26, 27, 28, 30, Jul 1, 3, 4, 5, 6, 7, 8, 10, 11, 12, 13, 15, 17, 18,
  19, 20, 21, 22, 24, 25, 28, 29, Aug 2, 4, 7, 10, 11, 14, 16, 17, 21, 22, 25,
  28, 29, 30, Sep 2, 4, 5, 6, 7, 8, 9, 11, 13, 14, 15, 16, 18, 19; 1759: HAY,
  Jan 12, Mar 29, Apr 2, 5, MARLY, 16, 17, May 19, 21, 22, 23, 24, 25, 26, 28,
  29, Jun 4, 5, 6, 7, 8, 19, 20, 22, 25, 29, Jul 3, 5, 7, 10, 12, 14, 17, 19,
  21, 24, Aug 16; 1760: MARLY, Jun 3, 4, 5, 6, 7, 9, 10, 11, 12, 13, 14, 16,
  17, Jul 9, 19, 24, 25, 26, 28, 29, 30, Aug 11, 13, 14, 15, 16, 20; 1761: HAY,
  Apr 29, Jul 14, 15, 16, 17, 18, 20, 22, 23, 24, 25, Aug 1, 4, 6, 8, 11, 12,
  25, 27, 29; 1763: KING'S, Mar 24, Apr 21, May 9; 1770: RANELAGH, May 28,
  MARLY, Jun 16, 19, 23, 26, 30, Jul 3, 5, 7, 10, 12, 14, 24, 31, Aug 7, 14,
  16, 18, 23, 25, Sep 4, 6, 11, 15, 18, 20; 1771: DL, Apr 12, MARLY, May 23,
  Jun 4, 6, 11, 13, 18, 20, 25, Jul 18, 23, 25, 30, Aug 1, 8, Sep 3; 1772:
  MARLY, Aug 20, 25; 1773: MARLY, Jul 22, 27, Aug 12, Sep 16; 1774: MARLY, Jul
  23, 28, Aug 1, 11, 16, 17, 31, Sep 5, 7, 13; 1776: KING'S, Apr 23, MARLY, May
  23, 25, 30; 1783: CG, Feb 14
--Strattaggemma, La; or, The Stratagem (burletta), 1759: MARLY, Jul 26, 27, 28,
  30, 31, Aug 1, 2, 3, 4, 6, 7, 8, 9, 10, 11, 13, 14, 15, 17, 18, 20, 21, 22,
  23, 24, 25, 27, 28, 29, 30, 31, Sep 1, 3, 5, 6, 7, 8, 10, 11, 12, 13; 1760:
  MARLY, Jun 18, 19, 20, 21, 23, 24, 27, Jul 2, 3, 4, 5, 7, 8, 31, Aug 1, 2,
  25, 26
--Studente a la Moda, Lo (opera), 1754: CG, Jan 15, 18, 21, 26, Feb 6
Periander. See Tracy, John.
Pericles, Prince of Tyre. See Shakespeare, William.
Perico, Carlo, 1770: GRP, Dec 10
Perignon, Mme Gervais (dancer), 1786: KING'S, Dec 23; 1787: KING'S, Jan 6, 20,
  Feb 13, Mar 8, 22, May 19, Jun 14
Perin (Perrine, Perune, Peryng), Anne (actor), 1691: DL, Mar 0; 1694: DL, Sep
  0; 1695: LIF, Dec 0; 1696: LIF, Mar 0, Jun 0, Oct 0, Nov 14; 1697: LIF, Jun
  0; 1698: LIF, Mar 0
Perin, Carey (actor), 1674: LIF, Mar 0; 1677: DL, Mar 0, 17, Jun 0; 1678: DL,
  Feb 0, Mar 0; 1681: DL, Oct 0; 1682: DL, Mar 11, Nov 28; 1683: DG, Jul 0,
  NONE, Sep 0, DL, Nov 12, Dec 0; 1685: DLORDG, Jan 20; 1686: DG, Mar 4; 1693:
  DL, Feb 0
Perin, John (actor), 1680: BF, Aug 31
Perjured Husband, The. See Centlivre, Susannah.
Perjured Love, The; or, The Broken Heart (play, anon), 1732: DL, Nov 17
Perjured Nun, The. See Brewer, Anthony.
Perjured Prince, The; or, The Martyred General (droll), 1728: BFB, Aug 24;
  1732: BFB, Aug 23
Perjuror, The. See Bullock, Christopher.
Perkin Warbeck. See Ford, John.
Perkins (actor), 1735: TC, May 28, LIF, Aug 22
Perkins (actor), 1756: DL, May 5; 1770: HAY, Dec 14; 1771: HAY, Apr 20
Perolini (singer), 1756: KING'S, Mar 6, Apr 5
Perolla and Izadora. See Cibber, Colley.
Perplexed Couple, The. See Molloy, Charles.
Perplexed Husband, The (pantomime), 1748: CG, Apr 20
Perplexed Lovers, The. See Centlivre, Susannah.
Perplexities, The. See Hull, Thomas.
Perrin, Pierre, 1674: DL, Mar 30

--Ariadne; or, The Marriage of Bacchus, 1674: NONE, Jan 5, DL, Mar 30
Perrott (coal merchant), 1790: DL, Nov 3
Perrott, Margaret Jemima, Lady (actor), 1797: HAY, Sep 18; 1798: HAY, Apr 23;
  1799: HAY, Jan 28; 1800: HAY, Feb 3
Perrott, Sir Richard (baronet), 1797: HAY, Sep 18; 1798: HAY, Apr 23; 1799:
  HAY, Jan 28
Perry (actor), 1740: CG, Oct 10; 1741: CG, Jan 5, Feb 24, Dec 9; 1744: CG, Dec
  13
Perry (gallery office keeper), 1795: DL, Jun 5; 1796: DL, Jun 15; 1797: DL, Jun
  13; 1798: DL, Jun 16; 1799: DL, Jul 3; 1800: DL, Jun 13
Perry (musician), 1734: DL/HAY, Mar 2, HAY, Apr 3
Perry (singer), 1783: CG, May 6
Perry, Christopher (actor), 1741: CG, Dec 9; 1746: JS, Oct 2, NWMF, 6
Perry, James (actor), 1758: DL, Jun 22, Oct 17, 30, CG, Nov 1, 14, DL, Dec 18;
  1759: DL, Jan 3, CG, Feb 20, DL, 26, CG, Mar 13, 20, 27, Apr 7, May 1, DL,
  11, CG, 11, DL, 14, 15, 18, CG, Sep 28, Oct 5, DL, 12, CG, Nov 5, DL, 10, 27,
  CG, 28, DL, Dec 1, CG, 10, 12, DL, 28; 1760: CG, Jan 12, 31, Mar 6, 25, Apr
  8, May 14, Sep 22, Oct 2, 10, Dec 6; 1761: CG, Jan 28, Mar 3, 24, 25, 26, May
  5, Sep 14, 25, Oct 5, 13, 31, Nov 4, Dec 11, 28; 1762: CG, Jan 12, Mar 23,
  29, Apr 13, 20, 24, 27, 29, May 7, 14, 21, Sep 22, 24, 27, Oct 2, 4, 6, 9,
  13, 14, 25, Nov 3, 15, 30, Dec 4; 1763: CG, Feb 14, Apr 15, 25, May 9, 11,
  14, Sep 21, 23, 26, 30, Oct 7, 10, 26, Nov 4, 26, Dec 9, 26; 1764: CG, Jan
  17, Feb 17, Mar 29, May 9, 15, 18, Sep 19, 21, 24, 26, Oct 5, 8, 15, Nov 1,
  3, 5, 15, 16; 1765: CG, Jan 21, Mar 26, Apr 19, 24, May 2, 3, 13, Sep 18, 20,
  30, Oct 2, 3, 5, 7, 8, 15, 16, 22, 23, 26, Nov 15, 21, 22, 27, Dec 10, 20;
  1766: CG, Jan 31, Mar 3, Apr 15, 29, May 3, Sep 26, Oct 1, 6, 8, 15, 21, 22,
  25, 30, Nov 4, 14, 18, 27; 1767: CG, Jan 26, Feb 14, 28, Mar 2, 21, 23, Apr
  24, 25, May 12, 13, 15, 26, 27, Sep 14, 16, 17, 18, 21, 22, 23, 25, Oct 16,
  26, 29, 30, Nov 4, 7, 18, 20, 23, Dec 8, 28; 1768: CG, Jan 9, 27, Feb 5, 25,
  Mar 17, Apr 9, 20, 25, 27, May 4, 13, 23, Sep 19, 20, 22, 26, 28, Oct 5, 7,
  17, 22, 24, 25, 26, Nov 4, 9, 24; 1769: CG, Jan 2, Feb 21, 25, Mar 13, 29,
  Apr 6, 14, 17, 19, May 3, 5, 16, 22, 23, 25, Sep 22, 25, 27, 29, Oct 4, 6, 7,
  18, 24, Nov 1, 4, 10, 17, Dec 1, 2, 19, 29; 1770: CG, Jan 3, 11, 19, Feb 3,
  5, 16, 22, Mar 3, 5, 22, 24, 29, 31, May 7, 9, 10, 12, Oct 1, 5, 8, 11, 12,
  16, 19, 23, 25, 26, Nov 5, 14, 29, 30, Dec 3, 6; 1771: CG, Feb 2, Mar 12, Apr
  5, 9, 20, 23, 29, 30, May 1, 4, 6, 30, Sep 25, 30, Oct 2, 25; 1772: CG, Feb
  19, 20, 24, Mar 2, 7, 14, 21, 24, 30, Apr 7, 11, 21, May 9, 12, 29, Oct 5,
  14, 17, 23, 24, 29, Nov 2, 4, 6, 17, Dec 5, 14; 1773: CG, Jan 16, Feb 6, 10,
  23, Mar 22, 30, Apr 16, 19, May 4, 7, 10, 14, 17, 20, 28; 1774: CG, May 24
Perry, Mrs (actor), 1766: CG, Nov 5; 1770: CG, Apr 25, Dec 26, 28; 1771: CG,
  Jan 21; 1775: CG, May 11
Perseo. See Sacchini, Antonio Maria Gasparo.
Perseus and Andromeda. See Theobald, Lewis.
Perseval. See Percival.
Perseverance. See Oulton, Walley Chamberlain.
Persia, King of, 1703: DL, Apr 19
Persian Ambassadors, 1781: CG, May 7, 12, DL, 22
Persian Dance (dance), 1774: KING'S, Jan 29
Persian Princess, The. See Theobald, Lewis.
Persius, 1685: BF, Aug 26
Pert Country Maid (dance), 1781: KING'S, Jan 13, 16, 23, 29, Feb 10, Mar 8, 15,
  Apr 24
Pertici, Caterina (singer), 1748: KING'S, Nov 8
Pertici, Pietro (singer), 1748: KING'S, Nov 8
Peruvian, The (Fair Peruvian, The) (opera, anon), 1786: CG, Mar 16, 18, 20, 21,
  23, 27, 28
Pervil, Thomas (auctioneer), 1757: CG, Apr 26; 1758: CG, Mar 13
Pervil, Young (actor), 1712: SML, Jun 4, 11, 18
Pervil's Auction House, 1760: CG, Apr 22
Pervill (boxkeeper), 1710: DL, May 18
Peryng, Mrs. See Perrin, Anne.
Pescatore, Leonardo (composer), 1746: DT, Mar 14
--Forza de l'Amore, La (musical), 1746: DT, Mar 14
Pescatrici, La. See Bertoni, Fernando Giuseppe.
Pescetti, Giovanni Battista (composer), 1737: KING'S, Feb 12; 1738: KING'S, Jan
  28; 1739: CG, Mar 10, HAY, Dec 1; 1740: HAY, May 10; 1741: HIC, Apr 24,
  KING'S, Oct 31; 1742: KING'S, Apr 20; 1754: KING'S, Feb 28
--Angelica and Medoro (opera), 1739: CG, Mar 10, 17, 24, Apr 11, May 10
--Busiri, Overo il Trionfo D'Amore (opera), 1740: HAY, May 10, 13, 17, 20
--Conquista del Vello D'Oro, La (opera), 1738: KING'S, Jan 28, 31, Feb 4, 7,
  14, 18, 21, May 23
--Demetrius (opera), 1737: KING'S, Feb 12, 15, 19, 22, 26, Mar 5, 8, 12, 15,

19, 22, 26, 29, Apr 2
--Diana and Endymion (musical), 1739: HAY, Dec 1, 4, 8, 11
Peter I, Czar, 1698: YB, Feb 16
Peterborough, Dean of. See Freeman, S.
Peters (actor), 1729: FLR, Nov 29, Dec 1, HAY, 18; 1736: DL, Oct 5, Dec 4, 20;
    1737: DL, Feb 10, Apr 19, BF, Aug 23, SF, Sep 7, DL, Oct 28; 1748: BFSY, Aug
    24; 1749: BFY, Aug 23
Peters (actor), 1772: DL, Dec 16
Peters, Hugh (chaplain), 1668: BRI/COUR, Dec 2
Peters, Rev Matthew William (scene designer), 1785: CG, Dec 20
Peters, Miss (actor), 1782: HAY, May 6
Peters, Mrs (actor), 1729: FLR, Nov 29, Dec 1; 1748: BFLYY, Aug 24, SFLYYW, Sep
    7, BHB, Oct 1; 1749: BFC, Aug 23, BF/SFP, Sep 7
Peterson (actor), 1730: GF, Oct 12, 27, Nov 5, 30, Dec 4, 30; 1731: HAY, Feb
    17, Mar 12, 24, May 12, SFGT, Sep 8; 1740: GF, Nov 27, 28, Dec 4, 5, 6, 8,
    10, 11; 1741: GF, Jan 15, 20, Feb 5, 10, 14, Mar 3, 7, 16, Apr 6, 27, TC, Aug
    4, GF, Sep 14, SF, 14, GF, 16, 18, 25, 28, Oct 2, 7, 9, 16, 19, 28, Nov 4, 9,
    27, 30, Dec 9, 26, 29; 1742: GF, Jan 5, 18, 26, 27, Feb 3, Mar 27, Apr 1, 6,
    May 19, 24, SOU, Sep 27, JS, Nov 9, LIF, 29, Dec 1, 3, 6, 13, 27, 28, 30;
    1743: LIF, Jan 10, 14, 21, Feb 2, 9, 14, 17, SOU, 18, LIF, Mar 17, 24, Apr 4,
    5, HAY, 14; 1748: BFSY, Aug 24
Peterson, Mrs (actor), 1735: YB, Mar 21; 1741: GF, Apr 6
Pether (beneficiary), 1736: CG, May 13
Petit (actor), 1779: HAY, Dec 27
Petit (house servant), 1758: DL, Apr 27
Petit (musician), 1732: LIF, Mar 10, May 10; 1733: HIC, Apr 27, TC, Jul 30;
    1736: HAY, Feb 20
Petit (tailor), 1772: DL, Dec 2
Petit Savoyard (dance), 1762: DL, May 12
Petit Scaramouche (dance), 1742: DL, Feb 1, 3, 4
Petit, Mme (dancer), 1751: CG, Dec 4; 1752: CG, Jan 16, Apr 25; 1756: CG, May
    19; 1757: DL, Oct 29; 1758: DL, Oct 20; 1759: DL, May 15
Petite Bergere (dance), 1760: CG, Apr 23; 1761: CG, Apr 22; 1762: CG, Apr 28;
    1763: CG, Apr 29
Petits Dances (dance), 1705: DL, Dec 17
Petits Riens (dance), 1781: KING'S, Dec 11, 20; 1782: KING'S, Jan 1, 29, 31,
    Feb 5, 21
Petre, Miss (actor), 1728: HAY, Nov 8; 1729: HAY, Apr 30, May 1
Petrie (Petreo, Petro) (dancer), 1760: HAY, Jun 2; 1764: CG, Jan 14; 1766: CG,
    Nov 18; 1767: CG, Apr 27, Oct 17; 1769: CG, Nov 4; 1772: CG, May 1; 1773: CG,
    Apr 24, KING'S, Oct 23
Petrosellini, Giuseppe (librettist), 1798: KING'S, Mar 10
Petry (musician), 1733: DL, Dec 31
Petticoat Plotter, The. See Hamilton, Newburgh.
Pettit (actor), 1729: HAY, Jan 25
Petto (musician), 1703: YB, Jan 28
Pettour (dancer), 1703: DL, Jan 2
Petty, Mrs (actor), 1676: DG, Dec 0; 1681: DG, Nov 0, DG/IT, 22; 1682: DG, Jan
    23, Mar 0; 1683: DG, May 31
Petty's Playhouse, 1735: TC, Aug 4; 1736: TCP, Aug 4
Pewter Platter (public house), 1760: HAY, Aug 15
Phaedra and Hippolytus. See Smith, Edmund.
Phaeton. See Paradies, Domenico.
Phaeton; or, The Fatal Divorce. See Gildon, Charles.
Pharnaces. See Bononcini, Giovanni; Bate, Henry.
Pharo Table, The. See O'Keeffe, John.
Phebe (beneficiary), 1755: DL, Apr 29
Phebe. See Coffey, Charles.
Phebe, Mrs (actor), 1736: YB, Apr 26
Phelimoguffinocarilocarneymacframe's Description of a Man of War and a Sea
    Fight (entertainment), 1782: HAY, Mar 21
Phenix. See Phoenix.
Phenix, Le. See Delosne de Monchesney.
Philadelphia, College of, 1763: DL, Apr 27
Philantropos (author), 1751: CG, Nov 19
Philaster. See Fletcher, John.
Philip of Macedon. See Lewis, David.
Philipps, Thomas (actor), 1796: CG, May 10, Oct 6, 10, 18, 20, 24, Nov 24, Dec
    19; 1797: CG, Jan 3, 25, Feb 10, 18, Mar 6, HAY, Jul 3, 6, Aug 14, Sep 4;
    1798: CG, May 23
Philips, Ambrose, 1712: DL, Mar 17; 1722: DL, Feb 19; 1723: DL, Feb 15
--Briton, The, 1722: DL, Feb 19, 20, 22, 24, 26, 27, Mar 1, 13, Apr 3; 1744:

657

JS, Apr 25
--Distressed Mother, The, 1712: DL, Mar 17, 18, 20, 22, 24, 25, 27, 29, Sep 27,
  Oct 18, Nov 25, Dec 22; 1713: DL, Feb 10, Apr 13, Oct 24; 1714: DL, Apr 1;
  1715: DL, Feb 19, Mar 7, May 9, Dec 2; 1716: DL, Feb 16, Oct 23; 1717: DL,
  Jan 15; 1718: DL, May 20; 1719: DL, Apr 17, 25, Jun 17; 1720: DL, Apr 23;
  1721: DL, Jan 21; 1722: DL, Apr 13, Oct 18; 1723: DL, Jan 19, Mar 30, Nov 27;
  1724: DL, Jan 27, Feb 29, Oct 20, Dec 5; 1725: DL, Feb 20, Oct 26; 1726: DL,
  Jan 4, Feb 19, Apr 14; 1727: DL, Jan 16, Mar 13, Apr 14, Oct 24; 1728: DL,
  Oct 8, Nov 16, 23; 1729: DL, Jan 16, Mar 4, Apr 17, Sep 18, Nov 11, Dec 8;
  1730: DL, Nov 20; 1731: DL, Feb 3, GF, 15, 16, 25, DL, May 13, GF, Dec 7;
  1732: DL, Jun 9, Nov 7; 1733: DL, Jan 10, GF, 17; 1734: DL, Feb 8, GF, 18,
  Apr 26, Dec 12; 1735: CG/LIF, Jan 9, 10, 16, CG, Nov 13, Dec 10; 1736: CG,
  Jan 23, Feb 4, GF, 20, DL, Mar 23, CG, Oct 15, Dec 31; 1737: DL, Apr 16, CG,
  May 6, DL, 7, CG, Oct 7; 1738: CG, Jan 12, DL, Apr 22, CG, Oct 31, Dec 9;
  1739: CG, Dec 4; 1740: DL, Jan 19, CG, Feb 13, DL, Mar 15, GF, Nov 26; 1741:
  CG, Feb 17, DL, Dec 14; 1742: DL, Feb 5, CG, Nov 29, Dec 18; 1743: CG, Feb
  26, Apr 13, DL, 29; 1744: CG, Feb 23, DL, Oct 17, HAY, 20; 1745: DL, Jan 11;
  1747: CG, Mar 19, Apr 4, 7, 20, DL, 25, CG, May 1; 1748: DL, Mar 10, 15;
  1749: CG, Jan 28, 31, Feb 1, 3, 9, 11, 13, 14, 16, 24, 25, DL, Apr 5, CG, Nov
  16; 1750: CG, Jan 10, SOU, 25, CG, Feb 3, DL, 7, CG, Dec 18, 19, 20, 22;
  1751: CG, Jan 12, Feb 4, Apr 17, May 10, DL, Dec 10; 1752: DL, Apr 22; 1753:
  CG, Mar 26, Apr 30; 1754: CG, Jan 10, 12, 15, 17, 19, Feb 7, 16, 19, Mar 14,
  23, Apr 25, DL, Oct 29, 31, Nov 25; 1755: CG, Feb 4, DL, Apr 16, CG, 23;
  1756: CG, Apr 6; 1757: CG, Jan 5, 7, DL, Nov 15, CG, Dec 9, DL, 14; 1760: DL,
  May 3; 1762: CG, Apr 3; 1764: DL, May 3, 24, Nov 23, Dec 8, 11, 17, 22, 29;
  1765: DL, Feb 9, 19, Apr 25, Nov 15, 16, 30, Dec 18; 1766: DL, Feb 10; 1767:
  DL, May 4, CG, Oct 29, Nov 12; 1768: CG, Apr 26, Oct 7; 1769: CG, Mar 28;
  1771: HAY, Apr 4, DL, May 6; 1772: DL, Mar 21; 1775: DL, Jan 4, 7, CG, 7, 9,
  DL, 9, CG, 11, 14, 16, DL, 16, CG, 20, DL, Feb 6, CG, 6, 28, Mar 25, DL, 30,
  CG, Apr 3, DL, May 4, Oct 14, CG, 17, DL, Dec 9; 1776: DL, Mar 2, CG, May 11,
  17, Oct 2, DL, 22, Dec 2; 1777: DL, Sep 27, Dec 31; 1778: CG, Nov 18, 19, 20,
  24, Dec 23; 1779: CG, Jan 2, Mar 15, Apr 12; 1781: DL, Mar 27; 1782: CG, Mar
  14, Oct 31; 1784: CG, Feb 19; 1786: CG, Jan 31, Feb 3, 6, DL, Mar 4, 16, Dec
  6; 1787: CG, Apr 14; 1793: CG, Jan 14, Dec 20; 1794: DL, Apr 25, 26, Oct 25;
  1795: DL, Nov 13, CG, Dec 15; 1796: DL, Jan 29, CG, Dec 10, DL, 21
--Humphrey, Duke of Gloucester, 1723: DL, Feb 15, 16, 18, 19, 20, 21, 22, 23,
  25, Mar 6
Philips, J (beneficiary), 1760: HAY, Jun 2
Philips, Joan
--Pair-Royal of Coxcombs, The, 1678: NONE, Sep 0
Philips, Katherine, 1663: NONE, May 0; 1664: ATCOURT, Jan 0, LIF, Mar 8; 1668:
  ATCOURT, Feb 4; 1669: BRIDGES, Feb 15
--Horace, 1668: ATCOURT, Feb 4; 1669: BRIDGES, Jan 16, 18, 19, 20, 21, NONE,
  Feb 10, BRIDGES, 15
Philips, Mlle (dancer), 1797: CG, Nov 4
Philips, Mrs (actor), 1742: DL, Apr 20; 1743: DL, Jan 17; 1755: DL, Nov 8, 15
Phillboy (dancer), 1693: NONE, Sep 0
Phillidor, Francois Andre Danican (composer), 1754: HAY, Jan 31, SOHO, Mar 28;
  1773: DL, Nov 2; 1779: HAY, Aug 14; 1791: KING'S, May 19
--Power of Harmony, The (musical), 1754: HAY, Jan 31, SOHO, Mar 28
Phillimore (singer), 1797: DL, Dec 9; 1798: Feb 24, Dec 4, 29, 31
Phillimore, John (actor), 1776: HAY, Oct 7; 1777: DL, Dec 6; 1778: DL, Jan 24,
  Mar 31, Apr 21, May 14, 19, 23, Sep 24, 26, Oct 16, Nov 2, Dec 21, 22; 1779:
  DL, Jan 8, 16, Feb 8, Mar 15, 16, May 10, 21, Sep 18, CG, 20, DL, 23, 25, Oct
  5, 7, 30, Nov 3, Dec 13, 27, 29; 1780: DL, Jan 3, 24, 26, Apr 3, 5, 7, 17,
  26, 29, May 2, 5, 10, 16, Sep 16, 19, 21, 23, Oct 3, 5, 10, 11, 17, 19, 23,
  Nov 3, 4, 8, 9, 13, 22, 24, 27, Dec 1, 4, 6, 27; 1781: DL, Jan 2, 9, 16, Feb
  12, Mar 19, Apr 24, May 1, 15, 23, Sep 18, 20, 25, Oct 12, 16, 18, 19, 26,
  Nov 5, 10, 13; 1782: DL, Jan 3, 4, 22, Apr 6, 8, 24, 25, 27, May 3, 7, 9, 10,
  14, 18, Sep 17, 20, 24, 28, Oct 3, 5, 18, 29, 30, Nov 1, 4, 8, 16, 26, Dec
  11, 14, 26; 1783: DL, Jan 3, 10, 29, Feb 8, 12, 18, 22, Mar 6, 10, Apr 23,
  May 2, 5, 12, 16, HAY, Jun 2, DL, Sep 23, 27, 30, Oct 11, 13, 14, 17, 18, 20,
  22, 24, Nov 8, 15, 18, 20, 22, 27, Dec 2, 5, 13, 19, 22; 1784: DL, Jan 3, 7,
  10, 13, 23, Mar 6, Apr 1, 19, 24, 26, May 3, 7, 10, 14, Sep 18, 21, 23, 30,
  Oct 5, 9, 11, 12, 19, 23, 26, 27, Nov 3, 5, 9, 17, 19, 20, 22, 25, Dec 2;
  1785: DL, Jan 6, 12, 14, 19, 20, Feb 21, Mar 28, 30, Apr 1, 11, 20, 22, 25,
  26, 27, May 9, 11, 13, 26, HAY, Sep 16, DL, 20, 22, 24, 27, 29, Oct 6, 8, 15,
  17, 20, 25, 27, 31, Nov 1, 7, 8, 12, 17, 18, 21, 26, Dec 1, 3, 8, 26; 1786:
  DL, Jan 24, Feb 18, Mar 9, 25, 27, 28, Apr 4, 6, 20, May 25, Sep 16, 19, 23,
  Oct 3, 5, 7, 10, 14, 16, 19, 21, 23, 24, 25, 28, Dec 5, 13, 19, 26, 30; 1787:
  DL, Jan 4, 18, 29, Feb 7, 16, 26, Mar 8, 27, Apr 10, 13, May 7, 16, 19, 21,
  25, Jun 1, 7, 8, Sep 18, 20, 29, Oct 2, 3, 6, 9, 11, 13, 18, 24, 26, 30, Nov

3, 5, 6, 8, 10, 16, 20, 21, 24, Dec 7, 10, 26; 1788: DL, Jan 1, 2, 8, 21, 22,
31, Feb 7, Mar 3, 13, 29, Apr 8, 11, 14, 15, 19, 28, May 1, 6, 14, 21, 23,
Jun 2, 6, HAY, 10, 11, 16, 30, Jul 2, 4, 10, 24, Aug 2, 5, 9, 22, 25, 26, 27,
29, DL, Sep 13, 25, 27, 30, Oct 2, 4, 7, 9, 14, 22, 28, Nov 1, 4, 5, 6, 10,
17, 28, 29, Dec 1, 6, 9, 17, 18, 22; 1789: DL, Jan 1, 6, 7, 10, 13, 17, 19,
Feb 7, 16, 28, Mar 9, 17, 21, 23, Apr 4, 14, 21, 30, May 1, 5, 11, 22, 23,
27, 28, Jun 4, Sep 12, 15, 17, 19, 22, 24, 29, Oct 1, 3, 13, 15, 28, 31, Nov
4, 5, 7, 13, 21, 30, Dec 17, 26; 1790: DL, Feb 3, 10, 15, 23, Mar 2, 8, 22,
Apr 7, 14, 23, May 4, 7, 14, 15, 18, 27, 31, Jun 3, 4, Oct 7, 11, 14, 18, 19,
20, 21, 23, 25, 26, 27, Nov 1, 3, 4, 10, 30, Dec 1, 7, 14, 27; 1791: DL, Jan
10, 11, Mar 21, 22, 28, Apr 4, 5, 28, 29, 30, May 10, 11, 14, 20, HAY, Jun 6,
8, 13, 16, 17, DLKING'S, Sep 22, 24, 27, 29, Oct 1, 3, 15, 25, 31, Nov 1, 2,
4, 5, 9, 11, 14, 15, 16, 29, 30, Dec 12, 13; 1792: DLKING'S, Jan 6, 7, 11,
14, 21, 24, 28, 31, Feb 2, 4, 11, 14, 18, 23, 27, Mar 1, 6, 13, 17, 19, 26,
29, Apr 12, 20, 27, May 23, 31, Jun 15, DL, Sep 15, 18, 22, 25, 29, Oct 4,
11, 13, 18, 31, Nov 2, 5, 10, 15, 21, 26, 27, Dec 8, 10, 13, 15, 17, 21, 26,
27, 28, 31; 1793: DL, Jan 4, 5, 7, 16, 29, Feb 5, 9, 12, 16, 23, 26, Mar 2,
7, 9, 18, Apr 6, 18, May 7, 9, 10, 15, 17, 24, 27, Jun 3, 4; 1794: DL, Apr
21, 25, 29, May 1, 3, 16, 22, 30, Jun 6, 9, 12, 16, Sep 18, 23, 27, Oct 4,
11, 21, 27, 28, 31, Nov 5, 7, 12, 14, 15, 18, 22, 24, 29, Dec 5, 9, 12, 16,
19, 20, 30; 1795: DL, Jan 20, 22, 26, Feb 5, 6, 12, 28, Mar 3, 14, 21, Apr
16, May 1, 6, 12, 20, 22, 26, Jun 3, Oct 1, 8, 12, 15, 19, 20, 21, 22, 27,
30, Nov 2, 6, 7, 10, 11, 16, 19, 20, 26, Dec 10, 11, 18, 21, 28; 1796: DL,
Jan 7, 12, 18, 23, Feb 1, 5, 8, 13, 15, 29, Mar 12, 31, Apr 2, 9, 12, 13, 18,
25, 26, 27, 29, 30, May 9, 11, 12, 13, Jun 3, 4, 7, 13, Sep 22, 24, 29, Oct
13, 15, 19, Nov 1, 2, 5, 8, 9, 10, 17, 18, 22, 23, 26, 28, Dec 2, 5, 9, 10,
23, 26, 30; 1797: DL, Jan 7, 10, 12, 21, Mar 4, 20, Apr 3, 4, 6, 18, 24, May
3, 15, 23, 24, 31, Jun 5, 7, 12, 15, Nov 8; 1798: DL, Jan 16, Feb 1, Oct 6,
Nov 14, Dec 17; 1799: DL, Jan 19, Feb 4, Mar 2, Jul 3
Phillimore, Mrs (wardrobe keeper), 1794: DL, Sep 23; 1798: DL, Jun 13
Phillipe (actor), 1725: HAY, Mar 29
Phillips (actor), 1704: DL, Jul 7, Aug 2, 16; 1705: DL, Jun 12; 1706: DL, Apr 8
Phillips (actor), 1744: DL, Oct 11, 19, 30, Nov 2, 6; 1745: DL, Jan 16, 25, Apr
30; 1746: GF, Feb 10, May 1, DL, Aug 4, 6, 11; 1749: HAY, Feb 10; 1753: DL,
Sep 27, Oct 6, 18, 20, Nov 8, 14, 26, Dec 26; 1754: DL, Jan 7, Feb 5, Mar 14,
30, May 4, Jul 2, Oct 10, 12, 18, 23, 25, Nov 7, 11, 22; 1755: DL, Jan 22,
Apr 25, Oct 3, 13, 17, 27, 31, Nov 1, 22, Dec 5, 11; 1756: DL, Mar 16, 29,
Apr 10, 29, May 17, Sep 25, Oct 5, 19, Nov 10, 12, 15, 18, Dec 13, 27, 30;
1757: DL, Mar 7, May 2, Sep 27, 29, Oct 13, HAY, Nov 2, DL, 8, Dec 1; 1758:
DL, Jan 11, 27, Feb 4, May 2, 4, 5, 12, 16, 18, Jun 22, Sep 19, 21, 23, Oct
7, 18, Nov 1, 7, 16, Dec 16, 21, 28; 1759: DL, Jan 20, Feb 6, 12, 26, Mar 1,
13, 20, Apr 2, 7, May 11, 14, 16, Jul 12, Sep 22, 27, Oct 2, 6, 9, 11, 22,
23, 27, 30, Nov 9, 17, 22; 1760: DL, Jan 19, Mar 24, 25, Apr 17, 22, 28, 29,
May 7, 16, Jun 19, Jul 29, Sep 30, Oct 3, 15, 23, Nov 17, 26, Dec 29, 30;
1761: DL, Apr 3, 6, 17, 21, 28, May 4, 5, 7, Sep 10, 12, 14, 18, 19, 26, Oct
1, 3, 7, 10, 29, Nov 14, 18; 1762: DL, Jan 11, 23, Feb 20, Mar 20, Apr 22,
May 4, 10, 17, 19, 26, Sep 18, 21, Oct 5, 14, Nov 2, 3, 6, 10, 18, Dec 1;
1763: DL, Apr 16, 22, May 7, 31, Oct 24, Nov 2, Dec 17; 1764: DL, Jan 14, 27,
Apr 14, May 8, Sep 20, Oct 2, 18; 1765: DL, Apr 13, May 8; 1766: DL, Apr 22,
Dec 17; 1767: DL, Jan 24, May 4; 1768: MARLY, Aug 4; 1769: HAY, Feb 28
Phillips (contortionist), 1732: BF, Aug 22
Phillips (dancer), 1695: DG, Jun 25
Phillips (dancer), 1733: DL, May 24; 1734: DL, Apr 29; 1736: DL, Jan 12, CG,
23, DL, Mar 22, 23, Apr 8, 12, 15, 16, 29, 30, May 3, 4, 7, 11, 13, 18, 22,
24, 25, Jun 2, Aug 31, Sep 4, 25, 28, 30, Oct 2, 5, 12, 16, 18, 19, 21, 22,
23, 25, 29, 30, Nov 1, 2, 3, 8, 10, 13, 23, Dec 4, 9, 10, 14, 17, 20; 1737:
DL, Jan 4, 27, Feb 5, 8, 14, 18, 22, Mar 2, 4, 7, 12, 14, Apr 13, 19, 26, 29,
May 2, 4, Nov 11, 12, 14, 15; 1738: DL, Jan 24, 27, 28, Feb 3, 4, 6, 11, 14,
21, Apr 13, 14, 17, 21, 27, May 3, 5, 6, 9, 10, 11, 15, 17, 26, 27, 29, 30,
31, Sep 12, Oct 3, 5, 7, 10, 16, 21, 25, 26, 27, Nov 22, 29, 30; 1739: CG,
Aug 2, TC, 8, CG, 10, 21, BF, 27, SF, Sep 8, CG, Oct 3; 1740: TCLP, Aug 4,
BFLP, 23, SF, Sep 9, SOU, Oct 9, CG, 23, 31, Nov 7, 18, 19; 1741: DL, Oct 28,
29, 31, Nov 11, Dec 4, 19; 1742: DL, Jan 12, 23, Feb 5, 6, Apr 22, 26, 27,
28, CG, 29, DL, 30, May 1, 4, 8, GF, 10, 12, DL, 13, 15, 17, 24, 27, BFPY,
Aug 25, SF, Sep 8, SOU, 27, DL, 30; 1743: LIF, Apr 6
Phillips (dancer), 1744: CG, Feb 28, JS, Apr 25, CG, May 1; 1746: CG, Feb 18,
Jun 11, 16, 20, 27, SOU, Aug 18, SFHP, Sep 8, SOU, Oct 7, 16, 20, 27; 1747:
SOU, Jan 21, Apr 27, SF, Sep 15, 24, SOU, Oct 5; 1748: SOU, Jan 19, CG, Mar
3, 28, Apr 20, SOU, Aug 1, BFP, 24, SFP, Sep 7, SOU, 26, CG, Oct 27, Dec 26,
27; 1749: CG, Mar 11, Apr 3, 12, 17, 29, BF/SFP, Aug 23, CG, Nov 24; 1750:
SFP, Sep 7, CG, Dec 26; 1751: SF, Sep 9, 18, CG, 27, Dec 4; 1752: CG, Apr 28,
29, May 2, 4, 6, 7, 8, SFP, Sep 21, 22, CG, Oct 26, SOU, Nov 24; 1753: SFP,

Sep 18; 1754: CG, May 1, SFP, Sep 18; 1755: SOU, Jan 13, 20, SF, Sep 18;
1756: CG, Dec 17; 1757: CG, Apr 27, May 4, 12, Oct 26; 1761: CG, Jan 6; 1762:
CG, Dec 31
Phillips (prologuist), 1714: DL, Apr 27
Phillips (singer, dancer), 1770: HAY, May 21, Jun 5, DL, 7, HAY, Aug 1, 24;
1771: DL, May 15, HAY, Jun 5, CG, 6, HAY, Jul 24, Aug 19, Sep 2, CG, Nov 12,
Dec 11; 1772: CG, Jan 27, Feb 24, HAY, Mar 16, CG, Apr 20, May 2, 14, DL, 26,
CG, 28, Nov 14; 1773: DL, May 21, MARLY, Jul 15, 22, 29, Aug 12, 25, 26, 27,
Sep 3; 1775: DL, May 12; 1780: HAY, Nov 13
Phillips' Booth, 1739: TC, Aug 8, SF, Sep 8; 1748: BFP, Aug 24, SFP, Sep 7, 8,
9, 10, 12; 1749: BF/SFP, Aug 23, 24, 25, 26, 28, Sep 7, 8, 9, 11, 12, SFP,
15, SOU, 18; 1750: SFP, Sep 7, 8, 10, 12, 13; 1751: SF, Sep 9; 1752: SFP, Sep
21, 22; 1753: SFP, Sep 18, 20, 22, 24, 27; 1754: SFP, Sep 18, 19, 20, 21, 23,
24; 1756: SF, Sep 18, 20
Phillips-Lee Booth, 1742: SF, Sep 8
Phillips-Yates Booth, 1742: BFPY, Aug 25, SF, Sep 8
Phillips, Anna Maria (singer, actor), 1780: DL, Nov 11; 1781: DL, Apr 21, May
5, 7, 25, Sep 22, Oct 12, 19, 22, 27, Nov 13, Dec 13; 1782: DL, Apr 20, May
18, Oct 26, Nov 2, 5, Dec 19; 1783: DL, Jan 29, Feb 7, Mar 14, 24, Apr 22,
26, May 5, 12, 14, 20, Oct 30, Nov 18, Dec 2, 5; 1784: DL, Jan 3, 7, 31, Feb
5, 17, 24, Mar 8, 30, Apr 1, 16, 26, May 3, 21, Sep 25, Oct 19, Nov 1, 4, 8,
9, 12, 13, 16, 22, 26, Dec 18; 1785: DL, Jan 12, 17, Feb 2, 8, 11, Mar 28,
30, Apr 8, 14, 18, Mar 3, Oct 11
Phillips, Captain (beneficiary), 1725: LIF, Jan 13
Phillips, Claudius (musician), 1709: SH, Aug 25; 1710: SH, Mar 22; 1717: DL,
May 31
Phillips, Constantia (author), 1749: BFCB, Aug 23
Phillips, Edward, 1730: DL, Feb 10; 1733: LIF/CG, Apr 27, DL, May 5; 1739: DL,
Dec 31
--Britons Strike Home; or, The Sailors' Rehearsal (farce), 1739: DL, Dec 31;
1740: BFFPT, Aug 23; 1779: DL, Mar 27
--Chambermaid, The, 1730: DL, Feb 10
--Devil in a Wood, The; or Harlequin Skeleton (farce), 1752: NWLS, Nov 16
--Livery Rake, The; or, The Intriguing Servant (or, The Disappointed Country
Lass) (ballad opera), 1733: DL, May 5, Oct 8, DL/HAY, 15, 17; 1734: DL, Jan
8, 9, 10, 14; 1735: DL, Apr 29; 1736: DL, May 25
--Mock Lawyer, The, 1733: CG/LIF, Apr 26, LIF/CG, 27, CG, Oct 18, 19, Dec 11,
12, 13, 15, 17, 19, 28, 31; 1734: CG, Jan 4, 16, 23, Feb 20, Apr 22, 27, May
2, 6, 10, 13; 1735: YB, Mar 19, CG, May 8, CG/LIF, 26; 1736: CG, Mar 15, Apr
5; 1737: CG, Mar 10, 14, May 10, 12, 20, Oct 10, 12; 1738: CG, Apr 5, May 8,
Oct 2; 1740: DL, Mar 20
--Royal Chace, The; or, Merlin's Cave (Harlequin Skeleton) (pantomime), 1736:
CG, Jan 23, 24, 26, 27, 28, 29, 31, Feb 2, 3, 4, 5, 6, 7, 9, 10, 11, 12, 13,
14, 16, 17, 18, 20, 21, 27, 28, Mar 1, 4, 5, 13, Apr 3, 26, Jun 3, 8; 1737:
CG, Feb 11, 14, 15, 17, 18, 21, 24, 26, 28, Mar 1, 3, 5, 8, 29, Apr 16, May
26; 1738: CG, Feb 13, 16, 18, 20, 21, 23, 27, 28, Mar 4, 6, 11, Apr 13, 26,
May 4, Oct 28, 30, 31, Nov 4, 6, 7, 10, 15, 17, Dec 7, 28, 29; 1739: CG, Jan
1, 4, 11, 12, 13, Feb 12, 19, 20, 24, 26, 27, Mar 1, 3, 29, Apr 5, 12, Jun 1,
5, BFHCL, Aug 23; 1741: CG, Jan 21, 22, 23, 24, 26, 31, Feb 2, 3, 6, 7, 9,
17, 19, 23, 26, Mar 5, 19, Apr 1, Oct 15, 16, 17, 19, 20, 29, 31, Nov 5, 24,
Dec 23, 30; 1743: CG, Feb 4, 7, 9, 10, 11, 21, 24, 28, Mar 3, 10, Apr 8, 11,
13, 18, May 20, 23, Dec 20, 21, 22, 23, 27, 28, 29, 30, 31; 1744: CG, Jan 2,
5, 6, 9, 13, 28, Feb 2, 3, 6, 7, 13, 28, Mar 15, 26, Apr 3, 6, 10, 13, 26,
28, May 16, 25, Oct 22, 26, 27, 29, Nov 5, 6, 7, 10, 13, 15, Dec 18, 20, 26;
1745: CG, Jan 10, 12, 22, 24, Mar 7, 19, Oct 29, 30, Nov 1, 4, 5, 7, 13, 21;
1746: CG, Jan 1, 2, 3, 10, 11, 13, 15, 17, 21, Feb 4, 5, 8, Mar 11, Apr 7,
10, 26, Jun 9, Dec 19, 22, 26, 27; 1747: CG, Jan 14, Mar 2, Dec 26, 28, 29;
1748: CG, Jan 7, 8, 12, 16, 25, 27, 29, Feb 1, 5, 10, 13, 20, 23, 27, Nov 16,
18, 19, 21, 22, 25, 26, 29, 30, Dec 1, 26, 27; 1749: CG, Jan 4, 7, 9, 12, 24,
Mar 11, 16, 18, Oct 24, 25, 27, Nov 3, 4, 11, 21, 22; 1750: CG, Dec 20, 21,
27, 28; 1751: CG, Jan 5, 7, 10, 18, 23, Feb 7, 13, Mar 19, Apr 25, Oct 28,
29, 30, 31, Nov 6, 7, 9; 1752: CG, Jan 3, 9, 16, Feb 8, Apr 15, Oct 18, 19,
23, 25, Dec 28; 1753: CG, Jan 2, 4, 10, 12, Dec 15, 22, 27, 29; 1754: CG, Jan
8, 10, 12, 15, 19, Feb 5, 7, 14, 19, Mar 2, 7, 14, Apr 15, Nov 5, 6, 11, 14,
21, 25, 28, 29, 30, Dec 26, 27, 31; 1755: CG, Jan 1, 22, 24, 27, May 2, Oct
22, 23, 25, 28, 29, 31, Nov 4, 6, 10, 13, 28, 29, Dec 1, 4, 26, 27, 29, 30;
1756: CG, Jan 21, Mar 20, May 19, 21, Oct 21, 23, 27, 30, Nov 3, 4, 6, 9, 10,
12, 13, 15, 20, 26, Dec 18, 22, 28, 31; 1757: CG, Oct 12, 14, 26, 28, Nov 10,
14, 19, 23; 1758: CG, Jan 18, Apr 8, Oct 6, 13, 20, 24, 28, 31, Nov 4, 18,
25, 28, Dec 15, 26, 30; 1759: CG, Jan 5, Feb 23, Nov 5; 1760: CG, Oct 15, 16,
17, 18, 25; 1765: CG, Oct 28, 29, 30, 31, Nov 1, 11, 13, 14, 18, 19, 22, 23,
25, 27, 28, Dec 3, 4, 5, 7, 10, 12, 14, 16, 18, 26, 27, 28; 1766: CG, Apr 24,

May 12, Oct 25, 28, 30, Nov 4, 8; 1767: CG, Oct 17, 19, 20, 23, 24, 26, 29,
30, Nov 19, Dec 1, 26, 30; 1768: CG, Jan 4, Feb 15, 22, Mar 14, Apr 11, May
3, 12, 27, Jun 1, Sep 24, 26, Oct 3, 8; 1769: CG, Jan 6, 31, Feb 3, 4, 6, 9,
13, 14, 20, 21, 25, 28, Mar 4, 7, 27, Apr 6, 20, 29, May 4, 11, 22, 24, Oct
23, 27, 30, Nov 3, Dec 21; 1770: CG, Nov 12, 19, 21, Dec 3, 13, 17, 19; 1771:
CG, Apr 18; 1772: CG, Jan 31, Feb 1, 3, 4, 5, 6, 7, 8, 17, 18, 19, 20, 21,
24, Mar 23, Nov 2, 30, Dec 1, 4; 1777: CG, Apr 23, 24, May 1, 3, 8, 16, 26,
Oct 1, 3, 6, 8; 1781: CG, May 7, 14, 21; 1783: CG, Apr 22, May 19, 23; 1785:
HAMM, Jul 25; 1788: CG, May 12, 16; 1793: DL, Apr 20; 1798: CG, Jun 2
--Stage Mutineers, The; or, A Playhouse To Be Let (ballad opera), 1733: CG, Jul
27, 31, Aug 2, 3, 7, 9, 10, 14, 16, 17, 20, 21; 1735: LIF, Jul 23, 25, Aug 29
Phillips, Lucy (actor), 1786: HAMM, Jun 28, 30, Jul 5, 7, 10, 19, 26
Phillips, Master (dancer), 1751: SF, Sep 9, 18
Phillips, Miss (actor), 1755: CG, Dec 15; 1756: CG, Feb 5, May 3
Phillips, Miss (dancer), 1792: DL, Nov 21, Dec 27; 1793: DL, Jun 7, 10; 1794:
DL, May 16, Oct 27, Dec 20, 23; 1795: DL, Feb 12, Jun 1
Phillips, Mr and Mrs (beneficiaries), 1748: SOU, Aug 1
Phillips, Mrs (actor), 1733: HAY, Apr 18
Phillips, Mrs (actor, singer), 1739: BFH, Aug 23, BF, 27, SF, Sep 8; 1740:
TCLP, Aug 4, BFLP, 23, BFHC, 23, SF, Sep 9, SOU, Oct 9; 1741: GF, May 6, BFH,
Aug 22, DL, Oct 31, Nov 11, 12; 1742: DL, Mar 20, Apr 26, BFPY, Aug 25, DL,
Sep 11, SOU, 21, 27; 1743: SOU, Mar 30; 1745: GF, Oct 28, 31, Nov 4, 6, 11,
18, 19, 22, 23, 26, GF, 26, 27, 28, 29, Dec 2, 4, 11, 16, 23, CG, 27,
GF, 27, 28, 30; 1746: GF, Jan 2, 3, 13, 15, 17, 20, 27, 31, Feb 3, 10, 18,
Mar 15, 20, May 1, SFHP, Sep 8, SOU, 25, Oct 7, 16, 20; 1747: DL, Jan 24, SF,
Sep 15, 24; 1748: SOU, Aug 1, BFP, 24, SFP, Sep 7, SOU, 26, Oct 10, CG, Nov
12, 19, 21; 1749: CG, Jan 3, 26, Apr 12, BF/SFP, Aug 23; 1750: SOU, Jan 25,
SFP, Sep 7; 1752: CG, Oct 26; 1755: DL, Oct 8
Phillips, Mrs (lodging householder), 1746: GF, Feb 10
Phillips, Mrs (prologuist), 1706: QUEEN'S, Apr 6
Phillips, R (dancer), 1792: DL, Dec 27
Phillips, R (publisher), 1799: DL, Apr 23, HAY, Jun 15
Phillips, Thomas (scene painter), 1793: CG, Oct 2, Dec 19; 1794: CG, Sep 22,
Nov 17, Dec 26; 1795: CG, Apr 6, DL, Jun 5, CG, Dec 21; 1796: CG, Mar 15, Apr
9, Oct 24, 29, Nov 5, Dec 19; 1797: CG, Feb 18, Mar 16, Oct 2, Nov 24, Dec
26; 1798: CG, Feb 12, Mar 31, Apr 9, May 28, Oct 15, Nov 12, Dec 11; 1799:
CG, Jan 29, Apr 19, Sep 23, Nov 14, Dec 23; 1800: CG, Jan 16, May 1
Phillips, Thomas, 1734: DL/HAY, Mar 21; 1736: HAY, May 26
--Love and Glory, 1733: DL/HAY, Nov 9; 1734: DL/HAY, Mar 21, 28, DL, Apr 29
--Rival Captains, The; or, The Impostor Unmasked, 1736: HAY, May 26, 31, Jun 1,
2, 11, 17, 21, Jul 2
Phillips, William, 1722: LIF, Feb 13; 1724: LIF, Apr 14
--Belisarius, 1724: LIF, Apr 14, 15, 16, 17, 18, 20, Nov 24; 1725: LIF, Jan 28;
1758: DL, Jan 11
--Hibernia Freed, 1722: LIF, Feb 13, 15, 17, 19, 20, 22, Mar 17
--Revengeful Queen, The, 1698: DL, Jun 0
Phillips' Theatre, 1748: SOU, Sep 26
Phillpot, Mrs (actor), 1731: SF/BFMMO, Aug 26
Philoclea. See Morgan, MacNamara.
Philodamus. See Bentley, Dr Richard.
Philosophe Marie, Le. See Destouches.
Philosophic Contracted Contractors (beneficiaries), 1745: GF, Feb 4
Philotas. See Frowde, Philip.
Phipps (actor), 1720: BFBL, Aug 23; 1721: LIF, Oct 21, 26, Nov 13, 25, 29, Dec
12, 18; 1722: LIF, Feb 2, Mar 15, 29, May 7, Jun 1, 13, Sep 29, Oct 1, 6, 18,
19, 20, 24, 30, 31, Nov 13, 17, Dec 14, HAY, 17, LIF, 21; 1723: LIF, Jan 11,
May 18, Jun 6
Phipps, Henry (prologuist), 1785: DL, Jan 27
Phiz Oratory (entertainment), 1731: LG, Mar 8, CRT, 10
Phlum, Mme (singer), 1791: KING'S, May 12
Phoebe at Court. See Arne, Dr Thomas A.
Phoebe. See Coffey, Charles, Phebe.
Phoebus sinketh in the West (song), 1757: HAY, Oct 21
Phoenix (actor), 1736: HAY, Apr 29; 1743: BFGA, Aug 23; 1744: MF, Jun 7; 1748:
BFLYY, Aug 24, SFLYYW, Sep 7, BHB, Oct 1, NWC, Dec 29; 1758: DL, Jun 22
Phoenix Court, 1794: HAY, Jun 2
Phoenix Fire Office, 1789: CG, Apr 2; 1797: CG, Apr 29; 1800: CG, Apr 4
Phoenix, The; or, Anacreontics Renovated (musical interlude, anon), 1796: DL,
May 27
Phormio. See Terence.
Phusimimesis; or, Resemblances of Nature (play), 1781: CG, May 7, 14
Phyllis whose heart was unconfined (song), 1681: DG, Jan 0

Physick Lies a Bleeding. See Brown, Thomas.
Piano Forte (music), <u>1767</u>: CG, May 16; <u>1771</u>: HAY, Apr 12; <u>1797</u>: DL, May 18;
    <u>1800</u>: CG, Mar 21, DL, Jun 5
Piano Forte Concerto (music), <u>1772</u>: MARLY, Aug 28; <u>1778</u>: CG, Mar 6, 13, 25, Apr
    8; <u>1781</u>: KING'S, Mar 15; <u>1784</u>: HAY, Apr 27; <u>1785</u>: DL, Mar 11; <u>1790</u>: CG, Feb
    24, DL, Mar 3, 26; <u>1791</u>: KING'S, May 19; <u>1792</u>: CG, May 22; <u>1793</u>: KING/HAY,
    Feb 15, 22, CG, Mar 15, May 16; <u>1794</u>: CG, Apr 25; <u>1796</u>: CG, Feb 12, 19, Mar
    4, 16; <u>1797</u>: CG, Mar 15, 17, 22, 24, Apr 5, 7, HAY, Aug 3; <u>1798</u>: CG, Mar 2,
    9, 14, 16; <u>1799</u>: CG, Feb 13, Mar 6; <u>1800</u>: CG, Feb 28, Mar 21, Apr 4
Piano Forte Sonata (music), <u>1799</u>: CG, May 15, 23, Jun 12; <u>1800</u>: CG, Mar 19
Piano Forte, Violin and Violoncello Trio (music), <u>1789</u>: KING'S, Jun 11
Piantafugo (actor), <u>1752</u>: CT/HAY, Mar 17, 21, Apr 1, May 5; <u>1753</u>: HAY, Mar 13,
    22
Piantanida (musician), <u>1739</u>: KING'S, Apr 19; <u>1742</u>: DL, Oct 21, 22, 26, Nov 9,
    12, 16, 17, 20, Dec 2, 9, 10, 13, 20; <u>1743</u>: DL, Jan 1, 10, 11, 12, 17, Feb 8,
    14, Apr 7, 11, 22, 25, May 23
Piatti (singer), <u>1769</u>: KING'S, Sep 5, Nov 7; <u>1770</u>: KING'S, Mar 22, Jun 12
Piatti, Sga (singer), <u>1766</u>: KING'S, Oct 21, Nov 25; <u>1767</u>: KING'S, Jan 31, Oct
    27; <u>1769</u>: KING'S, Sep 5, Nov 7; <u>1770</u>: KING'S, Feb 2
Piazza, <u>1725</u>: DL, Nov 16; <u>1750</u>: DL, Mar 19; <u>1752</u>: CG, Mar 30; <u>1753</u>: DL, Dec 20;
    <u>1754</u>: DL, Nov 22; <u>1755</u>: CG, Feb 19; <u>1758</u>: DL, Mar 13; <u>1759</u>: DL, Apr 19; <u>1761</u>:
    DL, Feb 27; <u>1762</u>: DL, Feb 26, CG, Apr 1, DL, 2; <u>1765</u>: CG, Apr 15; <u>1778</u>: CG,
    May 2; <u>1782</u>: CG, Apr 23, HAY, Aug 28, CG, Sep 23; <u>1783</u>: CG, May 7, HAY, Aug
    26; <u>1784</u>: CG, Apr 26, Jun 14, HAY, Aug 24; <u>1785</u>: CG, Apr 11, HAY, Aug 23;
    <u>1786</u>: CG, Apr 18, HAY, Aug 25; <u>1787</u>: CG, Apr 10, HAY, Aug 28; <u>1788</u>: CG, Mar
    26, HAY, Aug 27; <u>1789</u>: CG, Apr 20; <u>1790</u>: DL, May 12; <u>1792</u>: CG, Apr 21,
    DLKING'S, May 17, HAY, Aug 15, CG, Sep 17, Oct 1; <u>1793</u>: CG, Apr 25, HAY, Aug
    27; <u>1794</u>: CG, Apr 29, HAY, Aug 28, CG, Sep 15; <u>1795</u>: CG, May 1, DL, 28, HAY,
    Aug 25; <u>1796</u>: CG, Apr 5, DL, May 31, HAY, Sep 1; <u>1797</u>: CG, May 9, DL, 30,
    HAY, Aug 24, CG, Dec 6; <u>1798</u>: CG, May 8, HAY, Aug 28; <u>1799</u>: CG, Apr 30, HAY,
    Aug 27; <u>1800</u>: CG, May 6, HAY, Aug 29
Piccadilly, <u>1743</u>: CG, Apr 16; <u>1746</u>: HIC, Mar 10, NWSM, Jul 28; <u>1756</u>: DL, Nov
    12; <u>1774</u>: KING'S, Nov 8; <u>1777</u>: KING'S, May 1; <u>1778</u>: HAY, Apr 9, KING'S, May
    28; <u>1779</u>: KING'S, Mar 11, Apr 15, CG, 24, DL, May 5, HAY, Aug 27; <u>1780</u>:
    KING'S, Apr 13, 20, DL, 21, HAY, Aug 31; <u>1781</u>: CG, Mar 27, KING'S, Apr 26,
    DL, 26, 30; <u>1782</u>: CG, Mar 18, KING'S, Apr 30, May 27; <u>1783</u>: KING'S, Mar 27;
    <u>1784</u>: DL, May 20, KING'S, Jun 17; <u>1785</u>: HAY, Apr 8, KING'S, 28; <u>1786</u>: KING'S,
    Mar 30, Apr 27, CG, May 5, DL, 24; <u>1787</u>: CG, Mar 26, Apr 27; <u>1788</u>: CG, Mar
    10, Apr 18; <u>1789</u>: CG, Mar 28, May 12; <u>1791</u>: CG, Apr 11; <u>1792</u>: CG, Mar 26;
    <u>1793</u>: CG, Mar 18, May 2; <u>1794</u>: CG, Apr 7, May 10; <u>1795</u>: CG, Mar 16, May 7;
    <u>1796</u>: CG, Mar 14, Apr 19, HAY, Sep 28; <u>1797</u>: CG, May 4, DL, Jun 12; <u>1798</u>: CG,
    Apr 18; <u>1799</u>: CG, Apr 12, May 15; <u>1800</u>: CG, Apr 19, May 13, KING'S, 29
Piccini, Niccolo (composer), <u>1763</u>: KING'S, Apr 25; <u>1764</u>: KING'S, Feb 21; <u>1766</u>:
    KING'S, Nov 25, CG, Dec 3; <u>1767</u>: KING'S, Jan 31, Feb 24, Nov 7; <u>1768</u>: KING'S,
    Jan 9, HAY, Feb 24, KING'S, Mar 10, Aug 13, Dec 13; <u>1769</u>: KING'S, Nov 7;
    <u>1770</u>: KING'S, Feb 27, CG, Apr 4, MARLY, Aug 28, KING'S, Dec 29; <u>1771</u>: CG, Mar
    6, KING'S, Apr 25, May 16, 23; <u>1772</u>: CG, Apr 8; <u>1773</u>: HAY, Mar 17; <u>1775</u>:
    KING'S, May 23; <u>1776</u>: DL, Mar 20, Sep 21; <u>1777</u>: KING'S, Apr 1, 29, Dec 16;
    <u>1778</u>: KING'S, Mar 26, Apr 2; <u>1779</u>: KING'S, Nov 27; <u>1780</u>: KING'S, Apr 13, May
    25, Nov 28; <u>1781</u>: KING'S, Feb 22; <u>1782</u>: KING'S, Feb 7; <u>1784</u>: KING'S, Feb 24,
    26; <u>1786</u>: KING'S, Feb 14, May 4; <u>1787</u>: CG, May 15; <u>1789</u>: KING'S, May 28;
    <u>1794</u>: KING'S, Dec 20
--Accomplished Maid, The (opera), <u>1766</u>: CG, Dec 2, 3, 4, 5, 8, 10, 15, 17, 18,
    22, 31; <u>1767</u>: CG, Jan 2, 9, 14, 16
--Barone di Torre Forte, Il, <u>1781</u>: KING'S, Feb 22, 24, 27, Mar 1, 6, 10, 13,
    17, 20, 24, 27, 31, Apr 5, May 10, 15, 26, 29
--Buona Figliuola Maritata, La (opera), <u>1767</u>: KING'S, Jan 31, Feb 7, 17, Mar 3,
    17, 21, Apr 9, May 5, 26; <u>1768</u>: KING'S, Jan 9, 12; <u>1771</u>: KING'S, May 16, Jun
    8
--Buona Figliuola, La (opera), <u>1766</u>: KING'S, Nov 25, Dec 2, CG, 3, KING'S, 9,
    13, 16, 23, 27; <u>1767</u>: KING'S, Jan 3, 6, 13, 20, 27, Feb 3, 10, 24, Mar 10,
    24, 31, Apr 7, 21, 28, May 9, 12, 23, 30, Jun 2, 13, 20; <u>1768</u>: KING'S, Jan
    26, 29, Feb 2, 9, 16, Mar 8, Apr 12, 30, May 7, Jun 14, Aug 13, 16, Dec 31;
    <u>1769</u>: KING'S, Jan 3, 7, 24, Feb 28, Mar 28, Apr 4, 18, May 23; <u>1770</u>: KING'S,
    Mar 13, 20, CG, Apr 4, KING'S, 23, May 22, Jun 19, Dec 29; <u>1771</u>: KING'S, Jan
    3, 22, Feb 5, Mar 19, Apr 2, May 7, 23, 28, Jun 22, 29; <u>1772</u>: KING'S, Apr 9,
    May 12, 19, 28; <u>1773</u>: KING'S, Jun 1; <u>1774</u>: KING'S, Mar 17, Dec 13, 20, 23;
    <u>1775</u>: KING'S, Jan 31, Feb 4, 14, 21, 28, Mar 21, Apr 6, May 11, Jun 6, Dec
    12, 19; <u>1776</u>: KING'S, Apr 9, 16, May 28, Jun 18; <u>1777</u>: KING'S, Apr 29; <u>1778</u>:
    KING'S, Apr 2, 30, May 28; <u>1779</u>: KING'S, Apr 29, May 4, 11; <u>1780</u>: KING'S, May
    25, Jun 27, Nov 28; <u>1782</u>: KING'S, Jan 10, 15, 29, Feb 7, 14, May 23, Jun 5,
    6, 8; <u>1783</u>: KING'S, Jun 3; <u>1785</u>: KING'S, Apr 28; <u>1789</u>: KING'S, May 28; <u>1790</u>:

HAY, Mar 25; 1791: KING'S, May 23; 1796: KING'S, May 5
--Caio Mario (opera), 1776: KING'S, Apr 20, 27, May 4, 11
--Contadine Bizzarre, Le (opera), 1769: KING'S, Nov 7, 14, 21, 28, Dec 5
--Death of Abel, The (oratorio), 1768: HAY, Feb 24, 26; 1769: HAY, Feb 15;
    1770: CG, Apr 4; 1771: CG, Mar 6; 1773: CG, Mar 26
--Donna di Spirito, La (opera), 1775: KING'S, May 23, 30, Jun 17
--Donne Vindicate, Le (opera), 1768: KING'S, Dec 13, 17, 20, 23
--Schiava, La (opera), 1766: KING'S, Oct 21; 1767: KING'S, Nov 7, 10, 17, 21,
    24; 1768: KING'S, Jan 2, 5, 19, Feb 13, Mar 15, 22, Apr 16, May 3, Aug 20,
    Sep 27; 1769: KING'S, Jan 10, 21, Mar 14, May 16, Jun 13; 1770: KING'S, Feb
    22, 27, Mar 6, Apr 24, Jun 26; 1771: KING'S, Apr 25, 27, May 14, 21, 23, Jun
    22; 1772: KING'S, Mar 12, 14, 21, Apr 4; 1777: KING'S, Apr 1, 10, 22; 1780:
    KING'S, Apr 13, 18, 20, 25; 1784: KING'S, Feb 24, Mar 2
--Sesostri (opera), 1768: KING'S, Mar 10
--Vittorina (opera), 1777: KING'S, Dec 16, 23
Pickel, Mr and Mrs (spectators), 1759: CG, Oct 22
Pickering, Edward (spectator), 1661: BF, Aug 31
Pickering, Mrs (spectator), 1665: ATCOURT, Feb 2
Pickering, Roger (author), 1755: DL, Mar 13, Dec 19
Pico (dancer), 1773: KING'S, Oct 23
Picq (dancer), 1741: CG, Dec 15, 28, 30; 1742: CG, Jan 4, 5, 8, 11, 14, 18, 21,
    25, Feb 6, 10, 12, 25, Mar 18, 22, 29, Apr 5, 19, 20, 21, 28, Sep 29, Oct 1,
    Nov 5, Dec 9, 14, 15, 17, 21; 1743: CG, Mar 8, Apr 2, 6, 7, 8, 25, Dec 20,
    26; 1744: CG, Jan 14, Feb 14, Mar 3, 15, Apr 7, Oct 10, 22, 31, Dec 8; 1745:
    CG, Jan 1, 14, 25, Mar 28, Apr 2, 18, 24, May 6, 7, 10, Oct 4, 16, 29, Dec
    20; 1746: DL, Feb 6, Apr 25, CG, Dec 27; 1747: CG, Mar 26
Picture of a Modern Fine Lady (entertainment), 1794: HAMM, Mar 24; 1795: WLWS,
    Jun 19
Picture of a Playhouse, A. See Bucks have at ye all.
Picture of Paris, The. See Bonnor, Charles.
Picture, The. See Massinger, Phillip.
Picture, The; or, Cuckold in Conceit. See Miller, James.
Piddington (coach maker), 1762: CG, Apr 23
Pidgeon (doorkeeper), 1736: GF, May 3; 1741: GF, May 6
Pidgeon's Coffee House, 1735: GF, Apr 24
Piece, Dr
--Nump's Courtship; or, Love Makes the Painter, 1758: HAY, Jan 16, 18
Piedmontese Mountaineer (dance), 1768: DL, Nov 3, 5
Piele, John (violoncellist), 1797: CG, Mar 3; 1798: CG, Feb 23; 1799: CG, Feb 8
Piele, Mary, Mrs John (singer), 1791: CG, Mar 11, 18, 23, 25, Apr 13
Pieltain, Dieudonne Pascal (violinist, composer), 1782: DL, Feb 20; 1785: HAY,
    Feb 23; 1790: CG, Oct 4
Pieltain, Sga (actor, singer), 1789: KING'S, Jan 24, Apr 4, May 28; 1791: CG,
    Feb 26, Mar 10
Pieppo (Pepo) (musician), 1718: LIF, May 20, Nov 6, 27, SH, Dec 23; 1719: LIF,
    Apr 16; 1723: DL, Mar 20
Pierce (actor), 1729: BLA, Sep 30
Pierce (actor), 1763: HAY, Sep 5; 1764: HAY, Jul 30, Aug 20, Sep 1; 1766:
    KING'S, Aug 18; 1767: HAY, Jun 22; 1769: HAY, May 15, 26, 29; 1771: HAY, Apr
    15, May 15, 20, Jun 7, 14; 1772: HAY, May 22, 27, Jun 8, Aug 10, Sep 17;
    1773: HAY, May 26, 31, Jun 14, 18, 28, Jul 2, Sep 3; 1774: HAY, Jun 6, 8, 17,
    27, Sep 12; 1775: HAY, May 26, Jul 31, Aug 16, Sep 4; 1776: HAY, May 31, Jul
    10, Aug 2
Pierce (actor), 1781: HAY, Jun 16, Jul 23, Aug 22, 24, 29; 1782: HAY, Jun 4,
    Jul 5, Aug 5, 8, 13; 1783: HAY, Jul 5, Aug 1
Pierce (beneficiary), 1747: DL, May 11
Pierce (spectator), 1666: ATCOURT, Oct 29; 1667: NONE, Jul 13; 1668: ATCOURT,
    Jan 13; 1669: BRIDGES, Apr 17
Pierce (taverner), 1751: DL, Dec 17
Pierce, James (surgeon, spectator), 1666: ATCOURT, Oct 29; 1667: NONE, Jul 13;
    1668: ATCOURT, Jan 13; 1669: BRIDGES, Apr 17
Pierce, Miss (actor), 1767: CG, Nov 7; 1768: CG, Feb 13
Pierce, Mrs (spectator), 1661: SALSBURY, Mar 26, VERE, Oct 9; 1664: BRIDGES,
    Aug 18; 1667: BRIDGES, Jan 23, 24, Aug 12, NONE, Oct 26, BRIDGES, Dec 30;
    1668: LIF, Jan 6, Mar 26, May 4
Piercy (house servant), 1771: DL, May 30; 1772: DL, Jun 9; 1773: DL, Jun 1;
    1776: DL, May 20
Piercy (instrumentalist), 1798: HAY, Jan 15
Piercy, Miss (actor), 1761: DL, Mar 28
Pierot Arlequin (pantomime, anon), 1726: HAY, Apr 25
Pierot Grand Vizier; With The Turkish Ceremony of the Bourgeois Gentilhomme
    (pantomime, anon), 1725: HAY, Mar 18

Pierot le Furieux (pantomime, anon), 1722: HAY, Mar 15
Pierot Maitre Valet et L'Opera de Campagne; ou, La Critique de l'Opera de Paris
  (play), 1719: LIF, Jan 29, Feb 3
Pierpont Row, 1780: CII, Mar 17
Pierrepoint, Gervase (spectator), 1700: DLORLIF, Jan 23
Pierrette (dance), 1726: DL, Mar 21, 24, 31, Apr 15, May 4, 5, 6, 9, 23, 25,
  Dec 12, 29; 1727: DL, Feb 8, Apr 10, 19, 20, 21, 22, 24, 25, May 1, 8, Sep
  26; 1728: DL, Feb 27, Mar 14, 21, May 1, 3, 7, 8, 13, 16, 17, 22, Nov 8;
  1729: DL, Jan 31, Mar 18, 25, Apr 9, 21; 1730: DL, Apr 14, 15, 24, May 4, Sep
  15, 24, Oct 22; 1732: DL, Jun 6, 23; 1738: DL, Apr 21, 22, 24, 26, May 1, 2,
  11, 18, 19, 24, 25, 30, 31; 1739: DL, Apr 2, 28, May 31; 1740: DL, Apr 28
Pierrot and French Peasant (dance), 1729: HAY, Jun 11
Pierrot and Pierrette (dance), 1726: HAY, Apr 13; 1730: LIF, Apr 29, DL, May 2,
  BFOF, Aug 20; 1732: GF, Dec 13, 18, 29; 1733: GF, Jan 11, 12, 23, Mar 1, Apr
  17, 24, 30, May 3, 16, HAY, 28, GF, Sep 12, 14, 17, 21, 28, Oct 1, 9, 15, DL,
  Dec 13; 1735: GF/HAY, Feb 13, Mar 28, Apr 7, May 2, HAY, 26
Pierrot Courting a Bottle (dance), 1724: HAY, Mar 9
Pierrot Dance (dance), 1723: LIF, Nov 28, Dec 12; 1724: LIF, Mar 23, 26, Apr 6,
  8; 1725: HAY, Apr 14, LIF, May 19, Dec 16; 1726: LIF, Apr 11, 15, 18, 19, 25,
  26, 27, 29, May 4, 17, Jul 15, 22; 1727: LIF, Feb 8, 9, Mar 11, 13, 16, 23,
  DL, 23, LIF, Apr 3, 5, 6, 10, 12, 17, 19, 24, 27, May 3, DL, 5, LIF, 8, 10,
  12, 17, 19, Sep 15, 20, Oct 2, 17, 26, Nov 1; 1728: LIF, Jan 8, Mar 9, 18,
  21, Apr 1, 6, 23, 24, 29, May 3, 18, Oct 21, 23, Dec 12, 31; 1729: LIF, Jan
  13, Mar 10, 17, 20, 27, Apr 10, 11, 15, 24, DL, May 8, LIF, 20, 22, HAY, Jun
  18, BFF, Aug 23, LIF, Oct 20, GF, Nov 29, Dec 1, 2, 16, HAY, 27, 29; 1730:
  GF, Jan 1, 3, 6, 13, 19, 22, Mar 10, 12, 14, LIF, 17, GF, 17, Apr 6, 7, LIF,
  10, 13, GF, 16, LIF, 27, 30, May 1, 4, 9, GF, 13, DL, 27, GF, Jun 1, 16, 19,
  BFPG/TC, Aug 1, LIF, Sep 23, Oct 7, 19; 1731: LIF, Jan 4, Mar 22, 25, Apr 1,
  23, 24, 26, 29, May 1, 5, Oct 13, 20, GF, Dec 4, LIF, 7, 14; 1732: LIF, Jan
  5, 19, GF, 26, LIF, Feb 9, GF, 29, HAY, Mar 23, GF, 30, LIF, Apr 13, 14, 17,
  18, GF, 19, 21, 24, LIF, 24, 27, GF, 27, LIF, 28, May 2, 8, 9, 17, RIW/HAY,
  Sep 4, 11, 12, LIF/CG, 25, Oct 2, 9, Nov 14, Dec 15; 1733: LIF/CG, Jan 12,
  15, 27, Feb 2, GF, 2, LIF/CG, 3, CG, 8, GF, 12, LIF/CG, Mar 28, 29, Apr 2,
  GF, 6, 20, 25, 27, LIF/CG, May 3, GF, 5, LIF/CG, 8, GF, 11, 15, CG, Jun 26,
  Sep 20, 25, 29, Oct 4, GF, 16, 18, 19, DL, 19, GF, 24, 26, CG, 31, GF, 31,
  CG, Nov 1, GF, 2, DL, Dec 7, GF, 8, 11, 15, 19; 1734: GF, Jan 11, 28, Feb 5,
  DL/LIF, Mar 11, DL/HAY, 12, 18, 19, 23, 25, 28, 30, DL/LIF, Apr 1, DL, 4, 29,
  GF, May 1, DL/HAY, 1, GF, 6, 8, 13, CG, 15, DL, 16, 21, DL/HAY, 22, GF, 22,
  DL/HAY, 23, LIF, 23, HAY, 27, LIF, 29, HAY, Jun 19, 21, 24, 28, Jul 10, 19,
  LIF, Aug 20, DL, Sep 19, 24, Oct 3, 8, GF, 14, DL, 23, 24, Nov 7, Dec 4, 9,
  11, GF, 28; 1735: GF, Jan 6, 7, DL, 17, 18, 21, 28, 29, Feb 4, 6, 13, 14, GF,
  Mar 17, 29, Apr 9, 10, DL, 11, 14, GF, 16, 17, CG/LIF, 17, DL, 22, 25,
  GF/HAY, 25, DL, May 7, CG, 8, DL, 17, Jun 9, Jul 1, GF/HAY, 15, 18, 22, Aug
  1, BF, 23, GF, Sep 10, YB/HAY, 17, GF, 26, DL, Oct 1, GF, 3, CG, 3, 6, 13,
  15, 28, Nov 11, GF, 12, CG, 13, GF, 14, CG, 19, GF, 25, CG, 28, GF, 29, CG,
  Dec 2, GF, 10, CG, 12, GF, 13, 15, HAY, 17; 1736: HAY, Feb 2, 16, CG, Mar 15,
  16, 22, 23, 30, LIF, 31, CG, Apr 5, 6, DL, 8, CG, 12, GF, 13, DL, 16, GF, 17,
  28, CG, 29, DL, 30, CG, May 1, 3, GF, 6, CG, 10, DL, 15, CG, 17, DL, 20, CG,
  20, 25, BFHC, Aug 23, DL, 26, LIF, Nov 13, 18, 27, Dec 3, CG, 6, 30; 1737:
  CG, Jan 28, Feb 1, Mar 14, 19, LIF, 21, CG, 28, LIF, Apr 12, 14, CG, 15, LIF,
  18, CG, 19, 22, LIF, 25, CG, 26, LIF, 27, 29, 30, May 2, CG, 2, 3, LIF, 5,
  CG, 6, LIF, 6, 7, DL, 13, CG, 16, LIF, 18, DL, 19, 20, 25, CG, 31; 1738: CG,
  Mar 13, 20, 21, 23, Apr 4, 5, 6, 7, 10, 11, 15, 18, 21, May 5, DL, 13, CG,
  15, DL, 17, 22, 23, BFH, Aug 23; 1739: DL, Mar 17, CG, 22, DL, 26, CG, 26,
  27, DL, 27, CG, Apr 3, 24, 25, 27, 30, May 1, DL, 1, CG, 2, 4, DL, 5, 9, CG,
  9, DL, 11, 14, CG, 14, 15, DL, 16, CG, 17, 18, DL, 19, CG, 21, DL, 22, 23,
  CG, 23, 24, 25, 28, DL, 28, CG, 29, DL, 30, CG, 30, DL, Oct 9, 16, 18, 22,
  26, 27, 31, Dec 8, 10, 12, 14, 19; 1740: DL, Jan 7, Feb 16, 18, Apr 10, 17,
  May 2, 5, 7, 9, 12, 14, 15, 16, 17, 19, 20, 21, 22, 26, 28, 29; 1741: GF, Jan
  20, Feb 2, CG, Apr 22, 23, 25, 27, May 4, 5, 8, 11, 14, Oct 27, Nov 2, DL,
  14, Dec 3; 1742: GF, Feb 2, 6, 16, CG, Mar 29, GF, Apr 20; 1749: DL, May 2;
  1750: CG, Jan 8, Apr 18, 25; 1751: CG, May 1; 1752: CG, Apr 15, DL, May 1,
  CG, 4, 6, 7; 1753: DL, Mar 26, CG, May 1, 2, 10, 21; 1754: DL, May 4, 13, 14,
  15, 16, 17, 20, 21; 1755: HAY, Aug 21, 25, 28, Sep 9, 11, 15; 1762: CG, May
  13; 1769: DL, Jan 18; 1771: HAY, Jul 5
Pierson (treasurer), 1740: DL, Apr 25; 1741: DL, Apr 13; 1742: DL, Apr 6; 1743:
  DL, Apr 7
Pieto (beneficiary), 1723: HAY, Apr 4
Pietro (dancer), 1751: DL, Oct 18, Nov 5, Dec 26, 30; 1752: DL, Jan 18, 21, 27,
  Feb 4, 5, Mar 5, 14, 16, 17, Apr 9, 11, 13, 16, 22, 27, 28, 29, May 5, Oct
  12, 17, 26, Nov 2, 16, 28; 1753: DL, Apr 27, May 2; 1754: KING'S, Nov 9
Pietro (Piettero), Sga (dancer), 1751: DL, Oct 18, Nov 15, 23, Dec 20, 26, 30;

<u>1752</u>: DL, Jan 20, 21, 28, Feb 5; <u>1755</u>: DL, Nov 8, 15
Pietro (singer, musician), <u>1707</u>: YB, May 23; <u>1710</u>: PCGR, Jun 14; <u>1715</u>: GRT, Apr 25; <u>1717</u>: HIC, Mar 27, May 3; <u>1719</u>: HIC, Feb 18, MTH, Apr 29, HIC, May 7; <u>1722</u>: NONE, Mar 2, DL, Apr 21
Pietro, Master (dancer), <u>1752</u>: DL, Mar 16, Apr 9, 11, 13, 16; <u>1755</u>: DL, Nov 1, 4, 8
Pietro, Sg and Sga (dancers), <u>1751</u>: DL, Oct 15, Nov 19
Piety in Pattens. See Foote, Samuel, A Sentimental Comedy.
Piffet (musician), <u>1762</u>: HAY, Mar 16, CG, 23
Pig, The; or, Advice to the Critics (oration), <u>1757</u>: HAY, Aug 11
Pigeon (actor), <u>1731</u>: SFGT, Sep 8
Pigeon, The (song), <u>1783</u>: CG, May 7, 9, 10, 14; <u>1785</u>: HAMM, Jul 15
Piggot (spectator), <u>1759</u>: DL, Oct 27; <u>1760</u>: CG, Feb 16
Pigmalion; or, The Statue Metamorphosed (dance), <u>1734</u>: CG, Jan 14, 15, 16, 17, 18, 19, 21, 22, Feb 14, 18, 22, Mar 9, 11, 12, 18, 19, 21, 26, Apr 2, 6, 16, 17, 18, 27, May 1, 7, 8, CG/LIF, Nov 29; <u>1735</u>: CG/LIF, Mar 13, 22, Apr 8, 14, 24; <u>1746</u>: CG, Apr 9, 11, 14, 17, 18, 25, Jun 9; <u>1748</u>: CG, Apr 28; <u>1750</u>: DL, Oct 31, Nov 2, 3, 5, 6, 9, 12, 14, 17, 20, 22, 24, 27, Dec 1, 17, 21; <u>1751</u>: DL, Feb 13, CG, Apr 12, 18, May 16, 17, Sep 25, 28, Oct 11, 17, Nov 4; <u>1752</u>: CG, Jan 21, Mar 14, Apr 15; <u>1758</u>: HAY, Jan 25; <u>1775</u>: KING'S, Oct 31, Nov 4, 16, 18, 28, Dec 5; <u>1776</u>: KING'S, Jan 20, 27, Feb 17, 24, 29, Mar 2, 7, 9, 14, 28, Jun 8
Pigmy Revels, The. See Messink, James.
Piguenit (treasurer), <u>1770</u>: MARLY, Aug 14; <u>1771</u>: MARLY, Aug 27; <u>1772</u>: MARLY, Aug 20, 25; <u>1773</u>: MARLY, Jul 27; <u>1774</u>: MARLY, Aug 18
Piguenit, D J (composer), <u>1776</u>: CG, Apr 16
--Don Quixote (entertainment), <u>1776</u>: CG, Apr 16
Pilbrow (singer), <u>1794</u>: DL, May 16, Jun 21, Oct 27, Dec 20; <u>1795</u>: DL, Jan 19
Pilbrow (Pilborough) (ticket deliverer), <u>1781</u>: CG, May 26; <u>1782</u>: CG, May 29; <u>1783</u>: CG, Jun 4; <u>1784</u>: CG, May 29; <u>1786</u>: CG, Jun 1; <u>1787</u>: CG, Jun 2; <u>1788</u>: CG, May 27; <u>1789</u>: CG, Jun 13; <u>1790</u>: CG, Jun 8; <u>1791</u>: CG, Jun 9; <u>1792</u>: CG, Jun 1
Pile, Mrs (actor), <u>1736</u>: HAY, Jun 26; <u>1748</u>: BFLYY, Aug 24, SFLYYW, Sep 7, BHB, Oct 1
Pilfold (pit office keeper), <u>1768</u>: CG, May 28, 30; <u>1769</u>: CG, May 20, 22; <u>1770</u>: CG, May 18, 21; <u>1771</u>: CG, May 25; <u>1772</u>: CG, May 23; <u>1773</u>: CG, May 22; <u>1774</u>: CG, May 7; <u>1775</u>: CG, May 30; <u>1776</u>: CG, May 21; <u>1777</u>: CG, May 23; <u>1778</u>: CG, May 21; <u>1779</u>: CG, May 15; <u>1780</u>: CG, May 24; <u>1781</u>: CG, May 25; <u>1782</u>: CG, May 28; <u>1783</u>: CG, May 31; <u>1784</u>: CG, May 22; <u>1786</u>: CG, May 27; <u>1787</u>: CG, May 19; <u>1788</u>: CG, May 15; <u>1794</u>: CG, May 31
Pilgrim (dance), <u>1774</u>: CG, Apr 16, May 13, 25; <u>1775</u>: CG, May 3, 4, 23, 27, Sep 27, Oct 6, 27, Nov 3, 11, 14, 24; <u>1776</u>: CG, Mar 9, 11, 12, Apr 13, May 22, Oct 9, 29, Nov 16, 22, Dec 19; <u>1777</u>: CG, Oct 3; <u>1779</u>: CG, Oct 8, Nov 3; <u>1780</u>: CG, Mar 29, Apr 29, Nov 6, Dec 7
Pilgrim, The. See Fletcher, John.
Pilkington (box-office keeper), <u>1746</u>: DL, May 9
Pilkington (sheriff), <u>1682</u>: DG, Mar 0
Pilkington, Thomas (Lord Mayor), <u>1689</u>: CITY, Oct 29
Pilon, Frederick, <u>1778</u>: CG, Nov 4; <u>1779</u>: CG, Feb 22, Apr 12, Sep 27; <u>1780</u>: CG, Feb 2, Apr 21, Jun 26, Oct 19, DL, Nov 22, CG, Dec 28; <u>1781</u>: CG, Mar 8, May 10, HAY, Jul 9, CG, Oct 5, 13; <u>1782</u>: DL, May 18; <u>1783</u>: DL, Feb 8; <u>1784</u>: CG, Oct 29, Dec 27; <u>1785</u>: CG, Mar 29, HAY, Jul 26; <u>1786</u>: CG, Nov 18; <u>1787</u>: CG, Dec 15; <u>1788</u>: CG, Jun 4; <u>1793</u>: CG, Apr 8
--Aerostation; or, The Templar's Stratagem (farce), <u>1784</u>: CG, Oct 29, 30, Nov 1, 2, 5, 12, 17, 23
--Barataria; or, Sancho Turned Governor (farce), <u>1785</u>: CG, Mar 29, Apr 13, 18, 20, 27, 28, May 2, 3, 9, 14, 19, 25, Sep 26, Nov 3, 11, Dec 2; <u>1786</u>: CG, Mar 7, 14, 23, 28, Nov 14, Dec 11, 18; <u>1787</u>: CG, Feb 27, Mar 24, May 12, Oct 29; <u>1788</u>: CG, Apr 16, Nov 20; <u>1789</u>: CG, Mar 7, May 28; <u>1790</u>: CG, Apr 24; <u>1791</u>: CG, Mar 5; <u>1792</u>: CG, Jun 2, Oct 24; <u>1793</u>: CG, Dec 18; <u>1795</u>: CG, Apr 29; <u>1796</u>: CG, Sep 26; <u>1797</u>: CG, Jun 9, Nov 20
--Deaf Lover, The (farce), <u>1779</u>: CG, Sep 27; <u>1780</u>: CG, Feb 2, 3, 7, 8, 10, 12, 14, 15, 24, 26, 29, Mar 2, 30, Apr 14, 28, May 12, 18, 19, 24, 26, Sep 18, 29, Dec 1, 28; <u>1781</u>: CG, Mar 13, May 25, Sep 26, Oct 24, Nov 17; <u>1783</u>: DL, Nov 18, 24, Dec 6, 10, 23; <u>1784</u>: DL, Feb 4, Apr 24, May 8, 25; <u>1785</u>: DL, May 9; <u>1790</u>: DL, Jan 19, 23, 28, Feb 3, 6, 20, Mar 8, May 6, Dec 14, 21; <u>1791</u>: DL, Jan 12, CG, 26, Feb 9, 26, DL, Mar 7, 28, Apr 25, CG, May 26; <u>1792</u>: DLKING'S, Jan 5, 18, CG, Feb 2, May 10, DL, Dec 4; <u>1793</u>: DL, Jan 23, Feb 25, May 31, HAY, Jun 12, 29, Jul 19, Oct 8, Nov 23, 27, Dec 11; <u>1794</u>: CG, Feb 22, HAY, Jul 17, 26, DL, Dec 23, 29; <u>1795</u>: HAY, Jun 20, Jul 25, Aug 8, 15, Sep 2; <u>1796</u>: DL, Jun 11, 15, HAY, 30, Jul 5, Aug 12, 29, CG, Nov 19; <u>1797</u>: CG, Feb 22, HAY, Jun 15, Jul 19, Aug 15, DL, Nov 11; <u>1798</u>: HAY, Jun 12, 19, Jul 2,

21, Aug 22, Sep 12, CG, Nov 10; 1799: DL, May 25; 1800: DL, Jan 4, HAY, Aug
14, Sep 11
--Device, The; or, The Deaf Doctor (farce), 1779: CG, Sep 27, 29; 1780: CG, Feb
2
--Fair American, The (opera), 1782: DL, May 18, 20, 21, 22, 23, 24, 25; 1783:
DL, Feb 7, 8, 11, 14, Apr 22, May 8
--He Would be a Soldier, 1786: CG, Nov 18, 20, 21, 23, 25, 28, 30, Dec 2, 5, 7,
9, 12, 14; 1787: CG, Jan 9, 12, 16, 19, 22, 25, Feb 1, 6, Apr 10, 20, May 25,
Sep 26, Nov 29; 1788: CG, May 5; 1789: CG, Apr 15, Jun 4; 1791: CG, May 19,
Sep 21, 28; 1794: CG, Mar 6, 8, 13, May 16; 1795: CG, Feb 4, Apr 24
--Humours of an Election, The; or, Court and Country (farce), 1780: CG, Oct 19,
20, 21, 23, 24, 25, 26, 30, Nov 3, 7, 8, Dec 6, 22, 26; 1782: HAY, Jun 12
--Illumination; or, The Glaziers Conspiracy (Gazette Extraordinary) (prelude),
1779: CG, Apr 12, 27, May 3, 4, 10, 12, 13, 20; 1780: CG, Apr 21; May 6, 8,
10
--Invasion, The; or, A Trip to Brighthelmstone (Alarmed at Brighthelmstone)
(farce), 1778: CG, Nov 4, 5, 6, 7, 9, 10, 11, 12, 14, 16, 17, 19, 20, 21, 24,
25, 26, 27, 28, Dec 4, 5, 16, 18, 22, 26; 1779: CG, May 4, Sep 20, Nov 29,
Dec 21; 1793: CG, Apr 8, 9, 27, Oct 21
--Liverpool Prize, The (farce), 1779: CG, Feb 20, 22, 23, 25, 27, Mar 1, 2, 4,
6, 8, 23, Apr 5, 8, 14, 29, May 8, 15, 21, Sep 22, Oct 1
--Siege of Gibraltar, The (farce), 1780: CG, Apr 25, 26, 27, May 2, 4, 9, 11,
15, 22, 29
--Thelyphthora; or, More Wives than One (farce), 1781: CG, Mar 8, 10
Pilotti, Elizabetta (singer), 1713: QUEEN'S, Jan 10, Apr 25; 1714: KING'S, Nov
16, Dec 30; 1715: KING'S, Apr 2, GRT, May 9; 1716: KING'S, Feb 1; 1717:
KING'S, Jan 5, Feb 16, May 2
Pilsbury (ticket deliverer), 1787: DL, Jun 4; 1788: DL, Jun 6; 1789: DL, Jun
10; 1790: DL, May 29; 1791: DL, May 31; 1792: DLKING'S, Jun 13; 1793: DL, May
31; 1795: DL, Jun 4; 1796: DL, Jun 15; 1797: DL, Jun 15; 1798: DL, Jun 9
Pimlico, 1782: CG, Apr 24; 1795: DL, May 29; 1796: DL, Jun 2, HAY, Sep 17;
1797: DL, Jun 2; 1798: DL, Jun 6; 1799: DL, Apr 25
Pimmaglione. See Cimadoro, Giambattista.
Pinacci, Giovanni Battista (singer), 1731: KING'S, Dec 7; 1732: KING'S, Jan 15,
Feb 15, Mar 25, May 23, Jun 10
Pinart (beneficiary), 1725: HAY, Apr 9
Pinchbeck (actor), 1741: JS, Sep 29, DL, Oct 9
Pinchbeck, Edward (critic, manager), 1747: HAY, Apr 28; 1750: JS, Jan 25
Pinchbeck, Edward, (toyshop proprietor), 1741: JS, Nov 9; 1742: JS, Apr 19;
1744: JS, Mar 16, HAY, Apr 26; 1750: DL, Feb 21
Pindar, John (actor), 1794: HAY, Feb 25, Mar 31, Jul 8, 11, 12, 17, 18, 19, 22,
Aug 4, 11, 13, 20, 23, 27, Sep 3
Pindar, Peter (lyricist, composer), 1793: CG, May 1, 16; 1794: CG, May 26
Pindarick Ode on New Year's Day (song), 1691: ATCOURT, Jan 1
Pindarique Ode, A (song), 1690: ATCOURT, Nov 4
Pine, Sim (actor), 1751: DL, Mar 7
Pinetti, 1785: HAY, Feb 21
Pinkeman. See Penkethman.
Pinkyman. See Penkethman.
Pinner, George (actor), 1742: JS, May 31; 1743: JS, Jan 5; 1746: NWMF, Oct 6,
SOU, 16, GF, 27, 28, 29, 31, Nov 4, 6, 7, 13, 14; 1748: HAY, May 2, BFSY, Aug
24; 1749: NWLS, Feb 27, BFC, Aug 23; 1755: HAY, Sep 3, 9, 11, 15
Pinny, Mrs (house servant), 1742: DL, May 13
Pinto (violinist), 1798: CG, Feb 23
Pinto, Charles (musician), 1759: DL, Mar 30; 1761: SOHO, Jan 28; 1762: DL, Mar
5, KING'S, May 11; 1764: DL, Jan 16, KING'S, Apr 12, DL, 27, May 9; 1766: CG,
Feb 21, KING'S, Apr 10; 1767: KING'S, Jan 23, DL, Apr 6; 1768: KING'S, Feb 5;
1769: KING'S, Feb 3, HAY, 22, MARLY, Aug 24; 1773: HAY, Apr 19
Pinto, Charlotte, Mrs Thomas (singer), 1785: HAY, Mar 15, CG, Apr 22, 26; 1786:
HAY, May 12
Pinto, George Frederic (violinist), 1797: DL, May 18; 1798: CG, Feb 23, Mar 9
Pinto, Miss (actor), 1779: DL, Mar 23
Pinto, Mrs Charles (singer), 1766: CG, Nov 12, 15, Dec 1, 3, 20, 31; 1767:
KING'S, Jan 23, CG, 29, Feb 11, 14, 17, Mar 6, 30, Apr 21, 29, May 5, 11,
CHAPEL, 13, CG, Sep 18, Oct 13, 20, 22, 30, Nov 4, Dec 2, 14; 1768: KING'S,
Feb 5, CG, Mar 22, 24, May 5, 11, 13, 24, Sep 24, Oct 7, 13, 18, 22, Nov 25,
Dec 12; 1769: CG, Jan 14, Feb 1, Mar 7, 18, MARLY, Aug 10, 17, CG, Sep 18,
25, 27, 29, Nov 24, 28, Dec 5; 1770: CG, Jan 5, Apr 21, May 4, 5, 9, 17;
1771: CG, Apr 6
Pinto, Thomas (violinist), 1798: CG, Feb 23
Pious orgies (song), 1786: DL, Mar 22; 1787: DL, Feb 23; 1788: DL, Feb 8; 1789:
DL, Mar 18, CG, 20; 1790: DL, Feb 26, CG, Mar 26; 1791: DL, Mar 23; 1792:

KING'S, Feb 24; 1793: CG, Feb 15, KING/HAY, 15, 22, 27, CG, Mar 13; 1794: CG,
   Mar 7, DL, Apr 10; 1795: CG, Mar 4; 1796: CG, Mar 16; 1797: CG, Mar 31; 1798:
   CG, Mar 28; 1799: CG, Feb 15; 1800: CG, Mar 19
Piovene, Agostino, 1724: KING'S, Oct 31
Piozzi, Hester Lynch (epiloguist), 1788: DL, Mar 29; 1797: DL, May 1
Piping Pedlar (dance), 1785: CG, Nov 10, 11, 12, Dec 7; 1786: CG, Jan 6, Feb 2,
   7, 13, 18, 27, Apr 28, Oct 2, 12; 1787: CG, May 15, Nov 29; 1788: CG, Apr 19,
   Oct 21; 1789: CG, May 2; 1790: CG, Mar 23
Pipo (musician), 1719: HIC, Feb 13, MTH, Apr 29, DL, Nov 24; 1721: KING'S, Apr
   15; 1722: DL, Mar 14
Pipo's scholar (musician), 1719: MTH, Apr 29
Pippard (beneficiary), 1717: SH, Dec 23
Piramo e Tisbe. See Rauzzini, Venanzio; Bianchi Jr, Francesco.
Pirate's life (song), 1798: CG, Oct 15
Pirates, The. See Cobb, James.
Pirates' Dance (dance), 1774: DL, Apr 22; 1775: DL, Apr 22, 25, 29, May 2, 16,
   20, 22, 23, 26; 1777: HAY, Jun 19; 1782: HAY, Jun 11
Pirhame et Thisbe (dance), 1774: KING'S, Nov 8, 19
Pirker (Pircher), Sga (singer), 1746: KING'S, Nov 4; 1747: KING'S, Apr 14, Nov
   14; 1748: HAY, Jan 12, 29, KING'S, Mar 1, Apr 5
Pirkins (musician), 1758: MARLY, Aug 21
Piron, Alexis
--Gustave Vasa; or, Gustavus the Great, King of Sweden, 1735: GF/HAY, Feb 5
Pirro. See Paisiello, Giovanni.
Pisard (actor), 1728: HAY, Feb 21
Piscina, Maria Rosa (singer), 1711: QUEEN'S, Nov 21
Piso's Conspiracy (play, anon), 1675: DL, Aug 0
Pitchford (musician), 1713: HAW, Jun 27; 1715: CL, Jun 13; 1717: LIF, Oct 14
Pitel, Francoise (actor), 1677: ATCOURT, Dec 17
Piternesso, Miss (actor), 1736: LIF, Mar 31
Pitman (dancer), 1798: CG, Mar 19
Pitrot, Antoine (dancer), 1773: KING'S, Nov 20, 30, Dec 7; 1774: KING'S, Jan
   29, Feb 17, Mar 8, Apr 14, 19, 28, May 12; 1784: KING'S, May 20
Pitrot, Carolina (dancer), 1786: KING'S, Jan 24, Feb 18, Mar 11, 23, Apr 1, Jun
   1, 6, Jul 1
Pitt (actor), 1728: LIF, Jan 17, 29, May 22, Jun 25, Jul 2, 5, 19, BFHM, Aug
   24; 1729: LIF, Jan 13, Mar 4, Apr 23, 26, May 12, 14, Sep 19; 1730: LIF, Mar
   21, May 21, 23, SOU, Sep 24, LIF, Oct 7, 12
Pitt (actor), 1774: HAY, Apr 4
Pitt (ticket deliverer), 1794: CG, Jun 4; 1795: CG, Jun 4; 1796: CG, May 21;
   1797: CG, May 25, Jun 21; 1799: CG, Jun 4; 1800: CG, Jun 4
Pitt, Ann (actor), 1745: DL, Jan 12, 16, Mar 30, May 8, Nov 30; 1746: DL, Jan
   17, Mar 13, Apr 11, 21, 23, May 1, 14, Sep 23, 27, 30, Oct 11, 31, Dec 6, 20,
   26; 1747: DL, Feb 7, 25, Mar 3, 16, Apr 25, May 1; 1748: DL, Sep 13, 20, 22,
   Oct 12, 13, Nov 7, 12, 28, Dec 21, 28; 1749: DL, Jan 23, 25, 27, Feb 4, Apr
   29, May 2, 5, 6, 8, 12, Sep 16, 19, 20, 26, Oct 14, 24, Nov 27, Dec 2, 12,
   18, 26, 28; 1750: DL, Jan 22, Mar 13, 24, Apr 26, Sep 11, 15, 22, Oct 26, 30,
   Nov 14, Dec 14; 1751: DL, Jan 5, 10, 12, 17, 22, 26, 28, Feb 2, Mar 16, Apr
   25, 29, May 3, 13, 18, CG, Sep 27, Oct 29, Nov 7, 22; 1752: CG, Jan 6, 28,
   Feb 6, Apr 1, 28, Sep 20, Oct 14, 18, Dec 2, 5, 7, 12, 13, 14, 23; 1753: CG,
   Jan 8, 16, 22, Feb 6, 7, 13, Mar 20, Apr 5, 28, May 14, Sep 10, 12, 14, 17,
   24, Oct 1, 3, 5, 8, 10, 17, 22, Nov 2, 7, 22, 26, Dec 5; 1754: CG, Feb 12,
   Mar 18, Apr 20, 22, 23, 24, May 7, 8, 13, 18, Sep 16, 18, 20, 25, 27, 30, Oct
   2, 4, 7, 9, 14, 15, 16, Nov 1, 6, 12, 14, 20; 1755: CG, Jan 21, Feb 8, 18,
   Apr 10, 11, 18, May 2, 15, 19, 22, Oct 1, 3, 6, 10, 14, 16, 17, 18, 20, 21,
   22, 23, 27, 31, Nov 3, 21, Dec 3, 4, 12; 1756: CG, Jan 21, Feb 19, 20, Mar
   20, 25, 27, Apr 20, May 1, 10, 17, 21, Sep 20, 22, 27, Oct 1, 4, 6, 8, 13,
   14, 20, 21, 22, 25, 28, Nov 8, 11, 13, 16, 17, 22, Dec 1, 10, 17, 29; 1757:
   CG, Jan 8, Apr 15, 27, May 2, 4, 5, 6, Sep 14, 16, 21, 23, 26, 28, Oct 5, 10,
   12, 13, 15, 19, 20, 22, 28, 31, Nov 5, 9, 18, 26, Dec 7, 8; 1758: CG, Jan 28,
   Feb 21, Mar 11, 29, Apr 3, 24, Sep 18, 20, 22, 25, Oct 4, 6, 9, 13, 20, 24,
   25, Nov 1, 3, 9, 16, 18, 21, Dec 9; 1759: CG, Jan 4, Feb 1, Mar 5, 22, 27,
   Apr 7, May 1, 8, 23, Sep 24, DL, Oct 27, CG, Nov 24, 28, Dec 6, 7, 10, 13,
   18, 28, 29; 1760: CG, Jan 14, 16, 31, Feb 14, Mar 17, 24, Apr 8, 24, 25, 29,
   May 2, 8, 12, 19, Sep 22, 29, Oct 6, 8, 10, 13, 14, 17, 20, 23, Nov 18; 1761:
   CG, Jan 2, 6, 28, Feb 17, Mar 25, Apr 6, 21, May 11, Sep 9, 11, 14, 16, 18,
   23, 25, 28, 30, Oct 2, 5, 7, 9, 13, 14, 20, 26, Nov 13, Dec 11; 1762: CG, Jan
   28, Apr 21, 30, May 13, Sep 22, 24, Oct 1, 2, 4, 5, 14, 16, 19, 20, 21, 25,
   Nov 1, 16, Dec 18, 23, 27; 1763: CG, Jan 26, Mar 21, Apr 12, 15, 25, May 20,
   Sep 19, 21, 23, 26, 28, Oct 8, 10, 12, 14, 15, 19, 21, 24, 26, Nov 10, 18,
   Dec 9; 1764: CG, Jan 9, 20, 26, 28, Feb 1, 9, 15, Mar 20, 27, Apr 7, May 1,
   Sep 17, 21, 24, 26, 28, Oct 3, 5, 10, 16, 17, 18, 20, 27, Nov 1, 8, 16; 1765:

CG, Jan 8, 31, Mar 21, Apr 19, 24, 30, Sep 16, 20, 25, 27, Oct 2, 5, 7, 8, 10, 11, 12, 15, 16, 19, 26, 30, 31, Nov 19, 27, Dec 3, 12, 26; 1766: CG, Feb 6, 11, Mar 15, Apr 2, 21, 25, 26, Sep 22, Oct 6, 10, 16, 21, 22, 23, 25, 28, Nov 8, 15, 18, 25, 27, Dec 6, 16, 20, 30; 1767: CG, Mar 21, Apr 11, May 5, 14, 21, 22, Sep 15, 17, 18, 19, 22, 25, 26, Oct 8, 9, 13, 19, Nov 6, 10, 27, 28, Dec 8, 26; 1768: CG, Jan 29, Feb 1, Mar 8, Apr 27, May 5, 11, 13, 24, Jun 1, HAY, 10, 17, 23, 29, Jul 8, 25, 27, Aug 8, CG, Sep 19, 23, 24, 26, 29, 30, Oct 6, 7, 8, 10, 11, 15, 21, Nov 4, 16, Dec 21; 1769: CG, Feb 25, Apr 7, 24, 28, May 23, Sep 18, 20, 22, 29, 30, Oct 3, 6, 14, 18, Nov 2, 3, 4, 8, 11, 29, Dec 1, 7, 19, 20, 29; 1770: CG, Jan 27, Feb 23, Mar 20, 23, 31, Apr 20, 25, May 5, 7, Sep 28, Oct 1, 2, 8, 11, 13, 18, 25, Nov 16, 23, Dec 12, 17; 1771: CG, Jan 25, 26, Apr 23, 30, May 1, 3, 7, 27, Sep 23, 27, Oct 2, 4, 25, 28, Nov 1, 8, 16, Dec 7, 9, 18; 1772: CG, Jan 4, 27, Feb 22, Mar 30, 31, Apr 4, 22, 28, May 14, 15, 19, 25, Jun 1, Sep 25, 30, Oct 1, 13, 14, 23, 30, Nov 2, 6, 14, Dec 22, 28; 1773: CG, Mar 20, 22, 27, Apr 13, 16, 23, 27, May 3, 6, 10, 18, 19, 22, 28, Sep 20, 22, 29, Oct 6, 22, 23, 25, 27, 28, Dec 1, 7, 17; 1774: CG, Jan 3, 15, 29, Feb 7, Mar 15, Apr 5, 23, May 6, Sep 23, 28, 30, Oct 5, 7, 13, 14, 21, 27, Nov 1, 2, 3, 12, 19, Dec 1, 6, 20, 27; 1775: CG, Feb 18, Mar 30, Apr 28, May 2, 4, 9, 17, Jun 1, Sep 25, 27, Oct 4, 9, 16, 18, 19, 20, 31, Nov 4, 7, 21, 24, Dec 7, 23; 1776: CG, Jan 5, Feb 5, 9, 26, Mar 5, 19, 30, Apr 10, 26, 27, 30, May 10, 13, 14, Sep 23, 27, 30, Oct 4, 7, 9, 16, 25, Nov 1, 2, 4, 12, 15, 19, 26, Dec 2, 4; 1777: CG, Jan 3, DL, 4, Apr 14, 22, 28, May 2, 5, 6, 7, 14, DL, Sep 20, CG, 22, 24, 26, 29, Oct 8, 17, Nov 3, 12, 21, Dec 19; 1778: CG, Jan 29, Feb 6, 24, 26, Mar 2, 14, Apr 21, 25, 28, May 4, 9, 11, 13, 16, 21, 25, Sep 18, 21, 30, Oct 2, 5, 7, 9, 15, 17, 21, 26, 27, 29, Nov 4, 14, Dec 8, 10, 11, 12, 19; 1779: CG, Jan 2, 13, 26, Feb 13, Mar 9, Apr 12, 24, 26, 27, 29, May 3, 10, 15, 18, Sep 20, 24, 27, Oct 1, 11, 13, 16, 18, 23, Nov 8, 9, 12, 13, 16, 22, 23, 30, Dec 1, 3, 11, 16, 29; 1780: CG, Jan 18, 25, Feb 8, 12, Apr 12, 19, 21, 27, May 5, 12, 19, Sep 21, 22, Oct 2, 6, 23, 24, 31, Nov 1, 22, 27, Dec 5, DL, 20, 23, CG, 28; 1781: CG, Jan 10, 13, 25, Feb 15, Mar 8, Apr 18, 20, 21, 28, May 2, Sep 17, 21, 24, Oct 3, 13, 16, 23, 27, Nov 7, 9, 28, Dec 8, 11, 17, 26; 1782: CG, Jan 11, 18, Apr 4, 9, 17, 20, 24, 30, May 3, 11, 20, 28, Sep 23, 25, 30, Oct 2, 4, 7, 9, 15, 17, 22, 23, Nov 6, 18, 30, Dec 6, 30, 31; 1783: CG, Apr 1, Sep 17, 22, 26, Oct 6, 8, 11, 16, 17, 24, Nov 6, 10, Dec 6, 20; 1784: CG, Jan 7, Mar 6, 20, 27, Apr 27, May 1, 10, 11, 12, 26, 28, 29, Sep 21, 22, 24, 29, Oct 1, 4, 12, 25, 27, 28, 30, Nov 13, 20, Dec 1, 22, 28; 1785: CG, Mar 5, 29, Apr 8, May 18, Sep 19, 21, 26, 30, Oct 7, 12, 19, 27, Nov 1, 14, 29, Dec 8, 14, 15, 22; 1786: CG, Jan 28, Mar 4, 11, Apr 24, May 9, 29, Oct 19, 23, Nov 14, 15, 22, 24, 29, Dec 12, 23; 1787: CG, Jan 2, 31, May 1, 9, 16, 21, Sep 17, 19, 21, 24, Oct 1, 3, 11, 29, Nov 5, 20, 23, Dec 21, 26; 1788: CG, Jan 15, Mar 1, 29, Apr 1, 8, DL, Jun 10, CG, Sep 15, 22, Oct 8, 13, 24, Nov 7, 12, 20, DL, 24, CG, 28; 1789: CG, Jan 3, Apr 4, Jun 2, Sep 14, Oct 9, 20, Nov 2, Dec 10; 1790: CG, Mar 8, 22, 27, Apr 21, 24, 29, May 5, 7, 11, Sep 13, Oct 1, 13, 30, Nov 6, 25, Dec 11; 1791: CG, Jan 3, 12, Feb 11, Mar 5, 12, May 2, Jun 1, 3, 6, Sep 21, 26, Oct 5, Nov 15, 24, Dec 3; 1792: CG, Feb 8, 28, Jun 2
Pitt, Harriett (dancer), 1763: CG, Apr 30, Dec 8; 1764: CG, Mar 27, Apr 14, 27, 28, May 1, 3, 5, 9, 11, 12, 14, 16, 23, 24, 25, Dec 12; 1765: CG, Mar 26, Apr 9, 10, 12, 17, 29, 30, May 3, 7, 8, 22, 23, Nov 15; 1766: CG, Mar 18, Apr 8, 9, 12, 21, 30, May 7, 16, Nov 20, Dec 23; 1768: CG, May 24
Pitt, Master (dancer), 1741: CG, May 1, DL, 13
Pitt, Mrs (singer), 1776: DL, Oct 18, Nov 25, Dec 10; 1777: DL, Jan 1, Apr 22; 1778: DL, Jan 5, May 23
Pitt, Mrs (ticket deliverer), 1797: CG, Jun 2; 1798: CG, May 19; 1799: CG, May 21
Pittard, Joseph (actor), 1749: JS, Dec 27; 1754: HAY/SFB, Sep 26; 1755: HAY, Sep 9, 11, 15; 1757: CG, May 25, HAY, Sep 28; 1758: DL, Jan 12, HAY, 12, 16, 18; 1767: CG, Mar 4
Pittcarn, Master (actor), 1759: HAY, May 10
Pittore Parigino, Il. See Cimarosa, Domenico.
Pitts (spectator), 1697: LIF, Feb 19, 27
Piu amabile belta (song), 1751: KING'S, Apr 16
Pix, Mary, 1701: LIF, Mar 0; 1703: LIF, Nov 0; 1704: LIF, Nov 13; 1705: QUEEN'S, May 0; 1706: QUEEN'S, Jun 0; 1709: DL, May 28
--Adventures in Madrid, 1706: QUEEN'S, Jun 0
--Beau Defeated, The; or, The Lucky Younger Brother, 1700: LIF, Mar 0
--Conquest of Spain, The, 1705: QUEEN'S, May 0
--Czar of Muscovy, The, 1701: LIF, Mar 0
--Deceiver Deceived, The, 1697: LIF, Nov 0; 1698: NONE, Sep 0
--Different Widows, The; or, Intrigue a la Mode, 1703: LIF, Nov 0
--Double Distress, The, 1701: LIF, Mar 0
--False Friend, The; or, The Fate of Disobedience, 1699: LIF, May 0

668

--French Beau, The, 1698: NONE, Sep 0
--Ibrahim, the Thirteenth Emperour of the Turks, 1696: DL, May 0; 1702: DL, Oct
   20; 1704: DL, Jan 8, Feb 18; 1715: LIF, Mar 14, 15
--Innocent Mistress, The, 1697: LIF, Jun 0
--Queen Catharine; or, The Ruins of Love, 1698: LIF, Jun 0
--Spanish Wives, The; or, The Governor of Barcelona, 1696: DG, Aug 0; 1699: DL,
   Feb 2; 1703: DL, Jul 14; 1711: DL, Jun 26; 1726: LIF, Aug 12, 16
Pizarre; ou, La Conquete du Perou (dance), 1797: KING'S, Feb 7, 11, 14, 21, 25,
   Jul 4
Pizarro. See Sheridan, Richard Brinsley.
Pla (musician), 1769: HAY, Feb 9
Placido (equilibrist), 1766: HAY, Oct 27
Placido, Master (acrobat), 1766: HAY, Oct 27
Placido, Sga (equilibrist), 1766: HAY, Oct 27
Plague on both your Houses (entertainment), 1794: CG, May 13
Plaida (tumbler), 1767: SW, Jun 13
Plain Dealer, The. See Wycherley, William.
Plain Truth (song), 1728: LIF, Mar 28
Plain, Miss (actor), 1782: HAY, Jan 14
Plaisirs Provincials Basque (dance), 1732: DL, Apr 24
Plank (ticket deliverer), 1789: CG, Jun 13; 1790: CG, Jun 8; 1791: CG, Jun 9;
   1792: CG, Jun 1
Planxty (song), 1792: CG, Apr 21, HAY, Aug 15; 1793: CG, Mar 18; 1794: CG, May
   23, HAY, Aug 28; 1797: CG, May 20; 1799: CG, May 13, Jun 6
Plas, the two (musicians), 1754: DL, Mar 27
Platonic Wife, The. See Griffith, Elizabeth.
Platonick Lady, The. See Centlivre, Susannah.
Platonick Love; or, The Innocent Mistake (play, anon), 1718: LIF, Nov 24
Platt (actor, dancer), 1789: CG, Dec 26; 1790: CG, Jan 23, HAY, Jun 25, Aug 11,
   CG, Oct 4; 1791: CG, May 2, 7, Jun 13, HAY, Jul 1, CG, Nov 12, Dec 22; 1792:
   CG, Oct 8, Dec 26; 1793: CG, Mar 11, Oct 18, Nov 16; 1795: CG, Feb 19, May 1,
   Dec 21; 1796: CG, Jan 4, Mar 15, Apr 8, 9, 20, May 10; 1798: CG, Mar 19, Apr
   30, Sep 17, Oct 11, 15, 25, Nov 9, Dec 8, 11; 1799: CG, Jan 29, Mar 2, 5, 25,
   Apr 13, May 13, 25, Jun 4, Sep 18, Oct 21, 25, Dec 23; 1800: CG, Feb 10, Mar
   4, 25, 27, Apr 5, 23, 29, May 1, 7, 27, Jun 2, 13
Platt (carpenter), 1760: CG, Mar 29
Platt, Bart (singer), 1720: SOU, Oct 3; 1725: BF, Aug 23; 1730: GF, Jun 29;
   1731: SFLH, Sep 8; 1732: GF, Apr 24; 1746: SFLY, Sep 8; 1747: BFH, Aug 22;
   1748: SOU, Sep 26, Oct 10; 1749: JS, Mar 15, 21, BF/SFP, Aug 23, Sep 7; 1751:
   SF, Sep 9, 18; 1752: SOU, Sep 29; 1756: BFSI, Sep 3
Platt, Master (singer), 1796: CG, Dec 19; 1797: CG, Jun 5; 1798: CG, Nov 12;
   1799: CG, Apr 13; 1800: CG, Feb 10
Platt, Miss (actor), 1748: SOU, Sep 26; 1749: JS, Mar 15, BF/SFP, Aug 23; 1763:
   HAY, Jul 18, Aug 1
Platt, Mrs S J (actor), 1768: DL, Oct 18, 25, 28, Nov 17, Dec 6, 12; 1769: DL,
   Jan 20, Mar 11, 28, Apr 3, 10, Sep 19, Nov 2, 8, 23, 28, Dec 13, 16; 1770:
   DL, Jan 6, 10, 15, 16, 19, Feb 21, Mar 3, 26, 27, May 9, 14, 29, 30, Jun 7,
   Sep 25, Oct 4, 9, 12, 16, 17, 25, 31, Nov 16, 17, 24, Dec 13, 21, 31; 1771:
   DL, Mar 16, Apr 1, 2, 6, 15, May 27, Sep 26, Oct 5, 15, 17, 25, 26, 29, Nov
   22, 28; 1772: DL, Jan 3, 9, 15, 20, Feb 17, 21, 26, Mar 26, Apr 6, 22, 25,
   29, May 12, HAY, Jun 8, Jul 6, 15, Aug 10, 26, Sep 8, 17, DL, 19, Oct 6, 13,
   16, 21, 28, Nov 12, 28, Dec 2, 17, 21, 22, 26; 1773: DL, Feb 11, 17, 25, 27,
   Mar 23, Apr 1, 3, 21, May 6, HAY, 17, DL, 19, 24, HAY, 28, 31, Jun 4, 14, 18,
   Jul 2, 16, 21, 26, Aug 4, 11, 27, Sep 3, 17, DL, 25, Oct 5, 6, 9, 11, 13, 19,
   Nov 9, 15, 26, Dec 16, 27, 30; 1774: DL, Jan 5, 18, 19, 20, Feb 15, Mar 10,
   12, 14, 19, 26, Apr 21, 25, 26, 28, HAY, May 16, DL, 20, HAY, Jun 6, 13, 15,
   17, 27, Jul 6, 15, Aug 26, Sep 5, 6, 12, DL, 17, 27, 29, Oct 8, 21, Nov 1, 4,
   7, 8, 11, 18, 29, 30, Dec 7; 1775: DL, Jan 2, 4, 21, Feb 23, Mar 18, 25, Apr
   24, 29, May 6, 10, 12, HAY, 19, 24, Jun 5, 7, 12, 16, Jul 14, 31, Aug 9, 28,
   Sep 4, 16, 18, DL, 23, 28, 30, Oct 7, 10, 14, 21, 26, 28, 30, Nov 9, 14, 18,
   Dec 2, 6, 19; 1776: DL, Jan 13, Mar 18, 23, 25, Apr 22, 24, May 7, 11, 13,
   HAY, 20, 22, 28, 31, DL, Jun 3, HAY, 12, 19, Jul 1, 3, 5, 8, Aug 2, 14, 16,
   19, Sep 16, 20, DL, 21, 28, Oct 18, 19, 22, 25, Nov 5, 9, Dec 28, 31; 1777:
   DL, Jan 28, Feb 20, 24, Mar 20, Apr 3, 17, 22, 29, HAY, May 28, Jun 19, Jul
   7, 15, 30, Aug 9, 19, 25, 28, Sep 17, 19; 1778: HAY, May 21, Jun 1, 3, 8, Aug
   6, 21, CG, Sep 28, Oct 5, Dec 8, 12; 1779: CG, Jan 2, 22, Feb 11, Mar 20, Apr
   21, 28, May 3, Oct 13, Nov 1, 10, 19, 23, Dec 11; 1780: CG, Jan 18, 25, Sep
   25, Oct 9, 24, Nov 24, 25, Dec 27; 1781: CG, Jan 18, Feb 24, Mar 24, May 10,
   DL, 18, CG, Oct 5, 16, 31, Dec 5; 1782: CG, Jan 7, 9, Feb 9, 14, Oct 2, 3,
   14, 19, 21, 22, 26, Nov 2, Dec 2, 7; 1783: CG, Jan 1, 3, 28, Feb 25, Mar 29,
   Apr 1, Oct 13, 14, 20, 21, 28, 31, Nov 8, 24, 27, Dec 6; 1784: CG, Jan 7, 16,
   Feb 5, 12, 20, Mar 6, 22, Apr 26, May 11, 18, Jun 14, Sep 21, Oct 11, 18, 27,

28, 30, Nov 29, 30, Dec 13; 1785: CG, Mar 29, Apr 2, 6, 11, 12, Sep 21, 28,
  30, Oct 10, 14, 27, 28, Nov 2, 14, 19, 29; 1786: CG, Feb 4, 11, 16, Mar 6,
  11, Apr 18, 19, 24, May 15, 19, 26, 29, Sep 20, 25, Oct 23, 30, Nov 13, 24,
  Dec 15, 20; 1787: CG, Jan 4, 26, 27, 31, Feb 6, Mar 27, Apr 11, 27, 30, May
  11, Sep 24, Oct 1, 3, 19, 22, 31, Nov 2, 16, 20, Dec 10; 1788: CG, Jan 11,
  14, 18, 21, Feb 4, 25, Mar 1, 10, 24, Apr 1, Sep 22, 24, Oct 29, Nov 1, 10,
  21, 26, Dec 1, 26; 1789: CG, Apr 4, 20, 28, 30, May 19, 29, Jun 2, Sep 14,
  16, 18, 23, 25, 30, Nov 7, 12, 19, 20, 23, Dec 11, 31; 1790: CG, Jan 20, Mar
  22, 27, Apr 21, Sep 13, 29, Oct 11, 18, 23, Dec 2, 10, 28; 1791: CG, May 5,
  Jun 1, Sep 12, 17, 19, 26, 30, Oct 17, 20, 21, 24, 27, Nov 4, Dec 2; 1792:
  CG, Mar 31, Apr 10, 12, May 19, Jun 2, Sep 21, Oct 5, 8, 15, 19, 24, Nov 5,
  6, 12; 1793: CG, Jan 9, 14, Mar 4, Sep 17, 25, 27, 30, Oct 7, 8, 9, 14, 18,
  22, Nov 23, Dec 5, 7, 18, 20; 1794: CG, Jan 6, Feb 5, 26, Mar 17, May 6, 7,
  16, Sep 15, 19, Oct 1, 3, 8, 14, 15, Dec 6, 8, 18; 1795: CG, Mar 14, 16, 17,
  19, 28, Apr 7, 8, 22, 23, 25, 29, May 9, 29, Sep 14, 16, 23, 25, Oct 8, 15,
  16, 19, 24, Nov 9, 16, 27, Dec 4, 15; 1796: CG, Jan 6, 7, 11, 13, Feb 2, Apr
  19, 22, May 3, Jun 6, Sep 12, 21, 26, Oct 14, 21, Nov 5, 21, 24, Dec 10, 17;
  1797: CG, Jan 4, Feb 20, Apr 8, 19, May 4, 16, Jun 2, Sep 20, 22, 25, 29, Oct
  2, 4, 6, 11, Nov 2, 11, 15, 20, 21; 1798: CG, Jan 4, 5, Mar 22, 31, Apr 19,
  May 8, 30, Sep 17, 19, 21, 26, 28, Oct 3, 8, Nov 21; 1799: CG, Mar 16, Apr 9,
  13, May 6, Sep 23, 27, 30, Oct 2, 7, 11, 14, 18, 31, Nov 8
Platto, Don (beneficiary), 1753: HAY, Apr 5
Plautus, 1730: WS, Jan 15; 1733: DL/HAY, Dec 12; 1734: DL/HAY, Jan 9, DL, Oct
  8, CG/LIF, 9, Nov 2, DL, 23, Dec 31; 1735: DL, Apr 16, Oct 2, Dec 15; 1736:
  DL, Jan 31, Feb 19, May 6, Oct 25, Nov 30, Dec 18; 1737: DL, May 24, Sep 17;
  1738: DL, Feb 11, Apr 11, May 12, Nov 2, 10, Dec 23; 1739: DL, Jan 15; 1792:
  HAY, Aug 31
--Amphitryo, 1730: WS, Jan 15
Play is the Plot, The. See Breval, John.
Play of Love (song), 1725: LIF, Mar 18, Apr 2, 30; 1726: LIF, Apr 13, 26, May
  4, 13, Jun 17
Playhouse Act, 1737: HAY, Feb 19; 1745: DL, Apr 6
Playhouse Glee (song), 1793: CG, Dec 19; 1794: CG, Jun 13, Sep 22
Playhouse Passage, 1737: DL, Apr 23; 1740: CG, Mar 27, Apr 23; 1742: DL, Feb
  24, Mar 20, CG, 22, DL, 22, Apr 29; 1797: CG, Dec 6
Playhouse To Be Let, The. See Davenant, Sir William.
Pleasant Marriage, The (play, anon), 1726: KING'S, Oct 28
Pleasant Month of May (song), 1734: LIF, Oct 1
Pleaseaway (actor), 1755: HAY, Sep 11, 15
Pleasure my former ways resigning (song), 1789: CG, Mar 20, Apr 3; 1790: DL,
  Feb 24, CG, 26, DL, Mar 12; 1791: CG, Mar 23, DL, Apr 13; 1792: CG, Mar 2;
  1793: CG, Mar 6, KING/HAY, 13; 1794: DL, Mar 14, Apr 2, 11; 1795: KING'S, Mar
  13, CG, 13; 1796: CG, Feb 24, Mar 2; 1797: CG, Mar 15; 1800: CG, Mar 14
Pleasure's a Golden Reign (song), 1756: CG, Apr 19
Pleasures of Spring (dance), 1762: CG, Feb 12, 19, 23, Mar 18, 20, 23, 25, Apr
  1, 3, 13, 14, 23, May 6, 11, 12, 14, 19, 20, 21, Dec 2, 6, 15, 22
Pleasures of the Chace (song), 1791: CG, May 19; 1792: CG, May 15
Pleasures of the Town, The (puppetry), 1748: CG, Mar 28
Pleasures of the Town, The. See Fielding, Henry.
Pledge of Love; or, British Tar's Farewell (song), 1798: CG, May 15, 25
Plenius, Miss (singer), 1763: MARLY, Jun 28
Pleyel, Ignaz Joseph (composer), 1788: CG, Dec 13; 1789: CG, Nov 24, DL, 24;
  1790: CG, Mar 8, DL, Apr 16, CG, May 13, DL, Oct 4, CG, 4; 1791: PAN, Dec 31;
  1793: CG, Mar 11; 1794: HAY, Aug 18, CG, Dec 26; 1795: HAY, Mar 4, CG, Apr 9;
  1799: KING'S, Mar 26
Pliemess, Miss (singer), 1759: DL, Mar 23
Plinne (ticket deliverer), 1798: CG, Jun 5; 1799: CG, May 29; 1800: CG, Jun 11
Plomer, Mrs (actor), 1724: LIF, Jul 21, Aug 11, SOU, Sep 24; 1725: LIF, Feb 27,
  May 10, BF, Aug 23; 1731: GF, Feb 12, 17, 27, Mar 2, 22, Apr 8, 10, 26, 27,
  28, May 7, 14, 17, Jun 8, BFB, Aug 26
Plomer, Mrs (actor), 1788: HAY, Jun 12, 23, Jul 1, 31, Aug 13, Sep 3, 13; 1789:
  HAY, May 18, 27, Jun 3, 5, 12, Jul 7, Aug 11; 1796: CG, May 10
Plot and No Plot; or, Hanging Better than Marriage (entertainment), 1735: GF,
  Feb 17
Plot and no Plot, A. See Dennis, John.
Plot, The. See Kelly, John.
Plots of Harlequin, The (pantomime, anon), 1724: HAY, Feb 20
Plotting Lovers, The; or, The Old One Tricked at Last (farce, anon), 1743: SF,
  Sep 8
Plough and Harrow Tavern, 1786: HAMM, Aug 5
Plowman (dance), 1759: CG, Nov 21, 23; 1760: CG, Jan 4, 12, Feb 12, 16, Mar 3,
  17

Plowman, Henry (actor), 1738: CG, Dec 6; 1740: CG, Nov 7
Plummer (boxkeeper), 1744: DL, May 14; 1745: DL, May 6; 1746: DL, May 14; 1747:
   DL, May 4; 1748: CG, Apr 26; 1749: CG, Nov 30, Dec 4; 1753: CG, May 18; 1754:
   CG, May 17; 1755: CG, May 19; 1756: CG, May 21
Plumptre, Anne (author), 1799: CG, Apr 12, DL, May 24
Plumtree St, 1735: CG/LIF, May 12; 1737: CG, May 10
Plutarch, 1692: NONE, Feb 12
Pluto furens & vinctus; or, The raging devil bound (play), 1669: NONE, Jan 5
Plym, Miss (actor), 1763: DL, Oct 19, Nov 4; 1764: DL, Jan 18, 25, Feb 14, 21,
   Mar 3, 26, Apr 14, May 1, 2, 22, Sep 18, 25, Oct 4, 6, 22, 23, 25, Nov 9, 17,
   Dec 13, 18; 1765: DL, Jan 1, 3, 15, 18, 23, Mar 7, Apr 11, May 3, 14, 18, 22,
   Sep 19, 21, 24, Oct 15, 18, 23, 24, Nov 14, Dec 7; 1766: DL, Jan 6, 23, 28,
   29, Feb 20, Mar 15, 17, 20, 22, Apr 9, 16, 18, 25, May 3, 5, 6, 10, 19, 20,
   21, 22, Sep 20, 27, Oct 9, 10, 16, 17, 18, 21, 23, Nov 17, 18, 20, 28, Dec
   10, 13; 1767: DL, Jan 2, 24, 31, Feb 7, 12, Mar 30, 31, Apr 6, 21, 30, May 21
Plymouth In An Uproar. See Neville, Edward.
Plymouth Theatre, 1794: CG, Sep 24
Pochee (dancer), 1755: DL, Nov 8, 15
Pocock (spectator), 1760: DL, Oct 2
Poem in Praise of Virtue (entertainment), 1702: SH, May 7
Poem upon God's Omnipresence (entertainment), 1702: CC, May 21
Poem upon Music (entertainment), 1702: SH, Jan 31
Poem upon the Reformation of Poetry (entertainment), 1702: SH, May 7
Poet Buskin will give Chocolate, The (entertainment), 1748: HAY, Apr 13
Poetaster, The. See Jonson, Ben.
Poetess, The (play, anon), 1667: BRIDGES, Oct 7
Poetic Exordium (entertainment), 1773: KING'S, Nov 20
Poetical Address (entertainment), 1777: CHR, Jun 18; 1797: DL, Apr 8
Poetical Composition (entertainment), 1800: CG, Jun 12
Poetical Epistle from Shakespear, A (poetry), 1752: DL, Apr 17
Poetry and Music Descriptive of a Day (entertainment), 1791: CG, May 31
Poictiers. See Poitier.
Point at Herqui, The. See Cross, John Cartwright.
Point of Honour, The. See Kemble, Charles.
Poitier (Poictiers), Charles (dancer), 1739: CG, Dec 15; 1740: HAY, Apr 8, May
   15; 1742: DL, Apr 19, May 7; 1754: CG, Nov 26, 27; 1755: CG, Mar 17, Apr 15,
   18, 21, 22, 25, 28; 1756: KING'S, Mar 30, DL, May 3, CG, Oct 23; 1757: CG,
   Apr 16, 18, 23, 25, 26; 1758: CG, Apr 11; 1759: CG, Oct 15, 17, Nov 21, Dec
   5, 10, 11; 1760: CG, Jan 16, 18, Feb 16, Mar 3, 18, Apr 11, 17, May 28, Sep
   22, 29, Oct 20, Nov 28, Dec 11, 20, 22, 23, 31; 1761: CG, Jan 8, 9, 20, 22,
   Feb 2, 28, Mar 24, 26, 30, Apr 1, 6, 10, May 1, 25; see also Charles, Master
Poitier Jr's scholar (dancer), 1755: CG, Apr 15
Poitier, Charles and Jenny (dancer), 1742: DL, Apr 3; 1749: KING'S, Mar 7
Poitier, Jenny (dancer), 1742: DL, Apr 19, May 7; 1748: KING'S, Nov 8; 1750:
   HAY, Mar 1, 7, 13; 1754: HAY, May 29; 1755: DL, Feb 3, CG, Apr 15, DL, Sep
   27; 1762: CG, Oct 1, 4, 8, 26, Nov 1, 15, 29, Dec 30; 1763: CG, Jan 24, 28,
   Feb 24, Mar 15, Apr 15, 18, May 9; 1764: CG, Feb 22, Mar 3, 22, 24, Apr 2, 7,
   9, May 21, 26, Sep 21, Oct 1, 27, Nov 16; 1765: CG, Jan 15, 31, Feb 15, Mar
   14, 21, Apr 12, 26, 29, May 6, Oct 3, 7, 8, 12, 14, 22; 1766: CG, Feb 5, Apr
   9, CHAPEL, 30, CG, Oct 10, 14, 21, Nov 15, 21, Dec 3; 1767: CG, Feb 14, 21,
   Apr 11, 20, 21, 27, May 5
Poitier, Michael (dancer), 1726: HAY, Mar 24, 28, Apr 13, 14, 18, 22, 25, 27,
   May 2, 6, 9, KING'S, Sep 28, Nov 1, 5, 19, 23, 26, Dec 3, 10, 17, 21; 1727:
   LIF, Jan 10, 31, Feb 3, 7, 8, 9, 13, Mar 11, 13, 16, 20, 23, Apr 3, 5, 10,
   12, 17, 19, 21, 24, 26, 27, May 3, 8, 12, 15, 17, 18, 19, 22, Jun 7, Sep 13,
   15, 20, 29, Oct 2, 12, 17, 26, Nov 1, 9, 16, 23, Dec 19; 1728: LIF, Jan 8,
   Mar 9, 14, 18, 21, 25, Apr 1, 6, 22, 23, 24, 29, May 3, 6, 8, 13, 15, 18, 20;
   1729: LIF, Oct 20, 24, Nov 1, 4, 11, 20, Dec 17, 19; 1730: LIF, Jan 2, Mar
   17, 21, Apr 10, 13, 22, 24, 27, 30, May 1, 4, 18, Sep 23, 25, Oct 7, 9, 19,
   Nov 7, Dec 3, 5, 15; 1731: LIF, Jan 4, 23, Mar 22, 25, Apr 1, 3, 22, 23, 24,
   26, 29, May 1, 3, 13, Jun 7, Oct 4, 13, 20, Nov 6, 18, Dec 7, 14; 1732: LIF,
   Jan 5, 19, Feb 9, Apr 13, 14, 17, 18, 24, 25, 28, May 1, 2, 5, 8, 9, 10, 17,
   LIF/CG, Sep 25, Oct 2, 4, 9, 13, 30, Nov 8, 9, 14, 16, 24, Dec 8, 12, 15,
   CG/LIF, 16, 19, LIF/CG, 27; 1733: CG/LIF, Jan 4, LIF/CG, 11, 12, 15, 27, 31,
   Feb 2, 3, 5, 6, CG, 8, LIF/CG, Mar 12, CG, 27, LIF/CG, 28, 29, Apr 11, CG,
   May 1, LIF/CG, 7, CG, Sep 20, 25, 29, Oct 4, 11, 13, 31, Nov 1, 12; 1734: DL,
   Feb 4, 25, DL/LIF, Mar 11, DL/HAY, 12, 18, 19, 23, 25, 28, 30, DL/LIF, Apr 1,
   DL, 4, 15, LIF, 26, DL, 29, DL/HAY, May 1, DL, 15, Sep 19, 24, Oct 3, 5, 8,
   10, 28, Nov 4, 5, 8, 11, 15, 18, 20, 22, Dec 2, 7, 26; 1735: DL, Jan 1, 4, 8,
   Feb 8, 24, 26, Mar 3, May 21, 26, 30, Jun 2, 5, 9, LIF, 12, DL, Sep 1, 9, Oct
   1, 22, 27, 28, Nov 3, 5, 8, 15, 17, 29, Dec 3, 8, 17, 29; 1736: DL, Jan 3,
   Feb 2, 4, 6, 9, 11, 12, 28, Mar 3, 23, 27, Apr 1, 13, 30, May 3, 5, 12, 15,

31, Aug 26, Sep 4, 7, 23; 1737: DL, Apr 2; 1738: CG, Mar 20, DL, Sep 12, Nov
   8, Dec 16, 18, 22; 1739: DL, Mar 1, Apr 3, 7, 14, May 10, 11, 12, 17, 18, 19,
   22, 23, 25, CG, Oct 10, 15, 27, 31, Nov 6, 7, 8, 14, 15, 20, 21, Dec 1, 4, 6,
   10, 14, 15, 17, 18; 1740: HAY, Apr 8; 1742: DL, Apr 3, 19, May 7; 1748:
   KING'S, Nov 8; 1754: CG, Dec 3; 1755: CG, Jan 4, Feb 8, 15, Mar 15, 18, Apr
   2, 24, 30; 1757: CG, Jan 10, 28, Apr 16, 29, 30, May 4, 9, 17, 19; 1758:
   KING'S, Apr 4, CG, 11; 1759: CG, Apr 27, Nov 30; 1760: CG, Jan 12, 16, Feb
   12, Mar 20, Apr 10, 11, 17, May 8, Sep 22, Oct 20, Dec 17; 1761: CG, Jan 2,
   Feb 12, Mar 2, Apr 9, May 20, 25; 1762: CG, Apr 23; 1763: CG, Nov 3; 1764:
   CG, Oct 18; 1767: KING'S, Jan 23
Poland St, 1777: DL, Apr 22; 1779: DL, May 17; 1788: CG, Jan 28, Apr 30; 1789:
   CG, Jan 26, May 20; 1790: CG, Jun 2; 1791: PAN, Mar 24, May 9, Jun 16; 1792:
   CG, Feb 28, May 22, HAY, Dec 26
Poland, 1700: LIF, Sep 25; 1734: DL, Nov 4
Polichinelles (dance), 1733: DL/HAY, Dec 3, 19
Polichinelli (puppetry), 1666: MOORFLDS, Aug 22, 29, Sep 1; 1667: CC, Mar 20,
   Apr 8, Oct 24; 1668: LIF, May 2, BF, Aug 31
Polidoro. See Vanneschi, Francesco.
Polifemo. See Porpora, Nicola.
Polish Ballet (dance), 1774: KING'S, Mar 24
Polish Ballet, Grand (dance), 1734: DL, Dec 21, 26; 1735: DL, Jan 1, 3, 22
Polish Dance (dance), 1734: DL/HAY, Mar 12, 16; 1735: GF/HAY, Feb 6; 1738: DL,
   May 5, 6, 9; 1747: DL, Nov 2, 3, 7, 9, 11, 25, 26; 1748: DL, Jan 23, Mar 26;
   1780: CG, Dec 5
Polish Dance, Grand (dance), 1738: DL, Jan 28, Feb 3, 8, 11, 14
Polite Conversation. See Swift, Jonathan.
Politic Maid (dance), 1742: LIF, Nov 29
Politic Queen, The. See Davenport, Robert.
Politic Whore, The; or, The Conceited Cuckhold (play, anon), 1679: NONE, Sep 0
Politician Cheated, The. See Greene, Alexander.
Politician Reformed, The. See R, T.
Politics on Both Sides (ballad opera, anon), 1735: LIF, Jul 30
Poll of Plymouth (song), 1793: CG, Dec 6; 1796: CG, May 20
Pollar (merchant), 1758: CG, Feb 7
Pollard, Mrs (actor), 1787: DL, Feb 7; 1792: HAY, Apr 16
Pollet, Mrs (actor), 1710: GR, Jun 21, Jul 29, Aug 10, Sep 11
Polleti (artificial flower seller), 1795: CG, Jan 28
Pollett (dancer), 1730: GF, Sep 28, 30, Oct 5, Nov 11; 1733: GF, Apr 20; 1736:
   CG, Nov 23
Pollett's son (dancer), 1726: LIF, Apr 25
Pollock (ticket deliverer), 1794: CG, May 31
Pollock, Mrs (actor), 1792: CG, Nov 24; 1793: CG, Jan 14, Oct 2, 10, Dec 20;
   1794: CG, Jun 16
Pollone, Clara (singer), 1779: KING'S, Feb 23, Apr 29; 1781: KING'S, Jun 5;
   1782: KING'S, Nov 2, Dec 19; 1783: KING'S, Jan 7, 14, 25, 28, Feb 27, Mar 6,
   27, May 1, Jun 3, 14; 1784: KING'S, Dec 18; 1785: KING'S, Jan 25, Apr 2, May
   28
Polly Honeycomb. See Colman the elder, George.
Polly Willis (song), 1746: GF, Mar 17, DL, 18
Polly. See Gay, John.
Polomba, A, 1754: CG, Jan 18
--Violante, La (burletta), 1754: CG, Jan 18
Polonaise (dance), 1725: DL, Mar 18, 31, LIF, Apr 20, 26, 28, May 1, DL, 10,
   LIF, 12, 19, 21, 24, Oct 1, 19, 22, Nov 8, 11, 18, 22, 24, DL, 25; 1726: DL,
   Apr 15, 18, 28, May 9, 11, LIF, 16, DL, 23, LIF, Oct 12; 1727: DL, Mar 23,
   Apr 24; 1728: DL, Apr 1; 1729: DL, Mar 13, Apr 23, May 14; 1730: LIF, Mar
   17, Apr 10, DL, 29; 1734: DL/HAY, Mar 18, 19, 25, 28, 30, Apr 1, 2, DL, Dec
   28, 31; 1735: DL, Jan 18, 21, 23, 25, 28, Feb 3, 4; 1736: LIF, May 19, CG,
   25, 31, DL, Oct 18, 19, 23, 26, 28, Nov 1; 1738: DL, Feb 20, 21, 28, Apr 11,
   29, May 1, 2, 3, 16; 1777: KING'S, Nov 4, 8, 18, Dec 16; 1778: KING'S, Jan 3,
   24, 31, Feb 7, 10, Mar 10, 21, 24, Jun 13; 1786: HAY, Jun 21, 28, Jul 5
Polonaise Ballet, Grand (dance), 1736: DL, Oct 12
Poluscenicon. See Wild, James.
Polwart on the Green (song), 1730: LIF, May 21, 25, Jun 1
Pomfret, Countess of, 1760: DL, Dec 23
Pompeati, Sga (singer), 1746: KING'S, Jan 7, 28, Mar 25, May 13
Pompey. See Waller, Edmund.
Pond (ticket holder), 1755: CG, Dec 19
Pond, Miss (actor), 1755: CG, Dec 15, 19
Pond's (public house), 1773: DL, May 12
Pons Coffee House, 1746: DL, Dec 30
Ponsonby, Mrs (actor), 1785: HAY, Feb 10

672

Pont-de-Veyle, Antoine deFeriol comte de, 1798: CG, Feb 13, Apr 27
--Complaisant, Le, 1798: CG, Feb 13
--Somnambule, La; or, Sleep Walker, 1798: CG, Apr 27
Ponta (musician), 1772: KING'S, Feb 21, CG, Mar 6, DL, 11, 18, HAY, 23, DL, 25,
    HAY, 30, Apr 6, CG, 10, HAY, 27
Pontack's Tavern, 1749: DL, Feb 2
Pontifex, Mrs (beneficiary), 1757: SOHO, Feb 1
Ponto, Giovanni (horn player), 1788: DL, Mar 5, 7, KING'S, May 22
Pony Races (dance), 1776: CG, May 3; 1778: CG, Apr 21, 27, 28, May 1, 7, 13;
    1782: CG, Apr 17; 1783: CG, Apr 28, May 10, 13; 1784: CG, Apr 28, May 1, 4,
    7; 1785: CG, Apr 25; 1786: CG, May 4
Pooke, Mrs (singer), 1762: HIC, Feb 12
Poole, Martha Frances Caroline (singer), 1787: KING'S, May 1, 19; 1790: CG, Feb
    19, 24, 26, Mar 3, 17, 19, 26; 1791: CG, Mar 11, 18, 23, 25, 30, Apr 6, 13,
    15; 1793: KING/HAY, Feb 15, 20, 22, 27, Mar 6, 13, 15, 20, 22, CG, Oct 9, 12,
    26, Nov 2, 7, 18, 28, Dec 7, 17; 1794: CG, Jan 21, Feb 22, Apr 25, 29, May 2,
    13, 22, 24, 26, Sep 22, 24, 26, 29, Oct 7, 20, 30, Nov 15; 1795: CG, Feb 20,
    27, Mar 4, 9, Apr 28, May 29; 1797: CG, Mar 3, 10, 15, 17, 22, 24, 31; 1798:
    HAY, Jan 15, CG, Feb 23, 28, Mar 2, 9, 14, 28, 30; 1799: HAY, Jan 24, CG, Mar
    13, 15, HAY, 29, CG, Apr 6, May 3
Poor Harle in the Sudds at Last (farce, anon), 1739: TC, Aug 6
Poor Hillario, once so jolly (song), 1783: CG, Nov 8
Poor Jack; or, The sweet little cherub (song), 1789: DL, May 28, Jun 5, CG, 8,
    10; 1790: DL, Mar 23, Apr 6, May 19, 20, 28, Jun 3, CG, Dec 1; 1791: CG, Sep
    19; 1792: HAY, Nov 26; 1793: CG, May 21; 1794: CG, Apr 12; see also Life of
    Poor Jack; Go patter to lubbers
Poor Man's Comfort, The. See Daborne, Robert.
Poor Old Drury!!! See Cobb, James.
Poor Old Hay-Market. See Colman the younger, George.
Poor Orra come from distant shore (song), 1799: CG, Mar 16, Apr 18
Poor Orra tink on Yanco dear (song), 1791: CG, Jun 6, 7, 8, 10, 13
Poor Pierot Married. See Roger, Harlequin Happy.
Poor Recruit (song), 1792: DLKING'S, May 29
Poor Sailor, The. See Bernard, John.
Poor Soldier, The. See O'Keeffe, John.
Poor Thomas Day (song), 1780: HAY, Aug 24; 1781: CG, Apr 25, DL, 25; 1783: CG,
    May 21; 1784: DL, Mar 30, Apr 12, CG, 24, May 14, DL, 21, CG, 25; 1785: CG,
    Apr 18; 1787: HAY, Aug 21; 1788: HAY, Aug 22; 1789: CG, May 5, 29, Jun 12;
    1790: CG, Apr 21, May 24
Poor Vulcan. See Dibdin, Charles.
Pope (actor), 1789: KHS, Sep 16
Pope (wigmaker), 1749: DL, Apr 1, Nov 30; 1750: DL, Mar 31; 1751: DL, Apr 15,
    May 2; 1752: DL, Apr 4; 1754: DL, Apr 4; 1755: DL, Apr 10; 1756: DL, Apr 8;
    1757: DL, Apr 19; 1758: DL, Apr 17; 1759: DL, Apr 16
Pope John VIII (play), 1745: HAY, Mar 4
Pope, Alexander (actor, author), 1785: CG, Jan 8, 19, Feb 4, 28, Mar 7, Apr 12,
    23, May 23, Oct 17, Nov 9, Dec 1, 14; 1786: CG, Jan 2, 31, Feb 4, 23, 25, May
    5, 15, 20, Sep 20, 25, Oct 2, 4, 6, 12, 21, Nov 27, Dec 20; 1787: CG, Jan 6,
    8, 26, Feb 10, Mar 26, 31, Apr 11, 14, DL, 17, CG, 27, May 21, 22, 23, Sep
    24, 28, Oct 1, 5, 31, Nov 5, 9, 19, 20, Dec 3, 10, 17, 27, 28; 1788: CG, Jan
    2, 3, 9, 10, 11, 14, Feb 4, Mar 10, 24, Apr 8, 11, 18, 29, Sep 15, Oct 8, 10,
    18, 27, 29, Nov 1, 27, DL, Dec 16, CG, 19, 26, 29; 1789: CG, Jan 10, Apr 30,
    May 8, 12, 14, 22, Jun 8; 1792: CG, Sep 21, Oct 1, 15, Nov 3, 12, 24, 28, Dec
    1, 20; 1793: CG, Jan 14, 21, 29, Mar 4, 18, Apr 15, 18, 24, May 2, 24, Sep
    30, Oct 1, 2, 4, 8, 14, 17, 22, 25, 28, 30, Nov 13, 18, Dec 19, 20; 1794: CG,
    Jan 6, 13, Feb 18, Mar 17, 25, Apr 7, May 10, 19, 21, 26, Sep 17, 22, Oct 1,
    6, 7, 14, 15, 23, Nov 8, 19, Dec 6, 10; 1795: CG, Jan 6, 19, 31, Feb 21, Mar
    7, 16, Apr 6, 22, 23, 24, May 2, 7, 13, 25, Jun 3, Sep 14, 28, Oct 14, 15,
    16, 22, 23, Nov 4, 6, Dec 15, 21, 22, 31; 1796: CG, Jan 8, 13, 23, Mar 14,
    Apr 19, 20, 26, May 12, 17, 28, Jun 7, Sep 16, 26, 30, Oct 10, 13, 24, Nov 5,
    7, Dec 10, 22, 31; 1797: CG, Jan 7, 10, Feb 20, Mar 4, 14, 20, 23, 30, Apr
    29, May 4, 17, 31, Sep 27, Oct 2, 12, 13, 16, Dec 18, 23, 27; 1798: CG, Jan
    4, 5, 11, 24, Feb 9, 13, Mar 22, 31, Apr 10, 11, 18, 27, May 5, 18, 22, 28,
    30, Sep 21, 28, Oct 1, 11, Nov 7; 1799: CG, Jan 12, Mar 16, Apr 12, DL, 20,
    CG, 26, May 6, 15, 24, Jun 7, HAY, 15, 22, CG, Sep 16, 23, 25, 30, Oct 4, 9,
    10, 11, 16, 17, 25, 29, 31, Nov 7, 11, 14; 1800: CG, Jan 13, 16, 20, Feb 5,
    8, Apr 5, 19, 22, 24, May 2, 13, 28, Jun 2
--Count of Burgundy, The, 1799: CG, Apr 12
Pope, Alexander (poet, author), 1679: DG, May 0; 1711: DL, Nov 20; 1713: DL,
    Apr 14; 1732: YB, Apr 20; 1733: LIF/CG, Feb 10, DL/HAY, Dec 18; 1739: DL, Feb
    13; 1746: DL, Mar 13; 1747: DL, May 14; 1750: DL, Mar 22; 1752: DL, Dec 23;
    1753: DL, Apr 10; 1754: CG, Jan 21; 1755: HAY, Feb 13, DL, Nov 18; 1756: HAY,

Mar 18, Apr 1; <u>1760</u>: HAY, Feb 15; <u>1767</u>: DL, Jan 24, May 4; <u>1768</u>: CG, Oct 24; <u>1769</u>: HAY, Feb 23; <u>1772</u>: DL, Jun 10; <u>1773</u>: DL, Mar 22, Jun 2; <u>1774</u>: DL, Jun 2; <u>1775</u>: DL, May 27; <u>1776</u>: DL, Jun 10, CHR, Oct 7; <u>1797</u>: HAY, Dec 4; <u>1799</u>: HAY, Mar 29

Pope, Alexander and Maria Anne, <u>1798</u>: CG, Apr 18

Pope, Elizabeth, Mrs Alexander (the first) (actor), <u>1785</u>: CG, Nov 7; <u>1786</u>: CG, May 5, Sep 18, 25, 29, Oct 6, 12, 25, 30, Nov 15, 18, 29, Dec 15; <u>1787</u>: CG, Jan 4, 8, 15, Feb 10, Mar 15, 26, 27, 31, Apr 14, 16, 18, 19, 25, 27, May 21, 23, Sep 17, 26, Oct 1, 5, 10, 12, 22, 29, 31, Nov 9, 19, 22, 28, 30, Dec 28; <u>1788</u>: CG, Jan 1, 3, 9, 10, 18, 29, Mar 10, 15, 24, 28, Apr 8, 18, 23, 25, May 2, 7, Sep 19, 24, Oct 10, 15, 17, 18, 29, Nov 12, 21, 26, Dec 19, 26, 27, 31; <u>1789</u>: CG, Jan 15, Mar 5, 28, Apr 14, 15, 28, May 14, 19, 26, Jun 16, Sep 16, 25, Oct 9, 12, 16, Nov 6, 10, 16, 20, 21, 30, Dec 5, 11, 31; <u>1790</u>: CG, Jan 22, 23, 29, Feb 11, 25, Mar 22, Apr 14, 20, May 12, 18, 24, Sep 15, 17, 29, Oct 4, 6, 8, 13, 15, 18, 29, Nov 1, 4, 8, 11, Dec 2, 28, 31; <u>1791</u>: CG, Apr 5, 11, 16, May 2, 10, 11, 18, 19, 24, Jun 1, 6, Sep 16, 17, 19, 20, 21, Oct 3, 7, 10, 12, 24, Nov 29, Dec 3, 26; <u>1792</u>: CG, Feb 6, Mar 26, 31, Apr 10, 12, May 2, 11, 19, 30, Sep 24, 28, Oct 1, 5, 15, 17, 27, 29, 31, Nov 3, 7, 10, 12, 24, 28, Dec 1; <u>1793</u>: CG, Jan 14, 29, Mar 4, 18, Apr 8, 18, 22, 23, May 2, 24, Sep 16, 17, 20, 23, 27, 30, Oct 1, 4, 9, 10, 14, 17, 19, 23, Nov 1, 13, 19, 21, Dec 19, 20, 30; <u>1794</u>: CG, Jan 3, 13, 14, 22, Feb 5, Mar 25, Apr 7, 12, May 6, 10, 19, 24, 26, Sep 15, 17, 19, 22, 29, Oct 3, 6, 15, 23, Nov 20, 21, Dec 6; <u>1795</u>: CG, Jan 6, 12, 24, 29, Mar 16, 19, 28, Apr 24, May 2, 13, 14, 25, 27, Sep 14, 30, Oct 2, 7, 14, 16, 19, 22, 30, Nov 27, Dec 4, 7, 15, 21, 22, 26; <u>1796</u>: CG, Jan 6, 8, 13, Mar 14, Apr 19, 22, May 12, 24, 27, 28, Jun 6, Sep 12, 26, 30, Oct 5, 17, 24, 26, Dec 10, 17, 19, 21, 28, 31; <u>1797</u>: CG, Jan 4, 10

Pope, Jane (actor, author), <u>1749</u>: DL, Nov 30; <u>1755</u>: DL, Dec 18; <u>1756</u>: DL, May 5, Sep 25, Dec 3; <u>1757</u>: DL, May 6; <u>1759</u>: DL, Oct 27, Nov 7, Dec 31; <u>1760</u>: DL, Mar 6, Apr 9, 29, Jun 19, Oct 11, 22, 23, Nov 17, Dec 5, 19; <u>1761</u>: DL, Apr 28, Sep 10, 19, Oct 10; <u>1762</u>: DL, Jan 7, 15, Mar 6, 22, Apr 1, 27, May 7, Sep 23, 25, Oct 9, 12, 13, Nov 12, Dec 1, 10, 22; <u>1763</u>: DL, Feb 3, Mar 22, Apr 6, 11, May 19, Sep 17, 20, 22, 27, Oct 8, Nov 4, 8, Dec 5; <u>1764</u>: DL, Jan 3, 27, Feb 9, 29, Mar 3, Apr 10, Sep 15, 18, Oct 2, 6, 25, Nov 17; <u>1765</u>: DL, Jan 24, Feb 4, 7, Mar 18, Apr 11, May 13, 15, 17, Sep 14, 17, 19, Oct 3, 11, 18, 24, Nov 14, 16, Dec 7; <u>1766</u>: DL, Feb 20, Mar 15, Apr 1, 4, 16, 25, 26, May 6, 20, Sep 20, 25, Oct 9, 17, 21, 23, 25, Nov 8, 17, 18, 28, Dec 29, 30; <u>1767</u>: DL, Jan 24, Feb 9, 21, CG, Mar 16, DL, Apr 6, 21, 27, 29, Sep 12, 18, 23, 25, 26, CG, Oct 5, DL, 15, 20, 23, 28, Nov 6, 11, 16, 28, Dec 1, 4, 17, 19; <u>1768</u>: DL, Feb 12, Mar 17, 19, Apr 7, 9, 14, May 6, 24, Sep 20, 23, 24, 26, 27, 28, Oct 5, 6, 15, 20, 25, Nov 1, 21, Dec 1; <u>1769</u>: DL, Jan 6, 20, Feb 13, Mar 29, 31, Apr 3, May 1, CG, 2, DL, 9, 22, Sep 16, 19, 21, 30, Oct 6, 11, 14, 17, Nov 8, 14, 16, 23, Dec 6, 8, 21; <u>1770</u>: DL, Jan 6, 8, 12, 25, Feb 3, 7, 8, 13, Mar 13, CG, 22, DL, 27, May 10, 17, Sep 22, 25, 29, Oct 2, 4, 6, 12, 13, 18, Nov 3, 13, 21, 23, 28, Dec 4, 6, 17, 19, 29, 31; <u>1771</u>: DL, Jan 2, 23, Feb 21, Mar 11, 18, 21, Apr 2, 5, 9, 13, 19, May 10, 14, Sep 21, 26, 28, Oct 8, 12, 15, 17, 19, 22, 24, 26, 29, Nov 1, 6, 8, 11, 22, 25, 26, 28, Dec 3, 4, 11, 21, 30, 31; <u>1772</u>: DL, Jan 11, Feb 4, 17, Mar 23, Apr 4, 20, 21, May 14, 22, 27, Sep 24, 29, Oct 6, 13, 14, 16, 17, Nov 3, 6, 12, 16, 27, Dec 15, 29; <u>1773</u>: DL, Jan 19, 29, Feb 10, 11, 25, Mar 23, 30, Apr 1, May 17, 24, Sep 18, 28, Oct 2, 5, 8, 11, 13, 18, 19, 20, 25, 28, Nov 9, 24, Dec 20, 21, 30, 31; <u>1774</u>: DL, Jan 13, 19, 26, Mar 21, Apr 19, May 7, 20, Jun 2, Sep 17, 20, 24, 29, Oct 5, 20, 28, Nov 1, 3, 4, 7, 10, 17, 22, 30, Dec 1, 19; <u>1775</u>: DL, Jan 18, Mar 18, 28, Apr 8, 17, 19, 22, May 10, 20; <u>1776</u>: DL, Oct 5, 9, 15, 25, Nov 7, 9, 19, 28, 29, Dec 18, 31; <u>1777</u>: DL, Jan 1, Feb 20, Mar 31, Apr 22, May 8, Sep 25, 27, Oct 9, 22, 31, Nov 14, 29, Dec 11; <u>1778</u>: DL, Jan 22, 23, Feb 10, 24, Mar 5, Apr 9, 21, 27, Sep 17, Oct 1, 6, 13, 19, 21, Nov 4, 28, Dec 11, 19, 22; <u>1779</u>: DL, Jan 2, 7, Mar 11, 15, Apr 5, 16, 28, May 15, 25, Jun 1, Sep 21, 23, 25, 28, Oct 7, 9, 12, 19, 21, 30, Dec 2, 8, 29; <u>1780</u>: DL, Jan 11, 26, Mar 4, 28, Apr 19, Sep 16, Oct 3, 5, 10, 11, 14, 20, 31, Nov 8, 10, 22, Dec 1, 7, 8, 19; <u>1781</u>: DL, Jan 6, Feb 17, Apr 16, 28, May 10, Sep 20, 27, 29, Oct 6, 12, 13, 18, Nov 6, 7, 21, Dec 13; <u>1782</u>: DL, Jan 22, Feb 25, Apr 1, May 3, 8, 10, Sep 17, 19, 26, Oct 1, 29, Nov 7, Dec 5; <u>1783</u>: DL, Jan 10, 24, Feb 12, Apr 3, May 2, 5, Sep 16, 27, Oct 2, 24, Nov 20, 28, Dec 2, 12; <u>1784</u>: DL, Jan 7, 10, 28, Feb 14, Mar 30, May 17, Sep 23, 30, Oct 11, 14, 18, 26, 28, Nov 22, Dec 3, 10, 11, 22; <u>1785</u>: DL, Jan 6, Feb 21, Apr 4, 20, May 11, 26, Sep 20, 29, Oct 4, 6, 25, 26, 31, Nov 18, 26, Dec 5; <u>1786</u>: DL, Jan 14, Mar 27, Apr 19, 26, May 17, 25, Sep 16, 23, 26, 28, Oct 7, 10, 12, 26, 30, Nov 14, Dec 11, 19, 26; <u>1787</u>: DL, Jan 18, 24, Mar 12, Apr 11, May 21, 23, Jun 1, Sep 20, 22, 25, Oct 2, 9, 13, 15, 20, 24, Nov 6, 29; <u>1788</u>: DL, Jan 2, 25, Feb 7, 25, Apr 2, 10, 11, May 7, 14, 21, 22, Jun 6, Sep 27, Oct 4, 7, 9, 11, 22, Nov 12, 19; <u>1789</u>: DL, Jan 1, 26, Feb 26, Apr 16, 20, Sep 15, 19, 22, 26, Oct 3,

24, Dec 1; 1790: DL, Jan 1, Feb 18, Mar 2, 22, Apr 7, 30, Sep 16, Oct 12, 19,
20, 23, 25, 27, Nov 2, 10, 17, Dec 1; 1791: DL, Apr 27, May 10, 19, DLKING'S,
Sep 27, Oct 3, 10, 20, 25, Nov 1, 5, 8, 22, 29, Dec 2, 6; 1792: DLKING'S, Apr
10, 20, May 17, 29, DL, Sep 15, 27, Oct 9, 13, 15, 16, 20, 31, Nov 17, Dec
10, 27; 1793: DL, Jan 3, Feb 25, Mar 7, 14, Apr 3, 25, Jun 1; 1794: DL, Apr
25, May 17, Jun 4, 10, 12, 17, 25, 26, Sep 18, 20, 30, Oct 20, 29, Nov 7, 12,
29, Dec 10, 12, 13, 19; 1795: DL, Jan 5, 23, Feb 9, 12, Apr 17, 24, May 12,
26, Sep 17, 26, Oct 20, Nov 5, 7, 12, 14, 26, Dec 9; 1796: DL, Jan 23, Feb 1,
20, Apr 13, 26, May 5, 13, Jun 4, 6, 8, 14, Sep 20, 27, Oct 4, 8, 15, 17, 19,
25, Nov 1, 8, 28, Dec 29; 1797: DL, Jan 7, 10, 27, May 8, 12, 15, 24, Sep 19,
23, 28, Oct 7, 14, 19, 21, Nov 2, 9, 10, 11, 14, 20, 24, 28; 1798: DL, Jan
25, Mar 8, May 11, 19, 24, Sep 20, 25, Oct 6, 20, Nov 10, 26, Dec 5, HAY, 17;
1799: DL, Jan 8, 11, Feb 14, Mar 2, 9, Apr 8, 17, 19, 22, 24, May 9, Oct 1,
5, 8, 17, 22, 29, Nov 16, Dec 7, 26; 1800: DL, Feb 12, Apr 28, May 10, 16
--Young Couple, The, 1767: DL, Apr 21
Pope, Maria Anne, Mrs Alexander (the second) (actor), 1797: CG, Jan 26, 27, 28,
Feb 18; 1798: CG, Jan 11, 26, 29, Feb 2, 8, 13, Mar 19, 20, Apr 9, 17, 18,
30, May 7, 15, 22, 23, 28, 29, 30, 31, Jun 1, 5, Oct 1, 8, 15, Nov 7, Dec 8,
17; 1799: CG, Jan 12, Feb 4, Mar 16, Apr 8, 9, 12, 16, 19, 27, May 15, 24,
Jun 10, Sep 16, 25, Oct 4, 7, 9, 14, 16, 21, 29, 31, Nov 7, Dec 16; 1800: CG,
Jan 16, Feb 3, Apr 19, 24, 30, May 10, 13, 27, Jun 2
Pope, Master (actor), 1755: DL, Nov 8; 1756: DL, Dec 3; 1759: DL, Apr 5; 1762:
DL, Mar 29; 1765: DL, Feb 4
Pope, Richard (critic), 1696: NONE, Apr 2
Pope's Head Alley, 1752: DL, Dec 22; 1756: DL, Dec 21
Pope's Head Tavern, 1718: LIF, Apr 18; 1734: TB, Jan 26
Pope's Nuncio, 1687: CITY, Oct 29
Pope's Universal Prayer (music), 1755: HAY, Feb 13
Popish chapel (theatre), 1687: ATCOURT, Jan 30
Poplin, Miss (dancer), 1749: DL, Nov 9; 1750: DL, Jan 18, Apr 27, Nov 27; 1751:
DL, Nov 5; 1753: DL, Apr 25, Dec 19; 1755: DL, Nov 8, Dec 18; 1756: DL, Sep
25
Popple, William, 1675: ATCOURT, Jul 24; 1734: CG, Jan 9; 1735: CG, Apr 25
--Double Deceit, The, 1735: CG, Apr 25, 28; 1736: CG, Feb 26
--Lady's Revenge, The; or, The Rover Reclaimed, 1734: CG, Jan 9, 10, 11, 12,
Feb 8
Popplewell (actor), 1784: HAY, Dec 13
Populous cities please (song), 1791: CG, Mar 18, 30; 1792: CG, Feb 24; 1794:
CG, Mar 21
Pordage, Samuel, 1673: DG, Oct 28; 1770: DL, Mar 20; 1774: CG, Mar 14
--Herod and Mariamne, 1671: LIF, Sep 0; 1673: DG, Oct 28; 1675: DG, Jun 23;
1676: DG, Oct 11
--Siege of Babylon, The, 1677: DG, Sep 0
--Troades, 1659: NONE, Sep 0
Porponians, Society of, 1735: YB, Sep 18
Porpora, Nicola (composer), 1733: LIF, Dec 29; 1734: LIF, Feb 5, Mar 12, 16,
Apr 8, May 11; 1735: KING'S, Feb 1, 28, May 3, 6, GF/HAY, Jul 15; 1736:
KING'S, Jan 24, May 4; 1743: KING'S, Feb 22
--Aeneas (opera), 1734: LIF, May 11, 14, 18, 21, 24, 28, Jun 15
--Ariadne in Naxus (opera), 1733: PM, Dec 24, LIF, 29; 1734: LIF, Jan 1, 5, 8,
12, 15, 19, 22, 26, 29, Feb 2, 19, 23, DL/HAY, Mar 30, LIF, Apr 20, 23, 25,
27, 30, May 4, 7, 31, Jun 4, 8, 11, CG, Nov 27, 30, Dec 4, 7, 11
--David (oratorio), 1734: LIF, Mar 12, 16, 20, 27, Apr 3, 8, 10; 1735: KING'S,
Feb 28, Apr 1, 3
--Feast of Hymen, The (musical), 1736: KING'S, May 4, 8, 11, 15
--Ferdinando (opera), 1734: LIF, Feb 5, 9, 12, 16, 28
--Iphigenia (opera), 1735: KING'S, May 3, 6, 10, 13, 20
--Mithridates (opera), 1735: KING'S, Dec 16; 1736: KING'S, Jan 24, 27, 31, Feb
3
--Polifemo (opera), 1735: KING'S, Feb 1, 4, 8, 11, 15, 18, 22, 25, Mar 4, 8,
11, 25, 29, Jun 7, Oct 28, Nov 1, 4
--Temistocle (opera), 1743: KING'S, Feb 22, 26, Mar 1, 5, 8, 12, 15, 19
Port de Mer, Le (play, anon), 1720: KING'S, May 3; 1722: HAY, Jan 29, Feb 17
Porta, Giovanni
--Numitor (opera), 1720: KING'S, Apr 2, 5, 9, 19, 23, May 26, Jun 25
Portal (boxkeeper), 1782: DL, May 30; 1783: DL, May 29; 1784: DL, May 26; 1785:
DL, May 25; 1786: DL, May 31; 1787: DL, Jun 6; 1788: DL, Jun 10; 1789: DL,
Jun 6; 1790: DL, Jun 3; 1791: DL, Jun 1; 1792: DLKING'S, Jun 16; 1793: DL,
Jun 10; 1795: DL, May 30; 1796: DL, Jun 14; 1797: DL, Jun 14; 1798: DL, Jun
15; 1799: DL, Jul 4; 1800: DL, Jun 17
Portal, Abraham (author), 1778: DL, Feb 19
--Cady of Bagdad, The (opera), 1778: DL, Feb 17, 19, 21, 23

675

--Indiscreet Lover, The, <u>1768</u>: KING'S, May 12
Portenza. See Potenza.
Porter (actor), <u>1680</u>: DG, Feb 2; <u>1701</u>: LIF, Nov 0; <u>1785</u>: HAY, Feb 10
Porter St, <u>1750</u>: DL, Jan 9
Porter, Mary (actor), <u>1698</u>: LIF, Jun 0; <u>1699</u>: LIF, Nov 7, Dec 18; <u>1700</u>: LIF,
   Feb 0; <u>1701</u>: LIF, Jan 0, Mar 0, Apr 0, Nov 0, Dec 0; <u>1702</u>: LIF, Jun 0; <u>1703</u>:
   LIF, Jan 0, Mar 0, Apr 28, Nov 0, 1; <u>1704</u>: LIF, Jan 13, Feb 24, DL, Mar 6,
   LIF, 25; <u>1705</u>: LIF/QUEEN, Oct 30, QUEEN'S, Dec 27; <u>1706</u>: QUEEN'S, Jan 3, Feb
   21, Apr 5, 26, Jun 0, Nov 7, 18, Dec 7, 11, 27, 30; <u>1707</u>: QUEEN'S, Jan 4, 9,
   25, Feb 3, 4, May 2, 26, Jun 20, 25, 27, Jul 22, 26, 30, Aug 1, 12, 19; <u>1708</u>:
   DL/QUEEN, Feb 5, DL, 9, 19, DL/QUEEN, 21, DL, Mar 25, Apr 10, 22, DL/QUEEN,
   May 27, Jun 22, DL, 24, 26, Jul 1, 3, 8, 10, 13, 20, 27, Aug 4, Oct 19, Dec
   14, 18, 28, 30, 31; <u>1709</u>: DL, Jan 10, 11, 25, 27, 29, Feb 1, 3, 12, Mar 12,
   29, Apr 5, 9, 25, 26, May 3, 18, QUEEN'S, Sep 22, 24, 27, 29, Oct 1, 4, 8,
   11, 17, 22, 25, 28, 29, Nov 4, 8, 11, 12, 15, 19, Dec 5, 12; <u>1710</u>: QUEEN'S,
   Jan 5, 19, Mar 4, 27, Apr 17, 20, May 3, 6, 15, 16, 25, 29, Jun 5, 9,
   DL/QUEEN, Oct 7, Nov 6, 7, 8, 9, 11, 13, 14, 16, 17, 18, DL, 20, 21, 23, Dec
   1, 4, 5, 7, 12, 14, 16, 21, 22, 26, 30; <u>1711</u>: DL, Jan 9, 20, 27, Feb 15, 22,
   Mar 3, Apr 19, 21, DL/QUEEN, May 11, DL, 21, DL/QUEEN, 29, DL, Jun 29, Jul
   27, Aug 31, Sep 22, 27, 29, Oct 2, 4, 13, 19, 20, 22, 29, Nov 3, 7, 8, 9, 24,
   29, Dec 3, 10; <u>1712</u>: DL, Jan 1, Mar 17, Apr 28, SML, May 21, Jun 11, 18, DL,
   Sep 20, 25, Oct 13, 15, 17, 20, 21, 29, 30, Nov 1, 3, 7, 25, 28; <u>1713</u>: DL,
   Jan 6, 10, 15, 29, Feb 13, 19, Mar 14, Apr 13, 14, May 11, 12, 21, Jun 5, Oct
   13, 23, Nov 16, 19, 28; <u>1714</u>: DL, Jan 5, Feb 2, Apr 5, May 14, 17, 26, Jun
   18, 29, Jul 2, 20, Oct 26, Nov 15, 24, 26, 27, Dec 6, 20; <u>1715</u>: DL, Jan 5,
   15, 22, 24, 25, Feb 19, 21, 22, 25, 28, Mar 8, 14, 28, Apr 2, 20, May 17, 24,
   Jun 24, Jul 1, 6, Oct 22, Nov 9, 12, 19, Dec 6, 9, 12, 17, 20, 30, 31; <u>1716</u>:
   DL, Jan 5, 10, 13, 21, Feb 9, Apr 12, 16, May 9, Oct 6, 9, 11, 12, 13, 16,
   17, 23, 24, Nov 1, 2, 13, Dec 5, 15, 17, 29; <u>1717</u>: DL, Jan 4, 24, 26, 29, Feb
   2, 22, 25, Mar 1, 18, Apr 8, 11, 29, May 2, 10, Jun 18, Sep 28, Oct 1, 3, 9,
   11, 14, 16, 21, 24, 26, 28, Nov 13, 19, 20, 23, 25, 30, Dec 6, 31; <u>1718</u>: DL,
   Jan 27, Feb 13, 14, 22, Mar 8, 17, 18, 22, May 13, 20, 23, 29, Sep 20, Oct 2,
   4, 7, 8, 15, 20, 21, 24, 25, 27, 31, Nov 8, 13, 24, 27, Dec 1, 2, 3, 13, 16,
   19; <u>1719</u>: DL, Jan 3, 9, 24, Feb 14, Mar 16, Apr 1, 11, 29, May 8, 13, Sep 12,
   15, 17, 19, Oct 3, 7, 13, 14, 17, 21, 27, 28, 31, Nov 7, 10, 11, 17, 18, 20,
   21, 24, 26, Dec 5, 8, 11; <u>1720</u>: DL, Jan 1, 5, 8, Feb 2, 17, Mar 10, Apr 21,
   May 30, Nov 18, 19, 21, 22, 26, 29, Dec 1, 2, 6, 29, 31; <u>1721</u>: DL, Jan 10,
   17, 19, 23, 24, Feb 3, Mar 13, 16, 23, Apr 11, 13, 14, 18, May 13, Sep 9, 12,
   16, 23, 30, Oct 5, 14, 18, 19, 23, 28, 31, Nov 3, 8, 11, 13, 14, 16, 18, Dec
   1, 12, 28; <u>1722</u>: DL, Jan 1, 6, 16, 26, Feb 19, Mar 12, Apr 13, 17, May 2, 22,
   Sep 8, 15, 18, 25, Oct 6, 11, 15, 17, 18, 19, 22, 23, 27, 31, Nov 1, Dec 22,
   26; <u>1723</u>: DL, Jan 8, 21, 23, Feb 6, 7, 15, 28, Mar 2, 11, 21, Apr 1, 22, May
   10, Sep 17, 19, 28, Oct 12, 15, 21, 22, 26, 29, 31, Nov 1, 2, 7, 9, 12, 19,
   Dec 20; <u>1724</u>: DL, Jan 15, 27, Feb 6, 12, 22, Mar 16, Apr 8, 15, May 14, Sep
   12, 15, Oct 8, 10, 17, 20, 21, 22, 27, 31, Nov 6, 7, 13, 14, 16, 21, 27, Dec
   3, 7, 9, 18, 22; <u>1725</u>: DL, Jan 25, 27, Feb 1, 9, Mar 11, Apr 20, 24, May 8,
   31, Sep 9, 11, 25, 28, Oct 5, 13, 15, 16, 20, 21, 22, 26, Nov 1, 6, 10, 20,
   22, 27, 29, Dec 18; <u>1726</u>: DL, Jan 22, Feb 2, Mar 7, Apr 23, May 3, 11, 12,
   18, Sep 6, 17, 22, 27, Oct 11, Nov 9, 12, 15, 16, 19, Dec 3, 12, 13, 15, 17,
   21; <u>1727</u>: DL, Jan 5, 16, 21, 25, 27, Feb 4, 9, 23, Mar 16, Apr 17, 29, May
   26, Sep 23, 26, 28, 30, Oct 5, 7, 13, 14, 18, 20, 21, 23, 26, Nov 27, 28, 30,
   Dec 5, 13; <u>1728</u>: DL, Jan 3, 10, Feb 16, Mar 11, 14, Apr 1, May 1, 23, Sep 7,
   12, 17, 21, 28, Oct 1, 5, 8, 15, 21, 23, 28, 31, Nov 2, 9, Dec 6, 16, 26;
   <u>1729</u>: DL, Jan 1, 20, Feb 1, 22, 24, Mar 13, Apr 17, May 3, Sep 11, 13, 18,
   25, 27, 30, Oct 7, 11, 14, 25, 28, 31, Nov 1, 6, 12, 17, 21, 29; <u>1730</u>: DL,
   Jan 9, 21, 24, 26, Apr 2, 10, 14, 27, May 4, 18, Sep 12, 15, 19, 22, 26, Oct
   1, 3, 17, 22, 24, Nov 16, 20, 24, 25, Dec 11, 26; <u>1731</u>: DL, Jan 5, 27, Feb
   17, 22, Mar 18, 22, 29, Apr 3, 8, 10, May 10, 13, Dec 18; <u>1732</u>: DL, Mar 2;
   <u>1733</u>: DL, Jan 25, 31, Feb 5, Mar 8, 31; <u>1734</u>: DL, Mar 7; <u>1735</u>: DL, Jan 8, 23,
   Feb 7, CG, Nov 19, Dec 3, 10, 17; <u>1736</u>: CG, Jan 7, 21, 28, Feb 11, 23, DL,
   Nov 11, 18, 22, 23, CG, 27; <u>1737</u>: DL, Jan 19, Feb 5, 18, 24, 26; <u>1738</u>: DL,
   Apr 6, 22, 28; <u>1741</u>: CG, Jan 15, 28, Feb 5, 12, 17, 26, Mar 5, 19, Dec 17;
   <u>1742</u>: CG, Feb 4, 15, Mar 13, 18; <u>1743</u>: CG, Feb 14
Porter, Mrs (payee), <u>1750</u>: DL, Feb 8
Porter, Thomas, <u>1662</u>: NONE, Sep 0, LIF, Oct 18; <u>1664</u>: BRIDGES, Mar 7; <u>1667</u>:
   BRIDGES, Aug 12
--Carnival, The, <u>1664</u>: BRIDGES, Mar 7
--French Conjuror, The, <u>1677</u>: DG, Jun 0
--Villain, The; or, The Officers in Winter Quarters, <u>1662</u>: LIF, Oct 18, 20, 21,
   22, 23, 24, 25, ATCOURT, 27, LIF, 28, Dec 26; <u>1663</u>: LIF, Jan 1; <u>1667</u>:
   ATCOURT, Jan 1, LIF, Oct 24; <u>1671</u>: DG, Dec 27; <u>1676</u>: DG, Oct 27; <u>1688</u>:
   ATCOURT, Jan 31; <u>1693</u>: NONE, Sep 0; <u>1698</u>: NONE, Sep 0; <u>1702</u>: LIF, Nov 9;

1703: LIF, Jun 14; 1704: LIF, Jul 4; 1710: QUEEN'S, May 11, 15, DL/QUEEN, Nov
   13; 1711: DL/QUEEN, Jan 12
--Witty Combat, The; or, The Female Victor, 1662: NONE, Sep 0
Porter, Walsh, 1797: DL, Oct 7; 1798: CG, May 12
--Chimney Corner, The, 1797: DL, Oct 3, 7, 9, 10, 12
--Voluntary Contributions (interlude), 1798: CG, May 12, 17
Portland Chapel, 1782: KING'S, Mar 19; 1789: CG, May 5
Portland Place, 1790: CG, Apr 29; 1791: CG, May 10
Portland St, 1791: HAY, Mar 7
Portland, Lady. See Bentinck, Jane.
Portman Square, 1781: KING'S, May 10; 1783: KING'S, Feb 13; 1784: CG, Mar 13;
   1785: KING'S, Apr 21; 1790: DL, Mar 22; 1791: DL, Mar 22; 1792: DLKING'S, Apr
   16; 1793: DL, Apr 22; 1795: DL, May 4; 1796: DL, Apr 25; 1797: DL, May 29,
   HAY, Sep 18; 1798: HAY, Apr 23, DL, 30; 1799: HAY, Jan 28; 1800: HAY, Feb 3
Portman, Lady Elizabeth (spectator), 1669: LIF, Jan 15
Portmore, Countess of (patron), 1735: KING'S, Mar 15
Portogallo, Marcos Antonio (composer), 1796: KING'S, Mar 15; 1800: KING'S, Jun
   17
--Due Gobbi, I (Confusione nata della Somiglianza, La) (opera), 1796: KING'S,
   Mar 15, 19, 29, Apr 2, 5, 12, May 10
--Principe Spazzacamino, Il, 1800: KING'S, Jun 17
Portrait, Le (farce, anon), 1734: HAY, Oct 30, GF/HAY, Dec 27; 1735: HAY, Apr
   23
Portrait, The. See Colman the elder, George.
Portraits a la Mode (dance), 1774: CG, Dec 1
Portsdown Hill, 1799: CG, Oct 7
Portsmouth St, 1791: CG, May 19
Portsmouth Theatre, 1782: CG, Dec 31; 1783: DL, Oct 7
Portsmouth, Duchess of. See Keroualle, Louise de.
Portsmouth, 1757: DL, May 11; 1794: HAY, Aug 18, 20; 1796: CG, Apr 12, 20, May
   12, 28; 1799: CG, Oct 7
Portugal Row, 1725: LIF, Feb 24
Portugal St, 1778: HAY, Feb 9
Portugal, King of, 1703: LIF, Jun 14; 1712: MA, May 21; 1716: DL, Jun 6
Portugal, 1747: DL, May 16
Portuguese Envoy, 1703: LIF, Jun 14
Porus. See Handel, George Frederic.
Posi. See Pozzi.
Positive Man, The. See O'Keeffe, John.
Posso Contar L'Arene (song), 1716: KING'S, May 2
Postilion Dance (dance), 1782: DL, Apr 15, Oct 10; 1784: DL, May 15, Sep 16
Posture Masters (actor), 1728: BFY, Aug 24, SFY, Sep 6
Posture-Boy (actor), 1741: BF, Aug 22
Postures (entertainment), 1702: LIF, Dec 29; 1718: LIF, Dec 5, 26; 1732: BF,
   Aug 22; 1738: BFH, Aug 23
Postzug, Der. See Ayrenhoff, Cornelius Hermann von.
Potenza, Pasquale (singer), 1757: KING'S, Sep 20; 1758: KING'S, Jan 10, 31, Apr
   6, 18, 26, Nov 11; 1759: KING'S, Jan 16, Mar 12
Potpourri (dance), 1790: CG, Jul 6
Potter (boxkeeper), 1758: CG, May 9; 1759: CG, May 24; 1760: CG, May 15, 28,
   Sep 22; 1761: CG, May 13; 1762: CG, May 19; 1763: CG, May 25; 1764: CG, May
   25; 1765: CG, May 16; 1766: CG, May 14; 1767: CG, May 21; 1768: CG, Jun 1, 4;
   1769: CG, May 16, 18; 1770: CG, May 23, 26; 1771: CG, May 23; 1772: CG, May
   26; 1773: CG, May 25; 1774: CG, May 17; 1776: CG, May 11; 1777: CG, May 15
Potter (composer), 1763: DL, Dec 26
Potter (duellist), 1684: DLORDG, Oct 29
Potter (hatter), 1749: DL, Nov 24; 1750: DL, Feb 19
Potter, Henry, 1733: GF, Feb 5
--Decoy, The; or, The Harlot's Progress (ballad opera), 1733: GF, Feb 5, 6, 8,
   10
Potter, John (author)
--Choice of Apollo, The (musical), 1765: HAY, Mar 11
--Rites of Hecate, The; or, Harlequin from Harlequin (pantomime), 1763: DL, Dec
   24, 26, 27, 28, 29, 30, 31; 1764: DL, Jan 2, 3, 4, 5, 6, 7, 9, 10, 11, 12,
   13, 14, 16, 17, 18, 19, 20, 21, 23, 24, 25, 26, 27, 28, 31, Feb 1, 2, 3, 4,
   6, 7, 11, 14, 17, 20, 21, 23, 25, 29, Mar 10, May 7; 1765: DL, Jan 22, 23,
   Feb 2, May 10
Potter, John (proprietor), 1749: HAY, Jan 16, DL, 18, 19, 20
Potter, Mrs (actor), 1729: DL, Nov 19
Pottinger, J (printer), 1760: DL, Jan 1
Potts (singer), 1793: HAY, Dec 26; 1796: DL, Sep 29, Oct 19; 1797: DL, Jan 7,
   May 18, Nov 8; 1798: DL, Jan 16, Feb 20; 1799: DL, Jan 19, 28; 1800: CG, Jan

16, Feb 10

Potts, Sophia (singer), <u>1760</u>: CG, Sep 22; <u>1767</u>: CG, Jan 31, Apr 21; <u>1770</u>: CG,
Mar 24, Apr 26; <u>1771</u>: CG, Apr 24, Nov 8, Dec 14, 16, 23; <u>1772</u>: CG, Jan 17,
18, Feb 28

Poulet, Le. See Carmontelle.

Poultney (actor), <u>1780</u>: HAY, Apr 5

Poultry, <u>1745</u>: DL, Apr 1; <u>1749</u>: CG, Jan 17, Apr 28

Pour forth no more (song), <u>1791</u>: CG, Mar 18, 30; <u>1793</u>: CG, Mar 6; <u>1794</u>: CG, Mar
12, DL, Apr 9; <u>1795</u>: CG, Mar 13; <u>1796</u>: CG, Feb 26; <u>1797</u>: CG, Mar 22; <u>1798</u>:
CG, Mar 2; <u>1799</u>: CG, Feb 15; <u>1800</u>: CG, Feb 28

Pourceaugnac and Grilletta. See Orlandini, Giuseppe Maria.

Pourceaugnac, De (play), <u>1721</u>: HAY, Apr 20, 24

Poussin, Isabella, Mrs Joseph (actor), <u>1775</u>: CG, Sep 25, Oct 4, 9, 17, 30, Nov
4, 10, 13, 21, 30, Dec 1, 9, 21, 23; <u>1776</u>: CG, Jan 15, 24, May 13, 20, Oct 2,
7, 11, 17, 25, Nov 2, 7, 11, 13, 19, Dec 26; <u>1777</u>: CG, Jan 3, Mar 31, Apr 14,
28, May 5, 7, 13, HAY, 15, CG, 20, 24, HAY, 28, Jun 2, 9, 25, 26, Jul 15, 18,
Aug 7, 19, 25, Sep 19, CG, 24, 29, Oct 6, 8, Nov 7, 19; <u>1778</u>: CG, Jan 15, 20,
29, Feb 23, 28, Mar 16, 28, 30, Apr 22, 27, May 11, HAY, 21, 22, Jun 1, 8,
12, Jul 1, Aug 21, Sep 7, CG, 21, Oct 2, 5, 21, 26, Nov 19, Dec 1, 11, 26;
<u>1779</u>: CG, Jan 2, 11, 19, Mar 20, 27, Apr 5, 27, HAY, Jun 17, 18, Jul 1, 16,
17, 20, 31, Aug 17, 27, 31, CG, Sep 20, 24, 27, Nov 8, 13, 16, 22, 23, 30,
Dec 2, 31; <u>1780</u>: CG, Jan 7, Feb 8, 22, 24, Mar 18, May 12, 19, 24, HAY, 30,
Jun 2, 5, 9, 13, 14, 23, 26, Jul 1, 6, Aug 12, 14, 17, CG, Sep 18, 21, Oct 3,
10, 11, 19, 21, 23, 26, Nov 14, 24, 25, Dec 4, 12, 15; <u>1781</u>: CG, Jan 4, 10,
Feb 15, HAY, Jul 18, 21, Aug 15, Sep 4, CG, 24, 28, Oct 18, 19, 20, Nov 24,
Dec 5, 17, 18, 31; <u>1782</u>: CG, Jan 3, 4, 5, 8, 18, Feb 9, Mar 14, 19, Apr 12,
17, May 20, 28, HAY, Jun 4, 6, 11, 15, 22, Jul 16, Aug 9, 13, 26, 27, Sep 18,
CG, 27, Oct 2, 3, 7, 8, 23, 31, Nov 1, 6, 18, Dec 6, 12, 27; <u>1783</u>: CG, Feb
19, Mar 29, 31, May 3, HAY, 31, Jun 2, CG, 4, HAY, 6, 13, 18, Jul 2, Aug 20,
22, 27, CG, Sep 22, Oct 6, 8, 10, 15, Dec 6, 31; <u>1784</u>: CG, Jan 9, 13, 16, Feb
19, 23, Mar 16, May 11, 26, HAY, 28, CG, 29, HAY, Jun 2, Jul 24, 28, Sep 13,
CG, 24, 28, Oct 1, 4, 18, 25, 29, Nov 11, Dec 28; <u>1785</u>: CG, Jan 21, Feb 4,
Mar 5, 29, HAY, May 30, Jun 2, 7, 17, 24, Jul 11, 26, Aug 16, Sep 16; <u>1786</u>:
CG, Jan 18, HAY, Jun 14, 21, 26, 28, 29, Jul 13, 19, Aug 17; <u>1787</u>: HAY, May
16, 21, 23, 25, Jun 14, 16, 18, 23, 27, Jul 25, Sep 8; <u>1788</u>: HAY, Jun 10, 11,
16, 25, Jul 24, Aug 4, 9; <u>1789</u>: HAY, May 18, 25, Jun 19, 22, 29, 30

Povey, John (spectator), <u>1686</u>: ATCOURT, Feb 16

Povy, Thomas (spectator), <u>1667</u>: LIF, Sep 12

Powel (dancer), <u>1786</u>: HAY, Mar 6

Powel-Yates Booth, <u>1726</u>: SFPY, Sep 8

Powel, Cordal (author), <u>1796</u>: DL, Jan 18

Powel, John (treasurer), <u>1744</u>: DL, May 5; <u>1745</u>: DL, Apr 27; <u>1747</u>: DL, Apr 11,
Sep 17, 19, 22, 24, 26, 29, Oct 1, 3, 6, 8, 10, 13, 15, 17, 20, 21, 22, 23,
24, 26, 27, 28, 29, 30, 31, Nov 2, 3, 4, 5, 6, 7, 9, 10, 11, 12, 13, 14, 16,
17, 18, 19, 20, 21, 23, 24, 25, 27, 28, 30, Dec 1, 2, 3, 4, 5, 7, 8, 9, 10,
11, 12, 14, 15, 16, 17, 18, 19, 21, 22, 23, 26, 28, 29, 30, 31; <u>1748</u>: DL, Jan
1, 2, 4, 5, 6, 7, 8, 9, 11, 12, 13, 14, 15, 16, 18, 19, 20, 21, 22, 23, 25,
26, 27, 28, 29, Feb 1, 2, 3, 4, 5, 6, 8, 9, 10, 11, 12, 13, 15, 16, 18, 19,
20, 22, 23, 24, 25, 27, 29, Mar 1, 3, 5, 7, 8, 10, 12, 14, 15, 17, 19, 21,
22, 24, 26, 28, 29, 31, Apr 2, 11, 12, 13, 14, 15, 16, 18, 19, 20, 21, 22,
23, 25, 26, 27, 28, 29, 30, May 2, 4, 5, 6, 9, 11, 13, 16, 17, 18, 20, 25,
Sep 10, 13, 15, 17, 20, 22, 24, 27, 29, Oct 1, 4, 6, 8, 11, 13, 14, 15, 18,
19, 20, 21, 22, 25, 26, 27, 28, 29, 31, Nov 1, 2, 3, 4, 5, 7, 8, 9, 10, 11,
12, 14, 15, 16, 17, 18, 19, 21, 22, 23, 24, 25, 26, 28, 29, 30, Dec 1, 2, 3,
5, 6, 7, 8, 9, 10, 12, 13, 14, 15, 16, 17, 19, 20, 21, 22, 23, 26, 27, 28,
29, 30, 31; <u>1749</u>: DL, Jan 2, 3, 4, 5, 6, 7, 9, 10, 11, 12, 13, 14, 16, 17,
18, 19, 20, 21, 23, 24, 25, 26, 27, 28, 31, Feb 1, 2, 3, 4, 6, 7, 9, 11, 13,
14, 16, 18, 20, 21, 23, 25, 27, 28, Mar 2, 4, 6, 7, 9, 11, 13, 14, 16, 18,
20, 27, 28, 29, 30, Apr 1, 3, 4, 5, 6, 7, 8, 10, 11, 12, 13, 14, 15, 17, 18,
19, 20, 21, 22, 24, 25, 26, 28, 29, May 1, 2, 5, 6, 8, 9, 10, 11, 12, 13, 16

Powel, Miss (actor), <u>1777</u>: CHR, Jul 2, 21, 23; <u>1778</u>: HAY, Jul 1

Powel, Mrs (actor), <u>1741</u>: BFH, Aug 22

Powel, Mrs (householder), <u>1779</u>: DL, May 7

Powel, Sparks (actor), <u>1789</u>: CG, Sep 14, 16, 23, 25, Oct 2, 9, 12, 13, 16, 20,
21, 24, 28, 31, Nov 2, 6, 10, 11, 12, 14, 16, 20, 21, 24, 27, Dec 21, 26;
<u>1790</u>: CG, Jan 23, 27, 29, Feb 11, 23, Mar 18, 22, 27, Apr 7, 14, 24, May 5,
6, 7, 18, 26, 31, Jun 1, 4, Sep 13, 15, Oct 1, 6, 8, 11, 13, 18, 19, 20, 27,
29, Nov 4, 8, 23, 25, 27, 30, Dec 2, 6, 10, 11, 14, 18, 28; <u>1791</u>: CG, Jan 3,
12, 26, Feb 16, Mar 5, 14, Apr 16, 28, May 2, 3, 11, 14, 28, Jun 1, 6, Sep
12, 14, 19, 20, 23, 26, 28, 30, Oct 3, 6, 10, 12, 13, 17, 21, 24, 28, Nov 2,
15, 19, 24, 25, Dec 3, 15, 21, 22; <u>1792</u>: CG, Jan 12, Feb 2, 6, 18, 25, Mar 6,
26, 31, Apr 10, 14, May 5, 9, 10, 11, 15, 17, 18, 19, Jun 1, 2, Sep 17, 19,

21, 26, 28, Oct 1, 5, 8, 10, 12, 15, 17, 19, 24, 26, 27, 29, Nov 3, 5, 10,
12, 19, Dec 1, 5, 21, 26; 1793: CG, Jan 2, 9, 21, 23, 25, 29, 31, Feb 25, Mar
4, Apr 4, 15, 18, 24, 25, 30, May 1, 4, 8, 10, 11, 15, 21, Jun 6, 7, 10, 12,
Sep 16, 17, 18, 20, 23, 25, 27, 30, Oct 1, 3, 4, 7, 8, 9, 10, 11, 15, 16, 19,
24, 25, 30, Nov 1, 2, 9, 11, 13, 18, 23, 30, Dec 17, 18, 28; 1794: CG, Jan 3,
21, 24, Feb 1, 22, 24, Mar 6, 17, 25, Apr 10, 12, 29, May 13, 14, 22, 23, 27,
28, 29, Jun 5, 11, Sep 15, 17, 19, 22, 24, 26, 29, Oct 1, 3, 6, 7, 8, 17, 29,
30, Nov 12, 15, Dec 6, 10, 30; 1795: CG, Jan 31, Feb 3, 4, 5, 14, 21, Mar 5,
16, 17, 28, Apr 8, 23, 24, 29, May 1, 8, 13, 14, 19, 21, 25, 29, 30, Jun 1,
3, 6, 12, 13, 16, Sep 14, 16, 18, 21, 23, 30, Oct 5, 7, 8, 14, 15, 16, 19,
23, 24, Nov 6, 9, 23, 27, Dec 4, 5, 7, 9, 14, 29, 31; 1796: CG, Jan 6, 8, Mar
14, 15, 30, Apr 1, 13, 15, 19, 20, 29, May 10, 12, 18, 20, 28, Jun 1, Sep 12,
14, 17, 19, 21, 26, 28, 30, Oct 3, 6, 14, 17, 20, 21, 24, Nov 3, 5, 7, 19,
Dec 1, 9, 26, 31; 1797: CG, Jan 7, Feb 18, Mar 13, Apr 8, 19, May 4, 9, 17,
23, 27, 31, Jun 2, 5, 12, 13, 21, Sep 20, 22, 25, 27, 29, Oct 2, 6, 11, 13,
21, Nov 2, 3, 7, 8, 11, 13, 15, 20, Dec 28; 1798: CG, Jan 5, Feb 5, 6, 9, 12,
Mar 20, 31, Apr 10, 16, 18, 19, 20, 27, May 1, 8, 12, 14, 16, 22, 28, 30, Jun
2, Sep 17, 19, 26, Oct 1, 3, 8, 11, 15, 19, 22; 1799: CG, May 21
Powel, W (actor, dancer), 1789: CG, Dec 21; 1790: CG, Jan 23, Nov 15, Dec 20
Powell (actor), 1729: BFRP, Aug 25; 1742: BFPY, Aug 25
Powell (actor), 1745: GF, May 1, Dec 2
Powell (actor), 1779: HAY, Mar 15, Dec 27; 1780: HAY, Mar 28; 1781: HAY, Mar
26, Oct 16; 1783: HAY, Dec 15; 1784: HAY, Feb 23, Nov 16
Powell (actor, singer), 1794: DL, Oct 31; 1795: DL, Feb 12; 1796: DL, Jan 11;
1797: HAY, Sep 18
Powell (boxkeeper), 1739: CG, May 25; 1740: CG, May 19; 1741: CG, May 6; 1742:
CG, May 17; 1743: CG, May 3; 1744: CG, May 7; 1745: CG, May 10; 1746: CG, May
3; 1747: CG, May 16; 1748: CG, May 4
Powell (office keeper), 1760: CG, Jan 28; 1761: CG, Nov 4
Powell (scene painter), 1799: CG, Dec 23
Powell (singer), 1751: HAY, Dec 20
Powell (ticket deliverer), 1786: DL, May 26; 1788: DL, Jun 5; 1794: DL, Mar 19
Powell and Co (merchants), 1759: CG, Oct 30; 1767: DL, May 29
Powell, Charles (composer), 1695: NONE, Sep 0
Powell, Charles (servant), 1701: YB, Jun 18
Powell, Charles Stuart (actor), 1788: CG, Apr 26; 1789: HAY, May 18, 25, 29,
Jun 1, 3, 19, 22, Aug 5, CG, Sep 14, 25, 30, Oct 9, 12, Nov 7, 13, 14, 20,
27, Dec 10, 11, 21; 1790: CG, Jan 22, 23, Feb 4, 8, 23, Mar 8, 13, Apr 7, 20,
28, Jun 4, HAY, 18, 19, Jul 5, Sep 4, CG, 13, 15, Oct 20, Nov 15, Dec 10, 20;
1791: CG, Feb 2, Apr 11, 16, May 3, 10, 11, 20, Jun 15, HAY, Jul 14, 30, Aug
18, 31, CG, Sep 26, Oct 6, 12, Dec 2, 3, 21, 22; 1792: CG, Feb 6, 18, May 10,
12
Powell, Elizabeth, Mrs William (renter), 1769: CG, Jul 3; 1772: CG, Feb 18
Powell, George (actor, author), 1670: BRI/COUR, Dec 0; 1682: DL, Nov 16; 1687:
DG, Mar 0, ATCOURT, Apr 25; 1688: DG, Apr 0, DL, May 3, NONE, Sep 0; 1689:
NONE, Sep 0, DL, Nov 7, 20, Dec 4; 1690: DL, Jan 0, DLORDG, 16, Mar 0, NONE,
Sep 0, DL, 0, Oct 0, Nov 0, Dec 0; 1691: DL, Jan 0, Mar 0, NONE, Sep 0; 1692:
DLORDG, Oct 13, DL, Nov 0; 1693: DL, Feb 0, Mar 0, Apr 0, DG, May 0, DL, Oct
0; 1694: DL, Jan 0, Feb 0, Mar 21, Apr 0, DG, May 0, DL, Sep 0; 1695: DG, Apr
0, DL, 1, DLANDLIF, May 0, DL, 0, Sep 0, Oct 0, Nov 0, DG, 0; 1696: DL, Feb
0, Mar 0, Apr 0, May 0, DG, Jun 0, DL, Sep 0, DG, Oct 0, Nov 21; 1697: DL,
Jan 0, DG, Jun 0, DL, Sep 0, NONE, 0; 1698: DL, Feb 0, Mar 0, May 5, DL/ORDG,
Nov 0, DL, Dec 0; 1699: DL, Apr 0, Nov 28, Dec 0; 1700: DL, Feb 19, Apr 29,
Jul 9; 1701: LIF, Aug 0, Nov 0, Dec 0; 1702: LIF, Jun 0, Dec 31; 1703: LIF,
Jan 0, Feb 0, Apr 28, May 0, 21, Sep 21, 28, Oct 5, Nov 0; 1704: LIF, Jan 13,
Feb 24, DL, Mar 6, LIF, 25, ATCOURT, Apr 24, DL, Jun 17, 19, 21, Dec 7; 1705:
QUEEN'S, Apr 14, LIF, Aug 1; 1707: DL, Feb 20, Mar 11, Nov 22, 25, 26, 28,
29, Dec 2, 10, 11, 17, 27, 30; 1708: DL, Jan 1, 7, 9, 15, 31, Feb 9, 14, 19,
QUEEN/DL, Mar 4, DL, 9, 25, 27, Apr 14, 15, 19, DL/QUEEN, 24, DL, 27, May 21,
Jun 5, Aug 28, 31, Sep 3, 4, 7, 9, 11, 14, 16, 18, 21, 23, Oct 23, Dec 18,
21; 1709: DL, Jan 1, 3, 7, 10, 17, 18, 21, 26, Feb 11, 16, 19, 26, Mar 5, 17,
21, Apr 11, 14, May 2, 3, 7, Jun 2, Sep 6, Nov 23, 24, 25, 26, 28, 30, Dec 6,
7, 9, 10, 14, 22, 29, 31; 1710: DL, Jan 3, 14, 18, 20, 21, 23, 25, 26, 28,
31, Feb 14, 16, 18, 25, Mar 11, 14, 16, Apr 15, 21, May 26, GR, Jun 28, Jul
1, 6, 10, 12, 15, 20, 29, Aug 3, 5, 10, 12, 14, 19, 24, 26, 28, Sep 7, 9, 11,
20, 23, 28, 30, DL, Nov 25, 30, Dec 4, 7, 9, 18; 1711: DL, Jan 18, DL/QUEEN,
Feb 8, DL, 10, DL/QUEEN, 17, DL, 24, DL/QUEEN, 26, DL, 27, Mar 17, 20, Apr
17, 21, DL/QUEEN, May 1, 3, DL, 18, Jul 3, 10, 24, Sep 29, Oct 8, 9, 16, 20,
26, 27, 29, 30, 31, Nov 3, 10, 24, 27, Dec 3, 8, 13, 21; 1712: DL, Mar 17,
Apr 7, 29, May 12, SML, 21, DL, Jun 2, Jul 1, 11, 29, Aug 1, 5, 12, Oct 2, 7,
8, 11, 14, 17, 21, 23, 28, Nov 4, 25, 26; 1713: DL, Jan 5, 15, 29, Feb 19,
Mar 9, 16, 28, Apr 14, Jun 18, 19, Nov 27; 1714: DL, Jan 26, Mar 29, May 3,

7, 17, Jun 4, 14, 18; 1718: YB, Mar 5, DL, Jul 25
--Alphonso, King of Naples, 1669: BRIDGES, Jan 12; 1690: DL, Dec 0
--Brutus of Alba; or, Augusta's Triumph, 1696: DG, Oct 0
--Cornish Comedy, The, 1696: DG, Jun 0
--Imposture Defeated; or, A Trick to Cheat the Devil, 1697: DL, Sep 0
--Treacherous Brothers, The, 1682: DL, Nov 16; 1690: DL, Jan 0; 1695: NONE, Sep
   0; 1698: NONE, Sep 0
--Very Good Wife, A, 1693: DL, Apr 0
Powell, James, 1797: DL, Oct 28
--Narcotic, The, 1797: DL, Oct 28
Powell, Jane, Mrs William (actor), 1789: DL, Sep 12, Oct 10, 31, Nov 7, 30, Dec
   14; 1790: DL, Jan 1, Mar 8, May 15, 26, Oct 14, 21, Nov 3, 5; 1791: DL, May
   10, 14, DLKING'S, Sep 27, Oct 4, Nov 4, 7, 14, Dec 6, 12; 1792: DLKING'S, Jan
   24, 26, 27, 30, 31, Mar 13, 26, 29, 31, Apr 12, May 8, 15, 19, DL, Sep 20,
   Oct 4, Nov 5, Dec 7, 13, 21; 1793: DL, Jan 16, Feb 5, 9, 14, 23, 25, Mar 9,
   18, Apr 23, 27, May 24, Jun 5, 7; 1794: DL, Apr 25, 26, May 1, CG, 14, DL,
   14, CG, 28, DL, Jun 14, 24, Sep 23, Oct 14, 25, 28, 30, Nov 14, 15, 18, 29,
   Dec 9, 12, 30; 1795: DL, Feb 28, Mar 3, 21, May 2, 29, Jun 6, Sep 22, Oct 5,
   12, Nov 6, 23, Dec 10, 14; 1796: DL, Jan 29, Feb 15, Mar 19, 29, Apr 2, 18,
   20, May 12, 23, 27, Sep 22, 29, Oct 3, 6, 22, 24, Nov 5, 15, 23, Dec 9, 21;
   1797: DL, Jan 2, 14, 17, 20, Feb 1, 3, 7, 16, 22, Mar 14, 16, 20, May 1, CG,
   23, DL, 25, Jun 12, Sep 19, 30, Oct 5, 12, Nov 4, 15, 17, 23, 25, Dec 14;
   1798: DL, Mar 8, 17, May 11, 19, 21, 30, Jun 5, Sep 20, 25, 29, Oct 2, 4, 9,
   27, Nov 6, 16, 26, Dec 19, 29; 1799: DL, Feb 4, Mar 2, Apr 13, 22, 23, May 1,
   20, Sep 17, 19, 24, 26, 28, Oct 3, 7, 21, 31, Nov 8, 16, 25, 29, Dec 7, 9,
   26; 1800: DL, Apr 29, May 19, Jun 18
Powell, John (actor), 1698: DL, May 3
Powell, John (actor), 1798: DL, Oct 20, Nov 10, 22, Dec 28; 1799: DL, Jan 8,
   11, 31, Feb 26, Mar 26, Apr 17, 23, May 4, 24, Jun 28, Jul 1, 4, Oct 5, 29,
   Nov 14, Dec 2, 11, 30; 1800: DL, Jan 14, 18, Feb 10, 24, Mar 11, Apr 29, May
   16, Jun 12, 17
Powell, John (renter), 1758: CG, Feb 28; 1759: CG, Oct 5, 27
Powell, Martin (actor), 1670: BRI/COUR, Dec 0; 1673: LIF, Mar 0, Dec 0; 1674:
   LIF, Mar 0, DL, May 16, NONE, Sep 0; 1675: DL, May 10, Aug 0; 1676: DL, Jan
   29; 1677: DL, Mar 0, 17, May 5, Jun 0; 1678: DL, Feb 0, Mar 0; 1681: DL, Oct
   0; 1682: DL, Mar 11, OXFORD, Jul 10, DL, Nov 16; 1685: DLORDG, Jan 20; 1686:
   DG, Mar 4, NONE, Sep 0; 1687: ATCOURT, Apr 25; 1688: DG, Apr 0, DL, May 3;
   1695: DL, Dec 0
Powell, Mary Ann, Mrs Charles Stuart (actor), 1789: HAY, May 18, 27, 29, Jun 3,
   5, 10, 12, 24, Jul 29, Aug 1, 11, 28, Sep 14, 18, Oct 12, 14, Nov 7, 9, 10,
   Dec 5; 1790: CG, Mar 27, Apr 7, 29, May 11, HAY, Jun 14, 18, 22, 26, Jul 5,
   7, Aug 6, 12, 13, 20, 21, 27, CG, Sep 13, Oct 6, Nov 3, 6, 26, Dec 17; 1791:
   HAY, Jun 16, 18, 23, Jul 7, 15, 30, Aug 5, 9, 16, 18, 24, 31, Sep 1, CG, 26,
   Oct 3, 10; 1792: CG, Jan 25, 31, Feb 18, 28, Mar 31, Apr 12, May 10, HAY, Jun
   15, 18, 23, Jul 7, 24, 25, Aug 9, 14, 17, CG, Sep 17, Oct 8, 19, 24, 29, Dec
   13, 26; 1793: CG, Jan 25, Apr 8, 9, 24, 25, Jun 10, 11, HAY, 12, 14, 15, 17,
   21, 26, 29, Jul 1, 5, 10, 15, 18, Aug 3, 6, 7, 12, 16, 26, 30, Sep 10, 11,
   Oct 21, 30, Nov 4, 5, 19, 30, Dec 2, 23, 30; 1794: HAY, Jan 11, 14, Feb 15
Powell, Miss (actor), 1787: HAY, Mar 12
Powell, Mrs (actor), 1686: DL, Apr 0; 1695: DL, Sep 0, DG, Nov 0; 1696: DL, Feb
   0, Jul 0, Sep 0, Nov 21, DL/DL, Dec 0; 1697: DL, Jan 0, DL/DL, Mar 0, DL, May
   31, DG, Jun 0, DL, Jul 0, Sep 0; 1698: DL, Feb 0, Mar 0, Jun 0, Dec 0; 1699:
   DL, Nov 28, Dec 0; 1700: DL, Mar 0, Jul 9, Nov 23; 1701: DL, Feb 4; 1702: DL,
   Nov 0; 1703: DL, Jan 27, Apr 10, Jun 23; 1705: DL, Jan 18, Mar 29, Apr 23;
   1707: QUEEN'S, Feb 17, Mar 8, 27, Jul 10, 18, 22, 26, Aug 12, DL/QUEEN, Oct
   20, QUEEN'S, 21, DL/QUEEN, 22, 23, 31, Nov 10, 11; 1708: DL, Feb 3, 6,
   DL/QUEEN, 21, DL, Mar 8, 13, DL/QUEEN, Apr 8, DL, 10, 13, 14, 17, 26, May 21,
   Jun 15, 17, DL/QUEEN, 22, DL, 24, Jul 20, Aug 4, 28, 31, Sep 3, 4, 9, 16, 18,
   25, Oct 5, 9, 13, 15, 22, 25, Dec 28, 29, 31; 1709: DL, Jan 1, 27, Feb 2, Apr
   11, 16, 29, 30, May 3, 24, 26, 31, QUEEN'S, Sep 27, Oct 6, 8, 25, 28, Nov 9,
   19; 1710: QUEEN'S, Apr 27, May 29, Jun 1, GR, 28, Jul 1, 6, 20, 22, Aug 17,
   26, Sep 9, DL/QUEEN, Nov 8, 15, 16, DL, Dec 4, 11; 1711: DL, Jan 9, Mar 5,
   May 10, 15, 22, Jun 26, 29, Jul 27, Aug 3, 24, Sep 22, Oct 12, 22, Nov 1, 23,
   26, Dec 10, 18; 1712: DL, Jan 1, Jun 2, Oct 13, 22, Dec 12; 1713: DL, Jan 26,
   Mar 3, Jun 12; 1714: DL, Jan 28, Mar 31, Jun 16
Powell, Mrs (renter), 1769: CG, Jul 3; 1772: CG, Feb 18
Powell, Mrs (taverner), 1757: DL, Dec 14
Powell, Thomas (actor), 1777: CG, May 29
Powell, Widow (beneficiary), 1749: CG, Apr 25
Powell, William (actor, manager), 1763: DL, Oct 8, 20, Nov 21, 22, Dec 1, 3;
   1764: DL, Jan 7, 16, 18, Feb 14, 20, Mar 3, 20, 27, 31, Apr 2, 7, 10, 12, 24,
   25, May 10, 16, Oct 6, 9, 15, 19, 23, 31, Nov 9, 17, 24, Dec 8; 1765: DL, Jan

2, 15, 24, Feb 6, Mar 16, 19, 25, 26, Apr 20, May 11, Sep 21, Oct 2, 3, 8,
12, 15, 18, 22, 25, Nov 11, 15, 20, 25, Dec 3; 1766: DL, Jan 6, 8, Feb 13,
20, 25, Mar 11, 18, 20, 22, Apr 9, 19, May 5, KING'S, Aug 13, 25, DL, Sep 27,
Oct 8, 16, 17, 21, 29, Nov 4, 8, 17, 24, 26, Dec 2, 6, 13; 1767: DL, Jan 24,
31, Feb 7, 9, 21, Mar 24, 28, 30, 31, Apr 28, May 4, 8, 20, CG, Jun 9, Sep 14,
15, 16, 17, 18, 22, 23, 25, Oct 5, 8, 16, 19, 22, 24, 26, 29, 31, Nov 4, 10,
11, 18, 23, 27, Dec 5, 8, 28; 1768: CG, Jan 9, 20, 29, Feb 20, Mar 7, 10, 17,
Apr 11, 25, May 10, Jun 4, Sep 20, 26, 28, 30, Oct 4, 5, 6, 8, 12, 15, 17,
24, 26, Nov 9, 17, 19, 24, 26, Dec 3, 22; 1769: CG, Feb 16, 18, 20, Apr 4, 5,
7, 20, 24, May 3, Jul 3; 1771: DL, Sep 21; 1775: DL, Nov 24
Powell, William (prompter), 1791: DL, Jun 4; 1794: DL, Mar 19, Apr 24, 25, 26,
28, 29, 30, May 1, 2, 3, 5, 6, 7, 8, 9, 12, 13, 14, 15, 16, 17, 19, 20, 22,
23, 24, 26, 27, 28, 29, 30, Jun 2, 4, 6, 9, 10, 12, 13, 14, 16, 17, 18, 19,
20, 21, 23, 24, 25, 26, 27, 28, Jul 2, 3, 4, 5, Sep 16, 18, 20, 23, 25, 27,
30, Oct 2, 4, 6, 7, 9, 11, 13, 14, 16, 18, 21, 22, 23, 27, 28, 29, 30, 31,
Nov 1, 3, 4, 5, 6, 7, 8, 10, 11, 12, 13, 14, 17, 18, 19, 20, 21, 22, 24, 25,
27, 28, 29, Dec 1, 2, 4, 5, 6, 8, 9, 10, 11, 12, 13, 15, 16, 17, 18, 19, 20,
22, 23, 26, 27, 29, 30; 1795: DL, Jan 1, 2, 3, 5, 6, 7, 8, 9, 10, 12, 13, 15,
16, 17, 19, 20, 21, 22, 23, 24, 26, 28, 29, 31, Feb 2, 3, 4, 5, 6, 7, 9, 10,
12, 13, 14, 16, 17, 19, 21, 23, 24, 26, 28, Mar 2, 5, 7, 10, 12, 14, 16, 17,
19, 21, 23, Jun 5; 1796: DL, Jun 15; 1797: DL, Jun 15; 1798: DL, Jun 9; 1799:
DL, Jul 3; 1800: DL, Jun 13
Power of Gold (song), 1748: JS, May 30
Power of Harmony (song), 1776: CG, Mar 6
Power of Harmony, The. See Phillidor, Francois Andre Danican.
Powerful Guardians (song), 1748: DL, Apr 15, HAY, Dec 9
Powers, James (actor, dancer), 1791: CG, Dec 22; 1792: CG, Oct 8; 1793: CG, Mar
11; 1795: CG, Dec 23; 1796: CG, Jan 9, Dec 19; 1797: CG, May 26; 1798: CG,
Oct 15, 25, Dec 11; 1799: CG, Jan 14, 29, Mar 2, 25, Dec 23; 1800: CG, Mar 4
Powlen (actor), 1733: HAY, Mar 27
Powlett, Lady W (spectator), 1716: DL, Apr 9
Powney (stationer), 1749: DL, Nov 24; 1750: DL, Feb 19; 1767: DL, Jan 16; 1772:
DL, Jan 10, Feb 19; 1773: DL, Jan 27, Oct 29; 1774: DL, Feb 22, Jun 2; 1775:
DL, Jan 10, May 27, Nov 24; 1776: DL, Jan 26, Mar 25, Jun 10
Powre (actor), 1678: DL, Feb 0
Pox upon this Cursed Life (song), 1681: DG, Jan 0
Poynter (actor), 1749: HAY, May 19
Poyton, Miss (actor), 1788: HAY, Apr 9
Pozzi, Anna (singer), 1776: KING'S, Nov 2, 23; 1777: KING'S, May 24; 1778:
KING'S, Jan 20, Nov 24, 28, Dec 22; 1779: KING'S, Jan 23, Feb 23, Mar 25, Apr
29, May 15, 29, Nov 27, Dec 14; 1780: KING'S, Jan 22, Feb 8, Mar 9, Apr 13,
22, May 9, 25, 31; 1793: KING'S, Feb 26
Pozzi, Antonio (singer), 1778: KING'S, Apr 9
Pozzi (Posi), Carlo (composer), 1789: KING'S, May 9; 1794: KING'S, Feb 1
Pragmatical Jesuit New-leven'd, The. See Carpenter, Richard.
Praise of Bacchus (song), 1791: CG, Mar 25; 1792: CG, Mar 7; 1793: KING/HAY,
Mar 6; 1794: CG, Mar 14, DL, Apr 11
Praise of Good English Beer (song), 1736: CG, Apr 12, Jun 4; 1738: CG, Apr 11;
see also Of English Brown Beer
Praise the Lord (song), 1755: SOHO, Mar 11; 1789: CG, Mar 6, DL, 20; 1790: CG,
Feb 24; 1791: CG, Mar 18, Apr 15; 1792: CG, Feb 24; 1794: CG, Apr 9, DL, 11;
1797: CG, Mar 17
Prati, Alessio (composer), 1790: CG, Mar 8
Pratt, Mrs (actor), 1671: BRIDGES, Jun 0
Pratt, Samuel Jackson, 1774: CG, Oct 20; 1776: DL, Jun 1; 1778: DL, Apr 20;
1781: DL, Nov 27; 1782: DL, Nov 16; 1783: DL, Jan 29; 1787: HAY, Jul 19
--Fair Circassian, The, 1781: DL, Nov 27, 28, 29, 30, Dec 1, 3, 4, 6, 7, 8, 10,
12, 26; 1782: DL, Jan 3, 12, 15, 25, Feb 9, 18, Apr 2, 13
--Joseph Andrews (farce), 1778: DL, Apr 20
--School for Vanity, The, 1783: DL, Jan 29
Precaution Inutile, La. See Fatouville, Nolant de.
Precaution Inutile, Le; ou, Arlequin Gentilhomme Normand (pantomime), 1719:
KING'S, Feb 14, Mar 2; 1721: HAY, Jan 26, Feb 23
Precieuses Ridicules, Les. See Moliere.
Prefatory Address to the Anti-Gallicans (entertainment), 1756: NWGF, Mar 18
Prejudice of Fashion, The (farce, anon), 1776: HAY, Oct 7; 1779: HAY, Feb 22
Prelleur (composer), 1731: GF, May 13; 1733: GF, May 7; 1734: ST, Mar 22, GF,
May 14, Dec 10; 1735: GF, Jan 24, Oct 15; 1741: GF, Mar 3, Apr 20
--Contending Deities, The (masque), 1733: GF, May 7; 1735: GF, Apr 18
Prelot (dancer), 1776: DL, Nov 1
Prelude on the Happy Recovery of His Majesty, A (music), 1789: DL, Feb 27
Preludio, A. See Colman the elder, George.

Premier Navigateur, Le; ou, Force de l'Amour (dance), 1786: KING'S, Mar 23, Apr
4, 18, 20, 25, May 2, 9
Prendergrass (pit office keeper), 1786: KING'S, Dec 23; 1787: KING'S, Mar 17,
Dec 8; 1788: KING'S, Apr 5
Prentis (singer), 1759: DL, Dec 12; 1760: DL, Apr 14, May 14, HAY, Jun 2
Prepare, prepare (song), 1691: NONE, Sep 0
Prescott St, 1733: GF, Apr 30
Presgrove (dancer), 1734: GF, Feb 11, Apr 19; 1735: GF, Jan 24, Feb 4, Sep 19,
Oct 15
Preso al Caro amato Cido (song), 1745: CG, Apr 10
Press Gang; or, The Sailor's Farewell (dance), 1756: DL, Oct 13, 16, 18, 26,
Nov 6
Press Gang, The. See Carey, Henry, Nancy.
Pressley (actor), 1781: HAY, Oct 16; 1782: HAY, Jan 14, Nov 25; 1783: HAY, Sep
17
Preston (actor), 1764: DL, Oct 20, Nov 26, Dec 31; 1765: DL, May 16, HAY, Jun
10, 24, Jul 8, 15, 17, 31, Aug 8, 30; 1775: DL, Feb 27; 1776: DL, Jun 10
Preston (singer), 1675: ATCOURT, Feb 15
Preston and Son (music publishers), 1794: CG, Dec 26
Preston, Lord. See Graham, Richard.
Preston, Mrs (dancer), 1752: DL, Nov 22, 28; 1753: DL, Mar 24, May 5, 18, Dec
19; 1754: DL, Feb 7, 16; 1755: DL, Oct 8, Nov 8, 22; 1756: DL, Oct 18; 1757:
DL, May 4; 1758: DL, Oct 12, Dec 26; 1759: DL, Oct 24; 1760: DL, Feb 7, 11,
Mar 13, May 29, Oct 2, 7
Presumptuous Love. See Taverner, William.
Preswitz (spectator), 1693: DL, Jan 16
Pretenders, The; or, Kensington Gardens. See Leigh, John.
Pretenders, The; or, The Town Unmasked. See Dilke, Thomas.
Pretti, Paulo (composer), 1732: HIC, Mar 31
Pretty Gentleman, The; or, Softness of Manners, The (essay), 1747: CG, Mar 19
Preux (dancer), 1674: DL, Mar 30
Prevot (Prevost), Miss (dancer), 1792: DL, Nov 21; 1793: DL, Apr 8; 1795: CG,
Apr 6
Pria che la doglia (song), 1713: QUEEN'S, Apr 25
Price (actor), 1735: HAY, Aug 4
Price (actor), 1764: HAY, Jul 13
Price (actor), 1780: CII, Feb 29, Mar 6, 13, 27, Apr 5, 19
Price (beneficiary), 1718: LIF, Jul 9; 1719: LIF, Jun 3; 1720: LIF, May 24
Price (carpenter), 1747: CG, Apr 20
Price (dancer), 1740: TC, Aug 4, BF/WF/SF, 23; 1743: SF, Sep 8
Price (dancer), 1795: HAY, Mar 4, CG, Oct 26, Nov 16, Dec 21; 1796: CG, Jan 4,
Feb 12
Price (musician), 1675: ATCOURT, Feb 15
Price (singer), 1786: HAMM, Jun 5, 7, 28, 30, Jul 5, 7, 10, 19, 21, 24, 26
Price (smith), 1747: CG, May 22
Price (ticket seller), 1792: HAY, Oct 15
Price, Elizabeth (actor), 1685: DG, Jul 0, DL, Aug 0; 1686: DG, Mar 4
Price, Jacob (musician), 1730: GF, Jun 11
Price, Joseph (actor), 1661: LIF, Aug 24, LIF/MT, Oct 21; 1662: LIF, Mar 1,
NONE, Sep 0, LIF, 30, Oct 18; 1663: LIF, Jan 8, Oct 0, Dec 22; 1664: LIF, Mar
0, Sep 10; 1672: DG, Jan 31; 1676: DG, Aug 0
Price, Miss (actor, dancer), 1729: DL, May 26; 1730: HAY, Nov 16, Dec 21, 28;
1731: HAY, Jan 15, 18, 20, Feb 10, 26, Mar 10, Apr 22, May 12, SFGT, Sep 8;
1732: HAY, May 12, BFMMO, Aug 23; 1733: DL, Feb 12, Mar 26, 31, Apr 16, 20,
May 7, 14, BFMMO, Aug 23
Price, Mrs (actor), 1676: DG, May 25; 1678: DG, Jan 17, Apr 5, May 28, Jun 0,
Nov 0; 1679: DG, May 0, Dec 0; 1680: DG, Jun 0; 1682: DG, Jan 0
Price, Mrs (actor), 1752: DL, Oct 26, Nov 22, 28; 1753: DL, Jan 1, 9, Feb 7,
May 25; 1755: HAY, Sep 1, 11, 15
Price, Mrs (beneficiary), 1721: LIF, Jun 7
Price, Mrs (haberdasher), 1771: DL, Dec 16
Price, Mrs (house servant), 1740: CG, Dec 12
Price, Richard (actor), 1661: LIF, Dec 16
Price, Robert (correspondent), 1741: KING'S, Dec 19
Prichard, Sir William (Lord Mayor), 1682: CITY, Oct 30
Pride of the Sea (song), 1794: CG, May 9
Prideaux, Miss (actor), 1788: HAY, Jul 7, 10, 24, Aug 22, 25; 1789: HAY, May
25, DL, Oct 3; 1790: HAY, Jun 14, 18
Priere apres Souper (dance), 1789: HAY, Jul 27, Aug 17
Priest (dancer), 1667: LIF, Aug 15
Priest, Josias (dancing master), 1689: CHELSEA, Dec 0; 1690: DG, Jun 0; 1691:
DG, May 0; 1692: DG, May 2

Prime Minister, 1733: HAY, Mar 22
Primrose Girl (song), 1796: CG, May 16
Primrose Green. See King, Matthew Peter.
Primrose, Captain (commander of playhouse guards), 1691: NONE, Dec 17
Primroses deck the banks (song), 1787: DL, May 18; 1793: KING/HAY, Feb 15, DL,
   May 24
Prince (beneficiary), 1728: HAY, Apr 30
Prince (dancer), 1693: NONE, Sep 0; 1701: LIF, Oct 21; 1703: LIF, Jun 8, 11;
   1704: LIF, Jul 4, Aug 9; 1705: LIF, Jan 25; 1706: QUEEN'S, Jan 18, 22, 23;
   1710: DL, Mar 25, May 16, 23; 1712: DL, Apr 29, May 6, 26, 29, 30, Jun 10,
   12, 19, Aug 5; 1713: DL, May 27, Jun 1, 5, 9, 12, 18, 19; 1714: DL, May 3,
   31, Jun 9, 11, 14, 18, Jul 13, 16, 20; 1715: DL, Mar 19, Apr 19, May 13, 20,
   24, Jun 2, 6, 28, Jul 8, Aug 2, Oct 14, 31, Nov 2, 11, 14, 23, 30; 1716: DL,
   Apr 9, 21, May 31, Jun 6, 15, Jul 12, 17, 24, 26, Aug 16, Oct 18, 29, 31, Dec
   13; 1717: DL, Jan 3, Feb 6, 13, Mar 2, 28, Apr 4, May 20, 21, 29, Jun 3, 6,
   Jul 16, Aug 6, Oct 30, Nov 8; 1718: DL, Jan 21, Apr 15, 29, May 7, 21; 1724:
   RI, Jun 27
Prince (house servant), 1753: CG, May 21; 1754: CG, May 18; 1755: CG, May 20;
   1756: CG, May 24
Prince (linen draper), 1751: DL, Apr 23
Prince and Old England for ever (song), 1791: CG, May 18
Prince and Princess, 1714: KING'S, Dec 11, DL, 16, KING'S, 18, DL, 30; 1720:
   KING'S, May 11, RI, Aug 29
Prince Eugene's March (dance), 1749: HAY, Jan 7
Prince Frederick yacht, 1718: DL, Apr 25
Prince of Agra, The. See Addington, Sir William.
Prince of Orange's Coffee House, 1746: HAY, Apr 23; 1753: KING'S, Apr 30, DL,
   Dec 21; 1756: CG, Dec 8
Prince of Wales' Minuet (dance), 1734: HAY, Aug 21; 1778: CG, May 22; 1780: CG,
   May 18; 1782: KING'S, Jan 26, Feb 2
Prince of Wales' Saraband (dance), 1731: DL, Mar 22; 1734: HAY, Aug 21; 1735:
   DL, May 17; 1737: CG, Apr 25, May 13
Prince Travestie, Le; ou, L'Illustrie Avanturier; or, Harlequin an Innocent
   Traytor (pantomime, anon), 1735: HAY, Feb 17
Prince Unable to Conceal His Pain (song), 1746: KING'S, Mar 25; 1748: KING'S,
   Apr 5; 1751: CG, Apr 23; 1789: CG, Mar 20, Apr 3; 1790: DL, Feb 24, CG, Mar
   8, DL, 17, CG, 19, DL, 24, CG, 26; 1791: CG, Mar 25; 1792: CG, Mar 7, KING'S,
   28, 30; 1793: KING/HAY, Feb 15, 27; 1794: CG, Mar 14, DL, 26, Apr 4; 1799:
   CG, Mar 15
Prince, Mrs (actor), 1696: LIF, Mar 0, Oct 0, Dec 0; 1697: LIF, Jun 0, Nov 0;
   1698: LIF, Jan 0, Apr 0; 1699: LIF, Dec 18; 1700: LIF, Feb 0, Mar 0, 5; 1701:
   LIF, Jan 0, Aug 0, Nov 0; 1702: LIF, Jun 0, Dec 31; 1703: LIF, Feb 0, Mar 0,
   Apr 28, May 0, Jun 8, Nov 0; 1704: LIF, Feb 2, Mar 25, 30
Prince, the, 1661: LIF, Dec 16; 1677: ATCOURT, Nov 10, DG, 15; 1688: DL, May
   15; 1692: CITY, Oct 29; 1715: DL, Jan 5, 7, KING'S, 8, 15, DL, 27, KING's,
   Apr 9; 1716: DL, Mar 13, KING'S, May 15, DL, 18; 1717: SF, Sep 20, LIF, Oct
   7, DL, 15, 18, 23, Nov 4, 22, LIF, 25; 1718: DL, Apr 16, 22, NONE, May 31,
   Jun 6, RI, Jul 28, Aug 23, DL, Nov 6, LIF, 7, DL, 20, Dec 2, 15, LIF, 19;
   1719: DL, Jan 9, LIF, 22, Feb 5, DL, 21, KING'S, 26, DL, Mar 3, 5, 31, Oct
   26, 29, LIF, Nov 2, 7, DL, 20; 1720: LIF, Jan 11, DL, 22, LIF, Feb 26,
   KING'S, Apr 27, May 31, Jun 9, DL, Nov 2; 1721: LIF, Jan 12, KING'S, Mar 7,
   DL, May 15, KING'S, 24, DL, Oct 25, LIF, Dec 14; 1722: KING'S, Apr 25, May 9;
   1723: KING'S, Jan 22, LIF, Apr 22, DL, Nov 20, Dec 13; 1724: KING'S, Jan 11,
   DL, 17, KING'S, Feb 20, DL, Mar 5; 1725: LIF, Nov 6, DL, 10, 17; 1726:
   KING'S, Oct 21; 1728: DL, Dec 11, 12; 1729: DL, Jan 8, LIF, 11, DL, 16, Feb
   5, LIF, 6, DL, Nov 1, LIF, 11, 18, DL, Dec 27; 1730: DL, Jan 8, 12, LIF, Feb
   12, 19, KING'S, 21, LIF, 26, DL, Mar 9, KING'S, 31, LIF, Apr 2, 9, HAY, May
   14, DL, Aug 19, Nov 19, LIF, Dec 16, KING'S, 19; 1731: KING'S, Feb 13, 20,
   LIF, Mar 11, 18, 25, DL, 30, KING'S, Apr 6, 10, 20, LIF, 27, KING'S, May 1,
   LIF, 6, KING'S, 8, 18, HC, Oct 18, LIF, 29, KING'S, Nov 13, DL, 17, LIF, 18,
   DL, 29, KING'S, 30, Dec 4, 11, DL, 16, 22; 1732: LIF, Jan 7, KING'S, 8, 18,
   DL, 19, KING'S, 25, 29, DL, Feb 2, 9, KING'S, 15, 19, 22, 26, DL, Mar 2, 16,
   KING'S, 25, Apr 25, May 2, 16, Jun 20, 24, Nov 4, 7, 25, DL, 30, KING'S, Dec
   12, DL, 14, KING'S, 16, 19, CG/LIF, 21, KING'S, 26, 30; 1733: CG/LIF, Jan 3,
   KING'S, 13, Feb 6, DL, 22, KING'S, Mar 3, 17, 31, Apr 24, May 29, Jun 5, Nov
   20, Dec 4; 1734: DL/HAY, Apr 24, LIF, Jun 15, KING'S, Dec 10; 1735: RI, Aug
   16, DL, Dec 3, 17; 1736: KING'S, May 15; 1737: HAY, Apr 18; 1746: DL, Dec 5;
   1747: DL, Oct 23, Nov 10; 1750: DL, Jan 3, 6, Feb 9
Prince's Bow, The (satiric print), 1788: HAY, Apr 29
Prince's Court, 1751: DL, Dec 18
Prince's daughter (dancer), 1703: LIF, Jun 11
Princes applaud (song), 1791: CG, Mar 25; 1792: CG, Mar 7; 1794: CG, Mar 14

Princes Edward and George, 1746: CG, Dec 12; see also Highness
Princes St, 1757: DL, May 11; 1759: DL, Mar 30; 1786: DL, May 9; 1799: HAY, Aug
   15
Princes, the, 1674: NONE, Dec 14; 1749: DL, Jan 2
Princess Ann's Chaconne (dance), 1735: CG/LIF, May 9
Princess Elizabeth, The; or, The Rise of Judge Punch (entertainment), 1726:
   SFPY, Sep 8; 1727: BF, Aug 23; 1743: NONE, Jan 31
Princess of Cleve, The. See Lee, Nathaniel.
Princess of Georgia, The. See Craven, Elizabeth Baroness.
Princess of Parma, The. See Smith, Henry.
Princess of Saxe Gotha (dance), 1738: DL, May 22
Princess of Wales' Dance (dance), 1737: LIF, May 4, 7
Princess of Wales' Minuet and Gavotte (dance), 1795: DL, Jun 1
Princess St, 1777: HAY, Sep 18
Princess, The. See Killigrew, Thomas.
Princess, the, 1660: ATCOURT, Nov 19; 1677: DG, Nov 15; 1688: DL, May 15; 1692:
   CITY, Oct 29; 1697: YB, Feb 24; 1700: DLORLIF, Jan 20; 1715: DL, Jan 5, 7,
   KING'S, 8, 15, DL, 27, Feb 10, 15, KING'S, 19; 1716: KING'S, May 15; 1718:
   DL, Jul 18, RI, 28; 1719: DL, Feb 21; 1720: KING'S, May 31, DL, Nov 2; 1721:
   KING'S, May 24, DL, Oct 25; 1722: KING'S, May 9; 1723: KING'S, Jan 22, LIF,
   Apr 22, DL, Nov 20, Dec 13; 1724: KING'S, Jan 11, DL, 17, KING'S, Feb 20, DL,
   Mar 5; 1725: DL, Nov 10, 17; 1726: KING'S, Oct 21, Nov 7, 12; 1727: DL, Nov
   7, KING'S, Dec 26; 1728: DL, Jan 27, LIF, Feb 22, KING'S, Mar 9, 12, 30, Apr
   2, May 7, DL, Nov 20, 30, Dec 11, 12; 1729: DL, Jan 16, Feb 5, LIF, 11, 12,
   DL, Mar 13, RI, Aug 6, LIF, Nov 11; 1730: KING'S, Mar 17, 31, KG, Oct 22, DL,
   Dec 10, 17; 1731: DL, Jan 7, KING'S, Feb 9, DL, 25, Mar 30, KING'S, May 25,
   29, Nov 16, 30, DL, Dec 21, 28; 1732: DL, Feb 9, Oct 28, KING'S, Dec 2, 5, 9;
   1733: DL, Mar 5, KING'S, Apr 10, Jun 9, Nov 10, 13; 1734: KING'S, Mar 13;
   1736: KING'S, May 15; 1750: DL, Jan 6; 1751: DL, Oct 28; 1757: DL, Dec 30;
   1759: DL, Jan 22; 1764: DL, Jan 23; 1787: DL, Jan 9; 1797: CG, Jun 13
Princesses Amelia and Anne, 1716: DL, Apr 10
Princesses Amelia and Caroline, 1728: KING'S, Mar 19, DL, Nov 30; 1729: LIF,
   Feb 11, RI, Aug 6; 1730: DL, Jan 8, 12, KING'S, Dec 1, LIF, 3; 1731: KING'S,
   Feb 20, Mar 20, May 8, DL, Sep 18; 1732: LIF/CG, Oct 28; 1734: KING'S, Jul 6,
   HAY, Nov 1, CG/LIF, 9, HAY, 14, CG/LIF, 25, KING'S, Dec 10; 1735: CG, Jan 8,
   KING'S, Feb 1, HAY, 3, 10, CG/LIF, May 1; 1736: KING'S, Jan 24, CG, Feb 25,
   Jun 2
Princesses Amelia, Anne and Caroline, 1725: KING'S, Dec 28; 1726: KING'S, May
   31
Princesses Amelia, Caroline and Louisa, 1731: KING'S, Apr 20; 1735: HAY, Apr
   28; 1740: CG, Sep 29, Oct 25, Nov 13, 27, Dec 4, 11; 1741: DL, Jan 24, Mar
   19, CG, Apr 2, Oct 8, DL, Dec 2; 1742: DL, Jan 13, 20, Feb 4, 10, 18, 24, Mar
   11, 25, May 31, Sep 23, Oct 9, 20, Nov 4, 16, 24, Dec 8, 16, 31; 1743: DL,
   Jan 5, 19, 26, Feb 9, Mar 1, Apr 6, 12, May 3, 13
Princesses Amelia, Caroline, Louisa and Maria, 1735: GF/HAY, May 15
Princesses Amelia, Caroline, Louisa and Mary, 1730: DL, Dec 17; 1733: LIF/CG,
   Jan 23; 1734: DL, Mar 7; 1735: GF/HAY, Apr 21, CG, Nov 19; 1738: DL, Nov 10,
   24, 27; 1739: CG, Jan 11, Mar 22, DL, Sep 20, CG, Nov 3, 10, 24, Dec 1, 22
Princesses Amelia, Louisa and Mary, 1733: DL, Feb 27; 1734: GF/HAY, Nov 22;
   1735: DL, Oct 1
Princesses Anne and Mary, 1674: ATCOURT, Dec 15
Princesses Caroline and Louisa, 1730: KING'S, Nov 21; 1766: CG, Sep 24; 1767:
   DL, May 28
Princesses Caroline and Mary, 1732: KING'S, Dec 2
Princesses Caroline, Louisa and Mary, 1732: RI, Jul 22; 1735: DL, Sep 15, Oct
   29; 1736: CG, Jan 14, 29, Feb 5, DL, 11, CG, 26; 1738: DL, Nov 3
Princesses Louisa and Mary, 1729: BFR, Aug 25; 1732: TC, Aug 17; 1734: GF/HAY,
   Dec 27; 1735: GF/HAY, Jan 8, HAY, Mar 27, GF/HAY, Apr 7; 1738: CG, Mar 23
Princesses Royal and Amelia, 1732: DL, Apr 19, KING'S, May 2
Princesses Royal and Caroline, 1731: KING'S, Jan 16, Feb 6, 23, DL, Mar 4,
   KING'S, Dec 4; 1732: KING'S, Mar 18
Princesses, the, 1675: ATCOURT, Feb 16; 1717: DL, Mar 19, May 29; 1718: HC, Sep
   23, Oct 1; 1719: KING'S, Feb 12, Mar 5, RI, Aug 3; 1720: KING'S, Mar 24, Apr
   5; 1723: RI, Sep 2; 1724: LIF, Mar 10; 1726: KING'S, Jan 15, Mar 8, 15; 1728:
   DL, Nov 6, 13; 1729: LIF, Jan 11, DL, 28, Mar 6, BFR, Aug 26, DL, Oct 28, Nov
   12, 26; 1730: KING'S, Feb 14, LIF, 19, KING'S, 21, DL, Mar 19, KING'S, 31,
   DL, Apr 2, LIF, 9, KING'S, Dec 15, 19; 1731: KING'S, Jan 23, Feb 13, 16, 27,
   Mar 9, 16, DL, 18, LIF, 25, KING'S, Apr 6, 10, May 1, LIF, 6, KING'S, 11, HC,
   Oct 18, KING'S, Nov 13, 16, LIF, 18, KING'S, 23, 30, Dec 11; 1732: LIF, Jan
   7, KING'S, 8, 11, 18, 22, 25, 29, Feb 15, 19, 22, 26, DL, Mar 2, 16, KING'S,
   25, Apr 1, Jun 20, 24, GF, Oct 11, KING'S, Nov 4, 7, 25, DL, 30, KING'S, Dec
   12, DL, 14, KING'S, 16, 19, CG/LIF, 21, KING'S, 26, DL, 27, KING'S, 30; 1733:

CG/LIF, Jan 3, KING'S, 13, 27, Feb 6, 20, DL, 22, KING'S, Mar 3, 17, 27, 31,
Apr 24, May 1, 22, 29, Jun 5, HAY, 8, DL, Oct 27, KING'S, Nov 6, 13, 20, Dec
4; 1734: KING'S, Jan 5, 12, 29, Feb 2, 5, 12, DL, 13, KING'S, 19, Mar 12, CG,
21, KING'S, May 24, LIF, Jun 15, DL, Sep 19, GF/HAY, Nov 6, Dec 18; 1735:
KING'S, Oct 28, CG, Nov 8, KING'S, 25, DL, 26, Dec 31; 1736: DL, Jan 8, CG,
Feb 23, May 12, 15, HAY, Jun 2, DL, Nov 4, CG, 13, Dec 8; 1737: KING'S, May
17, 31, CG, Jun 1; 1739: KING'S, Jan 16, CG, 20, LIF, Dec 13; 1741: DL, Dec
19; 1742: DL, Feb 16; 1787: CG, Jun 15; 1789: CG, Apr 15, Jun 9; 1791: CG,
Jun 13; 1792: CG, Jun 2; 1793: CG, Apr 15
Princeton, 1765: DL, Jan 1
Principe Spazzacamino, Il. See Portogallo, Marcos Antonio.
Pring, Jacob Cubitt (singer), 1786: DL, Mar 3, 29; 1793: CG, Mar 20
Pringle, John (correspondent), 1754: CG, Nov 9
Prior (builder), 1772: DL, Sep 22
Prior, Matthew (author, poet), 1685: DLORDG, Jan 15; 1690: ATCOURT, Nov 4;
1695: WS, Dec 0; 1698: LIF, Nov 0; 1700: LIF, Jan 9; 1711: YB, Jul 16; 1717:
DL, May 11; 1720: HIC, Feb 2; 1749: CG, Mar 31; 1774: CG, Apr 13; 1775: DL,
Apr 20; 1779: HAY, Oct 18; 1780: HAY, Sep 5; 1781: DL, Apr 23; 1782: DL, Apr
·24
Prisoner at Large, The. See O'Keeffe, John.
Prisoner, The (dance), 1735: GF/HAY, Mar 28
Prisoner, The. See Rose, John.
Prisonnier, Le. See Duval, Alexandre Vincent Pineu.
Pritchard (actor), 1734: JS, May 23; 1736: LIF, Mar 31, CG, May 17, BFFH, Aug
23
Pritchard (office keeper), 1741: DL, May 25; 1742: DL, May 24; 1743: DL, May
24, Sep 13; 1744: DL, May 15; 1745: DL, May 7; 1746: DL, May 9; 1747: DL, May
15; 1748: DL, May 16; 1749: DL, May 5; 1750: DL, May 8
Pritchard, Hannah Mary (actor), 1756: DL, Oct 9, 22, 23, Nov 8, 16, 29, Dec 11;
1757: DL, Jan 10, Mar 22, Apr 18, 25, 28, 29, 30, May 20, Sep 17, Oct 7, 20,
Nov 8; 1758: DL, Jan 28, Mar 11, Apr 14, 25, May 1, Sep 23, 28, 30, Oct 18,
19, 24, Dec 20, 26, 28; 1759: DL, Jan 29, Feb 3, Mar 20, Apr 18, 19, 26, May
19, Jun 28, Sep 25, Oct 11, 23, Nov 2, 30, Dec 26; 1760: DL, Jan 24, Feb 8,
Mar 20, Apr 7, 9, 28, 29, 30, Sep 20, 30, Oct 14, 18, 25, Nov 19, Dec 2, 11,
22; 1761: DL, Jan 31, Feb 12, Apr 8, 10, 20, 27, May 13; 1763: DL, Nov 15
Pritchard, Hannah, Mrs William (actor), 1733: BF, Aug 23, BFFH, Sep 4, DL/HAY,
26, Oct 10, 15, 17, 20, 22, 29, Nov 24, 27, Dec 6, 12, 15, HAY, 26; 1734:
DL/HAY, Jan 12, HAY, Feb 12, DL/HAY, Mar 12, Apr 1, LIF, 26, DL/HAY, 30,
BFFO, Aug 24, DL, Sep 12, 14, 28, Oct 3, 5, 10, 19, 21, 25, Nov 22, 25; 1735:
DL, Jan 11, 13, 20, 22, 23, Feb 4, 5, 25, Mar 6, Apr 15, 28, May 6, 7, 10,
LIF, Jun 12, DL, Jul 1, GF/HAY, 15, 18, 22, Aug 1, DL, Sep 25, Oct 4, 23, 28,
Nov 6, 7, 10, 22, Dec 6; 1736: DL, Jan 12, Feb 5, 9, 20, 28, Mar 13, 23, 25,
27, Apr 12, 13, May 6, 11, 18, 25, 26, 27, LIF, Jun 16, RI, Aug 21, BFFH, 23,
DL, 26, Sep 11, 16, 23, Oct 9, 12, 13, 20, 22, 25, 29, Nov 3, 12, 19, 23, Dec
7, 17, 20, 21, 31; 1737: DL, Jan 29, Feb 5, 19, 28, Mar 1, Apr 15, 27, May 3,
4, 18, 19, Aug 30, Sep 1, 3, 6, 10, 15, 27, Oct 1, 8, 13, 21, 24, 25, 27, Nov
11, 12, 15, 16; 1738: DL, Jan 25, Feb 21, 27, 28, Mar 20, 21, Apr 21, 26, 27,
May 5, 8, 13, 23, 25, 26, Sep 9, 23, 30, Oct 16, 17, 25, 27, Nov 3, 9, 11,
25, 30, Dec 26; 1739: DL, Jan 3, 8, 11, 16, 22, 31, Feb 1, 3, Mar 13, 20, Apr
9, 28, May 17, 19, 28, Sep 1, 4, 6, 8, 11, 20, Oct 3, 6, 8, 9, 11, 17, 23,
24, 25, 26, 27, 29, Nov 7, 16, Dec 8, 10, 14, 17, 20, 22; 1740: DL, Jan 3,
16, Feb 7, 13, Mar 17, 20, 25, Apr 12, 14, 16, 19, 22, 23, May 23, 26, Sep 9,
11, 13, 16, 18, 20, 25, 27, 30, Oct 2, 7, 9, 10, 11, 17, 23, 28, 29, Nov 1,
6, 10, 24, 27, 29, Dec 9, 18, 20; 1741: DL, Jan 6, 15, Feb 14, Mar 14, 31,
Apr 14, 29, May 1, 13, 14, 21, 25, CG, Sep 21, 23, 25, 30, Oct 5, 8, 13, 15,
20, 29, 31, Nov 7, 11, 19, 23, 27, Dec 9, 11, 12, 16, 18; 1742: CG, Jan
19, 23, Feb 3, 15, 16, Mar 6, 20, 27, May 1, 4, DL, Sep 16, 18, 28, 30, Oct
5, 18, Nov 3, 16, 19, Dec 8, 14; 1743: DL, Jan 3, 27, Feb 17, Mar 3, 14, 15,
Apr 7, 20, 22, May 4, 10, 11, 24, 26, LIF, Jun 3, DL, Sep 13, CG, Dec 31;
1744: CG, Jan 4, 5, 7, 12, 14, 24, 28, Feb 3, 7, 23, 28, Mar 3, 8, 12, 13,
30, 31, Apr 2, 10, 13, 18, May 25, Sep 19, 21, 24, 26, 28, Oct 1, 3, 5, 10,
15, 16, 18, DL, 19, CG, 20, 22, 24, 26, 29, 31, Nov 1, 5, 7, 8, 12, 21, 27,
28, 29, Dec 6, 11, 17, 21, 26, 28; 1745: CG, Jan 1, 2, 7, DL, 14, CG, 14, 18,
Feb 9, 15, Mar 11, 14, 25, 28, Apr 2, 17, 20, 23, 26, May 13, Sep 23, 25, 27,
30, Oct 2, 4, 7, 9, 11, 14, 18, 29, 31, Nov 4, 7, 8, 9, 11, 12, 14, 15, 16,
22, 23, 25, 26, 28, 30, Dec 2, 5, 6, 10, 12, DL, 17; 1746: CG, Jan 2, 25, Feb
3, 5, 6, 8, Mar 10, 13, Apr 1, 3, 7, 21, 23, DL, 25, CG, 28, Jun 20, Sep 29,
Oct 1, 3, 4, 6, 10, 13, 15, 20, 24, 29, Nov 1, 3, 4, 8, 13, 18, 24, 26, Dec
2, DL, 5, CG, 10, 11, 18, 19, 22, 26, 29; 1747: CG, Jan 2, 17, 26, 27, 29,
31, Feb 2, 12, 28, Mar 12, 14, DL, 19, CG, 23, 26, Apr 4, 20, 27, May 20, 29,
DL, Nov 21, 23, 24, 26, CG, Dec 1, DL, 4, 5; 1748: DL, Jan 2, 6, 12, 15, 18,
27, Feb 13, Mar 10, 12, 19, Apr 21, 27, 28, HAY, Jun 3, DL, Sep 13, 15, 17,

20, 22, 24, 27, 29, Oct 1, 4, 19, 28, 29, Nov 1, 2, 9, 14, Dec 10, 21, 28;
1749: DL, Jan 13, 20, Feb 1, 6, Mar 11, Apr 5, 8, 11, 15, 26, May 16, Sep 19,
20, 22, 28, Oct 3, 10, 17, 18, 23, 26, 28, 30, Nov 2, 4, 9, 15, 16, 21, 27,
Dec 11, 15, 16; 1750: DL, Jan 22, 31, Feb 7, 24, Mar 12, 13, 19, 26, Apr 2,
5, Sep 15, 18, 21, 22, 25, 27, Oct 1, 13, 15, 16, 19, 20, 22, 23, 26, 30, Nov
3, 5, 7, 8, 12, 13, 15, 28, Dec 3, 14; 1751: DL, Jan 7, 15, 24, Feb 2, 4, 9,
14, Mar 11, Apr 10, 26, 29, May 1, Sep 14, 17, 18, 19, 21, 24, 26, Oct 2, 3,
9, 11, 14, Nov 4, 7, 28, Dec 10, 26, 30; 1752: DL, Jan 6, 28, Feb 5, 17, Mar
7, 9, 12, Apr 3, 10, 17, 21, 27, Sep 16, 23, 26, 28, 30, Oct 7, 10, 19, 21,
23, 26, Nov 4, 22, 25, Dec 7, 19, 29; 1753: DL, Jan 3, 8, Feb 6, 7, Mar 19,
20, Apr 2, 25, 30, May 18, 22, 25, Sep 13, 15, 20, 25, 27, 29, Oct 3, 6, 13,
16, 18, 20, 23, 24, 30, Nov 1, 5, 7, 8, 14, Dec 1, 22; 1754: DL, Feb 12, Mar
18, 21, 26, Apr 20, May 10, 28, Sep 21, 24, Oct 1, 3, 10, 16, 18, 23, 25, 29,
Nov 4, 11, 22, 30, Dec 7, 9, 13; 1755: DL, Jan 25, Feb 25, CG, Mar 12, DL,
13, 20, Apr 15, May 6, Sep 16, 20, 25, Oct 2, 3, 4, 10, 23, 24, 28, Nov 1, 4,
6, 22, Dec 11, 18; 1756: DL, Jan 1, 21, Feb 24, Mar 23, 27, 30, Apr 26, 28,
May 5, 10, 14, Sep 21, 23, 25, 30, Oct 2, 5, 7, 9, 13, 14, 16, 19, 23, 29,
Nov 2, 4, 17, Dec 30; 1757: DL, Jan 24, Mar 7, 21, 22, 24, 29, Apr 18, 29,
30, Sep 13, 15, 20, 24, 27, Oct 4, 7, 15, 18, 26, Nov 1, 4, 22, Dec 8; 1758:
DL, Jan 19, 27, Feb 4, 21, Mar 11, 16, May 1, 4, Jun 1, Sep 19, 21, 26, Oct
12, 18, 21, 27, 30, Nov 1, 2, 4, 7, 13, 17, 23, Dec 13, 28; 1759: DL, Feb 1,
15, Mar 20, Apr 26, 30, May 11, Jun 28, Sep 27, 29, Oct 4, 5, 9, 11, 12, 16,
19, 22, 25, 27, Nov 1, 2, 5, 9; 1760: DL, Jan 1, 19, 24, Feb 8, Mar 18, 20,
Apr 9, 22, May 8, 16, Oct 9, 10, 11, 14, 15, 17, 23, Nov 17, 27, Dec 2; 1761:
DL, Jan 3, 23, 28, Feb 12, Mar 12, 25, 28, Apr 24, 28, 29, May 1, 18, Sep 12,
15, 17, 21, 25, 26, 30, Oct 10, 14, 16, 24, 27, 31, Nov 4, 18, Dec 11, 30;
1762: DL, Jan 7, 27, 29, Mar 15, 19, 20, 30, Apr 14, 22, May 17, Sep 18, 30,
Oct 5, 6, 8, 13, 14, 23, Nov 1, 4, 18, 26, Dec 1, 11; 1763: DL, Jan 17, 19,
Feb 3, Mar 14, 19, Apr 9, 20, May 14, 16, Sep 17, 20, 24, Oct 12, 17, 24, Nov
4, 7, 8, 29, Dec 10; 1764: DL, Jan 4, 9, 14, 23, Feb 18, Mar 20, Apr 24, Sep
20, 27, 29, Oct 2, 13, 18, 24, Nov 5, 27, Dec 18; 1765: DL, Jan 15, Feb 4,
Mar 16, 26, Apr 8, 22, 29, May 20, Sep 19, Oct 14, 28, Dec 3; 1766: DL, Jan
6, 13, 24, Mar 15, Apr 7, 12, 14, Sep 23, Oct 7, 31; 1767: DL, Jan 24, Feb
17, Mar 7, 21, Apr 6, 11, May 16, 23, 28, Sep 15, 17, 19, 26, Oct 20, Dec 5;
1768: DL, Jan 9, Feb 4, Mar 17, Apr 14, 25, Aug 18
Pritchard, Master (actor), 1792: HAY, Oct 15
Pritchard, Mrs David (actor), 1796: DL, May 31
Pritchard, William (treasurer, author), 1736: DL, Feb 28; 1748: DL, Apr 27;
   1749: DL, Apr 26; 1750: DL, Apr 25; 1751: DL, Apr 30; 1752: DL, Apr 17; 1753:
   DL, Apr 30; 1754: DL, Apr 30; 1755: DL, Feb 11, Apr 23; 1756: DL, Apr 28;
   1757: DL, Apr 30; 1758: DL, Apr 28; 1759: DL, May 10; 1760: DL, Apr 30; 1761:
   DL, Apr 29; 1762: DL, May 5; 1763: DL, Jan 3
--Fall of Phaeton, The; With Harlequin a Captive, 1736: DL, Feb 28, Mar 1, 2,
   3, 4, 5, 6, 8, 9, 13, 16, 18, 27, 30, Apr 17, 26, 27, 28, May 1, 5, 10, 24,
   26, 29, Nov 13, 15, 16, 18, 19, 20, 23, 24, 25, 26, 27, 29, 30, Dec 1, 2, 7,
   8, 11, 13, 15, 16, 18; 1737: DL, Jan 6, 10, 11, 12, 13, 18, 19, 21, 22, 24,
   27, Apr 12, 18, 21, 22, 28, May 3, Oct 8, 22, 24, Nov 9, 18; 1738: DL, Jan
   13, 14, 16, Dec 7, 16, 20, 21; 1739: DL, Oct 26, 27, 29, 30, 31, Nov 1, 2, 3,
   5, 6, 8, 10, 13, 20, Dec 12, 14
Pritchard's Warehouse, 1754: DL, Mar 18, Apr 30; 1755: DL, Apr 23; 1756: DL,
   Mar 23, Apr 28; 1757: DL, Mar 22, Apr 18, 30
Pritchett, Mrs (actor), 1723: HAY, Apr 15
Prithee Susan (song), 1787: HAY, Aug 14, 21
Priva del caro Sposo (song), 1741: HIC, Apr 24
Privot, Mlle (dancer), 1799: DL, Dec 17
Prize, The. See Hoare, Prince.
Procession to the Monument of the Lunns (dance), 1754: HAY, Aug 8
Procope, D M (Dr), 1734: GF/HAY, Dec 27
--Arlequin Balourd; or, Harlequin a Blunderer, 1719: KING'S, Feb 16, 19, 24,
   26; 1720: KING'S, Mar 19; 1734: GF/HAY, Dec 27, 28; 1735: GF/HAY, Jan 2, Feb
   14, Mar 28, May 15
Prodigal Reformed, The. See Jacob, Hildebrand.
Prodigal Son, The. See Arnold, Dr Samuel.
Prodigal Son, The (Careful Father, The; or, The Extravagant Son) (droll), 1746:
   GF, May 1
Prodigal Son, The; or, The Libertine Reclaimed (play, anon), 1724: BFL, Aug 22
Prodigal, The. See Waldron, Francis Godolphin.
Prodigal, The; or, Recruits for the Queen of Hungary. See Odell, Thomas.
Progers (spectator), 1667: LIF, Sep 12
Progress of Poesy, The (ode), 1800: CG, Jun 16
Projects, The. See Kemble, John Philip.
Prologue on Everybody (entertainment), 1782: CG, Apr 23

Prologue to the Apprentice (entertainment), <u>1767</u>: CG, May 19
Prologue to the Court (entertainment), <u>1659</u>: NONE, Sep 0
Prologue to the Institution of the Theatrical Fund (entertainment), <u>1790</u>: CG,
   May 20
Prologue to the King (entertainment), <u>1660</u>: ATCOURT, Aug 16
Prologue to the Merchants of London (entertainment), <u>1734</u>: GF, Mar 28, May 6
Prologue to the Players (entertainment), <u>1689</u>: NONE, Sep 0
Prologue to the Queen (entertainment), <u>1693</u>: NONE, Sep 0
Prologue to the University of Oxford (entertainment), <u>1673</u>: NONE, Jul 0; <u>1674</u>:
   OXFORD, Jul 0; <u>1680</u>: NONE, Sep 0; <u>1703</u>: DL, Jul 16
Promesse del Ciels, Le. See Mattei, Sga Colomba.
Prometheus (pantomime, anon), <u>1775</u>: CG, Dec 26, 27, 28, 29, 30; <u>1776</u>: CG, Jan
   1, 5, 12, 16, 18, 19, 20, 22, 23, 24, 25, 26, 27, 29, 31, Feb 1, 2, 3, 5, 6,
   7, 8, 12, 16, 19, Mar 4, 25, Apr 15, 20, 22, Dec 26
Promptwell, Peter (correspondent), <u>1744</u>: DL, Nov 3
Prophecy, The. See Busby, Thomas.
Prophet, The. See Bentley, Dr Richard.
Prophetess, The. See Fletcher, John.
Prophetic Raptures (song), <u>1791</u>: DL, Mar 11
Prophetic Visions (song), <u>1789</u>: DL, Mar 20; <u>1794</u>: DL, Mar 21, Apr 4, 11
Prospect Place, <u>1796</u>: CG, Apr 22
Prosser (dancer), <u>1781</u>: CG, May 19; <u>1782</u>: CG, May 10; <u>1783</u>: CG, May 29; <u>1784</u>:
   CG, May 11; <u>1785</u>: CG, May 24
Protee avec la Critique des Comediens Francois (play, anon), <u>1725</u>: HAY, Feb 23
Proteo Novello, Il (pantomime, anon), <u>1727</u>: KING'S, Mar 16
Protestant Cause (song), <u>1758</u>: HAY, Mar 16
Protestant Exhortation (song), <u>1680</u>: CITY, Oct 29
Protestation (song), <u>1739</u>: DL, May 11, 23, 25
Proteus (musical dramatic poem), <u>1741</u>: HIC, Apr 17
Proteus. See Woodward, Henry.
Proud Woman (song), <u>1715</u>: LIF, Aug 23
Prova Dell' Opera, La. See Paisiello, Giovanni.
Prove Sono (song), <u>1749</u>: KING'S, Mar 21
Provencale (Provenzale, Provincial), <u>1730</u>: DL, May 4; <u>1733</u>: GF, Apr 20, 30;
   <u>1739</u>: DL, Sep 20, 22, 29, Oct 2, 3, 4, 6, Dec 14, 18, 19; <u>1740</u>: DL, Feb 11,
   Mar 4, 6, May 2, 5, 14, Nov 27; <u>1741</u>: DL, Jan 8, 9, Mar 7, 10, 19, Apr 9, 30,
   CG, Dec 15, 18, 19, 21, 22, 23, 26; <u>1742</u>: CG, Jan 4, 16, 25, Feb 12, 13, 15,
   23, Mar 1, 6, 15, Apr 8, 19, 24, May 15, 20, 25, Jun 2, Oct 1, Nov 5, 13, 16,
   18, 19, Dec 11, 14, 16, 18, 23; <u>1743</u>: CG, Feb 3, Mar 5, 15, Apr 5; <u>1744</u>: CG,
   Oct 10, 16, 18; <u>1751</u>: DL, Apr 11, 16; <u>1752</u>: DL, Mar 14, Apr 15; <u>1763</u>: CG, Feb
   24, Apr 8, May 7, HAY, Aug 5, 8, 10, 11, 12, 22, DL, Oct 14, 17, 19, 20, 22,
   26, Nov 1, 9, 11, 14, 15, 21, 30, Dec 7, 14, 21; <u>1764</u>: DL, Feb 1, 13, 18, Mar
   17, 24, 26, Apr 24, 27, May 1, 2, 17, 18, 21, Sep 18, Oct 11; <u>1768</u>: CG, Mar
   1, 3, 10, 14, Apr 6, 12, May 9, Nov 23, Dec 22; <u>1769</u>: CG, Apr 26; <u>1770</u>: CG,
   Sep 28; <u>1772</u>: KING'S, Feb 4, Mar 3, CG, May 29, KING'S, Jun 3, 9, 11, 20;
   <u>1774</u>: KING'S, Jan 11, Mar 24, CG, Sep 28, Oct 4, 5, 12, 20, 21, 26, Nov 1,
   Dec 22; <u>1777</u>: KING'S, Feb 4, HAY, Aug 22; <u>1778</u>: DL, Jan 28, Feb 19, KING'S,
   Mar 3, 10, 17, 31, Apr 28, 30, May 12, HAY, 18, 27, KING'S, 30, HAY, Jun 1,
   KING'S, 5, HAY, 5, 11, 12, 16, 30; <u>1779</u>: HAY, May 31; <u>1780</u>: HAY, Aug 4; <u>1785</u>:
   DL, Sep 22, Oct 13, 18; <u>1786</u>: KING'S, Apr 27, DL, May 8; <u>1791</u>: KING'S, Apr
   14, 26, May 7; <u>1795</u>: DL, May 26
Provencale Dance, Grand (dance), <u>1752</u>: DL, Feb 4, 6, 15, 24, 25, Apr 1, 2, 3;
   <u>1774</u>: DL, Dec 8, 13, 16, 20, 23, 31; <u>1775</u>: DL, Jan 6, 11, 16, 27, Feb 2, 9,
   10, 14, 15, 23, Mar 6, 21, 25, 30, Apr 3, 24, May 1, 4, 5, 9; <u>1776</u>: DL, Mar
   19, Apr 23
Provenzale (Provenrali), Sga (dancer), <u>1758</u>: KING'S, Apr 4; <u>1759</u>: KING'S, Nov
   13; <u>1760</u>: KING'S, Jan 15, Mar 1, HAY, 27, KING'S, Apr 17, May 31; <u>1765</u>:
   KING'S, Dec 3
Provert, Mlle (actor), <u>1791</u>: KING'S, May 19
Provident Damsel (song), <u>1738</u>: DL, May 13
Provident Wife, The; or, The Doctor's the Disease (play), <u>1732</u>: DL, Nov 17
Provincial Sailors (dance), <u>1758</u>: CG, Apr 8, 19, 24, 27; <u>1761</u>: CG, May 8, 11
Provision for the Convent (dance), <u>1792</u>: DLKING'S, Jun 7
Provo (beneficiary), <u>1718</u>: TEC, Mar 19
Provocation!, The. See Byrn, James.
Provoked Husband, The. See Cibber, Colley.
Provoked Wife, The. See Vanbrugh, Sir John.
Provost (actor), <u>1697</u>: DL, Jul 0
Provost, Mlle (dancer), <u>1716</u>: DL, Apr 11
Prudhomme (Proudhomme), Mlle (dancer), <u>1753</u>: DL, Nov 1, 5, 8, 10, 16, 17, 21,
   27
Prudom, Maria (singer, actor), <u>1776</u>: KING'S, Nov 5, Dec 14; <u>1777</u>: KING'S, Feb

4, Apr 1, 17, 29, May 20, 24, Nov 4, 8, Dec 16; 1778: KING'S, Jan 20, Feb 7, Mar 3, Apr 2, 4, May 5, 30; 1779: KING'S, Dec 14; 1780: KING'S, Feb 8, Apr 13, May 9, 25, DL, Nov 11, KING'S, 25, 28, Dec 19, DL, 27; 1781: KING'S, Jan 23, Feb 8, 22, DL, Mar 2, KING'S, 8, DL, 30, KING'S, 31, Apr 3, 5, DL, 30, KING'S, May 12, Jun 5, 23, DL, Oct 6, 12, 19, 22, KING'S, Nov 17, Dec 18; 1782: DL, Feb 15, KING'S, Mar 7, 16, May 25
Pruet (actor), 1689: DL, Nov 7
Prunella. See Estcourt, Richard.
Prussia, King of, 1703: YB, Jul 27; 1704: LIF, Apr 4; 1724: DL, Jun 13; 1755: HAY, Apr 18; 1756: SOHO, Feb 2, Mar 16; 1758: CG, Jan 24, HAY, Mar 13; 1791: CG, Nov 21
--Charlottenburg Festegiante (pastoral), 1755: HAY, Apr 18; 1756: SOHO, Feb 2, Mar 16; 1760: SOHO, Feb 14
Prussian Camp (dance), 1757: DL, Dec 23, 28; 1758: DL, Jan 7, 9, 10, 11, 12, 20, 25, 27, 31, Feb 4, 11, 14, 20, Mar 9, 14, 28, Apr 6, 15, 21, May 8, 26, Dec 14, 19, 23, 26, 29; 1759: DL, Jan 15, 31, Feb 22, Mar 1, 3, 13, 17, May 4; 1760: DL, Nov 17, 18, 20, 22, 26, 28; 1763: DL, Dec 17, 20; 1767: DL, Feb 26
Prussian Festival, The (interlude, anon), 1791: CG, Nov 21, 22, 23, 24, 25, 28, 30, Dec 1, 12, 14, 15, 16, 19
Prussian Rope Makers (dance), 1759: CG, Apr 27, May 16, 18
Prussian Sailors (dance), 1758: CG, Apr 20, DL, Jun 1, 22
Prussians' March to Bohemia (dance), 1757: HAY, Jun 17, Sep 2, 28
Pryer (turner), 1775: DL, Nov 2, Dec 18; 1776: DL, Jan 16, 26, Mar 25, Jun 10
Prynn, William (author), 1699: DLLIF, Sep 12
Psalm CVI (entertainment), 1702: CC, May 21
Psalm CXXXIX (entertainment), 1702: CC, May 21
Psiche (dance), 1772: DL, Apr 24
Psyche Debauched. See Duffett, Thomas.
Psyche; or, Love's Mistress. See Shadwell, Thomas.
Ptolomy. See Handel, George Frederic.
Pudding and Dumbling Song (song), 1698: DG, Feb 7
Pudding Lane, 1749: BBT, Mar 1
Pudsey, Mrs (renter), 1758: CG, Mar 11
Puffupandyke, Mynheer (actor), 1753: HAY, Mar 13, May 3
Pugh, Charles John (scene designer), 1787: DL, Nov 8; 1788: DL, Nov 18, CG, Dec 26; 1790: CG, Jun 8, Dec 20; 1791: CG, Jun 9, Sep 17, Oct 20, Dec 21; 1792: CG, Dec 1, 20; 1793: CG, Mar 11, Dec 19; 1794: CG, Sep 22; 1797: DL, Dec 14; 1798: CG, May 28
Pugnani, Gaetano (composer), 1767: KING'S, Oct 27; 1769: KING'S, Apr 8; 1773: KING'S, Mar 30, May 3
--Apollo Ed Issea (opera), 1773: KING'S, Mar 30, Apr 1, 3, 13, 17, May 3
--Nanetta E Lubino (opera), 1769: KING'S, Apr 8, 11, 15, 22, 25, 29, May 2, 9, Jun 17
Puisans, Les (dance), 1735: CG, Dec 31
Puisieux, Mlle (dancer), 1791: PAN, Feb 17, 26, Mar 22
Pull Away (song), 1799: CG, Apr 19; 1800: CG, Apr 19
Pullen (actor), 1731: HAY, Mar 10; 1732: HAY, Mar 17, 23, Apr 27, May 8, 10, TC, Aug 4, HAY, Nov 29; 1733: HAY, Feb 14, Mar 14, 20, 26, Apr 18; 1734: HAY, Aug 16, 22; 1736: HAY, Feb 16, 19, Mar 5, Apr 26, 29, May 3, Jun 26, Jul 30; 1737: HAY, Mar 21, Apr 13
Pullen (house servant), 1767: CG, May 18; 1768: CG, Jun 3, 4; 1769: CG, May 19, 22
Pullen, Mrs (actor), 1728: HAY, Nov 30, Dec 23; 1729: BFRP, Aug 25; 1730: HAY, Mar 18; 1731: HAY, Mar 10; 1732: HAY, Mar 10, 17, 31, May 8, 10, 15, TC, Aug 4, HAY, Nov 29; 1733: HAY, Feb 14, Mar 14
Pulley, John Griffin (actor), 1777: HAY, May 15, Sep 3, DL, Oct 7, Nov 24, Dec 13; 1778: DL, Jan 1, Feb 24, May 19, Sep 17, 29, CG, Oct 5, DL, 26, 27; 1779: DL, Mar 13, 25, Sep 25; 1780: DL, Jan 24, Apr 3, Oct 23, Dec 6; 1781: DL, May 18, Sep 18, Nov 5; 1782: DL, May 16; 1792: CG, Feb 28
Pulley, Mary (actor), 1777: DL, Dec 27; 1778: DL, Jan 2, May 8; 1779: DL, May 1; 1780: DL, Jan 21, Apr 29, Sep 19; 1781: DL, May 11; 1782: DL, May 14; 1783: DL, May 8, 21
Pulley, Master (actor), 1774: DL, Sep 22, HAY, 30, DL, Nov 25; 1775: DL, Mar 20, 23, Oct 3, Dec 7; 1776: DL, Feb 10, Mar 11, 23, May 11, 24, Oct 12, 18, 29, Nov 6, 25
Pulli, P (composer), 1750: KING'S, Apr 10; 1754: KING'S, Feb 28
Pullin, Widow (beneficiary), 1770: CG, May 18
Pulmon, Mrs (singer), 1718: LIF, Dec 9, SH, 23; 1719: LIF, Mar 5, CGR, 18, LIF, Apr 9, 11, 23, 25, May 1, 12, 19, 28
Pulteney, Colonel, 1738: HAY, Oct 9
Pultney (spectator), 1733: LIF/CG, Feb 10

Punch and Harlequin (dance), 1722: LIF, Apr 24, May 10; 1723: LIF, May 23;
   1727: LIF, May 8
Punch and his Wife (dance), 1724: DL, May 13
Punch in Love with Dame Ragonde (dance), 1735: GF/HAY, Apr 7, HAY, May 26;
   1737: CG, Mar 19, Apr 2
Punch's Dance (dance), 1715: LIF, Jul 21; 1725: HAY, Apr 14; 1726: DL, Jan 27;
   1733: DL/HAY, Oct 3, 12, 19, 24, Nov 14, 23; 1734: BFHBH, Aug 24; 1737: DL,
   May 19, 24, 25, 30, 31, Jun 11; 1738: DL, Mar 21, CG, Apr 10, DL, 21, 22, 24,
   26, 27, May 16, 17, 23, 25, 26, 27, 31, BFH, Aug 23, DL, Oct 7, 27, Dec 28;
   1739: DL, Jan 24, Mar 26, 27, Apr 3, 5, 10, 12, 27, 30, May 3, 5, 8, 11, 16,
   18, 19, 22, 23, 26; 1740: DL, Jan 8, Feb 12, 16, Mar 6, 8, May 13, 16; 1750:
   DL, May 2; 1752: DL, Sep 19; 1754: DL, May 4, SFH, Sep 19
Punch's Defeat; or, Harlequin Triumphant (dance), 1748: HAY, Apr 14, 15, 16
Punch's Oratory; or, The Pleasures of the Town (puppetry), 1730: TC, Aug 1
Punch's Song (song), 1741: GF, Mar 12; 1792: CG, Dec 26, 27
Punchanello (dance), 1704: DL, Jun 29, Jul 1, Nov 27; 1705: DL, Jan 1; 1715:
   LIF, Oct 1, 10, 15, 22
Punchanello and Scaramouch (dance), 1715: LIF, Oct 3
Punchanello, Harlequin and Dame Ragonde (dance), 1716: LIF, Jan 7, Mar 5, Apr
   2, Oct 18
Punchanello's Encounter with the Pig (pantomime), 1732: HAY, May 12
Punchinello (puppet show), 1671: NONE, Feb 3
Puntiglio Amoroso, Il. See Galuppi, Baldassare.
Pupille Amobile (song), 1749: KING'S, Mar 21
Puppetry (entertainment), 1662: CG, May 9, 23, ATCOURT, Oct 8, CC, Nov 10;
   1663: NONE, Aug 6; 1666: MOORFLDS, Aug 22, 29, Sep 1; 1667: CC, Mar 20, Apr
   8, Aug 21, Oct 24; 1695: DG, Nov 0; 1726: BFY, Aug 26, SFPY, Sep 8; 1727: BF,
   Aug 23; 1729: SF, Sep 12; 1734: DL, Jan 23; 1773: CG, Mar 15, HAY, Aug 23
Puppille care (song), 1754: KING'S, Feb 28
Pur di Cesti (song), 1731: GF, Jan 13
Purcell Dialogue (song), 1737: LIF, May 4, 17
Purcell, Daniel (composer), 1690: DLORDG, Jan 16; 1695: DG, Apr 0; 1696: DL,
   Jan 0, Feb 0, May 0, DG, Aug 0, Oct 0; 1697: DL, Feb 0, DG, Jun 0, NONE, Sep
   0; 1698: DL, Mar 0, YB, May 25, DL, Jun 0, YB, 7, DL/ORDG, Nov 0, SH, 22;
   1699: YB, Jan 4, DL, May 0, NONE, Sep 0, DL, Nov 28, YB, Dec 13; 1700: DL,
   Feb 19, Mar 0; 1704: DL, Jan 4; 1710: DL, May 26
Purcell, Henry (composer), 1680: DG, Sep 0, DL, Dec 0; 1681: DL, Oct 0, Dec 0;
   1683: NONE, Sep 0, MS, Nov 22; 1684: NONE, Sep 0; 1685: DG, Jul 0; 1688:
   ATCOURT, Feb 6, DG, Apr 0; 1689: DLORDG, May 28, NONE, Aug 5, DL, Nov 7;
   1690: MTH, Mar 27, ATCOURT, Apr 30, DG, Jun 0, NONE, Sep 0, DL, 0, Oct 0,
   DL/IT, 21, DLORDG, Nov 0; 1691: DG, May 0, NONE, Sep 0, DL, Dec 0, DLORDG, 0;
   1692: DL, Jan 0, Apr 0, ATCOURT, 30, DG, May 2, DL, Jun 0, DLORDG, Aug 24,
   NONE, Sep 0, DL, Nov 8, SH, 22; 1693: DL, Feb 0, Mar 0, Apr 0, ATCOURT, 30,
   DG, May 0, NONE, Sep 0, DL, Oct 0; 1694: DL, Jan 0, ATCOURT, 1, DG, 10, YB,
   25, DL, Feb 0, Apr 0, ATCOURT, 30, DG, May 0, NONE, Sep 0, DL, 0, SH, Nov 22;
   1695: DG, Apr 0, DL, 1, Sep 0, Oct 0, Nov 0, DG, 0; 1696: YB, Jan 13, DL, Apr
   0; 1697: YB, Mar 3, LW, Aug 18; 1698: YB, May 28, PEPYSS, 30; 1699: DLLIF,
   Dec 25; 1700: LIF, Feb 0; 1701: YB, Mar 10, DG, Apr 11, YB, Jun 18; 1702: YB,
   Feb 9, DL, Dec 29; 1703: DL, Feb 12, May 24, LIF, Jun 14, DL, Jul 1, 3, Oct
   16, Dec 11; 1704: DL, Jan 4, 18, LIF, 29, Feb 1, DL, 3, 4, Mar 14, 23, 28,
   YB, 29, LIF, Apr 8, YB, 20, LIF, 29, DL, May 25, 27, 31, LIF, Jun 6, CC, 7,
   DL, 13, 21, 29, Jul 5, YB, Nov 16, DL, Dec 6; 1705: DL, Jan 11, 15, 26, Feb
   5, 14, YB, Mar 7, DL, Apr 30, May 16, 22, QUEEN'S, 24, 28, DL, Jun 5, 9, 16,
   Jul 3, RIW, 14, HAW, Aug 18, DL, Sep 27, LIF, Oct 12, DL, Nov 6, Dec 10, 15,
   31; 1706: DL, Jan 1, 4, 12, 14, 24, Feb 12, 16, 23, Mar 2, 5, 12, 26, Apr 2,
   Jun 22, DG, Nov 23; 1707: DL, Jan 21, Nov 22, 25, Dec 10; 1708: SH, Mar 26;
   1709: HA, Sep 3, 19, DL, Dec 15, 29; 1710: DL, May 26; 1711: SH, Apr 11, May
   9, GR, Sep 8; 1712: SH, May 14; 1714: SH, May 27, DL, Jul 2, Dec 20; 1715:
   LIF, Jan 17, 25, Mar 24, DL, May 17, 24, Jul 19, Aug 5, 9, 19, LIF, Oct 6,
   Nov 1, 11; 1716: LIF, May 2, DL, 30, Jun 19, 26, Jul 10, 24; 1717: LIF, Apr
   11, DL, May 22, LIF, Dec 27; 1718: LIF, Apr 5, 24, DL, May 21, Jul 25, GLOBE,
   Dec 3; 1719: DL, Jun 2; 1720: DL, Jun 7, Oct 19; 1722: DL, Oct 29; 1724: LIF,
   Dec 12; 1725: DL, May 17, Oct 29; 1726: DL, Jan 8, IT, Feb 2, HAY, 24, LIF,
   Jul 5; 1728: LIF, Mar 9; 1729: DL, Jun 13, Oct 30, CRT, Dec 5; 1730: GF, Apr
   14, DL, Dec 3, GF, 19; 1731: GF, Jan 13, LIF, Apr 8, May 3, DL, 12; 1732:
   HIC, Mar 31, DL, Apr 19; 1733: LIF/CG, Mar 30, DL, Nov 26; 1734: GF, May 3;
   1735: GF, Dec 17; 1736: CG, Apr 12, LIF, Sep 28; 1737: CG, Mar 10, 14, 26,
   LIF, Apr 2, CG, 11, LIF, 12, 14, CG, 18, 19, 21, 22, LIF, May 4, CG, 5, LIF,
   10, Jul 26; 1738: CG, Apr 11, 12, 18; 1739: DL, Jan 3, CG, May 17, Dec 10;
   1741: GF, Feb 19, DL, Dec 10; 1742: GF, May 10; 1745: CG, Mar 14, Oct 18;
   1747: DL, Apr 22; 1748: CG, Apr 15; 1752: DL, Mar 21; 1756: CG, Apr 19; 1757:
   DL, May 7; 1758: CG, Feb 1; 1761: DL, May 11; 1762: CG, Feb 17; 1763: CG, Mar

4, May 9, Oct 3; 1764: CG, Oct 1; 1765: CG, Oct 3; 1766: CG, Nov 21; 1770:
DL, Dec 13; 1772: DL, May 6; 1776: CG, Nov 14, Dec 27; 1778: HAY, Jul 30;
1779: DL, Feb 26, Mar 12, CG, May 13, HAY, 31; 1780: DL, Feb 18, CG, Nov 24;
1781: DL, Mar 14, CG, Apr 3, 18; 1782: DL, Mar 15, CG, May 6; 1784: DL, Mar
24, Nov 9, 22; 1785: DL, Oct 17, Dec 8; 1786: DL, Dec 5, CG, 26; 1787: CG,
Nov 5; 1788: CG, Dec 13; 1789: DL, Feb 27, Mar 20, Oct 13, CG, Nov 24, DL,
24; 1790: DL, Mar 17, May 31, CG, Jun 2, 3, DL, Oct 11; 1791: DL, Apr 1, 13,
DLKING'S, Nov 9; 1792: CG, Mar 7, KING'S, 30, CG, Apr 18, DL, Dec 13; 1793:
CG, Feb 15, KING/HAY, 15, CG, 20, 22, Mar 1, KING/HAY, 6, CG, 6, 8, 13, 15,
20, 22, Apr 24, HAY, Nov 19; 1794: CG, Mar 12, DL, 14, CG, 26, May 7; 1795:
CG, Mar 4, 18, Apr 24, DL, May 27; 1796: CG, Feb 26, Mar 16; 1797: DL, Feb
22, CG, Mar 24, 31, May 31, DL, Dec 9; 1798: CG, Feb 28, Mar 9, 14, 30; 1799:
CG, Feb 20, Mar 1, 13, DL, May 4, HAY, Sep 16, DL, Nov 14; 1800: CG, Mar 14,
21
--Aeneas and Dido (opera), 1704: LIF, Jan 29, Apr 8
--Cupid and Bacchus (masque), 1707: DL, Jan 21, Feb 11; 1715: LIF, Mar 24, Apr
22; 1739: CG, Dec 10, 11
Purden, Mrs (actor), 1719: DL, May 19; 1720: DL, May 14, CGR, Jun 22, LIF, Oct
13, Nov 2, 29, Dec 22; 1721: LIF, Jan 19, Feb 6, 8, May 10, 11, Nov 13, 16,
17, Dec 11; 1722: LIF, Oct 9, 16, 22, 23, 29, Nov 7, Dec 27; 1723: LIF, Jan
2, 3, Mar 30, Apr 23, May 13, Oct 4, 9, 18, 25, 29, Nov 1, 12, 26; 1724: LIF,
Mar 16, 23, Apr 27, May 4, 13, 27, Jul 3, 21, Sep 28, Oct 12, 23; 1728: HAY,
Oct 15, 26, Nov 14, 19, Dec 7; 1729: HAY, Jan 10, 31, Feb 25, Mar 27, 29, May
2, 7, 26, Jun 14, BFLH, Aug 23, SF, Sep 15, GF, Oct 31, Nov 3, 5, 6, 11, 12;
1730: GF, Jan 5, 13, 26, Feb 10, 16, 24, Apr 6, 8, 15; 1731: GF, Oct 8, 13,
18, 25, 27, Nov 1, 6, 17, 19, 20, Dec 4, 6, 28; 1732: GF, Mar 7, Apr 28, Oct
4, 7, 10, 11, 17, 18, Dec 18, 20; 1733: GF, Jan 8, 12, 13, 18, 24, Feb 5, 20,
Mar 28, SF/BFLH, Aug 23; 1734: SFL, Sep 7, HAY, Oct 7, GR, Nov 4; 1741: BFLW,
Aug 22
Purdon, Edward (critic), 1759: DL, Oct 13
Pure (actor), 1771: HAY, May 22, Aug 28
Puritan, The. See Middleton, Thomas.
Puritanical Justice, The; or, The Beggars Turned Thieves (play, anon), 1697:
NONE, Sep 0
Puritans, 1668: BRIDGES, Sep 4
Purkins (ticket deliverer), 1796: CG, Jun 4; 1797: CG, Jun 8; 1798: CG, Jun 5;
1799: CG, Jun 4
Purkiss (actor), 1785: HAY, Apr 25
Purney, Laserre (trumpeter), 1792: CG, Feb 24; 1793: CG, Feb 15; 1794: CG, Mar
7; 1795: CG, Feb 20; 1796: CG, Feb 12; 1797: CG, Mar 3; 1798: CG, Feb 23;
1799: CG, Feb 8; 1800: CG, Feb 28
Purryer (instrumentalist), 1798: HAY, Jan 15
Purse, The. See Cross, John Cartwright.
Purser, John (actor), 1784: DL, May 3
Purser, William (boxkeeper), 1786: DL, May 29; 1787: DL, Jun 1, 4; 1788: DL,
Jun 10; 1789: DL, Jun 9, 10; 1790: DL, May 29, Jun 3; 1791: DL, May 31; 1796:
DL, Jun 10; 1797: DL, Jun 13; 1798: DL, Jun 2
Purseval. See Percival.
Push about the Jorum (song), 1777: CG, Mar 10; 1780: CG, Mar 29; 1781: CG, Feb
26, Apr 3; 1782: CG, Feb 26
Put thy Trust in God (song), 1789: DL, Mar 25
Pye Corner, 1719: BFPM, Aug 24; 1720: BFPMJ, Aug 23; 1722: BFLSH, Aug 25; 1733:
BFAP, Aug 23
Pye Tavern, 1724: PT, Nov 30
Pye, Henrietta, 1771: DL, May 10
--Capricious Lady, The, 1771: DL, May 10
Pye, Henry James, 1794: CG, May 19; 1799: CG, Jun 12; 1800: DL, Jan 25
--Adelaide, 1800: DL, Jan 25, 27, 29
--Birthday Ode (entertainment), 1799: CG, Jun 12
--Siege of Meaux, The, 1794: CG, May 19, 22, 27, 29, Jun 10
Pygmalion (dance), 1760: CG, Apr 11, 17; 1784: KING'S, Mar 25
Pygmalion (song), 1797: KING'S, Jun 8
Pygmalion. See Rousseau, Jean Jacques.
Pynn (actor), 1767: HAY, May 29, Jun 5, 8, Jul 2, Aug 5, 25, Sep 9, 18
Pyramids (entertainment), 1715: YB, May 28
Pyramus and Thisbe. See Leveridge, Richard; Lampe, John Frederick.
Pyrander. See Johnson, Nathaniel.
Pyrrhic Dance (dance), 1733: GF, Nov 29, 30, Dec 1, 3, 4, 6, 7, 21; 1734: GF,
Jan 23, Mar 11; 1794: CG, Nov 17
Pyrrhus and Demetrius. See Haym, Nicolino Francesco.
Pyrrhus, King of Epirus. See Hopkins, Charles.

Q, Nathaniel. See Cue, Nathaniel.
Quack Doctor, The (song), 1799: HAY, Aug 17
Quack Doctor's Speech (entertainment), 1744: HAY, Apr 26
Quacks, The; or, Love's the Physician. See Swiny, Owen.
Quacks, The; or, The Credulous Man. See Foot, Jesse.
Quadrille, Grand (dance), 1773: KING'S, Apr 27, May 28, Jun 8
Quadrilles (dance), 1773: DL, Mar 27, 30; 1776: CG, May 3; 1778: CG, May 16;
   1779: KING'S, Jun 15, 19; 1780: CG, May 16; 1782: KING'S, Feb 2, CG, Apr 2,
   27, May 25; 1783: CG, May 24; 1787: KING'S, Jan 20
Quaker, Mrs (taverner), 1752: DL, Apr 20
Quaker, The. See Dibdin, Charles.
Quaker's Dance (dance), 1703: DL, Mar 13; 1704: DL, Aug 16
Quaker's Opera, The. See Walker, Thomas.
Quaker's Sermon (entertainment), 1740: SOU, Oct 9; 1746: GF, Feb 10; 1755: SOU,
   Jan 20
Quaker's Song (song), 1724: RI, Jul 4
Quaker's Wedding, The; or, The Passionate Mistress (play, anon), 1719: LIF, Oct
   22, 24, Nov 2, Dec 4; 1720: LIF, Jan 23; 1721: LIF, May 10, 30
Qual Nocchiero (song), 1750: KING'S, Apr 10
Quan (Qualm, Quarme), Mrs (actor), 1751: DL, Ma0 7
Quando Saprai chi Sono (song), 1763: KING'S, Apr 25
Quanto Assano (song), 1738: DL, Apr 12
Quanto Dolce Quanto Care (song), 1733: DL/HAY, Oct 20, 25; 1734: DL, Apr 4,
   DL/HAY, May 3
Quantz, Johann Joachim (composer), 1733: DL, Oct 22; 1734: HIC, Apr 8; 1754:
   KING'S, Mar 12; 1755: HAY, Apr 18
Quarrel of the Alphabet (song), 1796: CG, Apr 26
Quarreling Lovers Reconciled (dance), 1742: CG, Apr 21
Quarter Deck, The; or, Half an Hour's Festivity (interlude, anon), 1798: CG,
   May 8
Quarter of an Hour before Dinner, A. See Rose, John.
Quarter Staff Dance (dance), 1710: DL, Mar 11
Quatres Arlequins par Magie, Les (pantomime, anon), 1721: HAY, Mar 20; 1725:
   HAY, Mar 8; 1726: HAY, May 9
Quatro e quatro otto (song), 1792: DLKING'S, Apr 19
Quay (house servant), 1743: CG, May 11
Quebec St Hospital, 1766: CG, Dec 26
Quebec St, 1766: CG, Dec 23
Queen Ann St, 1780: KING'S, Mar 9, May 31; 1791: PAN, Apr 14; 1792: DLKING'S,
   Jun 11; 1793: DL, May 23
Queen Bess; or, The Spanish Armada (song), 1798: CG, Mar 15, May 8; see also
   Brave Betty was a maiden queen
Queen Betty was a famous Queen (song), 1798: CG, Feb 9
Queen Caroline (dance), 1757: CG, Apr 27
Queen Catharine. See Pix, Mary.
Queen Court, 1742: DL, Mar 15; 1743: DL, Mar 14; 1744: DL, Mar 13; 1746: DL,
   Apr 29; 1788: DL, May 14
Queen Dowager, 1669: NONE, Sep 3; 1687: CITY, Oct 29; 1689: ATCOURT, Nov 15;
   1692: DG, Jan 7
Queen Elizabeth's Troubles and the History of Eighty Eight. See Heywood,
   Thomas.
Queen Mab. See Woodward, Henry.
Queen Mab; or, The Fairies' Jubilee (song), 1770: DL, Apr 28; 1772: DL, May 22
Queen Mary's Lamentation (song), 1784: DL, Apr 14; 1793: CG, May 16; 1794: DL,
   Apr 11
Queen Minuet (dance), 1741: DL, Apr 4
Queen of Arragon, The. See Habington, William.
Queen of Corinth, The. See Fletcher, John.
Queen of Spain, The. See Lampe, John Frederick.
Queen Row, 1798: DL, Jun 6
Queen Square, 1743: CG, Mar 24; 1744: CG, Apr 4; 1778: DL, Apr 6; 1782: CG, May
   1, DL, 3; 1788: DL, May 14
Queen St, 1707: DS, Jul 22; 1724: HT, Mar 13; 1759: DL, May 10; 1763: CG, Mar
   19; 1772: DL, Sep 29; 1782: HAY, Jan 14, KING'S, Apr 18; 1787: DL, May 8
Queen Tragedy Restored. See Hoper, Mrs.
Queen, the, 1660: ATCOURT, Nov 19; 1662: THAMES, Aug 23, ATCOURT, Oct 2, Nov
   17, Dec 1; 1663: ATCOURT, Jan 5, SH, 6; 1666: ATCOURT, Oct 11, 29, BRIDGES,
   Dec 20; 1667: NONE, Feb 12, BRIDGES, Apr 15, ATCOURT, Nov 15, 16; 1668:
   BRIDGES, Jan 20, ATCOURT, Feb 4, BRIDGES, May 18, ATCOURT, 29, BRIDGES, Jun

12, ATCOURT, Sep 28, BRIDGES, Nov 6, LIF, Dec 29; <u>1669</u>: BRIDGES, Jan 2, 21,
ATCOURT, Feb 22; <u>1670</u>: ATCOURT, Apr 6; <u>1671</u>: ATCOURT, Feb 9, Nov 14, DG, 15;
<u>1674</u>: DL, Nov 9, DG, Dec 2; <u>1675</u>: DG, Jan 8, 22, DL, 25, Apr 23, May 4, 7,
DG, Sep 0; <u>1676</u>: CITY, Oct 30; <u>1680</u>: DG, Nov 1; <u>1681</u>: DG, Apr 18, ATCOURT,
Nov 15; <u>1682</u>: DG, Nov 9, DL, 16, 25, Dec 1, 30; <u>1683</u>: DLORDG, Jan 11, 18;
<u>1684</u>: DLORDG, Nov 3; <u>1685</u>: DLORDG, Jan 13, 15, 20, 22, 27, Apr 28, DL, May
11, DLORDG, 30, DG, Jun 3, ATCOURT, Oct 10, DLORDG, 20, DL, Dec 19, DLORDG,
30; <u>1686</u>: DL, Feb 4, DLORDG, 8, 11, ATCOURT, 16, DLORDG, Apr 8, May 6, 10,
Oct 6, 13; <u>1687</u>: DLORDG, Jan 20, Apr 6, CITY, Oct 29; <u>1689</u>: DLORDG, May 28,
31, DL, Nov 7, Dec 4; <u>1690</u>: ATCOURT, Jan 1, DL/IT, Oct 21, DG, Nov 17; <u>1691</u>:
DL, Feb 4, OXFORD, Jun 30, DLORDG, Oct 10; <u>1692</u>: DG, Jan 7, DL, Feb 9, Apr 0,
NONE, 9, ATCOURT, 30, SF, Sep 13, CITY, Oct 29, NONE, Nov 14; <u>1693</u>: DG, Feb
16, ATCOURT, May 0, OXFORD, Jul 7; <u>1694</u>: DL, Jan 13; <u>1696</u>: DL, Dec 0; <u>1702</u>:
CC, Apr 25, May 25; <u>1703</u>: RIW, Aug 12; <u>1705</u>: RIW, Jul 14; <u>1710</u>: QUEEN'S, Jul
19; <u>1727</u>: DL, Sep 28, Nov 7, KING'S, Dec 5; <u>1728</u>: DL, Jan 27, KING'S, Feb 17,
LIF, 22, KING'S, Mar 9, 12, DL, 14, KING'S, 19, 30, Apr 2, May 7, DL, Nov 13,
20, 30, Dec 11; <u>1729</u>: LIF, Jan 16, DL, 28, Feb 5, Mar 6, 13, RI, Jul 26, DL,
Oct 28, Nov 12, 19, 26, KING'S, Dec 13; <u>1730</u>: KING'S, Feb 14, LIF, 19, 26,
KING'S, 28, Mar 17, DL, 19, Apr 2, Oct 28, Dec 10, 17; <u>1731</u>: KING'S, Mar 9,
DL, 11, KING'S, 16, DL, 18, KING'S, 20, LIF, 25, KING'S, 27, Apr 6, 10, 20,
May 1, 18, DL, Nov 12, LIF, 18, KING'S, Dec 4; <u>1732</u>: KING'S, Apr 15, SJP, 27,
KING'S, May 9, 16, Jun 17, 20, 24, DL, Sep 8; <u>1733</u>: KING'S, Mar 31, May 29,
Jun 5, Nov 6; <u>1734</u>: KING'S, Feb 2, 5, CG/LIF, Sep 30; <u>1735</u>: CG, Jan 8, LIF,
Feb 27, CG, Jul 2, DL, Sep 15, Oct 1; <u>1736</u>: CG, Jun 2, Nov 10, 13, Dec 8,
KING'S, 11; <u>1737</u>: KING'S, Jan 1, May 17; <u>1739</u>: CG, Jan 11; <u>1760</u>: CG, Sep 25;
<u>1761</u>: DL, Jul 27; <u>1762</u>: KING'S, Jan 16, DL, Sep 30, Oct 14, 21, Nov 12, Dec
16; <u>1763</u>: DL, Oct 20, Nov 10; <u>1764</u>: DL, Feb 2; <u>1767</u>: CG, Jan 1, DL, 2, CG,
Mar 6, DL, May 7, CG, Dec 28; <u>1768</u>: DL, Oct 20; <u>1769</u>: CG, Jan 2, DL, 12, Feb
9, Oct 12, 25, Nov 16; <u>1770</u>: CG, Jan 3, DL, Mar 8, Sep 27, Oct 10, 24, Dec
12; <u>1771</u>: DL, Jan 9; <u>1772</u>: CG, Jan 6; <u>1773</u>: CG, Jan 5, DL, Apr 21; <u>1774</u>: CG,
Jan 14, DL, Jun 2; <u>1775</u>: DL, Mar 10, Oct 5, Nov 22; <u>1776</u>: DL, Jan 20; <u>1787</u>:
CG, Dec 12; <u>1789</u>: CG, Apr 15, DL, Dec 16
Queen's Allemande (dance), <u>1782</u>: KING'S, Feb 2
Queen's Arms Tavern, <u>1715</u>: SF, Sep 5; <u>1720</u>: SOU, Oct 3; <u>1721</u>: SF, Sep 8; <u>1724</u>:
  SF, Sep 7; <u>1726</u>: SFSE, Sep 8; <u>1735</u>: SFLT, Sep 4; <u>1749</u>: BBT, Mar 1
Queen's Birthday Song (song), <u>1694</u>: ATCOURT, Apr 30; <u>1704</u>: LIF, Jul 24
Queen's Birthday, <u>1690</u>: ATCOURT, Apr 30; <u>1693</u>: ATCOURT, Apr 30
Queen's Buildings, <u>1781</u>: DL, May 9; <u>1782</u>: DL, May 1
Queen's Coronation Song (song), <u>1702</u>: SH, May 1
Queen's Court, <u>1785</u>: HAY, Apr 26
Queen's Garden, <u>1698</u>: RICHMOND, Aug 8
Queen's Head Coffee House, <u>1751</u>: DL, Apr 29
Queensberry, Marquis and Duke of. See Douglas, William.
Quel Ciglio che mesto (song), <u>1757</u>: KING'S, Mar 24
Quelch, Mrs (actor), <u>1755</u>: HAY, Sep 3, 9, 11, 15
Quelch, William (actor), <u>1755</u>: HAY, Sep 1, 3, 9, 11, 15
Quella fiamma (song), <u>1753</u>: KING'S, Apr 30
Quercioli, Sga (singer), <u>1767</u>: KING'S, Oct 27; <u>1768</u>: KING'S, Mar 10
Queroulle, Henrietta, Countess of Pembroke, <u>1675</u>: ATCOURT, Feb 15
Quest' alma sventurata (song), <u>1789</u>: DL, Mar 25; <u>1791</u>: CG, Apr 6
Questo core amato bene (song), <u>1750</u>: KING'S, Apr 10; <u>1758</u>: KING'S, Apr 6
Quick, John (actor), <u>1766</u>: HAY, Jun 18, 26, Jul 1, 8, 15, 23, 31, KING'S, Aug
13, 18, 20, HAY, 21, KING'S, 29, HAY, Sep 2, KING'S, 9, 13; <u>1767</u>: HAY, May
29, Jun 4, 5, 8, CG, 9, HAY, 17, 22, Jul 6, Aug 7, 12, 25, 27, Sep 4, 7, CG,
14, 21, Oct 5, 9, Nov 7, 20, 23, 28, Dec 8, 14; <u>1768</u>: CG, Jan 6, 9, 16, 29,
Feb 13, Apr 7, 19, 20, 29, May 27, Jun 3, 4, Oct 4, 10, 24, Dec 22, 23; <u>1769</u>:
CG, Jan 19, 28, Mar 6, Apr 1, 21, 22, May 12, 20, 23, 25, Oct 2, 6, 7, 11,
16, Nov 3, 15, 21, Dec 1, 2, 19, 29; <u>1770</u>: CG, Jan 6, 18, 27, Feb 3, 12, Mar
20, Apr 5, 24, May 7, 22, 28, Oct 1, 8, 12, 17, 19, 23, Nov 17, 30, Dec 12,
26; <u>1771</u>: CG, Jan 1, 4, 12, 26, Feb 9, 11, 21, Apr 3, 6, 12, 22, 24, 29, 30,
May 1, 6, 9, 15, 22, Sep 23, 27, Oct 2, 4, 11, 14, 15, 19, 22, Nov 2, 5, 21,
Dec 7, 14, 18; <u>1772</u>: CG, Jan 4, 27, Feb 24, Mar 5, 23, 31, Apr 21, 29, May 4,
8, 12, 13, 22, 23, 26, 29, Sep 21, 23, 25, Oct 7, 14, 16, 26, 28, Dec 5, 11,
28; <u>1773</u>: CG, Jan 4, 20, 28, Feb 6, 10, 17, Mar 15, 22, Apr 17, 23, 27, May
3, 4, 6, 8, 10, 19, Sep 22, 24, 29, Oct 5, 8, 9, 15, 22, 23, Nov 6, 16, 20,
26, 27, Dec 3, 7, 17, 23; <u>1774</u>: CG, Jan 3, 14, 29, Feb 9, Mar 12, 15, 22, 26,
Apr 5, 9, 12, 23, 26, May 2, Sep 21, 23, 26, 28, 30, Oct 11, 13, 14, 15, 21,
26, Nov 1, 4, 8, 12, 19, 24, Dec 1, 2, 6, 12, 27; <u>1775</u>: CG, Jan 17, 21, Feb
23, Mar 13, 20, Apr 19, 22, May 2, 4, 9, 17, 18, Jun 1, Sep 20, 22, 25, 27,
29, Oct 6, 9, 11, 13, 17, 19, 20, Nov 1, 3, 4, 9, 21, 28, 30, Dec 2, 7, 9,
21, 23, 29; <u>1776</u>: CG, Jan 5, 15, 24, Feb 22, 26, Mar 5, 21, 30, Apr 16, 19,
27, May 6, 10, 13, Sep 23, 25, 30, Oct 11, 15, 16, 17, 25, 29, 31, Nov 4, 7,

8, 9, 14, 15, 19, 20, 26, Dec 2, 4, 27; 1777: CG, Feb 5, Mar 17, Apr 7, 14, 28, May 2, 12, Sep 22, 24, Oct 6, 8, 15, 16, 21, 23, 29, Nov 3, 12, 18, 19, 20, Dec 5, 19; 1778: CG, Jan 15, 20, 29, Feb 2, 4, 24, 26, 28, Mar 9, Apr 25, 27, May 5, 6, 9, 11, 12, 22, Sep 18, 21, 28, DL, 29, CG, Oct 2, 5, 7, 12, 15, 16, 23, 27, 29, Nov 4, 23, Dec 1, 11, 19, 21; 1779: CG, Jan 2, 11, 21, 22, 25, 26, Feb 22, Apr 26, 27, May 3, 10, 13, 15, Sep 20, 22, 27, Oct 1, 8, 13, 18, 29, Nov 11, 13, 22, 23, 25, 27, 30, Dec 1, 11, 16, 17, 31; 1780: CG, Jan 7, 18, Feb 1, 5, 22, Mar 18, 29, Apr 3, 7, 12, 19, 21, 25, 27, May 1, 3, 23, 24, Sep 18, 20, 22, Oct 3, 10, 13, 19, 21, 23, 24, 26, Nov 1, 2, 4, 8, 22, 25, 27, Dec 9, 12, 15, 16; 1781: CG, Jan 10, 12, 13, 18, 25, Feb 15, 24, Mar 8, 24, 31, Apr 18, 28, 30, Sep 17, 19, 21, 26, 28, Oct 3, 10, 11, 27, 30, 31, Nov 2, 8, 12, 23, 28, Dec 5, 8, 18, 31; 1782: CG, Jan 4, 11, 22, Feb 2, 9, Mar 16, 19, Apr 1, 4, 10, 17, 20, May 6, 7, 11, 14, 20, 28, Sep 23, 25, 27, 30, Oct 2, 4, 8, 9, 16, 18, 23, 29, Nov 1, 2, 6, Dec 6; 1783: CG, Jan 17, Feb 19, 22, 25, Mar 3, Apr 1, 23, May 9, 10, 17, 19, Jun 3, Sep 17, 19, 26, Oct 2, 3, 8, 9, 11, 15, 16, 21, 24, 28, 31, Nov 6, 8, 19, Dec 5, 6; 1784: CG, Jan 7, 9, 14, Feb 13, Mar 16, 27, Apr 13, 17, 26, 27, May 4, 7, 8, 10, 11, 12, 17, 26, 29, Sep 17, 20, 21, 22, 24, 28, Oct 1, 8, 12, 18, 29, 30, Nov 6, 10, 11, 13, 16, 20, 25, 30, Dec 3, 14, 28; 1785: CG, Jan 8, 21, Feb 7, 21, Mar 5, 19, 29, 30, Apr 2, 11, 12, May 4, 6, 7, 12, 13, 18, 26, Sep 19, 23, 26, 28, 30, Oct 3, 5, 7, 12, 14, 17, 19, 21, 22, 26, Nov 1, 2, 3, 9, 10, 14, 19, 21, 22, 29, Dec 5, 7, 8, 14, 22, 28, 30; 1786: CG, Jan 3, DL, 5, CG, 6, 7, 20, 28, Feb 1, 4, 7, 13, 16, 17, 18, Mar 11, 18, Apr 1, 4, 18, 20, 24, May 6, 9, 11, 13, 20, 26, HAY, Jul 25, CG, Sep 18, 29, Oct 4, 9, 12, 16, 19, 21, Nov 14, 15, 18, 22, 23, 24, 25, 30, Dec 1, 6, 21, 30; 1787: CG, Jan 2, 4, 6, 11, 26, 27, Feb 10, Mar 12, 15, 27, Apr 11, 16, 25, 26, 27, May 1, 9, 14, 21, 22, Sep 19, 21, 26, 28, Oct 1, 3, 5, 10, 11, 17, 18, 19, 29, Nov 7, 8, 14, 22, 23, 28, Dec 5, 10, 15, 22; 1788: CG, Jan 3, 4, 10, 11, 15, 28, Feb 4, 9, 14, 23, 25, Mar 1, 11, 15, 24, 26, 28, 29, Apr 1, 2, 8, 11, 26, 29, May 12, Sep 15, 17, 22, 24, 26, Oct 1, 3, 7, 8, 15, 17, 18, 21, 22, 24, 29, Nov 1, 6, 7, 20, 22, 27, 28, Dec 13, 30, 31; 1789: CG, Jan 2, 15, 20, 28, Feb 3, 6, 11, 21, Mar 5, 28, 31, Apr 4, 14, 15, 30, May 2, 5, 8, 14, 15, 19, 26, Jun 2, 3, 5, 16, Sep 16, 18, 28, 30, Oct 2, 7, 13, 16, 17, 20, 21, 24, 28, 30, 31, Nov 6, 11, 12, 13, 14, 16, 20, 24, 27, Dec 2; 1790: CG, Jan 13, 22, 23, Mar 8, 13, 18, 22, 27, Apr 6, 7, 12, 20, 21, 24, May 6, 11, 13, 18, Jun 1, 16, Sep 15, Oct 1, 5, 12, 13, 15, 19, 20, 23, Nov 3, 11, 19, 30, Dec 6, 8, 11, 14, 17, 28; 1791: CG, Jan 14, Feb 2, Mar 5, 12, 14, Apr 16, 28, 30, May 2, 5, 10, 11, 18, 19, 20, 24, 31, Jun 1, 6, Sep 12, 14, 16, 17, 20, 21, 23, 28, 30, Oct 3, 6, 12, 13, 17, 20, 21, 27, Nov 1, 2, 5, 7, 15, 19, 25, 26, 29, Dec 2, 8, 10, 13, 15; 1792: CG, Jan 6, Feb 2, 6, 8, 18, 23, Mar 22, 31, Apr 10, 18, May 2, 5, 10, 11, 15, 18, 22, 29, 30, Jun 2, Sep 17, 19, 20, 21, 26, Oct 3, 5, 10, 12, 17, 18, 19, 24, 26, 27, 31, Nov 3, 5, 6, 7, 10, 24, Dec 1, 5; 1793: CG, Jan 2, 9, 25, 29, Feb 11, 12, 14, Apr 4, 8, 15, 18, 24, May 8, 10, 15, 24, 27, Jun 5, 12, Sep 16, 17, 18, 20, 25, 27, Oct 1, 2, 3, 4, 5, 8, 9, 10, 11, 15, 17, 18, 19, 21, 22, 23, 25, 29, 30, Nov 1, 2, 5, 9, 12, 16, 22, 23, Dec 5, 6, 7, 9, 17, 18; 1794: CG, Jan 3, 21, 22, Feb 5, 22, 24, 26, Mar 18, Apr 7, 12, 23, 25, 29, May 2, 13, 14, 16, 22, 26, 27, 28, Sep 24, 26, 29, Oct 1, 3, 7, 8, 10, 14, 21, 23, 30, Nov 11, 12, 17, 19, 20, 21, Dec 6, 10, 30, 31; 1795: CG, Jan 2, 3, 6, 8, 23, 24, 29, 31, Feb 14, Mar 16, 19, Apr 8, 22, 24, 28, 29, May 1, 2, 13, 18, 19, 20, 25, Jun 2, Oct 5, 7, 8, 14, 15, 19, 22, 24, Nov 4, 7, 25, 27, Dec 4, 9, 22, 29, 31; 1796: CG, Jan 2, 18, 23, Mar 14, 19, 30, Apr 1, 5, 12, 13, 15, 19, 20, 23, 29, May 6, 10, 12, 23, 28, Jun 6, 7, Sep 12, 14, 16, 17, 19, 23, 26, 28, 30, Oct 3, 5, 6, 14, 17, 18, 20, 21, 29, Nov 7, 19, Dec 22, 31; 1797: CG, Jan 3, 4, 7, 10, Feb 20, Mar 4, 16, Apr 8, 19, 25, 29, May 6, 9, 17, 18, 22, 31, Jun 1, 2, 8, 10, 13, Oct 16, 21, 28, 31, Nov 1, 3, 4, 10, 11, 15, 20, 21, 23, Dec 8, 12, 16, 18, 23, 28; 1798: CG, Jan 9, 11, Feb 6, 12, 13, Mar 20, 31, Apr 10, 11, 13, 16, 18, 19, 21, 25, 28, 30, May 2, Jun 5; 1799: DL, May 9; 1800: CG, Jun 12, 13
Quidnunc and Pamphlet (interlude, anon), 1798: HAY, Apr 21
Quiet, Mlle (dancer), 1705: DL, Dec 17
Quilici, Gaetano (singer), 1754: CG, Nov 18; 1758: KING'S, Nov 11, Dec 16; 1759: KING'S, Jan 16, Nov 13; 1760: KING'S, Jan 15, Mar 1, SOHO, 13, HAY, 27, KING'S, Apr 17, HIC, 29, KING'S, May 31, HAY, Jun 5, KING'S, Aug 25, Nov 22, Dec 16; 1761: KING'S, Jan 6, SOHO, 21, KING'S, Feb 7, Mar 9, Apr 28; 1762: CHAPEL, May 18; 1763: KING'S, Feb 19, Apr 25, HAY, Jun 9; 1764: CG, Jun 5; 1765: KING'S, Dec 3
Quin (dancer), 1798: CG, Feb 2
Quin, James (actor), 1715: DL, Feb 4, 23, Apr 20, May 10, Jun 28, Aug 9, Dec 6; 1716: DL, Jan 3, Mar 6, May 1, Jul 19, Aug 9, Oct 24, Nov 7, Dec 17, 27; 1717: DL, Jan 5, 12, 16, Feb 15, May 9, 10, 15, 30, Jul 16, Aug 6, 13, 22, SF, Sep 9, DL, Oct 16, Nov 18, 19; 1718: LIF, Jan 7, 11, Feb 1, 13, 18, Mar 1, 11, Apr 18, NONE, Jul 10, LIF, Sep 26, 29, 30, Oct 1, 4, 8, 11, 16, 18,

Nov 1, 4, 13, Dec 6; 1719: LIF, Jan 3, 16, 31, Feb 21, 28, Mar 19, 30, Apr 17, 20, Oct 2, 7, 13, 17, 31, Nov 5, 7, 18, 19, 24; 1720: LIF, Feb 11, 23, 29, Mar 12, Apr 26, May 11, 17, 19, Jun 7, 9, Oct 1, 8, 13, 15, 18, 20, 22, Nov 1, 2, 10, 15, 19, Dec 1, 8, 21, 27, 31; 1721: LIF, Jan 4, 7, 10, 17, 19, 28, Feb 6, 9, 25, Mar 4, 11, 18, Apr 1, 13, 19, 21, 25, May 5, Sep 23, 27, 29, Oct 5, 7, 10, 12, 14, 19, 20, 21, 24, 25, 26, 28, Nov 2, 4, 9, 11, 16, 18, 25, Dec 2, 12, 18, 28; 1722: LIF, Jan 9, 13, 22, Feb 13, Mar 5, 8, 15, 29, Apr 3, May 7, Sep 29, Oct 2, 4, 11, 13, 18, 19, 20, 23, 24, 27, 30, 31, Nov 1, 2, 3, 5, 7, 8, 12, 14, 17, 22, 29, 30, Dec 1, 7, 10, 14, 21, 31; 1723: LIF, Jan 3, 11, 18, Feb 1, 22, Mar 21, Apr 16, 23, 27, May 3, Sep 28, 30, Oct 2, 9, 10, 24, 25, 31, Nov 1, 2, 4, 14, 16, 18, 19, 21, 26, 28, Dec 2, 7; 1724: LIF, Feb 24, Mar 16, 19, 23, 26, 28, Apr 9, 14, 22, 28, 29, May 2, 19, 27, Jun 3, Sep 23, 28, Oct 7, 9, 14, 22, 27, Nov 3, 4, 6, 12, 17, 18, 20, 24, 26; 1725: LIF, Jan 4, 11, 16, 19, Mar 11, 18, 31, Apr 5, 14, 20, 23, 26, Sep 24, 29, Oct 1, 4, 11, 13, 15, 16, 25, 28, Nov 2, 4, 8, 9, 11, 17, 18, 29, 30, Dec 2, 6, 7, 15; 1726: LIF, Jan 7, Feb 19, Mar 19, 24, Apr 2, 22, May 3, 4, 11, Sep 12, 14, 19, 21, 26, 28, Oct 3, 12, 17, Nov 2, 4, 8, 10, 11, 14, 18, 21, 30, Dec 14; 1727: LIF, Jan 4, 9, 16, Feb 2, 7, Mar 23, Apr 19, May 2, 22, Sep 11, 13, 15, 18, 20, 25, 27, Oct 9, 19, 21, 26, 31, Nov 4, 16, 17; 1728: LIF, Jan 8, Mar 14, May 8, 11, 15, 18, 20, Sep 16, 18, 30, Oct 1, 7, 21, 23, Nov 1, 4, 11, 19, 20, Dec 7, 28, 31; 1729: LIF, Jan 13, Feb 6, 7, 10, 22, Mar 3, 4, 10, Apr 8, 15, 16, May 15, Sep 12, 17, 19, 22, 24, 26, 29, Oct 3, 6, 8, 10, 13, 20, 24, 31, Nov 4, 8, 13, 22, 25, Dec 15; 1730: LIF, Jan 26, Mar 19, Apr 10, 20, 22, May 6, 11, 15, 20, Jun 1, Sep 16, 18, 21, 23, Oct 5, 14, 19, 27, Nov 2, 3, 4, 6, 13, 23, Dec 3; 1731: LIF, Jan 4, 8, 11, 13, 21, Feb 3, 27, Mar 13, 15, 18, 22, Apr 3, 5, 22, May 1, 3, 5, 17, 20, 25, Sep 17, 20, 22, 27, 29, Oct 1, 6, 11, 13, 18, 25, 27, Nov 2, 4, 17, Dec 1, 6, 8, 9, 11, 15, 31; 1732: LIF, Jan 18, 19, 28, Feb 14, 28, Mar 21, 23, 25, Apr 10, 13, 18, 24, 27, 29, May 9, 18, RIW/HAY, Sep 11, CG/LIF, 22, LIF/CG, 25, 27, 29, Oct 4, 6, 9, 11, 16, LIF, 18, LIF/CG, 20, 21, 25, 27, 28, 30, Nov 1, 3, 4, 9, 11, 13, 18, 22, Dec 4, 7, 15; 1733: LIF/CG, Jan 1, 15, CG, Feb 8, LIF/CG, 10, Mar 15, CG, 27, LIF/CG, 31, Apr 2, CG, 4, LIF/CG, 10, 11, 12, 13, 17, CG, May 1, LIF/CG, 10, 24, CG, Sep 15, 20, 22, 25, 29, Oct 2, 4, 6, 9, 11, 13, 18, 20, 23, 26, 27, 31, Nov 1, 3, 5, 8, 9, 14, 16, 19, 21, 28, 30, Dec 3, 4, 15, 17, 20; 1734: CG, Jan 12, 18, Mar 5, 12, 18, 28, Apr 6, 16, May 13, 17, DL, Sep 10, 14, 24, 28, Oct 3, 5, 9, 12, 25, 26, Nov 4, 8, Dec 6, 7, 14, 27; 1735: DL, Jan 13, 23, Feb 4, 10, 25, Mar 10, 13, 22, Apr 23, May 13, 14, Sep 1, 6, 11, 18, 20, 25, 27, 30, Oct 7, 11, 25, 27, 30, Nov 1, 4, 7, 12, 17, 21, 24, 29, Dec 6; 1736: DL, Feb 9, 20, Mar 11, May 20, 26, Aug 26, Sep 4, 18, 21, 23, Oct 5, 7, 9, 12, 13, 19, 21, 27, Nov 2, 3, 4, 6, 11, 13, 19, 20, 22, Dec 14, 23; 1737: DL, Jan 6, 10, 14, 17, Feb 5, 7, 28, Mar 1, 10, 12, 15, 22, Sep 1, 8, 15, 20, 22, Oct 1, 6, 11, 19, 20, 21, 27, 31, Nov 1, 4, 12, 14, 17; 1738: DL, Jan 5, 11, 14, 19, 23, 31, Feb 16, 28, Mar 4, 16, Apr 6, 28, 29, May 3, 6, Sep 7, 12, 14, 16, 19, 21, 26, 30, Oct 12, 13, 17, 19, 20, 26, 31, Nov 4, 8, 20, 21, 30, Dec 6; 1739: DL, Feb 1, 13, Mar 8, 17, 31, May 1, Sep 1, 13, 18, 21, 24, Oct 4, 5, 6, 10, 13, 17, 19, 20, 22, 25, Nov 3, 5, 8, 10, 12, 17, 19, 20, 28, Dec 10, 22, 31; 1740: DL, Jan 3, Feb 23, Mar 13, 20, 25, 27, Apr 23, May 20, 29, 30, Sep 6, 16, 23, 25, 27, Oct 4, 7, 9, 13, 14, 15, 16, 29, Nov 1, 4, 10, 11, 19, 27, Dec 8, 10, 15, 18, 20; 1741: DL, Jan 6, Feb 14, Mar 10, 14, 17, Apr 16, May 13; 1742: CG, Mar 25, Sep 22, 29, Oct 1, 4, 6, 9, 11, 13, 15, 18, 19, 21, 25, 26, 27, Nov 3, 4, 11, 13, 15, 20, 25, 29, DL, Dec 1, CG, 15, 21; 1743: CG, Jan 5, 18, Mar 7, Oct 28, Nov 28, Dec 3, 8, 9, 10, 12, 13, 14, 15, 16, 17, 19, 20, 21, 27, 31; 1744: CG, Jan 2, 5, 7, 11, 14, 18, 24, Feb 3, 7, 23, Mar 3, 8, 12, 13, Apr 10, Sep 19, 21, 24, 26, 28, Oct 1, 5, 8, 15, 16, 18, 20, 22, 24, 26, 31, Nov 1, 5, 7, 9, 12, 21, 22, 28, Dec 5, 6, 12, 14, 21; 1745: CG, Jan 14, 18, Feb 11, 15, DL, Mar 9, CG, 11, Apr 20, 26, DL, Oct 24; 1746: DL, Oct 4, CG, 20, 24, Nov 1, 4, 6, 8, 13, 14, 17, 18, 26, 28, DL, Dec 5, CG, 6, 17, 19, 22, 29; 1747: CG, Jan 2, 20, 27, Feb 10, 11, 26, 28, Mar 2, 5, 7, 17, 26, Apr 4, 9, 20, May 8; 1748: CG, Apr 6, 16, 22, May 3, Sep 21, 23, 28, 30, Oct 3, 10, 14, 17, 21, 22, 24, 25, 28, Nov 4, 11, 16, 24, 26, Dec 1, DL, 10, CG, 10, 20; 1749: LEI, Jan 7, CG, 11, 13, 28, Feb 2, 23, 27, Mar 2, 14, 31, Apr 5, May 4, Sep 25, Oct 2, 4, 6, 9, 12, 16, 18, 19, 25, 26, Nov 1, 2, 4, 8, 9, 11, 16, 18, Dec 16; 1750: CG, Jan 18, 23, 31, Feb 5, Mar 12, 13, 17, 20, 27, Apr 23, DL, Oct 1, CG, 16, 17, 19, 20, 22, 24, 26, Nov 1, 5, 8, 12, 19, 22, 24, Dec 1, 4, 18; 1751: CG, Jan 1, 3, 19, Feb 5, 9, 16, 23, Mar 11, Apr 16, May 1; 1752: CG, Mar 16; 1753: CG, Mar 19, DL, Oct 30; 1762: HAY, May 1; 1763: HAY, Jun 20, 22, Jul 18, Aug 1, 10; 1766: DL, Jan 21, CG, Feb 7; 1773: CG, Oct 23

Quin, Mrs (actor), 1732: RIW/HAY, Sep 11

Quin, Mrs. See Marshall, Anne.

Quin, Simeon Michael (actor), 1756: DL, Aug 12

Quinault, J B, 1686: DLORDG, Feb 11

--Cadmus et Hermione (opera), 1686: DLORDG, Feb 11
--Maitre Etourdi, Le; ou, Les Fourberies d'Arlequin, 1718: LIF, Nov 21, 26;
   1719: LIF, Feb 5
Quinault, Mlle (dancer), 1734: CG/LIF, Dec 30; 1735: CG/LIF, Feb 13, CG, Nov 6
Quintetto, Grand (song), 1788: KING'S, May 15, Jun 3
Quintilian (rhetorician), 1753: CG, Nov 14
Quinto Fabio. See Bertoni, Fernando Giuseppe.
Quontz. See Quantz.
Quoz (song), 1789: HAY, Aug 27

R, Dr, 1754: HAY, Dec 18, 23
R, E (epiloguist), 1676: DG, Sep 0; 1677: DG, Feb 0
R, Mrs P (house servant), 1760: CG, Sep 22
R, Sir T, (commissioner, spectator), 1738: HAY, Oct 9
R, T, 1774: DL, Mar 1
--Politician Reformed, The, 1774: DL, Mar 1
R, Tom (actor), 1661: NONE, Sep 0
Raban (coal merchant), 1773: CG, Oct 26
Raban and Kime (coal merchants), 1771: CG, Oct 29; 1772: CG, Dec 2
Rabbit Seller (dance), 1769: DL, Dec 28, 30; 1770: DL, Jan 16, Feb 13, 15, Mar
   27, Apr 2, Oct 10, 22, Nov 8
Rablus (candle man), 1798: DL, Nov 10
Race (wigmaker), 1752: DL, Apr 14
Race Horse (song), 1788: DL, May 8; 1792: DLKING'S, May 29
Racine, Jean, 1699: DL, Dec 0; 1722: HAY, Jan 8, 29, Feb 5; 1735: HAY, Apr 16;
   1736: DL, Mar 23; 1778: CG, Mar 23
--Andromaque, 1722: HAY, Jan 4
--Brittanicus, 1722: HAY, Feb 5
--Iphigenie en Aulide, 1778: CG, Mar 23
--Mithridate, 1722: HAY, Jan 29
Racket (tailor), 1772: DL, Mar 26; 1773: DL, Feb 27; 1774: DL, Dec 9; 1776: DL,
   Mar 16, Jun 10
Racquet Court, 1777: CG, May 29
Radamistus. See Handel, George Frederic.
Radcliffe, Ann (novelist), 1794: CG, May 28
Radicatti, Sga (dancer), 1762: KING'S, Mar 20; 1766: KING'S, Nov 25; 1767:
   KING'S, Feb 24, Apr 30, May 2, 14; 1768: KING'S, Mar 10, May 5, Dec 10; 1769:
   KING'S, Sep 5; 1771: KING'S, Jun 1, Dec 10; 1772: KING'S, Feb 4, Mar 3
Radley, Eleanor (actor), 1768: DL, Oct 26, Dec 21; 1769: DL, Jan 24, Feb 18,
   Mar 31, Apr 1, 3, 20, 27, CG, 28, DL, May 2, Sep 23, 30, Oct 2, 4, 10, 14,
   Nov 2, Dec 6; 1770: DL, Jan 4, 16, Feb 8, Mar 20, 31, May 2, 4, 7, 29, Jun 7,
   HAY, Sep 20, DL, 25, 27, Oct 2, 3, 16, 19, 25, 29, Nov 1, 3, 14, 20, 23, 29,
   Dec 13, 21; 1771: DL, Mar 7, 16, 23, Apr 4, 19, May 7, 11, 14
Radnor (actor), 1732: HAY, Mar 17
Radnor, Mrs (actor), 1732: HAY, Mar 17
Rae (beneficiary), 1778: HAY, Apr 29; 1785: HAY, Jan 24
Raeburn, James (actor), 1784: HAY, Feb 9; 1785: HAY, Jan 24
Raeburn, Mrs James (actor), 1784: HAY, Feb 9; 1785: HAY, Jan 24
Raft, The. See Cross, John Cartwright.
Raftor, Catherine (actor, singer), 1728: DL, Oct 12, Nov 15; 1729: DL, Jan 2,
   7, 20, Feb 6, Apr 10, 12, 22, May 1, 3, 14, 28, Jun 13, 20, 24, Jul 25, Aug
   5, Sep 20, Oct 27, 30, Nov 21, Dec 8, 10; 1730: DL, Jan 9, Feb 10, Mar 30,
   Apr 11, 16, 18, 20, 24, 28, May 13, 15, 27, Sep 15, Oct 28, Nov 25, 30, Dec
   1, 3, 4; 1731: DL, Feb 8, Mar 15, 20, Apr 1, 19, 22, 26, 27, May 6, 12, 13,
   Jun 7, 11, 25, 30, Jul 6, 20, 23, 27, Aug 3, 6, 11, 16, 18, 20, Sep 30, Oct
   2, 16, 23, 30, Nov 1, 11, 15, 23, Dec 2, 16, 27, 29; 1732: DL, Jan 1, Feb 1,
   Mar 11, Apr 1, 17, 19, 20, May 1, 3, 8, 9, 12, 17, 25, 29, Jun 1, 23, Jul 11,
   28, Aug 1, 4, 17, 21, 22, Sep 8, 19, 21, 23, 28, Oct 3, 14, 26, 31, Nov 6, 7,
   13, Dec 6, 9, 11, 16, 22, 26; 1733: DL, Jan 11, 12, 19, 20, 29, Feb 6, 10,
   12, 17, 26, Mar 5, 26, 29, 31, Apr 4, 6, 13, 16, 19, 23, 24, May 2, 5, 7, 9,
   15, 21, Sep 24, 28, Oct 1; 1734: DL/LIF, Mar 11
Raftor, James (actor), 1733: DL, May 5, 7, Nov 14, Dec 17; 1734: DL, Jan 19,
   Apr 15, DL/HAY, May 24, DL, Sep 24, Oct 21, Nov 8; 1735: DL, Jan 22, Feb 25,
   Apr 21, May 15, Jun 9, LIF, 12, DL, Sep 6, 9, 11, 15, 30, Oct 7, Nov 15, 20,
   21, 22, 29; 1736: DL, Jan 12, Mar 25, LIF, Apr 14, DL, May 25, Aug 26, Sep 7,
   Oct 12, 18, Nov 22, Dec 31; 1737: DL, Jan 6, May 19, Sep 8, Oct 25, 27; 1738:
   DL, Jan 9, 19, 25, 26, Feb 16, 23, Apr 27, May 3, 13, 31, Sep 7, 23, Oct 11,
   25, Nov 4, 11, 15, 30, Dec 8, 15, 19; 1739: DL, Jan 3, 16, Mar 13, Apr 27,
   May 12, 15, 19, 25, 28, Sep 1, 6, 22, 26, Oct 4, 8, 13, 15, 20, 22, 29, Nov

8, 15, 16, Dec 8, 11; 1740: DL, Jan 3, 8, Feb 6, 13, Mar 17, 27, Apr 12, 15, 16, 22, 24, May 2, 9, 14, 20, Sep 11, 27, Oct 15, 23, Nov 10, 11, 24, 29, Dec 18; 1741: DL, Feb 24, Mar 14, 30, 31, Apr 24, 28, 29, Sep 8, 10, 17, 19, 24, Oct 6, 9, 31, Nov 16, 20, 21, Dec 19; 1742: DL, Mar 8, 9, 29, Apr 24, 28, May 10, 20, 27, 31, Sep 14, 16, 25, 30, Oct 2, 7, 13, Nov 12; 1743: DL, Feb 10, Apr 4, 29, May 6; 1744: CG, Apr 28; 1745: CG, May 29, DL, Nov 25, 30, Dec 20; 1746: DL, Jan 24, Apr 10, 15, Sep 27, 30, Oct 7, 18, Nov 8, Dec 11, 30; 1747: DL, Mar 7, 28, Apr 29, Sep 17, Dec 16; 1748: DL, Jan 6, Feb 3, Mar 28, May 2, Oct 15, 29, Nov 29; 1749: DL, Jan 25, Feb 2, May 1, 12, 16, Sep 26; 1750: DL, Jan 4, Apr 26, May 10, Sep 11, 28, Oct 30; 1751: DL, Jan 12, Mar 16, May 3, Sep 7, 12; 1752: DL, Apr 24, Oct 14, Dec 8, 20; 1753: DL, May 4, 21, Sep 8, 11, Oct 16; 1754: DL, May 14, Sep 14, Oct 14, 16; 1755: DL, Apr 19, Sep 23, Oct 17; 1756: DL, May 18, 20, Nov 18; 1757: DL, Apr 11, May 10, Sep 10, 29; 1758: DL, May 11, 17, Jun 22, Nov 16; 1759: DL, May 7, 22, Oct 30; 1760: DL, May 6, Oct 3; 1761: DL, Sep 14; 1762: DL, Nov 10; 1763: DL, May 9, 31, Nov 19; 1764: DL, May 14; 1765: DL, Apr 13, May 14, Nov 25; 1766: DL, May 9; 1767: DL, Jan 24, May 25; 1768: DL, May 24; 1769: DL, May 16; 1770: DL, May 23

Rag Fair, 1737: HAY, Mar 8
Rage, The. See Reynolds, Frederick.
Ragway (musician), 1675: ATCOURT, Feb 15
Rainaud (householder), 1732: LIF, Apr 13
Rainbow Coffee House, 1743: LIF, Mar 3; 1750: DL, Nov 28; 1751: DL, Mar 7, Dec 18; 1752: DL, Dec 19; 1753: DL, Dec 11; 1756: CG, Dec 8; 1758: CG, Jul 6; 1763: DL, Apr 27; 1772: CG, May 6
Rainel (dancer), 1757: HAY, Dec 26
Rainsford (actor), 1780: HAY, Sep 25
Rainsford, Mrs, 1794: CG, May 22
--Speechless Wife, The, 1794: CG, May 22
Rainton (Renton) (dancer), 1725: DL, Apr 27, May 10, Sep 14, Nov 16; 1726: DL, Mar 31, Apr 15, 21, May 3, 5, 9, 10, Jun 3, Oct 1, Nov 2; 1727: DL, Apr 18, Oct 5, 6, 7, 12; 1728: DL, Feb 21, Mar 19, 28, 30, Apr 4, 8, 11, 24, 25, May 1, 9, 15, 16, 22, 23, Jun 13, Sep 12, 17, 19, Oct 18, 21, 24, 30, Nov 15; 1729: DL, Feb 14, Mar 13, 22, 24, Apr 23, 30, May 8, 14, 21, 26, 28, Jun 24, Nov 3, Dec 8, 10, 12, 26; 1730: DL, Jan 1, Apr 10, 11, 13, 14, 18, 22, 23, 24, 25, 27, 29, 30, May 1, 2, 4, 11, 13, 15, 18, 19, 27, Sep 15, 17, 24, Oct 1, 8, 10, 22, 28, Nov 19, 30, Dec 3, 4; 1731: DL, Jan 23, 27, Feb 8, Mar 15, 25, Apr 1, 5, 8, 19, 21, 22, 26, 27, 29, May 3, 5, 6, 7, 10, 12, 17, 19, Jun 7, Jul 20, 23, SF/BFFHH, Aug 24, DL, Sep 25, Oct 26, Nov 11, 22, 25, Dec 2, 15; 1733: DL, May 21, BFCGBH, Aug 23, DL, Oct 10, Nov 7, 26; 1734: DL, Feb 4, DL/HAY, Mar 21, DL, Apr 15, 29, BFHBH, Aug 24, DL, Oct 5, 10, 22; 1735: LIF, Jun 12, DL, Oct 31; 1736: DL, Jan 12, May 20; 1737: DL, May 19, 21; 1739: DL, May 28, Dec 26; 1740: DL, Feb 14, Apr 11; 1741: DL, May 15
Rainton (house servant), 1756: DL, Apr 19; 1757: DL, May 13; 1758: DL, Apr 29
Rainton (householder), 1740: CAC, Mar 12
Rainton Jr (dancer), 1724: DL, Jan 27, Dec 18, 21, 30; 1725: DL, Jan 25, 29, Feb 9, Mar 4, 18, 31, Apr 2, 5, 7, 15, 19, 21, 23, 28, 29, 30, May 3, 4, 5, 11, 12, 19, 21, Sep 9, 25, Oct 7, 12, 14, 15, 19, 23, 25, 28, Nov 3, 25, Dec 4, 6, 16; 1726: DL, Jan 5, 24, 25, Feb 8, 11, Mar 17, 24, 28, Apr 18, 19, 21, 22, 23, 25, 26, 27, 28, 29, 30, May 2, 4, 7, 11, 12, 13, 16, 17, 19, 20, 23, 25, Jun 3, Sep 13, 15, 20, 29, Oct 1, 6, 15, 27, Nov 23, 30, Dec 6, 7, 12, 14, 17, 30; 1727: DL, Feb 8, 10, 18, 20, 27, Mar 23, Apr 6, 7, 8, 12, 14, 17, 20, 22, 24, 25, 26, 28, May 1, 2, 4, 8, 10, 15, 17, 19, 22, 24, 26, Oct 6, Nov 14; 1728: DL, May 10; 1730: DL, Oct 28, Dec 4; 1731: DL, Oct 16; 1734: DL, Apr 15
Rainton, Miss (dancer), 1725: DL, Oct 14
Raisin, Mlle (actor), 1677: ATCOURT, Dec 17
Rake Reformed, The; or, The Happy Lovers (play, anon), 1752: SFGT, Sep 18, 19, 20, 21, 22
Rake, The (play), 1747: CG, Jan 12
Rakes of Mallow (dance), 1780: CG, May 23; 1781: CG, May 1, 19
Rakestraw (Redstraw) (actor), 1722: LIF, Mar 15, May 7; 1723: MO, Apr 15
Rakestraw, Widow (beneficiary), 1723: LIF, May 18
Ralph, James, 1730: GF, Jan 26, Apr 2; 1731: GF, Feb 1; 1734: DL, Jan 3; 1741: DL, Feb 24; 1743: DL, Dec 12; 1744: DL, Apr 3; 1758: NONE, Mar 1
--Astrologer, The; or, The Pretended Transformation, 1736: HAY, Mar 24, 31; 1744: DL, Apr 3, 5
--Cornish Squire, The, 1734: DL, Jan 3, 4, 8, 9, 10, 23
--Fall of the Earl of Essex, The, 1731: GF, Feb 1, 2, 3, 4
--Fashionable Lady, The; or, Harlequin's Opera, 1730: GF, Apr 2, 3, 4, 11, 13, 18, 21, 22, 23, May 28, Jun 2, 17, Jul 27, Nov 11, Dec 4; 1731: GF, May 4
--Lawyer's Feast, The, 1743: DL, Dec 12, 13, 14, 16

Ralph's Ramble (entertainment), 1766: DL, Apr 19, 22
Ram Tavern, 1789: KHS, Sep 16
Ramage, Master (dancer), 1796: CG, Dec 19; 1797: CG, Jun 5; 1798: CG, Nov 12,
    Dec 11; 1799: CG, Jan 29, Mar 25, Apr 13; 1800: CG, Feb 10, May 1
Ramah Droog. See Cobb, James.
Ramble to Bath (entertainment), 1796: CG, May 6
Rambling Justice, The. See Leanerd, John.
Rambling Lovers, The; or, A New Way to Play an Old Game (farce, anon), 1740:
    BFH, Aug 23
Ramondon, Louis (singer), 1705: DL, Apr 13, 18, Jul 18, 25, Sep 22, Oct 2, 16,
    Nov 7, 9, Dec 26, 31; 1706: DL, Jan 3, 4, 14, 21, 28, Feb 1, Mar 2, 5, 11,
    26, 27, 30, Apr 2, 17, May 25, Jun 18, 20, DL/DG, Nov 2; 1707: DL, Mar 27,
    Nov 22, 25, 28, 29, DL/QUEEN, Dec 6; 1708: QUEEN'S, Dec 14; 1709: QUEEN'S,
    Mar 2; 1710: QUEEN'S, Jul 26
Rampant Alderman, The. See Marmion, Shackerley.
Rampany (singer), 1698: YB, Mar 28, Apr 15
Rampini, Giacomo (composer), 1792: DLKING'S, May 23
Ramsay, Allan, 1746: JS, Nov 12; 1752: HAY, Jan 31; 1755: HAY, Jun 30; 1756:
    HAY, Apr 8, 19; 1766: DL, Apr 22, HAY, May 19; 1768: HAY, Dec 19; 1770: HAY,
    Mar 19; 1772: HAY, Sep 21; 1774: DL, May 9; 1777: HAY, Oct 13; 1781: DL, Oct
    29; 1782: HAY, Jan 21, Mar 18, DL, Oct 16; 1783: DL, Sep 20; 1784: HAY, Feb
    9; 1798: CG, Apr 28
--Gentle Shepherd, The; or, Patie and Roger, 1732: YB, Nov 30; 1746: JS, Nov
    12, Dec 1, 3, 10, 18; 1747: JS, Jan 5, 15, 29, Apr 1; 1752: HAY, Jan 10, 27,
    31, Feb 5, 11, 20, 25, Mar 3, 7, 14, 19, 31, Apr 2, 8, 15, 22; 1755: HAY, Jun
    30; 1756: HAY, Apr 8, 19, Jun 3; 1757: HAY, Apr 22; 1758: HAY, Jan 27, Mar
    13, Apr 28; 1759: HAY, Jun 8; 1760: HAY, Feb 21, Mar 13, Apr 18, May 2, 30,
    Sep 1, Dec 19; 1761: HAY, Mar 9, May 11, Jun 2, Dec 16; 1762: HAY, Feb 19,
    Apr 28, Jul 28, Sep 17, Dec 8; 1763: HAY, Mar 8, May 3, Sep 15; 1764: HAY,
    Jan 24, Apr 9, Sep 17, Dec 12; 1765: HAY, May 16; 1766: DL, Apr 22, HAY, May
    19; 1768: HAY, Feb 22, Dec 19; 1769: HAY, Feb 27, Dec 18; 1770: HAY, Mar 19;
    1771: HAY, Jan 7; 1772: HAY, Sep 21, Dec 21; 1774: DL, May 9; 1775: HAY, Feb
    20, Nov 20; 1776: HAY, Oct 7; 1777: HAY, Apr 22; 1778: HAY, Sep 17; 1779:
    HAY, Jan 11, Mar 8; 1780: HAY, Jan 17, Sep 25; 1782: HAY, Mar 18, Apr 9;
    1784: HAY, Feb 9; 1785: HAY, Jan 24; 1791: HAY, Sep 26, Dec 12; 1792: HAY,
    Oct 22
Ramsey, Miss (actor), 1780: HAY, Sep 25; 1782: HAY, Mar 18
Ramsey, Mrs (actor), 1746: DL, Jan 29
Randall (actor), 1781: HAY, Mar 26; 1785: HAY, Jan 31; 1789: WHF, Nov 9, 11
Randall (pit doorkeeper), 1719: LIF, May 29; 1720: LIF, May 30; 1721: LIF, May
    26; 1722: LIF, May 19; 1723: LIF, May 29; 1724: LIF, May 29; 1725: LIF, May
    21
Randall (singer), 1715: DL, Jul 19, Aug 5, 19, LIF, Oct 22, Nov 1, 5, 10, 18,
    Dec 12; 1716: LIF, Jan 7, Feb 3, Mar 3, 6, 10, 15, 17, Apr 11
Randall (singer), 1762: DL, May 17
Randall (ticket holder), 1743: CG, May 11
Randall Coffee House, 1756: DL, Apr 24
Randall, John (actor), 1732: CR, Feb 23, JS, May 23, YB, Jul 8
Randall, Miss (actor), 1779: HAY, May 10
Randall, Rachael (publisher), 1782: DL, Oct 10
Randall, W (printer), 1779: DL, Jan 8
Randoll, Margaret (renter), 1758: CG, Feb 28
Randoll, Robert (renter), 1758: CG, Feb 28
Randolph, Thomas, 1668: LIF, Aug 20; 1683: NONE, Sep 0; 1748: CG, Mar 5, 14;
    1749: CG, Mar 9
--Amyntas; or, The Impossible Dowry, 1683: NONE, Sep 0
--Jealous Lovers, The, 1668: LIF, Aug 20
--Muses' Looking Glass, The, 1748: CG, Mar 5, 14; 1749: CG, Mar 9
Ranelagh House, 1757: RANELAGH, Jun 9; 1768: DL, Jun 21
Ranelagh Masquerade (entertainment), 1785: HAY, Jul 13
Ranelagh, 1749: DL, Apr 25; 1752: DL, Dec 23; 1767: RANELAGH, Jun 1, MARLY, 8;
    1770: RANELAGH, Oct 3, DL, Dec 7; 1774: HAY, Jun 7; 1790: CG, Jul 6
Ranger (author), 1753: DL, Dec 26
Ranieri (singer), 1754: KING'S, Jan 29
Ranoe, Miss (actor), 1783: CG, Dec 5; 1784: CG, Sep 27, Oct 11, 28, 29, Dec 13;
    1785: CG, May 13, Sep 21, Dec 2, 5
Ransom, Morland and Hammersley (bankers), 1784: KING'S, Dec 18; 1786: KING'S,
    Jan 24, Dec 23; 1787: KING'S, Dec 8; 1789: KING'S, Jan 10; 1790: HAY, Jan 7;
    1791: PAN, Dec 17; 1793: KING'S, Jan 26; 1798: HAY, Aug 18
Raoul Barbe Bleue. See Sedaine, Michel Jean.
Raoul Sire De Crequi. See Boutet de Monvel, Jacques Marie.
Rape of Europa by Jupiter, The (play, anon), 1693: NONE, Sep 0

Rape of Helen, The. See Breval, John.
Rape of Lucrece, The. See Heywood, Thomas.
Rape of Proserpine, The. See Theobald, Lewis.
Rape Upon Rape. See Fielding, Henry.
Rape, The. See Brady, Nicholas.
Rapinere (contortionist), 1738: BFH, Aug 23
Rapture, The (song), 1744: HAY, Apr 20; 1772: CG, May 6
Rare en Tout. See Roche-Guilhen, Mme de la.
Raro Raro (song), 1800: CG, Jun 6
Rary Shew. See Foote, Samuel.
Rash (French horn player), 1733: HIC, Apr 20
Rash (viola player), 1753: KING'S, Apr 30; 1758: CHAPEL, Apr 27
Rash stripling (song), 1798: CG, Apr 9
Rasserani i mesta rai (song), 1754: KING'S, Feb 28
Rasserena il mest Ciglio (song), 1746: DL, Apr 12; 1748: KING'S, Apr 5
Ratchford (dancer), 1779: CG, Nov 11, 15, Dec 29; 1780: CG, Apr 17, May 23;
    1781: CG, May 18; 1782: CG, Apr 1, 2, 17, 27, Oct 9; 1783: CG, Apr 22, May
    10, 23, 24, 26, Nov 19; 1784: CG, Apr 28, HAY, Jul 13, CG, Oct 6; 1785: CG,
    Mar 17, HAY, Aug 31, CG, Oct 7, Nov 12; 1786: CG, Mar 4, May 27, Oct 2, Dec
    12; 1787: CG, Jun 5, Sep 28; 1788: CG, Jan 21, May 12, 30, HAY, Jun 27, Aug
    8, 13, 15, CG, Dec 26; 1789: CG, Mar 16, Jun 5, 8, Sep 21, Dec 21; 1790: CG,
    Jan 23, Apr 8, May 27, Oct 4, 20, Nov 6, 15; 1791: CG, May 2, 3, 26, Jun 6,
    Sep 20, Dec 22; 1792: CG, Apr 10, May 12, Oct 8, 15, Dec 26; 1793: CG, Mar
    11, Dec 19; 1794: CG, Jun 10; 1795: CG, Jun 17; 1796: CG, May 10
Ratchford, Mr and Mrs (dancers), 1784: CG, May 11; 1786: CG, May 27; 1787: CG,
    Feb 8; 1788: CG, Mar 28; 1792: CG, Oct 10
Ratchford, Mrs E (dancer), 1780: CG, Sep 25; 1781: CG, Feb 13, Oct 16, 20;
    1782: CG, Apr 1, 2, 27, Oct 8, Dec 20; 1783: CG, May 24, 29; 1784: CG, Mar 6,
    8, May 11, 21, Oct 8, 27; 1785: CG, Apr 18, May 24, Nov 23; 1786: CG, May 30,
    Dec 12, 23; 1787: CG, Feb 9, May 19, Jun 5; 1788: CG, Feb 4, Mar 29, May 30,
    Nov 7, Dec 13, 26; 1789: CG, Feb 19, Mar 28, May 7, 28, Jun 6, 8, Sep 16, Nov
    19; 1790: CG, Feb 4, May 27, Oct 4, 20, Dec 20; 1791: CG, Jun 6, Oct 6, Dec
    21, 22; 1792: CG, Apr 10, May 12, Oct 8, 18, 19, 29, Dec 26; 1793: CG, Mar
    11, Apr 8, Oct 2, Dec 7, 19; 1794: CG, Jun 10; 1795: CG, Jun 17, Nov 9; 1796:
    CG, Jun 3
Ratcliff Cross, 1750: DL, Nov 28; 1752: DL, Dec 20
Ratcliff Highway, 1735: YEB, Dec 22; 1752: DL, Dec 20; 1782: HAY, Mar 18
Ratcliffe (physician), 1756: DL, Feb 9
Ratcliffe, Mrs (actor), 1720: SFLH, Sep 5; 1721: BF/SF, Aug 24; 1722: HAY, Dec
    17; 1723: HAY, Jan 31, Feb 13, Mar 14, Apr 15, 22, HA, Jul 22
Rathband (actor), 1675: NONE, Sep 0
Rathbone Place, 1740: HIC, Mar 31; 1742: LIF, Jan 29; 1767: CG, Mar 30; 1777:
    CG, Apr 16, 18, 23, DL, 29; 1778: CG, Apr 21, 24, 29, DL, May 9; 1779: DL,
    Apr 6, CG, 17, DL, May 8; 1780: CG, Apr 18; 1782: DL, Mar 19, CG, Apr 17, 19,
    HAY, Sep 3; 1783: HAY, Aug 29; 1784: DL, Mar 27, CG, Apr 14, 23, 24; 1785:
    DL, Mar 17; 1787: KING'S, May 24, HAY, Jul 27; 1788: KING'S, Mar 6, DL, Apr
    4, 7; 1789: KING'S, Jun 11; 1790: DL, Feb 1; 1791: DL, Feb 5; 1792: DLKING'S,
    May 30, HAY, Oct 15; 1793: KING'S, Feb 19, DL, Mar 11; 1796: CG, May 6, DL,
    27; 1797: CG, May 19; 1798: CG, May 15
Rathom (singer), 1768: DL, Nov 1
Rational Rosciad, The (pamphlet), 1767: DL, Feb 11
Ratto de la Sposa, Il. See Guglielmi, Pietro.
Ratto delle Sabine, Il; or, The Rape of the Sabines (dance), 1782: KING'S, Dec
    12, 14, 17, 31; 1783: KING'S, Jan 4, 7, 16, 18, 21, Feb 11
Rauber, Die. See Schiller, Johann.
Rauzzini, Venanzio (singer, composer), 1774: KING'S, Nov 8, Dec 3; 1775:
    KING'S, Jan 14, 26, Feb 7, Mar 16, 23, Apr 22, May 6, Oct 31, Nov 7; 1776:
    KING'S, Feb 6, 15, 29, CHAPEL, Apr 3, KING'S, 20, May 14, 18, Nov 2, Dec 14;
    1777: KING'S, Jan 21, Mar 1, 13, 15, May 24, Jul 5; 1781: KING'S, Mar 29, Jun
    5, 21, Nov 17; 1782: KING'S, Mar 16; 1783: KING'S, Apr 29; 1784: KING'S, Feb
    17, Mar 18, Apr 15, May 8; 1786: CG, Mar 14; 1787: KING'S, May 1; 1790: CG,
    Mar 8; 1792: CG, Apr 17, May 9
--Ali D'Amore, L' (opera), 1776: KING'S, Feb 29, Mar 7, 14; 1777: KING'S, Mar
    13, 20, Jul 5
--Creusa in Delfo (opera), 1783: KING'S, Apr 29, May 3
--Eroe Cinese (opera), 1782: KING'S, Mar 16, 23, Apr 2, 6, 13, 20, May 2, 4, 9,
    14, Jun 18; 1784: KING'S, Feb 17, 21, 28
--Piramo e Tisbe (cantata), 1775: KING'S, Mar 16, 23, Apr 22, May 6, 13, 20,
    27, Jun 10, 24; 1776: KING'S, May 14, 16, Dec 14, 17, 21; 1781: KING'S, Mar
    29, Apr 3, 7, 17, 21, 24, 26, 28, May 8, Jun 21
--Regina di Golconda, La (Alina) (opera), 1784: KING'S, Mar 18, 23, 27, 30, Apr
    3, 13, 20, 22, 27, May 1, 8, 15, 25, Jun 8

--Vestale, La; or, L'Amore Protetto dal Cielo (opera), 1776: KING'S, Feb 6, 10, 17, 24, Mar 2, 9, 23, 30, Apr 13, 30; 1787: KING'S, Apr 17, May 1, 12, 19
Ravenscroft (musician), 1730: GF, Jun 29, 30; 1731: GF, Jan 14, 16, May 7, 15; 1736: GF, Apr 26; 1741: GF, Apr 30; 1742: GF, Apr 22; 1743: LIF, Mar 24; 1745: GF, Apr 26; 1746: GF, Mar 11; 1747: GF, Feb 25
Ravenscroft, Edward, 1672: DG, Jul 4, LIF, Nov 0; 1673: LIF, Jun 30; 1677: NONE, Sep 0, DL, Oct 0; 1678: NONE, Sep 0; 1679: DL, Mar 0; 1680: DG, Mar 0; 1694: DL, Sep 0; 1696: LIF, Nov 14; 1720: DL, Jul 28; 1721: DL, Aug 11, LIF, Dec 11; 1722: LIF, Mar 27, May 3; 1748: DL, Oct 29; 1758: CG, Nov 9
--Anatomist, The; or, The Sham Doctor, 1696: LIF, Nov 14, 16, 17, 18, 19, 20; 1704: LIF, Jan 29, Feb 17, Apr 18; 1706: ATCOURT, Feb 5; 1710: DL, Jan 12, 13, 17, Feb 8, May 11; 1714: LIF, Dec 27, 28; 1715: LIF, Jan 6, Nov 4; 1716: LIF, Jan 2, 25, Apr 4, Aug 15, Nov 14; 1717: LIF, May 24, Dec 20; 1718: LIF, Jan 21, Apr 18; 1721: LIF, Apr 24; 1723: HAY, Apr 22; 1727: LIF, Mar 25, Apr 4, May 5, Dec 22; 1730: LIF, Feb 9, 10, 17, Mar 7, 12, Apr 1, 16, May 2, 22, Oct 29, Dec 28; 1731: LIF, Jan 27, Feb 25, Jun 4, Dec 2; 1732: LIF, Feb 11, Mar 18, May 19, LIF/CG, Dec 5; 1735: GF/HAY, Aug 1; 1736: CG, Mar 6; 1741: GF, Feb 14, 17, May 2; 1742: GF, Jan 18, 21, Feb 9, Mar 22, May 12; 1743: DL, Nov 18, 19, 22, 23, 24, Dec 1, 7, 10, 21, 26, 27, 29, 30; 1744: DL, Jan 4, Mar 10, 13, Apr 21, 30, May 1, 15, 21, Sep 18, 25, Oct 2, 9, 13, Dec 13, 17, 20, 27; 1745: DL, Jan 1, 12, Mar 14, Apr 24, 25, 27, Nov 19, 23, 27, Dec 6, 21, 27; 1746: DL, Jan 10, 14, 27, Feb 3, 6, 11, 24, 27, Apr 16, 19, 24, 26, 29, May 1, 8, 9, 12, 16, Sep 23, Oct 9, 21, 29, GF, Nov 13, 14, DL, 14, GF, 17, 18, DL, 21, GF, 28, DL, 28, GF, Dec 1, DL, 11; 1747: DL, Jan 1, 22, 31, Feb 7, 24, GF, 25, 26, DL, Apr 27, May 7, 13, 18, Sep 26, Oct 22, 29, Nov 5, 13, 30, Dec 14, 28; 1748: DL, Jan 4, 19, 29, Feb 6, Apr 30, May 6, 16, 20, Sep 15, 24, 27, Oct 6, 27, Nov 4, 19, 28, Dec 8, 15, 29; 1749: DL, Jan 17, 23, Feb 4, 16, Mar 30, Apr 1, 26, May 2, 8, 16, Sep 19, 23, Oct 11, 20, 30, Nov 7, 22, Dec 1, 30; 1750: DL, Jan 1, 19, 27, Feb 5, Apr 7, 18, May 1, 22, Sep 11, 25, Oct 18, 24, 29, Nov 2, 21, 29, Dec 10, 21; 1751: DL, Apr 16, 22, 27, May 13, NWLS, Sep 5, DL, 10, 20, 21, Oct 10, 22, 29, Nov 5, 11, 14, Dec 11, 18; 1752: DL, Jan 27, Feb 11, 13, 25, Mar 14, 31, May 5, Sep 19, 26, Oct 13, Nov 2, 15, 20, Dec 9; 1753: DL, Feb 26, May 12, Sep 11, 27, Oct 16, Dec 18; 1754: DL, Jan 17, Feb 2, Mar 26, May 17, Sep 17, Oct 1, 24; 1755: DL, Jan 27, Mar 6, May 5, 6, 23, Sep 13, 25, Oct 13, 23, Nov 10, Dec 2, 9, 23; 1756: DL, Feb 17, 25, Apr 21, May 8, 13, Sep 21, 30, Oct 9, 28, Nov 16, 24; 1757: DL, Feb 2, Sep 10, Oct 1, Nov 3, 10, 24; 1758: DL, Jan 27, May 9, Sep 16, Oct 3, Nov 2, 16, Dec 2; 1759: DL, Sep 29, Nov 10, Dec 1; 1760: DL, Mar 13; 1771: DL, Apr 15, 22, May 1, 6, Oct 17; 1772: DL, Mar 10, Jun 5, HAY, Jul 15, 20, Aug 3; 1773: DL, Feb 27; 1774: DL, Jan 5, 13, Sep 27, Oct 15, Dec 20; 1775: DL, Feb 17; 1776: DL, Jun 3; 1779: DL, Mar 18; 1786: CG, Dec 21, 23; 1791: DL, Jan 19, 22, 25, Feb 4, 10
--Canterbury Jests, The; or, A Bargain Broken, 1694: DL, Sep 0
--Careless Lovers, The, 1672: LIF, Nov 0; 1673: DG, Mar 12
--Dame Dobson; or, The Cunning Woman, 1683: DG, May 31
--English Lawyer, The, 1677: DL, Dec 0; 1683: NONE, Sep 0
--Innocent Wife, The; or, The Merry Cuckolds, 1736: SF, Sep 7
--Italian Husband, The, 1697: LIF, Nov 0
--King Edgar and Alfreda, 1677: NONE, Sep 0, DL, Oct 0
--London Cuckolds, The, 1681: DG/IT, Nov 22; 1682: DG/IT, Feb 2, DL, Nov 25, Dec 14; 1687: NONE, Sep 0; 1694: DLORDG, Sep 12; 1696: NONE, Sep 0; 1700: DL, Oct 29; 1702: DL, Aug 20; 1704: DL, Aug 4, Sep 29, Oct 30; 1706: QUEEN'S, Aug 23, Oct 29, Dec 27; 1707: QUEEN'S, Jan 23, Jun 13, Jul 18, 31; 1708: DL, Jun 15, Jul 8, Aug 28, 31; 1709: DL, Jan 25, Apr 26; 1710: QUEEN'S, Jun 5; 1712: DL, Aug 8, 15, 22; 1714: DL, Jun 29; 1715: LIF, Feb 14, 23, Nov 30, Dec 27; 1716: LIF, Jan 19, Mar 1, May 8, Oct 16; 1717: LIF, Dec 11; 1718: LIF, Jan 1, Feb 11, May 9; 1720: DL, Jul 26, 28, Aug 11; 1721: DL, Jul 4, Aug 11, LIF, Dec 11, 13, 26; 1722: LIF, Jan 12, Mar 27, May 3, DL, Jun 19, LIF, Oct 29, Nov 28, Dec 26; 1723: LIF, Feb 14, Oct 29, Dec 4, 19; 1724: LIF, Mar 9, May 26, Oct 12, 29; 1725: LIF, Apr 13, Oct 29, Nov 6, Dec 27; 1726: LIF, Oct 29, Dec 27; 1727: LIF, Feb 10, Nov 1, Dec 26; 1728: LIF, Nov 22; 1729: LIF, Jan 16, Oct 29; 1730: LIF, Nov 30, Dec 26; 1731: LIF, Jan 20, Mar 9, Jun 7, Nov 12, Dec 27; 1732: LIF, Feb 2, May 29; 1733: CG, Oct 29, Nov 23, Dec 27; 1734: CG/LIF, Oct 29; 1735: CG/LIF, Feb 1, CG, Oct 29, Dec 29; 1726: CG, Oct 29, Dec 28; 1737: CG, Apr 12, Oct 29; 1738: CG, Oct 30, Dec 27; 1739: CG, Oct 29; 1740: CG, Oct 29; 1741: CG, Jan 1, Oct 29; 1742: CG, Jan 1, Oct 29, Dec 27; 1743: CG, Oct 29, Dec 26; 1744: CG, Oct 29, Dec 27; 1745: CG, Oct 29, Dec 27; 1746: CG, Oct 29; 1747: CG, Oct 29; 1748: CG, Oct 29, DL, 29; 1749: DL, Oct 30, CG, 30, DL, Nov 1; 1750: DL, Oct 29, CG, 29, DL, 29; 1751: DL, Feb 12, Oct 29, CG, 29; 1752: CG, Nov 9, DL, 9; 1753: CG, Nov 9; 1755: CG, Nov 10; 1756: CG, Nov 9; 1757: CG, Nov 9; 1758: CG, Nov 9; 1764: DL, Apr 12; 1782: CG, Apr 10, 12

--Mamamouchi; or, The Citizen Turned Gentleman, 1672: DG, Jul 4, 8, 17, Aug 16,
   29, Oct 3, LIF, Nov 0; 1674: DG, Sep 0, ATCOURT, Nov 3
--Scaramouch a Philosopher; Harlequin a School-Boy, Bravo, Merchant and
   Magician, 1677: DL, May 5
--Wrangling Lovers, The; or, The Invisible Mistress, 1676: DG, Jul 25
Rawle (singer), 1794: DL, Oct 31
Rawlings, Thomas A (violinist), 1791: CG, Mar 11
Rawlins (dancer), 1771: GROTTO, Aug 30; 1775: HAY, Feb 2, Nov 20
Rawlins (Rawlings) (house servant), 1738: CG, Apr 29; 1743: CG, Apr 9; 1744:
   CG, Apr 14; 1745: CG, Apr 16; 1748: CG, Apr 12; 1749: CG, Apr 22; 1750: CG,
   Apr 27; 1751: CG, May 4; 1752: CG, May 2; 1753: CG, May 5; 1754: CG, Apr 27;
   1756: CG, May 19; 1757: CG, May 19; 1758: CG, Apr 22; 1759: CG, May 18; 1760:
   CG, May 3, Sep 22; 1762: CG, May 13; 1763: CG, May 14; 1764: CG, May 12;
   1765: CG, May 16; 1766: CG, May 15
Rawlins (singer), 1715: LIF, Feb 28, Mar 31, Apr 4, 9, 23, 28, 29, May 2, 6,
   13, Jun 3, 14, Oct 15; 1716: DL, Jan 9, 20
Rawlins Jr, Thomas, 1678: DG, Mar 0; 1782: HAY, Aug 13
--Tom Essence; or, The Modish Wife, 1676: DG, Aug 0
--Tunbridge Wells; or, A Day's Courtship, 1678: DG, Mar 0; 1782: HAY, Aug 13
Rawlinson (doorkeeper), 1760: CG, Sep 22
Rawlinson (house servant), 1741: DL, May 21
Rawlinson, Mrs (actor), 1748: HAY, Mar 30; 1750: HAY, Feb 16, 26, Mar 13
Rawlinson, Mrs (singer), 1727: LIF, Jan 9
Raworth, Master (actor), 1763: DL, Nov 23, 26; 1764: DL, Feb 24, Sep 22; 1766:
   MARLY, Sep 26; 1767: CG, Nov 4; 1769: KING'S, Jun 1
Ray (draper), 1776: DL, Jan 5, Mar 25
Ray (woolen draper), 1746: DL, Apr 29; 1754: DL, Feb 22
Ray, Jack (actor, singer), 1712: SML, Jun 4, 11, 18; 1715: DL, Jun 17; 1717:
   LIF, Nov 30, Dec 9; 1718: DL, Apr 14, 29, May 22, Jun 27, Nov 26, 28; 1719:
   DL, Jan 28, May 9, Jun 9, Jul 3, Aug 4; 1720: DL, Jan 20, May 31, Jul 26, Dec
   17; 1721: DL, May 29, SFHL, Sep 2; 1722: DL, May 26; 1723: DL, Jan 9, May 22,
   Nov 12; 1724: DL, May 12; 1725: DL, Feb 20, Apr 21, May 14; 1726: DL, May 17,
   Jun 3, Oct 1; 1727: DL, Feb 8, May 17, BF, Aug 21, DL, Sep 23, Oct 5, 6, Dec
   13; 1728: DL, Jan 2, 3, Mar 19, Sep 21, Oct 18, 30, Nov 12, 15; 1729: DL, Jan
   7, Feb 6, Mar 11, May 8, 14, 28, HAY, Jul 26, DL, Aug 16, HAY, 19, BFR, 25,
   SF, Sep 8, SOU, 23, LIF, Oct 22, 30, Nov 1, Dec 3, 27; 1730: LIF, Jan 2, 19,
   Apr 2, 13, 20, May 18, BFLH, Aug 31, SFG, Sep 8, SOU, 24, LIF, Oct 5, 9, 12,
   23, 27, Nov 10, 13, 23, Dec 4, 15; 1731: LIF, Mar 22, Apr 3, 24, May 5, Jun
   7, Sep 20, 27, Oct 1, 11, Nov 2, 13, 17, 18, Dec 9; 1732: LIF, Feb 3, Mar 23,
   May 3, 8, 9, LIF/CG, Oct 30, Nov 1, 14, 18, 24, CG/LIF, Dec 26; 1733: CG/LIF,
   Jan 22, 25, LIF/CG, Mar 29, CG, May 1, LIF/CG, 10, 14, CG, Jun 26, Sep 22,
   27, Oct 11, 26, 27, 31, Nov 1; 1734: CG, Jan 1, 25, Feb 21, 26, Mar 28, May
   8, GF, Sep 18, 25, Oct 28, Nov 7, 8, 12, Dec 20, 23; 1735: GF, Mar 6, 29, Apr
   17, 23, 30, HAY, Aug 4, GF, Oct 15, 20, Nov 6, 10, 20, 21, 26, Dec 5, 8;
   1736: GF, Feb 7, 9, Mar 4, 20, LIF, Jul 1, BFHC, Aug 23, LIF, Oct 9; 1737:
   DL, Feb 10, Mar 10, May 19, Aug 30, Sep 3, 17, 20, 22, 24, Oct 11, 20, 21,
   24, Nov 1; 1738: DL, Jan 26, 31, Feb 23, 28, May 1, 3, 6, 17, BFP, Aug 23,
   DL, Sep 14, 16, Oct 20, 21, 23, 25, 30, Nov 2, 4, 8, 9, 20; 1739: DL, Jan 1,
   9, 27, Feb 7, Mar 13, 22, Apr 12, 28, May 11, 14, 28, 30, Sep 1, 6, 8, Oct 4,
   10, 13, 16, 17, 20, Nov 5, 19, 20, Dec 10, 17, 22, 26; 1740: DL, Jan 3, 14,
   Feb 8, 13, Mar 4, 11, 13, 20, 29, Apr 12, 14, 16, 22, May 13, 23, Sep 6, 9,
   11, 16, 23, 30, Oct 13, 14, 15, 17, Nov 4, 6, 10, 19, 24, 27, 28, Dec 3, 6,
   18, 20, 26; 1741: DL, Apr 24, May 15, 25, Sep 5, 8, 17, 19, 24, Oct 6, 8, 9,
   10, 15, 20, 31, Nov 4, 20, 21, Dec 7, 19; 1742: DL, Jan 4, 8, 23, Mar 9, Apr
   21, 24, May 6, 7, 8, 10, 12, 14, Sep 14, 18, 25, 30, Oct 2, 7, 13, 18, 26,
   Nov 3, 4, 12, 16, 27, Dec 14; 1743: DL, Jan 27, 28, Feb 10, Mar 14, Apr 4,
   May 10, Sep 17, 22, 24, 29, Oct 4, 8, 13, 15, 22, 25, Nov 3, 4, 12, 17, 18,
   23, 29, Dec 9, 15, 17; 1744: DL, Jan 7, 13, 27, Apr 9, 10, May 4, 16, 22, Sep
   15, 18, Oct 2, 9, 19, 22, 24, 30, Nov 3, 5, 16, Dec 11, 19; 1745: DL, Jan 4,
   11, Feb 20, May 7, Sep 26, Oct 10, 12, 15, Nov 1, 15, 22, 23, 26, Dec 5, 13,
   20; 1746: DL, Jan 2, 8, 14, Apr 10, 11, 23, 29, May 3, 9, Sep 23, Oct 2, 27,
   31, Nov 4, 5, 21, Dec 11, 26, 30; 1747: DL, Jan 2, 15, Mar 16, 28, Apr 11,
   May 1, 5, Sep 15, 22, Oct 24, 29, Nov 6, 16, Dec 16, 26; 1748: DL, Feb 3, Mar
   19, Apr 12, May 4, Sep 13, 17, 20, 29, Oct 13, 14, 18, 28, 29, Nov 1, 3, 14,
   29; 1749: DL, Jan 9, 26, Mar 29, May 8, Sep 19, 20, 21, 28, Oct 3, 17, Nov
   16, Dec 12; 1750: DL, Jan 1, 4, Apr 19, May 3, Sep 22, 25, Oct 26, Nov 3, 7,
   8, 13; 1751: DL, Jan 12, 26, Apr 9, 25, 29, May 2, 17, Sep 10, 12, 14, 17,
   18, 26, Oct 11; 1752: DL, Apr 7, 8, 17, 23, 27
Ray, Mrs (actor), 1732: HAY, Mar 17
Rayman (actor), 1783: HAY, Aug 13
Raymond (actor), 1790: HAY, Sep 29
Raymond (actor), 1799: DL, Sep 26; 1800: DL, Jan 1, Feb 3, Mar 11, Apr 17, CG,

29, DL, Jun 11
Raymond (dancer), 1720: DL, Oct 17; 1724: DL, May 12
Raymond (dancer), 1776: CHR, Oct 9; 1781: KING'S, Nov 17, 28; 1782: KING'S, Feb
    2, 21, Mar 7
Raymond and Agnes. See Farley, Charles.
Raymond, Miss (actor), 1789: DL, Apr 4, May 19, Jun 3
Rayn (actor), 1741: CG, Dec 7
Raynard (actor), 1737: BF, Aug 23, SF, Sep 7
Rayner (Reyner) (dancer), 1741: DL, Nov 11; 1742: DL, Jan 6, Mar 4; 1746: BF,
    Aug 23
Rayner (supplier), 1766: CG, Dec 9
Rayner, Miss (dancer), 1741: DL, Oct 12, 27, Nov 4, 11, 28, Dec 4, 14, 18;
    1742: DL, Jan 6, Feb 18, Mar 4; 1745: JS, Sep 3; 1750: NWC, Apr 16; 1752: DL,
    Oct 12, 17, 26, Nov 2, 16, 22, 28; 1753: DL, May 5
Rayner, Mrs (actor), 1728: HAY, Aug 22, Dec 23; 1729: BFRP, Aug 25
Rayner, William (actor, singer), 1764: CG, Jan 16; 1765: CG, Oct 28; 1766: CG,
    Oct 25, Nov 18; 1767: CG, Oct 17; 1768: CG, Dec 26; 1769: CG, Nov 4; 1770:
    CG, Dec 19, 26; 1771: CG, Jan 1, Feb 21, Oct 15; 1772: CG, Feb 17, 25, Oct
    16; 1774: CG, Apr 11, May 23; 1775: CG, Nov 24, Dec 8, 15, 29; 1776: CG, Jan
    5; 1777: CG, Oct 3, Nov 25; 1778: CG, May 15, Oct 14, 22; 1779: CG, Oct 6,
    15; 1783: CG, Apr 22; 1784: CG, Jan 29, Sep 20; 1785: CG, Nov 2; 1786: CG,
    Apr 26; 1787: CG, Jan 31; 1789: CG, Dec 21; 1790: CG, Jan 23, Oct 4, Nov 15,
    Dec 20; 1791: CG, Jun 6, Dec 22; 1792: CG, Oct 8, Dec 26, 27; 1793: CG, Mar
    11, Dec 19; 1795: CG, May 12, Oct 26, Nov 16; 1796: CG, Mar 15, Oct 24, Dec
    19; 1397: CG, Feb 18; 1798: CG, Oct 15, 25; 1799: CG, May 13
Raynolds (actor), 1730: HAY, Oct 21
Raynor-Pullen Booth, 1729: BFRP, Aug 25
Raynor-Walker Booth, 1732: TC, Aug 17
Raynsford, Sir George (author), 1681: DL, Dec 0
Re Alla Caccia, Il. See Alessandri, Felice.
Re Pastore, Il. See Hasse, Johann Adolph.
Re Teodoro in Venezia, Il. See Paisiello, Giovanni.
Read (actor), 1739: DL, Jan 27, Feb 26, Mar 19, 24, 29
Read (actor), 1758: HAY, Jan 16
Read (scale maker), 1774: CG, Mar 22
Read (ticket deliverer), 1772: CG, May 29
Read, Alexander (actor), 1662: ATCOURT, Nov 1
Read, Benjamin, 1758: CG, Mar 9
Read, Mrs (actor), 1779: HAY, Mar 8; 1781: HAY, Nov 12; 1782: HAY, Jan 14, 21
Reading (actor), 1709: HA, Jul 30, SH, Nov 30; 1715: LIF, Jan 25, Feb 9, Mar 3,
    May 18, Oct 6, 18, Nov 1; 1716: LIF, Mar 10, Apr 11, May 2, Oct 29, 30, Nov
    28; 1717: LIF, Oct 31, Nov 12
Reading, John (composer), 1799: CG, Mar 13
Reading, John (singer), 1684: DLORDG, Dec 0; 1694: DG, May 0; 1695: LIF, Apr
    30, Dec 0; 1696: LIF, Jun 0, Nov 14; 1697: LIF, Jun 0
Reading, Mrs (actor), 1736: HAY, Feb 16; 1737: HAY, Mar 5
Reading, Mrs (musician), 1709: HA, Sep 3
Reading, Mrs (singer), 1724: BT, Jan 29, BPT, Feb 21
Reading, Thomas (attorney), 1736: HAY, Feb 16; 1737: HAY, Mar 5
Real (actor), 1767: CG, May 18; 1768: CG, Nov 25; 1769: CG, Sep 25, Oct 2, 23;
    1774: CG, Apr 7, May 24
Real (ticket deliverer), 1782: CG, May 16; 1783: CG, May 29; 1784: CG, May 11
Reapers (dance), 1761: HAY, Jul 30, Aug 3, 6
Reason's Music Room, 1700: YB, Dec 11
Reasonable Animals, The (entertainment), 1720: KING'S, Mar 17, 19, 26, Jun 9
Reasonable Lover (song), 1750: DL, May 4
Reasons why David Garrick should not appear on the Stage (pamphlet), 1759: DL,
    Oct 23
Rebecca. See Smith, John Christopher.
Rebour (actor), 1742: CG, Jan 8
Rebow, J M, 1772: DL, Apr 23
Receipt Tax, The. See Dent, John.
Recitativo (song), 1795: KING'S, Feb 27
Reconciliation. See Kotzebue, August Friedrich Ferdinand von.
Recorder Office, 1793: CG, Feb 15; 1794: CG, Mar 7
Recovery, The (play, anon), 1673: DG, Sep 27
Recreation (dance), 1784: HAY, Aug 28
Recrue des Houssars (dance), 1742: DL, Dec 11, 14, 16, 17, 21, 23, 27
Recrue par Force, La; or, The Kidnappers (dance), 1783: KING'S, Mar 13
Recruiting Officer, The. See Farquhar, George.
Recruiting Serjeant, The (dance), 1785: CG, Oct 7, Nov 10, 23
Recruiting Serjeant, The. See Bickerstaff, Isaac.

Recruits (dance), 1772: CG, May 1, Nov 17, 21, 25, 27, Dec 2, 5; 1774: CG, Feb
    17, May 13, 19
Rector (dancer), 1735: DL, Oct 1, 7, 22, Nov 17, 20, 25, Dec 18; 1736: DL, Feb
    28, Mar 22, May 14, Sep 7, Oct 2, 12, Nov 13; 1737: DL, Feb 10, Apr 30, May
    3, 4, 5, 9, Oct 27, Nov 7, 10; 1738: DL, Jan 19, 24, 28, Apr 12, May 6, 12,
    22, Sep 23, Oct 3, 30, Dec 15; 1739: DL, Feb 5, Mar 10, Apr 26, May 2, 9, 15,
    23, 26, Sep 8, 13, 26, Oct 10, Nov 22, 28, Dec 6, 19; 1740: DL, Jan 5, 15,
    Feb 13, Apr 11, May 7; 1741: DL, May 1; 1743: DL, May 4; 1744: DL, May 1, CG,
    Oct 10, 22; 1745: CG, May 6, Oct 29; 1746: CG, Apr 5, Dec 19; 1747: CG, May
    13
Rectus (author), 1766: CG, Feb 21
Red Cross Knight (song), 1800: CG, Apr 26, May 2, 6, 20, Jun 2, 5, HAY, Sep 3
Red Cross Knights, The. See Holman, Joseph George.
Red Lion Square, 1739: DL, Apr 3; 1740: DL, Apr 9, May 15; 1743: DL, Mar 22;
    1744: CG, Mar 28, HAY, Apr 23, DL, May 14; 1745: GF, Feb 26, CG, Mar 28;
    1746: CG, Mar 17; 1747: CG, Mar 26; 1748: CG, Mar 21; 1750: DL, Mar 24; 1751:
    DL, Apr 10, May 14; 1754: DL, Mar 28; 1755: DL, Apr 2; 1788: DL, May 8; 1790:
    DL, May 19; 1791: DL, May 17; 1792: DLKING'S, May 29; 1795: DL, Jun 2; 1796:
    DL, Jun 3; 1797: DL, Jun 8; 1798: DL, Jun 8; 1799: DL, May 17; 1800: DL, Jun
    4
Red Lion St, 1742: DL, Apr 1; 1744: CG, Apr 20; 1745: GF, Feb 26, Mar 18; 1746:
    GF, Mar 4; 1787: ROY, Jul 3
Red Lion Tavern, 1735: CG/LIF, Apr 24; 1740: CG, Apr 14; 1751: CG, Apr 19
Redding. See Reading.
Reddish, James (correspondent), 1774: DL, Jan 13
Reddish, Mary Ann, Mrs Samuel (actor), 1767: DL, Oct 26, Nov 11, 13, 26, Dec 1,
    19; 1768: DL, Jan 6, 14, 29, Mar 17, Apr 12, May 3, Sep 22, 28, Oct 3, 11,
    14, 15, 21, Nov 10, Dec 28; 1769: DL, Apr 28, May 16, Sep 28, Oct 6, 16, Nov
    17, 21, 24, Dec 1, 14, 23, 26; 1770: DL, Jan 2, 4, 15, 25, Mar 24, May 3, 15,
    Sep 22, Oct 6, 31, Nov 3, 14, 15, 28, Dec 29; 1771: DL, Mar 9, 16, 18, Apr
    17, May 3, Sep 26, Oct 9, 24, 25, 30, 31, Nov 2, 14, 18, 23, 26, 28, 29;
    1772: DL, Jan 4, Feb 4, 5, 7, Apr 25, Jun 10; 1776: DL, Dec 14, 16
Reddish, Samuel (actor), 1767: DL, Sep 18, 21, 23, Oct 10, 21, 23, 27, 30, Nov
    4, 5, 13, 19, 21, Dec 5; 1768: DL, Jan 6, 23, Feb 20, Mar 17, Apr 6, 12, 16,
    25, 27, Sep 22, 28, 30, Oct 3, 8, 10, 13, 14, 17, 26, Nov 4, 17, 24, Dec 17,
    28; 1769: DL, Jan 12, Feb 4, 23, Mar 29, 31, Apr 28, Sep 21, 23, 26, 28, Oct
    5, 7, 13, 14, 18, Nov 4, 11, 13, 21, 23, 24, 27, Dec 4, 13, 20, 23; 1770: DL,
    Jan 2, 4, 25, Feb 1, 3, 7, 27, Mar 3, 27, 31, May 15, 18, 30, Sep 22, Oct 4,
    5, 6, 9, 12, 13, 15, 16, 17, 20, 22, 25, 31, Nov 5, 6, 10, 14, 15, 24, 28,
    Dec 5, 13; 1771: DL, Jan 12, 19, Feb 21, Mar 16, 18, Apr 2, 3, 5, 9, 23, 29,
    May 3, Sep 26, 28, Oct 3, 5, 15, 25, 26, 28, 29, 31, Nov 4, 14, 15, 18, 21,
    23, 26, 27, 29, Dec 11; 1772: DL, Jan 7, 20, Feb 21, 26, Mar 23, 28, 30, Apr
    6, 25, May 12, 30, Jun 10, Sep 19, Oct 10, 13, 15, 23, 28, 30, 31, Nov 4, 7,
    12, Dec 8, 30; 1773: DL, Jan 4, 26, Feb 2, 8, 9, 10, 11, 16, 25, 27, Mar 9,
    16, 23, 25, 30, Apr 16, 23, May 10, 13, 14, Sep 21, 25, 30, Oct 5, 8, 9, CG,
    30, DL, Nov 4, 6, 20, 26, Dec 3, 10, 11, 18; 1774: DL, Jan 22, 26, Feb 2, 15,
    19, 21, Mar 12, 15, 19, 26, Apr 21, 26, 28, May 4, 14, 18, 20, Sep 27, Oct 1,
    6, 12, 13, 21, 26, 27, 29, Nov 1, 4, 22, Dec 9, 19; 1775: DL, Jan 2, 21, Feb
    17, Mar 6, 13, 18, 23, 25, 30, Apr 1, 6, 29, May 11, 15, 27, Sep 26, 28, Oct
    5, 7, 10, 12, 24, 25, 28, 30, Nov 1, 3, 4, 18, Dec 2, 7, 16, 19, 29; 1776:
    DL, Jan 3, Feb 1, Mar 12, 23, Apr 17, 26, May 13, 27, Jun 5, Sep 24, 28, Oct
    3, 8, 9, 10, 12, Nov 4, 6, 12, 15, 19, 23, 25, 29, Dec 14, 17, 31; 1777: DL,
    Jan 16, Feb 3, 24, Mar 31, Apr 11, 17; 1778: CG, Oct 12, 24; 1779: CG, May 5
Redemption. See Handel, George Frederic.
Redfern (boxkeeper), 1719: LIF, May 13; 1721: LIF, May 18; 1722: LIF, May 8;
    1723: LIF, May 17; 1724: LIF, May 12; 1725: LIF, May 11; 1726: LIF, May 20;
    1727: LIF, May 18
Redfern, Mrs (boxkeeper), 1728: LIF, May 29; 1729: LIF, May 15; 1730: LIF, May
    28; 1731: LIF, May 31; 1732: LIF, May 12; 1735: CG/LIF, May 26
Redhead (mercer), 1759: CG, Dec 1
Redhead and Co (silk mercers), 1760: CG, Dec 10
Redhead, Miss (actor), 1793: DL, Jan 23, May 31; 1794: DL, Apr 21, 26, 28, May
    16, 22, Jun 9, Sep 27, Oct 7, 27, 31, Nov 15, Dec 20; 1795: DL, Jan 19, 21,
    Feb 6, 12, Mar 14, May 6
Redman, Samuel (actor), 1741: BFLW, Aug 22; 1749: BFC, Aug 23, CG, Sep 27, Oct
    2, 9, 16, 19, 26, Nov 1, 8, 9, 17, Dec 20; 1750: CG, Jan 5, Feb 1, 20, Mar 1,
    26, Apr 26, 27, Oct 12, 17, 20, 25, 26, Nov 12, 22, 24, 29; 1751: CG, Feb 28,
    Apr 16, May 7, Sep 23, 27, Oct 9, 11, Nov 21, 22; 1752: CG, Mar 16, 17, 30,
    Apr 28, 30, May 4, Sep 22, Oct 2, 9, 18, 24, 27, 30, Nov 28, Dec 11, 13;
    1753: CG, Jan 22, Feb 7, 12, Mar 19, May 7, 8, 14, 18, Sep 12, 14, 17, 21,
    26, Oct 3, 5, 27, 30, 31, Nov 1, 12, 22; 1754: CG, Jan 22, Mar 9, 25, Apr 15,
    20, May 14, 17, 21, Sep 16, 20, 25, 30, Oct 2, 17, 18, 24, 29, Nov 4, 20, Dec

10, 13; 1755: CG, Jan 10, 28, Mar 6, Apr 8, May 9, Oct 6, 16, 17, 20, 27, Nov
4, 12, 13, 14, 17, 22, Dec 3, 4, 12; 1756: CG, Jan 6, Mar 18, May 5, Sep 22,
27, 29, Oct 4, 6, 11, 13, 19, 23, 25, 28, Nov 4, 16, 22, 24, 29, Dec 7, 10;
1757: CG, Jan 11, 27, Feb 16, May 10, 20, Sep 16, 28, Oct 5, 8, 10, 13, 20,
Nov 2, 4, 5, 7, 11, 16, 26, Dec 1, 7, 10; 1758: CG, Mar 9, 13, Apr 14, 17,
May 8, Sep 22, Oct 4, 6, 9, 20, 23, 30, Nov 1, 3, 4, 7, 21; 1759: CG, Feb 1,
Mar 17, 20, Apr 7, 28, May 11, 18, Oct 10, Nov 5, 28, Dec 6, 7, 10, 31; 1760:
CG, Jan 31, HAY, Feb 15, CG, 28, Mar 18, Apr 8, 12, May 2, 5, 12, Sep 22, 24,
29, Oct 1, 10, 18, 23, 25, Dec 9; 1761: CG, Mar 5, Apr 2, 17, 27, Sep 14, 25,
28, Oct 3, 9, 13, Nov 4; 1762: CG, Jan 5, Feb 15, 22, Apr 27, May 5, 7, 13,
Sep 22, 24, 27, Oct 4, 12, Nov 1; 1763: CG, Jan 14, Feb 3, May 9, 14, Sep 21,
26, Nov 4, 26; 1764: CG, Jan 26, Feb 1, Mar 27, 29, Apr 2, Sep 19, 28, Nov 5,
15, 30; 1765: CG, Jan 14, Apr 11, May 9, Sep 18, Oct 14, 28; 1766: CG, Jan
31, Mar 17, Apr 8, May 6, 9, Oct 1, 6, 17, 21, 30, 31, Nov 4; 1767: CG, Mar
21, May 20, Sep 14, 26, Oct 19; 1768: CG, Feb 20, Apr 25, May 31, Nov 16, 17;
1769: CG, Jan 2, May 17, Dec 29; 1770: CG, Feb 12, May 2, 25, Nov 16; 1771:
CG, Jan 12, May 28; 1772: CG, Apr 30; 1773: CG, Nov 27; 1774: CG, Apr 4, May
13; 1775: CG, May 8
Redstraw. See Rakestraw.
Reed (actor), 1739: DL, Apr 10, 14, May 5, 14, Sep 11, 22, Oct 4, 10, 18, 29,
Nov 21, Dec 10, 31; 1740: DL, Jan 3, 15, Feb 13, Mar 20, 29, Apr 16, 17, 29,
30, May 14
Reed (actor), 1758: HAY, Jan 16
Reed (author, rope maker), 1761: DL, Apr 25
Reed (ticket deliverer), 1768: CG, May 28, 30; 1769: CG, May 20, 23; 1770: CG,
May 18, 19, 23; 1773: CG, May 28; 1775: CG, May 27
Reed, Grace (actor), 1760: DL, Oct 20, Nov 27, Dec 17; 1761: DL, Jan 23, Apr
25, May 29, Sep 12; 1762: DL, May 6, 13, Sep 28; 1763: HAY, Jul 18, 22, Aug
5, 11, Sep 5, 7; 1769: HAY, May 15, 19, 22, 24, 26, Jun 28, Jul 12, Aug 25,
28, 30, Sep 12
Reed, Isaac (diarist), 1754: DL, Nov 22; 1762: HAY, Sep 6; 1764: HAY, Jun 28;
1766: KING'S, Aug 8; 1770: HAY, Aug 1
Reed, Joseph, 1754: CG, May 15; 1758: CG, Jul 6; 1767: DL, Mar 28; 1768: DL,
Feb 11; 1769: CG, Jan 14, Apr 1; 1771: CG, May 27; 1772: HAY, Sep 17; 1776:
CG, Mar 19
--Dido, The Queen of Carthage, 1767: DL, Mar 28, 31, Apr 2, 4, 6, 9, May 7, 14;
1768: DL, Feb 11; 1792: DLKING'S, May 23, 25, 28, Jun 2, 11; 1797: DL, Apr 28
--Imposters, The; or, A Cure for Credulity, 1776: CG, Mar 19
--Madrigal and Truletta, 1758: CG, Jul 6; 1771: HAY, Sep 18; 1772: HAY, Sep 17
--Register Office, The, 1761: DL, Apr 25, 27, May 1, 7; 1764: DL, Apr 12; 1767:
DL, May 6, 13, 14, 18, 20, 22, 25, 26, 27, 29, Jun 1, Nov 12, 25, Dec 8, 17;
1768: DL, Feb 2, 11, 12, 13, 15, Apr 7, 26, May 10; 1769: DL, May 1, 3, 8,
Oct 10, Dec 20; 1770: DL, Jan 24, Dec 20; 1771: DL, Jan 10, 23, HAY, 28, DL,
Feb 28, Apr 29, May 11, Oct 15, Dec 9, 21; 1772: DL, May 12, HAY, Sep 17, DL,
Oct 13, Nov 30, Dec 15, 26; 1773: DL, Apr 16, May 31, HAY, Jul 28, Aug 6, DL,
Oct 8; 1774: DL, Jan 6, Mar 14, Apr 6, May 3, Jun 2, Nov 7, Dec 5; 1775: DL,
Jan 5, HAY, Sep 19, 20, 21; 1776: CG, Apr 27; 1777: DL, Mar 31, Apr 22, May
6; 1778: DL, Jan 22; 1779: DL, Jun 1; 1781: DL, Apr 28, May 24
--Tom Jones (opera), 1768: CG, Dec 16; 1769: CG, Jan 14, 16, 17, 18, 19, 20,
23, 24, Feb 1, 2, 9, 14, 28, Apr 1; 1770: CG, May 1; 1771: CG, Apr 12
Reed, Mrs (actor), 1734: CG/LIF, Nov 7; 1736: YB, Apr 26
Reed, Mrs (actor), 1770: HAY, May 16, 18, Jun 5, 22, 25, 27, Aug 1, Oct 1;
1773: CG, May 28
Reel (dance), 1768: CG, Dec 12, 17, 21, 22; 1769: CG, Jan 5, 16, 24, Feb 18,
Mar 31; 1770: CG, Mar 29, 31, Apr 7, 17, 23, 26, Nov 3, 6, 8; 1771: CG, Mar
9, 12, Apr 8, Oct 30, Nov 5, Dec 21; 1772: CG, Mar 23; 1774: CG, Oct 28, Nov
1, 2, 5, 18, 29, Dec 23; 1775: CG, Jan 24, Feb 3; 1777: HAY, Apr 22; 1782:
HAY, Mar 18; 1784: HAY, Feb 9; 1792: CG, May 12; 1795: DL, Jun 1, 8
Rees Jr (actor), 1798: CG, Jun 2; 1799: CG, May 28
Rees, Owen (publisher), 1782: CG, Mar 16; 1788: CG, May 22; 1798: DL, Mar 24,
CG, Nov 12, 23, Dec 8; 1799: CG, Jan 12, Apr 8, 27, Oct 31; 1800: CG, Feb 8,
Mar 25
Rees, Thomas David (actor), 1788: CG, May 14; 1789: HAY, May 29, Jun 22, Jul
31, Aug 12, 25; 1790: HAY, Aug 4, CG, Nov 23, Dec 20; 1791: CG, Feb 3, Apr
16, 28, May 3, 16, 31, Sep 19, Oct 12, Nov 15, Dec 2, 21, 22; 1792: CG, Feb
2, 18, Mar 6, 26, 31, Apr 18, May 10, Sep 17, Oct 8, 17, 24, 26, 27, Nov 3,
5, Dec 13, 20, 22; 1793: CG, Jan 25, Mar 23, Apr 4, 8, 18, 24, May 1, 4, 10,
30, Sep 16, Oct 2, 9, 10, 16, 21, Nov 1, 2, 25, 30, Dec 5; 1794: CG, Jan 14,
Feb 13, 22, 26, Mar 18, Apr 12, 23, May 7, 9, 22, 26, Sep 17, 26, 29, Oct 3,
23, 29; 1795: CG, Feb 3, Mar 5, 19, Apr 6, 8, 23, May 20, 25, 27, Jun 11, 12,
Sep 14, 18, 21, 30, Oct 2, 5, 7, 8, 9, 15, 16, 19, 24, 26, Nov 9, 16, 25, 27,
Dec 5, 7, 9, 21, 26; 1796: CG, Jan 4, 23, Mar 14, 15, 30, Apr 9, 16, 19, 23,

26, 29, May 11, 16, Jun 2, 4, 7, Sep 12; 1797: CG, Feb 27, May 22, Sep 18,
22, 25, Oct 2, 11, 25, Nov 2, 3, 8, 11, 13, 15, 21, Dec 26; 1798: CG, Jan 11,
Feb 13, Mar 20, 27, 31, Apr 9, 27, 28, 30, May 1, 12, 15, 16, Jun 2, 7, Sep
17, 19, 21, 28, Oct 3, 11, 30, Nov 7, 9, 17, 20; 1799: CG, Jan 5, 26, Mar 16,
Apr 3, 6, 18, 23, 26, May 7, 13, 15, 28, Jun 1, 7, Sep 18, 20, 23, 27, 30,
Oct 2, 4, 10, 25, 29, 31, Nov 9, 13, 14, Dec 9, 30; 1800: CG, Jan 16, Mar 27,
Apr 5, 23, 24, 30, May 12, 15, 22, Jun 5, 12, 13
Reeve, W (publisher), 1749: DL, Jan 3, 20, Feb 23; 1750: DL, Feb 26, Mar 6;
1751: DL, Dec 17; 1754: DL, Mar 4
Reeve, William (actor, composer), 1786: CG, May 22; 1788: DL, Jun 2; 1789: CG,
Apr 14, HAY, May 18, CG, 28, HAY, Jun 1, DL, 3, HAY, 12, 23, Jul 1, 29, 31,
Aug 10, 11, 28, CG, Sep 14, 16, 18, Oct 2, 12, 20, 23, Nov 30, Dec 21; 1790:
CG, Mar 8, 27, Apr 6, 12, 21, 22, 30, May 3, 6, 24, Jun 4, Sep 13, Oct 4, 6,
8, 13, 19, Nov 15, Dec 8, 11, 20; 1791: CG, Feb 24, Apr 16, May 2, 3, 14, 16,
17, 18, 26, 31, Jun 6, Oct 3, 20; 1792: CG, Feb 28, Mar 6, Apr 17, Oct 25;
1793: CG, Mar 11, Apr 25, Oct 2, Dec 19; 1794: CG, Feb 6, HAY, 8, CG, May 1,
9, 26, 28, DL, Jul 2, HAY, Aug 22, Sep 3, CG, Oct 14, Nov 17, Dec 26; 1795:
HAY, Mar 4, CG, Apr 24, May 6, DL, 19, CG, Jun 16, HAY, Aug 18, 25, CG, Dec
21; 1796: CG, May 16, HAY, Sep 1, DL, Nov 5, CG, 5, Dec 19; 1797: CG, Feb 18,
Mar 16, Apr 8, May 9, 31, HAY, Jun 29, CG, Oct 9, Nov 13, 24, Dec 26; 1798:
CG, Feb 12, Mar 19, 31, Apr 9, Nov 12; 1799: CG, Mar 2, Apr 13, 16, 19, Jun
6, DL, Oct 3, CG, 24, Nov 14; 1800: CG, Feb 10, Mar 4, May 1, Jun 2
Reeves (actor), 1744: HAY, Jun 29
Reeves (musician), 1771: MARLY, Jun 27, Jul 13, Aug 3, 22, Sep 3, 5, 10, 12, 17
Reeves, Anne (actor), 1670: BRI/COUR, Dec 0; 1671: BRIDGES, Dec 7; 1672: LIF,
Apr 0, Jun 0, Nov 0
Reeves, Thomas (actor), 1668: NONE, Sep 0, BRIDGES, Dec 18
Reeves' scholar (musician), 1771: MARLY, Sep 3
Reflections on Theatrical Expression (pamphlet), 1755: DL, Mar 13, Dec 19
Reformation, The. See Arrowsmith, Joseph.
Reformed in Time. See Heartwell, Henry.
Reformed Wife, The. See Burnaby, William.
Refusal, The. See Cibber, Colley.
Regent, The. See Greatheed, Bertie.
Reggio, Pietro (composer), 1674: DG, Apr 30; 1680: EVELYN, Sep 23; 1684:
FALKLAND, Jul 25
Regina di Golconda, La. See Rauzzini, Venanzio.
Reginelli (singer), 1746: KING'S, Nov 4; 1747: KING'S, Apr 14; 1748: KING'S,
Mar 26, Apr 5, 26
Register Office, The. See Reed, Joseph.
Regnard, Jean Francois, 1719: KING'S, Mar 14; 1721: HAY, Dec 5; 1725: HAY, Jan
11, 20; 1748: DL, Mar 22
--Amoureuses Follies, 1725: HAY, Apr 19
--Arlequin Homme a Bonne Fortune (farce), 1718: LIF, Dec 26; 1721: HAY, Feb 10;
1726: HAY, Apr 20
--Attendez Moy sous L'Orme, 1720: KING'S, May 6, 9; 1721: HAY, Jan 20, Dec 29;
1722: HAY, Mar 1; 1725: HAY, Jan 4; 1735: HAY, Jan 10, GF/HAY, Apr 21
--Baguette de Vulcain, La; ou, L'Arlequin Chevalier Errant (farce), 1718: LIF,
Nov 28; 1721: HAY, Jan 9, Feb 7, Dec 19; 1725: HAY, Apr 26; 1734: HAY, Nov 13
--Democrite Amoureux, 1721: HAY, Dec 12; 1725: HAY, Feb 1
--Divorce du Mariage, Le (farce), 1725: HAY, Apr 21
--Divorce, Le; ou, Les Fourberies d'Arlequin, 1734: HAY, Nov 8
--Filles Errantes, Les, 1719: LIF, Jan 8; 1725: HAY, Jan 22, Apr 22; 1735: HAY,
Jan 1, 6, Mar 29
--Foire de St Germain, La, 1718: LIF, Nov 7, 12; 1720: KING'S, May 16; 1721:
HAY, Jan 2, Apr 10; 1725: HAY, Jan 8
--Folies Amoureuses, Les (farce), 1719: KING'S, Mar 14; 1720: KING'S, May 17;
1721: HAY, Feb 6, 25; 1722: HAY, Jan 12; 1725: HAY, Jan 27, Apr 19; 1735:
HAY, Mar 13, GF/HAY, May 5
--Harlequin a Man of Good Fortune (pantomime), 1720: KING'S, Mar 22
--Joueur, Le, 1720: KING'S, May 6; 1721: HAY, Jan 16, Feb 9, Dec 7; 1722: HAY,
Mar 1; 1725: HAY, Jan 11, 20, Apr 23; 1734: HAY, Dec 13; 1735: HAY, Mar 14
--Legatoire Universel, Le, 1721: HAY, Feb 7, Dec 18; 1725: HAY, Apr 26, May 10;
1748: DL, Mar 22
--Menechmes, Les; ou, Les Freves Jumeau, 1721: HAY, Dec 5; 1722: HAY, Jan 9
--Retour Impreuevu, Le, 1722: HAY, Apr 5
--Serenade, La (farce), 1720: KING'S, May 20; 1721: HAY, Jan 10, Apr 12; 1722:
HAY, Feb 5, 22; 1725: HAY, Jan 15, Apr 28
Regulus. See Crowne, John; Havard, William.
Rehearsal of Kings, A; or, The Projecting Gingerbread Baker (play, anon), 1737:
HAY, Feb 19, Mar 8, 9, 11, 14, 15, 17
Rehearsal, The. See Villiers, George.

Rehearsal, The; or, Bayes in Petticoats. See Clive, Catherine.
Reid (actor), 1748: BF, Aug 24, SFBCBV, Sep 7
Reid, Mrs (actor), 1784: HAY, Feb 9
Reilly (actor), 1781: HAY, Nov 12
Rein, Miss (tailor), 1794: DL, Dec 20; 1795: DL, Feb 12, May 6, Oct 21, Nov 23;
   1796: DL, Jan 18, Mar 12, Apr 2, 30, Nov 9, Dec 26; 1798: DL, Jan 16, Oct 6;
   1799: DL, Jan 19, May 24, Oct 14, Dec 11; 1800: DL, Mar 11, Apr 29
Reinagle, Joseph (violinist), 1790: CG, Feb 19
Reinagle, Miss (pianist), 1800: CG, Mar 19
Reinhold, Frederick Charles (actor, singer), 1752: DL, Feb 5, Oct 12; 1753: DL,
   Oct 17; 1754: DL, May 15; 1755: DL, Feb 3; 1767: DL, Jan 24; 1768: HAY, Mar
   4; 1769: HAY, Feb 22, CG, Oct 30, Nov 4, Dec 15, 19; 1770: CG, Jan 5, 17, Feb
   23, 24, Apr 3, HAY, May 3, CG, 4, 9, MARLY, Jun 16, Jul 17, 24, 31, Aug 7,
   14, 21, 28, CG, Oct 2, 5, 8, 15, 23, Nov 12, 14, 22, Dec 13, 26, 27; 1771:
   CG, Jan 1, 8, 11, 25, Apr 8, 18, 19, CHAPEL, 27, MARLY, May 23, CG, 30,
   MARLY, Jul 2, 4, 6, 9, 11, 13, 16, 18, 27, Aug 3, 8, 15, 20, CG, Oct 25, Nov
   1, 5, 8, 9, 11, 12, Dec 11; 1772: CG, Jan 27, 31, Feb 1, 4, Mar 23, 31, Apr
   23, MARLY, Aug 20, 25, 28, Sep 1, CG, 30, Oct 7, 14, 17, Nov 2, 30, Dec 26;
   1773: CG, Jan 18, 25, Feb 6, 26, Mar 3, 19, 20, 22, 27, Apr 3, 13, 20, MARLY,
   May 27, Jul 8, 15, 22, 29, Aug 26, 27, Sep 3, CG, 29, Oct 6, 16, 23, Nov 6,
   25, 26, Dec 13, 16; 1774: CG, Feb 7, 11, 17, Mar 12, 19, 26, CHAPEL, 26, CG,
   Apr 8, 13, 29, 30, May 3, MARLY, Jun 16, 18, 30, Jul 23, Aug 1, Sep 3, CG,
   21, 23, 28, Oct 13, 15, 19, 21, Nov 1, 19, 29, Dec 1, 27; 1775: CG, Jan 21,
   DL, Mar 10, CG, 30, Apr 1, 4, 25, DL, May 11, CG, 15, Sep 20, 22, 25, 27, Oct
   16, 17, 18, 19, CHAPEL, Nov 23, CG, Dec 26; 1776: STRAND, Jan 23, CG, Feb 12,
   26, DL, Mar 1, CG, 16, 25, CHAPEL, Apr 2, CG, 9, 16, May 6, 13, Sep 25, Oct
   7, 9, 15, 25, Nov 9, 14, Dec 2, 4, 6, 23, 31; 1777: CG, Jan 4, 18, 25, Feb
   14, 25, Mar 1, 4, 19, Apr 14, 18, 28, Sep 22, 26, 29, Oct 15, 21, 29, 30, Nov
   25, Dec 3; 1778: CG, Jan 8, Feb 4, 23, Mar 30, Apr 21, May 6, 12, 22, Sep 18,
   28, Oct 22, 26, 27; 1779: CG, Jan 4, 25, Feb 13, Mar 20, 22, Apr 5, 10, 17,
   22, 30, May 10, Oct 6, 16, 18, Nov 8, 30, Dec 17, 18, 29, 31; 1780: CG, Jan
   1, 7, 10, 18, Feb 5, Mar 11, 14, DL, 17, CG, 27, 29, Apr 3, 7, 10, 11, 12,
   18, 19, 25, 27, May 23, Sep 20, Oct 2, 3, 23, Nov 13, 15, 25, Dec 9, 12, 16,
   29; 1781: CG, Jan 1, 13, DL, Mar 2, CG, 3, DL, 30, CG, 31, Apr 3, 25, May 1,
   2, 5, 7, Sep 21, 24, 26, DL, Oct 12, CG, 13, 24, 25, 27, 30, 31, Nov 7, 12,
   24, 28, Dec 5, 6, 17; 1782: CG, Feb 2, DL, 15, CG, 23, DL, Mar 16, CG, Apr 9,
   17, 19, 26, May 6, Sep 25, 27, 30, Oct 7, 9, 23, Nov 2, 6, 18, 22, Dec 6, 27;
   1783: CG, Jan 23, Feb 14, Mar 3, DL, 14, CG, Apr 23, May 6, 12, 16, 24, Sep
   17, 19, 22, 26, Oct 1, 6, 11, 16, 21, 24, 28, Nov 8, Dec 6, 23; 1784: CG, Jan
   13, 14, DL, Feb 27, Mar 5, CG, 23, Apr 24, 26, 27, May 7, 19, 22; 1785: DL,
   Feb 11; 1787: DL, Feb 23, Mar 7; 1788: DL, Feb 8, 20, 22, Mar 5; 1789: DL,
   Feb 27, Mar 6, 18, 20, 25; 1790: DL, Feb 19, 24, 26, Mar 5, 10, 17; 1791: DL,
   Mar 16, 23, Apr 1, 13; 1792: KING'S, Feb 24, 29, Mar 7, 14, 23, 28, 30; 1798:
   CG, Feb 23, 28, Mar 2, 9, 14, 28, 30
Reinhold, Mrs (beneficiary), 1751: DL, Dec 20; 1753: DL, May 12; 1773: CG, Apr
20
Reinhold, Thomas (actor, singer), 1734: KING'S, Apr 2; 1735: CG, Mar 28; 1736:
   CG, May 12, Dec 8; 1737: CG, Jan 12, Feb 16, Mar 23, May 18, Oct 26; 1738:
   CG, Sep 15, Dec 9; 1739: CG, Mar 10, KING'S, Apr 4, DL, Sep 18, Oct 27, Nov
   20, LIF, Dec 13, DL, 17, 26; 1740: DL, Jan 15, Feb 14, HIC, 22, LIF, 27, DL,
   Mar 8, LIF, 26, HIC, 27, DL, 29, HIC, Apr 2, DL, 11, HIC, 18, 25, DL, May 13,
   14, LIF, Nov 22, CG, Dec 16; 1741: LIF, Jan 10, CG, 21, 23, Feb 17, 28, Apr
   24, Oct 29; 1742: CG, Jan 8, DL, Apr 17, CG, 23, 28, 30, May 5, Oct 9, Dec
   21; 1743: CG, Jan 8, Feb 4, 18, Mar 8, 23, Apr 16, Dec 3, 20; 1744: CG, Jan
   14, Feb 10, 14, 24, Mar 2, 3, 15, 28, 29, 30, Apr 2, 6, 7, 12, 16, 17, 19,
   30, KING'S, Jun 9, CG, Oct 1, 22, KING'S, Nov 3, CG, Dec 8, 29; 1745: CG, Jan
   1, 5, KING'S, 5, CG, 7, 14, 25, KING'S, Mar 27, CG, Apr 3, 10, 16, Sep 27,
   DL, 28, CG, Oct 29, Nov 14, 15; 1746: CG, Jan 1, 8, 25, Feb 14, Apr 8, 18,
   DL, Nov 7, Dec 15; 1747: DL, Jan 10, Mar 7, 10, CG, Apr 1, DL, 6, 9, Dec 3;
   1748: CG, Mar 9, 23, DL, Apr 20, Nov 14, Dec 26; 1749: CG, Feb 10, DL, 21,
   HIC, Apr 21, DL, Oct 17, Dec 20; 1750: DL, Jan 1, Feb 9, 15, CG, Mar 16, DL,
   Apr 26, Oct 1, 30, Nov 13, Dec 13, 18; 1751: DL, Feb 23, May 14, 22; 1754:
   DL, May 15; 1758: CHAPEL, Apr 27, MARLY, Jun 8, 10, 27, Jul 29, Aug 21, 22,
   Sep 18; 1759: DL, Jan 3, Mar 20, MARLY, May 10, Jul 26, Aug 9, DL, Sep 25,
   27, Oct 12, Nov 17, Dec 1, 14, 31; 1760: MARLY, Jun 18, Aug 11, 20; 1761:
   HAY, Jun 23, 27, 30, Jul 14, 17, 18, 28, Aug 6, 13, 22; 1765: DL, Feb 15
Reinholds (actor), 1783: HAY, Sep 17
Rejoice greatly (song), 1793: KING/HAY, Feb 20; 1794: DL, Mar 19; 1798: CG, Mar
30
Rejoice O Judah (song), 1799: CG, Mar 1
Rejoicing Night (entertainment), 1771: DL, Oct 21
Relapse, The. See Vanbrugh, Sir John.

Relation of His Majesties Entertainment Passing through the City of London to
   His Coronation (pageant), 1661: NONE, Apr 22
Relfe, John (composer), 1792: KING'S, Mar 28; 1794: CG, May 26
Relief of Williamstadt, The. See Goodwin, Thomas.
Relieve thy Champion (song), 1798: CG, Mar 14
Religious Rebel, The; or, The Pilgrim Prince (play, anon), 1670: NONE, Sep 0
Remdemi il figlio mio (song), 1762: KING'S, Mar 1
Remember us O Lord (song), 1789: DL, Mar 20
Remperino, Sga (dancer), 1754: HAY, Jul 11
Remy (actor), 1784: HAY, Jan 21
Renaudin (harpist), 1777: CG, Feb 26
Rendezvous (dance), 1797: KING'S, May 11, 13, 25, Jun 15
Rendezvous Gallant (dance), 1742: CG, Dec 17, 20, 22, 23, 30, 31; 1743: CG, Jan
   3, 5, 7, 17, 19, 21, 24, Feb 2, Mar 3, 10, Apr 4, 8, 21, 27, May 2, 11, 23
Rendezvous Interrompus, Les; ou, Arlequin Docteur Domestique (pantomime, anon),
   1725: HAY, Apr 1
Rendezvous, The (interlude, anon), 1797: CG, May 20; 1800: CG, Apr 15, 17
Rendi il sereno al ciglio (song), 1786: DL, Mar 10; 1787: KING'S, Mar 1; 1789:
   CG, Apr 3; 1790: CG, Feb 24, DL, Mar 12; 1791: CG, Mar 11, Apr 13; 1792: CG,
   Feb 24, Mar 23; 1795: KING'S, Feb 27
Renegado, The. See Massinger, Phillip.
Rennoldson (actor), 1767: MARLY, Sep 18, CG, Nov 4
Renos, Mlle (actor, dancer), 1741: CG, Nov 26, Dec 28; 1742: CG, Jan 8, 21, Feb
   22, May 8
Renton. See Rainton.
Renton, Charles (singer), 1707: DL, Nov 29; 1711: RIW, Jul 21, GR, Sep 8; 1712:
   DL, Aug 5; 1713: DL, Jun 5; 1714: DL, Jun 18; 1715: DL, Apr 19, May 13, Jun
   6, Jul 1, 15, 19, 26, Aug 5; 1716: DL, May 16, Jun 9, Jul 31; 1718: DL, Apr
   23, May 7, 21, 30; 1719: DL, May 14; 1723: DL, Jul 16
Reparation, The. See Andrews, Miles Peter.
Repley, Thomas (renter), 1758: CG, Mar 6
Reply to Garrick, 1743: DL, Dec 12, 19
Representation of the late battle in the Mediterranean, 1744: MF, May 4
Reprisal, The. See Smollett, Dr Tobias.
Reprizal, The; or, Titt for Tatt (dance), 1739: CG, Oct 15, 25, 27, 31, Nov 1,
   3, 8, 13, 14, Dec 3, 8
Rerriminonies (dancer), 1754: HAY, Jul 4, Aug 15
Resolution of the Two Kings of Brentford (song), 1733: LIF/CG, Apr 11
Resta (composer), 1751: KING'S, Apr 16
Resta Ingrata (song), 1791: CG, Apr 6
Restier (dancer), 1765: KING'S, Jan 5
Restless, in thought disturbed (song), 1695: LIF, Sep 0
Restoration and Adventures of Harlequin, The (pantomime, anon), 1757: BFG, Sep
   5, 6
Restoration of the King of Bantum (entertainment), 1748: CG, Mar 28
Restoration, The. See Villiers, George.
Resurrection, The. See Arnold, Dr Samuel.
Retaliation. See Macnally, Leonard.
Retired from mortal's sight (song), 1680: DL, Dec 0; 1681: DL, Dec 0
Retour de la Foire, La. See Gherardi.
Retour des Matelotes (dance), 1776: KING'S, Mar 19, 26, Apr 9, 16, 23, Jun 18
Retour Impreuevu, Le. See Regnard, Jean Francois.
Return from a Tiger Hunt (entertainment), 1798: CG, Nov 12; 1799: CG, Jan 21,
   Oct 24
Return from the Universities of Parnassus (entertainment), 1775: DL, Apr 19
Return O God of Hosts (song), 1745: CG, Apr 10; 1746: KING'S, Mar 25; 1747: ST,
   Apr 29; 1751: KING'S, Apr 16; 1753: KING'S, Apr 30; 1755: KING'S, Mar 17;
   1797: CG, Mar 10, 22; 1798: CG, Mar 14; 1799: CG, Mar 1, 15; 1800: CG, Mar 19
Return of Jemmy (dance), 1799: DL, May 2
Return, The (song), 1754: DL, May 2
Reunion des Amours, La (farce, anon), 1734: HAY, Nov 1
Reuse (musician), 1718: YB, Dec 10
Reveil du Bonheur (dance), 1784: KING'S; Feb 3, 7, 17, 26, Mar 4, 11, 30, Apr
   15, May 13, Jun 10
Revel Masque. See The Festival.
Revellers (dance), 1734: DL/HAY, Feb 20, Mar 5, 9, 12, 19, 23, 25, 26, Apr 1,
   DL, 4, 22, 25, DL/HAY, 26, 27, May 1, DL, 21, DL/HAY, 22, 23, LIF, 29, DL,
   Sep 7, 10, 12, 19, 24, Oct 3, 9, 23, 24, Nov 7, 15, 16, 19, Dec 9, 17; 1735:
   DL, Jan 11, 16, 17, Feb 13, 14, Mar 10, Apr 28, Oct 1, Nov 3, 4, 5, 6, 12,
   28, Dec 2, 6, 10, 12, 16, 17, 26, 31; 1736: DL, Feb 2, 4, 11, 14, 16, Mar 11,
   20, 29, Apr 5, 6, 15, May 6, 18, 22, Jun 23, Oct 15, 16, 19, 21, Nov 2, 3,
   12; 1746: CG, Apr 17

Revenge for Honour. See Glapthorne, Henry.
Revenge of Bussy D'Ambois. See Chapman, George.
Revenge, The. See Young, Edward.
Revenge, The; or, A Match in Newgate. See Behn, Aphra.
Revenge, Timotheus cries (song), 1741: DL, May 28; 1752: KING'S, Mar 24; 1784:
    CG, Apr 27; 1791: CG, Mar 25; 1792: CG, Mar 7; 1794: CG, Mar 14
Revengeful Queen, The. See Phillips, William.
Revet, Edward (actor, author), 1662: ATCOURT, Nov 1
--Town Shifts, The; or, The Suburb-Justice, 1671: LIF, Mar 15
Review, The. See Colman the younger, George.
Revived Anacreontics, The (interlude, anon), 1800: CG, May 6
Reviving Judah (song), 1795: CG, Mar 18
Revolt of Capua. See Southerne, Thomas.
Revolution of Sweden, The. See Trotter, Catherine.
Rewards of Virtue, The. See Fountain, John.
Reygle (house servant), 1753: DL, May 16
Reymers, Charles (printer), 1756: DL, Mar 9
Reynald (dancer), 1767: CG, Apr 27
Reynault (dancer), 1746: NWMF, Oct 6
Reynell, H (publisher), 1777: KING'S, Apr 1; 1779: KING'S, May 29; 1781:
    KING'S, Dec 11; 1782: KING'S, Apr 9, May 25, Nov 2; 1783: KING'S, Jan 7, Feb
    18, 27, Mar 6, 27, Apr 29, Nov 29, Dec 16; 1784: KING'S, Jan 6, 17, Feb 17,
    24, Mar 18, Apr 15, Jun 12; 1785: KING'S, Jan 4; 1788: KING'S, Jan 29; 1790:
    HAY, Jan 7, Feb 2, 27; 1791: PAN, Feb 17, Mar 1, 19, Apr 14, Jun 2, 16, Dec
    17; 1792: HAY, Feb 28, Mar 31, Apr 12; 1796: KING'S, Jul 23
Reyner. See Rayner.
Reynhold (actor), 1731: HAY, Mar 24
Reynolds (actor), 1728: HAY, Aug 9, Oct 15, 26, Nov 19; 1729: HAY, Jan 10, 31,
    Feb 25, Mar 29, May 7, 26, 29, Jun 14, 17, Jul 16, 23, 26, DL, Aug 16, HAY,
    19, BFR, 25, 26, SF, Sep 8, HAY, Nov 12, 15, 22, 29, Dec 18; 1730: HAY, Jan
    8, 21, 29, Feb 6, 12, 18, Mar 11, 12, 20, 30, Apr 20, 24, May 1, Jun 17, 23,
    27, Jul 17, TC, Aug 1, 11, BFR, 22, Sep 4, SFP, 9, SF, 14, HAY, 18, Oct 21,
    23, 26, Nov 9, 13, 16, 20, 30, Dec 9, 14, 28; 1731: HAY, Jan 13, 14, 15, 18,
    20, Feb 3, 10, 26, Mar 10, 15, 17, 24, Apr 22, May 10, 12
Reynolds (actor), 1749: BF/SFP, Aug 23; 1762: DL, Nov 23
Reynolds (actor), 1769: KING'S, Apr 5, MARLY, Aug 17; 1776: HAY, May 2
Reynolds (actor), 1784: HAY, Mar 8
Reynolds (beneficiary), 1747: DL, May 18
Reynolds (oil merchant), 1767: DL, Jan 16, Apr 4
Reynolds (pit office keeper), 1786: KING'S, Dec 23; 1787: KING'S, Mar 17
Reynolds (supplier), 1750: DL, Mar 22
Reynolds Crane Co, 1752: DL, Apr 6
Reynolds, Ann (actor), 1765: HAY, Jun 10, 24, Jul 8, 15, 17, Aug 8, 9, 21, 30;
    1766: DL, Sep 23, 30, Oct 18, 25, Dec 10, 12; 1767: DL, Jan 2, 23, 24, Feb 7,
    SW, Jun 13, DL, Sep 12, 22, Nov 10, 20, 21, 26, 28; 1768: DL, Jan 23, Apr 4,
    6, 9, HAY, Aug 8
Reynolds, Frederick, 1786: CG, Mar 14, Dec 20; 1789: CG, May 15; 1790: CG, May
    6, DL, Nov 17; 1791: CG, Oct 3, Nov 5; 1793: CG, Feb 15, 20, 22, Mar 6, 8,
    Apr 18; 1794: CG, Oct 23; 1795: CG, Jan 31, Nov 7; 1796: CG, Oct 29; 1797:
    DL, Apr 19, Oct 21; 1798: CG, Dec 8, 17; 1799: CG, Oct 31
--Cheap Living, 1797: DL, Oct 17, 21, 24, 26, 28, 31, Nov 1, 3
--Crusade, The, 1790: CG, May 6, 8, 10, 12, 14, 17, 19, 21, 25, 28, Jun 5, 9,
    14, Oct 19, 29; 1791: CG, Oct 3, 6, 10, 17, 31, Nov 8, 16
--Dramatist, The; or, Stop Him Who Can, 1789: CG, May 15, 21, 23, Oct 7, 14,
    21, 27, Nov 4, 11, 18, 25, Dec 3, 9, 16, 23; 1790: CG, Jan 1, 8, 14, 21, 25,
    Feb 2, 6, 10, 13, 16, 20, 23, 27, Mar 4, 9, 15, 23, Apr 9, 15, 23, 28, May
    20, Jun 4, Oct 26, Nov 3, 10, 17, 24, Dec 8, 30; 1791: CG, Jan 20, Sep 12,
    Oct 5, 29, Dec 12; 1792: CG, Feb 13, Nov 6, 27; 1793: CG, Oct 18, Dec 18;
    1795: CG, Jan 10, 23, Jun 8, Sep 16, Dec 30; 1796: CG, Jun 1, Sep 23, Dec 20;
    1797: CG, Sep 20; 1799: CG, Oct 18, Dec 31; 1800: CG, May 23
--Eloisa, 1786: CG, Dec 18, 20, 21, 22; 1787: CG, Feb 10
--Fortune's Fool, 1796: CG, Oct 29, 31, Nov 1, 3, 4, 5, 8, 9, 10, 11, 12, 14,
    15, 17, 18, 26, Dec 2, 6, 14, 29; 1797: CG, Jan 25
--How to Grow Rich, 1793: CG, Apr 18, 20, 22, 23, 26, 27, 29, 30, May 4, 6, 7,
    9, 11, 13, 14, 17, 20, 22, 25, 28, 29, Oct 2, 24; 1795: CG, May 25; 1800: CG,
    Apr 5
--Laugh When You Can, 1798: CG, Dec 8, 10, 11, 12, 14, 17, 19, 21, 22, 27, 29;
    1799: CG, Jan 1, 3, 5, 9, 26, Feb 1, 11, 25, Mar 11, 28, May 17, Jun 4, Sep
    16; 1800: CG, May 30
--Management, 1799: CG, Oct 31, Nov 1, 2, 4, 5, 6, 8, 9, 12, 13, 15, 16, 19,
    21, 22, 23, 25, 26, 27, 28, 29, Dec 11, 13, 17, 20; 1800: CG, Jan 1, Mar 31
--Notoriety, 1791: CG, Nov 5, 7, 8, 11, 14, 16, 18, 21, 23, 25, 30, Dec 7, 14,

16; <u>1792</u>: CG, Jan 4, 12, 14, 17, 25, 31, Feb 8, 11, 16, Apr 28, Oct 26, Dec
21; <u>1793</u>: CG, Jan 23, Feb 4, Oct 24, 29; <u>1794</u>: CG, Jan 1, Dec 31; <u>1796</u>: CG,
Jan 2
--Rage, The, <u>1794</u>: CG, Oct 23, 24, 28, 29, 31, Nov 3, 5, 7, 11, 13, 14, 15, 24,
25, 26, 27, 28, Dec 1, 2, 3, 4, 5, 11, 12, 13, 15, 16, 17, 20, 23; <u>1795</u>: CG,
Jan 15, 17, 21, 28, Feb 19, Mar 12, Apr 6, Oct 7, Nov 3; <u>1800</u>: CG, Apr 30
--Speculation, <u>1795</u>: CG, Nov 7, 9, 10, 11, 12, 13, 14, 16, 17, 18, 19, 20, 21,
24, 26, 28, Dec 1, 3, 5, 8, 10, 12, 17, 19; <u>1796</u>: CG, Jan 5, 9, 12, 16, 19,
21, Feb 6, Mar 15, 29, May 13; <u>1800</u>: CG, May 17
--Werter, <u>1786</u>: CG, Mar 14, 25, Apr 3, 22, May 1, 12, Oct 26; <u>1789</u>: CG, Jun 8,
Dec 21; <u>1795</u>: CG, Dec 23
--Will, The, <u>1797</u>: DL, Apr 19, 20, 21, 22, 24, 25, 26, 27, 29, May 2, 4, 5, 16,
20, 31, Sep 21, Oct 27; <u>1798</u>: DL, Jan 20, Feb 14; <u>1799</u>: DL, Dec 2, 6; <u>1800</u>:
DL, Jan 15, Feb 8, Apr 23
Reynolds, George Nugent, <u>1797</u>: CG, Feb 18
--Bantry Bay (music), <u>1797</u>: CG, Feb 18, 20, 22, 23, 25, 28, Mar 7, 9, 13, 14,
May 6
Reynolds, J, <u>1757</u>: CRT, Feb 7
Reynolds, Sir Joshua (painter), <u>1769</u>: CG, Dec 2; <u>1770</u>: DL, Apr 30; <u>1771</u>: HAY,
Jun 26; <u>1775</u>: DL, Mar 27; <u>1785</u>: DL, Nov 18
Reynolds, Miss (actor), <u>1776</u>: HAY, May 2, CHR, Sep 25, 27, Oct 14, 18; <u>1778</u>:
CG, Apr 30
Reynolds, Miss C (actor), <u>1776</u>: CHR, Sep 25
Reynolds, Mrs (actor), <u>1784</u>: HAY, Mar 8
Reynolds, Mrs (supplier), <u>1749</u>: DL, Dec 21; <u>1750</u>: DL, Jan 9, 23, Feb 22, Apr 26
Reynolds, Mrs Richard (actor), <u>1736</u>: CG, Oct 27, Nov 3, 11
Reynolds, Sarah Maria (actor), <u>1787</u>: CG, May 3; <u>1788</u>: CG, Oct 16, Nov 6; <u>1789</u>:
CG, Feb 24, May 2, 14
Reynolds' Booth, <u>1729</u>: BFR, Aug 25, 26, SF, Sep 8, SOU, 23; <u>1730</u>: TC, Aug 1,
BFR, 22, Sep 4
Reynoldson (singer), <u>1776</u>: DL, Oct 18, Nov 25; <u>1779</u>: CG, Apr 17; <u>1783</u>: CG, May
6; <u>1789</u>: DL, Dec 26; <u>1790</u>: CG, Feb 19, 24, 26, Mar 3, DL, Apr 16, Oct 26;
<u>1791</u>: DLKING'S, Oct 15, Nov 5; <u>1792</u>: DLKING'S, May 23; <u>1794</u>: DL, May 16, 23,
Jun 12, Oct 31
Rhadamisthe et Zenobie. See Crebillon, Prosper.
Rhapsody on the Death of a late Noble Commander (entertainment), <u>1760</u>: HAY, Feb
14
Rhenos, Mlle. See Renos, Mlle.
Rhodes, John (composer), <u>1795</u>: DL, Jun 4; <u>1796</u>: DL, Jun 11; <u>1799</u>: DL, Feb 5,
May 22; <u>1800</u>: DL, Jun 13
Rhodes, John (manager), <u>1659</u>: NONE, Sep 0; <u>1660</u>: COCKPIT, Feb 4, Jul 28; <u>1706</u>:
YB, Mar 25; <u>1711</u>: SH, May 21; <u>1718</u>: HA, Feb 19, CDS, Mar 14
Rhodes, Mrs (actor), <u>1729</u>: HAY, Nov 12, 18, FLR, Dec 1, HAY, 5
Rhodes, Richard
--Flora's Vagaries (Figaries), <u>1663</u>: BRIDGES, Nov 0, 3; <u>1664</u>: BRIDGES, Aug 8,
NONE, Nov 0; <u>1667</u>: ATCOURT, Feb 14, BRIDGES, Oct 5; <u>1668</u>: BRIDGES, Feb 18;
<u>1669</u>: NONE, Sep 0; <u>1676</u>: NONE, Sep 0; <u>1715</u>: DL, Jul 26
Ribarwarle (actor), <u>1728</u>: HAY, Feb 21
Ricard (actor), <u>1752</u>: CG, Mar 30, May 4, 5, Sep 22, Oct 21, 30, Dec 9, 11, 13;
<u>1753</u>: CG, Mar 19, May 5, 7, 8, 18
Ricci, Francesco (dancer), <u>1777</u>: DL, Apr 5
Ricci, Sga (dancer), <u>1776</u>: DL, Oct 24, Nov 6, 7, 26, Dec 4, 18; <u>1777</u>: DL, Jan
9, 17, Feb 10, Apr 5, 14, 22
Ricciarelli, Giuseppe (singer), <u>1754</u>: KING'S, Nov 9; <u>1755</u>: KING'S, Mar 17, Apr
12, Dec 9; <u>1756</u>: KING'S, Feb 10, Mar 15, DL, Apr 2, KING'S, 5, 6, 10; <u>1757</u>:
KING'S, Jan 18, Mar 24, DL, 25, KING'S, Apr 30, May 24, 31; <u>1758</u>: DL, Mar 10
Riccoboni, Luigi (author), <u>1759</u>: DL, Sep 22
Riccoloni, Lelio
--Arlequin Cartouche; ou, Les Voleurs, <u>1722</u>: HAY, Jan 12, 16, 19, 25, Feb 1, 2,
19, Mar 29; <u>1725</u>: HAY, Apr 12, 21, 23
Rice (boxkeeper), <u>1792</u>: DLKING'S, Jun 16; <u>1793</u>: DL, Jun 7; <u>1794</u>: KING'S, May 15
Rice (dancer), <u>1720</u>: LIF, Apr 29
Rice (musician), <u>1755</u>: CG, Apr 26; <u>1756</u>: DL, Aug 12; <u>1760</u>: DL, Apr 22, HAY, 30,
CG, May 1, DL, 14
Rice, Alexander (box-bookkeeper), <u>1779</u>: HAY, May 31, Oct 13; <u>1781</u>: HAY, May 30;
<u>1782</u>: HAY, Mar 4, Jun 3; <u>1783</u>: HAY, May 31, Dec 15; <u>1784</u>: HAY, Mar 22, May
28; <u>1785</u>: HAY, Jan 24, Feb 7, 10; <u>1786</u>: HAY, Jun 9; <u>1787</u>: HAY, Mar 12, May
16; <u>1788</u>: HAY, Jun 10; <u>1789</u>: HAY, May 18; <u>1790</u>: HAY, Jun 14, Oct 13; <u>1791</u>:
HAY, Jun 6, Oct 24; <u>1792</u>: HAY, Feb 6, Jun 15, Oct 15; <u>1793</u>: HAY, Jun 11, Sep
19, Dec 16; <u>1794</u>: HAY, Jan 27, May 22, Jul 8; <u>1795</u>: HAY, Jun 9, Sep 21; <u>1796</u>:
HAY, Jun 11; <u>1797</u>: HAY, Feb 9, Jun 12; <u>1798</u>: HAY, Jan 15, Jun 12, Aug 18, Dec
17; <u>1799</u>: HAY, Jan 24, Apr 17, Jun 15, Oct 21; <u>1800</u>: HAY, Jun 13

Rice, Mrs (actor), 1725: LIF, Nov 23, Dec 16; 1726: LIF, Jan 14, May 26, Jun
    17, 24, Jul 5, 22, Aug 2, 12, Sep 30, Oct 3, 19, Nov 10, 14, 30; 1727: LIF,
    Feb 13, Mar 13, Apr 5, 10, 19, May 4, Sep 11, Oct 12, Nov 9; 1728: LIF, Jan
    29, Apr 24, May 22, Jul 2, Aug 2, Nov 23; 1729: LIF, Jan 18, Apr 16, 19, May
    7, BFB, Aug 25, LIF, Sep 29, Oct 15, 30, Nov 4; 1730: RI, Jun 24, 27, Jul 5,
    LIF, Sep 25, Oct 23, Nov 7, 10; 1731: LIF, Jan 21, Apr 26, RI, Jul 22, BFB,
    Aug 26, LIF, Oct 4, 18, Nov 6; 1732: LIF, May 24, 26, RI, Aug 17, BFB, 23
Rich mines of hot love are rooted here (song), 1695: LIF, Dec 0
Rich, Christopher M (proprietor), 1695: DG, Apr 0, DL, 1; 1697: DL, Jan 0;
    1700: DLLIF, Feb 0; 1701: DL, Dec 0; 1704: DL, Feb 5, Dec 16; 1709: DL, May
    5; 1718: LIF, Apr 16; 1720: LIF, Feb 5; 1721: LIF, Apr 11; 1722: LIF, Mar 3,
    Apr 16; 1723: LIF, Mar 18, 19, May 1; 1724: LIF, May 1, Jun 5; 1759: CG, Oct
    5; 1760: CG, Sep 22; 1761: CG, Sep 24
Rich, Henry (pit office keeper), 1715: LIF, Jul 8; 1716: LIF, Jun 22; 1717:
    LIF, May 27
Rich, J B (treasurer of Lying-In Hospital), 1769: CG, Jan 10; 1770: CG, Jan 27;
    1771: CG, Dec 31
Rich, John (actor, proprietor, manager, pantomime writer), 1714: LIF, Dec 18;
    1715: LIF, Oct 22, Nov 10; 1716: LIF, Feb 21, Dec 18; 1717: LIF, Apr 29, May
    30, DL, Sep 28, LIF, Oct 25, Dec 6; 1718: LIF, Mar 29; 1719: LIF, Jan 9, Mar
    21; 1720: LIF, Jan 23, Feb 5, Mar 19, Dec 15; 1721: LIF, Mar 30, Apr 12, Oct
    10, Dec 18; 1722: LIF, Mar 12; 1723: LIF, Feb 11, 20, Mar 25, 26, Apr 17, Oct
    14; 1724: LIF, Jan 7, 10, 14, Apr 11, May 21; 1725: LIF, Jan 23, 27, Feb 1,
    Mar 20; 1726: LIF, Jan 17, 20, 24, Feb 19; 1727: LIF, Feb 7, 16, 27, DL, Oct
    26; 1728: LIF, Feb 28; 1729: LIF, Feb 10, Dec 5, 9; 1730: LIF, Jan 5, 12, Feb
    12, Oct 1, KG, 22; 1731: LIF, Jan 9, 16; 1732: LIF, Feb 26, May 13, LIF/CG,
    Dec 26; 1733: LIF/CG, Jan 15, CG/LIF, Apr 26, DL, Jun 9; 1735: CG, Apr 28,
    Dec 18; 1736: CG, Oct 1; 1737: CG, Mar 24, YB, Apr 14; 1738: CG, Nov 13;
    1740: CG, Feb 6, 12, 16; 1741: DL, Dec 4, 7; 1742: CG, Mar 1, 25; 1743: DL,
    Oct 6; 1744: KING'S, Jun 9; 1745: DL, Dec 9, CG, 21; 1746: CG, Nov 6; 1747:
    CG, Feb 12, 28, Mar 26; 1748: CG, Mar 5, Nov 7; 1749: CG, Feb 10, DL, May 16,
    CG, Sep 25, 29, Dec 23; 1750: DL, Feb 7, CG, Mar 1, Apr 18, May 4, DL, Sep 8;
    1751: CG, Jan 25; 1752: DL, Feb 11, Nov 6, CG, Dec 8, DL, 14; 1753: DL, May
    21, CG, Oct 10, 24, Nov 10; 1754: CG, Jan 18, 22, 29, Feb 11, 28; 1755: CG,
    Sep 29; 1756: DL, Apr 8; 1757: CG, Oct 28; 1758: CG, Feb 25, NONE, Mar 1, CG,
    Apr 10, DL, 14, CG, 20, DL, Sep 16, Nov 10; 1759: CG, Apr 10, DL, Oct 2, CG,
    5, 18, 20, DL, 23, CG, 30, Nov 13, 14, Dec 5, 6, 12, 21, 22; 1760: CG, Jan 7,
    26, Feb 4, 11, 23, Mar 4, 6, 15, 17, DL, 20, CG, 29, Apr 12, 28, DL, May 5,
    CG, 19, Sep 22, Oct 10, Nov 28, Dec 2, 16, 31; 1761: CG, Jan 6, 10, 14, 20,
    Feb 2, 3, 21, Mar 14, 23, Apr 4, May 8, 25, DL, Jun 18, CG, 23, DL, Jul 27,
    CG, Sep 12, 24, DL, 30, CG, Oct 23, Nov 3, 26, DL, 26; 1767: CG, Jan 1, May
    23, Sep 14; 1768: CG, May 2; 1770: CG, Feb 15; 1773: CG, Oct 28; 1778: CG,
    Oct 14; 1782: DL, Oct 28; 1792: CG, Dec 20; 1793: CG, Dec 19; 1796: CG, Mar
    15, Oct 24; 1798: CG, May 28; see also Lun
--Fair, The (pantomime), 1750: CG, Feb 7, 8, 9, 10, 12, 13, 14, 15, 16, 17, 19,
    20, 21, 22, 23, 24, 26, 27, Mar 1, 3, 5, 6, 8, 10; 1752: CG, Nov 2, 3, 4, 6,
    7, 8, 9, 10, 11, 13, 14, 15, 16, 17, 18, 20, 21, 22, 23, 24, 25, 27, 28, 29,
    30, Dec 1, 2, 4; 1753: DL, Oct 9; 1759: CG, Dec 7, 8, 10, 11, 13, 14, 15, 17,
    19, 20, 22, 26, 27, 28, 29, 31; 1760: CG, Jan 1, 2, 3, 7, 9, 10, 11, 14, 15,
    24, 28, Feb 1, 4, 6, 7, 9, 13, 18, 19, 23, 25, 26, 28, Mar 1, 4, 11, 13, 15,
    29, May 10, 20, 22, 26; 1761: CG, Oct 13, 14, 15, 16, 17, 19, 20, 21, 22, 24,
    26, 27, 28, 29, 30, 31, Nov 2, 3, 4, 5, 6, 7, 9; 1773: CG, Oct 11, 28, 29,
    Nov 1, 2, 3, Dec 16; 1774: CG, Mar 22, Apr 26, May 6, 24
Rich, John and Christopher M, 1716: LIF, Feb 9; 1717: LIF, Oct 25, Nov 1, 8,
    15, 22, 29, Dec 11, 13, 27; 1718: LIF, Jan 1, 3, 8, 10, 17, 29, 31, Feb 7,
    Nov 7, 12, 14, 19, 21, 28, Dec 3, 5, 12, 17, 26; 1719: LIF, Jan 9, Feb 4, Apr
    1; 1720: LIF, Feb 10, Apr 20, 22, 27; 1721: LIF, Jan 19, Mar 9
Rich, Lady (spectator), 1734: KING'S, Apr 2; 1735: KING'S, Mar 15
Rich, Mrs (actor), 1759: CG, Oct 5
Rich, Mrs (payee), 1773: CG, Jan 6
Rich, Mrs, and Co (landlords), 1772: CG, Nov 12; 1773: CG, Oct 25
Rich, Priscilla, Mrs John, 1761: CG, May 8, Nov 26; 1796: CG, Jun 7
Rich, Sir Robert, 1743: BFFP, Aug 23
Richard (actor), 1751: CG, Nov 22; 1752: CG, Apr 28; 1775: HAY, Sep 20
Richard Coeur de Lion (dance), 1788: KING'S, May 22
Richard Coeur de Lion. See Macnally, Leonard; Burgoyne, Lieutenant-General
    John.
Richard I, King of England. See Handel, George Frederic.
Richard II. See Shakespeare, William.
Richard III. See Shakespeare, William.
Richard Plantagenet (narrative poem), 1792: HAY, Apr 16
Richards (actor), 1723: HAY, Dec 12; 1724: HAY, Feb 20; 1729: HAY, Dec 18;

1730: HAY, Jan 21; 1736: HAY, Jan 19, SF, Sep 7; 1740: GF, Oct 29, Nov 1, 21;
  1741: GF, Jan 22, BFH, Aug 22; 1744: HAY, Sep 27, 29
Richards (actor), 1782: HAY, Nov 25; 1791: HAY, Oct 24; 1798: HAY, Mar 26
Richards (author)
--Device, The; or, The Marriage-Office (opera), 1777: CG, May 5
Richards (laceman), 1784: DL, Apr 21
Richards, B, 1775: DL, May 27
Richards, D (house servant), 1772: DL, Jun 10; 1773: DL, Jun 2; 1774: DL, Jun
  2; 1775: DL, May 27; 1779: DL, Mar 26
Richards, David (violinist), 1779: DL, Feb 19; 1780: DL, Feb 16, 18, 23, 25,
  Mar 1, 3, 8, 10, 15, 17; 1781: DL, Mar 2; 1782: DL, Feb 15; 1783: DL, Mar 26;
  1784: DL, Feb 27; 1785: DL, Feb 11; 1789: CG, Feb 27
Richards, Elizabeth Rebecca (actor), 1789: CG, Nov 13, Dec 10
Richards, John (actor), 1661: LIF, Aug 24; 1662: LIF, Mar 1, Sep 30; 1665: LIF,
  Apr 3; 1672: DG, Jan 31; 1676: DG, Jul 3, 25, Aug 0, Nov 4, Dec 0; 1677: DG,
  Mar 24, May 31, Jun 0, Jul 0, Sep 0; 1678: DG, Jan 0, 17, May 28; 1679: DG,
  Apr 0; 1680: DG, Jan 0, Jun 0; 1681: DG, Jan 0, DG/IT, Nov 22; 1682: DG, Jan
  0, Mar 0; 1683: DG, May 31, Jul 0
Richards, John Inigo (scene painter), 1760: CG, Feb 1, Mar 8; 1768: CG, Mar 15;
  1769: CG, Oct 27; 1770: CG, Jan 27, Feb 2, MARLY, Sep 4; 1771: HAY, Jan 28,
  MARLY, Sep 3, DL, Oct 19, CG, Nov 27; 1772: CG, May 26; 1773: CG, Jan 12;
  1774: CG, Jan 13, Nov 19; 1775: CG, Apr 24, Dec 26; 1776: CG, Nov 14, Dec 26;
  1777: CG, May 5; 1778: CG, Sep 18; 1779: CG, Jan 4, Feb 23, 27, Mar 20, Nov
  30; 1780: CG, Apr 25, Dec 29; 1781: CG, Oct 1, Nov 28, Dec 26; 1782: CG, Oct
  10, Nov 25; 1783: CG, Jan 18, Sep 22, Dec 23; 1784: CG, Jan 29, Sep 20, Dec
  27; 1785: CG, Sep 19, Oct 13, Dec 20; 1786: CG, Dec 26; 1787: CG, Nov 5, Dec
  26; 1788: CG, May 22, Nov 1, Dec 26; 1789: CG, Apr 13, Dec 21; 1790: CG, Sep
  29, Nov 15, Dec 20; 1791: CG, Feb 26, Oct 20, Dec 10, 21; 1792: CG, Nov 3,
  Dec 1; 1793: CG, Feb 25, Dec 19; 1794: CG, Feb 22, Apr 10, Sep 22, Oct 30,
  Dec 26; 1796: CG, Mar 15, Apr 9, Oct 24, 29, Nov 19; 1797: CG, Apr 25, Nov
  24, Dec 26; 1798: CG, Feb 12, May 28, Nov 12, Dec 11; 1799: CG, May 13, Nov
  14; 1800: CG, Jan 16, Feb 8
Richards, Miss (ticket deliverer), 1783: DL, May 23; 1784: DL, May 15
Richards, William (author), 1681: NONE, Sep 0; 1687: DL, May 12
--Christmas Ordinary, The, 1659: NONE, Sep 0; 1681: NONE, Sep 0
Richards, William (teacher), 1741: GF, Feb 5
Richardson (actor), 1675: ATCOURT, Feb 15
Richardson (actor), 1772: HAY, Dec 21
Richardson (composer), 1788: CG, Dec 26
Richardson (dancer), 1793: CG, Mar 11
Richardson (director), 1729: BOS, Jan 21
Richardson (stationer), 1786: DL, May 1
Richardson, Elizabeth, 1779: DL, Apr 28
--Double Deception, The, 1779: DL, Apr 27, 28, 30, May 6, 12, 27; 1780: DL, Jan
  26, 29
Richardson, John (actor), 1793: CG, Nov 12, 19, 22, 28, 30, Dec 7, 9, 12, 17,
  19, 27; 1794: CG, Jan 11, Feb 19, 22, Apr 7, 12, 25, 30, May 2, 7, 21, 22,
  23, 24, 30, Jun 5, Sep 22, 26, Oct 1, 7, 10, 15, 17, 20, 21, 23, 29, Nov 7,
  11, 12, Dec 26; 1795: CG, Jan 2, Feb 21, Mar 28, Apr 24, May 13, 14, 27, 30,
  Jun 12, Sep 14, 21, 25, 28, Oct 7, 14, 16, 19, 22, 24, Nov 14, 25, 27, Dec 7,
  9, 21, 22, 31; 1796: CG, Jan 4, 13, Mar 15, 17, 30, Apr 9, 20, May 16, 18,
  20, 23, 24, 27, 28, Jun 2, Oct 7
Richardson, Joseph, 1792: DLKING'S, Apr 20; 1794: DL, Jul 2
--Fugitive, The, 1792: DLKING'S, Apr 18, 20, 23, 27, May 2, 4, 7, 9, 11, 12,
  14, 16, 18, 21, DL, Oct 13, 22, 25, Nov 17, Dec 7, 19; 1793: DL, Jan 14, Feb
  7; 1796: DL, Feb 1
Richardson, Mrs (actor), 1690: DL, Dec 0; 1691: DL, Jan 0, Mar 0, DG, May 0,
  DL, Dec 0; 1692: DL, Feb 0
Richardson, Mrs (actor), 1710: GR, Sep 11
Richardson, Richard (landholder), 1768: CG, Jun 1
Richardson, Thomas (actor, dancer), 1733: DL, Oct 24, Nov 13, 14, Dec 7; 1734:
  DL, Jan 19, DL/HAY, Mar 30, LIF, Apr 15, DL/HAY, 20, JS, May 31, YB, Jul 8,
  BFHBH, Aug 24, GF, Nov 13, 18, CG/LIF, 29, GF, Dec 16; 1735: GF, Jan 3, 24,
  Feb 4, Mar 17, 24, May 3, LIF, Aug 22, GF, Sep 15, Oct 3, 6, 10, 20, 27, Nov
  4, CG, 6, GF, 14, CG, 15, GF, 20, 24, 26, CG, 28, Dec 2, GF, 5, 8, 17; 1736:
  CG, Jan 21, 23, GF, Feb 5, 9, 17, CG, Mar 2, 6, GF, 9, 18, 29, Apr 8, 28, CG,
  29, BFFH, Aug 23, SF, Sep 7, LIF, 28, Oct 5, CG, 8, 20, LIF, 26, CG, Nov 3,
  LIF, 4, 6, CG, 9, LIF, 16, 18, 20, 24, CG, 26, LIF, 27, Dec 3, 7, 8, 16, 17,
  22, 31; 1737: LIF, Jan 19, CG, 28, LIF, Feb 1, CG, 14, LIF, Mar 1, CG, 7, 24,
  LIF, 29, 31, Apr 14, 18, 25, CT, 29, LIF, May 4, 7, CG, 12, LIF, Jun 15, CG,
  Sep 30, Oct 3, 5, 12; 1738: CG, Feb 13, Apr 4, 7, 27, May 6, 8, 10, 11, 15,
  Oct 4, 20, 23, 26, 28, 30, Nov 8, 13, 18, Dec 6, 9; 1739: CG, Jan 3, 6, 8,

15, 16, 20, Feb 15, Mar 2, 5, Apr 23, 25, 26, 27, May 1, 2, 4, 5, 7, 8, 9,
10, 14, 16, 23, Sep 22, Oct 2, 3, 15, Nov 1, 23, 26, Dec 1, 4, 10, 17; 1740:
CG, Jan 8, Feb 12, Mar 24, Apr 9, 23, May 2, 5, 7, 9, 13, 14, 19, 20, 27, 29,
Sep 26, Oct 8, 10, 22, 23, 29, Dec 29; 1741: CG, Jan 5, 21, Feb 10, 17, 24,
28, Apr 2, 22, 23, 25, 27, 30, May 1, 2, 4, 5, 7, 8, 11, 14, Sep 28, Oct 17,
24, GF, Nov 9, CG, 26, Dec 22, 28, 30; 1742: CG, Jan 8, 21, Feb 22, Mar 9,
Apr 27, 30, May 5, 10, Oct 9, 15, 16, 25, Dec 28; 1743: CG, Jan 8, Feb 4, Mar
8, Apr 21, TCD/BFTD, Aug 4, CG, Oct 3; 1748: BFP, Aug 24, SFP, Sep 7; 1757:
HAY, Oct 31
Richardson, Van (musician), 1698: YB, Feb 16
Richardson, William (critic), 1772: CG, Mar 5
Richemont, Mlle (dancer), 1740: BFH, Aug 23
Riches, Miss (dancer), 1798: DL, Oct 6, Nov 14, Dec 6; 1799: DL, Jan 19, Feb 5,
Oct 14; 1800: DL, Mar 11
Richman, Mrs, Masquerade Warehouse, 1791: HAY, Oct 24
Richmond Heiress, The. See D'Urfey, Thomas.
Richmond Maggot (dance), 1734: CG/LIF, Sep 20, 25, Oct 7, 14, 23, 26, 31, Nov
1, 19, 25, Dec 5, 12; 1735: CG/LIF, Jan 14, 17, Mar 25, Apr 9, 15, 18, May 2,
CG, 6, 8, CG/LIF, 9, 12, 13, 15, 16, 19, 20, 22, 27, GF, Nov 3, 12, 14, 15,
19, 28, Dec 4, 6, 8, 10, 12, 15; 1736: GF, Feb 4, 5, 16, Mar 25, Apr 1, 6,
12, 28, May 6, 10, LIF, Oct 5, Dec 15; 1737: LIF, Jan 5
Richmond Primrose Girl (song), 1795: CG, May 14, Jun 6
Richmond Terrace, 1789: DL, Apr 20
Richmond Theatre, 1730: RI, Oct 20; 1735: RI, Aug 16; 1773: HAY, Sep 18; 1777:
DL, Jan 28; 1778: HAY, Aug 21; 1787: HAY, Mar 12, May 18; 1789: CG, Oct 28;
1790: CG, Dec 11; 1791: HAY, Oct 24; 1793: CG, Nov 12; 1795: DL, Jan 26;
1798: DL, Feb 17, Nov 10
Richmond Wells. See Williams, John.
Richmond Wells, 1701: RIW, Sep 8; 1721: RI, Oct 23; 1732: RIW/HAY, Sep 12
Richmond, Duchess of. See Stuart, Frances.
Richmond, Duchess of, 1729: LIF, Dec 17; 1780: DL, May 24
Richmond, Duke and Duchess of, 1723: GR, Dec 5
Richmond, Duke of. See Lennox, Charles.
Richmond, Duke of, 1729: GF, Dec 10; 1732: GF, Mar 6; 1735: KING'S, Mar 15;
1789: DL, Apr 20; see also Dukes
Richmond, Mlle (dancer), 1739: SF, Sep 8
Richmond, 1697: RICHMOND, Sep 20; 1698: RICHMOND, Aug 8; 1714: SOU, Nov 1;
1718: NONE, May 31, RI, Jul 19, SF, Sep 6; 1719: RI, Jun 6, Aug 3; 1723: RI,
Sep 2; 1724: RI, Jun 22, Aug 3; 1725: DL, Sep 20; 1729: RI, Aug 6; 1730: HAY,
Jun 4; 1731: LIF, Jun 8; 1732: LIF, Jul 3, DL, Nov 24; 1748: DL, Oct 12;
1753: DL, Oct 9; 1774: DL, May 6; 1777: DL, May 28; 1783: DL, May 12; 1793:
HAY, Dec 23; 1796: HAY, Mar 28, DL, Apr 29, CG, May 27; 1799: CG, Nov 11
Richter (musician), 1773: KING'S, Feb 5
Richter, John (beneficiary), 1729: YB, Feb 4; 1734: HIC, Mar 8; 1735: YB, Feb
14; 1741: HIC, Mar 5
Ricimero. See Galuppi, Baldassare; Bianchi, Giovanni Battista.
Rickaby, Thomas (publisher), 1797: DL, Feb 9, CG, Apr 25, DL, Sep 21, CG, Dec
16; 1798: CG, Nov 12, Dec 11
Riddle, Robert (actor), 1779: HAY, Jan 11, Mar 8; 1780: HAY, Jan 17, Sep 25
Ridgely (beneficiary), 1710: YB, Apr 17
Ridgway (actor), 1792: HAY, Apr 16
Ridgway, James (publisher), 1790: DL, Nov 17; 1791: HAY, Jun 25, Aug 13, Sep 2;
1799: DL, May 24, CG, 25, HAY, Jun 20, DL, 26, 29, Jul 1; 1800: DL, Mar 11,
HAY, Jun 16
Ridiculous Guardian, The. See Hasse, Johann Adolph.
Ridler (hosier), 1755: DL, Dec 16
Ridotto (entertainment), 1722: KING'S, Feb 15, Mar 6; 1768: HAY, Feb 15
Ridotto al'Fresco. See Cibber, Theophilus, Harlot's Progress.
Ridout, Isaac (actor), 1731: DL, Nov 25; 1732: DL, Mar 21, May 4, 12, 29, Jun
9, Aug 1, 4, 15, 17, Nov 4, Dec 14, 18, 22; 1733: DL, Feb 15, Apr 19, May 3,
5, 7, 15, BFMMO, Aug 23, DL/HAY, Oct 5, 6, 10, 12, 15, Dec 17, 19, 20; 1734:
DL/HAY, Feb 22, DL, Apr 22, HAY, May 27, BFHBH, Aug 24, CG/LIF, Sep 27, Oct
2, 9, 14, 18, 19, Nov 14, 25, Dec 26; 1735: CG/LIF, Jan 4, 25, May 9, 27, CG,
Oct 25, Nov 10, 17, 22; 1736: CG, Jan 9, Mar 27, LIF, Apr 16, CG, May 8, 17,
Sep 20, 29, Oct 6, Nov 1, 23; 1737: CG, Feb 26, Mar 31, Apr 11, 14, May 3,
20, 31, LIF, Jun 15, Jul 26, Aug 2, 5, CG, Sep 16, 30, Oct 22, Nov 2; 1738:
CG, Jan 13, 19, 25, 26, Feb 6, 16, 23, Mar 13, 25, Apr 10, 24, Sep 18, Oct
20, 24, Nov 6, DL, 13, 17, 18, 20, 29, 30, Dec 18; 1739: DL, Mar 10, 17, Apr
27, May 10, 16, 18, Sep 11, 14, 18, 21, 22, 24, Oct 6, 8, 9, 10, 13, 16, 17,
18, 20, Nov 5, 12, 15, 19, 20, 21, Dec 10, 26, 31; 1740: DL, Jan 3, 17, Feb
13, 14, Mar 11, Apr 17, 22, May 9, 14, 20, Sep 13, Oct 4, 13, 14, 15, Nov 1,
4, 10, 13, 19, 24, 27, 28, Dec 6, 8, 18, 20; 1741: DL, Jan 15, Feb 14, Mar

17, 21, 31, Apr 3, 27, Sep 19, 22, Oct 8, 9, 10, 12, 15, 20, 21, Nov 2, 4,
11, 18, 21, Dec 16, 19; 1742: DL, Jan 22, Feb 11, 13, Mar 9, 27, 29, Apr 19,
24, 28, 30, May 3, 12, 28, CG, Oct 11, 13, 15, Nov 4, 20, 25; 1743: CG, Jan
5, SOU, Feb 18, 25, CG, Mar 12, Apr 26, 28, Sep 21, 28, Oct 12, 17, 19, 28,
Nov 4, 16, 19, Dec 3, 8, 12, 17; 1744: CG, Jan 14, 24, Feb 3, 28, Mar 3, 8,
12, 13, Apr 26, May 9, 14, Sep 19, 26, Oct 1, 3, 5, 8, 10, 15, 18, 20, 24,
31, Nov 1, 5, 12, 21, 22, Dec 6, 17, 29; 1745: CG, Jan 14, Feb 11, 15, Mar
11, Apr 1, 17, 20, 23, 25, 26, 29, Sep 25, Oct 4, 7, 9, 14, 16, 31, Nov 4,
14, 15, 18, 22, 23, 28, Dec 7, 10, 13; 1746: CG, Jan 2, 7, 11, 13, Feb 8, Mar
4, 10, 13, Apr 1, 3, 7, 21, 23, Sep 29, Oct 3, 4, 10, 20, 24, 27, Nov 1, 4,
6, 11, 13, 26, Dec 2, 6, 17, 19, 20, 26, 29; 1747: CG, Jan 20, 26, 29, 31,
Feb 2, 3, Mar 7, 17, 26, Nov 13, 16, 23, Dec 4, 9, 15, 28; 1748: CG, Jan 2,
11, 12, 14, 16, 19, 27, 29, Feb 10, 15, Mar 14, Apr 11, 18, 21, 22, 29, Sep
21, 23, 28, 30, Oct 3, 10, 14, 17, 22, 25, 28, Nov 4, 9, 15, 16, 24, 26, Dec
1, 9, 10, 20, 22; 1749: CG, Jan 2, 11, 13, 28, Feb 23, Mar 2, 4, 9, 14, 31,
Apr 5, 7, 10, 21, May 4, Sep 25, 27, Oct 2, 4, 6, 9, 12, 16, 18, 19, 25, 26,
Nov 1, 3, 4, 8, 9, 11, 16, 18, 21, 23, Dec 8, 16, 28; 1750: CG, Jan 4, 16,
18, 23, 31, Feb 2, 5, Mar 1, 17, 20, 27, Apr 5, 23, 28, May 3, Sep 24, 28,
Oct 13, 16, 17, 18, 20, 22, 25, 26, Nov 5, 8, 12, 19, 22, 24, 29, Dec 1, 4,
10, 14, 18, 21; 1751: CG, Jan 1, 19, Feb 16, 23, Mar 16, Apr 10, 16, 19, 22,
27, May 1, 9, Sep 23, 25, Oct 7, 8, 9, 11, 21, 22, Nov 4, 6, 14, 16, 18, 21,
22, Dec 5, 16; 1752: CG, Jan 3, 28, Mar 3, 7, 17, 30, Apr 10, 15, 24, 28, 30,
Sep 22, 25, 29, Oct 4, 6, 9, 11, 12, 16, 19, 21, 23, 24, 30, Nov 1, 4, 7, 10,
16, 22, 23, 27, 28, Dec 9, 12, 13, 14, 19, 21, 27; 1753: CG, Jan 8, Feb 6,
12, Mar 20, 26, Apr 14, 23, May 7, 8, 11, 18, Sep 14, 17, 21, 24, 26, Oct 1,
8, 10, 17, 22, 24, 27, 30, 31, Nov 1, 5, 7, 12, 14, 20, 28, 30, Dec 26; 1754:
CG, Jan 10, 22, Feb 12, 23, Mar 9, 23, 25, Apr 2, 6, 17, 24, May 2, 7, 15,
Sep 18, 20, 23, 25, 27, Oct 2, 4, 7, 11, 14, 17, 18, 22, 24, 26, 29, Nov 1,
6, 7, 16, 20, 23, 27, 28, Dec 10, 13, 30; 1755: CG, Jan 4, 7, 10, 14, 28, Feb
4, 8, 18, 20, Mar 6, 18, Apr 2, 4, 8, 9, 10, 14, 15, 18, May 7, 15, Sep 29,
Oct 1, 3, 6, 8, 10, 14, 16, 20, 22, 24, 27, 30, Nov 7, 12, 13, 14, 17, 19,
21, 29, Dec 3, 4, 11; 1756: CG, Jan 6, 15, Feb 5, 9, 18, 19, 26, Mar 18, 23,
30, Apr 6, 20, 29, May 17, Sep 20, 24, 27, 29, Oct 1, 4, 6, 8, 11, 12, 15,
18, 19, 21, 22, 23, 25, 26, 28, 30, Nov 1, 11, 17, 22, Dec 7, 10; 1757: CG,
Jan 5, 14, 27, 28, Feb 9, 16, 19, Mar 14, Apr 27, Sep 14, 16, 23, 28, 30, Oct
5, 7, 8, 10, 12, 14, 15, 17, 19, 20, 21, 22, 27, Nov 2, 5, 7, 11, 16, 18, 23,
Dec 1, 5, 7, 9, 10, 14, 20; 1758: CG, Jan 11, 27, Feb 1, Mar 13, 14, 16, 27,
29, Apr 10, 14, 17, Sep 18, 20, 25, 27, Oct 4, 13, 14, 20, 23, 25, 26, 27,
30, Nov 1, 2, 7, 13, 14, 16, 21, 23, Dec 2, 18; 1759: CG, Jan 4, 11, 12, Feb
1, 15, Mar 3, 17, 24, 27, Apr 5, 7, 21, 28, May 8, 9, DL, 30, CG, Sep 24, 26,
28, Oct 5, Nov 23, 26, 28, 30, Dec 5, 12, 15, 17, 18, 19, 20, 28, 31; 1760:
CG, Jan 4, 9, 14, 24, 31, Feb 7, 28, Mar 6, 17, 18, 20, 25, Apr 7, 8, 17, 18,
24, 29, May 2, 8, Sep 22, 29, Oct 1, 6, 10, 14, 17, 18, 20, 25, Nov 18, 22,
Dec 2, 9, 22, 31; 1761: CG, Jan 7, 23, May 25, Dec 28
Ridout, Mary, Mrs Isaac (actor), 1741: DL, Dec 22, 28; 1742: DL, Jan 22, 25,
27, 29, Feb 1, 3, 13, Mar 2, 27, Apr 5, 24, 28, May 12, Sep 11, 16, 21, 25,
Oct 2, 5, 7, 13, 16, 25, Nov 1, 19, Dec 21, 22; 1743: DL, Jan 27, 28, Apr 7,
27, 29, 30, May 12, 16, 23, LIF, Jun 3, DL, Sep 15, 17, 20, 24, 29, Oct 1, 4,
6, 11, 20, 22, Nov 3, 8, 12, 17, 18, 23, 26, 29, Dec 1, 6, 12, 17; 1744: DL,
Mar 12, Apr 17, 18, 23, May 4, 11, 15, 22, Sep 15, 18, 20, 27, 29, Oct 2, 6,
9, 19, 27, 30, Nov 1, 2, 16, Dec 11, 19, 27; 1745: DL, Jan 4, 8, Mar 4, 14,
30, Apr 19, 24, May 1, 6, 7, 9, Sep 19, 21, 24, 26, Oct 3, 5, 8, 10, 15, 17,
19, Nov 4, 14, 22, 23, 26, 28, Dec 10, 12, 17, 20; 1746: DL, Apr 17, May 3,
12, Sep 23, Oct 4, 23, Nov 4, 21, Dec 1, 20, 30; 1747: DL, Mar 12, 23, Apr
22, May 5, 18, Sep 15, Nov 7, Dec 30; 1748: DL, Jan 22, Feb 3, Mar 10, 22,
CG, Sep 21, 23, 30, Oct 3, 10, 27, Nov 4, 11, 15; 1749: CG, Jan 25, Feb 6,
Mar 4, 29, 31, Apr 5, 11, 21, Oct 6, 11, 16, Nov 1, 3, 17, 21, 23, Dec 7, 28;
1750: CG, Jan 18, Mar 20, Apr 24, Sep 26, Oct 13, 15, 18, 20, 24, Nov 19, Dec
14; 1751: CG, Apr 22, May 16, Sep 23, Nov 6, 7, 18, 21, 26, Dec 10; 1752: CG,
Jan 3, 6, Mar 3, Apr 4, 30, May 4, Sep 20, Oct 9, 16, Nov 7, 29, Dec 11, 13,
14, 19, 27; 1753: CG, Feb 7, 12, Mar 20; 1756: DL, Jan 22
Riemschneider, Goffredo Giovanni (singer), 1729: KING'S, Dec 2; 1730: KING'S,
Feb 24, Apr 4
Rigadone Provencale (dance), 1736: DL, Apr 3, May 8; 1742: CG, Feb 26, Mar 25,
27, 30, Apr 20, 22, May 1, 11, 18
Rigadoon (dance), 1733: HAY, May 28; 1734: GF, Apr 19; 1736: CG, Apr 26, DL,
May 20; 1752: CG, Mar 19; 1753: DL, May 12; 1771: DL, Apr 22; 1776: CG, May
3; 1782: CG, Apr 27
Rigg (smith), 1749: DL, Nov 27
Riggs (musician), 1737: DL, Feb 1, Mar 22; 1741: DL, Jan 23
Right. See Wright.
Righteous Heaven (song), 1790: CG, Feb 26

Rights of Women, The (interlude, anon), 1792: CG, May 8, HAY, Aug 9
Riley (actor), 1783: HAY, Jun 6, 18, 27, Jul 4, 26, Aug 13, 29; 1784: HAY, Jun
    1, 2, 14, Jul 8, 12, 14, 20, 24, 28, 29, Aug 2, 19, Sep 2, 6, 13, 17; 1785:
    HAY, May 30, Jun 4, 7, 21, Jul 19, Aug 31, Sep 9; 1786: HAY, Jun 14, 23, Jul
    14, 18, 21
Riley, G (publisher), 1780: DL, May 24
Riley, Sarah (actor), 1784: HAY, Jun 14; 1785: HAY, Jul 19, Aug 4; 1786: HAY,
    Jun 13, 20, Jul 18
Rinaldo and Armida (dance), 1782: KING'S, Feb 23, 26, 28, Mar 14, 23, Apr 2, 6,
    13, 30, May 27, Jun 22
Rinaldo and Armida. See Dennis, John.
Rinaldo da Capua (composer), 1742: KING'S, Nov 2; 1748: KING'S, Nov 8
--Comedia in Comedia, La (burletta), 1748: KING'S, Nov 8, 12, 15, 26; 1749:
    KING'S, Jan 3, 7, 10, Mar 11, Jun 3
Rinaldo e Leonora (dance), 1800: KING'S, May 29, 30, Jun 7, 10, 24, Jul 12, 29
Rinaldo. See Handel, George Frederic; Sacchini, Antonio Maria Gasparo.
Ring and Pearl (residence), 1755: DL, Apr 26
Ring, The; or, Love Me for Myself. See Pavilion, The.
Rio che tumido ingrossa londa (song), 1714: QUEEN'S, Jun 23
Ripe Fruit. See Stuart, Charles.
Riposo del Campo, Il; or, The Recreations of the Camp (dance), 1783: KING'S,
    Mar 13, 15, 18, 20, 22, 25, 29, Apr 1, 5, 12, 24, May 3, 6, 10, 13, Jun 3,
    21, 28
Rippard (beneficiary), 1718: SH, Dec 23
Rise Glory Rise (song), 1733: DL/HAY, Oct 6; 1734: LIF, Aug 20; 1735: GF, Apr
    22, Oct 13, Nov 15; 1741: DL, Oct 24; 1744: DL, Dec 26; 1745: DL, Apr 25, Nov
    11, 15, 27; 1747: DL, Mar 21; 1750: CG, Apr 30, MARLY, Aug 16; 1752: CG, Mar
    9; 1754: DL, Mar 28, Apr 1; 1774: DL, Apr 15
Rise, Jephtha (song), 1791: CG, Mar 11
Rise, O God (song), 1789: DL, Mar 20
Rising Sun (public house), 1758: HAY, Jan 27; 1767: CG, Mar 31
Risk (actor), 1784: HAY, Feb 9
Ristori, Giovanni Alberto (composer), 1737: CG, Apr 13
Ristorini (singer), 1770: KING'S, May 19, Nov 17; 1771: KING'S, Feb 8, 9, Mar
    14, May 14; 1773: KING'S, Feb 5, CG, 26, Mar 3, 19
Ristorini, Sga (singer), 1770: KING'S, Nov 6, Dec 29; 1771: KING'S, Mar 14, May
    21, 28
Rites of Hecate, The. See Potter, John.
Ritorn' al Caro Bene (song), 1749: KING'S, Mar 21
Ritter (musician), 1774: KING'S, Feb 10
Riva (correspondent), 1729: KING'S, Dec 9
Rival Beaux, The; or, The Lover's Quarrel (play, anon), 1750: SFB, Sep 8, 10,
    SF, 11, SFB, 12
Rival Candidates, The. See Bate, Henry.
Rival Captains, The. See Phillips, Thomas.
Rival Clowns (dance), 1784: HAY, Apr 30, May 10; 1785: HAY, Feb 7, 21, 28, Mar
    7, 14, Apr 11
Rival Father, The. See Hatchett, William.
Rival Favourites, The. See Schomberg, Ralph.
Rival Fools, The. See Cibber, Colley.
Rival Kings, The. See Banks, John.
Rival Knights, The. See Bithmere, Augustin.
Rival Ladies, The. See Dryden, John.
Rival Lovers; or, The Gamester Bit, 1742: UM, Oct 4; 1748: BFP, Aug 24
Rival Milliners, The. See Drury, Robert.
Rival Modes, The. See Smythe, James Moore.
Rival Nymphs (dance), 1783: CG, May 24, 30, Nov 19; 1784: CG, Mar 18, Apr 21,
    30, May 15, 21, Oct 6, 13; 1785: CG, Mar 17
Rival Pierrots (dance), 1726: HAY, May 9
Rival Queans, The. See Cibber, Colley.
Rival Queens, The. See Lee, Nathaniel.
Rival Queens, The; or, Drury-Lane and Covent-Garden. See Holcroft, Thomas.
Rival Sisters, The. See Murphy, Arthur.
Rival Sisters, The; or, The Violence of Love. See Gould, Robert.
Rival Soldiers, The. See O'Keeffe, John.
Rival Suppose, Le. See Saint-Foix, Germain Francois Poulain de.
Rival Widows, The. See Cooper, Elizabeth.
Rivali Delusi, I. See Sarti, Giuseppe.
Rivals, The (dance), 1726: LIF, Apr 18; 1784: HAY, Jul 13, Sep 8
Rivals, The. See Davenant, Sir William; Sheridan, Richard Brinsley.
Rivals, The; or, The Happy Despair (entertainment), 1728: HAY, Feb 21, 23, 26,
    28, Mar 8, 13, 15, 20, 22, 27, Apr 3, 10, May 6

Rivaux Genereux (dance), 1798: KING'S, Mar 6, 13, May 15, Jun 16
River (printer), 1751: DL, Mar 19
Rivers (actor), 1781: CII, Mar 15, 27, 30, Apr 5, 9
Rivers (author), 1692: DL, Mar 0
Rivers (house servant), 1737: CG, May 19; 1738: CG, May 16; 1739: CG, May 29;
    1741: CG, May 8; 1742: CG, May 18; 1743: CG, May 11
Rivers, Mrs (actor), 1785: CG, Dec 5, 26; 1786: CG, Jan 4, May 15; 1787: HAY,
    Apr 30; 1789: HAY, Jun 30, Jul 30
Rivers, Widow, 1744: CG, May 14
Rivington (actor), 1780: HAY, Sep 25
Rivington (printer), 1766: CHAPEL, Apr 30
Rizzi, Marco (scene painter), 1710: QUEEN'S, Mar 23
Rizzio, David (composer), 1736: HIC, Apr 19; 1762: DL, May 11; 1785: CG, May
    12; 1786: CG, Oct 16; 1788: CG, Nov 6; 1789: CG, Sep 28; 1791: CG, May 18;
    1796: CG, Nov 5
Roach, J (publisher), 1794: CG, Apr 29; 1798: HAY, Jul 6
Roach, Miss (spectator), 1753: CG, Mar 24
Roach, Mrs (actor), 1773: HAY, Sep 20; 1778: HAY, Mar 23, Apr 30
Roachley, Mrs (actor), 1774: HAY, Sep 17
Road to Ruin, The. See Holcroft, Thomas.
Roades, Robert (musician), 1699: YB, Mar 29
Roan (actor), 1732: RIW/HAY, Sep 4
Roast Beef of Old England (song), 1735: CG/LIF, Apr 15, LIF, 19, CG/LIF, 22,
    May 2, 5, DL, 20, YB, Jun 3, LIF, Jul 11, 16, Aug 1, 22, 25, 29; 1736: HAY,
    Jan 14, LIF, Apr 2; 1738: CG, Apr 11, May 2, 10, HAY, Oct 9; 1739: CG, Apr
    27, May 18, 23; 1741: CG, May 6; 1742: CG, Mar 15; 1743: CG, Feb 23; 1751:
    CT, Dec 3; 1756: CG, May 14; 1757: CG, May 13; 1758: HAY, Mar 16, 1767: CG,
    Jun 9
Roast Beef of Old England, The; or, The Antigallican (dance), 1758: CG, Apr 20,
    May 4, 5; 1759: CG, Apr 21
Robbers, The; or, Harlequin Trapped by Colombine (entertainment), 1724: LIF,
    Mar 2
Robbins, Mrs (actor), 1718: LIF, Jan 4
Robe, Jane, 1723: LIF, Apr 23
--Fatal Legacy, The, 1723: LIF, Apr 23, 24, 26
Robens, John (composer), 1696: DG, Oct 0
Roberdeau, John Peter, 1791: HAY, Jun 20; 1792: CG, May 8; 1795: DL, May 29
--St Andrew's Festival; or, The Game at Goff, 1795: DL, May 29
Robert, J (publisher), 1749: DL, Feb 1
Robert, Mrs (beneficiary), 1726: HIC, Apr 1
Roberts (payee), 1772: CG, Jan 6
Roberts (spectator), 1700: LIF, Jan 29
Roberts (ticket deliverer), 1768: CG, May 28, DL, 30, CG, 30; 1769: DL, May 19,
    CG, 20, 22; 1770: CG, May 19, 22, DL, 28, 30; 1771: CG, May 25, DL, 28; 1772:
    CG, May 29, DL, Jun 5; 1773: CG, May 28, DL, 31; 1774: CG, May 24, DL, 26;
    1775: DL, May 24, CG, 27; 1776: DL, May 17, CG, 21; 1777: CG, May 23; 1778:
    CG, May 21; 1779: CG, May 15; 1780: CG, May 24; 1781: CG, May 25; 1782: CG,
    May 28; 1783: CG, May 31; 1784: CG, May 22; 1786: CG, May 31; 1787: CG, May
    19; 1788: CG, May 15; 1789: CG, Jun 6; 1792: CG, May 29; 1794: CG, May 31;
    1795: CG, Jun 13; 1796: CG, Jun 6; 1797: CG, May 25; 1798: CG, May 19; 1799:
    DL, May 4, CG, Jun 4; 1800: CG, Jun 10
Roberts, C (beneficiary), 1762: DL, May 18; 1765: DL, May 22; 1766: DL, May 19;
    1768: DL, May 25; 1769: DL, May 22
Roberts, C (shoemaker), 1771: DL, May 25, Oct 8, Dec 13; 1772: DL, May 13, Jun
    10; 1773: DL, Feb 9, Jun 2
Roberts, Elizabeth (actor), 1732: DL, Jun 1
Roberts, Ellis (actor, singer, dancer), 1722: DL, Feb 19, May 26; 1723: DL, Jan
    9, May 28, Jul 5, HA, 22, DL, Oct 24, Dec 5; 1724: RI, Jul 4, 13, 18, BFP,
    Aug 22, SF, Sep 5, DL, Dec 9; 1725: DL, Feb 1, BF, Aug 23, DL, Oct 21, Nov
    29; 1726: DL, Feb 2, May 11, 18; 1728: HAY, Feb 16, DL, Sep 14, Oct 12; 1729:
    DL, Jan 2, 11, 20, 31, May 7, 8, 16, Jun 13, 27, Jul 18, 25, BFLH, Aug 23,
    SF, Sep 15, DL, 20, 23, Nov 4, 21; 1730: DL, Jan 9, 26, Feb 28, Apr 29, May
    11, 13, 14, 27, GF, Jun 12, DL, Sep 24, 29, Oct 6, 20, HAY, Nov 9, 13, 16,
    30, Dec 7, 9, 17, 21; 1731: GF, May 7, DL, 12, Jun 7, 22, Jul 20, 23, Aug 6,
    SF/BFFHH, 24, DL, Sep 25, Oct 5, 16; 1732: DL, Apr 28, May 3, 4, 6, 8, GF,
    18, DL, 25, 29, Jun 1, 9, 23, Aug 1, 4, 15, 17, Sep 19, 21, 23, 28, 30, Oct
    5, 17, 26, Nov 4, 6, 14, 17, Dec 6, 11, 18, 20, 26; 1733: DL, Jan 8, 10, 25,
    26, Feb 3, 12, Mar 8, 15, 31, Apr 4, 27, 30, May 1, 3, 5, GF, 5, DL, 7, 9,
    10, 14, GF, 18, DL, 21, SF/BFLH, Aug 23, BFMMO, 23, DL, Sep 28, Oct 1,
    DL/HAY, 15, DL, 17, DL/HAY, 29, DL, 31, Nov 5, 14, DL/HAY, 24, DL, 26,
    DL/HAY, 26, Dec 3, DL, 5, 7, 11, 17, 21; 1734: DL/HAY, Jan 28, DL, Mar 7,
    DL/HAY, 21, HAY, Apr 3, 5, 17, DL, 29, GF, May 17, HAY, Jun 19, Aug 21, SFL,

Sep 7, CG/LIF, 23, 30, LIF, Oct 1, DL, 5, CG/LIF, 9, DL, 10, CG/LIF, 11, LIF,
12, CG/LIF, 14, 18, 19, DL, 22, CG/LIF, Nov 4, 28; 1735: DL, Mar 3, YB, 21,
DL, Apr 7, GF, May 6, DL, 6, 7, 9, 14, 20, 22, 23, 29, Jun 3, LIF, 12, DL,
Oct 31; 1736: DL, Jan 12, CG, 21, 23, HAY, Mar 5, CG, 27, LIF, 31, Apr 2, CG,
12, LIF, 16, HAY, 27, 29, CG, May 1, 3, DL, 3, GF, 4, CG, 6, 10, 11, DL, 13,
CG, 13, 14, 17, 24, HAY, 27, CG, Jun 3, 4, BFFH, Aug 23, DL, Oct 5, CG, 8,
20, DL, Dec 20; 1737: CG, Feb 14, HAY, Mar 5, CG, 10, HAY, 14, 21, CG, 26,
HAY, Apr 13, CG, 14, May 3, DL, 4, CG, 5, 12, LIF, 18, DL, 23, CG, Sep 26,
30, Oct 3; 1738: CG, Jan 3, Feb 13, Mar 14, Apr 11, 13, 19, May 5, 10, Aug
22, Oct 6, 28, Nov 18, 22, Dec 4, 5, 6, 7, 9, 11, 29; 1739: CG, Jan 6, 19,
20, Feb 10, 16, Mar 6, 20, 29, Apr 12, 26, May 4, 7, 14, 17, 18, Sep 5, 7,
14, 15, 21, 22, 27, 29, Oct 1, 3, 10, 22, 25, 26, 30, Nov 1, 5, 6, 7, 9, 20,
28, Dec 6, 10, 19, 21; 1740: CG, Jan 15, Feb 12, Mar 11, Apr 9, 14, 18, 21,
30, May 5, 23, Jun 5, Sep 19, 22, 26, Oct 1, 8, 10, Nov 4, 6, 20, Dec 4, 10;
1741: CG, Jan 5, 15, 21, 23, Feb 14, 17, 19, 24, Mar 2, 9, 12, Apr 7, 8, 9,
10, 13, 30, May 1, 2, 4, 11, 14, BFH, Aug 22, CG, Oct 17, 21, 24, Nov 7, Dec
3, 8, 9, 11, 16, 17, 18, 28; 1742: CG, Jan 2, 12, Mar 15, Apr 22, 23, May 3,
5, Oct 9, Dec 21; 1743: CG, Feb 24, Mar 8, 19, Apr 12, Dec 3; 1744: CG, Jan
14, Mar 3, Apr 12, Oct 1, Nov 3, Dec 8, 26, 29; 1745: CG, Jan 5, 12, 14, 25,
Apr 27, Sep 27, Nov 14, 15, Dec 13, GF, 28; 1746: CG, Jan 8, Apr 12, Nov 6,
Dec 29; 1747: CG, Mar 26, May 4, Nov 23; 1748: CG, Jan 27, Apr 13, 19, Dec
10; 1749: CG, Apr 18, May 4, Oct 12, Nov 23; 1750: CG, Mar 27, Apr 21, Oct
29, Nov 8, 24; 1751: CG, Apr 16, 27, May 3, Sep 30, Dec 9; 1752: CG, May 2,
Oct 10; 1753: CG, Apr 14, Oct 10; 1754: CG, Apr 18, May 2, Nov 16, 20; 1755:
CG, Apr 26, Oct 20, Nov 17; 1756: CG, May 4, 10, Oct 4, 6; 1757: CG, May 11,
Dec 7, 10; 1758: CG, Mar 7, Apr 10, 29, DL, May 17, CG, Nov 1; 1759: CG, May
5, DL, 28; 1760: CG, Jan 18, Apr 8, 17, May 6, DL, 12, 13, CG, Sep 29, Dec
11; 1761: CG, Apr 2, May 6, DL, 20, 21, CG, Sep 25, 26, Oct 13; 1762: CG, May
4, DL, 20, CG, Sep 22, Oct 8; 1763: CG, Jan 24, Apr 13, May 2, DL, 17, CG,
Sep 21, Nov 15; 1764: CG, Jan 4, May 4, DL, 21; 1765: CG, May 9, DL, 22;
1766: DL, May 19; 1767: DL, Jan 9, Feb 10, Jun 1; 1771: HAY, Apr 15
Roberts, Frank (musician), 1675: ATCOURT, Feb 15; 1693: ATCOURT, Apr 30; 1698:
   ROBERTS, Mar 23, YB, 30, DLLIF, Dec 13
Roberts, Henry (engraver), 1737: HAY, May 2
Roberts, James, 1794: HAY, Aug 18
--Rule Britannia! (entertainment), 1794: HAY, Aug 18, 19, 25, Sep 1, 4, 10
Roberts, John (actor), 1732: DL, Jan 28, May 17, Jun 1, Aug 21; 1734: HAY, Aug
   21; 1737: HAY, May 2; 1739: CG, May 17; 1742: CG, May 14
Roberts, Miss (actor), 1734: GF, Sep 25, Nov 18; 1735: GF, May 3, Nov 6; 1736:
   HAY, May 5; 1737: LIF, Apr 2, HAY, May 2, LIF, 7
Roberts, Miss (actor), 1770: HAY, Nov 21, Dec 19; 1771: HAY, Jan 28
Roberts, Mr and Mrs (beneficiaries), 1730: DL, May 18
Roberts, Mrs (actor), 1724: RI, Jun 29, Jul 4, 11, 13, BFP, Aug 22
Roberts, Mrs (actor), 1748: SFP, Sep 7; 1750: DL, Apr 19; 1770: DL, Nov 3, 8
Roberts, Mrs (actor), 1791: HAY, Oct 24
Roberts, Mrs John (actor, singer), 1729: DL, Feb 6, May 12, 16, 30, Jun 13,
   BFF, Aug 23, DL, Dec 30; 1730: DL, Feb 10, 14, 28, Mar 30, Apr 15, 20, May
   18, 21, BFOF, Aug 20, SFOF, Sep 9, DL, Oct 28, Nov 25, 30, Dec 4; 1731: DL,
   Mar 20, Apr 19, 26, May 1, 12, Aug 11, SF/BFMMO, 26, Sep 8, GF, 27, Oct 6, 8,
   11, 13, 18, 25, Nov 4, 5, 6, 8, 11, 13, 15, 18, 20, 22, Dec 6, 7, 8, 9, 13,
   20, 21, 28; 1732: GF, Jan 6, Feb 2, 19, 21, 29, Mar 4, 7, 16, 20, 27, 28, 30,
   Apr 10, 12, 17, 18, 19, 21, 27, 28, May 3, 4, 10, 15, Oct 6, 7, 9, 12, 14,
   16, 17, 18, Nov 3, 10, 27, 28, Dec 18, 20, 22; 1733: GF, Jan 1, 17, 18, 20,
   24, 27, Feb 5, 12, 13, 19, Mar 5, 6, 8, Apr 2, 3, 6, 11, 13, 16, 23, 24, May
   5, DL, 7, BFCGBH, Aug 23, Sep 4, GF, 14, 21, 27, Oct 3, 4, 8, 9, 11, 12, 15,
   18, 19, 22, 24, 25, 26, Nov 5, 7, 10, 13, 14, 27, Dec 13, 15, 26, 28; 1734:
   GF, Jan 3, 14, 19, 31, Feb 5, 7, 11, Mar 5, 18, 19, 25, Apr 18, 19, 24, 26,
   27, May 1, 3, 6, 10, 15, 16, HAY, Jun 3, 5, 7, 12, 17, 24, 28, Jul 5, 19, 26,
   31, Aug 7, 14, 16, LIF, 20, HAY, 22, BFRLCH, 24, Sep 2, GF, 9, RI, 12, GF,
   18, 20, 25, Nov 4, 6, 7, 11, 12, 13, 18, 22, 25, 27, Dec 2, 6, 12, 13, 16,
   20, 31; 1735: GF, Jan 1, 2, 6, 10, 13, 20, 24, Feb 6, 11, 22, 24, 25, Mar 10,
   13, 20, 29, DL, Apr 29, GF, May 8, 15, Sep 10, 15, 24, 26, Oct 6, 8, 15, 27,
   Nov 3, 4, 10, 11, 12, 14, 15, 19, 20, 24, 26, Dec 3, 4, 6, 8; 1736: GF, Jan
   29, Feb 4, 5, 10, 11, 12, 13, 16, 17, Mar 18, 20, 22, 25, 29, Apr 8, 16, 17,
   28, 29, CG, May 4, GF, 5, 13, LIF, Jun 8, Oct 23, 26, 28, Nov 4, 6, 9, 11,
   13, 16, 18, 24, 26, 27, 29, Dec 3, 7, 16, 20, 22, 31; 1737: LIF, Jan 10, 21,
   24, Feb 12, 14, 21, Mar 1, 21, 24, 26, 29, Apr 2, 12, 18, 21, 27, 29, 30, May
   2, 4, 6, 17, Jun 15, DL, Sep 20, 22, 29, Oct 1, 8, 20, 31, Nov 19; 1738: DL,
   Jan 14, Feb 2, 4, 8, Apr 26, May 2, 3, 6, 25, 29, Sep 14, 19, 21, 30, Oct 3,
   26, 30, Nov 4, 11, 20, Dec 12; 1739: DL, Jan 15, 31, Mar 10, 17, 27, 31, Apr
   12, 23, 30, May 14, Oct 9, 10, 13, 17, 18, 19, 20, Nov 5, Dec 22; 1740: DL,
   Jan 5, 19, Mar 13, 27, Apr 22, May 6, 9, 30, Sep 16, Oct 4, 15, 16, Nov 4, 8,

10, 19, Dec 6, 8; 1741: DL, Mar 30, Sep 24, Oct 20, Nov 4, 16, Dec 8, 14, 16, 19; 1742: DL, Feb 5, Mar 16, Apr 22, 24, Oct 13, 16, Nov 4, 8, 22; 1743: DL, Jan 10, 11, 27, Feb 4, Mar 3, 24, Apr 29, May 2, Sep 24, 27, 29, Oct 1, 4, 8, 15, 22, 27, Nov 4, 17, 24, Dec 15, 17, 19; 1744: DL, Jan 12, Mar 12, Apr 2, 23, May 11, HAY, Oct 20, DL, Nov 19
Roberts, Percy (actor), 1782: HAY, Sep 21, Dec 30
Roberts, Thomas (versifier), 1797: HAY, Feb 9
Robertson (actor), 1780: HAY, Apr 5
Robertson (beneficiary), 1767: DL, May 30
Robertson (prompter), 1758: CG, Apr 25; 1760: CG, Sep 22, Oct 25
Robertson, Mrs (actor), 1716: LIF, Apr 3; 1717: LIF, May 16, Nov 23, 26, Dec 12; 1718: LIF, Apr 19, May 3, Jul 24, Nov 11; 1719: LIF, Jan 16, Feb 7, 28, Nov 12, 21, 24, 26, Dec 31; 1720: LIF, Jan 11, 26, Feb 17, Mar 28, Apr 28
Robin Goodfellow; or, The Rival Sisters (pantomime, anon), 1738: DL, Oct 30, 31, Nov 1, 2, 3, 4, 6, 7, 8, 9, 11, 13, 14, 15, 16, 17, 18, 20, 21, 22, 23, 24, 25, 28, Dec 12, 13, 19, 22, 23, 26, 27, 29; 1739: DL, Feb 7, 8, 12, 23, Oct 10, 11, 12, 13, 16, 17, 18, 19, 20, 22, Nov 21, Dec 21, 27; 1740: DL, Jan 1, 3, 28, Feb 2, Oct 14, 15, 16, 17, Nov 1, 6, 10, 12, Dec 26; 1741: DL, Jan 7, 9; 1744: DL, Nov 7, 8, 9, Dec 11, 12, 14, 15, 26, 29, 31; 1745: DL, Jan 2, 4, 7
Robin Gray (dance), 1785: KING'S, Apr 14, 21, May 3, 7, Jun 28, Jul 2
Robin Hood. See Mendez, Moses; Macnally, Leonard.
Robin Hood (song), 1755: DL, May 2
Robin Hood and Little John (droll, anon), 1717: BF, Aug 26; 1730: BFLH, Aug 24, 31, SFG, Sep 8
Robin Hood Theatre, 1756: LRRH, Jan 28, 31, Feb 4, LRRH/PCR, 11
Robins (actor), 1780: HAY, Apr 5
Robins, Miss (actor), 1774: DL, Dec 1, 21, 22; 1775: DL, Jan 14, Mar 21, Oct 28, Nov 25, Dec 9
Robins, Mrs (actor), 1718: LIF, Feb 3, DL, Dec 3; 1719: DL, Jan 16, May 21
Robinson (actor), 1742: JS, Nov 8; 1744: MFHNT, May 1
Robinson (actor), 1778: CG, May 5
Robinson (actor), 1780: HAY, Nov 13
Robinson (actor), 1796: HAY, Feb 22
Robinson (beneficiary), 1715: DL, Jun 2; 1716: DL, May 30; 1717: DL, May 22; 1718: DL, May 21; 1719: DL, May 14; 1722: DL, May 22; 1724: DL, May 6
Robinson (beneficiary), 1762: HIC, Feb 12
Robinson (beneficiary), 1775: CG, May 27; 1776: CG, May 22; 1777: CG, May 24; 1778: CG, May 22; 1779: CG, May 19; 1780: CG, May 26; 1781: CG, May 26; 1782: CG, May 29; 1783: CG, Jun 4; 1784: CG, May 29
Robinson (dancer), 1706: HAW, Aug 10, 17
Robinson (dancer), 1755: DL, Nov 8, 12
Robinson (gallery doorkeeper), 1753: DL, May 17; 1754: DL, May 17, 21; 1755: DL, May 15; 1756: DL, May 18; 1757: DL, May 17; 1758: DL, May 16; 1760: DL, May 12; 1761: DL, May 25; 1762: DL, May 25; 1763: DL, May 13; 1764: DL, May 21, 22; 1765: DL, May 21; 1766: DL, May 21; 1768: DL, May 25; 1769: DL, May 22; 1770: DL, Jun 1; 1771: DL, May 30; 1772: DL, Jun 9; 1773: DL, Jun 2; 1774: DL, May 27; 1775: DL, May 18; 1776: DL, May 20; 1777: DL, Jun 4
Robinson (householder), 1755: DL, Apr 16
Robinson (musician), 1776: CHR, Oct 16
Robinson (organist), 1755: SOHO, Jan 16
Robinson (sub-treasurer), 1735: DL, May 23; 1736: DL, May 21; 1737: DL, May 25
Robinson (ticket deliverer), 1799: DL, Jul 2; 1800: DL, Jun 13
Robinson (wine merchant), 1766: CG, Nov 20
Robinson and Co (ornament maker), 1772: CG, Nov 28
Robinson Crusoe. See Sheridan, Richard Brinsley.
Robinson, Anastasia (singer), 1713: QUEEN'S, Jun 9, 20; 1714: QUEEN'S, Jan 27, Mar 4, Apr 3, 10, 24, May 1, 29, Jun 23, KING'S, Oct 23, Nov 20, Dec 11, 30; 1715: KING'S, Feb 26, HIC, Mar 31, KING'S, Apr 9, May 25, Jun 11; 1716: KING'S, Feb 16, Mar 3, 10, Apr 18; 1717: KING'S, Jan 5, Feb 2, 16, Mar 21, Apr 11; 1718: KING'S, Mar 15, Apr 5, LIF, Jun 20; 1719: KING'S, Feb 21, 28, Mar 21, DL, Oct 1, 3, Nov 24; 1720: DL, Feb 2, Mar 8, KING'S, Apr 2, 27, DL, May 17, KING'S, 30; 1721: KING'S, Mar 28, Apr 15, May 20, Jun 14, Dec 9; 1722: KING'S, Jan 10, Feb 15, 22, Mar 6; 1723: BUH, Jan 11, KING'S, 12, Feb 19, DL, Mar 20, KING'S, 30, May 14, Nov 27; 1724: KING'S, Jan 14, Feb 20, Apr 18, May 21; 1725: DL, Mar 18, Dec 8; 1726: DL, Jan 1, 8, 18, Feb 11, Apr 25, 28, Oct 1, Nov 24; 1727: DL, May 24; 1729: LIF, Mar 19, DL, 26
Robinson, Ann Turner (singer), 1720: KING'S, Apr 2, 27, May 30; 1723: DL, Mar 20; 1729: DL, Mar 26; 1732: KING'S, May 2
Robinson, Captain (spectator, wounded in fight), 1751: DL, Sep 21
Robinson, G G and J (publishers), 1778: HAY, Jun 10; 1781: CG, Oct 13; 1784: HAY, Aug 2, CG, Dec 14; 1785: CG, Apr 2, HAY, Aug 4, CG, Oct 22, 26, Nov 10;

1786: CG, May 20, HAY, Jun 20, CG, Nov 18, DL, 25; 1787: CG, Feb 10, DL, Mar
12, CG, May 22, Jun 15, HAY, Aug 4, CG, Oct 11, DL, Nov 10; 1788: DL, Jan 31,
HAY, Jul 2, 10, CG, Nov 28; 1789: HAY, Jul 15; 1790: HAY, Jun 26, Jul 06, CG,
Nov 11; 1791: CG, Feb 4, HAY, Jul 9, CG, Dec 3; 1793: CG, Jan 29; 1794: DL,
Jun 9, Nov 1; 1795: CG, May 2; 1796: DL, Jan 23; 1797: CG, Mar 4, DL, Apr 19,
May 1, HAY, Aug 15, DL, Oct 21; 1798: DL, Jan 25, CG, Feb 13, HAY, Jun 23,
Jul 21, CG, Oct 11; 1799: CG, Mar 16, Nov 14, 30
Robinson, George (masonic treasurer), 1732: HAY, Apr 19
Robinson, Hannah Henrietta (actor), 1778: HAY, Jan 26, Mar 24, Apr 30; 1779:
HAY, Feb 22; 1780: HAY, Mar 28; 1782: CG, Dec 31; 1783: CG, Jan 27, Feb 24,
25, Apr 23, May 7, 9
Robinson, J (printer), 1749: DL, Apr 1, Dec 4; 1750: DL, Nov 28; 1756: DL, May
18
Robinson, Sir John (Lord Mayor), 1662: CITY, Oct 29
Robinson, Mary, Mrs Thomas (actor, author), 1776: DL, Dec 10; 1777: DL, Feb 17,
24, Apr 10, Sep 30, Oct 7, 9, Dec 15; 1778: DL, Jan 10, Apr 9, 20, 23, 30,
May 23, Sep 19, Oct 15, 26, Nov 11, 14, Dec 21; 1779: DL, Feb 3, 8, 11, Apr
13, 14, 21, May 10, 15, Jun 1, Sep 18, 25, Oct 9, 23, Nov 6, 8, 9, 17, 18,
20, Dec 27; 1780: DL, Jan 28, 29, Apr 1, 3, 7, 17, 18, May 4, 24, 31; 1794:
DL, Jul 2, Nov 29
--Lucky Escape, The (opera), 1778: DL, Apr 30
--Nobody (farce), 1794: DL, Nov 10, 18, 20, 25, 26, 28, 29, Dec 1, 5, 6
Robinson, Master (actor), 1739: KING'S, Apr 4
Robinson, Miss (actor), 1773: DL, Oct 22
Robinson, Miss (actor, musician, dancer), 1722: DL, May 22; 1724: DL, Dec 18,
21, 30; 1725: DL, Jan 25, 29, Feb 9, Mar 4, 31, Apr 2, 5, 7, 15, 19, 21, 23,
27, 28, 29, 30, May 3, 4, 5, 10, 11, 12, 19, 21, Sep 9, 14, 25, Oct 2, 7, 12,
14, 15, 18, 23, 25, 28, Nov 3, 16, 25, Dec 4, 6, 16, 21; 1726: DL, Jan 5, 24,
25, Feb 8, 11, Mar 17, 24, 28, 31, Apr 15, 18, 19, 21, 22, 23, 26, 27, 28,
29, 30, May 2, 3, 4, 5, 7, 9, 10, 11, 12, 13, 16, 19, 20, 23, 25, Jun 3, Sep
13, 15, 20, 29, Oct 4, 6, 15, 27, Nov 2, 23, 30, Dec 6, 7, 12, 14, 17, 26,
30; 1727: DL, Feb 8, 10, 18, 20, 27, Mar 23, Apr 6, 7, 8, 10, 12, 18, 19, 20,
22, 24, 25, 26, 28, May 1, 2, 3, 4, 8, 10, 15, 17, 19, 22, 26, 31, Oct 23,
Nov 14, 22; 1728: DL, Feb 21, Mar 30, Apr 24, 25, May 1, 6, 17, 22, Jun 13,
Sep 12, 19, 26, Oct 10, 17, 18, 21, 24, 30, 31, Nov 7, 8, 12, 15; 1729: DL,
Jan 27, 31, Feb 25, Mar 13, 18, 25, 27, Apr 10, 19, 22, 23, 30, May 1, 2, 14,
Jun 13, 20, Sep 23, Oct 9, 25, 30, Nov 3, 22, Dec 8, 10, 12; 1730: DL, Jan 9,
Apr 10, 14, 16, 20, 22, 24, 25, 29, 30, May 1, 2, 11, 13, 15, 18, 19, 27, Sep
15, 26, 29, Oct 8, 10, 22, 28, Nov 30, Dec 3, 4; 1731: DL, Jan 23, 27, Feb
17, 22, Mar 15, 25, 29, Apr 1, 5, 8, 19, 21, 22, 26, May 19, Sep 23, Oct 16,
26, Nov 11, 22, 25, Dec 2, 15, 28, 29; 1732: DL, Feb 2, Mar 4, 6, 23, 27, 30,
Apr 17, 18, 19, 21, 22, 24, 25, 26, 27, 28, 29, May 1, 2, 3, 4, 6, 9, 12,
KING'S, Jun 10, DL, Sep 23, Oct 17, 19, 21, 26, Nov 7, 8, 10, 14, 25, Dec 26;
1733: DL, Jan 11, 17, 23, 25, 31, Feb 2, 12, 22, 26, Mar 5, 15, 26, 28, 29,
HAY, 29, DL, 31, Apr 4, 16, 24, 30, May 1, 2, 3, 5, 7, 9, 14, 18, 21, DL/HAY,
Sep 26, Oct 3, 6, 12, 13, 25, 27, Nov 1, 8, 12, 14, 15, 17, HAY, 19, DL/HAY,
24, 26, 28, Dec 1, 3, 5, 12, HAY, 13, DL/HAY, 20, 22, 28, 31; 1734: DL/HAY,
Jan 1, 7, 10, 12, 16, 23, 28, 29, Feb 4, 6, HAY, 12, DL/HAY, 20, Mar 4, 5, 9,
12, 16, 18, 19, 26, 30, Apr 1, 2, DL, 4; 1735: YB, Mar 21; 1741: TC, Aug 4;
1744: KING'S, Jun 9, Nov 3; 1745: KING'S, Jan 5, Mar 1, 27, CG, Apr 10,
KING'S, May 4; 1762: HIC, Feb 12
Robinson Jr, Miss (dancer), 1725: DL, Jan 9, Apr 30, May 10, 12, Oct 16; 1726:
DL, May 9, 11, Jun 3, Nov 2, Dec 30; 1727: DL, Feb 21, 27, Apr 22, 24, May 1,
12, Sep 9, Nov 14; 1728: DL, Jan 5, Feb 16, 21, 27, Mar 2, 16, 19, 21, 25,
Apr 1, May 9, 13, 15, 17, 20, 23, Jun 13, Sep 17, Oct 15, 18, 21, Nov 15;
1729: DL, Jan 2, 14, Mar 10, May 5, 26, Jun 20, 24, Aug 7
Robinson Sr, Miss (dancer), 1728: DL, Apr 1, 4, 8, 11, 23, May 9, 10, 13, 15,
16, 22, Sep 17, Nov 15; 1729: DL, Jan 14, Mar 10, 22, 24, May 5, 26
Robinson, Misses Sr and Jr (dancers), 1728: DL, May 15
Robinson, Mrs (actor), 1696: LIF, Nov 14, Dec 0
Robinson, Mrs (actor), 1771: DL, Nov 14; 1772: DL, Oct 15, Nov 28; 1773: DL,
Jan 19, Feb 2, 18, Oct 22, 30, Nov 24, Dec 15, 16; 1774: DL, Jan 22
Robinson, Mrs (actor), 1780: CII, Mar 27, Apr 5, 19; 1784: HAY, Jan 21; 1785:
HAY, Mar 15
Robinson, Mrs William, 1778: DL, May 26
Robinson, Robert (scene painter), 1700: DL, May 16
Robinson, Sir Thomas (renter), 1758: CG, Mar 16
Robinson, Widow, 1737: CG, Jan 17
Robinson, 1787: HAY, Aug 17
--Test of Love, The (farce), 1787: HAY, Aug 17
Robley (householder), 1785: CG, Apr 25
Robson (music porter), 1791: CG, Jun 14; 1792: CG, Jun 1; 1794: CG, Jun 16;

1795: CG, Jun 13; 1796: CG, Jun 3; 1797: CG, May 27; 1798: CG, May 31; 1799: CG, May 22; 1800: CG, Jun 7

Robson (paper hanger), 1795: CG, Oct 24

Robson (pit doorkeeper), 1768: CG, May 28, 30; 1769: CG, May 20, 22; 1770: CG, May 19, 22; 1771: CG, May 27; 1772: CG, May 29; 1773: CG, May 28; 1774: CG, May 14; 1775: CG, May 30; 1776: CG, May 22; 1777: CG, May 24; 1778: CG, May 22; 1779: CG, May 19; 1780: CG, May 26; 1781: CG, May 26; 1782: CG, May 29; 1783: CG, Jun 4; 1784: CG, May 29; 1786: CG, May 31; 1787: CG, May 28; 1788: CG, May 17; 1789: CG, Jun 16; 1790: CG, Jun 12; 1791: CG, Jun 9; 1792: CG, May 29; 1794: CG, Jun 14; 1795: CG, Jun 17; 1796: CG, Jun 4; 1797: CG, Jun 8; 1798: CG, Jun 5; 1799: CG, Jun 8; 1800: CG, Jun 10

Robson (ticket deliverer), 1799: DL, Jul 2; 1800: DL, Jun 13

Robson, Horatio Edgar, 1784: CG, May 10; 1786: CG, May 9; 1788: HAY, Aug 22; 1789: CG, Mar 31; 1793: CG, Apr 25

--Look before You Leap (farce), 1788: CG, Apr 11, HAY, Aug 22; 1789: CG, Mar 31

--Money at a Pinch; or, The Irishman's Frolicks, 1793: CG, Apr 25

--Too Loving by Half (opera), 1784: CG, May 10

Robson, James (publisher), 1777: DL, Mar 11; 1780: DL, Nov 22; 1788: DL, Mar 29; 1793: CG, Nov 13

Robson, Thomas (actor), 1770: HAY, May 28, Jun 18, 22, Jul 9, Aug 8, Oct 5; 1771: HAY, May 15, 17, 22, 23, 27, 29, Jun 5, 7, 10, Jul 1, 5, 10, 15, 24, Aug 19, 28, Sep 2, 16; 1772: HAY, May 18, 27, Jun 5, 8, 10, 15, 22, 29, Jul 10, 15, 27, Aug 4, 10, Sep 8; 1776: CG, Oct 7, 17, 25, 31, Nov 9, 13, 14, 18, 30, Dec 18, 27; 1777: CG, Jan 1, 4, Feb 25, Apr 7, 16, 28, May 2, 5, 7, Oct 15, 30, Nov 1, 6, Dec 3, 10, 20; 1778: CG, Jan 3, 15, 20, 21, 27, Feb 4, 6, 10, 23, 25, 26, 28, Mar 23, 30, Apr 7, 22, 29, May 5, 7, 9, 11, 15, Sep 25, 28, Oct 26, 31, Nov 4, 21, Dec 1, 2, 17, 21, 26; 1779: CG, Jan 2, 11, 19, 22, Feb 2, 18, 22, Mar 4, Apr 5, 13, 21, 24, 26, 30, May 3, 6, 13, Sep 20, 24, 27, Oct 1, 6, 16, 20, 23, Nov 1, 8, 10, 13, 19, 22, 23, 25, 26, 30, Dec 7, 11, 16, 18, 23, 29, 31; 1780: CG, Jan 12, 18, 25, Feb 2, 5, 8, 17, 22, Mar 14, 27, 29, Apr 1, 19, 21, 25, 28, May 24, Jun 1, Sep 18, 21, Oct 2, 3, 4, 9, 13, 19, 23, 24, 26, 30, Nov 1, 4, 8, 10, 13, 15, 24, 28, Dec 9, 15, 16, 27; 1781: CG, Jan 13, 31, Mar 8, 24, Apr 2, 3, May 7, 16, Sep 17, 19, 24, 26, HAY, Oct 16, CG, 23, 25, 30, 31, Nov 2, 5, 7, 12, 28, Dec 5, 8, 10, 11, 17, 20, 31; 1782: CG, Jan 4, 7, 9, Feb 5, 9, Mar 19, Apr 1, 4, 9, 10, 12, 24, May 6, 7, 11, 20; 1783: HAY, Sep 17; 1784: HAY, Jan 21; 1786: HAY, Jul 25

Roch, Elizabeth (actor), 1676: DL, Jan 29

Roche (actor), 1778: HAY, Apr 29

Roche-Guilhen, Mme de la, 1677: ATCOURT, May 22

--Rare en Tout, 1677: ATCOURT, May 29, DG, Jun 0

Roche, Mrs (actor), 1773: HAY, Sep 18; 1777: HAY, Oct 9

Rochefort, Jean Baptiste (composer), 1790: CG, Oct 4

Rochester Theatre, 1799: CG, Sep 18

Rochester, Bishop of, 1661: LIF, Dec 16

Rochester, Earl of. See Wilmot, John.

Rochester, Lady. See Wilmot, Elizabeth Mallet.

Rochetti, Gaetano Phillipo (singer, dancer), 1724: LIF, Nov 21; 1725: LIF, Jan 5, 21, Mar 15, 18, Apr 5, 12, 15, May 27, Nov 13; 1726: HAY, Mar 4, LIF, Sep 23, Nov 19, 26, Dec 9; 1727: LIF, Feb 13, Apr 24, 27, Sep 29, Nov 9; 1728: LIF, May 15, Oct 14; 1729: LIF, Jan 18, HIC, Apr 30, LIF, Nov 1, 4; 1730: LIF, May 14, Jun 12, Oct 9, Nov 7, Dec 15, 30; 1731: LIF, Mar 26, Apr 3, May 20, Sep 27, Oct 4, Nov 13, 18, Dec 1, 29; 1732: LIF, Apr 28, LIF/CG, Oct 30, Nov 8, 24; 1733: LIF/CG, Apr 20, May 3; 1734: CG, Jan 25, Feb 13, LIF, 26, CG, Apr 26, LIF, May 11; 1735: CG/LIF, Apr 7; 1739: CG, Mar 10, May 10, Dec 4, 10; 1740: HAY, Jan 22, Mar 15, May 10; 1741: CG, Jan 21; 1744: HIC, May 16

Rochfort (dancer), 1757: CG, Dec 10; 1758: CG, Feb 1, Apr 28, Oct 14, Nov 16, 23; 1759: CG, Dec 10; 1760: CG, Jan 16, 18, Apr 17, Sep 22, Oct 20, Dec 11; 1761: CG, Mar 9, Apr 2, May 25, Sep 16, 21, 26; 1762: CG, May 11; 1772: DL, Oct 23

Rochfort (Rotchford) (dancer), 1786: KING'S, Jun 1, 20, Jul 1, HAY, 3

Rock, Edward Anthony (actor), 1786: CG, Nov 15, 21, Dec 11; 1787: CG, Jan 27, Apr 30, Jun 5, Sep 17, 24, Oct 1, 3, 22, 31, Nov 5, 9, Dec 3, 21; 1788: CG, Jan 21, Feb 9, Mar 1, 11, 26, Apr 23, May 12, 13, 14, Jun 3, Sep 15, 17, 22, Oct 1, 8, 13, Nov 6, 10, 12, 17, 22, 27, Dec 15, 26, 27, 29; 1789: CG, Jan 23, Feb 3, 6, 21, Mar 3, 31, Apr 4, 14, 20, 21, 30, May 2, 12, 20, Jun 5, 16, 18, Sep 14, 23, 25, Oct 2, 7, 9, 12, 20, 23, 24, 30, 31, Nov 2, 7, 10, 11, 13, Dec 2, 21; 1790: CG, Jan 18, 22, 23, Feb 11, Mar 1, 8, 13, 18, 27, Apr 16, May 6, 7, 27, Jun 4, 12, Jul 16, Sep 13, 17, 29, Oct 1, 4, 6, 11, 13, 15, 19, 30, Nov 4, 11, 15, 26, Dec 11, 20, 22; 1791: CG, Jan 3, 14, 15, Apr 16, 28, May 2, 5, 6, 14, 26, Jun 1, HAY, 20, Jul 4, 15, 20, 30, Aug 2, 13, 16, 24, Sep 2, CG, 17, 20, 23, 26, 30, Oct 10, 12, 19, 21, Nov 4, 9, 15, 24, 29, Dec 2, 22, 26; 1792: CG, Feb 18, 23, 28, Mar 6, 31, Apr 10, 12, 18, May 1,

718

28, Sep 20, 24, 26, Oct 5, 8, 10, 24, 26, 29, Nov 3, 10, 24, Dec 13, 15, 26;
    1793: CG, Jan 1, 2, 9, 25, Mar 23, Apr 4, 8, May 4, 10, 27, Jun 6, Sep 17,
    25, 30, Oct 1, 2, 4, 7, 12, 16, 21, 23, 30, Nov 1, 2, 7, 18, 19, 23, 30, Dec
    5, 6, 17, 19; 1794: CG, Jan 2, 22, Feb 22, 26, Apr 29, May 6, 23, 26, Jun 11,
    Sep 15, 19, 22, 24, 26, Oct 3, 20, 22, 30; 1795: CG, Jan 29, 31, Feb 3, 4,
    14, Mar 16, 19, Apr 8, May 22, 29, Jun 6, 12
Rock, Mrs (actor), 1787: CG, Dec 26; 1788: CG, Mar 24, Oct 10, 22, Nov 7, 20,
    26, Dec 31; 1789: CG, Feb 11, Apr 4, 15, 20, 30, May 8, Oct 13, 23, Nov 12,
    20, 27, 28, Dec 31; 1790: CG, Apr 21, 24, May 5, Jun 11, Jul 16, Sep 17, 29,
    Oct 4, 13, 20, Nov 1; 1791: CG, Jan 12, 14, 26, Mar 5, 12, 14, Apr 11, 28,
    May 6, 19, 24, Jun 14, Sep 14, 16, 21, 23, 28, Oct 6, 27, Dec 3, 21, 22;
    1792: CG, Feb 2, 8, May 12, 15, Jun 2, Sep 19, 21, 26, 28, Oct 8, 10, 19, 24,
    29, Dec 20, 26; 1793: CG, Apr 8, 15, Jun 12
Rodelinda. See Handel, George Frederic.
Rodney, Admiral Sir George Brydges, 1781: DL, Mar 31
Rodogune. See Corneille, Pierre.
Rodolfe (musician), 1770: KING'S, Mar 1, CG, 2, KING'S, 8, 22
Roe Buck (public house), 1754: DL, Mar 27
Roebuck (actor), 1756: BFSI, Sep 3
Roehampton, 1744: DL, Apr 28
Roffe (house servant), 1769: CG, May 19; 1770: CG, May 18; 1771: CG, May 28;
    1773: CG, May 19
Roffey (dancer, actor), 1794: DL, Oct 9, 22, Nov 6, 10, Dec 20; 1795: DL, Jan
    19, Feb 12, Jun 5, Oct 21, 30; 1796: DL, Jan 18, Jun 10, KING'S, Jul 7, 12,
    DL, Oct 1, 29, Nov 9, Dec 26; 1797: DL, Jun 5, 10; 1798: DL, Jan 16, Feb 20,
    May 16, 21, Oct 6, Nov 14, Dec 6; 1799: DL, Jan 19, Feb 5, Oct 14, 21; 1800:
    DL, Mar 10, 11, 31
Roffey, Mrs (actor), 1797: DL, Jan 4, 7, 19, 20, 27, Feb 1, 7, 9, 16, 23, Mar
    4, May 19, 29, Jun 10, Sep 21, 23, 26, Oct 5, 12, 26, Nov 8, 17, 18, Dec 9;
    1798: DL, Jan 16, Feb 20, May 11, Sep 20, 22, Oct 2, 6, 11, Nov 10, 14, 26,
    29, Dec 4, 29; 1799: DL, Jan 19, Mar 2, May 24, Sep 17, Oct 1, 8, 14, 19, 31,
    Nov 14, Dec 11; 1800: DL, Jan 1, Mar 4, 11, Apr 29, May 19
Rogeir, Mrs (actor, dancer), 1721: DL, Aug 1, 4, 8, 15, LIF, Oct 3, 17, Nov 13,
    18, Dec 11, 12, 14, 18; 1722: LIF, Jan 1, 13, 15, Mar 13, 29, 31, Apr 6, 11,
    20, 24, 26, May 2, 7, 8, 10, 18, 25, Jun 1, Oct 2, 16, 19, 22, 24, 29, 30,
    31, Nov 7, 15, 16, Dec 13, 14, 21, 31; 1723: LIF, Jan 11, Feb 13, 19, Mar 25,
    Apr 27, May 6, 15, 18, Oct 7, 10, 16, 19, 25, 29, Nov 2, 8, 12, 16, 18, 19,
    22, 27, 28, Dec 3, 9, 11, 20; 1724: LIF, Jan 3, 4, Mar 2, 16, 23, 28, Apr 6,
    7, 8, 10, 21, 22, 23, 24, 27, 28, May 2, 4, 5, 12, 13, 15, 16, 18, 19, 20,
    22, 25, 27, 28, 29, Jun 3, Nov 3, 10
Roger (actor), 1777: CHR, Jun 20
Roger (choreographer)
--Diana and Acteon (pantomime), 1730: DL, Apr 23; 1734: GF, Apr 19, May 3
--Harlequin Grand Volgi (pantomime), 1735: DL, Sep 15, 16, Nov 13; 1738: DL,
    Jan 24, 25, 28, 31, Feb 1, 2, 3, 4, 11, 13, 14, May 24, Oct 3, 5, 7, Nov 10;
    1739: DL, Nov 22, 23, 24, 26, 27, Dec 5, 13, 18, 28; 1740: DL, Jan 2, 4, 12,
    TC, Aug 4; 1744: DL, Jan 17, 18, 20, 21, 23, 25
--Harlequin Happy and Poor Pierrot Married (pantomime), 1728: DL, Mar 11, 12,
    19, Apr 6, 9, 13, 22, 26, May 11, 20, 24, 31, Oct 18, Nov 1; 1729: DL, Jan
    13, 15, 18, 25, 28, Feb 1, 4, Mar 8, Nov 19, 27; 1736: DL, Dec 4, 6
Roger (dancer), 1742: DL, May 1; 1745: DL, Dec 17; 1746: DL, Mar 3, Apr 2, 26;
    1747: DL, Jan 24, May 5; 1748: DL, May 6, Oct 15; 1749: DL, Jan 27, Apr 10;
    1750: DL, Nov 13, 27; 1751: DL, May 4, Dec 26; 1752: DL, Jan 28, HAY, Apr 2,
    DL, May 1; 1753: DL, May 12; 1754: DL, May 15; 1757: DL, May 10; 1758: DL,
    May 11; 1763: HAY, Aug 8
Roger (dancer, actor), 1720: KING'S, May 3, Jun 9; 1721: HAY, Feb 21, 27, Mar
    6, 23; 1725: HAY, Jan 22, Feb 5, Mar 8, 18, Apr 9, 14, 16, May 7, DL, Sep 28,
    Oct 19, 25, 28, Nov 16, 19, Dec 6; 1726: DL, Feb 11, Mar 21, 24, 31, Apr 13,
    15, May 4, 5, 6, 9, 13, 19, 20, 23, 25, Jun 3, Sep 20, 29, Oct 1, 11, 15, 27,
    Nov 2, 15, 30, Dec 7, 12, 29, 30; 1727: DL, Feb 8, 20, 27, Mar 23, Apr 6, 7,
    8, 10, 12, 15, 17, 19, 20, 21, 22, 24, 25, May 1, 5, 8, 22, Sep 26, Oct 6,
    12, 19, 30, Nov 1, 14, 21; 1728: DL, Feb 21, 27, Mar 14, 19, 21, Apr 6, 9,
    26, May 1, 3, 6, 7, 8, 11, 13, 16, 17, 20, 22, Oct 10, 18, 30, Nov 8, 15;
    1729: DL, Jan 13, 27, 31, Mar 13, 15, 18, 22, 25, 27, Apr 9, 19, 22, 25, May
    2, 8, Nov 3, Dec 8, 10, 12, 26; 1730: DL, Apr 4, 11, 13, 14, 15, 18, 22, 23,
    24, 25, 29, 30, May 1, 2, 4, 11, 13, 15, 19, 21, 27, Sep 15, 17, 24, Oct 8,
    10, 22, 28, Nov 6, 19, 23, Dec 4; 1731: DL, Jan 11, Mar 30, Apr 27, Dec 4;
    1733: HAY, May 28; 1734: GF, Apr 19
Roger a Coverly (dance), 1702: LIF, Dec 29
Roger and Dolly (song), 1715: DL, Jul 1, 15
Roger, Miss (actor), 1745: DL, Dec 4
Roger, Mrs (dancer), 1728: DL, Oct 18; 1730: DL, Apr 23, May 15; 1732: DL, Feb

22, Mar 21, Aug 1
Roger, Young (actor), 1726: DL, Feb 26
Roger's Courtship to Dolly (song), 1736: HAY, Jul 7
Roger's Wedding (masque), 1710: QUEEN'S, Apr 11
Rogers (actor), 1697: DL, Feb 0, Jul 0, Sep 0
Rogers (actor), 1715: LIF, Jun 23, Oct 11, 24, Dec 12; 1716: LIF, Apr 3, May
   11; 1717: LIF, Jan 8, 28, Feb 11, Apr 6, Nov 14, Dec 14; 1718: LIF, Apr 29,
   Jul 24; 1720: LIF, Jun 2, DL, Dec 17; 1721: DL, May 20, SF, Sep 8; 1722: LIF,
   Feb 13; 1724: LIF, Jun 3; 1725: LIF, May 22
Rogers (actor), 1735: HAY, Dec 13
Rogers (actor), 1770: HAY, Oct 1
Rogers (actor), 1782: HAY, Mar 4
Rogers (beneficiary), 1731: DL, Apr 10; 1732: DL, May 17; 1733: DL, May 10;
   1734: LIF, May 9; 1738: DL, May 31; 1739: DL, May 30; 1741: DL, May 15; 1743:
   LIF, Mar 14
Rogers (composer), 1670: NONE, Sep 0
Rogers (haberdasher), 1773: CG, Oct 18
Rogers (ticket deliverer), 1800: DL, Jun 14
Rogers, Benjamin (composer), 1782: CG, Nov 25; 1783: CG, Jan 18; 1791: CG, May
   18; 1798: CG, Mar 9; 1799: CG, Mar 1
Rogers, Elizabeth (actor), 1760: DL, Apr 23, May 1, Jun 19, Oct 9; 1761: DL,
   Jan 31, Sep 14, 25, 26, Dec 11, 28; 1762: DL, Apr 28, May 4, 5, 6, 22, Oct 5,
   Nov 3, 5, 10, 23, 27, Dec 10; 1763: DL, Jan 14, 27, Mar 21, Apr 30, Oct 4,
   24, 28, Nov 23, 26, 29, Dec 20; 1764: DL, Jan 4, 18, Feb 14, 20, May 4, 23,
   24, 29, Sep 18, 20, 22, 25, Oct 23, Nov 9, 13, 27, Dec 26; 1765: DL, Feb 15,
   Mar 7, 18, Apr 13, 16, 22, Sep 21, 24, Oct 8, 14, Dec 14; 1766: DL, Jan 24,
   Mar 20, 22, May 5, 7, Sep 23, 27, Oct 28, 29, Dec 4; 1767: DL, Jan 2, Feb 7,
   Mar 24, Apr 7, 11, 29, May 8, 12, 27, Sep 12, 15, 17, 22, Nov 21, Dec 2;
   1768: DL, Jan 14, May 3, 5, 11, Sep 27, 29, Oct 11, Dec 30; 1769: DL, Mar 13,
   May 2, Sep 26, Oct 4, 9, 14, Nov 13, Dec 30; 1770: DL, Jan 19, May 5, 7, 10,
   Oct 3, 25, Nov 3, 19, 29, Dec 13; 1771: DL, Feb 21, Mar 7, 12, Apr 2, 9, May
   8, 10, Sep 24, Oct 1, 3, 19, 24, 28, Nov 2, 11, 25, 30, Dec 2, 4, 11, 12;
   1772: DL, Jan 4, 11, Mar 7, 12, 21, Apr 4, May 8, 12, 30, Jun 10
Rogers, Jane (actor), 1692: DL, Nov 0; 1693: DL, Feb 0, DG, May 0; 1694: DL,
   Mar 21, Sep 0; 1695: DG, Apr 0, DL, Sep 0, Oct 0, Nov 0, Dec 0; 1696: DL, Jan
   0, Feb 0, Mar 0, Apr 0, May 0, Jul 0, Nov 21; 1697: DL, Jan 0, Feb 0, May 8,
   31; 1698: DL/ORDG, Nov 0, DL, Dec 0; 1699: DL, Apr 0, May 0, Nov 28, Dec 0;
   1700: DL, Feb 19, Mar 0, Jul 9; 1701: DL, Feb 4, Mar 1, Apr 0, May 12, 31,
   Dec 0; 1702: DL, Jan 0, Feb 0, Nov 0, Dec 0, 14; 1703: DL, Jan 27, Jun 4, 23,
   Dec 2; 1704: DL, Jan 26, Feb 24, May 0, Jun 19; 1705: DL, Feb 26, Jun 12, Jul
   25, Nov 20; 1706: DL, Mar 25, Apr 8; 1707: DL/QUEEN, Oct 18, QUEEN'S, 21,
   DL/QUEEN, 25, Nov 1, QUEEN'S, 6, QUEEN/DL, 8, DL/QUEEN, 18, 20, QUEEN/DL, Dec
   6, QUEEN'S, 13, DL/QUEEN, 27, 31; 1708: DL, Jan 31, Feb 4, 7, 9, 19, Mar 8,
   9, 15, 18, 22, Apr 17, 19, 26, 27, 29, Aug 28, Sep 7, 11, 14, 18, 23, 25, 28,
   30, Oct 7, 12, 15, 18, 26, Dec 22, 30; 1709: DL, Jan 8, 17, 29, Feb 5, 16,
   26, Mar 5, 14, 19, 21, 22, 28, 31, Apr 30, May 12, 18, Jun 2; 1710: QUEEN'S,
   Jan 12, 19, 21, 25, Feb 4, 16, 18, 27, Mar 4, 11, 20, 27, Apr 20, May 6, 15,
   19, 25, Jun 13, Jul 21, DL/QUEEN, Oct 4, 5, Nov 6, 13, 14, DL, 20, 25, 27,
   30, Dec 9, 14, 15, 22; 1711: DL, Jan 15, 16, Feb 19, 22, Apr 20, DL/QUEEN,
   May 11, DL, 22, Jul 3, Aug 17, Sep 25, 27, Oct 2, 4, 8, 23, 24, Nov 2, 8, 12,
   23, 24, 29, Dec 3; 1712: DL, Mar 17, May 9, Jun 19, Jul 1, 18, 22, Aug 19,
   Sep 30, Oct 6, 7, 10, 21, 28, Nov 1; 1713: DL, Feb 13, May 11, Oct 13, Nov
   11; 1714: DL, Apr 16, Oct 26, Nov 3, 24; 1715: LIF, Jan 1, 4, 14, Feb 3, 5,
   Mar 14, 26, Apr 18, 30, May 18, 24, Sep 28, 29, Oct 7, 10, 12; 1716: LIF, Jan
   7, Feb 21, Mar 6, Jul 11, Oct 23, Nov 5, 9, 26, Dec 1, 4; 1717: LIF, Jan 8,
   28, Feb 11, Mar 11, 16, 30, Oct 15, 17, 24, 26, Nov 6, 11, 14, 16, 19, 20,
   21, 26, Dec 3, 7, 10; 1718: LIF, Feb 22, Mar 1, Sep 26, 29, Oct 4, 6, 8, 15,
   18
Rogers, John (petitions King), 1660: NONE, Aug 7
Rogers, Master (dancer), 1757: DL, May 6; 1758: DL, Jan 13, May 11; 1759: DL,
   May 4, Sep 25, Oct 24, Dec 7; 1760: DL, Feb 7, Mar 22, Oct 7; 1761: DL, Jun
   16, HAY, 23, DL, Jul 2, 27, HAY, 30, Aug 3, DL, Sep 12, 14, Oct 17, Dec 28;
   1762: DL, Feb 6, May 11, Oct 13; 1763: CG, Apr 25, HAY, Jun 9, 20, Jul 4, 20,
   Aug 1, 5, 22, Sep 3, 7; 1764: CG, Jan 20, Mar 20, May 3, HAY, Jun 26, Jul 5,
   Aug 6, Sep 1, 3, 5, 11; 1765: DL, May 15; 1766: DL, May 7
Rogers, Master (musician), 1770: MARLY, Aug 21
Rogers, Masters (dancers), 1759: DL, May 9; 1760: DL, Apr 23; 1761: HAY, Jun 27
Rogers, Miss (actor), 1715: LIF, Mar 14, 31, Apr 18, May 6, 13, 21, Oct 22, Nov
   29, Dec 12; 1716: LIF, Apr 27, May 4, Jul 11, Oct 18, Nov 5, 26, Dec 1; 1717:
   LIF, Mar 11, 16, 18, Apr 27, May 18, Jul 10
Rogers, Miss (actor), 1716: LIF, Feb 21
Rogers, Miss (dancer), 1727: LIF, Apr 6; 1729: LIF, Jan 1, Dec 3; 1730: LIF,

May 1, 21, 25, Jun 1; 1731: LIF, Apr 5, May 26, Dec 30; 1732: LIF, Jan 5, 7,
Feb 28, Apr 12, 18, May 4, 5, 9, 10, 15, LIF/CG, Dec 8, 12, CG/LIF, 26, 28;
1733: CG/LIF, Jan 4, 9, LIF/CG, 16, 18, 19, 23, 29, Feb 5, 6, Mar 12, 15,
CG/LIF, 26, CG, 27, LIF/CG, 28, 29, 31, Apr 11, 12, 20, 21, 23, 24, 25, 27,
CG, May 1, 4, LIF/CG, 7, 8, CG, 11, LIF/CG, 14, 15, CG, 16, LIF/CG, 19, 23,
24, 29, Jun 1, CG, 26, Jul 6, 27, 31, Sep 20, 25, 29, Oct 6, 13, 18, 25, 26,
27, 31, Nov 10, 12, 23, Dec 7, 28; 1734: CG, Jan 17, 25, Feb 26, Mar 11, 16,
Apr 1, 24, 25, 29, 30, May 4, 17, BFRLCH, Aug 24, RI, Sep 12, CG/LIF, 20, 25,
Oct 2, 7, 9, 14, 23, 26, 31, Nov 1, 12, 19, 25, Dec 5, 12, 19, 30; 1735:
CG/LIF, Jan 13, 14, 17, Feb 3, 13, 22, Mar 11, 15, 25, Apr 9, 10, 11, 14, 15,
17, 18, 22, 24, 29, May 1, 2, 5, CG, 6, 8, CG/LIF, 9, 12, 13, 15, 16, 19, 20,
22, 26, 27, Jun 2, LIF, Aug 29, CG, Sep 26, 29, Oct 3, 13, 17, Nov 6, 11, 19,
28, Dec 2, 12, 18, 30; 1736: CG, Jan 1, 9, 10, 17, 23, Feb 23, 24, 26, Mar 6,
11, 16, 23, 25, 30, Apr 5, 6, 10, 12, 15, LIF, 16, CG, 30, May 1, 3, 4, LIF,
5, CG, 6, 8, 10, 11, 14, 17, LIF, 19, CG, 20, 24, 25, 27, 31, Jun 4, 14;
1737: CG, Jan 14, 25, Feb 14, Mar 15, Apr 28; 1738: CG, Feb 13, Apr 3, Oct 2,
28; 1739: CG, Sep 22, Oct 2, 3, 26, Nov 23, 26, Dec 10; 1740: BFLP, Aug 23;
1741: JS, Sep 29
Rogers, Miss (dancer), 1800: CG, Jun 11, 13
Rogers, Mrs (actor, dancer), 1728: LIF, Jan 29; 1732: DL, Apr 28, TC, Aug 4,
  BFMMO, 23; 1733: LIF/CG, Mar 17; 1739: CG, Oct 15, Dec 4; 1740: CG, Jan 10
Rogers, Mrs (supplier), 1749: DL, Nov 10, 23, Dec 7
Rogers, Samuel (poet), 1795: DL, Apr 27; 1797: DL, Apr 19
Rogers, Sukey (dancer), 1730: LIF, May 21, 25, Jun 1; 1732: LIF, May 2, 15;
  1734: BFRLCH, Aug 24; 1735: CG/LIF, Mar 11
Rogers, Susanna (actor), 1729: LIF, Jan 1
Rogers, Widow (beneficiary), 1722: LIF, Jul 19
Rogers's, two Miss (dancer), 1764: DL, May 23
Rogier (dancer), 1714: HIC, Feb 1
Rogier, Claudio (actor), 1713: HAYGR, Apr 7; see also Claudio
Roland (dancer), 1734: GF/HAY, Dec 27; 1736: DL, Apr 3, LIF, 20, DL, May 8
Roland, Anne (dancer), 1735: DL, Nov 18, 19, 20, 22, 26, 27, 28, Dec 3, 4, 12,
  16, 17, 22, 26, 27, 31; 1736: DL, Jan 3, 6, 7, 8, 9, Feb 2, 9, 10, 11, 14,
  18, 21, 28, Mar 3, 11, 23, 25, 27, Apr 3, 17, May 8, 11, 19, Jun 23; 1739:
  CG, Sep 25, 28, Oct 1, 3, 23, 26, 27, 31, Nov 1, 3, 6, 7, 8, 10, 13, 14, 15,
  21, 23, 24, 26, 28, Dec 1, 10, 13, 17, 19, 21, 22; 1740: CG, Jan 25, Feb 2,
  6, 7, Mar 27, Apr 18, 23
Roland, Catharine (dancer), 1734: DL, Oct 28, Nov 4, 5, 8, 11, 14, 15, 18, 20,
  22, 23, 30, Dec 2, 6, 7, 26; 1735: DL, Jan 1, 8, Feb 8, May 21, 26, 30, Jun
  2, 5, 9, LIF, 12, DL, Sep 9, 15, 18, Oct 22, 27, 28, 29, Nov 3, 4, 5, 8, 10,
  15, 17, 18, 19, 20, 29, Dec 1, 2, 3, 4, 6, 8, 10, 16, 17, 29, 31; 1736: DL,
  Jan 2, 3, 6, 7, 8, 9, 29, Feb 2, 4, 5, 6, 9, 10, 11, 12, Mar 23, 27, Apr 1,
  3, 12, 13, 17, LIF, 20, DL, 26, 27, May 5, 8, 12, 14, 15, 31, Sep 7, 11, 16,
  21, 23, 28, LIF, 28, Oct 5, DL, 5, LIF, 9, DL, 12, 15, 16, LIF, 21, DL, 26,
  28, Nov 1, 4, 6, 9, 11, 13, 16, 22, 29, 30, Dec 1, LIF, 7, DL, 11, LIF, 16,
  DL, 23, 30; 1737: DL, Jan 18, 29, Feb 1, LIF, 1, DL, 3, 8, 10, 16, Mar 5, 7,
  12, 14, LIF, 21, 26, 31, Apr 2, DL, 2, 11, LIF, 19, DL, 22, LIF, 27, DL, 30,
  LIF, May 4, 10, CG, Oct 26, 27, Nov 8, 9, 10, 11, 12, 16; 1738: DL, Jan 3,
  CG, 3, 20, 21, 25, 28, 31, Feb 2, 3, 8, 9, 10, 13, 14, Mar 2, 7, 13, 14, 16,
  18, 20, 21, 23, Apr 5, 6, 7, 10, 12, 15, 17, 19, 20, 22, 24, 25, May 2, 6,
  10, 11, DL, Oct 12, CG, 13, 16, 18, DL, 19, CG, 23, 26, 28, Nov 2, DL, 8, CG,
  13, 18, DL, 30, CG, Dec 5, 6, DL, 8, CG, 9, 11, DL, 11, 16, 18, 20, 22; 1739:
  DL, Jan 2, CG, 3, DL, 6, CG, 8, DL, 13, CG, 15, DL, 16, CG, 18, Feb 9, 15,
  24, Mar 5, 13, 15, 19, 20, 22, 26, 27, Apr 3, 7, 9, DL, 14, CG, 14, 23, 25,
  26, 27, 30, May 3, 5, DL, 10, 11, 12, 14, 17, 19, 22, 23, 25, 26, 31, CG, Sep
  22, Oct 10, 15, 27, 31, Nov 6, 7, 8, 9, 10, 14, 15, 20, 21, Dec 1, 6, 8, 10,
  12, 14, 15, 17, 18, 19, 21; 1740: CG, Feb 12, Mar 18, 24, 25, HAY, Apr 8, CG,
  9, 14, 16, 23, 25, 28, 29, 30, May 5, 13, 14, 16, 20, 21, 27, 29, Oct 13, 15,
  25, Nov 13, 27, Dec 4, 11, 12, 19, 22; 1741: CG, Jan 6, 7, 8, 10, 15, 27, Feb
  24, Mar 9, 17, Apr 2, 28; 1742: DL, Apr 3, 19, May 7, LIF, Nov 24, 26, Dec 3,
  13, 27; 1743: LIF, Jan 7, Feb 17, Mar 3, 8, 22, Apr 7
Roland, Mlle and Anne (dancers), 1736: DL, Apr 3
Roland, Mme (dancer), 1741: CG, Apr 17; 1749: KING'S, Mar 7; 1750: HAY, Feb 21,
  Mar 7, 13; 1755: CG, Dec 5
Rolar (actor), 1737: DL, Oct 25
Rolland (musician), 1760: CG, Sep 22
Rolles (ticket deliverer), 1782: CG, May 29; 1783: CG, May 31; 1784: CG, May
  22; 1786: CG, May 31; 1787: CG, May 30; 1788: CG, Jun 4; 1789: CG, Jun 5;
  1790: CG, Jun 12; 1791: CG, Jun 14
Rollet (dancer), 1766: DL, Oct 11, Dec 8; 1767: DL, Jan 24, Mar 17, Nov 16;
  1768: DL, Apr 6; 1772: DL, Dec 9; 1773: DL, May 3
Rolli, Paolo Antonio, 1720: KING'S, Apr 2, May 30, Nov 19; 1721: KING'S, Feb 1,

Apr 15, May 20, Dec 9; 1722: KING'S, Jan 10, Feb 22; 1723: KING'S, Mar 30;
     1726: KING'S, Mar 12, May 5; 1727: KING'S, Jan 31, Nov 11; 1729: KING'S, Dec
     9; 1733: LIF, Dec 29; 1734: LIF, Mar 12, May 11; 1735: KING'S, Feb 1, May 3;
     1737: KING'S, Apr 25, 26, Oct 29; 1740: HAY, Jan 22, Mar 15; 1741: LIF, Jan
     10, KING'S, Nov 10, Dec 12; 1742: KING'S, Apr 20; 1744: KING'S, Jan 31, Apr
     3, 24
--Arsaces (opera), 1737: KING'S, Oct 29, Nov 1; 1738: KING'S, May 9
--Cyrus; or, Odio ed Amore (opera), 1721: KING'S, May 20, 24, 31, Jun 2, 10,
     17, 21, Jul 1; 1722: KING'S, Nov 17, 20, 24, 27, Dec 1
--Meraspe o L'Olimpiade (pastiche), 1742: KING'S, Apr 20, 24, 27, May 1, 4, 8,
     11, 15; 1745: CG, Apr 10
--Mutius Scaevola (pastiche), 1721: KING'S, Apr 15, 19, 22, 26, 29, May 3, 6,
     13, 17, Jun 7; 1722: KING'S, Oct 27, 31, Nov 3, 7, 10, 13
Rollo, Duke of Normandy. See Fletcher, John, The Bloody Brother.
Rolls Office, 1752: CG, Dec 12
Rolt, Captain (spectator), 1667: BRIDGES, Apr 20, Dec 11; 1668: BRIDGES, May 18
Rolt, Miss (payee), 1772: DL, Oct 10
Rolt, Richard, 1748: DL, Mar 10; 1754: HAY, May 29; 1764: DL, Nov 2; 1769: CG,
     Dec 15
--Almena (opera), 1764: DL, Nov 2, 6, 8, 10, 16, 19, 23, 26, 30; 1765: DL, Apr
     23; 1766: DL, Feb 6, 7, 18
--Amintas (opera), 1769: CG, Dec 15, 21, 22; 1770: HAY, May 3
Romagnezi, 1722: HAY, Feb 26, Mar 5, 8, 12
Romaine (lecturer), 1767: DL, May 7
Roman Actor, The. See Massinger, Phillip, The History and Fall of Domitian.
Roman and English Comedy, The (criticism), 1747: DL, Mar 2, NONE, 27
Roman Bride's Revenge, The. See Gildon, Charles.
Roman comedy, 1752: HAY, Jan 2, CT/HAY, Feb 6; 1773: DL, Mar 22
Roman Concerto (music), 1753: HAY, Mar 15
Roman Empress, The. See Joyner, William.
Roman Father, The. See Whitehead, William.
Roman Generals, The. See Dover, John.
Roman habits, 1692: NONE, Jan 19; 1722: GR, Oct 27; 1723: CH, Aug 15; 1734:
     HAY, Jun 3
Roman Maid, The. See Hurst, Robert.
Roman Ovation (song), 1768: CG, Apr 20; 1785: CG, Oct 17; 1786: CG, Oct 21;
     1787: CG, Dec 3; 1788: CG, Dec 29
Roman Sacrifice, The. See Shirley, William.
Roman Virgin, The. See Webster, John.
Romance of an Hour, The. See Kelly, Hugh.
Romance of the Forest, The (novel), 1794: CG, May 28
Romani, Sga (singer), 1771: KING'S, Feb 8, 9
Romano, Pietro Castrucci (beneficiary), 1719: YB, Mar 20
Romano, Victoria Albergotti (beneficiary), 1713: HIC, Apr 9
Romantic Lady, The (play, anon), 1672: DG, Mar 13
Romanzini, Maria Teresa (actor, singer), 1781: KING'S, Jun 5, DL, Oct 19; 1782:
     DL, May 10; 1783: DL, Feb 18; 1786: DL, Oct 24; 1787: DL, Jan 26, 29, Feb 15,
     Apr 13, 18, 23, Jun 2, Oct 4, Nov 1, 3, 8; 1788: DL, Jan 26, 28, Feb 21, 25,
     Mar 26, May 1, 6, 8, 9, 30, Sep 13, 18, 23, Oct 9, 14, 16, 23, 25, 28, Nov 1,
     17, 18, Dec 20; 1789: DL, Feb 18, 20, Mar 9, Apr 14, 21, May 19, 22, 27, 28,
     Jun 3, 9, Sep 26, Oct 1, 10, 13, 15, 22, 24, 26, 28, Nov 4, 7, 13, 24, Dec 7,
     9; 1790: DL, Jan 6, 19, Feb 11, 18, 24, Mar 10, 12, 17, 19, 24, Apr 5, 16,
     24, May 18, 31, Jun 1, Sep 11, 30, Oct 4, 11, 26, 28, Nov 19, 20, 24, Dec 9
Rome Opera, 1785: KING'S, Apr 16
Rome, 1687: ATCOURT, Jan 30; 1689: DLORDG, Apr 0; 1696: LIF, Feb 0; 1698: DL,
     Jul 9; 1699: LIF, Dec 0; 1702: DL, Dec 22; 1703: YB, Mar 5, DL, Nov 10; 1713:
     CA, Mar 20; 1716: HIC, Mar 14, 15; 1752: CT/HAY, Mar 21; 1757: CG, Mar 11;
     1761: HAY, Apr 29; 1784: KING'S, Dec 18; 1785: KING'S, Jan 25; 1788: KING'S,
     Jan 15; 1797: KING'S, Nov 28; 1798: KING'S, Mar 10
Rome's Follies. See N, N.
Romeo and Juliet. See Shakespeare, William.
Romney, Earl of. See Sidney, Henry.
Romp, The. See Lloyd, T A.
Rompereau, Mlle (actor), 1753: HAY, Mar 13
Romulus and Hersillia; or, The Sabine War (play, anon), 1682: DG, Aug 10
Ronaldson (machinist), 1800: HAY, Jul 2
Roncaglia, Francesco (singer), 1777: KING'S, Nov 8; 1778: KING'S, Feb 7, Mar 5,
     Apr 4, May 30; 1780: KING'S, Dec 2, 23; 1781: KING'S, Jan 23, Mar 8, 29, Jun
     5, 23
Rondeau (dance), 1782: CG, May 25
Rondo (song), 1770: MARLY, Sep 20; 1774: KING'S, Mar 17; 1775: HAY, Mar 9;
     1791: KING'S, May 23; 1796: CG, Apr 15, 22, May 3; 1799: CG, May 15

Rone (translator), 1772: HAY, Sep 17
Roofey. See Roffey.
Rooker, Edward (actor), 1749: NWLS, Feb 27; 1750: NWC, Apr 16; 1752: DL, Dec 8;
   1753: DL, May 11, 21; 1754: DL, May 16; 1755: DL, Oct 17, Nov 8, 27; 1756:
   DL, Feb 11, May 11, Oct 19, Nov 10, 18; 1757: DL, May 5, Sep 29, Oct 13, 31,
   Dec 16; 1758: DL, Mar 13, Apr 27, May 3, Jun 22, Sep 19, 30, Oct 5, 20, Nov
   16, 27; 1759: DL, Jan 4, May 2, Oct 4, 6, 16, 30, Nov 22, 26, Dec 7; 1760:
   DL, Jan 1, Apr 22, Oct 2, 3, 7; 1761: DL, Mar 14, Apr 17, Sep 14, 17, Oct 15,
   22, Nov 3, Dec 28; 1762: DL, Oct 5, 15, Nov 5, 10, 23; 1763: DL, Jan 5, Apr
   29, Sep 22, Oct 4, 28, Dec 26; 1764: DL, Jan 18, May 7, Sep 25, Oct 20, Nov
   9, 13, Dec 26; 1765: DL, Jan 22, Apr 18, Sep 24, Oct 5; 1766: DL, Jan 6, Apr
   30, May 5, Sep 27, Oct 29, Dec 4; 1767: DL, Jan 24, Apr 23, May 8, Sep 15,
   17, 23, Dec 2, 26; 1768: DL, Apr 19, Sep 8, 20, Oct 10, 11, Dec 5, 7, 30;
   1769: DL, Apr 12, 21, Sep 26; 1770: DL, May 5, Oct 13, Nov 17; 1771: DL, Apr
   6, May 3, Oct 21, Dec 26; 1772: DL, Mar 26, May 16, Oct 3, 21, Nov 18, Dec
   26; 1773: DL, May 8, Sep 21, 25, Nov 25; 1774: DL, Mar 14, Apr 30, Sep 29,
   Oct 14
Rooker, Michael (scene painter, machinist), 1779: HAY, Jul 1, 31, Aug 31; 1780:
   HAY, Jul 8, Sep 2; 1781: HAY, May 30, Jul 9, 18, Aug 8, Sep 4; 1782: HAY, Jun
   3, Aug 17; 1783: HAY, Jun 5, 30; 1785: HAY, Aug 31; 1786: HAY, Jul 3, Aug 12;
   1787: HAY, Aug 4; 1788: HAY, Aug 5; 1789: HAY, May 18, Aug 11; 1790: HAY, Jul
   16, Sep 4; 1791: HAY, Jul 30; 1792: HAY, Jul 25; 1793: HAY, Aug 3, Sep 19;
   1794: HAY, Jul 21, 26, Aug 9, 18; 1795: HAY, Jun 20, Jul 31; 1796: HAY, Jun
   25, Sep 1; 1797: HAY, Jul 8, Aug 9, 15; 1798: HAY, Jun 20, 29, 30; 1799: HAY,
   Jul 9, Aug 13; 1800: HAY, Jun 17
Rooker, Widow (beneficiary), 1775: DL, May 10
Roome (librettist), 1731: DL, Feb 8
Roope, Mrs (actor), 1781: CG, Oct 31; 1782: CG, Apr 24, HAY, Jun 15
Rope Dancers, 1696: SF, Sep 5; 1697: BF, Aug 24; 1698: BF, Aug 25, SF, Sep 17;
   1700: BF, Aug 0; 1701: BF, Aug 25; 1702: BFGB, Aug 24, BFBF, 24; 1704: MF,
   May 1; 1705: BF, Aug 27; 1706: BF, May 1; 1713: TEC, Nov 26; 1735: CG, Dec 18
Rope Dancing (entertainment), 1701: MF, May 1, BF, Aug 25; 1702: BFBF, Aug 24,
   BFGB, 24; 1703: DG, Apr 30, MF, May 0, YB, Jul 27, BFG, Aug 23; 1705: BF, Aug
   27, LIF/QUEN, Oct 11; 1706: MF, May 1; 1710: GR, Sep 7; 1713: TEC, Nov 26;
   1716: SF, Sep 25; 1720: LIF, Jun 6; 1722: SF, Sep 22; 1723: RI, Sep 2; 1728:
   HAY, Apr 3; 1732: HAY, Feb 16, RIW/HAY, Sep 6; 1745: GF, Apr 15, 22; 1746:
   HIC, Feb 3; 1756: BFGR, Sep 3
Roper, A (publisher), 1697: DG, Jul 1
Roper, Captain (started fight), 1776: DL, Feb 3
Rosa, Laura (singer), 1758: KING'S, Jan 10, 31, Nov 11; 1759: KING'S, Jan 16,
   Nov 13; 1760: KING'S, Jan 15, Mar 1, Apr 17, HIC, 29, KING'S, May 31; 1765:
   KING'S, Dec 3
Rosa, Salvator (artist), 1793: HAY, Dec 2
Rosalie (song), 1799: CG, May 24
Rosalind (singer), 1788: DL, Oct 7
Rosalinda. See Smith, John Christopher.
Rosamond (actor), 1736: DL, Jan 12, HAY, Apr 29, DL, Sep 7, Oct 12, Dec 4
Rosamond. See Addison, Joseph.
Rosania. See Shirley, James.
Rosciad, The (poem), 1749: DL, Nov 1; 1750: DL, Nov 28; 1761: DL, Mar 14; 1762:
   DL, Feb 12; 1763: DL, Sep 17
Rosco, James (actor), 1729: BFR, Aug 25, SF, Sep 8, DL, Nov 12, Dec 10; 1730:
   DL, Jan 26, Mar 30, Apr 20, May 18, HAY, Jun 23, 27, Jul 7, TC, Aug 1, BFR,
   22, Sep 4, SFLH, 8, DL, Oct 3, GF, 19, 30, Nov 5, 6, 12, 18, 24, 26, 30, Dec
   1, 4, 7, 8, 9, 21, 28, 30; 1731: GF, Jan 20, 23, 27, Feb 1, 15, 22, Mar 15,
   18, 22, 25, 27, Apr 8, 20, 21, 27, 28, HAY, May 3, 7, GF, 11, 14, 20, Jun 2,
   SF/BFFHH, Aug 24, SF, Sep 8, SFLH, 8, GF, 27, Oct 11, 13, 25, 26, 27, Nov 1,
   4, 5, 6, 8, 11, 13, 15, 16, 18, 19, 20, 22, 26, Dec 1, 4, 8, 9, 13, 20, 21,
   28, 30; 1732: GF, Jan 29, Feb 2, 21, Mar 7, 20, 27, 28, Apr 12, 13, 27, 28,
   May 3, 4, RI, Aug 17, BFB, 23, GF, Oct 2, 5, 6, 7, 9, 10, 11, 12, 13, 16, 17,
   18, 24, Nov 2, 3, 4, 8, 18, 28, Dec 1, 18; 1733: GF, Jan 1, 8, 18, 20, 24,
   27, Feb 5, 13, 19, 20, Mar 15, 17, 28, Apr 2, 3, 11, 13, 17, 19, May 8, 14,
   23, 29, BF, Aug 23, GF, Sep 10, 14, 17, 19, 24, 25, 27, 28, Oct 3, 4, 5, 8,
   10, 15, 19, 22, 23, 26, Nov 5, 8, 10, 13, 29, Dec 10, 13, 15, 26, 31; 1734:
   GF, Jan 3, 10, 14, 19, 31, Feb 7, 11, Mar 28, Apr 18, May 15, 17, 20, HAY,
   Jun 7, 17, 19, 21, 24, 28, Jul 5, BFFO, Aug 24, GF, Sep 9, 16, 20, 25, Oct
   16, 17, 18, 21, Nov 4, 7, 18, 22, 25, 27, 29, Dec 2, 6, 11, 12, 13, 16, 20;
   1735: GF, Jan 1, 4, 10, 11, 13, Feb 5, 6, 8, 22, Mar 10, 17, 24, 29, Apr 9,
   22, May 3, 8, Sep 10, 17, 19, 22, Oct 3, 6, 8, 10, 15, 27, Nov 3, 4, 6, 10,
   11, 19, 20, 21, 24, 25, 26, Dec 3, 6, 8, 17; 1736: GF, Jan 29, Feb 4, 5, 9,
   10, 17, Mar 9, 25, 29, Apr 1, 8, 16, 17, 27, May 5, 13, LIF, Oct 5, 9, 12,
   19, 23, 26, 28, Nov 4, 6, 9, 13, 16, 18, 20, 24, 26, 29, Dec 3, 7, 16, 20,

22; <u>1737</u>: LIF, Jan 10, DL, Feb 5, LIF, 21, Mar 1, Apr 18, 25, 27, May 2, 4,
6, Jun 15, Jul 26, Aug 2, 5, Sep 7, CG, 16, 19, 23, 26, 28, 30, Oct 14, 22,
Nov 2, 4, 9, 17, 18; <u>1738</u>: CG, Jan 3, 17, 18, 25, 31, Feb 6, 13, 16, 23, Mar
13, 14, 25, Apr 7, 17, 22, 24, 25, May 3, 10, Sep 15, 20, 22, 25, 29, Oct 6,
9, 11, 14, 16, 21, 24, 31, Nov 4, 7, 9, 13, 15, 20, 27, 29, Dec 2, 4, 5, 15,
18; <u>1739</u>: CG, Jan 4, 8, 16, 17, 20, 22, Feb 10, 12, 14, 16, 19, 26, Mar 3,
13, Apr 12, 23, May 1, 2, 4, 7, 25, 28, Sep 5, 7, 12, 14, 15, 17, Oct 3, 4,
5, 9, 10, 22, 23, 25, 26, 30, Nov 2, 5, 6, 13, 17, 20, Dec 1, 4, 6, 10, 15,
19, 21; <u>1740</u>: CG, Jan 15, 17, Feb 2, Mar 11, 18, 25, 27, Apr 9, 14, May 3, 5,
7, 9, 12, 14, Jun 5, Sep 19, 24, 26, 29, Oct 1, 3, 6, 8, 23, 31, Nov 4, 6,
10, 20, Dec 4, 5, 13; <u>1741</u>: CG, Jan 2, 6, 7, 12, 15, 21, 22, 23, 27, 28, 29,
Feb 5, 7, 12, 14, 17, 24, 26, Mar 7, 10, 12, 16, Apr 1, 10, 23, 27, May 1, 4,
11, Sep 21, 23, 25, Oct 2, 5, 7, 8, 10, 13, 15, 21, 24, 30, Nov 4, 9, 11, 23,
26, 27, 30, Dec 5, 7, 11, 17, 18; <u>1742</u>: CG, Jan 2, 23, Feb 4, 5, 18, 22, 25,
Mar 13, 18, Apr 1, May 5, 7, Sep 22, 29, Oct 1, 4, 6, 9, 11, 13, 15, 18, 21,
25, 26, 27, 28, Nov 3, 4, 11, 13, 20, 25, 29, 30, Dec 7, 15, 21, 22; <u>1743</u>:
CG, Jan 5, Apr 9, 20, 26, May 4, 5, Sep 21, 26, 28, 30, Oct 3, 5, 7, 12, 17,
19, 24, 26, 28, 31, Nov 2, 4, 16, 18, 19, 21, 28, 30, Dec 3, 8, 12, 17, 19,
27, 31; <u>1744</u>: CG, Jan 5, 11, 14, 24, Feb 3, 7, 14, 23, 28, Mar 8, 12, 13, Apr
19, 24, 27, 28, 30, May 14, Sep 19, 24, 26, 28, Oct 1, 3, 5, 8, 10, 15, 16,
18, 20, 22, 24, 31, Nov 1, 5, 7, 9, 21, 22, 24, 27, 28, Dec 10, 13, 21, 26,
28, 29; <u>1745</u>: CG, Jan 1, 5, Feb 11, 15, Mar 11, Apr 4, 20, 26, May 13, Sep
23, 25, Oct 4, 7, 11, 14, 16, Nov 4, 7, 15, 18, 22, 28, 30, Dec 2, 5, 6, 12,
13; <u>1746</u>: CG, Jan 2, 7, 11, 13, 23, Feb 3, 5, 8, 17, 24, Mar 13, 15, Apr 3,
7, 21, 23, Oct 15, 17, 29, 31, Nov 4, 6, 11, 14, 17, 18, 26, 28, Dec 4, 6,
17, 19, 20, 26, 29; <u>1747</u>: CG, Jan 20, 26, 28, 29, Feb 3, 6, Mar 7, 17, Apr 4,
9, May 11, 22, Oct 31, Nov 13, 23, Dec 4, 9, 15, 17, 28; <u>1748</u>: CG, Jan 7, 9,
12, 14, 16, 27, 29, Feb 10, 23, 27, Mar 14, Apr 11, 16, 18, 21, 22, 25, 27,
29, May 6
Rosco, Miss (actor), <u>1757</u>: DL, Feb 9
Rose (house servant), <u>1768</u>: CG, May 28, 30; <u>1769</u>: CG, May 19, 22; <u>1770</u>: CG, May
18, 22; <u>1772</u>: CG, May 19
Rose and Colin. See Dibdin, Charles.
Rose Boree et Ziphirs (dance), <u>1741</u>: DL, Apr 7, 9
Rose Coffee House, <u>1784</u>: HAY, Jan 21
Rose et Colas. See Sedaine, Michel Jean.
Rose St, <u>1680</u>: DG, Jan 0
Rose Tavern, <u>1744</u>: DL, May 4, 17; <u>1747</u>: DL, Apr 20, May 16; <u>1748</u>: DL, Apr 29;
<u>1749</u>: CG, Apr 28; <u>1758</u>: DL, Jan 30; <u>1763</u>: DL, Jan 19; <u>1770</u>: DL, May 5
Rose, Henry (beneficiary), <u>1741</u>: HAY, Feb 18
Rose, John, <u>1788</u>: HAY, Aug 2; <u>1792</u>: HAY, Sep 6, DL, Oct 18; <u>1793</u>: HAY, Aug 12;
<u>1797</u>: DL, May 13
--Caernarvon Castle; or, The Birth of the Prince of Wales, <u>1793</u>: HAY, Aug 12,
14, 15, 17, 19, 21, 24, 31
--Fairy Festival, The (interlude), <u>1797</u>: DL, May 13, 15, 16, 31, Jun 14
--Family Compact, The (farce), <u>1792</u>: HAY, Sep 6, 7, 13
--Prisoner, The (musical), <u>1792</u>: DL, Oct 18, 20, 22, 23, 24, 25, 29, 31, Nov 1,
2, 7, 8, 13, 17, Dec 5, 7, 11, 13, 19, 20, 26; <u>1793</u>: DL, Jan 9, 17, Feb 18,
Mar 4, 18, Apr 3; <u>1796</u>: DL, Sep 29, Oct 4, 11, Nov 1, 29, Dec 3; <u>1797</u>: DL,
May 18, 26; <u>1798</u>: DL, May 31; <u>1799</u>: DL, May 7
--Quarter of an Hour before Dinner, A; or, Quality Binding (farce), <u>1788</u>: HAY,
Aug 2, 5, 6, 7, 8, 12, 20, 23, 28, 30, Sep 1, 5, 9, 11; <u>1789</u>: HAY, May 20,
Jun 15, Aug 11, 17; <u>1790</u>: HAY, Jun 18, 24, Jul 2, 13, 20, 24, 29, Aug 4, 7,
Sep 2; <u>1791</u>: HAY, Jun 16, 29, Jul 7, 14, 16, 25, 27, Aug 3, 8, 11, 29, Sep 9;
<u>1793</u>: HAY, Jul 4, 9, 18, 23, 24, 31, Aug 5, 8, 12, Sep 10, 21, 28, Nov 23;
<u>1794</u>: HAY, Jan 14, 22, Feb 15, Apr 1, Jul 9, 25, Aug 20; <u>1795</u>: DL, Jun 1,
HAY, 13, 15, 19, Jul 10, 21, 31, Aug 13, 24, Sep 3; <u>1796</u>: HAY, Jun 29, Jul 2,
9, 20, Sep 2; <u>1797</u>: HAY, Jun 17, Jul 5, 7, 14, 21, Aug 1, 11, Sep 5; <u>1798</u>:
HAY, Jun 13, 19, Jul 2, 23
Rose, Miss (actor), <u>1769</u>: HAY, Jun 21, Aug 7, 14, 29, 31, Sep 19; <u>1770</u>: HAY,
Sep 27, Dec 19; <u>1771</u>: HAY, Mar 4, Apr 4, 20
Rose, Miss (dancer), <u>1779</u>: KING'S, Mar 25
Rose, Mme. See Didelot, Marie Rose.
Rose, Mrs, <u>1771</u>: HAY, Apr 4
Rose, The. See Arne, Dr Thomas A.
Roseingrave, Thomas (composer), <u>1717</u>: YB, Jun 14; <u>1720</u>: LIF, Feb 10, KING'S,
May 30; <u>1733</u>: CG, May 1; <u>1736</u>: DL, Apr 22
Roselli, Agrippino (singer), <u>1794</u>: KING'S, Apr 26, May 15; <u>1795</u>: KING'S, Dec
12; <u>1796</u>: KING'S, Jan 5, 19, Feb 9, Mar 10, Apr 7, May 24; <u>1800</u>: KING'S, Feb
8, Apr 15, May 22
Rosenbach, A S W (bookseller), <u>1747</u>: DL, Sep 15
Rosenberg, Francis (musician), <u>1726</u>: HIC, Mar 25; <u>1727</u>: HIC, Mar 15

Rosiere de Salency (dance), <u>1782</u>: KING'S, Mar 19, 21, Apr 2, 13, 16; <u>1785</u>:
  KING'S, Mar 3
Rosilind Castle (song), <u>1777</u>: HAY, Apr 22
Rosina. See Brooke, Francis.
Rosine, Mlle (dancer), <u>1794</u>: KING'S, Dec 6, 20; <u>1795</u>: KING'S, Jan 20, May 14
Rosmira. See DeGiardini, Felice.
Rosoman (actor, dancer), <u>1735</u>: BF, Aug 23; <u>1738</u>: SFH, Sep 5; <u>1739</u>: WF, Aug 31;
  <u>1740</u>: TC, Aug 4, BF/WF/SF, 23; <u>1742</u>: LIF, Dec 27; <u>1743</u>: LIF, Feb 17, MF, May
  9, TCY, Aug 4, BFYWR, 23, SF, Sep 8
Rosoman (author), <u>1792</u>: CG, Dec 20
Rosoman, Mrs (actor), <u>1743</u>: BFYWR, Aug 23, SF, Sep 8
Ross (actor), <u>1730</u>: HAY, Sep 18
Ross (ticket deliverer), <u>1750</u>: CG, May 7; <u>1752</u>: CG, May 7; <u>1753</u>: CG, May 21;
  <u>1754</u>: CG, May 18; <u>1755</u>: CG, May 20; <u>1756</u>: CG, May 24; <u>1757</u>: CG, May 20; <u>1758</u>:
  CG, May 12; <u>1759</u>: CG, May 25; <u>1760</u>: CG, May 19; <u>1761</u>: CG, May 15; <u>1762</u>: CG,
  May 21
Ross (ticket deliverer), <u>1795</u>: DL, Jun 5; <u>1796</u>: DL, Jun 15; <u>1797</u>: DL, Jun 13;
  <u>1798</u>: DL, Jun 16; <u>1799</u>: DL, Jul 2; <u>1800</u>: DL, Jun 13
Ross, Anne (actor), <u>1788</u>: CG, May 16
--Cottagers, The (opera), <u>1788</u>: CG, May 16
Ross, David (actor), <u>1751</u>: DL, Oct 1, 3, 5, 7, 10, 14, CG, 16, DL, 29, Nov 5,
  7, 8, 29, Dec 26; <u>1752</u>: DL, Jan 3, Feb 22, Mar 9, 31, Apr 10, 20, 21, Sep 21,
  26, Oct 3, 11, 12, 16, Nov 4, 28, 30, Dec 19; <u>1753</u>: DL, Jan 9, 22, Feb 6, Apr
  9, Sep 15, 18, Oct 2, 3, 6, 10, 12, 20, 31, Nov 5, 26, Dec 26; <u>1754</u>: DL, Feb
  25, Mar 19, Apr 2, 20, Sep 19, 24, Oct 5, 8, 10, 12, 21, 29, 30, Nov 4, 6,
  Dec 9; <u>1755</u>: DL, Jan 22, Apr 8, 28, May 1, 6, 15, 23, Sep 27, Oct 7, 10, 31,
  Nov 4, 17, 26, Dec 5, 6, 18; <u>1756</u>: DL, Jan 12, Feb 10, 27, Apr 6, 30, May 14,
  17, Sep 18, 25, Oct 16, 21, Nov 4, 11, 23, 24, Dec 11, 15; <u>1757</u>: DL, Jan 18,
  24, Feb 5, 22, Mar 28, Apr 13, CG, Oct 3, DL, 6, CG, 8, 15, 22, 26, Nov 4, 7,
  14, 16, 26, Dec 1; <u>1758</u>: CG, Feb 1, Mar 28, May 3, 4, 18, Sep 29, Oct 2, 4,
  6, 13, 14, 23, 24, 25, 27, 30, Nov 1, 4, 7, 14, 23, Dec 2, 18, 19; <u>1759</u>: CG,
  Jan 4, Feb 15, Mar 20, 24, Apr 21, May 7, 8, 14, Oct 1, Nov 5, 23, 28, 30,
  Dec 5, 7, 8, 15, 17, 18, 19, 21, 22; <u>1760</u>: CG, Jan 24, Feb 7, 28, Mar 20, 25,
  Apr 8, 17, May 12, Sep 22, 29, Oct 1, 8, 10, 11, 14, 15, 17, 18, 23, Nov 22,
  29, Dec 2, 11, 31; <u>1761</u>: CG, Jan 7, Feb 16, 17, Mar 3, 5, 9, 24, Apr 1, 2, 6,
  13, 21, 27, May 11, 25, Sep 14, 18, 23, 25, 26, 28, Oct 1, 3, 6, 7, 10, 13,
  20, 21, 24, 26, 27, Nov 4, 6, 9, Dec 11, 30; <u>1762</u>: CG, Feb 3, 22, Mar 2, 20,
  23, Apr 19, May 7, 11, 14, Sep 20, 22, 24, 27, 30, Oct 1, 2, 6, 8, 12, 19,
  20, Nov 1, 5, 8, 15, 16, 29, 30, Dec 4, 22; <u>1763</u>: CG, Jan 8, 14, 28, Feb 14,
  Mar 21, Apr 25, Sep 21, 26, 30, Oct 3, 5, 7, 12, 14, 15, 18, 20, 21, 24, Nov
  4, 10, 15, 16, 26, Dec 16, 27; <u>1764</u>: CG, Jan 9, 17, 28, Feb 1, 9, 13, Mar 24,
  29, May 7, 9, 11, 21, 23, 26, Sep 19, 21, 26, 28, Oct 1, 3, 10, 12, 17, 19,
  20, 22, 24, 25, 29, 30, Nov 5, 6, 7, 15, 16, 20, 24, 29, 30, Dec 7, 21; <u>1765</u>:
  CG, Jan 14, Mar 19, 26, May 11, 15, Sep 16, 18, 20, 23, 25, 27, Oct 3, 7, 9,
  10, 11, 14, 22, 28, 30, Nov 13, 19, 22, 27, 28, Dec 3, 10; <u>1766</u>: CG, Jan 9,
  31, Feb 5, Mar 15, 20, 31, Apr 18, May 2, 6, 13, Oct 6, 8, 14, 16, 21, 30,
  31, Nov 4, 7, 8, 11, 18, 19, 21, Dec 4, 6, 9, 10, 16, 20, 30; <u>1767</u>: CG, Jan
  2, 23, 31, Feb 14, 28, Mar 28, 31, Apr 6, 11, 24, May 18, 20, 25; <u>1770</u>: HAY,
  May 18, 30, Jun 18, Jul 25, Aug 22, 31, CG, Sep 24, Oct 10, 18, 23, 29, Nov
  15; <u>1771</u>: CG, Jan 28, Feb 23, Sep 28, Oct 7, Nov 2, Dec 21, 30; <u>1772</u>: CG, Jan
  15, Feb 1, DL, Mar 18, 23, CG, 23, Dec 11; <u>1773</u>: CG, Jan 14, 25, Feb 3, Mar
  20, Apr 17, May 6, Oct 23; <u>1777</u>: CG, Oct 6, Nov 1, 6; <u>1778</u>: CG, Feb 10, 13,
  16, 17
Ross, John (composer), <u>1795</u>: DL, May 2, 26
Ross, Mary (dancer), <u>1770</u>: DL, Apr 27, 28, May 30, Jun 4, Dec 7; <u>1771</u>: DL, Jan
  15, Feb 4, Apr 5, 16, 22, May 16, 27; <u>1772</u>: DL, Apr 24; <u>1773</u>: DL, Apr 1;
  <u>1774</u>: CG, Sep 28; <u>1775</u>: CG, May 12, 26, Oct 16, 17, Nov 18, Dec 7; <u>1776</u>: CG,
  May 3, 15, HAY, Oct 7; <u>1777</u>: CG, May 9, Oct 1; <u>1778</u>: CG, Apr 20, May 16, Oct
  14; <u>1779</u>: CG, May 3, DL, 14, CG, 21, Nov 9, Dec 29
Ross, Miss (actor), <u>1760</u>: DL, Jun 19
Ross, Mrs (actor), <u>1776</u>: CHR, Sep 23, 25, 27, 30, Oct 2, 4, 7, 9
Ross, Mrs (haberdasher), <u>1771</u>: DL, Oct 8
Rossennaw, Ninetta de (actor), <u>1754</u>: CG, Nov 18
Rossi, Antonio (singer), <u>1777</u>: KING'S, Nov 4, Dec 16; <u>1778</u>: KING'S, Jan 20, Mar
  3, 26, Apr 2, May 5, Nov 24, Dec 22; <u>1779</u>: KING'S, Feb 23, Apr 29, May 15
Rossi, Giacomo, <u>1711</u>: QUEEN'S, Feb 24; <u>1712</u>: QUEEN'S, May 3, Nov 22
--Hercules (opera), <u>1712</u>: QUEEN'S, May 3, 7, 10, Jun 4, 11
Rossi, Joseph (dancer), <u>1781</u>: HAY, Aug 8; <u>1782</u>: HAY, Jun 3; <u>1783</u>: HAY, Jun 5;
  <u>1785</u>: HAY, Feb 14, 21
Rossi, Margherita (dancer), <u>1782</u>: KING'S, Nov 30, Dec 12, 17; <u>1783</u>: KING'S, Jan
  11, Feb 13, 15, Mar 13, Apr 10, May 1, 31, Jun 28, Nov 29, Dec 6, 16, 27, 30;
  <u>1784</u>: KING'S, Jan 3, 17, Feb 3, 7, 14, 26, Mar 2, 6, 18, 20, 25, Apr 24, May

13, 20, Jun 1, 15, Dec 18; 1785: KING'S, Jan 1, 11, 22, Feb 5, 12, 26, Mar 3, 12, 17, Apr 7, 14, 21, May 12, Jun 18, 25, 28; 1786: KING'S, Mar 23; 1792: CG, Oct 25, 27, Nov 16, 24, Dec 20, 26; 1793: CG, Mar 11, 23, Apr 15, May 3, 4, 10, 27, Sep 16, Oct 18, Nov 19, Dec 19; 1794: CG, Feb 6, 25, Apr 7, 12, May 9, 23, 26, Sep 22, 26, Oct 14, 20, 29, Dec 26; 1795: CG, Feb 19, 26, Mar 14, KING'S, 26, CG, Apr 6, 28, May 1, 12, 13, 16, 29, Jun 6; 1796: CG, Apr 8
Rossignol, Gaetano a la (bird imitator), 1775: CG, Jan 6, DL, Feb 1, CG, 28, Mar 13, 16, 20
Rostand Sabotier (dance), 1734: DL/LIF, May 3
Rosy Bowers (song), 1704: DL, May 25, Jun 29; 1726: DL, Jan 8; 1730: GF, Apr 14; 1732: DL, Apr 19, May 3; 1737: CG, Mar 14, Apr 11, 12, 19; 1748: CG, Apr 15; 1779: DL, Mar 12; 1790: DL, May 31; see also From Rosy Bowers
Rosy Morn with Crimson Dye (song), 1778: DL, Mar 6
Rosy Morning (song), 1735: GF, Nov 19
Rotation Office, 1777: CHR, Jul 23
Rotchford. See Rochfort.
Rotherhithe, 1776: CHR, Oct 7; 1777: HAY, Feb 11, CHR, Jul 23; 1778: CHR, Jun 26
Rothery (dancer), 1784: HAY, Mar 8
Rotrou, Jean de
--Heureux Naufrage, L'; or, Harlequin Supposed Colombine and Colombine Supposed Harlequin, 1721: HAY, Jan 23, Feb 25, Mar 2; 1726: HAY, Apr 11, May 6; 1734: HAY, Nov 15; 1735: HAY, Feb 18, Mar 27
Rotterdam, 1737: DL, Aug 30
Roubiliac, Louis Francois (sculptor), 1760: CG, Dec 23; 1794: CG, Sep 22; 1798: CG, May 28
Rouchi, Abbe (spectator), 1682: DL, Nov 28, 30
Rouend, Mlle (dancer), 1755: DL, Nov 8
Round Court, 1738: CG, Aug 22; 1756: DL, Jan 23
Round Tower, The. See Cross, John Cartwright.
Roundelay (entertainment), 1784: HAY, Sep 17; 1795: CG, Jan 12
Roundheads, The. See Behn, Aphra.
Rouse us next to martial Deeds (song), 1790: CG, Feb 26
Rouse ye Gods of the Main (song), 1703: HA, May 18
Rousesini (musician), 1719: CGR, Mar 18
Roussau (dancer), 1723: HAY, Jan 31, Mar 14, Dec 16; 1724: HAY, Mar 9
Roussau's scholars (dancer), 1724: HAY, Mar 9
Rousseau (dancer), 1791: PAN, Feb 17, 26
Rousseau, Jacques (scene designer), 1686: DLORDG, Feb 11
Rousseau, Jean Jacques, 1759: DL, Jan 1; 1766: DL, Jan 23, Nov 21; 1767: DL, Jan 31; 1770: MARLY, Jul 17; 1784: KING'S, Mar 25; 1793: CG, Mar 18; 1796: CG, Nov 5
--Devin du Village, 1767: DL, Jan 31
--Pygmalion (monodrama), 1793: CG, Mar 18; 1794: CG, May 10
Rousseau, Mlle (dancer), 1791: PAN, Feb 17, 26, Mar 22
Rousselet, Mlle (dancer), 1755: DL, Nov 8, 15; 1756: DL, May 20; 1757: DL, May 4; 1758: DL, Apr 27; 1759: CG, Apr 27, May 16; 1761: DL, May 5
Rout, The. See Hill, John.
Rovedino, Carlo (singer), 1777: KING'S, Mar 13; 1778: KING'S, Mar 10, Nov 24, 28; 1779: KING'S, Jan 23, Feb 23, Mar 25, May 15, Dec 14; 1780: KING'S, Jan 22, Feb 8, Mar 28, Apr 8, 22; 1793: KING'S, Jan 26, Feb 5, 26, Mar 19, May 14, Jun 11, 25; 1794: KING'S, Jan 11, Feb 1, Mar 1, 18, Apr 1, 26, May 15, 17, Jun 5, Dec 6, 20; 1795: KING'S, Jan 27, Feb 7, 20, 27, Mar 13, 21, 28, Apr 14, 30, May 26, Jun 23, 30, Dec 12; 1796: KING'S, Jan 5, 19, Feb 9, 16, Mar 10, 29, Apr 7, 16, May 5, Jun 14, 18, Jul 23, Nov 26, Dec 6, 20; 1797: KING'S, Jan 7, 10, Feb 14, 25, Mar 7, 11, Apr 27, Jun 8, 10, Jul 18, Nov 28, Dec 9, 12, 20; 1798: KING'S, Jan 23, 27, Feb 20, 24, Mar 22, Apr 10, 21, 26, May 10, Dec 8, 11, 26, 29; 1799: KING'S, Jan 1, 5, 22, Feb 16, Apr 9, 13, 20, May 14, 30, Jun 15; 1800: KING'S, Jan 11, Feb 8, 18, Mar 4, 18, Apr 24, May 13, 22, Jun 17, 21, 28
Rovedino, Sga (singer), 1778: KING'S, Mar 26
Rovedino, Stefania (singer), 1799: KING'S, May 30; 1800: KING'S, Feb 18, Apr 15, May 22, Jun 17, 28
Rover (dancer), 1728: DL, Sep 26; 1730: DL, Apr 10
Rover, The (dance), 1736: DL, Jan 3, 5, 6, 7, 8, 9, 10, Feb 12, 13, 14, 17, 18, Mar 23, 25, Apr 8, 10, 12, 29, 30, May 4, 11, 14, 20, Oct 2, 5, 22, 25, 29, 30, Nov 17
Rover, The. See Behn, Aphra.
Rover, The, Part II. See Behn, Aphra.
Row, The (song), 1793: CG, Apr 25, HAY, Aug 27; 1797: CG, May 11
Rowe (musician), 1726: IT, Feb 2
Rowe (singer), 1792: CG, Feb 28

Rowe, Elizabeth (author), 1758: HAY, Mar 9
Rowe, Mrs (beneficiary), 1729: LIF, May 8
Rowe, Mrs (house servant), 1759: DL, May 7
Rowe, Nathaniel (prologuist), 1702: DL, Feb 0
Rowe, Nicholas, 1700: LIF, Dec 0; 1701: LIF, Dec 0; 1702: DL, Feb 0; 1703: LIF,
    May 0; 1704: LIF, Dec 4; 1705: LIF/QUEN, Feb 22, QUEEN'S, Nov 23; 1707:
    DL/QUEEN, Nov 25; 1709: DL, Apr 7; 1714: DL, Feb 2; 1715: DL, Apr 20, LIF,
    May 16, Dec 14; 1717: DL, Dec 6; 1719: DL, Aug 11; 1720: DL, Jun 14; 1721:
    DL, Jun 2, Nov 4, 6, 14; 1722: DL, Jan 25, Nov 5, 6; 1723: HAY, Dec 16; 1724:
    HAY, Jan 3, 13, 16; 1725: DL, Nov 12, 13, Dec 11; 1726: DL, Jan 19, Sep 8;
    1733: LIF/CG, Apr 17, DL/HAY, Oct 29, Nov 5, 6; 1734: DL/HAY, Jan 17, Mar 30,
    Apr 19, DL, Nov 4; 1735: DL, Jan 21, Mar 4, Nov 4, 5; 1736: CG, Apr 15, DL,
    Nov 4, 5; 1737: HAY, Mar 3, DL, Nov 4, 7; 1738: DL, Apr 29, Oct 12, 14, 16,
    Dec 18; 1739: CG, Jan 4, 5, 9, 18, Mar 15, Oct 6; 1742: CG, Oct 21; 1749: DL,
    Feb 1; 1756: CG, Mar 23; 1767: CG, Oct 24; 1773: CG, May 7; 1776: DL, Nov 4;
    1777: DL, Nov 4; 1778: CG, Nov 4; 1780: CG, Nov 4, DL, 4; 1781: CG, Nov 5;
    1782: CG, Nov 4; 1783: CG, Nov 4
--Ambitious Stepmother, The, 1700: LIF, Dec 0; 1706: QUEEN'S, Dec 6; 1715: LIF,
    Dec 14, 30; 1722: DL, Jan 25, 26; 1759: DL, Jan 31, Feb 1, 5, 7, 8, 9, 10,
    19, Apr 3
--Biter, The, 1704: LIF, Dec 4
--Fair Penitent, The, 1703: LIF, May 0, Jun 8; 1715: LIF, Aug 18, 23, Nov 3;
    1716: LIF, Apr 7; 1718: LIF, Jan 11, 16, Mar 15; 1719: CGR, Mar 20, DL, Aug
    11; 1720: DL, Jun 14; 1721: DL, Jun 2; 1723: HAY, Dec 16, 17; 1724: HAY, Jan
    3, Mar 12; 1725: DL, Nov 12, 13, 15, Dec 11; 1726: DL, Jan 19, Mar 8, May 17,
    Sep 8; 1727: DL, Mar 4, 11, Apr 11, Dec 9; 1728: DL, May 2, Oct 22, Dec 17;
    1729: DL, Feb 11, Mar 25, GF, Dec 8, DL, 10, 20; 1730: GF, Jan 15, 24, DL,
    Feb 19, 21, Mar 19, GF, May 27, HAY, Jul 7, GF, Oct 27, DL, Dec 5, HAY, 7;
    1731: GF, Jan 22, Apr 29, WINH, Jun 21, DL, Oct 12; 1732: DL, Mar 21, Sep 14;
    1733: LIF/CG, Apr 17, HAY, Jul 12; 1734: GF, Mar 5, DL/HAY, 30, Apr 19, HAY,
    Jun 19, Aug 21, RI, Sep 2; 1735: YB, Sep 18; 1736: CG, Mar 15, GF, 23, Apr 5,
    CG, 15; 1737: YB, Jan 31, CG, Feb 11, 24, Apr 2, Nov 15; 1738: CG, Feb 3, DL,
    Apr 29, CG, Nov 18; 1739: CG, Jan 27, Oct 6, DL, Nov 3; 1740: DL, Mar 27, GF,
    Nov 20; 1741: GF, Apr 7, JS, Jun 16, GF, Dec 2, 3, 9, 12, 28; 1742: GF, Jan
    16, 22, Feb 11, 22, 27, Apr 19, May 24, CG, Oct 21, 23, Nov 6, Dec 10; 1743:
    LIF, Jan 21, CG, 25, LIF, Mar 8, CG, 14, DL, 24, CG, Apr 12, DL, 18, 30, CG,
    May 20, DL, Dec 20; 1744: CG, Feb 7, JS, Mar 28, CG, 29, DL, Apr 21, MF, Jun
    11, CG, Sep 28, DL, Oct 20, 31, Nov 21; 1745: GF, Jan 24, DL, Feb 7, JS, Mar
    8, DL, 11, Apr 6, 30, GF, May 6, DL, Dec 12, JS, 26; 1746: DL, Jan 29, CG,
    Nov 14, 15, 17, 19, 20, 21, 22, 27, 29, Dec 1, 16, GF, 31; 1747: CG, Mar 24,
    30, GF, Apr 11, CG, May 7, 27; 1748: DL, Feb 1, 2, 4, 6, Mar 22, Apr 26, SOU,
    Jul 4, CG, Oct 10, 12, DL, 21, 22, Nov 24; 1749: DL, Jan 24, Feb 27, CG, Mar
    6, DL, 31, HAY, Apr 18, JS, Jul 3, DL, Oct 21, HAY, 26, DL, Nov 25, Dec 6;
    1750: CG, Mar 20, DL, 22, NWSM, Aug 20, HAY, Nov 10, DL, 28; 1751: CG, Jan
    19, 21, DL, 21, CG, 23, 31, Apr 11, DL, 26, CG, May 14, 15, DL, Nov 8, 9, 11,
    15, 22, HAY, Dec 20, DL, 23; 1752: CG, Apr 24, May 11, 13, DL, Oct 11, Nov 7,
    CG, 22; 1753: DL, Feb 1, CG, 15, Mar 24, DL, Apr 26, CG, 27, DL, Oct 31, Nov
    3, CG, 30, HIC, Dec 31; 1754: HIC, Jan 2, DL, 4, Mar 28, CG, Apr 29, DL, Nov
    6; 1755: DL, May 14; 1756: DL, Jan 12, Apr 3, Nov 23; 1757: CG, Feb 21, 24,
    28, Mar 24, Apr 22; 1758: CG, Apr 12; 1760: DL, Apr 11, Nov 20, 29, Dec 4, 6,
    19; 1761: DL, Jan 2, Mar 30; 1762: CG, Mar 27; 1763: DL, Mar 15, Apr 8; 1764:
    DL, Apr 9, Nov 17, 21; 1765: DL, Mar 7, 28, May 2, Oct 15, 16, 19; 1766: HAY,
    Apr 30, KING'S, Sep 15, DL, Oct 16, CG, Nov 7, 11, 13, DL, 15, CG, Dec 2, DL,
    8; 1767: CG, Apr 27, DL, 28, CG, Oct 22, 24, Nov 20, Dec 7; 1768: CG, Oct 12;
    1769: DL, Mar 18, Apr 19, CG, May 4, DL, Oct 10, Nov 11; 1770: DL, Jan 6, Apr
    21, HAY, Jul 9, 13, 18, 30, Sep 1, DL, Oct 20, 27, CG, Nov 15, 19; 1771: CG,
    Jan 16, HAY, 28, DL, Apr 26, CG, Oct 25, Nov 2, DL, 12; 1772: CG, Mar 17, DL,
    Oct 6; 1773: DL, Jan 5, May 4, Oct 26; 1774: CG, Feb 26, Mar 1, 5, 10; 1775:
    CG, Feb 11, 14, DL, Oct 28, CG, Nov 10; 1776: DL, Jan 16, CG, Apr 24, 29, May
    8, DL, Oct 3; 1777: CHR, Jun 18; 1778: CG, Feb 16; 1779: CG, Apr 6, 14, Oct
    4; 1780: CII, Mar 17, CG, Oct 18; 1781: CG, Jan 2, Mar 12, CII, 27; 1782: CG,
    Jan 1, HAY, Aug 26, Sep 2, CG, 27, DL, Nov 29, Dec 2, 6, 23, HAY, 30; 1783:
    DL, Jan 4, 14, 20, Feb 10, CG, 17, DL, 21, 28, Mar 22, Apr 5, May 1, 22, Oct
    21; 1784: CG, Jan 3, 10, DL, Feb 24, Nov 16; 1785: CG, Apr 12, May 2, HAMM,
    Jul 27; 1786: DL, Feb 15, Nov 18, CG, 27, Dec 29; 1787: DL, Jan 5, Apr 16;
    1788: DL, Nov 11; 1789: CG, Dec 14; 1792: DLKING'S, Jan 31, CG, Nov 3; 1793:
    DL, Apr 23; 1794: CG, Feb 18, 20, Nov 8, 17, Dec 26; 1795: DL, Mar 2, 3, CG,
    Nov 6; 1796: DL, Nov 23; 1799: CG, Nov 14
--Jane Shore, 1714: DL, Feb 2, 3, 4, 5, 6, 8, 9, 11, 13, 15, 16, 18, 20, 23,
    25, Mar 1, 4, 16, Apr 20, Sep 25, Nov 6, Dec 11; 1715: DL, Feb 23, May 17,
    Oct 18; 1716: DL, Jan 2, May 12, Nov 1, 30; 1717: TC, Aug 5, 6, 7, 8, 9, 10,
    12, 13, DL, Nov 30; 1718: DL, Jan 11, Mar 6, Oct 21, Dec 30; 1719: BFPM, Aug

24, DL, Dec 5; <u>1720</u>: DL, Mar 26; <u>1721</u>: DL, Feb 3, Apr 1, Nov 14; <u>1722</u>: HAY,
Jun 28; <u>1723</u>: DL, Jan 8, SF, Sep 5, DL, Nov 30; <u>1724</u>: HAY, Mar 2, DL, 12, Apr
25, Dec 22; <u>1727</u>: DL, Feb 9, Mar 16, BF, Aug 21, DL, Nov 27, Dec 28; <u>1729</u>:
DL, Oct 11, GF, Nov 7, Dec 16; <u>1730</u>: DL, Apr 15, GF, Jul 13, Dec 5; <u>1731</u>: DL,
Mar 22, GF, Nov 18; <u>1732</u>: DL, Aug 15; <u>1733</u>: GF, Feb 12, DL, Apr 13, BFMMO,
Aug 23, DL/HAY, Oct 29; <u>1734</u>: DL/HAY, Jan 17, GF, Mar 19, HA, Aug 20, GF, Nov
11; <u>1735</u>: CG/LIF, Jan 25, 27, GF, 31, CG/LIF, Feb 7, May 13, YB/HAY, Sep 17,
YB, 26, YB/HAY, 29, CG, Dec 3; <u>1736</u>: CG, Jan 14, HAY, Feb 11, GF, 16, CG, Mar
9, Nov 26; <u>1737</u>: CG, Jan 28, Oct 27; <u>1738</u>: CG, Jan 28, Oct 18; <u>1739</u>: CG, Jan
10, DL, Mar 17, CG, Nov 22; <u>1740</u>: GF, Nov 3; <u>1741</u>: GF, Feb 9, CG, 26, GF, May
2, Sep 23; <u>1742</u>: CG, Mar 18, Apr 3; <u>1743</u>: LIF, Feb 11, DL, Mar 3, 15, Apr 9,
12, 19, CG, Oct 3, DL, Nov 24; <u>1744</u>: HAY, Feb 15, GF, Dec 21, 28, CG, 28;
<u>1745</u>: MF, May 6, 10, GF, Dec 6; <u>1746</u>: CG, Dec 18, 20; <u>1747</u>: CG, Jan 2, 3, 5,
6, 8, 9, 10, 12, 16, Mar 12, 23, HAY, 24, Apr 20, CG, 27, May 29, SF, Sep 24;
<u>1748</u>: DL, Jan 2, 4, 5, 8, 9, 11, 29, Mar 14, Apr 21, HAY, May 2, CG, Oct 21,
DL, Nov 2, HAY, 14, CG, Dec 3, 5, 19, JS, 26, CG, 28; <u>1749</u>: NWMF, Jan 5, 10,
CG, Feb 7, SOU, 20, CG, Mar 13, JS, 15, DL, 16, Apr 4, SOU, Sep 18, CG, Nov
2, Dec 12, JS, 27; <u>1750</u>: CG, Jan 6, SOU, Mar 5, CG, Apr 21, DL, Oct 18, 19,
CG, Nov 1, 2, DL, 19, Dec 22; <u>1751</u>: CG, Jan 29, Feb 14, DL, Mar 19, CG, 21,
Apr 8, DL, 15, CG, 23, DL, 25, Oct 14, CG, 23, 25, 26, 31; <u>1752</u>: DL, Jan 7,
CG, Nov 10, 15; <u>1753</u>: CG, Feb 3, Mar 22, Apr 12, DL, 30, CG, May 9, DL, Dec
22; <u>1754</u>: DL, Jan 5, Mar 18, CG, 23, 28, DL, Apr 29, Nov 30; <u>1755</u>: DL, Apr
14, CG, 15, DL, Nov 6; <u>1756</u>: DL, Apr 6; <u>1757</u>: CG, Feb 26, DL, Mar 21, Apr 25,
Nov 1; <u>1758</u>: DL, Mar 11, Apr 25, Nov 2; <u>1759</u>: CG, Apr 5, 16, HAY, May 10, CG,
14, DL, Dec 20; <u>1760</u>: CG, Jan 24, 28, Feb 13, DL, Apr 14; <u>1761</u>: DL, Jan 8,
29, Mar 14, CG, Apr 13, DL, May 23, 30, Sep 18, Oct 28; <u>1762</u>: CG, Feb 3, DL,
Apr 3, Oct 16, 21; <u>1763</u>: DL, Jan 7; <u>1764</u>: CG, Feb 13, Mar 5, DL, Apr 12, 28,
May 14, CG, 23, Oct 22, DL, 26, CG, Dec 26; <u>1765</u>: CG, May 24, Oct 9, Dec 16;
<u>1766</u>: DL, Apr 7, May 9, Oct 24, CG, Dec 10; <u>1767</u>: DL, May 2, 29, HAY, Jul 6,
CG, Oct 16, 17, Nov 11, 28; <u>1768</u>: CG, Mar 26, Apr 18, 23, Sep 28, DL, Oct 1,
CG, 1, Nov 12, DL, 24, 26; <u>1769</u>: CG, Jan 27, Apr 5, May 5, DL, 19, CG, Oct
26, Nov 10, 25, DL, Dec 13; <u>1770</u>: CG, Jan 12, Feb 17, DL, May 21, HAY, Nov
16, CG, 29, Dec 10; <u>1771</u>: CG, Jan 8, Apr 13, 25, Nov 5, DL, 21, CG, Dec 3;
<u>1772</u>: CG, Feb 4, Mar 7, May 1, DL, 5, CG, Oct 5, 7, 12, 17, 24, Nov 6, Dec
14, 23; <u>1773</u>: CG, Jan 8, Feb 5, 18, 20, May 14, Oct 11, 28, DL, Nov 6, 8, 12,
22, Dec 6, 17; <u>1774</u>: CG, Jan 3, 10, Apr 6, May 9, DL, Oct 25, Nov 1, 17, 21,
CG, Dec 15, 17, 21; <u>1775</u>: CG, Jan 26, DL, Feb 10, CG, Apr 8, 17, DL, Oct 5,
12; <u>1776</u>: DL, Jan 9, Feb 24, Sep 24, Nov 12, 23; <u>1777</u>: CHR, Jun 25; <u>1778</u>:
HAY, Feb 9, CG, 10, DL, Apr 20, CHR, Jun 1, CG, Oct 31, Nov 2, 7, 12, 16, 28,
Dec 7, 14, 21, 30; <u>1779</u>: CG, Feb 15, 22, Mar 27, HAY, Dec 20; <u>1780</u>: CG, Jun
1, Oct 4, DL, 17, Nov 6, CG, Dec 19; <u>1781</u>: CG, Jan 8, Mar 8, 31, Apr 23, Dec
10; <u>1782</u>: CG, Jan 21, 23, 28, Apr 1, 26, DL, Nov 8, 11, 23, Dec 18; <u>1783</u>: DL,
Jan 6, 9, 11, 18, 23, CG, 27, DL, Feb 1, 13, Mar 8, Apr 1, CG, 29, DL, 30,
May 3, 13, 19, Oct 11; <u>1784</u>: CG, Jan 31, DL, Feb 6, May 6, Oct 5, 23; <u>1785</u>:
DL, Apr 7, HAMM, Jul 4, DL, Nov 8, CG, Dec 14, 20; <u>1786</u>: DL, Feb 8, 20, CG,
Jun 1, HAY, 20, CG, Oct 6, 13, Dec 26; <u>1787</u>: DL, May 7, CG, Jun 5, HAY, Aug
29, CG, Nov 9, DL, 16, CG, Dec 26; <u>1788</u>: DL, Jan 19, Mar 13, HAY, Sep 9, DL,
Nov 28; <u>1789</u>: DL, Feb 24, CG, May 15, Nov 30; <u>1790</u>: CG, Dec 27; <u>1791</u>: DL, Mar
21, CG, Dec 26; <u>1792</u>: DLKING'S, Jan 24, DL, Dec 21; <u>1793</u>: DL, Jan 26, May 11,
CG, Dec 19; <u>1794</u>: DL, Oct 9, 14, Dec 13; <u>1795</u>: DL, Apr 11, Oct 5, CG, 22, 29;
<u>1796</u>: DL, Jan 22, Apr 14, Sep 22, Oct 17; <u>1797</u>: DL, Feb 14, CG, Dec 27; <u>1798</u>:
DL, Mar 13, 17, CG, 19, DL, Sep 20; <u>1799</u>: DL, Jan 19, Apr 20, CG, Nov 7, DL,
25, CG, Dec 26; <u>1800</u>: DL, Apr 17
--Lady Jane Gray, <u>1715</u>: DL, Apr 20, 21, 22, 23, 25, 26, 27, 29, May 2, 12, Oct
18; <u>1716</u>: DL, Feb 11; <u>1731</u>: GF, Dec 30, 31; <u>1732</u>: GF, Jan 1, 19, Mar 21, Apr
25, Oct 5, 27, Nov 22; <u>1733</u>: GF, Sep 19; <u>1734</u>: GF, Jan 29, Feb 25, Oct 11;
<u>1735</u>: GF, Feb 8, Mar 25; <u>1738</u>: DL, Oct 12, 14, 16, Dec 18; <u>1740</u>: GF, Nov 24;
<u>1742</u>: DL, Mar 15; <u>1745</u>: DL, Nov 11, 12; <u>1749</u>: CG, Dec 16, 18, 19, 20, 21, 22,
23; <u>1750</u>: CG, Jan 5, Feb 1, Mar 13, Apr 26; <u>1751</u>: CG, Jan 1, 22, Feb 2, Apr
9, May 8; <u>1752</u>: DL, Feb 6, 7, Apr 9, CG, Oct 12, Nov 2; <u>1753</u>: DL, Feb 22, CG,
Dec 18, 19; <u>1755</u>: CG, Apr 21, May 7, Dec 11; <u>1756</u>: CG, Feb 3; <u>1762</u>: DL, Oct
15, 20, 22, Nov 23; <u>1773</u>: CG, Apr 19, May 7; <u>1774</u>: CG, May 11, Dec 9
--Royal Convert, The (Ethelinda), <u>1707</u>: DL/QUEEN, Nov 25, QUEEN'S, 26, 27, 28,
29, Dec 1; <u>1708</u>: DL/QUEEN, Jan 3; <u>1724</u>: HAY, Jan 13, 16, Feb 20, Mar 16;
<u>1739</u>: CG, Jan 4, 5, 9, 18, Mar 15; <u>1762</u>: CG, Nov 15, 17, 20, 25, Dec 1, 7;
<u>1763</u>: CG, May 17, Oct 3, Nov 5, Dec 14; <u>1764</u>: CG, Jan 3, 31, Apr 9, May 1,
Oct 1, Nov 2; <u>1765</u>: CG, Jan 26, May 16, 17, Oct 3, 7, Nov 23; <u>1766</u>: CG, Feb
10, Nov 21; <u>1776</u>: CG, Nov 8, 14, 18, Dec 3
--Tamerlane, <u>1701</u>: LIF, Dec 0; <u>1702</u>: LIF, Jun 22; <u>1704</u>: LIF, Apr 6; <u>1705</u>: LIF,
Jan 13; <u>1706</u>: QUEEN'S, Mar 4, Nov 19; <u>1708</u>: DL, Apr 15; <u>1710</u>: DL, Feb 25, Mar
7, GR, Sep 30; <u>1715</u>: LIF, May 13, 16, 26, Oct 15; <u>1716</u>: DL, Nov 5, 6, 7, 8,
9, 10, 15, Dec 6, 27; <u>1717</u>: DL, Mar 16, Apr 29, Nov 4, 5; <u>1718</u>: DL, Jan 29,

LIF, Feb 1, Mar 11, DL, Apr 28, LIF, Oct 8, DL, Nov 4, LIF, 4, DL, 5; 1719:
DL, Jan 1, Mar 12, May 4, Nov 4, 5; 1720: DL, Apr 2, Nov 4, 5; 1721: SOU, Feb
6, DL, 11, LIF, Apr 25, Oct 14, DL, Nov 4, LIF, 4, DL, 6, GR, Dec 15; 1722:
GR, Apr 14, LIF, May 15, DL, 21, Nov 5, LIF, 5, DL, 6, LIF, 6; 1723: LIF, Feb
2, May 15, DL, Nov 4, LIF, 4, 5, DL, 5; 1724: KING'S, Oct 17, 31, Nov 3, DL,
4, LIF, 4, 5, DL, 4, KING'S, 7, 10, 14, 17, 21, 24, 28; 1725: DL, May 1,
KING'S, 1, 4, 8, DL, Nov 4, LIF, 4, DL, 5, LIF, 5; 1726: DL, Nov 4, LIF, 4,
DL, 5, LIF, 5; 1727: DL, Feb 16, Mar 25, May 11, MH, Jun 7, LIF, Nov 4, DL,
4, LIF, 6, DL, 6; 1728: DL, Feb 13, May 29, HAY, Jul 1, DL, Sep 14, Nov 4,
LIF, 4, DL, 5; 1729: DL, Feb 4, Mar 26, HAY, May 2, DL, 5, GF, Nov 4, DL, 4,
LIF, 4, DL, 5, LIF, 5, DL, Dec 31; 1730: DL, May 7, LIF, Jun 4, DL, Nov 4,
LIF, 4, GF, 5, DL, 5, LIF, 5, GF, 9, 21; 1731: DL, Jan 19, GF, Feb 12, Mar
25, KING'S, Nov 1, GF, 4, DL, 4, LIF, 4, DL, 5, GF, 5, LIF, 5, KING'S, 13,
16, 20, DL, Dec 28; 1732: GF, Mar 28, DL, Nov 4, LIF/CG, 4, GF, 4, 6, LIF/CG,
6, GF, 7, 11, Dec 30; 1733: HAY, Feb 20, BFCGBH, Aug 23, Sep 4, DL/HAY, Oct
27, GF, Nov 5, DL, 5, DL/HAY, 5, CG, 5, GF, 6, DL/HAY, 6, CG, 6; 1734: YB,
Jul 8, GR, Nov 4, DL, 4, GF, 4, CG/LIF, 4, GF, 5, GR, 5, DL, 5, CG/LIF, 5, 6,
Dec 27; 1735: DL, Jan 21, Mar 4, GF, Apr 14, Nov 4, CG, 4, DL, 4, CG, 5, GF,
5, DL, 5, GF, 6, 22; 1736: LIF, Nov 4, CG, 4, DL, 4, 5, CG, 5; 1737: CG, Nov
4, DL, 4, 5, CG, 5, DL, 7; 1738: CG, Jul 21, Sep 1, Nov 4, DL, 4, 6, CG, 6,
DL, 7; 1739: CG, Nov 5, DL, 5, 6; 1740: GF, Nov 4, DL, 4, CG, 4, GF, 5, DL,
5; 1741: GF, Nov 4, CG, 4, DL, 4, 5, CG, 5; 1742: CG, Nov 4, DL, 4, CG, 5;
1743: DL, Nov 4, CG, 4, DL, 5; 1744: DL, Nov 5, CG, 5, 6, DL, 6, 10, 22, 26,
30; 1745: JS, Jan 14, CG, Nov 4, DL, 4, CG, 5, DL, 5; 1746: DL, Nov 4, GF, 4,
CG, 4, 5, GF, 5, CG, 12; 1747: RL, Jan 27, BFH, Aug 22, DL, Nov 4, 5; 1748:
CG, Nov 4, DL, 4, CG, 5, DL, 5; 1749: DL, Nov 4, CG, 4, DL, 6, CG, 6; 1750:
NWSM, May 10, CG, Nov 5, DL, 5, 6, CG, 6, 7; 1751: CG, Apr 11, Nov 4, DL, 4,
CG, 5, DL, 5; 1752: HAY, Mar 12, CG, Nov 4, DL, 4, CG, 6; 1753: DL, Nov 5,
CG, 5, 6; 1754: CG, Mar 21, Apr 20, DL, Nov 4, CG, 4; 1755: DL, Nov 4, CG, 4;
1756: DL, Nov 4, CG, 4; 1757: DL, Nov 4, CG, 4, DL, 5; 1758: DL, Nov 4, CG,
4, 6; 1759: CG, Nov 5, DL, 5; 1760: DL, May 3; 1761: CG, Nov 4, DL, 4, CG, 5;
1762: DL, Nov 4, CG, 5; 1763: DL, Nov 4, CG, 4; 1764: DL, Apr 12, CG, Nov 5,
DL, 5; 1765: DL, Nov 11; 1766: CG, Nov 4, DL, 4; 1767: DL, Nov 4, CG, 4, 5,
DL, 5, 30; 1768: CG, Nov 4, DL, 4; 1769: CG, Nov 4, DL, 4, CG, 6, DL, 6;
1770: CG, Jan 15, 29, DL, Nov 5, CG, 5, DL, 7; 1771: DL, Nov 4, CG, 4, DL, 5,
CG, 6; 1772: DL, May 20, CG, Nov 4, DL, 4; 1773: DL, May 14, CG, Nov 4, DL,
4, 5; 1774: DL, Nov 4, CG, 4; 1775: DL, Nov 4, CG, 4, 6; 1776: CG, Nov 4, DL,
4, 5; 1777: DL, Apr 26, Nov 4, CG, 4; 1778: CG, Nov 4; 1780: CG, May 1, Nov
4, DL, 4; 1781: CG, Nov 5; 1782: CG, Nov 4; 1783: CG, Nov 4, 5; 1784: CG, Nov
4, Dec 27; 1786: HAY, Mar 6; 1787: DL, Dec 31; 1788: HAY, Dec 22; 1789: CG,
Mar 27; 1790: CG, Nov 4; 1797: DL, Feb 3, 6, 8, 14, 17, 20, 24, Mar 2, 7, 25,
Nov 4, 29
--Ulysses, 1705: QUEEN'S, Nov 23, 24, 26, 27, 28, 30, Dec 1, 6, 8, 15; 1706:
QUEEN'S, Feb 19; 1742: JS, May 31; 1749: DL, Feb 1; 1756: CG, Mar 22, 23
Rowland (beneficiary), 1736: HIC, Apr 20, May 10
Rowland (pit doorkeeper), 1719: LIF, May 29; 1720: LIF, May 30; 1721: LIF, May
29; 1722: LIF, May 25; 1723: LIF, May 24; 1724: LIF, May 27; 1725: LIF, May
20; 1726: LIF, May 24; 1728: LIF, May 18; 1729: LIF, May 20; 1730: LIF, Jun 1
Rowland (tenant), 1767: DL, Jun 1; 1772: DL, Jun 10; 1773: DL, Jun 2; 1774: DL,
Jun 2; 1775: DL, Apr 6; 1776: DL, Feb 5
Rowland, Mrs (dancer), 1756: CG, Apr 22, 27
Rowlands (spectator), 1747: GF, Feb 25
Rowlands, 1746: GF, Mar 11
Rowley, Mrs (actor), 1743: CG, Oct 31; 1744: CG, Jan 18, Apr 21, Nov 29; 1745:
CG, Apr 6, 20, May 2, Nov 13, 22; 1746: CG, Feb 24, Mar 15, Apr 15, Dec 8,
17; 1747: CG, Feb 11, May 12; 1748: HAY, Feb 29
Rowley, William, 1660: NONE, Sep 0; 1661: NONE, Sep 0; 1662: REDBULL, Jan 22;
1689: NONE, Sep 0
--All's Lost by Lust (Rape Revenged, The; or, The Spanish Revolution), 1661:
REDBULL, Mar 23, LIF, Jul 4, 9; 1689: NONE, Sep 0
--Birth of Merlin, The; or, The Child Has Found His Father, 1661: NONE, Sep 0;
1736: TCP, Aug 4, SFL, Sep 7
--Changeling, The. See Middleton, Thomas.
--Cure for a Cuckold. See Webster, John.
--Maid in the Mill, The. See Fletcher, John.
--Mayor of Quinborough, The. See Middleton, Thomas.
--Noble Gentleman, The. See Fletcher, John.
--Shoemaker's a Gentleman, A, 1662: REDBULL, Jan 22; 1674: NONE, Sep 0; 1677:
DL, Jan 1
--Spanish Gypsies, The. See Middleton, Thomas.
Rowney (beneficiary), 1736: HAY, Jul 14
Rowson (gunsmith), 1771: CG, Dec 12; 1773: CG, Dec 27; 1774: CG, May 14

Rowson (ticket deliverer), 1782: CG, May 10; 1783: CG, May 29; 1784: CG, May
    11; 1786: CG, May 18; 1787: CG, May 28; 1788: CG, Jun 4; 1789: CG, Jun 5
Rowson, Elizabeth (dancer, actor), 1781: CG, May 1, Dec 13; 1782: CG, Feb 21,
    Apr 2, May 10; 1785: CG, May 28, HAY, Aug 31, CG, Sep 23, Dec 26; 1786: CG,
    Apr 24, May 4, 18, 23, 24, 26, Sep 18, Oct 9, Nov 18, 20, 25, Dec 21; 1787:
    CG, Apr 16, May 9, 11, 23, 28, Sep 17, 26, Oct 10, 12, 17, 18, 31, Nov 7, 28,
    Dec 3, 17; 1788: CG, Jan 7, 14, Mar 28, May 29, Jun 4, HAY, Aug 5, 11, CG,
    Sep 22, Oct 17, Nov 6, 7, Dec 29; 1789: CG, Mar 28, Apr 14, 15, 30, May 5,
    22, Jun 5, 8, 16, Sep 14, Oct 2, 7, 12, Nov 12, 21, 23, 28, Dec 9, 31; 1790:
    CG, Feb 4, 11, 23, Mar 1, 22, Apr 14, May 5, 27, Jun 1, Sep 13, 17, Oct 1, 4,
    6, 11, 13, 20, 25, Nov 20
Rowson, Jane (dancer), 1791: CG, Dec 22; 1792: CG, Oct 8
Rowson, Mrs (dancer), 1795: CG, Nov 16
Rowson, Susanna, Mrs William (actor), 1792: HAY, Oct 15
Rowson, William (actor), 1788: HAY, Aug 5; 1791: CG, Dec 2, 21, 22; 1792: CG,
    Jan 16, 23, Feb 2, 28, Mar 31, Apr 12, May 9, 10, 12, Oct 8, 10, 15, 24, 27,
    29, Nov 22, 23, Dec 26; 1793: CG, Mar 11, Apr 8, May 30
Roxana. See Handel, George Frederic.
Roxana's Epilogue (entertainment), 1792: HAY, Oct 15
Roy. See Royer.
Royal Academy of Music, 1674: DL, Mar 30; 1719: KING'S, Nov 27, 30, Dec 2;
    1720: KING'S, Apr 2, Nov 23; 1723: KING'S, Jan 19, Mar 12, 23, Jun 4; 1726:
    KING'S, Feb 1
Royal Academy, 1773: DL, Nov 8
Royal Amazon, The. See Pepusch, John Christopher, Thomyris Queen of Scythia.
Royal Bounty (prize money), 1735: KING'S, Aug 20
Royal Captive, The (play, anon), 1767: HAY, Sep 18
Royal Captives, The (play, anon), 1729: HAY, Mar 27
Royal Chace, The. See Phillips, Edward.
Royal Champion, The; or, St George for England (droll), 1728: SFLH, Sep 6
Royal Circus, 1781: DL, Oct 19; 1786: HAY, Jun 9, 14; 1789: DL, May 22; 1791:
    DLKING'S, Dec 31; 1797: CG, Nov 24; 1798: CG, May 28, Jun 6, Oct 15; 1800:
    CG, May 27, Jun 13
Royal Clemency. See The Deserter of Naples.
Royal Convert, The. See Rowe, Nicholas.
Royal Cuckold, The. See Vergerius, Paul.
Royal Exchange Office, 1771: CG, Nov 29; 1772: CG, Mar 17; 1773: CG, Dec 1;
    1774: CG, Mar 19; 1797: CG, Apr 29
Royal Exchange, 1690: HUGHS, Jan 8, GB, Oct 10; 1731: SUN, Nov 30; 1737: LH,
    Jan 26; 1742: GF, Apr 24; 1745: DL, Apr 16; 1746: CG, Jan 24, Mar 13; 1748:
    DL, Mar 12; 1749: CG, Apr 28; 1750: DL, Jan 11, Apr 4; 1751: DL, Mar 7, May
    14; 1752: DL, Nov 15, CG, Dec 12, DL, 19; 1755: DL, Apr 28; 1756: CRT, Oct
    28; 1757: DL, May 6; 1758: HAY, Jan 27, CG, Jul 6; 1762: CG, May 6; 1766: CG,
    Nov 18; 1772: CG, Dec 2; 1773: CG, Mar 29; 1787: CG, Jun 15
Royal Family, 1718: NONE, May 31; 1720: KING'S, Nov 19, Dec 28; 1723: RH, Sep
    2; 1728: DL, Dec 11; 1729: KING'S, Dec 13; 1730: KING'S, Nov 3, DL, 12,
    KING'S, 17; 1731: LIF, May 6, DL, Jun 14, Jul 9, Oct 19, GF, 30, KING'S, Nov
    27; 1732: KING'S, May 6, DL, Nov 24, KING'S, 28; 1733: DL, Jan 31, KING'S,
    Feb 3, 10, DL, Apr 26, KING'S, Oct 30, Nov 10, CG, 29; 1734: GF, Feb 11,
    KING'S, Mar 5, 13, GF, 15, KING'S, 23, 28, Jul 3, Oct 29; 1735: LIF, Feb 27,
    DL, Nov 5, 15; 1736: CG, Feb 26, DL, Mar 3, KING'S, May 8, CG, Nov 10, LIF,
    19; 1737: KING'S, Jan 1; 1743: CG, Mar 2; 1747: DL, Dec 9; 1749: CG, Dec 15;
    1761: DL, Sep 14; 1773: DL, Feb 26; 1793: CG, Jan 16, Nov 20
Royal Fireworks Music (music), 1749: VAUX, Apr 21
Royal Flight, The; or, The Conquest of Ireland (play, anon), 1689: NONE, Sep 0
Royal Foundation, 1736: WS, Feb 6
Royal Gardens, 1729: RI, Aug 6; 1733: PM, Dec 24
Royal Garland, The (entertainment), 1768: CG, Oct 10, 11, 12, 14
Royal Hero, The; or, Lover of His Country (droll, anon), 1744: MFHNT, May 1
Royal Incorporated Artists of Great Britain (entertainment), 1772: MARLY, Aug
28
Royal King, and The Loyal Subject, The. See Heywood, Thomas.
Royal Marriage, 1733: GF, Nov 12; 1734: CG, Mar 12; 1736: GF, Apr 30
Royal Merchant, The. See Fletcher, John, The Beggar's Bush.
Royal Mischief, The. See Manley, Mary.
Royal Oak, The. See Latham, John.
Royal Revenge, The; or, The Princely Shepherd (Valentine and Orson) (play),
    1722: SFW, Sep 5, SOU, 25; 1724: SF, Sep 5
Royal Shepherd, The. See Rush, George.
Royal Shepherdess, The. See Shadwell, Thomas.
Royal Slave, The. See Cartwright, William.
Royal Slave, The; or, A Wife for ye All (play, anon), 1753: SFP, Sep 18, 20,

22, 24
Royal Suppliants, The. See Delap, John.
Royalist, The. See D'Urfey, Thomas.
Royalist's March (music), 1794: CG, May 7
Royall (house servant), 1758: DL, May 9; 1760: DL, May 3
Royalty Coffee House, 1787: HAY, Mar 12
Royalty Theatre, 1778: CG, Feb 17; 1787: ROY, Jul 3, HAY, Aug 29, DL, Sep 18;
   1788: DL, Jun 2; 1789: CG, May 28; 1793: HAY, Jun 15; 1796: ROY, Mar 7; 1798:
   CG, Jun 7, HAY, Sep 17
Royer (dancer), 1747: DL, Nov 2, 13, 16
Royer (ticket deliverer), 1788: CG, Jun 4
Royer, Lawrence (actor), 1726: HAY, Feb 24; 1730: HAY, Dec 17; 1733: HAY, Feb
   20; 1734: HAY, Oct 10
Royer, Miss (actor), 1743: LIF, Jan 7, Feb 14, 17, Apr 11; 1744: HAY, Dec 26;
   1745: DL, Oct 17, Nov 30, Dec 30; 1746: DL, Mar 4, 13, Apr 19, Jun 9, 13, Sep
   30, Oct 23; 1747: DL, Feb 10, May 1, Dec 12; 1748: DL, Jan 9, 22, May 2, Oct
   15; 1749: DL, May 16, Sep 26
Royer, Pierre (scene painter), 1772: DL, Oct 17; 1773: DL, Sep 25; 1774: DL,
   Sep 24, Oct 15, Nov 5; 1775: DL, Sep 30
Rozier Jr (dancer), 1786: KING'S, Mar 23
Rubinelli, Giovanni Battista (singer), 1786: KING'S, May 4, 25, Dec 23; 1787:
   KING'S, Mar 1, 15, 22, 29, Apr 17, May 1, 12
Rubridge, Mrs (actor), 1715: LIF, Oct 24, Nov 14; 1716: LIF, Apr 27, Aug 3;
   1717: LIF, May 16
Ruby (house servant, lobby doorkeeper), 1747: CG, May 22; 1750: CG, May 7;
   1760: CG, Sep 22
Ruckholt House, 1743: DL, May 16, NWLS, Nov 1; 1746: DL, May 2
Rudd (dancer), 1774: CG, May 18; 1775: CG, May 26; 1776: CG, May 3, 11; 1777:
   CG, May 9
Rudd, John (boxkeeper), 1723: HAY, Mar 14; 1724: HAY, Mar 12; 1725: HAY, Apr 14
Rudd, Mrs (fruit woman), 1748: DL, Mar 28
Rudyard (actor), 1743: TCD/BFTD, Aug 4
Rudyard, Mrs (actor), 1743: TCD/BFTD, Aug 4
Ruffian boy (entertainer), 1742: BF, Aug 26
Ruge, Phillipo (organist), 1752: CT/HAY, Mar 21
Rugg, Thomas (spectator), 1660: NONE, Sep 13
Ruggle, George, 1662: ATCOURT, Nov 1
--Ignoramus, The; or, The English Lawyer, 1662: ATCOURT, Nov 1; 1704: LIF, Jul
   10; 1716: DL, Jun 19, 21; 1717: DL, Jun 27; 1720: DL, Jul 19; 1731: WS, Jan
   28; 1736: LIF, Nov 29, 30, Dec 1, 2, 9
Rule a Wife and Have a Wife. See Fletcher, John.
Rule Britannia (song), 1751: DL, Feb 26; 1755: DL, Apr 2, 3, CG, 9, DL, 10, 24,
   CG, May 12; 1756: CG, May 6; 1757: HAY, Oct 17; 1763: MARLY, Jun 28; 1776:
   DL, Nov 9; 1777: DL, Jun 4; 1781: CG, May 1, DL, 10; 1782: CG, May 17; 1783:
   DL, May 2, Sep 27; 1785: DL, Jan 6; 1793: CG, Jan 16, KING/HAY, Feb 15, CG,
   Apr 11, 24, Jun 10, Dec 4, 18; 1794: CG, Mar 7, 12, 14, 21, 26, 28, Apr 2, 7,
   23, 25, May 9, Jun 11, 13, KING'S, 23, 24, CG, Nov 26; 1795: CG, Apr 28, May
   13, DL, 18, CG, 27, DL, Jun 3; 1796: CG, Mar 17, Apr 12, 15, 22, May 3, 28,
   Jun 2, Oct 24; 1797: KING'S, Mar 4, CG, 24, 31, Apr 7, May 2, 11, 20, DL, Oct
   16, CG, 16, 18, 20; 1798: CG, Apr 24, May 9, Jun 4, DL, Oct 2; 1799: CG, Feb
   20, May 3, 14, Jun 1, 3, HAY, Sep 2, 9; 1800: CG, Mar 21, Apr 30, May 22
Rule Britannia! See Roberts, James.
Rum Duke and the Queer Duke, The; or, A Medley of Mirth and Sorrow (play,
   anon), 1730: TC, Aug 1, 11
Rumball (boxkeeper), 1737: DL, May 27; 1738: DL, May 30; 1739: DL, May 31;
   1740: DL, May 22; 1742: DL, May 25
Rumford (house servant), 1769: CG, Jan 2; 1773: CG, Jan 5
Rumler (householder), 1778: DL, May 4; 1782: CG, Apr 27
Rummer Tavern, 1749: CG, Apr 28; 1750: DL, Feb 21
Rumny, Lord (spectator), 1697: LIF, Feb 27
Rump, The. See Tatham, John.
Rumsey, Mrs (charwoman), 1760: CG, Sep 22
Runaway, The. See Cowley, Hannah.
Rundell (actor), 1791: HAY, Dec 26
Rundell, Francis (actor), 1776: DL, Apr 19; 1778: CG, Nov 9; 1779: CG, Jan 14,
   Feb 3, 12, Mar 22
Running Footman (dance), 1723: LIF, Nov 16, 19, 27, Dec 2, 9; 1724: LIF, Mar
   23, Apr 24, May 4, 20, 22, RI, Jul 4, 11, LIF, Oct 16, 23; 1725: LIF, Jan 4,
   Apr 7, 28; 1726: LIF, Mar 10, 21, Apr 11, 20, 22; 1728: LIF, Mar 9; 1729:
   HAY, Dec 27; 1730: GF, Feb 7, HAY, Mar 20, GF, Oct 5; 1731: GF, Apr 1, DL,
   May 3; 1732: HAY, Mar 23; 1733: LIF/CG, Mar 30; 1735: HAY, Sep 29; 1736: HAY,
   Feb 19; 1742: DL, Apr 28, 29, 30, May 1, 3, 4, 8, GF, 10, DL, 13, 15, 18, 22,

731

24, 27; 1745: DL, May 8; 1750: DL, Oct 20, 22, 23, 26, 29, 30, 31, Nov 12,
  15; 1751: DL, Apr 26, May 6; 1755: DL, Apr 24, May 3, 15; 1764: DL, May 4, 10
Rupert St, 1778: KING'S, Apr 30; 1783: KING'S, May 8
Rupert, Prince (spectator), 1666: ATCOURT, Oct 18; 1667: BRIDGES, May 1; 1672:
  DG, Jul 4; 1674: CITY, Oct 29; 1680: ATCOURT, Feb 20; 1682: DL, Nov 29
Rural Amusements (dance), 1772: CG, Apr 24; 1773: CG, Feb 6, 8
Rural Assembly (dance), 1742: CG, Jan 21, 22, 23, 25, Feb 6, 10, 13, 20, 22,
  27, Mar 2, 4, 9, 13, 20, 23, Apr 1, 3, 5, 10, May 8, 13, 15, 20, 25, Jun 2
Rural Ballet (dance), 1776: CG, Oct 23
Rural Courtship (dance), 1758: HAY, Jan 12
Rural Dance (dance), 1733: GF, Dec 28; 1750: DL, Jan 4; 1753: DL, May 18; 1758:
  HAY, Jan 25; 1760: CG, Dec 20, 22; 1776: CG, Dec 26; 1777: CG, Jan 1, 10, 21,
  May 20; 1778: CG, Nov 23; 1779: CG, Oct 8, Nov 5
Rural Dance in Honour of Flora (dance), 1746: DL, May 2
Rural Dialogue (song), 1732: WINH, May 27
Rural Grace (dance), 1777: DL, Oct 2, 9, 14, 18, 31, Nov 14, Dec 3, 26; 1778:
  DL, Jan 6, 9, 13, May 13
Rural Love (dance), 1764: CG, Dec 12, 27, 29; 1765: CG, Jan 2, 4, 9, 10, 11,
  14, 16, 24, 26, Feb 2, 11, 18, 21, 25, 26, 28, Mar 9, 12, 19, 25, 28, Apr 20,
  23, 30, May 1, 6, 7, 13, 15, 16, 24, Nov 15, 16, 20, 21, 30, Dec 2, 17, 19,
  21; 1766: CG, Jan 27, 29, Feb 1, 4, 13, 25, Mar 3, 17, 18, 22, Apr 1, 3, 4,
  9, 11, 14, 17, 18, 19, 22, 23, 26, May 6, 7, 16, Nov 20, Dec 1, 3, 5, 12, 16,
  18, 31; 1767: CG, Jan 15, 21, Apr 27, May 7, 11, 14; 1769: CG, Sep 25, 30,
  Nov 2
Rural Love; or, The Merry Shepherd (pastoral opera, anon), 1732: DL, Aug 4
Rural Masquerade (entertainment), 1790: CG, Nov 23; 1793: CG, May 21; 1794: CG,
  Apr 12, Oct 29; 1795: CG, Oct 7; 1797: CG, Oct 2; 1799: CG, Mar 16, Dec 9
Rural Merriment (dance), 1774: CG, Dec 9; 1775: CG, Feb 4, 7, 15, 21, Mar 21,
  27, Apr 28, Dec 20, 21; 1776: CG, Feb 13, 14, 15, Apr 13, 25, May 2, 7; 1780:
  CG, Oct 25, Nov 23, Dec 7; 1783: CG, May 29; 1784: CG, May 11; 1786: CG, May
  30
Rural Modes, The (dance), 1727: DL, Jan 24
Rural Sports (dance), 1780: KING'S, Apr 22, May 12, 20, 27, Jun 24, Jul 1;
  1781: KING'S, Jan 23, Feb 10, Mar 15, 24, 27, May 10
Rural Sports, The; With the Stratagems of Harlequin (pantomime, anon), 1740:
  DL, Oct 27, 28, 29, 30
Ruses de l'Amour (dance), 1783: KING'S, May 1, 8; 1794: KING'S, Apr 1, 26, May
  29
Rush (boxkeeper), 1750: DL, Jan 9; 1764: DL, Feb 24, Mar 1, Nov 28, 30
Rush (composer), 1768: HAY, Jul 8
Rush, George
--Royal Shepherd, The (opera), 1764: DL, Feb 24, 27, Mar 1, 2, 5, 8, 12, 15,
  19, Apr 5; 1769: CG, Dec 15
Russ (doorkeeper), 1763: CG, May 26
Russel (landlord), 1750: DL, Jan 5
Russel (singer), 1787: RLSN, Mar 26, 27, 29, 30, 31
Russel (singer), 1798: CG, Nov 12, Dec 11, 26; 1799: CG, Jan 21, 29, Mar 25,
  Apr 2, 13, 24, 25, May 4, Oct 24
Russel Court, 1706: DL, Jun 18; 1738: DL, May 16; 1740: DL, Apr 10; 1751: DL,
  May 1; 1758: CG, Jul 6; 1766: DL, Sep 23; 1799: HAY, Apr 17; 1800: HAY, Jun
  13
Russel St, 1672: BRIDGES, Jan 25; 1735: LIF, Aug 22; 1736: CG, May 3; 1737: DL,
  May 7; 1738: DL, May 9; 1739: DL, May 5; 1740: CAC, Mar 12; 1741: DL, Sep 5;
  1742: DL, Feb 1, GF, Apr 22, DL, 24; 1743: DL, Apr 9, 18; 1744: DL, May 17,
  Dec 13; 1745: DL, Apr 25; 1747: DL, Apr 20; 1748: DL, Apr 29; 1749: DL, Apr
  1, 10, May 16; 1750: DL, Mar 22, 31, Sep 8; 1751: DL, Feb 5, Mar 7, Apr 15,
  May 1, 2; 1752: DL, Jan 24, Mar 21, Apr 4, Dec 20; 1753: DL, Mar 27, Apr 10;
  1754: DL, Apr 4, 17, May 7; 1755: DL, Mar 22, Apr 10, 24, 26; 1756: DL, Apr
  8; 1757: DL, Feb 17, Apr 12, 19, 28; 1758: DL, Jan 26, Apr 17; 1759: DL, Apr
  16, 20, Jul 12; 1760: DL, Jan 8, Apr 11; 1772: DL, Oct 30; 1777: HAY, Feb 11;
  1778: CG, Apr 4; 1779: DL, Apr 14, CG, May 4; 1780: CG, Mar 27; 1782: CG, Apr
  23, HAY, Aug 28; 1784: CG, Apr 21; 1787: DL, Feb 2; 1791: HAY, Aug 19; 1793:
  DL, May 9; 1794: DL, Sep 16; 1795: DL, Sep 17; 1797: DL, Sep 19
Russel, Lord William (patron), 1794: DL, Jul 2
Russel's Triumph (song), 1771: GROTTO, Aug 30
Russell (actor), 1734: LIF, Oct 12, CG/LIF, Nov 19; 1736: HAY, Jun 26
Russell (clothier), 1766: DL, Dec 19; 1771: DL, Dec 6
Russell (composer), 1701: DG, Mar 21
Russell (singer), 1729: HAY, Mar 29, May 26, Jun 14, Jul 19, 28, Aug 2, BFR,
  25, SF, Sep 8; 1730: GF, Jun 2
Russell (singer), 1739: KING'S, Jan 16; 1740: HIC, Jan 4, Feb 1, 22, LIF, 27,
  HIC, Mar 27, 28, Apr 2, 18, 25; 1741: HAY, Mar 13; 1744: HAY, Apr 4

Russell (ticket deliverer), <u>1734</u>: HAY, Aug 16
Russell, Katherine (spectator), <u>1692</u>: DL, Nov 9
Russell, Lady Margaret (spectator), <u>1692</u>: DL, Nov 9
Russell, Miss (dancer), <u>1714</u>: LIF, Dec 22, 28; <u>1715</u>: LIF, Jan 6, 7, 10, 13, 20,
    25, Feb 1, 3, 5, 22, Mar 3, 10, 15, 21, 22, 26, Apr 2, 4, 18, 19, 22, 25, 28,
    29, 30, May 2, 3, 9
Russell, Mrs (actor), <u>1729</u>: LIF, Jan 18, HAY, May 9, 29
Russell, Mrs (ticket deliverer), <u>1747</u>: CG, May 22
Russell, Mrs Samuel (actor), <u>1775</u>: HAY, Mar 23; <u>1776</u>: HAY, Sep 18, CHR, 23, Oct
    4, 11, 16; <u>1777</u>: CHR, Jun 18, 20, 23, 27, 30, Jul 2, 23, HAY, Oct 9, 13;
    <u>1778</u>: CHR, May 25, 29, Jun 3, 8, 9, 10, 15, 18, 19, 22, 24, 26; <u>1781</u>: HAY,
    Jan 22; <u>1790</u>: HAY, Sep 29
Russell, Samuel (actor, manager), <u>1776</u>: CHR, Oct 4, 7, 9, 11, 14, 16, 18; <u>1777</u>:
    CHR, Jun 18, 20, 23, 27, 30, Jul 2, 21, 23, HAY, Oct 9; <u>1778</u>: CHR, May 25,
    27, 29, Jun 1, 3, 8, 9, 10, 15, 18, 19, 22, 24, 26; <u>1781</u>: HAY, Jan 22
Russell, Samuel Thomas (actor, imitator), <u>1775</u>: HAY, Mar 23; <u>1776</u>: HAY, Sep 18,
    CHR, 23, HAY, 23, CHR, 30, Oct 2, 4, 7, 9, 14, 16; <u>1777</u>: CHR, Jul 23; <u>1778</u>:
    HAY, Jan 26; <u>1779</u>: HAY, Dec 20; <u>1795</u>: DL, Jan 22, Sep 22, 24, Oct 8, Nov 6,
    20, Dec 10, 30; <u>1796</u>: DL, Jan 18, 22, Apr 2, May 16, 17, 30, Jun 2, 8, 11,
    Nov 2, 5, 8, 11, 28, Dec 1; <u>1797</u>: DL, Jan 17, 27, Mar 20, Apr 19, 27, May 12,
    15, 19, 23, 27, Jun 2, 5, 8, 10, Sep 21, 23, 26, 30, Oct 17, 23, Nov 7, 10,
    11, 13, 14, 15, 17, 18, 20, 23, 24, 25, 27, 28, Dec 2, 7, 19, 26; <u>1798</u>: DL,
    Jan 9, Feb 9, 13, May 16, 19, 24, Jun 6, 8, Sep 18, 20, 29, Oct 6, 9, Nov 10,
    Dec 4, HAY, 17, DL, 21; <u>1799</u>: DL, Jan 11, 31, Feb 23, 26, Apr 5, 24, 25, May
    3, 9, 18, 24, 27, Jun 10, 29, Jul 1, 2
Russell, William (organist), <u>1800</u>: CG, Jun 16
Russia, Emperour of, <u>1774</u>: KING'S, Jan 15
Russia, <u>1744</u>: MF, Jan 25
Russian Ambassador, <u>1681</u>: DLORDG, Dec 18; <u>1682</u>: DLORDG, Jan 10, DG, 11, DL, 13,
    DG, Mar 0; <u>1698</u>: DL, Jul 9; <u>1707</u>: QUEEN'S, Jun 10; <u>1755</u>: DL, Feb 5
Russian Light Infantry and Cossack Camp (dance), <u>1778</u>: CG, May 9
Russian Melodies (music), <u>1790</u>: CG, Mar 8
Russian Minuet (dance), <u>1787</u>: HAY, Jul 30, Sep 13; <u>1789</u>: DL, May 19, Jun 13;
    <u>1791</u>: DL, Apr 29
Russian Sailor (dance), <u>1735</u>: DL, Jan 9, 18, 23, Feb 4, 6, 27, Mar 10, 13, 17,
    20, 24, 27, 29, Apr 25, Nov 15, 27, Dec 10, 22; <u>1736</u>: DL, Jan 29, Feb 2, 5,
    13, Apr 10, May 5, 22; <u>1737</u>: DL, Mar 10, 12, 15, 22, Apr 23, 26, May 14, 16,
    24, 25, 27; <u>1738</u>: DL, Jan 21, Feb 1, 6, 9, Apr 29, May 1, 10, 12, 18; <u>1739</u>:
    DL, Apr 24, 27, May 1; <u>1740</u>: DL, Apr 25, 30; <u>1746</u>: SOU, Oct 7, 27
Ruth. See Handel, George Frederic.
Rutherford, John (proprietor), <u>1767</u>: CG, Jun 9; <u>1768</u>: CG, Mar 1, Jun 4
Rutherford, Lord Thomas (spectator), <u>1664</u>: BRIDGES, Sep 28
Ruthin, Lord Grey of. See Yelverton, Henry.
Rutland, Countess of. See Manners, Katherine.
Rutland, Earl of. See Manners, John.
Rutter, Margaret (actor), <u>1660</u>: NONE, Sep 0; <u>1661</u>: VERE, Dec 16; <u>1662</u>: ATCOURT,
    Nov 1; <u>1663</u>: VERE, Mar 0, NONE, Sep 0; <u>1666</u>: NONE, Sep 0, ATCOURT, Dec 10,
    BRIDGES, 27; <u>1667</u>: BRI/COUR, Feb 0, BRIDGES, Apr 16; <u>1668</u>: BRIDGES, Sep 14;
    <u>1669</u>: BRIDGES, Feb 6, Apr 17; <u>1671</u>: BRIDGES, Mar 0; <u>1675</u>: DL, Jan 12, 25, Aug
    0; <u>1677</u>: DL, Mar 0, Oct 0
Rutti, Miss (dancer), <u>1727</u>: KING'S, Apr 25
Ryan-Legar-Chapman-Hall Booth, <u>1734</u>: BFRLCH, Aug 24, Sep 2
Ryan, Anthony (actor), <u>1736</u>: CG, Mar 27, May 13, Nov 15; <u>1737</u>: CG, Feb 26, Mar
    24, Apr 14, May 3, 6, Sep 16, Oct 10; <u>1738</u>: CG, Feb 6, 13, 23, Mar 13, Apr
    14, 17, 25, Oct 6, 16, 21, 23, 26, Nov 6, 13, 25, 29, Dec 2, 5; <u>1739</u>: CG, Feb
    9, Mar 3, Apr 2, 25, May 7, 10, 16, 17, 23, 25, Sep 27, 29, Oct 22, 25, Nov
    10, Dec 7, 10, 19, 21; <u>1740</u>: CG, Jan 15, Mar 11, 24, 27, Apr 21, May 2, 3, 12
Ryan, Lacy (actor, author), <u>1710</u>: GR, Jul 1, 17, 29, Aug 3; <u>1711</u>: DL, Feb 3,
    Mar 17, DL/QUEEN, Jun 5, DL, Aug 3, 17, Oct 12, Nov 12; <u>1712</u>: DL, May 26;
    <u>1713</u>: DL, Jan 29, Feb 19, Apr 14, May 12, Jun 12; <u>1714</u>: DL, Jan 5, May 17,
    Jun 4, 14, 25, 29, Jul 13, 20; <u>1715</u>: DL, Feb 21, Mar 26, Apr 20, May 3, 18,
    31, Jun 6, 28, Oct 13, Nov 19, Dec 6; <u>1716</u>: DL, Jan 13, Feb 3, Mar 6, Apr 2,
    21, 28, Aug 9, Oct 6, 22, 24, Dec 17, 27; <u>1717</u>: DL, Jan 24, 26, 31, Feb 25,
    Apr 29, May 2, 10, 11, 30, Jun 10, Jul 16, Aug 6, 9, 13, 22, SF, Sep 9, DL,
    Oct 1, 14, 16, 22, 25, Nov 19; <u>1718</u>: LIF, Mar 1, 11, Apr 19, Jun 20, NONE,
    Jul 12, LIF, Sep 30, Oct 1, 3, 4, 6, 8, 11, 16, 18, Nov 1, 11, 13, 24, Dec 6;
    <u>1719</u>: LIF, Jan 16, Feb 7, 26, 28, Oct 2, 7, 10, 13, 15, 17, 31, Nov 7, 12,
    19, 21, 26, Dec 10; <u>1720</u>: LIF, Jan 7, 11, 26, Feb 11, 13, 26, 29, Mar 12, 17,
    Apr 2, 18, May 4, 11, 17, 19, Jun 7, Oct 1, 8, 13, 15, 20, 22, Nov 1, 2, 3,
    10, 18, 19, 22, 29, Dec 1, 8, 17, 21, 22, 27, 31; <u>1721</u>: LIF, Jan 7, 10, 17,
    19, 28, Feb 6, 9, 14, 25, Mar 4, 11, 18, 27, Apr 1, 13, 19, 21, 25, May 10,
    Sep 23, 27, 29, Oct 3, 5, 7, 10, 14, 17, 20, 21, 24, 25, 26, 28, Nov 2, 4,

13, 16, 18, 24, 25, 29, Dec 2, 11, 12, 18; <u>1722</u>: LIF, Jan 9, 13, 22, Feb 2,
13, Mar 5, 8, 15, 29, May 4, Oct 4, 6, 9, 11, 13, 16, 19, 20, 22, 23, 24, 27,
29, 30, 31, Nov 1, 2, 3, 5, 7, 8, 14, 16, 17, 22, 29, 30, Dec 1, 5, 7, 10,
14; <u>1723</u>: LIF, Jan 3, 11, 12, 18, Feb 1, 16, 22, Mar 11, Apr 16, 23, May 3,
Sep 28, 30, Oct 2, 7, 9, 10, 14, 18, 24, 25, 29, Nov 1, 2, 4, 12, 14, 16, 19,
21, 26, Dec 2, 7; <u>1724</u>: LIF, Feb 24, Mar 16, 19, 23, 26, 28, Apr 9, 14, 28,
May 19, Jun 3, Sep 23, 28, Oct 7, 9, 12, 14, 22, 30, Nov 3, 4, 6, 12, 18, 20,
24, 25, 26; <u>1725</u>: LIF, Jan 4, 11, 16, 19, Feb 27, Mar 11, 13, 31, Apr 5, 23,
26, May 12, 19, 20, Sep 24, 29, Oct 1, 4, 13, 15, 16, 19, 23, 26, 28, Nov 2,
4, 6, 8, 9, 11, 12, 17, 18, 23, 30, Dec 2, 3, 6, 8, 15; <u>1726</u>: LIF, Jan 7, Feb
19, Mar 19, 21, 24, Apr 2, 11, 22, May 3, 4, 11, Sep 12, 14, 19, 21, 26, Oct
3, 12, 17, 24, Nov 2, 4, 8, 10, 11, 14, 18, 21, Dec 14; <u>1727</u>: LIF, Jan 4, 16,
Feb 2, 7, Mar 13, Apr 7, 10, 17, 19, May 2, 9, 22, Sep 11, 15, 18, 25, 27,
Oct 9, 19, 21, 26, 31, Nov 1, 4, 16, 17, Dec 14, 16; <u>1728</u>: LIF, Jan 17, Mar
9, 14, 18, 21, 28, Apr 1, 4, 6, 22, 26, 30, May 11, 18, 23, Sep 16, 18, 30,
Oct 1, 7, 21, 23, Nov 1, 4, 11, 19, 20, Dec 5, 7, 28, 31; <u>1729</u>: LIF, Jan 13,
16, Feb 6, 7, 10, 22, Mar 3, 4, 10, 17, Apr 8, 10, 11, 15, 16, 17, May 3, Sep
12, 17, 19, 22, 24, 26, 29, Oct 3, 6, 8, 10, 13, 20, 22, 24, 29, 31, Nov 4,
7, 8, 13, 14, 22, 25, Dec 15; <u>1730</u>: LIF, Jan 19, Mar 9, Apr 6, 20, May 6, 7,
15, 18, 20, Jun 1, Sep 16, 18, 21, 23, Oct 5, 7, 12, 14, 19, 26, 27, 30, Nov
2, 3, 4, 13, 23, Dec 3; <u>1731</u>: LIF, Jan 4, 8, 9, 11, 13, 20, 21, Feb 3, 27,
Mar 15, 22, Apr 3, 5, 22, 26, May 1, 5, 10, 17, 20, 25, Sep 17, 20, 22, 27,
29, Oct 1, 6, 11, 18, 20, 25, 27, Nov 2, 4, 8, 12, 17, 25, Dec 1, 3, 6, 8, 9,
11, 15; <u>1732</u>: LIF, Jan 18, 19, 26, 28, Feb 15, 28, Mar 23, 25, Apr 10, 13,
18, 27, 29, May 1, 9, CG/LIF, Sep 22, LIF/CG, 25, 27, 29, Oct 4, 6, 9, 11,
16, LIF, 18, LIF/CG, 21, 23, 25, 27, 30, Nov 1, 3, 4, 7, 11, 13, 14, 17, 18,
22, Dec 4, 7, 14, 15; <u>1733</u>: LIF/CG, Jan 1, 15, CG, Feb 8, LIF/CG, Mar 15, CG,
27, LIF/CG, 29, 30, 31, Apr 2, CG, 4, LIF/CG, 10, 11, 13, CG, May 2, LIF/CG,
7, 10, 24, Jun 1, CG, Sep 15, 20, 22, 25, 27, 29, Oct 2, 4, 6, 9, 11, 13, 18,
19, 20, 23, 25, 26, 27, 29, 31, Nov 1, 3, 5, 8, 9, 14, 16, 19, 21, 26, 30,
Dec 3, 8, 15, 17, 20, 31; <u>1734</u>: CG, Jan 9, 12, 18, Feb 14, Mar 5, 18, 28, Apr
16, 18, May 13, 17, BFRLCH, Aug 24, Sep 2, CG, 2, RI, 9, CG/LIF, 18, 20, 23,
25, 30, Oct 7, 9, 11, 14, 16, 18, 19, 25, 29, Nov 4, 11, 14, 25, 28, Dec 5,
26; <u>1735</u>: CG/LIF, Jan 9, 17, 21, 25, 31, Feb 3, 4, 11, LIF, 12, CG/LIF, 13,
15, 22, LIF, Mar 3, CG/LIF, 13, 15, 18, 20, 24, CG, Apr 25, CG/LIF, May 1, 2,
CG, 6, CG/LIF, 19, CG, Sep 12, 16, 17, 19, 24, 29, Oct 3, 8, 10, 13, 15, 17,
20, 24, 25, 29, 31, Nov 1, 4, 6, 7, 8, 10, 13, 15, 17, 22, 29, Dec 8, 15;
<u>1736</u>: CG, Jan 8, Feb 21, 26, Mar 9, 18, 20, 22, 27, 29, Apr 13, 29, May 3,
13, 17, 20, Sep 15, 17, 20, 24, 27, Oct 1, 4, 6, 8, 11, 13, 15, LIF, 18, CG,
20, 23, 29, 30, Nov 1, 4, 8, 11, 15, 22, 25, 26, 29, Dec 9, 20; <u>1737</u>: CG, Jan
10, 17, Feb 3, 7, 14, 15, 26, Mar 14, 17, 24, Apr 14, 26, May 31, LIF, Sep 7,
CG, 16, 21, 23, 26, 28, Oct 3, 5, 7, 10, 12, 17, 21, 22, 26, 27, 29, 31, Nov
1, 4, 9, 14, 18, 19; <u>1738</u>: CG, Jan 3, 6, 9, 13, 17, 18, 25, 26, 31, Feb 6,
13, 16, 23, Mar 13, 14, 18, 20, 25, Apr 7, 10, 17, 22, 25, DL, 26, CG, May
18, Jul 21, Sep 15, 18, 22, 25, 27, Oct 2, 4, 6, 9, 13, 14, 16, 18, 21, 23,
24, 26, 30, 31, Nov 2, 4, 7, 9, 11, 15, 17, 20, 22, 23, 24, 27, 28, 29, 30,
Dec 2, 4, 7, 12; <u>1739</u>: CG, Jan 15, 17, 23, Feb 9, 10, 24, 26, Mar 3, 13, 20,
Apr 5, 10, 12, 25, May 1, 30, Aug 21, 31, Sep 7, 10, 12, 14, 15, 17, 19, 21,
27, 28, 29, Oct 2, 3, 5, 8, 10, 22, 23, 25, 26, 29, Nov 2, 5, 9, 10, 17, 20,
22, 27, 28, Dec 1, 4, 6, 10, 15, 19, 21, 29; <u>1740</u>: CG, Jan 12, 15, Mar 11,
18, 27, Apr 14, May 9, 27, Jun 5, Sep 19, 22, 24, 26, 29, Oct 3, 8, 22, 24,
25, 27, 29, 31, Nov 1, 4, 6, 7, 20, Dec 4, 5, 13, 19; <u>1741</u>: CG, Jan 2, 6, 7,
12, 15, 21, 27, Feb 14, 17, 23, 26, Mar 12, 16, 30, Apr 9, 11, 15, 17, 22,
24, May 1, 4, 11, 12, Sep 21, 23, 25, 28, 30, Oct 2, 5, 7, 8, 10, 13, 15, 20,
21, 24, 26, 29, 31, Nov 4, 7, 9, 11, 23, 26, 27, Dec 1, 9, 11, 17, 18; <u>1742</u>:
CG, Jan 23, Feb 3, 4, 10, 15, 25, 27, Mar 13, 15, 18, Apr 24, May 1, 5, 7,
Sep 22, 29, Oct 1, 4, 6, 9, 11, 15, 16, 18, 19, 21, 25, 26, 27, 28, 29, Nov
3, 4, 11, 13, 15, 20, 22, 25, 29, 30, Dec 7, 15, 22; <u>1743</u>: CG, Jan 5, Feb 9,
17, Mar 17, Apr 9, May 4, 5, Sep 21, 23, 26, 28, 30, Oct 3, 5, 7, 12, 14, 17,
21, 24, 26, 28, 29, 31, Nov 2, 4, 16, 19, 21, 28, 30, Dec 3, 8, 12, 16, 17,
19, 27, 31; <u>1744</u>: CG, Jan 4, 7, 11, 14, 24, Feb 3, 7, 23, Mar 3, 8, 12, 13,
Apr 19, Sep 19, 21, 24, 28, Oct 1, 3, 5, 8, 15, 16, 18, 20, 22, 26, 29, 31,
Nov 1, 5, 7, 9, 12, 21, 22, 27, 28, 29, Dec 5, 6, 11, 13, 21, 26, 28; <u>1745</u>:
CG, Jan 2, 4, 7, 14, 18, 23, Feb 9, 11, 15, Mar 11, 18, Apr 23, 25, May 6,
13, Sep 23, 25, 27, Oct 2, 4, 7, 9, 11, 14, 16, 29, 31, Nov 4, 7, 8, 9, 12,
13, 14, 15, 18, 19, 28, Dec 2, 5, 6, 12, 13; <u>1746</u>: CG, Jan 2, 7, 11, 13, Feb
3, 5, 6, 8, Mar 10, 13, 15, Apr 3, 7, 21, 23, Jun 11, 27, Sep 29, Oct 1, 3,
4, 6, 8, 10, 15, 24, 27, 29, Nov 1, 4, 6, 8, 11, 13, 14, 17, 18, 26, 28, Dec
6, 10, 17, 22, 29; <u>1747</u>: CG, Jan 2, 20, 29, 31, Feb 3, 11, 12, Mar 7, 17, DL,
19, CG, 24, 26, 30, Apr 2, 4, 20, Nov 11, 13, 16, 18, 23, Dec 1, 4, 9, 15,
17, 28; <u>1748</u>: CG, Jan 2, 7, 8, 9, 12, 14, 15, 16, 27, Feb 10, 15, Mar 5, 14,
Apr 11, 13, 16, 18, 21, 22, 26, Sep 21, 23, 28, 30, Oct 3, 7, 10, 14, 17, 21,

734

22, 24, 25, 27, 28, 29, Nov 1, 3, 4, 9, 11, 16, 24, 26, 28, Dec 1, 9, 10, DL,
10, CG, 20, 22, 26; 1749: CG, Jan 2, 11, 13, 25, 28, Feb 6, 23, Mar 2, 9, 14,
29, 31, Apr 5, 7, 15, 21, May 4, Sep 25, 27, 29, Oct 4, 6, 9, 11, 12, 16, 18,
19, 23, 25, 26, 27, 30, Nov 1, 2, 4, 8, 9, 11, 16, 18, 24, Dec 7, 8, 16, 27;
1750: CG, Jan 16, 18, 23, 31, Feb 2, 5, 20, Mar 12, 17, 19, 27, Apr 5, 23,
Sep 26, DL, Oct 1, CG, 15, 16, 17, 18, 19, 20, 22, 24, 25, 26, 29, Nov 1, 5,
8, 12, 19, 22, 24, 28, 30, Dec 1, 4, 10, 14, 21; 1751: CG, Jan 1, 3, Feb 1,
9, 23, Mar 14, 21, Apr 8, 10, 16, May 1, 9, 16, Sep 23, 25, Oct 11, 22, 25,
29, Nov 4, 6, 7, 11, 14, 16, 21, 22, 26, Dec 5, 10, 16, 26; 1752: CG, Jan 3,
18, 21, 28, Mar 3, 7, 16, 17, 30, Apr 4, 15, 28, 30, May 4, Sep 20, 22, 25,
29, Oct 4, 6, 9, 12, 14, 16, 19, 23, 27, 30, 31, Nov 4, 7, 9, 10, 16, 23, 27,
28, Dec 8, 9, 11, 13, 14, 19, 27; 1753: CG, Feb 6, 12, Mar 19, 20, May 3, 7,
8, Sep 10, 14, 21, 24, Oct 1, 3, 8, 17, 27, DL, 30, CG, 30, 31, Nov 1, 5, 7,
9, 12, 28, Dec 26; 1754: CG, Mar 9, 23, Apr 1, 6, 17, May 2, 3, 7, Sep 18,
20, 23, 27, Oct 4, 7, 9, 14, 16, 17, 18, 24, 26, 29, Nov 4, 16, 27, Dec 10,
13; 1755: CG, Jan 4, 10, 14, 28, Feb 18, Mar 12, Apr 4, 7, 8, 9, 10, 15, 23,
May 7, 15, Oct 1, 8, 14, 18, 21, 22, 27, Nov 4, 10, 12, 17, 21, 26, Dec 3,
11; 1756: CG, Feb 9, 26, Mar 18, 22, 27, Apr 3, 20, May 8, 20, Sep 20, Oct 1,
6, 8, 11, 15, 20, 23, 26, Nov 4, 9, 11, 15; 1757: CG, Jan 27, Feb 16, Mar 29,
May 16, Sep 14, 21, 23, 26, 30, Oct 5, 8, Nov 4, 5, 7, 9, 11, 16, 18, Dec 5,
9, 10; 1758: CG, Mar 14, 29, Apr 10, 14, 17, Sep 18, 20, 22, 25, Oct 2, 23,
26, 27, 30, Nov 2, 3, 4, 9; 1759: CG, Feb 1, 12, 15, Mar 29, Apr 2, 5, May 3,
7, 11, 15, Sep 26, Nov 5, Dec 6, 10, 19, 28; 1760: CG, Feb 7, Mar 18, Apr 14;
1761: CG, Apr 7
--Cobler's Opera, The; or, The Amours of Billingsgate (musical), 1728: LIF, Apr
26; 1729: LIF, Mar 17, Apr 9, 10, 24; 1731: GF, Apr 20, DL, Jun 11, 15, Jul
2; 1733: GF, Apr 25; 1734: HAY, Aug 22; 1739: CG, Apr 24, May 3
Ryan, Master (actor), 1736: CG, Mar 18, May 13; 1739: CG, Sep 10, 21
Ryan, Widow (beneficiary), 1761: CG, Apr 7
Ryder (actor), 1782: HAY, Nov 25; 1783: HAY, Dec 15; 1784: HAY, Feb 9; 1785:
HAY, Jan 31, Apr 25; 1792: HAY, Feb 20, Nov 26; 1799: WRSG, May 17
Ryder, Corbet (actor), 1798: DL, Nov 29, Dec 5, 7, HAY, 17, DL, 29; 1799: DL,
Jan 2, 19, Mar 2, 11, May 20, 24, Jun 26, Jul 3, 5, Sep 19, Oct 8, 10, 19,
31, Nov 6, 16; 1800: DL, Mar 11, 27, 31, Apr 5, 29, May 2, 3, Jun 12, 13, 18
Ryder, Mary (actor), 1790: CG, Apr 16, HAY, Jun 22
Ryder, Rose (actor), 1790: CG, Apr 16, HAY, Aug 6
Ryder, Thomas (actor, playwright), 1768: DL, Apr 12; 1782: HAY, Nov 25; 1786:
CG, Oct 25, Nov 13, 15, 22, 29, Dec 12, 21, 30; 1787: CG, Jan 2, 6, Mar 27,
Apr 16, 25, 26, 27, 30, May 1, 22, Sep 17, 19, Oct 10, 11, 12, 18, Nov 2, 5,
30, Dec 10, 15; 1788: CG, Jan 5, 14, 21, 29, Mar 1, 11, 15, Apr 8, 14, 23,
May 12, Sep 19, Oct 3, 7, 8, Nov 6, 10, 12, 18, 21, 28, Dec 13, 27, 31; 1789:
CG, Mar 5, 28, 31, Apr 4, 20, 29, 30, May 5, 7, 8, 19, 26, Jun 5, 8, 16, Sep
28, 30, Oct 6, 9, 24, 31, Nov 2, 7, 19, 30, Dec 5, 10; 1790: CG, Jan 13, Feb
4, 6, 11, 23, 25, Mar 18, Apr 6, 16, 20, 21, May 5, 7, Jun 4, HAY, 22, 26,
Jul 16, 22, Aug 6, 11, Sep 4, CG, 15, 17, Oct 8, 13, 15, Nov 4, 11, 19; 1791:
CG, Jun 10
--Like Master Like Man, 1767: HAY, Sep 21; 1768: DL, Apr 12, 27, May 7, 24;
1773: DL, Mar 30, Apr 28, May 10
--Opposition (farce), 1790: HAY, Aug 6
--Such Things Have Been (farce), 1789: CG, Mar 31, Jun 17
Rye (house servant), 1784: CG, May 22; 1786: CG, Jun 1; 1787: CG, Jun 2; 1788:
CG, May 30; 1789: CG, Jun 13; 1790: CG, Jun 8; 1791: CG, Jun 9; 1792: CG, May
29; 1794: CG, Jun 12; 1796: CG, Jun 6; 1797: CG, Jun 6; 1798: CG, Jun 5;
1799: CG, May 29; 1800: CG, Jun 4
Ryley (singer), 1760: CG, Jan 18, Dec 11; 1762: CG, Nov 3, 15; 1763: CG, May
17, Oct 3; 1764: CG, Jan 3, Oct 1; 1765: CG, Oct 3, 7, 22; 1766: CG, Oct 21,
Nov 21; 1767: CG, Feb 14, Sep 25, Oct 30, Nov 5
Rymer, Thomas, 1677: DL, Oct 0; 1682: NONE, Sep 0
--Edgar; or, The English Merchant, 1677: NONE, Sep 0, DL, Oct 0
Rymon, Mynheer (dancer), 1728: HAY, Apr 3
Rymos (actor), 1735: LIF, Aug 22

S hai pieta (song), 1714: QUEEN'S, May 1
S, J
--Converts, The; or, The Folly of Priest-Craft, 1689: NONE, Sep 0
S, T (author), 1766: KING'S, Sep 13
Sa Ga Yean Qua Rash Tow, King of the Marquas, 1710: QUEEN'S, Apr 28; see also
American Indians; Indian Kings, American
Sabatini (dancer), 1755: DL, Feb 3, Apr 1

Sabatini Jr (dancer), 1755: DL, Feb 3, Apr 1, 22
Sabatini, Sg and Sga (dancers), 1754: DL, Oct 22, 23, Nov 4, 5; 1755: DL, Apr
   1, 10, 22
Sabatini, Sg, Sga, and Jr (dancers), 1755: DL, Mar 17, Apr 3, 24
Sabatini, Sga (dancer), 1754: DL, Nov 15, 16, 19, 21, 25, 26, 28, Dec 7, 12,
   16, 26; 1755: DL, Feb 3
Sabotiers (dance), 1741: DL, Jan 16, 17, Feb 9, Apr 1; 1742: LIF, Dec 6; 1743:
   LIF, Jan 7; 1750: DL, Apr 28; 1754: CG, Mar 30, Apr 29; 1756: CG, Apr 22;
   1762: CG, Apr 19, 22, 26, DL, Oct 13, 15
Sabotiers de Piemont, Les (dance), 1741: CG, Apr 20
Sabotiers Tyrolese (dance), 1752: CG, Oct 28, Nov 16; 1753: CG, Feb 1, 12, Mar
   8, 15, 17, 27
Sabrina (opera), 1737: KING'S, Apr 25, 26, 30, May 3, 7, 10, 14, 17, 21, 31,
   Jun 7, 11, 14, Nov 19
Saby (house servant), 1787: CG, Jun 2; 1788: CG, May 27; 1789: CG, Jun 5; 1790:
   CG, May 29; 1791: CG, Jun 2; 1792: CG, May 25
Sacchini, Antonio Maria Gasparo (composer), 1771: KING'S, Mar 14; 1773: KING'S,
   Jan 19, May 6, Nov 20; 1774: KING'S, Jan 29, Apr 19, HIC, May 9; 1775:
   KING'S, Jan 14, Feb 7, Nov 7; 1776: KING'S, Mar 12, DL, 20; 1777: CG, Mar 19,
   KING'S, Nov 8, CG, 18; 1778: KING'S, Feb 7, Mar 5, Apr 9, May 5, Nov 24;
   1779: DL, Mar 12, KING'S, 25, May 13, Dec 14; 1780: KING'S, Feb 8, Apr 22,
   Dec 23; 1781: KING'S, Jan 23, Jun 23; 1782: KING'S, Mar 2, CG, Dec 31; 1784:
   KING'S, Feb 26, CG, Apr 17; 1785: DL, Dec 8; 1786: KING'S, Jan 24, Feb 14,
   Mar 11, 21, DL, May 2, CG, Dec 26; 1787: CG, Apr 24, Nov 5; 1788: CG, Dec 13;
   1789: CG, Jan 26, DL, Feb 27, Mar 6, 20, 25, CG, May 20, Nov 24; 1790: CG,
   Mar 8; 1791: PAN, Feb 17, CG, Apr 6, HAY, Jun 25; 1792: CG, Feb 28, Mar 7,
   May 22, DLKING'S, 23, CG, 28, Nov 3; 1793: CG, Sep 16; 1797: KING'S, Jan 10;
   1799: KING'S, Mar 26, DL, May 24
--Amore Soldato, L' (opera), 1778: KING'S, May 5, 12, 19, 26, Jun 2, 9, 16, 23;
   1780: KING'S, Feb 8, 15, 22, Mar 7, 14, 28, Apr 1, 4, 11
--Armida (opera), 1774: KING'S, Nov 8, 19, 22, 26, Dec 6; 1775: KING'S, Jan 7,
   14, 17, 21, 28, Mar 16, 23, Apr 22; 1780: KING'S, Apr 22
--Avaro Deluso, L' (opera), 1778: KING'S, Nov 24, Dec 1, 8, 15; 1779: KING'S,
   May 13; 1783: KING'S, Jun 14, 21
--Cid, Il (opera), 1773: KING'S, Jan 19, 23, 26, 29, Feb 2, 6, 9, 13, 16, 20,
   23, 27, Mar 4, 6, 16, 20, Apr 19, 24, 27, May 1, Jun 3, 19
--Contadina in Corte, La (opera), 1771: KING'S, Mar 14; 1779: KING'S, Dec 14,
   21, 23, 28; 1780: KING'S, Jan 1, 11, 25, Feb 1; 1782: KING'S, Mar 2, 5, 9,
   19, Apr 2, 4, 16, 23, 27, 30, May 7, 11, 21, Jun 1, 5
--Creso (opera), 1758: KING'S, Apr 4, 11, May 6
--Didone (opera), 1775: KING'S, Nov 7, 11, 18, 25, Dec 2, 9, 16, 30; 1776:
   KING'S, Jan 13, 20, 27
--Enea e Lavinia (opera), 1779: KING'S, Mar 25, 27, Apr 10, 17, 24, May 1, 8,
   11, 21
--Erifile (opera), 1778: KING'S, Feb 7, 14, 21, 28, Mar 7, 14, 21, 28; 1789:
   CG, May 20
--Euriso, 1781: KING'S, Jun 23, 26, 30, Jul 3
--Evelina (Arvire et Evelina) (opera), 1797: KING'S, Jan 10, 14, 17, 21, 24,
   28, 31, Feb 4, 18, 28, Mar 7, Apr 1, 4, 8, Dec 12, 16, 30; 1798: KING'S, Jan
   6, Feb 6
--Isola D'Amore, L' (opera), 1776: KING'S, Mar 12, 16, 19, 26, Apr 23, Jun 6
--Lucio Vero (opera), 1773: KING'S, Nov 20, 23, 27, 30, Dec 4, 11, 18; 1774:
   KING'S, Jan 1, 4, 8, 15, 22, 25, Feb 24, Mar 24, Apr 28, May 12
--Mitridate (opera), 1781: KING'S, Jan 23, 27, 29, Feb 3, 10, 17, Mar 3
--Motezuma (opera), 1775: KING'S, Feb 7, 11, 18, 25, Mar 4, 11, 25, Apr 1, 8,
   29, May 16
--Nitteti (opera), 1774: KING'S, Apr 19, 23, 26, 30
--Perseo (opera), 1774: KING'S, Jan 29, Feb 1, 5, 8, 12, 17, 19, 22, 26, Mar 1,
   5, 12, 17, 19, 26, Apr 7, May 7, 28, Jun 23; 1786: KING'S, Mar 21, 28, Apr 1,
   8, 22, 29
--Rinaldo (opera), 1780: KING'S, Apr 22, 29, May 6, 12, 20, 27, Jun 3, 10, 17,
   24, Dec 23, 30; 1781: KING'S, Jan 2, 6, 13, 16, 20, Feb 8
--Tamerlano (opera), 1773: KING'S, May 6, 8, 11, 15, 22, Jun 5
--Trionfo della Costazza, Il (serenata), 1774: HIC, May 9
Sack Posset. See Smart, Christopher.
Sackville, Charles, Earl of Dorset, Lord Buckhurst, 1666: ATCOURT, Oct 18;
   1667: NONE, Jul 13, BRIDGES, Aug 26, NONE, Oct 26; 1668: LIF, Feb 6; 1670:
   BRIDGES, Mar 0, May 0; 1676: DL, Dec 11; 1690: DG, Jun 0; 1692: NONE, Jan 19
Sackville, Edward, Major General (author), 1691: DL, Dec 0
Sackville, Mary Compton, Countess of Dorset, 1686: NONE, Jan 7
Sackville, Tufton, 9th Earl of Thanet, 1797: DL, Oct 27
Sacred Music (music), 1762: CHAPEL, May 18

Sacred Ode (song), <u>1763</u>: CG, Mar 4, DL, Apr 27
Sacred Truth (song), <u>1789</u>: DL, Mar 20
Sacrifice (song), <u>1704</u>: DL, Jan 4, Mar 28
Sacrifice of Iphigenia, The (oratorio, anon), <u>1750</u>: NWC, Apr 16
Sacrifice, The. See Fane, Sir Francis.
Sacrifice, The; or, The Death of Abel. See Arne, Dr Thomas A.
Sad Shepherd. See Jonson, Ben.
Sadee, Hadgee Mahomet (Algerian ambassador), <u>1732</u>: LIF, Jan 21
Sadler (house servant), <u>1739</u>: CG, May 29; <u>1742</u>: CG, May 18; <u>1743</u>: CG, May 11;
    <u>1746</u>: CG, May 7; <u>1747</u>: CG, May 22
Sadler (mercer), <u>1775</u>: DL, Nov 4
Sadler (singer), <u>1754</u>: HAY, May 29, Nov 28; <u>1757</u>: HAY, Aug 31, Sep 8, 14
Sadler, Anthony
--Subjects Joy for the King's Restoration, <u>1659</u>: NONE, Sep 0
Sadler, John (actor), <u>1786</u>: HAMM, Jul 5, 10, 19, 24, 26, Aug 5; <u>1796</u>: HAY, Feb
    22
Sadler, Miss (actor), <u>1797</u>: HAY, Dec 4
Sadler's Wells, <u>1743</u>: SW, Apr 11; <u>1744</u>: DL, May 11; <u>1746</u>: DL, May 2; <u>1750</u>: DL,
    Dec 26; <u>1751</u>: DL, Apr 22; <u>1752</u>: CG, Nov 2; <u>1756</u>: SW, Oct 9; <u>1761</u>: CG, Oct 9;
    <u>1767</u>: SW, Jun 13, DL, Sep 29; <u>1771</u>: DL, Oct 9; <u>1785</u>: HAY, Aug 8; <u>1789</u>: DL,
    Dec 26; <u>1790</u>: DL, Mar 23, CG, Nov 4; <u>1794</u>: HAY, Jul 28; <u>1797</u>: CG, Oct 20;
    <u>1798</u>: CG, Apr 28
Safely go in Joy and Peace (song), <u>1789</u>: DL, Mar 20
Saffry, Mrs (booth holder), <u>1682</u>: BF, Aug 24
Sage, Mrs L A (actor), <u>1773</u>: CG, Apr 24; <u>1780</u>: CG, Apr 27
Saggion (Saggioni, Saioni, Sajoni), Gioseppe (composer, musician), <u>1703</u>: DL,
    Jan 23, Feb 1, LIF, Jun 1; <u>1704</u>: YB, Apr 20, Nov 16; <u>1706</u>: DL, Jan 29; <u>1707</u>:
    YB, Apr 4
Saggione, Maria Gallia (singer), <u>1708</u>: QUEEN'S, Mar 20; <u>1710</u>: YB, Mar 29
Sailor and Country Girl (dance), <u>1732</u>: LIF, Mar 27
Sailor and his Lass (dance), <u>1720</u>: DL, May 20
Sailor and his Wife (dance), <u>1707</u>: DL, Feb 24; <u>1732</u>: GF, Jan 21, 25
Sailor and Mistress (dance), <u>1731</u>: LIF, Mar 15; <u>1739</u>: CG, Oct 27, Nov 3
Sailor Boy capering on Shore (song), <u>1796</u>: CG, Apr 29
Sailor Caught Napping (dance), <u>1787</u>: CG, Jun 5
Sailor's Carousal, The; or, Saturday Night at Sea. See Starboard Watch.
Sailor's Consolation (song), <u>1798</u>: DL, May 7
Sailor's Festival, The; or, All Alive at Portsmouth (interlude, anon), <u>1793</u>:
    CG, May 10, 24, Jun 3; <u>1794</u>: CG, Apr 7, 25, May 6, 20, 21; <u>1795</u>: CG, May 13
Sailor's Jig (dance), <u>1712</u>: DL, May 30
Sailor's Joke (song), <u>1795</u>: HAY, Mar 4
Sailor's Journal (song), <u>1796</u>: DL, Jun 3, HAY, Aug 23; <u>1797</u>: DL, Jun 8; <u>1798</u>:
    DL, May 7; <u>1799</u>: CG, May 3, Jun 3; <u>1800</u>: CG, May 7, 20, 30
Sailor's life's a life of woe (song), <u>1790</u>: CG, Nov 26, Dec 1; <u>1791</u>: CG, Sep
    19, 26; <u>1792</u>: CG, May 19; <u>1793</u>: CG, May 21; <u>1794</u>: CG, Apr 12, Oct 29; <u>1795</u>:
    CG, Jun 5, Oct 7; <u>1797</u>: CG, Oct 2; <u>1799</u>: CG, Mar 16, Dec 9
Sailor's life's the life for me (song), <u>1791</u>: CG, May 18
Sailor's Lullaby (song), <u>1794</u>: CG, May 9
Sailor's Opera, The (musical, anon), <u>1731</u>: DL, May 12; <u>1737</u>: HAY, May 3, 5, 9,
    11
Sailor's Pledge of Love (song), <u>1798</u>: CG, Jun 4
Sailor's Prize, The; or, May-Day Wedding (interlude, anon), <u>1795</u>: CG, May 1, 8;
    <u>1797</u>: CG, May 2; <u>1798</u>: CG, Apr 24; <u>1799</u>: CG, Apr 30
Sailor's Sheet Anchor, The (interlude, anon), <u>1783</u>: HAY, Sep 17
Sailor's Wedding, The; or, The Humours of Wapping (musical, anon), <u>1731</u>: GF,
    Apr 21, 27, May 4, 10, 11, 13, 14; <u>1732</u>: GF, May 4; <u>1739</u>: BFH, Aug 23
Sailors' Ballet, Grand (dance), <u>1737</u>: DL, Apr 11, 22, 30
Sailors' Dance (dance), <u>1710</u>: GR, Jul 24; <u>1730</u>: LIF, Mar 21, May 18, 21; <u>1731</u>:
    DL, May 12; <u>1732</u>: LIF, Apr 12, GF, 19, 20, 21, Oct 11, 13, 14, 16, 17, 23,
    24, 25, 27, 28, 30, Nov 2, 4, 8, 13, 15, 17, 23, 24, Dec 15, 18, 29; <u>1733</u>:
    GF, Jan 11, 12, 13, 23, Feb 2, HAY, May 26, GF, Oct 22; <u>1735</u>: CG, Nov 19, DL,
    26, CG, 28, Dec 2, 12, 18, 31; <u>1736</u>: CG, Jan 2, 19, HAY, 19, Feb 2, CG, Mar
    2, 15, 27, Apr 8, 12, 17, 27, 29, 30, May 1, 3, 4, 10, 13, 24, 27, Jun 4;
    <u>1737</u>: CG, Mar 15, 17; <u>1738</u>: CG, Mar 14, 23, DL, May 17, 26; <u>1740</u>: CG, Feb 2,
    TCLP, Aug 4; <u>1741</u>: DL, Apr 9, Oct 15, 16, 17, 19, 20, 24, 29, 31, Nov 21, 27,
    Dec 2, 7, 11; <u>1742</u>: DL, Jan 12, 19, CG, Apr 27, 30; <u>1743</u>: LIF, Jan 3, Mar 22;
    <u>1747</u>: DL, Apr 2, 4; <u>1756</u>: DL, Feb 17, Mar 22, 23, 27, 29, Apr 20, 22, 26;
    <u>1763</u>: CG, Dec 8; <u>1776</u>: DL, Nov 9; <u>1779</u>: CG, Apr 21; <u>1780</u>: CG, Mar 27, Apr 1,
    Sep 18, Oct 2, Dec 12; <u>1781</u>: CG, Apr 2, DL, 25, 26, CG, May 1, DL, 7, 10;
    <u>1783</u>: DL, Sep 27; <u>1785</u>: DL, Jan 6; <u>1791</u>: CG, Jun 3; <u>1795</u>: DL, Jun 3; <u>1797</u>:
    DL, Nov 9
Sailors' Dance, Grand (dance), <u>1730</u>: LIF, Apr 6, 27; <u>1737</u>: DL, Apr 2; <u>1744</u>: DL,

Oct 11, 13
Sailors' Hornpipe (dance), 1746: GF, Feb 10; 1749: DL, Dec 26
Sailors' Pageant (entertainment), 1771: DL, Oct 21
Sailors' Rendezvous (song), 1747: DL, Nov 17, 18, 19, 20, 21, Dec 2; 1748: DL, Apr 12, 25
Sailors' Return (dance), 1769: HAY, Aug 14, 25, Sep 4, 6
Sailors' Revels (dance), 1748: DL, Oct 29, Nov 25, Dec 26, 28; 1749: DL, Apr 12; 1771: DL, May 20, Jun 1, Oct 8, 15, 23, 24, 26, Nov 28, Dec 5, 16, 17, 18, 30; 1772: DL, Jan 28, 31, Feb 4, 8, 17, Mar 23, 30, Apr 7, 11, 20, 21, 22, 25, May 1, 2, 4, 7, 21, 22, 27, 29, Jun 5, 9, Sep 19, Dec 1; 1773: DL, Apr 12, 13, 16, 17, 23, May 25, Jun 1, Sep 28, Nov 27, Dec 9; 1774: DL, Jan 24, 28, Mar 14, 19, 26, Apr 15, May 17, 20, 24, 28, Sep 20, 27, Oct 18, 20, Dec 1, 21; 1775: DL, Apr 20, May 11, 19, 24, Dec 20, 21; 1776: DL, Feb 14, Mar 7, Apr 12, 29, May 10, 11, 14, 17, 20, Sep 26; 1778: DL, Apr 25, May 2, 4; 1786: DL, Apr 24, 25
Sailors' Revels at Portsmouth, The; or, British Glory (dance), 1778: CG, May 2, 11, 15, 16, 20
Sailors' Song (song), 1720: DL, Aug 16; 1730: LIF, Apr 17; 1747: DL, Nov 16; 1748: DL, Apr 25, SFLYYW, Sep 7; 1756: DL, Apr 10, May 6; 1760: DL, May 29
St Alban's St, 1709: H&P, Jun 18; 1731: STA, Aug 9; 1777: KING'S, Mar 20; 1784: HAY, Mar 22; 1792: DLKING'S, May 8; 1793: DL, May 9; 1796: KING'S, Apr 21; 1797: KING'S, Apr 27; 1800: KING'S, May 22
St Albans, Duke of. See Beauclerk, Charles.
St Amand (actor), 1749: HAY, Nov 14; 1750: DL, May 22
St Amand, Mlle (dancer), 1791: KING'S, Mar 31, Apr 12, May 5, 19, 23, Jun 28, CG, Oct 20, Nov 21, Dec 21, 22; 1792: CG, Jan 11, 25, 28, Feb 28, Apr 10, May 10, 19, 24, 28; 1793: CG, Oct 15, 18, Nov 12, Dec 19; 1794: CG, Jan 21, Feb 25, Apr 12, May 23, Sep 22, 26, Oct 1, 29; 1795: CG, Feb 19, 26, Apr 6, 28, May 1, 12, 16, 29, Jun 6, Sep 21, Oct 2, 7, 8, 12, 23, 26, Nov 9, 13, 16, 25, Dec 21; 1796: CG, Jan 4, Mar 15, Apr 8, 9, 12, 15, May 10, 30, Jun 3, 6, Oct 24, Nov 5, Dec 19; 1797: CG, Feb 18, Mar 16, Apr 8, May 22, Jun 9, Oct 2, 9, 16, 18, Nov 4, Dec 26; 1798: CG, Feb 9, Apr 9, 19, 30, May 5, 28, Jun 2; 1799: CG, Mar 14
St Andree (choreographer), 1675: ATCOURT, Feb 15, DG, 27
St Andrew Tavern, 1776: HAY, Oct 7; 1777: HAY, Oct 13; 1782: HAY, Mar 18; 1784: HAY, Feb 9
St Andrew's Festival. See Roberdeau, John Peter.
St Ann's, 1784: DL, Apr 14; 1785: HAY, Aug 2; 1786: DL, Apr 25, HAY, Aug 3; 1788: DL, Apr 24
St Bennet's Hill, 1777: CHR, Jul 23
St Brides Church, 1694: ATCOURT, Dec 9; 1756: DL, Feb 9
St Cecilia's Song (song), 1694: YB, Jan 15, Feb 5; 1698: YB, May 10; 1699: YB, Dec 13
St Ceciliae. See Union of the Three Sister Arts.
St Cecily; or, The Converted Twins (play, anon), 1666: BRIDGES, Mar 19
St Charles Theatre, Naples, 1795: KING'S, Feb 20
St Clement Danes, 1711: SH, Nov 22; 1718: NONE, Jul 30; 1729: DL, Jan 6
St Clement's Chop House, 1767: DL, Apr 4, May 4, Oct 28
St Clement's Church, 1678: EB, Nov 22, 25; 1679: EB, Jan 9; 1718: DL, Jul 25; 1736: YB, Apr 29; 1749: DL, Jan 20; 1750: DL, Feb 26, Mar 6; 1751: DL, May 2; 1753: DL, Dec 21
St Colombe (beneficiary), 1713: HIC, May 14
St David's Day. See Dibdin, Thomas John.
St David's Day; or, The Village Revels, The (dance), 1781: CG, May 1, 2, 16, 18, 19, Dec 13; 1782: CG, Apr 27, May 1
St Dunstan's Church, 1739: DL, Oct 29; 1747: DL, Mar 19; 1750: DL, Oct 1
St Everimont (machinist), 1710: GR, Jul 22
St Foix, Germain Francois Poulain de, 1780: CG, Nov 25; 1783: HAY, Aug 12
St George and the Dragon (droll, anon), 1686: BF, Aug 0
St George, Emilia Olivia, Duchess of Leinster, 1790: DL, May 8
St George's Church, 1695: SF, Sep 0; 1696: SF, Sep 5; 1698: SF, Sep 17; 1717: SF, Sep 25; 1723: SF, Sep 5; 1724: SF, Sep 5
St George's Day; or, Britons Rejoice (entertainment, anon), 1789: CG, Apr 30
St George's Fields, 1771: GROTTO, Jun 22; 1772: DL, Apr 24, GROTTO, Aug 17; 1789: DL, Apr 2; 1790: HAY, Oct 13; 1791: DL, Mar 24; 1792: DLKING'S, Mar 19
St George's Hospital, 1746: CG, Nov 18; 1757: CG, Oct 19; 1759: CG, Nov 16; 1760: CG, Nov 25; 1761: CG, Nov 10; 1767: DL, Apr 21; 1772: DL, May 1; 1773: DL, Apr 15; 1774: DL, Apr 5; 1775: DL, Mar 30; 1776: DL, Jun 10
St George's Parish, 1745: MF, May 2
St George's Row, 1790: DL, May 1
St Germain, Count of (composer), 1745: HAY, Feb 9
St Giles in the Fields, 1787: DL, Dec 8

St Giles, 1772: DL, Apr 24; 1787: HAY, Mar 12
St Giles' Jig (dance), 1732: DL, Aug 11, 19
St Giles's Scrutiny, The. See Baddeley, Robert.
St Helena. See Thompson, Edward.
St Helene (musician), 1732: HIC, May 10
St James' Chapel, 1795: CG, Feb 27; 1796: CG, Feb 12
St James' Church, 1743: CG, Apr 16
St James' Coffee House, 1744: DL, Apr 2; 1745: DL, Apr 16; 1750: DL, Jan 11;
    1751: DL, Dec 18; 1753: KING'S, May 12, DL, 22; 1756: DL, Nov 12; 1758: DL,
    Mar 10
St James' Guard Chamber (theatre), 1668: ATCOURT, Oct 14
St James' Market, 1744: HAY, Sep 29; 1751: DL, May 2; 1777: DL, May 6; 1787:
    HAY, Mar 12
St James' Palace, 1670: ATCOURT, Apr 6; 1678: DL, Feb 0; 1697: YB, Mar 24;
    1699: STJAMES, Sep 0, ATCOURT, Nov 4; 1704: DL, Feb 8, LIF, 19, DL, 29, LIF,
    Mar 21, ATCOURT, Apr 24, DL, 25; 1707: DL, Apr 3; 1711: GR, Sep 8; 1730:
    KING'S, Oct 9; 1731: GF, Mar 16; 1732: SJP, Apr 26; 1757: DL, Dec 29; 1778:
    DL, Nov 18; 1799: CG, Jun 12
St James' Parish, 1675: FT, Feb 4; 1727: MH, Jun 7; 1734: YB, Dec 12; 1745: CG,
    Feb 20; 1751: DL, Feb 27; 1752: CG, Apr 8; 1753: DL, Feb 6; 1762: HIC, Feb
    12; 1765: KING'S, Apr 24; 1779: CG, May 18; 1780: CG, Mar 29; 1784: HAY, Feb
    9; 1797: CG, Jun 13
St James' Park, 1702: CC, May 25; 1749: DL, Apr 27; 1750: DL, Mar 28; 1764: CG,
    Jun 5; 1769: CG, Feb 1
St James' Square, 1678: DL, Feb 0; 1739: DL, Apr 24; 1740: DL, Mar 22; 1765:
    KING'S, Apr 24; 1784: DL, Apr 16; 1790: HAY, Apr 29; 1793: DL, Jun 1; 1796:
    KING'S, Mar 10; 1799: DL, Jun 26
St James' St, 1737: DL, Mar 5; 1742: DL, Mar 20, CG, Apr 1; 1744: DL, Apr 2,
    KING'S, Nov 3; 1749: CG, Apr 28; 1750: DL, Jan 11, May 21, Nov 28; 1753: DL,
    May 22; 1756: DL, Nov 12, CG, Dec 8; 1758: DL, Mar 10; 1767: HAY, Aug 26;
    1768: DL, Jun 21; 1770: HAY, Mar 12; 1777: KING'S, Nov 4; 1785: HAY, Feb 7;
    1787: CG, Jun 15
St John, Henry, Viscount Bolingbrake (epiloguist), 1668: LIF, May 6; 1698: LIF,
    Jan 0; 1701: LIF, Dec 0
St John, John, 1789: DL, Mar 21, Nov 13
--Island of St Marguerite, The (opera), 1789: DL, Nov 13, 14, 16, 17, 18, 20,
    21, 23, 27, 30, Dec 7, 9, 14, 18, 21; 1790: DL, Jan 1, 6, 8, 9, 13, 15, 18,
    20, 22, 25, Feb 3, 5, 12, 22, Apr 5, 24, May 8, 26, Oct 11, Nov 19, 24, Dec
    3; 1791: DL, Feb 3, 23, May 5, 25, 30; 1798: HAY, Aug 23
--Mary, Queen of Scots, 1789: DL, Mar 21, 24, 28, 31, Apr 4, 18, 23, 27, May 9;
    1792: DLKING'S, Mar 13; 1793: DL, Feb 9; 1796: DL, Feb 15, Dec 28; 1797: DL,
    Jan 2
St John, Mrs (singer), 1755: SF, Sep 18
St John's St, 1660: NONE, Aug 20; 1661: REDBULL, Mar 23, Aug 22
St John's, 1664: REDBULL, Apr 25
St Katherine's, 1732: GF, Feb 7
St Laurence Pounctneys, 1665: MTS, Mar 0
St Ledger, Catherine M (actor), 1799: CG, Nov 7, 14, Dec 23; 1800: CG, Apr 29,
    May 29
St Leger (dancer), 1755: DL, Nov 8, 15
St Leger, Mlle (dancer), 1703: DL, Feb 18
St Luce (dancer), 1729: HAY, Jun 3, 11, 14, 18, BFF, Aug 23, LIF, Nov 15, 20,
    Dec 16; 1730: LIF, Jan 2, 26, Apr 10, 24, 27, 29, May 9, HAY, Jul 17, 28, TC,
    Aug 1, 11, BFOF, 20
St Malo, 1776: DL, Feb 27
St Margaret's Fair, 1660: SF, Sep 13
St Margaret's Hill, 1711: SOU, Feb 6
St Mark's, 1750: DL, Apr 20
St Martin's Charity School, 1767: DL, Feb 18, Mar 26; 1772: DL, Jan 2, Feb 18;
    1773: DL, Feb 11, 16; 1774: DL, May 19; 1775: DL, May 12; 1776: DL, May 17
St Martin's Church, 1760: DL, Jan 8; 1772: DL, May 20; 1773: DL, May 19; 1779:
    HAY, May 10
St Martin's Churchyard, 1751: DL, Feb 27; 1753: DL, Dec 11
St Martin's Court, 1746: DL, Apr 8
St Martin's Lane, 1683: DL, Jan 19; 1735: CAT, Jun 19; 1740: CR, Feb 29; 1744:
    CR, Mar 21, DL, Apr 4; 1745: CG, Mar 6, Apr 26; 1746: DL, Dec 30; 1752: DL,
    Apr 2; 1758: DL, Mar 29; 1760: CG, Mar 24; 1761: CG, Mar 14; 1780: HAY, Aug
    17; 1788: CG, Apr 16, DL, May 6; 1790: DL, May 20, CG, Jun 3; 1791: DL, May
    18, HAY, Aug 16; 1792: DLKING'S, May 10; 1795: HAY, Apr 22
St Martin's Parish, 1700: LIF, Jun 28; 1745: MF, May 2, DL, Oct 24; 1752: DL,
    Apr 22; 1759: DL, Jan 1; 1760: CG, Jan 4; 1766: DL, Nov 6, 12; 1767: DL, Jan
    26, Mar 21, Apr 4, May 21, 28; 1771: DL, Oct 15, Nov 1; 1772: DL, Feb 21, Apr

7, May 5, 12, Oct 28, Nov 9; 1773: DL, Jan 26, Apr 20, 27, Sep 28, Nov 30;
  1774: DL, Jan 7, Mar 8, Apr 21, 29, May 30, Jun 2, Nov 7; 1775: DL, Apr 3,
  May 5, Oct 23; 1784: DL, Nov 17; 1789: DL, Oct 21
St Martin's St, 1742: CG, Apr 21; 1779: HAY, Aug 17, Oct 13; 1784: DL, May 7,
  CG, 10, DL, 20; 1785: DL, May 6; 1790: HAY, May 20; 1791: KING'S, May 26;
  1794: HAY, Jun 2
St Martini (Martini) (oboist), 1729: HIC, May 21; 1730: LIF, May 13; 1732: HIC,
  Mar 20; 1733: HIC, Apr 20, LIF, May 7, 13; 1740: DL, Mar 27, Apr 17; 1741:
  KING'S, Mar 14
St Nicholas (actor), 1739: CG, May 14
St Pancras Churchyard, 1767: CG, May 23
St Pancras Parish, 1744: HAY, May 10; 1796: DL, May 20
St Patrick, 1732: CL, Mar 17
St Patrick's Day. See Sheridan, Richard Brinsley.
St Paul's Cathedral, 1793: KING/HAY, Feb 15; 1797: CG, Dec 19; 1798: CG, Feb 28
St Paul's Choir, 1789: DL, Feb 27
St Paul's Churchyard, 1698: CLARK'S, Apr 1; 1744: DL, Apr 2; 1751: DL, Mar 7;
  1753: DL, Oct 30; 1756: DL, Jan 22; 1758: DL, Feb 3; 1765: CG, Jan 21; 1766:
  CHAPEL, Apr 30
St Paul's Parish, 1661: CITY, Oct 29; 1672: WF, Dec 30; 1760: CG, Jan 4, SOHO,
  18; 1762: HIC, Feb 12
St Paul's School, 1751: DL, Jan 11
St Peter's, Rome, 1752: CT/HAY, Mar 21
St Petersburgh Opera, 1797: KING'S, Jan 17
St Petersburgh, 1789: KING'S, Jun 11
St Pierre (dancer), 1798: KING'S, Apr 19, DL, May 9; 1799: KING'S, May 2, DL,
  Jun 28; 1800: DL, Jun 2
St Sepulchre's Church, 1762: DL, Jan 29
St Serfe, Thomas, 1667: LIF, Oct 5
--Tarugo's Wiles; or, The Coffee House, 1667: LIF, Oct 5, 7, 8, 15
Saint-Foix, Germain Francois Poulain de
--Colonie, La, 1780: CG, Nov 25
--Isle Sauvage, L', 1780: CG, Nov 25
--Rival Suppose, Le, 1783: HAY, Aug 12
Saintquient, Mrs (dancer), 1742: LIF, Dec 3, 13
Saioni. See Saggion.
Saiz (singer), 1749: KING'S, Mar 21
Saiz, Angelica (singer), 1748: KING'S, Nov 8; 1749: KING'S, Mar 21
Sajoni. See Saggion.
Sala (dancer), 1786: KING'S, Dec 23; 1787: KING'S, Jan 20, Mar 13, Jun 14, Dec
  8; 1788: KING'S, Jan 29, Mar 13, May 15; 1789: KING'S, Jan 10, 31, Mar 3, 19
Sala, Anna (singer), 1786: KING'S, Mar 11
Sala, Sga (dancer), 1782: KING'S, Nov 2, 9, 14, 30, Dec 19, 31
Salatri, Philippo (singer), 1714: KING'S, Oct 23
Sale, John (singer), 1789: CG, Feb 27, Mar 6, 20, Apr 3; 1790: CG, Feb 19, 24,
  26, Mar 3, 17, 19, 26; 1791: CG, Mar 11, 18, 23, 25, Apr 15; 1796: CG, Feb
  12, 17, 24, 26; 1797: CG, Mar 3; 1798: HAY, Jan 15, CG, Feb 23, Mar 2, 14,
  28, 30; 1799: HAY, Jan 24, CG, Feb 8, 15, 20, Mar 1, 13, 15; 1800: CG, Feb
  28, Mar 5, 21
Sale, John Bernard (singer), 1799: CG, Feb 8
Salieri, Antonio (composer), 1786: KING'S, Mar 11; 1788: CG, Dec 13; 1789: CG,
  Nov 24; 1791: DL, Jan 1, May 3, DLKING'S, Sep 29; 1792: CG, Apr 17, DLKING'S,
  May 23; 1798: KING'S, Mar 10
--Cifra, La (Dama Pastorella, La) (opera), 1798: KING'S, Mar 10, 13, 20
--Scuola de Gelosi, La (opera), 1786: KING'S, Mar 7, 11, 14, 18, 25, 28, Apr 4,
  27, May 2, 9, 16, Jun 6
Salimbeni, Giovanna (singer), 1791: PAN, Feb 17, Mar 1, Apr 14, Jun 2, 25;
  1792: HAY, Feb 14, Mar 27, 31; 1796: KING'S, Dec 6, 20; 1797: KING'S, Jan 7,
  Apr 18, 27, Jun 8
Salisbury (spectator), 1660: COCKPIT, Oct 11
Salisbury Court, 1660: NONE, Aug 20, SALSBURY, Nov 15; 1661: SALSBURY, Jan 29,
  Mar 2, VERE, 11, SALSBURY, 25, 26, Apr 6, Sep 9, LIF, Nov 4; 1671: LIF, Nov
  18; 1672: DG, Feb 6; 1751: DL, May 14
Salisbury Square, 1787: CG, Jun 15
Salisbury St, 1740: CG, Mar 11; 1743: DL, May 4; 1780: HAY, Jul 24
Salisbury, Cathedral Church of, 1772: DL, Mar 6
Salisbury, Marquis of. See Cecil, James.
Salisbury, 1665: BF, Aug 7; 1737: HAY, Mar 5; 1762: DL, Oct 25; 1795: CG, Feb
  20, Mar 11
Salle Sr (dancer), 1717: LIF, May 11
Salle, Francis (dancer, actor), 1716: LIF, Oct 23, 25, 27, 30, 31, Nov 1, 5, 8,
  10, 12, 15, 16, 19, 21, 22, 24, 28, 30, Dec 1, 5, 6, 7, 8, 10, 11, 15, 20,

22, 26, 29, 31; 1717: LIF, Jan 4, 7, 10, 11, 14, 15, 17, 21, 22, 25, 31, Feb
1, 2, 6, 21, 25, 26, Mar 2, 5, 18, 25, 30, Apr 8, 23, 27, May 11, 16, Jun 1,
KING'S, 5, LIF, 7, 10; 1719: LIF, Jan 13, KING'S, Feb 12, Mar 2, RI, Jun 6;
1725: LIF, Oct 23, 25, 30, Nov 2, 3, 8, 11, 17, 22, 29, 30, Dec 2, 8, 16;
1726: LIF, Jan 3, 5, 14, Mar 10, 19, 21, 28, Apr 2, 11, 13, 15, 18, 19, 20,
21, 22, 25, 26, 27, 29, 30, May 3, 4, 10, 12, 13, 17, 19, 20, 25, Sep 16, 19,
26, 30, Oct 3, 5, 19, 24, 31, Nov 9, 14, 21, 30, Dec 3; 1727: LIF, Jan 31,
Feb 3, 7, 9, 13, Mar 11, 13, 20, 23, Apr 3, 5, 6, 7, 10, 14, 17, 26, May 3,
4, 8, 9, 10, 15, 17, 18, 19, 30, Sep 22, Oct 12, Nov 7, 9, 17; 1728: LIF, Mar
25, Apr 22, Oct 21, 23, 26, Nov 23, Dec 12, 31; 1729: LIF, Jan 13, 16, 18,
31, Feb 6, Mar 10, 17, 20, 27, Apr 8, 10, 11, 15, 17, 19, 21, 24, 26, 29, May
1, 3, 7, 8, 12, 14, 15, 19, 20, 22, Oct 3, 6, 10, 15, 20, 22, 24, 28, Nov 4,
Dec 17; 1730: LIF, Jan 2, Mar 17, 21, Apr 6, 8, 10, 17, 24, 27, May 9, 14,
21, Jun 4, Sep 21, 25, Oct 1, 7, 19, 27, 30, Nov 3, 6, 7, 23, Dec 3, 5, 7, 9,
11, 15, 30; 1731: LIF, Jan 11, 19, 23, Mar 15, 18, 22, 25, 29, Apr 1, 3, 5,
8, 21, 22, 24, 26, 28, 29, May 1, 5, 7, 12, 13, 14, 19, 20, 21, 24, 26, 28,
Jun 7, Oct 4, 11, 15, 20, 27, Nov 2, 6, 18, 25, Dec 1, 7, 14, 29, 30; 1732:
LIF, Jan 5, 22, 28, Feb 7, Mar 9, 23, Apr 10, 11, 12, 13, 17, 21, 24, 27, May
24, Jun 9; 1733: CG, May 4; 1734: CG, May 7; 1735: GF/HAY, Mar 18
Salle, Marie (dancer, actor), 1716: LIF, Oct 23, 25, 27, 30, 31, Nov 1, 5, 8,
10, 12, 15, 16, 19, 21, 22, 24, 28, 30, Dec 1, 5, 6, 7, 8, 10, 11, 15, 20,
22, 26, 29, 31; 1717: LIF, Jan 4, 7, 10, 11, 14, 15, 17, 21, 22, 25, 31, Feb
1, 2, 6, 21, 25, 26, Mar 2, 5, 18, 25, 30, Apr 8, 23, 27, May 11, 16, Jun 1,
KING'S, 5, LIF, 7, 10; 1719: KING'S, Feb 12, Mar 2, RI, Jun 6; 1725: LIF, Oct
23, 25, 30, Nov 2, 8, 11, 17, 27, 30, Dec 3, 14, 16; 1726: LIF, Jan 3, 5, 14,
Mar 10, 19, 21, 28, Apr 2, 11, 13, 18, 20, 21, 22, 27, 29, May 3, 10, 12, 13,
19, 20, 25, Sep 19, 30, Oct 3, 19, 31, Nov 14, 21, 30; 1727: LIF, Jan 31, Feb
3, 7, 9, 13, Mar 11, 13, 20, 23, Apr 3, 5, 6, 7, 10, 14, 17, 26, 27, May 3,
4, 8, 9, 10, 15, 17, 18, 19; 1728: LIF, Jan 29; 1730: LIF, Nov 23, 26, Dec 3,
5, 9, 12, 31; 1731: LIF, Jan 4, 22, 23, Mar 4, 6, 8, 15, 18, 22, 25, 29, 30,
Apr 5, 21, 22, 24, 26, 29, May 3, Jun 1; 1733: CG, Nov 8, 13, 15, 26, 28, 29,
30, Dec 1, 3, 8, 10, 12, 15, 17, 20, 22, 28, 29, 31; 1734: CG, Jan 2, 3, 4,
7, 9, 10, 11, 12, 14, Feb 14, 18, 22, 26, Mar 5, 7, 11, 12, 16, 18, 19, 21,
25, 28, Apr 1, 2, 16, 17, 18, 19, 22, 26, 27, 30, May 1, 2, 3, 4, 6, 7, 24,
CG/LIF, Nov 9, 18, 21, 29, Dec 12, 14, 26; 1735: CG/LIF, Jan 13, 14, 17, Mar
13, 15, DL, 17, CG/LIF, 20, 22, 24, 25, Apr 8, 9, 10, 11, 14, 15, 18, 24, 29,
May 1, 2, 9; 1736: BFFH, Aug 23
Salle, Mons and Mlle (dancers), 1716: LIF, Oct 18; 1718: LIF, Dec 19
Salle's scholar (dancer), 1729: LIF, May 14
Sally (song), 1717: DL, Aug 6, 13, 16, 20, 23
Sally in our Alley (song), 1792: DLKING'S, May 29; 1793: CG, Jun 10, 12; 1794:
CG, Apr 25, May 9, 21, 24; 1795: CG, Apr 24, May 16, DL, 27, Jun 2, CG, 12;
1796: CG, May 10; 1797: CG, May 16, 24, DL, Jun 8; 1798: CG, Jun 1; 1799: CG,
Apr 23, May 13, Jun 1, 6; 1800: CG, Apr 30, May 13, 20
Sallybotino (actor), 1754: HAY/SFB, Sep 13
Salomon, Giuseppe (dancer, choreographer), 1746: DL, Dec 3, 4, 17, 27, 29;
1747: DL, Jan 5, 21, 22, Feb 9, 11, 13, 16, 18, 20, 27, Mar 3, 5, 12, 14, 17,
19, 23, 26, 30, 31, Apr 6, 7, 10, 11, 20, 21, 22, 23, 25, 27, 29
Salomon, Johann Peter (violinist, composer), 1781: CG, Mar 23; 1795: CG, Apr 6,
9; 1798: KING'S, Mar 3; 1799: KING'S, May 30; 1800: CG, Apr 2
Salomon's son (dancer), 1746: DL, Nov 21, Dec 3, 4, 8, 16, 17, 27, 29; 1747:
DL, Jan 5, 22, 26, 31, Feb 4, 7, 16, 18, 27, Mar 5, 14, 17, 19, 23, 26, 30,
31, Apr 6, 7, 10, 20, 22, 23, 27, 29
Salpietro, Sga (singer), 1779: KING'S, May 15; 1780: KING'S, May 25; 1781:
KING'S, Dec 11; 1782: KING'S, Jan 15, Mar 2, Apr 9; 1783: KING'S, Jan 25, 28,
Feb 13
Salt (householder), 1743: CG, Mar 14
Salt Box (entertainment), 1751: CT, Dec 3; 1752: CT/HAY, Feb 11, Mar 17, 21;
1753: BFSY, Sep 3
Salt Box Dissertation (entertainment), 1753: HAY, Jan 9
Salt Box Oration (entertainment), 1751: HAY, Dec 27; 1752: CT/HAY, Jan 7, 14,
31, May 5, HAY, Dec 7, 18; 1754: HAY, Sep 10
Saltarella (dance), 1708: DL/QUEEN, Feb 21
Salter (beneficiary), 1718: CL, Mar 21; 1721: LIF, May 19; 1722: SH, Mar 9;
1723: SH, Mar 13
Saltero (music), 1748: KING'S, Apr 26
Salutation Tavern, 1747: CG, Apr 20; 1786: HAMM, Aug 5
Salvagni, Sga (singer), 1774: KING'S, Mar 17
Salvai, Madalena (singer), 1720: KING'S, Dec 28; 1721: KING'S, Feb 1, Mar 28,
Apr 15, May 20, Jun 14, Dec 9; 1722: KING'S, Jan 10, Feb 15, 22, Mar 6
Salve Regina (song), 1739: HAY, Dec 15; 1741: HIC, Apr 3, 10; 1744: KING'S, Mar
28

Salvi, Antonio, 1725: KING'S, Feb 13; 1729: KING'S, Dec 2; 1735: CG, Jan 8;
    1737: KING'S, Jan 1, CG, 12, May 18, KING'S, Oct 29
Salvini, Sga (actor), 1796: CG, May 10
Salway, Thomas (actor, singer, dancer), 1724: LIF, Mar 3, 10, 28, Apr 9, May 5;
    1725: LIF, Jan 21, Mar 29, Apr 14, 16, May 3, 24, Nov 13, Dec 2, 4; 1726:
    LIF, Jan 14, Mar 21, Apr 11, 22, May 9, Jun 17, 21, 24, Jul 1, 5, 15, 19, 22,
    26, 29, Aug 19, 23, Sep 23, 26, 30, Oct 7, 24, Nov 19; 1727: LIF, Feb 13, Mar
    13, 20, 23, Apr 17, May 3, 10, 18, 19, Sep 29, Oct 12, Nov 9, 17; 1728: LIF,
    Mar 9, 25, 27, Apr 23, 24, 29, May 2, 8, 13, 16, Jun 25, Jul 2, Nov 23; 1729:
    LIF, Jan 18, Apr 23, 30, May 6, BFB, Aug 25, LIF, Sep 19, Oct 3, 15, Nov 1,
    4, Dec 3; 1730: LIF, Jan 2, Mar 16, Apr 15, 20, 23, May 1, 13, 14, 23, 27,
    RI, Jun 27, Jul 16, LIF, Sep 21, 25, Oct 7, 9, Nov 7, 10, Dec 15; 1731: LIF,
    Feb 3, 27, Mar 22, 26, Apr 1, 3, 5, 8, 23, 24, 26, May 3, 6, 10, 14, 20, 21,
    RI, Jul 1, 15, 22, BFB, Aug 26, LIF, Sep 27, Oct 4, 13, Nov 6, 13, 18, Dec 1;
    1732: LIF, Jan 10, 26, Feb 21, Mar 10, 20, 23, 30, Apr 11, 18, 27, 28, May 2,
    4, 8, 17, 22, LIF/CG, Oct 6, 9, LIF, 18, LIF/CG, 27, 30, Nov 8, 11, 24,
    CG/LIF, Dec 16, LIF/CG, 27; 1733: LIF/CG, Jan 18, Feb 5, 10, Mar 29, 30, Apr
    3, 10, 11, 13, 21, 25, 27, CG, May 1, LIF/CG, 3, 19, CG/LIF, 28, LIF/CG, 29,
    CG, Jun 26, 29, Jul 6, BF, Aug 23, BFFH, Sep 4, CG, 17, 22, 25, 27, 29, Oct
    9, 11, 13, 18, 27, Nov 3, 14, 23, 28, 30, Dec 3, 7, 20; 1734: CG, Jan 1, 9,
    25, Feb 13, 26, Mar 5, 16, 28, Apr 1, 18, 29, 30, May 7, 13, BFFO, Aug 24,
    DL, Sep 14, 24, 28, Oct 3, 5, 8, 10, 14, 21, 22, 29, Nov 1, 8, 20, 22, Dec
    12; 1735: DL, Jan 6, 22, 23, Feb 5, 25, Mar 3, 22, Apr 7, 11, 15, 21, May 6,
    8, 10, 14, 20, Jun 9, Jul 1, GF/HAY, 15, 22, HAY, Aug 12, GF/HAY, 21, DL, Sep
    1, 4, 6, 11, 25, Oct 7, 21, 27, 30, 31, Nov 10, 12, 15, 19, 22, 25, 27; 1736:
    DL, Jan 12, Feb 20, 28, Mar 3, 11, 20, 25, 27, LIF, Apr 9, DL, 22, May 3, 25,
    LIF, Jun 16, BFFH, Aug 23, CG, Sep 15, 17, 20, 22, Oct 4, 8, 20, 27, Nov 3,
    15, 26; 1737: CG, Jan 25, Feb 14, 15, 26, Mar 14, 15, 17, 28, 31, Apr 12, 18,
    22, 26, 28, 29, May 3, 5, 9, 16, 31, LIF, Jul 26, Aug 2, 5, CG, Sep 16, 21,
    23, Oct 7, 10, 26, Nov 2, 9; 1738: CG, Jan 3, Feb 6, 13, 16, Mar 13, 14, 20,
    Apr 5, 7, 11, 12, 13, 17, 18, 22, 24, 25, May 2, 10, 12, Jun 27, 30, Jul 11,
    Aug 29, Sep 15, 22, 25, Oct 2, 4, 6, 23, 26, 28, Nov 13, 18, 29, Dec 2, 4, 6,
    9; 1739: CG, Jan 6, 8, 15, 20, Feb 23, 24, Mar 20, Apr 24, 27, May 1, 8, 17,
    18, 25, 28, Aug 29, 31, Sep 7, 10, 21, 22, 27, Oct 1, 2, 3, 10, 20, 22, 25,
    26, 30, 31, Nov 1, 2, 7, 9, 10, 13, 16, 20, Dec 1, 6, 10, 12, 14, 15, 17, 18;
    1740: CG, Jan 5, 10, 15, 22, Feb 12, Mar 18, Apr 9, 16, 28, 30, May 9, 21,
    Jun 5, Sep 19, 22, 26, Oct 1, 6, 10, 22, Nov 10, Dec 29; 1741: CG, Jan 2, 5,
    21, 23, 27, Feb 16, 17, 24, 28, Mar 2, 9, 30, Apr 10, 13, 16, 17, 18, 24, 25,
    30, May 12, Sep 28, 30, Oct 2, 8, 15, 17, 21, 24, Nov 26, 30; 1742: CG, Jan
    26, 27, Feb 13, 25, Mar 6, 15, Apr 22, 26, 28, 30, May 3, 4, 5, 6, 7, 14, 17,
    Oct 9, 16, 25, 26; 1743: CG, Jan 8, Feb 4, Mar 1
Sam's Coffee House, 1750: DL, Nov 28; 1752: DL, Apr 22; 1756: DL, Nov 12; 1759:
    CG, May 8
Sambuccio (dancer), 1754: HAY, Jul 11, Aug 15, Sep 10
Samford. See Sandford.
Sampieri (singer), 1780: KING'S, Apr 22; 1781: KING'S, Apr 5, Jun 5, 23
Sampson, Mrs (actor), 1740: DL, Nov 24
Sampson, William, 1668: LIF, Aug 20
Sams (actor), 1744: HAY, May 16
Samson (actor), 1746: DL, Jan 2
Samson Agonistes. See Milton, John.
Samson. See Handel, George Frederic.
Samuel, Solomon (haberdasher), 1750: DL, Mar 3
San Prigioniero (song), 1746: KING'S, Mar 25
Sanchy (spectator), 1661: LIF, Dec 2; 1662: LIF, Apr 2
Sanders (actor), 1732: HAY, Nov 29
Sanders (actor), 1757: HAY, Oct 31
Sanders, Mrs (actor), 1712: DL, Nov 7
Sanderson (machinist), 1753: DL, May 10; 1754: DL, Apr 19; 1755: DL, May 1;
    1756: DL, May 11; 1757: DL, May 19; 1760: DL, Apr 28; 1763: DL, Apr 29; 1764:
    DL, Jan 16, May 7; 1766: DL, Jan 24
Sanderson, James (composer), 1798: CG, Oct 15
Sanderson, Mrs (actor, singer), 1731: DL, Nov 19; 1732: LIF/CG, Oct 4, 13, 30,
    Nov 8, 24, Dec 27; 1733: CG/LIF, Jan 25, LIF/CG, May 3, CG, Oct 11; 1734: CG,
    Jan 25, Feb 13, Mar 16, LIF, Apr 15, JS, May 31
Sandford (author), 1723: HAY, Dec 12
--Female Fop, The; or, The False One Fitted, 1723: HAY, Dec 12, 13, 31
Sandford (wardrobe keeper), 1730: GF, Jun 17; 1731: GF, May 17
Sandford, P (printer), 1791: CG, May 6
Sandford, Samuel (actor), 1661: LIF, Dec 16; 1662: LIF, Mar 1, Oct 18, ATCOURT,
    Nov 1; 1663: LIF, Jan 8, Feb 23, Oct 0, ATCOURT, Dec 10; 1664: LIF, Mar 0,
    Aug 13, Sep 10, Nov 5; 1665: LIF, Apr 3; 1668: LIF, Mar 26; 1669: LIF, Dec

742

14; <u>1670</u>: LIF, Apr 0; <u>1671</u>: LIF, Jan 10, Mar 6, 15, Jun 0, NONE, Sep 0, DG,
Nov 0; <u>1672</u>: DG, Jul 4, Aug 3; <u>1673</u>: DG, Feb 18, May 0; <u>1675</u>: DG, May 28, Sep
0; <u>1676</u>: DG, Jan 10, Nov 4, Dec 0; <u>1677</u>: DG, Feb 12, May 31, Jul 0; <u>1678</u>: DG,
Jan 0, Jun 0, Sep 0, Nov 0; <u>1682</u>: DL, Nov 28; <u>1688</u>: DL, Feb 0, May 3; <u>1689</u>:
DL, Nov 20, Dec 4; <u>1690</u>: DLORDG, Mar 0, NONE, Sep 0, DL, 0, NONE, 0, DL, Oct
0, DL/IT, 21, DL, Nov 0; <u>1691</u>: DG, May 0, NONE, Sep 0; <u>1692</u>: DL, Jan 0, Apr
0, Jun 0, DLORDG, Oct 13, DL, Nov 8; <u>1693</u>: DL, Apr 0, NONE, Sep 0; <u>1694</u>:
NONE, Jul 0; <u>1695</u>: LIF, Apr 30; <u>1697</u>: LIF, Feb 20, Nov 0; <u>1698</u>: LIF, Jan 0;
<u>1704</u>: LIF, Jul 4
Sandham (dancer), <u>1712</u>: DL, May 30, Jun 10; <u>1714</u>: DL, May 17, 31, Jun 9, 14;
<u>1715</u>: LIF, Jan 7, 14, 25, Feb 1, 3, 9, 22, 26, Mar 1, 3, 26, Apr 22, DL, May
20, Jun 2; <u>1719</u>: LIF, Jan 9, Apr 29, May 7, 13, 21, 25, 28, 29, Jun 3, 25,
Oct 26, 27; <u>1720</u>: LIF, Apr 29, Nov 18, 19, Dec 6, 14, 26; <u>1721</u>: LIF, Feb 1,
21, 28, Apr 26, 29, May 1; <u>1722</u>: LIF, Apr 24, 28, May 25; <u>1726</u>: DL, Feb 11,
May 5, Nov 2; <u>1727</u>: DL, Nov 14; <u>1728</u>: HAY, Nov 14; <u>1729</u>: HAY, Feb 11, 25, Jul
5, GF, Nov 8, 14, 25, Dec 12, 15, 17; <u>1730</u>: GF, Jan 20, 24, Feb 6, 7, Mar 2,
9, 10, 14, 21, Apr 2, 3, 7, 10, 14, 16, 20, 24, May 13, 28, Jun 1, 3, 12, 16,
17, 25, 30, BFPG/TC, Aug 1, 24, GF, Sep 18, Nov 6, 11; <u>1731</u>: GF, Mar 18, 23,
Apr 1, 26, May 4, 7, 13, Jun 2; <u>1732</u>: HAY, Jul 26, GF, Oct 14, 28, 30, Nov 2,
8, 9, 17, 18, 23, Dec 20; <u>1733</u>: GF, Mar 12, HAY, 14, GF, Apr 20, May 23, Nov
12, 29, Dec 28; <u>1734</u>: GF, Jan 8, 28, 31, Feb 11, Mar 11, 18, Apr 19, May 6,
7, 22, Oct 28, Nov 18
Sandham Jr (dancer), <u>1720</u>: LIF, Mar 8, Apr 28, 29, May 7, 10, 11, 12, 23, 24,
30, Dec 6; <u>1721</u>: LIF, May 1; <u>1722</u>: LIF, Mar 3, Apr 28, SF, Sep 22; <u>1726</u>: DL,
Apr 15, 23, May 18, Dec 30; <u>1727</u>: DL, Feb 27, Apr 27, May 8; <u>1729</u>: HAY, Feb
11; <u>1732</u>: GF, Jan 15, Oct 16, 18
Sandham, Miss (actor, dancer), <u>1721</u>: LIF, May 1; <u>1722</u>: LIF, Mar 3, Apr 28, SF,
Sep 22; <u>1726</u>: DL, May 18; <u>1727</u>: DL, Apr 27, May 8; <u>1729</u>: GF, Nov 25, Dec 12,
15, 17; <u>1730</u>: GF, Jan 24, Feb 6, 7, 23, Mar 2, 7, 9, 10, 14, 21, Apr 7, 10,
14, 16, 24, Jun 1, 3, 12, 16, 25, 30, Jul 17, Sep 18, 28, Oct 21, 23, Nov 6;
<u>1731</u>: GF, May 10, Oct 18, 20, 25, 26, 27, Nov 1, 3, 4, 23, 25; <u>1732</u>: GF, Jan
15, HAY, Jul 26, GF, Nov 24, 25, 27, 29, 30, Dec 13, 15, 20; <u>1733</u>: GF, Jan
10, 11, 12, 13, 24, Feb 2, 5, 12, 13, HAY, 14, GF, Mar 1, 12, HAY, 14, GF,
Apr 13, HAY, 18, GF, 20, 27, May 3, 4, 8, 9, 10, 11, 16, 18, 22, 23, Sep 25,
27, Oct 9, 15, 16, 17, 26, Nov 9, 12, Dec 14, 20, 26, 28; <u>1734</u>: GF, Jan 8,
10, 11, 14, 19, 24, 26, 28, Feb 2, 5, 11, Apr 18, 19, 24, 26, May 7, 8, 16,
17, Sep 25, Oct 16, 17, 28, Dec 2, 12, 31; <u>1735</u>: GF, Jan 10, 13, 24, Mar 6,
YB/HAY, Sep 24, CG, Oct 3, 17, Nov 6; <u>1736</u>: CG, Jan 1, 5, 9, 10, 23, Feb 23,
Mar 6, 11
Sandham, Miss and Jr (dancers), <u>1721</u>: LIF, May 18, 22; <u>1722</u>: LIF, Apr 28, SF,
Sep 5, 22; <u>1724</u>: HAY, Jan 20
Sandham's children (dancer), <u>1725</u>: DL, Dec 20; <u>1726</u>: DL, Jan 27, Apr 27, May 5,
18, 25
Sandhill, <u>1777</u>: CG, May 20; <u>1778</u>: CG, May 16; <u>1779</u>: CG, May 8
Sandoni, Pietro (composer), <u>1716</u>: KING'S, May 26; <u>1721</u>: KING'S, Jul 5; <u>1735</u>:
KING'S, Apr 8
--Issipile (opera), <u>1735</u>: KING'S, Apr 8, 12, 15, 19
Sands (actor), <u>1785</u>: HAY, Jul 13; <u>1788</u>: HAY, Aug 5
Sandum, Mrs (actor), <u>1749</u>: BF/SFP, Aug 23
Sandwich, Lord. See Montagu, Edward.
Sandys and Co (colormen), <u>1772</u>: DL, Feb 5, Jun 10; <u>1773</u>: DL, Jan 21; <u>1774</u>: DL,
Jun 2
Sanford, Sir Richard (spectator), <u>1698</u>: DLORLIF, Jul 13, DLLIF, Dec 13
Sani, Domenico (composer), <u>1737</u>: KING'S, Mar 26
--Didone Abbandonata da Enea; or, Dido Forsaken by Aeneas, <u>1726</u>: KING'S, Dec 17
--Impresario, The (interlude), <u>1737</u>: KING'S, Mar 26, 29, Apr 2, 16, May 10
Sans Cullote (song), <u>1794</u>: HAMM, Mar 24
Sansom (beneficiary), <u>1760</u>: DL, Jul 29
Sant (dancer), <u>1732</u>: DL, Dec 18; <u>1733</u>: DL, Jan 17; <u>1737</u>: HAY, May 5
Santhilla (musician), <u>1748</u>: SOU, Oct 24
Santimore, Mrs (actor), <u>1751</u>: DL, Dec 26
Santini, Sga (singer), <u>1735</u>: KING'S, Nov 25
Santlow, Hester (actor, dancer), <u>1706</u>: DL, Feb 28, Mar 5, 7, 9, 16, 25, 28, Apr
2, 13, 16, Jun 28, Jul 5, DG, 9, Nov 1, DL/DG, 2, DL, 30, Dec 7, 17, 21;
<u>1707</u>: DL, Mar 3, 8, 11, 20, 25, Apr 3, May 24, Jun 2, Nov 11, 22, 29,
DL/QUEEN, Dec 9, DL, 27; <u>1708</u>: DL, Jan 3, 10, DL/QUEEN, Feb 7, 21; <u>1709</u>:
QUEEN'S, Apr 12, DL, Dec 3, 15, 17, 27; <u>1710</u>: DL, Jan 2, 3, 11, 12, 17, 19,
20, 28, 31, Feb 4, 7, 14, 15, 25, Mar 6, 11, 14, 23, 25, Apr 1, 12, 18, May
3, Jun 6, DL/QUEEN, Nov 9, 11, 17, DL, 23, Dec 2, 5, 7, 12, 21, 30; <u>1711</u>: DL,
Jan 19, 20, 27, Feb 22, Apr 7, DL/QUEEN, 12, DL, Sep 27, Oct 6, 16, 27, Nov
3, 6, 7, 9, 29; <u>1712</u>: DL, Jan 19, QUEEN'S, Mar 22, DL, May 2, 20, Sep 23;
<u>1713</u>: DL, Oct 7, 21, Nov 19, 25; <u>1714</u>: DL, Mar 13, Apr 27, 30, May 5, 7, 10,

12, 17, 19, 21, 26, 31, Jun 2, 4, 9, 11, 14, 16, 18, Oct 6, 11, 22, 25, **Nov**
11, 24, 25, Dec 1, KING'S, 4, DL, 9, 16; 1715: DL, Feb 4, 11, 12, 22, 28, Mar
5, 14, 17, 19, 21, Apr 19, 28, 30, May 10, 18, 20, Jun 2, 3, 6, Oct 13, 14,
24, 29, Nov 4, 5, 12, 17, 19, 22, 23, 29, Dec 5, 17, 20, 31; 1716: DL, Jan 7,
14, 17, 23, 26, Feb 9, 18, 25, Mar 3, 8, Apr 2, 7, 9, 26, May 14, 25, 30, 31,
Jun 6, 15, Oct 2, 4, 6, 9, 18, 19, 22, 27, Nov 3, 12, 14, 26, Dec 5, 13, 27;
1717: DL, Jan 3, 5, 31, Feb 6, 13, 19, 25, Mar 2, 7, 14, 25, Sep 28, Oct 9,
10, 12, 16, 22, 24, 30, Nov 1, 7, 13, 22, 25, 27, Dec 3, 4; 1718: DL, Jan 7,
14, 21, 23, 28, 29, 31, Feb 10, Mar 1, 4, 18, 25, Apr 25, May 2, 6, 7, 8, 13,
14, 15, 16, 22, Jun 6, Sep 20, 25, 27, Oct 2, 7, 10, 15, 17, 18, 22, 24, 28,
29, Nov 4, 11, 12, 14, 17, 25, Dec 10, 11, 13, 15, 19, 22; 1719: DL, Jan 29,
Feb 7, 12, Mar 16, 19, 30, Apr 9, 11, 14, 16, 17, 18, 20, 21, 23, 30, May 2,
5, 8, 9, 11, 12, 13, 19, 21, 27, 30, Jul 31, Sep 24; 1720: DL, Feb 5
Santlow, Miss (actor), 1772: DL, Sep 24
Santoli, Sga (dancer), 1766: KING'S, Nov 25
Saper bramate (song), 1786: DL, Jan 14
Saphio (composer), 1799: CG, Apr 19
Sapho et Phaon (dance), 1797: KING'S, Apr 6, May 11, 13, 16, 18, 20, 23, 27,
Jun 2, 6, 8
Sapredella (dance), 1785: KING'S, Feb 24
Sapsford, Mrs (actor), 1705: DL, Apr 23; 1706: DL, Apr 8; 1710: GR, Jun 15, Jul
3, 12, 27, 29, Aug 7, 10, 19, Sep 9, 11, 20
Saraband (dance), 1714: DL, May 3, 14; 1722: DL, May 22; 1723: DL, Jul 19, 23,
26, 30; 1724: DL, Apr 29, LIF, May 5, 8, DL, 14, LIF, 16, 19, 27, 28, Jun 2;
1725: DL, Mar 31, LIF, Apr 26, May 6, 19; 1726: LIF, Apr 14, 30, DL, May 6,
11, LIF, 17, 19, 26; 1727: DL, May 5; 1728: DL, May 3; 1729: DL, Apr 28;
1730: LIF, Apr 25, May 13, 21; 1731: LIF, Apr 5, 22, May 3, 7, 10, 17, 26,
31, Jun 2, Sep 22, Oct 13, Dec 17; 1732: LIF, Feb 9, May 1, DL, 10, 25,
LIF/CG, Sep 27, Oct 2, GF, 14, 16, LIF/CG, 16, GF, 18, 28, 30, Nov 2, 9, 17,
18, 23; 1733: LIF/CG, Jan 12, 15, 18, 19, 20, 27, Feb 2, CG, 8, Mar 27, DL,
Apr 30, May 5; 1734: CG, May 14, 16, HAY, Jun 19, Aug 14, LIF, 20, HAY, 22;
1736: HAY, Jul 7; 1737: DL, Nov 2, 7; 1738: DL, Feb 25, May 19, 31; 1739: DL,
Apr 26, May 11, 30; 1740: DL, May 21, CG, 23; 1742: CG, Feb 13
Sarbelloni, Pietro (singer), 1761: KING'S, Apr 28
Sardinia, King of, 1721: DL, Oct 31; 1733: LIF, May 7
Sargeant (actor), 1779: HAY, Mar 19; Oct 13
Sarjant and son (house servants), 1767: CG, May 25; 1768: CG, May 30; 1769: CG,
May 15; 1770: CG, May 21
Sarjant, Charles (box-book and housekeeper), 1758: CG, Nov 27; 1759: CG, Apr
21, May 4, 8, 14, Sep 24, Oct 11; 1760: CG, Jan 4, 12, Feb 18, Mar 24, Apr 7,
22, May 6, 28, Sep 22; 1761: CG, Mar 3, May 18, Sep 7, Oct 3; 1762: CG, Mar
20, 22, 25, May 6, 17, Sep 20, Dec 22; 1763: CG, Mar 19, May 20, Sep 19;
1764: CG, May 23, Sep 17; 1765: CG, Apr 15, May 3, 11, Sep 16; 1766: CG, Mar
15, 17, May 7, 13, Sep 24, Oct 28, Nov 6, Dec 20; 1767: CG, Mar 21, 23, 24,
30, 31, Apr 6, May 25, Sep 14, Nov 30, Dec 9; 1768: CG, Jun 2, 4, Sep 19;
1769: CG, May 17, Sep 18; 1770: CG, Mar 2, May 25, Sep 24; 1771: CG, Feb 15,
May 13, Oct 18, 29; 1772: CG, Feb 6, Mar 6, Apr 2, May 6, 18, Oct 5, 19;
1773: CG, Jan 21, Feb 26, Apr 23, May 17, Sep 20, Oct 13, Dec 21; 1774: CG,
Jan 7, 12, 24, May 5, 9, Sep 19; 1775: CG, May 22, Jun 1, Sep 20; 1776: CG,
Feb 23, May 13, Sep 23; 1777: CG, Feb 14, May 19, Sep 22; 1778: CG, May 18;
1779: CG, Apr 29; 1780: CG, May 24; 1781: CG, May 25; 1782: CG, May 28; 1783:
CG, May 31; 1784: CG, May 22
Sarjant, James (trumpeter), 1789: CG, Feb 27; 1790: CG, Feb 19, Mar 3; 1791:
CG, Mar 11; 1792: CG, Feb 24, Mar 9; 1793: CG, Feb 15; 1794: CG, Mar 7, Apr
11; 1795: CG, Feb 20; 1796: CG, Feb 12; 1797: CG, Mar 3; 1798: CG, Feb 23
Sarny (dancer), 1755: DL, Nov 8
Saro qual e il torrente (song), 1763: KING'S, Apr 25
Sarti, Giuseppe (composer), 1778: KING'S, Nov 28; 1781: CG, Jan 31; 1782:
KING'S, Nov 14; 1783: KING'S, Mar 6, Nov 29; 1784: KING'S, Jan 6, Mar 4, Apr
15; 1785: KING'S, Feb 24; 1786: CG, May 2; 1787: DL, Apr 20; 1788: KING'S,
Apr 5; 1789: KING'S, Jan 24, DL, Mar 6, Nov 24; 1791: DL, Apr 1, 6, PAN, 14,
DL, 15; 1792: KING'S, Mar 28, 30, DLKING'S, May 23, DL, Oct 18; 1793: KING'S,
Feb 26, Mar 19, Jun 11; 1794: KING'S, Feb 1, Mar 1, DL, Dec 20; 1795: KING'S,
Jun 16, DL, Oct 30; 1796: DL, Apr 30, Sep 29; 1797: KING'S, Nov 28; 1798:
KING'S, Dec 8; 1799: CG, Apr 19; 1800: KING'S, Apr 15
--Alessandro e Timoteo (opera), 1800: KING'S, Apr 15, 19, 22, 26, May 6, 10,
24, 27, Jun 7, 14, Jul 8
--Contadini Bizzarri, I (opera), 1794: KING'S, Feb 1, 4, 8, 11, 15, 18, 22, 25,
Mar 4, 11, 15, Apr 5, 8, 12; 1797: KING'S, Jun 8
--Gelosie Villane, Le (opera), 1784: KING'S, Apr 15, 17, May 4; 1794: KING'S,
Feb 1; 1797: KING'S, Jun 8, 20, Jul 18
--Giulio Sabino (opera), 1788: KING'S, Apr 5, 10, 12, 15, 17, 19, 22, 29, May

3, 31, Jun 28; 1789: DL, Mar 6
--Idalide (opera), 1791: PAN, Apr 7, 14, 16, 30, May 7, 10, 21, 28, Jun 10, 21,
   25, Jul 16, DLKING'S, Nov 19, CG, Dec 2; 1796: DL, Jun 9
--Ipermestra (opera), 1797: KING'S, Nov 28, Dec 2, 5
--Medonte (opera), 1782: KING'S, Nov 12, 14, 19, 23, 30, Dec 12, 14; 1783:
   KING'S, Jan 11, 21, Feb 11, Jun 19; 1798: KING'S, Dec 8, 11, 15, 22; 1799:
   KING'S, Jan 12, Feb 19, Mar 5
--Mitridate a Sinope (opera), 1781: CG, Jan 31
--Nozze di Dorina, Le (opera), 1793: KING'S, Feb 26, Mar 2, 5, 9, 12, 16, Apr
   9, 23, 30, May 7, Jun 25, 29; 1795: KING'S, Jun 16, 23
--Odenato and Zenobia (opera), 1793: KING'S, Jun 11, 15
--Rivali Delusi, I (Fra Due Litigante Il Terzo Gode) (opera), 1784: KING'S, Jan
   6, 10, 13, 20, 27, Feb 3, 7, 10, 14, 26, Mar 9, 11, 20, 25, May 13, 18, Jun
   1, 3, 10, 29, Jul 3; 1785: KING'S, Jan 4, 11, 20, Feb 22, Mar 3, Apr 14;
   1793: KING'S, Feb 26
Sartori, Angiola (singer), 1761: KING'S, Oct 13, Nov 10; 1762: KING'S, May 11;
   1763: KING'S, Nov 26; 1764: KING'S, Feb 21
Satan's Address to the Sun (entertainment), 1799: HAY, Sep 16
Satchell, Elizabeth (actor), 1780: CG, Sep 21, Nov 25; 1781: CG, Jan 9, 13, Mar
   24, Apr 28, 30, May 10, Sep 17, 24, Oct 5, Nov 17, Dec 31; 1782: CG, Jan 11,
   22, Feb 9, Mar 19, Apr 10, 20, 23, Oct 3, 4, 7, 8, 19, Nov 1, 29, Dec 14, 17;
   1783: CG, Jan 28, Apr 1, 7, 23, 25, 26, May 17, 19, 23, 24, Sep 22, 24, 26,
   Oct 3, 8, 9, 13, 20, Nov 4, 24, Dec 23, 27, 29; 1784: CG, Jan 19, May 27
Satchell, Susanna (actor), 1783: CG, May 17
Satire on All Trades (song), 1723: DL, Aug 6, 9; 1731: GF, Mar 18
Satires Puny (dance), 1742: DL, Jan 6, 7, 9, 11, 14, 18, 21, 25, 27, Feb 6, 10,
   19, 22, Mar 1, 4, 6, 11
Satirical Dialogue Humbly addressed to the Gentlemen who Deformed the play of
   Othello (pamphlet), 1751: DL, Mar 19
Saturday Night (song), 1795: CG, Oct 26
Saturday Night at Sea (song), 1798: CG, May 28
Saturday Night at Sea; or, Tars at Anchor (interlude, anon), 1799: CG, May 28;
   1800: CG, Apr 19
Satyrist, The (entertainment), 1799: CG, May 14
Satyrs and Nymphs (dance), 1740: CG, Dec 20; 1741: CG, Jan 2
Saul (actor), 1775: HAY, Mar 23, Oct 30; 1776: CHR, Sep 23, Oct 2, 11
Saul. See Handel, George Frederic.
Sauley, Mary (actor), 1782: HAY, Mar 21, May 6
Saulnier (dancer), 1787: KING'S, Dec 8; 1788: KING'S, Jan 29, Mar 13, May 15;
   1789: KING'S, Jan 10, 31, Mar 3, 19, CG, Jul 11
Saulnier, Mlle (dancer), 1789: KING'S, Mar 17, 31, Apr 28, May 14
Saunder (carpenter), 1752: DL, Apr 13
Saunders (actor), 1769: CG, Dec 1; 1770: CG, Jan 8, 27, Feb 5, Mar 20, Apr 25,
   HAY, May 16, 21, CG, 24, HAY, Jul 25, Aug 1, 8, 31, CG, Oct 2, 11; 1771: CG,
   Nov 1, 14; 1772: CG, Jan 4, 21, Apr 28, Jun 1, Sep 21, 30, Oct 16, Nov 21;
   1773: CG, Feb 18, 27, Mar 15, May 4, 8, 24
Saunders (actor, singer), 1793: HAY, Aug 3, 12, 15, Oct 10, Nov 19; 1794: HAY,
   Jul 17, 18, 21, 24, Aug 27
Saunders (doorkeeper), 1738: DL, May 31; 1739: DL, May 31; 1740: DL, May 19;
   1741: DL, May 25; 1742: DL, May 24; 1743: DL, May 24; 1744: DL, May 22; 1745:
   DL, May 13; 1746: DL, May 9; 1747: DL, May 15; 1748: DL, May 16; 1749: DL,
   May 16; 1752: DL, Apr 30
Saunders (equilibrist), 1759: CG, Oct 20, Dec 10; 1760: CG, Apr 19, May 26,
   HAY, Jun 2
Saunders, Charles
--Tamerlane the Great, 1681: DL, Mar 0
Saunders, Master (actor), 1770: HAY, Aug 13, 22
Saunders, Miss (actor), 1782: HAY, Sep 21
Saunders, Miss (dancer), 1738: DL, Oct 30; 1739: DL, Feb 7, Oct 10; 1744: CG,
   Jan 19; 1748: SOU, Oct 10
Saunders, Miss (singer), 1799: DL, Jan 19, 23, May 24, Oct 14, Nov 14, Dec 11,
   28; 1800: DL, Jan 1, Mar 11, Apr 29
Saunders, Mrs (actor), 1707: DL/QUEEN, Oct 18, 22, Nov 1, 11, 18; 1708:
   DL/QUEEN, Jan 1, DL, Feb 6, DL/QUEEN, 21, DL, Mar 15, 16, Apr 10, DL/QUEEN,
   21, May 19, DL, 21, Jun 26, DL/QUEEN, Jul 15, DL, Aug 4, 31, Sep 16, Dec 14,
   20, 22, 28, 30; 1709: DL, Jan 4, 8, Mar 4, May 12, QUEEN'S, Oct 11, 17, 22,
   28, 29, Nov 15, 19, Dec 12; 1710: QUEEN'S, Apr 10, May 1, 29, Jun 1, 9, DL,
   Nov 21, 27, 28, Dec 1, 4, 5, 12, 21; 1711: DL, Jan 9, 18, 19, 26, DL/QUEEN,
   Feb 5, DL, 10, 15, Mar 8, Apr 7, May 15, Jul 27, Sep 22, Oct 19, 22, 24, Nov
   1, 9, 27, Dec 8; 1712: DL, Jan 19, May 29, Aug 1, 26, Oct 10, 14, 15, 17, 30;
   1713: DL, Jan 14, Mar 3, May 12, Jun 23, Nov 19, 25; 1714: DL, Apr 27, May
   19, 28, Nov 26; 1715: DL, Jan 15, Feb 15, 28, Apr 2, 30, May 7, 18, 20, Jun

24, 28, Jul 1, 6, Oct 13, Dec 9, 17, 30; 1716: DL, Jan 3, 7, 23, 25, 26, Feb
1, 9, 18, Mar 10, Apr 26, Jun 15, Sep 29, Oct 12, 19, 24, 27, Nov 2, 12, 14,
26, 27, Dec 4, 5, 14; 1717: DL, Jan 9, 31, Mar 14, Apr 29, May 2, 30, Oct 1,
10, 21, 22, Nov 13, 27, Dec 4; 1718: DL, Jan 7, 20, 27, Feb 14, 19, Mar 24,
Apr 5, 14, 19, May 28, Oct 10, 11, 17, 22, 28, 30, Nov 18, 24, 25, 26, 28,
Dec 10, 19; 1719: DL, Apr 16, Sep 24, 29, Oct 10, 14, 15, 23, Nov 2, 3, 10,
16, 23, Dec 2, 28; 1720: DL, Jan 1, 12, 13, Feb 5, Mar 19, Apr 23, Jun 2, Sep
10, 13, 15, 24, 29, Oct 3, 6, 15, 17, Nov 11, 12, 18, 21; 1721: DL, Jan 13,
25, 27, Apr 13, 14
Saunders, Mrs (actor), 1768: HAY, Jun 17, 27, 29, Jul 6, 13, 27, Aug 8, 24;
1770: HAY, May 18, 28, Jun 22, 25, 27, Jul 9, Aug 1, 29, 31, Sep 13
Saunders, Mrs (actor), 1790: CG, Jul 16
Saunders, Mrs (actor), 1798: WRSG, Jun 8; 1799: DL, Feb 4, WRSG, May 17
Saunders, Richard (actor), 1682: DL, Feb 4, Mar 11, Nov 28; 1683: DG, May 31,
Jul 0, NONE, Sep 0, DL, Nov 12, Dec 0; 1684: DL, Mar 0, DLORDG, Aug 0; 1685:
DLORDG, Jan 20, DL, Aug 0; 1686: DG, Mar 4, NONE, Sep 0
Saunderson, L (payee), 1776: DL, Jan 8
Saunderson, Mary (actor), 1661: LIF, Jun 28, Aug 24, Dec 16; 1662: LIF, Mar 1,
Apr 2, Sep 30, Oct 18, ATCOURT, 27, Dec 1
Saunderson, Sir William (supporter), 1735: CG/LIF, Mar 24
Sauny the Scot. See Shakespeare, William, The Taming of the Shrew.
Saut de la Panche, Le (entertainment), 1720: KING'S, Apr 26
Sauvages (dance), 1773: KING'S, May 1, Jun 3, 5
Savage Dance (dance), 1748: DL, Mar 24; 1799: DL, May 1
Savage Hunters (dance), 1775: DL, Oct 20, 21, 28, 30, Nov 1, 2, 4, 15, 17, 18,
20, 22, 24, 25, Dec 2; 1776: DL, Feb 10, 13, 20, 22, 27, Apr 13, 17, 19, 26,
Jun 1, Oct 24, 26, Nov 1, 6; 1777: DL, Jan 9, Apr 5; 1778: DL, Mar 24, 28,
Apr 9
Savage, Richard (author, actor), 1698: LIF, Nov 0; 1718: DL, Jun 17; 1723: DL,
Jun 12, Jul 5, Oct 2; 1731: DL, Feb 17; 1777: CG, Feb 1
--Love in a Veil, 1718: DL, Jun 17, 20, 24, Jul 22; 1784: DL, Apr 19
--Sir Thomas Overbury, 1723: DL, Jun 12, 14, 19, Oct 2; 1777: CG, Feb 1, 3, 5,
6, 8, 13, 17, 20, 27, Apr 2, 8, May 3, 15, Sep 24, Nov 25
Savage, The (play, anon), 1727: LIF, Feb 27, Mar 6
Savage, William (actor, singer), 1735: CG, Apr 16; 1737: CG, Feb 16, ST, Mar 8,
CT, May 2; 1738: KING'S, Jan 3; 1739: KING'S, Apr 4; 1740: DL, Nov 19, LIF,
22, DL, 28, Dec 3, 10; 1741: LIF, Jan 10, DL, Mar 17, 24, 30, May 5, 15, 28;
1743: CG, Feb 18; 1744: CR, Mar 21; 1745: CG, Mar 6; 1757: CHAPEL, May 5, CG,
Oct 22; 1775: CG, Mar 18
Savage's scholars (singers), 1755: DL, Feb 3
Savery (house servant), 1790: CG, Jun 12; 1791: CG, Jun 14; 1792: CG, Jun 1;
1794: CG, Jun 14; 1795: CG, Jun 10
Savetiers, Les. See Sabotiers.
Savigny, John Horatio (actor), 1770: CG, Nov 1, Dec 4, 18; 1771: CG, Feb 23,
Apr 13, May 9, Oct 2, 11, 18, Dec 11; 1772: CG, Feb 1, Mar 21, DL, 23, CG,
Apr 25, May 11; 1773: CG, Feb 3; 1774: CG, Apr 21; 1775: HAY, Mar 23; 1791:
HAY, Dec 26
Savile Row, 1793: HAY, Aug 20
Saville, George, Lord Halifax, 1665: NONE, May 4; 1669: BRIDGES, Feb 27
Saville, Henry (spectator), 1665: NONE, May 4; 1668: ATCOURT, Feb 4; 1669:
BRIDGES, Mar 4; 1676: DL, Dec 11; 1677: ATCOURT, Dec 17
Saville, John (singer), 1777: CG, Feb 14, Mar 19; 1790: CG, Feb 19, 24, 26, Mar
3, 17, 19, 26
Savoi, Gasparo (singer), 1766: KING'S, Jan 25, Apr 10, 26, Oct 21, Nov 25;
1767: KING'S, Jan 31, Oct 27; 1768: KING'S, Mar 10; 1770: KING'S, Mar 8, 22,
May 19; 1771: KING'S, Jan 10, Feb 8, 9, 28; 1772: KING'S, Feb 21, HAY, Mar
30, Apr 6, 27; 1773: KING'S, Feb 5; 1775: KING'S, Oct 31, Nov 7, Dec 12;
1776: KING'S, Jan 9, Feb 6, 29, Mar 28, Apr 20, May 14, 18, Nov 2, 5, Dec 14;
1777: KING'S, Jan 21, Feb 4, Mar 1, 13, 15, Apr 1, 17, 29, May 3, 24
Savoy (dancer), 1781: CG, May 1
Savoy, Prince Eugene of, 1712: SH, Jan 21
Savoy, 1748: HAY, Dec 9; 1755: DL, Sep 27
Savoyard (singer), 1754: HAY, Dec 9
Savoyard Travellers (dance), 1749: DL, Nov 9, 10, 11, 13, 14, 15, 17, 18, 20,
21, 23, Dec 29; 1750: DL, Jan 3, 18, 20, 26, Feb 3, 6, 9, 17, Mar 17, Apr 16,
27; 1751: DL, Nov 5, 6, 7, 11, 16, 28, Dec 5, 10, 23; 1753: DL, Dec 19; 1762:
DL, Apr 24
Savoyards, The; or, Madame Catherina (dance), 1763: CG, Apr 15
Savoyards' Dance (dance), 1741: CG, Feb 14, 17; 1742: CG, May 1, 15, 20, 25,
Jun 2, Dec 18, 20, 23; 1743: CG, Jan 17; 1747: DL, Dec 14, 15, 19; 1748: DL,
Jan 1, 6, 7, 12, 13, 19, 23, 25, 26, 28, Feb 3, 6, Mar 8, 22, 29, Apr 12, 13,
14, 15, 19, 22, 25, 26, 27, 28, 29, May 2, 4, 5, 9, 17, 20, Sep 20, 22, Oct

1, 6, 11, 15, 19, 25, 29, 31, Nov 3, 10, 26, 28; 1749: DL, Jan 20, 23, 28,
    Feb 20, Mar 18, 20, 31, Apr 1, 3, 5, 7, 10, 11, 14, 28, May 1, 11, 12, Dec
    13, 14, 18, 23; 1751: DL, Apr 26; 1753: CG, Dec 10, 13, 14, 27; 1756: CG, May
    18, 20; 1758: CG, Apr 8, 13, 19; 1780: DL, May 2; 1794: CG, Feb 25, Apr 24,
    Jun 6, Sep 26; 1796: CG, Apr 12, Jun 3; 1798: CG, Apr 30, Jun 4
Sawney is a bonny, bonny lad (song), 1694: YB, Jan 25
Sawyer (actor, singer), 1793: CG, Oct 2, 24, Nov 28; 1794: CG, Oct 22; 1795:
    CG, Apr 24, Sep 21, Nov 30; 1796: CG, Sep 19, 26, Oct 6; 1797: CG, Feb 18,
    May 18, Nov 2; 1798: CG, Mar 19, Oct 8, Nov 12, Dec 11, 15; 1799: CG, Jan 14,
    DL, Feb 4, 9, Mar 2, CG, Apr 2, 9, 13, May 4, DL, 24, CG, Sep 30, Oct 7, DL,
    14, Nov 14, Dec 11, CG, 23; 1800: DL, Jan 1, CG, Feb 10, DL, Mar 11, 13, Apr
    29, May 3, HAY, Jul 10, 18, 25, Aug 14, 29, Sep 1, 11
Sawyer, Master (singer), 1798: CG, Nov 12; 1799: CG, Apr 13; 1800: CG, Jan 16,
    Feb 10
Saxe Gotha, Augusta, Princess of, 1796: CG, Feb 12
Saxe Gotha, Duke of (spectator), 1742: DL, Feb 13
Saxe Gotha, Princess of, 1736: CG, Apr 29
Say (chandler), 1789: CG, Nov 2
Say, Bonny Lass, will you carry a wallet? (song), 1786: CG, May 22; 1788: DL,
    May 6, HAY, Aug 13; 1791: CG, May 6, 27
Say, Bonny Lass, will you lie in a Barrack (verse), 1791: CG, May 19
Say, Bonny Lass, will you lie in a Garrat (song), 1791: CG, May 19
Say, cruel Amoret (song), 1691: DL, Dec 0
Sayer (spectator), 1693: DL, Jan 16
Sca Don Giovanni Libertino (entertainment), 1726: KING'S, Dec 21
Scacciato dal suo nido (song), 1726: DL, Apr 28; 1735: LIF, Jun 19
Scacia (composer), 1733: HIC, Apr 27
Scaliger, Joseph Guste (critic), 1715: KING'S, Jun 25
Scalkavy (house servant), 1774: CG, Jan 14
Scalzi, Carlo (singer), 1733: KING'S, Oct 30, Nov 13, Dec 4; 1734: KING'S, Jan
    26, Mar 13, Apr 27, May 18
Scanderbeg. See Havard, William.
Scaramouch a Philosopher. See Ravenscroft, Edward.
Scaramouch and Countryman (dance), 1729: SOU, Oct 14
Scaramouch and Dame Ragonde (dance), 1716: LIF, Dec 1
Scaramouch and French Peasant (dance), 1715: LIF, Jun 14
Scaramouch and Harlequin (dance), 1703: YB, Feb 5; 1715: DL, May 31; 1718: DL,
    May 13; 1724: HIC, Dec 21; 1731: GF, May 17
Scaramouch and Scaramouchette (dance), 1735: HAY, May 26
Scaramouch Dance (dance), 1704: DL, Jan 13; 1706: QUEEN'S, Feb 4, 9, Mar 25,
    DL, Jun 28, QUEEN'S, 29, LIF/QUEN, Aug 10, HAW, 17; 1709: DL, Dec 15; 1710:
    DL, Jan 12, 31, Mar 25, Apr 12, May 23, 30, GR, Aug 5, 17; 1711: GR, Sep 13;
    1712: DL, May 30, Jun 10, GR, Jul 19; 1713: DL, Jun 10; 1715: LIF, Feb 5, 9,
    22, Mar 14, 21, Apr 18, May 16, DL, Jun 2, LIF, 7, Jul 8, Aug 23; 1716: LIF,
    Aug 15; 1717: GLOBE, Jan 18, DL, Apr 24; 1718: LIF, May 6, 29; 1719: LIF, Apr
    9, 29, May 7, 13, 21, 25, Jun 3; 1720: LIF, Feb 22, May 24; 1723: HAY, Apr
    15; 1725: DL, May 19; 1726: DL, Apr 15, 23, May 18; 1728: HAY, Nov 14; 1730:
    GF, Jan 20, Apr 7, Sep 30; 1731: GF, Mar 18, Apr 1, May 13, 17; 1733: HAY,
    Mar 14, DL/HAY, Dec 12, HAY, 13, DL/HAY, 19; 1734: GF, Mar 18; 1735: GF/HAY,
    Apr 7; 1736: HAY, Feb 19, 20, LIF, Mar 31; 1738: BFH, Aug 23; 1739: DL, May
    30, TC, Aug 8, BF, 27, SF, Sep 8; 1747: SF, Sep 24; 1748: CG, Dec 26, 27;
    1761: CG, Jan 6; 1764: DL, Oct 13, 23, 26, Nov 8, Dec 13; 1777: KING'S, Feb 4
Scaramouch Dance to Faranoll's Ground (dance), 1704: LIF, Jun 26
Scaramouch Dance, Grand (dance), 1740: TCLP, Aug 4
Scaramouch, Harlequin and Punch (dance), 1703: DL, Jun 30, Dec 13
Scaramouch, Harlequin and Punch Comic Dance, Grand (dance), 1726: LIF, Apr 19,
    21
Scaramouch Man and Woman (dance), 1703: DL, Feb 12
Scaramouch Pedant Scrupuleux; ou, L'Escolier (farce), 1719: KING'S, Mar 14;
    1721: HAY, Feb 16
Scaramouch Persecute par Arlequin Faux Diable (pantomime), 1725: HAY, May 3
Scaramouch Scapin; or, The Old Miser Caught in a Sack (droll), 1742: BFHC, Aug
    25
Scaramouchio, Senior. See Fiorelli, Tiberio.
Scarborough, 1742: CG, Feb 23
Scarlatti, Alessandro (composer), 1706: DL, Jan 12; 1709: QUEEN'S, May 28, Jun
    9; 1710: QUEEN'S, Apr 25; 1712: QUEEN'S, Mar 22, Nov 12; 1719: HIC, May 1;
    1720: HIC, Sep 1; 1721: KING'S, Mar 28; 1724: HIC, Mar 20; 1732: LIF, Apr 28;
    1742: KING'S, Apr 20; 1757: KING'S, Mar 24
--Telemachus (musical), 1732: LIF, Apr 28
Scarlatti, Domenico (composer), 1718: HIC, Mar 26; 1720: KING'S, May 30
--Narcissus (opera), 1720: KING'S, May 30, Jun 2, 11, 15, 18

Scarlatti, Francisco (composer), 1719: HIC, May 1; 1720: HIC, Sep 1
Scarpettini, Gaetano (beneficiary), 1727: HIC, Feb 17; 1728: YB, Mar 8; 1729: HIC, Mar 7; 1730: HIC, Mar 13; 1731: HIC, Mar 5; 1732: HIC, Apr 26; 1736: HIC, Mar 15
Scarr (payee), 1773: DL, Feb 9
Scarron, Paul (author), 1758: CG, Nov 9
Scarsdale, Earl of. See Leke, Robert.
Scawen, John, 1786: CG, Dec 6; 1790: HAY, Jul 16
--Girl in Style, The (farce), 1786: CG, Dec 6, 7
--New Spain; or, Love in Mexico (opera), 1790: HAY, Jul 16, 19, 21, 23, 27, Aug 3, 9, 12, 14
Scene from two great Tragic Actresses (entertainment), 1788: CG, Apr 25; 1789: CG, May 15
Scene of Bedlam, New (entertainment), 1749: BFCB, Aug 23
Scene of the Monkey (entertainment), 1719: LIF, Feb 5, KING'S, Mar 16, 19
Schellenbergen, Mme, 1769: CG, Jun 6
Schellinks, Will (spectator), 1662: COCKPIT, Jan 20, REDBULL, 22, 25, LIF, 29, VERE, Feb 6, 11, 13, LIF, 15, VERE, Mar 22, REDBULL, 25, Apr 28, COCKPIT, Oct 21; 1663: LIF, Mar 9, NONE, 16
Schemers, The. See Mayne, Jasper.
Schemes of Harlequin, The; or, Mons Le Saxe's Disappointment (pantomime, anon), 1746: BF, Aug 23
Scheming Jockey and Fortune Teller (dance), 1787: DL, Jun 1, HAY, 13, 16, 20, 27
Scheroli (Shiroli) (singer), 1773: KING'S, Oct 23, Nov 20, Dec 7; 1774: KING'S, Jan 11, 29, Feb 10, 24, Mar 8, 17, Apr 19, May 17, Jun 3
Scherza il Nocchier (song), 1734: HIC, Jul 10; 1749: KING'S, Mar 21
Scherza Quest' Alma Mia (song), 1745: CG, Apr 10
Schiava, La. See Piccini, Niccolo.
Schiavi per Amore, Gli (dance), 1787: HAY, Aug 7, 13
Schiavi per Amore, Gli. See Paisiello, Giovanni.
Schiavonetti, Elizabetta Pilotti (singer), 1710: QUEEN'S, Nov 22, 25; 1711: QUEEN'S, Jan 10, Feb 24, Apr 28, Dec 12; 1712: QUEEN'S, Feb 27, Apr 5, Nov 22, Dec 10; 1713: QUEEN'S, Feb 26; 1715: KING'S, Feb 26, May 25; 1716: KING'S, Apr 18, May 9
Schickhard, John Christian (musician), 1732: TTT, Mar 10
Schiller, Johann Christoph Friedrich von, 1799: HAY, Aug 21
--Rauber, Die, 1799: HAY, Aug 21
Schindlerin, Sga (singer), 1774: KING'S, Nov 8, Dec 3; 1775: KING'S, Jan 14, 26, Feb 7, Mar 23, May 20; 1776: KING'S, May 14, 16
Schinotti (singer), 1782: KING'S, Nov 2, 14, Dec 19; 1783: KING'S, Jan 7, Feb 18, 27, Mar 6, 27, Apr 29, Jun 14, 19, Nov 29, Dec 16; 1784: KING'S, Jan 6, Feb 24, Mar 4, 25, Apr 15, Jun 12, Dec 18; 1785: KING'S, Jan 4, 25, Mar 3, 15, Apr 2, May 28; 1786: KING'S, Jan 24, Feb 14, Mar 11, 16, 21, 30, May 4, 25
Schinotti, Teresa (singer), 1783: KING'S, Dec 16; 1784: KING'S, Jan 6, Feb 24, Mar 18, Apr 15, May 8, Jun 12, Dec 18; 1785: KING'S, Jan 4, 25, Apr 2, 16, May 28; 1786: KING'S, Apr 6, Dec 23; 1787: KING'S, Jan 9, Mar 1, 8, 29, Apr 17, 24, May 1; 1788: KING'S, Jan 15, Feb 5, Mar 4, Apr 5, May 8, 15; 1791: PAN, Jun 16, 25; 1792: HAY, Feb 28; 1794: KING'S, Jan 11, May 17
Schlaiblin, Christian Benjamin (librettist), 1748: HAY, Dec 9
Schneider and Otto (furriers), 1772: CG, Jan 27
Schoelcher (composer), 1743: KING'S, Nov 15
Schola, Adamo (musician), 1728: HAY, Apr 3
Schomberg, Meinhardt, Duke of Leinster (Linster) (spectator), 1694: DG, Jan 10
Schomberg, Dr Ralph, 1768: HAY, Aug 24; 1769: CG, Mar 11
--Rival Favourites, The; or, The Death of Bucephalus the Great, 1769: CG, Mar 4, 7, 11
School Boy, The. See Cibber, Colley.
School for a Wife, A; or, The Lucky Adventure (play, anon), 1750: NWSM, May 1; 1757: BFB, Sep 5, 6
School for Arrogance, The. See Holcroft, Thomas.
School for Fathers, A. See Bickerstaff, Isaac.
School for Grey-Beards, A. See Cowley, Hannah.
School for Guardians, The. See Murphy, Arthur.
School for Ladies, A; or, The Levee of Lovers (play, anon), 1780: HAY, Apr 5
School for Lovers, The. See Whitehead, William.
School for Prejudice, The. See Dibdin, Thomas John, Liberal Opinions.
School for Rakes, The. See Griffith, Elizabeth.
School for Scandal Scandalized, The. See Kemble, John Philip.
School for Scandal, The. See Sheridan, Richard Brinsley.
School for Vanity, The. See Pratt, Samuel Jackson.

School for Widows, A. See Cumberland, Richard.
School for Wives, The. See Kelly, Hugh.
School for Women, A. See Moliere, L'Ecole des Femmes.
School of Anacreon (song), 1753: DL, Mar 27; 1754: DL, May 7, Sep 14, Oct 3, 8,
    10, Nov 26, 28, Dec 4; 1755: CG, May 8; 1756: CG, Apr 19, May 13, 14; 1757:
    HAY, Oct 21
School of Compliments. See Shirley, James, Love Tricks.
School of Eloquence, The. See Cowley, Hannah.
School (Professor) of Folly, The (play, anon), 1718: LIF, Jan 3, 8, 10
School of Lovers, The. See LeSage, Alain Rene.
School of Shakespeare, The; or, Humours and Passions (lecture), 1774: DL, Mar
    9, DT, 16, DL, 23, MARLY, Jul 6; 1781: HAY, Aug 7, 17; 1796: HAY, Aug 30
Schoolding (actor), 1715: LIF, Feb 3, 16, May 18, Jun 2, Oct 4, 11; 1716: LIF,
    Mar 24, Apr 3, Jul 25; 1717: LIF, May 23, Nov 19; 1718: LIF, Jan 7, SF, Sep
    5, AC, 24; 1720: SFLH, Sep 5
Schoolding, Miss (dancer), 1714: LIF, Dec 22, 28; 1715: LIF, Jan 4, 7, 8, 10,
    14, 25, Feb 1, 2, 5, 9, Mar 1, 3, 10, 21, 26, Apr 4, 9, 19, 22, Oct 24, 26,
    28, 29, 31, Nov 4, 10, 12, 14, 15, 16, 22, 25, 26, 28, 29, 30, Dec 13, 17,
    30; 1716: LIF, Jan 3, 11, 18, 27, Feb 3, 16, 27, 28, Mar 19, Apr 5, 6, 9, 30,
    May 10, 18, 24, Jun 1, 12, Jul 25, Aug 3, Oct 4, 10, 12, 23, 25, 29, 30, 31,
    Nov 5, 8, 9, 14, 15, 16, 28, 29, Dec 17, 18, 21, 29, 31; 1717: LIF, Jan 4, 7,
    10, 11, 14, 22, 31, Feb 2, 6, 11, Mar 18, 30, Apr 4, 23, 27, 29, May 10, 11,
    16, 23, 27, 28, Jun 1, 7, Oct 5, 14, 15, 17, 25, Nov 1, 8, 15, 22, Dec 6, 11;
    1718: LIF, Jan 1, 3, 24, Apr 16, May 15, Jun 4, Aug 6, Sep 29, Oct 3, 9, 28,
    31, Nov 10, 13, 17, 24, 29, Dec 1, 8, 22; 1719: LIF, Jan 9, 13, 14, Feb 9,
    24, Mar 19, Apr 3, 8, 9, 10, 28, 29, 30, May 7, 13, 19, 25, 28, RI, Sep 5
Schoolding Jr, Miss (actor, dancer), 1715: LIF, May 18; 1717: LIF, Apr 29, May
    7, Nov 22, Dec 6; 1718: LIF, Jan 3
Schoolmaster (dance), 1775: DL, May 8, Sep 26
Schram, Christopher (violoncellist), 1790: CG, Feb 19
Schreibepult, Das. See Kotzebue, August Friedrich Ferdinand von.
Schroder, Friedrich Ludwig, 1799: DL, Apr 8
--Zwillingsbruder, Die, 1799: DL, Apr 8
Schroeder, H B (composer), 1797: DL, Jun 12
Schubert (trombonist), 1793: KING/HAY, Feb 15
Schultz (actor), 1784: HAY, Feb 23
Schultz (musician), 1741: HAY, Mar 13
Schulz, Johann Abraham Peter (composer), 1799: KING'S, Mar 26
Schuster, Joseph (composer), 1786: KING'S, Feb 14; 1792: DLKING'S, May 23
Schutz (spectator), 1759: DL, Oct 27; 1760: CG, Mar 28
Schutz Jr (spectator), 1759: DL, Oct 27
Schutz, Baron (royal accountant), 1747: CG, May 20
Schutz, Colonel (spectator), 1729: DL, Nov 1
Schwartz (bassoonist), 1782: DL, Mar 1
Schweitzer (dancer), 1791: PAN, Feb 17, 26
Schweitzer, L A Ein (correspondent), 1769: DL, Feb 2
Schweitzer, Mme (dancer), 1791: PAN, Feb 17
Scidmore. See Scudamore.
Scipio Africanus. See Beckingham, Charles.
Scipio. See Handel, George Frederic.
Scipio's Triumph; or, The Siege of Carthage (farce, anon), 1730: BFR, Aeg 22
Scipione in Cartagine. See Galuppi, Baldassare.
Scobell (spectator), 1700: DLORLIF, Jan 23
Scoglio d'immota fronte (song), 1726: DL, Apr 28
Scola dei Maritati, La. See Martin y Soler, Vicente.
Scolari, Giuseppi (composer), 1780: KING'S, Nov 25
--Arcifanfano, L' (opera), 1780: KING'S, Nov 25
Scorn tho' Beauty frowns to tremble (song), 1696: LIF, Nov 14
Scorned Envy here's nothing (song), 1695: DG, Apr 0
Scornful Lady, The. See Fletcher, John.
Scorpion, The (play, anon), 1748: HAY, Apr 14, 15, 16
Scot, Mrs (actor), 1718: LIF, Apr 30
Scotch Air (song), 1736: HIC, Apr 19; 1751: DL, May 4; 1771: CG, Mar 16, MARLY,
    Aug 27, 29, GROTTO, 30, Sep 3, 9; 1774: HAY, Feb 25; 1776: CG, Oct 23; 1777:
    CG, May 14; 1780: CG, Feb 5, HAY, Jun 2; 1785: KING'S, Mar 17; 1793: CG, Apr
    25; 1794: DL, Apr 11
Scotch Ballad (song), 1728: LIF, Mar 18, 27, Apr 29, Jul 12; 1729: HAY, Mar 29;
    1730: DL, Apr 28; 1735: CG/LIF, Mar 29; 1780: CG, May 12; 1797: HAY, Dec 4
Scotch Ballet, Grand (dance), 1750: CG, Jan 31, Feb 1, Mar 19, 31, Sep 26, Oct
    13, 15, 16, 17, Dec 22; 1751: CG, Jan 3, Mar 21, Apr 8, 12, 17, 18, 26, 29,
    May 10, Oct 9; 1752: CG, Mar 19, Apr 6, 13, May 13, Dec 16, 18; 1753: CG, Jan
    6, 10, Feb 6, Mar 19, 22, 26, 29, Apr 2, 5, 7, 9, 10, 12, 14, 23, 24, 30, May

       2, 7, 9, 14, 15
Scotch Batallion, <u>1686</u>: DLORDG, May 6
Scotch Cantata (song), <u>1754</u>: DL, May 10; <u>1768</u>: HAY, Dec 19
Scotch Dance (dance), <u>1702</u>: DL, Aug 20; <u>1703</u>: DL, Feb 12; <u>1704</u>: LIF, Mar 28,
    Apr 1, 8, 17, 28, Jun 26; <u>1705</u>: LIF/QUEN, Dec 26; <u>1706</u>: QUEEN'S, Jan 2, 7,
    14; <u>1717</u>: LIF, May 23; <u>1718</u>: LIF, May 15; <u>1719</u>: LIF, Apr 27; <u>1720</u>: DL, May
    25; <u>1721</u>: DL, Mar 23, Apr 10; <u>1722</u>: DL, Apr 12, May 9, 22, 25; <u>1723</u>: DL, May
    15, Aug 9, Oct 3; <u>1724</u>: DL, Apr 29, May 12, 14; <u>1725</u>: LIF, Mar 11, 13, Apr 5,
    7, 10, 14, 22, 30, May 1, 4, 5, 6, 10, 11, 12, 14, 18, 19, 20, 24, Oct 4, Nov
    24; <u>1726</u>: LIF, Jan 3, 5, Apr 26, 27, May 2, 3, 10, 14, 18, 23, 24, 30, Jun
    24, Aug 16, 19, 23, Sep 14, 19, Oct 19, Nov 30; <u>1727</u>: LIF, Feb 9, Mar 11, 23,
    Apr 7, May 3, 4, Oct 2, 17; <u>1728</u>: LIF, Mar 21, 25, 28, Apr 1, 6, 22, 23, 24,
    May 11, 22, 23, 30, Jun 25, Dec 31; <u>1729</u>: LIF, Jan 13, Mar 20, Apr 12, 15,
    16, 22, 23, 24, May 6, 9, 13, 15, 20, 22, 23, BFB, Aug 25; <u>1730</u>: LIF, Apr 24, 27,
    May 11, 27, 28, Sep 23, Oct 19; <u>1731</u>: LIF, Jan 11, 19, Mar 15, 25, Apr 26,
    May 5, 19, 21, 24, 25, Sep 22, GF, Oct 8, LIF, 27, DL, Dec 28; <u>1732</u>: LIF, Feb
    9, HAY, Mar 8, DL, 27, GF, 30, Apr 1, 14, 17, LIF, 24, DL, 27, LIF, May 3, 5,
    8, DL, 9, LIF, 9, 11, 15, 16, 17, 18, DL, Aug 15, 17, GF, Oct 7, DL, 14, GF,
    17, 18, 19, 23, 24, 26, DL, 26, GF, 28, 30, Nov 2, DL, 8, GF, 13, 14, DL, 14,
    GF, 15, 21, 23, 25, 30, Dec 15; <u>1733</u>: LIF/CG, Jan 16, 23, CG, 24, LIF/CG, 27,
    29, 31, Feb 1, 3, 5, 6, Mar 12, DL, 15, CG, 27, LIF/CG, 28, DL, 29, LIF/CG,
    29, 30, 31, Apr 2, 3, 10, 12, 13, GF, 16, LIF/CG, 17, 18, 19, 20, 21, 23, 24,
    25, 27, 30, CG, May 1, 2, LIF/CG, 3, CG, 4, GF, 5, 7, LIF/CG, 8, DL, 9, GF,
    10, LIF/CG, 10, GF, 11, 14, LIF/CG, 14, CG, 16, GF, 16, CG, 17, LIF/CG, 18,
    21, 23, CG/LIF, 28, LIF/CG, 29, 31, Jun 1, CG, Aug 9, 14, 16, 17, 21, GF, Sep
    12, CG, 22, 27, 29, Oct 4, 6, GF, 12, 15, CG, 18, 26, GF, 30, CG, 31, GF, 31,
    Nov 1, 2, 6, 8, 9, 10, CG, 16, 20, GF, 26, CG, Dec 4, GF, 8, CG, 10, 12, 15,
    GF, 18, 19, 20, 27, 29, CG, 29, 31; <u>1734</u>: CG, Jan 4, GF, 7, 8, 9, 12, DL, 14,
    16, GF, 18, DL, 22, GF, 22, CG, 22, GF, 24, 26, Feb 2, 5, CG, 22, Mar 11, 12,
    18, 25, 26, 28, Apr 6, GF, 18, CG, 18, 19, GF, 19, CG, 22, 24, GF, 24, 26,
    CG, 30, GF, May 1, CG, 2, GF, 3, CG, 6, GF, 7, 8, DL/HAY, 8, CG, 13, GF, 15,
    DL, 16, GF, 16, 17, 20, DL, 21, DL/HAY, 22, GF, 22, LIF, 23, DL/HAY, 23, HAY,
    27, JS, 31, GF, Sep 13, 16, 18, CG/LIF, 20, 27, Oct 9, 14, 23, Nov 12, 25,
    GF, Dec 2, 4, CG/LIF, 5, GF, 6, 9, 10, CG/LIF, 12, GF, 12; <u>1735</u>: CG/LIF, Jan
    13, GF, 13, CG/LIF, 17, GF, 17, CG/LIF, Feb 3, Mar 11, 13, GF, 13, CG/LIF,
    15, GF, 17, CG/LIF, 18, 20, 22, 24, 25, GF, 27, 29, CG/LIF, 29, Apr 8, GF, 9,
    CG/LIF, 10, GF, 10, CG/LIF, 14, 15, GF, 16, CG/LIF, 17, 18, GF, 22, 24, 28,
    29, CG/LIF, 29, GF, 30, May 1, GF/HAY, 1, CG/LIF, 1, 2, GF, 2, CG/LIF, 5, CG,
    6, GF, 15, CG/LIF, 16, DL, 17, CG/LIF, 19, GF/HAY, Jun 2, Jul 18, GF, Sep 10,
    24, 26, CG, 29, HAY, 29, CG, Oct 3, 13, 15, HAY, 24, GF, Nov 3, CG, 11, 13,
    GF, 15, Dec 1, 4, 5, 6, 11, 12, CG, 18; <u>1736</u>: CG, Jan 9, HAY, 14, CG, 17, 19,
    HAY, 19, GF, Feb 4, 5, 6, 10, 17, HAY, 19, CG, 23, 24, 26, Mar 11, 16, 20,
    22, 23, 29, GF, 29, Apr 1, CG, 1, GF, 8, 12, 28, May 4, CG, 8, 20, DL, 25,
    27, 28, CG, Sep 29, Oct 4, LIF, 5, CG, 6, 27, Nov 11, 23, Dec 6, 13; <u>1737</u>:
    CG, Jan 7, Mar 14, LIF, 21, CG, 24, LIF, 26, CG, 28, LIF, 31, Apr 2, CG, 14,
    15, DL, May 13, Nov 10, 11, 12, 14, 15; <u>1738</u>: CG, Mar 13, 23, Apr 5, 6, 7,
    10, 15, 17, DL, May 6, CG, Nov 13, Dec 5, 11; <u>1739</u>: CG, Jan 3, 6, Feb 9, Mar
    22, Apr 7, 14, 26, 27, 30, DL, May 25, CG, Sep 25, DL, Oct 16, 18, 22, CG,
    23, DL, 24, 25, 26, 27, 29, 31, CG, Nov 3, 6, DL, 10, 20, CG, 24, 26, Dec
    17; <u>1740</u>: DL, Jan 5, 7, 8, 11, 14, Feb 2, 5, 7, 11, 16, 19, 21, CG, Mar 18,
    24, 25, Apr 23, 25, 29, 30, Sep 29, Nov 13, Dec 11; <u>1741</u>: CG, Jan 8, GF, Mar
    12, CG, Apr 2, GF, 6, 7, 16, CG, 28, May 1, DL, 25, CG, Nov 30, Dec 9, 11,
    16; <u>1742</u>: GF, Feb 6, 13, 16, 25, Mar 25, CG, Apr 1, 3, 5, GF, 6, 22, 26, DL,
    May 3, CG, 8, 15, 20, 25, Jun 2; <u>1743</u>: LIF, Mar 8, 14, CG, Apr 6, DL, May 14,
    26, CG, Oct 3, 26, Nov 24, 25, Dec 6, 8, 9, 10, 12, 15, 16; <u>1744</u>: CG, Mar 8,
    13, 28, 29, 30, Apr 2, 24, 27, 28, 30, Oct 12, 15, Nov 2, 9, 27, 29, Dec 3,
    11, 14; <u>1745</u>: CG, Jan 3, Apr 19, 20, May 1, 2, 7, 8, 10, 13, 14; <u>1746</u>: GF,
    Oct 27; <u>1747</u>: GF, Feb 16; <u>1749</u>: DL, Jan 18, 20, 21, 23, 24, 25, 27, 31, Feb
    2, 3, 4, 16, 18, Mar 14, 30, Apr 8, 14, 22, CG, 24; <u>1750</u>: CG, Apr 17; <u>1751</u>:
    DL, Apr 26, CG, May 1, 4; <u>1752</u>: DL, Apr 27, May 1, 5; <u>1753</u>: DL, May 1, 4, 12,
    18; <u>1757</u>: CG, Apr 26, HAY, Sep 8, 14, Oct 3; <u>1758</u>: HAY, Jan 25; <u>1763</u>: DL, Apr
    25; <u>1765</u>: CG, Apr 29, May 10; <u>1786</u>: DL, Jan 5
Scotch Dance, Grand (dance), <u>1749</u>: DL, Oct 31, Nov 3; <u>1750</u>: DL, Jan 31, Feb 1,
    5, 8, CG, Apr 18, 20, DL, 20, CG, 21, 23, 24, DL, May 21, 22
Scotch Dialogue (song), <u>1733</u>: CG, May 2, LIF/CG, 24; <u>1740</u>: TCLP, Aug 4; <u>1746</u>:
    DL, Mar 10, Apr 4, 7, 10, 11, 21
Scotch Divertissement (entertainment), <u>1793</u>: CG, May 4, 25, 30; <u>1799</u>: CG, Jun 4
Scotch Duet (song), <u>1788</u>: DL, May 26; <u>1792</u>: CG, May 28
Scotch Ghost, The; or, Little Fanny's Love (dance), <u>1796</u>: DL, Oct 29, 31, Nov
    1, 8, 12, 14, 16, 18, 23, 25, 28, 30, Dec 1, 7, 8, 12, 14, 19, 21, 22; <u>1797</u>:
    DL, Jan 4, 5, 6, 9, 11, 16, 18, 19, 23, 25, 26, 27, Feb 1, 2, 3, 6, 10, 13,
    15, 16, 17, 20, 22, Mar 2, 16, 20, 23, 27, 30, Apr 3, 17, 19, 21, 24, 26, 28,

                                    750

May 3, 4, 5, 10, 12, 26, 30, Jun 5, 9, 12, 14, 16; 1798: DL, Dec 6, 8, 11,
    12, 18, 21; 1799: DL, Jun 28, 29, Dec 2, 17, 19; 1800: DL, Feb 8, 12, Mar 8,
    May 21, 26, Jun 3, 9, 12, 13
Scotch Harp (music), 1717: CORH, Apr 26
Scotch Highlander (dance), 1719: LIF, Apr 7; 1722: LIF, Apr 26
Scotch Jig (dance), 1729: LIF, Mar 27, Apr 19
Scotch Lass (dance), 1721: DL, Jun 6
Scotch Lilt (dance), 1724: DL, Apr 7, 8
Scotch Measure (dance), 1749: CG, Apr 24; 1750: CG, Apr 28, 30
Scotch Music (music), 1743: DL, Dec 3; 1770: HAY, Nov 21; 1778: HAY, Sep 17;
    1779: HAY, Jan 11, May 10; 1780: HAY, Jan 17; 1791: CG, Oct 20; 1794: CG, Feb
    6, Oct 14; 1797: CG, Apr 8
Scotch nobility, 1723: KING'S, Feb 9; 1784: HAY, Feb 9
Scotch Overture (music), 1774: DL, May 9; 1779: HAY, Jan 11; 1780: HAY, Jan 17,
    Sep 25; 1788: CG, Nov 10
Scotch Pas de Deux (dance), 1800: CG, May 23, Jun 11
Scotch performers, 1718: AC, Sep 24; 1732: DL, Aug 11
Scotch Reel (dance), 1783: DL, Sep 20; 1784: DL, Mar 30; 1785: KING'S, Apr 14;
    1786: HAY, Jul 6; 1787: HAY, Jul 28; 1790: DL, Jun 2; 1795: KING'S, Mar 26;
    1796: CG, Jun 6; 1799: CG, Apr 18
Scotch Sailor (dance), 1736: GF, May 4
Scotch Sonata (music), 1748: DL, Oct 25, 29, Nov 3, 9, 12, 18, 23, 25, 26
Scotch Song (song), 1700: DL, Jul 6; 1702: DL, Dec 8; 1704: LIF, Apr 28, 29;
    1729: FLR, Dec 1; 1731: LG, Mar 8, CRT, 10, GF, Jun 1; 1743: IT, Dec 26;
    1750: CG, Apr 19; 1753: HAY, Apr 14; 1754: HAY, Feb 2, Aug 27; 1756: HAY, Apr
    8, 19; 1757: HAY, Apr 22, Aug 11, 22, 24, Sep 2, 8, 28, Oct 3; 1758: HAY, Jan
    25, 27, Apr 28; 1760: HAY, Feb 21, Sep 8; 1762: HAY, Sep 17; 1769: HAY, Feb
    27; 1774: HAY, Sep 17; 1784: HAY, Aug 3; 1791: CG, May 18
Scotch Song in Praise of a Highland Laird (song), 1704: LIF, Apr 28
Scotch Sword Dance (dance), 1733: DL, Dec 31
Scotch Whim (dance), 1703: DL, Jun 19; 1704: LIF, Aug 9
Scotch Woman (dance), 1732: DL, May 6
Scotland, 1680: DG, Feb 0, DL, Mar 0; 1682: DG, Apr 21, May 31; 1714: DL, Jun
    16; 1746: DL, Mar 3; 1761: BFY, Aug 31; 1770: CG, Oct 23
Scots Presbytery, 1757: CG, Mar 14
Scott (actor), 1715: LIF, Oct 28, Nov 30; 1716: LIF, Jan 4, Apr 3; 1717: LIF,
    May 23, Dec 12; 1718: LIF, Oct 6; 1719: LIF, Feb 7, May 25
Scott (actor), 1743: JS, Mar 16; 1744: MF, Jun 11; 1747: GF, Jan 16
Scott (actor), 1773: DL, Dec 27; 1774: DL, Jan 19
Scott (copper laceman), 1750: DL, Jan 4; 1767: DL, Jan 23, 24; 1771: CG, Nov
    26, DL, Dec 12; 1772: DL, Jun 10, CG, Nov 20, DL, Dec 8; 1773: DL, Mar 1, CG,
    2, DL, Jun 2, Nov 19; 1774: DL, Jan 7, CG, 20, DL, 21, CG, Apr 19, DL, Jun 2,
    Oct 20; 1775: DL, Jan 10, Feb 23, May 27; 1776: DL, Jan 26, Jun 10
Scott (householder), 1737: CG, Jan 24
Scott (singer), 1748: JS, Dec 26
Scott (singer), 1767: DL, Jan 24
Scott, Anne, Duchess of Monmouth, 1665: ATCOURT, Feb 2; 1668: ATCOURT, Jan 13,
    Feb 4
Scott, Isabella (actor), 1744: DL, May 8
Scott, Isabella, Mrs John (actor, singer), 1757: CG, Mar 11; 1758: CG, Feb 22,
    Mar 1; 1764: DL, Apr 26; 1767: HAB, Dec 10; 1768: DL, Aug 18; 1769: DL, Apr
    15, HAY, 18, DL, 21, 22, 26, May 1, CG, 2, DL, 5, 17, 22, KING'S, Jun 1, DL,
    Sep 23, 30, Oct 2, Nov 6, 8, 9, 20, 23, 28, Dec 6, 8, 18, 30; 1770: DL, Jan
    4, HAY, Mar 12, DL, 29, Apr 5, 26, HAY, May 4, DL, 15, Jun 7, Sep 22, Oct 4,
    12, 13, 25, 29, Nov 5, 9, 12, 14, 17, 19, 29, Dec 13; 1771: DL, Jan 22, Feb
    9, Mar 16, Apr 4, 8, 9, HAY, 12, DL, 19, 27, May 25, CG, Jun 6, DL, Sep 24,
    26, Oct 8, 10, 21, 22, 26, 29, Nov 4, 25, Dec 2, 6, 26; 1772: DL, Mar 6, 26,
    28, Apr 2, 25, May 4, 6, Sep 19, 29, Oct 1, 3, 20, Nov 4, 9, 12, 18, Dec 30;
    1773: DL, Feb 11, 25, Apr 19, HAY, 23, DL, May 10, 12, 14, HAY, Sep 20, DL,
    21, Oct 9, 25, Nov 4, 25, Dec 3, 27; 1774: HAY, Feb 18, 23, 25, DL, Mar 15,
    19, Apr 4, 12, May 20, 28, Jun 2, Sep 27, 29, Oct 1, 5, 14, Nov 4, 5, 25, 29,
    Dec 26; 1775: DL, Feb 1, 4, Mar 21, 23, Apr 27, May 1, 3, 10, Sep 26, Oct 7,
    17, 21, 28, Nov 1, 4, 10, 28, Dec 7, 26; 1776: DL, Feb 8, 10, Mar 26, Apr 9,
    20, May 18, 22, Oct 9, 18, 25, 26, Nov 7, 25, Dec 5, 10; 1777: DL, Jan 1, 4,
    Feb 20, Apr 22
Scott, James, Duke of Monmouth, 1662: ATCOURT, Nov 17; 1665: ATCOURT, Feb 2;
    1668: ATCOURT, Jan 13; 1674: CITY, Oct 29; 1675: ATCOURT, Feb 15, 16; 1680:
    DG, Feb 2; 1682: DLORDG, Jul 18, DG, Aug 16, DL, Nov 28; 1685: DG, Jun 3, 13
Scott, John (actor), 1779: HAY, Dec 20; 1784: HAY, Mar 8; 1785: DL, Jan 26;
    1790: CG, Oct 25; 1791: HAY, Oct 24; 1792: DLKING'S, Jun 15; 1793: DL, Jun 6;
    1796: DL, Jun 10; 1797: DL, Jun 15; 1798: DL, Jun 16; 1799: DL, Jul 3; 1800:
    DL, Jun 14

Scott, Major John (spectator), 1790: DL, Nov 17
Scott, Miss (actor), 1754: HAY, May 29; 1758: CG, Mar 3; 1764: DL, Nov 28
Scott, Miss (dancer), 1737: DL, Nov 2, 7; 1738: DL, Apr 17, May 5, 22; 1739:
    CG, Apr 7, DL, 26, May 12; 1741: DL, Mar 31, Apr 13, 14, May 2, 13, Dec 19;
    1742: DL, May 3, Dec 1, 13; 1743: LIF, Jan 7, 10, Feb 14, 17, Mar 17, Apr 5,
    DL, Sep 15, Oct 13, Nov 23; 1744: DL, Mar 29, May 8; 1746: DL, Jan 31, Feb 6,
    Mar 10
Scott, Miss (dancer), 1761: DL, Jun 19, Aug 8
Scott, Miss I (actor), 1754: HAY, May 29
Scott, Miss J (actor), 1743: LIF, Feb 14
Scott the elder, Miss (dancer), 1737: CG, Jan 24; 1738: DL, Feb 25; 1739: DL,
    May 12, 30
Scott the younger, Miss (dancer), 1737: CG, Jan 24, DL, Nov 2, 7; 1738: DL, May
    22, 23; 1739: DL, May 12, 30
Scott, Misses (dancers), 1736: CG, Sep 17, Oct 4, 6, Dec 6; 1737: CG, Jan 24,
    Mar 19, Apr 2, May 5, 12, DL, Nov 2, 7; 1738: DL, May 22; 1739: DL, May 12,
    30; 1742: DL, May 3, LIF, Dec 27; 1743: LIF, Mar 17; 1744: DL, Feb 3, Apr 9,
    May 8; 1745: CT, Jan 14, HAY, Apr 1
Scott, Mrs (house servant), 1790: DL, May 29; 1791: DL, May 31; 1795: DL, Jun 5
Scott, Thomas
--Mock Marriage, The, 1695: DL, Sep 0; 1696: DL, Jul 0, NONE, Sep 0
--Unhappy Kindness, The; or, A Fruitless Revenge, 1696: DL, Jul 0
Scott, William (featherman), 1760: CG, Sep 22; 1767: CG, Feb 2
Scotti, Teresa (singer), 1764: KING'S, Nov 24; 1765: KING'S, Jan 26, Mar 2, 21,
    28; 1766: KING'S, Apr 10, 26, May 3
Scottish Dal Karl (dance), 1734: CG, May 17
Scovell (musician), 1760: CG, Sep 22; 1769: CG, May 18
Scovelli, Gaetano (singer), 1782: KING'S, Nov 14; 1783: KING'S, Jan 7, Feb 18,
    Mar 6, Apr 10, 29, May 31
Scowrers, The. See Shadwell, Thomas.
Scrase, Henry (actor), 1750: DL, Sep 22, 25, 28, Oct 15, 30, Nov 13; 1751: DL,
    May 3, Sep 10, 14, 18, 20; 1752: DL, Jan 28, Feb 6, Apr 21, 22, Sep 19, Oct
    13, 16, 20, 23, 25, 26, Dec 7, 8; 1753: DL, Feb 22, May 5, 8, 18, 21, Oct 3,
    16; 1754: DL, Jan 15, 23, Feb 20, Mar 25, May 6, 9, Sep 24, Oct 10, 11, 16,
    Nov 11, Dec 13; 1755: DL, Apr 8, 26, Oct 4, 7, 8, 10, 17, 27, Nov 8, 15;
    1756: DL, Feb 9, May 1, 10, 15, 27, Sep 25, Oct 16, Nov 18; 1757: DL, Jan 27,
    May 9, Sep 29, Oct 4, 25; 1758: DL, May 2, 8, Oct 30, Nov 4, 8, 16, Dec 26;
    1759: DL, Jan 3, Feb 1, May 11, 21, 23, Jul 12, Sep 25, 29, Oct 12, 30, Nov
    3, 5, 17, Dec 1, 20, 31; 1760: DL, Feb 21, Mar 4, Apr 22, 28, May 3, 8, Oct
    3, Nov 27, Dec 17; 1761: DL, Jan 8, Apr 29, May 29, Sep 14, 15, 18, Oct 31,
    Nov 12, 21, 28, Dec 11; 1762: DL, Feb 8, 20, Mar 15, 18, Apr 30, May 13, 17,
    Sep 25; 1763: DL, Jan 17
Scrase, Patty Ann (actor), 1783: CG, Sep 19, Oct 1
Screven, Richard (actor), 1779: HAY, Dec 27; 1780: HAY, Jan 3
Scriver, Master (actor), 1774: CG, Nov 19, Dec 26
Scroop, Lord (rebel), 1746: DL, Aug 4
Scroope, Sir Car (author), 1676: DG, Mar 11; 1678: DL, Feb 0
Scrope (killed), 1675: DG, Aug 28
Scrub, Young (actor), 1711: PU, May 14
Scrub's Trip to the Jubilee (entertainment), 1769: HAY, Sep 19; 1770: HAY, Oct
    15; 1771: HAY, Aug 12, 19; 1772: DL, Apr 27, May 2, 11, HAY, Sep 17; 1773:
    DL, May 24; 1788: HAY, Sep 30
Scudamore (actor), 1746: HAY, Apr 30; 1748: HAY, Apr 30
Scudamore, Barnabas (actor), 1695: LIF, Sep 0; 1696: LIF, Mar 0, Oct 0, Dec 0;
    1697: LIF, Feb 20, Jun 0; 1698: LIF, Jan 0, Jun 0, Nov 0; 1699: LIF, Feb 0,
    Apr 0, May 0; 1700: LIF, Jan 9, Apr 0
Scullough (actor), 1739: BF, Aug 27, SF, Sep 8; 1746: DL, May 16
Scuola de Gelosi, La. See Salieri, Antonio.
Se Amor provaste mei (song), 1757: KING'S, Mar 24
Se constanta per timore (song), 1792: CG, Mar 7
Se Fosse il mio Diletto (song), 1748: KING'S, Apr 5; 1764: KING'S, Mar 29
Se l'arco (music), 1730: GF, May 28, Jun 2, 30; 1735: GF, Oct 10
Se l'arco Strali (song), 1729: LIF, Mar 5; 1733: LIF/CG, Apr 20, CG, May 1;
    1735: GF/HAY, Aug 21
Se mei turbo (song), 1733: DL/HAY, Dec 1; 1734: DL/HAY, Jan 10; 1735: GF, Apr
    22
Se mi Foglie (song), 1732: LIF, Apr 19
Se non avate O Dio! (song), 1789: DL, Mar 6
Se non Timor allata (song), 1751: KING'S, Apr 16
Se perde l'usignolo (song), 1752: KING'S, Mar 24
Se Pieta (song), 1726: DL, Apr 28
Se spoze (song), 1755: KING'S, Mar 17

Se Spuntan Vezzoze (song), 1748: CG, Apr 21
Se ti perdo (song), 1791: CG, Dec 10; 1792: CG, May 22; 1793: KING/HAY, Mar 13
Se torna il gelo usato (song), 1750: KING'S, Apr 10
Se Unsolo (song), 1729: LIF, Mar 5
Se vedi nascere (song), 1751: KING'S, Apr 16
Sea Ballad (song), 1798: CG, Apr 24
Sea Captains, The (play, anon), 1674: DG, Mar 18
Sea Compass (music), 1715: SH, Jun 30
Sea Fight (entertainment), 1780: CII, Feb 29
Sea Nymphs hourly ring his knell (song), 1793: KING/HAY, Feb 15
Sea Song (song), 1782: CG, May 20; 1791: CG, May 28, Jun 1; 1793: CG, Jun 6;
    1795: CG, Jan 14, May 16; 1796: HAY, Sep 1; 1797: HAY, May 10
Sea Song of Ninety-Two (song), 1766: CG, Apr 15; 1767: CG, May 19
Sea storm (cantata), 1779: HAY, Mar 17
Sea Storm (song), 1793: CG, May 3; 1794: CG, May 9; 1796: CG, Apr 12, 20, May
    16, Jun 1; 1797: CG, May 22; see also Storm, The; Cease, rude Boreas
Sea Voyage, The. See Fletcher, John.
Seabrook (actor), 1799: WRSG, May 17
Seabrook, Master (singer), 1798: WRSG, Jun 8
Seacciata del suo nido (song), 1729: DL, Mar 26
Seagoe's Coffee House, 1750: DL, Nov 28; 1752: DL, Nov 15
Seagrove, Mrs (actor), 1695: DL, Oct 0
Seale, Elizabeth (actor), 1718: DL, Jun 11, Aug 1, 15; 1719: DL, Dec 11; 1720:
    DL, May 14, CGR, Jun 22; 1721: DL, May 26; 1722: DL, Apr 17, May 25, Sep 18;
    1723: DL, Jan 7, May 13, Jul 5; 1724: DL, Feb 14, May 8, Nov 19; 1725: DL,
    Jan 5, May 8, Oct 2; 1729: HAY, May 2, GF, Nov 8, 11, 17, 20, 24, Dec 1, 3;
    1730: GF, Jan 5, 13, 22, 26, Feb 9, 10, Mar 12, Apr 6, 7, 15, 28, May 26
Sealy (dancer), 1760: DL, Oct 24
Seaman Who of Wars may Tell (song), 1796: CG, Apr 12, May 28
Seaman's Lamentation for the Loss of the Royal Charlette (entertainment), 1800:
    CG, Apr 29
Search after Scrubs (entertainment), 1767: DL, May 9; 1768: DL, Apr 15
Search round the world (song), 1790: CG, Feb 26, Mar 19; 1792: KING'S, Mar 7
Searle (author), 1744: DL, May 9
Searle's Coffee House, 1752: CG, Dec 12
Second (dancer), 1782: CG, Oct 8, 9; 1783: DL, Oct 4, 9, 18, Nov 8; 1784: DL,
    Apr 12
Second Part of Bartholomew Fair, The (poem), 1686: BF, Aug 0
Second Thought is Best. See Hough, J.
Second Thoughts are Best. See Cowley, Hannah.
Second, Sarah, Mrs John (actor), 1792: CG, Feb 24, Mar 2, 7, 9, 14, 21; 1796:
    CG, Oct 17, Nov 3, 19; 1800: CG, Feb 28, Mar 5, 14, 19, 21
Secret Love. See Dryden, John.
Secret Tribunal, The. See Boaden, James.
Secret, The. See Morris, Edward.
Secrets of Peace, The (song), 1696: LIF, Apr 0
Secrets Worth Knowing. See Morton, Thomas.
Secular Masque, The. See Dryden, John.
Secundus, Scriblerus, 1731: HAY, Mar 24
Secure within her sea-girt Reign (song), 1800: DL, Jun 5
Sedaine, Michel Jean, 1778: CG, Sep 18; 1786: CG, Oct 16, DL, 24; 1787: DL, Nov
    8; 1788: HAY, Aug 18; 1797: DL, Feb 9; 1798: DL, Jan 16
--Comte D'Albert et sa Suite, Le, 1797: DL, Feb 9
--Femmes Vengees, Les, 1778: CG, Sep 18
--Gageure Imprevue, La, 1788: HAY, Aug 18
--Raoul Barbe Bleue, 1798: DL, Jan 16
--Rose et Colas, 1778: CG, Sep 18
Seddon, Mrs. See Siddons, Sarah.
Sedgley, Benoni (taverner), 1754: DL, Apr 4
Sedgwick (beneficiary), 1747: SOU, Oct 22
Sedgwick, Thomas (singer, actor), 1787: DL, Oct 25; 1788: DL, Oct 9, 16, 23,
    25, Nov 17, 18; 1789: DL, Jan 3, Mar 9, Apr 17, May 19, 22, 28, Jun 3, 12,
    Sep 26, Oct 10, 13, 22, 24, 27, 28, Nov 13, 24, Dec 7, 9, 26; 1790: DL, Jan
    20, 22, 23, 25, 26, Apr 16, 23, May 14, 15, 19, 20, 31, CG, Jun 16, DL, Sep
    11, Oct 4, 11, 26, Dec 8; 1791: DL, Jan 18, Feb 10, Apr 28, May 3, 6, 13, 18,
    19, DLKING'S, Sep 22, 24, 27, 29, Oct 15, 29, 31, Nov 2, 5, 8, 9, 12, 25, 30,
    Dec 7, 31; 1792: DLKING'S, Jan 18, Feb 18, KING'S, 24, Mar 23, 28, 30,
    DLKING'S, Apr 10, 19, 21, May 8, 10, 23, Jun 1, DL, Sep 18, 20, 25, 27, Oct
    9, 11, 13, 18, 30, 31, Nov 21, Dec 13, 14, 26; 1793: DL, Jan 2, 23, KING/HAY,
    Feb 15, 20, 27, DL, Mar 7, KING/HAY, 8, 15, DL, May 7, 10, 21, HAY, Aug 6,
    Oct 22, Nov 5, 19, 30, Dec 16; 1794: HAY, Feb 24, Apr 3, DL, 21, 25, 26, 28,
    May 3, 9, 12, 16, 19, 22, 29, Jun 9, 16, Jul 2, 4, HAY, 11, 17, 18, 19, 24,

26, Aug 1, 18, 22, 27, Sep 4, 8, DL, 16, 23, 27, Oct 7, 14, 20, 27, 31, Nov
3, 12, 15, Dec 20; 1795: DL, Jan 26, 28, Feb 7, 17, May 1, 2, 27, 28, 29, Jun
3, Sep 17, 29, Oct 27, 30, Nov 4, 7, 9, 11, 23, Dec 14, 18, 30; 1796: DL, Jan
7, 18, Mar 12, Apr 25, 30, May 25, 27, Jun 3, 7, Oct 1, 10, 11, 22, 24, Nov
5, 10, 26, 28, Dec 5, 26; 1797: DL, Jan 9, 20, Feb 9, 16, 22, Mar 6, May 19,
22, 23, Jun 6, Sep 23, 26, Oct 5, 16, 19, 23, Nov 7, 9, 20, 24, Dec 9; 1798:
DL, Jan 16, Feb 20, May 11, 21, 23, 24, 31, Jun 7, Sep 18, Oct 2, 6, 11, 16,
Nov 26; 1799: DL, Jan 19, Feb 19, Mar 2, 11, Apr 5, 19, 25, May 1, 4, 7, 8,
24, Jun 28, Nov 6, 13, 14, Dec 4, 11; 1800: DL, Jan 1, Feb 12, Mar 11, 24,
Apr 19, 29, May 21, 23, 29, Jun 3, 6, 7, 11
Sedgwicke (merchant), 1739: DL, May 7
Sedley (Sidly), Sir Charles, 1664: BRIDGES, Oct 4; 1668: BRIDGES, Jan 11, LIF,
Feb 6, BRIDGES, May 7, 18; 1669: BRIDGES, Mar 6; 1687: DLORDG, Mar 26; 1692:
ATCOURT, Apr 30; 1693: DL, Mar 0
--Bellamira; or, The Mistress, 1676: NONE, Sep 0; 1687: DLORDG, Mar 26, DL, May
12
--Grumbler, The, 1754: DL, Apr 30, May 2, 7; 1773: CG, May 8
--Mulberry Garden, The, 1668: BRIDGES, Jan 11, May 7, 18, 20, NONE, Jun 29;
1674: NONE, Sep 0
Seduction. See Holcroft, Thomas.
See from the Silent Groves (song), 1726: LIF, Mar 31, May 4; 1730: GF, Apr 16;
1738: DL, May 17, 29; 1739: DL, Mar 27, Apr 28; 1740: DL, Apr 9; 1741: DL,
May 5, Nov 9, 13, Dec 23, 28; 1742: DL, Jan 1, 11, 22, Feb 4, 12, 25, Mar 1,
4, 9
See her awful domes (song), 1789: DL, Mar 20
See Hercules how smiles yon myrtle plain (song), 1752: KING'S, Mar 24
See how fair Corinna lies (song), 1684: DL, Apr 0
See if You Like It; or, 'Tis All a Mistake (play, anon), 1734: CG/LIF, Oct 9,
11, 14, Nov 2
See the conquering hero comes (song), 1776: CHR, Oct 7; 1789: CG, Apr 3; 1790:
DL, Mar 17; 1792: CG, Mar 9; 1793: CG, Mar 6; 1794: DL, Mar 12, CG, 12, DL,
14, Apr 2; 1796: CG, Mar 16; 1797: CG, Mar 31; 1800: CG, Mar 19
See the course throng'd with gazers (song), 1794: CG, May 26; see also High
mettled racer
See the godlike youth advance (song), 1790: DL, Mar 17
See the proud Chief (song), 1794: DL, Apr 4
See Vulcan, Jealousie, Jealousie appears (song), 1696: LIF, Nov 14
See where repenting Celia lyes (song), 1694: DL, Apr 0
Seede, Mrs (beneficiary), 1760: CG, Dec 16
Seedo (composer), 1729: HAY, Apr 12, Jun 11, SF, Sep 8; 1732: DL, May 3, Jun 9,
Oct 17; 1733: DL, May 21; 1734: DL/HAY, Feb 20, Mar 5, 9, HIC, Apr 5, HA, Sep
11, GF, 25, Oct 17; 1735: GF/HAY, May 2
--Venus, Cupid and Hymen (masque), 1733: DL, May 21
Seedo, Maria (dancer, singer), 1727: LIF, Sep 29, Oct 12; 1728: LIF, Mar 27,
Sep 30, Oct 14; 1729: LIF, Feb 6, Mar 12, 19; 1730: LIF, Jan 2, Mar 16, Apr
23, Sep 21, 25, Oct 1, 9, Nov 7, Dec 11, 15, 30; 1731: LIF, May 20, Sep 27,
Oct 4, 15, Nov 6, 13, 18, Dec 1; 1732: LIF, Apr 28, HAY, Nov 16; 1733: DL,
May 21
Seeing is Believing. See Jodrell, Richard Paul.
Segantini, Livia (singer), 1763: KING'S, Feb 19
Segatti, Maria (singer), 1733: LIF, Dec 29; 1734: LIF, Feb 26, May 11, KING'S,
Oct 29; 1735: KING'S, Feb 1, Apr 8, HIC, 11, KING'S, May 3; 1736: HIC, Jan
21, Mar 12, KING'S, Apr 13
Sei si trove in Lacci stretto (song), 1753: KING'S, Apr 30
Seil pianto mio fastante (song), 1741: HIC, Apr 24
Sejanus. See Jonson, Ben; Gentleman, Francis.
Selectation Tavern, 1745: CG, May 8
Selima and Azor. See Collier, Sir George.
Sellano (music), 1730: GF, May 13
Selves (singer), 1759: CG, Feb 2
Selwin (actor), 1734: HAY, Jun 24
Semele. See Handel, George Frederic.
Semini, Mlle (actor), 1784: CG, Jan 29
Semiramide Reconosciuta, La. See Hasse,Johann Adolph; Cocchi, Gioacchino.
Semiramide. See Bianchi Jr, Francesco.
Semiramis (dance), 1784: KING'S, May 20, 29, Jun 5
Semiramis (opera, anon), 1733: KING'S, Oct 30, Nov 3, 6, 10
Semiramis. See Ayscough, George Edward.
Senauki (spectator), 1734: CG/LIF, Sep 23, LIF, Oct 1, DL, 4, GF, 5, HAY, 7,
GF, 11, LIF, 12, DL, 14, GF, 17
Seneca, 1685: NONE, Sep 0
--Troas, 1685: NONE, Sep 0

Senesino, Francisco Bernardi (singer), 1720: KING'S, Nov 19, Dec 28; 1721:
   KING'S, Feb 1, Mar 28, Apr 15, May 20, Jun 14, Jul 5, Dec 9; 1722: KING'S,
   Feb 15, 22, Mar 6, Oct 31, Nov 3; 1723: KING'S, Jan 12, Feb 19, Mar 30, May
   14, Nov 27; 1724: KING'S, Jan 14, Feb 20, Apr 18, May 21, Oct 31, Dec 1;
   1725: KING'S, Jan 2, Feb 13, Apr 10, May 11; 1726: KING'S, Jan 15, May 5, Jun
   11; 1727: KING'S, Jan 7, 31, May 6, Nov 11, CR, 22; 1728: KING'S, Feb 17, Apr
   30; 1729: HIC, Apr 16, HAY, Jun 10; 1730: KING'S, Oct 9, Nov 3; 1731: KING'S,
   Feb 2, Apr 6, Dec 7; 1732: KING'S, Jan 15, Feb 15, Mar 25, May 2, 23, Jun 10,
   Nov 4, CRT, 20; 1733: KING'S, Jan 27, Mar 17, Jun 9, HIC, 15, LIF, Dec 29;
   1734: LIF, Feb 26, May 11, KING'S, Oct 29, PM, Nov 29; 1735: KING'S, Feb 1,
   Apr 8, May 3, Nov 25; 1736: KING'S, Jan 24, Apr 13, CG, Nov 27; 1747: KING'S,
   Nov 12; 1748: KING'S, Mar 8; 1754: KING'S, Mar 12; 1758: KING'S, Nov 11;
   1759: KING'S, Jan 16, Nov 13; see also Bernardi, Francisco
Senocrita. See Perez, Davide.
Sentimental Comedy, A. See Foote, Samuel.
Sentimental Spouter, The; or, Young Actor's Companion, 1774: DL, Apr 4
Sentir si Dire (song), 1734: DL/HAY, Jan 26
Sento ch' in Seno (song), 1782: KING'S, May 23; 1783: KING'S, May 1
Separate Maintenance, The. See Colman the elder, George.
September the Thirteenth proud Bourbon may mourn (song), 1784: CG, Mar 30; see
   also Memorable 13th of September
Sequedilla (dance), 1783: KING'S, Apr 10, 26, May 8; 1786: KING'S, Apr 27, May
   16
Sequel to Auld Robin Gray (song), 1783: HAY, Aug 1
Sequel to the Opera of Flora, The. See Hippisley, John.
Seraglio, The. See Dibdin, Charles.
Serasini (singer), 1754: KING'S, Jan 29, Feb 28
Seratina, Domenica (singer), 1758: MARLY, Jun 8, 10, 27, Jul 29, Aug 21, 22,
   Sep 18; 1759: HAY, Jan 12, MARLY, May 10, Jul 26, Aug 9, DL, Dec 14; 1760:
   MARLY, Jun 3, 18, Jul 2, 24; 1761: HAY, Jun 27, 30, Jul 14, 18, 28, Aug 11,
   13, 22
Serbo in petto (song), 1792: KING'S, Mar 14
Serenade (song), 1717: YB, Jun 14; 1735: GF/HAY, Jan 2; 1790: DL, Jan 15, Jun 3
Serenade (song), 1726: KING'S, Dec 10; 1727: KING'S, Mar 2
Serenade Interrompuee, La (dance), 1778: KING'S, Feb 24, Mar 3, 17, 28, 31, Apr
   11, 30, May 5, 26, 28, Jun 2, 5, 13; 1779: KING'S, May 15, 25, Jun 29; 1780:
   KING'S, Apr 20; see also Serenata Spagnola Interrota, La
Serenade, Grand (song), 1797: CG, May 23
Serenade, La. See Regnard, Jean Francois.
Serenade, The (dance), 1761: CG, Feb 28; 1777: CG, Apr 26, 30, May 3, 12, 15
Serenata (music), 1721: KING'S, Mar 28; 1737: CG, Mar 11; 1740: LIF, Nov 8;
   1701: DT, Feb 19; 1744: LIF, Dec 11; 1751: HAY, Feb 5; 1761: KING'S, Jun 3;
   1762: DL, Mar 17, KING'S, Jun 5; 1765: MARLY, Aug 6; 1773: CG, Mar 20; 1776:
   MARLY, May 27
Serenata Spagnola Interrota, La (dance), 1780: KING'S, May 9, 16; see also
   Serenade Interrompuee, La
Serene (dancer), 1702: DL, Aug 22
Sergeant (householder), 1776: CHR, Sep 23
Seriman, Abate Conte Zaccaria de (librettist), 1777: KING'S, Mar 15
Serious Air (song), 1782: DL, May 10
Serious Ballet (dance), 1734: DL, Nov 20; 1735: DL, Nov 8, CG, Dec 31; 1736:
   CG, Apr 8; 1739: CG, Sep 15; 1740: CG, May 7, Oct 6, DL, Dec 26; 1741: CG,
   Apr 2, DL, 20, 21, 29; 1743: DL, Apr 25, May 9, 12, 14, 20, CG, Oct 3, Dec
   13; 1772: KING'S, Nov 14, Dec 1, 5; 1773: KING'S, Jan 2, 5, 12, 15, Feb 9,
   Mar 16, 23; 1774: KING'S, Jan 29, Feb 22, Mar 12, CG, Apr 15, KING'S, 23, May
   10, 17; 1775: KING'S, Apr 22, 25, May 6, 30; 1776: KING'S, Jan 9, Feb 27, Apr
   25, May 30, Dec 10, 14; 1777: KING'S, Feb 25, Mar 1, 4, 8, 13, 15, Apr 12,
   19, 22, 26, 29, May 6, 8, 15, 20, 24, 27, 31, Jun 3, 7, 10, 17, 21, 24, 28,
   Jul 5, Dec 9, 13, 20, 23; 1778: KING'S, Jan 3, 17, 20, 24, 27, 31, Feb 3, 10,
   Apr 30, May 12, 19; 1780: KING'S, Jan 22, Feb 19, Mar 9, 18, Apr 1, 4, 8, 11,
   22, May 2, 9, 16, 20, 25, 27, Jun 24, Jul 1
Serious Ballet and Chaconne, Grand (dance), 1773: KING'S, Jan 5, Feb 20, 23,
   27, Nov 30, Dec 7
Serious Ballet, Grand (dance), 1735: DL, Oct 28, 29, Nov 3, 4, 15, 19; 1736:
   DL, Feb 21, May 19; 1740: DL, Dec 27; 1741: DL, Jan 1, 6, 24, Feb 3, 19, Mar
   7, Apr 2, May 6; 1742: DL, Oct 5, 8, 13, 15, 19, 20, 23, 28, 29, Nov 2, 4, 5,
   6, 15, 16; 1743: DL, Jan 10, Feb 14, Apr 20, 22; 1772: KING'S, Dec 8; 1773:
   KING'S, Jan 2, 5, 19, Feb 2, 20, 23, 27, Mar 18, Nov 20, 23, 30, Dec 7; 1774:
   KING'S, Feb 5, 12, Mar 8, 12; 1776: KING'S, Apr 18, Nov 2, 9, 12, 16, 30, Dec
   7, 17, 21; 1777: KING'S, Jan 4, 11, 17; 1779: KING'S, Nov 27; 1780: KING'S,
   Feb 8, 15, Mar 9, 18, Apr 13, 18, 25, 27, May 12, Dec 16, 19; 1781: KING'S,
   Jan 16, Mar 15, Apr 5, May 15, Jun 23

Serious Consideration on Plays (pamphlet), 1763: DL, Jan 1
Serious Dance (dance), 1703: YB, Feb 5; 1716: LIF, Oct 18, 23, 30, Nov 1, 24,
    28, 29; 1717: LIF, Jan 11, Feb 1, Dec 2; 1718: LIF, Jan 7, 16, Feb 20, Mar
    18, DL, Apr 22, May 20, 23, Nov 8; 1719: DL, Apr 14; 1720: DL, Oct 17; 1724:
    DL, Dec 21; 1725: LIF, May 5; 1726: HAY, Apr 14, DL, May 18, KING'S, Nov 1;
    1727: KING'S, Mar 23, Apr 8, LIF, 21, DL, May 17; 1729: LIF, Apr 22, May 14,
    DL, Nov 21; 1732: DL, Mar 16, LIF, Apr 13; 1734: DL, Nov 4, 11; 1735: DL, May
    30, Jun 2, 5, LIF, 12; 1736: CG, Jan 7, DL, Feb 11, 14, CG, Mar 20, DL, Apr
    12, CG, May 14, DL, 15, CG, 18, Nov 9, LIF, 16; 1737: CG, Jan 24, DL, Mar 5,
    CG, 19, LIF, 26, DL, Apr 2, CG, 2, DL, 23, CG, May 5, LIF, 10, DL, 11, CG,
    12, LIF, Jun 15, CG, Oct 12, DL, Nov 2, 7; 1738: CG, Apr 25, 28, 29, May 1,
    DL, 2, CG, 3, 5, 6, 8, 11, 12, 16, 18, Oct 20, 23, Nov 8, 13, Dec 5, 6; 1739:
    CG, Jan 8, 15, Feb 9, DL, Mar 6, 8, CG, Apr 24, 25, DL, 26, May 1, CG, 2, 17,
    23, Sep 5, Nov 3, Dec 15; 1740: CG, Apr 18, DL, 24, CG, 29, May 12, 20; 1741:
    CG, Mar 7, DL, Apr 25, May 2; 1742: DL, Mar 22, 23, 27, 30, Apr 19; 1743: DL,
    Mar 10, LIF, 22, CG, Apr 18, DL, May 4, 6; 1744: DL, Jan 19, 28, Apr 4, CG,
    4, 9, 12, 16, 17; 1745: DL, Jan 22, 26, Feb 6, Mar 16, CG, Apr 2, 18; 1753:
    DL, Apr 24; 1754: DL, Apr 26; 1755: CG, Apr 15; 1756: DL, Oct 13; 1759: CG,
    Apr 27; 1761: CG, Apr 22; 1762: CG, Apr 23, DL, 28, CG, 28, May 7; 1763: HAY,
    Jul 27, Aug 1, 3, Sep 7; 1767: CG, Apr 27, May 27, 28, HAY, Jul 8, 15, 22,
    24, 27, Sep 4, 7, 12, CG, 16, 17, 18, HAY, 21, CG, Nov 23; 1770: CG, Apr 20;
    1772: CG, Apr 24
Serious Dance, Grand (dance), 1728: LIF, Apr 30; 1734: DL, Nov 15; 1745: DL,
    Sep 26, 28, Oct 1, Dec 6; 1773: KING'S, Jan 26, Mar 30; 1774: DL, Apr 22
Serious Disuasion from Frequenting the Playhouse, A (pamphlet), 1776: DL, Jan 1
Serious Divertissement (dance), 1776: KING'S, Jan 27
Serious Enquiry into the nature and effects of the Stage (essay), 1765: DL, Jan
    1
Serjeant (actor), 1742: JS, Nov 8
Serjeant (drill master), 1779: DL, Nov 6
Serjeant Jr (musician), 1774: HAY, Mar 25
Serres, Dominique Michael (scene painter), 1773: DL, Nov 8
Serres, Lucretia, Mrs Dominique Michael (actor), 1795: CG, Oct 5, 24, Nov 6,
    Dec 21, 23; 1796: CG, Feb 2, Apr 5, 15, May 3, 16
Serva Amorosa, La. See Goldoni, Carlo.
Serva Padrona, La. See Pergolesi, Giovanbattista; Paisiello, Giovanni.
Servandoni, Jean Nicholas (scene painter), 1747: CG, Apr 4, 20, May 22; 1749:
    CG, Dec 21; 1750: CG, Jan 8, 15, 22, Feb 5, 12, 19, 26, Mar 1, 5, 12, 19, Apr
    2, 7, 16, 23, 30, May 7; 1758: CG, Mar 13; 1769: CG, Nov 4, 6; 1770: CG, Oct
    15; 1774: CG, Jan 3, Sep 23
Servants' Revel (entertainment), 1733: BFAP, Aug 23
Serve Rivali, Le. See Traetta, Tommaso.
Servi (musician), 1756: HAY, Mar 25
Servi (singer), 1770: KING'S, Jun 12
Service (actor), 1791: HAY, Sep 26, Dec 12; 1792: HAY, Oct 22, Dec 26
Servitore di due Padroni, Il. See Goldoni, Carlo.
Sesostri. See Piccini, Niccolo.
Sesostris. See Sturmy, John.
Sespone a perdersi (song), 1757: KING'S, Mar 24
Sestini, Andrew (actor, singer), 1783: HAY, Sep 9; 1784: HAY, Aug 17, 26; 1785:
    HAY, Aug 9; 1787: HAY, May 16; 1788: HAY, Aug 5
Sestini, Giovanna (singer), 1774: KING'S, Dec 13; 1775: KING'S, Mar 7, 30, Apr
    6, May 23, Oct 31, Nov 7, Dec 12; 1776: KING'S, Jan 9, Mar 12, 28, 30, Apr
    23, May 7, 30, Nov 5; 1777: KING'S, Feb 4, Mar 4, Apr 1, 17, 29, May 20;
    1778: KING'S, Nov 24, Dec 22; 1779: KING'S, Apr 29, May 15; 1780: KING'S, May
    25, Nov 25, 28, Dec 19; 1781: KING'S, Feb 22, Apr 5, Jun 5; 1782: KING'S, Jan
    10, Apr 9, May 23, CG, Nov 2, 8; 1783: CG, Jan 23, Feb 14, KING'S, Jun 3,
    HAY, Jul 16, Aug 28, Sep 9, CG, Oct 2, 16, 28; 1784: CG, Mar 13, HAY, Aug 10,
    17; 1785: CG, Mar 12, HAY, Jun 18, 28, 29, Jul 20, Aug 9; 1786: KING'S, Jan
    24, Mar 7, 11, 16, May 20, HAY, Jun 9, 29, Jul 3, 11, Aug 10, 12; 1787:
    KING'S, Jan 9, Feb 17, Apr 24, 26, May 1, HAY, Jun 25, Jul 2, 13, 16, Aug 3,
    KING'S, Dec 8; 1788: KING'S, Feb 5, 21, Mar 4, CG, Apr 25; 1789: KING'S, Mar
    24, May 2, 9, CG, 15, KING'S, 28; 1790: HAY, Jan 7, Feb 2, Mar 25, CG, Apr
    29, HAY, May 27; 1791: KING'S, Apr 16, 26, May 12, 19, 23, 24, Jun 2
Sestini, Vincenzio (tailor), 1775: KING'S, Oct 31, Nov 7; 1776: KING'S, Apr 20;
    1777: KING'S, Apr 17; 1784: KING'S, Dec 18; 1785: KING'S, May 12; 1793:
    KING'S, Feb 26, Apr 23; 1794: KING'S, Apr 26; 1795: KING'S, Mar 26, Jun 20;
    1796: KING'S, Dec 13; 1797: KING'S, Apr 6; 1799: KING'S, Mar 26; 1800:
    KING'S, Apr 15
Sesto Furio (song), 1723: KING'S, Feb 19; 1732: KING'S, Mar 25
Sethona. See Dow, Alexander.
Settle, Elkanah, 1667: BRIDGES, Nov 16; 1669: LIF, Jun 14; 1673: DG, Jul 3,

LIF, Dec 0; <u>1674</u>: DG, Nov 26; <u>1675</u>: DG, Feb 27, May 28; <u>1679</u>: DG, May 0;
<u>1680</u>: DL, Jun 2; <u>1681</u>: NONE, Sep 0; <u>1682</u>: DL, Mar 11; <u>1691</u>: CITY, Oct 29;
<u>1692</u>: CITY, Oct 29; <u>1693</u>: CITY, Oct 30; <u>1694</u>: DL, Mar 21, CITY, Oct 29; <u>1695</u>:
CITY, Oct 29; <u>1698</u>: CITY, Oct 29; <u>1699</u>: DL, Mar 18, CITY, Oct 30; <u>1701</u>: DL,
May 12; <u>1711</u>: DL, Aug 17; <u>1717</u>: LIF, May 3
--Ambitious Slave, The; or, A Generous Revenge, <u>1681</u>: NONE, Sep 0; <u>1694</u>: DL,
Mar 21
--Cambyses, King of Persia, <u>1666</u>: NONE, Sep 0; <u>1671</u>: LIF, Jan 10, OXFORD, Jul
0; <u>1674</u>: NONE, Sep 0; <u>1691</u>: NONE, Sep 0
--City Ramble, The; or, A Playhouse Wedding, <u>1711</u>: DL, Aug 17, 21, 28
--Conquest of China by the Tartars, The, <u>1675</u>: DG, May 28, Jun 22; <u>1697</u>: NONE,
Sep 3, Dec 0
--Distressed Innocence; or, The Princess of Persia, <u>1690</u>: DL, Oct 0
--Empress of Morocco, The, <u>1673</u>: DG, Jul 3, LIF, Dec 0, DG, 6; <u>1674</u>: DG, Nov
26; <u>1682</u>: DG, Jul 8; <u>1686</u>: NONE, Sep 0; <u>1697</u>: NONE, Sep 0; <u>1701</u>: DL, Aug 23;
<u>1704</u>: DL, Aug 2, 9, 15, Oct 5; <u>1708</u>: DL, Jul 10
--Fairy Queen, The, <u>1692</u>: DG, May 2, Jun 13; <u>1693</u>: DG, Feb 16; <u>1703</u>: DL, Feb 1;
<u>1704</u>: DL, Jan 4; <u>1711</u>: SH, Apr 11, May 9, PU, 14
--Fatal Love; or, The Forced Inconstancy, <u>1680</u>: DL, Sep 0
--Female Prelate, The; or, The History of Pope Joan, <u>1679</u>: DG, May 0; <u>1680</u>: DL,
May 31, DG, Jun 0, DL, 1, 2, DG, Nov 1; <u>1688</u>: NONE, Sep 0
--Glory's Resurrection, <u>1698</u>: CITY, Oct 29
--Heir of Morocco, The; With the Death of Gayland, <u>1682</u>: DL, Mar 11; <u>1693</u>:
NONE, Sep 0; <u>1704</u>: DL, Aug 9; <u>1708</u>: DL, Sep 7; <u>1709</u>: DL, Jan 19
--Ibrahim, The Illustrious Bassa, <u>1668</u>: BRIDGES, Jun 20; <u>1669</u>: LIF, Jun 14;
<u>1674</u>: DG, Nov 26; <u>1675</u>: DG, Feb 27; <u>1676</u>: DG, Mar 0; <u>1693</u>: NONE, Sep 0
--Love and Revenge, <u>1674</u>: DG, Nov 9, Dec 9
--New Athenian Comedy, The, <u>1692</u>: NONE, Sep 0
--Pastor Fido; or, The Faithful Shepherd, <u>1668</u>: LIF, Aug 20; <u>1676</u>: DG, Dec 0;
<u>1688</u>: NONE, Sep 0; <u>1693</u>: NONE, Sep 0; <u>1706</u>: DG, Oct 30; <u>1707</u>: DL, Jan 7;
<u>1711</u>: GR, May 21
--Siege of Troy, The (droll), <u>1724</u>: SF, Aug 28, Sep 7; <u>1726</u>: BFS, Aug 24,
BFLHS, 24, SFLH, Sep 8; <u>1734</u>: SFL, Sep 7; <u>1735</u>: SFLP, Sep 4; <u>1747</u>: BFLYW, Aug
22, SF, Sep 9, BHB, 26
--Virgin Prophetess, The; or, The Fate of Troy, <u>1701</u>: DL, May 12, 15, 19, 20;
<u>1703</u>: DL, Dec 27; <u>1704</u>: DL, Feb 7, Jul 26; <u>1705</u>: DL, Nov 12
--World in the Moon, The, <u>1697</u>: DG, Jun 0, LIF, 0, DG, 15, Jul 1; <u>1702</u>: DL, Oct
23; <u>1703</u>: DL, Jun 22
Settre (linen draper), <u>1743</u>: LIF, Mar 14
Settre and Co (mercers), <u>1776</u>: DL, Mar 9
Settree, Joseph (dancer), <u>1751</u>: CG, May 1; <u>1752</u>: CG, Apr 15; <u>1753</u>: CG, May 1;
<u>1754</u>: CG, Apr 27, May 4, HAY/SFB, Sep 26; <u>1755</u>: HAY, Feb 10, Sep 1, 3, 11,
15; <u>1757</u>: CG, May 25, HAY, Jun 17, Jul 5, Aug 31, Oct 3, 17, Nov 7; <u>1758</u>: CG,
Apr 20, DL, Nov 27; <u>1759</u>: DL, May 4, 15, Nov 8, Dec 7; <u>1760</u>: DL, Jun 19, Oct
7; <u>1761</u>: DL, May 5, Sep 17, Oct 23; <u>1762</u>: DL, Apr 21, Oct 5; <u>1763</u>: DL, Jan 3;
<u>1772</u>: CG, May 1; <u>1773</u>: DL, Feb 10, CG, Apr 24, May 26
Settree, Master (dancer), <u>1750</u>: CG, Apr 18; <u>1757</u>: CG, May 25, HAY, Jun 17, Jul
5, Aug 24, 31, Sep 2, 8, 14, 28, Oct 3, 12, 17, 31, Nov 2; <u>1758</u>: HAY, Jan 12,
25, Mar 6, CG, Apr 20, DL, Jun 1, Sep 16; <u>1759</u>: DL, May 9, 15, Jul 12, Dec
12; <u>1761</u>: DL, May 5
Settree's Cap Warehouse, <u>1757</u>: CG, Apr 25
Setwell (actor), <u>1799</u>: CG, Jun 12
Seven Dials, <u>1719</u>: BR, Apr 2
Seven Stars (public house), <u>1742</u>: DL, Apr 21; <u>1743</u>: DL, Apr 14; <u>1746</u>: DL, Mar
22; <u>1751</u>: CG, Nov 19
Seven Stars Coffee House, <u>1700</u>: BF, Aug 0
Seventeen Hundred and Eighty One. See Wilson, Richard.
Several (beneficiary), <u>1766</u>: DL, Feb 20; <u>1768</u>: DL, May 23
Seward (puppeteer), <u>1742</u>: UM, Apr 26
Sewell, George, <u>1718</u>: LIF, Feb 3; <u>1719</u>: LIF, Jan 16, Nov 7, Dec 10; <u>1720</u>: LIF,
Feb 20
--Lottery, The, <u>1720</u>: LIF, Feb 20
--Sir Walter Raleigh (Life and Death of Sir Walter Raleigh), <u>1719</u>: LIF, Jan 16,
17, 19, 21, 23, 24, 26, 28, Feb 2, 6, Mar 10, Apr 1, May 28, Oct 31; <u>1720</u>:
LIF, Jan 9, Feb 6, May 14; <u>1721</u>: LIF, Jan 17; <u>1722</u>: LIF, Apr 21; <u>1729</u>: LIF,
Sep 17, Dec 19; <u>1734</u>: HAY, Aug 21; <u>1739</u>: DL, Sep 24, 25, 26, 27, 28, 29, Oct
1, 2, Nov 27; <u>1789</u>: DL, Dec 14
Sewett, Master (actor), <u>1771</u>: HAY, Jul 24, Sep 18
Sextus Quintilius (entertainment), <u>1733</u>: GF, Nov 28; <u>1734</u>: GF, May 15
Seymour (doorkeeper), <u>1760</u>: CG, Sep 22
Seymour (ticket deliverer), <u>1780</u>: CG, May 24; <u>1781</u>: CG, May 25; <u>1782</u>: CG, May
28; <u>1783</u>: CG, May 31; <u>1784</u>: CG, May 22

Seymour, Edward Hickey (actor), 1787: CG, Oct 1; 1788: DL, Jun 4, Oct 14, 16
Seymour, Mrs (actor), 1677: DG, Sep 0; 1678: DG, Jan 0, Apr 5, Jun 0; 1679: DG, Mar 0, Sep 0
Seymour, Mrs (actor), 1717: DL, Aug 22; 1718: DL, Jun 17, Jul 11, Aug 12, 15, LIF, Oct 11, 16, 18, 31, Nov 24, Dec 6; 1719: LIF, Jan 16, 31, Feb 7; 1720: LIF, Feb 29, Mar 12, 21, Apr 18, 27, May 5, Oct 8, 11, 13, 15, 20, 22, Nov 2, 10, 15, 19, 29, Dec 1, 8, 17, 27, 31; 1721: LIF, Jan 7, 10, 17, 19, Feb 9, 25, Mar 4, 11, 16, 18, 27, Apr 13, 21, 25, 29, May 5, 12, 16, 23, 25, 30, Sep 23, 27, 29, Oct 3, 5, 7, 10, 12, 14, 17, 19, 20, 21, 24, 26, Nov 2, 4, 9, 11, 16, 18, 25, Dec 2, 12, 18; 1722: LIF, Jan 9, 13, 22, Feb 13, Mar 5, 8, 15, Apr 13, May 4, 7, 25, Jun 13, Aug 1, Oct 2, 4, 11, 12, 13, 18, 19, 20, 23, 24, 26, 27, 30, 31, Nov 1, 2, 3, 5, 7, 8, 12, 16, 17, 22, 29, 30, Dec 1, 7, 10, 14, 15, 21, 31; 1723: LIF, Jan 18, Feb 22, Mar 18, 21, Apr 2, 13, Jul 10
Seynor (actor), 1732: HAY, Mar 23
Sfogati o Ciel sereno (song), 1754: KING'S, Feb 28
Sganarell. See Vanbrugh, John, The Cuckold in Conceit.
Sgombra dall' Anima (song), 1729: HIC, Apr 30
Shade (householder), 1795: HAY, Apr 22
Shade, John (boxkeeper), 1781: DL, May 5; 1782: DL, Apr 27; 1783: DL, May 26; 1784: DL, May 27; 1785: DL, May 27; 1786: DL, Jun 2; 1787: DL, Jun 8; 1788: DL, Jun 12; 1789: DL, Jun 12; 1790: DL, Jun 5; 1791: DL, Jun 1; 1792: DLKING'S, Jun 16; 1793: DL, Jun 10; 1795: DL, May 30; 1796: DL, Jun 14
Shade, Thomas (boxkeeper), 1777: DL, Jun 6; 1778: DL, May 25; 1779: DL, Jun 1; 1780: DL, Apr 29, May 25; 1781: DL, May 25; 1782: DL, May 30; 1783: DL, May 29; 1784: DL, May 26; 1785: DL, May 25; 1786: DL, May 31; 1787: DL, Jun 6; 1788: DL, Jun 10; 1789: DL, Jun 6; 1790: DL, Jun 3; 1791: DL, Jun 1; 1792: DLKING'S, Jun 16; 1793: DL, Jun 10; 1795: DL, Jun 6; 1796: DL, Jun 13; 1797: DL, Jun 16; 1798: DL, Jun 14
Shadows of Shakespeare (entertainment), 1787: HAY, Jul 19
Shadwell (ticket deliverer), 1760: CG, Apr 7
Shadwell, Ann Gibbs (actor), 1664: LIF, Sep 10; 1665: LIF, Apr 3; 1668: LIF, Feb 6, May 2; 1670: LIF, Nov 0; 1671: LIF, Mar 6, Jun 0, DG, Nov 0; 1672: DG, Jan 31, Aug 3, Nov 4; 1675: NONE, Sep 0; 1676: DG, May 25, Jun 8, Aug 0; 1678: DG, Jan 0; 1680: DG, Jan 0; 1681: DG, Mar 0; 1690: DG, Jun 0
Shadwell, Charles, 1710: DL, Feb 25; 1713: DL, Jan 29, Jun 9; 1721: LIF, Dec 29
--Fair Quaker of Deal, The; or, The Humours of the Navy, 1710: DL, Feb 25, 27, 28, Mar 2, 4, 6, 13, 18, 25, Apr 1, 11, May 3, Jun 2, GR, Jul 12, 17, 24, DL, Dec 7, 8, 26; 1711: DL, Feb 6, May 31, GR, Jul 26, DL, Oct 16; 1712: DL, Mar 10, May 23, Nov 26; 1713: DL, Feb 24, May 29, Jun 9, Oct 7; 1714: DL, Feb 1, Apr 24; 1715: LIF, Jan 7, 13, Feb 7, May 21, Dec 12; 1717: LIF, May 21, Dec 28, 30; 1718: LIF, Jan 13, DL, 21, LIF, May 29, Oct 3, 21, DL, Dec 15; 1719: LIF, Mar 16, May 26, Nov 5, 12; 1720: LIF, Jan 21, Apr 19, DL, Aug 16, Oct 28, LIF, Nov 18; 1721: LIF, Jan 13, DL, Aug 4, LIF, Nov 13, Dec 5, 29; 1722: LIF, Jun 1, Oct 22; 1723: LIF, Nov 12; 1724: LIF, Jan 7, 28, Jun 2, Oct 30; 1725: LIF, Jan 27, May 14, Nov 12; 1726: LIF, Feb 11; 1730: GF, Mar 30, 31, LIF, May 18, GF, Jun 19, LIF, Oct 12, DL, 20, 30, GF, Nov 10; 1731: GF, Mar 23, May 14, DL, Jun 4, GF, Nov 8; 1732: LIF, Jan 26, GF, Apr 28, LIF/CG, Dec 14; 1737: CG, Nov 9, 10, 11; 1738: CG, Jan 2, Apr 15, May 16, Sep 22, Dec 14; 1739: CG, Jan 12, Feb 15, 20, May 5, Oct 26; 1740: CG, Feb 12, May 26, Oct 20, Nov 12; 1741: CG, Jan 2, Apr 25; 1742: CG, Feb 25, Mar 8, Apr 19, May 21; 1743: CG, May 4, Nov 19; 1746: CG, Jan 7, GF, 13, 14, 24, CG, Feb 4, GF, Mar 18; 1748: CG, Apr 13; 1752: CG, Apr 28, Dec 13, 28; 1755: DL, Oct 7, 9, 11, 15, 20, Nov 8, 26, Dec 10, 22, 27; 1756: DL, Jan 14, Feb 7, 21, Apr 19, Sep 28, Oct 18, Dec 29; 1757: DL, Mar 10, May 13, Dec 27; 1758: DL, Mar 28, May 18; 1759: DL, May 16; 1760: DL, May 16; 1766: CG, Apr 15; 1767: CG, May 19; 1768: CG, Mar 15; 1772: DL, May 12; 1773: DL, Nov 9, 10, 11, 16, 19, 23, 30, Dec 4, 8, 14, 30; 1774: DL, Mar 15, 21, Apr 6, 16, May 2, Sep 29, Oct 31, Nov 9, Dec 27; 1775: DL, Apr 1, 18; 1776: DL, Apr 22, Nov 9; 1777: DL, Apr 30, Jun 4; 1779: CG, Apr 21; 1781: DL, May 10; 1783: DL, May 2, Sep 27; 1785: DL, Jan 6
--Humours of the Army, The; or, The Female Officer, 1713: DL, Jan 29, 31, Feb 2, 3, 4, 5; 1746: DL, Apr 23, 26, 30, Dec 26, 31; 1747: DL, Feb 26
--Irish Hospitality; or, Virtue Rewarded, 1766: DL, Mar 15
--Merry Wives of Broad Street, The, 1713: DL, Jun 9
Shadwell, Thomas, 1668: LIF, Feb 6, BRIDGES, Sep 19; 1669: LIF, Feb 23, 25, Apr 16, Jun 14; 1670: NONE, Sep 0, LIF, Dec 10; 1671: NONE, Oct 26; 1674: DG, Apr 30, Nov 26; 1675: DG, Jun 12, 25; 1676: DG, May 25; 1678: DG, Jan 0; 1682: DG, Mar 0; 1687: DL, May 12; 1688: DL, Apr 0, May 12; 1689: NONE, Sep 0; 1692: NONE, Jan 19, DL, Feb 0, NONE, May 14, Oct 0, DL, Nov 0, COURT, 5; 1702: DL, Jul 11; 1703: LIF, Oct 5, DL, Dec 30; 1704: DL, Jan 5, 10, Feb 1, 17, Mar 2, Jul 1, Aug 16; 1710: DL, Mar 21; 1711: DL, May 22, Aug 7, 10, Oct 12, 22; 1712: DL, May 26, Jul 8; 1713: DL, Jun 12, Dec 16; 1714: DL, Jan 1,

Apr 19, Nov 29; <u>1715</u>: DL, Jul 8, Nov 11; <u>1716</u>: DL, Jun 28, LIF, 29, Dec 22;
<u>1717</u>: LIF, Mar 4, May 18, DL, Aug 22, LIF, Oct 21; <u>1720</u>: DL, Aug 18, Oct 21,
26; <u>1721</u>: DL, Feb 10, May 9, Oct 30; <u>1722</u>: DL, Apr 6, Oct 29; <u>1723</u>: DL, Jan
23, May 24, Nov 8; <u>1724</u>: DL, Jan 6, May 18; <u>1725</u>: DL, Jan 20, Nov 3; <u>1736</u>:
DL, Sep 23, 25, 28, 30, Oct 2, 26, Dec 11, 28; <u>1737</u>: LIF, Jul 26; <u>1744</u>: HAY,
Oct 11; <u>1786</u>: CG, May 13
--Amorous Bigot, The; with the second part of Teague O'Divelly, <u>1690</u>: DL, Mar 0
--Bury Fair, <u>1689</u>: DL, Apr 0; <u>1702</u>: DL, Jul 11; <u>1708</u>: DL, Apr 10, 12, Jun 3,
Dec 31; <u>1716</u>: LIF, Oct 10, 12
--Don John; or, The Libertine Destroyed, <u>1675</u>: DG, Jun 12, 14, 15, 25; <u>1676</u>:
DG, May 25, Oct 5; <u>1682</u>: DG, May 18; <u>1688</u>: NONE, Sep 0; <u>1691</u>: NONE, Sep 0;
<u>1697</u>: DL, Mar 27; <u>1701</u>: DL, Jun 11; <u>1703</u>: DL, Nov 5, Dec 22; <u>1704</u>: LIF, May
1, 9, DL, 27, Sep 22; <u>1705</u>: DL, Feb 5, Dec 31; <u>1706</u>: DG, Nov 23; <u>1707</u>: DL,
Nov 25; <u>1708</u>: DL, Jul 3, Sep 28; <u>1709</u>: DL, Jan 10, Dec 9, 14; <u>1710</u>: GR, Jul
8; <u>1711</u>: SH, May 9, DL, 21, Jun 19, Jul 24, GR, Aug 6, DL, Oct 29, Dec 28;
<u>1712</u>: DL, Mar 11, Aug 19, Oct 29; <u>1713</u>: DL, Jun 3, Oct 9; <u>1714</u>: DL, Jan 27,
Jul 2, Dec 20; <u>1717</u>: DL, May 8, 31; <u>1718</u>: DL, Aug 20; <u>1719</u>: DL, Jun 2; <u>1720</u>:
DL, Jan 22, Feb 29, Apr 18, Jun 7, Aug 2, 20, Oct 19; <u>1721</u>: DL, Feb 13, May
30, Aug 9; <u>1722</u>: DL, Apr 6, Jul 3, Oct 29; <u>1723</u>: DL, Jan 29, Jun 3; <u>1724</u>: DL,
Dec 26; <u>1725</u>: DL, Jan 1, May 17, Oct 29, Dec 27; <u>1726</u>: DL, Jun 3, Oct 29;
<u>1727</u>: DL, Jan 18, Oct 16; <u>1728</u>: DL, Jan 6, Oct 30, Dec 18; <u>1729</u>: DL, Feb 13,
Apr 7; <u>1730</u>: DL, Jan 1, 22, Apr 3, Nov 23; <u>1731</u>: DL, Jun 11, Nov 16; <u>1733</u>:
DL, Jan 1, Feb 2; <u>1734</u>: BFRLCH, Aug 24, Sep 2; <u>1740</u>: DL, Feb 13, 14, 21, Apr
11
--Epsom Wells, <u>1672</u>: ATCOU/DG, Dec 2, DG, 3, 4, ATCOU/DG, 27; <u>1673</u>: DG, Dec 5;
<u>1676</u>: DG, Sep 23; <u>1680</u>: ATCOURT, Feb 20; <u>1682</u>: DG, Jun 17; <u>1686</u>: NONE, Sep 0;
<u>1692</u>: NONE, Sep 0; <u>1697</u>: NONE, Sep 0; <u>1708</u>: DL, Dec 18, 20, 27; <u>1709</u>: DL, Jan
20, Feb 10, Mar 4, Apr 25, Jun 7, QUEEN'S, Oct 17, Nov 25; <u>1710</u>: QUEEN'S, Apr
12, GR, Jul 20, DL, Dec 1; <u>1712</u>: DL, Feb 23, Oct 15; <u>1713</u>: DL, Jun 9, Dec 16;
<u>1715</u>: DL, Apr 2, Dec 9; <u>1724</u>: DL, Mar 24, Apr 6, May 22; <u>1726</u>: LIF, Jul 22,
26
--Humourists, The, <u>1668</u>: LIF, Feb 6; <u>1670</u>: LIF, Dec 10, 12, 13, 14, 15, 16;
<u>1671</u>: LIF, Jan 10, 14; <u>1690</u>: NONE, Sep 0
--Hypocrite, The, <u>1669</u>: LIF, Jun 14
--Lancashire Witches, The, <u>1681</u>: DG, Sep 0; <u>1690</u>: NONE, Sep 0; <u>1694</u>: DLORDG,
Feb 0; <u>1697</u>: DL, May 27; <u>1702</u>: DL, Dec 22; <u>1703</u>: DL, Oct 29, Dec 1; <u>1704</u>: DL,
Jan 6, Feb 11, Apr 18, Aug 10; <u>1705</u>: DL, Oct 29; <u>1707</u>: QUEEN'S, Jul 1, 3, 15,
25, Aug 7, 21, DL/QUEEN, Oct 29, QUEEN'S, Nov 17; <u>1708</u>: DL/QUEEN, Jun 22,
DL,Sep 4; <u>1710</u>: DL, Mar 11, 20, Apr 14; <u>1711</u>: DL, Aug 3, 7, 14, Oct 12; <u>1712</u>:
DL, May 26, Jul 8; <u>1713</u>: DL, Jun 12; <u>1714</u>: DL, Jan 1, Mar 31, Jul 16, Nov 16;
<u>1715</u>: DL, Jul 8, Aug 2, Nov 11; <u>1716</u>: DL, Jun 28, Dec 13; <u>1717</u>: DL, Feb 6,
Apr 24, Jul 4, Oct 29; <u>1718</u>: DL, Jun 13, Nov 7; <u>1720</u>: DL, Jun 8, Jul 14, Aug
18, Oct 25; <u>1721</u>: DL, Jul 25, Aug 18, Oct 30; <u>1722</u>: DL, Jun 26; <u>1723</u>: DL, Jun
4; <u>1724</u>: DL, May 13, Oct 29; <u>1727</u>: DL, Apr 3, Oct 30; <u>1728</u>: DL, Dec 2
--Miser, The, <u>1672</u>: BRIDGES, Jan 0; <u>1704</u>: DL, Jun 5, Aug 16
--Psyche; or, Love's Mistress, <u>1704</u>: DL, Jun 9, 21
--Royal Shepherdess, The, <u>1669</u>: LIF, Feb 23, 25, 26, 27, Mar 1, 2, 3, 4; <u>1690</u>:
NONE, Sep 0
--Scowrers, The, <u>1690</u>: DL, Dec 0; <u>1696</u>: NONE, Sep 0; <u>1717</u>: DL, Aug 22
--Squire of Alsatia, The, <u>1688</u>: DL, Apr 0, May 3, 4, 5, 6, 8, 9, 10, 11, 12,
13, 15, 16, 17, NONE, Sep 0; <u>1689</u>: IT, Nov 1; <u>1691</u>: NONE, Sep 0; <u>1698</u>: NONE,
Sep 0; <u>1703</u>: DL, Dec 29, 30; <u>1704</u>: DL, Jan 3, 5, 10, 17, Feb 1, 9, 17, Mar 2,
27, Apr 19, Jun 5, Jul 1, Sep 13, Nov 14; <u>1705</u>: DL, Jan 3, Apr 16, Oct 25,
Dec 14; <u>1706</u>: DL, Feb 11; <u>1707</u>: DL, Jun 4, Nov 6; <u>1708</u>: DL, Apr 26, Oct 25;
<u>1709</u>: DL, Mar 22; <u>1711</u>: DL, May 22, Nov 23; <u>1712</u>: DL, Oct 20; <u>1713</u>: DL, Nov
16; <u>1714</u>: DL, Apr 19, Nov 29; <u>1715</u>: LIF, Mar 21, 26, May 3, Jun 3, Nov 9, Dec
15; <u>1716</u>: LIF, Mar 17, Jun 1, Dec 22; <u>1717</u>: LIF, Mar 4, 26, May 18, Oct 21;
<u>1718</u>: LIF, Jan 8; <u>1719</u>: LIF, Apr 17, May 11, Nov 24; <u>1720</u>: LIF, Jan 8, Mar
15, May 27, DL, Oct 20, 21, 22, 26, Nov 28; <u>1721</u>: DL, Feb 10, May 9; <u>1722</u>:
LIF, Apr 3, Dec 21; <u>1723</u>: LIF, Jan 16, DL, 23, 24, Feb 12, LIF, May 7, DL,
24, Nov 8, LIF, 25; <u>1724</u>: DL, Jan 6, LIF, Feb 6, DL, May 18, LIF, 27, Oct 27;
<u>1725</u>: DL, Jan 20, Mar 30, LIF, Apr 10, DL, Nov 3, LIF, 29; <u>1726</u>: LIF, Jan 1,
May 6; <u>1727</u>: LIF, Oct 23; <u>1728</u>: LIF, Jan 8; <u>1730</u>: LIF, May 11; <u>1734</u>: CG, Apr
6, 15, 23, May 3; <u>1735</u>: CG/LIF, May 16, Jun 11; <u>1736</u>: RI, Aug 14, DL, Sep 23,
25, 28, 30, Oct 2, 26, Dec 11, 28; <u>1737</u>: DL, Apr 13, May 6, Oct 21; <u>1738</u>: DL,
Mar 13, May 17; <u>1739</u>: CG, May 7, 12, DL, Dec 10, 29; <u>1740</u>: DL, Feb 15, Apr
18, May 22; <u>1744</u>: CG, Feb 28, May 2, Oct 10; <u>1746</u>: CG, Dec 26; <u>1748</u>: DL, Dec
28; <u>1749</u>: DL, Dec 18; <u>1758</u>: DL, May 2; <u>1760</u>: DL, May 5; <u>1763</u>: CG, Nov 18, 21,
24, 28, Dec 1, 13, 20; <u>1764</u>: CG, Mar 3; <u>1765</u>: CG, Jan 8, Dec 12; <u>1766</u>: CG,
Mar 13, Oct 23, Dec 13; <u>1767</u>: CG, Jan 7, Mar 12
--Sullen Lovers, The; or, The Impertinents, <u>1668</u>: LIF, May 2, 4, 5, 6, 8, Jun
24, Aug 29, Dec 29; <u>1669</u>: LIF, Apr 14; <u>1670</u>: DOVER, May 19; <u>1671</u>: LIF, Nov

18; <u>1672</u>: MT, Nov 1; <u>1677</u>: DG, Jul 28; <u>1692</u>: NONE, Sep 0; <u>1703</u>: LIF, Sep 27, Oct 5
--True Widow, A, <u>1678</u>: DG, Mar 21; <u>1688</u>: NONE, Sep 0
--Virtuoso, The, <u>1675</u>: DG, Jun 12; <u>1676</u>: DG, May 25, Jun 2; <u>1690</u>: NONE, Sep 0; <u>1700</u>: LIF, Sep 25; <u>1705</u>: LIF, Mar 31
--Volunteers, The; or, The Stock Jobbers, <u>1692</u>: DL, Nov 0; <u>1711</u>: DL, Jul 27, 31, Aug 10, Oct 22
--Woman Captain, The; or, A Usurer Turned Soldier, <u>1679</u>: DG, Sep 0, Oct 0; <u>1686</u>: NONE, Sep 0; <u>1703</u>: LIF, Oct 25; <u>1704</u>: LIF, Feb 23; <u>1710</u>: DL, Mar 21, 28; <u>1716</u>: LIF, Jun 29, Jul 4, 18, Oct 8; <u>1717</u>: LIF, Jan 14; <u>1737</u>: LIF, Jul 22, 26; <u>1744</u>: HAY, Oct 11
Shadwell, <u>1758</u>: CG, Jul 6
Shadwell's Coffee House, <u>1751</u>: DL, May 14
Shady Blest Retreat (song), <u>1775</u>: CG, May 13
Shaftesbury, Countess of, <u>1749</u>: CG, Feb 10
Shaftesbury, Lord. See Cooper, Anthony Ashley.
Shaftoe (gallery keeper), <u>1721</u>: LIF, Jun 6; <u>1724</u>: LIF, Jun 2; <u>1725</u>: LIF, May 24
Shaftoe, Mary (actor), <u>1729</u>: LIF, Jan 1
Shaftoe, Mrs (beneficiary), <u>1729</u>: LIF, May 20
Shake the dome and pierce the sky (song), <u>1789</u>: DL, Mar 20; <u>1790</u>: DL, Mar 5; <u>1791</u>: DL, Apr 1; <u>1792</u>: KING'S, Mar 14, 23; <u>1793</u>: KING/HAY, Mar 15; <u>1794</u>: DL, Mar 21; <u>1799</u>: CG, Feb 20
Shakespeare Coffee House, <u>1774</u>: CG, Jan 29; <u>1788</u>: HAY, Sep 30
Shakespeare Pageant (entertainment), <u>1769</u>: CG, Oct 7
Shakespeare Society, <u>1755</u>: CG, Feb 19; <u>1756</u>: DL, Jan 28; <u>1757</u>: CG, Jan 13, Dec 23; <u>1759</u>: CG, Mar 7
Shakespeare, Cento in honor of (entertainment), <u>1757</u>: DL, May 6
Shakespeare, Elogium upon (entertainment), <u>1752</u>: DL, Mar 31, Apr 21, 23
Shakespeare, Epitaph to the Memory of (entertainment), <u>1752</u>: DL, Mar 31, Apr 21
Shakespeare, Ode in Honor of (entertainment), <u>1756</u>: DL, Apr 1, 6; <u>1757</u>: DL, Apr 12; <u>1758</u>: DL, Mar 31; <u>1759</u>: DL, Apr 5; <u>1770</u>: HAY, Nov 21; <u>1775</u>: CG, Apr 4; <u>1780</u>: CG, Mar 14; <u>1788</u>: DL, May 1; <u>1791</u>: CG, Apr 30, May 31; <u>1796</u>: CG, May 16, 19; <u>1799</u>: HAY, Jan 24
Shakespeare, William, <u>1661</u>: LIF, Aug 24, NONE, Sep 0; <u>1662</u>: LIF, Feb 15; <u>1663</u>: LIF, Jan 6, Dec 22; <u>1667</u>: LIF, Nov 7; <u>1668</u>: LIF, Aug 20; <u>1672</u>: BRIDGES, Jan 0; <u>1692</u>: DG, May 2; <u>1693</u>: DL, Mar 0; <u>1699</u>: DLLIF, Sep 12, DL, Dec 0; <u>1700</u>: LIF, Jan 9, 28, Feb 0, DLLIF, 0, DL, Apr 29; <u>1701</u>: LIF, Jan 0; <u>1702</u>: LIF, Sep 24, Oct 7; <u>1704</u>: DL, Apr 4, Sep 16, Nov 17; <u>1707</u>: DL, Apr 16; <u>1709</u>: QUEEN'S, Sep 15; <u>1710</u>: GR, Jul 15, QUEEN'S, 26, GR, Sep 7; <u>1711</u>: DL/QUEEN, May 3; <u>1712</u>: DL, Jan 7, 11, Apr 5, 8, 24, 25, May 12, Nov 5, 15, JULIUS, Dec 11; <u>1713</u>: DL, Mar 16, Apr 6, May 4, Sep 22, 26, Oct 17, 27, 31, Dec 8, 19; <u>1714</u>: DL, Jan 14, 19, 23, Mar 20, Jun 18, 25, Oct 7, 9, 21, 30, Dec 4; <u>1715</u>: DL, Jan 15, 22; <u>1716</u>: DL, Jan 7, 18, Oct 2, 13, 20, Nov 19, Dec 1, 26; <u>1717</u>: DL, Jan 14, Feb 1, 21, Mar 4, LIF, Apr 11, DL, 27, May 2, 21, 24, Aug 13, 16, Sep 28, LIF, Oct 5, DL, 5, 8, LIF, 9, DL, 15, 22, LIF, 25, Nov 30, DL, Dec 31; <u>1718</u>: LIF, Jan 3, DL, Feb 22, Apr 17, LIF, 23, DL, May 1, 16, Jun 11, Jul 8, Aug 1, Sep 20, 27, 30, Nov 13, 25, 27, LIF, Dec 13, DL, 20; <u>1719</u>: DL, Jan 10, Apr 6, May 6, 7, Jul 28, Sep 19, Oct 10, 22, LIF, Nov 14, 21, DL, 28, Dec 26; <u>1720</u>: DL, Jan 2, 5, Feb 11, Mar 14, 28, LIF, Apr 9, DL, May 3, 11, Sep 17, 24, SOU, Oct 10, LIF, 22, 24, DL, 24, LIF, 25, 26, 29, DL, Nov 2, LIF, 10, 11, DL, 15, LIF, 17, 24, Dec 3, DL, 6, LIF, 8, 9, 10, 12, 13, DL, 15, LIF, 15, DL, 17, 19, 31; <u>1721</u>: LIF, Jan 2, DL, 12, LIF, 23, DL, 26, LIF, 26, Feb 9, 10, 11, 18, 27, DL, Mar 4, LIF, 9, DL, 11, LIF, 11, 13, 25, 27, Apr 10, DL, May 6, 13, Jun 27, Aug 22, Sep 16, 26, 30, LIF, Oct 7, 10, 17, 21, 31, DL, 31, LIF, Nov 3, 14, 15, DL, 18, LIF, 25, 27, DL, Dec 1, LIF, 7, 9, DL, 9, 16, 19, LIF, 22; <u>1722</u>: LIF, Jan 1, DL, 2, 3, LIF, 4, 10, 19, DL, Feb 1, LIF, Mar 3, 26, Apr 6, 11, May 1, DL, 5, LIF, 9, DL, 10, 14, LIF, 28, DL, Sep 22, 25, LIF, 29, Oct 13, 19, 20, 25, Nov 15, Dec 8, DL, 26, LIF, 29; <u>1723</u>: DL, Jan 1, 7, 9, LIF, 10, 12, 14, 29, Feb 11, Mar 21, DL, Apr 15, LIF, 18, 19, DL, 20, LIF, 27, May 3, 14, 18, 21, 31, DL, Jun 6, Jul 5, RI, Sep 2, DL, 28, LIF, 30, DL, Oct 8, LIF, 10, DL, 19, 22, LIF, 24, DL, 29, LIF, 31, Nov 14, 21, DL, Dec 5, LIF, 31; <u>1724</u>: DL, Jan 7, Feb 8, Apr 8, LIF, 9, 28, DL, May 6, 12, LIF, 13, 20, 29, DL, Sep 12, LIF, 28, DL, Oct 22, 27, 30, LIF, Nov 14, 18, 26, DL, Dec 19, 29; <u>1725</u>: DL, Jan 2, LIF, 19, DL, Feb 18, LIF, Mar 11, DL, 18, Apr 13, 26, LIF, May 10, 25, DL, Sep 4, LIF, 24, DL, Oct 5, LIF, 16, 28, DL, 30, LIF, Dec 2, DL, 8, LIF, 15, 31; <u>1726</u>: LIF, Jan 5, Apr 22, 25, DL, May 5, 7, LIF, 17, Sep 21, 26, DL, Nov 16, LIF, 18; <u>1727</u>: LIF, Jan 4, 10, DL, 24, Feb 21, 25, LIF, Mar 13, Apr 17, DL, May 22, Sep 7, 9, LIF, 18, DL, 30, LIF, Oct 19, DL, 26, 27, 28, 31, Nov 2, 3, 7, 8, 15, LIF, 17, DL, 24, Dec 13, 29; <u>1728</u>: DL, Mar 18, May 1, 8, 14, LIF, 15, DL, 23, LIr, 23, DL, Sep 28, LIF, 30, DL, Oct 18, LIF, Nov 1, 19, 20, Dec 19; <u>1729</u>: LIF, Jan 13, 31, Feb 1, 25, DL, Mar 29, Apr 11, 18, 21, 23, LIF, 26, 28, DL, May 6, 7, 26, 28,

LIF, Sep 12, DL, 20, LIF, 22, DL, 23, 25, LIF, Oct 3, 10, DL, 30, LIF, Nov
13, 17, 22, DL, 27, LIF, 29, DL, Dec 18, LIF, 30, DL, 30; <u>1730</u>: DL, Jan 7,
Feb 12, GF, Apr 24, DL, May 2, LIF, 14, DL, 19, LIF, 28, GF, Jun 3, HAY, 27,
LIF, Sep 21, DL, 29, LIF, Nov 7, 13, DL, 24, 30, Dec 1, GF, 10, LIF, 30;
<u>1731</u>: LIF, Feb 2, GF, 6, LIF, Apr 28, DL, May 4, LIF, 17, DL, 17, 18, 19, Jun
7, RI, Jul 8, DL, Sep 18, LIF, 27, 29, Oct 6, GF, 25, Nov 1, DL, 13, LIF, 13,
DL, 15, LIF, 17, 24, DL, Dec 1, 2, LIF, 31; <u>1732</u>: LIF, Jan 15, GF, 29, Feb 1,
LIF, 8, 12, GF, Mar 4, 30, LIF, May 3, DL, 5, LIF, 8, DL, Aug 4, 17, Sep 28,
GF, Oct 2, 11, DL, 19, LIF/CG, 25, 30, CG, Dec 13, GF, 20, 22, DL, 26; <u>1733</u>:
LIF/CG, Jan 12, DL, 24, CG/LIF, 25, LIF/CG, Apr 21, DL, 30, GF, May 3, DL, 7,
RI, Aug 20, BFCGBH, Sep 4, GF, 25, DL/HAY, Oct 10, 12, GF, 26, DL/HAY, Nov
12, CG, 14, DL, 14, DL/HAY, 17, CG, 19, DL/HAY, 21, 22, DL, 24, DL/HAY, 26,
Dec 8, CG, 20, DL, 27; <u>1734</u>: CG, Jan 7, DL/HAY, 16, 19, HAY, Feb 1, CG, 6,
Mar 19, DL/HAY, Apr 17, 20, May 4, 17, DL, Sep 10, CG/LIF, 18, DL, 24, Oct 4,
CG/LIF, 9, DL, 14, 15, GF, 16, DL, 16, 29, CG/LIF, Nov 2, DL, 8, 9, YB, 19,
DL, Dec 4, 6, 7, 9, 10, 11, 18, 27, 30; <u>1735</u>: DL, Jan 18, CG/LIF, 24, DL, Feb
7, 13, 22, 25, 27, Mar 1, GF, Apr 29, DL, May 5, 8, 13, Sep 1, 6, 11, 18, 27,
Oct 1, YB, 6, DL, 21, 22, 27, Nov 1, 21, 24, 27, Dec 5, 8, 9, CG, 27, DL, 30;
<u>1736</u>: CG, Feb 18, DL, 25, Mar 11, 20, Apr 16, CG, 26, DL, May 10, 13, 19, 20,
21, 29, 31, Sep 4, 9, 21, Oct 5, 7, 9, 19, 28, Nov 9, 18, 19, LIF, 20, DL,
27, Dec 4, 16, 20, 23, 27; <u>1737</u>: DL, Jan 6, 10, 13, 17, 21, 24, Feb 3, 7, 10,
CG, 15, 17, DL, 17, 21, 26, CG, 26, DL, Mar 1, LIF, 1, HAY, 3, DL, 3, HAY, 4,
CG, 5, DL, 7, LIF, 10, DL, 10, 14, LIF, 14, 17, DL, 21, CG, 21, DL, Apr 11,
LIF, 11, DL, 14, 21, 25, LIF, 25, DL, 28, CG, 29, HAY, May 4, CG, 5, LIF, 10,
18, DL, 23, LIF, Sep 7, CG, 16, DL, 22, 24, Oct 6, 20, Nov 1, CG, 2, 3, 7,
DL, 10; <u>1738</u>: CG, Jan 3, DL, 4, 12, 13, CG, 17, DL, 19, 23, 26, 31, CG, Feb
2, 6, 7, DL, 8, CG, 8, 9, 10, 11, 13, DL, 13, CG, 14, 16, 20, 21, 23, 25, DL,
25, CG, 28, Mar 2, 9, 13, DL, 16, CG, 20, Apr 3, 8, 10, DL, 12, CG, 13, 14,
DL, 28, May 1, 3, CG, 4, DL, 6, 11, 22, 23, CG, Jun 27, DL, Sep 7, 14, 16,
21, 26, 30, CG, Oct 6, DL, 13, 20, 23, Nov 13, 17, 20, CG, 29, 30, Dec 2, 4,
5, DL, 12, 14, 19, CG, 21, 22, DL, 22, CG, 29; <u>1739</u>: DL, Jan 1, CG, 11, 20,
DL, 25, 31, Feb 10, CG, 13, 19, DL, Mar 6, CG, 8, 19, DL, 29, CG, Apr 10, DL,
27, May 17, Sep 1, 18, 26, CG, 27, DL, Oct 10, 13, 17, 20, CG, 22, 23, 25,
Nov 17, DL, 19, 26, CG, Dec 6, DL, 11, 17, 20; <u>1740</u>: DL, Jan 2, 14, CG, Mar
11, DL, 20, 29, Apr 7, CG, 21, DL, 23, 30, May 9, 30, Sep 16, CG, 26, DL, Oct
13, 14, 15, CG, 24, Nov 5, Dec 13, DL, 20, 22, 26, 27, 29, 30, 31; <u>1741</u>: DL,
Jan 1, 2, 3, 5, 7, 8, 9, 10, 12, 13, 14, 15, GF, 15, CG, 16, GF, 16, DL, 17,
GF, 17, DL, 19, GF, 19, DL, 20, GF, 21, DL, 21, 22, 23, GF, 23, 24, DL, 26,
GF, 26, CG, 27, DL, 27, 28, 29, Feb 5, 6, CG, 10, DL, 14, 16, 17, 19, 21, 23,
GF, 25, DL, 25, 26, 28, Mar 2, 3, CG, 5, GF, 7, DL, 7, GF, 9, DL, 9, GF, 10,
DL, 10, 12, GF, 14, DL, 14, 16, GF, 17, DL, 19, 21, GF, 21, 30, Apr 3, DL, 7,
CG, 9, DL, 10, 14, 15, 17, 18, 20, 21, 23, 30, May 11, 13, CG, 15, DL, 18,
20, Sep 10, 19, GF, 28, DL, Oct 9, CG, 10, DL, 15, CG, 15, GF, 15, CG, 20,
DL, Nov 2, 11, CG, 11, Dec 9, GF, 9, DL, 21; <u>1742</u>: DL, Jan 22, GF, Apr 19,
CG, May 5, DL, Sep 11, 14, CG, 22, Oct 9, Nov 11, DL, 16, CG, 20, 25; <u>1743</u>:
LIF, Jan 10, DL, 21, LIF, 27, DL, Feb 10, BFFP, Aug 23, CG, Sep 21, DL, Nov
29, Dec 15; <u>1744</u>: DL, Jan 7, CG, 24, DL, Mar 1, 10, CG, Apr 19, 20, DL, May
22, HAY, Aug 28, Sep 11, CG, 26, Oct 20, DL, 30, CG, 31, HAY, Nov 1, CG, Dec
13; <u>1745</u>: CG, Jan 25, GF, Feb 14, CG, 15, DL, 15, 20, GF, Apr 15, CG, 25, Sep
23, 25, 27, Nov 18, GF, Dec 2, 4, DL, 5, GF, 19; <u>1746</u>: DL, Jan 31, CG, Feb 8,
Mar 13, Apr 1, 7, DL, 11, 15, May 9, CG, Jun 20, DL, Aug 4, BF, 23, DL, Sep
23, GF, Oct 29, CG, Dec 19, 29; <u>1747</u>: GF, Jan 2, DL, 15, GF, 16, DL, Mar 16,
GF, Apr 6, DL, Sep 15, Nov 2, Dec 14, 16, 26, 31; <u>1748</u>: DL, Jan 6, Mar 19,
CG, Apr 13, DL, 19, 23, SFP, Sep 7, DL, 17, CG, Oct 14, DL, 28, CG, Nov 11,
DL, 14, 19; <u>1749</u>: BBT, Mar 1, DL, Sep 21, Oct 17, CG, 18; <u>1750</u>: DL, Jan 2, 6,
CG, 16, Mar 27, DL, Sep 21, Oct 1, CG, 8, DL, 9, 11, 15, Nov 13, Dec 17;
<u>1751</u>: HAY, Feb 5, CG, 23, DL, Mar 16, CG, Dec 9; <u>1752</u>: DL, Jan 28, CG, Feb 8,
DL, 8, CG, Mar 4, DL, 31, Apr 21, 23, Oct 16, Nov 18, 27; <u>1753</u>: CG, Apr 12,
DL, May 18, Oct 3, CG, 22, DL, Dec 26; <u>1754</u>: CG, Jan 21, DL, 23, CG, Feb 23,
HAY, Mar 4, DL, 18, CG, 25, DL, Jul 2, HAY, 23, DL, Sep 24, Nov 11, CG, Dec
10; <u>1755</u>: CG, Jan 15, DL, Feb 3, Sep 18, Oct 4, 10, 29, Nov 1; <u>1756</u>: DL, Jan
21, 23, Feb 9, 11, 24, Apr 1, 6, May 4, CG, 17, DL, Sep 30, Oct 9, 16, 28,
Nov 19; <u>1757</u>: CG, Mar 12, DL, Apr 1, Sep 24, Oct 4, 19, 20, Nov 10, 22; <u>1758</u>:
DL, Mar 11, CG, Apr 17, Nov 2, 3; <u>1759</u>: DL, Jan 3, CG, Feb 15, DL, Apr 17,
Oct 12; <u>1760</u>: DL, Dec 23; <u>1761</u>: CG, Mar 30, DL, Nov 28; <u>1762</u>: CG, Mar 22, Apr
24, DL, Oct 16, Dec 21; <u>1763</u>: DL, Feb 1, CG, Mar 17, DL, Nov 22, 23; <u>1764</u>:
CG, Mar 26; <u>1765</u>: CG, Feb 18; <u>1766</u>: DL, Apr 12, CG, May 6; <u>1767</u>: DL, Mar 28,
CG, Apr 24, DL, May 28, Oct 22; <u>1768</u>: DL, Mar 15, CG, Apr 20, 28, Nov 26;
<u>1769</u>: HAY, Sep 11, DL, 19, 30, Oct 14; <u>1770</u>: DL, May 1, 11; <u>1771</u>: CG, Apr 24,
Nov 12; <u>1772</u>: DL, Mar 2, CG, May 4, Nov 6, DL, Dec 18; <u>1773</u>: CG, Oct 23;
<u>1774</u>: DL, Jan 19, Feb 1, HG, Aug 19, CG, Sep 19, Nov 19; <u>1775</u>: CG, Apr 4, DL,
Nov 6, Dec 23, 26, CG, 29; <u>1776</u>: DL, Mar 20; <u>1777</u>: DL, Jan 4, Mar 8, HAY, Jul

18, CG, Sep 29; <u>1778</u>: DL, Apr 27; <u>1779</u>: DL, Apr 19, Nov 20, HAY, Dec 27;
<u>1780</u>: CG, Mar 14, DL, Apr 13, 21, Sep 16, Oct 19, Dec 12; <u>1781</u>: HAY, Aug 7,
DL, Sep 25; <u>1782</u>: DL, Sep 24; <u>1785</u>: DL, Feb 2, KING'S, Mar 17, DL, May 10,
HAY, Jul 26, CG, Nov 8, DL, 18; <u>1786</u>: CG, May 13, DL, Dec 21; <u>1789</u>: DL, Sep
22, Oct 13; <u>1790</u>: CG, Nov 27; <u>1791</u>: CG, Jun 6; <u>1792</u>: DLKING'S, Feb 18, HAY,
Apr 16; <u>1793</u>: CG, Oct 9; <u>1794</u>: CG, Sep 29; <u>1795</u>: CG, Apr 24, HAY, Sep 21, CG,
Oct 19, Dec 22; <u>1796</u>: CG, Mar 14, Apr 2, May 16; <u>1799</u>: HAY, Jun 15; <u>1800</u>: CG,
Apr 15
--All's Well that Ends Well, <u>1669</u>: BRIDGES, Jan 12; <u>1741</u>: GF, Mar 7, 9, 10, 14,
17, 21, 30, Apr 3, Sep 28; <u>1742</u>: DL, Jan 22, 23, 25, 27, Feb 16, 19, 20, 22,
23, 25, 26, 27, Mar 23; <u>1743</u>: LIF, Jan 27, Feb 2, 4; <u>1746</u>: CG, Apr 1, DL, 10;
<u>1750</u>: DL, Dec 17; <u>1756</u>: DL, Feb 24, Mar 2, 8; <u>1757</u>: DL, Nov 22, 30; <u>1758</u>: DL,
Jan 14, May 5; <u>1762</u>: DL, Oct 16, 18, 20, 23, Nov 25, CG, 29, Dec 2, 6; <u>1763</u>:
CG, Jan 4, Feb 5, Mar 5, Apr 29, Oct 7; <u>1764</u>: CG, Mar 15, May 18, Nov 6;
<u>1767</u>: CG, Jan 23; <u>1772</u>: CG, May 8, Dec 3, 8, 31; <u>1774</u>: CG, Sep 19; <u>1785</u>: HAY,
Jul 26, 28; <u>1794</u>: DL, Nov 3, 4, 5, 17, 18, 20, 21, Dec 10, 11, 12
--Antony and Cleopatra, <u>1669</u>: BRIDGES, Jan 12; <u>1677</u>: DG, Feb 12, 13, 14, DL,
Mar 17; <u>1695</u>: NONE, Sep 0; <u>1759</u>: DL, Jan 3, 4, 5, 9, 12, 16, 18, 31, May 18,
22
--As You Like It, <u>1669</u>: BRIDGES, Jan 12; <u>1723</u>: DL, Jan 9; <u>1740</u>: DL, Dec 20, 22,
23, 26, 27, 29, 30, 31; <u>1741</u>: DL, Jan 1, 2, 3, 5, 7, 8, 9, 10, 12, 13, 14,
28, 29, Feb 6, Mar 10, 24, GF, Apr 10, DL, 14, 15, 25, May 11, 20, CG, Oct
15, DL, 15, 16, CG, 16, DL, 17, CG, 17, 19, DL, 19, 28, CG, 28, DL, Nov 10,
28, CG, Dec 3, DL, 21; <u>1742</u>: CG, Jan 8, DL, 16, CG, 22, DL, Feb 1, CG, 13,
DL, Mar 9, 11, Apr 8, JS, 19, CG, 23, DL, May 20, Sep 14, Oct 14, 27, Nov 30,
Dec 21; <u>1743</u>: DL, Jan 6, Apr 19, 21, 22, May 23; <u>1744</u>: CG, Jan 5, 6, 9, 10,
13, 21, KING'S, 31, CG, Feb 11, 25, Mar 27, Apr 20, May 23, Sep 26, Nov 2,
15, Dec 19; <u>1745</u>: CG, Jan 29, Apr 24, Sep 25, DL, Dec 5, 31; <u>1746</u>: CG, Jan
21, DL, Apr 8, CG, Dec 19; <u>1747</u>: CG, Jan 1, Mar 9, Apr 23, DL, Oct 31, Nov 2,
26; <u>1748</u>: DL, Feb 25, Mar 8, May 16, CG, Nov 11; <u>1750</u>: DL, Oct 15, Nov 28,
Dec 6; <u>1751</u>: DL, Jan 3; <u>1752</u>: DL, Apr 21, Nov 25, Dec 14, 26; <u>1753</u>: DL, Jan
17, 31, Mar 13, Apr 23, Sep 13, CG, Oct 22, DL, Nov 20; <u>1754</u>: CG, May 21, Sep
25; <u>1755</u>: DL, Feb 8, 18, Apr 29, May 13, Sep 18, Nov 14; <u>1756</u>: CG, May 17,
Nov 22; <u>1757</u>: CG, May 3, Oct 10, DL, Nov 19; <u>1758</u>: CG, Jan 21, DL, May 12,
Sep 16, CG, Nov 21; <u>1759</u>: DL, Feb 6, CG, Dec 11; <u>1760</u>: DL, May 7, Oct 7;
<u>1761</u>: DL, Apr 16, Sep 28; <u>1762</u>: DL, May 12, CG, Nov 3; <u>1763</u>: DL, Jan 14;
<u>1764</u>: CG, Jan 16; <u>1766</u>: KING'S, Sep 13; <u>1767</u>: DL, Oct 22, 27, Nov 10; <u>1768</u>:
DL, Mar 26, Apr 13, Oct 13; <u>1769</u>: DL, May 6, Oct 12, 13; <u>1770</u>: DL, May 9, Oct
9, Nov 22; <u>1771</u>: DL, Apr 1, CG, 5, DL, May 8, Oct 1, 23, Dec 17; <u>1772</u>: DL,
Apr 9, Jun 5, Nov 17; <u>1773</u>: DL, Apr 19, Nov 2; <u>1774</u>: DL, Mar 17, Oct 1, 13,
19, Dec 13, CG, 20; <u>1775</u>: CG, Jan 24, Feb 1, Mar 28, DL, Apr 18, CG, 29, May
13, DL, 20, Sep 26, Oct 13, 18, 24; <u>1776</u>: CG, Feb 5, Mar 19, DL, Apr 12, CG,
May 7, DL, 10, Oct 9, CG, Nov 12; <u>1777</u>: DL, May 3, Dec 3; <u>1778</u>: CG, Feb 24,
DL, May 14, Sep 26; <u>1779</u>: DL, Jan 11, Jun 1, CG, Sep 24, Dec 17, 22; <u>1780</u>:
DL, Jan 28, Apr 7, May 2, 22, Oct 5, 20; <u>1782</u>: CG, Jan 22, DL, Apr 11, 27,
Jun 1, Sep 28, Oct 17, Nov 5; <u>1783</u>: CG, May 17, HAY, Jul 4, 9, 12, DL, Oct
16; <u>1784</u>: CG, Sep 17, DL, Oct 26; <u>1785</u>: DL, Apr 30, May 7, 14, 18; <u>1786</u>: CG,
Feb 7, DL, 18, Jun 7; <u>1787</u>: DL, Apr 13, May 29, ROY, Jun 20, DL, Nov 6; <u>1788</u>:
DL, Oct 2, 7, Nov 13, Dec 17; <u>1789</u>: CG, Feb 11, DL, 20, Mar 10, Jun 6, 13,
Sep 22, CG, Nov 20, Dec 1; <u>1790</u>: DL, Feb 27, Mar 6, Apr 28, CG, Oct 20, DL,
27, CG, Nov 9, 15, Dec 3; <u>1791</u>: CG, Jan 8, 18, Feb 3, 7, DL, Mar 17, Apr 29,
May 28, CG, Sep 23, DLKING'S, Oct 3, CG, 6, DLKING'S, Nov 15, Dec 13; <u>1792</u>:
DLKING'S, Apr 9, Jun 7, CG, Oct 10; <u>1793</u>: DL, Mar 4, May 3, CG, 30; <u>1794</u>: DL,
Apr 24, 25, Jun 11, 18, 20, Oct 29; <u>1795</u>: DL, Jan 21, Feb 7, Nov 12; <u>1796</u>:
DL, Jan 5, HAY, Aug 30; <u>1797</u>: DL, May 12, Oct 7; <u>1798</u>: DL, Feb 9; <u>1799</u>: DL,
Feb 14, 21, 28, Apr 4, 15, 25, May 17, Oct 1, 15, Nov 21; <u>1800</u>: DL, Feb 24,
Apr 16
--Comedy of Errors, The, <u>1669</u>: BRIDGES, Jan 12; <u>1671</u>: NONE, Sep 0; <u>1741</u>: DL,
Nov 11, 12, 13, 14, Dec 10; <u>1762</u>: CG, Apr 24; <u>1770</u>: CG, Apr 26; <u>1779</u>: CG, Jan
22, 27, Feb 1, 6, 9, 20, Apr 21, May 4, 21, Oct 29, Dec 14; <u>1780</u>: CG, Jan 6,
May 16; <u>1781</u>: CG, Jan 18, Feb 8, Mar 20, May 22; <u>1785</u>: CG, Dec 30; <u>1786</u>: CG,
Jan 12, 25, Feb 24, May 24; <u>1788</u>: CG, Jan 4; <u>1789</u>: CG, Jan 2, Mar 16, 23, May
29; <u>1790</u>: CG, Apr 7, Jun 1, 10; <u>1791</u>: CG, May 31; <u>1792</u>: CG, May 18; <u>1793</u>: CG,
Apr 15, Jun 3, 5, Oct 8, 26; <u>1794</u>: CG, Jan 7, 16, May 17, Nov 19; <u>1795</u>: CG,
Jan 10, Mar 17, Apr 8, Dec 31; <u>1796</u>: CG, Apr 22; <u>1797</u>: CG, Jan 7, Apr 26;
<u>1798</u>: CG, Apr 10, Jun 2
--Coriolanus, <u>1669</u>: BRIDGES, Jan 12; <u>1698</u>: NONE, Sep 0; <u>1718</u>: LIF, Dec 13, 15,
16; <u>1719</u>: NONE, Mar 26; <u>1720</u>: LIF, Nov 24, Dec 26; <u>1721</u>: LIF, Apr 10, Oct 31;
<u>1722</u>: LIF, Jan 1
--Cymbeline; or, The Fatal Wager, <u>1669</u>: BRIDGES, Jan 12; <u>1697</u>: NONE, Sep 0;
<u>1702</u>: LIF, Sep 24, Oct 7; <u>1717</u>: DL, Sep 28, LIF, Oct 5, 9, 12, 25, Nov 30,
Dec 26; <u>1718</u>: LIF, Mar 18, Apr 23, Oct 23, Nov 15; <u>1719</u>: LIF, Feb 23; <u>1720</u>:

LIF, Jan 7, 20, Mar 14, Jun 9, Nov 3; 1737: CG, Feb 15, 17, 21, May 5; 1738:
CG, Mar 20; 1744: HAY, Nov 8, 10; 1746: CG, Apr 7, 10; 1759: CG, Feb 15, 17,
19, 20, 21, 22, Apr 19; 1761: DL, Nov 28, 30, Dec 1, 2, 3, 5, 7, 8, 10, 16,
19; 1762: DL, Jan 6, 12, Feb 8, 25, Mar 25, Apr 28, Oct 29, Nov 8, Dec 8;
1763: DL, Jan 15, Mar 10, Apr 6, 28, Dec 1, 3, 6, 8, 19, 23; 1764: DL, Jan
24, Feb 6, Mar 26, Apr 27, May 11, Oct 9, Nov 14, Dec 14; 1765: DL, Feb 8,
Mar 30, May 3, Nov 20; 1766: DL, Jan 8, Feb 5, Apr 22, May 6, Oct 21, Nov 12,
29, Dec 11; 1767: DL, Jan 24, Apr 6, 27, May 26, Oct 10, 13, 19, Nov 17, CG,
Dec 28, 31; 1768: CG, Jan 8, DL, 18, 29, CG, Mar 19, Apr 9, 18, DL, 26, CG,
May 9, Jun 4, Sep 20, DL, Oct 10, CG, 21, DL, 22, 24, 27, 29, Nov 3, CG, 21;
1769: DL, Jan 23, CG, Mar 7, 9, 11, DL, 27, Apr 7, CG, 25, May 8, DL, 9, CG,
16, DL, Sep 23, Nov 17, Dec 12, 28; 1770: DL, Jan 18, CG, 19, 22, DL, Mar 12,
CG, Apr 18, DL, 30, May 15, CG, 17, DL, Jun 1, Sep 22, CG, Oct 16, Nov 21,
DL, Dec 1, 6, 8; 1771: DL, Jan 5, CG, 23, DL, Mar 4, CG, Apr 16, 26, DL, 27,
Sep 26, Dec 5; 1772: CG, Jan 1, Apr 11, DL, May 7, CG, 9, DL, Sep 19; 1773:
CG, Jan 16, DL, Feb 8, CG, 12, DL, May 31, Sep 21, CG, Nov 12, 15, 17, 25,
Dec 6, 15; 1774: DL, Jan 28, CG, Feb 5, DL, Apr 5, May 23, Sep 27, Oct 18,
Dec 17; 1775: DL, Apr 22, 27, 29, May 2, CG, 20, DL, Nov 1; 1776: DL, Apr 27,
29, Oct 26, Nov 12; 1777: DL, Oct 31; 1778: DL, Feb 19, CG, Oct 24; 1779: CG,
Apr 20, May 5, 21; 1780: DL, Apr 18; 1782: HAY, Aug 9; 1783: DL, Feb 18, 25;
1784: DL, Jan 3, CG, Oct 18, DL, Nov 19; 1785: DL, Nov 21; 1786: CG, Jan 6;
1787: DL, Jan 29, Feb 1, 3, 5, 8, Mar 20, CG, Apr 27, DL, May 24, Nov 5;
1788: DL, Jan 10, Nov 15; 1792: CG, May 19; 1793: CG, Nov 18, 22; 1794: CG,
Oct 7, 10, Nov 10; 1795: CG, Jan 1; 1797: DL, Mar 6; 1800: CG, May 13
--Hamlet, 1660: SALSBURY, Dec 12; 1661: LIF, Aug 24, VERE, Nov 26, 27, LIF, Dec
5; 1663: LIF, Mar 9, May 28; 1668: LIF, Aug 31; 1674: DG, Dec 2; 1675: NONE,
Sep 0; 1682: NONE, Sep 0; 1686: ATCOURT, Apr 30; 1694: NONE, Sep 0; 1695: DL,
May 0, DLANDLIF, 0; 1703: DL, Oct 23, Nov 13; 1704: DL, Feb 8, Apr 6, Oct 7,
Nov 4; 1705: DL, Jan 31, Jul 7, Nov 6, 28; 1706: DL, Apr 25, Jun 18, QUEEN'S,
Oct 19, Dec 10; 1707: QUEEN'S, Jan 11, Apr 28, Jun 18, Nov 22; 1708: DL, Jan
15, DL/QUEEN, May 24, DL, Jun 11, Sep 9; 1709: DL, Jan 22, May 7, Jun 3,
QUEEN'S, Sep 20, Nov 4; 1710: QUEEN'S, Jan 2, DL, Feb 14, 23, QUEEN'S, Apr
27, DL, May 9, GR, Jul 1, QUEEN'S, 26, DL/QUEEN, Nov 11; 1711: DL/QUEEN, Mar
24, May 3, GR, Jul 30, Aug 9, DL, Oct 27; 1712: QUEEN'S, Feb 27, Mar 1, 4, 8,
11, 15, 18, DL, Apr 25, Oct 4, Nov 4, Dec 20; 1713: DL, Oct 17, Dec 19; 1714:
DL, Mar 20, Apr 23, Dec 4; 1715: DL, Jan 22, Feb 1, Mar 26, May 27, LIF, Jun
30, Jul 14, Sep 27, DL, Nov 12, Dec 22; 1716: DL, Mar 12, LIF, Apr 16, DL,
21, Jun 5, LIF, Oct 6, DL, 6, LIF, Nov 10; 1717: DL, Jan 12, LIF, Feb 2, Mar
25, DL, Apr 8, LIF, 25, May 27, DL, Sep 28; 1718: DL, Feb 1, LIF, May 3, DL,
Sep 20, Dec 20; 1719: LIF, Feb 26, Mar 30, Apr 30, DL, Sep 12, LIF, Oct 17,
Nov 16; 1720: DL, Jan 2, LIF, Feb 3, 20, DL, Mar 14, LIF, 22, Apr 2, DL, 30,
LIF, May 30, Oct 1, 27, DL, Nov 10, Dec 31; 1721: LIF, Jan 9, Feb 27, DL, Mar
16, May 12, Sep 30, LIF, Nov 25, DL, Dec 9, LIF, 22; 1722: LIF, Jan 29, DL,
Feb 1, Apr 24, Sep 15, LIF, Oct 13, DL, Dec 15; 1723: LIF, Feb 9, Apr 18, DL,
20, Sep 28, LIF, Nov 14, DT, 26, Dec 6, DL, 21; 1724: LIF, Apr 23, DL, 24,
Sep 12, LIF, Nov 26, DL, Dec 19; 1725: DL, Jan 22, Mar 15, LIF, Apr 28, DL,
Sep 11, LIF, Oct 28; 1726: DL, Jan 1, Mar 10, Apr 18, LIF, 25, May 25, Sep 9,
DL, Nov 12, Dec 22; 1727: LIF, Jan 4, Mar 13, DL, Apr 15, LIF, May 15, DL,
Sep 23, LIF, Oct 21, Dec 8; 1728: DL, Feb 24, LIF, Mar 5, 18, May 15, DL, Sep
21, LIF, Nov 1, Dec 19; 1729: DL, Mar 18, LIF, Apr 23, Sep 22, Nov 17; 1730:
GF, Jan 9, 10, 21, DL, 24, GF, Feb 21, LIF, Apr 15, GF, 20, May 14, Jun 30,
Jul 29, DL, Sep 12, GF, 25, LIF, Nov 13, GF, 18, Dec 18; 1731: LIF, Jan 5,
DL, 16, GF, Feb 19, LIF, Apr 28, Sep 18, LIF, Nov 17; 1732: LIF, Jan 29,
DL, Feb 12, GF, 26, 29, DL, Mar 11, GF, Apr 14, LIF, May 3, CG/LIF, Sep 22,
GF, Oct 24, DL, Nov 11, GF, 20, 21; 1733: DL, Jan 5, 8, CG/LIF, 22, DL, 29,
Feb 13, GF, Mar 8, CG/LIF, Apr 9, GF, 18, DL, 25, May 11, GF, 21, CG, Sep 22,
GF, 28, DL/HAY, Oct 17, CG, Nov 17, DL/HAY, 17, GF, Dec 12; 1734: CG, Jan 3,
Feb 21, GF, Apr 22, CG, May 14, GF, Sep 16, CG/LIF, 18, GF, Oct 17, CG/LIF,
31, Dec 14, GF, 23; 1735: GF, Feb 27, DL, Mar 10, GF, Apr 24, HAY, Jul 10,
CG, Sep 12, GF, 19, Oct 10, DL, Nov 1, Dec 5, GF, 5; 1736: CG, Jan 17, GF,
Feb 9, CG, Mar 13, DL, 20, LIF, Apr 16, DL, May 10, Sep 4, CG, Oct 23, DL,
Nov 9, LIF, Dec 13, DL, 20; 1737: LIF, Jan 6, CG, 13, DL, 27, CG, Apr 25,
LIF, May 2, DL, 23, Sep 17, 24; 1738: CG, Jan 17, DL, 23, CG, Apr 13, DL, May
1, Sep 7, CG, Oct 14, DL, 23, Dec 14; 1739: DL, Jan 25, CG, Feb 13, Apr 10,
DL, May 16, Sep 1, CG, Nov 17, DL, 26; 1740: DL, Jan 23, Apr 26, May 23, Sep
6, CG, Oct 24, DL, Nov 26, GF, Dec 4, 22; 1741: GF, Feb 26, DL, Mar 21, GF,
Apr 24, DL, May 5, Sep 19, GF, Oct 14, CG, 20, DL, Nov 18, GF, Dec 9, DL, 31;
1742: GF, Jan 15, DL, 26, CG, Feb 18, DL, Mar 15, May 3, CG, 20, Nov 11, DL,
16, 18, 20, 23, 25, 29, Dec 2, 4, 7, 10, 30; 1743: DL, Jan 5, 13, 22, Feb 5,
Mar 5, CG, May 9, Sep 21, Nov 5, Dec 14, DL, 15, 23; 1744: DL, Feb 11, Mar 5,
27, CG, 31, Apr 3, DL, May 18, HAY, Jun 12, 29, Jul 3, 6, DL, Oct 22, Nov 9,
GF, 27, 28, DL, Dec 13, GF, 13; 1745: DL, Jan 5, 28, GF, Mar 23, CG, Apr 26,

Sep 23, DL, Oct 12, GF, Nov 27, DL, 29, GF, Dec 28; 1746: GF, Jan 31, DL, May
7, CG, Jun 13, Sep 29, Oct 22, Nov 10, GF, Dec 3, 4; 1747: GF, Jan 29, Mar
12, DL, 24, 26, GF, Apr 7, DL, 11, 29, Sep 22, 24, Oct 23, Nov 24, CG, Dec 9;
1748: DL, Jan 21, CG, Feb 23, DL, Mar 1, 3, CG, 31, Apr 2, DL, 18, CG, 27,
DL, Sep 24, Oct 14, Dec 16, 17; 1749: DL, Jan 5, 26, HAY, 28, BBT, Mar 1, DL,
29, CG, Sep 27, DL, Oct 3, 23, 27, Nov 17, 20, CG, Dec 15; 1750: DL, Jan 2,
3, CG, Feb 15, DL, Mar 15, Apr 19, Sep 25, CG, Oct 25, DL, Nov 29, CG, Dec
11; 1751: CG, Apr 20, DL, 23, May 17, SF, Sep 18, DL, 18, CG, Oct 11, DL, 21;
1752: CG, Jan 4, DL, Apr 7, CG, 10, 20, DL, Oct 21, 23, Nov 17, CG, 28, DL,
Dec 20; 1753: CG, Apr 2, DL, May 1, Oct 16, CG, 30; 1754: DL, Jan 17, CG, Mar
5, Apr 19, DL, Oct 16, CG, 24, Nov 2, DL, 22; 1755: CG, Jan 16, SOU, 20, CG,
Mar 3, DL, 20, CG, Apr 4, 25, DL, Oct 4, CG, Nov 12, DL, Dec 2; 1756: DL, Feb
14, CG, Mar 8, Apr 5, DL, 20, May 20, 27, Sep 30, Nov 3, Dec 13; 1757: CG,
Feb 16, Mar 22, DL, May 3, CG, 4, DL, Sep 24, CG, Oct 8, 29, DL, Nov 29;
1758: CG, Jan 20, Feb 28, DL, Mar 30, Apr 8, CG, 24, May 18, DL, 29, Sep 26,
CG, Oct 30; 1759: CG, Jan 2, Feb 27, DL, Apr 17, CG, 30, DL, May 23, Sep 29,
Nov 27; 1760: CG, Mar 18, Apr 16, DL, 21, May 10, CG, Oct 1, DL, Nov 27, Dec
10, CG, 22; 1761: CG, Feb 7, DL, Mar 9, Apr 9, CG, 24, DL, Jun 3, Sep 15, CG,
Oct 10, DL, 13, Nov 24, CG, Dec 22; 1762: DL, Jan 19, May 4, CG, 7, Sep 27,
DL, Oct 6, Nov 6; 1763: DL, Apr 4, 29, CG, May 18, DL, Sep 20, Oct 26; 1764:
DL, Feb 11, CG, Mar 29, DL, May 16, CG, Sep 19, DL, 27, CG, Nov 13, DL, 22,
Dec 12; 1765: DL, Feb 16, Apr 27, CG, Sep 18, Nov 11; 1766: DL, Jan 13, Apr
28, CG, May 12, DL, Sep 23, CG, Oct 30, DL, Nov 7; 1767: CG, Jan 26, May 11,
DL, 28, Sep 15, Nov 9; 1768: DL, Jan 13, Feb 29, Apr 4, CG, 25, DL, May 31,
Sep 17, Oct 17; 1769: CG, Jan 2, DL, Feb 3, CG, 16, 27, Mar 31, Apr 18, DL,
21, HAY, Aug 7, Sep 1, DL, 19, Oct 28, CG, Nov 27; 1770: CG, Jan 8, Feb 5,
DL, May 2, CG, 22, HAY, 23, DL, Oct 3, CG, Dec 3; 1771: CG, Apr 29, DL, May
30, CG, Sep 25, DL, Nov 9, Dec 23; 1772: DL, Jan 8, Feb 5, CG, Apr 21, Oct
26, DL, Dec 18, 21, 23; 1773: DL, Jan 1, CG, 4, Feb 1, DL, 10, CG, May 19,
Oct 18, Nov 22; 1774: DL, Feb 8, CG, May 3, DL, 6, Oct 4, Dec 2, 12; 1775:
CG, Jan 3, Feb 20, DL, Oct 23, Nov 29, Dec 8, CG, 29; 1776: DL, Apr 27, May
30, Oct 15, CG, 17, DL, 23, Nov 12, 30; 1777: DL, Jan 1, Feb 3, 5, 8, May 5,
HAY, Jun 26, 27, Jul 3, 4, 10, 21, Aug 4, Sep 6, 15, 18, DL, 30, Oct 4, 23,
Nov 3, Dec 6, 29; 1778: DL, Feb 17, 19, Mar 17, Sep 19, CG, Oct 12, DL, 16,
Dec 15; 1779: DL, Jan 11, 12, Feb 6, CG, Apr 26, DL, Sep 18, Oct 30, CG, Nov
22; 1780: DL, Jan 17, Apr 21, CG, 25, HAY, Aug 17, DL, Sep 16, CG, Oct 26;
1781: CG, Jan 1, DL, Mar 1, CG, 19, DL, May 24, Sep 25, Nov 2, CG, Dec 31;
1782: DL, Jan 17, CG, Feb 4, DL, Sep 24, CG, Nov 1, Dec 9, DL, 11; 1783: DL,
Feb 6, Mar 24, CG, Jun 3, HAY, 6, DL, Sep 30, Oct 2, CG, 3, DL, 4, 6, 13, CG,
23, DL, 28, CG, 29, DL, Nov 15, 25, Dec 27; 1784: DL, Jan 6, 19, Mar 8, HAY,
Sep 13, CG, 20, DL, 21, Nov 1; 1785: DL, Jan 11, CG, Feb 15, Apr 22, HAY, Jun
24, Jul 13, CG, Sep 23, DL, Nov 17, Dec 28; 1786: DL, May 15, HAMM, Jun 30,
DL, Sep 19; 1787: DL, Jan 11, HAY, May 18, 21, DL, Sep 18, Oct 29, Dec 3, 31;
1788: DL, Jun 4, Sep 16, 30; 1789: HAY, Jun 1, CG, Nov 16; 1790: DL, Jan 4,
CG, Jun 2, 7, Dec 6, 13; 1791: CG, Oct 17; 1792: CG, Nov 5, Dec 27; 1793: CG,
Oct 9, 16, 21, 30, Nov 4, 15, Dec 16; 1794: CG, Jan 9, 28, Feb 21, May 10,
Sep 29, Oct 13, Dec 29; 1795: CG, Jan 12, HAY, Aug 18, CG, Oct 19, 26, Nov 2;
1796: CG, Mar 28, DL, Apr 29, May 12, 27, Jun 2, HAY, Aug 11, CG, Sep 12, DL,
Oct 24, 31, Nov 7, 21, Dec 5; 1797: DL, May 3, 25, CG, Sep 25, DL, 26, 28,
Oct 5, 9, 16, 23, Nov 13, 27; 1798: DL, Jan 24, Feb 8, 15, Mar 1, 20, Apr 24,
CG, 28, DL, May 14, HAY, Sep 3, CG, 17, 24, DL, Oct 4, 16; 1799: DL, Feb 11,
18, Apr 18, May 7, Sep 19, Oct 10, 28, Nov 4, 11, Dec 3; 1800: DL, Jan 13
--Henry IV, Part I, 1660: REDBULL, Aug 14, VERE, Nov 8, Dec 31; 1661: VERE, Jun
4; 1667: BRIDGES, Nov 2; 1668: BRIDGES, Jan 7, Sep 18; 1669: BRIDGES, Jan 12;
1699: DL, Dec 0; 1700: LIF, Jan 9, 28, DLLIF, Feb 0; 1704: LIF, Nov 6, 9, DL,
25, 28; 1705: DL, Jan 5, Dec 15, 19; 1706: QUEEN'S, Oct 26, Nov 6, Dec 4, 26;
1707: DL/QUEEN, Nov 18, 19; 1708: DL/QUEEN, Jan 24, DL, Oct 28; 1709: DL, Jan
1, Mar 10; 1710: QUEEN'S, May 4, DL/QUEEN, Nov 14, DL, Dec 2; 1711: DL, May
8, Nov 6, DL/QUEEN, 14; 1712: DL, Apr 7; 1713: DL, May 18; 1714: DL, Jun 2;
1715: DL, Feb 12, 14, LIF, Apr 4; 1716: DL, Mar 3, LIF, 15, Apr 17, DL, May
11, Oct 2, LIF, 20, Dec 12; 1717: LIF, May 2, DL, 21, Oct 15; 1718: DL, Jan
2, LIF, 7, DL, May 16, Sep 27, LIF, 30; 1719: DL, Jan 10, LIF, Apr 4, DL, May
7, LIF, Oct 2, DL, 22; 1720: LIF, Feb 9, Apr 29, DL, Sep 17, SOU, Oct 10, DL,
Nov 15; 1721: LIF, Jan 28, DL, Sep 26, LIF, Oct 28, Nov 3, Dec 9; 1722: DL,
Jan 2, LIF, Apr 6, Sep 29; 1723: LIF, Jan 12, Apr 17, DL, May 11, LIF, 21,
DL, Oct 8, LIF, 24, Dec 5; 1724: DL, Feb 7, LIF, Mar 7, May 20, DL, Oct 3,
LIF, Nov 7; 1725: LIF, Jan 19, Mar 18, DL, Apr 1, LIF, 20, DL, Sep 18, LIF,
Oct 16, DL, Dec 14; 1726: LIF, Jan 5, 29, DL, May 7, LIF, 17, Sep 21; 1727:
LIF, Jan 10, Sep 18; 1728: DL, Sep 10, LIF, Nov 19, DL, 28, Dec 30; 1729: DL,
Jan 28, LIF, Mar 22, Oct 10, Nov 29; 1730: LIF, Apr 22, Sep 25, DL, Dec 31;
1731: DL, Mar 8, HAY, May 3, 5, LIF, Sep 29, Oct 29, GF, Nov 1, 2, LIF, Dec
31; 1732: GF, Jan 29, Feb 1, Mar 4, 30, DL, Apr 17, LIF, May 8, GF, Oct 2, 3,

DL, 17, LIF/CG, Nov 25, GF, Dec 20; 1733: DL, Feb 3, LIF/CG, Apr 10, GF, May
3, Sep 25, DL/HAY, Oct 10, Nov 12, 21, CG, 30; 1734: DL/HAY, Jan 16, CG, 21,
Mar 21, DL/HAY, Apr 17, GF, 29, DL/HAY, May 2, 17, HAY, 27, RI, Jun 27, DL,
Sep 21, 24, Oct 4, GF, 16, CG/LIF, Nov 14, DL, Dec 30; 1735: CG/LIF, Jan 20,
Apr 17, GF, 29, DL, Sep 11, Nov 15; 1736: LIF, Apr 14, DL, May 17, Oct 7,
LIF, Nov 20, 22, DL, 27; 1737: DL, Jan 17, CG, Apr 14, DL, 18, Sep 22; 1738:
DL, Jan 12, CG, Feb 13, 16, Apr 5, DL, Sep 14, Nov 17, CG, Dec 2, DL, 19;
1739: DL, Mar 6, CG, May 4, Sep 27, Oct 20, DL, Nov 19; 1740: DL, Apr 25, Oct
13, GF, Nov 28, Dec 18; 1741: DL, Jan 26, CG, 27, DL, Apr 6, GF, 21, DL, Oct
9; 1742: DL, Apr 27, CG, Oct 25, Dec 11; 1743: CG, Jan 21, DL, Feb 10, CG,
Mar 12, LIF, 17, DL, Apr 29, CG, Dec 12; 1744: DL, May 22, CG, Oct 8; 1745:
CG, Jan 12, GF, Mar 26, Apr 17, Dec 2, 3; 1746: CG, Jan 11, DL, May 9, SOU,
Oct 20, GF, 29, 30, Nov 3, 10, CG, Dec 6, 8, 9, 10, 12, 13; 1747: GF, Jan 2,
DL, 15, 16, 17, 19, CG, Mar 28; 1748: CG, Apr 22, 25, Oct 17, Dec 6; 1749:
CG, Jan 10, Feb 27, Apr 13, Oct 26; 1750: CG, Jan 3, Mar 19, Nov 12, 13, 14,
15; 1751: CG, Jan 11, Feb 2, 8, 21, Mar 9, DL, 19; 1752: CG, Mar 16; 1753:
CG, Mar 19; 1754: CG, Jan 21; 1755: CG, Apr 10, 12, May 3, Oct 14, Nov 6, Dec
1; 1756: CG, Jan 5, May 10, Oct 8, Nov 24; 1757: CG, Jan 25, Apr 23, Oct 5,
Nov 17, Dec 15; 1758: CG, Jan 12, Apr 11, DL, 21, CG, May 16, Oct 4, 21, Nov
29; 1759: CG, Jan 5, May 1, Nov 28; 1760: CG, Jan 7, Feb 9, Apr 9, DL, 28,
CG, May 16, Oct 10, Dec 5, 19; 1761: CG, Jan 15, Mar 28, Sep 14; 1762: DL,
Apr 30, CG, May 4, Sep 24, DL, 25, Oct 2; 1763: CG, Sep 26, DL, Nov 9, 16;
1764: CG, Jan 25, Sep 26, DL, Oct 17, Nov 8; 1765: DL, May 21, CG, Nov 27;
1766: DL, Jan 9, Apr 12; 1767: DL, May 8; 1769: DL, Oct 23, CG, Dec 29; 1770:
DL, Jan 9, Feb 24; 1774: DL, Jan 19, CG, Mar 15, Apr 8, 30, May 7; 1775: CG,
May 17; 1776: CG, May 10, HAY, Sep 17; 1777: HAY, Feb 11, Jul 24, 28, 31, Aug
2, 13, 21, Sep 13, DL, Oct 17, 21, HAMM, 28, DL, Nov 5, 10, 20, Dec 10, 30;
1778: DL, Jan 21, Mar 21, Sep 22, Oct 30, Dec 28; 1779: DL, Jan 20, 22, CG,
Apr 24, DL, May 19, HAY, Aug 24, CG, Oct 23, Nov 24, DL, Dec 20, CG, 21;
1780: DL, Jan 14, Feb 12, May 23, CG, Sep 25, DL, Oct 2, CG, 2; 1781: HAY,
Aug 22, CG, Dec 11; 1782: CG, Jan 29, May 1, Nov 30; 1783: CG, Jan 4, May 29,
Oct 17, Nov 17; 1784: CG, Jan 12, May 25, Sep 29, Oct 29; 1785: CG, Sep 26,
Oct 22; 1786: HAY, Jul 21, CG, Nov 22, Dec 18; 1787: CG, Nov 5, Dec 31; 1788:
CG, Oct 8; 1789: CG, Jan 12, Nov 2; 1790: CG, Feb 22, Apr 30; 1791: CG, Jan
3, HAY, Jun 20, 29, DLKING'S, Nov 7, CG, 24, DLKING'S, Dec 5; 1792: HAY, Aug
6, 10, 30, Sep 3, 12; 1795: CG, Dec 9, 14, 16; 1796: CG, Jan 11, 18, Apr 1,
18, May 9, HAY, Aug 18, 30, CG, Oct 20; 1797: CG, Jan 2, Sep 18, Nov 1, DL,
25; 1798: CG, Feb 5; 1799: CG, Dec 30
--Henry IV, Part II, 1669: BRIDGES, Jan 12; 1720: DL, Dec 17, 19, 20, 21, 22,
30; 1722: DL, May 5; 1727: DL, Feb 21, 25, 27, Mar 14, Sep 9; 1728: DL, Oct
18, Dec 3, 30; 1729: DL, Feb 5, May 7, Sep 23, Dec 30; 1730: DL, Feb 12, Sep
29, Dec 4; 1731: DL, Mar 16, May 19, Oct 14, Dec 6; 1732: DL, Jan 15, Apr 18,
Oct 19, Nov 15; 1733: DL, Jan 6, May 7, DL/HAY, Oct 12, Nov 22, Dec 8; 1734:
DL/HAY, Jan 19, Apr 18, May 4; 1735: DL, Apr 11, May 8; 1736: DL, Mar 11, Apr
1, May 20, Oct 9, Dec 4, 17; 1737: DL, Jan 21, Oct 20; 1738: DL, Jan 13, CG,
Feb 16, 20, DL, Sep 16, Oct 13, CG, Dec 4; 1739: DL, Nov 20, CG, Dec 6; 1740:
CG, Feb 6, DL, Oct 14; 1741: DL, Jan 27; 1742: CG, Feb 12, 20, May 7, Oct 26,
Dec 29; 1743: CG, Feb 7; 1744: CG, Jan 11, DL, 27, CG, Mar 1, Apr 27, Nov 9,
Dec 1; 1745: CG, Feb 8, Apr 1; 1746: CG, Jan 13; 1747: GF, Apr 6; 1749: CG,
Mar 2, 11, 16, 18, Apr 8, Nov 8, Dec 9; 1750: CG, Jan 17, Apr 7, Nov 22, 23;
1751: CG, Jan 18, Mar 12; 1754: CG, Jan 21, DL, Jul 2; 1758: DL, Mar 13, Apr
1, 4; 1761: CG, Dec 11, 12, 14, 15, 17, 18, 19, 21, 23, 26, 31; 1762: CG, Jan
4, 9, 18, 21, 26, Feb 10, 27, Mar 11, 18, May 24, Oct 2, 23, DL, Nov 1, 2, 3,
4, 5, 11, 15, Dec 3, CG, 31; 1763: DL, Jan 10, Apr 15; 1764: DL, Jan 18, 21,
Feb 10, May 12, Nov 9, Dec 21; 1766: DL, May 5, CG, Oct 6, 7, 9, 11, 13, Dec
29; 1767: DL, May 8; 1770: DL, Jan 19, 26, Feb 2; 1773: CG, Apr 27, Nov 4;
1777: DL, Nov 24, 27, Dec 15; 1778: DL, Sep 29, Oct 24; 1779: DL, Jun 1;
1784: CG, Oct 30
--Henry V, 1664: LIF, Aug 13, 17, BRIDGES, Sep 14, 28, NONE, Nov 0; 1666:
ATCOURT, Dec 28; 1667: NONE, Feb 13, Aug 10, BRIDGES, Oct 19; 1668: LIF, Jul
6; 1676: NONE, Sep 0; 1723: DL, Dec 5, 6, 7, 9, 10, 26; 1735: GF, Nov 26, 27,
28, 29, Dec 1, 2, 3; 1736: GF, Feb 5, Apr 13, TC, Aug 4; 1738: CG, Feb 23,
25, 27, 28, Mar 6, Apr 3, May 4, Dec 5, 22; 1739: CG, Jan 11, Mar 19, Oct 20;
1740: CG, Mar 11; 1744: CG, Apr 19, 20; 1745: CG, Apr 25, Nov 18, Dec 11;
1746: CG, Jan 1, Mar 6, JS, 12, CG, May 1, DL, Aug 4; 1747: DL, Apr 24, Dec
14, 16, 17, 18, 31; 1748: DL, Oct 13; 1750: CG, Jan 16, Feb 19, 24, Nov 29,
30; 1752: CG, Mar 30; 1754: CG, Apr 17, May 8; 1755: CG, Feb 18, Dec 3; 1756:
CG, May 7; 1757: CG, Nov 5, 24, 28, Dec 28; 1758: CG, Apr 13; 1759: CG, Feb
1, Apr 25, Dec 28; 1760: CG, May 5, Nov 18, Dec 2; 1761: CG, Jan 1, May 1,
22, Nov 13, 14, 16, 17, 18, 19, 20, 21, 23, 24, 25, 26, 27, 28, 30, Dec 1, 2,
3, 4, 5, 7, 8, 9, 29; 1762: CG, Jan 1, Apr 12, Oct 16; 1764: CG, Feb 15;
1766: CG, Sep 22, 24, 29, Oct 1, 3, 17, Nov 17, Dec 27; 1767: CG, Apr 23, Sep

22, 24; 1768: CG, Nov 4, 22; 1769: CG, Sep 22; 1770: CG, May 16, Oct 25, Nov 26, Dec 28; 1771: CG, Apr 11; 1773: CG, Jan 6; 1778: CG, May 11, 18, Sep 21; 1779: CG, Jan 1, Sep 20; 1782: CG, May 20; 1789: DL, Oct 1, 5, 12, 19, 26, Nov 2, 9, 16, 23, Dec 7, 28; 1790: DL, May 11, Oct 7; 1791: DLKING'S, Oct 17, 31, Nov 28; 1792: DL, Sep 25, Oct 29; 1793: HAY, Sep 24; 1794: DL, Sep 20, 23, Oct 6; 1798: CG, Feb 14
--Henry VI, Part I, 1668: LIF, Aug 20; 1681: DG, Apr 0; 1738: CG, Mar 13
--Henry VI, Part II, 1668: LIF, Aug 20
--Henry VI, Part III, 1668: LIF, Aug 20
--Henry VIII (with John Fletcher), 1660: SALSBURY, Dec 12; 1663: LIF, Dec 10, 22, 23, 26, 28, 29, 30, 31; 1664: ATCOURT, Jan 0, LIF, 1, BRIDGES, 27, LIF, Feb 8; 1668: LIF, Dec 30; 1672: DG, Sep 3; 1675: DG, Nov 0; 1700: DLLIF, Feb 0, LIF, Nov 23, 25; 1705: QUEEN'S, May 3; 1707: QUEEN'S, Feb 15, 27; 1708: DL, Mar 11; 1709: DL, Jan 26; 1716: DL, Nov 19, 20, 21, 23, 24, Dec 8, 26; 1717: DL, Feb 21, Mar 4, May 24, Oct 5, Dec 2; 1718: DL, Apr 17, Sep 30, HC, Oct 1; 1719: DL, Apr 6, 20, Nov 28; 1720: DL, Mar 28, May 11; 1721: DL, Jan 12, May 13, Oct 31, Dec 19; 1722: DL, May 22, Sep 25; 1723: DL, Jan 1, May 28, Oct 22; 1724: DL, Jan 1, Apr 8, Oct 22, Dec 29; 1725: DL, Apr 13, LIF, Oct 30, Nov 1, Dec 14; 1726: LIF, Apr 22, Oct 31; 1727: LIF, Feb 2, DL, Oct 26, 27, 28, 30, 31, Nov 2, 3, 7, 8, 10, 11, 13, 15, 16, 17, 22, 24, Dec 13; 1728: DL, May 14, Sep 28, Oct 29, Dec 11; 1729: DL, Feb 20, Apr 11, 18, Sep 25, Dec 18; 1730: DL, May 19, Sep 22, Nov 27; 1731: DL, Feb 1, May 4, 18, Nov 13, 29; 1732: DL, Jan 4, Apr 11, Nov 13, Dec 13; 1733: DL, Feb 5, Mar 26, May 28, Nov 14, 15, 19, 24, Dec 27; 1734: DL/HAY, Apr 20, DL, Oct 14, 15, 29, Dec 27; 1735: DL, Feb 7, Oct 27, Dec 30; 1736: DL, May 5, 13, 31, Oct 19, Dec 30; 1737: DL, Feb 26; 1738: DL, May 6, 22, Nov 20, Dec 22; 1739: DL, Feb 10, Apr 27, May 17, Oct 20, Dec 20; 1740: DL, Jan 2, Apr 30, May 30, Nov 10; 1741: DL, Apr 18, 21; 1742: DL, Apr 24, SF, Sep 16; 1743: DL, Apr 5; 1744: CG, Jan 24, 25, 26, 27, Feb 4, Apr 12, May 10, Oct 20, Dec 29; 1745: CG, Mar 5, Apr 16, May 4, DL, Nov 22, GF, Dec 19, DL, 26; 1746: DL, Jan 1, CG, Dec 29; 1747: CG, Mar 3, May 14; 1749: CG, May 4, 5; 1751: CG, Apr 16; 1752: DL, Apr 10, 24, 29, Sep 26, Oct 9, 24, Dec 2; 1753: DL, Feb 5, 28, CG, Apr 12, DL, May 2, Oct 6, 11, Nov 9, Dec 17; 1754: DL, Apr 15, May 9, Oct 10, Nov 1; 1755: DL, Mar 31, Apr 19, May 19, Dec 18, 26; 1756: DL, Jan 6, May 4, 11, Sep 25, Nov 9; 1757: DL, Feb 17, May 10, Sep 27, Nov 28, Dec 16; 1758: DL, Apr 28, May 9, Sep 21, Nov 9; 1759: DL, May 18, 22, Oct 22; 1760: DL, Apr 8, May 26; 1761: DL, May 1, 23, 26, Jun 4, Sep 28, 30, Oct 2, 3, 5, 6, 8, 9, 10, 23, Nov 2; 1772: CG, Nov 6, 7, 9, 11, 13, 16, 18, 20, Dec 21; 1773: CG, Jan 1, 18, 29, Feb 10, 15, 27, Mar 23, May 21, Sep 22, Oct 8, Nov 9, Dec 22; 1774: CG, Feb 14, Mar 21, Apr 25, 26, May 6, Oct 15, Nov 14, Dec 29; 1775: CG, Nov 9; 1776: CHR, Sep 25, CG, Nov 25; 1777: HAY, Aug 29, Sep 4, 5; 1778: HAY, Jun 19, 25, Jul 2, 8, Aug 14, 25, CG, Oct 16; 1779: HAY, Aug 24; 1780: CG, Oct 30; 1781: CG, Apr 16; 1782: CG, May 13, Dec 30; 1783: CG, Jan 6, May 26, Nov 10; 1784: CG, Jan 5; 1785: CG, Apr 8; 1787: CG, Mar 26, May 14, Nov 19; 1788: DL, Nov 25, 29, Dec 2, 6, 13, 20, 27; 1789: DL, Jan 3, 10, 20, 24, Feb 3, Apr 29; 1792: DLKING'S, Mar 26, Apr 17; 1793: DL, Mar 9, May 14, CG, 24; 1794: DL, Apr 29, May 1, 14, Oct 16, 18, Dec 9; 1795: DL, Nov 6; 1796: DL, Jan 1, 15, HAY, Aug 30; 1799: CG, May 15
--Julius Caesar, 1669: BRIDGES, Jan 12; 1672: BRIDGES, Jan 0; 1676: DL, Dec 4; 1683: NONE, Sep 0; 1687: ATCOURT, Apr 18; 1690: NONE, Sep 0; 1694: NONE, Sep 0; 1695: DL, May 0; 1704: LIF, Feb 14; 1706: QUEEN'S, Mar 14; 1707: QUEEN'S, Jan 14, 15, Apr 1; 1709: DL, Dec 22; 1710: DL, Apr 22, GR, Sep 7; 1712: SPS, Feb 12, DL, Apr 5, 8, 24, Nov 15, DL, Dec 11; 1713: DL, Jan 20, Mar 16, Apr 6, May 4, Sep 26, Oct 27; 1714: DL, Jan 23, Apr 12, Oct 9; 1715: DL, Jan 24, May 13, Nov 24; 1716: DL, Mar 22, May 24, Oct 20, LIF, 27, Nov 8; 1717: LIF, Jan 3, Apr 4, DL, 27, LIF, May 3, Nov 7, DL, 16; 1718: LIF, Mar 1, 17, Nov 1, DL, 13, LIF, 25; 1719: DL, Jan 28, Apr 24, LIF, 25, Nov 19; 1720: LIF, Apr 9, Nov 1; 1721: DL, Jan 26, Mar 4, Apr 26, LIF, May 25, DL, Oct 3; 1722: DL, Jan 16, LIF, Oct 18, DL, 19; 1723: LIF, Jan 10, DL, Feb 13, May 9, LIF, 14, DL, Sep 24, LIF, Oct 31, Dec 31; 1724: DL, Jan 11, KING'S, Feb 20, 22, 25, 29, Mar 3, 7, 10, 14, 21, 24, YB, 27, KING'S, 28, Apr 7, 11, HAY, May 8, DL, Sep 19; 1725: DL, Jan 2, KING'S, 2, 5, 9, 12, 16, 19, 23, 26, Feb 2, 6, 9, LIF, Mar 11, DL, Apr 3, LIF, May 22, DL, Jun 18, Sep 30, LIF, Dec 15; 1726: DL, Jan 26, Apr 16, 28, LIF, Nov 11; 1727: DL, Apr 5, May 31, Oct 3; 1728: DL, Jan 4, HAY, Feb 16, LIF, Nov 20; 1729: LIF, Nov 13; 1730: KING'S, Jan 17, 24, 27, 31, Feb 3, 7, 14, 17, 21, Mar 21, 31; 1732: KING'S, Feb 1, 5, 8, 12, GF, Dec 1, 2, 4, 5, 6, 7, 9, 11, 12, 13, 14, 26; 1733: GF, Jan 3, 22, Apr 6, May 15, Sep 10, Oct 10; 1734: GF, Jan 21, Feb 14, Apr 1, Sep 20, DL, Nov 8, 9, 11, 12, 13, Dec 4; 1735: DL, Jan 18, GF, Mar 13, DL, Sep 1, Oct 1, CG, Nov 22, DL, Dec 9; 1736: DL, Apr 16, May 19, CHE, 24, 26, 28, DL, 29, Sep 21, Oct 28; 1737: DL, Jan 24, Feb 17, Apr 28; 1738: DL, Jan 19, Feb 8, Apr 28, Sep 21, Nov 29, Dec 12; 1739: DL, Mar 29, Oct 10, Dec 11; 1740: DL, Jan 17, Mar

13, HIC, 31, DL, Oct 4, Dec 19; 1741: DL, Feb 24, Apr 3, Nov 16, Dec 17;
1742: CG, Nov 20, Dec 20; 1743: CG, Jan 22, Feb 15, Dec 8; 1744: CG, Jan 3,
19, Apr 18, Oct 31, Nov 10; 1745: CG, Feb 2; 1747: DL, Mar 28, Apr 2, CG, 20,
DL, 30; 1748: CG, Nov 24, 25, Dec 8; 1749: CG, Oct 19, Nov 28; 1750: CG, Jan
12, Nov 24, 26, 27, Dec 27; 1751: CG, Feb 19, Mar 7, May 1; 1753: CG, May 7,
14; 1754: CG, Mar 9, 12, 16; 1755: CG, Jan 28; 1758: CG, Apr 14; 1766: CG,
Jan 31, Feb 3, 7, 24; 1767: CG, Apr 25; 1769: HAY, Sep 11; 1773: CG, May 4,
15; 1780: DL, Jan 24, 25, Feb 2, 15, 19, Mar 11, Apr 27; 1789: DL, Mar 20
--King John, 1669: BRIDGES, Jan 12; 1736: NONE, Sep 7; 1737: DL, Feb 11, CG,
26, Mar 1, 3, HAY, 4, CG, 5, 8, 22, 29, Apr 16, Sep 16; 1738: CG, Feb 2, Mar
2, Apr 8, Nov 29; 1739: CG, Mar 8, Oct 20, 22; 1741: CG, Apr 9; 1745: DL, Feb
15, 20, 21, 22, 23, 25, 26, 28, Mar 2; 1747: DL, Mar 16; 1749: BFC, Aug 23,
24, 25, 26, 28; 1751: CG, Feb 23, 25, 26, 28, Mar 2, 4, Apr 25; 1754: DL, Jan
23, 24, 26, 28, 31, Feb 2, 6, 8, Mar 16; 1758: CG, Apr 17; 1760: CG, Dec 9,
10, 17, DL, 17, 20, CG, 23, DL, 23; 1761: CG, Jan 3, DL, Apr 2, CG, Dec 30;
1762: CG, Jan 2, 6, 20, 27, Feb 13; 1764: CG, Dec 21; 1765: DL, Apr 25; 1766:
DL, Mar 20, Apr 11, CG, May 6, Oct 31, Nov 3, 5; 1767: DL, Feb 7, 20, CG, May
28, Sep 23, Dec 22; 1769: CG, May 3; 1770: HAY, Aug 3, 13, 30; 1774: DL, Feb
2, 4, 9, 11; 1775: CG, Dec 1, 15; 1777: DL, Nov 29, Dec 2; 1778: DL, Jan 1;
1783: CG, Mar 29, DL, Dec 10, 13, 16; 1784: CG, Jan 16; 1785: DL, Feb 2, Nov
22; 1792: DLKING'S, Mar 1; 1793: DL, Feb 12; 1795: DL, Mar 12, 14, Dec 18
--King Lear, 1660: SALSBURY, Dec 12; 1664: LIF, Jan 0; 1675: DG, Jun 29; 1681:
DG, Mar 0; 1687: ATCOURT, May 9; 1688: ATCOURT, Feb 20, NONE, Sep 0; 1699:
DL, Feb 3; 1702: DL, Oct 30; 1703: DL, Oct 9, 27, Dec 21; 1704: DL, Nov 15;
1705: DL, Jul 13; 1706: QUEEN'S, Apr 30, LIF/QUEN, Aug 13, QUEEN'S, Oct 30;
1708: DL, Jan 1, Oct 21; 1709: DL, Apr 27; 1710: QUEEN'S, Feb 4, DL, Nov 30;
1711: DL, Apr 28, GR, Sep 6, DL, Nov 10; 1712: DL, Feb 26, Oct 23; 1713: DL,
Jan 8, May 11, Nov 21; 1714: DL, Apr 26, Dec 9, 18; 1715: DL, Jan 4, Nov 29;
1716: DL, Jun 1; 1717: DL, Jan 5, Nov 14; 1718: DL, Mar 1, Sep 25, Nov 20;
1719: DL, Nov 19; 1720: DL, Jan 9, Apr 7, Oct 1, LIF, 15, Nov 5, DL, 24, LIF,
Dec 31; 1721: LIF, Jan 24, DL, Feb 21, LIF, Mar 16, Apr 12, May 15, Sep 23,
DL, Oct 7, LIF, Nov 30, DL, Dec 30; 1722: LIF, Jan 16, DL, Apr 26, LIF, Jun
2, DL, Sep 29, LIF, Nov 3, Dec 20, 29; 1723: DL, May 14, LIF, 27, DL, Oct
5, LIF, Nov 30; 1724: DL, Jan 4, LIF, Mar 28, DL, Apr 27, LIF, May 15, DL,
Sep 24, LIF, Oct 31; 1725: DL, Jan 5, LIF, Apr 23, May 25, Sep 24, DL, Dec
22; 1726: LIF, Feb 16, Mar 26, May 13, Sep 21, 23, Nov 18, DL, Dec 20; 1727:
LIF, Apr 3, Jun 1, Sep 11, DL, 16, LIF, Oct 19, Dec 30; 1728: LIF, Sep 16;
1729: DL, Jan 11, Jul 11, LIF, Sep 12, Dec 30; 1730: GF, Apr 1, May 26, LIF,
28, GF, Jun 18, Jul 7, LIF, Sep 16, GF, Oct 9, DL, Nov 28, GF, Dec 8; 1731:
LIF, Jan 28, Mar 13, DL, Jun 15, LIF, Oct 6; 1732: LIF, Feb 8, LIF/CG, Oct
27, CG, Dec 13; 1733: GF, Mar 17, LIF/CG, Apr 21, GF, 23, DL, 30, GF, Nov 10,
CG, 14; 1734: CG, Jan 14, GF, May 10, Nov 29; 1735: GF, Feb 15, CG/LIF, Apr
10, May 7, Jun 6, DL, Sep 27, Nov 24, CG, Dec 20; 1736: CG, Jan 8, Feb 24,
Nov 8; 1737: DL, Jan 10, CG, Feb 7, Sep 28; 1738: CG, Oct 21; 1739: CG, Mar
3, DL, 8; 1741: CG, Jan 7, 20; 1742: GF, Mar 11, 13, 18, 20, 27, 30, Apr 8,
10, May 1, 12, 19, DL, 28, Oct 26, Nov 9, 24, Dec 13, CG, 15, 16; 1743: LIF,
Jan 10, 14, DL, 15, CG, 17, LIF, 24, 26, DL, Feb 1, CG, 8, DL, Mar 12, CG,
Apr 25, 28, DL, Oct 25, Dec 13, CG, 27, DL, 31; 1744: DL, Feb 14, Mar 8, Apr
20, May 24, Oct 24, Dec 8, CG, 13; 1745: DL, Jan 23, Mar 14, GF, May 2, 9;
1746: CG, Jun 11, Oct 27, Dec 4; 1747: GF, Mar 2, DL, Oct 20, 30, Nov 14, Dec
23; 1748: DL, Feb 29, Mar 1, Apr 22, 23, May 2, 3, CG, Oct 3, 4, DL, 8, SOU,
24, DL, 26, Dec 31; 1749: DL, May 10, Oct 13, Nov 8; 1750: DL, Jan 25, Nov 1;
1751: DL, Nov 2, 4; 1752: DL, Jan 17, Mar 3, Apr 6, CG, Oct 16, 17, DL, Nov
3, 20; 1753: DL, Apr 12, CG, May 14, DL, 22, 23, Nov 15, 22; 1754: DL, Feb
18; 1755: DL, Mar 4, 11, May 23, CG, Nov 17, DL, Dec 4, 9; 1756: DL, Feb 12,
CG, 26, 28, Mar 1, 2, 6, 9, 13, DL, May 19, CG, Oct 15, DL, 28, 30; 1757: CG,
Mar 1, 21, DL, Apr 1, Nov 10, 12, 17, CG, Dec 1, DL, 5, CG, 5; 1758: CG, Jan
10, Feb 11, 18, Mar 16, Apr 7, DL, Oct 25; 1759: DL, Nov 10, 15, 28; 1760:
DL, Jan 5; 1761: DL, May 28, Dec 23; 1762: DL, Apr 17, Nov 19, Dec 31; 1763:
DL, May 5, 6, 12; 1764: CG, May 7, 23, Oct 29, Nov 27, Dec 3, 31; 1765: DL,
Jan 2, 5, CG, 7, DL, 9, 12, Feb 1, CG, Mar 19, DL, 25, Apr 17, CG, May 2, DL,
23, CG, Sep 23, DL, Oct 22, Nov 23, CG, Dec 19; 1766: DL, Jan 11, CG, Mar 4,
DL, Apr 5, CG, 23, DL, 29, KING'S, Aug 25, 29, DL, Oct 29, CG, Nov 19, 24;
1767: CG, Jan 19, Mar 9, DL, Apr 23, CG, May 13, DL, 20, HAY, Jul 15, DL, Oct
21, 24, CG, Nov 26; 1768: CG, Feb 20, Mar 7, DL, Apr 8, CG, 20, 21, 28, Nov
17, Dec 20; 1769: CG, Jan 11, 21, Apr 12, May 1, DL, Sep 21, Oct 7; 1770: DL,
Jan 11, 15, Feb 21, Mar 8, 13, HAY, Jun 18, Sep 11, CG, Oct 29, DL, 31; 1771:
CG, Jan 14, Apr 26, DL, Nov 23, CG, Dec 30; 1772: CG, May 21; 1773: CG, Jan
25, DL, Feb 2, 6, CG, 15, DL, 17, 19, CG, May 8, DL, 26; 1774: DL, Mar 12,
23, Apr 25, May 17, CG, Nov 24, 26; 1776: CG, Feb 22, 27, Mar 23, DL, May 13,
21, Jun 8; 1777: CG, Oct 6, 13, Nov 4, 10, Dec 29; 1778: CG, Feb 2, 5, DL,
Apr 30, CHR, Jul 30, HAY, Sep 17, CG, 28, Oct 19, Nov 9; 1779: DL, Mar 22,

Apr 14, May 4, CG, Nov 19; <u>1780</u>: CG, Jan 3, Feb 21, Dec 27; <u>1781</u>: CG, Jan 22,
Mar 26, Oct 31, Nov 2, 12, 14; <u>1783</u>: CG, Jan 1, Feb 24, Oct 20; <u>1784</u>: CG, Jan
5, Mar 30; <u>1786</u>: CG, Mar 6, HAMM, Jul 28; <u>1788</u>: DL, Jan 21, 24, 29, Mar 1, 8,
May 15; <u>1789</u>: CG, Nov 23; <u>1790</u>: CG, Jan 4, 11, 18, Feb 1, 15, Apr 19, Jun 8,
Oct 11, Nov 22; <u>1791</u>: CG, Jan 10, Oct 17, Nov 4; <u>1792</u>: DLKING'S, Feb 27, Mar
6; <u>1793</u>: DL, Feb 16; <u>1794</u>: CG, Jan 6, 20, 31, Apr 21, May 12, DL, Dec 5, 8,
9, 13; <u>1795</u>: CG, Jan 19, Feb 17, Sep 28, DL, Nov 20; <u>1796</u>: CG, Apr 25, Oct
10; <u>1797</u>: CG, Nov 20; <u>1799</u>: CG, Oct 29
--Love's Labour Lost, <u>1669</u>: BRIDGES, Jan 12
--Macbeth, <u>1660</u>: SALSBURY, Dec 12; <u>1664</u>: NONE, Nov 0, LIF, 5; <u>1666</u>: ATCOURT,
Dec 17, LIF, 28; <u>1667</u>: LIF, Jan 7, Apr 19, Oct 16, Nov 6; <u>1668</u>: LIF, Aug 12,
Dec 21; <u>1669</u>: LIF, Jan 15; <u>1670</u>: LIF, Nov 5; <u>1673</u>: DG, Feb 18, LIF, Apr 0,
DG, Aug 20, LIF, Dec 0; <u>1675</u>: DG, Aug 28; <u>1676</u>: DG, Oct 2, 18; <u>1680</u>: DL, Jun
2, DG, 2; <u>1682</u>: DG, Feb 16; <u>1686</u>: DLORDG, Feb 8, NONE, Sep 0; <u>1694</u>: NONE, Sep
0; <u>1696</u>: NONE, Sep 0; <u>1702</u>: DL, Nov 21; <u>1703</u>: DL, Jun 17, Nov 27; <u>1704</u>: DL,
Jan 1, 25, Feb 29, Apr 25, Jun 27, Dec 2, 29; <u>1705</u>: DL, Apr 17, Nov 13, Dec
29; <u>1706</u>: DL, Feb 5; <u>1707</u>: DL, Jan 23, 31, Apr 16, Nov 28, DL/QUEEN, Dec 27,
29; <u>1708</u>: QUEEN'S, Jan 10, DL/QUEEN, Apr 24, DL, Sep 14, Oct 16; <u>1709</u>: DL,
Jan 6, May 20, QUEEN'S, Nov 28, 30, Dec 17, 27; <u>1710</u>: QUEEN'S, Mar 20, Apr
24, GR, Jul 15, DL/QUEEN, Nov 18; <u>1711</u>: DL/QUEEN, Jan 13, Apr 5, DL, Oct 20,
Dec 22; <u>1712</u>: DL, Mar 6, Jun 5, Oct 25, Nov 22; <u>1713</u>: DL, Jan 24, Jun 5, Sep
22, Dec 8; <u>1714</u>: DL, Jan 19, Jun 18, Oct 21; <u>1715</u>: LIF, Mar 3, 8, 17, 28, Oct
18, 29, Dec 17; <u>1716</u>: DL, Jan 10, LIF, Apr 13, May 24, DL, Oct 13, LIF, 30;
<u>1717</u>: LIF, Jan 1, DL, 14, Feb 1, LIF, Mar 28, DL, May 9, LIF, 13, DL, Oct 8,
Dec 31; <u>1718</u>: LIF, Jan 3, Mar 3, DL, May 1, LIF, Nov 13, DL, 27, LIF, Dec 29;
<u>1719</u>: DL, Jan 13, LIF, Feb 16, DL, Apr 4, LIF, May 12, DL, 15, Sep 19, LIF,
Oct 13, Dec 18, DL, 26; <u>1720</u>: LIF, Feb 15, Mar 17, Apr 18, DL, May 3, Nov 2,
LIF, 19, DL, Dec 29; <u>1721</u>: LIF, Feb 1, DL, Sep 16, LIF, Oct 26, DL, Dec 16;
<u>1722</u>: DL, May 10, LIF, Oct 20, Dec 11, DL, 26; <u>1723</u>: LIF, Jan 29, DL, Apr 15,
LIF, May 18, DL, 27, LIF, Sep 30, DL, Oct 29, Dec 28; <u>1724</u>: DL, May 6, LIF,
13, Sep 28, DL, Oct 27; <u>1725</u>: DL, Feb 18, LIF, Mar 20, DL, Apr 26, LIF, Oct
1, DL, 5, LIF, Dec 2, 31; <u>1726</u>: LIF, Apr 12, DL, May 5, LIF, Sep 26, DL, Nov
16, Dec 28; <u>1727</u>: LIF, Apr 3, DL, 4, Sep 28, 30, LIF, Nov 17; <u>1728</u>: DL, May
8, LIF, Sep 30, Dec 3, DL, 6; <u>1729</u>: LIF, Jan 31, Feb 25, Apr 28, DL, May 6,
LIF, Oct 3, DL, 28, LIF, Nov 20; <u>1730</u>: LIF, Jan 1, DL, May 2, LIF, 14, Sep
21, DL, Nov 24, LIF, Dec 30; <u>1731</u>: DL, Apr 6, May 17, GF, 20, LIF, Sep 27,
DL, Dec 1, LIF, 29; <u>1732</u>: LIF, Feb 3, DL, May 5, LIF, 12, DL, Sep 28, LIF/CG,
Oct 30; <u>1733</u>: DL, Jan 15, CG/LIF, 25, GF, Feb 19, Apr 9, LIF/CG, May 3, GF,
22, CG, Oct 11, Nov 12; <u>1734</u>: CG, Jan 1, GF, 31, Feb 1, 4, CG, 13, Mar 19,
May 24, GF, Nov 7, 8, Dec 9; <u>1735</u>: GF, Apr 23, DL, Oct 21, 22, CG, Nov 15,
DL, 27, CG, Dec 27; <u>1736</u>: CG, Jan 21, Feb 18, Apr 26, DL, Sep 9, CG, Oct 20,
DL, Nov 18, Dec 23; <u>1737</u>: CG, Feb 1, DL, 7, CG, Mar 21, DL, May 19, CG, Oct
4; <u>1738</u>: CG, Jan 3, DL, 31, CG, Apr 14, Oct 6, DL, 20, CG, Dec 29; <u>1739</u>: DL,
Jan 1, CG, 20, Jun 5, DL, Sep 18, CG, Oct 25, DL, Dec 17; <u>1740</u>: CG, Jan 1,
DL, Mar 29, CG, Apr 21, May 10, DL, 13, CG, Sep 26, Nov 5, DL, 27, Dec 3, GF,
10, 27; <u>1741</u>: CG, Mar 5, DL, 30, Oct 8, Nov 30; <u>1742</u>: DL, Apr 19, CG, May 5,
Oct 9, 30; <u>1743</u>: CG, Jan 1, Feb 3, Mar 1, Apr 7, Dec 3, 29; <u>1744</u>: DL, Jan 7,
9, 10, 11, 14, 16, 18, 20, 21, 25, 26, 31, CG, Feb 9, DL, Mar 3, CG, Apr 13,
DL, 14, CG, May 1, Oct 1, 12, DL, 30, Nov 19, CG, 19, DL, Dec 10; <u>1745</u>: DL,
Jan 25, GF, Mar 9, 16, CG, Nov 15, Dec 21; <u>1746</u>: CG, Jan 14, 22, Jun 27, DL,
Oct 31, Nov 7, 8, 10, 11, 24, Dec 27; <u>1747</u>: GF, Jan 5, 6, 8, 14, 28, DL, Feb
5, Mar 14, GF, 16, DL, May 1; <u>1748</u>: DL, Mar 19, Apr 2, 27, May 13, Oct 28,
Dec 19; <u>1749</u>: DL, Jan 16, Mar 6, Apr 7, May 16, CG, Oct 12, DL, 17, Nov 13,
18, CG, Dec 14, DL, 30; <u>1750</u>: DL, Jan 29, CG, Mar 13, Apr 16, DL, 23, CG, Nov
8, DL, 13, 14, 16; <u>1751</u>: CG, Jan 15; <u>1752</u>: DL, Jan 28, 29, Feb 8, CG, 8, Mar
17, DL, 30, CG, Apr 20, DL, Oct 16, CG, 30, DL, 30, Nov 18, Dec 4; <u>1753</u>: DL,
May 7, Oct 3, Nov 13; <u>1754</u>: DL, Jan 14, May 6, Sep 24, Nov 2, CG, 16; <u>1755</u>:
DL, Mar 6, CG, Apr 4, DL, May 1, CG, 5, DL, Oct 10, CG, Nov 17, Dec 8, 26;
<u>1756</u>: CG, Apr 8, Oct 6, DL, 16, CG, Nov 10, Dec 28; <u>1757</u>: DL, Feb 24, CG, Mar
26, DL, Apr 16, Oct 4, CG, Dec 10, DL, 17; <u>1758</u>: CG, Mar 7, May 1, DL, 3, Oct
30; <u>1759</u>: DL, Mar 12, CG, May 14, DL, Oct 12; <u>1760</u>: CG, Apr 17; <u>1761</u>: CG, Apr
2, DL, 29, CG, May 25, DL, Oct 31, Nov 12; <u>1762</u>: DL, Jan 9, CG, Mar 25, DL,
Apr 15, 29, CG, May 11, DL, 15; <u>1763</u>: DL, Jan 17, Mar 17, Apr 13, May 2, 20,
Nov 29; <u>1764</u>: DL, Feb 28, May 11, CG, 21, DL, Nov 27; <u>1765</u>: DL, Feb 26, Apr
22, CG, May 11, Oct 14, DL, 28, Dec 20; <u>1766</u>: DL, Apr 2, CG, May 15; <u>1767</u>:
DL, Mar 21, May 13; <u>1768</u>: DL, Jan 14, CG, 20, 27, DL, Feb 4, 8, CG, 16, Apr
5, DL, 25, Sep 22, CG, Oct 17, Nov 10, Dec 23; <u>1769</u>: DL, Jan 24, CG, Mar 6,
Apr 3, 24, May 23, Dec 19; <u>1770</u>: CG, Jan 3, DL, 4, CG, 11, Feb 7, 14, Apr 23,
Oct 8, DL, Nov 14, CG, Dec 14; <u>1771</u>: CG, Apr 15, May 9, 20; <u>1772</u>: CG, Jan 27,
Mar 2, Apr 6, DL, 25, CG, 28, Jun 1, DL, 9; <u>1773</u>: CG, Mar 22, Apr 20, May 10,
DL, 10, CG, Oct 22, 23, 30, Nov 6, 13; <u>1774</u>: DL, Mar 9, CG, Apr 13, 26, 29;
<u>1775</u>: DL, Mar 23, CG, Oct 19, DL, Dec 4, 5, 7; <u>1776</u>: DL, Jan 1, 19, May 24,

Nov 25, CG, Dec 2, DL, 26, 30; 1777: DL, Apr 22; 1778: DL, Jan 5, 12, CG, 19,
DL, Mar 31, Apr 30, CG, May 6, HAY, Sep 7, 9, DL, 24, Nov 26, Dec 29; 1779:
DL, Apr 7, CG, Oct 18, 25, 30, Nov 29, Dec 28; 1780: CG, Apr 17, 24, DL, 26,
CG, 27, DL, May 3, CG, Oct 23, Nov 20, DL, Dec 6, 26; 1781: CG, Jan 15, Mar
5, May 9, DL, Nov 5, CG, Dec 17; 1782: CG, Jan 14, DL, Feb 5, CG, Mar 21, DL,
May 15, CG, 20, 27, Nov 18, Dec 23; 1783: CG, Oct 6, Nov 17, Dec 18; 1784:
CG, Feb 9, Oct 4, Nov 12, 15, 22, Dec 30; 1785: DL, Feb 2, 4, 7, 12, 15, 19,
22, 26, Mar 5, 15, KING'S, 17, DL, 31, Apr 19, CG, May 3, DL, 10, Oct 1, 29,
Nov 19; 1786: CG, Jan 18, DL, Mar 2, 16, 18, Apr 22, CG, May 29, DL, Oct 9,
Dec 2; 1787: DL, Apr 19, Jun 2, CG, Oct 1, DL, Nov 3, CG, 16; 1788: DL, Mar
10, May 29, Oct 16, 21, Nov 22, Dec 23; 1789: DL, Jan 31, Mar 30, Apr 28, CG,
Oct 12, 19; 1790: CG, Feb 8, May 3, Oct 6, Nov 26; 1791: CG, Jan 17, Oct 10;
1792: CG, Jan 6, 23, DLKING'S, Feb 18, Mar 20, CG, Oct 22, 29, Nov 9, DL, Dec
26; 1793: DL, Apr 16, May 8, CG, Sep 30, Oct 28, Dec 9, 27; 1794: CG, Feb 3,
DL, Apr 21, 22, 23, 24, 28, 30, May 2, 5, 7, 12, 19, 26, Jun 2, CG, Sep 22,
DL, Oct 6, 7, CG, Nov 4, 6, DL, 11, Dec 6; 1795: CG, Mar 9, DL, Apr 7, 25,
CG, May 18, Jun 10, Sep 14, DL, 29, Nov 9, CG, 30, DL, Dec 23; 1796: DL, Apr
11, CG, Sep 26, DL, Oct 10, CG, Nov 14, DL, Dec 13, 28; 1797: DL, Feb 20, Mar
14, Nov 7, Dec 11; 1798: DL, Mar 6, Jun 4, Sep 18, CG, Dec 15; 1799: DL, Apr
2, CG, May 14, Sep 30, Oct 28; 1800: CG, Apr 15
--Measure for Measure, 1660: SALSBURY, Dec 12; 1662: LIF, Feb 15; 1700: LIF,
Feb 0; 1706: QUEEN'S, Apr 26; 1720: LIF, Dec 8, 9, 10, 12, 13; 1721: LIF, Jan
2, 23, Mar 25, Oct 10, Nov 27, Dec 14; 1722: LIF, Nov 2; 1723: LIF, Jan 14,
Apr 19; 1724: LIF, Jan 4, 16, Feb 13, Apr 9, May 29, Nov 14; 1725: LIF, Feb
11; 1726: LIF, Jan 19, Mar 7; 1727: LIF, Jan 14, Mar 20, May 25; 1729: LIF,
Jan 13, Feb 1, Apr 26, Nov 22; 1730: LIF, Jan 17, Nov 7; 1731: LIF, Feb 2,
May 17, Nov 13; 1732: LIF, Jan 15, LIF/CG, Oct 25; 1733: LIF/CG, Jan 12, CG,
Nov 19; 1734: CG, Feb 6; 1737: DL, Mar 10, Apr 21, Nov 1; 1738: DL, Jan 26,
Apr 12; 1742: CG, Nov 25, 26, Dec 4; 1743: CG, Jan 4, Feb 1, 21, Mar 8, Apr
11; 1744: CG, Jan 14, 23, Apr 4, Nov 1; 1745: CG, Apr 6; 1746: DL, Apr 11,
CG, Dec 17; 1748: CG, Nov 26, 30, Dec 31; 1749: DL, Jan 9, CG, Mar 31, Oct
25; 1750: CG, Jan 15, Dec 4; 1755: DL, Feb 15, 20, 22, 27, Apr 9; 1756: DL,
Nov 19, Dec 30; 1757: DL, Jan 10, 19, Mar 1, May 20, Sep 22, Oct 31; 1758:
DL, Apr 29, Oct 10, 17, Dec 1; 1759: DL, Jan 29; 1770: CG, Feb 12, 15, 22,
May 12; 1771: CG, Jan 12, 18, 21, Feb 2, May 13, Oct 9, 23; 1772: CG, Feb 19;
1775: DL, Mar 18, Apr 20, Nov 18; 1776: DL, Jan 10, May 14, Oct 19; 1777: CG,
Jan 8, DL, Nov 13; 1778: DL, Oct 20; 1779: DL, Nov 16; 1780: DL, Jan 6, CG,
Oct 11; 1781: CG, Jan 17; 1782: CG, Jan 5, Feb 7, Dec 12; 1783: DL, Nov 3, 5,
7, 11; 1784: DL, Feb 4; 1785: DL, Oct 22, Nov 2; 1794: DL, Dec 1, 3, 27, 29,
30, 31; 1795: DL, Jan 6, 13, 27, Feb 26, Mar 7, 17, Apr 18, Dec 11; 1796: DL,
Nov 5; 1797: DL, Jan 11, Mar 28, Nov 17; 1798: DL, Mar 3, Oct 27; 1799: DL,
Jan 10, 12, 17, Apr 9, Nov 29
--Merchant of Venice, The, 1669: BRIDGES, Jan 12; 1741: DL, Feb 14, 16, 17, 19,
21, 23, 26, 28, Mar 2, 3, 7, 9, 12, 16, 19, Apr 7, 10, 23, 30, May 18, 29,
Nov 2, 3, 7, 17, Dec 2, 22; 1742: DL, Jan 9, 11, 20, Mar 6, 18, Apr 23, May
7, Sep 11, 23, Oct 25, Nov 27; 1743: DL, Jan 21, Apr 15, JS, 25, DL, May 20;
1744: HAY, Feb 23, CG, Mar 13, Apr 7, 26, DL, May 4, Dec 19, 20; 1745: DL,
Jan 1, 18, Feb 4, Mar 4, CG, Apr 23, DL, 27, May 13, Nov 23, Dec 6; 1746: DL,
Jan 10, Feb 8, CG, Mar 10, DL, 22, CG, Apr 26, DL, 29, May 3, Sep 23, Nov 6,
12; 1747: DL, Jan 29, Feb 9, 23, 27, Mar 19, May 16, Sep 15, Oct 27; 1748:
DL, Jan 1, May 9, Nov 3; 1749: DL, Jan 10, Apr 14, Sep 21, Oct 20; 1750: DL,
Feb 21, 22, May 4, Sep 8, CG, Oct 18, Nov 16; 1751: CG, Jan 2, May 6, DL, Sep
10, CG, Nov 16, 20, 23, Dec 3, 30; 1752: DL, Jan 21, CG, Feb 7, Apr 3, 29,
DL, May 2, Sep 19, CG, Oct 6, DL, Nov 9, CG, 21; 1753: CG, Jan 4, DL, 11, CG,
26, Apr 23, DL, Sep 8; 1754: CG, Apr 6, DL, 16, CG, May 9, DL, 15, CG, Sep
23, Oct 30; 1755: CG, May 2, Oct 8, Dec 2; 1756: DL, Apr 22, Oct 26, Dec 23;
1757: DL, Apr 20, CG, Sep 30, Dec 6; 1758: DL, Dec 18; 1759: DL, Jan 13, 19,
CG, May 3, DL, Dec 12, 13; 1760: CG, May 7, DL, 17; 1761: CG, Jan 10, 17, Feb
26, Mar 12, Apr 4, May 4, Sep 21; 1764: CG, Apr 10; 1765: CG, Apr 9; 1767:
CG, Apr 6, Oct 6, 7, 10, 14, 21, 28, Nov 21, Dec 10; 1768: CG, Jan 1, 22, 25,
Feb 29, DL, Mar 24, CG, Apr 6, 12, DL, 16, Sep 30, Nov 5, Dec 20; 1769: DL,
Jan 7, 26, Mar 30, May 3, 19, Oct 5, 26, Dec 2; 1770: CG, Mar 27, Apr 5, DL,
May 29, Oct 22, Dec 21; 1771: CG, Apr 3, DL, 24, CG, May 7, HAY, Sep 20, DL,
Oct 3, CG, 22, 24, 26, 29, 31; 1772: DL, Jan 11, May 2, CG, 13; 1773: DL, Jan
4, Feb 5, CG, Apr 16, 17, May 24, Oct 5, 14, 23, Nov 18; 1774: DL, May 14,
MARLY, Jul 6; 1775: HAY, Mar 23, CG, May 18, 29, Oct 6, 27, DL, Dec 29; 1776:
DL, Jan 2, CG, Apr 13, Oct 29, Nov 22, Dec 19; 1777: CG, Jan 15, Feb 15, Mar
22, Apr 19, HAY, Jun 11, 12, 16, 18, Jul 8, 23, Aug 15, DL, Oct 14, 16, CG,
16, 28, DL, Nov 7; 1778: CG, Jan 28, Mar 24, Apr 21, 24, CHR, Jul 30, DL, Oct
17; 1779: DL, Jan 19, CG, Feb 25, DL, May 14, CG, Nov 11, 20, 27, Dec 4;
1780: CG, Jan 8, 28, Apr 5, 29, May 12, HAY, Aug 24, CG, Nov 2, 6, 9, 16, 23,
30, Dec 7, 14; 1781: CG, Feb 13, 20, Apr 20, Nov 8, 15, Dec 4; 1782: CG, Jan

31, Apr 8, Oct 29, Dec 3, HAY, 30; 1783: CG, Feb 13, DL, 22, Mar 1, Apr 26,
CG, 30, Dec 5, 16; 1784: DL, Jan 22, 24, CG, Mar 18, DL, 22, CG, Jun 10, Nov
3, 10; 1785: CG, Feb 14; 1786: CG, Feb 10, 18, 27, DL, Apr 6, 20, 29, May 13,
HAMM, Jun 9, CG, Oct 12, Dec 19; 1787: CG, Feb 8, HAY, Jul 27, DL, Nov 24,
CG, Dec 20; 1788: DL, Jan 5, CG, 10, DL, 12, CG, 24, DL, Feb 1, CG, 14, 16,
Apr 3, Oct 18; 1789: DL, Jan 17, CG, Feb 18, May 7, Nov 6; 1790: CG, May 1,
HAY, Jun 22; 1792: HAY, Feb 20, DLKING'S, Mar 10; 1793: DL, Mar 5; 1795: DL,
Mar 10, HAY, Aug 3; 1796: CG, May 12, HAY, Jun 16, 21, Aug 6, 30, CG, Sep 30,
Oct 7, DL, Dec 16; 1797: DL, Jan 20, Feb 11, HAY, Aug 28, 29, CG, Nov 3, DL,
Dec 2, 13; 1798: CG, May 18, HAY, Aug 29, Sep 5, DL, Nov 13; 1799: HAY, Apr
17, CG, Jun 7, DL, Oct 30, Nov 8, 21; 1800: DL, Apr 21, May 19
--Merry Wives of Windsor, The, 1660: REDBULL, Aug 14, VERE, Nov 9, Dec 5; 1661:
VERE, Sep 25; 1667: BRIDGES, Aug 15; 1669: BRIDGES, Jan 12; 1675: DL, Dec 17;
1691: DL, Dec 31; 1704: ATCOURT, Apr 24, LIF, May 18; 1705: QUEEN'S, Apr 23,
LIF/QUEN, Dec 13; 1720: LIF, Oct 22, 24, 25, 26, 29, Nov 8, 17, Dec 3, 15,
29; 1721: LIF, Jan 14, 26, 27, Feb 16, Mar 9, 30, Apr 28, May 3, Jun 8, Oct
21, Nov 15, Dec 7, 28; 1722: LIF, Jan 4, 19, Feb 1, Mar 3, 26, Apr 11, May 1,
28, Oct 19, 25, Dec 8, 29; 1723: LIF, Feb 11, Mar 21, Apr 20, 27, May 31, Oct
19, Nov 22, Dec 14; 1724: LIF, Jan 1, 8, 22, Feb 10, Mar 2, 24, Apr 28, RI,
Aug 3, LIF, Oct 24, Nov 18, 23; 1725: LIF, Jan 1, 21, Feb 8, Apr 16, May 10,
Oct 21, Nov 19, Dec 30; 1726: LIF, Jan 15, 24, Feb 18, Mar 14, Apr 28, Sep
30, Dec 2; 1727: LIF, Feb 20, Apr 11, May 22, Sep 29, Nov 9, 29; 1728: LIF,
Oct 14, Nov 29, Dec 28; 1729: LIF, Jan 22, Apr 9, May 12, Oct 15, Nov 15;
1730: LIF, Jan 10, Feb 7, GF, Mar 17, 19, LIF, Apr 10, GF, 24, LIF, May 15,
Oct 9, GF, 30, LIF, Nov 26, GF, Dec 10; 1731: LIF, Jan 8, Feb 1, GF, 6, LIF,
Mar 4, 29, May 19, RI, Jul 8, LIF, Oct 4, GF, 25, LIF, Nov 24, Dec 8; 1732:
LIF, Feb 12, GF, Mar 4, LIF, Apr 12, LIF/CG, Oct 6, GF, 11, LIF/CG, Nov 28,
GF, Dec 22; 1733: LIF/CG, Jan 18, 23, Apr 16, May 19, CG, Sep 29, GF, Oct 26,
CG, Nov 20, Dec 21; 1734: CG, Jan 25, GF, Feb 20, Oct 9, DL, Dec 6, 7, 9, 10,
11, 18; 1735: GF, Jan 29, DL, Feb 13, May 13, GF, Nov 11, DL, 21; 1736: CG,
Mar 18, DL, May 21; 1737: LIF, Jan 3, DL, 6, Feb 3, CG, Mar 24, Apr 29; 1738:
DL, May 3, 18; 1739: CG, Apr 25, DL, Oct 13; 1740: CG, Mar 27, Apr 17, DL,
23, CG, May 29, DL, Oct 15, GF, Nov 15, Dec 20; 1741: CG, Jan 5, 16, Feb 10,
GF, Apr 17, CG, May 4, Oct 10, GF, 15, CG, Nov 16, Dec 10; 1742: CG, Jan 29,
Mar 23, Apr 21, Oct 27, Dec 3; 1743: CG, Jan 27, Feb 22, Mar 22, DL, Nov 29,
CG, Dec 19; 1744: CG, Jan 20, Feb 18, Apr 6, May 16, Oct 22, Nov 24; 1745:
GF, Mar 28; 1746: CG, Feb 3, Nov 18; 1747: GF, Jan 9, 13, CG, Mar 16; 1748:
CG, Jan 12, Mar 21, Oct 14, 31, Nov 10, Dec 17, 30; 1749: CG, Jan 27, Mar 9,
Apr 1, Oct 18, Nov 13, Dec 6, 29; 1750: CG, Jan 24, Mar 26, DL, Sep 22, CG,
Oct 22, Dec 6; 1751: CG, Jan 25; 1753: DL, May 18; 1754: CG, Jan 21, DL, Feb
20, CG, May 7, DL, 10, Dec 13; 1755: DL, Jan 10, May 2, CG, 15, Oct 22, Nov
11, Dec 17, 18, 31; 1756: CG, Feb 13, May 5, DL, 10, CG, Sep 20, Oct 29, Nov
25; 1757: CG, Jan 6, Apr 19, Sep 23, Nov 8; 1758: CG, Jan 7, Apr 22, Sep 25,
Oct 31; 1759: CG, Jan 16, Apr 26, Sep 26, Dec 10, 29; 1760: CG, Jan 11, DL,
Apr 22, CG, Oct 17; 1761: CG, Feb 12, Apr 16, Sep 23, Oct 15; 1762: CG, Jan
7, Apr 3, May 8, DL, 17, CG, Oct 20, Nov 18; 1763: CG, Nov 10; 1764: DL, Jan
4, CG, 21, Mar 8, Oct 17, Nov 28; 1765: CG, Jan 23, Oct 30; 1766: DL, Jan 24,
CG, Nov 8; 1768: DL, Jan 9, CG, Oct 4, 8, 13, Dec 14; 1769: DL, Dec 16, 29;
1771: DL, May 27; 1772: DL, Jan 15; 1777: HAY, Sep 3, 9; 1778: DL, Feb 24,
25, 28, Mar 9, Apr 2, Sep 17, Nov 6; 1779: DL, Jan 26, May 3, CG, Nov 13, Dec
7, 22; 1780: CG, Jan 21, Apr 28, Nov 1; 1781: CG, Jan 24, 26, Mar 3, 20, 22,
Apr 25, HAY, Aug 24, CG, Dec 8; 1782: CG, Jan 25, Apr 27, May 21, Oct 17;
1783: CG, Jan 18, Feb 14, 22, May 21, Oct 11, Dec 30; 1784: DL, Jan 10, 13,
27, CG, Mar 23, May 4, DL, 14, Oct 11, CG, Nov 13, Dec 11; 1785: CG, Apr 30,
May 24, Nov 1; 1786: CG, Nov 29; 1787: CG, Jan 18, Feb 3, Apr 13, Jun 2, Sep
17, Nov 26; 1788: DL, May 21, Sep 27, CG, Nov 12, DL, Dec 11; 1789: CG, Oct
9, Dec 4; 1790: CG, May 29, Oct 13; 1792: CG, May 12; 1796: CG, Mar 14, 28,
Apr 4, 16, 27, DL, Jun 8, CG, Nov 7, Dec 28; 1797: CG, Feb 13, Sep 27, Nov 1,
9; 1798: CG, Feb 12
--Midsummer Night's Dream, A, 1662: VERE, Sep 29; 1669: BRIDGES, Jan 12; 1755:
DL, Feb 3, Oct 29; 1763: DL, Nov 22, 23, 24, 25, 26; 1777: HAY, Jul 18
--Much Ado about Nothing, 1660: SALSBURY, Dec 12; 1662: LIF, Feb 15; 1690:
NONE, Sep 0; 1721: LIF, Feb 9, 10, 11; 1737: DL, Feb 28, Mar 3, 5, 7, 14, 21,
CG, Nov 2, 3, 7; 1739: CG, May 25; 1746: CG, Mar 13, 22, Apr 14; 1748: DL,
Nov 14, 15, 16, 17, 18, 19, 21, 22, 30, Dec 16; 1749: DL, Jan 19, Feb 3, 28,
Mar 30, Apr 29, May 16, Sep 28, Oct 5, Nov 3, 30; 1750: DL, Jan 27, Feb 23,
Mar 29, Oct 9, Nov 7, 23; 1751: DL, Apr 11, 25, Oct 11, Nov 1, 27; 1752: DL,
Jan 8, 23, Mar 19, Apr 9, Oct 19, Nov 13; 1753: DL, Jan 4, 17, Mar 26, Sep
27, Nov 21; 1754: DL, Jan 12, Mar 30, Apr 30, Nov 22, Dec 11; 1755: DL, Jan
9, 24, Apr 12, Nov 1, 15; 1756: DL, Jan 5, Feb 23, Apr 10, May 27, 28, Oct
19, Nov 29, 30, Dec 4, 18; 1757: DL, Mar 19, Apr 23, Nov 8, Dec 21; 1758: DL,
Apr 5, Sep 23, Dec 23; 1759: DL, Feb 26, Mar 27, Oct 23, Dec 15; 1760: DL,

May 23, Sep 30, Dec 16; <u>1761</u>: DL, Feb 9, Apr 13, Oct 1; <u>1762</u>: DL, Jan 5, Apr
27; <u>1763</u>: DL, Mar 1, Apr 16; <u>1764</u>: DL, Jan 27, Feb 7; <u>1765</u>: DL, Nov 14, 22;
<u>1766</u>: DL, Feb 11, Oct 23; <u>1767</u>: DL, Oct 28; <u>1768</u>: DL, Oct 20; <u>1769</u>: DL, Nov
14; <u>1770</u>: DL, Nov 13; <u>1771</u>: DL, May 24, Oct 17; <u>1772</u>: DL, Feb 28, Nov 3;
<u>1773</u>: DL, Oct 28; <u>1774</u>: DL, Apr 18, Oct 28, CG, Nov 8, 16, Dec 10; <u>1775</u>: DL,
Jan 10, CG, Sep 29, DL, Nov 6, 8, 10, 16, 22; <u>1776</u>: DL, Feb 12, Apr 16, May
7, 9; <u>1777</u>: CG, Oct 15; <u>1778</u>: DL, Feb 10, 11, 17, May 6, Nov 4; <u>1779</u>: DL, Jan
5, May 5, 29, CG, Dec 31; <u>1780</u>: CG, Jan 11, Feb 17, Apr 22, Oct 19, Dec 30;
<u>1781</u>: CG, Mar 15, May 3, Oct 10, Dec 5; <u>1783</u>: CG, Feb 19, DL, Mar 3, CG, Apr
25, May 5; <u>1784</u>: CG, Jan 9; <u>1785</u>: CG, Jan 21, 26, 27, Nov 2; <u>1786</u>: CG, Jan
24; <u>1787</u>: CG, Apr 11, HAY, May 25, Aug 17, CG, Nov 7; <u>1788</u>: CG, Jan 25, Apr
14, DL, 30; <u>1789</u>: CG, Jan 20, DL, Nov 27, Dec 9, 18, 26; <u>1790</u>: DL, Jan 6, Feb
3, May 12; <u>1792</u>: DL, Nov 2, Dec 27; <u>1793</u>: DL, Jan 10, CG, Sep 18; <u>1794</u>: CG,
Jan 15, DL, Jun 19, 20, CG, Nov 12; <u>1797</u>: DL, Jan 12, Mar 23, CG, Oct 6, 9,
Dec 14; <u>1798</u>: CG, Mar 15, May 14, DL, 24, HAY, Aug 21, DL, Oct 11; <u>1799</u>: DL,
Feb 2, Jul 4, Oct 12, Nov 5
--Othello (Moor of Venice, The), <u>1660</u>: REDBULL, Aug 14, COCKPIT, Oct 11, VERE,
Dec 8; <u>1661</u>: NONE, Sep 0; <u>1669</u>: BRIDGES, Jan 12, Feb 6; <u>1675</u>: DL, Jan 25;
<u>1676</u>: DL, Jan 12; <u>1680</u>: NONE, Sep 0; <u>1682</u>: DL, Nov 16; <u>1683</u>: DLORDG, Jan 18;
<u>1685</u>: DLORDG, May 30, ATCOURT, Nov 24; <u>1686</u>: DLORDG, Feb 6, ATCOURT, Nov 10;
<u>1690</u>: NONE, Sep 0; <u>1694</u>: NONE, Sep 0; <u>1695</u>: DL, May 0; <u>1703</u>: LIF, May 21;
<u>1704</u>: LIF, Feb 19, Apr 27, LIF/QUEN, Nov 25; <u>1705</u>: LIF/QUEN, Mar 3, Jun 2,
QUEEN'S, Dec 22; <u>1707</u>: QUEEN'S, Jan 28, May 9; <u>1708</u>: DL, Oct 9; <u>1709</u>: DL, Mar
24, Apr 7, QUEEN'S, Sep 15; <u>1710</u>: DL, Jan 21, May 18, GR, Jun 19, QUEEN'S,
22; <u>1711</u>: DL, Jan 18, Apr 24, GR, Jul 21, 30, DL, Nov 27; <u>1712</u>: DL, May 22,
Oct 14; <u>1713</u>: DL, Jan 27, Mar 26, Oct 3; <u>1714</u>: DL, Jan 14, Oct 7; <u>1715</u>: DL,
Jan 15; <u>1716</u>: DL, Jan 7, 18, May 1, Dec 1; <u>1717</u>: DL, Feb 9, May 2, Oct 22;
<u>1718</u>: DL, Feb 8, Nov 25; <u>1719</u>: DL, May 6, Oct 10; <u>1720</u>: DL, Feb 11, LIF, Mar
12, 19, DL, Apr 28, LIF, May 21, DL, Sep 24, LIF, Oct 20, DL, 24; <u>1721</u>: LIF,
Jan 5, Feb 23, DL, Mar 11, LIF, Sep 29, Nov 14, DL, 18; <u>1722</u>: LIF, Jan 10,
DL, Mar 27, LIF, May 9, DL, Sep 22, LIF, Nov 1; <u>1723</u>: LIF, Jan 15, Apr 30,
Oct 2, DL, 19; <u>1724</u>: DL, Apr 20, Sep 26; <u>1725</u>: DL, Mar 18, Jun 14, Sep 4,
LIF, Dec 6, DL, 8; <u>1726</u>: LIF, Feb 3, DL, Apr 27, Sep 3; <u>1727</u>: DL, Sep 7, LIF,
Oct 6; <u>1728</u>: LIF, Oct 7, DL, 12, Dec 28; <u>1729</u>: LIF, Feb 3, Mar 13, DL, 29,
Sep 20; <u>1730</u>: DL, Jan 7, GF, Jun 3, HAY, 27, LIF, Oct 14, GF, 19, Nov 4, 25,
DL, Dec 1, HAY, 17; <u>1731</u>: LIF, Mar 8, GF, 16, LIF, Sep 17, DL, Nov 15, GF,
26, 30; <u>1732</u>: GF, Jan 22, LIF, 24, GF, Feb 16, Mar 6, LIF, Apr 13, GF, 17,
May 19, DL, Aug 4, 17, LIF/CG, Oct 4, GF, 13, Nov 16, DL, Dec 4; <u>1733</u>: CG,
Jan 13, GF, Apr 2, LIF/CG, 3, GF, May 7, 16, LIF/CG, 31, CG, Sep 15, GF, Oct
5, CG, Nov 10, DL/HAY, 26; <u>1734</u>: CG, Jan 5, GF, 9, 25, HAY, Feb 1, CG, Mar 2,
DL, Apr 29, DL/HAY, May 2, DL, 13, CG, 22, DL, Sep 10, GF, Oct 4, DL, 16,
CG/LIF, 19, 21, 23, 24, 26, Nov 2, 18, YB, 19, 29, CG/LIF, Dec 19; <u>1735</u>: GF,
Jan 4, CG/LIF, 24, DL, Feb 22, YB, Mar 19, GF, 27, LIF, Apr 19, CG/LIF, May
9, DL, Sep 6, GF, 10, CG, Oct 3, Dec 6; <u>1736</u>: DL, Mar 4, CG, 30, DL, Oct 5,
Dec 16; <u>1737</u>: DL, Jan 13, CG, Mar 14, Apr 21, LIF, Sep 7, DL, Oct 6, Nov 10;
<u>1738</u>: DL, Jan 4, Feb 25, CG, Apr 10, DL, May 11, CG, Jun 27, Jul 7, DL, Sep
26, Nov 13; <u>1739</u>: DL, Sep 21, Dec 13, CG, 19; <u>1740</u>: CG, Mar 10, DL, Sep 27,
GF, Oct 23, Nov 14, DL, Dec 16; <u>1741</u>: GF, Jan 29, DL, Sep 10, Oct 26, CG, Dec
9; <u>1742</u>: CG, Apr 26, DL, May 6, CG, Sep 22, 24, 27, Nov 23, Dec 2, 13; <u>1743</u>:
CG, Feb 5, 17, 24, Apr 2, 4, May 17, Nov 28, 29; <u>1744</u>: CG, Jan 12, HAY, 21,
Feb 6, 13, 20, 23, Mar 2, DL, 10, CG, Apr 2, HAY, 26, CG, May 25, HAY, Sep
22, CG, Oct 16, Nov 3; <u>1745</u>: GF, Feb 6, SMMF, 11, 18, 20, CG, Mar 2, DL, 7,
9, GF, 21, CG, Apr 18, DL, 25, GF, May 7, DL, Oct 1, GF, Nov 29; <u>1746</u>: CG,
Apr 3, DL, 9, CG, Jun 20, JS, Oct 2, DL, 4, 7, 9, 11, 14, 17, 18, 21, 28, Nov
26, CG, 28, HAY, Dec 4, DL, 5, GF, 8, 9, CG, 31; <u>1747</u>: DL, Jan 1, Feb 4, GF,
20, DL, 24, Apr 4, 10, Sep 26, Oct 22, SOU, 22, DL, Dec 11; <u>1748</u>: CG, Jan 9,
11, DL, 15, Feb 10, CG, Apr 6, 11, DL, 20, HAY, 30, DL, Oct 4, CG, 28, DL,
Nov 23; <u>1749</u>: DL, Jan 6, Mar 9, CG, Oct 4, HAY, 17, DL, Nov 2, 22, 24, Dec 1;
<u>1750</u>: DL, Mar 10, JS, Jul 23, CG, Oct 17, Dec 1, 3; <u>1751</u>: CG, Feb 5, 9, DL,
Mar 6, 7, 8, CG, 11, DL, 19, CG, Apr 19, NWLS, Sep 5, CG, Oct 9, HAY, Dec 28;
<u>1752</u>: CG, Jan 7, Feb 1, DL, Mar 12, Apr 14, CG, 17, Oct 24, NWLS, Nov 16, CG,
Dec 1; <u>1753</u>: DL, Feb 26, Apr 2, CG, 5, Oct 27; <u>1754</u>: CG, Jan 8, Apr 1, Oct
18, 19, 21, Nov 15, Dec 5; <u>1755</u>: CG, Jan 24, May 8, HAY, Sep 1, 3, 6; <u>1756</u>:
CG, Mar 15, 16, 18, Apr 26, Oct 11, Nov 18, 20, 23, 25, 26; <u>1757</u>: CG, Jan 11,
Mar 7, May 7, Nov 16, Dec 12; <u>1758</u>: CG, Feb 21, Apr 4, Oct 23; <u>1759</u>: CG, Jan
17, DL, May 14, CG, 17, Dec 19; <u>1760</u>: CG, Apr 22, Oct 18; <u>1761</u>: CG, Jan 17,
DL, Mar 28, Apr 30, CG, Jun 23, Oct 13, DL, 17, 19, Dec 14; <u>1762</u>: CG, Oct 12;
<u>1764</u>: DL, Mar 31, Apr 12, 14, 28, May 24; <u>1765</u>: CG, Jan 14, DL, Mar 19, Apr
10, May 10, CG, 13, Oct 28; <u>1766</u>: DL, Feb 13, Apr 1, KING'S, Aug 8, 11, Sep
3, 17, DL, Dec 6; <u>1767</u>: DL, May 9, HAY, Jun 30, Jul 24, Sep 2, 21, DL, Oct
29, 31; <u>1768</u>: DL, Jan 28, CG, Apr 15, DL, May 5, Oct 31; <u>1769</u>: DL, Jan 28,
HAY, Feb 28, DL, Apr 17, HAY, Aug 30, DL, Nov 18, Dec 20; <u>1770</u>: DL, Mar 17,

Apr 24, HAY, Oct 1, DL, Nov 10; 1771: CG, Jan 28, Dec 21; 1772: DL, Jan 7,
CG, 25, DL, Oct 31; 1773: DL, Mar 20, 22, Apr 29, Nov 20, CG, 27, 29; 1774:
DL, Apr 12, CG, Dec 15; 1775: CG, Feb 9, DL, Oct 17, 19, Dec 28; 1777: DL,
Apr 11, CG, 16, CHR, Jul 21, CG, Nov 1, 14; 1779: CG, Mar 4, DL, Oct 16, Nov
1, 10; 1780: DL, Jan 8, May 11, HAY, Jul 24, 31, Aug 4, CG, Nov 10, DL, 29;
1781: CII, Mar 17; 1782: DL, Apr 23, Oct 1; 1783: CG, Sep 24, 29, Dec 27;
1784: DL, May 21, CG, Sep 27; 1785: DL, Mar 8, 12, 29, Apr 5, 21, CG, 23, May
16, HAY, Sep 9, DL, 17, Oct 10; 1786: HAY, Jul 14; 1787: DL, Jan 23, CG, Oct
12, 15, DL, 27; 1788: CG, Apr 18; 1789: CG, Oct 16, 26, DL, Nov 30; 1790: CG,
May 15, Nov 8; 1791: DL, Mar 28; 1792: HAY, Feb 6, DLKING'S, 14, Apr 25, CG,
Oct 1, DL, Dec 28; 1793: DL, Apr 20, CG, Sep 23, HAY, Oct 21; 1794: CG, May
21, Sep 17, DL, Nov 17, 18; 1795: CG, Apr 24; 1796: CG, Oct 24, Dec 12; 1797:
DL, Mar 20, HAY, Sep 4, DL, Nov 23; 1798: CG, Oct 15; 1799: CG, Oct 4; 1800:
DL, Jun 18
--Pericles, Prince of Tyre, 1659: NONE, Sep 0; 1660: SALSBURY, Dec 12; 1738:
CG, Aug 1, 4
--Richard II, 1669: BRIDGES, Jan 12; 1680: DL, Dec 0; 1681: DL, Jan 18; 1719:
LIF, Nov 21, Dec 10, 11, 12, 14, 19; 1720: LIF, Jan 2, 25; 1721: LIF, Jan 7,
Feb 4, Oct 24; 1738: CG, Feb 6, 7, 8, 9, 10, 11, 14, 21, Mar 9, May 2, Nov
30, Dec 1, 21; 1739: CG, Feb 19, Oct 20, 23
--Richard III, 1669: BRIDGES, Jan 12; 1671: NONE, Sep 0; 1691: NONE, Sep 0;
1699: DL, Dec 0; 1704: DL, Apr 4; 1705: DL, Mar 31; 1710: QUEEN'S, Jan 28,
Mar 27, May 13; 1713: DL, Feb 14, 26, Apr 27; 1714: DL, Jan 2, Feb 27, Apr
17, Oct 15; 1715: DL, Jan 27, Dec 6; 1717: DL, Jan 1, Nov 9; 1718: DL, Mar
15; 1719: DL, Feb 12, Sep 26; 1720: DL, Feb 13, May 19, Dec 3; 1721: LIF, Mar
11, 13, 27, Oct 7, Dec 16, DL, 26; 1722: DL, May 14, LIF, Oct 4, Nov 15;
1723: DL, Mar 9, LIF, Oct 10; 1724: LIF, Apr 30, Oct 22; 1725: DL, Feb 6,
LIF, May 1, DL, 10, LIF, Nov 9; 1726: LIF, Oct 17, DL, Nov 3, LIF, Dec 29;
1727: DL, Jan 17, LIF, Dec 21; 1728: LIF, Jan 3, DL, May 23, HAY, Aug 19, DL,
Nov 6, 20; 1730: DL, Nov 10, HAY, Dec 21; 1731: LIF, Nov 15; 1732: GF, Mar
20, 25, May 11, DL, Oct 14, Nov 17; 1733: DL, Feb 12, GF, Apr 11, 12, DL, Oct
17, Nov 2, CG, Dec 15, 26; 1734: DL, Jan 22, GF, Mar 18, May 8, CG, 16, SOU,
Oct 7, DL, 26, 28, GF, Dec 6, CG/LIF, 26; 1735: DL, Jan 7, Feb 5, CG/LIF, Apr
8, DL, Oct 25; 1736: CG, Jan 3, DL, May 26, Sep 18, Dec 1; 1737: DL, Jan 3,
Oct 1; 1738: DL, Feb 13, May 23, Sep 30; 1739: DL, Jan 31, Oct 17, CG, 20;
1740: DL, Jan 14, Sep 16; 1741: GF, Feb 10, DL, 12, CG, Oct 13, 14, GF, 19,
20, 21, 22, 24, 26, 27, Nov 2, 23, 26, CG, Dec 8, GF, 15, DL, 19, GF, 23, DL,
28; 1742: GF, Mar 6, Apr 21, DL, 30, GF, May 5, 14, 21, DL, 31, Oct 13, CG,
13, 14, DL, 15, 23, 28, Nov 5, 11, CG, Dec 4, 6, DL, 20, LIF, 27, 28; 1743:
DL, Jan 3, LIF, 3, 5, 7, DL, 10, LIF, 14, DL, 19, CG, 25, 28, DL, Feb 14, CG,
Mar 7, Apr 8, DL, 16, May 3, TCY, Aug 4, CG, Sep 28, Nov 14, Dec 10, DL, 17;
1744: CG, Jan 2, DL, 3, HAY, Feb 15, DL, 18, CG, Mar 26, Apr 5, DL, 7, May 7,
31, CG, Oct 24, DL, Nov 3, GF, Dec 5, 6, 7, 8, DL, 15, GF, 20; 1745: CG, Jan
8, DL, 12, GF, 19, DL, Feb 12, Mar 5, GF, 18, CG, Apr 22, GF, 30, CG, Nov 28,
GF, Dec 16, 17, 26; 1746: GF, Jan 2, DL, 8, 9, GF, Mar 3, DL, Apr 22, 29, CG,
Jun 16, Oct 20, 31, GF, Nov 11, Dec 17, 26, CG, 30; 1747: GF, Feb 6, Mar 26,
DL, Nov 6, CG, Dec 28; 1748: DL, Jan 27, CG, Feb 29, HAY, Apr 20, DL, 30,
SOU, Sep 26, DL, 29, Dec 23; 1749: DL, Mar 4, JS, 21, DL, Apr 6, May 16, CG,
Oct 2, SOU, 16, DL, Nov 16, 18; 1750: CG, Jan 1, DL, Feb 19, HAY, Mar 15, CG,
Apr 2, Oct 26, DL, Nov 8; 1751: DL, Feb 16, May 7, NWLS, Aug 6, 7, DL, Sep
26, 27, Oct 1, 5, CG, Nov 22, DL, 26, CG, Dec 26; 1752: DL, Jan 15, Feb 3,
11, Apr 1, CG, 18, May 5, Sep 22, DL, 30, NWLS, Nov 23, DL, 24, CG, Dec 28;
1753: CG, Jan 6, DL, 18, Feb 23, Apr 7, May 9, CG, 18, Sep 21, DL, 25, SFP,
27, DL, Oct 26, Nov 28, Dec 18; 1754: DL, Jan 9, CG, Apr 2, DL, May 2, CG,
Sep 20, DL, Oct 1, 24, CG, 26, Nov 14, Dec 28, DL, 28; 1755: CG, Apr 17, DL,
26, Oct 23, Dec 8; 1756: DL, Feb 25, Sep 21, Oct 22; 1757: DL, Jan 4, CG, 27,
29, Feb 1, 3, 4, 8, 10, DL, Mar 5, May 9, Sep 13, Oct 28, CG, Nov 11; 1758:
CG, Mar 13, DL, May 9, Oct 12; 1759: DL, Feb 27, CG, May 11, DL, Oct 19;
1760: DL, May 1, 22, 31, Oct 9, 13, Nov 19, 21; 1761: CG, Mar 30, DL, Apr 21,
CG, May 5, 21, DL, 29, Sep 26, Oct 21, CG, Dec 28; 1762: DL, Jan 2, CG, 5, 8,
11, 14, 16, 19, 23, Feb 8, 20, Mar 6, 16, Apr 3, DL, May 6, CG, 10, 18, DL,
Oct 5, CG, 9, Nov 26, DL, Dec 18, 23; 1763: DL, Jan 11, Oct 24, Nov 18, CG,
Dec 26; 1764: DL, Feb 4, CG, 20, DL, May 10, CG, 15, DL, Sep 20, CG, Oct 8,
DL, Nov 12, CG, 12, DL, 13; 1765: CG, Jan 1, DL, 4, Mar 11, CG, May 3, DL, 8,
CG, Sep 30, DL, Oct 14, CG, Nov 18; 1766: CG, Jan 6, Mar 10, Apr 21, Sep 26,
Oct 20, 24, 27, Nov 10, Dec 26; 1767: DL, Apr 11, May 11, CG, 27, DL, Sep
17, CG, Nov 7, 30, Dec 29; 1768: CG, Apr 11, DL, 12, CG, May 31, Sep 22, DL,
29, CG, Oct 19, Nov 5; 1769: DL, Jan 12, CG, Mar 27, DL, May 16, CG, 18, HAY,
Aug 14, Sep 6, CG, Oct 4, 28, DL, Nov 13, CG, Dec 28; 1770: CG, Jan 26, DL,
Apr 20, May 16, CG, Sep 26, Oct 26, Dec 31; 1771: DL, Apr 2, CG, May 4, Oct
15, Nov 25, Dec 16; 1772: CG, Feb 3, May 12, DL, 30, Jun 2, HAY, Sep 17, CG,
28, Oct 19, Dec 30; 1773: CG, May 20, Oct 4, Dec 6, 9, 20; 1774: CG, Jan 1,

26, May 10, DL, Sep 22, HAY, 30, CG, Oct 22, 29, DL, 29, CG, Nov 7, Dec 5,
31; 1775: CG, Apr 18, DL, 28, May 15, CG, 25, DL, 26, CG, Jun 1, DL, Oct 3,
Nov 7, Dec 12; 1776: CG, Jan 1, DL, May 27, Jun 3, 5, CHR, Oct 4, DL, 10, 12,
CG, Nov 4, 11, DL, Dec 6; 1777: HAY, Aug 7, 8, 11, Sep 17, DL, Oct 7, 11, CG,
Nov 7; 1778: HAY, Mar 24, DL, May 8, 26, CHR, Jun 26, CG, Oct 5, DL, 26, Nov
23, CG, Dec 7; 1779: DL, Jan 4, 9, May 18, Sep 25, CG, Nov 1, Dec 6; 1780:
CG, Jan 10, CII, Mar 6, DL, Apr 10, May 12, HAY, Jul 1, CG, Oct 9, DL, 23,
CG, Dec 26; 1781: DL, Mar 8, CII, 30, DL, May 18, Sep 18; 1782: CG, Jan 7,
HAY, Mar 4, CG, Oct 14, Dec 16; 1783: DL, Feb 12, Mar 10, Sep 23, CG, Oct 13,
Nov 3, DL, 6, 10, Dec 15, HAY, 15, CG, 29, DL, 29; 1784: DL, Jan 12, HAY, Sep
17, CG, Oct 11, DL, Nov 5; 1785: CG, Jan 12, 17, Sep 21, DL, Nov 7, CG, Dec
5; 1786: CG, Sep 20; 1787: DL, Dec 10, 17; 1788: DL, Jan 14, 16, Feb 18, Apr
17, Oct 14, Nov 10, Dec 29; 1789: DL, Jan 12, Sep 12, CG, 25, 28, Oct 5, 23,
DL, Nov 12, CG, Dec 8; 1790: DL, Jan 4, CG, Mar 1, Apr 6, Oct 18, DL, 21, 28;
1791: HAY, Aug 24, CG, Oct 24, DLKING'S, Nov 14; 1792: DLKING'S, Feb 7, HAY,
Apr 16, CG, Oct 15, DL, Nov 5, 12, CG, Dec 26; 1793: HAY, Aug 6, Sep 30, CG,
Oct 14, HAY, Dec 23; 1794: HAY, Feb 25, Aug 27, CG, Oct 15; 1795: CG, Jun 10,
Oct 16; 1796: HAY, Aug 30, CG, Nov 5, DL, 9; 1797: CG, Jun 2, Oct 2; 1798:
HAY, Apr 21, CG, May 4, DL, Sep 25, Oct 22, Nov 19; 1799: DL, Jan 18, CG, May
6, Sep 23, DL, Oct 1, 7, Nov 18
--Romeo and Juliet, 1660: SALSBURY, Dec 12; 1662: LIF, Mar 1; 1744: HAY, Aug
28, Sep 11, 12, 14, 17, 19, 29, Oct 2, 4, 13, 22, Nov 1, Dec 17, 26; 1748:
DL, Nov 19, 29, Dec 1, 2, 3, 5, 6, 7, 8, 9, 10, 12, 13, 14, 15, 16, 20, 30;
1749: DL, Jan 12, Feb 1, Mar 2, Apr 1, 14, CG, Dec 12; 1750: CG, Feb 1, Mar
1, 3, 5, 6, 8, Apr 18, DL, Sep 28, CG, 28, 29, DL, 29, Oct 1, CG, 1, 2, DL,
2, CG, 3, DL, 3, CG, 4, DL, 4, 5, CG, 5, 6, DL, 6, 8, CG, 8, DL, 9, CG, 9,
DL, 10, CG, 10, DL, 11, CG, 11, DL, 12, Nov 20, 21, 26, CG, Dec 8, 15, 17,
DL, 18; 1751: CG, Jan 17, 26, DL, 31, Feb 9, CG, 11, DL, 13, Mar 16, CG, 18,
Apr 30, May 14, 17, 21, DL, Sep 20, 28, CG, Oct 7, 15, DL, 19, CG, 23, Nov 2,
12, DL, 18, Dec 16, CG, 21, 31; 1752: CG, Jan 15, 23, DL, 25, 27, CG, 31, Feb
8, 10, DL, 22, 29, CG, Mar 23, DL, 31, May 7, CG, 11, DL, Oct 13, 20, CG, 21,
DL, 24, 25, CG, 25, DL, Nov 10, CG, 13, 18, 24, Dec 6, 18; 1753: CG, Jan 1,
DL, 24, CG, Feb 5, DL, Mar 29, CG, May 4, DL, 8, CG, 19, 26, DL, Oct 4, 5,
CG, 10, 11, 12, 13, 15, 18, DL, 19, CG, 23, 25, Nov 3, 7, 8, 24, Dec 3, 8,
18; 1754: CG, Jan 5, DL, 15, CG, 21, DL, Feb 11, HAY, Mar 4, CG, 18, Apr 15,
May 16, 22, DL, Oct 11, 26, CG, Nov 20, Dec 26, 27; 1755: SOU, Jan 13, 16,
DL, Feb 7, HAY, 10, CG, Apr 3, 11, May 14, DL, Oct 8, CG, 20, 29, Nov 5, DL,
11, CG, Dec 6, 27, 29, 30; 1756: CG, Jan 1, Feb 14, 24, Mar 20, DL, Apr 1,
CG, 21, May 12, Oct 4, DL, 9, 11, 12, 15, CG, 16, DL, 18, 20, 26, Nov 16, CG,
Dec 30; 1757: CG, Jan 1, Feb 12, DL, Apr 28, CG, May 5, 23, DL, Sep 17, Oct
1, Nov 24, CG, Dec 7, 16, 27; 1758: CG, Feb 14, Mar 27, DL, 31, CG, May 12,
15, DL, Sep 28, 30, Oct 6, 13, 28, CG, Nov 1, 8, 30, DL, Dec 8, 26, CG, 26;
1759: CG, Jan 6, Feb 26, DL, Apr 5, CG, 17, DL, May 10, CG, 22, DL, Sep 25,
Oct 24, Dec 26; 1760: DL, Feb 7, Mar 22, CG, 22, DL, Apr 7, CG, 8, 30, DL,
May 6, CG, 20, DL, Sep 20, CG, 29, Oct 3, DL, 20, CG, Nov 20, Dec 5, 6, DL,
26; 1761: CG, Jan 13, Mar 24, DL, Apr 6, CG, 10, DL, 13, 20, May 5, CG, 20,
DL, Sep 8, CG, 25, Oct 28, DL, Nov 7, Dec 26; 1762: DL, Jan 25, CG, Feb 25,
Mar 13, DL, 27, CG, Apr 13, 22, DL, May 13, CG, Sep 22, DL, 28, CG, Oct 18,
DL, 27, Dec 4; 1763: DL, Jan 1, CG, 24, DL, Mar 5, Apr 22, CG, May 26, Sep
21, DL, Oct 31, Nov 25, CG, Dec 29; 1764: CG, Apr 2, May 12, DL, 21, CG, Sep
21, DL, 22, CG, Oct 27, DL, 29; 1765: DL, Jan 7, CG, 21, Mar 25, Apr 29, DL,
May 6, 16, Sep 17, CG, Oct 7, Nov 25, DL, Dec 23, CG, 23; 1766: DL, Jan 6,
CG, Feb 20, Apr 8, 28, DL, May 2, CG, 19, KING'S, Aug 18, 20, DL, Sep 30, Oct
4, CG, 21, DL, Dec 26; 1767: CG, Feb 16, Mar 17, Apr 20, DL, May 18, CG, 20,
DL, 30, HAY, Jun 22, DL, Sep 21, CG, 25, 28, Oct 8, 12, Nov 16, DL, Dec 22;
1768: CG, Jan 4, DL, Apr 11, CG, 29, DL, May 30, CG, Sep 26, Nov 26, 28, 29,
30, Dec 1, 2; 1769: CG, Jan 6, Apr 15, DL, May 1, CG, 9, DL, Oct 2, CG, 6;
1770: CG, Jan 1, Apr 28, DL, May 8, Oct 29, Nov 1; 1771: CG, Apr 30, DL, May
25, CG, 28, DL, Oct 10, CG, 25, Dec 17; 1772: CG, Feb 24, Mar 16, May 2, DL,
Oct 1, 3, 10, CG, Nov 2; 1773: CG, Jan 1, May 17, Oct 25, Dec 13; 1774: CG,
Feb 9, Oct 13; 1775: CG, Sep 25, Oct 2, 9, Nov 7, DL, Dec 26, CG, 27; 1776:
DL, May 22, CG, Oct 7, 14, 21, Nov 8, DL, Dec 10, 12, 21, 27; 1777: CG, Sep
29; 1778: CG, Jan 12, Feb 23, DL, May 23, CHR, Jun 10, DL, Oct 16, CG, 26,
DL, Nov 9, CG, Dec 28; 1779: CG, Apr 19, Nov 8, DL, Dec 27; 1780: CII, Mar
13; 1781: DL, May 1, HAY, Aug 17, CG, Sep 24, Oct 1, 8, 15, Nov 12; 1782: DL,
Apr 22, 25, CG, Oct 7, Dec 26; 1783: CG, Sep 22, Oct 27; 1784: CG, Jan 19,
Apr 12, Oct 25, 26, Nov 1, 5, 8, 19, 26, Dec 6, 29; 1785: CG, Jan 31, Mar 28,
Apr 18, Nov 14, 17, 21, 25, 28, Dec 19; 1786: CG, Jan 23, Feb 20, Apr 17,
HAMM, Jul 12, CG, Oct 23, Dec 11; 1787: CG, Jan 29, RLSN, Mar 31, DL, May 7,
CG, Sep 24, Nov 12; 1788: CG, Jan 7, Sep 22, 29, Oct 6, 13, 20, Nov 3, DL,
17, 18, CG, Dec 22; 1789: DL, May 11, CG, Sep 14, 21, Nov 9, Dec 7, 28; 1790:
CG, Sep 13, Oct 25; 1791: CG, Sep 26, Nov 28; 1792: CG, Jan 16, Oct 8, 22,

Nov 19, 26; <u>1793</u>: CG, Jan 7, Oct 7, Nov 11; <u>1794</u>: CG, Apr 30, Oct 20, 22, 27;
<u>1795</u>: CG, Jan 5, 26, Sep 21, Oct 12, Nov 23; <u>1796</u>: DL, Apr 25, 28, CG, May
17, DL, 20, HAY, Sep 7, CG, 19, Oct 27, DL, Dec 30; <u>1797</u>: DL, Feb 13, CG, Nov
2, 6, 13, 27, Dec 19; <u>1798</u>: CG, Jan 1, 8, 22, 29, Mar 12, May 7, Oct 8; <u>1799</u>:
CG, May 10, Oct 7, Nov 18, Dec 9
--Taming of the Shrew, The; or, Sauny the Scot, <u>1662</u>: REDBULL, Jan 22; <u>1667</u>:
BRIDGES, Apr 9, Nov 1; <u>1669</u>: BRIDGES, Jan 12; <u>1697</u>: NONE, Sep 0; <u>1704</u>: DL,
Jul 5, Oct 20; <u>1707</u>: QUEEN'S, Jul 4, Aug 5, Oct 15; <u>1708</u>: DL, Jun 19; <u>1711</u>:
DL, Jul 10; <u>1712</u>: DL, Feb 6, Jul 4; <u>1714</u>: DL, Jul 13; <u>1716</u>: LIF, Jun 20, 27,
Jul 25, Oct 22; <u>1717</u>: LIF, Jun 12, Nov 13; <u>1719</u>: LIF, Dec 21, 29; <u>1720</u>: LIF,
Feb 8; <u>1723</u>: KAT, Dec 4, CT, 10, AVT, 31; <u>1724</u>: PY, Apr 20; <u>1725</u>: LIF, Apr 7,
May 18; <u>1735</u>: DL, May 5, GF, Dec 8, 9, 10, 12, 13, 15; <u>1736</u>: GF, Feb 23, LIF,
Nov 18; <u>1754</u>: DL, Mar 18
--Tempest, The; or, The Enchanted Island, <u>1660</u>: SALSBURY, Dec 12; <u>1667</u>: LIF,
Nov 7, 8, 9, 11, 12, 13, 14, 26, Dec 12; <u>1668</u>: LIF, Jan 6, Feb 3, Mar 14,
BRIDGES, 25, LIF, Apr 13, 30, BRIDGES, May 7, LIF, 11; <u>1669</u>: LIF, Jan 21, Feb
19; <u>1670</u>: LIF, Sep 20, Nov 14; <u>1674</u>: DG, Apr 30, May 16, Jun 4, 20, Sep 0,
Nov 11, 17, 18, DL, 19, DG, 28; <u>1675</u>: DG, Feb 27; <u>1676</u>: DG, Sep 25; <u>1677</u>: DG,
Nov 5, 15; <u>1682</u>: DG, Jan 11, Feb 1; <u>1684</u>: NONE, Aug 0; <u>1689</u>: NONE, Sep 0;
<u>1691</u>: NONE, Sep 0; <u>1694</u>: NONE, Sep 0; <u>1697</u>: DG, May 25; <u>1698</u>: DL, Jul 5;
<u>1700</u>: DL, May 30, Jun 28, LIF, 28; <u>1701</u>: DL, Jan 1, Feb 7, Mar 4; <u>1702</u>: LIF,
Oct 13; <u>1703</u>: LIF, Dec 1; <u>1704</u>: DL, Jun 19; <u>1706</u>: DL, Mar 5, Dec 26; <u>1707</u>:
DL, Jan 1, 21, Feb 13, Nov 20, Dec 27; <u>1708</u>: DL, Jul 29; <u>1710</u>: DL, Jan 20,
24, Feb 2, 10, Apr 13, May 12, GR, Jul 10; <u>1712</u>: DL, Jan 7, 8, 10, 11, 15,
17, 24, Feb 1, 15, Mar 15, Apr 21, May 10, Nov 5, 21, Dec 26; <u>1713</u>: DL, Jan
1, Feb 6, Apr 7, Jun 23, Nov 5, Dec 26, 28; <u>1714</u>: DL, Mar 30, Jun 4, Nov 25,
Dec 3, 13; <u>1715</u>: DL, Jan 1, 20, Feb 2, 18, Apr 18, Jun 10, Jul 12, Aug 16,
Nov 18; <u>1716</u>: DL, Jan 6, Apr 25, Jun 8, Jul 31, Aug 7, 23, Dec 28; <u>1717</u>: DL,
Feb 12, Apr 22, Jun 10, Dec 5; <u>1718</u>: DL, Jun 11, Aug 1, Dec 11; <u>1719</u>: DL, Feb
9, Mar 30, Jul 21; <u>1720</u>: DL, Jan 6, Apr 20, Jun 24, Aug 9, Dec 26; <u>1721</u>: DL,
May 20, Aug 22; <u>1722</u>: DL, Jan 3, Mar 26, Jun 12; <u>1723</u>: DL, Jan 7, Jun 6;
<u>1724</u>: DL, Jan 7, Apr 14, May 25, Oct 30; <u>1725</u>: DL, Jan 6, May 24, Oct 30;
<u>1726</u>: DL, Jan 6; <u>1727</u>: DL, Jan 24, May 22, Dec 29; <u>1729</u>: DL, Jan 2, 3, 6, Feb
12, May 28, Oct 30; <u>1730</u>: DL, Jan 6, Nov 30, Dec 17; <u>1731</u>: DL, Jan 13, GF,
Jun 2, DL, 7, Dec 2, 29; <u>1732</u>: DL, Dec 26; <u>1733</u>: DL, Jan 24, May 29, Nov 26,
27, 28, 29, 30, Dec 3, 19, 28; <u>1734</u>: DL, Jan 1, 29, May 15, Oct 22, Nov 15;
<u>1735</u>: DL, Feb 14, Oct 31; <u>1737</u>: DL, Feb 10, 11, 12, 14, 15, Apr 11, 14, 25;
<u>1739</u>: DL, Dec 26, 27; <u>1740</u>: DL, Jan 4, May 14, Nov 28; <u>1741</u>: DL, May 15;
<u>1745</u>: GF, Feb 14, 15, 16, 18, 19, 20, 21, 22, 23, Mar 5, Apr 15, Dec 4, 5,
26; <u>1746</u>: DL, Jan 31, Feb 1, 4, 5, 18, GF, 25, DL, May 19; <u>1747</u>: GF, Jan 16,
19, 20, Feb 9, 26, Apr 4, DL, Dec 26, 28, 29; <u>1748</u>: DL, Apr 11, SFP, Sep 7,
8, 9, 10, 12; <u>1749</u>: DL, May 16, BF/SFP, Aug 23, 24, 25, 26, 28; <u>1750</u>: DL, Jan
1, 2, 3, 5, 17, 19, Feb 12, Apr 27; <u>1756</u>: DL, Feb 11, 13, 18, 20, 26, Mar 16;
<u>1757</u>: DL, Oct 19, 20, 21, 24, 27, Nov 1, 7, 9, 11, 14, 16, 21, 23, Dec 5, 19,
26; <u>1758</u>: DL, Jan 21, Feb 13, Mar 27, Apr 24, Oct 24, Nov 20, Dec 27; <u>1759</u>:
DL, Mar 5, Apr 16; <u>1760</u>: DL, Dec 11, 27; <u>1761</u>: DL, Feb 2, Mar 24, May 8;
<u>1762</u>: DL, Mar 1, Apr 12, Oct 30, Nov 9; <u>1763</u>: DL, Apr 7, May 3, Nov 15, Dec
9; <u>1765</u>: DL, May 1; <u>1766</u>: DL, Feb 3, Apr 30, May 14; <u>1767</u>: DL, Apr 4, May 5;
<u>1768</u>: DL, Apr 22; <u>1769</u>: DL, Mar 16, 27, May 2, 5, Oct 9, Nov 20, Dec 27;
<u>1770</u>: DL, Apr 17, May 23, Nov 19; <u>1771</u>: DL, Apr 15, May 28, Dec 2, 21; <u>1772</u>:
DL, May 26; <u>1773</u>: DL, May 12; <u>1774</u>: DL, Apr 4, Dec 26; <u>1775</u>: DL, May 18;
<u>1776</u>: DL, May 18, CG, Dec 27, 30, 31; <u>1777</u>: DL, Jan 4, 6, 10, 13, CG, 13, DL,
18, 23, 25, CG, 27, DL, 31, Feb 4, CG, 13, DL, 18, Mar 3, 15, Apr 4, 14, 25,
May 2, 7, CG, 19, DL, 30, Sep 20, Nov 14, CG, 25, DL, Dec 26; <u>1778</u>: DL, Jan
6, May 15, Nov 2, 27; <u>1779</u>: DL, Feb 1, May 8, CG, 13, DL, Nov 3, 12, Dec 30;
<u>1780</u>: DL, Mar 13, Apr 24, Sep 23, Dec 12; <u>1781</u>: DL, Jan 3, Nov 13; <u>1782</u>: DL,
Feb 12, Apr 6; <u>1784</u>: DL, Nov 9, 18; <u>1785</u>: DL, Jan 10, 18, Mar 28, Apr 28, May
10, Oct 17, Nov 10, 24; <u>1786</u>: DL, Mar 7, Dec 5, 27; <u>1787</u>: DL, Jan 9, Jun 4;
<u>1789</u>: DL, Oct 13, 17, 20, 27, Nov 3, 10, WHF, 11, DL, 17, Dec 21, 30; <u>1790</u>:
DL, Jan 11, 18, 25, Feb 22, Apr 24, Oct 11, Nov 24; <u>1791</u>: DL, May 5, 30,
DLKING'S, Nov 9, 14, 25, Dec 14, 27; <u>1792</u>: DLKING'S, Apr 12, May 8, DL, Dec
13; <u>1793</u>: DL, Jan 2, KING/HAY, Feb 15, DL, May 7, HAY, Nov 19, Dec 5, 26;
<u>1794</u>: HAY, Jan 4; <u>1797</u>: DL, Feb 22, 28, Mar 18, Dec 9, 23; <u>1798</u>: DL, Feb 24,
Jun 5; <u>1799</u>: DL, May 4, Nov 14, 28
--Timon of Athens; or, The Man Hater, <u>1668</u>: LIF, Aug 20; <u>1678</u>: DG, Jan 0; <u>1687</u>:
NONE, Sep 0; <u>1693</u>: NONE, Sep 0; <u>1695</u>: NONE, Sep 0; <u>1697</u>: DL, Jan 2, Nov 26;
<u>1701</u>: DL, Jan 17; <u>1703</u>: DL, May 24, Jul 5, Dec 11; <u>1704</u>: LIF, Jan 27, DL, Feb
21, Mar 28, Dec 6; <u>1705</u>: DL, Jan 26, LIF, Oct 19; <u>1706</u>: DL, Jan 1, Jun 22;
<u>1707</u>: DL, Jan 9, Feb 11, QUEEN'S, Jun 27, Jul 16, DL, Oct 29, Dec 10; <u>1708</u>:
DL, Jul 1; <u>1709</u>: DL, Dec 10, 29; <u>1710</u>: DL, May 5; <u>1711</u>: CLK, Feb 6, DL/QUEEN,
17, SH, Apr 11, May 9, DL/QUEEN, Jun 22, GR, Aug 27, DL, Oct 30; <u>1712</u>: CLKCS,
Feb 6, DL, May 17; <u>1714</u>: DL, May 17, Jun 16; <u>1715</u>: LIF, Mar 24, Apr 22, Nov

11, DL, 17, 22, Dec 27; 1716: DL, Feb 28, LIF, May 2, DL, 16, Oct 18, LIF,
Nov 22; 1717: DL, Jan 29, LIF, Mar 23, DL, Oct 11; 1718: LIF, Jan 10, Feb 27,
DL, May 2; 1719: DL, Nov 24; 1720: DL, May 20, Oct 18, Dec 8; 1721: DL, May
24, Oct 10; 1722: DL, May 29; 1723: DL, May 20, Dec 30; 1724: DL, May 5, Nov
17; 1725: DL, Jan 21, Mar 29, May 11, Nov 26; 1726: DL, Feb 12, May 23; 1729:
DL, Apr 23, May 26, Nov 27; 1730: DL, Oct 31, Dec 18; 1731: DL, Oct 21; 1732:
DL, Jan 6; 1733: DL, Apr 18, CG, May 1, LIF/CG, 29, DL, Nov 23; 1734: CG, Mar
28, May 15; 1735: DL, Sep 18, Dec 8; 1736: DL, Feb 25, GF, 27, 28, Mar 5, DL,
Nov 19, Dec 27; 1737: DL, Feb 21; 1740: DL, Mar 20, Apr 7; 1741: GF, Mar 19,
DL, May 13; 1745: CG, Apr 20, Nov 22, Dec 30; 1771: DL, Dec 4, 7, 9, 11, 12,
14, 19, 28; 1772: DL, Jan 2, 10, 18, Feb 6, 21; 1786: CG, May 13
--Titus Andronicus; or, The Rape of Lavinia, 1678: NONE, Sep 0; 1686: NONE, Sep
0; 1704: DL, Aug 23, Sep 16, Nov 17; 1717: DL, Aug 13, 16, 20, 23; 1718: DL,
Jul 8; 1719: DL, Jul 28; 1720: LIF, Dec 21, 30; 1721: LIF, Feb 7, DL, Jun 27;
1722: LIF, Aug 1; 1724: LIF, Mar 19, Apr 25
--Troilus and Cressida; or, Truth Found Too Late, 1668: LIF, Aug 20; 1679: DG,
Apr 0; 1681: NONE, Sep 0; 1694: NONE, Sep 0; 1697: LIF, Oct 28; 1709: DL, Jun
2; 1720: LIF, Nov 10, 11, 12; 1721: LIF, Feb 18; 1723: LIF, Mar 21, May 3,
25, Nov 21; 1733: CG, Dec 19, 20; 1734: CG, Jan 7
--Twelfth Night; or, What You Will, 1660: SALSBURY, Dec 12; 1661: LIF, Sep 11;
1663: LIF, Jan 6; 1669: LIF, Jan 20; 1741: DL, Jan 15, 17, 19, 20, 21, 22,
23, Feb 5, Apr 20; 1746: DL, Apr 15, 18; 1747: DL, Dec 31; 1748: DL, Jan 6,
7, Nov 9; 1749: DL, Jan 7, Oct 28; 1751: DL, Jan 7, 11; 1752: DL, Jan 6, 22;
1753: DL, Jan 8, 27; 1754: DL, Jan 7, 24, Feb 12; 1755: DL, Jan 6, Feb 5;
1763: DL, Oct 19, 28; 1764: DL, Jan 6, Apr 12; 1771: DL, Dec 10, 13, 18, 20,
27; 1772: DL, Jan 1, 6, 13, Feb 3, 19, Mar 3, CG, 31, DL, Apr 24, May 1, CG,
5, 26, DL, 29, Oct 8, Dec 22, 31; 1773: DL, Jan 6, Feb 16, Apr 1, May 15, Dec
4, 10; 1774: DL, Apr 5, 30; 1775: DL, Jan 6, 11, Apr 4, 26, May 23, 26; 1776:
DL, Jan 6, 11, Apr 10, Sep 21, Oct 24; 1777: CG, Mar 17, DL, 17, Apr 28, Oct
18; 1778: DL, Jan 3, Mar 24, May 8, Oct 24, Nov 10; 1779: DL, Jan 6, Oct 23,
Dec 21, 31; 1780: DL, Apr 29, May 20; 1782: HAY, Aug 15, 30, DL, Sep 21, Oct
19; 1783: DL, Jan 1, CG, May 7, 14; 1784: DL, May 3; 1785: DL, Nov 11, 16,
23, 28, Dec 6, 16; 1786: DL, Jan 3, Mar 6, Apr 17, May 1, 9, Oct 21, Nov 23;
1787: DL, Jan 16, May 9; 1788: DL, Apr 8, 25, May 27, Oct 4, 18, 24, Nov 26;
1789: DL, Mar 19, May 13, 21; 1790: DL, Feb 10, Apr 9, 21, 26, Nov 3, Dec 8;
1791: DL, Jan 27, Feb 16, 25, DLKING'S, Nov 4; 1792: DLKING'S, Feb 20, May 1,
31; 1793: DL, May 24; 1794: DL, Nov 13, 14; 1795: DL, Apr 22, May 30, Nov 19;
1796: DL, Jan 12; 1797: DL, May 17; 1798: DL, Feb 13; 1799: DL, Feb 23
--Two Gentlemen of Verona, 1669: BRIDGES, Jan 12; 1735: YB, Oct 6; 1762: DL,
Dec 21, 22, 28, 30; 1763: DL, Jan 4, 6, 25, Feb 2; 1784: CG, Apr 13, 28;
1790: DL, Jan 15, 20, Jun 3
--Two Noble Kinsmen. See Fletcher, John.
--Winter's Tale, The, 1669: BRIDGES, Jan 12; 1741: GF, Jan 15, 16, 17, 19, 21,
23, 24, 26, Apr 10, CG, Nov 11, 12, 13, 14; 1742: CG, Jan 21; 1756: DL, Jan
21, 23, 24, 26, 27, 28, 29, 31, Feb 2, 3, 4, Mar 13, 20, Apr 28; 1757: DL,
Mar 24, Apr 21, May 24; 1758: DL, Mar 11, Apr 26; 1765: DL, Mar 26, Apr 26;
1768: DL, Mar 15; 1771: CG, Apr 24, May 9; 1772: CG, May 4; 1774: CG, Mar 12,
DL, Apr 12, CG, Nov 19, 21; 1777: HAY, Jul 18; 1779: DL, Nov 19, 20, 23, 26,
29, Dec 1, 3, 11; 1780: DL, Jan 1, 11, 22, Feb 10, Mar 30, Apr 12, May 18,
24, Oct 19; 1781: DL, Jan 23, 29; 1783: CG, May 19, Oct 9, Dec 23; 1784: CG,
May 10; 1785: DL, Apr 18, CG, May 7, DL, Nov 7, 18, Dec 29; 1786: DL, Oct 24;
1787: DL, Jan 9, 15, May 3, CG, 21; 1788: CG, Apr 11, DL, May 1, CG, 3, DL,
Jun 11, Sep 16, Dec 12; 1789: CG, May 22, DL, Jun 9; 1790: CG, Feb 11, Nov
27; 1792: CG, May 11; 1795: CG, Dec 22
Shakespeare's Club (Ladies), 1737: HAY, Mar 4
Shakespeare's Head Tavern, 1737: DL, May 7; 1745: CG, May 3; 1746: CG, Apr 24;
1750: DL, Mar 6; 1753: CG, Jan 12; 1756: DL, Jan 28, CG, Mar 10; 1757: CG,
Jan 13, DL, Mar 2, CG, Dec 23; 1759: CG, Mar 7; 1760: CG, Feb 27; 1771: CG,
May 10; 1773: CG, May 20
Shakespeare's Loadsters (song), 1797: CG, May 20
Shakespeare's Seven Ages (entertainment), 1751: DL, Apr 10; 1760: CG, May 14;
1764: DL, Apr 3; 1765: DL, Apr 20; 1769: DL, Apr 12; 1770: DL, May 14; 1772:
DL, Mar 24, Apr 7; 1776: DL, Mar 14; 1778: HAY, Mar 23; 1781: CII, Apr 9;
1790: CG, Feb 11; 1792: HAY, Sep 5; 1796: DL, Apr 29, May 5
Shakleton (actor), 1748: HAY, May 2
Shall I in Mamre's fertile plain (song), 1789: CG, Mar 6; 1790: CG, Feb 24, DL,
Mar 17; 1791: CG, Mar 11; 1792: KING'S, Feb 29, CG, Mar 7; 1793: CG, Mar 6;
1794: CG, Mar 12, DL, 21, Apr 9; 1795: CG, Mar 13; 1797: CG, Mar 10; 1798:
CG, Mar 14, 30; 1799: CG, Feb 15, Mar 13; 1800: CG, Mar 5
Sham Conjurer, The. See Lampe, John Frederick.
Sham Lawyer, The. See Drake, J.
Sham Physician, The; or, Trick for Trick (play, anon), 1753: SFGT, Sep 18, 19,

20, 21

Sham Pilgrims, The (farce, anon), <u>1734</u>: DL, Jan 3
Shamrock, The. See O'Keeffe, John.
Shane (upholsterer), <u>1760</u>: CG, Apr 19; <u>1772</u>: CG, Feb 26
Shapman (actor), <u>1736</u>: CG, Jan 9
Sharlarno (music), <u>1737</u>: SH, Mar 11
Sharp (actor), <u>1791</u>: HAY, Oct 24
Sharp, Elizabeth, Mrs Michael (actor), <u>1778</u>: DL, Sep 17, 26, Oct 19, 20, Nov 4,
    9, Dec 19; <u>1779</u>: CG, Jan 25, DL, May 3, 26, Sep 18, Oct 7, 9, 19, 21, Nov 5,
    15, Dec 13, 28; <u>1780</u>: DL, Jan 28, Mar 4, 7, Apr 17, 19, 26, May 17, Oct 3,
    10, 28, 31, Nov 4, 9, 10, 18, 27, Dec 4, 6, 19; <u>1781</u>: DL, Jan 6, Feb 3, 17,
    Mar 8, Apr 16, May 2, 10, 18, Sep 18, 27, Oct 13, Nov 5, 7, Dec 14; <u>1782</u>: DL,
    May 1, 3, 7, 8, 10, 11, 14, 29
Sharp, Francis (double bass player), <u>1792</u>: CG, Feb 24; <u>1793</u>: CG, Feb 15; <u>1794</u>:
    CG, Mar 7
Sharp, John (instrumentalist), <u>1794</u>: CG, Mar 7; <u>1795</u>: CG, Feb 20; <u>1796</u>: CG, Feb
    12; <u>1797</u>: CG, Mar 3; <u>1798</u>: CG, Feb 23; <u>1799</u>: CG, Feb 8; <u>1800</u>: CG, Feb 28
Sharp, Joseph (instrumentalist), <u>1796</u>: CG, Feb 12; <u>1797</u>: CG, Mar 3; <u>1798</u>: CG,
    Feb 23; <u>1799</u>: CG, Feb 8; <u>1800</u>: CG, Feb 28
Sharp, Master (violinist), <u>1797</u>: DL, May 18
Sharp, Michael (oboist), <u>1779</u>: HAY, Mar 17, 24; <u>1783</u>: CG, May 16; <u>1791</u>: CG, Mar
    11; <u>1794</u>: CG, Mar 7; <u>1795</u>: CG, Feb 20; <u>1796</u>: CG, Feb 12; <u>1797</u>: CG, Mar 3;
    <u>1798</u>: CG, Feb 23; <u>1799</u>: CG, Feb 8; <u>1800</u>: CG, Feb 28
Sharp, Miss (actor), <u>1738</u>: CG, Apr 7, May 3, Jun 30, Jul 11; <u>1742</u>: JS, Apr 7
Sharp, Miss (actor), <u>1775</u>: DL, Oct 24, Nov 24; <u>1776</u>: DL, Mar 23, Apr 29, May 22
Sharp, Miss (singer), <u>1793</u>: CG, Feb 15, Mar 6, 8, 13, 20
Sharp, Mrs (actor), <u>1734</u>: DL/HAY, Feb 28, Mar 12
Sharp, William (violoncellist), <u>1794</u>: CG, Mar 7; <u>1796</u>: CG, Feb 12; <u>1797</u>: CG,
    Mar 3; <u>1798</u>: CG, Feb 23; <u>1799</u>: CG, Feb 8; <u>1800</u>: CG, Feb 28
Sharpe, Ann (actor), <u>1778</u>: HAY, Aug 21
Sharpe, Mrs (singer), <u>1780</u>: CG, May 6, Sep 25; <u>1781</u>: CG, Apr 20, Oct 16, 20;
    <u>1784</u>: CG, Nov 8, 12, 22; <u>1786</u>: CG, Jan 18
Sharpe, Mrs (ticket deliverer), <u>1777</u>: CG, May 15; <u>1778</u>: CG, May 14; <u>1779</u>: CG,
    Apr 29; <u>1780</u>: CG, May 23; <u>1781</u>: CG, May 3; <u>1782</u>: CG, May 8; <u>1783</u>: CG, May 28;
    <u>1784</u>: CG, May 15
Sharper's Last Shift, The (farce, anon), <u>1781</u>: HAY, Jan 22
Sharpers, The. See Gardiner, Matthew.
Sharpless (actor), <u>1768</u>: HAY, Oct 7; <u>1769</u>: HAY, May 15, 26, 29, Jun 2, 5, Jul
    12, Aug 7, 11, 14, 30, Sep 11, 19; <u>1770</u>: HAY, Mar 17
Sharratt (Sherratt, Sherrard) (house servant), <u>1768</u>: CG, May 28, Jun 4; <u>1769</u>:
    CG, May 20, 25; <u>1770</u>: CG, May 18, 26, HAY, Nov 21; <u>1771</u>: CG, May 27; <u>1772</u>:
    CG, May 23; <u>1773</u>: CG, May 22; <u>1774</u>: CG, May 7; <u>1784</u>: DL, May 22; <u>1785</u>: DL,
    May 21; <u>1786</u>: DL, May 29; <u>1787</u>: DL, Jun 4; <u>1788</u>: DL, Jun 5; <u>1789</u>: DL, Jun 10;
    <u>1790</u>: DL, May 29; <u>1791</u>: DL, May 31; <u>1792</u>: DLKING'S, Jun 15; <u>1793</u>: DL, Jun 6
Shatford, James (actor), <u>1784</u>: HAY, Jan 21, Feb 23, Mar 8; <u>1787</u>: ROY, Jun 20
Shatford, Thomas (actor), <u>1779</u>: HAY, Mar 15; <u>1781</u>: CII, Mar 27
Shatterel (Shoterel, Shetterel, Shotrell), Edward (actor), <u>1660</u>: COCKPIT, Oct 8
Shatterel, Robert (actor), <u>1659</u>: NONE, Sep 0; <u>1660</u>: NONE, Sep 0, COCKPIT, Oct
    8, REDBULL, Nov 5, VERE, 17, Dec 3; <u>1663</u>: VERE, Mar 0, NONE, Sep 0; <u>1665</u>:
    BRIDGES, Jan 14; <u>1666</u>: BRIDGES, Mar 19, NONE, Sep 0, BRIDGES, Dec 7, ATCOURT,
    10; <u>1667</u>: BRIDGES, Apr 16, Oct 5, Nov 2; <u>1668</u>: BRIDGES, Jun 12, Sep 14, Nov
    6; <u>1669</u>: BRIDGES, May 6; <u>1675</u>: DL, Jan 12, Apr 23, May 10
Shatterel, William (actor), <u>1660</u>: REDBULL, Nov 5
Shaw (actor), <u>1760</u>: HAY, Jun 28; <u>1761</u>: DL, Jul 21, CG, Oct 19, Nov 3, 10; <u>1762</u>:
    CG, May 14; <u>1767</u>: DL, Feb 2, May 26
Shaw (beneficiary), <u>1710</u>: DL, Apr 20
Shaw (liaison), <u>1733</u>: DL, Jun 9
Shaw (singer), <u>1703</u>: DL, Oct 16
Shaw, Anthony (violinist), <u>1788</u>: CG, Dec 26; <u>1792</u>: KING'S, Feb 24
Shaw, John (dancer), <u>1715</u>: LIF, Feb 1, Jul 21, Sep 29, Oct 1, 3, 5, 6, 13, 14,
    15, 22, 24, 26, 29, Nov 4, 10, 12, 14, 15, 18, 22, 25, 26, 28, 29, Dec 13,
    17, 21, 28, 30; <u>1716</u>: LIF, Jan 11, 19, 27, Feb 2, 3, 16, 27, 28, Apr 6, 9,
    21, 30, May 8, 18, Nov 5, 8, 9, 14, 16, 22, 28, 29, Dec 17, 29, 31; <u>1717</u>: DL,
    Apr 9, LIF, 22, 25, 29, DL, May 6, LIF, 18, 21, 23, DL, Oct 9, 12, 25, 29,
    Nov 1, 8, 22, Dec 3; <u>1718</u>: DL, Jan 7, 14, 21, 23, 27, 28, 31, Feb 6, 10, Mar
    4, 18, 25, 31, May 2, 6, 7, 8, 13, 14, 15, 16, 19, 21, 22, 27, 29, 30, Jun 6,
    Oct 2, 7, 10, 15, 20, 22, 24, 28, Nov 4, 6, 11, 12, 14, 17, Dec 10, 15, 19;
    <u>1719</u>: DL, Jan 7, 29, Feb 7, 12, Mar 12, 16, 19, Apr 9, 11, 14, 16, 17, 18,
    20, 21, 23, 24, 30, May 2, 4, 5, 8, 9, 11, 12, 13, 14, 15, 18, 21, 30, Sep
    17, 29, Oct 12, 15, 20, 26, 29, Nov 3, 6, 25, Dec 4, 7; <u>1720</u>: DL, Jan 12, 14,
    Feb 1, 10, 29, Mar 15, 28, 31, Apr 19, 25, 26, 28, May 6, 9, 10, 12, 17, 19,
    20, 21, 23, 24, 25, 30, Jun 6, Sep 13, 20, 22, Oct 22, 31, Nov 8, 22, Dec 9,

14; <u>1721</u>: DL, Feb 7, 9, Mar 13, 16, 25, 30, Apr 10, 11, 12, 14, 15, 17, 25, May 31, Jun 6, Sep 12, Oct 13, 16, 18, Nov 13, 27, Dec 18, 29; <u>1722</u>: DL, Jan 8, 10, 19, Mar 10, 15, 27, Apr 5, 9, 10, 18, 24, 26, 27, 28, 30, May 4, 5, 7, 8, 9, 11, 16, 19, 23, 24, 28, 29, 30, Sep 27, Oct 5, 10, 12, 25, 29, 30, Dec 4, 11, 27; <u>1723</u>: DL, Jan 18, 21, 29, Feb 5, Mar 21, 25, Apr 18, 29, May 2, 4, 8, 9, 10, 13, 15, 16, 17, 21, 24, 30, Oct 1, 3, 25, Nov 1, 20, 21, 22, 23, 26; <u>1724</u>: DL, Jan 27, Feb 10, 20, 27, Mar 5, 9, 16, 26, Apr 7, 13, 15, 17, 18, 22, 29, May 2, 4, 8, 9, 12, 18, Sep 15, Oct 16, Nov 14; <u>1725</u>: DL, Apr 12, Dec 8; <u>1726</u>: DL, Apr 20

Shaw, Mrs (actor, singer), <u>1700</u>: DL, Feb 19; <u>1702</u>: DL, Oct 20; <u>1703</u>: DL, May 13, Jun 4; <u>1704</u>: DL, Jul 11

Shaw, Mrs Thomas (actor, singer), <u>1784</u>: HAY, Feb 9; <u>1788</u>: DL, May 8, Jun 5, Sep 13, Nov 17; <u>1789</u>: DL, May 22, Jun 13, Sep 24, 26, Oct 13, Nov 13, 14, 17, Dec 26; <u>1790</u>: DL, Jan 13, Apr 9, May 20, 26, Oct 11, 21; <u>1791</u>: DLKING'S, Sep 27, Oct 15, 18; <u>1792</u>: DLKING'S, Feb 7, 18, Mar 29, May 21, 23, DL, Sep 29, Oct 4, 11, Nov 21, Dec 13, 19, 20, 26, 27; <u>1793</u>: DL, Jan 10, Mar 7, Apr 22, May 21, Jun 5

Shaw, R (actor, singer), <u>1779</u>: DL, Dec 27; <u>1781</u>: DL, May 1; <u>1782</u>: HAY, Mar 18, Apr 9; <u>1789</u>: HAY, Aug 11, DL, Nov 14; <u>1790</u>: DL, Jan 8, 25, HAY, Jun 15; <u>1791</u>: HAY, Sep 26, DLKING'S, Oct 1, 15, Nov 16, HAY, Dec 12; <u>1792</u>: DLKING'S, Feb 18, Mar 26, 29, May 23, DL, Oct 11, 13, 18, HAY, 22, DL, Nov 21, Dec 26; <u>1793</u>: KING/HAY, Mar 6, DL, 7

Shaw Jr, Thomas (violinist, composer), <u>1786</u>: DL, Mar 10, 24, Apr 5, May 26; <u>1787</u>: DL, Feb 23, Mar 7, 21, Jun 1; <u>1788</u>: DL, Feb 8; <u>1789</u>: DL, Feb 27, Mar 6, 18, 20, 25, Nov 13, CG, Dec 21; <u>1790</u>: DL, Feb 19, Oct 11, CG, Nov 15; <u>1791</u>: DL, Mar 11, 16, Apr 13, DLKING'S, Dec 31; <u>1792</u>: KING'S, Feb 24, Mar 23, 28, 30; <u>1793</u>: DL, Jan 23, KING/HAY, Feb 15, DL, May 10, HAY, Aug 16, CG, Oct 2, HAY, Nov 30; <u>1794</u>: DL, Mar 12; <u>1797</u>: DL, Feb 11, Oct 7; <u>1798</u>: DL, Mar 24; <u>1800</u>: DL, Apr 29

--New Anthem, <u>1792</u>: KING'S, Mar 23, 28, 30

Shawford, Joseline (dancer), <u>1735</u>: HAY, Sep 29; <u>1736</u>: HAY, Jan 14, 19, Feb 16, 19, 20, CG, Sep 22; <u>1740</u>: GF, Oct 29, Nov 6, Dec 12, 15; <u>1741</u>: GF, Jan 27, Feb 14, 19, Mar 3, 19; <u>1743</u>: DL, Oct 13; <u>1744</u>: DL, Feb 16, Oct 17; <u>1745</u>: DL, Jan 14, May 8; <u>1746</u>: DL, Mar 3, Apr 2, 25, May 7; <u>1747</u>: DL, Jan 24, May 12, Nov 2, 13, 16; <u>1748</u>: DL, May 6, 16, BF, Aug 24, SFBCBV, Sep 7, DL, Oct 15, 27; <u>1749</u>: DL, Feb 21, May 2, BFY, Aug 23, DL, Oct 11, 18, 24, Nov 9, 27, Dec 28; <u>1750</u>: DL, Jan 1, 3, 17, 19, Feb 12, 19, Apr 5, 27, May 3, Nov 13, 27; <u>1751</u>: DL, May 8, Dec 26; <u>1752</u>: DL, Jan 28, May 1; <u>1753</u>: DL, May 12, Nov 26; <u>1754</u>: DL, May 7, 15; <u>1755</u>: DL, May 5, 15, Nov 8; <u>1756</u>: DL, May 13; <u>1757</u>: DL, May 18; <u>1758</u>: DL, May 11; <u>1759</u>: DL, May 22; <u>1760</u>: DL, May 13; <u>1761</u>: DL, May 21; <u>1762</u>: DL, May 20

Shawford, Master (dancer), <u>1740</u>: GF, Dec 4, 5, 12, 15; <u>1748</u>: DL, May 6; <u>1749</u>: DL, May 2, 9, Oct 24, Nov 9, 27, 29, Dec 2; <u>1750</u>: DL, Jan 1, May 2, 3, 8, Nov 27; <u>1751</u>: DL, May 8, 13, Dec 26; <u>1752</u>: DL, May 1, 2, 4

Shawford, Master and Miss (dancers), <u>1751</u>: DL, May 8

Shawford, Miss (dancer), <u>1748</u>: DL, May 6; <u>1749</u>: DL, Oct 11, 24, Nov 9, 27, 29; <u>1750</u>: DL, Apr 5, May 3, Nov 27; <u>1751</u>: DL, May 4, Dec 26; <u>1752</u>: DL, Apr 23, 27, May 1, 2, 4; <u>1753</u>: DL, Jan 1, May 1, 14, 17

Shawford, Mr and Miss (dancers), <u>1753</u>: DL, May 12

Shawford, Mrs (dancer), <u>1747</u>: DL, Jan 24, Nov 2, 13, 16; <u>1748</u>: BF, Aug 24, SFBCBV, Sep 7; <u>1749</u>: DL, Feb 23, BFY, Aug 23, DL, Sep 26, Oct 11, 18, 24, Nov 9; <u>1750</u>: DL, Jan 1, Apr 5, May 3, Nov 27; <u>1751</u>: DL, May 8, Dec 26

She comes my goddess comes (song), <u>1697</u>: DL, Sep 0

She Couldn't Help It (entertainment), <u>1792</u>: CG, Apr 28

She Gallant, The; or, Recruits for the King of Prussia (play, anon), <u>1759</u>: CG, Mar 20

She Gallant, The; or, Square-Toes Outwitted. See O'Keeffe, John.

She Gallants, The; or, Once a Lover and Always a Lover. See Granville, George.

She Stoops to Conquer. See Goldsmith, Oliver.

She sung whilst from her eye ran down (song), <u>1796</u>: DL, Apr 2

She that will but now discover (song), <u>1780</u>: CG, Apr 10; <u>1781</u>: CG, Apr 3, 25; <u>1782</u>: CG, May 6

She Ventures and He Wins (play, anon), <u>1695</u>: LIF, Sep 0, DL, 0

She Would and She Would Not (dance), <u>1758</u>: CG, Apr 12

She Would and She Would Not. See Cibber, Colley.

She Would if She Could. See Etherege, Sir George.

She's Eloped! See O'Keeffe, John.

She's Jealous of Herself (play, anon), <u>1670</u>: LIF, Oct 20

Sheark, Widow (beneficiary), <u>1759</u>: CG, Dec 18

Shebbeare, John (critic), <u>1758</u>: DL, Jan 12; <u>1767</u>: CG, Mar 4

Sheene (actor), <u>1782</u>: HAY, Mar 21

Sheep Shearers (dance), <u>1764</u>: DL, Mar 8, 12, 15, 19, Apr 5

Sheep Shearing Song (song), 1741: GF, Apr 10; 1762: DL, Jan 27; 1774: CG, Mar 12, DL, Apr 12, May 7, CG, Nov 19; 1778: HAY, Apr 29; 1779: DL, Nov 20; 1780: DL, Oct 19; 1785: HAY, Jan 24, DL, Apr 18, Nov 18; 1786: DL, Oct 24; 1788: DL, Jun 11, Sep 16; 1789: DL, Jun 9; 1798: CG, May 12
Sheep Shearing, The. See Colman the elder, George; Morgan, MacNamara, Florizel and Perdita.
Sheer Lane, 1744: TB, Feb 29
Sheffer (actor), 1729: HAY, Jan 25
Sheffer, Thomas (beneficiary), 1741: HAY, Feb 18
Sheffield, John, Earl of Mulgrave, Lord Normanby (actor), 1673: DG, Jul 3; 1676: DL, Dec 11; 1677: DL, Jul 0; 1698: DLLIF, Dec 13; 1794: DL, Jul 2
Shelbourne, Miss (actor), 1779: HAY, Mar 15; 1782: HAY, Mar 4; 1786: HAY, Mar 6, Dec 18; 1787: HAY, Mar 12
Sheldon, Ed (spectator), 1694: NONE, Jan 11
Sheldon, Sir Joseph (Lord Mayor), 1675: CITY, Oct 29
Shell House, 1741: CG, Mar 30
Shelmerdine (box-bookkeeper), 1799: KING'S, Jun 17
Shelton (actor), 1738: CG, Aug 1
Shelton, Mrs (house servant), 1740: CG, Nov 12
Shenan (dancer), 1674: DL, Mar 30
Shenstone, William (poet), 1741: CG, Jan 12, 16, DL, Feb 6; 1749: DL, Feb 20; 1773: CG, May 1
Shepard, Charles (actor), 1710: GR, Jun 19, 21, 24, Jul 1, 3, 10, 12, 20, 22, 27, Aug 3, Sep 20, 28, 30; 1715: DL, Feb 23, Apr 20, Jun 6, 28, Jul 1, Aug 9; 1716: DL, May 25; 1717: DL, Jan 12, May 22, Jun 24, Aug 6, 9, 22, SF, Sep 9; 1718: DL, Feb 19, May 1, Aug 8, RI, 9, 11, DL, 12; 1719: DL, Jan 28, May 13, Jun 9, RI, Jul 6, BFPM, Aug 24, DL, Sep 19, 22, Oct 7, 15, 21, 27, 30, Nov 16, 18, 30; 1720: DL, Jan 13, Feb 10, May 6, 20, Jul 7, BFPMJ, Aug 23, DL, Sep 20, 22, Oct 4, 5, 17, Nov 1, 2, 7, 11, 16, Dec 8, 14, 17; 1721: DL, Jan 27, Mar 23, Apr 14, May 3, 26, 29, Jul 28, Aug 1, 4, 18, BF/SF, 24, DL, Sep 12, 16, 21, Oct 2, 6, 10, 17, 18, 21, 23, 24, 27, Nov 1, 30; 1722: DL, Jan 9, May 1, RI, Jul 23, DL, Sep 13, 18, Oct 8, 15, 24, 25, 26, Nov 7, Dec 5, 17, 26; 1723: DL, Jan 7, Apr 30, May 15, 20, 23, 27, Jun 4, Sep 14, 17, 19, 26, Oct 9, 23, 24, 28, 29, Nov 1, 6, 15, 18, Dec 30; 1724: DL, Jan 23, Apr 18, 28, 30, Sep 15, 22, Oct 8, 14, 28, 29, Nov 2, 6, 10, 16, 19, 28, Dec 7, 18; 1725: DL, Jan 4, Feb 3, Apr 21, 23, 30, May 8, 11, Sep 9, 25, 28, Oct 2, 7, 14, 15, 18, 25, 27, 28, Nov 8, 29, Dec 7, 9; 1726: DL, Jan 3, 12, Apr 21, May 23, 25, Sep 15, 17, 22, Oct 6, 11, 18, 20, 22, Nov 9, 26, Dec 7, 12, 14, 21; 1727: DL, Jan 20, Feb 11, 21, Apr 8, 19, 28, May 2, 8, 22, Sep 9, 12, 21, 26, 28, Oct 5, 7, 19, 20, 30, Nov 9, Dec 4; 1728: DL, Jan 5, Mar 9, Apr 2, 29, May 8, 17, Sep 12, Oct 21, 23, 24, 25, 28, 31, Nov 8; 1729: DL, Jan 2, 20, 21, 22, 29, Feb 3, Apr 23, May 3, 6, 7, Sep 13, 23, 30, Oct 2, 4, 14, 16, 21, 23, Nov 6, 7, 8, 18, 21, 25, 27, 28, Dec 2, 3; 1730: DL, Jan 3, Apr 29, Sep 29, Oct 6, 8, 10, 20, Nov 16, 25, Dec 2; 1731: DL, Feb 8, Mar 29, Apr 1, 8, 21, 27, May 3, 10, 17, 19, Jun 7, 11, Jul 20, Aug 11, Sep 21, 23, 25, 28, 30, Oct 7, 9, 19, 21, 30, Nov 6, 8, 9, 10, Dec 2, 17; 1732: DL, Feb 10, 11, Mar 23, Apr 11, 25, 27, May 8, 12, Jun 1, 23, Sep 8, 19, 21, 23, 26, 28, 30, Oct 12, 21, 28, Nov 7, 9, 13, 14, 21, 24, Dec 6, 9, 14; 1733: DL, Jan 26, 29, Apr 4, 6, 9, 18, 24, May 1, 9, 24, 29, Jun 4, DL/HAY, Sep 26, Oct 5, 6, 10, 12, 15, 19, 22, Nov 15, Dec 5, 10, 12, 17, 19, 20, 22, HAY, 26; 1734: HAY, Feb 12, DL/HAY, Mar 12, 25, Apr 1, 18, DL, 22, DL/HAY, 26, May 3, DL, 15, Sep 12, 19, 24, 28, Oct 8, 14, 17, 19, 22, 25, 30, Nov 2, 8, 16, 20, Dec 6; 1735: DL, Jan 6, 11, 20, GF/HAY, 21, DL, 22, 28, 29, Feb 4, 25, Apr 11, 14, 21, May 1, 10, 14, Jun 9, Jul 1, Sep 4, 6, 11, 15, 18, Oct 4, 21, 23, 24, 27, 28, 31, Nov 3, 10, 19, 20, 21, 22, Dec 6; 1736: DL, Jan 3, Feb 5, 9, Mar 11, Apr 12, May 4, Aug 26, Sep 7, 9, 16, 18, 23, 28, Oct 9, 18, 19, 22, 23, 29, 30, Nov 1, 12, 15, 19, 23, Dec 17, 21; 1737: DL, Jan 6, 26, Feb 28, Mar 1, 10, 17, 29, Apr 27, May 6, Aug 30; 1738: DL, Nov 3, 8, 18, 20, 25, 27, 29, 30, Dec 9, 26; 1739: DL, Jan 1, 2, 3, 4, 8, 13, 16, 26, Feb 1, 3, Mar 10, 20, Apr 3, May 4, 8, 25, Sep 4, 11, 18, 22, Oct 3, 6, 8, 9, 10, 11, 15, 18, 20, 23, 24, 27, Dec 10, 26; 1740: DL, Jan 3, 8, 12, 16, Feb 7, 13, Mar 17, 20, 25, 29, Apr 22, 29, May 6, 13, 19, 26, Sep 9, 13, 18, 20, 30, Oct 2, 4, 10, 11, 14, 28, 29, Nov 1, 6, 7, 10, 13, 19, 27, 28, Dec 6, 18; 1741: DL, Jan 15, Mar 14, 31, Apr 28, May 13, 21, 25, Sep 5, 17, 22, Oct 6, 8, 20, 21, 23, Nov 16, Dec 7, 12, 16; 1742: DL, Jan 6, Feb 13, Mar 8, Apr 5, 24, 27, May 26; 1743: DL, Apr 5; 1744: DL, May 4
Shepard, F (beneficiary), 1739: DL, May 30
Shepard, Mrs (actor), 1710: GR, Jun 21, Jul 8, 10, 12, 20, 27, Aug 26, Sep 1, 9, 23, 28, 30; 1717: SF, Sep 14; 1718: RI, Aug 2, 9, 11
Shepheard (singer), 1675: ATCOURT, Feb 15
Shepheard (treasurer), 1732: GF, Apr 27; 1733: GF, Apr 25; 1734: GF, May 1; 1735: GF, Apr 23; 1736: GF, Apr 17; 1741: GF, Apr 13; 1742: GF, Apr 26; 1743:

LIF, Mar 22
Shepherd (actor), 1745: GF, Oct 28, Nov 4, 11, 18, 19, Dec 2, 5, 6, 11, 19;
    1746: GF, Jan 1, 13, 22
Shepherd (actor), 1777: HAY, Oct 13; 1778: HAY, Feb 9, Apr 9
Shepherd (beneficiary), 1737: LIF, Apr 28; 1738: CG, Apr 28
Shepherd (draper), 1766: DL, Dec 30
Shepherd and Shepherdess (dance), 1720: DL, Apr 26; 1722: LIF, May 18; 1724:
    HAY, Mar 9, LIF, Apr 27, May 15, 20; 1725: LIF, Mar 18, Nov 2, 8, 11, 17, 18,
    24; 1726: LIF, Mar 10, 28, 31, Apr 18, 21, 22, 29, May 3, 11, 12, 16, 17, DL,
    18, LIF, 19, 24, 25, 30, Sep 19, Oct 19; 1727: LIF, Feb 9, Apr 26, May 4, 18;
    1729: LIF, Jan 13; 1730: GF, Apr 6, LIF, 27, GF, Sep 28; 1731: LIF, May 6;
    1733: CG, Nov 29, 30, Dec 10, 12, 28, 29; 1734: CG, Jan 4, Feb 22, Mar 12,
    25, Apr 18, 19, 22, 30; 1735: GF/HAY, Feb 5, CG/LIF, Mar 29; 1736: CG, Apr 5,
    6; 1740: DL, Feb 13, Apr 11, Oct 31, Nov 1, 7, 8, 10, 11, Dec 19, 29; 1741:
    DL, Jan 10, Feb 19, 24, Mar 5, Apr 2, 4, 6, 7, 16, 18, 22, 27; 1754: CG, Apr
    24; 1781: DL, Apr 25, May 7, 10
Shepherd, what art thou pursuing? (song), 1748: CG, Mar 31; 1791: DL, Apr 1,
    CG, 13; 1792: KING'S, Feb 29; 1794: DL, Mar 26; 1798: CG, Mar 28
Shepherd, Edward (attorney), 1738: GF, Sep 16; 1745: MF, May 2
Shepherd's Artifice, The. See Dibdin, Charles.
Shepherd's Bush Fair, 1748: HAY, Apr 18
Shepherd's Frolic (dance), 1771: DL, Apr 6, May 16, 17, 20, 22
Shepherd's Invitation (song), 1744: HAY, Jan 19
Shepherd's Lottery, The. See Mendez, Moses.
Shepherd's Market, 1742: UM, Apr 26; 1745: NWMF, Feb 7; 1746: NWSM, Jul 28;
    1748: NWSM, May 3, Nov 30, Dec 26, 29; 1749: NWSM, May 1, 3, 4, 5, 6, 8, 10,
    15, 16; 1750: NWSM, May 1, 10; 1752: HAY, Mar 31
Shepherd's Mount (dance), 1735: DL, Feb 18, 22, Mar 17, Apr 15, 19, 22, 29, Oct
    1; 1736: DL, Apr 10, 13, 17, 26, 27, May 11; 1738: DL, Mar 3
Shepherd's Wedding (dance), 1777: CG, Feb 15, 17, Apr 19, May 20, Sep 24, 26,
    Oct 16, 28; 1778: CG, Sep 21; 1779: CG, Oct 13, Nov 11, 20; 1780: CG, Apr 5,
    Oct 3, 13, Nov 2, 22, 23, 30, Dec 23; 1781: CG, Feb 13, 15, 20, Apr 20, Sep
    26; 1787: HAY, Aug 14, 21; 1788: DL, May 6
Shepherd's Whim (dance), 1774: HAY, Aug 10
Shepherdess and Faux Aveugle (dance), 1764: HAY, Jul 30, Aug 3, 6, Sep 11
Shepherdess of Cheapside, The. See Cobb, James.
Shepherdess of the Alps, The. See Dibdin, Charles.
Shepherdesses (dance), 1764: DL, Jan 13, 19, Mar 15, 19, 29, Apr 10
Shepherds, I have lost my love (song), 1784: DL, May 18
Shepherds, two (musicians), 1732: LIF, Feb 25
Shepherds' Dance (dance), 1733: LIF/CG, Apr 30, GF, May 14; 1734: CG, May 8;
    1745: DL, Jan 26, 29, Feb 2, 4, 13, 14, Mar 4; 1746: DL, Mar 10; 1748: DL,
    Apr 15; 1751: CG, May 1; 1752: CG, Apr 15; 1787: HAY, May 23
Shepherds' Holiday (dance), 1729: GF, Nov 25, Dec 2, 10, 11, 18, 19, 20, 31;
    1730: GF, Jan 6, 13, Mar 17, 19, Apr 10, 24, Jun 3, 12, 30; 1754: DL, Oct 8,
    12, 15, 29, Nov 7, 12, Dec 4; 1755: DL, Feb 17, 20; 1759: DL, Oct 6, 17, Nov
    13, 16, 30, Dec 20
Shepherds' Music (music), 1714: DL, Jul 2, Dec 20; 1719: DL, Jun 2; 1720: DL,
    Feb 29, Jun 7, Oct 19; 1722: DL, Oct 29; 1725: DL, May 17, Oct 29
Shepley, W (spectator), 1660: VERE/RED, Nov 20; 1661: VERE, Mar 28
Sheppard, James (architect), 1731: LIF, Jan 16
Shepperson and Reynolds (publishers), 1794: CG, Feb 5
Sheppey, Thomas (actor), 1659: NONE, Sep 0; 1660: COCKPIT, Aug 18, REDBULL, Nov
    5; 1661: SALSBURY, Feb 23, Mar 1
Sherborn, Mrs (actor), 1777: DL, Mar 1, Sep 23
Sherburn (singer), 1694: NONE, Sep 0; 1696: LIF, Nov 14
Sherburn, Mrs (actor), 1710: DL, Feb 25, GR, Sep 11; 1711: DL, Feb 3, Mar 10,
    May 21, 22, DL/QUEEN, Jun 5, DL, 19, Jul 6, Aug 17, 31, Sep 29, Oct 13, 18,
    29, Nov 10, 12, 23, Dec 13; 1712: DL, Jun 5, 9, 10, 19
Sherburne, Sir Edward
--Troades; or, The Royal Captives, 1678: NONE, Sep 0
Sheridan, Elizabeth (songwriter), 1784: DL, Oct 5; 1787: DL, May 11
Sheridan, Frances, 1763: DL, Dec 10; 1767: DL, Apr 21
--Discovery, The, 1763: DL, Feb 3, 4, 5, 7, 8, 9, 10, 11, 12, 14, 15, 19, 22,
    26, Mar 3, 12, Apr 26; 1767: DL, Apr 21; 1776: DL, Jan 20, 22, 24, 26, 29,
    Feb 7; 1779: DL, Jan 25, Feb 3, 5, 27, Mar 8, Apr 9, Nov 9; 1780: DL, Mar 7,
    Oct 28; 1782: CG, Nov 29, Dec 4, 20; 1783: CG, Jan 10
--Dupe, The, 1763: DL, Dec 6, 9, 10, 12, 13
Sheridan, Richard Brinsley (proprietor, dramatist), 1775: CG, Jan 17, 28, Mar
    18, May 2, Nov 21; 1776: DL, Jan 19, Sep 21, Oct 9, 10, 15, 18, Nov 1, 5, 19,
    23, 29, Dec 14; 1777: DL, Jan 16, CG, Feb 1, DL, 24, CG, Apr 23, DL, May 8,
    9, Oct 9, 22; 1778: DL, Apr 22, Oct 15, Nov 28; 1779: DL, Jan 8, Mar 11, CG,

779

May 6, KING'S, 15, DL, Oct 30, CG, Dec 9; <u>1780</u>: DL, Jan 3, Mar 4, May 24, Sep
19, Dec 19; <u>1781</u>: DL, Jan 29, Nov 27, Dec 13; <u>1782</u>: DL, May 10, Sep 26; <u>1785</u>:
HAY, Sep 2; <u>1788</u>: CG, Mar 28; <u>1789</u>: CG, Apr 14; <u>1791</u>: DLKING'S, Jan 4, Oct 3;
<u>1792</u>: DLKING'S, Jan 30, HAY, Nov 26; <u>1793</u>: DL, Jan 24, CG, Apr 11; <u>1794</u>: CG,
May 9, DL, Jul 2, Sep 30, Oct 2; <u>1795</u>: DL, Feb 26, Apr 24; <u>1796</u>: DL, Jun 9,
HAY, Sep 28, DL, Nov 29; <u>1797</u>: DL, Mar 6, Apr 8; <u>1798</u>: DL, Apr 23, HAY, Aug
23; <u>1799</u>: DL, May 24, Dec 28
--Camp, The (music), <u>1778</u>: DL, Oct 15, 16, 17, 19, 20, 21, 23, 24, 26, 27, 28,
29, 30, 31, Nov 2, 3, 4, 5, 6, 7, 9, 10, 11, 12, 13, 14, 16, 17, 18, 20, 21,
23, 25, 26, 27, 28, Dec 3, 4, 7, 9, 10, 14, 17, 22, 26, 29, 30; <u>1779</u>: DL, Feb
9, 11, 12, 13, 15, 25, Mar 1, 15, Apr 12, 14, May 3, Nov 6, 13, 16, Dec 14,
17, 27; <u>1780</u>: DL, Feb 19, 26, 29, CII, Mar 27, DL, May 10, Oct 17, 23, Nov 8,
13, 25, Dec 23; <u>1781</u>: DL, Jan 22, Apr 16, 24, Sep 25, Oct 9; <u>1783</u>: DL, Mar 6,
13, Apr 23, Nov 20, Dec 11; <u>1784</u>: DL, Apr 30; <u>1800</u>: CG, Apr 22
--Cape St Vincent; or, British Valour Triumphant (entertainment), <u>1794</u>: DL, Jul
2; <u>1797</u>: DL, Mar 6, 7, 9, 11, 14, 16, 20, 23, 27, Apr 17
--Critic, The; or A Tragedy Rehearsed (burlesque), <u>1779</u>: DL, Oct 30, Nov 1, 2,
3, 4, 5, 8, 9, 10, 11, 12, 15, 20, 22, 23, 24, 26, 27, 29, 30, Dec 1, 3, 9,
10, 11, 23, 27; <u>1780</u>: DL, Jan 1, 11, 18, 22, 25, 28, Feb 3, 10, 12, 15, 24,
28, Mar 2, 6, 16, 27, 30, Apr 10, 12, 17, 21, May 1, 11, 15, 18, 27, Oct 5,
19, 25, Nov 6, 14, 21, 24, Dec 11, 13, 15, 21, 29; <u>1781</u>: DL, Jan 9, 12, 23,
26, Mar 8, Apr 17, May 1, 21, Sep 29, Oct 12, 25; <u>1782</u>: DL, Jan 1, Feb 7, Mar
18, Apr 3, May 13, 23, 25, Dec 20; <u>1783</u>: HAY, Aug 29; <u>1785</u>: CG, Feb 17, 21,
DL, 21, Mar 7, 10, 19, Apr 4, Sep 20, Oct 4, 10, 31, Dec 12; <u>1786</u>: DL, Feb
27, May 6, 30, Sep 23, Oct 5, Dec 19; <u>1788</u>: DL, Apr 10, 19, 24, 29, Oct 7,
Nov 8, 14, Dec 18; <u>1789</u>: DL, Jan 20, 24, Feb 3, May 7, 15; <u>1790</u>: DL, Oct 27,
Nov 13, 20, 27, Dec 4, 11, 18; <u>1791</u>: DL, Jan 1, Feb 16, Mar 2, 8, 17, 31, Apr
7, DLKING'S, Oct 3, 31; <u>1792</u>: DLKING'S, Apr 10; <u>1794</u>: DL, Dec 12, 19; <u>1795</u>:
DL, Jan 19; <u>1796</u>: DL, Apr 13; <u>1797</u>: DL, May 12, Jun 1, 9; <u>1798</u>: DL, May 24,
Jun 8; <u>1800</u>: CG, Apr 30
--Duenna, The; or, The Double Elopement (opera), <u>1775</u>: CG, Nov 20, 21, 22, 23,
24, 25, 27, 28, 29, 30, Dec 2, 4, 5, 6, 7, 9, 11, 12, 13, 14, 16, 18, 20, 21,
23; <u>1776</u>: CG, Jan 2, 3, 4, 6, 8, 9, 10, 11, 13, 16, 18, 20, 22, 23, 25, 27,
29, Feb 1, 3, 6, 8, 10, 13, 14, 15, 19, 20, 24, 29, Mar 2, 7, 9, 11, 12, 14,
21, 26, 28, Apr 8, 11, 12, 17, 18, 23, 25, 30, May 2, 9, 16, 20, 23, 27, 30,
Jun 1, Nov 9, 13, 16, 19, 20, 27, 30, Dec 7, 14, 21, 28; <u>1777</u>: CG, Jan 4, 9,
14, 21, 24, 28, Feb 4, 10, 18, Apr 4, 9, 11, 15, May 1, 16, 26, Oct 29, Nov
5, 11, 15, Dec 31; <u>1778</u>: CG, Jan 6, 13, 14, 19, 27, Feb 2, 9, 14, 20, 25, Mar
3, 9, 17, 26, Apr 9, 23, May 4, 25, Oct 23, 29, Nov 5, 11, 14, 18, Dec 5, 15,
29; <u>1779</u>: CG, Jan 16, 28, Feb 4, 18, 25, Apr 15, May 7, KING'S, 15, CG, 24,
Sep 22, 29, Oct 6, 22, 30, Nov 9, 17, 26, Dec 8, 10, 23; <u>1780</u>: CG, Jan 1, Mar
27, Apr 11, May 5, Sep 20, 27, Oct 20, Nov 3, 18, Dec 8, 28; <u>1781</u>: CG, Feb
26, Apr 17, May 4, HAY, Aug 15, CG, Sep 26, Oct 10, 22, Nov 10, 16, Dec 7,
13, 19; <u>1782</u>: CG, Feb 2, 26, Apr 4, 30, May 15, Oct 9, 16, 30, Dec 5; <u>1783</u>:
CG, Feb 18, May 28, Oct 21; <u>1784</u>: CG, Jan 14, 21, Feb 4, 14, Apr 27, Oct 8,
Nov 3; <u>1785</u>: CG, Apr 5, 20, May 17, HAMM, Jul 25, CG, Sep 19, Nov 5, Dec 8,
16; <u>1786</u>: CG, Mar 7, 13, Apr 6, May 2, 8, 16, 29, Jun 5, Oct 2, 9, 27, Dec 8;
<u>1787</u>: CG, Mar 17, Apr 21, 26, May 15, Jun 4, Oct 11, Dec 22; <u>1788</u>: CG, Jan 5,
12, 16, 22, Feb 9, Mar 1, 13, Apr 16, Jun 2, Oct 1, 28, Dec 18; <u>1789</u>: CG, Jan
9, Mar 14, Jun 11, Oct 31, Nov 17; <u>1790</u>: CG, Jan 2, 19, Mar 6, Apr 10, Oct
12, 26; <u>1791</u>: CG, Nov 1, Dec 8, 20, 28; <u>1792</u>: CG, May 17, Sep 19, Dec 22, 29;
<u>1793</u>: CG, Jan 16, Jun 8, Nov 5, Dec 14, 31; <u>1794</u>: CG, Oct 21; <u>1795</u>: CG, Jan
22, DL, May 18; <u>1796</u>: CG, May 23, Sep 14; <u>1797</u>: CG, May 20, 29, Jun 21; <u>1798</u>:
CG, Apr 21, 25; <u>1800</u>: CG, Jun 13
--Glorious First of June, The (with James Cobb) (entertainment), <u>1794</u>: DL, Jun
21, 25, 26, 28, Jul 2, 3, 4, 5, 7, Oct 11, 14, 18; <u>1797</u>: DL, Mar 6
--Pizarro, <u>1780</u>: DL, May 24; <u>1799</u>: DL, May 23, 24, 25, 27, 28, 29, 31, Jun 1,
3, 4, 5, 6, 7, 8, 10, 11, 12, 13, 14, 15, 17, 18, 19, 20, 21, 22, 24, 25, 26,
27, 28, 29, Jul 1, Dec 11, 13, 16, 18, 20, 21, 23, 28, 31; <u>1800</u>: DL, Jan 4,
7, 10, 14, 17, 20, 24, 28, 31, Feb 4, 7, 11, 14, 18, 21, 25, 27, Mar 1, 3,
11, 29, Apr 5, 19, 22, 24, 26, May 17, 20
--Rivals, The, <u>1775</u>: CG, Jan 17, 18, 28, 31, Feb 2, 4, 7, 8, 10, 13, 15, 17,
22, 27, Apr 27, May 2, 3, 8, Nov 1; <u>1776</u>: CG, Apr 30; <u>1777</u>: DL, Jan 16, 17,
21, 27, Feb 7, 15, 22, Mar 10, 11, Apr 3, 9, May 1; <u>1778</u>: DL, Mar 12, May 12,
19, Nov 20; <u>1779</u>: DL, Apr 13, May 5; <u>1780</u>: DL, Feb 5, 22, Apr 22, May 17, Nov
2; <u>1781</u>: DL, Apr 3, May 2; <u>1788</u>: CG, Mar 28, Apr 4, May 2; <u>1789</u>: CG, Apr 14;
<u>1790</u>: DL, Apr 14, 26, May 3, 10, 17, 24, Sep 16, Nov 1, 8, 15, 22, 29, Dec 6,
20; <u>1791</u>: DL, Jan 31, Feb 14, 28, Mar 10, Apr 26, May 24, DLKING'S, Oct 1,
15, 29, Nov 12, Dec 7; <u>1792</u>: DLKING'S, Mar 19, Apr 13, CG, May 2, DLKING'S,
10, CG, 24, HAY, Aug 2, DL, Sep 22, Oct 23, CG, Nov 7; <u>1793</u>: CG, May 2, DL,
13, CG, 31; <u>1794</u>: CG, May 9, DL, Jul 2, Nov 4, 5, 26; <u>1795</u>: DL, Jan 31, Feb
16, Apr 24, May 28, Oct 22, CG, 30, DL, Nov 24; <u>1796</u>: DL, May 3, 24, HAY, Sep

28, DL, Nov 8, Dec 31; 1797: DL, Jan 24, Feb 15, 18, CG, 27, Jun 12, DL, Nov
24, 30; 1798: DL, May 16, CG, 31, HAY, Sep 10, DL, Nov 10; 1799: DL, Jan 9,
Feb 1, Oct 5, Nov 7; 1800: DL, Jan 6, 9, Feb 15, Mar 6, CG, May 20
--Robinson Crusoe; or, Harlequin Friday (pantomime), 1781: DL, Jan 29, 31, Feb
1, 2, 3, 5, 6, 7, 8, 9, 10, 12, 13, 14, 15, 16, 23, 24, 26, 27, Mar 1, 3, 5,
6, 12, 13, 17, 20, 22, 24, 29, Apr 2, 5, 7, 19, 20, May 3, 14, 28, 29, Sep
20, 22, Oct 2, 4, 11, 15, 17, 18, 20, 23, 27, Nov 24, Dec 1, 4, 10, 26, 31;
1782: DL, Feb 7, 12, 18, Mar 4, 11, Apr 1, 11, 25, May 6, 14, 15, 20, Sep 20,
21, 26, Oct 7, 14, 24, 28, Nov 4, 11, 25, Dec 2, 9, 16; 1783: DL, Apr 21, May
8, Sep 23, Oct 6, 9, 30; 1785: HAMM, Jul 27; 1786: HAMM, Jul 10; 1788: DL,
Dec 20, 23, 29; 1789: DL, Jan 1, 5, 8, 10, 12, 15, 19, 20, 26, Feb 2, 18;
1796: DL, Dec 26, 27, 28, 29, 30, 31; 1797: DL, Jan 2, 3, 4, 5, 6, 7, 9, 13,
16, 20, 23, 26, 31, Feb 6; 1799: DL, May 1
--St Patrick's Day; or, The Scheming Lieutenant, 1775: CG, May 2, 6, 9, 15, 25,
Jun 1, Sep 25, Oct 2, 9, 11, 14, 19, Nov 8, 23; 1776: CG, Apr 23, 26, May 14,
17; 1777: CG, Nov 3, 5, 8, 11, Dec 10; 1778: CG, Jan 23, Feb 20, May 6, Dec
19; 1779: CG, Feb 11; 1780: CG, Nov 22, 29, Dec 21, 27; 1781: CG, Mar 26, May
26; 1782: CG, Oct 15, 25, 30, Nov 13, 29; 1783: CG, Oct 28, Nov 6; 1784: CG,
Apr 30, Oct 12, 22, Dec 8; 1785: CG, Sep 19; 1786: CG, Mar 16; 1788: CG, Feb
12; 1796: CG, Apr 1, May 4
--School for Scandal, The, 1777: DL, May 8, 9, 10, 12, 13, 14, 16, 19, 20, 21,
22, 23, 24, 26, 27, 29, 31, Jun 3, 5, 7, Oct 22, 24, 25, 29, Nov 1, 6, 12,
15, 19, 21, 22, 26, 28, Dec 1, 5, 9, 12, 16, 17, 23; 1778: DL, Jan 7, 9, 13,
15, 19, 28, Feb 3, 4, 13, 16, 18, 20, 23, 26, Mar 3, 7, 10, 14, 19, 23, 26,
28, Apr 4, 22, 24, 29, May 7, 20, 28, Oct 6, 10, 22, 29, Nov 5, 12, 19, 24,
Dec 3, 10, 17, 31; 1779: DL, Jan 5, 7, 14, 21, 28, Feb 4, 11, 18, 25, Mar 4,
9, 18, Apr 8, 15, 22, 29, 30, May 13, 20, 24, Jun 3, Sep 21, Oct 14, 22, Nov
6, 18, 25, Dec 22; 1780: DL, Jan 15, 27, Feb 14, 29, Mar 9, 28, Apr 5, 20,
May 1, 8, 15, 19, Oct 14, 21, Nov 7, 30, Dec 14, 22; 1781: DL, Jan 5, 19, Feb
5, 13, 26, Mar 5, 26, Apr 2, 7, 28, May 28, Sep 27, Oct 9, 20, Nov 1, 14, 26,
Dec 5, 31; 1782: DL, Jan 31, Feb 21, Mar 19, 23, Apr 3, 16, 26, May 17, Sep
26, Oct 22, 24, Nov 15, Dec 10; 1783: DL, Jan 7, 22, Apr 3, 25, May 15; 1784:
DL, Apr 19, Oct 18, Nov 8, 30, Dec 13; 1785: DL, Jan 31, Feb 14, Mar 14, 30,
May 2, 30, HAY, Sep 2, DL, 20, Dec 3, 19; 1786: DL, Jan 11, Feb 24, Apr 24,
May 5, 24, Sep 16, Oct 14, Nov 20; 1787: DL, Jan 4, 19, 31, Feb 12, 26, RLSN,
Mar 26, DL, Apr 9, May 2, 14, Sep 18, Oct 13, Nov 1, Dec 4; 1788: DL, Jan 2,
28, Feb 11, Apr 2, 23, Jun 9, HAY, Aug 25; 1790: DL, Oct 23, Nov 10, 18, Dec
2, 9, 16, 23, 30; 1791: DL, Feb 9, 17, Mar 3, 7, 31, Apr 7, DLKING'S, Sep 24,
27, Oct 11, 26, Nov 23, Dec 3, 10; 1792: DLKING'S, Feb 15, Mar 3, DL, Sep 15,
Oct 30, Nov 13, Dec 5, 18; 1793: DL, Jan 17, Feb 18, May 10, Jun 4; 1794:
HAMM, Mar 24, DL, Nov 8, 11, 12, 19, Dec 3; 1795: DL, Jan 21, 22, 28, Feb 10,
17, Sep 26, Oct 15, 28; 1796: DL, Jan 20, Mar 31, Apr 2, 4, Jun 3, Sep 27,
Nov 3, Dec 14; 1797: DL, Jan 19, Feb 9, 25, Mar 21, Apr 8, May 29, Jun 5, 9,
Sep 19, Oct 17; 1798: CG, Mar 31, Apr 27, DL, May 18; 1799: DL, Jan 5, 8, 15,
Feb 7, Apr 10; 1800: DL, Jan 2, Feb 12, May 16, 27, Jun 10, HAY, Aug 12
--Trip to Scarborough, A, 1777: DL, Feb 24, 25, 27, Mar 1, 4, 6, 8, 18, 22, Apr
2, 4, 8, May 12; 1778: DL, Dec 21; 1779: DL, Jan 13, Mar 11, Nov 18, 30;
1780: DL, Jan 10, 21, Feb 24, Apr 19, Nov 17; 1781: DL, Feb 2, Mar 3, Oct 25;
1782: DL, Feb 14, Oct 8; 1783: DL, May 16, Nov 21; 1784: DL, Mar 29, May 25;
1785: DL, Jan 22; 1786: DL, Jan 9, 10, 13, 31, Mar 16, May 8, 22, Sep 26, Oct
31, Nov 28, Dec 29; 1787: DL, Jan 6, 20, May 16, Dec 28; 1788: DL, Apr 16,
Jun 7, Sep 23, Oct 6, Nov 20; 1789: DL, Apr 15, May 2, 25; 1790: DL, Feb 15,
Apr 20, May 21, Oct 18, Dec 17; 1791: DL, Jan 17, Feb 23, Apr 14, DLKING'S,
Oct 10, Dec 20; 1792: DLKING'S, May 3; 1793: DL, Apr 17, May 22; 1794: DL,
Dec 3, 5, 17; 1795: DL, Jan 6, Apr 28, Nov 10, Dec 26; 1796: DL, Feb 18, Mar
5, 17, Apr 1, Oct 28, Dec 17; 1797: DL, May 23; 1798: DL, Jan 23, Feb 27;
1799: DL, Feb 23, 25, Jul 1; 1800: DL, Jan 18, Feb 19, Apr 18, Jun 13
--Wonders of Derbyshire, The; or, Harlequin in the Peak, 1779: DL, Jan 5, 8, 9,
11, 12, 13, 15, 16, 18, 19, 20, 21, 22, 23, 25, 26, 27, 28, 29, Feb 1, 2, 3,
4, 5, 6, 16, 18, 22, 23, 27, Mar 2, 6, 8, 9, Apr 8, 15, Sep 30, Oct 7, 28,
Nov 15, Dec 7, 16, 29
Sheridan, Thomas (actor, playwright), 1743: DL, Oct 4; 1744: CG, Mar 31, Apr 5,
10, 13, 18, May 1, DL, Oct 20, 23, Nov 5, Dec 13; 1745: DL, Mar 5, 18, Apr
25, 30; 1746: GF, Jan 21, BFYB, Aug 25; 1747: CG, Apr 15; 1748: DL, Apr 2;
1754: CG, Oct 24, 26, 28, 30, Nov 4, 7, 16, 20, 23, 27, Dec 10; 1755: CG, Jan
7, 10, 14, 28, Feb 4, 13, 20, Mar 6, 22; 1758: DL, Oct 27, CG, Nov 3; 1759:
DL, Oct 8; 1760: CG, Feb 18, DL, Oct 9, 18, 22, Nov 20, 27, Dec 17, 19; 1761:
DL, Jan 3, Mar 28, Apr 21, 23, 29, CG, Dec 22; 1763: DL, Feb 3, Mar 12; 1768:
CG, Apr 20; 1769: HAY, Feb 2, 23, Aug 7, 14, 30, Sep 1, 11; 1770: DL, May 14,
HAY, 23, Jul 9, Aug 8, 22, Sep 3; 1773: CG, Oct 23; 1775: CG, Oct 2, 21, 28,
Nov 4, 10, Dec 1, 8, 29; 1776: CG, Jan 1, Mar 5; 1778: DL, Dec 19
--Brave Irishman, The; or, Captain O'Blunder, 1746: GF, Jan 31, BFYB, Aug 25;

781

1755: CG, Mar 22; 1770: DL, May 14; 1779: HAY, May 10
--Irishman in London, The, 1755: CG, Mar 22
Sherman (actor), 1705: DL, Jun 12
Sherman (beneficiary), 1749: HAY, Jun 1
Sherman (boxkeeper), 1710: DL, May 18
Sherman, Miss (actor), 1773: CG, Oct 9, Nov 4, 8; 1774: CG, Mar 10, 14, Apr 23,
    May 6, Oct 20, 31, Dec 26
Sherno delli astri egioco (song), 1753: KING'S, Apr 30
Sherrard St, 1778: KING'S, Apr 9; 1780: KING'S, May 25; 1787: KING'S, Mar 15;
    1795: KING'S, May 28
Sherrard. See Sharratt.
Sherratt. See Sharratt.
Sherry, Katharine (actor), 1772: DL, Apr 25, Jun 9; 1773: DL, Feb 2, May 6, Sep
    23, 30, Oct 8, 26, Nov 26, Dec 3; 1774: DL, Jan 28, Feb 2, Mar 12, 26, Apr
    29, Sep 27, Oct 13, 14, Nov 3, 11, 24, Dec 17; 1775: DL, Mar 23, May 6, Oct
    7, 11, 20, 25, 26, 28, Nov 1, 7, Dec 7; 1776: DL, Jan 13, Apr 8, May 13, HAY,
    20, 22, 28, Jun 19, Jul 8, Aug 19, Sep 2, DL, Oct 18, 22, 26, 30, Nov 5, 25,
    29, Dec 31; 1777: DL, Apr 22, May 8, Sep 27, Oct 22, 31, Nov 29; 1778: DL,
    Jan 5, 23, Feb 2, Mar 5, Apr 20, May 4, HAY, 18, Jul 30, DL, Sep 24, Oct 6,
    8, 13, 19, Nov 18, Dec 8; 1779: DL, Feb 20, Mar 16, 22, May 1, HAY, 31, Jun
    18, Jul 16, 31, Aug 9, DL, Sep 21, 30, Oct 2, 12, 19, Nov 5, 11; 1780: DL,
    Jan 24, Apr 17, 18, 26, May 24, HAY, Jul 10, 15, 24, Aug 17, DL, Oct 12, 14,
    25, 26, 31, Dec 7, 15, 21, 26; 1781: DL, Jan 9, Feb 12, 16, Mar 27, Apr 17,
    HAY, Jun 16, Jul 18, 23, Aug 7, DL, Sep 27, Oct 2, 4, 13, 30, Nov 5, 6; 1782:
    DL, Jan 26, May 18, HAY, Jun 4, 15, 29, Jul 16, Aug 9, DL, Sep 18, 26
Sherwin, Master (actor), 1736: HAY, Apr 29, May 5
Sherwin's Booth, 1726: BFS, Aug 24
Sherwood (actor), 1671: LIF, Mar 6, 15; 1673: DG, Mar 12
Sherwood (house servant), 1797: DL, Jun 13; 1798: DL, Jun 9; 1799: DL, Jul 2;
    1800: DL, Jun 13
Shetterel. See Shatterel.
Sheward, Mrs (taverner), 1756: DL, Jan 22
Shield, William (composer), 1778: DL, May 1, HAY, Aug 17; 1779: CG, Apr 27, Sep
    27; 1780: CG, Feb 2, Apr 25, HAY, Sep 5, CG, Oct 30; 1781: DL, Apr 23, CG,
    Oct 27, DL, Nov 10; 1782: CG, Mar 16, DL, Apr 24, CG, Nov 25, Dec 31; 1783:
    CG, Jan 18, Apr 7, Nov 4, 8, Dec 23; 1784: DL, Jan 7, CG, 29, Mar 20, Apr 17,
    May 7, HAY, Aug 2, CG, Sep 20, DL, 23, CG, Oct 12, Nov 16, Dec 14, 27; 1785:
    CG, Apr 1, 12, May 12, HAMM, Jul 25, CG, Oct 13, 17, Nov 10, Dec 20; 1786:
    CG, Feb 17, May 2, 11, HAMM, Jul 7, 10, CG, Oct 16, Dec 1, 26; 1787: CG, Mar
    12, Apr 10, 24, DL, May 4, CG, Oct 31, Nov 5, DL, Dec 26; 1788: CG, Apr 1,
    May 22, Nov 1, 6, 10, Dec 13, 26; 1789: CG, May 6, 20, DL, Jun 3, CG, Sep 28,
    Nov 24, Dec 21; 1790: CG, Mar 8, HAY, Apr 29, CG, May 6, Jun 3, Oct 4, 19,
    Nov 4, 15, Dec 20; 1791: CG, Feb 11, 26, May 2, 5, 18, 20, Jun 6, Oct 3, 20,
    Dec 10; 1792: CG, Apr 12, Oct 19, 25, Nov 3, Dec 20; 1793: CG, Feb 25, Mar
    11, 23, May 1, 3, 11, Sep 16, Oct 2, 9, Nov 18, Dec 7, 19; 1794: CG, Feb 6,
    22, Apr 10, May 1, 2, 9, 16, 26, Sep 17, 22, 24, 26, 29, Oct 14, 30, Nov 17,
    Dec 26; 1795: CG, Jan 31, HAY, Mar 4, CG, 16, Apr 23, 24, 28, May 1, 6, 16,
    19, Jun 16, Sep 28, Oct 19, Nov 9, 16, 18; 1796: CG, Feb 2, Mar 14, 15, Apr
    1, 9, 15, May 10, 16, Sep 12, Oct 5, 7, 24, Nov 19; 1797: CG, Apr 8, May 2,
    11, 18, 20, 31, DL, Jun 6, CG, Sep 25, Oct 18, Dec 16; 1798: CG, Apr 21, DL,
    May 23, CG, 28, HAY, Aug 28, CG, Sep 17; 1799: CG, Apr 6, May 13; 1800: CG,
    Apr 15, May 22, DL, 29
Shields (house servant), 1767: CG, Dec 28
Ship and Anchor Tavern, 1754: DL, Apr 4
Ship Tavern, 1734: GR, Nov 4; 1742: DL, Apr 21; 1746: GF, Mar 11; 1750: DL, Nov
    28; 1751: DL, Apr 23; 1752: DL, Dec 20; 1755: DL, Nov 18; 1767: CG, Oct 17;
    1776: CHR, Oct 7, 18; 1789: WHF, Nov 9
Shipman, Thomas
--Henry III of France Stabbed by a Fryer, 1672: LIF, Mar 0, NONE, Sep 0
Shipton, John (trustee), 1717: SH, Feb 27
Shipwreck, The. See Mackenzie, Henry; Arnold, Samuel James.
Shipwreck, The; or, French Ingratitude. See Byrn, James.
Shipwreck, The; or, Perseus and Andromeda (entertainment), 1717: DL, Apr 2, 6,
    9; 1718: DL, Nov 15
Shipwreck, The; or, The Distressed Lovers (dance), 1756: DL, Oct 13
Shipwreck, The; or, Walking Statue (interlude), 1789: WHF, Nov 11
Shipwrecked Lovers, The; or, Friendly Perfidy Punished (play, anon), 1759: BFY,
    Sep 3, BF, 4, 5
Shipwrecked Sailors (song), 1795: HAY, Mar 4, DL, May 19
Shireborn. See Sherburn.
Shireburn, Frances (actor), 1727: DL, Apr 18, May 3, BF, Aug 21, DL, Oct 12,
    Dec 7; 1728: DL, Mar 30, May 14, 17, 20, BFHM, Aug 24, DL, Oct 3, 5, 23, 28,

782

Nov 8, 15; <u>1729</u>: DL, Jan 11, Feb 3, 6, May 7, 12, 14, Jun 13, Jul 18, 25,
BFF, Aug 23, DL, Sep 23, 27, Oct 14, 22, Nov 3, 6, Dec 3, 5, 10, 17; <u>1730</u>:
DL, Mar 30, Apr 10, 14, 20, May 11, Sep 15, 19, 29, Oct 20, Nov 25, 28, 30;
<u>1731</u>: DL, Jan 20, Feb 8, Mar 29, Apr 19, May 17, 19, Jun 11, Jul 6, 23, Sep
21, 30, Oct 9, 30, Nov 1, 23, 25; <u>1732</u>: DL, Feb 11, Mar 21, 23, Apr 1, 21,
27, 28, May 3, 4, 8, Oct 10, Nov 7, 14, 18, 20, Dec 6, 9, 11, 18; <u>1733</u>: DL,
Jan 10, 26, Mar 28, Apr 4, 19, 30, May 5, 14, CG, Jul 6, DL/HAY, Oct 3, 6,
10, 12, 15, 22, 25, Nov 9, 23, Dec 5, 12, 22, HAY, 26; <u>1734</u>: DL/HAY, Feb 22,
Mar 25, 28, 30, Apr 17, 18, DL, 22, DL/HAY, 26, 30, HAY, Jun 3, 14, 19, 24,
28, Jul 5, 19, Aug 7, LIF, 20, DL, Sep 12, 19, 24, 26, 28, Oct 5, 8, 9, 12,
23, 25, Nov 2, 16, 22, Dec 6, 16; <u>1735</u>: DL, Jan 20, 22, 23, 25
Shirley (beneficiary), <u>1784</u>: CG, May 29
Shirley (dancer), <u>1717</u>: DL, Nov 7; <u>1718</u>: DL, May 27
Shirley, George (actor), <u>1671</u>: BRIDGES, Jun 0, Dec 7; <u>1674</u>: LIF, Mar 0
Shirley, James, <u>1660</u>: NONE, May 29, Sep 0; <u>1662</u>: VERE, Mar 11; <u>1666</u>: NONE, Sep
0; <u>1668</u>: BRIDGES, Jul 11, LIF, Aug 20; <u>1669</u>: BRIDGES, Jan 12; <u>1692</u>: DL, Mar
0; <u>1715</u>: LIF, Feb 3; <u>1757</u>: DL, Dec 5, 22; <u>1772</u>: DL, Oct 30; <u>1786</u>: CG, Apr 24;
<u>1790</u>: CG, Jan 22
--Andromana; or, The Merchant's Wife, <u>1659</u>: NONE, Sep 0; <u>1670</u>: NONE, Sep 0
--Ball, The; or, French Dancing Master, <u>1662</u>: VERE, Mar 11
--Bird in a Cage, The, <u>1668</u>: LIF, Aug 20
--Brothers, The, <u>1662</u>: VERE, Jul 7; <u>1663</u>: IT, Nov 2; <u>1669</u>: BRIDGES, Jan 12
--Cardinal, The, <u>1662</u>: VERE, Jul 23, ATCOURT, Oct 2; <u>1667</u>: LIF, Feb 0, BRIDGES,
Aug 24; <u>1668</u>: BRIDGES, Apr 27; <u>1669</u>: BRIDGES, Jan 12
--Chabot Admiral of France, <u>1668</u>: LIF, Aug 20
--Changes, The; or, Love in a Maze, <u>1662</u>: VERE, May 17, 22; <u>1663</u>: BRIDGES, Jun
10; <u>1665</u>: IT, Feb 2; <u>1667</u>: BRIDGES, May 1; <u>1668</u>: BRIDGES, Feb 7, Apr 28;
<u>1674</u>: DL, May 11, Nov 24
--Constant Maid, The, <u>1660</u>: NONE, Sep 0; <u>1666</u>: NONE, Sep 0
--Court Secret, The, <u>1664</u>: BRIDGES, Aug 18
--Doubtful Heir, The, <u>1669</u>: BRIDGES, Jan 12
--Gamester, The, <u>1670</u>: LIF, Mar 10
--Gentleman of Venice, The, <u>1670</u>: LIF, Jan 7
--Grateful Servant, The, <u>1666</u>: NONE, Sep 0; <u>1669</u>: LIF, Feb 20
--Hyde Park, <u>1668</u>: BRIDGES, Jul 11, 14
--Impostor, The, <u>1669</u>: BRIDGES, Jan 12
--Love Tricks; or, The School of Compliments, <u>1666</u>: NONE, Sep 0; <u>1667</u>: ATCOURT,
May 9, LIF, Aug 5; <u>1668</u>: LIF, Jan 7; <u>1671</u>: LIF, Feb 17
--Love's Cruelty, <u>1660</u>: REDBULL, Aug 14, VERE, Nov 15; <u>1662</u>: VERE, Feb 6; <u>1667</u>:
BRIDGES, Dec 30; <u>1668</u>: BRIDGES, Apr 14
--Opportunity, The, <u>1660</u>: VERE, Nov 26
--Rosania; or, Love's Victory, <u>1669</u>: BRIDGES, Jan 12
--Sisters, The, <u>1668</u>: NONE, Sep 0; <u>1669</u>: BRIDGES, Jan 12
--Traitor, The, <u>1660</u>: REDBULL, Aug 14, Nov 6, VERE, 22; <u>1661</u>: VERE, Oct 10;
<u>1665</u>: BRIDGES, Jan 13; <u>1667</u>: BRIDGES, Oct 2; <u>1674</u>: DL, Oct 20; <u>1692</u>: DL, Mar
0
--Wedding, The, <u>1660</u>: REDBULL, Aug 14; <u>1661</u>: VERE, Jan 9
--Witty Fair One, The, <u>1666</u>: NONE, Sep 0
--Young Admiral, The, <u>1661</u>: LIF, Jul 4, 8, NONE, 13; <u>1662</u>: ATCOURT, Nov 20
Shirley, Mrs (actor), <u>1778</u>: HAY, Dec 28
Shirley, Robert (critic), <u>1696</u>: NONE, Jan 21; <u>1697</u>: LIF, Mar 13
Shirley, William, <u>1739</u>: CG, Jan 17; <u>1745</u>: DL, Apr 15; <u>1750</u>: DL, Jan 6; <u>1758</u>:
DL, Apr 14; <u>1777</u>: DL, Dec 18
--Edward the Black Prince; or, The Battle of Poictiers, <u>1750</u>: DL, Jan 6, 8, 9,
10, 12, 13, 15, 16, 17; <u>1778</u>: CG, May 15; <u>1783</u>: DL, Oct 20, 22, 25, 29, Dec
1, 30; <u>1784</u>: DL, Jan 9, Mar 22, May 19; <u>1796</u>: ROY, Mar 7
--King Pepin's Campaign, <u>1745</u>: DL, Apr 15, 16, 19
--Parracide, The; or, Innocence in Distress, <u>1739</u>: CG, Jan 17, 19
--Roman Sacrifice, The, <u>1777</u>: DL, Dec 18, 19, 20, 22
Shiroli. See Scheroli.
Shlagel, Frederick (beneficiary), <u>1749</u>: HAY, Apr 19
Shoe Lane, <u>1660</u>: NONE, Sep 0; <u>1784</u>: HAY, Feb 9
Shoemaker (dance), <u>1763</u>: DL, May 31; <u>1771</u>: HAY, May 17, 20, 22, 23, Jun 5, 7,
10, Aug 26
Shoemaker's a Gentleman, A. See Rowley, William.
Sholet, Mlle (dancer), <u>1771</u>: KING'S, Jun 1
Shoneman, Conrado (beneficiary), <u>1716</u>: HIC, Dec 20
Shooting a Deserter (entertainment), <u>1799</u>: DL, Apr 25
Shore, John (musician), <u>1693</u>: ATCOURT, May 0; <u>1697</u>: RICHMOND, Sep 20, 27; <u>1698</u>:
ROBERTS', Mar 23; <u>1699</u>: YB, Jan 4
Shore, Richard (booth holder), <u>1681</u>: BF, Aug 0
Shore, Serjeant (trumpeter), <u>1752</u>: DL, Dec 2

783

Short (actor), 1694: NONE, Sep 0
Short (house servant), 1731: LIF, May 24; 1732: LIF, May 9; 1733: LIF/CG, May
    8; 1735: CG, May 8; 1736: CG, May 6; 1737: CG, Apr 25; 1738: CG, Apr 29;
    1739: CG, Nov 7; 1744: CG, Apr 9
Short (singer), 1704: LIF, Jun 30, Jul 10, 24; 1705: LIF, Jan 25
Short (singer), 1776: DL, Nov 25
Short (supernumerary), 1776: DL, Feb 24, May 13, Jun 8
Short Notice of Farewells (entertainment), 1797: DL, May 1
Short, Miss (actor), 1731: LIF, May 24; 1741: CG, Sep 25, Oct 24, Nov 9, 27;
    1742: CG, Jan 8, May 11, Nov 30, Dec 21, 28
Short's scholar (musician), 1724: LIF, Apr 30
Shorter (painter), 1772: DL, Mar 14
Shorter, Sir John (Lord Mayor), 1687: CITY, Oct 29
Shotter (house servant), 1796: CG, May 21; 1797: CG, Jun 2; 1798: CG, May 18;
    1799: CG, May 17; 1800: CG, Jun 4
Shotter, Mrs (house servant), 1795: CG, Jun 17
Should I not lead a happy life (song), 1696: LIF, Jun 0
Shove (stationer), 1770: CG, May 29
Showers (musician), 1691: SH, Nov 23
Shrewsbury, Duchess of, 1720: KING'S, Apr 26
Shrewsbury, Lord. See Talbot, Francis.
Shropshire (brush merchant), 1768: CG, May 26; 1771: CG, Dec 12; 1772: CG, Oct
    26; 1773: CG, Nov 2; 1774: CG, Apr 14
Shudale (tailor), 1750: CG, Mar 13
Shuman (musician), 1757: HAY, Sep 12
Shurley. See Shirley.
Shuter (doorkeeper), 1777: CG, May 24; 1778: CG, May 21; 1779: CG, May 19;
    1780: CG, May 26; 1781: CG, May 26; 1782: CG, May 29; 1783: CG, Jun 4; 1784:
    CG, May 29; 1786: CG, Jun 1; 1787: CG, May 31; 1788: CG, May 31; 1789: CG,
    Jun 5; 1790: CG, May 29; 1791: CG, Jun 2; 1792: CG, May 25; 1794: CG, Jun 16
Shuter, Edward (actor, author), 1745: CG, Apr 15, DL, Jun 5; 1746: CG, Feb 5,
    Jun 13, 27, GF, Nov 6, 7, 13, 14, 18, 19, 21, 26, 27, 28, Dec 2, 3, 5, 9, 10,
    11, 12, 17, 18, 22, 31; 1747: GF, Jan 2, 5, 9, 16, 26, Feb 2, 3, 5, Mar 2, 5,
    9, 10, 12, 17, 19, 24, HAY, Apr 22, DL, Oct 29, Nov 2, 10, 25, Dec 5; 1748:
    DL, Jan 12, 18, 22; 1749: HAY, Apr 3, May 15, BFY, Aug 23, DL, Sep 19, Oct
    19, Nov 8, 27, Dec 9, 12, 20, 26, 28, 30; 1750: DL, Jan 1, 18, 22, 27, 29,
    Feb 10, 22, Mar 13, 17, Apr 9, 19, 30, May 10, HAY, Jul 26, DL, Sep 8, 11,
    13, 18, 21, 22, Oct 15, 16, 22, 26, 29, 30, Nov 1, 3, 7, 13, 14, 15, 24, Dec
    14, 26, 31; 1751: DL, Jan 3, 7, 12, 18, 21, 23, Feb 2, 14, Mar 12, 14, 16,
    Apr 22, 23, 25, 29, May 1, 18, Sep 10, 12, 13, 14, 17, 18, 21, 24, Oct 2, 9,
    11, 16, 22, 29, Nov 2, 7, 16, 29, Dec 14, 26; 1752: DL, Jan 1, 6, 11, 28, Mar
    10, Apr 3, 6, 10, 27, Sep 16, 19, 26, 28, 30, Oct 3, 5, 10, 11, 12, 16, 19,
    21, 23, 26, Nov 3, 22, 27, 30, Dec 7, 8, 18, 19, 20, 29; 1753: DL, Jan 1, 8,
    13, 15, 17, 22, Feb 6, 19, Mar 22, Apr 3, 12, 14, 25, 30, May 2, 21, CG, Sep
    17, 26, Oct 1, 8, 22, 30, Nov 2, 12, 26, Dec 26; 1754: CG, Feb 12, Mar 18,
    25, 28, Apr 2, 6, 17, May 17, DL, Jul 2, CG, Sep 18, 23, 25, 30, Oct 2, 7,
    11, 14, 15, 17, 23, 24, 29, 31, Nov 1, 6, Dec 10, 30; 1755: CG, Jan 8, 10,
    14, Feb 8, Mar 18, Apr 2, 4, 7, 10, 11, 14, 16, 18, May 5, 12, 15, Oct 1, 3,
    6, 8, 10, 11, 14, 16, 21, 22, 23, 24, 27, 31, Nov 3, 7, 12, 14, 21, Dec 5;
    1756: CG, Feb 3, 19, 21, 26, Mar 22, 25, 29, 30, Apr 3, 6, 23, 29, May 10,
    11, 17, 20, Sep 20, 22, 24, 27, 29, Oct 1, 6, 8, 11, 14, 15, 16, 18, 21, 22,
    26, Nov 13, 16, 17, 22, Dec 1, 10, 17, 20; 1757: CG, Jan 27, 28, Feb 16, 19,
    Mar 21, 26, Apr 18, 27, May 4, 25, BF, Sep 3, CG, 14, 21, 23, 26, 28, 30, Oct
    5, 8, 10, 12, 13, 17, 19, 21, 22, 28, Nov 1, 5, 23, 29, Dec 5, 8, 14; 1758:
    CG, Jan 28, Feb 1, 14, 21, Mar 9, 11, 13, 14, 28, 29, Apr 3, 11, May 10,
    BFYS, Sep 6, CG, 18, 20, 22, 25, 27, 29, Oct 2, 4, 9, 13, 14, 16, 18, 20, 24,
    25, 26, 30, Nov 2, 7, 9, 16, 18, 21, 23, Dec 9; 1759: CG, Jan 4, Feb 1, Mar
    3, 5, 19, 22, 24, 26, 27, Apr 7, 20, 21, 23, May 3, 5, 7, 11, 12, 17, 23,
    BFS, Sep 3, CG, 24, 26, 28, Oct 1, 3, 8, 11, 12, 13, 15, 22, 30, Nov 28, 30,
    Dec 8, 10, 11, 14, 17, 18, 20, 22, 28; 1760: CG, Jan 4, 9, 14, 16, 31, Feb
    14, 28, Mar 6, 17, 18, 20, 24, Apr 16, 18, 24, 29, May 2, 7, 8, 12, 23, BFS,
    Sep 3, 4, SF, 13, CG, 22, Oct 1, 2, 6, 8, 10, 11, 13, 14, 17, 20, 21, Nov 18,
    25, 29, Dec 19, 22; 1761: CG, Jan 6, 7, 10, Feb 17, Mar 5, 25, 26, DL, 26,
    CG, 26, 30, Apr 1, 2, 13, 16, 17, 20, 22, 27, May 4, 8, 11, BFG, Sep 1, CG,
    9, 11, 14, 16, 18, 21, 23, 25, 26, Oct 2, 3, 7, 10, 12, 13, 14, 17, 24, 26,
    31, Nov 6, 9, 13, Dec 11; 1762: CG, Jan 12, 28, Feb 15, 22, Mar 20, 22, 29,
    30, Apr 16, 19, 21, 24, 27, 28, 30, May 3, 11, 13, Sep 20, 24, 27, 29, 30,
    Oct 1, 2, 5, 11, 14, 16, 20, 25, 28, Nov 3, 8, 12, 15, 16, 29, Dec 8, 27;
    1763: CG, Jan 8, 14, 26, Feb 1, 14, Mar 21, Apr 5, 12, 15, 18, 25, 30, May 9,
    16, 18, Sep 19, 23, 26, 28, 30, Oct 5, 7, 8, 10, 11, 12, 14, 15, 18, 19, 21,
    22, 24, 26, Nov 3, 10, 15, 18, 22, 23, 26; 1764: CG, Jan 5, 9, 16, 26, Feb 1,
    9, 11, 15, 22, Mar 20, 27, 29, Apr 10, 14, 27, 28, May 3, 7, 11, 18, Sep 17,

19, 21, 24, 26, 28, Oct 1, 3, 5, 10, 11, 12, 16, 17, 18, 20, 23, 24, 25, 26,
29, Nov 1, 6, 7, 8, 15, 16, 29, 30, Dec 12, 29; 1765: CG, Jan 8, 10, 31, Feb
18, Mar 18, Apr 9, 11, DL, 15, CG, 19, 24, May 2, 15, HAY, Jun 10, Jul 8, 15,
17, 29, 31, Aug 8, 21, 30, CG, Sep 16, 18, 20, 23, 25, 27, Oct 2, 3, 4, 5, 8,
10, 11, 12, 15, 17, 26, 30, 31, Nov 12, 13, 19, 20, 21, 22, 27, 28, Dec 3, 6,
12, 26; 1766: CG, Jan 9, Feb 5, 6, Mar 15, 18, 22, Apr 2, 7, 15, 19, 21, 25,
26, May 13, 16, HAY, Jun 18, Jul 1, 8, 15, 18, 23, 31, KING'S, Aug 13, 18,
20, HAY, 21, KING'S, 27, 29, HAY, Sep 2, KING'S, 9, 12, 13, CG, 22, Oct 6, 8,
10, 14, 15, 16, 18, 22, 23, 25, 28, 30, Nov 1, 8, 11, 14, Dec 3, 6, 9, 16,
20, 23, 30; 1767: CG, Jan 1, 10, 23, 28, 29, 31, Feb 20, 21, 28, Mar 24, Apr
6, DL, 20, 21, CG, May 5, 15, 19, DL, 27, HAY, 29, Jun 4, 5, 8, CG, 9, HAY,
10, 7, 10, CG, 14, 17, 18, 19, 21, 22, 26, Oct 5, 6, 8, 13, 16, 22, 27, Nov
17, DL, 20, CG, 27, Dec 14, 26; 1768: DL, Jan 11, CG, 20, 29, DL, Feb 4, CG,
5, DL, 12, CG, 25, DL, Mar 10, CG, 21, Apr 12, DL, 16, CG, 20, 25, 27, 29,
30, May 5, DL, 5, CG, 11, 24, 27, 30, Sep 19, 21, 23, 24, 27, 29, 30, Oct 4,
7, 10, 12, 14, 15, Nov 4, 16, 25, Dec 16; 1769: CG, Jan 2, 14, 25, Mar 4, 11,
16, 29, Apr 1, 7, 12, 24, May 1, 16, 17, Sep 18, 20, 22, 25, 27, 29, Oct 2,
3, 5, 6, 7, 17, 27, Nov 3, 11, 17, 27, 29, Dec 22, 29; 1770: CG, Jan 3, 5,
Feb 23, Mar 17, 20, 26, 27, 29, Apr 5, 20, 25, May 1, 7, 9, 10, 14, 19, Sep
26, 28, Oct 2, 12, 13, 19, 25, 27, Nov 2, 8, 16, 17, 22, Dec 3, 13, 21; 1771:
CG, Jan 25, 26, Mar 18, Apr 2, 3, 6, 10, 12, 23, 29, May 3, 4, 25, Sep 25,
Oct 4, 19, 22, 30, Nov 1, 7, 8, 16, 18, 26, Dec 4, 6, 18, 23; 1772: CG, Jan
4, 15, 25, Feb 22, Mar 5, DL, 23, CG, 24, 28, Apr 4, DL, 24, CG, May 29, HAY,
Aug 4, 10, CG, Sep 21, 25, 30, Oct 9, 12, 13, 14, 16, 26, 29, Nov 6, 12, 14,
28, Dec 3, 5, 15, 22, 28; 1773: CG, Jan 6, 7, 14, 28, Mar 15, 20, 23, Apr 13,
16, 17, 23, 27, May 3, 6, 22, 24, 28, Sep 20, 22, 24, 29, Oct 1, 5, 8, 15,
18, 21, 22, 27, Nov 20, 23, Dec 1, 3, 17, 18, 23; 1774: CG, Jan 5, 15, 29,
Feb 7, 15, 17, Mar 12, 15, Apr 5, 7, 12, 18, 19, 23, May 24, Sep 19, 21, 23,
28, 30, Oct 5, 7, 14, 15, 21, 26, 27, Nov 1, 2, 3, 4, 8, 12, 29, Dec 2, 6,
12, 20; 1775: CG, Jan 3, 17, Mar 28, Apr 19, 28, May 9, 17, 18, 27, Sep 27,
29, Oct 4, Nov 3, Dec 5; 1776: DL, Feb 14, CG, May 10, 22, HAY, Sep 16, 17,
18, 20, 23; 1778: CHR, Jun 24; 1780: HAY, Nov 13; 1782: HAY, Aug 27
--Cure of the Spleen; or, Shuter's Warehouse, 1760: BFS, Sep 3; 1761: BFG, Sep
   1, 2, 3, 4, 5, 7
--English Mirror, The; or, Fun at the Fair, 1760: BFS, Sep 3, 4, 5, 6
Shuter's Booth, 1759: BFS, Sep 3, BF, 4, 5, 6, SFS, 18, 19, 20, 21; 1760: BFS,
   Sep 3, 4, 5, 6, SF, 18, 19, 20, 22
Shuter's Warehouse. See Shuter, Edward, Cure of the Spleen.
Shutze, Daniel (horn player), 1794: CG, Mar 7, 21; 1795: CG, Feb 20, Mar 4;
   1796: CG, Feb 12
Shylock's Plot (entertainment), 1776: MARLY, May 27
Si Caro Cara Si (song), 1728: LIF, Mar 28, Apr 23, 24, May 8, 29, HAY, Aug 9;
   1729: DL, Mar 26, HIC, Apr 30; 1731: GF, May 13
Si lieto e si conteno (song), 1714: QUEEN'S, May 1
Si t'intendo (song), 1714: QUEEN'S, May 1
Sibblis (actor), 1736: LIF, Apr 2
Sibilla (singer), 1773: MARLY, Aug 10
Sibilla, Sga (singer), 1745: DL, Jan 17, 31, Feb 15, Apr 3, 15; 1746: DL, Jan
   31, Apr 30, Nov 7; 1747: DL, Jan 10, May 5, KING'S, Nov 14; 1748: CG, Mar 23,
   HAY, Dec 9; 1749: CG, Feb 10
Sicilian Dance (dance), 1732: LIF, Mar 9, 21, 30, Apr 13, 17, 19, 22, 25, 26,
   May 8, 9, 11, 15, LIF/CG, Nov 14, 16, 21; 1733: CG/LIF, Jan 9, LIF/CG, 11,
   12, 19, 20, Feb 2, CG, 8, LIF/CG, Apr 30, May 3
Sicilian Peasant (dance), 1743: DL, Mar 10, 19, 21, 24, Apr 6, 8, 12, 13, 21,
   22, 28, 30, May 18, 19; 1757: CG, Dec 17; 1758: CG, Jan 17, Feb 21, 28, Mar
   7, 16, 28, 29, 30, Apr 3, 4, 5, 12; 1762: CG, Nov 24, 25, 26, 27, 29, Dec 1,
   3, 10, 11, 13, 23, 29, 30; 1763: CG, Jan 5, 7, 15, 18, 21, 22, 25, 29, Feb
   10, 12, 17, 21, Mar 14, 24, Apr 4, 14, 15, 19, 20, 23, 28, May 2, 3, 6, 12,
   19, 28, Oct 5, 7, 8, 10, 13, 22, 25, 29, Nov 3, 12, 17, 22, 29, Dec 1, 3, 5;
   1764: CG, Jan 19, Apr 26, HAY, Jun 26, 29, Jul 23, Aug 24, Sep 3, 12, CG, Oct
   1, 4, 17, 31, Nov 1, 17, 23, 26, Dec 1, 27; 1765: CG, Jan 24, Mar 11, 16, 26,
   Apr 22, May 3, Nov 26; 1766: CG, Mar 11, 22, Apr 8, 12, 25, 30, May 1, 8;
   1767: CG, Apr 11, 24, 30, Nov 23, Dec 9; 1768: CG, Feb 11
Sicilian Romance, The. See Siddons, Henry.
Sicilian Usurper, The. See Tate, Nahum.
Siddons, Henry (actor, playwright), 1782: DL, Oct 10; 1790: HAY, Aug 11; 1794:
   CG, May 28
--Modern Breakfast; or, All Asleep at Noon (interlude), 1790: HAY, Aug 11, 27
--Sicilian Romance, The; or, The Apparition of the Cliffs, 1794: CG, May 28,
   Jun 2, 6, 9, 10, 18
Siddons, Sarah, Mrs William (actor), 1775: DL, Nov 16, Dec 29; 1776: DL, Jan 2,

13, Feb 1, 3, 15, Apr 15, 29, May 23, 27; 1782: DL, Oct 10, 28, 30, Nov 8,
14, 16, 29, Dec 9, 14; 1783: DL, Mar 18, 22, May 3, 17, Jun 5, Oct 8, 11, 14,
17, 21, 24, Nov 3, CG, 13, DL, 22, Dec 10, 22; 1784: DL, Mar 6, 9, 18, Apr
24, May 4, 8, Oct 5, 9, 12, 19, 23, 27, 30, Nov 3, 16, 17, 20, CG, 29, DL,
Dec 2; 1785: DL, Jan 14, CG, 19, DL, 27, Feb 2, 19, Mar 8, 31, Apr 14, 30,
May 18, Sep 17, 22, 24, 29, Oct 1, 6, 8, 13, 15, 20, 22, 27, Nov 8, 12, 18,
22, 26; 1786: DL, Feb 11, 15, 18, 23, CG, 25, DL, Mar 4, 9, 16, 25, Apr 6,
May 15, Jun 7, Oct 3, 5, 9, 12, 16, 19, 23, Nov 18, 22, Dec 6, 19, 21; 1787:
DL, Jan 23, 29, Feb 10, Mar 8, 29, Apr 14, May 3, 7, 19, 29, CG, Oct 1, DL,
6, 11, 18, 27, 30, Nov 3, 6, 16, 20, 24, 27, Dec 11; 1788: DL, Jan 3, 8, 19,
21, 31, Mar 13, 29, Apr 3, CG, 8, 25, DL, May 5, Oct 16, 28, Nov 1, 4, 6, 11,
15, 25, 28, Dec 9; 1789: DL, Jan 6, 10, 13, 17, 20, Feb 7, 16, Mar 10, 17,
21, 27, KING'S, Apr 21, DL, May 4, 11, CG, 15, 23, DL, Sep 22; 1790: CG, Apr
29, HAY, Aug 18, CG, Oct 20, DL, Dec 7, 14; 1791: CG, Feb 11, DL, Mar 21, 28,
Apr 4, CG, May 10, DL, 14, HAY, Aug 27; 1792: DLKING'S, Jan 21, 24, 28, 31,
Feb 4, 7, 11, 14, 18, 23, Mar 1, 6, 10, 13, 17, 26, 31, Apr 28, May 5, DL,
Dec 17, 21, 26, 28, 31; 1793: DL, Jan 4, 7, 29, Feb 5, 9, 12, 16, 23, 26, Mar
2, 5, 9, 12, 18, Apr 23, 27, May 28; 1794: DL, Apr 21, 26, May 1, 19, 20, 22,
Jun 6, HAY, Aug 20, DL, Oct 2, 4, 7, CG, 7, DL, 9, 11, 14, 18, 21, 25, 28,
Nov 15, 18, 25, 29, Dec 12, 16, 30; 1795: DL, Mar 3, 10, 14, 21, Apr 14, 27,
29, May 2, HAY, Aug 29, DL, Sep 19, 24, 29, Oct 5, 12, 19, 21, Nov 6, 16, 20,
23, Dec 11, 18; 1796: DL, Jan 29, Feb 15, 20, Apr 18, 20, 29, May 2, 16, Sep
22, 24, Oct 3, 6, 10, 13, 22, Nov 2, 5, 9, 15, 23, 28, 29, Dec 9, 16, 21;
1797: DL, Jan 2, 20, Feb 3, Mar 14, 20, Apr 28, May 1, CG, 4, DL, Oct 30, Nov
4, 7, 9, 15, 17, 21, 23, 24, Dec 2, 8; 1798: DL, Mar 17, 24, Apr 23, 30, Sep
15, 18, 20, Oct 27, Nov 6, 13, Dec 3, 20, 27, 29; 1799: HAY, Feb 25, DL, Apr
23, 24, May 20, 24, 29, Nov 22, 25, 27, 29, Dec 9, 11, 30; 1800: DL, Jan 25,
Apr 21, 29, May 3, 5, 6, 7, 9
Siddons, 1768: CG, Oct 24
Side Drum (music), 1731: GF, Jan 16; 1751: HAY, Dec 27; 1752: CT/HAY, Jan 7, 14
Sidly. See Sedley.
Sidney (spectator), 1661: VERE, Jan 8
Sidney, Henry, Earl of Romney (spectator), 1680: DG, Feb 2, DGORDL, 19
Sidney, Laurence (entertainer), 1777: CHR, Jul 21; 1787: RLSN, Mar 26, 27, 28,
29, 30, 31
Sidney, Mrs (actor), 1796: HAY, Feb 22, Mar 28, Apr 27; 1797: HAY, Jan 23, May
10
Siege and Surrender of Mons, The (play, anon), 1690: NONE, Sep 0
Siege de Cythere (dance), 1791: PAN, May 9, 17, 21, 24, Jun 2, 14, 16, 30
Siege of Acre, The (interlude, anon), 1800: CG, May 7
Siege of Aquileia, The. See Home, John.
Siege of Babylon, The. See Pordage, Samuel.
Siege of Barcelona, The; or, The Soldier's Fortune (droll), 1706: BF, Aug 27
Siege of Belgrade, The. See Cobb, James.
Siege of Berwick, The. See Jerningham, Edward.
Siege of Bethulia, The (droll), 1720: SFLW, Sep 5; 1721: BFLGB, Aug 24; 1729:
BFLH, Aug 23, SF, Sep 15; 1730: BFLH, Aug 24, 31
Siege of Cartagena, The (exhibit), 1741: SF, Sep 7
Siege of Constantinople, The. See Payne, Henry Nevil.
Siege of Curzola, The. See O'Keeffe, John.
Siege of Damascus, The. See Hughes, John.
Siege of Gibraltar, The. See Pilon, Frederick.
Siege of Meaux, The. See Pye, Henry James.
Siege of Memphis, The. See D'Urfey, Thomas.
Siege of Namur, 1698: BF, Aug 25
Siege of Quebec, The; or, Harlequin Engineer (pantomime, anon), 1760: CG, May
14
Siege of Rhodes, Part II, The. See Davenant, Sir Willim.
Siege of Rhodes, The. See Davenant, Sir William.
Siege of Sinope, The. See Brooke, Frances.
Siege of Troy (song), 1791: CG, May 17; 1794: CG, May 7
Siege of Troy, The. See Minns, Mrs; Settle, Elkanah.
Siege of Urbin, The. See Killigrew, William.
Siete barhere amata Stello (song), 1758: KING'S, Apr 6
Siface. See Grossi, Giovanni Francesco.
Sifare (pastiche), 1767: KING'S, Mar 5, Dec 8, 12, 15, 19, 22
Sigh no more Ladies (song), 1789: HAY, Aug 25, DL, Dec 9; 1790: CG, Apr 21, DL,
May 20, HAY, Aug 20; 1791: CG, May 18; 1792: DL, Nov 2; 1797: DL, Jan 12, Mar
23; 1798: DL, May 24, HAY, Aug 21, DL, Oct 11; 1799: DL, Oct 12; 1800: CG,
May 17
Sighs. See Hoare, Prince.
Sign of the Globe (alehouse), 1749: HAY, Nov 17

Sign of the Holy Lamb (public house), 1748: CG, Apr 13
Sign of the Shoe and Slap (cobblers), 1667: BF, Sep 4
Sign of the Sun (milliner), 1750: DL, Mar 22
Signor Dottore, Il. See Fischietti, Domenico.
Silent Woman, The. See Jonson, Ben.
Silla. See Anfossi, Pasquale.
Silvain. See Marmontel, Jean Francois.
Silver St, 1745: HAY, Apr 1; 1751: DL, May 14; 1788: KING'S, May 22; 1789:
  KING'S, Mar 19, Jun 15, CG, Jul 2
Silver Tankard, The. See Craven, Elizabeth Baroness.
Silvester (actor), 1776: DL, May 18; 1777: DL, Jun 2; 1778: HAY, Apr 29, May
  18, Aug 27; 1790: HAY, Sep 29; 1791: HAY, Oct 24; 1792: HAY, Nov 26; 1798:
  CG, Nov 12, Dec 11, 26; 1799: CG, May 4, Oct 24; 1800: CG, Jan 16
Silvia's Revenge; or, The Berbadoes Fortune (play, anon), 1725: HAY, Dec 27
Silvie (dance), 1774: KING'S, Dec 3, 10, 13, 17; 1775: KING'S, Feb 14, 25, 28,
  Mar 4, Apr 4, 6, 8, 18, May 30
Simmonds (actor), 1768: CG, Jun 4; 1771: HAY, Mar 4, Apr 20
Simmonds, Miss (actor), 1771: HAY, Mar 4, Apr 15, 20; 1775: HAY, Feb 2, Mar 23
Simmonds, Miss (actor), 1790: HAY, Sep 29
Simmonds, Mrs (actor), 1742: BFPY, Aug 25
Simmons, Miss (actor), 1781: HAY, Mar 26
Simmons, Samuel (actor), 1783: CG, Nov 4; 1784: HAY, Sep 17, CG, Oct 11; 1785:
  HAY, Jul 13, CG, Sep 21, Nov 21, Dec 1; 1786: CG, Jun 2, HAY, Sep 4, CG, 20,
  Nov 23; 1787: CG, Jun 5; 1788: CG, Mar 29, May 24, Oct 3, 27, Dec 26; 1789:
  CG, Feb 3, Jun 5, Sep 25, Oct 16; 1790: CG, Jan 22, May 29, Oct 18, 27, Nov
  15, Dec 8; 1791: CG, Apr 16, Jun 2, Sep 16, Oct 12, 24, Dec 21, 22; 1792: CG,
  Feb 18, Mar 31, May 25, Oct 8, 15, 24, 27, Dec 26; 1793: CG, Apr 18, May 27,
  Sep 30, Oct 14, Dec 19, 26, 30; 1794: CG, May 26, Jun 10, 14, Sep 22, Oct 23,
  Dec 6, 26; 1795: CG, Mar 19, Apr 23, May 12, 14, Jun 6, 12, 13, Sep 14, Oct
  7, 8, 15, 23, Nov 9, 16, Dec 7, 21; 1796: CG, Jan 4, 23, 25, Feb 1, 18, Mar
  15, 19, 30, Apr 9, 16, 23, May 31, Sep 12, 16, 17, 19, 23, 26, Oct 6, 7, 24,
  25, 29, Nov 5, 7, 19, 21, Dec 1, 19, 27; 1797: CG, Jan 3, 10, Feb 18, Mar 14,
  16, Apr 8, 18, 19, 25, 26, 27, May 8, 18, 22, 23, 26, 31, Jun 9, 13, Sep 22,
  27, 29, Oct 2, 6, 9, 16, 25, 31, Nov 2, 4, 7, 8, 10, 13, 15, 17, 18, 20, 23,
  Dec 12, 16, 19, 26; 1798: CG, Feb 5, 6, 10, 20, Mar 19, 31, Apr 9, 13, 20,
  24, 30, May 1, 7, 8, 12, 15, 28, 29, Jun 2, Sep 17, 19, Oct 8, 15, 25, 29,
  30, 31, Nov 1, 10, 20, Dec 8, 11; 1799: CG, Jan 14, 17, 25, 29, Mar 5, 16,
  25, Apr 3, 6, 13, 19, 26, 30, May 3, 4, 7, 13, 22, 24, 25, 28, Jun 4, 6, 7,
  Sep 16, 18, 20, 23, 27, Oct 7, 21, 25, 31, Nov 9, 14, 18, 30, Dec 2, 4, 9,
  23, 27; 1800: CG, Jan 11, 29, Feb 3, 4, 10, 19, Mar 8, 25, 27, Apr 5, 17, 22,
  30, May 12, 17, 23, 27, 28, 30, Jun 2, 7
Simms (actor), 1746: GF, Oct 29; 1748: SFP, Sep 7
Simnel, Lambert (pretender), 1745: GF, Dec 19
Simon (actor), 1754: DL, Oct 10
Simon (author), 1791: CG, May 10; 1792: DLKING'S, Apr 16
--National Prejudice, 1791: CG, May 10
--Village Coquette, The (farce), 1792: DLKING'S, Apr 16
Simon, Mrs (actor), 1749: BFC, Aug 23
Simon, Richard (pretender supporter), 1745: GF, Dec 19
Simonet (dancer), 1776: KING'S, Nov 2, 30; 1777: KING'S, Jan 17, Feb 25, Mar
  15, May 1, 8, Nov 4, Dec 9; 1778: KING'S, Feb 24, Mar 3, 10, 31, Apr 4, Jun
  5, Nov 24, 28; 1779: KING'S, Mar 25, Apr 15, May 15, 29, Jun 15; 1780:
  KING'S, Apr 20, Nov 25, Dec 16; 1781: KING'S, Jan 13, 23, Feb 22, Mar 29, Apr
  26, Jun 5, Jul 3, Nov 17; 1782: KING'S, Feb 2, 7, 23, Apr 11, 30, Nov 2;
  1783: KING'S, Feb 18, May 1; 1784: KING'S, Mar 11; 1785: HAY, Apr 15, KING'S,
  Jun 18; 1788: KING'S, May 29; 1797: CG, Nov 25
Simonet (payee), 1775: DL, May 25
Simonet, Leonore (dancer), 1779: KING'S, Feb 23, Mar 2, 25, Nov 27; 1780:
  KING'S, Jan 22; 1785: HAY, Feb 14, Apr 15, 29, Aug 11; 1786: KING'S, Jun 6;
  1787: HAY, Aug 6; 1789: CG, Dec 21; 1791: PAN, Feb 17, Mar 19, 22, 24, May 9,
  17, Jun 10; 1792: HAY, Apr 14
Simonet, Leonore and Rosine (dancers), 1784: KING'S, Mar 18, Apr 20; 1785: HAY,
  Feb 14, 21, Apr 15, 29, May 30, 31, Jun 1, 27, Jul 6, 13, 28, Aug 31; 1786:
  KING'S, Jan 24, Feb 18, 25, Mar 11, 21, Apr 1, May 23, HAY, Jun 12, 19, 22,
  30, Jul 3, 17, Aug 2, 12, Sep 4; 1787: KING'S, Jan 6, Feb 13, Mar 8, 22, HAY,
  Jun 25, Jul 2, Aug 7, 14, 17, 21, KING'S, Dec 8; 1788: KING'S, Jan 12, 29,
  Feb 21, 28, Mar 13, Apr 3, May 31, HAY, Aug 5, Sep 30; 1789: KING'S, Jan 10,
  31, Mar 3, 19, 31, HAY, May 22, 25, KING'S, 26, HAY, Jul 8, 27, CG, Nov 13,
  Dec 21; 1790: CG, Jan 29, Apr 8, May 24; 1791: PAN, Dec 17; 1792: HAY, Feb
  14, Mar 10, Apr 14
Simonet, Mme (dancer), 1776: KING'S, Nov 2, 30, Dec 17; 1777: KING'S, Feb 4,
  Mar 15, May 1, 20, 24, Nov 4, Dec 9; 1778: KING'S, Jan 20, 31, May 28, Jun 5,

Nov 24, 28, Dec 22; <u>1779</u>: KING'S, Mar 25, Apr 15, Jun 15, 26, Dec 14; <u>1780</u>: KING'S, Jan 22, Feb 15, Apr 20, 22, May 9, 12, 25, 27, Nov 25, Dec 16, 19; <u>1781</u>: KING'S, Jan 23, Feb 10, 22, Mar 15, 27, 29, Apr 26, Jun 5, Jul 3, Dec 11; <u>1782</u>: KING'S, Jan 10, 26, 31, Feb 2, 23, Mar 12, Apr 11, 30, May 2, 7, 16, Jun 1, 3, 5, Nov 2; <u>1783</u>: KING'S, Feb 15, Mar 6, 13, 20, Apr 10, May 1, 10, 31, Jun 3, 28, Nov 29, Dec 6, 27; <u>1784</u>: KING'S, Jan 17, Feb 3, 7, 14, 26, Mar 11, 18, 20, Apr 24, May 20; <u>1791</u>: PAN, Feb 17
Simonet, Mons and Mme (dancers), <u>1776</u>: KING'S, Nov 2; <u>1777</u>: KING'S, Jan 21, Feb 4, May 1, 24, Jul 5, Nov 4, 15; <u>1778</u>: KING'S, May 26, 28; <u>1779</u>: KING'S, Feb 23; <u>1782</u>: KING'S, May 9
Simonet, Rosine (dancer), <u>1777</u>: CG, Nov 11; <u>1778</u>: CG, May 22, Nov 10; <u>1779</u>: KING'S, Apr 15, Dec 14; <u>1780</u>: DL, Feb 28, KING'S, Apr 22, CG, 18, KING'S, 27, DL, Oct 18, Nov 11; <u>1781</u>: KING'S, Jan 23, Nov 20; <u>1782</u>: KING'S, Feb 2, 28, Mar 19, May 16, Dec 10; <u>1783</u>: KING'S, Apr 10; <u>1784</u>: KING'S, Mar 11; <u>1785</u>: HAY, Feb 14, Mar 10, Aug 11; <u>1786</u>: KING'S, Jun 6; <u>1787</u>: KING'S, Mar 13, May 19; <u>1788</u>: KING'S, May 29; <u>1789</u>: HAY, Jul 16, CG, Dec 31; <u>1791</u>: PAN, Feb 17, Mar 19, 22, Jun 10; <u>1792</u>: HAY, Apr 14; <u>1796</u>: DL, Dec 26
Simonet, Theresa (dancer), <u>1781</u>: KING'S, Apr 26; <u>1782</u>: KING'S, Apr 30; <u>1783</u>: KING'S, May 1; <u>1785</u>: KING'S, May 12
Simonetti, Lodovico (singer), <u>1786</u>: KING'S, Mar 21, 30, Apr 8, May 4, 20
Simonin (dancer), <u>1769</u>: KING'S, Sep 5; <u>1770</u>: KING'S, Mar 10; <u>1775</u>: KING'S, Jan 7
Simons (actor), <u>1746</u>: GF, Oct 29
Simons (actor), <u>1770</u>: HAY, Mar 19
Simons, Master (dancer), <u>1749</u>: DL, Nov 9, 27, 29
Simpkinson (actor, singer), <u>1778</u>: HAY, Sep 7; <u>1779</u>: CG, Apr 17, May 6, 21, HAY, Jun 17, CG, Sep 24; <u>1780</u>: CG, May 6, 18, HAY, 30, CG, Sep 25, Oct 27; <u>1781</u>: CG, Apr 23, 25, May 19, HAY, Aug 15, 22, CG, Sep 24, Oct 19, 20, 27
Simple Story, A. See Inchbald, Elizabeth.
Simpson (acrobat), <u>1706</u>: BF, Aug 27
Simpson (actor), <u>1733</u>: HAY, Mar 20; <u>1735</u>: LIF, Aug 29
Simpson (actor), <u>1743</u>: LIF, Mar 14; <u>1744</u>: HAY, May 16, Jun 29, DL, Oct 2, 30, Nov 3; <u>1745</u>: DL, Jan 16, Feb 11, 20, Mar 7, 14, Apr 24, 27, 30, May 8, Oct 12, 15, Nov 30, Dec 13; <u>1746</u>: DL, Jan 8, 10, Apr 9, 11, 12, 14, 15, 22, 23, 30, May 14, Sep 23, 27, 30, Oct 23, 31, Nov 1, Dec 5; <u>1747</u>: DL, Feb 2, 7, Mar 16, 23, Apr 11, May 1, 4, Sep 15, 22, 26, Oct 29, Nov 6, 16, Dec 16; <u>1748</u>: DL, Jan 6, Mar 19, 22, May 6, Sep 24, 29, Oct 4, 19, 28, 29, Nov 28, 29; <u>1749</u>: DL, Jan 9, May 1, BFC, Aug 23, DL, Oct 3, 17, Nov 2, Dec 9, 18, 20; <u>1750</u>: DL, Jan 6, 27, Mar 15, Apr 2, 19, 30, May 3, 8, Sep 25, 27, 28, Oct 15, 19, 22, 24, 30, Nov 5, 13, 23, Dec 3; <u>1751</u>: DL, May 3, 14, Sep 10, 18, Oct 7, 11, 14, 17, 29, Nov 4; <u>1752</u>: DL, Jan 28, Feb 6, 13, Mar 5, Apr 6, 14, 21, 22, 24, 28, May 5, Sep 16, 19, 26, Oct 3, 16, 19, 23, 28, Nov 4, Dec 8; <u>1753</u>: DL, Jan 1, 5, Feb 22, Mar 3, Apr 25, May 7, 12, 18, 21, Sep 11, Oct 2, 3, 6, 16, 25, 31, Nov 5, 26, Dec 22, 26; <u>1754</u>: DL, Jan 23, May 10, 20, Sep 14, 24, Oct 11, 14, 16, 21, Nov 4, 13, 22, 30; <u>1755</u>: DL, Jan 25, Mar 15, 18, Apr 25, 28, Sep 20, 23, Oct 4, 10, 17, Nov 1, 4, 6, 17; <u>1756</u>: DL, Jan 1, 10, Feb 24, JS, Mar 18, DL, 29, May 5, 18, Sep 25, Oct 16, 19, Nov 4, 17, 18; <u>1757</u>: DL, Jan 18, Feb 5, May 6
Simpson (actor, dancer), <u>1795</u>: KING'S, Mar 26, CG, Oct 26, Dec 21; <u>1796</u>: CG, Jan 4, Mar 15, Jun 4, KING'S, Jul 7, 12, CG, Oct 24, Dec 19; <u>1797</u>: KING'S, Apr 6, CG, 8, 27, May 22, Jun 5, 9, Oct 9, 16, Nov 24; <u>1798</u>: CG, Feb 12, Mar 19, May 28; <u>1799</u>: CG, Jan 29, Mar 2, 4
Simpson (musician), <u>1758</u>: KING'S, Apr 6; <u>1759</u>: CG, Nov 30; <u>1761</u>: SOHO, Jan 28; <u>1762</u>: DL, Mar 5, 26, KING'S, May 11, HAY, 20; <u>1763</u>: KING'S, Apr 25, CG, Oct 13, 25, Dec 8; <u>1764</u>: CG, Jan 19, HAY, Nov 13; <u>1765</u>: CG, Jan 28; <u>1768</u>: HAY, Feb 19, 24, Mar 9, 16, CG, Dec 7; <u>1769</u>: HAY, Feb 10, Mar 10, CG, Oct 10; <u>1770</u>: CG, Feb 24, May 29; <u>1771</u>: CG, Oct 15; <u>1772</u>: CG, Jan 29, Dec 4; <u>1774</u>: CG, Jan 18, Mar 7; <u>1776</u>: STRAND, Jan 23
Simpson (ticket seller), <u>1745</u>: DT, Mar 14
Simpson (wine seller), <u>1770</u>: CG, Apr 2
Simpson, Elizabeth (actor), <u>1744</u>: HAY, May 16; <u>1745</u>: GF, Mar 12, 25; <u>1748</u>: DL, Sep 27; <u>1749</u>: DL, Jan 9, Oct 26; <u>1750</u>: DL, Jan 22, Apr 30, Nov 2; <u>1751</u>: DL, Sep 26, Oct 17; <u>1752</u>: DL, Jan 3, Mar 9, Apr 17, 23, Nov 6, 18, 30, Dec 8, 18; <u>1753</u>: DL, Feb 3, Mar 22, May 4, 7, 17, 21, Sep 22, 29, Oct 9, 31; <u>1754</u>: DL, Apr 30, May 10, 13, Sep 14; <u>1755</u>: DL, Apr 25, Nov 8, 15; <u>1756</u>: DL, Apr 29, May 5; <u>1757</u>: DL, Sep 29; <u>1758</u>: DL, May 10, Nov 13; <u>1759</u>: DL, May 21, 23, Sep 27, Oct 11, 16; <u>1760</u>: DL, May 7, Jun 19, Oct 23, Dec 29; <u>1761</u>: DL, Feb 12, 14, May 13, 27, Sep 19, Oct 24, Dec 28; <u>1762</u>: DL, Apr 14, May 14, Nov 26; <u>1763</u>: DL, Mar 14, May 7; <u>1764</u>: DL, May 15; <u>1765</u>: DL, May 15; <u>1766</u>: DL, May 3, 10; <u>1767</u>: DL, Jan 24, May 22, Sep 26, Dec 1; <u>1768</u>: DL, May 10, Oct 28; <u>1769</u>: DL, May 16, Oct 6; <u>1770</u>: DL, Feb 21, May 3, 23, Nov 24; <u>1771</u>: DL, Apr 15, Oct 28; <u>1772</u>: DL, Jun 1; <u>1773</u>: DL, May 8, 21; <u>1774</u>: DL, Apr 19, May 16

Simpson, James (viola player), 1792: CG, Feb 24; 1793: CG, Feb 15, Oct 2, 12,
    28; 1794: CG, Mar 7; 1795: CG, Feb 20, 27; 1796: CG, Feb 12; 1797: CG, Mar 3,
    10, 16, May 26; 1798: CG, Jun 2
Simpson, John (actor), 1786: HAMM, Jun 28, 30, Jul 5, 7, 10, HAY, Dec 18; 1787:
    HAY, Jan 8, Mar 12, RLSN, 26, 27, 28, 29, 30, 31, HAY, Apr 30, ROY, Jun 20;
    1788: HAY, Apr 9, Dec 22; 1794: HAY, Jun 2
Simpson, John and Juliana (actors), 1787: RLSN, Mar 31; 1794: HAY, Jun 2
Simpson, Juliana, Mrs John (actor), 1787: RLSN, Mar 26, 27, 28, 29, 30; 1794:
    HAY, Jun 2
Simpson, Master (actor), 1752: DL, Nov 8; 1753: DL, Jan 1, 15, 17, 18, Feb 19,
    Apr 9, 25, May 7, Sep 25, Oct 2, Nov 14; 1754: DL, Jan 23, Feb 20, May 10,
    Oct 1, 12, 21, Dec 5, 13; 1755: DL, Apr 25, 28, Oct 10, 23, 27, Nov 8, 22,
    Dec 18; 1756: DL, May 10, Sep 21, 25, Oct 16, 18, Nov 24, Dec 3; 1757: DL,
    May 2, 6, Sep 13, Oct 4, HAY, 31; 1758: DL, May 10, 12, Oct 12, 30, Nov 3,
    27, Dec 7; 1759: DL, Apr 5, May 23, Oct 12, 19, Nov 24; 1780: CII, Mar 27,
    Apr 19
Simpson, Master and Miss (dancers), 1756: DL, May 5; 1758: DL, May 10
Simpson, Miss (actor), 1753: DL, May 7, 21, Nov 17; 1754: DL, May 10; 1755: DL,
    Apr 28, Oct 17, Nov 8, Dec 18; 1756: DL, May 5, Sep 25, Nov 18, Dec 3; 1757:
    DL, Apr 18, May 6, 9; 1758: DL, May 10, 11, 12, Oct 12, 19, Nov 16, Dec 7;
    1759: DL, Apr 5, 7, May 9, 11, 21, 23, Oct 19, 25, 30; 1760: DL, Mar 20, May
    1, 7; 1763: DL, May 31; 1766: DL, May 7; 1767: DL, Jan 24, May 14, 15, 22,
    Oct 9, 22, Dec 12, 19; 1768: DL, Jan 4, Mar 15, 17, 26, Apr 6, May 10; 1778:
    DL, Jan 17, Mar 16, May 19, Sep 24, Oct 22; 1779: DL, Jan 8, May 15, 25, Sep
    21, 30, Oct 9, Dec 27; 1780: DL, Apr 26, 29, Sep 16, 28, Oct 17, 19, 30, Nov
    13, 15, Dec 6; 1781: DL, May 1, 17, Sep 18, 25, Oct 6, 12, 29, Nov 5, 21, 27,
    Dec 11, 13; 1782: DL, Jan 3, Feb 16, Mar 21, Apr 24, May 10, 13, 18, Sep 18,
    Oct 1, 5, 10, 12, 14, 18, Nov 1, 6, 7, Dec 5, 26; 1783: DL, Feb 7, Mar 3, 6,
    15, 17, May 12, Sep 25, Oct 7, 11, 20, 22, Nov 3, Dec 2, 16; 1784: DL, Apr
    14, May 7, 15, Sep 16, 23, Oct 12, 23; 1785: DL, Jan 12, 13, Feb 2, Apr 14,
    26, Dec 26; 1786: DL, Apr 6
Simpson, Mr and Elizabeth (actors), 1756: DL, May 5; 1757: DL, May 6
Simpson, Mr, Elizabeth, and Master (actors), 1754: DL, May 10
Simpson, R (actor), 1786: HAY, Dec 18; 1787: HAY, Jan 8, Mar 12; 1797: DL, Oct
    5, Nov 4, 8, 25, Dec 21; 1798: DL, Jan 16, 24, 26
Simpson, Thomas (actor), 1695: DL, Sep 0, Nov 0, Dec 0; 1696: DL, Feb 0, May 0,
    DG, Jun 0, DL, Nov 21; 1697: DL, Feb 0, Jul 0; 1698: DL, Mar 0, Jun 0; 1699:
    DLLIF, Sep 12, DL, Dec 0; 1700: DL, Apr 29, Oct 0, Dec 9; 1701: DL, Feb 4,
    Apr 0, May 12, Dec 0; 1702: DL, Nov 0, Dec 0
Simpson's Music Shop, 1745: DL, Apr 16; 1746: HIC, Mar 10
Sims (actor), 1792: HAY, Oct 15
Sims, Sarah (actor, singer), 1797: CG, Oct 20, Nov 2, 13, 24, Dec 18, 26; 1798:
    CG, Feb 12, 26, Apr 9, 16, Sep 17, 28, Oct 1, 3, 8, 25, 31, Nov 5, 12, 17,
    Dec 15, 26; 1799: CG, Jan 14, Apr 2, 6, 9, 13, 19, 30, May 6, 14, 24, 25, Jun
    3, 5, 6, 7, Sep 18, 23, 25, 30, Oct 4, 7, 16, 24, 25, Nov 9, 11, 14, Dec 10,
    23; 1800: CG, Jan 16, 18, Feb 10, Mar 4, 25, 27, Apr 5, 15, May 1, 2, 7, 10,
    20, 23, 24, Jun 12
Simson (actor), 1768: DL, Oct 31
Simsons, Henry (composer), 1698: CLARK'S, Apr 1
Sin not, O King (song), 1790: DL, Mar 17; 1791: DL, Apr 1; 1792: KING'S, Feb
    29; 1794: CG, Apr 11, DL, 11; 1800: CG, Mar 19
Since by Man came Death (song), 1793: KING/HAY, Feb 20; 1794: DL, Mar 19
Since from my dear (song), 1694: DG, Jan 10
Since the Race of Time Began (song), 1753: CG, May 10
Since Times are so bad (song), 1694: DG, May 0; 1702: DL, Dec 8, 22; 1715: LIF,
    Jan 17; 1716: LIF, Apr 25; 1718: LIF, May 1, 20; 1723: DL, Jul 23; 1728: LIF,
    Apr 29; 1730: LIF, Apr 15, May 27; 1731: LIF, Apr 8, May 3; 1733: LIF/CG, Mar
    30; 1734: GF, May 3; 1737: CG, Apr 12, 18, 22, LIF, May 4, CG, 5; 1738: CG,
    Apr 11, 12, 18, May 2, 12, Dec 6; 1739: CG, May 17, 25
Sincero Astelli (song), 1732: LIF, Apr 19
Sinclair (actor), 1779: HAY, Jan 11, May 10; 1791: HAY, Dec 12; 1792: HAY, Feb
    6
Sincock (actor), 1778: HAY, Jan 26; 1791: HAY, Sep 26
Sincock, Master (singer), 1797: HAY, Jan 23, May 10, Aug 3
Sincock, Mrs (actor), 1791: HAY, Sep 26; 1796: HAY, Apr 27; 1797: HAY, Jan 23,
    26, May 10
Sing all ye Muses (song), 1694: DG, May 0; 1702: DL, Dec 8; 1716: LIF, Mar 6;
    1717: LIF, Apr 4; 1742: GF, May 10; 1757: DL, May 7; 1761: DL, May 11
Sing then my Muse (song), 1736: DL, May 4
Sing unto God (song), 1790: DL, Mar 24
Sing unto the Lord (song), 1740: HIC, Apr 2; 1790: CG, Mar 3; 1792: CG, Mar 9,
    KING'S, 23, 28, 30; 1793: KING/HAY, Feb 22

Sing ye Druids, all your voices raise (song), 1695: DL, Sep 0
Sing ye to the Lord (song), 1789: DL, Mar 18, CG, 27; 1790: DL, Feb 26; 1791:
    DL, Mar 23; 1792: CG, Mar 2, KING'S, 21; 1793: CG, Feb 15, Mar 13; 1794: DL,
    Mar 12, CG, 14, DL, 14, Apr 2, CG, 9; 1795: KING'S, Feb 27, CG, 27, Mar 25;
    1797: CG, Mar 10; 1798: CG, Mar 14, 30; 1800: CG, Mar 5
Singer (actor), 1782: HAY, Nov 25
Singleton (actor), 1744: GF, Nov 29, 30, Dec 4, 18, 26; 1748: HAY, Mar 30, NWC,
    Apr 4, BFSY, Aug 24; 1749: NWLS, Feb 27, BFC, Aug 23
Singleton (bookkeeper), 1747: CG, May 19; 1748: CG, May 5
Singleton, John (musician), 1660: ATCOURT, Nov 19; 1675: ATCOURT, Feb 15
Singleton, Mrs (supernumerary), 1773: CG, May 21
Singleton, Thomas (house servant), 1769: CG, May 20, 22; 1770: CG, Feb 10, 15,
    20, 24, Mar 20, May 3, 17, 24, 28; 1771: CG, May 27, DL, Nov 15; 1772: CG,
    May 29; 1773: CG, May 28; 1774: CG, Apr 26, May 24
Sion now her head shall raise (song), 1797: CG, Mar 31
Siprutini (musician), 1762: DL, Feb 26, HAY, Mar 16, Apr 22, May 20; 1765: HAY,
    Mar 11
Sir Anthony Love. See Southerne, Thomas.
Sir Barnaby Whigg. See D'Urfey, Thomas.
Sir Courtly Nice. See Crowne, John.
Sir Harry Wildair. See Farquhar, George.
Sir Hercules Buffoon. See Lacy, John.
Sir John Cockle at Court. See Dodsley, Robert.
Sir John Falstaff in Masquerade. See Johnson, Samuel.
Sir John Oldcastle (farce, anon), 1742: BFPY, Aug 25
Sir Martin Marall. See Dryden, John.
Sir Patient Fancy. See Behn, Aphra.
Sir Peevy Pet (farce, anon), 1737: HAY, Mar 17
Sir Popular Wisdom; or, The Politician (play, anon), 1677: DG, Nov 17
Sir Roger deCoverley. See Dorman, Joseph.
Sir Solomon Single. See Caryll, John.
Sir Sydney Smith (song), 1799: CG, Oct 7
Sir Thomas Callico. See Crowne, John.
Sir Thomas Overbury. See Savage, Richard.
Sir Walter Raleigh. See Sewell, George.
Sir Watkins Delight (music), 1757: DL, Mar 31
Sir you're a comical fellow (song), 1791: CG, May 17
Sirbace. See Galuppi, Baldassare.
Siri Brahe. See Gustavas III.
Siri Brahe; oder, Die Neugierigen. See Gruttschreiber, J A.
Siris (dance master), 1705: DL, Nov 23
Sirmen, Sga Lombardini (musician), 1771: KING'S, Jan 10, Feb 8, CG, 15, 20,
    KING'S, 28, Mar 21, CHAPEL, Apr 27, KING'S, May 14, 17, 25, 28; 1772: KING'S,
    Feb 21, CG, Mar 6, 11, 20, HAY, 23, CG, Apr 10; 1773: KING'S, Jun 1
Siroe. See Handel, George Frederic; Hasse, Johann Adolph; Lampugnani, Giovanni
    Battista.
Sisigambis, Queen of Syracus (play, anon), 1699: NONE, Sep 0
Sister, The. See Lennox, Charlotte.
Sisters of the Tuneful Strain (song), 1775: CG, Apr 4
Sisters, The. See Shirley, James.
Sitting by yonder river side (song), 1678: DG, Jan 17
Six Days' Adventure, The. See Howard, Edward.
Sixfold Hornpipe (dance), 1772: CG, Apr 27, May 11, 16, 21; 1773: CG, Apr 28,
    May 3; 1774: CG, May 12, 18
Sixth Double Note Solo (music), 1707: YB, May 23
Skating Dance (dance), 1723: LIF, Oct 29, Dec 2, 13; 1724: LIF, Jan 3, Mar 2,
    Apr 30, Oct 30, Nov 11; 1728: LIF, Mar 25; 1730: LIF, Mar 21; 1731: LIF, Mar
    15
Skeate (spectator), 1711: CLK, Feb 6; 1712: CLKCS, Feb 6
Skeffington, Mrs (beneficiary), 1758: CG, Dec 22
Skeggs (musician), 1757: CG, May 6; 1758: HAY, Dec 28; 1760: HAY, Apr 30
Skeleton Dance (dance), 1740: SOU, Oct 9
Skeleton, The (pantomime), 1783: CG, May 19
Skerrett (actor), 1794: HAMM, Mar 24
Sketch of a Fine Lady's Return from a Rout. See Clive, Catherine.
Sketch of the Fashions. See Belles have at ye all.
Skewball, Peter (author), 1748: HAY, Jun 3
Skiddy (beneficiary), 1731: STA, Aug 9
Skillern, Thomas (violinist), 1796: CG, Feb 12; 1797: CG, Mar 3; 1798: CG, Feb
    23; 1799: CG, Feb 8
Skimmington (entertainment), 1729: LIF, May 6; 1730: LIF, Apr 20
Skinner (alderman), 1797: DL, Oct 27

Skinner, Charlotte (actor), 1750: HAY, Nov 10
Skinner, J (witness), 1735: GF/HAY, Mar 18, Apr 25
Skinners, Company of, 1663: CITY, Oct 29; 1671: CITY, Oct 30; 1689: CITY, Oct 29
Skippers (dance), 1712: DL, Jun 9
Skipwith, Sir Thomas (proprietor), 1694: NONE, Jul 0; 1699: DLORLIF, Feb 20
Skjoldebrand, Anders Fredrik Count, 1795: CG, Jun 3
--Herman von Unna, 1795: CG, Jun 3
Skyo (actor), 1792: HAY, Nov 26
Slack Rope (entertainment), 1701: MF, May 1, BF, Aug 25; 1702: BFGB, Aug 24; 1705: BF, Aug 27; 1713: TEC, Nov 26; 1766: HAY, Oct 27; 1798: CG, May 28
Slack Rope Vaulting (entertainment), 1710: GR, Sep 7
Slack, Miss (actor), 1764: DL, Nov 28; 1765: DL, Feb 15, Mar 2, Apr 26; 1768: DL, Nov 23
Slade, Betty (actor), 1668: BRIDGES, Jun 12; 1671: BRIDGES, Mar 0; 1672: LIF, Apr 0; 1675: DL, May 10
Slade, John, 1756: DL, Aug 12
--Love and Duty, 1756: DL, Aug 12
Slape, Master (actor, singer), 1798: CG, Nov 12, Dec 11; 1799: CG, Apr 13; 1800: CG, Jan 16, Feb 10, May 17
Slater (actor), 1750: SFP, Sep 7; 1758: CG, May 12; 1759: CG, May 25; 1760: CG, May 19, Sep 22; 1761: CG, May 15; 1762: CG, May 21
Slaughter (actor), 1762: HAY, Oct 25
Slaughter (wardrobe keeper), 1767: DL, Jan 24
Slaughter, Mrs (actor), 1671: DG, Nov 0
Slaughter, Mrs (tavern keeper), 1771: DL, Oct 15, Dec 5; 1772: DL, Jan 28, Jun 10, Dec 16
Slaughter's Coffee House, 1744: DL, Apr 4; 1752: DL, Apr 22; 1758: DL, Mar 29; 1760: CG, Mar 24; 1761: CG, Mar 14; 1791: HAY, Aug 16; 1795: HAY, Apr 22
Slave in Chains (dance), 1785: DL, May 5
Slave in Love (dance), 1788: DL, Oct 4
Slaves of Conquering Bacchus (dance), 1784: KING'S, Jan 17
Slaves' Dance (dance), 1725: LIF, Oct 25; 1727: LIF, Sep 20, Dec 19; 1764: DL, Apr 25, May 9; 1779: CG, Dec 16
Sledge, Miss (actor), 1757: CG, Jan 28, Feb 4, May 10, Oct 17; 1758: CG, Mar 11, Apr 8; 1759: CG, Mar 3, Apr 28; 1760: CG, Jan 9, 18, Feb 8, 14, Mar 17, May 8, Sep 22, Dec 11; 1761: CG, Mar 30, Apr 17, Sep 26, Oct 17, Nov 9; 1762: CG, Feb 22, Apr 27, Oct 4, 8; 1763: CG, May 16; 1764: CG, May 21; 1766: CG, Oct 17
Sledge, Mrs (householder), 1785: CG, Apr 23
Sleep, poor youth (song), 1694: DG, May 0
Sleep, shepherd, sleep (song), 1697: DL, Sep 0
Slezack (instrumentalist), 1799: CG, Feb 8; 1800: CG, Feb 28
Slighted Maid, The. See Stapylton, Sir Robert.
Slim (actor), 1754: DL, Jul 2
Slingsby, Barbara, Lady Arundel, 1700: DLORLIF, Jan 20
Slingsby, Henry (master of the mint, proprietor), 1674: SLINGSBY, Dec 2; 1675: SLINGSBY, Jan 19; 1679: SLINGSBY, Nov 20
Slingsby, Lady (actor), 1670: LIF, Jan 0; 1677: DG, May 12; 1680: DG, Sep 0, Dec 8; 1681: DG, Mar 0, Apr 0; 1682: DG, Jan 0, Aug 10, 12, DL, Nov 28; 1683: DG, May 31, NONE, Sep 0; 1685: DL, Aug 0; see also Lee, Mary
Slingsby, Simon (dancer, ballet master), 1764: DL, Sep 29, Nov 20; 1765: DL, Apr 27; 1766: KING'S, Nov 25; 1767: KING'S, Apr 30, May 2; 1768: KING'S, May 5, Dec 10; 1769: KING'S, Sep 5, Nov 28; 1770: KING'S, Feb 6; 1772: KING'S, Feb 4, Mar 3, Apr 28, May 5, 9, 14, 16, 23, 28, Jun 3, 11, Nov 14, 21, Dec 5, 8; 1773: KING'S, Jan 2, 5, 12, Feb 2, 16, 20, 25, Mar 9, 16, 18, 23, 30, Apr 1, 17, 24, 29, May 22, 25, 28, Jun 1, 8, 19; 1774: KING'S, Mar 24, DL, Nov 5, 18, Dec 7, 8, 9, 12, 17; 1775: DL, Mar 13, 30, Apr 1, 6, May 25, 27, Oct 20, Nov 28; 1776: DL, Feb 27, Mar 2, 19, Apr 23, Jun 10, Oct 9, 24, Nov 6, 7, Dec 18; 1777: DL, Feb 13, Sep 20; 1778: DL, Jan 28, Mar 24, Apr 9, KING'S, Nov 24, Dec 22; 1779: KING'S, Feb 23, Mar 2, 25, Apr 15, Jun 15, Nov 27, Dec 14; 1780: KING'S, Jan 22, Feb 8, 15, Apr 8, 13, May 9, 12, 16, 20, 27, Nov 25; 1781: KING'S, Jan 23, Feb 22, Mar 29, May 10, Jun 5, Jul 3, Nov 17, Dec 11; 1782: KING'S, Feb 2, 7, 16, Mar 9, May 2, 9, Jun 3, Nov 2, Dec 12; 1783: KING'S, Jan 11, Feb 13, 15, Mar 13, 22, 27, Apr 10, 12, May 3, 10, 31, Jun 3, 14, 19, 28, Nov 29, Dec 6, 16, 27; 1784: KING'S, Jan 17, Feb 3, 26, Mar 2, 18, 20, 25, May 11, 13, Jun 1; 1785: KING'S, Jan 11, Mar 17, Apr 21
Slip, The. See Bullock, Christopher.
Sloper, George (master carpenter), 1783: CG, May 31; 1789: CG, Dec 21; 1790: CG, Jan 23, Nov 15; 1793: CG, Sep 23; 1794: CG, Jun 13, Sep 22; 1795: CG, Apr 6, Jun 12, Sep 21, Dec 21; 1796: CG, Jun 2, Sep 17, Dec 19; 1797: CG, Mar 16, Jun 12, Oct 2, Nov 24, Dec 26; 1798: CG, Feb 12, Apr 9, May 28, Jun 4, Oct 8,

Nov 12; 1799: CG, Jan 29, Apr 19, May 13, Jun 6, Sep 23, Dec 23; 1800: CG, Jun 5

Sloper, William (ran off with Susannah Arne Cibber), 1766: DL, Jan 30

Sloping Rope (entertainment), 1701: BF, Aug 25

Small (singer), 1800: CG, Apr 2

Small Pox Hospital, 1753: KING'S, Mar 2

Small Talk. See Topham, Edward.

Smalley, Miss (actor), 1798: DL, Jun 5

Smallwood, Henry (constable), 1776: CG, May 22; 1777: CG, May 24; 1778: CG, May 22; 1779: CG, May 19; 1780: CG, May 26; 1781: CG, May 26; 1782: CG, May 29; 1783: CG, Jun 4; 1784: CG, May 29

Smart (musician), 1771: GROTTO, Aug 30, Sep 3

Smart (ticket deliverer), 1795: CG, Jun 13; 1796: CG, Jun 3; 1797: CG, May 27; 1798: CG, May 29; 1799: CG, May 29; 1800: CG, Jun 4

Smart, Charles Frederick (double-bass player), 1798: HAY, Jan 15

Smart, Christopher, 1749: DL, Nov 24; 1750: DL, Jan 3; 1751: DL, Mar 7; 1752: CT/HAY, Mar 21, May 5, HAY, Dec 14, DL, 23; 1753: DL, Jan 13; 1755: CG, Dec 5; 1759: DL, Feb 3; 1760: CG, Sep 22; 1764: KING'S, Apr 3; 1775: DL, May 27

--Adventures of Fribble, The, 1754: HAY, Mar 30, Apr 1, 22, 25, May 2, 6

--Aethiopian Concert (entertainment), 1754: HAY, Nov 8, 11, 14, 28, Dec 2, 9

--British Roratory, The; or, Mrs Midnight's New Carnival Concert, 1754: HAY, Jul 4, 5, 9, 11, 13, 16, 17, 18, 23, 26, Aug 1, 6, 8, 13, 15, 20, 27, 29, BFSIY, Sep 3, HAY, 10, HAY/SFB, 13, 17, 26, Oct 1

--Je Ne Sca Quoi, La; or, Wooden Spoons a la Mode, 1753: BFSY, Sep 3, 5, 6

--Mrs Midnight's Caudle (entertainment), 1752: HAY, May 21, 23; 1754: HAY, Apr 22, 25

--Mrs Midnight's Concert and Oratory 1760: HAY, Feb 14, Apr 30

--Mrs Midnight's Grand Concert (entertainment), 1752: CT, Mar 7; 1754: HAY, Apr 22, 25, May 2, 6

--Mrs Midnight's Rout (entertainment), 1755: HAY, Feb 10

--Old Woman's Oratory, The (entertainment), 1751: CT, Dec 3, HAY, 27, 30; 1752: HAY, Jan 2, CT/HAY, 7, 14, 21, 31, Feb 4, 6, 11, 13, 18, 22, 29, CT, Mar 7, CT/HAY, 12, 17, 21, HAY, 28, CT/HAY, Apr 1, 4, 7, 11, 14, 16, 18, 21, 27, May 2, 5, 7, 9, HAY, 12, Dec 7, 8, 9, 11, 12, 13, 14, 15, 16, 18, 19, 20, 21, 22, 23, 26, 28, 29, 30; 1753: HAY, Jan 2, 4, 6, 9, 11, 13, 16, 18, 20, 23, 25, 27, 31, Feb 1, 3, 6, 8, 10, 13, 15, 17, 20, 21, 22, 23, 24, 26, 27, 28, Mar 1, 3, 6, 8, 10, 13, 15, 22, 24, 27, 29, 31, Apr 5, 7, 10, 14, 25, May 3; 1754: HAY, Mar 4, 7, 9, 11, 14, 16, 25, 28, 30, Apr 1, HAY/SFB, Sep 19, 20, 21, 23, 24; 1758: HAY, May 18, Jun 1

--Sack Posset, 1754: HAY, Sep 10

Smart, George (violinist), 1798: HAY, Jan 15

Smart Jr, George Thomas (organist), 1798: HAY, Jan 15

Smart, Henry (violinist), 1788: HAY, Jan 15

Smeaton (actor), 1692: DL, Jan 0; 1695: DG, Nov 0; 1696: DL, Feb 0, DL/DL, Dec 0; 1697: DL, Jan 0, DL/DL, Mar 0, DL, Sep 0; 1705: LIF/QUEN, Feb 22

Smeltzer (haberdasher), 1773: DL, Dec 10

Smeton. See Smeaton.

Smile then with a beam divine (song), 1697: DG, Jun 0

Smiling Dawn (song), 1753: CG, Apr 12, May 9; 1784: CG, Apr 27, May 17; 1790: CG, Feb 26, DL, Mar 10; 1791: CG, Mar 23; 1792: CG, Mar 2, KING'S, 23; 1793: KING/HAY, Mar 13; 1794: DL, Mar 21, Apr 2; 1795: KING'S, Mar 13; 1796: CG, Feb 24; 1798: CG, Mar 9; 1799: CG, Feb 20; 1800: CG, Mar 19

Smiling Hour (song), 1748: CG, Apr 15; 1749: CG, Apr 18

Smiling love to thee belong (song), 1781: DL, Mar 10

Smirk, Robert (scene painter), 1782: CG, Nov 25; 1783: CG, Jan 18; 1796: CG, Mar 15, Oct 24

Smith (actor), 1697: DL, Sep 0; 1701: DL, Feb 4, May 12, Dec 0; 1707: DL, Oct 25; 1708: DL, Feb 9, Apr 15, 19, May 31, Jun 26, Jul 27, Sep 3, 21, 25, Oct 9; 1709: DL, Feb 5

Smith (actor), 1770: HAY, Jun 18, Jul 9, 25, Aug 8, 31, Oct 5

Smith (actor), 1787: HAY, Jan 8, Mar 12; 1778: HAY, Apr 9, Sep 30; 1790: HAY, Sep 29; 1792: HAY, Nov 26; 1799: WRSG, May 17

Smith (actor, dancer), 1715: LIF, Jan 7, 11, Feb 3, 5, Apr 30, May 2, 24, Sep 28, 29, Oct 4, 10, 11, 12, 24, Dec 12; 1716: LIF, Jan 4, Feb 21, May 2, Jul 11, Aug 3, Nov 10; 1717: LIF, Jan 8, 22, 28, Mar 30, May 13, Jul 10, Nov 11, 14, 19, 20, Dec 10, 14; 1718: LIF, Jan 7, 11, Feb 18, Apr 23, 30, Jun 20, Sep 30, Oct 11, Nov 13; 1719: LIF, Jan 16, Feb 21, Apr 20, BFBL, Aug 24, LIF, Oct 2, 7, 13, Nov 3, 5, 7, 17, 19, Dec 10; 1720: LIF, Jan 7, Feb 11, Apr 26, May 14, 17, Jun 7; 1721: LIF, May 8; 1722: LIF, Apr 6, Jun 1, 13, BFLSH, Aug 25; 1723: LIF, Jan 1, SH, Apr 3, LIF, 23, May 8, HA, Jul 22, LIF, Sep 28; 1724: LIF, Jul 3, 21, 31; 1725: SH, Mar 10; 1726: LIF, Aug 9, 16, 19, 23; 1727: LIF, Feb 3, 13, 27, BF, Aug 21, LIF, Sep 27, Nov 9, Dec 11; 1728: LIF, Jan

29, HAY, May 8, LIF, Jun 25, Jul 2, 19, Aug 2, BFB, 24, HAY, Oct 26, Nov 14,
Dec 7; 1729: HAY, Jan 10, LIF, 18, HAY, 27, 31, Mar 29, May 2, 7, 29, Jun 17,
Jul 16, DL, Aug 16, HAY, 19, BFF, 23, BFB, 25, GF, Oct 31, Nov 3, LIF, 4, GF,
4, 10, 11, 12, 19, 20, 21, 24, Dec 1, 20; 1730: LIF, Jan 2, GF, 5, 9, Feb 24,
Mar 30, Apr 2, 6, 7, May 22, 28, Jun 1, RI, 24, GF, 26, RI, 27, GF, Jul 1,
RI, 16, BFPG, Aug 20, BFOF, 20, SFOF, Sep 9, GF, 16, 18, 21, 25, 30, Oct 2,
5, 14, 19, 21, 24, 31, Nov 2, 5, LIF, 7, GF, 10, 11, 26, 27, 30, LIF, Dec 15,
GF, 21; 1731: GF, Jan 2, Mar 2, LIF, Apr 2, 3, GF, 5, May 5, HAY, 6, GF, 7,
14, 17, Jun 1, 2, 3, 8, 9, RI, Jul 1, 8, BFB, Aug 26, LIF, Oct 4, GF, 8, 26,
Nov 1, 4, 6, 8, 11, 12, LIF, 18, GF, 26, Dec 6, 20, 28; 1732: GF, Mar 20,
LIF, 22, GF, Apr 19, LIF, 27, BFB, Aug 23, GF, Oct 2, 17, RI, 17, LIF/CG, Nov
8, 24, GF, Dec 1, 29; 1733: BFCGBH, Aug 23, Sep 4; 1734: CG, Feb 26, May 7,
JS, 31, BFHBH, Aug 24, BFRLCH, 24, RI, Sep 26, CG/LIF, Dec 30; 1735: YB, Mar
19, LIF, Jul 16, 30, Aug 6, 22, Sep 5, YB/HAY, 17, 24, Oct 1, CG, Nov 6, 15,
22, Dec 27; 1736: HAY, Mar 5, CG, 27, LIF, 31, CG, Apr 6, HAY, 26, 29, CG,
May 17, 24, HAY, Jul 30, BFHC, Aug 23, CG, Oct 8; 1737: HAY, Mar 21, CG, May
6; 1738: CG, Nov 18; 1739: CG, Sep 5, 22, Oct 2, 26, Nov 20, Dec 10; 1740:
CG, Jan 15, Feb 12, Mar 25, May 9, Sep 24, Oct 3, 10; 1741: CG, Jan 5, 23,
Feb 24, HIC, Apr 24, BFH, Aug 22, CG, Oct 24, Nov 7, 26, Dec 4, JS, 28; 1742:
CG, Jan 8, JS, Apr 7, CG, May 3, 4, BFPY, Aug 25, CG, Dec 21; 1743: CG, Mar
8, TCD/BFTD, Aug 23; 1744: CG, Jan 14, JS, Mar 16, MFHNT, May 1, MF, 3, Jun
7, HAY, 29, CG, Oct 31, Dec 8; 1745: GF, May 1, CG, Nov 14; 1746: GF, Mar 3,
CG, Apr 17, BFWF, Aug 25, SFW, Sep 8; 1747: GF, Mar 10, BFC, Aug 22; 1748:
CG, Feb 25, Mar 28, Apr 21, May 6, BFP, Aug 24, SFP, Sep 7, SFLYYW, 7, CG,
26, Oct 17; 1749: HAY, Apr 29, May 2, 29, BF/SFP, Aug 23, BFCB, 23, BF/SFP,
Sep 7, CG, Oct 20, Nov 23; 1750: HAY, Feb 9, 16, 26, DL, Mar 3, CG, 17, Oct
12, 29, Nov 6; 1751: CG, Sep 27, 30, DL, Nov 23; 1752: DL, May 6, 7, 8, SFB,
Sep 22, CG, Oct 10, 18

Smith (beneficiary), 1705: YB, Jan 4; 1707: QUEEN'S, Jun 25; 1710: QUEEN'S, May
25; 1718: YB, Mar 26
Smith (boxkeeper, box-office keeper), 1751: DL, May 9; 1752: DL, May 4; 1753:
DL, May 14; 1754: DL, May 20; 1755: DL, May 12; 1756: DL, May 13; 1757: DL,
May 16; 1758: DL, May 15; 1759: DL, May 24; 1760: DL, May 14; 1761: DL, May
14; 1762: DL, May 21; 1763: DL, May 16; 1764: DL, May 18; 1765: DL, May 20;
1766: DL, May 16, Sep 25
Smith (canvas dealer), 1782: DL, Mar 14; 1783: DL, Nov 5
Smith (dancer), 1793: CG, Mar 11
Smith (householder), 1780: DL, May 6
Smith (musician), 1694: SMITH'S, Nov 17
Smith (musician), 1708: SH, Feb 4; 1711: SH, Apr 11; 1712: SH, May 14
Smith (musician), 1772: DL, Apr 24; 1773: DL, Apr 13
Smith (payee), 1758: CHAPEL, Apr 27
Smith (pit office keeper), 1785: DL, May 20; 1786: DL, May 26, Sep 30; 1787:
DL, Jun 1; 1788: DL, Jun 5; 1789: DL, Jun 10; 1790: DL, Jun 2; 1792:
DLKING'S, Jun 15; 1793: DL, Jun 6; 1796: DL, Jun 10; 1797: DL, Jun 15; 1798:
DL, Jun 2; 1799: DL, Jul 2; 1800: DL, Jun 13, 14
Smith (singer), 1797: CG, Dec 26; 1798: CG, Mar 19, 31, Apr 21, Nov 12, Dec 11;
1799: CG, Jan 14, Mar 2, 4, Apr 13, 23, 24, 25, May 4, Dec 23; 1800: CG, Jan
16, Feb 10
Smith (spectator), 1662: LIF, Apr 2
Smith and Co (coal merchants), 1777: DL, Oct 24
Smith, Adam (singer, composer), 1771: HAY, Mar 11, Apr 1, GROTTO, Jun 22, Aug
8, 30, Sep 3, 9; 1775: HAY, Feb 2
Smith, Augustus (composer), 1773: DL, Oct 11
Smith, Betty (beneficiary), 1723: HAY, Jan 31, Apr 22; 1726: HAY, Mar 2; 1729:
HIC, Feb 10; 1730: HIC, Feb 27; 1731: HIC, Mar 26
Smith, C (actor), 1754: CG, May 7; 1755: CG, May 15, Oct 17, 22, Nov 8; 1756:
CG, Sep 20, 22, Nov 8; 1757: CG, Sep 23, Oct 13, Nov 18; 1758: CG, Sep 25,
Oct 9; 1759: CG, Sep 26, Oct 10; 1760: CG, May 10, Sep 22, 24, Oct 17, 20;
1761: CG, Sep 16, 23; 1762: CG, Oct 4; 1763: CG, Jan 26; 1764: CG, Oct 17;
1765: CG, Oct 30; 1766: CG, Nov 8; 1768: CG, Feb 25; 1769: CG, Nov 4; 1771:
CG, Sep 28
Smith, Captain (mariner), 1752: CG, Dec 27
Smith, Charles (author), 1798: CG, Oct 11
--Day at Rome, A (farce), 1798: CG, May 7, 11, Oct 11
Smith, Charles (upholsterer), 1794: DL, May 1
Smith, Charlotte, 1799: CG, Apr 27
--What is She?, 1799: CG, Apr 27, 29, May 1, 2, 9, 20
Smith, Edmund, 1707: QUEEN'S, Apr 21; 1754: CG, Nov 7; 1775: CG, Feb 21
--Phaedra and Hippolytus, 1707: QUEEN'S, Apr 18, 21, 22, 25, 26; 1722: HAY, Jan
8; 1723: LIF, Jan 18, 19, 22, Feb 6, May 4; 1726: DL, Dec 3, 5, 31; 1745: JS,
Mar 26; 1751: DL, Nov 23, 28, 30, Dec 3, 5, 7, 12; 1752: DL, Feb 1, Apr 2;

1754: CG, Nov 4, 5, 6, 7, 8, DL, Dec 9; 1755: DL, Jan 8, Mar 8; 1756: CG, Feb
  5, Nov 1; 1757: DL, Dec 8; 1774: DL, Mar 24, Apr 21, 27; 1775: CG, Feb 21,
  23; 1780: HAY, Jun 26, 30; 1785: CG, Mar 3
Smith, Sir Edward (spectator), 1696: DLORDG, Oct 12; 1697: DLDG, Oct 6; 1698:
  DLDG, Oct 10; 1699: DL, Oct 6
Smith, Elizabeth (concessionaire), 1775: KING'S, Nov 7
Smith, Fr (musician), 1758: CHAPEL, Apr 27
Smith, G (actor), 1776: CHR, Oct 16
Smith, George (equilibrist), 1798: CG, May 28
Smith, Henrietta, Mrs Walter (actor), 1786: HAY, Jul 13, 25, Aug 17
Smith, Henry (author)
--Princess of Parma, The, 1699: LIF, Apr 0
Smith, Henry (beneficiary), 1754: HAY, Nov 28
Smith, I (beneficiary), 1704: LIF, Jul 14
Smith, J (actor), 1736: HAY, Aug 2
Smith, J (actor), 1776: CHR, Sep 23, 25, 30, Oct 2, 4, 7, 9, 11, 14, 16, 18
Smith, Sir James (Lord Mayor), 1684: CITY, Oct 29
Smith, Sir Jeremy (spectator), 1669: BRIDGES, Mar 4
Smith, John (actor), 1747: RL, Jan 27
Smith, John (author)
--Cytherea; or, The Enamouring Girdle, 1676: NONE, Sep 0
Smith, Sir John (play dedicated to), 1696: DL, Feb 0
Smith, John (supernumerary), 1771: CG, Nov 13; 1772: CG, Mar 9, 21, 26, May 30,
  Nov 3
Smith, John Christopher (musician, composer), 1732: LIF, Nov 20; 1733: LIF, Apr
  16; 1740: HIC, Jan 4, Feb 22; 1741: HAY, Feb 3; 1754: CHAPEL, May 15; 1755:
  DL, Feb 3, Mar 14, Oct 29; 1756: DL, Feb 11; 1760: DL, Dec 13; 1762: DL, Feb
  3; 1764: DL, Mar 16; 1772: DL, Mar 6; 1774: DL, Mar 2; 1776: CG, Dec 27;
  1779: CG, May 13
--Paradise Lost (oratorio), 1760: CG, Feb 29, Mar 5; 1761: CG, Feb 18; 1774:
  DL, Feb 25, Mar 2
--Rebecca (oratorio), 1761: CG, Mar 4
--Rosalinda (musical), 1740: HIC, Jan 4, 11, 18, 25, Mar 27, Apr 18, 25; 1744:
  KING'S, Jan 31, Feb 4, 7, 11, HAY, 14, KING'S, 18, 25, 28, Mar 3, 31
--Teraminta (opera), 1732: LIF, Nov 20, 23, 30
--Ulysses (opera), 1733: LIF, Apr 16
Smith, John Stafford (composer), 1794: CG, May 23
Smith, Joseph (house servant), 1758: CG, May 12; 1759: CG, May 25; 1761: CG,
  May 15
Smith, Joseph (organ builder), 1800: CG, Mar 21
Smith, Justice (judge), 1777: CHR, Jul 23
Smith, Maria, Mrs Theodore (actor, singer), 1771: HAY, Sep 18; 1772: HAY, Dec
  21; 1773: DL, Feb 8; 1774: HAY, Jun 7; 1775: DL, Mar 20, Apr 20; 1776: DL,
  Dec 12, 26, 31; 1777: DL, Jan 1, 4, Feb 24, Apr 22, 29, May 28; 1778: DL, Sep
  24, Nov 2; 1779: DL, May 21, Nov 3, Dec 27; 1780: DL, Apr 3, 26, Sep 19, 23,
  Dec 6; 1781: DL, Mar 10, May 1, Nov 13; 1782: DL, Feb 1, 2, Apr 25; 1783: DL,
  May 12, Dec 2; 1784: DL, Nov 9; 1785: DL, Jan 12, 20, Feb 2, Apr 14
Smith, Martha (beneficiary), 1747: GF, Mar 17
Smith, Mary (actor), 1778: CG, Oct 21
Smith, Miss (actor), 1711: DL, Dec 3
Smith, Miss (actor), 1728: DL, Nov 15; 1730: GF, Oct 16, 26, Nov 6, 10, 24, 26,
  Dec 1, 11, 16; 1731: GF, Jan 5, 25, 26, Feb 6, 8, 15, 22, Mar 1, 2, 8, 13,
  SFGT, Sep 8
Smith, Miss (actor), 1746: GF, Mar 4
Smith, Miss (actor), 1748: NWC, Apr 4
Smith, Miss (actor), 1768: DL, Sep 26
Smith, Miss (actor), 1792: HAY, Oct 15
Smith, Miss (actor, dancer), 1716: LIF, May 2, Jun 12, 29, Jul 13, 18, 27, Aug
  3, Oct 10, 25, 26, Nov 1, 9, 14, 15, 21, 22, 28, Dec 12, 17, 18, 21, 29, 31;
  1717: LIF, Jan 4, 7, 14, 15, 25, 31, Feb 2, 6, 25, 26, Apr 8, 25, May 10, 13,
  16, 18, 20, 23, 27, 28, Jun 1, 7, 12, 28, Jul 5, Oct 5, 7, 14, 15, 22, Nov 2,
  5, 8, 15, 20, 22, Dec 2, 6, 11; 1718: LIF, Jan 1, 2, 4, 9, 15, 16, 21, 24,
  27, Feb 4, Mar 1, 8, 10, Apr 15, 16, 24, 30, May 6, 15, Jun 4, 27, Jul 18,
  Aug 6, DL, Oct 8, 14, 27, 28, Nov 6, 12, 14, 17, 19, 21, 24, 28, Dec 10, 15;
  1719: DL, Jan 7, 8, 29, Feb 3, 7, 12, Mar 19, Apr 9, 11, 16, 18, May 8, 12,
  13, Jun 5, 9, 16, Jul 31, Sep 15, Oct 12, 15, 16, 19, 26, 30, Nov 3, 6, 9,
  18, 23, 25; 1720: DL, Jan 13, Feb 5, Mar 28, 29, 31, Apr 5, 9, 25, May 12,
  16, 17, 18, 19, 21, 26, 27, 31, Jun 1, 2, 7, 10, Jul 7, 14, 21, Sep 13, 20,
  27, Oct 6, 25, 31, Nov 8, 23, Dec 7, 9, 14; 1721: DL, Feb 7, 9, Mar 30, Apr
  10, 11, 12, 25, 29, May 1, 5, 10, 11, 16, 29, 31, Jun 16, 20
Smith, Miss (dancer), 1762: DL, Nov 23
Smith, Miss (dancer), 1792: DL, Dec 27

Smith, Miss (dancer, actor), <u>1730</u>: HAY, Jan 8, 29, May 1, Jun 23, SF, Sep 14, HAY, Oct 23, Nov 16, 18, 30
Smith, Miss (dancer, actor), <u>1792</u>: CG, Dec 26; <u>1793</u>: CG, Mar 11, Oct 2, 22, Nov 19; <u>1794</u>: CG, Oct 3, 7; <u>1795</u>: CG, Feb 19, Oct 26, Nov 9, 16; <u>1796</u>: CG, Apr 8, 9, May 10
Smith, Miss (singer), <u>1763</u>: MARLY, Jun 28
Smith, Miss (spectator), <u>1760</u>: CG, Mar 1, DL, 10
Smith, Mrs (actor), <u>1705</u>: DL, Jan 18
Smith, Mrs (actor), <u>1728</u>: HAY, Nov 19
Smith, Mrs (actor), <u>1741</u>: SF, Sep 14; <u>1742</u>: JS, Apr 7; <u>1743</u>: TCD/BFTD, Aug 23; <u>1744</u>: JS, Mar 16, MFHNT, May 1, MF, 3, Jun 7; <u>1746</u>: NWMF, Oct 6, SOU, 7; <u>1749</u>: NWC, Nov 27; <u>1750</u>: NWC, Apr 16, HAY, Jul 26, SFYW, Sep 7
Smith, Mrs (actor), <u>1778</u>: HAY, Jan 26; <u>1794</u>: HAMM, Mar 24
Smith, Mrs (beneficiary), <u>1715</u>: GRT, Mar 23; <u>1719</u>: HIC, Feb 18; <u>1724</u>: HAY, Mar 9
Smith, Mrs (ticket deliverer), <u>1757</u>: DL, May 13; <u>1758</u>: DL, May 9; <u>1759</u>: DL, May 7
Smith, Mrs (ticket deliverer), <u>1791</u>: DL, May 31
Smith, Mrs and Miss (ticket deliverers), <u>1795</u>: DL, Jun 4
Smith, Mrs J (singer), <u>1776</u>: DL, Oct 18, Nov 25, Dec 26; <u>1777</u>: DL, Sep 20; <u>1778</u>: DL, Jan 5, May 23
Smith, Mrs S (actor), <u>1772</u>: DL, Dec 26; <u>1773</u>: DL, Sep 25; <u>1774</u>: DL, Apr 19; <u>1775</u>: DL, Mar 23, Apr 17
Smith, P (actor), <u>1769</u>: CG, Dec 29
Smith, R (actor), <u>1744</u>: MF, Jun 7
Smith, Rev (beneficiary), <u>1760</u>: CG, Dec 9, 11
Smith, Richard (actor), <u>1752</u>: CG, Dec 11; <u>1753</u>: CG, May 5, 14; <u>1754</u>: CG, Feb 12, Mar 9, Apr 25, May 4, 15, Sep 16, 25, Oct 2, 15, 29; <u>1755</u>: CG, Jan 8, 28, Feb 20, Mar 6, Apr 25, May 9, 12, Oct 6, 27, Nov 5, 10, 21, Dec 3, 27; <u>1756</u>: CG, Mar 30, May 5, Sep 27, Oct 4, 16, Nov 9, 24, Dec 10; <u>1757</u>: CG, Jan 27, Feb 19, Mar 31, Apr 30, May 4, 27, Sep 21, 28, Oct 5, 8, 19, 21, 22, Nov 5, 9, 11, Dec 7; <u>1758</u>: CG, Jan 11, Apr 3, 14, 17, May 2, Oct 4, 20, Nov 1, 9, 16; <u>1759</u>: CG, Jan 4, 12, Feb 1, 14, Apr 7, 26, May 3, 11, Sep 26, Oct 10, Nov 28, Dec 6; <u>1760</u>: CG, Jan 4, Feb 14, 26, Apr 8, May 2, 5, Sep 22, 24, Oct 8, 10, 17, Nov 18, Dec 9; <u>1761</u>: CG, Jan 28, Apr 2, 29, May 5, Sep 14, Oct 23, Dec 11, 28, 30; <u>1762</u>: CG, Jan 7, 28, Feb 17, 22, Mar 2, 20, 27, Apr 24, 30, May 5, Sep 20, 24, 27, Oct 8, 9, 20, Nov 3, 8; <u>1763</u>: CG, Feb 14, May 9, 11, Sep 26, Oct 7, 17, Nov 10, 15, Dec 9, 26; <u>1764</u>: CG, Feb 1, Mar 8, 10, 20, 27, May 4, 11, 14, 21, Sep 21, Oct 8, 15, 17, 25, Nov 3, 7, Dec 21; <u>1765</u>: CG, Apr 19, 24, May 2, 7, Sep 16, 18, 30, Oct 3; <u>1766</u>: CG, Jan 6, 31, Mar 20, Apr 8, 26, 29, May 2, 6, Sep 26, Oct 1, 6, 21, 28, 31, Nov 8, 11; <u>1767</u>: CG, Jan 31, Feb 14, Mar 2, Apr 24, May 12, 25, Sep 14, 16, 19, 21, Oct 7, 9, 16, 30, Nov 4, 7, 10, 23, Dec 8; <u>1768</u>: CG, Jan 9, 13, 16, 29, Feb 1, 25, Apr 25, 29, May 6, Jun 4, Sep 22, 28, 29, Nov 4, 24; <u>1769</u>: CG, Jan 2, 24, Apr 4, May 5, 8, 11, Sep 20, 30, Oct 4, 7, 26, Nov 1, 4, Dec 11, 20, 29; <u>1770</u>: CG, Jan 12, 25, Feb 12, 17, 24, Mar 24, Apr 18, 24, 26, May 11, 14, Sep 26, Oct 5, 10, 17, 23, 25, Nov 5, 29, 30, Dec 4; <u>1771</u>: CG, Jan 12, 26, Feb 9, Apr 30, May 3, 8, Sep 23, 25, 27, Oct 7, 14, 15, 18, Nov 4, 5, 9, 16, 26, Dec 17, 23; <u>1772</u>: CG, Jan 1, Mar 7, 23, Apr 7, 11, May 13, Sep 25, 28, Nov 4, 6, Dec 11; <u>1773</u>: CG, Jan 1, 7, 28, Mar 30, Apr 19, May 1, 10, 15, Nov 12, Dec 11, 21, 23; <u>1774</u>: CG, Jan 13, 26, Mar 15, Apr 6, 7, 9, May 10, 11; <u>1778</u>: CG, Jan 20, 21, Feb 2, 23, Mar 14, 30, Apr 11, May 11, 12, Oct 14, 16, 24, Dec 26; <u>1779</u>: CG, Jan 13, Mar 22, Apr 17, 29, Nov 22; <u>1780</u>: CG, Jan 17, 19, Feb 2, May 17, Jun 1, Oct 6, 9, 26, Nov 14; <u>1781</u>: CG, May 19; <u>1782</u>: CG, Mar 19
Smith, Robert (actor), <u>1747</u>: RL, Jan 27
Smith, Robert (composer), <u>1667</u>: BRIDGES, Sep 25; <u>1672</u>: BRIDGES, Jan 0, LIF, Apr 0, DG, Jul 4, Aug 3, LIF, Nov 0, DG, 4; <u>1673</u>: DG, Feb 6, LIF, May 0, DG, 0
Smith, Robert Archibald (violinist), <u>1793</u>: KING'S, Jun 18
Smith, Sarah (actor), <u>1759</u>: DL, May 21, Oct 31; <u>1760</u>: DL, Jun 19, Oct 20; <u>1761</u>: DL, Apr 23, CG, Jun 23, HAY, Aug 22; <u>1762</u>: DL, May 18; <u>1764</u>: DL, May 11, Sep 25; <u>1766</u>: DL, Feb 1, May 19; <u>1767</u>: DL, Jan 24, May 1, Sep 26; <u>1768</u>: DL, Feb 27, Apr 27, Oct 10, 19, Nov 17, Dec 3; <u>1769</u>: DL, Feb 4, HAY, 28, DL, Apr 18, Sep 21; <u>1770</u>: DL, Mar 3, 26, May 8, Oct 13, 25, Nov 17, 20, HAY, Dec 14; <u>1771</u>: DL, Jan 2, 31; <u>1772</u>: DL, Feb 1, Apr 22, HAY, Sep 18, DL, Oct 20, Nov 6, 21, Dec 2, 18; <u>1773</u>: DL, Jan 9, Feb 1, HAY, 26, DL, Mar 29, Apr 20, May 12, 19, Jun 2, Sep 18, 23, 28, 30, Oct 9, 16, Nov 2, Dec 27; <u>1774</u>: DL, Jan 19, Feb 8, Apr 4, 12, 14, 15, May 3, 7, Jun 2, Sep 20, 24, Oct 1, 4, 5, 11, Nov 5, Dec 26; <u>1775</u>: DL, Feb 27, Mar 2, 23, Apr 17, 22, 27, May 2, 11, 27, Sep 23, 30, Oct 5, 7, 10, 23, 27, Nov 11; <u>1776</u>: DL, Feb 8, 17, Mar 11, 25, 26, Apr 9, 20, May 2, 18, 20, Jun 10
Smith, T (actor), <u>1736</u>: HAY, Jun 26, Aug 2
Smith, T (singer), <u>1778</u>: HAY, Mar 31

Smith, Theodore (composer), 1773: DL, Nov 25; 1776: DL, Apr 9; 1777: HAY, Jul 18
Smith, Thomas (actor), 1761: CG, Jun 23; 1767: CG, Oct 19, Nov 18; 1768: CG, Feb 20, 25, Apr 29, May 27, Jun 4, Sep 30, Nov 17; 1769: CG, May 19
Smith, Thomas (singer), 1755: DL, May 5
Smith, Thomson (payee), 1773: DL, Feb 9; 1775: DL, Nov 13
Smith, Tom (dancer), 1771: HAY, Aug 12
Smith, Walter (actor), 1777: HAY, Sep 13
Smith, William (actor), 1662: LIF, Sep 30, ATCOURT, Nov 1; 1663: LIF, Jan 8, Feb 23, Oct 0, Dec 22; 1664: LIF, Mar 0, Aug 13, Sep 10, Nov 5; 1665: LIF, Apr 3; 1666: NONE, Nov 14; 1667: LIF, Mar 7, Aug 15, Oct 24; 1668: LIF, Feb 6, 11, May 2, NONE, Sep 0; 1670: LIF, Apr 0, NONE, Sep 0, LIF, 20, Nov 0; 1671: LIF, Jan 10, Jun 0, Sep 0, DG, Nov 0; 1672: DG, Jan 31, Aug 3, Nov 4, ATCOU/DG, Dec 2; 1673: DG, Feb 18, Mar 12, Jul 3; 1674: DG, Nov 9; 1675: DG, May 28, NONE, Sep 0; 1676: DG, Mar 0, 11, May 25, Jun 8, Jul 3, 25, Aug 0, Nov 4, Dec 0; 1677: DG, Feb 12, Mar 24, May 12, 31, Sep 0; 1678: DG, Jan 0, 17, Apr 5, May 28, Jun 0, Sep 0, Nov 0; 1679: DG, Mar 0, Apr 0, May 0, Sep 0, Oct 0; 1680: DG, Jan 0, Feb 0, Jun 0, Sep 0, Nov 1, Dec 8; 1681: DG, Jan 0, Mar 0, Apr 0, Nov 0, DG/IT, 22; 1682: DG, Jan 23, Feb 9, Mar 0, Apr 21, DLORDG, Oct 9, ATCOURT, Nov 15, DL, 16, 28; 1683: DL, Jan 19, DG, Jul 0, NONE, Sep 0, DL, Nov 12; 1684: DL, Apr 0; 1686: DL, Nov 29; 1687: ATCOURT, Apr 25; 1688: NONE, Sep 0; 1689: NONE, Sep 0; 1691: NONE, Sep 0; 1695: LIF, Apr 30, Dec 0, 28
Smith, William (actor), 1753: CG, Jan 8, Feb 8, 13, 21, Mar 10, Apr 7, Sep 12, Oct 22, Nov 5, 20, 22, 26, Dec 11; 1754: CG, Jan 10, 22, Feb 12, 23, Mar 26, Apr 20, 24, 26, May 2, 13, Sep 16, 25, HAY/SFB, Oct 10, CG, 15, 22, Nov 4, 6, 7, 27, HAY, 28, CG, 28, HAY, Dec 2; 1755: CG, Jan 10, 28, Feb 8, 18, 24, Mar 1, 6, 22, Apr 3, 8, 9, 10, 15, 18, 28, May 14, Sep 29, Oct 10, 11, 14, 20, 27, 31, Nov 4, 7, 13, 15, 19, 22, Dec 4, 5, 12; 1756: CG, Jan 15, Feb 5, 19, 26, Mar 22, 23, 25, Apr 3, 27, May 3, 7, 17, Sep 29, Oct 12, 13, 14, 15, 18, 21, 23, 25, 27, 28, 30, Nov 1, 4, 17, 22, 29, Dec 1, 7, 17; 1757: CG, Jan 8, 25, 28, Feb 9, 19, 21, Mar 14, 22, May 16, Oct 5, 7, 10, 12, 14, 17, 19, 20, 21, 27, 28, 31, Nov 2, 5, 14, 26, Dec 1, 5, 14, 15, 20; 1758: CG, Jan 11, 27, Feb 1, Mar 9, 14, 16, 27, Apr 10, 12, Nov 2, 3, 4, 7, 13, 14, 16, 20, 21, 23; 1759: CG, Jan 12, 15, 16, Feb 1, 7, 15, Mar 3, 5, 6, 22, 24, 27, Apr 5, 7, 20, 21, 28, May 25, DL, 29, CG, Sep 28, Oct 3, 5, Nov 5, 23, 26, 30, Dec 5, 8, 11, 20, 28; 1760: CG, Jan 4, 9, 14, 18, 24, 31, Feb 28, 29, Mar 8, 17, 18, 25, Apr 18, 29, May 19, HAY, Jun 28, CG, Sep 22, Oct 6, 13, 25, Nov 18, 22, 29, Dec 9, 11; 1761: CG, Jan 2, Feb 6, 16, 17, Mar 3, 4, 5, 9, 25, 26, 30, Apr 13, 17, 22, May 8, Sep 9, 26, Oct 1, 2, 3, 5, 7, 17, 23, 24, 27, 31, Nov 2, 4, 13, 27, Dec 28, 30; 1762: CG, Jan 28, Feb 3, 15, Mar 13, 22, 23, Apr 19, 21, 24, 26, May 4, 13, Sep 20, 24, 30, Oct 1, 5, 6, 8, 9, 14, 16, 21, 25, Nov 3, 5, 15, 30; 1763: CG, Jan 14, 28, Feb 1, Mar 17, Apr 25, May 9, 14, Sep 19, 23, 26, 28, Oct 3, 5, 10, 14, 15, 17, 18, 20, 26, Nov 4, 15, 16, 18, Dec 26, 27; 1764: CG, Jan 9, 16, 17, 26, Feb 11, 13, 15, Mar 26, Apr 28, May 7, Sep 17, 24, 26, Oct 1, 5, 8, 11, 15, 19, 20, 22, 24, 25, 29, 30, Nov 1, 5, 7, 8, 16, 24, 30, Dec 11, 21; 1765: CG, Jan 8, 14, 21, Feb 18, Mar 14, Apr 11, 16, May 15, Sep 16, 20, 23, 25, 30, Oct 2, 3, 5, 8, 9, 10, 16, 17, 22, 23, 28, 31, Nov 13, 27, Dec 10, 12, 26; 1766: CG, Jan 9, 31, Feb 6, Mar 17, 31, Apr 1, 14, 15, 18, 19, May 2, 6, 13, Sep 22, Oct 20, 22, 23, 28, 31, Nov 4, 7, 11, 17, 19, 21, 25, 27, 28, Dec 4, 9, 10, 16, 23, 30; 1767: CG, Jan 10, 31, Feb 14, Mar 2, 21, 23, 28, Apr 10, 24, 25, May 11, 19, HAY, Jun 4, 5, 22, 26, Jul 2, 6, 31, Aug 5, 21, 25, 27, Sep 4, 7, 9, 16, CG, 17, HAY, 18, CG, 19, 21, 22, 23, 26, Oct 19, 22, 30, Nov 4, 7, 17, 18, 27, Dec 8, 28, 31; 1768: CG, Jan 7, Feb 19, 20, Mar 2, 17, 19, 24, Apr 9, 13, 20, May 10, 27, Sep 20, 21, 22, 29, Oct 5, 6, 12, 14, 15, Nov 4, 8, 16, 17, 19, Dec 3, HAY, 19, CG, 22; 1769: CG, Jan 2, 27, Feb 18, HAY, 28, CG, Mar 13, 14, 17, 28, 29, Apr 7, May 3, Sep 20, 22, 27, 30, Oct 4, 5, 6, 18, 24, 26, Nov 1, 4, 23, 27, 29, Dec 2, 19, 22, 29; 1770: CG, Jan 19, Feb 3, 16, 24, DL, Mar 2, HAY, 17, CG, 20, 22, 24, 26, 29, 31, Apr 30, May 8, HAY, 23, 28, 30, Jun 1, 15, Aug 24, CG, Sep 24, 26, HAY, Oct 5, CG, 8, 12, 13, 16, 18, 19, 25, 27, 29, Nov 5, 15, 23, 29, Dec 3, 4, HAY, 14; 1771: CG, Feb 9, Mar 12, 14, Apr 5, 9, HAY, 20, CG, 24, 25, 30, Sep 25, 27, Oct 4, 14, 15, 18, 25, Nov 2, DL, 2, CG, 4, 5, 7, 11, 16, 19, 26, Dec 6, 9, 11, 30; 1772: CG, Jan 1, 2, 27, DL, Feb 4, CG, Mar 5, HAY, 16, CG, 21, DL, 23, CG, 24, 30, Apr 4, 7, May 4, HAY, 22, 27, Jun 29, Jul 6, 10, Aug 10, Sep 17, 18, CG, 28, Oct 5, 14, 16, 23, 26, 30, Nov 2, 4, 12, 14, 21; 1773: CG, Jan 6, 7, 16, 25, 28, Feb 23, Mar 6, 22, 30, Apr 3, 16, 19, 28, May 1, 4, 7, Oct 4, 6, 11, 18, 21, 23, 25, Nov 4, 8, 12, 20, 23, Dec 1, 4, 7, 11, 18, 21, 23; 1774: CG, Jan 5, Feb 11, Mar 12, 14, 15, 22, Apr 11, 13, 19, May 11, DL, 13, MARLY, Jun 30, Sep 3, HAY, 21, DL, 22, 27, Oct 4, 15, Nov 1, 4, 11, 25, Dec 9, 19; 1775: DL, Jan 4, 21, 25, Feb 17, Mar 7, 18, 20, 21, 23, Apr 21, 24, May 1, 12, 13, 17, Oct 3, 5, 11, 12, 14, 21,

23, 26, Nov 1, 3, 4, 14, 18, Dec 2, 7; 1776: DL, Jan 27, Feb 10, 15, Mar 11,
12, 14, 18, 21, 23, 28, 30, Apr 24, May 16, Sep 24, 28, Oct 1, 10, 12, 19,
22, 23, 25, 26, 29, Nov 4, 5, 16, 19, 25, Dec 14, 18, 31; 1777: DL, Jan 28,
Feb 7, 24, Mar 10, Apr 16, May 8, Sep 23, 27, Oct 9, 17, 22, 28, 31, Nov 4,
13, 18, 29, Dec 11, 18; 1778: DL, Jan 2, 5, 10, 23, Feb 24, Mar 26, 30, Apr
20, May 8, Sep 17, CG, 21, DL, 22, 24, 26, Oct 6, 15, 19, 20, 23, 26, 27, 28,
CG, Nov 4, DL, 14, 16, 18, 28, Dec 11, 21; 1779: CG, Jan 19, DL, 23, Feb 8,
Mar 15, 16, 25, Apr 12, Sep 18, 21, 25, 28, Oct 2, 19, 30, Nov 5, 17, 18, 20,
24, Dec 13, 20; 1780: DL, Jan 24, Mar 4, 9, Apr 17, 18, 26, Oct 14, 19, 23,
25, 26, 31, Nov 1, 3, 4, 6, 10, 13, 17, 27, Dec 6, 8, 15, 19; 1781: DL, Jan
6, Feb 12, 17, Mar 26, 27, Apr 24, May 5, Sep 18, 25, 27, 29, Oct 13, 18, 19,
25, 27, 30, Nov 5, 7, 21, 27; 1782: DL, Jan 26, Feb 25, Mar 16, 18, Apr 30,
May 8, 10, Sep 18, 19, 24, 26, Oct 8, 10, 29, Nov 2, 8, 16, 22, Dec 5; 1783:
DL, Jan 10, Feb 18, Mar 10, 18, 25, May 22, Sep 23, Oct 8, 11, 24, Nov 3, 20,
21, 27, Dec 2, 10; 1784: DL, Jan 3, 10, 16, 28, Feb 3, Mar 6, 25, May 5, Sep
18, 23, 28, Oct 11, 12, 18, 23, Nov 3, 5, 16, 17, 19, 22, 23, 25, Dec 2;
1785: DL, Jan 14, 22, Feb 2, Mar 15, Apr 14, 18, 20, 27, May 3, 11, 24, Sep
20, 24, 27, 29, Oct 1, 20, 22, 27, 31, Nov 7, 8, 18, 21, 22, 26, Dec 7, 30;
1786: DL, Jan 9, 14, Feb 23, Mar 4, 7, 9, 21, May 24, HAY, Jul 25, DL, Sep
16, 26, 28, Oct 9, 12, 24, 26, 28, Nov 15; 1787: DL, Jan 18, 29, Mar 20, May
7, 19, 21, 23, 30, Sep 20, Oct 11, 13, 20, 24, Nov 3, 5, 16, 20, Dec 6, 7,
10, 28; 1788: DL, Jan 2, Mar 10, May 6, 14, 21, 23, Jun 9; 1798: DL, May 18
Smith, William (actor), 1778: HAY, Jan 26, Feb 9, Mar 24, 31; 1779: HAY, Feb
22, Mar 15, Oct 18, Dec 27; 1780: HAY, Jan 3, Mar 28; 1782: HAY, Jan 21;
1784: HAY, Jan 21, Feb 9, 23, Mar 8, 22, Dec 13; 1786: HAMM, Jun 5, 7, 28,
30, Jul 5, 7, 10, 24, 26; 1788: HAY, Aug 27
Smith, Sir William Sidney (admiral), 1796: CG, Apr 15; 1798: DL, May 21; 1800:
CG, May 7
Smith, Young (actor), 1728: BFHM, Aug 24
Smithfield Rounds, 1722: BFPMB, Aug 25; 1726: BFY, Aug 26; 1727: BF, Aug 23
Smithfield, 1682: BF, Aug 23; 1689: BF, Aug 26; 1698: BF, Aug 25; 1699: BF, Aug
23, DLLIF, Sep 12; 1701: MF, May 1, BF, Aug 25; 1705: BF, Aug 27; 1717: BF,
Aug 24; 1719: BFPM, Aug 24; 1720: BFPMJ, Aug 23, BFBL, 23; 1724: BFP, Aug 22;
1725: BF, Aug 23; 1730: BFPG, Aug 20; 1731: CRT, Mar 10; 1735: BF, Aug 23;
1742: BFHC, Aug 25; 1743: BFHC, Aug 23; 1745: DL, Apr 17; 1746: DL, Feb 26,
BF, Aug 23; 1749: BFC, Aug 23, BFY, 23, BFH, 23, BFY, 24, 25, BFYT, 26, BFY,
28; 1753: DL, Oct 9; 1757: BF, Sep 3; 1758: BFDVW, Sep 2; 1759: BFY, Sep 3,
BF, 5; 1762: DL, Jan 29, BFY, Sep 3
Smiths are good Fellows (song), 1782: HAY, Aug 17; 1783: HAY, Jun 30; 1785:
HAY, Jul 13
Smithson (actor), 1749: SOU, Jan 9
Smock Alley Theatre, Dublin, 1749: DL, Mar 31, HAY, Oct 17; 1767: DL, Nov 19;
1777: HAY, Oct 6; 1778: CG, May 5, HAY, Jul 2; 1779: DL, Mar 23, CG, Apr 30,
HAY, Oct 13; 1781: CG, May 10, Oct 16; 1782: CG, Mar 16, HAY, Nov 25; 1783:
DL, Nov 6, Dec 10; 1784: DL, Jan 22, HAY, Mar 22; 1785: CG, May 12; 1786: CG,
Feb 13, HAY, Mar 6, Aug 29, CG, Sep 18, Oct 25, DL, 30, CG, Nov 14; 1787: CG,
Oct 12; 1788: DL, Oct 28, Nov 5; 1791: CG, Feb 16; 1792: CG, Feb 28
Smollett, Dr Tobias, 1749: CG, Feb 14; 1750: CG, Mar 1; 1757: DL, Jan 22; 1769:
HAY, Feb 27; 1771: DL, Apr 1; 1773: DL, Mar 1; 1785: CG, Apr 1
--Alceste (opera), 1749: CG, Feb 14; 1750: CG, Mar 1
--Israelites, The; or, The Pampered Nabob (farce), 1785: CG, Apr 1
--Reprisal, The; or, The Tars of Old England, 1757: DL, Jan 22, 24, 25, 26, 27,
29, Feb 1, 3, 21, Apr 25, 27, May 5; 1759: DL, Apr 7; 1762: DL, Mar 27, May
17, BFY, Sep 3; 1771: DL, Apr 1, 3; 1777: CG, Oct 21, 22, 23, 27, 31; 1779:
CG, Jan 25, Feb 13, 15; 1784: HAY, Feb 23; 1793: CG, Apr 24
Smug Upon Tuesday (song), 1713: DL, Jun 17; 1718: DL, Jun 13, Nov 7; 1723: DL,
Aug 2, 6; 1724: RI, Jun 27; 1732: GF, Apr 28
Smuggler Foiled. See Tit for Tat (epilogue).
Smugglers, The. See Birch, Samuel.
Smuglers, The. See Odell, Thomas.
Smyrna Coffee House, 1753: DL, Dec 21; 1759: CG, May 8; 1763: DL, Apr 27; 1765:
DL, Dec 18
Smyth (dancer), 1675: ATCOURT, Feb 15
Smyth, John, 1690: NONE, Sep 0
--Win Her and Take Her; or, Old Fools will be Medling, 1690: NONE, Sep 0
Smyth, Miss (actor), 1783: HAY, Sep 17
Smythe, James Moore, 1727: DL, Jan 27
--Rival Modes, The, 1727: DL, Jan 27, 28, 31, Feb 1, 2, 3
Smythies, Mrs (actor), 1725: LIF, May 14, Nov 27; 1726: LIF, Jan 14, Mar 26,
May 13
Snagg, R (printer), 1780: HAY, Oct 30
Snelson (2nd gallery office keeper), 1786: KING'S, Dec 23; 1787: KING'S, Mar

17, Dec 8; 1788: KING'S, Apr 5
Snider (Snyder) (actor), 1732: HAY, Mar 13, Apr 24, Nov 16; 1733: HAY, Jun 4,
   DL, Nov 7, 26; 1734: DL, Jan 19, Feb 4, DL/HAY, Mar 21, DL, Apr 29; 1744:
   HAY, Apr 16
Snip's Humorous Description of the Camp (entertainment), 1790: CII, Apr 5
Snivley and Davis (worsted lacemen), 1771: CG, Nov 29
Snow (singer), 1693: ATCOURT, Apr 30; 1698: YB, May 10
Snow, Jonathan (beneficiary), 1757: HAY, May 2
Snow, Miss (dancer), 1765: CG, May 10, HAY, Jun 10
Snow, Robert (actor), 1791: CG, Oct 7; 1796: CG, Oct 6; see also Hargrave
Snow, Valentine (musician), 1734: DT, Mar 22; 1735: HAY, Jan 31, TB, Apr 24;
   1736: YB, Mar 4; 1737: LIF, Jan 20, Feb 1, HIC, Mar 24; 1740: HIC, Mar 19;
   1741: HIC, Feb 5, HAY, 26, CT, Mar 13, GF, Apr 28; 1744: SH, Feb 9; 1745:
   HAY, Feb 20; 1748: HAY, Dec 9; 1752: DL, Dec 2
Snowfields, 1752: SOU, Nov 24
Snowhill, 1743: DL, Jan 3; 1772: DL, Mar 17; 1792: HAY, Nov 26
Snuff Box, The. See Heard, William.
So che per Gioco (song), 1750: KING'S, Apr 10
So fair young Caelia's Charms (song), 1697: DL, Feb 0
So shall the Lute and Harp (song), 1760: DL, May 14; 1789: CG, Mar 27
So well Corinna likes the joy (song), 1695: LIF, Dec 0
So when the last (song), 1794: CG, Apr 11
Soaper. See Soper.
Socco (actor), 1749: BBT, Mar 1
Social Songsters, The (interlude, anon), 1800: CG, Apr 26, May 2
Soderini (musician), 1758: MARLY, Aug 21; 1766: CG, Mar 5
Sodi (dancer), 1743: KING'S, Jan 29; 1746: CG, Feb 6, 7, 8, 13, 15, 18, 20, 24,
   25, 27, Mar 1, 3, 6, 10, 11, 20, 22, 31, Apr 1, 5, 9, 11, 14, 17, 19, 22, 26,
   29, 30
Sodi, Pietro (dancer), 1761: CG, Mar 9, Apr 25, Sep 14, 21, 23, 26, Dec 10;
   1762: CG, Jan 28, Feb 2, 12, Apr 16, 17, 19, Oct 1, 7, 8, Nov 1, Dec 2; 1763:
   CG, Feb 3, Apr 15, May 26, KING'S, Nov 26; 1764: KING'S, Feb 21, Mar 31;
   1766: KING'S, Jan 25, Mar 13, Nov 25; 1773: CG, Apr 24
Sofonisba. See Vento, Mathias.
Sofonisbe. See Gluck, Christoph Willibald von.
Soft Music, let my humble lay (song), 1800: DL, Jun 10
Softly rise (song), 1790: CG, Mar 17, 19, 26; 1792: CG, Mar 9, KING'S, 28, 30;
   1793: KING/HAY, Mar 13; 1794: CG, Mar 14, DL, Apr 2; 1795: CG, Mar 18; 1796:
   CG, Feb 26; 1797: CG, Mar 17; 1798: CG, Mar 9; 1799: CG, Feb 20; 1800: CG,
   Mar 19
Softly sweet (song), 1751: CG, Apr 23; 1790: DL, Feb 24, CG, Mar 3; 1791: CG,
   Mar 25; 1792: CG, Mar 7, KING'S, 14; 1793: CG, Mar 8; 1794: CG, Mar 14; 1798:
   CG, Mar 28; 1799: CG, Feb 8, Mar 6, 15
Soho Square, 1685: OLDFIELD, Dec 30; 1726: CLAR, Nov 14; 1738: GF, Jul 26;
   1742: LIF, Jan 29, DL, Apr 5; 1772: CG, Dec 19; 1773: DL, Dec 21; 1777: DL,
   Dec 30; 1779: CG, Dec 22; 1793: DL, May 30; 1799: CG, Apr 26; 1800: CG, May 2
Soho, 1740: DL, Apr 24; 1741: DL, Apr 4; 1742: DL, Apr 28; 1743: DL, Apr 20,
   May 18; 1744: DL, Apr 9, 23, HAY, Dec 11; 1746: DT, Mar 14; 1748: DL, Mar 7;
   1752: DL, Mar 14, Apr 20; 1753: DL, Mar 24, 26; 1754: SOHO, Mar 26, 28,
   KING'S, Apr 2, 25; 1755: SOHO, Jan 16, Mar 11; 1756: SOHO, Feb 2, Mar 16;
   1757: SOHO, Feb 1, Mar 14; 1758: SOHO, Mar 31, KING'S, Apr 6; 1760: SOHO, Jan
   18, Feb 14; 1761: SOHO, Jan 21, 28, Apr 15; 1762: SOHO, Feb 9, CG, Mar 22;
   1763: CG, Mar 19; 1764: HAY, Nov 13; 1765: HAY, Feb 21; 1771: HAY, May 2;
   1774: DL, Feb 24; 1777: HAY, Sep 18; 1778: DL, May 14; 1779: DL, May 15;
   1782: HAY, Mar 4; 1785: HAY, Jan 24, DL, Apr 7, KING'S, May 19, HAY, Aug 2;
   1786: DL, Apr 25, May 25, HAY, Aug 3; 1787: CG, Mar 27, DL, Apr 25, HAY, Aug
   7, 10, 21; 1788: DL, Apr 21, HAY, Aug 15, 20; 1789: DL, Apr 30, HAY, Aug 10;
   1790: DL, Apr 14, CG, May 5, HAY, Aug 13, 31; 1791: CG, Feb 15, HAY, Mar 7,
   DL, Apr 5, CG, May 14, HAY, Jul 26, Aug 31; 1792: DLKING'S, Mar 29, CG, Apr
   14, HAY, Aug 20; 1793: DL, Apr 8, CG, 17, May 3, HAY, Aug 30; 1794: HAY, Jan
   27, CG, May 13, HAY, Sep 3; 1795: DL, Apr 16, CG, May 8, DL, 20, HAY, Aug 10;
   1796: HAY, Sep 7; 1797: HAY, Sep 4; 1798: CG, Apr 24, KING'S, May 10, DL, Jun
   7, HAY, Sep 7; 1799: DL, Apr 18, KING'S, 18, CG, 19, HAY, Aug 17; 1800:
   KING'S, May 8
Soiree a la Mode (dance), 1775: CG, Dec 7, 16, 18, 23; 1776: CG, Mar 7, 12, 21,
   26, Apr 23; 1777: CG, Nov 3, Dec 11; 1778: CG, Mar 21, 24, Apr 2, Oct 23, Nov
   10
Soiree Provencale (dance), 1787: DL, Jan 13, 29
Sol ti chiedo O spero amato (song), 1753: KING'S, Apr 30
Solard (actor), 1725: HAY, May 7
Soldano Generoso, Il. See Bertoni, Fernando Giuseppe.
Soldier and a Sailor (song), 1695: LIF, Apr 30

Soldier for me (song), 1783: DL, Apr 7; 1784: DL, Apr 12, 21, May 20; 1785: DL,
    Apr 1
Soldier take off thy Wine (song), 1780: HAY, Aug 24
Soldier Tired of War's Alarms (song), 1771: CG, Mar 16, DL, May 8, 10, MARLY,
    Aug 15, 20, 27, 29, GROTTO, 30, Sep 3, MARLY, 5, GROTTO, 9, MARLY, 12; 1772:
    DL, May 25, CG, Dec 19; 1774: CG, May 12, HAY, Jun 7; 1775: CG, Mar 21; 1776:
    DL, Apr 20, CG, May 11; 1777: DL, Apr 17; 1778: HAY, Feb 9, Mar 24; 1781: DL,
    Apr 21; 1782: DL, Apr 20, CG, May 4, HAY, 6, DL, 8; 1783: DL, Apr 22; 1784:
    DL, Apr 14, 26, May 17; 1785: DL, Mar 30, CG, Apr 6, HAY, 26, Aug 2; 1786:
    DL, Apr 24; 1787: CG, Apr 21, ROY, Jun 20; 1788: DL, Mar 5, 12, CG, Jun 3;
    1789: HAY, Feb 23, DL, Mar 20; 1790: DL, Mar 5; 1791: CG, Mar 18, 25, Apr 13,
    15; 1792: KING'S, Mar 14, CG, 14, 21; 1793: KING/HAY, Mar 15, 20; 1794: CG,
    Mar 21, DL, Apr 11; 1795: CG, Mar 13, 27; 1796: HAY, Feb 22, CG, Mar 16;
    1797: CG, May 24; 1798: Mar 2, 28; 1799: CG, Feb 20, Mar 1, 15; 1800: CG,
    Mar 21, May 22, Jun 2, DL, 7, 17, HAY, Aug 26
Soldier's Festival, The; or, The Night before Battle (interlude, anon), 1790:
    CG, Apr 21; 1791: CG, May 3, 9, 16, 31; 1792: CG, Apr 18; 1793: CG, Apr 24,
    May 1, 2, 16; 1794: CG, May 7; 1800: CG, Apr 23, May 10, 13, 17
Soldier's Fortune, The. See Otway, Thomas.
Soldier's Grave (Of all Sensations Pity brings), 1790: CG, Nov 23, Dec 1
Soldier's Song (song), 1798: CG, Apr 24
Soldier's Stratagem, The (play, anon), 1719: RI, Aug 31, Sep 5
Solemn Dirge (song), 1753: KING'S, May 12; 1754: DL, Mar 27
Soliloquy on Life Death and Immortality (entertainment), 1789: KHS, Sep 16
Solimano (pastiche), 1758: KING'S, Jan 31, Feb 7, 14, 21, Mar 4, Apr 18, 25,
    May 4, 20, Jun 3; 1765: KING'S, May 14, 18, 21, 23, Jun 1, 15, 22
Solitudini Amate (song), 1729: DL, Mar 26
Solo pieta vi chiedo (song), 1713: QUEEN'S, Apr 25
Solomon. See Boyce, Dr William; Handel, George Frederic.
Solomon. See Salomon.
Solyman the Magnificent (tale), 1782: CG, Dec 20; 1784: CG, Mar 6, Oct 27;
    1785: CG, Nov 23; 1787: CG, Feb 9; 1789: CG, Feb 19, Nov 19; 1792: CG, Oct 3;
    1797: CG, Nov 18; 1800: CG, Jun 13
Some Considerations on the establishment of the French Strollers (book), 1749:
    DL, Nov 2
Some happy soul come down and tell (song), 1672: DG, Aug 3
Somebody (song), 1796: CG, May 20; 1797: CG, Jun 5
Somers Town, 1798: DL, May 23; 1799: DL, Apr 18, HAY, Aug 20; 1800: DL, May 21
Somerset Coffee House, 1750: DL, Jan 11; 1752: DL, Dec 19; 1767: VAUX, May 25,
    DL, Jun 3
Somerset House, 1697: STRAND, Jun 17; 1698: RICHMOND, Aug 8; 1699: YB, May 12;
    1751: DL, May 2; 1755: DL, Feb 5; 1758: NONE, Mar 21; 1760: DL, Oct 13
Somerset St, 1790: DL, Mar 22; 1791: DL, Mar 22; 1792: DLKING'S, Apr 16; 1793:
    DL, Apr 22; 1795: DL, May 4; 1796: DL, Apr 25; 1797: DL, May 29; 1798: DL,
    Apr 30
Somerset, Henry, Duke of Beaufort, 1687: CITY, Oct 29
Somerset, Henry, Marquis of Worcester (spectator), 1675: ATCOURT, Jun 7; 1677:
    DL, Mar 17; 1681: DLORDG, Nov 12
Somerville, Mrs (actor), 1787: HAY, Mar 26; 1792: HAY, Nov 26
Sommerford, John (sawyer, near casualty), 1739: CG, Feb 6
Sommers (actor), 1762: HAY, May 1; 1763: HAY, Jul 18, Aug 5
Somnambule, La. See Pont-de-Veyle, Antoine de Feriol comte de.
Son Confusa Pastorella (song), 1731: LIF, Mar 26; 1748: KING'S, Apr 5; 1749:
    KING'S, Mar 21
Son Perfetta cacciatrice (song), 1792: DLKING'S, Apr 19
Son Priginiero (song), 1737: DL, Jan 14
Son Qual Nave (song), 1738: DL, Apr 12
Son Regina (song), 1779: DL, Mar 12
Son sventurato (song), 1750: KING'S, Apr 10
Son-in-Law, The. See O'Keeffe, John.
Song began from Jove (song), 1791: CG, Mar 25; 1792: CG, Mar 7; 1794: CG, Mar
    14
Song for Every Body, A (interlude, anon), 1800: HAY, Sep 3
Song of Diana (song), 1746: CG, Mar 10, 13, 17, 18, Apr 9, 16, 21
Song of Moses, The. See Linley Jr, Thomas.
Song on the Defeat of the Rebels (song), 1746: CG, Apr 25
Song on the Naval Victories (song), 1798: CG, Nov 7
Song on the Taking of Martinico (song), 1762: HAY, Apr 22
Song upon Everybody (song), 1754: HAY, Dec 9
Sono imbrogliato gia (song), 1792: KING'S, Feb 29
Sons of Anacreon, The; or, The Convivial Coterie (interlude, anon), 1785: DL,
    Apr 18, May 5, 6, 16, 19, HAY, Aug 19, 26, Sep 16; 1786: DL, Apr 4, May 9;

1787: DL, Apr 9, 27, May 22; 1788: HAY, Aug 22; 1789: CG, Apr 21, May 5, 14,
   29, HAY, Aug 10; 1790: DL, May 20; 1791: DL, May 18, HAY, Aug 26; 1792:
   DLKING'S, Apr 10, 19; 1795: DL, May 27; 1796: DL, May 27; 1798: DL, May 23
Soothed with the sound (song), 1791: CG, Mar 25; 1792: CG, Mar 7; 1794: CG, Mar
   14
Soper (actor, singer), 1758: SOHO, Apr 1
Soper, Master (actor), 1759: CG, Feb 2, May 4
Sophie, Mlle (dancer), 1774: KING'S, Dec 13; 1775: KING'S, Jan 17, Apr 18, 22,
   25, May 16, 30, Jun 6, 17, 24, Oct 31, Nov 7; 1776: KING'S, Jan 9, 20, Feb 3,
   6, 13, 24, Mar 12, 19, 28, Apr 18, 25, May 30, Jun 8
Sophocles, 1714: MEG, Apr 1; 1773: CG, Feb 2
--Oedipus Tyrannus, 1714: MEG, Apr 1, 3; 1773: CG, Feb 2
Sophonisba. See Thomson, James.
Sophonisba; or, Hannibal's Overthrow. See Lee, Nathaniel.
Sophy, The. See Denham, Sir John.
Sorbelloni, Pietro (singer), 1760: KING'S, Aug 25, Nov 22, Dec 16; 1761:
   KING'S, Jan 6, Feb 7
Sorge nell' alma mia (song), 1755: KING'S, Mar 17
Sorin (Sorein, Surrein) (dancer), 1697: LIF, Jun 0; 1703: DL, Oct 7; 1705: LIF,
   Oct 8; 1716: DL, Apr 4, 11, 20, May 7, 10, 12; 1736: HAY, Feb 20
Sorosini, Sga (singer), 1725: KING'S, Apr 10, May 11
Sorrows of Charlotte at the Tomb of Werter (song), 1785: CG, Apr 6
Sortemia Tiranna, La (song), 1746: KING'S, Mar 25
Sosarmes. See Handel, George Frederic.
Sot, The. See Arne, Dr Thomas A.
Sotheby. See Southby.
Sotheby, William (prologuist), 1800: DL, Jan 25
Souchart, Mrs (beneficiary), 1766: CG, May 12
Soulart (actor), 1725: HAY, Apr 19
Souls Warfare (play, anon), 1671: NONE, Sep 0
Sound an alarm (song), 1789: DL, Mar 6; 1790: DL, Mar 12, CG, 19; 1791: CG, Mar
   30, Apr 15; 1793: CG, Feb 15, KING/HAY, Mar 13; 1794: CG, Mar 7, DL, 21, Apr
   11; 1795: CG, Feb 20; 1796: CG, Mar 16; 1798: CG, Mar 28, 30; 1799: CG, Feb
   15, Mar 13; 1800: CG, Mar 5
Sound Fame (music), 1726: HAY, Feb 24
South Briton, The (play, anon), 1774: CG, Apr 12
South Sea Ballad (song), 1722: LIF, Feb 10
Southampton Buildings, 1787: HAY, Mar 12; 1792: HAY, Oct 15
Southampton Place, 1800: DL, May 30, HAY, Aug 23
Southampton Row, 1735: CG/LIF, Apr 14; 1736: CG, Apr 5; 1738: CG, Mar 21; 1739:
   CG, Mar 26; 1740: CG, Mar 24; 1791: DL, Apr 26; 1792: DLKING'S, Apr 9; 1795:
   DL, Apr 22; 1796: DL, May 3
Southampton St, 1744: DL, Mar 1; 1748: DL, Apr 2; 1749: DL, Jan 18, 20, Apr 3;
   1750: CG, Mar 27, DL, Apr 2, KING'S, May 16; 1751: DL, May 20; 1752: DL, Mar
   12; 1754: CG, Feb 26; 1755: DL, Nov 18; 1756: DL, Dec 15; 1757: DL, Dec 17;
   1758: CG, Jul 6; 1763: DL, Sep 17; 1765: DL, Apr 25; 1772: DL, Mar 3, 23;
   1777: DL, Apr 10; 1789: DL, May 8; 1797: CG, Jun 9; 1798: CG, May 24, 30
Southampton Theatre, 1800: CG, Jan 7
Southby, 1683: DL, Nov 12; 1697: DLORLIF, Feb 0
--Timoleon; or, The Revolution, 1697: DLORLIF, Feb 0
Southerne, Thomas, 1690: DL, Sep 0; 1691: DL, Dec 0; 1693: NONE, Jan 0, DL, Feb
   0, Mar 0, DLORDG, Nov 0; 1694: DL, Feb 0, Mar 21, NONE, 22; 1695: DL, Nov 0;
   1696: DL, Jan 0, NONE, 21, DL, Apr 0; 1700: NONE, Apr 11; 1704: DL, Jun 29;
   1719: DL, Nov 21, Dec 11, 12, 15; 1722: LIF, Jan 20, DL, Feb 5, 10, May 16;
   1723: DL, Jan 16; 1726: LIF, Feb 19; 1733: DL/HAY, Nov 23; 1734: DL/HAY, Jan
   7, DL, Oct 5; 1735: DL, Feb 17; 1736: DL, Oct 12; 1737: DL, Feb 5; 1738: DL,
   Feb 28, CG, Apr 24, Sep 20, DL, Nov 9; 1739: CG, Jan 24; 1741: CG, Jan 22,
   Apr 1, Oct 5, GF, 23; 1742: CG, Nov 13, DL, Dec 14; 1745: CG, Oct 4; 1757:
   DL, Dec 2, 10, 19; 1767: HAY, Sep 18; 1769: DL, Mar 11, Nov 28; 1770: CG, Mar
   31
--Disappointment, The; or, The Mother in Fashion, 1684: DL, Apr 0; 1685:
   DLORDG, Jan 27
--Fatal Marriage, The; or, The Innocent Adultery, 1680: DG, Feb 0; 1694: DL,
   Feb 0, Mar 21, NONE, 22; 1703: DL, May 13, Oct 16; 1704: DL, Feb 28, Apr 3,
   Jun 29; 1705: QUEEN'S, Nov 17; 1706: QUEEN'S, Apr 15, Oct 25; 1707: QUEEN'S,
   Jun 25; 1708: DL, Sep 18; 1709: DL, Feb 1, QUEEN'S, Oct 8; 1710: QUEEN'S, May
   19, GR, Jun 21, DL/QUEEN, Nov 14; 1711: DL/QUEEN, May 1; 1712: DL, Feb 5, GR,
   May 21; 1714: DL, Nov 12; 1716: LIF, Jan 7, 27, May 18, Nov 9; 1717: DL, Jun
   18, LIF, Oct 26; 1718: DL, Feb 13, May 13; 1719: DL, May 8, Nov 1; 1720: DL,
   Jan 14, May 9, Nov 22, Dec 10; 1721: DL, Feb 7, May 19, Oct 5; 1722: DL, Feb
   10, May 30; 1723: DL, Feb 6, May 25, Nov 23; 1724: DL, Feb 6, Nov 9; 1725:
   DL, Jan 25, Nov 23; 1726: DL, May 11, Dec 13; 1727: DL, Jan 11, Feb 13, Dec

5; <u>1728</u>: DL, May 11, Nov 19; <u>1729</u>: DL, Feb 24, May 9, Oct 31; <u>1730</u>: DL, May
18, Dec 10; <u>1734</u>: CG, Mar 18, Apr 4, May 4, CG/LIF, Oct 14, CG, Dec 9; <u>1735</u>:
DL, Jan 23, Feb 17, CG, Oct 20, Dec 13; <u>1736</u>: CG, Feb 11, GF, Mar 9, 11, 13,
May 3; <u>1737</u>: DL, Feb 5; <u>1741</u>: CG, Jan 15, GF, Mar 12; <u>1742</u>: CG, Mar 13; <u>1744</u>:
DL, Apr 10, 19, May 2; <u>1747</u>: GF, Mar 19; <u>1750</u>: DL, Mar 13, 27; <u>1751</u>: DL, Apr
29; <u>1752</u>: DL, Apr 20; <u>1755</u>: CG, Apr 18; <u>1756</u>: CG, Feb 19, May 13, Nov 17;
<u>1757</u>: DL, Dec 2, 3, 5, 6, 7, 9, 10, 12, 15, 19, 20, 26, 29; <u>1758</u>: DL, Jan 6,
18, Feb 3, Apr 17, May 6, 23
--Fate of Capua, The, <u>1700</u>: LIF, Apr 0, NONE, 11
--Loyal Brother, The; or, The Persian Prince, <u>1682</u>: DL, Feb 4
--Maid's Last Prayer, The; or, Any Rather than Fail, <u>1693</u>: DL, Feb 0
--Money the Mistress, <u>1726</u>: LIF, Feb 19, 21, 22
--Oroonoko; or, The Royal Slave, <u>1695</u>: DL, Nov 0; <u>1696</u>: DL, Jan 0, Nov 6; <u>1697</u>:
DL, Apr 23, Jun 12; <u>1698</u>: DL, Jul 9, NONE, Sep 0; <u>1702</u>: DL, Jul 7; <u>1703</u>: DL,
Jan 2, Apr 27, Jun 19, Oct 21, Nov 15; <u>1704</u>: DL, Jan 7, Apr 27, Jun 7, Sep
30, Oct 25; <u>1706</u>: DL, Jan 22, May 21; <u>1707</u>: DL, Feb 4, QUEEN'S, Mar 24; <u>1708</u>:
DL, Apr 19; <u>1709</u>: DL, Mar 21, Dec 2; <u>1710</u>: QUEEN'S, Jan 7, DL, Apr 21, GR,
Jun 26, DL, Dec 9, 19; <u>1711</u>: DL, Jul 6, Oct 8; <u>1712</u>: DL, May 20, Oct 7; <u>1713</u>:
DL, Feb 17, Oct 6, Dec 31; <u>1714</u>: DL, Jun 11, Oct 13; <u>1715</u>: LIF, Jan 24, Feb
3, 26, Oct 20, DL, Dec 16; <u>1716</u>: DL, Feb 1, LIF, Apr 5, Oct 13; <u>1717</u>: DL, Jan
9, 25, LIF, Mar 30, Jun 7, Nov 20, DL, 28; <u>1718</u>: DL, Apr 5, Jun 4, RI, Aug
30, DL, Oct 11; <u>1719</u>: DL, Feb 3, Apr 7, Oct 8, Dec 28; <u>1720</u>: LIF, Feb 13, 23,
Mar 24, Apr 7, DL, 9, LIF, May 19, Jun 2, DL, Oct 6, LIF, 8, DL, Nov 17, LIF,
Dec 7; <u>1721</u>: LIF, Feb 14, DL, Mar 28, LIF, Apr 29, DL, May 10, Sep 14, LIF,
Nov 11, 24; <u>1722</u>: LIF, Jan 20, DL, Feb 5, May 16, Sep 11, LIF, Dec 31; <u>1723</u>:
DL, Jan 16, LIF, Feb 16, SOU, 18, DL, May 21, Sep 21, LIF, Nov 18, Dec 12;
<u>1724</u>: LIF, Jan 25, DL, Feb 3, Mar 21, LIF, Apr 21, DL, Oct 1, LIF, Nov 17,
DL, Dec 28; <u>1725</u>: LIF, Jan 26, DL, Mar 1, Apr 22, LIF, May 6, DL, Sep 16,
LIF, Oct 25, DL, Dec 3; <u>1726</u>: LIF, Feb 2, DL, May 10, Sep 13; <u>1727</u>: LIF, Feb
7, Sep 20, Dec 19; <u>1728</u>: DL, Sep 19, Nov 26, HAY, Dec 7; <u>1729</u>: HAY, Feb 25,
DL, Mar 24, GF, Nov 11, Dec 12; <u>1730</u>: GF, Jan 23, LIF, 26, Mar 9, GF, 21,
LIF, May 13, GF, 29, Jun 2, Jul 1, LIF, Sep 28, GF, Nov 27, DL, Dec 9, 22;
<u>1731</u>: GF, Apr 8, DL, May 7, LIF, Oct 13, DL, Nov 22, GF, Dec 13; <u>1732</u>: GF,
Feb 10, May 9, LIF/CG, Nov 9, GF, 27; <u>1733</u>: GF, Jan 23, Apr 27, CG, May 16,
Aug 2, DL, Oct 8, GF, 9, SOU, 18, DL/HAY, Nov 23, CG, Dec 4, DL, 7; <u>1734</u>:
DL/HAY, Jan 7, DL, 31, GF, Apr 18, HAY, Jun 12, GF, Sep 11, DL, Oct 5, HAY,
10; <u>1735</u>: DL, Jan 3, GF, 14, YB, Mar 10, GF, 18, Apr 15, 30, DL, May 1,
CG/LIF, 5, GF, Sep 15, DL, Nov 7, GF, 15, 17, 18; <u>1736</u>: DL, Jan 10, Mar 1,
LIF, Apr 2, CG, 8, DL, Oct 12, LIF, Nov 27, CG, Dec 2; <u>1737</u>: CG, Jan 24, May
13, Sep 19; <u>1738</u>: DL, Feb 28, CG, Apr 24, Sep 20, DL, Nov 9; <u>1739</u>: CG, Jan
24, DL, Sep 8, CG, Oct 4, Dec 22; <u>1740</u>: DL, Feb 18, Sep 11, SOU, Oct 9, GF,
20, Dec 30; <u>1741</u>: CG, Jan 22, Apr 1, Oct 5, GF, 23, JS, Nov 30, GF, Dec 21;
<u>1742</u>: GF, Jan 23, CG, Feb 2, GF, 16, Apr 22, DL, May 12, CG, Nov 13, DL, Dec
14; <u>1743</u>: JS, Feb 2, DL, May 2, Sep 29; <u>1744</u>: DL, Dec 11, GF, 15; <u>1745</u>: CG,
Oct 4, GF, Nov 28; <u>1746</u>: SOU, Oct 29, GF, Dec 10, 16; <u>1747</u>: DL, Apr 22; <u>1748</u>:
CG, Jan 16, Apr 20, Nov 15, NWSM, 30; <u>1749</u>: CG, Feb 2, Mar 7, 28, May 3, Nov
3; <u>1750</u>: CG, Feb 21; <u>1751</u>: CG, Apr 22, DL, Oct 22, 23, 24, 25, 30, Nov 13,
CG, 18, DL, 25, Dec 28; <u>1752</u>: DL, Jan 13, CG, Apr 6, DL, 13, Oct 5, Nov 2;
<u>1753</u>: DL, Jan 16, Oct 10, Nov 19; <u>1754</u>: CG, Apr 24, DL, Sep 19; <u>1755</u>: DL, May
5, Oct 13, 14, 16, Nov 20, Dec 29; <u>1756</u>: DL, Jan 2, May 1, Nov 12; <u>1757</u>: DL,
Feb 28, May 17, CG, Oct 15, Nov 25; <u>1758</u>: CG, Jan 26; <u>1759</u>: CG, May 8, DL,
Dec 1, 3, 4, 6, 8, 10, 11, 28; <u>1761</u>: CG, May 11, Oct 20; <u>1762</u>: DL, Apr 14,
Oct 7; <u>1763</u>: DL, May 2; <u>1764</u>: DL, Apr 25, May 9, Oct 15, 27; <u>1766</u>: CG, Apr
25, DL, Dec 2; <u>1767</u>: HAY, Sep 18; <u>1769</u>: DL, Mar 11, Apr 15, CG, 17, 24, DL,
Nov 28, Dec 5, 15; <u>1770</u>: DL, Apr 27, CG, May 7, HAY, Aug 31; <u>1771</u>: HAY, Mar
4, CG, Apr 23, May 9, Oct 2, 21, Dec 20; <u>1772</u>: CG, Jan 9, May 22; <u>1774</u>: DL,
Oct 27, 31; <u>1776</u>: CHR, Oct 2; <u>1778</u>: CG, May 9, DL, 19; <u>1779</u>: CG, May 3, Dec
16, 27; <u>1781</u>: DL, May 17, Oct 29, Nov 12; <u>1782</u>: DL, Jan 8, Mar 12; <u>1783</u>: DL,
Mar 17; <u>1784</u>: DL, Jan 1; <u>1785</u>: CG, Jan 8, 10, May 23, Nov 9, Dec 3; <u>1786</u>: CG,
May 30; <u>1788</u>: CG, Mar 24; <u>1789</u>: DL, Oct 31; <u>1790</u>: DL, May 28; <u>1792</u>: CG, May
30; <u>1793</u>: HAY, Dec 30; <u>1794</u>: HAY, Jan 6; <u>1795</u>: CG, Dec 21, 28
--Revolt of Capua, <u>1700</u>: NONE, Apr 11
--Sir Anthony Love; or, The Rambling Lady, <u>1690</u>: DL, Sep 0; <u>1691</u>: DL, Dec 0
--Spartan Dame, The, <u>1719</u>: DL, Nov 21, Dec 11, 12, 14, 15, 16, 17, 18, 19, 21,
22
--Wives' Excuse, The; or, Cuckolds Make Themselves, <u>1690</u>: DL, Sep 0; <u>1691</u>: DL,
Dec 0
Southland, Thomas
--Ungrateful Favourite, The, <u>1663</u>: NONE, Sep 0
Southsea Coffee House, <u>1752</u>: CG, Dec 12
Southwark Fair; or, The Sheep Shearing (play, anon), <u>1729</u>: SF, Sep 8
Southwark Fair, <u>1660</u>: SF, Sep 10; <u>1665</u>: BF, Aug 7; <u>1668</u>: SF, Sep 21; <u>1680</u>:

BF/SF, Aug 0; 1692: SF, Sep 13; 1695: SF, Sep 0; 1696: DG, Aug 0, SF, Sep 5;
1714: SF, Aug 31; 1717: SF, Sep 20, LIF, Dec 30; 1718: RI, Aug 23, 30; 1719:
DL, May 23; 1722: DL, Sep 8; 1728: LIF, Sep 23; 1735: DL, Sep 1; 1736: SFL,
Sep 7; 1741: SF, Sep 11; 1747: BHB, Sep 26; 1748: BHB, Oct 1; 1749: SF/SF,
Sep 7; 1750: SFP, Sep 7; 1751: SF, Sep 9; 1752: SF, Sep 16; 1757: SF, Sep 17;
1759: SFS, Sep 18; 1760: SF, Sep 18; 1761: SFW, Sep 19
Southwark, 1660: SF, Sep 13; 1682: SF, Sep 12; 1690: NONE, Sep 8; 1693: SF, Sep
7; 1698: SF, Sep 17; 1711: SOU, Feb 6; 1714: SOU, Nov 1; 1717: NONE, Sep 12,
SF, 25; 1721: GG, Mar 22; 1723: SOU, Sep 24; 1725: SF, Sep 8; 1730: SOU, Sep
24; 1732: SOU, Dec 18; 1733: SF/BFLH, Aug 23; 1736: SOU, Sep 20; 1737: HAY,
Mar 8; 1740: BF/WF/SF, Sep 8; 1741: GF, Apr 23; 1746: GF, Feb 10, SOU, Nov 3,
HAY, 27; 1748: SOU, Jul 4, Aug 1, SFP, Sep 7, SFBCBV, 7, SFLYYW, 7, 8,
SFBCBV, 8, 9, SFLYYW, 9, SFBCBV, 10, SFLYYW, 12, SFBCBV, 12, 13, SFLYYW, 13,
SOU, Oct 10, 12, 24, 31; 1749: SOU, Jan 2, 9, 26, Feb 13, 20, DL, Apr 5,
SFGT, Sep 16, SOUGT, 25, SOU, Oct 2, 4, 9; 1750: SOU, Jan 25, Mar 5, DL, 22,
May 7, SFYW, Sep 7, SFB, 8, SFYW, 8, SFB, 10, SFYW, 10, 11, 12, SFY, 14;
1751: DL, Mar 14, SF, Sep 7, 9, 10, 11, 16, 17, 18; 1752: DL, Apr 10, SFGT,
Sep 18, 19, 20, SFP, 21, 22, SFB, 22; 1753: SFP, Sep 18; 1755: SOU, Jan 13,
16, 20, 27; 1756: ACAD, Dec 15; 1758: CG, Jul 6; 1760: SF, Sep 13, 19; 1789:
KHS, Sep 16
Southwell, Edward (spectator), 1685: BF, Aug 26
Southwell, Sir Robert, 1679: BF, Sep 3; 1685: BF, Aug 26, ATCOURT, Oct 10;
1686: ATCOURT, Feb 16
Sowdon, John (actor), 1747: CG, Dec 4; 1748: CG, Jan 9, Feb 29, DL, Sep 22, Oct
19, 28, Nov 4; 1749: DL, Jan 13, Feb 6, Apr 5, Oct 17, Nov 4, 15, 21; 1750:
DL, Jan 3, 6, 9, Feb 7, 24, Mar 5, 22, Apr 2, 11, Oct 13, 19, 22, 30, Nov 5,
13; 1751: DL, Jan 5, 7, 16, 21, Feb 2, 23, Mar 11, 14, Apr 29, Oct 14, Nov 4,
Dec 10; 1752: DL, Jan 6, 28, Apr 6, 10; 1767: HAY, Jun 4, 17, 19, 30, Jul 6,
8, 15, 31, Aug 14, 21, Sep 16, 18, 21; 1768: HAY, Jun 23, Jul 8, 13, Aug 19;
1769: HAY, May 24, 29, Jun 21, Aug 7, 14, 25, 30, Sep 11; 1770: HAY, May 18,
23, 28, 30, Aug 24, 31; 1771: DL, Jan 1
Sowdon, Thomas (ticket seller), 1749: DL, Apr 5; 1750: DL, Mar 22; 1752: DL,
Apr 10
Spackman (actor), 1741: BFH, Aug 22, JS, Nov 9; 1742: JS, Apr 7
Spackman, Mrs (actor), 1743: LIF, Apr 5; 1744: JS, Dec 10
Spagnola, Sga (singer), 1765: KING'S, Nov 23, Dec 10; 1766: KING'S, Jan 25, Apr
19
Spagnoletti, Paolo Diana (violinist), 1799: DL, Jul 1
Spain, King of, 1701: DL, Jan 31
Spalding (actor), 1694: NONE, Sep 0
Spandau (musician), 1773: KING'S, Feb 5, CG, 26, Mar 3, 5, KING'S, 18, CG, 19,
26, KING'S, Apr 12, HAY, 19
Spaniards Dismayed, The; or, True Blue for Ever. See Carey, Henry, Nancy.
Spanier in Peru, Die. See Kotzebue, August Friedrich Ferdinand von.
Spanish Ambassador, 1732: DL, Nov 21; 1733: HAY, Jun 11; 1735: KING'S, Mar 15;
1738: HAY, Oct 9; 1739: DL, Sep 25
Spanish Ballet, Grand (dance), 1782: HAY, Aug 17
Spanish Barber, The. See Colman the elder, George.
Spanish Beauties (dance), 1740: BFHC, Aug 23
Spanish Bull-baiting (vaudeville), 1789: KHS, Sep 16
Spanish Coal Heaver (dance), 1768: CG, Apr 16
Spanish Curate, The. See Fletcher, John.
Spanish Dance (dance), 1704: DL, Nov 27; 1711: GR, Sep 13; 1712: SH, Dec 8;
1715: LIF, Jan 6, May 16, Jul 21, Sep 30, Oct 22, DL, 24; 1716: LIF, Mar 24,
Oct 25, 26, 29, 31, Dec 22; 1717: LIF, Apr 8, KING'S, 11, LIF, May 13; 1718:
LIF, Jan 27, DL, Jun 13, Jul 18, LIF, Sep 26, DL, Nov 7, LIF, 10; 1724: LIF,
Oct 12; 1725: LIF, Nov 2, Dec 3; 1726: DL, May 9, LIF, 11, DL, 13, LIF, 26;
1727: DL, Apr 10, 19, May 1, LIF, 9; 1728: DL, Apr 1, 8, May 7, Oct 21; 1729:
DL, Apr 28, May 26, Oct 9; 1732: LIF, Apr 22; 1733: DL, Jan 23, Apr 16,
LIF/CG, May 7; 1758: DL, Apr 10, 11, CG, 11, DL, Oct 14, 17, 19, 20, Nov 1,
13, 15, 17, 23, 24, Dec 4, 12, 18; 1759: DL, May 18; 1767: HAY, Jul 17; 1775:
CG, Nov 21, 22, 23, 25, 27, 28, 29, 30, Dec 2, 4, 5, 6, 9, 11
Spanish Dance, Grand (dance), 1715: LIF, May 24; 1726: LIF, Apr 21; 1730: DL,
Apr 24; 1731: DL, May 12; 1774: DL, Apr 22; 1775: DL, May 8
Spanish Fandango (dance), 1796: CG, May 10; 1797: CG, Oct 9, 12; 1798: CG, Apr
23
Spanish Fryar, The. See Dryden, John.
Spanish Gypsies, The. See Middleton, Thomas.
Spanish habits, 1754: DL, Nov 4, 7
Spanish Lady, The. See Hull, Thomas.
Spanish Lovers (dance), 1779: HAY, Aug 18
Spanish mannner, 1754: DL, Nov 4, 7

Spanish music (music), 1795: KING'S, May 28
Spanish Rivals, The. See Lonsdale, Mark.
Spanish Rogue, The. See Duffett, Thomas.
Spanish Scaramouch (dance), 1721: LIF, May 5
Spanish Serenade (dance), 1786: HAY, Sep 1
Spanish Song (song), 1701: RIW, Aug 11
Spanish Wives, The. See Pix, Mary.
Spara il Pastor contente (song), 1750: CG, Mar 29
Sparite o Pensieri (song), 1729: LIF, Mar 5
Sparkes, Mrs (actor), 1776: HAY, Oct 7
Sparks (actor), 1739: CG, Apr 12, 30, DL, May 18
Sparks (brazier), 1757: DL, Apr 14
Sparks and Co (lacemen), 1775: DL, Nov 6
Sparks, Frances, Mrs Richard (actor), 1788: HAY, Apr 9
Sparks, Hugh (actor), 1797: DL, Dec 5, 21; 1798: DL, Feb 16, May 24, Jun 2, 7,
   12, Sep 15, 18, 25, Oct 4, 11, 16, 20, Nov 14, 22, 29, Dec 4, HAY, 17, DL,
   19, 29; 1799: DL, Jan 2, 19, Apr 24, 27, May 3, 4, 16, 24, Jun 26, Sep 19,
   21, 24, Oct 3, 7, 8, 10, 17, 19, 26, Nov 6, 25; 1800: DL, Jan 18, Mar 11, 20,
   27, 31, Apr 28, 29, Jun 11, 18
Sparks, Isaac (actor), 1745: DL, Sep 19, 24, 26, Oct 8, Nov 22, 25, Dec 5, 13,
   30; 1746: DL, Jan 14, 17, 31, Feb 13, Mar 3, Apr 4, 9, 11, 15, 21, 23, May 9,
   14, 19, Sep 23, 30, Oct 14, 23, Nov 5, 21, Dec 20, 26; 1747: DL, Jan 15, Mar
   30, Apr 25, 30, May 15, Oct 17, Nov 2, 6, Dec 16, 26; 1748: DL, Jan 12, Mar
   22, Apr 14, 28, May 2; 1749: CG, Mar 7, 14, May 4, Oct 2, 25, 27, Nov 3, 4,
   8, 9, 18; 1750: CG, Feb 2; 1768: CG, Dec 30; 1769: HAY, May 15, 24, 26, Jun
   5, 7, 16, Jul 12, Aug 7, 11, 14, 25, Sep 11, DL, Nov 2, 20; 1770: DL, May 14,
   HAY, 16, 18, 23, 28, Jun 22, 25, 27, Jul 25, Aug 24, 31, Sep 20, DL, Nov 19;
   1771: DL, May 7; 1773: CG, Oct 30
Sparks, James (actor), 1776: CHR, Sep 25, Oct 14; 1779: HAY, Jan 11, Feb 22,
   Mar 8, May 10; 1782: HAY, Sep 21, Nov 25
Sparks, Luke (actor), 1745: DL, Sep 24, Oct 22, Nov 9, 11, 22, Dec 5, 17; 1746:
   DL, Jan 8, 10, 14, 18, 29, 31, Apr 9, 14, 21, Sep 23, 27, Nov 5, 7, 15, Dec
   15, 26; 1747: DL, Jan 15, Feb 2, 16, Mar 12, 16, 19, 28, Sep 15, 22, Oct 3,
   Nov 4, 13, 17, Dec 16; 1748: DL, Jan 6, 18, Feb 13, Mar 19, Apr 18, 28, Sep
   17, 24, 29, Oct 4, 13, CG, 17, 22, 24, 25, 28, Nov 4, 9, 15, 16, 24, 26, 28,
   Dec 1, 9, 10, 20, 22, 26; 1749: CG, Jan 11, 13, 25, Feb 23, Mar 6, 11, 29,
   31, Sep 27, Oct 4, 11, 12, 19, 26, Nov 11, 23, Dec 8, 16, 26, 28; 1750: CG,
   Jan 4, 16, 18, 23, 31, Feb 5, 20, Mar 1, 12, 17, 20, 26, 27, Apr 3, 23, Sep
   28, Oct 15, 17, 18, 19, 23, 24, 25, 26, 27, 31, Nov 5, 8, 12, 22, 24, 29, Dec
   1, 4, 14; 1751: CG, Jan 1, 3, 16, 19, Feb 16, 23, Mar 16, Apr 10, 11, 16, 22,
   May 1, Oct 7, 9, 11, 17, 21, 25, Nov 4, 6, 7, 14, 16, 18, 21, 22, 28, Dec 5,
   16; 1752: CG, Jan 18, 28, Mar 7, 16, 17, 30, Apr 15, 24, 30, May 4, Sep 20,
   22, Oct 6, 12, 14, 16, 21, 24, 27, 30, 31, Nov 3, 4, 7, 10, 22, 27, 28, Dec
   9, 11, 12, 19, 21, 27; 1753: CG, Jan 8, Feb 6, 12, 21, Mar 10, 19, 26, Apr
   27, May 7, 18, Sep 10, 21, Oct 3, 10, 22, 27, 30, Nov 1, 5, 12, 14, 20, 22,
   28, 30, Dec 11, 26; 1754: CG, Jan 10, 22, Feb 23, Mar 9, 23, 25, 26, Apr 6,
   17, 20, 24, 26, Sep 20, 23, 25, 27, Oct 9, 14, 16, 17, 18, 24, Nov 1, 4, 16,
   20, 27, 28, Dec 10, 13, 30; 1755: CG, Jan 4, 10, 20, 28, Feb 4, 18, 20, 24,
   Mar 6, 17, 18, 22, Apr 2, 4, 8, 9, 10, 15, 29, May 7, 8, Sep 29, Oct 8, 11,
   14, 16, 18, 20, 21, 24, 27, 30, Nov 4, 7, 12, 13, 14, 17, 19, 22, Dec 3, 5,
   11, 12; 1756: CG, Jan 15, Feb 3, 9, 26, Mar 18, 22, 29, 30, Apr 1, 3, 6, 29,
   30, May 3, 17, Sep 29, Oct 4, 6, 8, 11, 12, 13, 15, 18, 20, 22, 23, 25, 26,
   27, 30, Nov 4, 13, 22, 29, Dec 7, 10; 1757: CG, Jan 5, 11, 14, 27, Feb 16,
   21, Mar 14, 31, Apr 27, May 16, Sep 21, 26, 30, Oct 3, 5, 7, 8, 10, 15, 21,
   27, Nov 2, 4, 5, 11, 14, 16, 26, Dec 1, 5, 7, 9, 10, 14, 20; 1758: CG, Jan
   11, 24, 27, Feb 1, Mar 9, 13, 14, 16, 29, Apr 10, 11, 12, 14, 17, Sep 22, 29,
   Oct 2, 4, 6, 16, 23, 24, 25, 26, DL, 27, CG, 27, 30, Nov 1, 2, 3, 4, 7, 14,
   21, 23, Dec 2, 18; 1759: CG, Jan 11, 12, Feb 1, 15, Mar 20, 24, 26, 27, Apr
   5, 7, 21, 28, May 3, 8, 11, Sep 28, Oct 1, 11, Nov 5, 23, 26, 28, 30, Dec 5,
   6, 7, 8, 11, 12, 19, 20, 21, 22, 28; 1760: CG, Jan 4, 24, 31, Feb 7, 14, 28,
   Mar 18, 20, 22, 25, Apr 8, 17, 18, 22, 24, 29, May 7, Sep 22, 29, Oct 1, 6,
   8, 10, 13, 15, 18, 23, 25, Nov 18, 22, 24, 29, Dec 9, 18, 22, 31; 1761: CG,
   Jan 7, 10, Feb 16, Mar 3, 5, 25, 30, Apr 2, 3, 6, 7, 13, 21, May 8, 11, 25,
   Sep 9, 14, 16, 18, 21, 25, 28, 30, Oct 1, 3, 5, 6, 10, 12, 13, 19, 20, 23,
   24, 27, Nov 2, 4, 9, 10, 13, Dec 11, 28, 30; 1762: CG, Jan 12, 22, Apr 3, Sep
   20, 22, 24, 27, 29, 30, Oct 2, 6, 12, 14, 16, 21, 25, Nov 3, 5, 15; 1763: CG,
   Apr 11, Sep 21, 23, 26, Oct 3, 5, 10, 17, 18, Dec 14; 1764: CG, Jan 16, Feb
   15, Mar 27, 29, Apr 9, 10, May 7, 9, 21, 22, Sep 19, 21, 26, Oct 1, 5, 15,
   24, 25, 29, Nov 1, Dec 7, 21; 1765: CG, Mar 12, 25, 30, Apr 9, May 11
Sparks, Mrs (ticket deliverer), 1762: CG, Apr 3
Sparks, Richard (actor), 1771: DL, May 7
Sparks, Sarah, Mrs Hugh (actor), 1797: DL, Oct 26, Nov 18; 1798: DL, Jan 10,

25, Feb 3, May 18, 30, Jun 5, 6, Oct 13, 16, 30, Nov 22, 29, HAY, Dec 17, DL, 29; 1799: DL, Jan 8, Apr 8, 17, 22, May 1, 9, 16, Sep 21, Oct 19, 22, Nov 2, Dec 7, 17; 1800: DL, Feb 12, Jun 5, 7, 9, 13, 18
Sparling (beneficiary), 1724: HAY, Feb 20; 1725: LIF, May 22
Sparling, Mrs (actor), 1730: HAY, Mar 12
Sparring Match (entertainment), 1788: CG, Dec 30; 1789: CG, Jan 5, 27
Sparrow (actor), 1776: CHR, Sep 25; 1782: HAY, Nov 25; 1783: HAY, Sep 17
Sparroworth, Miss (actor), 1756: BFSI, Sep 3
Spartan Dame, The. See Southerne, Thomas.
Spartan Ladies, The. See Carlell, Lodowick.
Spavan (printer), 1750: DL, Feb 1
Speak ye who best can tell (song), 1787: DL, Feb 23; 1789: DL, Mar 18; 1790: DL, Feb 26; 1791: DL, Mar 23; 1792: KING'S, Feb 24; 1793: KING/HAY, Feb 22; 1794: DL, Apr 10
Speare, Master (singer), 1796: CG, Dec 19; 1797: CG, Jun 5; 1798: CG, Nov 12; 1799: CG, Apr 13; 1800: CG, Jan 16, Feb 10
Speculation. See Reynolds, Frederick.
Speech of Old Time to the People of Great Britain (entertainment), 1751: HAY, Dec 27; 1757: HAY, Sep 28
Speechless Wife, The. See Rainsford, Mrs.
Speechly (singer), 1793: CG, Nov 28; 1794: CG, Oct 22; 1795: CG, Jan 31
Speed the Plough. See Morton, Thomas.
Speer (house servant), 1742: DL, Apr 24
Spellman, Mrs (actor), 1733: SF/BFLH, Aug 23
Speltra (musician), 1736: HIC, Jan 21
Speme Amabile, La (song), 1762: KING'S, May 11
Spence (singer), 1791: DL, Mar 11, 23, Apr 1, 13
Spence. See Moore, Edward.
Spencer (actor), 1740: CG, Oct 31
Spencer (music scribe), 1749: DL, Dec 30
Spencer (payee), 1772: DL, Oct 3
Spencer (proprietor), 1729: WINH, Jul 19
Spencer (tavern keeper), 1792: HAY, Oct 15
Spencer, Anne, Lady Sunderland, 1668: BRIDGES, Dec 18
Spencer, Charles (actor), 1781: CII, Mar 15; 1782: HAY, Dec 30
Spencer, Dorothy, Dowager Countess of Sunderland, 1680: DG, Feb 2, DGORDL, 19
Spencer, George John, 2nd Earl Spencer, 1797: KING'S, May 18, CG, Jun 14
Spencer, Captain James (deceased naval officer), 1751: DL, Dec 18
Spencer, Lady Georgina (subject of poem), 1748: CG, Feb 11
Spencer, Miss (singer), 1759: DL, Dec 31; 1760: DL, Apr 14, May 19; 1767: RANELAGH, Jun 1; 1770: CG, Jan 17
Spencer, Mrs (actor), 1671: LIF, Sep 0; 1675: DG, May 28
Spencer, Mrs (actor), 1797: CG, Oct 13, Nov 2, 18, 20, Dec 20, 27; 1798: CG, Jan 11, 24, 26, 29, Feb 2, 8, Mar 19, Apr 9, May 7, 29; see also Campion, Maria Anne
Spencer, Mrs James (beneficiary), 1751: DL, Dec 18
Spencer, Robert, Lord Sunderland, 1680: DG, Feb 2; 1683: DLORDG, Aug 14; 1697: NONE, Jun 4
Spencer, William Barber (actor), 1780: DL, May 12, Sep 19; 1781: DL, May 22, HAY, Jun 22, 29; 1782: DL, Jan 3, May 14, 15, HAY, Jun 18, Aug 17, DL, Nov 4, Dec 4, 26; 1783: DL, Jan 29, Feb 22, Mar 3, May 8, 12, HAY, Jun 7, 30, DL, Sep 23, Oct 13, Nov 8, Dec 2, 5; 1784: DL, Jan 7, 13, May 3, 7, 8, HAY, Jul 8, 19, Aug 10, DL, Sep 23, Oct 12, Nov 10; 1785: DL, Jan 12, 20, Apr 20, May 11, Sep 27, Oct 18, 26, Dec 1, 26; 1786: DL, Mar 4, 9, 11, May 25, Sep 21, Oct 24; 1787: DL, Jan 13, Mar 29, May 3, 16, 30, Sep 18, 22, Oct 26, Nov 8, 10, 21, 27, Dec 12, 26; 1788: DL, Feb 7, Mar 3, 29, Apr 14, May 21, 23, Sep 13, 27, 30, Nov 21, Dec 6, 22; 1789: DL, Jan 13, Jun 8, Sep 12, Oct 22; 1790: DL, Feb 8, 9, May 31, Sep 14, Oct 16; 1791: DL, Jan 10, May 23
Spendthrift, The. See Draper, Matthew.
Spendthrift, The; or, A Christmas Gambol. See Kenrick, Dr William.
Spendthrift, The; or, The Female Conspiracy. See Foote, Samuel.
Spenser, Edmund (author), 1746: CG, Feb 14
Sper il Fostore (song), 1748: CG, Mar 28
Sperai Vicino al lido (song), 1762: KING'S, May 11
Speranza mi dice albore (song), 1714: QUEEN'S, May 1, Jun 23
Speranze della Terra, Le. See Cocchi, Gioacchino.
Sperati (violoncellist), 1789: CG, Feb 27; 1790: CG, Feb 19
Speres, Mrs (actor), 1767: DL, Jan 24
Speziale, Lo. See Fischietti, Domenico.
Spezza lo Stral piagato (song), 1749: KING'S, Mar 21
Spicer (musician), 1675: ATCOURT, Feb 15
Spicer, Mrs (actor), 1723: LIF, Oct 31; 1724: LIF, May 19, 25

Spightful Sister, The. See Bailey, Abraham.
Spiletta, Nicolina (singer), 1753: CG, Dec 17; 1755: HAY, Feb 3, 17; 1756: CG,
   Jan 12, Feb 2; 1758: MARLY, Jun 10: 1764: KING'S, Nov 27; 1774: KING'S, Dec
   13; 1775: KING'S, Mar 7, 30, May 23; see also Giordani, Nicolina
Spiller (actor), 1734: SFL, Sep 7
Spiller-Baron Egleton Booth, 1726: SFSE, Sep 8
Spiller-Lee Booth, 1719: BFSL, Aug 24
Spiller, James (actor), 1709: DL, Dec 6, 9, 30; 1710: DL, Jan 9, 14, 31, Feb
   11, Mar 27, Apr 10, GR, Jun 21, Jul 1, 3, 10, 12, 20, 22, 27, 29, Aug 3, 7,
   12, 19, 28, Sep 9, 11, 23; 1711: DL, Oct 25, Dec 31; 1712: DL, Jun 5; 1713:
   DL, Jan 6, 29, Feb 9, May 12, Nov 25, Dec 2; 1715: LIF, Jan 4, 7, 8, Feb 2,
   3, 16, Mar 26, Apr 20, 21, May 17, Jun 7, 14, Aug 3, 10, 11, Sep 29, Oct 4,
   5, 7, 10, 12, 24, 28, Dec 12; 1716: LIF, Jan 4, 24, Feb 3, Mar 19, Apr 11,
   19, 21, Jul 4, 6, 13, Aug 3, 17, Oct 17, 20, 29, Nov 5, 10, 13, 26, Dec 4;
   1717: LIF, Jan 8, Feb 11, Apr 13, 22, 24, May 10, 16, 17, 18, Jun 7, 25, Jul
   10, SF, Sep 9, 25, LIF, Oct 15, 17, 21, 24, 28, Nov 4, 5, 6, 11, 22, 26, Dec
   7, 12, 21, 28; 1718: LIF, Jan 2, 7, 10, 24, Feb 3, Mar 8, 13, Apr 19, 23, May
   1, 20, Jun 4, 20, 27, 30, Jul 4, RI, Jul 19, LIF, 24, RI, 26, NONE, 30, LIF, Aug
   6, RI, 9, 11, 16, SF, Sep 5, AC, 24, LIF, 29, 30, Oct 3, 6, 9, 11, 15, 18,
   21, 28, 31, Nov 11, 24; 1719: LIF, Jan 9, Feb 7, 21, 28, Mar 16, 30, Apr 2,
   3, 4, Oct 10, 13, 15, 17, 20, 29, Nov 3, 5, 12, 13, 17, 18, 21, 23, 24, 26,
   Dec 30; 1720: LIF, Jan 7, 11, 22, 26, Feb 9, 11, 22, 23, Mar 28, 29, 31, Apr
   20, 26, BCA, Sep 23, LIF, Oct 1, 8, 11, 15, 18, 22, 31, Nov 3, 4, 10, 15, 29,
   Dec 1, 7, 8, 17, 22, 26, 27, 31; 1721: LIF, Jan 7, 13, 19, 25, 27, 28, Feb 6,
   16, Apr 1, 10, 12, 18, 24, 25, May 5, 10, Sep 23, 27, Oct 3, 12, 19, 21, 25,
   28, 31, Nov 9, 11, 13, 18, 25, 27, 29, Dec 2, 11, 18; 1722: LIF, Jan 1, 9,
   13, 15, Feb 2, Mar 5, 8, 15, 29, 31, Apr 3, 13, 20, 27, May 4, Jun 2, Jul 27,
   Aug 3, BFLSH, 25, LIF, Sep 29, Oct 1, 2, 6, 9, 11, 12, 13, 16, 18, 19, 22,
   24; 1723: LIF, Jan 10, Feb 9, 15, SOU, Sep 25, LIF, 30, Oct 9, 14, 18, 19,
   22, 24, 25, 29, 31, Nov 2, 12, 14, 16, 18, 19, 28, Dec 3, 19; 1724: LIF, Jan
   4, Mar 10, 23, 26, 28, Apr 6, 7, 28, 29, May 7, 8, 25, 27, Jun 3, 23, 30, Sep
   23, SOU, 24, LIF, 25, 28, Oct 5, 7, 9, 12, 23, 27, 30, Nov 3, 6, 11, 13, 17,
   18, 26; 1725: LIF, Jan 4, 11, 16, 19, 21, Mar 11, 13, 29, Apr 5, 7, 13, 14,
   17, 22, 23, 26, 28, May 1, 19, 21, Sep 24, Oct 1, 11, 13, 16, 21, 23, 25, 28,
   Nov 2, 6, 8, 11, 12, 13, 23, 24, 29, 30, Dec 2, 3, 7, 8, 15, 16; 1726: LIF,
   Jan 14, Mar 21, Apr 11, 18, 26, May 3, 4, 25, SFSE, Sep 8, LIF, 14, 21, 23,
   26, 28, 30, Oct 19, 24, 29, Nov 2, 10, 11, 18, 21, 30; 1727: LIF, Jan 4, 9,
   Feb 3, 7, 13, Mar 20, Apr 5, 7, 10, 28, May 4, 9, BF, Aug 22, LIF, Sep 13,
   18, 20, 25, 27, 29, Oct 2, 9, 12, 17, 19, 21, 26, 27, 31, Nov 1, 9, 16, 17,
   Dec 11, 14, 16; 1728: LIF, Jan 8, 29, Mar 9, 14, 25, 28, Apr 1, 4, 6, 23, 26,
   30, May 11, 15, Sep 16, 18, 30, Oct 1, 14, 21, Nov 1, 11, 19, 20, 23; 1729:
   LIF, Jan 16, 18, Apr 23
Spiller, Mrs (actor), 1709: DL, Dec 17; 1710: DL, Jan 2, 31, Feb 25, Mar 27,
   Apr 10, GR, Jun 15, 19, 21, 28, Jul 1, 3, 6, 8, 12, 15, 20, 22, 27, 29, Aug
   3, 7, 10, 12, 24, Sep 11, 23; 1712: DL, Nov 7; 1713: DL, Jan 6; 1715: LIF,
   Jan 7, 8, Feb 2, 3, 16, Mar 26, Apr 30, May 17, Aug 3, 10, Sep 28, 29, Oct 7,
   10, 12, 24, Dec 12; 1716: LIF, Jan 4, Apr 27, May 21, Jul 4, 11, Aug 3, Oct
   10, Dec 1, 4; 1717: LIF, Apr 13, May 18, Jul 10, TC, Aug 5, SF, Sep 14, LIF,
   Oct 17, Nov 19, 20, 26, 28, Dec 3, 7, 9, 10, 14; 1718: LIF, Jan 2, 11, 14,
   Feb 18, Apr 19, Jun 20, 30, Jul 24, RI, Aug 2, 9, 11, SF, Sep 5, AC, 24, LIF,
   29; 1719: LIF, Jan 3, Feb 7, 21, 28, Mar 31, Apr 2, Oct 2, 5, 7, 10, 13, 15,
   17, Nov 5, 12, 17, 18, 21, 23, 24, 26, Dec 10; 1720: LIF, Feb 26, Nov 1, Dec
   8; 1721: LIF, Feb 21, Mar 11, Apr 1, 13, Nov 13, 18, Dec 11, 18; 1722: LIF,
   Mar 29, Apr 6, May 4, Jun 13, BFLSH, Aug 25; 1723: HA, Jul 22; 1724: BFL, Aug
   22; 1727: BF, Aug 22; 1729: BFLH, Aug 23, SF, Sep 15, PLR, Nov 29, Dec 1;
   1730: BFLH, Aug 31; 1731: TC, Aug 4, 12, SFLH, Sep 8; 1733: SF/BFLH, Aug 23;
   1740: BFLP, Aug 23
Spilsbury (house servant), 1755: DL, May 15; 1758: DL, May 9, 17; 1760: DL, May
   13
Spilsbury (treasurer), 1763: KING'S, Nov 26; 1764: KING'S, Jan 24, Apr 5
Spilsbury, Master (dancer), 1755: DL, Nov 8
Spilsbury, T (publisher), 1779: HAY, Jul 31
Spinacuta (equilibrist), 1766: HAY, Oct 27
Spinnage, Major, 1764: KING'S, Jan 24
Spinning Wheel Dance (dance), 1724: LIF, Jul 14, 29; 1726: LIF, Jun 21
Spinning Wheel Dialogue (song), 1704: LIF, Oct 16; 1706: DL, Apr 3; 1727: LIF,
   Mar 23; 1728: LIF, Apr 29, May 2
Spinsters' Lottery (dance), 1796: CG, Apr 9
Spirit of Contradiction, The (play, anon), 1760: CG, Mar 6, 8, 10
Spirito Folletto, Lo; or, The Hobgoblin by Argentina (entertainment), 1726:
   KING'S, Dec 3; 1727: KING'S, Feb 16
Spirits' Dance (dance), 1754: HAY/SFB, Sep 19; 1765: DL, May 1; 1777: DL, Jan

805

4, Apr 14, 25, May 2, Sep 20; <u>1778</u>: DL, Nov 2; <u>1779</u>: DL, Nov 3; <u>1780</u>: DL, Mar
   13, Apr 24, Sep 23, Dec 12; <u>1781</u>: DL, Nov 13; <u>1784</u>: DL, Nov 9; <u>1785</u>: DL, Oct
   17; <u>1786</u>: DL, Dec 5
Spirits' Dance, Grand (dance), <u>1733</u>: DL, Nov 26; <u>1734</u>: DL, May 15
Spittalfields, <u>1741</u>: GF, Apr 17; <u>1742</u>: GF, Apr 20; <u>1749</u>: BBT, Mar 1; <u>1776</u>:
   STRAND, Jan 23
Spleen, The. See Colman the elder, George.
Spofforth, Reginald (actor, singer, composer), <u>1792</u>: CG, Dec 31; <u>1793</u>: CG, Jan
   1, 3, Oct 2, Nov 28, Dec 19; <u>1794</u>: CG, Sep 22, Oct 22, Dec 26; <u>1795</u>: CG, Jan
   31, Feb 14, Apr 9, May 14, Jun 6, Dec 21; <u>1796</u>: CG, Mar 15, 17, Apr 9, May
   10, 16, Oct 7, 24, Dec 10
Spoiled Child, The. See Bickerstaff, Isaac.
Spoke (householder), <u>1782</u>: HAY, Jan 14
Spoonatissima (actor), <u>1752</u>: HAY, Dec 7
Spoonatissima, Sga (actor), <u>1753</u>: HAY, Mar 13, 29, May 3; <u>1760</u>: HAY, Sep 8
Spooner (box-office keeper), <u>1776</u>: CHR, Sep 27
Sports of the Green (dance), <u>1779</u>: CG, Apr 28, May 7; <u>1781</u>: CG, May 1, 8, 9,
   Oct 24, 30
Sportsman Deceived (dance), <u>1779</u>: DL, Dec 10, 20, 28, 30, 31
Sportsman's snug little cot (song), <u>1796</u>: CG, May 6, 16, 24
Sportsmen's Return (dance), <u>1784</u>: DL, Mar 8, 11, 30, Apr 19, 26, May 3, 7, 20,
   21, Sep 16, 18, 23, 25, Oct 2, 14, 26, Nov 19; <u>1785</u>: DL, Apr 8
Sposa Fedele, La (pastiche), <u>1775</u>: KING'S, Oct 31, Nov 4, 16, 21, 28, Dec 5,
   23; <u>1776</u>: KING'S, Apr 18
Sposa in Equivoco, La. See Bianchi Jr, Francesco.
Spotted snakes (song), <u>1793</u>: KING/HAY, Mar 15; <u>1794</u>: CG, May 23, 26
Spouter, The. See Murphy, Arthur.
Spouting Club (entertainment), <u>1776</u>: MARLY, May 25, 27, 30, Jun 1, 8, Aug 3,
   10; <u>1784</u>: HAY, Dec 13
Spozzi (dancer), <u>1786</u>: KING'S, Jan 24, Feb 18, Mar 23
Spragg, William (beneficiary), <u>1738</u>: CG, Nov 8
Sprat, Thomas, Bishop of Rochester, <u>1661</u>: LIF, Dec 16
Spread Eagle (book seller), <u>1750</u>: DL, Dec 10
Spriggs, Rhoda, Mrs James (actor), <u>1791</u>: CG, May 19, Jun 13
Sprigs of Laurel. See O'Keeffe, John.
Spring Garden, <u>1727</u>: SG, Mar 8; <u>1736</u>: DL, May 22; <u>1741</u>: CG, Mar 30; <u>1749</u>: DL,
   Mar 7; <u>1764</u>: CG, Jun 5; <u>1767</u>: VAUX, May 25
Spring St, <u>1797</u>: HAY, Sep 18; <u>1798</u>: HAY, Apr 23; <u>1799</u>: HAY, Jan 28; <u>1800</u>: HAY,
   Feb 3
Spring, The. See Harris, James.
Spur St, <u>1790</u>: CG, Jun 16
Squibb (actor), <u>1764</u>: CG, Dec 12; <u>1765</u>: CG, Jan 4, Apr 27, May 1, 16, Oct 3, 7,
   22, Nov 13, Dec 6, 9, 23, 27; <u>1766</u>: CG, Apr 18, Oct 21, 25, Nov 18, 21, 29,
   Dec 6; <u>1767</u>: CG, Mar 30, Apr 29
Squibb (spectator), <u>1700</u>: DLORLIF, Apr 20
Squibb, Mrs (actor), <u>1768</u>: CG, May 10, 13
Squire (chorus singer), <u>1771</u>: DL, Nov 14; <u>1772</u>: DL, Jan 10
Squire Badger. See Arne, Dr Thomas A.
Squire Basinghall; or, The Cheapside Beau (play, anon), <u>1735</u>: LIF, Jul 23, 25,
   30, Aug 1, 6, 8, 22, Sep 5
Squire Brainless. See Hill, Aaron.
Squire Lubberly (farce, anon), <u>1739</u>: CHE, May 8
Squire of Alsatia, The. See Shadwell, Thomas.
Squire Oldsapp. See D'Urfey, Thomas.
Squire Outwitted (Marquis Desapointe, Le) (dance), <u>1780</u>: KING'S, Dec 2, 9, 12
Squire Trelooby. See Congreve, William.
Squire, <u>1779</u>: HAY, Dec 20
Stabat Mater (music), <u>1756</u>: DL, Apr 2; <u>1758</u>: DL, Mar 10; <u>1759</u>: CG, May 4; <u>1770</u>:
   KING'S, Mar 8, Jun 12; <u>1771</u>: KING'S, Feb 28; <u>1776</u>: CG, Mar 6
Stables (house servant), <u>1760</u>: CG, Sep 22; <u>1771</u>: CG, Sep 28
Stace, Machell (publisher), <u>1798</u>: DL, Nov 14; <u>1799</u>: HAY, Jul 30, Aug 15
Stacey (colorman), <u>1772</u>: DL, Oct 16; <u>1774</u>: DL, Oct 20, Nov 25; <u>1775</u>: DL, Feb
   23; <u>1776</u>: DL, Jan 26, Jun 10; <u>1777</u>: DL, Jan 20
Stacie, John (author), <u>1734</u>: DL, Feb 11
Stacy (actor), <u>1776</u>: CHR, Sep 25
Stacy (householder), <u>1777</u>: CG, May 6; <u>1784</u>: CG, May 8
Stael, Anne Louis Germaine, Mme de (novelist), <u>1782</u>: DL, Oct 10
Stafford (glass man), <u>1772</u>: DL, Jan 6, Jun 10; <u>1775</u>: DL, May 27
Stafford Theatre, <u>1795</u>: DL, Jan 31
Stafford, John (epiloguist), <u>1684</u>: DL, Apr 0
Stafford, Lady (correspondent), <u>1739</u>: DL, Jan 4
Stafford, Lord. See Howard, William.

Stafford, Mrs (householder), 1737: LIF, Apr 27
Stag (musician), 1732: DL, Apr 25
Stag Hunt with Real Stag (entertainment), 1793: CG, Apr 1
Stage (framing for), 1772: DL, Sep 29
Stage Coach Opera, The (musical, anon), 1730: DL, May 13, 27, Nov 19; 1732: GF,
    May 11
Stage Coach, The. See Farquhar, George.
Stage Mutineers, The. See Phillips, Edward.
Stage Policy Detected, or some Select Pieces of Theatrical Secret History Laid
    Open (pamphlet), 1744: DL, Nov 19
Stageldoir, James (actor, property man), 1783: DL, May 23; 1784: DL, May 24;
    1785: DL, May 23; 1786: DL, May 26; 1789: DL, Nov 13, 14; 1790: DL, Jan 8;
    1793: HAY, Oct 10, Dec 26; 1796: DL, Jun 11
Stageldoir, Jane (actor, dancer, singer), 1780: DL, Sep 28; 1781: DL, May 25;
    1783: DL, Apr 26; 1784: DL, Apr 14, 28, Nov 26; 1785: DL, Sep 27; 1786: DL,
    Jan 5, 6, Mar 9, Dec 5; 1787: DL, May 30, 31; 1788: DL, Jan 25, Feb 1, Mar 3,
    6, 10, Apr 8, 16, May 6, 30, Jun 2, 3, 6, Sep 18, Oct 20, Dec 4; 1789: DL,
    Sep 12, Oct 13, Nov 7, 13, 17, 20, Dec 26; 1790: DL, Jan 22, Feb 5, 18; 1794:
    DL, May 16, Jan 9, Sep 27, Oct 22, 27, Nov 15, Dec 20; 1795: DL, Jan 19, Feb
    6, 12, May 6
Stageldoir, Martha (actor, dancer, singer), 1776: DL, Sep 21, Oct 29; 1777: DL,
    Mar 31, Apr 22; 1778: DL, Jan 22; 1779: DL, Jun 1, Oct 23; 1780: DL, Sep 28,
    30; 1781: DL, May 24, KING'S, Jun 5, DL, Oct 19, 22, Dec 17; 1782: DL, Jan 3,
    11, Apr 5, 6, 18, 25, 29, May 8, 10; 1783: DL, Sep 18, 27, Oct 9, 13, Nov 4,
    8; 1784: DL, Apr 12, Oct 7, 12, Nov 4, 9, 22; 1785: DL, Jan 6, 20, May 20,
    Sep 22, 27, Oct 11, 17, 18, Nov 7, 21, Dec 26; 1786: DL, Jan 16, Feb 23, Apr
    24, 28, Jun 6, Sep 28, 30, Oct 12, Nov 25, Dec 5, 28; 1787: DL, Jan 26, 29,
    May 11, 22, 25, Sep 27, 29, Oct 4, 6, 11, 12, Nov 5, 29, Dec 26; 1788: DL,
    Jan 25, 26, Mar 3, Oct 2, 13, Nov 10, 17, 19, Dec 22; 1789: DL, Jan 12, Apr
    15, May 7, 22, 27, Jun 9
Stageldoir, Martha and Jane (dancers), 1776: DL, Apr 15, Dec 17; 1777: DL, Apr
    23, Oct 17; 1778: DL, May 8, Sep 19, 29; 1779: DL, Jan 8, Apr 17, May 18, Sep
    30, Oct 25, Nov 20, 22, 26, Dec 10, 17, 27; 1780: DL, Jan 7, Apr 19, May 4,
    Sep 19, 21, 30, Oct 19, Dec 12; 1781: DL, Jan 23, Apr 3, May 1, 7, 17, Sep
    15, 20, Oct 4, 12, 29, Nov 5, 17, Dec 1; 1782: DL, Jan 4, 5, 11, 21, Feb 19,
    23, Mar 7, 14, Apr 6, May 10, Sep 17, 20, 21, Oct 3, 16; 1783: DL, Apr 26,
    May 2, Sep 20, 23, Nov 8; 1784: DL, Jan 3, May 14, 17, Oct 18; 1785: DL, Feb
    2, Mar 7, Apr 14; 1786: DL, Feb 23, May 2, Jun 1, Sep 28; 1787: DL, Feb 15,
    May 9, 30, 31, Oct 26, Nov 1, 21, 23; 1788: DL, Jan 5
Stageldoir, Mary (actor, dancer, singer), 1782: DL, Oct 5; 1783: DL, Feb 18,
    Mar 10, Apr 28, May 7, Sep 20, 23, Oct 4, 7, 13, 18, Nov 8, 20; 1784: DL, Jan
    3, 7, 13, Mar 20, Apr 21, May 7, 22, 24, Sep 21, 23, Oct 7, 14, 18, Nov 5,
    19, Dec 3; 1785: DL, Jan 11, 20, Apr 8
Stageldoir, Mary, Martha and Jane (dancers), 1779: DL, May 18
Stageldoir, Mrs (payee), 1774: NONE, Dec 24
Stagg, Mrs (beneficiary), 1712: DR, Feb 27
Staggins, Isaack (musician), 1675: ATCOURT, Feb 15
Staggins, Nicholas (composer), 1670: BRI/COUR, Dec 0; 1672: LIF, Apr 0; 1675:
    ATCOURT, Feb 15, Jul 24; 1676: DL, Jan 29, DG, Mar 11; 1677: ATCOURT, May 22;
    1693: ATCOURT, Nov 4; 1697: YB, Mar 24, May 13
Stainer (music scribe), 1775: DL, Oct 23; 1776: DL, Mar 11
Stamford Theatre, 1800: HAY, Jun 27
Stamford, Thomas (secretary, Lock Hospital), 1767: CG, Dec 23; 1768: HAY, Feb
    15
Stamitz, Carl (viola player, composer), 1777: CG, Feb 19; 1778: CG, Mar 18, 25;
    1779: KING'S, Mar 25; 1782: CG, Nov 25; 1783: CG, Jan 18; 1795: HAY, Mar 4
Stamma, Louis (critic), 1767: DL, Jan 16
Stammering Glee (song), 1793: CG, Dec 19, 20; see also Goody Groaner
Stamp, Sir Thomas (Lord Mayor), 1691: CITY, Oct 29
Stamper, F (printer), 1751: DL, Mar 19
Stamper, Francis (actor), 1763: CG, Apr 15, May 7, 9, 18, Sep 26
Stampigli, S (librettist), 1730: KING'S, Feb 24
Stand around (by), my brave boys (song), 1745: DL, Nov 14, 18
Stand to your guns, my hearts of oak (song), 1778: DL, May 14; 1779: CG, Dec
    22; 1781: HAY, Jan 22, CG, May 7, DL, 7; 1783: CG, May 19, HAY, Aug 1, 29;
    1784: DL, May 20; 1785: DL, Apr 25, May 11, 12; 1786: DL, May 8; 1787: DL,
    Apr 25, May 14; 1789: CG, May 22; 1790: CG, Apr 20; 1791: CG, Jun 10; 1794:
    CG, May 2
Stand to your guns, our cannons thunder (song), 1798: CG, Oct 15
Standen (actor), 1756: DL, Aug 12
Standen (ticket deliverer), 1787: DL, Jun 4; 1788: DL, Jun 6; 1789: DL, Jun 10;
    1790: DL, May 29; 1791: DL, May 31, CG, Jun 9; 1792: CG, May 29; 1794: CG,

Jun 10; <u>1795</u>: CG, May 30; <u>1796</u>: CG, Jun 4; <u>1797</u>: CG, Jun 8; <u>1798</u>: CG, May 29; <u>1800</u>: CG, Jun 11

Standen, Master (actor), <u>1794</u>: CG, Oct 10; <u>1795</u>: CG, May 6, 29, Oct 2; <u>1796</u>: CG, Apr 23, May 18, Jun 4, Sep 12, Dec 15; <u>1797</u>: CG, Apr 8, 19, Jun 8, Oct 2, 13; <u>1798</u>: CG, Feb 9, Oct 1, 15, Nov 12; <u>1799</u>: CG, May 3; <u>1800</u>: CG, Jan 16, Apr 17, Jun 11

Standen, Miss (actor), <u>1790</u>: CG, Oct 18; <u>1791</u>: CG, Feb 11, HAY, Jun 23, 30, Aug 24, Sep 26, CG, Oct 24, 28, DLKING'S, Nov 14; <u>1792</u>: CG, Mar 26, HAY, Jun 15, Jul 25, CG, Oct 15; <u>1793</u>: CG, Jan 21, Mar 18, Jun 5, Sep 17, Oct 14, 28, Nov 23, 27; <u>1794</u>: CG, May 10, 28, Oct 8, 15; <u>1795</u>: CG, Feb 21, 23, Apr 24, 28, May 1, 14, Sep 18, Oct 16, Dec 7; <u>1796</u>: CG, Apr 20, 29, Nov 5; <u>1797</u>: CG, Oct 2; <u>1798</u>: CG, Feb 9; <u>1799</u>: CG, Jan 29, Mar 25

Standen, Mrs (actor), <u>1756</u>: DL, Aug 12

Standen, Mrs (actor), <u>1778</u>: HAY, Sep 18

Standford (actor), <u>1670</u>: LIF, Nov 0

Stanhope St, <u>1736</u>: DL, May 14; <u>1738</u>: DL, May 19; <u>1778</u>: HAY, Mar 24, Apr 29, Aug 21; <u>1791</u>: DL, May 20; <u>1792</u>: DLKING'S, Jun 7

Stanhope, Colonel (spectator), <u>1698</u>: DL, May 3

Stanhope, Francis (trustee), <u>1733</u>: DL, Jun 4

Stanhope, Mrs (renter), <u>1750</u>: DL, Jan 31

Stanhope, Phillip Dormer, 4th Earl of Chesterfield, <u>1746</u>: CG, Nov 6; <u>1758</u>: DL, Jan 12

Stanhope, Phillip, 5th Earl of Chesterfield, <u>1797</u>: KING'S, May 18, CG, Jun 14, Nov 25

Stanley, C (actor), <u>1792</u>: HAY, Nov 26

Stanley, Charles John (organist), <u>1753</u>: KING'S, Mar 2, HAY, Apr 2; <u>1754</u>: KING'S, Apr 25; <u>1756</u>: DL, Apr 2; <u>1757</u>: RANELAGH, Jun 9; <u>1758</u>: KING'S, Mar 6, DL, 10; <u>1759</u>: SOHO, Mar 1, CG, May 4, RANELAGH, Jun 13, HAM, Aug 13, DL, Dec 1; <u>1760</u>: CG, Feb 22, 29, KING'S, Apr 15; <u>1761</u>: CG, Feb 6, DL, Oct 26; <u>1762</u>: CG, Feb 26, SOHO, Apr 21; <u>1763</u>: CG, Feb 18; <u>1764</u>: CG, Mar 9; <u>1765</u>: CG, Feb 22; <u>1766</u>: CG, Feb 21, 26; <u>1767</u>: CG, Mar 6, Apr 10; <u>1768</u>: CG, Feb 19, Mar 2, Apr 9; <u>1769</u>: CG, Mar 17; <u>1770</u>: DL, Mar 2, 7; <u>1771</u>: DL, Feb 15, HAY, Apr 12; <u>1772</u>: DL, Mar 6, Apr 24; <u>1773</u>: DL, Mar 3, 10, 17, 24, Apr 13; <u>1774</u>: DL, Feb 23, May 13; <u>1775</u>: DL, Mar 3, 8, 10, 15, 24, Apr 18, CHAPEL, Nov 23; <u>1776</u>: DL, Feb 23, Mar 1, 6, 15, 22, 29, CHAPEL, Apr 2, DL, 11; <u>1777</u>: DL, Feb 14; <u>1778</u>: DL, Mar 6, Apr 10; <u>1779</u>: DL, Feb 19, Mar 12, 19, 26; <u>1780</u>: DL, Feb 11; <u>1781</u>: DL, Mar 2; <u>1782</u>: DL, Feb 15, 20, 27, HAY, Mar 21, DL, 22; <u>1783</u>: DL, Mar 14; <u>1784</u>: DL, Mar 12, Apr 2; <u>1785</u>: DL, Mar 18, Oct 4; <u>1787</u>: DL, Mar 28

Stanley, Dorothea, Countess of Derby, <u>1661</u>: ATCOURT, Feb 25; <u>1675</u>: ATCOURT, Feb 15

Stanley, John (composer), <u>1736</u>: GF, Feb 10; <u>1742</u>: DL, Mar 20; <u>1743</u>: DL, Apr 20, May 11, 16; <u>1747</u>: CG, Apr 24; <u>1748</u>: CG, Mar 8, 31; <u>1752</u>: DL, Apr 25; <u>1760</u>: DL, Nov 17

--Zimri (oratorio), <u>1760</u>: CG, Mar 12; <u>1761</u>: CG, Feb 20

Stanmore, Miss (actor), <u>1769</u>: CG, Nov 11, Dec 26

Stannard (actor), <u>1780</u>: HAY, Nov 13; <u>1781</u>: HAY, Jan 22, Aug 29; <u>1783</u>: HAY, Dec 15; <u>1784</u>: HAY, Jan 21, Mar 8; <u>1788</u>: HAY, Aug 5; <u>1794</u>: DL, Oct 31; <u>1796</u>: DL, Jan 11

Stannard Jr (actor), <u>1784</u>: HAY, Mar 8

Stanyan, Abraham (spectator), <u>1700</u>: LIF, Jan 9

Staple of News. See Jonson, Ben.

Staples Inn, <u>1750</u>: DL, Nov 28

Staples, J (printer), <u>1758</u>: DL, Jan 11

Staples, Master (dancer), <u>1777</u>: DL, May 15; <u>1778</u>: DL, May 8

Stapylton, Sir Robert, <u>1663</u>: LIF, Aug 0

--Slighted Maid, The, <u>1663</u>: ATCOURT, Feb 23, LIF, 23, May 29; <u>1668</u>: LIF, Jul 28

--Stepmother, The, <u>1663</u>: LIF, Aug 0, Oct 0, ATCOURT, Dec 10

--Tragedy of Hero and Leander, The, <u>1667</u>: NONE, Sep 0

Star (residence), <u>1747</u>: DL, Apr 4

Star and Anchor Tavern, <u>1736</u>: CG, Apr 30

Star Tavern, <u>1759</u>: DL, Apr 16

Starboard Watch (Sailor's Carousal, The; or, Saturday Night at Sea), <u>1798</u>: CG, May 28, 30

Starke, Mariana, <u>1788</u>: HAY, Aug 9; <u>1790</u>: CG, May 5

--British Orphan, The, <u>1790</u>: CG, May 5

--Sword of Peace, The; or, A Voyage of Love, <u>1788</u>: HAY, Aug 9, 12, 14, 16, 19, 23; <u>1789</u>: HAY, Jun 30, Jul 2, 7, Aug 20

--Widow of Malabar, The, <u>1790</u>: CG, May 5; <u>1791</u>: CG, Jan 12, 14, 19, 26, Feb 2, 9, 16, 23, May 6, Sep 23; <u>1792</u>: CG, May 15; <u>1794</u>: CG, Jun 5; <u>1795</u>: CG, Dec 26; <u>1796</u>: CG, Jan 4, May 2; <u>1798</u>: CG, May 23

Starke, Richard John Hughes (epiloguist), <u>1790</u>: CG, May 5; <u>1791</u>: CG, Jan 12

Starkey, Mrs (dancer), <u>1742</u>: NWC, Dec 27

Starkey, Richard (beneficiary), 1745: GF, May 3; 1746: GF, Feb 25; 1747: GF, Jan 29
Stars Acres, 1778: DL, Apr 25, HAY, Aug 27; 1780: CG, Apr 21
State Lungi Sol per poco (song), 1763: KING'S, Apr 25
State of Innocence, The. See Dryden, John.
States General Ambassador, 1716: DL, Apr 13
Statesman Foiled, The. See Dossie, Robert.
Stationers' Hall, 1687: MS, Nov 22; 1691: SH, Nov 23; 1697: SH, Nov 22; 1698: SH, Nov 22; 1699: SH, Nov 22; 1708: YB, Jan 21, SH, Feb 4; 1709: GO, Nov 21; 1737: HAY, May 16; 1744: SH, Feb 9; 1758: DL, Jan 11; 1767: CG, Mar 4
Statue Animated, The (dance), 1762: CG, Feb 2, 5
Statue Dance (dance), 1771: KING'S, May 23, Jun 15, HAY, Sep 16; 1772: KING'S, Apr 25, May 5, 12
Statues (dancer), 1726: KING'S, Oct 21
Statues Animees, Les (dance), 1756: CG, Mar 2, 4, 8, 11, 16, 22, 29, 30, Apr 5, 8; 1800: KING'S, Jan 28; see also Animated Statue
Statute Dance (dance), 1784: CG, Apr 28, May 22; 1785: HAMM, Jul 1; 1789: HAY, Jun 5; 1792: CG, Apr 21; 1797: CG, May 24, Nov 15; 1798: CG, May 17
Staunton, Richard Collet (actor), 1780: HAY, Jul 6; 1781: HAY, May 31, Jun 1, 7, 16, Jul 9, Aug 1, 7, 8, 21, 22, 24, 29; 1782: HAY, Jun 3, 10, 11, 12, 20, Jul 16, Aug 5, 9, 13, 15, 16, 26, DL, Nov 7; 1783: DL, Mar 6, 20, Apr 7, 26, May 2, 12, 20, Sep 16, 27, Oct 7, 20, 30, Nov 14, 20, Dec 2, 10, 11; 1784: DL, Jan 7, 9, 10, 20, 31, Feb 24, Apr 14, 28, May 3, 17, 20, HAY, Aug 5, DL, Sep 21, 23, Nov 2; 1785: DL, Jan 12, 14, 17, 20, 24, 27, Feb 1, 8, Apr 1, 6, 20, 22, 26, May 3, 5, 6, 7, 26, Oct 26, 27, Nov 8, 11, 17, 18, 22, Dec 26, 29; 1786: DL, Jan 5, Mar 25, May 9, 10, 26, Sep 19, 23, Oct 7, 19, 21, 23, Nov 25, Dec 6; 1787: DL, Jan 13, 29, Mar 29, May 16, Jun 4, Sep 18, 29, Oct 6, 18, Nov 5, 22, Dec 10, 14, 19, 26; 1788: DL, Jan 5, 16, 21, 22, 31, Mar 24, Apr 3, 17, May 14
Stay, shepherd, stay (song), 1791: DL, Apr 1; 1792: KING'S, Feb 29; 1794: DL, Mar 26
Stayley, G (critic), 1748: DL, Feb 13
Stead (ticket deliverer), 1785: HAMM, Jul 2
Stede, John (prompter), 1717: LIF, May 17; 1718: LIF, May 20; 1721: LIF, May 10; 1723: LIF, May 15; 1724: LIF, Apr 27; 1725: LIF, Apr 28; 1726: LIF, May 3; 1727: LIF, May 22; 1732: LIF, May 2; 1733: CG, May 2, DL, Jun 9; 1736: CG, Jun 4; 1740: CG, May 16; 1741: CG, May 14; 1743: CG, Apr 28; 1744: CG, May 2; 1745: CG, May 7; 1746: CG, Apr 29; 1747: CG, May 12; 1748: CG, Apr 29; 1749: CG, Apr 22; 1750: CG, Apr 27; 1751: CG, May 7; 1752: CG, May 4; 1753: CG, May 9; 1754: CG, Apr 30; 1755: CG, May 1; 1756: CG, May 13; 1757: CG, May 12, Nov 28; 1758: CG, May 4; 1759: CG, May 1; 1760: CG, Mar 17, May 15, Sep 22; 1761: CG, Apr 21; 1762: CG, Apr 30; 1763: CG, Apr 30; 1764: CG, May 1; 1765: CG, Apr 30; 1766: CG, Apr 23; 1767: CG, May 1; 1768: CG, May 12
Stede, Mary (dancer), 1768: CG, Feb 23, Apr 23, May 12, Jun 3; 1769: CG, May 19; 1770: CG, May 18; 1771: CG, May 8, 25; 1772: CG, May 1, 23; 1773: CG, Apr 15, 24, May 22; 1774: CG, May 7, 12, 16
Stede, Mrs (beneficiary), 1729: LIF, Apr 26
Stede, Mrs (house servant), 1742: CG, May 21
Stedman and Bewley (linen drapers), 1771: CG, Dec 2; 1772: CG, Dec 8; 1773: CG, Dec 2
Steel (mercer), 1750: DL, Jan 15
Steel (singer), 1773: MARLY, Sep 3; 1778: HAY, Sep 7; 1783: HAY, Jun 30
Steel, Mrs (actor), 1734: LIF, Oct 1; 1735: YB, Mar 21; 1740: GF, Nov 4, 12, 18, 19, 20, 24, 26, 27, 29, Dec 1, 2, 4, 6, 10, 12, 15; 1741: GF, Jan 15, 22, 27, Feb 2, 10, 14, 28, Mar 7, 19, Apr 10, BFH, Aug 22, GF, Sep 18, 23, 28, Oct 2, 7, 9, 16, 19, 23, 28, Nov 30, Dec 9, 10; 1742: GF, Jan 1, 4, Apr 22
Steele, Sir Richard, 1701: DL, Dec 0; 1703: DL, Dec 2; 1705: DL, Apr 23, QUEEN'S, Dec 27; 1711: DL, Apr 26; 1713: DL, May 11, Dec 9; 1714: DL, Sep 21; 1715: DL, Feb 28, YB, May 28, Oct 31; 1716: DL, Jan 12, Feb 10; 1718: HC, Sep 23, DL, Dec 3; 1719: NONE, Mar 26, DL, Nov 21; 1720: DL, Feb 20, Mar 3, LIF, Apr 22, DL, May 31; 1721: LIF, Jan 23, DL, Oct 17, 18, Dec 20; 1722: DL, Jan 8, Apr 16, Oct 20, 22, 25, Nov 7, Dec 17; 1723: DL, Mar 26; 1728: YB, Mar 8, MDS, Apr 3; 1729: DL, Nov 10; 1730: DL, Apr 17, Nov 3, 25; 1731: LIF, May 12, RI, Jul 22; 1732: DL, Mar 23, Apr 21, 27, Nov 14; 1733: DL, Jan 26, Apr 4, GF, 30, DL/HAY, Oct 15, GF, 29, 31, DL/HAY, Nov 8; 1734: DL/HAY, Jan 24, Mar 25, Apr 2, 16, 26, DL, Oct 25, Nov 2, Dec 13; 1735: DL, Jan 17, 24, Feb 3, Mar 24, Apr 29, Jun 5; 1736: DL, Feb 9, Mar 3, 15, Apr 12, CG, 17, DL, May 3, Aug 26, 31, Sep 16, CG, Oct 22, DL, Nov 16, Dec 15; 1737: CG, Jan 8, DL, Feb 1, Mar 29, Apr 30, CG, May 12, DL, Nov 12; 1738: CG, Jan 7, 16, DL, 27, Feb 27, CG, Oct 11, Dec 6; 1739: CG, Jan 8, DL, Feb 2, 5, CG, May 8, Sep 5, Nov 1, 6; 1740: CG, Jan 10, Mar 20; 1741: CG, Mar 9; 1742: DL, Sep 16, CG, 29; 1743: DL, Sep 13; 1744: CG, Jan 18, DL, May 21, Sep 27; 1745: DL, May 8;

1746: DL, Apr 4; 1747: DL, May 8; 1758: HAY, Jan 16; 1787: CG, Dec 5; 1789:
CG, Jan 28, Apr 30; 1791: CG, Oct 13; 1792: DLKING'S, Mar 19; see also
Bickerstaffe, Isaac
--City Nymphs, The; or, The Accomplished Fools, 1705: DL, Apr 23
--Conscious Lovers, The, 1722: DL, Nov 7, 8, 9, 10, 12, 13, 14, 15, 16, 17, 19,
20, 21, 22, 23, 24, 26, 27, 28, 30, Dec 5, 10, 12, 14, 18, 28; 1723: DL, Feb
26, Mar 12, Apr 4, 30, Sep 14; 1724: DL, Feb 18, Apr 22, Nov 19; 1725: DL,
Apr 5, 27; 1726: DL, Jan 3, Feb 24, Mar 31, Apr 29; 1727: DL, Feb 11, Mar 2,
Apr 10, Sep 21; 1728: MDS, Apr 3; 1729: DL, Nov 6, 8, 10; 1730: GF, Jan 13,
14, Apr 16, LIF, Nov 23, 24, 25, Dec 2; 1731: LIF, Jan 7, 23, Mar 11, Apr 5,
May 12, RI, Jul 22, LIF, Sep 20, Dec 14; 1732: LIF, Feb 19, Apr 25, LIF/CG,
Nov 18; 1733: GF, Jan 18, 19, Feb 2, DL, Apr 4, 28, CG, May 17, GF, 18; 1734:
GF, Mar 25, DL/HAY, Apr 26, May 24, DL, Oct 25; 1735: GF, Jan 13, DL, 17, Mar
24, CG/LIF, Apr 14, GF, 17, DL, 29, CG/LIF, May 23, DL, Jun 5, CG, Oct 22,
Nov 28; 1736: CG, Jan 6, DL, Feb 9, 10, 11, 12, 13, 14, 16, Mar 3, 15, Apr
13, GF, 16, 30, CG, May 1, Jun 1, DL, Aug 26, 31, CG, Oct 22, DL, Dec 15;
1737: CG, Jan 8, DL, Feb 1, CG, Mar 17, DL, 17, 22, Apr 22, CG, May 12, DL,
Sep 13, CG, Oct 24, DL, Nov 12; 1738: CG, Jan 7, 16, DL, 27, Feb 27, CG, Mar
21, May 3, Oct 11, Dec 6; 1739: CG, Jan 8, DL, Feb 1, 2, 5, CG, May 8, Sep 5,
Nov 1; 1740: CG, Jan 4, 17, Mar 20, DL, 25, Apr 19, May 15, Sep 20, CG, Oct
23, GF, Nov 10, CG, 18; 1741: CG, Mar 9, GF, Apr 2, CG, 7, DL, 8, CG, May 2,
Dec 11; 1742: CG, Jan 5, Feb 23, Mar 11, DL, Apr 5, CG, 30, DL, May 22, Sep
16, CG, 29, DL, Oct 21, CG, Nov 27, DL, Dec 17; 1743: CG, Jan 26, Mar 24, DL,
Apr 25, CG, 25, DL, May 18, Sep 13, CG, Oct 24, DL, Dec 12; 1744: CG, Jan 18,
Mar 30, Apr 24, DL, May 17, Sep 27, HAY, Oct 4, 6, 9, 18, DL, 25, Nov 17, CG,
28, DL, Dec 28; 1745: CG, Feb 1, DL, 5, Apr 22, CG, 30, DL, Oct 5, Nov 6, CG,
Dec 2; 1746: CG, Jan 16, GF, Mar 10, CG, 17, Apr 15, DL, 30, CG, Nov 17, GF,
Dec 18; 1747: GF, Feb 23, CG, 28, DL, Mar 12, 19, 31, Apr 7, CG, 22, DL, May
11, Nov 7, Dec 3, 30; 1748: DL, Jan 26, Feb 16, Apr 15, May 4, Oct 6, 31, CG,
Nov 28; 1749: DL, Jan 2, Apr 3, CG, 18, DL, May 1, CG, Oct 23, 27, 28, DL,
Nov 28, Dec 4, 16; 1750: DL, Feb 6, 16, Apr 20, CG, 30, DL, Sep 27, CG, Oct
23, Dec 5; 1751: CG, Feb 1, Apr 12, DL, 24, CG, May 2, DL, 22, Oct 1, 3, 4,
16, Nov 20; 1752: DL, Jan 4, CG, 18, 24, DL, Feb 11, CG, Mar 12, Apr 3, 27,
DL, 28, Sep 16, Oct 12, CG, 31, Nov 11, DL, 15, CG, 29, Dec 4, DL, 28; 1753:
CG, Jan 23, Apr 25, DL, May 14, Oct 12, Nov 16, Dec 21; 1754: DL, Jan 11, CG,
Mar 26, DL, Apr 6, CG, May 3, DL, 4, Oct 5; 1755: DL, Jan 11, CG, Mar 22, DL,
Apr 21, CG, 22, DL, May 3, Sep 27, CG, Dec 5, DL, 13; 1756: DL, Jan 16, CG,
Feb 16, DL, May 3, Nov 11; 1757: DL, Jan 11, May 6, CG, 16, DL, Oct 6, CG,
Nov 14, DL, 26, CG, Dec 15; 1758: CG, Apr 25, DL, 27, 29, CG, Oct 2, Nov 20,
Dec 22; 1759: CG, Jan 10, DL, 20, CG, Feb 12, Mar 29, DL, May 9, CG, 10, DL,
Oct 2, 6, Nov 8, CG, Dec 8; 1760: CG, Jan 3, DL, 3, CG, 14, DL, Mar 15, CG,
22, Apr 21, DL, 26, CG, May 9, DL, 27, Jul 29, CG, Nov 29, DL, Dec 30; 1761:
CG, Feb 14, DL, Apr 11, 25, CG, May 6, DL, 21, Sep 10, Oct 12, CG, 24; 1762:
DL, Jan 4, CG, May 6, DL, 8, CG, Sep 30, DL, Oct 9, CG, Nov 22, DL, Dec 14;
1763: CG, Oct 5, 13, DL, Dec 13, 14, 31; 1764: CG, Feb 8, DL, Oct 4, CG, 24;
1765: DL, Jan 14, Feb 2, Oct 23, CG, Nov 13, 14; 1766: DL, Apr 4, CG, 22, DL,
May 16, KING'S, Sep 9, 12, 13, DL, Nov 20, CG, Dec 9; 1767: CG, May 15, 26,
HAY, Aug 14, DL, Nov 20, Dec 19; 1768: DL, May 10, Oct 18; 1769: DL, Jan 9,
Apr 1, CG, 7, May 16, DL, Nov 8, Dec 22; 1770: DL, Feb 1, 3, Oct 12; 1771:
DL, Oct 29; 1772: DL, Apr 7; 1773: DL, Feb 11, CG, May 22, DL, 25; 1774: CG,
Oct 7DL, Jan 24; 1703: DL, May 28, Oct 26, Nov 1, Dec 2, 15; 1705: DL, Dec
12; 1708: DL, Mar 18; 1709: DL, Mar 31; 1710: QUEEN'S, Jan 12, Feb 6, 8, DL,
Dec 14; 1711: DL, Feb 9, Apr 26, Nov 8; 1712: DL, Jan 14, May 30, Nov 12;
1713: DL, Apr 8, May 11, Dec 9; 1715: DL, Feb 22, Nov 21; 1716: DL, Feb 9,
Apr 30, Dec 11; 1717: DL, Oct 16; 1718: DL, Feb 12, May 27; 1721: DL, Apr 13,
May 26, Oct 18, Dec 20; 1722: DL, Apr 16, Oct 22, Dec 17; 1723: DL, May 7,
Nov 1; 1724: DL, Jan 3, May 19, Nov 6; 1725: DL, Jan 19, May 5, Oct 15, Dec
20; 1726: DL, May 13, Sep 22, Dec 29; 1727: DL, May 4, Oct 20; 1728: DL, Feb
26, May 13, Oct 23; 1729: DL, Jan 10, May 8, Oct 14; 1730: DL, Jan 2, Apr 17,
Nov 25; 1731: DL, Feb 4, Nov 26; 1732: DL, Jan 24, Mar 23, Apr 21, Nov 14;
1733: GF, Oct 15, 16, 25, 29, 30, 31, Nov 1, 9; 1734: GF, Jan 7, Feb 15,
DL/HAY, Mar 25, Apr 16, GF, May 22, Nov 27; 1735: GF, Jan 18, Feb 10, CG, Dec
31; 1736: CG, Jan 1, 2, 9, 29, Mar 25, GF, Apr 1, CG, 17, May 31, RI, Jul 31,
CG, Sep 29; 1737: CG, Feb 8, Mar 10, LIF, Apr 27, CG, May 2, Sep 30, Nov 12;
1739: CG, Feb 16, Mar 1, Apr 26, Nov 6; 1740: CG, Jan 10, DL, Apr 22, CG, 30,
Nov 14; 1741: CG, Jan 23, Apr 23, May 14; 1742: CG, Jan 2, 15, Feb 8, May 8;
1743: CG, Oct 19; 1745: CG, Jan 1, Nov 11, 20; 1746: GF, Jan 27, 28, CG, Mar
4, GF, 22; 1747: CG, Jan 26, GF, Mar 9; 1748: CG, Jan 29; 1749: DL, Jan 13,
14, Feb 25, Nov 21; 1750: CG, Feb 22, DL, Apr 30, CG, May 3, DL, Oct 22, Nov
27; 1751: DL, Jan 4; 1753: CG, Sep 26, 28, Oct 19, Dec 7, 18, 19; 1754: CG,
Feb 9, Mar 19, Apr 23, Oct 2, 25; 1755: CG, Jan 21, Oct 6, Nov 15; 1756: CG,
May 11, Sep 27, Nov 5; 1757: CG, May 19, Sep 28; 1758: CG, Apr 21, Oct 20;

1760: DL, Feb 8, 11, 12, 18, Mar 18, CG, May 2, DL, 5; 1762: CG, Feb 22, DL,
Mar 15, May 5; 1764: CG, Feb 1, DL, 18, CG, Nov 29; 1768: DL, Apr 14; 1770:
DL, Apr 3, May 4; 1771: DL, Mar 21, May 4, 29; 1772: DL, May 13; 1773: CG,
Apr 23; 1774: CG, Apr 23; 1775: DL, Apr 8; 1776: CG, May 13; 1777: DL, Mar
13, 20, Apr 15; 1779: CG, Apr 27; 1780: CG, May 3, 19; 1781: CG, Feb 15, May
16; 1784: CG, May 26; 1786: CG, Jan 7; 1787: CG, Jan 6; 1789: CG, Apr 30;
1793: CG, Oct 25; 1794: CG, Dec 10; 1799: DL, Apr 17
--Conscious Lovers, The, 1722: DL, Nov 7, 8, 9, 10, 12, 13 , 19, 25, Nov 17;
1775: CG, Jan 10, DL, May 10, CG, 11, DL, Oct 21, 28, 30; 1776: CG, Jan 5,
Apr 24, May 11, DL, Oct 24, 25, CG, Nov 4, 6, DL, Dec 17; 1777: CG, Oct 8,
Nov 4; 1778: CG, Mar 12, Dec 11; 1779: CG, Sep 27; 1781: DL, Jan 6; 1782: DL,
May 8, Sep 19, CG, Oct 23, DL, Nov 29, Dec 19; 1783: DL, Feb 20, Oct 7, CG,
8; 1784: DL, Jan 7, CG, Oct 1, DL, Nov 4; 1786: CG, Mar 11, HAY, Jul 13;
1787: CG, Mar 27; 1788: CG, Feb 4, 11, Mar 6, Nov 1, 19; 1789: CG, Feb 24,
Sep 18; 1790: CG, Oct 23, Nov 19; 1791: CG, Oct 20, Dec 22; 1792: CG, Oct 12,
Nov 21; 1793: CG, Oct 5; 1794: CG, Nov 22, 29; 1795: CG, Apr 29; 1796: DL,
Dec 20; 1797: DL, Jan 3, CG, Nov 18; 1798: CG, Jan 10, Feb 2, 8
--Gentleman, The, 1719: DL, Nov 21; 1720: DL, Feb 20
--Lying Lover, The; or, The Lady's Friendship, 1703: DL, Dec 1, 2, 3, 4, 6, 7,
8; 1746: DL, Apr 4, 8, 19, May 1
--Tender Husband, The; or, The Accomplished Fools, 1705: DL, Apr 23, 24, 25,
26, 28, May 19, Jun 23, Oct 24, Nov 15, Dec 20; 1706: DL, Jan 16, Feb 26, May
30, Jun 6, QUEEN'S, Dec 7, 9; 1707: QUEEN'S, Feb 21, 25, DL/QUEEN, Nov 11;
1708: DL/QUEEN, Feb 5, May 27; 1709: DL, Jan 27; 1710: QUEEN'S, Jan 5, DL, 5,
QUEEN'S, 26; 1711: DL, Jan 11, May 10, Dec 18; 1712: DL, Nov 3; 1714: DL, Jan
28, Apr 9; 1715: DL, Feb 28, Apr 7, Oct 31; 1716: DL, Jan 12, Feb 10, May 15,
23, Nov 27; 1717: DL, Mar 7; 1718: DL, Jan 7, Apr 23, Oct 30; 1719: DL, Jan
31, May 18, Oct 15, Dec 29; 1720: DL, May 31; 1721: DL, Jan 27, Oct 17; 1722:
DL, Jan 8, Apr 9, Oct 25; 1723: DL, Jan 18, Mar 26, Nov 18; 1724: DL, Feb 4,
Nov 2; 1725: DL, Feb 15, Apr 17, Oct 28, Dec 29; 1726: DL, Apr 30, Oct 18,
Nov 30; 1727: DL, Oct 19, Dec 11; 1728: DL, Apr 4, Oct 24; 1729: DL, Jan 14,
Mar 8, Apr 28, Oct 21; 1730: DL, Jan 19, Apr 20, GF, Nov 6, 7; 1732: GF, Mar
27, DL, Apr 27, GF, May 12, DL, Dec 28; 1733: GF, Jan 1, 2, 5, DL, 26, GF,
Mar 1, Apr 4, 30, DL, May 2, GF, 29, Oct 4, DL/HAY, 15, Nov 8; 1734: DL/HAY,
Jan 24, Apr 24, May 8, GF, 16, Oct 3, DL, Nov 2, Dec 13; 1735: DL, Jan 24,
Feb 3, GF, 6; 1736: DL, Apr 12, GF, 17, DL, May 3, RI, Jul 24, DL, Sep 16,
Nov 16; 1737: DL, Mar 29, LIF, Apr 20, DL, 30; 1738: CG, Nov 20, 21, DL, 25,
Dec 1, 27; 1739: CG, Jan 29, Apr 23, May 30, DL, Oct 27, CG, Dec 1; 1740: DL,
Jan 7, Feb 11, CG, 21, Oct 11, DL, 28; 1741: DL, Oct 23, CG, Nov 27; 1742:
GF, Jan 29, DL, 29, CG, Feb 11, DL, 16, 18, CG, May 12, DL, 13, Sep 21, Dec
29; 1743: DL, Oct 20; 1745: DL, Dec 9, 10; 1750: DL, Nov 24; 1751: DL, Nov
16; 1758: HAY, Jan 16; 1760: CG, Mar 17, DL, Apr 24, CG, 25; 1764: CG, Apr
10; 1770: DL, Mar 27; 1772: DL, Apr 6; 1775: DL, Mar 27; 1783: DL, Apr 28,
May 21, Sep 20, Dec 17; 1787: CG, Nov 23, 26, Dec 5, 7, 12; 1788: CG, Jan 15;
1789: CG, Jan 28, Apr 17; 1791: CG, Oct 13; 1792: DL, Oct 20, CG, 24, DL, Nov
1, 16; 1794: CG, Feb 24
Steele's Great Room, 1728: YB, Apr 10
Steer (house servant), 1795: CG, Jun 13
Steevens, George (editor), 1748: DL, Apr 23; 1771: HAY, Jun 26
Stefani, Abbot (composer), 1721: KING'S, Jul 5; 1731: ACA, Jan 14; 1732: HIC,
Mar 31
Steffani, Agostino
--Arminius (opera), 1714: QUEEN'S, Mar 4, 6, 11, 13, 18, 20, Apr 10, May 1, 29,
KING'S, Oct 23, 26, Dec 11, 15, 22; 1715: KING'S, Mar 26
Steffkins, Christian (musician), 1675: ATCOURT, Feb 15
Steffkins, Mrs Christian (beneficiary), 1715: SH, May 5
Stefford, 1734: DL, Feb 2
Steibelt, Daniel (composer), 1798: CG, Dec 11
Stella and Flavia (song), 1743: DL, Apr 6, 7, 9, 20, JS, 25, DL, May 4
Stennet (haberdasher), 1773: CG, Oct 18
Stephanie, Gottlieb, 1788: DL, Oct 25
--Doktor und Apotheker, 1788: DL, Oct 25
Stephen St, 1777: DL, May 6
Stephens. See Stevens.
Stephens (actor), 1775: CG, Dec 26: 1776: CG, Feb 15
Stephens (lawyer), 1773: DL, Jun 2
Stephens (mason), 1771: CG, Nov 5; 1772: DL, Jun 10; 1773: CG, Jan 19; 1774:
DL, Jun 2; 1776: DL, Jun 10
Stephens (ticket deliverer), 1752: CG, Apr 10
Stephens, John (secretary, Marine Society), 1757: DL, May 11; 1759: DL, Mar 30
Stephens, Mary (actor), 1774: CG, May 10, 17, 20, Nov 19, Dec 7, 9, 14, 27;
1775: CG, Jan 2, Apr 29

811

Stephens, Miss (actor, singer), 1798: DL, Nov 29, Dec 11; 1799: DL, May 24, Jun
    28, Oct 12, 19, Nov 6, Dec 13, 17; 1800: DL, Jan 21, Feb 1, 17, Mar 11, Apr
    29, Jun 7, 17
Stephens, Mrs (actor), 1700: DL, Mar 0; 1701: DL, May 31
Stephens, Mrs (actor), 1732: LIF, Apr 18; 1735: CG/LIF, Feb 22
Stephens, Mrs (actor), 1755: CG, Oct 17, Dec 3, 5; 1756: CG, Feb 26, Apr 29,
    May 5, Sep 22, Oct 15; 1757: CG, Feb 19, May 10, 16, Oct 13, 19, Nov 5, 7,
    14, Dec 5; 1758: CG, Jan 11, Feb 1, Apr 22, Oct 2, 9, Nov 16, 23; 1759: CG,
    Feb 1, May 1, 7, Oct 10, 13, Nov 30, Dec 8; 1760: CG, Jan 14, 24, Feb 14, Apr
    25, May 5, 12, Sep 22, 24, Nov 18, 29; 1761: CG, Apr 20, 21, 27, Sep 7, Nov
    13; 1762: CG, Mar 22, Apr 17, 24, May 5, 6, 12, Sep 30, Oct 2, 4, 16, Nov 29,
    Dec 8; 1763: CG, Feb 1, Apr 13, May 7, Sep 28, 30, Oct 5, 7, 22, Nov 3, 22,
    25; 1764: CG, Jan 6, 21, Feb 15, 22, Apr 28, May 5, 7, Oct 5, 11, 18, 23, 24,
    29, Nov 6, 30; 1765: CG, Jan 28, Apr 11, 27, May 3, Sep 23, Oct 15, 17; 1766:
    CG, Feb 5, Mar 17, Apr 25, 29, Sep 22, Oct 8, 14, Nov 19, Dec 9, 20, 23;
    1767: CG, Jan 23, May 4, 11, Sep 22, Oct 13, 23, 27, 29, Nov 7, 13, 23, Dec
    8; 1768: CG, Feb 11, 13, 20, Apr 5, 13, 19, May 26, 27, DL, Sep 8, CG, Nov 4,
    DL, Dec 14, 17; 1769: DL, Mar 18, Apr 24, 25, May 16, 20, 22, Oct 7, 10, 23,
    31, Nov 2, 11, 15, 16, 27, Dec 4, 6, 8, 16, 20; 1770: DL, Feb 24, Mar 1
Stephens, Samuel (actor), 1734: CG/LIF, Oct 19, 23, 31, Nov 4, 7, 28; 1735:
    CG/LIF, Jan 4, 9, 25, Feb 15, Mar 13, 15, Apr 10, 17, LIF, 19, CG/LIF, May 5,
    CG, Sep 12, Oct 3, 25, Nov 1, 4, 8, 10, 13, 15, 22; 1736: CG, Mar 15, 27, 30,
    LIF, Apr 2, CG, 8, LIF, 16, CG, 26, May 17, Sep 27, Oct 6, 20, Nov 1, Dec 2;
    1737: CG, Feb 15, 24, 26, Apr 14, 21, May 3, 6, 31, LIF, Jul 26, Aug 2, 5,
    Sep 7, CG, 16, 19, Oct 22, 28, Nov 15; 1738: CG, Jan 3, 26, Feb 6, 13, 16,
    23, Mar 13, 20, 25, Apr 19, 24, May 2, 3, Jun 27, 30, Jul 7, 11, Aug 1, 22,
    29, Sep 18, 20, 25, Oct 6, 24, Nov 6, 9, 29, 30, Dec 2, 4, 5; 1739: CG, Jan
    27, Feb 2, 10, 24, Apr 3, 25, May 2, 7, 11, 17, 23, DL, 31, CG, Sep 21, 27,
    29, Oct 4, 6, 10, 22, 23, 25, Nov 6, Dec 6, 19; 1740: CG, Jan 15, Mar 11, 27,
    Apr 18, DL, May 19, CG, Jun 5, Sep 19, 26, DL, Oct 13, 14, 15, 17, CG, 31,
    Nov 7, DL, 19, CG, Dec 13, DL, 26; 1741: CG, Jan 22, 27, 28, Mar 9, 12, Apr
    13, May 4, DL, 25, BFLW, Aug 22, CG, Sep 25, Oct 2, 5, 7, 10, 13, 15, 20, 21,
    Nov 4, 11, Dec 17, 18; 1742: CG, Jan 2, Feb 2, Mar 18, Apr 10, 26, May 5, 7,
    DL, 24, CG, Oct 4, 9, 13, 25, 26; 1743: CG, Apr 25, May 9, LIF, Jun 3, CG,
    Sep 21, 28, Oct 26, Nov 4, Dec 3, 12; 1744: CG, Jan 5, 11, 24, Mar 29, 30,
    Apr 19, 20, DL, May 22
Stephens, Zachariah (witness), 1767: DL, Jan 2
Stephenson (house servant), 1768: CG, Jun 3, 4; 1769: CG, May 19, 20; 1770: CG,
    May 19, 24; 1771: CG, May 25; 1772: CG, May 29; 1774: CG, May 14, 24; 1775:
    CG, May 30; 1776: CG, May 22; 1777: CG, May 24; 1778: CG, May 22; 1779: CG,
    May 19; 1780: CG, May 26; 1781: CG, May 26; 1782: CG, May 29; 1783: CG, Jun
    4; 1784: CG, May 29
Stephenson (householder), 1777: KING'S, Apr 10
Stephenson (scene designer), 1675: DG, Feb 27
Stephenson, Joseph (guard), 1773: CG, Jan 22; 1774: CG, Jan 11
Stephkins (musician), 1675: ATCOURT, Feb 15
Stepmother, The. See Stapylton, Sir Robert.
Stergess (stage hand), 1760: CG, May 26
Sterling, James, 1735: GF, Dec 17; 1736: GF, Jan 29, Mar 3
--Parracide, The, 1736: GF, Jan 29, 31, Feb 2, 3, Mar 3
Sterling, Miss (actor), 1772: HAY, Sep 21
Sterling, Nancy, Mrs James (actor), 1723: LIF, Oct 2, 4, 7, Nov 4, 14, 19, 21;
    1724: LIF, Mar 19, 23, Apr 22, 29, May 18, Jun 1, SF, Sep 2
Sterne, Everard (actor), 1787: RLSN, Mar 26, 27, 28, 29, 30, 31; 1795: HAY, Mar
    11
Sterne, John (murderer), 1760: HAY, Aug 15
Sterne, Mrs Everard (actor), 1787: RLSN, Mar 26, 27, 28, 29, 30, 31
Stevens (actor), 1728: HAY, Apr 3; 1729: HAY, Jan 31; 1733: HAY, Jul 26, CG,
    27, Aug 14
Stevens (actor), 1745: DL, Oct 12, 19, Nov 4, 22, Dec 17; 1746: DL, Jan 18, 20;
    1748: JS, Jun 14, HAY, Sep 5, JS, Dec 26; 1750: NWSM, Aug 20
Stevens (actor), 1761: DL, Oct 31; 1762: DL, Apr 28, May 17, Sep 25, Nov 3, Dec
    22; 1763: DL, Jan 7, 15, 17, Apr 13, Nov 9, 29, Dec 26; 1764: DL, Jan 18, Feb
    8, May 1; 1768: DL, May 24; 1769: DL, Apr 17
Stevens (actor), 1778: HAY, Mar 24; 1785: HAY, Mar 15
Stevens (dancer), 1795: CG, Dec 21; 1796: CG, Jan 4
Stevens (singer), 1762: DL, Jan 15
Stevens (tenant), 1767: DL, Mar 23; 1772: DL, May 4
Stevens (ticket deliverer), 1772: DL, Jun 1; 1774: DL, May 16; 1775: DL, May 19
Stevens (ticket deliverer), 1792: DLKING'S, Jun 15; 1793: DL, Jun 6; 1797: DL,
    Jun 13; 1798: DL, Jun 9; 1799: DL, Jul 2; 1800: DL, Jun 13
Stevens, Captain (actor), 1751: DL, Mar 7; 1760: DL, Jan 12

Stevens, Captain and Mrs, <u>1751</u>: DL, Mar 7
Stevens, George Alexander (actor, author), <u>1753</u>: CG, Nov 12; <u>1754</u>: CG, Feb 12,
    23, Mar 9, 25, Apr 20, May 8, 21, Oct 17, Nov 4, 6, 27, Dec 10; <u>1755</u>: HAY,
    Jan 8, 28, CG, 28, Feb 20, Mar 6, May 12; <u>1760</u>: CG, Mar 20; <u>1762</u>: DL, Jan 15;
    <u>1765</u>: CG, Mar 18; <u>1766</u>: HAY, Feb 25; <u>1770</u>: CG, Jan 5; <u>1771</u>: CG, Apr 5; <u>1773</u>:
    DL, May 12, HAY, Aug 11; <u>1776</u>: CHR, Oct 9; <u>1777</u>: HAY, Mar 11, Oct 9; <u>1780</u>:
    CG, Jun 26, HAY, Oct 30, Nov 6; <u>1788</u>: HAY, Aug 22; <u>1790</u>: CG, Feb 11; <u>1791</u>:
    CG, May 2; <u>1794</u>: CG, May 26; <u>1797</u>: CG, May 22; <u>1798</u>: CG, May 23; <u>1799</u>: CG,
    Jun 1; <u>1800</u>: CG, Apr 15
--Cabinet of Fancy, The; or, Evening Exhibition (entertainment), <u>1780</u>: HAY, Oct
    30, Nov 1, 3, 6, 7, 8
--Course of Comic Lectures, A, <u>1755</u>: HAY, Jan 8, 13
--Court of Alexander, The (opera), <u>1770</u>: CG, Jan 3, 5, 6, 8, 9, 10, 11, 12
--French Flogged, The; or, The English Sailors in America, <u>1759</u>: BFS, Sep 3,
    BF, 4, 5, 6, SFS, 18, 19, 20, 21; <u>1777</u>: HAY, Oct 9
--Lecture on Heads, A (entertainment), <u>1765</u>: CG, Mar 18; <u>1766</u>: JS, Jan 6; <u>1769</u>:
    HAY, Mar 28; <u>1770</u>: CG, Jan 5; <u>1777</u>: HAY, Mar 11, 13, 15, 17, 19, 21, 31, Apr
    2, 4, 7, 9, 12, 16, 21, 23, 25, 30, May 5; <u>1780</u>: CG, Jun 26, 29, Jul 3, 6;
    <u>1781</u>: HAY, Mar 14, 16; <u>1785</u>: HAY, Aug 2; <u>1788</u>: HAY, Aug 22; <u>1789</u>: DL, May 22;
    <u>1790</u>: HAY, Oct 13; <u>1798</u>: CG, May 23
--Trip to Portsmouth, A, <u>1773</u>: HAY, Aug 11, 13, 16, 18, 20, 25, 27, Sep 1, 6,
    10, 13, 15, 17; <u>1774</u>: HAY, Sep 5, 6, 12; <u>1775</u>: HAY, Sep 4, 18
Stevens, Henry (spectator), <u>1680</u>: ATCOURT, Feb 20
Stevens, J (house servant), <u>1772</u>: DL, Jun 10, Sep 26, Oct 10; <u>1773</u>: DL, Jun 2,
    Sep 25, Dec 10; <u>1774</u>: DL, Sep 24; <u>1775</u>: DL, Sep 26
Stevens, John, <u>1745</u>: GF, Apr 18
--Modern Wife, The; or, The Virgin Her Own Rival, <u>1745</u>: GF, Apr 18, 19
Stevens, Miss (actor), <u>1746</u>: CG, Feb 24, Apr 23; <u>1748</u>: CG, Apr 14, 29; <u>1749</u>:
    HAY, Apr 29, May 26; <u>1750</u>: HAY, Feb 16
Stevens, Miss (actor), <u>1786</u>: HAMM, Jun 5
Stevens, Mrs (actor), <u>1751</u>: DL, Mar 7
Stevens, Priscilla (actor), <u>1730</u>: BFOF, Aug 20, SFOF, Sep 9, LIF, Oct 30, Dec
    4, 5; <u>1731</u>: HAY, Mar 17, LIF, Nov 2, 6, 25, Dec 3; <u>1732</u>: LIF, Jan 7, Feb 14,
    Mar 25, HAY, May 12, LIF, 22, 24, 31, LIF/CG, Oct 4, 16, 23, 28, Nov 7, 8, 9,
    Dec 7, 15, 27, 28; <u>1733</u>: LIF/CG, Feb 5, Mar 26, CG, 27, LIF/CG, 29, Apr 19,
    25, CG, May 1, LIF/CG, 7, 24, Jun 1, CG, Jul 27, Aug 2, Sep 15, 20, 27, Oct
    4, 6, 9, 13, 19, 26, 29, 31, Nov 8, 26, 28, Dec 4, 7, 8, 31; <u>1734</u>: CG, Jan
    23, Feb 14, 26, Mar 5, 28, Apr 1, 25, May 9, 10, 17, Sep 2, CG/LIF, 20, Oct
    7, 11, LIF, 12, CG/LIF, 14, 16, 25, 29, Nov 1, 7, 21, 25, Dec 5; <u>1735</u>:
    CG/LIF, Jan 6, 17, 23, Feb 4, LIF, 12, Mar 3, CG/LIF, 15, 29, Apr 21, CG, 25,
    CG/LIF, May 1, 2, 5, CG, Sep 17, 19, 24, 26, Oct 8, 13, 17, 20, 24, 29, Nov
    6, 7, 8, Dec 15, 31; <u>1736</u>: CG, Jan 23, Feb 10, 21, 26, Mar 15, 22, 29, Apr 8,
    17, LIF, May 5, CG, 20, Sep 17, 20, 24, 27, 29, Oct 1, 25, 29, 30, Nov 29,
    Dec 2, 9; <u>1737</u>: CG, Jan 10, 17, 21, Feb 14, Mar 10, 21, 31, Apr 11, 21, 26,
    28, May 16, 31, LIF, Jul 26, Sep 7, CG, 19, 30, Oct 3, 12, 17, 21, 28, 29,
    31, Nov 2, 14; <u>1738</u>: CG, Jan 3, 13, 25, 26, 31, Feb 2, Mar 18, Apr 6, 12, 24,
    25, Sep 20, Oct 4, 6, 20, 26, Nov 11, 15, 20, 22, 24, 29, Dec 7; <u>1739</u>: CG,
    Feb 2, 16, 24, Mar 13, Apr 14, May 2, Aug 2, 21, Sep 14, 15, 22, 25, Oct 2,
    3, 4, 5, 6, 8, 22, 25, Nov 6, 10, 28, Dec 1; <u>1740</u>: CG, Jan 3, 12, Apr 25, May
    2, 13, Sep 22, 26, Oct 1, 6, 22, 25, 27, Nov 20, Dec 6, 19; <u>1741</u>: CG, Jan 6,
    22, 23, Mar 30, Apr 1, 2, 3, 9, 22, Sep 28, 30, Oct 2, 7, 24, 31, Dec 1, 16;
    <u>1742</u>: CG, Jan 2, 19, 23, Feb 3, 4, Mar 13, Apr 24, May 5, Oct 16, 18, 21, 28,
    Nov 13, 15, 22; <u>1743</u>: CG, Jan 1, 18, Feb 9, Mar 15, Apr 12, May 5, Sep 23,
    26, 30, Oct 10, 14, 17, 19, 21, 28, Nov 16, Dec 3; <u>1744</u>: CG, Jan 4, 24, Feb
    7, Apr 12, Sep 21, 28, Oct 1, 3, 18, 20
Stevens, Richard John Samuel (composer), <u>1789</u>: DL, Dec 9; <u>1790</u>: CG, May 5, DL,
    20, HAY, Aug 20, CG, Oct 23; <u>1791</u>: CG, Jan 12, May 18, Jun 3; <u>1792</u>: KING'S,
    Mar 28; <u>1793</u>: KING/HAY, Mar 13, 15; <u>1794</u>: CG, May 23; <u>1795</u>: HAY, Mar 4; <u>1797</u>:
    DL, Jan 12; <u>1798</u>: DL, May 23, 24, HAY, Aug 21, DL, Oct 11; <u>1799</u>: DL, Oct 12
Stevens, William (actor), <u>1775</u>: HAY, Oct 30; <u>1776</u>: HAY, May 20, 22, 27, 28, 31,
    DL, Jun 10, HAY, 14, 19, Jul 5, 8, 10, 24, 29, Sep 6, 16, 17, 20, CG, Dec 27;
    <u>1777</u>: CG, Feb 1, HAY, Mar 13, CG, May 5, 9, HAY, 28, 30, Jun 26, 30, Jul 7,
    15, 18, 30, Aug 7, 14, 18, 30, Sep 3, 18; <u>1778</u>: CG, Jan 19, 20, Feb 2, 23,
    May 6, 7, HAY, 21, 22, Jun 11, 19, Jul 11, 30, Aug 6, 15, 17, 19, 20, 27, Sep
    2, 8, CG, Oct 14, 26; <u>1779</u>: CG, Apr 5, 23, 24, May 3, DL, 18, HAY, Jun 2, 4,
    10, 12, 18, Jul 15, Aug 9, 13, 14, 18, 24, 31, CG, Sep 27, Oct 6, 20, Nov 25;
    <u>1780</u>: CG, Jan 7, Feb 2, 26, Apr 25, HAY, Jun 2, 6, 13, 24, 28, 29, Jul 8, 29,
    Aug 5, 10, 12, 17, 24, Sep 2, 5, 8, 11, CG, 18, 25, Oct 6, 10, 13, 19, Nov 4,
    15, 25; <u>1781</u>: CG, Mar 3, Apr 28, 30, May 7, 16, HAY, 30, Jun 1, 9, 11, 15,
    16, Jul 2, 9, Aug 1, 7, 8, 15, 22, 29, Sep 4, 12, CG, 17, 24, 26, Oct 1, 13,
    16, 20, 23, Nov 2, 21, 24, Dec 5, 26; <u>1782</u>: CG, Mar 19, Apr 1, 10, 20, DL,
    May 4, CG, 11, 15, 17, 27, HAY, Jun 3, 4, 6, 10, 11, 12, 13, 20, 24, Jul 5,

813

17, Aug 9, 13, 15, 17, 27, CG, Sep 30, Oct 3, 4, 7, 19, 22, 23, Nov 2, 4, 8,
12, 19, HAY, 25, CG, 25, 27, 30; 1783: CG, Feb 25, Apr 1, 22, May 14, 19, 21,
23, HAY, 31, Jun 3, CG, 4, HAY, 4, 5, 6, 13, 18, 20, 30, Jul 5, Aug 1, 27,
CG, Sep 22, 26, Oct 1, 6, 10, 14, 16, 17, 28, 31, Nov 25, Dec 6; 1784: CG,
Jan 6, 7, 13, 14, 29, Feb 9, 28, Mar 9, 16, Apr 13, 26, May 8, 11, 18, 19,
26, HAY, 28, CG, 29, HAY, 29, Jun 1, 2, 25, Jul 8, 19, 27, Aug 16, 20, 24,
Sep 13, CG, 17, 20, 21, 28, 29, Oct 22, 25, 28, Dec 14, 22, 27, 28; 1785: CG,
Feb 21, Mar 29, 30, Apr 1, 6, HAY, 25, CG, May 7, 18, 24, HAY, 30, Jun 3, 7,
14, Jul 1, CG, Sep 23, 26, 28, 30, Oct 3, 12, 17, 26, Nov 1, 7, 29, Dec 7,
22; 1786: CG, Jan 7, Feb 1, 11, Mar 13, Apr 20, 24, May 13, 17, 26, Sep 29,
Oct 9, 16, 18, 28, Nov 22, Dec 11, 15; 1787: CG, Jan 2, Feb 20, Apr 16, 21,
May 11, 15, 23, Jun 2, Sep 17, 19, 21, Nov 5, 30, Dec 10; 1788: CG, Jan 2,
18, 28, Feb 23, Mar 11, Apr 1, May 12, 14, Jun 2, Oct 1, 8, 10, Nov 10, 12,
22, 26, Dec 18, 20, 26; 1789: DL, Jun 3, CG, 5; see also Castephens
Stevens, Young, 1733: HAY, Feb 14
Stevenson (actor), 1785: HAMM, Jun 17, 27, Jul 2, 4, 8, 27
Stevenson (boxkeeper), 1795: DL, May 30; 1796: DL, Jun 14; 1797: DL, Jun 14;
   1798: DL, Jun 15; 1799: DL, Jul 4; 1800: DL, Jun 17
Stevenson, J (publisher), 1786: KING'S, Mar 30; 1788: KING'S, Apr 5, May 8;
   1789: KING'S, Apr 4
Stevenson, John Andrew (composer), 1793: CG, May 3
Stevenson, Joseph (music porter), 1766: CG, Dec 18; 1767: CG, Mar 7; 1771: DL,
   Sep 28; 1773: CG, May 28; 1774: CG, May 24
Stevenson, Miss (singer), 1786: CG, Oct 21; 1787: CG, May 19
Steventon, Mrs (actor), 1791: HAY, Sep 26
Steward (dancer), 1740: BFH, Aug 23
Steward (equilibrist), 1752: SFGT, Sep 18, 19
Steward, Elizabeth (correspondent), 1699: DLORLIF, Feb 20, LIF, Mar 4, Nov 7,
   26, DL, Dec 14; 1700: LIF, Mar 12, NONE, Apr 11
Steward, Mrs (spectator), 1667: LIF, Feb 4
Stewart, James (actor, playwright), 1772: HAY, Sep 21; 1775: HAY, Feb 20; 1777:
   HAY, Oct 13; 1779: HAY, Jan 11; 1780: HAY, Jan 17, Sep 25; 1782: HAY, Mar 18;
   1798: HAY, Apr 23
--Exciseman Tricked, The (farce), 1782: HAY, Mar 18
--Students, The; or, The Humours of St Andrews (farce), 1777: HAY, Oct 13;
   1779: HAY, Jan 11; 1780: HAY, Jan 17; 1782: HAY, Mar 18
Stewart, Miss (actor), 1772: HAY, Sep 21; 1776: HAY, Sep 18, 20, CG, Nov 30
Stewart, Mrs (actor), 1736: HAY, Feb 16
Stewart, Thomas (actor, playwright), 1780: HAY, Sep 25; 1784: HAY, Feb 23;
   1785: HAY, Jan 24
--Double Amour, The, 1780: HAY, Sep 25; 1785: HAY, Jan 24; 1791: HAY, Sep 26
Stewart's (Stuart's) Rents, 1744: JS, Mar 28; 1748: HAY, Nov 14
Stewart's China Shop, 1782: HAY, Mar 18
Stichel, Mrs (actor), 1792: HAY, Oct 22
Stiff Rope (entertainment), 1710: GR, Sep 7; 1713: TEC, Nov 26
Stiles (actor), 1677: DL, Jun 0
Still I'm grieving still lamenting (song), 1693: NONE, Sep 0; 1694: DL, Feb 0
Still the Lark finds repose (song), 1786: DL, Apr 24; 1787: CG, May 9; 1789:
   DL, Apr 17
Stillingfleet, Benjamin (author), 1760: CG, Feb 29; 1774: DL, Mar 2
Stitchbury (actor, singer), 1736: GF, Feb 24, Mar 4, LIF, Dec 31; 1737: LIF,
   Feb 1, May 4; 1741: GF, Mar 3, Apr 2, 30; 1742: GF, Feb 3, May 10, 18, LIF,
   Dec 6; 1746: GF, Mar 15
Stivaux, Mme (dancer), 1757: HAY, Dec 26
Stock (actor), 1786: CG, Oct 6, Nov 15
Stockdale (haberdasher), 1773: DL, Dec 22
Stockdale (musician), 1715: LIF, May 9
Stockdale, John (publisher), 1782: HAY, Aug 5, DL, Nov 5; 1783: HAY, Aug 13;
   1800: DL, Jan 25
Stockdale, Mrs (actor), 1715: LIF, Jun 2
Stockley, Mrs (house servant), 1735: CG/LIF, May 26
Stockport Theatre, 1795: CG, Oct 19
Stockton (musician), 1758: CHAPEL, Apr 27; 1760: CG, Sep 22
Stockwell Conjurer, 1772: CG, Jan 31, Feb 8
Stockwell, Elizabeth, 1709: QUEEN'S, Sep 15
Stockwell, 1746: SOU, Nov 3
Stodherd's Academy, 1734: YB, Dec 12
Stokes (actor), 1772: HAY, Sep 17, 18; 1776: CHR, Sep 25, 27, Oct 16; 1777:
   CHR, Jun 25; 1778: CHR, May 27, Jun 26; 1780: HAY, Sep 25; 1781: CII, Mar 15
Stokes (actor), 1800: HAY, Jul 2
Stokes, James (assistant prompter), 1793: DL, May 31; 1795: DL, Jun 5; 1797:
   DL, Jun 12; 1798: DL, Jun 13; 1799: DL, May 16

Stokes, Mrs (actor), 1731: HAY, Mar 24
Stolen Heiress, The. See Centlivre, Susannah.
Stone (actor), 1735: TC, May 28, YB, Jul 17
Stone Eater, The. See Stuart, Charles.
Stone Guest, The; or, Don John the Libertine (play, anon), 1726: KING'S, Dec 21
Stone, Anne (actor), 1719: LIF, Nov 13, 18, 24, 26; 1720: LIF, Jan 4, 11, 21,
    Feb 3, 26, 29, Mar 28, Apr 26, May 3, 17, 23, Oct 1, 18, 22, Nov 18, Dec 8;
    1721: LIF, Jan 31, Feb 21, Mar 11, Apr 19, May 4, 10, 29, Oct 3, 5, 7, 12,
    21, Nov 10, 11, 25, Dec 18; 1722: LIF, Jan 13
Stone, Richard (frame maker), 1759: CG, Nov 20
Stonecastle (actor), 1734: JS, May 29; 1735: YB, Mar 21
Stonnell, Mrs (coffee house keeper), 1742: CG, Feb 23
Stoppelaer (Stopelar, Stoplear), Michael (actor, singer), 1729: SF, Sep 8, BLA,
    30, HAY, Nov 12, 15, 22, Dec 18; 1730: HAY, Jan 8, 21, Feb 6, 23, Mar 11, 20,
    30, Apr 20, Jun 17, 23, 27, Jul 17, TC, Aug 1, BFR, 22, Sep 4, HAY, 18, Oct
    21, 26, Nov 13, 16, GF, Dec 16, 28; 1731: GF, Jan 23, Mar 1, 8, 15, 18, Apr
    1, 20, 29, May 11, DL, Jul 6, 20, 23, Aug 6, 11, 16, 18, 20, BFB, 26, DL, Sep
    25, 30, Oct 2, 16, 30, Nov 25; 1732: DL, Jan 1, Feb 1, Apr 12, 17, 28, May 1,
    8, 9, 12, 29, Jun 23, Aug 1, 4, 17, BF, 22, DL, Sep 8, 19, 23, 28, Oct 14,
    GF, 26, DL, 31, GF, Nov 3, DL, 6, 7, GF, 8, DL, 17, GF, 24, Dec 1, DL, 6, 16,
    GF, 20, DL, 22; 1733: GF, Jan 20, 27, DL, 29, GF, Feb 5, DL, 12, GF, 13, DL,
    26, GF, Mar 5, DL, 28, 31, Apr 6, GF, 19, DL, 19, GF, 27, DL, May 2, 7, 9,
    21, BFCGBH, Aug 23, Sep 4, GF, 10, DL, 24, 26, GF, 27, DL, 28, Oct 1, GF, 8,
    9, DL, 12, GF, 19, DL, 22, 24, Nov 7, GF, 10, DL, 13, 26, Dec 5, 26; 1734:
    DL, Jan 3, 8, GF, 11, DL, 15, 19, 28, GF, 31, DL, Feb 4, GF, 5, 11, DL/LIF,
    Mar 11, DL/HAY, 16, 21, 25, GF, Apr 1, LIF, 4, 15, DL, 15, 22, DL/HAY, 26,
    GF, 27, DL/HAY, 27, DL, May 15, LIF, 29, BFFO, Aug 24, CG, Sep 2, GF, 11,
    CG/LIF, 20, 23, Oct 2, 9, 18, GF, Nov 7, CG/LIF, 11, GF, 18, CG/LIF, 19, Dec
    5, 19, GF, 21, CG/LIF, 30; 1735: CG/LIF, Jan 3, CG, 8, GF, 24, CG/LIF, Feb
    13, Mar 11, Apr 11, 15, 22, GF, 23, 28, May 3, CG/LIF, 26, Jun 2, HAY, Aug
    26, CG, Sep 12, 26, 29, Oct 1, 13, 17, 20, Nov 6, 15, 18, Dec 2, 11; 1736:
    CG, Jan 1, 9, 21, 23, Mar 15, 18, 27, Apr 6, 30, May 4, LIF, 5, CG, 6, 13,
    17, 18, 20, LIF, Jun 16, DL, Sep 4, 7, 9, CG, 20, DL, 23, 28, CG, 29, DL, Oct
    5, 9, 12, 16, 18, 20, 25, CG, 25, DL, Nov 13, 22, 23, Dec 20; 1737: DL, Jan
    29, CG, Feb 3, DL, 10, 19, CG, Mar 15, DL, 29, Apr 12, CG, 28, DL, 29, May 2,
    4, CG, 9, DL, 17, 18, 19, 27, CG, Sep 21, 30, Oct 28; 1738: CG, Jan 3, Feb
    16, 23, Mar 25, Apr 7, 27, Jun 27, 30, Aug 29, Oct 6, 20, Dec 4, 5; 1739:
    KING'S, Jan 16, CG, 20, Feb 10, 16, Mar 20, Apr 12, 25, May 7, 16, 21, Sep
    22, Oct 2, 25, Nov 6, 10; 1740: CG, Jan 15, Feb 2, Mar 11, DL, 17, CG, 24,
    DL, Apr 16, 21, 24, CG, 28, May 5, 9, DL, 13, 14, CG, Sep 26, Oct 1, 3, Nov
    6, Dec 4, 13; 1741: CG, Jan 23, 27, Mar 5, May 1, 12, Oct 13, 24, Nov 7, 26,
    30, Dec 4, 16; 1742: CG, Jan 2, 29, Feb 18, Apr 26, May 3, 4, 5, 7, 14, Oct
    9, 27, Nov 11; 1743: CG, Jan 18, Apr 29, May 2, 5, Sep 30, Oct 19, Nov 7, Dec
    3, 8, 9, 14, 19; 1744: CG, Jan 11, 14, 24, Feb 28, Mar 13, May 7, Sep 24, Oct
    10, 15, 20, 22, Nov 1, 8, 9, 10, Dec 12, 17; 1745: CG, Apr 4, 23, 26, May 3,
    13, Sep 23, 30, Oct 16, Dec 5, 10; 1746: CG, Jan 2, 9, 13, Feb 3, 6, 24, Mar
    10, 13, May 1, Jun 16, 27, Sep 29, Oct 3, 6, Nov 18, Dec 11, 17, 26, 29;
    1747: CG, Jan 26, 29, Feb 2, Mar 17, May 22, Oct 31, Nov 16, 23, Dec 9, 28;
    1748: CG, Jan 12, 15, 27, 29, Feb 27, Mar 24, 28, Apr 21, 22, 29, Sep 23, 26,
    Oct 14, 17, Nov 16, 24, 26; 1749: CG, Jan 2, Mar 2, 29, Apr 11, May 4, Sep
    27, Oct 18, 19, 20, Nov 8, 9, 17; 1750: CG, Jan 15, Feb 22, Mar 17, 27, Apr
    17, Oct 12, 22, 25, Nov 6, 22, 24, 29, Dec 4; 1751: CG, May 8; 1752: CG, Feb
    18, Mar 17, 30, Apr 13, 29, Oct 2, 6, 9, 30, Nov 28, 30; 1753: CG, Jan 6, 22,
    Feb 7, Mar 24, May 1, 7, Sep 12, 26, Oct 3, 5, 30, 31, Nov 26; 1754: CG, Feb
    12, Mar 9, Apr 6, May 7, 9, DL, Jul 2, CG, Sep 16, 23, 30, Oct 2, 15, 24, 28,
    29, Nov 5, 6, 13, Dec 10, 13, 30; 1755: CG, Jan 28, Apr 4, 24, May 6, 9, 15,
    Oct 6, 8, 17, 22, 31, Nov 3, 8, 12, 13, 14, 29, Dec 3, 4; 1756: CG, May 11,
    Sep 20, 22, 27, 29, Oct 6, 21, 26, 28, Nov 8, 13, 24, Dec 1, 7, 10; 1757: CG,
    Jan 11, Feb 9, 16, May 9, 27, Sep 23, 26, 28, 30, Oct 5, 8, 12, 13, 14, 20,
    28, Nov 2, 5, 9, 18, Dec 8; 1758: CG, Feb 1, Apr 14, May 5, 18, Sep 25, Oct
    4, 9, 20, 24, 30, Nov 3, 13, 23; 1759: CG, Feb 1, Mar 5, Apr 7, 28, May 3,
    17, DL, Jun 19, CG, Sep 26; 1760: CG, Jan 7, 31, Feb 25, Mar 18, Apr 15, 18,
    May 7, 9, Sep 22, Oct 1, 10, 17, 25, Dec 1; 1761: CG, Jan 10, Apr 20, 28, Jun
    23, Sep 21; 1762: CG, May 8; 1763: CG, May 18; 1764: CG, May 18; 1765: CG,
    May 15; 1766: CG, May 3; 1767: CG, May 19; 1768: CG, Feb 25, Apr 20, 25, May
    26, 27, Oct 4, Dec 22; 1769: CG, Jan 2, May 11, 17, Nov 27; 1770: CG, Feb 12,
    May 17, Dec 3, 26, 29; 1771: CG, Jan 12, May 16, Sep 25; 1772: CG, May 14,
    Oct 26, Nov 6; 1773: CG, Mar 15, May 18, Oct 18; 1774: CG, May 6; 1775: CG,
    May 11; 1776: CG, May 11; 1777: CG, May 15
Stoppelaer Jr (actor), 1734: BFFO, Aug 24
Stoppelaer, Mrs (actor), 1760: CG, May 9; 1761: CG, Apr 28
Storace, Anna Selina (singer), 1777: CG, Feb 14, KING'S, Mar 13, CG, 21,

815

KING'S, Jul 5; <u>1787</u>: KING'S, Apr 24, May 24, Dec 8; <u>1788</u>: KING'S, Jan 12, 15, Feb 5, Mar 4, 6, May 15; <u>1789</u>: CG, Feb 27, Mar 6, 20, 27, Apr 3, KING'S, 21, May 9, Jun 11, DL, Nov 24; <u>1790</u>: DL, Feb 1, 19, 24, 26, HAY, 27, DL, Mar 5, 10, 12, 17, 24, 26, Apr 16, CG, 29, HAY, Jun 3, 10, DL, Sep 11, Oct 4; <u>1791</u>: DL, Jan 1, Feb 5, 10, May 3, DLKING'S, Sep 22, 27, 29, Oct 15; <u>1792</u>: DLKING'S, May 30, DL, Sep 18, 20, Oct 9, 11, Nov 21; <u>1793</u>: KING'S, Jan 26, Feb 26, DL, Mar 11, KING'S, May 14, Jun 25, HAY, Aug 30, Sep 30, Oct 22, Nov 23, Dec 16; <u>1794</u>: DL, Mar 12, 19, 26, 28, HAY, 29, DL, Apr 2, 4, 9, 10, 11, 26, May 3, 12, 13, 16, Jul 2, Oct 20, 21, 27, 28, 29, Nov 3, Dec 20; <u>1795</u>: DL, Jan 13, 26, Apr 18, May 6, 18, Sep 17, 19, 22, Oct 6, 30, Nov 11, 16; <u>1796</u>: DL, Feb 20, Mar 12, 19, 28, Apr 30, May 9, 25, Jun 9; <u>1797</u>: KING'S, Mar 14, Apr 18, CG, 26, DL, May 22, CG, Jun 21

Storace, Stephen (musician, composer), <u>1759</u>: HAY, Jan 12, Mar 29; <u>1770</u>: MARLY, Aug 7; <u>1771</u>: MARLY, Aug 8, 20; <u>1772</u>: MARLY, Aug 31, Sep 2; <u>1787</u>: DL, Apr 20, KING'S, 24, CG, Oct 31; <u>1788</u>: KING'S, Feb 5, Mar 4, DL, Oct 25; <u>1789</u>: KING'S, May 9, DL, Nov 24; <u>1790</u>: DL, Jan 14, Apr 16, Oct 4; <u>1791</u>: DL, Jan 1, May 3, CG, 10, DLKING'S, Sep 22, 29, Oct 15, Dec 31; <u>1792</u>: DLKING'S, May 23, DL, Oct 11, Nov 21; <u>1793</u>: DL, Jan 23, KING'S, 26, CG, Feb 20, KING'S, 26, DL, Mar 11, KING'S, May 14, HAY, Nov 23, Dec 16; <u>1794</u>: DL, Mar 12, Apr 25, 26, May 1, 3, CG, 9, DL, 9, 12, 13, 16, 17, Jun 9, Jul 2, Sep 27, Oct 27, Dec 20; <u>1795</u>: HAY, Mar 4, Jun 11, Sep 2, DL, Oct 1, 30; <u>1796</u>: DL, Mar 12, Apr 30, May 9, 25, HAY, Jun 25, Aug 29; <u>1797</u>: DL, Feb 16, CG, Mar 31, DL, Jun 6, HAY, Aug 14; <u>1798</u>: DL, May 23, HAY, Jul 16, Sep 17; <u>1799</u>: HAY, Jul 27; <u>1800</u>: DL, Jan 1, HAY, Aug 7

--Cameriera Astuta, La (opera), <u>1788</u>: KING'S, Mar 4, 6, 8, 15, 29, Apr 1, 26

Store St, <u>1769</u>: CG, Dec 22; <u>1770</u>: CG, Dec 22; <u>1772</u>: DL, Dec 19; <u>1778</u>: CG, May 23; <u>1780</u>: HAY, Aug 2, CG, Dec 22; <u>1785</u>: HAY, Feb 10; <u>1788</u>: DL, Apr 14; <u>1789</u>: DL, May 5; <u>1790</u>: DL, Apr 20; <u>1791</u>: DL, Apr 28; <u>1792</u>: DLKING'S, Apr 12; <u>1796</u>: DL, Apr 29; <u>1797</u>: DL, May 24; <u>1798</u>: DL, May 18; <u>1799</u>: DL, Apr 24

Storer, Charles (actor), <u>1747</u>: CG, Nov 23, Dec 9, 19, 28; <u>1748</u>: CG, Jan 16, 27, 29, Mar 28, Apr 11, 13, 15, 21, 22, 27, 29, BF, Aug 24, SFBCBV, Sep 7; <u>1761</u>: CG, Jun 23, Sep 21, Oct 19, Nov 4, Dec 11

Storer, Elizabeth, Mrs Charles (actor, singer), <u>1747</u>: DL, Mar 16, Apr 29, CG, Oct 31, Nov 16, 24, Dec 9, 15, 17, 19; <u>1748</u>: CG, Jan 12, 15, Mar 3, 8, 14, 21, 24, 28, 31, Apr 6, 12, 15, 18, 20, 21, 23, 28, 29; <u>1752</u>: CG, Feb 6, 11, Mar 17, Apr 13, 18; <u>1761</u>: SOHO, Jan 28, CG, Mar 25, Oct 3

Storer, Maria (actor), <u>1779</u>: CG, Oct 16

Storey, Mrs (actor), <u>1730</u>: HAY, Sep 18

Storey, <u>1757</u>: CG, Apr 18

Storey's Gate, <u>1751</u>: DL, Dec 18

Storm, The (song), <u>1774</u>: CG, Apr 26; <u>1778</u>: DL, Apr 6; <u>1781</u>: CG, Apr 25, May 7; <u>1794</u>: CG, May 26; <u>1795</u>: CG, Apr 28, May 7, 8, 13, 14, 16, 21, 25, 27, Jun 2, 5, 8; <u>1796</u>: CG, Apr 29, May 26; <u>1797</u>: CG, May 2, 9, 11, 19, 20, 23, Jun 1, DL, 6, CG, 10, 13; <u>1798</u>: CG, Apr 21; <u>1799</u>: CG, Apr 6, Jun 1; <u>1800</u>: CG, Apr 15, Jun 12; see also Sea Storm; Cease, rude Boreas

Storm, The. See Fletcher, John, The Sea Voyage.

Story (actor), <u>1799</u>: HAY, Jun 28, Jul 16, 24, Aug 21, Sep 2, 16

Story of Lord Hoppergollop's Cook and Gardener's Ghost (monologue), <u>1797</u>: CG, May 16

Story of the Dog (entertainment), <u>1796</u>: CG, May 17

Story, Miss (actor, dancer), <u>1740</u>: DL, Jan 15, Apr 29, May 22, Oct 14, 27, Nov 17, Dec 4, 26; <u>1741</u>: DL, Apr 27, May 12, 28, Oct 12, 21, 31, Nov 4, 11, 21, Dec 4, 12, 14; <u>1742</u>: DL, Jan 6, Feb 24, Mar 13, Apr 20, LIF, Dec 3, 13, 27; <u>1743</u>: LIF, Apr 7; <u>1744</u>: DL, Oct 2, 17; <u>1745</u>: DL, Jan 14, May 8

Stot, Jane, Mrs John (actor), <u>1756</u>: CG, Nov 18

Strada del Po, Anna (singer), <u>1729</u>: KING'S, Dec 2; <u>1730</u>: KING'S, Feb 24, Mar 21, Apr 4, May 19, Nov 3; <u>1731</u>: KING'S, Feb 2, Apr 6, Dec 7; <u>1732</u>: KING'S, Jan 15, Feb 15, Mar 25, May 2, 23, Jun 10, Nov 4, CRT, 20; <u>1733</u>: KING'S, Jan 27, Mar 3, 17, Oct 30, Nov 13, Dec 4; <u>1734</u>: KING'S, Jan 26, Mar 13, Apr 2, 27, May 18, CG/LIF, Nov 9; <u>1735</u>: CG, Jan 8, Mar 5, 28, Apr 1, 16; <u>1736</u>: CG, Feb 19, May 12, Nov 27, Dec 1, 8; <u>1737</u>: CG, Jan 12, Feb 16, Mar 9, 23, May 18

Stradiotti, Sga (singer), <u>1714</u>: HIC, Apr 29, KING'S, Oct 23, Nov 16

Strafford, Earl of (spectator), <u>1738</u>: CG, Jan 18

Strafford, Lord, <u>1663</u>: SH, Jan 6

Strahan (house servant), <u>1788</u>: CG, May 24; <u>1789</u>: CG, Jun 5; <u>1790</u>: CG, May 29; <u>1791</u>: CG, Jun 2; <u>1792</u>: CG, May 25; <u>1794</u>: CG, Jun 16; <u>1795</u>: CG, Jun 13; <u>1796</u>: CG, Jun 3; <u>1797</u>: CG, May 27; <u>1798</u>: CG, May 31; <u>1799</u>: CG, May 22; <u>1800</u>: CG, Jun 7

Strahan, A (publisher), <u>1800</u>: HAY, Jul 15

Strahan, G (printer), <u>1745</u>: DL, Apr 1

Strahan, John (publisher), <u>1785</u>: CG, Dec 14

Strahan, William (publisher), <u>1777</u>: DL, Mar 13; <u>1781</u>: DL, Oct 19

Straight Rope (entertainment), 1732: RIW/HAY, Sep 8, 11, 15
Strand Lane, 1798: DL, Jun 6
Strange (actor), 1763: DL, Oct 8, 17, 27, Nov 4, 30, Dec 10; 1764: DL, Feb 11,
   Mar 20, May 16, Oct 6, 17, 19, 31, Nov 9, 13, 22, Dec 19; 1765: DL, Jan 3, 8,
   Apr 13, 30, May 14, Sep 14, Oct 2, 9, 12, 14, Nov 11, 16, 25, Dec 7, 14;
   1766: DL, Jan 9, 13, 20, 24, Feb 5, 13, 20, 22, Mar 10, 17, 18, 22, Apr 7, 9,
   12, 16, May 9, Sep 20, 23, 25, 27, Oct 8, 18, 24, 25, 28, Nov 4, 7, 8, 26,
   Dec 2, 4, 6, 13; 1767: DL, Jan 24, Feb 7, 21, Mar 24, 28, 30, Apr 11, May 1,
   4, 14, 25, HAY, Jun 5, 10, 12, 22, 26, 30, Jul 31, Aug 5, 12, 21, 25, 27, DL,
   Sep 15, 16, 17, HAY, 18, 21, DL, 23, 26, Oct 9, 14, 22, Nov 4, 11, 13, Dec 7,
   15, 26; 1768: DL, Jan 6, 9, Mar 15, 21, Apr 9, 14, May 11, HAY, Jun 8, Jul
   13, 27, DL, Sep 8, 17, 20, 26, 29, Oct 10, 11, 13, 20, 21, 28, 31, Nov 4, 17,
   24, Dec 17, 19, 23; 1769: DL, Jan 20, Feb 23, Mar 11, 16, 28, 29, Apr 3, 7,
   May 3, 10, 12, 15, HAY, 22, 24, 26, Jun 2, Jul 12, Aug 7, 9, 14; 1770: HAY,
   Oct 29
Strange, Mrs (actor), 1733: HAY, Mar 20, 27, Apr 18
Stranger, The. See Thompson, Benjamin.
Strangers at Home, The. See Cobb, James.
Strangeways, Lady Susan (married), 1764: DL, Apr 7
Stratagem, The. See Farquhar, George, The Beaux' Stratagem.
Stratagems of Harlequin, The; or, The Peasant Tricked (pantomime, anon), 1729:
   SF, Sep 15; 1730: BFLH, Aug 24, 31, SFG, Sep 8; 1756: SFW, Sep 18, 20, SF, 21
Stratford (payee), 1769: CG, Oct 27
Stratford upon Avon, 1769: DL, Sep 30, CG, Oct 7, DL, 13, 14; 1780: CG, Mar 14;
   1784: CG, May 7; 1788: DL, May 1
Stratford, Thomas, 1784: DL, Aug 20, 28, HAY, Sep 17; 1785: DL, Dec 1
--Lord Russel, 1784: DL, Aug 20, 25, 27, 28, 1785: DL, Dec 1
Strathpays (music), 1791: CG, May 18
Strato, 1769: CG, Dec 15
Strattaggemma, La. See Pergolesi, Giovanbattista.
Stravaganti, Gli (pastiche), 1766: KING'S, Oct 21, 25, 28, Nov 4, 11, 18; 1767:
   KING'S, Mar 21, May 14, 19, Jun 27
Strawberry (householder), 1738: DL, May 16
Strawberry Hill, 1781: CG, Nov 17
Street (ticket deliverer), 1787: DL, Jun 4
Street, James (actor, singer), 1791: CG, Oct 20; 1792: CG, Feb 28, May 25, DL,
   Oct 13, CG, Dec 26, 29, 31; 1793: CG, Feb 25, Sep 23, Oct 2, 9, 24, Nov 19,
   28, Dec 17, 19; 1794: CG, Feb 22, Mar 10, 22, 31, Sep 22, 26, 29, Oct 22, Dec
   26; 1795: CG, Jan 12, 31, Mar 14, 16, Apr 24, May 14, 16, Jun 6, Sep 14, 21,
   Oct 12, 15, 19, 24, Nov 4, 9, Dec 21, 23; 1796: CG, Jan 4, 23, Feb 2, Mar 15,
   Apr 5, 9, 15, 19, 26, Jun 6, Sep 12, 16, 19, 26, Oct 6, 7, 14, 24, 29, Nov
   19, Dec 12, 19, 27; 1797: CG, Jan 10, 11, Feb 13, 18, Mar 16, Apr 8, 19, 25,
   May 6, 11, 18, 19, Jun 13, Sep 18, 25, Oct 16, 18, 31, Nov 2, 8, 24, Dec 18,
   23, 26; 1798: CG, Feb 9, 12, Mar 17, 19, 31, Apr 9, 16, 21, 23, May 8, 28,
   29, Jun 2, 7, Sep 17, 21, 26, Oct 3, 8, 11, 15, 25, 31, Nov 10, 12, Dec 11,
   15, 26; 1799: CG, Jan 21, 29, Mar 2, 25, Apr 2, 6, 9, 13, 16, 19, 23, 26, May
   3, 4, 13, 15, 21, 28, Jun 1, 3, 6, 7, Sep 16, 18, 25, 30, Oct 2, 7, 16, 24,
   31, Nov 9, 11, 14, Dec 5, 10, 16, 23, 30; 1800: CG, Jan 16, Feb 8, 10, Mar 4,
   25, Apr 5, 17, May 1, 6, 23, 29
Street, Miss (dancer), 1761: HAY, Jun 23, 27, Jul 30, Aug 3; 1763: HAY, Jul 27,
   Aug 1, 3, 5, 11, 15, 22, 24, Sep 3, 5, 7, DL, Oct 14, Nov 10, 23, 26; 1764:
   DL, Jan 13, Feb 24, May 23, HAY, Jun 26, 28, 29, Jul 10, 23, 27, 30, Aug 24,
   Sep 1; 1765: HAY, Jun 10, 19, Jul 8, 19, Aug 7, 8, 9, 21, 28; 1766: HAY, Jun
   20, Jul 15, KING'S, Aug 27; 1768: HAY, May 30, Jul 27, Aug 1, 19, Sep 13;
   1769: HAY, May 15, Jul 12, Aug 9, 14, 25, 29; 1770: HAY, May 9
Streeter, Robert (scene designer), 1670: BRI/COUR, Dec 0; 1671: BRI/COUR, Feb
   10
Streeton, J (criminal), 1770: HAY, Aug 1
Strensham (actor), 1736: HAY, Mar 5
Strephon and Delia (pastoral, anon), 1746: NWC, Sep 15
Strephon's Return; or, The British Hero (interlude), 1746: DL, May 2
Stretched in a dark and dismal grove (song), 1695: LIF, Aug 0
Strike the Harp in praise of Bragela (song), 1798: CG, Apr 27; 1800: CG, May
   17, DL, Jun 5
Strike the Viol (song), 1694: ATCOURT, Apr 30
Stringellow (casualty), 1749: BF/SFP, Aug 23
Stripping Dance (dance), 1716: DL, May 31; 1718: DL, Apr 15; 1719: DL, May 5;
   1722: DL, Apr 12; 1724: LIF, May 4, 5, 12, 19
Strollers, The. See Breval, John.
Strollger (beneficiary), 1730: GF, Jul 6
Strong cemented walls (song), 1799: CG, Mar 1
Strong is the Heart (song), 1789: DL, Mar 20

Strong, John (musician), 1675: ATCOURT, Feb 15
Stroud (musician), 1747: GF, Mar 24
Strutt (bookseller), 1794: HAY, Jun 2
Strutt (tailor), 1773: CG, Nov 16
Strutton (actor), 1766: HAY, Jun 18, KING'S, Aug 20
Stuart (actor), 1785: HAMM, Jul 25
Stuart (beneficiary), 1752: HAY, Apr 8
Stuart (publisher), 1786: KING'S, Mar 30
Stuart (ticket deliverer), 1794: CG, Jun 16
Stuart and Stevenson (publishers), 1786: KING'S, May 25
Stuart, Ann (actor), 1779: CG, Feb 22, Mar 20, Oct 1, 13, Nov 8, Dec 11, 21;
    1780: CG, Feb 2, 22, Apr 8, 20, May 12, Sep 18, Oct 3, 6, 23, 24, Nov 25, Dec
    16, 27; 1781: CG, Jan 17, Mar 8, Apr 28, HAY, Aug 15, CG, Sep 24, Oct 16, 31,
    Nov 12, Dec 17; 1782: CG, Jan 4, 5, 9, 18, 22, Feb 9, Mar 11, 19, May 22, 27,
    Oct 3, 7, 8, 18, 22, Nov 18, 27, Dec 12, 14, 27; 1783: CG, Jan 1, 8, May 9,
    17, 24, Sep 22, Oct 3, 6, 14, 20, Nov 8, Dec 23; 1784: CG, Jan 7, 14, 29, Feb
    13, 20, 23, Mar 16, 27, Apr 26, Sep 17, 20, 21, 22, 24, Oct 4, 6, 18, 25, Nov
    2, 16, 30, Dec 4; 1785: CG, Jan 14, Mar 5, May 4, Sep 23, 26, 28, 30, Oct 5,
    10, 17, 19, 22, 29, Nov 4, 7, 14, 19, 29, Dec 1, 5, 7, 8, 22; 1786: CG, Jan
    18, 31, Feb 7, 8, 16, Mar 6, 14, Apr 18, 24, 28, May 9, 13, Sep 18, 25, 29,
    Oct 2, 21, 23, 26, Nov 13, 14, 18, 20, Dec 5, 12; 1787: CG, Jan 4, 26, Feb 6,
    13, Mar 15, 27, Apr 14, 27, 30, May 9, 21, 23, Jun 11, Sep 21, 24, 26, Oct 1,
    3, 10, 22, 29, Nov 2, 22, 28, Dec 3; 1788: CG, Jan 2, 5, 11, 14, 17, 21, 29,
    Feb 4, Mar 11, 26, 28, Apr 8, 11, 14, 23, Sep 15, 17, 19, 22, 24, 26, Oct 3,
    10, 15, 17, 24, 27, 29, Nov 20, 21, Dec 1, 29; 1789: CG, Jan 15, Feb 3, 11,
    21, Mar 3, 5, 28, 31, Apr 14, 15, 30, May 2, 20, 22, Jun 2, 8, Sep 14, 16,
    23, 30, Oct 2, 12, 20, 21, 23, 24, 30, Nov 12, 19, 20, Dec 2, 5, 10, 11, 14;
    1790: CG, Jan 13, 23, Feb 4, 25, Mar 18, 22, 27, May 5, 11, Sep 13, 15, Oct
    1, 6, 8, 15, 20, 27, Nov 3, 19, 26, 30, Dec 11, 17, 20, 28; 1791: CG, Jan 12,
    15, Feb 16, Apr 11, May 2, 5, 6, 11, Jun 6, Sep 14, 20, 21, 26, 30, Oct 3, 6,
    10, 20, 21, 27, 28, Nov 15, 25, 29, Dec 3, 10, 15, 21, 22; 1792: CG, Feb 6,
    23, 28, Mar 6, 10, 22, 31, Apr 12, 17, 18, May 2, 11, Sep 20, 21, Oct 3, 5,
    8, 10, 12, 17, 18, 19, 26, 29, Nov 3, 7, 10, 14, Dec 31; 1793: CG, Jan 9, 14,
    21, 25, Apr 11, 15, 18, 20, May 15, Sep 16, 17, 23, 25, 27, 30, Oct 2, 3, 7,
    9, 10, 11, 12, 15, 16, 17, 22, 23, 24, 25, 29, Nov 1, 2, 9, 11, 12, 16, 19,
    28, Dec 6, 7, 9, 20; 1794: CG, Jan 3, Feb 10, May 6, 22, Sep 19, 22, 26, 29,
    Oct 1, 14, 20, 23, 30, Nov 7, Dec 6; 1795: CG, Jan 8, 29, 31, Feb 3, 14, Mar
    19, Apr 7, 8, 24, May 14, Jun 6, 10, Sep 14, 21, 23, 30, Oct 5, 8, 15, 19,
    24, 30, 31, Nov 14, 30
Stuart, Anne Hyde, Duchess of York, 1662: ATCOURT, Feb 11; 1666: ATCOURT, Oct
    11; 1667: BRIDGES, Apr 15; 1671: NONE, Apr 1; 1673: DG, Dec 6; 1675: BF, Sep
    3; 1682: DG, Aug 4
Stuart, Charles, 1777: CG, Apr 16; 1779: CG, Apr 27; 1781: HAY, Aug 22, 29;
    1783: HAY, Aug 28; 1785: DL, May 24; 1786: HAY, Aug 3; 1787: DL, May 3, 16;
    1788: DL, May 14; 1791: HAY, Aug 13
--Box-Lobby Loungers (interlude), 1787: DL, May 16, 21
--Cobler of Castlebury, The (farce), 1779: CG, Apr 27
--Damnation; or, The Play-House Hissing-Hot (interlude), 1781: HAY, Aug 29
--Distressed Baronet, The (farce), 1787: DL, May 3, 11, 12, 15, 17, 21, Nov 27,
    30
--Experiment, The, 1777: CG, Apr 16
--Gretna Green (farce), 1783: HAY, Aug 28, 30, Sep 2, 4, 6, 8, 9, 11, 13, 15;
    1784: CG, Mar 30, HAY, May 31, Jun 5, 10, 17, Aug 5, 11; 1785: HAY, Jul 20,
    26, Aug 2, 3, 5, 10, 26, 29, Sep 2; 1786: HAY, Jul 11, 21, 22, 26, Aug 2, 28;
    1787: HAY, Jul 12, 13, 31, Aug 25, Sep 6, 13; 1788: HAY, Aug 13, 22, 23, Sep
    4; 1789: HAY, May 27, Jul 7, Aug 25; 1790: HAY, Jun 29, Jul 15, Aug 17, 18,
    30; 1791: HAY, Jun 23, 28, Jul 11, 23, Aug 30; 1792: HAY, Jul 14, Aug 11;
    1795: HAY, Jul 30, Aug 5, 12, 20, Sep 10; 1796: HAY, Jun 18, 27, Jul 1, Aug 9
--Irishman in Spain, The (farce), 1791: HAY, Aug 13, Sep 2, 3, 9
--Ripe Fruit; or, The Marriage Act, 1781: HAY, Aug 22, 24
--Stone Eater, The (interlude), 1788: DL, May 14, 22
Stuart, Daniel (printer), 1787: KING'S, Jan 9, Feb 17, Mar 1, Apr 24, May 1,
    Dec 8; 1788: KING'S, Jan 15, Feb 5, Mar 4; 1790: HAY, May 27; 1798: KING'S,
    Dec 26
Stuart, Elizabeth, 1663: ATCOURT, Feb 9; 1664: ATCOURT, Jul 14; 1668: ATCOURT,
    Dec 18
Stuart, Frances, Duchess of Richmond (spectator), 1680: DG, Sep 0
Stuart, Henry, Duke of Gloucester, 1660: NONE, Sep 13
Stuart, Lady Mary (spectator), 1664: BRIDGES, Sep 14
Stuart, Miss (actor), 1735: YB, Mar 19
Stuart, Miss (actor), 1795: DL, Feb 12, May 7, Oct 30, Nov 11, Dec 10; 1796:
    DL, Jan 8, 18, Mar 12, Apr 30, May 13, CG, 17, DL, Jun 7; 1797: DL, Apr 28,

May 15, 19, 24, 31, Jun 15, HAY, Sep 9, DL, Oct 3, 21; 1798: DL, Mar 24, HAY,
  Aug 27, DL, Sep 15, 22, Oct 22; 1799: DL, Feb 26, Apr 22, Sep 21, Nov 27, Dec
  7
Stuart, Mrs (actor, singer), 1793: HAY, Nov 5, 19, 30, Dec 14, 26; 1794: HAY,
  Jan 4, Feb 13, CG, Mar 7
Stubborn church division, folly, and ambition (song), 1693: DL, Apr 0
Stubbs (timber merchant), 1761: CG, Jan 9; 1771: CG, Oct 24
Studente a la Moda, Lo. See Pergolesi, Giovanbattista.
Students, The. See Stewart, James.
Sturbridge Fair, 1665: BF, Aug 7; 1666: NONE, Aug 3
Sturember, Countess of, (spectator), 1723: KING'S, Feb 23
Sturgeon (ticket deliverer), 1791: CG, Jun 14; 1792: CG, May 29; 1794: CG, Jun
  16; 1795: CG, Jun 13; 1796: CG, Jun 3; 1797: CG, Jun 2; 1798: CG, May 29;
  1799: CG, May 21; 1800: CG, Jun 10
Sturgess (actor), 1740: BF/WF/SF, Aug 23; 1748: BFLYY, Aug 24, SFLYYW, Sep 7,
  BHB, Oct 1, SOU, 31, JS, 31, NWC, Dec 26, 29; 1749: SOU, Jan 2, 9
Sturmy, John, 1722: LIF, Jan 22, Dec 15; 1728: LIF, Jan 17
--Compromise, The; or, Faults on both Sides (play), 1722: LIF, Dec 15, 17, 18
--Love and Duty; or, The Distressed Bride, 1722: LIF, Jan 22, 23, 24, 25, 26,
  27, Dec 17, 18
--Sesostris; or, Royalty in Disguise, 1728: LIF, Jan 17, 18, 19, 20, 22, 23,
  26, 27
Sturpesi (tumbler), 1766: HAY, Oct 27
Sturt (actor), 1751: DL, May 13; 1752: DL, May 1; 1753: DL, May 11; 1754: DL,
  May 16; 1755: DL, Nov 8; 1756: DL, May 7; 1757: DL, May 9
Sturt (drunken exhibitionist), 1796: DL, Apr 2
Stuttering Master of Music (entertainment), 1727: KING'S, Mar 16
Style, Miss (actor), 1789: HAY, Aug 1
Styles (actor), 1677: DL, Mar 0
Subjects Joy for the King's Restoration. See Sadler, Anthony.
Subligne, Mlle (author), 1703: DL, Apr 19
Submission, The (dance), 1717: LIF, Feb 21, 25
Subscription, The (song), 1745: DL, Nov 4, 5, 6, 7, 9, 11, 12, 13, 21, 23, 25,
  26, Dec 4, 5, 6, 7, 10, 16
Successful Pirate, The. See Johnson, Charles.
Successful Strangers, The. See Mountfort, William.
Such Things Are. See Inchbald, Elizabeth.
Such Things Have Been. See Ryder, Thomas.
Suckling, Sir John, 1662: VERE, Sep 24; 1667: BRIDGES, Jan 24
--Aglaura, 1659: NONE, Sep 0; 1661: VERE, Dec 28; 1662: VERE, Feb 27, Sep 24;
  1667: ATCOURT, May 16; 1668: BRIDGES, Jan 10; 1669: BRIDGES, Jan 12; 1674:
  DL, Nov 16
--Brenoralt; or, The Discontented (Contented) Colonel, 1661: VERE, Jul 23, Oct
  26; 1662: VERE, May 12; 1667: BRIDGES, Aug 12, Oct 18; 1668: BRIDGES, Mar 5;
  1669: BRIDGES, Jan 12
--Goblins, The, 1667: BRIDGES, Jan 24, May 22, Nov 21; 1669: BRIDGES, Jan 12
Suertt, Mrs (householder), 1743: CG, Nov 17
Suett, Master (singer), 1799: HAY, Aug 13, 22, Sep 5, 16; 1800: DL, May 23, Jun
  5, 10, HAY, Aug 7
Suett, Richard (actor, singer, composer), 1771: GROTTO, Jun 22, Aug 8; 1780:
  DL, Oct 7, 26, Nov 10, Dec 1, 27; 1781: DL, Jan 16, 29, Mar 10, Apr 25, May
  15, Sep 20, Oct 6, 22, 29, Nov 10, 15, 20, 29, Dec 6, 13; 1782: DL, Jan 3,
  22, 26, 29, 31, Mar 7, 14, Apr 12, 15, 17, 18, 24, May 3, 7, 16, 18, 20, 30,
  Sep 18, 19, 20, 24, Oct 5, 16, 26, Nov 1, 4, 12, 27, 30, Dec 11, 26; 1783:
  DL, Jan 25, Feb 7, Mar 17, 20, Apr 24, 26, May 12, Sep 16, 18, 20, 23, 30,
  Oct 2, 7, 13, 14, 28, Nov 14, 18, Dec 5, 12, 13; 1784: DL, Jan 1, 17, Feb 3,
  10, 24, Mar 30, Apr 12, 16, 26, 28, May 3, 10, Sep 18, 25, 30, Oct 12, 18,
  19, Nov 2, Dec 3; 1785: DL, Jan 5, 6, 11, 17, 20, 27, Feb 2, 8, Apr 1, 8, 11,
  18, 20, 22, 25, 28, May 3, 9, 11, HAY, Sep 16, DL, 17, 27, Oct 1, 11, 13, 20,
  27, Nov 11, 18, 21, Dec 7, 30; 1786: DL, Jan 5, 24, Feb 18, 23, Mar 27, 28,
  Apr 4, May 1, 2, Sep 19, 23, 28, 30, Oct 9, 10, 14, 17, 21, 24, Nov 15, 30,
  Dec 6, 19, 26, 28; 1787: DL, Jan 11, 13, 18, 24, 26, Apr 9, 25, 27, May 3,
  16, 30, Jun 1, Sep 18, 20, 25, 29, Oct 3, 26, 30, Nov 3, 6, 7, 8, 10, 24, 27,
  29, Dec 6, 14, 17, 19; 1788: DL, Jan 22, 26, Feb 7, Mar 31, Apr 8, 11, 14,
  21, 23, May 1, 6, 7, 8, 12, 14, 22, 23, 30, Jun 2, 6, Sep 13, 16, 18, 23, 27,
  30, Oct 2, 4, 13, 16, 20, 22, 25, Nov 1, 8, 12, 25, Dec 3, 6, 11, 12, 22;
  1789: DL, Jan 7, 8, 17, 23, 26, Feb 7, 18, 28, Mar 9, 23, Apr 4, 14, May 1,
  7, 11, 23, 27, Jun 3, 5, Sep 12, 15, 17, 19, 22, 24, 26, Oct 1, 8, 15, 22,
  24, 26, 27, 31, Nov 7, 13, 21, 24, Dec 3, 5, 7, 10, 17, 23; 1790: DL, Jan 15,
  Feb 10, 18, 23, 27, Mar 2, 8, 13, 18, 22, Apr 9, 16, 27, 28, May 4, 7, 11,
  14, 26, 27, 31, Jun 1, 4, Sep 11, 16, Oct 2, 4, 7, 11, 14, 16, 19, 25, 27,
  Nov 2, 3, 30, Dec 3, 11; 1791: DL, Jan 1, 10, 11, 25, Feb 10, Mar 4, 22, 24,

819

Apr 5, 30, May 3, 6, 11, 16, 19, 26, DLKING'S, Sep 22, 27, 29, Oct 1, 3, 4,
15, 25, 31, Nov 3, 4, 5, 10, 11, 12, 16, 17, 30, Dec 5, 26, 31; 1792:
DLKING'S, Jan 6, 9, 11, Feb 2, 7, 11, 27, Mar 10, 13, 17, 20, 26, 29, 31, Apr
10, 16, 19, May 1, 29, Jun 4, 7, 13, 15, DL, Sep 15, 18, 19, 20, 25, 29, Oct
4, 9, 11, 13, 15, 16, 18, 20, Nov 14, 16, 21, 26, 27, 29, Dec 3, 8, 14, 15,
21, 22, 27, 28; 1793: DL, Jan 17, 21, 23, Feb 21, 23, 25, Mar 5, 7, 9, 11,
Apr 3, 5, 8, 25, 29, May 7, 10, 21, 22, 24, Jun 1, 5, 10, HAY, 11, 12, 14,
15, 17, 18, 21, 25, 29, Jul 9, 13, 15, 18, Aug 6, 12, 26, 27, 30, Sep 13, 19,
21, 24, 26, 30, Oct 1, 7, 8, 10, 15, 18, 22, 24, 29, 30, Nov 5, 9, 16, 19,
22, 23, 30, Dec 7, 14, 16, 30; 1794: HAY, Jan 14, 21, 27, Feb 8, 22, Mar 13,
29, DL, Apr 21, 25, 26, 28, May 1, 3, 8, 9, 12, 13, 16, 19, 23, Jun 4, 9, 13,
16, 17, 23, 24, 26, 27, Jul 2, 7, HAY, 8, 9, 14, 17, 18, 19, 22, 26, 29, Aug
4, 9, 12, 13, 18, 29, Sep 1, 3, 6, 13, DL, 16, HAY, 17, DL, 18, 20, 23, 27,
Oct 7, 14, 18, 20, 27, Nov 3, 14, Dec 12, 13, 20, 30; 1795: DL, Jan 7, 16,
22, 26, 27, 31, Feb 6, 9, 12, 28, Mar 10, Apr 16, 17, 23, 24, May 1, 6, 9,
12, 18, 19, 29, 30, Jun 3, HAY, 9, 10, 11, 12, 13, 15, 16, 18, 20, 22, Jul 1,
6, 8, 20, 22, 25, 30, 31, Aug 3, 7, 10, 14, 18, 21, 25, 29, Sep 2, DL, 17,
19, 22, 24, 26, 29, Oct 1, 3, 6, 8, 15, 20, 27, 30, Nov 5, 6, 11, 14, 16, 19,
26, Dec 1, 2, 7, 10, 11, 12, 17, 18, 19, 22, 30; 1796: DL, Jan 23, Feb 1, 20,
27, Mar 12, Apr 13, 18, 26, 30, May 5, 11, 13, 17, 25, 27, Jun 6, 8, HAY, 11,
13, 14, 15, 16, 17, 18, 20, 22, 24, 25, 30, Jul 5, 6, 7, 8, 9, 12, 14, 15,
18, 23, 26, 30, Aug 3, 8, 10, 11, 13, 18, 24, 26, 29, Sep 1, 3, 7, 17, DL,
20, 22, 27, 29, Oct 1, 3, 4, 6, 8, 10, 11, 13, 15, 17, 19, 24, Nov 1, 5, 10,
18, 22, 26, 28, Dec 5, 6, 7, 10, 16, 20; 1797: DL, Jan 7, 10, 12, 14, 17, Feb
1, 9, 16, 21, 22, Mar 6, Apr 19, 24, 27, 28, May 8, 15, 17, 25, Jun 7, 12,
HAY, 16, 17, 20, 22, 23, 24, 26, 28, 29, Jul 3, 8, 15, Aug 4, 8, 9, 10, 14,
15, 19, 24, 28, Sep 4, 8, 9, 11, DL, 19, 21, 23, 26, 28, 30, Oct 5, 7, 12,
14, 16, 17, 19, 21, 23, 28, 31, Nov 2, 4, 7, 9, 11, 13, 15, 17, 20, 23, 25,
28, Dec 2, 9, 11, 21; 1798: DL, Jan 9, 13, 16, 23, 25, Feb 3, 12, 13, 20, Mar
8, 24, May 7, 15, 19, 23, 24, 30, 31, Jun 12, HAY, 13, 14, 15, 18, 20, 21,
23, 27, 28, 29, 30, Jul 6, 13, 14, 16, 21, Aug 3, 4, 6, 14, 16, 21, 23, 27,
29, Sep 3, 10, DL, 15, 18, 22, 25, 27, 29, Oct 2, 4, 6, 8, 9, 11, 15, 20, 27,
30, Nov 3, 13, 14, 22, 26, 28, 29, Dec 4, 5, 11, HAY, 17, DL, 19, 21; 1799:
DL, Jan 8, 17, 19, 31, Feb 4, 23, Mar 2, Apr 5, 8, 17, 18, 19, 22, CG, 23,
DL, 27, May 3, 4, 7, 8, 24, 27, 28, Jun 10, HAY, 15, 17, 18, DL, 18, HAY, 19,
21, 24, 25, 29, Jul 2, 4, 5, 6, 9, 10, 12, 13, 16, 19, 20, 27, 30, Aug 5, 10,
13, 15, 17, 21, 22, 24, 27, Sep 2, 16, DL, 17, 19, 21, 24, 26, 28, Oct 3, 8,
12, 14, 17, 19, 22, 26, 31, Nov 2, 6, 7, 8, 12, 13, 14, 16, 27, 29, Dec 2,
17; 1800: DL, Jan 1, 21, Feb 1, 12, Mar 11, 17, Apr 28, May 1, 20, 21, 29,
Jun 6, 10, 11, HAY, 14, 18, 19, 20, 24, 27, 28, Jul 1, 5, 7, 15, 26, Aug 5,
7, 8, 12, 14, 19, 20, 23, 29, Sep 1, 3, 4, 5
Suffolk St, 1668: ATCOURT, Jan 13; 1755: DL, Dec 16; 1777: HAY, Jun 16, KING'S,
Jul 5; 1778: KING'S, Mar 19, HAY, May 18, Sep 2; 1779: HAY, May 31, Aug 13;
1780: HAY, Aug 8, 22, 30; 1782: DL, Apr 22, HAY, Aug 16, 27; 1783: HAY, Aug
27; 1784: HAY, Mar 3, CG, 30, HAY, Aug 26; 1785: DL, Mar 28; 1786: DL, Apr 4;
1787: KING'S, Mar 29, CG, Apr 28; 1788: KING'S, Feb 28, Mar 13, HAY, Aug 13,
22; 1789: KING'S, May 14, HAY, Aug 25, 31; 1790: HAY, Jan 7, CG, Apr 13, HAY,
15, Sep 6; 1791: CG, Apr 28, HAY, Aug 24, Sep 5; 1792: DLKING'S, Apr 19, HAY,
Aug 22, Sep 10; 1793: DL, May 7, HAY, Aug 20, Sep 9; 1794: HAY, Aug 27, Sep
8; 1795: DL, May 19, HAY, Aug 18, Sep 7; 1796: DL, May 21, HAY, Sep 9; 1797:
DL, May 27, HAY, Aug 3, Sep 11; 1798: DL, Jun 5, HAY, Aug 9, 18, Sep 10;
1799: DL, Jul 1, HAY, Aug 10, Sep 9; 1800: HAY, Aug 2, Sep 8
Suffolk, Countess of (spectator), 1729: DL, Dec 27
Suffolk, Countess of. See Howard, Barbara.
Sugar Loaf (shop), 1742: GF, Apr 8
Suicide, The. See Colman the elder, George.
Sullen Lovers, The. See Shadwell, Thomas.
Sullivan, Daniel (actor, singer), 1743: DL, Feb 2, HAY, Mar 24, DL, Apr 15, May
23, Oct 13, 15, 18, 22, 25, 27, 28, Nov 15, 23, 24, 26; 1744: HAY, Jan 19,
23, CG, Feb 10, 24, Mar 2, HAY, Apr 16; 1745: HAY, Feb 14, Apr 1; 1746: DL,
Nov 7, Dec 15; 1747: DL, Mar 7, 16, 28, Apr 6, 21, 25, 30, Oct 29; 1748: DL,
Apr 15, 18
Sultan and Sultaness (dance), 1720: LIF, Feb 24
Sultan, The (masque), 1726: LIF, Oct 5, Nov 9, Dec 3; 1727: LIF, Jan 2, Feb 11,
Apr 14, Nov 7, 21; 1728: LIF, Oct 9, Nov 5; 1729: LIF, Oct 28, Nov 21; 1730:
LIF, Jan 27, Dec 11; 1731: LIF, Jan 18, May 20, Dec 1; 1732: LIF, Mar 6
Sultan, The. See Arne, Dr Thomas A.
Sultan, The; or, A Peep into the Seraglio. See Bickerstaff, Isaac.
Sultana (dance), 1728: DL, Jan 5, Mar 21, May 9, 15, Jun 13; 1729: DL, May 26,
Jun 20, 24, Aug 7, Dec 8; 1730: DL, Apr 25, 29, May 13, 19; 1732: DL, Apr 25
Sultaness, The. See Johnson, Charles.
Sumbel, Mary Stephens, Mrs Joseph (actor), 1799: HAY, Feb 25, Apr 17, CG, Jun

Summer Amusement. See Andrews, Miles Peter.
Summer's Tale, The. See Cumberland, Richard.
Summers (actor), 1759: MARLY, Aug 9; 1763: HAY, Sep 5, 7; 1769: HAY, May 15,
    22, 24, 26, 29, Jun 2, 7, Aug 7, 14, 25, Sep 11
Summers, Master (actor), 1761: DL, May 29; 1763: HAY, Aug 11, Sep 7
Summers, Robert (actor), 1778: HAY, Sep 18
Sumner (doorkeeper), 1742: DL, May 15
Sun Ale House, 1718: LIF, Jun 20, NONE, Jul 12
Sun Fire Office, 1749: DL, Dec 22; 1760: CG, Jan 10; 1767: DL, Jan 5; 1772: CG,
    Mar 19; 1773: DL, Jan 6, CG, Mar 29; 1774: CG, Apr 5
Sun Tavern, 1730: TC, Aug 10; 1731: SUN, Nov 30; 1738: DL, Mar 16; 1739: DL,
    Mar 8, May 5; 1740: DL, Mar 13; 1741: GF, Apr 22; 1746: DL, Mar 1; 1758: CG,
    Jul 6; 1787: HAY, Mar 12
Sunderland (actor), 1740: BFLP, Aug 23, SF, Sep 9
Sunderland, Dowager Countess of. See Spencer, Dorothy.
Sunderland, Lady. See Spencer, Anne.
Sunderland, Lord. See Spencer, Robert.
Sunshine after Rain. See Dibdin, Thomas John.
Supple (actor), 1784: DL, Aug 20
Supplement, The (lecture), 1766: HAY, Feb 25
Suppliants. See Aeschylus.
Suppose we sing a Catch (song), 1780: HAY, Aug 24
Sure an't the World a Masquerade (song), 1790: CG, Nov 23; 1791: CG, Sep 19;
    1793: CG, May 21; 1794: CG, Apr 12, Oct 29; 1795: CG, Oct 7; 1797: CG, Oct 2;
    1799: CG, Mar 16, 27, Dec 9
Surel (actor, author), 1728: DL, Dec 6; 1729: DL, Mar 15, May 8, Dec 26; 1730:
    DL, May 15, Oct 1, 28, Nov 3; 1731: LIF, May 10; 1733: DL, Oct 10
--Cheats of Harlequin, The; or, The Farmer Outwitted (pantomime), 1729: DL, May
    8
Surely he hath borne (song), 1793: KING/HAY, Feb 20; 1794: DL, Mar 19
Surmont (actor), 1798: DL, Sep 25, Oct 4, 11, 27, Nov 16, Dec 4, HAY, 17; 1799:
    DL, Jan 19, Feb 4, 23, 28, Mar 2, 16, Apr 2, 4, 18, May 17, 20, 24, Jun 15,
    Sep 19, 28, Oct 1, 3, 7, 12, 21, Nov 12, 16, 25, 29, Dec 2, 11, 19, 26, 30,
    31; 1800: DL, Jan 1, 4, 9, 10, 18, 20, Feb 7, 10, 12, 14, 18, Mar 11, 20, 27,
    29, 31, Apr 15, 24, 25, 28, 29, May 6, 17, Jun 11
Surprisal, The. See Howard, Sir Robert.
Surprise (dance), 1773: DL, Apr 1, 14
Surprise de l'Amour, La. See Marivaux, Pierre Carlet de Chamblain de.
Surprize de Daphnis et Cephise, La (dance), 1778: KING'S, Mar 31, Apr 4, 7, 21,
    May 2, 5, 9, 16, 23, 30, Jun 5, 13, 20
Surrein. See Sorin.
Surrender of Calais, The. See Colman the younger, George.
Surrender of Trinidad, The. See Cross, John Cartwright.
Surrey, 1728: MDS, Apr 3; 1746: SOU, Nov 3
Surry St, 1762: CG, Mar 25; 1798: DL, Jun 6
Susan's Complaint (song), 1730: GF, Apr 6
Susanna. See Handel, George Frederic.
Suspicious Husband Criticized, The. See Macklin, Charles.
Suspicious Husband, The. See Hoadly, Benjamin.
Sussex, Countess of. See Fitzroy, Anne.
Sussex, Lord. See Lennard, Thomas.
Sussex, 1686: DLORDG, Dec 14
Sutherland, John (musician), 1766: CG, Nov 13, 22, 28; 1767: CG, Oct 12, Nov 6
Sutton (actor), 1742: GF, May 18
Sutton (actor), 1761: CG, Jan 13, 24
Sutton (actor), 1780: HAY, Nov 13
Sutton (goldsmith), 1772: CG, Nov 24
Sutton (householder), 1778: DL, May 11
Sutton, Mrs (dancer), 1772: DL, Oct 23, 30, Nov 18, Dec 26; 1773: DL, Mar 27,
    Apr 24, May 14, Sep 18, 21, 25, Oct 9, Nov 9, 25, Dec 27; 1774: DL, Jan 22,
    Apr 4, 12, 20, 28, Sep 17, 27, 29, Oct 5, 14, 31, Nov 1, 5; 1775: DL, Jan 2,
    Mar 28, Apr 28, Sep 30, Oct 3, 11, 17, 18, Nov 1, 10, 11, 28, Dec 11, 12, 19;
    1776: DL, Mar 19, 25, Apr 22, 23, Jun 10, Oct 1, 26, 31, Nov 9, 26, Dec 10,
    18; 1777: DL, Jan 17, Feb 10, Apr 19, May 15; 1778: DL, May 8; 1779: CG, May
    8; 1785: DL, Oct 17, 18, 24, Dec 26; 1786: DL, Jan 5, Feb 23, Apr 24, May 19,
    Jun 6
Svenalo traditor (song), 1729: HIC, Apr 30
Sventurata in van mi lagno (song), 1777: KING'S, Mar 20
Swabian Peasants Procession and Dance (dance), 1798: CG, Dec 11; 1799: CG, May
    4
Swaine (actor), 1770: HAY, Nov 21

Swains I Scorn (song), 1741: JS, Nov 9
Swallow (song), 1737: CG, Apr 18
Swallow St, 1742: HAY, Jun 16
Swan (mercer), 1767: DL, Feb 6
Swan Inn Yard, 1753: BFSY, Sep 3, 5, 6; 1754: BFSIY, Sep 3, 4, 5, 6; 1755: BF, Sep 6
Swan Tavern, 1728: CRT, Dec 18; 1731: ST, Oct 21; 1737: ST, Mar 8; 1739: DL, May 1; 1743: TCD/BFTD, Aug 4; 1744: DL, Dec 12; 1745: DL, Apr 17; 1746: DL, Feb 26; 1752: DL, Dec 20; 1753: DL, Dec 21; 1755: BF, Sep 3, 4; 1756: BFSI, Sep 3, 4, 6; 1757: BFB, Sep 5, 6; 1758: CG, Jul 6; 1776: CHR, Oct 9
Swartzs (singer), 1733: KING'S, Mar 17
Sweden, Christina, Queen of, 1680: EVELYN, Sep 23
Sweden, King of, 1720: KING'S, May 6
Sweden, 1668: ATCOURT, Feb 4; 1680: EVELYN, Sep 23
Swedish Dal Karl (dance), 1715: LIF, Sep 30; 1716: LIF, May 7, Jun 12, Oct 22; 1717: LIF, Apr 23, Jun 12; 1718: DL, Mar 25; 1721: DL, Mar 20; 1722: DL, May 29; 1724: DL, May 4, LIF, 8, 22, Jul 14, 29, SOU, Sep 24; 1726: LIF, Jun 17, 21; 1728: LIF, Jul 2, Aug 2; 1733: CG, May 2, Jun 29, Aug 14, 17, 21, Sep 25, 27, Oct 4, 6, Nov 1, Dec 4, 11, 28; 1734: CG, May 9, 10, 14, 15, 16
Swedish Dal Karl and His Wife (dance), 1715: LIF, May 9, 10, 13, 18, Jun 1, 7
Swedish Dance (dance), 1715: LIF, Apr 2; 1718: DL, May 27; 1719: DL, May 2
Swedish Gardeners (dance), 1743: HAY, Mar 23; 1749: DL, Dec 19, 20; 1750: DL, Jan 26, 27, Feb 2, 6, 8, 22, Apr 19, 25, 30, May 2, 4; 1762: CG, Oct 7, 20, 21, Dec 18
Swedish Peasant (dance), 1710: DL, Jan 26
Swedish Pellarke (dance), 1728: HAY, Nov 1
Sweep the strings (song), 1790: CG, Feb 26; 1794: CG, Mar 26
Sweet (beneficiary), 1707: YB, Jan 27
Sweet Bird (song), 1742: DL, Mar 8, 20, 30, Apr 21, 28; 1759: DL, Oct 16; 1764: DL, Apr 27, May 9; 1770: CG, Apr 21; 1782: DL, Feb 15; 1788: CG, Jan 28; 1789: CG, Jan 26, DL, Mar 6, CG, Apr 4, May 6; 1790: CG, Feb 26, Jun 2; 1791: CG, Mar 18, DL, Apr 13; 1792: CG, Feb 28, Mar 3, KING'S, 14, 28, CG, Apr 25, May 28; 1793: KING/HAY, Mar 6, CG, 20; 1794: DL, Mar 12, CG, 21, DL, Apr 9, CG, 11; 1795: CG, Mar 25; 1796: CG, Feb 17, 26, Apr 15, Nov 3; 1797: CG, Mar 17; 1798: CG, Feb 28, Mar 28; 1799: CG, Mar 1; 1800: CG, Feb 28
Sweet Echo (song), 1738: DL, May 15; 1745: DL, Jan 14, 24; 1749: DL, Oct 11; 1750: DL, Oct 13; 1752: DL, Nov 29; 1758: DL, Nov 3; 1760: CG, Jan 18, Dec 11; 1763: CG, Nov 15; 1765: CG, Oct 22; 1767: CG, Feb 14; 1771: MARLY, Aug 20, 27, GROTTO, 30, Sep 3; 1775: DL, May 1; 1776: CG, Oct 7; 1777: CG, Feb 25, Oct 30, DL, Dec 15; 1778: DL, Sep 17; 1779: CG, Mar 22, DL, Apr 6, 13, May 1; 1780: CG, Feb 17, HAY, Jun 24, DL, Oct 10, CG, Nov 13; 1781: HAY, Aug 28, DL, Sep 27, CG, Oct 23; 1783: DL, Apr 7, CG, May 16, DL, Oct 7; 1784: CG, Jun 10, HAY, Jul 28, DL, Oct 7; 1785: CG, Mar 7, Apr 5, Sep 23; 1786: CG, Apr 1, DL, May 15; 1787: CG, Mar 31, HAY, Jul 21, Aug 14, 21, DL, Oct 4; 1788: CG, Feb 5, Mar 10, HAY, Jun 12, DL, Oct 23; 1789: DL, Oct 21; 1790: DL, Dec 8; 1791: CG, May 27, Sep 23, DLKING'S, Oct 29; 1792: DL, Sep 27; 1793: CG, Apr 11, HAY, Sep 2, CG, Oct 29; 1794: HAY, Aug 27; 1795: DL, May 27, CG, Jun 10, Nov 27; 1796: CG, May 25; 1797: CG, Jan 10, DL, May 23, HAY, Sep 4, 16, DL, Nov 24; 1798: HAY, Aug 9; 1800: HAY, Aug 26, Sep 16
Sweet, If You Love Me Smiling Turn (song), 1733: BFFH, Sep 4
Sweet is the Breath of Morn (song), 1773: CG, May 6
Sweet Lillies of the Valley (song), 1797: DL, Jun 8; 1798: DL, May 23; 1799: DL, May 17
Sweet Little Girl that I love, The (song), 1796: CG, May 28
Sweet Little Taffline. See Little Taffline.
Sweet, O sweet! (song), 1786: DL, May 24
Sweet Passion of Love (song), 1777: CHR, Jun 30; 1784: DL, May 12; 1790: CG, May 13
Sweet Poll of Plymouth (song), 1786: HAMM, Jul 10
Sweet Willy O (song), 1775: CG, Apr 4
Sweet's Coffee House, 1751: DL, Dec 18
Sweetest Bard that Ever Sung (song), 1769: CG, Oct 7; 1775: CG, Apr 4
Sweeting's Alley, 1745: DL, Apr 16; 1763: DL, Apr 27
Sweetlips, Miss (actor), 1756: BFSI, Sep 3
Swendall, James (actor), 1778: HAY, Mar 23, 31, Apr 9, 29; 1787: ROY, Jun 20; 1797: DL, May 27; 1799: HAY, Jun 15
Swift (bookseller), 1784: DL, Apr 16
Swift Wing'd Vengeance Nerve my Arm (song), 1771: GROTTO, Aug 30
Swift, Jonathan, 1713: DL, Apr 6; 1723: KING'S, Feb 2; 1728: LIF, Feb 15, Mar 20; 1740: DL, Apr 23; 1751: DL, Oct 30; 1753: DL, Feb 1; 1754: HAY, Dec 16; 1791: CG, May 2
--Polite Conversation, 1740: DL, Apr 23

Swift, Mrs (haberdasher), 1750: DL, Apr 17, 19
Swindall. See Swendall.
Swindlers, The. See Baddeley, Robert.
Swiny, Owen (proprietor, author), 1703: DL, Apr 23, Oct 15; 1704: DL, Apr 6,
    Jun 21; 1706: QUEEN'S, Dec 16; 1708: QUEEN'S, Dec 14; 1710: QUEEN'S, Mar 18,
    DL, Nov 20; 1713: QUEEN'S, Jan 10, 14; 1726: LIF, Nov 19; 1735: DL, Feb 26;
    see also MacSwiney, Owen
--Quacks, The; or, Love's the Physician, 1705: DL, Mar 22, 29, Apr 9, 10, 19,
    May 31, Jun 28, Jul 10; 1745: DL, Mar 30
Swiss Dance (dance), 1706: DL, Jun 25; 1740: CG, Apr 25, May 16, 20, 21, Jun 5,
    Sep 19, 24, 29, Oct 1, 3, 8, 23, 31, Nov 3, 13, 15, Dec 2, 5, 9, 11, 13, 30;
    1741: CG, Jan 3, 17, 27, 28, 29, Feb 2, 23, Mar 5, 30, Apr 1, 7, 10, 11, May
    14, DL, Sep 26, 29, Oct 9, 24, Nov 21, 27, Dec 1, 2, 4, 9, 11, 12, 19, 26,
    29; 1742: DL, Jan 19, 23, Feb 2, 8, 13, 25, Mar 9, 18, Apr 22, May 18, 27;
    1746: DL, Apr 16, 21, 24, May 12; 1758: DL, Nov 2, 4, 7, 14, 16, 29, Dec 2,
    9; 1759: DL, Feb 21, Apr 26, May 2, Nov 8, 9, 12, 14; 1762: DL, Feb 6, 15
Swiss performers, 1755: DL, Nov 8
Swiss, the little (dancer), 1749: DL, Apr 14, May 5, 8, 11, 12, Oct 28, 30, Nov
    10; 1750: DL, Jan 18, Apr 18, 20, 27, HAY, Jul 26, DL, Oct 15, 17, 22, 29,
    Nov 17, 27, Dec 12, 26; 1751: DL, Jan 1, 2, 3, 10, 22, Feb 1, Apr 8, 9, 10,
    12, 22, 26, 29, May 2, 4, 9, 10, Oct 16, 18, 29, Nov 5, Dec 17; 1752: DL, Mar
    16, 30, Apr 2, 8, 16, 17, 21, 23, 27, 30, May 2, 4, 5, 12, Sep 28, Oct 12,
    19; 1753: DL, Jan 1, 15, 17, Feb 6, 19, Apr 12, 24, May 4, 7, Sep 11, 13, 15,
    Oct 17, Nov 14, Dec 11; 1754: DL, Feb 1, 5, Oct 31, Dec 5; 1755: DL, Apr 29,
    Nov 22; 1756: DL, Oct 18
Swithin's Alley, 1745: DT, Mar 14; 1746: HIC, Mar 10
Swop, The (farce, anon), 1789: HAY, Jun 19, 22
Sword Dance (dance), 1707: HA, Aug 1; 1711: GR, May 21; 1724: HIC, Dec 21
Sword of Peace, The. See Starke, Mariana.
Sword that is drawn (song), 1786: DL, Mar 10; 1788: DL, Feb 8; 1789: DL, Mar
    18; 1790: DL, Feb 26; 1791: DL, Mar 23; 1792: KING'S, Feb 24; 1793: KING/HAY,
    Feb 22; 1794: DL, Apr 10
Sword-Blade Coffee House, 1753: DL, Dec 21
Swords, Mrs William (actor, singer), 1784: HAY, Sep 17; 1785: CG, Oct 19, Nov
    21; 1786: CG, Apr 24
Swords, T and J (publishers), 1799: CG, May 18
Swords, William (actor), 1778: HAY, Dec 28; 1779: HAY, Jan 11, Mar 8, 15, May
    10; 1780: HAY, Nov 13; 1781: HAY, Nov 12; 1782: HAY, Jan 14, 21, May 6, Jun
    3, 10, 12, Jul 16, Aug 5, 9, 13, 16, 17, Sep 16, 21; 1783: HAY, Jun 9, 18,
    20, 30, Aug 23, 28, Sep 17; 1784: HAY, Mar 8, Apr 30, May 29, Jun 1, 2, 19,
    Jul 6, 8, 28, Aug 2, 10, 24, 26, 28; 1785: HAY, Apr 25, May 28, 30, Jun 21,
    23, 24, Jul 1, 11, 19, 20, 28, Aug 2, 6, 23, 24, 25, 31, CG, Sep 21, 26, 30,
    Oct 5, 12, 17, 22, Nov 10, 21, 29, Dec 19, 26; 1786: CG, Jan 7, Feb 17, Mar
    18, Apr 24, HAY, Jun 12, 14, 16, 26, 29, Jul 8, 11, 12, Aug 10, 12, 17, Sep
    4, 9, CG, Oct 12, 16, 23, Nov 22, 29, Dec 11; 1787: CG, Jan 27, Mar 27, May
    11, HAY, Jun 14, 18, 20, 22, 25, Jul 13, 19, 23, 27, Aug 4, 17, 21, 29, Sep
    1; 1788: HAY, Aug 5; 1791: HAY, Sep 26; 1792: HAY, Oct 22
Sworms (musician), 1758: CHAPEL, Apr 27
Sybars. See Cibber.
Sycamore Shade (song), 1771: DL, May 8
Sydly. See Sedley.
Sydney, Grace (actor), 1799: CG, Sep 18, 20, 23, 30, Oct 7, 21, 24, Nov 9, Dec
    23; 1800: CG, Jan 16, Feb 10, Mar 1, 8, 25, May 1, 17, 23
Sydney, Mrs (actor), 1784: HAY, Nov 16, Dec 13
Sydney, Sir Philip, 1791: DLKING'S, Dec 31
--Arcadia, 1791: DLKING'S, Dec 31
Sykes, Major (actor), 1784: DL, Aug 20
Sykes, Mrs (haberdasher), 1772: DL, Nov 3; 1773: DL, Sep 23
Sylphide, La. See Biancolelli, Pierre Francoise Dominique.
Sylphs, The; or, Harlequin's Gambols (pantomime), 1774: CG, Jan 3, 4, 5, 6, 8,
    10, 11, 13, 15, 17, 18, 19, 20, 21, 22, 25, 26, 27, 28, 29, Feb 5, 7, 8, 9,
    10, 11, 12, 14, 19, 24, 28, Mar 3, 5, 7, 8, 12, 17, Apr 4, 8, 26, May 24, Sep
    23, 26, 30, Oct 3, 4, 7, 10, 12, 13, 14, 17, 18, 24; 1786: HAMM, Jul 24;
    1796: CG, Mar 15, Oct 24
Sylvester (machinist), 1800: HAY, Jul 2
Sylvester Daggerwood. See Colman the younger, George.
Sylvester, Mrs (householder), 1748: KING'S, Nov 29
Sylvia, don't Refuse your Bloom (song), 1742: DL, Feb 15
Sylvia, wilt thou waste thy Prime (song), 1742: DL, Feb 16, 17
Sylvia. See Lillo, George.
Sylvie (dance), 1787: KING'S, Mar 22, May 1
Sylvius, 1751: SF, Sep 18

Symonds. See Simmonds.
Symmonds (actor), _1722_: DL, May 29; _1723_: DL, Jun 3 _1728_: HAY, Oct 15; _1731_:
    SFGT, Sep 8; _1744_: MFHNT, May 1
Symmonds, Mrs (actor), _1777_: CHR, Jun 25
Symmons. See Symmonds.
Symonds (house servant), _1768_: CG, Jun 3; _1769_: CG, May 6, 8; _1770_: CG, May 18,
    21; _1771_: CG, May 22; _1772_: CG, May 29; _1773_: CG, May 28; _1774_: CG, May 24;
    _1775_: CG, May 30; _1776_: CG, May 21; _1777_: CG, May 23
Symonds, H D (publisher), _1788_: DL, May 14
Symonds, H D and Cawthorn, G (publishers), _1798_: CG, Oct 11
Symonds, Miss (actor), _1793_: CG, Nov 23
Symone (dancer), _1792_: HAY, Nov 26
Symons (spectator), _1678_: DL, Mar 19
Symphony, Grand (music), _1784_: HAY, May 10
Sympson. See Simpson.
Syrens, The. See Thompson, Edward.
Syrian Princes (spectators), _1722_: LIF, May 18; _1730_: HAY, Apr 22
Syrmen. See Sirmen.

T, B (letter writer), _1768_: CG, Mar 15
T, I (author), _1661_: NONE, Sep 0
T, S (letter writer), _1749_: DL, Feb 1
Tabatier (actor), _1729_: LIF, Apr 8
Tableau du Mariage, Le (play, anon), _1725_: HAY, Feb 15; _1726_: HAY, May 9
Tableau Parlant, Le. See Anseaume, Louis.
Tacet, Joseph (musician), _1755_: HAY, Feb 13; _1756_: HAY, Mar 25; _1757_: KING'S,
    Mar 24; _1758_: DL, Mar 10; _1759_: CG, May 4; _1761_: SOHO, Jan 28; _1766_: KING'S,
    Apr 10; _1769_: HAY, Feb 9; _1770_: KING'S, Feb 2, Jun 12; _1771_: KING'S, Feb 8;
    _1772_: KING'S, Feb 21, HAY, Mar 23; _1773_: KING'S, Feb 5; _1774_: KING'S, Feb 10,
    HAY, Mar 18; _1775_: KING'S, Mar 8, 10, 24, 29, Apr 5
Tack and Half Tack (song), _1799_: HAY, Sep 2, 12
Tady (actor), _1671_: NONE, Sep 0
Taffy and Griddy (song), _1790_: CG, Nov 23; _1791_: CG, Sep 19; _1793_: CG, May 21;
    _1794_: CG, Apr 12; _1799_: CG, Dec 9; see also Abergavenny is fine
Tagg in Tribulation!. See Dibdin, Thomas John.
Tagnoni, Madelena (singer), _1764_: KING'S, Feb 21, Mar 27
Tailleurs (dance), _1753_: CG, Dec 10, 13, 14, 22, 27, 29; _1754_: CG, Mar 18, 19,
    21, 23, 25, 28, Apr 1, 2, 6, 16, 29, May 7, 10; _1757_: HAY, Oct 3, 17, Nov 2
Tailors (dance), _1757_: HAY, Aug 31, Sep 2, 8; _1762_: CG, Jan 7, 12, 14, 15, 16,
    18, 19, 21, 23, 26, Feb 8, 9, 20, Mar 6, 16, Apr 16, 20, 24, 27, 30, May 1,
    3, 4, 5, 7, 10, 13, 18, 21, 24; _1774_: DL, Apr 28, May 5, 7
Tailors, The; A Tragedy for Warm Weather (burlesque, anon), _1767_: HAY, Jul 2,
    3, 7, 9, 13, 17, 29, Aug 12, 19, 25, Sep 1; _1776_: HAY, Sep 16; _1777_: HAY, May
    28, Jun 2, Aug 1; _1778_: HAY, May 21, 25, Jun 8, 9; _1779_: HAY, Jun 4, 9, Jul
    14, 21, 28, Sep 7, 16; _1780_: HAY, Jul 29; _1782_: HAY, Nov 25; _1785_: DL, Apr 20
Tajana, Giovanni (singer), _1791_: KING'S, Apr 26, May 14, 24, Jun 2
Take not a woman's anger ill (song), _1695_: DL, Oct 0
Taking of Cape Breton, The (entertainment), _1758_: BFYS, Sep 2, SFW, 18, 19, 20,
    21
Talbot (spectator), _1669_: LIF, Feb 18
Talbot Court, _1758_: CG, Jul 6
Talbot, Catherine (spectator), _1747_: CG, Apr 15
Talbot, Francis, Lord Shrewsbury, _1669_: BRIDGES, Mar 4
Talbot, J (translater), _1685_: NONE, Sep 0
Talbot, Montague (actor), _1794_: CG, Jan 13, May 28; _1799_: DL, Apr 27; _1800_: DL,
    Feb 12, Apr 29, May 10, 12, Jun 18
Talbot, Mrs (actor), _1730_: SOU, Sep 24, HAY, Oct 21; _1732_: HAY, Apr 27, BF, Aug
    22; _1733_: HAY, Feb 21, Mar 19, BFCGBH, Aug 23, Sep 4; _1734_: HAY, Jun 3, 7,
    17, 21, 24, Jul 5, 10, 26, 31, Aug 14, 16, BFFO, 24; _1735_: LIF, Jul 25, 30,
    Aug 1, 6, 22, 25, Sep 2, YB/HAY, Oct 1, HAY, Dec 13; _1736_: HAY, Jan 19, LIF,
    Mar 3, 24, HAY, Apr 26, LIF, 29, HAY, Jun 26, Jul 30, BFFH, Aug 23; _1737_:
    HAY, Mar 2; _1739_: BFHCL, Aug 23; _1740_: BFHC, Aug 23; _1744_: HAY, Apr 20, May
    10; _1750_: HAY, Feb 9, 16, Mar 13, Apr 9, DL, Nov 23
Talbot's Coffee House, _1737_: HAY, Mar 2
Tale of a Cock and a Bull (song), _1756_: DL, Mar 30
Tale of a Tubb. See Jonson, Ben.
Tale of Edwin and Angelina (song), _1788_: DL, May 6
Talisman, The (farce, anon), _1784_: HAY, Jan 21
Tally ho! (song), _1778_: DL, Apr 28; _1779_: DL, Apr 13, May 1, 3, 10; _1780_: CII,

Apr 5, DL, 11, 13, May 5; 1781: DL, Apr 24, 25; 1782: DL, Apr 16, CG, 27, May
1, 11; 1783: CG, May 16, 19, 23, DL, 23, CG, 26, Jun 3; 1784: DL, Mar 30, Apr
12, May 3, 5, 7, 21, CG, 25; 1785: CG, Apr 8, DL, May 19; 1786: DL, Apr 18;
1787: CG, May 9; 1788: CG, Apr 25
Tambour Dance of Moors (dance), 1728: DL, Sep 19; 1730: DL, Apr 14; 1731: DL,
May 12
Tambour de Basque Concerto (music), 1754: HAY, Jul 4, Sep 10, HAY/SFB, 19
Tambourina, Sga (actor), 1760: HAY, Feb 14
Tambourine (dance), 1731: LIF, Jan 4, DL, 23, LIF, Mar 18, DL, Apr 5, LIF, 5,
DL, 19, LIF, 21, DL, 22, 26, LIF, 26, 29, May 26, DL, Sep 23, Nov 11, LIF,
Dec 30; 1732: LIF, Jan 5, 7, GF, 11, 21, 25, Feb 14, 28, DL, Mar 30, GF, 30,
LIF, Apr 12, DL, 19, GF, 20, DL, 26, GF, May 1, DL, 1, LIF, 4, GF, 4, LIF, 5,
9, GF, 10, LIF, 10, GF, 11, 12, LIF, 15, GF, 15, 17, 18, 22, 23, Oct 10, 11,
13, DL, 21, GF, 25, DL, 26, GF, Nov 4, 6, DL, 8, GF, 8, 11, 13, 21, LIF/CG,
Dec 8, 9, 12, CG/LIF, 26, 28; 1733: CG/LIF, Jan 4, 9, LIF/CG, 16, 18, 19, 20,
23, CG, 24, LIF/CG, 29, Feb 5, 6, GF, 13, LIF/CG, Mar 12, 15, 17, CG/LIF, 26,
CG, 27, LIF/CG, 29, 31, Apr 11, 12, 20, 21, 23, 24, 25, 27, CG, May 1, 4,
LIF/CG, 7, 8, GF, 9, CG, 11, LIF/CG, 14, 15, CG, 16, LIF/CG, 19, 23, 24, 29,
Jun 1, CG, Sep 20, 25, 29, Oct 6, DL, 12, 15, GF, 18, CG, 18, GF, 19, 22, 23,
24, CG, 26, DL, 31, CG, 31, DL/HAY, Nov 15, CG, 23, DL/HAY, 28, Dec 5, DL, 7,
GF, 8, 11, DL/HAY, 12, HAY, 13, GF, 15, 19; 1734: GF, Jan 2, 8, DL/HAY, 10,
GF, 10, 14, 24, CG, Apr 24, 25, 29, 30, May 4, 9, 10, 13, 14, 15, 16, GF, 17,
CG, 17, GF, 20, CG/LIF, Sep 25, Oct 7, 9, 23, 26, 31, Nov 1, 12, 18, 19, 21,
Dec 5, 12, 26, GF/HAY, 28, 30; 1735: CG/LIF, Feb 3, Mar 11, Apr 11, 22, 29,
May 1, CG, 8, CG/LIF, 12, 13, 15, 20, 22, 26, 27, LIF, Aug 29, DL, Nov 10,
Dec 10, 31; 1736: DL, Jan 6, 7, 8, 9, CG, 9, 17, DL, 29, Feb 5, 6, 10, CG,
23, 24, 26, Mar 23, 25, DL, 27, CG, 30, DL, Apr 1, CG, 5, 6, 10, 12, DL, 13,
LIF, 16, DL, 17, 26, 27, CG, 30, May 1, 3, DL, 5, LIF, 5, CG, 6, 10, DL, 14,
CG, 14, 17, LIF, 19, CG, 24, 25, 31, DL, 31, Sep 7, 11, 16, 21, 28, Oct 5,
12, 15, 16, Nov 6, 29, 30, Dec 1; 1737: DL, Jan 29, Feb 1, 3, 8, Mar 12, LIF,
May 10; 1738: DL, Mar 20, 25, CG, Apr 6, DL, 12, 13, 14, 21, 22, 26, May 9,
Oct 26; 1739: DL, Jan 24, CG, Mar 26, Apr 14, 23, DL, May 11, 12, 14, 17, 25,
26, 30, 31, Sep 13, CG, 17, DL, 18, CG, 19, DL, 20, 22, 25, 29, CG, Oct 2,
DL, 2, 3, 4, 6, 8, 11, 12, 15, CG, 15, 27, DL, 31, Nov 1, 3, 19, 23, 26, Dec
8, 10, 15, 21, CG, 22, DL, 22, CG, 26; 1740: DL, Jan 1, 8, 11, CG, 12, DL,
14, CG, 15, 17, 19, 22, 24, 25, DL, 31, Feb 1, 2, CG, 2, DL, 4, CG, 7, DL,
12, 14, 15, Mar 10, CG, 11, DL, 17, 20, 22, 24, 27, Apr 7, 10, 14, 15, 16,
17, 19, 21, 22, 24, 25, 26, 28, May 2, 6, CG, 7, DL, 7, 8, CG, 9, DL, 9, 12,
13, 15, 17, 19, 20, 21, 22, 23, 26, 29, Oct 4, 7, 9, 10, 13, Nov 12, Dec 30;
1741: DL, Jan 2, 6, 24, Feb 3, CG, 14, 17, DL, 24, CG, Mar 2, DL, 5, 7, 9,
14, CG, 19, DL, 21, 30, CG, 30, DL, 31, Apr 1, 2, CG, 3, DL, 6, 7, CG,
14, DL, 14, CG, 15, DL, 20, 21, 22, CG, 24, DL, 24, CG, 25, DL, 27, CG, 28,
DL, 30, May 1, CG, 2, DL, 2, 4, 5, 6, 7, 9, 14, CG, 15, DL, 15, 21, 22, 23,
26, CG, Oct 30, DL, Dec 8, 9, CG, 15, DL, 16, CG, 30; 1742: CG, Jan 7, 16,
Feb 6, 9, 10, 23, 26, Mar 13, 18, 22, Apr 1, DL, 19, CG, Oct 4, 25, Nov 9,
Dec 1, 2, 7, 10, 11, 13, 14, 16, 18; 1743: CG, Feb 4, Mar 22, Apr 5, 6, 12,
13, 19, May 4, DL, 26; 1744: CG, Apr 9, DL, May 21; 1746: DL, Jan 10, 13, 17,
24, GF, Oct 27; 1747: DL, Dec 23, 30; 1748: DL, Jan 1, 7, 12, 13, 19, 23, 28,
Feb 11, 12, Mar 3, 8, 14, Apr 14, 16, 21, 26, May 11, 17, 25; 1750: CG, Jan
8, 9, 31, Apr 3, 17, 19, 21, 24, DL, 26, CG, 28, Dec 22; 1751: CG, Jan 3;
1752: DL, Mar 16; 1758: CG, Mar 30, Apr 13, 25, 28, May 4, 5; 1759: CG, Apr
27, May 16; 1762: DL, Apr 24, May 3; 1763: DL, Feb 17, May 4, 19; 1764:
KING'S, Mar 10, 20, 29, CG, May 5, KING'S, 15, HAY, Jul 5, 10, 27, DL, Sep
29, Oct 2, 11, CG, 15, DL, 16, CG, 16, 17, DL, 17, CG, 18, DL, 19, 20, 22,
24, 25, 27, 30, Nov 1, CG, 2, DL, 3, 8, 9, CG, 9, DL, 10, 12, CG, 15, DL, 16,
19, 23, CG, Dec 6, 7, DL, 8, 11; 1765: DL, Jan 11, CG, 19, DL, 23, 26, 28,
31, CG, Feb 4, DL, 8, 11, 12, 25, 28, Mar 4, CG, 5, 7, DL, 19, CG, 21, DL,
28, CG, Apr 8, DL, 8, CG, 9, DL, 9, CG, 10, 11, 12, 13, 15, 16, 17, DL, 18,
19, 23, 26, 27, 30, May 3, 6, 10, CG, 11; 1766: DL, Jan 23, Mar 20, Apr 8,
17, 22, 25, 28, May 2, 10, 13; 1767: CG, Apr 27, KING'S, 30, CG, May 12, 15,
25, 27, HAY, Jul 17, 20, CG, Oct 10, 14, 21, Nov 19, 21, 24, Dec 18; 1768:
KING'S, May 5; 1769: CG, Mar 14, Apr 27; 1770: DL, Apr 20, CG, May 1, 10;
1771: KING'S, Jun 1; 1772: CG, May 1, DL, 5, CG, 13, 15, 18, HAY, Jun 15;
1773: DL, Apr 22, HAY, Jun 30, Jul 5, 7, 9, 12, 21, Aug 4, 23, Sep 3, 9, 14;
1774: HAY, Jun 3, 10; 1775: DL, Mar 30, HAY, Jul 10, 12, 14, 26, Aug 7, 16,
23, 30, Sep 7, 12; 1776: HAY, Jun 12, 14, 24, Jul 22, 29, Aug 2, 12; 1778:
CG, May 2, HAY, Jun 24, Jul 3; 1779: CG, Apr 28, HAY, Jun 2, 7, 9, 18; 1780:
CG, May 16; 1781: HAY, Jun 1, Jul 16; 1782: HAY, Aug 24; 1788: CG, May 28;
1789: CG, Oct 21, Nov 6, 7, 20; 1790: CG, Feb 11, Mar 22, Apr 14
Tambourine (music), 1800: CG, Mar 21, DL, Jun 2, 3
Tambourine Matelote (dance), 1740: DL, Dec 4, 10; 1741: DL, Jan 7, 9, 15, 21,
23, 29, Feb 7, Mar 7, 14, 21, 31, Apr 2, 28, 30, May 2, 25

Tame, Mrs (actor), 1743: LIF, Apr 9, HAY, 15
Tamer Tamed, The. See Fletcher, John, The Woman's Prize.
Tamerlane the Great. See Saunders, Charles.
Tamerlane. See Rowe, Nicholas.
Tamerlano. See Sacchini, Antonio Maria Gasparo.
Taming of the Shrew, The. See Shakespeare, William.
Tamo Tanto (music), 1728: LIF, Mar 18, 21, May 30; 1729: LIF, May 8
Tancred and Sigismunda. See Thomson, James.
Tanfield Court, 1799: HAY, Sep 2; 1800: CG, Apr 26, HAY, Sep 10
Tanner actor), 1792: HAY, Feb 20
Tanner of York. See Arthur, John, Lucky Discovery.
Tannett, B (actor), 1773: HAY, Jun 4, MARLY, Sep 3; 1777: HAY, Oct 9
Tantara Rara, Rogues All! See O'Keeffe, John.
Tantini, Anna (dancer), 1779: KING'S, Nov 27, Dec 14; 1780: KING'S, Jan 22, Feb
   15, Apr 1, 11, 22, May 2, 9, 25, 27, Nov 25; 1781: KING'S, Jan 13, 23, Feb
   22, DL, Mar 12, KING'S, 29, DL, May 14, KING'S, Jun 26, Jul 3
Tantivy, the welkin resounds (song), 1785: CG, Apr 18, 25, May 4; 1786: CG, May
   22
Tape (dancer), 1720: LIF, Apr 29
Taphouse of the Wells, 1745: GF, Feb 4; 1746: GF, Feb 17, 20, Mar 4, 11
Tapsford, Mrs (actor), 1705: DL, Jul 25
Tarantula, La; or, The Merry Bedlamites (dance), 1783: CG, May 9
Tarare et Irza (dance), 1799: KING'S, May 2, 4, Jun 11, 15, 22
Tarchi, Angelo (composer), 1786: KING'S, May 4; 1787: KING'S, Apr 17; 1789:
   KING'S, Jan 24, Feb 28, May 9, Jun 2; 1790: HAY, Apr 29; 1791: KING'S, Apr
   26; 1793: KING'S, Jun 11
--Disertore, Il (opera), 1789: KING'S, Feb 28, Mar 3, 7, 10, 14, 17, 19, 21,
   Apr 2, May 2, 19, 21
--Generosita d'Alessandro, La (opera), 1789: KING'S, Jun 2, 6, 9, 13, 16, CG,
   27, 30, Jul 7; 1790: HAY, Apr 29, May 1, 4, 8, 11, 13, 15, 18, Jun 5, 12, CG,
   22, Jul 10
--Virginia (opera), 1786: KING'S, May 4, 6, 13, 16, 18, 23, Jun 13, 15, 22, 24,
   Jul 8; 1787: KING'S, Mar 15, 22, Apr 17, 21, Jun 5, 9
Taretti (singer), 1774: KING'S, Mar 17
Tarewoo (Terrywoo) (song), 1775: HAY, Feb 20, Nov 20
Tariot (dancer), 1760: CG, May 28, HAY, Jun 2, KING'S, Nov 22, Dec 16; 1761:
   KING'S, Jan 6, Feb 7, Mar 9
Tariot, Master (dancer), 1760: HAY, Jun 2
Tariot, Mr and Mrs (dancers), 1759: CG, Oct 13
Tariot, Mrs (dancer), 1760: HAY, Jun 2
Tarr, Mrs (singer), 1730: GF, Oct 31
Tars at Torbay; or, Sailors on Saturday Night (interlude, anon), 1799: HAY, Sep
   2, 9, 12, 16
Tars of Old England, The; or, Humours of Greenwich Fair (pantomime, anon),
   1799: CG, May 14
Tartars (dance), 1767: DL, Nov 5; 1768: CG, Apr 16, May 5, Oct 4, 22, 25, Nov
   3, 11; 1769: CG, Jan 18, 23, Mar 18, 29, Dec 7, 13; 1770: CG, Mar 22, Apr 7,
   May 3, Oct 3, 4, 6; 1771: CG, Mar 2, 21, Apr 5, 12, 16, 27, Sep 27, Oct 31;
   1772: CG, Nov 24, 26, Dec 4; 1773: KING'S, May 6, 11, 22, 28, Jun 5, 8
Tartars' Festival (dance), 1764: DL, Nov 2
Tartuffe. See Moliere.
Tarugo's Wiles. See St Serfe, Thomas.
Tasca, Luigi (singer), 1784: KING'S, Jan 6, Feb 24, Mar 4, 25, Apr 15, Jun 12,
   Dec 18; 1785: KING'S, Jan 4, 25, Mar 17, Apr 2, 28, May 28; 1786: KING'S, Feb
   11, 14, Mar 11, 16, 21, May 20
Tasca, Santa (singer), 1736: KING'S, Jan 24
Tassie, Mrs (actor), 1785:HAY, Jan 24
Tasso, Torquato, 1659: NONE, Sep 0; 1697: NONE, Sep 0; 1794: CG, May 30
--Aminta, 1697: NONE, Sep 0
Tassoni (dancer), 1762: KING'S, Mar 20, CG, Oct 8, 23, Nov 1; 1763: CG, Jan 26,
   Apr 21, DL, Oct 28; 1764: DL, Mar 10, 19, 26, May 4, Sep 25, Dec 14; 1765:
   DL, Feb 8, May 10, 11, 15, 16, Sep 24, Oct 8; 1766: DL, Jan 6, May 7, Sep 23,
   27, Nov 11; 1767: DL, Jan 24, Apr 4, SW, May 13, DL, 13, 18, SW, Jun 13, DL,
   Sep 12; 1768: DL, Apr 6, May 4, Aug 18, Oct 10; 1769: DL, Mar 13, May 5, 9,
   HAY, 15, Aug 14, 25, DL, Sep 23, Dec 30; 1770: DL, May 15; 1772: DL, May 6;
   1773: DL, May 10; 1774: KING'S, Jan 29
Tassoni's scholar (dancer), 1772: DL, May 13; 1773: DL, Jan 14, Apr 3
Taste a la Mode (play, anon), 1736: DL, May 13, 31
Taste and Feeling (play, anon), 1790: HAY, Aug 13; 1791: HAY, Jul 7
Taste. See Foote, Samuel.
Taste; or, Frolicks of Fancy (interlude), 1790: DL, May 18
Taswell, James (actor), 1729: HAY, Mar 29, May 13; 1739: DL, Jan 16, Mar 3, 6,

31, Apr 10, 14, 28, May 2, 5, 15, 16, Sep 8, 22, 26, Oct 10, 17, Nov 10, 15,
19, 23, Dec 31; 1740: DL, Jan 3, Feb 7, 13, Mar 20, 22, 25, Apr 15, 17, 23,
26, May 7, 8, 9, 22, 26, 28, Sep 6, 11, 13, 16, 18, 20, 27, 30, Oct 4, 9, 10,
13, 14, 15, 23, 28, Nov 7, 13, 19, 27, 28, Dec 2, 6, 8, 15, 18, 20; 1741: DL,
Feb 14, Mar 14, 31, Apr 3, May 12, 13, 21, BFLW, Aug 22, DL, Sep 8, 10, 15,
19, 22, Oct 6, 8, 9, 15, 21, 23, 27, 31, Nov 2, 11, 16, 21, Dec 7, 12, 19;
1742: DL, Jan 6, Feb 12, Mar 22, 29, Apr 5, 24, 26, May 3, 6, 11, 13, 26, Sep
11, 14, 16, 21, Oct 2, 13, 16, 18, 30, Nov 16, 19; 1743: DL, Jan 28, Feb 10,
17, Mar 14, 21, SOU, 30, DL, Apr 29, May 12, LIF, Jun 3, DL, Sep 15, 17, 20,
22, 24, 27, 29, Oct 4, 11, 13, 15, 20, 22, 25, Nov 8, 12, 17, 18, 23, 26, 29,
Dec 6, 12, 15, 16, 17; 1744: DL, Jan 7, 27, Feb 21, Mar 10, 12, Apr 2, 9, 17,
28, May 1, 22, Sep 15, 18, 20, 27, 29, Oct 2, 6, 9, 19, 22, 30, Nov 3, 6, Dec
11, 19; 1745: DL, Jan 4, 8, Feb 2, 11, 14, Apr 19, May 13, Sep 26, 28, Oct 5,
8, 10, 12, 15, 17, Nov 1, 14, 18, 22, 23, 28, Dec 10, 11, 13, 31; 1746: DL,
Jan 2, 3, 8, 10, 14, 18, Feb 6, 24, Mar 17, Apr 14, 23, 30, May 16, Sep 23,
25, 27, 30, Oct 2, 11, 14, 23, 27, 31, Nov 5, 7, 21, 22, Dec 1, 26, 29; 1747:
DL, Mar 3, 7, 12, 23, 24, 28, 30, May 1, Sep 15, 22, Oct 1, 17, 21, 24, 29,
Nov 2, 6, 7, 16, 25, Dec 16, 26; 1748: DL, Jan 6, 12, 22, Feb 3, Mar 19, Apr
11, 28, May 4, BFSY, Aug 24, DL, Sep 13, 15, 20, 22, 24, 29, Oct 6, 13, 19,
27, 28, Nov 1, 3, 7, 14, 23, 29, Dec 26, 28; 1749: DL, Jan 2, 9, 18, Apr
29, May 1, 5, 11, Sep 16, 19, 20, 21, 28, Oct 3, 14, 17, 19, 30, Nov 9, 15,
28, Dec 9, 12, 18, 20, 28; 1750: DL, Jan 1, Mar 29, Apr 19, 27, 30, HAY, Jul
26, DL, Sep 25, 27, Oct 26, Nov 14, 30, Dec 14, 28, 31; 1751: DL, Jan 3, 4,
5, 16, 26, Apr 25, 27, May 6, Sep 10, 12, 13, 14, 17, 18, Oct 3, 11, 17, 22,
Nov 29; 1752: DL, Jan 1, 11, Feb 3, Mar 10, Apr 3, 6, 9, 10, 21, 27, May 2,
Sep 19, 26, Oct 5, 12, 19, 21, 23, 30, Nov 8, 25, 27, 30, Dec 8, 18, 29;
1753: DL, Jan 3, 22, Mar 26, Apr 14, 25, 28, May 17, 18, 21, Sep 13, 27, Oct
6, 9, 10, 12, 16, 20, Nov 1, 6, 8, 14; 1754: DL, Jan 16, Feb 13, 20, Mar 19,
23, Apr 30, May 7, Sep 19, 26, Oct 5, 10, 12, 16, 25, 30, Nov 11, 22, Dec 13;
1755: DL, Jan 15, Feb 18, 22, Mar 20, Apr 24, Sep 13, 18, 27, Oct 3, 4, 7,
Nov 1, 20, 22, Dec 1, 5, 6, 11, 18; 1756: DL, Mar 30, Apr 19, 24, May 5, 10,
20, 24, 28, Sep 25, 30, Oct 5, 13, 19, Nov 6, 11, 19, 23; 1757: DL, Jan 12,
Feb 28, Mar 7, 19, Apr 22, May 2, 3, 9, 19, 20, Sep 15, 24, 27, Oct 6, 8, 13,
19, Nov 8, 19; 1758: DL, Jan 27, 28, Feb 4, Mar 30, Apr 27, Sep 16, 19, 21,
23, 26, Oct 3, 17, 27, Nov 1, 7, 24, Dec 18; 1759: DL, Jan 8
Tate, Nahum, 1680: DL, Dec 0, 3; 1681: DL, Jan 18; 1684: ATCOURT, Feb 11; 1690:
DL, Dec 0; 1693: ATCOURT, Jan 1, 2, Apr 30, Nov 4; 1698: DL/ORDG, Nov 0;
1699: ATCOURT, Nov 4; 1702: SH, Jan 31, May 7; 1723: DL, Jun 25, 28, Aug 6;
1729: DL, Jul 11; 1731: DL, Jun 15; 1735: DL, Sep 27, Nov 24; 1737: DL, Jan
10; 1753: DL, Apr 12; 1756: CG, Feb 26; 1768: CG, Apr 28; 1774: CG, Nov 24
--Brutus of Alba; or, The Enchanted Lovers, 1678: DG, Jun 0
--Cuckolds-Haven; or, An Alderman No Conjurer, 1685: DG, Jul 0
--Dido and Aeneas, 1689: CHELSEA, Dec 0
--Duke and no Duke, A, 1684: DLORDG, Aug 0, Nov 3, Dec 9; 1693: ATCOURT, Jan 2;
1704: LIF, Feb 12, 15, 22; 1705: QUEEN'S, Nov 16; 1710: QUEEN'S, Aug 16;
1712: DL, May 16, Dec 5; 1715: LIF, Aug 3, 4, Oct 14; 1718: RI, Aug 25; 1719:
DL, Dec 4, 7, 9; 1723: DL, Jun 25, 28, Jul 12, Aug 6; 1724: RI, Jul 4, Aug 3;
1729: DL, Jul 11, 18, 22, Aug 5; 1731: DL, Jun 15; 1732: LIF, Jan 1, 3, 4, 6,
21, Feb 10, Mar 2, 16, May 13, LIF/CG, Nov 24; 1733: LIF/CG, Feb 5, LIF, Apr
28; 1734: CG, Feb 23, Mar 14; 1735: CG/LIF, Feb 10, Mar 8; 1736: CG, Jan 26;
1740: CG, Feb 23, 25, 28, Mar 4, Apr 7, Oct 16, 30; 1741: CG, Feb 28; 1743:
CG, Apr 26; 1744: CG, May 14; 1746: CG, Jan 23, 25, 27, 28, Feb 3, 15, 20,
Mar 13, Apr 4, 28, May 5, Oct 29, Nov 1, 7, 12, 17, Dec 10; 1749: DL, Dec 26,
27, 29; 1750: DL, Jan 5, 15, 16, 17, 20, 24, 26, Feb 12, 14, 19, Apr 16, 20,
May 4, 7, Oct 13, 20, 25, 29, Nov 3, 5, 12, 19, Dec 8, 18, 20; 1751: DL, Feb
13, 19, Apr 11, 25, Oct 4, 8, 14, Nov 7, 14, Dec 14; 1752: DL, Mar 17, 19,
21, Apr 11, 15, 16, 29, Sep 30, Oct 9; 1753: DL, Mar 26, May 5, 22, 23, Oct
13, Dec 13, 19; 1754: DL, Feb 18, 23, Mar 12, Sep 21; 1755: DL, Mar 1, Apr 1,
Sep 23, Nov 3; 1756: CG, Apr 29, May 3, 4, 11, 13, 17, 18, Sep 22, DL, Nov
26, CG, Dec 8, 10; 1757: CG, Jan 1, 27, Feb 18, 28, Mar 22, Apr 26, Oct 13,
DL, 26, CG, Nov 2, 25, 29, Dec 21, 27; 1758: CG, Jan 9, Mar 30, May 1, 11,
DL, Sep 21, CG, Oct 9, 19, DL, 28, CG, Nov 6, 11, 30, Dec 20, DL, 29, CG, 29;
1759: CG, Jan 6, 8, 19, Feb 20, DL, 20, CG, Apr 28, May 16, Sep 28, Oct 17,
25, Nov 2, 9, 17; 1760: CG, Jan 4, 12, Feb 16, Apr 12, May 5, 9, Oct 2, DL,
3, 9, 25, CG, Nov 18, DL, 24, CG, Dec 18, 30; 1761: CG, Jan 24, Mar 31, DL,
Apr 10, 15, CG, May 18, Sep 21; 1762: CG, Apr 20, May 14, DL, Nov 4; 1763:
CG, Sep 30; 1764: CG, Jan 3, Oct 5; 1765: CG, Jan 9, Apr 8, Oct 2, Nov 26;
1767: CG, May 15, HAY, Jul 22, 24, 27, 31, Aug 5, Sep 10; 1768: CG, Apr 27,
May 31; 1770: CG, May 9, Oct 12, Dec 6; 1775: CG, Dec 9, 11, 12; 1776: CG,
Jan 2, 8, Feb 15, 24, Mar 11, May 3, HAY, Sep 20, CG, Nov 13, 27; 1784: DL,
May 3, 10, 14; 1786: CG, Apr 18, 26, May 31; 1787: CG, Feb 6; 1788: DL, May
14, 22, Jun 3, CG, Dec 1, 13; 1789: HAY, Aug 27; 1797: CG, Apr 8, HAY, Aug 14

--Ingratitude of a Common-Wealth, The; or, The Fall of Caius Marius Coriolanus, 1681: DL, Dec 0; 1682: DL, Jan 14
--Loyal General, The, 1679: DG, Dec 0
--Sicilian Usurper, The, 1680: DL, Dec 0, 13; 1681: DL, Jan 18; 1689: NONE, Sep 0
--Tyrant of Sicily, The, 1681: DL, Jan 18, 19
Tatham, John, 1659: CITY, Oct 29; 1660: CITY, Oct 29; 1663: CITY, Oct 29
--Aqua Triumphalis (pageant), 1662: THAMES, Aug 23
--Londinium Triumphans, 1663: CITY, Oct 29
--London's Triumph (pageant), 1659: CITY, Oct 29; 1661: CITY, Oct 29; 1662: CITY, Oct 29; 1664: CITY, Oct 29; 1676: CITY, Oct 30; 1677: CITY, Oct 29
--Neptune's Address to His Most Sacred Majesty Charles the Second, 1661: NONE, Apr 22
--Royal Oak, The, 1660: CITY, Oct 29
--Rump, The; or, The Mirrour of the Late Times, 1660: DC, Jun 0, NONE, Sep 0; 1661: NONE, Jul 13
Tatlers, The. See Hoadly, Benjamin.
Tatteratro, Sga (musician), 1753: BFSY, Sep 3
Tattnel (actor), 1704: LIF, Feb 2
Tattoo (musician), 1759: CG, Dec 10; 1761: CG, Oct 13
Taubman, Matthew, 1685: CITY, Oct 29; 1686: CITY, Oct 29; 1687: CITY, Oct 29; 1688: CITY, Oct 28; 1689: CITY, Oct 29
--London's Anniversary Festival (pageant), 1688: CITY, Oct 28
--London's Annual Triumph (pageant), 1685: CITY, Oct 29
--London's Glory Represented by Time, Truth and Fame, 1660: CITY, Jul 5
--London's Great Jubilee (pageant), 1689: CITY, Oct 29
--London's Triumph; or, The Goldsmith's Jubilee (pageant), 1687: CITY, Oct 29
--London's Yearly Jubilee (pageant), 1686: CITY, Oct 29
Tauranac's Wine Vault, 1756: DL, May 1
Tavern Bilkers, The (dance), 1720: HOUN, Jun 13; 1729: LIF, Apr 8
Tavern Bilkers, The (droll, anon), 1733: GF, Jan 13, 15, 16, 17, 18, 31, Feb 3, Apr 3, Sep 24, 25, Oct 5, 8, 17, Dec 12, 14; 1734: GF, Jan 21, Feb 7; 1749: JS, Mar 29
Taverner, William, 1704: DL, May 0; 1708: DL, Jun 5; 1713: DL, Jan 6; 1716: LIF, Mar 10; 1717: LIF, Feb 11, Dec 3; 1719: LIF, Feb 28; 1747: DL, Mar 3; 1778: HAY, May 18; 1795: CG, May 1
--Artful Husband, The, 1717: LIF, Feb 11, 12, 14, 15, 18, 19, 21, 22, 23, Mar 2, Apr 1, 8, 24, May 11, 17, Oct 24; 1718: LIF, Feb 14, Mar 8, Apr 3, Jun 4; 1721: LIF, Apr 18, May 5; 1747: DL, Mar 3, 5, 10, 26, May 4; 1795: CG, May 1
--Artful Wife, The, 1717: LIF, Nov 30, Dec 3, 4, 5; 1778: HAY, May 18
--Every Body Mistaken, 1716: LIF, Mar 10, 12, 13
--Faithful Bride of Granada, The, 1704: DL, May 0
--Female Advocates, The, 1713: DL, Jan 6
--Maid's the Mistress, The, 1708: DL, Jun 5, 8; 1737: LIF, Mar 21
--Presumptuous Love, 1716: LIF, Mar 10, 12, 13
--Tis Well if it Takes, 1719: LIF, Feb 28, Mar 2, 3, 7, Apr 3, May 13
Tavistock Row, 1753: DL, Mar 26, Apr 26; 1754: DL, Feb 22, Apr 24; 1755: DL, Apr 11; 1778: CG, Mar 24; 1780: CG, Apr 5, DL, 7; 1784: CG, May 20; 1786: CG, Mar 30; 1787: CG, May 5; 1788: CG, Apr 28; 1790: CG, Apr 14; 1791: CG, Apr 30; 1794: CG, May 28
Tavistock St, 1716: LIF, Apr 11; 1718: LIF, Mar 4; 1724: LIF, Apr 9; 1726: LIF, Apr 13; 1728: LIF, Mar 28; 1730: LIF, Apr 15; 1731: LIF, Apr 8; 1733: LIF/CG, Apr 11; 1735: DL, Mar 29, CG/LIF, Apr 15; 1736: CG, Apr 12, 30; 1737: CG, Jan 24, DL, May 18; 1748: DL, Apr 2; 1749: DL, Apr 3; 1750: DL, Apr 2; 1751: DL, Apr 17; 1753: DL, Apr 2; 1754: DL, Mar 18, 25; 1755: DL, Mar 15, Apr 23; 1756: DL, Mar 23, Apr 28; 1757: DL, Mar 22, 26, Apr 18, 30; 1760: DL, Mar 24; 1777: CG, May 2; 1779: DL, Apr 7, May 3; 1780: DL, Apr 4; 1782: DL, Apr 24; 1784: CG, May 4; 1786: CG, May 9, 22; 1789: CG, May 28; 1790: CG, May 26; 1791: CG, Jun 3; 1794: CG, May 23
Tavistock, Marquis of (renter), 1766: DL, Oct 31
Tax on Old Maids (song), 1786: HAMM, Jul 24
Taxes, The. See Bacon, Dr Phanuel.
Taylor (actor), 1764: HAY, Jun 26, Jul 6, 12, 23, Aug 20, Sep 1; 1765: MARLY, Aug 6; 1766: MARLY, Sep 26
Taylor (actor), 1776: CHR, Oct 14; 1778: HAY, Sep 17, 18
Taylor (actor), 1798: CG, Apr 20
Taylor (actor, dancer), 1729: HAY, May 7; 1731: TCY, Aug 9, SF, Sep 8; 1732: WINH, May 27, UM, Jun 19; 1734: YB, Apr 24, SFG, Sep 7, GF, Oct 16, 28, Nov 18, Dec 20; 1735: GF, May 3, BF, Aug. 23, LIF, Sep 2, 5, DL, 15, 30, Oct 7, 30, Nov 15, 20, Dec 6; 1736: DL, Jan 12, Dec 27; 1737: CG, Nov 8; 1738: CG, Dec 8; 1739: CG, Dec 8, 13; 1741: GF, May 4, BFTY, Aug 22, CG, Dec 9, 11; 1743: LIF, Jan 3, 7

Taylor (boxkeeper), 1720: LIF, May 10; 1721: LIF, May 22; 1722: LIF, May 24;
    1723: LIF, May 23; 1724: LIF, May 19; 1725: LIF, May 18; 1726: LIF, May 14;
    1728: LIF, May 30; 1729: LIF, May 22
Taylor (carpenter), 1797: DL, Oct 16
Taylor (first gallery keeper), 1728: DL, May 22; 1729: DL, May 9; 1730: DL, May
    7; 1731: DL, May 13; 1732: DL, May 10; 1733: DL, May 23; 1734: DL/HAY, May
    22; 1735: DL, May 29; 1736: DL, May 27; 1737: DL, May 24; 1738: DL, May 27;
    1739: DL, May 23; 1740: DL, May 29; 1741: DL, May 27; 1742: DL, May 27; 1743:
    DL, May 18
Taylor (linen draper), 1799: HAY, Apr 17
Taylor (taverner), 1773: DL, Dec 28
Taylor (ticket deliverer), 1744: CG, Apr 21
Taylor, Elizabeth (actor), 1770: HAY, Mar 19; 1771: GROTTO, Jun 22
Taylor, Elizabeth (dancer), 1787: DL, Jun 4; 1791: CG, Dec 22; 1792: CG, Apr 12
Taylor, George Thomas (bassoonist), 1795: CG, Feb 20; 1796: CG, Feb 12; 1797:
    CG, Mar 3; 1798: CG, Feb 23; 1799: CG, Feb 8; 1800: CG, Feb 28
Taylor, Hannah Henrietta, Mrs William Perkins (actor), 1787: DL, Sep 29, Oct
    26, Nov 5, 29, Dec 8, 10, 26; 1788: DL, Jan 10, 19, Mar 31, Apr 21, 28
Taylor, John (actor), 1794: HAY, Jun 2
Taylor, John (author), 1788: HAY, Aug 26; 1790: JAY, Aug 11, CG, Nov 23; 1791:
    CG, Apr 5, 16; 1793: CG, Nov 23; 1795: CG, Mar 19, DL, Apr 17, Jun 3; 1797:
    CG, Mar 6, DL, Apr 19, CG, 29, HAY, Sep 18, DL, Oct 21; 1798: CG, Mar 17, Apr
    17, DL, May 19, CG, Oct 11, Dec 8, HAY, 17; 1799: CG, Jan 12, HAY, Jul 30,
    Aug 21, CG, Oct 31, Nov 30; 1800: DL, Jan 25, May 10, Jun 18
Taylor, Joseph (actor), 1661: LIF, Aug 24
Taylor, Mary (actor), 1789: HAY, May 25, Jun 5, 12, 22, Jul 29, Aug 10, 11, 25,
    28, Sep 8, 15; 1790: HAY, Jun 14, 15, 22, 25, 26, Aug 4, 10, 30; 1791: HAY,
    Jun 8, 16, 25, 28, Jul 28, 30, Aug 16, 31; 1792: HAY, Jun 18, 23, 29, 30, Jul
    16, 25, 31, Aug 9
Taylor, Miss (actor), 1744: HAY, May 16, Jun 29
Taylor, Miss (actor), 1776: CHR, Sep 23, 27, 30, Oct 2, 4, 7, 9, 11, 16, 18;
    1778: CHR, Jul 30
Taylor, Miss (dancer), 1765: DL, May 22; 1768: DL, May 13, 23
Taylor, Mrs (actor), 1723: HAY, Apr 15, 22; 1724: LIF, May 28; 1728: HAY, Oct
    15; 1731: BFLH, Aug 24, SFLH, Sep 8; 1741: BFH, Aug 22
Taylor, Mrs (actor), 1789: WHF, Nov 9, 11; 1791: HAY, Dec 12, 26; 1792: HAY,
    Feb 6
Taylor, Raynor (composer), 1778: HAY, Jul 31
Taylor, William (proprietor), 1783: KING'S, May 20; 1791: PAN, Apr 12; 1795:
    KING'S, Mar 28
Te Deum Laudamus (anthem), 1702: SH, May 7, CC, 21
Te Deum. See Handel, George Frederic.
Te Deum, Grand. See Paisiello, Giovanni.
Tea a la Mode. See Wilkinson, Tate.
Tea. See Foote, Samuel.
Teague's Ramble to London (entertainment), 1771: HAY, Jan 28; 1776: CHR, Oct
    18; 1781: DL, May 7, 10, 15; 1789: CG, Jun 8
Teano. See Teno.
Tears and Triumphs of Parnassus (song), 1760: DL, Nov 17, 18, 20, 25
Tears are my daily Food (song), 1789: DL, Mar 25
Tears such as tender fathers shed (song), 1791: DL, Mar 11; 1792: CG, Mar 9;
    1793: CG, Feb 22, Mar 20; 1794: DL, Mar 12, 14, CG, 26, DL, Apr 11; 1795: CG,
    Mar 25; 1796: CG, Feb 26; 1797: CG, Mar 31; 1799: CG, Feb 8, Mar 6, 13
Teasdale (haberdasher), 1772: CG, Jan 3
Ted Blarney (song), 1779: HAY, Aug 17
Tedeschi, Sga (singer), 1741: KING'S, Oct 31; 1742: KING'S, Jan 19, Mar 2
Tedeschini, Christian (singer), 1760: KING'S, Nov 22; 1761: KING'S, Jan 6,
    SOHO, 21, KING'S, Mar 9, Apr 28
Tee Yee Neen Ho Go Row (Emperor of the Six Nations), 1710: QUEEN'S, Apr 28; see
    also American Princes; Cherokee Chiefs; Indian Kings, American
Teede (musician), 1758: CHAPEL, Apr 27
Telasco and Amgahi; or, The Peruvian Nuptials (dance), 1800: DL, May 14
Telegraph, The. See Dent, John.
Telemachus in the Island of Calypso (dance), 1791: PAN, Mar 19, 22, 24, Apr 2,
    5, 12, 14, 16, May 31, Jun 23, Jul 9
Telemachus. See Scarlatti, Allessandro.
Telemaco. See Traetta, Tommaso.
Telemaque (dance), 1799: KING'S, Mar 26, 30, May 4, 7, DL, 8, KING'S, 10, Jun
    17, 29, Jul 16; 1800: KING'S, Jun 17, 19, 21, Jul 1
Tell me, Belinda, prithee do (song), 1697: DL, Jan 0
Tell me, Gentle Shepherd, Where (song), 1744: HAY, Apr 20
Tell me, lovely shepherd (song), 1793: KING/HAY, Feb 27

Tell me no more I am deceived (song), 1684: DLORDG, Aug 0
Tell me no more I am deceived (song), 1693: DL, Feb 0
Tell me, Silvia, why so sad? (song), 1777: CG, Apr 29
Tell me, Thyrsis, all your anguish (song), 1682: DL, Nov 28
Tell me what a thing is love (song), 1691: NONE, Sep 0
Tell Me Why, My Charming Fair (song), 1705: DL, Feb 8; 1711: GR, Sep 8
Tell my Strephon that I die (song), 1679: DG, Dec 0
Tell Truth and Shame the Devil. See Dunlap, William.
Tellier (actor), 1719: LIF, Jan 13
Temista di Mare (music), 1724: HAY, May 8
Temistocle. See Porpora, Nicola.
Tempest of War (song), 1763: DL, Apr 9, 11
Tempest, The. See Shakespeare, William.
Tempest, The; or, The Happy Shipwreck (dance), 1774: KING'S, Apr 19
Tempio della Gloria, Il. See Cocchi, Gioacchino.
Templars, the, 1739: DL, Jan 4
Temple (boxkeeper), 1730: GF, Jun 25; 1732: GF, May 19; 1733: GF, May 22
Temple (ticket holder), 1737: LIF, May 10
Temple Bar, 1696: BF, Aug 0; 1723: KAT, Dec 4; 1730: DL, Dec 3; 1731: DT, Apr
    23; 1736: DT, Apr 16; 1737: DT, Mar 7; 1741: GF, May 7; 1742: GF, Apr 22, JS,
    Oct 12; 1744: TB, Feb 29, DL, Mar 10; 1745: DL, Apr 16; 1747: HAY, Apr 25;
    1749: CG, Apr 28; 1750: DL, Feb 22, CG, Nov 5; 1751: DL, Feb 4; 1752: DL, Jan
    16, Dec 19, 23; 1754: DL, Apr 4, Dec 16; 1756: LRRH, Jan 28, 31, Feb 4,
    LRRH/PCR, 11; 1763: DL, Apr 27; 1774: DL, Mar 9
Temple Beau, The. See Fielding, Henry.
Temple Exchange Coffee House, 1744: DL, Apr 2, May 14; 1746: CG, Jan 24; 1751:
    DL, May 14, Dec 18; 1752: DL, Dec 19; 1754: DL, Dec 16
Temple Lane, 1778: CG, May 19; 1779: CG, May 13
Temple of Dulness, The. See Arne, Dr Thomas A.
Temple of Jupiter (dance), 1748: NWC, Apr 4
Temple of Love, The. See Motteux, Peter Anthony.
Temple of Taste (entertainment), 1752: CG, Feb 22, 24, 26, 28, Mar 4, 11
Temple Rake. See Drury, Robert, Rival Milliners.
Temple, Lady. See Osborne, Dorothy.
Temple, Mrs (actor, dancer), 1693: NONE, Sep 0; 1695: DL, Dec 0; 1696: DL, Feb
    0, DG, Jun 0, DL, Sep 0, DL/DL, Dec 0; 1697: DL, Sep 0; 1698: DL, Feb 0, Mar
    0; 1700: DL, Feb 19, Mar 0, Jul 9, Dec 9; 1703: DL, Jun 23; 1705: DL, Mar 29,
    Jul 25; 1706: DL, Apr 0; 1707: DL, Oct 25
Temple, 1759: DL, Mar 23; 1799: HAY, Sep 2; 1800: CG, Apr 26, HAY, Sep 10
Templer, Mrs (actor), 1728: LIF, Dec 7; 1729: BF, Aug 26, LIF, Sep 12, 17, Dec
    15; 1730: LIF, Jan 19, Apr 2, May 23, RI, Jun 27, Jul 16, LIF, Sep 16, Oct
    27, Nov 25, Dec 4; 1731: LIF, Jan 13, Feb 27, Apr 3, RI, Jul 1, 8, 15, 22,
    SF/BFFHH, Aug 24, LIF, Oct 6; 1732: LIF, Feb 21, Apr 10, May 15, 22, RI, Aug
    17, BF, 22, LIF/CG, Oct 23, 27, Nov 17, 18, Dec 14, CG/LIF, 16; 1733: LIF/CG,
    Jan 18, Feb 5, Apr 16, 17, CG, May 17, CG/LIF, 28, CG, Sep 29, Oct 29, Nov
    14, 19, Dec 1, 5, 31; 1734: CG, Jan 4, 17, RI, Jun 27, CG/LIF, Sep 23, 25,
    RI, 26, CG/LIF, 27, Oct 7, LIF, 12, CG/LIF, 29, Nov 7, 11; 1735: CG/LIF, Feb
    15, Mar 11, 13, Apr 10, 23, CG, 25, LIF, 30, CG/LIF, May 1, CG, Oct 1, 17,
    29, Nov 7, 28, Dec 2; 1736: CG, Jan 8, Feb 26, Mar 15, LIF, 31, CG, May 10,
    27, Jun 14, Sep 17, 27, Oct 15, LIF, 18, CG, 22, 29, Nov 8, 9, 23; 1737: CG,
    Jan 10, Feb 15, 24, Mar 15, Apr 14, May 6, Oct 3, 5, 7, 21, 24, 29, Nov 2,
    15; 1738: CG, Jan 26, 31, Mar 20, Sep 27, Oct 11, 21, 30, 31, Nov 15; 1739:
    CG, Feb 9, 24, Mar 3, May 17
Templeton, Mrs (actor), 1784: CG, Jan 29, Sep 20; 1785: CG, Sep 30
Templeton, Mrs (ticket deliverer), 1780: CG, May 23
Tenauki (spectator), 1734: CG/LIF, Oct 25
Tench, Fisher (dancer), 1729: LIF, May 9, 14, 19, HAY, 26; 1730: DL, Apr 28,
    May 15, Oct 28, Nov 3, Dec 4; 1731: DL, Jun 7, Aug 6, 20, SF/BFFHH, 24, Sep
    8, DL, Oct 16, Nov 25; 1732: DL, Feb 22, Mar 4, 21, Apr 17, 21, 25, 26, 28,
    May 1, 2, 3, 6, 12, Sep 23, 28, Oct 19, Nov 8, 17, Dec 6, 14, 26; 1733: DL,
    Jan 23, Feb 12, Mar 26, 31, Apr 16, 20, GF, May 5, DL, 5, 7, BF, Aug 23,
    BFCGBH, 23, Sep 4, DL/HAY, 26, Oct 3, 6, 12, 19, 24, 25, 27, 29, Nov 1, 8,
    14, 15, HAY, 19, DL/HAY, 23, 24, 26, Dec 1, 3, 10, HAY, 13, DL/HAY, 19, 20,
    22, 28, 31; 1734: DL/HAY, Jan 2, 7, 12, 23, 29, Feb 7, DL, Apr 15, DL/HAY,
    27, DL, 29, May 15, DL/HAY, 22, 23, HAY, 27, LIF, 29, HAY, Jun 3, 5, BFHBH,
    Aug 24, GF, Sep 11, 13, 16, Oct 14, 16, 28, Dec 2, 3, 4, 5, 6, 12, 28, 31;
    1735: GF, Jan 6, 7, 13, 24, Mar 6, 13, 17, 27, 29, Apr 10, 21, 22, 24, 28,
    30, May 1, 2, 5, CG, Sep 26, Oct 3, 13, 17, Nov 6, 11, 15, 19, 28, Dec 2, 12,
    18; 1736: CG, Jan 1, 9, 10, 21, 23, Feb 23, 24, 26, Mar 2, 6, 11, 16, Apr 29,
    May 6, 8, 11, LIF, 19, CG, 20, 27, 31, Jun 4, 14, Sep 22, 29, Oct 4, 6, 8,
    20, 27, Nov 3, 23, 26, Dec 28; 1737: CG, Feb 14, Mar 24, 28, Apr 15, LIF, Jul
    26, Aug 2, 5, 9, CG, Sep 26, Oct 3, 7; 1738: CG, Jan 21, 25, Feb 2, 3, 13,

Mar 2, 7, 13, 16, 18, 21, Apr 5, 11, 12, 17, 19, 21, 24, 25, 26, 27, May 1,
    2, 3, 5, 10, 11, 12, 15, 16, 18
Tench, Henry (actor), 1731: DL, Aug 6, Nov 25; 1732: DL, Mar 21; 1733: DL, May
    3, BFCGBH, Aug 23, DL/HAY, Oct 5, Nov 26; 1734: DL/HAY, Jan 12, 29, HAY, Feb
    12, DL/HAY, 22, Mar 23, 30, DL, Apr 15, DL/HAY, 26, HAY, Jul 10
Tench, Miss (singer), 1747: GF, Jan 5
Tender Husband, The. See Steele, Sir Richard.
Tender Husband, The; or, The Artfull Wife (play, anon), 1754: SFY, Sep 18, 19,
    20, 21, 23, 24
Tenducci, Giusto Ferdinando (singer), 1758: KING'S, Nov 11, Dec 16; 1759:
    KING'S, Jan 16, Nov 13; 1760: KING'S, Jan 15, Mar 1, SOHO, 13, HAY, 27,
    KING'S, Apr 17, HIC, 29, HAY, Jun 5; 1761: SOHO, Jan 28, DL, Feb 27,
    RANELAGH, Jun 12; 1762: CG, Feb 2, DL, 26, Mar 3, 5, HAY, 16, CG, Apr 3, HAY,
    22, CHAPEL, May 18, HAY, 20, RANELAGH, Jun 11, 16, CG, Nov 1, 15; 1763: CG,
    Jan 24, Feb 24, DL, Apr 27, CG, May 3, HAY, Jun 9, CG, Oct 3, 15, Dec 12, 29;
    1764: CHAPEL, Feb 29, KING'S, Apr 5, CG, May 2, Nov 23, KING'S, 24; 1765:
    KING'S, Jan 26, Feb 15, Mar 2, 28, CG, May 1, KING'S, Dec 3; 1767: DL, Jun 3;
    1769: CG, Dec 15, 22; 1770: KING'S, Feb 2, HAY, Mar 12, KING'S, 29, CG, Apr
    7, HAY, May 3, CG, 4; 1771: KING'S, Jan 10, Feb 2, 8, 9, 28, Mar 12; 1777:
    DL, Feb 10, 13, CG, 14, Mar 19, DL, Dec 15; 1785: KING'S, May 12, CG, 12,
    KING'S, 19; 1786: CG, Oct 16; 1787: CG, Mar 12
Tenducci, Sga (actor), 1760: SOHO, Feb 14
Teniers, David (painter), 1759: DL, Jan 4; 1761: DL, Nov 3
Tennant, Miss (singer), 1800: CG, Feb 28, Mar 5, 14, 19, 21
Tennis Court, 1697: HIC, Dec 9; 1707: HIC, Apr 2; 1708: DL, Sep 7; 1734: JS,
    Apr 22, May 23; 1741: JS, Feb 20, May 11, 19; 1750: JS, Jan 25
Teno (actor), 1729: DL, Jun 24; 1730: DL, Oct 28, Nov 30, Dec 4; 1731: DL, Jun
    7, SF/BFMMO, Aug 26, Sep 8; 1732: BFMMO, Aug 23; 1733: DL, May 21, BFMMO, Aug
    23, DL/HAY, Oct 6, Dec 20; 1734: DL/HAY, Mar 16, GR, Nov 4
Teno (singer), 1707: SH, Nov 12; 1709: HA, Jul 30, SH, Aug 25, HA, Sep 3; 1710:
    YB, Apr 17, HA, Jul 22; 1711: RIW, Jul 21, GR, Sep 8; 1715: SH, Apr 6, DL,
    May 13, Jul 19, Aug 5; 1716: SH, Mar 14; 1719: DL, May 14
Teno, Miss (beneficiary), 1740: DL, May 28
Teno, Theodosia (actor, dancer), 1717: DL, Oct 10, 12, Nov 7; 1718: DL, Jan 21,
    23, Feb 6, Mar 31, Apr 28, May 6, 8, 13, 15, 16, 19, 29, 30, Jun 6, 13, 27,
    Jul 11, 18, Aug 1, 12, 15, 20, Oct 8, 14, 15, 20, 22, 24, 27, 29, Nov 4, 6,
    7, 14, 17, 19, 21, 24, 28, Dec 10, 19; 1719: DL, Jan 7, 8, 29, Feb 12, Mar
    16, Apr 11, 16, 18, 20, 21, 23, May 4, 7, 8, 9, 13, 18, 19, 21, 30, Jun 5,
    16, Jul 31, Sep 15, 22, 29, Oct 12, 15, 16, 19, 26, 30, Nov 9, 23, 25, 27,
    Dec 28; 1720: DL, Jan 13, Feb 1, 5, 12, 29, Mar 15, 29, Apr 9, 19, 25, 26,
    28, May 5, 9, 11, 12, 17, 18, 19, 21, 24, 27, 30, 31, Jun 1, 2, 6, 10, 21,
    Jul 7, 14, 21, 28, Aug 4, Sep 20, 22, 27, Oct 6, 7, 13, 22, 25, 31, Nov 23,
    30, Dec 7, 9, 14; 1721: DL, Jan 20, Feb 7, 23, Mar 7, 13, Apr 10, 11, 12, 25,
    29, May 1, 5, 8, 9, 10, 16, 19, 29, 31, Jun 16, 20, 27, Aug 1, 4, 8, 18, Sep
    14, 19, Oct 13, 16, 24, Nov 17, 27, Dec 18, 20, 22, 29; 1722: DL, Jan 5, 10,
    19, 24, Mar 10, 28, Apr 5, 10, 18, 25, 27, 30, May 1, 4, 5, 7, 9, 11, 15, 26,
    28, 29, Jun 19, 26, Jul 10, Sep 20, 27, Oct 5, 9, 10, 12, 16, 29, 30, Dec 4;
    1723: DL, Jan 3, 18, 21, Feb 5, 28, Mar 21, 25, Apr 29, May 2, 4, 8, 9, 15,
    16, 17, 21, 30, Jun 6, 25, Jul 12, 16, 19, 23, 26, 30, Aug 2, 6, 9, 12, 16,
    Sep 21, Oct 1, 9, 28, Nov 1, 14, 16, 18, 20, 21, 22, 23, 26, Dec 31; 1724:
    DL, Jan 3, 27, Feb 10, 11, 17, Mar 9, 16, Apr 7, 10, 11, 13, 15, 18, 22, 28,
    May 1, 2, 4, 8, 9, 12, 14, 16, 18, 22, Sep 17, Oct 8, 10, 14, 16, 29, Nov 2,
    10, 14, 21, 23, 27, Dec 7; 1725: DL, Jan 29, Feb 4, 20, Mar 31, Apr 2, 5, 15,
    16, 19, 21, 22, 23, 27, 29, 30, May 1, 3, 4, 8, 11, 21, Sep 7, 14, 16, 25,
    28, Oct 7, 12, 14, 15, 18, 19, 23, 25, 28, Nov 2, 6, 16, 19, 22, 29, Dec 6,
    13, 16; 1726: DL, Jan 22, 25, Feb 11, Mar 17, 21, Apr 18, 19, 21, 22, 25, 26,
    29, May 2, 7, 11, 12, 13, 20, 23, Sep 10, 13, 17, 20, 27, 29, Oct 1, 6, 11,
    13, 18, 27, Nov 2, 15, 26, Dec 6, 7, 12, 14, 17, 30; 1727: DL, Jan 20, Feb 8,
    10, 18, 20, 27, Mar 23, Apr 6, 8, 15, 17, 18, 19, 20, 21, 26, 27, 29, May 2,
    4, 5, 8, 10, 15, 17, 22, 24, 26, Sep 14, 19, Nov 14
Teno's scholar (singer), 1710: HA, Jul 22, 27; 1715: DL, May 24
Tent, Mrs (actor), 1730: HAY, Jan 16
Teodolinda. See Andreozzi, Gaetano.
Teraminta. See Smith, John Christopher.
Teredellas, Domenico (composer), 1746: KING'S, Dec 6; 1747: KING'S, Mar 24;
    1750: KING'S, Apr 10; 3753: KING'S, Apr 30
--Bellerephon, 1747: KING'S, Mar 24, 28, 31, Apr 4, 7, 11, 21, 25, 28, May 2
--Mitridate (opera), 1746: KING'S, Dec 2, 6, 9, 13, 16, 20, 23, 27, 30; 1747:
    KING'S, Jan 3, 6, 10, May 9, 16, 23, 30
Terence, 1687: DLORDG, Mar 26; 1717: WS, Apr 23, DL, Jul 9; 1721: WS, Nov 21;
    1722: WS, Jan 23; 1724: WS, Nov 13; 1727: WS, Dec 14; 1732: CL, May 10, FUL,
    Nov 13, CL, 22; 1733: ACDL, Mar 14; 1734: SS, Apr 10, YB, Dec 12; 1736: WS,

831

Feb 6, Dec 3; 1743: LIF, Feb 28, WS, Nov 25; 1749: HAY, May 27, Jun 24; 1751:
  CHA, May 24
--Adelphi, 1724: WS, Nov 13; 1734: WS, Feb 28
--Andria, 1721: WS, Nov 21; 1722: GR, Oct 27, 29; 1732: CL, May 10; 1734: SS,
  Apr 10; 1735: WS, Dec 5; 1736: WS, Feb 6; 1745: WS, Jan 11; 1749: HAY, May
  27, Jun 24
--Eunuch, The, 1717: DL, Jul 9, 11; 1722: WS, Jan 23, 26; 1732: FUL, Nov 13,
  15, 17, CL, 22, WS, Dec 8; 1733: WS, Feb 6, ACDL, Mar 14; 1734: KING'S, Jan
  26; 1736: WS, Dec 3; 1739: CL, Feb 12; 1751: CHA, May 24
--Phormio, 1717: WS, Apr 23; 1727: WS, Dec 14; 1728: WS, Jan 15; 1730: CHA, Apr
  22, May 1; 1734: YB, Dec 12; 1743: WS, Nov 25
Tergi il pianto (song), 1779: DL, Mar 12
Terodat (actor), 1749: HAY, Nov 14; 1750: DL, May 22
Terpsichore (dance), 1741: DL, Apr 1, 14
Terpsicore. See Handel, George Frederic.
Terrace, 1777: CG, Mar 17; 1793: CG, May 15
Terrier (dancer), 1759: CG, Dec 10; 1760: CG, Jan 16, Apr 11
Terrier, Mrs (dancer), 1759: CG, Dec 10; 1760: CG, Jan 16
Terriot (dancer), 1760: CG, Jan 18
Terriot, Master (dancer), 1760: HAY, Jun 5
Terriot, Miss (dancer), 1760: CG, Jan 18
Terriot, Mrs (dancer), 1760: CG, Jan 18
Terry Woo. See Tarewoo.
Terry's (ordinary), 1767: DL, Oct 22
Terryll (spectator), 1668: BRIDGES, Dec 18; 1669: BRIDGES, Jan 16, 29, NONE,
  Feb 10
Terzetto (dance), 1760: HAY, Jun 5; 1764: KING'S, Mar 10, 20, 29, May 15
Terzetto (song), 1791: KING'S, Apr 16
Tesoro, Il. See Mazzinghi, Joseph.
Test of Love, The. See Robinson.
Tetley, Master (dancer), 1761: HAY, Jun 23, Jul 30, Aug 3; 1767: DL, Jan 24
Tetley, Miss (dancer), 1761: HAY, Jun 23, 27, Jul 30, Aug 3; 1762: DL, Nov 23;
  1764: KING'S, Mar 10, 20, 29, 31, May 5, DL, Oct 20; 1765: DL, Apr 16, 23,
  May 2, 11, 13, 15, 16, 18, 21, Oct 5, 8; 1766: DL, Apr 30, May 9, 10, 19, 20,
  Sep 23; 1767: DL, Mar 17, Apr 4, 27, May 15, 27, 30, Jun 1, Sep 12, 17; 1768:
  DL, Apr 6, 28, May 9, 25, Aug 18, Dec 7; 1769: DL, Mar 13, Apr 18, Dec 30;
  1770: DL, May 5, Dec 12
Tett, Benjamin (actor), 1791: CG, Oct 20; 1792: CG, Feb 28, DLKING'S, May 23;
  1793: CG, Sep 23, Oct 2, 24, Nov 28; 1794: DL, May 16, Jun 21, CG, Oct 22,
  DL, 27, Dec 20; 1795: DL, Jan 19, CG, Apr 24, Sep 21, Oct 15, DL, 30, Nov 11,
  CG, 30, DL, Dec 10, CG, 21; 1796: DL, Jan 8, 11, Mar 3, 12, Apr 30, CG, Sep
  19, 26, DL, 29, CG, Oct 6, DL, 19, CG, Dec 19; 1797: DL, Jan 7, 20, CG, Feb
  18, DL, May 18, CG, 18, Oct 16, Nov 2, DL, 8, CG, Dec 26; 1798: DL, Jan 16,
  Feb 20, Oct 6, CG, 8, 15, Nov 12, DL, 14, 26, Dec 4, CG, 11, 15, 26, DL, 29,
  31; 1799: DL, Jan 19, CG, 21, DL, 28, CG, 29, DL, Feb 4, CG, 11, DL, Mar 2,
  CG, Apr 2, 3, 9, DL, 16, CG, 23, DL, 23, 29, CG, May 4, DL, 24, CG, Sep 30,
  Oct 7, DL, 14, CG, 24, DL, Nov 14, Dec 11, CG, 23; 1800: DL, Jan 1, CG, 16,
  DL, Mar 11, 13, Apr 29
Teuzzone. See Ariosti, Attilio.
Teyfer (Teyfey) (gallery doorkeeper), 1724: LIF, May 26; 1725: LIF, May 25
Thais led the way (song), 1791: CG, Mar 25; 1792: CG, Mar 7; 1794: CG, Mar 14
Thamas Kouli Kan, The Persian Hero; or, The Distress'd Princess (farce, anon),
  1741: BFTY, Aug 22
Thames and Augusta (song), 1731: SFLH, Sep 8
Thames River, 1662: THAMES, Aug 23; 1684: THAMES, Jan 24
Thames St, 1702: PR, Jun 30
Thanet, Earl of. See Sackville, Tufton.
Thanks to my Brethren (song), 1789: CG, Mar 27
Thanksgiving Day Music (music), 1748: HAY, Dec 9
That you alone my heart possess (song), 1698: NONE, Sep 0
Thatched House Tavern, 1749: CG, Apr 28; 1750: DL, Nov 28; 1768: DL, Jun 21;
  1770: HAY, Mar 12; 1773: CG, Dec 23; 1787: CG, Jun 15
Theatre Coffee House, 1740: DL, May 2; 1742: DL, Feb 24; 1780: HAY, Jul 27
Theatre Tavern, 1732: GF, Nov 29; 1733: GF, Apr 20
Theatre, The (play, anon), 1720: LIF, Apr 22, 23
Theatrical Campaign, The (pamphlet), 1767: DL, Jan 1
Theatrical Candidates, The. See Garrick, David.
Theatrical Disquisitions; or, a Review of the late Riot at Drury Lane Theatre
  (pamphlet), 1763: DL, Feb 1
Theatrical Entertainments Consistent with Society, Morality and Religion
  (pamphlet), 1767: DL, Jan 1
Theatrical Fund, 1767: CG, Dec 9, 10; 1769: CG, Dec 19, 20; 1770: DL, May 24

Theatrical Glee (song), 1784: CG, May 7
Theatrical Manager, The (book), 1751: DL, Jan 1
Theatricus (critic), 1776: DL, May 27
Theatricus, C V (critic), 1766: DL, Jan 6
Theatricus, G F (critic), 1765: DL, Dec 23; 1766: DL, Jan 6, 8, Mar 11
Their bodies are buried in Peace (song), 1786: DL, Mar 10; 1789: DL, Mar 18;
   1790: DL, Feb 26; 1791: DL, Mar 23; 1792: KING'S, Feb 24; 1793: KING/HAY, Feb
   22; 1794: DL, Apr 10
Their looks are such that mercy flows (song), 1695: DG, Apr 0
Their sound is gone (song), 1793: KING/HAY, Feb 20; 1794: DL, Mar 19
Thelwall (silk mercer), 1777: DL, Mar 11; 1778: DL, Mar 30; 1779: DL, Mar 16
Thelwall, John (prologuist), 1794: CG, Feb 5
Thelyphthora. See Pilon, Frederick.
Themistocles, the Lover of His Country. See Madden, Samuel.
Then, beautious nymph, look from above (song), 1694: DLORDG, Feb 0
Then come, kind Damon (song), 1697: DG, Jun 0
Then round about the starry throne (song), 1789: CG, Mar 27; 1790: CG, Feb 26;
   1791: CG, Mar 11; 1792: CG, Mar 2; 1793: CG, Mar 6; 1794: CG, Mar 12; 1795:
   CG, Mar 25; 1796: CG, Feb 24, 26, Mar 2; 1797: CG, Mar 15; 1798: CG, Mar 2;
   1799: CG, Feb 20; 1800: CG, Mar 5
Then sent he Moses (song), 1794: DL, Apr 10
Then shall be brought to pass (song), 1793: KING/HAY, Feb 20; 1794: DL, Mar 19
Then shall the Eyes (song), 1793: KING/HAY, Feb 20; 1794: DL, Mar 19
Then, undaunted Briton (song), 1793: KING/HAY, Mar 13
Then when the Sun (song), 1789: CG, Apr 3
Theobald, Lewis, 1708: DL, May 31; 1715: LIF, Oct 24; 1716: LIF, Feb 21; 1718:
   LIF, Jan 14, Mar 22; 1719: LIF, Feb 28, Nov 21, Dec 10; 1724: LIF, Feb 24;
   1725: LIF, Jan 21; 1726: LIF, Jan 14; 1727: LIF, Jan 16, Feb 13, DL, Dec 13;
   1731: LIF, Apr 3; 1733: CG, Apr 4; 1734: DL, Dec 12; 1739: CG, Apr 10, DL,
   Sep 26; 1740: CG, Dec 13; 1741: CG, Apr 9, HAY, 16, CG, May 15; 1742: LIF,
   Jan 29; 1745: DL, Jan 17; 1767: CG, Apr 24; 1770: DL, May 11; 1778: CG, Oct
   14; 1791: CG, Jun 6
--Apollo and Daphne; or, The Burgomaster Tricked, 1726: LIF, Jan 14, 15, 17,
   18, 19, 20, 21, 22, 24, 25, 26, 27, 28, 29, Feb 1, 2, 3, 4, 5, 7, 8, 9, 10,
   11, 12, 14, 15, 16, 17, 18, 24, 26, 28, Mar 1, 3, 5, 7, 8, 12, 14, 15, 17,
   22, 26, 29, Sep 30, Oct 14, 26, Nov 12, 17, Dec 2; 1727: LIF, Jan 7, 14, 28,
   Feb 4, May 23, Jun 1, Oct 12, 13, 14, 20, Nov 4, 22, Dec 20, 27; 1728: LIF,
   Jan 3, 27, Nov 23, 25, Dec 16, 26, 27, 28; 1729: LIF, Feb 5, Mar 29, Oct 15,
   17, 25, 29, Nov 15, 18, 22, Dec 12, 20, 26; 1730: LIF, Jan 24, 28, Sep 25,
   28, Oct 29, 31, Nov 5, Dec 12, 14, 16, 17; 1731: LIF, Mar 23, 27, Nov 6, 9,
   11, Dec 2, 4, 21, 28, 31; 1732: LIF, Jan 7, 11, 13, 25, 29, Feb 2, 3, 14, 28,
   May 26, LIF/CG, Oct 4, 6, 11, 20, 27, Nov 1, 4, 6, 17, 18, 22, Dec 27, 28;
   1733: CG, Oct 13, 16, 20, 23, 25, 27, 29, Nov 3, 5, 6, 10, 17, 24, 27, 29,
   Dec 1, 7, 14, 18, 22, 26, 27; 1734: CG, Jan 1, 2, 5, 8, 24, Apr 1; 1735: CG,
   Oct 17, 18, 20, 22, 24, 29, 31, Nov 4, 5; 1736: CG, Jan 1, 5, 6, 7, 8, 10,
   14, 15, Nov 3, 4, 5, 8, 15, Dec 30; 1737: CG, Feb 7; 1739: CG, Oct 3, 4, 5,
   6, 8, 9, 27, Nov 12, 16, Dec 28, 29; 1748: CG, Mar 3, 5, 7, 10, 12, 15, 17,
   19, 22, 26, 29, Apr 2, 11, 12, 19, 23, 25, 26, Oct 27, 29, 31, Nov 1, 3, 5,
   9, 10, 11, 15, Dec 2, 3, 5, 9, 17, 19, 20, 23, 28, 29, 30, 31; 1749: CG, Jan
   2, 25, 26, 27, 28, 31, Feb 1, 2, 3, 4, 6, 7, 9, HAY, 10, CG, 11, 13, 14, 16,
   18, 20, 21, 23, 25, 28, Mar 2, 7, 27, 28, Apr 1, 6, 8, 13, 15, 26, May 9, 11,
   Oct 30, 31, Nov 7; 1750: CG, Nov 29, 30, Dec 26, 29, 31; 1751: CG, Jan 8, 9,
   11, 16, 22, 25, Feb 8, 12, 15, 19, 21, 26, 28, Mar 2, 5, 7, 9, 12, Dec 4, 5,
   6, 7, 11, 12, 17, 18, 21, 23, 28, 31; 1752: CG, Jan 7, 11, 13, 15, 17, 23,
   Oct 26, 27, Nov 1, Dec 26, 30; 1753: CG, Jan 1, 3; 1762: CG, Jan 28, 29, Feb
   1, 3, 4, 6, 11, 15, 17, 18, 22, 25, Mar 1, 2, 4, 8, 9, Apr 15, 20, May 11;
   1768: CG, Dec 26, 27, 28, 29, 30, 31; 1769: CG, Jan 2, 3, 4, 5, 7, 9, 10, 11,
   12, 13, 21, 24, 25, 26, 27, 28; 1778: CG, Oct 14
--Death of Hannibal, The, 1739: DL, Sep 26
--Double Falsehood, The; or, The Distressed Lovers, 1727: DL, Dec 13, 14, 15,
   16, 18, 19, 20, 21, 22, 26; 1728: DL, Jan 9, Mar 18, May 1; 1729: DL, Apr 21;
   1740: CG, Dec 13, 15; 1741: CG, May 15; 1767: CG, Apr 24, May 6; 1770: DL,
   Mar 31, May 11; 1791: CG, Jun 6
--Fatal Secret, The, 1733: CG, Apr 4, 5, 6
--Happy Captive, The, 1741: HAY, Apr 16, 23; 1742: LIF, Jan 29; 1745: DL, Jan
   17
--Harlequin Captive, 1744: MFDSB, May 1
--Harlequin Sorcerer (pantomime), 1725: LIF, Jan 21, 22, 23, 25, 26, 27, 28,
   29, Feb 1, 2, 3, 4, 5, 6, 8, 9, 11, 13, 15, 16, 18, 20, 22, 23, Mar 16, Apr
   3, 6, 27, May 26, Nov 13, 15, 16, Dec 4, 18, 20, 21, 30; 1726: LIF, Jan 1,
   Apr 16, Sep 23, Oct 7, Dec 9, 12, 19, 21, 22, 26, 27, 28, 29; 1727: LIF, Jun
   7, Sep 29, Oct 4, 28, Dec 22, 26; 1728: LIF, Oct 14, 16, Nov 8; 1729: LIF,

Apr 18, 21, 29, Nov 1, 11, 14; 1730: LIF, Oct 9, 16; 1731: LIF, Mar 4, 6, 8,
Nov 13, 16, Dec 8, 11, 13; 1732: LIF, Jan 8, 10, 21, 24, 26, Feb 26; 1741:
TC, Aug 4; 1752: CG, Feb 1, 11, 13, 15, 17, 18, 20, 22, 24, 25, 27, 29, Mar
2, 3, 5, 10, 21, 31, Apr 2, 4, 7, 9, 11, 14, 16, 21, 23, 27, May 1, 9, 11,
15, DL, Dec 26; 1753: CG, Jan 13, 15, 16, 17, 18, 19, 20, 22, 23, 24, 25, 26,
27, 29, 31, Feb 1, 2, 3, 5, 7, 8, 9, 10, 12, 13, 14, 15, 16, 17, 19, 20, Mar
6, 13, 20, 27, Apr 3, 26, May 4, 16, 19, 23, 26, Oct 15, 16, 17, 19, 20, 22,
24, 26, 27, 29, 31, Nov 1, 2, 5, 6, 7, 8, 9, 10, 12, 13, 17, 21, 23, 26, 27,
28, 29, Dec 26, 28; 1754: CG, Jan 1, 3, 17, Feb 9, 16, 21, Mar 5, 9, 12, 16,
19, 21, Apr 16, May 10, 22, Dec 2, 4, 6, 28; 1755: CG, Jan 2, 6, 9, 13, 17,
20; 1757: CG, Jan 8, 10, 12, 13, 15, 17, 18, 19, 20, 21, 22, 24, 25, 26, Feb
2, 3, 4, 5, 7, 9, 15, 17, 19, 22, 26, Mar 3, 5, 8, 10, 12, Apr 11, May 5, 7,
23, 24, Sep 30, Oct 3, 5, 7, 8, 10, 15, 17, 25, 26, 29, 31, Nov 9, 12, 15,
26, Dec 1, 3, 26; 1758: CG, Jan 7, 11, 14, 17, 19, 23, 25, Mar 27, Apr 1, 6,
15, 18, 25, May 6, 12, 15, 16, 18, Dec 23, 27, 28; 1759: CG, Jan 1, 4, 10,
13, 17, 20, Feb 1, 7, 10, 12; 1762: CG, Oct 23, Nov 1, 3, 4, 5, 6, 8, 9, 11,
16, 18, 22, 23, 30, Dec 2, 4, 6, 27, 28; 1763: CG, Jan 4, 6, 8, 11, 12, 13,
14, 17, 20, Oct 14, 15, 17, 18, 19, 21, 24, 31, Nov 4, 5, 7, 9, 14, 16, 21,
26, 28, 30, Dec 2, 6, 10, 13, 17, 20, 26, 27, 28; 1764: CG, Apr 26, Nov 5, 6,
8, 9, 12, 13, 15, 19, 20, 22, 28, 29, 30, Dec 3, 4, 10; 1765: CG, Jan 15, 17,
18, 22, 23, 28, 29, Feb 15, Apr 25, May 9, 17; 1772: CG, Dec 26, 28, 29, 30,
31; 1773: CG, Jan 1, 2, 4, 5, 6, 7, 8, 9, 11, 12, 14, 16, 19, 20, 21, 22, 23,
25, 27, 28, Feb 1, 3, 4, 5, 11, 15, 16, 18, 19, 22, Mar 20, 29, Apr 21, May
5, 6, 7, 12, 13, 17, 21, 28, 31, Oct 6, 7, 11, 20, Dec 16; 1774: CG, Apr 26,
May 6; 1780: CG, Dec 29; 1789: CG, Dec 21; 1790: CG, Nov 15; 1793: CG, Oct 2;
1796: CG, Mar 15, Oct 24; 1798: CG, Jun 2; 1799: CG, May 13
--Lady's Triumph, The, 1718: LIF, Mar 22, 24, 25, 27, Apr 1, 14, 17, Jun 2
--Merlin; or, The Devil of Stonehenge (pantomime), 1734: DL, Dec 12, 13, 14,
16, 17, 18; 1739: WF, Aug 31
--Orestes, 1731: LIF, Mar 30, Apr 3, 6, 10, 19, 20, 27
--Pan and Syrinx, 1718: LIF, Jan 14, 18, 23, 25, 28, Feb 8, 13, 15, 27, Mar 6,
17, May 9, 22, Oct 17, 27; 1726: LIF, Oct 24, 28, Nov 2, 10
--Perfidious Brother, The, 1716: LIF, Feb 21, 23, 25, 27
--Perseus and Andromeda; or, The Cheats of Harlequin (or, The Flying Lovers),
1728: DL, Nov 14, 15, 16, 18, 19, 20, 21, 22, 23, 25, 26, 27, 28, 29, 30, Dec
2, 3, 4, 5, 6, 7, 9, 10, 12, 13, 14, 16, 17, 18, 19, 20, 26, 27, 28, 30, 31;
1729: DL, Jan 23, 24, Feb 3, 13, 22, 25, Mar 15, 17, 22, 24, Apr 7, 16, 26,
29, Oct 25, Nov 1, 12, 15; 1730: DL, Jan 1, 2, LIF, 2, 3, 5, 6, 7, 8, 9, 10,
12, 13, 14, 15, 16, 17, Feb 3, 4, 5, 6, 7, 9, 10, 12, 14, 16, 17, 19, 21, DL,
23, LIF, 23, 24, DL, 24, LIF, 26, DL, 26, LIF, 28, Mar 2, 3, 5, 7, 10, 12,
14, 30, Apr 1, 3, 4, 7, 9, 11, 14, 16, 18, 21, 28, May 2, 5, 8, 12, 19, 22,
26, Jun 3, 8, 12, TC, Aug 10, SFY, Sep 8, LIF, Dec 15, 18, 19, 21, 22; 1731:
LIF, Feb 12, 13, 15, 16, 17, 18, 19, 20, 22, 23, 24, 25, 26, Mar 16, 20, GF,
Apr 1, LIF, Jun 1, Nov 18, 19, 20, 22, 23, 24, DL, 25, 26, 27, Dec 4, 6, 7,
9, LIF, 18, 20; 1732: LIF, Jan 1, 3, 4, 6, 7, DL, 26, LIF, Feb 10, 11, 12,
24, Mar 2, 16, 18, DL, 21, 25, Apr 10, LIF, May 13, 19, Jun 2, LIF/CG, Nov
24, 25, 27, 28, 29, Dec 2, 5; 1733: LIF/CG, Mar 26, 27, LIF, Apr 28; 1734:
CG, Jan 25, 26, 28, 29, 31, Feb 1, 2, 4, 5, 6, 7, 8, 9, 11, 12, 16, 19, 23,
May 22; 1735: CG/LIF, Feb 13, 14, 15, 17, 18, Mar 8, 10, 17, Apr 7; 1736: CG,
Mar 6, 8, 9, Nov 25, 26, 29, 30, Dec 2, 4, 9, 10, 14, 29, 31; 1737: CG, Jan
1, 3, 4, Feb 4, 10; 1739: CG, Jan 20, 22, 23, 24, 25, 26, 27, 29, 31, Feb 1,
2, 3, 5, 6, 7, 8, 13, 17, 28, Mar 2, 6, 12, Apr 2, 14, BFHCL, Aug 23, CG, Dec
4, 5, 7, 20; 1740: CG, Jan 10, 12, 19, 22, 24, 26, 29, 31, Feb 4, 9; 1741:
CG, Feb 28, Mar 3, Apr 3, 24, Nov 26, 27, 28, Dec 1, 3, 4, 5, 7, 8, 10, 12,
18, 22, 26, 31; 1742: CG, Jun 2; 1743: CG, Jan 8, 10, 11, 12, 13, 14, 15, 18,
20, 22, Feb 1, 8, 12, 15, 19, 26, Mar 1, 5, 12, 19, Apr 5, 16, 19, 23, May
17; 1749: CG, Nov 23, 24, 25, 27, 28, 29, Dec 1, 2, 4, 5, 6, 7, 8, 9, 11, 12,
13, 14, 15, 16, 18, 19, 20, 21, 22, 23, 26, 27, 28, 29, 30; 1750: CG, Jan 1,
2, 3, 4, 5, 6, 8, 9, 10, 11, 12, 13, 15, 16, 17, 18, 19, 20, 22, 23, 24, 25,
26, 27, 29, 31, Feb 1, 2, 3, 5, 6, Mar 13, 15, 22, 24, Apr 7, 16, 18, 20, May
10, Oct 29, 30, 31, Nov 3, 7, 9, 15, 16, 19, 20, 22, 23, 28, Dec 12, 14, 19;
1751: CG, Jan 1, 2, 24, 28, Feb 1, 2, 6, Mar 14, Apr 9, May 15, Sep 30, Oct
2, 4, 5, 8, 12, 14, 16, 19, 22, 24, Nov 1, Dec 13, 14, 19, 26; 1752: CG, Jan
1, 6, 8, 20, Oct 10, 11, 14, 16, 17, 20; 1764: CG, Jan 14, 16, 17, 18, 19,
20, 21, 23, 24, 25, 26, 27, 28, 31, Feb 1, 2, 3, 4, 6, 7, 8, 9, 10, 11, 13,
14, 15, 16, 17, Mar 3, 5, 6, 8, 10, 13, 15, May 19, Oct 18, 19, 20, 22, 24,
25, 26, 30, Dec 19, 20, 21, 22, 26, 28, 31; 1765: CG, Jan 1, 3, 5, 8, 12, Oct
9, 10, 11, 14, 16, 17, 18, 21, 23, 24, 26, Dec 23; 1766: CG, Jan 6, 8, May
13, 19; 1767: CG, Jan 29, May 23, Sep 19, 25, 28, Oct 8; 1778: CG, Oct 14;
1780: CG, Dec 29
--Persian Princess, The; or, The Royal Villain, 1708: DL, May 31, Jun 1
--Rape of Proserpine, The; or, The Birth and Adventures of Harlequin

(pantomime), <u>1727</u>: LIF, Feb 7, 13, 14, 16, 18, 20, 21, 23, 25, 27, 28, Mar 2,
4, 6, 7, 9, 14, 18, 21, 25, Apr 4, 8, 11, 13, 15, 18, 22, May 5, 25, 26, Jun
5, 9, 14, Nov 9, 10, 11, 13, 14, 15, 18, 20, 24, 25, 27, 28, 29, 30, Dec 1,
2, 4, 5, 6; <u>1728</u>: LIF, Jan 5, 10, 11, 13, 16; <u>1729</u>: LIF, Jan 18, 20, 22, 23,
25, Feb 8, Mar 15, 18, 22, 25, Apr 14, Nov 4, 5, 8, 10, 20, 24, Dec 16, 19;
<u>1730</u>: LIF, Nov 7, 9, 14, 16, 17, 18, 19, 21, 26, 27, 28, 30, Dec 1, 3, 8, 10,
26, 28; <u>1731</u>: LIF, Jan 1, 2, Feb 1, 2, 10, Mar 13, Jun 4, Oct 4, 8, 29, 30,
Dec 15, 16, 27; <u>1732</u>: LIF, Jan 14, 15, Feb 16, 17, 18, 19, Mar 4, 11, 13, 14,
Apr 15, 20, May 24, LIF/CG, Nov 8, 9, 10, 11, 13; <u>1733</u>: LIF/CG, Jan 1; <u>1734</u>:
CG/LIF, Dec 30, 31; <u>1735</u>: CG/LIF, Jan 1, 2, 3, 4, 6, 7, 9, 10, 16, 20, 21,
23, 24, 25, 27, 28, 31, Feb 1, 8, 10, 11, Mar 4, 27, May 23, 30, Jun 6, 11,
17, CG, Nov 6, 7, 8, 12, 17, 18, 19, 21, 22, 24, 26, 27, 29, Dec 1, 3, 4, 6,
8, 13, 15, 26, 27, 30; <u>1736</u>: CG, Oct 8, 11, 13, 15, LIF, 18, CG, 22, 23, 25,
29, 30, Nov 1, 17, 18, 22, Dec 16, 18, 20, 21, 27; <u>1737</u>: CG, Jan 8, 20, 25,
27; <u>1738</u>: CG, Nov 18, 20, 21, 22, 23, 24, 25, 27, 28, 29, 30, Dec 1, 2, 4,
26, 27, 30; <u>1739</u>: CG, Jan 18, Feb 16, 21, 22, 23, Mar 31, Sep 22, 25, 27, 29,
Oct 26, 29, Nov 2, 5, 17, 22, 27, 29, Dec 26, 27; <u>1740</u>: CG, Jan 3; <u>1742</u>: CG,
Jan 5, 8, 9, 12, 14, 15, 19, Feb 1, 2, 8, Mar 11, Apr 6, May 8, 21, Dec 21,
27, 28, 29; <u>1743</u>: CG, Jan 1, 4, 6, 25, 29, Feb 5, 17, 22, Mar 8, 15, 26, Apr
4, 7, 21, 26, 28; <u>1744</u>: CG, Jan 14, 17, 18, 20, 21, 23, Feb 1, 11, Apr 5, 7,
14, 24, Dec 8, 12, 15, 19, 21, 27, 28; <u>1745</u>: CG, Jan 15, 21, Feb 14, Apr 17,
29, Nov 14, 16, 18, 29, Dec 3, 4, 12, 27; <u>1746</u>: CG, Jan 9, 20, Apr 1, 15, 22,
Nov 24, 26, Dec 2, 6; <u>1759</u>: CG, Mar 1, 3, 5, 6, 8, 10, 12, 13, 15, 17, 31,
Apr 16, 19, 26, May 9, 22, 29, Nov 24, 26, 28; <u>1760</u>: CG, Jan 16, Apr 7, 11,
May 13, 21, 23, 28, Oct 20, 22, 23, 24, 25, Dec 8, 12, 17, 26, 27, 29; <u>1761</u>:
CG, Jan 1, 5, 7, 12, 15, 19, 22, 23, 26, Feb 12, 16, 23, Mar 2, 5, 10, 23,
28, Apr 9, 11, 14, 30, May 2, 7, 20, 21, 22, 25, Sep 11, 16, 23, 24, 28, 29,
Oct 2, 5, 7; <u>1763</u>: CG, Jan 26, 27, 28, Feb 1, 3, 5, 7, 9, 11, 15, 22, 28, Mar
12, Apr 25, May 23; <u>1769</u>: CG, Nov 4, 6, 7, 8, 9, 10, 11, 13, 14, 15, 16, 17,
18, 20, 22, 23, 24, 25, 27, 28, 29, 30, Dec 1, 18, 26, 27, 28, 29, 30; <u>1770</u>:
CG, Jan 1, 2, 4, 13, 15, 16, Apr 16, 18, 30, May 7, 8, 14, 21, Oct 15, 16,
18, 19, 20, 22, 29, Nov 5, 9, 20, 28, Dec 8; <u>1778</u>: CG, Oct 14; <u>1780</u>: CG, Dec
29; <u>1797</u>: CG, Jun 9; <u>1798</u>: CG, Jun 2
Theobald's Road, <u>1781</u>: DL, May 11
Theodora. See Handel, George Frederic.
Theodore, Mme (dancer), <u>1781</u>: KING'S, Nov 17, Dec 11; <u>1782</u>: KING'S, Jan 10, 29,
Feb 2, 7, 21, 23, Mar 19, Apr 11, 30, May 2, 9, 16, 25, Jun 3, 15, Nov 2, 19,
Dec 12; <u>1783</u>: KING'S, Jan 11, 16, 25, Feb 13, 15, Mar 13, 20, 27, Apr 10, May
1, 6, 8, 31, Jun 3, 14, 28, Dec 6, 16; <u>1784</u>: KING'S, Jan 17, Feb 3, 7, 14,
26, Mar 6, 11, 18, 25, Apr 24, May 13, 20, 29, Jul 3; <u>1791</u>: PAN, Feb 17, Mar
19; see also D'Auberval, Mme Jean
Theodosius. See Lee, Nathaniel.
Theorbo, Great (music), <u>1707</u>: HIC, Apr 2
There beneath a lowly shade (song), <u>1789</u>: DL, Mar 18; <u>1790</u>: DL, Feb 26; <u>1791</u>:
DL, Mar 11, 23, 25; <u>1792</u>: KING'S, Feb 24; <u>1793</u>: KING/HAY, Feb 22; <u>1794</u>: DL,
Apr 10
There in myrtle shades (song), <u>1791</u>: CG, Mar 25
There in old Arden's inmost shade (song), <u>1776</u>: DL, Mar 20
There is one black and solemn hour (song), <u>1686</u>: DL, Jan 0
There let Hymen oft appear (song), <u>1791</u>: CG, Mar 18, 30; <u>1792</u>: CG, Feb 24;
<u>1794</u>: CG, Mar 21
There let the pealing organ (song), <u>1792</u>: CG, Mar 21
There the silvered waters roam (song), <u>1796</u>: DL, May 25; <u>1797</u>: DL, Jun 6; <u>1798</u>:
DL, May 23; <u>1799</u>: DL, Apr 19, May 7
There was a jolly beggar (song), <u>1683</u>: DL, Dec 0
There was an Irish lad (song), <u>1795</u>: CG, May 16
There were shepherds (song), <u>1790</u>: DL, Mar 24; <u>1793</u>: KING/HAY, Feb 20; <u>1794</u>:
DL, Mar 19
There's my Thumb, I'll ne'er beguile ye (song), <u>1780</u>: HAY, Sep 25
There's no pleasing all (song), <u>1790</u>: DL, Apr 5
There's not a swain on the plain (song), <u>1693</u>: DLORDG, Dec 0
There's nothing so fatal as Woman (song), <u>1688</u>: DG, Apr 0
Therefore with joy (song), <u>1792</u>: KING'S, Mar 23, 28, 30
These are thy glorious works (song), <u>1794</u>: DL, Apr 10
These as they change (song), <u>1794</u>: DL, Apr 4
These delights if thou canst give (song), <u>1791</u>: CG, Mar 18; <u>1792</u>: CG, Feb 24,
Mar 21; <u>1794</u>: CG, Mar 21
These des Dames, Le (play, anon), <u>1721</u>: HAY, Apr 12
These pleasures melancholy give (song), <u>1792</u>: CG, Mar 21
Theseus. See Handel, George Frederic.
Thespian Advice (monologue), <u>1795</u>: HAY, Mar 4
Thespian Panorama, The; or, Three Hours Heart's Ease (entertainment, anon),

1795: HAY, Mar 4, 11, 13, 18, 20, DL, May 19
Thespis (pamphlet), 1766: DL, Nov 7, Dec 5; 1767: DL, Jan 16
They say there is an echo here (song), 1781: CG, Apr 3; 1782: CG, May 6, 20;
    1783: CG, May 19, HAY, Aug 1; 1784: DL, Apr 26, May 21; 1785: CG, Apr 18
They tell us that you mighty powers above (song), 1695: DG, Apr 0
They've Bit the Old One. See Cross, John Cartwright.
Thierry and Theodorat. See Fletcher, John.
Thierry, Jacques (spectator), 1662: COCKPIT, Jan 20, REDBULL, 22, 25, LIF, 29,
    VERE, Feb 6, 11, 13, LIF, 15, VERE, Mar 22, REDBULL, 25, Apr 28, COCKPIT, Oct
    21; 1663: LIF, Mar 9, NONE, 16
Thimble's Flight from the Shopboard (farce, anon), 1789: HAY, Aug 25; 1790:
    HAY, Aug 4
Thinne, Henry (spectator), 1680: DGORDL, Feb 19
This bleak and frosty Morning (song), 1792: CG, Dec 26; 1793: CG, Nov 19
This fond Sorrow (song), 1796: DL, Jun 9
This is the life of a frolicksome fellow (song), 1787: HAY, Mar 12
This Life is like a Country Dance (song), 1800: CG, Apr 26, May 2, 15
This new Creation (song), 1790: CG, Feb 24
Thomas (actor), 1723: HAY, Dec 12; 1724: HAY, Feb 5, 27; 1728: HAY, Oct 26;
    1732: UM, Jun 19; 1733: MEG, Sep 28; 1735: YB/HAY, Sep 29
Thomas (actor), 1776: CHR, Oct 4, 7, 9; 1780: HAY, Nov 13; 1782: HAY, Nov 25;
    1797: HAY, Dec 4
Thomas (butcher), 1799: HAY, Apr 17
Thomas (organist), 1772: CG, Apr 20
Thomas (singer), 1796: CG, Oct 6; 1797: CG, Feb 18, Apr 25, May 18, Dec 26;
    1798: CG, Nov 12, Dec 11, 26; 1799: CG, Jan 14, 21, 29, Mar 2, 25, Apr 2, 3,
    13, 23, May 4, 28, Jun 7, Sep 30, Oct 7, 24, Dec 10, 23; 1800: CG, Jan 16,
    Feb 10, Mar 4, Apr 5, May 1, HAY, Jul 16, 18, 21, Aug 29, Sep 1, 11
Thomas (ticket deliverer), 1799: CG, Jun 8
Thomas and Henry (song), 1732: LIF, May 4, 15
Thomas and Sally. See Bickerstaff, Isaac.
Thomas Day. See Poor Thomas Day.
Thomas, Elizabeth (actor), 1794: HAY, May 22
Thomas, Joseph (musician), 1733: SH, Mar 19; 1734: SH, Mar 28
Thomas, Master (actor), 1799: WRSG, May 17
Thomas, Miss (actor), 1782: HAY, Mar 4
Thomas, Miss (singer), 1753: DL, Mar 1, 22, Apr 27, Sep 13, Oct 6, 31, Nov 9;
    1754: DL, Jan 14, Mar 23, 28, Apr 17, May 6, 13, 15, 16, 17, 18, 22, Sep 24,
    Oct 3; 1755: DL, Mar 17, Apr 19, 26, 29, May 9, HAY, Dec 15; 1756: SOHO, Mar
    16; 1757: DL, May 11; 1762: CG, Feb 2, DL, 26, Mar 3, 5, RANELAGH, Jun 11;
    1771: MARLY, Jun 4, 6, 11, 13, 18, 20, 25, 27, Jul 6, 18, 23, 27, 30, Aug 3,
    8
Thomas, Mrs (actor), 1723: HAY, Dec 12
Thomas, Mrs (actor), 1729: HAY, Jan 31, Feb 25, Mar 28, 29, May 7, 26, 29, Jun
    14, 17, Jul 26, BFR, Aug 25, SF, Sep 8, SOU, 23, GF, Oct 31, Nov 3, 4, 6, 12,
    14, 17, 20, Dec 3, 12, 15, 17, 20; 1730: GF, Jan 5, 12, 13, Feb 9, Mar 10,
    12, 14, 21, Apr 2, 6, 7, 16, 25, 28, May 22, 26, 27, 28, Jun 2, 12, 18, 19,
    23, 25, 29, Jul 1, 6, 17, BFPG/TC, Aug 1, BFPG, 31, GF, Sep 16, 18, 21, 23,
    30, Oct 5, 12, 14, 20, 24, 26, 31, Nov 5, 6, 10, 11, 17, 19, 23, 27, Dec 1,
    7, 8, 11, 12, 15, 16, 30; 1731: GF, Jan 13, 20, 27, Feb 15, Mar 1, 2, 8, 15,
    22, Apr 1, 20, 27, 28, May 5, 7, 14, 17, Jun 1, 2, 3, TC, Aug 4, 12, SOU, Sep
    28
Thomas, Tobias (actor), 1696: DL, Sep 0; 1697: NONE, Sep 0, DL, 0; 1698: DL,
    Feb 0, Mar 0, Jun 0, DL/ORDG, Nov 0; 1699: DL, Dec 0; 1700: DL, Feb 19, Apr
    29, Oct 0; 1701: DL, Feb 4, Dec 0; 1704: DL, May 0
Thomaso. See Killigrew, Thomas.
Thompson (actor), 1778: HAY, Feb 9, Mar 23, 24, 31, Apr 29; 1781: CII, Mar 27,
    30, Apr 5; 1782: HAY, Mar 4; 1783: HAY, Jun 2, Dec 15; 1784: HAY, Jan 21;
    1785: HAY, Jan 24, 31; 1792: HAY, Feb 6
Thompson (beneficiary), 1776: CHR, Oct 4
Thompson (box-office keeper), 1777: DL, Apr 19; 1778: DL, May 4; 1779: DL, May
    7; 1780: DL, May 9; 1781: DL, May 16; 1782: Dl, May 13; 1783: DL, May 16;
    1784: DL, May 14; 1790: DL, May 29; 1799: DL, Jun 5
Thompson (dancer), 1796: DL, Oct 1, 19, 29, Nov 9, 26; 1797: DL, Jun 10
Thompson (musician), 1675: ATCOURT, Feb 15
Thompson (payee), 1790: DL, Oct 19
Thompson (ticket deliverer), 1777: CG, May 3, 9; 1778: CG, May 14; 1779: CG,
    Apr 22; 1784: CG, May 24; 1791: DL, May 31; 1792: DLKING'S, Jun 15; 1793: DL,
    Jun 6; 1795: DL, Jun 5, CG, 15; 1796: CG, Jun 6, DL, 15; 1797: CG, Jun 2, 6,
    DL, 10; 1798: CG, May 18, 19, Jun 5; 1799: CG, May 21, Jun 4, 8; 1800: CG,
    May 23, Jun 7
Thompson, Benjamin, 1794: DL, Oct 28; 1798: DL, Mar 24

--Stranger, The, <u>1798</u>: DL, Mar 17, 24, 26, 27, 29, 31, Apr 10, 11, 12, 14, 16,
    17, 19, 20, 23, 26, 28, May 1, 3, 4, 5, 8, 12, 15, 17, 22, 25, Jun 18, HAY,
    Aug 23, DL, Sep 15, Oct 29, 31, Nov 3, 8, 15, 21, 23, 28, Dec 12; <u>1799</u>: DL,
    Jan 7, 23, Mar 30, Apr 6, CG, 12, DL, 30, Nov 27, Dec 5; <u>1800</u>: DL, Jan 11,
    21, Feb 3, Mar 4, Apr 1
Thompson, Edward, <u>1766</u>: DL, Apr 16; <u>1767</u>: CG, Sep 14; <u>1773</u>: DL, Nov 9, 23;
    <u>1776</u>: CG, Feb 26, DL, Oct 9, 10, 15, CG, Nov 14; <u>1777</u>: DL, May 28, CG, Oct 17
--Hobby Horse, The, <u>1766</u>: DL, Apr 16
--St Helena; or, The Isle of Love (farce), <u>1777</u>: DL, May 28, 29
--Seraglio. See Dibdin, Charles.
--Syrens, The, <u>1776</u>: CG, Feb 26, 27, Mar 5, Apr 10, 24, 29, May 11, DL, Oct 9
Thompson, James (actor), <u>1766</u>: CG, Nov 25; <u>1767</u>: CG, Feb 19, HAY, Jul 2, 15,
    22, 31, Aug 5, Sep 12, 16; <u>1768</u>: CG, Apr 20; <u>1770</u>: CG, Apr 24, May 19, Oct
    23, Dec 29; <u>1771</u>: CG, Jan 1, Feb 6, 21, Apr 29, May 1, 15, 22, Sep 23, 25,
    30, Oct 2, 15, 19, DL, 31, CG, Nov 4, 7, DL, 16, CG, 28, Dec 10, 11, DL, 13,
    CG, 19, 20; <u>1772</u>: DL, Jan 10, CG, 21, 27, Feb 17, CG, 25, Mar 7, 10, 24, DL,
    Apr 20, CG, May 11, 13, 19, 22, DL, 25, CG, 28, Oct 13, Nov 6, Dec 5, 8;
    <u>1773</u>: CG, Feb 15, 23, Mar 15, 22, Apr 16, 19, 28, May 1, 10, 24, Sep 22, Oct
    4, 5, 8, 16, 23, 25, 27, 28, Nov 4, 8, 9, 16, 23, 25, 27, Dec 11; <u>1774</u>: CG,
    Jan 1, 3, 26, 29, Feb 11, Mar 15, 22, Apr 7, 11, 19, May 10, 16, Sep 19, 23,
    Oct 5, 7, 10, 11, 19, 20, 24, Nov 1, 4, 8, 19, 24, 29, Dec 3, 17, 20, 26, 27;
    <u>1775</u>: CG, Jan 23, Feb 21, 23, 24, Mar 2, 30, Apr 8, 22, 28, May 2, 4, 17, 18,
    20, HAY, Sep 19, CG, 29, Oct 6, 9, 12, 13, 18, 19, 23, 30, Nov 1, 13, 14, 22,
    27, 28, Dec 1, 5, 7, 9, 21, 23, 26; <u>1776</u>: CG, Jan 5, DL, 5, CG, 15, Feb 15,
    22, Mar 16, 18, 19, Apr 17, 19, 29, 30, May 1, 2, 10, 27, Sep 23, 27, 30, Oct
    4, 11, 17, 24, 25, 29, 31, Nov 4, 8, 13, 14, 30, Dec 2, 18, 26, 27; <u>1777</u>: CG,
    Feb 1, 22, Apr 14, 28, May 2, 5, Sep 22, 24, 29, Oct 6, 10, 15, 16, 20, 23,
    Nov 4, 6, 12, 13, 19, 21, 27, Dec 10, 26; <u>1778</u>: CG, Jan 15, 20, 21, Feb 2,
    10, 11, 13, 16, 23, 25, Mar 7, 10, 23, 31, Apr 22, 27, May 5, 6, 11, 13, 15,
    Sep 28, Oct 2, 14, 23, 29, 31, Nov 21, Dec 1, 2, 3, 8, 11, 12, 17, 26; <u>1779</u>:
    CG, Jan 4, 5, 6, 14, 19, 22, Feb 2, 8, 12, Apr 6, 8, 12, 23, 24, 26, 30, May
    3, 6, 10, 12, 15, 20, Sep 20, 22, 24, 27, Oct 1, 18, 20, 23, Nov 1, 9, 10,
    11, 13, 16, 19, 22, 23, 25, 30, Dec 1, 16, 18, 31; <u>1780</u>: CG, Jan 7, 17, Feb
    1, 2, 22, Mar 14, 18, 29, Apr 11, 12, 21, 25, 27, May 10, 25, 26, Sep 18, 20,
    21, 22, Oct 2, 3, 4, 9, 10, 11, 13, 19, 21, 23, 26, Nov 2, 4, 6, 14, 24, 27,
    Dec 5, 12, 15, 27, 29; <u>1781</u>: CG, Jan 4, 10, 15, 31, Mar 3, Apr 2, 21, 26, 28,
    May 7, 10, 16, 19, Sep 17, 24, 26, 28, Oct 5, 13, 16, 27, 31, Nov 5, 8, 9,
    17, Dec 5, 10, 11, 17, 18, 20, 26, 31; <u>1782</u>: CG, Jan 3, 5, 7, 8, 10, 18, 22,
    Mar 19, Apr 10, 17, 20, May 6, 11, 15, 20, 21, 28, 29, Sep 23, Oct 3, 4, 7,
    10, 14, 19, 21, 23, 29, 31, Nov 1, 2, 6, 8, 12, 18, 19, Dec 2, 12, 14, 19,
    31; <u>1783</u>: CG, Jan 1, Feb 19, Mar 29, Apr 1, 22, 23, 26, May 14, 16, 17, 19,
    22, 23, 27, Sep 22, 24, 26, Oct 1, 3, 6, 8, 9, 10, 11, 13, 14, 15, 20, 28,
    Nov 4, DL, 12, CG, 13, 27, Dec 5, 6, 8, 11, 26, 31; <u>1784</u>: CG, Jan 9, 13, 16,
    23, 26, 29, 31, Feb 5, 12, 19, 20, 23, Mar 1, 4, 6, 16, 22, 23, Apr 13, 27,
    May 4, 7, 8, 10, 11, 20, 26, HAY, 28, CG, 29, HAY, Jun 1, Aug 18, CG, Sep 17,
    20, 27, 28, Oct 1, 4, 11, 18, 22, 25, 27, 28, Nov 4, 10, 13, 16, 29, Dec 13,
    14, 22, 27, 28, 29; <u>1785</u>: CG, Jan 8, 14, 19, 21, Feb 4, 5, 8, 21, 28, Mar 3,
    7, 8, 15, 19, 29, 30, Apr 22, May 6, 7, 11, 12, Sep 21, 23, 26, 28, Oct 3, 5,
    10, 12, 14, 17, 22, 26, 27, 28, Nov 1, 2, 7, 9, 10, 14, 29, 30, Dec 1, 7, 10,
    14, 16, 22, 26, 27; <u>1786</u>: CG: Jan 3, 14, 18, 20, 31, Feb 1, 7, 8, 11, 13, 16,
    17, 18, 21, 23, 25, 28, Mar 6, 11, Apr 4, 18, 19, 20, 24, 26, May 6, 10, 15,
    23, 24, DL, 26, CG, Sep 20, 25, 27, 29, Oct 2, 6, 12, 23, 28, 30, Nov 13, 14,
    15, 18, 29, Dec 15, 23, 30; <u>1787</u>: CG, Jan 2, 11, 15, 31, Feb 6, 10, 13, 20,
    Mar 1, 5, 27, 31, Apr 10, 11, 16, 24, 25, 26, 27, 30, May 11, 14, 21, 22, 23,
    24, 25, Sep 17, 19, 21, 24, 26, 28, Oct 1, 5, 10, 11, 12, 22, 29, 31, Nov 2,
    7, 8, 9, 14, 20, 28, 30, Dec 10, 15, 27, 28; <u>1788</u>: CG, Jan 2, 3, 10, 14, 18,
    21, 25, Feb 4, 5, 14, 23, Mar 1, 10, 11, 15, 24, 26, 28, 29, Apr 1, 5, 14,
    30, May 12, 14, 22, 28, Sep 17, 22, Oct 1, 7, 10, 17, 18, 22, 27, 28, 29, Nov
    1, 10, 12, 20, 21, 22, 26, 28, Dec 1, 26, 30, 31; <u>1789</u>: CG, Jan 3, 20, 21,
    Feb 3, 10, 11, 14, 17, 21, Mar 28, Apr 14, 15, 23, 27, 30, May 2, 5, 6, 15,
    18, 19, 22, 23, 26, 28, Jun 5, 8, 15, 16, 17, Sep 14, 18, 21, 23, 25, 28, 30,
    Oct 6, 7, 9, 12, 13, 16, 24, 31, Nov 6, 9, 12, 13, 14, 16, 19, 20, 21, 24,
    27, 30, Dec 10, 21, 26, 29, 31; <u>1790</u>: CG, Jan 23, Feb 4, 11, Mar 13, 22, 27,
    Apr 7, 14, 20, 24, 29, May 5, 6, 7, 11, 18, Jun 4, 10, Sep 17, 29, Oct 1, 4,
    5, 6, 13, 15, 18, 19, 20, 23, 27, Nov 1, 3, 4, 6, 8, 15, 19, 23, 25, Dec 2,
    6, 11, 14, 23, 31; <u>1791</u>: CG, Jan 12, 26, Feb 2, 4, 11, 16, Mar 5, 14, Apr 5,
    11, 16, 28, 30, May 2, 3, 5, 11, 19, 20, Jun 10, 13, Sep 12, 16, 17, 19, 21,
    23, 30, Oct 3, 5, 6, 7, 10, 12, 17, 20, 21, 24, 28, Nov 7, 9, 19, 26, 29, Dec
    3, 15, 26; <u>1792</u>: CG, Feb 2, 18, 25, Mar 6, 10, 22, 26, Apr 10, 17, 18, May 2,
    5, 10, 15, 30, Jun 2, Sep 17, 21, 24, 26, 28, Oct 5, 10, 12, 15, 18, 19, 24,
    26, 27, 29, 30, Nov 3, 5, 6, 7, 10, 12, Dec 1, 5, 26; <u>1793</u>: CG, Jan 2, 9, 21,
    29, Feb 25, Mar 4, Apr 4, 11, 18, 24, 30, May 8, 10, 27, Jun 6, 10, Sep 17,

18, 20, 23, 25, 27, 30, Oct 1, 2, 5, 8, 9, 11, 12, 14, 16, 18, 23, 24, 29,
Nov 1, 2, 11, 12, 13, 15, 18, 22, 23, Dec 17, 18, 19, 30; 1794: CG, Jan 2, 3,
14, 22, 24, Feb 1, 22, 26, Mar 10, 17, 25, 31, May 2, 9, 14, 19, 23, 26, 28,
Jun 5, 11, Sep 15, 17, 22, 24, 26, Oct 1, 3, 15, 17, 20, 30, Nov 12, 15, Dec
6; 1795: CG, Jan 29, 31, Feb 5, 6, 14, 21, HAY, Mar 11, CG, 14, 16, 19, Apr
7, 8, 23, 25, 29, May 6, 8, 12, Jun 3, 4, 8, 10, Sep 14, 16, 21, 23, 25, 30,
Oct 5, 8, 9, 15, 16, 19, 22, 23, 24, 30, Nov 6, 7, 9, 16, 18, 27, Dec 5, 9,
21, 26; 1796: CG, Jan 4, 5, 9, 13, 23, 26, 28, Feb 1, 16, Mar 14, 15, 19, 30,
Apr 9, 19, 20, May 6, 21, 24, 28, Jun 2, 3, Sep 12, 14, 16, 19, 21, 23, 26,
30, Oct 5, 6, 7, 10, 13, 14, 20, 21, 24, 25, 26, 29, Nov 5, 7, 19, 21, 24,
Dec 1, 9, 17, 19; 1797: CG, Jan 4, 10, Feb 27, Mar 4, 13, 16, Apr 8, 19, 29,
May 4, 9, 16, 31, Jun 1, 8, 12, 13, Sep 18, 20, 22, 25, 27, 29, Oct 2, 4, 6,
11, 12, 13, 21, 23, 31, Nov 2, 3, 4, 8, 11, 13, 15, 18, 20, 22, 23, Dec 23,
27; 1798: CG, Jan 5, 11, Feb 6, 9, 12, 13, 20, Mar 20, 27, 31, Apr 19, 27,
May 4, 12, 15, 23, 30, 31, Jun 2, 6, 11, Sep 17, 19, 21, 26, 28, Oct 1, 3, 5,
8, 11, 25, 31, Nov 1, 6, 7, 9, 10, 12, 17, 20, 21, 22, Dec 8, 26; 1799: CG,
Jan 12, 28, Mar 16, Apr 9, 12, 13, 16, 23, 26, May 3, 6, 7, 13, 15, 22, 31,
Jun 1, 5, 7, 12, Sep 16, 18, 20, 23, 25, 27, 30, Oct 2, 9, 10, 14, 17, 18,
24, 25, 29, 31, Nov 7, 8, 9, 14, 30, Dec 16, 23, 30; 1800: CG, Jan 16, 29,
Feb 15, Mar 17, 27, Apr 5, 17, 22, 23, 24, 29, May 13, 17, 20, 27, Jun 2, 10,
13
Thompson, Jane (singer), 1766: CG, Dec 3; 1767: KING'S, Jan 23, CG, Apr 21,
CHAPEL, May 13, CG, Sep 16, 25, Oct 8, 22, 23, 26, 27, 30, Nov 18, Dec 2, 28,
31; 1768: CG, Jan 6, 20, KING'S, Feb 5, CG, Apr 11, May 13, 24, Sep 19, 20,
21, 26, 30, Oct 5, 17, 22, Nov 25, Dec 26; 1769: CG, Jan 21, HAY, Feb 28, CG,
Apr 5, 29, HAY, Aug 31, CG, Sep 20, 25, 27, 29, Oct 6, 20, Nov 2, 4, 7, 8,
10, 24; 1770: CG, Jan 3, 5, 13, 20, 23, Mar 8, 29, 31, Apr 7, 18, 25, May 8,
MARLY, Jun 16, Jul 17, RANELAGH, 20, MARLY, 24, Aug 7, 14, 28, CG, Sep 24,
26, 28, Oct 5, 8, 15, 16, 29, Nov 22; 1771: CG, Mar 14, Apr 6, 30, MARLY, May
23, CG, 30, MARLY, Jun 27, Jul 18, 27, Aug 3, 8, 10, Sep 12, 17, DL, Dec 6;
1772: HAY, Mar 16, DL, 23, MARLY, Aug 20, 25, 28, Sep 1, 7; 1773: MARLY, May
27, Jul 8, 15, 22, 29, Aug 26, 27, Sep 3, CG, 27, Oct 21, 23, Nov 12, Dec 8,
13; 1774: CG, Jan 29, Feb 7, 17, Mar 12, Apr 7, HAY, Jun 7, Aug 8, MARLY, 18,
HAY, Sep 6, 19, 30
Thompson, Mary Anne (actor, singer), 1791: HAY, Dec 12; 1792: HAY, Feb 20;
1798: HAY, Mar 26
Thompson, Mrs (actor), 1733: HAY, Mar 19; 1736: HAY, Feb 16; 1738: DL, Jan 11,
13, 19, 20, 28, Feb 1, 3, 6, 23, Mar 4, 9, 13, 14, 16, 23, Apr 21, 22, 24,
26, May 1, 2, 6, 11, 18, 19, 22, 24, 25, 30, 31, Oct 30; 1739: DL, Feb 28,
Mar 3, 10, 13, Apr 10, 12, May 2, 26, Sep 8, 13, 26, Oct 15, 19, 26, Nov 1,
28; 1740: DL, Jan 5, 29, Feb 13, Apr 11, 29, Oct 13, 14, 15, 16, 27, 31, Dec
4, 10, 13, 19, 26; 1741: DL, Mar 17, Apr 22, Oct 12, 21, 27, Nov 11, 28, Dec
14, 18; 1742: DL, Jan 6, Mar 13, May 8, Sep 21; 1743: DL, Feb 4, 11, Nov 8,
10, 26; 1744: DL, Feb 1, 3, Oct 2, 17, HAY, Dec 17; 1745: DL, Dec 17; 1747:
DL, Jan 24, Nov 2, 13, 16
Thompson, Mrs (dancer), 1796: DL, Oct 1, 29, Nov 1, 16
Thompson, Mrs (spectator), 1661: VERE, Jun 27
Thompson, Ned (casualty), 1748: DL, Mar 21
Thompson, Samuel, Ann and Peter (music publishers), 1786: CG, Mar 18
Thompson, T (actor), 1729: LIF, Oct 3; 1730: LIF, Jan 2, May 14, Sep 21, Dec
15; 1731: LIF, Apr 24, May 28, Sep 27, Nov 18; 1732: LIF, May 17, LIF/CG, Oct
30, Nov 24; 1733: LIF/CG, May 14; 1734: CG, Jan 25, Feb 26, HAY, Jun 5; 1735:
CG/LIF, Jan 3, Feb 13, Mar 27, May 19, CG, Nov 6; 1736: CG, Mar 6, May 10,
Oct 8, 20; 1737: CG, May 6, BF, Aug 23, SF, Sep 7; 1738: CG, Jan 3, Apr 27,
Oct 4, 6, Nov 18, Dec 9; 1739: CG, Jan 3, 6, 15, 20, Mar 2, DL, 15, CG, 27,
May 8, 11, 21, 28, 29, BFH, Aug 23, CG, Oct 25, Dec 4, 10; 1740: CG, Feb 12,
Apr 30, Sep 26, Oct 10; 1741: CG, Jan 5, Feb 24, 28, Apr 24, Oct 24, Nov 7,
26, Dec 28; 1742: CG, May 5, Oct 9; 1743: CG, Jan 8, Apr 29, Dec 3; 1744: CG,
Mar 3, Apr 21, Oct 1, Dec 29; 1745: CG, Jan 14, DL, Mar 20, CG, May 6, Nov
15; 1746: CG, Jan 8, Apr 30, Jun 27, Dec 29; 1747: CG, Mar 26, May 15; 1748:
BF, Aug 24, BFLYY, 24, SFLYYW, Sep 7, SFBCBV, 7, BHB, Oct 1; 1749: CG, Jan 9,
18
Thompson, William (gallery keeper), 1677: DL, Dec 12
Thoms. See Toms.
Thomson. See Thompson.
Thomson (beneficiary), 1722: HIC, Feb 14
Thomson (boxkeeper), 1734: CG, May 16; 1740: CG, May 13; 1741: CG, May 11;
1745: DL, Mar 28
Thomson (singer), 1798: DL, Jan 16, Feb 20, Apr 16
Thomson (smith), 1772: DL, Feb 4, Jun 10; 1773: DL, Jun 2; 1774: DL, Jan 7, Jun
2, Nov 25; 1775: DL, Feb 23, May 27; 1776: DL, Mar 16, Apr 11, Jun 10
Thomson, E (beneficiary), 1739: CG, May 9

Thomson, James, 1730: DL, Feb 28; 1738: DL, Apr 6; 1745: DL, Mar 18; 1749: CG,
  Jan 13, 17; 1751: DL, Feb 23, Mar 8; 1754: CG, Dec 10; 1755: CG, Jan 15;
  1758: CG, Nov 2, 3; 1765: CG, Feb 18; 1775: CG, Mar 18; 1778: CG, Oct 28;
  1781: DL, Nov 10
--Agamemnon, 1738: DL, Apr 6, 7, 8, 10, 15, 18, 19, 20, 25
--Coriolanus, 1749: CG, Jan 9, 11, 13, 14, 16, 17, 18, 19, 20, 21, 23, 24, Feb
  1; 1754: DL, Nov 11, 13, 15, 18, 20, 23, 27, 29, CG, Dec 10, 11, 12, 14, 18,
  21; 1755: CG, Jan 15, 27, Mar 31, DL, Apr 22; 1758: CG, Mar 14, Apr 20, Nov
  2, 3; 1759: CG, Feb 3; 1760: CG, Apr 18; 1765: CG, Feb 18; 1768: CG, Apr 20;
  1775: DL, Dec 26
--Edward and Eleonora, 1739: CG, Mar 27; 1775: CG, Mar 18, 27, Apr 6, 26, May
  1, Nov 14, Dec 19; 1776: CG, May 3; 1796: DL, Oct 22
--Sophonisba, 1730: DL, Feb 28, Mar 2, 3, 5, 7, 9, 10, 12, 14, 17, 19; 1731:
  YB, Apr 7, 9, GF, May 21, Jun 1; 1733: CG, Jul 6, 10; 1735: CG/LIF, Mar 15;
  1745: JS, Jun 4
--Tancred and Sigismunda, 1745: DL, Mar 18, 19, 21, 23, 25, 26, 28, Apr 1, 2;
  1747: GF, Feb 16, 18, Mar 3; 1749: DL, Mar 7; 1752: DL, Feb 10, 13, 15, Mar
  14, Apr 18; 1755: DL, Mar 18; 1756: DL, Jan 10, 13, 15, 19, Mar 22, Apr 8;
  1758: DL, Apr 7, CG, Oct 14, 16, 18, 28, Nov 28, Dec 13; 1759: CG, Mar 10,
  15, DL, Apr 19, May 21, Nov 30, CG, Dec 15; 1760: CG, Jan 16, DL, Mar 3, May
  15, CG, Dec 2, 4; 1761: DL, Jan 31, May 13, Sep 24, CG, Oct 21; 1762: CG, Mar
  15, DL, 18, Oct 12, Nov 30; 1763: DL, Sep 27, Dec 30; 1764: DL, Oct 16, Dec
  19; 1765: DL, Oct 9, Nov 21; 1767: DL, Oct 14, 16; 1769: DL, Oct 21, 26, 31;
  1770: CG, Feb 16, 19, Mar 1, May 3; 1771: DL, Apr 23, May 1; 1773: DL, May
  13, Sep 30; 1777: CG, Apr 14, 21, May 14; 1778: CG, Mar 7, Apr 27, Oct 28;
  1779: CG, Jan 29, Feb 3, Mar 2; 1784: CG, Mar 1, DL, Apr 24, 27, 29, May 1,
  8, HAY, Jul 12, 14, 19, 24, DL, Oct 27; 1785: DL, Apr 23, HAY, Jun 16, DL,
  Oct 6; 1786: DL, Oct 5; 1788: DL, Dec 1; 1789: CG, Jan 10, 16; 1791: CG, Dec
  21; 1794: HAY, May 22
Thomson, John (actor), 1797: KING'S, May 18, CG, Jun 14
Thomson, Mrs (actor), 1784: HAY, Mar 8, Nov 16; 1794: HAY, May 22
Thomson, Thomas
--English Rogue, The, 1667: NONE, Sep 0
--Life of Mother Shipton, The, 1668: NURSERY, Sep 0; 1669: NONE, Sep 0; 1670:
  NONE, Sep 0
Thomyris, Queen of Scythia. See Pepusch, John Christopher.
Thoral (actor), 1735: SOU, Apr 7
Thorley (wax chandler), 1783: DL, Nov 27
Thorman. See Thurmond.
Thorne (scene painter), 1785: HAY, Apr 25, HAMM, Jul 25; 1794: CG, Dec 26;
  1795: CG, Dec 21; 1796: CG, Dec 19; 1797: CG, Mar 16; 1799: CG, Jan 29
Thorne (sceneman), 1761: CG, Oct 3
Thornhill (spectator), 1791: DLKING'S, Sep 27
Thornhill, Dr (beneficiary), 1720: SOU, Oct 3
Thornhill, Mrs (actor), 1720: LIF, Mar 28
Thornowets, Miss (actor, singer), 1729: GF, Dec 9, 10, 18, 20, 30; 1730: GF,
  Jan 1, 21, 22, 23, 24, Feb 6, 7, 12, 23, Mar 2, 7, 9, 10, 12, 14, 17, 19, 21,
  30, 31, Apr 6, 10, 16, 20, 24, May 13, 14, 18, 27, Jun 1, 12, 16, 25; 1735:
  GF, Dec 17; 1736: GF, Feb 20, LIF, Sep 30, Oct 12, 21, Dec 7, 30, 31
Thornton, Bonnell, 1759: CG, Apr 10; 1768: MARLY, Jul 28; 1774: HAY, Mar 15
--Timotheus, 1774: HAY, Mar 15
Thornton, Henry Ford (actor), 1795: HAY, Apr 22
Thornton, Margaret (actor), 1779: CG, Feb 13, Mar 20, Apr 7, 30; 1780: DL, Apr
  11
Thornton, Martha (actor), 1786: CG, May 9, 22
Thou art gone up (song), 1793: KING/HAY, Feb 20; 1794: DL, Mar 19
Thou didst blow (song), 1793: KING/HAY, Feb 15, 27
Thou hast stole away from me Mary (song), 1782: DL, May 1; 1784: DL, May 21
Thou joy of all hearts (song), 1675: DG, Jun 12
Thou shalt break them (song), 1793: KING/HAY, Feb 20; 1794: DL, Mar 19
Thou shalt bring them in (song), 1790: CG, Feb 24; 1791: CG, Mar 25; 1792: CG,
  Mar 16; 1793: CG, Mar 6; 1794: CG, Apr 9; 1796: CG, Mar 2; 1797: CG, Mar 24;
  1798: CG, Mar 14; 1799: CG, Feb 20, Mar 13
Thou Soft-Flowing Avon (song), 1775: CG, Apr 4
Though Bacchus may boast (song), 1790: CG, Jun 3
Though born in a Stable a Man's not a Horse (song), 1795: HAY, Mar 4
Though Crimes from Death and Torture Fly (song), 1775: CG, Apr 4
Though Hurricanes rattle (song), 1795: CG, Mar 16, May 16; 1796: CG, Apr 1, May
  26; see also May our Navy Old England forever protect; Our Laws, Constitution
  and King
Though I'm no Dancing Master (Kitty Grogan) (song), 1792: CG, May 15; 1794: CG,
  May 26

Though over all mankind (song), <u>1698</u>: DL, Mar 0
Though pleasure swells (song), <u>1797</u>: CG, Mar 31
Though Strange, tis True; or, Love's Vagaries (pastoral farce), <u>1732</u>: LIF, Mar 23
Though the Fate of Battle on Tomorrow wait (song), <u>1783</u>: CG, May 19; <u>1791</u>: CG, Jun 6
Though you make no return to my passion (song), <u>1693</u>: DL, Feb 0
Thrale, Hester Lynch (prologuist), <u>1781</u>: DL, Feb 17
Threadneedle St, <u>1690</u>: MTH, Mar 27; <u>1752</u>: DL, Apr 22; <u>1773</u>: DL, Jan 6
Three and the Deuce, The. See Hoare, Prince.
Three Children on the Ice (entertainment), <u>1724</u>: LIF, Nov 4
Three Hours after Marriage. See Gay, John.
Three Old Women Weatherwise. See Carey, Henry.
Three Queens Tavern, <u>1742</u>: DL, Apr 26; <u>1743</u>: DL, May 4
Three Tun Court, <u>1755</u>: DL, Nov 18
Three Tuns and Bull-Head Tavern, <u>1732</u>: TTT, Mar 3, 10
Three Tuns Tavern, Aldgate, <u>1750</u>: DL, Feb 21
Three Tuns Tavern, <u>1736</u>: GF, Mar 25; <u>1742</u>: GF, Apr 20
Three Weeks after Marriage. See Murphy, Arthur.
Three Years I've bade sweet Home adieu (song), <u>1798</u>: CG, Oct 15
Threshers (dance), <u>1758</u>: CG, Oct 14, Nov 27; <u>1759</u>: CG, Jan 8, 16, 29, Feb 3, 5, 8, Mar 22, 29, Apr 2, 3, 5, 25, 28, May 15, 17, 23, DL, Jul 12, CG, Oct 5, 13, 23; <u>1760</u>: CG, Jan 5, Apr 12, 18, May 6, 8, 9
Thrice happy the Monarch (song), <u>1791</u>: DL, Apr 1
Thrift St, <u>1748</u>: DL, Mar 7; <u>1752</u>: DL, Mar 14; <u>1753</u>: DL, Mar 24; <u>1765</u>: HAY, Feb 21
Throckmorton, Lady (correspondent), <u>1739</u>: HAY, Dec 1
Throgmorton St, <u>1742</u>: GF, Apr 24
Through the Land so Lovely Blooming (song), <u>1752</u>: KING'S, Mar 24
Through the Wood, Laddie (song), <u>1765</u>: HAY, Aug 8; <u>1766</u>: DL, Apr 21, 22; <u>1767</u>: HAY, Sep 7; <u>1796</u>: DL, May 13
Throw Physick to the Dogs! See Lee, Henry.
Throwsters Opera, The (play, anon), <u>1731</u>: GF, Jun 2
Thumoth, Burk (musician), <u>1730</u>: GF, May 13, 22, 28, Jun 2, 30; <u>1731</u>: HIC, Apr 9, DT, 23, HAY, May 10, STA, Aug 9; <u>1732</u>: HIC, Apr 5, GF, 27, May 4, HAY, Jun 1, BF, Aug 22; <u>1733</u>: HAY, Feb 28, HIC, Mar 16, GF, Apr 13, HAY, May 26, DL, Oct 22; <u>1734</u>: HIC, Apr 8; <u>1735</u>: HAY, Apr 28; <u>1736</u>: DL, May 22; <u>1738</u>: HAY, Mar 3; <u>1742</u>: DL, Sep 16; <u>1743</u>: DL, Jan 4, 6, 7, 15, 17, 19, 22, 25, 27, 29, Feb 1, 5, SOU, Mar 30, DL, Apr 9, 11, 12, 13, 15, 16, 20, 27, 29, May 2, 23, 24, 26; <u>1744</u>: SH, Feb 9, HAY, 20, Oct 4, 18, Nov 5, DL, Dec 12; <u>1747</u>: DL, Feb 9
Thunder Ode (music), <u>1773</u>: CG, Mar 19, 20
Thura (spectator), <u>1694</u>: BF, Sep 5, DLORDG, 12
Thurmond (householder), <u>1760</u>: CG, Sep 22
Thurmond, John (actor, author), <u>1695</u>: LIF, Dec 0; <u>1696</u>: LIF, Mar 0, Oct 0; <u>1697</u>: LIF, Nov 0; <u>1698</u>: LIF, Mar 0, May 0, Jun 0, Nov 0; <u>1699</u>: LIF, Feb 0, Apr 0, May 0; <u>1700</u>: LIF, Mar 0; <u>1708</u>: DL/QUEEN, Jun 4, DL, Jul 10, Sep 7, 9, 14, 18, 23, 25, 28, 30, Oct 2, 9, 23, Dec 21; <u>1709</u>: DL, Feb 5, Mar 19, May 2, Jun 2, QUEEN'S, Sep 27, Oct 1, 8, 29, 31, Nov 4; <u>1710</u>: QUEEN'S, Apr 26, May 15, GR, Jun 15, 19, 21, 24, 28, Jul 1, 3, 8, 12, 15, Aug 3, QUEEN'S, 16, GR, Sep 7, 9, DL/QUEEN, Nov 13, 14, 18, DL, 21, Dec 9, 16; <u>1711</u>: DL, Jan 19, DL/QUEEN, Feb 8, QUEEN'S, May 2, DL, 21, Jul 6, Oct 31; <u>1712</u>: DL, May 6, 29, Jun 9, 12, Oct 29, Nov 28; <u>1715</u>: DL, May 10, LIF, 16, 24, Oct 6, 7, 22, 24, 28, Nov 12, 22, 29, Dec 17, 21; <u>1716</u>: LIF, Jan 4, Apr 16, DL, May 11, Oct 2, LIF, Dec 29; <u>1717</u>: DL, May 11, Jun 3, LIF, 12, DL, Aug 6, 13, Oct 15, 24, 25, LIF, Dec 2, 11; <u>1718</u>: LIF, Jan 4, DL, 13, Feb 12, Mar 1, LIF, 8, DL, 8, Apr 23, LIF, 24, DL, 25, LIF, 28, 30, May 6, DL, 20, 29, Jun 11, 17, Jul 1, 8, Aug 20, Sep 25, 27, Oct 7, 17, 20, 25, 27, 30, Nov 28, Dec 1, 3, 20; <u>1719</u>: DL, Jan 8, Feb 12, Mar 7, Apr 9, 21, May 19, Jun 9, 26, Sep 12, 22, Oct 21, 22, 24, 26, Nov 11, 23, Dec 4, 11; <u>1720</u>: DL, Jan 9, Feb 17, Apr 5, 29, May 6, Jun 2, Sep 17, 20, 22, Oct 1, 12, 13, 21, Nov 1, 22, Dec 12, 14, 17; <u>1721</u>: DL, Mar 2, 16, Apr 13, 18, 26, 29, May 2, Jun 27, Aug 1, 8, Sep 21, 26, 30, Oct 2, 3, 5, 7, 12, 13, 18, 24, Nov 3, 4, 7, Dec 12, 22, 28; <u>1722</u>: DL, Jan 10, 26, Feb 19, Apr 17, 27, May 1, 22, 29, Sep 13, 15, 29, Oct 8, 9, 10, 11, 19, 22, 23, Dec 3, 4, 22; <u>1723</u>: DL, Jan 9, 23, Feb 4, 6, 15, Mar 11, May 1, 11, 13, 30, Sep 24, 26, 28, Oct 5, 8, 9, 15, 30, 31, Nov 8, 21, Dec 5; <u>1724</u>: DL, Apr 27, Sep 12, 19, 22, 24, Oct 8, Nov 6; <u>1725</u>: DL, Jan 4, 9, 20, 25, Feb 1, 9, Mar 18, Apr 15, 20, 22, 30, Sep 11, 16, 18, 30, Oct 5, 12, 13, 15, 18, 21, 27, Nov 3, Dec 22; <u>1726</u>: DL, Jan 5, Apr 27, May 18, Sep 3, 13, 20, 22, Oct 15, 22, Nov 12, 16, Dec 7, 20; <u>1727</u>: DL, Feb 4, Apr 8, 22, 24, 29, Sep 7; <u>1733</u>: DL, Jun 9
--Apollo and Daphne; or, Harlequin's Metamorphoses (pantomime), <u>1725</u>: DL, Feb 20, 22, 23, 25, 27, Mar 1, 2, 6, 9, 13, 16, 20, 29, 30, Apr 1, 3, 6, 10;

<u>1726</u>: DL, Feb 11, 12, 14, 15, 16, 17, 18, 19, 21, 22, 24, 26, 28, Mar 1, 5,
8, 12, 15, 19, 22, 26, 29, Apr 2, 11, 12, 13, 14, Nov 2, 3, 7, 10, 14, 18,
22, Dec 9, 13; <u>1727</u>: DL, Feb 9, 13, 14, Nov 14; <u>1729</u>: DL, Dec 10
--Dumb Farce, The, <u>1719</u>: DL, Feb 12, 24, 26, 28, Mar 2, 30, Apr 1, 4, 8, 13,
18, 25, 28, Oct 9
--Escapes of Harlequin, The (pantomime), <u>1751</u>: SF, Sep 17, 19
--Harlequin Doctor Faustus (pantomime), <u>1723</u>: DL, Nov 26, 27, 28, 29, 30, Dec
2, 3, 4, 11, 12, 13, 14, 16, 17, 18, 19, 26, 27, 28; <u>1724</u>: DL, Jan 1, 10, 31,
Feb 5, 29, Mar 2, 3, 7, 10, 12, 14, 17, 19, 21, 24, 28, Apr 6, 9, 20, May 13,
22, Oct 1, 3, 6, 9, 13, 15, 23, 26, Nov 9, 12, 17, 20, 24, Dec 17, 28; <u>1725</u>:
DL, Jan 1, 8, 16, 21, 26, 28, Feb 6, 11, HAY, Mar 8, 15, DL, Apr 14, HAY, 14,
DL, May 5, 20, 27, 31, Jun 3, 7, 11, Nov 9, 11, 18, 23, 26, Dec 3, 10,
14, 27, 28, 31; <u>1726</u>: DL, Jan 7, 10, 28, Jun 3, Oct 1, 4, 8, 25, 29, Nov 24,
25, 29, Dec 2, 15, 19, 26, 27; <u>1727</u>: DL, Jan 23, 26, Feb 6, 7, May 12, 31,
Jun 2, Oct 6, 10, 13, 16, 18, 24, 25; <u>1728</u>: DL, Jan 6, Mar 9, 23, May 17, 29,
Oct 23, 30, Dec 11; <u>1729</u>: DL, Feb 14, 18, Mar 4, Apr 17, 18, May 5, 21, 30,
Jun 20, Nov 6, 7, 8, 26, Dec 26, 29; <u>1730</u>: DL, Jan 21, 22, 23, Apr 3, 4, 21,
Oct 1, 6, 17, Nov 23, 27; <u>1733</u>: DL, Oct 10, 12, 15, 17, 19, 22, 31, Dec 1;
<u>1737</u>: CG, Oct 4; <u>1740</u>: SF, Sep 9; <u>1766</u>: CG, Nov 18, 19, 20, 21, 22, 24, 25,
26, 27, 28, 29, Dec 1, 2, 4, 6, 8, 9, 10, 11, 13, 19, 20, 30; <u>1767</u>: CG, Jan
1, 2, 3, 5, 6, 7, 8, 19, 20, 22, 23, 26, 27, Feb 13, 16, 20, 26, 27, Mar 2,
3, 9, 10, 14, 17, 21, 26, Apr 2, May 1, 8, 9, 26, Oct 5, 7, 9, 12, 13, 15,
Nov 2, 6, Dec 4, 7, 12; <u>1768</u>: CG, Mar 15, Apr 4, 15, 21, May 2, 5, 23, 28,
Oct 24, 27, 31, Nov 7, 8, 9, 11, 14, 18, 21, Dec 7, 12, 14; <u>1769</u>: CG, Jan 19,
Apr 10, 18, 21, 24, May 1, 3, 19, 20, Oct 2; <u>1771</u>: CG, Apr 22, May 4, 13, 15,
21, 27; <u>1772</u>: CG, Mar 23, 26, Apr 2, 30, May 14, Jun 1; <u>1773</u>: CG, Nov 23, 25,
29, 30, Dec 1, 6, 10, 14, 15, 27, 28
--Harlequin Shepard (pantomime), <u>1724</u>: DL, Nov 28, 30, Dec 1, 2, 3, 4, 26
--Harlequin's Triumph (pantomime), <u>1727</u>: DL, Feb 27, 28, Mar 2, 4, 6, 7, 11,
14, 18, 21, 25, Apr 3, 4, 5, 11, 13, 21
--Miser, The; or, Wagner and Abericock, <u>1726</u>: DL, Dec 30, 31; <u>1727</u>: DL, Jan 2,
3, 4, 5, 6, 7, 9, 10, 11, 12, 13, 14, 16, 17, 18, 19, 21
Thurmond, John Jr (actor, dancer), <u>1708</u>: DL, Aug 31, Sep 9; <u>1709</u>: DL, May 2;
<u>1710</u>: QUEEN'S, Mar 16, GR, Jun 15, 21, Jul 1, 3, 6, QUEEN'S, Aug 16; <u>1711</u>:
GR, Sep 13, COH, Dec 20; <u>1715</u>: LIF, Jun 7, 30, Jul 5, 12, 14, 27, Aug 3, 10,
11, 17, 23, Oct 3, 5, 12, 13, 14, 24, 26, 28, 29, Nov 4, 9, 10, 14, 15, 16,
18, 25, 26, 28, 29, Dec 13, 28, 30; <u>1716</u>: LIF, Jan 11, 19, Feb 27, 28, Apr 5,
6, 9, 30, May 18, 24, Jun 1, 4, 12, 20, 29, Jul 13, 18, 25, 27, Aug 3, 10,
15, Oct 4, 10, 25, 26, 30, Nov 1, 9, 14, 21, 22, Dec 12, 17, 18, 21, 31;
<u>1717</u>: LIF, Jan 4, 7, 15, 22, 25, 31, Feb 2, 6, 25, 26, DL, Mar 1, LIF, 2, 30,
Apr 4, 8, 22, 25, 29, May 10, 13, 16, 18, 20, 21, 23, 27, 28, Jun 7, Oct 5,
7, 14, 15, 22, 25, 29, Nov 1, 2, 5, 8, 9, 15, 20, 22, 23, 25, Dec 6, 9, 10,
26, 27; <u>1718</u>: LIF, Jan 1, 2, 4, 9, 10, 15, 16, 21, 24, 27, Feb 4, Mar 3, 8,
10, 13, 18, 20, Apr 16, 24, May 3, 6, 15, 20, Jun 4, DL, Oct 8, 14, 22, 24,
27, 28, 29, Nov 6, 12, 14, 19, 21, 24, 28, Dec 10, 15; <u>1719</u>: DL, Jan 7, 8,
29, Feb 3, 7, 12, Mar 16, 19, Apr 9, 11, 16, 18, 20, 21, 25, May 4, 11, 12,
30, Jun 5, 9, 16, Jul 21, 31, Sep 15, Oct 12, 14, 15, 16, 19, 20, 30, Nov 3,
6, 9, 16, 18, 23, 25, 27, Dec 4, 7, 28; <u>1720</u>: DL, Jan 13, Feb 1, 5, Mar 28,
29, 31, Apr 9, 25, 29, May 5, 11, 12, 17, 18, 19, 24, 25, 26, 27, 31, Jun 1,
2, 6, 7, 10, Sep 27, Oct 6, 13, 25, 31, Nov 8, 23, 30, Dec 7, 9, 14; <u>1721</u>:
DL, Feb 9, Mar 13, Apr 10, 11, 12, 14, May 1, 8, 10, 16, 17, 19, 23, 31, Jun
27, Sep 14, 19, Oct 13, 16, Nov 27, Dec 18, 20, 29; <u>1722</u>: DL, Jan 19, 24, Mar
27, 28, Apr 5, 10, 27, May 1, 5, 7, 11, 15, 19, 24, 26, 28, 30, Sep 27, Oct
9, 10, 12, 29, 30, Dec 4, 27; <u>1723</u>: DL, Jan 3, 18, 21, 29, Feb 5, Mar 21, 25,
May 2, 4, 8, 13, 15, 16, 17, 21, Oct 1, 28, Nov 1, 21, 23, 26, Dec 31; <u>1724</u>:
DL, Jan 3, 27, Feb 4, 11, 17, 20, 27, Mar 16, 26, Apr 7, 11, 15, 18, 20, 22,
29, May 2, 8, 12, 16, 18, Nov 14, 28, Dec 9; <u>1725</u>: DL, Feb 4, 20, Mar 15, 18,
31, Apr 2, 5, 14, 16, 19, 21, 30, May 1, 3, 10, 21, Sep 14, 25, 28, Oct 2, 7,
12, 19, 20, 23, 25, Nov 1, 16, Dec 13, 16; <u>1726</u>: DL, Jan 24, 25, Feb 2, 11,
Mar 17, 21, 24, 28, 31, Apr 12, 15, 19, 21, 22, 23, 26, 27, 29, 30, May 2, 3,
4, 7, 11, 12, Sep 6, 29, Oct 1, 11, Nov 2, Dec 6, 12, 30; <u>1727</u>: DL, Feb 8,
20, 27, Apr 11, 17, Oct 6, Nov 14; <u>1728</u>: DL, Mar 7, 16, 25, Apr 24, 25, 30,
May 2, 10, 22, Oct 30, Nov 15; <u>1729</u>: DL, Mar 15, Apr 17, May 14, 26, 28, Dec
10, 11, 26; <u>1730</u>: DL, Apr 11, 14, 15, 16, 18, 21, 24, 27, 29, May 1, 11, 19,
Oct 1, 10, 28, Nov 23, Dec 4; <u>1731</u>: DL, Apr 10, May 7, Oct 16, Nov 22, 25,
Dec 15, 28; <u>1732</u>: DL, Feb 2, 22, Mar 4, 21, Apr 17, 18, 21, 22, 26, 27, 28,
29, May 1, 2, 3, 6, 12, Sep 23, 28, GF, Dec 20, 27; <u>1733</u>: GF, Jan 6, 10, 13,
Feb 15, Mar 1, 12, 26, 30, Apr 10, 16, May 3, 23, 24, Sep 21, 24, Nov 7, 12,
29, Dec 10, 17; <u>1734</u>: GF, Jan 5, 14, Feb 11, Mar 11, 21, DL, Oct 5, 10, 17,
21, 22; <u>1735</u>: DL, Mar 3, Apr 7, 25, 26, Sep 15, Nov 15, Dec 6; <u>1736</u>: DL, Apr
6, May 1, Sep 7, 9, Nov 13, 23, Dec 6; <u>1737</u>: DL, Jan 27, Feb 10, Apr 11;
<u>1793</u>: CG, Dec 19

841

Thurmond, Miss (actor), 1749: DL, Jan 13
Thurmond, Sarah, Mrs John Jr (actor, singer), 1715: LIF, Jun 23, Jul 8, Aug 3,
    10, 11, Oct 5, 7, 24; 1716: LIF, Jan 3, Apr 24, 27, Jun 29, Jul 25, Aug 3,
    Oct 10, 22; 1717: LIF, Jan 10, 14, Feb 11, Apr 8, 25, May 16, Oct 15, 17, 24,
    26, Nov 9, 13, 16, 26, Dec 3, 7, 9, 28; 1718: LIF, Jan 11, 14, Feb 1, 3, 18,
    Mar 8, 22, Apr 5, 19, 23, 24, May 6, DL, Nov 8; 1719: DL, Jan 9, 16, Feb 14,
    Mar 7, 31, Apr 1, May 4, 11, 13, 19, Jun 9, 12, 26, Sep 17, Oct 10, 23, 30,
    31, Nov 11, 20, Dec 2, 8, 26; 1720: DL, Feb 5, Mar 28, May 30, Jun 7, 11, 30,
    Sep 13, 22, 24, Oct 3, 4, 6, 8, 13, Nov 1, 2, 4, 10, 18, 26, Dec 1, 8; 1721:
    DL, Jan 13, 24, Mar 20, Apr 26, Aug 1, 8, Sep 12, 14, 16, 21, Oct 3, 6, 10,
    Nov 7, 18; 1722: DL, Feb 8, Mar 3, 6, 27, Apr 10, 17, 27, May 21, 23, Sep 11,
    13, 18, 22, Oct 2, 16, 20, 23, 24, 30, 31, Nov 5, 7; 1723: DL, Jan 9, 23, Feb
    6, Mar 21, May 1, 10, 13, 20, 21, Sep 14, 17, 21, 24, 26, Oct 15, 16, 19, Nov
    4, 6, 8, 9, 14, 19, Dec 5, 30; 1724: DL, Feb 22, Mar 26, Apr 24, 27, 28, May
    14, 20, 22, Sep 15, 19, 22, 26, Oct 14, 24, 28, Nov 4, 19, 27, Dec 3; 1725:
    DL, Jan 20, 25, Feb 1, Mar 18, Apr 20, 22, May 11, 19, 21, Sep 4, 9, 16, 21,
    30, Oct 7, 14, 21, Nov 3, 4, 8, 22, Dec 7, 13, 18; 1726: DL, Jan 3, 22, Mar
    17, May 11, 12, 18, 23, Sep 3, 13, Oct 6, 11, Nov 4; 1727: DL, Feb 4, 8, 11,
    Mar 23, May 5, 15, 19, Sep 7, 12, 21, 26, Oct 3, 9, Nov 4, 21, Dec 5; 1728:
    DL, Jan 2, 3, 5, 10, Mar 16, May 10, 16, Sep 7, 12, 14, 17, 19, Oct 5, 12,
    25, Nov 2, 7, 12, 14; 1729: DL, Jan 7, 29, Feb 6, 10, 11, 27, Mar 18, 20, Apr
    22, 23, May 9, 12, 14, Sep 11, 13, 20, 27, Oct 2, 23, 31, Nov 4, 8, 14, 17,
    24, 25, 27, 28, Dec 8, 10; 1730: DL, Feb 10, Apr 8, May 1, Sep 17, 19, Oct 3,
    6, 20, 22, Dec 1, 11; 1731: DL, Jan 20, Mar 20, 22, 25, Apr 1, 8, 10, 19, May
    3, 7, 10, Sep 18, 25, 28, Oct 9, 19, 21, Nov 1, 5, 8, 10, 15, 22, Dec 1, 3,
    18; 1732: DL, Feb 10, 11, Mar 11, Apr 1, Sep 19, 21, 26, 30, Oct 3, GF, 18,
    19, 20, 21, 23, Nov 3, 4, 8, 10, 13, 24, 28, Dec 1; 1733: GF, Jan 8, 24, Feb
    12, Mar 6, 28, 30, Apr 3, 17, May 4, 5, Sep 10, 14, 17, 21, 24, 27, Oct 3, 8,
    15, 22, 23, 24, Nov 5, 13, 29, Dec 17, 18, 26, 28, 31; 1734: GF, Jan 11, 14,
    Feb 7, 11, Mar 19, May 15, DL, Sep 7, 10, 12, 14, 26, 28, Oct 3, 5, 9, 12,
    14, 21, 24, 26, Nov 4, 8, 16, Dec 14; 1735: DL, Jan 13, 23, Mar 6, 20, Apr
    25, Sep 1, 4, 6, 9, 13, 18, 20, 23, 25, 30, Oct 4, 7, 24, 25, 27, 30, Nov 3,
    4, 7, 10, 12, 29; 1736: DL, Mar 13, 22, Apr 15, 29, May 26, Sep 7, 11, 14,
    18, 21, 23, Oct 12, 13, 19, 27, 29, 30, Nov 1, 2, 3, 4, 6, 11, 19, 20, 23,
    Dec 14; 1737: DL, Jan 6, Feb 5, 18, Mar 12, 19, Apr 15, May 2, 5, Sep 1
Thursday in the Morn the Nineteenth of May (song), 1795: CG, May 25; 1797: CG,
    May 20; 1799: CG, Apr 16; see also Battle of La Hogue, The
Thurston (doorkeeper), 1751: DL, Sep 17
Thurston, Joseph (author), 1731: HAY, Jan 20
Thus all our Lives (song), 1669: LIF, Feb 25
Thus at Height of Love We Live (song), 1705: QUEEN'S, May 28
Thus Damon knocked at Celia's door (song), 1699: DL, Nov 28
Thus for Man the Woman fair (song), 1800: CG, Jun 2
Thus long ago (song), 1791: CG, Mar 25; 1792: CG, Mar 7; 1794: CG, Mar 14
Thus mighty Eastern Kings (song), 1739: DL, May 15
Thus night oft see me (song), 1794: CG, Mar 21
Thus saith the Lord (song), 1793: KING/HAY, Feb 20; 1794: DL, Mar 19
Thus we view (song), 1790: DL, Mar 10
Thy Genius lo! (song), 1689: DL, Nov 7
Thy glorious deeds (song), 1790: DL, Mar 5
Thy rebuke hath broken His heart (song), 1793: KING/HAY, Feb 20; 1794: DL, Mar
    19
Thy right hand O Lord (song), 1789: CG, Mar 20; 1795: CG, Mar 25; 1797: CG, Mar
    10
Thyestes. See Wright, John.
Thynne, Miss (actor), 1736: DL, Dec 31; 1737: DL, Oct 21, 25; 1738: DL, Sep 23,
    Oct 30, Dec 15; 1739: DL, Apr 25, May 3, 28, Sep 6, 26, Oct 1, 10, 15, Dec
    11, 26; 1740: DL, Feb 13, Apr 14, 28, May 9; 1742: BFHC, Aug 25
Thyrsis unjustly you complain (song), 1687: DL, May 12
Thyrsis. See Oldmixon, John.
Ti con solo (song), 1729: DL, Mar 26
Ti parli in seno amore (song), 1754: KING'S, Feb 28
Ti stringo o mio diletto (song), 1713: QUEEN'S, Apr 25; 1714: QUEEN'S, May 1,
    29
Tibaldi (composer), 1711: GR, Aug 27
Tibson, S (publisher), 1800: KING'S, Feb 18
Tice (house servant), 1795: DL, Jun 5; 1796: DL, Jun 15; 1797: DL, Jun 13;
    1798: DL, Jun 9; 1799: DL, Jul 3; 1800: DL, Jun 14
Tichfield St, 1782: KING'S, Mar 19; 1789: DL, Apr 14
Tickell, Mrs (actor), 1769: CG, Oct 7
Tickell, Richard, 1778: DL, Oct 15; 1781: DL, Oct 29, Nov 3, Dec 13; 1782: DL,
    Feb 25; 1783: DL, Sep 20; 1787: DL, Apr 20; 1792: DLKING'S, Apr 20

--Carnival of Venice, The, <u>1781</u>: DL, Dec 13, 14, 15, 17, 18, 19, 20, 21, 22, 27, 28, 29; <u>1782</u>: DL, Jan 7, 8, 10, 11, 14, 18, 23, 28, Feb 11, Apr 2, 5, May 6
--Gentle Shepherd, The, <u>1781</u>: DL, Oct 29, 30, 31, Nov 1, 2, 3, 5, 6, 7, 8, 9, 14, 16, 21, 23, 26, 28, 30, Dec 3, 5, 8, 12, 27, 28; <u>1782</u>: DL, Jan 26, Feb 2, 5, 9, 23, 26, Mar 5, 9, 12, Apr 4, May 1, 8, 11, Oct 16, 19, 29, Nov 16, 29, Dec 5; <u>1783</u>: DL, Jan 29, Apr 28, May 7, 9, 23, Sep 20, 27, Oct 18, 25, Nov 21, Dec 20, 29; <u>1784</u>: DL, Feb 13, Apr 13, Oct 18, 29, Dec 9, 22, 31; <u>1785</u>: DL, Jan 7, 19, Apr 5, May 21; <u>1786</u>: DL, Feb 23, Mar 13, 23, May 19, 26, Jun 3, 8, Sep 28, Oct 19, Nov 22, Dec 2; <u>1787</u>: DL, Mar 12; <u>1789</u>: DL, May 27, Jun 5; <u>1790</u>: DL, Jun 1; <u>1794</u>: CG, May 23; <u>1796</u>: DL, Jun 8
Tickell, Thomas (author), <u>1715</u>: YB, May 28; <u>1718</u>: HC, Sep 23
Tidd (billsticker), <u>1760</u>: CG, Sep 22
Tiddy Doll, <u>1754</u>: HAY, Dec 18, 23
Tidswell, Charlotte (actor), <u>1783</u>: DL, Jan 24, Mar 18, Apr 10, 24, 28, May 10, 12, 14, 23, Sep 16, 20, Oct 24, Nov 8, Dec 2, 12; <u>1784</u>: DL, Jan 7, 13, 23, Mar 29, Apr 14, May 3, 10, 15, 17, 24, Sep 16, 23, Oct 26, Nov 3, Dec 22; <u>1785</u>: DL, Jan 12, 14, 20, 27, Mar 17, Apr 20, 25, 27, May 20, Sep 22, 24, 27, 29, Oct 4, 6, 24, 25, 26, Dec 1, 26; <u>1786</u>: DL, Jan 14, 19, Mar 4, 9, 28, May 26, Sep 19, 28, Oct 7, 12, 25, Nov 29, Dec 2, 6; <u>1787</u>: DL, Jan 24, Feb 2, 7, Mar 3, 8, 12, 29, Apr 14, May 3, 16, 19, 31, Jun 1, Sep 18, Oct 2, 9, 18, 20, 30, Nov 6, 21, 27, Dec 7, 8, 10, 11, 15, 26; <u>1788</u>: DL, Jan 21, Mar 13, Apr 15, 21, 25, May 5, 6, 14, Jun 3, 6, Sep 25, 30, Oct 4, 9, 22, 25, Nov 4, 5, 10, 24, Dec 17, 18, 19; <u>1789</u>: DL, Jan 6, 10, 13, 19, 21, Feb 7, Mar 2, 21, May 11, Jun 4, Sep 17, 19, 24, 29, Oct 3, 20, Nov 5, Dec 2, 14; <u>1790</u>: DL, Jan 6, 19, 20, Feb 3, Mar 2, 6, 8, 22, Apr 9, 14, May 7, 12, 14, 15, 18, 27, 29, Sep 14, Oct 14, 16, 20, 23, Nov 4, Dec 1, 3, 14; <u>1791</u>: DL, Jan 25, May 10, 14, 19, 20, DLKING'S, Sep 24, Oct 8, Nov 1, 10, 11, 21, 22, 30, Dec 2, 12; <u>1792</u>: DLKING'S, Jan 5, 25, Feb 8, 11, 18, 27, Mar 3, 8, 13, 31, Apr 10, May 15, 17, 31, Jun 7, 14, 15, DL, Sep 18, 22, 25, 27, 29, Oct 9, 15, 18, 20, 27, Nov 2, 5, Dec 3, 4, 8, 10, 26, 31; <u>1793</u>: DL, Jan 18, Feb 5, 9, 23, Mar 2, 14, Apr 22, May 1, 17, 22, Jun 1, 5, HAY, Oct 8, 15, Nov 6, Dec 26, 30; <u>1794</u>: HAY, Jan 4, 11, 14, 20, Feb 1, Mar 31, DL, Apr 21, 26, 28, 29, May 6, 8, 17, 19, 30, Jun 10, 12, 14, 16, 24, 25, 28, HAY, Jul 17, Aug 6, 11, 20, Sep 3, DL, 16, 20, 30, Oct 7, 25, Nov 1, 7, 15, 26, 29, Dec 12, 16, 20, 30; <u>1795</u>: DL, Jan 20, 22, 23, Feb 6, 9, 10, 12, 28, Apr 24, 27, May 1, 12, 29, Jun 3, HAY, 9, 16, 17, 19, Jul 25, Aug 18, DL, Sep 17, 22, 24, 29, Oct 3, 12, 19, 21, 30, Nov 5, 10, 11, 16, 20, Dec 1, 2, 11, 12, 14, 19; <u>1796</u>: DL, Jan 16, 18, 23, 29, Feb 15, 29, Mar 5, 10, 12, Apr 2, 13, 18, 25, 26, 29, May 3, 13, Jun 4, 6, 8, 11, 13, HAY, 18, 30, Jul 15, 30, Aug 11, Sep 7, 8, DL, 20, 24, 29, Oct 3, 4, 8, 10, 11, 13, 15, 17, 19, 24, 25, 27, 28, Nov 1, 2, 5, 9, 16, 22, 28, Dec 7, 9, 20, 21, 26, 30; <u>1797</u>: DL, Jan 2, 12, 17, 20, 24, 27, Feb 1, Mar 16, 21, Apr 1, 6, 19, 24, 27, 28, May 8, 12, 15, Jun 12, 13, Sep 19, 21, 23, 28, 30, Oct 5, 12, 14, 19, 23, Nov 7, 9, 10, 11, 14, 15, 17, 18, 21, 23, 28, Dec 8, 21; <u>1798</u>: DL, Jan 4, 9, 23, Feb 3, Mar 8, Apr 30, May 7, 11, 24, 29, 30, Jun 5, 6, 12, 13, Sep 15, 18, 20, 22, 25, 29, Oct 2, 6, 8, 9, 11, 13, 20, 27, 30, Nov 6, 10, 16, 22, 28, 29, HAY, Dec 17, DL, 29; <u>1799</u>: DL, Jan 11, 31, Feb 4, 26, Apr 5, 8, 18, 22, 24, 27, May 1, 4, 16, 20, Jun 10, Jul 1, Sep 17, 19, 26, 28, Oct 1, 3, 7, 8, 12, 17, 19, 21, 29, Nov 2, 12, 14, 29, Dec 7, 9; <u>1800</u>: DL, Jan 4, 14, 18, Mar 13, 17, Apr 29, May 3, 12, 19, Jun 9, 12, 13
Tien (Dutch spectator), <u>1689</u>: BF, Aug 26
Tifer. See Tyfer.
Tight Irish Boy, The (song), <u>1797</u>: CG, May 9, Sep 29; <u>1799</u>: CG, Jan 25, Oct 25
Tight Little Island (song), <u>1799</u>: CG, Apr 16, May 14, 18, 25, 31, Jun 1, 3, 7; <u>1800</u>: CG, Apr 15, 19, 23, May 2, 6, 10
Tight Little Lads of the Ocean (song), <u>1800</u>: CG, Apr 22
Tigrane (opera), <u>1746</u>: KING'S, Mar 4
Tigrane (pastiche), <u>1767</u>: KING'S, Oct 27, 31, Nov 14, 28, Dec 1
Tigreardo Disdegno, La (music), <u>1729</u>: LIF, Mar 5, DL, 26
Tildsley (house servant), <u>1800</u>: DL, Jun 14
Tillemans (scene painter), <u>1726</u>: DL, Dec 30
Tillman (gallery keeper), <u>1722</u>: LIF, May 28; <u>1723</u>: LIF, Jun 6; <u>1724</u>: LIF, May 26; <u>1725</u>: LIF, May 25; <u>1726</u>: LIF, May 12
Tiltyard Coffee House, <u>1745</u>: CT, Jan 14; <u>1751</u>: DL, Dec 18; <u>1778</u>: CG, May 8
Timanthes. See Hoole, John.
Timbertoe (dancer), <u>1752</u>: HAY, May 21, 23, Dec 18; <u>1753</u>: HAY, Mar 13, 31, Apr 5, 10, BFSY, Sep 3, 5; <u>1754</u>: HAY, Mar 7, 11, 30, Apr 1, 22, May 2
Time and Truth. See Handel, George Frederic, Triumph of Time and Truth.
Time has not thinned my flowing Hair (song), <u>1783</u>: DL, May 14; <u>1784</u>: DL, Mar 30, Apr 12; <u>1787</u>: HAY, Aug 14; <u>1800</u>: CG, May 15
Times, The. See Griffith, Elizabeth.
Timido Pelegrino (song), <u>1732</u>: LIF, Apr 19

Timkins (boxkeeper), 1796: CG, Jun 6
Timoleon. See Martyn, Benjamin.
Timoleon; or, The Revolution. See Southby.
Timon in Love. See Kelly, John.
Timon le Misantrope. See Lisle de la Drevetiere, L F.
Timon of Athens. See Shakespeare, William.
Timotheus (author), 1768: KING'S, Nov 3, 8
Timotheus placed on high (song), 1792: CG, Mar 7; 1794: CG, Mar 14
Timotheus. See Thornton, Bonnell.
Tindal (dancer), 1740: BFH, Aug 23
Tindal, Charles (actor), 1761: CG, Apr 25, Nov 13, Dec 11; 1762: CG, Jan 20,
    Feb 15, Mar 23, Apr 13, 24, May 1, 6, Oct 2, 12, 16, Nov 3; 1763: CG, Feb 14,
    May 9, 17, Nov 4, 16, Dec 9; 1764: CG, Feb 15, May 9, 16, Oct 19, Nov 3, 5,
    Dec 21; 1765: CG, Jan 14, Mar 26, Apr 16, May 11, 15, 16, HAY, Jun 10, 24,
    Jul 15, 31, Aug 9, 21, Sep 11; 1767: CG, May 8
Tinker (spectator), 1748: DL, Sep 27
Tinker's Glee (song), 1794: CG, Dec 26; 1795: CG, Dec 21; 1796: CG, Jan 4
Tinker's Travels (entertainment), 1775: HAY, Feb 20
Tinney, John (print seller), 1754: CG, Jan 21
Tinsdale (haberdasher), 1772: CG, Feb 24
Tinte, Rosa (dancer), 1775: KING'S, Oct 31, Nov 7, 16, 28; 1776: KING'S, Jan 9,
    Feb 3, 13, 24, Mar 19, Apr 25, May 30, CG, Oct 23, Nov 23, Dec 26; 1777: CG,
    Feb 18, Apr 4, 26, May 3, 20, Oct 1, Nov 3, 11, 25; 1778: CG, Jan 28, Feb 23,
    Apr 20, 21, May 7, 9, Oct 14, 16, 22, 23, KING'S, Nov 24, 28, Dec 22; 1779:
    KING'S, Jan 29, Feb 23, Mar 25, CG, Apr 22, May 3, DL, 14, KING'S, 15, Jun 15
Tioli (dancer), 1760: DL, Oct 14, Dec 13; 1761: DL, Jan 24, Apr 18
Tiperary, 1744: HAY, Dec 26
Tippee against Twaddle (song), 1785: HAY, Feb 12
Tippety witchet (song), 1794: CG, May 16, HAY, Aug 23
Tippling Philosopher (song), 1720: LIF, Mar 19, 22, 24, Apr 2, 28; 1724: LIF,
    Mar 23, 26; 1725: LIF, Apr 10; 1735: CG/LIF, Mar 15, 18, 25, Apr 15; 1736:
    CG, May 13
Tippoo Saib. See Lonsdale, Mark.
Tippy Bob (song), 1792: HAY, Nov 26; 1796: CG, Apr 15, 22, May 3
Tiranni Mici Pensieri (song), 1729: LIF, Mar 5
Tirenello (dancer), 1754: HAY, Aug 15
Tirolisi, Le (dance), 1740: CG, Nov 28
Tirrell (house servant), 1800: DL, Jun 14
Tirrevette (actor), 1722: LIF, Jan 13
Tis a mighty fine thing (song), 1792: CG, May 15
Tis a Wise Child Knows its Father. See Waldron, Francis Godolphin.
Tis All a Farce. See Allingham, John Till.
Tis an Ill Wind Blows Nobody Good; or, The Road to Odiham (play), 1788: DL, Apr
    14
Tis death alone (song), 1688: DG, Apr 0
Tis done, thus I exert (song), 1791: DL, Apr 1, CG, 13; 1792: KING'S, Feb 29,
    CG, Mar 9; 1794: DL, Mar 26
Tis Generous Wine (song), 1789: DL, Mar 20
Tis health that gives birth (song), 1789: DL, Apr 17
Tis in vain to tell me I am deceived (song), 1696: DG, Oct 0
Tis Joy to wound a Lover (song), 1734: HAY, Aug 16
Tis Liberty, dear Liberty (song), 1748: CG, Feb 13, 20, Mar 28, Apr 20, 21, 27,
    JS, Dec 26; 1790: DL, Mar 17; 1794: DL, Apr 4
Tis mighty wine inspires us (song), 1789: DL, Mar 20; 1790: DL, Mar 17; 1791:
    DL, Apr 1
Tis Pity She's a Whore. See Ford, John.
Tis Sultry Weather, Pretty Maid (song), 1715: LIF, Aug 3, 10
Tis Well if it Takes. See Taverner, William.
Tis Well It's No Worse. See Bickerstaff, Isaac.
Tis well; six times (song), 1799: CG, Mar 1
Tis Wine was made to rule the Day (song), 1742: GF, Feb 2
Tisdale, Mrs (actor), 1769: HAY, May 22
Tit for Tat (dance), 1735: DL, Feb 15, 17
Tit for Tat (song), 1747: DL, Nov 16
Tit for Tat. See Colman the elder, George.
Tit for Tat; or, A Dish of the Auctioneer's Own Chocolate. See Woodward,
    Henry.
Tit for Tat; or, The Comedy and Tragedy of War. See Charke, Charlotte.
Tit for Tat; or, The Kiss Returned (dance), 1749: BFY, Aug 23
Tit for Tat; or, The Smuggler Foiled at his Own Weapon (epilogue), 1749: HAY,
    May 15, 19, 26, Jun 1
Tito Manlio. See Abos, Girolamo; Cocchi, Gioacchino.

Titus. See Veracini, Francis.
Titus and Berenice. See Otway, Thomas.
Titus Andronicus. See Shakespeare, William.
Titus Manlius (opera), 1717: KING'S, Apr 4, 13, 27, May 4, 11, 25, Jun 29
Tiverton Fire, 1731: DL, Dec 3
To all you Ladies now at Land (song), 1797: HAY, May 10
To Arms (song), 1691: NONE, Sep 0; 1695: DL, Sep 0; 1739: DL, Oct 24, CG, 30,
   31, Nov 3; 1744: CG, Mar 15, 28, 29, 30, Apr 2, 12, 16, 17, 30; 1756: CG, May
   6; 1791: CG, May 3, 16; 1792: CG, Apr 18; 1793: CG, Feb 15, KING/HAY, 15, CG,
   20, 22, Mar 1, 6, 8, 13, 15, 20, 22, Apr 24; 1794: CG, May 7; 1797: CG, May
   31; 1798: CG, Feb 9, 28, Mar 9; 1800: CG, Apr 23
To Arms; or, The British Recruit. See Hurlstone, Thomas.
To Batchelor's Hall (song), 1790: CG, Nov 23; 1791: CG, Sep 19; 1793: CG, May
   21; 1794: CG, Apr 12, Oct 29; 1795: CG, Oct 7; 1797: CG, Oct 2; 1798: CG, Apr
   28
To be jovial and gay (song), 1791: CG, May 17, 28
To be sure I don't love in my heart (song), 1795: CG, May 25
To be sure she don't like a brisk Irish lad (song), 1791: CG, May 18
To Beauty devoted (song), 1713: QUEEN'S, Apr 25; 1714: QUEEN'S, May 29, Jun 23
To double the sports (song), 1696: LIF, Nov 14
To keep my gentle Jessy (song), 1774: MARLY, Jul 6; 1781: CG, Nov 8
To me you made a thousand vows (song), 1695: DL, Oct 0
To meet her, May, the Queen of Love comes here (song), 1696: LIF, Nov 14
To Miss Raftor, on her Success in the Part of Polly in The Beggar's Opera
   (poem), 1732: DL, Jul 25
To Mr Betterton, Acting Oedipus King of Thebes (poem), 1696: LIF, Jul 0
To Mr Giffard, Master of the New Theatre in Goodman's-Fields, on closing the
   Season (poem), 1733: GF, Jun 22
To Mr Giffard, on his Reviving the Play of Julius Caesar (poem), 1733: GF, Jan
   24
To Mr Giffard, on the New Theatre in Goodman's Fields (poem), 1732: GF, Nov 13
To Mr Walker, upon his Choice of Alexander the Great, for his Benefit (poem),
   1732: LIF, Apr 10
To Mrs Sybilla, on her Acting the Goddess of Dullness (poem), 1745: DL, Jan 17
To non fugaste (song), 1764: KING'S, Mar 29
To pensive years resign your pining (song), 1698: DL, Mar 0
To Song and Dance (song), 1784: CG, Apr 27, May 17; 1790: DL, Mar 10
To Sylvia (song), 1744: HAY, Jan 19
To the Duchess of Newcastle with his Emilia (poem), 1671: NONE, Sep 0
To the Duke on His Return (poem), 1682: DL, May 29
To thee, O gentle sleep (song), 1745: CG, Nov 4; 1751: DL, Nov 4; 1754: DL, Nov
   4; 1769: DL, Nov 4; 1776: DL, Nov 4; 1777: DL, Nov 4; 1778: CG, Nov 4; 1780:
   CG, May 1, Nov 4, DL, 4; 1781: CG, Nov 5; 1783: CG, Nov 4; 1784: CG, Nov 4;
   1788: HAY, Dec 22; 1797: DL, Feb 6
To thy brave sons (song), 1800: CG, Jun 16
To treble the pleasures with regular measures (song), 1696: LIF, Nov 14
To welcome mirth and harmless glee (song), 1798: DL, Mar 24, Sep 15, Oct 31;
   1799: DL, Apr 6, Nov 27; 1800: DL, Mar 4
Toast, Knights of the, 1700: LIF, Jan 9
Toast, The (song), 1757: DL, Mar 31
Tobacco Box, The; or, The Soldier's Farewell (song), 1782: HAY, Sep 18; 1785:
   HAY, Jul 19, Aug 26; 1786: CG, May 10, HAY, Jul 18; 1790: CG, Apr 20; 1791:
   CG, Jun 6, 7, 8, HAY, Oct 24
Tobacco Box, The; or, The Soldier's Pledge of Love (interlude, anon), 1782:
   HAY, Aug 13, 14, 15
Tobacco Roll, 1746: GF, Mar 3
Tobacconist, The. See Gentleman, Francis.
Tobin (dancer), 1732: RIW/HAY, Sep 4, 11, 12
Toby, Old (actor), 1724: WINH, Apr 13
Toby's brown jug (song), 1785: DL, May 11
Todd, James (actor), 1736: CG, Mar 27, SF, Sep 7, CG, Oct 4
Todi, Luiggia (singer), 1777: KING'S, Nov 4, Dec 16; 1778: KING'S, Mar 3, 26,
   Apr 2, May 5
Todlen Hame (song), 1798: CG, Apr 28
Toe (singer), 1752: CT/HAY, Apr 1, 18, May 5; 1753: HAY, Mar 31, Apr 10; 1758:
   HAY, May 18
Tofts, Katherine (singer), 1703: DL, Nov 30, Dec 14, LIF, 21; 1704: DL, Jan 4,
   18, LIF, Feb 1, DL, 5, 22, LIF, Mar 7, DL, 14; 1705: DL, Jan 16, Apr 28, Jun
   16, 23, 26, Nov 10; 1706: DL, Mar 30, Jun 14, Jul 5, DG, 9, Oct 24, 30,
   DL/DG, Nov 21, DL, Dec 5; 1707: DL, Mar 4, 13, Apr 1, Nov 15, DL/QUEEN, Dec
   6, DL, 18; 1708: QUEEN'S, Feb 26, Dec 14; 1709: QUEEN'S, Jan 22, 29, Mar 2,
   17, 22

Together let us range the fields (song), 1791: CG, Apr 6, 13, Dec 10; 1792: CG, Mar 7, 14, 21; 1793: CG, Mar 6, KING/HAY, 6, CG, 20; 1794: CG, Mar 26, DL, Apr 9; 1797: CG, May 31; 1799: CG, Mar 1, 13, Apr 6, May 3, Jun 6; 1800: CG, Mar 19, May 22

Tokely, James (actor), 1798: DL, Mar 24, Jun 5, HAY, 28, DL, Sep 29, Nov 22; 1799: HAY, Jun 15, 18, DL, Sep 26, Oct 3, Nov 22

Tollard (tumbler), 1723: RI, Sep 2

Tollet's Grounds (dance), 1702: DL, Jun 9, Aug 20; 1703: DL, May 28; 1704: DL, Aug 15; 1716: DL, Apr 19; 1718: DL, May 30; 1719: DL, May 4; 1720: DL, May 20, Jun 6; 1721: DL, May 19; 1723: LIF, Apr 27, May 6, 15, DL, Nov 20; 1724: DL, Feb 10, LIF, Apr 6, 27, May 2, 15, 16, 18, 25, 28, 29, Jun 3, SOU, Sep 24; 1726: LIF, Apr 30, Jul 1, 5, 29, Aug 2; 1727: LIF, Apr 10; 1729: BFB, Aug 25; 1730: GF, Jan 24, Feb 12, Mar 7, LIF, May 1, 6, 20, 23, Jun 1, GF, 4, LIF, Jul 3; 1731: LIF, Sep 22, Oct 27, GF, Dec 11, LIF, 14; 1732: LIF/CG, Sep 27, Oct 16, LIF, 18, LIF/CG, Nov 21, Dec 15, CG/LIF, 28; 1733: LIF/CG, Apr 20, 21

Tollet's Grounds (music), 1732: GF, May 11; 1733: HAY, Feb 28

Tollett, Henrietta Maria (actor, dancer), 1726: HAY, Feb 24; 1731: SF, Sep 8, SOU, 28, GF, Oct 25, 29, Nov 1, 4, 5, 6, 8, 11, 23, 24, 25, Dec 3, 4, 6, 7, 9, 11, 13, 16, 20, 29; 1732: GF, Jan 15, 25, 26, Feb 2, 19, 21, 29, Mar 7, 23, 27, 28, 30, Apr 18, 19, 24, 27, May 10, 17; 1733: GF, Sep 21, Oct 8, 9, 19, 24, 25, Dec 8, 18, 26, 27, 31; 1734: GF, Jan 10, 14, 19, Feb 11, Apr 18, 26, May 7, 20, BFRLCH, Aug 24, GF, Sep 9, 11, 13, Oct 14, 16, 18, 21, 23, Nov 13, Dec 12; 1735: GF, Jan 3, 10, 11, 24, Feb 4, 22, Mar 10, Apr 9, 12, May 6, 8, Sep 12, 15, 17, 22, 24, Oct 6, 8, 27, Nov 3, 14, 21, 24, 25, 26, Dec 17; 1736: GF, Mar 18, Apr 28, May 13, LIF, Sep 28, Oct 9, 12, 26, Nov 6, 13, 26, 27, 29, Dec 3, 7, 17, 30, 31; 1737: LIF, Jan 10, 20, 21, Feb 21, Mar 15, 29, Apr 2, 27, May 4, 6, DL, Oct 25; 1738: DL, Jan 19, 26, Feb 2, 11, 18, 23, 28, Mar 21, Apr 17

Tollett, Thomas (composer), 1692: DL, Jan 0, NONE, Sep 0

Tolomeo (pastiche), 1761: KING'S, Dec 21; 1762: KING'S, Jan 2, 9, 16, 23, 25, 29, Feb 6, 13, 20, 27, Mar 9, 29, Apr 20

Tolson, Francis, 1719: DL, Jun 26
--Earl of Warwick, The; or, The British Exile, 1719: DL, Jun 26, 30, Jul 3

Tolve, Francesco (singer), 1736: KING'S, Nov 23; 1737: KING'S, Jan 8, Feb 12, Apr 12, May 24

Tom Bowling (song), 1790: CG, Dec 1; 1799: CG, Apr 19; see also Here a sheer hulk

Tom Essence. See Rawlins Jr, Thomas.

Tom Jones (novel), 1749: CG, Mar 29

Tom Jones. See Reed, Joseph.

Tom Thumb. See Fielding, Henry; O'Hara, Kane.

Tom Tough (song), 1799: DL, Apr 8

Tom's Coffee House, 1697: DLORLIF, Sep 15, DL, Oct 16; 1741: GF, Dec 2; 1742: GF, Mar 18, DL, 20, GF, Apr 22; 1743: LIF, Mar 14, DL, Apr 29; 1744: DL, Apr 2; 1745: DL, Apr 25; 1746: CG, May 2; 1753: DL, May 22; 1755: DL, Mar 22; 1757: DL, Apr 12, Dec 21; 1758: DL, Mar 10; 1760: DL, Apr 11; 1761: DL, Mar 30

Tombeau de Maitre Andre, Le. See Biancolelli, Louis.

Tombs of Westminster (entertainment), 1766: DL, Apr 2, 5, 28, May 6, 12; 1767: DL, Apr 20, 21, May 2, 5; 1782: HAY, Aug 28, Sep 3; 1783: CG, May 7, HAY, Aug 26; 1786: CG, May 6, 22, HAMM, Jul 24; 1788: CG, Jun 3; 1791: CG, Apr 28

Tomich, Francesco (composer), 1794: KING'S, May 31

Tomkins (actor), 1799: DL, May 1, Nov 6

Tomkins, John (doorkeeper), 1723: HAY, Apr 15

Tomkins, Miss (actor), 1750: SFP, Sep 7

Tomkis, Thomas
--Albumazar, 1668: LIF, Feb 22; 1747: DL, Sep 22, Oct 3, 6, 8, 10, 13, 17, Nov 17; 1748: DL, Apr 13; 1773: DL, Oct 19, 21, 25, 27, Nov 3, Dec 30

Tomkyn's Coffee House, 1755: CG, Feb 19

Tomkyns and Co (wine merchants), 1766: CG, Oct 10, Nov 20

Tomlings (house servant), 1752: DL, May 2; 1757: DL, May 20

Tomlins (actor), 1791: HAY, Oct 24

Tomlinson (actor, house servant), 1747: DL, May 14; 1749: DL, May 11; 1750: DL, May 10; 1751: DL, May 9; 1752: DL, May 2; 1753: DL, May 17; 1754: DL, May 21; 1755: DL, May 15; 1760: DL, May 12; 1761: DL, May 8, 20; 1762: DL, May 18; 1763: DL, May 13; 1764: DL, May 17; 1765: DL, May 17; 1766: DL, May 14; 1767: DL, May 27; 1768: DL, May 13, 23; 1769: DL, May 17; 1770: DL, May 28; 1771: DL, May 25; 1772: DL, Jun 3; 1773: DL, Jan 1, May 28; 1774: DL, May 24; 1775: DL, May 23; 1776: DL, May 18; 1777: DL, May 30; 1778: DL, May 22; 1779: DL, May 29; 1780: DL, May 23; 1781: DL, May 25

Tomlinson, Kellom (choreographer), 1743: CG, Apr 9

Tomlinson, Richard (musician), 1681: ATCOURT, Nov 15
Tomo, Adomo (spectator), 1738: DL, Feb 21
Tomorrow; or, The Mars (song), 1799: CG, Apr 30, May 15
Tomosein (dancer), 1741: TC, Aug 4
Tompion (watch maker), 1676: DG, Jun 2
Tompson (actor), 1797: HAY, May 10
Toms (actor), 1700: DL, Feb 19, Mar 0, Jul 9, Nov 23, Dec 9; 1701: DL, Feb 4,
    Mar 1, May 12, Dec 0; 1702: DL, Nov 0; 1703: DL, Dec 2; 1704: DL, Jan 26;
    1705: DL, Jun 12; 1706: DL, Apr 0
Toms (actor), 1790: CG, Oct 4; 1795: CG, Sep 21, Oct 16, 19, Dec 15, 26; 1796:
    CG, Jan 5, 6, 13, Mar 14, Apr 26, 29, May 20, Sep 12, 17, 19, Oct 6, 10, 13,
    14, 20, 21, 24, 29, Nov 5, 7, 14, Dec 9, 10, 20, 21, 22, 26, 29; 1797: CG,
    Jan 25, Feb 27, May 6, 17, Jun 10, 14, Sep 18, 20, 22, 25, 27, 29, Oct 6, 11,
    12, 31, Nov 2, 3, 8, 20, Dec 12, 18, 27; 1798: CG, Jan 5, Feb 9, Apr 19, May
    4, 16, 23, 30, 31
Toms (composer), 1766: CG, Dec 3, 15, 22, 29; 1767: CG, Jan 16; 1770: CG, Mar
    2, Apr 16; 1772: CG, Feb 3, Mar 6
Tomson. See Thompson.
Ton, The. See Wallace, Eglantine.
Tonioli, Girolamo (librettist), 1784: KING'S, Jun 12; 1791: PAN, Jun 16
Tonneliers de Strasbourg, Les (dance), 1752: DL, Oct 17, 18, 19, 21
Tonson and Draper (booksellers), 1754: DL, Feb 28, Mar 11
Tonson, J and R (printers), 1747: CG, Mar 7; 1749: CG, Mar 3, DL, Apr 13; 1750:
    DL, Oct 11; 1751: DL, Dec 4; 1754: DL, Mar 12; 1756: DL, Jan 23; 1757: DL,
    Dec 19; 1758: CG, Feb 3; 1759: CG, Mar 9, 14; 1762: CG, Mar 19; 1763: CG, Feb
    18; 1764: CG, Mar 30
Tonson, Jacob (printer), 1684: NONE, Aug 0; 1696: LIF, Feb 0; 1697: NONE, Dec
    0; 1698: DLLIF, May 12; 1720: KING'S, Feb 18
Tony Aston's Medley (entertainment), 1716: GLOBE, Dec 28; 1717: GLOBE, Jan 4,
    7, 9, 11, 14, 16, 18, 21, 23, 25, 28, 31, Feb 1, 4, 6, 14, 15, 18, 20, 22,
    25, Mar 1, 11, 13, 15, 18, 29, Apr 1, 3, 8, 10, 12, 16, 18, 22, 23; 1718:
    GLOBE, Dec 3, 26; 1734: BLO, Jan 16, TB, 26
Tony Lumpkin in Town. See O'Keeffe, John.
Tony Lumpkin's Adventures in a Trip to London (entertainment), 1777: CG, Apr
    28; 1781: CG, Apr 18
Tony Lumpkin's Ramble through London (entertainment), 1778: CG, May 5
Tony Lumpkin's Ramble to Town (interlude, anon), 1792: CG, Apr 10
Too Civil by Half. See Dent, John.
Too justly alas (song), 1671: DG, Nov 0
Too Loving by Half. See Robson, Horatio Edgar.
Too Soon, O Gentle Youth (song), 1764: DL, May 10
Tooanahowi, John (American Indian visitor), 1734: LIF, Aug 20, DL, Oct 4, GF,
    5, HAY, 7, GF, 11, LIF, 12, DL, 14, GF, 17, CG/LIF, 25; see also American
    Princes; Indian Kings, American
Toogood, Miss (actor), 1756: CG, Apr 28; 1757: CG, Apr 27; 1758: CG, Apr 19;
    1759: CG, Apr 25
Toogood, Sarah (actor, dancer), 1747: DL, May 5; 1750: DL, Nov 27, Dec 26, 31;
    1751: DL, Jan 10, 22, Feb 21, May 4, 9, Oct 2, 9, 16, 28, 29, Dec 26; 1752:
    DL, Jan 1, Mar 9, 10, Apr 25, Sep 28, Oct 10, Nov 8, 22, 27; 1753: DL, Mar
    22, May 4, Oct 9, 13, 17, 18, 31; 1754: DL, Jan 23, May 13, Sep 14, Oct 31;
    1755: CG, Apr 23, DL, 29, May 8, Sep 19
Tooke, Horne (instigator), 1770: DL, Mar 5
Toole (actor), 1745: GF, Feb 14, Apr 15, May 1, Dec 4; 1746: GF, Feb 20, Mar
    22; 1747: GF, Jan 16
Toosey, William (pit office keeper), 1787: KING'S, Dec 8; 1788: KING'S, Apr 5
Top of the Tree, The; or, A Tit Bit for a Nice Palate (pantomime, anon), 1739:
    BFHCL, Aug 23
Topers, The; or, The Sons of Bacchus (music), 1738: CG, Mar 14
Topham, Edward, 1779: HAY, Jul 17; 1780: DL, Dec 4; 1781: DL, Mar 10, HAY, Jul
    9; 1782: DL, Dec 11; 1784: DL, Feb 14, HAY, Sep 2, DL, Oct 28, Dec 22; 1785:
    DL, Apr 15, HAY, Jul 9, CG, Oct 22; 1786: CG, Apr 24, May 11; 1787: CG, May
    1; 1788: CG, Apr 8; 1791: CG, Jun 15; 1792: CG, Apr 28; 1794: CG, Oct 23;
    1795: CG, Jan 31; 1796: CG, Jan 23, Apr 9, Sep 16
--Bonds without Judgement; or, The Loves of Bengal, 1787: CG, May 1, 2, 10, 24,
    29, Jun 1, 4, 6, 12, Oct 11
--Deaf Indeed (farce), 1780: DL, Dec 4
--Fool, The (farce), 1785: DL, Apr 15, HAY, Jul 29, CG, Dec 14, 15, 16, 19;
    1786: CG, Feb 13, Mar 20, 21, HAMM, Jul 26
--Small Talk; or, The Westminster Boy (farce), 1786: CG, May 11
Topham, H (Jr) (dancer), 1718: DL, Aug 12, 20; 1720: LIF, Mar 7, 26, Apr 29,
    30, May 11, 12, 23, 24, 25, 30, Jun 6; 1724: DL, Jan 27, May 2, 14, Nov 14;
    1725: DL, May 6; 1733: DL, Sep 24, Oct 10, 24, 31, Nov 7, 13, 15, 23, 26, Dec

5, 11; <u>1734</u>: DL, Jan 15, 19, Feb 4, DL/LIF, Mar 11, DL/HAY, 18, 21, Apr 1,
  DL/LIF, 1, HAY, 5, DL, 15, DL/HAY, 26, DL, 29, May 15, 16, LIF, 23, HAY, 27,
  JS, 31, GF, Sep 25, DL, Oct 5, 10, GF, 17, 28; <u>1735</u>: GF, Jan 24, Mar 6, May
  2, 3, GF/HAY, Jul 15, 22, Aug 1, HAY, 4, 12, GF/HAY, 21, LIF, 25, GF, Nov 6,
  17, HAY, Dec 13, 17, GF, 17; <u>1736</u>: GF, Feb 20, Mar 3, HAY, 5, GF, Apr 26,
  HAY, 29; <u>1740</u>: SF, Sep 9
Topham, John (dancer), <u>1717</u>: DL, Oct 25, 29, Nov 8, 22, Dec 3; <u>1718</u>: DL, Jan 7,
  14, 21, 27, 28, Feb 6, 10, Mar 18, Apr 25, 28, 29, May 2, 6, 7, 13, 15, 16,
  19, 21, 22, 27, 29, 30, Jun 6, 13, 27, Jul 18, Aug 12, 20, Oct 2, 7, 8, 14,
  15, 18, 20, 22, 24, 27, 29, Nov 4, 6, 7, 12, 14, 17, 19, 21, 24, 28, Dec 10,
  19; <u>1719</u>: DL, Jan 7, 8, 29, Feb 12, Mar 16, 19, Apr 11, 14, 16, 18, 20, 21,
  23, 24, 30, May 2, 4, 7, 9, 15, 18, 19, 21, 30, Jun 5, 9, 16, Jul 3, 21, Sep
  15, 29, Oct 12, 15, 16, 19, 26, 30; <u>1720</u>: LIF, Apr 29; <u>1722</u>: DL, Sep 27, Oct
  5, 9, 10, 12, 29; <u>1723</u>: DL, Jan 3, 21, 29, Mar 21, 25, Apr 29, May 8, 9, 13,
  15, 21, 25, Oct 25, 28, Nov 23, Dec 31; <u>1724</u>: DL, Jan 3, Feb 4, 11, 17, 20,
  27, Mar 9, 16, 26, Apr 7, 11, 13, 15, 18, May 4, 9, 12, 18, Nov 2, 14, 23;
  <u>1725</u>: DL, Jan 29, Feb 4, 20, 22, Mar 31, Apr 2, 15, 16, 19, 21, 23, 24, 27,
  29, 30, May 3, 4, 11, Sep 25; <u>1733</u>: DL, Nov 26, 27
Topham, Thomas (singer, strong man), <u>1734</u>: HIC, Jul 10, LIF, Sep 6; <u>1735</u>: HAY,
  Mar 22; <u>1741</u>: DL, May 26
Topham's Concert Room, <u>1729</u>: YB, Feb 21, Apr 15; <u>1730</u>: YB, Feb 20, Mar 6
Topping (actor), <u>1737</u>: HAY, Mar 21, Apr 13
Topsham, Mrs (haberdasher), <u>1772</u>: CG, Dec 26
Torinese, Checo (dancer), <u>1742</u>: DL, Nov 8, 13, 17, 19, 22, 26, 30, Dec 1, 11,
  21, 31; <u>1743</u>: DL, Jan 14, Feb 3, 26, Mar 10, 19, 24, Apr 8, May 16
Tormenting passion leave my breast (song), <u>1694</u>: DLORDG, Feb 0
Torna mi a Vegbeggiar (song), <u>1736</u>: DL, Dec 15, 16
Torre di Rezzonico (Brizzonie), Count Gaston della (translator), <u>1800</u>: KING'S,
  Apr 15
Torregiani, Paolo (singer), <u>1789</u>: KING'S, Jan 10, 24, Mar 24, Apr 4, Jun 11;
  <u>1790</u>: HAY, Jan 7, Feb 2, Apr 6, 29, May 27, 29, Jun 3; <u>1794</u>: KING'S, Feb 1,
  Mar 1, Apr 1, 26, 29, May 17, 29, Jun 5, Dec 6; <u>1795</u>: KING'S, Jan 10, 27, Feb
  7
Toscano (actor), <u>1749</u>: HAY, Nov 14; <u>1750</u>: DL, May 22
Tosi (musician), <u>1693</u>: YB, Oct 30, Nov 2
Total eclipse (song), <u>1745</u>: CG, Apr 10; <u>1789</u>: CG, Mar 6; <u>1790</u>: CG, Feb 24;
  <u>1791</u>: CG, Mar 11, DL, 11; <u>1792</u>: CG, Mar 2, KING'S, 14; <u>1793</u>: KING/HAY, Feb
  15, CG, Mar 6; <u>1794</u>: CG, Mar 12, DL, 21; <u>1795</u>: CG, Feb 27, KING'S, Mar 13,
  CG, 25; <u>1796</u>: CG, Feb 24; <u>1797</u>: CG, Mar 10, 22, Apr 7; <u>1798</u>: CG, Mar 14;
  <u>1799</u>: CG, Mar 13; <u>1800</u>: CG, Feb 28
Toten (house servant), <u>1758</u>: CG, May 12; <u>1759</u>: CG, May 25; <u>1760</u>: CG, May 19,
  Sep 22; <u>1761</u>: CG, May 15
Tothill Fields, <u>1733</u>: DL/HAY, Nov 16; <u>1776</u>: CG, Feb 27
Tottenham Court Booth, <u>1717</u>: TC, Aug 5
Tottenham Court Fair, <u>1739</u>: TC, Aug 6, 8; <u>1740</u>: TCLP, Aug 4; <u>1743</u>: TCD/BFTD,
  Aug 23; <u>1748</u>: HAY, Apr 18
Tottenham Court Road, <u>1746</u>: DL, May 2; <u>1769</u>: CG, Dec 22; <u>1770</u>: CG, Dec 22;
  <u>1772</u>: DL, Dec 19; <u>1777</u>: DL, May 6; <u>1778</u>: CG, May 23; <u>1779</u>: CG, May 5; <u>1780</u>:
  HAY, Aug 2, CG, Dec 22; <u>1791</u>: DL, May 20; <u>1793</u>: CG, May 15, 24, DL, Jun 1;
  <u>1794</u>: CG, May 16, HAY, Aug 23; <u>1795</u>: CG, May 14, HAY, Aug 21; <u>1796</u>: CG, Apr
  26, HAY, Aug 18; <u>1797</u>: CG, May 31, DL, Nov 25; <u>1798</u>: DL, May 30, HAY, Aug 21;
  <u>1799</u>: DL, May 3, HAY, Aug 13; <u>1800</u>: DL, May 23, 30, HAY, Aug 8, 23
Tottenham Court, <u>1730</u>: BFPG/TC, Aug 1, 24; <u>1731</u>: TCY, Aug 9; <u>1733</u>: TC, Jul 30;
  <u>1735</u>: TC, Aug 4; <u>1736</u>: TCP, Aug 4; <u>1738</u>: TC, Aug 7; <u>1743</u>: TCY, Aug 4,
  TCD/BFTD, 4; <u>1744</u>: HAY, May 10; <u>1782</u>: HAY, Jan 14
Touch at Old Times, A; or, No Days better than Our Own (entertainment), <u>1788</u>:
  DL, Apr 21; <u>1799</u>: CG, Apr 16, 30, Jun 1
Touch of the Times, A; or, A Ramble Through London (Humours of London, The)
  (entertainment), <u>1788</u>: DL, Apr 21, HAY, Aug 20
Touchbury (actor), <u>1735</u>: GF, Dec 17; <u>1736</u>: GF, Feb 20, Mar 3, Apr 16, May 4,
  LIF, Sep 28, Oct 21, Dec 7, 17; <u>1741</u>: GF, Feb 19, Mar 3
Touchstone of Invention, The. See Brownsmith, John.
Touchstone, The. See Dibdin, Charles.
Tour in Wales, A (play, anon), <u>1779</u>: HAY, Jul 24
Tourneur, Cyril, <u>1662</u>: REDBULL, Jan 22
--Nobleman, The; or, The Great Man, <u>1662</u>: REDBULL, Jan 22
Tower Division, <u>1748</u>: HAY, Apr 18
Tower Hill, <u>1724</u>: HT, Mar 13; <u>1749</u>: CG, Apr 28
Tower Song (song), <u>1799</u>: CG, May 14
Tower St, <u>1663</u>: LIF, Feb 23
Towers (dancer), <u>1735</u>: DL, Oct 7, Nov 20; <u>1736</u>: DL, Jan 12, May 3, 13, 24
Town Airs, The (play, anon), <u>1723</u>: HAY, Sep 23

Town and Country (song), 1796: DL, Jun 3; 1797: DL, Jun 8; 1798: DL, Jun 8
Town before You, The. See Cowley, Hannah.
Town Crier (song), 1796: HAY, Sep 1; 1797: HAY, Aug 10; 1799: DL, May 4, 7
Town Fop, The. See Behn, Aphra.
Town Miss, The; or, The Miser Outwitted (puppet show), 1752: SFB, Sep 22
Town Rakes, The (song), 1696: DL, Feb 0
Town Shifts, The. See Revet, Edward.
Town, The (criticism), 1748: DL, Mar 10
Townley, Blayney, 1754: CG, Nov 9
Townley, James, 1765: DL, Feb 4
--False Concord, 1764: CG, Mar 20
--High Life below Stairs, 1759: DL, Oct 31, Nov 1, 2, 3, 5, 6, 7, 8, 9, 12, 13,
14, 16, 17, 21, 27, Dec 4, 6, 8, 10, 20, 29; 1760: DL, Jan 10, 19, Feb 11,
15, Mar 17, 22, Apr 15, 23, 28, May 7, 22, Sep 30, Oct 17, 18, Dec 4; 1761:
DL, Jan 5, 14, Mar 27, 31, Apr 21, 29, May 8, 29, Sep 8, Oct 31, Dec 8; 1762:
DL, Feb 17, Mar 18, Apr 3, May 5, Nov 10; 1763: DL, Jan 20, 24, Feb 15, Mar
10, Apr 4, 19, Oct 29, Dec 13, 14; 1764: DL, Mar 24, Apr 7, 25, May 3, 16,
Oct 26, Nov 1, 5, Dec 11, 19; 1765: DL, Feb 12, Mar 16, Apr 25, May 8, Sep
21, Oct 4, Nov 13; 1766: DL, Apr 7, May 6, Dec 15, 20, 22; 1767: DL, Jan 24,
Mar 3, 23, 26, 31, Apr 24, 25, May 5, Oct 14, 21, Dec 21; 1768: DL, Feb 9,
Mar 3, 12, May 6, Sep 27, Dec 20; 1769: DL, Jan 16, Apr 15, May 9, 17, 20,
Sep 16; 1770: DL, May 16, 30, Nov 21, Dec 26; 1771: DL, Jan 11, 25, Mar 12,
18, Apr 19, May 20, Sep 21, Nov 18; 1772: DL, Jan 21, 31, Apr 7, May 21, Sep
24, Oct 20, Dec 10, 22; 1773: DL, Feb 23, Mar 13, Apr 12, Sep 18, Oct 12, Dec
17; 1774: DL, Jan 3, Feb 22, May 27, Oct 5, Nov 15; 1775: DL, Feb 16, May 23;
1776: DL, Mar 18, CHR, Oct 16, CG, Nov 30, Dec 7, 10, 20; 1777: CG, Feb 1,
DL, Nov 14, 20, Dec 3; 1778: CHR, Jun 18; 1779: DL, Jan 7, 14, Feb 8, Mar 22,
Dec 8; 1780: HAY, Mar 28, DL, May 25, Sep 16, Oct 24, Dec 16; 1783: DL, Oct
2, 16; 1784: DL, Jan 2, Mar 30, May 5, 18, Oct 14, Nov 24, 29; 1785: DL, Jan
6, 15, Feb 15, Apr 12, May 13, Sep 29, Nov 15; 1786: DL, Sep 26, Oct 23, Nov
24, Dec 7; 1787: CG, Apr 27, DL, Sep 22, Oct 23, Nov 10, Dec 13; 1788: DL,
Jan 24, Feb 26, CG, Apr 14, DL, 15, CG, 21, DL, May 23, Oct 4, 16, Dec 16;
1789: DL, Jan 9, Feb 20, Mar 21, Jun 8, Dec 1, 15; 1790: DL, Jan 29; 1791:
DL, Jan 26, CG, Apr 11, DL, May 19, DLKING'S, Nov 22, 26; 1792: DLKING'S,
Jan 20, Feb 4, 16, Apr 27, May 18, Jun 2, 6, DL, Oct 6, 9, Nov 19; 1794: DL,
Jun 25, 30, Jul 3; 1795: DL, Jan 5, 23; 1796: CG, Mar 14, DL, Jun 4, Sep 20;
1797: DL, Jun 16, HAY, Aug 5, DL, Nov 14; 1798: CG, Apr 27, May 15, DL, Jun
9, HAY, Aug 30, Sep 5, DL, 20, HAY, Dec 17; 1799: DL, Feb 12, Mar 9, Apr 12,
May 18, Jun 17, Jul 3, HAY, Aug 26, DL, Oct 1, Nov 8, Dec 17; 1800: DL, Jun
12
Townly (actor), 1744: HAY, Apr 6, May 10, 16, Jun 29, GF, Dec 11, 12, 19; 1745:
GF, Feb 20, Mar 7, 21
Townly, Mrs (actor), 1744: HAY, May 10
Townsend, Edward Evans (actor, singer), 1793: CG, Nov 14, 18, Dec 7, 9, 14, 19,
21, 23, 27, 30, 31; 1794: KING'S, Jan 11, CG, 11, 14, 15, 27, Feb 6, 22, Apr
7, 25, 30, May 2, 9, 23, 24, 28, Jun 2, 3, 5, 6, Sep 17, 22, 24, 26, Oct 1,
3, 7, 10, 14, 17, 20, 21, 29, 30, Nov 7, 11, 12, 15; 1795: CG, Jan 2, 12, Mar
14, 16, 19, Apr 8, 24, 28, May 1, 13, 14, 16, 22, 25, 27, 29, Jun 6, 10, 13,
16, Sep 14, 16, 18, 21, 23, 28, Oct 2, 5, 7, 8, 12, 15, 22, 23, 26, 30, 31,
Nov 6, 9, 14, 16, 27, 30, Dec 5, 7, 18, 21; 1796: CG, Jan 4, 13, Mar 14, 15,
17, 19, 30, Apr 9, 12, 15, 26, 29, 30, May 16, 18, 20, 23, 28, Jun 2, 4, Sep
14, 17, 19, 21, 23, 26, 30, Oct 3, 5, 6, 7, 17, 21, 24, Nov 5, 7, 12, Dec 15,
19, 21, 31; 1797: CG, Jan 2, 10, Feb 13, 18, 27, Apr 8, 19, 26, May 9, 17,
18, 22, 30, Jun 2, 6, 8, 13, Sep 20, 22, 27, 29, Oct 2, 4, 6, 16, 18, 20, 24,
31, Nov 1, 2, 8, 10, 24, Dec 19, 26, 28; 1798: CG, Jan 1, Feb 9, Mar 15, 31,
Apr 9, 16, 18, 21, 24, May 1, 9, 10, 12, 14, 15, 16, 18, 23, 25, 28, 31, Jun
4, 5, 7, Sep 19, 26, 28, Oct 5, 8, 11, 15, 25, 31, Nov 1, 7, 12, 14, 21, Dec
8, 11, 15; 1799: CG, Jan 5, 14, 22, 26, 29, Mar 2, 16, 25, Apr 6, 9, 12, 16,
19, 27, 30, May 3, 4, 7, 13, 14, 15, 18, 24, 25, 28, 31, Jun 1, 3, 6, 7, 8,
DL, Jul 2, CG, Sep 16, 20, 23, 25, 27, 30, Oct 4, 7, 21, 24, 30, Nov 9, 13,
Dec 2, 7, 9, 10; 1800: CG, Jan 16, Feb 19, Mar 1, 4, 17, 25, Apr 5, 15, 17,
19, 22, 23, 30, May 1, 2, 6, 7, 10, 15, 17, 20, 22, 27, 29, 30, Jun 2, 5, 6,
11, DL, 13
Townsend, Elizabeth, Mrs Edward Evans (actor), 1795: CG, May 8, Sep 16, 18, 23,
Oct 2, 9, 15, Nov 6, Dec 15, 26, 29; 1796: CG, Jan 6, 8, Apr 13, 29, May 12,
20, 24, Jun 2, 7
Townsend, G S (actor), 1796: CG, Oct 5
Townsend, Miss (spectator), 1767: CG, Jan 1
Townshend, Colonel (spectator), 1729: DL, Nov 6, Dec 27
Townshend, Lady Ethelreda (correspondent), 1744: KING'S, Jun 22
Toy Shop, The. See Dodsley, Robert.
Toy, The. See O'Keeffe, John.

Traci Amanti, I. See Cimarosa, Domenico.
Tracy, John, <u>1731</u>: LIF, Jan 13
--Periander, <u>1731</u>: LIF, Jan 13, 14, 15, 16, 25
Trade and Navigation (song), <u>1738</u>: CG, Apr 11
Trader's Dance (dance), <u>1745</u>: SMMF, Jul 11
Tradesman, a (actor), <u>1741</u>: GF, Apr 6
Tradge (actor), <u>1734</u>: JS, May 23
Traetta (Tragetta), Tommaso Michele Francesco Savario (composer), <u>1763</u>: KING'S,
   Apr 25; <u>1769</u>: KING'S, Jun 3; <u>1773</u>: HAY, May 5; <u>1776</u>: KING'S, Dec 2; <u>1777</u>:
   KING'S, Jan 21, Mar 1, 15, May 20; <u>1780</u>: KING'S, Dec 19
--Germondo (opera), <u>1776</u>: KING'S, Dec 2; <u>1777</u>: KING'S, Jan 4, 21, 25, Feb 1, 8,
   15
--Serve Rivali, Le (Capricci del Sesso, I) (opera), <u>1769</u>: KING'S, Jun 3, 6, 10;
   <u>1777</u>: KING'S, May 13, 20, 27, Jun 3, 10, 14, 24, 28; <u>1780</u>: KING'S, Dec 19;
   <u>1781</u>: KING'S, Jan 9, Feb 6, 13, 20
--Telemaco (opera), <u>1777</u>: KING'S, Mar 15, 22, Apr 5, 12, 19, 26, May 3, 10
Traffieri, Giuseppe (dancer), <u>1781</u>: KING'S, Jan 13, 23, Feb 22, DL, Mar 12,
   KING'S, 29, DL, Apr 30, KING'S, Jun 5, Jul 3
Trafford (tavern keeper), <u>1744</u>: DL, May 17
Tragedy a la Mode. See Foote, Samuel, Taste.
Tragedy of Hero and Leander, The. See Stapylton, Sir Robert.
Tragedy of Nero, The. See Lee, Nathaniel.
Tragedy of Sertorius, The. See Bancroft, John.
Tragical Cantata of the Mare that Lost Her Shoe (song), <u>1730</u>: DL, May 21
Traitant de France, Le (play, anon), <u>1722</u>: HAY, Feb 8
Traitor to Himself, The; or, Man's Heart his Greatest Enemy (interlude), <u>1677</u>:
   NONE, Sep 0
Traitor, The. See Shirley, James.
Traitor, The; or, Tragedy of Amidea. See Bullock, Christopher.
Trakebarne Gran Mogol (pastiche), <u>1766</u>: KING'S, Nov 1, 8, 15, 22, 29, Dec 6;
   <u>1767</u>: KING'S, Jan 24
Trame Deluse, Le. See Cimarosa, Domenico.
Trampwell, Mrs (actor), <u>1757</u>: HAY, Aug 29, Sep 2
Transfigurations (dance), <u>1735</u>: GF/HAY, Mar 28
Transformation. See Bonnor, Charles.
Transporting Charmer (song), <u>1734</u>: HIC, Jul 10
Trapp, Joseph, <u>1703</u>: DL, Jul 16; <u>1704</u>: LIF, Jan 13, Dec 2; <u>1798</u>: CG, Apr 17
--Abra Mule; or, Love and Empire, <u>1704</u>: LIF, Jan 13, 14, 15, 17, 18, 20, 21,
   22, 24, 25, 28, Feb 10, Mar 20, Apr 3, 25, Dec 2, 12; <u>1710</u>: DL, Jan 26; <u>1711</u>:
   DL, Mar 20; <u>1721</u>: LIF, Mar 18, 20, 23, Apr 26, Nov 2, 28; <u>1722</u>: LIF, May 19,
   Oct 27, Nov 26; <u>1723</u>: LIF, May 17; <u>1726</u>: LIF, Apr 2, May 9; <u>1735</u>: CG/LIF, Feb
   15, 17, 18, Mar 11, Apr 18; <u>1736</u>: CG, Mar 27; <u>1741</u>: CG, Mar 12, Apr 13; <u>1744</u>:
   CG, Mar 8
--Curiosity, <u>1798</u>: CG, Apr 17, May 12
Trappolin, The Supposed Prince. See Cokayne, Sir Aston.
Trau, Schau, Wem. See Brandes, Johann Christian.
Travellers in Switzerland, The. See Bate, Henry.
Travels of Cosmo the Third, The (entertainment), <u>1669</u>: BRIDGES, Apr 15, LIF,
   20, BRIDGES, 24, LIF, May 10, BRIDGES, 24
Travels of Trudge (entertainment), <u>1798</u>: CG, Apr 24
Travers, John (composer), <u>1779</u>: DL, Mar 12; <u>1786</u>: CG, Dec 26; <u>1787</u>: CG, Nov 5
Tre Cicisbei Ridicoli, Li. See Ciampi, Lorenzo.
Tre Gobbi Rivali, I (opera), <u>1761</u>: KING'S, Mar 9
Treacherous Brothers, The. See Powell, George.
Treachery and Ingratitude. See Byrn, James, The Shipwreck.
Treatise on the Art of Dancing, A, <u>1762</u>: CG, Mar 3
Treatise on the Passions, A (criticism), <u>1747</u>: CG, May 12; <u>1752</u>: DL, Jan 25
Trebbi, Giuseppe (singer), <u>1775</u>: KING'S, Oct 31, Dec 12; <u>1776</u>: KING'S, Jan 9,
   27, Feb 6, 15, 29, Mar 12, 14, 28, Apr 20, 23, May 14, 18, Nov 2, 5; <u>1777</u>:
   KING'S, Jan 21, Feb 4, Mar 1, 13, 15, Apr 1, 10, 17, 29, May 20, 24; <u>1779</u>:
   KING'S, Nov 27, Dec 14; <u>1780</u>: KING'S, Jan 22, Feb 8, Mar 9, Apr 13, 22, May
   9, 25, 31, Nov 25, 28, Dec 19; <u>1781</u>: KING'S, Jan 23, Feb 8, 22, Mar 8, 29,
   Apr 5, Jun 5, 23
Treble Harp Concerto (music), <u>1734</u>: DL/HAY, Mar 2
Trecothick (alderman), <u>1763</u>: DL, Apr 27
Trefusis, Joseph (actor), <u>1689</u>: DL, Nov 20; <u>1690</u>: DL, Nov 0, Dec 0; <u>1692</u>: DL,
   Jan 0; <u>1693</u>: DL, Apr 0; <u>1694</u>: DG, May 0, DL, Sep 0; <u>1695</u>: LIF, Apr 30; <u>1696</u>:
   LIF, Mar 0, Apr 0, Jun 0; <u>1697</u>: LIF, Jun 0, Nov 0, ATCOURT, 4; <u>1698</u>: LIF, Mar
   0
Trelany, Sir Jonathan (spectator), <u>1678</u>: DL, Mar 19
Tremende oscure atroci (song), <u>1745</u>: CG, Apr 10; <u>1755</u>: KING'S, Mar 17
Tremoille, Duchess de la (correspondent), <u>1661</u>: ATCOURT, Feb 25

Trentham, Lord (correspondent), 1749: HAY, Nov 22
Trentham, Lord (rioter), 1749: HAY, Nov 14, 17, 22, 29
Trento, Vittorio (composer), 1796: DL, Oct 1
Tresham, Henry (painter), 1791: PAN, Feb 17
Trevor, George (beneficiary), 1711: CLH, Apr 25
Trevor, John (dancer), 1675: ATCOURT, Feb 15
Trevor, Mrs (actor, singer), 1800: CG, Jan 16, Mar 25, May 1, 24
Trew (actor), 1780: CG, Nov 24; 1781: CG, Sep 24; 1782: CG, Mar 14, Apr 26;
    1783: CG, May 24
Trial of Conjugal Love, The. See Jacob, Hildebrand.
Trial of Fanny Phantom (entertainment), 1763: HAY, May 11
Trial of Skill, A (entertainment), 1664: REDBULL, May 30
Trial Scenes of the Cock Lane Ghost (play, anon), 1762: BFY, Sep 3
Trials of the Heart (play, anon), 1799: DL, Apr 24
Triangle (music), 1800: CG, Mar 21
Trick for Trick. See Fabian, R.
Trick for Trick; or, An Odd Affair between Harlequin, his Associates and the
    Vintner of York (farce), 1739: TC, Aug 6
Trick for Trick; or, The Debauched Hypocrite. See D'Urfey, Thomas.
Trick upon Trick. See Kemble, John Philip.
Trick upon Trick; or, Harlequin Statue. See Yarrow, Joseph.
Tricks of Harlequin, The; or, The Doctor Defeated (pantomime, anon), 1723: DL,
    Jul 2, 9, 12, 23, 26, Aug 2, 9
Tricks of Pierrot (dance), 1764: CG, May 22
Triffusis. See Trefusis.
Trifle (song), 1731: GF, Mar 18
Trimuer (actor), 1728: HAY, Feb 21
Trio Jovial (song), 1740: CG, Apr 16
Trio of True Happiness (song), 1741: CG, Apr 10
Triomphante, La (dance), 1726: HAY, Apr 27
Triomphe D'Euthime sur Le Genie de Liba, Le (dance), 1775: KING'S, Oct 31, Nov
    4, 7, 11, 18, 21, 25, 28
Triomphe de Cupidon, Le; ou, Les Nymphes Vaincrues par l'Amour (dance), 1797:
    KING'S, May 25
Triomphe de l'Amour Conjugal, Le (Alceste) (dance), 1782: KING'S, Jan 10, 12,
    15, 19, 26, Feb 2, 7, 9, 12, 14, 16, 19, Mar 2, 12, 16, 19, Apr 6, 25, 27,
    May 27
Triomphe de la Folie (dance), 1791: PAN, May 3, 14, Jun 2, 18, 23
Triomphe de la Magie (dance), 1772: KING'S, May 12, 19, 23, 26, Jun 3; 1776:
    KING'S, May 30
Triomphe de Themis (dance), 1797: KING'S, Dec 20, 23, 26; 1798: KING'S, Jan 16,
    Mar 22, 24, 31, May 10
Trionfo d'Amore, Il (serenata), 1740: HIC, Dec 19, 26; 1741: HIC, Jan 2, 9, Mar
    20
Trionfo d'Amore, Il. See Bottarelli, F.
Trionfo D'Arianna, Il. See Anfossi, Pasquale.
Trionfo del Tempo e Della Verita, Il. See Handel, George Frederic.
Trionfo del Tempo, Il (oratorio), 1757: CG, Mar 11
Trionfo della Continenza, Il. See Galuppi, Baldassare.
Trionfo della Costanza, Il. See Anfossi, Pasquale.
Trionfo della Costazza, Il. See Sacchini, Antonio Maria Gasparo.
Trionfo della Gloria, Il (opera), 1759: KING'S, Jan 31
Trionfo di Camilla, Il. See Ciampi, Lorenzo.
Trip to Calais, A. See Foote, Samuel.
Trip to Carrickfergus (entertainment), 1761: CG, Mar 26
Trip to Portsmouth, A. See Stevens, George Alexander.
Trip to Scarborough, A. See Sheridan, Richard Brinsley.
Trip to Scotland, A. See Whitehead, William.
Trip to the Nore, A. See Franklin, Andrew.
Triple Harp (music), 1771: CG, Apr 24; 1776: CG, Apr 22
Triple Hornpipe (dance), 1769: CG, Apr 8; 1774: CG, Apr 15; 1780: CG, May 23;
    1783: DL, Nov 4, 6, 22; 1784: DL, Feb 14; 1790: DL, Mar 23; 1791: HAY, Jun
    17, 20; 1793: CG, May 10; 1794: CG, Apr 7; 1795: CG, May 13, Jun 17; 1797:
    CG, Oct 18, Nov 9; 1798: CG, Feb 9
Tripoline Ambassador, 1700: DL, Nov 21, Dec 27; 1715: LIF, Feb 19, 22; 1728:
    HAY, Oct 24, DL, Nov 1, LIF, 23; 1744: CG, Mar 15; 1759: DL, Oct 22; 1760:
    CG, Jan 11; 1661: DL, Apr 16; 1767: RANELAGH, Jun 1
Triquet, Major John (beneficiary), 1741: GF, Apr 17
Tristram Shandy. See Macnally, Leonard.
Triulzi (singer), 1746: KING'S, Nov 4; 1747: KING'S, Apr 14
Triumph of Britannia Over the Four Parts of the World, The (dance), 1728: HAY,
    Oct 24, DL, Nov 1, LIF, 23; 1741: BFH, Aug 22

Triumph of Cupid (dance), <u>1787</u>: ROY, Jul 3
Triumph of Honour, The. See Beaumont, Francis.
Triumph of Hymen, The. See Marinari, Gaetano.
Triumph of Julius Caesar (dance), <u>1787</u>: KING'S, Mar 1
Triumph of Love (dance), <u>1760</u>: KING'S, Mar 24; <u>1776</u>: DL, Nov 7, Dec 12; <u>1777</u>:
    DL, Jan 9, 10, 13, 24, Feb 10, 13, 24, Apr 7, 9, May 30; <u>1796</u>: DL, Oct 1, 3,
    4, 6, 11, 13, 18, 22, 26
Triumph of Love in the Temple of Apollo, The (entertainment), <u>1754</u>: BFSIY, Sep
    3, 4, 5, 6; <u>1777</u>: DL, Jan 9
Triumph of Mirth, The. See King, Thomas.
Triumph of Peace, The. See Dodsley, Robert.
Triumph of Time and Truth, The. See Handel, George Frederic.
Triumph of Truth, The (music), <u>1789</u>: DL, Feb 27, Mar 4, 20
Triumph of Wine (song), <u>1794</u>: CG, May 26; see also What tho' from Venus Cupid
    sprung
Triumphant Queen of Hungary, The; or, The French Defeated (play, anon), <u>1743</u>:
    BFGA, Aug 23
Triumphant Widow, The. See Cavendish, William.
Triumphs of Archery (entertainment), <u>1795</u>: CG, Dec 21, 28
Triumphs of Hibernia, The. See Pasquale.
Triumphs of Hymen; and, the Landing of the Queen (droll), <u>1761</u>: SFW, Sep 19, 21
Triumphs of London, The. See Jordan, Thomas.
Triumphs of Love and Honour, The. See Cooke, Thomas.
Triumphs of Love, The (pastiche), <u>1712</u>: QUEEN'S, Nov 12, 15; <u>1728</u>: LIF, Nov 23;
    <u>1729</u>: LIF, Oct 15; <u>1733</u>: CG, Oct 13
Triumphs of Virtue, The (play, anon), <u>1697</u>: DL, Feb 0
Troades. See Pordage, Samuel.
Troades; or, The Royal Captives. See Sherburne, Sir Edward.
Troas (beneficiary), <u>1748</u>: HAY, Jan 29
Troas (musician), <u>1726</u>: LIF, May 11
Troas. See Seneca.
Troche, Gervaise (dancer), <u>1791</u>: PAN, Feb 17, Mar 19, 22, 24, May 9, 17, Jun 10
Troilus and Cressida. See Shakespeare, William.
Trois Freres Riveaux, Les. See La Font, Joseph de.
Trois Sultanes (dance), <u>1796</u>: KING'S, Feb 13, 20, Mar 1, 5, 10, 29
Trompeur Trompe, Le (dance), <u>1797</u>: KING'S, Apr 25
Trott (doorkeeper), <u>1735</u>: CG/LIF, May 26; <u>1741</u>: CG, May 7; <u>1742</u>: CG, May 18;
    <u>1743</u>: CG, May 11; <u>1744</u>: CG, May 14; <u>1745</u>: CG, May 15; <u>1746</u>: CG, May 7; <u>1747</u>:
    CG, May 22; <u>1748</u>: CG, May 6; <u>1749</u>: CG, May 3; <u>1750</u>: CG, May 7; <u>1751</u>: CG, May
    14; <u>1752</u>: CG, May 7; <u>1753</u>: CG, May 21; <u>1754</u>: CG, May 18; <u>1755</u>: CG, May 20;
    <u>1756</u>: CG, May 24; <u>1757</u>: CG, May 20; <u>1758</u>: CG, May 12; <u>1759</u>: CG, May 25; <u>1760</u>:
    CG, May 19; <u>1761</u>: CG, May 15; <u>1762</u>: CG, May 21; <u>1763</u>: CG, May 26
Trott, Widow (beneficiary), <u>1764</u>: CG, May 12; <u>1766</u>: CG, May 15; <u>1767</u>: CG, May
    18; <u>1768</u>: CG, May 27, 28; <u>1769</u>: CG, May 6, 8; <u>1770</u>: CG, May 18, 21; <u>1771</u>: CG,
    May 22; <u>1772</u>: CG, May 23; <u>1773</u>: CG, May 22; <u>1774</u>: CG, May 7; <u>1775</u>: CG, May 30
Trotter (actor), <u>1775</u>: HAY, Feb 2; <u>1776</u>: HAY, May 2; <u>1777</u>: CHR, Jun 18, 20, 25,
    27, 30, Jul 2, 21, 23
Trotter, Catherine, <u>1698</u>: LIF, Jun 0; <u>1700</u>: DL, Nov 23; <u>1701</u>: DL, Feb 4; <u>1706</u>:
    QUEEN'S, Feb 11
--Agnes de Castro, <u>1695</u>: DL, Dec 0
--Fatal Friendship, <u>1698</u>: LIF, May 0
--Love at a Loss; or, Most Votes Carry It, <u>1700</u>: DL, Nov 23
--Revolution of Sweden, The, <u>1706</u>: QUEEN'S, Feb 7, 11, 12, 14, 16
--Unhappy Penitent, The, <u>1701</u>: DL, Feb 4
Trotter, Miss. See Truster, Miss.
Trotter, Mrs (actor), <u>1777</u>: CHR, Jul 23
Trout (actor), <u>1696</u>: LIF, Jun 0, Nov 14; <u>1697</u>: LIF, Jun 0; <u>1700</u>: LIF, Jan 9,
    Mar 0; <u>1701</u>: LIF, Jan 0; <u>1703</u>: LIF, Nov 0; <u>1704</u>: LIF, Feb 2, Mar 25, Dec 4;
    <u>1707</u>: QUEEN'S, Jan 4, Feb 18
Trout. See Trott.
Trouton (merchant), <u>1762</u>: CG, Mar 25
Trowa (musician), <u>1758</u>: CHAPEL, Apr 27
Trowell (actor), <u>1774</u>: HAY, Sep 21
Trowell, Miss (actor), <u>1770</u>: HAY, May 28, Jun 18, 27, Jul 25, Aug 1, 8, 22, 31,
    Sep 27, Oct 5
Trowion (ticket deliverer), <u>1791</u>: CG, May 26
Trudge's Exordium on the Quay (entertainment), <u>1798</u>: CG, Apr 24
True and Famous History of Semiramis, Queen of Babylon: or, The Woman Wears the
    Breeches (droll), <u>1725</u>: BF, Aug 23
True Blue (song), <u>1742</u>: CG, Apr 23
True Blue. See Carey, Henry, Nancy.
True Briton, The. See Cranke.

True Courage (song), 1799: CG, May 3
True, Famous and Ancient History of King Saul, and the Witch of Endor, The
    (droll), 1721: SFHL, Sep 2
True Friends. See Dibdin, Thomas John.
True Glory (song), 1798: DL, May 7
True State of the Differences Subsisting (pamphlet), 1768: CG, Mar 1
True Widow, A. See Shadwell, Thomas.
True-Born Irishman. See Macklin, Charles, Irish Fine Lady.
True-Born Scotsman, The. See Macklin, Charles.
Trueman (actor), 1756: SFB, Sep 20
Trueman (actor), 1794: DL, Apr 21, 28, May 1, 3, 16, 30, Jun 9, 14, 24, 25, Sep
    18, 23, 27, Oct 11, 31, Nov 1, 5, 8, 11, 13, 15, 18, 29, Dec 5, 6, 9, 16, 19,
    20, 23, 30; 1795: DL, Jan 3, 23, 26, 28, 31, Feb 2, 3, 6, 28, Mar 5, 9, 14,
    21, Apr 16, 22, May 1, 6, 12, 22, 28, Jun 1, 3, Sep 17, 19, 22, 24, 29, Oct
    1, 6, 10, 12, 15, 19, 21, 27, 30, Nov 6, 10, 11, 17, 19, 20, 21, 23, Dec 2,
    10, 11, 18, 23, 28, 30; 1796: DL, Jan 13, 18, 23, 25, Feb 15, 20, Mar 12, Apr
    2, 18, 26, 29, 30, May 2, 9, 11, 13, 17, 20, 23, Jun 1, 4, 8, HAY, 11, DL,
    13, HAY, 13, 14, 15, 16, 17, 20, 22, 25, 29, 30, Jul 2, 5, 6, 8, 9, 12, 14,
    15, 21, 23, Aug 8, 11, 12, 18, 23, 29, Sep 1, 3, 5, 7, DL, 20, 22, 24, 27,
    29, Oct 3, 4, 6, 10, 13, 17, 19, 22, 24, 27, 28, Nov 5, 9, 10, 15, 18, 26,
    28, Dec 9, 16, 26; 1797: DL, Jan 13, 17, 20, 27, Feb 1, 2, 3, 7, 9, 16, 21,
    Mar 20, Apr 24, May 1, 12, 17, 24, Jun 6, 9, HAY, 13, 15, DL, 15, HAY, 16,
    17, 19, 20, 21, 22, 23, 24, 26, 27, 29, Jul 6, 8, 10, 13, 14, 15, 31, Aug 5,
    9, 14, 15, 24, 28, 30, Sep 1, 4, 8, 11, DL, 19, 21, 23, 28, Oct 3, 5, 7, 12,
    21, 28, 30, Nov 2, 4, 7, 9, 11, 14, 15, 17, 21, 23, 24, 25, Dec 2, 8, 11, 12,
    14, 21, 27; 1798: DL, Jan 16, 25, Feb 1, 13, 20, 27, Mar 17, Apr 14, May 7,
    9, 14, 21, 24, 30, Jun 7, HAY, 12, DL, 12, HAY, 13, DL, 14, HAY, 15, 16, 18,
    19, 20, 21, 23, 29, 30, Jul 4, 5, 6, 13, 14, 16, 17, 21, 25, 30, Aug 3, 6, 7,
    11, 14, 21, 28, 29, 30, 31, Sep 3, 7, DL, 15, 18, 20, 22, 25, 27, 29, Oct 4,
    6, 11, 13, 15, 16, 18, 20, 27, Nov 12, 13, 14, 16, 20, 26, 29, Dec 3, 4, 17,
    19, 27; 1799: DL, Jan 8, 10, 11, 17, 19, 31, Feb 4, 14, 23, Mar 2, 11, Apr 5,
    25, 27, May 3, 7, 8, 20, 24, 30, 31, HAY, Jun 15, 21, 24, 27, DL, Jul 2, 4,
    5, HAY, 5, 6, 9, 12, 16, 19, 20, 22, 23, 26, 27, Aug 5, 10, 13, 20, 21, 22,
    26, 27, 28, Sep 2, 13, DL, 17, 19, 21, 24, 28, Oct 1, 3, 5, 7, 12, 14, 19,
    21, 31, Nov 6, 8, 22, 25, 29, Dec 11; 1800: DL, Jan 24, 28, Feb 7, 12, 14,
    18, Mar 11, 13, 25, 27, 29, Apr 5, 17, 21, 29, May 10, 12, 16, 19, 23, 29,
    Jun 5, 11, HAY, 16, DL, 17, HAY, 19, 20, 27, 28, Jul 1, 2, 7, 15, 25, 26, Aug
    7, 12, 14, 20, 23, 26, 27, 29, Sep 1, 3
Trueman, Thomas (actor), 1800: HAY, Jul 21, Aug 22, Sep 16
Truly Happy Man (song), 1749: CG, Apr 14; 1750: CG, Mar 29; 1751: CG, Apr 24
Trumpet (music), 1697: LW, Jul 21; 1702: PR, Jun 30, LIF, Dec 29; 1703: YB, Feb
    24, HA, May 18, LIF, Jun 11, 14; 1705: LIF, Jan 25; 1709: HA, Jul 30, SH, Nov
    30; 1710: SH, Mar 22; 1712: GR, May 19, B&S, Nov 24, SH, Dec 30; 1713: CA,
    Mar 20, HIC, Apr 9, SH, May 12; 1714: QUEEN'S, May 1; 1715: LIF, Mar 31;
    1719: YB, Dec 19; 1720: LIF, Mar 12, DL, May 24; 1721: HIC, Mar 1; 1724: YB,
    Mar 27; 1725: LIF, Mar 18; 1729: HIC, Apr 30; 1730: GF, May 22; 1731: HIC,
    Apr 9, DT, 23, LIF, 29, HAY, May 10, STA, Aug 9; 1732: HIC, Mar 27; 1733: DL,
    May 21, DL/HAY, Oct 6; 1735: HAY, Jan 31, LIF, Sep 5; 1737: HIC, Mar 24, CG,
    Apr 25, 28; 1738: DL, Mar 21; 1740: DL, May 14, 21; 1741: HIC, Feb 5, HAY,
    26, GF, Mar 12, CT, 13; 1744: SH, Feb 9, TB, 29; 1748: HAY, Dec 9; 1775: HAY,
    May 1; 1778: HAY, Dec 28; 1790: CG, Mar 3; 1792: CG, Feb 24, Mar 9; 1794: DL,
    Mar 14, 19, CG, Apr 11
Trumpet and Flute (music), 1707: YB, Mar 26
Trumpet and German Flute (music), 1714: SH, Apr 6; 1733: HAY, Feb 28; 1738:
    HAY, Mar 3
Trumpet and Hautboy (music), 1709: HA, Jul 30
Trumpet and Violin (music), 1706: YB, Mar 18; 1712: OS, Nov 28
Trumpet Cantata (music), 1730: LIF, May 7
Trumpet Concerto (music), 1722: DL, Mar 14, HAY, May 11; 1729: HIC, Apr 30;
    1731: HAY, May 10; 1732: LIF, Mar 10, GF, Apr 27, May 4, HAY, Jun 1; 1733:
    GF, Apr 13, HAY, May 26; 1752: CT/HAY, Jan 7; 1770: MARLY, Jul 17; 1771: CG,
    May 15, GROTTO, Aug 30, Sep 3, 9; 1772: CG, Apr 9; 1774: HAY, Mar 25; 1779:
    HAY, Mar 19, 26, CG, Apr 29
Trumpet Concerto, Grand (music), 1734: HIC, Apr 8; 1748: HAY, Dec 9
Trumpet Gregorian Song (song), 1740: DL, May 13
Trumpet Minuet (music), 1738: DL, Feb 28
Trumpet on the Violin (music), 1725: HIC, Mar 19
Trumpet shall sound (song), 1786: DL, Mar 24; 1792: KING'S, Mar 30; 1793:
    KING/HAY, Feb 20; 1794: DL, Mar 19; 1795: CG, Mar 27; 1798: CG, Mar 30; 1799:
    CG, Feb 13
Trumpet Solo (music), 1706: HAW, Aug 17
Trumpet Sonata (music), 1703: HA, May 18; 1709: SH, May 26; 1710: SH, Mar 22;

Tunbridge Wells Theatre, 1724: CT, Nov 24; 1775: HAY, Feb 2; 1786: DL, Dec 6;
  1796: DL, Oct 11
Tunbridge Wells. See Rawlins Jr, Thomas.
Tunbridge, 1701: LIF, Aug 0
Tune your harps (song), 1751: KING'S, Apr 16; 1789: CG, Mar 20; 1790: CG, Mar
  3; 1793: KING/HAY, Mar 13, CG, 13; 1794: CG, Mar 7, Apr 9; 1795: CG, Feb 20,
  Mar 4; 1797: CG, Mar 31; 1799: CG, Feb 15, Mar 1; 1800: CG, Mar 19
Tunis, 1733: DL, Oct 22, DL/HAY, Nov 1
Tunisian ambassador (spectator), 1722: LIF, May 4; 1734: CG, Mar 28, GF, Apr 4,
  May 3
Tunstall (actor), 1789: KHS, Sep 16, WHF, Nov 9, 11
Tunstall, Mrs (actor), 1789: KHS, Sep 16, WHF, Nov 9, 11
Turbaned Turk who scorns the world (song), 1795: CG, May 25; 1796: CG, Apr 5;
  1797: CG, May 9; 1799: CG, Apr 26
Turber, Captain (shareholder), 1750: DL, Jan 22
Turbutt-Dove Booth, 1743: TCD/BFTD, Aug 23
Turbutt-Yates Booth, 1741: BFTY, Aug 22
Turbutt, Benjamin (actor), 1735: HAY, Aug 26, DL, Nov 13
Turbutt, P (actor), 1734: DL, Oct 21
Turbutt, Robert (actor), 1733: BFMMO, Aug 23, DL, Oct 1, Nov 5, 13, 14, 26, Dec
  5, 7, 11, 17, 21; 1734: DL, Jan 8, 19, 31, Feb 4, 11, Mar 7, DL/HAY, 30,
  DL/LIF, Apr 1, HAY, 5, DL, 15, LIF, May 9, DL, 13, 15, LIF, 23, HAY, 27, Jun
  3, 5, 7, 12, 19, 24, 28, Jul 19, 26, 31, Aug 7, 14, 16, 22, DL, Sep 24, 28,
  Oct 5, 8, 14, 19, 21, 22, Nov 8, 20, 25; 1735: DL, Jan 22, Feb 25, Mar 6, 10,
  22, Apr 28, May 6, 10, 14, 20, LIF, Jun 12, DL, Jul 1, GF/HAY, 15, 22, Aug 1,
  HAY, 12, GF/HAY, 21, HAY, 26, DL, Sep 9, 11, 15, 18, Oct 2, 7, 25, 31, Nov 6,
  12, 15, 19, 29, Dec 4; 1736: DL, Jan 3, 12, Feb 20, 28, LIF, Apr 14, DL, 15,
  May 25, LIF, Jun 16, RI, Aug 21, DL, 26, Sep 7, 18, Oct 5, 12, 20, 25, Nov
  13, 15, 19, 22, Dec 17, 31; 1737: DL, Jan 14, 26, 29, Feb 19, Mar 3, 15, May
  5, 17, 19, 21, Sep 1, 3, 8, 17, 22, 29, Oct 1, 13, 21, 25, 27, Nov 11, 12,
  15; 1738: DL, Jan 11, 19, 25, 26, 31, Feb 2, 16, 23, 28, Mar 25, Apr 13, 17,
  27, May 6, 8, 17, Sep 7, 12, 14, 23, 30, Oct 3, 11, 16, 18, 19, 20, 25, 27,
  28, Nov 2, 4, 9, 11, 14, 18, 25, 30, Dec 6, 11, 15, 26; 1739: DL, Jan 1, 3,
  8, 13, 16, 18, 27, Feb 3, 12, 23, Mar 3, 8, 19, 20, 27, 31, Apr 5, 10, 25,
  28, 30, May 1, 14, 15, 16, 17, 18, 19, 22, 28, Sep 1, 6, 8, 13, 15, 18, 22,
  24, 26, 27, Oct 4, 5, 8, 11, 13, 15, 16, 17, 23, 24, 27, 29, Nov 5, 10, 15,
  16, 19, 20, 21, 22, Dec 8, 10, 11, 14, 15, 26, 31; 1740: DL, Jan 3, 18, Feb
  7, Mar 11, 17, 20, 29, Apr 15, 17, 21, May 2, 6, 9, 12, 13, 14, 15, 17, Sep
  11, 16, 23, 27, Oct 2, 4, 7, 10, 13, 14, 15, 16, 23, 27, 28, Nov 4, 6, 7, 13,
  19, 24, 27, 28, Dec 15, 18, 20; 1741: DL, Jan 15, Feb 2, 14, Mar 30, 31, Apr
  29, May 12, 13, 21, 22, Jun 4, BFTY, Aug 22, DL, Sep 8, 10, 17, 19, 24, Oct
  8, 9, 10, 15, 21, 23, 31, Nov 4, 11, 16, 21, Dec 1, 7, 8, 19; 1742: DL, Jan
  4, 6, 22, Feb 12, Mar 22, 27, 29, Apr 24, 30, May 4, 12, 28, 31, Sep 11, 14,
  16, 21, 25, 30, Oct 2, 5, 7, 9, 13, 26, Nov 3, 4, 8, 16, 19, Dec 8, 14; 1743:
  DL, Jan 11, 27, 28, Feb 4, 10, 17, 21, Mar 14, 21, SOU, 30, DL, Apr 7, 8, 15,
  21, 29, May 5, 7, LIF, Jun 3, DL, Nov 4, 5, 15, 17, 18, 23, 29, Dec 6, 10,
  12, 13, 15, 16, 17; 1744: DL, Jan 7, 12, 17, 27, Feb 3, 21, Mar 10, 12, Apr
  2, 6, 9, 10, 17, 23, 25, 26, 30, May 14, 22, Sep 18, 22, 29, Oct 2, 13, 19,
  22, 24, 25, 27, 30, Nov 1, 3, 5, 6, 12; 1745: DL, Jan 4, 5, 7, Feb 11, 13,
  20, Mar 30, Apr 17, 26, Sep 21, 28, Oct 5, 12, 15, 19, Nov 1, 20, 22, 25, 28,
  30, Dec 10, 11, 13, 16; 1746: DL, Jan 24, Feb 26
Turene (beneficiary), 1785: HAMM, Jul 11
Turin Opera, 1761: SFT, Sep 21; 1785: KING'S, Jan 8
Turin, 1782: KING'S, May 25; 1789: KING'S, Jan 24
Turk, and No Turk (play), 1785: HAY, Jul 7, 9, 11, 12, 14, 15, 18, 21, 23, 25,
  27, Aug 25, Sep 5; 1786: HAY, Aug 15
Turk's Head (public house), 1736: HAY, Apr 6; 1756: DL, Jan 22; 1760: DL, Oct
  13
Turk's Head Coffee House, 1757: DL, Dec 14
Turk's Head Tavern, 1753: DL, Mar 26; 1758: KING'S, Apr 6
Turkey Cock (dance), 1719: RI, Jun 6
Turkey Cock Music (music), 1702: LIF, Dec 29; 1704: LIF, Jul 24
Turkish Ambassador, 1746: GF, Feb 10; 1794: CG, Jun 3, 13; 1795: CG, May 6;
  1798: CG, May 9, 23; 1800: CG, May 17, DL, Jun 3
Turkish Ballet (dance), 1773: KING'S, Apr 29
Turkish Ceremony (entertainment), 1720: KING'S, Apr 29, May 10; 1721: HAY, Feb
  27; 1735: HAY, Jan 13
Turkish Coffee House (dance), 1763: KING'S, Dec 13; 1764: KING'S, Jan 10, 14,
  Feb 25, Mar 10, 20, Apr 10
Turkish Dance (dance), 1723: DL, Jun 6; 1724: DL, Mar 26; 1726: DL, Mar 31, Apr
  15, HAY, 27, DL, 27, May 3; 1727: DL, Apr 25, May 3, 10, 15; 1728: DL, May
  10, 15, 22; 1729: DL, May 8; 1730: GF, Feb 23, Mar 2, 7, 9, 17, Apr 7; 1737:

DL, Mar 10, 14, Apr 2, 13, 23, 28, 29, 30, May 13, Jun 11; <u>1738</u>: DL, Apr 12,
13, May 2, 3, 8, 17; <u>1739</u>: DL, Mar 22, 26, 27, Apr 3, May 14, 25, Sep 22, Oct
4, 5, 6, 9; <u>1744</u>: DL, Apr 6, 13; <u>1745</u>: DL, Mar 16; <u>1749</u>: CG, Oct 28, Dec 23;
<u>1765</u>: CG, May 9; <u>1768</u>: DL, Nov 16, 21; <u>1772</u>: KING'S, Mar 31, Apr 4, 9, 25,
May 26
Turkish Dance, Grand (dance), <u>1726</u>: DL, May 4; <u>1744</u>: DL, Oct 2, 9; <u>1760</u>:
KING'S, Mar 24; <u>1772</u>: KING'S, May 9, 19; <u>1773</u>: DL, Apr 24
Turkish Entertainment (entertainment), <u>1710</u>: DL, Feb 2
Turkish Music (music), <u>1749</u>: CG, Oct 28
Turkish performers, <u>1726</u>: KING'S, Nov 5, 19; <u>1727</u>: KING'S, Mar 2; <u>1732</u>: LIF,
Feb 25
Turkish Pirate, The; or, Descent on the Grecian Coast (dance), <u>1746</u>: DL, Dec
27, 29, 31; <u>1747</u>: DL, Jan 2, 5, 8, 12, 14
Turkish Seraglio (dance), <u>1742</u>: DL, Oct 25, 27, 28, 29, Nov 1, 3, 6, 12, 15,
26, 27
Turner (actor), <u>1778</u>: HAY, Sep 17; <u>1781</u>: HAY, Jan 22, Mar 26; <u>1790</u>: CG, Oct 4;
<u>1791</u>: HAY, Dec 12; <u>1792</u>: HAY, Dec 26
Turner (actor), <u>1798</u>: CG, Dec 15
Turner (actor, singer), <u>1718</u>: LIF, Jan 24; <u>1722</u>: HAY, Jun 28; <u>1728</u>: HAY, Oct
15, Nov 19, Dec 30; <u>1729</u>: HAY, Jan 10; <u>1735</u>: SOU, Apr 7, TC, May 28, LIF, Jul
11, 16, 30, HAY, Aug 4, LIF, 6, 22, 25, Sep 2, 5, YB/HAY, 17, 24, Oct 1;
<u>1736</u>: HAY, Apr 26, 29; <u>1749</u>: DL, Nov 23; <u>1755</u>: HAY, Sep 1, 9, 11, 15; <u>1757</u>:
BFG, Sep 5; <u>1761</u>: CG, Jun 23; <u>1764</u>: HAY, Jul 13
Turner (beneficiary), <u>1740</u>: CG, Dec 19
Turner (musician), <u>1774</u>: DL, Mar 24
Turner (prologuist), <u>1785</u>: CG, Dec 20
Turner (scene designer), <u>1783</u>: HAY, Aug 13
Turner (singer), <u>1706</u>: DL, Mar 30; <u>1707</u>: DL/QUEEN, Dec 6; <u>1708</u>: QUEEN'S, Dec
14; <u>1715</u>: DL, Oct 28, Nov 10, 18, 23; <u>1716</u>: DL, Jan 12, 20, 23, 27, Apr 2,
12, 17, May 14, 16, 18, 30, Jun 5, 6, 9, 19, 26, Jul 3, 19, 24, 31, Aug 9,
Oct 4, 22, 30, Nov 26, Dec 28; <u>1717</u>: DL, Jan 2, 9, Feb 4, 15, SH, Mar 27, DL,
30, Apr 23, HIC, May 3, DL, 22, 30, Jul 4
Turner, Ann (actor), <u>1719</u>: KING'S, Feb 28, Mar 21, DL, Oct 1
Turner, Betty (Cousin Betty) (spectator), <u>1668</u>: LIF, Mar 26; <u>1669</u>: BRIDGES, Mar
9
Turner, Jane (spectator), <u>1668</u>: BRIDGES, Apr 21, LIF, May 7
Turner, John (spectator), <u>1669</u>: LIF, Feb 18
Turner, Madam (spectator), <u>1663</u>: MT, Feb 2
Turner, Miss (actor), <u>1735</u>: YB, Mar 19; <u>1745</u>: DT, Mar 14
Turner, Miss (actor), <u>1782</u>: HAY, May 6
Turner, Miss (singer), <u>1754</u>: SOHO, Mar 26; <u>1755</u>: SOHO, Mar 11
Turner, Mrs (actor), <u>1735</u>: HAY, Dec 13; <u>1743</u>: HAY, Apr 15
Turner, Mrs (dancer), <u>1728</u>: HAY, Oct 15, Nov 14, 19, Dec 7; <u>1729</u>: HAY, May 26
Turner, Robert (actor), <u>1660</u>: REDBULL, Nov 5; <u>1663</u>: LIF, Feb 23
Turner, Robert (singer), <u>1674</u>: DG, Apr 30, May 16; <u>1675</u>: ATCOURT, Feb 15; <u>1693</u>:
ATCOURT, Apr 30
Turner, Theophilia (The) (spectator), <u>1663</u>: MT, Feb 2; <u>1669</u>: LIF, Jan 15, Feb
1, 18
Turner, Dr William (composer), <u>1675</u>: DG, Jun 12; <u>1676</u>: DG, Nov 4, Dec 0; <u>1677</u>:
DG, May 31; <u>1698</u>: YB, May 4; <u>1702</u>: SH, Jan 31; <u>1709</u>: SH, Nov 30; <u>1714</u>: CL,
Apr 9
Turnpike Gate, The. See Knight, Thomas.
Turnpike, <u>1730</u>: BFPG/TC, Aug 1; <u>1779</u>: CG, May 5
Turns upon One Foot Three Hundred Times (entertainment), <u>1710</u>: GR, Aug 17
Turtle (house servant), <u>1782</u>: CG, May 29; <u>1783</u>: CG, Jun 4; <u>1784</u>: CG, May 29;
<u>1786</u>: CG, Jun 1; <u>1787</u>: CG, May 30; <u>1788</u>: CG, May 31; <u>1789</u>: CG, Jun 16
Tuscan Treaty, The. See Bond, William.
Tuscany, Cosmo Prince of (spectator), <u>1669</u>: BRIDGES, May 24
Tutchin, John, <u>1684</u>: NONE, Sep 0
--Unfortunate Shepherd, The, <u>1684</u>: NONE, Sep 0
Tuteur Trompe, Le (dance), <u>1783</u>: KING'S, Jan 11, 16, 25, 28, Feb 4, 13, 15, Mar
4, 6, 15, 27, Apr 1, 10, 24, 26, 29, May 3, 6, 31, Jun 3, 6, 14, 19, 21, 28;
<u>1784</u>: KING'S, Mar 25, May 8, 11, 29, Jun 29, Jul 3; <u>1785</u>: KING'S, Jan 1, 15,
Feb 24; <u>1789</u>: KING'S, Jun 15, CG, Jul 2; <u>1790</u>: CG, Apr 8; see also Guardian
Outwitted
Tutor Burlato, Il. See Paisiello, Giovanni.
Tutor for the Beaus, A. See Hewitt, John.
Tutor, The. See Hasse, Johann Adolph.
Tutore e la Pupilla, Il (pastiche), <u>1762</u>: KING'S, Nov 13, 20, 27, 29, Dec 6,
13, 20; <u>1763</u>: KING'S, Jan 1, 15, 24, Feb 14, Mar 14, 24, May 9
Twa bonny lads were Sawney and Jockey (song), <u>1682</u>: DG, Jan 23
Twaddle (song), <u>1785</u>: CG, May 7, HAMM, Jul 6

Twaites, Miss (actor), 1797: HAY, Dec 4
Twaits, William (actor, singer), 1798: WRSG, Jun 8; 1799: WRSG, May 17
Twangdillo (actor), 1753: HAY, Mar 13; 1760: HAY, Feb 14
Twanglyre, Shadrach (actor), 1774: HAY, Mar 15
Twas at the royal feast (song), 1790: CG, Mar 26; 1791: CG, Mar 25; 1792: CG,
    Mar 7; 1794: CG, Mar 14, DL, Apr 9
Twas early one morning (song), 1694: DG, May 0
Twas in the good ship Rover (song), 1790: CG, Nov 23; 1791: CG, Sep 19; 1793:
    CG, May 21; 1794: CG, Apr 12, Oct 29; 1795: CG, Oct 7; 1797: CG, Oct 2; see
    also Greenwich Pensioner
Twas in the month of May (song), 1697: NONE, Sep 0
Twas in the solemn midnight hour (song), 1799: HAY, Jul 30, Aug 24; 1800: HAY,
    Jun 18
Twas when the seas were roaring (song), 1782: CG, May 6; 1784: HAY, Aug 10;
    1797: CG, Apr 19
Twas within a Furlong (song), 1695: DL, Sep 0
Twas you, Sir (song), 1783: HAY, May 31; 1788: HAY, Sep 2
Tweedale, Miss (actor), 1787: CG, Nov 14, 22, 28, Dec 26; 1788: CG, Jan 18, 23,
    Feb 4, Mar 26, Apr 2, May 23, Sep 17, Oct 1, 15, 17, 27, Nov 1, 26, Dec 27;
    1789: CG, Mar 28, May 8, Jun 17
Tweedside (song), 1792: CG, May 11
Twelfth Night. See Shakespeare, William.
Twice Married and a Maid Still; or, Bedding Makes the Bargain Fast (play,
    anon), 1717: SF, Sep 9, 14
Twiford (Twyford), Mrs (actor), 1676: DG, Mar 11; 1677: DG, May 12; 1682: DG,
    Jan 23; 1683: DG, May 31, DL, Dec 0; 1684: DLORDG, Aug 0; 1685: DG, Jul 0,
    DL, Aug 0; 1686: DL, Jan 0, DG, Mar 4, NONE, Sep 0; 1688: NONE, Sep 0
Twiggle and a Friz, A (song), 1789: CG, Dec 21
Twikins (house servant), 1794: CG, Jun 16
Twin Rivals, The. See Farquhar, George.
Twin Venturers, The (farce, anon), 1710: DL, May 17
Twins, The. See Lewis, Matthew Gregory.
Twisdale, Mrs (actor), 1769: HAY, Jul 12
Twiselton (musician), 1713: CA, Mar 20
Twist (Twyste), Dolly (dancer), 1763: HAY, Aug 22; 1766: CG, Nov 18; 1767: CG,
    Apr 27, May 9, 26; 1770: CG, Jan 27, Oct 1, 5, Nov 23, Dec 19, 26; 1771: CG,
    Jan 1, Feb 21, Mar 16, Apr 12, 22, May 8, Sep 30, Oct 11, 15, 28, 30; 1772:
    CG, Feb 27, Mar 23, Apr 24, May 1, Sep 23, 28, 30, Oct 13, 16, 17, 28, Nov 4,
    5, 6, 17, 21, Dec 26; 1773: CG, Mar 4, 16, 20, Apr 24, 29, May 12, 26, Sep
    22, Oct 5, 6, 13, 16, 21, 23, 25, 27, 28, Nov 10, 25, Dec 7, 8, 13, 23; 1774:
    CG, Jan 3, 7, Feb 17, Mar 12, Apr 11, 15, 16, May 4, 13
Twist, Charlotte (supernumerary), 1770: CG, Apr 26
Twist, Dolly and Sukey (dancers), 1760: HAY, Jun 2; 1763: CG, Jan 26; 1769: CG,
    Nov 4
Twist, Mary (supernumerary), 1770: CG, Apr 26
Twist, Miss (actor), 1777: HAY, Jun 9, Jul 14, 18, 24, Aug 22, 29; 1778: CG,
    Jan 8, May 1, HAY, 22, Jun 12, 19, 25, Jul 9, 22, Aug 3, 7, Sep 7; 1779: HAY,
    Jun 7, 17, Aug 24, 31, Sep 7; 1780: HAY, May 30, Jun 3, 13, 24, Aug 31
Twist, Sukey (dancer), 1757: CG, May 25, HAY, Jun 17, Jul 5, Aug 24, 31, Sep 2,
    8, 14, 28, Oct 3, 12, 17, 31, Nov 2; 1758: HAY, Jan 12, 25, Mar 6, CG, Apr
    20, DL, Jun 1, Sep 16; 1759: DL, May 9, 15, Jul 12; 1760: DL, Jun 19; 1761:
    CG, May 8, HAY, Jun 23, 27, Jul 30, Aug 3, 22, CG, Sep 21, Oct 10; 1762: CG,
    Apr 17, Dec 8; 1763: CG, Feb 2, Mar 12, 26, May 13, 18, 20, Oct 12, 22, Nov
    3, Dec 8; 1764: CG, Mar 26, Apr 2, 5, 7, 10, 12, 24, May 7, 18, 22, Oct 18,
    23, 27, Dec 12; 1765: CG, Mar 14, 26, May 9, 15, 20, 24, Oct 4, 7, Nov 12,
    15; 1766: CG, Apr 25, 29, May 6, 9, 14, HAY, Sep 2, Oct 25, Nov 15, 18,
    20; 1767: CG, Jan 31, Feb 7, Apr 27, 29, May 7, 9, 20; 1768: CG, Sep 27, Oct
    7, 24; 1769: CG, Jan 19, Sep 27, Oct 2, Nov 11, Dec 5; 1770: CG, Mar 8, Apr
    21, May 1, 3, 5, 23
Twistings and Twinings; or, Tea's the Twaddle (interlude, anon), 1785: HAY, Feb
    12
Twistleton, Charlotte Anne Frances, Mrs Thomas James (actor), 1794: CG, Feb 1,
    18, Mar 17, Apr 21, 30, May 6
Two Blue Posts Tavern, 1792: HAY, Oct 15
Two Connoisseurs, The. See Hayley, William.
Two Gentlemen of Verona, The. See Shakespeare, William.
Two Misers, The. See O'Hara, Kane.
Two Noble Kinsmen. See Fletcher, John.
Two Red Lamps (residence), 1765: DL, Mar 18
Two Sisters (play, anon), 1769: CG, Jan 31
Two Socias, The (play, anon), 1792: HAY, Aug 29, 31
Two Strings to Your Bow. See Jephson, Robert.

Two to One. See Colman the younger, George.
Tyburn Road, 1743: NONE, Jan 31
Tyburn Turnpike, 1790: DL, May 1
Tyburn, 1770: HAY, Aug 1
Tyfer (beneficiary), 1723: LIF, Jun 6; 1731: LIF, May 21; 1741: CG, May 8
Tyfer (house servant), 1739: CG, May 29; 1740: CG, May 27
Tyldesley (boxkeeper), 1737: DL, May 31; 1738: DL, May 19
Tyldsley, Mrs (seamstress), 1766: DL, Oct 23
Tyler, Miss (actor), 1748: BF, Aug 24, SFBCBV, Sep 7
Tymms (singer), 1755: HAY, Sep 11
Tynte, Miss (actor), 1725: DL, Jan 20, Feb 13, May 6, 19, Sep 9, Nov 3; 1726:
    DL, May 7, Oct 11; 1727: DL, May 17; 1728: HAY, Jun 20, LIF, 25
Tyrannic Love. See Dryden, John.
Tyranny Triumphant (criticism), 1743: DL, Oct 6
Tyrant of Sicily, The. See Tate, Nahum.
Tyrant, The (play, anon), 1722: HAY, Dec 31; 1723: HAY, Jan 10
Tyrants would in impious throngs (song), 1789: CG, Mar 20; 1790: CG, Feb 24,
    DL, Mar 10; 1791: DL, Apr 1; 1792: CG, Mar 2, KING'S, 23; 1793: CG, Mar 6;
    1794: CG, Mar 12, DL, 26; 1795: CG, Mar 25; 1796: CG, Feb 24; 1797: CG, Mar
    31; 1798: CG, Mar 30; 1800: CG, Mar 5
Tyrants, ye in vain conspire (song), 1790: DL, Mar 10; 1791: DL, Apr 1; 1792:
    KING'S, Mar 23; 1793: CG, Mar 6; 1797: CG, Mar 31; 1798: CG, Mar 30
Tyrawley, Lord, 1765: KING'S, Jan 25
Tyre, T (printer), 1751: DL, Dec 17
Tyrolean Dance (dance), 1740: CG, Dec 30; 1741: CG, Jan 2, 3, 8, 10, 17, 29,
    Feb 23, Mar 5, 16, 31; 1742: CG, Feb 6, 9, 10, 27, Mar 1, 2, 4, 9, DL, Sep
    21, 23, 25, 28, 30, Oct 2, 5, 7, 8, Nov 29, Dec 7, 29; 1743: DL, Mar 15, May
    6, 9, 11, 13, 18, 20
Tyrolese (dance), 1763: CG, Mar 8
Tyrolese Amusements (dance), 1768: DL, Nov 2, 4
Tyrolese Peasants (dance), 1764: CG, Dec 12, 27; 1765: CG, Jan 4
Tyrolese Wedding (dance), 1763: KING'S, Dec 13
Tyrwhitt, Thomas (MP), 1797: KING'S, May 18, CG, Jun 14
Tythe Pig, The. See Byrn, James.

Uccellatori, Gli (pastiche), 1770: KING'S, Dec 18, 22; 1771: KING'S, Jan 1, 8,
    19, 26, 29, Feb 2, 19, Mar 12, Apr 9, 23
Uccellatrice, L'. See Jomelli, Niccolo.
Ugly Club, The. See Iliff, Edward Henry.
Uhl, Antony (musician), 1735: HIC, Feb 21
Ulysses. See Rowe, Nicholas; Smith, John Christopher.
Unanimity; or, War, Love and Loyalty (interlude, anon), 1798: CG, Jun 4
Uncle (actor), 1792: HAY, Apr 16, Jul 4
Undaunted Britons (song), 1793: KING/HAY, Mar 6, 20
Under Ground Lodging (song), 1798: CG, Apr 24
Under sweet Friendship's Name (song), 1779: HAY, Mar 17
Under the branches of a spreading tree (song), 1677: DG, May 31
Under the Greenwood Tree (song), 1742: CG, Apr 28, May 3
Underhill (Undril), Cave (actor), 1660: REDBULL, Nov 5; 1661: LIF, Aug 15, 24,
    Sep 11, Dec 16; 1662: LIF, Mar 1, NONE, Sep 0, ATCOURT, Nov 1; 1663: LIF, Jan
    6, 8, Feb 23, Oct 0, ATCOURT, Dec 10, LIF, 22; 1664: LIF, Mar 0, NONE, Apr
    27, LIF, Aug 13, Sep 10; 1667: LIF, Aug 15, Nov 7; 1668: LIF, Mar 26; 1669:
    LIF, Dec 14; 1670: LIF, Apr 0, Nov 0; 1671: LIF, Mar 6; 1672: DG, Jul 4, Nov
    4, ATCOU/DG, Dec 2; 1673: DG, May 0; 1674: DG, Apr 30; 1675: NONE, Sep 0;
    1676: DG, Jan 10, May 25, Jul 25, Nov 4, Dec 0; 1677: DG, Mar 24; 1678: DG,
    Jan 0, Apr 5, May 28, Jun 0, Nov 0; 1679: DG, Mar 0, Apr 0, Sep 0, Oct 0;
    1680: DG, Jan 0, Nov 1; 1681: DG, Jan 0, Nov 0, DG/IT, 22; 1682: DG, Jan 0,
    23, DL, Nov 28; 1683: DG, Jul 0, NONE, Sep 0; 1685: DLORDG, Jan 20, NONE, Feb
    6, DL, May 9; 1686: DL, Jan 0, NONE, Sep 0; 1687: DG, Mar 0; 1688: DL, Feb 0,
    May 3, NONE, Sep 0; 1689: DL, Apr 0, Nov 20, Dec 4; 1690: DL, Jan 0, DLORDG,
    Mar 0, DL, 0, NONE, Sep 0; 1691: DL, Jan 0, Apr 0, NONE, Sep 0; 1692: DL, Jun
    0; 1693: DL, Feb 0, Mar 0, Apr 0, DG, May 0; 1694: DL, Jan 0, Feb 0, DG, May
    0, DL, Sep 0; 1695: LIF, Apr 30, Dec 0; 1696: LIF, Apr 0, Jun 0, Oct 0, Nov
    14, Dec 0; 1697: LIF, May 0, Jun 0; 1698: LIF, Mar 0; 1699: LIF, Dec 18;
    1700: LIF, Mar 5, Nov 23; 1702: LIF, Oct 13; 1704: LIF, Feb 8, ATCOURT, 28,
    LIF, Mar 21; 1705: LIF, Mar 31; 1706: QUEEN'S, Dec 5; 1707: QUEEN'S, Jan 20,
    May 28; 1709: DL, Jun 3; 1710: DL, Feb 23, May 12, GR, Aug 26
Underwood, William (machinist), 1798: DL, Jan 16, Oct 6; 1799: DL, Jan 19, May
    24, Oct 14, Dec 11; 1800: DL, Mar 11, Apr 29

Unfortunate Couple, The. See Filmer, Edward.
Unfortunate Dutchess of Malfey, The; or, The Unnatural Brothers. See Webster,
    John, The Duchess of Malfi.
Unfortunate Lovers, The. See Davenant, Sir William.
Unfortunate Shepherd, The. See Tutchin, John.
Unfortunate Usurper, The (play, anon), 1662: NONE, Sep 0
Ungrateful Favourite, The. See Southland, Thomas.
Ungrateful Lovers, The. See Davenant, Sir William, The Unfortunate Lovers.
Unguarded lies the wishing maid (song), 1696: LIF, Apr 0
Unhappy Choice, An. See Webster, John, The Duchess of Malfi.
Unhappy Favourite, The. See Banks, John.
Unhappy Kindness, The. See Scott, Thomas.
Unhappy Libertine, The (farce, anon), 1731: SOU, Jun 11
Unhappy Marriage (droll, anon), 1694: BF, Sep 5
Unhappy Penitent, The. See Trotter, Catherine.
Unhappy Vow-Breaker (novel), 1694: NONE, Mar 22
Unicorn (residence), 1745: DL, Mar 11; 1747: DL, Mar 16
Union Coffee House, 1746: GF, Jan 15, 22; 1750: DL, Jan 11; 1752: DL, Nov 15;
    1758: CG, Jul 6
Union Court, 1776: KING'S, Nov 2; 1777: KING'S, Nov 4; 1778: KING'S, Nov 24;
    1779: KING'S, Nov 27; 1781: KING'S, Jun 5, Nov 17; 1788: KING'S, Feb 7; 1789:
    KING'S, Jan 10; 1794: HAMM, Mar 24
Union Dance (dance), 1707: DL, Mar 8, Apr 3; 1718: AC, Sep 24; 1724: RI, Jul 4,
    11; 1736: GF, May 6
Union des Bergeres, L' (dance), 1794: KING'S, Mar 1, 4, 8, 11, 22
Union of the Three Sister Arts, The; or, St Cecilliae (entertainment), 1723:
    LIF, Nov 22, 23, 25, 30, Dec 5, 13, 18; 1724: LIF, Jan 2; 1725: LIF, Apr 15,
    Nov 22, 29
Union of the Two Nations (dance), 1724: RI, Jun 27
Union Pipe and Pedal Harp (music), 1794: HAY, Jun 2
Union Pipes (music), 1795: CG, Mar 5; 1798: CG, May 5; 1799: CG, Jan 31
Union Pipes and Harp (music), 1791: CG, Oct 24, Dec 19; 1792: CG, May 28, 31
Union Pipes and Harp Duet (music), 1792: CG, May 28, Oct 25; 1794: CG, May 26
Union Pipes and Harp Medley (music), 1799: CG, Jan 29
Union Pipes Solo (music), 1794: CG, May 26; 1798: CG, May 28
Union St, 1750: DL, Feb 21; 1783: KING'S, Nov 29; 1792: HAY, Oct 15
Union, The; or, St Andrew's Day (interlude), 1791: CG, May 18
United Englishmen (song), 1798: HAY, Aug 14, 16, 23, Sep 7; 1800: CG, Apr 19,
    May 30
United Kingdoms, The. See Howard, Henry.
Uniti a Lupi (song), 1755: KING'S, Mar 17
Universal Gallant, The. See Fielding, Henry.
Universal Monarch Defeated, The; or, The Queen of Hungary Triumphant (puppet
    show), 1742: BF, Aug 26
Universal Motion (play, anon), 1662: LI, Jan 3
Universal Passion, The. See Miller, James.
Universal Prayer, The. See Barbandt, Charles.
Unjustly Phillis, you accuse your slave (song), 1695: NONE, Sep 0
Unlucky Lover, The; or, The Merry London Cuckolds (play, anon), 1717: DL, Jul
    16, 18, Aug 9
Unnatural Brother, The. See Filmer, Edward.
Unnatural Combat, The. See Massinger, Phillip.
Unnatural Mother (play, anon), 1699: LIF, Sep 0
Unnatural Parents, The; or, The Fair Maid of the West (droll), 1726: SFSE, Sep
    8; 1727: BF, Aug 22; 1735: TC, Aug 4, 18, SFLT, Sep 4; 1748: BFLYY, Aug 24,
    SFLYYW, Sep 7, 8, 9, 10, 12, 13, BHB, Oct 1; 1749: NWSM, May 1, 3, 4, 5, 6,
    8; 1755: SFG, Sep 18, 19, 20, 22
Unto which of the (song), 1793: KING/HAY, Feb 20; 1794: DL, Mar 19
Unwinn, Mrs. See Urwin, Mrs.
Unzer, Johann Christoph, 1798: HAY, Jun 23
--Diego und Leonore, 1798: HAY, Jun 23
Uphill, Susanna (actor), 1669: BRIDGES, Jun 24; 1671: BRIDGES, Jun 0; 1672:
    LIF, Apr 0; 1673: LIF, Mar 0; 1674: DL, May 16; 1675: DL, May 10, DG, Aug 28,
    DL, Nov 17
Upholsterer, The. See Murphy, Arthur.
Upper Brook St, 1787: HAY, Mar 12
Upper Charlotte St, 1779: DL, Apr 6
Upper Gallery, The (poem), 1753: DL, Feb 1
Upper James St, 1779: HAY, Aug 10; 1784: HAY, Mar 8; 1788: KING'S, May 8; 1789:
    KING'S, Apr 2
Upper Mews Gate, 1795: DL, May 21; 1796: DL, May 13; 1797: DL, May 23; 1798:
    DL, May 24; 1799: DL, May 9; 1800: DL, Jun 3

Upper Moorfields, 1724: WINH, Apr 13; 1731: UM, Apr 19; 1732: UM, Jun 19; 1742: UM, Apr 26, Oct 4
Upper Queen St, 1776: CHR, Oct 2
Upper Seymour St, 1781: KING'S, May 10; 1783: KING'S, Feb 13; 1784: CG, Mar 13; 1785: KING'S, Apr 21
Upper Shadwell, 1746: GF, Mar 11
Upper St, 1780: CII, Mar 17
Ups and Downs of Life (song), 1792: CG, May 18, 28
Upsdell, Mrs (actor), 1797: HAY, Jul 6
Upton (actor), 1791: HAY, Dec 26
Upton, James (author), 1749: DL, May 1
Upton, William (versifier), 1786: HAY, Jul 28
Urban, Sylvanus, 1751: DL, Oct 30
Urbani, Valentino (singer), 1708: QUEEN'S, Dec 14; 1709: QUEEN'S, Mar 2; 1710: QUEEN'S, Jan 10, Mar 23; 1711: QUEEN'S, Feb 24, Apr 11, May 5; 1712: QUEEN'S, Nov 22, Dec 10; 1713: QUEEN'S, Feb 26, Apr 11, Jun 9
Urquhart, David Henry
--Election, The (interlude), 1784: CG, May 17
Ursula, the Cook Maid's Rapture (entertainment), 1733: BFAP, Aug 23
Urwin (Unwinn), Mrs (actor), 1695: DL, Sep 0; 1696: DG, Jun 0
Usefulness of Dramatic Interludes, The (pamphlet), 1744: DL, Jan 2; 1745: CG, Feb 1
Usher (actor), 1739: DL, Oct 30, Nov 20; 1740: DL, Jan 15, Apr 30, Oct 27; 1743: DL, Oct 22, Nov 4, 8, 12, 17, Dec 6; 1744: DL, Jan 27, Feb 21, Oct 2, 19, Dec 13; 1745: DL, Feb 20, Mar 5, 30, Apr 30, Nov 19, 22, 30, Dec 5, 13; 1746: DL, Jan 2, 8, 25, Mar 10, 13, Apr 4, 14, 15, 21, 23, May 7, 9, 14, Sep 23, 27, 30, Oct 2, 18, 23, 31, Nov 1, 4, 7, Dec 26; 1747: DL, Jan 3, 15, 24, Feb 2, 7, Mar 3, 7, 16, 23, 28, Apr 11, 28, May 15, Sep 22, 24, Oct 29, Nov 2, 4, 6, 13, 16, 25, Dec 5, 16, 17; 1748: DL, Jan 6, 18, Mar 22, Apr 28, BF, Aug 24, SFBCBV, Sep 7, DL, 13, 17, 22, 24, 27, 29, Oct 1, 8, 12, Nov 2, 4, 9, 12, 29, Dec 26; 1749: DL, Jan 9, Feb 6, Mar 7, Apr 29, May 1, Sep 16, 19, 28, Oct 3, 10, 11, 13, 19, 26, 28, Nov 2, 4, 16, Dec 18, 20, 26, 28; 1750: DL, Jan 6, 22, 31, Feb 10, Apr 30, CG, Oct 25, 26, Nov 1, 5, 8, 12, 22, 24, 29, Dec 10; 1751: CG, Jan 19, Mar 7, Apr 16, May 2, Oct 7, 11, 21, 25, Nov 4, 22; 1752: CG, Mar 7, 9, 16, 17, 30, Apr 24, 28, May 4, Sep 22, Oct 4, 11, 16, 21, 30, Nov 4, 7, 10, 23, 28, Dec 9, 11, 12, 13, 14; 1753: CG, Jan 8, 22, 25, 26, Feb 7, 21, Mar 19, 20, 24, Apr 23, May 7, 11, 18, Sep 17, 21, 24, Oct 5, 10, 17, 30, Nov 5, 7, 20, 28, 30, Dec 11; 1754: CG, Jan 22, Mar 9, 23, Apr 26, 30, May 2, 8, 14, DL, Sep 24, Oct 24, Nov 7, Dec 17, 28; 1755: DL, Mar 20, Apr 15, 16, Oct 7, 10, 17, 23, Nov 11, 12, 28, Dec 4, 5, 18, 23; 1756: DL, Feb 14, Mar 29, Sep 21, 28, 30, Oct 5, 9, 13, 16, 28, Nov 6, 17, 18, 24, Dec 10, 15; 1757: DL, Jan 3, 22, 26, Feb 5, 17, Mar 24, Apr 29, 30, May 10, Sep 13, 17, 20, 24, 29, Oct 4, 13, 15, 19, Nov 10, 15, Dec 3, 27; 1758: DL, Jan 24, Mar 13, 30, Apr 3, May 1, 26
Usher, Howard (actor), 1774: DL, Oct 14, 27, 28, Nov 3, 8, 24, 25, Dec 17, 27; 1775: DL, Jan 2, 4, Feb 17, Mar 2, 18, 23, Apr 8, 17, 24, May 4, Sep 23, 28, Oct 11, 14, 20, 21, 23, 31, Nov 3, 6, 18, 27, Dec 7, 19; 1776: DL, Feb 10, 12, Mar 23, Apr 8, 22; 1778: HAY, Jun 19, Jul 30, Sep 10, 18; 1779: HAY, May 31, Jul 16, 17, 31, Aug 17, 24, Sep 8; 1780: HAY, May 30, Jun 6, 9, 14, 23, Jul 10, 15, 24, Aug 24, 26, Sep 2, 5, 11; 1781: HAY, May 30, Jun 1, 16, 21, Jul 18, 23, Aug 7, 28, Sep 1, 10; 1782: HAY, Jun 3, 4, 6, 11, 12, 15, 18, Jul 5, 16, 17, Aug 9, 13, 17, Sep 16, Dec 30; 1783: HAY, May 31, Jun 2, 4, 7, 18, 30, Jul 4, 5, Aug 1, 20, 27; 1784: HAY, Jun 1, 2, 5, 25, Jul 19, 27, Aug 9, 10, 18, 19, Sep 13, 17; 1785: HAY, Jun 2, 17, 21, 24, Jul 11, 19, 21, Aug 19, 24, 31, Sep 9; 1786: HAY, Jun 13, 21, 22, 28, Jul 7, 13, 14, 21, 28, Aug 25, 29, Sep 9; 1787: HAY, May 16, 23, 25, Jun 14, 27, Jul 19, 25, 27, Aug 4, 28; 1788: HAY, Jun 10, 11, 19, 23, Jul 10, 14, Aug 5, 18, 20, Sep 3; 1789: HAY, May 18, 27, Jun 1, 5, 19, 22, 25, 29, Jul 3, 4, Aug 5, 11; 1790: HAY, Jun 14, 15, 16, 18, 19, 22, 28, Jul 5, 22, 28, Sep 4, 13; 1791: HAY, Jun 10, 13, 18, 20, Jul 1, 8, 15, 20, 30, Aug 5, 24, 31, Sep 12; 1792: HAY, Jun 19, 20, 23, 26, Jul 3, 9, Aug 2, 6, 9, 22; 1793: HAY, Jun 13, 14, 17, 29, Jul 1, 5, 6, 9, 19, 25, Aug 3, 6, 12, 27, Sep 10, 19, 21, 24, 28, 30, Oct 4, 8, 21, 29, Nov 6, 16, 19, Dec 14, 30; 1794: HAY, Jan 14, Jul 8, 9, 10, 11, 16, 17, 21, 22, Aug 4, 9, 11, 12, Sep 1, 3, 10, 17; 1795: HAY, Jun 9, 10, 11, 12, 13, 15, 18, 27, Jul 1, 16, 22, 31, Aug 14, Sep 21; 1796: HAY, Jun 14, 16, 22, 25, 29, 30, Jul 6, 7, 9, 11, 15, 21, 26, Aug 9, 11, 18, Sep 3, 7; 1797: HAY, Jun 12, 13, 15, 16, 20, 21, 23, 24, 28, Jul 3, 10, Aug 4, 9, 15, Sep 2, 4, 11; 1798: HAY, Jun 16, 18, 19, 20, 23, 30, Jul 14, Aug 3, 4, 21, Sep 3; 1799: HAY, Jun 15, 17, 18, 20, 25, 29, Jul 2, 9
Usher, Miss (actor), 1800: DL, Jun 14
Usher, Mrs (actor), 1772: DL, May 5
Usurer, The; or, Harlequin's Last Shift (pantomime, anon), 1733: HAY, Feb 23

Usurier Gentilhomme et les Vendanges de Suresne, L' (play), 1722: HAY, Jan 15,
    Feb 2
Usurpator Innocente, L'. See Federici, Vincenzo.
Usurper, The. See Howard, Edward.
Ut Pictura Poesis! See Colman the younger, George.
Utrecht (peace of), 1772: DL, Mar 11
Uttini, Vincenzo (singer), 1783: KING'S, Nov 29, Dec 16; 1784: KING'S, Apr 15,
    May 4, 8
Uxbridge, 1747: CG, Mar 26; 1758: CG, Nov 27; 1759: CG, Nov 28, Dec 22

Vacances des Procureurs, Les. See D'Ancourt, Florent Carton.
Vachon (musician), 1772: HAY, Apr 27
Vagrant Act, 1737: DL, Mar 29
Vaillant, Paul (publisher, printer), 1743: DL, Mar 3; 1744: DL, Mar 1, 5; 1749:
    DL, Jan 18, 20; 1756: CG, Feb 12, DL, Dec 15; 1757: DL, Feb 17, Dec 17
Vain is Beauty's gaudy Flower (song), 1761: KING'S, Mar 12; 1764: CG, May 8;
    1789: DL, Mar 20
Vain your Triumph (song), 1790: CG, Feb 24
Valcour (payee), 1775: DL, Oct 27
Valcour, Miss (dancer), 1758: DL, Apr 27, Nov 3, Dec 8, 26; 1759: DL, Apr 18,
    May 15
Vale, J (secretary, Choral Society), 1798: HAY, Jan 15
Valentine's Day. See Heard, William.
Valentini (singer), 1707: DL, Mar 8, Apr 1, HIC, 2, DL/QUEEN, Dec 6, DL, 18;
    1708: QUEEN'S, Feb 26, Apr 17; 1709: QUEEN'S, Feb 16; 1710: QUEEN'S, Mar 18,
    28; 1713: QUEEN'S, Jan 10, Apr 25, May 6; 1714: QUEEN'S, Jan 9, 27, Mar 4,
    Apr 24, May 1, 29; 1715: HIC, Mar 31
Valentinian. See Fletcher, John.
Valeriano, Cavaliero (singer), 1712: QUEEN'S, Nov 22, Dec 10; 1713: QUEEN'S,
    Jan 10, Apr 25; see also Pellegrini
Valescchi, Marianna (singer), 1763: KING'S, Feb 19, HAY, Jun 9
Valesciene (composer), 1734: HAY, May 27
Valiant Cid, The. See Corneille, Pierre.
Vallois (D'Vallois), Jovan de (dancer), 1732: LIF, Apr 13, May 1, DL, Jul 28,
    Aug 1, 4, 11, 15, 17, 19, 22, GF, Oct 9, 10, 11, 12, 13, 14, 16, 17, 18, 19,
    27, 30, Dec 15, 27; 1733: GF, Jan 6, 10, 13, 23, Feb 2, 12, 15, Mar 1, 12,
    26, 29, Apr 6, 10, 17, 18, 20, 24, 25, 27, 30, May 3, 5, 10, 11, 15, 16, 22,
    23, 24, HAY, 28, CG, Jun 26, Jul 31, BFMMO, Aug 23, GF, Sep 12, 17, 19, 20,
    21, 24, 25, 28, Oct 1, 3, 9, 11, 12, 15, 16, 18, 19, 22, 24, 26, 29, 31, Nov
    1, 2, 6, 7, 8, 12, 26, 29, Dec 8, 10, 11, 15, 18, 19, 20, 21, 26, 27, 28;
    1734: GF, Jan 2, 7, 8, 9, 10, 11, 18, 19, 22, 24, 28, 31, Feb 2, 5, 11, Mar
    11, Apr 18, 19, 24, 26, May 1, 6, 7, 8, 13, 15, 16, 17, 20, 22, BFRLCH, Aug
    24, GF, Sep 9, 18, 20, Oct 14, 28, Dec 2, 5, 6, 12, 28; 1735: GF, Jan 6, 7,
    13, 17, 24, Mar 6, 13, 17, 27, 29, Apr 9, 10, 16, 17, 22, 30, GF/HAY, Jul 15,
    18, 22, Aug 1, GF, Sep 10, 12, 24, 26, Oct 3, 15, Nov 6, 12, 14, 17, 19, 25,
    29, Dec 3, 4, 5, 6, 8, 9, 10, 11, 13, 15, 17; 1736: GF, Feb 6, 11, 17, 20,
    Mar 3, 18, 20, 22, 25, Apr 1, 6, 8, 12, 13, 17, 27, 28, May 5, 6, 10, LIF,
    Jun 18, Sep 30, Oct 5, 9, 21, Nov 13, 18, 27, Dec 3, 7, 16, 22; 1737: LIF,
    Jan 5, Feb 1, Mar 21, 31, Apr 2, 12, 14, 18, 21, 25, 27, 28, 29, 30, May 2,
    4, 5, 6, 7, 17, 18, DL, Nov 10; 1738: DL, Jan 24, 28, Apr 12, 17, May 5, 6,
    13, 17, 22, 23
Vallois, Catharine (actor, dancer), 1748: CG, Sep 26, Oct 19, 27; 1749: CG, Jan
    26, Mar 9, Oct 20; 1750: CG, Oct 12; 1752: CG, Nov 8; 1753: CG, Sep 12; 1754:
    CG, Sep 16; 1755: CG, Oct 17; 1756: CG, Sep 22; 1757: CG, Apr 15, 22, May 12,
    HAY, Sep 8, 14; 1758: CG, Mar 30, Apr 14, 25, 28, 29, May 4, 5, Sep 25, Oct
    6, Nov 16, 23; 1759: HAY, Apr 18, CG, May 7, HAY, 10, CG, 11, Sep 26, Dec 7;
    1760: CG, Apr 17, May 12, Sep 22, Oct 17, 23; 1761: CG, Mar 30, Apr 20, 27,
    Sep 23, 28, Dec 10, 28; 1762: CG, Feb 2, Apr 23, May 5, Oct 7, 9, Nov 1, 5,
    Dec 2; 1763: CG, Feb 24, Sep 26, Oct 8, Dec 6, 22, 26; 1764: CG, Jan 20, Mar
    20, May 3, 5, 21, HAY, Jun 26, 28, Jul 5, Aug 6, Sep 5, 11, CG, Oct 3, 4, Nov
    5, Dec 21; 1765: CG, Jan 1, 31, Feb 4, 11, Mar 11, Apr 18, 23, 29, May 2, Sep
    25, 30, Oct 28; 1766: CG, May 2, Sep 22, 26, Nov 18; 1767: CG, Jan 29, Feb
    14, 21, Apr 2, May 16, Sep 19, Oct 5, 8, 17, 24, 30, Nov 7, 26; 1768: CG, Jan
    5, 6, 23, Mar 7, 8, 12, Apr 13, May 13, 24, Sep 19, 20, Oct 24, Nov 4, 18,
    Dec 12, 26; 1769: CG, Jan 19, Feb 1, 4, 20, Mar 6, 30, DL, Apr 5, CG, 13, May
    10, 23, Sep 25, 29, Nov 4, 10, Dec 2, 27, 29, 30; 1770: CG, Jan 5, Feb 3, Mar
    13, 29, Apr 25, 27, 30, May 1, 9, 14, Oct 1, 19, Nov 3, Dec 13; 1771: CG, Jan
    15, Apr 12, 22, May 1, Oct 2, 7, 19, Nov 1, 8, 28, Dec 11, 19, 21; 1772: CG,
    Mar 23, 26, Apr 9, May 9, Sep 23, Oct 9, 16, 30, Nov 4, 5, 21, Dec 26; 1773:

CG, Jan 23, Feb 6, Apr 3, May 26, Sep 20, Oct 5, 6, 7, 9, 21, 28, 30, Nov 10, 12, 18, 20, 25, 26, Dec 13, 16; 1774: CG, Jan 3, Feb 11, Apr 11, 15, Sep 23, Oct 3, 7, 13, 15, 20, 28, Nov 4, 8, 9, 19, 29, Dec 2, 20, 27; 1775: CG, Feb 1, Sep 25, 29, Oct 19, Nov 16, Dec 26; 1776: CG, Jan 24, Feb 12, Mar 25, May 13, 20, Oct 7, 15, 31, Nov 9, 20, Dec 2, 26, 27; 1777: CG, Jan 22, Apr 23, 25, 28, Sep 29, Nov 4, 25; 1778: CG, Jan 15, 21, 28, Mar 9, Apr 24, May 2, 6, 16, Oct 14, 22, 26, Nov 25, 27; 1779: CG, Jan 4, Feb 13, Mar 20, Apr 28, May 10, 13, Sep 22, Oct 6, 18, 22, Nov 8, 9, 23, Dec 29; 1780: CG, Feb 5, Apr 17, 27, May 8, 10, Sep 20, 27, Oct 11, 23, Dec 9, 23; 1781: CG, Feb 23
Vallois, Jovan and Mrs de (dancers), 1732: GF, Oct 4, 5, 7, Dec 13, 18, 29; 1733: GF, Jan 11, 12, Feb 13, Apr 3, 18, 25, HAY, May 28, CG, Jun 29, Aug 2, 9, BFMMO, 23.
Vallois, Mrs Jovan de (actor, dancer), 1732: GF, Oct 9, 12, 13, 14, 17, 18, 19, 30, Dec 20; 1733: GF, Jan 10, 24, Feb 5, Apr 20, HAY, May 28, CG, Aug 14, BFMMO, 23, GF, Oct 17, 22, 29, Nov 1, 8, 12, Dec 26, 28; 1734: GF, Jan 8, 14, 28, Feb 11, Apr 19, BFRLCH, Aug 24, GF, Oct 28; 1735: GF, Jan 10, 24, Mar 6, 13, 25, HAY, Aug 12, GF, Oct 15, Nov 17, Dec 17; 1736: GF, Feb 17, 20, Mar 3; 1738: DL, May 6, 22, Sep 26, Oct 3, 10, 30, Dec 15; 1739: DL, Jan 12, Feb 5, Mar 10, May 28, Sep 6, 8, 13, 26, Oct 10, 19, 26, Nov 1, 22, 28, Dec 6, 11, 19; 1740: DL, Jan 5, 15, Feb 13; 1741: GF, Feb 19, BFH, Aug 22, GF, Oct 9, 16, Nov 9, 30, Dec 28; 1742: GF, Jan 5, 13, 14, 27, Feb 8, BFHC, Aug 25, LIF, Nov 26, Dec 3, 13; 1743: LIF, Jan 7, Feb 14, 17
Vallois' scholar (dancer), 1732: GF, Oct 10; 1735: GF/HAY, Jul 15
Vallouis (Vallouy), Niel, Mme Simonin (dancer), 1774: KING'S, Nov 8, Dec 3; 1775: KING'S, Feb 7, 14, 25, Mar 7, 23, Apr 4, 6, 8, 18, 22, 25, May 6, 20, 25, 30, Jun 6, 17, 24; 1776: KING'S, Jan 20, Feb 24, Mar 28, Apr 25, Nov 2, 12, Dec 10; 1777: KING'S, Mar 15
Vallouis, Simonin (dancer), 1774: KING'S, Nov 8, Dec 3; 1775: KING'S, Jan 21, Feb 7, 14, 21, 25, Mar 7, 23, Apr 4, 6, 8, 18, 22, 25, May 25, 27, 30, Jun 6, 17, 24; 1776: KING'S, Jan 20, Feb 24, Mar 28, Apr 25, Nov 2, 12, Dec 17; 1777: KING'S, Jan 21, Feb 4, Mar 15, May 8, 20, 31
Vallouis, Simonin and Niel (dancers), 1774: KING'S, Dec 13; 1775: KING'S, Jan 17, Feb 7, Apr 8, May 11, 25; 1776: KING'S, Apr 30, May 4, 7, Jun 6, 8; 1777: KING'S, May 8
Vallouis le Cadet, Simonin (dancer), 1775: KING'S, Jan 7, Apr 22, 25, Jun 24; 1776: KING'S, Nov 2, 12, Dec 14, 17; 1777: KING'S, Jan 17, 21, Feb 4, 25, Mar 15, May 1, 8, 20, 24, Jul 5, Nov 4, 15, Dec 9; 1778: KING'S, Feb 7, 24, Mar 3, Apr 4
Vanbraken (Van Brockin) (actor), 1710: GR, Aug 21, 24, Sep 1
VanBright (musician), 1675: ATCOURT, Feb 15
Vanbrugh (Vanbroog, Vanbrook), Sir John, 1699: LIF, Dec 18, DLLIF, 25; 1700: NONE, Apr 11, DL, 29; 1702: DL, Feb 0; 1704: LIF, Mar 30; 1705: DL, Mar 22, LIF/QUEN, Oct 30, QUEEN'S, Dec 27; 1707: QUEEN'S, Mar 22; 1719: LIF, Apr 2; 1720: KING'S, Feb 18; 1721: DL, Mar 23, LIF, Apr 24, Oct 19, DL, 23, Nov 9; 1722: DL, Jan 12; 1723: LIF, Feb 18, Mar 19, Oct 22, Dec 3; 1724: RI, Jun 22, LIF, Oct 14, 16, Nov 21; 1725: LIF, May 4, Nov 24, Dec 16, 17, 18, 20; 1726: LIF, Jan 4, 17, Mar 19, Apr 15, 20, May 11, 20, Oct 19, 21, 24, 28, Nov 12, Dec 5; 1727: LIF, Jan 7, 11, 13, Feb 9, Mar 21, DL, Apr 21, LIF, May 3, DL, Oct 5, Nov 9, LIF, 10, 18, 27, DL, 29, LIF, Dec 1; 1728: DL, Jan 10, LIF, 11, 13, Mar 25, DL, 25, Apr 8, LIF, 30, May 6, 18, DL, Oct 21, LIF, 23, Nov 2, DL, 8, 13, LIF, Dec 12, 16; 1729: LIF, Feb 8, 22, Mar 25, Apr 17, DL, 22, LIF, 24, 29, DL, May 2, LIF, 6, 8, 19, 20, DL, Sep 30, LIF, Oct 6, DL, 16, LIF, 31, Nov 14, 24, DL, Dec 17, 29; 1730: LIF, Jan 15, Feb 6, 12, 14, 19, Mar 16, Apr 8, DL, 8, 13, LIF, 17, 29, 30, May 9, Oct 16, 26, 31, Nov 9, 28, Dec 3, 16, 19, 22; 1731: DL, Jan 11, LIF, 11, Feb 13, 17, 20, Mar 15, DL, 25, LIF, Apr 8, 21, DL, 27, LIF, May 26, 28, 31, DL, Sep 23, LIF, Oct 8, 22, Nov 11, 16, 19, DL, 19, LIF, Dec 13, 20; 1732: LIF, Jan 18, DL, 28, LIF, Feb 9, 15, 16, 18, 28, Mar 27, 30, DL, Apr 14, 22, May 10, LIF, 11, 15, DL, Sep 30, LIF/CG, Oct 2, Nov 3, 13, DL, 16, LIF/CG, 17, DL, 21, 30; 1733: DL, Jan 3, CG, 24, LIF/CG, 31, HAY, Mar 7, DL, 12, GF, 30, CG, May 4, GF, 14, DL, 18, LIF/CG, 18, RI, Sep 10, DL, 26, DL/HAY, Oct 6, CG, 16, 20, DL/HAY, Nov 3, CG, 8, DL/HAY, Dec 1, CG, 3, 6, 7, GF, 13, 14, CG, 18, 21, 29, 31; 1734: DL, Jan 3, CG, 17, 22, DL, 23, CG, 26, DL/HAY, 26, CG, Feb 1, 20, DL/HAY, Mar 11, DL/HAY, 19, 30, CG, Apr 18, DL, 22, DL/LIF, May 3, CG/LIF, Oct 7, DL, 17, 21, Nov 7, Dec 2; 1735: DL, Jan 25, CG/LIF, 31, Mar 22, Apr 18, DL, 23, CG/LIF, May 19, DL, 23, Jun 3, YB, Jul 17, GF/HAY, Aug 8, CG, Oct 10, 17, DL, 24, CG, Dec 15, DL, 16; 1736: CG, Jan 27, Feb 2, 5, 9, Mar 1, 11, DL, Apr 17, CG, 27, 28, May 25, Jun 4, DL, Sep 7, CG, Oct 4, Nov 22; 1737: CG, Jan 4, Mar 7, DL, May 4, CG, Sep 21, DL, Oct 8, 13, 15, CG, Nov 1, 8, DL, 17, 18; 1738: DL, Jan 5, CG, 23, 31, DL, Feb 1, CG, Mar 7, 18, DL, Apr 21, CG, May 15, DL, 29, Sep 9, Oct 10, 24, Nov 8, 11, 21, CG, 23, 24, DL, 24, 30, Dec 15; 1739: DL, Jan 4, 12, CG, 15, DL, 24, Feb 26, CG, Mar 5, DL, May 5, 9, CG, Aug 2, 31, Sep

14, DL, Oct 4, CG, 5, 24, Nov 3; <u>1740</u>: DL, Jan 3, CG, 12, DL, Mar 8, CG, Sep
22, Oct 8, DL, Nov 11; <u>1741</u>: CG, Jan 10, 17, Apr 17, DL, Oct 6, CG, 8, 24,
Dec 14; <u>1742</u>: CG, May 4, Nov 3, DL, 12, LIF, Dec 3; <u>1744</u>: CG, Feb 1, Dec 12;
<u>1745</u>: CG, Nov 19; <u>1748</u>: HAY, Apr 25; <u>1751</u>: DL, Mar 19, CG, Apr 24, Nov 13;
<u>1752</u>: CG, Jan 28, Mar 3; <u>1753</u>: CG, Jan 22, Feb 6; <u>1764</u>: CG, Nov 8; <u>1766</u>: DL,
Jan 23; <u>1768</u>: DL, Apr 12; <u>1770</u>: CG, Mar 20; <u>1773</u>: DL, Mar 30, CG, Apr 27;
<u>1774</u>: DL, Mar 15, Dec 19; <u>1777</u>: DL, Feb 24; <u>1778</u>: DL, Dec 19; <u>1784</u>: HAY, Aug
6; <u>1785</u>: HAY, Dec 26; <u>1787</u>: DL, Oct 26; <u>1789</u>: DL, Oct 24; <u>1790</u>: CG, Feb 11,
Oct 15; <u>1791</u>: CG, Nov 29; <u>1792</u>: CG, Nov 10
--Aesop, <u>1696</u>: DL/DL, Dec 0; <u>1697</u>: DL/DL, Jan 22, May 24, DL, Dec 9; <u>1702</u>: DL,
Oct 26; <u>1703</u>: DL, Nov 10; <u>1704</u>: DL, Jan 21, Oct 27; <u>1705</u>: DL, Mar 31, Nov 27,
30; <u>1706</u>: DL, Feb 21; <u>1708</u>: DL, Mar 16; <u>1710</u>: DL, Dec 5; <u>1712</u>: DL, Feb 14,
Oct 24; <u>1713</u>: DL, Jan 28; <u>1715</u>: DL, Jan 14, Mar 15, Dec 5; <u>1716</u>: DL, Jan 31,
Apr 18, Nov 16; <u>1717</u>: DL, Nov 7; <u>1718</u>: DL, Nov 10; <u>1719</u>: DL, Oct 12; <u>1720</u>:
DL, Oct 14, Dec 7; <u>1723</u>: DT, Nov 1; <u>1724</u>: DL, Nov 3, CT, 24, DL, 28, DT, Dec
2; <u>1725</u>: LIF, Nov 13, 15, 16, Dec 7; <u>1726</u>: LIF, Jan 14, Feb 4, Oct 7, DL, Nov
25; <u>1727</u>: LIF, Jan 9, Feb 18, Mar 7, Sep 13; <u>1728</u>: DL, Nov 22; <u>1730</u>: LIF, Jan
15, Feb 12, Nov 6; <u>1731</u>: LIF, Feb 24, GF, Jun 9, LIF, Dec 13; <u>1732</u>: LIF, Feb
18, LIF/CG, Oct 20; <u>1733</u>: HAY, Mar 7, DL, Sep 24, 26; <u>1734</u>: CG, Jan 26; <u>1736</u>:
HAY, Feb 20; <u>1738</u>: DL, Jan 5, 6, 7, 9, Nov 8, Dec 15; <u>1739</u>: DL, Feb 26, Oct
4; <u>1740</u>: DL, Jan 12, GF, Oct 25; <u>1742</u>: CG, May 4, 15; <u>1743</u>: DL, Oct 22, 28,
CG, Dec 9; <u>1744</u>: DL, Jan 19, CG, Feb 1, 20, Dec 12, 22; <u>1745</u>: GF, Jan 21, 22;
<u>1748</u>: CG, Jan 21, Feb 27; <u>1751</u>: DL, Mar 19; <u>1753</u>: CG, Jan 22; <u>1758</u>: DL, Dec
19, 28; <u>1759</u>: DL, Jan 1, 4, 8, 10, Feb 13, 21; <u>1778</u>: DL, Dec 19
--Aesop, Part II, <u>1697</u>: DL/DL, Mar 0
--City Wives' Confederacy, The (Confederacy, The), <u>1705</u>: LIF/QUEN, Oct 30, 31,
Nov 1, 2, 6, QUEEN'S, 15, LIF/QUEN, Dec 4, 26; <u>1706</u>: LIF/QUEN, Jan 15, 24,
Jun 12, QUEEN'S, Dec 11; <u>1709</u>: DL, Dec 17, 19; <u>1710</u>: DL, Jan 2, 11, May 30,
GR, Sep 11, DL, Nov 23, 24; <u>1711</u>: DL, Feb 2, Nov 7; <u>1712</u>: DL, Dec 19; <u>1713</u>:
DL, Dec 11; <u>1715</u>: LIF, Jan 8, 17, 21, Feb 1; <u>1716</u>: LIF, Jan 12, 24, Feb 20,
May 7, Nov 12; <u>1719</u>: LIF, Apr 2; <u>1720</u>: LIF, Mar 28; <u>1725</u>: LIF, Dec 16, 17,
18, 20, 21; <u>1726</u>: LIF, Jan 4, 17, Feb 17, Mar 10, Apr 20, Oct 26, Dec 5;
<u>1727</u>: LIF, Jan 7, Feb 21, Apr 5, May 3, Jun 9, Sep 22, Oct 28, Dec 1; <u>1728</u>:
LIF, Jan 10, Mar 25, May 6, Nov 2, Dec 30; <u>1729</u>: LIF, Apr 24, Nov 24; <u>1730</u>:
LIF, Jan 28, Feb 14, Apr 30, Oct 31, Dec 19; <u>1731</u>: LIF, Feb 17, Apr 21, May
28, Nov 11; <u>1732</u>: LIF, Feb 16, Mar 30, May 11, LIF/CG, Oct 2; <u>1733</u>: LIF/CG,
Jan 31, May 18, CG, Oct 16, Dec 7; <u>1734</u>: CG, Feb 20, DL/LIF, Mar 11, CG, Apr
25, DL/LIF, May 3; <u>1735</u>: CG/LIF, May 15; <u>1736</u>: CG, Mar 1, LIF, 24, May 19;
<u>1737</u>: CG, Jan 21, DL, Oct 8, 13, 15, 18, Nov 18; <u>1738</u>: DL, Feb 1, May 29, Nov
11, 24; <u>1739</u>: DL, Jan 12, Dec 8, 15; <u>1740</u>: DL, May 7, Oct 23; <u>1741</u>: DL, Feb
9, Apr 9, May 4; <u>1742</u>: DL, Mar 22, CG, 29, DL, Apr 3; <u>1743</u>: LIF, Mar 14, CG,
Nov 18; <u>1744</u>: CG, Dec 10, 20; <u>1745</u>: CG, May 14, Nov 30; <u>1746</u>: CG, Jan 4, Feb
15, DL, 24, 27, Apr 3, May 1, CG, 5, DL, Nov 22; <u>1747</u>: DL, Jan 22, Feb 23,
Apr 2, May 8, Oct 1; <u>1748</u>: DL, May 18, Sep 15; <u>1749</u>: DL, Nov 9, Dec 19; <u>1750</u>:
DL, Nov 12; <u>1751</u>: DL, Feb 12, CG, Apr 19, 24, Nov 13, 27; <u>1752</u>: CG, Jan 8,
Feb 25, DL, Apr 29, CG, Oct 10; <u>1753</u>: DL, Jan 3, CG, 24, Nov 2, 21, Dec 21;
<u>1754</u>: CG, May 20, Sep 30, Dec 3; <u>1755</u>: CG, Oct 23; <u>1756</u>: CG, May 24, Nov 16;
<u>1757</u>: CG, May 18; <u>1759</u>: DL, Oct 27, 29, 31, Nov 7; <u>1760</u>: DL, Jan 9, Feb 6,
14, May 9, Nov 17, Dec 13; <u>1761</u>: DL, May 16, Oct 10; <u>1762</u>: CG, May 13, DL,
20, Dec 1; <u>1763</u>: DL, May 9, Nov 8; <u>1764</u>: DL, Jan 5, CG, 26, Feb 2, Nov 8;
<u>1765</u>: CG, Jan 15, DL, May 17, CG, Oct 31; <u>1767</u>: CG, Sep 26, Oct 9; <u>1768</u>: CG,
Jan 6, Jun 2, Nov 16; <u>1769</u>: CG, May 20, DL, Dec 8; <u>1770</u>: CG, Nov 16; <u>1771</u>:
CG, May 25; <u>1778</u>: DL, Apr 9; <u>1781</u>: HAY, Aug 21; <u>1782</u>: DL, Nov 7, Dec 16;
<u>1783</u>: DL, May 23; <u>1784</u>: DL, Mar 23, Dec 10, 17; <u>1785</u>: DL, Jan 11, Feb 1, Apr
6, May 16, HAY, Jun 11, 14, DL, Dec 5; <u>1786</u>: DL, Nov 14; <u>1787</u>: DL, May 28;
<u>1788</u>: DL, May 22, Oct 24, Nov 19, 24, Dec 10, 26; <u>1789</u>: DL, Jan 2, 9, 23, Mar
12, 26, May 18, Jun 12; <u>1790</u>: DL, Mar 2, May 8, Oct 20, Nov 16, Dec 13; <u>1791</u>:
DL, Feb 2, 14, Mar 14, Apr 28, May 16, DLKING'S, Oct 20, 27, Nov 3, 18, Dec
17, 28; <u>1792</u>: DLKING'S, Jan 25, Mar 8, Apr 18; <u>1793</u>: DL, Mar 14, HAY, Oct 22,
28, Nov 12, Dec 21; <u>1794</u>: DL, Dec 9, 10; <u>1795</u>: DL, Jan 15, 27, Nov 14; <u>1796</u>:
DL, Feb 16, Oct 8, Nov 24, Dec 15; <u>1797</u>: DL, Nov 11; <u>1798</u>: DL, Jan 18, Feb 20
--Country House, The, <u>1698</u>: DL, Jan 18, NONE, Sep 0; <u>1703</u>: DL, Jan 23; <u>1705</u>:
DL, Jun 16, 28; <u>1715</u>: LIF, Jan 14, 17, 18, 20, Feb 1, 10, 11, 15, 25, Mar 1,
Jun 1, 2, Oct 14, 17, Nov 28, Dec 31; <u>1716</u>: LIF, Nov 14; <u>1718</u>: LIF, Jun 27;
<u>1721</u>: LIF, Apr 24, Nov 24, Dec 6; <u>1722</u>: LIF, Jan 11; <u>1723</u>: LIF, Feb 18, 19,
20, 21, Mar 19, May 2, Jun 3, Oct 22, Dec 3; <u>1724</u>: LIF, Apr 6, Jun 4, Nov 10;
<u>1725</u>: LIF, Oct 22, Nov 24; <u>1726</u>: LIF, Oct 19; <u>1727</u>: LIF, Feb 16, Mar 21, Nov
24, 25; <u>1728</u>: LIF, May 6, Dec 12; <u>1729</u>: LIF, Mar 25, Apr 18, 29, May 19, 20;
<u>1730</u>: LIF, Jan 2, 3, 5, Feb 19; <u>1731</u>: LIF, Jan 26, Nov 19; <u>1732</u>: LIF, Feb 9,
15, Mar 27; <u>1733</u>: CG, Dec 3, 6, 10, 21, 29; <u>1734</u>: CG, Jan 17, DL/HAY, Mar 30,
CG/LIF, Oct 7; <u>1735</u>: CG/LIF, Jan 14, Apr 18, 22, May 5; <u>1736</u>: CG, Mar 11;
<u>1737</u>: CG, Mar 28, Apr 11, 22; <u>1739</u>: CG, Apr 25, May 7, 9, Nov 3; <u>1740</u>: CG,

May 16; <u>1742</u>: CG, May 7, 15, Dec 7; <u>1746</u>: CG, Dec 3; <u>1758</u>: CG, Apr 3; <u>1760</u>: CG, Mar 24, Apr 25

--Cuckold in Conceit, The; or, Sganarell, <u>1707</u>: QUEEN'S, Mar 22; <u>1709</u>: DL, May 25, Jun 4

--False Friend, The, <u>1702</u>: DL, Feb 0; <u>1710</u>: QUEEN'S, Mar 4, 7; <u>1715</u>: DL, Nov 5, 7, 25; <u>1720</u>: HOUN, Jun 13; <u>1724</u>: RI, Jun 22, LIF, Oct 14, 16, 17, Nov 21; <u>1725</u>: LIF, Feb 13, Mar 15, May 4, Nov 3; <u>1726</u>: LIF, Feb 5, Mar 5, May 11, Nov 12; <u>1727</u>: LIF, Jan 11, Feb 23, Oct 14, Nov 10; <u>1728</u>: LIF, Jan 16; <u>1729</u>: LIF, Feb 8, 22, Mar 29, May 6, Oct 31; <u>1730</u>: LIF, Jan 12, Apr 17, Oct 16, Nov 28, Dec 3; <u>1731</u>: LIF, Feb 20, Mar 16, May 26, Oct 8; <u>1732</u>: LIF, Jan 18, Mar 14, LIF/CG, Nov 3; <u>1733</u>: RI, Sep 10, CG, Nov 8; <u>1734</u>: CG, Jan 22; <u>1735</u>: CG, Dec 15; <u>1736</u>: CG, Feb 2, 5, Apr 28, RI, Aug 28; <u>1738</u>: CG, May 18, Apr 29, Nov 24; <u>1739</u>: CG, Jan 26, Dec 29; <u>1748</u>: HAY, Apr 25; <u>1752</u>: CG, Jan 28, 29, Feb 13; <u>1753</u>: CG, Feb 6; <u>1767</u>: DL, Mar 31; <u>1789</u>: DL, Oct 21, 24, 28

--Mistake, The; or, The Wrangling Lovers, <u>1705</u>: QUEEN'S, Dec 10, 27, 28, 29, 31; <u>1706</u>: QUEEN'S, Jan 1, 2, 16, 23, Mar 25; <u>1710</u>: DL, Feb 11, Mar 9, 27, GR, Aug 19, Sep 1; <u>1715</u>: LIF, Jan 5, 10, Nov 2; <u>1726</u>: LIF, Oct 24, 28; <u>1727</u>: LIF, Jan 13, Feb 9, 25, Oct 12, Nov 27; <u>1728</u>: LIF, Jan 11, Apr 30, Dec 16; <u>1729</u>: LIF, Apr 17, May 8, Nov 14; <u>1730</u>: LIF, Jan 8, Feb 6, Apr 8, May 9, Oct 26, Dec 22; <u>1731</u>: LIF, Jan 11, Feb 13, Apr 8, May 31, Oct 22, Dec 20; <u>1732</u>: LIF, Feb 15, May 15, LIF/CG, Nov 17; <u>1733</u>: CG, Jan 24, GF, Dec 13, 14, 15, 19, CG, 31; <u>1734</u>: CG, Feb 1, GF, 22, Dec 13; <u>1735</u>: GF, Jan 23, 24, May 1, WF, Aug 23, CG, Oct 17, 18; <u>1736</u>: CG, Jan 27, Mar 8, May 25; <u>1738</u>: CG, Jan 31, Mar 4, May 5, Nov 15; <u>1739</u>: CG, Feb 1, May 24, Oct 5, Nov 29; <u>1740</u>: CG, Feb 15, 26, Oct 15; <u>1741</u>: CG, Jan 6, May 7, Oct 24, Dec 5; <u>1742</u>: CG, Feb 19, Apr 22; <u>1743</u>: CG, Oct 14; <u>1744</u>: CG, Feb 21; <u>1745</u>: CG, Nov 19; <u>1752</u>: CG, Mar 3, 5; <u>1755</u>: DL, Mar 13, Apr 5, 18, May 10; <u>1756</u>: DL, Mar 30, May 4; <u>1757</u>: DL, Apr 14; <u>1758</u>: DL, May 4; <u>1760</u>: DL, Mar 20, Apr 16; <u>1761</u>: DL, Apr 28; <u>1762</u>: DL, Mar 20, Apr 22, 26, Oct 14, 19; <u>1763</u>: DL, Apr 25; <u>1764</u>: DL, Jan 14, 19, Feb 18, 22, Oct 18, 19; <u>1765</u>: DL, Oct 31; <u>1766</u>: CG, Feb 6, 11, May 14; <u>1767</u>: HAY, Sep 21; <u>1768</u>: DL, Apr 12; <u>1770</u>: HAY, Dec 14; <u>1780</u>: CG, Oct 21, 27, Dec 22; <u>1781</u>: CG, Jan 5, May 1; <u>1786</u>: CG, Jan 17, 20; <u>1790</u>: CG, Feb 11, Oct 15; <u>1791</u>: CG, Nov 29; <u>1792</u>: CG, Nov 10

--Provoked Wife, The, <u>1697</u>: LIF, Apr 0; <u>1706</u>: QUEEN'S, Jan 19, 21, 22, Mar 11, 27; <u>1710</u>: DL, Feb 11; <u>1711</u>: GR, Aug 30, Sep 3; <u>1715</u>: LIF, Dec 21, 22; <u>1716</u>: LIF, Jan 3, Feb 4, Mar 3, 22, Apr 23, Jun 4, Oct 26; <u>1717</u>: LIF, Jan 10, 29, Mar 19, May 7, Oct 7, Dec 9, 21; <u>1718</u>: LIF, Jan 20, Mar 4, Apr 15; <u>1719</u>: LIF, Jan 3, 31, Mar 5, Apr 20; <u>1720</u>: LIF, Apr 28, Nov 15, Dec 20; <u>1721</u>: LIF, May 17, Oct 19, Nov 7; <u>1722</u>: LIF, Nov 12, Dec 12; <u>1723</u>: LIF, May 6; <u>1724</u>: LIF, Apr 22; <u>1725</u>: LIF, Apr 2; <u>1726</u>: DL, Jan 11, 12, 13, 14, 15, 17, 18, Feb 1, 9, Mar 3, LIF, 19, Apr 15, DL, 26, LIF, May 20, DL, Sep 15, LIF, Oct 21, DL, Nov 1, Dec 27; <u>1727</u>: DL, Apr 26, Nov 9, LIF, 18; <u>1728</u>: LIF, Jan 13, DL, Mar 25, LIF, May 18, Oct 23, DL, Nov 8, 13; <u>1729</u>: DL, Jan 17, LIF, Mar 18, Apr 22, DL, 22, LIF, Oct 6, DL, 16, Dec 17; <u>1730</u>: LIF, Mar 16, DL, Apr 8, 28, LIF, 29, Nov 9, Dec 16, DL, 19; <u>1731</u>: DL, Jan 11, LIF, Mar 15, DL, 25, Apr 27, LIF, May 3, DL, Sep 23, LIF, Nov 16, DL, 19; <u>1732</u>: DL, Jan 28, LIF, Feb 28, DL, Apr 22, LIF/CG, Nov 13, DL, 21, 30; <u>1733</u>: DL, Jan 3, Feb 26, LIF/CG, Mar 28, CG, May 4, Oct 20, Dec 18; <u>1734</u>: CG, Apr 18, May 13, DL, Dec 2; <u>1735</u>: CG/LIF, Jan 31, Mar 22, DL, Apr 23, CG/LIF, May 19, CG, Oct 10; <u>1736</u>: CG, Feb 9, Apr 27, Nov 22; <u>1737</u>: CG, Jan 4, DL, Mar 12, CG, Apr 22, DL, 23, CG, Sep 21, Nov 8, DL, 17; <u>1738</u>: CG, Jan 23, Mar 7, DL, Apr 21, CG, May 15, DL, Oct 24, Nov 21; <u>1739</u>: CG, Jan 15, DL, 24, CG, Mar 5, DL, May 9, Nov 8; <u>1740</u>: DL, Feb 19, Apr 14, CG, 14, DL, May 20, CG, Oct 8, DL, Nov 11; <u>1741</u>: CG, Jan 10, Apr 17, DL, May 1, CG, Oct 8, DL, Nov 20, Dec 3, CG, 14; <u>1742</u>: DL, Jan 8, 13, Feb 24, Mar 13, CG, 15, DL, Apr 29, May 24, CG, Nov 3, DL, 12, Dec 1, CG, 8; <u>1743</u>: CG, Apr 15, DL, May 12, CG, Oct 7, Nov 25, Dec 13, 22; <u>1744</u>: DL, Jan 13, 23, CG, Apr 23, DL, May 15, CG, Oct 26, DL, Nov 16, 19, 28, 29, Dec 4, CG, 31; <u>1745</u>: DL, Jan 2, CG, 5, DL, Feb 1, 6, GF, Mar 14, 25, Apr 4, DL, 20, May 9, CG, Sep 27, DL, Nov 26; <u>1746</u>: CG, Jan 18, DL, 23, May 8, CG, Nov 8, Dec 5, GF, 11; <u>1747</u>: GF, Jan 12, CG, 27, Mar 19, May 5, DL, 5, Nov 10, 11, 28, Dec 15; <u>1748</u>: DL, Jan 13, 14, Feb 11, CG, 15, DL, Mar 21, Apr 25, CG, May 3, 4, Sep 21, Oct 11, DL, 18, Dec 22; <u>1749</u>: DL, Feb 2, CG, 18, 20, Mar 9, DL, 14, Apr 11, CG, 20, Sep 25, Oct 14, DL, 23, Nov 7, CG, Dec 4, DL, 15; <u>1750</u>: CG, Jan 26, DL, Feb 16, Mar 27, CG, 31, DL, Apr 3, CG, 6, DL, May 7, CG, Oct 16, DL, 20, CG, Nov 10, Dec 13; <u>1751</u>: CG, Feb 7, DL, 18, Apr 16, CG, 18, DL, Sep 24, Oct 26, Dec 18; <u>1752</u>: DL, Jan 14, Apr 8, CG, Oct 4, DL, 7, CG, Nov 17, Dec 16; <u>1753</u>: DL, Jan 9, CG, 27, May 10, DL, 16, CG, Sep 24, Oct 26, DL, Nov 7; <u>1754</u>: DL, Jan 8, Apr 2, CG, 18, DL, May 27, CG, Sep 27; <u>1755</u>: DL, Jan 17, Feb 8, Apr 1, 30, Oct 27, Nov 13; <u>1756</u>: DL, Jan 7, Nov 2; <u>1757</u>: DL, Jan 13, Mar 3, Oct 12, Dec 1; <u>1758</u>: DL, Jan 17, Apr 10, Oct 14; <u>1759</u>: DL, Jan 13, 19, 31, Feb 22, Apr 30, Oct 26, Dec 18; <u>1760</u>: DL, Feb 15, May 20, Dec 2; <u>1761</u>: DL, Apr 3, Sep 23, Nov 3; <u>1762</u>: DL, Feb 3, Mar 16, CG, Apr 19, DL, 23,

29, Sep 29; <u>1763</u>: DL, Jan 12, CG, 28, Feb 7, 28, Mar 12, DL, Apr 18, CG, May
13, Oct 20, Dec 31; <u>1764</u>: CG, Oct 30; <u>1765</u>: DL, Jan 23, CG, May 7, DL, Dec 5,
13; <u>1766</u>: DL, Jan 23, CG, Apr 18, DL, Oct 10; <u>1767</u>: DL, Feb 3, Sep 25, Nov
25; <u>1768</u>: DL, Feb 18, Sep 8, Dec 14; <u>1769</u>: DL, Oct 10, Dec 30; <u>1770</u>: DL, Apr
2, Nov 20, Dec 28; <u>1771</u>: HAY, Jun 5, DL, Nov 22; <u>1772</u>: DL, Jan 3, May 21, Oct
14, Dec 4; <u>1773</u>: DL, Feb 23, Oct 30, Dec 2; <u>1774</u>: DL, Apr 7, Nov 16; <u>1775</u>:
DL, Jan 6, Oct 31; <u>1776</u>: DL, Jan 31, Feb 5, Apr 30; <u>1777</u>: HAY, Sep 10, 12,
18, Oct 9, CG, 23; <u>1778</u>: DL, Apr 27, HAY, Sep 2, 4, CG, 25; <u>1779</u>: CG, Jan 9,
Feb 8, Apr 22, HAY, Aug 18; <u>1780</u>: CG, Mar 14; <u>1786</u>: DL, May 17, CG, Oct 25,
28; <u>1787</u>: CG, Jan 1, 23, May 19, Nov 30; <u>1788</u>: CG, Jan 1; <u>1791</u>: HAY, Dec 26;
<u>1796</u>: HAY, Aug 8, 16
--Relapse, The; or, Virtue in Danger, <u>1696</u>: DL, Nov 21, 23, 24, 25, 26, 27;
<u>1698</u>: DL, Jan 5; <u>1700</u>: DL, Feb 10; <u>1701</u>: DL, Jan 9; <u>1702</u>: DL, Nov 13; <u>1703</u>:
DL, May 15, Jul 1, Oct 22, Nov 23; <u>1705</u>: DL, Feb 26, Mar 24, Jul 18, Sep 22,
Nov 29; <u>1706</u>: DL/DG, Nov 2, DG, 28; <u>1707</u>: DL, Jan 27; <u>1708</u>: DL, Jan 26, Jun
17, Oct 26; <u>1709</u>: DL, Feb 2; <u>1710</u>: QUEEN'S, Jan 21, DL, Feb 11, QUEEN'S, 28,
GR, Sep 9, 20, DL, Dec 15; <u>1711</u>: GR, Aug 4, DL, Nov 2; <u>1715</u>: DL, Nov 26, 28,
Dec 12; <u>1716</u>: DL, Feb 3, May 8, Oct 16; <u>1717</u>: DL, Jan 3, 8, Apr 1, May 20,
Nov 20; <u>1718</u>: DL, Jan 24, Mar 13, May 19, Oct 2, Dec 18; <u>1719</u>: DL, Jan 7, Apr
7, 29, Oct 7, Dec 3; <u>1720</u>: DL, Jan 29, Apr 4; <u>1721</u>: DL, Jan 6, Mar 23, May 3,
Jun 1, Oct 23, Nov 9; <u>1722</u>: DL, Jan 12, Mar 10, Apr 20, Oct 15, Nov 2; <u>1723</u>:
DL, Feb 1, Mar 14, May 22, Sep 19, Dec 31; <u>1724</u>: DL, Feb 11, Apr 13, Oct 15,
Dec 7; <u>1725</u>: DL, Mar 11, Apr 16, May 31, Sep 25, Dec 16; <u>1726</u>: DL, Feb 28,
Mar 28, May 2, Sep 17, Nov 23; <u>1727</u>: DL, Feb 18, 20, Apr 21, Oct 5, Nov 29;
<u>1728</u>: DL, Mar 7, Apr 8, Oct 21, Dec 16; <u>1729</u>: DL, Mar 11, May 2, Sep 30, Dec
29; <u>1730</u>: DL, Apr 13, Nov 11, Dec 8; <u>1731</u>: DL, May 10, Nov 17; <u>1732</u>: DL, Feb
10, Apr 14, May 10, Sep 30, Nov 16; <u>1733</u>: DL, Mar 12, GF, 30, 31, May 14, DL,
18, DL/HAY, Oct 6, Nov 3, Dec 1; <u>1734</u>: DL/HAY, Jan 26, Mar 19, DL, Apr 22,
GF, 24, May 15, DL, Oct 17, Nov 7, Dec 5; <u>1735</u>: GF, Mar 29, DL, Jun 3, YB,
Jul 17, DL, Oct 24, Dec 16; <u>1736</u>: DL, Mar 25, Apr 17, CG, 29, Jun 4, DL, Sep
7, CG, Oct 4; <u>1737</u>: CG, Mar 7, DL, May 4, CG, Nov 1; <u>1738</u>: CG, Jan 20, DL,
Mar 2, CG, Apr 28, DL, May 5, Sep 9, Oct 10, CG, Nov 23; <u>1739</u>: DL, Jan 4, CG,
Mar 2, DL, 26, CG, May 14, Aug 2, 31, Nov 9; <u>1740</u>: CG, Apr 18, DL, 29, CG,
May 13, DL, Sep 30, Nov 25, GF, Dec 8, 9; <u>1741</u>: CG, Mar 30, GF, Apr 6, DL,
May 26, Sep 15, Oct 6, 24, Dec 23; <u>1742</u>: CG, Jan 4, 7, 18, DL, Feb 8, 15, Mar
16, CG, Apr 24, DL, May 13, Oct 18, CG, Nov 22, LIF, Dec 3, DL, 9; <u>1743</u>: LIF,
Apr 7, CG, May 3, DL, 14, Oct 15, 18, Nov 12, Dec 3; <u>1744</u>: DL, Mar 31, HAY,
Apr 6, 9, DL, 13; <u>1745</u>: CG, Jan 2, 19, Apr 2, GF, 6, CG, May 7, Nov 9, DL,
14, 15, 27; <u>1746</u>: CG, Jan 9, GF, Feb 10, CG, 25, GF, Mar 6, DL, Apr 7, CG,
16, Oct 3, GF, Dec 12; <u>1747</u>: DL, Jan 2, CG, Feb 7, May 13, Nov 16, Dec 30;
<u>1748</u>: CG, Mar 29, May 2, DL, Sep 13, Nov 25; <u>1749</u>: CG, Jan 2, Feb 28, Apr 15,
DL, May 2, Sep 19, Oct 25; <u>1750</u>: DL, Jan 11, Feb 8, May 1, Sep 15; <u>1751</u>: DL,
Sep 14, Dec 31; <u>1752</u>: DL, May 4, Oct 21; <u>1753</u>: DL, May 15, Nov 8; <u>1754</u>: DL,
Jan 1, CG, Feb 12, DL, May 21, Oct 18, CG, Nov 6, 29; <u>1755</u>: CG, Apr 26, DL,
Nov 22; <u>1756</u>: DL, Oct 5; <u>1758</u>: DL, Nov 1; <u>1763</u>: CG, Apr 25, May 7, 23, Oct
15, Dec 17; <u>1764</u>: CG, Feb 17, Apr 7, May 14, Nov 16; <u>1765</u>: CG, Jan 10, 12,
25, Apr 26, Sep 20, Dec 4; <u>1766</u>: CG, Mar 1, May 7; <u>1770</u>: CG, Mar 20; <u>1773</u>:
CG, Apr 27; <u>1777</u>: DL, Feb 24; <u>1784</u>: HAY, Aug 6
Vanbrughe (singer), <u>1718</u>: YB, Mar 5; <u>1719</u>: CGR, Mar 18
Vandeput, Sir George (candidate for Parliament), <u>1749</u>: HAY, Nov 14
Vanderbank, James (actor), <u>1750</u>: CG, Nov 20
Vanderhoff, Mynheer (tumbler), <u>1734</u>: BFHBH, Aug 24
VanderHuff (actor), <u>1737</u>: BF, Aug 23, SF, Sep 7
Vandermere, John Byron (actor), <u>1768</u>: HAY, Jun 8, 22, 23, 29, Jul 6, 27, Aug 1,
8, 19, 24, Sep 13, 19; <u>1769</u>: HAY, Feb 28, May 15, 17, 24, 26, 29, Jun 2, 5,
Jul 12, Aug 7, 9, 21, 25, 28, 29, 30, 31, Sep 1, 4, 8, 11; <u>1770</u>: HAY, May 16,
18, 23, 28, Jun 5, 22, Jul 20, Aug 1, 24, Sep 27, Oct 1, 5; <u>1771</u>: HAY, May
15, 17, 23, 27, 29, 31, Jun 5, 7, 10, 14, 21, 26, Jul 1, 3, 5, 10, 15, 24,
Aug 19, Sep 2, 16, 18, 19, 20
Vandersluys (dancer), <u>1746</u>: CG, Apr 17; <u>1747</u>: CG, Dec 26; <u>1748</u>: CG, Mar 3
Vandersluys, Aleda (dancer), <u>1745</u>: CG, Nov 14, 25, 26, Dec 27; <u>1746</u>: CG, Apr 5,
7, 8, 17; <u>1747</u>: CG, Apr 23, May 4; <u>1748</u>: CG, Mar 3, 14; <u>1750</u>: DL, Nov 8
Vanderstop, Cornelius, <u>1777</u>: HAY, Oct 13
--Gentle Shepherd, The, <u>1777</u>: HAY, Oct 13
Vandervelt, Mrs (actor), <u>1720</u>: LIF, Jan 11
VanDyke (painter), <u>1757</u>: DL, Jan 1; <u>1783</u>: DL, Sep 30
VanEsch (composer), <u>1791</u>: KING'S, Apr 11; <u>1795</u>: DL, Jun 1
Vanfleet, Mynheer (dancer), <u>1733</u>: GF, May 8
Vangable (tumbler), <u>1745</u>: GF, Apr 15, 16
Vanguard, The; or, British Tars Regaling after Battle (interlude, anon), <u>1799</u>:
CG, May 3, Jun 1, 3
Vanhout (actor), <u>1753</u>: BFGI, Sep 4

Vanhuyck (house servant), 1747: CG, May 19
Vanneschi, Francesco (manager, composer), 1741: KING'S, Oct 31, Nov 10; 1742:
   KING'S, Jan 19, Mar 2; 1743: KING'S, Jan 1; 1745: HAY, Feb 9; 1746: KING'S,
   Jan 7, Mar 4; 1747: KING'S, Jan 17, Mar 24; 1749: KING'S, May 20; 1753:
   KING'S, Nov 13; 1754: KING'S, May 11; 1756: KING'S, Feb 10, 17; 1757: KING'S,
   May 31, Sep 20; 1758: KING'S, Apr 22; 1759: KING'S, May 19
--Polidoro (pastiche), 1742: KING'S, Jan 19, 23, 26, Feb 2, 6, 9, 13, 16
Vanni Parti (song), 1726: DL, Apr 28
VanRymsdyck (dancer), 1772: HAY, Sep 18
VanTromp, Admiral (spectator, hissed), 1675: NONE, Jan 0
Vanture, Y (actor), 1728: HAY, Feb 21
Varcan col' Vento istesso (song), 1751: KING'S, Apr 16
Vardill (versifier), 1789: CG, Apr 28
Variety. See Griffith, Richard.
Variety, The. See Cavendish, William.
Varley (plumber), 1771: CG, Nov 18; 1773: CG, Jan 18; 1774: CG, May 10; 1776:
   CG, May 22; 1777: CG, May 23; 1778: CG, May 22; 1779: CG, May 19; 1780: CG,
   May 26; 1781: CG, May 26; 1782: CG, May 29; 1783: CG, Jun 4; 1784: CG, May
   29; 1786: CG, May 30; 1787: CG, May 28; 1788: CG, May 17; 1789: CG, Jun 13;
   1791: CG, Jun 9; 1792: CG, Jun 1
Varney (stage doorkeeper), 1752: DL, May 5; 1753: DL, May 18, Sep 8, Dec 11,
   21; 1754: DL, Mar 23, 27, May 22, Sep 14; 1755: DL, Mar 19, May 8, Sep 13;
   1756: DL, Apr 3, May 8, Aug 12, Sep 18, Nov 12; 1757: DL, Feb 22, Mar 25, 26,
   28, Apr 14, 27, May 5, 6, 11, 14, Sep 5, 10, Dec 14, 21; 1758: DL, Mar 2, 3,
   7, 10, 16, 29, Apr 10, 11, 17, 21, 24, May 12, Sep 16; 1759: DL, Mar 30, Apr
   16, May 19, Jul 12, Sep 22; 1760: DL, May 19, Sep 20; 1761: DL, Feb 27, Mar
   4, 30, Apr 1, 30, May 16
Vascour, Mr and Mrs (payees), 1774: DL, Oct 29
Vashon (musician), 1774: DL, Feb 18
Vaucanson (machinist), 1742: LIF, Dec 27
Vaudemont, Prince, 1698: YB, Mar 28, Apr 15
Vaughan (actor), 1731: GF, Nov 4; 1732: DL, Aug 1; 1734: BFRLCH, Sep 2, CG/LIF,
   Nov 14; 1735: CG/LIF, Jan 20
Vaughan (beneficiary), 1726: LIF, May 17
Vaughan (householder), 1746: CG, Mar 13; 1748: DL, Mar 12
Vaughan (spectator), 1682: DG, Apr 27
Vaughan, Amy (payee), 1767: DL, Jan 16
Vaughan, Henry (actor), 1750: DL, Sep 22; 1751: DL, Oct 29; 1752: DL, Nov 22;
   1753: DL, May 18, Oct 13; 1754: DL, Jul 2; 1756: DL, Jan 2, May 10, Sep 18;
   1757: CG, May 27
Vaughan, Henry (actor, dancer), 1739: DL, Jan 8; 1740: DL, Jan 15, 16, Apr 17,
   May 23, Oct 20, 21, 22, GF, 24, DL, 24, GF, 29, DL, Nov 3, GF, 4, DL, 7, 15,
   GF, 15, DL, 18, GF, 21, 22, DL, 24, GF, 25, 29, Dec 1, DL, 4, GF, 6, 8, DL,
   9, GF, 10, 12, 15, DL, 18, 19; 1741: GF, Jan 20, 27, Feb 2, 5, 9, 10, 16, 19,
   DL, 24, GF, Mar 3, 16, DL, Apr 3, GF, 17, DL, 22, May 12, TC, Aug 4, BFLW,
   22, BFTY, 22, GF, Sep 14, SF, 14, GF, 16, 23, 25, 30, Oct 2, 5, 9, CG, 13,
   15, GF, 16, 19, 28, Nov 6, 9, CG, Dec 4, GF, 9, 15; 1742: GF, Jan 1, 27, Feb
   3, Mar 1, CG, 27, GF, Apr 6, 21, 29, CG, May 4, GF, 5, 18, DL, Oct 13; 1743:
   SOU, Feb 18, 25, CG, Nov 7, Dec 8; 1744: CG, Apr 6, HAY, May 16, Jun 29, CG,
   Oct 15, 31, Nov 7, 8, Dec 17, GF, 26; 1745: CG, Apr 4, DL, 4, 27, 30, CG, May
   29, Sep 25, 30, Oct 16, DL, 17, Dec 5, 6, 9, CG, 10, DL, 20, 30; 1746: CG,
   Jan 7, 13, DL, 13, CG, 17, Feb 3, 17, 24, Apr 17, 22, 29, Nov 18, 26, Dec 11;
   1747: CG, Feb 2, 6, 12, Mar 17, DL, Sep 17, Dec 5, 26; 1748: BF, Aug 24,
   SFBCBV, Sep 7, DL, 22, 24, 27, Oct 6, 14, 15, 18, 19, 27, 29, Nov 7, 14, 29;
   1749: DL, Jan 2, 7, 9, 10, 13, 26, Feb 21, Mar 29, Oct 14, 26, Nov 9, 28;
   1750: DL, Feb 10, Apr 30, Sep 13, 27, 28, Oct 15, 16, 22, 30, Nov 7, 14, Dec
   31; 1751: DL, Jan 5, 23, 26, Feb 14, May 22, Sep 13, Oct 3, 9, 17, Nov 29,
   Dec 26; 1752: DL, Jan 1, Apr 3, 4, 7, 27, Sep 16, Oct 12, 23, Nov 8, 25, 27,
   30, Dec 8, 29; 1753: DL, Jan 5, Apr 14, May 3, 17, 21, Sep 13, 22, Oct 9, 12,
   16, Nov 19; 1754: DL, Feb 5, Apr 30, May 9, Jul 2, Sep 26, Oct 10, 12, 16,
   30, Nov 7, 11; 1755: DL, Feb 18, 22, May 5, Sep 13, Oct 4, 7, 17, Nov 8, 15,
   26, Dec 6, 11; 1756: DL, Jan 2, 21, Feb 17, Mar 23, May 11, 14, Sep 18, 25,
   28, 30, Oct 13, 15, 21, Nov 18, 19, Dec 27; 1757: DL, Feb 5, Mar 7, Apr 27,
   May 2, Sep 20, 24, 29, Oct 8, 15, 19, 29, Dec 22, 27; 1758: DL, Jan 27, Apr
   18, 25, Sep 26, Oct 3, 17, 24, Nov 7, 16, Dec 18, 28; 1759: DL, Mar 20, 26,
   31, Apr 27, May 11, 16, Jul 12, Sep 29, Oct 2, 4, 9, 27, 30, Nov 13, 24, Dec
   12, 31; 1760: DL, Feb 8, Mar 4, Apr 9, 22, 28, 30, May 8, 16, Jun 19, Jul 29,
   Oct 2, 3, 11, 15, 22, 25, Nov 27; 1761: DL, Apr 15, 17, CG, Jun 23, DL, Sep
   10, 14, 15, 17, Oct 20, 29, Nov 9, Dec 28; 1762: DL, Jan 7, 11, 23, Mar 15,
   Apr 1, 21, 30, May 7, 17, Sep 25, Oct 4, 5, 6, 25, 28, Nov 3, 5, 10, 12, 18,
   Dec 11, 27; 1763: DL, Jan 15, 18, Feb 24, May 31, Sep 20, 29, Oct 1, 4, Nov
   9, 30, Dec 14, 17, 26, 28; 1764: DL, Jan 4, 18, 20, Feb 18, 21, Apr 24, May

21, Sep 25, 27, Oct 4, 17, 20, 25, Nov 13; <u>1765</u>: DL, Jan 22, Feb 4, Apr 13,
May 11, 17, 18, 22, Oct 23, 24, Nov 16, Dec 3; <u>1766</u>: DL, Jan 9, 13, 24, 29,
May 3, 19, 21, 22; <u>1767</u>: DL, Jan 16; <u>1771</u>: HAY, Apr 15; <u>1772</u>: DL, Jun 10;
<u>1776</u>: DL, Jan 5, Mar 25, Apr 15
Vaughan, J Taylor (patron), <u>1794</u>: DL, Jul 2
Vaughan, Miss (actor), <u>1730</u>: GF, Jun 1, 5, 8, 9, 19, Jul 6, 17, 22, DL, Oct 20,
GF, Nov 10; <u>1732</u>: GF, Oct 2; <u>1733</u>: GF, Apr 30; <u>1744</u>: CG, Oct 3, Nov 7, Dec 8;
<u>1745</u>: CG, May 3, Oct 7, Nov 14, 26, 29, Dec 12, 13, 14; <u>1746</u>: CG, Feb 24, Mar
13, Apr 17, May 13, Oct 1, Nov 4, 26; <u>1747</u>: CG, Feb 2, 28
Vaughan, Miss M (dancer), <u>1730</u>: GF, May 27, Jun 1, 3, 5, 19, Jul 6, 17, DL, Nov
25, 30; <u>1733</u>: GF, Apr 30
Vaughan, Miss P (actor), <u>1730</u>: DL, Dec 11; <u>1731</u>: DL, Feb 8, Mar 20, Apr 26, May
12
Vaughan, Mrs (actor), <u>1748</u>: BF, Aug 24, SFBCBV, Sep 7, DL, Oct 15; <u>1749</u>: DL,
May 16
Vaughan, Mrs (haberdasher), <u>1772</u>: DL, Jan 6; <u>1773</u>: DL, Jan 21, Jun 2; <u>1774</u>: DL,
Jan 21, Jun 2; <u>1775</u>: DL, Jan 10, May 27; <u>1776</u>: DL, Jun 10
Vaughan, R (actor), <u>1751</u>: DL, Oct 11
Vaughan, Thomas, <u>1775</u>: CG, Mar 2; <u>1776</u>: DL, Nov 21; <u>1784</u>: DL, Oct 28; <u>1786</u>: DL,
Mar 9; <u>1787</u>: HAY, Jul 9; <u>1791</u>: HAY, Jul 9; <u>1793</u>: DL, Mar 18; <u>1794</u>: DL, Nov 1
--Hotel, The; or, The Double Valet (farce), <u>1776</u>: DL, Nov 21, 23, 25, 26, 28,
Dec 2, 4; <u>1777</u>: DL, Feb 1; <u>1791</u>: CG, Feb 16
--Love's Metamorphoses, <u>1776</u>: DL, Apr 15
Vaughan, W (boxkeeper), <u>1733</u>: CG, May 17; <u>1734</u>: CG, May 10; <u>1735</u>: CG, May 20;
<u>1736</u>: CG, May 24; <u>1737</u>: CG, May 16; <u>1738</u>: CG, May 15; <u>1739</u>: CG, May 23; <u>1740</u>:
CG, May 21; <u>1741</u>: CG, May 6; <u>1742</u>: CG, May 17; <u>1743</u>: CG, May 5; <u>1744</u>: CG, May
9; <u>1745</u>: CG, May 10; <u>1746</u>: CG, May 5; <u>1747</u>: CG, May 20; <u>1748</u>: CG, May 2;
<u>1749</u>: CG, May 1; <u>1750</u>: CG, May 3; <u>1751</u>: CG, May 13; <u>1752</u>: CG, May 6; <u>1753</u>:
CG, May 18; <u>1754</u>: CG, May 21; <u>1755</u>: CG, May 19; <u>1756</u>: CG, May 18; <u>1757</u>: CG,
May 17; <u>1758</u>: CG, May 9; <u>1759</u>: CG, May 24; <u>1760</u>: CG, May 16, Sep 22; <u>1761</u>:
CG, May 13; <u>1763</u>: CG, May 24; <u>1764</u>: CG, May 25; <u>1765</u>: CG, May 23; <u>1766</u>: CG,
May 14; <u>1767</u>: CG, May 21
Vaughan, William (actor), <u>1750</u>: DL, Sep 22, 28, Oct 22, 30, Nov 3, 12; <u>1751</u>:
DL, Jan 22, May 2, 17, Sep 14, 21, Oct 29; <u>1752</u>: DL, Jan 21, 23, 28, May 1,
Sep 19, Oct 3, 16, 19; <u>1753</u>: DL, Apr 30, May 9, 17, 18, 21, Sep 25, Oct 9,
23, Nov 1; <u>1754</u>: DL, Jan 10, 16, 23, Feb 5, 20, Jul 2, Nov 7, 11, 22, Dec 13;
<u>1755</u>: DL, Jan 15, Oct 15, 17, Dec 6, 19; <u>1756</u>: DL, Jan 21, Mar 27, May 7, 10,
15, Nov 6, Dec 10; <u>1757</u>: DL, May 23
Vaulting (entertainment), <u>1701</u>: BF, Aug 25; <u>1703</u>: DL, Apr 27, YB, Jul 27; <u>1705</u>:
BF, Aug 27; <u>1706</u>: BF, Aug 27; <u>1718</u>: LIF, Dec 30; <u>1719</u>: LIF, Jan 1, 6, 8, 15,
22, 29, Feb 3; <u>1724</u>: BFP, Aug 22
Vaulting on the Horse (entertainment), <u>1701</u>: LIF, Oct 21; <u>1702</u>: DL, Jul 7, Aug
22; <u>1703</u>: YB, Feb 5, DL, Apr 27, DG, 30, BFG, Aug 23; <u>1705</u>: LIF/QUEN, Oct 11;
<u>1710</u>: GR, Aug 26; <u>1717</u>: SF, Sep 25
Vaurinville (Vaurentille, Voirinville), Mlle (dancer), <u>1721</u>: HAY, Mar 6, Apr
20, LIF, 27; <u>1722</u>: HAY, Feb 19
Vaux, Miss (singer), <u>1746</u>: GF, Jan 24, Feb 13
Vaux, Mrs (dancer), <u>1755</u>: SOU, Jan 20, SF, Sep 18
Vauxhall Road, <u>1800</u>: CG, Jun 16
Vauxhall, <u>1736</u>: DL, May 22; <u>1737</u>: HAY, May 2; <u>1745</u>: DL, Sep 21; <u>1766</u>: DL, Oct
31; <u>1767</u>: VAUX, May 25, DL, Jun 3; <u>1777</u>: DL, Mar 15; <u>1778</u>: DL, Apr 28; <u>1781</u>:
CG, Apr 3; <u>1782</u>: DL, Apr 16; <u>1783</u>: DL, Apr 7; <u>1784</u>: DL, Apr 12, HAY, 27;
<u>1785</u>: DL, Apr 1; <u>1786</u>: DL, Apr 18, HAMM, Jul 24; <u>1787</u>: DL, May 10; <u>1793</u>: CG,
Oct 9; <u>1797</u>: CG, Jun 21; <u>1798</u>: CG, Apr 20
Veal (house servant), <u>1753</u>: DL, May 16; <u>1754</u>: DL, May 18; <u>1755</u>: DL, May 13;
<u>1756</u>: DL, May 17; <u>1757</u>: DL, May 20; <u>1758</u>: DL, May 18; <u>1759</u>: DL, May 30; <u>1760</u>:
DL, May 16; <u>1761</u>: DL, May 27; <u>1762</u>: DL, May 24; <u>1763</u>: DL, May 18; <u>1764</u>: DL,
May 19; <u>1765</u>: DL, May 18; <u>1766</u>: DL, May 20; <u>1767</u>: DL, May 29, Jun 1; <u>1768</u>:
DL, May 27; <u>1769</u>: DL, May 20; <u>1770</u>: DL, Jun 4; <u>1771</u>: DL, May 29
Veal, Mrs, <u>1772</u>: DL, Jun 10; <u>1775</u>: DL, May 26; <u>1776</u>: DL, Apr 20; <u>1777</u>: DL, Apr
25
Vecchi Burlati, I. See Anfossi, Pasquale.
Vedeste Mai Sulprato (song), <u>1729</u>: DL, Mar 26
Vedi Amor nel mio Sembiante (song), <u>1763</u>: KING'S, Apr 25
Vedie, Mlle (dancer), <u>1787</u>: KING'S, Dec 8; <u>1788</u>: KING'S, Jan 29, Mar 13, May
15; <u>1791</u>: PAN, Feb 17, 26, Mar 22, Jun 10; <u>1793</u>: KING'S, Feb 26
Vedrai Moror Costante (song), <u>1741</u>: HIC, Apr 24
Vegelini, Signori (musicians), <u>1714</u>: SH, May 27
Venables (actor), <u>1755</u>: HAY, Sep 9, 11, 15
Venables (actor), <u>1781</u>: HAY, Oct 16
Venables (householder), <u>1747</u>: DL, Mar 21
Venables, Ann (singer), <u>1772</u>: DL, Nov 12; <u>1773</u>: CG, Feb 26, Mar 3, 19, DL, Apr

867

Vendanges de Suresne, Les (play), 1721: HAY, Dec 26; 1722: HAY, Jan 1
Vendangeurs, Les (dance), 1728: LIF, Oct 21, Dec 31; 1729: LIF, Apr 11, 12, 16;
     1799: DL, May 8
Vendemmia, La. See Gazzaniga, Giuseppe.
Vendu (theatre), 1692: VENDU, Mar 10
Veneta Bella (song), 1731: LIF, Apr 29
Venetian Ambassador, 1669: BRIDGES, May 24; 1696: DG, Apr 29; 1707: DL, May 24
Venetian Carnival (entertainment), 1726: KING'S, Nov 5; 1732: DL, Jun 9; 1799:
     CG, Apr 30
Venetian Dance (dance), 1703: LIF, Jun 14; 1715: LIF, Apr 28, May 5, Oct 19;
     1716: LIF, May 31; 1723: DL, Nov 1; 1724: DL, Feb 10, May 4, LIF, 5; 1725:
     DL, Apr 7; 1726: LIF, May 9; 1727: KING'S, Mar 2; 1772: KING'S, Jan 14
Venetian Gardeners (dance), 1749: DL, Oct 24, 31, Nov 3; 1750: DL, Mar 22, 29,
     31, Apr 2, 21, 23; 1752: CG, Apr 18, 24; 1763: HAY, Aug 1, 3, 5, 8, 10, 11,
     12, 15, 22, 24, DL, Nov 10; 1764: HAY, Jun 29, Jul 5; 1765: CG, Sep 25, 27,
     30, Oct 2, 15, Dec 17, 21; 1766: CG, Jan 21, 23, 25, Feb 17, Apr 1, 23, 26,
     29; 1773: CG, Feb 6
Venetian Gondolier and Courtezan (dance), 1729: DL, Jun 24, Aug 7; 1735: DL,
     Dec 31; 1736: DL, Jan 2, 3, Apr 3, May 8; 1761: DL, Apr 18
Venetian Pantomime (entertainment), 1735: GF/HAY, Mar 28
Venetian Peasant (dance), 1720: DL, Mar 31; 1750: DL, Mar 13
Venetian Regatta (dance), 1776: HAY, Aug 19, 21, 23, 26, 28, 30, Sep 2, 4, 6,
     9, 10, 11, 12, 13, 14; 1777: HAY, Jun 11, 18, Jul 30
Venetian Song (song), 1726: KING'S, Dec 10; 1727: KING'S, Mar 2
Venetian Travellers (dance), 1766: DL, May 5, Sep 20
Vengeance de l'Amour, La (dance), 1798: KING'S, Mar 22, 24, Apr 21, 26, 28, May
     1, CG, Jun 11, KING'S, Jul 3
Venice Preserved. See Otway, Thomas.
Venice Theatre, 1799: CG, May 18
Venice, Doge of, 1702: LIF, Dec 29; 1731: ACA, Jan 14
Venice, 1709: QUEEN'S, Apr 2; 1710: QUEEN'S, Mar 23; 1715: KING'S, Jun 25;
     1720: KING'S, Apr 27; 1772: CG, Apr 8; 1777: KING'S, May 20; 1784: KING'S,
     Apr 15; 1785: KING'S, Feb 26; 1786: KING'S, Mar 11; 1788: KING'S, Apr 5;
     1792: HAY, Mar 31; 1794: KING'S, Dec 20; 1795: KING'S, Mar 21, May 14; 1796:
     KING'S, Feb 9; 1798: KING'S, Mar 22; 1800: KING'S, Feb 18, Jun 17
Venner (actor), 1673: LIF, Dec 0
Venor's Brother, Captain (spectator), 1755: DL, Nov 13
Vento, Mathias (composer), 1764: KING'S, Jan 10, Mar 29; 1765: KING'S, Mar 2;
     1766: KING'S, Jan 21, DL, Apr 15; 1767: KING'S, Apr 4; 1771: HAY, Apr 17;
     1772: KING'S, Nov 14; 1775: KING'S, Jan 14, Oct 31, Nov 16; 1776: KING'S, Jan
     9, Feb 6, Apr 20; 1777: KING'S, Mar 1; 1782: CG, Nov 2; 1788: CG, Apr 1;
     1789: CG, Mar 31, Sep 23
--Conquesta Del Massico, La (opera), 1767: KING'S, Apr 4, 11, 25, May 2, Jun 5
--Demofoonte (opera), 1765: KING'S, Mar 2, 5, 9, 12, 16, 19, 23, 30, Apr 13,
     16, 23, 29, May 7, 11, Jun 3, 8; 1766: KING'S, Mar 22, Apr 5, 8, 15, May 15,
     20
--Leucippo (opera), 1764: KING'S, Jan 10, 14, 21, 24, 28, 31, Feb 4, 7, 11, 14,
     Mar 29
--Sofonisba (opera), 1766: KING'S, Jan 21, 25, Feb 1, 6, 8, 11, 15, Mar 6, 8,
     11, 15, Apr 19, 29; 1772: KING'S, Nov 14, 17, 21, 24, 28, Dec 8, 12; 1773:
     KING'S, Jan 9
Venus and Adonis (dance), 1793: KING'S, Feb 26, Mar 2, 5, 9, 12, 16, 19, 23,
     Apr 2, 6, 9, 13, 16, 20
Venus and Adonis. See Blow, Dr John; Cibber, Colley.
Venus, Cupid and Hymen. See Seedo.
Venus laughing from the skies (song), 1790: DL, Mar 10, CG, 26
Venus Revenged (dance), 1763: CG, Dec 22, 23, 29, 30, 31; 1764: CG, Jan 2, 3,
     5, 7, 10, 13, Feb 18, 20, 21, 22, 23, 24, 27, 28, Mar 2, 12, 17, 31, Apr 3,
     9, 12, 14, 23, May 1, 2, 17, 22, 23, 24, 28
Vera Costanza, La. See Anfossi, Pasquale.
Veracini, Francis (musician, composer), 1714: QUEEN'S, Jan 23, HIC, Mar 17,
     QUEEN'S, Apr 3, HIC, 22; 1733: HIC, Apr 27, May 25; 1734: HIC, Mar 18, 25;
     1735: HIC, Apr 11, KING'S, Nov 25, Dec 16; 1737: KING'S, Apr 12; 1738:
     KING'S, Mar 14; 1741: LIF, Feb 28, HAY, Mar 9, 13, HIC, Apr 28; 1742: DL, Sep
     23, 25, 28, 30, Oct 2, 5, 7, 8, 9, 12, 13, 14, 15, 18, 19, 20, 23, Nov 2, 3,
     4, 6, 8; 1744: KING'S, Jan 31, Mar 20; 1748: KING'S, Apr 5
--Adriano (opera), 1735: KING'S, Nov 25, 29, Dec 2, 6, 9, 13, 16, 20, 27, 30;
     1736: KING'S, Feb 7, 10, 14, 17, 21, 24, 28, May 18, 22, 25, 29
--Errore di Solomone, L' (oratorio), 1744: KING'S, Mar 20, 22
--New Eclogue, A (musical), 1741: HAY, Mar 9
--Partenio (opera), 1738: KING'S, Mar 14, 18, 21, 25, Apr 4, 8, 11, Jun 6

--Titus (opera), <u>1737</u>: KING'S, Apr 12, 16, 19, 23
Verbruggen, John (actor), <u>1688</u>: DL, May 3, NONE, Sep 0; <u>1689</u>: NONE, Sep 0, DL,
    Nov 7, 20; <u>1690</u>: DL, Jan 0, Mar 0, NONE, Sep 0, DL, Oct 0, Dec 0; <u>1691</u>: DL,
    Mar 0, DG, May 0, NONE, Sep 0; <u>1692</u>: DL, Mar 0, Apr 0, Nov 0; <u>1693</u>: DL, Feb
    0, Mar 0, Oct 0; <u>1694</u>: DL, Jan 0, Feb 0, Mar 21, DG, May 0, DL, Sep 0; <u>1695</u>:
    DL, Sep 0, Oct 0, DG, Nov 0, DL, 0, Dec 0; <u>1696</u>: DL, Jan 0, Feb 0, Mar 0, Apr
    0, May 0, Jul 0, Sep 0, DG, Oct 0, NONE, 26, DL, Nov 21; <u>1697</u>: LIF, Feb 20,
    Apr 0, May 0, Jun 0, Sep 0, Nov 0; <u>1698</u>: LIF, Jan 0, Apr 0, May 0, Jun 0;
    <u>1699</u>: LIF, Feb 0, Apr 0, May 0, Nov 7, Dec 0, 18; <u>1700</u>: LIF, Jan 9, Feb 0,
    Mar 0, 5, Apr 0, Dec 0; <u>1701</u>: LIF, Jan 0, Mar 0, Aug 0, Dec 0; <u>1703</u>: LIF, Feb
    0, Apr 28, May 0, 21; <u>1704</u>: LIF, Jan 13, ATCOURT, Feb 7, Apr 24, LIF, Jun 8,
    Oct 2, Nov 13, Dec 4; <u>1705</u>: LIF/QUEN, Feb 22, DL, Jun 16, QUEEN'S, Nov 23;
    <u>1706</u>: QUEEN'S, Jan 3, Feb 21, LIF/QUEN, Apr 1, QUEEN'S, Oct 26, 30, Nov 19,
    21, 22, Dec 6, 10, 14, 27, 30; <u>1707</u>: QUEEN'S, Jan 14, 20, 28, 29, Feb 15, Mar
    1, 6, 8, 24, May 9, Jun 18, 20, 25, 27, Jul 22, 30, Aug 1, 19; <u>1708</u>: DL, Apr
    26
Verbruggen, Susannah (actor), <u>1691</u>: NONE, Sep 0; <u>1694</u>: DL, Feb 0, Apr 0, DG,
    May 0, DL, Sep 0; <u>1695</u>: DL, Sep 0, Oct 0, Nov 0, DG, 0, DL, Dec 0; <u>1696</u>: DL,
    Jan 0, Feb 0, Mar 0, Apr 0, May 0, DG, Aug 0, DL, Sep 0, Nov 21, 24, DL/DL,
    Dec 0; <u>1697</u>: DG, Jun 0, DL, Jul 0, NONE, Sep 0; <u>1698</u>: DL, Feb 0, Jun 0; <u>1699</u>:
    DL, Apr 0, Nov 28; <u>1700</u>: DL, Mar 0, Nov 23, Dec 9; <u>1701</u>: DL, Mar 1, Apr 0,
    May 31, Dec 0; <u>1702</u>: DL, Jan 0, Feb 0, Nov 26; <u>1703</u>: DL, Jan 27, Feb 18, Apr
    10; <u>1708</u>: DL, Apr 26; <u>1743</u>: DL, Apr 19
Verdi Prati (song), <u>1757</u>: KING'S, Mar 24; <u>1761</u>: KING'S, Mar 12; <u>1778</u>: DL, Mar
    27; <u>1779</u>: DL, Mar 12; <u>1781</u>: DL, Mar 28; <u>1786</u>: DL, Mar 10, 29; <u>1787</u>: KING'S,
    Mar 1; <u>1788</u>: DL, Feb 8; <u>1790</u>: DL, Feb 24; <u>1797</u>: CG, Mar 17
Vere St, <u>1660</u>: VERE, Nov 8, 27; <u>1661</u>: VERE, Mar 11, Sep 28, Oct 26; <u>1662</u>: VERE,
    Feb 6, 11, 13, Mar 22, 31; <u>1663</u>: BRIDGES, May 7, VERE, Jun 1, BRIDGES, Nov 3;
    <u>1724</u>: BT, Jan 29; <u>1739</u>: DL, May 1
Vergerius, Paul
--Royal Cuckold; or, Great Bastard, <u>1692</u>: NONE, Sep 0
Verginella (song), <u>1797</u>: CG, Jun 9
Verhuyck (Vanhuyck) (doorkeeper), <u>1738</u>: CG, May 8; <u>1739</u>: CG, May 28; <u>1740</u>: CG,
    May 19; <u>1741</u>: CG, May 5; <u>1742</u>: CG, May 11; <u>1743</u>: CG, May 9; <u>1744</u>: CG, May 11;
    <u>1745</u>: CG, May 14; <u>1746</u>: CG, May 6; <u>1747</u>: CG, May 19; <u>1748</u>: CG, May 5
Verhuyck, John (actor), <u>1729</u>: LIF, Jan 1; <u>1731</u>: HAY, Mar 24
Veritas (author), <u>1757</u>: CG, Apr 19
Vermeil, Mlle (dancer), <u>1748</u>: HAY, Apr 14
Vermilly (dancer), <u>1791</u>: KING'S, Mar 26, Apr 12, May 5, Jun 10, 25, 28
Vernells, the two Miss (entertainers), <u>1785</u>: HAY, Aug 2
Verner (beneficiary), <u>1713</u>: SH, Dec 3
Verneuil (actor), <u>1734</u>: GF/HAY, Dec 2, 9, HAY, 13, 20, 23, GF/HAY, 27, 30;
    <u>1735</u>: GF/HAY, Jan 8, 9, HAY, 13, GF/HAY, 16, Feb 5, HAY, Mar 24, Apr 16, May
    9, GF, 23
Verneuil, Mimi (dancer), <u>1734</u>: GF/HAY, Nov 20, Dec 9, HAY, 13, GF/HAY, 30;
    <u>1735</u>: GF/HAY, Feb 5, 13, HAY, Mar 24, Apr 16, GF/HAY, May 5
Verney. See Varney.
Verney, Edmund (spectator), <u>1677</u>: ATCOURT, May 29
Verney, Sir Grenvill (actor), <u>1668</u>: ATCOURT, Feb 4
Verney, John (spectator), <u>1675</u>: ATCOURT, Apr 22, DG, Aug 28; <u>1677</u>: ATCOURT, May
    29; <u>1679</u>: DG, Jun 21; <u>1688</u>: BF, Aug 0
Verney, Sir Ralph (spectator), <u>1670</u>: DOVER, May 11; <u>1675</u>: ATCOURT, Apr 22, DG,
    Aug 28; <u>1679</u>: DG, Jun 21
Vernon, Admiral, <u>1740</u>: TCLP, Aug 4, BFLP, 23, GF, Nov 12
Vernon, James, <u>1673</u>: ATCOURT, Aug 22
Vernon, Jane, Mrs Joseph (dancer), <u>1755</u>: DL, Feb 3, Sep 27, 30, Oct 8, Nov 4,
    8, 22, Dec 1, 13; <u>1756</u>: DL, Feb 11, May 3, 11, 13, Oct 12, 13, 18, 19, 21,
    Dec 20, 27; <u>1757</u>: DL, Mar 24, Apr 12, CG, 16, DL, 20, May 19, Sep 17, 29, Oct
    4, 7, 20, 29, Dec 23; <u>1758</u>: DL, Feb 21, Mar 11, May 9, Sep 30, Oct 10, 12,
    24, 30, Nov 2, 15, 27, Dec 14, 26; <u>1759</u>: DL, Jan 4, Feb 21, May 2, Sep 25,
    Oct 16, Nov 8, 22, 24, Dec 7, 31; <u>1760</u>: DL, Mar 13, Apr 17, May 10, 29, CG,
    Sep 22, 24, 29, Oct 3, Nov 28, Dec 11; <u>1761</u>: CG, Feb 28, Apr 2, 6, 8, 20, 23,
    May 18, HAY, Jun 23, Jul 18, Aug 6, CG, Sep 7, 14, 18, 25, 26; <u>1762</u>: CG, Jan
    28, Feb 2, 17, Mar 27, 30, Apr 19, 20, 23, May 11, BFY, Sep 3, CG, 22
Vernon, Joseph (actor, singer, songwriter), <u>1750</u>: DL, Dec 26; <u>1751</u>: DL, Feb 23,
    May 11, Sep 20, Oct 16, Nov 12, 13, 19; <u>1752</u>: DL, Jan 24, 28, Feb 5, 8, 10,
    Mar 21, Apr 3, 17, 20, 21, 30, May 4, Oct 11, 13, 16, Nov 28; <u>1753</u>: DL, Mar
    19, Apr 10, 27, May 1, 18, Sep 22, Oct 3, 4, 13, 20, Nov 1, 14; <u>1754</u>: DL, Jan
    23, 24, Feb 1, Mar 19, 23, 30, Apr 19, May 2, 15, Sep 17, 24, Oct 10, 11, 16,
    30, Nov 11; <u>1755</u>: DL, Feb 3, Mar 4, 17, Apr 11, 15, May 6, 9, Sep 27, Oct 18;
    <u>1756</u>: DL, Jan 3; <u>1757</u>: DL, Jan 28, Nov 7, 17, Dec 22; <u>1758</u>: DL, Jan 25, Feb
    13, 21, Mar 28, 30, Apr 1, 27, May 1, 2, 12, 15, 18, 23, Sep 16; <u>1759</u>: DL,

Oct 12; <u>1762</u>: DL, Sep 21, 29, Oct 4, 22, 25, 30, Nov 6, 11, 23, Dec 22; <u>1763</u>:
DL, Jan 14, Feb 24, Mar 1, 24, Apr 5, 9, 11, 13, 20, May 2, 3, 14, 17, 26,
31, Sep 17, Oct 15, 17, 19, 28, 31, Nov 15, 23, 29, Dec 26; <u>1764</u>: DL, Jan 21,
25, 27, Feb 24, Mar 24, 31, Apr 2, 5, 12, 14, 26, 27, May 12, Sep 15, 22, 25,
Oct 25, Nov 2, 7, HAY, 13, DL, 27, 28; <u>1765</u>: DL, Jan 22, Feb 15, Mar 2, 26,
Apr 11, 15, 22, 23, May 1, 7, 9, Sep 14, 17, 24, Oct 8, 28, Nov 14, 22, Dec
5, 16; <u>1766</u>: DL, Jan 23, Feb 3, 7, Mar 17, 20, Apr 2, 5, 8, 15, 22, 28,
CHAPEL, 30, DL, May 6, 12, Sep 20, 23, 25, 30, Oct 10, 11, 18, Nov 21; <u>1767</u>:
DL, Jan 2, KING'S, 23, DL, 24, Feb 7, CG, Mar 6, DL, 21, Apr 4, 7, 11, 20,
21, CG, 21, DL, May 2, 4, 5, CHAPEL, 13, DL, 13, 27, HAY, Aug 12, DL, Sep 12,
16, 21, 22, 25, Oct 22, 23, 28, Nov 23, Dec 7; <u>1768</u>: DL, Jan 14, KING'S, Feb
5, DL, 10, HAY, Mar 4, DL, 10, 15, 24, 26, Apr 22, 27, May 3, 4, CHAPEL, 25,
DL, Aug 18, Sep 8, 20, 22, 27, 28, 30, Oct 3, HAY, 7, DL, 13, 20, Nov 1, Dec
14; <u>1769</u>: DL, Jan 6, HAY, Feb 22, DL, Mar 13, 16, 27, Apr 3, KING'S, 5, DL,
7, 8, 24, May 1, 5, KING'S, Jun 1, DL, Sep 23, 30, Oct 2, 4, 5, 9, 10, 11,
13, 14, Nov 14, 18, Dec 6, 30; <u>1770</u>: DL, Jan 4, Feb 8, 13, Mar 22, 29, Apr
18, HAY, May 4, DL, 5, 26, Sep 22, 27, Oct 2, 3, 19, 22, 30, Nov 13, 19, 20,
22, 29, Dec 5, 13; <u>1771</u>: DL, Jan 22, Feb 9, Mar 7, 11, 18, 19, 23, Apr 9,
HAY, 12, DL, 12, 26, CHAPEL, 27, DL, 27, May 14, Sep 21, 24, Oct 1, 3, 8, 17,
19, Nov 22, 23, 26, Dec 2, 6, 10, 14, 16, 26; <u>1772</u>: DL, Jan 1, 11, Feb 4, Mar
23, 26, Apr 2, 29, Sep 22, 26, Oct 3, 8, 14, 20, 27, Nov 3, 5, 12, 17, Dec 2,
14; <u>1773</u>: DL, Jan 4, 9, Feb 1, HAY, 26, DL, Mar 9, 29, May 12, 17, Jun 2, Sep
18, 30, Oct 9, 13, 16, 28, 30, Nov 2, 9, 24, Dec 8, 10, 27; <u>1774</u>: DL, Jan 19,
HAY, Feb 18, 23, 25, DL, Mar 17, CHAPEL, 30, DL, Apr 4, 27, May 3, 7, 9, 10,
14, Sep 24, Oct 1, 5, 11, 19, 20, 28, Nov 5, 16, 19, Dec 26; <u>1775</u>: DL, Jan
11, Feb 1, Mar 2, 4, 28, Apr 17, 22, May 1, 2, 6, 27, Sep 23, 26, 30, Oct 5,
7, 10, 28, 31, Nov 6, Dec 15, 23, 29; <u>1776</u>: STRAND, Jan 23, DL, 29, Feb 1, 3,
CG, 23, DL, Mar 14, 25, CHAPEL, Apr 3, DL, 9, 10, 15, May 18, 20, 27, Jun 8,
Sep 21, 24, 26, Oct 9, 18, Nov 6, 7, 19, 20, Dec 5, 17; <u>1777</u>: DL, Jan 4, 8,
Feb 20, Mar 1, 15, 20, Apr 1, May 15, 19, Sep 25, Oct 2, 7, 9, 14, 18, 22,
23, 29, Nov 7, 12, Dec 3, 4, 26; <u>1778</u>: DL, Jan 17, Feb 10, CG, Mar 6, DL, 16,
30, Apr 2, 25, 27, 30, May 19, Sep 29, Oct 6, 10, 13, 17, CG, 23, DL, Nov 2,
4, 10, CG, 21, 23, DL, 28, Dec 21, 23; <u>1779</u>: DL, Jan 5, 11, HAY, Mar 3, 17,
DL, 23, 27, Apr 9, CG, 17, DL, May 19, Sep 21, CG, 22, Oct 8, DL, 9, 12, 19,
CG, 20, DL, 21, 23, 25, 26, Nov 3, 20, Dec 4, 22; <u>1780</u>: DL, Jan 3, CG, 8, 18,
DL, 28, Mar 14, Apr 3, 4, 14, CG, 18, DL, 26, 28, May 2, 12, Sep 16, 19, 21,
26, 28, Oct 3, 5, 10, 12, 14, 19, Nov 3, 11, 22, 28, Dec 19, 27; <u>1781</u>: DL,
Mar 31, May 4, Sep 22, 27, Oct 6, 9, 19; <u>1784</u>: HAY, Sep 17; <u>1797</u>: DL, May 24
Vernon, Miss (actor), <u>1784</u>: HAY, Mar 8
Vernon, Mrs (actor), <u>1791</u>: CG, Jan 27
Vernor (publisher), <u>1794</u>: DL, Oct 28
Vero non e che Sia (song), <u>1758</u>: KING'S, Apr 6
Verrio (painter), <u>1758</u>: DL, Apr 8
Versailles, Court of, <u>1780</u>: KING'S, Apr 20
Verses to the Memory of an Unfortunate Lady (entertainment), <u>1769</u>: HAY, Feb 23
Versohnung, Die. See Kotzebue, August Friedrich Ferdinand von.
Vertumnus (dance), <u>1740</u>: TCLP, Aug 4
Vertumnus and Pomona (dance), <u>1748</u>: DL, Oct 27, 31, Nov 1, 3, 5, 9, 12, 23, 25,
28; <u>1749</u>: DL, Jan 11
Vertumnus and Pomona. See Feilde, Matthew.
Very Good Wife, A. See Powell, George.
Very Woman, A. See Massinger, Phillip.
Vespasian. See Ariosti, Attilio.
Vestal Virgin, The. See Howard, Sir Robert.
Vestale, La; or, L'Amore Protetto dal Cielo. See Rauzzini, Venanzio.
Vestris, Gaetan Appoline Balthasar (dancer), <u>1781</u>: KING'S, Feb 22, Mar 15, 27,
29, Apr 26, May 17, Jun 5, Jul 3; <u>1782</u>: KING'S, Jan 8; <u>1783</u>: KING'S, Feb 15;
<u>1791</u>: KING'S, Apr 11, May 5, 10, 26, Jun 2, 4, 6, 10, 14, 17, 25, 28, Jul 9
Vestris, Marie Jean Augustin (dancer), <u>1780</u>: KING'S, Dec 16, 23; <u>1781</u>: KING'S,
Jan 23, Feb 22, Mar 29, Jun 5, Jul 3; <u>1783</u>: KING'S, Dec 6, 16; <u>1784</u>: KING'S,
Jan 17, Feb 3, 7, 14, 26, Mar 6, 11, 18, 25, Apr 24, CG, May 8, KING'S, 13,
20, 29, Jul 3; <u>1786</u>: KING'S, Jan 24, Feb 18, 25, Mar 11, 23, Apr 1, 27, May
23, Jun 1; <u>1787</u>: KING'S, Dec 8; <u>1788</u>: KING'S, Jan 12, 15, 29, Feb 21, 28, Mar
13, Apr 3, 19, 5, 28, Jul 9
Vestry Dinner (song), <u>1794</u>: CG, May 26; see also Churchwarden I have been
Veuve du Malabar, La. See LeMierre, Antoine Marin.
Vezian (author), <u>1719</u>: KING'S, Feb 16
Viaggiatori Felici, I. See Anfossi, Pasquale.
Viaggiatori Ridicoli, I. See Guglielmi, Pietro.
Vial (viola player), <u>1800</u>: CG, Feb 28
Vials (dancer), <u>1799</u>: CG, Apr 13, 25, Oct 21, Dec 23; <u>1800</u>: CG, Feb 10
Viblett (musician), <u>1675</u>: ATCOURT, Feb 15

Vice Chamberlain, 1720: DL, Mar 3; 1793: CG, Jan 23
Vice Reclaimed. See Wilkinson, Richard.
Vicende Della Sorte, La; or, The Turns of Fortune (pastiche), 1770: KING'S, Nov
  6, 17, 20, 27, Dec 11; 1771: KING'S, Apr 13
Vicenza, 1788: KING'S, May 8
Vico, Diana (singer), 1714: KING'S, Nov 16, Dec 30; 1715: KING'S, Feb 26, Mar
  26, Apr 30, GRT, May 16, KING'S, 25, Aug 27; 1716: KING'S, Feb 1, Mar 10, May
  26
Victim, The. See Johnson, Charles.
Victim, The; or, Achilles and Iphigenia in Aulis. See Dennis, John.
Victimes Cloitrees, Les. See Boutet de Monvel, Jacques Marie.
Victor (actor), 1734: LIF, Apr 18
Victor (dancer), 1791: KING'S, Mar 26, Apr 12, May 5, Jun 10, 25, 28
Victor, Benjamin (treasurer), 1745: DL, Mar 9; 1761: DL, May 1; 1762: DL, Nov
  23; 1763: DL, Jan 3, 25; 1764: DL, Nov 2; 1765: DL, Jan 24, Feb 4, 15; 1766:
  DL, Jan 6, Dec 17; 1772: DL, Jun 10; 1773: DL, Jun 2; 1774: DL, Jun 2; 1775:
  DL, May 27; 1776: DL, Feb 9, Jun 10
Victoria (beneficiary), 1727: KING'S, Mar 23
Victorious Love. See Walker, William.
Victory (ode), 1779: HAY, Mar 17, 19
Vidi, Mme (dancer), 1796: KING'S, Apr 21, DL, May 25, KING'S, Jul 7, 12
Vidini, Victoria (dancer), 1768: DL, Nov 16, 21, Dec 5, 10; 1769: DL, Jan 16,
  18, Feb 2, Sep 26, 30, Oct 14, 26, Nov 16, 20, 23, Dec 28; 1770: DL, Jan 18,
  Apr 25, May 24, Sep 22, 25, Oct 3, 4, 10, 30, Nov 12, 19; 1771: DL, Jan 1,
  Feb 4, Mar 4, 7, 12, Apr 22, May 24, Sep 21, Oct 26, Nov 18, Dec 4, 26; 1772:
  DL, Mar 21, 26, Apr 24, May 30, Sep 22, Oct 3, 6, Nov 12, Dec 4, 26; 1773:
  DL, Feb 25, Mar 27, Apr 22, May 4, 5, Sep 25, Oct 21; 1774: KING'S, Mar 24,
  CG, Oct 7, 15, Nov 19, Dec 1, 14, 16, 27; 1775: CG, Mar 30, May 12, 16, Oct
  13, 26, Nov 9, 18, 21, Dec 7, 26; 1776: CG, Jan 23, 24, Feb 12, 16, 17, Mar
  25, May 3, 6, DL, Oct 24, Nov 6, 7, Dec 4, 18; 1777: DL, Feb 10; 1778: CG,
  May 9; 1779: KING'S, Jan 23, Mar 25, Jun 26; 1782: HAY, Jul 11, Aug 17
Vie est un Songe, La. See Boissy, Louis de.
Viebar (musician), 1722: DL, Mar 14
Viebert, Mrs (spectator), 1760: CG, Mar 29
Vieni o morte a Consolatmi (song), 1714: QUEEN'S, May 29
Vienna Besieged (play, anon), 1686: BF, Aug 0
Vienna Court Theatre, 1787: DL, Apr 20; 1791: CG, Dec 10
Vienna National Theatre, 1800: CG, Mar 28
Vienna Opera, 1787: KING'S, Apr 24; 1791: DL, Mar 11
Vienna, 1703: DL, Apr 27, DG, 30; 1746: KING'S, Mar 11; 1753: HAY, Mar 1; 1773:
  KING'S, Mar 9; 1787: KING'S, Dec 8; 1789: KING'S, Jan 10, Jun 11; 1795:
  KING'S, Apr 30; 1797: KING'S, Apr 18; 1798: KING'S, Mar 10; 1800: CG, Mar 28,
  Apr 2
Vietch (ticket deliverer), 1780: HAY, Apr 5
Vigano, Maria, Mrs Salvatore (dancer), 1791: PAN, Feb 17, 26, May 9, Jun 10
Vigano, Salvatore (dancer), 1791: PAN, Feb 17, Mar 24, May 9, Jun 10
Vigano, Salvatore and Maria (dancers), 1791: PAN, May 17
Viganoni, Giuseppe (singer), 1781: KING'S, Dec 11; 1782: KING'S, Jan 10, Feb
  28, Mar 2, Apr 9, Nov 2, Dec 19; 1783: KING'S, Feb 27, Mar 27, Jun 3, 14;
  1796: KING'S, Mar 15, 29, Apr 7, 16, May 5, 24, Jun 14, Jul 23, Dec 6, 20;
  1797: KING'S, Jan 7, 10, Feb 14, 18, 25, Mar 11, 18, Apr 18, 27, Jun 8, 10,
  Jul 18, Nov 28, Dec 9, 12, 20; 1798: KING'S, Jan 2, 23, Feb 20, 24, Mar 10,
  22, Apr 10, 26, Jun 5, 19, Dec 8, 26, 29; 1799: KING'S, Jan 22, Mar 26, May
  14, 30; 1800: KING'S, Jan 11, Feb 18, Mar 18, Apr 24, May 6, 13, 22, Jun 17,
  21, 28
Vigo, 1702: DL, Dec 8, LIF, 11
Village Archers (dance), 1787: DL, Feb 24
Village Coquette, The. See Simon.
Village Dance (dance), 1729: DL, May 14, 26
Village Delight (song), 1787: HAY, Aug 21
Village Fete, The. See Cumberland, Richard.
Village Lawyer, The. See Colman the elder, George.
Village Opera, The. See Johnson, Charles.
Village Romps (dance), 1765: CG, Oct 19, 25, Nov 12, Dec 9, 20, 26; 1766: CG,
  Jan 7, 9, 14, 15, 16, 17, 18, 20, 22, 31, Feb 3, 7, 8, 18, Mar 15, Apr 2, 5,
  7, 10, 15, 16, 21, 28, 29, May 3, 9, 14, Oct 8, 10, 15, 18, 21, 22, Nov 13,
  14, 15, Dec 16, 20, 23; 1767: CG, Jan 10, 12, 13, Mar 23, 31, Apr 6, 7, 20,
  22, May 14
Villageoise (dance), 1742: CG, Oct 6, 11, 13, 14, 15, 18, 19, 21, Nov 5, 6, 26,
  30, Dec 2, 6, 7, 8
Villageoise Enlevee (dance), 1796: KING'S, May 12, 13
Villagers (dance), 1741: CG, Oct 24; 1756: CG, Mar 15, 16, 27, Apr 10, 20, 23,

24, 27, 30, May 13; 1777: CG, Jan 22, 25, Feb 5, Apr 16; 1778: CG, Jan 21,
Nov 27, Dec 10; 1779: CG, Apr 9; 1780: CG, Oct 11, 13, 16
Villagers, The. See Johnson, Charles.
Villain, The. See Porter, Thomas.
Villana Riconosciuta, La. See Cimarosa, Domenico.
Villanella Rapita, La. See Bianchi Jr, Francesco.
Villars (actor), 1748: BFP, Aug 24
Villars (actor), 1786: HAMM, Jun 5, 7; 1794: HAY, Jun 2
Villars, Mrs (actor), 1786: HAMM, Jun 5, 7
Villati (actor), 1755: HAY, Apr 18
Ville, Mons D'Ferrou (dancer), 1732: BF, Aug 22
Villeneuve (dancer), 1734: DL, Oct 21, 22, 25, 28, Nov 1, 16, 22, Dec 11, 12,
21, 26, GF/HAY, 27, DL, 31; 1735: DL, Jan 17, 18, 21, 28, Feb 5, 18, Mar 3,
15, 25, Apr 7, 11, 18, 25, 29, May 6, 7, 8, 9, 13, 14, 20, 22, 23, 29, 30,
Jun 3, 5, 11, LIF, 12, DL, Sep 15, 25, Oct 1, 4, 7, 22, Nov 6, 12, 15, 17,
20, 25, Dec 6, 18, 27; 1736: DL, Jan 3, 5, 6, 7, 9, Feb 2, 4, 14, 17, 18, 21,
24, 25, 27, 28, Mar 11, 20, 22, 23, 25, 27, 29, Apr 1, 5, 6, 8, 12, 13, 15,
16, 27, 29, May 4, 6, 7, 18, 20, 21, 22, 25, 27, 28, Jun 2, Sep 7, 9, Oct 2,
5, 12, 22, 28, 29, 30, Nov 2, 3, 6, 8, 10, 11, 12, 13, 17, 20, Dec 4, 9, 10,
17, 22; 1737: DL, Jan 5, Feb 14, 18, Mar 2, 4, 7, 10, 14, 15, 19, 21, Apr 2,
11, 13, 19, 26, 30, May 2, 4, 5, 6, 7, 11, 13, 14, 16, 18, 19, 20, 24, 25,
26, 27, 30, 31, Jun 11, LIF, Jul 26, Aug 2, 5, 9, CG, Oct 3, 7, 12, Nov 16;
1738: CG, Jan 3, 20, 21, 25, 28, 31, Feb 2, 3, 18, Mar 2, 7, 16, 18, 21, Apr
5, 11, 12, 17, 24, 25, 26, 27, 28, 29, May 1, 2, 3, 5, 6, 8, 10, 11, 12, 15,
16, 18, Sep 22, 27, Oct 4, 20, 23, 26, 28, 30, Nov 8, 13, 18, Dec 5, 6, 9,
11; 1739: CG, Jan 3, 6, 8, 15, 16, 20, Feb 9, 15, Mar 2, 5, 13, 15, 19, 22,
26, 27, Apr 2, 3, 7, 9, 23, 24, 25, 26, 27, 30, May 1, 2, 3, 4, 5, 7, 8, 9,
10, 11, 14, 16, 17, 18, 21, 23, Aug 21, 29, Sep 5, 7, 10, 12, 15, 22, 28, Oct
3, 15, 30, Nov 3, 6, 7, 8, 9, 10, 13, 14, 20, 21, 23, 24, 26, 28, Dec 1, 3,
4, 6, 8, 10, 12, 14, 17, 18, 19, 21, 29; 1740: CG, Jan 4, 5, 8, 15, 17, Feb
2, 6, 7, 12, Mar 10, 20, 24, 25, 27, Apr 9, 14, 16, 18, 23, 28, 29, May 2, 5,
7, 12, 13, 19, 20, 23, 27, Jun 5, Sep 19, 26, 29, Oct 3, 6, 8, 10, 22, 23,
29, 31, Nov 3, 7, 13, 15, 18, 19, 20, Dec 12, 19, 22, 29; 1741: CG, Jan 5, 7,
21, Feb 10, 14, 17, 24, 28, Mar 2, 12, 16, 30, Apr 2, 6, 7, 8, 9, 24, 28, Sep
28, Oct 17, 24, Nov 26, Dec 9, 15, 28, 30; 1742: CG, Jan 8, 21, 25, 26, Feb
6, 10, 22, May 1, 11, Sep 29, Oct 1, 6, 9, 11, 15, 16, 25, Nov 2, 23, Dec 18,
21, 30; 1743: CG, Jan 8, 19, Feb 4, Apr 9, 18, 23, May 20, Sep 26, 30, Oct 3,
26, Nov 24, Dec 17, 20; 1744: CG, Jan 14, Feb 13, 14, Mar 3, 15, Apr 14, 21,
24, Oct 10, 12, 22, 31, Dec 8; 1745: CG, Jan 1, 14, 25, Mar 28, Apr 19, May
2, 4, 7, Oct 4, 16, 29, Nov 14, 23, Dec 27; 1746: CG, Apr 9, 15, 17, May 13,
Jun 13, Dec 19, 31; 1747: CG, Mar 26, Apr 23, 29, May 13, Dec 26; 1748: CG,
Mar 3, 14, 28, Apr 19, 21, Oct 27; 1749: CG, Mar 9, Apr 15, 21, Nov 23; 1750:
CG, Apr 24, Oct 29, Dec 21, 26; 1751: CG, Jan 17, Apr 25, 26, Sep 30, Oct 28,
Nov 11, Dec 4; 1752: CG, Jan 16, Apr 22, Oct 10, 26, Dec 7; 1753: CG, Apr 10;
1754: CG, Apr 23; 1755: CG, Apr 22; 1756: CG, Apr 27
Villeneuve, Mlle (dancer), 1739: CG, Sep 17, 19, Oct 2
Villeneuve, Mrs (dancer), 1735: DL, Sep 15, Oct 7, 9, Nov 15, 20, Dec 6; 1736:
DL, Jan 3, Feb 28, Apr 13, May 13, 18, 25, Sep 7, 23, Oct 5, 12, Nov 8, 15,
Dec 31; 1737: DL, May 5, 9, 17; 1739: CG, Aug 10, Oct 3, 4, 15, Dec 4, 10;
1740: CG, Feb 12, May 12, BFHC, Aug 23, CG, Oct 10, 29, Nov 3, Dec 29; 1741:
CG, Jan 5, Feb 24, 28, Apr 2, Oct 21, 24, 30, Nov 7, 26, Dec 15, 28, 30;
1742: CG, Jan 2, 25, Sep 29, Oct 1, 25, Nov 2, Dec 21; 1743: CG, Mar 8, Dec
21; 1744: CG, Jan 14, Feb 14, Mar 3, Apr 6, Oct 10, 22, Dec 8; 1745: CG, May
2, 7, Nov 14, 26; 1746: CG, Apr 15, May 13, Jun 13, Dec 31; 1748: CG, Mar 3,
14, 28, Sep 26, Oct 27; 1749: CG, Mar 9; 1750: CG, Dec 21, 26; 1751: CG, Apr
25, Oct 28, Dec 4, 20; 1752: CG, Jan 16, Oct 26, Dec 7
Villeneuve's scholars (dancer), 1749: CG, Apr 21; 1754: CG, Apr 23
Villepierre, Mlle (dancer), 1734: CG/LIF, Dec 30; 1735: CG/LIF, Feb 22, Apr 17,
HAY, 23
Villers, Miss (actor), 1793: HAY, Aug 26
Villette (dancer), 1747: DL, May 16
Villiers (actor), 1749: HAY, Nov 14; 1750: DL, May 22
Villiers St, 1690: EC, Feb 24, YB, Mar 10, Sep 29; 1693: YB, Jun 17; 1738: CG,
Mar 2, YB, 26; 1739: DL, May 12; 1788: HAY, Aug 26; 1789: HAY, Aug 5; 1790:
DL, Apr 30; 1791: DL, May 5
Villiers, Densengencracolas (dancer), 1734: DL/LIF, May 3; 1736: HAY, Feb 11
Villiers, George, Duke of Buckingham, 1662: NONE, Sep 0; 1667: LIF, Jul 20;
1668: LIF, Feb 6; 1669: BRIDGES, Feb 27, Mar 4; 1671: BRIDGES, Dec 7, 14;
1676: DL, Dec 11; 1683: DLORDG, Feb 0; 1689: DLORDG, Apr 0; 1708: DL, Feb 24,
Apr 23; 1709: DL, Jan 18, QUEEN'S, Sep 27, Nov 18, Dec 5; 1710: DL/QUEEN, Oct
7; 1711: DL, Oct 6, 26; 1712: DL, Jan 1, Sep 23; 1713: DL, Oct 21; 1714: DL,
Jan 18, Nov 17; 1715: DL, Jan 17, Feb 25, Mar 17, Oct 27; 1717: DL, Jan 4,

Jun 3, Oct 24; <u>1718</u>: DL, Feb 3, Apr 1, Oct 27, Nov 17; <u>1719</u>: DL, Mar 16, Oct
28; <u>1720</u>: DL, Jan 4, Apr 5, Sep 27, Nov 23, Dec 28; <u>1721</u>: DL, Jun 6, Oct 13,
Nov 15; <u>1722</u>: DL, Jan 10, 15, May 7, Dec 3; <u>1723</u>: BUH, Jan 11, DL, 28, May
31, Oct 30; <u>1724</u>: DL, Feb 24, May 12, Nov 16, 18; <u>1725</u>: DL, Jan 29, Dec 9,
15; <u>1726</u>: DL, Nov 18; <u>1727</u>: DL, Jan 9; <u>1728</u>: DL, May 20; <u>1729</u>: DL, Jan 13,
Dec 1; <u>1730</u>: DL, Dec 2; <u>1731</u>: DL, Apr 30, Nov 9; <u>1732</u>: DL, Apr 25, Nov 8, Dec
15; <u>1736</u>: GF, Feb 7, 9; <u>1738</u>: CG, Apr 12; <u>1739</u>: CG, Oct 10, 27, 31, Nov 8,
14, 19, 21, DL, 23, 24, CG, 26, Dec 3, 18, 28; <u>1740</u>: CG, Jan 19, 26, Feb 4,
Jun 5, Sep 19, Nov 3, 17; <u>1741</u>: CG, Feb 16, 21, Mar 3, Apr 24, Oct 21, DL,
Nov 21; <u>1742</u>: GF, Feb 3, DL, Oct 7, LIF, Dec 6; <u>1744</u>: LIF, Dec 11; <u>1745</u>: CG,
Dec 13; <u>1748</u>: DL, Dec 10; <u>1752</u>: DL, Dec 5; <u>1791</u>: CG, Jun 1
--Rehearsal, The, <u>1662</u>: NONE, Sep 0; <u>1665</u>: BRIDGES, Apr 0; <u>1669</u>: BRIDGES, Mar
4, 6; <u>1671</u>: BRIDGES, Dec 7, 14; <u>1672</u>: DG, Sep 3; <u>1674</u>: DL, Dec 21, 28; <u>1682</u>:
NONE, Sep 0; <u>1686</u>: DLORDG, May 6; <u>1687</u>: DLORDG, Jan 3, 20; <u>1689</u>: DLORDG, Apr
0; <u>1691</u>: NONE, Sep 0; <u>1704</u>: DL, Nov 18, 21, Dec 1; <u>1705</u>: DL, Jan 4, Feb 2,
Nov 5; <u>1706</u>: DL, Jan 28, Dec 3; <u>1707</u>: DL, Jan 16, Mar 20, Nov 18; <u>1708</u>: DL,
Feb 12; <u>1709</u>: DL, Jan 18, QUEEN'S, Nov 18; <u>1710</u>: DL, Dec 18; <u>1711</u>: DL, Jan
29, Oct 26; <u>1712</u>: DL, Feb 25; <u>1717</u>: DL, Feb 7, 8, 9, 20, 23, Mar 21, 25, 28,
Oct 17; <u>1718</u>: DL, Feb 3, Nov 17; <u>1719</u>: DL, Nov 25; <u>1720</u>: DL, May 19, Sep 27,
Nov 23; <u>1721</u>: DL, Jan 18, Nov 15; <u>1722</u>: DL, Jan 15; <u>1723</u>: DL, Jan 28, Nov 29;
<u>1724</u>: DL, Mar 7, Nov 18; <u>1725</u>: DL, Jan 29, Nov 9; <u>1726</u>: DL, Nov 14; <u>1727</u>: DL,
Jan 2, 26, Dec 1; <u>1728</u>: DL, Mar 30, Nov 1, Dec 13; <u>1729</u>: DL, Sep 16; <u>1730</u>:
DL, Jan 23, Oct 29, Nov 19; <u>1731</u>: DL, Jan 18, Oct 26, Dec 15; <u>1732</u>: DL, Mar
4, Apr 25, Sep 8, Nov 8, Dec 15; <u>1733</u>: DL, Jan 17, May 30; <u>1734</u>: DL, Oct 31;
<u>1736</u>: DL, Jan 8, Feb 6; <u>1739</u>: CG, Oct 10, 11, 12, 13, 15, 16, 17, 18, 19, 20,
27, 31, Nov 8, 14, 19, 21, 23, 26, Dec 3, 14, 18, 28; <u>1740</u>: CG, Jan 5, 19,
26, Feb 4, 9, Mar 13, Apr 10, 15, 24, May 1, 8, 22, 30, Jun 5, 10, 13, Sep
19, Oct 18, Nov 3, 17, Dec 3, 18; <u>1741</u>: CG, Feb 16, 21, Mar 3, 14, 21, 31,
Apr 14, 24, 29, May 19, Oct 21, 22, DL, Nov 21, 23, 24, 26, 27, Dec 4, GF, 9,
DL, 26; <u>1742</u>: DL, Jan 25, CG, Feb 1, GF, 3, 4, 5, 6, DL, 6, GF, 8, 9, 10, 12,
13, 15, 17, 18, 20, 23, Mar 9, CG, 29, GF, Apr 28, May 7, DL, 26, Oct 7, 8,
20, Nov 2, LIF, Dec 6, DL, 7, LIF, 8, DL, 16; <u>1743</u>: DL, Jan 7, 17, 29, Feb 3,
28, Mar 7, Apr 4, 19, 30, May 6, Dec 6, 8, 9, 28; <u>1744</u>: DL, Mar 15, Apr 12,
May 28, Oct 19, Nov 19, Dec 6, 27; <u>1745</u>: GF, Jan 7, 8, 10, 14, 15, DL, 16,
GF, Feb 7, 8, DL, 14, 16, GF, Mar 14, DL, Dec 13, CG, 13, 19, 26; <u>1746</u>: DL,
Jan 24, CG, May 2, Nov 6, 7, Dec 18; <u>1747</u>: CG, Jan 13, GF, Mar 23, CG, Nov
23, 24; <u>1748</u>: CG, Feb 5; <u>1749</u>: DL, Dec 14, 20, 21, 22, 26; <u>1750</u>: DL, Jan 4,
Feb 14, Mar 15; <u>1752</u>: DL, Dec 5, 8, 9, 12, 13, 16; <u>1753</u>: DL, Feb 3, 26, May
21; <u>1754</u>: CG, Dec 30, 31; <u>1755</u>: CG, Jan 1, Feb 11, 25, Apr 14, 21, HAY, Sep
11, 15, DL, Oct 17, 18, Nov 5, 27, Dec 19; <u>1756</u>: DL, Feb 9, May 12, 15, Nov
18; <u>1757</u>: DL, Sep 29, Oct 22, Nov 25; <u>1758</u>: CG, Jan 24, DL, May 19, Sep 19,
Nov 16; <u>1759</u>: DL, May 25, Oct 30, Nov 23; <u>1760</u>: DL, Mar 13, May 2, Oct 3, Dec
12; <u>1761</u>: DL, May 22, Sep 14; <u>1762</u>: DL, Mar 2, Nov 10; <u>1763</u>: DL, Apr 21, HAY,
Aug 1, 11; <u>1764</u>: HAY, Aug 20; <u>1765</u>: DL, Apr 13, May 6, HAY, Aug 30; <u>1766</u>: DL,
Dec 4; <u>1767</u>: DL, Apr 25, CG, Sep 14, 15, Nov 26; <u>1768</u>: HAY, Sep 19; <u>1771</u>: DL,
Apr 6; <u>1772</u>: DL, Mar 26, 31, May 15, HAY, Aug 10, 24, 31, DL, Oct 21, 26, Dec
7; <u>1773</u>: DL, Apr 29, HAY, Jun 18, 23, Jul 19; <u>1774</u>: DL, Mar 14, Apr 8, HAY,
Jun 27, Jul 11, CG, Oct 11; <u>1775</u>: HAY, Jul 31, Aug 7; <u>1776</u>: DL, May 11, HAY,
Aug 2; <u>1777</u>: HAY, Aug 25, 27, DL, Dec 13, 16; <u>1778</u>: CG, Jan 20, Feb 2; <u>1782</u>:
CG, Mar 19; <u>1785</u>: CG, Sep 28, Oct 3, 5; <u>1792</u>: HAY, Aug 9
--Restoration, The; or, Right Will Take Place, <u>1683</u>: DLORDG, Feb 0
Villiers, Mary, Duchess of Buckingham, <u>1661</u>: ATCOURT, Feb 25; <u>1667</u>: ATCOURT,
Nov 16
Villiers, Miss (actor), <u>1781</u>: HAY, Nov 12
Vimonda. See McDonald, Andrew.
Vince, Widow (beneficiary), <u>1754</u>: DL, Dec 16
Vincent (actor), <u>1734</u>: CG, Jan 25, CG/LIF, Dec 30; <u>1735</u>: CG/LIF, Feb 13, CG,
Nov 6; <u>1736</u>: CG, Jan 23; <u>1738</u>: CG, Feb 13, Apr 13, Oct 28; <u>1739</u>: CG, Jan 20;
<u>1741</u>: CG, Nov 26
Vincent (actor), <u>1789</u>: HAY, Aug 11, DL, Nov 13, 14; <u>1790</u>: DL, Jan 8, HAY, Jun
15, 21
Vincent (actor, dancer), <u>1748</u>: CG, Mar 3, Oct 27; <u>1750</u>: HAY, Feb 26, CG, Oct
29, Dec 21, 26; <u>1751</u>: CG, Sep 30, Oct 28, Dec 4; <u>1752</u>: CG, Oct 10, 18, 26;
<u>1760</u>: CG, Oct 15
Vincent (dancer), <u>1761</u>: DL, Sep 25, 26, Oct 7, 20, 26, Nov 28, Dec 28; <u>1762</u>:
DL, Jan 15, Apr 24, May 3, 7, Sep 18, 21, 25, 28, Oct 7, 15, 21, 22, 27, 29,
30, Nov 5, 23; <u>1763</u>: DL, Jan 3, 14, Feb 17, 24, Mar 26, Apr 6, 16, 22, 30,
May 4, 17
Vincent, Charles (actor), <u>1777</u>: DL, Jan 22, Jun 6
Vincent, Elizabeth, Mrs Richard Sr (actor), <u>1738</u>: CG, Jan 2, 3, 6, 7, 10, 11,
17, 18, 20, 24, 25, 27, Feb 1, 2, 4, Mar 11, 13, 14, 18, Apr 5, 11, 17, 18,
20, 22, 24, 25, 26, May 18, Jun 27, 30, Jul 7, 11, 21, Aug 1, 22, 29, Sep 22,

25, 27, Oct 2, 6, 11, 14, 18, 20, 24, 26, 28, 30, Nov 2, 4, 7, 13, 17, 23,
24, 27, 28, 29, Dec 12; 1739: CG, Jan 8, 15, 16, 20, 22, Feb 9, 14, 16, 24,
26, Mar 13, 20, 27, Apr 3, 12, 23, 24, 25, May 1, 7, 17, 18, 23, 25, 28, Aug
2, 10, 21, 31, Sep 5, 7, 12, 14, 15, 17, 19, 21, 22, 29, Oct 2, 25, 26, 29,
30, Nov 5, 6, 9, 10, 13, 17, 20, Dec 6, 15, 17, 29; 1740: CG, Jan 12, 17, Feb
2, Mar 24, 27, Apr 9, 14, 25, 28, May 2, 5, 7, 9, 12, 27, Sep 22, 24, 26, 29,
Oct 1, 3, 8, 23, 24, 25, 29, 31, Nov 4, 6, 10, Dec 4, 19; 1741: CG, Jan 2,
12, 21, 23, 27, 29, Feb 7, 14, 19, Mar 2, Apr 3, 9, 11, 17, 21, 30, May 1, 2,
4, 5, 8, 11, 12, Sep 21, 23, 25, 28, 30, Oct 8, 10, 13, 15, 20, 29, 30, Nov
4, 23, 26, 30, Dec 7, 12, 18; 1742: CG, Jan 2, 19, 23, Feb 22, 25, 27, Apr 1,
6, May 21, Oct 6, 9, 19, 27, 28, 29, Nov 3, 4, 8, 11, 27, 30, Dec 7, 22;
1743: CG, Feb 9, 17, Mar 15, Apr 15, 21, 26, May 4, Sep 21, 23, 26, Oct 5, 7,
10, 12, 19, 21, 24, 31, Nov 2, 4, 7, 16, 17, 18, 19, 21, 25, 30, Dec 3, 16,
19, 27, 29; 1744: CG, Jan 7, Feb 9, 28, Apr 7, 23, 25, May 1, 14, Sep 19, 21,
26, Oct 1, 8, 10, 15, 22, 26, Nov 5, 7, 8, 21, 24, 27, 28, 29, 30, Dec 11,
13, 17, 21; 1745: CG, Jan 1, 4, 18, Feb 9, Mar 14, Apr 23, 25, May 1, 13, Sep
23, 25, 27, 30, Oct 2, 16, Dec 2, 4, 6, 10; 1746: CG, Jan 23, Feb 3, 4, 5, 6,
Mar 4, 10, 11, 15, 20, Apr 2, 3, 8, 18, 23, Jun 9, 11, 16, 23, 27, Sep 29,
Oct 1, 6, 8, 13, 24, 27, 29, Nov 1, 4, 8, 14, 17, 18, Dec 6, 10, 19, 20, 22,
26, 30; 1747: CG, Jan 26, 29, Feb 2, 3, 6, 11, 12, Mar 2, 17, May 20, Oct 31,
Nov 11, 13, 18; 1748: CG, Mar 14, 24, Apr 16, Sep 22; 1749: CG, Sep 25, 27,
Oct 16, 23, 26, 27, Nov 2, 4, 9, 11, 17, 18, 21, 23, Dec 7, 8, 26, 27, 28;
1750: CG, Jan 18, Feb 22, Mar 17, Apr 5, Sep 24, 26, Oct 13, 16, 18, 19, 20,
24, 26, 27, 31, Nov 8, 12, 28, Dec 1, 6, 10, 14, 21; 1751: CG, Jan 15, 19,
Feb 5, 7, 14, 23, Apr 10, 15, 16, 17, 20, 23, 24, May 8, 9, 16, Sep 23, 25,
28, Oct 8, 17, 19, 22, 29, Nov 6, 11, 12, 13, 16, 21, 22, 26, 28, Dec 10, 14;
1752: CG, Jan 3, 18, 28, 29, Mar 3, 7, 16, 17, 30, Apr 4, 21, 30, May 4, 7,
Sep 18, 22, 25, 29, Oct 2, 4, 6, 10, 11, 16, 19, 27, 30, 31, Nov 1, 3, 7, 9,
23, 27, Dec 8, 11, 13, 19, 27; 1753: CG, Jan 8, 22, Feb 6, 7, 12, 21, Mar 19,
20, Apr 27, May 11, Sep 12, 14, 17, 21, 24, 26, Oct 1, 5, 17, 22, 24, 25, 30,
31, Nov 1, 2, 7, 9, 12, 20, Dec 11; 1754: CG, Jan 22, Mar 9, 14, 18, 26, Apr
6, 17, 26, 29, May 2, 9, Sep 16, 18, 20, 23, 25, 27, 30, Oct 2, 4, 7, 11, 17,
23, 24, 30, Nov 16, Dec 7; 1755: CG, Jan 4, 7, 8, 15, 28, Feb 24, Mar 31, Apr
15, 18, Oct 1, 3, 6, 8, 11, 23, Nov 3, 10, 17, 19, 21, 22, 29, Dec 4, 11;
1756: CG, Jan 15, Feb 19, Apr 5, 20, 23, May 17, Sep 24, 27, 29, Oct 6, 16,
25, 26, 27, 28, 30, Nov 4, 9, 11, 16, 17, 19, 22, Dec 8; 1757: CG, Jan 8, Feb
9, Mar 14, Apr 23, May 10, 12, Sep 16, 28, 30, Oct 3, 5, 10, 12, 14, 19, 20,
21, 22, 31, Nov 3, 4, 7, 9, 11, 14, 18, 23, 26, Dec 1, 8, 9, 10, 14, 20;
1758: CG, Jan 20, 27, Feb 1, Mar 7, 11, 16, Apr 3, 10, 14, 17, 20, Sep 20,
27, 29, Oct 2, 4, 13, 14, 20, 25, 30, Nov 2, 4, 7, 9, 13, 14, 16, 21, 23, Dec
1, 18, 21; 1759: CG, Jan 3, 4, Feb 15, Mar 1, 17, Apr 17, 21, 23, May 2, 3,
7, 11, 14, 17, 24, Sep 24, Oct 3, 5, 30, Nov 5, 23, 28, 30, Dec 5, 8, 15, 18,
21, 31; 1760: CG, Jan 14, 28, Feb 5, 14, 28, Mar 17, 18, 24, 25, Apr 16, 18,
24, May 2, 7, 12, Sep 22, Oct 10, 14, 20, Nov 22, 29, Dec 9; 1761: CG, Jan 2,
10, 23, Feb 16, Mar 3, 25, 30, Apr 1, 13, 16, 24, May 8, Sep 7, 9, 11, 14,
16, 21, 30, Oct 1, 5, 10, 21, 22, 24, 26, 27, Nov 4, 6, Dec 28, 30; 1762: CG,
Feb 15, 22, Mar 20, 23, Apr 16, 19, 21, 24, May 6, 13, Sep 24, 29, Oct 6, 9,
11, 14, 19, Nov 3, 8, 12, 30; 1763: CG, Jan 8, 14, 19, 27, 28, Feb 1, 3, Mar
21, Apr 12, 15, 20, 25, May 9, Sep 19, 23, 26, 28, 30, Oct 8, 11, 15, 20, 21,
26, Nov 15, 16, 18, Dec 16, 26, 27; 1764: CG, Jan 16, 26, 27, Feb 9, Mar 8,
27, Apr 10, 24, 30, May 7, 9, 11, 25, Sep 24, 28, Oct 3, 5, 8, 10, 11, 12,
17, 19, 24, 25, 26, 29, 30, Nov 8, 16, Dec 21; 1765: CG, Jan 8, 21, 22, 24,
Mar 26, Apr 9, 26, May 7, Sep 16, 20, 23, 25, 27, 30, Oct 2, 11, 16, 17, 30,
31, Nov 19, 20, 21, 27, Dec 3, 6, 10, 12; 1766: CG, Jan 31, Feb 5, Mar 15,
31, Apr 1, 2, 10, 19, May 6, 16, Sep 26, Oct 8, 16, 23, 31, Nov 8, 11, 14,
18, 19, 25, 27, Dec 4, 6, 23, 30; 1767: CG, Jan 1, Feb 20, Mar 23, 24, 31,
Apr 6, 25, 27, May 2, 8, Sep 23, Nov 7, Dec 28; 1768: CG, Feb 29, Apr 6, 11,
12, 23, May 27, Sep 20, 22, Oct 7, Nov 4, 17, Dec 28; 1769: CG, Jan 25, Mar
27, Apr 13, 15, Sep 22, Oct 4, 17, 24, Nov 11; 1770: CG, Jan 19, Feb 16, Mar
20, 24, 27, Apr 24, May 5, 8, 14, Sep 26, Oct 10, 16, 25, 26, 29, Dec 17, 31;
1771: CG, Apr 9, May 7, 25, Oct 7, 15, 28, Nov 25, Dec 4, 11, 16, 30; 1772:
CG, Jan 1, Feb 3, Apr 7, May 15, Sep 28, Oct 13, 23; 1773: CG, Jan 16, 25,
Mar 30, May 4, 7, 20, 24
Vincent, Isabella, Mrs Richard Jr (actor, singer), 1760: DL, Sep 23, Oct 20,
Nov 17, Dec 13, 19; 1761: DL, Mar 30, Apr 9, 13, 28, 29, Sep 5, 8, Oct 26,
31, Nov 28; 1762: DL, Jan 27, Feb 3, Mar 6, 22, 23, Apr 3, 20, 21, May 7, 10,
11, 14, 15, 17, Sep 21, 28, 29, Oct 9, 22, 25, 29, 30, Nov 6, 23; 1763: DL,
Jan 17, Apr 18, Sep 17, Oct 28, 31, Nov 15, 23, 29, Dec 1, 26; 1764: DL, Feb
16, Apr 27, May 7, 9, Sep 15, 22, Oct 4, 9, Nov 2, 5, HAY, 13, DL, 27; 1765:
DL, Jan 1, Feb 2, 15, Mar 26, 30, Apr 22, 24, May 1, MARLY, Aug 6, DL, Sep
14, 17, 24, 26, Oct 28, Nov 20; 1766: DL, Jan 6, 21, Feb 3, 7, Apr 15, 21,
26, MARLY, Sep 26, DL, 27, 30, Oct 21; 1767: DL, Mar 21, Apr 4, 6, 22, May 1,

874

27, 28, Jun 1, MARLY, Sep 18
Vincent, Mary (actor), 1715: LIF, Jan 11, Jun 14, Aug 11, Sep 29, Oct 5, 7, 11,
    24, Nov 29; 1716: LIF, May 18, Jul 4; 1723: LIF, Oct 7, 9, 10, 14, 24, 29,
    Nov 1, 18, 19, 28; 1724: LIF, Feb 24, Apr 30, Jun 2, 23, RI, Jul 11, LIF, 14,
    RI, 18, SF, Sep 2, LIF, Oct 27, 30, Nov 3, 13, 25, 26; 1725: LIF, Feb 27, Mar
    31, Apr 7, 17, 22, Sep 29, Oct 26, 28, Nov 8, 12, 24, 29, Dec 3; 1726: LIF,
    Jan 5, 7, 14, Apr 29, Jun 17, 24, Jul 22, Aug 19, Sep 30, Oct 19, Nov 30;
    1727: LIF, Jan 4, Feb 13, Mar 20, Apr 5, May 4, 12, 15, 22, Oct 12, 21, Nov
    1, 9; 1728: LIF, Jan 8, 17, Mar 21, 25, Jul 19, Aug 2, Nov 1, 23; 1729: LIF,
    Jan 1, 16, 18, Feb 22, Apr 24, 25, May 15, Sep 22, Oct 15, 17, 29, 31, Nov 4,
    Dec 16; 1730: LIF, Apr 22, 30, May 11, Oct 12, 31, Nov 10, 13, Dec 3; 1731:
    LIF, Jan 20, May 7, 20, Nov 12, 17, Dec 1; 1732: LIF, Jan 18, 26, Mar 20, 30,
    Apr 19, LIF/CG, Oct 2, Nov 3; 1733: LIF/CG, Apr 24, CG, Oct 16, Nov 8; 1734:
    CG, Jan 25, Apr 23; 1735: CG/LIF, Feb 13
Vincent, Miss (actor), 1739: CG, Oct 22
Vincent, Miss (actor), 1770: HAY, Oct 5, Nov 21, Dec 14, 19; 1771: HAY, Mar 4
Vincent, Mrs (actor), 1677: DL, May 5
Vincent, Mrs and Elizabeth (actors), 1764: CG, Apr 24; 1765: CG, Apr 26; 1766:
    CG, Apr 19
Vincent, Richard (composer), 1789: CG, Dec 21; 1790: CG, Nov 15; 1792: CG, Dec
    20; 1793: CG, Oct 2; 1799: CG, May 13
Vincent, Richard (haberdasher), 1761: CG, Oct 5
Vincent, Richard (renter), 1758: CG, Mar 4
Vincent Sr, Thomas (harpsichordist), 1737: HIC, Mar 24
Vincent Jr, Thomas (oboist), 1743: KING'S, Mar 30; 1744: KING'S, Mar 28, HAY,
    Apr 4; 1745: HAY, Mar 23, CG, Apr 10; 1746: CG, Nov 17, 22; 1748: KING'S, Apr
    5; 1749: KING'S, Mar 21; 1750: KING'S, Apr 10; 1751: KING'S, Apr 16; 1752:
    KING'S, Mar 24; 1753: KING'S, Apr 30; 1754: KING'S, Feb 28; 1755: KING'S, Mar
    17; 1756: KING'S, Apr 5; 1757: KING'S, Mar 24; 1758: DL, Mar 10, SOHO, Apr 1,
    CG, 17, CHAPEL, 27; 1759: CG, Feb 2, DL, Mar 23, 30, CG, May 4; 1760: KING'S,
    Apr 24, CG, Sep 22; 1761: KING'S, Mar 12, CG, Oct 8, 28; 1764: CHAPEL, Feb
    29; 1765: KING'S, Nov 23; 1766: KING'S, Oct 21, CG, Dec 13; 1767: KING'S, Jan
    23, DL, 24, KING'S, May 9, CG, 23, KING'S, Oct 27; 1768: KING'S, Feb 20, Nov
    3; 1769: CG, Jun 6, KING'S, 29; 1770: CG, May 29; 1772: CG, Jan 29; 1775: DL,
    Mar 3, 8, 10, 17, 22, 24
Vinci, Leonardo (composer), 1725: KING'S, May 11; 1741: HIC, Apr 24; 1752:
    KING'S, Mar 24; 1754: KING'S, Feb 28; 1772: KING'S, May 23; 1779: HAY, Mar 3,
    10; 1793: KING/HAY, Feb 15; 1794: CG, May 26; 1800: CG, Mar 19
--Artaserse (opera), 1793: KING/HAY, Feb 15
--Elpidia; or, The Generous Rivals (opera), 1725: KING'S, May 11, 15, 18, 22,
    25, 29, Jun 1, 5, 8, 12, 15, 19, Nov 30, Dec 4, 7, 11
Vine St, 1746: GF, Mar 11; 1772: DL, Apr 24; 1778: HAY, Apr 9
Vine Tavern, 1737: HAY, May 2
Vinegar Yard, 1772: DL, Nov 9; 1776: DL, May 13; 1798: CG, Mar 31
Viner (musician), 1707: YB, May 23; 1710: YB, Mar 31
Vining, Miss (singer, dancer), 1798: DL, Jan 16, Feb 20, May 16, Oct 6, Nov 14,
    Dec 6; 1799: DL, Jan 19, Feb 5, Oct 14; 1800: DL, Mar 11, HAY, Jul 2
Vint (clothier), 1773: DL, Nov 24
Vint (perfumer), 1794: CG, May 28
Vintage Festival (dance), 1774: CG, Oct 7, 14, 18, 19, 20, 25, 26, 27, Nov 3,
    9, 11, 15, 17, 26, 29, Dec 2, 3; 1775: CG, Mar 18, Apr 4, 22, May 2, 18, Oct
    26, 28
Vintage, The (dance), 1746: DL, Dec 4, 5, 10, 12, 15, 17, 19, 22; 1747: DL, Jan
    16, 19; 1764: KING'S, Nov 24; 1766: DL, Oct 11, 13, 14, 17, 20, 22, 24, Nov
    1, 5, 13, Dec 4, 10, 12, 17, 22, 27, 29; 1767: DL, Feb 5, 21, 24, Mar 21, 30,
    31, Apr 6, 7, 11, May 6; 1769: DL, Mar 31
Vintner (house servant), 1735: LIF, May 21
Vintner in the Suds, The (play, anon), 1740: DL, Apr 25
Vintner Tricked, The (farce, anon), 1746: DL, Apr 9, 21
Vintner Tricked, The. See Ward, Henry.
Vintner's Escape, The; or, Good Luck at Last (farce, anon), 1733: HAY, May 12
Vintners Hall, 1660: VH, Apr 12
Viol d'Amore (music), 1716: KING'S, Jul 12; 1728: HIC, Mar 20; 1734: YB, Apr 5;
    1784: HAY, Apr 27
Viol d'Amore Concerto (music), 1768: HAY, Mar 3; 1778: CG, Mar 25, Apr 3
Viol d'Amore Solo (music), 1743: LIF, Mar 15; 1751: CT, Dec 3, HAY, 27; 1752:
    CT/HAY, Jan 7, 14, 31, Feb 4, 6
Viol de Vevere (music), 1724: HAY, Mar 18
Viol di Gamba (music), 1710: PCGR, Jun 14; 1767: KING'S, Mar 5
Viol di Gamba Solo (music), 1772: HAY, Mar 30, Apr 27
Viola (music), 1746: GF, Feb 10
Viola Concerto (music), 1760: HAY, Feb 15

875

Viola Obligato (music), 1788: KING'S, May 29
Violante, La. See Polomba, A.
Violante, Larini (dancer), 1734: GF, Apr 27
Violante, Mlle (rope dancer), 1726: HAY, Mar 28, Apr 25, 27, May 9; 1727: LIF,
    Apr 14; 1728: HAY, Feb 21, Mar 20; 1732: RIW/HAY, Sep 4, 8, 11, 12
Violante, Mme (dancer, proprietor), 1720: LIF, Jun 6, 9; 1726: HAY, Apr 14, 27,
    May 6, Jun 1, SF, Sep 7; 1728: HAY, Feb 21, Mar 8, 20; 1729: HAY, Apr 28;
    1732: RIW/HAY, Sep 4, 6, 8, 11, 12, 15
Violenta, Sga (dancer), 1720: KING'S, Apr 26, 29, May 3
Violette (Violetty), Eva Maria (dancer), 1746: KING'S, Mar 11, DL, Dec 3, 4,
    17, 27, 29; 1747: DL, Jan 5, 14, 16, 21, 22, Feb 9, 11, 13, 16, 18, 20, 27,
    Apr 23; 1749: DL, May 16, Sep 28
Violin (music), 1675: SLINGSBY, Jan 19; 1701: HAW, Sep 15; 1702: HAW, May 11,
    Jun 1, PR, 30, HAW, Jul 27; 1703: DL, Mar 13; 1709: HA, Jul 30, SH, Nov 30;
    1712: B&S, Nov 24, SH, Dec 30; 1713: TEC, Nov 26; 1719: HIC, Feb 13, CGR, Mar
    18; 1720: SH, Mar 9; 1721: YB, Feb 6, HIC, Mar 1, 3, 15; 1722: HAY, Jan 26,
    May 11; 1723: HIC, Mar 6, HAY, May 24; 1724: HIC, Apr 20, HAY, May 8; 1726:
    DL, May 9; 1727: CR, Nov 22; 1728: YB, Mar 13; 1729: DL, Jul 29; 1731: HIC,
    Feb 4, LIF, Apr 2, DL, Jun 25; 1732: LIF, Feb 25, May 10, HIC, 10, LIF, 10;
    1733: YB, Mar 8, SH, 19; 1734: YB, Mar 8, SH, 28; 1735: DL, Mar 3, TB, Apr
    24, DL, May 13; 1736: HIC, Jan 21, ST, Feb 11, MR, 11, HAY, 20, HIC, Apr 19;
    1737: ST, Mar 8, DT, 30; 1738: HAY, Mar 3; 1740: HIC, Feb 1, 22, Mar 27, 28,
    SOU, Oct 9; 1741: HIC, Jan 16, Feb 19, 27, Mar 5, 6, CT, 13, HIC, 13, Apr 28;
    1744: SH, Feb 9, HAY, Sep 5; 1745: CT, Jan 14, DT, Mar 14; 1748: HAY, Jan 29;
    1753: HAY, Apr 2; 1754: KING'S, Apr 25; 1755: SOU, Jan 20, HAY, 29; 1758:
    SOHO, Apr 1; 1759: CG, Feb 2, May 4; 1760: SOHO, Jan 18, Feb 14, HIC, Apr 29;
    1762: HAY, Mar 16; 1764: CHAPEL, Feb 29, KING'S, Apr 5, DL, 27, May 9; 1765:
    HAY, Mar 11; 1766: CG, Mar 5, CHAPEL, Apr 30; 1767: KING'S, Jan 23; 1768:
    HAY, Jun 3; 1769: CG, Feb 10, HAY, 15; 1770: CG, Mar 2, DL, 2, 7, CG, 7, DL,
    14, 21, 28, CG, 30, HAY, May 3, 4, MARLY, Sep 11, 21; 1771: DL, Feb 15, Mar
    8, CHAPEL, Apr 27, KING'S, May 14, 28, MARLY, Jun 27, Jul 18, Aug 22; 1772:
    DL, Mar 6, CG, 27, HAY, 30, CG, Apr 8, HAY, 27; 1773: HAY, Apr 23, HIC, May
    18; 1774: CHAPEL, Mar 30; 1775: CHAPEL, Nov 23; 1776: HAY, Feb 22, CG, 23,
    Mar 1, 6, 27, CHAPEL, Apr 2, 3; 1778: KING'S, Mar 5, CG, 6, DL, 6, CG, 11,
    DL, 11, CG, 13, DL, 13, CG, 18, DL, 18, CG, 20, DL, 20, 25, CG, 25, 27, DL,
    27, Apr 1, CG, 1, 3, KING'S, 4, CG, 8, 10; 1780: DL, Feb 16, 18, 23, 25, Mar
    1, 3, 8, 10, 15, 17; 1781: DL, Mar 2; 1782: DL, Feb 15; 1784: DL, Feb 27;
    1785: DL, Feb 11, 18, 23, 25; 1786: DL, Mar 10, Apr 5; 1787: DL, Feb 23;
    1788: DL, Feb 8, CG, May 28; 1789: DL, Feb 27, Mar 6, 18, 20, 25; 1790: DL,
    Feb 19, Mar 19, CG, Jun 2; 1791: DL, Mar 11, 16, Apr 13; 1792: CG, Feb 28,
    May 22; 1793: KING/HAY, Mar 6, CG, 20; 1794: CG, Mar 21, Apr 11; 1795: CG,
    Mar 13; 1796: CG, Feb 19, 26; 1797: DL, May 18; 1798: KING'S, Jan 9, CG, Feb
    28, Mar 28; 1799: CG, Mar 1; 1800: CG, Feb 28
Violin and Flute Concerto (music), 1716: LIF, May 7, 31, Oct 17; 1717: LIF, Mar
    1, Nov 11
Violin and Harp (music), 1799: KING'S, May 30
Violin and Harpsichord (music), 1734: HA, Sep 11
Violin and Little Flute Concerto (music), 1719: LIF, Jan 2
Violin and Lute Sonata (music), 1712: SH, Dec 8
Violin and Oboe Obligato (music), 1795: CG, May 19
Violin and Viola Duet (music), 1777: CG, Feb 19; 1778: CG, Mar 25; 1790: CG,
    May 13
Violin and Violoncello Concerto (music), 1775: KING'S, Mar 24
Violin and Violoncello Concerto Obligato (music), 1796: CG, Feb 12; 1797: CG,
    Mar 15
Violin Concertino (music), 1734: HA, Sep 11
Violin Concerto (music), 1716: DL, May 18; 1724: YB, Mar 27; 1726: HIC, Mar 30;
    1728: HIC, May 15; 1729: HAY, Jan 28; 1731: DL, Apr 24; 1732: CL, Mar 17, DL,
    Oct 12; 1733: HIC, Apr 27, DL, May 7; 1737: CT, May 2; 1741: HAY, Mar 13;
    1743: DL, May 23; 1744: HAY, Apr 4, DL, 6; 1745: DL, Apr 3; 1753: KING'S, Apr
    30, Nov 20; 1754: DL, Mar 27, CG, May 23; 1755: DL, Mar 14, KING'S, 17, DL,
    19; 1757: KING'S, Mar 24, DL, Apr 28; 1758: DL, Mar 3, KING'S, Apr 6; 1759:
    CG, Feb 2, DL, Mar 30; 1761: KING'S, Mar 12; 1762: DL, Mar 5, KING'S, May 11,
    CHAPEL, 18; 1763: CG, Feb 18, KING'S, Apr 25, DL, 27; 1764: KING'S, Apr 12;
    1765: KING'S, Feb 15; 1766: CG, Feb 14, RANELAGH, Jun 20; 1767: KING'S, Jan
    23, CHAPEL, May 13; 1768: CHAPEL, May 25, HAY, Jun 17, DL, 21, HAY, 23; 1769:
    HAY, Feb 10, CG, 15, 24, Mar 3, HAY, 10, MARLY, Aug 24; 1770: HAY, Mar 12,
    KING'S, 22, 29, CG, Apr 21, MARLY, Jul 17, Sep 4, 15; 1771: KING'S, Jan 10,
    Feb 8, CG, 15, KING'S, 28, Mar 21, HAY, Apr 12, CHAPEL, 27, KING'S, May 17,
    25, MARLY, Jul 13, GROTTO, Aug 30, Sep 3; 1772: KING'S, Feb 21, CG, Mar 6,
    11, 13, 18, 20, 25, Apr 1, 3, 10, HAY, 27; 1773: DL, Feb 26, Mar 5, CG, 19,
    26, DL, 26, MARLY, Jun 15; 1774: KING'S, Feb 10, DL, 18, HAY, 18, 23, 25, Mar

2, 11, 16, 18, 23, 25, MARLY, Jun 30; <u>1775</u>: KING'S, Jan 26, DL, Mar 3, 10,
KING'S, 10, DL, 15, KING'S, 17, DL, 17, 22, KING'S, 31, Apr 7, DL, 7; <u>1776</u>:
STRAND, Jan 23, KING'S, Feb 15, CG, 23, DL, 28, CG, 28, Mar 1, DL, 1, CG, 6,
DL, 6, CG, 8, 13, DL, 20, CG, 20, 22, DL, 27, CG, 27, HAY, Apr 18; <u>1777</u>: DL,
Feb 14, CG, 14, 19, 26, 28, Mar 14, 19, May 29; <u>1778</u>: CG, Mar 6, DL, 6, 11,
13, CG, 13, Apr 8, HAY, 30; <u>1779</u>: DL, Feb 19, HAY, Mar 3, DL, 12, HAY, 17,
19, 24, 26; <u>1780</u>: DL, Feb 11, 25, Mar 3, CG, Jun 1; <u>1781</u>: DL, Mar 2, CG, 23,
DL, Apr 6, KING'S, Jun 14; <u>1782</u>: DL, Feb 20, KING'S, May 9; <u>1784</u>: HAY, Mar 3,
Apr 27; <u>1786</u>: DL, Mar 24; <u>1787</u>: DL, Mar 7, 9, 21; <u>1789</u>: CG, Feb 27, Mar 6;
<u>1790</u>: DL, Feb 19, CG, 19, DL, 24, Mar 3, 10, CG, 12, DL, 12, 17, 24, CG, May
13, HAY, Sep 29; <u>1791</u>: DL, Mar 11, CG, 18, DL, 23, 30, CG, 30, DL, Apr 6, 13,
15, KING'S, May 19; <u>1792</u>: KING'S, Feb 24, 29; <u>1793</u>: CG, Feb 15, KING/HAY, 15,
20, CG, 20, KING/HAY, 27, CG, Mar 1, KING/HAY, 6, 8, CG, 13, KING/HAY, 15,
20, 22, Apr 11; <u>1794</u>: DL, Mar 12, 14, CG, 14, DL, 19, 21, 26, 28, Apr 2, 4,
9, 11, KING'S, May 15, HAY, 22, KING'S, Jun 3, 23; <u>1795</u>: CG, Mar 25, DL, May
18; <u>1796</u>: CG, Feb 19, Mar 4, KING'S, 10, CG, 18; <u>1798</u>: CG, Feb 23, Mar 9, 30;
<u>1799</u>: HAY, Jan 24; <u>1800</u>: CG, Mar 19, Apr 2, 4
Violin Concerto, Grand (music), <u>1799</u>: DL, Jul 1
Violin Obligato (music), <u>1774</u>: HAY, Feb 25; <u>1777</u>: CG, Mar 19; <u>1779</u>: KING'S, Mar
11; <u>1788</u>: KING'S, Feb 21; <u>1797</u>: KING'S, May 23
Violin Quintetto (music), <u>1797</u>: DL, May 18
Violin Serenata Concerto (music), <u>1798</u>: CG, Mar 2
Violin Solo (music), <u>1703</u>: DL, Apr 23, Nov 9, Dec 22; <u>1704</u>: DL, Jan 25, Feb 21,
Mar 30, Nov 18, 27, Dec 28; <u>1705</u>: HDR, Jan 2, RIW, Jul 14; <u>1709</u>: HA, Sep 3;
<u>1711</u>: WCH, Oct 17; <u>1712</u>: GR, May 19, SH, Dec 30; <u>1714</u>: HIC, Apr 22; <u>1715</u>:
HIC, Apr 6, LIF, May 13, GRT, Jul 23; <u>1716</u>: LIF, Jan 27, HIC, Mar 14; <u>1717</u>:
HIC, Apr 10, DL, May 22, 25, LIF, Oct 14; <u>1718</u>: LR, Dec 3; <u>1719</u>: LIF, Apr 16;
<u>1721</u>: LIF, May 2; <u>1722</u>: LIF, May 4; <u>1723</u>: SH, Mar 6; <u>1724</u>: HIC, Feb 26; <u>1726</u>:
HIC, Mar 26; <u>1730</u>: DL, Apr 24, 28; <u>1731</u>: GF, Jan 14, 16, LIF, May 12, DT, Jul
7; <u>1732</u>: LIF, Mar 10; <u>1733</u>: GF, Jan 18, 19, Feb 2, DL, Apr 4, HIC, 20, GF,
May 15, 18, HAY, Aug 20; <u>1734</u>: GF, Mar 25, Apr 18; <u>1735</u>: DL, Mar 24, CG/LIF,
24, SH, 28, HIC, Apr 17, GF, 23, 29, DL, 29, Jun 5; <u>1736</u>: DL, Feb 9, 10, 11,
14, HAY, 20, LIF, Mar 8, HIC, Apr 8, SH, 16, GF, 27, DL, May 7, LIF, Jun 16;
<u>1737</u>: DL, Feb 1, DT, Mar 16, DL, 22, HIC, 24; <u>1738</u>: DL, Jan 27, HAY, Mar 3,
CG, May 1; <u>1739</u>: CG, May 2; <u>1740</u>: HIC, Apr 11, 18, 25; <u>1741</u>: HIC, Feb 5, HAY,
26, KING'S, Mar 14, HIC, 17, GF, Apr 2, DL, 16; <u>1743</u>: CG, Mar 2, 18, 23, 25,
29, 31; <u>1744</u>: JS, Dec 10; <u>1745</u>: HAY, Feb 14, Apr 1; <u>1750</u>: HIC, May 18; <u>1754</u>:
HAY, Feb 13; <u>1755</u>: HAY, Feb 13; <u>1758</u>: DL, Mar 10, MARLY, Aug 21; <u>1759</u>: CG,
May 4, HAM, Aug 13; <u>1760</u>: HAY, Feb 15, CG, 27; <u>1761</u>: HAY, Jan 28, Feb 5, CG,
6, DL, May 6; <u>1762</u>: CG, Feb 26, Mar 23; <u>1763</u>: CG, May 13; <u>1764</u>: CG, Jun 5,
HAY, Nov 13; <u>1765</u>: KING'S, Jan 25; <u>1766</u>: KING'S, Apr 10; <u>1767</u>: CG, Feb 19,
HAB, Dec 10; <u>1768</u>: KING'S, Feb 5, HAY, 19, 24, Mar 4, 9, 16, 18; <u>1769</u>:
KING'S, Feb 3, CG, 17, HAY, Apr 18; <u>1770</u>: KING'S, Feb 2, Mar 8, MARLY, Aug
14, 28; <u>1771</u>: CG, Feb 20, KING'S, 28, May 14, MARLY, Jun 27, Aug 3, 22, Sep
3, 5, 10, 12, 17; <u>1772</u>: DL, Mar 13; <u>1773</u>: KING'S, Feb 5, CG, 26, HAY, 26, Mar
3, 5, CG, 5, HAY, 17; <u>1774</u>: HAY, Mar 9, PANT, Apr 4, HAY, Sep 16; <u>1776</u>:
KING'S, Feb 15, CG, Oct 23; <u>1785</u>: DL, Feb 23, Mar 16; <u>1798</u>: HAY, Jan 15
Violin Solo Concerto (music), <u>1770</u>: MARLY, Aug 7, 21
Violin Sonata (music), <u>1703</u>: DL, Nov 10, YB, Dec 11; <u>1704</u>: DL, Jan 1, 12, YB,
May 18; <u>1705</u>: DL, Oct 12; <u>1706</u>: DL, Jun 22; <u>1713</u>: SH, May 15; <u>1714</u>: QUEEN'S,
May 1; <u>1717</u>: DL, May 22; <u>1725</u>: HAY, Mar 18; <u>1729</u>: HAY, Jan 28
Violin, German Flute, Tenor and Piano Forte Quartetto (music), <u>1778</u>: CG, Mar 18
Violin, Oboe, Tenor and Violoncello Concertante (music), <u>1800</u>: CG, Mar 14
Violin, Oboe, Viola and Violoncello Concertante (music), <u>1799</u>: CG, Feb 15
Violin, Viola and Violoncello Trio (music), <u>1793</u>: CG, Mar 20
Violin, Violoncello and Tenor (music), <u>1790</u>: HAY, Apr 29
Violoncello (music), <u>1718</u>: SH, Dec 23; <u>1724</u>: HIC, Apr 17; <u>1732</u>: LIF, Feb 25,
HIC, Apr 24; <u>1736</u>: HIC, Apr 15; <u>1740</u>: HIC, Feb 1, 22, Mar 27, 28; <u>1741</u>: HIC,
Jan 16, Feb 19, 27, Mar 6, 13, Apr 28; <u>1743</u>: DL, Dec 1; <u>1744</u>: LIF, Dec 11;
<u>1745</u>: CT, Jan 14, DT, Mar 14; <u>1752</u>: CT/HAY, Jan 7; <u>1758</u>: SOHO, Apr 1; <u>1761</u>:
HAY, Feb 5; <u>1762</u>: HAY, Mar 16; <u>1772</u>: DL, Mar 6, CG, Apr 8; <u>1775</u>: KING'S, Mar
31; <u>1778</u>: KING'S, Apr 4; <u>1790</u>: DL, Feb 24, Mar 17; <u>1791</u>: DL, Mar 11, CG, 23;
<u>1792</u>: KING'S, Feb 29, CG, Mar 9; <u>1793</u>: CG, Feb 15, KING/HAY, 15, Mar 6, CG,
13, 20; <u>1794</u>: CG, Mar 7, 12, 14, 21, Apr 11; <u>1795</u>: CG, Feb 20, Mar 25,
KING'S, Jun 16; <u>1796</u>: CG, Mar 16; <u>1797</u>: CG, Mar 10, 31, DL, May 18; <u>1798</u>: CG,
Mar 9, 28, 30; <u>1799</u>: CG, Feb 8, 15, 20, Mar 15; <u>1800</u>: CG, Feb 28, Mar 19
Violoncello Concerto (music), <u>1736</u>: ST, Feb 11; <u>1737</u>: CT, May 2; <u>1742</u>: DL, Nov
22, 23, Dec 18, 22, 28, 30; <u>1743</u>: DL, Jan 1, 3, 4, 5, 6, 25, KING'S, Mar 30,
DL, May 5; <u>1744</u>: KING'S, Mar 28, HAY, Apr 4, DL, May 8, HAY, Nov 5; <u>1745</u>:
HAY, Apr 1; <u>1748</u>: HAY, Jan 12, 26, Feb 2; <u>1750</u>: DL, Mar 28, Apr 23; <u>1752</u>: DL,
Apr 29; <u>1753</u>: KING'S, Apr 30; <u>1754</u>: KING'S, Feb 28; <u>1755</u>: KING'S, Mar 17;
<u>1756</u>: KING'S, Apr 5; <u>1757</u>: KING'S, Mar 24; <u>1758</u>: KING'S, Apr 6; <u>1759</u>: CG, Feb

2; 1761: KING'S, Mar 12; 1762: DL, Feb 26, HAY, Apr 22, KING'S, May 11; 1763:
KING'S, Apr 25, DL, 27; 1764: KING'S, Apr 12, CG, Jun 5; 1765: HAY, Mar 11;
1769: HAY, Apr 18; 1770: KING'S, Feb 2, DL, Mar 16; 1771: KING'S, Mar 21;
1772: DL, Mar 13, 18, HAY, 23, DL, 27, HAY, 30, DL, Apr 3; 1773: KING'S, Feb
5; 1774: KING'S, Feb 10; 1775: KING'S, Jan 26, Mar 17, DL, 22, Apr 7; 1776:
KING'S, Feb 15; 1777: CG, Feb 14; 1779: DL, Feb 26, Mar 19; 1782: DL, Feb 15,
Mar 1; 1784: DL, Mar 5; 1786: DL, Mar 29; 1787: DL, Mar 21; 1788: DL, Feb 22;
1789: DL, Mar 25; 1790: DL, Mar 5; 1792: KING'S, Mar 7, 9, 21; 1793: CG, Mar
6; 1794: KING'S, May 15; 1796: CG, Feb 24; 1797: CG, Mar 3; 1798: CG, Mar 14;
1799: CG, Mar 1; 1800: CG, Mar 5
Violoncello Duet (music), 1772: HAY, Apr 27
Violoncello Solo (music), 1732: HIC, May 10; 1733: HIC, Apr 20, 27, LIF, May 7;
1734: HIC, Mar 22; 1735: HIC, Apr 17; 1736: HAY, Feb 19; 1740: HIC, Apr 11,
18, 25; 1741: KING'S, Mar 14, HIC, 17; 1745: HAY, Feb 14; 1748: HAY, Dec 9;
1751: CT, Dec 3, HAY, 27; 1752: CT/HAY, Apr 14, May 5; 1754: HAY, Feb 13;
1756: DL, Aug 12; 1761: HAY, Jan 28, Feb 26; 1762: HAY, May 20; 1764: HAY,
Nov 13; 1765: KING'S, Jan 25; 1770: KING'S, Mar 1, 8, DL, 14, 21, 28, CG, 30,
DL, Apr 6, HAY, May 4, KING'S, Jun 12; 1771: KING'S, Jan 10, Feb 8, DL, 15,
Mar 8, HAY, Apr 12; 1772: KING'S, Feb 21, DL, Mar 6, 11, CG, 11, DL, 18, CG,
18, DL, 20, 25, CG, 25, Apr 1, 10, HAY, 27; 1773: HAY, Mar 26; 1774: HAY, Feb
23, DL, 23, HAY, Mar 9, HIC, May 9; 1775: KING'S, Mar 22; 1777: CG, Mar 19;
1791: DL, Apr 13
Violoncello Sonata (music), 1770: KING'S, Mar 22, 29, HAY, May 3
Violoncello, Mock (music), 1759: HAY, Sep 21
Viotti, Giovanni Battista (violinist), 1789: CG, Feb 27; 1794: KING'S, Apr 26,
HAY, May 22; 1795: KING'S, Jan 3; 1796: KING'S, Dec 27; 1798: KING'S, Jan 9,
Mar 3
Vipont (proprietor), 1735: HA, Oct 1
Virgil, 1694: NONE, Jan 11; 1752: HAY, Dec 7
Virgin Martyr, The. See Dekker, Thomas.
Virgin Prophetess, The. See Settle, Elkanah.
Virgin Queen, The. See Dryden, John.
Virgin Queen, The; or, The Captive Princess. See Barford, Richard.
Virgin Unmasked, The. See Fielding, Henry.
Virgin's Wish, The (play, anon), 1755: BF, Sep 3, 4, 5, 6
Virginia. See Crisp, Henry; Tarchi, Angelo.
Virgins too (song), 1790: DL, Mar 17
Virtue its own Reward (entertainment), 1788: CG, May 2
Virtue my soul shall still embrace (song), 1790: CG, Mar 17
Virtuoso, The. See Shadwell, Thomas.
Virtuous Wife, The. See D'Urfey, Thomas.
Viscomica (author), 1766: KING'S, Oct 30
Visconti (composer), 1731: DL, May 19
Visconti, Caterina (singer), 1741: KING'S, Oct 31, Nov 10, Dec 12, 19; 1742:
KING'S, Jan 19, Mar 2, Apr 13, 20, Nov 2, Dec 4; 1743: KING'S, Jan 1, Feb 22,
Mar 30, Apr 5, Nov 15; 1744: KING'S, Jan 3, 31, Mar 28, Apr 3, 24; 1754:
KING'S, Jan 29, Feb 28; 1766: KING'S, Apr 10
Visions of the Soul, The. See Dunton, John.
Visiting Scene of 4 Aldermen's Ladies, A (droll, anon), 1707: DL, Apr 3
Vitalba (dancer), 1775: KING'S, Apr 22, 25, May 16, 27
Vittora, Sga. See Argentina, Sga.
Vittoria Corombona. See Webster, John, The White Devil.
Vittoria, La (cantata), 1794: KING'S, Jun 23, 24
Vittorina. See Piccini, Niccolo.
Vitturi, B (composer), 1746: KING'S, Mar 4
Viv non ti contendono (song), 1748: KING'S, Apr 5
Vivaldi, Antonio (composer), 1724: HAY, May 8; 1731: HIC, Feb 4, DL, Jul 23;
1732: DL, May 3, LIF, 10; 1733: GF, Apr 13, HAY, May 26, Jun 4, DL/HAY, Oct
20, HAY, Nov 19, DL/HAY, Dec 20; 1734: DL/HAY, Jan 4, 10, 26, Mar 2; 1735:
LIF, Jun 12, HAY, Oct 24
--Fifth Concerto, 1732: DL, May 3; 1733: GF, Apr 13, HAY, Jun 4, DL, Dec 31
--Grand Concerto Favorito, 1732: LIF, May 10
Viviani, Elena Croce (singer), 1716: KING'S, Feb 1, Mar 10, Apr 18; see also
Croce, Elena
Viviez (Vivier) Jr (ticket deliverer), 1758: CG, Apr 8
Viviez, Miss (dancer), 1755: CG, Apr 30; 1756: CG, May 19; 1757: CG, Apr 30,
HAY, Jun 17, Jul 5, CG, Dec 17; 1758: CG, Feb 1, Apr 8, 12, 14, 28, May 2,
Oct 14, Nov 16, 23; 1759: CG, Apr 28, Dec 10; 1760: CG, Jan 16, 18, Apr 12,
May 28, Oct 11, 20; 1761: CG, Mar 9, Apr 17, May 25, Sep 16, 21; 1762: CG,
Jan 28, Apr 17; 1764: CG, May 22; 1765: CG, May 22; 1766: CG, May 9; 1767:
CG, Apr 27, May 20
Vo Solcando (song), 1745: DL, Mar 16; 1752: KING'S, Mar 24; 1793: KING/HAY, Feb

15; 1794: CG, May 26; 1800: CG, Mar 19
Voelcher (haberdasher), 1761: CG, Feb 2, 28
Voglio Amor (song), 1755: KING'S, Mar 17
Voi leggete in ogni core (song), 1762: KING'S, Mar 1
Voirinville, Mlle. See Vaurinville, Mlle.
Voisenon, Claude Henri de Fusee de, 1786: CG, Mar 18
--Amitie a l'epreuve, L'. See Favart, Charles Simon.
Volage (dancer), 1741: JS, Oct 6
Volage Fixe (dance), 1792: HAY, Mar 10, 24, Jun 7
Volar, Mrs (actor), 1728: HAY, Feb 21
Volcano, The. See Dibdin, Thomas John.
Volgo Dubbiosa (song), 1746: KING'S, Mar 25
Vollan (actor), 1728: HAY, Feb 21
Vologeso (pastiche), 1759: KING'S, Nov 13, 17, 24, Dec 1, 8; 1760: KING'S, Jan
   12
Volpone. See Jonson, Ben.
Voltaire, Francois Marie Arouet de, 1722: HAY, Apr 10; 1731: SS, Nov 8; 1733:
   CHE, May 9; 1735: GF/HAY, Jan 9; 1736: DL, Jan 12, LIF, Jun 18, Oct 14; 1740:
   SS, Dec 10; 1744: DL, Apr 23, 25, 27; 1751: CG, Mar 16, Oct 21; 1755: DL, Dec
   19; 1757: CG, Mar 12; 1767: DL, Feb 23; 1769: CG, Mar 13; 1774: DL, Oct 15;
   1776: DL, Dec 14; 1781: CG, May 10; 1783: KING'S, Mar 13; 1795: DL, Apr 27
--Ecosseisse, L', 1767: DL, Feb 23
--Mahomet, 1744: DL, Apr 23
--Mort de Cesar, La, 1740: SS, Dec 10
--Nanine, 1781: CG, May 10
--Oedipe, 1722: HAY, Apr 10
--Orestes, 1769: CG, Mar 13; 1770: CG, Mar 22; 1774: DL, Oct 15
--Zaire, 1733: CHE, May 9, 10, 11; 1735: GF/HAY, Jan 9
Volumner (musician), 1701: YB, Mar 24
Voluntary Contributions. See Porter, Walsh.
Volunteers, The; or, Taylors to Arms! See Downing, George.
Volunteers, The; or, The Adventures of Roderick Random and His Friend Strap
   (farce, anon), 1748: BF, Aug 24, SFBCBV, Sep 7, 8, 9, 10, 12, 13
Volunteers, The; or, The Stock Jobbers. See Shadwell, Thomas.
Von (dancer), 1771: HAY, Apr 24
Vorei Poterti Amar (song), 1733: DL/HAY, Nov 22
Vortigern. See Ireland, William Henry.
Votary of Wealth, The. See Holman, Joseph George.
Voulez Vous (dance), 1732: LIF/CG, Nov 16
Vowell (actor), 1771: HAY, May 20, 22, 29, 31, Jun 3, 5, 14, Jul 1, 5, 10, Aug
   26, 28, Sep 18, 19, 20; 1772: HAY, May 18, 27, Jun 1, 8, Jul 3, 6, 8, 10, 15,
   Aug 10, Sep 8, 17, 18; 1774: HAY, Sep 21; 1777: CHR, Jun 18, 20, 23, 25, 27,
   30, Jul 2, 21, 23; 1780: HAY, Jan 3
Voyage to Cytherea (dance), 1740: DL, Jan 15, 16, 17, 18, 19, 21, 22, 23, Feb
   2, 5, 8, 9, 11, 12, 13, 14, 15, 16, 18, 19, 21, Apr 29, May 6; 1741: DL, Nov
   11
Vratz, Colonel Christopher (executed), 1682: DG, Mar 0
Vuoi Saper se tu mi piaci (song), 1748: KING'S, Apr 5
Vyner, Sir Robert (Lord Mayor), 1674: CITY, Oct 29

W (entrepreneur), 1772: DL, Sep 29
W, H (author), 1769: DL, Sep 16
W, M, 1661: NONE, Sep 0
--Marriage Broker, The; or, The Pander, 1661: NONE, Sep 0
W, S (author), 1749: DL, Feb 1
Waas. See Wass.
Wadderburn, Mrs (actor), 1723: HAY, Dec 12
Waddy, John (actor), 1796: CG, Oct 5, 10, 18, Nov 19, 22, Dec 1, 15, 31; 1797:
   CG, Jan 2, 3, 10, Feb 18, Mar 4, 16, May 2, 16, 26, Sep 18, 25, 27, Oct 2, 6,
   11, 16, 31, Nov 4, 18, 20, Dec 23; 1798: CG, Feb 9, 20, Mar 31, Apr 11, 13,
   17, 21, 28, 30, May 8, 15, 17, 22, 24, 30, Jun 5, Sep 17, 21, Oct 3, 15,
   Nov 14, 17, 20, 21, 22, Dec 26; 1799: CG, Jan 22, 26, Mar 5, 14, 16, 27, Apr
   2, 6, 8, 9, 26, May 6, 10, 15, 24, 28, 31, Jun 5, HAY, 19, 25, 27, 28, 29,
   Jul 1, 2, CG, Sep 16, 23, 30, Oct 2, 4, 7, 9, 11, 14, 16, 17, 18, 21, 24, 25,
   29, Nov 13, 30, Dec 7, 9, 16, 30; 1800: CG, Jan 16, 18, 29, Feb 8, Mar 27,
   Apr 30, May 13, 27, 28, 30, Jun 2, 4, 12, HAY, 13, 17
Wade (dancer), 1712: DL, Jun 9; 1713: DL, Jun 12; 1714: DL, May 31, Jun 9, 14;
   1715: DL, Feb 11, 28, Mar 17, 19, Apr 19, May 13, 20, 31, Jun 2, Oct 28, 31,
   Nov 2, 11, 14, 23, 30, Dec 5, 19, 30; 1716: DL, Jan 14; 1717: DL, Mar 2, Apr

2, Oct 25, 29, 30, Nov 8, 22, Dec 3; 1718: DL, Jan 7, 14, 21, 27, Mar 18, Apr 25, 28, 29, May 7, 8, 13, 16, 19, 21, 22, Jun 6, Oct 2, 7, 18, 29, Nov 4, 6, 12, 14, 17, 19, 24, 28, Dec 10; 1719: DL, Jan 7, 29, Feb 12, Mar 12, 16, Apr 18, May 9
Wade (dancer), 1732: GF, Apr 21
Wade, Colonel (renter), 1758: CG, Feb 23
Waft her, angels (song), 1790: CG, Mar 3; 1791: DL, Mar 25; 1792: KING'S, Mar 23, 30; 1793: CG, Mar 8; 1794: DL, Mar 12, 14; 1795: CG, Mar 13, 27; 1797: CG, Mar 10; 1799: CG, Feb 8, 20; 1800: CG, Mar 5
Waggoner, The (song), 1795: DL, May 19; 1797: DL, Jun 7
Waggoners, The (dance), 1761: CG, Feb 28, Apr 8, 11, 15, 17, 24, 25, 28
Waghorne (beneficiary), 1731: DT, Jun 4, Jul 7
Wainwright (apothocary), 1747: CG, Feb 26
Wainwright, Miss (actor), 1764: CG, Dec 12; 1765: CG, Jan 2
Waistkum (actor), 1749: CG, Apr 10, 12
Waite, Mrs (actor), 1782: HAY, Mar 21
Waiter (chemist), 1751: DL, May 1
Waiter Song (song), 1795: CG, Apr 24; 1796: CG, Apr 15, 22, May 3, 24, HAY, Aug 30
Wake (dance), 1768: DL, Feb 20, 29, Mar 7, 12, 15, 21, 24, 26, Apr 4, 8, 11, 12, 13, 14, 16, 23, 29, May 3, Sep 29, 30, Oct 1, 12, 24, 28, Dec 5, 16, 20; 1769: DL, Feb 1, 4, 6, Mar 29, 31, Apr 3, 4, 5, 11, 12, 20, 26, 29, May 1, 16, 18, 19, 22, 23, Oct 6; 1770: DL, May 2, 16, Jun 1
Wake, Sons of Odin (song), 1789: DL, Jun 3; 1790: DL, May 20; 1792: KING'S, Mar 28; 1793: KING/HAY, Mar 13, 15
Wake, thou son of dullness (song), 1780: CG, Feb 22
Wake, wake, Quivera (song), 1695: DG, Apr 0
Wakelin (beneficiary), 1749: HAY, May 16
Walcot, Miss (actor), 1797: DL, Nov 7; 1798: DL, Mar 22, Apr 28, Jun 5; 1799: DL, May 7
Walcot, Mrs (actor), 1785: HAY, Apr 26; 1797: DL, Sep 21, 28, Oct 3, 30, Nov 9, 11, 15, 25, Dec 14; 1798: DL, Jan 9, 23, 25, Feb 3, May 30, 31, Jun 6, 12, Sep 22, 27, 29, Oct 8, 30, Nov 22, 28, 29, Dec 3, 5; 1799: DL, Jan 31, Feb 26, Apr 8, 18, 24, May 3, Jun 10, Jul 1, Sep 17, 21, Oct 19, Nov 2, 6, 12, 14, 22, Dec 2, 17; 1800: DL, Jan 18, Feb 1, Mar 13, May 10, 21, Jun 5, 9
Walcup (ticket deliverer), 1799: CG, May 17
Walcup, Grace (actor), 1795: CG, Oct 24; 1798: CG, Mar 31, Apr 9
Walcup, Miss (actor, singer), 1795: CG, Jan 23, 31, May 14, Sep 14, 21, Oct 2, 19, 24, Nov 4, 16, 27, Dec 7; 1796: CG, Apr 9, 26, May 16, Sep 12, 19, 26, Oct 6, 7, Dec 19; 1797: CG, Feb 18, Apr 25, May 18, Sep 25, Oct 16, Nov 2, Dec 18, 26; 1798: CG, Feb 12, Sep 17, 19, Oct 8, 25, 31, Nov 1, 12, Dec 11, 15, 26; 1799: CG, Jan 14, 17, 29, Mar 2, 25, Apr 3, 12, 13, 19, May 4, 21
Walcup, Miss E (singer), 1796: CG, Apr 9, Oct 7
Waldegrave, James Earl of, 1767: CG, May 23
Walden, Richard (spectator), 1661: REDBULL, Mar 23, LIF, Jul 3, 4, 5, 8
Waldgrave (pensioner), 1767: DL, Jan 24
Waldron, Francis Godolphin (actor, playwright), 1769: DL, Oct 6, 14, 21, 23, 27, Nov 8, 29; 1770: DL, Feb 1, Mar 1, Apr 3, 16, May 8, 10, 14, 16, 17, Sep 29, Oct 3, 4, 5, 12, 15, 25, Nov 26, 29; 1771: DL, Jan 4, Mar 12, 21, Apr 20, 22, May 10, 20, Sep 28, Oct 5, 8, 10, 29, Nov 9, 13, Dec 7, 10; 1772: DL, Jan 1, 20, Mar 21, 28, Apr 20, May 4, 12, 13, Sep 22, 29, Oct 8, 16, 21, 28, 30, Nov 20, 30, Dec 26; 1773: DL, Feb 4, 11, May 15, 17, Sep 18, 25, Oct 5, 22, 25, Nov 2, 26, Dec 10, 18, 22, 23; 1774: DL, Jan 19, 21, Feb 1, 2, 3, 5, 12, Mar 15, 21, 22, Apr 9, 15, 21, May 7, 9, 10, 11, 19, Sep 20, Oct 12, 19, 24, 26, Nov 4, 17, 18, 24, Dec 19; 1775: DL, Jan 2, 11, Apr 8, 17, May 3, 5, 6, 10, 11, 12, 16, 17, 19, 20, 22, 25, Sep 26, Oct 11, 21, 24, 30, Nov 1, 4, 6, 14, 18, 21, 25, 30, Dec 4, 9, 29; 1776: DL, Jan 26, Mar 23, 25, 28, 30, Apr 10, 19, 20, 24, 25, May 4, 8, 11, 15, 20, 21, 22, HAY, Sep 17, DL, 24, 26, 28, Oct 9, 15, 23, 25, Nov 6, 29, Dec 10, 17; 1777: DL, Jan 1, 28, Feb 20, Mar 13, Apr 18, 29, May 28, Jun 2, Sep 23, 27, 30, Oct 14, 17, Nov 8, 24, 29, Dec 3, 4, 13; 1778: DL, Feb 2, 19, 21, 24, Mar 5, Apr 21, 30, May 9, 18, 22, 23, Sep 17, 19, 22, 26, 29, Oct 1, 13, 15, 31, Nov 18; 1779: DL, Jan 7, 8, 13, 23, 29, Mar 16, 22, Apr 5, 16, 28, May 8, 18, 25, Sep 18, 25, 30, Oct 2, 5, 7, 9, 12, 14, 28, 30, Nov 22, Dec 20, 27, 29, 31; 1780: DL, Jan 5, 11, 24, 26, Mar 14, Apr 4, May 2, 10, 25, Sep 16, 19, 21, 23, 28, Oct 2, 3, 5, 7, 11, 19; 1781: DL, Feb 15, Mar 10, 19, 27, May 1, 8, Sep 25, 29, Oct 12, 15, 30, Nov 6, 15, Dec 5, 27; 1782: DL, Jan 19, Apr 17, 18, 20, 24, 25, 27, May 3, 4, 11, CG, 21, 23, DL, Sep 20, 24, 28, Oct 3, 5, 19, 31, Nov 2, 4, 5, 26, 28, 30, Dec 7, 26; 1783: DL, Jan 27, Feb 12, 22, Mar 4, 6, 20, Apr 25, 26, 29, May 5, 12, 15, 30, Sep 23, 30, CG, Oct 3, DL, 4, 6, Nov 13, 18, 19, 20, 21, 27, 28, 29, Dec 2, 11; 1784: DL, Jan 7, 10, 13, Feb 12, Mar 29, Apr 16, 19, 21, May 10, Sep 21, 23, 25, Oct 11, 26, Nov 25, Dec 28; 1785: DL, Jan 6,

11, 12, 13, 14, 15, 20, 22, 28, Feb 21, Apr 1, 11, 20, May 12, 26, HAMM, Jun
17, 27, Jul 1, 2, 6, 8, 15, 22, 25, 26, 27, DL, Sep 20, Oct 13, 26, Nov 3,
14, 17, 18, Dec 1, 26, 30; 1786: DL, Jan 4, 6, 9, 16, Feb 18, Apr 20, May 17,
HAMM, Jun 5, 9, 30, Jul 5, 7, 10, 19, 24, HAY, 25, HAMM, 26, 28, Aug 5, DL,
Sep 19, 23, 26, Oct 25, 26, 27, 28, Nov 25, Dec 19, 26, 28, 30; 1787: DL, Jan
4, 12, 26, Mar 29, Apr 13, May 3, Sep 18, 25, 27, 29, Oct 6, 24, 26, Nov 1,
6, 14, 21, 24, Dec 7, 28; 1788: DL, Jan 2, 18, 22, 26, Feb 7, Apr 10, 11, 14,
May 1, 6, 14, 16, 21, 23, Jun 5, Sep 13, 23, 27, Oct 2, 7, Nov 5, 8, 17, 25,
Dec 31; 1789: DL, Jan 1, 13, 14, 17, Feb 18, 28, Apr 15, Jun 3, 4, 5, Sep 17,
19, 22, Oct 1, 3, 8, 24, 27, Nov 13, Dec 7; 1790: DL, Jan 19, Feb 13, 15, 18,
23, May 18, Jun 1, CG, Jul 16, DL, Oct 4, 7, 11, 12, 18, 19, 23, 27, Dec 14;
1791: DL, Apr 5, 12, 29, 30, May 31, DLKING'S, Sep 29, Oct 3, 10, 25, 31, Nov
1, 12, 23, Dec 27; 1792: DLKING'S, Jan 5, CG, 6, DLKING'S, 28, Feb 23, 27,
Mar 1, 10, 26, 29, Apr 10, Jun 4, 13, DL, Sep 15, 25, Oct 2, 4, 30, 31, Nov
10, Dec 4, 8, 14, 27, 28; 1793: DL, Jan 16, Feb 12, Mar 4, 5, 7, 9, 14, Apr
17, 22, 25, May 7, 10, HAY, Jun 17, Aug 12, 26, 28, Sep 5, 12, 19, 21, 24,
Oct 7, 9, 21, Dec 2, 10, 16; 1794: HAY, Jan 14, Feb 19, Mar 10, DL, Apr 25,
May 1, 5, 16, Jun 14, Jul 7, HAY, 17, Aug 9, 13, Sep 17, DL, 23, 27, Oct 29,
Nov 7, Dec 3, 5, 9, 12, 19; 1795: DL, Jan 22, Feb 6, 26, 28, Mar 10, 14, 16,
Apr 6, 18, May 29, Jun 6, HAY, 9, 13, Jul 1, 8, 25, Aug 3, Sep 4, 21, DL, Dec
10, 18, 26; 1796: DL, Jan 1, 4, 7, 14, 15, Mar 5, 19, 28, Apr 25, May 5, Jun
8, HAY, 11, 14, 16, 25, 30, Jul 8, 9, 11, 15, Aug 8, 11, 17, 30, Sep 5, 7,
16; 1797: HAY, Jun 12, 15, 23, 24, Aug 28, Sep 1, 16; 1798: HAY, Jun 15, 19,
23, Jul 14, Aug 21, 29, Sep 17; 1799: HAY, Jun 15, 26, Jul 2, Aug 22, Sep 16;
1800: HAY, Jun 19, 20, Aug 12, 14, Sep 16
--Contrast, The; or, The Jew and Married Courtezan, 1775: DL, May 12
--Heigho for a Husband, 1783: DL, May 12; 1794: HAY, Jan 7, 14, 15, 17, 20, 22,
25, 29, Feb 1, 4, 8, 15, 20, Apr 3, Jul 14, Aug 6, 18, Sep 12; 1795: HAY, Sep
21; 1796: HAY, Jul 30
--Imitation; or, The Female Fortune-Hunters, 1783: DL, May 12
--Love and Madness!, 1795: HAY, Sep 21
--Maid of Kent, The, 1773: DL, May 15, 17; 1774: DL, May 7, 19; 1795: HAY, Sep
21
--Prodigal, The (interlude), 1793: HAY, Dec 2, 3, 4, 6, 10, 12, 18; 1794: HAY,
Jan 17, 25, Feb 4, 19, Mar 24
--Tis a Wise Child Knows its Father, 1795: HAY, Sep 21
Waldron, Francis Godolphin and Mrs (actors), 1786: HAMM, Aug 8
Waldron, George (actor), 1793: HAY, Jun 11, 12, 17, 18, 21, 22, 24, 29, Jul 6,
9, 13, 20, Aug 3, 12, 16, 20, 27, Sep 10, 19, 21, 24, 26, 28, Oct 1, 4, 5, 8,
15, 21, 24, 29, 30, Nov 5, 6, 16, 23, Dec 7, 14, 17, 19, 26, 28; 1794: HAY,
Jan 3, 4, 11, 13, 14, 24, 31, Feb 5, 6, 22, 25, Mar 1, 17, Jul 8, 9, 10, 11,
14, 17, 18, 19, 21, 26, Aug 11, 12, 20, 27, Sep 17; 1795: HAY, Jun 9, 10, 11,
13, 15, Jul 1, 4, 8, 16, 20, 22, 25, 30, 31, Aug 3, 6, 14, 18, 20, 27, Sep 2,
21; 1796: HAY, Jun 11, 13, 14, 17, 18, 20, 22, 25, 29, 30, Jul 6, 8, 9, 14,
15, 21, 23, 26, 30, Aug 8, 10, 11, 13, 18, 20, 29, Sep 7; 1797: HAY, Jun 12,
13, 15, 16, 17, 19, 20, 21, 22, 23, 24, Jul 3, 4, 10, 15, Aug 1, 4, 5, 9, 15,
28, 31, Sep 14, 18; 1798: HAY, Jun 12, 13, 14, 15, 16, 18, 19, 20, 21, 23,
27, 30, Jul 14, 16, 21, 23, Aug 3, 9, 11, 21, 23, 25, 28, 29, Sep 3, 5, 12,
17
Waldron, Mrs Francis Godolphin (actor), 1778: HAY, Mar 31; 1785: HAY, Mar 15,
Apr 26; 1786: HAMM, Jul 5, 7, 10; 1787: HAY, Mar 12; 1788: HAY, Apr 9, Sep
30; see also Harlowe, Sarah
Wale, Samuel (scene painter), 1758: CG, Mar 13
Wales, Frederick Louis, Prince of, 1796: CG, Feb 12
Wales, Frederick, Prince of, 1751: DL, Mar 20; 1754: CG, Jan 3
Wales, Prince and Princess of, Wedding Anthem for (song), 1773: HAY, Mar 3
Wales, Prince and Princess of, 1714: KING'S, Oct 23, Nov 20, DL, 22, Dec 3;
1715: KING'S, Apr 23, DL, Jun 3; 1723: RI, Sep 2; 1725: KING'S, Dec 28; 1726:
KING'S, Jan 11, DL, Mar 7, KING'S, 8, 15, May 31, Sep 28, Oct 5, LIF, 24;
1736: KING'S, May 1, 4, DL, 5, KING'S, 8, DL, 12, CG, 12, KING'S, 18, DL, 19,
CG, Jun 2, KING'S, 15, DL, 23, LIF, Jul 1, RI, 24, 31, DL, Aug 26, Sep 23,
Oct 12, 20, CG, Nov 6, DL, 11, 18, LIF, 19, CG, 20, KING'S, 23, DL, Dec 3,
CG, 22, DL, 30; 1737: CG, Jan 12, KING'S, 25, DL, 27, CG, 29, DL, Feb 2, 16,
24, CG, Mar 2, DL, 5, 10, CG, 16, DL, 17, CG, 23, DL, Apr 27, KING'S, May 31,
CG, Jun 10, DL, 11, CG, 25, DL, Oct 4, 11, 27, Nov 4; 1738: DL, Jan 11, 25,
Feb 9, 18, 27, Mar 2, 9, 13, 20, 25, KING'S, 28, DL, Apr 17, 18, 19, 22, May
24, Sep 12, 23, Oct 3, 10, 13, Dec 12, 19; 1739: DL, Jan 9, 18, 26, Feb 6,
16, CG, 20, DL, 22, Mar 8, 10, Apr 12, KING'S, 17, DL, 24, 26, 27, CG, May 1,
DL, 2, CG, 12, DL, 18, Sep 11, 29, Oct 3, 12, 15, 23, 30, Nov 7, 14, 22, 30,
LIF, Dec 13, DL, 15, 22, 29; 1740: DL, Jan 12, 17, Feb 9, 14, CG, 16, DL, 26,
Mar 10, CG, 13, DL, 22, Apr 10, CG, 15, DL, 18, 21, 26, CG, May 10, DL, Oct
4, CG, 30; 1741: DL, Feb 3, CG, 6, 12, DL, 19, LIF, 21, CG, 28, Mar 2, DL,

10, 14, Apr 2, CG, 6, DL, 7, CG, 16, DL, 21, CG, 24, May 15, Oct 30, DL, Nov
6, CG, 11, Dec 30; 1742: CG, Jan 14, DL, 21, CG, 25, Feb 1, DL, 8, CG, 10,
15, 20, Mar 1, DL, 8, 22, CG, Apr 1, 5, KING'S, 13, CG, 21, DL, May 4, CG,
Sep 27, Oct 1, DL, 29, Nov 11, CG, 17, DL, 25; 1743: CG, Jan 27, Feb 3, 14,
DL, Mar 3, CG, 7, DL, 8, CG, 14, DL, 22, CG, Apr 6, 26, DL, May 5, CG, Oct 3,
DL, 11, CG, Dec 22; 1744: CG, Jan 16, Feb 1, 9, Mar 12, 13, 28, May 10, HAY,
Nov 2; 1745: DL, Jan 19, Feb 6, HAY, Mar 6, DL, 9, CG, 11, DL, 16, CG, 28,
May 4; 1746: CG, Jan 15, DL, Feb 6, CG, Apr 17, Jun 9, DL, Oct 17, CG, 24,
DL, 28, CG, Nov 14, 27, 28, Dec 5, 12; 1747: DL, Jan 14, CG, Feb 13, DL, 16,
CG, Apr 9, 30, May 14, DL, Dec 2, CG, 15; 1748: CG, Feb 3, DL, Mar 24, CG,
Oct 11, 25, Nov 10, Dec 21; 1749: CG, Feb 9, 27, May 4, DL, 12, 13, CHAPEL,
27, CG, Oct 12, Nov 28, Dec 16, DL, 21; 1750: DL, Apr 25, CG, Oct 2, Nov 8,
22, 29, Dec 6, 13, 20; 1751: CG, Jan 17, DL, 22, CG, 31, DL, Mar 8, CG, 16;
1796: CG, Feb 12
Wales, Prince of, 1697: STRAND, Jun 17; 1715: LIF, Oct 24, Dec 20; 1716: DL,
Nov 19, 22, Dec 6; 1717: DL, Mar 4; 1720: DL, Oct 19; 1726: LIF, Jan 21,
KING'S, Feb 8; 1729: DL, Jan 28, LIF, Feb 11, DL, Mar 6, 13, Apr 15, 22, HAY,
28, LIF, 29, RI, Jul 26, Aug 6, BFR, 26, LIF, Oct 1, 8, 22, DL, 28, LIF, Nov
4, DL, 6, 12, 26, LIF, Dec 8, 18; 1730: DL, Jan 29, LIF, Mar 17, KING'S, 17,
DL, 19, HAY, Apr 25, KING'S, May 23, RI, Oct 20, DL, 28, Nov 26, KING'S, Dec
1, DL, 10, KING'S, 15; 1731: DL, Jan 7, LIF, 14, KING'S, 23, Feb 9, 16, DL,
May 5, KING'S, 22, DL, Sep 18, KING'S, Nov 23, DL, Dec 8, 13, KING'S, 18,
LIF, 21, DL, 22; 1732: DL, Jan 5, D, 12, LIF, Mar 9, DL, 13, 27, KING'S, Jun
17, RI, Jul 22, SFLH, Sep 5, GF, Oct 11, DL, 28, LIF/CG, Nov 27, KING'S, Dec
5, CG/LIF, 20, 27; 1733: CG/LIF, Jan 1, DL, Feb 8, LIF/CG, 12, Mar 12,
KING'S, 27, DL, May 16, HAY, Jun 6, KING'S, Jul 5, DL, Sep 24, KING'S, Nov
13, DL/HAY, Dec 18, PM, 24; 1734: LIF, Jan 1, 5, 12, 29, IT, Feb 2, KING'S,
12, Mar 13, GF, 15, DL/HAY, 18, CG, 21, KING'S, 23, CG, Apr 1, 2, 6, DL/HAY,
18, KING'S, May 18, Jun 28, Nov 2, 5, PM, 29; 1735: KING'S, Feb 1, Mar 15,
CG/LIF, 20, Apr 24, HAY, 28, DL, Sep 15, KING'S, Oct 28, DL, Nov 19, 22, Dec
20, CG, 31; 1736: DL, Jan 5, CG, 12, 24, DL, 26, KING'S, 27, HAY, Mar 29, CG,
May 12; 1737: CGKING'S, Jul 5; 1740: CG, Nov 6, DL, 12, 17, CG, 20, 25, DL,
28, Dec 2, LIF, 13, CG, 16, DL, 18, 29; 1741: CG, Jan 2, DL, 6, CG, 13, DL,
16, CG, 21, DL, Dec 3; 1742: CG, Jan 14, Dec 9; 1743: NONE, Jul 13; 1744: CG,
Oct 12; 1745: DL, Mar 20; 1747: CG, Jan 2, Apr 4; 1749: DL, Jan 20; 1750: CG,
Jan 3, KING'S, 16, CG, Oct 2; 1751: DL, Feb 23, Oct 28; 1752: CG, Jan 14, Feb
8, 10, 24, DL, Apr 7, Nov 6, 18, CG, Dec 4, 30; 1753: DL, Feb 3, CG, 19, Apr
4, DL, 7, CG, Oct 25, DL, Nov 22, CG, Dec 27; 1754: CG, Jan 3, DL, 31, CG,
Oct 31, DL, Dec 12; 1755: CG, Dec 17, 18, DL, 31; 1756: DL, Jan 9, 29, CG,
Feb 4, DL, 26, Mar 4, CG, 16, Apr 30, DL, May 12, Oct 26, CG, Nov 6, DL, Dec
3, CG, 10, DL, 30; 1757: CG, Jan 28, Mar 1, 19, Apr 20, DL, Oct 22, CG, Nov
5, 25, DL, Dec 17; 1758: CG, Jan 6, DL, 11, CG, 28, Feb 4, DL, 6, 25, 28, Mar
4, Apr 19, CG, Dec 8; 1759: DL, Jan 12, 19, CG, Feb 3, DL, 10, 26, CG, Mar 3,
DL, 17, 31, CG, Apr 7, 19, DL, 23, 28, May 18, Jun 4, Dec 28; 1760: DL, Jan
5, CG, 5, DL, 29, CG, Feb 5, DL, 16, 28, Mar 10, CG, Apr 26, DL, May 2, 10,
31; 1761: CG, Jan 7, Nov 19; 1767: CG, Jan 29; 1768: CG, Jan 14, May 5; 1769:
CG, Feb 13; 1772: CG, Jan 20, MARLY, Sep 1, 7; 1776: DL, Dec 10; 1780: DL,
May 24, CG, 29; 1781: CG, May 28; 1782: KING'S, May 9; 1783: HAY, Aug 12;
1784: KING'S, Mar 25; 1786: CG, Sep 18; 1790: DL, Mar 26; 1791: HAY, Mar 7,
DLKING'S, Dec 31; 1792: DLKING'S, Apr 16, DL, Sep 25; 1793: DL, May 7, HAY,
Aug 12; 1794: DL, Apr 21, KING'S, May 15, DL, Jul 2; 1795: CG, Feb 27, Apr 6,
Jun 6; 1796: DL, Jan 18; 1797: HAY, May 10, KING'S, 18, CG, Jun 14, DL, Oct
27; 1799: CG, Apr 30; 1800: CG, Jun 12
Wales, Princess Dowager of, 1754: DL, Jan 1; 1761: KING'S, Nov 28; 1765:
KING'S, Nov 29; 1771: KING'S, Nov 29; 1772: CG, Jan 7, KING'S, Feb 8, 18
Wales, Princess of, 1715: SH, Jun 30; 1716: HIC, Jun 9; 1720: KING'S, May 26;
1721: KING'S, Apr 15; 1722: DL, Nov 16; 1726: KING'S, Feb 8; 1736: RI, Aug
21; 1737: HAY, Apr 18, LIF, 18; 1744: CG, Oct 12; 1747: CG, Jan 2, Apr 4;
1750: CG, Jan 3; 1752: CG, Nov 4; 1754: CG, Jan 3; 1755: CG, Jan 2, DL, 9,
CG, Mar 13, DL, Dec 31; 1756: CG, Jan 21; 1757: CG, Nov 5; 1758: CG, Jan 6,
28, Feb 4; 1760: CG, Jan 5, Feb 5, Apr 26, Dec 19; 1761: CG, Sep 24; 1770:
CG, Jan 6
Wales, 1733: DL, Dec 31; 1741: GF, Dec 23; 1755: DL, Sep 13; 1756: DL, Dec 30
Walford (actor), 1723: LIF, May 13; 1724: LIF, May 18, SF, Sep 2
Walgrave (actor), 1797: HAY, Sep 18
Walham Green, 1789: WHF, Nov 9
Walker (actor), 1749: BF/SFP, Aug 23, BFC, 23
Walker (bookseller), 1747: HAY, Apr 22
Walker (dancer), 1751: DL, May 6; 1753: DL, Apr 25, May 15, 17; 1754: DL, May
13, 15, 17, 18, 21, 22, HAY, Sep 10, DL, Nov 11, Dec 17; 1755: DL, Feb 22,
Apr 14, 24, 25, May 3, 5, 8, 12, 13, HAY, Sep 1, BF, 6, HAY, 9, 11, 15, DL,
Oct 17, 21, 24, 27, Nov 4, 6, 8, 15; 1756: DL, Jan 21, Feb 10, 24, 27, Apr

29, May 7, 15, 17, Aug 12, Nov 18, 19, Dec 6, 11, 15, 27; 1757: DL, Jan 7,
24, Feb 5, 9, 22, 24, Mar 19, 21, 24, May 4, 5, 7, 9, 12, 14, 16, 17, 19, 20,
Sep 10, 20, 29, Oct 4, 11, 15, Nov 1, 8, 22, Dec 3, 8, 22; 1758: DL, Jan 23,
Feb 1, Mar 16, Apr 7, 25, May 2, 8, 12, 15, 17, 18, Jun 1; 1759: DL, Feb 26,
May 11, 17, 19, 22, 29, 30; 1760: DL, May 6, 12, 13, 15; 1762: DL, May 18;
1763: DL, Jan 3, May 4, Nov 2; 1764: CG, May 1, DL, 14; 1765: DL, Apr 16, 23,
CG, 30, DL, May 2, 11, 13, 14, 15, 18, 21; 1766: CG, Apr 21, DL, May 9, 10,
20; 1767: DL, Jan 24, Apr 4, May 11, 15, 25, 30, Jun 1, Dec 26; 1768: DL, May
9, 24, 25, Sep 8, 20, Oct 10; 1769: DL, Apr 25, May 10, 16, 20; 1770: DL, Jan
8, May 4, 21, 23, Jun 4, Oct 13, Nov 17; 1771: DL, May 21, 22, 29; 1772: DL,
May 27, Jun 1, 10, Sep 22; 1773: DL, May 21, 25; 1774: DL, May 16, 23; 1775:
DL, May 8; 1776: DL, May 15, 24; 1777: DL, Apr 30; 1778: DL, May 18; 1779:
DL, May 21, Oct 5, Dec 2; 1780: DL, May 16, Sep 21; 1781: DL, May 23, Oct 15;
1782: DL, May 15; 1783: DL, May 21; 1784: DL, May 21; 1785: DL, May 19; 1786:
DL, Jun 6; 1787: DL, May 31; 1788: DL, Jun 3; 1789: DL, Jun 9; 1790: DL, Jun
2; 1791: DL, May 26
Walker (doorkeeper), 1739: DL, May 25; 1740: DL, May 19; 1741: DL, May 25;
  1742: DL, May 24; 1743: DL, May 26; 1744: DL, May 15
Walker (doorkeeper), 1794: CG, Jun 16; 1795: CG, Jun 13
Walker (mercer), 1774: CG, Apr 13
Walker (numberer), 1741: DL, May 23; 1742: DL, May 25; 1743: DL, May 23; 1744:
  DL, May 9; 1745: DL, May 9; 1746: DL, May 16
Walker (oil merchant), 1753: DL, Dec 11
Walker (tailor), 1780: HAY, Sep 25; 1781: HAY, Oct 16; 1782: HAY, Mar 18
Walker, Anthony (engraver), 1754: CG, Jan 21
Walker, John (actor), 1757: CG, May 27; 1760: HAY, Jun 2, CG, Oct 11; 1762: CG,
  Oct 25, 28, Nov 1, 3, 29, 30; 1763: CG, May 18, Oct 7, 10, Nov 5, 23, Dec 27;
  1764: CG, Jan 16, 28, Feb 1, Mar 27, 29, Sep 19, Nov 1, 6, 29; 1765: CG, Jan
  7, 26, Feb 18, Apr 16, May 24, HAY, Aug 30, CG, Sep 18, 23, Oct 3, 8, 14, 23,
  Nov 13, Dec 10, 28; 1766: CG, Jan 31, Feb 6, Apr 1, 7, 14, May 6, 13, Sep 22,
  Oct 22, 30, 31, Nov 4, 7, 11, 18, 19, 21, 28, Dec 9; 1767: CG, Jan 10, 23,
  28, Mar 21, Apr 24, 25
Walker, Miss (actor), 1779: HAY, Dec 27
Walker, Mr and Mrs, 1758: DL, Sep 16
Walker, Mrs (actor), 1741: DL, Sep 15
Walker, Mrs (actor), 1775: HAY, Nov 20
Walker, Mrs (dancer), 1755: HAY, Sep 4, BF, 6
Walker, Sybilla, Mrs John (actor), 1762: CG, Sep 29, Oct 13, Dec 8, 18, 23;
  1763: CG, Sep 21, Oct 22, 26, Nov 3; 1764: CG, Feb 11, May 15, Sep 24, 26,
  Oct 16, 23; 1765: CG, Mar 18, Apr 17, Sep 30, Oct 4, 16, Dec 20; 1766: CG,
  Jan 9, Apr 15, Oct 18, 29, Nov 27; 1767: CG, May 19
Walker, T, 1704: LIF, Jun 24
--Wit of a Woman, The, 1704: LIF, Jun 24, Aug 17
Walker, Thomas (actor), 1715: LIF, Jun 2, DL, Dec 12; 1716: DL, Feb 3, May 21,
  Aug 9, Oct 16, Dec 17, 27; 1717: DL, Jan 16, 24, May 10, 11, 24, Aug 13, Oct
  25, Nov 19, Dec 6; 1718: DL, Jan 11, 29, Feb 19, Mar 8, 13, Apr 28, Jun 27,
  Jul 8, NONE, 30, DL, Aug 15, Sep 25, Oct 2, 25, Nov 4, 12; 1719: DL, Jan 28,
  Mar 7, Apr 24, Jun 9, 12, 26, Oct 7, 13, 22, 27, Nov 6, 11, 17; 1720: DL, Jan
  2, 5, 13, Feb 11, 17, Apr 2, 28, Jun 6, Sep 17, 24, Oct 5, Nov 4, 10, 29, Dec
  6, 8, 17; 1721: DL, Jan 19, Mar 2, 20, 23, Apr 26, Jun 27, Aug 4, BFLGB, 24,
  SF, Sep 8, LIF, 23, 29, Oct 3, 5, 7, 12, 14, 17, 20, 28, Nov 4, 9, 11, 13,
  16, 18, 25, 29, Dec 1, 2, 11, 12, 18; 1722: LIF, Jan 13, Feb 2, 13, Mar 15,
  31, Apr 3, 6, 13, Jun 13, Aug 1, Sep 29, Oct 1, 2, 4, 6, 11, 12, 13, 16, 18,
  20, 22, 23, 24, 26, 29, 31, Nov 1, 3, 5, 7, 8, 12, 16, 17, 22, 29, Dec 1, 7,
  10, 14, 15, 21; 1723: LIF, Jan 11, Feb 9, 15, 22, Mar 30, Apr 18, 23, May 3,
  4, Sep 28, 30, Oct 2, 4, 7, 10, 14, 18, 22, 25, 29, 31, Nov 4, 12, 14, 21,
  26, 28, Dec 2, 7; 1724: LIF, Feb 24, Mar 16, 19, 23, 26, 28, Apr 14, 22, 29,
  May 19, 20, 27, Jun 3, 23, Jul 3, 21, 31, Aug 11, Sep 23, 28, Oct 7, 12, 14,
  22, 23, 27, 30, Nov 4, 12, 13, 20, 24, 25, 26; 1725: LIF, Jan 4, 11, 16, 19,
  Feb 27, Mar 11, 13, 29, 31, Apr 5, 7, 14, 23, May 19, 20, Sep 24, 29, Oct 1,
  4, 11, 13, 15, 16, 19, 23, 26, 28, Nov 2, 4, 6, 9, 11, 12, 17, 18, 23, 24,
  29, Dec 2, 3, 6, 7, 8, 15, 16; 1726: LIF, Jan 7, Feb 19, Mar 19, 21, 24, Apr
  11, 22, May 4, 11, 12, Sep 12, 14, 19, 21, 26, 28, Oct 3, 12, 17, 19, 24, Nov
  4, 8, 10, 11, 14, 18, Dec 14; 1727: LIF, Jan 4, 9, 16, Apr 5, 7, 10, 17, 19,
  May 2, 4, 9, 19, Sep 11, 13, 15, 18, 25, 27, Oct 2, 9, 17, 19, 21, 31, Nov 1,
  4, 17, Dec 11, 14, 16; 1728: LIF, Jan 8, 29, Mar 9, 21, 25, 28, Apr 1, 4, 6,
  24, 26, 29, 30, May 2, 11, 15, 18, 23, 29, Sep 16, 18, 30, Oct 1, 7, 21, 23,
  Nov 1, 4, 11, 19, 20, Dec 7, 31; 1729: LIF, Jan 16, Feb 6, 10, 22, Mar 3, 4,
  10, 24, Apr 10, 11, 15, 16, 17, 19, 24, 29, 30, May 1, 3, Sep 12, 17, 19, 22,
  24, 26, 29, Oct 3, 6, 8, 10, 13, 20, 22, 29, 30, 31, Nov 4, 7, 8, 13, 14, 25,
  Dec 3, 15, 27; 1730: LIF, Mar 31, Apr 20, 24, 30, May 6, 7, 11, 18, 20, 23,
  25, Jun 1, Sep 16, 18, 21, 23, Oct 5, 7, 12, 14, 19, 23, 26, 27, 30, 31, Nov

2, 3, 4, 10, 13, 23, Dec 3, 4; <u>1731</u>: LIF, Jan 4, 9, 13, 20, 21, Feb 3, 27,
Mar 15, Apr 1, 3, 26, May 1, 5, 6, 10, 20, 21, 25, Jun 2, Sep 17, 20, 22, 27,
29, Oct 6, 11, 18, 20, 25, 27, Nov 4, 8, 12, 17, 25, Dec 1, 3, 6, 9, 11;
<u>1732</u>: LIF, Jan 7, 10, 18, 19, 26, Feb 15, HAY, 16, LIF, 21, 28, HAY, Mar 8,
LIF, 20, 21, 23, 25, 30, Apr 10, 13, 24, 26, 27, 29, May 1, 9, CG/LIF, Sep
22, LIF/CG, 25, 27, 29, Oct 2, 4, 9, 11, LIF, 18, LIF/CG, 20, 23, 27, 30, Nov
3, 4, 7, 8, 9, 11, 13, 14, 17, 18, 22, Dec 4, 14, 15, CG/LIF, 16; <u>1733</u>: CG,
Feb 8, LIF/CG, 10, CG, Mar 27, LIF/CG, 30, Apr 2, CG, 4, CG/LIF, 9, LIF/CG,
10, 11, 12, 13, 17, CG, May 1, 2, LIF/CG, 7, 8, CG/LIF, 28, LIF/CG, Jun 1,
CG, 26, Jul 6, 31, Aug 2, 20, Sep 15, 17, 22, 25, 27, Oct 2, 4, 9, 11, 13,
16, 18, 19, 20, 23, 25, 26, 27, 29, Nov 3, 5, 8, 9, 14, 16, 19, 26, 28, 30,
Dec 3, 4, 8, 15, 17, 20, 31; <u>1734</u>: CG, Jan 9, 18, 23, Feb 14, Mar 18, 28, Apr
6, 18, May 13, 17, CG/LIF, Sep 18, 20, 23, 25, 27, Oct 7, 9, 11, 14, 19, 25,
29, Nov 1, 4, 7, 11, 14, 21, 25, 28, Dec 5, 26; <u>1735</u>: CG/LIF, Jan 17, 23, 31,
Feb 3, 4, 10, 11, LIF, 12, CG/LIF, 13, 15, LIF, Mar 3, CG/LIF, 13, 15, SOU,
Apr 7, CG/LIF, 9, 10, 17, LIF, 19, CG/LIF, 21, CG, 25, 28, CG/LIF, May 1, 2,
5, 13, 15, 20, LIF, 21, CG/LIF, 27, Jun 11, LIF, Jul 11, 16, 23, Aug 1, 6,
22, 29, CG, Sep 12, 16, 19, 26, 29, Oct 1, 3, 8, 10, 13, 15, 17, 20, 22, 24,
25, 29, 31, Nov 6, 7, 8, 10, 15, 22, 28, Dec 15, 27; <u>1736</u>: CG, Jan 8, 10, Feb
10, 26, Mar 9, 15, 18, 20, 22, 27, 29, LIF, Apr 2, CG, 3, 13, YB, 26, CG, 26,
29, May 1, 3, LIF, 5, CG, 17, 20, Jun 14, Sep 15, 22, 24, 27, Oct 1, 4, 6, 8,
11, 13, LIF, 18, CG, 20, 22, 25, 29, Nov 1, 3, 4, 8, 15, 22, 26, 29, Dec 29;
<u>1737</u>: CG, Jan 10, 13, 17, 21, 25, Feb 3, 7, 14, 15, 24, 26, Mar 14, 15, 31,
Apr 11, 14, 15, 28, May 3, DL, 27, CG, 31, Sep 16, 21, 23, 26, 28, Oct 5, 10,
12, 14, 17, 19, 21, 22, 24, 27, 28, 29, Nov 1, 4, 14, 15, 17, 18, 19; <u>1738</u>:
CG, Jan 3, 6, 17, 26, 31, Feb 6, 23, Mar 13, 18, 20, Apr 8, 10, 20, May 18,
Jul 21, Oct 21, 23, 24, 26, 28, 30, Nov 6, 7, 11, 17, 18, 23, 24, 27, 28, 29,
30, Dec 5, 7, 12, 15; <u>1739</u>: CG, Jan 15, 22, 23, Feb 20, Mar 3, Apr 5, 24, 28,
May 1, 2, 7, 17, 21, DL, 25, CG, Aug 2, 10, DL, Sep 14; <u>1740</u>: DL, May 17, GF,
Oct 18, 20, 22, 23, DL, 27, GF, 27, Nov 3, 4, 12, 17, 18, 20, 24, 26, 28, Dec
1, 2, 4, 6, 8, 10, 12, 31; <u>1741</u>: GF, Jan 15, 20, 27, 28, Feb 9, 10, Mar 12,
19, Apr 9, May 6; <u>1742</u>: GF, May 27
Walker, Thomas (actor, singer), <u>1790</u>: DL, Oct 26; <u>1791</u>: DLKING'S, Nov 5; <u>1792</u>:
DLKING'S, Mar 19, DL, Nov 21; <u>1793</u>: HAY, Jul 20, Aug 3, 12, 16, Sep 19, Oct
10, Nov 19; <u>1794</u>: DL, May 16, 22, CG, Jun 17, HAY, Jul 17, 18, 21, 24, Aug
27, DL, Oct 27, Dec 20; <u>1795</u>: DL, Jan 19, HAY, Jun 13, 20, Jul 31, DL, Oct
30, Nov 11, Dec 10; <u>1796</u>: DL, Jan 8, Apr 30, May 4, HAY, Jul 15, Aug 29, DL,
Sep 29, Oct 19, Dec 3; <u>1797</u>: DL, Jan 7, HAY, 23, DL, Feb 9, 10, HAY, Jun 23,
Jul 3, Aug 14, 24, 31, DL, Nov 8; <u>1798</u>: HAY, Jan 15, DL, 16, Feb 1, HAY, Jul
21, Aug 11, DL, Oct 6, Nov 14, Dec 4, 17, 29, 31; <u>1799</u>: HAY, Jan 24; <u>1800</u>:
CG, Jun 16
Walker, Thomas (author), <u>1728</u>: BFLHS, Aug 24; <u>1730</u>: GF, Feb 24; <u>1744</u>: NONE, Jun
5
--Fatal Villainy, The, <u>1730</u>: GF, Feb 24, 26, 28
--Quaker's Opera, The; or, The Escapes of Jack Sheppard (ballad opera), <u>1728</u>:
BFLHS, Aug 24, SFLHS, Sep 6, HAY, Oct 31, Nov 1, 5, 6
Walker, William (actor), <u>1768</u>: HAY, Jun 23, Jul 27, Aug 24, Dec 19; <u>1770</u>: HAY,
Mar 19, CG, May 19, 22; <u>1771</u>: HAY, Jan 7, CG, May 27, Nov 29; <u>1772</u>: CG, Feb
19, May 29, HAY, Aug 10, Sep 21; <u>1773</u>: CG, May 28; <u>1774</u>: CG, May 24, HAY, Jun
8, Aug 29, Sep 21; <u>1775</u>: HAY, Feb 20, May 15, 17, CG, 27, HAY, 29, Jun 5, Aug
16, Nov 20; <u>1776</u>: CG, May 22, HAY, Jun 14, Jul 10, Oct 7; <u>1777</u>: CG, May 23,
HAY, Jun 6, Aug 9, Oct 13; <u>1778</u>: CG, May 21, HAY, 21, Jun 8, Aug 27; <u>1779</u>:
CG, May 15, HAY, Aug 13, 28; <u>1780</u>: CG, May 24, HAY, Jun 6, Sep 11; <u>1781</u>: CG,
May 25, HAY, Jul 9, Aug 8; <u>1782</u>: CG, May 28, HAY, Jun 3, Sep 21; <u>1783</u>: CG,
May 31, HAY, Jun 5; <u>1784</u>: HAY, Feb 9, CG, May 22; <u>1785</u>: HAY, Aug 6; <u>1786</u>: CG,
Jun 2; <u>1787</u>: CG, May 30; <u>1788</u>: CG, Jun 4; <u>1789</u>: CG, Jun 5; <u>1790</u>: CG, May 29;
<u>1791</u>: CG, Jun 2, HAY, Sep 26, Dec 12; <u>1792</u>: CG, May 25, DLKING'S, Jun 13,
HAY, Oct 22, Dec 26
Walker, William, <u>1698</u>: DL, May 0; <u>1703</u>: LIF, Nov 1; <u>1747</u>: DL, Mar 30
--Marry or Do Worse; or, No Wit Like a Woman's, <u>1703</u>: LIF, Nov 1; <u>1747</u>: DL, Mar
30
--Victorious Love, <u>1698</u>: DL, May 0
Walker's Booth, <u>1722</u>: SFW, Sep 5, SOU, 25
Walking Statue, The. See Hill, Aaron.
Wall (house servant), <u>1797</u>: CG, Jun 2; <u>1798</u>: CG, May 29; <u>1799</u>: CG, Jun 8; <u>1800</u>:
CG, Jun 4
Wall, J (actor), <u>1671</u>: NONE, Sep 0
Wall, Mrs (actor), <u>1671</u>: NONE, Sep 0
Wall, Mrs (dancer), <u>1723</u>: LIF, Oct 7, 16, Nov 2, 8, 19, 22, Dec 3, 9, 11, 12,
16, 20; <u>1724</u>: LIF, Jan 3, 4, Mar 23, 28, Apr 6, 7, 8, 10, 21, 22, 23, 27, 28,
May 2, 4, 5, 8, 12, 13, 15, 16, 18, 19, 20, 22, 25, 26, 27, 28, 29, Jun 1, 3,
Sep 30, Oct 5, 9, 12, 14, 16, 23, 30, Nov 3, 10, 11, 13, 18, 27; <u>1725</u>: LIF,

Jan 4, 18, 21, Mar 11, 13, 18, 29, 31, Apr 7, 14, 15, 17, 20, 22, 23, 26, 28,
May 1, 5, 6, 7, 10, 12, 14, 17, 18, 19, 20, 21, 22, 24, 27, Sep 29, Oct 1, 4,
13, 19, 21, 22, Nov 3, 8, 9, 11, 12, 13, 18, 22, 24, 29, 30, Dec 8; 1726:
LIF, Jan 3, 14, Mar 21, Apr 18, 19, 20, 21, 22, 30, May 14, 16, 17, 19, 23,
26, 30, Oct 5; 1727: LIF, May 23
Wall, Mrs (singer), 1797: HAY, Jun 23, Aug 24
Wall, William (actor), 1671: NONE, Sep 0
Wallace, Eglantine, Lady, 1788: CG, Apr 8
--Ton, The; or, Follies of Fashion, 1788: CG, Apr 8, 10, 12
Wallace, Master (actor), 1755: DL, Apr 28; 1756: DL, May 5; 1760: DL, May 15
Wallace, Thomas Wogan (actor), 1778: HAY, Feb 9
Wallaker (actor), 1799: WRSG, May 17
Waller (actor), 1707: DL, Oct 18, 23, 25
Waller (actor), 1765: HAY, Jul 8, 15, 31, Aug 21
Waller (bookseller), 1746: CG, Jan 24
Waller (hosier), 1766: DL, Dec 26; 1767: DL, Feb 6; 1771: DL, Dec 12; 1772: DL,
Jun 10, Dec 8; 1773: DL, Nov 19; 1774: DL, Jan 21; 1775: DL, Dec 18; 1776:
DL, Jun 10
Waller (house servant), 1795: CG, Jun 17
Waller and Co (hosiers), 1773: DL, Jun 2; 1774: DL, Jun 2, Nov 18; 1775: DL,
May 27; 1776: DL, Jan 26; 1777: DL, Oct 24
Waller, Edmund, 1663: VERE, Mar 0; 1676: DL, Dec 11; 1755: DL, Feb 3
--Maid's Tragedy Altered, The, 1689: NONE, Sep 0
--Pompey, 1663: NONE, May 0, LIF, Aug 0; 1664: ATCOURT, Jan 0, LIF, Mar 8,
ATCOURT, Jul 14; 1672: DG, Jan 15, Mar 28
Wallingford House, 1664: BRIDGES, Sep 14
Wallington, Ben (music patron), 1672: WF, Dec 30
Wallis (actor), 1736: HAY, Feb 19, Mar 5, Apr 29, May 3, Aug 2, BFHC, 23; 1737:
HAY, Mar 7; 1740: GF, Oct 22, 23, 25, 29, 30, 31, Nov 3, 6, 19, 22, 28; 1741:
TC, Aug 4, BFLW, 22, BFH, 22, SF, Sep 14; 1742: BFPY, Aug 25
Wallis (actor), 1763: HAY, Sep 5, 7; 1776: DL, Jun 5
Wallis (dancer), 1762: DL, May 20; 1767: DL, Jan 24; 1771: DL, Nov 11; 1772:
DL, Jan 13, Nov 27; 1774: DL, Apr 11; 1775: DL, Feb 17, Oct 27; 1776: DL, Jan
25, Oct 15
Wallis (renter), 1750: DL, Feb 12
Wallis and Parker (bankers), 1778: KING'S, Nov 24
Wallis, Albany (attorney), 1776: DL, Oct 15
Wallis, Elizabeth (actor), 1795: CG, Apr 22
Wallis, Fielding (prologuist), 1789: CG, Jan 10
Wallis, J (publisher), 1795: HAY, Aug 29; 1796: DL, May 13
Wallis, Mrs (dresser), 1748: CG, Mar 29; 1760: CG, Sep 22
Wallis, Tryphosa Jane (actor), 1789: CG, Jan 10, 21, Feb 11, 19; 1794: CG, Oct
7, 14, 20, 30, Nov 8, 12, 22, Dec 6, 27; 1795: CG, Jan 19, 31, Feb 21, Mar
16, 19, Apr 6, 22, 23, 24, May 1, 2, 29, Jun 3, Sep 18, 21, 25, 28, Oct 14,
15, 23, 30, Nov 4, 7, 27, Dec 7, 22, 23; 1796: CG, Jan 23, Mar 19, 29, 30,
31, Apr 20, 26, May 6, DL, 25, CG, Sep 16, 19, 21, Oct 6, 10, 29, Nov 21, 24,
25, Dec 29; 1797: CG, Jan 5, 10, Feb 20, 24, 25, 27, Mar 4, 6, 16, Apr 8, 26,
May 6, 16, 17, 22, 24, Jun 7
Walloons, The. See Cumberland, Richard.
Walmesley, Gilbert (correspondent), 1746: CG, Nov 6
Walmisley, Thomas Forbes (singer), 1796: CG, Feb 17, 19
Walmsley, Thomas (scene painter), 1791: CG, Dec 21; 1792: CG, Dec 1, 20; 1793:
CG, Mar 11, Oct 2, Dec 19; 1794: CG, Feb 22, Sep 22, Nov 17, Dec 26; 1795:
KING'S, Mar 21, CG, Apr 6; 1798: CG, May 28
Walpole, Charlotte (actor), 1777: DL, Oct 2, 7, 14, Nov 11, 17, 19, Dec 15;
1778: DL, May 2, Sep 19, Oct 6, 15; 1779: DL, Jan 19, Mar 23, Apr 5, 16, 19
Walpole, Horace, 1736: GF, Jan 3, CG, Jun 9, Oct 1; 1741: KING'S, Oct 31, Nov
10, Dec 22; 1742: DL, May 6, KING'S, 25; 1743: CG, Feb 23, KING'S, Apr 19,
Aug 14; 1745: DL, Mar 28; 1746: DL, Oct 4, CG, Nov 4, DL, Dec 5; 1748: DL,
Feb 16, 25; 1751: DL, Feb 12; 1752: CT/HAY, May 5; 1755: DL, Feb 3; 1760: DL,
Nov 21, 24; 1761: DL, Mar 7, Jun 18, Jul 27; 1769: DL, Apr 24; 1773: CG, Mar
19; 1775: DL, Feb 17, CG, Mar 18; 1776: CG, Dec 6; 1777: DL, May 8, Dec 18;
1778: HAY, Jun 10; 1779: DL, Dec 2; 1780: DL, May 24, KING'S, Dec 16; 1781:
KING'S, Feb 22, CG, Nov 17; 1782: DL, Oct 28; 1786: DL, Dec 14; 1791: PAN,
Feb 17, KING'S, Mar 29; 1793: HAY, Dec 2; 1797: DL, Jan 20
--Nature Will Prevail (interlude), 1778: HAY, Jun 10, 15, 19, 22, Jul 9, 10,
Aug 22; 1779: HAY, May 31, Jun 7, Jul 2, 5, 8; 1780: HAY, Jun 2, 3, 12; 1782:
HAY, Jun 11, Sep 7, 9, 12; 1783: HAY, Jun 6, 23, Jul 1; 1784: HAY, Jun 22;
1785: HAY, Jun 15, Jul 9, Aug 2; 1786: HAY, Aug 12, Sep 6; 1788: DL, May 7
Walpole, Lady, 1776: DL, Jun 10
Walpole, Lord, 1776: DL, Jun 10
Walpole, Sir Robert, 1733: HAY, Mar 22; 1737: HAY, Apr 18

Walsh (actor), 1736: CG, Feb 19
Walsh, J (music publisher), 1748: DL, Mar 29; 1749: CG, Feb 28, Mar 31; 1752:
    CG, Feb 14; 1755: DL, Mar 14; 1756: DL, Feb 11
Walsh, John (renter), 1758: CG, Feb 23
Walsh, William (author), 1690: DLORDG, Nov 0; 1691: NONE, Aug 13; 1693: DL, Apr
    0, NONE, May 9, Dec 12; 1699: DLORLIF, Feb 20; 1704: LIF, Mar 30
--Gordian Knot Untied, The, 1690: DLORDG, Nov 0, DL, 0
Walsh, William (composer), 1800: CG, Jun 6
Walsh's Music Shop, 1744: DL, Apr 6, KING'S, Nov 3; 1745: DT, Mar 14; 1746:
    HIC, Mar 10; 1749: DL, Mar 16; 1750: DL, Mar 26; 1751: DL, Apr 12; 1754: DL,
    Mar 30
Walter, Elizabeth, Mrs Walter (actor), 1742: CG, Dec 22, 27; 1743: CG, Feb 17,
    22, Mar 15, Oct 5, 10, 29, Nov 2, 19, 21, Dec 19
Walter, Master (actor), 1798: DL, Jun 5
Walter, Mrs (dancer), 1725: DL, Feb 22, Mar 31, Apr 16, 19, 30, May 4, 6, Sep
    25, Oct 7, Nov 19, Dec 6, 16; 1726: DL, Jan 25, Feb 11, Mar 21, May 13, 16,
    18, 19, 23, 25, Oct 1, 27, Nov 2, 15, 23, 30, Dec 7, 14, 17, 30; 1727: DL,
    Feb 10, 18, 27, Mar 23, Apr 12, 17, 18, 20, 28, 29, May 2, 17, 24, 26, Sep
    26, Oct 5, 6, 7, 12, 19, Nov 1, 14, 21; 1728: DL, Mar 16, 19, 28, 30, Apr 30,
    May 1, 6, 23, Jun 13, Sep 12, Oct 10, 18, 30, Nov 15; 1729: DL, Mar 15, 22,
    May 6, 8, 14, 26, Nov 3; 1730: DL, Apr 13, 14, 23, 27, 29, 30, May 2, 4, 6,
    11, 15, 18, 19, 27, Sep 15, 17, 24, Oct 8, 10, 22, 28, Nov 19, Dec 3, 4;
    1731: DL, Jan 23, Mar 15, 25, Apr 1, 5, 8, 21, 22, 26, 27, 29, May 3, 5, 6,
    7, 10, 17, 19, 31, Jun 7, 11, Jul 13, Sep 23, Oct 16, 26, Nov 6, 11, 22, 25,
    Dec 2, 15, 28; 1732: DL, Feb 2, 11, 22, Mar 4, 16, 21, 30, Apr 17, 18, 21,
    22, 26, 27, 28, 29, May 1, 2, 3, 6, 8, 12, 29, Jun 6, 9, 23, 28, Jul 4, 7,
    Aug 1, 4, 11, 15, 17, 19, 22, Sep 23, Oct 12, 14, 17, 19, 21, 26, Nov 7, 8,
    10, 14, 17, 18, 20, Dec 11, 14, 18, 22, 26; 1733: DL, Jan 11, 23, 25, 31, Feb
    2, 12, 22, Mar 5, 8, 15, 26, 28, 29, 31, Apr 4, 16, 30, May 1, 5, 7, 9, 18,
    Sep 26, Oct 10, 12, 17, 19, 24, 31, Nov 2, 13, 23, 26, Dec 5, 7, 11; 1734:
    DL, Jan 22, Feb 4, 13, Mar 7, DL/LIF, 11, DL/HAY, 12, 16, 18, 19, 23, 25, 26,
    28, 30, DL/LIF, Apr 1, DL/HAY, 1, LIF, 15, DL, 15, 22, 25, DL/HAY, 26, 27,
    DL, 29, DL/HAY, May 1, DL/LIF, 3, DL/HAY, 3, 8, DL, 13, 15, DL/HAY, 22, 23,
    LIF, 29, DL, Sep 7, 10, 19, 24, 26, Oct 3, 8, 9, 10, 21, 22, 25, 28, Nov 1,
    7, 15, 16, 22, Dec 9, 11, 17, 19, 21, 26, 28, 31; 1735: DL, Jan 1, 11, 16,
    17, 18, 21, 23, 25, 28, Feb 3, 4, 5, 13, 14, 15, 17, 18, 22, 27, Mar 3, 10,
    13, 22, 25, 27, Apr 7, 11, 18, 25, 26, 28, 29, May 6, 7, 8, 9, 13, 14, 20,
    22, 23, 29, 30, Jun 3, 5, 11, Sep 1, 25, Oct 1, 4, 7, 22, 27, 31, Nov 3, 6,
    12, 15, 17, 20, 22, 25, 28, Dec 2, 4, 6, 10, 12, 16, 17, 18, 26, 27, 31;
    1736: DL, Jan 3, 5, 6, 7, 9, 12, Feb 2, 4, 11, 12, 13, 14, 17, 18, 21, 24,
    25, 27, 28, Mar 11, 20, 22, 23, 25, 27, 29, Apr 1, 5, 6, 8, 10, 12, 13, 15,
    16, 17, 26, 27, 28, 29, 30, May 4, 6, 7, 11, 14, 18, 20, 21, 22, 25, 27, 28,
    Jun 2, 23, Aug 26, 31, Sep 7, 11, 16, Oct 2, 5, 12, 15, 16, 18, 19, 21, 22,
    23, 26, 28, 29, 30, Nov 1, 2, 3, 5, 6, 8, 9, 10, 11, 12, 15, 17, 20, 23, Dec
    9, 10, 17, 22, 31; 1737: DL, Jan 5, Feb 10, 18, Mar 2, 4, 5, 7, 15, 19, 21,
    Apr 13, 19, 26, 30, May 2, 3, 4, 5, 6, 7, 11, 14, 16, 18, 20, 24, 25, 26, 27,
    30, 31, Oct 22, Nov 10; 1738: DL, Jan 19, 20, 24, 28, Feb 1, 6, 20, 21, 25,
    28, Mar 2, 4, 9, 13, 14, 16, 20, 21, 23, Apr 11, 17, 21, 22, 24, 26, 27, 29,
    May 1, 2, 3, 5, 6, 8, 9, 10, 12, 16, 19, Oct 10, 21, 30, Nov 8, 24, 27, 29,
    Dec 2, 5, 7, 11, 12, 14, 15, 16, 28, 30; 1739: DL, Jan 2, 3, 4, 6, 13, 16,
    17, 20, 24, Feb 5, 7, Apr 5, 9, 10, 12, 14, 24, 25, 26, 28, May 2, 3, 5, 7,
    9, 10, 15, Sep 6, 8, 13, 26, Oct 10, 15, 19, 26, Nov 1, 20, 22, 28, Dec 6,
    26; 1740: DL, Jan 5, 15, Feb 13, Mar 17, Apr 8, 11, 29, May 7, 8, 15, 22, Oct
    9, 13, 14, 15, 16, 17, 23, 27, 31, Nov 24, 28, Dec 4, 10, 13, 19, 26; 1741:
    DL, Jan 20, 26, Feb 2, Mar 17, May 1, 7, 12, Oct 12, 15, 17, 19, 21, 27, Nov
    11, 28, Dec 14, 18; 1742: DL, Jan 6, Feb 24, Mar 13, 22, Apr 26; 1743: DL,
    Feb 4, 11, May 2, 4, 14, Oct 13, 15, Nov 8, 10, 19, 23, 26; 1744: DL, Jan 19,
    Feb 1, 3, Apr 9, May 1, 5
Walter, William, 1789: CG, Feb 24
--Hide and Seek (farce), 1789: CG, Feb 20, 24, 26, Mar 2, 5, 9, 12
Walters (actor), 1756: BFSI, Sep 3; 1769: CG, May 20; 1770: CG, May 18, 23, Dec
    29; 1771: CG, Jan 1, Feb 21, May 22, Oct 15; 1772: CG, Feb 25, May 29, HAY,
    Jun 8, 24, Sep 17; 1773: CG, May 28; 1775: CG, May 8, HAY, 22, Jun 7, Jul 31,
    Aug 16, 21, Sep 4, 16, CG, Oct 13, Nov 18; 1776: CG, May 11, HAY, 20, 22, 27,
    28, 31, Jul 10, Aug 2, Sep 16, 18, 20; 1777: CG, Apr 7, May 15, CHR, Jun 20,
    23, 25, 27, Jul 2, 21, 23
Walters, Miss (actor), 1778: HAY, Dec 28
Walters, Mrs (beneficiary), 1767: CG, May 18; 1769: CG, May 19
Walton (actor), 1785: HAY, Apr 26
Walton (doorkeeper), 1773: DL, May 28; 1775: DL, May 23; 1776: DL, May 18;
    1777: DL, May 30
Walton, Miss (actor), 1777: HAY, Sep 18, Oct 9; 1778: HAY, May 18, Aug 27, Sep

2; <u>1779</u>: HAY, Aug 18
Waltz, Gustavus (singer), <u>1732</u>: HAY, Mar 13, Apr 24, May 17, Nov 16; <u>1733</u>: LIF,
    Apr 16, HAY, Jun 4, DL, Nov 7, KING'S, 13, DL, 26, KING'S, Dec 4; <u>1734</u>:
    KING'S, Jan 26, DL, Feb 4, KING'S, Mar 13, DL/HAY, 21, KING'S, Apr 2, DL, 15,
    KING'S, 27, DL, 29, May 15, KING'S, 18, CG/LIF, Nov 9; <u>1735</u>: CG, Jan 8, HIC,
    Feb 21, CG, Mar 5, Apr 1, 16; <u>1736</u>: DL, Apr 22, CG, May 12; <u>1737</u>: HIC, Apr 7;
    <u>1739</u>: KING'S, Jan 16, CG, Mar 10, KING'S, Apr 4, CG, Dec 10; <u>1740</u>: CG, Feb
    12, Apr 30, Sep 19, Oct 10; <u>1741</u>: CG, Jan 5, Feb 24, May 15, Sep 30, Oct 24,
    Nov 7, Dec 28; <u>1743</u>: DL, Feb 2; <u>1744</u>: HAY, Jan 19, Apr 16; <u>1745</u>: DL, Jan 17,
    31, HAY, Feb 14, DL, 15, Apr 15; <u>1748</u>: HAY, Jan 29, Dec 9; <u>1749</u>: CG, Oct 12,
    Nov 23; <u>1750</u>: CG, Oct 29, Nov 8; <u>1751</u>: CG, Apr 20, May 3; <u>1754</u>: CHAPEL, May
    15; <u>1758</u>: CHAPEL, Apr 27
Walwyn, B, <u>1781</u>: CG, Mar 24, Apr 20
--Chit Chat; or, The Penance of Polygamy (interlude), <u>1781</u>: CG, Apr 20, May 2,
    9
Wamsley, Mrs, Music Shop, <u>1746</u>: HIC, Mar 10
Wanby, Nathaniel, <u>1667</u>: BRIDGES, Apr 16
Wandering Gipsy (song), <u>1793</u>: CG, May 1; see also Gipsy Ballad
Wandering Jew, The. See Franklin, Andrew.
Wandering Prince of Troy, The (play, anon), <u>1744</u>: MFMCB, May 1
Wandering Sailor (song), <u>1791</u>: CG, Apr 28; <u>1795</u>: CG, May 27
Wandering Tar (song), <u>1794</u>: CG, May 9
Wandesford, Osborne Sidney, <u>1730</u>: HAY, Jan 21
--Fatal Love; or, The Degenerate Brother, <u>1730</u>: HAY, Jan 21, 22, Feb 2
Wane, Mrs (actor), <u>1739</u>: DL, Nov 3
Wansworth, <u>1728</u>: MDS, Apr 3
Wanton Breezes (song), <u>1745</u>: CG, Mar 14
Wanton God who Pierces Hearts (song), <u>1771</u>: MARLY, Aug 15, 27, 29, Sep 12;
    <u>1773</u>: CG, Mar 27; <u>1774</u>: MARLY, Sep 7; <u>1775</u>: HAY, Feb 16; <u>1782</u>: CG, Feb 26
Wanton Jesuit, The; or, Innocence Seduced (ballad opera, anon), <u>1732</u>: HAY, Mar
    17
Wanton Maid, The; or, Lover Outwitted (farce, anon), <u>1743</u>: BFGA, Aug 23
Wanton Trick, The; or, All Alive and Merry (play, anon), <u>1743</u>: TCY, Aug 4
Wanton Widow, The; or, The Fool in Fashion (play, anon), <u>1752</u>: SFP, Sep 21, 22
Waple, John (notary), <u>1749</u>: HAY, Nov 17
Wapping Landlady; or, Jack in Distress (dance), <u>1767</u>: CG, Apr 27, 28, May 2, 4,
    5, 6, 7, 11, 12, 13, 14, 18, 19, 20, 21, 22, 25, 26, 28; <u>1768</u>: CG, Apr 16,
    19, 23, 26, 27, May 3, 6, 7, 10, 11, 25; <u>1769</u>: CG, Apr 8, 11, 12, 13, 19, 21,
    24, 28, May 3; <u>1770</u>: CG, Apr 20, 24, 27, May 12, 25; <u>1771</u>: CG, Apr 12, 22,
    May 1, 7, 8, 9, 11, 17, 28; <u>1772</u>: CG, Apr 24, 27, May 11, 16, 21; <u>1773</u>: CG,
    Apr 24, 28, May 3, 26; <u>1774</u>: CG, Apr 15, May 12, 18; <u>1776</u>: CHR, Oct 18; <u>1777</u>:
    DL, May 15; <u>1783</u>: HAY, Sep 17; <u>1785</u>: CG, May 18, HAMM, Jul 8, CG, Nov 2, 3,
    7; <u>1786</u>: CG, Apr 26, May 17, 23; <u>1787</u>: CG, Jan 31, Feb 9, Apr 17, May 23, 28;
    <u>1788</u>: CG, Apr 1, May 7, Jun 4; <u>1789</u>: CG, Apr 14, Jun 16; <u>1790</u>: CG, Apr 16,
    Dec 2, 4; <u>1791</u>: CG, Jan 27, Sep 12; <u>1792</u>: CG, Nov 6; <u>1793</u>: CG, May 30, Sep
    17; <u>1794</u>: CG, Jun 10, 12; <u>1795</u>: CG, Jun 10
Wapping, <u>1695</u>: LIF, Apr 30; <u>1728</u>: DL, Jan 6; <u>1748</u>: NTW, Nov 16; <u>1776</u>: HAY, Oct
    7; <u>1777</u>: HAY, Oct 13; <u>1782</u>: HAY, Mar 18; <u>1784</u>: HAY, Feb 9
War Dance (dance), <u>1720</u>: YB, Apr 1; <u>1730</u>: LIF, Apr 22; <u>1790</u>: DL, Jun 1
War, he sung, is Toil and Trouble (song), <u>1739</u>: CG, Apr 26, May 18; <u>1742</u>: DL,
    Mar 20, GF, Apr 22, DL, 28, 30; <u>1745</u>: CG, Apr 27; <u>1791</u>: CG, Mar 25; <u>1792</u>: CG,
    Mar 7; <u>1794</u>: CG, Mar 14
War Musick (song), <u>1697</u>: LW, Jul 21
War-Whoop Chorus (entertainment), <u>1794</u>: DL, Dec 22
Warboys (actor), <u>1770</u>: CG, Jan 19
Warburton (householder), <u>1784</u>: HAY, Jul 27
Warburton, Master (dancer), <u>1787</u>: DL, Jun 4
Warcup, Edmund (spectator), <u>1697</u>: LIF, Feb 22
Ward (actor), <u>1734</u>: JS, May 23, YB, Jul 8; <u>1736</u>: LIF, Mar 31; <u>1737</u>: HAY, Mar
    21, Apr 13, DL, May 21; <u>1741</u>: DL, Sep 19, Oct 9, 15, Nov 11, 16; <u>1742</u>: JS,
    Apr 7; <u>1746</u>: GF, Feb 27; <u>1748</u>: CG, Oct 7, 28, 29; <u>1753</u>: DL, May 1; <u>1754</u>: DL,
    May 4
Ward (actor), <u>1766</u>: DL, Nov 8; <u>1767</u>: CG, Nov 4; <u>1770</u>: HAY, Nov 16, Dec 19;
    <u>1772</u>: HAY, Jun 29, Aug 10; <u>1773</u>: HAY, May 31, Jun 18, Jul 28, Aug 4, 11, 27,
    Sep 3; <u>1774</u>: HAY, Sep 30; <u>1775</u>: HAY, Sep 19
Ward (actor), <u>1776</u>: CHR, Sep 25
Ward (musician), <u>1760</u>: CG, Sep 22
Ward (ticket deliverer), <u>1799</u>: CG, Jun 8
Ward of the Castle, The. See Burke, Mrs.
Ward, A (publisher), <u>1776</u>: CG, Dec 6
Ward, Henry, <u>1736</u>: LIF, Mar 31
--Happy Lovers, The; or, The Beau Metamorphosed, <u>1736</u>: LIF, Mar 31

--Vintner Tricked, The, 1769: HAY, Jun 7, 12, 19, Jul 5, 12, Aug 4; 1770: HAY,
   May 23, Jul 13, Sep 1, 20, 27; 1771: HAY, Jul 12; 1772: HAY, Jul 8
Ward, John (actor), 1722: LIF, Nov 17; 1723: LIF, Feb 22, May 14; 1724: LIF,
   Mar 19, May 20, SOU, Sep 24; 1725: LIF, May 12; 1726: LIF, May 25
Ward, John (spectator), 1661: VERE, Jun 14; 1662: LI, Jan 3, NONE, Sep 0
Ward, Margaretta Priscilla (actor), 1764: CG, Apr 2, May 7; 1765: CG, Mar 26;
   1766: CG, Apr 8, 25; 1767: CG, Oct 5, 26, 31, Nov 6, 17; 1768: CG, Feb 5, Apr
   13, May 30, Sep 30, Oct 4, 6, 14, 25, Nov 16, HAY, Dec 19; 1769: CG, Apr 10,
   21, 22, 24, 29, May 17, Sep 30, Nov 1, 29, Dec 2, 22; 1770: CG, Jan 15, Feb
   3, Oct 1, 13, 19, 27, Nov 23, 30; 1771: CG, Apr 15, Sep 23, 27, 30
Ward, Master (actor), 1749: DL, Dec 26
Ward, Miss (dancer), 1769: DL, Apr 25, May 16, 20; 1770: DL, May 4
Ward, Mrs (actor), 1725: LIF, Oct 4, 23, Nov 6, 11; 1728: SFFR, Sep 6, LIF, 23,
   HAY, Oct 8; 1729: HAY, Feb 25, Mar 5, 28, LIF, Apr 24, SOU, Sep 23, BLA, 30,
   HAY, Nov 15, 18
Ward, Mrs (actor, dancer, singer), 1792: HAY, Oct 22; 1798: CG, Feb 12, Oct 15,
   Dec 11; 1799: CG, Mar 25, Apr 13
Ward, Sarah, Mrs Henry (actor), 1748: CG, Oct 3, 10, 21, 25, 27, 28, Nov 4, DL,
   Dec 10; 1749: CG, Jan 28, Feb 4, 6, 7, Mar 4, 9, 14, 29, Apr 3, 6, 7, 19, 20,
   21, DL, Sep 16, Oct 13, 21, Dec 8, 9, 12; 1750: DL, Jan 6, Feb 7, 24, Mar 19,
   20, 26, Sep 13, 18, Oct 1, 16, 22, 23, 29, Nov 5, 8; 1751: DL, Jan 24, Mar
   11, 12, 19, Apr 30, May 10, 14, Sep 13, 19, 26, Oct 9, Nov 8, 29, Dec 14, 26;
   1752: DL, Feb 17, Mar 19, Apr 6; 1753: DL, Oct 30; 1759: CG, Oct 18, 30, Nov
   20, 23, Dec 5, 7, 8, 12, 15, 19, 21; 1760: CG, Jan 4, 15, 18, 31, Feb 7, Mar
   6, 20, 25, Apr 7, 8, May 9, 20, Sep 22, Oct 15, 18, Nov 22, 29, Dec 9, 11,
   16, 31; 1761: CG, Jan 28, Feb 16, Mar 3, 9, 31, Apr 21, May 20, Sep 9, 11,
   18, 21, 23, 26, 30, Oct 2, 7, 24, Dec 30; 1762: CG, Jan 28, Feb 22, Mar 15,
   20, 23, 25, Apr 19, 21, 24, May 14, Sep 20, Oct 6, 8, 9, 11, 12, 14, 25, Nov
   5, 8, 15, 16, 18, 29, 30, Dec 4; 1763: CG, Jan 28, Feb 14, Mar 19, Oct 3, 7,
   8, 10, 12, 17, 18, 20, 24, Nov 4, 10, 15, Dec 16, 26, 27; 1764: CG, Jan 9,
   17, 26, Feb 1, 11, 13, Mar 29, Apr 2, DL, May 4, CG, 7, 9, 11, 21, 26, Sep
   19, Oct 1, 8, 12, 15, 17, 22, 25, 30, Nov 1, 5, 6, 7, 8, 29; 1765: CG, Jan
   14, Mar 26, Apr 11, May 11, Sep 16, 18, 25, 30, Oct 3, 8, 9, 14, 23, 28, 30,
   31, Nov 28, Dec 10, 26; 1766: CG, Mar 17, Apr 8, 18, May 13, 16, Sep 26, Oct
   14, 30, 31, Nov 4, 8, 11, 18, 21, 28; 1767: CG, Sep 21, Oct 5, 26, 31, Nov 7,
   Dec 5; 1768: CG, Jan 9, Feb 13, Mar 17, Apr 13, Sep 22, Nov 9; 1769: CG, Jan
   2, 28, Feb 18, Mar 13, 28, 29, Apr 1, Sep 25, Oct 4, Nov 27; 1770: CG, Jan 6,
   Feb 21, Apr 24, Sep 26, Oct 10, Dec 3; 1771: CG, Jan 4, Sep 23, 27, 30
Ward, Sarah, Mrs Thomas Achurch (actor), 1776: CG, Nov 14, Dec 18, 26; 1777:
   CG, May 5, 6; 1780: DL, Oct 17, Nov 1, 13, 27; 1782: DL, Oct 1, 22, Nov 7, 8,
   12, 26; 1783: DL, Jan 10, Apr 21, 28, May 2, 5, Sep 20, 27, Nov 3, 4, 6, 14,
   20, 27, 28, Dec 19, 29; 1784: DL, Jan 12, 17, Apr 19, 26, May 10, 21, Sep 18,
   Nov 2, 5, 11, 15, 17, 22, 23, 25; 1785: DL, Jan 6, 20, 27, Mar 7, Apr 11, 25,
   27, May 3, 6, Sep 20, 22, Oct 18, 22, 31, Nov 3, 9, 18, Dec 1, 7, 19, 21, 26;
   1786: DL, Jan 5, May 6, 8, 25, Jun 1, Oct 19, 26, 27, 28, Nov 14, 18, 20, 22,
   29, Dec 11, 13, 19, 26; 1787: DL, Jan 11, 13, Feb 8, Apr 14, May 7, 14, 19,
   21, 23, 30, Sep 22, 25, 29, Oct 2, 13, 15, 24, 30, Nov 5, 16, Dec 6, 11, 14,
   26, 31; 1788: DL, Jan 2, 8, 21, Mar 29, May 5, 6, 12, 14, 22, Jun 11, Sep 13,
   16, 18, 20, 27, Oct 11, 14, 20, 23, Nov 5, 8, 11, 12, 17, 19, 21, 28, Dec 9,
   17; 1789: DL, Jan 1, 6, Feb 7, Mar 17, 21, May 1, 2, 27, Jun 2, Sep 12, 15,
   17, 26, Oct 1, 3, 8, 10, Nov 7, 30, Dec 14; 1790: DL, Jan 1, Feb 8, 10, Mar
   2, 8, 20, May 18, Sep 14, Oct 4, 7, 12, 14, 20, 21, Nov 5, 10, Dec 1, 8;
   1791: DL, Jan 17, Feb 23, Mar 21, 28, 31, Apr 27, May 10, 13, DLKING'S, Sep
   24, 27, Oct 4, 6, 20, 25, 27, 29, 31, Nov 4, 5, 8, 11, 14, 29, Dec 1, 6;
   1792: DLKING'S, Feb 7, 8, 14, 23, Mar 6, 13, 17, 31, Apr 16, 20, May 24, DL,
   Sep 15, 20, 25, 27, Oct 13, 16, 31, Nov 1, 5, 16, Dec 28; 1793: DL, Jan 4, 7,
   Feb 9, 12, 16, 23, 28, Mar 14, Apr 22, 25, 29, May 22, 23; 1794: DL, Dec 12
Ward, Sophia, Mrs Thomas (actor), 1774: MARLY, Jul 2, 14, Aug 11, 18, Sep 3
Ward, Thomas Achurch (actor), 1776: CG, Oct 7, Nov 11, 25, 28, 30, Dec 2, 6,
   21; 1783: DL, Oct 18; 1784: DL, Jan 27, Feb 10, Mar 29, May 10
Ward, Thomas Achurch and Sarah, 1777: CG, May 6; 1784: DL, May 10
Ward, William (pugilist), 1789: CG, Jan 27
Warde, Sir Patience (Lord Mayor), 1680: CITY, Oct 29
Wardour St, 1764: HAY, Nov 13; 1785: HAY, Jan 24; 1786: DL, May 25
Ware (actor), 1729: HAY, Mar 29, May 9, 26, 29, Jun 14, 17; 1733: DL, Oct 10;
   1736: LIF, Oct 9, 19, 28, Nov 4, 13, 18, 27; 1738: CG, Jun 27, Jul 7; 1741:
   BFH, Aug 22; 1743: BFYWR, Aug 23
Ware (actor), 1776: CHR, Sep 25, Oct 14
Ware (dancer), 1788: CG, May 12
Ware (spectator), 1760: CG, Feb 2
Ware, George (composer), 1793: CG, Dec 19
Ware, J (violinist), 1800: CG, Feb 28

Ware, Master (violoncellist), 1797: DL, May 18
Ware, Mrs (actor), 1733: DL, Sep 28; 1736: LIF, Nov 11, 13, Dec 7, 17; 1737:
    CG, Nov 9; 1738: CG, Jan 13, 25, Feb 13, 23, Mar 13, 18, 25, Apr 22, Sep 18,
    22, 27, Oct 2, Nov 9, 24, Dec 2, 5; 1739: CG, Jan 15, Feb 10, Mar 20, May 21,
    Sep 7, 10, 27, Oct 26, Dec 29; 1740: CG, Mar 11, 25, Nov 6; 1741: CG, Jan 2,
    15, 27, Feb 14, May 11, 12
Ware, William Henry (violinist), 1789: CG, Jun 12; 1791: CG, Mar 11; 1794: CG,
    Dec 26; 1796: CG, Feb 19, HAY, Mar 4, May 21; 1797: CG, Mar 3; 1798: CG, Feb
    23; 1799: CG, Feb 8; 1800: CG, Feb 28
Ware, William Henry and J (violinists), 1788: CG, May 28
Wargrave, 1791: CG, Dec 21
Waring, Mrs (beneficiary), 1732: HAY, Mar 23, May 10
Warneck, Mrs (house servant), 1777: CG, May 15
Warner (actor), 1734: MEG, Sep 30; 1739: WF, Aug 31; 1740: TC, Aug 4, BF/WF/SF,
    23; 1741: TC, Aug 4, BFLW, 22, SF, Sep 14; 1743: MF, May 9, BFYWR, Aug 23,
    SF, Sep 8; 1745: NWC, Dec 30; 1746: HIC, Mar 10, BFWF, Aug 25, SFW, Sep 8,
    NWC, Oct 20; 1748: BFLYY, Aug 24, SFLYYW, Sep 7, BHB, Oct 1; 1750: NWC, Apr
    16, SFYW, Sep 7; 1755: SFG, Sep 18
Warner (lobby keeper), 1748: DL, May 16, Sep 17; 1749: DL, May 11, 16
Warner (viola player), 1758: CHAPEL, Apr 27
Warner-Fawkes Booth, 1746: BFWF, Aug 25
Warner, Captain (composer), 1793: CG, Apr 4
Warner, Mrs (actor), 1740: TC, Aug 4, BF/WF/SF, 23; 1743: BFYWR, Aug 23; 1745:
    NWC, Dec 30; 1747: SF, Sep 16; 1752: CT/HAY, Mar 21
Warner's Booth, 1746: SFW, Sep 8; 1756: SFW, Sep 18, 20, SF, 21; 1757: SF, Sep
    17, 19, 20, 21, 22; 1758: SFW, Sep 18, 19, 20, 21; 1761: SFW, Sep 19, 21
Warnuck, Widow (ticket deliverer), 1776: CG, May 11
Warrell, A (actor), 1790: CG, Jun 1; 1791: CG, Jun 13
Warrell, Mrs (actor, singer), 1790: CG, Feb 18, Mar 18, 20, May 13, 24, Jun 1,
    3, Sep 13, Oct 6, 13, Nov 2, 3, 26, Dec 20; 1791: CG, Jan 12, Mar 7, May 24,
    Jun 4, 6
Warren (actor), 1722: HAY, Jun 28
Warren (actor), 1746: SFW, Sep 8
Warren (actor), 1759: CG, Dec 10, 11; 1761: CG, Oct 13; 1762: CG, Nov 1, 3
Warren, Ann, Mrs Thomas (actor), 1785: CG, Dec 10; 1786: CG, Feb 4, 10, 16, Mar
    4, 11, Apr 8, 19, May 3, 4, 6, 26
Warren, Bernard (auctioneer), 1738: GF, Jul 26
Warren, Miss (actor), 1747: DL, Jan 26
Warren, Miss (singer), 1737: LIF, Sep 7
Warren, Mrs (singer), 1727: LIF, Mar 11, 13, 20, Apr 7, May 3, 4, 8, 17, 18,
    Jun 7; 1728: LIF, Mar 27, 28, Apr 23, 24, 26, 30, May 2, 3, 8, 11, 13, 16,
    18, 29, 30, Jun 19, 25, Jul 2, 12, Aug 2, Sep 20, 30, Nov 23; 1729: LIF, Mar
    17, Apr 25
Warren, William (violinist), 1794: CG, Mar 7; 1795: CG, Feb 20
Warriner (boxkeeper), 1731: LIF, Jun 2; 1732: LIF, May 16; 1734: CG, May 10;
    1735: CG/LIF, May 22; 1736: CG, May 18; 1737: CG, May 12; 1738: CG, May 11
Warring (accountant), 1759: CG, Sep 28
Warrior's Song (song), 1736: GF, Apr 8
Warriors' Dance (dance), 1735: GF/HAY, Mar 28; 1780: CG, Apr 10; 1781: CG, Apr
    3, 25
Warriors' Dance, Grand (dance), 1736: HAY, Feb 20; 1795: CG, Dec 21; 1796: CG,
    Jan 4
Warwell (actor), 1732: HAY, Mar 10, 17; 1733: DL, Oct 10, Nov 13, Dec 5; 1734:
    DL, Feb 4, HAY, Apr 5, DL, 23, LIF, May 17
Warwell, Mrs (supernumerary), 1770: CG, Mar 22
Warwhick (ticket deliverer), 1794: CG, Jun 14; 1795: CG, Jun 17; 1796: CG, Jun
    4; 1797: CG, Jun 8; 1798: CG, Jun 5; 1799: CG, May 29; 1800: CG, Jun 7
Warwick St Coffee House, 1753: DL, Dec 21
Warwick St, 1777: DL, Apr 5; 1792: HAY, Feb 20
Warwick, Mrs (charwoman), 1760: CG, Sep 22
Warwick, Susan (actor), 1736: CG, Oct 4
Warwickshire Lads and Lasses (song), 1775: CG, Apr 4
Wary Widow, The. See Higden, Henry.
Was ever nymph like Rosamond (song), 1733: DL/HAY, Oct 6, 13, 27, HAY, Nov 19,
    DL/HAY, Dec 31; 1734: DL/HAY, Feb 4, Mar 30, Apr 6, GF, May 8, DL, 13, HAY,
    Jun 5, 28, Jul 31, Aug 16, 21, YB, 28, DL, Oct 25; 1735: GF, Mar 17, LIF, Jun
    19, GF/HAY, Aug 21; 1741: DL, Apr 8, 20, 24, 27, May 2, 4, 12, 15, 26, 27,
    Dec 8, 9, 12, 16; 1742: DL, Jan 28, 29, Feb 10, 11, 16, 18, Mar 20, 27, 29;
    1743: DL, Apr 8, 21; 1744: HAY, Oct 18
Wass (singer), 1752: CG, Feb 26, KING'S, Mar 24; 1753: KING'S, Apr 30; 1754:
    HAY, Feb 11, CHAPEL, May 15; 1757: SOHO, Feb 1; 1758: HAY, Feb 2, CHAPEL, Apr
    27; 1759: SOHO, Mar 1

Wasted with sighs, I sighed and pined (song), 1691: NONE, Sep 0
Wat Tyler and Jack Straw (droll, anon), 1730: BFPG, Aug 20, 31, Sep 1
Wat Tyler; or, The State Menders (droll, anon), 1733: DL, Jan 19
Watchman's Song (song), 1736: GF, Apr 8
Water Lane, 1742: CG, Mar 27
Water Music (music by Handel), 1722: SH, Feb 9, LIF, Apr 4; 1724: LIF, Mar 19,
    Apr 25; 1729: HIC, Apr 16; 1730: DL, May 13, LIF, 14; 1731: GF, Mar 23, LIF,
    May 24, GF, Jun 3, LIF, 7; 1732: GF, Mar 30, LIF, Apr 13, DL, May 3, GF, 9,
    11, LIF, 18, DL, Jul 7, HAY, 26; 1733: HAY, Feb 28, LIF/CG, Mar 30, HAY, Apr
    23, LIF/CG, 25, CG, May 1, 2, LIF/CG, 7, 8, 24, CG, Aug 9; 1734: DL/HAY, Feb
    4, DL/LIF, Mar 11, LIF, Apr 26, DL/HAY, May 1, CG, 14, 15; 1735: CG/LIF, Mar
    15, CG, May 8, CG/LIF, 9, 12, LIF, 21, CG/LIF, 27, HAY, Dec 13; 1736: MR, Feb
    11, CG, Mar 27, LIF, 31, CG, May 11, 17, DL, 22, CG, Jun 4, YB, Dec 1; 1737:
    DL, May 4, CG, 16; 1738: CG, Apr 8, May 3, DL, 17; 1739: CG, May 15, 25, Nov
    7; 1740: DL, Apr 14, 22, May 17, 21, 26; 1741: CG, Mar 10, GF, 12, DL, Apr
    20, CG, May 14, Nov 30; 1742: CG, Apr 22, GF, 22, 29, HAY, Jun 16; 1743: LIF,
    Mar 15; 1744: HAY, Feb 15; 1745: DL, May 13; 1746: DL, May 8; 1748: HAY, Dec
    9; 1750: HAY, Oct 18; 1751: HAY, Dec 30; 1752: CT/HAY, Jan 7; 1757: HAY, Aug
    11, 31, Sep 2, 8, 28; 1762: CG, Apr 23; 1763: CG, Nov 3; 1780: HAY, Jul 8;
    1797: CG, Mar 24, 31; 1798: CG, Mar 28; 1799: CG, Feb 20, Mar 13; 1800: CG,
    Mar 14
Water Parted from the Sea (song), 1762: CG, Apr 3; 1771: CG, Mar 16, MARLY, Aug
    3, 15, GROTTO, 24, Sep 3; 1783: HAY, Sep 9; 1794: CG, May 2, 9, 23
Waterer (tenant), 1776: DL, Jun 10
Waterer (ticket deliverer), 1796: DL, Jun 15; 1797: DL, Jun 13; 1798: DL, Jun
    16; 1799: DL, Jul 2; 1800: DL, Jun 14
Waterer, Yearley (taverner), 1772: DL, Sep 29
Waterhouse, Master (actor), 1792: HAY, Jul 25
Waterhouse, William (actor), 1790: HAY, Jun 26, Jul 16, Aug 6, 18, 19, 20, Sep
    4, Oct 13
Waterman, Sir George (Lord Mayor), 1671: CITY, Oct 30
Waterman, The. See Dibdin, Charles.
Waterman's Dance (dance), 1727: DL, May 22; 1729: DL, May 28, Oct 30; 1731: GF,
    Jun 2; 1737: DL, Apr 11; 1739: DL, Dec 26; 1747: DL, Dec 26; 1782: CG, May
    10; 1787: CG, May 19
Waterman's Song (song), 1735: GF, Apr 9, May 2, 5
Waters (actor), 1739: BFB, Aug 23; 1746: NWC, Sep 15; 1749: NWLS, Feb 27
Waters (actor), 1772: HAY, May 25, 27, Jun 22, Jul 6, Aug 10
Waters (house servant), 1743: LIF, Jun 3
Waters (singer), 1675: ATCOURT, Feb 15
Waters (singer), 1745: GF, Oct 28
Waters (ticket deliverer), 1795: DL, Jun 5
Waters, Miss M A (actor, singer), 1798: CG, Nov 12, Dec 13, 26; 1799: CG, Feb
    20, Mar 1, 2, 5, 6, 13, 15, 16, Apr 9, 19, May 10, 14, 24, Jun 5, Sep 30, Oct
    7, 24, Nov 14; 1800: CG, Jan 16, 18, Mar 4, May 17, 22
Waters, Mrs (actor), 1739: BFB, Aug 23
Watford (upholder), 1738: DL, May 9; 1739: DL, May 5
Wathen (actor), 1729: HAY, Jan 31, Feb 25, Mar 29, May 7, 26, 29, Jun 14, 17,
    26; 1730: HAY, Jun 23, BFR, Aug 22, Sep 4, SF, 14, HAY, Oct 21, 26, Nov 30,
    Dec 7; 1731: HAY, Jan 13, 14, 18, Feb 3, 26, Mar 5, 17, 24, May 12, 17
Wathen, George (actor), 1793: HAY, Aug 20; 1795: DL, Jan 26, Feb 2, HAY, Mar 4,
    DL, May 19, HAY, Jun 10, 11, 12, 16, 18, 27, Jul 1, 20, 22, Aug 3, 18, 21,
    29, Sep 2, DL, 26, Oct 6, 8, 15, 20, Nov 10, 23, Dec 30; 1796: DL, Jan 18,
    22, Feb 20, 25, Mar 19, 28, May 13, 17, 23, 26, 27, 30, Jun 1, 3, 6, 7, HAY,
    11, DL, 13, HAY, 13, 15, 16, 17, 20, 22, 25, 29, Jul 6, 7, 8, 9, 14, 15, 21,
    23, 26, Aug 10, 18, 23, Sep 1, 5, DL, Oct 3, 15, 17, 19, 27, 28, Nov 5, Dec
    27; 1797: DL, Jan 7, 10, 31, Feb 9, 16, May 12, 15, 22, 26, Jun 6, 7, HAY,
    12, 13, 15, 16, 17, 19, 20, 21, 23, 24, 26, Jul 3, 13, 31, Aug 1, 2, 3, 9,
    17, 21, 23, 24, Sep 11, DL, 19, 23, 28, 30, Oct 19, 27, Nov 2, 8, 13, 18, 20,
    28, Dec 14; 1798: DL, Jan 4, 16, 22, 23, Feb 20, Apr 25, May 7, 23, 24, Jun
    5, 6, 7, HAY, 12, DL, 12, HAY, 14, 15, DL, 16, HAY, 18, 20, 21, Jul 6, 14,
    17, 20, 21, 23, 30, Aug 3, 20, 23, Sep 7, DL, 22, 25, 29, Oct 6, 13, Nov 6,
    20, Dec 4, 19, 21; 1799: DL, Jan 19, Feb 9, Mar 2, Apr 8, 17, 18, 19, May 1,
    24, 27, HAY, Jun 15, 17, 19, DL, 19, HAY, 21, 24, DL, 24, HAY, 25, DL, 25,
    HAY, Jul 2, DL, 3, 4, HAY, 10, 11, 12, 19, 23, Aug 5, 13, 17, 20, 21, 24, 26,
    27, 28, Sep 2, 16, DL, 17, Oct 8, 22, 31, Nov 6, 16, Dec 7, 19; 1800: DL, Jan
    18, Apr 28, 29, May 10, 21, 23, Jun 2, 3, HAY, 14, 17, 19, Jul 5, 7, 26, Aug
    5, 7, 8, 12, 19, 23, 26
Watkins (actor), 1743: TCD/BFTD, Aug 4
Watkins (actor), 1760: DL, May 6, Dec 17; 1761: DL, May 8, Jul 27, Sep 14, Nov
    9; 1762: DL, Mar 6, May 17, 26, Sep 25, Oct 7, 15, Nov 3, 10, 23, Dec 22;
    1763: DL, Jan 3, Feb 3, May 31, Sep 22, Oct 8, 27, Nov 30, Dec 10; 1764: DL,

Jan 4, May 11, 17, Oct 15, 20, 22, Nov 13, 14; 1765: DL, Apr 13, Oct 5, Dec
12, 14, 23; 1766: DL, Jan 6, 24, Feb 22, Mar 10, Apr 12, 16, May 13, Sep 27,
Oct 17, 22, 28, Dec 2, 4, 19; 1767: DL, Jan 24, Apr 11, May 1, 25, Sep 17,
Dec 5, 7, 26; 1768: DL, Jan 14, 15, 23, Feb 6, 11, May 24, Sep 8, 20, 26, Oct
10, Nov 17, 18; 1770: DL, Mar 3, May 7, 16, Oct 27, Nov 20; 1771: DL, Apr 6,
HAY, 20, DL, May 10, 27, Nov 11; 1772: DL, Jan 15, Nov 20, Dec 26; 1773: DL,
Sep 25, Nov 25; 1774: DL, Feb 9, Apr 19, Oct 14; 1775: DL, Jan 2
Watkins (optician), 1751: CG, Nov 19
Watkins, Ann (actor, dancer), 1780: HAY, Nov 13; 1782: DL, May 14
Watkins, Miss (dancer), 1764: DL, May 17; 1766: DL, May 13; 1767: DL, May 25;
    1768: DL, May 24; 1772: DL, Oct 3; 1773: DL, Dec 16; 1775: DL, Nov 3
Watkins, Mrs Simson (beneficiary), 1771: DL, May 21
Watkinson (actor), 1799: OCH, May 15
Wats (actor), 1675: DL, Apr 30
Watson (actor), 1715: LIF, Sep 30, Oct 11, 22; 1719: CGR, Mar 20; 1720: DL, Dec
17; 1721: DL, May 24, Oct 10, Dec 7; 1722: DL, Jan 5, Apr 4, May 11, Sep 20,
Oct 9, Dec 4; 1723: DL, Jan 23, Feb 15, May 20, Oct 1, 28, Nov 8, Dec 5;
1724: DL, Apr 18, 28, May 16, Sep 17, Oct 24; 1725: DL, Jan 4, 20, Apr 15,
20, 28, 30, May 21, Sep 7, 21, Oct 2, 12, 14, 27, Nov 3, Dec 13; 1726: DL,
Jan 5, Apr 29, May 18, Sep 3, 10, 20, Oct 6, 15, 22, Nov 26; 1727: DL, Feb 4,
8, 21, Apr 8, May 8, Sep 7, 9, 19, Oct 3, 9, 17, 30, Nov 1, 6; 1728: DL, Jan
2, 5, Apr 29, May 6, Sep 14, 26, Oct 10, 12, 25, Nov 2, 12; 1729: DL, Jan 21,
28, 31, Apr 30, May 3, 7, 14, 20, Jul 25, Sep 20, 23, Oct 2, 4, 9, 23, Nov 3,
4, 12, 17, 24, Dec 2; 1730: DL, Jan 3, 26, Apr 10, 29, Sep 17, 24, 29, Oct 6,
8, 20, Dec 1; 1731: DL, Jan 20, 27, Mar 15, HAY, 24, DL, Apr 1, 23, May 3, 7,
18, 19, Sep 21, 25, 28, 30, Oct 2, 5, 19, 30, Nov 5, 8, 10, 11, 15, 22, Dec
21; 1732: DL, Feb 3, 14, Apr 17, 25, 26, May 3, 5, Sep 30, Oct 3, 10, 17, Nov
4, 11, 13, 24, Dec 9; 1740: BFLP, Aug 23
Watson (boxkeeper), 1755: DL, May 3; 1763: DL, May 16; 1764: DL, May 18; 1765:
DL, May 20; 1766: DL, May 19, Sep 25; 1767: DL, Jun 1; 1768: DL, May 30;
1769: DL, May 19; 1770: DL, May 30, Jun 1; 1771: DL, May 28, Sep 26; 1772:
DL, Jun 5, Sep 24; 1773: DL, May 31, Sep 21; 1774: DL, May 26, 30, Sep 17;
1775: DL, May 24, CG, 27, DL, 27, Sep 26; 1776: DL, May 17; 1777: DL, Jun 2;
1778: DL, May 23; 1779: DL, May 28; 1780: DL, May 20; 1781: DL, May 24; 1782:
DL, May 29; 1783: DL, May 28; 1784: DL, May 25
Watson (citizen), 1759: DL, Oct 27
Watson (linen draper), 1752: DL, Apr 8
Watson (singer), 1792: CG, Feb 28
Watson (ticket deliverer), 1784: HAY, Feb 9
Watson, Brook (Lord Mayor), 1797: DL, Oct 27
Watson, George, 1795: CG, Feb 21
--England Preserved, 1795: CG, Feb 21, 23, 24, 26, 28, Mar 2, Apr 23; 1798: CG,
Feb 9, May 7, 11
Watson, Marmaduke (actor), 1660: REDBULL, Nov 5; 1661: NONE, Sep 0; 1668: NONE,
Sep 0, BRIDGES, Nov 6; 1670: BRIDGES, Aug 0, BRI/COUR, Dec 0; 1672: LIF, Apr
0; 1673: LIF, Mar 0, May 0, Dec 0; 1674: DL, May 16; 1675: DL, Jan 25, Apr
23; 1677: DL, Mar 0, 17, Jun 0; 1678: DL, Mar 0; 1682: DL, Nov 16; 1697: LIF,
Nov 0; see also Duke
Watson, Miss (singer), 1792: CG, Oct 19, 29; 1793: CG, Sep 30, Oct 7, Dec 7,
13, 27; 1800: HAY, Jul 2
Watson Jr, Miss (actor), 1784: HAY, Feb 23
Watson Sr, Miss (actor), 1784: HAY, Feb 23
Watson, Mlle (dancer), 1791: PAN, Feb 17
Watson, Mrs (actor), 1776: HAY, Sep 20
Watson, Mrs (actor), 1782: HAY, Apr 9; 1784: HAY, Feb 9
Watson, Robert (pugilist), 1789: CG, Jan 27
Watteau (dance), 1733: DL, Jan 23, May 2, 5, 21, DL/HAY, Oct 3, 5, 12, Nov 12,
14, Dec 3, 20; 1734: DL/HAY, Feb 6, Mar 9, 26; 1757: HAY, Jul 27
Watts (actor), 1733: HAY, Jun 4; 1746: CG, Oct 3; 1747: RL, Jan 27
Watts (actor), 1778: CHR, Jun 15, 18
Watts (actor), 1784: HAY, Mar 8, Dec 13; 1786: HAMM, Jun 5, 7, 28, 30, Jul 5,
7, 10, 19, 21, 24, 26; 1788: HAY, Sep 30; 1789: CG, Jun 16
Watts Jr (actor), 1786: HAMM, Jun 7
Watts, John (actor), 1780: HAY, Jun 12
Watts, John (printer, stationer), 1744: DL, Mar 1, Apr 27; 1745: CG, Feb 20,
Mar 6; 1749: DL, Feb 27; 1750: DL, Feb 14; 1752: CG, Mar 18; 1757: CG, Feb
25; 1758: CG, Feb 10; 1759: CG, Mar 23; 1764: CG, Mar 23
Watts, Louisa, Mrs John (actor, singer), 1787: CG, Sep 24, Oct 1, 22, Nov 2,
Dec 3; 1788: CG, Jan 14, Mar 24, Apr 1, May 12, Jun 3, Sep 22, Dec 26, 29;
1789: CG, May 20, Jun 8, 16, Sep 14, Oct 12; 1790: CG, Jan 23, Sep 13, Oct 6,
Nov 15, 26, Dec 4, 20; 1791: CG, Jun 6, Sep 12, 26, Oct 3, 10, Dec 21, 22;
1792: CG, Jan 6, 27, Feb 28, Apr 12, 17, May 10, 12, 19, Oct 8, 19, 27, 29,

Nov 6, 16, Dec 26; 1793: CG, Mar 11, 23, Sep 16, 17, 20, 30, Oct 2, 7, 9, 17,
    24, Nov 1, 9, 18, 28, Dec 19, 27; 1794: CG, Feb 22, Mar 6, Apr 30, May 9, 13,
    Jun 12, Sep 22, 26, 29; 1795: CG, Mar 19, Apr 7, 24, May 29, Jun 10, 16, Sep
    14, 21, Oct 2, 8, 19, Nov 9, 16, 27; 1796: CG, Apr 9, 20, 26, 29, May 10, 24,
    30, Sep 12, 19, 26, Oct 3, 6, 7, 17, 29, Nov 19, 24, Dec 1, 19, 21; 1797: CG,
    Feb 18, Mar 16, Apr 8, 19, 25, May 18, 26, 27, Jun 2, 9, Sep 25, Oct 2, 9,
    13, 16, 18, Nov 2, 24, Dec 8, 18, 19, 26; 1798: CG, Jan 31, Feb 9, 12, Mar
    19, 31, Apr 9, 13, May 7, Jun 1, 4, Sep 17, 28, Oct 8, 11, 15, 25, Nov 10,
    12, 20, 21, Dec 11, 15, 26; 1799: CG, Jan 17, 29, Mar 2, 16, 25, Apr 2, 9,
    13, 18, 23, May 22, 28, 31, Jun 4, 6, 8, Sep 18, 30, Oct 7, 21, 24, Nov 11,
    Dec 4, 9, 23; 1800: CG, Jan 10, 16, Mar 4, 25, Apr 5, 15, 29, 30, May 1, 23,
    27, Jun 2, 12, 13
Watts, Miss (actor), 1679: BRUSSELS, Oct 3
Wave from Wave (song), 1790: CG, Feb 26, Mar 19; 1793: CG, Mar 8; 1795: CG, Mar
    13; 1797: CG, Mar 31; 1798: CG, Mar 28; 1799: CG, Feb 20
Wavering Nymph, The. See Behn, Aphra.
Waves of the sea (song), 1790: CG, Mar 3; 1792: CG, Mar 9
Way (ticket deliverer), 1792: CG, Jun 1
Way of the World, The. See Congreve, William.
Way to Get Married, The. See Morton, Thomas.
Way to Get Un-Married, The. See Cross, John Cartwright.
Way to Keep Him, The. See Murphy, Arthur.
Wayland, L (printer), 1789: KING'S, Mar 24, May 9, Jun 2, 11; 1793: KING'S, Jan
    26; 1798: KING'S, Jun 5
Waylin (Weylin) (actor), 1764: CG, Nov 2, 5, 7; 1765: CG, May 11, 16, Oct 3,
    Nov 23
Ways and Means. See Colman the younger, George.
Wayte (office keeper), 1732: GF, May 12; 1733: GF, May 9; 1734: GF, May 15;
    1735: GF, May 1; 1736: GF, Apr 29; 1737: LIF, Apr 28
We be three poor Mariners (song), 1781: CG, Apr 25, May 4, 12; 1784: DL, Apr
    12; 1793: CG, May 10, 24; 1794: CG, Apr 7; 1795: CG, May 13
We bipeds made up of frail clay (song), 1791: CG, May 18
We come in bright array (song), 1789: CG, Apr 3; 1790: DL, Mar 10, CG, 19;
    1791: CG, Apr 15; 1792: CG, Mar 9; 1793: KING/HAY, Feb 15, CG, 15, KING/HAY,
    Mar 13, CG, 13, 22; 1794: CG, Mar 7, DL, 26, Apr 4; 1795: CG, Feb 20; 1796:
    CG, Feb 26; 1797: CG, Mar 10; 1798: CG, Mar 28; 1799: CG, Feb 20; 1800: CG,
    Mar 19
We come, ye guardians of our isle (song), 1799: CG, Oct 7
We hear the pleasing dreadful call (song), 1790: DL, Mar 12, CG, 19; 1791: CG,
    Mar 30, Apr 15; 1793: CG, Feb 15; 1794: CG, Mar 7, DL, 21; 1795: CG, Feb 20;
    1798: CG, Mar 28, 30; 1799: CG, Feb 15
We three archers be (song), 1786: CG, May 22
We will rejoice (song), 1789: DL, Mar 20
We worship God (song), 1790: DL, Mar 10
We're Gaily yet (song), 1746: CG, Apr 22, 28
We've bade the restless seas adieu (song), 1796: CG, Apr 12, May 12, 28; 1797:
    CG, Oct 18, 20
Wealth Outwitted. See Jordan, Thomas.
Weathercock, The. See Forrest, Theodosius.
Weaver, Elizabeth Farley (actor), 1660: NONE, Sep 0; 1661: NONE, Sep 0; 1663:
    NONE, Sep 0; 1664: NONE, Sep 0, BRIDGES, Nov 0; 1665: BRIDGES, Apr 0; 1667:
    BRIDGES, Jan 15; 1668: BRIDGES, Jan 11
Weaver, John (dancer), 1700: DL, Jul 6; 1701: LIF, Oct 21; 1702: LIF, Dec 29;
    1703: YB, Feb 5, DL, May 28; 1717: DL, Mar 2, Apr 2, 9, Oct 12, 25, 29, Nov
    8; 1718: DL, Jan 7, 27, Mar 6, 31, May 7, 16, Nov 12; 1719: DL, Apr 7, 20,
    Aay 4, 8, 11, 13, 14, Oct 16, 29, Nov 6, 23, 25; 1720: DL, Jan 12, 14, Feb 5,
    Mar 29, Apr 5, 19, 25, May 6, 9, 11, 12, 17, 20, 23, Jun 2, 6, Nov 23; 1721:
    DL, Feb 9, 23, Apr 10, 27; 1723: DL, May 30; 1728: DL, Mar 16, 19, 30, Apr
    23, Oct 18, Nov 1, 15; 1729: DL, Apr 25, 28, May 2; 1733: DL, Feb 15
--Orpheus and Eurydice (entertainment), 1718: DL, Mar 6, 8, 10, 17, Oct 25;
    1720: DL, Mar 21
Weaver, John, sons of (dancers), 1718: DL, Mar 31, May 13, 21
Weaver's Complaint against The Calico Madams (song), 1719: LIF, Nov 5
Webb (actor), 1777: HAY, May 1
Webb (actor), 1780: HAY, Jan 17
Webb (beneficiary), 1723: LIF, Apr 30
Webb (beneficiary), 1776: DL, Apr 26
Webb (house servant), 1739: CG, May 29; 1740: CG, May 27; 1741: CG, May 8;
    1742: CG, May 18
Webb (singer), 1779: CG, Apr 17
Webb (singer, chorus director), 1785: KING'S, May 12
Webb, Alexander (actor), 1788: HAY, Dec 22; 1789: DL, Sep 24, Oct 1, 31, Nov 5,

13, 24, Dec 14, 22, 26; 1790: DL, Jan 8, Feb 10, 13, 15, CG, 19, 24, 26, Mar
3, DL, 8, 22, Apr 19, May 4, 14, 15, 29, 31, Jun 2, 3, 5, Sep 11, Oct 7, 11,
14, 18, 25, 26, Nov 4, 17, Dec 7, 27, 29; 1791: DL, Jan 10, Mar 22, May 11,
19, 28, DLKING'S, Sep 29, Oct 4, 6, 31, Nov 5, 11, 16, 30; 1792: DLKING'S,
Jan 14, 18, 21, 28, Feb 18, Mar 17, 19, 29, Apr 12, 17, 21, 28, Jun 4, 15,
DL, Sep 18, 25, 29, Oct 2, 4, 9, 13, 18, Nov 10, 21, Dec 10, 17, 26; 1793:
DL, Jan 7, 16, Feb 25, 28, Mar 11, Apr 3, 17, 20, 22, 23, 29, May 7, 10, 14,
21, 29, 31, Jun 3, 4, 5, 6; 1794: DL, Apr 21, 26, 29, May 5, 8, 13, 16, 22,
23, 30, Jun 6, 9, 10, Jul 4, Sep 23, 27, Oct 4, 27, 31, Nov 11, 15, Dec 5,
12; 1795: DL, Jan 3, 20, 23, Feb 6, 12, 28, Mar 2, 9, Apr 14, 17, May 12, 22,
30, Jun 4, Sep 17, 19, 22, Oct 8, Nov 3, 10, 16, 20, 26, Dec 10, 12, 19;
1796: DL, Jan 11, 15, 18, 23, Feb 15, 27, 29, Mar 3, 12, Apr 2, 25, 30, May
2, 9, 13, 21, 23, 24, Jun 4, 8, 11, 13, Sep 22, 24, 27, Oct 1, 3, 4, 17, 19,
22, 24, 27, 28, Nov 1, 2, 5, 9, 10, 15, 18, 22, 23, Dec 9, 16, 23, 26; 1797:
DL, Jan 7, 10, 24, 27, Feb 1, 7, 9, Apr 1, 6, 19, 27, 28, May 2, 5, 15, 16,
Sep 21, 23, 26, Oct 3, 5, 12, 14, 21, 24, 28, 30, Nov 2, 4, 6, 11, 15, 17,
24, 25, Dec 19, 20, 21; 1798: DL, Jan 16, Feb 13, 27, Mar 8, 17, 24, 26, Apr
30, May 19, Jun 1, 9, Sep 18, 20, 25, 27, 29, Oct 2, 4, 8, 13, 20, Nov 6, 10,
Dec 4, 5, HAY, 17, DL, 21, 27, 29; 1799: DL, Jan 2, 8, 11, 19, Mar 2, 11, Apr
22, 25, 27, May 1, 3, 20, 24, Jul 2, Sep 17, 19, 24, Oct 7, 12, 17, 26, Nov
5, 6, 16, 25, Dec 5, 9, 11, 30; 1800: DL, Jan 4, 21, Feb 12, Mar 11, Apr 5,
28, May 10, 29, Jun 12, 17, 18
Webb, Edward (dancer), 1792: DL, Dec 27; 1798: CG, Oct 15; 1799: CG, Apr 13,
May 28, Jun 4, 12, Dec 23; 1800: CG, Jan 10, Feb 10, May 27
Webb, Ludia, Mrs Richard (actor), 1778: HAY, Jun 1, Jul 1, 9, 11, Aug 6, 21,
27, Sep 7; 1779: HAY, Jun 2, 4, 10, Jul 1, 5, Aug 13, 17, 27, 31, Sep 17, Nov
8, CG, 12; 1780: CG, Feb 12, 22, 24, 26, Apr 19, 22, May 10, 12, HAY, 30, Jun
5, 13, 14, 15, 29, Jul 8, 29, Aug 10, 29, 31, Sep 11, CG, 20, 21, Oct 3, 19,
24, 26, Nov 4, 10, 25, 27; 1781: CG, Jan 12, Feb 10, 15, 24, Mar 8, Apr 28,
May 5, HAY, Jun 5, 7, 8, 12, 16, 21, 26, Jul 6, 9, 23, Aug 7, 8, 15, 21, 22,
Sep 4, CG, 17, 26, Oct 3, 16, 30, Nov 2, 24; 1782: CG, Feb 2, Mar 16, Apr 9,
20, 30, May 17, HAY, Jun 3, 4, 6, 11, 12, 20, Jul 2, 5, 25, 30, Aug 6, 17,
27, Sep 18, 19, CG, 23, 27, Oct 2, 3, 4, 9, 16, 22, Nov 2, 4, 19; 1783: CG,
Jan 17, Feb 3, Apr 1, 22, May 13, 19, HAY, 31, Jun 10, 13, 18, 20, 30, Jul
26, 28, Aug 1, 8, 13, 22, 26, 28, CG, Sep 19, 26, Oct 2, 9, 10, 14, 21, Nov
19; 1784: CG, Jan 7, 13, Feb 13, Apr 26, 27, May 1, 7, 10, 11, 17, 19, HAY,
28, 29, Jun 1, 2, 4, 14, Jul 27, Aug 10, 17, 19, 20, 21, 24, 26, Sep 2, 6,
CG, 17, 21, 22, Oct 6, 8, 18, 29, Nov 6, 11, 16, Dec 4, 14, 22; 1785: CG, Jan
8, Feb 21, Mar 19, 29, Apr 1, 2, 6, 11, May 3, 26, HAY, 30, 31, Jun 2, 3, 4,
7, 11, 16, 18, 21, 28, Jul 9, 11, 19, 20, Aug 16, 23, 26, Sep 16, CG, 19, 26,
30, Oct 3, 5, 7, 14, 22, 26, 29, Nov 3, 4, 9, 21, 29; 1786: CG, Feb 1, 13,
17, 21, Apr 18, May 9, 11, HAY, Jun 9, 10, 12, 14, 16, 19, 23, 26, 28, 29,
Jul 7, 10, 18, 19, 21, Aug 12, 15, 28, 29, Sep 9, CG, 18, Oct 4, 9, Nov 14,
18, 23, 25, Dec 1, 5, 6, 23; 1787: CG, Jan 6, 26, 27, Feb 13, 20, Mar 27, Apr
16, 25, 26, May 22, HAY, Jun 14, 16, 18, 21, 23, 27, Jul 2, 13, 23, 25, 31,
Aug 3, 7, 14, 21, 28, Sep 8, CG, 21, 24, 26, 28, Oct 10, 11, 17, 18, 29, Nov
8, 14, Dec 5, 15, 22, 26; 1788: CG, Jan 11, Feb 4, 9, 25, 26, Mar 11, 15, 24,
28, 29, Apr 1, 2, 26, May 8, HAY, Jun 10, 11, 13, 16, 30, Jul 4, 10, 30, Aug
25, 27, 29, CG, Sep 17, 22, 26, Oct 1, 3, 7, 28, Nov 1, 20, Dec 13; 1789: CG,
Jan 8, 28, Feb 3, 4, 21, Mar 3, 28, 31, Apr 14, 15, 20, 30, May 5, 15, 22,
Jun 5, 16, HAY, 19, 22, 26, 29, Jul 4, 11, 29, Aug 1, 10, 27, Sep 2, CG, Oct
2, 7, 16, 23, 24, 30, 31, Nov 5, 21, 27, Dec 12; 1790: CG, Jan 13, Feb 23,
Mar 18, 27, Apr 16, 20, 24, May 7, 13, HAY, Jun 14, 16, 18, 19, 22, 26, Jul
5, 22, 30, Aug 2, 13, CG, Oct 1, 5, 12, 15, 23, 29, Nov 3, 4, 11, 30, Dec 8,
14, 17, 20; 1791: CG, Jan 14, 15, Feb 10, Mar 5, May 2, 3, 6, 18, 19, Jun 1,
HAY, 10, 13, 16, 17, 18, 20, 23, 25, Aug 5, 10, 13, 18, 19, CG, Sep 12, 14,
16, 17, 20, 21, 23, Oct 13, 20, 27, Nov 1, 5, 19, Dec 10; 1792: CG, Jan 19,
25, 31, Feb 2, 23, Mar 26, 31, Apr 10, May 2, 5, 10, 22, 30, Jun 2, HAY, 15,
19, 20, 27, 29, 30, Jul 9, 25, Aug 2, 6, 9, 15, 21, 23, 24, CG, Sep 19, 20,
21, 26, Oct 3, 10, 12, 19, DL, 23, CG, 24, 26, 27, Nov 6, 7; 1793: CG, Jan 2,
29, Apr 8, 25, May 27, Jun 5, 10, HAY, 13, 14, 17, 18, 21, 25, 29, Jul 6, 10,
15, Aug 20, 27, CG, Sep 17, Oct 1, 4, 5, 11, 12, 15, 18, 21, 22, 29, 30, Nov
2, 5, 9
Webb, Master (actor, dancer), 1791: CG, Dec 21, 23; 1792: HAY, Jul 25, CG, Oct
8; 1796: DL, Mar 12, 19, HAY, Aug 29; 1797: CG, Jun 9; 1799: CG, Mar 16, Apr
23
Webb, Miss (actor), 1779: HAY, Dec 27
Webb, Miss (actor), 1788: HAY, Jul 30; 1790: HAY, Jul 30
Webb, Miss (actor), 1798: CG, Dec 11; 1799: CG, Jan 14, Jun 6
Webb, Miss (dancer), 1795: CG, Nov 16
Webb, Mrs (actor), 1734: DL, Dec 26
Webb, Richard (actor), 1778: HAY, Jul 1, 11, Aug 6, Sep 2, 7; 1779: HAY, May

31, Jun 2, 4, 10, Aug 13; 1780: HAY, May 30, Jun 6, Jul 29, Aug 12, Sep 2,
    11, CG, Oct 2, 9, 13, 19, 21, 23, Nov 4, 22; 1781: HAY, May 30, Jun 1, 8, 16,
    21, Jul 6, 9, 23, Aug 8, 17, 21, Sep 4, CG, Nov 24, Dec 11, 17, 26; 1782: CG,
    Jan 7, 11, 22, Apr 30, HAY, Jun 3, 4, 6, 11, 12, 18, Jul 5, 16, Aug 9, 13,
    17, Sep 19, CG, Oct 14, 15, 22, Nov 18, Dec 16; 1783: CG, Mar 31, Apr 23, May
    9, 13, 17
Webbe (singer), 1767: MARLY, Sep 18, CG, Nov 4; 1774: KING'S, Jan 11; 1776: DL,
    Oct 18, Nov 25
Webbe, Samuel (composer), 1785: DL, May 3; 1790: CG, Mar 3; 1791: CG, Mar 18,
    Apr 15, DL, May 18; 1792: CG, Mar 7, 14, 21; 1793: KING/HAY, Feb 15, Mar 20;
    1794: CG, May 22; 1797: HAY, Aug 3
Webber (actor), 1792: HAY, Apr 16
Weber (ticket deliverer), 1798: DL, Jun 2
Weber, Francisco (musician), 1724: HAY, Apr 22; 1728: HIC, May 15
Webster (actor), 1729: HAY, Feb 11, 25, Mar 29, May 12, 26, 29, Jun 14
Webster (actor), 1770: HAY, Oct 15; 1776: CG, Feb 22, 27, Mar 16, 18, Apr 29
Webster (actor), 1780: HAY, Sep 25
Webster (house servant), 1769: CG, Jan 2; 1773: CG, Jan 5; 1776: CG, Jan 15
Webster (spectator), 1685: BF, Aug 26
Webster, Anthony (actor, singer), 1777: DL, Nov 8, Dec 15; 1778: DL, Jan 8, Mar
    6, 12, 27, Apr 7, 25, May 1, Sep 17, Oct 3, 15, Nov 20, 30; 1779: DL, Jan 16,
    29, Feb 19, Mar 11, 12, 22, 26, Apr 6, 17, Sep 18, Oct 5, 25, Nov 6, 19, Dec
    16; 1780: DL, Feb 11, Mar 17, 31
Webster, James (witness), 1745: CG, Feb 20
Webster, John, 1669: LIF, May 12; 1696: LIF, Mar 0
--Appius and Virginia, 1669: LIF, May 12
--Cure for a Cuckold, A (with William Rowley), 1660: NONE, Sep 0; 1696: LIF,
    Mar 0
--Duchess of Malfi, The, 1660: SALSBURY, Dec 12; 1662: LIF, Sep 30; 1668: LIF,
    Nov 25; 1672: DG, Jan 31; 1676: DG, Aug 0; 1686: ATCOURT, Jan 13; 1705: LIF,
    Oct 3; 1707: QUEEN'S, Jul 22, 23, Aug 8
--Roman Virgin, The; or, The Unjust Judge, 1669: LIF, May 12, 13, 14, 15, 17,
    18, 19, 20
--White Devil, The; or, Vittoria Corombona, 1661: VERE, Oct 2, 4, Dec 11; 1664:
    NONE, Sep 0; 1671: BRIDGES, Aug 0, NONE, Sep 0
Wedding Dance (dance), 1703: LIF, Jun 1, 11; 1714: DL, Jul 20; 1716: DL, Jul
    24; 1718: LIF, Oct 21, Dec 1; 1735: GF/HAY, May 5
Wedding Dance, Grand (dance), 1718: LIF, Oct 4, 9, Nov 10
Wedding Day (song), 1787: RLSN, Mar 26, 27
Wedding Day, The. See Fielding, Henry; Barthelemon, Francois Hippolyte;
    Inchbald, Elizabeth.
Wedding Night, The. See Carey, Henry; Cobb, James.
Wedding Ring, The. See Dibdin, Charles.
Wedding, The (music), 1701: LIF, Jun 24
Wedding, The. See Shirley, James; Hawker, Essex.
Weedon (actor), 1766: HAY, Jun 26, Jul 31, KING'S, Aug 13
Weedon, Cavendish (financier), 1702: SH, Jan 31, May 7, CC, 21
Weekly, Mrs (dancer, singer), 1724: DL, Jan 29, Feb 1, Apr 10, Oct 8, 10; 1725:
    DL, Apr 9, Nov 8
Weeks (actor), 1740: DL, Oct 14, 27, Nov 17, Dec 4, 26
Weeks, James (actor), 1729: LIF, Jan 1
Weeks, Master (dancer), 1732: LIF, Apr 12, May 5, 15; 1733: LIF/CG, Apr 30, CG,
    May 4, GF, 14; 1734: CG, May 8; 1736: DL, May 20
Weeks, Mrs (actor), 1780: CII, Feb 29, Mar 6, 13, 17, 27, Apr 5, 19
Weely (singer), 1712: SH, Mar 13; 1713: SH, Mar 12; 1717: SH, Mar 13, 27; 1723:
    BUH, Jan 11; 1726: IT, Feb 2
Weep, all ye nymphs (song), 1680: DG, Sep 0
Weep, Israel, weep (song), 1794: CG, Mar 26, Apr 11
Wegg (renter), 1766: DL, Nov 7; 1772: DL, Jun 5; 1773: DL, Feb 5, Jun 2, Dec
    22; 1774: DL, May 23, Nov 21; 1775: DL, May 12, Nov 10; 1776: DL, Apr 26
Weichsel (musician), 1758: CHAPEL, Apr 27
Weichsel, Charles (violinist, composer), 1778: CG, Mar 6, 18, 25; 1790: CG, Mar
    8, DL, 10, 12, 17, CG, Jun 2; 1791: CG, Mar 30; 1792: CG, Feb 28, May 22
Weichsel, Miss (actor), 1778: CG, Mar 6, 18, 25
Weichsel, Mrs Carl (singer), 1765: CG, Oct 9, 14, 22, 28, Nov 13, 23, 25, Dec
    23; 1766: CG, Feb 20, Mar 20, Apr 22, 24, May 13; 1769: KING'S, Apr 5, HAY,
    18; 1771: HAY, Apr 12, CHAPEL, 27, DL, 27; 1772: DL, Mar 6; 1773: DL, Feb 26,
    CR, Apr 14, HAY, 19; 1775: DL, Mar 10, KING'S, 24, CG, Nov 16; 1776: STRAND,
    Jan 23, CG, Feb 23, May 4; 1778: CG, Mar 6, 25
Weideman, Charles (musician), 1729: SH, Mar 14, DL, 26, LIF, Apr 30; 1733: SH,
    Mar 19; 1734: SH, Mar 28; 1737: DT, Mar 16; 1741: HIC, Jan 16, HAY, Feb 3,
    HIC, 27, Mar 6, 13, KING'S, 14; 1743: KING'S, Mar 30; 1744: KING'S, Mar 28;

1745: CG, Apr 10; 1746: KING'S, Mar 25
Weippert, John Michael (harpist), 1791: CG, Dec 19; 1792: CG, May 28, 31, Oct
    25; 1793: CG, Jun 6; 1794: CG, Feb 6, May 26, HAY, Jun 2, CG, 11, Nov 3;
    1795: CG, Mar 5, Apr 6, Oct 12, Dec 30; 1796: CG, Mar 14, Apr 9, May 18, Oct
    31; 1797: CG, Apr 8, 25, May 9, 18, 24, Nov 24, Dec 16; 1798: CG, Feb 14, Mar
    19, May 25, 28, HAY, Jul 21, CG, Oct 11; 1799: CG, Jan 29, 31, Feb 5, Mar 2,
    DL, May 9, CG, Jun 6, 12; 1800: CG, Mar 4, 31, May 17, Jun 13
Weirman, Miss (actor), 1764: CG, Oct 18, Nov 5; 1765: CG, Jan 15, Feb 15, May
    16
Welch Fair, 1739: WF, Aug 31; 1740: BF/WF/SF, Aug 29
Welch Heiress, The. See Jerningham, Edward.
Welch Opera, The. See Fielding, Henry.
Welch, Justice (constable), 1752: DL, Apr 13, TCJS, Aug 11; 1755: DL, Nov 18,
    19; 1760: HAY, Aug 15
Welch, Mrs (dancer), 1760: CG, Sep 22, Dec 11; 1761: CG, Mar 9, May 25, Sep 21,
    23, 26; 1762: CG, Jan 28
Welchman's Triumph (dance), 1742: GF, Jan 14, 15, Feb 10, 18, Mar 29, Apr 24,
    May 27
Welcome Mars (song), 1734: HIC, Jul 10
Welcome mighty King (song), 1786: DL, Mar 10; 1789: DL, Mar 18; 1790: CG, Feb
    24, DL, 26, Mar 17; 1791: DL, Mar 23; 1792: KING'S, Feb 24; 1793: KING/HAY,
    Feb 22; 1794: DL, Mar 12, 14, Apr 2, 10; 1800: CG, Mar 14
Welcome mortal to this place (song), 1683: DG, Jul 0
Welcome the Covert (song), 1790: CG, Apr 21, DL, May 20
Welcome to the Spring (song), 1777: CG, May 5
Weldon (musician), 1701: DG, Mar 21, May 6; 1702: SHG, May 12, YB, Jul 2, DL,
    7, HAW, 27; 1703: DL, Jun 22, RIW, Aug 12; 1704: DL, Jan 18, LIF, Feb 1, DL,
    22; 1713: CA, Mar 20; 1716: DL, Aug 7
Well (actor), 1791: HAY, Oct 24
Well Close Square, 1787: HAY, Mar 12, CG, Apr 21; 1788: CG, Jun 2
Well's Row, 1780: CII, Apr 19
Welldon (actor), 1780: HAY, Nov 13
Weller (actor), 1703: LIF, Nov 0; 1704: LIF, Mar 25, Nov 13; 1705: LIF/QUEN,
    Feb 22, LIF, Aug 1, QUEEN'S, Nov 23; 1707: DL, Apr 22; 1710: DL, Jan 14, Mar
    25; 1715: DL, Feb 23, Aug 9, Dec 6; 1716: DL, Jun 8; 1717: DL, May 31; 1718:
    DL, May 28
Weller (actor), 1759: CG, Dec 29; 1760: CG, Jan 28, Feb 19, Mar 18, May 12, 14,
    Sep 22, Nov 22, Dec 17; 1761: CG, Jan 28, Mar 25, 30, Apr 1, 17, 20, May 5,
    Sep 16, Oct 5, Dec 28; 1762: CG, Feb 17, May 7, Sep 27, Oct 14; 1763: CG, Jan
    4, 26, Apr 27, May 9, Oct 14, 26, Nov 10, 18, Dec 9; 1764: CG, Feb 1, Mar 29,
    Apr 28, May 12, 15, Sep 19, 24, Oct 8, 17, Nov 3, 5, Dec 22; 1765: CG, Jan 8,
    May 2, 10, Sep 20, Oct 15, 21, 28, Nov 11, Dec 21; 1766: CG, Jan 9, 17, 31,
    Apr 8, Oct 1, 15, 17, 21, 25, Nov 8, 18, Dec 12, 13, 16, 20, 23; 1767: CG,
    Jan 31, Feb 28, Mar 21, May 13, 15, 23, 26, Sep 19, 23, Oct 5, 9, 19, 24, 26,
    Nov 6, Dec 4
Weller, Ann (actor), 1770: DL, Jan 8, HAY, Mar 12, DL, Apr 18, May 4; 1772: DL,
    Sep 22, Dec 2; 1775: HAY, May 1, 15, 17, 29, 31, Jul 31, Aug 21, Sep 7, 20,
    21; 1776: HAY, Feb 22, CG, Mar 16, HAY, Sep 18; 1778: CG, Sep 18, Oct 17
Wellesley, Garret, Lord Mornington (composer), 1759: CG, Mar 28; 1784: CG, Apr
    17; 1794: HAY, Aug 18; 1796: CG, Nov 5
Wellman (actor), 1785: HAMM, Jun 17, 27, Jul 1, 2, 4, 6, 8, 15, 22, 25, 26, 27
Wellman, Mr and Mrs (actors), 1785: HAMM, Jul 15
Wellman, Mrs (actor), 1785: HAMM, Jun 17, 27, Jul 2, 4, 6, 8, 15, 22, 25, 26,
    27
Wellman, Mrs (beneficiary), 1717: LIF, May 28
Wells (actor), 1723: HAY, Feb 13; 1729: HAY, Nov 12, 15, 22, Dec 18; 1730: HAY,
    Jan 8, 21, Feb 6, 18, 23, Mar 11, 12, 30, Apr 20, Jun 23, Jul 3, BFR, Sep 4,
    SF, 14
Wells (actor), 1794: DL, Oct 27, Dec 20; 1795: DL, Jan 19, Oct 30; 1796: DL,
    Jan 18, Apr 4, Jun 10, Oct 1, 19, 29, Nov 9, Dec 26; 1797: DL, Jun 10; 1798:
    DL, Jan 16, Feb 20, May 16, Jun 2, Oct 6, Nov 14, Dec 6; 1799: DL, Jan 19,
    Feb 5, Jul 2, Oct 14, Nov 6; 1800: DL, Mar 11
Wells (boxkeeper), 1794: CG, Jun 17; 1795: CG, Jun 17; 1796: CG, Jun 6; 1797:
    CG, Jun 6; 1798: CG, May 29; 1799: CG, Jun 8; 1800: CG, Jun 11
Wells (casualty), 1758: DL, Dec 25
Wells (house servant), 1775: CG, May 30; 1776: CG, May 21; 1777: CG, May 23;
    1778: CG, May 21; 1779: CG, May 15; 1780: CG, May 24; 1781: CG, May 25; 1782:
    CG, May 28
Wells (musician), 1713: SH, Feb 23; 1714: SH, Feb 22; 1715: SH, May 2
Wells (taverner), 1758: CG, Jul 6
Wells Jr (actor), 1729: HAY, Dec 18; 1730: HAY, Jan 21, Mar 12, 20, 30
Wells St, 1779: CG, May 8; 1784: CG, May 21

Wells, John Wilmot (actor), <u>1798</u>: HAY, Dec 17
Wells, Mary Stephens, Mrs Ezra (actor), <u>1781</u>: HAY, Jun 1, 26, Aug 28, Sep 4,
  14, DL, 25, Oct 29, Nov 7; <u>1782</u>: DL, Jan 22, Apr 6, 12, 22, 30, CG, May 4,
  DL, 7, HAY, Jun 3, 4, 11, 15, Aug 12, 16, 23, 24, Sep 16, DL, 19, HAY, 20,
  DL, Oct 8, 16; <u>1783</u>: DL, Jan 3, 10, Mar 6, Apr 30, HAY, May 31, Jun 2, 4, 6,
  20, Jul 5, Aug 1, 15, 27, 29, DL, Sep 20, 25, Oct 16, 18, 24, 29, 31, Nov 20;
  <u>1784</u>: DL, Feb 14, Apr 12, 30, May 13, HAY, 28, Jun 2, 22, 25, Jul 6, 7, 20,
  Aug 5, 10, 20, 26, Sep 6, DL, 21, Oct 18, 30, Nov 19, 22, Dec 11; <u>1785</u>: DL,
  Jan 14, CG, Mar 12, DL, Apr 15, HAY, May 28, 30, Jun 6, 7, 9, 15, 16, 17, 18,
  29, Jul 9, 21, 29, Aug 2, 16, CG, Dec 14, 20, 29; <u>1786</u>: CG, Jan 2, 6, 31, Feb
  7, 18, Mar 4, Apr 18, 24, May 3, 11, 15, 20, 22, HAY, Jun 10, 12, 14, 15, 19,
  20, 21, Jul 8, 25, 28, Sep 9, CG, 18, 25, Oct 25, Nov 18, 22, Dec 6; <u>1787</u>:
  CG, Jan 12, Mar 31, Apr 18, 19, 25, May 1, 9, 22, 31, Sep 17, 21, 26, Oct 3,
  10, 11, 18, Nov 26, 30; <u>1788</u>: CG, Jan 2, 3, 29, Feb 5, Mar 25, Apr 8, 11, 25,
  29, Sep 15, 19, Oct 7, 15, 21, Nov 27, 28; <u>1789</u>: CG, Apr 4, 15, 20, May 6,
  15, 22, 23, Jun 16, Oct 7, 20, 24, 28, Nov 27, Dec 31; <u>1790</u>: CG, Jan 23, Feb
  25, Apr 9, 13, 21, 29, May 31, HAY, Jun 15, 16, 25, Jul 5, 7, Aug 3, 18, CG,
  Oct 1, 8, 19, Nov 3, Dec 11, 14; <u>1791</u>: CG, Feb 4, 15, 21, Mar 14, Apr 16, 30,
  May 2, 10, 19, 27, Jun 6, HAY, 13, CG, 15, HAY, 17, Jul 8, CG, Sep 12, 16,
  21, 23, Oct 12, Nov 5, 15, 19, Dec 13; <u>1792</u>: CG, Feb 8, 11, Apr 28, Jun 2,
  Sep 28, Oct 15, 17, 19, 26, 31, Nov 6, 14, 24, Dec 5, 28; <u>1793</u>: CG, Jan 25;
  <u>1795</u>: HAY, Mar 20, CG, May 6; <u>1799</u>: HAY, Apr 17, CG, Jun 12
Wells, Master (actor), <u>1796</u>: DL, Oct 3; <u>1798</u>: DL, Mar 24, Jun 5
Welman (dancer), <u>1726</u>: HAY, Apr 14, 18, 22, 25, 27, May 6, 9, KING'S, Dec 17;
  <u>1727</u>: KING'S, Mar 16
Welsch, Miss. See Welch, Mrs.
Welsh Air (song), <u>1751</u>: DL, May 4
Welsh Buffoon (dance), <u>1742</u>: GF, Apr 6, 22, 27, 29, LIF, Nov 29, Dec 3, 6, 13;
  <u>1743</u>: LIF, Jan 7, Feb 11, 17, 28, Mar 3, 8, 14; <u>1744</u>: GF, Dec 10
Welsh Cantata (song), <u>1789</u>: DL, May 15
Welsh Charity School, <u>1778</u>: CG, Dec 19; <u>1779</u>: DL, Dec 18
Welsh Harp (music), <u>1731</u>: GF, May 7, 17; <u>1753</u>: DL, Mar 27, CG, Apr 14; <u>1755</u>:
  CG, Apr 26; <u>1758</u>: CG, Apr 10; <u>1759</u>: CG, May 5; <u>1761</u>: CG, May 6; <u>1762</u>: CG, May
  4
Welsh Harp Concerto (music), <u>1737</u>: LIF, May 4; <u>1743</u>: LIF, Mar 15
Welsh Harp Lesson (entertainment), <u>1742</u>: DL, May 15
Welsh Harp Solo (song), <u>1733</u>: Dl, Dec 31; <u>1756</u>: DL, Aug 12
Welsh Harp Voluntary (music), <u>1730</u>: GF, Jun 30
Welsh Society, <u>1778</u>: HAY, Mar 31
Welsh Song (song), <u>1746</u>: SOU, Nov 6; <u>1759</u>: HAY, Oct 1; <u>1796</u>: HAY, Aug 30
Welsh Whimsical Song (song), <u>1740</u>: SOU, Oct 9
Welsh, James (actor, singer), <u>1792</u>: DL, Nov 2, 21, Dec 26; <u>1793</u>: DL, Jan 16,
  KING/HAY, Mar 6, DL, 7, KING/HAY, 13, 15, DL, May 10, HAY, Oct 10, Nov 19;
  <u>1794</u>: DL, Apr 21, 28, May 16, 30, Jun 9, 14, Sep 27, Oct 14, 27, 31, Nov 15,
  Dec 20; <u>1795</u>: DL, Feb 6, May 6, Sep 22, Oct 1, 30, Nov 11, 20, 23, Dec 10,
  18; <u>1796</u>: DL, Jan 18, Feb 27, Mar 12, Apr 30, Sep 29, Oct 19, Nov 9, Dec 26;
  <u>1797</u>: DL, Jan 7, 20, Feb 9, 16, Mar 6, May 18, 24
Welsh, James and Thomas (actors), <u>1793</u>: KING/HAY, Mar 13
Welsh, Thomas (actor, singer), <u>1792</u>: KING'S, Feb 24, 29, Mar 7, 14, 23, 28, 30,
  DLKING'S, May 23, DL, Oct 18; <u>1793</u>: DL, Jan 7, 23, KING/HAY, Feb 15, 20, 22,
  Mar 6, DL, 11, KING/HAY, 13, 15, DL, 19, KING/HAY, 22, DL, Apr 2, May 10, 14,
  22, 24, 27; <u>1794</u>: DL, Mar 12, 19, 26, Apr 2, 4, 9, 10, 11, 21, May 3, 12, 13,
  14, 19, Jun 9, Jul 2, Sep 18, 27, Oct 7, 11, 14, 31, Nov 3, 15, Dec 20; <u>1795</u>:
  DL, Jan 31, Feb 4, Mar 14, Apr 27, May 1, 2, 6, 19, 26, 27, 29, Jun 6, Sep
  19, 24, 29, Oct 1, 6, 30, Nov 23, Dec 4, 18; <u>1796</u>: DL, Jan 11, 18, Feb 1, Mar
  3, 12, Apr 13, 25, May 11, 13, 25, 27, 30, Jun 9, Sep 20, 24, 29, Oct 6, 10,
  Nov 5, 9, 10, 19, 28, Dec 6, 10, 20; <u>1797</u>: DL, Jan 5, 12, 14, Feb 6, 9, 16,
  22, Mar 6, 18, 23, 28, May 13, 18, 20, 23, 25
Welstead, Leonard, <u>1721</u>: LIF, Jan 23, 26; <u>1725</u>: DL, May 10; <u>1726</u>: LIF, Feb 19,
  DL, May 9, Jun 3, LIF, Dec 14
--Dissembled Wanton, The; or, My Son Get Money, <u>1726</u>: LIF, Dec 14, 15, 16, 19,
  21
Weltje, Louis (confectioner), <u>1777</u>: KING'S, Nov 4; <u>1785</u>: HAY, Feb 7
Wenceslaus (opera, anon), <u>1717</u>: KING'S, Mar 14, 16, May 13
Wenceslaus. See Handel, George Frederic.
Wendling (musician), <u>1772</u>: HAY, Mar 30, Apr 6, 27
Wenpicollo (actor), <u>1728</u>: HAY, Feb 21
Wentworth (actor), <u>1795</u>: DL, Nov 23; <u>1796</u>: DL, Jan 18, Feb 15, Mar 12, Apr 2,
  18, 20, 30, May 2, 9, Jun 4, 11, Oct 26, 28, Nov 9, 15, 18, Dec 26; <u>1797</u>: DL,
  Jan 7, 18, 20, Feb 3, 7, 9, 16, 23, May 24, Jun 15, Sep 23, 28, 30, Oct 5,
  14, 28, Nov 2, 4, 8, 9, 15, 28, Dec 14, 18; <u>1798</u>: DL, Jan 16, Feb 13, 20, 27,
  Mar 22, May 19, 21, 23, Jun 13, Sep 18, 25, 29, Oct 4, 6, 9, 20, 27, Nov 14,

19, 26, 29, Dec 4, 29; <u>1799</u>: DL, Jan 2, 11, 19, 23, Feb 23, Mar 16, Apr 19,
27, May 24, Sep 17, 19, 24, Oct 7, 8, 17, 19, 26, 31, Nov 6, 14, 16, 25, 29,
Dec 11, 30; <u>1800</u>: DL, Jan 1, 4, 18, Mar 11, Apr 29, Jun 18
Wentworth, Lady (correspondent), <u>1708</u>: QUEEN'S, Dec 11
Wentworth, Lady Henrietta, <u>1675</u>: ATCOURT, Feb 15
Wentworth, Lord (spectator), <u>1738</u>: CG, Jan 18; <u>1739</u>: DL, Jan 4
Wentworth, Lucy (spectator), <u>1737</u>: KING'S, Jan 8
Wentworth, Miss (actor), <u>1772</u>: HAY, May 18, 27, Jul 3, 6, 10, 27, Aug 4, 10,
Sep 8, 17
Wentworth, Miss S (actor, singer), <u>1795</u>: DL, Nov 23, Dec 4; <u>1796</u>: DL, Jan 11,
18, Mar 3, 12, Apr 30, Dec 2; <u>1797</u>: DL, Jan 7, Feb 8, 9, 16, 23, May 13, 24,
CG, Jun 14, DL, Sep 26, Oct 16, Nov 8, Dec 9, 23; <u>1798</u>: DL, Jan 16, Feb 20,
Mar 6, Jun 4, 13, Sep 18, 25, Oct 2, 6, Nov 14, 26, Dec 4, 29; <u>1799</u>: DL, Jan
19, Mar 2, Apr 2, May 4, 21, 24, Jul 4, 5, Sep 26, Oct 7, 12, 14, Nov 13, 14,
Dec 11; <u>1800</u>: DL, Jan 1, 11, Mar 11, Apr 29, Jun 9, 11
Wentworth, Mrs (actor), <u>1796</u>: DL, Nov 9; <u>1797</u>: CG, Jun 21
Wentworth, Peter, <u>1712</u>: QUEEN'S, Jan 9
Werenfels (moralist), <u>1744</u>: DL, Jan 2
Werter. See Reynolds, Frederick.
Wescomb (actor), <u>1733</u>: DL, Oct 1, 5
Wesley, Charles (organist), <u>1794</u>: CG, Mar 19
Wesley, Samuel (organist, composer), <u>1799</u>: CG, Feb 22; <u>1800</u>: CG, Apr 2
West (actor), <u>1724</u>: RI, Jun 27, 29, Jul 13
West (actor), <u>1734</u>: GF, Jan 19, 31, Feb 11, Nov 18, Dec 11
West (actor), <u>1759</u>: DL, May 28, Jun 19; <u>1760</u>: DL, May 12; <u>1761</u>: DL, May 20;
<u>1762</u>: DL, May 18; <u>1763</u>: DL, Jan 3, May 13; <u>1764</u>: DL, May 17; <u>1765</u>: DL, May
17; <u>1766</u>: DL, Jan 6, Apr 16, May 14, Sep 27, Oct 9; <u>1767</u>: DL, Jan 24, May 27
West (beneficiary), <u>1726</u>: LIF, May 26
West (beneficiary), <u>1797</u>: CG, Jun 8; <u>1798</u>: CG, May 19; <u>1799</u>: CG, Jun 4
West (critic), <u>1748</u>: CG, Mar 5
West (frame maker), <u>1748</u>: DL, Apr 20
West (householder), <u>1742</u>: DL, Feb 1, 24
West India Coffee House, <u>1749</u>: CG, Apr 28
West India Sufferers (beneficiaries), <u>1781</u>: KING'S, Feb 8
West Indian, The. See Cumberland, Richard.
West Indies, <u>1781</u>: KING'S, Feb 8, HAY, Mar 14; <u>1795</u>: HAY, Apr 22
West Smithfield, <u>1682</u>: BF, Aug 24; <u>1697</u>: BF, Aug 24; <u>1700</u>: BF, Aug 0; <u>1727</u>: BF,
Aug 22; <u>1732</u>: BF, Aug 22; <u>1741</u>: BFTY, Aug 22; <u>1742</u>: BFPY, Aug 25, BFG, 25,
BF, 26; <u>1743</u>: BFYWR, Aug 23, BFFP, 23, TCD/BFTD, 23, BFGA, 23; <u>1746</u>: BFWF,
Aug 25, BFLY, 25, BFYB, 25; <u>1749</u>: BF/SF, Aug 23, BFYT, 23, BFHG, 23, BFYT,
24, 25, 26, 28; <u>1753</u>: BFSY, Sep 3, 5, 6; <u>1754</u>: BFYJN, Sep 3, BFSIY, 3; <u>1755</u>:
BF, Sep 3, BFGT, 3, 5, BF, 6; <u>1756</u>: BFSI, Sep 3; <u>1757</u>: BFG, Sep 5, BFB, 5, 6;
<u>1759</u>: BFS, Sep 3; <u>1760</u>: BFG, Sep 3, 4, 5, 6; <u>1761</u>: BFY, Aug 31, BFG, Sep 1;
<u>1792</u>: HAY, Nov 26
West Wycombe, <u>1757</u>: SOHO, Feb 1
West, Gilbert (composer), <u>1771</u>: CG, Nov 12
West, James (dancer), <u>1768</u>: DL, Oct 11; <u>1770</u>: HAY, May 21, Jul 16, Aug 1, 8,
22, Sep 5; <u>1771</u>: HAY, May 15, 29, 31, Jun 17, 26, Jul 3, 10, Aug 21, 23, 26,
Sep 4; <u>1789</u>: DL, May 7; <u>1793</u>: CG, Oct 15, 18, Dec 19
West, Louisa Margaretta (dancer), <u>1768</u>: DL, Sep 27; <u>1769</u>: DL, Oct 4; <u>1770</u>: HAY,
May 21, Jul 16, Aug 1, 8, 22, Sep 5; <u>1771</u>: HAY, May 15, 17, 29, 31, Jun 17,
26, Jul 3, 10, Aug 21, 23, 26, Sep 4
West, Master and Miss (dancers), <u>1770</u>: DL, May 2, HAY, 16, Jun 11, Jul 4, 18;
<u>1771</u>: HAY, Jul 24, Aug 7, Sep 20; <u>1774</u>: CG, Sep 19
West, Mrs Thomas Wade (actor), <u>1776</u>: CHR, Sep 25, 30, Oct 2, 4, 7, 9, 18; <u>1777</u>:
HAY, Feb 11, May 1; <u>1778</u>: HAY, Jan 26, Mar 23, 24, Apr 30, CHR, May 25, 27,
29, Jun 3, 8, 9, 15, 18, 22, 24, HAY, Sep 17
West, Richard, <u>1726</u>: DL, Feb 2
--Hecuba, <u>1726</u>: DL, Feb 2, 3, 4
West, Thomas Wade (actor), <u>1775</u>: HAY, Mar 23; <u>1776</u>: HAY, May 2, CHR, Oct 4, 7;
<u>1777</u>: HAY, Feb 11, May 1, Oct 13; <u>1778</u>: HAY, Jan 26, Feb 9, Mar 23, 24, Apr
30, CHR, May 25, 27, 29, Jun 3, 8, 9, 10, 15, 19, 22, 24, 26, HAY, Sep 17
Westcoat (actor), <u>1787</u>: ROY, Jun 20
Westcombe, Mrs (actor), <u>1736</u>: LIF, Apr 19
Westenholt (actor), <u>1786</u>: HAMM, Jun 5, 7
Westley, Mrs (actor), <u>1736</u>: HAY, Jan 14
Westley, Thomas (house servant, treasurer), <u>1775</u>: DL, Dec 16; <u>1776</u>: DL, Jun 10;
<u>1782</u>: DL, Apr 26
Westminster Abbey, <u>1702</u>: SH, May 7; <u>1730</u>: DL, Oct 27; <u>1752</u>: DL, Mar 31, Apr 21;
<u>1755</u>: SOHO, Jan 16; <u>1762</u>: HIC, Feb 12; <u>1766</u>: DL, Feb 6; <u>1770</u>: HAY, Aug 1;
<u>1784</u>: CG, Apr 27; <u>1785</u>: DL, Feb 11; <u>1786</u>: DL, Mar 10; <u>1789</u>: CG, Mar 6; <u>1790</u>:
CG, Feb 19, 24, DL, 24, 26; <u>1791</u>: DL, Mar 23; <u>1793</u>: KING/HAY, Feb 22; <u>1796</u>:

CG, Feb 12; 1797: CG, Mar 3; 1798: CG, Feb 23; 1799: CG, Feb 8, HAY, Mar 29;
1800: CG, Feb 28
Westminster Bridge, 1758: CG, Jul 6; 1766: CG, Dec 16; 1767: DL, Dec 19; 1768:
CG, Dec 22; 1771: CG, Dec 21; 1774: CG, Dec 23; 1778: HAY, Mar 31
Westminster Charity, 1776: DL, Jan 20
Westminster Choir, 1789: DL, Feb 27; 1798: HAY, Jan 15; 1799: HAY, Jan 24
Westminster Division, 1748: HAY, Apr 18
Westminster Hall in an Uproar. See Dent, John, The Lawyer's Panic.
Westminster Hall, 1697: IT, Nov 1
Westminster New Lying-in Hospital, 1766: CG, Dec 16; 1767: DL, Dec 19; 1768:
CG, Dec 22; 1769: CG, Jan 10; 1770: DL, Dec 21; 1771: CG, Dec 21, 31; 1774:
CG, Dec 23; 1775: DL, Dec 22; 1778: HAY, Apr 30
Westminster School, 1695: WS, Dec 0; 1717: WS, Apr 23; 1720: HIC, Feb 2; 1727:
WS, Dec 14; 1730: WS, Jan 15; 1731: WS, Jan 28; 1732: WS, Dec 8; 1733: WS,
Feb 6; 1736: WS, Dec 3; 1752: HAY, Mar 12; 1774: DL, Jan 29
Westminster, 1661: CITY, Oct 29; 1683: CITY, Oct 29; 1700: BF, Jun 25; 1721:
HAY, Nov 18, WS, 21; 1722: WS, Jan 23; 1724: PY, Apr 20; 1731: YB, Apr 7,
HAY, Aug 20; 1733: HAY, Mar 29; 1742: JS, Oct 12; 1743: WS, Nov 25; 1744: CG,
Jan 19; 1745: DL, Apr 22, CG, Dec 19; 1746: SOU, Nov 3; 1749: HAY, Nov 22,
30; 1750: DL, Feb 21; 1752: TCJS, Aug 11; 1753: KING'S, Apr 30; 1758: KING'S,
Apr 6; 1759: CG, Feb 2; 1768: DL, Nov 23; 1777: CG, Mar 17, DL, Apr 23, CG,
May 10; 1778: CG, May 9; 1779: CG, May 1, DL, 11; 1780: KING'S, Mar 9, CG,
Apr 28, DL, May 5, KING'S, 31; 1782: HAY, Jan 14, DL, May 3, CG, 3; 1784:
HAY, Jul 24; 1785: HAY, Feb 24, CG, Apr 22, DL, May 5; 1786: DL, May 10, CG,
11, 13, HAY, Jul 14; 1787: CG, May 4, HAY, Jul 25; 1788: HAY, Sep 30; 1789:
HAY, Jul 31; 1793: CG, May 24, DL, Jun 1; 1795: DL, May 1; 1796: DL, May 11,
CG, Jun 7; 1797: DL, May 18, CG, 31; 1798: CG, May 30; 1799: HAY, Apr 17
Westmoreland Society, 1778: HAY, Mar 31
Weston (actor), 1795: WLWS, Jun 19
Weston (actor, imitator), 1787: HAY, Mar 12
Weston (schoolmaster), 1721: GR, Dec 15
Weston, John
--Amazon Queen, The; or, The Amours of Thalestris to Alexander the Great, 1666:
NONE, Sep 0
Weston, Martha (beneficiary), 1776: DL, Feb 14
Weston, Mrs Thomas (actor), 1763: HAY, Jun 29, Jul 1, Aug 17; 1764: HAY, Sep 1;
1766: HAY, Jul 18, 23, 31, Aug 21, KING'S, 27, 29, Sep 9; 1771: DL, Nov 15,
Dec 21; 1772: DL, Mar 17; 1773: HAY, May 26, DL, 29, HAY, 31, Jun 7, 18, Aeg
11, 27; 1774: DL, Feb 17, HAY, Jun 1, 6, 27, Jul 6, 11, Sep 19, 30; 1775:
HAY, May 26, Jul 31, Aug 21, Sep 4, 16, 19; 1776: HAY, Aug 26
Weston, Thomas (actor), 1759: HAY, Sep 28; 1760: HAY, Jun 28; 1761: DL, Jun 15,
Jul 2, 21, 27, Aug 8, Sep 15, Nov 10, Dec 28; 1762: DL, Jan 7, 29, Apr 30,
HAY, May 1, DL, 7, 17, HAY, Aug 23, 30; 1763: HAY, Jun 20, 27, Jul 6, 18, Aug
1, 5, Sep 5, 7, DL, Oct 1, Nov 9, 19, 30, Dec 17; 1764: DL, Jan 4, 18, Feb
18, May 7, 11, 22, HAY, Jun 13, 26, Jul 6, 16, 23, 30, Aug 20, 29, Sep 1;
1766: HAY, Jun 18, 26, Jul 1, 15, 18, 23, 31, KING'S, Aug 18, 20, HAY, 21,
KING'S, 27, Sep 9, 12, 17, DL, 30, Oct 4, 23, Nov 20, 28, Dec 4; 1767: DL,
Jan 24, Mar 7, May 7, 8, 19, HAY, 29, Jun 4, 5, 8, 10, 12, 17, 22, 30, Jul 2,
3, 6, 15, 22, Aug 5, 7, 10, 12, 14, 17, 21, 25, 27, 31, Sep 7, DL, 15, 21,
26, Oct 15, 28, Nov 20, 28, Dec 1, 12; 1768: DL, Apr 9, 22, May 6, HAY, 30,
Jun 10, 23, Jul 13, 18, 25, DL, Aug 18, HAY, 24, DL, Sep 23, 26, Oct 5, HAY,
7, DL, 15, 18, Nov 17, Dec 23; 1769: DL, Mar 28, 31, Apr 29, May 1, HAY, 15,
24, 29, Jun 2, 5, 21, Aug 16, 28, Sep 19, DL, 21, Dec 11; 1770: DL, Feb 2,
12, 13, Apr 26, HAY, May 16, 18, DL, 22, HAY, 23, 28, Jun 15, 22, Jul 25, Aug
24, 31, Oct 15; 1771: HAY, May 15, 17, 20, 22, 23, 29, 31, Jun 7, 12, 14, 21,
26, Jul 15, Aug 12, 19, 26, 28, Sep 13, DL, 26, 28, Oct 10, 19, 21, 28, 29,
Nov 2, 6, 8, 12, 14, 25, 26, 27, 28, Dec 11, 17; 1772: DL, Jan 3, 11, 20, Feb
8, Mar 5, 21, 23, 28, Apr 7, 20, 21, 24, 27, 29, HAY, May 18, 20, 22, 27, Jun
8, 10, 15, 29, Jul 27, Aug 4, 10, Sep 8, 17, DL, Oct 1, 3, 10, 16, 19, 21,
23, 29, Nov 6, Dec 8, 9, 18, 29; 1773: DL, Jan 8, 19, 20, 26, Feb 2, 3, 4, 6,
Apr 1, 3, 15, 17, HAY, May 17, 26, 28, 31, Jun 14, 18, Jul 21, 23, Aug 4, 11,
23, 27, 31, Sep 3, 17, DL, Oct 2, 5, 25, Nov 1, 8, 9, 24, Dec 11, 27; 1774:
DL, Jan 19, 28, Feb 3, 5, 9, 15, 19, Mar 14, 15, 26, Apr 7, 8, 9, 11, 25, 27,
May 2, 3, 5, 9, 12, HAY, 16, 30, Jun 1, DL, 2, HAY, 6, 8, 10, 27, Jul 15, Aug
8, 19, 26, 29, Sep 5, 6, 12, 16, DL, 17, HAY, 19, DL, 29, HAY, 30, DL, Oct 5,
6, 12, 14, 20, Nov 3, 4, 5, 7, Dec 17, 19; 1775: CG, Jan 6, DL, Feb 1, 2, 16,
21, Mar 7, 14, Apr 19, 21, 22, 24, HAY, May 15, 17, 19, 22, 26, 29, 31, Jun
5, 12, Jul 31, Aug 2, 16, 28, Sep 4, 7, 11, 16, 18, 19, 21, DL, Oct 3, 5, 10,
20, 28; 1776: DL, Jan 1, Feb 14, CG, Apr 27, HAY, Aug 26, DL, Sep 28; 1784:
HAY, Sep 17; 1785: HAY, Apr 26
Weston's Academy, 1723: GR, Nov 23
Weston's scholars (actors), 1722: GR, Apr 14, Oct 27, 29; 1723: GR, Nov 23, Dec

Westray, Juliana, Mrs Anthony (actor), <u>1788</u>: HAY, Sep 9
Westray, Miss (actor), <u>1770</u>: DL, Oct 29
Westwood (actor), <u>1670</u>: LIF, Sep 20, Nov 0; <u>1671</u>: LIF, Mar 15, Jun 0
Wetherhead (actor), <u>1782</u>: HAY, Dec 30
Wetherhill (actor), <u>1728</u>: BFHM, Aug 24
Wetherhill, Mrs (actor), <u>1728</u>: BFHM, Aug 24
Wetherilt (Wetherell), Henry (actor), <u>1720</u>: DL, Dec 17; <u>1722</u>: DL, May 18; <u>1728</u>:
    DL, Oct 30, Nov 15; <u>1730</u>: DL, May 15, 18, Oct 3, 22, 28, Nov 26, 30, Dec 4;
    <u>1731</u>: DL, Jan 20, Feb 8, Apr 30, May 8, 10, 12, 17, 19, Jun 7, 11, 22, Jul 6,
    13, 20, 23, Aug 6, 11, 18, SF/BFMMO, 26, DL, Sep 25, 30, Oct 16, 21, 30, Nov
    9, 10, 23, 25, Dec 1, 2, 21; <u>1732</u>: DL, Jan 1, Mar 21, 30, Apr 17, May 5, 6,
    12, BF, Aug 22, DL, Sep 19, 23, 28, 30, Oct 17, 26, 31, Nov 9, GF, 13, 15,
    25, 28, Dec 1, 27; <u>1733</u>: GF, Feb 19, Mar 6, 28, 30, Apr 2, 24, May 16, 29,
    Sep 10, 12, 17, 21, 25, 27, 28, Oct 5, 12, 15, 18, 22, 23, 24, 26, Dec 8, 31;
    <u>1734</u>: GF, Jan 10, 11, 14, 21, 31, Feb 11, Mar 28, May 15, BFFO, Aug 24, GF,
    Sep 13, 20, 25, Oct 14, 16, 17, 18, Nov 8, 13, 18, 27, Dec 2, 16, 20, 31;
    <u>1735</u>: GF, Jan 3, 4, 6, 8, 11, 20, 24, Feb 20, 24, 25, 27, Mar 13, 20, Apr 22,
    23, May 3, 6, 8, Sep 19; <u>1736</u>: LIF, Oct 9; <u>1737</u>: LIF, Feb 1, Mar 26, May 2
Wetherilt, Elizabeth, Mrs Henry (actor), <u>1721</u>: BF/SF, Aug 24, Sep 2, DL, Oct
    25; <u>1722</u>: DL, May 18, RI, Jul 23; <u>1723</u>: DL, May 14; <u>1724</u>: DL, May 20; <u>1725</u>:
    DL, May 17; <u>1726</u>: DL, May 10, Sep 13, 29, Oct 1, 11, 20, 27, Nov 11, Dec 17,
    30; <u>1727</u>: DL, Jan 20, Feb 21, 27, Apr 28, Sep 9, Oct 12, 30; <u>1728</u>: DL, Mar 9,
    Apr 2, Sep 19, Oct 3, 30; <u>1729</u>: DL, Jan 29, Feb 3, 17, 24, Apr 22, May 7, Sep
    23, Oct 16, 22, 23, 31, Nov 7, 28, Dec 2, 3, 4, 26; <u>1730</u>: DL, Feb 10, May 18,
    Sep 29, Oct 1, 6, 10; <u>1731</u>: DL, Apr 1, 21, May 7, 19, Jun 11, Aug 11,
    SF/BFMMO, 26, DL, Sep 30, Oct 7, 9, 30, Nov 6, 8, 10, 22; <u>1732</u>: DL, Jan 1,
    Apr 14, May 6, 10, Sep 30, Oct 12, GF, Nov 27, 29; <u>1733</u>: GF, Jan 1, 24, Feb
    15, Mar 17, 30, Apr 24, May 8, 29, Sep 21, Oct 4, 9, 11, 17, 22, 23, Dec 8,
    27, 31; <u>1734</u>: GF, Jan 18, 28, Feb 11, May 3, 15, Sep 11, Oct 16, 18, Nov 13,
    Dec 20; <u>1735</u>: GF, Jan 8, Feb 6, Mar 29, Apr 9, May 6, 8, 15, Sep 15, 22, Nov
    3, 10, 11, 14, 20, 25; <u>1736</u>: GF, Mar 9, 18, Apr 16, 17, LIF, Oct 9, 23, 26,
    Nov 20, 24, 27; <u>1737</u>: LIF, Mar 29, May 6
Wetherilt, Mrs Robert Jr (actor), <u>1734</u>: GF, May 3
Wetherilt Jr, Robert (actor), <u>1722</u>: SF, Sep 5; <u>1723</u>: DL, Jun 6; <u>1728</u>: DL, Jan
    10, Mar 19, Oct 18; <u>1729</u>: DL, Jun 20, Dec 26; <u>1730</u>: DL, Apr 23, May 18, Oct
    1, Nov 16; <u>1731</u>: DL, Aug 6, Oct 7, 19, Nov 1; <u>1732</u>: DL, May 3, GF, Dec 4;
    <u>1733</u>: GF, Apr 24
Wewitzer, Mary, Mrs Ralph (actor), <u>1783</u>: HAY, Jun 20
Wewitzer, Miss (actor), <u>1776</u>: CG, Nov 14, Dec 17; <u>1777</u>: CG, Apr 29, May 13;
    <u>1780</u>: HAY, Sep 2, CG, Nov 15; <u>1781</u>: CG, Mar 17, HAY, May 30, Aug 20, 24
Wewitzer, Miss (actor), <u>1782</u>: CG, Oct 18; <u>1784</u>: CG, Dec 14; <u>1788</u>: CG, Sep 22,
    Oct 17, 28; <u>1789</u>: CG, Jan 15, Feb 24, Mar 31, May 8, Jun 2
Wewitzer, Mrs Ralph (actor), <u>1794</u>: HAY, May 22
Wewitzer, Ralph (actor, pantomime writer), <u>1774</u>: CG, Sep 26, Oct 5, 11, 21, Nov
    1, Dec 12, 20; <u>1775</u>: CG, May 2, 17, 19, Oct 9, 13, 18, 31, Nov 1, 13, 21, Dec
    21, 23, 26; <u>1776</u>: CG, Jan 5, 15, Feb 12, Mar 4, Apr 29, 30, Sep 25, 27, Oct
    4, 11, 16, 17, 25, Nov 4, 9, 25, 26, 30, Dec 5, 27, 30; <u>1777</u>: CG, Jan 1, 3,
    8, Feb 22, Mar 31, Apr 16, 23, 28, 29, May 2, 5, 13, Oct 3, 10, 15, 17, 20,
    21, Nov 4, 18, 19, 21; <u>1778</u>: CG, Jan 15, 19, 20, 27, 29, Feb 11, 23, 25, 26,
    Mar 26, Apr 27, May 11, 13, Sep 23, 30, Oct 2, 7, 9, 14, 17, 21, 23, Nov 4,
    21, Dec 1, 11, 12, 15, 21; <u>1779</u>: CG, Jan 4, 22, 25, Feb 22, Mar 27, Apr 12,
    15, 24, 26, 27, 30, May 6, 18, Sep 20, 22, 24, 27, Oct 1, 6, 13, 15, 20, 23,
    Nov 4, 6, 13, 16, Dec 21; <u>1780</u>: CG, Feb 22, 26, Mar 18, Apr 7, 19, 20, 21,
    22, 24, 25, May 17, HAY, Jun 17, 24, Jul 8, 20, 24, Aug 2, Sep 7, CG, Nov 15,
    17, 18, 29, Dec 4, 5, 15, 27, 29; <u>1781</u>: CG, Jan 18, 24, Feb 24, Mar 24, Apr
    17, 21, 26, 28, May 7, 10, 25, HAY, 30, Jun 16, Jul 6, 9, Aug 8, 15, 22, 28,
    29, 31, CG, Sep 17, 19, 26, 28, Oct 5, 10, 13, 22, Nov 1, 7, Dec 12; <u>1782</u>:
    HAY, Jun 3, 6, 12, 13, 18, Jul 2, 5, Aug 8, 13, 17, 27, Sep 18, CG, 23, Oct
    3, 9, 15, 17, 18, 19, 23, Nov 1, 2, 12, 19, 25, Dec 30; <u>1783</u>: CG, Jan 1, 3,
    17, Apr 1, 12, 22, 26, May 13, 15, 17, 19, 20, 23, HAY, 31, Jun 2, 3, 5, CG,
    6, HAY, 7, 9, 12, 20, 21, 30, Jul 5, 26, Aug 1, 13, 19, 27, 29, CG, Sep 17,
    19, 26, Oct 1, 8, 11, 17, 20, 21, Nov 4, 6, 25, Dec 6; <u>1784</u>: CG, Jan 9, 14,
    23, 29, Feb 13, 20, Mar 9, Apr 13, 15, 26, 27, May 8, 10, 18, Jun 2, HAY, 9,
    14, Jul 6, 7, 8, 19, 24, 30, Aug 6, 20, 26, 30, Sep 6, 13, CG, 17, 21, 24,
    29, Oct 1, 8, 12, 18, 29, Nov 3, 13, 16, 30, Dec 1, 4, 14, 22, 27; <u>1785</u>: CG,
    Jan 14, 21, 27, Feb 7, 21, 24, Mar 19, 29, Apr 1, 2, 8, May 4, 7, 12, 18, 26,
    HAY, 28, 30, Jun 7, 9, 21, 22, 23, 24, 29, Jul 6, 13, 18, 26, Aug 16, 19, 31,
    Sep 3, CG, 19, 26, 28, 30, Oct 7, 10, 12, 14, 17, 20, 26, Nov 1, 2, 3, 10,
    22, 29, Dec 7, 14, 23, 26; <u>1786</u>: CG, Jan 5, 7, 14, 28, Feb 1, 7, Mar 6, 11,
    Apr 1, 18, 24, May 9, 11, 13, HAY, Jun 14, 19, 28, 30, Jul 3, 8, 13, 18, 21,
    24, 25, Aug 4, Sep 9, CG, 18, 29, Oct 9, 16, 21, 25, 31, Nov 13, 18, 22, 29,

Dec 1, 21, 23, 26; 1787: CG, Jan 2, 27, Feb 6, 13, 20, Apr 20, 24, 30, May 1,
14, 16, 21, HAY, Jun 13, 16, 20, 21, 22, 27, 28, Jul 23, 25, Aug 7, 28, CG,
Sep 17, 19, 21, 26, Oct 3, 11, 18, 19, Nov 2, 5, 7, 8, 16, 19, 22, 23, 24,
Dec 5, 22, 26; 1788: CG, Jan 5, 10, 14, 21, 28, 29, Feb 4, 25, Mar 11, 15,
24, 26, 28, 29, Apr 1, 2, 8, 23, May 14, HAY, Jun 10, 11, 13, 16, 19, 26, Jul
2, 3, 4, Aug 5, 9, 22, 25, 27, CG, Sep 15, 19, 26, Oct 1, 8, 15, 18, 22, Nov
1, 6, 11, 12, 21, 22, Dec 1; 1789: CG, Jan 20, 28, 31, Feb 3, 11, Mar 16, 28,
31, Apr 4, 14, 15, 20, 27, 30, May 5, 19, 20, 22, 28, 29, Jun 18; 1791: HAY,
Mar 7, Jun 6, 17, 18, 20, 23, Jul 1, 30, Aug 10, 13, 16, 19, Sep 2, DLKING'S,
27, Oct 4, Nov 12; 1792: DLKING'S, Jan 16, 28, Mar 15, 29, Apr 20, 28, May
17, 19, HAY, Jun 15, 22, 23, 29, Jul 7, 19, Aug 2, 6, 9, 15, 23, 31, Sep 5,
6, DL, 20, 25, Oct 4, 13, 18, Nov 10, 21, Dec 10, 14, 21, 22; 1793: DL, Jan
16, 23, Mar 11, 12, 19, Apr 3, 17, May 7, 10, 25, HAY, Jun 11, 12, 14, 17,
18, 21, 22, 24, 25, 26, 29, Jul 9, Aug 3, 27, 30, Sep 12, 13, 30, Oct 7, 8,
10, 15, 17, 29, Nov 5, 9, 13, 16, 29, 30, Dec 7, 10, 13, 14, 16, 17, 26, 30;
1794: HAY, Jan 4, 11, 14, 16, 21, 27, Feb 5, 10, 13, 15, 20, Mar 15, May 22;
1795: DL, Nov 11, 16, 26, Dec 2, 10, 18, 19, 26, 30; 1796: DL, Jan 11, 16,
23, Feb 1, 20, 27, Mar 3, 5, Apr 13, 26, May 9, 12, 17, 21, 25, 28, 31, Jun
6, 8, HAY, Sep 17, DL, 24, 27, 29, Oct 1, 6, 10, 19, 24, 28, Nov 1, 5, 18,
26, Dec 5, 29; 1797: DL, Jan 12, 17, 27, Feb 2, May 1, 8, 9, 12, 15, 23, 26,
27, 30, 31, Jun 7, 12, HAY, Aug 8, DL, Sep 19, 23, 30, Oct 3, 5, 7, 14, 16,
23, 28, Nov 4, 7, 9, 13, 27, Dec 11, 23; 1798: DL, Jan 4, 23, 24, 25, Mar 3,
8, 24, May 7, 11, 24, 29, 30, 31, Jun 5, 6, 7, 12, HAY, Aug 21, DL, Sep 15,
18, 22, Oct 4, 6, 15, 20, 27, Nov 22, Dec 4, HAY, 17, DL, 19, 21, 29; 1799:
DL, Jan 8, 31, Feb 11, Apr 8, 22, 30, May 1, 3, 7, Jun 29, Jul 1, 2, Sep 21,
Oct 3, 8, 10, 26, 31, Nov 6, 7, 13, 15, 27, 29; 1800: DL, Jan 11, 14, Feb 1,
12, 19, Apr 19, 24, 28, May 10, 27, Jun 11, 13
--Dumb Cake, The; or, The Regions of Fancy (pantomime), 1787: CG, Dec 26, 27,
28, 29, 31; 1788: CG, Jan 1, 2, 3, 4, 7, 9, 11, 12, 14, 16, 18, 22, 31, Feb
14, 18, 25
--Gnome, The; or, Harlequin Underground (with Invill), 1788: HAY, Aug 5, 6, 7,
8, 11, 30
--Magic Cavern, The; or, Virtue's Triumph (pantomime), 1784: CG, Dec 27, 28,
29, 30, 31; 1785: CG, Jan 1, 3, 4, 5, 6, 7, 8, 10, 11, 12, 13, 15, 17, 18,
19, 20, 21, 22, 24, 25, 26, 27, 28, 29, 31, Feb 4, 10, 19, 28, Mar 28, Apr 2,
May 2, Oct 13, 21, 31, Nov 5; 1789: CG, Dec 21; 1790: CG, Nov 15; 1793: CG,
Oct 2; 1796: CG, Mar 15, Oct 24; 1799: CG, May 13
Wewitzer, Sarah (singer), 1772: CG, Nov 4, 20, 21, Dec 26; 1773: CG, Feb 23,
Mar 4, 20, May 12, 21; 1774: MARLY, Jun 16, 18, 30, Jul 6, 23, Aug 1, 18, Sep
3, 7
Weybough, Francisco (musician), 1723: HIC, Mar 6
Weylin. See Waylin.
Weyman, Mary (actor), 1729: LIF, Jan 1
Weymouth St, 1790: CG, Apr 29; 1791: CG, May 10
Weymouth Theatre, 1795: CG, Apr 8, Sep 21; 1796: DL, May 2
Whalebone Warehouse, 1757: DL, Feb 22
Whaley (actor), 1671: LIF, Mar 15
Whalley, Thomas Sedgwick, 1799: DL, Apr 23
--Castle of Montval, The, 1799: DL, Apr 13, 20, 23, 26, 29, May 6, 10, 13, 15,
22
Whap'em Aw Wully (song), 1746: CG, Nov 3
Wharton, Anne, 1686: ATCOURT, Feb 3
--Love's Martyr; or, Wit Above Crowns, 1686: ATCOURT, Feb 3
Wharton, Thomas (riot sufferer), 1680: DG, Feb 2
What a Blunder. See Holman, Joseph George.
What an ungratefull devil moves you (song), 1696: DL, Jan 0
What boots it where thy soldier (song), 1793: KING/HAY, Mar 13
What D'ye Call It, The (dance), 1715: LIF, Dec 21, 28; 1716: LIF, Jan 3, 19,
May 10
What D'ye Call It, The. See Gay, John.
What is She? See Smith, Charlotte.
What passion cannot music raise (song), 1789: CG, Mar 6; 1790: CG, Mar 17;
1793: KING/HAY, Feb 15; 1794: CG, Mar 12; 1797: CG, Mar 22; 1800: CG, Mar 19
What shall he have who killed the Deer (song), 1784: CG, Apr 24; 1794: CG, May
23
What state of life can be so blest (song), 1694: DL, Jan 0
What tho' from Venus Cupid sprung (song), 1794: CG, May 26; see also Triumph of
Wine
What though I trace (song), 1790: DL, Mar 10, CG, 17, 26; 1791: DL, Mar 25;
1792: KING'S, Feb 29, Mar 28; 1793: CG, Feb 15; 1794: CG, Mar 7, DL, 12, 14,
Apr 2, 11; 1795: CG, Feb 20; 1796: CG, Feb 24, Mar 16; 1797: CG, Mar 31;
1798: CG, Mar 23; 1799: CG, Feb 8, 20, Mar 6, 13; 1800: CG, Mar 5, 21

What We Must All Come To. See Murphy, Arthur.
What's sweeter than the new blown rose (song), 1790: DL, Mar 5; 1791: DL, Apr
   1; 1792: KING'S, Mar 23, 30; 1793: CG, Mar 8, KING/HAY, 13; 1795: CG, Feb 20;
   1797: CG, Mar 22; 1798: CG, Mar 14, 28
What's That to You? (song), 1757: HAY, Sep 8
Whatley (house servant), 1769: CG, May 19, 23; 1770: CG, May 19; 1771: CG, May
   27; 1772: CG, May 23; 1773: CG, May 22
Wheat Sheaf Tavern, 1792: HAY, Oct 15
Wheatland (actor), 1793: CG, Apr 8
Wheatland, Isaac (musician), 1766: CG, Dec 19
Wheatley, Frederick (actor), 1797: CG, Sep 25, Oct 2, 21
Wheatley, Miss (actor, dancer), 1795: DL, Feb 16, May 6; 1797: DL, May 13, CG,
   Oct 31, Nov 2, 13, Dec 18, 19, 26; 1798: CG, Feb 9, Mar 19, Apr 9, 17, 20,
   28, May 23, 24, 28, Jun 6, Sep 17, Oct 5, 8, 11, Nov 12, Dec 11, 15, 26;
   1799: CG, Mar 2, 4, 5, 27, Apr 2, 9, 26, 30, May 14, 27, Jun 7, Sep 30, Oct
   7, 21, 24, Nov 11, Dec 7, 9, 10, 23; 1800: CG, Jan 16, Mar 4, 8, Apr 30, May
   1, 13, 17, Jun 2, 5, 13, HAY, Aug 14
Wheatley, Mrs (actor), 1782: HAY, Aug 26, CG, Sep 27; 1783: HAY, Jun 6, 30
Wheatsheaf (residence), 1737: LIF, Mar 24; 1754: DL, Mar 23; 1755: DL, Mar 17
Wheble (printer(, 1774: DL, Apr 4
Wheedler, The (song), 1732: GF, May 2, 12
Wheel of Fortune, The. See Cumberland, Richard.
Wheel of Fortune, The; or, The Fools Expectation (entertainment), 1698: DG, Oct
   18
Wheel of Life (song), 1728: LIF, Mar 28
Wheel of Life, The; or, Harlequin's Death (pantomime), 1727: BF, Aug 21
Wheel Turned to Some Tune, The (song), 1726: LIF, Apr 13, 26
Wheelbarrow, The (song), 1757: HAY, Aug 11, 22, 24
Wheeler, Eliza (actor, singer), 1784: CG, Sep 22, 24, Oct 4, 12, 25, Nov 16;
   1785: CG, Feb 1, Mar 15, 30, Apr 5, 6, May 25; 1786: CG, Jan 18, KING'S, 24,
   Mar 16, 30, May 20, 25
Wheeler, Frances (actor), 1781: DL, Oct 15, 29, Dec 6, 27; 1782: DL, Jan 22,
   Apr 11, 24, May 18, Sep 19, 28, Oct 5, 14, 16, Nov 16, 30, Dec 10, 11, 13;
   1783: DL, Jan 24, Feb 7, 22, May 5, 31, Sep 16, 18, 20, 25, CG, Oct 2, DL, 7,
   8, 16, 21, 30, Nov 18, 28, Dec 12, 22, 27; 1784: DL, Jan 3, 10, 14, 16, 22,
   Feb 10, CG, Mar 18, DL, Apr 14, 21, 26, May 5, 27
Wheeler, John (the first) (actor), 1769: HAY, May 15, 26, 29, Jun 2, 5, 7, 14,
   Jul 12, 17, Aug 7, 11, 14, 30, Sep 1, 11, DL, Oct 11, 13, 14, 21, 27, Nov 4,
   Dec 4, 16; 1770: DL, Jan 2, 27, Mar 24, Apr 20, HAY, May 16, DL, 22, HAY, 23,
   25, 28, Jun 5, 25, Jul 9, Aug 8, 24, 31, DL, Sep 27, Oct 9, 13, Nov 5, 17,
   28, Dec 5, 13; 1771: DL, Jan 19, Mar 11, Apr 3, 15, May 21, 27, Sep 21, 26,
   Oct 1, 5, 10, 15, 17, Nov 4, 11, 18, Dec 4, 10; 1772: DL, Jan 1, 15, Feb 21,
   26, 29, Mar 21, 26, 28, Apr 22, 29, May 4, 7, Jun 1, 10, Sep 22, 29, Oct 1,
   20, 21, 30, Nov 4, 7, 12, 17, Dec 22; 1773: DL, Jan 6, Feb 8, 27, Apr 3, 21,
   23, May 24, 28, Sep 18, 25, Oct 8, 19, 25, Nov 2, 4, 15, 20, Dec 30; 1774:
   DL, Jan 5, 6, 17, 19, Feb 2, 17, 19, Mar 14, 19, Apr 21, 25, May 10, 18, Sep
   27, Oct 1, 5, 8, 13, 26, 27, Nov 4, 7, 30, Dec 7; 1775: DL, Jan 2, 21, 23,
   Feb 17, Mar 18, 21, 25, 28, Apr 17, May 1, 12, 13, 16; 1777: DL, Apr 22
Wheeler, John (the second) (actor), 1782: HAY, Nov 25
When a Tar returns home (song), 1799: CG, Oct 7
When all the air shall ring (song), 1793: KING/HAY, Mar 13
When all the Attic Fire was fled (song), 1757: HAY, Aug 31, Sep 2, 5, 12
When Arthur first in court began (song), 1791: CG, May 17; 1792: CG, May 11;
   1800: CG, May 2
When Bacchus (song), 1761: KING'S, Mar 12
When Bibo went down (song), 1789: CG, May 5, 29; 1791: CG, May 18; 1795: DL,
   May 19
When Britain first at Heaven's Command (song), 1745: DL, Apr 4; 1751: DL, Feb
   26; 1793: KING/HAY, Feb 15
When Britain first her Flag upreared (song), 1799: CG, Oct 7
When Britain from her sea girt shore (song), 1793: KING/HAY, Mar 13, 15
When daisies mead (song), 1793: CG, May 24; 1794: CG, Apr 7
When first Amintas charmed my heart (song), 1676: DG, Mar 11
When first I began, Sir, to ogle the Ladies (song), 1799: DL, Apr 19; 1800: DL,
   May 29
When first I saw the bright Aurelia's eyes (song), 1694: DG, Jan 10
When foaming waves contrary beat (song), 1795: CG, May 25; 1796: CG, Apr 5
When generous wine (song), 1787: CG, Oct 18; 1795: CG, May 27
When Gentle Parthenissa (song), 1760: CG, Mar 17
When his loud voice (song), 1786: DL, Mar 10; 1789: DL, Mar 18, CG, 27; 1790:
   CG, Feb 24, DL, 26; 1791: CG, Mar 11, DL, 23; 1792: KING'S, Feb 24, CG, Mar
   9; 1793: KING/HAY, Feb 22, CG, Mar 6; 1794: CG, Mar 12, DL, 21, Apr 4, 10;

1795: KING'S, Feb 27, CG, Mar 13, 25; 1796: CG, Feb 24, Mar 2; 1797: CG, Mar
    31; 1798: CG, Mar 30; 1799: CG, Feb 8
When I Drink My Heart Is Possessed (song), 1706: DL, Jan 7
When I languished and wished (song), 1697: LIF, Jun 0
When I was a little baby (song), 1783: CG, Feb 25
When in War on the Ocean (song), 1793: CG, Oct 2, 12
When Joseph was dead (song), 1794: DL, Apr 10
When Joshua (song), 1794: DL, Apr 10
When King David (song), 1794: DL, Apr 10
When love was a stranger (song), 1796: CG, Apr 12, May 12, 28
When my Money was gone (song), 1793: CG, May 24; 1794: CG, Apr 7; 1795: CG, May
    13; see also Disconsolate Sailor
When Myra Sings (song), 1729: DL, Mar 26
When on board our trim vessel (song), 1793: CG, May 10; 1794: CG, May 2; 1795:
    DL, May 19; 1797: DL, Jun 12
When Peace smiles around (song), 1799: CG, Oct 7
When Phoebus the tops of the hills does adorn (song), 1757: DL, Mar 31, CG, May
    3; 1781: CG, Apr 25, May 7; 1783: CG, May 17; 1784: CG, Apr 24, May 1
When sable Night (song), 1798: CG, Apr 21
When shall we three meet again? (song), 1780: CG, Apr 10
When spring has chac'd the winter's snow (song), 1787: CG, Oct 18
When storms the proud (song), 1789: DL, Mar 20; 1792: CG, Feb 24; 1793: CG, Mar
    8; 1798: CG, Mar 14
When sunny Beams (song), 1798: CG, Oct 15
When Sylvia was kind (song), 1690: DL, Dec 0
When the ear heard him (song), 1793: CG, Feb 15; 1794: DL, Apr 4, 11
When the earth was without form (song), 1786: DL, Mar 29; 1794: DL, Apr 10
When the seaman quits the shore (song), 1799: CG, Jun 7
When the sun (song), 1794: CG, Mar 21
When the time drew near (song), 1794: DL, Apr 10
When the world first knew creation (song), 1694: DG, May 0
When thou art absent (song), 1791: CG, May 20
When tis night and the mid watch is come. See Mid Watch.
When virtue forms (song), 1792: CG, May 15
When warlike Ensigns (song), 1794: DL, Apr 9
When will Stella kind and tender (song), 1697: LIF, Nov 0
When you dispense your influence (song), 1675: DG, Jun 12
Where art thou god of love (song), 1682: DG, Aug 10
Where e'er you walk (song), 1789: CG, Mar 6, DL, 18; 1790: CG, Feb 24, DL, 26;
    1791: DL, Mar 23, CG, 23; 1793: KING/HAY, Feb 22; 1799: CG, Mar 6; 1800: CG,
    Feb 28
Where is that towering spirit fled? (song), 1796: CG, Mar 14, Apr 1, May 18;
    1797: CG, May 24; see also Minstrel's Song
Where is this stupendous stranger? (song), 1786: DL, Mar 29; 1787: DL, Feb 23;
    1789: DL, Mar 18; 1790: DL, Feb 26; 1791: DL, Mar 23; 1792: KING'S, Feb 24;
    1793: KING/HAY, Feb 22; 1794: DL, Apr 10; 1795: CG, Mar 13; 1799: CG, Mar 6
Where shall I seek (song), 1791: DL, Apr 1, CG, 13; 1792: KING'S, Feb 29; 1793:
    CG, Mar 8; 1794: DL, Mar 26
Where the bee sucks (song), 1774: MARLY, Jul 6; 1787: DL, Mar 7, HAY, Aug 14,
    21; 1788: DL, Feb 22, Mar 5; 1794: CG, May 23
Where would coy Aminta run (song), 1684: ATCOURT, Feb 11
Wherever I am (song), 1670: BRI/COUR, Dec 0
Wherrit, Esther (dancer), 1729: LIF, Jan 1, May 14; 1730: LIF, Apr 25, May 1,
    7, 13, 21, 28; 1731: LIF, May 19, 25, 31, Jun 2, Oct 11, Nov 2, 25, Dec 14,
    GF, 17, 18, 20, 21, 22; 1732: GF, Jan 11, 15, LIF, 19, GF, 21, 25, 27, Feb 2,
    14, 15, 17, 22, 24, 28, Mar 4, 6, 7, 16, 25, 30, Apr 1, 12, 14, 15, 17, 18,
    20, 21, 26, 28, May 1, 2, 4, 10, 11, 12, 15, 17, 18, 19, 22, 23, TC, Aug 4,
    GF, Oct 4, 9, 10, 11, 13, 14, 16, 18, 25, 26, 27, 28, 30, Nov 2, 4, 6, 8, 9,
    11, 13, 14, 15, 17, 18, 21, 23, 24, 25, 27, 29, 30, Dec 13, 15, 20; 1733: GF,
    Jan 10, 11, 12, 13, 20, 23, 24, Feb 2, 5, 12, 13, 15, Mar 1, 12, 13, Apr 13,
    20, 27, 30, May 3, 4, 8, 9, 10, 11, 16, 18, 22, 23, Sep 25, 27, Oct 1, 4, 9,
    15, 16, 17, 18, 19, 22, 24, 26, 29, 30, 31, Nov 1, 2, 6, 7, 8, 9, 10, 12, 26,
    Dec 8, 11, 14, 15, 18, 19, 20, 26, 27, 28, 29, 31; 1734: GF, Jan 2, 7, 8, 9,
    10, 11, 12, 14, 18, 19, 22, 24, 26, 28, Feb 2, 5, 11, Mar 18, Apr 18, 19, 24,
    26, May 1, 6, 7, 8, 15, 16, 17, 20
Which is the Man? See Cowley, Hannah.
Whicherly. See Wycherley.
Whig and Tory. See Griffin, Benjamin.
While Phillis does drink (song), 1695: LIF, Dec 0
While the jolly grog (song), 1798: CG, Oct 15
Whilst Alexas lay prest (song), 1672: LIF, Apr 0
Whilst I with grief (song), 1689: DLORDG, May 28; 1693: NONE, Sep 0

Whilst wretched fools sneak up and down (song), 1699: DL, May 0
Whim (dance), 1703: LIF, Jun 14; 1733: DL/HAY, Oct 3, 12, 19, 24, Nov 14, 15,
     HAY, Dec 13, DL/HAY, 19; 1734: DL/HAY, Jan 2, GF, 26, 28, Feb 2, 5, Apr 18,
     24, May 8, 16, 17, HAY, 27, LIF, 29, GF, Dec 31; 1736: DL, Mar 25, 29, May
     15; 1748: HAY, Jan 25; 1769: CG, Apr 27, Nov 23, 30, Dec 6, 12, 14, 20; 1770:
     CG, Jan 19, 25, 26, Feb 22, Mar 15, 24, 27, Apr 3, 5, 21, 28, May 7, 26, Oct
     24, 31; 1771: CG, Mar 5, 23; 1772: CG, Mar 12, 21, 24, 28; 1773: CG, Apr 26,
     May 6, 8, 20; 1774: CG, Apr 16, May 4
Whim, The; or, The Hospital Fools (play, anon), 1770: HAY, Mar 17
Whim, The; or, The Merry Cheat (musical, anon), 1741: CG, Apr 17
Whims and Fancies (entertainment), 1800: CG, May 10
Whimsical Battle of the Greybeards, The; or, The Humourous History of a Covent
     Garden Adventure (droll, anon), 1761: SFT, Sep 21, 22
Whimsical Behavior of Choice Spirits (entertainment), 1761: CG, Apr 16
Whimsical Country Wedding (dance), 1710: GR, Sep 11
Whimsical Dance (dance), 1710: GR, Aug 5, 10, 19, 28, 29
Whimsical Death of Harlequin, The (pantomime, anon), 1716: DL, Apr 4, 6, 18,
     25, 27, May 2, 10, 12, 15
Whimsical Description of the Antients and Moderns (entertainment), 1765: DL,
     May 9
Whimsical Lovers, The (farce, anon), 1736: TC, Aug 4
Whimsical Song (song), 1702: LIF, Oct 21
Whip of Dunboyne (dance), 1702: DL, Dec 8; 1703: DL, Feb 12, DG, Apr 30, DL,
     Jun 16, 18; 1704: DL, Oct 20; 1706: DL, Jan 21; 1707: YB, Nov 19
Whistling Plowman (song), 1766: DL, May 13
Whitaker (actor), 1735: LIF, Jun 12, Aug 6, 22, 29, Sep 5, HAY, Dec 13; 1736:
     HAY, Feb 16
Whitaker (actor), 1752: CG, Oct 10; 1759: CG, Dec 10, 31; 1760: CG, Jan 18, Dec
     11; 1761: CG, Sep 26, Oct 13; 1762: CG, Mar 27
Whitaker (singer), 1784: CG, Oct 25, Nov 12; 1785: CG, Mar 28, May 3; 1786: CG,
     Jan 18
Whitaker, William
--Conspiracy, The; or, The Change of Government, 1680: DG, Mar 0
Whitby (actor), 1779: HAY, Oct 13
Whitcomb St, 1779: KING'S, May 13
White (actor), 1742: JS, May 31; 1744: JS, Dec 10; 1746: JS, Dec 29; 1749: BFC,
     Aug 23
White (actor), 1792: HAY, Oct 15
White (auctioneer), 1782: HAY, Jan 14
White (boxkeeper), 1703: DL, Jun 14; 1710: DL, Apr 15; 1711: SH, May 9; 1715:
     LIF, Jun 1; 1716: LIF, Jun 5; 1717: LIF, May 22; 1718: LIF, May 27; 1719:
     LIF, May 14; 1720: LIF, May 7; 1725: LIF, May 14
White (householder), 1756: HAY, Mar 25
White (violinist), 1800: CG, Feb 28
White Bear Tavern, 1777: KING'S, May 1
White Devil, The. See Webster, John.
White Hart Tavern, 1742: BFG, Aug 25; 1744: CG, Apr 20; 1749: DL, Feb 14; 1757:
     DL, Dec 21
White Head Theatre, 1702: WH, Jan 14
White Horse Inn, 1789: KHS, Sep 16, WHF, Nov 9
White Joke (dance), 1730: GF, Apr 28, May 19, 26, Jun 4, 17, 19, Jul 6, SOU,
     Sep 24; 1732: RIW/HAY, Sep 11
White Joke (song), 1730: GF, Jun 2, 29
White Lion Tavern, 1758: CG, Jul 6
White, Captain (shipper), 1758: DL, Oct 27
White, Edward (actor), 1752: CG, Dec 11; 1753: CG, Feb 7, Mar 24, May 14, Sep
     21, Oct 5, 10, 22, 27, 30, Nov 1, 12; 1754: CG, Mar 9, Apr 22, May 14, Sep
     20, 25, Oct 2, 15, 17, 18, 22, 24, Nov 4, 16, 20, Dec 10, 26, 30; 1755: CG,
     Jan 10, 28, Feb 18, 20, Mar 6, 18, Apr 30, May 7, Sep 29, Oct 6, 20, 27, Nov
     4, 12, 17, 19, 21, Dec 3, 4, 11; 1756: CG, Jan 15, 27, Feb 3, 26, Mar 18, 22,
     30, Apr 1, 6, 29, May 14, 17, 24, Sep 22, 27, Oct 4, 6, 11, 12, 15, 20, 25,
     28, 30, Nov 4, 22, Dec 10, 20; 1757: CG, Jan 14, 27, 28, Feb 16, 19, Mar 14,
     21, May 4, 13, 20, 25, Sep 21, 28, Oct 8, 10, 13, 15, 17, 19, 20, 21, 22, 27,
     Nov 4, 5, 11, 16, Dec 5, 6, 7, 10, 14, 20; 1758: CG, Jan 11, 27, Feb 1, Mar
     14, Apr 3, 14, 17, 22, 27, May 3, DL, Sep 16; 1762: CG, Sep 20, 24, 27, Oct
     2, 6, 8, 16, 19, Nov 3, 5, 12, 15, 29; 1763: CG, Feb 1, Mar 21, Apr 12, May
     9, 14, Sep 21, 26, 28, Oct 3, 17, 21, 26, Nov 4, 15, 18, 26, Dec 16; 1764:
     CG, Jan 9, 16, Feb 15, Mar 29, Apr 28, May 7, 9, 15, 18, 23, Sep 19, 24, 26,
     Oct 1, 10, 11, 15, 16, 17, 18, Nov 5, 7, 15, 27, Dec 21; 1765: CG, Jan 8, 21,
     29, Feb 18, Mar 26, May 3, 10, 17, 24, Sep 18, 20, 23, Oct 3, 4, 17; 1772:
     HAY, Dec 21
White, Eleanor (actor, dancer), 1759: CG, Apr 28; 1760: CG, Jan 16, 25, Feb 14,

Mar 17, Apr 7, May 3, 19, Sep 22, 24, Oct 20; <u>1761</u>: CG, Jan 6, Apr 20, Sep
16, 23, Oct 14; <u>1762</u>: CG, Oct 4, Dec 8, 10, 27; <u>1763</u>: CG, May 11, Oct 7, 26,
Nov 18, Dec 1; <u>1764</u>: CG, Sep 21, 24, Oct 23; <u>1765</u>: CG, Jan 8, May 2, Oct 3,
4, 16; <u>1766</u>: CG, Oct 18, Nov 27; <u>1767</u>: CG, Sep 18, Nov 28; <u>1768</u>: CG, Jan 29,
Feb 1, HAY, Jun 23, Jul 8, 27, Aug 8, 19, Oct 7; <u>1769</u>: CG, Feb 1, HAY, May
22, 26, Jun 5, Jul 12, Aug 7, 25, 28, CG, Oct 24; <u>1770</u>: CG, Jan 29, 31, HAY,
May 23, Jun 25, 27, Jul 25, Aug 1, 8, 24, Sep 27, CG, Dec 26; <u>1771</u>: CG, Jan
1, 15, Apr 12, 22, HAY, May 22, 31, Jun 5, 14, 26, Jul 1, 3, 10, Aug 26, Sep
2, 28; <u>1772</u>: CG, May 1, HAY, 18, 22, Jun 24, 29, Jul 10, 15, 27, Sep 17, 18,
CG, Oct 23; <u>1774</u>: CG, Jan 3, Apr 11, Sep 23, Nov 1, 19, Dec 27; <u>1775</u>: CG, Mar
30, Oct 31, Dec 21; <u>1776</u>: CG, Apr 30, Oct 11, 25, Nov 2, 30; <u>1777</u>: CG, Jan 3,
May 2, Oct 20, Nov 19; <u>1778</u>: CG, Feb 23, Mar 28, Oct 14, 17, Dec 1, 21; <u>1779</u>:
CG, Apr 21, HAY, Oct 18, CG, Nov 13; <u>1780</u>: CG, Jan 25, Feb 8, 22, 24, 26, Apr
25, Dec 15; <u>1781</u>: CG, Mar 8, 24; <u>1782</u>: CG, Dec 6; <u>1784</u>: CG, Jan 29, HAY, Mar
8, CG, Sep 20, 28; <u>1785</u>: CG, Feb 21, Oct 17; <u>1787</u>: CG, Apr 16; <u>1788</u>: CG, Nov
22, Dec 26; <u>1789</u>: CG, Dec 21; <u>1790</u>: CG, Jan 23, Mar 13
White, George (proprietor), <u>1791</u>: DL, Jun 4
White, James (boxkeeper, treasurer), <u>1741</u>: CG, May 4; <u>1742</u>: CG, May 10; <u>1743</u>:
CG, May 5; <u>1744</u>: CG, Apr 30; <u>1745</u>: CG, Apr 30; <u>1746</u>: CG, Apr 28; <u>1747</u>: CG,
May 6; <u>1748</u>: CG, Apr 27; <u>1749</u>: CG, Apr 17; <u>1750</u>: CG, Apr 25; <u>1751</u>: CG, Apr
29; <u>1752</u>: CG, Apr 24; <u>1753</u>: CG, May 7; <u>1754</u>: CG, May 6; <u>1755</u>: CG, May 5;
<u>1756</u>: CG, May 10
White, John (renter), <u>1758</u>: CG, Feb 23; <u>1759</u>: CG, Sep 28
White, Master (dancer), <u>1772</u>: DL, May 5
White, Miss (actor), <u>1757</u>: CG, Nov 2; <u>1758</u>: CG, Feb 11, Apr 8; <u>1759</u>: CG, Jan
29, Mar 20, Apr 28, Oct 8, 30; <u>1760</u>: CG, Mar 6, May 3
White, Miss (actor; <u>1746</u>: GF, Dec 5
White, Mrs (actor), <u>1741</u>: SF, Sep 14
White, Mrs (beneficiary), <u>1719</u>: LIF, May 28; <u>1721</u>: LIF, May 16; <u>1722</u>: LIF, Apr
20; <u>1723</u>: LIF, May 24; <u>1724</u>: LIF, May 18; <u>1725</u>: LIF, May 19
White, Mrs C (wardrobe keeper), <u>1760</u>: CG, Sep 22
White, Richard (publisher), <u>1795</u>: DL, Apr 17; <u>1797</u>: CG, Feb 18
White, Susan (renter), <u>1758</u>: CG, Apr 29
White's Chocolate House, <u>1742</u>: DL, Mar 20; <u>1744</u>: KING'S, Nov 3; <u>1750</u>: DL, May
21, 22; <u>1753</u>: DL, Feb 6; <u>1756</u>: DL, Nov 12
White's Coffee House, <u>1749</u>: HAY, Nov 20; <u>1751</u>: DL, Feb 27
Whitechapel, <u>1743</u>: LIF, Mar 22; <u>1744</u>: HAY, Apr 23; <u>1754</u>: NWLS, Mar 1; <u>1787</u>:
ROY, Jul 3
Whitefield, George (bishop), <u>1767</u>: HAY, Sep 4
Whitefriars, <u>1661</u>: SALSBURY, Jan 29, Feb 9, 23, Mar 1, 16, 19, Apr 1, 2; <u>1672</u>:
WF, Dec 30; <u>1673</u>: WF, Sep 4, Nov 20, Dec 22; <u>1674</u>: WF, Jan 12, Apr 20, Sep
29; <u>1675</u>: WF, Jan 26; <u>1748</u>: CG, Feb 8; <u>1778</u>: CG, May 19; <u>1779</u>: CG, May 13
Whitehall Bridge, <u>1662</u>: THAMES, Aug 23
Whitehall, <u>1660</u>: ATCOURT, Aug 0, Nov 19; <u>1661</u>: ATCOURT, Apr 20, NONE, 22,
ATCOURT, Dec 16; <u>1662</u>: THAMES, Aug 23, ATCOURT, Oct 8, Nov 17; <u>1663</u>: LIF, Oct
0, ATCOURT, Dec 10; <u>1664</u>: BRIDGES, Sep 28; <u>1665</u>: ATCOURT, Apr 20; <u>1666</u>:
ATCOURT, Oct 11, 29, Nov 5, BRIDGES, Dec 27, ATCOURT, 28; <u>1667</u>: ATCOURT, Oct
1, Nov 16; <u>1668</u>: ATCOURT, Sep 28, Nov 9, Dec 14; <u>1669</u>: ATCOURT, Feb 15, 22;
<u>1670</u>: ATCOURT, Nov 4; <u>1671</u>: ATCOURT, Feb 9, 20, Sep 19; <u>1672</u>: ATCOU/DG, Dec
2, 27; <u>1674</u>: DL, Mar 27, DG, May 16, ATCOURT, Sep 10; <u>1675</u>: ATCOURT, Jan 25,
NONE, Jun 20, ATCOURT, Jul 24, Sep 29; <u>1677</u>: ATCOURT, Feb 5, May 22, 29, Dec
17; <u>1681</u>: ATCOURT, Nov 15; <u>1683</u>: CITY, Oct 29; <u>1684</u>: ATCOURT, Feb 11; <u>1685</u>:
ATCOURT, Nov 24; <u>1686</u>: ATCOURT, Jan 27, Dec 1, 9, 15; <u>1687</u>: ATCOURT, Jan 5,
19, 26, May 16; <u>1688</u>: ATCOURT, Jun 18; <u>1689</u>: ATCOURT, Nov 4, 15, DLORDG, 28;
<u>1690</u>: ATCOURT, Jan 1, Nov 4; <u>1692</u>: DLORDG, Jul 14; <u>1693</u>: ATCOURT, May 0;
<u>1697</u>: ATCOURT, Feb 6; <u>1720</u>: DL, Mar 3; <u>1745</u>: CT, Jan 14, LIF, Oct 7; <u>1779</u>:
HAY, Aug 24; <u>1789</u>: DL, Apr 20; <u>1799</u>: HAY, Apr 17
Whitehead, Christopher (householder), <u>1660</u>: NONE, Sep 0
Whitehead, Paul (prologuist), <u>1767</u>: CG, Sep 14
Whitehead, William, <u>1750</u>: DL, Feb 24, Mar 5; <u>1754</u>: DL, Apr 20; <u>1757</u>: DL, Dec
27; <u>1758</u>: DL, Jan 26; <u>1762</u>: DL, Feb 10; <u>1770</u>: DL, Jan 6; <u>1771</u>: DL, Jan 12;
<u>1773</u>: CG, Apr 16; <u>1796</u>: CG, May 17
--Creusa, Queen of Athens, <u>1754</u>: DL, Apr 8, 20, 22, 23, 25, 27, May 1, 3, 8,
11; <u>1755</u>: DL, Feb 25, Mar 1, Apr 10; <u>1757</u>: DL, Apr 30, May 4; <u>1758</u>: DL, Jan
19, 26; <u>1759</u>: DL, Feb 15, 17
--Roman Father, The, <u>1750</u>: DL, Feb 24, 26, 27, Mar 1, 3, 5, 6, 8, 12, Apr 7,
24, May 8, 11; <u>1751</u>: DL, Mar 11, Apr 18, May 15; <u>1754</u>: DL, Apr 8, 20; <u>1757</u>:
DL, Dec 27; <u>1758</u>: DL, Jan 28, 31, Feb 2, 6, Apr 14; <u>1760</u>: DL, Apr 15; <u>1764</u>:
DL, Mar 27, Apr 14, May 8; <u>1765</u>: DL, Apr 20; <u>1767</u>: CG, Nov 18, 25, Dec 2;
<u>1768</u>: CG, Feb 13, 22, 23, Apr 11, Oct 5; <u>1769</u>: CG, Feb 3, Mar 14, Apr 11, May
15; <u>1770</u>: CG, Mar 29; <u>1775</u>: CG, Dec 8; <u>1776</u>: CG, Jan 22, 26, DL, Apr 24, Nov
16, 18, 21; <u>1777</u>: DL, Apr 1, Oct 28, 30; <u>1778</u>: CG, Nov 10; <u>1785</u>: CG, Oct 17,

20, 24, Nov 8, Dec 9; <u>1786</u>: CG, Jan 9, Feb 17, Oct 21; <u>1787</u>: CG, Feb 5, May
19, Dec 3; <u>1788</u>: CG, Jan 1, Dec 29; <u>1794</u>: DL, Nov 7, 10, 11, 13, 14, 15, 22,
25, Dec 2
--School for Lovers, The, <u>1762</u>: DL, Feb 10, 11, 12, 13, 15, 16, 17, 18, 19, 23,
27, Mar 4, 11; <u>1763</u>: DL, Mar 21; <u>1765</u>: DL, Mar 18, May 15, Oct 30, Nov 19;
<u>1766</u>: DL, Jan 27; <u>1767</u>: DL, Feb 19, May 7, Oct 8, Nov 23, Dec 31; <u>1768</u>: DL,
May 7, Oct 1, Nov 11; <u>1769</u>: DL, Nov 1; <u>1770</u>: DL, Oct 24; <u>1775</u>: DL, Oct 20,
24, Nov 2; <u>1776</u>: DL, Feb 2; <u>1794</u>: DL, Nov 12, Dec 15, 18, 19; <u>1795</u>: DL, Feb
24
--Trip to Scotland, A (farce), <u>1770</u>: DL, Jan 6, 8, 9, 11, 15, 17, 19, 23, 26,
Feb 2, 5, 9, Mar 5, 27, Apr 23, May 15, 23, Jun 4, Sep 25, Dec 21, 28; <u>1771</u>:
DL, Jan 16, Apr 5, 27, May 27, 29, Nov 22; <u>1772</u>: DL, Jan 23, Mar 30, Apr 22,
May 9, 13, 29, Jun 3, Oct 6, 22, Nov 26, Dec 19; <u>1773</u>: DL, Feb 19, Mar 2, CG,
Apr 16, DL, 21, May 14, Jun 2, Oct 13, 30, Dec 22; <u>1774</u>: DL, Jan 4, May 19,
25, Nov 1; <u>1775</u>: DL, Feb 24, May 17, Sep 30, Dec 22; <u>1776</u>: CHR, Oct 2; <u>1782</u>:
DL, Apr 15, Oct 10; <u>1783</u>: DL, Apr 10, May 1, 24; <u>1784</u>: DL, May 15, Sep 16
Whitely (actor), <u>1782</u>: HAY, Mar 21
Whitemore, Mrs (actor), <u>1800</u>: CG, Jan 16
Whiten (beneficiary), <u>1718</u>: HA, Feb 19
Whitfield, John (actor, author), <u>1774</u>: CG, Sep 26, 30, Oct 4, 10, 11, 13, 15,
19, 29, 31, Nov 2, 4, 8, 24, Dec 1, 6, 15, 20, 27; <u>1775</u>: CG, Jan 23, Feb 11,
Mar 2, May 2, 4, HAY, 15, CG, 17, 20, HAY, 22, 24, 26, 29, Jun 5, 7, Jul 7,
31, Aug 2, 9, 16, 28, Sep 4, 16, 18, 19, DL, 26, 30, Oct 3, 5, 10, 17, 28,
Nov 3, 4, 9, 23, Dec 2, 7, 26; <u>1776</u>: DL, Mar 7, 14, 18, 25, 28, Apr 19, 24,
29, May 11, 13, HAY, 20, 22, 28, 31, Jun 12, 14, 26, Jul 10, 29, Aug 2, Sep
2, CG, 23, 25, 27, Oct 2, 7, 8, 16, 17, 31, Nov 6, 8, 11, 14, 20, 21, 25, 26,
28, Dec 5, 6, 21; <u>1777</u>: CG, Jan 17, 25, Feb 1, 13, 22, 25, Mar 17, Apr 7, 14,
16, 28, May 2, 5, 13, 29, Sep 22, 24, 26, 29, Oct 1, 10, 15, 20, 21, 30, Nov
1, 7, 20, Dec 3, 5, 10, 26; <u>1778</u>: CG, Jan 15, 19, 20, 21, 29, Feb 6, 10, 23,
24, Mar 9, 30, 31, Apr 7, 11, 20, 21, 22, 25, 27, 29, 30, May 5, 6, 9, 11,
13, 15, 19, Sep 18, 21, 23, Oct 2, 7, 9, 12, 14, 15, 21, 22, 24, 26, Nov 4,
19, DL, 30, CG, Dec 15, 17, 21, 26; <u>1779</u>: CG, Jan 4, 18, 19, 21, 22, 25, Feb
22, 23, Mar 4, 20, 22, Apr 5, 13, 21, 24, May 3, 4, 10, 18, Sep 20, 22, 24,
Oct 1, 13, 18, 23, 29, Nov 1, 4, 6, 10, 13, 16, 22, 27, 30, Dec 1, 3, 7, 11,
16, 23, 31; <u>1780</u>: CG, Jan 12, 25, Feb 2, 17, 22, Mar 18, 29, Apr 7, 12, 21,
24, 25, 27, May 1, 3, 18, Sep 18, Oct 2, 3, 6, 9, 10, 18, 19, 21, 23, 24, 26,
30, 31, Nov 1, 4, 8, 10, 13, 14, 27, Dec 4, 12, 16; <u>1781</u>: CG, Jan 10, 12, 18,
31, Feb 14, 20, Mar 8, 13, Apr 18, 28, May 7, 11, 14, Sep 17, 19, 26, 28, Oct
3, 23, 31, Nov 2, 5, 9, 28, Dec 5, 8, 11, 17, 18, 20, 31; <u>1782</u>: CG, Jan 1, 7,
8, 10, 22, Feb 5, 9, 11, Mar 14, 16, 19, 21, Apr 1, 10, 12, 17, 23, May 3, 7,
11, 17, 20, 28, 29, Sep 23, 25, 27, 30, Oct 3, 7, 10, 14, 16, 18, 21, 31, Nov
1, 2, 4, 6, 8, 12, 14, 16, 18, 27, 30, Dec 2, 14, 19, 20, 27, 30; <u>1783</u>: CG,
Jan 3, Feb 19, 25, Mar 29, Apr 1, 7, 23, 25, 26, 30, May 3, 7, 9, 10, 17, 20,
HAY, Jun 4, CG, Sep 19, 22, 24, 26, Oct 1, 2, 3, 6, 10, 13, 15, 16, 17, 28,
31, Nov 4, 8, 10, 19, 27, Dec 6, 11, 26; <u>1784</u>: CG, Jan 3, 7, 9, 14, 16, 22,
Feb 5, 10, 13, 18, 19, 20, 23, Mar 4, 6, 18, 20, 22, Apr 13, 26, 27, May 4,
7, 8, 13, 17, 19, 29; <u>1786</u>: DL, Oct 7, 30, Nov 22, Dec 19; <u>1787</u>: DL, Jan 2,
CG, 11, DL, 13, 16, Feb 16, Apr 14, 19, 23, May 1, Sep 18, 22, Oct 4, 9, 18,
23, 26, 29, Dec 10, 11, 14; <u>1788</u>: DL, Jan 5, 21, 28, 31, Feb 7, Mar 29, 31,
Apr 8, 10, 14, 28, 30, May 5, 7, 23, 26, Sep 18, 20, 30, Oct 2, 4, 7, 9, 23,
Nov 4, 10, 17, 22, 25, 28, 29, Dec 15, 16, 29; <u>1789</u>: DL, Feb 7, 16, 20, 21,
24, Mar 21, 24, Apr 2, 4, 21, May 1, 19, Jun 4, 13, Sep 12, 26, Oct 1, 8, 10,
28, 31, Nov 6, 7, 24, 27, 30, Dec 1, 2, 5, 10; <u>1790</u>: DL, Feb 8, 10, 11, 23,
Mar 8, 18, 22, Apr 7, 9, 30, May 12, 27, 28, Jun 1, Sep 11, 14, 16, Oct 2, 4,
7, 14, 21, 23, 27, Nov 3, 5, Dec 14; <u>1791</u>: DL, Mar 28, May 10, 11, 31, Jun 1,
DLKING'S, Sep 22, Oct 3, 4, 6, 31, Nov 5, 7, 10, 11, 14, 22, Dec 2, 19; <u>1792</u>:
DLKING'S, Jan 7, 9, 18, Feb 11, 14, 18, 23, Mar 1, 6, 10, 13, 26, 29, 31, Apr
14, May 17, Jun 13, DL, Sep 18, 19, 20, 25, 27, 29, Oct 9, 16, Nov 2, 5, 27,
Dec 3, 10, 15, 21, 26, 28, 31; <u>1793</u>: DL, Jan 3, 16, 21, Feb 9, 12, 16, 21,
23, 25, 28, Mar 4, 5, 9, 11, Apr 9, 17, 25, May 4, 9, 11, 22, 30, Jun 1, 5;
<u>1794</u>: DL, Apr 21, 25, 29, May 1, 3, 7, 13, 19, Jun 12, 14, 23, 26, Sep 18,
20, 23, 30, Oct 7, 14, 18, 20, 28, 29, Nov 10, 13, 18, 24, Dec 12, 13, 16;
<u>1795</u>: DL, Jan 1, 20, 22, 23, Feb 9, 28, Mar 2, 10, 14, 21, Apr 15, 22, May 4,
28, 29, Jun 6, Sep 19, 22, 29, Oct 5, 19, 20, 21, Nov 6, 12, 20, 23, Dec 9,
18, 21; <u>1796</u>: DL, Jan 29, Feb 15, 29, Mar 8, 30, Apr 1, 2, 8, 12, 18, 19, 20,
25, 29, May 2, 13, 23, 24, 31, Jun 14, Sep 20, 22, 29, Oct 3, 10, 13, 22, 24,
Nov 1, 10, 22, 23, Dec 16, 29, 30; <u>1797</u>: DL, Jan 2, 12, 14, 17, 20, Feb 3, 7,
18, Mar 9, Apr 6, 27, 28, May 1, 12, 22, 30, CG, Oct 23, Nov 1, 2, 3, 9, 20,
23, 29, Dec 27, 28; <u>1798</u>: CG, Jan 4, 11, Feb 6, 9, 13, Apr 17, 20, 28, 30,
May 15, 16, 22, 30, Sep 17, 19, Oct 5, 8, 15, Nov 21, Dec 8; <u>1799</u>: CG, Jan
25, Apr 9, 12, May 15, 25, Sep 16, 18, 20, 30, Oct 2, 4, 7, 14, 29, 31, Nov
7, 11, Dec 4, 30; <u>1800</u>: CG, Feb 4, Mar 27, Apr 23, 30, May 10, 13, 23, 29,

30, Jun 7
Whitfield, John and Mary (actors), <u>1774</u>: CG, Oct 1
--Masonic Melange, A (interlude), <u>1795</u>: DL, May 28
Whitfield, Mary, Mrs John (actor), <u>1774</u>: CG, Sep 30, Oct 7, 20, Nov 8, 19, 24,
    Dec 27; <u>1775</u>: CG, Mar 30, Apr 17, 22, HAY, Aug 9, Sep 4, 16, 18, 19, 21, DL,
    23, 28, Oct 11, Nov 3, 9; <u>1776</u>: DL, Jan 26, Mar 12, HAY, May 22, Jul 29, Aug
    16, Sep 2, CG, Oct 15, 16, 24, 31, Nov 2, 7, Dec 26; <u>1777</u>: CG, Jan 3, 8, Feb
    6, 8, Apr 16, 24, May 2, 5, 13, Oct 1, Nov 17; <u>1778</u>: CG, Mar 23, Apr 2, May
    9, 13, Oct 9, 24, Dec 2; <u>1779</u>: CG, Jan 1, 9, 15, 21, Apr 10, 28, 29, May 1,
    3, 18, Sep 20, 24, Oct 1, 20, Dec 3, 16, 18, 31; <u>1780</u>: CG, Jan 7, 25, Feb 2,
    8, Mar 14, Apr 3, May 3, 16, 23, Sep 18, 21, Oct 11, 13, 19; <u>1781</u>: CG, Feb
    10, Mar 8, May 11, 22, Sep 26, Oct 16, 26, Nov 9, Dec 8; <u>1782</u>: CG, May 20,
    25, Sep 23, DL, 26, CG, Oct 3, 10, 22, Nov 8, 16; <u>1783</u>: CG, Feb 19, 24, 25,
    Mar 29, Apr 26, May 10, 12, 21, 22, 29, Jun 4, Sep 19, 24, Oct 11, 14, 20,
    28, 31; <u>1784</u>: CG, Mar 1, 4, 6, 16, Apr 3, May 7, 12, 26; <u>1787</u>: HAY, Jun 11,
    14, 28, Jul 3, 25; <u>1788</u>: HAY, Jun 17, Jul 12, 14; <u>1789</u>: HAY, May 18, Jun 8,
    30, Jul 15, Aug 5, 27; <u>1790</u>: HAY, Jun 14, 16, Aug 11, 16; <u>1791</u>: HAY, Jun 13,
    16, 17, Jul 26, Aug 2, 24, 29; <u>1792</u>: HAY, Jun 29, Jul 2, 4, Aug 2, 18, Sep 5;
    <u>1793</u>: HAY, Jun 17, 21, 22, Aug 6, 26
Whitfield, Mrs (dresser), <u>1760</u>: CG, Sep 22
Whitfield, Robert (wardrobe keeper, tailor), <u>1759</u>: CG, Dec 22; <u>1760</u>: CG, Apr
    10, May 28, Sep 22; <u>1761</u>: CG, Sep 28; <u>1771</u>: CG, Nov 9, 30; <u>1772</u>: CG, Jan 20,
    Feb 5, Mar 7, Apr 11, 22, Oct 19, Nov 20, Dec 4; <u>1773</u>: CG, Jan 21, Mar 2, Apr
    23, May 12, Oct 13; <u>1774</u>: CG, Jan 12, 24, Apr 13, 15; <u>1788</u>: CG, Jan 8; <u>1791</u>:
    HAY, Jul 30
Whither fairest? (song), <u>1791</u>: DL, Apr 1; <u>1792</u>: KING'S, Feb 29; <u>1794</u>: DL, Mar
    26
Whither my Love (song), <u>1796</u>: DL, Jun 9
Whitherilt, Mrs. See Wetherilt, Mrs.
Whiting (Whitein), Thomas (joiner), <u>1659</u>: CITY, Oct 29; <u>1660</u>: CITY, Oct 29;
    <u>1662</u>: THAMES, Aug 23
Whitlock, Elizabeth (actor), <u>1792</u>: HAY, Jun 18, 23
Whitlock, Mrs (supplier), <u>1775</u>: DL, Nov 17
Whitlow, Master (dancer), <u>1772</u>: DL, Jun 3; <u>1773</u>: DL, May 28; <u>1774</u>: DL, May 24
Whitmell (dancer), <u>1790</u>: CG, Mar 1, DL, Oct 26; <u>1791</u>: DL, May 26, DLKING'S, Nov
    5; <u>1792</u>: DLKING'S, Mar 19, Jun 13, HAY, 27, Jul 25, DL, Nov 21, Dec 27; <u>1793</u>:
    DL, May 31; <u>1794</u>: DL, May 16, Jun 9, Sep 27, Oct 27, Nov 10, Dec 20; <u>1795</u>:
    DL, Jan 19, Jun 4, Oct 30; <u>1796</u>: DL, Jan 18, Mar 12, 19, 28, Apr 4, Jun 10,
    Oct 1, 29, Nov 9, Dec 26; <u>1797</u>: DL, Jun 10; <u>1798</u>: DL, Jan 16, Feb 20, May 16,
    Jun 2, Oct 6, Nov 14, Dec 6; <u>1799</u>: DL, Jan 19, Feb 5, May 20, Jul 2, Oct 14,
    Nov 6, Dec 2; <u>1800</u>: DL, Jan 1, Mar 11, Jun 13
Whitmell, Master (dancer), <u>1792</u>: HAY, Jul 25
Whitmell, Miss (dancer), <u>1792</u>: DL, Dec 27
Whitmore Sr (actor, scene painter), <u>1799</u>: CG, Oct 21
Whitmore, James (actor), <u>1798</u>: CG, Sep 21, 26, 28, Oct 3, 11, 15, Nov 1, 12,
    Dec 26; <u>1799</u>: CG, Jan 16, 29, Mar 25, Apr 13, 23, May 13, 15, 28, Oct 2, 7,
    17, 21, 24, 28, Dec 16, 23; <u>1800</u>: CG, Feb 10, Mar 25, Apr 5, 23, May 7, 23,
    27, HAY, Jun 16, 19, Jul 15
Whitmore, John (dancer, actor), <u>1799</u>: CG, Oct 31; <u>1800</u>: CG, May 1
Whitmore, Mrs (actor), <u>1798</u>: CG, Oct 3, Nov 12, Dec 11, 26; <u>1799</u>: CG, Jan 14,
    29, Mar 25, Apr 3, 8, May 4, 23, 28, Oct 16, 21, 24, Nov 14, 30, Dec 3; <u>1800</u>:
    CG, Jan 16, Feb 10, Mar 25, Apr 5, 29, 30, May 1, 2, 5, 12, Jun 2, 3, 13,
    HAY, 14, 16, Aug 8, 19, Sep 3
Whitmore, Mrs (singer), <u>1798</u>: CG, Sep 17, Oct 8, Dec 15; <u>1799</u>: CG, Apr 9, Sep
    30, Oct 7
Whitmore, Samuel? (scene painter), <u>1800</u>: HAY, Jul 2, Sep 1
Whitmores, two (scene painters), <u>1799</u>: CG, Dec 23
Whitsun Festival, A (interlude, anon), <u>1800</u>: CG, Jun 2
Whitsun Holiday (dance), <u>1721</u>: DL, May 29; <u>1724</u>: DL, May 4; <u>1725</u>: DL, Apr 16;
    <u>1726</u>: DL, Apr 18, 25, May 11, 13, 23; <u>1727</u>: DL, Apr 20, May 10, 22; <u>1728</u>: DL,
    May 2; <u>1729</u>: DL, Mar 13; <u>1730</u>: DL, Apr 25
Whitsuntide; or, The Clown's Contention (entertainment), <u>1722</u>: LIF, May 17;
    <u>1724</u>: BPT, Apr 16
Whittaker (actor), <u>1780</u>: HAY, Apr 5, Nov 13
Whittey (ticket deliverer), <u>1777</u>: DL, May 30; <u>1778</u>: DL, May 22; <u>1779</u>: DL, May
    29
Whittingham (actor), <u>1743</u>: DL, Feb 10, 12, Apr 29
Whittington (ticket deliverer), <u>1778</u>: CG, May 14, 22; <u>1779</u>: CG, May 15; <u>1780</u>:
    CG, May 24; <u>1781</u>: CG, May 25
Whittington, Thrice Lord Mayor of London (droll, anon), <u>1718</u>: SF, Sep 5; <u>1731</u>:
    SFLH, Sep 8; <u>1732</u>: SFLHO, Sep 5; <u>1749</u>: BF/SF, Aug 23, 24, 25, 26, 28, SF/SF,
    Sep 7, BF/SF, 8, 9, 11, 12

906

Whittington's Cat (puppetry), 1668: SF, Sep 21; 1699: BF, Aug 30
Whittington's Feast. See Arne, Dr Thomas A.
Whitton, Tom (spectator), 1661: SALSBURY, Mar 26
Whittow (dancer), 1781: CG, May 1; 1788: DL, Jun 5; 1789: DL, Jun 10, Dec 26;
  1790: DL, Jan 16, Jun 2, Oct 26; 1791: DL, May 26
Whitty, Master (actor), 1784: DL, May 3
Whitty, Master J (actor), 1784: DL, May 3
Who can resist my Celia's charms (song), 1684: DLORDG, Aug 0
Who Pays the Reckoning? See Arnold, Samuel James.
Who trusts in God (song), 1794: DL, Mar 21
Who will buy my Heart (song), 1747: CG, Apr 24; 1748: CG, Mar 31
Who would not up to London come? (song), 1797: HAY, Aug 8
Who'd Have Thought It! See Cobb, James.
Who're Nice and Fair (song), 1741: JS, Nov 9
Who's the Dupe? See Cowley, Hannah.
Whore of Babylon the Devil and the Pope, The (droll, anon), 1685: BF, Aug 0
Why, Chloe, will you not perceive? (song), 1696: DG, Oct 0
Why do the Nations (song), 1793: KING/HAY, Feb 20; 1794: DL, Mar 14, 19
Why does the foolish world mistake (song), 1676: DG, Dec 0
Why does the God of Israel sleep? (song), 1745: CG, Apr 10; 1751: KING'S, Apr
  16; 1758: KING'S, Apr 6; 1789: DL, Mar 25; 1790: CG, Feb 26, Mar 19; 1791:
  DL, Mar 11, CG, 11; 1792: KING'S, Mar 23, 30; 1793: CG, Mar 8, 22; 1794: CG,
  Mar 12, DL, 14; 1795: CG, Mar 13; 1797: CG, Apr 7; 1798: CG, Mar 2; 1799: CG,
  Mar 15; 1800: CG, Mar 5
Why dost thou fly me (song), 1696: DG, Oct 0
Why should a foolish Marriage Vow (song), 1672: LIF, Apr 0
Why should men quarrel (song), 1695: DG, Apr 0
Why should Salem (song), 1795: CG, Mar 25
Why should the world mistake (song), 1694: DL, Mar 21
Why so full of grief (song), 1789: DL, Mar 25
Why swells my wavy burnished grain (song), 1796: DL, May 27
Wicklow Mountains, The. See O'Keeffe, John, The Lad of the Hills.
Widnel. See Wignell.
Widow and no Widow, A. See Jodrell, Richard Paul.
Widow Bewitched, The. See Mottley, John.
Widow Lovett (entertainment), 1784: HAY, Sep 17
Widow of Delphi, The. See Cumberland, Richard.
Widow of Malabar, The. See Starke, Mariana.
Widow Ranter, The. See Behn, Aphra.
Widow, The. See Middleton, Thomas.
Widow's Dialogue (song), 1718: DL, May 30
Widow's Tears, The. See Chapman, George.
Widow's Vow, The. See Inchbald, Elizabeth.
Widow's Wish, The; or, An Equippage of Lovers (farce, anon), 1746: MF, May 5
Widowed Wife, The. See Kenrick, Dr William.
Wiers, Dinnis, Mrs William (actor), 1760: DL, May 3
Wife for a Month, A. See Fletcher, John.
Wife for Any Man, A. See D'Urfey, Thomas.
Wife I Do Hate (song), 1671: BRIDGES, Mar 0
Wife in the Right, A. See Griffith, Elizabeth.
Wife of Bath, The. See Gay, John.
Wife to be Let, A. See Haywood, Eliza.
Wife Well Managed, A. See Centlivre, Susannah.
Wife's Relief, The. See Johnson, Charles.
Wigan (beneficiary), 1735: LIF, Apr 16
Wignell (Widnel, Wignal), John (actor), 1732: HAY, Apr 27, May 8, 10, 15, Jun
  1; 1733: CG, Oct 26, Nov 19, Dec 20; 1734: CG, Jan 4, 18, Mar 28, Apr 29, May
  3, 17, JS, 31, BFRLCH, Aug 24, CG, Sep 2, RI, 26, CG/LIF, 27, LIF, Oct 12,
  CG/LIF, 14, Nov 19, 21, 25, Dec 5, 26; 1735: CG/LIF, Jan 17, 20, Feb 3, 11,
  Mar 11, May 9, 13, 16, 26, 27, CG, Sep 24, 26, 29, Oct 1, 3; 1746: GF, Nov
  18, 19, 20, 21, 26, 27, 28, Dec 1, 2, 3, 9, 10, 11, 12, 15, 17, 18, 22, 29,
  31; 1747: GF, Jan 2, 5, 9, 16, 22, 26, Feb 2, 5, 25, Mar 2, 5, 9, 19; 1752:
  NWLS, Nov 16, 28, 30; 1753: CG, Sep 14, 21, 24, 26, Oct 3, 5, 24, 27, 31, Nov
  1, 12, 28; 1754: CG, Apr 2, 19, 22, 24, May 7, 13, Sep 20, 30, Oct 2, 4, 17,
  24, 26, Dec 10, 13, 26, 30; 1755: CG, May 13, 15, Oct 6, 20, 22, Nov 13, 17,
  21, 26, Dec 3, 4; 1756: CG, Jan 15, Mar 27, Apr 20, 29, May 17, Sep 20, 22,
  29, Oct 6, 25, 28, Nov 11, 24, Dec 1, 7, 10; 1757: CG, Jan 27, Feb 19, May
  16, 25, Sep 23, Oct 5, 13, 19, 20, 22, 28, Nov 2, 5, 7, 11, 18, Dec 10, 20;
  1758: CG, Mar 29, Apr 21, May 2, 5, Sep 20, 25, Oct 4, 20, 30, Nov 14, 16;
  1759: CG, Jan 4, Feb 1, Mar 5, 20, Apr 7, 28, May 3, 11, 17, DL, Jul 12, CG,
  Sep 26, Oct 5, 20, Nov 28; 1760: CG, Jan 7, 9, 31, Feb 26, Mar 18, 25, Apr
  17, May 2, 5, 12, DL, Jul 29, CG, Sep 22, 24, Oct 1, 10, 17, 25, Nov 18;

CG, May 19, 22; <u>1771</u>: CG, May 22; <u>1772</u>: CG, May 23; <u>1773</u>: CG, May 22; <u>1774</u>:
CG, May 7; <u>1775</u>: CG, May 23
Wilkinson, Isabella (equilibrist), <u>1755</u>: HAY, Jan 28; <u>1756</u>: SW, Oct 9; <u>1757</u>:
HAY, Oct 12, 17, 31, Nov 2, Dec 26; <u>1758</u>: HAY, Jan 25; <u>1761</u>: DL, Nov 3; <u>1762</u>:
DL, Jan 27, Nov 23; <u>1763</u>: DL, May 31; <u>1765</u>: DL, Mar 26, 30, May 16, Nov 14;
<u>1772</u>: DL, May 5, Oct 10
Wilkinson, Miss (actor), <u>1798</u>: HAY, Mar 26
Wilkinson, Richard, <u>1703</u>: DL, Jun 23
--Vice Reclaimed; or, The Passionate Mistress, <u>1703</u>: DL, Jun 23, 24, 25, 26, 28
Wilkinson, Rosemond (actor), <u>1786</u>: CG, Oct 4, 31, Nov 24, Dec 5, 11, 13, 26;
<u>1787</u>: CG, Jan 11, Feb 10, Mar 12, 27, 31, Apr 10, 16, 24, 30, May 1, 9, 21,
Oct 11
Wilkinson, Tate (actor), <u>1753</u>: DL, Nov 19; <u>1756</u>: DL, Oct 9; <u>1757</u>: CG, May 4;
<u>1758</u>: DL, Oct 17, 27; <u>1759</u>: DL, May 14, Oct 27, Nov 5; <u>1760</u>: DL, May 3, CG,
Nov 24, Dec 18; <u>1761</u>: CG, Mar 10, 26, May 4; <u>1763</u>: HAY, May 9, Jun 20, Jul 1,
6, Aug 1; <u>1764</u>: HAY, Jul 16, 23, Aug 20, 29, Sep 1; <u>1778</u>: CG, Jan 15, 19, 20,
29, Feb 6
--Tea a la Mode (entertainment), <u>1761</u>: CG, May 4
Wilks (actor), <u>1774</u>: HAY, Jan 24
Wilks (actor), <u>1780</u>: HAY, Nov 1; <u>1781</u>: HAY, Jun 26
Wilks, Mary (beneficiary), <u>1733</u>: DL, Feb 22
Wilks, Mary (patentee), <u>1733</u>: DL, Jun 4, 9; <u>1734</u>: DL, Feb 13
Wilks, Master (actor), <u>1746</u>: DL, Nov 7; <u>1747</u>: DL, Mar 23
Wilks, Mrs (actor), <u>1776</u>: CHR, Sep 23, 27, 30, Oct 2, 4, 7, 9, 11, 16; <u>1778</u>:
HAY, Jan 26
Wilks, Robert (actor), <u>1699</u>: DL, Nov 28, Dec 0; <u>1700</u>: DL, Mar 0, Apr 29, Jul 9,
Nov 23, Dec 9; <u>1701</u>: DL, Feb 4, Mar 1, Apr 0, DG, 11, May 6, DL, 12, DG, Jun
3, DL, Dec 0; <u>1702</u>: DL, Jan 0, Feb 0, Oct 20, Nov 0, 21, Dec 0, 14; <u>1703</u>: DL,
Jan 27, Feb 18, Mar 11, YB, 17, DL, Jun 4, 12, 19, 23, Oct 23, Dec 2; <u>1704</u>:
DL, Jan 26, Feb 2, 3, ATCOURT, 7, 28, DL, Mar 6, May 0, Jun 13, 15, 17, Jul
11, Dec 7; <u>1705</u>: DL, Jan 18, Feb 27, Apr 23, Jun 12, Jul 25, Oct 30, Nov 20,
Dec 3; <u>1706</u>: DL, Feb 12, Apr 0, 8, 16, QUEEN'S, Oct 26, Nov 2, 7, 9, 13, 14,
19, 20, 25, 29, Dec 2, 3, 5, 7, 13, 14, 16; <u>1707</u>: QUEEN'S, Jan 1, 4, 11, 13,
14, Feb 4, 14, 18, 22, Mar 1, 3, 8, 27, Apr 21, 28, 30, May 9, 26, Jun 2, 10,
DL/QUEEN, Oct 18, 20, QUEEN'S, 21, DL/QUEEN, 25, 27, 28, 31, Nov 1, QUEEN'S,
6, QUEEN/DL, 8, DL/QUEEN, 10, 11, 14, 15, 18, 19, 20, QUEEN'S, 22, DL/QUEEN,
25, QUEEN/DL, Dec 6, QUEEN'S, 13, DL/QUEEN, 27, 31; <u>1708</u>: DL/QUEEN, Jan 1,
QUEEN'S, 10, DL, 15, Feb 3, 4, 7, 14, 23, 24, 26, Mar 8, 9, 15, 18, DL/QUEEN,
23, DL, Apr 19, 22, 26, 27, 29, May 21, 31, Oct 7, 12, 13, 14, 15, 16, 19,
21, 22, 25, 26, Dec 14, 18, 22, 30; <u>1709</u>: DL, Jan 1, 4, 5, 8, 11, 15, 17, 18,
21, 22, 27, 29, Feb 5, 12, 24, 26, Mar 3, 5, 14, 15, 31, Apr 9, 14, 25, 30,
May 12, 18, Jun 2, QUEEN'S, Sep 22, 24, 27, 29, Oct 1, 4, 8, 11, 17, 21, 22,
25, 28, 29, 31, Nov 4, 5, 8, 9, 11, 12, 15, 18, 19, Dec 3, 12; <u>1710</u>: QUEEN'S,
Jan 2, 5, 7, 11, 12, 14, 18, 19, 21, Feb 4, 11, 13, 18, Mar 4, 11, 27, Apr
13, 19, 20, May 6, 15, 29, Jun 13, 22, Jul 6, 13, 19, 21, 26, DL/QUEEN, Oct
4, 5, 7, Nov 4, 6, 7, 8, QUEEN'S, 10, DL/QUEEN, 11, 13, 14, 15, 17, 18, DL,
20, 21, 25, 27, 28, 30, Dec 1, 2, 11, 12, 14, 15, 16, 18, 21, 22, 30; <u>1711</u>:
DL, Jan 9, 11, 15, 16, 19, 25, 26, 27, DL/QUEEN, Feb 8, DL, 15, 19, 22, Mar
3, 10, 22, Apr 3, 7, May 15, 22, Sep 22, 25, 27, Oct 2, 4, 6, 9, 10, 11, 13,
17, 18, 19, 20, 23, 24, 26, 27, 31, Nov 1, 2, 5, 6, 8, 9, 10, 12, 23, 29, Dec
3, 10, 13, 18, 31; <u>1712</u>: DL, Jan 19, Mar 17, Apr 29, May 6, Jun 12, Sep 20,
23, 25, 30, Oct 2, 4, 6, 8, 10, 11, 13, 16, 20, 22, 23, 30, Nov 1, 3, 7, 28,
Dec 27; <u>1713</u>: DL, Jan 10, 15, 19, 29, Feb 9, 13, 28, Mar 3, 9, 14, 16, Apr
14, May 11, 12, 18, Jun 5, 23, Oct 13, 22, Nov 9, 11, 16, 18, 19, 23, 28, Dec
2, 18; <u>1714</u>: DL, Jan 5, 26, 28, Feb 2, Mar 29, Apr 16, 23, 26, 27, May 3, 5,
21, 26, 28, Jun 2, 18, Sep 21, Oct 11, 22, 25, Nov 9, 15, 24, 26, 27, Dec 2,
4, 8, 9, 16, 21; <u>1715</u>: DL, Jan 5, 15, 24, Feb 4, 10, 12, 15, 22, 25, 28, Mar
8, 14, 21, 28, Apr 2, 19, May 17, 18, 24, YB, 28, DL, Oct 13, 22, Nov 9, 12,
19, 29, Dec 6, 9, 12, 17, 20, 30, 31; <u>1716</u>: DL, Jan 5, 7, 10, 11, 17, 21, 24,
25, 26, Feb 3, 9, 18, 21, 23, 25, Mar 3, 8, 10, 24, Apr 16, May 9, 11, Jun
15, Sep 29, Oct 2, 4, 6, 9, 11, 12, 13, 15, 16, 17, 19, 24, 25, 27, Nov 1, 2,
3, 13, 27, Dec 4, 5, 14, 15, 17, 27, 29; <u>1717</u>: DL, Jan 2, 4, 5, 24, 26, 31,
Feb 2, 25, Apr 8, 11, May 22, Jun 7, 14, 24, Sep 28, Oct 1, 9, 10, 14, 15,
16, 21, 24, 26, 28, Nov 8, 13, 18, 20, 23, 25, 30, Dec 3, 4, 6, 31; <u>1718</u>: DL,
Jan 7, 13, 20, 23, 27, 29, Feb 14, 22, Mar 1, 3, 8, 17, Apr 19, May 8, 14,
Jun 27, Jul 1, Sep 20, 25, 27, Oct 2, 8, 10, 15, 17, 20, 21, 22, 24, 25, 27,
28, 30, 31, Nov 4, 8, 13, 18, 24, 25, 29, Dec 2, 3, 10, 11, 13, 16, 19, 29;
<u>1719</u>: DL, Jan 16, 24, Feb 4, 14, Mar 7, Apr 11, 27, 29, May 11, Sep 12, 17,
19, 22, 24, 29, Oct 3, 7, 9, 13, 14, 15, 17, 20, 21, 22, 23, 24, 27, 28, 30,
31, Nov 3, 5, 10, 14, 16, 18, 19, 20, 21, Dec 2, 5, 11; <u>1720</u>: DL, Jan 1, 8,
12, 27, Feb 17, Mar 19, Apr 2, 30, May 23, Jun 2, Jul 7, BFPMJ, Aug 23, DL,
Sep 10, 13, 15, 17, 20, 22, 29, Oct 1, 4, 5, 8, 12, 15, 17, 20, 29, Nov 1, 2,

910

4, 7, 10, 11, 12, 18, 21, 29, Dec 1; 1721: DL, Jan 3, 10, 13, 16, 17, 23, 24,
25, 27, Feb 3, 14, Mar 2, 23, Apr 13, 14, 18, 26, May 12, 15, Sep 9, 12, 16,
19, 21, 26, 28, 30, Oct 2, 3, 4, 6, 7, 9, 11, 12, 13, 14, 17, 18, 19, 20, 21,
23, 24, 28, 31, Nov 1, 4, 8, 11, 13, 14, 16, 18, 25, 28, Dec 12, 22, 28;
1722: DL, Jan 5, 6, 9, Feb 19, Apr 14, 27, May 2, 5, 17, 22, Sep 8, 13, 15,
18, 20, 22, 25, 27, 29, Oct 2, 5, 8, 10, 11, 12, 13, 15, 16, 17, 19, 22, 24,
25, 26, 31, Nov 1, 5, 7, Dec 3, 4, 5, 7, 26; 1723: DL, Jan 8, 9, 17, 23, Feb
4, Mar 2, 11, 21, Apr 1, 18, May 10, 11, Sep 14, 17, 19, 24, 26, 28, Oct 1,
3, 5, 8, 9, 16, 18, 21, 22, 23, 29, 30, 31, Nov 1, 2, 4, 6, 8, 9, 14, 16, 18,
19, 21, Dec 5, 20; 1724: DL, Jan 15, Feb 15, 22, Apr 8, 15, 18, 25, 28, May
1, 15, 16, 22, Sep 12, 15, 17, 19, 22, 24, 29, Oct 8, 10, 14, 16, 17, 19, 21,
27, 28, Nov 2, 4, 6, 7, 10, 13, 16, 19, 21, 26, 27, Dec 7, 9; 1725: DL, Jan
9, 20, 27, Feb 3, 9, Apr 5, 15, May 8, 12, 21, 27, Jun 11, Sep 7, 9, 11, 14,
18, 25, 30, Oct 2, 5, 7, 9, 12, 13, 14, 15, 16, 18, 20, 22, 23, 25, 28, Nov
2, 4, 6, 8, 12, 22, 27, 29, Dec 7, 8, 9, 10, 13, 18, 22; 1726: DL, Jan 3, 5,
11, 22, 28, Sep 6, 8, 10, 15, 17, 20, 22, 24, 27, 29, Oct 6, 11, 13, 15, 18,
22, 27, Nov 4, 12, 15, 16, 19, 26, 29, Dec 7, 12, 14, 15, 17, 20, 21; 1727:
DL, Jan 5, 21, 25, 27, Feb 8, 23, Apr 24, May 8, Sep 12, 14, 16, 19, 23, 26,
28, 30, Oct 3, 5, 7, 12, 14, 17, 19, 20, 23, Nov 4, 9, 18, 22, 28, 30, Dec 4,
9, 13, 30; 1728: DL, Jan 2, 3, 5, 10, Feb 16, Mar 11, Apr 1, 2, 13, 29, May
1, 20, 23, Sep 7, 10, 12, 14, 17, 21, 26, Oct 3, 10, 15, 17, 21, 22, 23, 24,
25, 28, 31, Nov 2, 8, 12, 14, 25, Dec 4, 9, 12; 1729: DL, Jan 1, 2, 7, 13,
21, 22, 25, 29, 31, Feb 1, 15, 18, 22, 25, Mar 13, Apr 16, May 6, 7, 14, Sep
11, 13, 30, Oct 2, 4, 7, 9, 11, 14, 16, 21, 22, 25, 28, Nov 1, 3, 4, 6, 7, 8,
12, 17, 18, 19, 22, 24, 25, 28, 29, Dec 1, 4, 5, 10, 13, GF, 20, DL, 20;
1730: DL, Jan 3, 9, 21, 24, 26, Feb 28, Mar 19, Apr 14, 23, 30, May 4, Sep
12, 15, 17, 24, 26, Oct 1, 3, 6, 8, 17, 22, Nov 3, 14, 16, 24, 25, 26, 28,
Dec 2, 11, 26; 1731: DL, Jan 11, 16, 20, 27, Feb 17, 22, Mar 8, 15, 29, Apr
8, 21, May 3, 10, Sep 18, 21, 23, 25, 28, 30, Oct 2, 5, 9, 19, 30, Nov 1, 5,
6, 9, 10, 20, 23, 24, Dec 1, 7, 10, 18, 21, 22; 1732: DL, Jan 3, 7, 10, 14,
17, 19, 21, 22, 24, 26, 29, Feb 2, 10, 11, 14, Mar 23, 30, Apr 17, 24, 27,
28, 29, May 4, 5, Sep 14, 27, 28, Oct 14, 17, 31; 1733: DL, May 18, Jun 9;
1734: HAY, Jun 12, Aug 16, HA, Sep 2; 1743: DL, Oct 15; 1753: DL, Oct 30;
1768: DL, Aug 18
Wilks, Robert, On the Death of (poem), 1732: DL, Sep 30
Wilks, Thomas (author), 1759: CG, Mar 28
Wilks, William (boxkeeper), 1716: DL, Jun 5; 1718: DL, May 19; 1720: DL, May
    23; 1721: DL, Aug 9; 1723: DL, Jun 6
Wilks Jr, William (actor), 1715: DL, Oct 17, Dec 6; 1716: DL, Jan 23, Jul 12,
    Oct 29, Nov 12, 26; 1717: DL, Jan 12, Apr 23, May 17, Jul 2, Aug 6, 9, 22,
    Oct 3, 10, 25, Nov 6, 27; 1718: DL, May 6, 19, Jul 11, Aug 15, 20, Oct 22,
    Nov 19; 1719: DL, Jan 28, Apr 27, RI, Jul 6, DL, 21, BFPM, Aug 24, DL, Oct
    16, Nov 11; 1720: DL, Jan 13, Feb 5, Apr 30, Oct 3, 7, Dec 17; 1721: DL, Apr
    28, May 29, Jun 20, Jul 28, Aug 4, 8, 18, BF/SF, 24, DL, Oct 21, 23, 27, Nov
    17, 30; 1722: DL, Jan 31, Feb 1, Apr 10, 26, May 19, RI, Jul 23, DL, Sep 15,
    Oct 2, 15, 30, Dec 5, 7; 1723: DL, Jan 3, 7, May 2, 23, Jun 4, Jul 5, Aug 12,
    16, Sep 19, 28, Oct 9, 23, Nov 15, 22; 1724: DL, Feb 14, 17, Apr 24, May 22,
    SF, Sep 2, DL, Oct 24, 29, Nov 13, Dec 7; 1725: DL, Feb 3, 5, Apr 15; 1734:
    HAY, Jun 12, Aug 16
Will and No Will, A. See Macklin, Charles.
Will, The. See Reynolds, Frederick.
Will's Coffee House, 1697: DLORLIF, Sep 15; 1733: LIF/CG, Apr 2; 1736: CG, Mar
    22; 1749: DL, Apr 5; 1750: DL, Mar 22; 1751: DL, Mar 14; 1752: DL, Apr 10,
    Nov 15
Willems, Mrs (dancer, singer), 1772: CG, May 1, 23; 1773: CG, Jan 19, Feb 23,
    Apr 16, 24, 28, May 12, 31, Oct 15, Nov 9, 25, Dec 4, 13; 1774: CG, Jan 3,
    Feb 11, May 23, Sep 23, Oct 13, Nov 2, 19; 1775: CG, Feb 18, Sep 25, Oct 19,
    Dec 9, 26; 1776: CG, Mar 19, Apr 9, 19, May 6, Oct 7, 16, 25, Nov 7, 13, Dec
    2; 1777: CG, May 22, Sep 29; 1778: CG, Feb 2, Apr 27, May 6, Oct 7, 9, 26,
    Nov 4, Dec 21; 1779: CG, Apr 19, Sep 20, Oct 18, 25, Nov 8, 30, Dec 3, 29;
    1780: CG, Apr 7, 27, May 6, 12, 25, Oct 9, 13, 23; 1781: CG, Mar 8
Willes (satirized), 1767: HAY, Aug 25
Willet, Thomas, 1778: HAY, Jun 25
--Buxom Joan (burletta), 1778: HAY, Jun 25, 26, Jul 1, 7, 21, 23, 27, 31, Sep
    7; 1780: CG, Apr 22
Willett, Deborah (spectator), 1667: LIF, Oct 14, 15, BRIDGES, 18, 28, Nov 2,
    11, LIF, 13, BRIDGES, Dec 7; 1668: NURSERY, Jan 7, BRIDGES, 10, 11, LIF, Feb
    11, NURSERY, 24, BRIDGES, 27, LIF, Mar 26, BRIDGES, 28, Jun 19, LIF, 24,
    BRIDGES, 27, LIF, Jul 28, BRIDGES, Aug 1, BF, 29, LIF, 31, BRIDGES, Oct 12,
    LIF, 19
Willey, John (doorkeeper), 1800: DL, Jun 14
William and Nanny. See Goodenough, Richard Josceline.

William and Susan; or, The Sailor's Sheet-Anchor (interlude, anon), 1785: HAY,
    Aug 26
William III, 1689: NONE, Apr 11; 1690: ATCOURT, Nov 4; 1691: ATCOURT, Jan 1;
    1697: ATCOURT, Nov 4; 1702: NONE, Mar 0; 1716: DL, Nov 6; 1758: CG, Feb 4;
    1766: DL, Feb 20; 1772: MARLY, Jul 2; 1782: CG, Nov 4; see also Highness;
    King, the; Majesty
William St, 1795: DL, Jun 3; 1796: DL, Jun 7
William, Prince, 1728: DL, Nov 13, 20; 1731: KING'S, Nov 23, 30; 1732: TC, Aug
    17; 1746: CG, Nov 28; 1747: CG, May 14; 1748: CG, Dec 21; 1749: CG, Feb 27,
    May 4, Dec 16; 1750: CG, Mar 10, 12; 1752: CG, Dec 30; 1758: CG, Mar 22;
    1760: CG, Dec 19; 1765: DL, Dec 30; 1780: DL, Mar 13; see also Prince
Williames, Elizabeth, Mrs Matthew (actor), 1785: HAY, Feb 10; 1790: DL, Jun 5,
    Sep 11, 14, 16, Oct 4, 11, 23, 25, 27, Nov 1, 2; 1791: DL, Jan 25, Feb 15,
    Mar 4, May 3, 11, 31; 1798: HAY, Mar 26
Williames, Matthew (actor), 1779: DL, Nov 20; 1780: DL, Jan 3, 24, Apr 5, 21,
    29, May 2, 5, Sep 16, 19, 21, Oct 2, Nov 4, Dec 27; 1781: DL, Jan 16, Feb 17,
    Mar 6, 19, May 1, 10, 17, 22, Sep 15, 18, 22, 25, 27, Oct 4, 6, 11, 15, 19,
    20, 29, Nov 5, 20; 1782: DL, Jan 3, Feb 16, Mar 16, Apr 3, 20, 24, 25, May 8,
    11, 16, 29, Jun 1, Sep 20, 24, 26, 28, Oct 3, 5, 18, 26, Nov 1, 4, 16, 29,
    30, Dec 26; 1783: DL, Jan 25, Feb 22, Mar 3, 17, Apr 7, 21, 26, 28, May 2, 5,
    8, 12, 14, 20, Sep 18, 20, 23, 25, 27, 30, Oct 7, 13, 16, 20, 21, 30, Nov 4,
    18, Dec 2, 5, 10, 29; 1784: DL, Jan 1, 7, 13, 22, 31, Feb 24, Mar 16, 30, Apr
    1, 12, 16, 21, 26, 28, May 3, 7, 20, Sep 21, 23, 25, Oct 7, 12, 14, 18, 19,
    26, Nov 12, 16, 22, Dec 18, 28; 1785: DL, Jan 6, 12, 20, 24, 27, Feb 2, Mar
    28, Apr 1, 8, 11, 18, 20, 22, 27, May 3, 6, 11, Sep 20, 22, Oct 1, 11, 13,
    15, 26, Nov 1, 9, 17, 18, 22, Dec 8; 1786: DL, Jan 5, Feb 15, 18, Apr 4, 6,
    May 2, 9, 15, 17, Jun 1, 8, Sep 16, 19, Oct 7, 9, 24, 25, Nov 18, Dec 1, 2,
    5, 26, 28; 1787: DL, Jan 20, 26, Feb 1, Apr 9, 13, 20, 27, May 11, 22, Sep
    18, 27, Oct 13, 25, 26, 30, Nov 1, 3, 5, 6, 8, 24, Dec 17, 19, 26; 1788: DL,
    Jan 2, 22, 26, 31, Feb 7, 25, Mar 29, Apr 10, 22, 30, May 1, 6, 14, Jun 2,
    Sep 16, 23, 27, 30, Oct 2, 9, 14, 16, Nov 1, 4, 10, 11, 17, 25, 28, 29, Dec
    17, 22; 1789: DL, Jan 8, 13, 17, Feb 7, 16, 18, Mar 9, 21, Apr 14, 21, May
    15, 23, Jun 8, 9, Sep 12, 15, 22, 24, Oct 1, 13, 15, 22, 26, 28, 31, Nov 4,
    24, 27, Dec 9, 14; 1790: DL, Feb 10, 27, Mar 2, CG, Apr 20, DL, May 8, 11,
    14, 15, 18, 31, Sep 11, HAY, 15, DL, Oct 7, 11, 14, 20, 21, 25, 26, 27, Nov
    10, 30, Dec 13, 14; 1791: DL, Mar 4, 22, 24, Apr 27, May 11, 14, 26, Jun 4;
    1795: HAY, Mar 4; 1799: DL, Jul 3; 1800: DL, Jun 13, 14
Williams (actor), 1757: CG, May 20; 1766: HAY, Oct 27
Williams (actor), 1771: HAY, Mar 4, Apr 15; 1773: HAY, Sep 16, 18; 1774: HAY,
    Sep 19, 30; 1775: HAY, Feb 2, May 17, 19, 24, Jul 28, Aug 30, Sep 13, 16, 18,
    19; 1777: HAY, Oct 9; 1779: HAY, Oct 18, Dec 27; 1780: HAY, Mar 28, Nov 13;
    1781: HAY, Jan 22, Mar 26; 1782: HAY, Jan 14; 1783: HAY, Dec 15; 1784: HAY,
    Jan 21, CG, Jun 10; 1785: HAY, Sep 16; 1796: HAY, Feb 22; 1797: HAY, Dec 4
Williams (actor), 1799: CG, May 22, Jun 12; 1800: CG, Jun 7
Williams (citizen), 1760: DL, Jan 16
Williams (dancer), 1740: BFH, Aug 23; 1746: GF, Feb 17, 27, Mar 10, 18, NWC,
    Oct 20; 1747: GF, Jan 29, Mar 31, Apr 6
Williams (hairdresser), 1785: HAMM, Jul 15
Williams (musician), 1767: DL, Jan 3, 17, Mar 17, Jun 1; 1771: DL, Dec 10
Williams (tenant), 1750: DL, Apr 20; 1772: DL, Jun 10; 1773: DL, Jun 2; 1774:
    DL, Jun 2
Williams, Ann (beneficiary), 1756: DL, Jan 22
Williams, Celia (actor), 1777: CHR, Jun 18; 1780: HAY, Apr 5; 1782: HAY, Jan
    21, Mar 4, May 6; 1786: HAMM, Jun 5, 7, 30, Jul 5, 10, 19, 24, 26, Aug 5;
    1790: CG, Oct 19, 30, Nov 4, 12, 15, 18, Dec 20; 1791: CG, Jan 12, Mar 7, Apr
    9, 14, 30, May 24, 27, Jun 4; 1799: DL, May 24
Williams, Charles (actor), 1717: LIF, Jun 12, Nov 20, Dec 12, 14; 1718: LIF,
    Jan 2, 7, DL, Mar 8, May 1, Jun 17, Jul 8, 11, RI, Aug 2, 9, 11, DL, 12, 15,
    Oct 25, Dec 3; 1719: DL, Jan 28, Mar 7, May 7, Jun 9, 26, BFPM, Aug 24, DL,
    Oct 13, 16, 22, Dec 11; 1720: DL, Feb 17, May 11, Jul 7, BFPMJ, Aug 23, SFLH,
    Sep 5, DL, Nov 29, Dec 17; 1721: DL, Mar 2, 20, Apr 18, May 1, 29, Jun 20,
    27, Aug 4, 8, 18, BF/SF, 24, SFHL, Sep 2, DL, Oct 3, 10, 14, Nov 1, 3, 4, 8,
    25, Dec 28, 30; 1722: DL, Jan 5, 26, Feb 19, Apr 17, 19, 23, May 22, RI, Jul
    23, DL, Sep 29, Oct 11, 17, 19, 23, 26, 27, Nov 1, 5, 7, Dec 22; 1723: DL,
    Jan 9, Feb 15, Mar 2, Apr 22, 29, May 20, Jun 4, Sep 14, 24, Oct 5, 19, 26,
    31, Nov 4, 7, 15, Dec 5, HAY, 12, DL, 30; 1724: DL, Jan 15, HAY, Feb 5, DL,
    12, 14, 15, HAY, 18, DL, Apr 16, 22, RI, Jun 29, Jul 4, 11, 13, 18, BFP, Aug
    22, SF, Sep 5, DL, 19, 24, 26, Oct 24, 29, Nov 4, 13, 14, 19, 26, 27, Dec 9,
    18, 22; 1725: DL, Jan 25, Feb 1, 9, Apr 19, 20, 21, 22, 24, May 11, BF, Aug
    23, DL, Sep 4, 11, 16, 21, 28, 30, Oct 9, 13, 20, 21, Nov 1, 4, 12, 20, 22,
    Dec 22; 1726: DL, Jan 3, Feb 7, Apr 18, May 18, Aug 3, Sep 3, 6, 8, 13, Nov
    4, 9, 12, 16, 19, Dec 3, 20; 1727: DL, Jan 25, Feb 4, 11, 16, 21, Mar 16, Apr

17, 29, May 15, Sep 7, 9, 12, 16, 21, 23, 30, Oct 3, 9, 20, 21, 23, 30, Nov
1, 4, 27, 30, Dec 5, 9, 13, 30; 1728: DL, Jan 3, Apr 1, 13, May 1, 23, 29,
31, HAY, Aug 9, DL, Sep 14, 17, 19, 21, Oct 1, 5, 8, 12, HAY, 15, DL, 15, 22,
23, HAY, 26, DL, Nov 9, 14, HAY, 14, 19; 1729: DL, Jan 1, 7, 11, 15, 20, 25,
28, HAY, 31, DL, Feb 6, 22, 24, HAY, Mar 27, 29, DL, Apr 11, 14, HAY, May 2,
7, DL, 20, Sep 18, 20, 23, 27, BLA, 30, DL, Oct 7, 11, 14, 25, 28, 31, Nov 4,
8, 12, 21, 25, Dec 20, 27; 1730: DL, Jan 21, 24, 26, Feb 28, Mar 19, Apr 14,
15, 16, 20, 27, May 13, Sep 12, 15, 19, 26, 29, Oct 1, 20, 22, 24, Nov 20,
24, 25, 28, Dec 1; 1731: DL, Jan 20, 27, 28, May 31
Williams, Charles Hanbury (satirist), 1778: DL, Nov 30
Williams, Dan (beneficiary), 1700: YB, Dec 11
Williams, David (actor), 1678: DG, Sep 0; 1679: DG, Apr 0, NONE, Oct 0, DG, Dec
0; 1680: DG, Feb 0; 1681: DG, Apr 0; 1682: DG, Feb 9
Williams, Henry (bellringer), 1770: CG, Feb 6, 10, 15, 20, 24, Mar 20, May 3,
28
Williams, J (publisher), 1777: HAY, Oct 9; 1779: HAY, Oct 13
Williams, John (author), 1722: RI, Jul 23
--Richmond Wells; or, Good Luck at Last, 1722: RI, Jul 23
Williams, John (poet), 1798: DL, Jan 16
Williams, Joseph (actor), 1662: ATCOURT, Nov 1; 1671: LIF, Mar 15; 1675: NONE,
Sep 0; 1677: DG, May 12, Sep 0; 1678: DG, May 28, Nov 0; 1679: DG, Apr 0, May
0, Oct 0, Dec 0; 1680: DG, Jan 0, Feb 0, Jun 0, Sep 0, Nov 1, Dec 8; 1681:
DG, Jan 0, Mar 0, Apr 0, DG/IT, Nov 22; 1682: DG, Jan 0, 23, Mar 0, Apr 0;
1683: NONE, Sep 0; 1684: DLORDG, Aug 0; 1685: DLORDG, Jan 20, DG, Jul 0, DL,
Aug 0; 1686: DL, Jan 0, NONE, Sep 0; 1688: DL, Feb 0, NONE, Sep 0; 1689:
NONE, Apr 11, DL, Nov 7, 20, Dec 4; 1690: DL, Jan 0, DLORDG, 16, DL, Mar 0,
DLORDG, 0, NONE, Sep 0, DL, 0, DL/IT, Oct 21, DL, Nov 0, Dec 0; 1691: DG, May
0, NONE, Sep 0, DL, Dec 0; 1692: DL, Feb 0, Mar 0, Jun 0; 1693: DL, Mar 0,
Apr 0, ATCOURT, 30, NONE, Sep 0, DL, Oct 0; 1694: DL, Jan 0, Feb 0, NONE, Jul
0; 1695: DL, May 0, NONE, Sep 0, DL, Oct 0, Nov 0; 1696: DL, Jan 0, DG, Jun
0, DL, Jul 0; 1697: DL, Feb 0, DG, Jun 0; 1698: DL, Mar 0, Dec 0; 1699: LIF,
Dec 0; 1700: YB, Mar 20, DL, Nov 23; 1701: DL, Feb 4; 1703: DL, Jun 23; 1704:
DL, Jan 26, Jun 29; 1705: DL, Jun 12, Jul 25, Dec 3; 1706: DL, Apr 8; 1707:
DL, Apr 22
--Have at All; or, The Midnight Adventure, 1694: DL, Apr 0
Williams, Miss (actor), 1763: DL, Sep 29, Oct 4, Dec 26, 27; 1764: DL, Feb 24,
Nov 2; 1765: DL, May 8
Williams, Miss (actor, dancer), 1730: HAY, Mar 11, DL, Apr 14, 23, May 4, 15,
19, BFOF, Aug 20, SFOF, Sep 9, DL, Oct 28, Dec 4; 1731: DL, Feb 17, May 4,
Jun 11, Jul 20, 23, Aug 6, 16, SF/BFMMO, 26, DL, Sep 25, Oct 2, 16, Nov 25,
Dec 28; 1732: DL, Jan 1, Feb 22, Mar 21, Apr 24, 26, 28, May 2, 3, 4, 6, 12,
29, Jun 1, 9, 23, Aug 1, 4, 21, Sep 8, 19, 23, Oct 10, 19, 26, Nov 7, 8, 17,
Dec 11, 14, 18, 20, 22, 26; 1734: YB, Jul 8; 1741: BFLW, Aug 22
Williams, Mrs (actor), 1663: LIF, Feb 23, Oct 0, ATCOURT, Dec 10; 1666: NONE,
Oct 25; 1668: BRI/COUR, Dec 2
Williams, Mrs (actor), 1724: DL, Dec 9
Williams, Mrs (actor), 1749: HAY, Apr 29; 1750: HAY, Feb 16
Williams, Mrs (actor), 1773: HAY, Jun 2, 4, 14, Jul 2, 16, 21, 28, Aug 27, Sep
3, 16, 18, 20; 1774: HAY, May 16, 30, Jul 15, Aug 19, 26, Sep 2, 5, 19, CG,
23, HAY, 30; 1775: HAY, May 19, 22, Jun 5, Aug 2, Sep 7, 16, 19, 20, CG, 29,
Nov 7, 16, Dec 15; 1776: CG, Feb 16; 1779: HAY, Mar 15; 1784: HAY, Jan 21;
1786: HAMM, Jun 28
Williams, Mrs (beneficiary), 1706: YB, Dec 11
Williams, Mrs (beneficiary), 1772: CG, May 23
Williams, Mrs Thomas (beneficiary), 1701: YB, Mar 10
Williams, Rd, 1774: DL, Feb 17
Williams, Rev David (prologuist), 1772: DL, Mar 2; 1788: DL, Mar 29
Williams, Robert (actor), 1725: DL, May 17; 1726: DL, May 7; 1727: DL, May 22;
1729: BFF, Aug 23, SOU, Sep 23, GF, Oct 31, Nov 3, 4, 5, 6, 7, 8, 10, 11, 12,
15, 20, 21, 24, Dec 3, 9, 20; 1730: GF, Jan 5, 8, 9, 13, 19, 21, 26, Feb 7,
24, Mar 17, 30, Apr 2, 3, 6, 15, 27, 28, May 14, 18, 19, 22, 26, 28, Jun 1,
3, Jul 1, 6, BFPG/TC, Aug 1, BFPG, 20, GF, Sep 16, 18, 21, 25, 30, Oct 2, 5,
9, 14, 20, 24, 31, Nov 5, 10, 11, 12, 18, 24, 25, 27, 30, Dec 7, 16, 18, 21;
1731: GF, Jan 8, 9, 20, Feb 11, 12, 27, Apr 1, 20, 23, 27, May 4, 5, 7, 14,
Jun 1, 2, 8, Oct 8, 11, 26, 29, Nov 1, 4, 8, 12, 15, 16, 18, 19, 26, Dec 6,
13, 20, 30; 1732: GF, Mar 4, 20, 28, May 11, UM, Jun 19, GF, Oct 5, 9, 26,
30, Nov 27, Dec 1; 1733: GF, Jan 25, HAY, Mar 27, GF, Apr 11, May 9, 14, Sep
10, 12, MEG, 28, GF, Oct 3, 17; 1734: MEG, Sep 30; 1735: LIF, Jul 23, Aug 22;
1736: HAY, Apr 26; 1740: LIF, Mar 26; 1741: JS, Nov 9; 1743: TCD/BFTD, Aug 4;
1744: GF, Dec 3, HAY, 17; 1745: NWC, Dec 30; 1746: GF, Dec 29; 1747: GF, Jan
16; 1748: NWC, Dec 26; 1749: JS, Mar 27; 1750: HAY, Feb 9, 26, Mar 13; 1758:
CG, Feb 4, Mar 22; 1762: HAY, May 1, DL, 17

913

Williams, Rynwick (criminal), 1790: DL, May 11
Williams, Sir (spectators), 1661: CITY, Oct 29
Williams, William (actor), 1729: BFF, Aug 23, SF, Sep 8, SOU, 23, GF, Oct 31,
    Nov 3, 4, 5, 6, 7, 8, 10, 12, 14, 17, 24, Dec 1, 8, 20; 1730: GF, Jan 5, 9,
    Feb 10, Mar 5, 12, 30, Apr 2, 6, 7, 15, 20, 27, 28, May 12, 27, 28, Jun 3, 8,
    18, 23, Jul 1, BFPG/TC, Aug 1, BFPG, 20, GF, Sep 16, 21, 25, 30, Oct 2, 5, 9,
    14, 19, 21, 27, Nov 2, 6, 10, 11, 12, 19, 26, 27, Dec 1, 5, 14, 21; 1731: GF,
    Jan 7, Feb 8, 11, 15, 22, Mar 1, 2, 13, 22, 25, Apr 19, 20, May 5, 7, 14, 17,
    Jun 1
Williams, William (renter), 1758: CG, Mar 7
Williamson (actor), 1734: JS, May 23; 1747: RL, Jan 27; 1750: SFP, Sep 7
Williamson (dancer), 1779: DL, Oct 23; 1782: DL, Sep 20, 21, Oct 24, Dec 6;
    1783: DL, Feb 18, Sep 20, 23, 27, Oct 9, 13, Nov 4, 8; 1784: DL, Jan 3, 7,
    13, May 19, Sep 21, 23, Oct 18, Nov 19; 1785: DL, Jan 6, Oct 18, Nov 21, Dec
    26; 1786: DL, Jan 2, 5, Apr 20, May 22
Williamson (householder), 1765: HAY, Feb 21
Williamson, David (actor, singer), 1791: CG, Feb 26, Mar 7, Apr 28, 30, May 2,
    5, 6, 16, 18, 24, 26, 27, 31, Sep 17, 23, 28, Oct 3, 6, 10, 20, Nov 28, Dec
    14; 1792: CG, Jan 23, May 18; 1793: CG, Sep 18, 20, 25, 27, Oct 4, 7, 9, 10,
    18, 30, Nov 11; 1794: CG, Apr 30, Oct 22, Dec 6; 1795: CG, Jan 31, Feb 21,
    Mar 19, Apr 24, 29, May 1, 29, Jun 3, 6, 13, Sep 14, 18, 21, 25, 30, Oct 2,
    8, 19, 23, 24, 26, Nov 4, 9, 16, 25, 27, Dec 7, 9, 21, 23; 1796: CG, Jan 4,
    8, 13, 23, Mar 15, 30, Apr 9, 16, 20, 26, May 12, Jun 2, 7; 1798: CG, Jun 5;
    1799: CG, Jun 4; 1800: CG, Jun 3
Williamson, James Brown (actor, playwright), 1783: HAY, Jun 6, 13, 16, 20, Jul
    4, 5, 26, Aug 12, 13, 19, 20, 26, 27, 29; 1784: CG, Feb 11, HAY, Mar 22, May
    29, Jun 2, 14, Jul 6, 12, 20, 28, Aug 5, 6, 18, 24, Sep 2; 1785: HAY, May 28,
    Jun 2, 4, 6, 7, 16, Jul 9, 19, 23, 26, Aug 4, 11, 23; 1786: HAY, Jun 13, 15,
    16, 22, 23, Jul 8, 13, 18, 27, Aug 12, 14, 15, 29; 1787: HAY, May 16, 18, 25,
    Jun 11, 14, 18, 20, 21, 23, Jul 4, 25, 27, Aug 4, 28, 29; 1788: HAY, 14, 24,
    Aug 2, 9, 27, Sep 3; 1789: HAY, May 18, 20, 25, 27, 29, Jun 1, 3, 8, 17, 22,
    24, 30, Jul 15, 30, Aug 5, 10, 11, 27, Sep 2, 8; 1790: HAY, Jun 14, 15, 16,
    18, 25, 28, 30, Jul 7, Aug 11, 16; 1791: HAY, Jun 8, 13, 16, 17, 18, 20, 23,
    Jul 14, 15, 18, 22, 26, 30, Aug 2, 24; 1792: HAY, Jun 15, 18, 23, Jul 4, 7,
    16, 23, Aug 2, 6, 9, 23, 28, 31, Sep 5
--Lawyer, The, 1783: HAY, Aug 19
Williamson, Sir Joseph (spectator), 1673: ATCOURT, Aug 22
Williamson, Master (dancer), 1771: HAY, May 17
Williamson, Mrs (actor), 1730: HAY, Jun 23, 27, BFR, Aug 22, Sep 4, HAY, Dec 2;
    1731: SF/BFMMO, Sep 8; 1732: GF, Oct 9, 25, Dec 1; 1733: GF, Jan 8, 17, 24,
    Feb 5, Mar 5, Apr 3, 23, May 14, 15, SF/BFLH, Aug 23; 1740: GF, Dec 19; 1745:
    GF, Oct 28, Nov 4, 18, 19, 23; 1746: SOU, Oct 7; 1748: JS, Oct 31; 1749: SOU,
    Jan 2, 9; 1750: SFP, Sep 7; 1751: SF, Sep 9
Williamson, Mrs (beneficiary), 1724: LIF, Jun 3
Williamson, Thomas (chandler), 1766: CG, Oct 14
Willis (actor), 1735: SOU, Apr 7
Willis (actor), 1780: CII, Feb 29
Willis (beneficiary), 1733: DT, App 5
Willis (musician), 1758: CHAPEL, Apr 27
Willis (ticket deliverer), 1798: DL, Jun 2
Willis, Elizabeth, Mrs Richard (actor, dancer, singer), 1694: NONE, Sep 0;
    1696: DL, Feb 0, DG, Oct 0, DL/DL, Dec 0; 1697: LIF, Apr 0, May 0, Jun 0,
    ATCOURT, Nov 4; 1698: LIF, Mar 0; 1699: LIF, Dec 18; 1700: LIF, Mar 0, 5;
    1701: LIF, Jan 0, Apr 0; 1702: LIF, Dec 29; 1703: LIF, Mar 0, Nov 0; 1704:
    LIF, Apr 29, Jun 8, 30, Jul 10, 24; 1705: LIF, Jan 25, LIF/QUEN, Feb 22, Oct
    30; 1706: LIF/QUEN, Jan 25, QUEEN'S, Mar 7, Apr 15, 20, 26, 30, Jun 29,
    LIF/QUEN, Aug 16, BF, 27, QUEEN'S, Nov 25, Dec 11, 13; 1707: QUEEN'S, Jun 20,
    27; 1708: DL, Feb 6, 7, 26, Mar 13, 18, Apr 5, May 29, Aug 28, Oct 13, 22,
    Dec 28; 1709: DL, Jan 3, 11, Mar 17, 31, Apr 27, May 3, QUEEN'S, Sep 24, 27,
    Nov 19; 1710: QUEEN'S, Feb 11, May 3, 16, 18, DL/QUEEN, Nov 9, 15, DL, 23,
    Dec 30; 1711: DL, Jan 9, 25, DL/QUEEN, Mar 15, DL, Apr 7, DL/QUEEN, May 12,
    DL, 24, DL/QUEEN, 25, 29, DL, Aug 3, 17, 31, Sep 22, 27, Oct 6, 11, 12, Nov
    7; 1712: DL, Jun 5, Jul 8, Aug 1; 1713: DL, Jan 26, Feb 9, 13, 28, Jun 17,
    Dec 2, 18; 1714: DL, May 5, 21, 26, Jun 2, 18, 25, Jul 13, 16, 20, 27, Nov 9,
    Dec 8; 1715: DL, Feb 12, 15, 23, 25, Apr 19, May 13, 24, Jun 2, 6, 28, Jul 1,
    6, 8, 15, 19, 26, Aug 2, 5, Nov 5, 11, 14; 1716: DL, Jan 12, Feb 3, 18, 23,
    Mar 3, May 3, 9, 14, 16, 25, 30, Jun 6, 9, 19, Jul 12, 19, Oct 2, 9, 27, 29,
    31, Nov 3; 1717: DL, Jan 4, 16, May 14, 20, 29, Jun 6, 24, 27, Jul 4, 16, Aug
    6, 9, Oct 15, 24, 30, Nov 6, 8, 25; 1718: DL, Jan 23, Feb 14, Apr 19, 23, May
    21, 30, Jun 27, Jul 11, Aug 12, 15, 20, SF, Sep 3, DL, 27, Oct 15, 27, Nov 7,
    19, 26, Dec 1, 10, 19; 1719: LIF, Jan 3, Feb 7, Apr 2, 20, May 29, RI, Jun 6,
    BFBL, Aug 24, B-L, Sep 5, LIF, Oct 10, 29, Nov 3, 13; 1720: DL, Jan 4, 12,

Feb 3, Mar 31, May 4, Jun 30, Jul 7, Aug 4, BFPMJ, 23, DL, Sep 17, Oct 12,
Dec 2, 17; 1721: DL, Jan 16, 25, Apr 14, May 4, 29, Jul 28, BF/SF, Aug 24,
SFHL, Sep 2, DL, 12, 26, Oct 4, 13, 17, 21; 1722: DL, Jan 5, 10, Apr 30, RI,
Aug 20, BFPMB, 25, SF, Sep 5, DL, 18, SF, 22, DL, Oct 12, Dec 3, 5; 1723: DL,
Apr 1, May 11, 14, Jul 12, 16, 23, 26, Aug 2, 6, 9, 12, 16, Sep 17, Oct 8,
23, 24, 30; 1724: DL, May 1, 2, 6, RI, Jun 22, 27, 29, Jul 4, BFP, Aug 22,
SF, Sep 5, DL, 15, 29, Nov 10, 16; 1725: DL, Jan 27, Feb 3, Apr 21, 30, May
17, 24, BF, Aug 23, DL, Sep 9, 14, 18, Oct 19, 23, 25, Nov 27, Dec 9; 1726:
DL, May 23; 1727: DL, Mar 9, Apr 19, 20, May 2, 22, Sep 26, Dec 4; 1728: DL,
Apr 23, May 20, BFB, Aug 24, DL, Sep 10, 12; 1729: DL, Jan 13, 22, Apr 16,
May 7, 28, Jun 13, BF, Aug 26, DL, Sep 13, Nov 18, Dec 1; 1730: DL, Dec 2;
1731: DL, Apr 8, 19, Jul 6, 13, Dec 22; 1732: DL, Mar 30, Apr 17, May 4, Aug
4, 17, Sep 19, Oct 10, 17, 28; 1733: DL, Jan 22, Feb 22, Apr 24, May 14, Nov
15, Dec 21; 1734: DL/LIF, Mar 11, DL/HAY, May 1, YB, Jul 8, DL, Sep 7, 26;
1735: DL, Jan 22, 29, Apr 28, May 2, Sep 4, 13, Nov 6; 1736: DL, Oct 20, Dec
7, 10; 1737: DL, Mar 17, May 19, Aug 30; 1738: DL, Sep 28
Willis, Mary (actor, dancer), 1704: LIF, Jul 24; 1717: DL, Jun 10, Aug 6; 1723:
DL, Jan 7
Willis, Miss (actor), 1758: HAY, Jan 16; 1771: HAY, Sep 18
Willis, Miss (actor, dancer, singer), 1709: DL, Apr 27, QUEEN'S, Oct 1; 1710:
QUEEN'S, Jun 1, 5, Nov 10, DL, Dec 4; 1711: DL/QUEEN, Jan 12, DL, Mar 8, May
21, Jun 19, Jul 27, Aug 31, Sep 29, Oct 22, 24, 29, Nov 5, 12; 1712: DL, May
26, Jun 5, Jul 11, 22, Aug 1, 8, Oct 31; 1713: DL, Jan 14, 16, Jun 17, Sep
29; 1714: DL, May 24, 28, Jun 25; 1715: DL, May 18, 24, Jun 17, 28, Aug 9,
Oct 13; 1716: DL, Feb 3, May 3, Jul 19, Sep 29, Oct 12; 1717: DL, Feb 15, Mar
2, May 20, Aug 22, Oct 10, 12; 1718: DL, Jan 27, Feb 14, Mar 24, Apr 23, May
28, Jun 11, 13, 17, Jul 11, Aug 1, Oct 22, 28, 30, Nov 26, 28, Dec 11, 19;
1719: LIF, Jan 9, Feb 28, Mar 30, Apr 2, 20, Oct 17, 29, Nov 17; 1720: DL,
May 4, Jul 7, Sep 13, Dec 17; 1721: DL, Jan 27, May 29, Aug 4; 1722: DL, Oct
25; 1723: DL, Jun 4, Jul 16
Willis, Miss (dancer, singer), 1781: CG, May 19, Dec 17; 1782: CG, May 27, Nov
18; 1798: DL, Jan 16, Feb 20, May 16; 1800: DL, Mar 24, HAY, Jul 2
Willis, Mrs, and daughter, 1717: DL, May 20; 1718: DL, Apr 23
Willis, Mrs, older daughter of (singer), 1704: LIF, Jul 24
Willis, Mrs, two daughters of (singers), 1704: LIF, Jun 30
Willoughby, Lord. See Bertie, Robert.
Willoughby, Master (actor, singer), 1796: HAY, Aug 29; 1797: HAY, Jan 23, May
10
Willoughby, Mr and Mrs (citizens), 1769: DL, Feb 20
Willoughby, Mrs (actor), 1748: DL, Sep 27, Oct 18, Nov 28, Dec 21; 1749: DL,
Jan 25, Sep 20, Oct 23, 24, 26, Nov 27, Dec 7; 1750: DL, Jan 1, 22, Mar 13,
Oct 16, 20, 26, 30, Nov 7, 15, Dec 14; 1751: DL, Jan 12, 23, Apr 16, 29, May
1, 6, Sep 12, 17, 21, 24, Oct 9, 11, 17, 22, Nov 7; 1752: DL, Mar 9
Willoughby, Thomas (actor, singer), 1791: HAY, Jul 30, Aug 31, DLKING'S, Oct
15; 1792: DLKING'S, May 23, HAY, Jun 23; 1793: HAY, Jun 17, Jul 20, Oct 10,
Nov 19; 1794: DL, May 16, HAY, Jul 17, 18, 21, 24, Aug 27, DL, Oct 27, Dec
20; 1795: DL, Jan 19, HAY, Jul 31, Sep 21, DL, Oct 30, Nov 11, Dec 10; 1796:
DL, Jan 8, Mar 12, Apr 30, HAY, Jul 15, Aug 29, DL, Sep 29, Oct 19, Nov 9,
Dec 3; 1797: DL, Jan 7, HAY, 23, DL, Feb 9, 10, HAY, Jun 23, Aug 14, 15, 24,
DL, Nov 8; 1798: DL, Jan 16, Feb 20, HAY, Jun 30, Jul 21, Aug 11, DL, Oct 6,
Nov 14, Dec 4, 17, 29, 31; 1799: DL, Jan 19, 28, Feb 4, Mar 2, May 24, HAY,
Jul 9, 13, Aug 21, Sep 2, 9, DL, Oct 14, Nov 14, Dec 11, 28; 1800: DL, Jan 1,
Mar 11, 13, Apr 29, May 3, HAY, Jun 14, Jul 2, 21, Aug 14, 29, Sep 1, 11
Wills (actor), 1770: HAY, Oct 29
Wills (coffee house), 1697: DLORLIF, Sep 15
Wills (mercer), 1772: CG, Apr 21
Wills, Master (actor), 1749: DL, Dec 26
Wilmer (boxkeeper), 1715: LIF, May 26; 1717: LIF, May 30; 1718: LIF, May 27;
1719: LIF, May 26; 1720: LIF, May 7; 1721: LIF, May 18; 1722: LIF, May 8;
1723: LIF, May 17; 1724: LIF, May 12; 1725: LIF, May 11; 1726: LIF, May 20;
1727: LIF, May 18; 1728: LIF, May 29; 1729: LIF, May 15; 1730: LIF, May 28;
1731: LIF, May 31; 1732: LIF, May 16; 1733: CG, May 17; 1734: CG, May 10;
1735: CG/LIF, May 22; 1736: CG, May 27; 1737: CG, May 9; 1738: CG, May 12;
1739: CG, May 25
Wilmer (shoemaker), 1796: CG, Oct 19
Wilmot, Elizabeth Mallet, Lady Rochester, 1671: BRIDGES, Jan 2, NONE, Mar 4;
1718: LIF, Mar 28; see also Mallet, Elizabeth
Wilmot, John, Earl of Rochester, 1667: LIF, Feb 4; 1673: DG, Jul 3; 1674: NONE,
Sep 0; 1676: DL, Dec 11; 1677: ATCOURT, Dec 17; 1680: DG, Sep 0; 1683: DL,
Jan 19; 1684: ATCOURT, Feb 11; 1710: DL, Feb 1; 1711: DL, Apr 21
Wilmot, Mrs (actor), 1782: DL, Dec 26
Wilmott (actor), 1746: JS, Dec 29

Wilson (actor), 1715: DL, Dec 6; 1719: DL, Jan 28; 1720: DL, Dec 17; 1723: DL,
    Jan 9, Jul 5; 1729: HAY, Mar 28
Wilson (actor), 1748: BFLYY, Aug 24; 1749: SOU, Jan 2
Wilson (actor), 1775: HAY, Feb 20, Nov 20; 1776: HAY, Oct 7; 1779: HAY, Jan 11,
    Mar 8; 1780: HAY, Jan 17, CII, Feb 29, Mar 6, 13, 17, Apr 19, HAY, Sep 5;
    1782: HAY, Mar 18; 1785: HAY, Feb 12; 1786: HAMM, Jun 5, 7, 28, 30, Jul 5,
    10, 19, 24, 26; 1787: RLSN, Mar 26, 27, 28, 29, 30, 31; 1789: WHF, Nov 9;
    1791: HAY, Dec 12; 1792: HAY, Feb 6, Dec 26; 1795: WLWS, Jun 19; 1797: HAY,
    Jan 23, Dec 4
Wilson (actor), 1798: HAY, Mar 26
Wilson (boxkeeper), 1721: LIF, May 25
Wilson (boxkeeper), 1766: DL, May 13; 1769: DL, May 12; 1770: DL, May 16; 1774:
    DL, May 26; 1775: DL, May 24; 1776: DL, May 17; 1777: DL, Jun 2; 1778: DL,
    May 23; 1779: DL, May 28; 1780: DL, May 20; 1781: DL, May 24; 1782: DL, May
    29; 1783: DL, May 28; 1784: DL, May 25; 1785: DL, May 27; 1786: DL, Jun 2;
    1787: DL, Jun 8; 1788: DL, Jun 12; 1789: DL, Jun 12; 1790: DL, Jun 5; 1791:
    DL, May 28; 1792: DLKING'S, Jun 14; 1793: DL, Jun 7; 1795: DL, Jun 6; 1796:
    DL, Jun 13; 1797: DL, Jun 16; 1798: DL, Jun 14
Wilson (householder), 1739: DL, May 4
Wilson (watchmaker), 1777: CG, Mar 10
Wilson, D (printer), 1755: CG, Mar 13; 1763: DL, Feb 1
Wilson, Elizabeth, Mrs James (actor), 1783: DL, Oct 7, Nov 4, 18, 20, Dec 12,
    13; 1784: DL, Jan 1, 14, 22, 28, Feb 10, Apr 30, May 7, 15, 20, Sep 30, Oct
    26, 28, Nov 4, 13, Dec 7, 11, 14; 1785: DL, Jan 6, Feb 2, 8, Mar 30, Apr 11,
    15, 20, 25, 27, May 3, 9, Sep 22, Oct 13, 25, 26, Nov 18, Dec 26, 29; 1786:
    DL, Jan 14, 18, Feb 18, Mar 27, 28, Apr 6, 26, May 3, 17, 25, Jun 1, Sep 19,
    28, Oct 7, 10, Nov 18, 25, Dec 26, 28, 29; 1787: DL, Jan 13, Mar 12, 29, Apr
    9, 13, May 3, 4, 9, 16, 19, 23, 31, Jun 1, Sep 18, 22, 25, Oct 9, 20, 30, Nov
    6, 21, 27; 1788: DL, Jan 5, Feb 25, Mar 31, Apr 11, 14, 21, 28, May 1, 6, 7,
    14, Jun 6, Sep 18, 20, 27, 30, Oct 2, 9, 21, Nov 8, 12, 21, 29, Dec 31; 1789:
    DL, Jan 7, 8, 13, 17, Feb 26, Mar 2, Apr 4, May 11, 15, Jun 5, Sep 12, 15,
    22, 26, Oct 8, 22, Nov 21, 24, Dec 5, 8, 10, 23; 1790: DL, Jan 15, Feb 8, 11,
    13, 18, Mar 20, 27, Apr 14, 30, May 7, 11, 14, 18, 28, Jun 1, 5
Wilson, Francis (renter), 1758: CG, Mar 9
Wilson, James (actor), 1779: CG, Apr 27, Sep 24, Oct 18, Nov 8, 30; 1780: CG,
    Jan 17, Feb 1, Apr 1, 11, 21, 27, Oct 19, 20, 23, Nov 4, 7, 18, 25; 1781: CG,
    Jan 31, Feb 10, Apr 2, 3, 25, 28, May 10, 18, 19, Sep 17, 24, Oct 5, 13, 19,
    Nov 2, 5, 12, 24, Dec 11, 17, 28, 31; 1782: CG, Jan 11, Mar 19, Apr 17, May
    3, 6, 10, 11, 17, 22, 27, 28, HAY, Sep 16, 18, CG, Oct 2, 3, 4, 7, 16, 19,
    Nov 18, 28; 1783: DL, Oct 4, 11, 13, 17, 22, 24, Nov 8, 14, 20, 24, Dec 12,
    13, 22; 1784: DL, Jan 1, 7, 10, 13, 17, Mar 29, Apr 24, 26, May 3, CG, 18,
    DL, 21, CG, Jun 14, DL, Sep 23, Oct 9, 11, 12, 23, 27, Nov 2, 3, 9, 22; 1785:
    DL, Jan 12, 14, 17, 20, 27, Feb 2, 4, Apr 1, 11, 20, 25, 26, May 3, 5, 9, Sep
    22, 24, 27, 29, Oct 1, 6, 17, 26, Nov 11, Dec 26; 1786: DL, Jan 5, 14, 19,
    Mar 9, 25, 28, Apr 6, Sep 19, 23, 28, 30, Oct 3, 5, 7, 9, 19, Nov 25, Dec 5,
    7, 19, 26; 1787: DL, Jan 13, 20, May 3, 9, 16, 19, Sep 18, 20, 29, Oct 15,
    20, 26, 29, Nov 10, 21, 27, Dec 7, 14, 26; 1788: DL, Jan 8, 17, 31, Feb 5, 7,
    Mar 3, 29, Apr 4, 8, 14, 19, May 5, 14, 21, 22, Jun 2, Sep 25, 27, 30, Oct 7,
    9, 13, 20, Nov 1, 8, 10, 17, 28, Dec 1, 4, 22; 1789: DL, Jan 6, Mar 17, 21,
    28, Apr 15, Sep 15, 17, 29, Oct 1, 13, 27, 31, Nov 12, 13, 17, 20, Dec 17;
    1790: DL, Jan 8
Wilson, John (actor), 1729: LIF, Jan 1
Wilson, John (author), 1660: NONE, Sep 0; 1671: BRIDGES, May 0; 1672: WF, Dec
    30; 1673: DG, Jul 3; 1674: SLINGSBY, Dec 2; 1675: DG, Feb 27; 1685: DG, Jun
    3; 1691: DG, May 0; 1720: LIF, Nov 26, 28, Dec 2; 1721: LIF, Feb 17
--Andronicus Comenius, 1663: NONE, Sep 0
--Andronicus, 1660: NONE, Sep 0; 1669: BRIDGES, Jan 12
--Belphegor; or, The Marriage of the Devil, 1690: DG, Jun 0
--Cheats, The, 1663: VERE, Mar 0, NONE, 0; 1671: BRIDGES, May 0; 1683: NONE,
    Sep 0; 1692: NONE, Sep 0; 1720: LIF, Nov 26, 28, Dec 2; 1721: LIF, Feb 17,
    May 29
Wilson, John (composer), 1786: CG, Oct 16
Wilson, Master (actor), 1782: DL, Dec 26; 1783: DL, Mar 3, May 23
Wilson, Miss (actor), 1735: GF, Dec 17; 1736: GF, Feb 20, Mar 4, LIF, Sep 28,
    Oct 5, 21, Dec 31; 1737: LIF, Feb 1, Mar 24, Apr 30, Jun 15, DL, Oct 25, 27;
    1738: DL, Apr 26, May 17, Sep 23, 26, Oct 3, 20, 28, 30, Dec 15
Wilson, Miss (actor), 1777: CHR, Jun 18, 30
Wilson, Miss (actor), 1792: HAY, Oct 22
Wilson, Mrs (actor), 1723: LIF, Sep 28, 30, Oct 10, 18, 25; 1730: HAY, Mar 5;
    1731: WINH, Jun 21; 1738: DL, Oct 10; 1749: SOU, Jan 2
Wilson, Mrs (actor), 1796: HAY, Sep 28
Wilson, Richard (actor, playwright), 1770: HAY, Oct 29; 1772: HAY, Sep 21;

1774: HAY, May 30, Jun 3, 6, 8, 13, 15, 17, 22, 27, Jul 6, 13, 15, Aug 8, 19,
26, Sep 5, 6, 12, 17, 19, 21; 1775: HAY, May 15, 17, 19, 22, 24, 29, 31, Jun
7, 12, 16, Jul 12, 14, 19, 21, 31, Aug 2, 16, 21, 28, Sep 7, CG, Oct 2, 9,
11, 16, 20, 31, Nov 1, 9, 11, 13, 16, 21, 28, Dec 2; 1776: CG, Jan 15, Feb
26, Mar 19, Apr 27, 30, May 6, 13, HAY, Aug 26, CG, Sep 25, 27, Oct 9, 24,
31, Nov 2, 9, 25, 30, Dec 4, 27; 1777: CG, Jan 3, Mar 17, 31, Apr 28, 29, May
2, 5, Sep 26, Oct 3, 17, 20, 21, 23, 29, Nov 17, 18, Dec 5, 20; 1778: CG, Feb
6, 25, Apr 22, 25, 27, May 8, 11, 12, Sep 18, 21, 30, Oct 2, 7, 16, 17, 23,
24, 27, Nov 23, Dec 2; 1779: CG, Jan 4, 21, 25, 26, Feb 8, 13, 22, Mar 13,
20, 27, Apr 12, 21, 26, 27, May 3, 6, 10, 13, Sep 20, 22, 27, Oct 1, 6, 8,
13, Nov 12, 13, 22, 23, 27, Dec 18, 29; 1780: CG, Jan 7, HAY, 17, CG, 18, 29,
Feb 1, 2, 8, Apr 3, 7, 19, 21, 22, 24, 25, May 3, HAY, Jun 6, 12, 13, 14, 15,
24, 28, Jul 8, Aug 5, 8, 12, 17, 30, 31, CG, Sep 18, 20, 21, HAY, 25, CG, Oct
19, 21, 26, 30, 31, Nov 1, 4, 15, 25; 1781: CG, Jan 12, 13, 25, Feb 15, 24,
Mar 3, 8, 24, Apr 18, 20, 21, 28, 30, May 2, 10, HAY, 30, Jun 5, 7, 9, 12,
16, Jul 6, 9, 18, 23, 28, Aug 7, 8, 15, 17, 21, 22, 24, 28, 29, Sep 4, CG,
17, 21, 26, Oct 13, 27, Nov 2, 7, 24, 28, Dec 5, 8, 28; 1782: CG, Apr 30,
HAY, Jun 3, 4, 10, 12, 24, Jul 2, 5, 16, 30, Aug 1, 5, 13, 17, 27, Sep 16,
18, CG, Oct 22, 23, 31, Nov 1, 2, 8, 16, 25, Dec 5, 10, 30; 1783: CG, Jan 17,
18, Feb 3, 14, 22, 25, Apr 1, 7, 23, 25, 26, May 7, 9, 10, 15, HAY, Jun 10,
12, 16, 20, 30, Jul 26, Aug 1, 12, 13, 20, 26, 27, 28, 29, CG, Sep 17, 26,
Oct 1, 2, 3, 10, 11, 14, 16, 17, 21, 28, 31, Nov 4, 8, 10, 17, 19, 24, Dec 6;
1784: CG, Jan 13, 14, 29, Feb 12, 13, 18, HAY, Mar 10, 17, 31, CG, May 1, 18,
24, HAY, 28, 31, Jun 4, 19, 28, Jul 2, 3, 8, 30, Aug 6, 10, 17, 19, 20, 21,
24, 26, 28, Sep 2, 6, 13, CG, 17, 20, 21, 22, Oct 8, 12, 28, 29, 30, Nov 11,
13, 16, 20, Dec 1, 3, 10, 14, 22; 1785: CG, Jan 1, Feb 19, Mar 12, May 4, 7,
11, HAY, 28, 30, 31, Jun 3, 4, 6, 7, 11, 21, 22, 30, Jul 6, 22, Aug 9, 10,
16, 17, 19, 25, 26, Sep 2, 16, CG, 19, 23, 28, 30, Oct 3, 7, 10, 12, 14, 20,
21, 26, Nov 1, 3, 10; 1786: CG, Jan 20; 1790: CG, Sep 29, Oct 1, 5, 8, 12,
13, 15, 19, Nov 3, 4, 11, 23, 30, Dec 6, 10, 17, 18; 1791: CG, Jan 3, 7, 14,
15, 26, Feb 2, 4, Mar 3, 14, Apr 11, 16, 28, 30, May 2, 5, 6, 14, 18, 24,
HAY, Jun 13, 17, 23, 30, Jul 7, 14, 20, 22, 30, Aug 10, 16, 19, Sep 2, CG,
14, 19, 20, 23, 30, Oct 12, 13, 17, 27, Nov 1, 5, 7, 24, 26; 1792: CG, Jan
12, Feb 2, 18, 23, Mar 6, 22, 26, 31, Apr 18, 21, May 2, 7, 8, 11, 15, 17,
19, HAY, Jun 15, 19, 23, 27, 30, Jul 3, 9, 11, 14, 23, Aug 2, 9, 15, 22, 23,
CG, Sep 17, 19, 20, 21, 26, 28, Oct 3, 5, 18, 24, 26, 27, 31, Nov 2, 5, 10;
1793: CG, Mar 18; 1796: HAY, Sep 28
--Life and Death of Common Sense, The (prelude), 1782: HAY, Aug 13, 15, Sep 16
--Peep (Trip) into Elysium, A; or, Foote, Weston, and Shuter in the Shades
  (interlude), 1784: HAY, Aug 10, 13, 19, 26, Sep 2; 1785: HAY, Feb 12; 1791:
  HAY, Aug 10
--Seventeen Hundred and Eighty One; or, The Cartel at Philadelphia (prelude),
  1781: CG, Apr 28
Wilson, Sarah Maria (actor), 1775: HAY, May 19, Jun 5, 12, 16, Aug 21, 28, Sep
  4, 7, 11; 1776: CG, Apr 30, Nov 19, 30, Dec 16; 1777: CG, Feb 10, Mar 17, 31,
  Apr 18, 29, May 2, 5, 21, Oct 3, Nov 18; 1778: CG, Jan 29, Mar 31, Apr 22,
  25, Sep 30, Oct 5; 1779: CG, Apr 27, Sep 24, 27, Dec 7, 23, 29; 1780: CG, Jan
  8, 18, Feb 1, 2, Mar 18, Apr 3, 7, 19, 21, 22, 25, May 5, 25, HAY, Aug 5, 17,
  24, 26, 29, Sep 5, CG, 18, 22, Oct 10, 21, Nov 1, 4, 15, DL, 17; 1781: CG,
  Feb 10, 15, Mar 8, 24, Apr 2, 18, 20, 21, 28, May 10, HAY, Jun 7, 16, Jul 6,
  9, Aug 7, 8, 15, 21, 22, CG, Sep 21, 26, 28, Oct 5, 13, 16, 19, Nov 7, 24,
  Dec 8, 26; 1782: CG, Jan 4, 18, 25, Feb 9, Mar 16, Apr 4, 9, 10, DL, 17, CG,
  20, 23, 29, 30, May 6, 7, 11, 17, HAY, Jun 3, 7, 10, 11, Jul 2, 5, Aug 23,
  Sep 18, 19, 20, CG, 23, 25, 30, Oct 3, 4, 8, 9, 16, 17, 19, 22, Nov 2, 4, 8,
  16, 25, 27, Dec 3, 6, 14; 1783: CG, Feb 25, Apr 7, 23, 26, May 7, 9, 12, 14,
  Jun 4, HAY, 16, CG, Sep 17, 24, Oct 1, 2, 28, 31, Nov 8, 19, Dec 3, 5, 6, 26,
  30; 1784: CG, Jan 13, 23, 29, Feb 7, 18, Mar 16, 27, Apr 17, 26, May 4, 7, 8,
  19, Sep 17, 22, Oct 8, 12, Nov 2, Dec 20, 27; 1785: CG, Jan 6, 18, Feb 7, 8,
  17, 21, 24, Mar 5, 29, 30, Apr 2, 6, 11, 20, 25, 30, May 4, 6, 12, 13, Sep
  26, 28, 30, Oct 7, 14, 19, 21, 22, 26, Nov 1, 3, 7, 22, Dec 7, 8, 14, 26, 28;
  1786: CG, Jan 14, 20, Feb 1, 4, 11, 18, May 24
Wilson, W (publisher), 1784: CG, Nov 16
Wilson, William (composer), 1791: CG, May 18
Wilton, Charles Henry (violinist), 1785: HAY, Mar 16
Wiltshire (Wiltsher), John (actor, singer), 1675: DL, Aug 0; 1677: DL, Mar 0,
  17, May 5, Oct 0; 1678: DL, Feb 0, Mar 0; 1680: DG, Feb 0, Sep 0, Nov 1, Dec
  8; 1681: DG, Jan 0, Mar 0, Nov 0, DG/IT, 22; 1682: DG, Jan 0, Feb 9, Mar 0,
  NONE, Sep 0, DL, Nov 16, 28; 1683: DG, May 31, Jul 0, NONE, Sep 0, DL, Nov
  12, Dec 0; 1684: DL, Mar 0, Apr 0, DLORDG, Aug 0; 1691: NONE, Sep 0; 1694:
  NONE, Sep 0; 1696: LIF, Apr 0; 1697: ATCOURT, Nov 4
Win Her and Take Her. See Smyth, John.
Winch (musician), 1735: SH, Mar 28; 1736: DL, May 22; 1745: DT, Mar 14

Winchelsea, Countess of. See Finch, Anne.
Winchelsea, Lord. See Finch, Heneage.
Winchelsea, Mrs (actor), 1779: HAY, Oct 13
Winchester Cathedral, 1698: YB, Feb 16
Winchester, 1684: ATCOURT, Oct 29; 1794: CG, Mar 7
Wind blew fresh and fair (song), 1798: CG, Apr 9, May 28, Jun 4; 1799: CG, May
    13, 18, 28; 1800: CG, Jun 6
Wind, Mrs (actor), 1730: HAY, Mar 30
Windham, Sir William (spectator), 1733: LIF/CG, Feb 10
Windmill Hill, 1723: MO, Apr 15; 1724: WINH, Apr 13; 1729: WINH, Jul 19; 1731:
    WINH, Jun 21; 1732: WINH, May 27
Windmill St, 1750: HAY, Nov 10; 1772: DL, Sep 29; 1788: KING'S, May 15
Winds' Dance (dance), 1727: DL, May 22; 1729: DL, May 28, Oct 30; 1737: DL, Apr
    11; 1739: DL, Dec 26; 1747: DL, Dec 26; 1750: DL, Jan 1
Windsor (musician), 1798: HAY, Jan 15
Windsor Castle Inn, 1786: HAMM, Aug 5
Windsor Castle. See Pearce, William.
Windsor Castle, 1688: ATCOURT, Jul 0; 1696: LIF, Jul 0
Windsor Lady (song), 1785: HAY, Aug 23
Windsor, 1674: DG, May 16; 1683: WINDSOR, Aug 0; 1684: ATCOURT, Oct 29; 1687:
    NONE, Jul 24; 1688: ATCOURT, Jul 0, Sep 29; 1722: LIF, Jan 4; 1730: GF, Jun
    27; 1771: DL, Nov 11, CG, Dec 7; 1791: CG, May 28; 1793: CG, Apr 15; 1795:
    HAY, Apr 22
Wine cannot cure the pain I endure (song), 1791: CG, May 5, 20; 1792: CG, Apr
    12, May 5, 17
Wine-Office Court, 1702: LS, Jul 25
Wingate (actor), 1730: GF, Jun 29
Wingfield (actor), 1671: NONE, Sep 0; 1767: DL, Sep 18, Oct 6, 9; 1768: DL, Jan
    9, Mar 24
Winninton, Sir Francis (spectator), 1699: DLLIF, Apr 22
Winsor (householder), 1750: DL, Mar 8, Apr 25
Winsor Castle (residence), 1794: HAMM, Mar 24
Winstone, Richard (actor), 1732: DL, Aug 15, 17, GF, Oct 2, 12, 13, Nov 18, 27,
    Dec 1, 18; 1733: GF, Jan 24, 27, Feb 19, 20, Mar 5, 15, Apr 11, 17, 19, May
    3, 16, BFMMO, Aug 23, DL/HAY, Oct 5, 8, 10, 12, Nov 13, 28, Dec 10, 17, 19,
    20, HAY, 26; 1734: DL/HAY, Feb 11, 22, Mar 30, DL, Apr 15, DL/HAY, 27, LIF,
    May 9, DL, 13, DL/HAY, 17, HAY, 27, BFHBH, Aug 24, DL, Sep 14, 19, 24, 28,
    Oct 5, 8, 21, 22, 23, 26, Nov 8, 20, 25; 1735: DL, Jan 13, 23, 28, 29, Feb
    20, Mar 10, YB, 21, DL, Apr 21, May 2, 6, 22, Sep 11, 13, 15, 18, 20, Oct 9,
    11, 21, 23, 25, 27, 31, Nov 12, 15, 19, 20, 29, Dec 26; 1736: DL, Jan 3, Feb
    28, LIF, Apr 14, DL, 27, May 20, Sep 7, 9, 14, 18, 23, 28, Oct 5, 9, 12, 13,
    19, 20, 27, Nov 6, 8, 12, 13, 15, 19, 22, Dec 10, 17, 31; 1737: DL, Jan 10,
    14, 29, Feb 5, 19, 28, Mar 1, 15, 17, 29, May 9, 17, 20, 26, Oct 13, 20, 21,
    24, 25, 27, 31, Nov 1; 1738: DL, Jan 9, 11, 19, 26, 31, Feb 16, 28, Apr 13,
    17, 28, May 3, 6, 8, 13, 17, Sep 16, 19, 23, 28, Oct 3, 12, 16, 18, 20, 21,
    24, Nov 4, 8, 9, 20, 23, 25, 29, 30, Dec 15, 18, 19; 1739: DL, Jan 3, 8, 13,
    16, 24, 27, Feb 13, Mar 8, 10, 13, 17, Apr 5, 10, 14, 25, 28, 30, May 14, 18,
    25, 28, 31, Sep 6, 8, 11, 13, 18, Oct 8, 9, 10, 13, 15, 16, 17, 19, 20, 27,
    Nov 5, 8, 19, 20, Dec 8, 10, 11, 21, 26, 31; 1740: DL, Jan 3, 5, 8, 12, 17,
    Feb 7, 13, 14, 23, Mar 11, 20, Apr 8, 16, 17, 22, 29, May 2, 6, 14, 20, Sep
    9, 11, 13, 16, Oct 4, 13, 14, 15, 16, 17, 28, Nov 4, 7, 10, 11, 13, 17, 19,
    24, 27, 28, Dec 2, 6, 18, 20; 1741: DL, Jan 6, 15, Feb 2, 14, 24, Mar 14, 31,
    Apr 3, 28, May 13, Jun 4, BFH, Aug 22, DL, Sep 8, 10, 15, 17, 19, 22, Oct 8,
    9, 10, 15, 20, 21, 23, Nov 2, 4, 11, 16, 20, 21, Dec 4, 8, 14, 16, 19; 1742:
    DL, Jan 8, 22, Mar 9, 29, Apr 5, 20, 24, 27, 28, May 12, 28, Sep 11, 14, 16,
    21, 25, Oct 2, 7, 13, 15, 26, 28, Nov 3, 4, 8, 12, Dec 14, 22; 1743: DL, Jan
    11, 27, 28, Feb 4, 10, 14, Mar 3, Apr 18, 29, Sep 22, 24, 27, 29, Oct 1, 4,
    8, 11, 15, 20, 22, 25, 27, Nov 3, 4, 8, 17, 18, 23, 24, 29, Dec 9, 12, 17,
    19; 1744: DL, Jan 7, 13, 27, Mar 10, 12, Apr 2, 23, 25, 28, 30, May 22, Sep
    20, 27, Oct 2, 4, 9, 11, 13, 17, 19, 23, 24, 30, Nov 1, 3, 5, 9, 10, 24, Dec
    11, 20; 1745: DL, Jan 4, 8, Feb 20, Mar 7, 30, Apr 22, 29, May 8, Sep 19, 21,
    Oct 1, 5, 12, Nov 4, 9, 11, 18, 20, 22, 23, 28, 30, Dec 13, 26; 1746: DL, Jan
    3, 8, 14, 18, 21, Mar 3, 13, 18, Apr 5, 11, 15, 18, 23, May 8, 9, 16, 19, Jun
    11, Sep 23, 30, Oct 2, 4, 14, 23, Nov 4, 5, 7, Dec 15, 26, 30; 1747: DL, Jan
    3, 15, Feb 16, Mar 3, 7, 16, 24, 28, Apr 11, 27, 28, May 5, 6, Sep 15, 22,
    24, 26, Oct 15, 17, 20, 24, 30, Nov 2, 4, 6, 7, 10, 16, Dec 12, 16, 26; 1748:
    DL, Jan 2, 6, 18, Feb 3, Mar 10, 19, 22, Apr 11, 13, 28, May 3, 4, Sep 17,
    22, 24, 27, 29, Oct 1, 4, 6, 8, 13, 15, 18, 19, 28, Nov 2, 3, 4, 8, 9, 11,
    14, 25, 28, 29, Dec 21, 26; 1749: DL, Jan 2, 9, 13, 16, 18, 20, 25, Feb 21,
    Apr 5, 15, 28, May 9, 12, 16, Sep 16, 19, 26, 28, Oct 3, 13, 17, 18, 19, 26,
    28, Nov 2, 15, 16, 21, 27, 28, Dec 12, 20, 23, 26, 28; 1750: DL, Jan 6, 22,
    29, 31, Feb 7, Mar 26, 29, Apr 17, May 11, Sep 15, 18, 21, 22, 25, 27, 28,

Oct 15, 17, 19, 22, 24, 30, Nov 1, 5, 7, 8, 13, 14, 30, Dec 31; <u>1751</u>: DL, Jan
5, 7, 24, 26, Apr 29, May 1, 13, 17, Sep 7, 10, 12, 14, 17, 18, 20, 24, 26,
Oct 2, 3, 11, 17, 22, Nov 2, 4, 7, 29, Dec 10; <u>1752</u>: DL, Jan 1, 22, 28, Feb
6, 8, Mar 10, Apr 10, 14, 27, Sep 16, 19, 26, 28, 30, Oct 3, 5, 11, 13, 14,
19, 21, 23, 28, 30, Nov 3, 4, 8, 22, 25, 27, 30, Dec 7, 8, 18, 19, 29; <u>1753</u>:
DL, Jan 8, 13, Feb 22, Mar 3, 19, 26, Apr 14, May 2, 4, 7, 8, 18
Winter, Mrs (florist), <u>1767</u>: CG, Dec 19
Winter, Peter von (composer), <u>1800</u>: KING'S, Feb 18
--Due Fratelli Rivali, I (opera), <u>1800</u>: KING'S, Feb 18, 22, 25, Mar 8, 11, 15,
May 29, Jun 3, 10, Jul 22
Winter's Tale, The. See Shakespeare, William.
Winterly (pit doorkeeper), <u>1740</u>: CG, May 23; <u>1741</u>: CG, May 5
Wintersell (Wintersall, Wintershul, Winterson), William (actor), <u>1660</u>: NONE,
Sep 0, COCKPIT, Oct 8, REDBULL, Nov 5, VERE, 9, 17, Dec 0, 3; <u>1661</u>: NONE, Sep
0; <u>1663</u>: VERE, Mar 0, BRIDGES, May 7, NONE, Sep 0; <u>1665</u>: BRIDGES, Apr 0;
<u>1666</u>: NONE, Sep 0, BRIDGES, Dec 7, ATCOURT, 10; <u>1667</u>: BRIDGES, Apr 16, Oct
19, Nov 2; <u>1668</u>: BRIDGES, Apr 28, Jun 12, Sep 14, Dec 18; <u>1669</u>: BRIDGES, Apr
17, May 6; <u>1670</u>: BRI/COUR, Dec 0; <u>1671</u>: BRIDGES, Mar 0, Jun 0, Dec 7; <u>1672</u>:
LIF, Apr 0; <u>1673</u>: LIF, May 0; <u>1674</u>: DL, May 16; <u>1675</u>: DL, Apr 23, 30, May 10,
NONE, Sep 0, DL, Nov 17; <u>1676</u>: ATCOURT, May 29; <u>1678</u>: DL, Feb 0
Winterton (dresser), <u>1760</u>: CG, Sep 22
Winton (actor), <u>1775</u>: HAY, Feb 2
Wisdom of Solomon, The; or, The Two Harlots (opera, anon), <u>1723</u>: BFL, Aug 22
Wisdom of the Ancients (song), <u>1746</u>: CG, Apr 16
Wise (payee), <u>1774</u>: DL, Jan 21
Wise Man of the East, The. See Inchbald, Elizabeth.
Wise men flattering (song), <u>1758</u>: KING'S, Apr 6; <u>1792</u>: CG, Feb 24; <u>1793</u>: CG,
Mar 6; <u>1796</u>: CG, Mar 16; <u>1799</u>: CG, Feb 15, Mar 13; <u>1800</u>: CG, Feb 28
Wise Woman of Hogsdon, The. See Heywood, Thomas.
Wise, Widow (beneficiary), <u>1776</u>: CG, May 4; <u>1781</u>: CG, May 19; <u>1782</u>: CG, May 10
Wiseman, Jane, <u>1701</u>: LIF, Nov 0
--Antiochus the Great, <u>1701</u>: LIF, Nov 0; <u>1711</u>: QUEEN'S, Dec 12, 15, 19, 22;
<u>1712</u>: QUEEN'S, Jan 2, 5, 9, 19, Feb 2, 16, Apr 5, 12, 23, 30, May 14, 28, Jun
14; <u>1721</u>: LIF, Apr 13, 14, 15
Wish, The (opera, anon), <u>1775</u>: DL, Apr 22, May 2
Wishes, The. See Bentley, Dr Richard.
Wishing Cap (entertainment), <u>1773</u>: DL, Mar 23, 25, 29
Wit a la Mode (play, anon), <u>1672</u>: DG, Feb 28
Wit at Several Weapons. See Fletcher, John.
Wit in a Constable. See Glapthorne, Henry.
Wit of a Woman, The. See Walker, T.
Wit without Money. See Fletcher, John.
Wit's Last Stake. See King, Thomas.
Witaker, Mrs (haberdasher), <u>1774</u>: CG, Apr 7
Witch of Endor, The (play, anon), <u>1753</u>: SFP, Sep 18, 20, 22, 24
Witch of Sherwood (song), <u>1795</u>: CG, Dec 21
Witch of the Wood, The; or, The Nutting Girls (farce, anon), <u>1796</u>: CG, May 10
Witch of the Woods; or, A Woman without a Head (entertainment), <u>1759</u>: BFS, Sep
3
Witches Frolic, The (pantomime), <u>1789</u>: WHF, Nov 11
Witches Revels, The; or, The Birth of Harlequin (pantomime, anon), <u>1798</u>: CG,
Jun 2
Witches, The (song), <u>1800</u>: CG, Apr 15, May 6
Witches, The; or, A Trip to Naples. See Dance, James.
Witches, The; or, Harlequin Cherokee. See Dance, James.
Witches' Dance (dance), <u>1714</u>: DL, Jul 16
Witches' Music (music), <u>1707</u>: DL, Apr 16; <u>1713</u>: DL, Jun 5; <u>1720</u>: DL, Jul 14;
<u>1723</u>: DL, Jun 4; <u>1724</u>: DL, May 13, Oct 29; <u>1727</u>: DL, Apr 3, Oct 30; <u>1729</u>: DL,
Dec 2
With a jolly full Bottle (song), <u>1798</u>: CG, Feb 9, May 9, Jun 4; <u>1799</u>: CG, Apr
6, May 3, 28
With downcast looks (song), <u>1790</u>: DL, Feb 24; <u>1792</u>: CG, Mar 7; <u>1794</u>: CG, Mar 14
With Horns and Hounds (song), <u>1762</u>: CG, May 11; <u>1766</u>: CG, Apr 9; <u>1771</u>: MARLY,
Jul 18, Aug 8, 20, Sep 5, 12, 17; <u>1774</u>: HAY, Jun 7; <u>1781</u>: HAY, Aug 28; <u>1783</u>:
HAY, Aug 1
With lowly suit and plaintive ditty (song), <u>1795</u>: DL, May 18; <u>1796</u>: DL, May 25
With plaintive notes (song), <u>1790</u>: DL, Mar 17, 24; <u>1799</u>: CG, Feb 20
With pride we steer for Britain's Coast (song), <u>1795</u>: CG, May 6; <u>1796</u>: CG, Apr
12, May 12, 28; <u>1797</u>: CG, Oct 18, 20, 24
With Ravished ears (song), <u>1748</u>: DL, Apr 15; <u>1790</u>: CG, Mar 26; <u>1791</u>: CG, Mar
25; <u>1792</u>: CG, Mar 7, KING'S, 23; <u>1794</u>: CG, Mar 14
With Rosabel what joy to stray (song), <u>1796</u>: CG, Apr 12, May 28

With thee, the unsheltered moor (song), 1790: CG, Mar 17; 1794: CG, Mar 7
With this, this sacred charming wand (song), 1694: DG, May 0
Withers (actor), 1728: HAY, Aug 9, Oct 15, 26
Witherspoon, John (president of Princeton University), 1765: DL, Jan 1
Within a mile of Edinburgh (song), 1794: HAY, Aug 20; 1795: DL, Jun 2, 3
Within this happy World above (song), 1697: DG, Jun 0
Wits Led by the Nose. See Chamberlayne, William.
Wits, The. See Davenant, Sir William.
Witty (house servant), 1747: DL, May 11
Witty Combat, A. See Porter, Thomas.
Witty Fair One, The. See Shirley, James.
Witwe und das Reitpferd, Die. See Kotzebue, August Friedrich Ferdinand von.
Wives and Sweethearts (song), 1795: CG, May 27
Wives as they Were, and Maids as they Are. See Inchbald, Elizabeth.
Wives in Plenty!; or, The More the Merrier (opera, anon), 1793: HAY, Nov 23,
   25, 27, 29
Wives Revenged, The. See Dibdin, Charles.
Wives' Excuse, The. See Southerne, Thomas.
Wizard of the Silver Rock (pantomime), 1789: WHF, Nov 11
Woburn St, 1794: DL, Mar 12; 1795: HAY, Apr 22; 1797: DL, Sep 19
Woffington, Margaret (Peg) (actor, dancer), 1732: RIW/HAY, Sep 4; 1740: CG, Nov
   6, 10, 13, 15, 21, Dec 5, 6, 13, 29; 1741: CG, Jan 2, 7, 12, 15, 29, Feb 7,
   14, 24, Mar 2, 7, 9, 16, 30, Apr 3, 6, 7, 11, 15, 20, DL, Sep 8, 22, Oct 6,
   15, Nov 2, 11, 20, Dec 7, 16; 1742: DL, Jan 4, 6, 22, 23, 25, Feb 16, Mar 8,
   20, 22, May 28, Sep 14, Oct 2, 9, 12, 18, 26, Nov 12, 22, Dec 22; 1743: DL,
   Jan 17, 21, Feb 17, Mar 3, 17, 21, May 3, Nov 1, 3, 12, 26, 29, Dec 1, 12,
   15, 22; 1744: DL, Jan 13, Feb 21, Mar 12, Apr 3, 10, May 1, 4, 11, 14, 31,
   Sep 15, 18, 20, 27, Oct 2, 6, 9, 11, 13, 22, Nov 1, 2, 3, 16, Dec 19; 1745:
   DL, Jan 26, Feb 6, 11, Mar 12, 30, Apr 1, 18, 19, 20, Sep 19, 21, 24, 26, Oct
   5, 8, 10, 12, 15, 17, 22, 29, Nov 1, 14, 18, 20, 26, Dec 5, 11, 20; 1746: DL,
   Jan 2, 8, 18, Feb 24, Mar 10, 13, 17, 18, 22, Apr 4, 10, 11, 15, 21, 23, 28,
   Oct 2, 23, 25, 27, 31, Nov 1, 21, 28, Dec 11, 12, 26, 29, 30; 1747: DL, Jan
   2, 3, 15, 22, Feb 2, 3, 5, Mar 3, 19, 23, 30, Apr 20, 21, May 5, Sep 15, 17,
   19, 22, 24, 29, Oct 1, 3, 15, 17, 24, 29, Nov 2, 6, 10, 16, 17, Dec 4, 5, 26;
   1748: DL, Jan 12, 18, Feb 3, 13, 16, Mar 14, CG, Sep 21, 23, 28, 30, Oct 7,
   14, 17, 21, 29, Nov 3, 9, 11, 24, 26, 28, Dec 10, DL, 10, CG, 22, 26; 1749:
   CG, Jan 2, 13, 25, 28, Feb 6, Mar 4, 6, 29, 31, Apr 5, 7, 10, 11, 15, 20, 21,
   May 4, Sep 25, 29, Oct 2, 4, 6, 9, 11, 12, 16, 18, 19, 23, 25, 27, 30, Nov 1,
   2, 4, 16, 17, 21, 24, Dec 16; 1750: CG, Jan 4, 18, Mar 12, 17, 19, 27, Apr 5,
   May 10, DL, Oct 1, CG, 13, 15, 16, 18, 20, 22, 23, 24, 25, 27, 29, 31, Nov 1,
   5, 8, 19, 24, Dec 1, 4, 10, 13, 14, 18; 1751: CG, Jan 1, 3, Feb 7, 28, Apr
   16, 17, 24, May 1; 1753: DL, Oct 30; 1754: CG, Sep 20, Oct 21, 22, 28, 30,
   Nov 1, 4, 5, 6, 7, 9, 16, 28, Dec 10, 13; 1755: CG, Jan 4, 7, 8, 10, Feb 4,
   8, 20, Mar 12, 17, 22, Apr 2, 4, 8, 9, 15, 17, 18, May 1, 7, 15, Sep 29, Oct
   1, 8, 10, 16, 18, 21, 22, 23, 24, 27, Nov 4, 7, 12, 13, 17, 21, 22, 25, Dec
   4, 5, 11; 1756: CG, Jan 2, 6, 15, 17, Feb 5, 19, Mar 22, 23, 25, 30, Apr 6,
   8, 23, May 17, 26, Sep 20, 29, Oct 1, 6, 12, 14, 18, 19, 20, 21, 22, 23, 25,
   26, 28, Nov 1, 13, 16, 17, 22, 29, Dec 7, 10; 1757: CG, Jan 5, 8, 10, 14, 27,
   28, Feb 9, 16, 19, Mar 14, 24, 29, Apr 27, May 4; 1771: DL, Jan 1
Woffington, Polly (dancer), 1741: CG, Apr 20
Wogan, P (publisher), 1792: CG, Mar 26
Woidner (flutist), 1800: CG, Mar 19
Wolcot, John, 1786: CG, May 5; 1787: CG, Apr 24; 1790: CG, Apr 22; 1791: CG,
   May 6; 1792: CG, May 10; 1793: CG, Mar 6, May 1, 16; 1794: CG, May 26; 1795:
   CG, Mar 19
--Nina (farce), 1787: CG, Apr 24, May 15, 17, 24, 29, Jun 1, 6, 9, 12, 15;
   1793: CG, Nov 28, Dec 5
Wolf (actor), 1736: YB, Apr 26
Wolf (actor), 1770: DL, Jan 27, May 17
Wolf, The (song), 1790: CG, Apr 13; 1791: HAY, Aug 24; 1797: CG, May 11
Wolfall. See Woodfall.
Wolfe (actor), 1777: DL, Apr 24
Wolfe (furrier), 1773: CG, Apr 13
Wolfe, General James, 1760: HAY, Sep 8, SF, 18
Wolley, George (renter), 1758: CG, Feb 25
Wolloughan, Teady (author), 1761: DL, Apr 24
Wolseley, Robert (epiloguist), 1680: DG, Nov 1
Woman Captain, The. See Shadwell, Thomas.
Woman Captive, The (pantomime), 1725: HAY, Apr 19
Woman Hater, The. See Beaumont, Francis.
Woman Is a Riddle, A. See Bullock, Christopher.
Woman is a Weather Cock, The. See Field, Nathan.

Woman Made a Justice, The. See Betterton, Thomas.
Woman More Constant than Man; or, Diana and Harlequin Metamorphosed into
    Armenians (pantomime), 1727: KING'S, Feb 9
Woman Turned Bully, The; or, The Lover's Triumph (play, anon), 1675: DG, Mar
    24; 1758: BFYS, Sep 2, 5, 6
Woman Will Have Her Will, A (play, anon), 1713: DL, Feb 24, Jun 3
Woman's Prize, The. See Fletcher, John.
Woman's Revenge, A. See Bullock, Christopher.
Woman's Wit. See Cibber, Colley.
Women and Wine (song), 1748: HAY, Nov 22
Women Pleased. See Fletcher, John.
Women's Conquest, The. See Howard, Edward.
Wonder (singer), 1795: CG, Mar 13
Wonder of Nature, The (freak show), 1667: BF, Sep 4
Wonder. See Carey, Henry, The Honest Yorkshireman.
Wonder, The. See Centlivre, Susannah.
Wonders in the Sun, The. See D'Urfey, Thomas.
Wonders of Derbyshire, The. See Sheridan, Richard Brinsley.
Wood (actor), 1742: BFPY, Aug 25
Wood (actor), 1770: HAY, Dec 19
Wood (actor), 1785: HAY, Jan 31
Wood (casualty), 1750: CG, Feb 2
Wood (sub-treasurer), 1756: DL, May 4, 12, 15; 1757: DL, May 3; 1758: DL, May
    4; 1759: DL, May 16; 1760: DL, May 1; 1761: DL, May 4; 1762: DL, May 7
Wood (treasurer), 1715: LIF, May 13, Oct 24; 1716: LIF, May 10; 1717: LIF, May
    7; 1718: LIF, May 1; 1721: LIF, May 2; 1722: LIF, May 2; 1723: LIF, May 2;
    1724: LIF, Apr 28; 1725: LIF, Apr 30; 1726: LIF, May 4; 1727: LIF, May 3;
    1728: LIF, May 2; 1729: LIF, May 1; 1730: LIF, May 1; 1731: LIF, May 13;
    1732: LIF, May 5; 1733: CG, May 1; 1734: CG, May 1; 1735: CG/LIF, May 2;
    1736: CG, May 11; 1737: CG, May 5; 1738: CG, May 2; 1739: CG, Nov 1; 1741:
    CG, Oct 27
Wood (violinist), 1758: CHAPEL, Apr 27; 1760: CG, Sep 22
Wood Jr (violinist), 1758: CHAPEL, Apr 27
Wood Nymph (dance), 1705: LIF/QUEN, Oct 11
Wood St, 1742: DL, May 17; 1767: HAB, Dec 10
Wood, Anthony (author), 1661: LIF, Jul 3; 1671: NONE, Oct 26; 1678: NONE, Sep
    0; 1693: ATCOURT, Jan 2
Wood, Charles (actor, singer), 1779: HAY, Jun 7, 12, 17, Jul 1, 15, 20, Aug 14,
    Sep 17; 1780: HAY, Jun 5, 13, 15, 24, 28, Jul 1, 13, 14, 20, Aug 10, 17, 24,
    29, Sep 2; 1781: HAY, May 30, Jun 4, 9, 12, 16, 22, 26, Jul 9, 28, Aug 8, 15,
    17, 22, 24, 28, Sep 4, 11; 1782: HAY, Jun 3, 4, 10, 11, 18, Jul 2, 5, 30, Aug
    9, 16, 17, 23, 24, Sep 19; 1783: HAY, May 31, Jun 2, 5, 7, 10, 20, 27, 30,
    Jul 16, Aug 1, 15; 1786: HAY, Jul 25
Wood, J (boxkeeper), 1771: DL, May 28; 1772: DL, Jun 5; 1773: DL, May 31; 1774:
    DL, May 27; 1775: DL, May 18; 1776: DL, May 20, Jun 10; 1777: DL, Jun 4;
    1778: DL, May 26; 1779: DL, Jun 1; 1780: DL, May 25; 1781: DL, May 26; 1782:
    DL, May 31; 1784: DL, May 27; 1785: DL, May 26; 1786: DL, Jun 1; 1787: DL,
    Jun 7; 1788: DL, Jun 11; 1789: DL, Jun 11; 1790: DL, Jun 4; 1791: DL, May 28;
    1792: DLKING'S, Jun 14; 1793: DL, Jun 7; 1795: DL, Jun 6; 1796: DL, Jun 13;
    1797: DL, Jun 16; 1798: DL, Jun 14
Wood, John Francis (violinist), 1793: CG, Feb 15; 1794: CG, Mar 7; 1795: CG,
    Feb 20; 1796: CG, Feb 12; 1797: CG, Mar 3; 1798: CG, Feb 23; 1799: CG, Feb 8;
    1800: CG, Feb 28
Wood, Master (actor), 1773: MARLY, Sep 3
Wood, Miss (actor), 1729: HAY, Nov 12, 15, 22, Dec 18; 1730: HAY, Jan 8, 21,
    Feb 23, Mar 11
Wood, Miss (actor), 1778: CG, Oct 30; 1779: HAY, May 31, Jul 1, 2, 16, 17, Aug
    17, 31; 1780: HAY, Jun 6, 9, 13, Jul 15, 19, Sep 2; 1781: HAY, May 30, Jul 9,
    21, Aug 7, 8, Nov 12
Wood, Thomas (publisher), 1787: CG, Oct 15
Woodbridge, John (musician), 1738: CG, Apr 8
Woodbridge, Joseph (kettle drummer), 1733: HIC, Mar 16; 1735: DL, Jul 1,
    GF/HAY, 15; 1736: LIF, Mar 31; 1738: CG, Apr 8, May 3, DL, 17, CG, Dec 11;
    1739: CG, May 15, 25, Nov 7; 1740: DL, May 21; 1741: CG, Mar 10, DL, Apr 20,
    CG, May 14, DL, 28, CG, Nov 30; 1742: CG, Apr 22, GF, 22, 29; 1743: LIF, Mar
    15; 1745: GF, Mar 23, DL, May 13; 1746: DL, May 8, SOU, Sep 25; 1747: DL, May
    4; 1750: HAY, Oct 18; 1753: HAY, Mar 29, BFSY, Sep 3; 1754: HAY, Apr 25;
    1755: BFGT, Sep 3, SFG, 18; 1756: DL, Aug 12; 1757: HAY, Aug 3, Sep 8
Woodbridge, Mrs (musician), 1725: LIF, May 20
Woodbridge, Robert, 1793: CG, May 27
--Pad, The (farce), 1793: CG, May 27, Jun 10, HAY, 21, 24, Jul 2, Aug 2
Woodbridge, Thomas (beneficiary), 1737: SH, Mar 18

Woodburn (actor), 1734: DL/HAY, Feb 22, May 24, HAY, Jun 19, 24, Jul 26, 31,
    Aug 14, LIF, 20, HAY, 22, DL, Nov 8, 25; 1735: DL, Jan 22, May 22, LIF, Jun
    12, GF/HAY, Jul 18, 22, Aug 21, YB/HAY, Sep 17; 1736: HAY, May 7, 27; 1737:
    HAY, Mar 21, Apr 13, May 11, DL, Oct 25; 1738: DL, Feb 23, Oct 30, Nov 30;
    1739: DL, Feb 13, Mar 13, Apr 5, 14, May 9, 28, Sep 6, Oct 15, 27, Nov 15,
    20, Dec 11, 26, 31; 1740: DL, Jan 3, Feb 13, Mar 3, Apr 16, May 2, 9, 13, 22,
    Sep 23, 27, Oct 17, Nov 24, 28, 29, Dec 18; 1741: DL, Jan 15, May 12, 13, Sep
    8, 17, Oct 6, 31, Nov 2, 11, 18, 21, Dec 19, 28; 1742: DL, Jan 22, Mar 9, Apr
    19, 20, 24, 27, 30, May 4, 10, Sep 11, 14, 16, 18, 25, Oct 2, 7, 13, 16, Nov
    4, 12, 16; 1743: DL, Jan 27, Feb 4, 10, Mar 14, Apr 9, 29, LIF, Jun 3, DL,
    Sep 13, Dec 9, 15, 17, 19, 21, 26; 1744: DL, Jan 12, 13, 27, Feb 21, Mar 10,
    12, Apr 2, 9, 10, 17, 21, May 2, 4, 22, Sep 15, Oct 2, 4, 11, 19, 22, Nov 2,
    3, 5, 16, Dec 19; 1745: DL, Jan 8, 11, 14, Feb 20, Mar 7, Apr 15, 17, 29, 30,
    Oct 1, 10, Nov 4, 9, 11, 14, 18, 22, 23, 26, 30, Dec 5, 11, 13, 17, 20, 26;
    1746: DL, Jan 8, 18, 31, Feb 15, 22, Mar 10, Apr 30
Woodburn, Mrs (actor), 1740: DL, Nov 7, Dec 26; 1741: DL, May 12
Woodcock, Elizabeth, Lady Batten (spectator), 1661: VERE, Jun 27
Woodcock, Miss (actor), 1786: HAY, Mar 6
Woodcocke (composer), 1722: DL, Mar 14; 1734: GF, May 8
Woodcutters (dance), 1762: CG, Apr 30
Wooden Shoe Dance (dance), 1710: GR, Aug 17, 26; 1719: LIF, Jun 3; 1723: LIF,
    Nov 19, Dec 16; 1724: LIF, Apr 29, May 18; 1725: LIF, Apr 10, 26, May 3, 6,
    Oct 13, 25, Nov 9, 12, 18; 1726: LIF, Mar 10, 28, Apr 13, DL, 27, May 5, LIF,
    16, 23, 25, Oct 12; 1727: LIF, Feb 3, 7, Mar 11, Apr 7, May 4, 9, 15, 18, 22,
    Sep 13; 1728: LIF, May 23, 29; 1730: LIF, Apr 6, 24, HAY, Jul 22, 23, BFOF,
    Aug 20; 1731: LIF, Jan 11, 19, Apr 5, 22; 1732: LIF, Mar 20, Apr 13; 1733:
    HAY, May 28; 1734: GF, Jan 12, 22, HAY, Nov 7; 1735: GF/HAY, Mar 28, Apr 25;
    1736: CG, Apr 8, May 8, 17, BFHC, Aug 23, DL, Oct 2; 1737: DL, May 4, 5, 6,
    7, 9, 11, 13, 14, 16, 18, 19, 20, 24, 25, 26, 27, 30, 31, Jun 11; 1738: DL,
    Mar 3; 1739: DL, May 22, CG, Dec 22, 26; 1740: DL, Feb 19, CG, Mar 24, DL,
    Apr 21, May 5, 6, 7, 23, CG, Nov 18, 19, 20; 1741: CG, Jan 7, Mar 9, 10, 16,
    May 1, 5, DL, 13; 1743: BFFP, Aug 23; 1746: GF, Jan 31, Mar 4; 1747: DL, May
    16; 1749: DL, Dec 19, 20; 1750: DL, Mar 17, Apr 26, May 1; 1757: CG, Apr 16;
    1758: HAY, Jan 12, CG, Apr 11; 1761: CG, Dec 10; 1765: CG, Apr 30; 1773: DL,
    May 28, HAY, Jun 2; 1775: CG, May 12, 16
Wooden Walls of England (song), 1780: CG, Apr 11; 1790: CG, May 24; 1793:
    KING/HAY, Mar 15; 1798: CG, Feb 9
Woodeson (singer), 1693: ATCOURT, Apr 30
Woodfall, George (printer), 1750: DL, Oct 1; 1780: KING'S, Dec 2; 1785: KING'S,
    Jan 8
Woodfall, Henry (publisher), 1744: DL, Mar 1; 1747: CG, Feb 17, May 22; 1748:
    DL, Sep 27; 1754: CG, Jan 18, Feb 11, Mar 4; 1755: DL, Nov 13; 1758: CG, Feb
    23; 1760: CG, Jan 15, Mar 10, Apr 26, May 28; 1761: CG, Feb 7; 1763: CG, Oct
    15
Woodfall, Henry Sampson (prologuist), 1787: CG, May 22, Dec 15; 1788: CG, Jan
    14, Apr 29
Woodfall, Thomas (publisher), 1782: CG, Nov 2; 1783: CG, Nov 4; 1785: CG, Feb
    7, HAY, Jun 16; 1786: CG, Feb 17; 1787: CG, Jan 27, Oct 31; 1788: CG, Mar 1,
    Nov 6; 1789: CG, Feb 3, Mar 5; 1790: CG, Mar 8, HAY, Sep 4; 1791: CG, Mar 14,
    Apr 16; 1793: HAY, Jun 29; 1795: CG, Mar 19; 1796: CG, Apr 23, HAY, Jun 22,
    CG, Sep 12, Oct 7; 1797: HAY, Jun 12; 1798: CG, Feb 12, HAY, Jun 12; 1799:
    HAY, Jun 15; 1800: HAY, Jun 13
Woodfall, W (printer), 1791: CG, Dec 21; 1792: CG, Nov 3; 1794: CG, May 22
Woodfall, William (author), 1777: CG, Feb 1, 6, 20
Woodham, Joseph (violinist), 1794: CG, Mar 7; 1795: CG, Feb 20; 1796: CG, Feb
    12; 1797: CG, Mar 3; 1798: CG, Feb 23; 1799: CG, Feb 8; 1800: CG, Feb 28
Woodham, Master (singer), 1796: CG, Dec 19; 1797: HAY, Jan 23, CG, Jun 5
Woodhouse (actor), 1743: TCD/BFTD, Aug 23, SF, Sep 8
Woodhouse's Booth, 1742: SF, Sep 16
Woodman (actor), 1741: CG, Dec 9; 1743: DL, Feb 11
Woodman, Mary (actor), 1739: DL, Oct 10; 1740: DL, Jan 15, Feb 13, May 22, Oct
    14, 17, 27, 28, Nov 17, 24, Dec 4; 1741: DL, Jan 24, Feb 14, May 1, 9, 27,
    Sep 15, 17, 24, Oct 20, 23, Nov 2, 9, 21, Dec 9, 12, 17, 19, 22
Woodman, Mrs (actor), 1784: HAY, Dec 13
Woodman, Mrs (singer), 1771: CG, Jun 6, Nov 12, Dec 5, 7, 11, 23; 1772: CG, Feb
    26, Mar 10, Apr 29; 1773: MARLY, Sep 8, 11; 1775: HAY, Feb 2, Oct 30
Woodman, The. See Bate, Henry.
Woodmason (householder), 1787: HAY, Jul 21; 1788: HAY, Jul 23
Woodson (musician), 1760: CG, Sep 22
Woodward (actor), 1779: HAY, Oct 18; 1792: CG, Dec 20; 1793: CG, Dec 19
Woodward, C (actor), 1750: HAY, Jul 26
Woodward, Henry (actor, dancer, author), 1729: LIF, Jan 1; 1730: SFOF, Sep 9,

GF, 18, 28, Oct 5, 19, 21, 24, 30, HAY, Nov 9, 16, 20, GF, 24, 28, HAY, 30,
GF, Dec 4, HAY, 14, 17, 28, GF, 30; 1731: GF, Jan 26, 27, Mar 1, 15, May 4,
5, Jun 1, 2, 3, RI, Jul 1, 8, 22, SOU, Sep 28, GF, Oct 25, Nov 4, Dec 9;
1732: GF, Mar 28, Apr 21, May 10, TC, Aug 4, GF, Oct 11, 18, Nov 4; 1733: GF,
Jan 13, 18, Feb 19, 27, May 5, 10, Sep 14, 21, 24, 27, Oct 9, 17, 24, 26, Nov
5, 12, 13, Dec 8, 14, 26, 28; 1734: GF, Jan 8, 19, 25, 28, 31, May 7, 15, 20,
22, HAY, Jun 7, 17, 19, 24, Jul 5, 19, 26, 31, BFRLCH, Aug 24, GF, Sep 13,
Oct 14, 16, 28, Nov 7, 18, 22, Dec 2; 1735: GF, Apr 17, May 2, 3, 6, 15, Sep
10, 12, 19, 26, Oct 6, 8, 15, Nov 3, 4, 10, 11, 14, 24, 25, 26, Dec 4, 5, 8,
17; 1736: GF, Jan 29, Feb 5, 9, Mar 18, 25, 29, Apr 8, 16, 27, 28, May 5, 13,
LIF, Sep 28, Oct 5, 9, 12, 26, Nov 4, 6, 9, 11, 13, 18, 20, 24, 29, Dec 3,
20, 22; 1737: LIF, Feb 12, 14, 21, Mar 29, Apr 25, 27, May 2, 6, 17, DL, Nov
11; 1738: DL, Jan 13, Feb 2, 23, Apr 26, May 3, 5, 8, 9, 15, 17, 25, 26, 27,
Sep 16, 23, 28, Oct 27, Nov 3, 9, 13, 14, 17, 29, 30, Dec 9, 15, 26, 28;
1739: DL, Jan 8, 13, 22, 26, Feb 3, 5, Mar 10, 13, 19, 20, 22, 27, 29, 31,
Apr 10, 12, 25, 28, May 1, 2, 12, 15, Sep 4, 8, 11, 21, 22, 26, 27, Oct 10,
11, 13, 15, 18, 23, 24, 25, 26, 29, Nov 15, 16, 19, 20, 21, 22, 23, Dec 6,
10, 11, 14, 15, 19, 22, 26, 31; 1740: DL, Jan 3, 5, 15, 16, Feb 7, 18, Mar
13, 20, Apr 8, 15, 17, 18, 23, 29, May 6, 9, Sep 9, 11, 13, 23, 25, 27, 30,
Oct 2, 4, 10, 11, 13, 14, 15, 27, 29, Nov 6, 7, 13, 17, 28, 29, Dec 4, 6, 18,
19, 20, 26; 1741: DL, Jan 6, 15, Feb 2, Apr 3, 4, 20, May 13, 15, 21, 25, TC,
Aug 4, BFLW, 22, SF, Sep 14, CG, 25, 28, Oct 2, 10, 15, 20, 21, 26, 29, 30,
Nov 2, 7, 19, 23, 24, 26, Dec 1, 3, 4, 12, 18, 19; 1742: CG, Jan 2, 15, 23,
27, Feb 3, 22, 25, Mar 6, 13, 27, 30, Apr 1, 6, 19, 24, 26, May 4, 5, 7, Sep
22, Oct 6, 16, 19, 25, 26, 27, 28, 29, Nov 8, 11, 19, 20, 22, Dec 7, 15, 21;
1743: CG, Jan 8, 18, Feb 4, SOU, 18, 25, CG, Mar 8, 17, Apr 7, 11, May 4, 5,
17, 20, TCD/BFTD, Aug 23, CG, Sep 21, 26, 30, Oct 10, 19, 21, 29, Nov 16, 17,
19, 21, 25, 28, Dec 3, 8, 9, 12, 19, 20, 26, 27; 1744: CG, Jan 4, 7, 11, 14,
24, Feb 14, Apr 6, 19, 30, Sep 19, 21, 24, 26, Oct 1, 3, 5, 8, 10, 16, 20,
22, 29, 31, Nov 7, 9, 24, 30, Dec 8, 11, 12, 13, 21; 1745: CG, Jan 1, 2, 4,
23, Apr 17, 20, 23, 25, 26, Sep 23, 25, 27, Oct 2, 9, 11, 18, 29, Nov 2, 9,
11, 14, 15, 18, 22, 23, 25, 26, Dec 12, 13; 1746: CG, Jan 1, 7, 11, 15, 24,
25, Feb 3, 4, 5, 6, 17, Mar 18, Apr 1, 3, 4, 7, 9, 14, 16, 22, 23, 24, 28,
May 1, Sep 29, Oct 1, 3, 6, 10, 13, 15, 20, 27, Nov 1, 6, 18, 24, 26, 28, Dec
2, 6, 8, 10, 19, 20, 22, 27, 29, 31; 1747: CG, Jan 17, 26, 29, 31, Feb 3, 6,
12, Mar 17, Apr 20, May 22; 1748: DL, Sep 10, 13, 15, 17, 20, 22, 24, 27, Oct
1, 4, 6, 13, 19, 21, 29, Nov 1, 9, 11, 12, 28, 29, Dec 21, 26, 28; 1749: DL,
Jan 2, 9, 13, 18, 20, 25, HAY, Mar 10, DL, 18, Apr 6, 29, Sep 16, 19, 20, 28,
Oct 3, 5, 10, 18, 24, 26, 28, 30, Nov 9, 15, 21, 27, 28, Dec 2, 7, 9, 12, 18,
20, 26, 28; 1750: DL, Jan 4, 22, 26, Mar 15, 19, 26, 27, Apr 18, 19, May 11,
Sep 13, 15, 18, 21, 22, 25, 27, 28, Oct 13, 15, 16, 17, 22, 23, 26, 29, 30,
Nov 2, 3, 12, 14, 15, 24, Dec 11, 14, 26, 31; 1751: DL, Jan 5, 7, 26, Feb 2,
4, 21, Mar 12, 16, Apr 10, May 17, Sep 13, 14, 17, 18, 19, 20, 21, 24, 28,
Oct 2, 3, 4, 9, 11, 16, 17, 18, 29, Nov 16, 29, Dec 5, 26, 30; 1752: DL, Jan
1, 6, 7, 9, Feb 7, Mar 9, 10, Apr 3, 14, 21, 27, Sep 16, 23, 28, 30, Oct 3,
10, 12, 13, 21, 23, 26, 30, CG, Nov 2, DL, 6, 8, 11, 13, 16, 17, 18, 22, 25,
27, 30, Dec 8, 9, 13, 18, 23, 26, 29; 1753: DL, Jan 1, 2, 3, 8, 12, 13, 15,
22, Feb 19, Mar 20, 22, Apr 5, 25, 28, May 4, 17, 18, 25, Sep 20, 22, 29, Oct
3, 4, 9, 12, 13, 16, 17, 18, 19, 23, 24, 30, 31, Nov 1, 6, 8, 14, 20, 21, 26,
Dec 26; 1754: DL, Jan 7, 10, 16, Feb 1, 20, Mar 18, 19, 23, Apr 16, 17, Sep
17, 21, 26, 28, Oct 3, 5, 11, 12, 15, 16, 18, 22, 23, 25, 30, 31, Nov 5, Dec
5, 7, 13, 17; 1755: DL, Jan 6, 15, 20, 22, Feb 18, 22, CG, Mar 12, DL, 13,
20, Apr 2, 15, 19, Sep 13, 16, 18, 23, 25, 27, 30, Oct 2, 3, 4, 7, 8, 9, 21,
24, 31, Nov 6, 12, 22, 26, Dec 1, 5, 6, 11; 1756: DL, Jan 2, 10, 21, Feb 24,
Mar 25, 27, 30, Apr 3, 19, 20, May 5, Sep 18, 23, 28, Oct 2, 5, 7, 9, 14, 15,
18, 23, 29, Nov 1, 6, 11, 12, 13, 19, 26, Dec 3, 10, 15, 27; 1757: DL, Jan 3,
12, 22, Mar 7, 14, 22, 24, 28, Apr 12, 18, May 2, Sep 15, 17, 20, 22, Oct 6,
7, 8, 13, 18, 19, 20, 26, 27, 29, 31, Nov 1, 7, 19, 22, Dec 3, 8, 13, 22, 27;
1758: DL, Jan 13, 24, 27, Feb 4, 9, 11, 14, 20, Mar 11, 13, 16, 29, 30, Apr
29, May 2, 4, Sep 16, 19, Nov 10; 1762: CG, Apr 29, Oct 5, 13, 19, 21, 25,
28, Nov 1, 12, 15, 24, 29, Dec 27; 1763: CG, Jan 8, 17, 20, 24, 28, Feb 1,
14, Mar 15, 17, 21, Apr 12, 15, 20, 25, 30, May 9, Sep 19, 21, 23, 30, Oct 7,
10, 12, 15, 19, 20, 21, 26, Nov 10, 15, 18, 23, Dec 9, 10, 16; 1764: CG, Jan
9, 14, Mar 20, 27, Apr 10, 26, May 3, 15, Sep 17, 19, 21, 24, 26, 28, Oct 1,
3, 5, 10, 11, 12, 16, 18, 30, Nov 1, 3, 6, 7, 16; 1765: CG, Jan 8, 10, 21,
Mar 12, Apr 9, May 11, Sep 20, 23, 25, 27, 30, Oct 2, 5, 7, 8, 15, 16, 17,
26, Nov 12, 19, 21, 28, Dec 3, 12, 23; 1766: CG, Feb 6, 13, Mar 15, Apr 1, 2,
15, 18, May 8, 13, Oct 6, 8, 14, 15, 16, 18, 21, 22, 23, 25, 28, 29, Nov 1,
14, 18, 25, 27, Dec 6, 8, 23, 30; 1767: CG, Jan 10, 23, 28, Feb 20, Mar 21,
24, Apr 6, May 16, 19, 26, HAY, Sep 4, CG, 17, 18, 19, 21, 25, 26, Oct 5, 8,
DL, 9, CG, 10, 12, 16, 31, Nov 6, 7, 10, 27, 28, Dec 12, 26; 1768: CG, Jan 9,
29, Feb 5, Mar 8, 10, 12, 15, 24, Apr 21, 22, 23, May 5, 11, 27, DL, Aug 18,

CG, Sep 21, 23, 26, 28, 29, Oct 4, 6, 7, 10, 12, 15, 21, Nov 3, 16, Dec 16, 19, 22; 1769: CG, Jan 28, Mar 4, 7, 9, 11, 16, 28, 31, Apr 1, 4, 10, 19, May 6, 16, 17, Sep 20, 27, 29, 30, Oct 3, 5, 6, 7, 11, 17, 18, 24, Nov 3, 15, Dec 2, 7; 1770: CG, Jan 18, 27, Feb 3, 10, 12, Mar 20, 26, 31, Apr 5, 20, 25, 26, Sep 24, Oct 23; 1771: DL, Jan 1, HAY, May 17, 22, 27, 31, Jun 5, 10, 14, 21, 26, Aug 19, 26, 28, Sep 2, CG, Nov 7, 8, 11, 16, 21, 22, 30, Dec 4, 6, 7, 9, 17, 18, DL, 19, CG, 23; 1772: CG, Jan 4, 15, 21, 25, Feb 22, DL, Mar 23, CG, 23, 24, 31, Apr 4, 22, 25, May 8, 30, Sep 25, 28, Oct 1, 9, 12, 14, 23, 29, 30, Nov 2, 12, 28, Dec 3, 11, 22, 28; 1773: CG, Jan 14, Mar 20, 25, Apr 23, 27, May 6, Sep 20, 22, 24, 27, 29, Oct 1, 5, 6, 21, 25, 27, Nov 9, 16, 20, 23, Dec 7, 17, 18; 1774: CG, Jan 3, 5, 15, 29, Feb 8, 15, 28, Mar 12, 24, Apr 5, 22, 27, May 25, Sep 19, 21, Oct 5, 7, 13, 26, 27, Nov 2, 3, 19, 29, Dec 6, 12, 15; 1775: CG, Jan 17, Feb 23, Mar 20, Apr 8, 28, May 9, 12, 18, Sep 20, 25, Oct 4, 6, 18, 20, Nov 1, 3, 16, 22, 24, Dec 5, 9, 20, 21; 1776: CG, Jan 5, Feb 5, 9, Mar 19, 21, Apr 19, 27, 30, May 6, Sep 23, 25, Oct 4, 7, 11, 15, 24, 29, Nov 2, 4, 8, 12, 13, 15, 26, Dec 30; 1777: CG, Jan 7, 8, 13, Apr 10
--Fortunatus (pantomime), 1753: DL, Dec 26, 27, 28, 29, 31; 1754: DL, Jan 1, 2, 3, 4, 5, 7, 8, 9, 10, 11, 12, 14, 19, 22, 24, 26, Feb 1, 4, 7, 16, 19, 20, 21, Mar 14, 21, Apr 6, 15, 19, 29, May 27, 28, Oct 18, 19, 28, 29, Nov 23, 27, Dec 12; 1755: DL, Oct 3, 11, 15, 20, 25, 31, Nov 19, 20; 1756: DL, Mar 16, 20, Sep 28, Oct 5, 16, 25, Nov 2, 15, 25; 1759: DL, Jan 4, 6, 8, 10, 11, 13, 17, 19, 20, 29, Feb 12, 13, 14, Mar 5, 12, 15, Apr 3, 16, 17, May 2, 22, Oct 16, 18, 20, 23, 26, 29, Nov 19, 20, 23; 1761: DL, Nov 3, 4, 5, 25, Dec 4, 10, 19, 22; 1762: DL, Oct 15, 16, 18, 19, 21, 27, 28, 30, Nov 1, 2; 1763: DL, Jan 18, 25, Apr 29, May 19, 28, Sep 22, 24, 29, Oct 1, 24, Dec 15; 1764: DL, Apr 30, May 4, 10, 14, Oct 20, 22, 24, 25, 29, Nov 8, 9; 1765: DL, Apr 19, 20, May 1, 9, 14, Oct 5, 7, 10; 1766: DL, Apr 2, 8, 30, May 8, 15; 1767: DL, Sep 17, 19; 1768: DL, Nov 9, Dec 7, 8, 10, 13, 15, 26, 27, 28, 29; 1769: DL, Feb 2, 9, 21, Apr 27; 1770: DL, May 5; 1780: DL, Jan 3, 4, 5, 6, 7, 8, 10, 12, 13, 14, 15, 17, 19, 20, 21, 24, 27, 29, Feb 1, 2, 5, 7, 8, 14, 17, 21, 22, 29, Mar 4, 7, 9, 14, 18, 28, 29, 30, 31, Apr 8, May 2, 9, 12, Sep 19, Oct 2, Nov 4, Dec 7, 18, 28; 1781: DL, Jan 4, May 4; 1783: DL, Nov 8, 10, 12, 13, 14, 17, 25, 28, Dec 1, 3, 4, 8, 15, 17, 19, 26, 27; 1784: DL, Jan 1; 1789: DL, Dec 26
--Genii, The (pantomime), 1752: DL, Dec 26, 27, 28, 29, 30; 1753: DL, Jan 1, 2, 3, 4, 5, 6, 8, 9, 10, 11, 12, 13, 15, 16, 17, 18, 19, 20, 22, 23, 25, 26, 27, 29, 31, Feb 1, 2, 3, 5, 19, 20, 21, 22, 23, 24, 27, 28, Mar 2, 13, Apr 23, May 3, 8, 10, 19, 21, Nov 14, 16, 17, 21, 22, 23, 27, 29; 1754: DL, Dec 5, 6, 9, 10, 11, 13, 14, 26, 27, 28; 1755: DL, Nov 22, 25, 26, 29, Dec 1, 3, 5, 8, 10, 13, 22, 26, 27, 29; 1756: DL, Jan 1, Feb 7, 21, 24, Mar 2, 8, Apr 19, 27, May 4, Oct 18, 22, 27, Nov 5, 9, 17, 19, 22, 30; 1761: DL, Dec 28, 29, 30, 31; 1762: DL, Jan 1, 2, 4, 5, 6, 7, 8, 11, 12, 13, 14, 15, 16, 18, 19, 20, 21, 22, 23, 25, 26, 29, Feb 1, 5, 9, 20, 22, 23, 25, Mar 1, 4, 15, Apr 12, 13, 16, 29, 30, May 22, Nov 4, 5, 8, 9, 12, 13, 17, 18, 20; 1763: DL, Jan 6, 12, 13, Mar 7, 8, 17, Apr 14, May 23, Oct 4, 6, 11, 12, 14; 1764: DL, Nov 12, 13, 15, 20, 22, 24, 26, Dec 7, 10, 13, 14, 15, 18, 20, 21; 1773: DL, Nov 25, 26, 27, 29, 30, Dec 1, 3, 4, 7, 8, 10, 14, 16; 1774: DL, Jan 22, 25, 28, 29, Feb 4, 15, Mar 10, Apr 9, 11, May 10, Oct 14, 18, 19, 21, 25, Dec 3, 5, 8; 1775: DL, Dec 11, 19; 1776: DL, May 4; 1780: DL, May 5, 8, 17; 1789: DL, Dec 26
--Harlequin Ranger (pantomime), 1751: DL, Dec 2, 26, 27, 28, 30, 31; 1752: DL, Jan 1, 2, 3, 4, 6, 7, 8, 9, 10, 11, 13, 14, 15, 16, 18, 20, Feb 1, 4, 11, Mar 5, Apr 18, May 8, Nov 6, 7, 8, 9, 10, 11, 13, 14, 16, Dec 12, 14, 15; 1753: DL, Oct 9, 10, 12, 15; 1757: DL, Oct 29, 31, Nov 4, 5, 7, 8, 9, 11, 14, 19, 21, 22, 23, 26, 28, Dec 8, 16, 19, 26, 28; 1758: DL, May 3, 19, 26, Oct 20, 23, 24, 31, Nov 7, 10, 20, Dec 26, 30; 1759: DL, Oct 4, 9, 13, 22, 27, 30, Nov 26; 1760: DL, Oct 2, 4, Nov 29, Dec 1, 2, 3; 1761: DL, Sep 17, 23, 29, Oct 1, 15; 1762: DL, Oct 5, 7, 8, 11
--Harlequin's Jubilee (pantomime), 1769: CG, Oct 27; 1770: CG, Jan 27, 29, 31, Feb 1, 2, 3, 5, 6, 7, 8, 9, 10, 12, 13, 14, 15, 16, 17, 19, 20, 21, 22, 23, Mar 1, 3, 19, 20, 22, 24, May 3, 17, 24, 28, 29, Oct 1, 3, 4, 6, 8
--Lick at the Town, A, 1751: DL, Mar 16; 1752: CG, Apr 8
--Mercury Harlequin (pantomime), 1756: DL, Dec 27, 28, 29, 30, 31; 1757: DL, Jan 1, 3, 4, 5, 6, 7, 8, 10, 11, 12, 13, 14, 15, 19, 20, Feb 8, 14, 24, 28, Mar 1, 3, 17, 19, 29, Apr 11, 16, 20, 22, 23, May 4, 13, 26, Oct 7, 8, 14, 25, Nov 30, Dec 27; 1758: DL, Nov 27, 30, Dec 1, 5, 11, 19, 28; 1759: DL, Jan 1
--Proteus; or, Harlequin in China (pantomime), 1755: DL, Jan 4, 6, 7, 8, 9, 10, 11, 13, 14, 15, 16, 17, 18, 20, 21, 22, 23, 24, 25, 28, Feb 5, 8, 18, 22, 27, Mar 8, 31, Apr 9, 12, 17, 30, May 1, 7, 19
--Queen Mab (pantomime), 1750: DL, Dec 26, 27, 28, 29, 31; 1751: DL, Jan 1, 2, 3, 4, 5, 7, 8, 9, 10, 11, 12, 14, 15, 16, 17, 18, 19, 21, 22, 23, 24, 25, 26,

28, 29, 31, Feb 1, 14, 15, 18, 21, 27, Apr 8, 9, 17, 20, 24, May 11, 15, 18, 22, Oct 16, 18, 26, 31, Nov 1, 12, 13, 27; 1752: DL, Feb 5, 7, 10, 27, Mar 2, 30, Apr 7, May 7, Oct 12, 14, 21, 24, 25, 31, Nov 18, 21, 23, 25, 27, 29, Dec 6; 1753: DL, Oct 17, 18, 26, Nov 7, 9; 1754: DL, Oct 31, Nov 1, 4, 5, 9, 18, 20, 29, Dec 2; 1758: DL, Jan 13, 14, 16, 17, 19, 21, 23, 24, Feb 4, 7, 13, 16, 18, 20, Mar 27, 28, Apr 8, 15, May 29, Oct 5, 10, 18, 26, Nov 3, 4, 11, 13, 22, 25, Dec 8, 14, 15, 16, 22, 23, 27; 1759: DL, May 4, 9, 10, 25, Jun 4, Dec 7, 11, 17, 26, 28; 1760: DL, Apr 22, 25, Jun 3, Oct 7, 10, 15, 23, Dec 10; 1761: DL, Mar 14, Apr 17, May 5, 19, Jun 1, 4, Oct 22, 23, 29, Nov 9, 16, 19, Dec 12, 16, 21; 1764: DL, Dec 26, 27, 28, 29, 31; 1765: DL, Jan 1, 3, 4, 7, 8, 10, 11, 14, 17, 18, Feb 6, 7, 8, 11, 13, 16, 19, 26, Mar 12, 28, Apr 8, 9; 1766: DL, Oct 29, 30, Nov 1, 3, 4, 5, 6, 10, 11, 12, Dec 2, 9, 10, 11, 26, 27, 30; 1767: DL, Jan 1, 22, 23, Feb 4, 9, 11, 19, Apr 30, Sep 15, 16, 21, Nov 16; 1768: DL, Apr 23, Oct 11, Nov 9, 10, 11, 12, 14, 15, 16, 18, 19, 22, 23, 24, 25, 26, 29, Dec 1, 5, 7, 30; 1769: DL, Jan 2, 4, 7, 10, 13, 17, 18, 19, 26, 28, Apr 6, May 4, Sep 26, Oct 7, 11; 1770: DL, Apr 20, May 2; 1775: DL, Nov 11, 13, 15, 17, 20, 22, 23, 24, Dec 2, 11; 1778: DL, Jan 1, 2, 3, 5, 6, 8, 10, 12, 14, 16, 19, Feb 3, 4, 9, 18, Mar 5, 12, Apr 29, May 11, 13, Oct 8, Dec 2, 16; 1779: DL, Apr 22, Oct 5, 23; 1780: DL, Sep 30, Oct 7, Nov 9, Dec 9, 14, 30; 1781: DL, Jan 6; 1789: DL, Dec 26
--Tit for Tat; or, A Dish of the Auctioneer's Own Chocolate, 1749: DL, Mar 18, 28, 29, 31, Apr 8, 11, 26, May 16, SOU, Sep 18; 1754: HAY, Dec 18
Woodward, Mrs (actor), 1730: GF, Sep 16, HAY, 18, GF, 23, 28, Oct 5, 9, 14, 24, Nov 2, 6, HAY, 9, 16, 20, 30, Dec 7, 9, 17, 28; 1734: HAY, Jun 14, GF, Sep 11, 13, 16, 18, 25, Oct 14, 16, 17, 28, Dec 2, 3, 4, 5, 6, 12, 28, 31; 1735: GF, Jan 6, 7, 8, 10, 11, 13, 24, Feb 6, Mar 6, 13, 17, 25, 27, 29, Apr 9, 10, 17, 21, 22, 24, 28, 29, 30, May 1, 2, 5, 6, 15, GF/HAY, Jul 22, GF, Sep 12, 22, 24, Oct 3, 15, Nov 3, 12, 14, 15, 17, 19, 21, 28, Dec 4, 6, 8, 10, 12, 15, 17; 1736: GF, Feb 4, 5, 16, 20, Mar 3, 23, 25, Apr 1, 6, 12, 17, 28, May 6, 10, LIF, Jul 1, BFHC, Aug 23, LIF, Sep 30, Oct 5, 9, 21, Dec 7, 15, 16; 1737: LIF, Jan 5, Feb 1, DL, Oct 25; 1738: DL, Jan 19, 24, 28; 1739: DL, Sep 6, 13, CG, 29, DL, Oct 1, 10, 15, 26, Nov 1, 14, 28, CG, Dec 4, DL, 11, 15, CG, 29; 1740: DL, Jan 15, 29, Feb 13, CG, Mar 25, DL, Apr 22, CG, May 3, 7, 23, Oct 24, 31, GF, Nov 6, CG, Dec 22; 1741: CG, Mar 10, Apr 1, 22, Oct 5; 1742: CG, Feb 23, Mar 13, 27, Apr 1, 22, 26, 29, May 1, Sep 27, Oct 13, 19, 28, Nov 11, 13, 20, Dec 15, 27; 1743: CG, Jan 18, 26, Apr 9, 26, DL, Sep 17, CG, 21, 26, 28, Oct 3, 17, 24, Dec 8
Woody Vale (song), 1793: KING/HAY, Mar 22
Woodyer (housekeeper), 1721: LIF, May 5; 1722: LIF, May 25
Wooldridge (boxkeeper), 1793: DL, Jun 6; 1795: DL, Jun 6; 1796: DL, Jun 13; 1797: DL, Jun 16; 1798: DL, Jun 14; 1799: DL, Jul 3
Wooler (actor), 1769: HAY, Feb 28; 1770: HAY, Oct 29; 1771: HAY, Mar 4, Sep 20; 1772: HAY, Dec 21; 1774: HAY, Jan 24; 1775: HAY, Feb 2
Wooley (beneficiary), 1733: HAY, Feb 14
Wooley (house servant), 1768: CG, May 28, 30; 1769: CG, May 20, 23; 1770: CG, May 23; 1771: CG, May 27; 1772: CG, May 23; 1774: CG, May 24; 1775: CG, May 30; 1776: CG, May 21; 1777: CG, May 23; 1778: CG, May 21; 1779: CG, May 15
Woollams, Thomas (boxkeeper), 1778: DL, May 22; 1779: DL, May 29; 1780: DL, May 23; 1789: DL, Jun 10; 1790: DL, Jun 4; 1791: DL, May 28; 1792: DLKING'S, Jun 14; 1793: DL, Jun 5; 1795: DL, Jun 6; 1796: DL, Jun 13; 1797: DL, Jun 14; 1798: DL, Jun 15; 1799: DL, Jul 4; 1800: DL, Jun 17
Woollery, Frances Barnet (actor), 1784: HAY, Jul 12, 24, Aug 18; 1785: HAY, Feb 24, Jun 2, 16, 29, Jul 16, Aug 11, 31, Sep 2, 9; 1786: HAY, Jun 20, 22, Jul 3, 14, 27, Aug 29; 1787: HAY, May 25, Jun 18, 23, 28, Jul 3, 7, 25, Aug 1, 4, 29, Sep 5, 8
Woolley, Mrs (house servant), 1770: CG, May 18; 1773: CG, May 22
Woolwich, 1731: LIF, Jun 7
Worcester Theatre, 1790: DL, Apr 22
Worcester, Marchioness of, 1675: ATCOURT, Jun 7; 1677: DL, Mar 17; 1681: DLORDG, Nov 12
Worcester, Marquis of. See Somerset, Henry.
Worcester, 1707: YB, Apr 18; 1766: DL, Dec 3
Word for Nature, A. See Cumberland, Richard.
Word to the Wise, A. See Kelly, Hugh.
Wordsworth, William (actor), 1779: CG, Nov 12, Dec 22; 1780: CG, Feb 1, Mar 29, Apr 21, 22, 25, May 23
Worgan, James (composer), 1753: CG, Apr 5; 1761: SOHO, Apr 15; 1764: KING'S, Apr 3; 1767: CHAPEL, May 13; 1794: CG, May 7, 24
--Hannah (oratorio), 1764: KING'S, Apr 3
--Manasseh (oratorio), 1766: CHAPEL, Apr 30; 1767: CHAPEL, May 13
Work for a Cooper (dance), 1729: DL, Nov 14
World (prompter), 1733: GF, May 16; 1734: GF, May 16; 1735: GF, Apr 22; 1736:

GF, Apr 13
World as it Goes, The. See Cowley, Hannah.
World in a Village, The. See O'Keeffe, John.
World in the Moon, The. See Settle, Elkanah.
Worldly (dancer), 1742: LIF, Dec 6
Worley, Mary (actor), 1766: HAY, Jul 3, 8, 15, 31, KING'S, Aug 18, 25, 27, 29,
    Sep 5, 9, 12, 13, 15
Worley, Thomas (teacher), 1741: GF, May 1
Worm Doctor, The (farce, anon), 1736: LIF, Oct 9, 12, 14, 16, 19
Wormall (actor), 1770: CG, Jan 5
Worsdale (actor), 1752: DL, Jan 11, 13, 21; 1756: CG, Apr 23
Worsdale, James, 1735: DL, Feb 25, May 5; 1750: CG, Mar 27
--Cure for a Scold, A; or, The Taming of a Shrew, 1735: DL, Feb 25, 27, Mar 1,
    20, May 5; 1750: CG, Mar 27, Apr 26
Worse and Worse. See Digby, George.
Worsely (spectator), 1699: DLLIF, Apr 22
Worsley (actor), 1731: GF, Jun 2
Worthington, Mrs (actor), 1797: DL, Mar 6
Worthy is the Lamb (song), 1790: DL, Mar 5; 1791: DL, Apr 1; 1792: KING'S, Mar
    14, 21, 23, 30; 1793: KING/HAY, Feb 20; 1794: DL, Mar 19
Wortley (actor), 1780: CII, Feb 29, Mar 6, 13, 17, 27, Apr 5, 19
Wost (ticket deliverer), 1796: CG, Jun 4
Wotton (shoemaker), 1662: VERE, Sep 24; 1663: LIF, Jul 22, Oct 24, Dec 10
Would custom bid (song), 1786: DL, Mar 10
Would you gain the Tender Creature (song), 1737: DL, Jan 14, 15, 18; 1791: DL,
    Apr 1; 1792: KING'S, Feb 29, Mar 28; 1794: DL, Mar 26, Apr 2
Would you see the World in little (song), 1795: CG, Jan 12, 14, 19
Would you view the loveliest rose (song), 1783: CG, Nov 8
Wounded Gizzard (song), 1757: HAY, Sep 28
Wrangling Deities, The; or, Venus Upon Earth (farce, anon), 1741: BFLW, Aug 22
Wrangling Lovers, The (farce, anon), 1741: JS, Jun 16
Wrangling Lovers, The; or, Like Master Like Man. See Lyon, William.
Wrangling Lovers, The; or, The Invisible Mistress. See Ravenscroft, Edward.
Wrekin Tavern, 1792: HAY, Oct 15
Wren, Sir Christopher (architect), 1674: DG, Jun 20
Wrestling Dance (dance), 1730: LIF, Apr 25, May 9
Wretched lovers (song), 1790: DL, Mar 10; 1791: DL, Apr 1; 1792: KING'S, Feb
    29, CG, Mar 14, 21; 1794: DL, Mar 26; 1795: CG, Mar 13
Wrexell (musician), 1760: CG, Sep 22, Nov 28
Wrexham (mercer), 1727: DL, May 11; 1728: DL, May 23
Wrexham (secretary), 1734: DL/HAY, May 23
Wright (accountant), 1772: DL, Oct 19, Dec 9, 14; 1773: DL, Mar 9; 1775: DL,
    Jan 6, Feb 17, Nov 15
Wright (actor), 1713: DL, Jan 29; 1715: DL, Aug 9, Dec 6; 1720: DL, Dec 17;
    1721: LIF, Jan 10, DL, May 31; 1722: DL, May 25; 1723: DL, May 28; 1724: DL,
    May 21; 1725: DL, May 19; 1726: DL, May 23, Oct 1; 1727: DL, May 15, Oct 6;
    1728: DL, Mar 30, May 29, Oct 30, Nov 15; 1729: DL, May 21, Jun 13, 20, 27,
    Dec 26; 1730: DL, Apr 23, May 19, Oct 1, Nov 23, 30, Dec 4; 1731: DL, May 19,
    Jun 7, Aug 6, 11, SFGT, Sep 8, DL, Oct 16, 30, Dec 2; 1732: DL, Apr 21, May
    12, Aug 1, Dec 6, 26; 1733: DL, Mar 31, May 9, DL/HAY, Dec 17, 20; 1734: DL,
    Apr 15, 23, DL/HAY, 27, DL, May 15, LIF, 29, DL, Sep 19, Oct 21, 22, Nov 1;
    1735: DL, Jan 22, Feb 14, May 14, Jun 3, LIF, 12, GF/HAY, Jul 22, HAY, Aug
    12, GF/HAY, 21, DL, Sep 15, Oct 7, 31, Nov 20; 1736: DL, May 25, LIF, Jun 18,
    Oct 5, DL, 12, LIF, 14, 19, 28, Dec 20, DL, 31; 1737: LIF, Jan 19, Feb 12,
    14, 21, Mar 1, 15, 21, 24, Apr 18, 28, May 2, DL, 25, Sep 1, 8, 15, 20, 22,
    24, 27, 29, Oct 6, 19, 20, 21, 26, 27, Nov 1, 4, 11, 12, 14, 16; 1738: DL,
    Jan 19, 24, 31, Feb 10, Mar 2, 21, Apr 6, 17, 29, May 2, 6, 19, 23, Sep 7, 9,
    12, 14, 16, 21, 23, 26, Oct 3, 12, 17, 18, 19, 20, 26, Nov 1, 4, 9, 14, 20,
    Dec 6; 1739: DL, Jan 8, 15, 26, Feb 1, 3, 13, Mar 8, 10, 17, Apr 27, May 1,
    18, 28, Sep 1, 6, 8, 13, 18, 21, 22, 24, Oct 3, 5, 6, 9, 10, 11, 17, 18, 20,
    22, 23, 25, Nov 3, 5, 12, 16, 19, 20, 22, 23, 28, Dec 10, 31; 1740: DL, Jan
    5, Feb 23, Mar 13, 25, 27, Apr 23, May 2, 9, 21, 26, 30, Sep 6, 11, 16, 18,
    20, 25, 27, 30, Oct 4, 7, 11, 13, 14, 16, 17, 29, Nov 1, 4, 6, 8, 10, 13, 19,
    24, 27, Dec 6, 8, 10, 20; 1741: DL, Apr 13, 17, May 12, 14, BFH, Aug 22, DL,
    Oct 6, Nov 21, Dec 19; 1742: DL, Oct 7, 13, Nov 19; 1743: LIF, Jun 3, DL, Sep
    20, Nov 8, Dec 9; 1744: CG, Apr 21, DL, Sep 29, HAY, 29, DL, Oct 11, 19;
    1745: DL, May 13, Nov 18, Dec 13; 1746: DL, Apr 16, May 1, SFW, Sep 8, DL,
    30; 1747: DL, Mar 28, May 18; 1748: DL, Jan 18, Sep 17, Nov 29; 1749: BFY,
    Aug 23, DL, Dec 20; 1750: DL, May 10, SFP, Sep 7, DL, 28; 1751: DL, May 13
Wright (actor), 1778: CG, Jan 3; 1779: CG, May 8, 13
Wright (actor), 1779: HAY, Oct 18; 1786: HAY, Aug 3, Sep 5; 1791: HAY, Sep 26,
    Dec 12

Wright (casualty), 1753: DL, Apr 7
Wright (glazier), 1772: CG, Jan 3, Dec 3; 1774: CG, May 4
Wright (hospital treasurer), 1767: CG, Dec 23; 1772: CG, Dec 31
Wright and Co (bankers), 1791: PAN, Feb 17
Wright, Charlotte (actor, singer), 1779: DL, Feb 19, Mar 11, May 7, 24, Jun 3,
    Oct 5, 12; 1780: DL, Apr 14, 26, Oct 10, 19, Nov 4, 10, 11; 1781: DL, Mar 10,
    May 2, Sep 25, 27, Oct 12, 19; 1782: DL, Jan 23, Mar 16, Apr 15, 17, 24, 25,
    May 7, CG, 24, DL, 25, Sep 28, Oct 5, 10, 26, Nov 29, Dec 26; 1783: DL, Jan
    25, Mar 6, 15, Apr 7, May 9, 21
Wright, Christiana (actor, dancer), 1737: DL, May 25, Nov 7, 11, 12, 19; 1738:
    DL, Jan 20, Feb 28, Mar 13, 20, 21, 25, Apr 12, 13, 14, 21, 22, 24, 26, 29,
    May 3, 5, 8, 9, 10, 11, 13, 15, 17, 18, 19, 23, 24, 25, 26, 27, 29, 30, 31,
    BFH, Aug 23, DL, Oct 5, 7, 26, 27, 30, Nov 30, Dec 4, 16, 28; 1739: DL, Feb
    7, Mar 17, 26, 27, Apr 2, 3, 5, 10, 12, 27, 30, May 1, 3, 5, 8, 14, 16, 18,
    19, 22, 23, 25, 26, 31, Oct 10, 16, 18, 22, 24, 25, 26, 27, 29, 31, Nov 1, 2,
    10, 13, 20, 21, Dec 7, 12, 14, 28, 29; 1740: DL, Jan 5, 7, 8, 11, 14, Feb 2,
    5, 7, 11, 12, 15, 16, 18, 19, 21, Mar 6, 8, May 21, Oct 14, Dec 26; 1741: DL,
    May 14, Nov 28, Dec 14, 18; 1742: DL, Feb 18, May 25, Dec 7, 8, 11; 1743: CG,
    Mar 1, HAY, 23, DL, May 26, Dec 6, 10, 17; 1744: DL, May 23, Oct 2, 19, 27,
    Nov 3, Dec 10, 27
Wright, Elizabeth (actor, singer), 1761: DL, Jan 31, Apr 2, Oct 23, Dec 11;
    1763: DL, Nov 23, 26; 1764: DL, Jan 21, Feb 24, CHAPEL, 29, DL, Apr 5, 7, 28,
    May 10, Sep 22, Nov 2, 28; 1765: DL, Mar 2, Apr 23, Oct 8, Nov 16, Dec 14,
    16; 1766: DL, Feb 7, Mar 17, Apr 14, 22, Sep 23, 25, Oct 28, Nov 5, 14
Wright, Henry (scene keeper), 1673: LIF, Dec 0
Wright, John, 1662: VERE, Jul 23
--Thyestes, 1673: NONE, Sep 0; 1680: DL, Mar 0
Wright, Justice, 1772: CG, Oct 27
Wright, Mr and Christiana (actors), 1744: DL, May 23
Wright, Mrs (actor), 1670: LIF, Sep 20, Nov 0
Wright, Mrs (actor), 1769: HAY, Sep 19
Wright, Mrs (actor, singer), 1729: LIF, Feb 1, Mar 5, 12, 19, Apr 16; 1730:
    LIF, Jan 2, Mar 16, Apr 8, 15, 22, Nov 7, Dec 11, 15; 1731: LIF, Mar 26, Apr
    3, 8, 28, 29, May 12, 14, 20, 24, 26, 28, Oct 4, Nov 18, Dec 1; 1732: LIF,
    Mar 30, Apr 19, 28, May 5, 9, 15, 18, LIF/CG, Oct 30, Nov 8, 24; 1733:
    LIF/CG, Mar 15, KING'S, 17, LIF/CG, 29, Apr 11, LIF, 16, LIF/CG, 18, 20, CG,
    May 1, 2, LIF/CG, 3, 8, 24, CG, Oct 11, 13, Dec 7; 1734: CG, Jan 1, 25, Feb
    13, Mar 16, 18, 28, Apr 1, 25, May 1, 4, 9, 14, 15, CG/LIF, Dec 30; 1735:
    CG/LIF, Feb 13, Mar 20, Apr 21, May 2, CG, Oct 17, Nov 6, 15; 1736: CG, Jan
    1, 21, Mar 6, 18, Apr 17, May 6, 13, 17, Jun 4, Oct 8, 20, Nov 3, 26; 1737:
    CG, Apr 18, 21; 1738: CG, Nov 18; 1739: CG, Jan 20, DL, 24, Sep 13, CG, 22,
    Oct 3, DL, 23, CG, 26, DL, 27, Nov 1, 9, 20, 28, CG, Dec 4, 10; 1740: DL, Jan
    15, 19, 21, CG, Feb 12, DL, Mar 11, Apr 11, May 6, Sep 23, Oct 7, CG, 10, DL,
    11, 13, 15, 16, 17, 24, 27, Nov 17, 24, Dec 4, 10, 19; 1741: CG, Jan 5, DL,
    20, 26, Feb 2, CG, 24, 28, DL, Mar 17, CG, Apr 24, DL, 28, May 9, BFLW, Aug
    22, CG, Oct 7, 8, 15, 24, 30, Nov 7, 26, Dec 15, 28, 30; 1742: CG, Jan 8, 21,
    25, Feb 22, 25, Mar 23, Apr 24, May 8, Sep 29, Oct 1, 16, Nov 3, Dec 21;
    1743: CG, Jan 8, Mar 8, Apr 16, 23, May 4; 1744: CG, Jan 14, Mar 3, Dec 8;
    1745: CG, Jan 14, Nov 14; 1746: CG, Jan 8; 1747: CG, Mar 26; 1748: CG, Dec
    15; 1749: CG, Oct 12, Nov 23; 1750: CG, Mar 27, Oct 29, Nov 8; 1751: CG, Jan
    15; 1754: DL, May 4
Wright, Mrs (beneficiary), 1775: DL, May 10
Wright, Roger (actor, dancer), 1767: DL, Feb 11, Dec 5, 10; 1768: DL, Jan 23,
    May 24, Sep 20, 26, Oct 28, Nov 4, 15, Dec 30; 1769: DL, Jan 27, Apr 4, May
    4, 12, Sep 19, 21, 26, Oct 2, 5, 9, 14, 31, Nov 17, 23, 27, Dec 13, 23; 1770:
    DL, Jan 16, 19, 27, Mar 20, Apr 7, 17, 20, May 3, 4, 7, 9, 14, 16, 24, 29,
    Jun 1, 4, Sep 29, Oct 3, 13, 25, Nov 3, 14, 15, 17, 19, 30, Dec 5, 31; 1771:
    DL, Mar 7, 23, Apr 1, 2, 9, 13, 17, 23, 26, 27, May 1, 15, 22, 23, 30, Sep
    24, 26, 28, Oct 3, 19, Nov 11, 14, 21, Dec 2, 4, 10; 1772: DL, Jan 1, 4, 15,
    Feb 17, Mar 28, Apr 21, 22, 29, May 12, 26, 30, Sep 19, 29, Oct 10, 16, Nov
    3, 6, 9, 19, 20, Dec 2, 7, 8, 17, 26; 1773: DL, Jan 6, 21, Feb 4, 17, 27, Mar
    20, 23, Apr 1, 17, 21, 23, 24, 30, May 1, 4, 10, 11, 13, 17, 18, 28, Sep 21,
    25, 30, Oct 5, 9, 11, 14, 23, 25, 28, Nov 2, 6, 9, 15, 25, Dec 27, 30; 1774:
    DL, Jan 19, 25, Feb 2, 8, 9, 15, 19, Mar 14, 15, 17, 19, Apr 4, 12, 15, May
    10, 14, 20, 26, 28, Sep 17, 20, 22, 27, Oct 4, 5, 8, 11, 12, 14, 15, 21, 24,
    26, 27, 28, Nov 1, 4, 5, 7, 18, 30, Dec 2, 3, 7, 9, 19, 26; 1775: DL, Jan 2,
    13, 23, Feb 23, Mar 2, 18, 23, May 10, Sep 23, 26, 28, Oct 3, 7, 10, 11, 12,
    17, 23, Nov 1, 3, 4, 6, 9, 11, 18, 25, Dec 7, 11; 1776: DL, Jan 4, Feb 12,
    Mar 14, 25, 28, Apr 9, 10, 17, May 4, 6, 11, 18, HAY, Sep 17, DL, 21, 24, 26,
    28, Oct 1, 8, 10, 12, 18, 19, 23, 26, Nov 4, 6, 25, Dec 28; 1777: DL, Jan 1,
    Feb 17, Mar 1, Apr 25, May 9, Sep 23, 27, 30, Oct 7, 17, 18, 31, Nov 4, 10,
    13, 18, 24, 29, Dec 4, 18; 1778: DL, Jan 1, 5, Feb 2, 10, 24, Mar 16, 30, Apr

20, 27, May 11, Sep 17, 19, 22, 24, 29, Oct 1, 8, 10, 15, 20, 26, 28, 31, Nov
4, 10, Dec 11, 21, HAY, 28; <u>1779</u>: DL, Jan 8, 23, Feb 8, Mar 13, 16, 22, Apr
12, 23, May 10, 11, 15, 18, Sep 18, 21, 25, 28, 30, Oct 5, 9, 30, Nov 3, 24,
Dec 20, 22, 31; <u>1780</u>: DL, Jan 3, Apr 1, 3, 5, 18, May 2, 5, 9, 10, 12, Sep
16, 19, 21, 28, 30, Oct 11, 17, 23, 30, Nov 1, 3, 4, 27, 28, Dec 1, 8; <u>1781</u>:
DL, Jan 9, 29, May 4, Sep 18, 20, 25, 29, Oct 12, 24, 26, Nov 21; <u>1782</u>: DL,
Jan 3, Apr 5, May 3, 4, 7, 14, 18, Sep 18, 20, 24, Oct 5, 18, 30, Nov 4, 22,
26, Dec 5, 11, 14, 26; <u>1783</u>: DL, Jan 3, Feb 8, 18, Mar 6, 10, Apr 29, May 8,
12, 20, Sep 23, Oct 11, 13, 18, 22, 27, Nov 3, 8, 20, Dec 2, 12, 19; <u>1784</u>:
DL, Jan 3, 7, 10, 13, 16, 31, Feb 3, Mar 6, Apr 26, May 7, 10, 12, 17, Sep
23, Oct 11, 23, Nov 5, 9, 16, 19, 20, 23, Dec 3; <u>1785</u>: DL, Jan 12, 20, Feb
21, Apr 11, 20, 26, May 3, 5, 13, HAMM, Jun 17, 27, Jul 1, 2, 4, 6, 8, 15,
22, 25, 26, 27, DL, Sep 20, 27, Oct 8, 15, 17, 22, Nov 3, 7, 21, Dec 26, 29,
30; <u>1786</u>: DL, Apr 6, May 10, 17, Jun 1, HAMM, 5, 9, Jul 7, 10, 24, 26, Aug 5,
DL, Sep 23, Oct 3, 27
Wright, Thomas (actor), <u>1705</u>: DL, Jun 12
Wright, Thomas (author)
--No Fools Like Wits (Female Virtuosos, The), <u>1693</u>: DG, May 0; <u>1721</u>: LIF, Jan
10, 11, 12
Wright, William (abused spectator), <u>1742</u>: CG, Dec 18
Wrighten, Charlotte Sophia (actor), <u>1794</u>: DL, Apr 23, May 16, Jun 9, HAY, Jul
17, 18, 21, 24, 28, Aug 27
Wrighten, James (actor, prompter), <u>1769</u>: DL, Nov 27; <u>1770</u>: DL, Jan 16, 27, Feb
21, Mar 3, May 11, 15, 16, 17, 23, Oct 13, Nov 17, 24, 26; <u>1771</u>: DL, Jan 31,
Feb 1, Apr 5, 6, May 1, 8, Sep 24, Oct 15, Nov 11, Dec 2, 4, 10; <u>1772</u>: DL,
Jan 1, 4, Feb 21, Mar 5, 26, 28, Apr 22, Oct 21, 23, Dec 17, 18, 22, 26;
<u>1773</u>: DL, Feb 8, 18, Mar 30, Apr 3, 21, 30, May 1, 8, 12, 13, 25, Sep 25, 30,
Oct 23, Nov 15, 20, 25, Dec 27; <u>1774</u>: DL, Jan 19, Feb 2, 8, 9, 17, Mar 14,
22, Apr 4, 19, 25, 28, May 18, 20, Sep 20, Oct 4, 5, 14, 27, 31, Nov 4, 7,
Dec 7, 9, 26, 27; <u>1775</u>: DL, Jan 2, 3, 10, 21, Feb 1, 9, 17, 23, Apr 17, 18,
19, 22, 29, May 1, 3, 15, 17, 22, 23, 24, Sep 23, 26, 28, Oct 11, 17, 23, 28,
Nov 1, 3, 4, 6, 9, 18, 21, 23, 25, Dec 2, 11, 21, 26, 29; <u>1776</u>: DL, Jan 4,
Feb 12, Mar 7, 9, 18, 23, 28, Apr 10, 15, 22, May 11, 18, 20, Sep 21, 24, 26,
28, Oct 8, 10, 15, 19, 23, Nov 4, 9, 16, 25, 29, Dec 4, 6, 28; <u>1777</u>: DL, Jan
1, 4, 18, 31, Feb 17, 20, 24, Apr 11, 22, May 20, Jun 6, Sep 20, 25, 27, 30,
Oct 7, 14, 17, 18, 31, Nov 4, 13, 18, 29, Dec 4, 11, 13, 18; <u>1778</u>: DL, Jan
22, Feb 2, 10, 19, Mar 16, 30, Apr 27, May 21, 25, Sep 19, 22, 24, 26, 29,
Oct 1, 6, 15, 20, 21, 27, 31, Nov 2, 4, 9, 10, 16; <u>1779</u>: DL, Jan 5, 29, Feb
8, 18, Mar 11, 16, 22, 27, Apr 12, 19, May 18, Jun 1, Sep 18, 23, CG, 24, DL,
25, 28, Oct 5, 7, 16, 19, 23, 28, 30, Nov 3, Dec 2, 20, 28, 31; <u>1780</u>: DL, Jan
3, 18, 24, 27, Feb 8, Apr 3, 7, 14, 18, 20, 21, 29, May 2, 4, 10, 24, Sep 16,
19, 21, 23, 28, Oct 2, 3, 5, 10, 11, 12, 17, Nov 1, 3, 4, 9, 10, 13, 27, 29,
Dec 1, 8; <u>1781</u>: DL, Jan 6, 16, 19, Feb 26, 27, Mar 19, 27, 29, 31, Apr 24,
May 8, 17, 24, Sep 18, 20, 25, 29, Oct 12, 15, 19, 29, Nov 7, 13, 21, 27, 29,
Dec 27; <u>1782</u>: DL, Jan 19, 22, Mar 21, 23, Apr 6, 17, 23, 27, May 3, 8, 14,
29, Sep 17, 19, 20, 21, 24, 26, 28, Oct 1, 8, 10, 12, 30, Nov 1, 5, 7, 12,
22, 26, 30, Dec 5, 7, 26; <u>1783</u>: DL, Jan 10, Feb 18, 22, Mar 3, 6, 17, 18, 20,
24, Apr 21, 23, 29, May 2, 12, Sep 16, 25, 30, Oct 4, 7, 8, 13, 14, 31, Nov
3, 8, 13, 14, 18, 20, Dec 2, 10, 12, 19, 29; <u>1784</u>: DL, Jan 1, 3, 16, 17, Apr
16, 26, May 3, 17, 21, Sep 21, 23, 25, 30, Oct 12, 18, 19, 26, Nov 2, 4, 9,
13, 19, 23, Dec 10, 22, 28; <u>1785</u>: DL, Jan 11, 13, 14, 20, 24, 27, Feb 8, Mar
8, Apr 11, 20, 22, 25, May 3, 9, 24, HAY, Sep 2, DL, 17, 20, Oct 4, 13, 15,
17, 20, 22, 25, 26, 31, Nov 3, 9, 11, 17, 18, 21, 22, Dec 3, 5, 26, 30; <u>1786</u>:
DL, Jan 5, 16, Feb 18, 23, Mar 27, Apr 20, 28, May 17, Jun 1, Sep 16, 19, Oct
7, 12, 27, Nov 15, Dec 5, 19, 28; <u>1787</u>: DL, May 10, Sep 25; <u>1788</u>: DL, Apr 23,
24, May 6, HAY, Aug 25; <u>1789</u>: DL, May 19; <u>1790</u>: DL, Apr 23, Oct 27; <u>1791</u>: DL,
Feb 9, Apr 29, DLKING'S, Sep 27, Oct 3; <u>1792</u>: DLKING'S, Apr 13, May 7, HAY,
Jun 15; <u>1793</u>: DL, Jan 22, Apr 29, HAY, Aug 13
Wrighten, Mary (actor), <u>1794</u>: DL, Apr 23, May 16, Jun 9, HAY, Jul 17, 18, 21,
24, 28, Aug 27
Wrighten, Mary Ann, Mrs James (actor, singer), <u>1770</u>: DL, Feb 8, Apr 18, 28, Jun
7, Oct 19, Dec 7, 13; <u>1771</u>: DL, Jan 18, Feb 9, May 8, 10, Sep 21, 24, Oct 10,
19, 28; <u>1772</u>: DL, Mar 26, 28, Apr 20, 25, May 4, 18, 22, 25, Jun 9, Sep 29,
Oct 1, 3, Nov 9, 24, Dec 26, 30; <u>1773</u>: DL, Jan 9, 15, 20, Feb 1, 9, Mar 9,
27, 29, Apr 19, May 3, 10, 11, 12, 13, Jun 2, Sep 18, HAY, 20, DL, 25, 30,
Oct 9, Nov 2, 25, Dec 3, 27; <u>1774</u>: DL, Jan 19, Mar 17, 19, CHAPEL, 26, 30,
DL, Apr 4, 12, 15, 28, May 3, 9, Oct 1, 5, 11, 14, 19, Nov 1, 5, 25, Dec 9,
26; <u>1775</u>: DL, Feb 1, 28, Apr 22, 26, May 13, 17, Sep 23, 30, Oct 7, 10, 28,
Nov 9, 28, Dec 5, 12; <u>1776</u>: DL, Jan 26, Feb 1, 3, 10, 15, CG, 23, DL, Mar 14,
23, 25, Apr 9, 12, 15, May 16, 18, Sep 21, 24, 26, 28, Oct 1, 5, 10, 18, 29,
Nov 7, 21, 25, Dec 28; <u>1777</u>: DL, Jan 16, Mar 1, Apr 1, May 15, 19, Sep 23,
25, Oct 2, 7, 9, 29, Nov 8, 19, 22, Dec 4, 15; <u>1778</u>: DL, Jan 6, 8, 10, 12,

17, CG, Mar 6, DL, 12, 16, CG, 25, DL, 30, 31, Apr 20, 28, 30, May 1, Oct 3,
6, 10, 15, 22, Nov 14, 20, 28, Dec 5, 15, 21, 23; 1779: DL, Jan 29, CG, Feb
23, HAY, Mar 3, DL, 11, HAY, 17, DL, 25, Apr 10, 13, CG, 30, DL, May 18, 19,
Sep 18, 23, Oct 5, 9, 19, 21, 25, Nov 6, 17, 19, 27, Dec 4, 9, 22, 31; 1780:
DL, Feb 11, 22, 28, Mar 4, Apr 3, 7, 11, 14, 29, May 10, Sep 26, 28, Oct 5,
7, 10, 12, 17, Nov 1, 2, 3, 28, Dec 19, 27; 1781: DL, Apr 21, 24, 25, 26, May
5, 8, Sep 15, 22, 25, 27, Oct 6, 15, 19, 22, 24, 27, Nov 10, 20, 29, Dec 6,
13; 1782: DL, Mar 16, Apr 11, 15, 16, 18, 20, 24, May 10, 18, Sep 17, 18, 24,
28, Oct 3, 5, Nov 2, 12, 30, Dec 11, 26; 1783: DL, Jan 18, 29, Feb 7, Mar 6,
20, Apr 7, 26, 29, May 12, 20, 30, HAY, Aug 19, DL, Sep 16, 18, Oct 7, 9, 11,
13, Nov 4, 11, 18, 20, Dec 5, 23; 1784: DL, Jan 17, 31, Mar 8, 30, Apr 1, 12,
14, 16, 19, 28, May 13, 20, Sep 25, 30, Oct 7, 14, 21, 23, 26, Nov 1, 4, 12,
16, 26, Dec 18; 1785: DL, Jan 17, Feb 2, 19, Apr 1, 8, 14, 20, 25, Sep 17,
Oct 1, 11, 13, 15, 18, 27, Nov 1, 18, Dec 8, 26, 29; 1786: DL, Jan 6, Feb 18,
20, Apr 4, 6, 18, 24, CG, May 6, DL, 15, Sep 21, 23, Oct 3, 9, Nov 25, Dec 6;
1787: DL, Mar 3, Apr 19; 1788: CG, Apr 25; 1789: CG, May 23
Writ of Inquiry will be Executed on the Inquisitor General, A. See Foote,
Samuel.
Writing and Copying (vaudeville), 1789: KHS, Sep 16
Wroth, Mrs Thomas (beneficiary), 1702: LS, Jul 25
Wroth, Thomas (musician), 1702: LS, Jul 25
Wroughton (Rottan, Rotten), Richard (actor, manager), 1768: CG, Oct 24, Nov 5,
19, Dec 27; 1769: CG, Mar 29, May 4, 17, 18, 20, 23, Sep 18, 25, Oct 2, 4, 7,
18, Nov 1, 4, Dec 28, 29; 1770: CG, Jan 3, 4, 6, 26, Feb 12, 24, Mar 17, Apr
17, 18, 20, 24, 25, 30, May 8, 12, 19, Dec 26, 31; 1771: CG, Jan 12, 16, 23,
26, Feb 23, Mar 14, Apr 9, 16, 20, 24, 27, May 6, Sep 30, Oct 7, 9, 15, 26,
30, Nov 2, 4, 11, 26; 1772: CG, Jan 1, 2, 15, 25, 27, Feb 22, Mar 17, 21, 23,
30, 31, Apr 4, 7, 22, 25, May 4, 7, 11, Jun 1, Sep 21, 25, 28, Oct 19, Nov 4,
6, Dec 5, 11, 22; 1773: CG, Jan 7, 14, 16, Mar 20, 30, Apr 3, 23, 27, 28, May
1, 3, 4, 15, 20, 22, 28, Sep 20, 22, 27, Oct 4, 5, 8, 9, 15, 23, Nov 4, 8,
12, 18, 20, Dec 3, 4, 8, 9, 11, 21; 1774: CG, Jan 15, Feb 11, 26, Mar 14, Apr
6, 7, 12, 14, 21, 23, May 19, Sep 26, 28, 30, Oct 4, 7, 14, 15, 21, 24, 26,
27, 31, Nov 1, 3, 4, 8, Dec 3, 20, 26; 1775: CG, Jan 3, Feb 11, Mar 20, Apr
8, 24, 29, May 20, Sep 20, 22, 27, 29, Oct 4, 6, 9, 12, 13, 19, 20, 21, 23,
25, 30, Nov 3, 4, 9, 10, 13, 24, 28, Dec 1, 2, 8, 29; 1776: CG, Jan 5, 15,
24, Feb 5, 9, Mar 5, 18, 19, 30, Apr 19, 26, May 6, 10, 11, 13, Oct 15, 25,
29, 31, Nov 1, 2, 4, 8, 11, 14, 21, 25, 26, 28, Dec 5, 6, 17, 26; 1777: CG,
Jan 8, 25, Feb 1, 5, 22, Mar 17, Apr 7, 16, 28, May 7, 29, Sep 24, 26, 29,
Oct 1, 8, 10, 15, 16, 21, 23, 30, Nov 6, 7, 13, 27, Dec 3, 10, 15, 19, 26;
1778: CG, Jan 3, 15, 21, 29, Feb 6, 13, 16, 25, 28, Mar 2, 14, 30, Apr 7, 22,
25, 27, May 5, 6, 11, 15, 16, 19, Sep 18, 23, 25, Oct 2, 5, 9, 14, 16, 21,
22, 24, 26, 31, Nov 4, 10, 19, 21, Dec 3, 8, 11, 12, 17, 26; 1779: CG, Jan 4,
11, 13, 14, 18, 26, Feb 12, Mar 9, 27, Apr 5, 21, 24, 27, May 3, 6, 10, 15,
20, Sep 20, 27, Oct 1, 11, 13, 18, Nov 1, 4, 6, 8, 11, 13, 16, 23, 24, 25,
30, Dec 9, 11, 27, 31; 1780: CG, Jan 7, 12, 17, Feb 22, Mar 14, 18, DL, Apr
1, CG, 3, 7, 10, 12, 27, May 1, 24, Jun 1, Sep 18, Oct 2, 4, 6, 9, 10, 11,
13, 24, 30, 31, Nov 1, 2, 4, 8, 10, 14, Dec 12; 1781: CG, Jan 4, 10, 25, Feb
10, 14, 15, Apr 2, 3, 18, May 7, Sep 17, 19, 28, Oct 3, 23, Nov 5, 6, 8, 9,
14, 17, 20, 28, Dec 8, 10, 11, 18; 1782: CG, Jan 3, 4, 5, 7, 8, 11, Feb 5, 9,
Apr 2, 10, 12, 17, 20, May 3, 20, 28, 29, Sep 23, Oct 3, 4, 7, 8, 10, 14, 17,
18, 21, 23, 29, 31, Nov 14, 27, 29, 30, Dec 6, 12, 16, 27, 30, 31; 1783: CG,
Jan 17, 27, 28, Feb 25, Mar 29, 31, Apr 1, 8, 23, 26, May 7, 20, 22, Sep 22,
26, Oct 1, 8, 11, 13, 15, 17, 31, Nov 4, 8, 10, 13, 24, 27, Dec 5, 6, 11, 26,
27, 29, 31; 1784: CG, Jan 7, 14, 16, 22, 23, 26, 31, Feb 10, 11, 13, 19, 20,
23, Mar 4, 16, 20, 22, 29, Apr 13, 26, May 8, 13, 26, 29, Sep 21, 24, 28, 29,
Oct 1, 6, 11, 18, 30, Nov 4, 10, 11, 13, 29, Dec 3, 21, 28; 1785: CG, Jan 14,
Feb 8, Mar 5, 8, 15, 29, Apr 2, 8, 11, May 4, 6, 13, 18, 26, Sep 21, 28, Oct
3, 10, 12, 19, 22, 28, 29, Nov 1, 7, 19, Dec 7, 10, 14, 22, 28, 29; 1786: CG,
Jan 2, 3, 5, 6, 7, 14, Feb 1, 16, 18, Mar 4, 11, 14, Apr 4, 8, 18, 24, May 9,
13, 20, 26, HAY, Jul 25; 1787: DL, Sep 29, Oct 2, 4, 11, 18, 24, Nov 6, 10,
29, Dec 3, 10, 11, 14, 26; 1788: DL, Jan 5, 21, 31, Mar 29, 31, Apr 21, May
1, Sep 16, 18, 23, 27, Oct 2, 9, 16, Nov 8, 25, Dec 18; 1789: DL, Jan 17, 19,
26, Feb 2, 7, 16, 17, 19, 24, 26, 28, Mar 12, 17, 21, 24, Apr 2, 14, 20, 21,
May 1, 7, 23, 27, Jun 1, 2, 5, 13, Sep 12, 22, 26, Oct 8, 10, 24, Nov 5, 7,
21, Dec 2; 1790: DL, Jan 1, 15, Feb 11, 15, 23, Mar 2, 8, 22, 23, Apr 14, May
14, 18, 19, CG, Jun 16, DL, Sep 11, 16, Oct 4, 14, 18, Nov 4, 5, Dec 1; 1791:
DL, May 10, 20, DLKING'S, Oct 4, 10, Nov 5, 7, 11, 29, Dec 6, 12; 1792:
DLKING'S, Jan 18, Feb 8, 18, Mar 6, 10, 17, 26, 31, Apr 10, 13, 20, May 17,
Jun 13, DL, Sep 20, 29, Oct 13, 16, 20, 30, 31, Dec 10, 15, 26; 1793: DL, Jan
7, 9, Feb 16, 23, 25, Mar 5, 9, 18, Apr 3, 17, May 3, 4, 9, 10, Jun 1, 10;
1794: DL, Apr 21, 29, May 1, 8, 19, Jun 17, 19, 23, 26, Sep 16, 18, 20, Oct
7, 18, 28, Nov 11, 12, Dec 5, 6, 13, 30; 1795: DL, Jan 20, 21, Feb 10, 17,

Mar 10, Apr 16, May 12, 29, Sep 17, 26, 29, Oct 3, Nov 6, 10, 17, 20, 26, Dec
9, 11, 23; 1796: DL, Jan 5, Feb 1, 29, Mar 12, Apr 9, 11, 18, 20, 26, 28, 29,
May 2, 13, 23, Jun 8, Sep 20, 22, 27, Oct 3, 4, 10, 11, 24, 25, 28, Nov 1, 5,
9, 29, Dec 16, 20, 29; 1797: DL, Jan 10, Feb 7, 20, Apr 6, 8, 19, Jun 7, Sep
19, 21, Oct 5, 14, 27, Nov 2, 4, 7, 10, 17, 21, 25, Dec 2, 14; 1798: DL, Jan
16, 23, 25, Feb 3, 9, 17, Mar 8, 17, May 7, 11, 19, Jun 4, 8
Wurttemberg, Prince Frederick William of, 1797: DL, May 13
Wyan's Court, 1742: LIF, Jan 29
Wyatt (actor), 1785: HAY, Apr 25
Wyatt (ticket deliverer), 1789: CG, Jun 16; 1790: CG, Jun 12; 1791: CG, Jun 14;
    1792: CG, May 25; 1794: CG, Jun 12; 1795: CG, Jun 17; 1798: DL, Jun 9; 1799:
    DL, Jul 2; 1800: DL, Jun 14
Wyatt, Mrs (actor), 1675: DL, Jan 12
Wyber (ticket deliverer), 1799: DL, Jul 2
Wybrow, Mrs (actor), 1798: CG, Jun 6, Oct 15, 25, Nov 12, Dec 26; 1799: CG, Jan
    29, Mar 26, Apr 22, 29, May 13
Wych St, 1778: DL, Apr 21
Wycherley (Whicherly, Wicherley), William, 1672: DG, Feb 6; 1685: ATCOURT, Dec
    14; 1695: DL, Dec 0; 1701: LIF, Oct 1, 21; 1702: LIF, Dec 29; 1715: DL, May
    18, 23, Oct 13, LIF, Nov 19, 21, 29; 1716: LIF, Feb 10, DL, Apr 4, Sep 29,
    LIF, Dec 13; 1717: DL, Apr 23, Oct 10; 1718: DL, Jan 31, Mar 27, May 8, Aug
    15, 19, Oct 22; 1719: DL, Sep 29, Dec 9; 1720: DL, Feb 1, Apr 19, Sep 10, Nov
    3, Dec 13; 1721: DL, Jan 4, 5, 14, Mar 30, Oct 20, Dec 5; 1722: DL, Mar 30,
    May 18, 19, Oct 9, Dec 7; 1723: DL, May 15, Oct 28; 1724: DL, Jan 8; 1725:
    DL, Jan 4, May 7, Oct 2, LIF, 4, 6, DL, 27, Nov 17, LIF, 27, DL, Dec 30;
    1726: DL, Apr 21, LIF, Oct 3, Nov 16; 1727: DL, Apr 8, LIF, May 17; 1729: DL,
    May 14, Nov 3; 1733: LIF/CG, Jan 15, 16, 17, 29, DL, Apr 19, LIF/CG, 20, May
    23, CG, Nov 21; 1734: CG, Feb 18, Apr 19, CG/LIF, Oct 18; 1735: CG/LIF, Jan
    28, DL, Feb 4, Dec 6, CG, 8; 1736: CG, Feb 27, May 6, DL, 15, LIF, Oct 18;
    1737: DL, Oct 27, Nov 3; 1738: DL, Jan 14, 16, 20, 21, 24, Feb 6; 1765: DL,
    Apr 26; 1766: DL, Oct 25; 1768: CG, Apr 13; 1774: DL, Dec 19; 1776: CG, Dec
    16; 1782: HAY, Jan 21; 1786: CG, Apr 18, HAMM, Jun 28; 1792: HAY, Oct 15
--Country Wife, The, 1675: DL, Jan 12, 15; 1676: DL, May 16; 1683: NONE, Sep 0;
    1688: NONE, Sep 0; 1694: NONE, Sep 0; 1701: LIF, Oct 1, 21; 1702: LIF, Dec
    29; 1709: DL, Apr 14, 29; 1710: DL, Feb 14; 1715: DL, May 18, 23, Oct 13, 25,
    Dec 28; 1716: DL, Apr 4, Sep 29; 1717: DL, Apr 23, Oct 10; 1718: DL, Jan 31,
    Mar 27, May 8, Aug 15, 19, Oct 22; 1719: DL, May 21, Sep 29, Dec 9; 1720: DL,
    Feb 1, Apr 19, Sep 10, Nov 3, Dec 13; 1721: DL, Mar 30, Jun 13, Oct 20, Nov
    21; 1722: DL, Mar 30, May 19, Dec 7; 1723: DL, Mar 19; 1725: DL, Oct 2, LIF,
    4, 6, 8, DL, Nov 11, 17, LIF, 27, Dec 22; 1726: LIF, Jan 22, Feb 15, Mar 3,
    17, Apr 13, Oct 3, Nov 16, Dec 12; 1727: LIF, Feb 4, DL, 20, LIF, Mar 23, Apr
    21, DL, May 8, LIF, 17, Jun 5, Sep 11, DL, Oct 25, LIF, 25, Dec 9; 1728: LIF,
    May 30, Oct 16; 1729: DL, Feb 14, LIF, Mar 3, 20, May 7, DL, 14, LIF, 23, Sep
    19, DL, Nov 3; 1730: LIF, Jan 16, Apr 2, 27, Sep 18, DL, Nov 2, LIF, 27;
    1731: LIF, Jan 2, Mar 18, Apr 22, Jun 2, DL, Sep 21, LIF, Oct 27, Dec 17, DL,
    31; 1732: LIF, Feb 29, May 4, LIF/CG, Oct 9, Nov 16; 1733: LIF/CG, Jan 26,
    DL, Apr 19, CG, May 11, Oct 18, Nov 13, 29; 1734: CG, Feb 25, Apr 2, May 8,
    CG/LIF, Nov 11; 1735: DL, Feb 4, 6, CG/LIF, Apr 29, May 26, CG, Oct 6, DL,
    Dec 6; 1736: CG, Jan 15, DL, May 15, LIF, Oct 18; 1737: CG, Oct 5, DL, 27,
    Nov 3; 1739: CG, Feb 9, DL, May 1, Oct 6, Nov 14; 1740: DL, Apr 28, Nov 1,
    Dec 4; 1741: DL, May 9, 27, CG, Oct 31, Nov 2; 1742: CG, Jan 12, Nov 15, 16,
    19, Dec 1, 14, 30; 1743: CG, Jan 20, Feb 10, Mar 5, DL, Apr 7, CG, 20, DL,
    28, CG, Dec 16, 28; 1744: CG, Feb 13, Dec 5; 1745: CG, Feb 4, DL, 13, May 7,
    Nov 28; 1746: DL, Feb 13, May 19, Dec 20; 1747: CG, Feb 11, 26, Mar 12; 1748:
    DL, Nov 28; 1749: DL, Dec 7; 1753: CG, Mar 20, 27, DL, May 4, CG, Nov 7;
    1765: DL, Apr 26, 27, May 7, 13, 15, 20; 1766: DL, Apr 18, 21; 1768: CG, Apr
    13, May 4, HAY, Aug 15, 17, Sep 12, CG, Oct 25, Nov 28, Dec 3, 5; 1769: CG,
    Jan 14, Nov 1; 1776: CG, Dec 16, 21, 23, 28; 1777: CG, Jan 3, 28, 31, Feb 4,
    10, Apr 4, 9, 26, May 6; 1779: CG, Dec 23; 1782: CG, Nov 16; 1786: CG, Feb 7,
    8, 9, 11, 28, Mar 16, 18, Oct 2, 6, 18, Nov 17; 1787: CG, Feb 17
--Gentleman Dancing Master, The, 1672: DG, Feb 6; 1692: NONE, Sep 0
--Love in a Wood; or, St James's Park, 1671: BRIDGES, Mar 0; 1687: NONE, Sep 0;
    1693: NONE, Sep 0; 1718: DL, Aug 15, 19, 22; 1782: HAY, Jan 21
--Plain Dealer, The, 1676: DL, Dec 11, 13; 1677: NONE, Sep 0; 1680: NONE, Sep
    0; 1681: DL, Mar 0; 1682: NONE, Sep 0, DL, Nov 16; 1683: IT, Nov 1; 1685:
    ATCOURT, Dec 14; 1690: NONE, Sep 0; 1692: NONE, Mar 11; 1693: NONE, Sep 0;
    1698: DL, Jun 2; 1699: NONE, Sep 0; 1700: DL, Nov 27; 1701: DL, Jan 23; 1702:
    DL, Oct 31; 1703: DL, Nov 12; 1704: DL, Feb 25, Nov 27; 1705: DL, Feb 6, 24,
    Nov 16; 1715: LIF, Nov 19, 21, 29, Dec 13; 1716: LIF, Feb 10, Apr 21, 26, Jun
    22, Dec 13; 1718: DL, Aug 15, 19; 1721: DL, Jan 4, 5, 7, 9, 14, Dec 5; 1722:
    DL, May 18, Oct 9; 1723: DL, May 15, Oct 28; 1724: DL, Jan 8; 1725: DL, Jan
    4, May 7, Oct 27, Dec 30; 1726: DL, Apr 21; 1727: DL, Apr 8; 1733: LIF/CG,

Jan 15, 16, 17, 29, Apr 20, May 23, CG, Nov 21; 1734: BLO, Jan 16, CG, Feb
18, Apr 19, CG/LIF, Oct 18; 1735: CG/LIF, Jan 28, CG, Dec 8; 1736: CG, Feb
27, May 6; 1737: CG, Apr 26; 1738: DL, Jan 14, 16, 17, 18, 20, 21, 24, Feb 6;
1739: DL, Mar 31, Apr 2, 24, May 10, Nov 10; 1740: DL, Dec 15; 1743: CG, Jan
18, 19, 24; 1744: TB, Mar 22; 1765: DL, Dec 7, 9, 11, 14, 16, 17, 19, 21, 28;
1766: DL, Jan 10, 18, Feb 1, 6, Mar 17, 31, Apr 17, 21, Oct 9, 15, Dec 5, 17;
1767: DL, Feb 5, Apr 21, May 15, 25, Nov 28, Dec 30; 1768: DL, Apr 19, May
27, Oct 5, Dec 16; 1769: DL, Apr 11, Oct 17, Nov 10; 1770: DL, Oct 18; 1771:
DL, May 21, Oct 19; 1773: DL, Apr 30; 1775: DL, Dec 11; 1776: DL, Jan 11, May
3; 1778: DL, May 14; 1779: DL, May 15, Oct 9, 28; 1780: DL, Feb 8; 1783: DL,
Dec 12; 1786: CG, Apr 18, May 25; 1787: DL, Jun 1; 1788: DL, Jun 6; 1796: DL,
Feb 27, Mar 1, 7, Apr 6
Wye (proprietor, masquerade warehouse), 1792: HAY, Feb 6
Wykehamists, 1799: CG, Mar 13
Wylde. See Wild.
Wyler (ticket deliverer), 1800: DL, Jun 13
Wyn, Mrs. See Marshall, Anne.
Wynn (lawyer), 1767: DL, Feb 11
Wynn, Sir Watkin Williams, 1781: CG, May 1

Xeno (librettist), 1737: KING'S, Jan 8
Xerxes. See Cibber, Colley; Handel, George Frederic.
Ximena. See Cibber, Colley.
Ximene (musician), 1772: DL, Mar 6, 13

Yamacrow (Yamicraw) Indians (spectators), 1734: LIF, Aug 20, CG/LIF, Sep 23;
  see also American Princes; Indian Kings, American
Yankee Doodle (song), 1784: HAY, Jun 19; 1786: CG, Dec 26
Yard Arm & Yard Arm (song), 1798: CG, May 9
Yarrow, Joseph
Yarrow, Joseph (actor), 1736: HAY, Feb 19
--Cupid's Friendship; or, The Farmer Outwitted, 1770: CG, Mar 31; 1771: HAY,
  Mar 11, Apr 1, 24
--Harlequin Statue; or, The Country Farmer Deceived (pantomime), 1739: CG, Apr
  9; 1741: CG, Apr 6, 28; 1751: CG, May 1, 16, 21, SF, Sep 9; 1753: CG, Apr 25,
  May 3, 9; 1755: CG, Apr 23; 1756: CG, Apr 28, May 1; 1757: CG, Apr 23, 25,
  May 2, 3; 1758: CG, Apr 19, 21, 25; 1760: CG, Apr 23, 28, 29, May 1, 3, 6;
  1762: CG, Apr 28, May 12, 17; 1763: CG, Apr 27, May 2; 1765: CG, May 10, 20;
  1770: HAY, Feb 14, CG, Mar 31
--Trick upon Trick; or, Harlequin Statue (or, Vintner in the Suds) (farce),
  1743: MF, May 9, 10, BFYWR, Aug 23; 1747: SF, Sep 24; 1749: SOU, Jan 26,
  BFHG, Aug 23
Yarroway (timber merchant), 1792: DL, Oct 13
Yates (musician), 1765: HAY, Mar 11
Yates Jr's Booth, 1754: BFYJN, Sep 3
Yates Sr-Bennet Booth, 1746: BFYB, Aug 25
Yates Sr-Yates Jr Booth, 1732: SF, Sep 11; 1733: BFYY, Aug 23, SFYY, Sep 10;
  1735: BF, Aug 23
Yates-Shuter Booth, 1758: BFYS, Sep 2, 5, 6
Yates-Warner Booth, 1750: SFYW, Sep 7, 8, 10, 11, 12, 13
Yates-Warner-Hind Booth, 1735: WF, Aug 23
Yates-Warner-Rosoman Booth, 1742: UM, Oct 4; 1743: MF, May 9, 10, TCY, Aug 4,
  BFYWR, 23, SF, Sep 8
Yates, Elizabeth Mary, Mrs Richard (the second) (actor, booth keeper), 1740:
  GF, Oct 28, 29, 31, Nov 15, 21, 25, 27, 28, 29, Dec 1, 5, 6, 12, 15; 1741:
  GF, Jan 15, 27, 28, Feb 2, 10, 19, Mar 7, 16, Apr 15, 17, 27, BFTY, Aug 22,
  GF, Sep 14, 16, 21, 25, 28, Oct 2, 9, 12, 16, 19, Nov 6, 9, 27, 30, Dec 10,
  16, 29; 1742: GF, Jan 5, 27, Feb 3, Mar 22, 27, 29, Apr 19, 20, DL, Nov 3;
  1743: SOU, Feb 18, 25, Mar 30, DL, Sep 20, Oct 4, Nov 26; 1744: DL, Feb 13,
  Apr 4, Sep 20, 22, Oct 6, 22, Nov 1, 24; 1745: DL, Apr 30, Sep 21, Oct 12,
  17, Nov 18; 1746: DL, Sep 30, Oct 11; 1747: DL, Jan 3, Apr 11, Sep 22, 24,
  Oct 29, Nov 14, SOU, 16, DL, Dec 5, 12; 1748: DL, Jan 12, Feb 3, Apr 23, May
  2, 18, Sep 24, 27, Oct 1, 15, 28, NWC, Nov 21, DL, 28, NWC, Dec 26, 29; 1749:
  SOU, Jan 2, 9, DL, May 16, SOUGT, Sep 22, 25, DL, 26, Oct 3, BHB, 5, DL, 10,
  17, 26, NWC, Nov 27, DL, Dec 26; 1750: DL, Feb 10, 14, NWC, Apr 16, DL, 27,
  30, May 2, Sep 25, Oct 16, Nov 13; 1751: DL, Apr 22, May 1, 17, Sep 7, 17,

18, Oct 9, Nov 7, 27, JS, Dec 16, DL, 26; 1752: DL, Apr 9, Sep 16, Oct 23,
Nov 22, Dec 18; 1753: DL, May 16
Yates (Yeates), George (dancer), 1746: SFY, Sep 8, NWC, 25; 1747: SF, Sep 16;
1748: DL, Oct 27, SOU, 31, NWC, Nov 21, Dec 26, 29; 1749: SOU, Jan 2, 9, DL,
Feb 25, SOUGT, Sep 22, DL, Oct 12, 24, Nov 9, 27, 29; 1750: DL, Apr 5, Nov
27; 1751: DL, May 4, SF, Sep 17
Yates, J (beneficiary), 1746: NWC, Dec 22
Yates, Mary Ann, Mrs Richard (the second) (actor), 1756: DL, Dec 15; 1757: DL,
Feb 22, Apr 14, Nov 15, Dec 8; 1758: DL, Jan 24, Feb 1, 21, 25, 27, Mar 14,
16, 30, Apr 22, 25, May 17, Nov 2, 13, 14; 1759: DL, Jan 3, 17, Feb 8, Mar
26, Apr 7, 21, 23, 24, May 2, Oct 16, Nov 9, 17, Dec 20; 1760: DL, Jan 1, 11,
24, Feb 13, Mar 20, 24, 27, Apr 11, 14, 15, 26, 29, Jun 19, Oct 7, 8, Nov 18,
20, Dec 17; 1761: DL, Jan 8, 10, 28, 31, Feb 5, Mar 30, Apr 2, 14, May 30,
Jun 15, Jul 16, 21, Sep 12, 18, 21, 25, 28, 30, Oct 26, Nov 10, Dec 11, 17,
30; 1762: DL, Jan 15, Feb 10, 20, 22, Mar 6, 23, Apr 1, 3, Sep 30, Oct 11,
15, 16, Nov 1, 17, 29, Dec 6, 10, 13, 22; 1763: DL, Jan 14, 27, Feb 3, Mar
21, Apr 8, 11, 20, May 6, 19, Oct 8, 14, 17, 21, Nov 2, 7, 14, 22, Dec 5, 14,
20; 1764: DL, Jan 3, 7, 13, Feb 14, 29, Mar 3, 26, 27, 31, Apr 2, 7, 14, 26,
May 24, 29, Oct 11, 19, 24, 26, Nov 8, 14, 24, Dec 8; 1765: DL, Jan 3, 24,
Feb 4, 12, Mar 7, 12, 18, 19, 23, 25, 26, Apr 20, 29, Sep 21, 24, Oct 2, 11,
12, 15, 22, 23, 25, 30, Nov 11, 15, 20, Dec 3, 6, 7; 1766: DL, Jan 6, 11, Feb
13, Mar 11, 18, 20, 22, Oct 16, 18, 21, 24, 29, Nov 4, 19, 20, 24, Dec 5, 6,
13; 1767: DL, Jan 31, Feb 7, 9, 11, 19, Mar 24, 28, 30, 31, Apr 6, 9, 22, 29,
May 2, 4, 14, 20, Sep 12, CG, Oct 16, 17, 22, 24, DL, 27, CG, 29, Nov 10, 18,
23, Dec 5, 8; 1768: CG, Jan 20, Feb 20, Mar 17, 26, Apr 13, 25, Sep 20, 28,
30, Oct 1, 5, 7, 12, 17, 24, 26, Nov 8, 17, 19, Dec 3; 1769: CG, Mar 13, 29,
Apr 12, 17, Oct 26, 28, Nov 1, 15, 23, 29, Dec 2, 19, 20; 1770: CG, Jan 19,
26, Feb 7, 24, Mar 1, 3, 22, 24, 26, 27, 29, Apr 17, 19, May 17, Oct 5, 8,
12, 13, 16, 23, Nov 1, 15, 29, Dec 4; 1771: CG, Jan 12, 18, Feb 9, 23, Mar
12, 19, Apr 9, Sep 28, Oct 9, 11, 14, 18, Nov 2, 5, 11, Dec 11, 16, 17; 1772:
CG, Jan 24, 27, Feb 1, Mar 21, DL, 23, CG, 24, 30, 31, Apr 7, 11; 1773: CG,
Mar 6, Apr 19, KING'S, Nov 20; 1774: DL, Oct 15, 25, Nov 1, 11, 25, Dec 17;
1775: DL, Jan 4, 18, Feb 17, Mar 4, 6, 9, 18, 20, 23, 30, Apr 24, May 1, 27,
Oct 5, 12, 14, 18, 26, 28, KING'S, 31, DL, Nov 3, 14, 18, 21, Dec 7; 1776:
DL, Feb 10, Mar 11, 14, 18, 21, 28, May 16, Sep 24, Oct 3, 10, 12, 19, 22,
29, Nov 5, 16, Dec 14, 18, 19, 23, 30; 1777: DL, Feb 24, Mar 22, Apr 4, Sep
27, Oct 11, 28, Nov 13, 18, 29, Dec 11, 18; 1778: DL, Jan 24, CG, Feb 10, DL,
Mar 30, Apr 20, 28, Oct 1, 15, 20, 23, 27, CG, 31, Nov 10, 19, Dec 14; 1779:
CG, Jan 19, Feb 2, DL, Mar 11, 25, CG, Apr 5, DL, 7, 12, CG, 14, May 3, Oct
4, 13, DL, Nov 16, Dec 13; 1780: DL, Jan 6, Feb 8, CG, Jun 1, Sep 18, Oct 4,
11, 18, 21, 23, Nov 2, 14; 1781: CG, Jan 25, 31, Mar 24, DL, 27, CG, May 7,
14, 28, Sep 17, Dec 4, 10, 17, 20; 1782: CG, Jan 1, 5, 8, 11, Feb 5, Mar 14,
DL, 16, CG, Apr 12, Oct 21, 31, Nov 18, Dec 2, 12, 27; 1783: CG, Jan 27, Feb
13, 17, Mar 29, Apr 1, May 19; 1785: DL, May 24; 1787: CG, Oct 1
Yates, Miss (actor), 1731: TCY, Aug 9; 1732: WINH, May 27, UM, Jun 19; 1733:
MEG, Sep 28; 1734: MEG, Sep 30; 1744: DL, Feb 3, Apr 10, Oct 17, Nov 7, Dec
15, 27; 1745: DL, Apr 17, 30, Dec 13; 1746: DL, Apr 25; 1747: DL, Nov 6, 18,
Dec 16; 1748: DL, Jan 20, Sep 29, Oct 11, 13, 29; 1749: DL, BFC, Aug 23, DL, Nov
16, Dec 8, 20; 1750: DL, Mar 13, Sep 22, Nov 8; 1751: DL, Apr 29, Sep 26, Oct
7; 1752: DL, Sep 30, Oct 3, Dec 8; 1763: DL, Apr 8; 1764: DL, Jan 25
Yates, Mr and Mrs (actors), 1741: GF, Mar 16; 1747: SOU, Nov 16; 1749: BHB, Oct
5
Yates, Mrs (singer), 1667: NONE, Sep 9
Yates, Mrs and Mrs (actors), 1767: DL, Jan 24
Yates, Nancy (actor), 1734: MEG, Sep 30
Yates, Richard (actor, booth keeper, author), 1730: TC, Aug 10; 1731: UM, Apr
19, TCY, Aug 9; 1732: UM, Jun 19; 1733: MEG, Sep 28; 1734: MEG, Sep 30; 1736:
HAY, Jan 19, Mar 5, BFHC, Aug 23, LIF, Oct 5, 9, 23, Nov 13, 16, 29, Dec 7,
16, 22, 31; 1737: LIF, Feb 1, Mar 21, Apr 25, 27, 30, May 4, Jul 26, Aug 5,
Sep 7, CG, Nov 9; 1738: CG, Feb 16, Apr 25, May 18, Dec 4; 1739: CG, May 8,
10, 14, 15, 17, Aug 21, BFHCL, 23, WF, 31, DL, Sep 4, 20, 21, Oct 3, 4, 10,
11, 13, 24, 29, Nov 7, 15, 20, 21, 23, Dec 6, 31; 1740: DL, Jan 3, 15, Feb
13, Apr 12, 17, 22, 23, 25, 29, May 12, 17, 19, 20, 22, 23, TC, Aug 4,
BF/WF/SF, 23, BFHC, 23, DL, Sep 18, 23, Oct 2, 4, GF, 18, 20, 21, 22, 23, 24,
25, 28, 29, 30, 31, Nov 13, 15, 18, 19, 22, 25, 28, 29, Dec 1, 4, 6, 8, 10,
12; 1741: GF, Jan 15, 20, 27, 28, 29, Feb 2, 5, 6, 9, 14, 16, 19, Mar 3, 7,
16, 19, Apr 2, 6, 7, 8, 9, 13, 14, 15, 17, 27, 28, 30, BFTY, Aug 22, SF, Sep
11, GF, 14, 16, 21, 23, 25, 28, 30, Oct 2, 5, 9, 12, 13, 15, 16, 20, 23, 28,
Nov 2, 4, 9, 27, 30, Dec 9, 10, 16, 26; 1742: GF, Jan 4, 5, 14, 18, 26, 27,
Feb 2, 3, 16, 22, Mar 1, 22, 27, Apr 19, 20, BFPY, Aug 25, DL, Sep 18, 28,
Oct 7, 12, 16, 18, Nov 1, 16, Dec 22; 1743: DL, Jan 15, Feb 10, 17, SOU, 18,
DL, Mar 15, 22, SOU, 30, DL, Apr 8, 27, 29, May 10, LIF, Jun 3, SF, Sep 8,

DL, 17, 20, 22, 24, MEF, Oct 3, DL, 4, 11, 13, 20, 22, Nov 8, 12, 18, 23, 26, 29, Dec 1, 6, 15; 1744: DL, Jan 5, 7, 12, 17, 27, Feb 1, 13, Mar 12, Apr 2, 3, 6, 10, 13, 23, May 21, 22, Sep 15, 18, 20, 22, 29, Oct 2, 6, 9, 11, 13, 17, 19, 22, 24, 30, Nov 1, 2, 7, 10, 24, Dec 29; 1745: DL, Jan 5, 7, 10, Feb 13, Mar 7, 30, Apr 18, 19, May 1, Sep 24, 28, Oct 1, 3, 8, 10, 12, 17, Nov 1, 15, 18, 19, 25, 28, 30, Dec 11, 13, 30, HIC, 30; 1746: DL, Jan 17, HIC, Feb 3, DL, 24, Mar 3, HIC, 10, DL, 13, 17, Apr 4, 15, 21, 23, 25, MF, May 5, DL, 9, 16, SOU, Sep 17, DL, 23, 25, 27, 30, Oct 2, 4, 11, 23, Nov 7, 22, Dec 1, 26, 29; 1747: DL, Jan 2, 15, Mar 3, 7, 19, 24, 28, 30, Apr 11, 20, 29, SF, Sep 14, DL, 19, 22, 26, BHB, 26, DL, 29, Oct 1, 3, 17, 21, 24, Nov 10, SOU, 16, DL, 17, Dec 4, 5, 16; 1748: DL, Jan 6, 12, 18, 22, Feb 3, 9, 13, Mar 19, 22, 29, Apr 14, 15, BFSY, Aug 24, DL, Sep 10, 13, 15, 17, 20, 22, 24, Oct 1, 8, 13, 15, 18, 21, 28, 29, Nov 3, 7, 9, 17, 23, 28, Dec 21, 26, 28; 1749: DL, Jan 2, 9, SOU, 9, DL, 13, 18, 20, 25, Feb 21, 25, Mar 16, 27, Apr 3, 4, NWSM, May 1, DL, 1, NWSM, 3, 10, BFY, Aug 23, DL, Sep 16, 19, 20, 21, SOUGT, 22, DL, 26, Oct 3, BHB, 5, DL, 10, 11, 12, 14, 17, 19, 23, 24, 28, 30, Nov 2, 9, 15, 21, 27, Dec 7, 9, 12, 18, 20; 1750: DL, Jan 1, Mar 13, 22, 26, 27, NWC, Apr 16, DL, 19, HAY, Jul 26, DL, Sep 8, 11, 13, 15, 18, 22, 25, Oct 20, 22, 23, 26, 29, 30, Nov 2, 12, 13, 14, 15, 24, Dec 26; 1751: DL, Jan 5, 7, 12, 26, Feb 2, Mar 12, Apr 12, 15, 18, 29, May 1, Sep 7, 10, 12, 13, 14, 17, SF, 17, DL, 18, 21, 24, Oct 2, 17, 29, Nov 7, 16, 29, Dec 5, 14; 1752: DL, Jan 6, 11, 28, Feb 10, Mar 9, 12, Apr 3, Sep 19, 21, 28, Oct 3, 7, 10, 14, 16, 21, 23, 26, Nov 8, 30, Dec 8, 18, 19; 1753: DL, Jan 2, 3, 8, 13, 22, Mar 10, 20, Apr 2, 3, 5, 12, 24, 25, 30, May 4, 18, 21, Sep 8, 11, 13, 15, 22, 25, 29, Oct 3, 10, 16, 18, 20, 23, 24, Nov 1, 6, 7, 8, Dec 20, 29; 1754: DL, Jan 7, Feb 1, 5, 9, 20, Mar 18, 19, 23, 30, Apr 16, 30, May 14, 24, Sep 14, 17, 19, 24, 26, Oct 3, 12, 14, 15, 16, 18, 22, 23, 25, 30, Nov 7, 11; 1755: DL, Jan 6, 10, 15, 17, Feb 22, Mar 13, Apr 2, 4, 15, May 6, Sep 13, 16, 23, Oct 2, 3, 4, 7, 10, 13, 17, 24, 27, Nov 12, 22, 26, 28, Dec 1, 5, 6, 11; 1756: DL, Jan 2, 21, Feb 11, 12, 24, Mar 23, 25, 27, 29, 30, Apr 3, 10, 24, May 5, 10, 12, 14, 18, 24, Sep 18, 21, 28, 30, Oct 5, 7, 13, 14, 15, 16, 21, 23, 28, Nov 2, 3, 10, 12, 18, 19, 23, Dec 10, 15, 18, 27; 1757: DL, Jan 3, 17, 22, 26, Feb 5, Mar 7, 22, 24, 28, Apr 2, 11, 13, 14, 20, 21, 30, May 3, BF, Sep 3, DL, 10, 13, 15, 20, 22, 24, 29, Oct 4, 8, 12, 13, 15, 19, 20, 26, 27, 29, 31, Nov 2, 3, 15, 18, 22, Dec 3, 22, 27; 1758: DL, Jan 24, 27, Feb 4, 11, 20, Mar 11, 13, 16, 29, 30, Apr 3, 11, 18, 25, 29, May 2, 4, 17, Jun 22, Sep 16, 19, 26, Oct 3, 7, 10, 12, 14, 18, 24, 25, 27, 30, Nov 1, 7, 13, 16, 21, 23, 24, Dec 20, 23, 28; 1759: DL, Jan 13, 17, Feb 3, Mar 6, 20, 24, 26, 31, Apr 7, 27, May 11, 14, 16, 21, 28, BFY, Sep 3, DL, 22, 25, 27, 29, Oct 6, 9, 12, 16, 17, 19, 23, 26, 27, 30, 31, Nov 9, 13, 22, 24, 30, Dec 5, 31; 1760: DL, Jan 10, 19, Feb 8, Mar 20, 24, 27, 29, Apr 9, 11, 22, 28, 30, May 7, 8, 16, Jun 19, Jul 29, BFG, Sep 3, 4, BFS, 4, BFG, 4, 5, 6, DL, 23, 30, Oct 3, 7, 8, 10, 11, 15, 22, 23, 24, Nov 17, 27, Dec 2, 5, 11, 22; 1761: DL, Jan 10, Feb 12, Mar 23, 26, 27, 28, Apr 15, 24, 28, 29, May 18, Jun 15, Jul 2, Aug 8, Sep 5, 8, 10, 14, 15, 19, 23, 25, 28, 30, Oct 1, 7, 10, 14, 16, 17, 20, 21, 24, 27, 31, Nov 10, 18, 23, Dec 14, 17; 1762: DL, Jan 7, 11, 20, 27, 29, Mar 1, 6, 15, 20, 27, Apr 1, 22, 30, May 7, 10, 19, 26, Sep 23, 25, 29, Oct 2, 4, 6, 8, 9, 11, 12, 13, 14, 23, 25, 28, 30, Nov 2, 3, 10, 11, 12, 17, 18, 26, Dec 1, 11, 22; 1763: DL, Jan 14, 17, 18, 22, Feb 19, Mar 1, 14, 19, 24, Apr 9, 13, 23, May 2, 13, 14, 20, 31, Sep 17, 20, 22, 27, 29, Oct 1, 12, 13, 14, 19, 21, 29, Nov 1, 2, 8, 15, 19, 23, 26, 28, 29, Dec 10, 17; 1764: DL, Jan 3, 4, 9, 13, 14, 18, 23, 27, Feb 9, 18, 21, Mar 3, 26, 27, Apr 2, 10, 24, May 4, Sep 15, 18, 27, Oct 6, 13, 18, 20, 22, 26, Nov 3, 8, 9, 27, 28, Dec 13, 18; 1765: DL, Jan 3, 18, Mar 2, 19, 23, 26, Apr 20, May 1, 11, 17, 18, 22, 27, Sep 14, 17, 19, 21, 24, Oct 3, 11, 18, 28, 31, Nov 14, 16, Dec 5, 7; 1766: DL, Jan 13, 23, 24, 29, Feb 3, 20, Mar 11, 17, 18, Apr 1, 25, May 2, 5, 10, 20, 21, 22, Sep 20, 23, 25, Oct 7, 9, 10, 17, 18, 23, 31, Nov 17, 18, Dec 4, 10, 15, 29; 1767: DL, Feb 9, 21, 23, Mar 21, 28, 31, Apr 4, 11, 22, 25, May 4, 8, 27, 28, Sep 12, CG, Oct 5, DL, 30, CG, 31, Nov 10, Dec 8, 14, DL, 16, CG, 28, 31; 1768: CG, Jan 9, Feb 12, Mar 12, 24, 26, May 12, Sep 20, Oct 4, 20, Nov 3, 8, Dec 21; 1769: CG, Jan 28, Mar 29, Apr 4, 22, 27, Nov 15, 20, 23, Dec 2, 20; 1770: CG, Jan 6, 19, Feb 3, Mar 22, 27, 29, Apr 26, 28, Sep 24, 28, Oct 9, 16, 17, 19, Nov 16, Dec 17; 1771: CG, Jan 4, 12, Feb 9, Mar 19, Apr 1, May 7, 23, Oct 9, 11, 14, 18, 19, 28, 30, Nov 19, 21; 1772: CG, Jan 1, 25, DL, Mar 23, CG, 30, 31, Apr 22, May 6, 27; 1773: DL, Jan 19, Feb 2, CG, Mar 6, DL, Apr 3, 21, May 24, KING'S, Oct 23; 1774: DL, Mar 15; 1775: DL, Mar 4, May 5, Oct 2, 7, 26, Nov 23, Dec 1, 11; 1776: DL, Jan 13, 27, Feb 15, Mar 12, 21, Apr 13, May 7, Sep 21, Oct 1, Nov 5, 19, 29, Dec 31; 1777: DL, Jan 13, 28, May 8, Sep 23, Oct 9, 18, 22, Nov 24; 1778: DL, Jan 23, Mar 5, Sep 29, Oct 6, 13, 19, Nov 10, 28, Dec 11, 19, 22; 1779: DL, Jan 23, Mar 15, May 15, Sep 21, 28, Oct 7, 9, 12, 19, 23, Nov 5, 12, 20; 1780: DL, Mar 4, 18, Oct 3, 14, 19, 26, 31, Dec 7, 8, 19; 1781: DL, Mar 27, Sep 27, Oct 13, Nov 6, 21; 1782: DL,

933

Jan 22, 26, Apr 30, May 10, CG, Dec 6; 1783: CG, Jan 28, Apr 29, May 31;
    1786: CG, May 6
--Adventures of Timur Koran, The; or, The Favourite of the Sun, 1760: BFG, Sep
    3, 4, 5, 6
--British Tar's Triumph over M Soup-Maigre, The, 1761: BFY, Aug 31
--Fair Bride, The; or, The Unexpected Event, 1761: BFY, Aug 31, Sep 3, 4, 5, 7
Yates, Sarah, Mrs Thomas (actor), 1794: HAY, Mar 31, CG, May 30; 1797: HAY, Feb
    9; 1800: DL, Feb 22
Yates, Thomas (boxkeeper), 1677: DL, Dec 12, 26
Yates, W (beneficiary), 1761: DL, May 29; 1766: DL, May 2
Yates, Widow, Booth of, 1755: BF, Sep 4, 5
Yates' Booth, 1726: BFY, Aug 26; 1727: BF, Aug 23; 1728: BFY, Aug 24, SFY, Sep
    6; 1729: UM, Apr 7, 15, SF, Sep 12; 1730: SFY, Sep 8; 1731: TCY, Aug 9, BFYG,
    24; 1732: UM, Jun 19, BF, Aug 25; 1735: YEB, Dec 22; 1739: WF, Aug 31; 1740:
    TC, Aug 4, BF/WF/SF, 23, 29, Sep 8; 1744: MF, May 4; 1745: NWMF, May 13;
    1748: BFSY, Aug 24; 1749: BFYT, Aug 23, BFY, 23, BFYT, 24, BFY, 24, 25, BFYT,
    25, 26, 28, BFY, 28; 1750: SFY, Sep 14; 1752: SFB, Sep 22; 1754: SFY, Sep 18,
    19, 20, 21, 23, 24; 1762: BFY, Sep 3
Yates' Concert Hall, 1761: BFY, Aug 31, Sep 3, 4, 5, 7
Yatesmore (actor), 1786: HAMM, Jun 28, 30, Jul 5, 7, 10
Ye Brethren of the Ancient Craft (song), 1738: CG, May 1; 1739: DL, May 15
Ye Gentlemen of England (song), 1795: CG, Apr 28, DL, May 2, CG, 16, 27; 1796:
    CG, Mar 14, Apr 1, 15; 1797: HAY, May 10; 1798: CG, May 28; 1799: HAY, Sep 2
Ye men of Gaza (song), 1789: CG, Mar 27; 1790: DL, Feb 24, CG, Mar 3; 1791: CG,
    Mar 11; 1792: CG, Mar 9, KING'S, 23, 30; 1794: CG, Mar 12, DL, Apr 9; 1795:
    CG, Mar 13, 25; 1796: CG, Feb 26; 1797: CG, Mar 24; 1798: CG, Mar 9; 1799:
    CG, Mar 13
Ye nymphs and sylvan gods (song), 1694: DG, May 0; 1728: LIF, May 11; 1730:
    LIF, May 21, Jun 1
Ye sacred priests (song), 1758: KING'S, Apr 6; 1789: CG, Mar 20; 1790: CG, Feb
    24, DL, Mar 10; 1791: CG, Mar 11, DL, 25; 1792: CG, Mar 2, KING'S, 7; 1793:
    CG, Feb 15; 1794: CG, Mar 7, DL, Apr 4; 1795: CG, Mar 13; 1796: CG, Feb 24;
    1797: CG, Mar 17; 1798: CG, Mar 9; 1800: CG, Mar 5
Ye sons of Israel (song), 1786: DL, Mar 10; 1789: CG, Mar 6, DL, 18; 1790: CG,
    Feb 24, DL, 24, 26; 1791: CG, Mar 11, DL, 11, 23; 1792: KING'S, Feb 24, Mar
    7, CG, 9; 1793: KING/HAY, Feb 15, 22, CG, Mar 6; 1794: CG, Mar 12, DL, 12,
    14, CG, 26, DL, Apr 2, 10, CG, 11; 1795: CG, Mar 13; 1796: CG, Feb 26; 1797:
    CG, Mar 10; 1798: CG, Mar 14; 1799: CG, Feb 15
Ye southern breezes (song), 1790: CG, Mar 17, 19, 26; 1792: CG, Mar 9, KING'S,
    30; 1794: CG, Mar 14, DL, Apr 2; 1796: CG, Feb 26; 1797: CG, Mar 17; 1799:
    CG, Feb 20; 1800: CG, Mar 19
Ye verdant plains (song), 1791: DL, Apr 1; 1792: KING'S, Feb 29; 1794: DL, Mar
    26
Yeames, Mrs (actor), 1742: GF, Feb 1
Yeates. See Yates.
Yeates, Mrs (actor), 1754: DL, Feb 25, HAY, Nov 28; 1755: BF, Sep 3, 6, SFG, 18
Yellow Joke (dance), 1730: GF, Jun 29, 30
Yellow Stockings (dance), 1716: LIF, Mar 24
Yelverton, Barbara, Lady Longueville, 1700: DLORLIF, Jan 20
Yelverton, Frances, Lady Hatton, 1680: DG, Nov 1
Yelverton, Henry, Lord Grey of Ruthin, Viscount Longueville (spectator), 1691:
    DL, Dec 16; 1697: LIF, Mar 4
Yeoens, Miss (singer), 1792: CG, Apr 17
Yeoman of Kent, The. See Baker, Thomas, Tunbridge Walks.
Yield, no, no (song), 1696: LIF, Nov 14
Ynca, Oakecharinga Tiggwamtubby Tocholoo (spectator), 1719: LIF, Dec 21; see
    also Indian Kings, American; American Princes
Yo Heave Ho (song), 1799: CG, May 3, Jun 3
Yokney, Mrs (actor), 1668: NONE, Sep 0
Yonge (composer), 1731: DL, Feb 8
York (actor), 1744: HAY, Feb 6, GF, Dec 26; 1745: GF, Feb 14
York Buildings, 1686: ATCOURT, Jan 27; 1689: YB, Oct 17, Nov 11, 14; 1690: YB,
    Feb 3, EC, 24, YB, Mar 10, Sep 29; 1691: YB, Apr 13, Nov 9; 1692: YB, Nov 1;
    1693: YB, Jan 10, May 13, Jun 17, Nov 2, 27; 1694: YB, Jan 15, 25, Feb 5, 26,
    Nov 12; 1695: YB, Nov 25; 1697: YB, Jan 7, Feb 24, Mar 3, 17, 24, Apr 29, LW,
    May 5, YB, 13, Dec 16; 1698: YB, Jan 10, 17, Feb 10, 16, Mar 16, 28, 30, 31,
    Apr 15, 25, May 4, 10, 25, 28, 30, Jun 1, 7, Dec 22; 1699: YB, Jan 4, Mar 17,
    Apr 28, Dec 13; 1700: YB, Mar 19, 20, May 8, Jun 21, Dec 11; 1702: HAW, Jul
    27; 1708: SH, Feb 4; 1711: YB, May 24, QUEEN'S, Dec 26; 1712: DL, Jan 18;
    1735: YB/HAY, Sep 24; 1736: CG, Apr 27; 1737: YB, Jan 31; 1738: CG, Feb 13,
    Mar 2, YB, 26; 1739: DL, May 12; 1757: CG, Mar 22, Apr 15, DL, May 11; 1758:
    DL, Apr 8; 1779: DL, Mar 22, CG, Apr 20; 1780: CG, Mar 14; 1781: CG, Mar 31;

1782: CG, Mar 19; 1784: CG, Mar 23; 1785: CG, Mar 8; 1786: CG, Feb 25, Mar 14; 1787: CG, Apr 11; 1788: CG, Mar 28, HAY, Aug 26; 1789: HAY, Aug 5; 1790: DL, Apr 30; 1791: DL, May 5, CG, Jun 4; 1797: CG, Jun 10
York Comedians, 1770: DL, Oct 8
York St, 1691: YS, Nov 6; 1742: DL, Apr 29; 1743: DL, Apr 18; 1751: DL, Apr 20; 1756: DL, Mar 23, Apr 28; 1757: CG, Mar 31; 1782: CG, Apr 12, DL, 23; 1784: CG, Apr 16, DL, 30; 1791: DL, May 13, CG, Jun 4; 1792: DLKING'S, May 24; 1793: DL, May 22; 1794: DL, Mar 12; 1795: CG, May 19; 1796: CG, May 10; 1799: DL, Jun 26
York Theatre, 1773: HAY, Sep 16; 1775: DL, Oct 13; 1777: HAY, May 1, CG, Oct 8; 1778: CG, Jan 15; 1779: HAY, Jun 7, 18, Jul 16; 1780: CG, Oct 3, DL, 7, HAY, Nov 13; 1783: DL, Jan 6, HAY, Sep 17, CG, 19, Oct 5, HAY, Dec 15; 1785: DL, Oct 18; 1786: HAY, Mar 6, Jul 13, CG, Sep 25, Oct 4; 1787: HAY, Jul 19, DL, Sep 29; 1788: HAY, Jul 2; 1791: CG, Sep 21, Oct 3, HAY, Dec 26; 1797: HAY, Dec 4; 1798: CG, Sep 21, Oct 3; 1799: HAY, Jun 29, CG, Dec 9
York, Duchess of. See Frederica, Princess.
York, Duchess of. See Stuart, Anne Hyde.
York, Duke and Duchess of, 1661: ATCOURT, Apr 20; 1674: CITY, Oct 29; 1679: BRUSSELS, Oct 3; 1796: KING'S, Mar 10
York, Duke of. See James II.
York, Edward Augustus, Duke of, 1758: DL, Apr 8; 1760: CG, Apr 26; 1761: CG, Sep 24; 1767: CG, Jan 6, HAY, May 29, Jul 6, Aug 26, DL, Sep 28, 29, Nov 2, 3, CG, 4; see also Duke
York, Frederick Augustus, Duke of, 1791: HAY, Mar 7, CG, Nov 21; 1797: KING'S, May 18, CG, Jun 14, DL, Oct 27; 1800: CG, Jun 12; see also Duke
York, 1679: DG, May 0; 1690: MTH, Mar 27; 1773: HAY, Sep 16, 18; 1776: HAY, Apr 22, CG, Dec 6; 1780: CG, Mar 18; 1787: DL, May 7; 1792: CG, May 16; 1794: DL, Nov 15
Yorke, Philip, Lord Hardwicke (chief justice), 1733: HAY, Nov 19; 1756: DL, Feb 9
Yorkshire Jig (dance), 1784: HAY, Sep 17; 1785: HAY, Apr 26
Yorkshire Maggot (dance), 1740: CG, Dec 12, 19, 22; 1741: CG, Jan 7, 10, 27, Mar 17
Yorkshire Tale (song), 1731: GF, Apr 1
Yorkshire, 1770: DL, Oct 8
You all must have heard (song), 1792: CG, May 15
You are aw nodding (song), 1792: CG, May 15
You may feast your ears (song), 1792: CG, May 15
You never did hear of an Irishman's fear (song), 1791: CG, May 5
You Say 'Tis Love (song), 1715: DL, May 17
You take off good likenesses (song), 1798: CG, Apr 9
Youckney (Yokney), Elizabeth (actor), 1668: NONE, Sep 0
Young (actor), 1745: GF, Apr 15
Young (actor), 1787: RLSN, Mar 26, 27, 29, 30, 31
Young (beneficiary), 1714: SH, Jan 25
Young (beneficiary), 1733: YB, Mar 8; 1734: YB, Mar 8, MR, Dec 13; 1736: MR, Feb 11, YB, Apr 29
Young (duelist), 1695: DLORLIF, Jun 22
Young (ticket deliverer), 1786: CG, May 31; 1787: CG, Jun 2; 1788: CG, May 15; 1789: CG, Jun 6; 1790: CG, May 29; 1791: CG, Jun 2; 1792: CG, May 25; 1794: CG, Jun 12; 1795: CG, Jun 4; 1796: CG, May 21; 1797: CG, Jun 2; 1798: CG, May 19; 1799: CG, Jun 4; 1800: CG, Jun 10
Young Actor, The. See Colman the elder, George.
Young Admiral, The. See Shirley, James.
Young Chrysostome had virtue, sense (song), 1694: DG, May 0
Young Coquet, The (play, anon), 1705: DL, Jun 16, 28; 1706: DL, Mar 9
Young Couple, The. See Pope, Jane.
Young Henry (song), 1786: CG, May 9
Young I am, and yet unskilled (song), 1694: DL, Jan 0
Young Jamie loved me well (song), 1794: CG, May 26; see also Auld Robin Grey
Young King, The. See Behn, Aphra.
Young Men and Old Women. See Inchbald, Elizabeth.
Young Patagonians (dance), 1768: DL, Nov 7
Young Philander wooed me long (song), 1699: DL, May 0
Young Quaker, The. See O'Keeffe, John.
Young Strephon he has woo'd me long (song), 1697: DG, Jun 0
Young Strephon met me t'other Day (song), 1697: DG, Jun 0
Young Widow (entertainment), 1795: CG, May 27
Young William was a seaman true (song), 1798: CG, Apr 21, May 9, 28, Jun 2, 4; 1799: CG, Apr 6, 18, May 18, 28, Jun 1, 5, 6, 7, Dec 9; 1800: CG, May 13, 22, 30
Young, Anthony (organist), 1711: SH, Nov 22

Young, Arabella (actor), 1759: DL, May 21
Young, Cecilia (singer), 1730: DL, Mar 4, NONE, Oct 13; 1731: SH, Mar 4, LIF,
    Apr 2; 1732: HIC, Apr 24, May 3, HAY, Nov 14, 16, Dec 18; 1733: LIF, Feb 16,
    SH, 22, HAY, 27, YB, Mar 8, KING'S, 17, LIF, Apr 16, HIC, May 25, DL, Nov 26;
    1734: DL, Feb 4, YB, Mar 8, DL/HAY, 21, DT, 22, SH, 28, .DL, Apr 29, May 15,
    JS, 31, HIC, Jul 10, MR, Dec 13; 1735: CG, Jan 8, YB, Feb 28, CG, Mar 28, Apr
    1, 16; 1736: MR, Feb 11, YB, Apr 29, DL, Dec 15, 16; 1737: DL, Jan 14, 15,
    18, HIC, Apr 1; 1739: KING'S, Jan 16
Young, Cecilia and Isabella (singers), 1735: ST, Nov 26
Young, Edward, 1719: DL, Mar 7; 1721: DL, Apr 18; 1722: DL, Feb 13; 1732: HAY,
    May 24; 1736: HAY, Jan 19, 20; 1748: JS, May 30, HAY, Sep 5; 1753: DL, Mar 3,
    6, 10; 1756: CG, Mar 22; 1794: HAY, Jun 2
--Brothers, The, 1753: DL, Mar 3, 5, 6, 8, 10, 12, 15, 17
--Busiris, King of Egypt, 1719: DL, Mar 7, 9, 10, 14, 17, 21, Apr 2, 3, 15;
    1722: DL, Feb 12, 13; 1736: LIF, Mar 3; 1748: HAY, Sep 5; 1756: CG, Mar 22
--Revenge, The, 1721: DL, Apr 18, 19, 20, 21, 22, 24; 1722: HAY, Jun 21; 1723:
    HAY, Dec 23; 1724: HAY, Jan 8; 1732: HAY, May 24; 1736: HAY, Jan 19, 20;
    1737: YB, May 2; 1744: CG, Nov 12, 13, 14, 17, 20, Dec 4, 14, 18, 21; 1745:
    CG, Jan 10, 15, 22, Feb 7, Mar 19, HAY, Apr 24; 1746: GF, Oct 27, CG, Nov 13;
    1748: JS, May 30, CG, Nov 19, Dec 1; 1749: CG, Jan 7, HAY, May 16; 1750: CG,
    Jan 31, Apr 7; 1751: DL, Jan 11, CG, Feb 16, 18, Mar 14, DL, Oct 5, 10, 12,
    15, 31, Nov 19, Dec 17; 1752: DL, Jan 3, 11, Mar 5, Sep 21, CG, 29, Oct 2,
    DL, 18; 1753: CG, Jan 13, DL, May 10, Sep 18, Oct 22, Dec 28; 1754: DL, Oct
    8; 1755: CG, Jan 14, DL, May 3, CG, Nov 17, 26, 28; 1756: DL, Oct 27, Dec 18,
    27; 1757: DL, Feb 7, May 17; 1768: DL, Oct 14, 17, Nov 7, 14, Dec 29; 1769:
    DL, Sep 28, Oct 20; 1770: HAY, Mar 17; 1774: CG, Apr 21, May 25; 1777: DL,
    Apr 24, CG, May 7; 1778: CG, Jan 3; 1783: DL, Apr 24, CG, 26, DL, May 26;
    1784: DL, Jan 23; 1788: CG, Oct 3; 1789: DL, Jan 19, 22, May 6; 1791:
    DLKING'S, Dec 12; 1793: HAY, Oct 28, Nov 4; 1794: HAY, Jun 2; 1798: DL, Feb
    24, Oct 2; 1799: DL, Oct 3
Young, Elizabeth (dancer, singer), 1755: DL, Feb 3, Apr 19, Nov 12, Dec 18;
    1756: DL, Feb 10, 11, Apr 19, May 4, 13, Sep 25, Oct 13, Nov 23, 24, Dec 15,
    20; 1757: DL, Mar 24, 28, 31, Apr 15, 19, 20, May 2, 5, 9, 23, Sep 17, 27,
    Oct 20, Nov 4, Dec 2, 3, 21; 1758: DL, Jan 13, 24, Feb 21, Mar 11, 16, Apr 5,
    6, 27, May 2, Jun 22, Sep 21, 28, Oct 24, Nov 3, 4, 13, 25, Dec 14; 1759: DL,
    Jan 11, 13, 19, Feb 1, 14, 26, Mar 20, 29, Apr 2, 24, May 24, 28, Sep 25, 27,
    Oct 2, 16, 17, 22, Nov 5, 15, 17, 22, 24, Dec 1, 7, 31; 1760: DL, Feb 19, Apr
    16, May 8, Oct 10, 11, 20, Nov 17, Dec 1, 11, 13, 15, 27; 1761: DL, Jan 12,
    19, 23, 24, Mar 14, 30, Apr 13, 14, 18, 29, May 1, 11, 27, Jun 1, Sep 5, 8,
    10, 25, 30, Oct 7, 14, 26, 29, 31, Nov 16; 1762: DL, Jan 4, 15, 27, Feb 3, 9,
    17, 20, Mar 1, 6, 27, Apr 14, 23, May 1, 6, 7, 19, 25, Sep 28, 29, Oct 7, 9,
    22, 25, 30, Nov 4, 23, 26, Dec 16, 28; 1763: DL, Jan 17, Feb 24, Mar 24, Apr
    5, 6, 7, 9, 13, 20, 23, 27, May 2, Oct 17, 28, 31, Nov 4, 15, 23, 29, Dec 14,
    26; 1764: DL, Jan 9, 21, Feb 24, Mar 31, Apr 12, 26, 30, May 1, Sep 22, 25,
    Oct 29, 30, Nov 27, 28, Dec 18; 1765: DL, Jan 14, Mar 2, 7, 26, Apr 22, May
    1, Sep 17, 24, Oct 8, 10, 23, 28, Nov 11; 1766: DL, Feb 3, 7, Apr 15, May 10,
    14, Sep 23, 30, Nov 4; 1767: DL, Mar 21, Apr 11, 23, May 5, Sep 12, 21, 23,
    Oct 10, 23, Nov 4, 20, Dec 7, 26; 1768: DL, Jan 14, Mar 15, 17, Apr 22, 27,
    May 4, Sep 8, 17, 20, 22, Oct 10, 18, Nov 1, 4; 1769: CG, Apr 5, DL, 12, CG,
    27, DL, Sep 23, Nov 4, 13, 23; 1771: DL, Oct 31, Nov 22; 1772: DL, Jan 1, 4,
    Feb 21, Mar 30, May 12, Sep 19, Oct 14, 16; 1773: DL, Nov 6; 1774: DL, Feb
    15, Mar 19, Oct 8, 26; 1776: DL, Jan 27, Mar 18, Apr 10
Young, Esther (actor, singer), 1736: MR, Feb 11, DL, Apr 22; 1737: DT, Mar 30,
    CG, Oct 26; 1738: CG, Sep 15, Oct 9, Dec 9; 1739: CG, Feb 9, Apr 28, May 8,
    Aug 29, 31, Sep 21, Oct 10, 31, Dec 10, 15; 1740: CG, Jan 1, Feb 12, Apr 30,
    Jun 5, Sep 19, 26, Oct 10, 22, Dec 29; 1741: CG, Jan 5, Feb 16, 24, Apr 10,
    18, TC, Aug 4, CG, Sep 28, 30, Oct 21, 24; 1742: CG, Apr 30, May 5; 1743: DL,
    Feb 2, HAY, Mar 24; 1744: HAY, Jan 19, CG, Feb 10, 14, Mar 2, 3, HAY, Apr 16;
    1745: DL, Jan 14, 17, 31, Feb 15, Apr 3, 15; 1746: DL, Jan 31, Mar 3, CG, Apr
    18, May 2, 3, Jun 9, 23, 27, Nov 3, 6, Dec 29; 1747: CG, Apr 25; 1748: CG,
    Jan 8, 26, Mar 28, Apr 13, Sep 26, Oct 7, 27, 28, 29, HAY, Dec 9, CG, 10, 21;
    1749: CG, Mar 29, 31, Apr 5, 11, May 4, Sep 25, 29, Oct 12, 16, 19, 20, Nov
    23, 24; 1750: CG, Mar 27, 31, Apr 5, 19, 26, 30, Sep 24, Oct 12, 13, 29, Nov
    8, 19, Dec 21, 26; 1751: CG, Mar 1, Apr 16, 18, 20, May 3, 14, Sep 23, 25,
    27, 30, Oct 18, Nov 11, Dec 4; 1752: CG, Feb 11, Mar 17, Apr 20, Sep 18, Oct
    4, 6, 10, 21, 23, 26, 30, Dec 7; 1753: CG, Jan 6, Feb 10, 12, May 2, Sep 12,
    17, Oct 10, Dec 5; 1754: CG, Mar 25, Apr 17, 25, 26, May 3, 4, 15
Young, Isabella (actor, singer), 1734: MR, Dec 13; 1735: YB, Feb 28; 1736: MR,
    Feb 11, DL, Apr 22; 1737: DT, Mar 30, CG, Oct 26; 1738: DL, Oct 4
Young, Isabella (actor, singer), 1754: CG, Apr 26, May 3, HAY, 29, CG, Sep 16,
    25, Oct 2, 7, Nov 16, 20, Dec 30; 1755: CG, Apr 9, 15, 24, 28, DL, May 9, CG,
    Sep 29, Oct 10, 17, 20, 21, Nov 15, 17; 1756: CG, Apr 24, May 5, 9, Sep 22,

936

24, Oct 4, 6, Nov 13, DL, Dec 20; 1757: SOHO, Feb 1, CG, Mar 11, 24, May 6,
Sep 23, 26, Oct 13, Dec 7, 10; 1758: HAY, Feb 2, CG, 22, Mar 1, 3, 13, 30,
SOHO, Apr 1, CG, 13, 21, CHAPEL, 27, CG, Sep 27, Oct 4, 9, 24, Nov 1, 23, 27;
1759: CG, Mar 24, Apr 7, 30, HAM, Aug 13, CG, Oct 1, 10, Nov 30; 1760: CG,
Jan 18, 31, Feb 14, 29, Mar 18, Apr 8, 9, 17, 28, Sep 22, 24, 29, Oct 8, Dec
11; 1761: CG, Jan 3, KING'S, Mar 12, CG, Apr 2, 14, 27, Sep 16, 18, 25; 1762:
CG, May 4, 11, CHAPEL, 18, CG, Dec 4; 1763: CG, Apr 23; 1764: KING'S, Nov 24;
1765: KING'S, Jan 26, Mar 2, 28; 1766: RANELAGH, Jun 20, KING'S, Oct 21, Nov
25; 1767: CG, Mar 6; 1769: DL, Mar 11, 13, Apr 1
Young, Isabella and Esther (singers), 1737: DT, Mar 30; 1738: CG, Apr 15
Young, John (actor), 1662: LIF, Sep 30, Oct 18, ATCOURT, 27; 1663: LIF, Jan 8,
Feb 23, Oct 0, ATCOURT, Dec 10, LIF, 22; 1664: LIF, Aug 13, Sep 10; 1665:
LIF, Apr 3; 1667: LIF, Aug 15, Oct 16; 1668: LIF, Feb 6, ATCOURT, May 29;
1670: LIF, Sep 20, Nov 0; 1671: LIF, Jan 10, Mar 6, Jun 0, DG, Nov 0; 1672:
DG, Jan 31, Aug 3; 1675: NONE, Sep 0; 1676: DG, Aug 0
Young, Mrs (actor, dancer), 1725: DL, May 14, Oct 2; 1726: DL, Feb 11, May 6,
Nov 2, Dec 7, 30; 1727: DL, Feb 27, Mar 23, May 8, Nov 14; 1728: DL, Mar 19,
30, Apr 28
Young, Polly (actor), 1762: CG, Sep 30, Oct 8, Nov 1, 5, 15; 1763: CG, Jan 24,
Apr 23, May 2, DL, 27, CG, Sep 21, Oct 3, 5, 13, 14, Nov 4, 15, 28; 1764: CG,
Mar 27, May 8, 21; 1765: HAY, Mar 11, KING'S, Apr 29; 1766: DL, Apr 15
Young, Thomas (actor), 1760: CG, Sep 22; 1761: CG, Oct 13, Dec 11; 1762: CG,
Jan 12, Feb 15, HAY, May 1, CG, 12, 14, Sep 24, Oct 8, Nov 15; 1763: CG, Feb
14, May 9, 18; 1765: DL, Sep 26; 1771: HAY, Jan 28; 1774: CG, Mar 15, Oct 1,
5, 14, 22, 28, Nov 1, Dec 22; 1775: CG, May 16, Sep 25, 29, Oct 16, 17, 21,
23, 25, Nov 9, 10, 13, 24, Dec 1, 5, 9, 26; 1776: CG, Jan 1, 13, 15, Feb 13,
22, Mar 7, 16, 18, 30, Apr 17, 19, 27, 30, May 1, 2, 13, 14, 27; 1777: CHR,
Jun 18, 23, 30
Younge (Yonge), Elizabeth (singer), 1768: DL, Oct 22, 24, Nov 3, 24, Dec 17;
1769: DL, Apr 7, Oct 2, 21, 30, Nov 4, 9, 27, Dec 13, 23; 1770: DL, Jan 16,
18, 25, Mar 3, 27, 31, Apr 3, 17, 21, May 15, 24, Sep 22, Oct 4, 6, 8; 1771:
DL, Sep 26, 28, Oct 15, 19, 26, 29, Nov 8, 21, 22, 25, 26, Dec 10; 1772: DL,
Jan 4, Mar 5, 17, 23, 28, Apr 6, 11, 22, May 6, 13, 19, 20, 22, 25, 30, Jun
5, Oct 8, 15, 23, 24, 28, 29, 30, 31, Nov 12, 27, Dec 8, 17, 28; 1773: DL,
Jan 13, 16, 27, Feb 11, 18, 25, Mar 23, Apr 3, 17, 21, 30, May 6, 10, 14, 17,
26, 27, Sep 21, 25, Oct 2, 9, 20, 30, Nov 13, 15, 25, Dec 10, 11, 13; 1774:
DL, Jan 22, Mar 15, 19, 22, 26, Apr 4, 5, 7, 12, 28, May 4, 5, 7, 17, 20, 23,
27, Sep 22, 27, Oct 1, 12, 13, 20, 21, 27, Nov 1, 4, 16, Dec 9; 1775: DL, Jan
2, 4, 11, 21, Mar 21, 25, 28, Apr 18, 21, May 1, 6, 10, 12, Sep 26, 28, Oct
10, 12, 13, 14, 17, 18, 21, 25, 31, Nov 1, 4, 21, Dec 2, 11, 19; 1776: DL,
Jan 27, Feb 15, Mar 4, 12, 18, 28, Apr 12, 17, 19, 24, May 13, 23, Sep 21,
24, 28, Oct 1, 5, 8, 9, 12, 22, 25, 26, Nov 1, 4, 5, 6, 19, 29, Dec 17; 1777:
DL, Jan 22, 28, Mar 11, 13, Apr 11, 17, Sep 23, 27, Oct 9, 14, 18, 31, Nov 4,
Dec 3, 18; 1778: DL, Jan 5, 10, 24, Feb 24, Mar 5, 12, 16, 30, Apr 20, 23,
27, Sep 17, 24, 26, CG, 28, DL, Oct 1, 13, CG, 16, DL, 17, 24, Nov 10, 14,
16, 20, 28, 30, Dec 18, 19; 1779: DL, Jan 23, Feb 8, Mar 13, 15, 16, 22, Apr
10, 12, 19, 27, CG, May 6, Nov 10, 13, 19, Dec 9, 11, 17, 31; 1780: CG, Jan
7, 12, 25, Feb 22, Mar 18, Apr 3, 10, May 1, Oct 4, 10, 19, 24, 30, Nov 1, 4,
8, 10, 24, Dec 27; 1781: CG, Jan 4, Feb 10, 24, Mar 24, 27, May 7, 10, 14,
18, Sep 19, 28, Oct 3, 5, 13, 26, 30, Nov 5, 8, 17, 20, Dec 5, 8, 10, 20;
1782: CG, Jan 3, 10, 22, 31, Feb 9, Mar 18, 19, Apr 12, 27, Oct 3, 8, 10, 18,
19, 23, 29, 31, Dec 2, 3, 5, 14, 19, 30; 1783: CG, Jan 1, 28, Feb 8, Mar 31,
Apr 5, May 7, 17, Jun 6, Oct 31, Nov 8, 10, 24, Dec 6, 31; 1784: CG, Jan 7,
9, 14, 26, 29, 31, Feb 5, 19, 23, Mar 16, 18, 22, May 8, Jun 10, Sep 17, 21,
24, 28, Oct 1, 18, 25, 28, Nov 10, 12, 26, Dec 3, 14; 1785: CG, Jan 8, 18,
Feb 4, 28, Mar 7, 8, Apr 2, 8, 13, 18, 23, May 2, 4, 13; 1790: CG, Mar 22
Younge, Miss (singer), 1739: CG, Sep 7, Oct 20, Dec 10; 1746: CG, Dec 31; 1747:
CG, Mar 26, Apr 25, Nov 23, Dec 11; 1758: CG, Feb 1
Younger (dancer), 1721: DL, Feb 9
Younger Brother, The. See Behn, Aphra.
Younger Brother, The; or, The Sham Marquis (play, anon), 1719: LIF, Feb 7, 9,
10
Younger, Elizabeth (actor, dancer), 1706: DL, Mar 27; 1711: DL, Jan 29, Feb 27;
1712: SML, May 21, Jun 11, 18, DL, Sep 30; 1713: DL, Jan 29, May 25; 1714:
DL, May 3, 14, 21, 26, 31, Jun 14, 25, 29; 1715: DL, Feb 4, 15, 23, Mar 8,
May 3, 18, 20, YB, 28, DL, Jun 17, Jul 1, Aug 19, Oct 13, 14, 29, Nov 5, 14,
17, 22, Dec 5, 17, 30; 1716: DL, Jan 11, 14, 23, 25, 26, Feb 1, 18, Apr 2,
21, 26, May 1, 9, 14, 18, 25, Jun 6, 15, Sep 29, Oct 9, 18, 22, Nov 3, 12,
14, 26, Dec 4, 10, 13; 1717: DL, Jan 2, 3, 9, 26, Feb 2, 6, 19, Mar 2, 14,
28, May 6, 10, 11, 15, 16, 17, 20, 24, 29, 30, Jun 3, 6, 10, 18; 1718: DL,
Jan 14, 20, 31, Mar 4, 18, 20, 31, Apr 3, 5, 19, 26, 28, May 2, 6, 7, 13, 14,
15, 16, 19, 21, 22, 27, 28, 29, 30, Jun 6, Oct 2, 7, 11, 15, 18, 20, 22, Nov

937

4, 12, 18, 28, Dec 2, 10; <u>1719</u>: DL, Apr 17, 24, May 2, 4, 5, 11, 15, Sep 29,
Oct 3, 9, Nov 3, 6, 7, 16, 21, 23, 30; <u>1720</u>: DL, Jan 1, 12, Feb 5, May 10,
12, 20, 26, Jun 6, Sep 10, 15, 29, Oct 3, 4, 5, 12, 17, 20, Nov 7, 11, 17,
21, 22, Dec 5, 9, 14; <u>1721</u>: DL, Jan 17, 18, 23, 25, Feb 9, Mar 13, 30, Apr
11, 12, 14, 17, 25, 29, May 1, 5, 8, 10, 19, 24, 29, Jun 13, Sep 12, 14, 19,
Oct 2, 4, 5, 12, 13, 14, 16, 18, 20, Nov 1, 13, 25, 27, 28, Dec 12, 18, 20,
22; <u>1722</u>: DL, Jan 8, 9, 10, 24, Feb 19, Mar 10, Apr 5, 9, 10, 14, 19, 24, 26,
27, 28, May 4, 5, 16, 23, 24, 28, Sep 20, Oct 2, 8, 10, 12, 13, 24, 26, 29,
30, Nov 7, 28, Dec 3, 4, 7, 27; <u>1723</u>: DL, Mar 11, 16, Apr 4, 19, May 2, 7, 8,
13, 15, 22, 23, 24, Sep 14, 19, 21, Oct 1, 9, 25, 28, 30, Nov 1, 2, 8, 9, 15,
16, 18, 20, 21, 26; <u>1724</u>: DL, Feb 4, 6, 10, 17, 20, 27, Mar 5, 26, Apr 7, 11,
13, 15, 17, 18, 29, May 1, 4, 8, 9, 12, 16, 18, 22; <u>1725</u>: DL, Apr 5, LIF, Oct
4, 13, 25, Nov 3, 11, 29, Dec 6, 7, 8, 16; <u>1726</u>: LIF, Jan 7, 14, Feb 19, Mar
10, 19, 21, Apr 11, 27, May 3, 4, 13, 14, Sep 12, 14, 30, Oct 3, 24, Nov 2,
4, 10, 18, 19, Dec 14; <u>1727</u>: LIF, Jan 9, 16, Feb 7, 13, Mar 11, 20, Apr 5,
10, May 2, 9, 18, 30, Sep 11, 13, 15, 20, 22, 25, 27, Oct 2, 12, 17, 19, Nov
4, 9, 16, Dec 14; <u>1728</u>: LIF, Jan 8, 17, Mar 9, 11, 25, Apr 22, 23, 26, 30,
May 11, 18, 30, Sep 16, 18, Oct 7, 21, 23, Nov 4, Dec 7, 28, 31; <u>1729</u>: LIF,
Mar 3, 13, 15, 17, 20, Apr 8, 11, 15, 16, 17, 21, 24, 26, 30, Sep 12, 19, 24,
29, Oct 6, 8, 15, 22, Nov 4, 7, 14, 25; <u>1730</u>: LIF, Jan 2, 19, 26, Mar 12, 17,
21, Apr 2, 7, 20, 30, May 15, 18, 27, Jun 1, Sep 16, 18, 23, 25, Oct 26, 27,
31, Nov 4, 6, 7, 23, Dec 15; <u>1731</u>: LIF, Jan 4, 8, 13, 21, 23, Feb 3, Mar 8,
11, 15, 22, 25, Apr 1, 3, 5, 21, 22, 26, May 1, 3, 5, 21, Sep 17, 20, 22, Oct
1, 4, 6, 13, 18, 20, 27, Nov 2, 4, 6, 18, 25, Dec 8, 11, 15; <u>1732</u>: LIF, Jan
10, Feb 14, 15, 28, Mar 9, 23, 25, 30, Apr 12, 13, 26, 27, May 9, LIF/CG, Sep
25, 27, Oct 2, 4, 6, 9, 16, 20, 21, 23, 27, Nov 1, 4, 8, 11, 13, 14, 17, 18,
22, 24, Dec 7, 14, 15, 27; <u>1733</u>: LIF/CG, Jan 15, 23, Mar 12, 15, 26, CG, 27,
LIF/CG, Apr 11, 17, May 24, Jun 1, CG, Sep 20, 25, 27, Oct 4, 6, 9, 13, 16,
18, 19, 20, 26, 31, Nov 1, 3, 5, 10, 14, 21, Dec 3, 7, 8, 19, 31; <u>1734</u>: CG,
Jan 5, 9, 11, 12, 18, 25, Feb 14, Mar 5, 11, 18, Apr 1, 6, 16, May 10; see
also Bicknell, Mrs, sister of
Younger, Joseph (actor, prompter), <u>1760</u>: CG, Dec 27; <u>1761</u>: CG, Feb 14, Mar 6,
Apr 24, May 25, Sep 23; <u>1762</u>: CG, Apr 3, 26; <u>1763</u>: CG, Apr 23; <u>1764</u>: CG, May
7; <u>1765</u>: CG, May 3, 15; <u>1766</u>: CG, Apr 25, Sep 24; <u>1767</u>: CG, Nov 16, Dec 26;
<u>1768</u>: CG, Jan 14, Feb 16, Apr 20, 23, May 2, Dec 3, 14, 16; <u>1769</u>: CG, Jan 17,
31, DL, Feb 15, CG, 25, Mar 18, Apr 17, 24, Oct 12, Nov 25, Dec 4; <u>1770</u>: CG,
Jan 3, Feb 23, Apr 30; <u>1771</u>: CG, Apr 11, 15, 18, 22, 29, 30, May 4, Sep 25,
30, Nov 11, Dec 16; <u>1772</u>: CG, Jan 16, 22, Mar 5, 21, Apr 7, 27, May 19, 25,
Sep 21, Nov 3, Dec 7; <u>1773</u>: CG, Feb 3, 4, 19, Mar 13, Apr 21, 27, May 17, 20,
28, Sep 24, 27, Nov 5, 16, Dec 29; <u>1774</u>: CG, Jan 1, 8, 12, 27, Apr 11, May 4,
DL, 6, CG, 12, DL, 25; <u>1777</u>: DL, Apr 26, HAY, Jun 11, Jul 24, Aug 7, 29, Sep
15; <u>1779</u>: CG, Apr 30; <u>1781</u>: DL, Apr 7; <u>1782</u>: DL, Mar 23
Younger, Mrs (actor), <u>1761</u>: CG, Apr 24, Sep 9, 18, Oct 7; <u>1762</u>: CG, Apr 29, May
8, Sep 20, Oct 1, 6, Nov 16, Dec 8, 10; <u>1763</u>: CG, Apr 23, Oct 15, Dec 9;
<u>1764</u>: CG, Jan 5, Feb 1
Your harps and cymbals sound (song), <u>1793</u>: CG, Mar 8
Your voices tune (song), <u>1792</u>: CG, Mar 7; <u>1794</u>: CG, Mar 14

Zadock the Priest (song), <u>1775</u>: DL, Mar 17; <u>1777</u>: CG, Mar 21; <u>1791</u>: DL, Mar 11;
<u>1792</u>: KING'S, Mar 28; <u>1793</u>: CG, Mar 13; <u>1794</u>: CG, Mar 7, DL, 12, CG, Apr 9;
<u>1795</u>: CG, Feb 20, KING'S, Mar 13, CG, 27; <u>1796</u>: CG, Feb 12; <u>1797</u>: CG, Mar 17;
<u>1799</u>: CG, Feb 15
Zaffaroni, Filippo (scene designer), <u>1795</u>: KING'S, Jun 20
Zaire. See Voltaire.
Zall, Hellend (musician), <u>1741</u>: HIC, Mar 17
Zamperini, Anna (singer), <u>1766</u>: KING'S, Oct 21, Nov 25; <u>1767</u>: KING'S, Jan 31,
Feb 24, Apr 2; <u>1769</u>: KING'S, Nov 7; <u>1770</u>: KING'S, Mar 20, Apr 23
Zamperini, Antonia (singer), <u>1767</u>: KING'S, Apr 2; <u>1769</u>: KING'S, Nov 7
Zamperini, Giandomenico (singer), <u>1766</u>: KING'S, Oct 21; <u>1767</u>: KING'S, Apr 2,
May 2; <u>1769</u>: KING'S, Sep 5; <u>1770</u>: KING'S, Mar 13
Zamperini, Maria (singer), <u>1767</u>: KING'S, Apr 2
Zanaida. See Bach, Johann Christian.
Zanca (singer), <u>1771</u>: KING'S, Jan 22, Mar 14, May 16, 28
Zanoni, Angelo (singer), <u>1714</u>: KING'S, Dec 30; <u>1715</u>: KING'S, Feb 26, Mar 26,
GRT, May 9, 16
Zappino (actor), <u>1754</u>: HAY/SFB, Sep 13
Zara. See Hill, Aaron.
Zary, Don Venturo (Moroccan ambassador), <u>1710</u>: QUEEN'S, May 4; <u>1714</u>: SH, Apr 6
Zelie. See Genlis, Stephanie Felicite Ducrest de Saint Aubin, Comtesse de.

Zelindra. See Killigrew, William.

Zelma. See Hayley, William.

Zelmane. See Mountfort, William.

Zemira and Azor (dance), 1787: KING'S, Feb 13, 17, 20, 24, 27, May 17

Zemira e Azor. See Gretry, Andre Ernest Modeste.

Zeno (Zano), Apostolo (librettist), 1711: QUEEN'S, Dec 12; 1712: QUEEN'S, Feb 27; 1715: KING'S, Feb 26; 1724: KING'S, Dec 1; 1725: KING'S, May 11; 1727: KING'S, Jan 7, Oct 21; 1730: KING'S, Apr 4; 1731: KING'S, Jan 12; 1732: KING'S, May 23; 1733: KING'S, Dec 4; 1738: KING'S, Jan 3, Feb 25; 1742: KING'S, Nov 2; 1743: KING'S, Feb 22

--Alessandro Severo (pastiche), 1738: KING'S, Feb 25, 28, Mar 4, 7, 11, May 30

Zenobia in Palmira. See Anfossi, Pasquale.

Zenobia of Armenia. See Mount-Edgcumbe, Richard.

Zenobia. See Cocchi, Gioacchino; Murphy, Arthur.

Zibber. See Cibber.

Zimri. See Stanley, John.

Zingara, La. See Barthelemon, Francois Hippolyte.

Zingari in Fiera, I. See Paisiello, Giovanni.

Zingis. See Dow, Alexander.

Zingoni, Giovan Battista (singer), 1763: KING'S, Feb 19, Apr 25, HAY, Jun 9

Zobeide. See Cradock, Joseph.

Zoffany, Johann (painter), 1770: DL, Apr 30; 1782: KING'S, May 27

Zonca, Giambattista (singer), 1761: KING'S, Oct 13, Nov 10; 1762: KING'S, May 11

Zoraida. See Hodson, William.

Zorinski. See Morton, Thomas.

Zoroastres. See Boyle, Roger.

Zouch, Rev H, 1761: DL, Mar 7

Zuchelli, Alessandro (dancer, ballet master), 1775: CG, Nov 21, Dec 26; 1776: CG, Jan 5, 31, Feb 3, 16, 19, Mar 25, May 6, KING'S, Nov 2, Dec 7, 17; 1777: KING'S, Feb 25, Mar 15, Apr 12, May 20, Nov 4, Dec 9; 1778: DL, Oct 3, KING'S, Nov 24; 1779: KING'S, Jan 23, Mar 2, 25, DL, May 17, KING'S, Nov 27, Dec 14; 1780: KING'S, Apr 11, May 9, Dec 2; 1781: KING'S, Feb 22, Jun 5, Jul 3, DL, Oct 4, 19, Nov 17, Dec 11, 17, 27; 1782: DL, Jan 3, 5, 21, Feb 19, 23, Mar 7, Apr 6, 29, May 8, 10, 29, KING'S, Nov 2, 9, Dec 12; 1783: KING'S, Jan 11, Feb 15, Mar 13, Apr 10, May 1, 31, Jun 28, Dec 6; 1784: KING'S, Jan 17, Mar 11, 18, 25, May 13, 20, Dec 18; 1785: KING'S, Jan 1, 11, Feb 5, Mar 3, May 12, Jun 18; 1789: KING'S, Jun 15

Zuchelli, Alessandro and Sga (dancers), 1775: CG, Oct 2, 11, 12, 13, Nov 4; 1776: CG, Feb 12, Mar 5, May 3, KING'S, Nov 2, 12, Dec 7; 1777: KING'S, Jan 21, Feb 4, May 1, 24, Nov 4, 15, Dec 16; 1778: KING'S, Feb 24, Mar 31, Apr 4, May 19, DL, Oct 3, Nov 2, Dec 11, KING'S, 22, 29; 1779: KING'S, Feb 23, Mar 25, Apr 15, May 15, Jun 15, 19, DL, Sep 28, Nov 20, KING'S, 27, Dec 14; 1780: KING'S, Jan 22, Feb 15, DL, 24, 28, KING'S, Apr 13, 22, May 2, 9, DL, Oct 18, KING'S, Nov 25, Dec 2, 16; 1781: DL, Jan 2, 18, KING'S, 23, DL, 31, Feb 3, KING'S, 22, Mar 29, DL, Apr 25

Zuchelli, Sga Alessandro (dancer), 1775: CG, Nov 21; 1776: CG, Jan 31, Feb 19, Mar 4, May 6, KING'S, Nov 2, Dec 17; 1777: KING'S, Jan 4, Feb 25, Mar 15, Apr 12, May 20, Jun 17, 21, 24, Jul 5, Nov 4; 1778: KING'S, Nov 24; 1779: KING'S, Jan 23, 29, Feb 2, 6, Mar 2, 25; 1780: KING'S, Apr 11, May 9, DL, Nov 11; 1781: KING'S, Feb 22, Jun 5, Jul 3

Zwillingsbruder, Die. See Schroder, Friedrich Ludwig.

Zwingman, Johann Nicolaus (trombonist), 1792: KING'S, Feb 24; 1793: KING/HAY, Feb 15; 1798: HAY, Jan 15